# Table of Contents

# Table of Contents *continued*

# Introduction

**WELCOME TO THE 78TH EDITION OF *THE NATIONAL HOCKEY LEAGUE OFFICIAL GUIDE & RECORD BOOK***, the definitive statistical record of the NHL. This year's book pays special attention to Olympic hockey. For the fourth time since 1998, the NHL's regular-season schedule has been structured to provide a break so that top players can travel to Vancouver and play for their nations' Olympic teams from February 16 to 28, 2010. The previous three Olympic hockey competitions have seen six different teams reach the gold medal final. In Nagano (1998), the Czech Republic defeated Russia; in Salt Lake City (2002), Canada defeated the USA; while in Torino (2006), Sweden defeated Finland. It seems likely that there will be some repeat participation in the gold medal game for the first time since NHLers have taken part in the tournament. Olympic hockey schedules for both men's and women's competition are found on page 15. Olympic scoring statistics for active NHL players begin on page 19. Goaltenders' Olympic results are found on page 20.

As always, if it has happened in this League, or if it's about to happen, it's in the *Guide*. The 2009 Stanley Cup playoffs are covered in depth. This was a terrific playoff year with 10 of 15 series being decided in six or seven games. The Final was a rematch of 2008 and saw the Detroit Red Wings win the first two games, then lead the series three games to two before the Pittsburgh Penguins won games six and seven by identical 2-1 scores. The Penguins are led by their young stars from captain Sidney Crosby to playoff MVP Evgeni Malkin, goaltender Marc-Andre Fleury and others. As individuals and as a team, they grew during these playoffs and will be a challenge for their opponents going forward. Their roster is stacked with elite players still in their early 20s. Beginning on page 113, the *NHL Guide*'s four-page Penguins club section includes their roster listing players' ages, every Pittsburgh draft choice for the last 15 seasons, club records, all-time coaching, captains' and general managers' histories, retired numbers and all-time records vs. other clubs. Every NHL club has a similar section. Listed alphabetically, these begin with Anaheim Ducks on page 21 and conclude with the Washington Capitals on page 137. Key off-season signings and acquisitions are found top left on the first page of each club.

On 2008-09, three players—Washington's Alex Ovechkin and Pittsburgh's Evgeni Malkin and Sidney Crosby—reached the 100-point plateau. Only Ovechkin scored 50-or-more goals (with 56) while seven players—Jeff Carter, Zach Parise, Ilya Kovalchuk, Thomas Vanek, Marian Hossa, Rick Nash and Eric Staal—scored 40 or more. Ovechkin, who won his second consecutive Hart Trophy as League MVP in 2008-09, now ranks fifth in career goals-per-game average for players with a minimum of 200 goals, which is remarkable given that he has never played in one of the NHL's high-scoring eras. In addition, two veteran players with U.S. Olympic experience, Keith Tkachuk and Doug Weight, joined the exclusive 1,000-point club in 2008-09. An all-time list of 50-goal and 100-point seasons begins on page 202. All of the NHL's 1,000-point scorers beginning with Gordie Howe are listed on page 209. Individual NHL Records begin on page 172, with special attention paid to the history of the League's all-time scoring marks on page 170. Detailed statistics for 2008-09 begin on page 141.

New Jersey's Martin Brodeur set a career record for goaltender wins in 2009, surpassing Patrick Roy's mark of 551. Brodeur now leads with 557 wins and sits just behind Roy in games played (Roy has 1,029; Brodeur 999). He also became the second goaltender to record his 100th NHL regular-season shutout and trails Terry Sawchuk for the career lead 103 to 101. Goaltending records are found on page 182 and a photo of Brodeur celebrating his career wins record leads off the New Jersey club section on page 89.

This was also the fourth season of the shootout in the NHL, the result of which is that games can no longer end with the score tied. The shootout again proved popular with fans and created some surprising category leaders. Wojtek Wolski of the Colorado Avalanche led the NHL in shootout goals scored with 10 on 12 shots and in shootout scoring percentage at 83.3%, while the New York Rangers won 10 of 16 shootout games led by goaltender Henrik Lundqvist, who won nine games in the shootout and stopped 30 of 40 shots faced. Atlanta's Johan Hedberg led all goaltenders with a .923 shootout save percentage, stopping 12 of 13 shots faced. Complete team and individual shootout statistics are found on page 149. Updated single-season and all-time shootout records are found in the Regular-Season Record Book. Team shootout records are found on page 169. Individual shootout scoring records are on page 175; goaltending shootout records are on page 182.

As always in the *NHL Guide & Record Book*, every one of the more than 6,000 players who have appeared in an NHL game, plus more than 1,000 prospects who have yet to do so, are in this book, either in the Prospect Register (279), Active Player Register (352), Goaltender Register (585), Retired Players Index (610), regular-season or playoff Record Books (172 and 246), Award Winners (215), All-Star Teams (232) or Hockey Hall of Fame sections (239). A special tribute to the 2009 inductees to the Hockey Hall of Fame is found on page 657 and winners of the NHL's Player of the Week and Month Awards for 2008-09 are listed on page 656. A register of free agent signings begins on page 658 and a trade register is found on page 660.

A key to the abbreviations and symbols used in individual player and goaltender data panels, along with useful information on how to use the Registers, is found on page 278. Late additions are found on page 609 and each NHL club's minor-pro affiliates are found on page 14. A list of league abbreviations used in the Prospect, Player and Goaltender Registers is found on page 662 and a useful table on page 222 breaks down U.S. and Canadian-born draftees by state or province of birth. Players from 20 states and seven provinces were drafted in 2009.

As always, our thanks to readers, correspondents and members of the media who take the time to comment on the *Guide & Record Book*. Thanks as well to the people working in the communications departments of the NHL's member clubs and to their counterparts in minor pro, junior, college and European hockey.

Best wishes for an enjoyable 2009-10 season.

**ACCURACY REMAINS THE *GUIDE & RECORD BOOK*'S TOP PRIORITY.**

We appreciate comments and clarification from our readers. Please direct these to:


- Ralph Dinger — Senior Managing Editor, 194 Dovercourt Road, Toronto, Ontario M6J 3C8. e-mail: ralph.dda@sympatico.ca.
- Greg Inglis — 1185 Avenue of the Americas, New York, New York 10036 . . . or . . .
- David Keon — 50 Bay Street, 11th Floor, Toronto, Ontario, M5J 2X8


Your involvement makes a better book.

# NATIONAL HOCKEY LEAGUE

**New York**, 1185 Avenue of the Americas, New York, NY 10036,
212/789-2000, Fax: 212/789-2020, PR Fax: 212/789-2080

**Montréal**, 1800 McGill College Avenue, Suite 2600, Montréal, Québec, H3A 3J6
514/841-9220, Fax: 514/841-1070

**Toronto**, 50 Bay Street, 11th Floor, Toronto, Ontario, M5J 2X8
416/359-7900, Fax: 416/981-2779

**Executive**

Commissioner .......... Gary B. Bettman
Deputy Commissioner .......... William Daly
Chief Operating Officer .......... John Collins
Senior Executive Vice President of Hockey Operations .......... Colin Campbell

# NHL Critical Dates 2009-10

**September**

| | |
|---|---|
| 5 | Opening Day of Rookie Camp |
| 12 | Opening Day of NHL Training Camps |
| 14 | Pre-season schedule begins |
| 14 | Kraft Hockeyville Game – NY Islanders vs. Vancouver Canucks (Terrace, B.C.) |
| 28 | Victoria Cup – Chicago Blackhawks vs. HC Davos (Zurich, Switzerland) |
| 28 | NHL Premiere Challenge (exhibition) Florida Panthers vs. Tappara Tampere (Tampere, Finland) |
| 29 | Victoria Cup - Chicago Blackhawks vs. Zurich Lions (Zurich, Switzerland) |
| 29 | NHL Premiere Challenge (exhibition) St. Louis Blues vs. Linkoping (Linkoping, Sweden) |
| 30 | NHL Premiere Challenge (exhibition) Detroit Red Wings vs. Farjestad (Karlstad, Sweden) |
| 30 | NHL Premiere Challenge (exhibition) Florida Panthers vs. Jokerit (Helsinki, Finland) |
| 30 | Opening Day Rosters set (3:00 p.m. ET) |

**October**

| | |
|---|---|
| 1 | Hockey Fights Cancer Awareness Month |
| 1 | Opening Night - 92nd NHL Regular Season begins |
| 1 | San Jose @ Colorado - Joe Sakic's number #19 retired |
| 2 | NY Rangers at Pittsburgh (Stanley Cup Banner raising) |
| 2 | NHL Premiere - Chicago vs. Florida (Helsinki, Finland) |
| 2 | NHL Premiere - Detroit vs. St. Louis (Stockholm, Sweden) |
| 3 | NHL Premiere - Chicago vs. Florida (Helsinki, Finland) |
| 3 | NHL Premiere - Detroit vs. St. Louis Blues (Stockholm, Sweden) |
| 3 | All 30 teams in action |
| 22 | Lester Patrick Award luncheon (New York, NY) Inductees: Jim Devellano, Mark Messier, Mike Richter |
| 24 | All 30 teams in action |

**November**

| | |
|---|---|
| 4-7 | U20 4 Nations Cup |
| 7 | Hockey Hall of Fame Game (Detroit Red Wings at Toronto Maple Leafs) |
| 8 | Hockey Hall of Fame Legends Game (Canada vs. World) |
| 9 | Hockey Hall of Fame Induction Ceremony (Toronto, ON) Inductees: Brett Hull, Brian Leetch, Luc Robitaille, Steve Yzerman (Player category); Lou Lamoriello (Builder category) |

**December**

| | |
|---|---|
| 1 | Signing deadline for Group 2 free agents |
| 19-27 | Holiday Roster Freeze in effect. For all players on an NHL active roster, injured reserve, or players with non-roster and injured non-roster status as of midnight, local time, December 19, a roster freeze shall apply through midnight local time December 27, with respect to waivers, trades and loans, subject to the exceptions provided for in CBA Article 16.10. |
| 24-25 | No scheduled practices - dressing rooms closed |
| 26 – Jan. 5 | IIHF World U20 Championship (Saskatoon & Regina, Canada) |

**January**

| | |
|---|---|
| 1 | 2010 Bridgestone NHL Winter Classic, Fenway Park, Boston (Philadelphia at Boston) |
| 29-31 | Hockey Weekend Across America (USA Hockey) |
| 30 | CBC's Hockey Day in Canada (Host: Stratford, ON) Montreal at Ottawa, Vancouver at Toronto, Edmonton at Calgary |
| 31 | 2009 Stanley Cup Final rematch – Detroit at Pittsburgh |

**February**

| | |
|---|---|
| 1 | Hockey is for Everyone Month |
| 14 | Last NHL games before Olympic break |
| 12-28 | 2010 Winter Olympics (Vancouver, Canada) |
| 16 | Olympic Hockey tournament begins (GM Place) |
| 22 | 30th Anniversary of 'Miracle on Ice' game (1980) |
| 26 | Olympic Bronze medal game |
| 28 | Olympic Gold medal game |

**March**

| | |
|---|---|
| 2 | NHL Regular season resumes after Olympic break |
| 3 | Trade deadline (3:00 p.m. ET) |

**April**

| | |
|---|---|
| 8-10 | NCAA Frozen Four (Ford Field, Detroit) |
| 11 | Last day of 2009-10 regular season |
| 13-23 | IIHF U18 World Championship (Mogileu & Bobruisk, Belarus) |
| 14 | Stanley Cup Playoffs begin |

**May**

| | |
|---|---|
| 1-9 | 2010 Royal Bank Cup (Dauphin, MB) |
| 7-23 | IIHF World Championship (Germany) |
| 24-29 | NHL Combine (Toronto, ON) |

**June**

| | |
|---|---|
| 18 | Last possible day for 2009 Stanley Cup Final |
| TBA | Deadline for first club-elected salary arbitration (later of June 15 or 48 hours after the conclusion of the Stanley Cup Final, 5:00 p.m. ET) |
| TBA | 2010 NHL Awards |
| TBA | NHL Entry Draft Media Day - Top Prospects Media Lunch & Clinic |
| TBA | NHL Entry Draft |

**July**

| | |
|---|---|
| 1 | Free Agency period begins |
| 5 | Deadline for player-elected salary arbitration (5:00 p.m. ET) |
| 6 | Deadline for club-elected salary arbitration (5:00 p.m. ET) |
| 20 – Aug. 4 | Salary arbitration hearings held |

**August**

| | |
|---|---|
| 6 | Deadline for salary arbitration decisions to be rendered |

# BOARD OF GOVERNORS

CHAIRMAN OF THE BOARD – JEREMY M. JACOBS

VICE CHAIR – TOM HICKS

## Anaheim Ducks

Michael Schulman........................................ Governor
Tim Ryan........................................Alternate Governor
Bob Murray........................................Alternate Governor

## Atlanta Thrashers

Bruce Levenson........................................Governor
Don Waddell........................................Alternate Governor
J. Rutherford Seydel, II........................................Alternate Governor
Ed Peskowitz........................................Alternate Governor

## Boston Bruins

Jeremy M. Jacobs........................................Governor
Charles Jacobs........................................Alternate Governor
Jeremy Jacobs, Jr........................................Alternate Governor
Louis Jacobs........................................Alternate Governor
Harry J. Sinden........................................Alternate Governor
Peter Chiarelli........................................Alternate Governor
Cam Neely........................................Alternate Governor

## Buffalo Sabres

B. Thomas Golisano........................................ Governor
Lawrence Quinn........................................Alternate Governor
Daniel J. DiPofi........................................Alternate Governor
Darcy Regier........................................Alternate Governor

## Calgary Flames

N. Murray Edwards........................................Governor
Harley N. Hotchkiss........................................Alternate Governor
Ken King........................................Alternate Governor
Alvin Libin........................................Alternate Governor
Darryl Sutter........................................Alternate Governor

## Carolina Hurricanes

Peter Karmanos, Jr........................................Governor
Jim Rutherford........................................Alternate Governor
Michael Amendola........................................Alternate Governor
Jason Karmanos........................................Alternate Governor

## Chicago Blackhawks

W. Rockwell Wirtz........................................Governor
Robert J. Pulford........................................Alternate Governor
John A. Ziegler, Jr........................................Alternate Governor
John McDonough........................................Alternate Governor

## Colorado Avalanche

Stan Kroenke........................................Governor
Pierre Lacroix........................................Alternate Governor
Paul Andrews........................................Alternate Governor
Mark Waggoner........................................Alternate Governor
Greg Sherman........................................Alternate Governor

## Columbus Blue Jackets

John P. McConnell........................................Governor
Mike Priest........................................Alternate Governor
Scott Howson........................................Alternate Governor

## Dallas Stars

Tom Hicks........................................Governor
Jeffrey Cogen........................................Alternate Governor
Tom Hicks, Jr........................................Alternate Governor
Brett Hull........................................Alternate Governor

## Detroit Red Wings

Michael Ilitch........................................Governor
Jim Devellano........................................Alternate Governor
Ken Holland........................................Alternate Governor
Christopher Ilitch........................................Alternate Governor
Steve Yzerman........................................Alternate Governor
Rob Carr........................................Alternate Governor

## Edmonton Oilers

Daryl Katz........................................Governor
Cal Nichols........................................Alternate Governor
Patrick LaForge........................................Alternate Governor
Kevin Lowe........................................Alternate Governor

## Florida Panthers

Alan Cohen........................................Governor
Bill Torrey........................................Alternate Governor
Michael Yormark........................................Alternate Governor
Cliff Viner........................................Alternate Governor

## Los Angeles Kings

Timothy J. Leiweke........................................Governor
Philip F. Anschutz........................................Alternate Governor
Luc Robitaille........................................Alternate Governor

## Minnesota Wild

Craig Leopold........................................Governor
Phil Falcone........................................Alternate Governor
Jac Sperling........................................Alternate Governor

## Montréal Canadiens

George Gillett, Jr........................................Governor
Pierre Boivin........................................Alternate Governor
Jeff Joyce........................................Alternate Governor
Fred Steer........................................Alternate Governor
Foster Gillett........................................Alternate Governor
Bob Gainey........................................Alternate Governor

## Nashville Predators

David Freeman........................................Governor
Herbert Fritch........................................Alternate Governor
Ed Lang........................................Alternate Governor
David Poile........................................Alternate Governor

## New Jersey Devils

Lou Lamoriello........................................Governor
Jeff Vanderbeek........................................Alternate Governor
Michael Gilfillan........................................Alternate Governor

## New York Islanders

Charles Wang........................................Governor
Roy Reichbach........................................Alternate Governor
Arthur J. McCarthy........................................Alternate Governor
Michael J. Picker........................................Alternate Governor
Garth Snow........................................Alternate Governor
Chris Dey........................................Alternate Governor

## New York Rangers

James L. Dolan........................................ Governor
Glen Sather........................................Alternate Governor
Hank Ratner........................................Alternate Governor
Scott O'Neil........................................Alternate Governor

## Ottawa Senators

Eugene Melnyk........................................Governor
Sheldon Plener........................................Alternate Governor
Cyril Leeder........................................Alternate Governor
Erin Crowe........................................Alternate Governor
Bryan Murray........................................Alternate Governor

## Philadelphia Flyers

Edward M. Snider........................................Governor
Philip I. Weinberg........................................Alternate Governor
Peter Luukko........................................Alternate Governor
Paul Holmgren........................................Alternate Governor

## Phoenix Coyotes

Wayne Gretzky........................................Alternate Governor
Doug Moss........................................Alternate Governor
Don Maloney........................................Alternate Governor

## Pittsburgh Penguins

Ken Sawyer........................................Governor
Ronald Burkle........................................Alternate Governor
Anthony Liberati........................................Alternate Governor
Ray Shero........................................Alternate Governor
David Morehouse........................................Alternate Governor
Mario Lemieux........................................Alternate Governor

## St. Louis Blues

Dave Checketts........................................Governor
Kenneth Munoz........................................Alternate Governor
John Davidson........................................Alternate Governor
Larry Pleau........................................Alternate Governor
Michael McCarthy........................................Alternate Governor

## San Jose Sharks

Greg Jamison........................................Governor
Kevin Compton........................................Alternate Governor
Doug Wilson........................................Alternate Governor

## Tampa Bay Lightning

Oren Koules........................................Governor
Len Barrie........................................Alternate Governor
Brian Lawton........................................Alternate Governor

## Toronto Maple Leafs

Larry Tanenbaum........................................Governor
Richard A. Peddie........................................Alternate Governor
Dale Lastman........................................Alternate Governor
Erol Uzumeri........................................Alternate Governor
Brian Burke........................................Alternate Governor

## Vancouver Canucks

Francesco Aquilini........................................Governor
Paolo Aquilini........................................Alternate Governor
Roberto Aquilini........................................Alternate Governor
Mike Gillis........................................Alternate Governor

## Washington Capitals

Ted Leonsis........................................Governor
Richard M. Patrick........................................Alternate Governor
George McPhee........................................Alternate Governor

## Commissioner and League Presidents

**Gary B. Bettman**

Gary B. Bettman took office as the NHL's first Commissioner on February 1, 1993. Since the League was formed in 1917, there have been five League Presidents.

| NHL President | Years in Office |
|---|---|
| Frank Calder | 1917-1943 |
| Mervyn "Red" Dutton | 1943-1946 |
| Clarence Campbell | 1946-1977 |
| John A. Ziegler, Jr. | 1977-1992 |
| Gil Stein | 1992-1993 |

### Hockey Hall of Fame

Brookfield Place
30 Yonge Street
Toronto, Ontario M5E 1X8
Phone: 416/360-7735
Executive Fax: 416/360-1501
Resource Centre Fax: 416/360-1316
www.hhof.com

William C. Hay – Chairman and Chief Executive Officer
Jeff Denomme – President, C.O.O. and Treasurer
Craig Baines – Vice President, Operations
Peter Jagla – Vice President, Marketing
Phil Pritchard – Vice President and Curator
Ron Ellis – Director, Public Affairs and Assistant to the President
Kelly Massé – Manager, Corporate & Media Relations
Craig Campbell – Manager, Resource Centre & Archives
Steve Ozimec – Manager, Special Events & Hospitality
Jackie Schwartz – Manager, Marketing & Promotions
Matt Manor and Dave Sanford – Photographers

### National Hockey League Players' Association

20 Bay Street, Suite 1700
Toronto, Ontario M5J 2N8
Phone: 416/313-2300
Fax: 416/313-2301
www.nhlpa.com

Paul Kelly – Executive Director
Ian Penny – General Counsel
Mike Ouellet – Chief of Business Affairs
Glenn Healy – Director, Player Affairs
Roland Lee – Director, Salary Cap & Marketplace and Associate Counsel
Matt Nussbaum – Associate Counsel, Labour
Roman Stoykewych – Associate Counsel, Labour
Adam Larry – Director, Licensing and Associate Counsel
Kim Murdoch – Director, Player Insurance & Pensions
Richard Smit – Director, Finance & HRR
Devin Smith – Director, Marketing & Community Relations
Jonathan Weatherdon – Director, Communications
Tyler Currie – Director, International Affairs

# NHL On-Ice Officials

Total NHL Games and 2008-09 Games columns count regular-season games only.

## Referees

| # | Name | Birthplace | *Age | First NHL Game | Total NHL Games | 2008-09 Games |
|---|---|---|---|---|---|---|
| 15 | Stephane Auger | Montreal, Que. | 39 | Apr 1/00 | 529 | 73 |
| 44 | David Banfield | Halifax, N.S. | 30 | Mar 17/08 | 18 | 15 |
| 46 | Frances Charron | Ottawa, Ont. | 26 | ... | 0 | 0 |
| 41 | Chris Ciamaga | Buffalo, NY | 32 | Mar 22/08 | 16 | 15 |
| 10 | Paul Devorski | Guelph, Ont. | 51 | Oct 14/89 | 1187 | 73 |
| 19 | Gord Dwyer | Halifax, N.S. | 32 | Nov 19/05 | 241 | 73 |
| 2 | Kerry Fraser | Sarnia, Ont. | 57 | Apr 6/75 | 1828 | 73 |
| 27 | Eric Furlatt | Trois-Rivieres, Que. | 38 | Oct 8/01 | 459 | 73 |
| 30 | Mike Hasenfratz | Regina, Sask. | 43 | Oct 21/00 | 541 | 73 |
| 49 | Ghislain Hebert | Bathurst, NB | 28 | Mar 2/09 | 1 | 1 |
| 8 | Dave Jackson | Montreal, Que. | 45 | Dec 22/90 | 1046 | 73 |
| 25 | Marc Joannette | Verdun, Que. | 41 | Oct 1/99 | 582 | 73 |
| 18 | Greg Kimmerly | Toronto, Ont. | 45 | Nov 30/96 | 669 | 73 |
| 32 | Tom Kowal | Vernon, B.C. | 42 | Oct 29/99 | 467 | 73 |
| 40 | Steve Kozari | Penticton, B.C. | 36 | Oct 15/05 | 193 | 73 |
| 14 | Dennis LaRue | Savannah, GA | 50 | Mar 26/91 | 861 | 73 |
| 48 | Frederick L'Ecuyer | Trois-Rivieres, Que. | 32 | Oct 11/07 | 29 | 17 |
| 28 | Chris Lee | Saint John, N.B. | 39 | Apr 2/00 | 442 | 74 |
| 3 | Mike Leggo | North Bay, Ont. | 45 | Mar 3/98 | 659 | 73 |
| 6 | Dan Marouelli | Edmonton, Alta. | 54 | Nov 2/84 | 1557 | 73 |
| 26 | Rob Martell | Winnipeg, Man. | 46 | Mar 14/84 | [1]555 | 73 |
| 4 | Wes McCauley | Georgetown, Ont. | 37 | Jan 20/03 | 316 | 73 |
| 7 | Bill McCreary | Guelph, Ont. | 54 | Nov 3/84 | 1597 | 73 |
| 34 | Brad Meier | Dayton, OH | 42 | Oct 23/99 | 583 | 73 |
| 36 | Dean Morton | Peterborough, Ont. | 41 | Nov 11/00 | 144 | 73 |
| 13 | Dan O'Halloran | Essex, Ont. | 45 | Oct 1/95 | 738 | 73 |
| 9 | Dan O'Rourke | Calgary, Alta. | 37 | Oct 2/99 | [2]313 | 71 |
| 20 | Tim Peel | Toronto, Ont. | 43 | Oct 21/99 | 592 | 73 |
| 43 | Brian Pochmara | Detroit, MI | 33 | Dec 23/05 | 124 | 74 |
| 33 | Kevin Pollock | Kincardine, Ont. | 39 | Mar 28/00 | 589 | 73 |
| 37 | Kyle Rehman | Stettler, Alta. | 31 | Jan 22/08 | 17 | 14 |
| 5 | Chris Rooney | Boston, MA | 34 | Nov 22/00 | 486 | 74 |
| 38 | Francois St. Laurent | Greenfield Park, Que. | 32 | Nov 10/05 | 66 | 18 |
| 45 | Justin St. Pierre | Dolbeau, Que. | 37 | Nov 9/05 | 245 | 73 |
| 11 | Kelly Sutherland | Richmond, BC | 38 | Dec 19/00 | 525 | 73 |
| 21 | Don Van Massenhoven | Parkhill, Ont. | 49 | Nov 11/93 | 961 | 73 |
| 29 | Ian Walsh | Philadelphia, PA | 37 | Oct 14/00 | 427 | 73 |
| 23 | Brad Watson | Regina, Sask. | 48 | Mar 7/96 | 688 | 73 |

[1] plus 1 game as a linesman. [2] plus 120 games as a linesman.

## Linesmen

| # | Name | Birthplace | *Age | First NHL Game | Total NHL Games | 2008-09 Games |
|---|---|---|---|---|---|---|
| 75 | Derek Amell | Port Colborne, Ont. | 41 | Oct 11/97 | 724 | 75 |
| 59 | Steve Barton | Vankleek Hill, Ont. | 38 | Nov 1/00 | 504 | 73 |
| 96 | David Brisebois | Sudbury, Ont. | 33 | Oct 11/99 | 461 | 74 |
| 74 | Lonnie Cameron | Victoria, B.C. | 45 | Oct 5/96 | 840 | 71 |
| 67 | Pierre Champoux | Ville St-Pierre, Que. | 46 | Oct 8/88 | 1291 | 71 |
| 50 | Scott Cherrey | Drayton, Ont. | 33 | Oct 6/07 | 121 | 75 |
| 76 | Michel Cormier | Trois-Rivieres, Que. | 35 | Oct 10/03 | 365 | 73 |
| 88 | Mike Cvik | Calgary, Alta. | 47 | Oct 8/87 | 1425 | 74 |
| 54 | Greg Devorski | Guelph, Ont. | 40 | Oct 9/93 | 1005 | 74 |
| 68 | Scott Driscoll | Seaforth, Ont. | 41 | Oct 10/92 | 1077 | 74 |
| 82 | Ryan Galloway | Winnipeg, Man. | 37 | Oct 17/02 | 388 | 73 |
| 66 | Darren Gibbs | Edmonton, Alta. | 43 | Oct 1/97 | 694 | 73 |
| 91 | Don Henderson | Calgary, Alta. | 41 | Mar 11/95 | 828 | 73 |
| 55 | Shane Heyer | Summerland, B.C. | 45 | Oct 6/88 | [3]1003 | 71 |
| 71 | Brad Kovachik | Woodstock, Ont. | 38 | Oct 10/96 | 808 | 74 |
| 86 | Brad Lazarowich | Vancouver, B.C. | 47 | Oct 9/86 | 1518 | 73 |
| 78 | Brian Mach | Little Falls, MN | 35 | Oct 7/00 | 568 | 73 |
| 90 | Andy McElman | Chicago Heights, IL | 48 | Oct 3/93 | 1010 | 73 |
| 89 | Steve Miller | Stratford, Ont. | 37 | Oct 11/00 | 556 | 74 |
| 97 | Jean Morin | Sorel, Que. | 46 | Oct 5/91 | 1118 | 72 |
| 93 | Brian Murphy | Dover, NH | 45 | Oct 7/88 | [4]1207 | 60 |
| 95 | Jonny Murray | Beauport, Que. | 35 | Oct 7/00 | 570 | 72 |
| 70 | Derek Nansen | Ottawa, Ont. | 38 | Oct 11/02 | 427 | 73 |
| 80 | Thor Nelson | Westminister, CA | 41 | Feb 16/95 | 724 | 71 |
| 77 | Tim Nowak | Buffalo, NY | 42 | Oct 8/93 | 1011 | 73 |
| 94 | Bryan Pancich | Great Falls, MT | 27 | ... | 0 | 0 |
| 79 | Mark Paré | Windsor, Ont. | 52 | Oct 11/79 | 2104 | 71 |
| 65 | Pierre Racicot | Verdun, Que. | 42 | Oct 12/93 | 1040 | 74 |
| 73 | Vaughan Rody | Winnipeg, Man. | 41 | Oct 8/00 | 540 | 71 |
| 52 | Dan Schachte | Madison, WI | 51 | Oct 6/82 | 1822 | 69 |
| 61 | Lyle Seitz | Brooks, Alta. | 40 | Oct 7/92 | [5]667 | 74 |
| 84 | Anthony Sericolo | Troy, NY | 41 | Oct 21/98 | 664 | 74 |
| 57 | Jay Sharrers | New Westminister, B.C. | 42 | Oct 6/90 | [6]927 | 68 |
| 92 | Mark Shewchyk | Waterdown, Ont. | 34 | Oct 9/03 | 364 | 74 |
| 56 | Mark Wheler | North Battleford, Sask. | 44 | Oct 10/92 | 1104 | 73 |

[3] plus 386 games as a referee. [4] plus 88 games as a referee. [5] plus 10 games as a referee. [6] plus 136 games as a referee.

– Age at start of 2009-10 season

# NHL History

**1917** — National Hockey League organized November 26 in Montreal following suspension of operations by the National Hockey Association of Canada Limited (NHA). Montreal Canadiens, Montreal Wanderers, Ottawa Senators and Quebec Bulldogs attended founding meeting. Delegates decided to use NHA rules.

Toronto Arenas were later admitted as fifth team; Quebec decided not to operate during the first season. Quebec players allocated to remaining four teams.

Frank Calder elected president and secretary-treasurer.

First NHL games played December 19, with Toronto only arena with artificial ice. Clubs played 22-game split schedule.

**1918** — Emergency meeting held January 3 due to destruction by fire of Montreal Arena which was home ice for both Canadiens and Wanderers.

Wanderers withdrew, reducing the NHL to three teams; Canadiens played remaining home games at 3,250-seat Jubilee rink.

Quebec franchise sold to P.J. Quinn of Toronto on October 18 on the condition that the team operate in Quebec City for 1918-19 season. Quinn did not attend the November League meeting and Quebec did not play in 1918-19.

**1919-20** — NHL reactivated Quebec Bulldogs franchise. Former Quebec players returned to the club. New Mount Royal Arena became home of Canadiens. Toronto Arenas changed name to St. Patricks. Clubs played 24-game split schedule.

**1920-21** — H.P. Thompson of Hamilton, Ontario made application for the purchase of an NHL franchise. Quebec franchise shifted to Hamilton with other NHL teams providing players to strengthen the club.

**1921-22** — Split schedule abandoned. First and second place teams at the end of full schedule to play for championship.

**1922-23** — Clubs agreed that players could not be sold or traded to clubs in any other league without first being offered to all other clubs in the NHL. In March, Foster Hewitt broadcasts radio's first hockey game.

**1923-24** — Ottawa's new 10,000-seat arena opened. First U.S. franchise granted to Boston for following season.

Dr. Cecil Hart Trophy donated to NHL to be awarded to the player judged most useful to his team.

**1924-25** — Canadian Arena Company of Montreal granted a franchise to operate Montreal Maroons. NHL now six team league with two clubs in Montreal. Inaugural game in new Montreal Forum played November 29, 1924 as Canadiens defeated Toronto 7-1.

Hamilton finished first in the standings, receiving a bye into the finals. But Hamilton players, demanding $200 each for additional games in the playoffs, went on strike. The NHL suspended all players, fining them $200 each. Stanley Cup finalist to be the winner of NHL semi-final between Toronto and Canadiens.

Prince of Wales and Lady Byng trophies donated to NHL.

Clubs played 30-game schedule.

**1925-26** — Hamilton club dropped from NHL. Players signed by new New York Americans franchise. Pittsburgh Pirates granted franchise.

Clubs played 36-game schedule.

**1926-27** — New York Rangers granted franchise May 15, 1926. Chicago Black Hawks and Detroit Cougars granted franchises September 25, 1926. NHL now ten-team league with an American and a Canadian Division.

Stanley Cup came under the control of NHL. In previous seasons, winners of the now-defunct Western or Pacific Coast leagues would play NHL champion in Cup finals.

Toronto franchise sold to a new company controlled by Hugh Aird and Conn Smythe. Name changed from St. Patricks to Maple Leafs.

Clubs played 44-game schedule.

The Montreal Canadiens donated the Vezina Trophy to be awarded to the team allowing the fewest goals-against in regular season play. The winning team would, in turn, present the trophy to the goaltender playing in the greatest number of games during the season.

**1930-31** — Detroit franchise changed name from Cougars to Falcons. Pittsburgh transferred to Philadelphia for one season. Pirates changed name to Philadelphia Quakers. Trading deadline for teams set at February 15 of each year. NHL approved operation of farm teams by Rangers, Americans, Falcons and Bruins. Four-sided electric arena clock first demonstrated.

**1931-32** — Philadelphia dropped out. Ottawa withdrew for one season. New Maple Leaf Gardens completed.

Clubs played 48-game schedule.

**1932-33** — Detroit franchise changed name from Falcons to Red Wings. Franchise application received from St. Louis but refused because of additional travel costs. Ottawa team resumed play.

**1933-34** — First All-Star Game played as a benefit for injured player Ace Bailey. Leafs defeated All-Stars 7-3 in Toronto.

**1934-35** — Ottawa franchise transferred to St. Louis. Team called St. Louis Eagles and consisted largely of Ottawa's players.

**1935-36** — Ottawa-St. Louis franchise terminated. Montreal Canadiens finished season with very poor record. To strengthen the club, NHL gave Canadiens first call on the services of all French-Canadian players for three seasons.

**1937-38** — Second benefit All-Star game staged November 2 in Montreal in aid of the family of the late Canadiens star Howie Morenz.

Montreal Maroons withdrew from the NHL on June 22, 1938, leaving seven clubs in the League.

**1938-39** — Expenses for each club regulated at $5 per man per day for meals and $2.50 per man per day for accommodation.

**1939-40** — Benefit All-Star Game played October 29, 1939 in Montreal for the children of the late Albert (Babe) Siebert.

**1940-41** — Ross-Tyer puck adopted as the official puck of the NHL. Early in the season it was apparent that this puck was too soft. The Spalding puck was adopted in its place.

On May 16, 1941, Arthur Ross, NHL governor from Boston, donated a perpetual trophy to be awarded annually to the player voted outstanding in the league. Due to wartime restrictions, the trophy was never awarded.

**1941-42** — New York Americans changed name to Brooklyn Americans.

**1942-43** — Brooklyn Americans withdrew from NHL, leaving six teams: Boston, Chicago, Detroit, Montreal, New York and Toronto. Playoff format saw first-place team play third-place team and second play fourth.

Clubs played 50-game schedule.

Frank Calder, president of the NHL since its inception, died in Montreal. Meryn "Red" Dutton, former manager of the New York Americans, became president. The NHL commissioned the Calder Memorial Trophy to be awarded to the League's outstanding rookie each year.

**1945-46** — Philadelphia, Los Angeles and San Francisco applied for NHL franchises.

The Philadelphia Arena Company of the American Hockey League applied for an injunction to prevent the possible operation of an NHL franchise in that city.

**1946-47** — Mervyn Dutton retired as president of the NHL prior to the start of the season. He was succeeded by Clarence S. Campbell.

Individual trophy winners and all-star team members to receive $1,000 awards.

Playoff guarantees for players introduced.

Clubs played 60-game schedule.

**1947-48** — The first annual All-Star Game for the benefit of the players' pension fund was played when the All-Stars defeated the Stanley Cup Champion Toronto Maple Leafs 4-3 in Toronto on October 13, 1947.

Criteria for awarding Art Ross Trophy changed. Now awarded to top scorer. Elmer Lach was its first winner.

Philadelphia and Los Angeles franchise applications refused.

National Hockey League Pension Society formed.

**1949-50** — Clubs played 70-game schedule.

First intra-league draft held April 30, 1950. Clubs allowed to protect 30 players. Remaining players available for $25,000 each.

**1951-52** — Referees included in the League's pension plan.

**1952-53** — In May of 1952, City of Cleveland applied for NHL franchise. Application denied. In March of 1953, the Cleveland Barons of the AHL challenged the NHL champions for the Stanley Cup. The NHL governors did not accept this challenge.

**1953-54** — The James Norris Memorial Trophy presented to the NHL for annual presentation to the League's best defenseman.

Intra-league draft rules amended to allow teams to protect 18 skaters and two goaltenders, claiming price reduced to $15,000.

**1954-55** — Each arena to operate an "out-of-town" scoreboard.

**1956-57** — Referees and linesmen to wear shirts of black and white vertical stripes. Standardized signals for referees and linesmen introduced.

**1960-61** — Canadian National Exhibition, City of Toronto and NHL reach agreement for the construction of a Hockey Hall of Fame on the CNE grounds. Hall opens on August 26, 1961.

**1963-64** — Player development league established with clubs operated by NHL franchises located in Minneapolis, St. Paul, Indianapolis, Omaha and, beginning in 1964-65, Tulsa. First universal amateur draft took place. All players of qualifying age (17) unaffected by sponsorship of junior teams available to be drafted.

**1964-65** — Conn Smythe Trophy presented to the NHL to be awarded annually to the outstanding player in the Stanley Cup playoffs.

Minimum age of players subject to amateur draft changed to 18.

**1965-66** — NHL announced expansion plans for a second six-team division to begin play in 1967-68.

**1966-67** — Fourteen applications for NHL franchises received.

Lester Patrick Trophy presented to the NHL to be awarded annually for outstanding service to hockey in the United States.

NHL sponsorship of junior teams ceased, making all players of qualifying age not already on NHL-sponsored lists eligible for the amateur draft.

**1967-68** — Six new teams added: California Seals, Los Angeles Kings, Minnesota North Stars, Philadelphia Flyers, Pittsburgh Penguins, St. Louis Blues. New teams to play in West Division. Remaining six teams to play in East Division.

Minimum age of players subject to amateur draft changed to 20.

Clubs played 74-game schedule.

Clarence S. Campbell Trophy awarded to team finishing the regular season in first place in West Division.

California Seals change name to Oakland Seals on December 8, 1967.

**1968-69** — Clubs played 76-game schedule.

Amateur draft expanded to cover any amateur player of qualifying age throughout the world.

**1970-71** — Two new teams added: Buffalo Sabres and Vancouver Canucks. These teams joined East Division: Chicago switched to West Division. Oakland Seals change name to California Golden Seals prior to season.

Clubs played 78-game schedule.

**1971-72** — Playoff format amended. In each division, first to play fourth; second to play third.

**1972-73** — Soviet Nationals and Canadian NHL stars play eight-game pre-season series. Canadians win 4-3-1.

Two new teams added. Atlanta Flames join West Division; New York Islanders join East Division.

**1974-75** — Two new teams added: Kansas City Scouts and Washington Capitals. Teams realigned into two nine-team conferences, the Prince of Wales made up of the Norris and Adams Divisions, and the Clarence Campbell made up of the Smythe and Patrick Divisions.

Clubs played 80-game schedule.

**1976-77** — California franchise transferred to Cleveland. Team named Cleveland Barons. Kansas City franchise transferred to Denver. Team named Colorado Rockies.

**1977-78** — Clarence S. Campbell retires as NHL president. Succeeded by John A. Ziegler, Jr.

**1978-79** — Cleveland and Minnesota franchises merge, leaving NHL with 17 teams. Merged team placed in Adams Division, playing home games in Minnesota.

Minimum age of players subject to amateur draft changed to 19.

**1979-80** — Four new teams added: Edmonton Oilers, Hartford Whalers, Quebec Nordiques and Winnipeg Jets.

Minimum age of players subject to entry draft changed to 18.

**1980-81** — Atlanta franchise shifted to Calgary, retaining "Flames" name.

**1981-82** — Teams realigned within existing divisions. New groupings based on geographical areas. Unbalanced schedule adopted.

**1982-83** — Colorado Rockies franchise shifted to East Rutherford, New Jersey. Team named New Jersey Devils. Franchise moved to Patrick Division from Smythe; Winnipeg moved to Smythe Division from Norris.

**1991-92** — San Jose Sharks added, making the NHL a 22-team league. NHL celebrates 75th Anniversary Season. The 1991-92 regular season suspended due to a players' strike on April 1, 1992. Play resumed April 12, 1992.

## NHL History *— continued*

**1992-93** — Gil Stein named NHL president (October, 1992). Gary Bettman named first NHL Commissioner (February, 1993). Ottawa Senators and Tampa Bay Lightning added, making the NHL a 24-team league. NHL celebrates Stanley Cup Centennial. Clubs played 84-game schedule.

**1993-94** — Mighty Ducks of Anaheim and Florida Panthers added, making the NHL a 26-team league. Minnesota franchise shifted to Dallas, team named Dallas Stars. Prince of Wales and Clarence Campbell Conferences renamed Eastern and Western. Adams, Patrick, Norris and Smythe Divisions renamed Northeast, Atlantic, Central and Pacific. Winnipeg moved to Central Division from Pacific; Tampa Bay moved to Atlantic Division from Central; Pittsburgh moved to Northeast Division from Atlantic.

**1994-95** — A lockout resulted in the cancellation of 468 games from October 1, 1994 to January 19, 1995. Clubs played a 48-game schedule that began January 20, 1995 and ended May 3, 1995. No inter-conference games were played.

**1995-96** — Quebec franchise transferred to Denver. Team named Colorado Avalanche and placed in Pacific Division of Western Conference. Clubs to play 82-game schedule.

**1996-97** — Winnipeg franchise transferred to Phoenix. Team named Phoenix Coyotes and placed in Central Division of Western Conference.

**1997-98** — Hartford franchise transferred to Raleigh. Team named Carolina Hurricanes and remains in Northeast Division of Eastern Conference.

**1998-99** — The addition of the Nashville Predators made the NHL a 27-team league and brought about the creation of two new divisions and a League-wide realignment in preparation for further expansion to 30 teams by 2000-2001. Nashville was added to the Central Division of the Western Conference, while Toronto moved into the Northeast Division of the Eastern Conference. Pittsburgh was shifted from the Northeast to the Atlantic, while Carolina left the Northeast for the newly created Southeast Division of the Eastern Conference. Florida, Tampa Bay and Washington also joined the Southeast. In the Western Conference, Calgary, Colorado, Edmonton and Vancouver make up the new Northwest Division. Dallas and Phoenix moved from the Central to the Pacific Division.

The NHL retired uniform number 99 in honor of all-time scoring leader Wayne Gretzky who retired at the end of the season.

**1999-2000** — Atlanta Thrashers added, making the NHL a 28-team league.

**2000-01** — Columbus Blue Jackets and Minnesota Wild added, making the NHL a 30-team league.

**2003-04** — First outdoor NHL game. 57,167 attend Heritage Classic at Edmonton's Commonwealth Stadium. Montreal defeated Edmonton 4-3, November 22, 2003.

**2004-05** — A lockout resulted in the cancellation of the season.

**2007-08** — NHL-record crowd of 71,217 fills Buffalo's Ralph Wilson Stadium on New Year's Day for the 2008 Winter Classic, the first NHL outdoor game in the United States. Sidney Crosby's shootout goal gives the Pittsburgh Penguins a 2-1 win over the Buffalo Sabres.

**2008-09** — Third edition of NHL Winter Classic played at Wrigley Field in Chicago. Detroit defeated Chicago 6-4 before a crowd of 40,818.

# NHL Attendance

| | Regular Season | | Playoffs | | Total |
|---|---|---|---|---|---|
| Season | Games | Attendance | Games | Attendance | Attendance |
| 1967-68 | 444 | 4,938,043 | 40 | 495,089 | 5,433,132 |
| 1968-69 | 456 | 5,550,613 | 33 | 431,739 | 5,982,352 |
| 1969-70 | 456 | 5,992,065 | 34 | 461,694 | 6,453,759 |
| 1970-71 | 546 | 7,257,677 | 43 | 707,633 | 7,965,310 |
| 1971-72 | 546 | 7,609,368 | 36 | 582,666 | 8,192,034 |
| 1972-73 | 624 | 8,575,651 | 38 | 624,637 | 9,200,288 |
| 1973-74 | 624 | 8,640,978 | 38 | 600,442 | 9,241,420 |
| 1974-75 | 720 | 9,521,536 | 51 | 784,181 | 10,305,717 |
| 1975-76 | 720 | 9,103,761 | 48 | 726,279 | 9,830,040 |
| 1976-77 | 720 | 8,563,890 | 44 | 646,279 | 9,210,169 |
| 1977-78 | 720 | 8,526,564 | 45 | 686,634 | 9,213,198 |
| 1978-79 | 680 | 7,758,053 | 45 | 694,521 | 8,452,574 |
| 1979-80 | 840 | 10,533,623 | 63 | 976,699 | 11,510,322 |
| 1980-81 | 840 | 10,726,198 | 68 | 966,390 | 11,692,588 |
| 1981-82 | 840 | 10,710,894 | 71 | 1,058,948 | 11,769,842 |
| 1982-83 | 840 | 11,020,610 | 66 | 1,088,222 | 12,028,832 |
| 1983-84 | 840 | 11,359,386 | 70 | 1,107,400 | 12,466,786 |
| 1984-85 | 840 | 11,633,730 | 70 | 1,107,500 | 12,741,230 |
| 1985-86 | 840 | 11,621,000 | 72 | 1,152,503 | 12,773,503 |
| 1986-87 | 840 | 11,855,880 | 87 | 1,383,967 | 13,239,847 |
| 1987-88 | 840 | 12,117,512 | 83 | 1,336,901 | 13,454,413 |
| 1988-89 | 840 | 12,417,969 | 83 | 1,327,214 | 13,745,183 |
| 1989-90 | 840 | 12,579,651 | 85 | 1,355,593 | 13,935,244 |
| 1990-91 | 840 | 12,343,897 | 92 | 1,442,203 | 13,786,100 |
| 1991-92 | 880 | 12,769,676 | 86 | 1,327,920 | 14,097,596 |
| 1992-93 | 1,008 | 14,158,177[1] | 83 | 1,346,034 | 15,504,211 |
| 1993-94 | 1,092 | 16,105,604[2] | 90 | 1,440,095 | 17,545,699 |
| 1994-95 | 624[3] | 9,233,884 | 81 | 1,329,130 | 10,563,014 |
| 1995-96 | 1,066 | 17,041,614 | 86 | 1,540,140 | 18,581,754 |
| 1996-97 | 1,066 | 17,640,529 | 82 | 1,494,878 | 19,135,407 |
| 1997-98 | 1,066 | 17,264,678 | 82 | 1,507,416 | 18,772,094 |
| 1998-99 | 1,107 | 18,001,741 | 86 | 1,509,411 | 19,511,152 |
| 1999-2000 | 1,148 | 18,800,139 | 83 | 1,524,629 | 20,324,768 |
| 2000-01 | 1,230 | 20,373,379 | 86 | 1,584,011 | 21,957,390 |
| 2001-02 | 1,230 | 20,614,613 | 90 | 1,691,174 | 22,305,787 |
| 2002-03 | 1,230 | 20,408,704 | 89 | 1,636,120 | 22,044,824 |
| 2003-04 | 1,230 | 20,356,199 | 89 | 1,708,691 | 22,064,890 |
| 2004-05 | .... | .... | .... | .... | .... |
| 2005-06 | 1,230 | 20,854,169 | 83 | 1,530,405 | 22,384,574 |
| 2006-07 | 1,230 | 20,861,787 | 81 | 1,496,501 | 22,358,288 |
| 2007-08 | 1,230 | 21,236,255 | 85 | 1,587,054 | 22,823,309 |
| 2008-09 | 1,230 | 21,475,223 | 87 | 1,639,602 | 23,114,825 |

NHL Expansion: the NHL operated as a six-team league from 1942-43 to 1966-67. Six teams were added in 1967-68: California (later to move to Cleveland), Los Angeles, Minnesota (later to move to Dallas), Philadelphia, Pittsburgh and St. Louis. In 1970-71: Buffalo and Vancouver. In 1972-73: Atlanta (later to move to Calgary) and NYIslanders. In 1974-75: Kansas City (later to move to Colorado and then to New Jersey) and Washington. In 1979-80, Hartford (later to move to Carolina), Edmonton, Quebec (later to move to Colorado) and Winnipeg (later to move to Phoenix). In 1991-92, San Jose. In 1992-93, Ottawa and Tampa Bay. In 1993-94, Anaheim and Florida. In 1998-99, Nashville. In 1999-2000, Atlanta. In 2000-01, Columbus and Minnesota.

[1] Includes 24 neutral site games • [2] Includes 26 neutral site games
[3] Lockout resulted in the cancellation of 468 regular-season games.

# Major Rule Changes

**1910-11** — Game changed from two 30-minute periods to three 20-minute periods.

**1911-12** — National Hockey Association (forerunner of the NHL) originated six-man hockey, replacing seven-man game.

**1917-18** — Goalies permitted to fall to the ice to make saves. Previously a goaltender was penalized for dropping to the ice.

**1918-19** — Penalty rules amended. For minor fouls, substitutes not allowed until penalized player had served three minutes. For major fouls, no substitutes for five minutes. For match fouls, no substitutes allowed for the remainder of the game.

With the addition of two lines painted on the ice twenty feet from center, three playing zones were created, producing a forty-foot neutral center ice area in which forward passing was permitted. Kicking the puck was permitted in this neutral zone.

Tabulation of assists began.

**1921-22** — Goaltenders allowed to pass the puck forward up to their own blue line.

Overtime limited to twenty minutes.

Minor penalties changed from three minutes to two minutes.

**1923-24** — Match foul defined as actions deliberately injuring or disabling an opponent. For such actions, a player was fined not less than $50 and ruled off the ice for the balance of the game. A player assessed a match penalty may be replaced by a substitute at the end of 20 minutes. Match penalty recipients must meet with the League president who can assess additional punishment.

**1925-26** — Delayed penalty rules introduced. Each team must have a minimum of four players on the ice at all times.

Two rules were amended to encourage offense: No more than two defensemen permitted to remain inside a team's own blue line when the puck has left the defensive zone. A faceoff to be called for ragging the puck unless shorthanded.

Team captains only players allowed to talk to referees.

Goaltender's leg pads limited to 12-inch width.

Timekeeper's gong to mark end of periods rather than referee's whistle. Teams to dress a maximum of 12 players for each game from a roster of no more than 14 players.

**1926-27** — Blue lines repositioned to sixty feet from each goal-line, thereby enlarging the neutral zone and standardizing distance from blue line to goal.

Uniform goal nets adopted throughout NHL with goal posts securely fastened to the ice.

**1927-28** — To further encourage offense, forward passes allowed in defending and neutral zones and goaltender's pads reduced in width from 12 to 10 inches.

Game standardized at three twenty-minute periods of stop-time separated by ten-minute intermissions.

Teams to change ends after each period.

Ten minutes of sudden-death overtime to be played if the score is tied after regulation time.

Minor penalty to be assessed to any player other than a goaltender for deliberately picking up the puck while it is in play. Minor penalty to be assessed for deliberately shooting the puck out of play.

The Art Ross goal net adopted as the official net of the NHL.

Maximum length of hockey sticks limited to 53 inches measured from heel of blade to end of handle. No minimum length stipulated.

Home teams given choice of end to defend at start of game.

**1928-29** — Forward passing permitted in defensive and neutral zones and into attacking zone if pass receiver is in neutral zone when pass is made. No forward passing allowed inside attacking zone.

Minor penalty to be assessed to any player who delays the game by passing the puck back into his defensive zone.

Ten-minute overtime without sudden-death provision to be played in games tied after regulation time. Games tied after this overtime period declared a draw.

Exclusive of goaltenders, team to dress at least 8 and no more than 12 skaters.

## Major Rule Changes — *continued*

**1929-30** — Forward passing permitted inside all three zones but not permitted across either blue line.

Kicking the puck allowed, but a goal cannot be scored by kicking the puck in.

No more than three players including the goaltender may remain in their defensive zone when the puck has gone up ice. Minor penalties to be assessed for the first two violations of this rule in a game; major penalties thereafter.

Goaltenders forbidden to hold the puck. Pucks caught must be cleared immediately. For infringement of this rule, a faceoff to be taken ten feet in front of the goal with no player except the goaltender standing between the faceoff spot and the goal-line.

Highsticking penalties introduced.

Maximum number of players in uniform increased from 12 to 15.

**December 21, 1929** — Forward passing rules instituted at the beginning of the 1929-30 season more than doubled number of goals scored. Partway through the season, these rules were further amended to read, "No attacking player allowed to precede the play when entering the opposing defensive zone." This is similar to modern offside rule.

**1930-31** — A player without a complete stick ruled out of play and forbidden from taking part in further action until a new stick is obtained. A player who has broken his stick must obtain a replacement at his bench.

A further refinement of the offside rule stated that the puck must first be propelled into the attacking zone before any player of the attacking side can enter that zone; for infringement of this rule a faceoff to take place at the spot where the infraction took place.

**1931-32** — Though there is no record of a team attempting to play with two goaltenders on the ice, a rule was instituted which stated that each team was allowed only one goaltender on the ice at one time.

Attacking players forbidden to impede the movement or obstruct the vision of opposing goaltenders.

Defending players with the exception of the goaltender forbidden from falling on the puck within 10 feet of the net.

**1932-33** — Each team to have captain on the ice at all times. Maximum number of players in uniform reduced to 14 from 15.

If the goaltender is removed from the ice to serve a penalty, the manager of the club to appoint a substitute.

Match penalty with substitution after five minutes instituted for kicking another player.

**1933-34** — Number of players permitted to stand in defensive zone restricted to three including goaltender.

Visible time clocks required in each rink.

Two referees replace one referee and one linesman.

**1934-35** — Penalty shot awarded when a player is tripped and thus prevented from having a clear shot on goal, having no player to pass to other than the offending player. Shot taken from inside a 10-foot circle located 38 feet from the goal. The goaltender must not advance more than one foot from his goal-line when the shot is taken.

**1937-38** — Rules introduced governing icing the puck.

Penalty shot awarded when a player other than a goaltender falls on the puck within 10 feet of the goal.

**1938-39** — Penalty shot modified to allow puck carrier to skate in before shooting.

One referee and one linesman replace two referee system.

Blue line widened to 12 inches.

Maximum number of players in uniform increased from 14 to 15.

**1939-40** — A substitute replacing a goaltender removed from ice to serve a penalty may use a goaltender's stick and gloves but no other goaltending equipment.

**1940-41** — Flooding ice surface between periods made obligatory.

**1941-42** — Penalty shots classified as minor and major. Minor shot to be taken from a line 28 feet from the goal. Major shot, awarded when a player is tripped with only the goaltender to beat, permits the player taking the penalty shot to skate right into the goalkeeper and shoot from point-blank range.

One referee and two linesmen employed to officiate games.

For playoffs, standby minor league goaltenders employed by NHL as emergency substitutes.

**1942-43** — Because of wartime restrictions on train scheduling, regular-season overtime was discontinued on November 21, 1942.

Player limit reduced from 15 to 14. Minimum of 12 men in uniform abolished.

**1943-44** — Red line at center ice introduced to speed up the game and reduce offside calls. This rule is considered to mark the beginning of the modern era in the NHL.

**1945-46** — Goal indicator lights synchronized with official time clock required at all rinks.

**1946-47** — System of signals by officials to indicate infractions introduced.

Linesmen from neutral cities employed for all games.

**1947-48** — Goal awarded when a player with the puck has an open net to shoot at and a thrown stick prevents the shot on goal. Major penalty to any player who throws his stick in any zone other than defending zone. If a stick is thrown by a player in his defending zone but the thrown stick is not considered to have prevented a goal, a penalty shot is awarded.

All playoff games played until a winner determined, with 20-minute sudden-death overtime periods separated by 10-minute intermissions.

**1949-50** — Ice surface painted white.

Clubs allowed to dress 17 players exclusive of goaltenders.

Major penalties incurred by goaltenders served by a member of the goaltender's team instead of resulting in a penalty shot.

**1950-51** — Each team required to provide an emergency goaltender in attendance with full equipment at each game for use by either team in the event of illness or injury to a regular goaltender.

**1951-52** — Home teams to wear basic white uniforms; visiting teams basic colored uniforms.

Goal crease enlarged from 3 × 7 feet to 4 × 8 feet.

Number of players in uniform reduced to 15 plus goaltenders.

Faceoff circles enlarged from 10-foot to 15-foot radius.

**1952-53** — Teams permitted to dress 15 skaters on the road and 16 at home.

**1953-54** — Number of players in uniform set at 16 plus goaltenders.

**1954-55** — Number of players in uniform set at 18 plus goaltenders up to December 1 and 16 plus goaltenders thereafter. Teams agree to wear colored uniforms at home and white uniforms on the road.

**1956-57** — Player serving a minor penalty allowed to return to ice when a goal is scored by opposing team.

**1959-60** — Players prevented from leaving their benches to enter into an altercation. Substitutions permitted providing substitutes do not enter into altercation.

**1960-61** — Number of players in uniform set at 16 plus goaltenders.

**1961-62** — Penalty shots to be taken by the player against whom the foul was committed. In the event of a penalty shot called in a situation where a particular player hasn't been fouled, the penalty shot to be taken by any player on the ice when the foul was committed.

**1964-65** — No body contact on faceoffs.

In playoff games, each team to have its substitute goaltender dressed in his regular uniform except for leg pads and body protector. All previous rules governing standby goaltenders terminated.

**1965-66** — Teams required to dress two goaltenders for each regular-season game. Maximum stick length increased to 55 inches.

**1966-67** — Substitution allowed on coincidental major penalties.

Between-periods intermissions fixed at 15 minutes.

**1967-68** — If a penalty incurred by a goaltender is a co-incident major, the penalty to be served by a player of the goaltender's team on the ice at the time the penalty was called. Limit of curvature of hockey stick blade set at $1^1/_2$ inches.

**1969-70** — Limit of curvature of hockey stick blade set at 1 inch.

**1970-71** — Home teams to wear basic white uniforms; visiting teams to wear basic colored uniforms.

Limit of curvature of hockey stick blade set at $^1/_2$ inch.

Minor penalty for deliberately shooting the puck out of the playing area.

**1971-72** — Number of players in uniform set at 17 plus 2 goaltenders.

Third man to enter an altercation assessed an automatic game misconduct penalty.

**1972-73** — Minimum width of stick blade reduced to 2 inches from $2^1/_2$ inches.

**1974-75** — Bench minor penalty imposed if a penalized player does not proceed directly and immediately to the penalty box.

**1976-77** — Rule dealing with fighting amended to provide a major and game misconduct penalty for any player who is clearly the instigator of a fight.

**1977-78** — Teams requesting a stick measurement to be assessed a minor penalty in the event that the measured stick does not violate the rules.

**1979-80** — Wearing of helmets made mandatory for players entering the NHL.

**1980-81** — Maximum stick length increased to 58 inches.

**1981-82** — If both of a team's listed goaltenders are incapacitated, the team can dress and play any eligible goaltender who is available.

**1982-83** — Number of players in uniform set at 18 plus 2 goaltenders.

**1983-84** — Five-minute sudden-death overtime to be played in regular-season games that are tied at the end of regulation time.

**1985-86** — Substitutions allowed in the event of co-incidental minor penalties. Maximum stick length increased to 60 inches.

**1986-87** — Delayed off-side is no longer in effect once the players of the offending team have cleared the opponents' defensive zone.

**1990-91** — The goal lines, blue lines, defensive zone face-off circles and markings all moved one foot out from the end boards, creating 11 feet of room behind the nets and shrinking the neutral zone from 60 to 58 feet.

**1991-92** — Video replays employed to assist referees in goal/no goal situations. Size of goal crease increased. Crease changed to semi-circular configuration. Time clock to record tenths of a second in last minute of each period and overtime. Major and game misconduct penalty for checking from behind into boards. Penalties added for crease infringement and unnecessary contact with goaltender. Goal disallowed if puck enters net while a player of the attacking team is standing on the goal crease line, is in the goal crease or places his stick in the goal crease.

**1992-93** — No substitutions allowed in the event of coincidental minor penalties called when both teams are at full strength. Minor penalty for attempting to draw a penalty ("diving"). Major and game misconduct penalty for checking from behind into goal frame. Game misconduct penalty for instigating a fight. High sticking redefined to include any use of the stick above waist-height. Previous rule stipulated shoulder-height.

**1993-94** — High sticking redefined to allow goals scored with a high stick below the height of the crossbar of the goal frame.

**1996-97** — Maximum stick length increased to 63 inches. All players must be clear of the attacking zone prior to the puck being shot into that zone. The opportunity to "tag-up" and return into the zone has been removed.

**1998-99** — The league instituted a two-referee system with each team to play 20 regular-season games with two referees and a pair of linesmen. Goal line moved to 13 feet from end boards. Goal crease altered to extend one foot beyond each goal post (eight feet across in total. Sides of crease squared off, extending 4'6". Only the top of the crease remains rounded. Only the top of the crease remains rounded.

**1999-2000** — Each team to play 25 home and 25 road games using the two-referee system. Crease rule revised to implement a "no harm, no foul, no video review" standard. Teams to play with four skaters and a goaltender in regular-season overtime. If a goal is scored in regular-season overtime, the winner is awarded two points and the loser one point. In no goal is scored in overtime, both teams are awarded one point.

**2000-01** — All games to be played using the two-referee system.

**2002-03** — "Hurry-up" faceoff and line-change rules implemented.

**2003-04** — Home teams to wear basic colored uniforms; visiting teams to wear basic white uniforms. Maximum length of goaltender's pads set at 38 inches.

**2005-06** — The NHL adopted a comprehensive package of rule changes that included the following:

Goal line moved to 11 feet from end boards; blue lines moved to 75 feet from end boards, reducing neutral zone from 54 feet to 50 feet. Center red line eliminated for two-line passes. "Tag-up" off-side rule reinstituted. This rule was previously used from 1986-87 through 1995-96. Goaltender not permitted to play the puck outside a designated trapezoid-shaped area behind the net. A team that ices the puck will not be permitted to make any player substitutions prior to the ensuing faceoff. A player who instigates a fight in the final five minutes of regulation time or at any time of overtime will receive a minor, a major, a misconduct and an automatic one-game suspension. The size of goaltender equipment has been reduced by approximately 11 percent. If a game remains tied after five minutes of overtime, a shootout will be conducted to determine a winner.

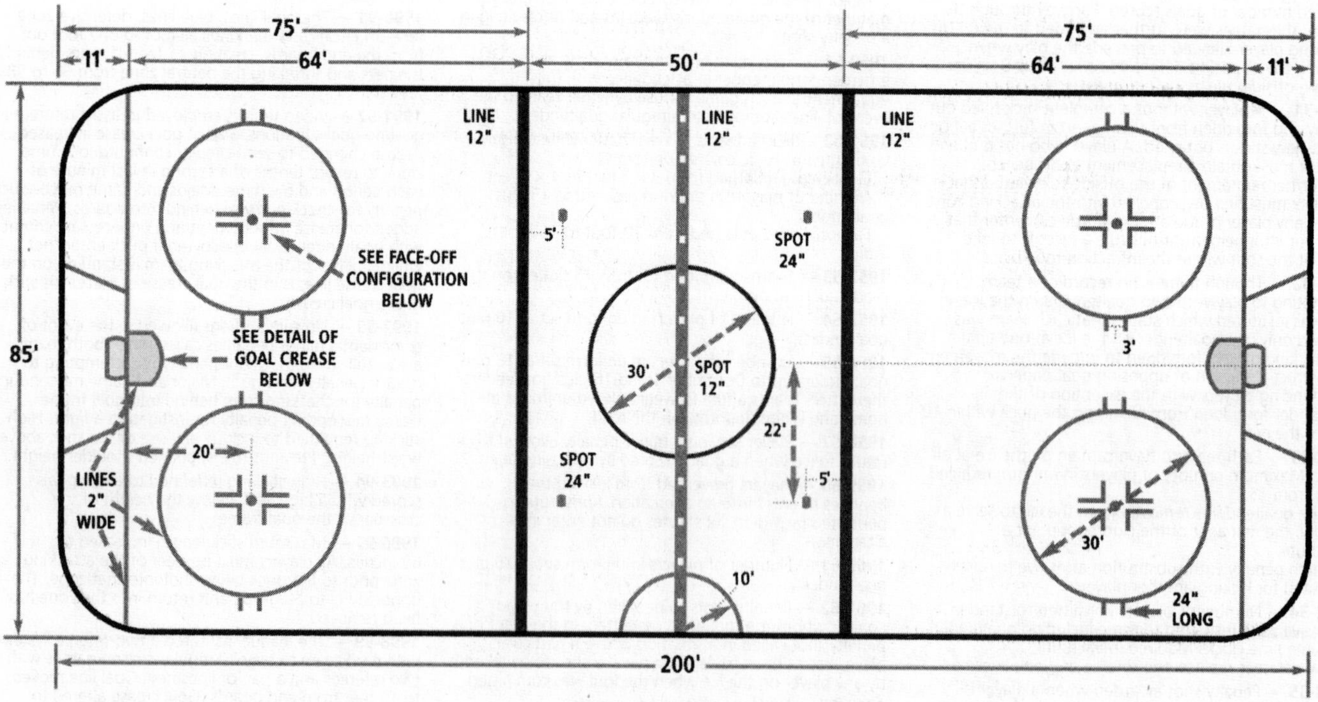


## NHL RINK DIMENSIONS

## FACEOFF CONFIGURATION

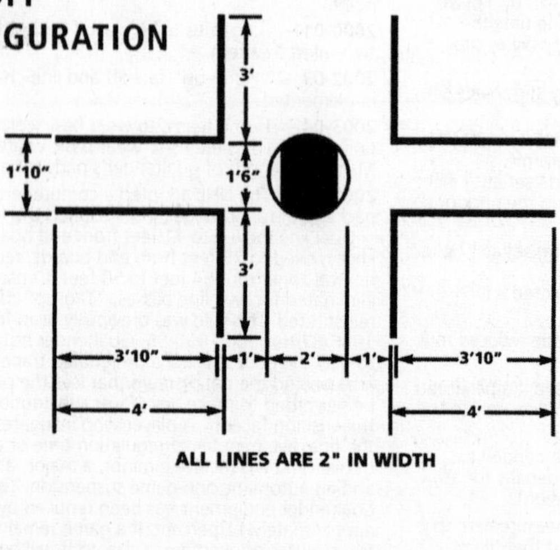


ALL LINES ARE 2" IN WIDTH

## CREASE DIMENSIONS

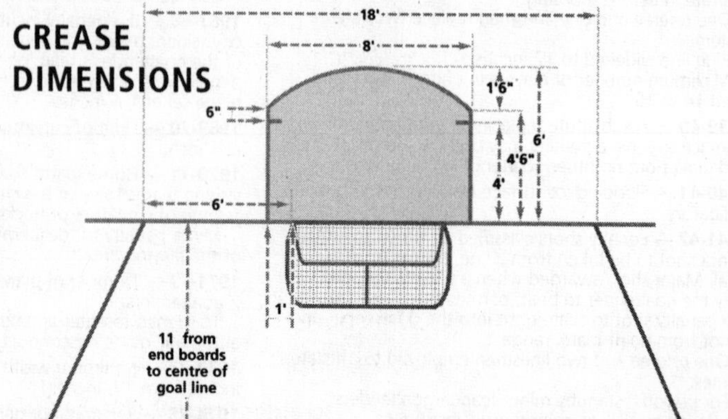

# NHL League and Team Websites

National Hockey League.........www.nhl.com
*(includes links to official team and League sites)*

NHL Site for Kids.......................www2.nhl.com/kids
NHL Merchandise Shop.............shop.nhl.com
NHL Job Postings .......................hockeyjobs.nhl.com
Hockey Fights Cancer................www.hockeyfightscancer.com
NHL Auctions .............................nhlauctions.typepad.com

## Official NHL Team Websites:

Anaheim ...................................www.ducks.nhl.com
Atlanta......................................www.thrashers.nhl.com
Boston ......................................www.bruins.nhl.com
Buffalo......................................www.sabres.nhl.com
Calgary .....................................www.flames.nhl.com
Carolina ....................................www.hurricanes.nhl.com
Chicago ....................................www.blackhawks.nhl.com
Colorado...................................www.avalanche.nhl.com
Columbus ................................www.bluejackets.nhl.com
Dallas........................................www.stars.nhl.com
Detroit .....................................www.redwings.nhl.com
Edmonton.................................www.oilers.nhl.com
Florida......................................www.panthers.nhl.com
Los Angeles ..............................www.kings.nhl.com
Minnesota.................................www.wild.nhl.com
Montreal ..................................www.canadiens.nhl.com
Nashville .................................www.predators.nhl.com
New Jersey................................www.devils.nhl.com
NY Islanders.............................www.islanders.nhl.com
NY Rangers...............................www.rangers.nhl.com
Ottawa ....................................www.senators.nhl.com
Philadelphia .............................www.flyers.nhl.com
Phoenix....................................www.coyotes.nhl.com
Pittsburgh ...............................www.penguins.nhl.com
St. Louis ..................................www.blues.nhl.com
San Jose...................................www.sharks.nhl.com
Tampa Bay ...............................www.lightning.nhl.com
Toronto ...................................www.mapleleafs.nhl.com
Vancouver................................www.canucks.nhl.com
Washington .............................www.capitals.nhl.com

**To order the *NHL Official Guide & Record Book* and other books about hockey:**

**www.nhlofficialguide.com**

# NHL Clubs' Minor-League Affiliations, 2009-10

| NHL Club | Minor-League Affiliates |
|---|---|
| **Anaheim** | Bakersfield Condors (ECHL) |
| **Atlanta** | Chicago Wolves (AHL)<br>Gwinnett Gladiators (ECHL) |
| **Boston** | Providence Bruins (AHL)<br>Reading Royals (ECHL) |
| **Buffalo** | Portland Pirates (AHL) |
| **Calgary** | Abbotsford Heat (AHL) |
| **Carolina** | Albany River Rats (AHL)<br>Florida Everblades (ECHL) |
| **Chicago** | Rockford IceHogs (AHL)<br>Toledo Walleye (ECHL) |
| **Colorado** | Lake Erie Monsters (AHL)<br>Charlotte Checkers (ECHL) |
| **Columbus** | Syracuse Crunch (AHL) |
| **Dallas** | Texas Stars (AHL)<br>Idaho Steelheads (ECHL) |
| **Detroit** | Grand Rapids Griffins (AHL)<br>Toledo Walleye (ECHL) |
| **Edmonton** | Springfield Falcons (AHL)<br>Stockton Thunder (ECHL) |
| **Florida** | Rochester Americans (AHL)<br>Florida Everblades (ECHL) |
| **Los Angeles** | Manchester Monarchs (AHL)<br>Ontario (CA) Reign (ECHL) |
| **Minnesota** | Houston Aeros (AHL) |
| **Montreal** | Hamilton Bulldogs (AHL)<br>Cincinnati Cyclones (ECHL) |
| **Nashville** | Milwaukee Admirals (AHL)<br>Cincinnati Cyclones (ECHL) |
| **New Jersey** | Lowell Devils (AHL)<br>Trenton Devils (ECHL) |
| **NY Islanders** | Bridgeport Sound Tigers (AHL)<br>Utah Grizzlies (ECHL)<br>Odessa Jackalopes (CHL) |
| **NY Rangers** | Hartford Wolf Pack (AHL)<br>Charlotte Checkers (ECHL) |
| **Ottawa** | Binghamton Senators (AHL)<br>Elmira Jackals (ECHL) |
| **Philadelphia** | Adirondack Phantoms (AHL)<br>Kalamazoo Wings (ECHL) |
| **Phoenix** | San Antonio Rampage (AHL)<br>Las Vegas Wranglers (ECHL) |
| **Pittsburgh** | Wilkes-Barre/Scranton Penguins (AHL)<br>Wheeling Nailers (ECHL) |
| **St. Louis** | Peoria Rivermen (AHL)<br>Alaska Aces (ECHL) |
| **San Jose** | Worcester Sharks (AHL)<br>Kalamazoo Wings (ECHL)<br>China Sharks (Asia League Ice Hockey) |
| **Tampa Bay** | Norfolk Admirals (AHL) |
| **Toronto** | Toronto Marlies (AHL)<br>Reading Royals (ECHL) |
| **Vancouver** | Manitoba Moose (AHL)<br>Victoria Salmon Kings (ECHL) |
| **Washington** | Hershey Bears (AHL)<br>South Carolina Stingrays (ECHL) |

# NHL Players at the 2006 Olympic Winter Games

For the fourth time since 1997-98, the NHL's 2009-10 regular season will be interrupted in order to allow the League's players to represent their countries at the Olympic Winter Games in Vancouver. Since NHL players began to participate in the Olympics, this will mark the first time that the Winter Games have been held in an NHL city. (Calgary hosted the Games in 1988, ten years before NHL participation.)

Twelve teams, divided into three groups of four, will play for Olympic gold. Each team will play the three opponents in its group from Feb. 16 to Feb. 21. Canada, USA Switzerland and Norway will compete in Group A.; Russia, the Czech Republic, Slovakia and Latvia in Group B; and Sweden, Finland, Belarus and Germany in Group C.

At the conclusion of the Preliminary Round, all 12 teams will be ranked in one group. The top four teams will advance to the quaterfinals. The remaining teams play a single Qualification Playoff on Feb. 23: 5 vs.12, 6 vs.11, 7 vs.10 and 8 vs.9. The four winners qualify for the quarterfinals. Single-game playoffs will then determine the winner of the quarterfinals (Feb. 24), the semifinals (Feb. 26), the bronze medal game (Feb. 27) and the gold medal game (Feb. 28).

## 2010 Men's Olympic Hockey Schedule

*Start times listed in Pacific Standard Time (PST).*
*EST is +3 local time in Vancouver.*
*Europe is +9 local time in Vancouver.*

**Preliminary Round** (round robin)

| | | | | |
|---|---|---|---|---|
| Feb. 16 | USA | vs. | Switzerland | noon |
| | Canada | vs. | Norway | 4:30 pm |
| | Russia | vs. | Latvia | 9:00 pm |
| Feb. 17 | Finland | vs. | Belarus | noon |
| | Sweden | vs. | Germany | 4:30 pm |
| | Czech Republic | vs. | Slovakia | 9:00 pm |
| Feb. 18 | USA | vs. | Norway | noon |
| | Switzerland | vs. | Canada | 4:30 pm |
| | Slovakia | vs. | Russia | 9:00 pm |
| Feb. 19 | Belarus | vs. | Sweden | noon |
| | Czech Republic | vs. | Latvia | 4:30 pm |
| | Finland | vs. | Germany | 9:00 pm |
| Feb. 20 | Norway | vs. | Switzerland | noon |
| | Latvia | vs. | Slovakia | 4:30 pm |
| | Germany | vs. | Belarus | 9:00 pm |
| Feb. 21 | Russia | vs. | Czech Republic | noon |
| | Canada | vs. | USA | 4:45 pm |
| | Sweden | vs. | Finland | 9:00 pm |

**Qualification Playoff Round** (single elimination)

| | | |
|---|---|---|
| Feb. 23 | Qualification Playoff Game 1 | noon |
| | Qualification Playoff Game 2 | 4:30 pm |
| | Qualification Playoff Game 3 | 7:00 pm |
| | Qualification Playoff Game 3 | 9:00 pm |

Note: If in Qualification Round, USA to play at noon; Canada to play at 4:30 pm.

**Playoff Round** (single elimination)

| | | |
|---|---|---|
| Feb. 24 | Quarterfinal 1 | noon |
| | Quarterfinal 2 | 4:30 pm |
| | Quarterfinal 3 | 7:00 pm |
| | Quarterfinal 4 | 9:00 pm |

Note: If qualified, USA to play at noon or 9:00 pm; If qualified, Canada to play at 4:30 pm.

| | | |
|---|---|---|
| Feb. 26 | Semifinal | noon |
| | Semifinal | 6:30 pm |
| Feb. 27 | Bronze Medal Game | 7:00 pm |
| Feb. 28 | Gold Medal Game | 12:15 pm |

## 2010 Women's Olympic Hockey Schedule

*Start times listed in Pacific Standard Time (PST).*
*EST is +3 local time in Vancouver.*
*Europe is +9 local time in Vancouver.*

**Preliminary Round** (round robin)

| | | | | |
|---|---|---|---|---|
| Feb. 13 | Sweden | vs. | Switzerland | noon |
| | Canada | vs. | Slovakia | 5:00 pm |
| Feb. 14 | USA | vs. | China | noon |
| | Finland | vs. | Russia | 4:30 pm |
| Feb. 15 | Switzerland | vs. | Canada | 2:30 pm |
| | Sweden | vs. | Slovakia | 7:00 pm |
| Feb. 16 | Russia | vs. | USA | 2:30 pm |
| | Finland | vs. | China | 7:00 pm |
| Feb. 17 | Canada | vs. | Sweden | 2:30 pm |
| | Slovakia | vs. | Switzerland | 7:00 pm |
| Feb. 18 | USA | vs. | Finland | 2:30 pm |
| | China | vs. | Russia | 7:00 pm |

**Playoff Round** (single elimination)

| | | |
|---|---|---|
| Feb. 20 | Placement Game 1 | 2:30 pm |
| | Placement Game 2 | 7:00 pm |

Note: If qualified, Canada to play at 7:00 pm.

| | | |
|---|---|---|
| Feb. 22 | Semifinal | noon |
| | Placement Game 3 | 2:00 pm |
| | Semifinal | 5:00 pm |
| | Placement Game 4 | 7:00 pm |

Note: If qualified, USA to play at noon; Canada at 5:00.

**Finals**

| | | |
|---|---|---|
| Feb. 25 | Bronze Medal Game | 11:00 am |
| | Gold Medal Game | 3:30 pm |

### Cumulative Medal Standings, Women's Olympic Hockey, 1998-2006

| | G | S | B | Total | Last Medal |
|---|---|---|---|---|---|
| 1. Canada | 2 | 1 | 0 | 3 | Gold 06 |
| 2. USA | 1 | 1 | 1 | 3 | Bronze 06 |
| 3. Sweden | 0 | 1 | 1 | 2 | Silver 06 |
| 4. Finland | 0 | 0 | 1 | 1 | Bronze 98 |

### Cumulative Medal Standings, Men's Olympic Hockey, 1924-2006

| | G | S | B | Total | Last Medal |
|---|---|---|---|---|---|
| 1. USSR/Russia* | 8 | 2 | 2 | 12 | Bronze 02 |
| 2. Canada | 6 | 4 | 2 | 12 | Gold 02 |
| 3. USA | 2 | 6 | 1 | 9 | Silver 02 |
| 4. Czechoslovakia/Czech Rep. | 1 | 4 | 4 | 9 | Bronze 06 |
| 5. Sweden | 2 | 2 | 4 | 8 | Gold 06 |
| 6. Great Britain | 1 | 0 | 1 | 2 | Gold 36 |
| 7. Finland | 0 | 2 | 2 | 4 | Silver 06 |
| 8. W. Germany | 0 | 0 | 2 | 2 | Bronze 76 |
| 9. Switzerland | 0 | 0 | 2 | 2 | Bronze 48 |

** Soviet Union/Russia played as the Unified Team in 1992.*

## Torino, Italy • 2006

### Men

#### Preliminary Round

**Group A**

| Team | GP | W | L | T | GF | GA | Pts |
|---|---|---|---|---|---|---|---|
| Finland | 5 | 5 | 0 | 0 | 19 | 2 | 10 |
| Switzerland | 5 | 2 | 1 | 2 | 10 | 12 | 6 |
| Canada | 5 | 3 | 2 | 0 | 15 | 9 | 6 |
| Czech Republic | 5 | 2 | 3 | 0 | 14 | 12 | 4 |
| Germany | 5 | 0 | 3 | 2 | 7 | 16 | 2 |
| Italy | 5 | 0 | 3 | 2 | 9 | 23 | 2 |

**Group B**

| Team | GP | W | L | T | GF | GA | Pts |
|---|---|---|---|---|---|---|---|
| Slovakia | 5 | 5 | 0 | 0 | 18 | 8 | 10 |
| Russia | 5 | 4 | 1 | 0 | 23 | 11 | 8 |
| Sweden | 5 | 3 | 2 | 0 | 15 | 12 | 6 |
| United States | 5 | 1 | 3 | 1 | 13 | 13 | 3 |
| Kazakhstan | 5 | 1 | 4 | 0 | 9 | 16 | 2 |
| Latvia | 5 | 0 | 4 | 1 | 11 | 29 | 1 |

**Quarterfinals**

| | | | |
|---|---|---|---|
| Sweden | 6 | Switzerland | 2 |
| Finland | 4 | USA | 3 |
| Russia | 2 | Canada | 0 |
| Czech Republic | 3 | Slovakia | 1 |

**Semifinals**

| | | | |
|---|---|---|---|
| Sweden | 7 | Czech Republic | 3 |
| Finland | 4 | Russia | 0 |

**Bronze Medal game**

| | | | |
|---|---|---|---|
| Czech Republic | 3 | Russia | 0 |

**Gold Medal game**

| | | | |
|---|---|---|---|
| Sweden | 3 | Finland | 2 |

### 2006 Final Rankings, Men

1. Sweden
2. Finland
3. Czech Republic
4. Russia
5. Slovakia
6. Switzerland
7. Canada
8. United States
9. Kazakhstan
10. Germany
11. Italy
12. Latvia

### 2006 Scoring Leaders

| Player | Team | GP | G | A | PTS | PIM |
|---|---|---|---|---|---|---|
| Teemu Selänne | Finland | 8 | 6 | 5 | 11 | 4 |
| Saku Koivu | Finland | 8 | 3 | 8 | 11 | 12 |
| Daniel Alfredsson | Sweden | 8 | 5 | 5 | 10 | 4 |
| Marián Hossa | Slovakia | 6 | 5 | 5 | 10 | 4 |
| Ville Peltonen | Finland | 8 | 4 | 5 | 9 | 6 |
| Olli Jokinen | Finland | 8 | 6 | 2 | 8 | 2 |
| Jere Lehtinen | Finland | 8 | 3 | 5 | 8 | 0 |
| Mats Sundin | Sweden | 8 | 3 | 5 | 8 | 4 |
| Martin Straka | Czech Rep. | 8 | 2 | 6 | 8 | 6 |
| Pavel Datsyuk | Russia | 8 | 1 | 7 | 8 | 10 |

### 2006 Goaltending Leaders

(Minimum 150 Mins)

| Player | Team | GP | Min | GA | SO | GAA |
|---|---|---|---|---|---|---|
| Antero Niittymaki | Finland | 6 | 359 | 8 | 3 | 1.34 |
| Evgeni Nabokov | Russia | 7 | 359 | 8 | 3 | 1.34 |
| David Aebischer | Switz. | 4 | 200 | 7 | 0 | 2.10 |
| Peter Budaj | Slovakia | 3 | 179 | 6 | 0 | 2.01 |
| Martin Brodeur | Canada | 4 | 239 | 8 | 0 | 2.01 |

## Salt Lake City, Utah, USA • 2002

### Men

#### Preliminary Round

**Group A**

| Team | GP | W | L | T | GF | GA | Pts |
|---|---|---|---|---|---|---|---|
| Germany | 3 | 3 | 0 | 0 | 10 | 3 | 6 |
| Latvia | 3 | 1 | 1 | 1 | 11 | 12 | 3 |
| Austria | 3 | 1 | 2 | 0 | 7 | 9 | 2 |
| Slovakia | 3 | 0 | 2 | 1 | 8 | 12 | 1 |

**Group B**

| Team | GP | W | L | T | GF | GA | Pts |
|---|---|---|---|---|---|---|---|
| Belarus | 3 | 2 | 1 | 0 | 5 | 3 | 4 |
| Ukraine | 3 | 2 | 1 | 0 | 9 | 5 | 4 |
| Switzerland | 3 | 1 | 1 | 1 | 7 | 9 | 3 |
| France | 3 | 0 | 2 | 1 | 6 | 10 | 1 |

#### Final Round

**Group C**

| Team | GP | W | L | T | GF | GA | Pts |
|---|---|---|---|---|---|---|---|
| Sweden | 3 | 3 | 0 | 0 | 14 | 4 | 6 |
| Czech Rep. | 3 | 1 | 1 | 1 | 12 | 7 | 3 |
| Canada | 3 | 1 | 1 | 1 | 8 | 10 | 3 |
| Germany | 3 | 0 | 3 | 0 | 5 | 18 | 0 |

**Group D**

| Team | GP | W | L | T | GF | GA | Pts |
|---|---|---|---|---|---|---|---|
| USA | 3 | 2 | 0 | 1 | 16 | 3 | 5 |
| Finland | 3 | 2 | 1 | 0 | 11 | 8 | 4 |
| Russia | 3 | 1 | 1 | 1 | 9 | 9 | 3 |
| Belarus | 3 | 0 | 3 | 0 | 6 | 22 | 0 |

**Quarterfinals**

| | | | |
|---|---|---|---|
| Belarus | 4 | Sweden | 3 |
| Russia | 2 | Czech Republic | 1 |
| USA | 5 | Germany | 0 |
| Canada | 2 | Finland | 1 |

**Semifinals**

| | | | |
|---|---|---|---|
| Canada | 7 | Belarus | 1 |
| USA | 3 | Russia | 2 |

**Bronze Medal game**

| | | | |
|---|---|---|---|
| Russia | 7 | Belarus | 2 |

**Gold Medal game**

| | | | |
|---|---|---|---|
| Canada | 5 | USA | 2 |

### 2002 Final Rankings, Men

| | |
|---|---|
| 1 | Canada |
| 2 | USA |
| 3 | Russia |
| 4 | Belarus |
| 5-8 | Czech Republic |
| 5-8 | Finland |
| 5-8 | Germany |
| 5-8 | Sweden |
| 9 | Latvia |
| 10 | Ukraine |
| 11 | Switzerland |
| 12 | Austria |
| 13 | Slovakia |
| 14 | France |

### 2002 Scoring Leaders

| Player | Team | GP | G | A | PTS | PIM |
|---|---|---|---|---|---|---|
| Mats Sundin | Sweden | 4 | 5 | 4 | 9 | 10 |
| Brett Hull | USA | 6 | 3 | 5 | 8 | 6 |
| John LeClair | USA | 6 | 6 | 1 | 7 | 2 |
| Joe Sakic | Canada | 6 | 4 | 3 | 7 | 0 |
| Marian Hossa | Slovakia | 2 | 4 | 2 | 6 | 0 |
| J-J Aeschlimann | Switzerland | 4 | 3 | 3 | 6 | 2 |
| Philippe Bozon | France | 4 | 3 | 3 | 6 | 2 |
| Len Soccio | Germany | 7 | 3 | 3 | 6 | 8 |
| Mario Lemieux | Canada | 5 | 2 | 4 | 6 | 0 |
| Steve Yzerman | Canada | 6 | 2 | 4 | 6 | 2 |
| Nicklas Lidstrom | Sweden | 4 | 1 | 5 | 6 | 0 |
| Mike Modano | USA | 6 | 0 | 6 | 6 | 0 |

### 2002 Goaltending Leaders

(Minimum 150 Mins)

| Player | Team | GP | Min | GA | SO | GAA |
|---|---|---|---|---|---|---|
| Martin Gerber | Switzerland | 3 | 157 | 4 | 0 | 1.52 |
| Martin Brodeur | Canada | 5 | 300 | 9 | 0 | 1.80 |
| Dominik Hasek | Czech Rep. | 4 | 239 | 8 | 0 | 2.01 |
| Mike Richter | USA | 4 | 240 | 9 | 1 | 2.34 |
| N. Khabibulin | Russia | 6 | 359 | 14 | 1 | 2.34 |
| Tommy Salo | Sweden | 3 | 179 | 7 | 0 | 2.35 |

## Nagano, Japan • 1998

### Men

#### Preliminary Round

#### Group A

| Team | GP | W | L | T | GF | GA | Pts |
|---|---|---|---|---|---|---|---|
| Kazakhstan | 3 | 2 | 0 | 1 | 14 | 11 | 5 |
| Slovakia | 3 | 1 | 1 | 1 | 9 | 9 | 3 |
| Italy | 3 | 1 | 2 | 0 | 11 | 11 | 2 |
| Austria | 3 | 0 | 1 | 2 | 9 | 12 | 2 |

#### Group B

| Team | GP | W | L | T | GF | GA | Pts |
|---|---|---|---|---|---|---|---|
| Belarus | 3 | 2 | 0 | 1 | 14 | 4 | 5 |
| Germany | 3 | 2 | 1 | 0 | 7 | 9 | 4 |
| France | 3 | 1 | 2 | 0 | 5 | 8 | 2 |
| Japan | 3 | 0 | 2 | 1 | 5 | 10 | 1 |

#### Final Round

#### Group A

| Team | GP | W | L | T | GF | GA | Pts |
|---|---|---|---|---|---|---|---|
| Canada | 3 | 3 | 0 | 0 | 12 | 3 | 6 |
| Sweden | 3 | 2 | 1 | 0 | 11 | 7 | 4 |
| USA | 3 | 1 | 2 | 0 | 8 | 10 | 2 |
| Belarus | 3 | 0 | 3 | 0 | 4 | 15 | 0 |

#### Group B

| Team | GP | W | L | T | GF | GA | Pts |
|---|---|---|---|---|---|---|---|
| Russia | 3 | 3 | 0 | 0 | 15 | 6 | 6 |
| Czech Rep. | 3 | 2 | 1 | 0 | 12 | 4 | 4 |
| Finland | 3 | 1 | 2 | 0 | 11 | 9 | 2 |
| Kazakhstan | 3 | 0 | 3 | 0 | 6 | 25 | 0 |

#### Quarterfinals

| | | | |
|---|---|---|---|
| Canada | 4 | Kazakhstan | 1 |
| Czech Republic | 4 | USA | 1 |
| Finland | 2 | Sweden | 1 |
| Russia | 4 | Belarus | 1 |

#### Semifinals

*Note: SO = Shootout*

| | | | |
|---|---|---|---|
| Czech Republic | 2 | Canada | 1 (SO) |
| Russia | 7 | Finland | 4 |

#### Bronze Medal game

| | | | |
|---|---|---|---|
| Finland | 3 | Canada | 2 |

#### Gold Medal game

| | | | |
|---|---|---|---|
| Czech Republic | 1 | Russia | 0 |

#### 1998 Final Rankings, Men

1 Czech Republic
2 Russia
3 Finland
4 Canada
5–8 USA
5–8 Sweden
5–8 Belarus
5–8 Kazakhstan
9 Germany
10 Slovakia
11 France
12 Italy
13 Japan
14 Austria

#### 1998 Scoring Leaders

| Player | Team | GP | G | A | PTS | PIM |
|---|---|---|---|---|---|---|
| Teemu Selanne | Finland | 5 | 4 | 6 | 10 | 8 |
| Saku Koivu | Finland | 6 | 2 | 8 | 10 | 4 |
| Pavel Bure | Russia | 6 | 9 | 0 | 9 | 2 |
| Alex. Koreshkov | Kazakhstan | 7 | 3 | 6 | 9 | 2 |
| Phillipe Bozon | France | 4 | 5 | 2 | 7 | 4 |
| K. Shafranov | Kazakhstan | 7 | 4 | 3 | 7 | 6 |
| Dominik Lavoie | Austria | 4 | 5 | 1 | 6 | 8 |
| Jere Lehtinen | Finland | 6 | 4 | 2 | 6 | 2 |
| Alexei Yashin | Russia | 6 | 3 | 3 | 6 | 0 |
| Serge Poudrier | France | 6 | 2 | 4 | 6 | 4 |
| Sergei Fedorov | Russia | 6 | 1 | 5 | 6 | 8 |

#### 1998 Goaltending Leaders

(Minimum 150 Mins)

| Player | Team | GP | Min | GA | SO | GAA |
|---|---|---|---|---|---|---|
| Dominik Hasek | Czech Rep. | 6 | 369 | 6 | 2 | 0.97 |
| Patrick Roy | Canada | 6 | 369 | 9 | 1 | 1.46 |
| M. Shtalenkov | Russia | 5 | 290 | 8 | 0 | 1.65 |
| Tommy Salo | Sweden | 4 | 238 | 9 | 0 | 2.27 |
| Dusty Imoo | Japan | 3 | 189 | 8 | 0 | 2.54 |
| Mike Rosati | Italy | 4 | 215 | 12 | 0 | 3.35 |

## Lillehammer, Norway • 1994

#### Group A

| Team | GP | W | L | T | GF | GA | PTS |
|---|---|---|---|---|---|---|---|
| Finland | 5 | 5 | 0 | 0 | 25 | 4 | 10 |
| Germany | 5 | 3 | 2 | 0 | 11 | 14 | 6 |
| Czech Rep. | 5 | 3 | 2 | 0 | 16 | 11 | 6 |
| Russia | 5 | 3 | 2 | 0 | 20 | 14 | 6 |
| Austria | 5 | 1 | 4 | 0 | 13 | 28 | 2 |
| Norway | 5 | 0 | 5 | 0 | 5 | 19 | 0 |

#### Group B

| Team | GP | W | L | T | GF | GA | PTS |
|---|---|---|---|---|---|---|---|
| Slovakia | 5 | 3 | 0 | 2 | 26 | 14 | 8 |
| Canada | 5 | 3 | 1 | 1 | 17 | 11 | 7 |
| Sweden | 5 | 3 | 1 | 1 | 23 | 13 | 7 |
| USA | 5 | 1 | 1 | 3 | 21 | 17 | 5 |
| Italy | 5 | 1 | 4 | 0 | 15 | 31 | 2 |
| France | 5 | 0 | 4 | 1 | 11 | 27 | 1 |

#### Quarterfinals

| | | | |
|---|---|---|---|
| Canada | 3 | Czech Rep. | 2 |
| Finland | 6 | USA | 1 |
| Sweden | 3 | Germany | 0 |
| Russia | 3 | Slovakia | 2 |

#### Semifinals

| | | | |
|---|---|---|---|
| Canada | 5 | Finland | 3 |
| Sweden | 4 | Russia | 3 |

#### Bronze Medal Game

| | | | |
|---|---|---|---|
| Finland | 4 | Russia | 0 |

#### Gold Medal Game

*Note: SO = Shootout*

| | | | |
|---|---|---|---|
| Sweden | 3 | Canada | 2 (SO) |

#### 1994 Final Standings

1. Sweden
2. Canada
3. Finland
4. Russia
5. Czech Republic
6. Slovakia
7. Germany
8. USA
9. Italy
10. France
11. Norway
12. Austria

#### 1994 Scoring Leaders

| Player | Team | GP | G | A | PTS | PIM |
|---|---|---|---|---|---|---|
| Ziggy Palffy | Slovakia | 8 | 3 | 7 | 10 | 8 |
| Miroslav Satan | Slovakia | 8 | 9 | 0 | 9 | 0 |
| Peter Stastny | Slovakia | 8 | 5 | 4 | 9 | 9 |
| Hakan Loob | Sweden | 8 | 4 | 5 | 9 | 2 |
| Gates Orlando | Italy | 7 | 3 | 6 | 9 | 41 |
| Patrik Juhlin | Sweden | 8 | 7 | 1 | 8 | 16 |
| Jiri Kucera | Czech Rep. | 8 | 6 | 2 | 8 | 4 |
| Marty Dallman | Austria | 7 | 4 | 4 | 8 | 8 |
| Mika Nieminen | Finland | 8 | 3 | 5 | 8 | 0 |
| David Sacco | USA | 8 | 3 | 5 | 8 | 12 |
| Peter Forsberg | Sweden | 8 | 2 | 6 | 8 | 6 |

## Albertville, France • 1992

#### Group A

| Team | GP | W | L | T | GF | GA | PTS |
|---|---|---|---|---|---|---|---|
| USA | 5 | 4 | 0 | 1 | 18 | 7 | 9 |
| Sweden | 5 | 3 | 0 | 2 | 22 | 11 | 8 |
| Finland | 5 | 3 | 0 | 1 | 22 | 11 | 7 |
| Germany | 5 | 2 | 3 | 0 | 11 | 12 | 4 |
| Italy | 5 | 1 | 4 | 0 | 18 | 24 | 2 |
| Poland | 5 | 0 | 5 | 0 | 4 | 30 | 0 |

#### Group B

| Team | GP | W | L | T | GF | GA | PTS |
|---|---|---|---|---|---|---|---|
| Canada | 5 | 4 | 1 | 0 | 28 | 9 | 8 |
| Unified Team* | 5 | 4 | 1 | 0 | 32 | 10 | 8 |
| Czech. | 5 | 4 | 1 | 0 | 25 | 15 | 8 |
| France | 5 | 2 | 3 | 0 | 14 | 22 | 4 |
| Switzerland | 5 | 1 | 4 | 0 | 13 | 25 | 2 |
| Norway | 5 | 0 | 5 | 0 | 7 | 38 | 0 |

* Soviet Union/Russia played as Unified Team in 1992.

#### Medal Round

*Note: SO = Shootout*

| | | | |
|---|---|---|---|
| Canada | 4 | Germany | 3 (SO) |
| Czechoslovakia | 3 | Sweden | 1 |
| USA | 4 | France | 1 |
| Unified Team | 6 | Finland | 1 |

#### Semifinals

| | | | |
|---|---|---|---|
| Canada | 4 | Czechoslovakia | 2 |
| Unified Team | 5 | USA | 2 |

#### Bronze Medal Game

| | | | |
|---|---|---|---|
| Czechoslovakia | 6 | USA | 1 |

#### Gold Medal Game

| | | | |
|---|---|---|---|
| Unified Team | 3 | Canada | 1 |

#### 1992 Final Rankings

1. Unified Team
2. Canada
3. Czechoslovakia
4. USA
5. Sweden
6. Germany
7. Finland
8. France
9. Norway
10. Switzerland
11. Poland
12. Italy

#### 1992 Scoring Leaders

| Player | Team | GP | G | A | PTS | PIM |
|---|---|---|---|---|---|---|
| Joe Juneau | Canada | 8 | 6 | 9 | 15 | 5 |
| Andrei Khomutov | Unified | 8 | 7 | 7 | 14 | 2 |
| Robert Lang | Czech. | 8 | 5 | 8 | 13 | 8 |
| Teemu Selanne | Finland | 8 | 7 | 4 | 11 | 6 |
| Eric Lindros | Canada | 8 | 5 | 6 | 11 | 5 |
| H. Jarvenpaa | Finland | 8 | 5 | 6 | 11 | 14 |
| V. Bykov | Unified | 8 | 4 | 7 | 11 | 2 |
| Yuri Khmylev | Unified | 8 | 4 | 6 | 10 | 4 |
| Mika Nieminen | Finland | 8 | 4 | 6 | 10 | 6 |
| N. Borschevsky | Unified | 8 | 7 | 2 | 9 | 0 |

## Calgary, Alberta, Canada • 1988

#### Group A

| Team | GP | W | L | T | GF | GA | PTS |
|---|---|---|---|---|---|---|---|
| Finland | 5 | 3 | 1 | 1 | 22 | 8 | 7 |
| Sweden | 5 | 2 | 0 | 3 | 23 | 10 | 7 |
| Canada | 5 | 3 | 1 | 1 | 17 | 12 | 7 |
| Switzerland | 5 | 3 | 2 | 0 | 19 | 10 | 6 |
| Poland | 5 | 0 | 4 | 1 | 3 | 13 | 1 |
| France | 5 | 1 | 4 | 0 | 10 | 41 | 0 |

#### Group B

| Team | GP | W | L | T | GF | GA | PTS |
|---|---|---|---|---|---|---|---|
| Soviet Union | 5 | 5 | 0 | 0 | 32 | 10 | 10 |
| W. Germany | 5 | 4 | 1 | 0 | 19 | 12 | 8 |
| Czech. | 5 | 3 | 2 | 0 | 23 | 14 | 6 |
| USA | 5 | 2 | 3 | 0 | 27 | 27 | 4 |
| Austria | 5 | 0 | 4 | 1 | 12 | 29 | 1 |
| Norway | 5 | 0 | 4 | 1 | 11 | 32 | 1 |

#### Final Round

| Team | GP | W | L | T | GF | GA | PTS |
|---|---|---|---|---|---|---|---|
| Soviet Union | 5 | 4 | 1 | 0 | 25 | 7 | 8 |
| Finland | 5 | 3 | 1 | 1 | 18 | 10 | 7 |
| Sweden | 5 | 2 | 1 | 2 | 15 | 16 | 6 |
| Canada | 5 | 2 | 2 | 1 | 17 | 14 | 5 |
| W. Germany | 5 | 1 | 4 | 0 | 8 | 26 | 2 |
| Czech. | 5 | 1 | 4 | 0 | 12 | 22 | 2 |

#### 1988 Final Rankings

1. Soviet Union
2. Finland
3. Sweden
4. Canada
5. W. Germany
6. Czechoslovakia
7. USA
8. Switzerland
9. Austria
10. Poland
11. France
12. Norway

#### 1988 Scoring Leaders

| Player | Team | GP | G | A | PTS | PIM |
|---|---|---|---|---|---|---|
| Vladimir Krutov | Soviet Union | 8 | 6 | 9 | 15 | 0 |
| Igor Larionov | Soviet Union | 8 | 4 | 9 | 13 | 4 |
| V. Fetisov | Soviet Union | 8 | 4 | 9 | 13 | 6 |
| Corey Millen | USA | 6 | 6 | 5 | 11 | 4 |
| Dusan Pasek | Czech. | 8 | 6 | 5 | 11 | 8 |
| Sergei Makarov | Soviet Union | 8 | 3 | 8 | 11 | 10 |
| Erkki Lehtonen | Finland | 8 | 4 | 6 | 10 | 2 |
| Anders Eldebrink | Sweden | 8 | 4 | 6 | 10 | 4 |
| Igor Liba | Czech. | 8 | 4 | 6 | 10 | 8 |
| Gerd Truntschka | W. Germany | 8 | 3 | 7 | 10 | 10 |
| Raimo Helminen | Finland | 7 | 2 | 8 | 10 | 4 |

## Sarajevo, Yugoslavia • 1984

#### Group A

| Team | GP | W | L | T | GF | GA | PTS |
|---|---|---|---|---|---|---|---|
| Soviet Union | 5 | 5 | 0 | 0 | 42 | 5 | 10 |
| Sweden | 5 | 3 | 1 | 1 | 34 | 15 | 7 |
| W. Germany | 5 | 3 | 1 | 1 | 27 | 17 | 7 |
| Poland | 5 | 1 | 4 | 0 | 16 | 37 | 2 |
| Italy | 5 | 1 | 4 | 0 | 15 | 31 | 2 |
| Yugoslavia | 5 | 1 | 4 | 0 | 8 | 37 | 2 |

#### Group B

| Team | GP | W | L | T | GF | GA | PTS |
|---|---|---|---|---|---|---|---|
| Czech. | 5 | 5 | 0 | 0 | 38 | 7 | 10 |
| Canada | 5 | 4 | 1 | 0 | 24 | 10 | 8 |
| Finland | 5 | 2 | 2 | 1 | 27 | 19 | 5 |
| USA | 5 | 1 | 2 | 2 | 16 | 17 | 4 |
| Austria | 5 | 1 | 4 | 0 | 13 | 37 | 2 |
| Norway | 5 | 0 | 4 | 1 | 15 | 43 | 1 |

#### Final Round

| Team | GP | W | L | | GF | GA | PTS |
|---|---|---|---|---|---|---|---|
| Soviet Union | 3 | 3 | 0 | 0 | 16 | 1 | 6 |
| Czech. | 3 | 2 | 1 | 0 | 6 | 2 | 4 |
| Sweden | 3 | 1 | 2 | 0 | 3 | 12 | 2 |
| Canada | 3 | 0 | 3 | 0 | 0 | 10 | 0 |

#### Consolation Round

| Team | GP | W | L | T | GF | GA | PTS |
|---|---|---|---|---|---|---|---|
| W. Germany | 1 | 1 | 0 | 0 | 7 | 4 | 2 |
| USA | 1 | 1 | 0 | 0 | 7 | 4 | 2 |
| Finland | 1 | 0 | 1 | 0 | 4 | 7 | 0 |
| Poland | 1 | 0 | 1 | 0 | 4 | 7 | 0 |

#### 1984 Final Rankings

1. Soviet Union
2. Czechoslovakia
3. Sweden
4. Canada
5. W. Germany
6. Finland
7. USA
8. Poland

#### 1984 Scoring Leaders

| Player | Team | GP | G | A | PTS | PIM |
|---|---|---|---|---|---|---|
| Erich Kuhnhackl | W. Germany | 6 | 8 | 6 | 14 | 12 |
| Peter Gradin | Sweden | 7 | 9 | 4 | 13 | 6 |
| N. Drozdetski | Soviet Union | 7 | 10 | 2 | 12 | 2 |
| V. Fetisov | Soviet Union | 7 | 3 | 8 | 11 | 8 |
| Petri Skriko | Finland | 6 | 6 | 4 | 10 | 8 |
| Vladimir Ruzicka | Czech. | 7 | 4 | 6 | 10 | 0 |
| R. Summanen | Finland | 6 | 4 | 6 | 10 | 4 |
| Darius Rusnak | Czech. | 7 | 4 | 6 | 10 | 6 |
| Jiri Hrdina | Czech. | 7 | 4 | 6 | 10 | 10 |
| Vincent Lukac | Czech. | 7 | 4 | 5 | 9 | 2 |
| Viktor Tjumenev | Soviet Union | 6 | 0 | 9 | 9 | 2 |

## Lake Placid, NY, USA • 1980

#### Red Division

| Team | GP | W | L | T | GF | GA | PTS |
|---|---|---|---|---|---|---|---|
| Soviet Union | 5 | 5 | 0 | 0 | 51 | 11 | 10 |
| Finland | 5 | 3 | 2 | 0 | 26 | 18 | 6 |
| Canada | 5 | 3 | 2 | 0 | 28 | 12 | 6 |
| Poland | 5 | 2 | 3 | 0 | 15 | 23 | 4 |
| Holland | 5 | 1 | 3 | 1 | 16 | 43 | 3 |
| Japan | 5 | 0 | 4 | 1 | 7 | 36 | 1 |

#### Blue Division

| Team | GP | W | L | T | GF | GA | PTS |
|---|---|---|---|---|---|---|---|
| Sweden | 5 | 4 | 0 | 1 | 26 | 7 | 9 |
| USA | 5 | 4 | 0 | 1 | 25 | 10 | 9 |
| Czech. | 5 | 3 | 2 | 0 | 34 | 16 | 6 |
| Romania | 5 | 1 | 3 | 1 | 13 | 29 | 3 |
| W. Germany | 5 | 1 | 4 | 0 | 21 | 30 | 2 |
| Norway | 5 | 0 | 4 | 1 | 9 | 36 | 1 |

#### Final Round

| Team | GP | W | L | T | GF | GA | PTS |
|---|---|---|---|---|---|---|---|
| USA | 3 | 2 | 0 | 1 | 10 | 7 | 5 |
| Soviet Union | 3 | 2 | 1 | 0 | 16 | 8 | 4 |
| Sweden | 3 | 0 | 1 | 2 | 7 | 14 | 2 |
| Finland | 3 | 0 | 2 | 1 | 7 | 11 | 1 |

#### 1980 Final Rankings

1. USA
2. Soviet Union
3. Sweden
4. Finland
5. Czechoslovakia
6. Canada

7. Poland
8. Holland
9. Romania
10. W. Germany
11. Norway
12. Japan

### 1980 Scoring Leaders

| Player | Team | GP | G | A | PTS | PIM |
|---|---|---|---|---|---|---|
| Milan Novy | Czech. | 6 | 7 | 8 | 15 | 0 |
| Peter Stastny | Czech. | 6 | 7 | 7 | 14 | 6 |
| Jaroslav Pouzar | Czech. | 6 | 8 | 5 | 13 | 8 |
| Alexander Golikov | Soviet Union | 7 | 7 | 6 | 13 | 6 |
| Jukka Porvari | Finland | 7 | 7 | 4 | 11 | 4 |
| Boris Mikhailov | Soviet Union | 7 | 6 | 5 | 11 | 2 |
| Vladimir Krutov | Soviet Union | 7 | 6 | 5 | 11 | 4 |
| Sergei Makarov | Soviet Union | 7 | 5 | 6 | 11 | 2 |
| Marian Stastny | Czech. | 6 | 5 | 6 | 11 | 4 |
| Mark Johnson | USA | 7 | 5 | 6 | 11 | 6 |

## Innsbruck, Austria • 1976

### Group A

| Team | GP | W | L | T | GF | GA | PTS |
|---|---|---|---|---|---|---|---|
| Soviet Union | 5 | 5 | 0 | 0 | 40 | 11 | 10 |
| Czech. | 5 | 3 | 2 | 0 | 17 | 10 | 6 |
| W. Germany | 5 | 2 | 3 | 0 | 21 | 24 | 4 |
| Finland | 5 | 2 | 3 | 0 | 19 | 18 | 4 |
| USA | 5 | 2 | 3 | 0 | 15 | 21 | 4 |
| Poland | 5 | 0 | 5 | 0 | 9 | 37 | 0 |

### Group B

| Team | GP | W | L | T | GF | GA | PTS |
|---|---|---|---|---|---|---|---|
| Romania | 5 | 4 | 1 | 0 | 23 | 15 | 8 |
| Austria | 5 | 3 | 2 | 0 | 18 | 14 | 6 |
| Japan | 5 | 3 | 2 | 0 | 20 | 18 | 6 |
| Yugoslavia | 5 | 3 | 2 | 0 | 22 | 19 | 6 |
| Switzerland | 5 | 2 | 3 | 0 | 24 | 22 | 4 |
| Bulgaria | 5 | 0 | 5 | 0 | 19 | 38 | 0 |

### 1976 Final Rankings

1. Soviet Union
2. Czechoslovakia
3. W. Germany
4. Finland
5. USA
6. Poland
7. Romania
8. Austria
9. Japan
10. Yugoslavia
11. Switzerland
12. Bulgaria

### 1976 Scoring Leaders

| Player | Team | GP | G | A | PTS | PIM |
|---|---|---|---|---|---|---|
| Vladimir Shadrin | Soviet Union | 5 | 6 | 4 | 10 | 0 |
| Alexander Maltsev | Soviet Union | 5 | 5 | 5 | 10 | 0 |
| Victor Shalimov | Soviet Union | 5 | 5 | 5 | 10 | 2 |
| Erich Kuhnhackl | W. Germany | 5 | 5 | 5 | 10 | 10 |
| Valeri Kharlamov | Soviet Union | 5 | 3 | 6 | 9 | 6 |
| Ernst Kopf | W. Germany | 5 | 3 | 5 | 8 | 2 |
| Vladimir Petrov | Soviet Union | 5 | 4 | 3 | 7 | 8 |
| A. Yakushev | Soviet Union | 5 | 3 | 4 | 7 | 2 |
| Bob Dobek | USA | 5 | 3 | 4 | 7 | 4 |
| Lorenz Funk | W. Germany | 5 | 2 | 5 | 7 | 4 |
| Victor Zhluktov | Soviet Union | 5 | 1 | 6 | 7 | 2 |

## Sapporo, Japan • 1972

### Group A

| Team | GP | W | L | T | GF | GA | PTS |
|---|---|---|---|---|---|---|---|
| Soviet Union | 5 | 4 | 0 | 1 | 33 | 13 | 9 |
| USA | 5 | 3 | 2 | 0 | 18 | 15 | 6 |
| Czech. | 5 | 3 | 2 | 0 | 26 | 13 | 6 |
| Sweden | 5 | 2 | 2 | 1 | 17 | 13 | 5 |
| Finland | 5 | 2 | 3 | 0 | 14 | 24 | 4 |
| Poland | 5 | 0 | 5 | 0 | 9 | 39 | 0 |

### Group B

| Team | GP | W | L | T | GF | GA | PTS |
|---|---|---|---|---|---|---|---|
| W. Germany | 4 | 3 | 1 | 0 | 22 | 10 | 6 |
| Norway | 4 | 3 | 1 | 0 | 16 | 14 | 6 |
| Japan | 4 | 2 | 1 | 1 | 17 | 16 | 5 |
| Switzerland | 4 | 0 | 2 | 2 | 9 | 16 | 2 |
| Yugoslavia | 4 | 0 | 3 | 1 | 9 | 17 | 1 |

### 1972 Final Rankings

1. Soviet Union
2. USA
3. Czechoslovakia
4. Sweden
5. Finland
6. Poland
7. W. Germany
8. Norway
9. Japan
10. Switzerland
11. Yugoslavia

### 1972 Scoring Leaders

| Player | Team | GP | G | A | PTS | PIM |
|---|---|---|---|---|---|---|
| Valeri Kharlamov | Soviet Union | 5 | 9 | 6 | 15 | 2 |
| V. Nedomansky | Czech. | 5 | 6 | 3 | 9 | 0 |
| Vladimir Vikulov | Soviet Union | 5 | 5 | 4 | 9 | 0 |
| Craig Sarner | USA | 5 | 4 | 5 | 9 | 0 |
| Kevin Ahearn | USA | 5 | 4 | 3 | 7 | 0 |
| Alexander Maltsev | Soviet Union | 5 | 4 | 3 | 7 | 0 |
| Anatoli Firsov | Soviet Union | 5 | 2 | 5 | 7 | 0 |
| Yuri Blinov | Soviet Union | 5 | 3 | 3 | 6 | 0 |
| Jiri Kochta | Czech. | 5 | 3 | 3 | 6 | 0 |
| Richard Farda | Czech. | 5 | 1 | 5 | 6 | 0 |

## Grenoble, France • 1968

### Group A

| Team | GP | W | L | T | GF | GA | PTS |
|---|---|---|---|---|---|---|---|
| Soviet Union | 7 | 6 | 1 | 0 | 48 | 10 | 12 |
| Czech. | 7 | 5 | 1 | 1 | 33 | 17 | 11 |
| Canada | 7 | 5 | 2 | 0 | 28 | 15 | 10 |
| Sweden | 7 | 4 | 2 | 1 | 23 | 18 | 9 |
| Finland | 7 | 3 | 3 | 1 | 17 | 23 | 7 |
| USA | 7 | 2 | 4 | 1 | 23 | 28 | 5 |
| W. Germany | 7 | 1 | 6 | 0 | 13 | 39 | 2 |
| E. Germany | 7 | 0 | 7 | 0 | 13 | 48 | 0 |

### Group B

| Team | GP | W | L | T | GF | GA | PTS |
|---|---|---|---|---|---|---|---|
| Yugoslavia | 5 | 5 | 0 | 0 | 33 | 9 | 10 |
| Japan | 5 | 4 | 1 | 0 | 27 | 12 | 8 |
| Norway | 5 | 3 | 2 | 0 | 15 | 15 | 6 |
| Romania | 5 | 2 | 3 | 0 | 22 | 23 | 4 |
| Austria | 5 | 1 | 4 | 0 | 12 | 27 | 2 |
| France | 5 | 0 | 5 | 0 | 9 | 32 | 0 |

### 1968 Final Rankings

1. Soviet Union
2. Czechoslovakia
3. Canada
4. Sweden
5. Finland
6. USA
7. W. Germany
8. E. Germany
9. Yugoslavia
10. Japan
11. Norway
12. Romania
13. Austria
14. France

### 1968 Scoring Leaders

| Player | Team | GP | G | A | PTS | PIM |
|---|---|---|---|---|---|---|
| Anatoli Firsov | Soviet Union | 7 | 12 | 4 | 16 | 4 |
| Vladimir Vikulov | Soviet Union | 7 | 2 | 10 | 12 | 2 |
| Vyatch. Starshinov | Soviet Union | 7 | 6 | 6 | 12 | 2 |
| Victor Populanov | Soviet Union | 7 | 6 | 6 | 12 | 10 |
| Josef Golonka | Czech. | 7 | 4 | 6 | 10 | 8 |
| Jan Hrbaty | Czech. | 7 | 2 | 7 | 9 | 2 |
| Fran Huck | Canada | 7 | 4 | 5 | 9 | 10 |
| Marshall Johnston | Canada | 7 | 2 | 6 | 8 | 4 |
| Jack Morrison | USA | 7 | 2 | 6 | 8 | 10 |
| V. Nedomansky | Czech. | 7 | 5 | 2 | 7 | 4 |

## Innsbruck, Austria • 1964

### Group A

| Team | GP | W | L | T | GF | GA | PTS |
|---|---|---|---|---|---|---|---|
| Soviet Union | 7 | 7 | 0 | 0 | 54 | 10 | 14 |
| Sweden | 7 | 5 | 2 | 0 | 47 | 16 | 10 |
| Czech. | 7 | 5 | 2 | 0 | 38 | 19 | 10 |
| Canada | 7 | 5 | 2 | 0 | 32 | 17 | 10 |
| USA | 7 | 2 | 5 | 0 | 29 | 33 | 4 |
| Finland | 7 | 2 | 5 | 0 | 10 | 31 | 4 |
| W. Germany | 7 | 2 | 5 | 0 | 13 | 49 | 4 |
| Switzerland | 7 | 0 | 7 | 0 | 9 | 57 | 0 |

### Group B

| Team | GP | W | L | T | GF | GA | PTS |
|---|---|---|---|---|---|---|---|
| Poland | 7 | 6 | 1 | 0 | 40 | 13 | 12 |
| Norway | 7 | 5 | 2 | 0 | 40 | 19 | 10 |
| Japan | 7 | 4 | 2 | 1 | 35 | 31 | 9 |
| Romania | 7 | 3 | 3 | 1 | 31 | 28 | 7 |
| Austria | 7 | 3 | 3 | 1 | 24 | 28 | 7 |
| Yugoslavia | 7 | 3 | 3 | 1 | 29 | 37 | 7 |
| Italy | 7 | 2 | 5 | 0 | 24 | 42 | 4 |
| Hungary | 7 | 0 | 7 | 0 | 14 | 39 | 0 |

### 1964 Final Rankings

1. Soviet Union
2. Sweden
3. Czechoslovakia
4. Canada
5. USA
6. Finland
7. W. Germany
8. Switzerland
9. Poland
10. Norway
11. Japan
12. Romania
13. Austria
14. Yugoslavia
15. Italy
16. Hungary

### 1964 Scoring Leaders

| Player | Team | GP | G | A | PTS | PIM |
|---|---|---|---|---|---|---|
| Sven Tumba | Sweden | 7 | 8 | 3 | 11 | 0 |
| Ulf Sterner | Sweden | 7 | 6 | 5 | 11 | 0 |
| Victor Yakushev | Soviet Union | 7 | 7 | 3 | 10 | 0 |
| Boris Mayorov | Soviet Union | 7 | 7 | 3 | 10 | 0 |
| Jiri Dolana | Czech. | 7 | 7 | 3 | 10 | 0 |
| Vy. Starshinov | Soviet Union | 7 | 7 | 3 | 10 | 6 |
| Josef Cerny | Czech. | 7 | 5 | 5 | 10 | 2 |
| A. Andersson | Sweden | 7 | 7 | 2 | 9 | 8 |
| K. Loktev | Soviet Union | 7 | 4 | 5 | 9 | 8 |
| Gary Dineen | Canada | 7 | 3 | 6 | 9 | 10 |

## Squaw Valley, CA, USA • 1960

### Group A

| Team | GP | W | L | T | GF | GA | PTS |
|---|---|---|---|---|---|---|---|
| Canada | 2 | 2 | 0 | 0 | 24 | 3 | 4 |
| Sweden | 2 | 1 | 1 | 0 | 21 | 5 | 2 |
| Japan | 2 | 0 | 2 | 0 | 1 | 38 | 0 |

### Group B

| Team | GP | W | L | T | GF | GA | PTS |
|---|---|---|---|---|---|---|---|
| Soviet Union | 2 | 2 | 0 | 0 | 16 | 4 | 4 |
| W. Germany | 2 | 1 | 1 | 0 | 4 | 9 | 2 |
| Finland | 2 | 0 | 2 | 0 | 5 | 12 | 0 |

### Group C

| Team | GP | W | L | T | GF | GA | PTS |
|---|---|---|---|---|---|---|---|
| USA | 2 | 2 | 0 | 0 | 19 | 6 | 4 |
| Czech. | 2 | 1 | 1 | 0 | 23 | 6 | 2 |
| Australia | 2 | 0 | 2 | 0 | 2 | 30 | 0 |

### Final Round

| Team | GP | W | L | T | GF | GA | PTS |
|---|---|---|---|---|---|---|---|
| USA | 5 | 5 | 0 | 0 | 29 | 11 | 10 |
| Canada | 5 | 4 | 1 | 0 | 31 | 12 | 8 |
| Soviet Union | 5 | 2 | 2 | 1 | 24 | 19 | 5 |
| Czech. | 5 | 2 | 3 | 0 | 21 | 23 | 4 |
| Sweden | 5 | 1 | 3 | 1 | 19 | 19 | 3 |
| W. Germany | 5 | 0 | 5 | 0 | 5 | 45 | 0 |

### Consolation Round

| Team | GP | W | L | T | GF | GA | PTS |
|---|---|---|---|---|---|---|---|
| Finland | 4 | 3 | 0 | 1 | 50 | 11 | 7 |
| Japan | 4 | 2 | 1 | 1 | 32 | 22 | 5 |
| Australia | 4 | 0 | 4 | 0 | 8 | 57 | 0 |

### 1960 Final Rankings

1. USA
2. Canada
3. Soviet Union
4. Czechoslovakia
5. Sweden
6. W. Germany
7. Finland
8. Japan
9. Australia

### 1960 Scoring Leaders

| Player | Team | GP | G | A | PTS | PIM |
|---|---|---|---|---|---|---|
| Fred Etcher | Canada | 7 | 9 | 12 | 21 | 0 |
| Bobby Attersley | Canada | 7 | 6 | 12 | 18 | 4 |
| Bill Cleary | USA | 7 | 7 | 7 | 14 | 2 |
| Bill Christian | USA | 7 | 2 | 11 | 13 | 2 |
| G. Samolenko | Canada | 7 | 8 | 4 | 12 | 0 |
| Lars E. Lundvall | Sweden | 7 | 8 | 4 | 12 | 2 |
| Vaclav Panucek | Czech. | 7 | 7 | 5 | 12 | 0 |
| John Mayasich | USA | 7 | 7 | 5 | 12 | 2 |
| Nisse Nilsson | Sweden | 7 | 7 | 5 | 12 | 4 |
| V. Alexandrov | Soviet Union | 7 | 7 | 5 | 12 | 8 |
| Butch Martin | Canada | 7 | 6 | 6 | 12 | 14 |
| Ronald Petersson | Sweden | 7 | 4 | 8 | 12 | 2 |

## Cortina d'Ampezzo, Italy • 1956

### Group A

| Team | GP | W | L | T | GF | GA | PTS |
|---|---|---|---|---|---|---|---|
| Canada | 3 | 3 | 0 | 0 | 30 | 1 | 6 |
| W. Germany | 3 | 1 | 1 | 1 | 9 | 6 | 3 |
| Italy | 3 | 0 | 1 | 2 | 5 | 7 | 2 |
| Austria | 3 | 0 | 2 | 1 | 2 | 32 | 1 |

### Group B

| Team | GP | W | L | T | GF | GA | PTS |
|---|---|---|---|---|---|---|---|
| Czech. | 2 | 2 | 0 | 0 | 12 | 6 | 4 |
| USA | 2 | 1 | 1 | 0 | 7 | 4 | 2 |
| Poland | 2 | 0 | 2 | 0 | 3 | 12 | 0 |

### Group C

| Team | GP | W | L | T | GF | GA | PTS |
|---|---|---|---|---|---|---|---|
| Soviet Union | 2 | 2 | 0 | 0 | 15 | 4 | 4 |
| Sweden | 2 | 1 | 1 | 0 | 7 | 10 | 2 |
| Switzerland | 2 | 0 | 2 | 0 | 8 | 16 | 0 |

### Final Round

| Team | GP | W | L | T | GF | GA | PTS |
|---|---|---|---|---|---|---|---|
| Soviet Union | 5 | 5 | 0 | 0 | 25 | 5 | 10 |
| USA | 5 | 4 | 1 | 0 | 26 | 12 | 8 |
| Canada | 5 | 3 | 2 | 0 | 23 | 11 | 6 |
| Sweden | 5 | 1 | 3 | 1 | 10 | 17 | 3 |
| Czech. | 5 | 1 | 4 | 0 | 20 | 30 | 2 |
| W. Germany | 5 | 0 | 4 | 1 | 6 | 35 | 1 |

### Consolation Round

| Team | GP | W | L | T | GF | GA | PTS |
|---|---|---|---|---|---|---|---|
| Italy | 3 | 3 | 0 | 0 | 21 | 7 | 6 |
| Poland | 3 | 2 | 1 | 0 | 12 | 10 | 4 |
| Switzerland | 3 | 1 | 2 | 0 | 12 | 8 | 2 |
| Austria | 3 | 0 | 3 | 0 | 9 | 19 | 0 |

### 1956 Final Rankings

1. Soviet Union
2. USA
3. Canada
4. Sweden
5. Czechoslovakia
6. W. Germany
7. Italy
8. Poland
9. Switzerland
10. Austria

### 1956 Scoring Leaders

| Player | Team | GP | G | A | PTS | PIM |
|---|---|---|---|---|---|---|
| Jim Logan | Canada | 8 | 7 | 5 | 12 | 2 |
| Paul Knox | Canada | 8 | 7 | 5 | 12 | 2 |
| Vsevolod Bobrov | Soviet Union | 7 | 9 | 2 | 11 | 4 |
| Gerry Theberge | Canada | 8 | 9 | 2 | 11 | 8 |
| Jack McKenzie | Canada | 8 | 7 | 4 | 11 | 4 |
| John Mayasich | USA | 7 | 7 | 3 | 10 | 2 |
| Alexei Guryshev | Soviet Union | 7 | 7 | 2 | 9 | 0 |
| Vlastimil Bubnik | Czech. | 7 | 5 | 4 | 9 | 14 |
| George Scholes | Canada | 8 | 5 | 3 | 8 | 2 |

## Oslo, Norway • 1952

| Team | GP | W | L | T | GF | GA | PTS |
|---|---|---|---|---|---|---|---|
| Canada | 8 | 7 | 0 | 1 | 71 | 1 | 15 |
| USA | 8 | 6 | 1 | 1 | 43 | 21 | 13 |
| Sweden | 8 | 6 | 2 | 0 | 48 | 19 | 12 |
| Czech. | 8 | 6 | 2 | 0 | 47 | 18 | 12 |
| Switzerland | 8 | 4 | 4 | 0 | 40 | 40 | 8 |
| Poland | 8 | 2 | 5 | 1 | 21 | 56 | 5 |
| Finland | 8 | 2 | 6 | 0 | 21 | 60 | 4 |
| W. Germany | 8 | 1 | 6 | 1 | 21 | 53 | 3 |
| Norway | 8 | 0 | 8 | 0 | 15 | 46 | 0 |

### 1952 Final Rankings

1. Canada
2. USA
3. Sweden
4. Czechoslovakia
5. Switzerland
6. Poland
7. Finland
8. W. Germany
9. Norway

## St. Moritz, Switzerland • 1948

| Team | GP | W | L | T | GF | GA | PTS |
|---|---|---|---|---|---|---|---|
| Canada | 7 | 6 | 0 | 1 | 57 | 2 | 13 |
| Czech. | 7 | 6 | 0 | 1 | 76 | 15 | 13 |
| Switzerland | 7 | 5 | 2 | 0 | 62 | 17 | 10 |
| Sweden | 7 | 4 | 3 | 0 | 53 | 23 | 8 |
| Great Britain | 7 | 3 | 4 | 0 | 36 | 43 | 6 |
| Poland | 7 | 2 | 5 | 0 | 25 | 74 | 4 |
| Austria | 7 | 1 | 6 | 0 | 31 | 64 | 2 |
| Italy | 7 | 0 | 7 | 0 | 23 | 125 | 0 |

* USA also competed as an unofficial entry.

### 1948 Final Rankings

1. Canada
2. Czechoslovakia
3. Switzerland
4. Sweden
5. Great Britain
6. Poland
7. Austria
8. Italy

## Garmisch-Partenkirchen, Germany • 1936

### Group A

| Team | GP | W | L | T | GF | GA | PTS |
|---|---|---|---|---|---|---|---|
| Canada | 3 | 3 | 0 | 0 | 24 | 3 | 6 |
| Austria | 3 | 2 | 1 | 0 | 11 | 7 | 4 |
| Poland | 3 | 1 | 2 | 0 | 11 | 12 | 2 |
| Latvia | 3 | 0 | 0 | 3 | 3 | 27 | 0 |

### Group B

| Team | GP | W | L | T | GF | GA | PTS |
|---|---|---|---|---|---|---|---|
| Germany | 3 | 2 | 1 | 0 | 5 | 1 | 4 |
| USA | 3 | 2 | 1 | 0 | 5 | 2 | 4 |
| Italy | 3 | 1 | 2 | 0 | 2 | 5 | 2 |
| Switzerland | 3 | 1 | 2 | 0 | 1 | 5 | 2 |

### Group C

| Team | GP | W | L | T | GF | GA | PTS |
|---|---|---|---|---|---|---|---|
| Czech. | 3 | 3 | 0 | 0 | 10 | 0 | 6 |
| Hungary | 3 | 2 | 1 | 0 | 14 | 5 | 4 |
| France | 3 | 1 | 2 | 0 | 4 | 7 | 2 |
| Belgium | 3 | 0 | 3 | 0 | 4 | 20 | 6 |

### Group D

| Team | GP | W | L | T | GF | GA | PTS |
|---|---|---|---|---|---|---|---|
| Great Britain | 2 | 2 | 0 | 0 | 4 | 0 | 4 |
| Sweden | 2 | 1 | 1 | 0 | 2 | 1 | 2 |
| Japan | 2 | 0 | 2 | 0 | 0 | 5 | 0 |

### Group A Semifinal Round

| Team | GP | W | L | T | GF | GA | PTS |
|---|---|---|---|---|---|---|---|
| Great Britain | 3 | 2 | 0 | 1 | 8 | 3 | 5 |
| Canada | 3 | 2 | 1 | 0 | 22 | 4 | 4 |
| Germany | 3 | 1 | 1 | 1 | 5 | 8 | 3 |
| Hungary | 3 | 0 | 0 | 3 | 2 | 22 | 0 |

### Group B Semifinal Round

| Team | GP | W | L | T | GF | GA | PTS |
|---|---|---|---|---|---|---|---|
| USA | 3 | 3 | 0 | 0 | 5 | 1 | 6 |
| Czech. | 3 | 2 | 1 | 0 | 6 | 4 | 4 |
| Sweden | 3 | 1 | 2 | 0 | 3 | 6 | 2 |
| Austria | 3 | 0 | 3 | 0 | 1 | 4 | 0 |

### Final Round

| Team | GP | W | L | T | GF | GA | PTS |
|---|---|---|---|---|---|---|---|
| Great Britain | 3 | 2 | 0 | 1 | 7 | 1 | 5 |
| Canada | 3 | 2 | 1 | 0 | 9 | 2 | 4 |
| USA | 3 | 1 | 1 | 1 | 2 | 1 | 3 |
| Czech. | 3 | 0 | 3 | 0 | 0 | 14 | 0 |

### 1936 Final Rankings

1. Great Britain
2. Canada
3. USA
4. Czechoslovakia
5. Germany
5. Sweden
7. Hungary
7. Austria

## Lake Placid, NY, USA • 1932

| Team | GP | W | L | T | GF | GA | PTS |
|---|---|---|---|---|---|---|---|
| Canada | 6 | 5 | 0 | 1 | 32 | 4 | 11 |
| USA | 6 | 4 | 1 | 1 | 27 | 5 | 9 |
| Germany | 6 | 2 | 4 | 0 | 7 | 26 | 4 |
| Poland | 6 | 0 | 6 | 0 | 3 | 34 | 0 |

### 1932 Final Rankings

1. Canada
2. USA
3. Germany
4. Poland

## St. Moritz, Switzerland • 1928

### Group A

| Team | GP | W | L | T | GF | GA | PTS |
|---|---|---|---|---|---|---|---|
| Great Britain | 3 | 2 | 1 | 0 | 10 | 6 | 4 |
| France | 3 | 2 | 1 | 0 | 6 | 5 | 4 |
| Belgium | 3 | 2 | 1 | 0 | 9 | 10 | 4 |
| Hungary | 3 | 0 | 3 | 0 | 2 | 6 | 0 |

### Group B

| Team | GP | W | L | T | GF | GA | PTS |
|---|---|---|---|---|---|---|---|
| Sweden | 2 | 1 | 0 | 1 | 5 | 2 | 3 |
| Czech. | 2 | 1 | 1 | 0 | 3 | 5 | 2 |
| Poland | 2 | 0 | 0 | 1 | 4 | 5 | 1 |

### Group C

| Team | GP | W | L | T | GF | GA | PTS |
|---|---|---|---|---|---|---|---|
| Switzerland | 2 | 1 | 0 | 1 | 5 | 4 | 3 |
| Austria | 2 | 0 | 0 | 2 | 4 | 4 | 2 |
| Germany | 2 | 0 | 0 | 1 | 0 | 1 | 1 |

### Final Round

| Team | GP | W | L | T | GF | GA | PTS |
|---|---|---|---|---|---|---|---|
| Canada | 3 | 3 | 0 | 0 | 38 | 0 | 6 |
| Sweden | 3 | 2 | 1 | 0 | 7 | 12 | 4 |
| Switzerland | 3 | 1 | 2 | 0 | 4 | 17 | 2 |
| Great Britain | 3 | 0 | 3 | 0 | 1 | 21 | O |

### 1928 Final Rankings

1. Canada
2. Sweden
3. Switzerland
4. Great Britain
5. France
5. Czechoslovakia
5. Austria
8. Belgium
8. Poland
8. Germany
11. Hungary

## Chamonix, France • 1924

### Group A

| Team | GP | W | L | T | GF | GA | PTS |
|---|---|---|---|---|---|---|---|
| Canada | 3 | 3 | 0 | 0 | 85 | 0 | 6 |
| Sweden | 3 | 2 | 1 | 0 | 18 | 25 | 4 |
| Czech. | 3 | 1 | 2 | 0 | 14 | 41 | 2 |
| Switzerland | 3 | 0 | 3 | 0 | 2 | 53 | 0 |

### Group B

| Team | GP | W | L | T | GF | GA | PTS |
|---|---|---|---|---|---|---|---|
| USA | 3 | 3 | 0 | 0 | 52 | 0 | 6 |
| Great Britain | 3 | 2 | 1 | 0 | 34 | 16 | 4 |
| France | 3 | 1 | 2 | 0 | 9 | 42 | 2 |
| Belgium | 3 | 0 | 3 | 0 | 8 | 35 | 0 |

### Final Round

| Team | GP | W | L | T | GF | GA | PTS |
|---|---|---|---|---|---|---|---|
| Canada | 3 | 3 | 0 | 0 | 47 | 3 | 6 |
| USA | 3 | 2 | 1 | 0 | 32 | 6 | 4 |
| Great Britain | 3 | 1 | 2 | 0 | 6 | 33 | 2 |
| Sweden | 3 | 0 | 3 | 0 | 3 | 46 | 0 |

### 1924 Final Rankings

1. Canada
2. USA
3. Great Britain
4. Sweden
5. Czechoslovakia
5. France
7. Switzerland
7. Belgium

## Antwerp, Belgium • 1920

**(unofficial)**

*Hockey was played at the 1920 Summer Olympics in Antwerp, Belgium. This tournament is not counted in cumulative Winter Olympic Hockey statistics. The IIHF has declared it the first World Championship.*

### 1920 Final Rankings

1. Canada
2. USA
3. Czechoslovakia
4. Sweden
5. Switzerland

# Women's Olympic Results and Rankings, 2006 to 1998

## Torino, Italy • 2006

| | | | |
|---|---|---|---|
| Finland | 3 | Germany | 0 |
| Sweden | 3 | Russia | 1 |
| United States | 6 | Switzerland | 0 |
| Canada | 16 | Italy | 0 |
| Canada | 12 | Russia | 0 |
| United States | 5 | Germany | 0 |
| Sweden | 11 | Italy | 0 |
| Finland | 4 | Switzerland | 0 |
| Russia | 5 | Italy | 1 |
| Canada | 8 | Sweden | 1 |
| Germany | 2 | Switzerland | 1 |
| United States | 7 | Finland | 3 |

### Classification Round

| | | | |
|---|---|---|---|
| Russia | 6 | Suwitzerland | 2 |
| Germany | 5 | Italy | 2 |

### Semi-final Games

| | | | |
|---|---|---|---|
| Sweden | 3 | United States | 2 (SO) |
| Canada | 6 | Finland | 0 |

### Seventh-Place Game

| | | | |
|---|---|---|---|
| Switzerland | 11 | Italy | 0 |

### Fifth-Place Game

| | | | |
|---|---|---|---|
| Germany | 1 | Russia | 0 |

### Bronze Medal Game

| | | | |
|---|---|---|---|
| USA | 4 | Finland | 0 |

### Gold Medal Game

| | | | |
|---|---|---|---|
| Canada | 4 | Sweden | 1 |

### 2006 Final Rankings, Women

1 Canada
2 Sweden
3 USA
4 Finland
5 Germany
6 Russia
7 Switzerland
8 Italy

## Salt Lake City, Utah, USA • 2002

| | | | |
|---|---|---|---|
| Canada | 7 | Kazakhstan | 0 |
| Sweden | 3 | Russia | 2 |
| USA | 10 | Germany | 0 |
| Finland | 4 | China | 0 |
| Russia | 0 | Canada | 7 |
| Sweden | 7 | Kazakhstan | 0 |
| Finland | 3 | Germany | 1 |
| China | 1 | USA | 12 |
| Kazakhstan | 1 | Russia | 4 |
| USA | 5 | Finland | 0 |
| Germany | 5 | China | 5 |
| Canada | 11 | Sweden | 0 |

### Classification Round

| | | | |
|---|---|---|---|
| Russia | 5 | China | 0 |
| Germany | 4 | Kazakhstan | 0 |

### Semi-final Games

| | | | |
|---|---|---|---|
| Canada | 7 | Finland | 3 |
| USA | 4 | Sweden | 0 |

### Seventh-Place Game

| | | | |
|---|---|---|---|
| China | 2 | Kazakhstan | 1 (OT) |

### Fifth-Place Game

| | | | |
|---|---|---|---|
| Russia | 5 | Germany | 0 |

### Bronze Medal Game

| | | | |
|---|---|---|---|
| Sweden | 2 | Finland | 0 |

### Gold Medal Game

| | | | |
|---|---|---|---|
| Canada | 3 | USA | 2 |

### 2002 Final Rankings, Women

1 Canada
2 USA
3 Sweden
4 Finland
5 Russia
6 Germany
7 China
8 Kazakhstan

## Nagano, Japan • 1998

| | | | |
|---|---|---|---|
| Sweden | 0 | Finland | 6 |
| Canada | 13 | Japan | 0 |
| China | 0 | USA | 5 |
| Finland | 11 | Japan | 1 |
| USA | 7 | Sweden | 1 |
| Canada | 2 | China | 0 |
| Sweden | 3 | Canada | 5 |
| Japan | 1 | China | 6 |
| USA | 4 | Finland | 2 |
| China | 3 | Sweden | 1 |
| USA | 10 | Japan | 0 |
| Finland | 2 | Canada | 4 |
| Japan | 0 | Sweden | 5 |
| Finland | 6 | China | 1 |
| Canada | 4 | USA | 7 |

### Bronze Medal Game

| | | | |
|---|---|---|---|
| Finland | 4 | China | 1 |

### Gold Medal Game

| | | | |
|---|---|---|---|
| USA | 3 | Canada | 1 |

### 1998 Final Rankings, Women

1 USA
2 Canada
3 Finland
4 China
5 Sweden
6 Japan

# Olympic Results, Active NHL Players

| Medal | Name | Year | Team | GP | G | A | Pts | PIM |
|---|---|---|---|---|---|---|---|---|
| B | Afinogenov, Maxim | 2002 | RUS | 6 | 2 | 2 | 4 | 4 |
| | Afinogenov, Maxim | 2006 | RUS | 8 | 0 | 1 | 1 | 10 |
| | Alfredsson, Daniel | 1998 | SWE | 4 | 2 | 3 | 5 | 2 |
| | Alfredsson, Daniel | 2002 | SWE | 4 | 1 | 4 | 5 | 2 |
| G | Alfredsson, Daniel | 2006 | SWE | 8 | 5 | 5 | 10 | 4 |
| | Antropov, Nik | 2006 | KAZ | 5 | 1 | 0 | 1 | 4 |
| S | Aucoin, Adrian | 1994 | CAN | 4 | 0 | 0 | 0 | 2 |
| | Axelsson, P.J. | 2002 | SWE | 4 | 0 | 0 | 0 | 2 |
| G | Axelsson, P.J. | 2006 | SWE | 8 | 3 | 3 | 6 | 0 |
| G | Backman, Christian | 2006 | SWE | 8 | 1 | 2 | 3 | 6 |
| | Berard, Bryan | 1998 | USA | 2 | 0 | 0 | 0 | 0 |
| | Bertuzzi, Todd | 2006 | CAN | 6 | 0 | 3 | 3 | 6 |
| | Blake, Jason | 2006 | USA | 6 | 0 | 0 | 0 | 2 |
| | Blake, Rob | 1998 | CAN | 6 | 1 | 1 | 2 | 2 |
| G | Blake, Rob | 2002 | CAN | 6 | 1 | 2 | 3 | 2 |
| | Blake, Rob | 2006 | CAN | 6 | 0 | 1 | 1 | 2 |
| | Bouwmeester, Jay | 2006 | CAN | 6 | 0 | 0 | 0 | 0 |
| G | Brewer, Eric | 2002 | CAN | 6 | 2 | 0 | 2 | 0 |
| | Brind'Amour, Rod | 1998 | CAN | 6 | 1 | 2 | 3 | 0 |
| | Cajanek, Petr | 2002 | CZE | 4 | 0 | 0 | 0 | 0 |
| B | Cajanek, Petr | 2006 | CZE | 7 | 1 | 0 | 1 | 4 |
| | Chara, Zdeno | 2006 | SVK | 6 | 1 | 1 | 2 | 2 |
| | Chelios, Chris | 1984 | USA | 6 | 0 | 4 | 4 | 8 |
| | Chelios, Chris | 1998 | USA | 4 | 2 | 0 | 2 | 2 |
| S | Chelios, Chris | 2002 | USA | 6 | 1 | 0 | 1 | 4 |
| | Chelios, Chris | 2006 | USA | 6 | 0 | 1 | 1 | 2 |
| | Cole, Erik | 2006 | USA | 6 | 1 | 2 | 3 | 0 |
| | Conroy, Craig | 2006 | USA | 6 | 1 | 4 | 5 | 2 |
| B | Datsyuk, Pavel | 2002 | RUS | 6 | 1 | 2 | 3 | 0 |
| | Datsyuk, Pavel | 2006 | RUS | 8 | 1 | 7 | 8 | 10 |
| | Demitra, Pavol | 2002 | SVK | 2 | 1 | 2 | 3 | 2 |
| | Demitra, Pavol | 2006 | SVK | 6 | 2 | 5 | 7 | 2 |
| | Doan, Shane | 2006 | CAN | 6 | 2 | 1 | 3 | 2 |
| | Draper, Kris | 2006 | CAN | 6 | 0 | 0 | 0 | 0 |
| S | Drury, Chris | 2002 | USA | 6 | 0 | 0 | 0 | 0 |
| | Drury, Chris | 2006 | USA | 6 | 0 | 3 | 3 | 2 |
| | Dvorak, Radek | 2002 | CZE | 4 | 0 | 0 | 0 | 0 |
| | Ehrhoff, Christian | 2002 | GER | 7 | 0 | 0 | 0 | 8 |
| | Ehrhoff, Christian | 2006 | GER | 5 | 1 | 1 | 2 | 4 |
| | Elias, Patrik | 2002 | CZE | 4 | 1 | 1 | 2 | 0 |
| B | Elias, Patrik | 2006 | CZE | 1 | 0 | 0 | 0 | 2 |
| B | Erat, Martin | 2006 | CZE | 8 | 1 | 1 | 2 | 4 |
| B | Fedorov, Sergei | 1998 | RUS | 6 | 1 | 5 | 6 | 8 |
| B | Fedorov, Sergei | 2002 | RUS | 6 | 2 | 2 | 4 | 4 |
| | Fedotenko, Ruslan | 2002 | UKR | 1 | 1 | 0 | 1 | 4 |
| | Foote, Adam | 1998 | CAN | 6 | 0 | 1 | 1 | 4 |
| G | Foote, Adam | 2002 | CAN | 6 | 1 | 0 | 1 | 2 |
| | Foote, Adam | 2006 | CAN | 6 | 0 | 1 | 1 | 6 |
| | Frolov, Alexander | 2006 | RUS | 3 | 0 | 1 | 1 | 0 |
| | Gaborik, Marian | 2006 | SVK | 6 | 3 | 4 | 7 | 4 |
| G | Gagne, Simon | 2002 | CAN | 6 | 1 | 3 | 4 | 0 |
| | Gagne, Simon | 2006 | CAN | 6 | 1 | 2 | 3 | 6 |
| | Gionta, Brian | 2006 | USA | 6 | 4 | 0 | 4 | 2 |
| | Goc, Marcel | 2006 | GER | 5 | 1 | 0 | 1 | 0 |
| | Gomez, Scott | 2006 | USA | 6 | 1 | 4 | 5 | 10 |
| B | Gonchar, Sergei | 1998 | RUS | 6 | 0 | 2 | 2 | 0 |
| B | Gonchar, Sergei | 2002 | RUS | 6 | 0 | 0 | 0 | 2 |
| | Gonchar, Sergei | 2006 | RUS | 8 | 0 | 2 | 2 | 8 |
| | Guerin, Bill | 1998 | USA | 4 | 0 | 3 | 3 | 2 |
| S | Guerin, Bill | 2002 | USA | 6 | 4 | 0 | 4 | 4 |
| | Guerin, Bill | 2006 | USA | 6 | 1 | 0 | 1 | 0 |
| | Hagman, Niklas | 2002 | FIN | 4 | 1 | 2 | 3 | 0 |
| S | Hagman, Niklas | 2006 | FIN | 8 | 0 | 1 | 1 | 2 |
| | Hamrlik, Roman | 1998 | CZE | 6 | 1 | 0 | 1 | 2 |
| | Hamrlik, Roman | 2002 | CZE | 4 | 0 | 1 | 1 | 2 |
| | Handzus, Michal | 2002 | SVK | 2 | 1 | 0 | 1 | 6 |
| G | Havelid, Niclas | 2006 | SWE | 7 | 0 | 0 | 0 | 4 |
| | Havlat, Martin | 2002 | CZE | 4 | 3 | 1 | 4 | 27 |
| | Heatley, Dany | 2006 | CAN | 6 | 2 | 1 | 3 | 8 |
| | Hecht, Jochen | 1998 | GER | 4 | 1 | 0 | 1 | 6 |
| | Hecht, Jochen | 2002 | GER | 4 | 1 | 1 | 2 | 2 |
| | Hedican, Bret | 1992 | USA | 8 | 0 | 0 | 0 | 4 |
| | Hedican, Bret | 2006 | USA | 6 | 0 | 1 | 1 | 6 |
| G | Hejduk, Milan | 1998 | CZE | 4 | 0 | 0 | 0 | 2 |
| | Hejduk, Milan | 2002 | CZE | 4 | 1 | 0 | 1 | 0 |
| B | Hejduk, Milan | 2006 | CZE | 8 | 2 | 1 | 3 | 2 |
| B | Hemsky, Ales | 2006 | CZE | 8 | 1 | 2 | 3 | 2 |
| | Holmstrom, Tomas | 2002 | SWE | 4 | 1 | 0 | 1 | 0 |
| G | Holmstrom, Tomas | 2006 | SWE | 8 | 1 | 3 | 4 | 10 |
| | Hossa, Marcel | 2006 | SVK | 6 | 0 | 0 | 0 | 0 |
| | Hossa, Marian | 2002 | SVK | 2 | 4 | 2 | 6 | 0 |
| | Hossa, Marian | 2006 | SVK | 6 | 5 | 5 | 10 | 4 |
| G | Iginla, Jarome | 2002 | CAN | 6 | 3 | 1 | 4 | 0 |
| | Iginla, Jarome | 2006 | CAN | 6 | 2 | 1 | 3 | 4 |
| G | Jagr, Jaromir | 1998 | CZE | 6 | 1 | 4 | 5 | 2 |
| | Jagr, Jaromir | 2002 | CZE | 4 | 2 | 3 | 5 | 4 |
| B | Jagr, Jaromir | 2006 | CZE | 8 | 2 | 5 | 7 | 6 |
| | Johnsson, Kim | 2002 | SWE | 4 | 1 | 1 | 2 | 0 |
| S | Jokinen, Jussi | 2006 | FIN | 8 | 1 | 3 | 4 | 2 |
| | Jokinen, Olli | 2002 | FIN | 4 | 2 | 1 | 3 | 0 |
| S | Jokinen, Olli | 2006 | FIN | 8 | 6 | 2 | 8 | 2 |
| G | Jovanovski, Ed | 2002 | CAN | 6 | 0 | 3 | 3 | 4 |
| | Jurcina, Milan | 2006 | SVK | 6 | 0 | 1 | 1 | 8 |
| B | Kaberle, Frantisek | 2006 | CZE | 8 | 0 | 1 | 1 | 6 |
| | Kaberle, Tomas | 2002 | CZE | 4 | 0 | 1 | 1 | 2 |
| B | Kaberle, Tomas | 2006 | CZE | 8 | 2 | 2 | 4 | 2 |
| S | Kapanen, Niko | 2006 | FIN | 8 | 2 | 1 | 3 | 2 |
| S | Kariya, Paul | 1994 | CAN | 8 | 3 | 4 | 7 | 2 |
| G | Kariya, Paul | 2002 | CAN | 6 | 3 | 1 | 4 | 0 |
| | Knuble, Mike | 2006 | USA | 6 | 1 | 1 | 2 | 4 |
| S | Koivu, Mikko | 2006 | FIN | 8 | 0 | 0 | 0 | 6 |
| B | Koivu, Saku | 1994 | FIN | 8 | 4 | 3 | 7 | 12 |
| B | Koivu, Saku | 1998 | FIN | 6 | 2 | 8 | 10 | 4 |
| S | Koivu, Saku | 2006 | FIN | 8 | 3 | 8 | 11 | 12 |
| | Koltsov, Konstantin | 2002 | BLR | 2 | 0 | 0 | 0 | 0 |
| B | Kotalik, Ales | 2006 | CZE | 4 | 0 | 0 | 0 | 0 |
| B | Kovalchuk, Ilya | 2002 | RUS | 6 | 1 | 2 | 3 | 14 |
| | Kovalchuk, Ilya | 2006 | RUS | 8 | 4 | 1 | 5 | 31 |
| G | Kovalev, Alex | 1992 | RUS | 8 | 1 | 2 | 3 | 14 |
| B | Kovalev, Alex | 2002 | RUS | 6 | 3 | 1 | 4 | 4 |
| | Kovalev, Alex | 2006 | RUS | 8 | 4 | 2 | 6 | 4 |
| | Kozlov, Viktor | 2006 | RUS | 8 | 2 | 3 | 5 | 2 |
| G | Kronwall, Niklas | 2006 | SWE | 2 | 1 | 1 | 2 | 8 |
| B | Kuba, Filip | 2006 | CZE | 8 | 1 | 0 | 1 | 0 |
| | Kubina, Pavel | 2002 | CZE | 4 | 0 | 1 | 1 | 0 |
| B | Kubina, Pavel | 2006 | CZE | 8 | 1 | 1 | 2 | 12 |
| S | Kukkonen, Lasse | 2006 | FIN | 2 | 0 | 0 | 0 | 0 |
| S | Laaksonen, Antti | 2006 | FIN | 8 | 0 | 0 | 0 | 6 |
| B | Lang, Robert | 1992 | CZE | 8 | 5 | 8 | 13 | 8 |
| G | Lang, Robert | 1998 | CZE | 6 | 0 | 3 | 3 | 0 |
| | Lang, Robert | 2002 | CZE | 4 | 1 | 2 | 3 | 2 |
| B | Lang, Robert | 2006 | CZE | 8 | 0 | 4 | 4 | 4 |
| | Langenbrunner, J. | 1998 | USA | 3 | 0 | 0 | 0 | 4 |
| | Lecavalier, Vincent | 2006 | CAN | 6 | 0 | 3 | 3 | 16 |
| B | Lehtinen, Jere | 1994 | FIN | 8 | 3 | 0 | 3 | 0 |
| B | Lehtinen, Jere | 1998 | FIN | 6 | 4 | 2 | 6 | 2 |
| | Lehtinen, Jere | 2002 | FIN | 4 | 1 | 2 | 3 | 2 |
| S | Lehtinen, Jere | 2006 | FIN | 8 | 3 | 5 | 8 | 0 |
| | Leopold, Jordan | 2006 | USA | 6 | 1 | 0 | 1 | 4 |
| | Lidstrom, Nicklas | 1998 | SWE | 4 | 1 | 1 | 2 | 2 |
| | Lidstrom, Nicklas | 2002 | SWE | 4 | 1 | 5 | 6 | 0 |
| G | Lidstrom, Nicklas | 2006 | SWE | 8 | 2 | 4 | 6 | 2 |
| | Liles, John-Michael | 2006 | USA | 6 | 0 | 2 | 2 | 2 |
| S | Lydman, Toni | 2006 | FIN | 8 | 1 | 0 | 1 | 10 |
| B | Malik, Marek | 2006 | CZE | 8 | 0 | 0 | 0 | 8 |
| | Malkin, Evgeni | 2006 | RUS | 7 | 2 | 4 | 6 | 31 |
| | Marchant, Todd | 1994 | USA | 8 | 1 | 1 | 2 | 6 |
| | Markov, Andrei | 2006 | RUS | 8 | 1 | 2 | 3 | 6 |
| B | Markov, Danny | 2002 | RUS | 5 | 0 | 1 | 1 | 0 |
| | Markov, Danny | 2006 | RUS | 8 | 0 | 2 | 2 | 4 |
| | McCabe, Bryan | 2006 | CAN | 6 | 0 | 0 | 0 | 18 |
| | Meszaros, Andrej | 2006 | SVK | 6 | 0 | 2 | 2 | 4 |
| | Modano, Mike | 1998 | USA | 4 | 2 | 0 | 2 | 0 |
| S | Modano, Mike | 2002 | USA | 6 | 0 | 6 | 6 | 4 |
| | Modano, Mike | 2006 | USA | 6 | 2 | 0 | 2 | 6 |
| G | Modin, Fredrik | 2006 | SWE | 8 | 2 | 1 | 3 | 6 |
| | Nash, Rick | 2006 | CAN | 6 | 0 | 1 | 1 | 10 |
| | Naslund, Markus | 2002 | SWE | 4 | 2 | 1 | 3 | 0 |
| G | Niedermayer, Scott | 2002 | CAN | 6 | 1 | 1 | 2 | 4 |
| | Nieminen, Ville | 2002 | FIN | 4 | 0 | 1 | 1 | 2 |
| S | Nieminen, Ville | 2006 | FIN | 8 | 0 | 1 | 1 | 4 |
| G | Nolan, Owen | 2002 | CAN | 6 | 0 | 3 | 3 | 2 |
| S | Nummelin, Petteri | 2006 | FIN | 8 | 0 | 2 | 2 | 2 |
| S | Numminen, Teppo | 1988 | FIN | 6 | 1 | 4 | 5 | 0 |
| B | Numminen, Teppo | 1998 | FIN | 6 | 1 | 1 | 2 | 2 |
| | Numminen, Teppo | 2002 | FIN | 4 | 0 | 1 | 1 | 0 |
| S | Numminen, Teppo | 2006 | FIN | 8 | 1 | 2 | 3 | 2 |
| | Nylander, Michael | 1998 | SWE | 4 | 0 | 0 | 0 | 6 |
| | Nylander, Michael | 2002 | SWE | 4 | 1 | 2 | 3 | 0 |
| | Ohlund, Mattias | 1998 | SWE | 4 | 0 | 1 | 1 | 4 |

## Olympic Results, Active NHL Players *continued*

| Medal | Name | Year | Team | GP | G | A | Pts | PIM |
|---|---|---|---|---|---|---|---|---|
| | Ohlund, Mattias | 2002 | SWE | 4 | 0 | 2 | 2 | 2 |
| G | Ohlund, Mattias | 2006 | SWE | 6 | 0 | 2 | 2 | 2 |
| B | Olesz, Rostislav | 2006 | CZE | 8 | 0 | 0 | 0 | 2 |
| | Ovechkin, Alex | 2006 | RUS | 8 | 5 | 0 | 5 | 8 |
| G | Pahlsson, Samuel | 2006 | SWE | 8 | 2 | 2 | 4 | 8 |
| | Parrish, Mark | 2006 | USA | 6 | 0 | 0 | 0 | 4 |
| G | Peca, Michael | 2002 | CAN | 6 | 0 | 2 | 2 | 2 |
| B | Peltonen, Ville | 1994 | FIN | 8 | 4 | 3 | 7 | 0 |
| B | Peltonen, Ville | 1998 | FIN | 6 | 2 | 1 | 3 | 6 |
| S | Peltonen, Ville | 2006 | FIN | 8 | 4 | 5 | 9 | 6 |
| | Petrovicky, Ronald | 2006 | SVK | 6 | 1 | 0 | 1 | 2 |
| | Pock, Thomas | 2002 | AUT | 4 | 0 | 0 | 0 | 2 |
| | Ponikarovsky, Alexei | 2002 | UKR | 4 | 1 | 1 | 2 | 6 |
| S | Poti, Tom | 2002 | USA | 6 | 0 | 1 | 1 | 4 |
| | Pronger, Chris | 1998 | CAN | 6 | 0 | 0 | 0 | 4 |
| G | Pronger, Chris | 2002 | CAN | 6 | 0 | 1 | 1 | 2 |
| | Pronger, Chris | 2006 | CAN | 6 | 1 | 2 | 3 | 16 |
| B | Prospal, Vaclav | 2006 | CZE | 8 | 4 | 2 | 6 | 2 |
| S | Rafalski, Brian | 2002 | USA | 6 | 1 | 2 | 3 | 2 |
| | Rafalski, Brian | 2006 | USA | 5 | 0 | 2 | 2 | 0 |
| | Recchi, Mark | 1998 | CAN | 5 | 0 | 2 | 2 | 0 |
| | Redden, Wade | 2006 | CAN | 6 | 1 | 0 | 1 | 0 |
| | Regehr, Robyn | 2006 | CAN | 6 | 0 | 1 | 1 | 2 |
| | Richards, Brad | 2006 | CAN | 6 | 2 | 2 | 4 | 6 |
| | Roenick, Jeremy | 1998 | USA | 4 | 0 | 1 | 1 | 6 |
| S | Roenick, Jeremy | 2002 | USA | 6 | 1 | 4 | 5 | 2 |
| | Rolston, Brian | 1994 | USA | 8 | 7 | 0 | 7 | 8 |
| S | Rolston, Brian | 2002 | USA | 6 | 0 | 3 | 3 | 0 |
| | Rolston, Brian | 2006 | USA | 6 | 3 | 1 | 4 | 4 |
| | Ruutu, Jarkko | 2002 | FIN | 4 | 0 | 0 | 0 | 4 |
| S | Ruutu, Jarkko | 2006 | FIN | 8 | 0 | 0 | 0 | 31 |
| | Sakic, Joe | 2006 | CAN | 6 | 1 | 2 | 3 | 0 |
| | Salei, Ruslan | 1998 | BLR | 7 | 1 | 0 | 1 | 4 |
| | Salei, Ruslan | 2002 | BLR | 6 | 2 | 1 | 3 | 4 |
| | Salo, Sami | 2002 | FIN | 4 | 0 | 0 | 0 | 0 |
| S | Salo, Sami | 2006 | FIN | 6 | 1 | 3 | 4 | 0 |
| B | Samsonov, Sergei | 2002 | RUS | 6 | 1 | 2 | 3 | 4 |
| G | Samuelsson, Mikael | 2006 | SWE | 8 | 1 | 3 | 4 | 2 |
| | Satan, Miroslav | 1994 | SVK | 8 | 9 | 0 | 9 | 0 |
| | Satan, Miroslav | 2002 | SVK | 2 | 0 | 1 | 1 | 0 |
| | Satan, Miroslav | 2006 | SVK | 6 | 0 | 2 | 2 | 2 |
| | Schneider, Mathieu | 1998 | USA | 4 | 0 | 0 | 0 | 6 |
| | Schneider, Mathieu | 2006 | USA | 6 | 1 | 2 | 3 | 16 |
| | Schubert, Christoph | 2002 | GER | 7 | 0 | 1 | 1 | 6 |
| | Schubert, Christoph | 2006 | GER | 5 | 0 | 1 | 1 | 2 |
| G | Sedin, Daniel | 2006 | SWE | 8 | 1 | 3 | 4 | 2 |
| G | Sedin, Henrik | 2006 | SWE | 8 | 3 | 1 | 4 | 2 |
| | Seidenberg, Dennis | 2002 | GER | 7 | 1 | 1 | 2 | 8 |
| | Seidenberg, Dennis | 2006 | GER | 5 | 0 | 0 | 0 | 6 |
| | Selanne, Teemu | 1992 | FIN | 8 | 7 | 4 | 11 | 6 |
| B | Selanne, Teemu | 1998 | FIN | 5 | 4 | 6 | 10 | 8 |
| | Selanne, Teemu | 2002 | FIN | 4 | 3 | 0 | 3 | 2 |
| S | Selanne, Teemu | 2006 | FIN | 8 | 6 | 5 | 11 | 4 |
| | Shanahan, Brendan | 1998 | CAN | 6 | 2 | 0 | 2 | 0 |
| G | Shanahan, Brendan | 2002 | CAN | 6 | 0 | 1 | 1 | 0 |
| | Skoula, Martin | 2002 | CZE | 4 | 0 | 0 | 0 | 0 |
| | Skrastins, Karlis | 2002 | LAT | 1 | 0 | 0 | 0 | 0 |
| | Skrastins, Karlis | 2006 | LAT | 5 | 0 | 1 | 1 | 0 |
| G | Smyth, Ryan | 2002 | CAN | 6 | 0 | 1 | 1 | 0 |
| | Smyth, Ryan | 2006 | CAN | 6 | 0 | 1 | 1 | 4 |
| G | Spacek, Jaroslav | 1998 | CZE | 6 | 0 | 0 | 0 | 4 |
| | Spacek, Jaroslav | 2002 | CZE | 4 | 0 | 0 | 0 | 0 |
| B | Spacek, Jaroslav | 2006 | CZE | 8 | 0 | 1 | 1 | 0 |
| | St. Louis, Martin | 2006 | CAN | 6 | 2 | 1 | 3 | 0 |
| | Streit, Mark | 2002 | SUI | 4 | 1 | 1 | 2 | 0 |
| | Streit, Mark | 2006 | SUI | 6 | 2 | 1 | 3 | 6 |
| | Stumpel, Jozef | 2002 | SVK | 2 | 2 | 1 | 3 | 0 |
| | Stumpel, Jozef | 2006 | SVK | 3 | 0 | 0 | 0 | 0 |
| | Sturm, Marco | 1998 | GER | 2 | 0 | 0 | 0 | 0 |
| | Sturm, Marco | 2002 | GER | 5 | 0 | 1 | 1 | 0 |
| | Sulzer, Alexander | 2006 | GER | 5 | 0 | 1 | 1 | 2 |
| | Sundin, Mats | 1998 | SWE | 4 | 3 | 0 | 3 | 4 |
| | Sundin, Mats | 2002 | SWE | 4 | 5 | 4 | 9 | 10 |
| G | Sundin, Mats | 2006 | SWE | 8 | 3 | 5 | 8 | 4 |
| | Svatos, Marek | 2006 | SVK | 6 | 0 | 0 | 0 | 0 |
| | Sykora, Petr | 2002 | CZE | 4 | 1 | 0 | 1 | 0 |
| | Thornton, Joe | 2006 | CAN | 6 | 1 | 2 | 3 | 0 |
| B | Timonen, Kimmo | 1998 | FIN | 6 | 0 | 1 | 1 | 2 |
| | Timonen, Kimmo | 2002 | FIN | 4 | 0 | 1 | 1 | 2 |
| S | Timonen, Kimmo | 2006 | FIN | 8 | 1 | 4 | 5 | 2 |
| G | Tjarnqvist, Daniel | 2006 | SWE | 8 | 2 | 1 | 3 | 4 |
| | Tkachuk, Keith | 1992 | USA | 8 | 1 | 1 | 2 | 12 |
| | Tkachuk, Keith | 1998 | USA | 4 | 0 | 2 | 2 | 6 |
| S | Tkachuk, Keith | 2002 | USA | 5 | 2 | 0 | 2 | 2 |
| | Tkachuk, Keith | 2006 | USA | 6 | 0 | 0 | 0 | 8 |
| | Tyutin, Fedor | 2006 | RUS | 8 | 0 | 1 | 1 | 4 |
| | Vaananen, Ossi | 2002 | FIN | 2 | 0 | 1 | 1 | 0 |
| | Vishnevski, Vitaly | 2006 | RUS | 8 | 0 | 1 | 1 | 4 |
| | Visnovsky, Lubomir | 1998 | SVK | 3 | 0 | 0 | 0 | 2 |
| | Visnovsky, Lubomir | 2002 | SVK | 3 | 1 | 2 | 3 | 0 |
| | Visnovsky, Lubomir | 2006 | SVK | 6 | 1 | 1 | 2 | 0 |
| | Volchenkov, Anton | 2006 | RUS | 8 | 0 | 0 | 0 | 2 |
| B | Vyborny, David | 2006 | CZE | 8 | 1 | 3 | 4 | 0 |
| | Weight, Doug | 1998 | USA | 4 | 0 | 2 | 2 | 2 |
| S | Weight, Doug | 2002 | USA | 6 | 0 | 3 | 3 | 4 |
| | Weight, Doug | 2006 | USA | 6 | 0 | 3 | 3 | 4 |
| B | Yashin, Alexei | 1998 | RUS | 6 | 3 | 3 | 6 | 0 |
| B | Yashin, Alexei | 2002 | RUS | 6 | 1 | 1 | 2 | 0 |
| | Yashin, Alexei | 2006 | RUS | 8 | 1 | 3 | 4 | 4 |
| S | York, Mike | 2002 | USA | 6 | 0 | 1 | 1 | 0 |
| | Zednik, Richard | 2006 | SVK | 6 | 1 | 0 | 1 | 12 |
| | Zetterberg, Henrik | 2002 | SWE | 4 | 0 | 1 | 1 | 0 |
| G | Zetterberg, Henrik | 2006 | SWE | 8 | 3 | 3 | 6 | 0 |
| G | Zhitnik, Alexei | 1992 | RUS | 8 | 1 | 0 | 1 | 0 |
| B | Zhitnik, Alexei | 1998 | RUS | 6 | 0 | 2 | 2 | 2 |
| B | Zidlicky, Marek | 2006 | CZE | 7 | 4 | 1 | 5 | 16 |
| G | Zubov, Sergei | 1992 | RUS | 8 | 0 | 1 | 1 | 0 |

## Olympic Results, Active NHL Goaltenders

| Medal | Name | Year | Team | GPI | W | L | T | Mins | GA | SO | Avg |
|---|---|---|---|---|---|---|---|---|---|---|---|
| | Aebischer, David | 2002 | SUI | 2 | 1 | 0 | 0 | 81 | 6 | 0 | 4.43 |
| | Aebischer, David | 2006 | SUI | 4 | 1 | 0 | 2 | 200 | 7 | 0 | 2.10 |
| S | Backstrom, Niklas | 2006 | FIN | Did not play – backup goaltender | | | | | | | |
| | Brodeur, Martin | 1998 | CAN | Did not play – backup goaltender | | | | | | | |
| G | Brodeur, Martin | 2002 | CAN | 5 | 4 | 0 | 1 | 300 | 9 | 0 | 1.80 |
| | Brodeur, Martin | 2006 | CAN | 4 | 2 | 2 | 0 | 239 | 8 | 0 | 2.01 |
| B | Bryzgalov, Ilya | 2002 | RUS | Did not play – backup goaltender | | | | | | | |
| | Bryzgalov, Ilya | 2006 | RUS | 1 | 0 | 1 | 0 | 60 | 5 | 0 | 5.00 |
| | Budaj, Peter | 2006 | SVK | 3 | 2 | 1 | 0 | 179 | 6 | 0 | 2.01 |
| | DiPietro, Rick | 2006 | USA | 4 | 1 | 3 | 0 | 237 | 9 | 0 | 2.28 |
| | Esche, Robert | 2006 | USA | 1 | 0 | 1 | 0 | 59 | 5 | 0 | 5.10 |
| | Gerber, Martin | 2002 | SUI | 3 | 1 | 1 | 1 | 158 | 4 | 0 | 1.52 |
| | Gerber, Martin | 2006 | SUI | 3 | 1 | 2 | 0 | 160 | 11 | 1 | 4.13 |
| | Grahame, John | 2006 | USA | 1 | 0 | 0 | 1 | 60 | 3 | 0 | 3.00 |
| | Greiss, Thomas | 2006 | GER | 1 | 0 | 1 | 0 | 60 | 5 | 0 | 5.00 |
| | Hasek, Dominik | 1988 | CZE | 5 | 3 | 2 | 0 | 217 | 18 | 1 | 4.98 |
| G | Hasek, Dominik | 1998 | CZE | 6 | 5 | 1 | 0 | 369 | 6 | 2 | 0.97 |
| | Hasek, Dominik | 2002 | CZE | 4 | 1 | 2 | 1 | 239 | 8 | 0 | 2.01 |
| B | Hasek, Dominik | 2006 | CZE | 1 | 0 | 0 | 0 | 9 | 0 | 0 | 0.00 |
| | Hedberg, Johan | 1998 | SWE | Did not play – backup goaltender | | | | | | | |
| | Hedberg, Johan | 2002 | SWE | 1 | 1 | 0 | 0 | 60 | 1 | 0 | 1.00 |
| | Huet, Cristobal | 1998 | FRA | 2 | 1 | 1 | 0 | 120 | 5 | 0 | 2.50 |
| | Huet, Cristobal | 2002 | FRA | 3 | 0 | 2 | 1 | 179 | 10 | 0 | 3.36 |
| | Joseph, Curtis | 1998 | CAN | Did not play – backup goaltender | | | | | | | |
| G | Joseph, Curtis | 2002 | CAN | 1 | 0 | 1 | 0 | 60 | 5 | 0 | 5.00 |
| G | Khabibulin, Nikolai | 1992 | RUS | Did not play – backup goaltender | | | | | | | |
| B | Khabibulin, Nikolai | 2002 | RUS | 6 | 3 | 2 | 1 | 359 | 14 | 1 | 2.34 |
| | Khabibulin, Nikolai | 2006 | RUS | Did not play – backup goaltender | | | | | | | |
| S | Kiprusoff, Miikka | 2006 | FIN | Did not play – backup goaltender | | | | | | | |
| | Kolzig, Olaf | 1998 | GER | 2 | 2 | 0 | 0 | 120 | 2 | 1 | 1.00 |
| | Kolzig, Olaf | 2006 | GER | 3 | 0 | 1 | 2 | 179 | 8 | 0 | 2.68 |
| S | Legace, Manny | 1994 | CAN | Did not play – backup goaltender | | | | | | | |
| G | Lundqvist, Henrik | 2006 | SWE | 6 | 5 | 1 | 0 | 360 | 14 | 0 | 2.33 |
| | Luongo, Roberto | 2006 | CAN | 2 | 1 | 1 | 0 | 119 | 3 | 0 | 1.51 |
| | Markkanen, Jussi | 2002 | FIN | Did not play – backup goaltender | | | | | | | |
| | Nabokov, Evgeni | 2006 | RUS | 7 | 4 | 2 | 0 | 359 | 8 | 3 | 1.34 |
| S | Niittymaki, Antero | 2006 | FIN | 6 | 5 | 1 | 0 | 359 | 8 | 3 | 1.34 |
| S | Norrena, Fredrik | 2006 | FIN | 2 | 2 | 0 | 0 | 120 | 0 | 2 | 0.00 |
| | Tellqvist, Mikael | 2002 | SWE | Did not play – backup goaltender | | | | | | | |
| G | Tellqvist, Mikael | 2006 | SWE | 1 | 0 | 1 | 0 | 60 | 3 | 0 | 3.00 |
| | Turco, Marty | 2006 | CAN | Did not play – backup goaltender | | | | | | | |
| B | Vokoun, Tomas | 2006 | CZE | 7 | 3 | 4 | 0 | 342 | 14 | 1 | 2.46 |

# Anaheim Ducks

## 2008-09 Results: 42W-33L-4OTL-3SOL 91PTS.
## Second, Pacific Division

### Key Off-Season Signings/Acquisitions

**2009**

**June** 8 • Re-signed RW **Mike Brown.**

26 • Acquired RW **Joffrey Lupul**, D **Luca Sbisa**, Philadelphia's 1st-round picks in 2009 and 2010 and a conditional pick from Philadelphia for D **Chris Pronger** and C **Ryan Dingle.**

**July** 1 • Re-signed D **Scott Niedermayer** and C **Erik Christensen.**

7 • Re-signed C **Todd Marchant.**

8 • Signed C **Saku Koivu.**

9 • Signed D **Nick Boynton.**

10 • Signed D **Steve McCarthy.**

13 • Re-signed D **James Wisniewski.**

29 • Re-signed C **Petteri Nokelainen.**

### Year-by-Year Record

| | | Home | | | | Road | | | | Overall | | | | | | | | |
|---|---|---|---|---|---|---|---|---|---|---|---|---|---|---|---|---|---|---|
| **Season** | **GP** | **W** | **L** | **T** | **OL** | **W** | **L** | **T** | **OL** | **W** | **L** | **T** | **OL** | **GF** | **GA** | **Pts.** | **Finished** | **Playoff Result** |
| 2008-09 | 82 | 20 | 18 | .... | 3 | 22 | 15 | .... | 4 | 42 | 33 | .... | 7 | 245 | 238 | 91 | 2nd, Pacific Div. | Lost Conf. Semi-Final |
| 2007-08 | 82 | 28 | 9 | .... | 4 | 19 | 18 | .... | 4 | 47 | 27 | .... | 8 | 205 | 191 | 102 | 2nd, Pacific Div. | Lost Conf. Quarter-Final |
| **2006-07** | **82** | **26** | **6** | .... | **9** | **22** | **14** | .... | **5** | **48** | **20** | .... | **14** | **258** | **208** | **110** | **1st, Pacific Div.** | **Won Stanley Cup** |
| 2005-06* | 82 | 26 | 10 | .... | 5 | 17 | 17 | .... | 7 | 43 | 27 | .... | 12 | 254 | 229 | 98 | 3rd, Pacific Div. | Lost Conf. Championship |
| 2004-05* | .... | .... | .... | .... | .... | .... | .... | .... | .... | .... | .... | .... | .... | .... | .... | .... | | |
| 2003-04* | 82 | 19 | 11 | 7 | 4 | 10 | 24 | 3 | 4 | 29 | 35 | 10 | 8 | 184 | 213 | 76 | 4th, Pacific Div. | Out of Playoffs |
| 2002-03* | 82 | 22 | 10 | 7 | 2 | 18 | 17 | 2 | 4 | 40 | 27 | 9 | 6 | 203 | 193 | 95 | 2nd, Pacific Div. | Lost Final |
| 2001-02* | 82 | 15 | 19 | 5 | 2 | 14 | 23 | 3 | 1 | 29 | 42 | 8 | 3 | 175 | 198 | 69 | 5th, Pacific Div. | Out of Playoffs |
| 2000-01* | 82 | 15 | 20 | 4 | 2 | 10 | 21 | 7 | 3 | 25 | 41 | 11 | 5 | 188 | 245 | 66 | 5th, Pacific Div. | Out of Playoffs |
| 1999-2000* | 82 | 19 | 13 | 7 | 2 | 15 | 20 | 5 | 1 | 34 | 33 | 12 | 3 | 217 | 227 | 83 | 5th, Pacific Div. | Out of Playoffs |
| 1998-99* | 82 | 21 | 14 | 6 | .... | 14 | 20 | 7 | .... | 35 | 34 | 13 | .... | 215 | 206 | 83 | 3rd, Pacific Div. | Lost Conf. Quarter-Final |
| 1997-98* | 82 | 12 | 23 | 6 | .... | 14 | 20 | 7 | .... | 26 | 43 | 13 | .... | 205 | 261 | 65 | 6th, Pacific Div. | Out of Playoffs |
| 1996-97* | 82 | 23 | 12 | 6 | .... | 13 | 21 | 7 | .... | 36 | 33 | 13 | .... | 245 | 233 | 85 | 2nd, Pacific Div. | Lost Conf. Semi-Final |
| 1995-96* | 82 | 22 | 15 | 4 | .... | 13 | 24 | 4 | .... | 35 | 39 | 8 | .... | 234 | 247 | 78 | 4th, Pacific Div. | Out of Playoffs |
| 1994-95* | 48 | 11 | 9 | 4 | .... | 5 | 18 | 1 | .... | 16 | 27 | 5 | .... | 125 | 164 | 37 | 6th, Pacific Div. | Out of Playoffs |
| 1993-94* | 84 | 14 | 26 | 2 | .... | 19 | 20 | 3 | .... | 33 | 46 | 5 | .... | 229 | 251 | 71 | 4th, Pacific Div. | Out of Playoffs |

* Mighty Ducks of Anaheim

### 2009-10 Schedule

| | | | | | | | |
|---|---|---|---|---|---|---|---|
| **Oct.** | Sat. | 3 | San Jose | | Sun. | 3 | at Chicago |
| | Tue. | 6 | at Minnesota | | Tue. | 5 | Detroit |
| | Thu. | 8 | at Boston | | Thu. | 7 | St. Louis |
| | Sat. | 10 | at Philadelphia | | Sat. | 9 | at Nashville |
| | Sun. | 11 | at NY Rangers* | | Sun. | 10 | at Chicago |
| | Wed. | 14 | Minnesota | | Wed. | 13 | Boston |
| | Sat. | 17 | St. Louis | | Thu. | 14 | at Los Angeles |
| | Wed. | 21 | Dallas | | Sun. | 17 | Calgary* |
| | Sat. | 24 | Columbus | | Tue. | 19 | Buffalo |
| | Mon. | 26 | Toronto | | Thu. | 21 | at San Jose |
| | Fri. | 30 | Vancouver | | Sat. | 23 | at St. Louis |
| | Sat. | 31 | at Phoenix | | Tue. | 26 | at Atlanta |
| **Nov.** | Tue. | 3 | Pittsburgh | | Wed. | 27 | at Washington |
| | Thu. | 5 | Nashville | | Fri. | 29 | at Tampa Bay |
| | Sat. | 7 | Phoenix | **Feb.** | Mon. | 1 | at Florida |
| | Wed. | 11 | at New Jersey | | Wed. | 3 | Detroit |
| | Fri. | 13 | at Columbus | | Thu. | 4 | at Los Angeles |
| | Sat. | 14 | at Detroit | | Mon. | 8 | Los Angeles |
| | Mon. | 16 | at Pittsburgh | | Wed. | 10 | Edmonton |
| | Thu. | 19 | Tampa Bay | | Sat. | 13 | at Calgary |
| | Sat. | 21 | San Jose | | Sun. | 14 | at Edmonton* |
| | Mon. | 23 | Calgary | **Mar.** | Wed. | 3 | Colorado |
| | Wed. | 25 | Carolina | | Sat. | 6 | at Phoenix |
| | Fri. | 27 | Chicago* | | Sun. | 7 | Montreal* |
| | Sun. | 29 | Phoenix* | | Tue. | 9 | Columbus |
| **Dec.** | Tue. | 1 | Los Angeles | | Fri. | 12 | Nashville |
| | Thu. | 3 | at Dallas | | Sun. | 14 | San Jose* |
| | Fri. | 4 | at Minnesota | | Wed. | 17 | Chicago |
| | Sun. | 6 | Ottawa* | | Fri. | 19 | NY Islanders |
| | Tue. | 8 | Dallas | | Sun. | 21 | Colorado* |
| | Fri. | 11 | at Detroit | | Tue. | 23 | at Calgary |
| | Sat. | 12 | at Columbus | | Wed. | 24 | at Vancouver |
| | Wed. | 16 | at Vancouver | | Fri. | 26 | at Edmonton |
| | Thu. | 17 | at San Jose | | Mon. | 29 | Dallas |
| | Sat. | 19 | Phoenix* | | Wed. | 31 | at Colorado |
| | Tue. | 22 | at Colorado | **Apr.** | Fri. | 2 | Vancouver |
| | Wed. | 23 | at Phoenix | | Sat. | 3 | at Los Angeles |
| | Sat. | 26 | at San Jose | | Tue. | 6 | Los Angeles |
| | Tue. | 29 | Minnesota | | Thu. | 8 | at Dallas |
| | Thu. | 31 | at Dallas | | Fri. | 9 | at St. Louis |
| **Jan.** | Sat. | 2 | at Nashville | | Sun. | 11 | Edmonton* |

* Denotes afternoon game.

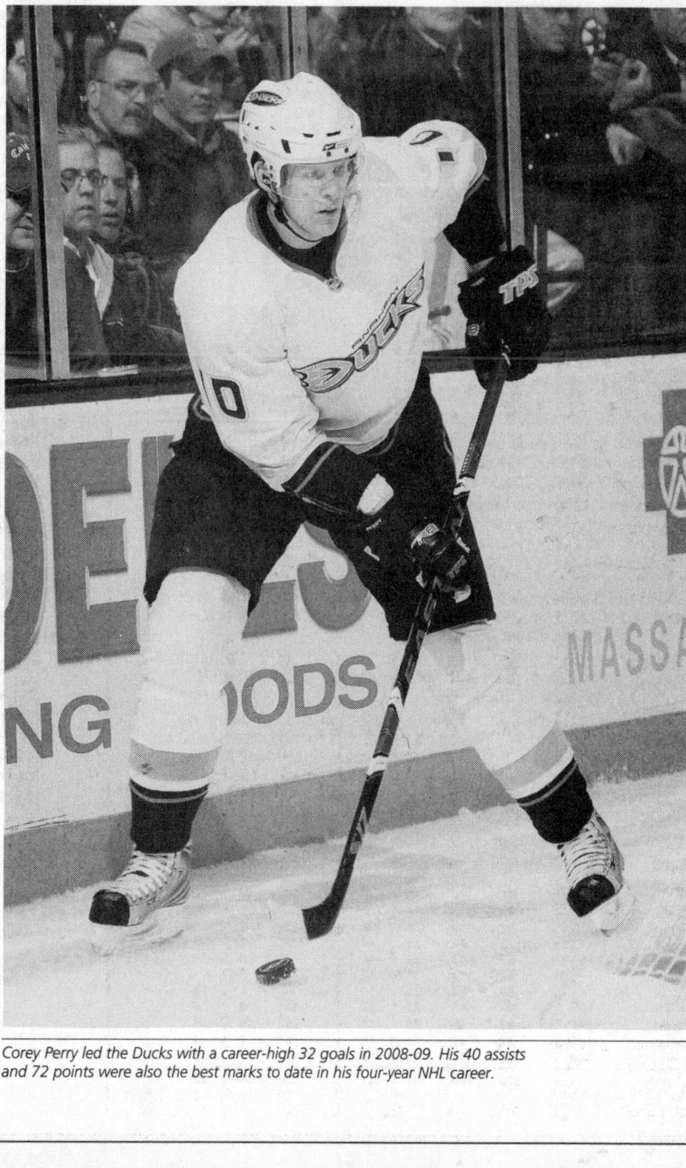


*Corey Perry led the Ducks with a career-high 32 goals in 2008-09. His 40 assists and 72 points were also the best marks to date in his four-year NHL career.*

**PACIFIC DIVISION**
**17th NHL Season**

**Franchise date:** June 15, 1993

# 2009-10 Player Personnel

| FORWARDS | HT | WT | S | Place of Birth | *Age | 2008-09 Club |
|---|---|---|---|---|---|---|
| BELESKEY, Matt | 6-0 | 208 | L | Windsor, Ont. | 21 | Anaheim-Iowa |
| BODIE, Troy | 6-4 | 215 | R | Portage La Prairie, Man. | 24 | Anaheim-Iowa |
| BROWN, Mike | 6-0 | 210 | R | Northbrook, IL | 24 | Vancouver-Anaheim |
| CARTER, Ryan | 6-2 | 202 | L | White Bear Lake, MN | 26 | Anaheim |
| CHRISTENSEN, Erik | 6-1 | 205 | L | Edmonton, Alta. | 25 | Atlanta-Anaheim |
| DESCHAMPS, Nicolas | 6-1 | 185 | L | Lasalle, Que. | 19 | Chicoutimi-Iowa |
| DONALLY, Ryan | 6-5 | 223 | L | Tecumseh, Ont. | 24 | Iowa |
| EBBETT, Andrew | 5-9 | 182 | L | Calgary, Alta. | 26 | Anaheim-Iowa |
| GETZLAF, Ryan | 6-4 | 221 | R | Regina, Sask. | 24 | Anaheim |
| KOIVU, Saku | 5-10 | 182 | L | Turku, Finland | 34 | Montreal |
| LUPUL, Joffrey | 6-1 | 205 | R | Fort Saskatchewan, Alta. | 26 | Philadelphia |
| MACENAUER, Maxime | 6-0 | 198 | L | Laval, Que. | 20 | Rouyn-Noranda-Shawinigan |
| MacMILLAN, Logan | 6-2 | 200 | L | Charlottetown, P.E.I. | 20 | Halifax-Rimouski |
| MARCHANT, Todd | 5-10 | 182 | L | Buffalo, NY | 36 | Anaheim |
| MILLER, Drew | 6-2 | 185 | L | Dover, NJ | 25 | Anaheim-Iowa |
| NOKELAINEN, Petteri | 6-1 | 191 | R | Imatra, Finland | 23 | Boston-Anaheim |
| PARROS, George | 6-5 | 231 | R | Washington, PA | 29 | Anaheim |
| PERRY, Corey | 6-3 | 209 | R | Peterborough, Ont. | 24 | Anaheim |
| RYAN, Bobby | 6-2 | 208 | R | Cherry Hill, NJ | 22 | Anaheim-Iowa |
| SELANNE, Teemu | 6-0 | 200 | R | Helsinki, Finland | 39 | Anaheim |
| SEXTON, Dan | 5-10 | 166 | R | Apple Valley, MN | 22 | Bowling Green |
| SHARP, MacGregor | 6-1 | 195 | R | Vancouver, B.C. | 24 | U. Minn-Duluth-Iowa |
| **DEFENSEMEN** | | | | | | |
| BICKEL, Stu | 6-4 | 215 | R | Chanhassen, MN | 22 | Iowa |
| BOYNTON, Nick | 6-2 | 220 | R | Nobleton, Ont. | 30 | Florida |
| BROOKBANK, Sheldon | 6-2 | 205 | R | Lanigan, Sask. | 28 | New Jersey-Anaheim |
| DEGRAY, John | 6-4 | 216 | L | Richmond Hill, Ont. | 21 | Iowa |
| EVANS, Brennan | 6-3 | 220 | L | North Battleford, Sask. | 27 | Iowa |
| FESTERLING, Brett | 6-1 | 214 | L | Quesnel, B.C. | 23 | Anaheim-Iowa |
| McCARTHY, Steve | 6-1 | 210 | L | Trail, B.C. | 28 | Ufa |
| McCUE, Matt | 6-1 | 218 | L | Cochrane, Alta. | 21 | Brandon-Medicine Hat |
| MIKKELSON, Brendan | 6-3 | 210 | L | Regina, Sask. | 22 | Anaheim-Iowa |
| MITERA, Mark | 6-3 | 211 | L | Royal Oak, MI | 21 | U. of Michigan-Iowa |
| NIEDERMAYER, Scott | 6-1 | 195 | L | Edmonton, Alta. | 36 | Anaheim |
| REGAN, Eric | 6-2 | 205 | R | Whitby, Ont. | 21 | Iowa |
| SALCIDO, Brian | 6-2 | 208 | L | Los Angeles, CA | 24 | Anaheim-Iowa |
| SBISA, Luca | 6-2 | 195 | L | Ozieri, Italy | 19 | Leth-Phi-Phi (AHL) |
| WHITNEY, Ryan | 6-4 | 219 | L | Boston, MA | 26 | Pit-Wilkes-Barre-Ana |
| WISNIEWSKI, James | 6-0 | 207 | R | Canton, MI | 25 | Chicago-Rockford-Anaheim |

| GOALTENDERS | HT | WT | C | Place of Birth | *Age | 2008-09 Club |
|---|---|---|---|---|---|---|
| GIGUERE, Jean-Sebastien | 6-1 | 201 | L | Montreal, Que. | 32 | Anaheim |
| HILLER, Jonas | 6-2 | 193 | R | Felben Wellhausen, Switz. | 27 | Anaheim |
| LEVASSEUR, Jean-Philippe | 6-1 | 205 | R | Victoriaville, Que. | 22 | Iowa |
| PIELMEIER, Timo | 6-0 | 194 | L | Deggendorf, West Germany | 20 | Shawinigan |

* – Age at start of 2009-10 season

## Randy Carlyle

### Head Coach

*Born: Sudbury, Ont., April 19, 1956.*

Randy Carlyle was hired as the head coach in Anaheim on August 1, 2005. In his first season behind the bench in 2005-06, he led the Ducks to the Western Conference Final. He led Anaheim to its first Stanley Cup championship in 2007.

Prior to joining Anaheim, Carlyle had served as the head coach of the Manitoba Moose, the Vancouver Canucks' primary development team. In all, Carlyle spent six seasons between 1996 and 2005 as head coach in Manitoba (both in the International and American Hockey Leagues) with his team posting an overall record of 222-159-52-7. He had the additional duties of general manager of the Moose from 1996 to 2000, and served as club president for the 2001-02 season. Carlyle helped the Moose to a 47-21-14 record for 108 points in 1998-99, for which he was named the IHL's general manager of the year.

Following the 2001-02 season, Carlyle joined the coaching staff of the Washington Capitals. He served as an assistant coach with Washington for two seasons (2002 to 2004), before rejoining Manitoba in 2004–05.

Carlyle played 17 seasons in the NHL with Toronto, Pittsburgh and Winnipeg. He appeared in 1,055 games and had 148 goals and 499 assists for 647 points. Known as a fiery, tough-nosed defenseman, he was selected to play in four NHL All-Star Games, winning the Norris Trophy as the league's top defenseman in 1981. At the conclusion of his playing career in 1993, Carlyle remained with the Winnipeg organization's hockey operations staff, eventually becoming an assistant coach for the 1995-96 season.

### Coaching Record

| | | | Regular Season | | | | Playoffs | | | |
|---|---|---|---|---|---|---|---|---|---|---|
| Season | Team | League | GC | W | L | O/T | GC | W | L | T |
| 1996-97 | Manitoba | IHL | 32 | 16 | 14 | 2 | .... | .... | .... | .... |
| 1997-98 | Manitoba | IHL | 82 | 39 | 36 | 7 | 3 | 0 | 3 | .... |
| 1998-99 | Manitoba | IHL | 82 | 47 | 21 | 14 | 5 | 2 | 3 | .... |
| 99-2000 | Manitoba | IHL | 82 | 37 | 31 | 14 | 2 | 0 | 2 | .... |
| 2000-01 | Manitoba | IHL | 82 | 39 | 31 | 12 | 13 | 6 | 7 | .... |
| 2004-05 | Manitoba | AHL | 80 | 44 | 26 | 10 | 14 | 6 | 8 | .... |
| **2005-06** | **Anaheim** | **NHL** | **82** | **43** | **27** | **12** | **16** | **9** | **7** | .... |
| **2006-07♦** | **Anaheim** | **NHL** | **82** | **48** | **20** | **14** | **21** | **16** | **5** | .... |
| **2007-08** | **Anaheim** | **NHL** | **82** | **47** | **27** | **8** | **6** | **2** | **4** | .... |
| **2008-09** | **Anaheim** | **NHL** | **82** | **42** | **33** | **7** | **13** | **7** | **6** | .... |
| | **NHL Totals** | | **328** | **180** | **107** | **41** | **56** | **34** | **22** | .... |

♦ Stanley Cup win.

# 2008-09 Scoring

* – rookie

## Regular Season

| Pos | # | Player | Team | GP | G | A | Pts | TOI | +/– | PIM | PP | SH | GW | S | % |
|---|---|---|---|---|---|---|---|---|---|---|---|---|---|---|---|
| C | 15 | Ryan Getzlaf | ANA | 81 | 25 | 66 | 91 | 20:07 | 5 | 121 | 9 | 0 | 2 | 227 | 11.0 |
| R | 10 | Corey Perry | ANA | 78 | 32 | 40 | 72 | 18:36 | 10 | 109 | 10 | 0 | 8 | 283 | 11.3 |
| D | 27 | Scott Niedermayer | ANA | 82 | 14 | 45 | 59 | 26:55 | –8 | 70 | 9 | 0 | 2 | 178 | 7.9 |
| R | 9 * | Bobby Ryan | ANA | 64 | 31 | 26 | 57 | 15:26 | 13 | 33 | 12 | 0 | 3 | 174 | 17.8 |
| R | 8 | Teemu Selanne | ANA | 65 | 27 | 27 | 54 | 16:29 | –3 | 36 | 16 | 0 | 5 | 186 | 14.5 |
| D | 25 | Chris Pronger | ANA | 82 | 11 | 37 | 48 | 26:56 | 0 | 88 | 4 | 0 | 2 | 196 | 5.6 |
| C | 48 * | Andrew Ebbett | ANA | 48 | 8 | 24 | 32 | 13:52 | 8 | 24 | 6 | 0 | 0 | 100 | 8.0 |
| C | 26 | Erik Christensen | ATL | 47 | 5 | 14 | 19 | 14:16 | –7 | 14 | 1 | 0 | 0 | 90 | 5.6 |
| | | | ANA | 17 | 2 | 7 | 9 | 11:55 | –2 | 6 | 1 | 0 | 0 | 32 | 6.3 |
| | | | Total | 64 | 7 | 21 | 28 | 13:38 | –9 | 20 | 2 | 0 | 0 | 122 | 5.7 |
| D | 34 | James Wisniewski | CHI | 31 | 2 | 11 | 13 | 19:15 | 6 | 14 | 1 | 0 | 0 | 70 | 2.9 |
| | | | ANA | 17 | 1 | 10 | 11 | 20:57 | 3 | 16 | 0 | 0 | 0 | 19 | 5.3 |
| | | | Total | 48 | 3 | 21 | 24 | 19:51 | 9 | 30 | 1 | 0 | 0 | 89 | 3.4 |
| D | 19 | Ryan Whitney | PIT | 28 | 2 | 11 | 13 | 24:34 | –15 | 16 | 1 | 0 | 0 | 42 | 4.8 |
| | | | ANA | 20 | 0 | 10 | 10 | 22:52 | 1 | 12 | 0 | 0 | 0 | 29 | 0.0 |
| | | | Total | 48 | 2 | 21 | 23 | 23:51 | –14 | 28 | 1 | 0 | 0 | 71 | 2.8 |
| L | 44 | Rob Niedermayer | ANA | 79 | 14 | 7 | 21 | 15:34 | –17 | 42 | 1 | 1 | 2 | 88 | 15.9 |
| C | 22 | Todd Marchant | ANA | 72 | 5 | 13 | 18 | 14:31 | –2 | 34 | 0 | 2 | 0 | 101 | 5.0 |
| R | 16 | George Parros | ANA | 74 | 5 | 5 | 10 | 6:15 | 8 | 135 | 0 | 0 | 0 | 47 | 10.6 |
| L | 18 | Drew Miller | ANA | 27 | 4 | 6 | 10 | 12:59 | 0 | 17 | 0 | 0 | 0 | 45 | 8.9 |
| C | 17 | Petteri Nokelainen | BOS | 33 | 0 | 3 | 3 | 9:40 | –1 | 10 | 0 | 0 | 0 | 30 | 0.0 |
| | | | ANA | 17 | 4 | 2 | 6 | 14:20 | 3 | 6 | 0 | 1 | 0 | 26 | 15.4 |
| | | | Total | 50 | 4 | 5 | 9 | 11:15 | 2 | 16 | 0 | 1 | 0 | 56 | 7.1 |
| C | 20 | Ryan Carter | ANA | 48 | 3 | 6 | 9 | 9:05 | 3 | 52 | 0 | 0 | 1 | 40 | 7.5 |
| D | 40 | Kent Huskins | ANA | 33 | 2 | 4 | 6 | 18:47 | 6 | 27 | 0 | 0 | 0 | 20 | 10.0 |
| D | 3 | Bret Hedican | ANA | 51 | 1 | 5 | 6 | 16:18 | –7 | 36 | 0 | 0 | 0 | 40 | 2.5 |
| D | 23 | Francois Beauchemin | ANA | 20 | 4 | 1 | 5 | 24:54 | –3 | 12 | 0 | 0 | 2 | 45 | 8.9 |
| D | 53 * | Brett Festerling | ANA | 40 | 0 | 5 | 5 | 16:40 | 5 | 18 | 0 | 0 | 0 | 15 | 0.0 |
| R | 13 * | Mike Brown | VAN | 20 | 0 | 1 | 1 | 5:29 | –5 | 85 | 0 | 0 | 0 | 6 | 0.0 |
| | | | ANA | 28 | 2 | 1 | 3 | 10:02 | –2 | 60 | 0 | 0 | 2 | 38 | 5.3 |
| | | | Total | 48 | 2 | 2 | 4 | 8:08 | –7 | 145 | 0 | 0 | 2 | 44 | 4.5 |
| D | 21 | Sheldon Brookbank | N.J. | 15 | 0 | 0 | 0 | 8:50 | 1 | 25 | 0 | 0 | 0 | 6 | 0.0 |
| | | | ANA | 29 | 1 | 3 | 4 | 13:50 | 3 | 51 | 0 | 0 | 0 | 24 | 4.2 |
| | | | Total | 44 | 1 | 3 | 4 | 12:07 | 4 | 76 | 0 | 0 | 0 | 30 | 3.3 |
| D | 60 * | Brendan Mikkelson | ANA | 34 | 0 | 2 | 2 | 13:56 | 0 | 17 | 0 | 0 | 0 | 19 | 0.0 |
| D | 55 * | Brian Salcido | ANA | 2 | 0 | 1 | 1 | 12:17 | 2 | 0 | 0 | 0 | 0 | 1 | 0.0 |
| D | 6 * | Nathan McIver | ANA | 18 | 0 | 1 | 1 | 9:23 | 2 | 36 | 0 | 0 | 0 | 5 | 0.0 |
| L | 64 * | Matt Beleskey | ANA | 2 | 0 | 0 | 0 | 11:09 | 0 | 0 | 0 | 0 | 0 | 0 | 0.0 |
| R | 50 * | Troy Bodie | ANA | 4 | 0 | 0 | 0 | 8:08 | 0 | 0 | 0 | 0 | 0 | 5 | 0.0 |

### Goaltending

| No. | Goaltender | GPI | Mins | Avg | W | L | OT | EN | SO | GA | SA | S% | G | A | PIM |
|---|---|---|---|---|---|---|---|---|---|---|---|---|---|---|---|
| 1 | Jonas Hiller | 46 | 2486 | 2.39 | 23 | 15 | 1 | 6 | 4 | 99 | 1217 | .919 | 0 | 0 | 0 |
| 35 | Jean-Sebastien Giguere | 46 | 2458 | 3.10 | 19 | 18 | 6 | 3 | 2 | 127 | 1274 | .900 | 0 | 0 | 4 |
| | **Totals** | **82** | **4988** | **2.83** | **42** | **33** | **7** | **9** | **6** | **235** | **2500** | **.906** | | | |

## Playoffs

| Pos | # | Player | Team | GP | G | A | Pts | TOI | +/– | PIM | PP | SH | GW | OT | S | % |
|---|---|---|---|---|---|---|---|---|---|---|---|---|---|---|---|---|
| C | 15 | Ryan Getzlaf | ANA | 13 | 4 | 14 | 18 | 24:08 | 3 | 25 | 1 | 0 | 0 | 0 | 25 | 16.0 |
| R | 10 | Corey Perry | ANA | 13 | 8 | 6 | 14 | 21:59 | 2 | 36 | 2 | 0 | 1 | 0 | 41 | 19.5 |
| D | 27 | Scott Niedermayer | ANA | 13 | 3 | 7 | 10 | 26:17 | 0 | 11 | 3 | 0 | 2 | 0 | 32 | 9.4 |
| D | 25 | Chris Pronger | ANA | 13 | 2 | 8 | 10 | 27:12 | 4 | 12 | 1 | 0 | 0 | 0 | 27 | 7.4 |
| R | 9 * | Bobby Ryan | ANA | 13 | 5 | 2 | 7 | 19:40 | 0 | 0 | 2 | 0 | 1 | 0 | 49 | 10.2 |
| R | 8 | Teemu Selanne | ANA | 13 | 4 | 2 | 6 | 15:08 | –2 | 4 | 2 | 0 | 1 | 0 | 31 | 12.9 |
| D | 19 | Ryan Whitney | ANA | 13 | 1 | 5 | 6 | 21:33 | –1 | 9 | 1 | 0 | 0 | 0 | 9 | 11.1 |
| C | 20 | Ryan Carter | ANA | 10 | 2 | 3 | 5 | 12:14 | 0 | 0 | 1 | 0 | 0 | 0 | 18 | 11.1 |
| L | 18 | Drew Miller | ANA | 13 | 2 | 1 | 3 | 16:08 | 1 | 2 | 0 | 0 | 1 | 0 | 23 | 8.7 |
| D | 34 | James Wisniewski | ANA | 12 | 1 | 2 | 3 | 20:22 | 0 | 10 | 0 | 0 | 0 | 0 | 16 | 6.3 |
| C | 48 * | Andrew Ebbett | ANA | 13 | 1 | 2 | 3 | 13:11 | –1 | 8 | 0 | 0 | 0 | 0 | 16 | 6.3 |
| L | 44 | Rob Niedermayer | ANA | 13 | 0 | 3 | 3 | 16:13 | 1 | 12 | 0 | 0 | 0 | 0 | 7 | 0.0 |
| C | 22 | Todd Marchant | ANA | 13 | 1 | 1 | 2 | 19:55 | 0 | 16 | 0 | 0 | 1 | 1 | 18 | 5.6 |
| C | 26 | Erik Christensen | ANA | 8 | 0 | 2 | 2 | 10:37 | –1 | 0 | 0 | 0 | 0 | 0 | 10 | 0.0 |
| R | 13 * | Mike Brown | ANA | 13 | 0 | 2 | 2 | 8:27 | 0 | 25 | 0 | 0 | 0 | 0 | 6 | 0.0 |
| D | 23 | Francois Beauchemin | ANA | 13 | 1 | 0 | 1 | 21:24 | 1 | 15 | 0 | 0 | 0 | 0 | 9 | 11.1 |
| D | 53 * | Brett Festerling | ANA | 1 | 0 | 0 | 0 | 14:34 | –1 | 0 | 0 | 0 | 0 | 0 | 0 | 0.0 |
| L | 12 | Josh Green | ANA | 5 | 0 | 0 | 0 | 5:53 | 0 | 0 | 0 | 0 | 0 | 0 | 2 | 0.0 |
| R | 16 | George Parros | ANA | 7 | 0 | 0 | 0 | 5:32 | 0 | 9 | 0 | 0 | 0 | 0 | 5 | 0.0 |
| C | 17 | Petteri Nokelainen | ANA | 9 | 0 | 0 | 0 | 8:42 | –1 | 2 | 0 | 0 | 0 | 0 | 2 | 0.0 |
| D | 21 | Sheldon Brookbank | ANA | 13 | 0 | 0 | 0 | 11:12 | –1 | 18 | 0 | 0 | 0 | 0 | 3 | 0.0 |

### Goaltending

| No. | Goaltender | GPI | Mins | Avg | W | L | EN | SO | GA | SA | S% | G | A | PIM |
|---|---|---|---|---|---|---|---|---|---|---|---|---|---|---|
| 35 | Jean-Sebastien Giguere | 1 | 17 | 0.00 | 0 | 0 | 1 | 0 | 0 | 6 | 1.000 | 0 | 0 | 0 |
| 1 | Jonas Hiller | 13 | 807 | 2.23 | 7 | 6 | 1 | 2 | 30 | 524 | .943 | 0 | 0 | 0 |
| | **Totals** | **13** | **827** | **2.32** | **7** | **6** | **2** | **2** | **32** | **532** | **.940** | | | |

# Club Records

## Team

(Figures in brackets for season records are games played; records for fewest points, wins, ties, losses, goals, goals against are for 70 or more games)

| | | |
|---|---|---|
| **Most Points** | **110** | 2006-07 (82) |
| **Most Wins** | **48** | 2006-07 (82) |
| **Most Ties** | **13** | 1996-97 (82), 1997-98 (82), 1998-99 (82) |
| **Most Losses** | **46** | 1993-94 (84) |
| **Most Goals** | **258** | 2006-07 (82) |
| **Most Goals Against** | **261** | 1997-98 (82) |
| **Fewest Points** | **65** | 1997-98 (82) |
| **Fewest Wins** | **25** | 2000-01 (82) |
| **Fewest Ties** | **5** | 1993-94 (84) |
| **Fewest Losses** | **20** | 2006-07 (82) |
| **Fewest Goals** | **175** | 2001-02 (82) |
| **Fewest Goals Against** | **191** | 2007-08 (82) |
| **Longest Winning Streak** | | |
| **Overall** | **7** | Feb. 20-Mar. 7/99 |
| **Home** | **10** | Feb. 17-Mar. 26/08 |
| **Away** | **7** | Nov. 28-Dec. 13/06 |
| **Longest Undefeated Streak** | | |
| **Overall** | **12** | Feb. 22-Mar. 19/97 (7 wins, 5 ties) |
| **Home** | **14** | Feb. 12-Apr. 9/97 (10 wins, 4 ties) |
| **Away** | **7** | Nov. 28-Dec. 13/06 (7 wins) |
| **Longest Losing Streak** | | |
| **Overall** | **8** | Oct. 12-30/96, Nov. 3-20/05 |
| **Home** | **8** | Jan. 10-Feb. 9/01 |
| **Away** | **7** | Oct. 8-Nov. 12/05 |
| **Longest Winless Streak** | | |
| **Overall** | **9** | Three times |
| **Home** | **11** | Jan. 5-Feb. 14/01 (8 losses, 3 ties) |
| **Away** | **13** | Nov. 1-Dec. 27/03 (11 losses, 2 ties) |
| **Most Shutouts, Season** | **9** | 2002-03 (82) |
| **Most PIM, Season** | **1,843** | 1997-98 (82) |
| **Most Goals, Game** | **8** | Jan. 21/98 (Fla. 3 at Ana. 8), Mar. 21/04 (Det. 6 at Ana. 8) |

## Individual

| | | |
|---|---|---|
| **Most Seasons** | **10** | Steve Rucchin, Teemu Selanne |
| **Most Games** | **647** | Teemu Selanne |
| **Most Goals, Career** | **352** | Teemu Selanne |
| **Most Assists, Career** | **391** | Teemu Selanne |
| **Most Points, Career** | **743** | Teemu Selanne (352G, 391A) |
| **Most PIM, Career** | **788** | Dave Karpa |
| **Most Shutouts, Career** | **31** | Jean-Sebastien Giguere |
| **Longest Consecutive Games Streak** | **275** | Samuel Pahlsson (Feb. 7/03-Apr. 7/07) |
| **Most Goals, Season** | **52** | Teemu Selanne (1997-98) |
| **Most Assists, Season** | **66** | Ryan Getzlaf (2008-09) |
| **Most Points, Season** | **109** | Teemu Selanne (1996-97; 51G, 58A) |
| **Most PIM, Season** | **285** | Todd Ewen (1995-96) |
| **Most Points, Defenseman, Season** | **69** | Scott Niedermayer (2006-07; 15G, 54A) |
| **Most Points, Center, Season** | **91** | Ryan Getzlaf (2008-09; 25G, 66A) |
| **Most Points, Right Wing, Season** | **109** | Teemu Selanne (1996-97; 51G, 58A) |
| **Most Points, Left Wing, Season** | **108** | Paul Kariya (1995-96; 50G, 58A) |
| **Most Points, Rookie, Season** | **57** | Bobby Ryan (2008-09; 31G, 26A) |
| **Most Shutouts, Season** | **8** | Jean-Sebastien Giguere (2002-03) |
| **Most Goals, Game** | **3** | Twenty-seven times |
| **Most Assists, Game** | **5** | Dmitri Mironov (Dec. 12/97), Teemu Selanne (Nov. 19/06), Ryan Getzlaf (Oct. 29/08) |
| **Most Points, Game** | **5** | Twelve times |

## General Managers' History

Jack Ferreira, 1993-94 to 1997-98; Pierre Gauthier, 1998-99 to 2001-02; Bryan Murray, 2002-03, 2003-04; Al Coates, 2004-05; Brian Burke, 2005-06 to 2007-08; Brian Burke and Bob Murray, 2008-09; Bob Murray, 2009-10.

## Coaching History

Ron Wilson, 1993-94 to 1996-97; Pierre Page, 1997-98; Craig Hartsburg, 1998-99, 1999-2000; Craig Hartsburg and Guy Charron, 2000-01; Bryan Murray, 2001-02; Mike Babcock, 2002-03 to 2004-05; Randy Carlyle, 2005-06 to date.

## Captains' History

Troy Loney, 1993-94; Randy Ladouceur, 1994-95, 1995-96; Paul Kariya, 1996-97; Paul Kariya and Teemu Selanne, 1997-98; Paul Kariya, 1998-99 to 2002-03; Steve Rucchin, 2003-04; Scott Niedermayer, 2005-06, 2006-07; Chris Pronger, 2007-08; Scott Niedermayer, 2008-09 to date.

# All-time Record vs. Other Clubs

## Regular Season

| | At Home | | | | | | | | On Road | | | | | | | | Total | | | | | | | |
|---|---|---|---|---|---|---|---|---|---|---|---|---|---|---|---|---|---|---|---|---|---|---|---|---|
| | GP | W | L | T | OL | GF | GA | PTS | GP | W | L | T | OL | GF | GA | PTS | GP | W | L | T | OL | GF | GA | PTS |
| Atlanta | 6 | 3 | 3 | 0 | 0 | 18 | 18 | 6 | 5 | 4 | 1 | 0 | 0 | 18 | 11 | 8 | 11 | 7 | 4 | 0 | 0 | 36 | 29 | 14 |
| Boston | 10 | 3 | 3 | 2 | 2 | 20 | 25 | 10 | 10 | 4 | 5 | 0 | 1 | 27 | 33 | 9 | 20 | 7 | 8 | 2 | 3 | 47 | 58 | 19 |
| Buffalo | 11 | 4 | 7 | 0 | 0 | 22 | 33 | 8 | 11 | 3 | 4 | 3 | 1 | 25 | 30 | 10 | 22 | 7 | 11 | 3 | 1 | 47 | 63 | 18 |
| Calgary | 34 | 20 | 8 | 6 | 0 | 110 | 84 | 46 | 33 | 11 | 21 | 1 | 0 | 76 | 95 | 23 | 67 | 31 | 29 | 7 | 0 | 186 | 179 | 69 |
| Carolina | 11 | 5 | 5 | 1 | 0 | 32 | 35 | 11 | 11 | 4 | 6 | 1 | 0 | 25 | 28 | 9 | 22 | 9 | 11 | 2 | 0 | 57 | 63 | 20 |
| Chicago | 30 | 18 | 8 | 3 | 1 | 84 | 62 | 40 | 32 | 15 | 14 | 2 | 1 | 80 | 85 | 33 | 62 | 33 | 22 | 5 | 2 | 164 | 147 | 73 |
| Colorado | 29 | 13 | 11 | 3 | 2 | 75 | 71 | 31 | 29 | 9 | 14 | 4 | 2 | 74 | 85 | 24 | 58 | 22 | 25 | 7 | 4 | 149 | 156 | 55 |
| Columbus | 16 | 9 | 4 | 1 | 2 | 46 | 38 | 21 | 16 | 8 | 8 | 0 | 0 | 40 | 43 | 16 | 32 | 17 | 12 | 1 | 2 | 86 | 81 | 37 |
| Dallas | 42 | 18 | 20 | 3 | 1 | 103 | 114 | 40 | 42 | 10 | 26 | 2 | 4 | 81 | 138 | 26 | 84 | 28 | 46 | 5 | 5 | 184 | 252 | 66 |
| Detroit | 30 | 12 | 14 | 4 | 0 | 78 | 84 | 28 | 30 | 3 | 21 | 3 | 3 | 61 | 104 | 12 | 60 | 15 | 35 | 7 | 3 | 139 | 188 | 40 |
| Edmonton | 34 | 17 | 14 | 2 | 1 | 94 | 92 | 37 | 33 | 12 | 18 | 0 | 3 | 71 | 82 | 27 | 67 | 29 | 32 | 2 | 4 | 165 | 174 | 64 |
| Florida | 11 | 4 | 6 | 1 | 0 | 29 | 33 | 9 | 9 | 3 | 3 | 2 | 1 | 22 | 27 | 9 | 20 | 7 | 9 | 3 | 1 | 51 | 60 | 18 |
| Los Angeles | 45 | 23 | 9 | 7 | 6 | 152 | 118 | 59 | 45 | 17 | 22 | 4 | 2 | 117 | 133 | 40 | 90 | 40 | 31 | 11 | 8 | 269 | 251 | 99 |
| Minnesota | 16 | 9 | 5 | 0 | 2 | 39 | 38 | 20 | 16 | 5 | 8 | 2 | 1 | 29 | 38 | 13 | 32 | 14 | 13 | 2 | 3 | 68 | 76 | 33 |
| Montreal | 9 | 4 | 5 | 0 | 0 | 28 | 28 | 8 | 10 | 4 | 4 | 2 | 0 | 30 | 31 | 10 | 19 | 8 | 9 | 2 | 0 | 58 | 59 | 18 |
| Nashville | 20 | 16 | 1 | 0 | 3 | 65 | 36 | 35 | 20 | 8 | 8 | 2 | 2 | 46 | 47 | 20 | 40 | 24 | 9 | 2 | 5 | 111 | 83 | 55 |
| New Jersey | 12 | 6 | 5 | 1 | 0 | 34 | 31 | 13 | 9 | 2 | 6 | 0 | 1 | 16 | 32 | 5 | 21 | 8 | 11 | 1 | 1 | 50 | 63 | 18 |
| NY Islanders | 10 | 2 | 4 | 3 | 1 | 22 | 29 | 8 | 10 | 4 | 5 | 1 | 0 | 27 | 26 | 9 | 20 | 6 | 9 | 4 | 1 | 49 | 55 | 17 |
| NY Rangers | 10 | 6 | 2 | 0 | 2 | 36 | 32 | 14 | 11 | 6 | 3 | 1 | 1 | 32 | 28 | 14 | 21 | 12 | 5 | 1 | 3 | 68 | 60 | 28 |
| Ottawa | 10 | 5 | 3 | 2 | 0 | 24 | 19 | 12 | 10 | 5 | 4 | 1 | 0 | 27 | 30 | 11 | 20 | 10 | 7 | 3 | 0 | 51 | 49 | 23 |
| Philadelphia | 11 | 4 | 4 | 2 | 1 | 38 | 40 | 11 | 9 | 2 | 4 | 3 | 0 | 17 | 25 | 7 | 20 | 6 | 8 | 5 | 1 | 55 | 65 | 18 |
| Phoenix | 42 | 26 | 11 | 3 | 2 | 130 | 102 | 57 | 41 | 22 | 12 | 2 | 5 | 123 | 111 | 51 | 83 | 48 | 23 | 5 | 7 | 253 | 213 | 108 |
| Pittsburgh | 9 | 6 | 3 | 0 | 0 | 32 | 26 | 12 | 11 | 2 | 7 | 2 | 0 | 32 | 37 | 6 | 20 | 8 | 10 | 2 | 0 | 64 | 63 | 18 |
| St. Louis | 30 | 14 | 14 | 2 | 0 | 86 | 85 | 30 | 30 | 11 | 12 | 3 | 4 | 80 | 92 | 29 | 60 | 25 | 26 | 5 | 4 | 166 | 177 | 59 |
| San Jose | 45 | 18 | 22 | 2 | 3 | 119 | 135 | 41 | 45 | 23 | 19 | 2 | 1 | 122 | 120 | 49 | 90 | 41 | 41 | 4 | 4 | 241 | 255 | 90 |
| Tampa Bay | 10 | 5 | 4 | 1 | 0 | 31 | 26 | 11 | 10 | 6 | 4 | 0 | 0 | 27 | 20 | 12 | 20 | 11 | 8 | 1 | 0 | 58 | 46 | 23 |
| Toronto | 12 | 6 | 5 | 1 | 0 | 39 | 28 | 13 | 17 | 3 | 10 | 4 | 0 | 35 | 55 | 10 | 29 | 9 | 15 | 5 | 0 | 74 | 83 | 23 |
| Vancouver | 33 | 11 | 12 | 7 | 3 | 89 | 98 | 32 | 34 | 13 | 19 | 2 | 0 | 84 | 110 | 28 | 67 | 24 | 31 | 9 | 3 | 173 | 208 | 60 |
| Washington | 11 | 6 | 3 | 1 | 1 | 35 | 31 | 14 | 10 | 6 | 4 | 0 | 0 | 28 | 17 | 12 | 21 | 12 | 7 | 1 | 1 | 63 | 48 | 26 |
| **Totals** | **599** | **293** | **215** | **58** | **33** | **1710** | **1591** | **677** | **599** | **225** | **292** | **49** | **33** | **1472** | **1713** | **532** | **1198** | **518** | **507** | **107** | **66** | **3182** | **3304** | **1209** |

## Playoffs

| | Series | W | L | GP | W | L | T | GF | GA | Last Mtg. | Rnd. | Result |
|---|---|---|---|---|---|---|---|---|---|---|---|---|
| Calgary | 1 | 1 | 0 | 7 | 4 | 3 | 0 | 17 | 16 | 2006 | CQF | W 4-3 |
| Colorado | 1 | 1 | 0 | 4 | 4 | 0 | 0 | 16 | 4 | 2006 | CSF | W 4-0 |
| Dallas | 2 | 1 | 1 | 12 | 6 | 6 | 0 | 27 | 34 | 2008 | CQF | L 2-4 |
| Detroit | 5 | 2 | 3 | 25 | 11 | 14 | 0 | 57 | 75 | 2009 | CSF | L 3-4 |
| Edmonton | 1 | 0 | 1 | 5 | 1 | 4 | 0 | 13 | 16 | 2006 | CF | L 1-4 |
| Minnesota | 2 | 2 | 0 | 9 | 8 | 1 | 0 | 21 | 10 | 2007 | CQF | W 4-1 |
| New Jersey | 1 | 0 | 1 | 7 | 3 | 4 | 0 | 12 | 19 | 2003 | F | L 3-4 |
| Ottawa | 1 | 1 | 0 | 5 | 4 | 1 | 0 | 16 | 11 | 2007 | F | W 4-1 |
| Phoenix | 1 | 1 | 0 | 7 | 4 | 3 | 0 | 17 | 17 | 1997 | CQF | W 4-3 |
| San Jose | 1 | 1 | 0 | 6 | 4 | 2 | 0 | 18 | 10 | 2009 | CQF | W 4-2 |
| Vancouver | 1 | 1 | 0 | 5 | 4 | 1 | 0 | 14 | 8 | 2007 | CSF | W 4-1 |
| **Totals** | **17** | **11** | **6** | **92** | **53** | **39** | **0** | **228** | **220** | | | |

## Playoff Results 2009-2004

| Year | Round | Opponent | Result | GF | GA |
|---|---|---|---|---|---|
| 2009 | CSF | Detroit | L 3-4 | 17 | 22 |
| | CQF | San Jose | W 4-2 | 18 | 10 |
| 2008 | CQF | Dallas | L 2-4 | 13 | 20 |
| **2007** | **F** | **Ottawa** | **W 4-1** | **16** | **11** |
| | CF | Detroit | W 4-2 | 16 | 17 |
| | CSF | Vancouver | W 4-1 | 14 | 8 |
| | CQF | Minnesota | W 4-1 | 12 | 9 |
| 2006 | CF | Edmonton | L 1-4 | 13 | 16 |
| | CSF | Colorado | W 4-0 | 16 | 4 |
| | CQF | Calgary | W 4-3 | 17 | 16 |

**Abbreviations: Round: F** - Final; **CF** – conference final; **CSF** – conference semi-final; **CQF** – conference quarter-final

## 2008-09 Results

| | | | |
|---|---|---|---|
| **Oct.** | 9 | at San Jose | 1-4 |
| | 12 | Phoenix | 2-4 |
| | 14 | at Los Angeles | 3-6 |
| | 15 | Edmonton | 2-3 |
| | 17 | San Jose | 4-0 |
| | 19 | Carolina | 1-3 |
| | 21 | at Toronto | 3-2† |
| | 24 | at Ottawa | 4-3 |
| | 25 | at Montreal | 6-4 |
| | 27 | at Columbus | 3-2 |
| | 29 | Detroit | 5-4* |
| | 31 | Vancouver | 6-7† |
| **Nov.** | 2 | Calgary | 3-2 |
| | 4 | at Los Angeles | 1-0* |
| | 5 | St. Louis | 5-2 |
| | 7 | Dallas | 2-5 |
| | 9 | Florida | 1-3 |
| | 14 | Nashville | 3-4* |
| | 16 | Los Angeles | 2-0 |
| | 19 | Washington | 4-6 |
| | 21 | at St. Louis | 2-3* |
| | 22 | at Dallas | 2-1† |
| | 24 | Colorado | 4-1 |
| | 28 | Chicago | 1-0 |
| | 30 | at Carolina | 4-1 |
| **Dec.** | 1 | at Detroit | 1-2 |
| | 3 | at Chicago | 2-4 |
| | 7 | Columbus | 5-3 |
| | 10 | St. Louis | 4-2 |
| | 11 | at San Jose | 0-2 |
| | 14 | Minnesota | 4-2 |
| | 16 | NY Rangers | 1-3 |
| | 19 | at Edmonton | 3-2† |
| | 22 | at Vancouver | 3-4 |
| | 23 | at Calgary | 3-4 |
| | 27 | at Dallas | 3-4* |
| | 28 | at St. Louis | 4-3 |
| | 31 | Columbus | 0-2 |
| **Jan.** | 2 | Philadelphia | 4-5† |
| | 4 | Phoenix | 2-0 |
| | 6 | Los Angeles | 3-1 |
| | 8 | at Los Angeles | 3-4 |
| | 9 | Tampa Bay | 3-4 |
| | 11 | New Jersey | 4-3 |
| | 14 | Detroit | 3-4 |
| | 16 | at Pittsburgh | 1-3 |
| | 17 | at Minnesota | 3-0 |
| | 20 | at NY Rangers | 2-4 |
| | 21 | at NY Islanders | 1-2 |
| | 27 | at Phoenix | 7-3 |
| | 28 | Chicago | 2-3 |
| | 31 | at Colorado | 4-3 |
| **Feb.** | 2 | Buffalo | 3-2 |
| | 4 | at Minnesota | 0-3 |
| | 5 | at Nashville | 2-4 |
| | 7 | at Calgary | 2-1 |
| | 11 | Calgary | 3-2* |
| | 15 | Atlanta | 4-8 |
| | 18 | Los Angeles | 3-4 |
| | 20 | at Detroit | 2-5 |
| | 21 | at Columbus | 5-2 |
| | 24 | at Buffalo | 3-2 |
| | 26 | at Boston | 0-6 |
| | 28 | at Dallas | 4-3 |
| **Mar.** | 3 | at Chicago | 2-3* |
| | 6 | Dallas | 2-3 |
| | 8 | Minnesota | 2-3 |
| | 11 | Vancouver | 4-3* |
| | 15 | San Jose | 0-1 |
| | 18 | Nashville | 4-3* |
| | 19 | at Phoenix | 3-2† |
| | 22 | Phoenix | 6-2 |
| | 24 | at Nashville | 2-1† |
| | 25 | at Colorado | 7-2 |
| | 27 | Edmonton | 3-5 |
| | 29 | Colorado | 4-1 |
| | 31 | at Edmonton | 5-3 |
| **Apr.** | 2 | at Vancouver | 6-5† |
| | 4 | at San Jose | 5-2 |
| | 5 | San Jose | 2-3 |
| | 10 | Dallas | 4-3† |
| | 11 | at Phoenix | 4-5† |

* – Overtime † – Shootout

## Entry Draft Selections 2009-1995

Name in bold denotes played in NHL.

**2009**

| Pick | |
|---|---|
| 15 | Peter Holland |
| 26 | Kyle Palmieri |
| 37 | Matt Clark |
| 76 | Igor Bobkov |
| 106 | Sami Vatanen |
| 136 | Radoslav Illo |
| 166 | Scott Valentine |

**2008**

| Pick | |
|---|---|
| 17 | Jake Gardiner |
| 35 | Nicolas Deschamps |
| 39 | Eric O'Dell |
| 43 | Justin Schultz |
| 71 | Josh Brittain |
| 83 | Marco Cousineau |
| 85 | Brandon McMillan |
| 113 | Ryan Hegarty |
| 143 | Stefan Warg |
| 208 | Nick Pryor |

**2007**

| Pick | |
|---|---|
| 19 | Logan MacMillan |
| 42 | Eric Tangradi |
| 63 | Maxime Macenauer |
| 92 | Justin Vaive |
| 93 | Steven Kampfer |
| 98 | Sebastian Stefaniszin |
| 121 | Mattias Modig |
| 151 | Brett Morrison |

**2006**

| Pick | |
|---|---|
| 19 | Mark Mitera |
| 38 | Bryce Swan |
| 83 | John Degray |
| 112 | **Matt Beleskey** |
| 172 | **Petteri Wirtanen** |

**2005**

| Pick | |
|---|---|
| 2 | **Bobby Ryan** |
| 31 | **Brendan Mikkelson** |
| 63 | Jason Bailey |
| 127 | Bobby Bolt |
| 141 | **Brian Salcido** |
| 197 | Jean-Philippe Levasseur |

**2004**

| Pick | |
|---|---|
| 9 | **Ladislav Smid** |
| 39 | Jordan Smith |
| 74 | Kyle Klubertanz |
| 75 | **Tim Brent** |
| 172 | Matt Auffrey |
| 203 | Gabriel Bouthillette |
| 236 | Matt Christie |
| 269 | **Janne Pesonen** |

**2003**

| Pick | |
|---|---|
| 19 | **Ryan Getzlaf** |
| 28 | **Corey Perry** |
| 86 | Shane Hynes |
| 90 | Juha Alen |
| 119 | Nathan Saunders |
| 186 | **Drew Miller** |
| 218 | Dirk Southern |
| 250 | **Shane O'Brien** |
| 280 | Ville Mantymaa |

**2002**

| Pick | |
|---|---|
| 7 | **Joffrey Lupul** |
| 37 | **Tim Brent** |
| 71 | Brian Lee |
| 103 | Joonas Vihko |
| 140 | George Davis |
| 173 | Luke Fritshaw |
| 261 | Francois Caron |
| 267 | Chris Petrow |

**2001**

| Pick | |
|---|---|
| 5 | **Stanislav Chistov** |
| 35 | **Mark Popovic** |
| 69 | Joel Stepp |
| 102 | **Timo Parssinen** |
| 105 | Vladimir Korsunov |
| 118 | Brandon Rogers |
| 137 | **Joel Perrault** |
| 170 | Jan Tabacek |
| 224 | **Tony Martensson** |
| 232 | **Martin Gerber** |
| 264 | **P. A. Parenteau** |

**2000**

| Pick | |
|---|---|
| 12 | **Alexei Smirnov** |
| 44 | **Ilya Bryzgalov** |
| 98 | **Jonas Ronnqvist** |
| 134 | Peter Podhradsky |
| 153 | Bill Cass |

**1999**

| Pick | |
|---|---|
| 44 | **Jordan Leopold** |
| 83 | **Niclas Havelid** |
| 105 | Alexandr Chagodayev |
| 141 | Maxim Rybin |
| 173 | Jan Sandstrom |
| 230 | **Petr Tenkrat** |
| 258 | Brian Gornick |

**1998**

| Pick | |
|---|---|
| 5 | **Vitaly Vishnevski** |
| 32 | **Stephen Peat** |
| 112 | Viktor Wallin |
| 150 | **Trent Hunter** |
| 178 | **Jesse Fibiger** |
| 205 | David Bernier |
| 233 | Pelle Prestberg |
| 245 | Andreas Andersson |

**1997**

| Pick | |
|---|---|
| 18 | **Michael Holmqvist** |
| 45 | **Maxim Balmochnykh** |
| 72 | Jay Legault |
| 125 | Luc Vaillancourt |
| 178 | Tony Mohagen |
| 181 | Mat Snesrud |
| 209 | Rene Stussi |
| 235 | Tommi Degerman |

**1996**

| Pick | |
|---|---|
| 9 | **Ruslan Salei** |
| 35 | **Matt Cullen** |
| 117 | Brendan Buckley |
| 149 | Blaine Russell |
| 172 | Timo Ahmaoja |
| 198 | Kevin Kellett |
| 224 | Tobias Johwelin |

**1995**

| Pick | |
|---|---|
| 4 | **Chad Kilger** |
| 29 | **Brian Wesenberg** |
| 55 | **Mike Leclerc** |
| 107 | **Igor Nikulin** |
| 133 | **Peter LeBoutillier** |
| 159 | Mike LaPlante |
| 185 | Igor Karpenko |

## Bob Murray

### Executive Vice President and General Manager

*Born: Kingston, Ont., November 26, 1954.*

Bob Murray was named executive vice president and general manager of the Anaheim Ducks on November 12, 2008 after 3 1/2 years as senior vice president of hockey operations. He was named to that original position on July 14, 2005. Murray's astute judgment of hockey talent and player evaluation were instrumental in several trades and acquisitions the Ducks made over his tenure, highlighted by a Stanley Cup championship in 2007.

Murray's responsibilities include overseeing all aspects of player development, playing a key role in the club's professional scouting efforts, contract negotiations and all matters relating to the National Hockey League. He has been instrumental in the organization's success at both the NHL and AHL level. Both the Ducks and American Hockey League's Portland Pirates made Conference Final appearances in 2006, making Anaheim the only organization to have both their NHL and AHL teams advance to their league's respective Conference Finals.

Prior to joining the Ducks, Murray worked as a professional scout with the Vancouver Canucks from 1999 to 2005 under then-general manager Brian Burke (1998 to 2004). Murray's scouting expertise helped to build teams that recorded 100+ point season two years in a row (2002-03 and 2003-04) and advanced to the Stanley Cup playoffs four seasons in a row (2001 to 20004). Before his stint in Vancouver, he served as a scouting consultant for Anaheim during the 1998-99 season.

Murray was a member of the Chicago Blackhawks organization for 25 years, serving as general manager from 1997 to 1999. He was promoted to the post after serving as assistant general manager under Bob Pulford for two seasons. Before joining upper management, Murray was named the director of player personnel in 1991 and was largely responsible for the club's entry draft selections over eight seasons.

Drafted by the Blackhawks in 1974, Murray spent his entire 1,008-game, 15-year career in a Chicago uniform. He became just the fourth player in Blackhawks history to reach the 1,000-game plateau. In addition, he became the first defenseman in club history to appear in 100 postseason contests, reaching the mark during the 1990 Stanley Cup playoffs. In all, Murray scored had 132 goals and 382 assists for 514 points, and currently ranks second in all-time points among Blackhawk defensemen. He was named to both the 1981 and 1983 NHL All-Star Games. Murray retired at the conclusion of the 1989-90 season. Known for his work ethic, intelligence and determination as a player, Murray remained with the organization as a professional scout following his retirement in 1990.

# Club Directory

Honda Center

**Anaheim Ducks**
Honda Center
2695 E. Katella Ave.
Anaheim, CA 92806
Phone **714/940-2900**
FAX 714/940-2953
Ticket Information 877/WILDWING
www.anaheimducks.com
**Capacity:** 17,174

**Executive Management**

| | |
|---|---|
| Owners | Henry and Susan Samueli |
| Chief Executive Officer | Michael Schulman |
| Executive Vice President/General Manager | Bob Murray |
| Executive Vice President/Chief Operating Officer | Tim Ryan |
| Senior Vice President, Hockey Operations | David McNab |
| Senior Vice President/Chief Marketing Officer | Bob Wagner |
| Vice President of Human Resources | Jay Scott |
| Vice President of Human Resources | Kim Kutcher |
| Vice President of Finance | Doug Heller |
| Senior Manager of Hockey Operations | Maureen Nyeholt |
| Exec. Asst. to the Executive V.P./COO | Cheryl Gorman |
| Exec. Asst. to the Senior V.P./CMO | Janet Conley |
| Administrative Assistant, Hockey Operations | Christina Morrow |

**Coaching Staff**

| | |
|---|---|
| Head Coach | Randy Carlyle |
| Assistant Coaches | Dave Farrish, Newell Brown |
| Goaltending Consultant | Pete Peeters |
| Video Coordinator | Joe Trotta |
| Strength & Conditioning Coach | Sean Skahan |
| Hockey Club Operations | |
| Director of Professional Scouting | Rick Paterson |
| Director of Amateur Scouting | Martin Madden |
| Assistant Director of Amateur Scouting | Alain Chainey |
| Scouting Staff | David Baseggio, Glen Cochrane, Jeff Crisp, Jan-Åke Danielson, Bob Ferguson, Casey Hankinson, Konstantin Krylov, Matt Laatsch, Donald Marier, Kevin Murray, Jim Sandlak |
| Head Athletic Trainer | Tim Clark |
| Assistant Athletic Trainer | Meaghan Beaudoin |
| Massage Therapist | James Partida |
| Equipment Manager | Doug Shearer |
| Assistant Equipment Manager | Chris Aldrich |
| Equipment Assistant | Chris Kincaid |
| Manager of Hockey Operations | Ryan Lichtenfels |
| Team Physicians | Dr. Ronald Glousman, Dr. Craig Milhouse |
| Oral Surgeon | Dr. Jeff Pulver |

**Broadcasting**

| | |
|---|---|
| Director of Broadcasting | Aaron Teats |
| Associate Producer | Bob Sipowich |
| Television, Fox Sports Prime Ticket (Cable), KDOC-TV | John Ahlers & Brian Hayward |
| Radio, KLAA AM 830 & Ducks Radio Network | Steve Carroll |
| Host/Producer | Kent French |

**Communications**

| | |
|---|---|
| Director of Media & Communications | Alex Gilchrist |
| Media & Communications Managers | Steve Hoem, Lauren O'Gorman |
| Game Night Communications Staff | Lisa Parris, Grant Young, Courtney Strayer, Larry Woodard, Jennifer Andrews |

**Community Relations**

| | |
|---|---|
| Director of Community Relations & Public Affairs | Wendy Yamagishi |
| Community Relations Managers | Jesse Tyler, Jennifer Walker |

**Entertainment**

| | |
|---|---|
| Director of Entertainment/Multi-Media | Rod Murray |
| Entertainment Manager | Chris Brown |
| Editor/Producer | Rich Cooley |
| Arena Vision Editor/Producer | Davin Maske |
| Producer / Associate Producer | Peter Uvalle / Gabriel Suarez |

**Fan Development**

| | |
|---|---|
| Director of Fan Development | Matt Savant |
| Senior Managers, School / Youth Hockey Programs | Joseph Hwang / Lynsie Estes |
| Fan Development Manager | Champ Baginski |

**Finance and Administration**

| | |
|---|---|
| Controller | Melody Martin |
| IT Manager | Mike Wing |
| Human Resources Managers | Wendy Mulhall, Donna Vass |
| Corporate Partnerships | |
| Director of Corporate Partnerships | Wendy Grover |
| Director of Corporate Sales | Tanya Mitchell |
| Director of Corporate Relations and Research | Alex Evezich |
| Senior Corporate Sales Managers | Bonner Paddock, Jamal Spears |

**Marketing**

| | |
|---|---|
| Director of Marketing | Tracie Jones |
| Senior Manager, Signature Programs and Events | Kris Loomis |
| Senior Media and Marketing Manager | Adam Mendelsohn |
| Marketing Managers | Shannon Ritter, Ryan Spillers, Jesse Chatfield |
| Signature Programs and Events Manager | Jamie Minkler |
| Designers, Senior / Junior | Mariana Stoopen / Patrick Boykin |

**Publications and New Media**

| | |
|---|---|
| Director of Publications and New Media | Adam Brady |
| Publications and New Media | Coordinator Matt Vevoda |

**Premium Sales and Service**

| | |
|---|---|
| Director of Premium Sales and Service | Jim Panetta |
| Premium Account Executives | Geoff Matthews, Timothy Thompson, Mark Eggering |
| Premium Services Manager | Jana Cannavo |

**Ticketing Department**

| | |
|---|---|
| Manager of Ticket Operations | James Bakken |
| Assistant Ticketing Manager | Jonas Calicdan |
| Assistant Manager, Premium Ticketing | Gina Bulgheroni |

**Ticket Sales and Customer Service**

| | |
|---|---|
| Director of Ticket Sales & Service | Lisa Johnson |
| Senior Manager of Season & Group Sales | Mike Morrow |
| Inside Sales Manager | Zach Hollins |

# Atlanta Thrashers

## 2008-09 Results: 35W-41L-5OTL-1SOL 76PTS.
## Fourth, Southeast Division

### Key Off-Season Signings/Acquisitions

**2009**

**June 8** • Re-signed C **Marty Reasoner.**

**26** • Selected C **Evander Kane** (Vancouver, WHL) fourth overall in the 2009 Entry Draft.

**July 1** • Acquired D **Pavel Kubina** and RW **Tim Stapleton** from Toronto for D **Garnet Exelby** and LW **Colin Stuart.**

**2** • Re-signed C **Chris Thorburn.**

**2** • Signed RW **Nik Antropov.**

**6** • Signed C **Jason Krog.**

**7** • Re-signed RW **Joey Crabb** and D **Nathan Oystrick.**

**8** • Re-signed C **Jim Slater.**

**13** • Signed RW **Anthony Stewart** and D **Noah Welch.**

**15** • Re-signed G **Kari Lehtonen.**

**16** • Re-signed RW **Colby Armstrong.**

**21** • Re-signed D **Boris Valabik.**

### 2009-10 Schedule

| | | | | | | | |
|---|---|---|---|---|---|---|---|
| **Oct.** | Sat. | 3 | Tampa Bay | | Tue. | 5 | at Pittsburgh |
| | Thu. | 8 | at St. Louis | | Thu. | 7 | NY Rangers |
| | Sat. | 10 | at Ottawa | | Sat. | 9 | Washington |
| | Fri. | 16 | at New Jersey | | Tue. | 12 | Ottawa |
| | Sat. | 17 | at Buffalo | | Thu. | 14 | Buffalo |
| | Tue. | 20 | at Montreal | | Sat. | 16 | at Carolina |
| | Thu. | 22 | Washington | | Mon. | 18 | at Florida |
| | Sat. | 24 | San Jose | | Tue. | 19 | Toronto |
| | Thu. | 29 | Washington | | Thu. | 21 | Carolina |
| | Sat. | 31 | at Ottawa* | | Sat. | 23 | at Tampa Bay |
| **Nov.** | Tue. | 3 | at Montreal | | Tue. | 26 | Anaheim |
| | Thu. | 5 | Columbus | | Thu. | 28 | at Philadelphia |
| | Sat. | 7 | at NY Islanders | | Sat. | 30 | at Nashville |
| | Sun. | 8 | St. Louis* | **Feb.** | Tue. | 2 | Tampa Bay |
| | Thu. | 12 | at NY Rangers | | Fri. | 5 | at Washington |
| | Fri. | 13 | Los Angeles | | Sat. | 6 | Florida |
| | Sun. | 15 | Edmonton* | | Wed. | 10 | at Colorado |
| | Thu. | 19 | Boston | | Fri. | 12 | at Minnesota |
| | Sat. | 21 | Pittsburgh | | Sat. | 13 | at Chicago |
| | Sun. | 22 | Tampa Bay* | **Mar.** | Tue. | 2 | Florida |
| | Wed. | 25 | at Detroit | | Thu. | 4 | NY Islanders |
| | Fri. | 27 | at Carolina | | Sat. | 6 | at Tampa Bay |
| | Sat. | 28 | Philadelphia | | Sun. | 7 | Carolina* |
| | Mon. | 30 | Florida | | Tue. | 9 | Nashville |
| **Dec.** | Thu. | 3 | NY Islanders | | Thu. | 11 | at Columbus |
| | Sat. | 5 | at Florida | | Fri. | 12 | NY Rangers |
| | Mon. | 7 | at Toronto | | Sun. | 14 | Phoenix* |
| | Wed. | 9 | at Calgary | | Tue. | 16 | Buffalo |
| | Thu. | 10 | at Vancouver | | Thu. | 18 | Ottawa |
| | Sat. | 12 | Montreal | | Sat. | 20 | Philadelphia |
| | Mon. | 14 | at NY Rangers | | Sun. | 21 | at Philadelphia |
| | Wed. | 16 | at Florida | | Tue. | 23 | Boston |
| | Thu. | 17 | Dallas | | Thu. | 25 | Toronto |
| | Sat. | 19 | New Jersey | | Sat. | 27 | at Carolina |
| | Mon. | 21 | Montreal | | Mon. | 29 | Carolina |
| | Wed. | 23 | at Boston | | Tue. | 30 | at Toronto |
| | Sat. | 26 | at Tampa Bay | **Apr.** | Thu. | 1 | at Washington |
| | Mon. | 28 | at New Jersey | | Sat. | 3 | at Pittsburgh* |
| | Wed. | 30 | at Boston | | Tue. | 6 | New Jersey |
| **Jan.** | Fri. | 1 | at Buffalo | | Fri. | 9 | at Washington |
| | Sat. | 2 | at NY Islanders | | Sat. | 10 | Pittsburgh |

* Denotes afternoon game.

**SOUTHEAST DIVISION**
**11th NHL Season**
**Franchise date:** June 25, 1997

### Year-by-Year Record

| | | Home | | | | Road | | | | Overall | | | | | | | | |
|---|---|---|---|---|---|---|---|---|---|---|---|---|---|---|---|---|---|---|
| **Season** | **GP** | **W** | **L** | **T** | **OL** | **W** | **L** | **T** | **OL** | **W** | **L** | **T** | **OL** | **GF** | **GA** | **Pts.** | **Finished** | **Playoff Result** |
| 2008-09 | 82 | 18 | 21 | .... | 2 | 17 | 20 | .... | 4 | 35 | 41 | .... | 6 | 257 | 280 | 76 | 4th, Southeast Div. | Out of Playoffs |
| 2007-08 | 82 | 19 | 19 | .... | 3 | 15 | 21 | .... | 5 | 34 | 40 | .... | 8 | 216 | 272 | 76 | 4th, Southeast Div. | Out of Playoffs |
| 2006-07 | 82 | 23 | 12 | .... | 6 | 20 | 16 | .... | 5 | 43 | 28 | .... | 11 | 246 | 245 | 97 | 1st, Southeast Div. | Lost Conf. Quarter-Final |
| 2005-06 | 82 | 24 | 13 | .... | 4 | 17 | 20 | .... | 4 | 41 | 33 | .... | 8 | 281 | 275 | 90 | 3rd, Southeast Div. | Out of Playoffs |
| 2004-05 | .... | .... | .... | .... | .... | .... | .... | .... | .... | .... | .... | .... | .... | .... | .... | .... | | |
| 2003-04 | 82 | 18 | 17 | 4 | 2 | 15 | 20 | 4 | 2 | 33 | 37 | 8 | 4 | 214 | 243 | 78 | 2nd, Southeast Div. | Out of Playoffs |
| 2002-03 | 82 | 15 | 19 | 4 | 3 | 16 | 20 | 3 | 2 | 31 | 39 | 7 | 5 | 226 | 284 | 74 | 3rd, Southeast Div. | Out of Playoffs |
| 2001-02 | 82 | 11 | 21 | 9 | 0 | 8 | 26 | 2 | 5 | 19 | 47 | 11 | 5 | 187 | 288 | 54 | 5th, Southeast Div. | Out of Playoffs |
| 2000-01 | 82 | 10 | 23 | 6 | 2 | 13 | 22 | 6 | 0 | 23 | 45 | 12 | 2 | 211 | 289 | 60 | 4th, Southeast Div. | Out of Playoffs |
| 1999-2000 | 82 | 9 | 26 | 3 | 3 | 5 | 31 | 4 | 1 | 14 | 57 | 7 | 4 | 170 | 313 | 39 | 5th, Southeast Div. | Out of Playoffs |

*In his first full season in 2008-09, Bryan Little scored 31 goals and led the Thrashers with an 18 percent shooting percentage that placed him third in the NHL.*

# 2009-10 Player Personnel

| FORWARDS | HT | WT | S | Place of Birth | *Age | 2008-09 Club |
|---|---|---|---|---|---|---|
| ANTROPOV, Nik | 6-6 | 230 | L | Ust-Kamenogorsk, USSR | 29 | Toronto-NY Rangers |
| ARMSTRONG, Colby | 6-2 | 195 | R | Lloydminster, Sask. | 26 | Atlanta |
| BOULTON, Eric | 6-1 | 225 | L | Halifax, N.S. | 33 | Atlanta |
| CRABB, Joey | 6-1 | 195 | R | Anchorage, AK | 26 | Atlanta-Chicago (AHL) |
| ESPOSITO, Angelo | 6-1 | 180 | L | Montreal, Que. | 20 | Montreal (QMJHL) |
| FORNEY, Michael | 6-2 | 185 | R | Thief River Falls, MN | 21 | Green Bay |
| GRATTON, Josh | 6-2 | 215 | L | Brantford, Ont. | 27 | Milwaukee-Phi-Phi (AHL) |
| HOLZAPFEL, Riley | 6-0 | 190 | L | Regina, Sask. | 21 | Chicago (AHL) |
| KAIP, Rylan | 6-1 | 195 | L | Wilcox, Sask. | 25 | Chicago (AHL) |
| KANE, Evander | 6-1 | 180 | L | Vancouver, B.C. | 18 | Vancouver (WHL) |
| KOVALCHUK, Ilya | 6-1 | 230 | R | Tver, USSR | 26 | Atlanta |
| KOZEK, Andrew | 5-10 | 190 | L | Revelstoke, B.C. | 23 | North Dakota-Chicago (AHL) |
| KOZLOV, Vyacheslav | 5-10 | 190 | L | Voskresensk, USSR | 37 | Atlanta |
| KROG, Jason | 5-11 | 185 | R | Fernie, B.C. | 33 | Vancouver-Manitoba |
| LaVALLEE, Jordan | 6-3 | 225 | L | Corvallis, OR | 23 | Atlanta-Chicago (AHL) |
| LITTLE, Bryan | 5-11 | 185 | R | Edmonton, Alta. | 21 | Atlanta |
| MACHACEK, Spencer | 6-1 | 185 | R | Lethbridge, Alta. | 20 | Atlanta-Chicago (AHL) |
| PEVERLEY, Rich | 6-0 | 185 | R | Guelph, Ont. | 27 | Nashville-Atlanta |
| POSPISIL, Tomas | 6-0 | 180 | R | Sumperk, Czech. | 22 | Chi (AHL)-Alb-Gwinnett |
| REASONER, Marty | 6-1 | 205 | L | Honeoye Falls, NY | 32 | Atlanta |
| SIDDALL, Matt | 6-1 | 210 | R | North Vancouver, B.C. | 25 | Chicago (AHL)-Gwinnett |
| SLATER, Jim | 6-0 | 200 | L | Petoskey, MI | 26 | Atlanta |
| STAPLETON, Tim | 5-9 | 160 | R | La Grange, IL | 27 | Toronto-Toronto (AHL) |
| STERLING, Brett | 5-7 | 175 | L | Los Angeles, CA | 25 | Atlanta-Chicago (AHL) |
| STEWART, Anthony | 6-2 | 240 | R | LaSalle, Que. | 24 | Florida |
| THORBURN, Chris | 6-3 | 225 | R | Sault Ste. Marie, Ont. | 26 | Atlanta |
| WHITE, Todd | 5-10 | 195 | L | Kanata, Ont. | 34 | Atlanta |
| **DEFENSEMEN** | | | | | | |
| BOGOSIAN, Zach | 6-2 | 200 | R | Massena, NY | 19 | Atlanta-Chicago (AHL) |
| DENNY, Chad | 6-3 | 225 | L | Sydney, N.S. | 22 | Chicago (AHL)-Gwinnett |
| ENSTROM, Tobias | 5-10 | 180 | L | Nordingra, Sweden | 24 | Atlanta |
| HAINSEY, Ron | 6-3 | 205 | L | Bolton, CT | 28 | Atlanta |
| KUBINA, Pavel | 6-4 | 245 | R | Celadna, Czech. | 32 | Toronto |
| KULDA , Arturs | 6-2 | 210 | L | Riga, Latvia | 21 | Chicago (AHL) |
| LEHMAN, Scott | 6-1 | 200 | L | Fort McMurray, Alta. | 23 | Atlanta-Chicago (AHL) |
| LEWIS, Grant | 6-3 | 205 | R | Pittsburgh, PA | 24 | Atlanta-Chicago (AHL) |
| OYSTRICK, Nathan | 6-0 | 210 | L | Regina, Sask. | 26 | Atlanta |
| POSTMA, Paul | 6-2 | 180 | R | Red Deer, Alta. | 20 | Calgary (WHL) |
| SALMELA, Anssi | 6-1 | 200 | L | Nokia, Finland | 25 | N.J.-Lowell (AHL)-Atl-Chi (AHL) |
| VALABIK, Boris | 6-7 | 240 | L | Nitra, Czech. | 23 | Atlanta-Chicago (AHL) |
| VERNACE, Michael | 6-2 | 200 | L | Toronto, Ont. | 23 | Colorado-Lake Erie |
| WELCH, Noah | 6-4 | 220 | L | Brighton, MA | 27 | Fla-Rochester-T.B. |

| GOALTENDERS | HT | WT | C | Place of Birth | *Age | 2008-09 Club |
|---|---|---|---|---|---|---|
| HEDBERG, Johan | 6-0 | 190 | L | Leksand, Sweden | 36 | Atlanta |
| LEHTONEN, Kari | 6-4 | 215 | L | Helsinki, Finland | 25 | Atlanta |
| MacINTYRE, Drew | 6-2 | 185 | L | Charlottetown, P.E.I. | 26 | Milwaukee |
| MANNINO, Peter | 6-0 | 200 | R | Farmington Hills, MI | 25 | NY Islanders-Bridgeport-Utah |
| PAVELEC, Ondrej | 6-2 | 215 | L | Kladno, Czech. | 22 | Atlanta-Chicago (AHL) |

* – Age at start of 2009-10 season

# 2008-09 Scoring

* – rookie

## Regular Season

| Pos | # | Player | Team | GP | G | A | Pts | TOI | +/– | PIM | PP | SH | GW | S | % |
|---|---|---|---|---|---|---|---|---|---|---|---|---|---|---|---|
| L | 17 | Ilya Kovalchuk | ATL | 79 | 43 | 48 | 91 | 21:48 | –12 | 50 | 12 | 0 | 6 | 275 | 15.6 |
| L | 13 | Vyacheslav Kozlov | ATL | 82 | 26 | 50 | 76 | 17:14 | –14 | 44 | 12 | 0 | 3 | 165 | 15.8 |
| C | 12 | Todd White | ATL | 82 | 22 | 51 | 73 | 18:03 | –9 | 24 | 12 | 1 | 0 | 150 | 14.7 |
| C | 10 | Bryan Little | ATL | 79 | 31 | 20 | 51 | 16:55 | –5 | 24 | 12 | 0 | 4 | 172 | 18.0 |
| C | 47 | Rich Peverley | NSH | 27 | 2 | 7 | 9 | 12:07 | –3 | 15 | 0 | 0 | 0 | 42 | 4.8 |
| | | | ATL | 39 | 13 | 22 | 35 | 18:49 | 16 | 18 | 2 | 1 | 5 | 75 | 17.3 |
| | | | Total | 66 | 15 | 29 | 44 | 16:05 | 13 | 33 | 2 | 1 | 5 | 117 | 12.8 |
| R | 20 | Colby Armstrong | ATL | 82 | 22 | 18 | 40 | 15:09 | 5 | 75 | 3 | 0 | 2 | 141 | 15.6 |
| D | 6 | Ron Hainsey | ATL | 81 | 6 | 33 | 39 | 22:22 | –16 | 32 | 4 | 0 | 0 | 148 | 4.1 |
| D | 39 | Tobias Enstrom | ATL | 82 | 5 | 27 | 32 | 23:31 | 14 | 52 | 2 | 1 | 1 | 86 | 5.8 |
| C | 19 | Marty Reasoner | ATL | 79 | 14 | 16 | 30 | 15:18 | 11 | 36 | 0 | 1 | 2 | 131 | 10.7 |
| C | 11 | Eric Perrin | ATL | 78 | 7 | 16 | 23 | 14:10 | –2 | 36 | 1 | 1 | 0 | 109 | 6.4 |
| D | 4 * | Zach Bogosian | ATL | 47 | 9 | 10 | 19 | 18:06 | 11 | 47 | 2 | 1 | 1 | 90 | 10.0 |
| C | 23 | Jim Slater | ATL | 60 | 8 | 10 | 18 | 11:14 | 0 | 52 | 0 | 2 | 0 | 94 | 8.5 |
| R | 27 | Chris Thorburn | ATL | 82 | 7 | 8 | 15 | 9:35 | –10 | 104 | 0 | 0 | 1 | 85 | 8.2 |
| L | 36 | Eric Boulton | ATL | 76 | 3 | 10 | 13 | 7:32 | –3 | 176 | 0 | 0 | 0 | 71 | 4.2 |
| D | 7 * | Nathan Oystrick | ATL | 53 | 4 | 8 | 12 | 15:44 | –2 | 50 | 0 | 0 | 0 | 43 | 9.3 |
| R | 42 * | Joey Crabb | ATL | 29 | 4 | 5 | 9 | 12:12 | –2 | 28 | 0 | 1 | 1 | 33 | 12.1 |
| L | 49 | Colin Stuart | ATL | 33 | 5 | 3 | 8 | 12:28 | 3 | 18 | 0 | 3 | 0 | 54 | 9.3 |
| D | 2 | Garnet Exelby | ATL | 59 | 0 | 7 | 7 | 16:43 | –2 | 120 | 0 | 0 | 0 | 42 | 0.0 |
| D | 25 * | Anssi Salmela | N.J. | 17 | 0 | 3 | 3 | 15:10 | 1 | 6 | 0 | 0 | 0 | 33 | 0.0 |
| | | | ATL | 9 | 1 | 2 | 3 | 17:31 | 0 | 2 | 1 | 0 | 0 | 8 | 12.5 |
| | | | Total | 26 | 1 | 5 | 6 | 15:58 | 1 | 8 | 1 | 0 | 0 | 41 | 2.4 |
| D | 48 * | Boris Valabik | ATL | 50 | 0 | 5 | 5 | 15:14 | –14 | 132 | 0 | 0 | 0 | 16 | 0.0 |
| R | 41 | Joe Motzko | ATL | 6 | 1 | 0 | 1 | 11:39 | 1 | 0 | 0 | 0 | 0 | 8 | 12.5 |
| L | 21 * | Brett Sterling | ATL | 6 | 1 | 0 | 1 | 13:53 | –3 | 2 | 0 | 0 | 0 | 11 | 9.1 |
| D | 40 * | Clay Wilson | CBJ | 5 | 0 | 1 | 1 | 9:25 | –2 | 0 | 0 | 0 | 0 | 9 | 0.0 |
| | | | ATL | 2 | 0 | 0 | 0 | 15:54 | –1 | 0 | 0 | 0 | 0 | 4 | 0.0 |
| | | | Total | 7 | 0 | 1 | 1 | 11:16 | –3 | 0 | 0 | 0 | 0 | 13 | 0.0 |
| D | 38 * | Grant Lewis | ATL | 1 | 0 | 0 | 0 | 15:29 | 0 | 0 | 0 | 0 | 0 | 1 | 0.0 |
| D | 51 * | Scott Lehman | ATL | 1 | 0 | 0 | 0 | 3:03 | 0 | 0 | 0 | 0 | 0 | 0 | 0.0 |
| L | 50 * | Jordan LaVallee | ATL | 2 | 0 | 0 | 0 | 6:39 | –1 | 0 | 0 | 0 | 0 | 1 | 0.0 |
| R | 46 * | Spencer Machacek | ATL | 2 | 0 | 0 | 0 | 8:11 | 0 | 0 | 0 | 0 | 0 | 1 | 0.0 |

## Goaltending

| No. | Goaltender | GPI | Mins | Avg | W | L | OT | EN | SO | GA | SA | S% | G | A | PIM |
|---|---|---|---|---|---|---|---|---|---|---|---|---|---|---|---|
| 32 | Kari Lehtonen | 46 | 2624 | 3.06 | 19 | 22 | 3 | 4 | 3 | 134 | 1498 | .911 | 0 | 1 | 6 |
| 1 | Johan Hedberg | 33 | 1717 | 3.49 | 13 | 12 | 3 | 3 | 0 | 100 | 875 | .886 | 0 | 0 | 2 |
| 31 | * Ondrej Pavelec | 12 | 599 | 3.61 | 3 | 7 | 0 | 2 | 0 | 36 | 301 | .880 | 0 | 0 | 0 |
| | **Totals** | **82** | **4981** | **3.36** | **35** | **41** | **6** | **9** | **3** | **279** | **2683** | **.896** | | | |

*Chosen third overall in the 2008 Entry Draft, Zach Bogosian jumped directly to the NHL in 2008-09. Injuries limited him to just 47 games.*

# Don Waddell

## Vice President and General Manager

*Born: Detroit, MI, August 19, 1958.*

As the only general manager in the history of the Atlanta Thrashers, Don Waddell has established a foundation for long-term success in Atlanta by infusing the club with solid veterans to support a talented young line-up. Waddell built a team that set club records in wins (43) and points (97) in 2006-07, winning the Southeast Division and reaching the playoffs for the first time.

Waddell came to the franchise on June 23, 1998 – almost a year to the day after the NHL granted Atlanta a team. He has built the core of the franchise through the NHL Entry Draft and by stockpiling impressive prospects. He made Ilya Kovalchuk the first Russian player selected first overall in the history of the Entry Draft. In the 2002 Entry Draft, Waddell made Kari Lehtonen of Finland the highest-selected European goaltender in NHL draft history.

Waddell has a long-standing relationship with USA Hockey as a player and in management, and served as assistant general manager for the 2004 World Championship and World Cup teams. He was general manager of the 2005 World Championship team and the 2006 Olympic team. His extensive organizational experience also includes having previously built two professional hockey franchises: the San Diego Gulls and the Orlando Solar Bears of the now-defunct International Hockey League. He's also no stranger to winning through his role as assistant general manager for the Stanley Cup champion Detroit Red Wings during the 1997-98 season.

Waddell's playing experience includes more than nine seasons of professional hockey, mostly in the IHL. He was drafted by the NHL's Los Angeles Kings in 1978 and spent three years with the organization from 1980 to 1983. During a successful amateur career, Waddell helped the U.S. national team win the gold medal at the 1983 B-Pool World Championships. He played Division I hockey at Northern Michigan University from 1976 to 1980, where he majored in business management.

### Coaching Record

| | | | Regular Season | | | | Playoffs | | | |
|---|---|---|---|---|---|---|---|---|---|---|
| Season | Team | League | GC | W | L | O/T | GC | W | L | T |
| 2002-03 | Atlanta | NHL | 10 | 4 | 5 | 1 | .... | .... | .... | .... |
| 2007-08 | Atlanta | NHL | 76 | 34 | 34 | 8 | .... | .... | .... | .... |
| | **NHL Totals** | | **86** | **38** | **39** | **9** | .... | .... | .... | .... |

## General Managers' History

Don Waddell, 1999-2000 to date.

## Captains' History

Kelly Buchberger, 1999-2000; Steve Staios, 2000-01; Ray Ferraro, 2001-02; no captain, 2002-03; Shawn McEachern, 2002-03, 2003-04; Scott Mellanby, 2005-06, 2006-07; Bobby Holik, 2007-08; no captain and Ilya Kovalchuk, 2008-09; Ilya Kovalchuk, 2009-10.

## Coaching History

Curt Fraser, 1999-2000 to 2001-02; Curt Fraser, Don Waddell and Bob Hartley, 2002-03; Bob Hartley, 2003-04 to 2006-07; Bob Hartley and Don Waddell, 2007-08; John Anderson, 2008-09 to date.

# Club Records

## Team

(Figures in brackets for season records are games played.)

| | | |
|---|---|---|
| Most Points | 97 | 2006-07 (82) |
| Most Wins | 43 | 2006-07 (82) |
| Most Ties | 12 | 2000-01 (82) |
| Most Losses | 57 | 1999-2000 (82) |
| Most Goals | 281 | 2005-06 (82) |
| Most Goals Against | 313 | 1999-2000 (82) |
| Fewest Points | 39 | 1999-2000 (82) |
| Fewest Wins | 14 | 1999-2000 (82) |
| Fewest Ties | 7 | 1999-2000 (82), 2002-03 (82) |
| Fewest Losses | 33 | 2005-06 (82) |
| Fewest Goals | 170 | 1999-2000 (82) |
| Fewest Goals Against | 243 | 2003-04 (82) |
| **Longest Winning Streak** | | |
| Overall | 6 | Mar. 6-16/09 |
| Home | 7 | Mar. 2-18/07 |
| Away | 4 | Jan. 13-Feb. 7/03, Nov. 3-21/07, Feb. 3-16/09 |
| **Longest Undefeated Streak** | | |
| Overall | 6 | Mar. 6-16/09 (6 wins) |
| Home | 7 | Mar. 2-18/07 (7 wins) |
| Away | 7 | Oct. 21-Nov. 13/00 (3 wins, 4 ties) |
| **Longest Losing Streak** | | |
| Overall | 12 | Jan. 24-Feb. 20/00 |
| Home | *11 | Jan. 24-Mar. 16/00 |
| Away | 10 | Oct. 6-Nov. 18/01, Feb. 16-Mar. 18/08 |
| **Longest Winless Streak** | | |
| Overall | 16 | Jan. 16-Feb. 20/00 (14 losses, 2 ties) |
| Home | *17 | Jan. 19-Mar. 29/00 (15 losses, 2 ties) |
| Away | 10 | Oct. 6-Nov. 18/01 (10 losses) |
| Most Shutouts, Season | 5 | 2005-06 (82), 2007-08 (82) |
| Most PIM, Season | 1,505 | 2003-04 (82) |
| Most Goals, Game | 9 | Nov. 12/05 (Atl. 9 at Car. 0) |

## Individual

| | | |
|---|---|---|
| Most Seasons | 7 | Ilya Kovalchuk |
| Most Games | 545 | Ilya Kovalchuk |
| Most Goals, Career | 297 | Ilya Kovalchuk |
| Most Assists, Career | 260 | Ilya Kovalchuk |
| Most Points, Career | 557 | Ilya Kovalchuk (297G, 260A) |
| Most PIM, Career | 532 | Jeff Odgers |
| Most Shutouts, Career | 14 | Kari Lehtonen |
| Longest Consecutive Games Streak | 202 | Vyacheslav Kozlov (Jan. 9/07-Apr. 11/09) |
| Most Goals, Season | 52 | Ilya Kovalchuk (2005-06), (2007-08) |
| Most Assists, Season | 69 | Marc Savard (2005-06) |
| Most Points, Season | 100 | Marian Hossa (2006-07; 43G, 57A) |
| Most PIM, Season | 226 | Jeff Odgers (2000-01) |
| Most Points, Defenseman, Season | 39 | Ron Hainsey (2008-09; 6G, 33A) |
| Most Points, Center, Season | 97 | Marc Savard (2005-06; 28G, 69A) |
| Most Points, Right Wing, Season | 100 | Marian Hossa (2006-07; 43G, 57A) |
| Most Points, Left Wing, Season | 98 | Ilya Kovalchuk (2005-06; 52G, 46A) |
| Most Points, Rookie, Season | 67 | Dany Heatley (2001-02; 26G, 41A) |
| Most Shutouts, Season | 4 | Kari Lehtonen (2006-07), (2007-08) |
| Most Goals, Game | 4 | Pascal Rheaume (Jan. 19/02), Ilya Kovalchuk (Nov. 11/05) |
| Most Assists, Game | 4 | Seven times |
| Most Points, Game | 5 | Seven times |

* NHL Record.

# All-time Record vs. Other Clubs

## Regular Season

| | At Home | | | | | | | | On Road | | | | | | | | Total | | | | | | | |
|---|---|---|---|---|---|---|---|---|---|---|---|---|---|---|---|---|---|---|---|---|---|---|---|---|
| | GP | W | L | T | OL | GF | GA | PTS | GP | W | L | T | OL | GF | GA | PTS | GP | W | L | T | OL | GF | GA | PTS |
| Anaheim | 5 | 1 | 4 | 0 | 0 | 11 | 18 | 2 | 6 | 3 | 3 | 0 | 0 | 18 | 18 | 6 | 11 | 4 | 7 | 0 | 0 | 29 | 36 | 8 |
| Boston | 18 | 8 | 10 | 0 | 0 | 55 | 54 | 16 | 18 | 6 | 7 | 2 | 3 | 61 | 64 | 17 | 36 | 14 | 17 | 2 | 3 | 116 | 118 | 33 |
| Buffalo | 18 | 12 | 3 | 1 | 2 | 61 | 53 | 27 | 18 | 8 | 10 | 0 | 0 | 50 | 80 | 16 | 36 | 20 | 13 | 1 | 2 | 111 | 133 | 43 |
| Calgary | 6 | 5 | 0 | 1 | 0 | 19 | 11 | 11 | 4 | 0 | 4 | 0 | 0 | 7 | 18 | 0 | 10 | 5 | 4 | 1 | 0 | 26 | 29 | 11 |
| Carolina | 28 | 7 | 15 | 3 | 3 | 77 | 95 | 20 | 28 | 10 | 14 | 1 | 3 | 82 | 90 | 24 | 56 | 17 | 29 | 4 | 6 | 159 | 185 | 44 |
| Chicago | 6 | 2 | 3 | 0 | 1 | 19 | 18 | 5 | 3 | 1 | 2 | 0 | 0 | 3 | 8 | 2 | 9 | 3 | 5 | 0 | 1 | 22 | 26 | 7 |
| Colorado | 6 | 2 | 2 | 1 | 1 | 13 | 16 | 6 | 6 | 4 | 2 | 0 | 0 | 19 | 20 | 8 | 12 | 6 | 4 | 1 | 1 | 32 | 36 | 14 |
| Columbus | 5 | 3 | 2 | 0 | 0 | 10 | 10 | 6 | 5 | 2 | 2 | 0 | 1 | 11 | 14 | 5 | 10 | 5 | 4 | 0 | 1 | 21 | 24 | 11 |
| Dallas | 5 | 0 | 4 | 0 | 1 | 12 | 21 | 1 | 6 | 1 | 5 | 0 | 0 | 9 | 13 | 2 | 11 | 1 | 9 | 0 | 1 | 21 | 34 | 3 |
| Detroit | 5 | 1 | 4 | 0 | 0 | 17 | 31 | 2 | 6 | 1 | 3 | 0 | 2 | 16 | 23 | 4 | 11 | 2 | 7 | 0 | 2 | 33 | 54 | 6 |
| Edmonton | 4 | 1 | 3 | 0 | 0 | 5 | 12 | 2 | 6 | 2 | 3 | 1 | 0 | 16 | 22 | 5 | 10 | 3 | 6 | 1 | 0 | 21 | 34 | 7 |
| Florida | 28 | 15 | 7 | 4 | 2 | 94 | 79 | 36 | 28 | 14 | 9 | 1 | 4 | 84 | 73 | 33 | 56 | 29 | 16 | 5 | 6 | 178 | 152 | 69 |
| Los Angeles | 5 | 2 | 3 | 0 | 0 | 13 | 18 | 4 | 6 | 2 | 4 | 0 | 0 | 22 | 32 | 4 | 11 | 4 | 7 | 0 | 0 | 35 | 50 | 8 |
| Minnesota | 4 | 1 | 3 | 0 | 0 | 11 | 16 | 2 | 4 | 0 | 3 | 1 | 0 | 6 | 13 | 1 | 8 | 1 | 6 | 1 | 0 | 17 | 29 | 3 |
| Montreal | 18 | 6 | 9 | 2 | 1 | 34 | 46 | 15 | 18 | 5 | 12 | 0 | 1 | 42 | 63 | 11 | 36 | 11 | 21 | 2 | 2 | 76 | 109 | 26 |
| Nashville | 6 | 3 | 0 | 1 | 2 | 19 | 17 | 9 | 5 | 2 | 3 | 0 | 0 | 13 | 17 | 4 | 11 | 5 | 3 | 1 | 2 | 32 | 34 | 13 |
| New Jersey | 18 | 5 | 11 | 2 | 0 | 39 | 65 | 12 | 18 | 8 | 8 | 1 | 1 | 40 | 52 | 18 | 36 | 13 | 19 | 3 | 1 | 79 | 117 | 30 |
| NY Islanders | 18 | 6 | 9 | 2 | 1 | 57 | 71 | 15 | 18 | 9 | 9 | 0 | 0 | 47 | 59 | 18 | 36 | 15 | 18 | 2 | 1 | 104 | 130 | 33 |
| NY Rangers | 18 | 8 | 9 | 0 | 1 | 54 | 60 | 17 | 18 | 10 | 6 | 1 | 1 | 51 | 50 | 22 | 36 | 18 | 15 | 1 | 2 | 105 | 110 | 39 |
| Ottawa | 18 | 7 | 10 | 1 | 0 | 61 | 68 | 15 | 18 | 6 | 11 | 1 | 0 | 50 | 80 | 13 | 36 | 13 | 21 | 2 | 0 | 111 | 148 | 28 |
| Philadelphia | 18 | 2 | 13 | 1 | 2 | 37 | 66 | 7 | 18 | 2 | 13 | 2 | 1 | 49 | 77 | 7 | 36 | 4 | 26 | 3 | 3 | 86 | 143 | 14 |
| Phoenix | 5 | 1 | 3 | 0 | 1 | 10 | 17 | 3 | 7 | 0 | 5 | 1 | 1 | 12 | 25 | 2 | 12 | 1 | 8 | 1 | 2 | 22 | 42 | 5 |
| Pittsburgh | 18 | 6 | 10 | 0 | 2 | 54 | 62 | 14 | 18 | 4 | 12 | 0 | 2 | 44 | 70 | 10 | 36 | 10 | 22 | 0 | 4 | 98 | 132 | 24 |
| St. Louis | 6 | 2 | 3 | 1 | 0 | 18 | 20 | 5 | 4 | 1 | 3 | 0 | 0 | 4 | 13 | 2 | 10 | 3 | 6 | 1 | 0 | 22 | 33 | 7 |
| San Jose | 5 | 1 | 3 | 1 | 0 | 8 | 16 | 3 | 6 | 0 | 5 | 1 | 0 | 11 | 24 | 1 | 11 | 1 | 8 | 2 | 0 | 19 | 40 | 4 |
| Tampa Bay | 28 | 17 | 6 | 3 | 2 | 93 | 74 | 39 | 28 | 10 | 13 | 1 | 4 | 73 | 100 | 25 | 56 | 27 | 19 | 4 | 6 | 166 | 174 | 64 |
| Toronto | 17 | 6 | 10 | 0 | 1 | 33 | 63 | 13 | 17 | 6 | 9 | 1 | 1 | 45 | 62 | 14 | 34 | 12 | 19 | 1 | 2 | 78 | 125 | 27 |
| Vancouver | 5 | 2 | 3 | 0 | 0 | 16 | 17 | 4 | 4 | 1 | 2 | 1 | 0 | 7 | 13 | 3 | 9 | 3 | 5 | 1 | 0 | 23 | 30 | 7 |
| Washington | 28 | 15 | 9 | 2 | 2 | 84 | 81 | 34 | 28 | 8 | 14 | 3 | 3 | 82 | 101 | 22 | 56 | 23 | 23 | 5 | 5 | 166 | 182 | 56 |
| **Totals** | **369** | **147** | **171** | **26** | **25** | **1034** | **1195** | **345** | **369** | **126** | **196** | **19** | **28** | **974** | **1294** | **299** | **738** | **273** | **367** | **45** | **53** | **2008** | **2489** | **644** |

## Playoffs

| | Series | W | L | GP | W | L | T | GF | GA | Last Mtg. | Rnd. | Result |
|---|---|---|---|---|---|---|---|---|---|---|---|---|
| NY Rangers | 1 | 0 | 1 | 4 | 0 | 4 | 0 | 6 | 17 | 2007 | CQF | L 0-4 |
| **Totals** | **1** | **0** | **1** | **4** | **0** | **4** | **0** | **6** | **17** | | | |

## Playoff Results 2009-2004

| Year | Round | Opponent | Result | GF | GA |
|---|---|---|---|---|---|
| 2007 | CQF | NY Rangers | L 0-4 | 6 | 17 |

**Abbreviations: Round: CQF** – conference quarter-final.

## 2008-09 Results

| Month | Day | Opponent | Score |
|---|---|---|---|
| Oct. | 10 | Washington | 7-4 |
| | 11 | at Florida | 2-3* |
| | 14 | Minnesota | 2-4 |
| | 16 | New Jersey | 0-1 |
| | 18 | Buffalo | 3-2† |
| | 21 | at Tampa Bay | 2-3* |
| | 24 | at Detroit | 3-5 |
| | 25 | at Boston | 4-5 |
| | 28 | Philadelphia | 0-7 |
| | 30 | at NY Rangers | 2-3 |
| Nov. | 1 | at New Jersey | 1-6 |
| | 2 | Florida | 5-3 |
| | 6 | NY Islanders | 4-3 |
| | 7 | at Buffalo | 5-4* |
| | 9 | at Carolina | 5-2 |
| | 14 | Carolina | 3-2 |
| | 16 | at Philadelphia | 3-4 |
| | 20 | Pittsburgh | 2-3 |
| | 22 | Columbus | 0-2 |
| | 25 | at Toronto | 6-3 |
| | 26 | at Washington | 3-5 |
| | 28 | Nashville | 3-4* |
| | 30 | St. Louis | 2-4 |
| Dec. | 2 | at Montreal | 4-5 |
| | 3 | at Ottawa | 1-5 |
| | 6 | at NY Islanders | 5-1 |
| | 10 | NY Rangers | 2-3* |
| | 12 | Boston | 3-7 |
| | 13 | at Boston | 2-4 |
| | 16 | at Ottawa | 4-1 |
| | 18 | Pittsburgh | 3-6 |
| | 20 | Tampa Bay | 4-3 |
| | 22 | Toronto | 2-6 |
| | 23 | at NY Islanders | 4-2 |
| | 26 | Carolina | 4-5 |
| | 28 | Boston | 1-2 |
| | 30 | at Toronto | 3-4* |
| | 31 | at Carolina | 1-3 |
| Jan. | 2 | Vancouver | 4-3† |
| | 4 | Tampa Bay | 1-4 |
| | 6 | at Pittsburgh | 1-3 |
| | 8 | at New Jersey | 4-0 |
| | 10 | at Florida | 4-8 |
| | 14 | Ottawa | 2-3 |
| | 16 | Toronto | 4-3* |
| | 17 | at Nashville | 7-2 |
| | 20 | Montreal | 4-2 |
| | 21 | at Philadelphia | 3-5 |
| | 27 | at Dallas | 0-2 |
| | 29 | NY Islanders | 4-5 |
| | 31 | at Carolina | 0-2 |
| Feb. | 3 | at NY Rangers | 2-1† |
| | 6 | New Jersey | 1-5 |
| | 8 | Philadelphia | 2-3 |
| | 10 | at Tampa Bay | 3-1 |
| | 11 | Chicago | 1-3 |
| | 15 | at Anaheim | 8-4 |
| | 16 | at Los Angeles | 7-6† |
| | 19 | at Phoenix | 3-4† |
| | 21 | at San Jose | 1-3 |
| | 24 | Colorado | 4-3 |
| | 26 | at Washington | 3-4 |
| | 28 | Carolina | 5-3 |
| Mar. | 3 | Florida | 3-4 |
| | 6 | Montreal | 2-0 |
| | 8 | Calgary | 5-2 |
| | 10 | at Colorado | 3-0 |
| | 12 | at Edmonton | 4-3* |
| | 14 | at Buffalo | 4-3† |
| | 16 | Washington | 5-1 |
| | 17 | at Pittsburgh | 2-6 |
| | 20 | Detroit | 3-6 |
| | 21 | at Tampa Bay | 4-3† |
| | 24 | at Montreal | 3-6 |
| | 26 | NY Rangers | 5-4† |
| | 28 | Ottawa | 6-3 |
| Apr. | 1 | Buffalo | 3-2* |
| | 3 | at Florida | 3-1 |
| | 5 | at Washington | 4-6 |
| | 7 | Washington | 2-4 |
| | 9 | Florida | 2-3 |
| | 11 | Tampa Bay | 6-2 |

* – Overtime † – Shootout

## Entry Draft Selections 2009-1999

Name in bold denotes played in NHL.

**2009**
Pick
4 Evander Kane
34 Carl Klingberg
45 Jeremy Morin
117 Edward Pasquale
120 Ben Chiarot
125 Cody Sol
155 Jimmy Bubnick
185 Levko Koper
203 Jordan Samuels-Thomas

**2008**
Pick
3 **Zach Bogosian**
29 Daultan Leveille
64 Danick Paquette
94 Vinny Saponari
124 Nicklas Lasu
154 Christopher Carrozzi
184 Zach Redmond

**2007**
Pick
67 **Spencer Machacek**
115 Niclas Lucenius
175 John Albert
205 Paul Postma

**2006**
Pick
12 **Bryan Little**
43 Riley Holzapfel
80 Michael Forney
135 Alex Kangas
165 Jonas Enlund
195 Jesse Martin
200 Arturs Kulda
210 Will O'Neill

**2005**
Pick
16 Alex Bourret
41 **Ondrej Pavelec**
49 Chad Denny
53 Andrew Kozek
116 **Jordan LaVallee**
135 Tomas Pospisil
187 Andrei Zubarev
207 Myles Stoesz

**2004**
Pick
10 **Boris Valabik**
40 **Grant Lewis**
76 **Scott Lehman**
106 Chad Painchaud
142 Juraj Gracik
186 Dan Turple
204 Miikka Tuomainen
237 Mitch Carefoot
270 Matt Siddall

**2003**
Pick
8 **Braydon Coburn**
110 Jim Sharrow
116 Guillaume Desbiens
136 Michael Vannelli
145 **Brett Sterling**
175 Mike Hamilton
203 Denis Loginov
239 **Tobias Enstrom**
269 Rylan Kaip

**2002**
Pick
2 **Kari Lehtonen**
30 **Jim Slater**
116 **Patrick Dwyer**
124 Lane Manson
144 Paul Flache
167 Brad Schell
198 **Nathan Oystrick**
230 Colton Fretter
236 Tyler Boldt
257 Pauli Levokari

**2001**
Pick
1 **Ilya Kovalchuk**
80 **Michael Garnett**
100 Brian Sipotz
112 Milan Gajic
135 **Colin Stuart**
189 **Pasi Nurminen**
199 Matt Suderman
201 Colin FitzRandolph
262 Mario Cartelli

**2000**
Pick
2 **Dany Heatley**
31 Ilja Nikulin
42 Libor Ustrnul
107 Carl Mallette
108 Blake Robson
147 Matt McRae
168 Zdenek Smid
178 Jeff Dwyer
180 **Darcy Hordichuk**
230 Samu Isosalo
242 Evan Nielsen
244 Eric Bowen
288 Mark McRae
290 **Simon Gamache**

**1999**
Pick
1 **Patrik Stefan**
30 **Luke Sellars**
68 **Zdenek Blatny**
98 David Kaczowka
99 Rob Zepp
128 **Derek MacKenzie**
159 Yuri Dobryshkin
188 Stephen Baby
217 **Garnet Exelby**
245 **Tommi Santala**
246 Raymond DiLauro

## John Anderson

### Head Coach

*Born: Toronto, Ont., March 28, 1957.*

The Atlanta Thrashers named John Anderson the fourth head coach in team history on June 20, 2008. Anderson led the Chicago Wolves, Atlanta's American Hockey League farm club, to the 2008 Calder Cup championship. It was his fifth championship in 13 seasons as a head coach in the minor leagues. Anderson spent 11 seasons as head coach of the Wolves, who have been the Thrashers' primary minor-league affiliate since 2001. During his tenure with Chicago, Anderson earned a 506-283-99 regular-season record, a 105-60 post-season record and captured two Calder Cup championships (2002, 2008,) and two Turner Cup titles (1998, 2000) when the team was a member of the International Hockey League. Anderson earned his first of five league titles as a head coach with the Quad City Mallards of the Colonial Hockey League in 1997.

Throughout his 13 seasons as a head coach in the minor leagues, Anderson's teams made the playoffs on 12 occasions, including 10 of his 11 seasons with the Wolves. Overall, he led his teams to the league finals eight times and advanced to the conference finals 10 times. He has won 40-or-more games in a season 10 times, including 50-or-more wins on four occasions, and has reached the 100-point mark seven times. He is also the Wolves all-time leader in regular-season wins (506) and playoff wins (105).

Under Anderson's leadership, the Wolves set several single-season team records, including 55 wins (1997-98); 114 points (1999-2000); 331 goals (2006-07); and 208 goals-against (2003-04). After the team joined the AHL in 2001, Anderson racked up 306 regular-season wins and led the squad to a 16-4 series record in the Calder Cup playoffs. Prior to joining the Wolves, Anderson led Quad City to the 1997 Colonial Cup championship. The previous season (1995-96), he began his coaching career with the Winston-Salem Mammoths, leading them to the Southern Hockey League finals. In July of 2007, Anderson made his international coaching debut when he led the United States squad to a gold medal at the World Jewish Cup in Metulla, Israel.

During his 12-year NHL playing career from 1977 to 1989, Anderson amassed 282 goals and 349 assists for 631 points in 814 games with the Toronto Maple Leafs (1977 to1985), Quebec Nordiques (1985-86) and Hartford Whalers (1986 to 1989). He also notched nine goals and 27 points in 37 career playoff games. Originally selected by the Maple Leafs in the first round, 11th overall, in the 1977 NHL Entry Draft, Anderson registered five 30-goal campaigns, including four straight from 1982 to 1985. His most productive season came in 1982-83, when he led Toronto with 80 points (31 goals, 49 assists) in 80 games.

After his NHL career, Anderson spent four full seasons in the minor leagues. With the New Haven Nighthawks in 1991-92, Anderson became the oldest player to win the AHL's MVP award at age 35. As a player/assistant coach with the San Diego Gulls of the IHL in 1992-93, he helped propel the club to an IHL-record 62 wins and a berth in the Turner Cup Finals.

# Club Directory

Philips Arena

**Atlanta Thrashers**
Centennial Tower
101 Marietta St.
Suite 1900
Atlanta, GA 30303
Phone **404/878-3800**
FAX 404/878-3765
www.atlantathrashers.com
**Capacity:** 18,545

**Ownership** .......... Atlanta Spirit, LLC
**Owners** .......... Bruce Levenson, Michael Gearon, Steve Belkin, Ed Peskowitz, Rutherford Seydel, Todd Foreman, Felix Riccio, Michael Gearon, Sr., Beau Turner

**Executive Management**
Executive Vice President and General Manager .......... Don Waddell
President of Philips Arena .......... Bob Williams
Executive Vice President and G.M. Hawks .......... Rick Sund
Senior Vice President of Sales and Marketing .......... Tracy White
Vice President and Chief Financial Officer .......... Phil Ebinger
V.P., Chief Legal Officer and Asst. G.M., Hawks .......... Scott Wilkinson

**Hockey Operations**
Associate General Manager .......... Rick Dudley
Vice President and Assistant General Manager .......... Larry Simmons
Director of Amateur Scouting and Player Development .......... Dan Marr
Director of Player Personnel .......... Mark Dobson
Senior Director of Team Services .......... Michele Zarzaca
Practice Facility Office Manager .......... Rachel Stamper

**Coaching**
Head Coach .......... John Anderson
Assistant Coaches .......... Randy Cunneyworth, Todd Nelson, Steve Weeks
Video Coach .......... Tony Borgford

**Scouting**
Head Scout .......... Marcel Comeau
Full-Time Scouts .......... Evgeny Bogdanovich, Bernd Freimuller, Mark Hillier, Tavis MacMillan, Peter Mahovlich, Bob Owen, John Perpich
Part-Time Scouts .......... Terry Brennan, Pat Carmichael, Freddie Jax

**Training**
Strength and Conditioning Coach .......... Ray Bear
Head Athletic Trainer .......... Tommy Alva
Assistant Athletic Trainer .......... Step Roberts
Massage Therapist .......... Inar Treiguts

**Equipment**
Head Equipment Manager .......... Bobby Stewart
Assistant Equipment Manager .......... Joe Guilmet
Equipment Assistant .......... Jim Guilmet

**Medical**
Team Physician and Orthopaedic Surgeon .......... Dr. Scott Gillogly
Assistant Team Physician and Internist .......... Dr. William Whaley
Primary Care Sports Medicine .......... Dr. Ched Garten
Oral and Maxillofacial Surgeon .......... Dr. Glenn Maron
Team Dentists .......... Dr. Lawrence Saltzman, Dr. Brett Silverman

**Public Releations**
Senior Director of Public Relations .......... Rob Koch
Director of Media Relations .......... Brian Potter
Media Relations Assistant .......... Rob Tillotson

### Coaching Record

| | | | Regular Season | | | | Playoffs | | | |
|---|---|---|---|---|---|---|---|---|---|---|
| Season | Team | League | GC | W | L | O/T | GC | W | L | T |
| 1995-96 | Winston-Salem | SHL | 60 | 30 | 23 | 7 | 9 | 4 | 5 | .... |
| 1996-97 | Quad City | CoHL | 74 | 51 | 20 | 3 | 15 | 11 | 4 | .... |
| 1997-98 | Chicago | IHL | 82 | 55 | 24 | 3 | 22 | 15 | 7 | .... |
| 1998-99 | Chicago | IHL | 82 | 49 | 21 | 12 | 10 | 6 | 4 | .... |
| 99-2000 | Chicago | IHL | 82 | 53 | 21 | 8 | 16 | 12 | 4 | .... |
| 2000-01 | Chicago | IHL | 82 | 43 | 32 | 7 | 16 | 9 | 7 | .... |
| 2001-02 | Chicago | AHL | 80 | 37 | 31 | 12 | 25 | 17 | 8 | .... |
| 2002-03 | Chicago | AHL | 80 | 43 | 25 | 12 | 9 | 3 | 6 | .... |
| 2003-04 | Chicago | AHL | 80 | 42 | 26 | 12 | 10 | 6 | 4 | .... |
| 2004-05 | Chicago | AHL | 80 | 49 | 24 | 7 | 18 | 12 | 6 | .... |
| 2005-06 | Chicago | AHL | 80 | 36 | 32 | 12 | .... | .... | .... | .... |
| 2006-07 | Chicago | AHL | 80 | 46 | 25 | 9 | 15 | 9 | 6 | .... |
| 2007-08 | Chicago | AHL | 80 | 53 | 22 | 5 | 24 | 16 | 8 | .... |
| **2008-09** | **Atlanta** | **NHL** | **82** | **35** | **41** | **6** | .... | .... | .... | .... |
| | **NHL Totals** | | **82** | **35** | **41** | **6** | .... | .... | .... | .... |

# Boston Bruins

## 2008-09 Results: 53W-19L-4OTL-6SOL 116PTS.
## First, Northeast Division

### Key Off-Season Signings/Acquisitions

**2009**

- **June** 2 • Re-signed C **David Krejci.**
- **July** 1 • Re-signed RW **Byron Bitz.**
- 1 • Signed C **Steve Bégin** and D **Johnny Boychuk.**
- 2 • Re-signed RW **Mark Recchi.**
- 20 • Re-signed D **Matt Hunwick.**
- 25 • Signed D **Derek Morris.**

### 2009-10 Schedule

| | | | | | | | |
|---|---|---|---|---|---|---|---|
| **Oct.** | Thu. | 1 | Washington | | Tue. | 5 | at Ottawa |
| | Sat. | 3 | Carolina | | Thu. | 7 | Chicago |
| | Thu. | 8 | Anaheim | | Sat. | 9 | NY Rangers* |
| | Sat. | 10 | NY Islanders | | Wed. | 13 | at Anaheim |
| | Mon. | 12 | Colorado* | | Thu. | 14 | at San Jose |
| | Fri. | 16 | at Dallas | | Sat. | 16 | at Los Angeles* |
| | Sat. | 17 | at Phoenix | | Mon. | 18 | Ottawa* |
| | Wed. | 21 | Nashville | | Thu. | 21 | Columbus |
| | Thu. | 22 | at Philadelphia | | Sat. | 23 | Ottawa* |
| | Sat. | 24 | at Ottawa | | Sun. | 24 | at Carolina* |
| | Thu. | 29 | New Jersey | | Fri. | 29 | at Buffalo |
| | Sat. | 31 | Edmonton* | | Sat. | 30 | Los Angeles |
| **Nov.** | Sun. | 1 | at NY Rangers* | **Feb.** | Tue. | 2 | Washington |
| | Tue. | 3 | at Detroit | | Thu. | 4 | Montreal |
| | Thu. | 5 | Montreal | | Sat. | 6 | Vancouver* |
| | Sat. | 7 | Buffalo | | Sun. | 7 | at Montreal* |
| | Tue. | 10 | Pittsburgh | | Tue. | 9 | at Buffalo |
| | Thu. | 12 | Florida | | Thu. | 11 | at Tampa Bay |
| | Sat. | 14 | at Pittsburgh | | Sat. | 13 | at Florida |
| | Mon. | 16 | NY Islanders | **Mar.** | Tue. | 2 | Montreal |
| | Thu. | 19 | at Atlanta | | Thu. | 4 | Toronto |
| | Fri. | 20 | at Buffalo | | Sat. | 6 | at NY Islanders* |
| | Mon. | 23 | at St. Louis | | Sun. | 7 | at Pittsburgh* |
| | Wed. | 25 | at Minnesota | | Tue. | 9 | at Toronto |
| | Fri. | 27 | New Jersey | | Thu. | 11 | at Philadelphia |
| | Sat. | 28 | Ottawa | | Sat. | 13 | at Montreal |
| **Dec.** | Wed. | 2 | Tampa Bay | | Mon. | 15 | at New Jersey |
| | Fri. | 4 | at Montreal | | Tue. | 16 | at Carolina |
| | Sat. | 5 | Toronto | | Thu. | 18 | Pittsburgh |
| | Thu. | 10 | Toronto | | Sun. | 21 | NY Rangers* |
| | Sat. | 12 | at NY Islanders | | Tue. | 23 | at Atlanta |
| | Mon. | 14 | Philadelphia | | Thu. | 25 | Tampa Bay |
| | Fri. | 18 | at Chicago | | Sat. | 27 | Calgary* |
| | Sat. | 19 | at Toronto | | Mon. | 29 | Buffalo |
| | Mon. | 21 | at Ottawa | | Tue. | 30 | at New Jersey |
| | Wed. | 23 | Atlanta | **Apr.** | Thu. | 1 | Florida |
| | Sun. | 27 | at Florida* | | Sat. | 3 | at Toronto |
| | Mon. | 28 | at Tampa Bay | | Mon. | 5 | at Washington |
| | Wed. | 30 | Atlanta | | Thu. | 8 | Buffalo |
| **Jan.** | Fri. | 1 | Philadelphia* | | Sat. | 10 | Carolina* |
| | Mon. | 4 | at NY Rangers | | Sun. | 11 | at Washington* |

* Denotes afternoon game.

**NORTHEAST DIVISION**
**86th NHL Season**

**Franchise date:** November 1, 1924

### Year-by-Year Record

| | | Home | | | | Road | | | | Overall | | | | | | | | |
|---|---|---|---|---|---|---|---|---|---|---|---|---|---|---|---|---|---|---|
| Season | GP | W | L | T | OL | W | L | T | OL | W | L | T | OL | GF | GA | Pts. | Finished | Playoff Result |
| 2008-09 | 82 | 29 | 6 | .... | 6 | 24 | 13 | .... | 4 | 53 | 19 | .... | 10 | 274 | 196 | 116 | 1st, Northeast Div. | Lost Conf. Semi-Final |
| 2007-08 | 82 | 21 | 16 | .... | 4 | 20 | 13 | .... | 8 | 41 | 29 | .... | 12 | 212 | 222 | 94 | 3rd, Northeast Div. | Lost Conf. Quarter-Final |
| 2006-07 | 82 | 18 | 19 | .... | 4 | 17 | 22 | .... | 2 | 35 | 41 | .... | 6 | 219 | 289 | 76 | 5th, Northeast Div. | Out of Playoffs |
| 2005-06 | 82 | 16 | 15 | .... | 10 | 13 | 22 | .... | 6 | 29 | 37 | .... | 16 | 230 | 266 | 74 | 5th, Northeast Div. | Out of Playoffs |
| 2004-05 | .... | .... | .... | .... | .... | .... | .... | .... | .... | .... | .... | .... | .... | .... | .... | .... | | |
| 2003-04 | 82 | 18 | 12 | 9 | 2 | 23 | 7 | 6 | 5 | 41 | 19 | 15 | 7 | 209 | 188 | 104 | 1st, Northeast Div. | Lost Conf. Quarter-Final |
| 2002-03 | 82 | 23 | 11 | 5 | 2 | 13 | 20 | 6 | 2 | 36 | 31 | 11 | 4 | 245 | 237 | 87 | 3rd, Northeast Div. | Lost Conf. Quarter-Final |
| 2001-02 | 82 | 23 | 11 | 2 | 5 | 20 | 13 | 4 | 4 | 43 | 24 | 6 | 9 | 236 | 201 | 101 | 1st, Northeast Div. | Lost Conf. Quarter-Final |
| 2000-01 | 82 | 21 | 12 | 5 | 3 | 15 | 18 | 3 | 5 | 36 | 30 | 8 | 8 | 227 | 249 | 88 | 4th, Northeast Div. | Out of Playoffs |
| 1999-2000 | 82 | 12 | 17 | 11 | 1 | 12 | 16 | 8 | 5 | 24 | 33 | 19 | 6 | 210 | 248 | 73 | 5th, Northeast Div. | Out of Playoffs |
| 1998-99 | 82 | 22 | 10 | 9 | .... | 17 | 20 | 4 | .... | 39 | 30 | 13 | .... | 214 | 181 | 91 | 3rd, Northeast Div. | Lost Conf. Semi-Final |
| 1997-98 | 82 | 19 | 16 | 6 | .... | 20 | 14 | 7 | .... | 39 | 30 | 13 | .... | 221 | 194 | 91 | 2nd, Northeast Div. | Lost Conf. Quarter-Final |
| 1996-97 | 82 | 14 | 20 | 7 | .... | 12 | 27 | 2 | .... | 26 | 47 | 9 | .... | 234 | 300 | 61 | 6th, Northeast Div. | Out of Playoffs |
| 1995-96 | 82 | 22 | 14 | 5 | .... | 18 | 17 | 6 | .... | 40 | 31 | 11 | .... | 282 | 269 | 91 | 2nd, Northeast Div. | Lost Conf. Quarter-Final |
| 1994-95 | 48 | 15 | 7 | 2 | .... | 12 | 11 | 1 | .... | 27 | 18 | 3 | .... | 150 | 127 | 57 | 3rd, Northeast Div. | Lost Conf. Quarter-Final |
| 1993-94 | 84 | 20 | 14 | 8 | .... | 22 | 15 | 5 | .... | 42 | 29 | 13 | .... | 289 | 252 | 97 | 2nd, Northeast Div. | Lost Conf. Semi-Final |
| 1992-93 | 84 | 29 | 10 | 3 | .... | 22 | 16 | 4 | .... | 51 | 26 | 7 | .... | 332 | 268 | 109 | 1st, Adams Div. | Lost Div. Semi-Final |
| 1991-92 | 80 | 23 | 11 | 6 | .... | 13 | 21 | 6 | .... | 36 | 32 | 12 | .... | 270 | 275 | 84 | 2nd, Adams Div. | Lost Conf. Championship |
| 1990-91 | 80 | 26 | 9 | 5 | .... | 18 | 15 | 7 | .... | 44 | 24 | 12 | .... | 299 | 264 | 100 | 1st, Adams Div. | Lost Conf. Championship |
| 1989-90 | 80 | 23 | 13 | 4 | .... | 23 | 12 | 5 | .... | 46 | 25 | 9 | .... | 289 | 232 | 101 | 1st, Adams Div. | Lost Final |
| 1988-89 | 80 | 17 | 15 | 8 | .... | 20 | 14 | 6 | .... | 37 | 29 | 14 | .... | 289 | 256 | 88 | 2nd, Adams Div. | Lost Div. Final |
| 1987-88 | 80 | 24 | 13 | 3 | .... | 20 | 17 | 3 | .... | 44 | 30 | 6 | .... | 300 | 251 | 94 | 2nd, Adams Div. | Lost Final |
| 1986-87 | 80 | 25 | 11 | 4 | .... | 14 | 23 | 3 | .... | 39 | 34 | 7 | .... | 301 | 276 | 85 | 3rd, Adams Div. | Lost Div. Semi-Final |
| 1985-86 | 80 | 24 | 9 | 7 | .... | 13 | 22 | 5 | .... | 37 | 31 | 12 | .... | 311 | 288 | 86 | 3rd, Adams Div. | Lost Div. Semi-Final |
| 1984-85 | 80 | 21 | 15 | 4 | .... | 15 | 19 | 6 | .... | 36 | 34 | 10 | .... | 303 | 287 | 82 | 4th, Adams Div. | Lost Div. Semi-Final |
| 1983-84 | 80 | 25 | 12 | 3 | .... | 24 | 13 | 3 | .... | 49 | 25 | 6 | .... | 336 | 261 | 104 | 1st, Adams Div. | Lost Div. Semi-Final |
| 1982-83 | 80 | 28 | 6 | 6 | .... | 22 | 14 | 4 | .... | 50 | 20 | 10 | .... | 327 | 228 | 110 | 1st, Adams Div. | Lost Conf. Championship |
| 1981-82 | 80 | 24 | 12 | 4 | .... | 19 | 15 | 6 | .... | 43 | 27 | 10 | .... | 323 | 285 | 96 | 2nd, Adams Div. | Lost Div. Final |
| 1980-81 | 80 | 26 | 10 | 4 | .... | 11 | 20 | 9 | .... | 37 | 30 | 13 | .... | 316 | 272 | 87 | 2nd, Adams Div. | Lost Prelim. Round |
| 1979-80 | 80 | 27 | 9 | 4 | .... | 19 | 12 | 9 | .... | 46 | 21 | 13 | .... | 310 | 234 | 105 | 2nd, Adams Div. | Lost Quarter-Final |
| 1978-79 | 80 | 25 | 10 | 5 | .... | 18 | 13 | 9 | .... | 43 | 23 | 14 | .... | 316 | 270 | 100 | 1st, Adams Div. | Lost Semi-Final |
| 1977-78 | 80 | 29 | 6 | 5 | .... | 22 | 12 | 6 | .... | 51 | 18 | 11 | .... | 333 | 218 | 113 | 1st, Adams Div. | Lost Final |
| 1976-77 | 80 | 27 | 7 | 6 | .... | 22 | 16 | 2 | .... | 49 | 23 | 8 | .... | 312 | 240 | 106 | 1st, Adams Div. | Lost Final |
| 1975-76 | 80 | 27 | 5 | 8 | .... | 21 | 10 | 9 | .... | 48 | 15 | 17 | .... | 313 | 237 | 113 | 1st, Adams Div. | Lost Semi-Final |
| 1974-75 | 80 | 29 | 5 | 6 | .... | 11 | 21 | 8 | .... | 40 | 26 | 14 | .... | 345 | 245 | 94 | 2nd, Adams Div. | Lost Prelim. Round |
| 1973-74 | 78 | 33 | 4 | 2 | .... | 19 | 13 | 7 | .... | 52 | 17 | 9 | .... | 349 | 221 | 113 | 1st, East Div. | Lost Final |
| 1972-73 | 78 | 27 | 10 | 2 | .... | 24 | 12 | 3 | .... | 51 | 22 | 5 | .... | 330 | 235 | 107 | 2nd, East Div. | Lost Quarter-Final |
| **1971-72** | **78** | **28** | **4** | **7** | .... | **26** | **9** | **4** | .... | **54** | **13** | **11** | .... | **330** | **204** | **119** | **1st, East Div.** | **Won Stanley Cup** |
| 1970-71 | 78 | 33 | 4 | 2 | .... | 24 | 10 | 5 | .... | 57 | 14 | 7 | .... | 399 | 207 | 121 | 1st, East Div. | Lost Quarter-Final |
| **1969-70** | **76** | **27** | **3** | **8** | .... | **13** | **14** | **11** | .... | **40** | **17** | **19** | .... | **277** | **216** | **99** | **2nd, East Div.** | **Won Stanley Cup** |
| 1968-69 | 76 | 29 | 3 | 6 | .... | 13 | 15 | 10 | .... | 42 | 18 | 16 | .... | 303 | 221 | 100 | 2nd, East Div. | Lost Semi-Final |
| 1967-68 | 74 | 22 | 9 | 6 | .... | 15 | 18 | 4 | .... | 37 | 27 | 10 | .... | 259 | 216 | 84 | 3rd, East Div. | Lost Quarter-Final |
| 1966-67 | 70 | 10 | 21 | 4 | .... | 7 | 22 | 6 | .... | 17 | 43 | 10 | .... | 182 | 253 | 44 | 6th, | Out of Playoffs |
| 1965-66 | 70 | 15 | 17 | 3 | .... | 6 | 26 | 3 | .... | 21 | 43 | 6 | .... | 174 | 275 | 48 | 5th, | Out of Playoffs |
| 1964-65 | 70 | 12 | 17 | 6 | .... | 9 | 26 | 0 | .... | 21 | 43 | 6 | .... | 166 | 253 | 48 | 6th, | Out of Playoffs |
| 1963-64 | 70 | 13 | 15 | 7 | .... | 5 | 25 | 5 | .... | 18 | 40 | 12 | .... | 170 | 212 | 48 | 6th, | Out of Playoffs |
| 1962-63 | 70 | 7 | 18 | 10 | .... | 7 | 21 | 7 | .... | 14 | 39 | 17 | .... | 198 | 281 | 45 | 6th, | Out of Playoffs |
| 1961-62 | 70 | 9 | 22 | 4 | .... | 6 | 25 | 4 | .... | 15 | 47 | 8 | .... | 177 | 306 | 38 | 6th, | Out of Playoffs |
| 1960-61 | 70 | 13 | 17 | 5 | .... | 2 | 25 | 8 | .... | 15 | 42 | 13 | .... | 176 | 254 | 43 | 6th, | Out of Playoffs |
| 1959-60 | 70 | 21 | 11 | 3 | .... | 7 | 23 | 5 | .... | 28 | 34 | 8 | .... | 220 | 241 | 64 | 5th, | Out of Playoffs |
| 1958-59 | 70 | 21 | 11 | 3 | .... | 11 | 18 | 6 | .... | 32 | 29 | 9 | .... | 205 | 215 | 73 | 2nd, | Lost Semi-Final |
| 1957-58 | 70 | 15 | 14 | 6 | .... | 12 | 14 | 9 | .... | 27 | 28 | 15 | .... | 199 | 194 | 69 | 4th, | Lost Final |
| 1956-57 | 70 | 20 | 9 | 6 | .... | 14 | 15 | 6 | .... | 34 | 24 | 12 | .... | 195 | 174 | 80 | 3rd, | Lost Final |
| 1955-56 | 70 | 14 | 14 | 7 | .... | 9 | 20 | 6 | .... | 23 | 34 | 13 | .... | 147 | 185 | 59 | 5th, | Out of Playoffs |
| 1954-55 | 70 | 16 | 10 | 9 | .... | 7 | 16 | 12 | .... | 23 | 26 | 21 | .... | 169 | 188 | 67 | 4th, | Lost Semi-Final |
| 1953-54 | 70 | 22 | 8 | 5 | .... | 10 | 20 | 5 | .... | 32 | 28 | 10 | .... | 177 | 181 | 74 | 4th, | Lost Semi-Final |
| 1952-53 | 70 | 19 | 10 | 6 | .... | 9 | 19 | 7 | .... | 28 | 29 | 13 | .... | 152 | 172 | 69 | 3rd, | Lost Final |
| 1951-52 | 70 | 15 | 12 | 8 | .... | 10 | 17 | 8 | .... | 25 | 29 | 16 | .... | 162 | 176 | 66 | 4th, | Lost Semi-Final |
| 1950-51 | 70 | 13 | 12 | 10 | .... | 9 | 18 | 8 | .... | 22 | 30 | 18 | .... | 178 | 197 | 62 | 4th, | Lost Semi-Final |
| 1949-50 | 70 | 15 | 12 | 8 | .... | 7 | 20 | 8 | .... | 22 | 32 | 16 | .... | 198 | 228 | 60 | 5th, | Out of Playoffs |
| 1948-49 | 60 | 18 | 10 | 2 | .... | 11 | 13 | 6 | .... | 29 | 23 | 8 | .... | 178 | 163 | 66 | 2nd, | Lost Semi-Final |
| 1947-48 | 60 | 12 | 8 | 10 | .... | 11 | 16 | 3 | .... | 23 | 24 | 13 | .... | 167 | 168 | 59 | 3rd, | Lost Semi-Final |
| 1946-47 | 60 | 18 | 7 | 5 | .... | 8 | 16 | 6 | .... | 26 | 23 | 11 | .... | 190 | 175 | 63 | 3rd, | Lost Semi-Final |
| 1945-46 | 50 | 11 | 5 | 4 | .... | 13 | 13 | 4 | .... | 24 | 18 | 8 | .... | 167 | 156 | 56 | 2nd, | Lost Final |
| 1944-45 | 50 | 11 | 12 | 2 | .... | 5 | 18 | 2 | .... | 16 | 30 | 4 | .... | 179 | 219 | 36 | 4th, | Lost Semi-Final |
| 1943-44 | 50 | 15 | 8 | 2 | .... | 4 | 18 | 3 | .... | 19 | 26 | 5 | .... | 223 | 268 | 43 | 5th, | Out of Playoffs |
| 1942-43 | 50 | 17 | 3 | 5 | .... | 7 | 14 | 4 | .... | 24 | 17 | 9 | .... | 195 | 176 | 57 | 2nd, | Lost Final |
| 1941-42 | 48 | 17 | 4 | 3 | .... | 8 | 13 | 3 | .... | 25 | 17 | 6 | .... | 160 | 118 | 56 | 3rd, | Lost Semi-Final |
| **1940-41** | **48** | **15** | **4** | **5** | .... | **12** | **4** | **8** | .... | **27** | **8** | **13** | .... | **168** | **102** | **67** | **1st,** | **Won Stanley Cup** |
| 1939-40 | 48 | 20 | 3 | 1 | .... | 11 | 9 | 4 | .... | 31 | 12 | 5 | .... | 170 | 98 | 67 | 1st, | Lost Semi-Final |
| **1938-39** | **48** | **20** | **2** | **2** | .... | **16** | **8** | **0** | .... | **36** | **10** | **2** | .... | **156** | **76** | **74** | **1st,** | **Won Stanley Cup** |
| 1937-38 | 48 | 18 | 3 | 3 | .... | 12 | 8 | 4 | .... | 30 | 11 | 7 | .... | 142 | 89 | 67 | 1st, Amn. Div. | Lost Semi-Final |
| 1936-37 | 48 | 9 | 11 | 4 | .... | 14 | 7 | 3 | .... | 23 | 18 | 7 | .... | 120 | 110 | 53 | 2nd, Amn. Div. | Lost Quarter-Final |
| 1935-36 | 48 | 15 | 8 | 1 | .... | 7 | 12 | 5 | .... | 22 | 20 | 6 | .... | 92 | 83 | 50 | 2nd, Amn. Div. | Lost Quarter-Final |
| 1934-35 | 48 | 17 | 7 | 0 | .... | 9 | 9 | 6 | .... | 26 | 16 | 6 | .... | 129 | 112 | 58 | 1st, Amn. Div. | Lost Semi-Final |
| 1933-34 | 48 | 11 | 11 | 2 | .... | 7 | 14 | 3 | .... | 18 | 25 | 5 | .... | 111 | 130 | 41 | 4th, Amn. Div. | Out of Playoffs |
| 1932-33 | 48 | 19 | 2 | 3 | .... | 6 | 13 | 5 | .... | 25 | 15 | 8 | .... | 124 | 88 | 58 | 1st, Amn. Div. | Lost Semi-Final |
| 1931-32 | 48 | 11 | 10 | 3 | .... | 4 | 11 | 9 | .... | 15 | 21 | 12 | .... | 122 | 117 | 42 | 4th, Amn. Div. | Out of Playoffs |
| 1930-31 | 44 | 16 | 1 | 5 | .... | 12 | 9 | 1 | .... | 28 | 10 | 6 | .... | 143 | 90 | 62 | 1st, Amn. Div. | Lost Semi-Final |
| 1929-30 | 44 | 21 | 1 | 0 | .... | 17 | 4 | 1 | .... | 38 | 5 | 1 | .... | 179 | 98 | 77 | 1st, Amn. Div. | Lost Final |
| **1928-29** | **44** | **15** | **6** | **1** | .... | **11** | **7** | **4** | .... | **26** | **13** | **5** | .... | **89** | **52** | **57** | **1st, Amn. Div.** | **Won Stanley Cup** |
| 1927-28 | 44 | 13 | 4 | 5 | .... | 7 | 9 | 6 | .... | 20 | 13 | 11 | .... | 77 | 70 | 51 | 1st, Amn. Div. | Lost Semi-Final |
| 1926-27 | 44 | 15 | 7 | 0 | .... | 6 | 13 | 3 | .... | 21 | 20 | 3 | .... | 97 | 89 | 45 | 2nd, Amn. Div. | Lost Final |
| 1925-26 | 36 | 10 | 7 | 1 | .... | 7 | 8 | 3 | .... | 17 | 15 | 4 | .... | 92 | 85 | 38 | 4th, | Out of Playoffs |
| 1924-25 | 30 | 3 | 12 | 0 | .... | 3 | 12 | 0 | .... | 6 | 24 | 0 | .... | 49 | 119 | 12 | 6th, | Out of Playoffs |

# 2009-10 Player Personnel

| FORWARDS | HT | WT | S | Place of Birth | *Age | 2008-09 Club |
|---|---|---|---|---|---|---|
| BEGIN, Steve | 6-0 | 192 | L | Trois-Rivieres, Que. | 31 | Montreal-Dallas |
| BERGERON, Patrice | 6-2 | 194 | R | Ancienne-Lorette, Que. | 24 | Boston |
| BITZ, Byron | 6-5 | 215 | R | Saskatoon, Sask. | 25 | Boston-Providence (AHL) |
| KESSEL, Phil | 5-11 | 180 | R | Madison, WI | 21 | Boston |
| KOBASEW, Chuck | 5-11 | 192 | L | Vancouver, B.C. | 27 | Boston |
| KREJCI, David | 6-0 | 177 | R | Sternberk, Czech. | 23 | Boston |
| LARMAN, Drew | 6-3 | 195 | R | Canton, MI | 24 | Rochester |
| LEHTONEN, Mikko | 6-5 | 203 | R | Espoo, Finland | 22 | Boston-Providence (AHL) |
| LoVECCHIO, Jeff | 6-2 | 198 | L | Arlington Heights, IL | 24 | (none) |
| LUCIC, Milan | 6-3 | 228 | L | Vancouver, B.C. | 21 | Boston |
| MARCHAND, Brad | 5-9 | 183 | L | Halifax, N.S. | 21 | Providence (AHL) |
| RECCHI, Mark | 5-10 | 195 | L | Kamloops, B.C. | 41 | Tampa Bay-Boston |
| RYDER, Michael | 6-0 | 192 | R | St. John's, Nfld. | 29 | Boston |
| SAVARD, Marc | 5-10 | 191 | L | Ottawa, Ont. | 32 | Boston |
| SOBOTKA, Vladimir | 5-11 | 193 | L | Trebic, Czech. | 22 | Boston-Providence (AHL) |
| STURM, Marco | 6-0 | 194 | L | Dingolfing, West Germany | 31 | Boston |
| THORNTON, Shawn | 6-2 | 217 | R | Oshawa, Ont. | 32 | Boston |
| WHEELER, Blake | 6-5 | 205 | R | Robbinsdale, MN | 23 | Boston |
| WHITFIELD, Trent | 5-11 | 209 | L | Estevan, Sask. | 32 | St. Louis-Peoria |

| DEFENSEMEN | HT | WT | S | Place of Birth | *Age | 2008-09 Club |
|---|---|---|---|---|---|---|
| BOYCHUK, Johnny | 6-2 | 225 | R | Edmonton, Alta. | 25 | Boston-Providence (AHL) |
| CHARA, Zdeno | 6-9 | 255 | L | Trencin, Czech. | 32 | Boston |
| FERENCE, Andrew | 5-11 | 189 | L | Edmonton, Alta. | 30 | Boston |
| HUNWICK, Matt | 5-11 | 190 | L | Warren, MI | 24 | Boston-Providence (AHL) |
| McQUAID, Adam | 6-4 | 197 | R | Charlottetown, P.E.I. | 22 | Providence (AHL) |
| MORRIS, Derek | 6-0 | 221 | R | Edmonton, Alta. | 31 | Phoenix-NY Rangers |
| PENNER, Jeff | 5-10 | 191 | L | Steinbach, Man. | 22 | Providence (AHL) |
| STUART, Mark | 6-2 | 213 | L | Rochester, MN | 25 | Boston |
| WIDEMAN, Dennis | 6-0 | 196 | R | Kitchener, Ont. | 26 | Boston |

| GOALTENDERS | HT | WT | C | Place of Birth | *Age | 2008-09 Club |
|---|---|---|---|---|---|---|
| RASK, Tuukka | 6-2 | 169 | L | Savonlinna, Finland | 22 | Boston-Providence (AHL) |
| SABOURIN, Dany | 6-4 | 200 | L | Val-d'Or, Que. | 29 | Pittsburgh-Springfield |
| THOMAS, Tim | 5-11 | 208 | L | Flint, MI | 35 | Boston |

* – Age at start of 2009-10 season

# 2008-09 Scoring

* – rookie

## Regular Season

| Pos | # | Player | Team | GP | G | A | Pts | TOI | +/- | PIM | PP | SH | GW | S | % |
|---|---|---|---|---|---|---|---|---|---|---|---|---|---|---|---|
| C | 91 | Marc Savard | BOS | 82 | 25 | 63 | 88 | 19:32 | 25 | 70 | 9 | 0 | 5 | 213 | 11.7 |
| C | 46 | David Krejci | BOS | 82 | 22 | 51 | 73 | 16:51 | 37 | 26 | 5 | 2 | 6 | 146 | 15.1 |
| R | 28 | Mark Recchi | T.B. | 62 | 13 | 32 | 45 | 16:53 | –15 | 20 | 2 | 0 | 1 | 97 | 13.4 |
| | | | BOS | 18 | 10 | 6 | 16 | 16:22 | –3 | 2 | 4 | 0 | 2 | 32 | 31.3 |
| | | | Total | 80 | 23 | 38 | 61 | 16:46 | –18 | 22 | 6 | 0 | 3 | 129 | 17.8 |
| R | 81 | Phil Kessel | BOS | 70 | 36 | 24 | 60 | 16:33 | 23 | 16 | 8 | 0 | 6 | 232 | 15.5 |
| R | 73 | Michael Ryder | BOS | 74 | 27 | 26 | 53 | 14:55 | 28 | 26 | 10 | 0 | 7 | 185 | 14.6 |
| D | 33 | Zdeno Chara | BOS | 80 | 19 | 31 | 50 | 26:04 | 23 | 95 | 11 | 0 | 3 | 216 | 8.8 |
| D | 6 | Dennis Wideman | BOS | 79 | 13 | 37 | 50 | 24:38 | 32 | 34 | 6 | 1 | 2 | 169 | 7.7 |
| L | 26 | * Blake Wheeler | BOS | 81 | 21 | 24 | 45 | 13:41 | 36 | 46 | 3 | 2 | 3 | 150 | 14.0 |
| R | 12 | Chuck Kobasew | BOS | 68 | 21 | 21 | 42 | 14:41 | 5 | 56 | 6 | 0 | 3 | 129 | 16.3 |
| L | 17 | Milan Lucic | BOS | 72 | 17 | 25 | 42 | 14:56 | 17 | 136 | 2 | 0 | 3 | 97 | 17.5 |
| C | 37 | Patrice Bergeron | BOS | 64 | 8 | 31 | 39 | 17:59 | 2 | 16 | 1 | 1 | 1 | 155 | 5.2 |
| L | 11 | P.J. Axelsson | BOS | 75 | 6 | 24 | 30 | 16:13 | –1 | 16 | 2 | 0 | 0 | 87 | 6.9 |
| D | 48 | * Matt Hunwick | BOS | 53 | 6 | 21 | 27 | 16:59 | 15 | 31 | 0 | 0 | 1 | 58 | 10.3 |
| D | 23 | Steve Montador | ANA | 65 | 4 | 16 | 20 | 16:12 | 14 | 125 | 0 | 0 | 0 | 100 | 4.0 |
| | | | BOS | 13 | 0 | 1 | 1 | 15:55 | 3 | 18 | 0 | 0 | 0 | 17 | 0.0 |
| | | | Total | 78 | 4 | 17 | 21 | 16:09 | 17 | 143 | 0 | 0 | 0 | 117 | 3.4 |
| C | 18 | Stephane Yelle | BOS | 77 | 7 | 11 | 18 | 13:16 | 6 | 32 | 1 | 0 | 2 | 72 | 9.7 |
| D | 45 | Mark Stuart | BOS | 82 | 5 | 12 | 17 | 15:24 | 20 | 76 | 0 | 0 | 1 | 61 | 8.2 |
| D | 21 | Andrew Ference | BOS | 47 | 1 | 15 | 16 | 21:31 | 7 | 40 | 1 | 0 | 0 | 72 | 1.4 |
| L | 16 | Marco Sturm | BOS | 19 | 7 | 6 | 13 | 16:01 | 9 | 8 | 4 | 0 | 0 | 45 | 15.6 |
| D | 34 | Shane Hnidy | BOS | 65 | 3 | 9 | 12 | 15:37 | 6 | 45 | 1 | 0 | 1 | 49 | 6.1 |
| L | 22 | Shawn Thornton | BOS | 79 | 6 | 5 | 11 | 10:02 | –2 | 123 | 0 | 0 | 2 | 136 | 4.4 |
| D | 44 | Aaron Ward | BOS | 65 | 3 | 7 | 10 | 19:01 | 16 | 44 | 0 | 1 | 0 | 53 | 5.7 |
| R | 61 | * Byron Bitz | BOS | 35 | 4 | 3 | 7 | 10:21 | 0 | 18 | 0 | 0 | 0 | 31 | 12.9 |
| C | 60 | Vladimir Sobotka | BOS | 25 | 1 | 4 | 5 | 10:32 | –10 | 10 | 0 | 0 | 0 | 19 | 5.3 |
| C | 47 | * Martin St. Pierre | BOS | 14 | 2 | 2 | 4 | 11:24 | –1 | 4 | 0 | 1 | 1 | 15 | 13.3 |
| D | 55 | * Johnny Boychuk | BOS | 1 | 0 | 0 | 0 | 14:48 | 0 | 0 | 0 | 0 | 0 | 0 | 0.0 |
| R | 68 | * Mikko Lehtonen | BOS | 1 | 0 | 0 | 0 | 16:14 | 0 | 0 | 0 | 0 | 0 | 1 | 0.0 |

### Goaltending

| No. | Goaltender | GPI | Mins | Avg | W | L | OT | EN | SO | GA | SA | S% | G | A | PIM |
|---|---|---|---|---|---|---|---|---|---|---|---|---|---|---|---|
| 40 | * Tuukka Rask | 1 | 60 | 0.00 | 1 | 0 | 0 | 0 | 1 | 0 | 35 | 1.000 | 0 | 0 | 0 |
| 30 | Tim Thomas | 54 | 3259 | 2.10 | 36 | 11 | 7 | 4 | 5 | 114 | 1694 | .933 | 0 | 1 | 6 |
| 35 | Manny Fernandez | 28 | 1644 | 2.59 | 16 | 8 | 3 | 1 | 1 | 71 | 791 | .910 | 0 | 0 | 2 |
| | **Totals** | **82** | **4987** | **2.29** | **53** | **19** | **10** | **5** | **7** | **190** | **2525** | **.925** | | | |

## Playoffs

| Pos | # | Player | Team | GP | G | A | Pts | TOI | +/- | PIM | PP | SH | GW | OT | S | % |
|---|---|---|---|---|---|---|---|---|---|---|---|---|---|---|---|---|
| C | 91 | Marc Savard | BOS | 11 | 6 | 7 | 13 | 19:35 | 2 | 4 | 3 | 0 | 2 | 0 | 17 | 35.3 |
| R | 73 | Michael Ryder | BOS | 11 | 5 | 8 | 13 | 15:45 | 4 | 8 | 1 | 0 | 1 | 0 | 25 | 20.0 |
| R | 81 | Phil Kessel | BOS | 11 | 6 | 5 | 11 | 15:55 | 7 | 4 | 0 | 0 | 0 | 0 | 38 | 15.8 |
| L | 17 | Milan Lucic | BOS | 10 | 3 | 6 | 9 | 15:13 | 12 | 43 | 0 | 0 | 0 | 0 | 20 | 15.0 |
| C | 46 | David Krejci | BOS | 11 | 2 | 6 | 8 | 17:17 | 6 | 2 | 0 | 0 | 1 | 0 | 26 | 7.7 |
| D | 6 | Dennis Wideman | BOS | 11 | 0 | 7 | 7 | 24:42 | 3 | 4 | 0 | 0 | 0 | 0 | 28 | 0.0 |
| R | 28 | Mark Recchi | BOS | 11 | 3 | 3 | 6 | 16:56 | 0 | 2 | 1 | 0 | 1 | 0 | 19 | 15.8 |
| R | 12 | Chuck Kobasew | BOS | 11 | 3 | 3 | 6 | 16:09 | 3 | 14 | 0 | 0 | 1 | 0 | 23 | 13.0 |
| C | 37 | Patrice Bergeron | BOS | 11 | 0 | 5 | 5 | 17:56 | 3 | 11 | 0 | 0 | 0 | 0 | 22 | 0.0 |
| D | 33 | Zdeno Chara | BOS | 11 | 1 | 3 | 4 | 25:10 | 1 | 12 | 1 | 0 | 1 | 0 | 28 | 3.6 |
| D | 23 | Steve Montador | BOS | 11 | 1 | 2 | 3 | 19:32 | 5 | 18 | 0 | 0 | 0 | 0 | 15 | 6.7 |
| R | 61 | * Byron Bitz | BOS | 5 | 1 | 1 | 2 | 11:27 | 0 | 2 | 0 | 0 | 0 | 0 | 4 | 25.0 |
| D | 34 | Shane Hnidy | BOS | 7 | 1 | 0 | 1 | 14:06 | –1 | 0 | 0 | 0 | 0 | 0 | 6 | 16.7 |
| L | 22 | Shawn Thornton | BOS | 10 | 1 | 0 | 1 | 9:06 | 0 | 6 | 0 | 0 | 0 | 0 | 14 | 7.1 |
| D | 44 | Aaron Ward | BOS | 11 | 1 | 0 | 1 | 19:40 | 4 | 2 | 0 | 0 | 0 | 0 | 6 | 16.7 |
| C | 18 | Stephane Yelle | BOS | 11 | 0 | 1 | 1 | 12:29 | –4 | 2 | 0 | 0 | 0 | 0 | 13 | 0.0 |
| L | 11 | P.J. Axelsson | BOS | 11 | 0 | 1 | 1 | 14:02 | –6 | 2 | 0 | 0 | 0 | 0 | 9 | 0.0 |
| D | 45 | Mark Stuart | BOS | 11 | 0 | 1 | 1 | 17:56 | 5 | 7 | 0 | 0 | 0 | 0 | 7 | 0.0 |
| D | 48 | * Matt Hunwick | BOS | 1 | 0 | 0 | 0 | 15:59 | 0 | 0 | 0 | 0 | 0 | 0 | 2 | 0.0 |
| D | 21 | Andrew Ference | BOS | 3 | 0 | 0 | 0 | 15:30 | 1 | 4 | 0 | 0 | 0 | 0 | 3 | 0.0 |
| L | 26 | * Blake Wheeler | BOS | 8 | 0 | 0 | 0 | 12:07 | 0 | 0 | 0 | 0 | 0 | 0 | 4 | 0.0 |

### Goaltending

| No. | Goaltender | GPI | Mins | Avg | W | L | EN | SO | GA | SA | S% | G | A | PIM |
|---|---|---|---|---|---|---|---|---|---|---|---|---|---|---|
| 30 | Tim Thomas | 11 | 680 | 1.85 | 7 | 4 | 1 | 1 | 21 | 323 | .935 | 0 | 1 | 0 |
| | **Totals** | **11** | **682** | **1.94** | **7** | **4** | **1** | **1** | **22** | **324** | **.932** | | | |

# Claude Julien

## Head Coach

*Born: Orleans, Ont., April 23, 1960.*

The Boston Bruins named Claude Julien the 28th head coach in club history on June 21, 2007. In his first season behind the bench in 2007-08, he guided the Bruins back to the playoffs for the first time since 2003-04. In 2008-09, the Bruins posted the best record in the Eastern Conference and were second overall in the NHL, earning Julien the Jack Adams Award for coach of the year. Julien joined the Bruins with four years of NHL head coaching experience. In his lone season with New Jersey, he held a record of 47-24-8 before being replaced on April 2, 2007 with three games remaining in the 2006-07 regular season. At the time he was replaced by the Devils, Julien's club was in first place in the Atlantic Division.

Prior to being named head coach of the Devils, Julien spent three seasons as the head coach of the Montreal Canadiens, serving from January 2003 until January of 2006. During his tenure with Montreal, Julien led the Canadiens to a record of 72-71-16 in 159 games.

Before joining the NHL coaching ranks, Julien spent four seasons with Hull of the Quebec Major Junior Hockey League and three campaigns with Hamilton of the American Hockey League. While with Hamilton, Julien was co-awarded the Louis A. R. Pieri Award as the league's outstanding coach during the 2002-03 season.

Julien has also coached at the international level, having served as an assistant coach to Team Canada at the 2006 World Championship after he led Team Canada to a bronze medal as a head coach at the 2000 World Junior Championship.

A defenseman, Julien's professional playing career spanned 12 seasons from 1981 to 1992, highlighted by stints with the Quebec Nordiques between 1984 and 1986.

### Coaching Record

| | | | Regular Season | | | | Playoffs | | | |
|---|---|---|---|---|---|---|---|---|---|---|
| Season | Team | League | GC | W | L | O/T | GC | W | L | T |
| 1996-97 | Hull | QMJHL | 70 | 48 | 19 | 3 | 14 | 12 | 2 | .... |
| | Hull | M-Cup | .... | .... | .... | .... | 5 | 3 | 2 | .... |
| 1997-98 | Hull | QMJHL | 70 | 32 | 37 | 1 | 11 | 6 | 5 | .... |
| 1998-99 | Hull | QMJHL | 70 | 23 | 38 | 9 | 23 | 15 | 8 | .... |
| 99-2000 | Hull | QMJHL | 72 | 42 | 24 | 6 | 15 | 9 | 6 | .... |
| 2000-01 | Hamilton | AHL | 80 | 28 | 41 | 11 | .... | .... | .... | .... |
| 2001-02 | Hamilton | AHL | 80 | 37 | 30 | 13 | 15 | 10 | 5 | .... |
| 2002-03 | Hamilton | AHL | 45 | 33 | 9 | 3 | .... | .... | .... | .... |
| **2002-03** | **Montreal** | **NHL** | **36** | **12** | **16** | **8** | .... | .... | .... | .... |
| **2003-04** | **Montreal** | **NHL** | **82** | **41** | **30** | **11** | **11** | **4** | **7** | .... |
| **2004-05** | **Montreal** | | | | SEASON CANCELLED | | | | | |
| **2005-06** | **Montreal** | **NHL** | **41** | **19** | **16** | **6** | .... | .... | .... | .... |
| **2006-07** | **New Jersey** | **NHL** | **79** | **47** | **24** | **8** | .... | .... | .... | .... |
| **2007-08** | **Boston** | **NHL** | **82** | **41** | **29** | **12** | **7** | **3** | **4** | .... |
| **2008-09** | **Boston** | **NHL** | **82** | **53** | **19** | **19** | **11** | **7** | **4** | .... |
| | **NHL Totals** | | **402** | **213** | **134** | **64** | **29** | **14** | **15** | .... |

# Coaching History

Art Ross, 1924-25 to 1927-28; Cy Denneny, 1928-29; Art Ross, 1929-30 to 1933-34; Frank Patrick, 1934-35, 1935-36; Art Ross, 1936-37 to 1938-39; Cooney Weiland, 1939-40, 1940-41; Art Ross, 1941-42 to 1944-45; Dit Clapper, 1945-46 to 1948-49; Georges Boucher, 1949-50; Lynn Patrick, 1950-51 to 1953-54; Lynn Patrick and Milt Schmidt, 1954-55; Milt Schmidt, 1955-56 to 1960-61; Phil Watson, 1961-62; Phil Watson and Milt Schmidt, 1962-63; Milt Schmidt, 1963-64 to 1965-66; Harry Sinden, 1966-67 to 1969-70; Tom Johnson, 1970-71, 1971-72; Tom Johnson and Bep Guidolin, 1972-73; Bep Guidolin, 1973-74; Don Cherry, 1974-75 to 1978-79; Fred Creighton and Harry Sinden, 1979-80; Gerry Cheevers, 1980-81 to 1983-84; Gerry Cheevers and Harry Sinden, 1984-85; Butch Goring, 1985-86; Butch Goring and Terry O'Reilly, 1986-87; Terry O'Reilly, 1987-88, 1988-89; Mike Milbury, 1989-90, 1990-91; Rick Bowness, 1991-92; Brian Sutter, 1992-93 to 1994-95; Steve Kasper, 1995-96, 1996-97; Pat Burns, 1997-98 to 1999-2000; Pat Burns and Mike Keenan, 2000-01; Robbie Ftorek, 2001-02; Robbie Ftorek and Mike O'Connell, 2002-03; Mike Sullivan, 2003-04 to 2005-06; Dave Lewis, 2006-07; Claude Julien, 2007-08 to date.

# Club Records

## Team

(Figures in brackets for season records are games played; records for fewest points, wins, ties, losses, goals, goals against are for 70 or more games)

| | | |
|---|---|---|
| **Most Points** | 121 | 1970-71 (78) |
| **Most Wins** | 57 | 1970-71 (78) |
| **Most Ties** | 21 | 1954-55 (70) |
| **Most Losses** | 47 | 1961-62 (70), 1996-97 (82) |
| **Most Goals** | 399 | 1970-71 (78) |
| **Most Goals Against** | 306 | 1961-62 (70) |
| **Fewest Points** | 38 | 1961-62 (70) |
| **Fewest Wins** | 14 | 1962-63 (70) |
| **Fewest Ties** | 5 | 1972-73 (78) |
| **Fewest Losses** | 13 | 1971-72 (78) |
| **Fewest Goals** | 147 | 1955-56 (70) |
| **Fewest Goals Against** | 172 | 1952-53 (70) |
| **Longest Winning Streak** | | |
| Overall | 14 | Dec. 3/29-Jan. 9/30 |
| Home | *20 | Dec. 3/29-Mar. 18/30 |
| Away | 8 | Feb. 17-Mar. 8/72, Mar. 15-Apr. 14/93 |
| **Longest Undefeated Streak** | | |
| Overall | 23 | Dec. 22/40-Feb. 23/41 (15 wins, 8 ties) |
| Home | 27 | Nov. 22/70-Mar. 20/71 (26 wins, 1 tie) |
| Away | 15 | Dec. 22/40-Mar. 16/41 (9 wins, 6 ties) |
| **Longest Losing Streak** | | |
| Overall | 11 | Dec. 3/24-Jan. 5/25 |
| Home | *11 | Dec. 8/24-Feb. 17/25 |
| Away | 14 | Dec. 27/64-Feb. 21/65 |
| **Longest Winless Streak** | | |
| Overall | 20 | Jan. 28-Mar. 11/62 (16 losses, 4 ties) |
| Home | 11 | Dec. 8/24-Feb. 17/25 (11 losses) |
| Away | 14 | Three times |
| **Most Shutouts, Season** | 15 | 1927-28 (44) |
| **Most PIM, Season** | 2,443 | 1987-88 (80) |
| **Most Goals, Game** | 14 | Jan. 21/45 (NYR 3 at Bos. 14) |

## Individual

| | | |
|---|---|---|
| **Most Seasons** | 21 | John Bucyk, Raymond Bourque |
| **Most Games** | 1,518 | Raymond Bourque |
| **Most Goals, Career** | 545 | John Bucyk |
| **Most Assists, Career** | 1,111 | Raymond Bourque |
| **Most Points, Career** | 1,506 | Raymond Bourque (395G, 1,111A) |
| **Most PIM, Career** | 2,095 | Terry O'Reilly |
| **Most Shutouts, Career** | 74 | Tiny Thompson |
| **Longest Consecutive Games Streak** | 418 | John Bucyk (Jan. 23/69-Mar. 2/75) |
| **Most Goals, Season** | 76 | Phil Esposito (1970-71) |
| **Most Assists, Season** | 102 | Bobby Orr (1970-71) |
| **Most Points, Season** | 152 | Phil Esposito (1970-71; 76G, 76A) |
| **Most PIM, Season** | 302 | Jay Miller (1987-88) |
| **Most Points, Defenseman, Season** | *139 | Bobby Orr (1970-71; 37G, 102A) |
| **Most Points, Center, Season** | 152 | Phil Esposito (1970-71; 76G, 76A) |
| **Most Points, Right Wing, Season** | 105 | Ken Hodge (1970-71; 43G, 62A), (1973-74; 50G, 55A) Rick Middleton (1983-84; 47G, 58A) |
| **Most Points, Left Wing, Season** | 116 | John Bucyk (1970-71; 51G, 65A) |
| **Most Points, Rookie, Season** | 102 | Joe Juneau (1992-93; 32G, 70A) |
| **Most Shutouts, Season** | 15 | Hal Winkler (1927-28) |
| **Most Goals, Game** | 4 | Twenty one times |
| **Most Assists, Game** | 6 | Ken Hodge (Feb. 9/71) Bobby Orr (Jan. 1/73) |
| **Most Points, Game** | 7 | Bobby Orr (Nov. 15/73; 3G, 4A) Phil Esposito (Dec. 19/74; 3G, 4A) Barry Pederson (Apr. 4/82; 3G, 4A) Cam Neely (Oct. 16/88; 3G, 4A) |

* NHL Record.

## Retired Numbers

| | | |
|---|---|---|
| 2 | Eddie Shore | 1926-1940 |
| 3 | Lionel Hitchman | 1925-1934 |
| 4 | Bobby Orr | 1966-1976 |
| 5 | Dit Clapper | 1927-1947 |
| 7 | Phil Esposito | 1967-1975 |
| 8 | Cam Neely | 1986-1996 |
| 9 | John Bucyk | 1957-1978 |
| 15 | Milt Schmidt | 1936-1955 |
| 24 | Terry O'Reilly | 1971-1985 |
| 77 | Raymond Bourque | 1979-2000 |

# All-time Record vs. Other Clubs

## Regular Season

| | At Home | | | | | | | | On Road | | | | | | | | Total | | | | | | | |
|---|---|---|---|---|---|---|---|---|---|---|---|---|---|---|---|---|---|---|---|---|---|---|---|---|
| | GP | W | L | T | OL | GF | GA | PTS | GP | W | L | T | OL | GF | GA | PTS | GP | W | L | T | OL | GF | GA | PTS |
| Anaheim | 10 | 6 | 4 | 0 | 0 | 33 | 27 | 12 | 10 | 5 | 3 | 2 | 0 | 25 | 20 | 12 | 20 | 11 | 7 | 2 | 0 | 58 | 47 | 24 |
| Atlanta | 18 | 10 | 4 | 2 | 2 | 64 | 61 | 24 | 18 | 10 | 7 | 0 | 1 | 54 | 55 | 21 | 36 | 20 | 11 | 2 | 3 | 118 | 116 | 45 |
| Buffalo | 122 | 67 | 40 | 14 | 1 | 442 | 361 | 149 | 123 | 43 | 61 | 15 | 4 | 354 | 442 | 105 | 245 | 110 | 101 | 29 | 5 | 796 | 803 | 254 |
| Calgary | 48 | 29 | 12 | 6 | 1 | 168 | 132 | 65 | 46 | 22 | 20 | 4 | 0 | 156 | 166 | 48 | 94 | 51 | 32 | 10 | 1 | 324 | 298 | 113 |
| Carolina | 86 | 49 | 29 | 7 | 1 | 295 | 230 | 106 | 84 | 40 | 34 | 9 | 1 | 290 | 277 | 90 | 170 | 89 | 63 | 16 | 2 | 585 | 507 | 196 |
| Chicago | 286 | 163 | 89 | 34 | 0 | 1031 | 812 | 360 | 288 | 96 | 145 | 45 | 2 | 774 | 930 | 239 | 574 | 259 | 234 | 79 | 2 | 1805 | 1742 | 599 |
| Colorado | 63 | 31 | 22 | 9 | 1 | 240 | 194 | 72 | 68 | 37 | 25 | 6 | 0 | 277 | 242 | 80 | 131 | 68 | 47 | 15 | 1 | 517 | 436 | 152 |
| Columbus | 3 | 2 | 1 | 0 | 0 | 10 | 7 | 4 | 5 | 2 | 1 | 0 | 2 | 18 | 10 | 6 | 8 | 4 | 2 | 0 | 2 | 28 | 17 | 10 |
| Dallas | 62 | 42 | 9 | 10 | 1 | 264 | 149 | 95 | 62 | 30 | 18 | 13 | 1 | 221 | 179 | 74 | 124 | 72 | 27 | 23 | 2 | 485 | 328 | 169 |
| Detroit | 289 | 155 | 90 | 43 | 1 | 1012 | 765 | 354 | 286 | 80 | 153 | 52 | 1 | 726 | 955 | 213 | 575 | 235 | 243 | 95 | 2 | 1738 | 1720 | 567 |
| Edmonton | 31 | 22 | 6 | 3 | 0 | 129 | 80 | 47 | 31 | 17 | 11 | 3 | 0 | 103 | 102 | 37 | 62 | 39 | 17 | 6 | 0 | 232 | 182 | 84 |
| Florida | 30 | 11 | 13 | 4 | 2 | 81 | 81 | 28 | 29 | 14 | 12 | 2 | 1 | 85 | 89 | 31 | 59 | 25 | 25 | 6 | 3 | 166 | 170 | 59 |
| Los Angeles | 63 | 44 | 12 | 6 | 1 | 289 | 178 | 95 | 62 | 34 | 21 | 7 | 0 | 232 | 216 | 75 | 125 | 78 | 33 | 13 | 1 | 521 | 394 | 170 |
| Minnesota | 5 | 0 | 5 | 0 | 0 | 5 | 16 | 0 | 4 | 1 | 3 | 0 | 0 | 8 | 13 | 2 | 9 | 1 | 8 | 0 | 0 | 13 | 29 | 2 |
| Montreal | 350 | 161 | 131 | 56 | 2 | 1030 | 947 | 380 | 349 | 101 | 199 | 47 | 2 | 823 | 1176 | 251 | 699 | 262 | 330 | 103 | 4 | 1853 | 2123 | 631 |
| Nashville | 6 | 3 | 2 | 1 | 0 | 17 | 10 | 7 | 8 | 4 | 2 | 0 | 2 | 18 | 21 | 10 | 14 | 7 | 4 | 1 | 2 | 35 | 31 | 17 |
| New Jersey | 64 | 34 | 17 | 8 | 5 | 242 | 198 | 81 | 61 | 29 | 17 | 11 | 4 | 188 | 158 | 73 | 125 | 63 | 34 | 19 | 9 | 430 | 356 | 154 |
| NY Islanders | 67 | 37 | 17 | 11 | 2 | 247 | 184 | 87 | 69 | 30 | 28 | 10 | 1 | 218 | 225 | 71 | 136 | 67 | 45 | 21 | 3 | 465 | 409 | 158 |
| NY Rangers | 306 | 164 | 96 | 42 | 4 | 1090 | 852 | 374 | 310 | 117 | 136 | 55 | 2 | 866 | 948 | 291 | 616 | 281 | 232 | 97 | 6 | 1956 | 1800 | 665 |
| Ottawa | 48 | 29 | 13 | 5 | 1 | 168 | 127 | 64 | 46 | 22 | 15 | 3 | 6 | 136 | 120 | 53 | 94 | 51 | 28 | 8 | 7 | 304 | 247 | 117 |
| Philadelphia | 84 | 48 | 22 | 11 | 3 | 302 | 236 | 110 | 81 | 37 | 33 | 10 | 1 | 243 | 264 | 85 | 165 | 85 | 55 | 21 | 4 | 545 | 500 | 195 |
| Phoenix | 32 | 22 | 5 | 4 | 1 | 138 | 96 | 49 | 31 | 15 | 13 | 3 | 0 | 105 | 102 | 33 | 63 | 37 | 18 | 7 | 1 | 243 | 198 | 82 |
| Pittsburgh | 86 | 61 | 17 | 6 | 2 | 376 | 242 | 130 | 88 | 38 | 34 | 15 | 1 | 313 | 301 | 92 | 174 | 99 | 51 | 21 | 3 | 689 | 543 | 222 |
| St. Louis | 61 | 35 | 15 | 9 | 2 | 252 | 170 | 81 | 61 | 24 | 24 | 9 | 4 | 206 | 194 | 61 | 122 | 59 | 39 | 18 | 6 | 458 | 364 | 142 |
| San Jose | 12 | 7 | 2 | 3 | 0 | 43 | 37 | 17 | 12 | 6 | 4 | 2 | 0 | 40 | 31 | 14 | 24 | 13 | 6 | 5 | 0 | 83 | 68 | 31 |
| Tampa Bay | 31 | 22 | 3 | 6 | 0 | 118 | 74 | 50 | 31 | 16 | 12 | 3 | 0 | 93 | 89 | 35 | 62 | 38 | 15 | 9 | 0 | 211 | 163 | 85 |
| Toronto | 313 | 170 | 94 | 47 | 2 | 1016 | 838 | 389 | 314 | 102 | 158 | 51 | 3 | 823 | 1044 | 258 | 627 | 272 | 252 | 98 | 5 | 1839 | 1882 | 647 |
| Vancouver | 53 | 39 | 7 | 7 | 0 | 219 | 124 | 85 | 53 | 28 | 17 | 8 | 0 | 212 | 171 | 64 | 106 | 67 | 24 | 15 | 0 | 431 | 295 | 149 |
| Washington | 64 | 38 | 15 | 9 | 2 | 230 | 167 | 87 | 63 | 30 | 19 | 12 | 2 | 209 | 181 | 74 | 127 | 68 | 34 | 21 | 4 | 439 | 348 | 161 |
| Defunct Clubs | 164 | 112 | 39 | 13 | 0 | 525 | 306 | 237 | 164 | 79 | 67 | 18 | 0 | 496 | 440 | 176 | 328 | 191 | 106 | 31 | 0 | 1021 | 746 | 413 |
| **Totals** | **2857** | **1613** | **831** | **376** | **37** | **10076** | **7701** | **3639** | **2857** | **1109** | **1292** | **415** | **41** | **8312** | **9161** | **2674** | **5714** | **2722** | **2123** | **791** | **78** | **18388** | **16862** | **6313** |

## Playoffs

| | Series | W | L | GP | W | L | T | GF | GA | Last Mtg. | Rnd. | Result |
|---|---|---|---|---|---|---|---|---|---|---|---|---|
| Buffalo | 7 | 5 | 2 | 39 | 21 | 18 | 0 | 139 | 130 | 1999 | CSF | L 2-4 |
| Carolina | 4 | 3 | 1 | 26 | 15 | 11 | 0 | 80 | 64 | 2009 | CSF | L 3-4 |
| Chicago | 6 | 5 | 1 | 22 | 16 | 5 | 1 | 97 | 63 | 1978 | QF | W 4-0 |
| Colorado | 2 | 1 | 1 | 11 | 6 | 5 | 0 | 37 | 36 | 1983 | DSF | W 3-1 |
| Dallas | 1 | 0 | 1 | 3 | 0 | 3 | 0 | 13 | 20 | 1981 | PRE | L 0-3 |
| Detroit | 7 | 4 | 3 | 33 | 19 | 14 | 0 | 96 | 98 | 1957 | SF | W 4-1 |
| Edmonton | 2 | 0 | 2 | 9 | 1 | 8 | 0 | 20 | 41 | 1990 | F | L 1-4 |
| Florida | 1 | 0 | 1 | 5 | 1 | 4 | 0 | 16 | 22 | 1996 | CQF | L 1-4 |
| Los Angeles | 2 | 2 | 0 | 13 | 8 | 5 | 0 | 56 | 38 | 1977 | QF | W 4-2 |
| Montreal | 32 | 8 | 24 | 163 | 64 | 99 | 0 | 403 | 494 | 2009 | CQF | W 4-0 |
| New Jersey | 4 | 1 | 3 | 23 | 8 | 15 | 0 | 60 | 68 | 2003 | CQF | L 1-4 |
| NY Islanders | 2 | 0 | 2 | 11 | 3 | 8 | 0 | 35 | 49 | 1983 | CF | L 2-4 |
| NY Rangers | 9 | 6 | 3 | 42 | 22 | 18 | 2 | 114 | 104 | 1973 | QF | L 1-4 |
| Philadelphia | 4 | 2 | 2 | 20 | 11 | 9 | 0 | 60 | 57 | 1978 | SF | W 4-1 |
| Pittsburgh | 4 | 2 | 2 | 19 | 9 | 10 | 0 | 62 | 67 | 1992 | CF | L 0-4 |
| St. Louis | 2 | 2 | 0 | 8 | 8 | 0 | 0 | 48 | 15 | 1972 | SF | W 4-0 |
| Toronto | 13 | 5 | 8 | 62 | 30 | 31 | 1 | 153 | 150 | 1974 | QF | W 4-0 |
| Washington | 2 | 1 | 1 | 10 | 6 | 4 | 0 | 28 | 21 | 1998 | CQF | L 2-4 |
| Defunct Clubs | 3 | 1 | 2 | 11 | 4 | 5 | 2 | 20 | 20 | | | |
| **Totals** | **107** | **48** | **59** | **530** | **252** | **272** | **6** | **1537** | **1557** | | | |

Calgary totals include Atlanta Flames, 1972-73 to 1979-80. Carolina totals include Hartford, 1979-80 to 1996-97.
Colorado totals include Quebec, 1979-80 to 1994-95. Dallas totals include Minnesota North Stars, 1967-68 to 1992-93.
New Jersey totals include Kansas City, 1974-75, 1975-76, and Colorado Rockies, 1976-77 to 1981-82.
Phoenix totals include Winnipeg, 1979-80 to 1995-96.

## Playoff Results 2009-2004

| Year | Round | Opponent | Result | GF | GA |
|---|---|---|---|---|---|
| 2009 | CSF | Carolina | L 3-4 | 17 | 16 |
| | CQF | Montreal | W 4-0 | 17 | 6 |
| 2008 | CQF | Montreal | L 3-4 | 15 | 19 |
| 2004 | CQF | Montreal | L 3-4 | 14 | 19 |

**Abbreviations: Round: F** - Final; **CF** - conference final; **CSF** - conference semi-final; **CQF** - conference quarter-final; **DSF** - division semi-final; **SF** - semi-final; **QF** - quarter-final; **PRE** - preliminary round.

## 2008-09 Results

| | | | |
|---|---|---|---|
| **Oct.** | 9 | at Colorado | 5-4 |
| | 11 | at Minnesota | 3-4 |
| | 15 | at Montreal | 3-4† |
| | 18 | at Ottawa | 4-2 |
| | 20 | Pittsburgh | 1-2† |
| | 21 | at Buffalo | 2-3† |
| | 23 | Toronto | 2-4 |
| | 25 | Atlanta | 5-4 |
| | 27 | at Edmonton | 1-0* |
| | 28 | at Vancouver | 1-0 |
| | 30 | at Calgary | 2-3 |
| **Nov.** | 1 | Dallas | 5-1 |
| | 6 | Toronto | 5-2 |
| | 8 | Buffalo | 3-1 |
| | 12 | at Chicago | 2-1† |
| | 13 | Montreal | 6-1 |
| | 15 | at NY Rangers | 2-3† |
| | 17 | at Toronto | 3-2 |
| | 19 | Buffalo | 7-4 |
| | 21 | Florida | 4-2 |
| | 22 | at Montreal | 3-2† |
| | 26 | at Buffalo | 2-3 |
| | 28 | NY Islanders | 7-2 |
| | 29 | Detroit | 4-1 |
| **Dec.** | 4 | at Tampa Bay | 3-1 |
| | 6 | at Florida | 4-0 |
| | 8 | Tampa Bay | 5-3 |
| | 10 | at Washington | 1-3 |
| | 12 | at Atlanta | 7-3 |
| | 13 | Atlanta | 4-2 |
| | 18 | Toronto | 8-5 |
| | 20 | Carolina | 4-2 |
| | 21 | at St. Louis | 6-3 |
| | 23 | at New Jersey | 2-0 |
| | 27 | at Carolina | 4-2 |
| | 28 | at Atlanta | 2-1 |
| | 30 | at Pittsburgh | 5-2 |
| **Jan.** | 1 | Pittsburgh | 4-2 |
| | 3 | Buffalo | 2-4 |
| | 6 | Minnesota | 0-1 |
| | 8 | Ottawa | 6-4 |
| | 10 | Carolina | 5-1 |
| | 13 | Montreal | 3-1 |
| | 15 | at NY Islanders | 2-1 |
| | 17 | at Washington | 1-2 |
| | 19 | St. Louis | 4-5† |
| | 21 | at Toronto | 4-3† |
| | 27 | Washington | 3-2* |
| | 29 | New Jersey | 3-4* |
| | 31 | NY Rangers | 1-0 |
| **Feb.** | 1 | at Montreal | 3-1 |
| | 4 | at Philadelphia | 3-1 |
| | 5 | at Ottawa | 4-3† |
| | 7 | Philadelphia | 3-4* |
| | 10 | San Jose | 2-5 |
| | 13 | at New Jersey | 0-1 |
| | 14 | at Nashville | 2-3† |
| | 17 | at Carolina | 5-1 |
| | 21 | at Florida | 0-2 |
| | 22 | at Tampa Bay | 3-4 |
| | 24 | Florida | 6-1 |
| | 26 | Anaheim | 6-0 |
| | 28 | Washington | 3-4* |
| **Mar.** | 3 | Philadelphia | 2-4 |
| | 5 | Phoenix | 1-2 |
| | 7 | Chicago | 5-3 |
| | 8 | at NY Rangers | 3-4 |
| | 10 | at Columbus | 0-2 |
| | 12 | Ottawa | 5-3 |
| | 14 | NY Islanders | 2-1 |
| | 15 | at Pittsburgh | 4-6 |
| | 19 | Los Angeles | 2-3* |
| | 22 | New Jersey | 4-1 |
| | 28 | at Toronto | 7-5 |
| | 29 | at Philadelphia | 4-3 |
| | 31 | Tampa Bay | 3-1 |
| **Apr.** | 2 | Ottawa | 2-1 |
| | 4 | NY Rangers | 1-0 |
| | 7 | at Ottawa | 2-3 |
| | 9 | Montreal | 5-4* |
| | 11 | at Buffalo | 1-6 |
| | 12 | at NY Islanders | 6-2 |

* – Overtime † – Shootout

# Entry Draft Selections 2009-1995

Name in bold denotes played in NHL.

**2009**
Pick
25 Jordan Caron
86 Ryan Button
112 Lane MacDermid
176 Tyler Randell
206 Ben Sexton

**2008**
Pick
16 Joe Colborne
47 Maxime Sauve
77 Michael Hutchinson
97 Jamie Arniel
173 Nick Tremblay
197 Mark Goggin

**2007**
Pick
8 Zach Hamill
35 Tommy Cross
130 Denis Reul
159 Alain Goulet
169 Radim Ostrcil
189 Jordan Knackstedt

**2006**
Pick
5 **Phil Kessel**
37 Yuri Alexandrov
50 **Milan Lucic**
71 Brad Marchand
128 Andrew Bodnarchuk
158 Levi Nelson

**2005**
Pick
22 **Matt Lashoff**
39 **Petr Kalus**
83 **Mikko Lehtonen**
100 **Jonathan Sigalet**
106 **Vladimir Sobotka**
154 Wacey Rabbit
172 Lukas Vantuch
217 Brock Bradford

**2004**
Pick
63 **David Krejci**
64 **Martins Karsums**
108 Ashton Rome
134 **Kris Versteeg**
160 **Ben Walter**
224 **Matt Hunwick**
255 Anton Hedman

**2003**
Pick
21 **Mark Stuart**
45 **Patrice Bergeron**
66 **Masi Marjamaki**
107 **Byron Bitz**
118 Frank Rediker
129 Patrik Valcak
153 Mike Brown
183 **Nate Thompson**
247 Benoit Mondou
277 Kevin Regan

**2002**
Pick
29 **Hannu Toivonen**
56 Vladislav Evseev
130 Jan Kubista
153 Peter Hamerlik
228 Dmitri Utkin
259 **Yan Stastny**
290 Pavel Frolov

**2001**
Pick
19 **Shaone Morrisonn**
77 Darren McLachlan
111 Matti Kaltiainen
147 Jiri Jakes
179 **Andrew Alberts**
209 **Jordan Sigalet**
241 **Milan Jurcina**
282 Marcel Rodman

**2000**
Pick
7 **Lars Jonsson**
27 **Martin Samuelsson**
37 **Andy Hilbert**
59 **Ivan Huml**
66 Tuukka Makela
73 **Sergei Zinovjev**
102 Brett Nowak
174 **Jarno Kultanen**
204 Chris Berti
237 **Zdenek Kutlak**
268 **Pavel Kolarik**
279 Andreas Lindstrom

**1999**
Pick
21 **Nick Boynton**
56 Matt Zultek
89 **Kyle Wanvig**
118 Jaakko Harikkala
147 Seamus Kotyk
179 Donald Choukalos
207 Greg Barber
236 John Cronin
247 **Mikko Eloranta**
264 Georgy Pujacs

**1998**
Pick
48 **Jonathan Girard**
52 **Bobby Allen**
78 **Peter Nordstrom**
135 **Andrew Raycroft**
165 Ryan Milanovic

**1997**
Pick
1 **Joe Thornton**
8 **Sergei Samsonov**
27 **Ben Clymer**
54 Mattias Karlin
63 **Lee Goren**
81 Karol Bartanus
135 Denis Timofeev
162 Joel Trottier
180 Jim Baxter
191 **Antti Laaksonen**
218 Eric Van Acker
246 **Jay Henderson**

**1996**
Pick
8 **Johnathan Aitken**
45 Henry Kuster
53 Eric Naud
80 Jason Doyle
100 **Trent Whitfield**
132 Elias Abrahamsson
155 Chris Lane
182 Thomas Brown
208 Bob Prier
234 Anders Soderberg

**1995**
Pick
9 **Kyle McLaren**
21 **Sean Brown**
47 **Paxton Schafer**
73 Bill McCauley
99 **Cameron Mann**
151 **Yevgeny Shaldybin**
177 **P.J. Axelsson**
203 Sergei Zhukov
229 Jonathon Murphy

## Captains' History

No captain, 1924-25 to 1926-27; Lionel Hitchman, 1927-28 to 1930-31; George Owen, 1931-32; Dit Clapper, 1932-33 to 1937-38; Cooney Weiland, 1938-39; Dit Clapper, 1939-40 to 1945-46; Dit Clapper and John Crawford, 1946-47; John Crawford 1947-48 to 1949-50; Milt Schmidt, 1950-51 to 1953-54; Milt Schmidt, Ed Sanford, 1954-55; Fern Flaman, 1955-56 to 1960-61; Don McKenney, 1961-62, 1962-63; Leo Boivin, 1963-64 to 1965-66; John Bucyk, 1966-67; no captain, 1967-68 to 1972-73; John Bucyk, 1973-74 to 1976-77; Wayne Cashman, 1977-78 to 1982-83; Terry O'Reilly, 1983-84, 1984-85; Raymond Bourque, Rick Middleton (co-captains) 1985-86 to 1987-88; Raymond Bourque, 1988-89 to 1999-2000; Jason Allison, 2000-01; no captain, 2001-02; Joe Thornton, 2002-03, 2003-04; Joe Thornton and no captain, 2005-06; Zdeno Chara, 2006-07 to date.

## General Managers' History

Art Ross, 1924-25 to 1953-54; Lynn Patrick, 1954-55 to 1964-65; Hap Emms, 1965-66, 1966-67; Milt Schmidt, 1967-68 to 1971-72; Harry Sinden, 1972-73 to 1999-2000; Harry Sinden and Mike O'Connell, 2000-01; Mike O'Connell, 2001-02 to 2005-06; Peter Chiarelli, 2006-07 to date.

# Peter Chiarelli

## General Manager

*Born: Nepean, Ont., August 5, 1964.*

Peter Chiarelli became just the seventh man in club history to hold the position of general manager when he was named to the post on May 26, 2006. He is in charge of every aspect of the team's hockey operations. He officially began his position in Boston on July 10, 2006 as a result of a league-arbitrated compensation agreement that saw the Bruins surrender a third-round draft pick in the 2006 NHL Entry Draft (Eric Gryba, 68th overall) to the Ottawa Senators. By his third season in Boston in 2008-09, the Bruins posted the best record in the Eastern Conference and were second overall in the NHL.

Chiarelli came to the Bruins after seven seasons with the Ottawa Senators, five as the director of legal relations and the last two as assistant general manager. He was involved in all aspects of that team's hockey operations, including contract research and negotiations, salary arbitration and all player personnel matters. He was also involved in overseeing Ottawa's top developmental affiliate, the Binghamtom Senators of the American Hockey League. The Senators had four 100+ point seasons during his tenure and never finished below 94 points, finished with the NHL's top record in 2002-03 (113 points) and the best record in the Eastern Conference in 2005-06 (113 points).

A native of the Ottawa area, Chiarelli played four seasons of college hockey at Harvard University where he served the team as captain and was a teammate of former Bruin Don Sweeney. He had 21 goals and 28 assists for 49 points with 70 penalty minutes in 109 career college games and earned his degree in Economics in 1987. He played professionally in Europe for one year before returning to school and obtaining his law degree from the University of Ottawa. He was admitted to the Ontario bar in 1993 and spent six years as a lawyer and player agent prior to joining the Senators front office in 1999.

# Club Directory

TD Garden

**Boston Bruins**
TD Garden
100 Legends Way
Boston, MA 02114
Phone **617/624-2327**
FAX 617/523-7184
www.bostonbruins.com
**Capacity:** 17,565

**Ownership**

| | |
|---|---|
| Owner & Governor, Boston Bruins; Chairman, NHL Board of Governors | Jeremy M. Jacobs |
| Principal, Boston Bruins | Charlie Jacobs |
| Alternate Governors | Charlie Jacobs, Jeremy Jacobs, Jr., Louis Jacobs, Harry Sinden, Peter Chiarelli, Cam Neely |
| Senior Advisor to the Owner | Harry Sinden |

**Executive**

| | |
|---|---|
| Vice President | Cam Neely |
| Vice President, Business Operations | Daniel J. Zimmer |
| Sr. Vice President, Sales and Marketing | Amy Latimer |
| Vice President, Finance | Jim Bednarek |
| Vice President, Marketing | Jen Compton |
| Vice President, Corporate Partnerships | Chris Johnson |
| Director of Administration | Dale Hamilton-Powers |
| Executive Secretary | Rita Brandano |
| Administrative Assistant | Karen Ondo |

**Hockey Operations**

| | |
|---|---|
| General Manager | Peter Chiarelli |
| Assistant General Manager | Jim Benning |
| Dir. of Hockey Operations & Player Development | Don Sweeney |
| Director of Player Personnel | Scott Bradley |
| Director of Amateur Scouting | Wayne Smith |
| Director of Collegiate Scouting | John Weisbrod |
| Scouting Staff | Mike Chiarelli, Adam Creighton, Scott Fitzgerald, Jack Higgins, Jukka Holtari, Denis LeBlanc, Dean Malkoc, Mike McGraw, Tom McVie, Svenake Svensson |
| Manager of Hockey Administration | Ryan Nadeau |
| Assistant to Hockey Administration | Matt Falconer |
| Team Road Services Coordinator | John Bucyk |

**Coaching**

| | |
|---|---|
| Head Coach | Claude Julien |
| Assistant Coaches | Doug Houda, Craig Ramsay, Geoff Ward |
| Goaltending Coach | Bob Essensa |
| Video Analyst | Brant Berglund |

**Medical, Training and Equipment**

| | |
|---|---|
| Strength & Conditioning Coach | John Whitesides |
| Athletic Trainer | Don DelNegro |
| Physical Therapist | Scott Waugh |
| Assistant Athletic Trainer & Massage Therapist | Derek Repucci |
| Equipment Manager | Mark Dumas |
| Assistant Equipment Managers | Keith Robinson, Mark Dumas II |
| Head Team Physician/Orthopedist | Dr. Peter Asnis |
| Team Psychologist | Dr. Frank Lodato |

**Communications and Community Relations**

| | |
|---|---|
| Director of Communications | Matthew Chmura |
| Director of Publications & Information | Heidi Holland |
| Director of Community Relations & Promotions | Kerry Collins |
| Director of Development, Boston Bruins Foundation | Bob Sweeney |
| Director of Interactive | Darrell Wood |
| Manager of Media Relations | Eric Tosi |
| Content Manager, BostonBruins.com | John Bishop |
| Event Manager, Boston Bruins Foundation | Sarah Higgins |
| Public Relations Coordinator | Kelly Mohr |
| Community Relations Coordinator | Liz Serpico |
| Coordinators, Boston Bruins Foundation | Erin McEvoy, Zach Fitzgerald |
| Administrative Assistant, Alumni Office | Mal Viola |

**Sales, Marketing and Retail**

| | |
|---|---|
| Senior Director, Premium Sales | Leah Leahy |
| Senior Director, The Premium Club | Dana Petrie |
| Director of Marketing | Chris DiPierro |
| Director of Ticket Sales | Leigh Castergine |
| Retail Director | Lauma Cerlins |
| Ticket Sales Manager | Mark Rodrigues |
| Marketing Manager | Liz d'Entremont |
| Game Presentation & Promotions Manager | Cole Parsons |
| Youth Hockey Development Manager | Lori DiGiacomo |
| Fan Relations Manager | Tamala Sweesy |
| Group Sales Manager | Chris Spano |
| Graphic Designer | Jason Petrie |
| Promotions Coordinator | Beth Anthony |
| Marketing Coordinator | Rachael Markovitz |
| Legends Sales Coordinator | Ben Mazza |
| Marketing & Media Strategist | MaryAnn Bagnoli |
| Senior Fan Relations Representative | John Hughes |
| Fan Relations Representatives | Nick Camara, Lindsay Corbo, Nikki Gulloti, Courtney McNeice, Kaitlin Rowe |
| Season Sales Account Executives | Sean Cummings, Matt Gulley, Tina Zettel |
| Group Sales Account Executives | Charlie Karoly, Briana Lynch, Caillin Miller |
| Ticket Sales Representatives | John Cadigan, Adam DiVincenzo, Lindsey Warren, Dan Weiner |

**Finance, Legal, Human Resources and Box Office**

| | |
|---|---|
| Controller | Rick McGlinchey |
| Senior Staff Accountant | Dan Eccles |
| Staff Accountant | Linda Bartlett |
| Payroll & Benefits Manager | Botin Bou |
| Assistant General Counsel | Matt Reece |
| Director of Human Resources | Joe Lawlor |
| Human Resources Generalist | Jamie Smith |
| Director of Ticket Operations | Matthew Whelan |
| Assistant Director of Ticket Operations | Jim Foley |
| Senior Box Office Analyst | Allyson Leonard |
| Ticket Office Receptionist | Jo-Ann Connolly-White |
| Business Analyst | Matt Synakowski |
| Assistant to V.P. of Business Operations | Nate Silverstein |

# Buffalo Sabres

## 2008-09 Results: 41W-32L-4OTL-5SOL 91PTS.
## Third, Northeast Division

### Key Off-Season Signings/Acquisitions

**2009**

**May 11** • Signed 2008 1st-round pick (12th overall) D **Tyler Myers.**
**July 1** • Signed D **Steve Montador.**
**11** • Signed D **Joe DiPenta.**
**15** • Re-signed RW **Patrick Kaleta.**
**20** • Re-signed D **Andrej Sekera** and LW **Clarke MacArthur.**
**Aug. 1** • Signed C **Cody McCormick.**

*Despite suffering a broken jaw in February, Thomas Vanek played 73 games for the Sabres in 2008-09 and ranked among the NHL leaders with 40 goals.*

### 2009-10 Schedule

|  |  |  |  |
|---|---|---|---|
| **Oct.** | Sat. | 3 | Montreal |
| | Thu. | 8 | Phoenix |
| | Sat. | 10 | at Nashville |
| | Tue. | 13 | Detroit |
| | Fri. | 16 | NY Islanders |
| | Sat. | 17 | Atlanta |
| | Wed. | 21 | at Florida |
| | Sat. | 24 | at Tampa Bay |
| | Wed. | 28 | at New Jersey |
| | Fri. | 30 | Toronto |
| | Sat. | 31 | at NY Islanders |
| **Nov.** | Wed. | 4 | NY Islanders |
| | Fri. | 6 | Philadelphia |
| | Sat. | 7 | at Boston |
| | Wed. | 11 | Edmonton |
| | Fri. | 13 | Calgary |
| | Sat. | 14 | at Philadelphia |
| | Wed. | 18 | Florida |
| | Fri. | 20 | Boston |
| | Sat. | 21 | at Ottawa |
| | Wed. | 25 | at Washington |
| | Fri. | 27 | at Philadelphia* |
| | Sat. | 28 | Carolina |
| | Mon. | 30 | at Toronto |
| **Dec.** | Thu. | 3 | Montreal |
| | Sat. | 5 | NY Rangers |
| | Mon. | 7 | New Jersey |
| | Wed. | 9 | Washington |
| | Fri. | 11 | Chicago |
| | Sat. | 12 | at NY Rangers |
| | Mon. | 14 | at Montreal |
| | Wed. | 16 | at Ottawa |
| | Fri. | 18 | Toronto |
| | Sat. | 19 | Pittsburgh |
| | Mon. | 21 | at Toronto |
| | Wed. | 23 | at Washington |
| | Sat. | 26 | Ottawa |
| | Sun. | 27 | at St. Louis* |
| | Tue. | 29 | Pittsburgh |
| **Jan.** | Fri. | 1 | Atlanta |
| | Sun. | 3 | at Montreal* |
| | Wed. | 6 | Tampa Bay |
| | Fri. | 8 | Toronto |
| | Sat. | 9 | Colorado |
| | Thu. | 14 | at Atlanta |
| | Sat. | 16 | at NY Islanders |
| | Mon. | 18 | at Phoenix* |
| | Tue. | 19 | at Anaheim |
| | Thu. | 21 | at Los Angeles |
| | Sat. | 23 | at San Jose |
| | Mon. | 25 | at Vancouver |
| | Wed. | 27 | New Jersey |
| | Fri. | 29 | Boston |
| **Feb.** | Mon. | 1 | at Pittsburgh |
| | Wed. | 3 | Ottawa |
| | Fri. | 5 | Carolina |
| | Sat. | 6 | at Columbus |
| | Tue. | 9 | Boston |
| | Thu. | 11 | at Carolina |
| | Sat. | 13 | San Jose |
| **Mar.** | Tue. | 2 | at Pittsburgh |
| | Wed. | 3 | Washington |
| | Fri. | 5 | Philadelphia |
| | Sun. | 7 | at NY Rangers |
| | Wed. | 10 | Dallas |
| | Fri. | 12 | Minnesota |
| | Sat. | 13 | at Detroit |
| | Tue. | 16 | at Atlanta |
| | Thu. | 18 | at Tampa Bay |
| | Sat. | 20 | at Florida |
| | Sun. | 21 | at Carolina* |
| | Wed. | 24 | Montreal |
| | Fri. | 26 | Ottawa |
| | Sat. | 27 | Tampa Bay |
| | Mon. | 29 | at Boston |
| | Wed. | 31 | Florida |
| **Apr.** | Thu. | 1 | at Toronto |
| | Sat. | 3 | at Montreal |
| | Tue. | 6 | NY Rangers |
| | Thu. | 8 | at Boston |
| | Sat. | 10 | at Ottawa |
| | Sun. | 11 | at New Jersey* |

* Denotes afternoon game.

### Year-by-Year Record

| Season | GP | Home W | Home L | Home T | Home OL | Road W | Road L | Road T | Road OL | Overall W | Overall L | Overall T | Overall OL | GF | GA | Pts. | Finished | Playoff Result |
|---|---|---|---|---|---|---|---|---|---|---|---|---|---|---|---|---|---|---|
| 2008-09 | 82 | 23 | 15 | .... | 3 | 18 | 17 | .... | 6 | 41 | 32 | .... | 9 | 250 | 234 | 91 | 3rd, Northeast Div. | Out of Playoffs |
| 2007-08 | 82 | 20 | 15 | .... | 6 | 19 | 16 | .... | 6 | 39 | 31 | .... | 12 | 255 | 242 | 90 | 4th, Northeast Div. | Out of Playoffs |
| 2006-07 | 82 | 28 | 10 | .... | 3 | 25 | 12 | .... | 4 | 53 | 22 | .... | 7 | 308 | 242 | 113 | 1st, Northeast Div. | Lost Conf. Championship |
| 2005-06 | 82 | 27 | 11 | .... | 3 | 25 | 13 | .... | 3 | 52 | 24 | .... | 6 | 281 | 239 | 110 | 2nd, Northeast Div. | Lost Conf. Championship |
| 2004-05 | .... | .... | .... | .... | .... | .... | .... | .... | .... | .... | .... | .... | .... | .... | .... | .... | | |
| 2003-04 | 82 | 21 | 13 | 4 | 3 | 16 | 21 | 3 | 1 | 37 | 34 | 7 | 4 | 220 | 221 | 85 | 5th, Northeast Div. | Out of Playoffs |
| 2002-03 | 82 | 18 | 16 | 5 | 2 | 9 | 21 | 5 | 6 | 27 | 37 | 10 | 8 | 190 | 219 | 72 | 5th, Northeast Div. | Out of Playoffs |
| 2001-02 | 82 | 20 | 16 | 5 | 0 | 15 | 19 | 6 | 1 | 35 | 35 | 11 | 1 | 213 | 200 | 82 | 5th, Northeast Div. | Out of Playoffs |
| 2000-01 | 82 | 26 | 12 | 3 | 0 | 20 | 18 | 2 | 1 | 46 | 30 | 5 | 1 | 218 | 184 | 98 | 2nd, Northeast Div. | Lost Conf. Semi-Final |
| 1999-2000 | 82 | 21 | 14 | 5 | 1 | 14 | 18 | 6 | 3 | 35 | 32 | 11 | 4 | 213 | 204 | 85 | 3rd, Northeast Div. | Lost Conf. Quarter-Final |
| 1998-99 | 82 | 23 | 12 | 6 | .... | 14 | 16 | 11 | .... | 37 | 28 | 17 | .... | 207 | 175 | 91 | 4th, Northeast Div. | Lost Final |
| 1997-98 | 82 | 20 | 13 | 8 | .... | 16 | 16 | 9 | .... | 36 | 29 | 17 | .... | 211 | 187 | 89 | 3rd, Northeast Div. | Lost Conf. Championship |
| 1996-97 | 82 | 24 | 11 | 6 | .... | 16 | 19 | 6 | .... | 40 | 30 | 12 | .... | 237 | 208 | 92 | 1st, Northeast Div. | Lost Conf. Semi-Final |
| 1995-96 | 82 | 19 | 17 | 5 | .... | 14 | 25 | 2 | .... | 33 | 42 | 7 | .... | 247 | 262 | 73 | 5th, Northeast Div. | Out of Playoffs |
| 1994-95 | 48 | 15 | 8 | 1 | .... | 7 | 11 | 6 | .... | 22 | 19 | 7 | .... | 130 | 119 | 51 | 4th, Northeast Div. | Lost Conf. Quarter-Final |
| 1993-94 | 84 | 22 | 17 | 3 | .... | 21 | 15 | 6 | .... | 43 | 32 | 9 | .... | 282 | 218 | 95 | 4th, Northeast Div. | Lost Conf. Quarter-Final |
| 1992-93 | 84 | 25 | 15 | 2 | .... | 13 | 21 | 8 | .... | 38 | 36 | 10 | .... | 335 | 297 | 86 | 4th, Adams Div. | Lost Div. Final |
| 1991-92 | 80 | 22 | 13 | 5 | .... | 9 | 24 | 7 | .... | 31 | 37 | 12 | .... | 289 | 299 | 74 | 3rd, Adams Div. | Lost Div. Semi-Final |
| 1990-91 | 80 | 15 | 13 | 12 | .... | 16 | 17 | 7 | .... | 31 | 30 | 19 | .... | 292 | 278 | 81 | 3rd, Adams Div. | Lost Div. Semi-Final |
| 1989-90 | 80 | 27 | 11 | 2 | .... | 18 | 16 | 6 | .... | 45 | 27 | 8 | .... | 286 | 248 | 98 | 2nd, Adams Div. | Lost Div. Semi-Final |
| 1988-89 | 80 | 25 | 12 | 3 | .... | 13 | 23 | 4 | .... | 38 | 35 | 7 | .... | 291 | 299 | 83 | 3rd, Adams Div. | Lost Div. Semi-Final |
| 1987-88 | 80 | 19 | 14 | 7 | .... | 18 | 18 | 4 | .... | 37 | 32 | 11 | .... | 283 | 305 | 85 | 3rd, Adams Div. | Lost Div. Semi-Final |
| 1986-87 | 80 | 18 | 18 | 4 | .... | 10 | 26 | 4 | .... | 28 | 44 | 8 | .... | 280 | 308 | 64 | 5th, Adams Div. | Out of Playoffs |
| 1985-86 | 80 | 23 | 16 | 1 | .... | 14 | 21 | 5 | .... | 37 | 37 | 6 | .... | 296 | 291 | 80 | 5th, Adams Div. | Out of Playoffs |
| 1984-85 | 80 | 23 | 10 | 7 | .... | 15 | 18 | 7 | .... | 38 | 28 | 14 | .... | 290 | 237 | 90 | 3rd, Adams Div. | Lost Div. Semi-Final |
| 1983-84 | 80 | 25 | 9 | 6 | .... | 23 | 16 | 1 | .... | 48 | 25 | 7 | .... | 315 | 257 | 103 | 2nd, Adams Div. | Lost Div. Semi-Final |
| 1982-83 | 80 | 25 | 7 | 8 | .... | 13 | 22 | 5 | .... | 38 | 29 | 13 | .... | 318 | 285 | 89 | 3rd, Adams Div. | Lost Div. Final |
| 1981-82 | 80 | 23 | 8 | 9 | .... | 16 | 18 | 6 | .... | 39 | 26 | 15 | .... | 307 | 273 | 93 | 3rd, Adams Div. | Lost Div. Semi-Final |
| 1980-81 | 80 | 21 | 7 | 12 | .... | 18 | 13 | 9 | .... | 39 | 20 | 21 | .... | 327 | 250 | 99 | 1st, Adams Div. | Lost Quarter-Final |
| 1979-80 | 80 | 27 | 5 | 8 | .... | 20 | 12 | 8 | .... | 47 | 17 | 16 | .... | 318 | 201 | 110 | 1st, Adams Div. | Lost Semi-Final |
| 1978-79 | 80 | 19 | 13 | 8 | .... | 17 | 15 | 8 | .... | 36 | 28 | 16 | .... | 280 | 263 | 88 | 2nd, Adams Div. | Lost Prelim. Round |
| 1977-78 | 80 | 25 | 7 | 8 | .... | 19 | 12 | 9 | .... | 44 | 19 | 17 | .... | 288 | 215 | 105 | 2nd, Adams Div. | Lost Quarter-Final |
| 1976-77 | 80 | 27 | 8 | 5 | .... | 21 | 16 | 3 | .... | 48 | 24 | 8 | .... | 301 | 220 | 104 | 2nd, Adams Div. | Lost Quarter-Final |
| 1975-76 | 80 | 28 | 7 | 5 | .... | 18 | 14 | 8 | .... | 46 | 21 | 13 | .... | 339 | 240 | 105 | 2nd, Adams Div. | Lost Quarter-Final |
| 1974-75 | 80 | 28 | 6 | 6 | .... | 21 | 10 | 9 | .... | 49 | 16 | 15 | .... | 354 | 240 | 113 | 1st, Adams Div. | Lost Final |
| 1973-74 | 78 | 23 | 10 | 6 | .... | 9 | 24 | 6 | .... | 32 | 34 | 12 | .... | 242 | 250 | 76 | 5th, East Div. | Out of Playoffs |
| 1972-73 | 78 | 30 | 6 | 3 | .... | 7 | 21 | 11 | .... | 37 | 27 | 14 | .... | 257 | 219 | 88 | 4th, East Div. | Lost Quarter-Final |
| 1971-72 | 78 | 11 | 19 | 9 | .... | 5 | 24 | 10 | .... | 16 | 43 | 19 | .... | 203 | 289 | 51 | 6th, East Div. | Out of Playoffs |
| 1970-71 | 78 | 16 | 13 | 10 | .... | 8 | 26 | 5 | .... | 24 | 39 | 15 | .... | 217 | 291 | 63 | 5th, East Div. | Out of Playoffs |

**NORTHEAST DIVISION**
**40th NHL Season**

**Franchise date:** May 22, 1970

# 2009-10 Player Personnel

| FORWARDS | HT | WT | S | Place of Birth | *Age | 2008-09 Club |
|---|---|---|---|---|---|---|
| CONNOLLY, Tim | 6-1 | 190 | R | Syracuse, NY | 28 | Buffalo |
| ELLIS, Matt | 6-0 | 212 | L | Welland, Ont. | 28 | Buffalo-Portland (AHL) |
| GAUSTAD, Paul | 6-5 | 225 | L | Fargo, ND | 27 | Buffalo |
| GRIER, Mike | 6-1 | 225 | R | Detroit, MI | 33 | San Jose |
| HECHT, Jochen | 6-1 | 199 | L | Mannheim, West Germany | 32 | Buffalo |
| KALETA, Patrick | 5-11 | 198 | R | Buffalo, NY | 23 | Buffalo |
| MacARTHUR, Clarke | 5-11 | 191 | L | Lloydminster, Alta. | 24 | Buffalo |
| MAIR, Adam | 6-1 | 208 | R | Hamilton, Ont. | 30 | Buffalo |
| McCORMICK, Cody | 6-3 | 215 | R | London, Ont. | 26 | Colorado |
| PAILLE, Daniel | 6-0 | 200 | L | Welland, Ont. | 25 | Buffalo |
| POMINVILLE, Jason | 6-0 | 186 | R | Repentigny, Que. | 26 | Buffalo |
| ROY, Derek | 5-9 | 188 | L | Ottawa, Ont. | 26 | Buffalo |
| STAFFORD, Drew | 6-2 | 216 | R | Milwaukee, WI | 23 | Buffalo |
| VANEK, Thomas | 6-2 | 208 | R | Vienna, Austria | 25 | Buffalo |
| **DEFENSEMEN** | | | | | | |
| LYDMAN, Toni | 6-1 | 210 | L | Lahti, Finland | 32 | Buffalo |
| MONTADOR, Steve | 6-0 | 210 | R | Vancouver, B.C. | 29 | Anaheim-Boston |
| PAETSCH, Nathan | 6-1 | 198 | L | Humboldt, Sask. | 26 | Buffalo |
| RIVET, Craig | 6-2 | 210 | R | North Bay, Ont. | 35 | Buffalo |
| SEKERA, Andrej | 6-0 | 197 | L | Bojnice, Czech. | 23 | Buffalo |
| TALLINDER, Henrik | 6-3 | 214 | L | Stockholm, Sweden | 30 | Buffalo |
| **GOALTENDERS** | **HT** | **WT** | **C** | **Place of Birth** | ***Age** | **2008-09 Club** |
| LALIME, Patrick | 6-3 | 189 | L | St-Bonaventure, Que. | 35 | Buffalo |
| MILLER, Ryan | 6-2 | 170 | L | East Lansing, MI | 29 | Buffalo |

* – Age at start of 2009-10 season

## Coaching History

Punch Imlach, 1970-71; Punch Imlach, Floyd Smith and Joe Crozier, 1971-72; Joe Crozier, 1972-73, 1973-74; Floyd Smith, 1974-75 to 1976-77; Marcel Pronovost, 1977-78; Marcel Pronovost and Billy Inglis, 1978-79; Scotty Bowman, 1979-80; Roger Neilson, 1980-81; Jim Roberts and Scotty Bowman, 1981-82; Scotty Bowman 1982-83 to 1984-85; Jim Schoenfeld and Scotty Bowman, 1985-86; Scotty Bowman, Craig Ramsay and Ted Sator, 1986-87; Ted Sator, 1987-88, 1988-89; Rick Dudley, 1989-90, 1990-91; Rick Dudley and John Muckler, 1991-92; John Muckler, 1992-93 to 1994-95; Ted Nolan, 1995-96, 1996-97; Lindy Ruff, 1997-98 to date.

## Captains' History

Floyd Smith, 1970-71; Gerry Meehan, 1971-72 to 1973-74; Gerry Meehan and Jim Schoenfeld, 1974-75; Jim Schoenfeld, 1975-76, 1976-77; Danny Gare, 1977-78 to 1980-81; Danny Gare and Gilbert Perreault, 1981-82; Gilbert Perreault, 1982-83 to 1985-86; Gilbert Perreault and Lindy Ruff, 1986-87; Lindy Ruff, 1987-88; Lindy Ruff and Mike Foligno, 1988-89; Mike Foligno, 1989-90; Mike Foligno and Mike Ramsey, 1990-91; Mike Ramsey, 1991-92; Mike Ramsey and Pat LaFontaine, 1992-93; Pat LaFontaine and Alexander Mogilny, 1993-94; Pat LaFontaine, 1994-95 to 1996-97; Donald Audette and Michael Peca, 1997-98; Michael Peca, 1998-99, 1999-2000; no captain, 2000-01; Stu Barnes. 2001-02, 2002-03; Miroslav Satan, Chris Drury, James Patrick, J.P. Dumont, Daniel Briere, 2003-04; Daniel Briere and Chris Drury, 2005-06, 2006-07; Jochen Hecht, Toni Lydman, Brian Campbell, Jaroslav Spacek, Jason Pominville, 2007-08; Craig Rivet, 2008-09 to date.

# Lindy Ruff

### Head Coach

*Born: Warburg, Alta., February 17, 1960.*

A former captain of the Sabres, Lindy Ruff was appointed as the club's 15th head coach on July 21, 1997. In 1999, he led the Sabres to the Stanley Cup Finals for just the second time in club history and in 2006 he guided the Sabres to the Eastern Conference Final and was rewarded with the Jack Adams Award as coach of the year. The Sabres won the Presidents' Trophy for finishing first overall in the NHL standings in 2006-07, recording 113 points and a franchise-record 53 wins. Ruff is the winningest coach in club history. As a player, Ruff was drafted 32nd overall by the Sabres in the 1979 Entry Draft. He played both defense and left wing in an NHL career that spanned 12 seasons including 608 regular-season games with Buffalo. He became a playing assistant coach with Rochester of the AHL in 1991-92 and San Diego of the IHL in 1992-93. Ruff's San Diego club set a pro hockey record with 62 wins. In 1993-94 he became an NHL assistant coach with the Florida Panthers.

**Coaching Record**

| | | | Regular Season | | | | Playoffs | | | |
|---|---|---|---|---|---|---|---|---|---|---|
| Season | Team | League | GC | W | L | O/T | GC | W | L | T |
| 1997-98 | Buffalo | NHL | 82 | 36 | 29 | 17 | 15 | 10 | 5 | .... |
| 1998-99 | Buffalo | NHL | 82 | 37 | 28 | 17 | 21 | 14 | 7 | .... |
| 99-2000 | Buffalo | NHL | 82 | 35 | 32 | 15 | 5 | 1 | 4 | .... |
| 2000-01 | Buffalo | NHL | 82 | 46 | 30 | 6 | 13 | 7 | 6 | .... |
| 2001-02 | Buffalo | NHL | 82 | 35 | 35 | 12 | .... | .... | .... | .... |
| 2002-03 | Buffalo | NHL | 82 | 27 | 37 | 18 | .... | .... | .... | .... |
| 2003-04 | Buffalo | NHL | 82 | 37 | 34 | 11 | .... | .... | .... | .... |
| 2004-05 | Buffalo | | SEASON CANCELLED | | | | | | | |
| 2005-06 | Buffalo | NHL | 82 | 52 | 24 | 6 | 18 | 11 | 7 | .... |
| 2006-07 | Buffalo | NHL | 82 | 53 | 22 | 7 | 16 | 9 | 7 | .... |
| 2007-08 | Buffalo | NHL | 82 | 39 | 31 | 12 | .... | .... | .... | .... |
| 2008-09 | Buffalo | NHL | 82 | 41 | 32 | 9 | .... | .... | .... | .... |
| | NHL Totals | | 902 | 438 | 334 | 130 | 88 | 52 | 36 | .... |

# 2008-09 Scoring

* – rookie

## Regular Season

| Pos | # | Player | Team | GP | G | A | Pts | TOI | +/- | PIM | PP | SH | GW | S | % |
|---|---|---|---|---|---|---|---|---|---|---|---|---|---|---|---|
| C | 9 | Derek Roy | BUF | 82 | 28 | 42 | 70 | 21:11 | –5 | 38 | 9 | 1 | 9 | 221 | 12.7 |
| R | 29 | Jason Pominville | BUF | 82 | 20 | 46 | 66 | 19:45 | –4 | 18 | 6 | 1 | 2 | 239 | 8.4 |
| L | 26 | Thomas Vanek | BUF | 73 | 40 | 24 | 64 | 17:11 | –1 | 44 | 20 | 2 | 5 | 211 | 19.0 |
| C | 19 | Tim Connolly | BUF | 48 | 18 | 29 | 47 | 19:07 | 12 | 22 | 5 | 1 | 5 | 126 | 14.3 |
| R | 21 | Drew Stafford | BUF | 79 | 20 | 25 | 45 | 15:37 | 3 | 29 | 9 | 0 | 0 | 183 | 10.9 |
| C | 17 | Dominic Moore | TOR | 63 | 12 | 29 | 41 | 17:18 | –1 | 69 | 4 | 1 | 1 | 132 | 9.1 |
| | | | BUF | 18 | 1 | 3 | 4 | 15:12 | –1 | 23 | 0 | 0 | 0 | 33 | 3.0 |
| | | | Total | 81 | 13 | 32 | 45 | 16:50 | –2 | 92 | 4 | 1 | 1 | 165 | 7.9 |
| D | 6 | Jaroslav Spacek | BUF | 80 | 8 | 37 | 45 | 22:16 | 2 | 38 | 4 | 0 | 0 | 130 | 6.2 |
| L | 41 | Clarke MacArthur | BUF | 71 | 17 | 14 | 31 | 13:50 | –4 | 56 | 5 | 0 | 0 | 108 | 15.7 |
| C | 28 | Paul Gaustad | BUF | 62 | 12 | 17 | 29 | 16:06 | 4 | 108 | 3 | 1 | 1 | 122 | 9.8 |
| C | 55 | Jochen Hecht | BUF | 70 | 12 | 15 | 27 | 17:23 | –9 | 33 | 3 | 1 | 1 | 173 | 6.9 |
| L | 20 | Daniel Paille | BUF | 73 | 12 | 15 | 27 | 11:54 | 0 | 20 | 0 | 0 | 2 | 80 | 15.0 |
| D | 52 | Craig Rivet | BUF | 64 | 2 | 22 | 24 | 20:14 | 4 | 125 | 1 | 0 | 0 | 80 | 2.5 |
| D | 5 | Toni Lydman | BUF | 80 | 3 | 20 | 23 | 21:46 | 0 | 70 | 0 | 0 | 0 | 99 | 3.0 |
| R | 61 | Maxim Afinogenov | BUF | 48 | 6 | 14 | 20 | 12:36 | –7 | 20 | 0 | 0 | 0 | 93 | 6.5 |
| C | 22 | Adam Mair | BUF | 75 | 8 | 11 | 19 | 10:34 | 4 | 95 | 0 | 0 | 1 | 75 | 10.7 |
| D | 44 | Andrej Sekera | BUF | 69 | 3 | 16 | 19 | 20:42 | –11 | 22 | 1 | 0 | 1 | 84 | 3.6 |
| D | 27 | Teppo Numminen | BUF | 57 | 2 | 15 | 17 | 17:30 | –4 | 22 | 1 | 0 | 1 | 34 | 5.9 |
| L | 37 | Matt Ellis | BUF | 45 | 7 | 5 | 12 | 8:49 | 4 | 12 | 0 | 0 | 2 | 73 | 9.6 |
| D | 10 | Henrik Tallinder | BUF | 66 | 1 | 11 | 12 | 18:25 | –2 | 36 | 0 | 0 | 1 | 35 | 2.9 |
| R | 36 | Patrick Kaleta | BUF | 51 | 4 | 5 | 9 | 8:55 | 1 | 89 | 0 | 0 | 0 | 35 | 11.4 |
| D | 38 | Nathan Paetsch | BUF | 23 | 2 | 4 | 6 | 12:11 | 3 | 25 | 0 | 0 | 0 | 21 | 9.5 |
| D | 34 | * Chris Butler | BUF | 47 | 2 | 4 | 6 | 16:43 | 11 | 18 | 0 | 0 | 1 | 36 | 5.6 |
| R | 25 | * Mark Mancari | BUF | 7 | 1 | 1 | 2 | 13:15 | –4 | 4 | 0 | 0 | 0 | 21 | 4.8 |
| C | 42 | * Nathan Gerbe | BUF | 10 | 0 | 1 | 1 | 13:36 | 3 | 4 | 0 | 0 | 0 | 24 | 0.0 |
| L | 76 | Andrew Peters | BUF | 28 | 0 | 1 | 1 | 4:01 | –2 | 81 | 0 | 0 | 0 | 10 | 0.0 |
| L | 58 | * Tim Kennedy | BUF | 1 | 0 | 0 | 0 | 11:04 | 0 | 0 | 0 | 0 | 0 | 1 | 0.0 |
| D | 17 | * Marc-Andre Gragnani | BUF | 4 | 0 | 0 | 0 | 15:23 | 2 | 2 | 0 | 0 | 0 | 3 | 0.0 |
| D | 4 | * Mike Weber | BUF | 7 | 0 | 0 | 0 | 14:10 | –3 | 19 | 0 | 0 | 0 | 2 | 0.0 |

## Goaltending

| No. | Goaltender | GPI | Mins | Avg | W | L | OT | EN | SO | GA | SA | S% | G | A | PIM |
|---|---|---|---|---|---|---|---|---|---|---|---|---|---|---|---|
| 32 | Mikael Tellqvist | 6 | 230 | 2.35 | 2 | 1 | 0 | 1 | 0 | 9 | 125 | .928 | 0 | 0 | 0 |
| 30 | Ryan Miller | 59 | 3443 | 2.53 | 34 | 18 | 6 | 6 | 5 | 145 | 1773 | .918 | 0 | 0 | 4 |
| 40 | Patrick Lalime | 24 | 1297 | 3.10 | 5 | 13 | 3 | 1 | 0 | 67 | 669 | .900 | 0 | 0 | 0 |
| | **Totals** | **82** | **4998** | **2.75** | **41** | **32** | **9** | **8** | **5** | **229** | **2575** | **.911** | | | |

*Though plagued by injuries once again, Tim Connolly averaged almost a point per game in 2008-09 and led the Sabres in plus-minus at +12.*

# Club Records

## Team

(Figures in brackets for season records are games played; records for fewest points, wins, ties, losses, goals, goals against are for 70 or more games)

| | | |
|---|---|---|
| **Most Points** | 113 | 1974-75 (80), 2006-07 (82) |
| **Most Wins** | 53 | 2006-07 (82) |
| **Most Ties** | 21 | 1980-81 (80) |
| **Most Losses** | 44 | 1986-87 (80) |
| **Most Goals** | 354 | 1974-75 (80) |
| **Most Goals Against** | 308 | 1986-87 (80) |
| **Fewest Points** | 51 | 1971-72 (78) |
| **Fewest Wins** | 16 | 1971-72 (78) |
| **Fewest Ties** | 5 | 2000-01 (82) |
| **Fewest Losses** | 16 | 1974-75 (80) |
| **Fewest Goals** | 190 | 2002-03 (82) |
| **Fewest Goals Against** | 175 | 1998-99 (82) |
| **Longest Winning Streak** | | |
| Overall | 10 | Jan. 4-23/84, Oct. 4-26/06 |
| Home | 12 | Nov. 12/72-Jan. 7/73, Oct. 13-Dec. 10/89 |
| Away | 10 | Dec. 10/83-Jan. 23/84, Oct. 4-Nov. 13/06 |
| **Longest Undefeated Streak** | | |
| Overall | 14 | Mar. 6-Apr. 6/80 (8 wins, 6 ties) |
| Home | 21 | Oct. 8/72-Jan. 7/73 (18 wins, 3 ties) |
| Away | 10 | Dec. 10/83-Jan. 23/84 (10 wins), Oct. 4-Nov. 13/06 (10 wins) |
| **Longest Losing Streak** | | |
| Overall | 8 | Jan. 25-Feb. 13/03 |
| Home | 6 | Oct. 10-Nov. 10/93, Mar. 3-Apr. 3/96 |
| Away | 7 | Oct. 14-Nov. 7/70, Feb. 6-27/71, Jan. 10-Feb. 3/96, Feb. 19-Mar. 21/09 |
| **Longest Winless Streak** | | |
| Overall | 12 | Nov. 23-Dec. 20/91 (8 losses, 4 ties), Oct. 25-Nov. 19/02 (10 losses, 2 ties) |
| Home | 12 | Jan. 27-Mar. 10/91 (7 losses, 5 ties) |
| Away | 23 | Oct. 30/71-Feb. 19/72 (15 losses, 8 ties) |
| **Most Shutouts, Season** | 13 | 1997-98 (82) |
| **Most PIM, Season** | *2,713 | 1991-92 (80) |
| **Most Goals, Game** | 14 | Jan. 21/75 (Wsh. 2 at Buf. 14), Mar. 19/81 (Tor. 4 at Buf. 14) |

## Individual

| | | |
|---|---|---|
| **Most Seasons** | 17 | Gilbert Perreault |
| **Most Games** | 1,191 | Gilbert Perreault |
| **Most Goals, Career** | 512 | Gilbert Perreault |
| **Most Assists, Career** | 814 | Gilbert Perreault |
| **Most Points, Career** | 1,326 | Gilbert Perreault (512G, 814A) |
| **Most PIM, Career** | 3,189 | Rob Ray |
| **Most Shutouts, Career** | 55 | Dominik Hasek |
| **Longest Consecutive Games Streak** | 776 | Craig Ramsay (Mar. 27/73-Feb. 10/83) |
| **Most Goals, Season** | 76 | Alexander Mogilny (1992-93) |
| **Most Assists, Season** | 95 | Pat LaFontaine (1992-93) |
| **Most Points, Season** | 148 | Pat LaFontaine (1992-93; 53G, 95A) |
| **Most PIM, Season** | 354 | Rob Ray (1991-92) |
| **Most Points, Defenseman, Season** | 81 | Phil Housley (1989-90; 21G, 60A) |
| **Most Points, Center, Season** | 148 | Pat LaFontaine (1992-93; 53G, 95A) |
| **Most Points, Right Wing, Season** | 127 | Alexander Mogilny (1992-93; 76G, 51A) |
| **Most Points, Left Wing, Season** | 95 | Rick Martin (1974-75; 52G, 43A) |
| **Most Points, Rookie, Season** | 74 | Rick Martin (1971-72; 44G, 30A) |
| **Most Shutouts, Season** | 13 | Dominik Hasek (1997-98) |
| **Most Goals, Game** | 5 | Dave Andreychuk (Feb. 6/86) |
| **Most Assists, Game** | 5 | Gilbert Perreault (Feb. 1/76), (Mar. 9/80), (Jan. 4/84); Dale Hawerchuk (Jan. 15/92); Pat LaFontaine (Mar. 19/92), (Dec. 31/92), (Feb. 10/93) |
| **Most Points, Game** | 7 | Gilbert Perreault (Feb. 1/76; 2G, 5A) |

* NHL Record.

## Retired Numbers

| | | |
|---|---|---|
| 2 | Tim Horton | 1972-1974 |
| 7 | Rick Martin | 1971-1981 |
| 11 | Gilbert Perreault | 1970-1987 |
| 14 | Rene Robert | 1971-1979 |
| 16 | Pat Lafontaine | 1991-1996 |
| 18 | Danny Gare | 1974-1981 |

# All-time Record vs. Other Clubs

## Regular Season

| | At Home | | | | | | | | On Road | | | | | | | | Total | | | | | | | |
|---|---|---|---|---|---|---|---|---|---|---|---|---|---|---|---|---|---|---|---|---|---|---|---|---|
| | GP | W | L | T | OL | GF | GA | PTS | GP | W | L | T | OL | GF | GA | PTS | GP | W | L | T | OL | GF | GA | PTS |
| Anaheim | 11 | 5 | 3 | 3 | 0 | 30 | 25 | 13 | 11 | 7 | 4 | 0 | 0 | 33 | 22 | 14 | 22 | 12 | 7 | 3 | 0 | 63 | 47 | 27 |
| Atlanta | 18 | 10 | 5 | 0 | 3 | 80 | 50 | 23 | 18 | 5 | 7 | 1 | 5 | 53 | 61 | 16 | 36 | 15 | 12 | 1 | 8 | 133 | 111 | 39 |
| Boston | 123 | 65 | 40 | 15 | 3 | 442 | 354 | 148 | 122 | 41 | 64 | 14 | 3 | 361 | 442 | 99 | 245 | 106 | 104 | 29 | 6 | 803 | 796 | 247 |
| Calgary | 46 | 28 | 13 | 5 | 0 | 192 | 133 | 61 | 48 | 18 | 19 | 11 | 0 | 149 | 161 | 47 | 94 | 46 | 32 | 16 | 0 | 341 | 294 | 108 |
| Carolina | 85 | 51 | 26 | 7 | 1 | 342 | 246 | 110 | 86 | 39 | 33 | 11 | 3 | 258 | 250 | 92 | 171 | 90 | 59 | 18 | 4 | 600 | 496 | 202 |
| Chicago | 54 | 33 | 14 | 7 | 0 | 202 | 139 | 73 | 53 | 19 | 28 | 6 | 0 | 142 | 169 | 44 | 107 | 52 | 42 | 13 | 0 | 344 | 308 | 117 |
| Colorado | 64 | 36 | 19 | 9 | 0 | 249 | 207 | 81 | 66 | 23 | 31 | 11 | 1 | 204 | 233 | 58 | 130 | 59 | 50 | 20 | 1 | 453 | 440 | 139 |
| Columbus | 6 | 2 | 4 | 0 | 0 | 14 | 18 | 4 | 3 | 0 | 2 | 1 | 0 | 6 | 8 | 1 | 9 | 2 | 6 | 1 | 0 | 20 | 26 | 5 |
| Dallas | 53 | 29 | 13 | 11 | 0 | 192 | 142 | 69 | 56 | 23 | 27 | 6 | 0 | 163 | 178 | 52 | 109 | 52 | 40 | 17 | 0 | 355 | 320 | 121 |
| Detroit | 54 | 33 | 13 | 8 | 0 | 229 | 161 | 74 | 57 | 19 | 32 | 5 | 1 | 163 | 208 | 44 | 111 | 52 | 45 | 13 | 1 | 392 | 369 | 118 |
| Edmonton | 31 | 11 | 13 | 7 | 0 | 111 | 113 | 29 | 31 | 7 | 21 | 3 | 0 | 87 | 123 | 17 | 62 | 18 | 34 | 10 | 0 | 198 | 236 | 46 |
| Florida | 31 | 21 | 7 | 3 | 0 | 92 | 58 | 45 | 29 | 14 | 14 | 1 | 0 | 81 | 78 | 29 | 60 | 35 | 21 | 4 | 0 | 173 | 136 | 74 |
| Los Angeles | 55 | 30 | 16 | 9 | 0 | 232 | 158 | 69 | 55 | 23 | 23 | 9 | 0 | 189 | 193 | 55 | 110 | 53 | 39 | 18 | 0 | 421 | 351 | 124 |
| Minnesota | 4 | 1 | 3 | 0 | 0 | 8 | 13 | 2 | 5 | 4 | 1 | 0 | 0 | 14 | 9 | 8 | 9 | 5 | 4 | 0 | 0 | 22 | 22 | 10 |
| Montreal | 117 | 63 | 32 | 19 | 3 | 366 | 309 | 148 | 118 | 41 | 64 | 12 | 1 | 346 | 431 | 95 | 235 | 104 | 96 | 31 | 4 | 712 | 740 | 243 |
| Nashville | 6 | 1 | 4 | 1 | 0 | 17 | 22 | 3 | 6 | 4 | 2 | 0 | 0 | 16 | 12 | 8 | 12 | 5 | 6 | 1 | 0 | 33 | 34 | 11 |
| New Jersey | 62 | 34 | 19 | 8 | 1 | 235 | 188 | 77 | 62 | 29 | 21 | 9 | 3 | 193 | 179 | 70 | 124 | 63 | 40 | 17 | 4 | 428 | 367 | 147 |
| NY Islanders | 69 | 38 | 21 | 9 | 1 | 233 | 192 | 86 | 69 | 30 | 29 | 9 | 1 | 193 | 191 | 70 | 138 | 68 | 50 | 18 | 2 | 426 | 383 | 156 |
| NY Rangers | 76 | 44 | 20 | 10 | 2 | 306 | 233 | 100 | 74 | 27 | 30 | 15 | 2 | 201 | 238 | 71 | 150 | 71 | 50 | 25 | 4 | 507 | 471 | 171 |
| Ottawa | 46 | 27 | 16 | 3 | 0 | 143 | 108 | 57 | 48 | 20 | 18 | 7 | 3 | 128 | 135 | 50 | 94 | 47 | 34 | 10 | 3 | 271 | 243 | 107 |
| Philadelphia | 71 | 36 | 26 | 8 | 1 | 240 | 201 | 81 | 75 | 20 | 42 | 12 | 1 | 194 | 260 | 53 | 146 | 56 | 68 | 20 | 2 | 434 | 461 | 134 |
| Phoenix | 33 | 21 | 6 | 5 | 1 | 133 | 83 | 48 | 31 | 15 | 14 | 2 | 0 | 96 | 93 | 32 | 64 | 36 | 20 | 7 | 1 | 229 | 176 | 80 |
| Pittsburgh | 79 | 38 | 20 | 17 | 4 | 296 | 214 | 97 | 79 | 21 | 39 | 18 | 1 | 241 | 294 | 61 | 158 | 59 | 59 | 35 | 5 | 537 | 508 | 158 |
| St. Louis | 54 | 30 | 18 | 6 | 0 | 207 | 171 | 66 | 51 | 14 | 28 | 7 | 2 | 127 | 183 | 37 | 105 | 44 | 46 | 13 | 2 | 334 | 354 | 103 |
| San Jose | 13 | 12 | 1 | 0 | 0 | 58 | 37 | 24 | 11 | 2 | 4 | 4 | 1 | 40 | 37 | 9 | 24 | 14 | 5 | 4 | 1 | 98 | 74 | 33 |
| Tampa Bay | 31 | 19 | 10 | 2 | 0 | 100 | 88 | 40 | 31 | 21 | 7 | 3 | 0 | 100 | 69 | 45 | 62 | 40 | 17 | 5 | 0 | 200 | 157 | 85 |
| Toronto | 84 | 53 | 24 | 6 | 1 | 332 | 221 | 113 | 82 | 38 | 29 | 12 | 3 | 284 | 242 | 91 | 166 | 91 | 53 | 18 | 4 | 616 | 463 | 204 |
| Vancouver | 54 | 28 | 18 | 8 | 0 | 195 | 157 | 64 | 53 | 16 | 26 | 11 | 0 | 163 | 197 | 43 | 107 | 44 | 44 | 19 | 0 | 358 | 354 | 107 |
| Washington | 64 | 40 | 18 | 6 | 0 | 252 | 169 | 86 | 64 | 38 | 17 | 9 | 0 | 226 | 164 | 85 | 128 | 78 | 35 | 15 | 0 | 478 | 333 | 171 |
| Defunct Clubs | 23 | 13 | 5 | 5 | 0 | 94 | 63 | 31 | 23 | 12 | 8 | 3 | 0 | 97 | 76 | 27 | 46 | 25 | 13 | 8 | 0 | 191 | 139 | 58 |
| **Totals** | **1517** | **852** | **447** | **197** | **21** | **5622** | **4273** | **1922** | **1517** | **590** | **684** | **212** | **31** | **4548** | **4936** | **1423** | **3034** | **1442** | **1131** | **409** | **52** | **10170** | **9209** | **3345** |

## Playoffs

| | Series | W | L | GP | W | L | T | GF | GA | Last Mtg. | Rnd. | Result |
|---|---|---|---|---|---|---|---|---|---|---|---|---|
| Boston | 7 | 2 | 5 | 39 | 18 | 21 | 0 | 130 | 139 | 1999 | CSF | W 4-2 |
| Carolina | 1 | 0 | 1 | 7 | 3 | 4 | 0 | 17 | 22 | 2006 | CF | L 3-4 |
| Chicago | 2 | 2 | 0 | 9 | 8 | 1 | 0 | 36 | 17 | 1980 | QF | W 4-0 |
| Colorado | 2 | 0 | 2 | 8 | 2 | 6 | 0 | 27 | 35 | 1985 | DSF | L 2-3 |
| Dallas | 3 | 1 | 2 | 13 | 5 | 8 | 0 | 37 | 39 | 1999 | F | L 2-4 |
| Montreal | 7 | 3 | 4 | 35 | 17 | 18 | 0 | 111 | 124 | 1998 | CSF | W 4-0 |
| New Jersey | 1 | 0 | 1 | 7 | 3 | 4 | 0 | 14 | 14 | 1994 | CQF | L 3-4 |
| NY Islanders | 4 | 1 | 3 | 21 | 8 | 13 | 0 | 62 | 70 | 2007 | CQF | W 4-1 |
| NY Rangers | 2 | 2 | 0 | 9 | 6 | 3 | 0 | 28 | 19 | 2007 | CSF | W 4-2 |
| Ottawa | 4 | 3 | 1 | 21 | 13 | 8 | 0 | 52 | 47 | 2007 | CF | L 1-4 |
| Philadelphia | 8 | 3 | 5 | 43 | 18 | 25 | 0 | 123 | 124 | 2006 | CQF | W 4-2 |
| Pittsburgh | 2 | 0 | 2 | 10 | 4 | 6 | 0 | 26 | 26 | 2001 | CSF | L 3-4 |
| St. Louis | 1 | 1 | 0 | 3 | 2 | 1 | 0 | 7 | 8 | 1976 | PRE | W 2-1 |
| Toronto | 1 | 1 | 0 | 5 | 4 | 1 | 0 | 21 | 16 | 1999 | CF | W 4-1 |
| Vancouver | 2 | 2 | 0 | 7 | 6 | 1 | 0 | 28 | 14 | 1981 | PRE | W 3-0 |
| Washington | 1 | 0 | 1 | 6 | 2 | 4 | 0 | 11 | 13 | 1998 | CF | L 2-4 |
| **Totals** | **48** | **21** | **27** | **243** | **119** | **124** | **0** | **730** | **727** | | | |

## Playoff Results 2009-2004

| Year | Round | Opponent | Result | GF | GA |
|---|---|---|---|---|---|
| 2007 | CF | Ottawa | L 1-4 | 10 | 15 |
| | CSF | NY Rangers | W 4-2 | 17 | 13 |
| | CQF | NY Islanders | W 4-1 | 17 | 11 |
| 2006 | CF | Carolina | L 3-4 | 17 | 22 |
| | CSF | Ottawa | W 4-1 | 16 | 13 |
| | CQF | Philadelphia | W 4-2 | 27 | 14 |

**Abbreviations: Round: F** - Final; **CF** - conference final; **CSF** - conference semi-final; **CQF** - conference quarter-final; **DSF** - division semi-final; **QF** - quarter-final; **PRE** - preliminary round.

Calgary totals include Atlanta Flames, 1972-73 to 1979-80.
Carolina totals include Hartford, 1979-80 to 1996-97.
Colorado totals include Quebec, 1979-80 to 1994-95.
Dallas totals include Minnesota North Stars, 1970-71 to 1992-93.
New Jersey totals include Kansas City, 1974-75, 1975-76, and Colorado Rockies, 1976-77 to 1981-82.
Phoenix totals include Winnipeg, 1979-80 to 1995-96.

## 2008-09 Results

| | | | |
|---|---|---|---|
| Oct. | 10 | Montreal | 2-1† |
| | 13 | at NY Islanders | 7-1 |
| | 15 | at NY Rangers | 3-1 |
| | 17 | Vancouver | 5-2 |
| | 18 | at Atlanta | 2-3† |
| | 21 | Boston | 3-2† |
| | 23 | at Minnesota | 4-3* |
| | 25 | at Colorado | 1-2† |
| | 27 | Ottawa | 2-5 |
| | 30 | Tampa Bay | 2-5 |
| Nov. | 1 | Washington | 5-0 |
| | 3 | at New Jersey | 2-0 |
| | 7 | Atlanta | 4-5* |
| | 8 | at Boston | 1-3 |
| | 12 | St. Louis | 4-3 |
| | 14 | Columbus | 1-6 |
| | 15 | at Pittsburgh | 2-5 |
| | 19 | at Boston | 4-7 |
| | 21 | Philadelphia | 0-3 |
| | 22 | NY Islanders | 2-4 |
| | 26 | Boston | 3-2 |
| | 28 | Pittsburgh | 4-3 |
| | 29 | at Montreal | 2-3 |
| Dec. | 1 | Nashville | 0-2 |
| | 4 | at Florida | 1-2 |
| | 6 | at Tampa Bay | 4-3 |
| | 8 | at Pittsburgh | 4-3 |
| | 10 | Tampa Bay | 4-2 |
| | 12 | Toronto | 1-2 |
| | 13 | at New Jersey | 4-2 |
| | 17 | New Jersey | 3-5 |
| | 19 | Los Angeles | 5-0 |
| | 20 | at Montreal | 3-4* |
| | 22 | Pittsburgh | 3-4* |
| | 26 | at Washington | 2-3 |
| | 27 | NY Islanders | 4-3† |
| | 30 | Washington | 2-4 |
| Jan. | 1 | at Toronto | 4-1 |
| | 3 | at Boston | 4-2 |
| | 6 | Ottawa | 4-2 |
| | 9 | NY Rangers | 2-1† |
| | 10 | at Detroit | 1-3 |
| | 14 | at Chicago | 1-4 |
| | 15 | at Dallas | 5-4† |
| | 17 | Carolina | 3-1 |
| | 19 | at Florida | 3-2† |
| | 21 | at Tampa Bay | 3-5 |
| | 27 | at Edmonton | 10-2 |
| | 28 | at Calgary | 2-5 |
| | 31 | at Phoenix | 2-0 |
| Feb. | 2 | at Anaheim | 2-3 |
| | 4 | Toronto | 5-0 |
| | 6 | Montreal | 3-2 |
| | 7 | at Ottawa | 2-3† |
| | 11 | Ottawa | 1-3 |
| | 13 | San Jose | 6-5† |
| | 15 | Carolina | 0-3 |
| | 17 | at Toronto | 4-1 |
| | 19 | at Philadelphia | 3-6 |
| | 21 | NY Rangers | 4-2 |
| | 24 | Anaheim | 2-3 |
| | 26 | at Carolina | 1-2† |
| | 28 | at NY Islanders | 0-2 |
| Mar. | 4 | Montreal | 5-1 |
| | 6 | Phoenix | 5-1 |
| | 7 | at Ottawa | 3-6 |
| | 10 | at Philadelphia | 2-5 |
| | 12 | Florida | 3-1 |
| | 14 | Atlanta | 3-4† |
| | 17 | at Ottawa | 2-4 |
| | 20 | Philadelphia | 4-6 |
| | 21 | at NY Rangers | 3-5 |
| | 25 | Florida | 5-3 |
| | 27 | Toronto | 5-3 |
| | 28 | at Montreal | 4-3† |
| Apr. | 1 | at Atlanta | 2-3* |
| | 3 | at Washington | 5-4* |
| | 4 | New Jersey | 2-3 |
| | 6 | Detroit | 1-4 |
| | 8 | at Toronto | 3-1 |
| | 9 | at Carolina | 5-1 |
| | 11 | Boston | 6-1 |

* – Overtime † – Shootout

## Entry Draft Selections 2009-1995

Name in bold denotes played in NHL.

**2009**
Pick
13 Zack Kassian
66 Brayden McNabb
104 Marcus Foligno
134 Mark Adams
164 Connor Knapp
194 Maxime Legault

**2008**
Pick
12 Tyler Myers
26 Tyler Ennis
44 Luke Adam
81 Corey Fienhage
101 Justin Jokinen
104 Jordon Southorn
134 Jacob Lagace
164 Nick Crawford

**2007**
Pick
31 T.J. Brennan
59 Drew Schiestel
89 Corey Tropp
139 Bradley Eidsness
147 Jean-Simon Allard
179 Paul Byron
187 Nick Eno
209 Drew Mackenzie

**2006**
Pick
24 Dennis Persson
46 Jhonas Enroth
57 **Mike Weber**
117 Felix Schutz
147 Alex Biega
207 Benjamin Breault

**2005**
Pick
13 Marek Zagrapan
48 Philip Gogulla
87 **Marc-Andre Gragnani**
96 **Chris Butler**
142 **Nathan Gerbe**
182 Adam Dennis
191 Vyacheslav Buravchikov
208 Matt Generous
227 Andrew Orpik

**2004**
Pick
13 **Drew Stafford**
43 **Michael Funk**
71 **Andrej Sekera**
145 Michal Valent
176 **Patrick Kaleta**
207 **Mark Mancari**
241 **Mike Card**
273 Dylan Hunter

**2003**
Pick
5 **Thomas Vanek**
65 Branislav Fabry
74 **Clarke MacArthur**
106 **Jan Hejda**
114 Denis Ezhov
150 Thomas Morrow
172 Pavel Voroshnin
202 **Nathan Paetsch**
235 Jeff Weber
266 Louis-Philippe Martin

**2002**
Pick
11 **Keith Ballard**
20 **Daniel Paille**
76 Michael Tessier
82 John Adams
108 Jakub Hulva
121 Marty Magers
178 Maxim Schevjev
178 Maxim Sheviev
208 **Radoslav Hecl**
241 **Dennis Wideman**
271 Martin Cizek

**2001**
Pick
22 **Jiri Novotny**
32 **Derek Roy**
50 **Chris Thorburn**
55 **Jason Pominville**
155 Michal Vondrka
234 Calle Aslund
247 Marek Dubec
279 Ryan Jorde

**2000**
Pick
15 Artem Kryukov
48 Gerard Dicaire
111 Ghyslain Rousseau
149 Denis Denisov
213 Vasily Bizyayev
220 **Paul Gaustad**
258 **Sean McMorrow**
277 Ryan Courtney

**1999**
Pick
20 **Barrett Heisten**
35 **Milan Bartovic**
55 **Doug Janik**
64 **Mike Zigomanis**
73 Tim Preston
117 Karel Mosovsky
138 **Ryan Miller**
146 Matt Kinch
178 Seneque Hyacinthe
206 Bret DeCecco
235 Brad Self
263 Craig Brunel

**1998**
Pick
18 **Dmitri Kalinin**
34 **Andrew Peters**
47 **Norm Milley**
50 **Jaroslav Kristek**
77 **Mike Pandolfo**
137 Aaron Goldade
164 **Ales Kotalik**
191 **Brad Moran**
218 **David Moravec**
249 Edo Terglav

**1997**
Pick
21 **Mika Noronen**
48 **Henrik Tallinder**
69 **Maxim Afinogenov**
75 Jeff Martin
101 Luc Theoret
128 Torrey DiRoberto
156 **Brian Campbell**
184 Jeremy Adduono
212 **Kamil Piros**
238 Dylan Kemp

**1996**
Pick
7 **Erik Rasmussen**
27 **Cory Sarich**
33 Darren Van Oene
54 Francois Methot
87 Kurt Walsh
106 Mike Martone
115 **Alexei Tezikov**
142 Ryan Davis
161 Darren Mortier
222 Scott Buhler

**1995**
Pick
14 **Jay McKee**
16 **Martin Biron**
42 Mark Dutiaume
68 Mathieu Sunderland
94 **Matt Davidson**
111 Marian Menhart
119 Kevin Popp
123 Daniel Bienvenue
172 Brian Scott
198 Mike Zanutto
224 **Rob Skrlac**

## General Managers' History

Punch Imlach, 1970-71 to 1977-78; John Anderson, 1978-79; Scotty Bowman, 1979-80 to 1985-86; Scotty Bowman and Gerry Meehan, 1986-87; Gerry Meehan, 1987-88 to 1992-93; John Muckler, 1993-94 to 1996-97; Darcy Regier, 1997-98 to date.

## Darcy Regier

### General Manager

*Born: Swift Current, Sask., November 27, 1957.*

Darcy Regier became the sixth general manager of the Buffalo Sabres on June 11, 1997 after a lengthy management apprenticeship in the New York Islanders organization. As a player, Regier played eight pro seasons, including part of the 1977-78 season with the Cleveland Barons and parts of the 1982-83 and 1983-84 campaigns with the New York Islanders.

He began his career as an administrator with the Islanders in 1984-85 and went on to serve in a variety of capacities including director of administration, assistant director of hockey operations, assistant coach and assistant general manager. He also served as an assistant coach with Hartford in 1991-92.

While with the Islanders, Regier benefited from working with talented managers and coaches including Bill Torrey and Al Arbour. As a minor pro player with Indianapolis of the CHL he became associated with another important influence on his hockey career, current Detroit Red Wing executive Jim Devellano.

# Club Directory

HSBC Arena

**Buffalo Sabres**
HSBC Arena
One Seymour H. Knox III Plaza
Buffalo, NY 14203
Phone **716/855-4100**
Fax 716/855-4110
Tickets, U.S.: 888/GO-SABRES
Canada: 888/669-GOAL
www.sabres.com
**Capacity:** 18,690

**Executive**
Owner . . . . . . . . . . B. Thomas Golisano
Managing Partner/Minority Owner . . . . . . . . . . Lawrence Quinn
Chief Operating Officer/Minority Owner . . . . . . . . . . Daniel DiPofi

**Hockey Department**
General Manager . . . . . . . . . . Darcy Regier
Director of Amateur Scouting . . . . . . . . . . Kevin Devine
Director of Pro Scouting . . . . . . . . . . Jon Christiano
Pro Scouts . . . . . . . . . . Dennis Miller, Ryan Vinz
Amateur Scouts . . . . . . . . . . Bo Berglund, Nik Fattey, Iouri Khmylev, Al MacAdam, Paul Merritt, Craig Benning, Kim Gellert, Eric Weissman
Director of Amateur Scouting Operations . . . . . . . . . . Scott Schranz
Assistant to the General Manager . . . . . . . . . . Mark Jakubowski
Coordinator of Hockey Operations . . . . . . . . . . Michael Bermingham

**Coaching Staff**
Head Coach . . . . . . . . . . Lindy Ruff
Associate Coach . . . . . . . . . . Brian McCutcheon
Assistant Coach . . . . . . . . . . James Patrick
Strength & Conditioning Coach . . . . . . . . . . Doug McKenney
Asst. Strength & Conditioning Coach . . . . . . . . . . Kevin Collins
Goaltender Coach . . . . . . . . . . Jim Corsi
Administrative Assistant Coach . . . . . . . . . . Corey Smith
Athletic Trainer . . . . . . . . . . Tim Macre
Equipment Managers / Asst. Mgr. . . . . . . . . . . Rip Simonick, Dave Williams / George Babcock
Massage Therapist . . . . . . . . . . Chuck Garlow

**Medical**
Medical Director . . . . . . . . . . Les Bisson, M.D.
Team Physicians . . . . . . . . . . Nicholas Aquino, M.D., William Hartrich, M.D., Mark Feinberg, M.D.
Oral Surgeon / Team Dentist . . . . . . . . . . Steven Jenson, DDS, David Croglio, DDS
Team Doctor Emeritus . . . . . . . . . . John L. Butsch, M.D.

**Legal**
Director of Legal Affairs & Human Resources . . . . . . . . . . Dave Zygaj
Finance and Administration
Director of Finance & Administration . . . . . . . . . . Chuck LaMattina
Accounting Manager . . . . . . . . . . Christine Ivansitz
Payroll & Human Resource Manager . . . . . . . . . . Birgid Haensel
Accounts Payable Clerk / Exec. Asst. . . . . . . . . . . Kim Binkley / Nadine Lawicki
IT Systems Engineer . . . . . . . . . . David Blaszak

**Broadcast**
Director of Broadcasting . . . . . . . . . . Chrisanne Bellas
TV Producer / Director . . . . . . . . . . Joe Pinter / Matt Gould
Lead Feature Editor / Photographer-Editor . . . . . . . . . . Drew Boeing / Mark Blaszak
Production Assistant . . . . . . . . . . Jason Wiese
Scoreboard Director/Editor . . . . . . . . . . Jeff Hill
Broadcast Team . . . . . . . . . . Rick Jeanneret (Play-by-Play), Harry Neale (Commentator), Kevin Sylvester (Studio Host), Mike Robitaille, Rob Ray (Analysts)

**Merchandise**
Director of Merchandise . . . . . . . . . . Mike Kaminska
Merchandise Mgrs, Inventory / Event Sales . . . . . . . . . . Glenn Barker / Jeff Smith
Store Manager . . . . . . . . . . Alec Moslow

**Marketing**
Director of Marketing . . . . . . . . . . Rob Kopacz
Director of Game Presentation . . . . . . . . . . Jenifer Dunford
Database Marketing Manager . . . . . . . . . . Tom Matheny
Promotions Coordinator . . . . . . . . . . Jacqueline Tollar
Game Presentation Coordinator . . . . . . . . . . Robert Neumann
Website Manager . . . . . . . . . . Scott Miner
Web Content Coordinator . . . . . . . . . . Erin Pollina
Director of Creative Services . . . . . . . . . . Frank Cravotta
Graphic Artist . . . . . . . . . . Vicki Sitek

**Public and Community Relations**
Director of Public Relations . . . . . . . . . . Michael Gilbert
Manager of Publications & Hockey Information . . . . Kevin Snow
Manager of Community Development . . . . . . . . . . Rich Jureller
Coordinator of Media Relations . . . . . . . . . . Chris Bandura
Community Relations Coordinator . . . . . . . . . . Teresa Belbas
Mascot Coordinator . . . . . . . . . . Ed Grudzinski
Graduate Assistant . . . . . . . . . . Tim Bulmer
Team Photographer . . . . . . . . . . Bill Wippert
Director of Alumni Relations . . . . . . . . . . Larry Playfair
Corporate & Community Relations Liaison . . . . . . . . . . Gilbert Perreault
Sales and Business Development
VP Sales & Business Development . . . . . . . . . . John Livsey
Senior Account Managers . . . . . . . . . . Joe Foy, Chris Luterek
Director of Corporate Fulfillment . . . . . . . . . . Rob Nugent
Director of Sales/Marketing – Rochester . . . . . . . . . . Gary Muxworthy

**Ticket Sales and Operations**
Director of Ticket Operations & Services . . . . . . . . . . John Sinclair
Account Services Manager . . . . . . . . . . Michael Tout
Box Office Mgr. / Coordinators . . . . . Marty Maloney / Gretchen Knott, Ryan Handley
Account Services Representatives . . . Roxanne Anderson, Andrea Keane, Lisa Jacobs, Melissa Rugg
Special Consultant . . . . . . . . . . Joe Crozier
Coordinator of Suite Services . . . . . . . . . . Michelle Mitchell

**HSBC Arena**
Director of Arena Operations . . . . . . . . . . Stan Makowski, Jr.
Director of Arena Services . . . . . . . . . . Thomas Ahern
Director of Event Booking . . . . . . . . . . Jennifer Van Rysdam
Arena Marketing Manager . . . . . . . . . . Tracey Penner
Director of Amateur Athletics . . . . . . . . . . Kevin Sylvester
Event Managers . . . . . . . . . . Matt Rabinowitz, Beth Guiliani Gatto
Mgr. of Technical Communications . . . . . . . . . . Mike Queeno, Ray Riel
Chief Engineer . . . . . . . . . . Lou Long
Building Services Manager . . . . . . . . . . Dennis Hooper
Security Manager . . . . . . . . . . Marc Brenner

## Key Off-Season Signings/Acquisitions

**2009**

**June 5** • Re-signed G **Curtis McElhinney.**

**23** • Named **Brent Sutter** head coach and **Dave Lowry**, **Ryan McGill**, and **Jamie McLennan** assistant coaches.

**27** • Acquired D **Jay Bouwmeester** from Florida for D **Jordan Leopold** and a 3rd-round pick in 2009.

**27** • Acquired RW **Brandon Prust** from Phoenix for D **Jim Vandermeer.**

**July 1** • Signed LW **Fredrik Sjostrom.**

**1** • Re-signed D **Adam Pardy.**

**7** • Re-signed C **Jamie Lundmark.**

**11** • Signed RW **Brian McGrattan.**

**16** • Claimed LW **Nigel Dawes** on waivers from Phoenix.

**30** • Re-signed C **Dustin Boyd.**

# Calgary Flames

## 2008-09 Results: 46W-30L-4OTL-2SOL 98PTS.
## Second, Northwest Division

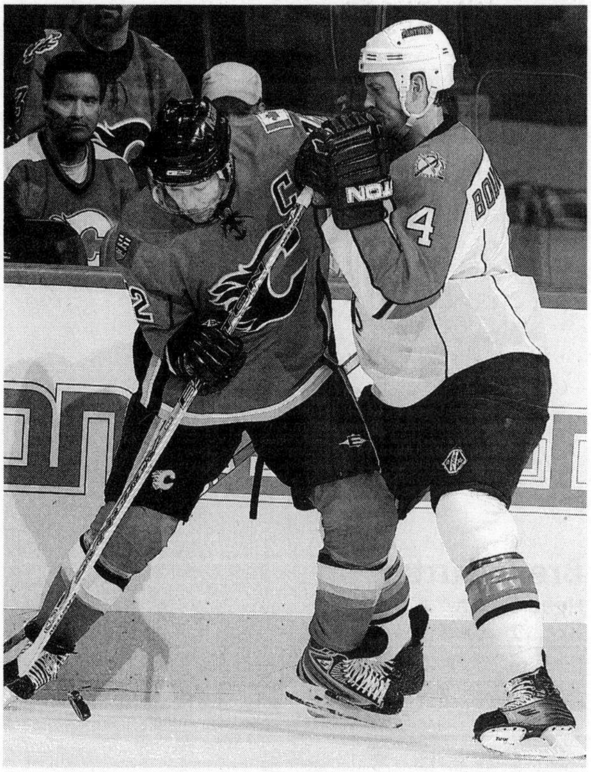

*A couple of native Albertans, Jarome Iginla and Jay Bouwmeester will now be teammates in Calgary. The Flames swung a deal to acquire the defenseman's rights from Florida before Bouwmeester became a free agent.*

## 2009-10 Schedule

| | | | | | | | |
|---|---|---|---|---|---|---|---|
| **Oct.** | Thu. | 1 | Vancouver | | Tue. | 5 | at Nashville |
| | Sat. | 3 | at Edmonton | | Wed. | 6 | at Minnesota |
| | Tue. | 6 | Montreal | | Fri. | 8 | Columbus |
| | Thu. | 8 | at Edmonton | | Sat. | 9 | at Vancouver |
| | Fri. | 9 | Dallas | | Mon. | 11 | Colorado |
| | Mon. | 12 | at Chicago | | Wed. | 13 | Pittsburgh |
| | Tue. | 13 | at Columbus | | Fri. | 15 | Nashville |
| | Fri. | 16 | Vancouver | | Sun. | 17 | at Anaheim* |
| | Tue. | 20 | Columbus | | Mon. | 18 | at San Jose |
| | Sat. | 24 | Edmonton | | Thu. | 21 | Chicago |
| | Wed. | 28 | Colorado | | Mon. | 25 | St. Louis |
| | Sat. | 31 | Detroit | | Wed. | 27 | at Dallas |
| **Nov.** | Wed. | 4 | at Dallas | | Thu. | 28 | at Phoenix |
| | Thu. | 5 | at St. Louis | | Sat. | 30 | Edmonton |
| | Sat. | 7 | NY Rangers | **Feb.** | Mon. | 1 | Philadelphia |
| | Tue. | 10 | at Montreal | | Wed. | 3 | Carolina |
| | Fri. | 13 | at Buffalo | | Fri. | 5 | at Florida |
| | Sat. | 14 | at Toronto | | Sat. | 6 | at Tampa Bay |
| | Tue. | 17 | Colorado | | Tue. | 9 | at Ottawa |
| | Thu. | 19 | Chicago | | Thu. | 11 | Dallas |
| | Sat. | 21 | at Los Angeles* | | Sat. | 13 | Anaheim |
| | Mon. | 23 | at Anaheim | **Mar.** | Wed. | 3 | Minnesota |
| | Wed. | 25 | Phoenix | | Fri. | 5 | New Jersey |
| | Fri. | 27 | at Detroit | | Sun. | 7 | at Minnesota* |
| | Sat. | 28 | at Columbus | | Tue. | 9 | at Detroit |
| | Mon. | 30 | at Nashville | | Thu. | 11 | Ottawa |
| **Dec.** | Thu. | 3 | at Phoenix | | Sun. | 14 | at Vancouver |
| | Sat. | 5 | at San Jose | | Mon. | 15 | Detroit |
| | Mon. | 7 | at Los Angeles | | Wed. | 17 | at Colorado |
| | Wed. | 9 | Atlanta | | Fri. | 19 | San Jose |
| | Fri. | 11 | Minnesota | | Sun. | 21 | at Minnesota* |
| | Sun. | 13 | at Colorado | | Tue. | 23 | Anaheim |
| | Tue. | 15 | at St. Louis | | Thu. | 25 | at NY Islanders |
| | Thu. | 17 | Los Angeles | | Sat. | 27 | at Boston* |
| | Sat. | 19 | Nashville* | | Sun. | 28 | at Washington* |
| | Wed. | 23 | St. Louis | | Wed. | 31 | Phoenix |
| | Sun. | 27 | Vancouver | **Apr.** | Fri. | 2 | at Colorado |
| | Mon. | 28 | at Edmonton | | Sun. | 4 | at Chicago* |
| | Wed. | 30 | Los Angeles | | Tue. | 6 | San Jose |
| | Thu. | 31 | Edmonton | | Thu. | 8 | Minnesota |
| **Jan.** | Sat. | 2 | Toronto* | | Sat. | 10 | at Vancouver |

* Denotes afternoon game.

## Year-by-Year Record

| | | Home | | | | Road | | | | Overall | | | | | | | | |
|---|---|---|---|---|---|---|---|---|---|---|---|---|---|---|---|---|---|---|
| **Season** | **GP** | **W** | **L** | **T** | **OL** | **W** | **L** | **T** | **OL** | **W** | **L** | **T** | **OL** | **GF** | **GA** | **Pts.** | **Finished** | **Playoff Result** |
| 2008-09 | 82 | 27 | 10 | .... | 4 | 19 | 20 | .... | 2 | 46 | 30 | .... | 6 | 254 | 248 | 98 | 2nd, Northwest Div. | Lost Conf. Quarter-Final |
| 2007-08 | 82 | 21 | 11 | .... | 9 | 21 | 19 | .... | 1 | 42 | 30 | .... | 10 | 229 | 227 | 94 | 3rd, Northwest Div. | Lost Conf. Quarter-Final |
| 2006-07 | 82 | 30 | 9 | .... | 2 | 13 | 20 | .... | 8 | 43 | 29 | .... | 10 | 258 | 226 | 96 | 3rd, Northwest Div. | Lost Conf. Quarter-Final |
| 2005-06 | 82 | 30 | 7 | .... | 4 | 16 | 18 | .... | 7 | 46 | 25 | .... | 11 | 218 | 200 | 103 | 1st, Northwest Div. | Lost Conf. Quarter-Final |
| 2004-05 | .... | .... | .... | .... | .... | .... | .... | .... | .... | .... | .... | .... | .... | .... | .... | .... | | |
| 2003-04 | 82 | 21 | 14 | 5 | 1 | 21 | 16 | 2 | 2 | 42 | 30 | 7 | 3 | 200 | 176 | 94 | 3rd, Northwest Div. | Lost Final |
| 2002-03 | 82 | 14 | 16 | 10 | 1 | 15 | 20 | 3 | 3 | 29 | 36 | 13 | 4 | 186 | 228 | 75 | 5th, Northwest Div. | Out of Playoffs |
| 2001-02 | 82 | 20 | 14 | 5 | 2 | 12 | 21 | 7 | 1 | 32 | 35 | 12 | 3 | 201 | 220 | 79 | 4th, Northwest Div. | Out of Playoffs |
| 2000-01 | 82 | 12 | 18 | 9 | 2 | 15 | 18 | 6 | 2 | 27 | 36 | 15 | 4 | 197 | 236 | 73 | 4th, Northwest Div. | Out of Playoffs |
| 1999-2000 | 82 | 20 | 14 | 6 | 1 | 11 | 22 | 4 | 4 | 31 | 36 | 10 | 5 | 211 | 256 | 77 | 4th, Northwest Div. | Out of Playoffs |
| 1998-99 | 82 | 15 | 20 | 6 | .... | 15 | 20 | 6 | .... | 30 | 40 | 12 | .... | 211 | 234 | 72 | 3rd, Northwest Div. | Out of Playoffs |
| 1997-98 | 82 | 18 | 17 | 6 | .... | 8 | 24 | 9 | .... | 26 | 41 | 15 | .... | 217 | 252 | 67 | 5th, Pacific Div. | Out of Playoffs |
| 1996-97 | 82 | 21 | 18 | 2 | .... | 11 | 23 | 7 | .... | 32 | 41 | 9 | .... | 214 | 239 | 73 | 5th, Pacific Div. | Out of Playoffs |
| 1995-96 | 82 | 18 | 18 | 5 | .... | 16 | 19 | 6 | .... | 34 | 37 | 11 | .... | 241 | 240 | 79 | 2nd, Pacific Div. | Lost Conf. Quarter-Final |
| 1994-95 | 48 | 15 | 7 | 2 | .... | 9 | 10 | 5 | .... | 24 | 17 | 7 | .... | 163 | 135 | 55 | 1st, Pacific Div. | Lost Conf. Quarter-Final |
| 1993-94 | 84 | 25 | 12 | 5 | .... | 17 | 17 | 8 | .... | 42 | 29 | 13 | .... | 302 | 256 | 97 | 1st, Pacific Div. | Lost Conf. Quarter-Final |
| 1992-93 | 84 | 23 | 14 | 5 | .... | 20 | 16 | 6 | .... | 43 | 30 | 11 | .... | 322 | 282 | 97 | 2nd, Smythe Div. | Lost Div. Semi-Final |
| 1991-92 | 80 | 19 | 14 | 7 | .... | 12 | 23 | 5 | .... | 31 | 37 | 12 | .... | 296 | 305 | 74 | 5th, Smythe Div. | Out of Playoffs |
| 1990-91 | 80 | 29 | 8 | 3 | .... | 17 | 18 | 5 | .... | 46 | 26 | 8 | .... | 344 | 263 | 100 | 2nd, Smythe Div. | Lost Div. Semi-Final |
| 1989-90 | 80 | 28 | 7 | 5 | .... | 14 | 16 | 10 | .... | 42 | 23 | 15 | .... | 348 | 265 | 99 | 1st, Smythe Div. | Lost Div. Semi-Final |
| **1988-89** | **80** | **32** | **4** | **4** | .... | **22** | **13** | **5** | .... | **54** | **17** | **9** | .... | **354** | **226** | **117** | **1st, Smythe Div.** | **Won Stanley Cup** |
| 1987-88 | 80 | 26 | 11 | 3 | .... | 22 | 12 | 6 | .... | 48 | 23 | 9 | .... | 397 | 305 | 105 | 1st, Smythe Div. | Lost Div. Final |
| 1986-87 | 80 | 25 | 13 | 2 | .... | 21 | 18 | 1 | .... | 46 | 31 | 3 | .... | 318 | 289 | 95 | 2nd, Smythe Div. | Lost Div. Semi-Final |
| 1985-86 | 80 | 23 | 11 | 6 | .... | 17 | 20 | 3 | .... | 40 | 31 | 9 | .... | 354 | 315 | 89 | 2nd, Smythe Div. | Lost Final |
| 1984-85 | 80 | 23 | 11 | 6 | .... | 18 | 16 | 6 | .... | 41 | 27 | 12 | .... | 363 | 302 | 94 | 3rd, Smythe Div. | Lost Div. Semi-Final |
| 1983-84 | 80 | 22 | 11 | 7 | .... | 12 | 21 | 7 | .... | 34 | 32 | 14 | .... | 311 | 314 | 82 | 2nd, Smythe Div. | Lost Div. Final |
| 1982-83 | 80 | 21 | 12 | 7 | .... | 11 | 22 | 7 | .... | 32 | 34 | 14 | .... | 321 | 317 | 78 | 2nd, Smythe Div. | Lost Div. Final |
| 1981-82 | 80 | 20 | 11 | 9 | .... | 9 | 23 | 8 | .... | 29 | 34 | 17 | .... | 334 | 345 | 75 | 3rd, Smythe Div. | Lost Div. Semi-Final |
| 1980-81 | 80 | 25 | 5 | 10 | .... | 14 | 22 | 4 | .... | 39 | 27 | 14 | .... | 329 | 298 | 92 | 3rd, Patrick Div. | Lost Semi-Final |
| 1979-80* | 80 | 18 | 15 | 7 | .... | 17 | 17 | 6 | .... | 35 | 32 | 13 | .... | 282 | 269 | 83 | 4th, Patrick Div. | Lost Prelim. Round |
| 1978-79* | 80 | 25 | 11 | 4 | .... | 16 | 20 | 4 | .... | 41 | 31 | 8 | .... | 327 | 280 | 90 | 4th, Patrick Div. | Lost Prelim. Round |
| 1977-78* | 80 | 20 | 13 | 7 | .... | 14 | 14 | 12 | .... | 34 | 27 | 19 | .... | 274 | 252 | 87 | 3rd, Patrick Div. | Lost Prelim. Round |
| 1976-77* | 80 | 22 | 11 | 7 | .... | 12 | 23 | 5 | .... | 34 | 34 | 12 | .... | 264 | 265 | 80 | 3rd, Patrick Div. | Lost Prelim. Round |
| 1975-76* | 80 | 19 | 14 | 7 | .... | 16 | 19 | 5 | .... | 35 | 33 | 12 | .... | 262 | 237 | 82 | 3rd, Patrick Div. | Lost Prelim. Round |
| 1974-75* | 80 | 24 | 9 | 7 | .... | 10 | 22 | 8 | .... | 34 | 31 | 15 | .... | 243 | 233 | 83 | 4th, Patrick Div. | Out of Playoffs |
| 1973-74* | 78 | 17 | 15 | 7 | .... | 13 | 19 | 7 | .... | 30 | 34 | 14 | .... | 214 | 238 | 74 | 4th, West Div. | Lost Quarter-Final |
| 1972-73* | 78 | 16 | 16 | 7 | .... | 9 | 22 | 8 | .... | 25 | 38 | 15 | .... | 191 | 239 | 65 | 7th, West Div. | Out of Playoffs |

* Atlanta Flames

**NORTHWEST DIVISION**
**38th NHL Season**

**Franchise date:** June 6, 1972

Transferred from Atlanta to Calgary, June 24, 1980.

# 2009-10 Player Personnel

| FORWARDS | HT | WT | S | Place of Birth | *Age | 2008-09 Club |
|---|---|---|---|---|---|---|
| BOURQUE, Rene | 6-2 | 213 | L | Lac La Biche, Alta. | 27 | Calgary |
| BOYD, Dustin | 6-0 | 198 | L | Winnipeg, Man. | 23 | Calgary-Quad City |
| CONROY, Craig | 6-2 | 193 | R | Potsdam, NY | 38 | Calgary |
| DAWES, Nigel | 5-8 | 190 | L | Winnipeg, Man. | 24 | NY Rangers-Phoenix |
| GLENCROSS, Curtis | 6-1 | 195 | L | Kindersley, Sask. | 26 | Calgary |
| IGINLA, Jarome | 6-1 | 207 | R | Edmonton, Alta. | 32 | Calgary |
| JOKINEN, Olli | 6-3 | 215 | L | Kuopio, Finland | 30 | Phoenix-Calgary |
| LANGKOW, Daymond | 5-10 | 183 | L | Edmonton, Alta. | 33 | Calgary |
| LUNDMARK, Jamie | 6-0 | 197 | R | Edmonton, Alta. | 28 | Calgary-Quad City |
| McGRATTAN, Brian | 6-4 | 235 | R | Hamilton, Ont. | 28 | Phoenix-San Antonio |
| MOSS, Dave | 6-3 | 200 | L | Livonia, MI | 27 | Calgary |
| NYSTROM, Eric | 6-1 | 193 | L | Syosset, NY | 26 | Calgary |
| PRUST, Brandon | 5-11 | 195 | L | London, Ont. | 25 | Calgary-Phoenix |
| SJOSTROM, Fredrik | 6-1 | 218 | L | Fargelanda, Sweden | 26 | NY Rangers |
| STUART, Colin | 6-2 | 205 | L | Rochester, MN | 27 | Atlanta-Chicago (AHL) |
| **DEFENSEMEN** | | | | | | |
| BOUWMEESTER, Jay | 6-4 | 214 | L | Edmonton, Alta. | 26 | Florida |
| GIORDANO, Mark | 6-0 | 203 | L | Toronto, Ont. | 25 | Calgary |
| KRONWALL, Staffan | 6-4 | 209 | L | Jarfalla, Sweden | 27 | Tor (AHL)-Wsh-Hershey |
| PARDY, Adam | 6-4 | 206 | L | Bonavista, Nfld. | 25 | Calgary |
| PHANEUF, Dion | 6-3 | 214 | L | Edmonton, Alta. | 24 | Calgary |
| REGEHR, Robyn | 6-3 | 225 | L | Recife, Brazil | 29 | Calgary |
| SARICH, Cory• | 6-4 | 207 | R | Saskatoon, Sask. | 31 | Calgary |
| STRALMAN, Anton | 6-1 | 200 | R | Tibro, Sweden | 23 | Toronto-Toronto (AHL) |

| GOALTENDERS | HT | WT | C | Place of Birth | *Age | 2008-09 Club |
|---|---|---|---|---|---|---|
| KIPRUSOFF, Miikka | 6-1 | 184 | L | Turku, Finland | 32 | Calgary |
| McELHINNEY, Curtis | 6-2 | 193 | L | London, Ont. | 26 | Calgary |

* – Age at start of 2009-10 season

# Brent Sutter

## Head Coach

*Born: Viking, Alta., June 10, 1962.*

General manager Darryl Sutter announced on June 23, 2009 that his brother Brent Sutter had been named head coach of the Calgary Flames. Brent Sutter joined the Flames after two seasons as the bench boss of the New Jersey Devils compiling a 97-56-11 (.625) record during the regular season, and an Atlantic Division title in 2008-09.

Prior to joining the Devils, Sutter spent eight seasons as owner, president, general manager, and head coach of the Red Deer Rebels of the Western Hockey League. During that time, he led the Rebels to a 314-194-68 (.604) record as the team's head coach. Sutter guided the Rebels to a WHL championship and Memorial Cup title in 2001, and three consecutive WHL Eastern Conference championships from 2001 to 2003. He was named as the WHL's top coach in 2001.

Internationally, Sutter has represented Canada twice as the head coach guiding the national junior team to consecutive 6-0-0 marks and gold medals at the 2005 and 2006 World Junior Championships. As a player, the Viking, Alberta native helped his country win the 1984, 1987, and 1991 Canada Cup titles. Sutter was also a member of Canada's 1986 bronze medal-winning World Championship team.

Sutter played 18 years in the NHL with the New York Islanders and Chicago Blackhawks. Originally the Islanders' first choice (17th overall) in the 1980 NHL Entry Draft, he recorded 363 goals and 466 assists for 829 points and 1,054 penalty minutes in 1,111 career regular-season games. Sutter scored an additional 30 goals and 44 assists for 74 points and 164 penalty minutes in 144 career playoff games. Along with current Flames director of player personnel and brother Duane Sutter, Brent Sutter was a member of New York Islanders 1982 and 1983 Stanley Cup championship teams, and served as captain from 1987 through 1991. Brent was traded to Chicago on October 25, 1991 and played seven more seasons, including three years under his brother Darryl. Brent retired on April 18, 1998.

Brent Sutter is the third youngest of seven Sutter brothers, six of whom played in the NHL. His son Brandon is a member of the Carolina Hurricanes, and was their first choice (11th overall) in the 2007 NHL Entry Draft.

### Coaching Record

| | | | Regular Season | | | | Playoffs | | | |
|---|---|---|---|---|---|---|---|---|---|---|
| Season | Team | League | GC | W | L | O/T | GC | W | L | T |
| 99-2000 | Red Deer | WHL | 72 | 32 | 31 | 9 | 4 | 0 | 4 | .... |
| 2000-01 | Red Deer | WHL | 72 | 54 | 12 | 6 | 22 | 16 | 6 | .... |
| | Red Deer | M-Cup | .... | .... | .... | .... | 4 | 3 | 1 | .... |
| 2001-02 | Red Deer | WHL | 72 | 46 | 18 | 8 | 23 | 14 | 9 | .... |
| 2002-03 | Red Deer | WHL | 72 | 50 | 17 | 5 | 23 | 14 | 9 | .... |
| 2003-04 | Red Deer | WHL | 72 | 35 | 22 | 15 | 19 | 10 | 9 | .... |
| 2004-05 | Red Deer | WHL | 72 | 36 | 26 | 10 | 7 | 3 | 4 | .... |
| 2005-06 | Red Deer | WHL | 72 | 26 | 40 | 6 | .... | .... | .... | .... |
| 2006-07 | Red Deer | WHL | 72 | 35 | 28 | 9 | 7 | 3 | 4 | .... |
| **2007-08** | **New Jersey** | **NHL** | **82** | **46** | **29** | **7** | **5** | **1** | **4** | .... |
| **2008-09** | **New Jersey** | **NHL** | **82** | **51** | **27** | **4** | **7** | **3** | **4** | .... |
| | **NHL Totals** | | **164** | **97** | **56** | **11** | **12** | **4** | **8** | .... |

# 2008-09 Scoring

* – rookie

## Regular Season

| Pos | # | Player | Team | GP | G | A | Pts | TOI | +/- | PIM | PP | SH | GW | S | % |
|---|---|---|---|---|---|---|---|---|---|---|---|---|---|---|---|
| R | 12 | Jarome Iginla | CGY | 82 | 35 | 54 | 89 | 21:36 | –2 | 37 | 10 | 0 | 4 | 289 | 12.1 |
| L | 13 | Mike Cammalleri | CGY | 81 | 39 | 43 | 82 | 17:33 | –2 | 44 | 19 | 0 | 6 | 255 | 15.3 |
| C | 21 | Olli Jokinen | PHX | 57 | 21 | 21 | 42 | 18:09 | –5 | 49 | 6 | 2 | 2 | 169 | 12.4 |
| | | | CGY | 19 | 8 | 7 | 15 | 21:02 | –7 | 18 | 3 | 0 | 1 | 67 | 11.9 |
| | | | Total | 76 | 29 | 28 | 57 | 18:53 | –12 | 67 | 9 | 2 | 3 | 236 | 12.3 |
| C | 22 | Daymond Langkow | CGY | 73 | 21 | 28 | 49 | 17:11 | 1 | 20 | 4 | 0 | 3 | 161 | 13.0 |
| C | 24 | Craig Conroy | CGY | 82 | 12 | 36 | 48 | 15:22 | 20 | 28 | 0 | 1 | 1 | 104 | 11.5 |
| D | 3 | Dion Phaneuf | CGY | 80 | 11 | 36 | 47 | 26:31 | –11 | 100 | 4 | 0 | 4 | 277 | 4.0 |
| R | 7 | Todd Bertuzzi | CGY | 66 | 15 | 29 | 44 | 18:36 | –13 | 74 | 6 | 0 | 4 | 127 | 11.8 |
| L | 17 | Rene Bourque | CGY | 58 | 21 | 19 | 40 | 16:05 | 18 | 70 | 0 | 1 | 0 | 149 | 14.1 |
| L | 20 | Curtis Glencross | CGY | 74 | 13 | 27 | 40 | 14:40 | 14 | 42 | 1 | 1 | 3 | 152 | 8.6 |
| R | 25 | Dave Moss | CGY | 81 | 20 | 19 | 39 | 13:35 | –5 | 22 | 8 | 0 | 4 | 194 | 10.3 |
| D | 33 | Adrian Aucoin | CGY | 81 | 10 | 24 | 34 | 22:17 | –8 | 46 | 3 | 0 | 3 | 126 | 7.9 |
| D | 40 | Jordan Leopold | COL | 64 | 6 | 14 | 20 | 18:09 | –10 | 18 | 1 | 0 | 1 | 82 | 7.3 |
| | | | CGY | 19 | 1 | 3 | 4 | 20:58 | –5 | 6 | 0 | 0 | 0 | 25 | 4.0 |
| | | | Total | 83 | 7 | 17 | 24 | 18:48 | –15 | 24 | 1 | 0 | 1 | 107 | 6.5 |
| C | 16 | Dustin Boyd | CGY | 71 | 11 | 11 | 22 | 12:52 | –11 | 10 | 1 | 1 | 3 | 74 | 14.9 |
| D | 6 | Cory Sarich | CGY | 76 | 2 | 18 | 20 | 17:52 | 12 | 112 | 0 | 0 | 0 | 57 | 3.5 |
| D | 5 | Mark Giordano | CGY | 58 | 2 | 17 | 19 | 16:12 | 2 | 59 | 2 | 0 | 0 | 82 | 2.4 |
| C | 45 | Jamie Lundmark | CGY | 27 | 8 | 8 | 16 | 13:58 | 2 | 17 | 0 | 0 | 0 | 50 | 16.0 |
| L | 23 | Eric Nystrom | CGY | 76 | 5 | 5 | 10 | 9:15 | –7 | 89 | 0 | 1 | 3 | 83 | 6.0 |
| D | 55 * | Adam Pardy | CGY | 60 | 1 | 9 | 10 | 14:59 | 3 | 69 | 0 | 0 | 0 | 38 | 2.6 |
| D | 28 | Robyn Regehr | CGY | 75 | 0 | 8 | 8 | 21:08 | 10 | 73 | 0 | 0 | 0 | 79 | 0.0 |
| D | 4 | Jim Vandermeer | CGY | 45 | 1 | 6 | 7 | 16:01 | 1 | 108 | 0 | 0 | 0 | 31 | 3.2 |
| C | 19 | Wayne Primeau | CGY | 24 | 0 | 4 | 4 | 10:22 | –3 | 14 | 0 | 0 | 0 | 22 | 0.0 |
| L | 27 | Andre Roy | CGY | 44 | 3 | 0 | 3 | 5:29 | –1 | 83 | 0 | 0 | 1 | 26 | 11.5 |
| D | 56 * | Matt Pelech | CGY | 5 | 0 | 3 | 3 | 13:16 | 1 | 9 | 0 | 0 | 0 | 4 | 0.0 |
| R | 59 * | David Van Der Gulik | CGY | 6 | 0 | 2 | 2 | 8:28 | –1 | 0 | 0 | 0 | 0 | 11 | 0.0 |
| C | 42 * | Brett Sutter | CGY | 4 | 1 | 0 | 1 | 8:03 | –2 | 2 | 0 | 0 | 0 | 6 | 16.7 |
| L | 63 | Warren Peters | CGY | 16 | 1 | 0 | 1 | 7:04 | –2 | 12 | 0 | 0 | 0 | 13 | 7.7 |
| D | 61 * | John Negrin | CGY | 3 | 0 | 1 | 1 | 9:59 | –2 | 2 | 0 | 0 | 0 | 3 | 0.0 |
| C | 60 * | Mikael Backlund | CGY | 1 | 0 | 0 | 0 | 10:44 | 0 | 0 | 0 | 0 | 0 | 1 | 0.0 |
| L | 62 * | Kris Chucko | CGY | 2 | 0 | 0 | 0 | 7:01 | 0 | 2 | 0 | 0 | 0 | 0 | 0.0 |
| L | 47 * | Kyle Greentree | CGY | 2 | 0 | 0 | 0 | 9:17 | –1 | 0 | 0 | 0 | 0 | 3 | 0.0 |

### Goaltending

| No. | Goaltender | GPI | Mins | Avg | W | L | OT | EN | SO | GA | SA | S% | G | A | PIM |
|---|---|---|---|---|---|---|---|---|---|---|---|---|---|---|---|
| 34 | Miikka Kiprusoff | 76 | 4418 | 2.84 | 45 | 24 | 5 | 3 | 4 | 209 | 2155 | .903 | 0 | 3 | 2 |
| 1 | * Curtis McElhinney | 14 | 518 | 3.59 | 1 | 6 | 1 | 3 | 0 | 31 | 280 | .889 | 0 | 0 | 2 |
| | **Totals** | **82** | **4964** | **2.97** | **46** | **30** | **6** | **6** | **4** | **246** | **2441** | **.899** | | | |

## Playoffs

| Pos | # | Player | Team | GP | G | A | Pts | TOI | +/- | PIM | PP | SH | GW | OT | S | % |
|---|---|---|---|---|---|---|---|---|---|---|---|---|---|---|---|---|
| C | 21 | Olli Jokinen | CGY | 6 | 2 | 3 | 5 | 19:24 | –1 | 4 | 0 | 0 | 0 | 0 | 23 | 8.7 |
| R | 12 | Jarome Iginla | CGY | 6 | 3 | 1 | 4 | 20:56 | –4 | 0 | 2 | 0 | 0 | 0 | 18 | 16.7 |
| L | 23 | Eric Nystrom | CGY | 6 | 2 | 2 | 4 | 10:56 | 1 | 0 | 0 | 0 | 1 | 0 | 8 | 25.0 |
| R | 25 | Dave Moss | CGY | 6 | 3 | 0 | 3 | 12:50 | 0 | 0 | 0 | 0 | 1 | 0 | 17 | 17.6 |
| D | 33 | Adrian Aucoin | CGY | 6 | 2 | 1 | 3 | 21:09 | –2 | 2 | 0 | 0 | 0 | 0 | 11 | 18.2 |
| L | 13 | Mike Cammalleri | CGY | 6 | 1 | 2 | 3 | 18:01 | 1 | 2 | 0 | 0 | 0 | 0 | 16 | 6.3 |
| D | 3 | Dion Phaneuf | CGY | 5 | 0 | 3 | 3 | 24:48 | 2 | 4 | 0 | 0 | 0 | 0 | 8 | 0.0 |
| C | 22 | Daymond Langkow | CGY | 6 | 0 | 3 | 3 | 17:06 | 4 | 2 | 0 | 0 | 0 | 0 | 12 | 0.0 |
| L | 20 | Curtis Glencross | CGY | 6 | 0 | 3 | 3 | 15:00 | –1 | 12 | 0 | 0 | 0 | 0 | 8 | 0.0 |
| R | 7 | Todd Bertuzzi | CGY | 6 | 1 | 1 | 2 | 17:24 | 4 | 8 | 0 | 0 | 0 | 0 | 9 | 11.1 |
| D | 55 * | Adam Pardy | CGY | 6 | 0 | 2 | 2 | 14:51 | –2 | 5 | 0 | 0 | 0 | 0 | 7 | 0.0 |
| C | 16 | Dustin Boyd | CGY | 5 | 1 | 0 | 1 | 9:51 | –2 | 0 | 0 | 0 | 0 | 0 | 5 | 20.0 |
| L | 17 | Rene Bourque | CGY | 5 | 1 | 0 | 1 | 17:06 | –2 | 22 | 0 | 0 | 0 | 0 | 12 | 8.3 |
| D | 6 | Cory Sarich | CGY | 5 | 0 | 1 | 1 | 18:43 | 3 | 4 | 0 | 0 | 0 | 0 | 4 | 0.0 |
| C | 24 | Craig Conroy | CGY | 6 | 0 | 1 | 1 | 12:35 | –2 | 0 | 0 | 0 | 0 | 0 | 5 | 0.0 |
| D | 40 | Jordan Leopold | CGY | 6 | 0 | 1 | 1 | 23:09 | 2 | 8 | 0 | 0 | 0 | 0 | 5 | 0.0 |
| D | 4 | Jim Vandermeer | CGY | 6 | 0 | 1 | 1 | 16:33 | –1 | 4 | 0 | 0 | 0 | 0 | 3 | 0.0 |
| D | 8 | Anders Eriksson | CGY | 2 | 0 | 0 | 0 | 18:42 | –1 | 0 | 0 | 0 | 0 | 0 | 2 | 0.0 |
| L | 27 | Andre Roy | CGY | 2 | 0 | 0 | 0 | 4:05 | –1 | 0 | 0 | 0 | 0 | 0 | 0 | 0.0 |
| C | 45 | Jamie Lundmark | CGY | 2 | 0 | 0 | 0 | 7:06 | –2 | 0 | 0 | 0 | 0 | 0 | 1 | 0.0 |
| L | 63 | Warren Peters | CGY | 4 | 0 | 0 | 0 | 7:03 | 2 | 0 | 0 | 0 | 0 | 0 | 2 | 0.0 |

### Goaltending

| No. | Goaltender | GPI | Mins | Avg | W | L | EN | SO | GA | SA | S% | G | A | PIM |
|---|---|---|---|---|---|---|---|---|---|---|---|---|---|---|
| 1 | * Curtis McElhinney | 1 | 34 | 1.76 | 0 | 0 | 0 | 0 | 1 | 10 | .900 | 0 | 0 | 0 |
| 34 | Miikka Kiprusoff | 6 | 324 | 3.52 | 2 | 4 | 1 | 0 | 19 | 164 | .884 | 0 | 0 | 2 |
| | **Totals** | **6** | **360** | **3.50** | **2** | **4** | **1** | **0** | **21** | **175** | **.880** | | | |

## Coaching History

Bernie Geoffrion, 1972-73, 1973-74; Bernie Geoffrion and Fred Creighton, 1974-75; Fred Creighton, 1975-76 to 1978-79; Al MacNeil, 1979-80 to 1981-82; Bob Johnson, 1982-83 to 1986-87; Terry Crisp, 1987-88 to 1989-90; Doug Risebrough, 1990-91; Doug Risebrough and Guy Charron, 1991-92; Dave King, 1992-93 to 1994-95; Pierre Page, 1995-96, 1996-97; Brian Sutter, 1997-98 to 1999-2000; Don Hay and Greg Gilbert, 2000-01; Greg Gilbert, 2001-02; Greg Gilbert, Al MacNeil and Darryl Sutter, 2002-03; Darryl Sutter, 2003-04 to 2005-06; Jim Playfair, 2006-07; Mike Keenan, 2007-08, 2008-09; Brent Sutter, 2009-10.

## Captains' History

Keith McCreary, 1972-73 to 1974-75; Pat Quinn, 1975-76, 1976-77; Tom Lysiak, 1977-78, 1978-79; Jean Pronovost, 1979-80; Brad Marsh, 1980-81; Phil Russell, 1981-82, 1982-83; Lanny McDonald, Doug Risebrough, 1983-84; Lanny McDonald, Doug Risebrough, Jim Peplinski, 1984-85 to 1986-87; Lanny McDonald, Jim Peplinski, 1987-88; Lanny McDonald, Jim Peplinski, Tim Hunter, 1988-89; Brad McCrimmon, 1989-90; alternating captains, 1990-91; Joe Nieuwendyk, 1991-92 to 1994-95; Theoren Fleury, 1995-96, 1996-97; Todd Simpson, 1997-98, 1998-99; Steve Smith, 1999-2000; Steve Smith and Dave Lowry, 2000-01; Dave Lowry; Bob Boughner and Craig Conroy, 2001-02; Bob Boughner and Craig Conroy, 2002-03; Jarome Iginla, 2003-04 to date.

# Club Records

## Team

(Figures in brackets for season records are games played; records for fewest points, wins, ties, losses, goals, goals against are for 70 or more games)

**Most Points** .............. **117** 1988-89 (80)
**Most Wins** ................. **54** 1988-89 (80)
**Most Ties** .................. **19** 1977-78 (80)
**Most Losses** ................ **41** 1996-97 (82), 1997-98 (82), 1999-2000 (82)
**Most Goals** ................ **397** 1987-88 (80)
**Most Goals Against** ......... **345** 1981-82 (80)
**Fewest Points** ............... **65** 1972-73 (78)
**Fewest Wins** ................ **25** 1972-73 (78)
**Fewest Ties** ................. **3** 1986-87 (80)
**Fewest Losses** ............... **17** 1988-89 (80)
**Fewest Goals** .............. **186** 2002-03 (82)
**Fewest Goals Against** ....... **176** 2003-04 (82)
**Longest Winning Streak**
**Overall** .................. **10** Oct. 14-Nov. 3/78
**Home** .................... **10** Nov. 7-Dec. 12/06
**Away** ..................... **7** Nov. 10-Dec. 4/88
**Longest Undefeated Streak**
**Overall** .................. **13** Nov. 10-Dec. 8/88 (12 wins, 1 tie)
**Home** .................... **18** Dec. 29/90-Mar. 14/91 (17 wins, 1 tie)
**Away** ..................... **9** Feb. 20-Mar. 21/88 (6 wins, 3 ties), Nov. 11-Dec. 16/90 (6 wins, 3 ties)
**Longest Losing Streak**
**Overall** .................. **11** Dec. 14/85-Jan. 7/86
**Home** ..................... **6** Dec. 5-31/98
**Away** ..................... **9** Dec. 1/85-Jan. 12/86
**Longest Winless Streak**
**Overall** .................. **11** Dec. 14/85-Jan. 7/86 (11 losses), Jan. 5-26/93 (9 losses, 2 ties)
**Home** .................... **10** Oct. 21-Dec. 4/00 (6 losses, 4 ties)
**Away** .................... **13** Feb. 3-Mar. 29/73 (10 losses, 3 ties)
**Most Shutouts, Season** ....... **11** 2003-04 (82)
**Most PIM, Season** ......... **2,643** 1991-92 (80)
**Most Goals, Game** ........... **13** Feb. 10/93 (S.J. 1 at Cgy. 13)

## Individual

**Most Seasons** ............... **13** Al MacInnis
**Most Games** ................ **942** Jarome Iginla
**Most Goals, Career** ......... **409** Jarome Iginla
**Most Assists, Career** ........ **609** Al MacInnis
**Most Points, Career** ......... **851** Jarome Iginla (409G, 442A)
**Most PIM, Career** ......... **2,405** Tim Hunter
**Most Shutouts, Career** ........ **27** Miikka Kiprusoff
**Longest Consecutive Games Streak** ............ **257** Brad Marsh (Oct. 11/78-Nov. 10/81)
**Most Goals, Season** .......... **66** Lanny McDonald (1982-83)
**Most Assists, Season** ......... **82** Kent Nilsson (1980-81)
**Most Points, Season** ........ **131** Kent Nilsson (1980-81; 49G, 82A)
**Most PIM, Season** .......... **375** Tim Hunter (1988-89)
**Most Points, Defenseman, Season** ................. **103** Al MacInnis (1990-91; 28G, 75A)
**Most Points, Center, Season** ................. **131** Kent Nilsson (1980-81; 49G, 82A)
**Most Points, Right Wing, Season** ................. **110** Joe Mullen (1988-89; 51G, 59A)
**Most Points, Left Wing, Season** .................. **90** Gary Roberts (1991-92; 53G, 37A)
**Most Points, Rookie, Season** .................. **92** Joe Nieuwendyk (1987-88; 51G, 41A)
**Most Shutouts, Season** ....... **10** Miikka Kiprusoff (2005-06)
**Most Goals, Game** ............ **5** Joe Nieuwendyk (Jan. 11/89)
**Most Assists, Game** ........... **6** Guy Chouinard (Feb. 25/81), Gary Suter (Apr. 4/86)
**Most Points, Game** ............ **7** Sergei Makarov (Feb. 25/90; 2G, 5A)

Records include Atlanta Flames, 1972-73 through 1979-80.

## Retired Numbers

| | | |
|---|---|---|
| **9** | Lanny McDonald | 1981-1989 |
| **30** | Mike Vernon | 1982-1994; 2000-02 |

# All-time Record vs. Other Clubs

## Regular Season

| | At Home | | | | | | | | On Road | | | | | | | | Total | | | | | | | |
|---|---|---|---|---|---|---|---|---|---|---|---|---|---|---|---|---|---|---|---|---|---|---|---|---|
| | GP | W | L | T | OL | GF | GA | PTS | GP | W | L | T | OL | GF | GA | PTS | GP | W | L | T | OL | GF | GA | PTS |
| Anaheim | 33 | 21 | 11 | 1 | 0 | 95 | 76 | 43 | 34 | 8 | 17 | 6 | 3 | 84 | 110 | 25 | 67 | 29 | 28 | 7 | 3 | 179 | 186 | 68 |
| Atlanta | 4 | 4 | 0 | 0 | 0 | 18 | 7 | 8 | 6 | 0 | 5 | 1 | 0 | 11 | 19 | 1 | 10 | 4 | 5 | 1 | 0 | 29 | 26 | 9 |
| Boston | 46 | 20 | 22 | 4 | 0 | 166 | 156 | 44 | 48 | 13 | 29 | 6 | 0 | 132 | 168 | 32 | 94 | 33 | 51 | 10 | 0 | 298 | 324 | 76 |
| Buffalo | 48 | 19 | 18 | 11 | 0 | 161 | 149 | 49 | 46 | 13 | 26 | 5 | 2 | 133 | 192 | 33 | 94 | 32 | 44 | 16 | 2 | 294 | 341 | 82 |
| Carolina | 30 | 22 | 6 | 2 | 0 | 143 | 92 | 46 | 30 | 14 | 11 | 5 | 0 | 108 | 100 | 33 | 60 | 36 | 17 | 7 | 0 | 251 | 192 | 79 |
| Chicago | 71 | 31 | 25 | 13 | 2 | 218 | 212 | 77 | 69 | 26 | 29 | 13 | 1 | 200 | 222 | 66 | 140 | 57 | 54 | 26 | 3 | 418 | 434 | 143 |
| Colorado | 62 | 31 | 19 | 9 | 3 | 217 | 178 | 74 | 62 | 22 | 27 | 11 | 2 | 195 | 223 | 57 | 124 | 53 | 46 | 20 | 5 | 412 | 401 | 131 |
| Columbus | 16 | 11 | 3 | 0 | 2 | 48 | 33 | 24 | 16 | 4 | 11 | 0 | 1 | 30 | 49 | 9 | 32 | 15 | 14 | 0 | 3 | 78 | 82 | 33 |
| Dallas | 70 | 37 | 17 | 14 | 2 | 224 | 170 | 90 | 70 | 24 | 34 | 11 | 1 | 212 | 249 | 60 | 140 | 61 | 51 | 25 | 3 | 436 | 419 | 150 |
| Detroit | 68 | 39 | 22 | 6 | 1 | 247 | 196 | 85 | 67 | 20 | 36 | 10 | 1 | 200 | 251 | 51 | 135 | 59 | 58 | 16 | 2 | 447 | 447 | 136 |
| Edmonton | 96 | 53 | 33 | 9 | 1 | 372 | 307 | 116 | 96 | 36 | 48 | 10 | 2 | 301 | 343 | 84 | 192 | 89 | 81 | 19 | 3 | 673 | 650 | 200 |
| Florida | 10 | 5 | 3 | 1 | 1 | 28 | 27 | 12 | 10 | 5 | 3 | 2 | 0 | 24 | 22 | 12 | 20 | 10 | 6 | 3 | 1 | 52 | 49 | 24 |
| Los Angeles | 102 | 62 | 28 | 12 | 0 | 447 | 328 | 136 | 99 | 41 | 47 | 9 | 2 | 340 | 360 | 93 | 201 | 103 | 75 | 21 | 2 | 787 | 688 | 229 |
| Minnesota | 25 | 19 | 2 | 3 | 1 | 71 | 47 | 42 | 26 | 13 | 9 | 1 | 3 | 52 | 61 | 30 | 51 | 32 | 11 | 4 | 4 | 123 | 108 | 72 |
| Montreal | 51 | 18 | 26 | 7 | 0 | 155 | 168 | 43 | 48 | 12 | 28 | 8 | 0 | 117 | 172 | 32 | 99 | 30 | 54 | 15 | 0 | 272 | 340 | 75 |
| Nashville | 20 | 10 | 5 | 3 | 2 | 61 | 48 | 25 | 21 | 7 | 13 | 1 | 0 | 50 | 73 | 15 | 41 | 17 | 18 | 4 | 2 | 111 | 121 | 40 |
| New Jersey | 43 | 28 | 6 | 8 | 1 | 184 | 112 | 65 | 47 | 28 | 16 | 3 | 0 | 168 | 132 | 59 | 90 | 56 | 22 | 11 | 1 | 352 | 244 | 124 |
| NY Islanders | 51 | 25 | 14 | 11 | 1 | 181 | 152 | 62 | 52 | 17 | 26 | 9 | 0 | 145 | 194 | 43 | 103 | 42 | 40 | 20 | 1 | 326 | 346 | 105 |
| NY Rangers | 50 | 28 | 11 | 10 | 1 | 220 | 151 | 67 | 54 | 24 | 23 | 5 | 2 | 189 | 182 | 55 | 104 | 52 | 34 | 15 | 3 | 409 | 333 | 122 |
| Ottawa | 13 | 8 | 4 | 1 | 0 | 46 | 29 | 17 | 12 | 4 | 5 | 3 | 0 | 31 | 30 | 11 | 25 | 12 | 9 | 4 | 0 | 77 | 59 | 28 |
| Philadelphia | 53 | 25 | 19 | 9 | 0 | 210 | 175 | 59 | 53 | 16 | 33 | 3 | 1 | 142 | 201 | 36 | 106 | 41 | 52 | 12 | 1 | 352 | 376 | 95 |
| Phoenix | 79 | 43 | 26 | 9 | 1 | 321 | 248 | 96 | 78 | 31 | 34 | 11 | 2 | 270 | 284 | 75 | 157 | 74 | 60 | 20 | 3 | 591 | 532 | 171 |
| Pittsburgh | 47 | 27 | 11 | 8 | 1 | 206 | 143 | 63 | 46 | 11 | 25 | 10 | 0 | 136 | 171 | 32 | 93 | 38 | 36 | 18 | 1 | 342 | 314 | 95 |
| St. Louis | 70 | 36 | 27 | 5 | 2 | 230 | 195 | 79 | 72 | 30 | 32 | 9 | 1 | 226 | 250 | 70 | 142 | 66 | 59 | 14 | 3 | 456 | 445 | 149 |
| San Jose | 40 | 23 | 13 | 4 | 0 | 141 | 109 | 50 | 42 | 21 | 16 | 4 | 1 | 123 | 127 | 47 | 82 | 44 | 29 | 8 | 1 | 264 | 236 | 97 |
| Tampa Bay | 12 | 6 | 5 | 0 | 1 | 40 | 35 | 13 | 11 | 5 | 5 | 1 | 0 | 41 | 37 | 11 | 23 | 11 | 10 | 1 | 1 | 81 | 72 | 24 |
| Toronto | 63 | 36 | 22 | 5 | 0 | 244 | 198 | 77 | 55 | 18 | 29 | 7 | 1 | 199 | 215 | 44 | 118 | 54 | 51 | 12 | 1 | 443 | 413 | 121 |
| Vancouver | 113 | 64 | 31 | 15 | 3 | 431 | 323 | 146 | 114 | 51 | 41 | 18 | 4 | 370 | 390 | 124 | 227 | 115 | 72 | 33 | 7 | 801 | 713 | 270 |
| Washington | 40 | 25 | 8 | 7 | 0 | 161 | 98 | 57 | 42 | 14 | 22 | 6 | 0 | 141 | 156 | 34 | 82 | 39 | 30 | 13 | 0 | 302 | 254 | 91 |
| Defunct Clubs | 13 | 8 | 4 | 1 | 0 | 51 | 34 | 17 | 13 | 7 | 3 | 3 | 0 | 43 | 33 | 17 | 26 | 15 | 7 | 4 | 0 | 94 | 67 | 34 |
| **Totals** | **1439** | **784** | **441** | **188** | **26** | **5337** | **4196** | **1782** | **1439** | **535** | **683** | **191** | **30** | **4413** | **5016** | **1291** | **2878** | **1319** | **1124** | **379** | **56** | **9750** | **9212** | **3073** |

## Playoffs

| | Series | W | L | GP | W | L | T | GF | GA | Last Mtg. | Rnd. | Result |
|---|---|---|---|---|---|---|---|---|---|---|---|---|
| Anaheim | 1 | 0 | 1 | 7 | 3 | 4 | 0 | 16 | 17 | 2006 | CQF | L 3-4 |
| Chicago | 4 | 2 | 2 | 18 | 9 | 9 | 0 | 53 | 54 | 2009 | CQF | L 2-4 |
| Dallas | 1 | 0 | 1 | 6 | 2 | 4 | 0 | 18 | 25 | 1981 | SF | L 2-4 |
| Detroit | 3 | 1 | 2 | 14 | 6 | 8 | 0 | 26 | 38 | 2007 | CQF | L 2-4 |
| Edmonton | 5 | 1 | 4 | 30 | 11 | 19 | 0 | 96 | 132 | 1991 | DSF | L 3-4 |
| Los Angeles | 6 | 2 | 4 | 26 | 13 | 13 | 0 | 112 | 105 | 1993 | DSF | L 2-4 |
| Montreal | 2 | 1 | 1 | 11 | 5 | 6 | 0 | 32 | 31 | 1989 | F | W 4-2 |
| NY Rangers | 1 | 0 | 1 | 4 | 1 | 3 | 0 | 8 | 14 | 1980 | PRE | L 1-3 |
| Philadelphia | 2 | 1 | 1 | 11 | 4 | 7 | 0 | 28 | 43 | 1981 | QF | W 4-3 |
| Phoenix | 3 | 1 | 2 | 13 | 6 | 7 | 0 | 43 | 45 | 1987 | DSF | L 2-4 |
| St. Louis | 1 | 1 | 0 | 7 | 4 | 3 | 0 | 28 | 22 | 1986 | CF | W 4-3 |
| San Jose | 3 | 1 | 2 | 20 | 10 | 10 | 0 | 68 | 57 | 2008 | CQF | L 3-4 |
| Tampa Bay | 1 | 0 | 1 | 7 | 3 | 4 | 0 | 14 | 13 | 2004 | F | L 3-4 |
| Toronto | 1 | 0 | 1 | 2 | 0 | 2 | 0 | 5 | 9 | 1979 | PRE | L 0-2 |
| Vancouver | 6 | 4 | 2 | 32 | 17 | 15 | 0 | 101 | 96 | 2004 | CQF | W 4-3 |
| **Totals** | **40** | **15** | **25** | **208** | **94** | **114** | **0** | **648** | **701** | | | |

## Playoff Results 2009-2004

| Year | Round | Opponent | Result | GF | GA |
|---|---|---|---|---|---|
| 2009 | CQF | Chicago | L 2-4 | 16 | 21 |
| 2008 | CQF | San Jose | L 3-4 | 17 | 19 |
| 2007 | CQF | Detroit | L 2-4 | 10 | 18 |
| 2006 | CQF | Anaheim | L 3-4 | 16 | 17 |
| 2004 | F | Tampa Bay | L 3-4 | 14 | 13 |
| | CF | San Jose | W 4-2 | 16 | 12 |
| | CSF | Detroit | W 4-2 | 11 | 12 |
| | CQF | Vancouver | W 4-3 | 19 | 16 |

**Abbreviations: Round: F** - Final; **CF** - conference final; **CSF** - conference semi-final; **CQF** - conference quarter-final; **DSF** - division semi-final; **SF** - semi-final; **QF** - quarter-final; **PRE** - preliminary round.

Carolina totals include Hartford, 1979-80 to 1996-97.
Colorado totals include Quebec, 1979-80 to 1994-95.
Dallas totals include Minnesota North Stars, 1972-73 to 1992-93.
New Jersey totals include Kansas City, 1974-75, 1975-76, and Colorado Rockies, 1976-77 to 1981-82.
Phoenix totals include Winnipeg, 1979-80 to 1995-96.

## 2008-09 Results

| | | | |
|---|---|---|---|
| **Oct.** | 9 | at Vancouver | 0-6 |
| | 11 | Vancouver | 4-5* |
| | 14 | Colorado | 5-4 |
| | 17 | Edmonton | 3-4 |
| | 18 | at Edmonton | 2-3 |
| | 21 | Washington | 2-1 |
| | 23 | at Nashville | 5-3 |
| | 25 | at Phoenix | 4-1 |
| | 28 | Colorado | 3-0 |
| | 30 | Boston | 3-2 |
| **Nov.** | 1 | at Los Angeles | 3-2 |
| | 2 | at Anaheim | 2-3 |
| | 4 | Phoenix | 2-4 |
| | 6 | Nashville | 7-6 |
| | 8 | at Columbus | 1-3 |
| | 9 | at Chicago | 1-6 |
| | 11 | Toronto | 4-3 |
| | 13 | at San Jose | 1-6 |
| | 18 | Colorado | 4-1 |
| | 20 | at Colorado | 1-0 |
| | 22 | Detroit | 2-5 |
| | 25 | Los Angeles | 6-2 |
| | 27 | at Vancouver | 4-3 |
| | 29 | Vancouver | 3-1 |
| **Dec.** | 2 | Dallas | 1-3 |
| | 5 | at St. Louis | 4-3* |
| | 7 | at NY Rangers | 3-0 |
| | 9 | at Montreal | 1-4 |
| | 10 | at Detroit | 3-4* |
| | 12 | Florida | 2-3† |
| | 16 | at St. Louis | 6-3 |
| | 17 | at Minnesota | 3-2* |
| | 19 | Chicago | 2-3* |
| | 23 | Anaheim | 4-3 |
| | 27 | Ottawa | 6-3 |
| | 29 | Minnesota | 2-1 |
| | 31 | Edmonton | 6-4 |
| **Jan.** | 3 | at Nashville | 3-2 |
| | 4 | at Chicago | 2-5 |
| | 6 | San Jose | 5-2 |
| | 8 | NY Islanders | 5-2 |
| | 13 | St. Louis | 3-1 |
| | 15 | at San Jose | 3-2 |
| | 17 | Phoenix | 3-4 |
| | 18 | at Colorado | 2-6 |
| | 21 | Columbus | 5-4† |
| | 28 | Buffalo | 5-2 |
| | 30 | Nashville | 3-1 |
| **Feb.** | 2 | at Colorado | 3-4 |
| | 3 | at Dallas | 1-3 |
| | 5 | Chicago | 2-5 |
| | 7 | Anaheim | 1-2 |
| | 9 | Montreal | 6-2 |
| | 11 | at Anaheim | 2-3* |
| | 12 | at Los Angeles | 2-0 |
| | 14 | at Phoenix | 7-5 |
| | 17 | Vancouver | 3-4† |
| | 19 | at Minnesota | 3-2* |
| | 21 | at Edmonton | 3-2† |
| | 24 | Columbus | 4-1 |
| | 27 | Minnesota | 4-1 |
| **Mar.** | 1 | Tampa Bay | 6-8 |
| | 3 | at Ottawa | 6-3 |
| | 5 | at Philadelphia | 5-1 |
| | 6 | at Carolina | 1-6 |
| | 8 | at Atlanta | 2-5 |
| | 10 | at New Jersey | 2-3 |
| | 12 | at Detroit | 6-5† |
| | 14 | at Toronto | 6-8 |
| | 18 | Dallas | 2-1 |
| | 20 | St. Louis | 2-3 |
| | 23 | Detroit | 5-3 |
| | 25 | at Pittsburgh | 0-2 |
| | 26 | at Columbus | 0-5 |
| | 28 | Minnesota | 3-2 |
| | 30 | San Jose | 1-2 |
| **Apr.** | 2 | at Dallas | 2-1 |
| | 3 | at Minnesota | 0-4 |
| | 6 | Los Angeles | 4-1 |
| | 7 | at Vancouver | 1-4 |
| | 10 | at Edmonton | 1-5 |
| | 11 | Edmonton | 4-1 |

* – Overtime † – Shootout

# Entry Draft Selections 2009-1995

Name in bold denotes played in NHL.

**2009**
Pick
23 Tim Erixon
74 Ryan Howse
111 Henrik Bjorklund
141 Spencer Bennett
171 Joni Ortio
201 Gaelan Patterson

**2008**
Pick
25 Greg Nemisz
48 Mitch Wahl
78 Lance Bouma
108 Nick Larson
114 T.J. Brodie
168 Ryley Grantham
198 Alexander Deilert

**2007**
Pick
24 **Mikael Backlund**
70 **John Negrin**
116 Keith Aulie
143 Mickey Renaud
186 C.J. Severyn

**2006**
Pick
26 Leland Irving
87 John Armstrong
89 Aaron Marvin
118 Hugo Carpentier
149 Juuso Puustinen
179 Jordan Fulton
187 Devin Didiomete
209 Per Jonsson

**2005**
Pick
26 **Matt Pelech**
69 Gord Baldwin
74 Dan Ryder
111 J.D. Watt
128 Kevin Lalande
158 **Matt Keetley**
179 **Brett Sutter**
221 Myles Rumsey

**2004**
Pick
24 **Kris Chucko**
70 **Brandon Prust**
98 **Dustin Boyd**
118 Aki Seitsonen
121 Kris Hogg
173 **Adam Pardy**
182 Fred Wikner
200 Matt Schneider
213 James Spratt
279 Adam Cracknell

**2003**
Pick
9 **Dion Phaneuf**
39 **Tim Ramholt**
97 Ryan Donally
112 Jamie Tardif
143 **Greg Moore**
173 Tyler Johnson
206 Thomas Bellemare
240 Cam Cunning
270 Kevin Harvey

**2002**
Pick
10 **Eric Nystrom**
39 Brian McConnell
90 **Matthew Lombardi**
112 Yuri Artemenkov
141 Jiri Cetkovsky
142 Emanuel Peter
146 Viktor Bobrov
159 Kristofer Persson
176 **Curtis McElhinney**
206 **David Van Der Gulik**
207 Pierre Johnsson
238 Jyri Marttinen

**2001**
Pick
14 **Chuck Kobasew**
41 Andrei Taratukhin
56 Andrei Medvedev
108 **Tomi Maki**
124 Yegor Shastin
145 James Hakewill
164 Yuri Trubachev
207 Garrett Bembridge
220 **Dave Moss**
233 Joe Campbell
251 Ville Hamalainen

**2000**
Pick
9 **Brent Krahn**
40 **Kurtis Foster**
46 **Jarret Stoll**
116 Levente Szuper
141 Wade Davis
155 **Travis Moen**
176 **Jukka Hentunen**
239 David Hajek
270 **Micki DuPont**

**1999**
Pick
11 **Oleg Saprykin**
38 Dan Cavanaugh
77 **Craig Anderson**
106 Roman Rozakov
135 Matt Doman
153 Jesse Cook
166 Cory Pecker
170 **Matt Underhill**
190 Blair Stayzer
252 Dmitri Kirilenko

**1998**
Pick
6 **Rico Fata**
33 **Blair Betts**
62 **Paul Manning**
102 Shaun Sutter
108 **Dany Sabourin**
120 Brent Gauvreau
192 Radek Duda
206 **Jonas Frogren**
234 Kevin Mitchell

**1997**
Pick
6 **Daniel Tkaczuk**
32 Evan Lindsay
42 **John Tripp**
51 Dmitri Kokorev
60 Derek Schutz
70 **Erik Andersson**
92 Chris St. Croix
100 **Ryan Ready**
113 Martin Moise
140 Ilja Demidov
167 Jeremy Rondeau
223 Dustin Paul

**1996**
Pick
13 **Derek Morris**
39 **Travis Brigley**
40 **Steve Begin**
73 Dmitri Vlasenkov
89 **Toni Lydman**
94 Christian Lefebvre
122 Josef Straka
202 Ryan Wade
228 **Ronald Petrovicky**

**1995**
Pick
20 **Denis Gauthier**
46 Pavel Smirnov
72 **Rocky Thompson**
98 Jan Labraaten
150 **Clarke Wilm**
176 Ryan Gillis
233 Steve Shirreffs

# Darryl Sutter
## General Manager
*Born: Viking, Alta., August 19, 1958.*

Darryl Sutter was named general manager of the Calgary Flames on April 11, 2003 after having joined the club as coach on December 28, 2002. In 2003-04, he led the team back to the playoffs after a seven-year absence and guided the club on a thrilling run to the seventh game of the Stanley Cup Finals. He stepped down as coach prior to the 2006-07 season.

Before joining the Flames, Sutter was the San Jose Sharks franchise leader in regular-season games coached (434) and wins (192). Prior to San Jose, Sutter coached Chicago for three years (1992 to 1995) and spent two seasons (1995 to 1997) with the Blackhawks as a consultant for special assignments. He spent the 1987-88 campaign as a Blackhawks assistant coach to Bob Murdoch and served as an associate coach for Mike Keenan during the 1990-91 and 1991-92 seasons. During his final season as associate coach, the Blackhawks advanced to the Stanley Cup Finals. Sutter spent two seasons coaching the Blackhawks' top development affiliate in the IHL, which played in Saginaw (1988-89) and in Indianapolis (1989-90). Under his leadership, the Indianapolis Ice won the Turner Cup championship. He was named IHL coach of the year.

As a player, Sutter was selected by Chicago in the ninth round, 179th overall, in the 1978 NHL Entry Draft. During his eight-year career with the Blackhawks from 1979 to 1987, he scored 279 points (161 goals, 118 assists) with 288 penalty minutes in 406 NHL career games. Sutter served as team captain with the Blackhawks for five seasons before he was forced to retire prematurely due to a series of injuries.

Darryl is a member of the famous Sutter hockey family that had six brothers who played in the NHL. Along with his brothers, Darryl is very involved in the Sutter Foundation, which raises money for non-profit organizations in Alberta.

### Coaching Record

| | | | Regular Season | | | | Playoffs | | | |
|---|---|---|---|---|---|---|---|---|---|---|
| Season | Team | League | GC | W | L | O/T | GC | W | L | T |
| 1992-93 | Chicago | NHL | 84 | 47 | 25 | 12 | 4 | 0 | 4 | .... |
| 1993-94 | Chicago | NHL | 84 | 39 | 36 | 9 | 6 | 2 | 4 | .... |
| 1994-95 | Chicago | NHL | 48 | 24 | 19 | 5 | 16 | 9 | 7 | .... |
| 1997-98 | San Jose | NHL | 82 | 34 | 38 | 10 | 6 | 2 | 4 | .... |
| 1998-99 | San Jose | NHL | 82 | 31 | 33 | 18 | 6 | 2 | 4 | .... |
| 99-2000 | San Jose | NHL | 82 | 35 | 30 | 17 | 12 | 5 | 7 | .... |
| 2000-01 | San Jose | NHL | 82 | 40 | 27 | 15 | 6 | 2 | 4 | .... |
| 2001-02 | San Jose | NHL | 82 | 44 | 27 | 11 | 12 | 7 | 5 | .... |
| 2002-03 | San Jose | NHL | 24 | 8 | 12 | 4 | .... | .... | .... | .... |
| 2002-03 | Calgary | NHL | 46 | 19 | 18 | 9 | .... | .... | .... | .... |
| 2003-04 | Calgary | NHL | 82 | 42 | 30 | 10 | 26 | 15 | 11 | .... |
| 2004-05 | Calgary | | | | SEASON CANCELLED | | | | | |
| 2005-06 | Calgary | NHL | 82 | 46 | 25 | 11 | 7 | 3 | 4 | .... |
| | **NHL Totals** | | **860** | **409** | **320** | **131** | **101** | **47** | **54** | .... |

# Club Directory

Pengrowth Saddledome

**Calgary Flames**
Pengrowth Saddledome
P.O. Box 1540 Station M
Calgary, Alberta T2P 3B9
Phone **403/777-2177**
FAX 403/777-2195
www.calgaryflames.com
**Capacity:** 19,289

Owners: . . . . . . . . N. Murray Edwards (Chairman), Harley N. Hotchkiss, Alvin G. Libin, Allan P. Markin, Jeff McCaig, Clayton H. Riddell

**Executive**
President & Chief Executive Officer . . . . . . Ken King
General Manager . . . . . . Darryl Sutter
Vice-President, Hockey Administration/CFO . . . . . . Michael Holditch
Vice-President, Building Operations . . . . . . Libby Raines
Vice President, Advertising, Sponsorship & Marketing
Jim Bagshaw
Vice-President, Sales . . . . . . Rollie Cyr
Vice-President, Communications . . . . . . Peter Hanlon
Vice-President, Business Development . . . . . . Jim Peplinski
Vice-President, Food and Beverage . . . . . . Mark Vaillant

**Hockey Club Personnel**
General Manager . . . . . . Darryl Sutter
Vice-President, Hockey Administration/CFO . . . . . . Michael Holditch
Director, Hockey Administration . . . . . . Mike Burke
Director, Player Personnel . . . . . . Duane Sutter
Director of Scouting . . . . . . Tod Button
Pro Scout/Player Development . . . . . . Ron Sutter
Amateur Scout/Player Development . . . . . . Tom Webster
Head Coach . . . . . . Brent Sutter
Assistant Coaches . . . . . . Dave Lowry, Ryan McGill, Jamie McLennan, Rob Cookson
Exec. Asst. to GM and Hockey Operations . . . . . . Brenda Koyich
Director of Amateur Scouting . . . . . . Mike Sands
Scouts . . . . . . Fred Devereaux, Juha Hautamaa, Steve Leach, Bob MacMillan, Robert Pulford, Greg Rejanen, Blair Reid, Anders Steen, Ritch Thibeau, Al Tuer
Team Services Manager . . . . . . Sean O'Brien

**Medical/Training Staff**
Strength & Conditioning Coach . . . . . . Rich Hesketh
Athletic Therapist . . . . . . Morris Boyer
Assistant Athletic Therapist . . . . . . Schad Richea
Equipment Manager . . . . . . Gus Thorson
Assistant Equipment Manager . . . . . . Mark DePasquale
Massage Therapist . . . . . . Bryan Lentz
Head Physician . . . . . . Dr. Kelly Brett
Team Physician/Sports Medicine . . . . . . Dr. Jim Thorne
Team Orthopedic Surgeons . . . . . . Dr. Nicholas Mohtadi,Dr. Richard Boorman
Team Dentist . . . . . . Dr. Bill Blair
Team Optometrist . . . . . . Dr. Derek Gaume
Dressing Room Attendant . . . . . . Jules Carriere

**Abbotsford Heat**
President . . . . . . Tom Mauthe
Head Coach . . . . . . Jim Playfair
Assistant Coaches . . . . . . Jared Bednar, Steve O'Rourke

**Communications**
Vice-President, Communications . . . . . . Peter Hanlon
Manager, Media Relations . . . . . . Sean Kelso
Administrative Assistant, Communications . . . . . . Bernie Hargrave

**Administration**
Exec. Asst. to President/CEO . . . . . . Judy O'Brien
Exec. Asst. to V.P. Hockey Admin/CFO . . . . . . Anita Cranston
Director, Finance . . . . . . Deniece Kennedy
Manager, Human Resources . . . . . . Betty Mah

**Marketing/Ticketing**
V.P. Advertising, Sponsorship & Marketing . . . . . . Jim Bagshaw
V.P. Sales . . . . . . Rollie Cyr
V.P. Business Development . . . . . . Jim Peplinski
Senior Director, Advertising . . . . . . Pat Halls
Director, Corporate Sponsorship . . . . . . Kevin Gross
Manager, Key Corporate Accounts . . . . . . Mark Stiles
Manager, Promotions . . . . . . Scott Matheson
Executive Assistant Marketing . . . . . . Yvette Mutcheson
Executive Assistant to V.P. of Sales . . . . . . Vicki Rinke
Director, Executive Suites . . . . . . Bob White
Sales Manager . . . . . . Mike Franco
Customer Service Manager . . . . . . Marc Leost
Director, Broadcast & Production . . . . . . Carlo Petrini
Manager, Game Entertainment . . . . . . Geordie Macleod
Director, Retail/FanAttic . . . . . . Brent Gibbs
Publishing Manager . . . . . . Laurie Wheeler
Website Manager . . . . . . Mike Board

**Pengrowth Saddledome**
V.P. Building Operations . . . . . . Libby Raines
V.P. Food and Beverage . . . . . . Mark Vaillant
Operations Manager . . . . . . George Greenwood
Director, Food Services . . . . . . Art Hernandez
Senior Food Services Manager . . . . . . Sheila Parisien
Security/Parking/Loss Prevention Manager . . . . . . Bob Godun

**Miscellaneous**
Radio Affiliate . . . . . . The FAN 960 (960 AM)
TV Affiliate . . . . . . Rogers Sportsnet, CBC-TV, Flames PPV, TSN

## General Managers' History

Cliff Fletcher, 1972-73 to 1990-91; Doug Risebrough, 1991-92 to 1994-95; Doug Risebrough and Al Coates, 1995-96; Al Coates, 1996-97 to 1999-2000; Craig Button, 2000-01 to 2002-03; Darryl Sutter, 2003-04 to date.

# Carolina Hurricanes

## 2008-09 Results: 45W-30L-2OTL-5SOL 97PTS.
## Second, Southeast Division

### Key Off-Season Signings/Acquisitions

**2009**

**June 29** • Re-signed LW **Jussi Jokinen.**
**July 1** • Re-signed LW **Erik Cole**, RW **Patrick Dwyer** and C **Michael Ryan.**
**2** • Re-signed C **Chad LaRose.**
**14** • Signed RW **Tom Kostopoulos.**
**15** • Signed D **Andrew Alberts.**
**23** • Re-signed C **Tuomo Ruutu.**
**24** • Acquired D **Aaron Ward** from Boston for RW **Patrick Eaves** and a 4th-round pick in the 2010 Entry Draft.

*Cam Ward ranked third in the NHL with a franchise-record 39 wins for the Hurricanes in 2008-09. His 2.44 goals-against average was also a career best and ranked him 11th in the NHL.*

### 2009-10 Schedule

|  |  |  |  |
|---|---|---|---|
| **Oct.** | Fri. | 2 | Philadelphia |
| | Sat. | 3 | at Boston |
| | Tue. | 6 | Tampa Bay |
| | Fri. | 9 | Florida |
| | Sat. | 10 | at Tampa Bay |
| | Wed. | 14 | Pittsburgh |
| | Sat. | 17 | at New Jersey |
| | Wed. | 21 | at NY Islanders |
| | Fri. | 23 | at Colorado |
| | Sat. | 24 | at Minnesota |
| | Wed. | 28 | St. Louis |
| | Sat. | 31 | at Philadelphia* |
| **Nov.** | Sun. | 1 | San Jose* |
| | Wed. | 4 | at Florida |
| | Fri. | 6 | Toronto |
| | Sat. | 7 | at Columbus |
| | Wed. | 11 | Los Angeles |
| | Fri. | 13 | NY Islanders |
| | Sun. | 15 | Minnesota* |
| | Tue. | 17 | at Montreal |
| | Thu. | 19 | Toronto |
| | Sat. | 21 | Tampa Bay |
| | Mon. | 23 | at Dallas |
| | Wed. | 25 | at Anaheim |
| | Fri. | 27 | Atlanta |
| | Sat. | 28 | at Buffalo |
| | Mon. | 30 | Washington |
| **Dec.** | Sat. | 5 | Vancouver* |
| | Mon. | 7 | at Pittsburgh |
| | Wed. | 9 | at New Jersey |
| | Fri. | 11 | at Washington |
| | Sat. | 12 | at Ottawa |
| | Wed. | 16 | Dallas |
| | Fri. | 18 | at Florida |
| | Sat. | 19 | Florida |
| | Mon. | 21 | NY Rangers |
| | Wed. | 23 | Montreal |
| | Sat. | 26 | Philadelphia |
| | Mon. | 28 | at Washington |
| | Thu. | 31 | NY Rangers |
| **Jan.** | Sat. | 2 | at NY Rangers* |
| | Thu. | 7 | at Nashville |
| | Fri. | 8 | Colorado |
| | Sun. | 10 | Ottawa* |
| | Tue. | 12 | at Toronto |
| | Thu. | 14 | at Detroit |
| | Sat. | 16 | Atlanta |
| | Mon. | 18 | Tampa Bay |
| | Thu. | 21 | at Atlanta |
| | Sat. | 23 | at Philadelphia* |
| | Sun. | 24 | Boston* |
| | Wed. | 27 | at NY Rangers |
| | Thu. | 28 | NY Islanders |
| | Sat. | 30 | Chicago |
| **Feb.** | Mon. | 1 | at Edmonton |
| | Wed. | 3 | at Calgary |
| | Fri. | 5 | at Buffalo |
| | Sat. | 6 | at NY Islanders |
| | Tue. | 9 | Florida |
| | Thu. | 11 | Buffalo |
| | Sat. | 13 | New Jersey |
| **Mar.** | Tue. | 2 | at Toronto |
| | Thu. | 4 | Ottawa |
| | Sat. | 6 | at Florida |
| | Sun. | 7 | at Atlanta* |
| | Wed. | 10 | at Washington |
| | Thu. | 11 | Pittsburgh |
| | Sat. | 13 | Phoenix |
| | Tue. | 16 | Boston |
| | Thu. | 18 | Washington |
| | Sat. | 20 | at Pittsburgh* |
| | Sun. | 21 | Buffalo* |
| | Tue. | 23 | at Tampa Bay |
| | Thu. | 25 | Washington |
| | Sat. | 27 | Atlanta |
| | Mon. | 29 | at Atlanta |
| | Wed. | 31 | at Montreal |
| **Apr.** | Thu. | 1 | at Ottawa |
| | Sat. | 3 | New Jersey |
| | Tue. | 6 | at Tampa Bay |
| | Thu. | 8 | Montreal |
| | Sat. | 10 | at Boston* |

* Denotes afternoon game.

### Year-by-Year Record

| | | Home | | | | Road | | | | Overall | | | | | | | | |
|---|---|---|---|---|---|---|---|---|---|---|---|---|---|---|---|---|---|---|
| **Season** | **GP** | **W** | **L** | **T** | **OL** | **W** | **L** | **T** | **OL** | **W** | **L** | **T** | **OL** | **GF** | **GA** | **Pts.** | **Finished** | **Playoff Result** |
| 2008-09 | 82 | 26 | 14 | .... | 1 | 19 | 16 | .... | 6 | 45 | 30 | .... | 7 | 239 | 226 | 97 | 2nd, Southeast Div. | Lost Conf. Final |
| 2007-08 | 82 | 24 | 13 | .... | 4 | 19 | 20 | .... | 2 | 43 | 33 | .... | 6 | 252 | 249 | 92 | 2nd, Southeast Div. | Out of Playoffs |
| 2006-07 | 82 | 21 | 16 | .... | 4 | 19 | 18 | .... | 4 | 40 | 34 | .... | 8 | 241 | 253 | 88 | 3rd, Southeast Div. | Out of Playoffs |
| **2005-06** | **82** | **31** | **8** | .... | **2** | **21** | **14** | .... | **6** | **52** | **22** | .... | **8** | **294** | **260** | **112** | **1st, Southeast Div.** | **Won Stanley Cup** |
| 2004-05 | .... | .... | .... | .... | .... | .... | .... | .... | .... | .... | .... | .... | .... | .... | .... | .... | | |
| 2003-04 | 82 | 13 | 18 | 8 | 2 | 15 | 16 | 6 | 4 | 28 | 34 | 14 | 6 | 172 | 209 | 76 | 3rd, Southeast Div. | Out of Playoffs |
| 2002-03 | 82 | 12 | 17 | 9 | 3 | 10 | 26 | 2 | 3 | 22 | 43 | 11 | 6 | 171 | 240 | 61 | 5th, Southeast Div. | Out of Playoffs |
| 2001-02 | 82 | 15 | 13 | 11 | 2 | 20 | 13 | 5 | 3 | 35 | 26 | 16 | 5 | 217 | 217 | 91 | 1st, Southeast Div. | Lost Final |
| 2000-01 | 82 | 23 | 15 | 3 | 0 | 15 | 17 | 6 | 3 | 38 | 32 | 9 | 3 | 212 | 225 | 88 | 2nd, Southeast Div. | Lost Conf. Quarter-Final |
| 1999-2000 | 82 | 20 | 16 | 5 | 0 | 17 | 19 | 5 | 0 | 37 | 35 | 10 | 0 | 217 | 216 | 84 | 3rd, Southeast Div. | Out of Playoffs |
| 1998-99 | 82 | 20 | 12 | 9 | .... | 14 | 18 | 9 | .... | 34 | 30 | 18 | .... | 210 | 202 | 86 | 1st, Southeast Div. | Lost Conf. Quarter-Final |
| 1997-98 | 82 | 16 | 18 | 7 | .... | 17 | 23 | 1 | .... | 33 | 41 | 8 | .... | 200 | 219 | 74 | 6th, Northeast Div. | Out of Playoffs |
| 1996-97* | 82 | 23 | 15 | 3 | .... | 9 | 24 | 8 | .... | 32 | 39 | 11 | .... | 226 | 256 | 75 | 5th, Northeast Div. | Out of Playoffs |
| 1995-96* | 82 | 22 | 15 | 4 | .... | 12 | 24 | 5 | .... | 34 | 39 | 9 | .... | 237 | 259 | 77 | 4th, Northeast Div. | Out of Playoffs |
| 1994-95* | 48 | 12 | 10 | 2 | .... | 7 | 14 | 3 | .... | 19 | 24 | 5 | .... | 127 | 141 | 43 | 5th, Northeast Div. | Out of Playoffs |
| 1993-94* | 84 | 14 | 22 | 6 | .... | 13 | 26 | 3 | .... | 27 | 48 | 9 | .... | 227 | 288 | 63 | 6th, Northeast Div. | Out of Playoffs |
| 1992-93* | 84 | 12 | 25 | 5 | .... | 14 | 27 | 1 | .... | 26 | 52 | 6 | .... | 284 | 369 | 58 | 5th, Adams Div. | Out of Playoffs |
| 1991-92* | 80 | 13 | 17 | 10 | .... | 13 | 24 | 3 | .... | 26 | 41 | 13 | .... | 247 | 283 | 65 | 4th, Adams Div. | Lost Div. Semi-Final |
| 1990-91* | 80 | 18 | 16 | 6 | .... | 13 | 22 | 5 | .... | 31 | 38 | 11 | .... | 238 | 276 | 73 | 4th, Adams Div. | Lost Div. Semi-Final |
| 1989-90* | 80 | 17 | 18 | 5 | .... | 21 | 15 | 4 | .... | 38 | 33 | 9 | .... | 275 | 268 | 85 | 4th, Adams Div. | Lost Div. Semi-Final |
| 1988-89* | 80 | 21 | 17 | 2 | .... | 16 | 21 | 3 | .... | 37 | 38 | 5 | .... | 299 | 290 | 79 | 4th, Adams Div. | Lost Div. Semi-Final |
| 1987-88* | 80 | 21 | 14 | 5 | .... | 14 | 24 | 2 | .... | 35 | 38 | 7 | .... | 249 | 267 | 77 | 4th, Adams Div. | Lost Div. Semi-Final |
| 1986-87* | 80 | 26 | 9 | 5 | .... | 17 | 21 | 2 | .... | 43 | 30 | 7 | .... | 287 | 270 | 93 | 1st, Adams Div. | Lost Div. Semi-Final |
| 1985-86* | 80 | 21 | 17 | 2 | .... | 19 | 19 | 2 | .... | 40 | 36 | 4 | .... | 332 | 302 | 84 | 4th, Adams Div. | Lost Div. Final |
| 1984-85* | 80 | 17 | 18 | 5 | .... | 13 | 23 | 4 | .... | 30 | 41 | 9 | .... | 268 | 318 | 69 | 5th, Adams Div. | Out of Playoffs |
| 1983-84* | 80 | 19 | 16 | 5 | .... | 9 | 26 | 5 | .... | 28 | 42 | 10 | .... | 288 | 320 | 66 | 5th, Adams Div. | Out of Playoffs |
| 1982-83* | 80 | 13 | 22 | 5 | .... | 6 | 32 | 2 | .... | 19 | 54 | 7 | .... | 261 | 403 | 45 | 5th, Adams Div. | Out of Playoffs |
| 1981-82* | 80 | 13 | 17 | 10 | .... | 8 | 24 | 8 | .... | 21 | 41 | 18 | .... | 264 | 351 | 60 | 5th, Adams Div. | Out of Playoffs |
| 1980-81* | 80 | 14 | 17 | 9 | .... | 7 | 24 | 9 | .... | 21 | 41 | 18 | .... | 292 | 372 | 60 | 4th, Norris Div. | Out of Playoffs |
| 1979-80* | 80 | 22 | 12 | 6 | .... | 5 | 22 | 13 | .... | 27 | 34 | 19 | .... | 303 | 312 | 73 | 4th, Norris Div. | Lost Prelim. Round |

* Hartford Whalers

**SOUTHEAST DIVISION**
**31st NHL Season**

**Franchise date:** June 22, 1979

Transferred from Hartford to Carolina, June 25, 1997.

# 2009-10 Player Personnel

| FORWARDS | HT | WT | S | Place of Birth | *Age | 2008-09 Club |
|---|---|---|---|---|---|---|
| ANGELIDIS, Mike | 6-1 | 210 | L | Woodbridge, Ont. | 24 | Albany |
| BLANCHARD, Nicolas | 6-1 | 200 | L | Granby, Que. | 22 | Albany |
| BOWMAN, Drayson | 6-1 | 190 | L | Grand Rapids, MI | 20 | Spokane |
| BOYCHUK, Zach | 5-10 | 185 | L | Airdrie, Alta. | 19 | Car-Lethbridge-Albany |
| BRIND'AMOUR, Rod | 6-1 | 205 | L | Ottawa, Ont. | 39 | Carolina |
| CHAPUT, Stefan | 6-0 | 190 | L | Montreal, Que. | 21 | Albany |
| COLE, Erik | 6-2 | 205 | L | Oswego, NY | 30 | Edmonton-Carolina |
| CULLEN, Matt | 6-1 | 200 | L | Virginia, MN | 32 | Carolina |
| DODGE, Nick | 5-10 | 185 | R | Oakville, Ont. | 23 | Albany |
| DWYER, Patrick | 5-11 | 175 | R | Spokane, WA | 26 | Carolina-Albany |
| GOERTZEN, Steven | 6-2 | 216 | R | Stony Plain, Alta. | 25 | Phoenix-San Antonio |
| HUGHES, Bobby | 5-10 | 180 | L | Richmond Hill, Ont. | 21 | Albany-Florida (ECHL) |
| JOKINEN, Jussi | 5-11 | 190 | L | Kalajoki, Finland | 26 | Tampa Bay-Carolina |
| KOSTOPOULOS, Tom | 6-0 | 201 | R | Mississauga, Ont. | 30 | Montreal |
| LaROSE, Chad | 5-10 | 181 | R | Fraser, MI | 27 | Carolina |
| PISTILLI, Matthew | 6-2 | 219 | R | Montreal, Que. | 20 | Shawinigan |
| REED, Harrison | 6-1 | 185 | R | Newmarket, Ont. | 21 | Albany-Florida (ECHL) |
| RUUTU, Tuomo | 6-0 | 205 | L | Vantaa, Finland | 26 | Carolina |
| RYAN, Michael | 6-1 | 188 | L | Boston, MA | 29 | Carolina-Albany |
| SAMSON, Jerome | 6-0 | 195 | R | Greenfield Park, Que. | 22 | Albany |
| SAMSONOV, Sergei | 5-8 | 188 | R | Moscow, USSR | 30 | Carolina |
| STAAL, Eric | 6-4 | 205 | L | Thunder Bay, Ont. | 24 | Carolina |
| SUTTER, Brandon | 6-3 | 183 | R | Huntington, NY | 20 | Carolina-Albany |
| TERRY, Chris | 5-10 | 190 | L | Brampton, Ont. | 20 | Plymouth |
| WALKER, Scott | 5-10 | 196 | R | Cambridge, Ont. | 36 | Carolina |
| WHITNEY, Ray | 5-10 | 180 | R | Fort Saskatchewan, Alta. | 37 | Carolina |
| **DEFENSEMEN** | | | | | | |
| ALBERTS, Andrew | 6-5 | 218 | L | Minneapolis, MN | 28 | Philadelphia |
| BABCHUK, Anton | 6-5 | 212 | R | Kiev, USSR | 25 | Carolina |
| BELLEMORE, Brett | 6-4 | 205 | R | Windsor, Ont. | 21 | Plymouth-Albany |
| BORER, Casey | 6-2 | 205 | L | Minneapolis, MN | 24 | Carolina-Albany |
| CARSON, Brett | 6-4 | 210 | R | Regina, Sask. | 23 | Carolina-Albany |
| CONBOY, Tim | 6-2 | 210 | R | Farmington, MN | 27 | Carolina-Albany |
| CORVO, Joe | 6-0 | 204 | R | Oak Park, IL | 32 | Carolina |
| FITZGERALD, Zach | 6-2 | 214 | L | Two Harbors, MN | 24 | Manitoba |
| GLEASON, Tim | 6-0 | 217 | L | Clawson, MI | 26 | Carolina |
| HARRISON, Jay | 6-4 | 211 | L | Oshawa, Ont. | 26 | Toronto-Zug |
| McBAIN, Jamie | 6-2 | 200 | R | Edina, MN | 21 | U. of Wisconsin-Albany |
| PITKANEN, Joni | 6-3 | 210 | L | Oulu, Finland | 26 | Carolina |
| RODNEY, Bryan | 6-0 | 195 | R | London, Ont. | 25 | Carolina-Albany |
| WALLIN, Niclas | 6-3 | 220 | L | Boden, Sweden | 34 | Carolina |
| WARD, Aaron | 6-2 | 209 | R | Windsor, Ont. | 36 | Boston |

| GOALTENDERS | HT | WT | C | Place of Birth | *Age | 2008-09 Club |
|---|---|---|---|---|---|---|
| LEIGHTON, Michael | 6-3 | 190 | L | Petrolia, Ont. | 28 | Carolina |
| MURPHY, Mike | 5-11 | 165 | L | Kingston, Ont. | 20 | Belleville |
| PETERS, Justin | 6-1 | 205 | L | Blyth, Ont. | 23 | Albany |
| WARD, Cam | 6-1 | 200 | L | Saskatoon, Sask. | 25 | Carolina |

* – Age at start of 2009-10 season

## Captains' History

Rick Ley, 1979-80; Rick Ley and Mike Rogers, 1980-81; Dave Keon, 1981-82; Russ Anderson, 1982-83; Mark Johnson, 1983-84; Mark Johnson and Ron Francis, 1984-85; Ron Francis, 1985-86 to 1990-91; Randy Ladouceur, 1991-92; Pat Verbeek, 1992-93 to 1994-95; Brendan Shanahan, 1995-96; Kevin Dineen, 1996-97, 1997-98; Keith Primeau, 1998-99; Keith Primeau and Ron Francis, 1999-2000; Ron Francis, 2000-01 to 2003-04; Rod Brind'Amour, 2005-06 to date.

# 2008-09 Scoring

* – rookie

## Regular Season

| Pos | # | Player | Team | GP | G | A | Pts | TOI | +/– | PIM | PP | SH | GW | S | % |
|---|---|---|---|---|---|---|---|---|---|---|---|---|---|---|---|
| L | 13 | Ray Whitney | CAR | 82 | 24 | 53 | 77 | 18:24 | 2 | 32 | 7 | 0 | 2 | 219 | 11.0 |
| C | 12 | Eric Staal | CAR | 82 | 40 | 35 | 75 | 21:02 | 15 | 50 | 14 | 1 | 8 | 372 | 10.8 |
| C | 15 | Tuomo Ruutu | CAR | 79 | 26 | 28 | 54 | 18:18 | 0 | 79 | 10 | 0 | 4 | 190 | 13.7 |
| C | 17 | Rod Brind'Amour | CAR | 80 | 16 | 35 | 51 | 18:58 | –23 | 36 | 6 | 1 | 1 | 135 | 11.9 |
| L | 14 | Sergei Samsonov | CAR | 81 | 16 | 32 | 48 | 17:19 | –8 | 28 | 3 | 0 | 3 | 155 | 10.3 |
| C | 8 | Matt Cullen | CAR | 69 | 22 | 21 | 43 | 16:48 | 11 | 20 | 4 | 2 | 2 | 139 | 15.8 |
| L | 26 | Erik Cole | EDM | 63 | 16 | 11 | 27 | 17:04 | –3 | 63 | 5 | 0 | 1 | 145 | 11.0 |
| | | | CAR | 17 | 2 | 13 | 15 | 19:35 | 3 | 10 | 0 | 0 | 0 | 33 | 6.1 |
| | | | Total | 80 | 18 | 24 | 42 | 17:37 | 0 | 73 | 5 | 0 | 1 | 178 | 10.1 |
| D | 77 | Joe Corvo | CAR | 81 | 14 | 24 | 38 | 24:19 | –1 | 18 | 8 | 1 | 6 | 213 | 6.6 |
| D | 33 | Anton Babchuk | CAR | 72 | 16 | 19 | 35 | 18:04 | 13 | 16 | 9 | 0 | 4 | 127 | 12.6 |
| D | 25 | Joni Pitkanen | CAR | 71 | 7 | 26 | 33 | 24:48 | 11 | 58 | 2 | 0 | 3 | 147 | 4.8 |
| C | 59 | Chad Larose | CAR | 81 | 19 | 12 | 31 | 15:08 | 6 | 35 | 0 | 2 | 4 | 171 | 11.1 |
| D | 4 | Dennis Seidenberg | CAR | 70 | 5 | 25 | 30 | 22:19 | –9 | 37 | 2 | 0 | 1 | 129 | 3.9 |
| L | 36 | Jussi Jokinen | T.B. | 46 | 6 | 10 | 16 | 15:38 | –8 | 16 | 2 | 0 | 0 | 64 | 9.4 |
| | | | CAR | 25 | 1 | 10 | 11 | 14:43 | –2 | 12 | 0 | 0 | 1 | 37 | 2.7 |
| | | | Total | 71 | 7 | 20 | 27 | 15:18 | –10 | 28 | 2 | 0 | 1 | 101 | 6.9 |
| R | 24 | Scott Walker | CAR | 41 | 5 | 10 | 15 | 13:19 | –4 | 39 | 1 | 0 | 0 | 71 | 7.0 |
| R | 44 | Patrick Eaves | CAR | 74 | 6 | 8 | 14 | 11:15 | 7 | 31 | 1 | 1 | 1 | 115 | 5.2 |
| L | 18 | Ryan Bayda | CAR | 70 | 5 | 7 | 12 | 10:27 | 2 | 26 | 0 | 0 | 0 | 62 | 8.1 |
| D | 6 | Tim Gleason | CAR | 70 | 0 | 12 | 12 | 20:39 | 3 | 68 | 0 | 0 | 0 | 61 | 0.0 |
| D | 7 | Niclas Wallin | CAR | 64 | 2 | 8 | 10 | 16:16 | –1 | 42 | 0 | 0 | 1 | 53 | 3.8 |
| D | 5 | Frantisek Kaberle | CAR | 30 | 1 | 7 | 8 | 14:03 | –4 | 8 | 1 | 0 | 0 | 28 | 3.6 |
| C | 16 | * Brandon Sutter | CAR | 50 | 1 | 5 | 6 | 8:49 | –1 | 16 | 0 | 0 | 0 | 57 | 1.8 |
| L | 20 | Dan LaCouture | CAR | 11 | 2 | 0 | 2 | 4:16 | –1 | 10 | 0 | 0 | 1 | 4 | 50.0 |
| C | 63 | * Dwight Helminen | CAR | 23 | 1 | 1 | 2 | 6:49 | –2 | 0 | 0 | 0 | 0 | 15 | 6.7 |
| D | 29 | * Bryan Rodney | CAR | 8 | 0 | 2 | 2 | 12:37 | –3 | 2 | 0 | 0 | 0 | 3 | 0.0 |
| C | 20 | Michael Ryan | CAR | 18 | 0 | 2 | 2 | 8:12 | –3 | 2 | 0 | 0 | 0 | 24 | 0.0 |
| R | 39 | * Patrick Dwyer | CAR | 13 | 1 | 0 | 1 | 8:33 | –2 | 0 | 0 | 0 | 0 | 9 | 11.1 |
| L | 28 | Wade Brookbank | CAR | 27 | 1 | 0 | 1 | 2:29 | 0 | 40 | 0 | 0 | 0 | 8 | 12.5 |
| C | 56 | * Jakub Petruzalek | CAR | 2 | 0 | 1 | 1 | 8:04 | 1 | 0 | 0 | 0 | 0 | 0 | 0.0 |
| D | 38 | Tim Conboy | CAR | 28 | 0 | 1 | 1 | 5:21 | –1 | 37 | 0 | 0 | 0 | 13 | 0.0 |
| L | 23 | * Zach Boychuk | CAR | 2 | 0 | 0 | 0 | 12:03 | 0 | 0 | 0 | 0 | 0 | 0 | 0.0 |
| D | 53 | * Casey Borer | CAR | 3 | 0 | 0 | 0 | 11:05 | 0 | 5 | 0 | 0 | 0 | 0 | 0.0 |
| D | 27 | * Brett Carson | CAR | 5 | 0 | 0 | 0 | 15:43 | –3 | 4 | 0 | 0 | 0 | 2 | 0.0 |

### Goaltending

| No. | Goaltender | GPI | Mins | Avg | W | L | OT | EN | SO | GA | SA | S% | G | A | PIM |
|---|---|---|---|---|---|---|---|---|---|---|---|---|---|---|---|
| 30 | Cam Ward | 68 | 3928 | 2.44 | 39 | 23 | 5 | 10 | 6 | 160 | 1901 | .916 | 0 | 1 | 4 |
| 49 | Michael Leighton | 19 | 1029 | 2.92 | 6 | 7 | 2 | 1 | 0 | 50 | 507 | .901 | 0 | 0 | 4 |
| | **Totals** | **82** | **4986** | **2.66** | **45** | **30** | **7** | **11** | **6** | **221** | **2419** | **.909** | | | |

## Playoffs

| Pos | # | Player | Team | GP | G | A | Pts | TOI | +/– | PIM | PP | SH | GW | OT | S | % |
|---|---|---|---|---|---|---|---|---|---|---|---|---|---|---|---|---|
| C | 12 | Eric Staal | CAR | 18 | 10 | 5 | 15 | 21:31 | –3 | 4 | 3 | 0 | 1 | 0 | 73 | 13.7 |
| L | 36 | Jussi Jokinen | CAR | 18 | 7 | 4 | 11 | 15:34 | –3 | 2 | 2 | 0 | 3 | 1 | 28 | 25.0 |
| C | 59 | Chad Larose | CAR | 18 | 4 | 7 | 11 | 17:47 | 0 | 16 | 0 | 0 | 0 | 0 | 51 | 7.8 |
| L | 13 | Ray Whitney | CAR | 18 | 3 | 8 | 11 | 18:35 | –9 | 4 | 0 | 0 | 1 | 0 | 55 | 5.5 |
| L | 14 | Sergei Samsonov | CAR | 17 | 5 | 3 | 8 | 15:48 | 2 | 6 | 0 | 0 | 0 | 0 | 28 | 17.9 |
| D | 25 | Joni Pitkanen | CAR | 18 | 0 | 8 | 8 | 26:28 | 0 | 16 | 0 | 0 | 0 | 0 | 46 | 0.0 |
| D | 77 | Joe Corvo | CAR | 18 | 2 | 5 | 7 | 25:27 | –7 | 4 | 1 | 0 | 1 | 0 | 52 | 3.8 |
| R | 24 | Scott Walker | CAR | 18 | 1 | 6 | 7 | 11:31 | –3 | 19 | 0 | 0 | 1 | 1 | 25 | 4.0 |
| C | 8 | Matt Cullen | CAR | 18 | 3 | 3 | 6 | 16:41 | 0 | 14 | 0 | 1 | 0 | 0 | 29 | 10.3 |
| D | 4 | Dennis Seidenberg | CAR | 16 | 1 | 5 | 6 | 22:25 | –5 | 16 | 0 | 0 | 0 | 0 | 18 | 5.6 |
| D | 6 | Tim Gleason | CAR | 18 | 1 | 4 | 5 | 20:28 | –2 | 32 | 0 | 0 | 1 | 1 | 11 | 9.1 |
| L | 26 | Erik Cole | CAR | 18 | 0 | 5 | 5 | 17:17 | –5 | 22 | 0 | 0 | 0 | 0 | 32 | 0.0 |
| L | 18 | Ryan Bayda | CAR | 15 | 2 | 2 | 4 | 6:20 | 2 | 18 | 0 | 0 | 0 | 0 | 17 | 11.8 |
| C | 15 | Tuomo Ruutu | CAR | 16 | 1 | 3 | 4 | 14:15 | –3 | 8 | 0 | 0 | 0 | 0 | 17 | 5.9 |
| C | 17 | Rod Brind'Amour | CAR | 18 | 1 | 3 | 4 | 15:22 | –5 | 8 | 0 | 0 | 0 | 0 | 29 | 3.4 |
| R | 44 | Patrick Eaves | CAR | 18 | 1 | 2 | 3 | 9:29 | –1 | 13 | 0 | 0 | 0 | 0 | 21 | 4.8 |
| R | 39 | * Patrick Dwyer | CAR | 2 | 0 | 1 | 1 | 4:47 | 1 | 0 | 0 | 0 | 0 | 0 | 0 | 0.0 |
| D | 5 | Frantisek Kaberle | CAR | 7 | 0 | 1 | 1 | 12:14 | 2 | 2 | 0 | 0 | 0 | 0 | 7 | 0.0 |
| D | 33 | Anton Babchuk | CAR | 13 | 0 | 1 | 1 | 16:02 | –5 | 10 | 0 | 0 | 0 | 0 | 21 | 0.0 |
| C | 63 | * Dwight Helminen | CAR | 1 | 0 | 0 | 0 | 3:08 | 0 | 0 | 0 | 0 | 0 | 0 | 0 | 0.0 |
| D | 38 | Tim Conboy | CAR | 3 | 0 | 0 | 0 | 4:22 | 0 | 9 | 0 | 0 | 0 | 0 | 0 | 0.0 |
| D | 7 | Niclas Wallin | CAR | 18 | 0 | 0 | 0 | 13:45 | 1 | 4 | 0 | 0 | 0 | 0 | 10 | 0.0 |

### Goaltending

| No. | Goaltender | GPI | Mins | Avg | W | L | EN | SO | GA | SA | S% | G | A | PIM |
|---|---|---|---|---|---|---|---|---|---|---|---|---|---|---|
| 30 | Cam Ward | 18 | 1101 | 2.67 | 8 | 10 | 3 | 2 | 49 | 576 | .915 | 0 | 0 | 0 |
| | **Totals** | **18** | **1109** | **2.81** | **8** | **10** | **3** | **2** | **52** | **579** | **.910** | | | |

# Paul Maurice

## Head Coach

*Born: Sault Ste. Marie, Ont., January 30, 1967.*

Paul Maurice was named head coach of the Carolina Hurricanes on December 3, 2008. After coaching the Toronto Maple Leafs for two seasons, he returned to a franchise where he was the winningest coach in history, having amassed 268 wins in his 674 regular-season games coached during first eight-plus seasons with the team from November 6, 1995, until December 15, 2003. After taking over the Hurricanes midway through the 2008-09 season, he led the team to the Eastern Conference Finals.

Maurice guided the Hurricanes to the 2002 Eastern Conference title and two Southeast Division crowns during his first stint as the team's head coach. He led the team to four consecutive winning seasons from 1999 to 2002. Prior to the 2003-04 season, Maurice was the longest-tenured head coach in the NHL after having originally been promoted from a Hartford Whalers assistant coach's position on November 6, 1995. At only 28 years old when he was first hired, Maurice was the league's youngest head coach, a distinction he maintained until the Boston Bruins hired Mike Sullivan on June 23, 2003.

Prior to joining the Whalers as an assistant coach during the summer of 1995, Maurice spent two seasons as head coach of the Ontario Hockey League's Detroit Jr. Red Wings. He led the team to the 1995 OHL championship and an appearance in the Memorial Cup. That season, he finished second in voting to Guelph's Craig Hartsburg for the Matt Leyden Trophy, which is annually awarded to the OHL's Coach of the Year.

Maurice played his junior hockey with the OHL's Windsor Spitfires (1984 to 1988). He was Philadelphia's 12th choice, 252nd overall, in the 1985 NHL Entry Draft but had his career cut short due to an eye injury and began coaching as an assistant with the Jr. Red Wings shortly thereafter.

### Coaching Record

| | | | Regular Season | | | | Playoffs | | | |
|---|---|---|---|---|---|---|---|---|---|---|
| Season | Team | League | GC | W | L | O/T | GC | W | L | T |
| 1993-94 | Detroit | OHL | 66 | 42 | 20 | 4 | 17 | 11 | 6 | .... |
| 1994-95 | Detroit | OHL | 44 | 18 | 4 | .... | 21 | 16 | 5 | .... |
| | Detroit | M-Cup | .... | .... | .... | .... | 5 | 3 | 2 | .... |
| **1995-96** | **Hartford** | **NHL** | **70** | **29** | **33** | **8** | .... | .... | .... | .... |
| **1996-97** | **Hartford** | **NHL** | **82** | **32** | **39** | **11** | .... | .... | .... | .... |
| **1997-98** | **Carolina** | **NHL** | **82** | **33** | **41** | **8** | .... | .... | .... | .... |
| **1998-99** | **Carolina** | **NHL** | **82** | **34** | **30** | **18** | **6** | **2** | **4** | .... |
| **99-2000** | **Carolina** | **NHL** | **82** | **37** | **35** | **10** | .... | .... | .... | .... |
| **2000-01** | **Carolina** | **NHL** | **82** | **38** | **32** | **12** | **6** | **2** | **4** | .... |
| **2001-02** | **Carolina** | **NHL** | **82** | **35** | **26** | **21** | **23** | **13** | **10** | .... |
| **2002-03** | **Carolina** | **NHL** | **82** | **22** | **43** | **17** | .... | .... | .... | .... |
| **2003-04** | **Carolina** | **NHL** | **30** | **8** | **12** | **10** | .... | .... | .... | .... |
| 2005-06 | Toronto | AHL | 80 | 41 | 29 | 10 | 5 | 1 | 4 | .... |
| **2006-07** | **Toronto** | **NHL** | **82** | **40** | **31** | **11** | .... | .... | .... | .... |
| **2007-08** | **Toronto** | **NHL** | **82** | **36** | **35** | **11** | .... | .... | .... | .... |
| **2008-09** | **Carolina** | **NHL** | **57** | **33** | **19** | **5** | **18** | **8** | **19** | .... |
| | **NHL Totals** | | **895** | **377** | **376** | **142** | **53** | **25** | **37** | .... |

# Club Records

## Team

(Figures in brackets for season records are games played; records for fewest points, wins, ties, losses, goals, goals against are for 70 or more games)

| | | |
|---|---|---|
| **Most Points** | 112 | 2005-06 (82) |
| **Most Wins** | 52 | 2005-06 (82) |
| **Most Ties** | 19 | 1979-80 (80) |
| **Most Losses** | 54 | 1982-83 (80) |
| **Most Goals** | 332 | 1985-86 (80) |
| **Most Goals Against** | 403 | 1982-83 (80) |
| **Fewest Points** | 45 | 1982-83 (80) |
| **Fewest Wins** | 19 | 1982-83 (80) |
| **Fewest Ties** | 4 | 1985-86 (80) |
| **Fewest Losses** | 22 | 2005-06 (82) |
| **Fewest Goals** | 171 | 2002-03 (82) |
| **Fewest Goals Against** | 202 | 1998-99 (82) |
| **Longest Winning Streak** | | |
| Overall | 9 | Oct. 22-Nov. 11/05, Dec. 31/05-Jan. 19/06, Mar. 18-Apr. 07/09 |
| Home | 12 | Feb. 20-Apr. 7/09 |
| Away | 6 | Nov. 10-Dec. 7/90 |
| **Longest Undefeated Streak** | | |
| Overall | 10 | Jan. 20-Feb. 10/82 (6 wins, 4 ties) |
| Home | 12 | Feb. 20-Apr. 7/09 (12 wins) |
| Away | 8 | Nov. 11-Dec. 5/96 (4 wins, 4 ties) |
| **Longest Losing Streak** | | |
| Overall | 9 | Feb. 19-Mar. 8/83 |
| Home | 7 | Dec. 27/02-Jan. 20/03 |
| Away | 13 | Dec. 18/82-Feb. 5/83 |
| **Longest Winless Streak** | | |
| Overall | 14 | Jan. 4-Feb. 9/92 (8 losses, 6 ties) |
| Home | 13 | Jan. 15-Mar. 10/85 (11 losses, 2 ties) |
| Away | 15 | Nov. 11/79-Jan. 9/80 (11 losses, 4 ties), Jan. 7-Mar. 2/03 (13 losses, 2 ties) |
| **Most Shutouts, Season** | 8 | 1998-99 (82) |
| **Most PIM, Season** | 2,354 | 1992-93 (84) |
| **Most Goals, Game** | 11 | Feb. 12/84 (Edm. 0 at Hfd. 11), Oct. 19/85 (Mtl. 6 at Hfd. 11), Jan. 17/86 (Que. 6 at Hfd. 11), Mar. 15/86 (Chi. 4 at Hfd. 11) |

## Individual

| | | |
|---|---|---|
| **Most Seasons** | 16 | Ron Francis |
| **Most Games** | 1,186 | Ron Francis |
| **Most Goals, Career** | 382 | Ron Francis |
| **Most Assists, Career** | 793 | Ron Francis |
| **Most Points, Career** | 1,175 | Ron Francis (382G, 793A) |
| **Most PIM, Career** | 1,439 | Kevin Dineen |
| **Most Shutouts, Career** | 20 | Arturs Irbe |
| **Longest Consecutive Games Streak** | 419 | Dave Tippett (Mar. 3/84-Oct. 7/89) |
| **Most Goals, Season** | 56 | Blaine Stoughton (1979-80) |
| **Most Assists, Season** | 69 | Ron Francis (1989-90) |
| **Most Points, Season** | 105 | Mike Rogers (1979-80; 44G, 61A), (1980-81; 40G, 65A) |
| **Most PIM, Season** | 358 | Torrie Robertson (1985-86) |
| **Most Points, Defenseman, Season** | 69 | Dave Babych (1985-86; 14G, 55A) |
| **Most Points, Center, Season** | 105 | Mike Rogers (1979-80; 44G, 61A), (1980-81; 40G, 65A) |
| **Most Points, Right Wing, Season** | 100 | Blaine Stoughton (1979-80; 56G, 44A) |
| **Most Points, Left Wing, Season** | 89 | Geoff Sanderson (1992-93; 46G, 43A) |
| **Most Points, Rookie, Season** | 72 | Sylvain Turgeon (1983-84; 40G, 32A) |
| **Most Shutouts, Season** | 6 | Arturs Irbe (1998-99), (2000-01) Kevin Weekes (2003-04) Cam Ward (2008-09) |
| **Most Goals, Game** | 4 | Jordy Douglas (Feb. 3/80) Ron Francis (Feb. 12/84) Eric Staal (Mar. 7/09) |
| **Most Assists, Game** | 6 | Ron Francis (Mar. 5/87) |
| **Most Points, Game** | 6 | Paul Lawless (Jan. 4/87; 2G, 4A) Ron Francis (Mar. 5/87; 6A), (Oct. 8/89; 3G, 3A) Eric Staal (Mar. 7/09; 4G, 2A) |

Records include Hartford Whalers, 1979-80 through 1996-97.

## Retired Numbers

| | | |
|---|---|---|
| 2 | Glen Wesley | 1994-2008 |
| 10 | Ron Francis | 1981-1991; 1998-2004 |

# All-time Record vs. Other Clubs

## Regular Season

| | At Home | | | | | | | | On Road | | | | | | | | Total | | | | | | | |
|---|---|---|---|---|---|---|---|---|---|---|---|---|---|---|---|---|---|---|---|---|---|---|---|---|
| | GP | W | L | T | OL | GF | GA | PTS | GP | W | L | T | OL | GF | GA | PTS | GP | W | L | T | OL | GF | GA | PTS |
| Anaheim | 11 | 6 | 4 | 1 | 0 | 28 | 25 | 13 | 11 | 5 | 5 | 1 | 0 | 35 | 32 | 11 | 22 | 11 | 9 | 2 | 0 | 63 | 57 | 24 |
| Atlanta | 28 | 17 | 8 | 1 | 2 | 90 | 82 | 37 | 28 | 18 | 6 | 3 | 1 | 95 | 77 | 40 | 56 | 35 | 14 | 4 | 3 | 185 | 159 | 77 |
| Boston | 84 | 35 | 38 | 9 | 2 | 277 | 290 | 81 | 86 | 30 | 49 | 7 | 0 | 230 | 295 | 67 | 170 | 65 | 87 | 16 | 2 | 507 | 585 | 148 |
| Buffalo | 86 | 36 | 38 | 11 | 1 | 250 | 258 | 84 | 85 | 27 | 50 | 7 | 1 | 246 | 342 | 62 | 171 | 63 | 88 | 18 | 2 | 496 | 600 | 146 |
| Calgary | 30 | 11 | 14 | 5 | 0 | 100 | 108 | 27 | 30 | 6 | 22 | 2 | 0 | 92 | 143 | 14 | 60 | 17 | 36 | 7 | 0 | 192 | 251 | 41 |
| Chicago | 31 | 15 | 12 | 4 | 0 | 102 | 96 | 34 | 31 | 11 | 16 | 3 | 1 | 88 | 120 | 26 | 62 | 26 | 28 | 7 | 1 | 190 | 216 | 60 |
| Colorado | 64 | 25 | 26 | 12 | 1 | 212 | 221 | 63 | 66 | 17 | 40 | 9 | 0 | 193 | 279 | 43 | 130 | 42 | 66 | 21 | 1 | 405 | 500 | 106 |
| Columbus | 6 | 4 | 2 | 0 | 0 | 16 | 17 | 8 | 4 | 2 | 2 | 0 | 0 | 10 | 10 | 4 | 10 | 6 | 4 | 0 | 0 | 26 | 27 | 12 |
| Dallas | 33 | 14 | 15 | 4 | 0 | 106 | 114 | 32 | 31 | 10 | 17 | 2 | 2 | 92 | 123 | 24 | 64 | 24 | 32 | 6 | 2 | 198 | 237 | 56 |
| Detroit | 32 | 18 | 13 | 1 | 0 | 108 | 91 | 37 | 32 | 7 | 17 | 7 | 1 | 88 | 124 | 22 | 64 | 25 | 30 | 8 | 1 | 196 | 215 | 59 |
| Edmonton | 31 | 12 | 12 | 7 | 0 | 120 | 103 | 31 | 32 | 7 | 20 | 5 | 0 | 93 | 124 | 19 | 63 | 19 | 32 | 12 | 0 | 213 | 227 | 50 |
| Florida | 40 | 26 | 11 | 3 | 0 | 127 | 102 | 55 | 41 | 15 | 16 | 8 | 2 | 98 | 121 | 40 | 81 | 41 | 27 | 11 | 2 | 225 | 223 | 95 |
| Los Angeles | 32 | 16 | 11 | 5 | 0 | 116 | 116 | 37 | 32 | 11 | 17 | 3 | 1 | 119 | 135 | 26 | 64 | 27 | 28 | 8 | 1 | 235 | 251 | 63 |
| Minnesota | 3 | 3 | 0 | 0 | 0 | 6 | 2 | 6 | 6 | 1 | 3 | 2 | 0 | 18 | 17 | 4 | 9 | 4 | 3 | 2 | 0 | 24 | 19 | 10 |
| Montreal | 86 | 34 | 38 | 13 | 1 | 251 | 293 | 82 | 83 | 25 | 49 | 7 | 2 | 246 | 323 | 59 | 169 | 59 | 87 | 20 | 3 | 497 | 616 | 141 |
| Nashville | 7 | 3 | 2 | 1 | 1 | 21 | 22 | 8 | 5 | 1 | 4 | 0 | 0 | 7 | 10 | 2 | 12 | 4 | 6 | 1 | 1 | 28 | 32 | 10 |
| New Jersey | 52 | 22 | 21 | 8 | 1 | 156 | 153 | 53 | 53 | 19 | 28 | 4 | 2 | 161 | 182 | 44 | 105 | 41 | 49 | 12 | 3 | 317 | 335 | 97 |
| NY Islanders | 53 | 27 | 20 | 5 | 1 | 187 | 169 | 60 | 52 | 25 | 21 | 4 | 2 | 152 | 153 | 56 | 105 | 52 | 41 | 9 | 3 | 339 | 322 | 116 |
| NY Rangers | 51 | 30 | 18 | 3 | 0 | 170 | 153 | 63 | 53 | 16 | 31 | 4 | 2 | 131 | 193 | 38 | 104 | 46 | 49 | 7 | 2 | 301 | 346 | 101 |
| Ottawa | 35 | 20 | 11 | 4 | 0 | 99 | 89 | 44 | 37 | 16 | 17 | 4 | 0 | 94 | 109 | 36 | 72 | 36 | 28 | 8 | 0 | 193 | 198 | 80 |
| Philadelphia | 52 | 15 | 25 | 9 | 3 | 162 | 189 | 42 | 51 | 13 | 28 | 5 | 5 | 132 | 190 | 36 | 103 | 28 | 53 | 14 | 8 | 294 | 379 | 78 |
| Phoenix | 32 | 15 | 11 | 6 | 0 | 108 | 93 | 36 | 33 | 16 | 15 | 2 | 0 | 123 | 120 | 34 | 65 | 31 | 26 | 8 | 0 | 231 | 213 | 70 |
| Pittsburgh | 56 | 28 | 23 | 5 | 0 | 206 | 197 | 61 | 54 | 21 | 25 | 6 | 2 | 194 | 210 | 50 | 110 | 49 | 48 | 11 | 2 | 400 | 407 | 111 |
| St. Louis | 33 | 14 | 17 | 2 | 0 | 98 | 100 | 30 | 33 | 10 | 19 | 3 | 1 | 95 | 120 | 24 | 66 | 24 | 36 | 5 | 1 | 193 | 220 | 54 |
| San Jose | 12 | 7 | 5 | 0 | 0 | 40 | 27 | 14 | 13 | 5 | 8 | 0 | 0 | 38 | 57 | 10 | 25 | 12 | 13 | 0 | 0 | 78 | 84 | 24 |
| Tampa Bay | 42 | 25 | 8 | 7 | 2 | 135 | 113 | 59 | 41 | 15 | 21 | 3 | 2 | 112 | 121 | 35 | 83 | 40 | 29 | 10 | 4 | 247 | 234 | 94 |
| Toronto | 45 | 23 | 15 | 6 | 1 | 172 | 147 | 53 | 44 | 22 | 16 | 5 | 1 | 155 | 145 | 50 | 89 | 45 | 31 | 11 | 2 | 327 | 292 | 103 |
| Vancouver | 30 | 13 | 12 | 5 | 0 | 97 | 101 | 31 | 32 | 10 | 14 | 6 | 2 | 87 | 113 | 28 | 62 | 23 | 26 | 11 | 2 | 184 | 214 | 59 |
| Washington | 64 | 25 | 27 | 10 | 2 | 185 | 193 | 62 | 62 | 21 | 36 | 4 | 1 | 160 | 209 | 47 | 126 | 46 | 63 | 14 | 3 | 345 | 402 | 109 |
| **Totals** | **1161** | **539** | **457** | **147** | **18** | **3745** | **3664** | **1243** | **1161** | **402** | **612** | **116** | **31** | **3384** | **4197** | **951** | **2322** | **941** | **1069** | **263** | **49** | **7129** | **7861** | **2194** |

## Playoffs

| | Series | W | L | GP | W | L | T | GF | GA | Last Mtg. | Rnd. | Result |
|---|---|---|---|---|---|---|---|---|---|---|---|---|
| Boston | 4 | 1 | 3 | 26 | 11 | 15 | 0 | 64 | 80 | 2009 | CSF | W 4-3 |
| Buffalo | 1 | 1 | 0 | 7 | 4 | 3 | 0 | 22 | 17 | 2006 | CF | W 4-3 |
| Colorado | 2 | 1 | 1 | 9 | 5 | 4 | 0 | 35 | 34 | 1987 | DSF | L 2-4 |
| Detroit | 1 | 0 | 1 | 5 | 1 | 4 | 0 | 7 | 14 | 2002 | F | L 1-4 |
| Edmonton | 1 | 1 | 0 | 7 | 4 | 3 | 0 | 19 | 16 | 2006 | F | W 4-3 |
| Montreal | 7 | 2 | 5 | 39 | 16 | 23 | 0 | 106 | 125 | 2006 | CQF | W 4-2 |
| New Jersey | 4 | 3 | 1 | 24 | 14 | 10 | 0 | 51 | 56 | 2009 | CQF | W 4-3 |
| Pittsburgh | 1 | 0 | 1 | 4 | 0 | 4 | 0 | 9 | 20 | 2009 | CF | L 0-4 |
| Toronto | 1 | 1 | 0 | 6 | 4 | 2 | 0 | 10 | 6 | 2002 | CF | W 4-2 |
| **Totals** | **22** | **10** | **12** | **127** | **59** | **68** | **0** | **323** | **368** | | | |

## Playoff Results 2009-2004

| Year | Round | Opponent | Result | GF | GA |
|---|---|---|---|---|---|
| 2009 | CF | Pittsburgh | L 0-4 | 9 | 20 |
| | CSF | Boston | W 4-3 | 16 | 17 |
| | CQF | New Jersey | W 4-3 | 17 | 15 |
| **2006** | **F** | **Edmonton** | **W 4-3** | **19** | **16** |
| | CF | Buffalo | W 4-3 | 22 | 17 |
| | CSF | New Jersey | W 4-1 | 17 | 10 |
| | CQF | Montreal | W 4-2 | 15 | 17 |

**Abbreviations: Round: F** - Final; **CF** - conference final; **CSF** - conference semi-final; **CQF** - conference quarter-final; **DSF** - division semi-final.

Calgary totals include Atlanta Flames, 1979-80.
Dallas totals include Minnesota North Stars, 1979-80 to 1992-93.
Phoenix totals include Winnipeg, 1979-80 to 1995-96.
Colorado totals include Quebec, 1979-80 to 1994-95.
New Jersey totals include Colorado Rockies, 1979-80 to 1981-82.

## 2008-09 Results

| | | | | | | | |
|---|---|---|---|---|---|---|---|
| **Oct.** | 10 | Florida | 6-4 | | 8 | at Florida | 2-4 |
| | 11 | at Tampa Bay | 4-3* | | 10 | at Boston | 1-5 |
| | 13 | Detroit | 1-3 | | 13 | at Ottawa | 1-5 |
| | 17 | at Los Angeles | 3-4* | | 15 | Toronto | 4-6 |
| | 19 | at Anaheim | 3-1 | | 17 | at Buffalo | 1-3 |
| | 23 | at Pittsburgh | 1-4 | | 19 | at Toronto | 2-0 |
| | 25 | at NY Islanders | 4-3 | | 20 | at Pittsburgh | 2-1 |
| | 28 | at Montreal | 2-3† | | 27 | at NY Rangers | 2-3 |
| | 30 | at St. Louis | 1-0 | | 29 | Tampa Bay | 3-2 |
| **Nov.** | 1 | Edmonton | 1-3 | | 31 | Atlanta | 2-0 |
| | 2 | Toronto | 6-4 | **Feb.** | 3 | at Vancouver | 3-4 |
| | 4 | at Toronto | 5-4* | | 5 | at San Jose | 4-3† |
| | 6 | at Washington | 2-3 | | 7 | at Phoenix | 7-2 |
| | 7 | Ottawa | 2-1 | | 12 | Florida | 0-5 |
| | 9 | Atlanta | 2-5 | | 14 | Columbus | 1-5 |
| | 12 | Washington | 1-5 | | 15 | at Buffalo • | 3-0 |
| | 14 | at Atlanta | 2-3 | | 17 | Boston | 1-5 |
| | 16 | Tampa Bay | 3-2† | | 19 | at NY Islanders | 6-2 |
| | 18 | Montreal | 2-1 | | 20 | Tampa Bay | 4-1 |
| | 21 | Phoenix | 5-2 | | 22 | Colorado | 5-2 |
| | 23 | Nashville | 2-5 | | 24 | at Ottawa | 2-4 |
| | 24 | at Florida | 2-3 | | 26 | Buffalo | 2-1† |
| | 26 | Philadelphia | 1-3 | | 28 | at Atlanta | 3-5 |
| | 28 | at Philadelphia | 3-2* | **Mar.** | 3 | at Washington | 5-2 |
| | 30 | Anaheim | 1-4 | | 6 | Calgary | 6-1 |
| **Dec.** | 4 | Pittsburgh | 2-5 | | 7 | at Tampa Bay | 9-3 |
| | 6 | Philadelphia | 1-2* | | 9 | NY Rangers | 3-0 |
| | 7 | Washington | 3-1 | | 11 | at Chicago | 2-3† |
| | 11 | at Philadelphia | 5-6† | | 12 | at Dallas | 2-3 |
| | 13 | at NY Rangers | 2-3† | | 14 | at Washington | 4-5† |
| | 16 | Montreal | 3-2 | | 18 | New Jersey | 4-2 |
| | 18 | Florida | 2-1* | | 20 | NY Islanders | 5-4 |
| | 20 | at Boston | 2-4 | | 21 | Washington | 4-1 |
| | 21 | at Montreal | 3-2* | | 23 | at Florida | 3-2* |
| | 23 | at Minnesota | 2-3 | | 25 | Ottawa | 2-1 |
| | 26 | at Atlanta | 5-4 | | 28 | at New Jersey | 2-1 |
| | 27 | Boston | 2-4 | **Apr.** | 2 | NY Rangers | 4-2 |
| | 31 | Atlanta | 3-1 | | 4 | Pittsburgh | 3-2* |
| **Jan.** | 2 | St. Louis | 2-1 | | 7 | NY Islanders | 9-0 |
| | 3 | at Tampa Bay | 3-2 | | 9 | Buffalo | 1-5 |
| | 6 | New Jersey | 3-2 | | 11 | at New Jersey | 2-3 |

* – Overtime † – Shootout

## Entry Draft Selections 2009-1995

Name in bold denotes played in NHL.

**2009**
Pick
27 Philippe Paradis
51 Brian Dumoulin
88 Mattias Lindstrom
131 Matt Kennedy
178 Rasmus Rissanen
208 Tommi Kivisto

**2008**
Pick
14 **Zach Boychuk**
45 Zac Dalpe
105 Michal Jordan
165 Mike Murphy
195 Samuel Morneau

**2007**
Pick
11 **Brandon Sutter**
72 Drayson Bowman
102 Justin McCrae
132 Chris Terry
162 Brett Bellemore

**2006**
Pick
63 Jamie McBain
93 Harrison Reed
123 Bobby Hughes
153 Stefan Chaput
183 Nick Dodge
213 Justin Krueger

**2005**
Pick
3 **Jack Johnson**
58 Nate Hagemo
64 Joe Barnes
94 Jakub Vojta
123 Ondrej Otcenas
145 Tim Kunes
159 Risto Korhonen
192 Nicolas Blanchard
198 Kyle Lawson

**2004**
Pick
4 **Andrew Ladd**
38 Justin Peters
69 **Casey Borer**
109 **Brett Carson**
137 Magnus Akerlund
202 Ryan Pottruff
235 Jonas Fiedler
268 Martin Vagner

**2003**
Pick
2 **Eric Staal**
31 **Danny Richmond**
102 Aaron Dawson
126 Kevin Nastiuk
130 Matej Trojovsky
137 **Tyson Strachan**
198 **Shay Stephenson**
230 Jamie Hoffmann
262 Ryan Rorabeck

**2002**
Pick
25 **Cam Ward**
91 Jesse Lane
160 Daniel Manzato
224 Adam Taylor

**2001**
Pick
15 Igor Knyazev
46 **Mike Zigomanis**
91 Kevin Estrada
110 Rob Zepp
181 Daniel Boisclair
211 Sean Curry
244 Carter Trevisani
274 Peter Reynolds

**2000**
Pick
32 **Tomas Kurka**
80 **Ryan Bayda**
97 **Niclas Wallin**
110 Jared Newman
181 J.D. Forrest
212 Magnus Kahnberg
235 Craig Kowalski
276 Troy Ferguson

**1999**
Pick
16 **David Tanabe**
49 **Brett Lysak**
84 **Brad Fast**
113 Ryan Murphy
174 **Damian Surma**
202 Jim Baxter
231 David Evans
237 Antti Jokela
259 Yevgeny Kurilin

**1998**
Pick
11 **Jeff Heerema**
70 Kevin Holdridge
71 **Erik Cole**
91 **Josef Vasicek**
93 **Tommy Westlund**
97 Chris Madden
184 Don Smith
208 **Jaroslav Svoboda**
211 Mark Kosick
239 Brent McDonald

**1997**
Pick
22 **Nikos Tselios**
28 **Brad DeFauw**
80 **Francis Lessard**
88 **Shane Willis**
142 Kyle Dafoe
169 Andrew Merrick
195 **Niklas Nordgren**
199 Randy Fitzgerald
225 **Kent McDonell**

**1996**
Pick
34 Trevor Wasyluk
61 Andrei Petrunin
88 **Craig MacDonald**
104 Steve Wasylko
116 Mark McMahon
143 Aaron Baker
171 **Greg Kuznik**
197 Kevin Marsh
223 **Craig Adams**
231 Ashkat Rakhmatullin

**1995**
Pick
13 **Jean-Sebastien Giguere**
35 Sergei Fedotov
85 **Ian MacNeil**
87 **Sami Kapanen**
113 Hugh Hamilton
165 **Byron Ritchie**
191 Milan Kostolny
217 **Mike Rucinski**

## Coaching History

Don Blackburn, 1979-80; Don Blackburn and Larry Pleau, 1980-81; Larry Pleau, 1981-82; Larry Kish, Larry Pleau and John Cuniff, 1982- 83; Jack Evans, 1983-84 to 1986-87; Jack Evans and Larry Pleau, 1987-88; Larry Pleau, 1988-89; Rick Ley, 1989-90, 1990-91; Jim Roberts, 1991-92; Paul Holmgren, 1992-93; Paul Holmgren and Pierre Maguire, 1993-94; Paul Holmgren, 1994-95; Paul Holmgren and Paul Maurice, 1995-96; Paul Maurice, 1996-97 to 2002-03; Paul Maurice and Peter Laviolette, 2003-04; Peter Laviolette, 2004-05 to 2007-08; Peter Laviolette and Paul Maurice, 2008-09; Paul Maurice, 2009-10.

## General Managers' History

Jack Kelley, 1979-80, 1980-81; Larry Pleau, 1981-82, 1982-83; Emile Francis, 1983-84 to 1988-89; Eddie Johnston, 1989-90 to 1991-92; Brian Burke, 1992-93; Paul Holmgren, 1993-94; Jim Rutherford, 1994-95 to date.

## Jim Rutherford

### President and General Manager

*Born: Beeton, Ont., February 17, 1949.*

Jim Rutherford, a former NHL goaltender, is the franchise's seventh general manager and the only general manager of the Carolina Hurricanes. Named to his position on June 28, 1994, Rutherford has always taken an aggressive approach towards improving the fortunes of the franchise through trades and the NHL entry draft. In 2002, the team reached the Stanley Cup Finals for the first time in history. The Hurricanes won the Stanley Cup in 2006.

A veteran of 13 NHL seasons, Rutherford began his professional goaltending career in 1969 as a first-round selection of the Detroit Red Wings. While playing for Detroit, Pittsburgh, Toronto and Los Angeles, Rutherford collected 14 career shutouts. For five seasons he also served as the Red Wings' player representative. Rutherford also played for Team Canada at the World Championships in Vienna in 1977 and Moscow in 1979.

After his playing days with the Red Wings, Rutherford joined Compuware to serve as the director of hockey operations for Compuware Sports Corporation. Rutherford gained a wealth of experience in youth hockey and junior programs. As a former player, coach, and general manager, his ability to develop players and produce winning programs is widely respected throughout the hockey community.

He started his management career by guiding Compuware Sports Corporation's purchase of the Windsor Spitfires of the Ontario Hockey League in April of 1984. During the next four years, Rutherford acted as general manager of the Spitfires. After the Spitfires advanced to the 1988 Memorial Cup finals, Rutherford led Compuware's efforts to bring the first American-based OHL franchise to Detroit on December 11, 1989. Rutherford was voted the 1987 executive of the year in both the OHL and the Canadian Hockey League and won the OHL executive of the year award again in 1988.

# Club Directory

RBC Center

**Carolina Hurricanes**
1400 Edwards Mill Rd.
Raleigh, NC 27607
Phone **919/467-7825**
FAX 919/462-0123
Tickets 1.866.NHL.CANES
www.carolinahurricanes.com
**Capacity:** 18,680

**Executive Management**

| | |
|---|---|
| Chief Executive Officer/Owner/Governor | Peter Karmanos, Jr. |
| President/General Manager | Jim Rutherford |
| Chief Financial Officer/Alternate Governor | Mike Amendola |
| Vice President/General Manager, RBC Center | Davin Olsen |
| Vice President/Assistant General Manager | Jason Karmanos |

**Hockey Operations**

| | |
|---|---|
| Head Coach | Paul Maurice |
| Associate Head Coach/Dir. of Player Personnel | Ron Francis |
| Assistant Coaches | Kevin McCarthy, Tom Rowe, Tom Barrasso |
| Director of Defensemen Development | Glen Wesley |
| Video Coach | Chris Huffine |
| Head Athletic Trainer/ Strength Conditioning Coach | Peter Friesen |
| Assistant Athletic Trainer | Jason Bailey |
| Equipment Managers | Wally Tatomir, Skip Cunningham, Bob Gorman |
| Director of Team Operations | Brian Tatum |
| Executive Assistant to the President/G.M. | Mari Jeter |
| Motivational Consultant/Mgr. Community Dev. | Doris E. Barksdale |
| Director of Amateur Scouting | Tony MacDonald |
| Amateur Scouts | Phil Horner, Bob Luccini, Bert Marshall, Mario Marois |
| Director of Pro Scouting | Marshall Johnston |
| Pro Scouts | Claude Larose, Ron Smith |
| European Scout | Robert Kron |
| Albany River Rats Head Coach/G.M. | Jeff Daniels |
| Albany River Rats Assistant Coach | Geordie Kinnear |

**Administration**

| | |
|---|---|
| Receptionists / General Office Assistant | Mary Lou Ruetz, Janet Davis / Angela Dennis |

**Arena Operations**

| | |
|---|---|
| Assistant General Manager, RBC Center | Larry Perkins |
| Marketing Manager | Crystal Pace |
| Guest Services Coordinator/Exec. Assistant | April Keeley |
| Security Manager / Parking Manager | Clinton Peterson / Mike Alexander |
| Event Services Manager | Steve Congress |
| Premium Services and Sales Manager | Suzanne Golden |
| Operations Manager | Dan McGowan |
| Facility Systems Manager | Rick Dunning |
| Arena Box Office Manager | Joe Sousa |
| Assistant Ticket Operations Manager | Chris Jovino |
| Arena Office Manager | Hilman Huskey |

**Broadcasting**

| | |
|---|---|
| Television Rightsholder | FS Carolinas |
| Radio Flagship | WCMC 99.9 FM The Fan |
| Television Play-by-Play / Analyst | John Forslund / Tripp Tracy |
| Radio Play-by-Play | Chuck Kaiton |

**Communications**

| | |
|---|---|
| Director of Media Relations | Mike Sundheim |
| Manager of Media Relations/Broadcast Coord. | Kyle Hanlin |
| Director of Community Relations | Doug Warf |
| Community Relations Coordinator | Katharine Kelley |
| Team Photographer | Gregg Forwerck |

**Finance/Information Technology**

| | |
|---|---|
| General Counsel/Senior Director of Finance | William Traurig |
| Accounts Payable / Receivable | Michael Arrington / Patty Hilliard, Temika Smith-Harris |
| Payroll/Human Resources Coordinator | Cyndy Coffey |
| Payroll Coordinator | Crystal DeDitius |
| Assistant to the CFO | Stacey Ustin |
| Director of Information Technology | Glenn Johnson |
| Client/Server Technologists | Dwight Baptist, Alex Byrd, Myatt Williams |

**Food and Beverage**

| | |
|---|---|
| Director of Food and Beverage | Chris Diamond |
| Concessions Manager | Rick Rhodes |
| Assistant Concessions Manager/ Group Coordinator | Barbara Couch |
| Chefs | Dennis Atkinson, Michael Flood, Andrew Booger, Kevin Heintz |
| Managers | Katrina Ryan, Skip Roach, Gary Berry, Jim O'Brien |

**Marketing**

| | |
|---|---|
| Director of Marketing and Brand Development | Ben Aycock |
| Dir. of Advertising Prod. & In-Game Marketing | Pete Soto |
| Director of Promotions and Fan Development | Jon Chase |
| Website Producer | Paul Branecky |
| Graphic Designers | Lauren Baxter, Andrew Roman |
| Youth and Amateur Hockey Coordinator | Paul Strand |
| Mascot Coordinator | George Brown |
| Marketing Coordinator | Laura Caso |
| Promotions/Fan Development Coordinator | Ryan O'Quinn |
| Producers, GaleForce/CanesVison/Wolfpack TV | Charles Graham, Don Sill |
| Web Prod., GaleForce/CanesVison/Wolfpack TV | Eric Bridenstine |
| Graphics Prod., GaleForce/CanesVison/Wolfpack TV | Stephen Rutherford |
| Mascot Coordinator | George Brown |
| Marketing Coordinator | Laura Caso |
| Promotions/Fan Development Coordinator | Ryan O'Quinn |

**Merchandise**

| | |
|---|---|
| Retail Operations Manager | James Blitch |

**Sales**

| | |
|---|---|
| Director of Corporate Sales | Mike Hurley |
| Senior Corporate Sales Executive | Rick Francis, Julia Zeigler |
| Corporate Sales Executives | Joe Fontanetta, Johnny Gill, Lindsey Moore |
| Director of Ticket Sales | Kyle Prairie |
| Manager of Sales and Client Services | Peterson Avetta |
| Account Executives, Business Development | Rich Davis, Michael Miller |
| Client Relations Representatives | Brooke Baragona, Ray Hall, Matt Horton |
| Hurricanes Group Sales Manager | Brian Kapusta |
| RBC Center Group Sales Manager | Brian Slais |
| Business Development Executive Group Sales | Greg Perna |

# Chicago Blackhawks

## 2008-09 Results: 46W-24L-5OTL-7SOL 104PTS.
## Second, Central Division

### Key Off-Season Signings/Acquisitions

**2009**

**June 30** • Re-signed C **Dave Bolland.**

**July 1** • Signed RW **Marian Hossa** and C **Tomas Kopecky.**

**2** • Signed C **John Madden.**

**6** • Re-signed RW **Troy Brouwer,** G **Corey Crawford,** LW **Ben Eager,** C **Colin Fraser** and D **Aaron Johnson.**

**7** • Re-signed D **Cam Barker.**

**8** • Re-signed LW **Kris Versteeg.**

**14** • Named **Stan Bowman** general manager.

### 2009-10 Schedule

| | | | |
|---|---|---|---|
| **Oct.** | Fri. | 2 | Florida† |
| | Sat. | 3 | at Florida† |
| | Thu. | 8 | at Detroit |
| | Sat. | 10 | Colorado |
| | Mon. | 12 | Calgary |
| | Wed. | 14 | Edmonton |
| | Thu. | 15 | at Nashville |
| | Sat. | 17 | Dallas |
| | Wed. | 21 | Vancouver |
| | Sat. | 24 | Nashville |
| | Mon. | 26 | Minnesota |
| | Thu. | 29 | at Nashville |
| | Fri. | 30 | Montreal |
| **Nov.** | Thu. | 5 | at Phoenix |
| | Fri. | 6 | at Colorado |
| | Mon. | 9 | Los Angeles |
| | Wed. | 11 | Colorado |
| | Fri. | 13 | Toronto |
| | Sun. | 15 | San Jose |
| | Thu. | 19 | at Calgary |
| | Sat. | 21 | at Edmonton |
| | Sun. | 22 | at Vancouver |
| | Wed. | 25 | at San Jose |
| | Fri. | 27 | at Anaheim* |
| | Sat. | 28 | at Los Angeles |
| **Dec.** | Tue. | 1 | Columbus |
| | Fri. | 4 | Nashville |
| | Sat. | 5 | at Pittsburgh |
| | Wed. | 9 | NY Rangers |
| | Fri. | 11 | at Buffalo |
| | Sun. | 13 | Tampa Bay |
| | Wed. | 16 | St. Louis |
| | Fri. | 18 | Boston |
| | Sun. | 20 | Detroit |
| | Tue. | 22 | San Jose |
| | Wed. | 23 | at Detroit |
| | Sat. | 26 | at Nashville |
| | Sun. | 27 | Nashville |
| | Tue. | 29 | at Dallas |
| | Thu. | 31 | New Jersey |
| **Jan.** | Sat. | 2 | at St. Louis |
| | Sun. | 3 | Anaheim |
| | Tue. | 5 | Minnesota |
| | Thu. | 7 | at Boston |
| | Sat. | 9 | at Minnesota |
| | Sun. | 10 | Anaheim |
| | Thu. | 14 | Columbus |
| | Sat. | 16 | at Columbus* |
| | Sun. | 17 | at Detroit* |
| | Tue. | 19 | at Ottawa |
| | Thu. | 21 | at Calgary |
| | Sat. | 23 | at Vancouver |
| | Tue. | 26 | at Edmonton |
| | Thu. | 28 | at San Jose |
| | Sat. | 30 | at Carolina |
| **Feb.** | Wed. | 3 | St. Louis |
| | Fri. | 5 | Phoenix |
| | Sat. | 6 | at St. Louis |
| | Tue. | 9 | Dallas |
| | Sat. | 13 | Atlanta |
| | Sun. | 14 | at Columbus* |
| **Mar.** | Tue. | 2 | at NY Islanders |
| | Wed. | 3 | Edmonton |
| | Fri. | 5 | Vancouver |
| | Sun. | 7 | Detroit |
| | Wed. | 10 | Los Angeles |
| | Sat. | 13 | at Philadelphia* |
| | Sun. | 14 | Washington |
| | Wed. | 17 | at Anaheim |
| | Thu. | 18 | at Los Angeles |
| | Sat. | 20 | at Phoenix |
| | Tue. | 23 | Phoenix |
| | Thu. | 25 | at Columbus |
| | Sun. | 28 | Columbus |
| | Tue. | 30 | at St. Louis |
| | Wed. | 31 | at Minnesota |
| **Apr.** | Fri. | 2 | at New Jersey |
| | Sun. | 4 | Calgary* |
| | Tue. | 6 | at Dallas |
| | Wed. | 7 | St. Louis |
| | Fri. | 9 | at Colorado |
| | Sun. | 11 | Detroit* |

* Denotes afternoon game. † Games played in Helsinki, FI.

### Year-by-Year Record

| | | Home | | | | Road | | | | Overall | | | | | | | | |
|---|---|---|---|---|---|---|---|---|---|---|---|---|---|---|---|---|---|---|
| Season | GP | W | L | T | OL | W | L | T | OL | W | L | T | OL | GF | GA | Pts. | Finished | Playoff Result |
| 2008-09 | 82 | 24 | 9 | .... | 8 | 22 | 15 | .... | 4 | 46 | 24 | .... | 12 | 264 | 216 | 104 | 2nd, Central Div. | Lost Conf. Final |
| 2007-08 | 82 | 23 | 16 | .... | 2 | 17 | 18 | .... | 6 | 40 | 34 | .... | 8 | 239 | 235 | 88 | 3rd, Central Div. | Out of Playoffs |
| 2006-07 | 82 | 17 | 20 | .... | 4 | 14 | 22 | .... | 5 | 31 | 42 | .... | 9 | 201 | 258 | 71 | 5th, Central Div. | Out of Playoffs |
| 2005-06 | 82 | 16 | 19 | .... | 6 | 10 | 24 | .... | 7 | 26 | 43 | .... | 13 | 211 | 285 | 65 | 4th, Central Div. | Out of Playoffs |
| 2004-05 | .... | .... | .... | .... | .... | .... | .... | .... | .... | .... | .... | .... | .... | .... | .... | .... | | |
| 2003-04 | 82 | 13 | 17 | 6 | 5 | 7 | 26 | 5 | 3 | 20 | 43 | 11 | 8 | 188 | 259 | 59 | 5th, Central Div. | Out of Playoffs |
| 2002-03 | 82 | 17 | 15 | 7 | 2 | 13 | 18 | 6 | 4 | 30 | 33 | 13 | 6 | 207 | 226 | 79 | 3rd, Central Div. | Out of Playoffs |
| 2001-02 | 82 | 28 | 7 | 5 | 1 | 13 | 20 | 8 | 0 | 41 | 27 | 13 | 1 | 216 | 207 | 96 | 3rd, Central Div. | Lost Conf. Quarter-Final |
| 2000-01 | 82 | 14 | 21 | 4 | 2 | 15 | 19 | 4 | 3 | 29 | 40 | 8 | 5 | 210 | 246 | 71 | 4th, Central Div. | Out of Playoffs |
| 1999-2000 | 82 | 16 | 19 | 5 | 1 | 17 | 18 | 5 | 1 | 33 | 37 | 10 | 2 | 242 | 245 | 78 | 3rd, Central Div. | Out of Playoffs |
| 1998-99 | 82 | 20 | 17 | 4 | .... | 9 | 24 | 8 | .... | 29 | 41 | 12 | .... | 202 | 248 | 70 | 3rd, Central Div. | Out of Playoffs |
| 1997-98 | 82 | 14 | 19 | 8 | .... | 16 | 20 | 5 | .... | 30 | 39 | 13 | .... | 192 | 199 | 73 | 5th, Central Div. | Out of Playoffs |
| 1996-97 | 82 | 16 | 21 | 4 | .... | 18 | 14 | 9 | .... | 34 | 35 | 13 | .... | 223 | 210 | 81 | 5th, Central Div. | Lost Conf. Quarter-Final |
| 1995-96 | 82 | 22 | 13 | 6 | .... | 18 | 15 | 8 | .... | 40 | 28 | 14 | .... | 273 | 220 | 94 | 2nd, Central Div. | Lost Conf. Semi-Final |
| 1994-95 | 48 | 11 | 10 | 3 | .... | 13 | 9 | 2 | .... | 24 | 19 | 5 | .... | 156 | 115 | 53 | 3rd, Central Div. | Lost Conf. Championship |
| 1993-94 | 84 | 21 | 16 | 5 | .... | 18 | 20 | 4 | .... | 39 | 36 | 9 | .... | 254 | 240 | 87 | 5th, Central Div. | Lost Conf. Quarter-Final |
| 1992-93 | 84 | 25 | 11 | 6 | .... | 22 | 14 | 6 | .... | 47 | 25 | 12 | .... | 279 | 230 | 106 | 1st, Norris Div. | Lost Div. Semi-Final |
| 1991-92 | 80 | 23 | 9 | 8 | .... | 13 | 20 | 7 | .... | 36 | 29 | 15 | .... | 257 | 236 | 87 | 2nd, Norris Div. | Lost Final |
| 1990-91 | 80 | 28 | 8 | 4 | .... | 21 | 15 | 4 | .... | 49 | 23 | 8 | .... | 284 | 211 | 106 | 1st, Norris Div. | Lost Div. Semi-Final |
| 1989-90 | 80 | 25 | 13 | 2 | .... | 16 | 20 | 4 | .... | 41 | 33 | 6 | .... | 316 | 294 | 88 | 1st, Norris Div. | Lost Conf. Championship |
| 1988-89 | 80 | 16 | 14 | 10 | .... | 11 | 27 | 2 | .... | 27 | 41 | 12 | .... | 297 | 335 | 66 | 4th, Norris Div. | Lost Conf. Championship |
| 1987-88 | 80 | 21 | 17 | 2 | .... | 9 | 24 | 7 | .... | 30 | 41 | 9 | .... | 284 | 328 | 69 | 3rd, Norris Div. | Lost Div. Semi-Final |
| 1986-87 | 80 | 18 | 13 | 9 | .... | 11 | 24 | 5 | .... | 29 | 37 | 14 | .... | 290 | 310 | 72 | 3rd, Norris Div. | Lost Div. Semi-Final |
| 1985-86 | 80 | 23 | 12 | 5 | .... | 16 | 21 | 3 | .... | 39 | 33 | 8 | .... | 351 | 349 | 86 | 1st, Norris Div. | Lost Div. Semi-Final |
| 1984-85 | 80 | 22 | 16 | 2 | .... | 16 | 19 | 5 | .... | 38 | 35 | 7 | .... | 309 | 299 | 83 | 2nd, Norris Div. | Lost Conf. Championship |
| 1983-84 | 80 | 25 | 13 | 2 | .... | 5 | 29 | 6 | .... | 30 | 42 | 8 | .... | 277 | 311 | 68 | 4th, Norris Div. | Lost Div. Semi-Final |
| 1982-83 | 80 | 29 | 8 | 3 | .... | 18 | 15 | 7 | .... | 47 | 23 | 10 | .... | 338 | 268 | 104 | 1st, Norris Div. | Lost Conf. Championship |
| 1981-82 | 80 | 20 | 13 | 7 | .... | 10 | 25 | 5 | .... | 30 | 38 | 12 | .... | 332 | 363 | 72 | 4th, Norris Div. | Lost Conf. Championship |
| 1980-81 | 80 | 21 | 11 | 8 | .... | 10 | 22 | 8 | .... | 31 | 33 | 16 | .... | 304 | 315 | 78 | 2nd, Smythe Div. | Lost Prelim. Round |
| 1979-80 | 80 | 21 | 12 | 7 | .... | 13 | 15 | 12 | .... | 34 | 27 | 19 | .... | 241 | 250 | 87 | 1st, Smythe Div. | Lost Quarter-Final |
| 1978-79 | 80 | 18 | 12 | 10 | .... | 11 | 24 | 5 | .... | 29 | 36 | 15 | .... | 244 | 277 | 73 | 1st, Smythe Div. | Lost Quarter-Final |
| 1977-78 | 80 | 20 | 9 | 11 | .... | 12 | 20 | 8 | .... | 32 | 29 | 19 | .... | 230 | 220 | 83 | 1st, Smythe Div. | Lost Quarter-Final |
| 1976-77 | 80 | 19 | 16 | 5 | .... | 7 | 27 | 6 | .... | 26 | 43 | 11 | .... | 240 | 298 | 63 | 3rd, Smythe Div. | Lost Prelim. Round |
| 1975-76 | 80 | 17 | 15 | 8 | .... | 15 | 15 | 10 | .... | 32 | 30 | 18 | .... | 254 | 261 | 82 | 1st, Smythe Div. | Lost Quarter-Final |
| 1974-75 | 80 | 24 | 12 | 4 | .... | 13 | 23 | 4 | .... | 37 | 35 | 8 | .... | 268 | 241 | 82 | 3rd, Smythe Div. | Lost Quarter-Final |
| 1973-74 | 78 | 20 | 6 | 13 | .... | 21 | 8 | 10 | .... | 41 | 14 | 23 | .... | 272 | 164 | 105 | 2nd, West Div. | Lost Semi-Final |
| 1972-73 | 78 | 26 | 9 | 4 | .... | 16 | 18 | 5 | .... | 42 | 27 | 9 | .... | 284 | 225 | 93 | 1st, West Div. | Lost Final |
| 1971-72 | 78 | 28 | 3 | 8 | .... | 18 | 14 | 7 | .... | 46 | 17 | 15 | .... | 256 | 166 | 107 | 1st, West Div. | Lost Semi-Final |
| 1970-71 | 78 | 30 | 6 | 3 | .... | 19 | 14 | 6 | .... | 49 | 20 | 9 | .... | 277 | 184 | 107 | 1st, West Div. | Lost Final |
| 1969-70 | 76 | 26 | 7 | 5 | .... | 19 | 15 | 4 | .... | 45 | 22 | 9 | .... | 250 | 170 | 99 | 1st, East Div. | Lost Semi-Final |
| 1968-69 | 76 | 20 | 14 | 4 | .... | 14 | 19 | 5 | .... | 34 | 33 | 9 | .... | 280 | 246 | 77 | 6th, East Div. | Out of Playoffs |
| 1967-68 | 74 | 20 | 13 | 4 | .... | 12 | 13 | 12 | .... | 32 | 26 | 16 | .... | 212 | 222 | 80 | 4th, East Div. | Lost Semi-Final |
| 1966-67 | 70 | 24 | 5 | 6 | .... | 17 | 12 | 6 | .... | 41 | 17 | 12 | .... | 264 | 170 | 94 | 1st, | Lost Semi-Final |
| 1965-66 | 70 | 21 | 8 | 6 | .... | 16 | 17 | 2 | .... | 37 | 25 | 8 | .... | 240 | 187 | 82 | 2nd, | Lost Semi-Final |
| 1964-65 | 70 | 20 | 13 | 2 | .... | 14 | 15 | 6 | .... | 34 | 28 | 8 | .... | 224 | 176 | 76 | 3rd, | Lost Final |
| 1963-64 | 70 | 26 | 4 | 5 | .... | 10 | 18 | 7 | .... | 36 | 22 | 12 | .... | 218 | 169 | 84 | 2nd, | Lost Semi-Final |
| 1962-63 | 70 | 17 | 9 | 9 | .... | 15 | 12 | 8 | .... | 32 | 21 | 17 | .... | 194 | 178 | 81 | 2nd, | Lost Semi-Final |
| 1961-62 | 70 | 20 | 10 | 5 | .... | 11 | 16 | 8 | .... | 31 | 26 | 13 | .... | 217 | 186 | 75 | 3rd, | Lost Final |
| **1960-61** | **70** | **20** | **6** | **9** | .... | **9** | **18** | **8** | .... | **29** | **24** | **17** | .... | **198** | **180** | **75** | **3rd,** | **Won Stanley Cup** |
| 1959-60 | 70 | 18 | 11 | 6 | .... | 10 | 18 | 7 | .... | 28 | 29 | 13 | .... | 191 | 180 | 69 | 3rd, | Lost Semi-Final |
| 1958-59 | 70 | 14 | 12 | 9 | .... | 14 | 17 | 4 | .... | 28 | 29 | 13 | .... | 197 | 208 | 69 | 3rd, | Lost Semi-Final |
| 1957-58 | 70 | 15 | 17 | 3 | .... | 9 | 22 | 4 | .... | 24 | 39 | 7 | .... | 163 | 202 | 55 | 5th, | Out of Playoffs |
| 1956-57 | 70 | 12 | 15 | 8 | .... | 4 | 24 | 7 | .... | 16 | 39 | 15 | .... | 169 | 225 | 47 | 6th, | Out of Playoffs |
| 1955-56 | 70 | 9 | 19 | 7 | .... | 10 | 20 | 5 | .... | 19 | 39 | 12 | .... | 155 | 216 | 50 | 6th, | Out of Playoffs |
| 1954-55 | 70 | 6 | 21 | 8 | .... | 7 | 19 | 9 | .... | 13 | 40 | 17 | .... | 161 | 235 | 43 | 6th, | Out of Playoffs |
| 1953-54 | 70 | 8 | 21 | 6 | .... | 4 | 30 | 1 | .... | 12 | 51 | 7 | .... | 133 | 242 | 31 | 6th, | Out of Playoffs |
| 1952-53 | 70 | 14 | 11 | 10 | .... | 13 | 17 | 5 | .... | 27 | 28 | 15 | .... | 169 | 175 | 69 | 4th, | Lost Semi-Final |
| 1951-52 | 70 | 9 | 19 | 7 | .... | 8 | 25 | 2 | .... | 17 | 44 | 9 | .... | 158 | 241 | 43 | 6th, | Out of Playoffs |
| 1950-51 | 70 | 8 | 22 | 5 | .... | 5 | 25 | 5 | .... | 13 | 47 | 10 | .... | 171 | 280 | 36 | 6th, | Out of Playoffs |
| 1949-50 | 70 | 13 | 18 | 4 | .... | 9 | 20 | 6 | .... | 22 | 38 | 10 | .... | 203 | 244 | 54 | 6th, | Out of Playoffs |
| 1948-49 | 60 | 13 | 12 | 5 | .... | 8 | 19 | 3 | .... | 21 | 31 | 8 | .... | 173 | 211 | 50 | 5th, | Out of Playoffs |
| 1947-48 | 60 | 10 | 17 | 3 | .... | 10 | 17 | 3 | .... | 20 | 34 | 6 | .... | 195 | 225 | 46 | 6th, | Out of Playoffs |
| 1946-47 | 60 | 10 | 17 | 3 | .... | 9 | 20 | 1 | .... | 19 | 37 | 4 | .... | 193 | 274 | 42 | 6th, | Out of Playoffs |
| 1945-46 | 50 | 15 | 5 | 5 | .... | 8 | 15 | 2 | .... | 23 | 20 | 7 | .... | 200 | 178 | 53 | 3rd, | Lost Semi-Final |
| 1944-45 | 50 | 9 | 14 | 2 | .... | 4 | 16 | 5 | .... | 13 | 30 | 7 | .... | 141 | 194 | 33 | 5th, | Out of Playoffs |
| 1943-44 | 50 | 15 | 6 | 4 | .... | 7 | 17 | 1 | .... | 22 | 23 | 5 | .... | 178 | 187 | 49 | 4th, | Lost Final |
| 1942-43 | 50 | 14 | 3 | 8 | .... | 3 | 15 | 7 | .... | 17 | 18 | 15 | .... | 179 | 180 | 49 | 5th, | Out of Playoffs |
| 1941-42 | 48 | 15 | 8 | 1 | .... | 7 | 15 | 2 | .... | 22 | 23 | 3 | .... | 145 | 155 | 47 | 4th, | Lost Quarter-Final |
| 1940-41 | 48 | 11 | 10 | 3 | .... | 5 | 15 | 4 | .... | 16 | 25 | 7 | .... | 112 | 139 | 39 | 5th, | Lost Semi-Final |
| 1939-40 | 48 | 15 | 7 | 2 | .... | 8 | 12 | 4 | .... | 23 | 19 | 6 | .... | 112 | 120 | 52 | 4th, | Lost Quarter-Final |
| 1938-39 | 48 | 5 | 13 | 6 | .... | 7 | 15 | 2 | .... | 12 | 28 | 8 | .... | 91 | 132 | 32 | 7th, | Out of Playoffs |
| **1937-38** | **48** | **10** | **10** | **4** | .... | **4** | **15** | **5** | .... | **14** | **25** | **9** | .... | **97** | **139** | **37** | **3rd, Amn. Div.** | **Won Stanley Cup** |
| 1936-37 | 48 | 8 | 13 | 3 | .... | 6 | 14 | 4 | .... | 14 | 27 | 7 | .... | 99 | 131 | 35 | 4th, Amn. Div. | Out of Playoffs |
| 1935-36 | 48 | 15 | 7 | 2 | .... | 6 | 12 | 6 | .... | 21 | 19 | 8 | .... | 93 | 92 | 50 | 3rd, Amn. Div. | Lost Quarter-Final |
| 1934-35 | 48 | 12 | 9 | 3 | .... | 14 | 8 | 2 | .... | 26 | 17 | 5 | .... | 118 | 88 | 57 | 2nd, Amn. Div. | Lost Quarter-Final |
| **1933-34** | **48** | **13** | **4** | **7** | .... | **7** | **13** | **4** | .... | **20** | **17** | **11** | .... | **88** | **83** | **51** | **2nd, Amn. Div.** | **Won Stanley Cup** |
| 1932-33 | 48 | 12 | 7 | 5 | .... | 4 | 13 | 7 | .... | 16 | 20 | 12 | .... | 88 | 101 | 44 | 4th, Amn. Div. | Out of Playoffs |
| 1931-32 | 48 | 13 | 5 | 6 | .... | 5 | 14 | 5 | .... | 18 | 19 | 11 | .... | 86 | 101 | 47 | 2nd, Amn. Div. | Lost Quarter-Final |
| 1930-31 | 44 | 13 | 8 | 1 | .... | 11 | 9 | 2 | .... | 24 | 17 | 3 | .... | 108 | 78 | 51 | 2nd, Amn. Div. | Lost Final |
| 1929-30 | 44 | 12 | 9 | 1 | .... | 9 | 9 | 4 | .... | 21 | 18 | 5 | .... | 117 | 111 | 47 | 2nd, Amn. Div. | Lost Quarter-Final |
| 1928-29 | 44 | 3 | 13 | 6 | .... | 4 | 16 | 2 | .... | 7 | 29 | 8 | .... | 33 | 85 | 22 | 5th, Amn. Div. | Out of Playoffs |
| 1927-28 | 44 | 2 | 18 | 2 | .... | 5 | 16 | 1 | .... | 7 | 34 | 3 | .... | 68 | 134 | 17 | 5th, Amn. Div. | Out of Playoffs |
| 1926-27 | 44 | 12 | 8 | 2 | .... | 7 | 14 | 1 | .... | 19 | 22 | 3 | .... | 115 | 116 | 41 | 3rd, Amn. Div. | Lost Quarter-Final |

**CENTRAL DIVISION**

**84th NHL Season**

**Franchise date:** September 25, 1926

# 2009-10 Player Personnel

| FORWARDS | HT | WT | S | Place of Birth | *Age | 2008-09 Club |
|---|---|---|---|---|---|---|
| ALIU, Akim | 6-2 | 200 | R | Okene, Nigeria | 20 | London-Sudbury-Rockford |
| BEACH, Kyle | 6-3 | 203 | R | Vancouver, B.C. | 19 | Everett-Leth-Rockford |
| BERTRAM, Dan | 5-11 | 182 | R | Calgary, Alta. | 22 | Rockford |
| BICKELL, Bryan | 6-4 | 223 | L | Bowmanville, Ont. | 23 | Rockford |
| BOIS, Danny | 6-1 | 202 | R | Thunder Bay, Ont. | 26 | Binghamton |
| BOLLAND, Dave | 6-0 | 181 | R | Toronto, Ont. | 23 | Chicago |
| BROPHEY, Evan | 6-1 | 203 | L | Kitchener, Ont. | 22 | Rockford |
| BROUWER, Troy | 6-2 | 213 | R | Vancouver, B.C. | 24 | Chicago-Rockford |
| BURISH, Adam | 6-1 | 200 | R | Madison, WI | 26 | Chicago |
| BYFUGLIEN, Dustin | 6-3 | 246 | R | Minneapolis, MN | 24 | Chicago |
| CULLEN, Mark | 5-11 | 190 | L | Moorhead, MN | 30 | Manitoba |
| DAVIS, Nathan | 6-1 | 193 | L | Cleveland, OH | 23 | Rockford |
| DOWELL, Jake | 6-0 | 202 | L | Eau Claire, WI | 24 | Chicago-Rockford |
| EAGER, Ben | 6-2 | 220 | L | Ottawa, Ont. | 25 | Chicago |
| FRASER, Colin | 6-1 | 188 | L | Surrey, B.C. | 24 | Chicago |
| HOBSON, Adam | 6-0 | 210 | L | Lund, Sweden | 22 | Rockford-Fresno-Gwinnett |
| HOSSA, Marian | 6-1 | 210 | L | Stara Lubovna, Czech. | 30 | Detroit |
| KANE, Patrick | 5-10 | 175 | L | Buffalo, NY | 20 | Chicago |
| KLINKHAMMER, Robert | 6-3 | 209 | L | Lethbridge, Alta. | 23 | Rockford |
| KOPECKY, Tomas | 6-3 | 200 | L | Ilava, Czech. | 27 | Detroit |
| LADD, Andrew | 6-2 | 198 | L | Maple Ridge, B.C. | 23 | Chicago |
| MacARTHUR, Pete | 5-10 | 180 | L | Clifton Park, NY | 24 | Rockford-Fresno |
| MADDEN, John | 5-11 | 190 | L | Barrie, Ont. | 36 | New Jersey |
| SHARP, Patrick | 6-1 | 197 | R | Winnipeg, Man. | 27 | Chicago |
| SKILLE, Jack | 6-1 | 198 | R | Madison, WI | 22 | Chicago-Rockford |
| TOEWS, Jonathan | 6-2 | 209 | L | Winnipeg, Man. | 21 | Chicago |
| VERSTEEG, Kris | 5-10 | 180 | R | Lethbridge, Alta. | 23 | Chicago |

| DEFENSEMEN | HT | WT | S | Place of Birth | *Age | 2008-09 Club |
|---|---|---|---|---|---|---|
| BARKER, Cam | 6-3 | 213 | L | Winnipeg, Man. | 23 | Chicago-Rockford |
| BRENNAN, Mike | 6-0 | 190 | R | Smithtown, NY | 23 | Rockford |
| CAMPBELL, Brian | 6-0 | 188 | L | Strathroy, Ont. | 30 | Chicago |
| CARLSSON, Jonathan | 6-1 | 198 | R | Uppsala, Sweden | 21 | Brynas |
| CONNELLY, Brian | 5-9 | 170 | L | Bloomington, MN | 23 | Colorado College-Rockford |
| DANIS-PEPIN, Simon | 6-7 | 217 | R | Gatineau, Que. | 21 | U. of Maine |
| HENDRY, Jordan | 6-0 | 196 | L | Nokomis, Sask. | 25 | Chicago-Rockford |
| HJALMARSSON, Niklas | 6-2 | 200 | L | Eksjo, Sweden | 22 | Chicago-Rockford |
| JOHNSON, Aaron | 6-1 | 211 | L | Port Hawkesbury, N.S. | 26 | Chicago-Rockford |
| KEITH, Duncan | 6-1 | 194 | L | Winnipeg, Man. | 26 | Chicago |
| PETIOT, Richard | 6-2 | 190 | L | Daysland, Alta. | 27 | Tor (AHL)-T.B.-Norfolk |
| SAWYER, Jean-Claude | 6-3 | 194 | L | Saint John, N.B. | 23 | Rockford-Fresno-Gwinnett |
| SEABROOK, Brent | 6-3 | 220 | R | Richmond, B.C. | 24 | Chicago |
| SOPEL, Brent | 6-1 | 211 | R | Calgary, Alta. | 32 | Chicago |

| GOALTENDERS | HT | WT | C | Place of Birth | *Age | 2008-09 Club |
|---|---|---|---|---|---|---|
| CRAWFORD, Corey | 6-2 | 183 | L | Montreal, Que. | 24 | Rockford-Chicago |
| FALLON, Joseph | 6-3 | 203 | L | Bemidji, MN | 24 | Rockford-Fresno-Gwinnett |
| HUET, Cristobal | 6-1 | 205 | L | St. Martin d'Heres, France | 34 | Chicago |
| NIEMI, Antti | 6-1 | 200 | L | Vantaa, Finland | 26 | Chicago-Rockford |
| RICHARDS, Alec | 6-4 | 190 | | Robbinsdale, MN | 22 | Yale |

* – Age at start of 2009-10 season

## Joel Quenneville

### Head Coach

*Born: Windsor, Ont., September 15, 1958.*

Joel Quenneville was named the 37th head coach in Chicago Blackhawks history on October 16, 2008. He originally joined the organization as a pro scout in September 2008. Quenneville has been a proven winner throughout his career as a head coach in the NHL, including seven seasons with the St. Louis Blues (1996 to 2004) and three with the Colorado Avalanche (2005 to 2008). In his first season behind the bench in Chicago, he led the Blackhawks to the Western Conference Final in just their second playoff appearance since the 1996-97 season.

One of only three men in the history of the NHL to have played in and coached 800 or more games, Quenneville is the winningest coach in Blues history, having compiled a 307-191-95 record. He was awarded the 2000 Jack Adams Trophy as the league's top coach. Quenneville was drafted by the Toronto Maple Leafs in the first round (21st overall) of the 1978 NHL Entry Draft. He spent 13 seasons as an NHL defenseman, netting 54 goals, 136 assists, 190 points and 705 penalty minutes in 803 career games with the Toronto Maple Leafs, Colorado Rockies, New Jersey Devils, Hartford Whalers and Washington Capitals.

Quenneville retired as an active player after the 1991-92 season, when he served as a player-coach for the American Hockey League's St. John's Maple Leafs. Quenneville broke into coaching with the AHL's Springfield Indians before serving as an assistant coach for the Quebec Nordiques/Colorado Avalanche organization for two and a half seasons. He helped Colorado capture the 1996 Stanley Cup in that position before accepting his first NHL head coaching job with St. Louis for the 1996-97 campaign.

#### Coaching Record

| | | | Regular Season | | | | Playoffs | | | |
|---|---|---|---|---|---|---|---|---|---|---|
| Season | Team | League | GC | W | L | O/T | GC | W | L | T |
| 1993-94 | Springfield | AHL | 80 | 29 | 38 | 13 | 6 | 2 | 4 | .... |
| **1996-97** | **St. Louis** | **NHL** | **40** | **18** | **15** | **7** | **6** | **2** | **4** | .... |
| **1997-98** | **St. Louis** | **NHL** | **82** | **45** | **29** | **8** | **10** | **6** | **4** | .... |
| **1998-99** | **St. Louis** | **NHL** | **82** | **37** | **32** | **13** | **13** | **6** | **7** | .... |
| **99-2000** | **St. Louis** | **NHL** | **82** | **51** | **19** | **12** | **7** | **3** | **4** | .... |
| **2000-01** | **St. Louis** | **NHL** | **82** | **43** | **22** | **17** | **15** | **9** | **6** | .... |
| **2001-02** | **St. Louis** | **NHL** | **82** | **43** | **27** | **12** | **10** | **5** | **5** | .... |
| **2002-03** | **St. Louis** | **NHL** | **82** | **41** | **24** | **17** | **7** | **3** | **4** | .... |
| **2003-04** | **St. Louis** | **NHL** | **61** | **29** | **23** | **9** | .... | .... | .... | .... |
| **2004-05** | **Colorado** | | | | SEASON CANCELLED | | | | | |
| **2005-06** | **Colorado** | **NHL** | **82** | **43** | **30** | **9** | **9** | **4** | **5** | .... |
| **2006-07** | **Colorado** | **NHL** | **82** | **44** | **31** | **7** | .... | .... | .... | .... |
| **2007-08** | **Colorado** | **NHL** | **82** | **44** | **31** | **7** | **10** | **4** | **6** | .... |
| **2008-09** | **Chicago** | **NHL** | **78** | **45** | **22** | **11** | **17** | **9** | **8** | .... |
| | **NHL Totals** | | **917** | **483** | **305** | **129** | **104** | **51** | **53** | .... |

# 2008-09 Scoring

* – rookie

## Regular Season

| Pos | # | Player | Team | GP | G | A | Pts | TOI | +/- | PIM | PP | SH | GW | S | % |
|---|---|---|---|---|---|---|---|---|---|---|---|---|---|---|---|
| R | 24 | Martin Havlat | CHI | 81 | 29 | 48 | 77 | 17:23 | 29 | 30 | 5 | 0 | 5 | 249 | 11.6 |
| R | 88 | Patrick Kane | CHI | 80 | 25 | 45 | 70 | 18:39 | –2 | 42 | 13 | 0 | 4 | 254 | 9.8 |
| C | 19 | Jonathan Toews | CHI | 82 | 34 | 35 | 69 | 18:37 | 12 | 51 | 12 | 0 | 7 | 195 | 17.4 |
| R | 32 * | Kris Versteeg | CHI | 78 | 22 | 31 | 53 | 17:02 | 15 | 55 | 6 | 4 | 3 | 139 | 15.8 |
| D | 51 | Brian Campbell | CHI | 82 | 7 | 45 | 52 | 22:34 | 5 | 22 | 4 | 0 | 1 | 108 | 6.5 |
| L | 16 | Andrew Ladd | CHI | 82 | 15 | 34 | 49 | 14:23 | 26 | 28 | 0 | 0 | 2 | 195 | 7.7 |
| C | 36 | Dave Bolland | CHI | 81 | 19 | 28 | 47 | 16:26 | 19 | 52 | 2 | 2 | 4 | 111 | 17.1 |
| R | 10 | Patrick Sharp | CHI | 61 | 26 | 18 | 44 | 17:58 | 6 | 41 | 9 | 0 | 4 | 184 | 14.1 |
| D | 2 | Duncan Keith | CHI | 77 | 8 | 36 | 44 | 25:34 | 33 | 60 | 2 | 1 | 1 | 173 | 4.6 |
| D | 25 | Cam Barker | CHI | 68 | 6 | 34 | 40 | 18:20 | –6 | 65 | 5 | 0 | 1 | 101 | 5.9 |
| R | 33 | Dustin Byfuglien | CHI | 77 | 15 | 16 | 31 | 14:52 | 7 | 81 | 3 | 0 | 4 | 202 | 7.4 |
| R | 22 * | Troy Brouwer | CHI | 69 | 10 | 16 | 26 | 15:05 | 7 | 50 | 4 | 1 | 0 | 126 | 7.9 |
| D | 7 | Brent Seabrook | CHI | 82 | 8 | 18 | 26 | 23:19 | 23 | 62 | 3 | 1 | 1 | 132 | 6.1 |
| C | 26 | Samuel Pahlsson | ANA | 52 | 5 | 10 | 15 | 18:30 | –16 | 32 | 1 | 0 | 1 | 74 | 6.8 |
| | | | CHI | 13 | 2 | 1 | 3 | 17:24 | –1 | 2 | 0 | 0 | 1 | 14 | 14.3 |
| | | | Total | 65 | 7 | 11 | 18 | 18:17 | –17 | 34 | 1 | 0 | 2 | 88 | 8.0 |
| C | 46 * | Colin Fraser | CHI | 81 | 6 | 11 | 17 | 10:53 | 3 | 55 | 0 | 1 | 0 | 67 | 9.0 |
| L | 55 | Ben Eager | CHI | 75 | 11 | 4 | 15 | 8:31 | 1 | 161 | 0 | 0 | 0 | 80 | 13.8 |
| D | 8 | Matt Walker | CHI | 65 | 1 | 13 | 14 | 16:37 | 7 | 79 | 0 | 0 | 0 | 83 | 1.2 |
| R | 37 | Adam Burish | CHI | 66 | 6 | 3 | 9 | 9:12 | 3 | 93 | 0 | 0 | 2 | 83 | 7.2 |
| D | 23 | Aaron Johnson | CHI | 38 | 3 | 5 | 8 | 14:08 | 19 | 33 | 0 | 0 | 1 | 27 | 11.1 |
| D | 4 * | Niklas Hjalmarsson | CHI | 21 | 1 | 2 | 3 | 14:59 | 4 | 0 | 0 | 0 | 0 | 15 | 6.7 |
| D | 5 | Brent Sopel | CHI | 23 | 1 | 1 | 2 | 13:48 | –4 | 8 | 0 | 0 | 1 | 15 | 6.7 |
| R | 11 * | Jack Skille | CHI | 8 | 1 | 0 | 1 | 9:26 | –3 | 5 | 0 | 0 | 0 | 14 | 7.1 |
| C | 49 * | Jake Dowell | CHI | 1 | 0 | 0 | 0 | 13:37 | 1 | 2 | 0 | 0 | 0 | 0 | 0.0 |
| C | 56 * | Tim Brent | CHI | 2 | 0 | 0 | 0 | 8:20 | 0 | 2 | 0 | 0 | 0 | 0 | 0.0 |
| L | 27 * | Pascal Pelletier | CHI | 7 | 0 | 0 | 0 | 9:08 | –4 | 0 | 0 | 0 | 0 | 7 | 0.0 |
| D | 6 | Jordan Hendry | CHI | 9 | 0 | 0 | 0 | 10:06 | –1 | 4 | 0 | 0 | 0 | 1 | 0.0 |

### Goaltending

| No. | Goaltender | GPI | Mins | Avg | W | L | OT | EN | SO | GA | SA | S% | G | A | PIM |
|---|---|---|---|---|---|---|---|---|---|---|---|---|---|---|---|
| 39 | Nikolai Khabibulin | 42 | 2467 | 2.33 | 25 | 8 | 7 | 1 | 3 | 96 | 1192 | .919 | 0 | 2 | 8 |
| 38 | Cristobal Huet | 41 | 2351 | 2.53 | 20 | 15 | 4 | 5 | 3 | 99 | 1087 | .909 | 0 | 0 | 2 |
| 31 | * Antti Niemi | 3 | 141 | 3.40 | 1 | 1 | 1 | 0 | 0 | 8 | 59 | .864 | 0 | 0 | 0 |
| | **Totals** | **82** | **4996** | **2.51** | **46** | **24** | **12** | **6** | **6** | **209** | **2344** | **.911** | | | |

## Playoffs

| Pos | # | Player | Team | GP | G | A | Pts | TOI | +/- | PIM | PP | SH | GW | OT | S | % |
|---|---|---|---|---|---|---|---|---|---|---|---|---|---|---|---|---|
| R | 24 | Martin Havlat | CHI | 16 | 5 | 10 | 15 | 15:34 | 0 | 8 | 0 | 0 | 1 | 1 | 35 | 14.3 |
| R | 88 | Patrick Kane | CHI | 16 | 9 | 5 | 14 | 16:35 | –9 | 12 | 2 | 0 | 0 | 0 | 34 | 26.5 |
| C | 19 | Jonathan Toews | CHI | 17 | 7 | 6 | 13 | 16:13 | –1 | 26 | 5 | 0 | 2 | 0 | 43 | 16.3 |
| C | 36 | Dave Bolland | CHI | 17 | 4 | 8 | 12 | 18:43 | –1 | 24 | 1 | 1 | 1 | 0 | 30 | 13.3 |
| R | 32 * | Kris Versteeg | CHI | 17 | 4 | 8 | 12 | 16:13 | –5 | 22 | 3 | 0 | 0 | 0 | 27 | 14.8 |
| D | 7 | Brent Seabrook | CHI | 17 | 1 | 11 | 12 | 26:00 | 0 | 14 | 1 | 0 | 0 | 0 | 36 | 2.8 |
| R | 10 | Patrick Sharp | CHI | 17 | 7 | 4 | 11 | 16:16 | –1 | 6 | 3 | 0 | 2 | 1 | 42 | 16.7 |
| D | 51 | Brian Campbell | CHI | 17 | 2 | 8 | 10 | 20:28 | 0 | 0 | 2 | 0 | 0 | 0 | 27 | 7.4 |
| R | 33 | Dustin Byfuglien | CHI | 17 | 3 | 6 | 9 | 17:10 | –2 | 26 | 1 | 0 | 0 | 0 | 40 | 7.5 |
| D | 25 | Cam Barker | CHI | 17 | 3 | 6 | 9 | 16:38 | –3 | 2 | 0 | 0 | 0 | 0 | 32 | 9.4 |
| D | 2 | Duncan Keith | CHI | 17 | 0 | 6 | 6 | 24:38 | 1 | 10 | 0 | 0 | 0 | 0 | 23 | 0.0 |
| R | 37 | Adam Burish | CHI | 17 | 3 | 2 | 5 | 11:02 | 3 | 30 | 0 | 0 | 1 | 0 | 23 | 13.0 |
| C | 26 | Samuel Pahlsson | CHI | 17 | 2 | 3 | 5 | 16:38 | –4 | 4 | 1 | 0 | 0 | 0 | 11 | 18.2 |
| L | 16 | Andrew Ladd | CHI | 17 | 3 | 1 | 4 | 12:54 | 3 | 12 | 0 | 0 | 1 | 1 | 35 | 8.6 |
| L | 55 | Ben Eager | CHI | 17 | 1 | 1 | 2 | 8:32 | –1 | 61 | 0 | 0 | 1 | 0 | 15 | 6.7 |
| D | 8 | Matt Walker | CHI | 17 | 0 | 2 | 2 | 15:21 | –4 | 14 | 0 | 0 | 0 | 0 | 15 | 0.0 |
| R | 22 * | Troy Brouwer | CHI | 17 | 0 | 2 | 2 | 11:50 | –1 | 12 | 0 | 0 | 0 | 0 | 24 | 0.0 |
| D | 4 * | Niklas Hjalmarsson | CHI | 17 | 0 | 1 | 1 | 16:37 | –2 | 6 | 0 | 0 | 0 | 0 | 10 | 0.0 |
| C | 46 * | Colin Fraser | CHI | 2 | 0 | 0 | 0 | 11:30 | 0 | 2 | 0 | 0 | 0 | 0 | 5 | 0.0 |

### Goaltending

| No. | Goaltender | GPI | Mins | Avg | W | L | EN | SO | GA | SA | S% | G | A | PIM |
|---|---|---|---|---|---|---|---|---|---|---|---|---|---|---|
| 39 | Nikolai Khabibulin | 15 | 881 | 2.93 | 8 | 6 | 3 | 0 | 43 | 421 | .898 | 0 | 0 | 0 |
| 38 | Cristobal Huet | 3 | 130 | 3.23 | 1 | 2 | 0 | 0 | 7 | 78 | .910 | 0 | 0 | 0 |
| 50 | * Corey Crawford | 1 | 16 | 3.75 | 0 | 0 | 0 | 0 | 1 | 7 | .857 | 0 | 0 | 0 |
| | **Totals** | **17** | **1034** | **3.13** | **9** | **8** | **3** | **0** | **54** | **509** | **.894** | | | |

## Stan Bowman

### General Manager

*Born: Montreal, Que., June 28, 1973.*

Stan Bowman was named general manager of the Chicago Blackhawks on July 14, 2009. Prior to being named to the position, Bowman had served for eight years in the Blackhawks operations department, including two seasons as assistant general manager from 2007 to 2009.

Bowman originally joined the Blackhawks in 2001, serving for four seasons as special assistant to the general manager before being promoted to director of hockey operations, a role he served in for two years (2005 to 2007). As assistant general manager, Bowman attended to the day-to-day administration of the Blackhawks' hockey operations department with his primary responsibilities including all CBA-related matters such as contract negotiations, free agency, salary arbitration, player movement and player assignment. He also tracked the progress of the Blackhawks prospects by working closely with the staff of the club's minor league affiliate in Rockford, while also assisting with player evaluation, prospect development and professional and amateur scouting.

Bowman played an integral part in the free agent signings of Marian Hossa, Tomas Kopecky and John Madden in 2009 and Brian Campbell and Cristobal Huet in 2008 while weighing in on the decision making that brought players such as Patrick Sharp, Kris Versteeg and Andrew Ladd to the club in trades.

Bowman graduated from the University of Notre Dame in 1995 with degrees in Finance and Computer Applications. He was born in Montreal where his father, legendary National Hockey League fixture and current Blackhawks senior advisor Scotty Bowman was coaching at the time.

# Club Records

## Team

(Figures in brackets for season records are games played; records for fewest points, wins, ties, losses, goals, goals against are for 70 or more games)

**Most Points** ............... **107** 1970-71 (78), 1971-72 (78)
**Most Wins** ................. **49** 1970-71 (78), 1990-91 (80)
**Most Ties** .................. **23** 1973-74 (78)
**Most Losses** ................ **56** 2005-06 (82)
**Most Goals** ................ **351** 1985-86 (80)
**Most Goals Against** ......... **363** 1981-82 (80)
**Fewest Points** ............... **31** 1953-54 (70)
**Fewest Wins** ................ **12** 1953-54 (70)
**Fewest Ties** .................. **6** 1989-90 (80)
**Fewest Losses** ............... **14** 1973-74 (78)
**Fewest Goals** ............. ***133** 1953-54 (70)
**Fewest Goals Against** ....... **164** 1973-74 (78)

**Longest Winning Streak**
**Overall** ..................... **9** Dec. 7-28/08
**Home** ...................... **13** Nov. 11-Dec. 20/70
**Away** ....................... **7** Dec. 9-29/64

**Longest Undefeated Streak**
**Overall** .................... **15** Jan. 14-Feb. 16/67 (12 wins, 3 ties), Oct. 29-Dec. 3/75 (6 wins, 9 ties)
**Home** ...................... **18** Oct. 11-Dec. 20/70 (16 wins, 2 ties)
**Away** ...................... **12** Nov. 2-Dec. 16/67 (6 wins, 6 ties)

**Longest Losing Streak**
**Overall** .................... **12** Feb. 25-Mar. 25/51
**Home** ...................... **10** Jan. 29-Mar. 21/28
**Away** ...................... **19** Nov. 10/03-Jan. 29/04

**Longest Winless Streak**
**Overall** .................... **21** Dec. 17/50-Jan. 28/51 (18 losses, 3 ties)
**Home** ...................... **15** Dec. 16/28-Feb. 28/29 (11 losses, 4 ties)
**Away** ...................... **22** Dec. 19/50-Mar. 25/51 (20 losses, 2 ties)

**Most Shutouts, Season** ....... **15** 1969-70 (76)
**Most PIM, Season** ......... **2,663** 1991-92 (80)
**Most Goals, Game** ........... **12** Jan. 30/69 (Chi. 12 at Phi. 0)

## Individual

**Most Seasons** ................ **22** Stan Mikita
**Most Games** ............. **1,394** Stan Mikita
**Most Goals, Career** .......... **604** Bobby Hull
**Most Assists, Career** ......... **926** Stan Mikita
**Most Points, Career** ....... **1,467** Stan Mikita (541G, 926A)
**Most PIM, Career** ......... **1,495** Chris Chelios
**Most Shutouts, Career** ........ **74** Tony Esposito
**Longest Consecutive Games Streak** ............ **884** Steve Larmer (Oct. 6/82-Apr. 15/93)
**Most Goals, Season** .......... **58** Bobby Hull (1968-69)
**Most Assists, Season** ......... **87** Denis Savard (1981-82, 1987-88)
**Most Points, Season** ........ **131** Denis Savard (1987-88; 44G, 87A)
**Most PIM, Season** .......... **408** Mike Peluso (1991-92)
**Most Points, Defenseman, Season** ................... **85** Doug Wilson (1981-82; 39G, 46A)
**Most Points, Center, Season** .................. **131** Denis Savard (1987-88; 44G, 87A)
**Most Points, Right Wing, Season** .................. **101** Steve Larmer (1990-91; 44G, 57A)
**Most Points, Left Wing, Season** .................. **107** Bobby Hull (1968-69; 58G, 49A)
**Most Points, Rookie, Season** ................... **90** Steve Larmer (1982-83; 43G, 47A)
**Most Shutouts, Season** ....... **15** Tony Esposito (1969-70)
**Most Goals, Game** ............ **5** Grant Mulvey (Feb. 3/82)
**Most Assists, Game** ........... **6** Pat Stapleton (Mar. 30/69)
**Most Points, Game** ............ **7** Max Bentley (Jan. 28/43; 4G, 3A), Grant Mulvey (Feb. 3/82; 5G, 2A)

* NHL Record.

## Retired Numbers

| | | |
|---|---|---|
| 1 | Glenn Hall | 1957-1967 |
| 3 | Pierre Pilote | 1955-68 |
| | Keith Magnuson | 1969-80 |
| 9 | Bobby Hull | 1957-1972 |
| 18 | Denis Savard | 1980-1990, 1995-1997 |
| 21 | Stan Mikita | 1958-1980 |
| 35 | Tony Esposito | 1969-1984 |

## General Managers' History

Major Frederic McLaughlin, 1926-27 to 1941-42; Bill Tobin, 1942-43 to 1953-54; Tommy Ivan, 1954-55 to 1976-77; Bob Pulford, 1977-78 to 1989-90; Mike Keenan, 1990-91, 1991-92; Mike Keenan and Bob Pulford, 1992-93; Bob Pulford, 1993-94 to 1996-97; Bob Murray, 1997-98, 1998-99; Bob Murray and Bob Pulford, 1999-2000; Mike Smith, 2000-01 to 2002-03; Mike Smith and Bob Pulford, 2003-04; Bob Pulford, 2004-05; Dale Tallon, 2005-06 to 2008-09; Stan Bowman, 2009-10.

# All-time Record vs. Other Clubs

## Regular Season

| | At Home | | | | | | | | On Road | | | | | | | | Total | | | | | | | |
|---|---|---|---|---|---|---|---|---|---|---|---|---|---|---|---|---|---|---|---|---|---|---|---|---|
| | GP | W | L | T | OL | GF | GA | PTS | GP | W | L | T | OL | GF | GA | PTS | GP | W | L | T | OL | GF | GA | PTS |
| Anaheim | 32 | 15 | 15 | 2 | 0 | 85 | 80 | 32 | 30 | 9 | 18 | 3 | 0 | 62 | 84 | 21 | 62 | 24 | 33 | 5 | 0 | 147 | 164 | 53 |
| Atlanta | 3 | 2 | 1 | 0 | 0 | 8 | 3 | 4 | 6 | 4 | 2 | 0 | 0 | 18 | 19 | 8 | 9 | 6 | 3 | 0 | 0 | 26 | 22 | 12 |
| Boston | 288 | 147 | 95 | 45 | 1 | 930 | 774 | 340 | 286 | 89 | 163 | 34 | 0 | 812 | 1031 | 212 | 574 | 236 | 258 | 79 | 1 | 1742 | 1805 | 552 |
| Buffalo | 53 | 28 | 18 | 6 | 1 | 169 | 142 | 63 | 54 | 14 | 33 | 7 | 0 | 139 | 202 | 35 | 107 | 42 | 51 | 13 | 1 | 308 | 344 | 98 |
| Calgary | 69 | 30 | 26 | 13 | 0 | 222 | 200 | 73 | 71 | 27 | 30 | 13 | 1 | 212 | 218 | 68 | 140 | 57 | 56 | 26 | 1 | 434 | 418 | 141 |
| Carolina | 31 | 17 | 10 | 3 | 1 | 120 | 88 | 38 | 31 | 12 | 15 | 4 | 0 | 96 | 102 | 28 | 62 | 29 | 25 | 7 | 1 | 216 | 190 | 66 |
| Colorado | 49 | 26 | 17 | 3 | 3 | 166 | 152 | 58 | 47 | 16 | 25 | 6 | 0 | 147 | 182 | 38 | 96 | 42 | 42 | 9 | 3 | 313 | 334 | 96 |
| Columbus | 25 | 14 | 8 | 1 | 2 | 76 | 61 | 31 | 26 | 11 | 11 | 1 | 3 | 81 | 83 | 26 | 51 | 25 | 19 | 2 | 5 | 157 | 144 | 57 |
| Dallas | 118 | 69 | 34 | 15 | 0 | 435 | 311 | 153 | 120 | 47 | 55 | 16 | 2 | 367 | 412 | 112 | 238 | 116 | 89 | 31 | 2 | 802 | 723 | 265 |
| Detroit | 353 | 160 | 138 | 51 | 4 | 1058 | 1003 | 375 | 350 | 103 | 212 | 33 | 2 | 870 | 1207 | 241 | 703 | 263 | 350 | 84 | 6 | 1928 | 2210 | 616 |
| Edmonton | 52 | 26 | 15 | 7 | 4 | 194 | 172 | 63 | 53 | 21 | 26 | 5 | 1 | 168 | 190 | 48 | 105 | 47 | 41 | 12 | 5 | 362 | 362 | 111 |
| Florida | 11 | 5 | 4 | 2 | 0 | 35 | 33 | 12 | 10 | 6 | 2 | 1 | 1 | 37 | 22 | 14 | 21 | 11 | 6 | 3 | 1 | 72 | 55 | 26 |
| Los Angeles | 83 | 40 | 33 | 9 | 1 | 286 | 238 | 90 | 82 | 36 | 37 | 8 | 1 | 271 | 282 | 81 | 165 | 76 | 70 | 17 | 2 | 557 | 520 | 171 |
| Minnesota | 16 | 5 | 9 | 1 | 1 | 33 | 48 | 12 | 16 | 4 | 9 | 0 | 3 | 37 | 49 | 11 | 32 | 9 | 18 | 1 | 4 | 70 | 97 | 23 |
| Montreal | 274 | 94 | 125 | 55 | 0 | 733 | 762 | 243 | 278 | 54 | 174 | 48 | 2 | 657 | 1075 | 158 | 552 | 148 | 299 | 103 | 2 | 1390 | 1837 | 401 |
| Nashville | 32 | 18 | 11 | 1 | 2 | 89 | 82 | 39 | 31 | 12 | 12 | 3 | 4 | 90 | 104 | 31 | 63 | 30 | 23 | 4 | 6 | 179 | 186 | 70 |
| New Jersey | 48 | 25 | 12 | 10 | 1 | 181 | 132 | 61 | 49 | 16 | 21 | 11 | 1 | 145 | 152 | 44 | 97 | 41 | 33 | 21 | 2 | 326 | 284 | 105 |
| NY Islanders | 50 | 26 | 18 | 5 | 1 | 165 | 168 | 58 | 48 | 14 | 19 | 15 | 0 | 143 | 168 | 43 | 98 | 40 | 37 | 20 | 1 | 308 | 336 | 101 |
| NY Rangers | 288 | 129 | 115 | 43 | 1 | 874 | 796 | 302 | 287 | 113 | 119 | 55 | 0 | 810 | 847 | 281 | 575 | 242 | 234 | 98 | 1 | 1684 | 1643 | 583 |
| Ottawa | 10 | 6 | 2 | 2 | 0 | 24 | 21 | 14 | 11 | 7 | 4 | 0 | 0 | 34 | 34 | 14 | 21 | 13 | 6 | 2 | 0 | 58 | 55 | 28 |
| Philadelphia | 62 | 27 | 16 | 19 | 0 | 212 | 176 | 73 | 63 | 16 | 36 | 11 | 0 | 162 | 207 | 43 | 125 | 43 | 52 | 30 | 0 | 374 | 383 | 116 |
| Phoenix | 56 | 31 | 14 | 10 | 1 | 209 | 141 | 73 | 58 | 23 | 28 | 5 | 2 | 182 | 184 | 53 | 114 | 54 | 42 | 15 | 3 | 391 | 325 | 126 |
| Pittsburgh | 62 | 40 | 11 | 10 | 1 | 244 | 163 | 91 | 60 | 23 | 29 | 7 | 1 | 194 | 215 | 54 | 122 | 63 | 40 | 17 | 2 | 438 | 378 | 145 |
| St. Louis | 133 | 75 | 39 | 18 | 1 | 482 | 379 | 169 | 130 | 48 | 62 | 17 | 3 | 396 | 433 | 116 | 263 | 123 | 101 | 35 | 4 | 878 | 812 | 285 |
| San Jose | 33 | 15 | 14 | 2 | 2 | 101 | 107 | 34 | 34 | 11 | 17 | 3 | 3 | 87 | 100 | 28 | 67 | 26 | 31 | 5 | 5 | 188 | 207 | 62 |
| Tampa Bay | 15 | 9 | 4 | 2 | 0 | 50 | 36 | 20 | 13 | 5 | 4 | 3 | 1 | 35 | 32 | 14 | 28 | 14 | 8 | 5 | 1 | 85 | 68 | 34 |
| Toronto | 319 | 157 | 120 | 42 | 0 | 971 | 832 | 356 | 317 | 99 | 164 | 54 | 0 | 832 | 1079 | 252 | 636 | 256 | 284 | 96 | 0 | 1803 | 1911 | 608 |
| Vancouver | 79 | 49 | 20 | 7 | 3 | 284 | 189 | 108 | 80 | 24 | 39 | 15 | 2 | 225 | 242 | 65 | 159 | 73 | 59 | 22 | 5 | 509 | 431 | 173 |
| Washington | 41 | 23 | 12 | 6 | 0 | 156 | 120 | 52 | 43 | 16 | 22 | 5 | 0 | 133 | 152 | 37 | 84 | 39 | 34 | 11 | 0 | 289 | 272 | 89 |
| Defunct Clubs | 139 | 79 | 40 | 20 | 0 | 408 | 268 | 178 | 140 | 52 | 67 | 21 | 0 | 316 | 346 | 125 | 279 | 131 | 107 | 41 | 0 | 724 | 614 | 303 |
| **Totals** | **2824** | **1387** | **996** | **410** | **31** | **9000** | **7677** | **3215** | **2824** | **932** | **1455** | **404** | **33** | **7758** | **9453** | **2301** | **5648** | **2319** | **2451** | **814** | **64** | **16758** | **17130** | **5516** |

## Playoffs

| | Series | W | L | GP | W | L | T | GF | GA | Last Mtg. | Rnd. | Result |
|---|---|---|---|---|---|---|---|---|---|---|---|---|
| Boston | 6 | 1 | 5 | 22 | 5 | 16 | 1 | 63 | 97 | 1978 | QF | L 0-4 |
| Buffalo | 2 | 0 | 2 | 9 | 1 | 8 | 0 | 17 | 36 | 1980 | QF | L 0-4 |
| Calgary | 4 | 2 | 2 | 18 | 9 | 9 | 0 | 54 | 53 | 2009 | CQF | W 4-2 |
| Colorado | 2 | 0 | 2 | 12 | 4 | 8 | 0 | 28 | 49 | 1997 | CQF | L 2-4 |
| Dallas | 6 | 4 | 2 | 33 | 19 | 14 | 0 | 120 | 118 | 1991 | DSF | L 2-4 |
| Detroit | 15 | 8 | 7 | 74 | 39 | 35 | 0 | 220 | 209 | 2009 | CF | L 1-4 |
| Edmonton | 4 | 1 | 3 | 20 | 8 | 12 | 0 | 77 | 102 | 1992 | CF | W 4-0 |
| Los Angeles | 1 | 1 | 0 | 5 | 4 | 1 | 0 | 10 | 7 | 1974 | QF | W 4-1 |
| Montreal | 17 | 5 | 12 | 81 | 29 | 50 | 2 | 185 | 261 | 1976 | QF | L 0-4 |
| NY Islanders | 2 | 0 | 2 | 6 | 0 | 6 | 0 | 6 | 21 | 1979 | QF | L 0-4 |
| NY Rangers | 5 | 4 | 1 | 24 | 14 | 10 | 0 | 66 | 54 | 1973 | SF | W 4-1 |
| Philadelphia | 1 | 1 | 0 | 4 | 4 | 0 | 0 | 20 | 8 | 1971 | QF | W 4-0 |
| Pittsburgh | 2 | 1 | 1 | 8 | 4 | 4 | 0 | 24 | 23 | 1992 | F | L 0-4 |
| St. Louis | 10 | 7 | 3 | 50 | 28 | 22 | 0 | 171 | 142 | 2002 | CQF | L 1-4 |
| Toronto | 9 | 3 | 6 | 38 | 15 | 22 | 1 | 89 | 111 | 1995 | CQF | W 4-3 |
| Vancouver | 3 | 2 | 1 | 15 | 9 | 6 | 0 | 47 | 43 | 2009 | CSF | W 4-2 |
| Defunct Clubs | 4 | 2 | 2 | 9 | 5 | 3 | 1 | 16 | 15 | | | |
| **Totals** | **93** | **42** | **51** | **428** | **197** | **226** | **5** | **1213** | **1349** | | | |

Calgary totals include Atlanta Flames, 1972-73 to 1979-80. Carolina totals include Hartford, 1979-80 to 1996-97.
Colorado totals include Quebec, 1979-80 to 1994-95. Dallas totals include Minnesota North Stars, 1967-68 to 1992-93.
New Jersey totals include Kansas City, 1974-75, 1975-76, and Colorado Rockies, 1976-77 to 1981-82.
Phoenix totals include Winnipeg, 1979-80 to 1995-96.

## Playoff Results 2009-2004

| Year | Round | Opponent | Result | GF | GA |
|---|---|---|---|---|---|
| 2009 | CF | Detroit | L 1-4 | 10 | 19 |
| | CSF | Vancouver | W 4-2 | 23 | 19 |
| | CQF | Calgary | W 4-2 | 21 | 16 |

**Abbreviations: Round: F** - Final; **CF** - conference final; **CSF** - conference semi-final; **CQF** - conference quarter-final; **DSF** - division semi-final; **SF** - semi-final; **QF** - quarter-final.

## 2008-09 Results

| | | | |
|---|---|---|---|
| **Oct.** | 10 | at NY Rangers | 2-4 |
| | 11 | at Washington | 2-4 |
| | 13 | Nashville | 2-3† |
| | 15 | Phoenix | 4-1 |
| | 18 | at St. Louis | 3-4† |
| | 19 | Vancouver | 4-2 |
| | 22 | Edmonton | 3-0 |
| | 25 | Detroit | 5-6† |
| | 27 | at Minnesota | 2-3 |
| | 31 | Dallas | 5-2 |
| **Nov.** | 1 | at Columbus | 4-3† |
| | 3 | Colorado | 6-2 |
| | 9 | Calgary | 6-1 |
| | 12 | Boston | 1-2† |
| | 14 | St. Louis | 3-4* |
| | 16 | San Jose | 5-6 |
| | 18 | at Phoenix | 3-2† |
| | 20 | at Dallas | 6-3 |
| | 22 | at Toronto | 5-4* |
| | 26 | at San Jose | 2-3* |
| | 28 | at Anaheim | 0-1 |
| | 29 | at Los Angeles | 2-5 |
| **Dec.** | 3 | Anaheim | 4-2 |
| | 6 | at Detroit | 4-5† |
| | 7 | Phoenix | 7-1 |
| | 10 | Ottawa | 2-0 |
| | 12 | at Colorado | 4-3 |
| | 14 | Columbus | 3-1 |
| | 16 | at Edmonton | 9-2 |
| | 19 | at Calgary | 3-2* |
| | 20 | at Vancouver | 3-1 |
| | 26 | Philadelphia | 5-1 |
| | 28 | at Minnesota | 4-1 |
| | 30 | at Detroit | 0-4 |
| **Jan.** | 1 | Detroit | 4-6 |
| | 4 | Calgary | 5-2 |
| | 6 | at Phoenix | 6-0 |
| | 8 | at Colorado | 1-2 |
| | 10 | at Nashville | 1-4 |
| | 11 | Nashville | 3-1 |
| | 14 | Buffalo | 4-1 |
| | 16 | NY Rangers | 2-3* |
| | 17 | at St. Louis | 2-1* |
| | 19 | Minnesota | 1-4 |
| | 21 | St. Louis | 0-2 |
| | 28 | at Anaheim | 3-2 |
| | 29 | at Los Angeles | 2-5 |
| | 31 | at San Jose | 4-2 |
| **Feb.** | 3 | at Edmonton | 3-1 |
| | 5 | at Calgary | 5-2 |
| | 7 | at Vancouver | 3-7 |
| | 11 | at Atlanta | 3-1 |
| | 13 | at St. Louis | 0-1 |
| | 14 | Dallas | 6-2 |
| | 17 | at Tampa Bay | 5-3 |
| | 19 | at Florida | 4-0 |
| | 21 | at Dallas | 3-1 |
| | 22 | Minnesota | 1-2 |
| | 24 | at Nashville | 3-5 |
| | 27 | Pittsburgh | 4-5* |
| **Mar.** | 1 | Los Angeles | 4-2 |
| | 3 | Anaheim | 3-2* |
| | 7 | at Boston | 3-5 |
| | 8 | Colorado | 1-5 |
| | 11 | Carolina | 3-2† |
| | 13 | Columbus | 3-5 |
| | 15 | NY Islanders | 2-4 |
| | 17 | at New Jersey | 2-3 |
| | 18 | at Columbus | 3-4* |
| | 20 | Edmonton | 4-5† |
| | 22 | Los Angeles | 4-1 |
| | 25 | San Jose | 6-5† |
| | 27 | New Jersey | 3-2* |
| | 29 | Vancouver | 0-4 |
| | 31 | at Montreal | 1-4 |
| **Apr.** | 1 | St. Louis | 3-1 |
| | 3 | Nashville | 3-1 |
| | 5 | at Columbus | 1-0* |
| | 7 | at Nashville | 4-2 |
| | 8 | Columbus | 3-4† |
| | 11 | at Detroit | 4-2 |
| | 12 | Detroit | 3-0 |

* – Overtime † – Shootout

## Entry Draft Selections 2009-1995

Name in bold denotes played in NHL.

### 2009

| Pick | |
|---|---|
| 28 | Dylan Olsen |
| 59 | Brandon Pirri |
| 89 | Daniel Delisle |
| 119 | Byron Froese |
| 149 | Marcus Kruger |
| 177 | David Pacan |
| 195 | Paul Phillips |
| 209 | David Gilbert |

### 2008

| Pick | |
|---|---|
| 11 | Kyle Beach |
| 68 | Shawn Lalonde |
| 132 | Teigan Zahn |
| 162 | Jonathan Carlsson |
| 169 | Ben Smith |
| 179 | Braden Birch |
| 192 | Joe Gleason |

### 2007

| Pick | |
|---|---|
| 1 | **Patrick Kane** |
| 38 | Bill Sweatt |
| 56 | Akim Aliu |
| 69 | Maxime Tanguay |
| 86 | Josh Unice |
| 126 | Joseph Lavin |
| 156 | Richard Greenop |

### 2006

| Pick | |
|---|---|
| 3 | **Jonathan Toews** |
| 33 | Igor Makarov |
| 61 | Simon Danis-Pepin |
| 76 | Tony Lagerstrom |
| 95 | Ben Shutron |
| 96 | Joe Palmer |
| 156 | Jan-Mikael Juutilainen |
| 169 | Chris Auger |
| 186 | Peter Leblanc |

### 2005

| Pick | |
|---|---|
| 7 | **Jack Skille** |
| 43 | **Michael Blunden** |
| 54 | Dan Bertram |
| 68 | Evan Brophey |
| 108 | **Niklas Hjalmarsson** |
| 113 | Nathan Davis |
| 117 | Denis Istomin |
| 134 | Brennan Turner |
| 167 | Joseph Fallon |
| 188 | Joe Charlebois |
| 202 | David Kuchejda |
| 203 | Adam Hobson |

### 2004

| Pick | |
|---|---|
| 3 | **Cam Barker** |
| 32 | **Dave Bolland** |
| 41 | **Bryan Bickell** |
| 45 | Ryan Garlock |
| 54 | Jakub Sindel |
| 68 | **Adam Berti** |
| 120 | Mitch Maunu |
| 123 | Karel Hromas |
| 131 | Trevor Kell |
| 140 | **Jake Dowell** |
| 165 | Scott McCulloch |
| 196 | **Petri Kontiola** |
| 214 | **Troy Brouwer** |
| 223 | Jared Walker |
| 229 | Eric Hunter |
| 256 | Matthew Ford |
| 260 | Marko Anttila |

### 2003

| Pick | |
|---|---|
| 14 | **Brent Seabrook** |
| 52 | **Corey Crawford** |
| 59 | **Michal Barinka** |
| 151 | **Lasse Kukkonen** |
| 156 | Alexei Ivanov |
| 181 | Johan Andersson |
| 211 | Mike Brodeur |
| 245 | **Dustin Byfuglien** |
| 275 | Michael Grenzy |
| 282 | **Chris Porter** |

### 2002

| Pick | |
|---|---|
| 21 | **Anton Babchuk** |
| 54 | **Duncan Keith** |
| 93 | Alexander Kojevnikov |
| 128 | **Matt Ellison** |
| 156 | **James Wisniewski** |
| 188 | Kevin Kantee |
| 219 | Tyson Kellerman |
| 251 | Jason Kostadine |
| 282 | **Adam Burish** |

### 2001

| Pick | |
|---|---|
| 9 | **Tuomo Ruutu** |
| 29 | **Adam Munro** |
| 59 | **Matt Keith** |
| 73 | **Craig Anderson** |
| 104 | Brent MacLellan |
| 115 | Vladimir Gusev |
| 119 | Alexei Zotkin |
| 142 | Tommi Jaminki |
| 174 | Alexander Golovin |
| 186 | Petr Puncochar |
| 205 | Teemu Jaaskelainen |
| 216 | Oleg Minakov |
| 268 | Jeff Miles |

### 2000

| Pick | |
|---|---|
| 10 | **Mikhail Yakubov** |
| 11 | **Pavel Vorobiev** |
| 49 | **Jonas Nordqvist** |
| 74 | **Igor Radulov** |
| 106 | Scott Balan |
| 117 | **Olli Malmivaara** |
| 151 | Alexander Barkunov |
| 177 | Michael Ayers |
| 193 | Joey Martin |
| 207 | Cliff Loya |
| 225 | Vladislav Luchkin |
| 240 | **Adam Berkhoel** |
| 262 | Peter Flache |
| 271 | **Reto Von Arx** |
| 291 | Arne Ramholt |

### 1999

| Pick | |
|---|---|
| 23 | **Steve McCarthy** |
| 46 | Dimitri Levinski |
| 63 | Stepan Mokhov |
| 134 | Michael Jacobsen |
| 165 | **Michael Leighton** |
| 194 | Mattias Wennerberg |
| 195 | Yorick Treille |
| 223 | Andrew Carver |

### 1998

| Pick | |
|---|---|
| 8 | **Mark Bell** |
| 94 | Matthias Trattnig |
| 156 | **Kent Huskins** |
| 158 | Jari Viuhkola |
| 166 | Jonathan Pelletier |
| 183 | **Tyler Arnason** |
| 210 | Sean Griffin |
| 238 | Alexandre Couture |
| 240 | Andrei Yershov |

### 1997

| Pick | |
|---|---|
| 13 | **Daniel Cleary** |
| 16 | **Ty Jones** |
| 39 | **Jeremy Reich** |
| 67 | Mike Souza |
| 110 | **Ben Simon** |
| 120 | Peter Gardiner |
| 130 | **Kyle Calder** |
| 147 | Heath Gordon |
| 174 | Jerad Smith |
| 204 | Sergei Shikhanov |
| 230 | Chris Feil |

### 1996

| Pick | |
|---|---|
| 31 | **Remi Royer** |
| 42 | **Jeff Paul** |
| 46 | Geoff Peters |
| 130 | Andy Johnson |
| 184 | Mike Vellinga |
| 210 | Chris Twerdun |
| 236 | Andrei Kozyrev |

### 1995

| Pick | |
|---|---|
| 19 | **Dmitri Nabokov** |
| 45 | **Christian Laflamme** |
| 71 | Kevin McKay |
| 82 | Chris Van Dyk |
| 97 | Pavel Kriz |
| 146 | Marc Magliarditi |
| 149 | Marty Wilford |
| 175 | Steve Tardif |
| 201 | **Casey Hankinson** |
| 227 | Mike Pittman |

## Coaching History

Pete Muldoon, 1926-27; Barney Stanley and Hugh Lehman, 1927-28; Herb Gardiner and Dick Irvin, 1928-29; Tom Shaughnessy and Bill Tobin, 1929-30; Dick Irvin, 1930-31; Bill Tobin, 1931-32; Emil Iverson, Godfrey Matheson and Tommy Gorman, 1932-33; Tommy Gorman, 1933-34; Clem Loughlin, 1934-35 to 1936-37; Bill Stewart, 1937-38; Bill Stewart and Paul Thompson, 1938-39; Paul Thompson, 1939-40 to 1943-44; Paul Thompson and Johnny Gottselig, 1944-45; Johnny Gottselig, 1945-46, 1946-47; Johnny Gottselig and Charlie Conacher, 1947-48; Charlie Conacher, 1948-49, 1949-50; Ebbie Goodfellow, 1950-51, 1951-52; Sid Abel, 1952-53, 1953-54; Frank Eddolls, 1954-55; Dick Irvin, 1955-56; Tommy Ivan, 1956-57; Tommy Ivan and Rudy Pilous, 1957-58; Rudy Pilous, 1958-59 to 1962-63; Billy Reay, 1963-64 to 1975-76; Billy Reay and Bill White, 1976-77; Bob Pulford, 1977-78, 1978-79; Eddie Johnston, 1979-80; Keith Magnuson, 1980-81; Keith Magnuson and Bob Pulford, 1981-82; Orval Tessier, 1982-83, 1983-84; Orval Tessier and Bob Pulford, 1984-85; Bob Pulford, 1985-86, 1986-87; Bob Murdoch, 1987-88; Mike Keenan, 1988-89 to 1991-92; Darryl Sutter, 1992-93 to 1994-95; Craig Hartsburg, 1995-96 to 1997-98; Dirk Graham and Lorne Molleken, 1998-99; Lorne Molleken and Bob Pulford, 1999-2000; Alpo Suhonen, 2000-01; Brian Sutter, 2001-02 to 2004-05; Trent Yawney, 2005-06; Trent Yawney and Denis Savard, 2006-07; Denis Savard, 2007-08; Denis Savard and Joel Quenneville, 2008-09; Joel Quenneville, 2009-10.

## Captains' History

Dick Irvin, 1926-27 to 1928-29; Duke Dukowski, 1929-30; Ty Arbour, 1930-31; Cy Wentworth, 1931-32; Helge Bostrom, 1932-33; Charlie Gardiner, 1933-34; no captain, 1934-35; Johnny Gottselig, 1935-36 to 1939-40; Earl Seibert, 1940-41, 1941-42; Doug Bentley, 1942-43, 1943-44; Clint Smith 1944-45; John Mariucci, 1945-46; Red Hamill, 1946-47; John Mariucci, 1947-48; Gaye Stewart, 1948-49; Doug Bentley, 1949-50; Jack Stewart, 1950-51, 1951-52; Bill Gadsby, 1952-53, 1953-54; Gus Mortson, 1954-55 to 1956-57; no captain, 1957-58; Ed Litzenberger, 1958-59 to 1960-61; Pierre Pilote, 1961-62 to 1967-68, no captain, 1968-69; Pat Stapleton, 1969-70; no captain, 1970-71 to 1974-75; Stan Mikita and Pit Martin, 1975-76; Stan Mikita, Pit Martin and Keith Magnuson, 1976-77; Keith Magnuson, 1977-78, 1978-79; Keith Magnuson and Terry Ruskowski, 1979-80; Terry Ruskowski, 1980-81, 1981-82; Darryl Sutter, 1982-83 to 1984-85; Darryl Sutter and Bob Murray, 1985-86; Darryl Sutter, 1986-87; no captain, 1987-88; Denis Savard and Dirk Graham, 1988-89; Dirk Graham, 1989-90 to 1994-95; Chris Chelios, 1995-96 to 1998-99; Doug Gilmour, 1999-2000; Tony Amonte, 2000-01, 2001-02; Alex Zhamnov, 2002-03, 2003-04; Adrian Aucoin and Martin Lapointe, 2005-06, 2006-07; no captain, 2007-08; Jonathan Toews, 2008-09 to date.

# Club Directory

United Center

**Chicago Blackhawks**
United Center
1901 W. Madison Street
Chicago, IL 60612
Phone **312/455-7000**
FAX 312/455-7041
www.chicagoblackhawks.com
**Capacity:** 17,717

**Management**
Chairman .... W. Rockwell "Rocky" Wirtz
President .... John F. McDonough
Senior Vice President, Business Operations .... Jay Blunk
General Manager .... Stan Bowman
Assistant General Manager .... Kevin Cheveldayoff
Senior Advisors, Hockey Operations .... Dale Tallon, Scotty Bowman
Sr. Director, Hockey Admin./Asst. to the Pres. .... Al MacIsaac

**Coaching Staff**
Head Coach .... Joel Quenneville
Assistant Coaches .... John Torchetti, Mike Haviland
Goaltending Coach .... Stephane Waite
Strength and Conditioning Coach .... Paul Goodman
Video Coach .... Brad Aldrich
Skating Coach .... Paul Vincent
Developmental Goaltending Coach .... Wade Flaherty

**Hockey Operations & Scouting**
Director, Player Personnel .... Marc Bergevin
G.M., Minor League Affiliations .... Mark Bernard
Director, Player Development .... Norm Maciver
Director, Amateur Scouting .... Mark Kelley
Director, Player Recruitment .... Ron Anderson
Chief Amateur Scout .... Michel Dumas
Director Team Services .... Tony Ommen
Scouting Coordinator .... Ian Gentile
Amateur Scouts .... Bruce Franklin, Tim Keon, Peter Nevin, Jad Ramsay
Head European Scout .... Niklas Blomgren
European Amateur Scouts .... Ryan Stewart, Karl Pavlik, Ruslan Shabanov
Pro Scouts .... Gord Donnelly, Jim Pappin, Steve Smith
European Pro Scout .... Mats Hallin

**Training/Equipment Staff**
Head Athletic Trainer .... Mike Gapski
Equipment Manager .... Troy Parchman
Massage Therapist .... Pawel Prylinski
Assistant Athletic Trainer .... Jeff Thomas
Assistant Equipment Manager .... Clinton Reif
Equipment Assistant .... Jim Heintzelman

**Medical**
Medical Staff .... Dr. Michael Terry (Head Team Physician – Orthopedics); Dr. William Harper (Head Team Internist – U. of Chicago Medical Center); Dr. Sherwin Ho (Team Physician – Orthopedics – U. of Chicago Medical Center), Dr. Martin Leland (Team Physician – Orthopedics – U. of Chicago Medical Center); Jim Gary (Team Therapist); Ari Levy, Todd Stern, Russ Baer, Anthony LaVacca, Martin Marcus, Louise Sclafani.

**Broadcasters**
TV Play-By-Play/Color .... Pat Foley/Eddie Olczyk
Radio Play-By-Play/Color .... John Wiedeman/Troy Murray
TV/Radio Studio Hosts .... Steve Konroyd/Judd Sirott, Jim Memolo

**Media Relations**
Director, Media Relations .... Brandon Faber
Manager, Media Relations .... Adam Rogowin
Coordinator, Media Relations .... Paul Kennedy

**Community Relations**
Sr. Director, Market Dev. & Community Affairs .... Pete Hassen
Director, Youth Hockey .... Annie Camins
Coordinators, Community Relations .... Elizabeth Queen, Brooke Scheyer
Youth Hockey Assistant .... Ashley Hinton
Mascot Coordinator .... Joe Doyle

**Corporate Sponsorships**
Sr. Director, Corporate Sponsorships .... Steve Waight
Manager, Client Services .... Kelly Smith
Account Execs., Corp. Sponsorships . Rich Sommers, Steve McNelley, Bart Miller, Sara Bailey
Coordinator, Market Research .... Mark McGuire, Jr.
Administrative Assistant, Client Services .... Kristin Ludden

**Executive Staff**
Sr. Exec. Asst. to G.M. / Hockey Ops. .... Julie Kavanaugh
Exec. Asst. to President .... Janelle Miller
Exec. Asst. to Sr. V.P., Business Ops. .... Kayla Kindred

**Finance**
Director, Finance .... TJ Skattum
Accounting Manager/Payroll Administrator .... Michael Dorsch/Patricia Walsh

**Human Resources**
Director, Human Resources .... Marie Sutera
Assistant, H.R./Office Coordinator .... Kyleen King/Jillian Smith

**Marketing and Business Development / Game Presentation**
Sr. Exec. Dir., Mktg. & Bus. Development .... Dave Knickerbocker
Executive Producer, Game Presentation .... Tom O'Grady
Manager, New Media and Advertising .... Patrick Dahl
Graphic Designer .... Chris Weibring

**New Media and Publications**
Director, New Media and Publications .... Adam Kempenaar
Coordinator, Publications .... John Sandberg
Assistant, New Media and Publications .... Brad Boron
Team Photographer .... Bill Smith
Web Contributor .... Harvey Wittenberg

**Ticketing**
Senior Executive Director .... Chris Werner
Executive Director .... James K. Bare
Director, Ticket Sales and Service .... Dan Rozenblat
Senior Manager, Customer Service .... Julie Lovins
Manager, Season Ticket Services .... Trisha Ithal
Manager, Group Sales .... Steve DiLenardi

# Colorado Avalanche

## 2008-09 Results: 32W-45L-1OTL-4SOL 69PTS.
## Fifth, Northwest Division

### Key Off-Season Signings/Acquisitions

**2009**

**June 3** • Named **Greg Sherman** general manager.
**4** • Named **Joe Sacco** head coach.
**19** • Named **Steve Konowalchuk** assistant coach and **Adam Deadmarsh** video/development coach.
**22** • Re-signed LW **Cody McLeod.**
**26** • Selected C **Matt Duchene** (Brampton, OHL) third overall in the 2009 Entry Draft.

**July 1** • Signed G **Craig Anderson** and LW **David Koci.**
**3** • Acquired D **Kyle Quincey**, D **Tom Preissing** and a 5th-round pick in 2010 from Los Angeles for LW **Ryan Smyth.**
**6** • Re-signed RW **David Jones.**
**10** • Re-signed D **Kyle Cumiskey.**

### 2009-10 Schedule

|  |  |  |  |
|---|---|---|---|
| **Oct.** | Thu. | 1 | San Jose |
| | Sat. | 3 | Vancouver* |
| | Thu. | 8 | at Nashville |
| | Sat. | 10 | at Chicago |
| | Mon. | 12 | at Boston* |
| | Tue. | 13 | at Toronto |
| | Thu. | 15 | at Montreal |
| | Sat. | 17 | at Detroit |
| | Wed. | 21 | at Minnesota |
| | Fri. | 23 | Carolina |
| | Sat. | 24 | Detroit |
| | Tue. | 27 | at Edmonton |
| | Wed. | 28 | at Calgary |
| | Fri. | 30 | at San Jose |
| **Nov.** | Sun. | 1 | at Vancouver |
| | Wed. | 4 | Phoenix |
| | Fri. | 6 | Chicago |
| | Sun. | 8 | Edmonton |
| | Wed. | 11 | at Chicago |
| | Sat. | 14 | Vancouver |
| | Tue. | 17 | at Calgary |
| | Wed. | 18 | at Edmonton |
| | Fri. | 20 | at Vancouver |
| | Mon. | 23 | Philadelphia |
| | Wed. | 25 | Nashville |
| | Fri. | 27 | at Minnesota* |
| | Sat. | 28 | Minnesota |
| | Mon. | 30 | at Tampa Bay |
| **Dec.** | Wed. | 2 | at Florida |
| | Thu. | 3 | at Pittsburgh |
| | Sat. | 5 | at Columbus |
| | Mon. | 7 | at St. Louis |
| | Wed. | 9 | Minnesota |
| | Fri. | 11 | Tampa Bay |
| | Sun. | 13 | Calgary |
| | Tue. | 15 | Washington |
| | Sat. | 19 | Columbus |
| | Mon. | 21 | at Minnesota |
| | Tue. | 22 | Anaheim |
| | Sat. | 26 | Dallas |
| | Wed. | 30 | at Ottawa |
| | Thu. | 31 | at Detroit |
| **Jan.** | Sat. | 2 | at Columbus |
| | Wed. | 6 | NY Islanders |
| | Fri. | 8 | at Carolina |
| | Sat. | 9 | at Buffalo |
| | Mon. | 11 | at Calgary |
| | Sat. | 16 | New Jersey* |
| | Mon. | 18 | Edmonton |
| | Fri. | 22 | Nashville |
| | Sun. | 24 | Dallas |
| | Thu. | 28 | Minnesota |
| | Fri. | 29 | at Dallas |
| | Sun. | 31 | NY Rangers |
| **Feb.** | Tue. | 2 | Columbus |
| | Thu. | 4 | at Nashville |
| | Sat. | 6 | Edmonton |
| | Mon. | 8 | St. Louis |
| | Wed. | 10 | Atlanta |
| | Fri. | 12 | Phoenix |
| | Sat. | 13 | at Los Angeles |
| **Mar.** | Mon. | 1 | Detroit |
| | Wed. | 3 | at Anaheim |
| | Thu. | 4 | at Phoenix |
| | Sat. | 6 | St. Louis |
| | Tue. | 9 | Vancouver |
| | Thu. | 11 | Florida |
| | Sun. | 14 | at Dallas* |
| | Tue. | 16 | at St. Louis |
| | Wed. | 17 | Calgary |
| | Sun. | 21 | at Anaheim* |
| | Mon. | 22 | at Los Angeles |
| | Wed. | 24 | Los Angeles |
| | Sat. | 27 | at Phoenix |
| | Sun. | 28 | at San Jose* |
| | Wed. | 31 | Anaheim |
| **Apr.** | Fri. | 2 | Calgary |
| | Sun. | 4 | San Jose |
| | Tue. | 6 | at Vancouver |
| | Wed. | 7 | at Edmonton |
| | Fri. | 9 | Chicago |
| | Sun. | 11 | Los Angeles* |

* Denotes afternoon game.

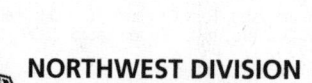

**NORTHWEST DIVISION**
**31st NHL Season**
**Franchise date:** June 22, 1979

Transferred from Quebec to Denver, June 21, 1995.

*Ryan Smyth (left) and Milan Hejduk each scored their 300th career goal in a 6-2 Colorado win over Calgary on January 18, 2009. Danny Gare and Ivan Boldirev are the only other teammates to both reach the milestone in the same game, doing it with the Detroit Red Wings back in 1983.*

### Year-by-Year Record

| | | Home | | | | Road | | | | Overall | | | | | | | | |
|---|---|---|---|---|---|---|---|---|---|---|---|---|---|---|---|---|---|---|
| **Season** | **GP** | **W** | **L** | **T** | **OL** | **W** | **L** | **T** | **OL** | **W** | **L** | **T** | **OL** | **GF** | **GA** | **Pts.** | **Finished** | **Playoff Result** |
| 2008-09 | 82 | 18 | 21 | .... | 2 | 14 | 24 | .... | 3 | 32 | 45 | .... | 5 | 199 | 257 | 69 | 5th, Northwest Div. | Out of Playoffs |
| 2007-08 | 82 | 27 | 12 | .... | 2 | 17 | 19 | .... | 5 | 44 | 31 | .... | 7 | 231 | 219 | 95 | 2nd, Northwest Div. | Lost Conf. Semi-Final |
| 2006-07 | 82 | 22 | 16 | .... | 3 | 22 | 15 | .... | 4 | 44 | 31 | .... | 7 | 272 | 251 | 95 | 4th, Northwest Div. | Out of Playoffs |
| 2005-06 | 82 | 25 | 10 | .... | 6 | 18 | 20 | .... | 3 | 43 | 30 | .... | 9 | 283 | 257 | 95 | 2nd, Northwest Div. | Lost Conf. Semi-Final |
| 2004-05 | .... | .... | .... | .... | .... | .... | .... | .... | .... | .... | .... | .... | .... | .... | .... | .... | | |
| 2003-04 | 82 | 19 | 14 | 6 | 2 | 21 | 8 | 7 | 5 | 40 | 22 | 13 | 7 | 236 | 198 | 100 | 2nd, Northwest Div. | Lost Conf. Semi-Final |
| 2002-03 | 82 | 21 | 9 | 8 | 3 | 21 | 10 | 5 | 5 | 42 | 19 | 13 | 8 | 251 | 194 | 105 | 1st, Northwest Div. | Lost Conf. Quarter-Final |
| 2001-02 | 82 | 24 | 12 | 4 | 1 | 21 | 16 | 4 | 0 | 45 | 28 | 8 | 1 | 212 | 169 | 99 | 1st, Northwest Div. | Lost Conf. Championship |
| **2000-01** | **82** | **28** | **6** | **5** | **2** | **24** | **10** | **5** | **2** | **52** | **16** | **10** | **4** | **270** | **192** | **118** | **1st, Northwest Div.** | **Won Stanley Cup** |
| 1999-2000 | 82 | 25 | 12 | 4 | 0 | 17 | 16 | 7 | 1 | 42 | 28 | 11 | 1 | 233 | 201 | 96 | 1st, Northwest Div. | Lost Conf. Championship |
| 1998-99 | 82 | 21 | 14 | 6 | .... | 23 | 14 | 4 | .... | 44 | 28 | 10 | .... | 239 | 205 | 98 | 1st, Northwest Div. | Lost Conf. Championship |
| 1997-98 | 82 | 21 | 10 | 10 | .... | 18 | 16 | 7 | .... | 39 | 26 | 17 | .... | 231 | 205 | 95 | 1st, Pacific Div. | Lost Conf. Quarter-Final |
| 1996-97 | 82 | 26 | 10 | 5 | .... | 23 | 14 | 4 | .... | 49 | 24 | 9 | .... | 277 | 205 | 107 | 1st, Pacific Div. | Lost Conf. Championship |
| **1995-96** | **82** | **24** | **10** | **7** | .... | **23** | **15** | **3** | .... | **47** | **25** | **10** | .... | **326** | **240** | **104** | **1st, Pacific Div.** | **Won Stanley Cup** |
| 1994-95* | 48 | 19 | 1 | 4 | .... | 11 | 12 | 1 | .... | 30 | 13 | 5 | .... | 185 | 134 | 65 | 1st, Northeast Div. | Lost Conf. Quarter-Final |
| 1993-94* | 84 | 19 | 17 | 6 | .... | 15 | 25 | 2 | .... | 34 | 42 | 8 | .... | 277 | 292 | 76 | 5th, Northeast Div. | Out of Playoffs |
| 1992-93* | 84 | 23 | 17 | 2 | .... | 24 | 10 | 8 | .... | 47 | 27 | 10 | .... | 351 | 300 | 104 | 2nd, Adams Div. | Lost Div. Semi-Final |
| 1991-92* | 80 | 18 | 19 | 3 | .... | 2 | 29 | 9 | .... | 20 | 48 | 12 | .... | 255 | 318 | 52 | 5th, Adams Div. | Out of Playoffs |
| 1990-91* | 80 | 9 | 23 | 8 | .... | 7 | 27 | 6 | .... | 16 | 50 | 14 | .... | 236 | 354 | 46 | 5th, Adams Div. | Out of Playoffs |
| 1989-90* | 80 | 8 | 26 | 6 | .... | 4 | 35 | 1 | .... | 12 | 61 | 7 | .... | 240 | 407 | 31 | 5th, Adams Div. | Out of Playoffs |
| 1988-89* | 80 | 16 | 20 | 4 | .... | 11 | 26 | 3 | .... | 27 | 46 | 7 | .... | 269 | 342 | 61 | 5th, Adams Div. | Out of Playoffs |
| 1987-88* | 80 | 15 | 23 | 2 | .... | 17 | 20 | 3 | .... | 32 | 43 | 5 | .... | 271 | 306 | 69 | 5th, Adams Div. | Out of Playoffs |
| 1986-87* | 80 | 20 | 13 | 7 | .... | 11 | 26 | 3 | .... | 31 | 39 | 10 | .... | 267 | 276 | 72 | 4th, Adams Div. | Lost Div. Final |
| 1985-86* | 80 | 23 | 13 | 4 | .... | 20 | 18 | 2 | .... | 43 | 31 | 6 | .... | 330 | 289 | 92 | 1st, Adams Div. | Lost Div. Semi-Final |
| 1984-85* | 80 | 24 | 12 | 4 | .... | 17 | 18 | 5 | .... | 41 | 30 | 9 | .... | 323 | 275 | 91 | 2nd, Adams Div. | Lost Conf. Championship |
| 1983-84* | 80 | 24 | 11 | 5 | .... | 18 | 17 | 5 | .... | 42 | 28 | 10 | .... | 360 | 278 | 94 | 3th, Adams Div. | Lost Div. Final |
| 1982-83* | 80 | 23 | 10 | 7 | .... | 11 | 24 | 5 | .... | 34 | 34 | 12 | .... | 343 | 336 | 80 | 4th, Adams Div. | Lost Div. Semi-Final |
| 1981-82* | 80 | 24 | 13 | 3 | .... | 9 | 18 | 13 | .... | 33 | 31 | 16 | .... | 356 | 345 | 82 | 4th, Adams Div. | Lost Conf. Championship |
| 1980-81* | 80 | 18 | 11 | 11 | .... | 12 | 21 | 7 | .... | 30 | 32 | 18 | .... | 314 | 318 | 78 | 4th, Adams Div. | Lost Prelim. Round |
| 1979-80* | 80 | 17 | 16 | 7 | .... | 8 | 28 | 4 | .... | 25 | 44 | 11 | .... | 248 | 313 | 61 | 5th, Adams Div. | Out of Playoffs |

* Quebec Nordiques

# 2009-10 Player Personnel

| FORWARDS | HT | WT | S | Place of Birth | *Age | 2008-09 Club |
|---|---|---|---|---|---|---|
| BURKI, Codey | 6-0 | 190 | L | Winnipeg, Man. | 21 | Johnstown-Lake Erie |
| DUCHENE, Matt | 5-11 | 200 | L | Haliburton, Ont. | 18 | Brampton |
| DUPUIS, Philippe | 6-0 | 196 | R | Laval, Que. | 24 | Colorado-Lake Erie |
| DURNO, Chris | 6-4 | 205 | L | Scarborough, Ont. | 28 | Colorado-Lake Erie |
| FRITSCHE, Tom | 5-11 | 183 | L | Parma, OH | 23 | Lake Erie |
| GALIARDI, T.J. | 6-2 | 190 | L | Calgary, Alta. | 21 | Colorado-Lake Erie |
| HAYDAR, Darren | 5-9 | 170 | R | Toronto, Ont. | 29 | Grand Rapids |
| HEJDUK, Milan | 6-0 | 190 | R | Usti nad Labem, Czech. | 33 | Colorado |
| HENDRICKS, Matt | 6-0 | 215 | L | Blaine, MN | 28 | Colorado-Lake Erie |
| HENSICK, T.J. | 5-10 | 185 | R | Lansing, MI | 23 | Colorado-Lake Erie |
| JONES, David | 6-2 | 210 | R | Guelph, Ont. | 25 | Colorado |
| KOCI, David | 6-6 | 238 | L | Prague, Czech. | 28 | Tampa Bay-St. Louis |
| LALONDE-McNICOLL, Cedric | 5-10 | 176 | L | Longueuil, Que. | 21 | Shawinigan |
| McLEOD, Cody | 6-2 | 210 | L | Binscarth, Man. | 25 | Colorado |
| MERCIER, Justin | 5-11 | 190 | L | Erie, PA | 22 | Miami U. |
| SERTICH, Marty | 5-9 | 165 | L | Roseville, MN | 26 | Lake Erie |
| STASTNY, Paul | 6-0 | 205 | L | Quebec City, Que. | 23 | Colorado |
| STEWART, Chris | 6-2 | 228 | R | Toronto, Ont. | 21 | Colorado-Lake Erie |
| STOA, Ryan | 6-3 | 200 | L | Bloomington, MN | 22 | U. of Minnesota |
| SVATOS, Marek | 5-10 | 185 | R | Kosice, Czech. | 27 | Colorado |
| TUCKER, Darcy | 5-10 | 178 | L | Castor, Alta. | 34 | Colorado |
| WILLSIE, Brian | 6-1 | 202 | R | Belmont, Ont. | 31 | Colorado-Lake Erie |
| WOLSKI, Wojtek | 6-3 | 210 | L | Zabrze, Poland | 23 | Colorado |
| YIP, Brandon | 6-1 | 180 | R | Vancouver, B.C. | 24 | Boston University |
| **DEFENSEMEN** | | | | | | |
| CLARK, Brett | 6-0 | 195 | L | Wapella, Sask. | 32 | Colorado |
| CUMISKEY, Kyle | 5-10 | 185 | L | Abbotsford, B.C. | 22 | Colorado-Lake Erie |
| FAHEY, Brian | 6-1 | 215 | R | Des Plaines, IL | 28 | Hartford |
| FOOTE, Adam | 6-2 | 220 | R | Toronto, Ont. | 38 | Colorado |
| GAUNCE, Cameron | 6-1 | 203 | L | Sudbury, Ont. | 19 | St. Michael's |
| HANNAN, Scott | 6-1 | 225 | L | Richmond, B.C. | 30 | Colorado |
| LILES, John-Michael | 5-10 | 185 | L | Indianapolis, IN | 28 | Colorado |
| MACIAS, Ray | 6-2 | 195 | R | Long Beach, CA | 23 | Col-Lake Erie-Johnstown |
| MONTGOMERY, Kevin | 6-1 | 185 | L | Rochester, NY | 21 | London-Lake Erie |
| O'NEILL, Wes | 6-4 | 215 | L | Windsor, Ont. | 23 | Col-Lake Erie-Johnstown |
| PELTIER, Derek | 5-11 | 190 | L | Plymouth, MN | 24 | Colorado-Lake Erie |
| PREISSING, Tom | 6-0 | 198 | R | Arlington Heights, IL | 30 | Los Angeles-Manchester |
| QUINCEY, Kyle | 6-2 | 207 | L | Kitchener, Ont. | 24 | Los Angeles |
| SALEI, Ruslan | 6-1 | 212 | L | Minsk, USSR | 34 | Colorado |
| SKINNER, Brett | 6-1 | 183 | L | Brandon, Man. | 26 | NYI-Bridgeport-Chi (AHL) |
| WILSON, Ryan | 6-1 | 207 | L | Windsor, Ont. | 22 | Quad City-Lake Erie |

| GOALTENDERS | HT | WT | C | Place of Birth | *Age | 2008-09 Club |
|---|---|---|---|---|---|---|
| ANDERSON, Craig | 6-2 | 180 | L | Park Ridge, IL | 28 | Florida |
| BUDAJ, Peter | 6-1 | 200 | L | Banska Bystrica, Czech. | 27 | Colorado |
| CANN, Trevor | 5-11 | 199 | L | Oakville, Ont. | 20 | Peterborough-London |
| WEIMAN, Tyler | 5-11 | 180 | L | Saskatoon, Sask. | 25 | Lake Erie |

* – Age at start of 2009-10 season

# 2008-09 Scoring

* – rookie

## Regular Season

| Pos | # | Player | Team | GP | G | A | Pts | TOI | +/- | PIM | PP | SH | GW | S | % |
|---|---|---|---|---|---|---|---|---|---|---|---|---|---|---|---|
| R | 23 | Milan Hejduk | COL | 82 | 27 | 32 | 59 | 19:55 | –19 | 16 | 10 | 1 | 2 | 211 | 12.8 |
| L | 94 | Ryan Smyth | COL | 77 | 26 | 33 | 59 | 20:17 | –15 | 62 | 10 | 1 | 3 | 257 | 10.1 |
| L | 8 | Wojtek Wolski | COL | 78 | 14 | 28 | 42 | 18:23 | –13 | 28 | 2 | 1 | 3 | 169 | 8.3 |
| D | 4 | John-Michael Liles | COL | 75 | 12 | 27 | 39 | 21:32 | –19 | 31 | 6 | 0 | 1 | 146 | 8.2 |
| C | 26 | Paul Stastny | COL | 45 | 11 | 25 | 36 | 21:14 | –9 | 22 | 7 | 0 | 2 | 118 | 9.3 |
| R | 40 | Marek Svatos | COL | 69 | 14 | 20 | 34 | 13:06 | –6 | 34 | 6 | 0 | 1 | 140 | 10.0 |
| C | 39 | Tyler Arnason | COL | 71 | 5 | 17 | 22 | 13:18 | –16 | 14 | 2 | 0 | 1 | 108 | 4.6 |
| C | 37 | T.J. Hensick | COL | 61 | 4 | 17 | 21 | 12:54 | –7 | 14 | 1 | 0 | 0 | 116 | 3.4 |
| D | 24 | Ruslan Salei | COL | 70 | 4 | 17 | 21 | 21:06 | –4 | 72 | 1 | 0 | 0 | 93 | 4.3 |
| L | 55 | Cody McLeod | COL | 79 | 15 | 5 | 20 | 11:34 | –11 | 162 | 0 | 0 | 3 | 118 | 12.7 |
| R | 42 * | Chris Stewart | COL | 53 | 11 | 8 | 19 | 12:19 | –18 | 54 | 1 | 1 | 1 | 98 | 11.2 |
| R | 14 | Ian Laperriere | COL | 74 | 7 | 12 | 19 | 13:50 | 0 | 163 | 0 | 0 | 0 | 61 | 11.5 |
| R | 16 | Darcy Tucker | COL | 63 | 8 | 8 | 16 | 14:06 | –13 | 67 | 2 | 0 | 1 | 94 | 8.5 |
| R | 54 | David Jones | COL | 40 | 8 | 5 | 13 | 12:43 | –8 | 8 | 1 | 0 | 1 | 47 | 17.0 |
| C | 28 | Ben Guite | COL | 50 | 5 | 7 | 12 | 12:43 | 2 | 30 | 0 | 0 | 1 | 63 | 7.9 |
| C | 19 | Joe Sakic | COL | 15 | 2 | 10 | 12 | 18:06 | –6 | 6 | 0 | 0 | 0 | 46 | 4.3 |
| D | 5 | Brett Clark | COL | 76 | 2 | 10 | 12 | 22:19 | –16 | 32 | 0 | 0 | 1 | 97 | 2.1 |
| R | 11 | Cody McCormick | COL | 55 | 1 | 11 | 12 | 9:36 | –5 | 92 | 0 | 0 | 0 | 66 | 1.5 |
| D | 22 | Scott Hannan | COL | 81 | 1 | 9 | 10 | 22:22 | –21 | 26 | 0 | 0 | 0 | 70 | 1.4 |
| D | 52 | Adam Foote | COL | 42 | 1 | 6 | 7 | 19:40 | –12 | 30 | 0 | 0 | 1 | 19 | 5.3 |
| L | 43 * | T.J. Galiardi | COL | 11 | 3 | 1 | 4 | 16:20 | –4 | 6 | 0 | 0 | 0 | 14 | 21.4 |
| D | 29 | Daniel Tjarnqvist | COL | 37 | 2 | 2 | 4 | 14:39 | 1 | 8 | 0 | 0 | 0 | 19 | 10.5 |
| R | 18 | Brian Willsie | COL | 42 | 1 | 3 | 4 | 11:47 | –6 | 14 | 0 | 0 | 0 | 59 | 1.7 |
| D | 47 * | Ray Macias | COL | 6 | 0 | 1 | 1 | 17:59 | 0 | 0 | 0 | 0 | 0 | 4 | 0.0 |
| D | 3 | Lawrence Nycholat | VAN | 14 | 0 | 1 | 1 | 9:41 | 3 | 6 | 0 | 0 | 0 | 8 | 0.0 |
| | | | COL | 5 | 0 | 0 | 0 | 10:32 | –2 | 0 | 0 | 0 | 0 | 1 | 0.0 |
| | | | Total | 19 | 0 | 1 | 1 | 9:54 | 1 | 6 | 0 | 0 | 0 | 9 | 0.0 |
| C | 45 | Chris Durno | COL | 2 | 0 | 0 | 0 | 6:01 | 0 | 0 | 0 | 0 | 0 | 3 | 0.0 |
| D | 62 * | Wes O'Neill | COL | 3 | 0 | 0 | 0 | 10:51 | –2 | 4 | 0 | 0 | 0 | 1 | 0.0 |
| L | 97 | Per Ledin | COL | 3 | 0 | 0 | 0 | 9:56 | –1 | 2 | 0 | 0 | 0 | 2 | 0.0 |
| C | 53 | Matt Hendricks | COL | 4 | 0 | 0 | 0 | 8:30 | 1 | 13 | 0 | 0 | 0 | 5 | 0.0 |
| D | 34 | Aaron MacKenzie | COL | 5 | 0 | 0 | 0 | 14:38 | 1 | 0 | 0 | 0 | 0 | 3 | 0.0 |
| D | 48 | Kyle Cumiskey | COL | 6 | 0 | 0 | 0 | 8:32 | –2 | 0 | 0 | 0 | 0 | 2 | 0.0 |
| C | 59 * | Philippe Dupuis | COL | 8 | 0 | 0 | 0 | 9:33 | –1 | 4 | 0 | 0 | 0 | 11 | 0.0 |
| D | 50 * | Derek Peltier | COL | 11 | 0 | 0 | 0 | 13:15 | –4 | 2 | 0 | 0 | 0 | 7 | 0.0 |
| D | 41 * | Michael Vernace | COL | 12 | 0 | 0 | 0 | 19:39 | –5 | 8 | 0 | 0 | 0 | 9 | 0.0 |

## Goaltending

| No. | Goaltender | GPI | Mins | Avg | W | L | OT | EN | SO | GA | SA | S% | G | A | PIM |
|---|---|---|---|---|---|---|---|---|---|---|---|---|---|---|---|
| 31 | Peter Budaj | 56 | 3232 | 2.86 | 20 | 29 | 5 | 5 | 2 | 154 | 1531 | .899 | 0 | 1 | 0 |
| 1 | Andrew Raycroft | 31 | 1722 | 3.14 | 12 | 16 | 0 | 4 | 0 | 90 | 836 | .892 | 0 | 0 | 2 |
| | **Totals** | **82** | **4990** | **3.04** | **32** | **45** | **5** | **9** | **2** | **253** | **2376** | **.894** | | | |

# Joe Sacco

## Head Coach

*Born: Medford, MA, February 4, 1969.*

Joe Sacco, former head coach of Colorado's American Hockey League affiliate, the Lake Erie Monsters, was named the 13th head coach in franchise history on June 4, 2009. Sacco moved into the Avalanche head coach position after four seasons with the organization serving both as assistant coach (Lowell 2005-06; Albany 2006-07) and head coach (Lake Erie 2007-08, 2008-09) with the club's American Hockey League affiliates.

Under Sacco's guidance, the Monsters finished with a 34-38-13 record (76 points) in 2008-09, posting eight more wins and 11 more points than they did in their inaugural season of 2007-08. Following the season, Sacco was tabbed as an assistant coach for Team USA at the 2009 Men's World Championship in Switzerland.

Sacco, a native of Medford, Massachusetts, played college hockey at Boston University where he appeared in 111 games over three seasons with the Terriers. He was a fourth-round draft pick (71st overall) by the Toronto Maple Leafs in the 1987 NHL Entry Draft and went on to play in 738 total games over a 13-year NHL career, which included stints with Toronto, Anaheim, the New York Islanders, Washington and Philadelphia. The right winger finished with 94 goals and 119 assists. Sacco also competed internationally with the United States at the 1992 Olympics in Albertville, France, where the team finished fourth. He would go on to play for Team USA in six World Championships, winning a bronze medal in 1996.

### Coaching Record

| | | | Regular Season | | | | Playoffs | | | |
|---|---|---|---|---|---|---|---|---|---|---|
| Season | Team | League | GC | W | L | O/T | GC | W | L | T |
| 2007-08 | Lake Erie | AHL | 80 | 26 | 41 | 13 | .... | .... | .... | .... |
| 2008-09 | Lake Erie | AHL | 80 | 34 | 38 | 8 | .... | .... | .... | .... |

## Coaching History

Jacques Demers, 1979-80; Maurice Filion and Michel Bergeron, 1980-81; Michel Bergeron, 1981-82 to 1986-87; Andre Savard and Ron Lapointe, 1987-88; Ron Lapointe and Jean Perron, 1988-89; Michel Bergeron, 1989-90; Dave Chambers, 1990-91; Dave Chambers and Pierre Page, 1991-92; Pierre Page, 1992-93, 1993-94; Marc Crawford, 1994-95 to 1997-98; Bob Hartley, 1998-99 to 2001-02; Bob Hartley and Tony Granato, 2002-03; Tony Granato, 2003-04; Joel Quenneville, 2004-05 to 2007-08; Tony Granato, 2008-09; Joe Sacco, 2009-10.

## Captains' History

Marc Tardif, 1979-80, 1980-81; Robbie Ftorek and Andre Dupont, 1981-82; Mario Marois, 1982-83 to 1984-85; Mario Marois and Peter Stastny, 1985-86; Peter Stastny, 1986-87 to 1989-90; Joe Sakic and Steven Finn, 1990-91; Mike Hough, 1991-92; Joe Sakic, 1992-93 to 2008-09.

# Club Records

## Team

(Figures in brackets for season records are games played; records for fewest points, wins, ties, losses, goals, goals against are for 70 or more games)

| | | |
|---|---|---|
| **Most Points** | 118 | 2000-01 (82) |
| **Most Wins** | 52 | 2000-01 (82) |
| **Most Ties** | 18 | 1980-81 (80) |
| **Most Losses** | 61 | 1989-90 (80) |
| **Most Goals** | 360 | 1983-84 (80) |
| **Most Goals Against** | 407 | 1989-90 (80) |
| **Fewest Points** | 31 | 1989-90 (80) |
| **Fewest Wins** | 12 | 1989-90 (80) |
| **Fewest Ties** | 5 | 1987-88 (80) |
| **Fewest Losses** | 16 | 2000-01 (82) |
| **Fewest Goals** | 212 | 2001-02 (82) |
| **Fewest Goals Against** | 169 | 2001-02 (82) |
| **Longest Winning Streak** | | |
| Overall | 12 | Jan. 10-Feb. 7/99 |
| Home | 10 | Nov. 26/83-Jan. 10/84, Mar. 6-Apr. 16/95 |
| Away | 7 | Jan. 10-Feb. 7/99 |
| **Longest Undefeated Streak** | | |
| Overall | 12 | Dec. 23/96-Jan. 20/97 (9 wins, 3 ties), Jan. 10-Feb. 7/99 (12 wins) |
| Home | 14 | Nov. 19/83-Jan. 21/84 (11 wins, 3 ties) |
| Away | 10 | Jan. 10-Mar. 3/99 (8 wins, 2 ties) |
| **Longest Losing Streak** | | |
| Overall | 14 | Oct. 21-Nov. 19/90 |
| Home | 8 | Oct. 21-Nov. 24/90 |
| Away | 18 | Jan. 18-Apr. 1/90 |
| **Longest Winless Streak** | | |
| Overall | 17 | Oct. 21-Nov. 25/90 (15 losses, 2 ties) |
| Home | 11 | Nov. 14-Dec. 26/89 (7 losses, 4 ties) |
| Away | 33 | Oct. 8/91-Feb. 27/92 (25 losses, 8 ties) |
| **Most Shutouts, Season** | 11 | 2001-02 (82) |
| **Most PIM, Season** | 2,104 | 1989-90 (80) |
| **Most Goals, Game** | 12 | Feb. 1/83 (Hfd. 3 at Que. 12), Oct. 20/84 (Que. 12 at Tor. 3), Dec. 5/95 (S.J. 2 at Col. 12) |

## Individual

| | | |
|---|---|---|
| **Most Seasons** | 20 | Joe Sakic |
| **Most Games** | 1,378 | Joe Sakic |
| **Most Goals, Career** | 625 | Joe Sakic |
| **Most Assists, Career** | 1,016 | Joe Sakic |
| **Most Points, Career** | 1,641 | Joe Sakic (625G, 1,016A) |
| **Most PIM, Career** | 1,562 | Dale Hunter |
| **Most Shutouts, Career** | 37 | Patrick Roy |
| **Longest Consecutive Games Streak** | 312 | Dale Hunter (Oct. 9/80-Mar. 13/84) |
| **Most Goals, Season** | 57 | Michel Goulet (1982-83) |
| **Most Assists, Season** | 93 | Peter Stastny (1981-82) |
| **Most Points, Season** | 139 | Peter Stastny (1981-82; 46G, 93A) |
| **Most PIM, Season** | 301 | Gord Donnelly (1987-88) |
| **Most Points, Defenseman, Season** | 82 | Steve Duchesne (1992-93; 20G, 62A) |
| **Most Points, Center, Season** | 139 | Peter Stastny (1981-82; 46G, 93A) |
| **Most Points, Right Wing, Season** | 103 | Jacques Richard (1980-81; 52G, 51A) |
| **Most Points, Left Wing, Season** | 121 | Michel Goulet (1983-84; 56G, 65A) |
| **Most Points, Rookie, Season** | 109 | Peter Stastny (1980-81; 39G, 70A) |
| **Most Shutouts, Season** | 9 | Patrick Roy (2001-02) |
| **Most Goals, Game** | 5 | Mats Sundin (Mar. 5/92), Mike Ricci (Feb. 17/94) |
| **Most Assists, Game** | 5 | Eight times |
| **Most Points, Game** | 8 | Peter Stastny (Feb. 22/81; 4G, 4A), Anton Stastny (Feb. 22/81; 3G, 5A) |

Records include Quebec Nordiques, 1979-80 through 1994-95.

## Retired Numbers

| | | |
|---|---|---|
| 3 | J.C. Tremblay* | 1972-1979 |
| 8 | Marc Tardif* | 1979-1983 |
| 16 | Michel Goulet* | 1979-1990 |
| 19 | Joe Sakic | 1988-2009 |
| 26 | Peter Stastny* | 1980-1990 |
| 33 | Patrick Roy | 1995-2003 |
| 77 | Raymond Bourque | 2000-2001 |

* Quebec Nordiques

# All-time Record vs. Other Clubs

## Regular Season

| | At Home | | | | | | | | On Road | | | | | | | | Total | | | | | | | |
|---|---|---|---|---|---|---|---|---|---|---|---|---|---|---|---|---|---|---|---|---|---|---|---|---|
| | GP | W | L | T | OL | GF | GA | PTS | GP | W | L | T | OL | GF | GA | PTS | GP | W | L | T | OL | GF | GA | PTS |
| Anaheim | 29 | 16 | 8 | 4 | 1 | 85 | 74 | 37 | 29 | 13 | 8 | 3 | 5 | 71 | 75 | 34 | 58 | 29 | 16 | 7 | 6 | 156 | 149 | 71 |
| Atlanta | 6 | 2 | 3 | 0 | 1 | 20 | 19 | 5 | 6 | 3 | 2 | 1 | 0 | 16 | 13 | 7 | 12 | 5 | 5 | 1 | 1 | 36 | 32 | 12 |
| Boston | 68 | 25 | 37 | 6 | 0 | 242 | 277 | 56 | 63 | 23 | 31 | 9 | 0 | 194 | 240 | 55 | 131 | 48 | 68 | 15 | 0 | 436 | 517 | 111 |
| Buffalo | 66 | 32 | 22 | 11 | 1 | 233 | 204 | 76 | 64 | 19 | 35 | 9 | 1 | 207 | 249 | 48 | 130 | 51 | 57 | 20 | 2 | 440 | 453 | 124 |
| Calgary | 62 | 29 | 21 | 11 | 1 | 223 | 195 | 70 | 62 | 22 | 31 | 9 | 0 | 178 | 217 | 53 | 124 | 51 | 52 | 20 | 1 | 401 | 412 | 123 |
| Carolina | 66 | 40 | 17 | 9 | 0 | 279 | 193 | 89 | 64 | 27 | 25 | 12 | 0 | 221 | 212 | 66 | 130 | 67 | 42 | 21 | 0 | 500 | 405 | 155 |
| Chicago | 47 | 25 | 14 | 6 | 2 | 182 | 147 | 58 | 49 | 20 | 26 | 3 | 0 | 152 | 166 | 43 | 96 | 45 | 40 | 9 | 2 | 334 | 313 | 101 |
| Columbus | 16 | 13 | 3 | 0 | 0 | 56 | 29 | 26 | 16 | 10 | 4 | 1 | 1 | 56 | 33 | 22 | 32 | 23 | 7 | 1 | 1 | 112 | 62 | 48 |
| Dallas | 49 | 26 | 12 | 7 | 4 | 172 | 126 | 63 | 49 | 17 | 25 | 5 | 2 | 137 | 165 | 41 | 98 | 43 | 37 | 12 | 6 | 309 | 291 | 104 |
| Detroit | 50 | 22 | 22 | 4 | 2 | 165 | 168 | 50 | 48 | 18 | 28 | 1 | 1 | 140 | 171 | 38 | 98 | 40 | 50 | 5 | 3 | 305 | 339 | 88 |
| Edmonton | 62 | 32 | 25 | 4 | 1 | 229 | 215 | 69 | 61 | 26 | 29 | 4 | 2 | 196 | 232 | 58 | 123 | 58 | 54 | 8 | 3 | 425 | 447 | 127 |
| Florida | 12 | 5 | 4 | 3 | 0 | 35 | 31 | 13 | 13 | 11 | 2 | 0 | 0 | 52 | 36 | 22 | 25 | 16 | 6 | 3 | 0 | 87 | 67 | 35 |
| Los Angeles | 50 | 26 | 21 | 3 | 0 | 204 | 169 | 55 | 51 | 18 | 27 | 5 | 1 | 171 | 201 | 42 | 101 | 44 | 48 | 8 | 1 | 375 | 370 | 97 |
| Minnesota | 26 | 17 | 7 | 2 | 0 | 77 | 60 | 36 | 25 | 11 | 7 | 1 | 6 | 72 | 66 | 29 | 51 | 28 | 14 | 3 | 6 | 149 | 126 | 65 |
| Montreal | 65 | 33 | 27 | 5 | 0 | 220 | 227 | 71 | 65 | 16 | 39 | 10 | 0 | 203 | 269 | 42 | 130 | 49 | 66 | 15 | 0 | 423 | 496 | 113 |
| Nashville | 20 | 11 | 6 | 2 | 1 | 54 | 42 | 25 | 20 | 9 | 6 | 3 | 2 | 61 | 56 | 23 | 40 | 20 | 12 | 5 | 3 | 115 | 98 | 48 |
| New Jersey | 36 | 18 | 14 | 4 | 0 | 126 | 102 | 40 | 38 | 14 | 20 | 4 | 0 | 125 | 154 | 32 | 74 | 32 | 34 | 8 | 0 | 251 | 256 | 72 |
| NY Islanders | 35 | 21 | 11 | 3 | 0 | 125 | 98 | 45 | 34 | 13 | 20 | 1 | 0 | 115 | 138 | 27 | 69 | 34 | 31 | 4 | 0 | 240 | 236 | 72 |
| NY Rangers | 36 | 20 | 13 | 3 | 0 | 147 | 133 | 43 | 36 | 12 | 20 | 4 | 0 | 102 | 141 | 28 | 72 | 32 | 33 | 7 | 0 | 249 | 274 | 71 |
| Ottawa | 17 | 13 | 3 | 1 | 0 | 75 | 49 | 27 | 19 | 8 | 8 | 3 | 0 | 66 | 54 | 19 | 36 | 21 | 11 | 4 | 0 | 141 | 103 | 46 |
| Philadelphia | 37 | 14 | 10 | 12 | 1 | 131 | 125 | 41 | 36 | 11 | 22 | 2 | 1 | 97 | 130 | 25 | 73 | 25 | 32 | 14 | 2 | 228 | 255 | 66 |
| Phoenix | 49 | 25 | 17 | 5 | 2 | 173 | 165 | 57 | 48 | 22 | 17 | 7 | 2 | 168 | 164 | 53 | 97 | 47 | 34 | 12 | 4 | 341 | 329 | 110 |
| Pittsburgh | 34 | 19 | 13 | 2 | 0 | 150 | 127 | 40 | 38 | 17 | 16 | 5 | 0 | 155 | 149 | 39 | 72 | 36 | 29 | 7 | 0 | 305 | 276 | 79 |
| St. Louis | 49 | 25 | 16 | 7 | 1 | 167 | 130 | 58 | 48 | 17 | 27 | 4 | 0 | 140 | 174 | 38 | 97 | 42 | 43 | 11 | 1 | 307 | 304 | 96 |
| San Jose | 31 | 17 | 9 | 4 | 1 | 106 | 66 | 39 | 32 | 18 | 12 | 1 | 1 | 108 | 89 | 38 | 63 | 35 | 21 | 5 | 2 | 214 | 155 | 77 |
| Tampa Bay | 15 | 10 | 3 | 2 | 0 | 58 | 33 | 22 | 14 | 5 | 8 | 1 | 0 | 37 | 40 | 11 | 29 | 15 | 11 | 3 | 0 | 95 | 73 | 33 |
| Toronto | 31 | 18 | 8 | 5 | 0 | 120 | 97 | 41 | 36 | 16 | 16 | 4 | 0 | 137 | 119 | 36 | 67 | 34 | 24 | 9 | 0 | 257 | 216 | 77 |
| Vancouver | 62 | 32 | 20 | 8 | 2 | 206 | 170 | 74 | 62 | 31 | 21 | 7 | 3 | 230 | 197 | 72 | 124 | 63 | 41 | 15 | 5 | 436 | 367 | 146 |
| Washington | 35 | 15 | 15 | 5 | 0 | 108 | 121 | 35 | 35 | 12 | 19 | 4 | 0 | 110 | 134 | 28 | 70 | 27 | 34 | 9 | 0 | 218 | 255 | 63 |
| **Totals** | **1161** | **601** | **401** | **138** | **21** | **4168** | **3592** | **1361** | **1161** | **459** | **551** | **123** | **28** | **3717** | **4084** | **1069** | **2322** | **1060** | **952** | **261** | **49** | **7885** | **7676** | **2430** |

## Playoffs

| | Series | W | L | GP | W | L | T | GF | GA | Last Mtg. | Rnd. | Result |
|---|---|---|---|---|---|---|---|---|---|---|---|---|
| Anaheim | 1 | 0 | 1 | 4 | 0 | 4 | 0 | 4 | 16 | 2006 | CSF | L 0-4 |
| Boston | 2 | 1 | 1 | 11 | 5 | 6 | 0 | 36 | 37 | 1983 | DSF | L 1-3 |
| Buffalo | 2 | 2 | 0 | 8 | 6 | 2 | 0 | 35 | 27 | 1985 | DSF | W 3-2 |
| Carolina | 2 | 1 | 1 | 9 | 4 | 5 | 0 | 34 | 35 | 1987 | DSF | W 4-2 |
| Chicago | 2 | 2 | 0 | 12 | 8 | 4 | 0 | 49 | 28 | 1997 | CQF | W 4-2 |
| Dallas | 4 | 2 | 2 | 24 | 14 | 10 | 0 | 66 | 62 | 2006 | CQF | W 4-1 |
| Detroit | 6 | 3 | 3 | 34 | 17 | 17 | 0 | 88 | 97 | 2008 | CSF | L 0-4 |
| Edmonton | 2 | 1 | 1 | 12 | 7 | 5 | 0 | 35 | 30 | 1998 | CQF | L 3-4 |
| Florida | 1 | 1 | 0 | 4 | 4 | 0 | 0 | 15 | 4 | 1996 | F | W 4-0 |
| Los Angeles | 2 | 2 | 0 | 14 | 8 | 6 | 0 | 33 | 23 | 2002 | CQF | W 4-3 |
| Minnesota | 2 | 1 | 1 | 13 | 7 | 6 | 0 | 34 | 28 | 2008 | CQF | W 4-2 |
| Montreal | 5 | 2 | 3 | 31 | 14 | 17 | 0 | 85 | 105 | 1993 | DSF | L 2-4 |
| New Jersey | 1 | 1 | 0 | 7 | 4 | 3 | 0 | 19 | 11 | 2001 | F | W 4-3 |
| NY Islanders | 1 | 0 | 1 | 4 | 0 | 4 | 0 | 9 | 18 | 1982 | CF | L 0-4 |
| NY Rangers | 1 | 0 | 1 | 6 | 2 | 4 | 0 | 19 | 25 | 1995 | CQF | L 2-4 |
| Philadelphia | 2 | 0 | 2 | 11 | 4 | 7 | 0 | 29 | 39 | 1985 | CF | L 2-4 |
| Phoenix | 1 | 1 | 0 | 5 | 4 | 1 | 0 | 17 | 10 | 2000 | CQF | W 4-1 |
| St. Louis | 1 | 1 | 0 | 5 | 4 | 1 | 0 | 17 | 11 | 2001 | CF | W 4-1 |
| San Jose | 3 | 2 | 1 | 19 | 10 | 9 | 0 | 51 | 52 | 2004 | CSF | L 2-4 |
| Vancouver | 2 | 2 | 0 | 10 | 8 | 2 | 0 | 40 | 26 | 2001 | CQF | W 4-0 |
| **Totals** | **43** | **25** | **18** | **243** | **130** | **113** | **0** | **715** | **684** | | | |

Calgary totals include Atlanta Flames, 1979-80.
Dallas totals include Minnesota North Stars, 1979-80 to 1992-93.
Phoenix totals include Winnipeg, 1979-80 to 1995-96.

## Playoff Results 2009-2004

| Year | Round | Opponent | Result | GF | GA |
|---|---|---|---|---|---|
| 2008 | CSF | Detroit | L 0-4 | 9 | 21 |
| | CQF | Minnesota | W 4-2 | 17 | 12 |
| 2006 | CSF | Anaheim | L 0-4 | 4 | 16 |
| | CQF | Dallas | W 4-1 | 18 | 15 |
| 2004 | CSF | San Jose | L 2-4 | 7 | 14 |
| | CQF | Dallas | W 4-1 | 19 | 10 |

**Abbreviations: Round: F** - Final; **CF** - conference final; **CSF** - conference semi-final; **CQF** - conference quarter-final; **DSF** - division semi-final.

Carolina totals include Hartford, 1979-80 to 1996-97.
New Jersey totals include Colorado Rockies, 1979-80 to 1981-82.

## 2008-09 Results

| | | | |
|---|---|---|---|
| **Oct.** | 9 | Boston | 4-5 |
| | 12 | at Edmonton | 2-3 |
| | 14 | at Calgary | 4-5 |
| | 16 | Philadelphia | 5-2 |
| | 18 | at Dallas | 5-4 |
| | 20 | at Los Angeles | 4-3 |
| | 23 | Edmonton | 4-1 |
| | 25 | Buffalo | 2-1† |
| | 28 | at Calgary | 0-3 |
| | 30 | Columbus | 2-4 |
| **Nov.** | 2 | San Jose | 3-5 |
| | 3 | at Chicago | 2-6 |
| | 6 | Minnesota | 1-3 |
| | 8 | Nashville | 1-0 |
| | 12 | at Vancouver | 2-1† |
| | 15 | at Edmonton | 3-2† |
| | 18 | at Calgary | 1-4 |
| | 20 | Calgary | 0-1 |
| | 22 | at Los Angeles | 4-3† |
| | 24 | at Anaheim | 1-4 |
| | 26 | St. Louis | 3-1 |
| | 28 | at Phoenix | 1-2 |
| | 29 | Tampa Bay | 4-3 |
| **Dec.** | 1 | at Minnesota | 6-5 |
| | 4 | at Nashville | 2-3 |
| | 5 | at Dallas | 1-2† |
| | 7 | Vancouver | 5-4† |
| | 9 | Los Angeles | 6-1 |
| | 12 | Chicago | 3-4 |
| | 15 | at Detroit | 3-2 |
| | 16 | at Philadelphia | 2-5 |
| | 18 | at Tampa Bay | 2-1† |
| | 21 | at Florida | 0-3 |
| | 23 | Phoenix | 5-4* |
| | 27 | Detroit | 4-3† |
| | 29 | Nashville | 5-1 |
| | 31 | at Phoenix | 1-3 |
| **Jan.** | 2 | Columbus | 1-6 |
| | 4 | Minnesota | 0-2 |
| | 6 | at Nashville | 2-1 |
| | 8 | Chicago | 2-1 |
| | 10 | Pittsburgh | 5-3 |
| | 13 | at Columbus | 3-4 |
| | 15 | at St. Louis | 2-5 |
| | 16 | Edmonton | 2-3 |
| | 18 | Calgary | 6-2 |
| | 21 | Los Angeles | 5-6 |
| | 27 | San Jose | 0-3 |
| | 29 | Toronto | 4-7 |
| | 31 | Anaheim | 3-4 |
| **Feb.** | 2 | Calgary | 4-3 |
| | 5 | Dallas | 3-2 |
| | 7 | at St. Louis | 1-4 |
| | 10 | at Columbus | 0-3 |
| | 11 | at Minnesota | 2-3 |
| | 13 | Montreal | 2-4 |
| | 15 | at Detroit | 6-5† |
| | 17 | Ottawa | 3-2* |
| | 20 | at Washington | 4-1 |
| | 22 | at Carolina | 2-5 |
| | 24 | at Atlanta | 3-4 |
| | 26 | at New Jersey | 0-4 |
| | 28 | at NY Rangers | 1-6 |
| **Mar.** | 2 | at NY Islanders | 2-4 |
| | 4 | Detroit | 2-3 |
| | 8 | at Chicago | 5-1 |
| | 10 | Atlanta | 0-3 |
| | 12 | Minnesota | 2-1† |
| | 14 | at Edmonton | 3-2* |
| | 15 | at Vancouver | 2-4 |
| | 17 | at Minnesota | 2-3† |
| | 19 | Edmonton | 1-8 |
| | 22 | at San Jose | 1-3 |
| | 25 | Anaheim | 2-7 |
| | 27 | Vancouver | 1-4 |
| | 29 | at Anaheim | 1-4 |
| **Apr.** | 1 | Phoenix | 0-3 |
| | 5 | at Vancouver | 4-1 |
| | 7 | at San Jose | 0-1† |
| | 9 | Dallas | 2-3† |
| | 11 | Vancouver | 0-1* |
| | 12 | St. Louis | 0-1 |

* – Overtime † – Shootout

# Entry Draft Selections 2009-1995

Name in bold denotes played in NHL.

**2009**
Pick
3 Matt Duchene
33 Ryan O'Reilly
49 Stefan Elliott
64 Tyson Barrie
124 Kieran Millan
154 Brandon Maxwell
184 Gus Young

**2008**
Pick
50 Cameron Gaunce
61 Peter Delmas
110 Kelsey Tessier
140 Mark Olver
167 Joel Chouinard
170 Jonas Holos
200 Nate Condon

**2007**
Pick
14 Kevin Shattenkirk
45 Colby Cohen
49 Trevor Cann
55 **T.J. Galiardi**
105 Brad Malone
113 Kent Patterson
135 Paul Carey
155 Jens Hellgren
195 Johan Alcen

**2006**
Pick
18 **Chris Stewart**
51 Nigel Williams
59 Codey Burki
81 Michael Carman
110 Kevin Montgomery
201 Billy Sauer

**2005**
Pick
34 Ryan Stoa
44 **Paul Stastny**
47 Tom Fritsche
52 Chris Durand
88 **T.J. Hensick**
124 **Ray Macias**
166 Jason Lynch
168 Justin Mercier
222 **Kyle Cumiskey**

**2004**
Pick
21 **Wojtek Wolski**
55 Victor Oreskovich
72 Denis Parshin
154 Richard Demen-Willaume
184 **Derek Peltier**
215 Ian Keserich
239 Brandon Yip
249 J.D. Corbin
281 Steve McClellan

**2003**
Pick
63 **David Liffiton**
131 David Svagrovsky
146 Mark McCutcheon
163 **Brad Richardson**
204 Linus Videll
225 Brett Hemingway
257 Darryl Yacboski
288 **David Jones**

**2002**
Pick
28 **Jonas Johansson**
61 **Johnny Boychuk**
94 Eric Lundberg
107 Mikko Kalteva
129 **Tom Gilbert**
164 **Tyler Weiman**
195 Taylor Christie
227 Ryan Steeves
258 Sergei Shemetov
289 Sean Collins

**2001**
Pick
63 **Peter Budaj**
97 **Danny Bois**
130 Colt King
143 Frantisek Skladany
144 **Cody McCormick**
149 Mikko Viitanen
165 Pierre-Luc Emond
184 Scott Horvath
196 **Charlie Stephens**
227 **Marek Svatos**

**2000**
Pick
14 **Vaclav Nedorost**
47 **Jared Aulin**
50 Sergei Soin
63 Agris Saviels
88 **Kurt Sauer**
92 Sergei Klyazmin
119 Brian Fahey
159 **John-Michael Liles**
189 Chris Bahen
221 Aaron Molnar
252 **Darryl Bootland**
266 Sean Kotary
285 Blake Ward

**1999**
Pick
25 **Mikhail Kuleshov**
45 **Martin Grenier**
93 **Branko Radivojevic**
112 Sanny Lindstrom
122 Kristian Kovac
142 Will Magnuson
152 **Jordan Krestanovich**
158 Anders Lovdahl
183 **Riku Hahl**
212 **Radim Vrbata**
240 **Jeff Finger**

**1998**
Pick
12 **Alex Tanguay**
17 **Martin Skoula**
19 **Robyn Regehr**
20 **Scott Parker**
28 **Ramzi Abid**
38 **Philippe Sauve**
53 **Steve Moore**
79 Evgeny Lazarev
141 K.C. Timmons
167 Alexander Ryazantsev

**1997**
Pick
26 Kevin Grimes
53 Graham Belak
55 **Rick Berry**
78 **Ville Nieminen**
87 **Brad Larsen**
133 Aaron Miskovich
161 **David Aebischer**
217 Doug Schmidt
243 Kyle Kidney
245 Stephen Lafleur

**1996**
Pick
25 **Peter Ratchuk**
51 **Yuri Babenko**
79 **Mark Parrish**
98 Ben Storey
107 Randy Petruk
134 Luke Curtin
146 **Brian Willsie**
160 Kai Fischer
167 **Dan Hinote**
176 **Samuel Pahlsson**
188 Roman Pylner
214 Matt Scorsune
240 Justin Clark

**1995**
Pick
25 **Marc Denis**
51 Nic Beaudoin
77 **John Tripp**
81 **Tomi Kallio**
129 **Brent Johnson**
155 John Cirjak
181 **Dan Smith**
207 Tomi Hirvonen
228 Chris George

# Club Directory

Pepsi Center

**Colorado Avalanche**
Pepsi Center
1000 Chopper Circle
Denver, CO 80204
Phone **303/405-1100**
FAX 303/893-0614
Press Box 303/575-1926
www.coloradoavalanche.com
**Capacity:** 18,007

**Executive**

| | |
|---|---|
| Owner & Governor | E. Stanley Kroenke |
| President & Alternate Governor | Pierre Lacroix |
| General Manager & Alternate Governor | Greg Sherman |
| Vice President of Hockey Op/Asst. G.M. | Craig Billington |
| Director of Player Personnel | Brad Smith |
| Director of Hockey Operations | Eric Lacroix |
| Executive Director of Hockey Administration | Charlotte Grahame |

**Coaching Staff**

| | |
|---|---|
| Head Coach | Joe Sacco |
| Assistant Coaches | Sylvain Lefebvre, Steve Konowalchuk |
| Video/Development Coach | Adam Deadmarsh |

**Training Staff**

| | |
|---|---|
| Head Athletic Trainer | Matthew Sokolowski |
| Assistant Athletic Trainer/Physical Therapist | Scott Woodward |
| Head Equipment Manager | Mark Miller |
| Assistant Equipment Managers | Kurt Harvey, Cliff Halstead |
| Inventory Manager | Wayne Flemming |
| Strength & Conditioning Coach | Paul Goldberg |
| Massage Therapist | Gregorio Pradera |

**Scouting Staff**

| | |
|---|---|
| Director of Amateur Scouting | Richard Pracey |
| Assistant Director of Amateur Scouting | Alan Hepple |
| Pro Scouts | Garth Joy, Terry Martin |
| Scouts | Anders Carlsson, Rick Lanz, Joni Lehto, Don Paarup, Guy Perron, Neil Shea |

**Communications/Team Services**

| | |
|---|---|
| Sr. V.P., Communications & Business Operations | Jean Martineau |
| Director of Media Services/Internet | Brendan McNicholas |
| Manager of Media Relations/Website | Craig Stancher |
| Team Services Coordinator | Erin DeGraff |

**Lake Erie Monsters (AHL affiliate)**

| | |
|---|---|
| G.M./Director of Player Development | David Oliver |
| Head Coach | David Quinn |
| Assistant Coach | Dan Laperriere |
| Head Athletic Trainer | Glenn Burke |
| Head Equipment Manager | Terry Geer |

**Team Information**

| | |
|---|---|
| Practice Facility | South Suburban Family Sports Center |
| Television Outlet | Altitude Sports & Entertainment Network |
| Radio | Altitude Radio Network (flagship: KCKK AM 1510) |

## General Managers' History

Maurice Filion, 1979-80 to 1987-88; Martin Madden, 1988-89; Martin Madden and Maurice Filion, 1989-90; Pierre Page, 1990-91 to 1993-94; Pierre Lacroix, 1994-95 to 2005-06; Francois Giguere, 2006-07 to 2008-09; Greg Sherman, 2009-10.

# Greg Sherman

## General Manager

*Born: Scranton, PA, March 30, 1970.*

Greg Sherman was named general manager of the Colorado Avalanche on June 3, 2009. At the time of his appointment, he had spent the last seven years as the team's assistant general manager and had been associated with the franchise for 13 years.

In his previous role, Sherman worked on contract negotiations, arbitration cases, salary cap management and matters concerning personnel at all levels of the organization. In addition, Sherman also served as a liaison between the Avalanche and its American Hockey League affiliate, the Lake Erie Monsters. He oversaw and coordinated all financial obligations of both clubs.

Born in Scranton, Pennsylvania and raised in Denver, Sherman has spent most of his life in Colorado. He attended the University of San Diego and received his Bachelor in Accountancy in May 1992.

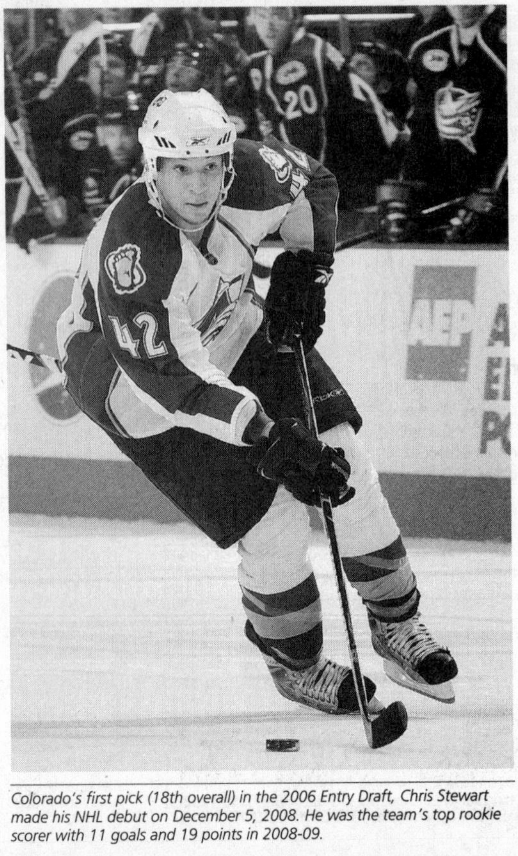

*Colorado's first pick (18th overall) in the 2006 Entry Draft, Chris Stewart made his NHL debut on December 5, 2008. He was the team's top rookie scorer with 11 goals and 19 points in 2008-09.*

# Columbus Blue Jackets

## Key Off-Season Signings/Acquisitions

**2009**

**July 1** • Signed C **Samuel Pahlsson** and G **Mathieu Garon.**
**3** • Re-signed LW **Rick Nash.**
**22** • Re-signed D **Marc Methot.**
**28** • Re-signed G **Dan LaCosta.**

## 2008-09 Results: 41W-31L-3OTL-7SOL 92PTS.
## Fourth, Central Division

### Year-by-Year Record

| | | Home | | | | Road | | | | Overall | | | | | | | | |
|---|---|---|---|---|---|---|---|---|---|---|---|---|---|---|---|---|---|---|
| **Season** | **GP** | **W** | **L** | **T** | **OL** | **W** | **L** | **T** | **OL** | **W** | **L** | **T** | **OL** | **GF** | **GA** | **Pts.** | **Finished** | **Playoff Result** |
| 2008-09 | 82 | 25 | 13 | .... | 3 | 16 | 18 | .... | 7 | 41 | 31 | .... | 10 | 226 | 230 | 92 | 4th, Central Div. | Lost Conf. Quarter-Final |
| 2007-08 | 82 | 20 | 14 | .... | 7 | 14 | 22 | .... | 5 | 34 | 36 | .... | 12 | 193 | 218 | 80 | 4th, Central Div. | Out of Playoffs |
| 2006-07 | 82 | 18 | 19 | .... | 4 | 15 | 23 | .... | 3 | 33 | 42 | .... | 7 | 201 | 249 | 73 | 4th, Central Div. | Out of Playoffs |
| 2005-06 | 82 | 23 | 18 | .... | 0 | 12 | 25 | .... | 4 | 35 | 43 | .... | 4 | 223 | 279 | 74 | 3rd, Central Div. | Out of Playoffs |
| 2004-05 | .... | .... | .... | .... | .... | .... | .... | .... | .... | .... | .... | .... | .... | .... | .... | .... | | |
| 2003-04 | 82 | 17 | 18 | 4 | 2 | 8 | 27 | 4 | 2 | 25 | 45 | 8 | 4 | 177 | 238 | 62 | 4th, Central Div. | Out of Playoffs |
| 2002-03 | 82 | 20 | 14 | 5 | 2 | 9 | 28 | 3 | 1 | 29 | 42 | 8 | 3 | 213 | 263 | 69 | 5th, Central Div. | Out of Playoffs |
| 2001-02 | 82 | 14 | 18 | 5 | 4 | 8 | 29 | 3 | 1 | 22 | 47 | 8 | 5 | 164 | 255 | 57 | 5th, Central Div. | Out of Playoffs |
| 2000-01 | 82 | 19 | 15 | 4 | 3 | 9 | 24 | 5 | 3 | 28 | 39 | 9 | 6 | 190 | 233 | 71 | 5th, Central Div. | Out of Playoffs |

## 2009-10 Schedule

| | | | | | | | |
|---|---|---|---|---|---|---|---|
| **Oct.** | Sat. | 3 | Minnesota | | Thu. | 31 | Nashville |
| | Mon. | 5 | at Vancouver | **Jan.** | Sat. | 2 | Colorado |
| | Thu. | 8 | at San Jose | | Tue. | 5 | at Vancouver |
| | Sat. | 10 | at Phoenix | | Thu. | 7 | at Edmonton |
| | Tue. | 13 | Calgary | | Fri. | 8 | at Calgary |
| | Sat. | 17 | Los Angeles | | Sun. | 10 | Dallas |
| | Tue. | 20 | at Calgary | | Tue. | 12 | at St. Louis |
| | Thu. | 22 | at Edmonton | | Thu. | 14 | at Chicago |
| | Sat. | 24 | at Anaheim | | Sat. | 16 | Chicago* |
| | Sun. | 25 | at Los Angeles | | Mon. | 18 | St. Louis |
| | Wed. | 28 | Phoenix | | Tue. | 19 | at Philadelphia |
| | Fri. | 30 | Pittsburgh | | Thu. | 21 | at Boston |
| **Nov.** | Sun. | 1 | at Washington* | | Sat. | 23 | at Minnesota |
| | Wed. | 4 | San Jose | | Tue. | 26 | Nashville |
| | Thu. | 5 | at Atlanta | | Thu. | 28 | Los Angeles |
| | Sat. | 7 | Carolina | | Sat. | 30 | at St. Louis |
| | Wed. | 11 | Detroit | **Feb.** | Tue. | 2 | at Colorado |
| | Fri. | 13 | Anaheim | | Thu. | 4 | Dallas |
| | Mon. | 16 | Edmonton | | Sat. | 6 | Buffalo |
| | Thu. | 19 | at Dallas | | Wed. | 10 | San Jose |
| | Sat. | 21 | at Nashville | | Fri. | 12 | Vancouver |
| | Mon. | 23 | at NY Rangers | | Sun. | 14 | Chicago* |
| | Tue. | 24 | at Montreal | **Mar.** | Tue. | 2 | Vancouver |
| | Thu. | 26 | at Ottawa | | Sat. | 6 | at San Jose |
| | Sat. | 28 | Calgary | | Mon. | 8 | at Los Angeles |
| | Mon. | 30 | St. Louis | | Tue. | 9 | at Anaheim |
| **Dec.** | Tue. | 1 | at Chicago | | Thu. | 11 | Atlanta |
| | Thu. | 3 | Toronto | | Sat. | 13 | St. Louis |
| | Sat. | 5 | Colorado | | Mon. | 15 | Edmonton |
| | Wed. | 9 | Florida | | Fri. | 19 | Minnesota |
| | Thu. | 10 | at Nashville | | Sat. | 20 | at Nashville |
| | Sat. | 12 | Anaheim | | Tue. | 23 | at New Jersey |
| | Mon. | 14 | Nashville | | Thu. | 25 | Chicago |
| | Tue. | 15 | at Minnesota | | Sat. | 27 | NY Islanders |
| | Thu. | 17 | Phoenix | | Sun. | 28 | at Chicago |
| | Sat. | 19 | at Colorado | | Tue. | 30 | Tampa Bay |
| | Mon. | 21 | at Phoenix | **Apr.** | Thu. | 1 | at Detroit |
| | Wed. | 23 | at Dallas | | Sat. | 3 | Washington |
| | Sat. | 26 | at Detroit | | Mon. | 5 | at St. Louis |
| | Mon. | 28 | Detroit | | Wed. | 7 | at Detroit |
| | Tue. | 29 | at NY Islanders | | Fri. | 9 | Detroit |

* Denotes afternoon game.

*Steve Mason began the 2008-09 season in the minors after knee surgery, but was recalled to Columbus on November 4, 2008. He went on to lead the NHL with 10 shutouts and win the Calder Trophy as rookie of the year.*

**CENTRAL DIVISION**
**10th NHL Season**

**Franchise date:** June 25, 1997

# 2009-10 Player Personnel

| FORWARDS | HT | WT | S | Place of Birth | *Age | 2008-09 Club |
|---|---|---|---|---|---|---|
| BLUNDEN, Michael | 6-4 | 207 | R | Toronto, Ont. | 22 | Rockford-Syracuse |
| BOLL, Jared | 6-2 | 210 | R | Charlotte, NC | 23 | Columbus |
| BRASSARD, Derick | 6-1 | 190 | L | Hull, Que. | 22 | Columbus |
| CHIMERA, Jason | 6-2 | 216 | L | Edmonton, Alta. | 30 | Columbus |
| DORSETT, Derek | 5-11 | 187 | R | Kindersley, Sask. | 22 | Columbus-Syracuse |
| FILATOV, Nikita | 6-0 | 172 | R | Moscow, USSR | 19 | Columbus-Syracuse |
| FRISCHMON, Trevor | 5-11 | 197 | L | Ham Lake, MN | 28 | Syracuse |
| HUSELIUS, Kristian | 6-1 | 179 | L | Osterhaninge, Sweden | 30 | Columbus |
| MacKENZIE, Derek | 5-11 | 185 | L | Sudbury, Ont. | 28 | Columbus-Syracuse |
| MODIN, Fredrik | 6-4 | 218 | L | Sundsvall, Sweden | 34 | Columbus |
| MURRAY, Andrew | 6-2 | 216 | L | Selkirk, Man. | 27 | Columbus |
| NASH, Rick | 6-4 | 218 | L | Brampton, Ont. | 25 | Columbus |
| PAHLSSON, Samuel | 6-0 | 204 | L | Ange, Sweden | 31 | Anaheim-Chicago |
| PELLETIER, Pascal | 5-11 | 197 | R | Labrador City, Nfld. | 26 | Chicago-Rockford |
| PICARD, Alexandre | 6-2 | 206 | L | Les Saules, Que. | 23 | Columbus-Syracuse |
| SESTITO, Tom | 6-5 | 226 | L | Utica, NY | 22 | Syracuse |
| TORRES, Raffi | 6-0 | 223 | L | Toronto, Ont. | 27 | Columbus |
| UMBERGER, R.J. | 6-2 | 215 | L | Pittsburgh, PA | 27 | Columbus |
| VERMETTE, Antoine | 6-1 | 197 | L | St-Agapit, Que. | 27 | Ottawa-Columbus |
| VORACEK, Jakub | 6-1 | 205 | L | Kladno, Czech. | 20 | Columbus |
| **DEFENSEMEN** | | | | | | |
| COMMODORE, Mike | 6-5 | 228 | R | Fort Saskatchewan, Alta. | 29 | Columbus |
| HEJDA, Jan | 6-3 | 218 | L | Prague, Czech. | 31 | Columbus |
| KLESLA, Rostislav | 6-3 | 220 | L | Novy Jicin, Czech. | 27 | Columbus |
| METHOT, Marc | 6-3 | 224 | L | Ottawa, Ont. | 24 | Columbus |
| ROY, Mathieu | 6-2 | 210 | R | St-Georges, Que. | 26 | Springfield |
| RUSSELL, Kris | 5-10 | 180 | L | Red Deer, Alta. | 22 | Columbus-Syracuse |
| SIGALET, Jonathan | 6-1 | 199 | L | Vancouver, B.C. | 23 | Syracuse |
| TYUTIN, Fedor | 6-3 | 216 | L | Izhevsk, USSR | 26 | Columbus |

| GOALTENDERS | HT | WT | C | Place of Birth | *Age | 2008-09 Club |
|---|---|---|---|---|---|---|
| GARON, Mathieu | 6-2 | 199 | R | Chandler, Que. | 31 | Edmonton-Pittsburgh |
| LaCOSTA, Dan | 6-2 | 194 | L | Labrador City, Nfld. | 23 | Columbus-Syracuse |
| LALANDE, Kevin | 6-0 | 175 | L | Kingston, Ont. | 22 | Quad City-Las Vegas-Syracuse |
| MASON, Steve | 6-4 | 212 | R | Oakville, Ont. | 21 | Columbus-Syracuse |

* – Age at start of 2009-10 season

# Ken Hitchcock

## Head Coach

*Born: Edmonton, Alta., December 17, 1951.*

Ken Hitchcock was named head coach of the Columbus Blue Jackets on November 22, 2006. In 2008-09 Columbus reached the playoffs for the first time in franchise history. In eight full seasons behind the bench before arriving in Columbus, Hitchcock led his teams to six division titles and guided the Dallas Stars to the Stanley Cup championship in 1999.

Hitchcock began his professional coaching career as an assistant coach with the Flyers from 1990 to 1993 before spending two-plus seasons as the head coach of the Kalamazoo Wings/Michigan K-Wings, International Hockey League affiliate of the Dallas Stars. He took over as head coach of the Stars midway through the 1995-96 season and in his first full season at the helm led them to the Central Division title. That year, Dallas became just the ninth team in NHL history to go from last place to first place in one season. Hitchcock holds Stars franchise records for career wins (277), playoff wins (47), regular-season winning percentage (.610) and playoff winning percentage (.588) and in 1998-99 led the club to franchise single season records for wins, points and highest winning percentage with a 51-19-12 record and 114 points.

On May 14, 2002, Hitchcock was named Flyers head coach and led the club to three-straight 100-point seasons, capturing the Atlantic Division title in 2003-04 and also advanced to the Eastern Conference Finals that year. The Edmonton, Alberta native has represented Canada at numerous international competitions, winning gold medals as an assistant/associate coach at the 2002 Salt Lake City Olympics, the 2004 World Cup of Hockey, the 2002 World Championship and the 1987 World Junior Championship. Prior to joining the professional ranks, Hitchcock was one of the winningest coaches in the history of the Western Hockey League with the Kamloops Blazers.

### Coaching Record

| | | | Regular Season | | | | Playoffs | | | |
|---|---|---|---|---|---|---|---|---|---|---|
| Season | Team | League | GC | W | L | O/T | GC | W | L | T |
| 1984-85 | Kamloops | WHL | 71 | 52 | 17 | 2 | 15 | 10 | 5 | .... |
| 1985-86 | Kamloops | WHL | 72 | 49 | 19 | 4 | 16 | 14 | 2 | .... |
| | Kamloops | M-Cup | .... | .... | .... | .... | 4 | 1 | 3 | .... |
| 1986-87 | Kamloops | WHL | 72 | 55 | 14 | 3 | 13 | 8 | 5 | .... |
| 1987-88 | Kamloops | WHL | 72 | 45 | 26 | 1 | 18 | 12 | 6 | .... |
| 1988-89 | Kamloops | WHL | 72 | 34 | 33 | 5 | 16 | 8 | 8 | .... |
| 1989-90 | Kamloops | WHL | 72 | 56 | 16 | 0 | 17 | 14 | 3 | .... |
| | Kamloops | M-Cup | .... | .... | .... | .... | 3 | 0 | 3 | .... |
| 1993-94 | Kalamazoo | IHL | 81 | 48 | 26 | 7 | 5 | 1 | 4 | .... |
| 1994-95 | Kalamazoo | IHL | 81 | 43 | 24 | 14 | 16 | 10 | 6 | .... |
| 1995-96 | Michigan | IHL | 40 | 19 | 10 | 11 | .... | .... | .... | .... |
| **1995-96** | **Dallas** | **NHL** | **43** | **15** | **23** | **5** | .... | .... | .... | .... |
| **1996-97** | **Dallas** | **NHL** | **82** | **48** | **26** | **8** | **7** | **3** | **4** | .... |
| **1997-98** | **Dallas** | **NHL** | **82** | **49** | **22** | **11** | **17** | **10** | **7** | .... |
| **1998-99♦** | **Dallas** | **NHL** | **82** | **51** | **19** | **12** | **23** | **16** | **7** | .... |
| **99-2000** | **Dallas** | **NHL** | **82** | **43** | **23** | **16** | **23** | **14** | **9** | .... |
| **2000-01** | **Dallas** | **NHL** | **82** | **48** | **24** | **10** | **10** | **4** | **6** | .... |
| **2001-02** | **Dallas** | **NHL** | **50** | **23** | **17** | **10** | .... | .... | .... | .... |
| **2002-03** | **Philadelphia** | **NHL** | **82** | **45** | **20** | **17** | **13** | **6** | **7** | .... |
| **2003-04** | **Philadelphia** | **NHL** | **82** | **40** | **21** | **21** | **18** | **11** | **7** | .... |
| **2004-05** | **Philadelphia** | | | | SEASON CANCELLED | | | | | |
| **2005-06** | **Philadelphia** | **NHL** | **82** | **45** | **26** | **11** | **6** | **2** | **4** | .... |
| **2006-07** | **Philadelphia** | **NHL** | **8** | **1** | **6** | **1** | .... | .... | .... | .... |
| | **Columbus** | **NHL** | **62** | **28** | **29** | **5** | .... | .... | .... | .... |
| **2007-08** | **Columbus** | **NHL** | **82** | **34** | **36** | **12** | .... | .... | .... | .... |
| **2008-09** | **Columbus** | **NHL** | **82** | **41** | **31** | **10** | **4** | **0** | **4** | .... |
| | **NHL Totals** | | **983** | **511** | **323** | **149** | **121** | **66** | **55** | .... |

♦ Stanley Cup win.

# 2008-09 Scoring

* – rookie

## Regular Season

| Pos | # | Player | Team | GP | G | A | Pts | TOI | +/– | PIM | PP | SH | GW | S | % |
|---|---|---|---|---|---|---|---|---|---|---|---|---|---|---|---|
| L | 61 | Rick Nash | CBJ | 78 | 40 | 39 | 79 | 21:09 | 11 | 52 | 6 | 5 | 5 | 263 | 15.2 |
| L | 20 | Kristian Huselius | CBJ | 74 | 21 | 35 | 56 | 19:31 | 1 | 44 | 5 | 0 | 2 | 212 | 9.9 |
| C | 29 | Jason Williams | ATL | 41 | 7 | 11 | 18 | 16:04 | –9 | 8 | 4 | 0 | 2 | 79 | 8.9 |
| | | | CBJ | 39 | 12 | 17 | 29 | 15:37 | 5 | 16 | 3 | 0 | 2 | 74 | 16.2 |
| | | | Total | 80 | 19 | 28 | 47 | 15:51 | –4 | 24 | 7 | 0 | 4 | 153 | 12.4 |
| C | 18 | R.J. Umberger | CBJ | 82 | 26 | 20 | 46 | 18:46 | –10 | 53 | 9 | 0 | 2 | 234 | 11.1 |
| C | 50 | Antoine Vermette | OTT | 62 | 9 | 19 | 28 | 18:03 | –12 | 42 | 2 | 0 | 0 | 141 | 6.4 |
| | | | CBJ | 17 | 7 | 6 | 13 | 19:29 | 5 | 8 | 1 | 1 | 1 | 33 | 21.2 |
| | | | Total | 79 | 16 | 25 | 41 | 18:21 | –7 | 50 | 3 | 1 | 1 | 174 | 9.2 |
| R | 93 | * Jakub Voracek | CBJ | 80 | 9 | 29 | 38 | 12:39 | 11 | 44 | 0 | 0 | 1 | 101 | 8.9 |
| C | 27 | Manny Malhotra | CBJ | 77 | 11 | 24 | 35 | 18:00 | 9 | 28 | 0 | 0 | 3 | 116 | 9.5 |
| D | 51 | Fedor Tyutin | CBJ | 82 | 9 | 25 | 34 | 23:30 | 1 | 81 | 5 | 1 | 0 | 167 | 5.4 |
| C | 16 | * Derick Brassard | CBJ | 31 | 10 | 15 | 25 | 14:25 | 12 | 17 | 3 | 0 | 1 | 59 | 16.9 |
| L | 33 | Fredrik Modin | CBJ | 50 | 9 | 16 | 25 | 16:52 | 2 | 28 | 2 | 0 | 0 | 113 | 8.0 |
| D | 22 | Mike Commodore | CBJ | 81 | 5 | 19 | 24 | 22:53 | 11 | 100 | 0 | 0 | 0 | 103 | 4.9 |
| L | 25 | Jason Chimera | CBJ | 49 | 8 | 14 | 22 | 16:14 | 8 | 41 | 1 | 0 | 1 | 115 | 7.0 |
| C | 19 | Michael Peca | CBJ | 71 | 4 | 18 | 22 | 14:06 | –6 | 58 | 0 | 0 | 2 | 74 | 5.4 |
| D | 8 | Jan Hejda | CBJ | 82 | 3 | 18 | 21 | 22:22 | 23 | 38 | 0 | 0 | 1 | 66 | 4.5 |
| D | 10 | Kris Russell | CBJ | 66 | 2 | 19 | 21 | 16:07 | –10 | 28 | 1 | 0 | 1 | 86 | 2.3 |
| L | 14 | Raffi Torres | CBJ | 51 | 12 | 8 | 20 | 12:05 | –4 | 23 | 2 | 0 | 6 | 74 | 16.2 |
| D | 3 | Marc Methot | CBJ | 66 | 4 | 13 | 17 | 17:57 | 7 | 55 | 0 | 0 | 0 | 58 | 6.9 |
| R | 40 | Jared Boll | CBJ | 75 | 4 | 10 | 14 | 8:53 | –6 | 180 | 1 | 0 | 0 | 73 | 5.5 |
| C | 17 | Andrew Murray | CBJ | 67 | 8 | 3 | 11 | 11:16 | –6 | 10 | 1 | 0 | 3 | 89 | 9.0 |
| D | 97 | Rostislav Klesla | CBJ | 34 | 1 | 8 | 9 | 20:58 | 2 | 38 | 0 | 0 | 0 | 30 | 3.3 |
| C | 12 | Jiri Novotny | CBJ | 42 | 4 | 3 | 7 | 13:20 | 4 | 14 | 0 | 1 | 0 | 56 | 7.1 |
| D | 5 | Christian Backman | CBJ | 56 | 2 | 5 | 7 | 15:39 | 5 | 32 | 1 | 0 | 1 | 54 | 3.7 |
| R | 15 | * Derek Dorsett | CBJ | 52 | 4 | 1 | 5 | 8:53 | –1 | 150 | 0 | 0 | 1 | 59 | 6.8 |
| C | 28 | * Nikita Filatov | CBJ | 8 | 4 | 0 | 4 | 8:07 | 3 | 0 | 0 | 0 | 1 | 10 | 40.0 |
| C | 77 | Chris Gratton | T.B. | 18 | 0 | 2 | 2 | 10:47 | –3 | 10 | 0 | 0 | 0 | 16 | 0.0 |
| | | | CBJ | 6 | 0 | 1 | 1 | 9:45 | 2 | 2 | 0 | 0 | 0 | 4 | 0.0 |
| | | | Total | 24 | 0 | 3 | 3 | 10:32 | –1 | 12 | 0 | 0 | 0 | 20 | 0.0 |
| C | 11 | Craig MacDonald | CBJ | 8 | 1 | 1 | 2 | 10:39 | 1 | 0 | 0 | 0 | 1 | 6 | 16.7 |
| D | 24 | * Aaron Rome | CBJ | 8 | 0 | 1 | 1 | 15:28 | 1 | 0 | 0 | 0 | 0 | 7 | 0.0 |
| L | 21 | Alexandre Picard | CBJ | 15 | 0 | 1 | 1 | 6:53 | –1 | 26 | 0 | 0 | 0 | 10 | 0.0 |
| D | 55 | Ole-Kristian Tollefsen | CBJ | 19 | 0 | 1 | 1 | 10:20 | –4 | 37 | 0 | 0 | 0 | 12 | 0.0 |
| L | 78 | Mike York | CBJ | 1 | 0 | 0 | 0 | 13:15 | 0 | 0 | 0 | 0 | 0 | 1 | 0.0 |
| C | 26 | Derek MacKenzie | CBJ | 1 | 0 | 0 | 0 | 7:15 | –1 | 2 | 0 | 0 | 0 | 1 | 0.0 |
| L | 43 | * Maksim Mayorov | CBJ | 3 | 0 | 0 | 0 | 5:44 | 0 | 0 | 0 | 0 | 0 | 1 | 0.0 |

### Goaltending

| No. | Goaltender | GPI | Mins | Avg | W | L | OT | EN | SO | GA | SA | S% | G | A | PIM |
|---|---|---|---|---|---|---|---|---|---|---|---|---|---|---|---|
| 30 | * Dan LaCosta | 3 | 156 | 1.54 | 2 | 0 | 0 | 0 | 1 | 4 | 80 | .950 | 0 | 0 | 0 |
| 1 | * Steve Mason | 61 | 3664 | 2.29 | 33 | 20 | 7 | 7 | 10 | 140 | 1658 | .916 | 0 | 0 | 2 |
| 30 | Fredrik Norrena | 8 | 323 | 3.16 | 1 | 3 | 2 | 0 | 0 | 17 | 133 | .872 | 0 | 0 | 0 |
| 34 | Wade Dubielewicz | 3 | 169 | 3.55 | 1 | 2 | 0 | 1 | 0 | 10 | 77 | .870 | 0 | 0 | 0 |
| 31 | Pascal Leclaire | 12 | 674 | 3.83 | 4 | 6 | 1 | 1 | 0 | 43 | 324 | .867 | 0 | 1 | 0 |
| | **Totals** | **82** | **5010** | **2.67** | **41** | **31** | **10** | **9** | **11** | **223** | **2281** | **.902** | | | |

## Playoffs

| Pos | # | Player | Team | GP | G | A | Pts | TOI | +/– | PIM | PP | SH | GW | OT | S | % |
|---|---|---|---|---|---|---|---|---|---|---|---|---|---|---|---|---|
| C | 18 | R.J. Umberger | CBJ | 4 | 3 | 0 | 3 | 16:21 | 0 | 0 | 2 | 0 | 0 | 0 | 9 | 33.3 |
| L | 61 | Rick Nash | CBJ | 4 | 1 | 2 | 3 | 20:51 | –4 | 2 | 0 | 0 | 0 | 0 | 13 | 7.7 |
| L | 20 | Kristian Huselius | CBJ | 4 | 1 | 1 | 2 | 17:52 | –4 | 4 | 1 | 0 | 0 | 0 | 11 | 9.1 |
| D | 10 | Kris Russell | CBJ | 4 | 1 | 1 | 2 | 16:40 | 0 | 2 | 0 | 0 | 0 | 0 | 5 | 20.0 |
| L | 14 | Raffi Torres | CBJ | 4 | 0 | 2 | 2 | 12:03 | –3 | 2 | 0 | 0 | 0 | 0 | 4 | 0.0 |
| L | 33 | Fredrik Modin | CBJ | 4 | 1 | 0 | 1 | 13:06 | –2 | 0 | 0 | 0 | 0 | 0 | 4 | 25.0 |
| D | 24 | * Aaron Rome | CBJ | 3 | 0 | 1 | 1 | 15:24 | 2 | 0 | 0 | 0 | 0 | 0 | 2 | 0.0 |
| L | 25 | Jason Chimera | CBJ | 4 | 0 | 1 | 1 | 13:21 | 0 | 2 | 0 | 0 | 0 | 0 | 11 | 0.0 |
| D | 97 | Rostislav Klesla | CBJ | 4 | 0 | 1 | 1 | 21:21 | 0 | 0 | 0 | 0 | 0 | 0 | 3 | 0.0 |
| C | 29 | Jason Williams | CBJ | 4 | 0 | 1 | 1 | 14:11 | –2 | 2 | 0 | 0 | 0 | 0 | 5 | 0.0 |
| R | 93 | * Jakub Voracek | CBJ | 4 | 0 | 1 | 1 | 12:06 | 0 | 8 | 0 | 0 | 0 | 0 | 12 | 0.0 |
| R | 40 | Jared Boll | CBJ | 1 | 0 | 0 | 0 | 5:17 | –2 | 0 | 0 | 0 | 0 | 0 | 1 | 0.0 |
| D | 8 | Jan Hejda | CBJ | 3 | 0 | 0 | 0 | 16:53 | –5 | 2 | 0 | 0 | 0 | 0 | 1 | 0.0 |
| R | 15 | * Derek Dorsett | CBJ | 3 | 0 | 0 | 0 | 9:11 | –1 | 2 | 0 | 0 | 0 | 0 | 7 | 0.0 |
| C | 19 | Michael Peca | CBJ | 4 | 0 | 0 | 0 | 12:39 | 1 | 2 | 0 | 0 | 0 | 0 | 4 | 0.0 |
| C | 27 | Manny Malhotra | CBJ | 4 | 0 | 0 | 0 | 17:53 | –2 | 0 | 0 | 0 | 0 | 0 | 4 | 0.0 |
| D | 22 | Mike Commodore | CBJ | 4 | 0 | 0 | 0 | 21:32 | –7 | 18 | 0 | 0 | 0 | 0 | 4 | 0.0 |
| C | 50 | Antoine Vermette | CBJ | 4 | 0 | 0 | 0 | 16:46 | –4 | 10 | 0 | 0 | 0 | 0 | 6 | 0.0 |
| D | 51 | Fedor Tyutin | CBJ | 4 | 0 | 0 | 0 | 23:15 | 0 | 0 | 0 | 0 | 0 | 0 | 3 | 0.0 |
| D | 3 | Marc Methot | CBJ | 4 | 0 | 0 | 0 | 16:15 | –3 | 2 | 0 | 0 | 0 | 0 | 1 | 0.0 |

### Goaltending

| No. | Goaltender | GPI | Mins | Avg | W | L | EN | SO | GA | SA | S% | G | A | PIM |
|---|---|---|---|---|---|---|---|---|---|---|---|---|---|---|
| 1 | * Steve Mason | 4 | 239 | 4.27 | 0 | 4 | 1 | 0 | 17 | 139 | .878 | 0 | 1 | 0 |
| | **Totals** | **4** | **240** | **4.50** | **0** | **4** | **1** | **0** | **18** | **140** | **.871** | | | |

## General Managers' History

Doug MacLean, 2000-01 to 2006-07; Scott Howson, 2007-08 to date.

## Coaching History

Dave King, 2000-01, 2001-02; Dave King and Doug MacLean, 2002-03; Doug MacLean and Gerard Gallant, 2003-04; Gerard Gallant, 2004-05, 2005-06; Gerard Gallant, Gary Agnew and Ken Hitchcock, 2006-07; Ken Hitchcock, 2007-08 to date.

# Club Records

## Team

(Figures in brackets for season records are games played.)

**Most Points** ................ **92** 2008-09 (82)
**Most Wins** ................. **41** 2008-09 (82)
**Most Ties** .................. **9** 2000-01 (82)
**Most Losses** ............... **47** 2001-02 (82)
**Most Goals** ............... **226** 2008-09 (82)
**Most Goals Against** ......... **279** 2005-06 (82)
**Fewest Points** .............. **57** 2001-02 (82)
**Fewest Wins** ............... **22** 2001-02 (82)
**Fewest Ties** ................ **8** 2001-02 (82), 2002-03 (82), 2003-04 (82)
**Fewest Losses** .............. **31** 2008-09 (82)
**Fewest Goals** ............. **164** 2001-02 (82)
**Fewest Goals Against** ....... **218** 2007-08 (82)
**Longest Winning Streak**
- **Overall** .................. **6** Mar. 24-Apr. 3/06
- **Home** .................... **6** Dec. 26/07-Jan. 15/08
- **Away** .................... **4** Dec. 2-12/06

**Longest Undefeated Streak**
- **Overall** .................. **6** Mar. 24-Apr. 3/06 (6 wins)
- **Home** .................... **6** Dec. 26/07-Jan. 15/08 (6 wins)
- **Away** .................... **4** Jan. 3-11/03 (3 wins, 1 tie), Dec. 2-12/06 (4 wins)

**Longest Losing Streak**
- **Overall** .................. **8** Nov. 17-Dec. 3/00, Mar. 3-18/04
- **Home** .................... **6** Oct. 12-Nov. 9/01
- **Away** .................... **9** Oct. 12-Nov. 20/05

**Longest Winless Streak**
- **Overall** .................. **9** Dec. 4-23/03 (8 losses, 1 tie)
- **Home** .................... **8** Oct. 4-Nov. 9/01 (6 losses, 2 ties), Dec. 4-31/03 (7 losses, 1 tie)
- **Away** ................... **14** Oct. 9-Dec. 23/03 (13 losses, 1 tie)

**Most Shutouts, Season** ....... **11** 2007-08 (82), 2008-09 (82)
**Most PIM, Season** ......... **1,505** 2002-03 (82)
**Most Goals, Game** ............ **8** Mar. 7/08 (CBJ 8 at Det. 2)

## Individual

**Most Seasons** ................ **8** Rostislav Klesla
**Most Games** ............... **543** David Vyborny
**Most Goals, Career** ......... **194** Rick Nash
**Most Assists, Career** ........ **204** David Vyborny
**Most Points, Career** ......... **355** Rick Nash (194G, 161A)
**Most PIM, Career** ......... **1,025** Jody Shelley
**Most Shutouts, Career** ........ **12** Marc Denis
**Longest Consecutive Games Streak** ............ **243** Jason Chimera (Oct. 9/05-Apr. 5/08)
**Most Goals, Season** .......... **41** Rick Nash (2003-04)
**Most Assists, Season** ......... **52** Ray Whitney (2002-03)
**Most Points, Season** ......... **79** Rick Nash (2008-09; 40G, 39A)
**Most PIM, Season** .......... **249** Jody Shelley (2002-03)
**Most Points, Defenseman, Season** .................. **45** Jaroslav Spacek (2002-03; 9G, 36A)
**Most Points, Center, Season** .................. **68** Andrew Cassels (2002-03; 20G, 48A)
**Most Points, Right Wing, Season** .................. **65** David Vyborny (2005-06; 22G, 43A)
**Most Points, Left Wing, Season** .................. **79** Rick Nash (2008-09; 40G, 39A)
**Most Points, Rookie, Season** .................. **39** Rick Nash (2002-03; 17G, 22A)
**Most Shutouts, Season** ....... **10** Steve Mason (2008-09)
**Most Goals, Game** ............ **4** Geoff Sanderson (Mar. 29/03)
**Most Assists, Game** ........... **5** Espen Knutsen (Mar. 24/01)
**Most Points, Game** ............ **5** Espen Knutsen (Mar. 24/01; 5A)
Geoff Sanderson (Mar. 29/03; 4G, 1A)
Andrew Cassels (Mar. 29/03; 1G, 4A)
David Vyborny (Feb. 28/04; 1G, 4A)

## Captains' History

Lyle Odelein, 2000-01, 2001-02; Ray Whitney, 2002-03; Luke Richardson, 2003-04; Luke Richardson and Adam Foote, 2005-06; Adam Foote, 2006-07; Adam Foote and Rick Nash, 2007-08; Rick Nash, 2008-09 to date.

## 2008-09 Results

| Month | Date | Opponent | Score |
|---|---|---|---|
| Oct. | 10 | at Dallas | 5-4* |
| | 11 | at Phoenix | 1-3 |
| | 14 | at San Jose | 2-5 |
| | 17 | Nashville | 5-3 |
| | 18 | at Nashville | 3-6 |
| | 21 | Vancouver | 4-2 |
| | 24 | NY Rangers | 1-3 |
| | 25 | at Minnesota | 1-2 |
| | 27 | Anaheim | 2-3 |
| | 30 | at Colorado | 4-2 |
| Nov. | 1 | Chicago | 3-4† |
| | 3 | at NY Islanders | 3-4* |
| | 5 | Edmonton | 5-4 |
| | 7 | Montreal | 4-3† |
| | 8 | Calgary | 3-1 |
| | 12 | Phoenix | 2-5 |
| | 14 | at Buffalo | 6-1 |
| | 15 | at Minnesota | 2-3† |
| | 18 | Edmonton | 2-7 |
| | 22 | at Atlanta | 2-0 |
| | 26 | Phoenix | 2-3 |
| | 28 | at Detroit | 3-5 |
| | 29 | Washington | 3-0 |
| Dec. | 1 | Vancouver | 3-2 |
| | 4 | at San Jose | 2-3 |
| | 6 | at Los Angeles | 0-3 |
| | 7 | at Anaheim | 3-5 |
| | 11 | Nashville | 2-1† |
| | 13 | NY Islanders | 3-1 |
| | 14 | at Chicago | 1-3 |
| | 17 | San Jose | 2-1* |
| | 18 | at Dallas | 5-6† |
| | 20 | at Phoenix | 0-2 |
| | 23 | Los Angeles | 0-3 |
| | 27 | Philadelphia | 3-0 |
| | 29 | at Los Angeles | 2-0 |
| | 31 | at Anaheim | 2-0 |
| Jan. | 2 | at Colorado | 6-1 |
| | 3 | at St. Louis | 2-5 |
| | 6 | at Detroit | 0-3 |
| | 9 | at Washington | 3-0 |
| | 10 | Minnesota | 4-2 |
| | 13 | Colorado | 4-3 |
| | 16 | New Jersey | 1-2 |
| | 18 | at Vancouver | 6-5† |
| | 20 | at Edmonton | 3-4 |
| | 21 | at Calgary | 4-5† |
| | 27 | Detroit | 3-2* |
| | 30 | Ottawa | 1-0 |
| | 31 | Dallas | 3-7 |
| Feb. | 3 | St. Louis | 2-4 |
| | 6 | at Pittsburgh | 1-4 |
| | 7 | San Jose | 3-2* |
| | 10 | Colorado | 3-0 |
| | 13 | Detroit | 3-2 |
| | 14 | at Carolina | 5-1 |
| | 16 | Dallas | 2-3† |
| | 18 | St. Louis | 4-3 |
| | 19 | at Toronto | 4-3† |
| | 21 | Anaheim | 2-5 |
| | 24 | at Calgary | 1-4 |
| | 26 | at Edmonton | 1-0 |
| Mar. | 1 | at Vancouver | 1-3 |
| | 3 | Los Angeles | 5-4 |
| | 5 | at Nashville | 2-4 |
| | 7 | at Detroit | 8-2 |
| | 10 | Boston | 2-0 |
| | 12 | Pittsburgh | 4-3† |
| | 13 | at Chicago | 5-3 |
| | 15 | Detroit | 0-4 |
| | 18 | Chicago | 4-3* |
| | 21 | at Florida | 3-1 |
| | 24 | at Tampa Bay | 1-2* |
| | 26 | Calgary | 5-0 |
| | 28 | at St. Louis | 3-4† |
| | 29 | St. Louis | 2-5 |
| | 31 | Nashville | 2-1 |
| Apr. | 4 | at Nashville | 4-5† |
| | 5 | Chicago | 0-1* |
| | 8 | at Chicago | 4-3† |
| | 10 | at St. Louis | 1-3 |
| | 11 | Minnesota | 3-6 |

* – Overtime † – Shootout

# All-time Record vs. Other Clubs

## Regular Season

| | At Home | | | | | | | | On Road | | | | | | | | Total | | | | | | | |
|---|---|---|---|---|---|---|---|---|---|---|---|---|---|---|---|---|---|---|---|---|---|---|---|---|
| | GP | W | L | T | OL | GF | GA | PTS | GP | W | L | T | OL | GF | GA | PTS | GP | W | L | T | OL | GF | GA | PTS |
| Anaheim | 16 | 8 | 7 | 0 | 1 | 43 | 40 | 17 | 16 | 6 | 7 | 1 | 2 | 38 | 46 | 15 | 32 | 14 | 14 | 1 | 3 | 81 | 86 | 32 |
| Atlanta | 5 | 3 | 2 | 0 | 0 | 14 | 11 | 6 | 5 | 2 | 3 | 0 | 0 | 10 | 10 | 4 | 10 | 5 | 5 | 0 | 0 | 24 | 21 | 10 |
| Boston | 5 | 3 | 2 | 0 | 0 | 10 | 18 | 6 | 3 | 1 | 2 | 0 | 0 | 7 | 10 | 2 | 8 | 4 | 4 | 0 | 0 | 17 | 28 | 8 |
| Buffalo | 3 | 2 | 0 | 1 | 0 | 8 | 6 | 5 | 6 | 4 | 2 | 0 | 0 | 18 | 14 | 8 | 9 | 6 | 2 | 1 | 0 | 26 | 20 | 13 |
| Calgary | 16 | 12 | 3 | 0 | 1 | 49 | 30 | 25 | 16 | 5 | 10 | 0 | 1 | 33 | 48 | 11 | 32 | 17 | 13 | 0 | 2 | 82 | 78 | 36 |
| Carolina | 4 | 2 | 2 | 0 | 0 | 10 | 10 | 4 | 6 | 2 | 4 | 0 | 0 | 17 | 16 | 4 | 10 | 4 | 6 | 0 | 0 | 27 | 26 | 8 |
| Chicago | 26 | 14 | 9 | 1 | 2 | 83 | 81 | 31 | 25 | 10 | 13 | 1 | 1 | 61 | 76 | 22 | 51 | 24 | 22 | 2 | 3 | 144 | 157 | 53 |
| Colorado | 16 | 5 | 10 | 1 | 0 | 33 | 56 | 11 | 16 | 3 | 12 | 0 | 1 | 29 | 56 | 7 | 32 | 8 | 22 | 1 | 1 | 62 | 112 | 18 |
| Dallas | 16 | 4 | 9 | 0 | 3 | 37 | 54 | 11 | 16 | 4 | 10 | 0 | 2 | 35 | 53 | 10 | 32 | 8 | 19 | 0 | 5 | 72 | 107 | 21 |
| Detroit | 26 | 8 | 12 | 1 | 5 | 55 | 83 | 22 | 25 | 6 | 17 | 0 | 2 | 60 | 92 | 14 | 51 | 14 | 29 | 1 | 7 | 115 | 175 | 36 |
| Edmonton | 16 | 4 | 8 | 3 | 1 | 38 | 56 | 12 | 16 | 4 | 10 | 0 | 2 | 34 | 53 | 10 | 32 | 8 | 18 | 3 | 3 | 72 | 109 | 22 |
| Florida | 3 | 1 | 2 | 0 | 0 | 6 | 9 | 2 | 5 | 3 | 2 | 0 | 0 | 15 | 14 | 6 | 8 | 4 | 4 | 0 | 0 | 21 | 23 | 8 |
| Los Angeles | 16 | 10 | 5 | 0 | 1 | 44 | 51 | 21 | 16 | 6 | 9 | 1 | 0 | 32 | 39 | 13 | 32 | 16 | 14 | 1 | 1 | 76 | 90 | 34 |
| Minnesota | 15 | 10 | 4 | 1 | 0 | 42 | 30 | 21 | 16 | 4 | 9 | 0 | 3 | 32 | 47 | 11 | 31 | 14 | 13 | 1 | 3 | 74 | 77 | 32 |
| Montreal | 3 | 1 | 2 | 0 | 0 | 7 | 9 | 2 | 5 | 3 | 1 | 1 | 0 | 9 | 6 | 7 | 8 | 4 | 3 | 1 | 0 | 16 | 15 | 9 |
| Nashville | 25 | 11 | 12 | 0 | 2 | 58 | 72 | 24 | 26 | 4 | 19 | 1 | 2 | 54 | 91 | 11 | 51 | 15 | 31 | 1 | 4 | 112 | 163 | 35 |
| New Jersey | 6 | 3 | 3 | 0 | 0 | 17 | 17 | 6 | 3 | 0 | 2 | 1 | 0 | 4 | 6 | 1 | 9 | 3 | 5 | 1 | 0 | 21 | 23 | 7 |
| NY Islanders | 6 | 5 | 0 | 1 | 0 | 20 | 11 | 11 | 4 | 2 | 1 | 0 | 1 | 14 | 15 | 5 | 10 | 7 | 1 | 1 | 1 | 34 | 26 | 16 |
| NY Rangers | 6 | 4 | 2 | 0 | 0 | 21 | 13 | 8 | 3 | 1 | 1 | 1 | 0 | 8 | 9 | 3 | 9 | 5 | 3 | 1 | 0 | 29 | 22 | 11 |
| Ottawa | 4 | 2 | 1 | 1 | 0 | 14 | 11 | 5 | 4 | 1 | 2 | 1 | 0 | 9 | 14 | 3 | 8 | 3 | 3 | 2 | 0 | 23 | 25 | 8 |
| Philadelphia | 5 | 1 | 2 | 2 | 0 | 10 | 10 | 4 | 3 | 0 | 2 | 1 | 0 | 5 | 10 | 1 | 8 | 1 | 4 | 3 | 0 | 15 | 20 | 5 |
| Phoenix | 16 | 7 | 8 | 1 | 0 | 40 | 39 | 15 | 16 | 4 | 8 | 3 | 1 | 36 | 48 | 12 | 32 | 11 | 16 | 4 | 1 | 76 | 87 | 27 |
| Pittsburgh | 5 | 3 | 0 | 0 | 2 | 20 | 13 | 8 | 5 | 1 | 4 | 0 | 0 | 13 | 21 | 2 | 10 | 4 | 4 | 0 | 2 | 33 | 34 | 10 |
| St. Louis | 25 | 12 | 8 | 2 | 3 | 66 | 66 | 29 | 26 | 6 | 15 | 1 | 4 | 61 | 95 | 17 | 51 | 18 | 23 | 3 | 7 | 127 | 161 | 46 |
| San Jose | 16 | 9 | 6 | 0 | 1 | 41 | 33 | 19 | 16 | 1 | 13 | 0 | 2 | 25 | 63 | 4 | 32 | 10 | 19 | 0 | 3 | 66 | 96 | 23 |
| Tampa Bay | 4 | 2 | 1 | 1 | 0 | 10 | 7 | 5 | 5 | 1 | 3 | 0 | 1 | 6 | 11 | 3 | 9 | 3 | 4 | 1 | 1 | 16 | 18 | 8 |
| Toronto | 2 | 1 | 1 | 0 | 0 | 6 | 7 | 2 | 5 | 1 | 3 | 1 | 0 | 9 | 16 | 3 | 7 | 2 | 4 | 1 | 0 | 15 | 23 | 5 |
| Vancouver | 16 | 7 | 6 | 2 | 1 | 41 | 52 | 17 | 16 | 5 | 10 | 0 | 1 | 43 | 61 | 11 | 32 | 12 | 16 | 2 | 2 | 84 | 113 | 28 |
| Washington | 6 | 2 | 2 | 0 | 2 | 17 | 19 | 6 | 4 | 1 | 2 | 1 | 0 | 10 | 11 | 3 | 10 | 3 | 4 | 1 | 2 | 27 | 30 | 9 |
| **Totals** | **328** | **156** | **129** | **18** | **25** | **860** | **914** | **355** | **328** | **91** | **196** | **15** | **26** | **727** | **1051** | **223** | **656** | **247** | **325** | **33** | **51** | **1587** | **1965** | **578** |

## Playoffs

| | Series | W | L | GP | W | L | T | GF | GA | Last Mtg. | Rnd. | Result |
|---|---|---|---|---|---|---|---|---|---|---|---|---|
| Detroit | 1 | 0 | 1 | 4 | 0 | 4 | 0 | 7 | 18 | 2009 | CQF | L 0-4 |
| **Totals** | **1** | **0** | **1** | **4** | **0** | **4** | **0** | **7** | **18** | | | |

## Playoff Results 2009-2004

| Year | Round | Opponent | Result | GF | GA |
|---|---|---|---|---|---|
| 2009 | CQF | Detroit | L 0-4 | 7 | 18 |

**Abbreviations: Round: CQF** – conference quarter-final.

# Entry Draft Selections 2009-2000

Name in bold denotes played in NHL.

**2009**

| Pick | |
|---|---|
| 21 | John Moore |
| 56 | Kevin Lynch |
| 94 | David Savard |
| 137 | Thomas Larkin |
| 167 | Anton Blomqvist |
| 197 | Kyle Neuber |

**2008**

| Pick | |
|---|---|
| 6 | **Nikita Filatov** |
| 37 | Cody Goloubef |
| 107 | Steven Delisle |
| 118 | Drew Olson |
| 127 | Matthew Calvert |
| 135 | Tomas Kubalik |
| 137 | Brent Regner |
| 157 | Cam Atkinson |
| 187 | Sean Collins |

**2007**

| Pick | |
|---|---|
| 7 | **Jakub Voracek** |
| 37 | Stefan Legein |
| 53 | Will Weber |
| 68 | Jake Hansen |
| 94 | **Maksim Mayorov** |
| 158 | Allen York |
| 211 | Trent Vogelhuber |

**2006**

| Pick | |
|---|---|
| 6 | **Derick Brassard** |
| 69 | **Steve Mason** |
| 85 | **Tom Sestito** |
| 113 | Ben Wright |
| 129 | Robert Nyholm |
| 136 | Nick Sucharski |
| 142 | Maxime Frechette |
| 159 | Jesse Dudas |
| 189 | **Derek Dorsett** |
| 194 | Matt Marquardt |

**2005**

| Pick | |
|---|---|
| 6 | **Gilbert Brule** |
| 55 | Adam McQuaid |
| 67 | **Kris Russell** |
| 101 | **Jared Boll** |
| 131 | **Tomas Popperle** |
| 177 | Derek Reinhart |
| 189 | Kirill Starkov |
| 201 | Trevor Hendrikx |

**2004**

| Pick | |
|---|---|
| 8 | **Alexandre Picard** |
| 46 | **Adam Pineault** |
| 59 | Kyle Wharton |
| 93 | **Dan LaCosta** |
| 96 | Andrey Plekhanov |
| 133 | Petr Pohl |
| 167 | Rob Page |
| 190 | Lennart Petrell |
| 198 | Justin Vienneau |
| 231 | Brian McGuirk |
| 233 | Matt Greer |
| 271 | Grant Clitsome |

**2003**

| Pick | |
|---|---|
| 4 | **Nikolai Zherdev** |
| 46 | **Dan Fritsche** |
| 71 | Dmitry Kosmachev |
| 103 | Kevin Jarman |
| 104 | **Philippe Dupuis** |
| 138 | Arsi Piispanen |
| 168 | **Marc Methot** |
| 200 | Alexander Guskov |
| 233 | Mathieu Gravel |
| 283 | Trevor Hendrikx |

**2002**

| Pick | |
|---|---|
| 1 | **Rick Nash** |
| 41 | **Joakim Lindstrom** |
| 65 | **Ole-Kristian Tollefsen** |
| 96 | Jeff Genovy |
| 98 | Ivan Tkachenko |
| 119 | Jekabs Redlihs |
| 133 | **Lasse Pirjeta** |
| 168 | Tim Konsorada |
| 184 | **Jaroslav Balastik** |
| 199 | **Greg Mauldin** |
| 225 | **Steven Goertzen** |
| 231 | Jaroslav Kracik |
| 263 | Sergei Mozyakin |

**2001**

| Pick | |
|---|---|
| 8 | **Pascal Leclaire** |
| 38 | **Tim Jackman** |
| 53 | Kiel McLeod |
| 85 | **Aaron Johnson** |
| 87 | Per Mars |
| 141 | **Cole Jarrett** |
| 173 | Justin Aikins |
| 187 | Artem Vostrikov |
| 204 | Raffaele Sannitz |
| 236 | Ryan Bowness |
| 242 | **Andrew Murray** |

**2000**

| Pick | |
|---|---|
| 4 | **Rostislav Klesla** |
| 69 | Ben Knopp |
| 133 | **Petteri Nummelin** |
| 138 | Scott Heffernan |
| 150 | Tyler Kolarik |
| 169 | Shane Bendera |
| 200 | Janne Jokila |
| 231 | Peter Zingoni |
| 278 | Martin Paroulek |
| 286 | **Andrej Nedorost** |
| 292 | Louis Mandeville |

# Scott Howson

## General Manager

*Born: Toronto, Ont., April 9, 1960.*

The Columbus Blue Jackets announced the signing of Scott Howson as the second general manager in franchise history on June 15, 2007. In 2008-09 he led the Blue Jackets to the playoffs for the first time in franchise history. Howson joined the Blue Jackets after spending seven years with the Edmonton Oilers. He joined the Oilers in June 2000 as assistant to the general manager and was named assistant general manager a year later. In that role, he was responsible for all aspects of the club's hockey administration, including player contracts, personnel decisions, the collective bargaining agreement, its American Hockey League affiliates and the salary cap.

During his six seasons with the Oilers, the club posted five-straight winning campaigns from 2000 to 2006, averaged 37 wins and 89 points per season, topped 90 points four times and advanced to the 2006 Stanley Cup Finals, where they were defeated in seven games by the Carolina Hurricanes.

Prior to his arrival in Edmonton, Howson spent six years with the club's AHL affiliates. As general manager of the Cape Breton Oilers from 1994 1o 1996, he oversaw the franchise's move to Hamilton in 1996 and was the Bulldogs' general manager from 1996 to 2000. During that time, he led Hamilton to a pair of berths in the Calder Cup Finals (1997, 2003) and a conference semifinals appearance in 2002.

Howson played three seasons in the Ontario Hockey League as a forward with the Kingston Canadiens from 1978 to 1981, serving as team captain and earning OHL All-Star honors. Following his junior career, he signed a free agent contract with the New York Islanders and spent the next five years playing at various levels throughout the organization.

During his rookie season in 1981-82, he was named the International Hockey League's rookie of the year after registering 55 goals and 65 assists for 120 points in 71 games with the Toledo Goaldiggers. He was the league's second-leading scorer that year and helped Toledo capture the league championship. Howson also won a Central Hockey League title with the Indianapolis Checkers in 1982-83. He made his NHL debut with the Islanders during the 1984-85 season and tallied 4 goals and one assist in eight games. He added a goal and two assists in 10 games the following season before retiring as a player at the end of the 1985-86 season. Howson received his bachelor's degree in 1987 from York University in Toronto and is a 1990 graduate of the university's Osgoode Hall Law School.

# Club Directory

Nationwide Arena

**Columbus Blue Jackets**
Nationwide Arena
200 W. Nationwide Blvd.
Columbus, Ohio 43215
Phone **614/246-4625**
FAX 614/246-4007
www.BlueJackets.com
**Capacity:** 18,144

**Ownership**

| | |
|---|---|
| Majority Owner/Governor | John P. McConnell |

**Executive Staff**

| | |
|---|---|
| President/Alternate Governor | Mike Priest |
| Sr. Vice President of Business Operations | Larry Hoepfner |
| Sr. Vice President General Counsel | Greg Kirstein |
| Vice President of Corporate Development | Cameron Scholvin |
| Vice President of Marketing | Marc Gregory |
| Vice President of Public Relations | Todd Sharrock |
| Chief Financial Officer | T.J. LaMendola |
| Vice President of Premium Seating Sales | Paul D'Aiuto |

**Hockey Operations**

| | |
|---|---|
| General Manager | Scott Howson |
| Assistant General Manager | Chris MacFarland |
| Director of Hockey Ops. & Player Personnel | Don Boyd |
| Director of Pro Scouting | Bob Strumm |
| Director of Amateur Scouting | Paul Castron |
| Assistant Director of Amateur Scouting | John Williams |
| Amateur Scouts | Sam McMaster, Brian Bates, Andrew Dickson |
| Pro Scout | Peter Dineen |
| Professional European Scout | Kjell Larsson |
| Regional Scouts | Rob Riley, Andrew Shaw, Artem Telepin, Milan Tichy |
| Video Scout | Bryan Stewart |
| Hockey Operations Coordinator | Julie Gamble |
| Assistant Video Scout | Scott Harris |
| Manager of Hockey Administration | Josh Flynn |

**Coaching Staff**

| | |
|---|---|
| Head Coach | Ken Hitchcock |
| Assistant Coaches | Gary Agnew, Gord Murphy, Claude Noel |
| Goaltending Coach | Dave Rook |
| Strength & Conditioning Coach | Barry Brennan |
| Development Coach | Tyler Wright |
| Video Coordinator | Dan Singleton |
| Performance Psychologist | Dr. Kimberley Amirault |

**Training & Equipment Staff**

| | |
|---|---|
| Head Athletic Trainer / Assistants | Mike Vogt / Mark Teeples, Chris Strickland |
| Equipment Manager / Assistant | Tim LeRoy / Jamie Healy |
| Equipment Assistant | Jason Stypinski |

**Business Operations**

| | |
|---|---|
| Director of Communications | Karen Davis |
| Director of Event Presentation/Production | Kimberly Kershaw |
| Director of Marketing & Fan Development | J.D. Kershaw |
| Director of Community Development | Wendy Bradshaw |
| Director of Creative Services | Jason Rothwell |
| Director of Human Resources | Kelley Walton |
| Senior Graphic Designer | Will Bennett |
| Graphic Designer | Sharon McMullen |
| Manager of Communications | Ryan Holtmann |
| Manager of Multimedia | Ryan Mulcrone |
| Managers, Partnership Marketing | Josh Hafer, Erin Gibbons, Becky Ackford |
| Premium Seating Relationship Manager | Rachel Mayfield |
| Corporate Sales Analyst | Craig Smith |
| Corp. Development Account Executives | Jerry Angel, A.J. Poole, Matt Tremblay |
| Premium Seating Manager | Amanda Horning |
| Managers of Production | David Bakalik, David Traube |
| Manager of Event Presentation | Lynn Truitt |
| Video Broadcast Engineer | Rick Shepherd |
| Graphics Coordinator | Andy Hookman |
| Payroll Manager | Christine Parthemore |
| Human Resources Assistant | Whitney Mitchell |
| Manager of Fan Development | Joel Siegman |
| Manager of Marketing | Nate Ferrall |
| Mgr. of Marketing, Youth & Amateur Hockey | Gordy Haggard |
| Partnership Activation Manager | Mike Kerrigan |
| Manager of Community Development | Kate Furman |
| Mascot Coordinator | Jason Zumpano |
| Administrative Assistant | April Lester |
| Legal Assistant | Rachel Phillips |
| Paralegal | Ken Erney |

**Finance**

| | |
|---|---|
| Controller | Jeremy Manly |
| Assistant Controller | Jason LaPlace |
| Staff Accountant | Nora Ludwig |
| Accounts Payable Coordinators | Beth Carpenter, Lindsay Rice |
| Director of Information Tech. | Jim Connolly |
| Manager of Information Tech. | John Gruber |
| Systems Analyst | Matthew DeStephen |
| Receptionist/Office Coordinator | Beth Carlisle |

**Ticket Operations**

| | |
|---|---|
| Director, Ticket Ops./Customer Service | Mark Morris |
| Director, Ticket Sales & Service | Joe Ondrejko |
| Manager, Season Ticket Sales & Service | Corey Rowe |
| Inside Sales Manager | Luke Burket |

**Broadcasting**

| | |
|---|---|
| Director of Broadcasting | Russ Mollohan |
| FS Ohio Play-by-Play / Color | Jeff Rimer/Bill Davidge |
| Radio Play-by-Play Announcer / Color | George Matthews/Bob McElligott |

# Dallas Stars

## 2008-09 Results: 36W-35L-5OTL-6SOL 83PTS.
### Third, Pacific Division

## Key Off-Season Signings/Acquisitions

**2009**

**May 31** • Named **Joe Nieuwendyk** general manager.
**June 11** • Named **Marc Crawford** head coach.
**30** • Re-signed RW **Jere Lehtinen.**
**July 2** • Signed D **Karlis Skrastins.**
**7** • Signed D **Jeff Woywitka.**
**8** • Acquired G **Alex Auld** from Ottawa for a 6th-round pick in 2010.
**8** • Re-signed D **Mark Fistric.**
**Aug. 4** • Named **Charlie Huddy** assistant coach.

*In his first full season in 2008-09, Loui Eriksson led the Stars (and ranked among the NHL leaders) with 36 goals. His 20.2 shooting percentage was second in the NHL behind Tampa Bay's Ryan Malone (21.0).*

## 2009-10 Schedule

|  |  |  |  |
|---|---|---|---|
| **Oct.** | Sat. | 3 | Nashville |
| | Tue. | 6 | at Edmonton |
| | Fri. | 9 | at Calgary |
| | Sun. | 11 | at Vancouver |
| | Wed. | 14 | Nashville |
| | Fri. | 16 | Boston |
| | Sat. | 17 | at Chicago |
| | Mon. | 19 | Los Angeles |
| | Wed. | 21 | at Anaheim |
| | Thu. | 22 | at Los Angeles |
| | Sat. | 24 | at St. Louis |
| | Wed. | 28 | Toronto |
| | Fri. | 30 | Florida |
| | Sat. | 31 | at Nashville |
| **Nov.** | Wed. | 4 | Calgary |
| | Fri. | 6 | Vancouver |
| | Sat. | 7 | at Minnesota |
| | Thu. | 12 | at San Jose |
| | Sat. | 14 | at Phoenix |
| | Wed. | 18 | at Detroit |
| | Thu. | 19 | Columbus |
| | Sat. | 21 | New Jersey |
| | Mon. | 23 | Carolina |
| | Wed. | 25 | St. Louis |
| | Fri. | 27 | at Phoenix |
| | Sat. | 28 | Tampa Bay |
| | Mon. | 30 | at Detroit |
| **Dec.** | Thu. | 3 | Anaheim |
| | Sat. | 5 | Edmonton* |
| | Tue. | 8 | at Anaheim |
| | Fri. | 11 | at San Jose |
| | Sat. | 12 | at Los Angeles |
| | Wed. | 16 | at Carolina |
| | Thu. | 17 | at Atlanta |
| | Sat. | 19 | Detroit* |
| | Mon. | 21 | San Jose |
| | Wed. | 23 | Columbus |
| | Sat. | 26 | at Colorado |
| | Tue. | 29 | Chicago |
| | Thu. | 31 | Anaheim |
| **Jan.** | Sat. | 2 | Vancouver* |
| | Tue. | 5 | at New Jersey |
| | Wed. | 6 | at NY Rangers |
| | Fri. | 8 | NY Islanders |
| | Sun. | 10 | at Columbus |
| | Tue. | 12 | at Philadelphia |
| | Thu. | 14 | at Montreal |
| | Sat. | 16 | Detroit* |
| | Mon. | 18 | Minnesota |
| | Thu. | 21 | at Vancouver |
| | Fri. | 22 | at Edmonton |
| | Sun. | 24 | at Colorado |
| | Wed. | 27 | Calgary |
| | Fri. | 29 | Colorado |
| | Sun. | 31 | Phoenix* |
| **Feb.** | Tue. | 2 | Minnesota |
| | Thu. | 4 | at Columbus |
| | Sat. | 6 | Phoenix* |
| | Tue. | 9 | at Chicago |
| | Thu. | 11 | at Calgary |
| | Sat. | 13 | at Phoenix |
| **Mar.** | Tue. | 2 | Los Angeles |
| | Thu. | 4 | St. Louis |
| | Sat. | 6 | at Pittsburgh* |
| | Mon. | 8 | at Washington |
| | Wed. | 10 | at Buffalo |
| | Fri. | 12 | Los Angeles |
| | Sun. | 14 | Colorado* |
| | Tue. | 16 | San Jose |
| | Thu. | 18 | Philadelphia |
| | Sat. | 20 | Ottawa* |
| | Sun. | 21 | Phoenix |
| | Tue. | 23 | at Nashville |
| | Thu. | 25 | at San Jose |
| | Sat. | 27 | at Los Angeles |
| | Mon. | 29 | at Anaheim |
| | Wed. | 31 | San Jose |
| **Apr.** | Fri. | 2 | Edmonton |
| | Sat. | 3 | at St. Louis |
| | Tue. | 6 | Chicago |
| | Thu. | 8 | Anaheim |
| | Sat. | 10 | at Minnesota |

* Denotes afternoon game.

## Year-by-Year Record

| | | Home | | | | Road | | | | Overall | | | | | | | | |
|---|---|---|---|---|---|---|---|---|---|---|---|---|---|---|---|---|---|---|
| **Season** | **GP** | **W** | **L** | **T** | **OL** | **W** | **L** | **T** | **OL** | **W** | **L** | **T** | **OL** | **GF** | **GA** | **Pts.** | **Finished** | **Playoff Result** |
| 2008-09 | 82 | 20 | 16 | .... | 5 | 16 | 19 | .... | 6 | 36 | 35 | .... | 11 | 230 | 257 | 83 | 3rd, Pacific Div. | Out of Playoffs |
| 2007-08 | 82 | 23 | 16 | .... | 2 | 22 | 14 | .... | 5 | 45 | 30 | .... | 7 | 242 | 207 | 97 | 3rd, Pacific Div. | Lost Conf. Championship |
| 2006-07 | 82 | 28 | 11 | .... | 2 | 22 | 14 | .... | 5 | 50 | 25 | .... | 7 | 226 | 197 | 107 | 3rd, Pacific Div. | Lost Conf. Quarter-Final |
| 2005-06 | 82 | 28 | 11 | .... | 2 | 25 | 12 | .... | 4 | 53 | 23 | .... | 6 | 265 | 218 | 112 | 1st, Pacific Div. | Lost Conf. Quarter-Final |
| 2004-05 | .... | .... | .... | .... | .... | .... | .... | .... | .... | .... | .... | .... | .... | .... | .... | .... | | |
| 2003-04 | 82 | 26 | 7 | 8 | 0 | 15 | 19 | 5 | 2 | 41 | 26 | 13 | 2 | 194 | 175 | 97 | 2nd, Pacific Div. | Lost Conf. Quarter-Final |
| 2002-03 | 82 | 28 | 5 | 6 | 2 | 18 | 12 | 9 | 2 | 46 | 17 | 15 | 4 | 245 | 169 | 111 | 1st, Pacific Div. | Lost Conf. Semi-Final |
| 2001-02 | 82 | 18 | 13 | 6 | 4 | 18 | 15 | 7 | 1 | 36 | 28 | 13 | 5 | 215 | 213 | 90 | 4th, Pacific Div. | Out of Playoffs |
| 2000-01 | 82 | 26 | 10 | 5 | 0 | 22 | 14 | 3 | 2 | 48 | 24 | 8 | 2 | 241 | 187 | 106 | 1st, Pacific Div. | Lost Conf. Semi-Final |
| 1999-2000 | 82 | 21 | 11 | 5 | 4 | 22 | 12 | 5 | 2 | 43 | 23 | 10 | 6 | 211 | 184 | 102 | 1st, Pacific Div. | Lost Final |
| **1998-99** | **82** | **29** | **8** | **4** | .... | **22** | **11** | **8** | .... | **51** | **19** | **12** | .... | **236** | **168** | **114** | **1st, Pacific Div.** | **Won Stanley Cup** |
| 1997-98 | 82 | 26 | 8 | 7 | .... | 23 | 14 | 4 | .... | 49 | 22 | 11 | .... | 242 | 167 | 109 | 1st, Central Div. | Lost Conf. Championship |
| 1996-97 | 82 | 25 | 13 | 3 | .... | 23 | 13 | 5 | .... | 48 | 26 | 8 | .... | 252 | 198 | 104 | 1st, Central Div. | Lost Conf. Quarter-Final |
| 1995-96 | 82 | 14 | 18 | 9 | .... | 12 | 24 | 5 | .... | 26 | 42 | 14 | .... | 227 | 280 | 66 | 6th, Central Div. | Out of Playoffs |
| 1994-95 | 48 | 9 | 10 | 5 | .... | 8 | 13 | 3 | .... | 17 | 23 | 8 | .... | 136 | 135 | 42 | 5th, Central Div. | Lost Conf. Quarter-Final |
| 1993-94 | 84 | 23 | 12 | 7 | .... | 19 | 17 | 6 | .... | 42 | 29 | 13 | .... | 286 | 265 | 97 | 3rd, Central Div. | Lost Conf. Semi-Final |
| 1992-93* | 84 | 18 | 17 | 7 | .... | 18 | 21 | 3 | .... | 36 | 38 | 10 | .... | 272 | 293 | 82 | 5th, Norris Div. | Out of Playoffs |
| 1991-92* | 80 | 20 | 16 | 4 | .... | 12 | 26 | 2 | .... | 32 | 42 | 6 | .... | 246 | 278 | 70 | 4th, Norris Div. | Lost Div. Semi-Final |
| 1990-91* | 80 | 19 | 15 | 6 | .... | 8 | 24 | 8 | .... | 27 | 39 | 14 | .... | 256 | 266 | 68 | 4th, Norris Div. | Lost Final |
| 1989-90* | 80 | 26 | 12 | 2 | .... | 10 | 28 | 2 | .... | 36 | 40 | 4 | .... | 284 | 291 | 76 | 4th, Norris Div. | Lost Div. Semi-Final |
| 1988-89* | 80 | 17 | 15 | 8 | .... | 10 | 22 | 8 | .... | 27 | 37 | 16 | .... | 258 | 278 | 70 | 3rd, Norris Div. | Lost Div. Semi-Final |
| 1987-88* | 80 | 10 | 24 | 6 | .... | 9 | 24 | 7 | .... | 19 | 48 | 13 | .... | 242 | 349 | 51 | 5th, Norris Div. | Out of Playoffs |
| 1986-87* | 80 | 17 | 20 | 3 | .... | 13 | 20 | 7 | .... | 30 | 40 | 10 | .... | 296 | 314 | 70 | 5th, Norris Div. | Out of Playoffs |
| 1985-86* | 80 | 21 | 15 | 4 | .... | 17 | 18 | 5 | .... | 38 | 33 | 9 | .... | 327 | 305 | 85 | 2nd, Norris Div. | Lost Div. Semi-Final |
| 1984-85* | 80 | 14 | 19 | 7 | .... | 11 | 24 | 5 | .... | 25 | 43 | 12 | .... | 268 | 321 | 62 | 4th, Norris Div. | Lost Div. Final |
| 1983-84* | 80 | 22 | 14 | 4 | .... | 17 | 17 | 6 | .... | 39 | 31 | 10 | .... | 345 | 344 | 88 | 1st, Norris Div. | Lost Conf. Championship |
| 1982-83* | 80 | 23 | 6 | 11 | .... | 17 | 18 | 5 | .... | 40 | 24 | 16 | .... | 321 | 290 | 96 | 2nd, Norris Div. | Lost Div. Final |
| 1981-82* | 80 | 21 | 7 | 12 | .... | 16 | 16 | 8 | .... | 37 | 23 | 20 | .... | 346 | 288 | 94 | 1st, Norris Div. | Lost Div. Semi-Final |
| 1980-81* | 80 | 23 | 10 | 7 | .... | 12 | 18 | 10 | .... | 35 | 28 | 17 | .... | 291 | 263 | 87 | 3rd, Adams Div. | Lost Final |
| 1979-80* | 80 | 25 | 8 | 7 | .... | 11 | 20 | 9 | .... | 36 | 28 | 16 | .... | 311 | 253 | 88 | 3rd, Adams Div. | Lost Semi-Final |
| 1978-79* | 80 | 19 | 15 | 6 | .... | 9 | 25 | 6 | .... | 28 | 40 | 12 | .... | 257 | 289 | 68 | 4th, Adams Div. | Out Of Playoffs |
| 1977-78* | 80 | 12 | 24 | 4 | .... | 6 | 29 | 5 | .... | 18 | 53 | 9 | .... | 218 | 325 | 45 | 5th, Smythe Div. | Out of Playoffs |
| 1976-77* | 80 | 17 | 14 | 9 | .... | 6 | 25 | 9 | .... | 23 | 39 | 18 | .... | 240 | 310 | 64 | 2nd, Smythe Div. | Lost Prelim. Round |
| 1975-76* | 80 | 15 | 22 | 3 | .... | 5 | 31 | 4 | .... | 20 | 53 | 7 | .... | 195 | 303 | 47 | 4th, Smythe Div. | Out of Playoffs |
| 1974-75* | 80 | 17 | 20 | 3 | .... | 6 | 30 | 4 | .... | 23 | 50 | 7 | .... | 221 | 341 | 53 | 4th, Smythe Div. | Out of Playoffs |
| 1973-74* | 78 | 18 | 15 | 6 | .... | 5 | 23 | 11 | .... | 23 | 38 | 17 | .... | 235 | 275 | 63 | 7th, West Div. | Out of Playoffs |
| 1972-73* | 78 | 26 | 8 | 5 | .... | 11 | 22 | 6 | .... | 37 | 30 | 11 | .... | 254 | 230 | 85 | 3rd, West Div. | Lost Quarter-Final |
| 1971-72* | 78 | 22 | 11 | 6 | .... | 15 | 18 | 6 | .... | 37 | 29 | 12 | .... | 212 | 191 | 86 | 2nd, West Div. | Lost Quarter-Final |
| 1970-71* | 78 | 16 | 15 | 8 | .... | 12 | 19 | 8 | .... | 28 | 34 | 16 | .... | 191 | 223 | 72 | 4th, West Div. | Lost Semi-Final |
| 1969-70* | 76 | 11 | 16 | 11 | .... | 8 | 19 | 11 | .... | 19 | 35 | 22 | .... | 224 | 257 | 60 | 3rd, West Div. | Lost Quarter-Final |
| 1968-69* | 76 | 11 | 21 | 6 | .... | 7 | 22 | 9 | .... | 18 | 43 | 15 | .... | 189 | 270 | 51 | 6th, West Div. | Out of Playoffs |
| 1967-68* | 74 | 17 | 12 | 8 | .... | 10 | 20 | 7 | .... | 27 | 32 | 15 | .... | 191 | 226 | 69 | 4th, West Div. | Lost Semi-Final |

* Minnesota North Stars

**PACIFIC DIVISION**
**43rd NHL Season**

**Franchise date:** June 5, 1967

Transferred from Minnesota to Dallas, June 9, 1993.

# 2009-10 Player Personnel

| FORWARDS | HT | WT | S | Place of Birth | *Age | 2008-09 Club |
|---|---|---|---|---|---|---|
| BARCH, Krys | 6-2 | 220 | L | Hamilton, Ont. | 29 | Dallas |
| BRUNNSTROM, Fabian | 6-2 | 203 | L | Jonstorp, Sweden | 24 | Dallas-Manitoba |
| ERIKSSON, Loui | 6-1 | 183 | L | Goteborg, Sweden | 24 | Dallas |
| LEHTINEN, Jere | 6-0 | 192 | R | Espoo, Finland | 36 | Dallas |
| MODANO, Mike | 6-3 | 210 | L | Livonia, MI | 39 | Dallas |
| MORROW, Brenden | 5-11 | 205 | L | Carlyle, Sask. | 30 | Dallas |
| NEAL, James | 6-3 | 206 | L | Whitby, Ont. | 22 | Dallas-Manitoba |
| OTT, Steve | 6-0 | 193 | L | Summerside, P.E.I. | 27 | Dallas |
| PETERS, Warren | 6-0 | 198 | L | Saskatoon, Sask. | 27 | Calgary-Quad City |
| PETERSEN, Toby | 5-10 | 197 | L | Minneapolis, MN | 30 | Dallas |
| RIBEIRO, Mike | 6-0 | 178 | L | Montreal, Que. | 29 | Dallas |
| RICHARDS, Brad | 6-0 | 192 | L | Murray Harbour, P.E.I. | 29 | Dallas |
| SAWADA, Raymond | 6-2 | 195 | R | Richmond, B.C. | 24 | Dallas-Manitoba |
| SUTHERBY, Brian | 6-3 | 209 | L | Edmonton, Alta. | 27 | Anaheim-Dallas |
| WANDELL, Tom | 6-1 | 183 | L | Sodertalje, Sweden | 22 | Timra-Dallas |
| **DEFENSEMEN** | | | | | | |
| DALEY, Trevor | 5-11 | 207 | L | Toronto, Ont. | 25 | Dallas |
| FISTRIC, Mark | 6-2 | 232 | L | Edmonton, Alta. | 23 | Dallas-Manitoba |
| GROSSMAN, Nicklas | 6-3 | 206 | L | Stockholm, Sweden | 24 | Dallas |
| HUTCHINSON, Andrew | 6-2 | 206 | R | Evanston, IL | 29 | Tampa Bay-Norfolk-Dallas |
| JANCEVSKI, Dan | 6-3 | 218 | L | Windsor, Ont. | 28 | Dallas-Hamilton |
| NISKANEN, Matt | 6-0 | 194 | R | Virginia, MN | 22 | Dallas |
| ROBIDAS, Stephane | 5-11 | 190 | R | Sherbrooke, Que. | 32 | Dallas |
| SKRASTINS, Karlis | 6-1 | 210 | L | Riga, Latvia | 35 | Florida |
| STAFFORD, Garrett | 6-0 | 200 | R | Los Angeles, CA | 29 | Dallas-Grand Rapids |
| VISHNEVSKIY, Ivan | 5-11 | 176 | L | Barnaul, USSR | 21 | Dallas-Peoria |
| WOYWITKA, Jeff | 6-2 | 217 | L | Vermilion, Alta. | 26 | St. Louis-Peoria |

| GOALTENDERS | HT | WT | C | Place of Birth | *Age | 2008-09 Club |
|---|---|---|---|---|---|---|
| AULD, Alex | 6-4 | 223 | L | Cold Lake, Alta. | 28 | Ottawa |
| TURCO, Marty | 5-11 | 185 | L | Sault Ste. Marie, Ont. | 34 | Dallas |

* – Age at start of 2009-10 season

# Marc Crawford

## Head Coach

*Born: Belleville, Ont., February 13, 1961.*

Dallas Stars general manager Joe Nieuwendyk announced on June 11, 2009 that the club had hired Marc Crawford as the 20th head coach in franchise history. At the time of his hiring, Crawford ranked as the 16th winningest coach in NHL history with 470 career victories, and had also coached the 15th most games in league history at 987, over 13 seasons with the Quebec Nordiques/Colorado Avalanche, Vancouver Canucks and Los Angeles Kings. He won the 1996 Stanley Cup championship with Colorado, as well as five division titles and had six seasons of 40-or-more wins. Crawford was the youngest recipient of the Jack Adams Trophy as NHL coach of the year, winning at age 34 with the Quebec Nordiques in 1995.

Crawford is the all-time winningest coach in Vancouver Canucks history with 246 wins over seven seasons from 1999 to 2006. The Canucks made the playoffs in four of his last five seasons as head coach. Crawford began his NHL coaching career with Quebec in 1994 and, after the Nordiques relocated to Denver in 1996, became the third-youngest coach in NHL history to win the Stanley Cup.

The native of Belleville, Ontario, served as the head coach for Team Canada at the 1998 Winter Olympic Games in Nagano, Japan, finishing first in its pool and advancing to the semifinals before losing to the eventual champions, Czech Republic. Crawford spent three seasons as the head coach of St. John's in the American Hockey League from 1991 to 1994, where he won the 1993 Louis A.R. Pieri Memorial Award as AHL coach of the year, and two campaigns with the Cornwall Royals of the Ontario Hockey League from 1989 to 1991.

Prior to beginning his coaching career, Crawford was selected in the fourth round (70th overall) of the 1980 Entry Draft by Vancouver, and skated in 176 career NHL games, all with the Canucks, recording 19 goals and 31 assists for 50 points. He made his NHL debut with Vancouver during the 1981-82 season, which he split between the Canucks and the Dallas Black Hawks of the Central Hockey League.

### Coaching Record

| | | | Regular Season | | | | Playoffs | | | |
|---|---|---|---|---|---|---|---|---|---|---|
| Season | Team | League | GC | W | L | O/T | GC | W | L | T |
| 1989-90 | Cornwall | OHL | 66 | 24 | 38 | 4 | 6 | 2 | 4 | .... |
| 1990-91 | Cornwall | OHL | 66 | 23 | 42 | 1 | .... | .... | .... | .... |
| 1991-92 | St. John's | AHL | 80 | 39 | 29 | 12 | 16 | 11 | 5 | .... |
| 1992-93 | St. John's | AHL | 80 | 41 | 26 | 13 | 9 | 4 | 5 | .... |
| 1993-94 | St. John's | AHL | 80 | 45 | 23 | 12 | 11 | 6 | 5 | .... |
| **1994-95** | **Quebec** | **NHL** | **48** | **30** | **13** | **5** | **6** | **2** | **4** | .... |
| **1995-96♦** | **Colorado** | **NHL** | **82** | **47** | **25** | **10** | **22** | **16** | **6** | .... |
| **1996-97** | **Colorado** | **NHL** | **82** | **49** | **24** | **9** | **17** | **10** | **7** | .... |
| **1997-98** | **Colorado** | **NHL** | **82** | **39** | **26** | **17** | **7** | **3** | **4** | .... |
| **1998-99** | **Vancouver** | **NHL** | **37** | **8** | **23** | **6** | .... | .... | .... | .... |
| **99-2000** | **Vancouver** | **NHL** | **82** | **30** | **29** | **23** | .... | .... | .... | .... |
| **2000-01** | **Vancouver** | **NHL** | **82** | **36** | **28** | **18** | .... | .... | .... | .... |
| **2001-02** | **Vancouver** | **NHL** | **82** | **42** | **30** | **10** | **6** | **2** | **4** | .... |
| **2002-03** | **Vancouver** | **NHL** | **82** | **45** | **23** | **14** | **14** | **7** | **7** | .... |
| **2003-04** | **Vancouver** | **NHL** | **82** | **43** | **24** | **15** | **7** | **3** | **4** | .... |
| **2004-05** | **Vancouver** | | | | SEASON CANCELLED | | | | | |
| **2005-06** | **Vancouver** | **NHL** | **82** | **42** | **32** | **8** | .... | .... | .... | .... |
| **2006-07** | **Los Angeles** | **NHL** | **82** | **27** | **41** | **14** | .... | .... | .... | .... |
| **2007-08** | **Los Angeles** | **NHL** | **82** | **32** | **43** | **7** | .... | .... | .... | .... |
| | **NHL Totals** | | **987** | **470** | **361** | **156** | **79** | **43** | **36** | .... |

♦ Stanley Cup win.

# 2008-09 Scoring

* – rookie

## Regular Season

| Pos | # | Player | Team | GP | G | A | Pts | TOI | +/– | PIM | PP | SH | GW | S | % |
|---|---|---|---|---|---|---|---|---|---|---|---|---|---|---|---|
| C | 63 | Mike Ribeiro | DAL | 82 | 22 | 56 | 78 | 20:57 | –4 | 52 | 7 | 0 | 1 | 163 | 13.5 |
| L | 21 | Loui Eriksson | DAL | 82 | 36 | 27 | 63 | 19:49 | 14 | 14 | 7 | 1 | 4 | 178 | 20.2 |
| C | 91 | Brad Richards | DAL | 56 | 16 | 32 | 48 | 20:28 | –4 | 6 | 5 | 0 | 2 | 180 | 8.9 |
| C | 29 | Steve Ott | DAL | 64 | 19 | 27 | 46 | 17:34 | 3 | 135 | 5 | 0 | 0 | 132 | 14.4 |
| C | 9 | Mike Modano | DAL | 80 | 15 | 31 | 46 | 18:18 | –13 | 46 | 4 | 0 | 4 | 197 | 7.6 |
| L | 18 | * James Neal | DAL | 77 | 24 | 13 | 37 | 15:52 | –11 | 51 | 9 | 0 | 2 | 171 | 14.0 |
| D | 5 | Matt Niskanen | DAL | 80 | 6 | 29 | 35 | 19:58 | –11 | 52 | 2 | 0 | 0 | 111 | 5.4 |
| C | 11 | Brendan Morrison | ANA | 62 | 10 | 12 | 22 | 13:51 | 0 | 16 | 1 | 0 | 2 | 82 | 12.2 |
| | | | DAL | 19 | 6 | 3 | 9 | 15:23 | 3 | 16 | 2 | 0 | 2 | 29 | 20.7 |
| | | | Total | 81 | 16 | 15 | 31 | 14:12 | 3 | 32 | 3 | 0 | 4 | 111 | 14.4 |
| L | 96 | * Fabian Brunnstrom | DAL | 55 | 17 | 12 | 29 | 11:37 | –8 | 8 | 4 | 0 | 5 | 81 | 21.0 |
| D | 3 | Stephane Robidas | DAL | 72 | 3 | 23 | 26 | 24:32 | 10 | 76 | 1 | 0 | 0 | 158 | 1.9 |
| D | 6 | Trevor Daley | DAL | 75 | 7 | 18 | 25 | 21:59 | 2 | 73 | 0 | 0 | 2 | 104 | 6.7 |
| R | 26 | Jere Lehtinen | DAL | 48 | 8 | 16 | 24 | 19:00 | 1 | 8 | 2 | 0 | 1 | 119 | 6.7 |
| C | 20 | Brian Sutherby | ANA | 17 | 3 | 3 | 6 | 7:11 | 6 | 19 | 0 | 0 | 0 | 17 | 17.6 |
| | | | DAL | 42 | 5 | 4 | 9 | 12:24 | –5 | 52 | 0 | 1 | 0 | 50 | 10.0 |
| | | | Total | 59 | 8 | 7 | 15 | 10:54 | 1 | 71 | 0 | 1 | 0 | 67 | 11.9 |
| L | 10 | Brenden Morrow | DAL | 18 | 5 | 10 | 15 | 21:21 | –4 | 49 | 2 | 0 | 0 | 52 | 9.6 |
| D | 55 | Darryl Sydor | PIT | 8 | 1 | 1 | 2 | 14:23 | 5 | 2 | 0 | 0 | 0 | 7 | 14.3 |
| | | | DAL | 65 | 2 | 11 | 13 | 18:41 | –2 | 16 | 0 | 0 | 0 | 66 | 3.0 |
| | | | Total | 73 | 3 | 12 | 15 | 18:13 | 3 | 18 | 0 | 0 | 0 | 73 | 4.1 |
| R | 37 | Mark Parrish | DAL | 44 | 8 | 5 | 13 | 11:16 | –3 | 18 | 4 | 0 | 3 | 46 | 17.4 |
| R | 25 | Chris Conner | DAL | 38 | 3 | 10 | 13 | 10:55 | –5 | 10 | 0 | 0 | 1 | 34 | 8.8 |
| L | 44 | Steve Begin | MTL | 42 | 6 | 4 | 10 | 10:51 | –5 | 27 | 0 | 0 | 1 | 65 | 9.2 |
| | | | DAL | 20 | 1 | 1 | 2 | 10:25 | –1 | 15 | 0 | 0 | 0 | 25 | 4.0 |
| | | | Total | 62 | 7 | 5 | 12 | 10:43 | –6 | 42 | 0 | 0 | 1 | 90 | 7.8 |
| D | 2 | Nicklas Grossman | DAL | 81 | 2 | 10 | 12 | 17:38 | –8 | 51 | 0 | 0 | 1 | 60 | 3.3 |
| C | 17 | Toby Petersen | DAL | 57 | 4 | 7 | 11 | 11:24 | 1 | 14 | 0 | 0 | 0 | 80 | 5.0 |
| R | 13 | Krys Barch | DAL | 72 | 4 | 5 | 9 | 6:27 | 1 | 133 | 0 | 0 | 1 | 27 | 14.8 |
| R | 22 | Landon Wilson | DAL | 27 | 2 | 6 | 8 | 9:13 | 5 | 21 | 0 | 0 | 0 | 34 | 5.9 |
| C | 39 | Joel Lundqvist | DAL | 43 | 1 | 5 | 6 | 10:48 | –9 | 20 | 0 | 0 | 1 | 32 | 3.1 |
| D | 27 | Andrew Hutchinson | T.B. | 2 | 0 | 0 | 0 | 14:43 | –5 | 0 | 0 | 0 | 0 | 2 | 0.0 |
| | | | DAL | 38 | 2 | 3 | 5 | 14:20 | –4 | 12 | 0 | 0 | 0 | 56 | 3.6 |
| | | | Total | 40 | 2 | 3 | 5 | 14:21 | –9 | 12 | 0 | 0 | 0 | 58 | 3.4 |
| D | 56 | Sergei Zubov | DAL | 10 | 0 | 4 | 4 | 24:17 | –4 | 0 | 0 | 0 | 0 | 15 | 0.0 |
| D | 28 | Mark Fistric | DAL | 36 | 0 | 4 | 4 | 15:56 | –1 | 42 | 0 | 0 | 0 | 35 | 0.0 |
| C | 23 | * Tom Wandell | DAL | 14 | 1 | 2 | 3 | 11:09 | –1 | 4 | 0 | 0 | 0 | 23 | 4.3 |
| D | 36 | Garrett Stafford | DAL | 3 | 0 | 2 | 2 | 18:00 | 0 | 0 | 0 | 0 | 0 | 5 | 0.0 |
| D | 59 | * Ivan Vishnevskiy | DAL | 3 | 0 | 2 | 2 | 19:33 | 1 | 2 | 0 | 0 | 0 | 9 | 0.0 |
| R | 12 | * Raymond Sawada | DAL | 5 | 1 | 0 | 1 | 8:41 | –1 | 0 | 0 | 0 | 0 | 2 | 50.0 |
| D | 4 | Dan Jancevski | DAL | 3 | 0 | 0 | 0 | 15:19 | 0 | 0 | 0 | 0 | 0 | 4 | 0.0 |

## Goaltending

| No. | Goaltender | GPI | Mins | Avg | W | L | OT | EN | SO | GA | SA | S% | G | A | PIM |
|---|---|---|---|---|---|---|---|---|---|---|---|---|---|---|---|
| 35 | Marty Turco | 74 | 4327 | 2.81 | 33 | 31 | 10 | 8 | 3 | 203 | 1993 | .898 | 0 | 5 | 18 |
| 33 | * Matt Climie | 3 | 185 | 2.92 | 2 | 1 | 0 | 0 | 0 | 9 | 85 | .894 | 0 | 0 | 0 |
| 31 | * Tobias Stephan | 10 | 438 | 3.70 | 1 | 3 | 1 | 1 | 0 | 27 | 208 | .870 | 0 | 1 | 0 |
| 41 | Brent Krahn | 1 | 20 | 9.00 | 0 | 0 | 0 | 0 | 0 | 3 | 9 | .667 | 0 | 0 | 0 |
| | **Totals** | **82** | **5005** | **3.01** | **36** | **35** | **11** | **9** | **3** | **251** | **2304** | **.891** | | | |

## Coaching History

Wren Blair, 1967-68; Wren Blair and John Muckler, 1968-69; Wren Blair and Charlie Burns, 1969-70; Jack Gordon, 1970-71 to 1972-73; Jack Gordon and Parker MacDonald, 1973-74; Jack Gordon and Charlie Burns, 1974-75; Ted Harris, 1975-76, 1976-77; Ted Harris, André Beaulieu and Lou Nanne, 1977-78; Harry Howell and Glen Sonmor, 1978-79; Glen Sonmor, 1979-80 to 1981-82; Glen Sonmor and Murray Oliver, 1982-83; Bill Mahoney, 1983-84, 1984-85; Lorne Henning, 1985-86; Lorne Henning and Glen Sonmor, 1986-87; Herb Brooks, 1987-88; Pierre Page, 1988-89, 1989-90; Bob Gainey, 1990-91 to 1994-95; Bob Gainey and Ken Hitchcock, 1995-96; Ken Hitchcock, 1996-97 to 2000-01; Ken Hitchcock and Rick Wilson, 2001-02; Dave Tippett, 2002-03 to 2008-09; Marc Crawford, 2009-10.

# Club Records

## Team

(Figures in brackets for season records are games played; records for fewest points, wins, ties, losses, goals, goals against are for 70 or more games)

**Most Points** ............... 114 1998-99 (82)
**Most Wins** ................. 53 2005-06 (82)
**Most Ties** ................. 22 1969-70 (76)
**Most Losses** ............... 53 1975-76 (80), 1977-78 (80)
**Most Goals** ................ 346 1981-82 (80)
**Most Goals Against** ......... 349 1987-88 (80)
**Fewest Points** .............. 45 1977-78 (80)
**Fewest Wins** ................ 18 1968-69 (76), 1977-78 (80)
**Fewest Ties** ................ 4 1989-90 (80)
**Fewest Losses** .............. 19 1998-99 (82)
**Fewest Goals** ............... 189 1968-69 (76)
**Fewest Goals Against** ....... 167 1997-98 (82)

**Longest Winning Streak**
**Overall** ................... 7 Mar. 16-28/80, Mar. 16-Apr. 2/97, Nov. 22-Dec. 5/97, Jan. 29-Feb. 11/08
**Home** ...................... 11 Nov. 4-Dec. 27/72
**Away** ...................... 7 Four times

**Longest Undefeated Streak**
**Overall** ................... 15 Dec. 6/98-Jan. 6/99 (12 wins, 3 ties)
**Home** ...................... 17 Jan. 23-Mar. 20/04 (13 wins, 4 ties)
**Away** ...................... 10 Jan. 12-Mar. 4/99 (8 wins, 2 ties), Dec. 27/02-Feb. 25/03 (7 wins, 3 ties)

**Longest Losing Streak**
**Overall** ................... 10 Feb. 1-20/76
**Home** ...................... 6 Jan. 17-Feb. 4/70, Feb. 21-Mar. 8/09
**Away** ...................... 8 Oct. 19-Nov. 13/75, Jan. 28-Mar. 3/88

**Longest Winless Streak**
**Overall** ................... 20 Jan. 15-Feb. 28/70 (15 losses, 5 ties)
**Home** ...................... 12 Jan. 17-Feb. 25/70 (8 losses, 4 ties)
**Away** ...................... 23 Oct. 25/74-Jan. 28/75 (19 losses, 4 ties)

**Most Shutouts, Season** ....... 11 2000-01 (82), 2002-03 (82)
**Most PIM, Season** ........... 2,313 1987-88 (80)
**Most Goals, Game** ............ 15 Nov. 11/81 (Wpg. 2 at Min. 15)

## Individual

**Most Seasons** ............... 20 Mike Modano
**Most Games** ................. 1,400 Mike Modano
**Most Goals, Career** ......... 543 Mike Modano
**Most Assists, Career** ........ 786 Mike Modano
**Most Points, Career** ......... 1,329 Mike Modano (543G, 786A)
**Most PIM, Career** ........... 1,883 Shane Churla
**Most Shutouts, Career** ....... 36 Marty Turco
**Longest Consecutive Games Streak** ............ 442 Danny Grant (Dec. 4/68-Apr. 7/74)
**Most Goals, Season** .......... 55 Dino Ciccarelli (1981-82), Brian Bellows (1989-90)
**Most Assists, Season** ......... 76 Neal Broten (1985-86)
**Most Points, Season** .......... 114 Bobby Smith (1981-82; 43G, 71A)
**Most PIM, Season** ............ 382 Basil McRae (1987-88)
**Most Points, Defenseman, Season** ............ 77 Craig Hartsburg (1981-82; 17G, 60A)
**Most Points, Center, Season** ............ 114 Bobby Smith (1981-82; 43G, 71A)
**Most Points, Right Wing, Season** ............ 106 Dino Ciccarelli (1981-82; 55G, 51A)
**Most Points, Left Wing, Season** ............ 99 Brian Bellows (1989-90; 55G, 44A)
**Most Points, Rookie, Season** ............ 98 Neal Broten (1981-82; 38G, 60A)
**Most Shutouts, Season** ........ 9 Ed Belfour (1997-98), Marty Turco (2003-04)
**Most Goals, Game** ............ 5 Tim Young (Jan. 15/79)
**Most Assists, Game** ........... 5 Murray Oliver (Oct. 24/71), Larry Murphy (Oct. 17/89), Brad Richards (Feb. 28/08)
**Most Points, Game** ............ 7 Bobby Smith (Nov. 11/81; 4G, 3A)

Records include Minnesota North Stars, 1967-68 through 1992-93.

## Retired Numbers

| | | |
|---|---|---|
| 7 | Neal Broten | 1980-1995, 1996-1997 |
| 8 | Bill Goldsworthy* | 1967-1976 |
| 19 | Bill Masterton* | 1967-1968 |

* Minnesota North Stars

# All-time Record vs. Other Clubs

## Regular Season

| | At Home | | | | | | | | On Road | | | | | | | | Total | | | | | | | |
|---|---|---|---|---|---|---|---|---|---|---|---|---|---|---|---|---|---|---|---|---|---|---|---|---|
| | GP | W | L | T | OL | GF | GA | PTS | GP | W | L | T | OL | GF | GA | PTS | GP | W | L | T | OL | GF | GA | PTS |
| Anaheim | 42 | 30 | 9 | 2 | 1 | 138 | 81 | 63 | 42 | 21 | 14 | 3 | 4 | 114 | 103 | 49 | 84 | 51 | 23 | 5 | 5 | 252 | 184 | 112 |
| Atlanta | 6 | 5 | 1 | 0 | 0 | 13 | 9 | 10 | 5 | 5 | 0 | 0 | 0 | 21 | 12 | 10 | 11 | 10 | 1 | 0 | 0 | 34 | 21 | 20 |
| Boston | 62 | 19 | 30 | 13 | 0 | 179 | 221 | 51 | 62 | 10 | 42 | 10 | 0 | 149 | 264 | 30 | 124 | 29 | 72 | 23 | 0 | 328 | 485 | 81 |
| Buffalo | 56 | 27 | 22 | 6 | 1 | 178 | 163 | 61 | 53 | 13 | 29 | 11 | 0 | 142 | 192 | 37 | 109 | 40 | 51 | 17 | 1 | 320 | 355 | 98 |
| Calgary | 70 | 35 | 22 | 11 | 2 | 249 | 212 | 83 | 70 | 19 | 35 | 14 | 2 | 170 | 224 | 54 | 140 | 54 | 57 | 25 | 4 | 419 | 436 | 137 |
| Carolina | 31 | 19 | 10 | 2 | 0 | 123 | 92 | 40 | 33 | 15 | 14 | 4 | 0 | 114 | 106 | 34 | 64 | 34 | 24 | 6 | 0 | 237 | 198 | 74 |
| Chicago | 120 | 57 | 46 | 16 | 1 | 412 | 367 | 131 | 118 | 34 | 68 | 15 | 1 | 311 | 435 | 84 | 238 | 91 | 114 | 31 | 2 | 723 | 802 | 215 |
| Colorado | 49 | 27 | 15 | 5 | 2 | 165 | 137 | 61 | 49 | 16 | 25 | 7 | 1 | 126 | 172 | 40 | 98 | 43 | 40 | 12 | 3 | 291 | 309 | 101 |
| Columbus | 16 | 12 | 2 | 0 | 2 | 53 | 35 | 26 | 16 | 12 | 2 | 0 | 2 | 54 | 37 | 26 | 32 | 24 | 4 | 0 | 4 | 107 | 72 | 52 |
| Detroit | 114 | 55 | 40 | 18 | 1 | 386 | 339 | 129 | 114 | 40 | 58 | 16 | 0 | 358 | 434 | 96 | 228 | 95 | 98 | 34 | 1 | 744 | 773 | 225 |
| Edmonton | 53 | 30 | 16 | 7 | 0 | 191 | 146 | 67 | 52 | 21 | 22 | 8 | 1 | 170 | 199 | 51 | 105 | 51 | 38 | 15 | 1 | 361 | 345 | 118 |
| Florida | 10 | 4 | 3 | 2 | 1 | 32 | 31 | 11 | 12 | 6 | 4 | 1 | 1 | 33 | 25 | 14 | 22 | 10 | 7 | 3 | 2 | 65 | 56 | 25 |
| Los Angeles | 99 | 61 | 24 | 13 | 1 | 369 | 259 | 136 | 97 | 35 | 38 | 19 | 5 | 286 | 319 | 94 | 196 | 96 | 62 | 32 | 6 | 655 | 578 | 230 |
| Minnesota | 16 | 12 | 2 | 1 | 1 | 61 | 36 | 26 | 16 | 8 | 7 | 0 | 1 | 34 | 41 | 17 | 32 | 20 | 9 | 1 | 2 | 95 | 77 | 43 |
| Montreal | 61 | 18 | 31 | 12 | 0 | 158 | 207 | 48 | 59 | 12 | 38 | 9 | 0 | 146 | 254 | 33 | 120 | 30 | 69 | 21 | 0 | 304 | 461 | 81 |
| Nashville | 20 | 16 | 4 | 0 | 0 | 58 | 27 | 32 | 20 | 8 | 11 | 1 | 0 | 43 | 53 | 17 | 40 | 24 | 15 | 1 | 0 | 101 | 80 | 49 |
| New Jersey | 47 | 28 | 13 | 6 | 0 | 171 | 120 | 62 | 45 | 19 | 23 | 3 | 0 | 134 | 155 | 41 | 92 | 47 | 36 | 9 | 0 | 305 | 275 | 103 |
| NY Islanders | 48 | 18 | 21 | 8 | 1 | 139 | 173 | 45 | 50 | 16 | 25 | 8 | 1 | 142 | 181 | 41 | 98 | 34 | 46 | 16 | 2 | 281 | 354 | 86 |
| NY Rangers | 63 | 21 | 31 | 11 | 0 | 199 | 228 | 53 | 64 | 17 | 36 | 11 | 0 | 170 | 216 | 45 | 127 | 38 | 67 | 22 | 0 | 369 | 444 | 98 |
| Ottawa | 12 | 7 | 5 | 0 | 0 | 46 | 32 | 14 | 11 | 6 | 3 | 0 | 2 | 30 | 27 | 14 | 23 | 13 | 8 | 0 | 2 | 76 | 59 | 28 |
| Philadelphia | 67 | 28 | 23 | 16 | 0 | 219 | 214 | 72 | 69 | 10 | 43 | 16 | 0 | 157 | 260 | 36 | 136 | 38 | 66 | 32 | 0 | 376 | 474 | 108 |
| Phoenix | 70 | 34 | 27 | 9 | 0 | 235 | 204 | 77 | 69 | 37 | 26 | 4 | 2 | 231 | 212 | 80 | 139 | 71 | 53 | 13 | 2 | 466 | 416 | 157 |
| Pittsburgh | 66 | 37 | 22 | 6 | 1 | 250 | 221 | 81 | 64 | 19 | 39 | 6 | 0 | 179 | 240 | 44 | 130 | 56 | 61 | 12 | 1 | 429 | 461 | 125 |
| St. Louis | 123 | 59 | 41 | 22 | 1 | 413 | 355 | 141 | 125 | 34 | 68 | 21 | 2 | 350 | 452 | 91 | 248 | 93 | 109 | 43 | 3 | 763 | 807 | 232 |
| San Jose | 44 | 20 | 17 | 4 | 3 | 116 | 108 | 47 | 45 | 27 | 15 | 1 | 2 | 126 | 105 | 57 | 89 | 47 | 32 | 5 | 5 | 242 | 213 | 104 |
| Tampa Bay | 12 | 7 | 4 | 1 | 0 | 42 | 33 | 15 | 15 | 11 | 2 | 2 | 0 | 41 | 25 | 24 | 27 | 18 | 6 | 3 | 0 | 83 | 58 | 39 |
| Toronto | 98 | 51 | 36 | 11 | 0 | 368 | 307 | 113 | 103 | 37 | 49 | 17 | 0 | 329 | 359 | 91 | 201 | 88 | 85 | 28 | 0 | 697 | 666 | 204 |
| Vancouver | 79 | 43 | 24 | 12 | 0 | 280 | 228 | 98 | 79 | 33 | 34 | 10 | 2 | 235 | 274 | 78 | 158 | 76 | 58 | 22 | 2 | 515 | 502 | 176 |
| Washington | 43 | 22 | 11 | 8 | 2 | 161 | 117 | 54 | 41 | 17 | 16 | 8 | 0 | 132 | 124 | 42 | 84 | 39 | 27 | 16 | 2 | 293 | 241 | 96 |
| Defunct Clubs | 33 | 19 | 8 | 6 | 0 | 123 | 86 | 44 | 32 | 10 | 16 | 6 | 0 | 84 | 105 | 26 | 65 | 29 | 24 | 12 | 0 | 207 | 191 | 70 |
| **Totals** | **1630** | **821** | **560** | **228** | **21** | **5527** | **4788** | **1891** | **1630** | **568** | **802** | **231** | **29** | **4611** | **5605** | **1396** | **3260** | **1389** | **1362** | **459** | **50** | **10138** | **10393** | **3287** |

## Playoffs

| | Series | W | L | GP | W | L | T | GF | GA | Last Mtg. | Rnd. | Result |
|---|---|---|---|---|---|---|---|---|---|---|---|---|
| Anaheim | 2 | 1 | 1 | 12 | 6 | 6 | 0 | 34 | 27 | 2008 | CQF | W 4-2 |
| Boston | 1 | 1 | 0 | 3 | 3 | 0 | 0 | 20 | 13 | 1981 | PRE | W 3-0 |
| Buffalo | 3 | 2 | 1 | 13 | 8 | 5 | 0 | 39 | 37 | 1999 | F | W 4-2 |
| Calgary | 1 | 1 | 0 | 6 | 4 | 2 | 0 | 25 | 18 | 1981 | SF | W 4-2 |
| Chicago | 6 | 2 | 4 | 33 | 14 | 19 | 0 | 118 | 120 | 1991 | DSF | W 4-2 |
| Colorado | 4 | 2 | 2 | 24 | 10 | 14 | 0 | 62 | 66 | 2006 | CQF | L 1-4 |
| Detroit | 4 | 0 | 4 | 24 | 8 | 16 | 0 | 50 | 72 | 2008 | CF | L 2-4 |
| Edmonton | 8 | 6 | 2 | 42 | 27 | 15 | 0 | 118 | 104 | 2003 | CQF | W 4-2 |
| Los Angeles | 1 | 1 | 0 | 7 | 4 | 3 | 0 | 26 | 21 | 1968 | QF | W 4-3 |
| Montreal | 2 | 1 | 1 | 13 | 6 | 7 | 0 | 37 | 48 | 1980 | QF | W 4-3 |
| New Jersey | 1 | 0 | 1 | 6 | 2 | 4 | 0 | 9 | 15 | 2000 | F | L 2-4 |
| NY Islanders | 1 | 0 | 1 | 5 | 1 | 4 | 0 | 16 | 26 | 1981 | F | L 1-4 |
| Philadelphia | 2 | 0 | 2 | 11 | 3 | 8 | 0 | 26 | 41 | 1980 | SF | L 1-4 |
| Pittsburgh | 1 | 0 | 1 | 6 | 2 | 4 | 0 | 16 | 28 | 1991 | F | L 2-4 |
| St. Louis | 12 | 6 | 6 | 66 | 34 | 32 | 0 | 197 | 187 | 2001 | CSF | L 0-4 |
| San Jose | 3 | 3 | 0 | 17 | 12 | 5 | 0 | 46 | 30 | 2008 | CSF | W 4-2 |
| Toronto | 2 | 2 | 0 | 7 | 6 | 1 | 0 | 35 | 26 | 1983 | DSF | W 3-1 |
| Vancouver | 2 | 0 | 2 | 12 | 4 | 8 | 0 | 23 | 31 | 2007 | CQF | L 3-4 |
| **Totals** | **56** | **28** | **28** | **307** | **154** | **153** | **0** | **897** | **910** | | | |

Calgary totals include Atlanta Flames, 1972-73 to 1979-80. Carolina totals include Hartford, 1979-80 to 1996-97.
Colorado totals include Quebec, 1979-80 to 1994-95.
New Jersey totals include Kansas City, 1974-75, 1975-76, and Colorado Rockies, 1976-77 to 1981-82.
Phoenix totals include Winnipeg, 1979-80 to 1995-96.

## Playoff Results 2009-2004

| Year | Round | Opponent | Result | GF | GA |
|---|---|---|---|---|---|
| 2008 | CF | Detroit | L 2-4 | 10 | 17 |
| | CSF | San Jose | W 4-2 | 15 | 11 |
| | CQF | Anaheim | W 4-2 | 20 | 13 |
| 2007 | CQF | Vancouver | L 3-4 | 12 | 13 |
| 2006 | CQF | Colorado | L 1-4 | 15 | 18 |
| 2004 | CQF | Colorado | L 1-4 | 10 | 19 |

**Abbreviations: Round: F** - Final;
**CF** - conference final; **CSF** - conference semi-final;
**CQF** - conference quarter-final;
**DSF** - division semi-final; **SF** - semi-final;
**QF** - quarter-final; **PRE** - preliminary round.

## 2008-09 Results

| | | | | | | | |
|---|---|---|---|---|---|---|---|
| **Oct.** | 10 | Columbus | 4-5* | | 15 | Buffalo | 4-5† |
| | 11 | at Nashville | 1-3 | | 17 | Los Angeles | 3-2† |
| | 15 | Nashville | 6-4 | | 19 | at Tampa Bay | 2-4 |
| | 16 | at St. Louis | 1-6 | | 21 | at Florida | 4-1 |
| | 18 | Colorado | 4-5 | | 27 | Atlanta | 2-0 |
| | 20 | at NY Rangers | 2-1 | | 29 | at Detroit | 4-2 |
| | 22 | at New Jersey | 0-5 | | 31 | at Columbus | 7-3 |
| | 23 | at NY Islanders | 5-3 | **Feb.** | 3 | Calgary | 3-1 |
| | 25 | Washington | 5-6* | | 5 | at Colorado | 2-3 |
| | 29 | Minnesota | 4-2 | | 6 | NY Rangers | 10-2 |
| | 31 | at Chicago | 2-5 | | 8 | Nashville | 4-1 |
| **Nov.** | 1 | at Boston | 1-5 | | 11 | Phoenix | 0-1 |
| | 7 | at Anaheim | 5-2 | | 13 | Vancouver | 2-1 |
| | 8 | at San Jose | 1-2 | | 14 | at Chicago | 2-6 |
| | 11 | at Los Angeles | 2-3† | | 16 | at Columbus | 3-2† |
| | 13 | Los Angeles | 2-3 | | 19 | Edmonton | 4-2 |
| | 15 | at Phoenix | 3-2 | | 21 | Chicago | 1-3 |
| | 20 | Chicago | 3-6 | | 23 | San Jose | 0-1 |
| | 22 | Anaheim | 1-2† | | 26 | St. Louis | 1-3 |
| | 24 | at Philadelphia | 3-4 | | 28 | Anaheim | 3-4 |
| | 26 | at Minnesota | 4-3 | **Mar.** | 1 | Pittsburgh | 1-4 |
| | 28 | San Jose | 2-6 | | 3 | at San Jose | 4-1 |
| | 30 | Edmonton | 4-3 | | 5 | at Los Angeles | 4-5* |
| **Dec.** | 2 | at Calgary | 3-1 | | 6 | at Anaheim | 3-2 |
| | 3 | at Edmonton | 2-5 | | 8 | Montreal | 1-3 |
| | 5 | Colorado | 2-1† | | 10 | at St. Louis | 2-5 |
| | 10 | Phoenix | 3-5 | | 12 | Carolina | 3-2 |
| | 12 | Detroit | 3-1 | | 14 | Minnesota | 3-2* |
| | 13 | at Nashville | 0-3 | | 17 | at Vancouver | 2-4 |
| | 16 | Phoenix | 2-1* | | 18 | at Calgary | 1-2 |
| | 18 | Columbus | 6-5† | | 21 | at San Jose | 2-5 |
| | 20 | at Ottawa | 4-5* | | 24 | Vancouver | 2-5 |
| | 23 | at Toronto | 8-2 | | 26 | Los Angeles | 0-1† |
| | 27 | Anaheim | 4-3* | | 28 | Florida | 3-6 |
| | 29 | San Jose | 1-3 | | 30 | at Phoenix | 5-6* |
| | 31 | New Jersey | 4-2 | | 31 | at Los Angeles | 3-2 |
| **Jan.** | 3 | at Edmonton | 1-4 | **Apr.** | 2 | Calgary | 1-2 |
| | 4 | at Vancouver | 3-2† | | 4 | St. Louis | 5-4* |
| | 8 | at Detroit | 1-6 | | 7 | at Minnesota | 1-3 |
| | 10 | at Phoenix | 0-1† | | 9 | at Colorado | 3-2† |
| | 12 | Detroit | 5-4* | | 10 | at Anaheim | 3-4† |

* – Overtime † – Shootout

## Entry Draft Selections 2009-1995

Name in bold denotes played in NHL.

**2009**
Pick
8 Scott Glennie
38 Alex Chiasson
69 Reilly Smith
129 Tomas Vincour
159 Curtis McKenzie

**2008**
Pick
59 Tyler Beskorowany
89 Scott Winkler
149 Philip Larsen
176 Matthew Tassone
209 Mike Bergin

**2007**
Pick
50 Nico Sacchetti
64 Sergei Korostin
112 Colton Sceviour
128 Austin Smith
129 Jamie Benn
136 Ondrej Roman
149 Michael Neal
172 Luke Gazdic

**2006**
Pick
27 **Ivan Vishnevskiy**
90 Aaron Snow
120 Richard Bachman
138 David McIntyre
150 Max Warn

**2005**
Pick
28 **Matt Niskanen**
33 **James Neal**
71 Richard Clune
75 Perttu Lindgren
146 **Tom Wandell**
160 Matt Watkins
223 Pat McGann

**2004**
Pick
28 **Mark Fistric**
34 Johan Fransson
52 **Raymond Sawada**
56 **Nicklas Grossman**
86 John Lammers
104 Fredrik Naslund
183 Trevor Ludwig
218 Sergei Kukushkin
248 Lukas Vomela
280 Matt McKnight

**2003**
Pick
33 **Loui Eriksson**
36 **Vojtech Polak**
54 **B.J. Crombeen**
99 Matt Nickerson
134 Alexander Naurov
144 Eero Kilpelainen
165 Gino Guyer
185 Francis Wathier
195 Drew Bagnall
196 Elias Granath
259 Niko Vainio

**2002**
Pick
26 Martin Vagner
32 Janos Vas
34 **Tobias Stephan**
42 Marius Holtet
43 **Trevor Daley**
78 Geoff Waugh
110 Jarkko A. Immonen
147 David Bararuk
180 Kirill Sidorenko
210 Bryan Hamm
243 Tuomas Mikkonen
273 Ned Havern

**2001**
Pick
26 **Jason Bacashihua**
70 Yared Hagos
92 Anthony Aquino
126 Daniel Volrab
161 **Mike Smith**
167 Michal Blazek
192 **Jussi Jokinen**
255 Marco Rosa
265 Dale Sullivan
285 Marek Tomica

**2000**
Pick
25 **Steve Ott**
60 **Dan Ellis**
68 **Joel Lundqvist**
91 Alexei Tereschenko
123 Vadim Khomitski
139 Ruslan Bernikov
162 Artem Chernov
192 Ladislav Vlcek
219 Marco Tuokko
224 **Antti Miettinen**

**1999**
Pick
32 **Michael Ryan**
66 **Dan Jancevski**
96 **Mathias Tjarnqvist**
126 Jeff Bateman
156 Gregor Baumgartner
184 Justin Cox
186 Brett Draney
215 **Jeff MacMillan**
243 Brian Sullivan
265 Jamie Chamberlain
272 Mikhail Donika

**1998**
Pick
39 **John Erskine**
57 **Tyler Bouck**
86 Gabriel Karlsson
153 **Pavel Patera**
173 **Niko Kapanen**
200 Scott Perry

**1997**
Pick
25 **Brenden Morrow**
52 **Roman Lyashenko**
77 **Steve Gainey**
105 Marcus Kristoffersson
132 Teemu Elomo
160 Alexei Timkin
189 Jeff McKercher
216 Alexei Komarov
242 **Brett McLean**

**1996**
Pick
5 **Ric Jackman**
70 **Jon Sim**
90 Mike Hurley
112 **Ryan Christie**
113 Yevgeny Tsybuk
166 Eoin McInerney
194 **Joel Kwiatkowski**
220 Nick Bootland

**1995**
Pick
11 **Jarome Iginla**
37 **Patrick Cote**
63 **Petr Buzek**
69 **Sergey Gusev**
115 Wade Strand
141 Dominic Marleau
173 Jeff Dewar
193 Anatoli Koveshnikov
202 Sergei Luchinkin
219 Stephen Lowe

## General Managers' History

Wren Blair, 1967-68 to 1973-74; Jack Gordon, 1974-75 to 1976-77; Lou Nanne, 1977-78 to 1987-88; Jack Ferreira, 1988-89, 1989-90; Bob Clarke 1990-91, 1991-92; Bob Gainey, 1992-93 to 2000-01; Bob Gainey and Doug Armstrong, 2001-02; Doug Armstrong, 2002-03 to 2006-07; Doug Armstrong and Brett Hull/Les Jackson, 2007-08; Brett Hull/Les Jackson, 2008-09; Joe Nieuwendyk, 2009-10.

## Joe Nieuwendyk

### General Manager

*Born: Oshawa, Ont., September 10, 1966.*

Joe Nieuwendyk was named general manager of the Dallas Stars on May 31, 2009. Nieuwendyk is considered by many to be one of the top up-and-coming hockey executives in the NHL. The former Stars player returned to Dallas from the Toronto Maple Leafs, where he served as special assistant to the general manager in 2008-09. Prior to joining the Leafs and after his 2006 retirement as a player, Nieuwendyk worked as a special consultant to the general manager with the Florida Panthers. He also helped lead Team Canada to a silver medal at the 2009 World Championship as assistant general manager.

A veteran of 20 seasons as a player in the National Hockey League, Nieuwendyk played seven with the Dallas Stars (1995 to 2002). He won the Stanley Cup for three different teams, in three different decades (Calgary in 1989, Dallas in 1999, New Jersey in 2003). Nieuwendyk was awarded the Conn Smythe Trophy as the Stanley Cup playoffs most valuable player in 1999 when he led Dallas in postseason scoring on their way to winning the Stanley Cup. The Whitby, Ontario, native played in 1,257 NHL games, scoring 564 goals and 562 assists for 1,126 points. He also appeared in 158 career playoff games, recording 116 points on 66 goals and 50 assists. Nieuwendyk played in 442 games for Dallas, scoring 178 goals and 162 assists for 340 points.

# Club Directory

**American Airlines Center**

**Dallas Stars**
Office Address:
2601 Ave. of the Stars
Frisco, TX 75034
Phone **214/387-5500**
FAX 214/387-5564
Ticket Information 214/GO STARS
www.dallasstars.com
**Capacity:** 18,532

| | |
|---|---|
| General Manager | Joe Nieuwendyk |
| Director, Scouting & Player Development | Les Jackson |
| Assistant General Manager | Frank Provenzano |
| Director, Player Personnel | Dave Taylor |
| General Manager, Texas Stars | Scott White |
| Head Coach | Marc Crawford |
| Assistant Coaches | Stu Barnes, Charlie Huddy |
| Goaltending Consultant | Andy Moog |
| Strength and Conditioning Coach | J.J. McQueen |
| Director, Team Services | Lesa Moake |
| Director, Amateur Scouting | Tim Bernhardt |
| Director, European Scouting | Kari Takko |
| Director, Professional Scouting | Doug Overton |
| Regional Scouts | Shane Churla, Jack Foley, Johan Garpenlov, Bob Gernander, Dennis Holland, Jiri Hrdina, Jimmy Johnston, Alex LePore, Paul McIntosh, Rickard Oquist, Butch Ott, Jim Pederson, Borys Protsenko, Shane Turner, Bobby Vermette |
| Head Athletic Trainer | David Zeis |
| Associate Athletic Trainer | Craig Lowry |
| Head Equipment Manager | Steve Sumner |
| Assistant Equipment Manager | Chris Davidson-Adams |
| Equipment Assistant | Dennis Soetaert |
| Massage Therapist | Cleo Bates |
| Asst. Strength and Conditioning Coach | Manny Hernando |
| Manager, Hockey Administration | Mark Janko |
| Executive Assistant, Hockey Operations | Pam Wenzel |

*James Neal was the Stars' second pick (33rd overall) in the 2005 Entry Draft. He scored 24 goals in 2008-09 to rank second among NHL rookies behind Anaheim's Bobby Ryan, who was picked second overall (behind Sidney Crosby) in the same draft.*

## Captains' History

Bob Woytowich, 1967-68; Moose Vasko, 1968-69; Claude Larose, 1969-70; Ted Harris, 1970-71 to 1973-74; Bill Goldsworthy, 1974-75, 1975-76; Bill Hogaboam, 1976-77; Nick Beverley, 1977-78; J.P. Parise, 1978-79; Paul Shmyr, 1979-80, 1980-81; Tim Young, 1981-82; Craig Hartsburg, 1982-83; Craig Hartsburg and Brian Bellows, 1983-84; Craig Hartsburg, 1984-85 to 1987-88; Curt Fraser, Bob Rouse and Curt Giles, 1988-89; Curt Giles, 1989-90, 1990-91; Mark Tinordi, 1991-92 to 1993-94; Neal Broten and Derian Hatcher, 1994-95; Derian Hatcher, 1995-96 to 2002-03; Mike Modano, 2003-04 to 2005-06; Brenden Morrow, 2006-07 to date.

# Detroit Red Wings

## 2008-09 Results: 51W-21L-6OTL-4SOL 112PTS.
## First, Central Division

### Key Off-Season Signings/Acquisitions

**2009**

**July** 6 • Re-signed LW **Ville Leino.**

8 • Signed D **Doug Janik.**

23 • Re-signed 2005 1st-round pick (19th overall) D **Jakub Kindl.**

28 • Signed D **Andy Delmore.**

**Aug.** 4 • Signed RW **Patrick Eaves.**

### 2009-10 Schedule

| Month | Day | Date | Opponent | Month | Day | Date | Opponent |
|---|---|---|---|---|---|---|---|
| **Oct.** | Fri. | 2 | at St. Louis† | | Tue. | 5 | at Anaheim |
| | Sat. | 3 | St. Louis† | | Thu. | 7 | at Los Angeles |
| | Thu. | 8 | Chicago | | Sat. | 9 | at San Jose |
| | Sat. | 10 | Washington | | Tue. | 12 | at NY Islanders |
| | Tue. | 13 | at Buffalo | | Thu. | 14 | Carolina |
| | Thu. | 15 | Los Angeles | | Sat. | 16 | at Dallas* |
| | Sat. | 17 | Colorado | | Sun. | 17 | Chicago* |
| | Thu. | 22 | at Phoenix | | Tue. | 19 | at Washington |
| | Sat. | 24 | at Colorado | | Thu. | 21 | at Minnesota |
| | Tue. | 27 | at Vancouver | | Sat. | 23 | Los Angeles |
| | Thu. | 29 | at Edmonton | | Tue. | 26 | Phoenix |
| | Sat. | 31 | at Calgary | | Wed. | 27 | at Minnesota |
| **Nov.** | Tue. | 3 | Boston | | Fri. | 29 | Nashville |
| | Thu. | 5 | San Jose | | Sun. | 31 | at Pittsburgh* |
| | Sat. | 7 | at Toronto | **Feb.** | Tue. | 2 | at San Jose |
| | Wed. | 11 | at Columbus | | Wed. | 3 | at Anaheim |
| | Thu. | 12 | Vancouver | | Sat. | 6 | at Los Angeles* |
| | Sat. | 14 | Anaheim | | Tue. | 9 | at St. Louis |
| | Wed. | 18 | Dallas | | Thu. | 11 | San Jose |
| | Fri. | 20 | Florida | | Sat. | 13 | Ottawa |
| | Sat. | 21 | at Montreal | **Mar.** | Mon. | 1 | at Colorado |
| | Mon. | 23 | at Nashville | | Wed. | 3 | Vancouver |
| | Wed. | 25 | Atlanta | | Fri. | 5 | Nashville |
| | Fri. | 27 | Calgary | | Sun. | 7 | at Chicago |
| | Sat. | 28 | at St. Louis | | Tue. | 9 | Calgary |
| | Mon. | 30 | Dallas | | Thu. | 11 | Minnesota |
| **Dec.** | Thu. | 3 | Edmonton | | Sat. | 13 | Buffalo |
| | Sat. | 5 | at New Jersey | | Mon. | 15 | at Calgary |
| | Sun. | 6 | at NY Rangers | | Fri. | 19 | at Edmonton |
| | Wed. | 9 | St. Louis | | Sat. | 20 | at Vancouver |
| | Fri. | 11 | Anaheim | | Mon. | 22 | Pittsburgh |
| | Sat. | 12 | at Nashville | | Wed. | 24 | St. Louis |
| | Mon. | 14 | Phoenix | | Fri. | 26 | Minnesota |
| | Thu. | 17 | Tampa Bay | | Sat. | 27 | at Nashville |
| | Sat. | 19 | at Dallas* | | Tue. | 30 | Edmonton |
| | Sun. | 20 | at Chicago | **Apr.** | Thu. | 1 | Columbus |
| | Wed. | 23 | Chicago | | Sat. | 3 | Nashville* |
| | Sat. | 26 | Columbus | | Sun. | 4 | at Philadelphia* |
| | Mon. | 28 | at Columbus | | Wed. | 7 | Columbus |
| | Thu. | 31 | Colorado | | Fri. | 9 | at Columbus |
| **Jan.** | Sat. | 2 | at Phoenix | | Sun. | 11 | at Chicago* |

* Denotes afternoon game. † Games played in Stockholm, SE.

### Year-by-Year Record

| Season | GP | Home W | Home L | Home T | Home OL | Road W | Road L | Road T | Road OL | Overall W | Overall L | Overall T | Overall OL | GF | GA | Pts. | Finished | Playoff Result |
|---|---|---|---|---|---|---|---|---|---|---|---|---|---|---|---|---|---|---|
| 2008-09 | 82 | 27 | 9 | .... | 5 | 24 | 12 | .... | 5 | 51 | 21 | .... | 10 | 295 | 244 | 112 | 1st, Central Div. | Lost Final |
| **2007-08** | **82** | **29** | **9** | .... | **3** | **25** | **12** | .... | **4** | **54** | **21** | .... | **7** | **257** | **184** | **115** | **1st, Central Div.** | **Won Stanley Cup** |
| 2006-07 | 82 | 29 | 4 | .... | 8 | 21 | 15 | .... | 5 | 50 | 19 | .... | 13 | 254 | 199 | 113 | 1st, Central Div. | Lost Conf. Championship |
| 2005-06 | 82 | 27 | 9 | .... | 5 | 31 | 7 | .... | 3 | 58 | 16 | .... | 8 | 305 | 209 | 124 | 1st, Central Div. | Lost Conf. Quarter-Final |
| 2004-05 | .... | .... | .... | .... | .... | .... | .... | .... | .... | .... | .... | .... | .... | .... | .... | .... | | |
| 2003-04 | 82 | 30 | 7 | 4 | 0 | 18 | 14 | 7 | 2 | 48 | 21 | 11 | 2 | 255 | 189 | 109 | 1st, Central Div. | Lost Conf. Semi-Final |
| 2002-03 | 82 | 28 | 6 | 5 | 2 | 20 | 14 | 5 | 2 | 48 | 20 | 10 | 4 | 269 | 203 | 110 | 1st, Central Div. | Lost Conf. Quarter-Final |
| **2001-02** | **82** | **28** | **7** | **5** | **1** | **23** | **10** | **5** | **3** | **51** | **17** | **10** | **4** | **251** | **187** | **116** | **1st, Central Div.** | **Won Stanley Cup** |
| 2000-01 | 82 | 27 | 9 | 3 | 2 | 22 | 11 | 6 | 2 | 49 | 20 | 9 | 4 | 253 | 202 | 111 | 1st, Central Div. | Lost Conf. Quarter-Final |
| 1999-2000 | 82 | 28 | 9 | 3 | 1 | 20 | 13 | 7 | 1 | 48 | 22 | 10 | 2 | 278 | 210 | 108 | 2nd, Central Div. | Lost Conf. Semi-Final |
| 1998-99 | 82 | 27 | 12 | 2 | .... | 16 | 20 | 5 | .... | 43 | 32 | 7 | .... | 245 | 202 | 93 | 1st, Central Div. | Lost Conf. Semi-Final |
| **1997-98** | **82** | **25** | **8** | **8** | .... | **19** | **15** | **7** | .... | **44** | **23** | **15** | .... | **250** | **196** | **103** | **2nd, Central Div.** | **Won Stanley Cup** |
| **1996-97** | **82** | **20** | **12** | **9** | .... | **18** | **14** | **9** | .... | **38** | **26** | **18** | .... | **253** | **197** | **94** | **2nd, Central Div.** | **Won Stanley Cup** |
| 1995-96 | 82 | 36 | 3 | 2 | .... | 26 | 10 | 5 | .... | 62 | 13 | 7 | .... | 325 | 181 | 131 | 1st, Central Div. | Lost Conf. Championship |
| 1994-95 | 48 | 17 | 4 | 3 | .... | 16 | 7 | 1 | .... | 33 | 11 | 4 | .... | 180 | 117 | 70 | 1st, Central Div. | Lost Final |
| 1993-94 | 84 | 23 | 13 | 6 | .... | 23 | 17 | 2 | .... | 46 | 30 | 8 | .... | 356 | 275 | 100 | 1st, Central Div. | Lost Conf. Quarter-Final |
| 1992-93 | 84 | 25 | 14 | 3 | .... | 22 | 14 | 6 | .... | 47 | 28 | 9 | .... | 369 | 280 | 103 | 2nd, Norris Div. | Lost Div. Semi-Final |
| 1991-92 | 80 | 24 | 12 | 4 | .... | 19 | 13 | 8 | .... | 43 | 25 | 12 | .... | 320 | 256 | 98 | 1st, Norris Div. | Lost Div. Final |
| 1990-91 | 80 | 26 | 14 | 0 | .... | 8 | 24 | 8 | .... | 34 | 38 | 8 | .... | 273 | 298 | 76 | 3rd, Norris Div. | Lost Div. Semi-Final |
| 1989-90 | 80 | 20 | 14 | 6 | .... | 8 | 24 | 8 | .... | 28 | 38 | 14 | .... | 288 | 323 | 70 | 5th, Norris Div. | Out of Playoffs |
| 1988-89 | 80 | 20 | 14 | 6 | .... | 14 | 20 | 6 | .... | 34 | 34 | 12 | .... | 313 | 316 | 80 | 1st, Norris Div. | Lost Div. Semi-Final |
| 1987-88 | 80 | 24 | 10 | 6 | .... | 17 | 18 | 5 | .... | 41 | 28 | 11 | .... | 322 | 269 | 93 | 1st, Norris Div. | Lost Conf. Championship |
| 1986-87 | 80 | 20 | 14 | 6 | .... | 14 | 22 | 4 | .... | 34 | 36 | 10 | .... | 260 | 274 | 78 | 2nd, Norris Div. | Lost Conf. Championship |
| 1985-86 | 80 | 10 | 26 | 4 | .... | 7 | 31 | 2 | .... | 17 | 57 | 6 | .... | 266 | 415 | 40 | 5th, Norris Div. | Out of Playoffs |
| 1984-85 | 80 | 19 | 14 | 7 | .... | 8 | 27 | 5 | .... | 27 | 41 | 12 | .... | 313 | 357 | 66 | 3rd, Norris Div. | Lost Div. Semi-Final |
| 1983-84 | 80 | 18 | 20 | 2 | .... | 13 | 22 | 5 | .... | 31 | 42 | 7 | .... | 298 | 323 | 69 | 3rd, Norris Div. | Lost Div. Semi-Final |
| 1982-83 | 80 | 14 | 19 | 7 | .... | 7 | 25 | 8 | .... | 21 | 44 | 15 | .... | 263 | 344 | 57 | 5th, Norris Div. | Out of Playoffs |
| 1981-82 | 80 | 15 | 19 | 6 | .... | 6 | 28 | 6 | .... | 21 | 47 | 12 | .... | 270 | 351 | 54 | 6th, Norris Div. | Out of Playoffs |
| 1980-81 | 80 | 16 | 15 | 9 | .... | 3 | 28 | 9 | .... | 19 | 43 | 18 | .... | 252 | 339 | 56 | 5th, Norris Div. | Out of Playoffs |
| 1979-80 | 80 | 14 | 21 | 5 | .... | 12 | 22 | 6 | .... | 26 | 43 | 11 | .... | 268 | 306 | 63 | 5th, Norris Div. | Out of Playoffs |
| 1978-79 | 80 | 15 | 17 | 8 | .... | 8 | 24 | 8 | .... | 23 | 41 | 16 | .... | 252 | 295 | 62 | 5th, Norris Div. | Out of Playoffs |
| 1977-78 | 80 | 22 | 11 | 7 | .... | 10 | 23 | 7 | .... | 32 | 34 | 14 | .... | 252 | 266 | 78 | 2nd, Norris Div. | Lost Quarter-Final |
| 1976-77 | 80 | 12 | 22 | 6 | .... | 4 | 33 | 3 | .... | 16 | 55 | 9 | .... | 183 | 309 | 41 | 5th, Norris Div. | Out of Playoffs |
| 1975-76 | 80 | 17 | 15 | 8 | .... | 9 | 29 | 2 | .... | 26 | 44 | 10 | .... | 226 | 300 | 62 | 4th, Norris Div. | Out of Playoffs |
| 1974-75 | 80 | 17 | 17 | 6 | .... | 6 | 28 | 6 | .... | 23 | 45 | 12 | .... | 259 | 335 | 58 | 4th, Norris Div. | Out of Playoffs |
| 1973-74 | 78 | 21 | 12 | 6 | .... | 8 | 27 | 4 | .... | 29 | 39 | 10 | .... | 255 | 319 | 68 | 6th, East Div. | Out of Playoffs |
| 1972-73 | 78 | 22 | 12 | 5 | .... | 15 | 17 | 7 | .... | 37 | 29 | 12 | .... | 265 | 243 | 86 | 5th, East Div. | Out of Playoffs |
| 1971-72 | 78 | 25 | 11 | 3 | .... | 8 | 24 | 7 | .... | 33 | 35 | 10 | .... | 261 | 262 | 76 | 5th, East Div. | Out of Playoffs |
| 1970-71 | 78 | 17 | 15 | 7 | .... | 5 | 30 | 4 | .... | 22 | 45 | 11 | .... | 209 | 308 | 55 | 7th, East Div. | Out of Playoffs |
| 1969-70 | 76 | 20 | 11 | 7 | .... | 20 | 10 | 8 | .... | 40 | 21 | 15 | .... | 246 | 199 | 95 | 3rd, East Div. | Lost Quarter-Final |
| 1968-69 | 76 | 23 | 8 | 7 | .... | 10 | 23 | 5 | .... | 33 | 31 | 12 | .... | 239 | 221 | 78 | 5th, East Div. | Out of Playoffs |
| 1967-68 | 74 | 18 | 15 | 4 | .... | 9 | 20 | 8 | .... | 27 | 35 | 12 | .... | 245 | 257 | 66 | 6th, East Div. | Out of Playoffs |
| 1966-67 | 70 | 21 | 11 | 3 | .... | 6 | 28 | 1 | .... | 27 | 39 | 4 | .... | 212 | 241 | 58 | 5th, | Out of Playoffs |
| 1965-66 | 70 | 20 | 8 | 7 | .... | 11 | 19 | 5 | .... | 31 | 27 | 12 | .... | 221 | 194 | 74 | 4th, | Lost Final |
| 1964-65 | 70 | 25 | 7 | 3 | .... | 15 | 16 | 4 | .... | 40 | 23 | 7 | .... | 224 | 175 | 87 | 1st, | Lost Semi-Final |
| 1963-64 | 70 | 23 | 9 | 3 | .... | 7 | 20 | 8 | .... | 30 | 29 | 11 | .... | 191 | 204 | 71 | 4th, | Lost Final |
| 1962-63 | 70 | 19 | 10 | 6 | .... | 13 | 15 | 7 | .... | 32 | 25 | 13 | .... | 200 | 194 | 77 | 4th, | Lost Final |
| 1961-62 | 70 | 17 | 11 | 7 | .... | 6 | 22 | 7 | .... | 23 | 33 | 14 | .... | 184 | 219 | 60 | 5th, | Out of Playoffs |
| 1960-61 | 70 | 15 | 13 | 7 | .... | 10 | 16 | 9 | .... | 25 | 29 | 16 | .... | 195 | 215 | 66 | 4th, | Lost Final |
| 1959-60 | 70 | 18 | 14 | 3 | .... | 8 | 15 | 12 | .... | 26 | 29 | 15 | .... | 186 | 197 | 67 | 4th, | Lost Semi-Final |
| 1958-59 | 70 | 13 | 17 | 5 | .... | 12 | 20 | 3 | .... | 25 | 37 | 8 | .... | 167 | 218 | 58 | 6th, | Out of Playoffs |
| 1957-58 | 70 | 16 | 11 | 8 | .... | 13 | 18 | 4 | .... | 29 | 29 | 12 | .... | 176 | 207 | 70 | 3rd, | Lost Semi-Final |
| 1956-57 | 70 | 23 | 7 | 5 | .... | 15 | 13 | 7 | .... | 38 | 20 | 12 | .... | 198 | 157 | 88 | 1st, | Lost Semi-Final |
| 1955-56 | 70 | 21 | 6 | 8 | .... | 9 | 18 | 8 | .... | 30 | 24 | 16 | .... | 183 | 148 | 76 | 2nd, | Lost Final |
| **1954-55** | **70** | **25** | **5** | **5** | .... | **17** | **12** | **6** | .... | **42** | **17** | **11** | .... | **204** | **134** | **95** | **1st,** | **Won Stanley Cup** |
| **1953-54** | **70** | **24** | **4** | **7** | .... | **13** | **15** | **7** | .... | **37** | **19** | **14** | .... | **191** | **132** | **88** | **1st,** | **Won Stanley Cup** |
| 1952-53 | 70 | 20 | 5 | 10 | .... | 16 | 11 | 8 | .... | 36 | 16 | 18 | .... | 222 | 133 | 90 | 1st, | Lost Semi-Final |
| **1951-52** | **70** | **24** | **7** | **4** | .... | **20** | **7** | **8** | .... | **44** | **14** | **12** | .... | **215** | **133** | **100** | **1st,** | **Won Stanley Cup** |
| 1950-51 | 70 | 25 | 3 | 7 | .... | 19 | 10 | 6 | .... | 44 | 13 | 13 | .... | 236 | 139 | 101 | 1st, | Lost Semi-Final |
| **1949-50** | **70** | **19** | **9** | **7** | .... | **18** | **10** | **7** | .... | **37** | **19** | **14** | .... | **229** | **164** | **88** | **1st,** | **Won Stanley Cup** |
| 1948-49 | 60 | 21 | 6 | 3 | .... | 13 | 13 | 4 | .... | 34 | 19 | 7 | .... | 195 | 145 | 75 | 1st, | Lost Final |
| 1947-48 | 60 | 16 | 9 | 5 | .... | 14 | 9 | 7 | .... | 30 | 18 | 12 | .... | 187 | 148 | 72 | 2nd, | Lost Final |
| 1946-47 | 60 | 14 | 10 | 6 | .... | 8 | 17 | 5 | .... | 22 | 27 | 11 | .... | 190 | 193 | 55 | 4th, | Lost Semi-Final |
| 1945-46 | 50 | 16 | 5 | 4 | .... | 4 | 15 | 6 | .... | 20 | 20 | 10 | .... | 146 | 159 | 50 | 4th, | Lost Semi-Final |
| 1944-45 | 50 | 19 | 5 | 1 | .... | 12 | 9 | 4 | .... | 31 | 14 | 5 | .... | 218 | 161 | 67 | 2nd, | Lost Final |
| 1943-44 | 50 | 18 | 5 | 2 | .... | 8 | 13 | 4 | .... | 26 | 18 | 6 | .... | 214 | 177 | 58 | 2nd, | Lost Semi-Final |
| **1942-43** | **50** | **16** | **4** | **5** | .... | **9** | **10** | **6** | .... | **25** | **14** | **11** | .... | **169** | **124** | **61** | **1st,** | **Won Stanley Cup** |
| 1941-42 | 48 | 14 | 7 | 3 | .... | 5 | 18 | 1 | .... | 19 | 25 | 4 | .... | 140 | 147 | 42 | 5th, | Lost Final |
| 1940-41 | 48 | 14 | 5 | 5 | .... | 7 | 11 | 6 | .... | 21 | 16 | 11 | .... | 112 | 102 | 53 | 3rd, | Lost Final |
| 1939-40 | 48 | 11 | 10 | 3 | .... | 5 | 16 | 3 | .... | 16 | 26 | 6 | .... | 91 | 126 | 38 | 5th, | Lost Semi-Final |
| 1938-39 | 48 | 14 | 8 | 2 | .... | 4 | 16 | 4 | .... | 18 | 24 | 6 | .... | 107 | 128 | 42 | 5th, | Lost Semi-Final |
| 1937-38 | 48 | 8 | 10 | 6 | .... | 4 | 15 | 5 | .... | 12 | 25 | 11 | .... | 99 | 133 | 35 | 4th, Amn. Div. | Out of Playoffs |
| **1936-37** | **48** | **14** | **5** | **5** | .... | **11** | **9** | **4** | .... | **25** | **14** | **9** | .... | **128** | **102** | **59** | **1st, Amn. Div.** | **Won Stanley Cup** |
| **1935-36** | **48** | **14** | **5** | **5** | .... | **10** | **11** | **3** | .... | **24** | **16** | **8** | .... | **124** | **103** | **56** | **1st, Amn. Div.** | **Won Stanley Cup** |
| 1934-35 | 48 | 11 | 8 | 5 | .... | 8 | 14 | 2 | .... | 19 | 22 | 7 | .... | 127 | 114 | 45 | 4th, Amn. Div. | Out of Playoffs |
| 1933-34 | 48 | 15 | 5 | 4 | .... | 9 | 9 | 6 | .... | 24 | 14 | 10 | .... | 113 | 98 | 58 | 1st, Amn. Div. | Lost Final |
| 1932-33* | 48 | 17 | 3 | 4 | .... | 8 | 12 | 4 | .... | 25 | 15 | 8 | .... | 111 | 93 | 58 | 2nd, Amn. Div. | Lost Semi-Final |
| 1931-32 | 48 | 15 | 3 | 6 | .... | 3 | 17 | 4 | .... | 18 | 20 | 10 | .... | 95 | 108 | 46 | 3rd, Amn. Div. | Lost Quarter-Final |
| 1930-31** | 44 | 10 | 7 | 5 | .... | 6 | 14 | 2 | .... | 16 | 21 | 7 | .... | 102 | 105 | 39 | 4th, Amn. Div. | Out of Playoffs |
| 1929-30 | 44 | 9 | 10 | 3 | .... | 5 | 14 | 3 | .... | 14 | 24 | 6 | .... | 117 | 133 | 34 | 4th, Amn. Div. | Out of Playoffs |
| 1928-29 | 44 | 11 | 6 | 5 | .... | 8 | 10 | 4 | .... | 19 | 16 | 9 | .... | 72 | 63 | 47 | 3rd, Amn. Div. | Lost Quarter-Final |
| 1927-28 | 44 | 9 | 10 | 3 | .... | 10 | 9 | 3 | .... | 19 | 19 | 6 | .... | 88 | 79 | 44 | 4th, Amn. Div. | Out of Playoffs |
| 1926-27*** | 44 | 5 | 16 | 0 | .... | 7 | 12 | 4 | .... | 12 | 28 | 4 | .... | 76 | 105 | 28 | 5th, Amn. Div. | Out of Playoffs |

* Team name changed to Red Wings. ** Team name changed to Falcons. *** Team named Cougars.

**CENTRAL DIVISION**
**84th NHL Season**

**Franchise date:** September 25, 1926

# 2009-10 Player Personnel

| FORWARDS | HT | WT | S | Place of Birth | *Age | 2008-09 Club |
|---|---|---|---|---|---|---|
| ABDELKADER, Justin | 6-1 | 215 | L | Muskegon, MI | 22 | Detroit-Grand Rapids |
| CLEARY, Daniel | 6-0 | 210 | L | Carbonear, Nfld. | 30 | Detroit |
| DATSYUK, Pavel | 5-11 | 194 | L | Sverdlovsk, USSR | 31 | Detroit |
| DRAPER, Kris | 5-10 | 188 | L | Toronto, Ont. | 38 | Detroit |
| EAVES, Patrick | 5-11 | 190 | R | Calgary, Alta. | 25 | Carolina |
| FILPPULA, Valtteri | 6-0 | 193 | L | Vantaa, Finland | 25 | Detroit |
| FRANZEN, Johan | 6-3 | 220 | L | Landsbro, Sweden | 29 | Detroit |
| HELM, Darren | 5-11 | 172 | L | Winnipeg, Man. | 22 | Detroit-Grand Rapids |
| HOLMSTROM, Tomas | 6-0 | 203 | L | Pitea, Sweden | 36 | Detroit |
| LEINO, Ville | 6-0 | 182 | L | Savonlinna, Finland | 25 | Detroit-Grand Rapids |
| MALTBY, Kirk | 6-0 | 193 | R | Guelph, Ont. | 36 | Detroit |
| WILLIAMS, Jason | 5-11 | 185 | R | London, Ont. | 29 | Atlanta-Columbus |
| ZETTERBERG, Henrik | 5-11 | 195 | L | Njurunda, Sweden | 28 | Detroit |

| DEFENSEMEN | HT | WT | S | Place of Birth | *Age | 2008-09 Club |
|---|---|---|---|---|---|---|
| DELMORE, Andy | 6-0 | 200 | R | LaSalle, Ont. | 32 | Hamburg |
| ERICSSON, Jonathan | 6-4 | 206 | L | Karlskrona, Sweden | 25 | Detroit-Grand Rapids |
| JANIK, Doug | 6-2 | 209 | L | Agawam, MA | 29 | Dal-Rockford-Mtl-Hamilton |
| KINDL, Jakub | 6-3 | 199 | L | Sumperk, Czech. | 22 | Grand Rapids |
| KOLOSOV, Sergei | 6-4 | 210 | L | Novopolotsk, Belarus | 23 | Grand Rapids |
| KRONWALL, Niklas | 6-0 | 189 | L | Stockholm, Sweden | 28 | Detroit |
| LEBDA, Brett | 5-9 | 195 | L | Buffalo Grove, IL | 27 | Detroit |
| LIDSTROM, Nicklas | 6-1 | 189 | L | Vasteras, Sweden | 39 | Detroit |
| LILJA, Andreas | 6-3 | 220 | L | Helsingborg, Sweden | 34 | Detroit |
| MEECH, Derek | 5-11 | 197 | L | Winnipeg, Man. | 25 | Detroit |
| RAFALSKI, Brian | 5-10 | 191 | R | Dearborn, MI | 36 | Detroit |
| STUART, Brad | 6-2 | 213 | L | Rocky Mtn. House, Alta. | 29 | Detroit |

| GOALTENDERS | HT | WT | C | Place of Birth | *Age | 2008-09 Club |
|---|---|---|---|---|---|---|
| HOWARD, Jimmy | 6-0 | 218 | L | Syracuse, NY | 25 | Detroit-Grand Rapids |
| LARSSON, Daniel | 6-0 | 180 | L | Boden, Sweden | 23 | Grand Rapids |
| OSGOOD, Chris | 5-10 | 178 | L | Peace River, Alta. | 36 | Detroit |

* – Age at start of 2009-10 season

# 2008-09 Scoring

* – rookie

## Regular Season

| Pos | # | Player | Team | GP | G | A | Pts | TOI | +/- | PIM | PP | SH | GW | S | % |
|---|---|---|---|---|---|---|---|---|---|---|---|---|---|---|---|
| C | 13 | Pavel Datsyuk | DET | 81 | 32 | 65 | 97 | 19:12 | 34 | 22 | 11 | 1 | 3 | 248 | 12.9 |
| C | 40 | Henrik Zetterberg | DET | 77 | 31 | 42 | 73 | 19:52 | 13 | 36 | 12 | 2 | 5 | 309 | 10.0 |
| R | 81 | Marian Hossa | DET | 74 | 40 | 31 | 71 | 17:47 | 27 | 63 | 10 | 0 | 8 | 307 | 13.0 |
| R | 93 | Johan Franzen | DET | 71 | 34 | 25 | 59 | 18:06 | 21 | 44 | 11 | 1 | 8 | 246 | 13.8 |
| D | 5 | Nicklas Lidstrom | DET | 78 | 16 | 43 | 59 | 24:49 | 31 | 30 | 10 | 0 | 4 | 180 | 8.9 |
| D | 28 | Brian Rafalski | DET | 78 | 10 | 49 | 59 | 23:10 | 17 | 20 | 5 | 0 | 1 | 141 | 7.1 |
| L | 26 | Jiri Hudler | DET | 82 | 23 | 34 | 57 | 13:39 | 7 | 16 | 6 | 0 | 2 | 155 | 14.8 |
| D | 55 | Niklas Kronwall | DET | 80 | 6 | 45 | 51 | 22:53 | 2 | 50 | 4 | 0 | 1 | 121 | 5.0 |
| R | 37 | Mikael Samuelsson | DET | 81 | 19 | 21 | 40 | 15:22 | 0 | 50 | 7 | 0 | 1 | 257 | 7.4 |
| R | 11 | Daniel Cleary | DET | 74 | 14 | 26 | 40 | 16:56 | 0 | 46 | 3 | 0 | 3 | 163 | 8.6 |
| C | 51 | Valtteri Filppula | DET | 80 | 12 | 28 | 40 | 16:06 | 9 | 42 | 1 | 0 | 1 | 129 | 9.3 |
| L | 96 | Tomas Holmstrom | DET | 53 | 14 | 23 | 37 | 15:15 | 18 | 38 | 8 | 0 | 1 | 75 | 18.7 |
| C | 82 | Tomas Kopecky | DET | 79 | 6 | 13 | 19 | 10:24 | –7 | 46 | 1 | 1 | 2 | 110 | 5.5 |
| C | 33 | Kris Draper | DET | 79 | 7 | 10 | 17 | 11:58 | –13 | 40 | 0 | 1 | 2 | 93 | 7.5 |
| D | 22 | Brett Lebda | DET | 65 | 6 | 10 | 16 | 13:38 | 9 | 48 | 0 | 0 | 1 | 69 | 8.7 |
| D | 23 | Brad Stuart | DET | 67 | 2 | 13 | 15 | 20:13 | –3 | 26 | 1 | 0 | 0 | 105 | 1.9 |
| D | 3 | Andreas Lilja | DET | 60 | 2 | 11 | 13 | 16:59 | 13 | 66 | 0 | 0 | 0 | 60 | 3.3 |
| R | 18 | Kirk Maltby | DET | 78 | 5 | 6 | 11 | 9:08 | –9 | 28 | 0 | 0 | 1 | 58 | 8.6 |
| L | 21 | * Ville Leino | DET | 13 | 5 | 4 | 9 | 12:42 | 5 | 6 | 0 | 0 | 1 | 17 | 29.4 |
| D | 14 | Derek Meech | DET | 41 | 2 | 5 | 7 | 10:02 | –12 | 12 | 0 | 0 | 0 | 44 | 4.5 |
| D | 52 | * Jonathan Ericsson | DET | 19 | 1 | 3 | 4 | 17:40 | –1 | 15 | 0 | 0 | 0 | 25 | 4.0 |
| R | 44 | Aaron Downey | DET | 4 | 1 | 1 | 2 | 5:12 | 0 | 7 | 0 | 0 | 0 | 2 | 50.0 |
| R | 25 | Darren McCarty | DET | 13 | 1 | 0 | 1 | 5:17 | –2 | 25 | 0 | 0 | 0 | 6 | 16.7 |
| C | 43 | * Darren Helm | DET | 16 | 0 | 1 | 1 | 12:25 | –7 | 4 | 0 | 0 | 0 | 29 | 0.0 |
| L | 8 | * Justin Abdelkader | DET | 2 | 0 | 0 | 0 | 9:17 | 0 | 0 | 0 | 0 | 0 | 2 | 0.0 |
| D | 24 | Chris Chelios | DET | 28 | 0 | 0 | 0 | 11:40 | 1 | 18 | 0 | 0 | 0 | 14 | 0.0 |

### Goaltending

| No. | Goaltender | GPI | Mins | Avg | W | L | OT | EN | SO | GA | SA | S% | G | A | PIM |
|---|---|---|---|---|---|---|---|---|---|---|---|---|---|---|---|
| 29 | Ty Conklin | 40 | 2246 | 2.51 | 25 | 11 | 2 | 4 | 6 | 94 | 1033 | .909 | 0 | 0 | 4 |
| 30 | Chris Osgood | 46 | 2663 | 3.09 | 26 | 9 | 8 | 0 | 2 | 137 | 1208 | .887 | 0 | 2 | 8 |
| 35 | * Jimmy Howard | 1 | 59 | 4.07 | 0 | 1 | 0 | 1 | 0 | 4 | 28 | .857 | 0 | 0 | 0 |
| | **Totals** | **82** | **4992** | **2.88** | **51** | **21** | **10** | **5** | **8** | **240** | **2274** | **.894** | | | |

## Playoffs

| Pos | # | Player | Team | GP | G | A | Pts | TOI | +/- | PIM | PP | SH | GW | OT | S | % |
|---|---|---|---|---|---|---|---|---|---|---|---|---|---|---|---|---|
| C | 40 | Henrik Zetterberg | DET | 23 | 11 | 13 | 24 | 22:09 | 13 | 13 | 4 | 0 | 0 | 0 | 82 | 13.4 |
| R | 93 | Johan Franzen | DET | 23 | 12 | 11 | 23 | 19:40 | 8 | 12 | 4 | 0 | 3 | 0 | 72 | 16.7 |
| D | 5 | Nicklas Lidstrom | DET | 21 | 4 | 12 | 16 | 25:38 | 11 | 6 | 3 | 0 | 1 | 0 | 59 | 6.8 |
| C | 51 | Valtteri Filppula | DET | 23 | 3 | 13 | 16 | 17:37 | 8 | 8 | 1 | 0 | 1 | 0 | 35 | 8.6 |
| R | 11 | Daniel Cleary | DET | 23 | 9 | 6 | 15 | 16:54 | 17 | 12 | 0 | 0 | 3 | 0 | 57 | 15.8 |
| R | 81 | Marian Hossa | DET | 23 | 6 | 9 | 15 | 18:38 | 5 | 10 | 2 | 1 | 1 | 0 | 100 | 6.0 |
| L | 26 | Jiri Hudler | DET | 23 | 4 | 8 | 12 | 13:27 | 4 | 6 | 2 | 0 | 1 | 0 | 36 | 11.1 |
| D | 28 | Brian Rafalski | DET | 18 | 3 | 9 | 12 | 22:26 | 11 | 11 | 3 | 0 | 1 | 0 | 24 | 12.5 |
| R | 37 | Mikael Samuelsson | DET | 23 | 5 | 5 | 10 | 15:08 | 7 | 6 | 0 | 0 | 2 | 1 | 79 | 6.3 |
| D | 23 | Brad Stuart | DET | 23 | 3 | 6 | 9 | 24:08 | 5 | 12 | 1 | 0 | 0 | 0 | 34 | 8.8 |
| D | 55 | Niklas Kronwall | DET | 23 | 2 | 7 | 9 | 23:23 | 4 | 33 | 2 | 0 | 0 | 0 | 32 | 6.3 |
| C | 13 | Pavel Datsyuk | DET | 16 | 1 | 8 | 9 | 20:05 | 5 | 9 | 1 | 0 | 0 | 0 | 52 | 1.9 |
| D | 52 | * Jonathan Ericsson | DET | 22 | 4 | 4 | 8 | 18:43 | 9 | 25 | 0 | 0 | 1 | 0 | 33 | 12.1 |
| L | 96 | Tomas Holmstrom | DET | 23 | 2 | 5 | 7 | 13:44 | –2 | 22 | 0 | 0 | 0 | 0 | 25 | 8.0 |
| D | 22 | Brett Lebda | DET | 23 | 0 | 6 | 6 | 13:20 | 8 | 22 | 0 | 0 | 0 | 0 | 19 | 0.0 |
| C | 43 | * Darren Helm | DET | 23 | 4 | 1 | 5 | 12:05 | 1 | 4 | 0 | 0 | 1 | 1 | 42 | 9.5 |
| L | 8 | * Justin Abdelkader | DET | 10 | 2 | 1 | 3 | 6:58 | 2 | 0 | 0 | 0 | 0 | 0 | 11 | 18.2 |
| L | 21 | * Ville Leino | DET | 7 | 0 | 2 | 2 | 8:43 | 2 | 0 | 0 | 0 | 0 | 0 | 7 | 0.0 |
| C | 33 | Kris Draper | DET | 8 | 1 | 0 | 1 | 8:36 | 0 | 0 | 0 | 0 | 0 | 0 | 6 | 16.7 |
| C | 82 | Tomas Kopecky | DET | 8 | 0 | 1 | 1 | 9:31 | 0 | 7 | 0 | 0 | 0 | 0 | 13 | 0.0 |
| R | 18 | Kirk Maltby | DET | 20 | 0 | 1 | 1 | 9:06 | –1 | 2 | 0 | 0 | 0 | 0 | 12 | 0.0 |
| D | 14 | Derek Meech | DET | 2 | 0 | 0 | 0 | 4:04 | 0 | 0 | 0 | 0 | 0 | 0 | 1 | 0.0 |
| D | 24 | Chris Chelios | DET | 6 | 0 | 0 | 0 | 7:21 | 0 | 2 | 0 | 0 | 0 | 0 | 4 | 0.0 |

### Goaltending

| No. | Goaltender | GPI | Mins | Avg | W | L | EN | SO | GA | SA | S% | G | A | PIM |
|---|---|---|---|---|---|---|---|---|---|---|---|---|---|---|
| 29 | Ty Conklin | 1 | 20 | 0.00 | 0 | 0 | 0 | 0 | 0 | 9 | 1.000 | 0 | 0 | 0 |
| 30 | Chris Osgood | 23 | 1406 | 2.01 | 15 | 8 | 1 | 2 | 47 | 637 | .926 | 0 | 2 | 2 |
| | **Totals** | **23** | **1432** | **2.01** | **15** | **8** | **1** | **2** | **48** | **647** | **.926** | | | |

# Mike Babcock

## Head Coach

*Born: Manitouwadge, Ont., April 29, 1963.*

Mike Babcock became the 26th coach in Detroit Red Wings history on July 14, 2005. In 2008, he led the Red Wings to the Stanley Cup. The Red Wings reached the Finals again in 2009 and have topped 50 wins during the regular season in each of Babcock's four years with the team.

Babcock brought a winning track record to Detroit from all levels of play, including college and junior hockey, the American Hockey League, the NHL and international hockey. He is the only man to coach Team Canada to victories at both the World Junior Championship (1997) and the senior World Championship (2004.) Prior to joining the Red Wings, he had spent two seasons with Anaheim, leading the team to the Stanley Cup finals in his first season behind the bench in 2002-03. He became the first rookie coach to reach the Finals since Florida's Doug MacLean in 1996. With a four-game sweep over Detroit in the first round of the playoffs, the Ducks became the first team since the 1952 Red Wings (over Toronto) to sweep a defending Stanley Cup champion.

Before joining Anaheim, Babcock spent two seasons as head coach of the Cincinnati Mighty Ducks (2000 to 2002), the primary development affiliate for both Detroit and Anaheim in the American Hockey League. He led the club to a franchise-best 41 wins and 95 points in 2000-01. Babcock moved to Cincinnati after a successful six-year run as the head coach of the Spokane Chiefs of the Western Hockey League (1994 through 2000). He was twice named WHL coach of the year (1996 and 2000) after taking the Chiefs to the league finals in both seasons. He began his WHL coaching career with the Moose Jaw Warriors in 1991-92. In Canadian university play, Babcock won a national championship and was named the coach of the year with the Lethbridge Pronghorns in 1993-94. In 1988, he was named head coach at Red Deer College in Red Deer, Alberta. He spent three seasons at the school, winning the Alberta college championship and coach of the year award in 1989.

Babcock played in the WHL for Saskatoon (1980-81) and Kelowna (1982-83), where he was team captain. In between, he spent a year at the University of Saskatoon. Babcock also played four years at McGill University (1983 to 1987), twice being named an All-Star defenseman. He earned his bachelor's degree in physical education and attended graduate school in sports psychology at McGill.

### Coaching Record

| | | | Regular Season | | | | Playoffs | | | |
|---|---|---|---|---|---|---|---|---|---|---|
| Season | Team | League | GC | W | L | O/T | GC | W | L | T |
| 1991-92 | Moose Jaw | WHL | 72 | 33 | 36 | 3 | 4 | 0 | 4 | .... |
| 1992-93 | Moose Jaw | WHL | 72 | 27 | 42 | 3 | .... | .... | .... | .... |
| 1993-94 | U of Lethbridge | CIAU | 28 | 19 | 7 | 2 | .... | .... | .... | .... |
| 1994-95 | Spokane | WHL | 72 | 32 | 36 | 4 | 11 | 6 | 5 | .... |
| 1995-96 | Spokane | WHL | 72 | 50 | 18 | 4 | 9 | 3 | 6 | .... |
| 1996-97 | Spokane | WHL | 72 | 35 | 33 | 4 | 9 | 4 | 5 | .... |
| 1997-98 | Spokane | WHL | 72 | 45 | 23 | 4 | 18 | 10 | 8 | .... |
| 1998-99 | Spokane | WHL | 72 | 19 | 44 | 9 | .... | .... | .... | .... |
| 99-2000 | Spokane | WHL | 72 | 47 | 19 | 6 | 20 | 15 | 5 | .... |
| 2000-01 | Cincinnati | AHL | 80 | 41 | 26 | 13 | 4 | 1 | 3 | .... |
| 2001-02 | Cincinnati | AHL | 80 | 33 | 33 | 14 | 3 | 1 | 2 | .... |
| **2002-03** | **Anaheim** | **NHL** | **82** | **40** | **27** | **15** | **21** | **15** | **6** | .... |
| **2003-04** | **Anaheim** | **NHL** | **82** | **29** | **35** | **18** | .... | .... | .... | .... |
| **2004-05** | **Anaheim** | | | | SEASON CANCELLED | | | | | |
| **2005-06** | **Detroit** | **NHL** | **82** | **58** | **16** | **8** | **6** | **2** | **4** | .... |
| **2006-07** | **Detroit** | **NHL** | **82** | **50** | **19** | **13** | **18** | **10** | **8** | .... |
| **2007-08♦** | **Detroit** | **NHL** | **82** | **54** | **21** | **7** | **22** | **16** | **6** | .... |
| **2008-09** | **Detroit** | **NHL** | **82** | **51** | **21** | **10** | **23** | **15** | **8** | .... |
| | **NHL Totals** | | **492** | **282** | **139** | **71** | **90** | **58** | **32** | .... |

♦ Stanley Cup win.

# Club Records

## Team

(Figures in brackets for season records are games played; records for fewest points, wins, ties, losses, goals, goals against are for 70 or more games)

| | | |
|---|---|---|
| **Most Points** | **131** | 1995-96 (82) |
| **Most Wins** | ***62** | 1995-96 (82) |
| **Most Ties** | **18** | 1952-53 (70), 1980-81 (80), 1996-97 (82) |
| **Most Losses** | **57** | 1985-86 (80) |
| **Most Goals** | **369** | 1992-93 (84) |
| **Most Goals Against** | **415** | 1985-86 (80) |
| **Fewest Points** | **40** | 1985-86 (80) |
| **Fewest Wins** | **16** | 1976-77 (80) |
| **Fewest Ties** | **4** | 1966-67 (70) |
| **Fewest Losses** | **13** | 1950-51 (70), 1995-96 (82) |
| **Fewest Goals** | **167** | 1958-59 (70) |
| **Fewest Goals Against** | **132** | 1953-54 (70) |
| **Longest Winning Streak** | | |
| **Overall** | **9** | Seven times |
| **Home** | **14** | Jan. 21-Mar. 25/65 |
| **Away** | ***12** | Mar. 1-Apr. 15/06 |
| **Longest Undefeated Streak** | | |
| **Overall** | **15** | Nov. 27-Dec. 28/52 (8 wins, 7 ties) |
| **Home** | **19** | Dec. 31/00-Apr.7/01 (17 wins, 2 ties) |
| **Away** | **15** | Oct. 18-Dec. 20/51 (10 wins, 5 ties) |
| **Longest Losing Streak** | | |
| **Overall** | **14** | Feb. 24-Mar. 25/82 |
| **Home** | **7** | Feb. 20-Mar. 25/82 |
| **Away** | **14** | Oct. 19-Dec. 21/66 |
| **Longest Winless Streak** | | |
| **Overall** | **19** | Feb. 26-Apr. 3/77 (18 losses, 1 tie) |
| **Home** | **10** | Dec. 11/85-Jan. 18/86 (9 losses, 1 tie) |
| **Away** | **26** | Dec. 15/76-Apr. 3/77 (23 losses, 3 ties) |
| **Most Shutouts, Season** | **13** | 1953-54 (70) |
| **Most. PIM, Season** | **2,393** | 1985-86 (80) |
| **Most Goals, Game** | **15** | Jan. 23/44 (NYR 0 at Det. 15) |

## Individual

| | | |
|---|---|---|
| **Most Seasons** | **25** | Gordie Howe |
| **Most Games** | **1,687** | Gordie Howe |
| **Most Goals, Career** | **786** | Gordie Howe |
| **Most Assists, Career** | **1,063** | Steve Yzerman |
| **Most Points, Career** | **1,809** | Gordie Howe (786G, 1,023A) |
| **Most PIM, Career** | **2,090** | Bob Probert |
| **Most Shutouts, Career** | **85** | Terry Sawchuk |
| **Longest Consecutive Games Streak** | **548** | Alex Delvecchio (Dec. 13/56-Nov. 11/64) |
| **Most Goals, Season** | **65** | Steve Yzerman (1988-89) |
| **Most Assists, Season** | **90** | Steve Yzerman (1988-89) |
| **Most Points, Season** | **155** | Steve Yzerman (1988-89; 65G, 90A) |
| **Most PIM, Season** | **398** | Bob Probert (1987-88) |
| **Most Points, Defenseman, Season** | **80** | Nicklas Lidstrom (2005-06; 16G, 64A) |
| **Most Points, Center, Season** | **155** | Steve Yzerman (1988-89; 65G, 90A) |
| **Most Points, Right Wing, Season** | **103** | Gordie Howe (1968-69; 44G, 59A) |
| **Most Points, Left Wing, Season** | **105** | John Ogrodnick (1984-85; 55G, 50A) |
| **Most Points, Rookie, Season** | **87** | Steve Yzerman (1983-84; 39G, 48A) |
| **Most Shutouts, Season** | **12** | Terry Sawchuk (1951-52), (1953-54), (1954-55) Glenn Hall (1955-56) |
| **Most Goals, Game** | **6** | Syd Howe (Feb. 3/44) |
| **Most Assists, Game** | ***7** | Billy Taylor (Mar. 16/47) |
| **Most Points, Game** | **7** | Carl Liscombe (Nov. 5/42; 3G, 4A), Don Grosso (Feb. 3/44; 1G, 6A), Billy Taylor (Mar. 16/47; 7A) |

* NHL Record.

## Retired Numbers

| | | |
|---|---|---|
| 1 | Terry Sawchuk | 1949-55, 57-64, 68-69 |
| 7 | Ted Lindsay | 1944-57, 64-65 |
| 9 | Gordie Howe | 1946-1971 |
| 10 | Alex Delvecchio | 1951-1973 |
| 12 | Sid Abel | 1938-43, 45-52 |
| 19 | Steve Yzerman | 1983-2006 |

# All-time Record vs. Other Clubs

## Regular Season

| | At Home | | | | | | | | On Road | | | | | | | | Total | | | | | | | |
|---|---|---|---|---|---|---|---|---|---|---|---|---|---|---|---|---|---|---|---|---|---|---|---|---|
| | GP | W | L | T | OL | GF | GA | PTS | GP | W | L | T | OL | GF | GA | PTS | GP | W | L | T | OL | GF | GA | PTS |
| Anaheim | 30 | 24 | 3 | 3 | 0 | 104 | 61 | 51 | 30 | 14 | 11 | 4 | 1 | 84 | 78 | 33 | 60 | 38 | 14 | 7 | 1 | 188 | 139 | 84 |
| Atlanta | 6 | 5 | 1 | 0 | 0 | 23 | 16 | 10 | 5 | 4 | 1 | 0 | 0 | 31 | 17 | 8 | 11 | 9 | 2 | 0 | 0 | 54 | 33 | 18 |
| Boston | 286 | 154 | 80 | 52 | 0 | 955 | 726 | 360 | 289 | 91 | 154 | 43 | 1 | 765 | 1012 | 226 | 575 | 245 | 234 | 95 | 1 | 1720 | 1738 | 586 |
| Buffalo | 57 | 33 | 18 | 5 | 1 | 208 | 163 | 72 | 54 | 13 | 33 | 8 | 0 | 161 | 229 | 34 | 111 | 46 | 51 | 13 | 1 | 369 | 392 | 106 |
| Calgary | 67 | 37 | 19 | 10 | 1 | 251 | 200 | 85 | 68 | 23 | 39 | 6 | 0 | 196 | 247 | 52 | 135 | 60 | 58 | 16 | 1 | 447 | 447 | 137 |
| Carolina | 32 | 18 | 7 | 7 | 0 | 124 | 88 | 43 | 32 | 13 | 18 | 1 | 0 | 91 | 108 | 27 | 64 | 31 | 25 | 8 | 0 | 215 | 196 | 70 |
| Chicago | 350 | 214 | 101 | 33 | 2 | 1207 | 870 | 463 | 353 | 142 | 155 | 51 | 5 | 1003 | 1058 | 340 | 703 | 356 | 256 | 84 | 7 | 2210 | 1928 | 803 |
| Colorado | 48 | 29 | 16 | 1 | 2 | 171 | 140 | 61 | 50 | 24 | 21 | 4 | 1 | 168 | 165 | 53 | 98 | 53 | 37 | 5 | 3 | 339 | 305 | 114 |
| Columbus | 25 | 19 | 4 | 0 | 2 | 92 | 60 | 40 | 26 | 17 | 6 | 1 | 2 | 83 | 55 | 37 | 51 | 36 | 10 | 1 | 4 | 175 | 115 | 77 |
| Dallas | 114 | 58 | 39 | 16 | 1 | 434 | 358 | 133 | 114 | 41 | 53 | 18 | 2 | 339 | 386 | 102 | 228 | 99 | 92 | 34 | 3 | 773 | 744 | 235 |
| Edmonton | 52 | 30 | 15 | 3 | 4 | 202 | 163 | 67 | 52 | 18 | 20 | 10 | 4 | 180 | 194 | 50 | 104 | 48 | 35 | 13 | 8 | 382 | 357 | 117 |
| Florida | 9 | 5 | 1 | 3 | 0 | 35 | 23 | 13 | 11 | 7 | 1 | 2 | 1 | 32 | 22 | 17 | 20 | 12 | 2 | 5 | 1 | 67 | 45 | 30 |
| Los Angeles | 87 | 43 | 31 | 13 | 0 | 338 | 294 | 99 | 88 | 31 | 42 | 14 | 1 | 276 | 334 | 77 | 175 | 74 | 73 | 27 | 1 | 614 | 628 | 176 |
| Minnesota | 16 | 11 | 3 | 1 | 1 | 60 | 37 | 24 | 16 | 10 | 2 | 2 | 2 | 46 | 37 | 24 | 32 | 21 | 5 | 3 | 3 | 106 | 74 | 48 |
| Montreal | 282 | 131 | 98 | 53 | 0 | 808 | 720 | 315 | 283 | 68 | 172 | 43 | 0 | 640 | 995 | 179 | 565 | 199 | 270 | 96 | 0 | 1448 | 1715 | 494 |
| Nashville | 32 | 22 | 4 | 2 | 4 | 117 | 72 | 50 | 31 | 15 | 12 | 2 | 2 | 89 | 89 | 34 | 63 | 37 | 16 | 4 | 6 | 206 | 161 | 84 |
| New Jersey | 42 | 27 | 13 | 2 | 0 | 172 | 132 | 56 | 41 | 11 | 21 | 9 | 0 | 105 | 139 | 31 | 83 | 38 | 34 | 11 | 0 | 277 | 271 | 87 |
| NY Islanders | 47 | 26 | 19 | 2 | 0 | 166 | 139 | 54 | 47 | 20 | 23 | 4 | 0 | 141 | 167 | 44 | 94 | 46 | 42 | 6 | 0 | 307 | 306 | 98 |
| NY Rangers | 287 | 166 | 76 | 45 | 0 | 1013 | 706 | 377 | 285 | 93 | 134 | 58 | 0 | 742 | 871 | 244 | 572 | 259 | 210 | 103 | 0 | 1755 | 1577 | 621 |
| Ottawa | 10 | 6 | 4 | 0 | 0 | 35 | 22 | 12 | 12 | 7 | 4 | 1 | 0 | 34 | 33 | 15 | 22 | 13 | 8 | 1 | 0 | 69 | 55 | 27 |
| Philadelphia | 61 | 33 | 18 | 10 | 0 | 219 | 187 | 76 | 59 | 13 | 35 | 11 | 0 | 169 | 236 | 37 | 120 | 46 | 53 | 21 | 0 | 388 | 423 | 113 |
| Phoenix | 59 | 31 | 20 | 8 | 0 | 230 | 193 | 70 | 57 | 25 | 18 | 14 | 0 | 188 | 168 | 64 | 116 | 56 | 38 | 22 | 0 | 418 | 361 | 134 |
| Pittsburgh | 67 | 41 | 13 | 12 | 1 | 262 | 186 | 95 | 67 | 19 | 44 | 4 | 0 | 200 | 281 | 42 | 134 | 60 | 57 | 16 | 1 | 462 | 467 | 137 |
| St. Louis | 125 | 61 | 44 | 17 | 3 | 452 | 370 | 142 | 125 | 45 | 57 | 20 | 3 | 358 | 401 | 113 | 250 | 106 | 101 | 37 | 6 | 810 | 771 | 255 |
| San Jose | 33 | 28 | 4 | 1 | 0 | 132 | 56 | 57 | 34 | 17 | 14 | 3 | 0 | 130 | 123 | 37 | 67 | 45 | 18 | 4 | 0 | 262 | 179 | 94 |
| Tampa Bay | 13 | 11 | 1 | 1 | 0 | 51 | 23 | 23 | 16 | 11 | 4 | 1 | 0 | 71 | 49 | 23 | 29 | 22 | 5 | 2 | 0 | 122 | 72 | 46 |
| Toronto | 324 | 169 | 107 | 46 | 2 | 975 | 796 | 386 | 317 | 105 | 164 | 47 | 1 | 848 | 1048 | 258 | 641 | 274 | 271 | 93 | 3 | 1823 | 1844 | 644 |
| Vancouver | 74 | 45 | 18 | 8 | 3 | 298 | 213 | 101 | 73 | 30 | 32 | 10 | 1 | 231 | 259 | 71 | 147 | 75 | 50 | 18 | 4 | 529 | 472 | 172 |
| Washington | 48 | 22 | 15 | 11 | 0 | 165 | 138 | 55 | 48 | 21 | 22 | 5 | 0 | 153 | 175 | 47 | 96 | 43 | 37 | 16 | 0 | 318 | 313 | 102 |
| Defunct Clubs | 141 | 76 | 40 | 25 | 0 | 430 | 307 | 177 | 141 | 49 | 63 | 29 | 0 | 364 | 375 | 127 | 282 | 125 | 103 | 54 | 0 | 794 | 682 | 304 |
| **Totals** | **2824** | **1575** | **832** | **390** | **27** | **9729** | **7459** | **3567** | **2824** | **997** | **1375** | **425** | **27** | **7918** | **9351** | **2446** | **5648** | **2572** | **2207** | **815** | **54** | **17647** | **16810** | **6013** |

## Playoffs

| | Series | W | L | GP | W | L | T | GF | GA | Last Mtg. | Rnd. | Result |
|---|---|---|---|---|---|---|---|---|---|---|---|---|
| Anaheim | 5 | 3 | 2 | 25 | 14 | 11 | 0 | 75 | 57 | 2009 | CSF | W 4-3 |
| Boston | 7 | 3 | 4 | 33 | 14 | 19 | 0 | 98 | 96 | 1957 | SF | L 1-4 |
| Calgary | 3 | 2 | 1 | 14 | 8 | 6 | 0 | 38 | 26 | 2007 | CQF | W 4-2 |
| Carolina | 1 | 1 | 0 | 5 | 4 | 1 | 0 | 14 | 7 | 2002 | F | W 4-1 |
| Chicago | 15 | 7 | 8 | 74 | 35 | 39 | 0 | 209 | 220 | 2009 | CF | W 4-1 |
| Colorado | 6 | 3 | 3 | 34 | 17 | 17 | 0 | 97 | 88 | 2008 | CSF | W 4-0 |
| Columbus | 1 | 1 | 0 | 4 | 4 | 0 | 0 | 18 | 7 | 2009 | CQF | W 4-0 |
| Dallas | 4 | 4 | 0 | 24 | 16 | 8 | 0 | 72 | 50 | 2008 | CF | W 4-2 |
| Edmonton | 3 | 0 | 3 | 16 | 4 | 12 | 0 | 43 | 58 | 2006 | CQF | L 2-4 |
| Los Angeles | 2 | 1 | 1 | 10 | 6 | 4 | 0 | 32 | 21 | 2001 | CQF | L 2-4 |
| Montreal | 12 | 7 | 5 | 62 | 29 | 33 | 0 | 149 | 161 | 1978 | QF | L 1-4 |
| Nashville | 2 | 2 | 0 | 12 | 8 | 4 | 0 | 29 | 21 | 2008 | CQF | W 4-2 |
| New Jersey | 1 | 0 | 1 | 4 | 0 | 4 | 0 | 7 | 16 | 1995 | F | L 0-4 |
| NY Rangers | 5 | 4 | 1 | 23 | 13 | 10 | 0 | 57 | 49 | 1950 | F | W 4-3 |
| Philadelphia | 1 | 1 | 0 | 4 | 4 | 0 | 0 | 16 | 6 | 1997 | F | W 4-0 |
| Phoenix | 2 | 2 | 0 | 12 | 8 | 4 | 0 | 44 | 28 | 1998 | CQF | W 4-2 |
| Pittsburgh | 2 | 1 | 1 | 13 | 7 | 6 | 0 | 34 | 24 | 2009 | F | L 3-4 |
| St. Louis | 7 | 5 | 2 | 40 | 24 | 16 | 0 | 125 | 103 | 2002 | CSF | W 4-1 |
| San Jose | 3 | 2 | 1 | 17 | 11 | 6 | 0 | 64 | 36 | 2007 | CSF | W 4-2 |
| Toronto | 23 | 11 | 12 | 117 | 59 | 58 | 0 | 321 | 311 | 1993 | DSF | L 3-4 |
| Vancouver | 1 | 1 | 0 | 6 | 4 | 2 | 0 | 22 | 16 | 2002 | CQF | W 4-2 |
| Washington | 1 | 1 | 0 | 4 | 4 | 0 | 0 | 13 | 7 | 1998 | F | W 4-0 |
| Defunct Clubs | 4 | 3 | 1 | 10 | 7 | 2 | 1 | 21 | 13 | | | |
| **Totals** | **111** | **65** | **46** | **563** | **300** | **262** | **1** | **1598** | **1421** | | | |

Calgary totals include Atlanta Flames, 1972-73 to 1979-80. Carolina totals include Hartford, 1979-80 to 1996-97.
Colorado totals include Quebec, 1979-80 to 1994-95. Dallas totals include Minnesota North Stars, 1967-68 to 1992-93.
New Jersey totals include Kansas City, 1974-75, 1975-76, and Colorado Rockies, 1976-77 to 1981-82.
Phoenix totals include Winnipeg, 1979-80 to 1995-96.

## Playoff Results 2009-2004

| Year | Round | Opponent | Result | GF | GA |
|---|---|---|---|---|---|
| 2009 | F | Pittsburgh | L 3-4 | 17 | 14 |
| | CF | Chicago | W 4-1 | 19 | 10 |
| | CSF | Anaheim | W 4-3 | 22 | 17 |
| | CQF | Columbus | W 4-0 | 18 | 7 |
| **2008** | **F** | **Pittsburgh** | **W 4-2** | **17** | **10** |
| | CF | Dallas | W 4-2 | 17 | 10 |
| | CSF | Colorado | W 4-0 | 21 | 9 |
| | CQF | Nashville | W 4-2 | 17 | 12 |
| 2007 | CF | Anaheim | L 2-4 | 17 | 16 |
| | CSF | San Jose | W 4-2 | 13 | 9 |
| | CQF | Calgary | W 4-2 | 18 | 10 |
| 2006 | CQF | Edmonton | L 2-4 | 17 | 19 |
| 2004 | CSF | Calgary | L 2-4 | 12 | 11 |
| | CQF | Nashville | W 4-2 | 12 | 9 |

**Abbreviations: Round: F** - Final; **CF** - conference final; **CSF** - conference semi-final; **CQF** - conference quarter-final; **DSF** - division semi-final; **SF** - semi-final; **QF** - quarter-final.

## 2008-09 Results

| | | | | | | | |
|---|---|---|---|---|---|---|---|
| **Oct.** | 9 | Toronto | 2-3 | | 12 | at Dallas | 4-5* |
| | 11 | at Ottawa | 3-2 | | 14 | at Anaheim | 4-3 |
| | 13 | at Carolina | 3-1 | | 15 | at Los Angeles | 4-0 |
| | 16 | Vancouver | 3-4* | | 17 | at San Jose | 5-6 |
| | 18 | NY Rangers | 5-4* | | 20 | at Phoenix | 3-6 |
| | 22 | at St. Louis | 4-3 | | 27 | at Columbus | 2-3* |
| | 24 | Atlanta | 5-3 | | 29 | Dallas | 2-4 |
| | 25 | at Chicago | 6-5† | | 31 | at Washington | 2-4 |
| | 27 | at Los Angeles | 4-3† | **Feb.** | 2 | St. Louis | 4-3† |
| | 29 | at Anaheim | 4-5* | | 4 | Phoenix | 5-4 |
| | 30 | at San Jose | 2-4 | | 7 | Edmonton | 8-3 |
| **Nov.** | 2 | at Vancouver | 3-2 | | 8 | at Pittsburgh | 3-0 |
| | 8 | New Jersey | 3-1 | | 10 | at Nashville | 5-3 |
| | 11 | Pittsburgh | 6-7* | | 12 | Minnesota | 4-2 |
| | 13 | at Tampa Bay | 4-3 | | 13 | at Columbus | 2-3 |
| | 14 | at Florida | 3-2 | | 15 | Colorado | 5-6† |
| | 17 | Edmonton | 4-0 | | 18 | Nashville | 6-2 |
| | 20 | at Edmonton | 4-3 | | 20 | Anaheim | 5-2 |
| | 22 | at Calgary | 5-2 | | 21 | at Minnesota | 2-5 |
| | 24 | at Vancouver | 2-3* | | 25 | San Jose | 4-1 |
| | 26 | Montreal | 1-3 | | 27 | Los Angeles | 2-1 |
| | 28 | Columbus | 5-3 | | 28 | at Nashville | 0-8 |
| | 29 | at Boston | 1-4 | **Mar.** | 3 | at St. Louis | 5-0 |
| **Dec.** | 1 | Anaheim | 2-1 | | 4 | at Colorado | 3-2 |
| | 4 | Vancouver | 6-5 | | 7 | Columbus | 2-8 |
| | 6 | Chicago | 5-4† | | 10 | Phoenix | 3-2* |
| | 10 | Calgary | 4-3* | | 12 | Calgary | 5-6† |
| | 12 | at Dallas | 1-3 | | 14 | at St. Louis | 5-2 |
| | 13 | at Phoenix | 5-4† | | 15 | at Columbus | 4-0 |
| | 15 | Colorado | 2-3 | | 17 | Philadelphia | 3-2 |
| | 18 | San Jose | 6-0 | | 20 | at Atlanta | 6-3 |
| | 20 | Los Angeles | 6-4 | | 23 | at Calgary | 3-5 |
| | 23 | St. Louis | 4-1 | | 24 | at Edmonton | 3-2 |
| | 26 | at Nashville | 2-3 | | 27 | NY Islanders | 0-2 |
| | 27 | at Colorado | 3-4† | | 29 | Nashville | 3-4 |
| | 30 | Chicago | 4-0 | **Apr.** | 2 | St. Louis | 4-5 |
| **Jan.** | 1 | at Chicago | 6-4 | | 5 | Minnesota | 3-2 |
| | 3 | at Minnesota | 3-2† | | 6 | at Buffalo | 4-1 |
| | 6 | Columbus | 3-0 | | 9 | Nashville | 3-4† |
| | 8 | Dallas | 6-1 | | 11 | Chicago | 2-4 |
| | 10 | Buffalo | 3-1 | | 12 | at Chicago | 0-3 |

* – Overtime † – Shootout

## Entry Draft Selections 2009-1995

Name in bold denotes played in NHL.

**2009**

| Pick | |
|---|---|
| 32 | Landon Ferraro |
| 60 | Tomas Tatar |
| 75 | Andrej Nestrasil |
| 90 | Gleason Fournier |
| 150 | Nick Jensen |
| 180 | Mitchell Callahan |
| 210 | Adam Almquist |

**2008**

| Pick | |
|---|---|
| 30 | Thomas McCollum |
| 91 | Max Nicastro |
| 121 | Gustav Nyquist |
| 151 | Julien Cayer |
| 181 | Stephen Johnston |
| 211 | Jesper Samuelsson |

**2007**

| Pick | |
|---|---|
| 27 | Brendan Smith |
| 88 | Joakim Andersson |
| 148 | Randy Cameron |
| 178 | Zack Torquato |
| 208 | Bryan Rufenach |

**2006**

| Pick | |
|---|---|
| 41 | Cory Emmerton |
| 47 | **Shawn Matthias** |
| 62 | Dick Axelsson |
| 92 | Daniel Larsson |
| 182 | Jan Mursak |
| 191 | Nick Oslund |
| 212 | Logan Pyett |

**2005**

| Pick | |
|---|---|
| 19 | Jakub Kindl |
| 42 | **Justin Abdelkader** |
| 80 | Christofer Lofberg |
| 103 | **Mattias Ritola** |
| 132 | **Darren Helm** |
| 137 | Johan Ryno |
| 151 | Jeff May |
| 175 | Juho Mielonen |
| 214 | Bretton Stamler |

**2004**

| Pick | |
|---|---|
| 97 | **Johan Franzen** |
| 128 | Evan McGrath |
| 151 | Sergei Kolosov |
| 162 | Tyler Haskins |
| 192 | Anton Axelsson |
| 226 | Steven Covington |
| 257 | Gennady Stolyarov |
| 290 | Nils Backstrom |

**2003**

| Pick | |
|---|---|
| 64 | **Jimmy Howard** |
| 132 | **Kyle Quincey** |
| 164 | Ryan Oulahen |
| 170 | Andreas Sundin |
| 194 | Stefan Blom |
| 226 | Tomas Kollar |
| 258 | Vladimir Kutny |
| 289 | Mikael Johansson |

**2002**

| Pick | |
|---|---|
| 58 | **Jiri Hudler** |
| 63 | **Tomas Fleischmann** |
| 95 | **Valtteri Filppula** |
| 131 | Johan Berggren |
| 166 | Logan Koopmans |
| 197 | Jimmy Cuddihy |
| 229 | **Derek Meech** |
| 260 | Pierre-Olivier Beaulieu |
| 262 | Christian Soderstrom |
| 291 | **Jonathan Ericsson** |

**2001**

| Pick | |
|---|---|
| 62 | Igor Grigorenko |
| 121 | **Drew MacIntyre** |
| 129 | Miroslav Blatak |
| 157 | Andreas Jamtin |
| 195 | Nick Pannoni |
| 258 | **Dmitri Bykov** |
| 288 | Francois Senez |

**2000**

| Pick | |
|---|---|
| 29 | **Niklas Kronwall** |
| 38 | **Tomas Kopecky** |
| 102 | Stefan Liv |
| 127 | Dmitri Semenov |
| 128 | Alexander Seluyanov |
| 130 | Aaron Van Leusen |
| 187 | Per Backer |
| 196 | Paul Ballantyne |
| 228 | Jimmie Svensson |
| 251 | Todd Jackson |
| 260 | Yevgeny Bumagin |

**1999**

| Pick | |
|---|---|
| 120 | Jari Tolsa |
| 149 | Andrei Maximenko |
| 181 | **Kent McDonell** |
| 210 | **Henrik Zetterberg** |
| 238 | Anton Borodkin |
| 266 | Ken Davis |

**1998**

| Pick | |
|---|---|
| 25 | **Jiri Fischer** |
| 55 | **Ryan Barnes** |
| 56 | Tomek Valtonen |
| 84 | Jake McCracken |
| 111 | Brent Hobday |
| 142 | Calle Steen |
| 151 | Adam DeLeeuw |
| 171 | **Pavel Datsyuk** |
| 198 | Jeremy Goetzinger |
| 226 | David Petrasek |
| 256 | Petja Pietilainen |

**1997**

| Pick | |
|---|---|
| 49 | **Yuri Butsayev** |
| 76 | **Petr Sykora** |
| 102 | **Quintin Laing** |
| 129 | John Wikstrom |
| 157 | **B.J. Young** |
| 186 | Mike Laceby |
| 213 | Steve Willejto |
| 239 | Greg Willers |

**1996**

| Pick | |
|---|---|
| 26 | **Jesse Wallin** |
| 52 | Aren Miller |
| 108 | Johan Forsander |
| 135 | Michal Podolka |
| 144 | Magnus Nilsson |
| 162 | Alexandre Jacques |
| 189 | Colin Beardsmore |
| 215 | Craig Stahl |
| 241 | Eugeny Afanasiev |

**1995**

| Pick | |
|---|---|
| 26 | **Maxim Kuznetsov** |
| 52 | **Philippe Audet** |
| 58 | **Darryl Laplante** |
| 104 | Anatoli Ustyugov |
| 125 | Chad Wilchynski |
| 126 | David Arsenault |
| 156 | Tyler Perry |
| 182 | Per Eklund |
| 208 | Andrei Samokhvalov |
| 234 | David Engblom |

# Club Directory

Joe Louis Arena

**Detroit Red Wings**
Joe Louis Arena
19 Steve Yzerman Drive
Detroit, MI 48226
Phone **313/394-7000**
FAX PR: 313/567-0296
Media Hotline: 313/396-7599
www.detroitredwings.com
**Capacity:** 20,066

| | |
|---|---|
| Owner/Governor | Mike Ilitch |
| Owner/Secretary-Treasurer | Marian Ilitch |
| President and CEO Ilitch Holdings/ Alternate Governor Red Wings | Christopher Ilitch |
| Senior Vice President/Alternate Governor | Jim Devellano |
| Executive Vice President/General Manager | Ken Holland |
| Vice President/Hockey | Steve Yzerman |
| Vice President/Assistant General Manager | Jim Nill |
| Senior Vice President of Business Affairs | Steven Violetta |
| Vice President Olympia Entertainment/ General Counsel Red Wings | Robert E. Carr |
| Director of Hockey Administration | Ryan Martin |
| Director of Player Development | Jiri Fischer |
| Head Coach | Mike Babcock |
| Assistant Coaches | Paul MacLean, Brad McCrimmon |
| Video Coach | Keith McKittrick |
| Goaltending Coach | Jim Bedard |
| Director of Pro Scouting | Mark Howe |
| Pro Scouts | Pat Verbeek, Glenn Merkosky |
| Director of Amateur Scouting | Joe McDonnell |
| Amateur Scouts | Bruce Haralson, Mark Leach, Dave Kolb, Jeff Finley |
| Director of European Scouting | Hakan Andersson |
| European Scouts | Vladimir Havluj, Evgeni Erfilov, Ari Vouri |
| Part-Time Scout | Marty Stein |
| Vice President of Finance | Paul MacDonald |
| Executive Assistant | Kathi Wyatt |
| General Accountant | Bridget Merritt |
| Administrative Assistant | Julie Dailey |
| Athletic Therapist | Piet Van Zant |
| Head Equipment Manager | Paul Boyer |
| Assistant Athletic Therapist | Russ Baumann |
| Assistant Equipment Managers | John Remejes, Adam Sheehan |
| Team Masseurs | Sergei Tchekmarev, Lynne Newman |
| Senior Director of Communications | John Hahn |
| Media Relations Manager | Todd Beam |
| Public Relations Coordinator | Lisa Hickok |
| Community Relations Coordinator | Kelli Kearly |
| Medical Director | Dr. Donald Weaver |
| Team Physicians | Dr. Anthony Colucci, Dr. Doug Plagens |
| Team Dentist | Dr. C.J. Regula |
| Team Photographer | Dave Reginek |
| Radio Announcers, 97.1 The Ticket | Ken Kal, Paul Woods |
| Television Announcers, Fox Sports Detroit | Ken Daniels, Mickey Redmond |

### Coaching History

Art Duncan and Duke Keats, 1926-27; Jack Adams, 1927-28 to 1946-47; Tommy Ivan, 1947-48 to 1953-54; Jimmy Skinner, 1954-55 to 1956-57; Jimmy Skinner and Sid Abel, 1957-58; Sid Abel, 1958-59 to 1967-68; Bill Gadsby, 1968-69; Bill Gadsby and Sid Abel, 1969-70; Ned Harkness and Doug Barkley, 1970-71; Doug Barkley and Johnny Wilson, 1971-72; Johnny Wilson, 1972-73; Ted Garvin and Alex Delvecchio, 1973-74; Alex Delvecchio, 1974-75; Doug Barkley and Alex Delvecchio, 1975-76; Alex Delvecchio and Larry Wilson, 1976-77; Bobby Kromm, 1977-78, 1978-79; Bobby Kromm and Ted Lindsay, 1979-80; Ted Lindsay and Wayne Maxner, 1980-81; Wayne Maxner and Billy Dea, 1981-82; Nick Polano, 1982-83 to 1984-85; Harry Neale and Brad Park, 1985-86; Jacques Demers, 1986-87 to 1989-90; Bryan Murray, 1990-91 to 1992-93; Scotty Bowman, 1993-94 to 1997-98; Dave Lewis, Barry Smith (co-coaches) and Scotty Bowman, 1998-99; Scotty Bowman, 1999-2000 to 2001-02; Dave Lewis, 2002-03 to 2004-05; Mike Babcock, 2005-06 to date.

## Ken Holland

### General Manager

*Born: Vernon, B.C., November 10, 1955.*

Ken Holland has served in the Red Wings front office since 1985, and has been the club's general manager since July 18, 1997. He has established himself as one of the most innovative and aggressive GMs in the National Hockey League. Detroit's Stanley Cup victory in 2008 marked the team's third championship under his leadership. Holland began his tenure as the club's general manager after serving as assistant general manager for the previous three seasons.

Holland oversees all aspects of hockey operations including all matters relating to player personnel, development, contract negotiations and player movements, though he now takes a less prominent role in the NHL draft than he did during his seven years as the club's director of amateur scouting.

At the conclusion of his playing days as a goaltender, spending most of his pro career at the American Hockey League level, Holland began his off-ice career in 1985 as a western Canada scout followed by five years as an amateur scouting director before promotions led to his current position as general manager.

A native of Vernon, British Columbia, Holland played in the junior ranks for Medicine Hat (WHL) in 1974-75. He was Toronto's 13th pick (188th overall) in the 1975 draft but never saw action with the Maple Leafs. Holland twice signed with NHL teams as a free agent — in 1980 with Hartford and 1983 with Detroit. He spent most of his pro career with AHL clubs in Binghamton and Springfield, along with Adirondack, but did appear in four NHL games, making his debut with Hartford in 1980-81 and playing three contests for Detroit in 1983-84.

### General Managers' History

Art Duncan and Duke Keats, 1926-27; Jack Adams, 1927-28 to 1961-62; Sid Abel, 1962-63 to 1969-70; Sid Abel and Ned Harkness, 1970-71; Ned Harkness, 1971-72 to 1973-74; Alex Delvecchio, 1974-75, 1975-76; Alex Delvecchio and Ted Lindsay, 1976-77; Ted Lindsay, 1977-78 to 1979-80; Jimmy Skinner, 1980-81, 1981-82; Jim Devellano, 1982-83 to 1989-90; Bryan Murray, 1990-91 to 1993-94; Jim Devellano (Senior Vice President), 1994-95 to 1996-97; Ken Holland, 1997-98 to date.

### Captains' History

Art Duncan, 1926-27; Reg Noble, 1927-28 to 1929-30; George Hay, 1930-31; Carson Cooper, 1931-32; Larry Aurie, 1932-33; Herbie Lewis, 1933-34; Ebbie Goodfellow, 1934-35; Doug Young, 1935-36 to 1937-38; Ebbie Goodfellow, 1938-39 to 1940-41; Ebbie Goodfellow and Syd Howe, 1941-42; Sid Abel, 1942-43; Mud Bruneteau, Flash Hollett, 1943-44; Flash Hollett, 1944-45; Flash Hollett and Sid Abel, 1945-46; Sid Abel, 1946-47 to 1951-52; Ted Lindsay, 1952-53 to 1955-56; Red Kelly, 1956-57, 1957-58; Gordie Howe, 1958-59 to 1961-62; Alex Delvecchio, 1962-63 to 1972-73; Alex Delvecchio, Nick Libett, Red Berenson, Gary Bergman, Ted Harris, Mickey Redmond and Larry Johnston, 1973-74; Marcel Dionne, 1974-75; Danny Grant and Terry Harper, 1975-76; Danny Grant and Dennis Polonich, 1976-77; Dan Maloney and Dennis Hextall, 1977-78; Dennis Hextall, Nick Libett and Paul Woods, 1978-79; Dale McCourt, 1979-80; Errol Thompson and Reed Larson, 1980-81; Reed Larson, 1981-82; Danny Gare, 1982-83 to 1985-86; Steve Yzerman, 1986-87 to 2005-06; Nicklas Lidstrom, 2006-07 to date.

# Edmonton Oilers

## 2008-09 Results: 38W-35L-5OTL-4SOL 85PTS.
## Fourth, Northwest Division

### Key Off-Season Signings/Acquisitions

**2009**

**May 26** • Named **Pat Quinn** head coach and **Tom Renney** associate coach.
**July 1** • Signed G **Nikolai Khabibulin.**
**1** • Re-signed D **Jason Strudwick.**
**21** • Re-signed D **Denis Grebeshkov.**
**29** • Re-signed LW **Liam Reddox** and C **Ryan Potulny.**

### Year-by-Year Record

| | | Home | | | | Road | | | | Overall | | | | | | | | |
|---|---|---|---|---|---|---|---|---|---|---|---|---|---|---|---|---|---|---|
| Season | GP | W | L | T | OL | W | L | T | OL | W | L | T | OL | GF | GA | Pts. | Finished | Playoff Result |
| 2008-09 | 82 | 18 | 17 | .... | 6 | 20 | 18 | .... | 3 | 38 | 35 | .... | 9 | 234 | 248 | 85 | 4th, Northwest Div. | Out of Playoffs |
| 2007-08 | 82 | 23 | 17 | .... | 1 | 18 | 18 | .... | 5 | 41 | 35 | .... | 6 | 235 | 251 | 88 | 4th, Northwest Div. | Out of Playoffs |
| 2006-07 | 82 | 19 | 19 | .... | 3 | 13 | 24 | .... | 4 | 32 | 43 | .... | 7 | 195 | 248 | 71 | 5th, Northwest Div. | Out of Playoffs |
| 2005-06 | 82 | 20 | 15 | .... | 6 | 21 | 13 | .... | 7 | 41 | 28 | .... | 13 | 256 | 251 | 95 | 3rd, Northwest Div. | Lost Final |
| 2004-05 | .... | .... | .... | .... | .... | .... | .... | .... | .... | .... | .... | .... | .... | .... | .... | .... | | |
| 2003-04 | 82 | 22 | 12 | 4 | 3 | 14 | 17 | 8 | 2 | 36 | 29 | 12 | 5 | 221 | 208 | 89 | 4th, Northwest Div. | Out of Playoffs |
| 2002-03 | 82 | 20 | 12 | 5 | 4 | 16 | 14 | 6 | 5 | 36 | 26 | 11 | 9 | 231 | 230 | 92 | 4th, Northwest Div. | Lost Conf. Quarter-Final |
| 2001-02 | 82 | 23 | 14 | 4 | 0 | 15 | 14 | 8 | 4 | 38 | 28 | 12 | 4 | 205 | 182 | 92 | 3rd, Northwest Div. | Out of Playoffs |
| 2000-01 | 82 | 23 | 9 | 7 | 2 | 16 | 19 | 5 | 1 | 39 | 28 | 12 | 3 | 243 | 222 | 93 | 2nd, Northwest Div. | Lost Conf. Quarter-Final |
| 1999-2000 | 82 | 18 | 11 | 9 | 3 | 14 | 15 | 7 | 5 | 32 | 26 | 16 | 8 | 226 | 212 | 88 | 2nd, Northwest Div. | Lost Conf. Quarter-Final |
| 1998-99 | 82 | 17 | 19 | 5 | .... | 16 | 18 | 7 | .... | 33 | 37 | 12 | .... | 230 | 226 | 78 | 2nd, Northwest Div. | Lost Conf. Quarter-Final |
| 1997-98 | 82 | 20 | 16 | 5 | .... | 15 | 21 | 5 | .... | 35 | 37 | 10 | .... | 215 | 224 | 80 | 3rd, Pacific Div. | Lost Conf. Semi-Final |
| 1996-97 | 82 | 21 | 16 | 4 | .... | 15 | 21 | 5 | .... | 36 | 37 | 9 | .... | 252 | 247 | 81 | 3rd, Pacific Div. | Lost Conf. Semi-Final |
| 1995-96 | 82 | 15 | 21 | 5 | .... | 15 | 23 | 3 | .... | 30 | 44 | 8 | .... | 240 | 304 | 68 | 5th, Pacific Div. | Out of Playoffs |
| 1994-95 | 48 | 11 | 12 | 1 | .... | 6 | 15 | 3 | .... | 17 | 27 | 4 | .... | 136 | 183 | 38 | 5th, Pacific Div. | Out of Playoffs |
| 1993-94 | 84 | 17 | 22 | 3 | .... | 8 | 23 | 11 | .... | 25 | 45 | 14 | .... | 261 | 305 | 64 | 6th, Pacific Div. | Out of Playoffs |
| 1992-93 | 84 | 16 | 21 | 5 | .... | 10 | 29 | 3 | .... | 26 | 50 | 8 | .... | 242 | 337 | 60 | 5th, Smythe Div. | Out of Playoffs |
| 1991-92 | 80 | 22 | 13 | 5 | .... | 14 | 21 | 5 | .... | 36 | 34 | 10 | .... | 295 | 297 | 82 | 3rd, Smythe Div. | Lost Conf. Championship |
| 1990-91 | 80 | 22 | 15 | 3 | .... | 15 | 22 | 3 | .... | 37 | 37 | 6 | .... | 272 | 272 | 80 | 3rd, Smythe Div. | Lost Conf. Championship |
| **1989-90** | **80** | **23** | **11** | **6** | .... | **15** | **17** | **8** | .... | **38** | **28** | **14** | .... | **315** | **283** | **90** | **2nd, Smythe Div.** | **Won Stanley Cup** |
| 1988-89 | 80 | 21 | 16 | 3 | .... | 17 | 18 | 5 | .... | 38 | 34 | 8 | .... | 325 | 306 | 84 | 3rd, Smythe Div. | Lost Div. Semi-Final |
| **1987-88** | **80** | **28** | **8** | **4** | .... | **16** | **17** | **7** | .... | **44** | **25** | **11** | .... | **363** | **288** | **99** | **2nd, Smythe Div.** | **Won Stanley Cup** |
| **1986-87** | **80** | **29** | **6** | **5** | .... | **21** | **18** | **1** | .... | **50** | **24** | **6** | .... | **372** | **284** | **106** | **1st, Smythe Div.** | **Won Stanley Cup** |
| 1985-86 | 80 | 32 | 6 | 2 | .... | 24 | 11 | 5 | .... | 56 | 17 | 7 | .... | 426 | 310 | 119 | 1st, Smythe Div. | Lost Div. Final |
| **1984-85** | **80** | **26** | **7** | **7** | .... | **23** | **13** | **4** | .... | **49** | **20** | **11** | .... | **401** | **298** | **109** | **1st, Smythe Div.** | **Won Stanley Cup** |
| **1983-84** | **80** | **31** | **5** | **4** | .... | **26** | **13** | **1** | .... | **57** | **18** | **5** | .... | **446** | **314** | **119** | **1st, Smythe Div.** | **Won Stanley Cup** |
| 1982-83 | 80 | 25 | 9 | 6 | .... | 22 | 12 | 6 | .... | 47 | 21 | 12 | .... | 424 | 315 | 106 | 1st, Smythe Div. | Lost Final |
| 1981-82 | 80 | 31 | 5 | 4 | .... | 17 | 12 | 11 | .... | 48 | 17 | 15 | .... | 417 | 295 | 111 | 1st, Smythe Div. | Lost Div. Semi-Final |
| 1980-81 | 80 | 17 | 13 | 10 | .... | 12 | 22 | 6 | .... | 29 | 35 | 16 | .... | 328 | 327 | 74 | 4th, Smythe Div. | Lost Quarter-Final |
| 1979-80 | 80 | 17 | 14 | 9 | .... | 11 | 25 | 4 | .... | 28 | 39 | 13 | .... | 301 | 322 | 69 | 4th, Smythe Div. | Lost Prelim. Round |

### 2009-10 Schedule

| Month | Day | Date | Opponent |
|---|---|---|---|
| **Oct.** | Sat. | 3 | Calgary |
| | Tue. | 6 | Dallas |
| | Thu. | 8 | Calgary |
| | Sat. | 10 | Montreal |
| | Mon. | 12 | at Nashville |
| | Wed. | 14 | at Chicago |
| | Fri. | 16 | Minnesota |
| | Mon. | 19 | Vancouver |
| | Thu. | 22 | Columbus |
| | Sat. | 24 | at Calgary |
| | Sun. | 25 | at Vancouver |
| | Tue. | 27 | Colorado |
| | Thu. | 29 | Detroit |
| | Sat. | 31 | at Boston* |
| **Nov.** | Mon. | 2 | at NY Islanders |
| | Thu. | 5 | NY Rangers |
| | Sun. | 8 | at Colorado |
| | Tue. | 10 | at Ottawa |
| | Wed. | 11 | at Buffalo |
| | Sun. | 15 | at Atlanta* |
| | Mon. | 16 | at Columbus |
| | Wed. | 18 | Colorado |
| | Sat. | 21 | Chicago |
| | Mon. | 23 | Phoenix |
| | Wed. | 25 | Los Angeles |
| | Fri. | 27 | San Jose |
| | Sat. | 28 | at Vancouver |
| **Dec.** | Thu. | 3 | at Detroit |
| | Sat. | 5 | at Dallas* |
| | Mon. | 7 | at Florida |
| | Wed. | 9 | at Tampa Bay |
| | Fri. | 11 | at St. Louis |
| | Tue. | 15 | Los Angeles |
| | Thu. | 17 | Nashville |
| | Sat. | 19 | Washington |
| | Mon. | 21 | St. Louis |
| | Wed. | 23 | at Minnesota |
| | Sat. | 26 | at Vancouver |
| | Mon. | 28 | Calgary |
| | Wed. | 30 | Toronto |
| | Thu. | 31 | at Calgary |
| **Jan.** | Sat. | 2 | at San Jose |
| | Tue. | 5 | Phoenix |
| | Thu. | 7 | Columbus |
| | Tue. | 12 | Nashville |
| | Thu. | 14 | Pittsburgh |
| | Sat. | 16 | at San Jose* |
| | Mon. | 18 | at Colorado |
| | Wed. | 20 | Vancouver |
| | Fri. | 22 | Dallas |
| | Tue. | 26 | Chicago |
| | Thu. | 28 | St. Louis |
| | Sat. | 30 | at Calgary |
| **Feb.** | Mon. | 1 | Carolina |
| | Wed. | 3 | Philadelphia |
| | Thu. | 4 | at Minnesota |
| | Sat. | 6 | at Colorado |
| | Mon. | 8 | at Phoenix |
| | Wed. | 10 | at Anaheim |
| | Thu. | 11 | at Los Angeles |
| | Sun. | 14 | Anaheim* |
| **Mar.** | Tue. | 2 | at Nashville |
| | Wed. | 3 | at Chicago |
| | Fri. | 5 | Minnesota |
| | Sun. | 7 | New Jersey |
| | Tue. | 9 | Ottawa |
| | Thu. | 11 | at Montreal |
| | Sat. | 13 | at Toronto |
| | Mon. | 15 | at Columbus |
| | Tue. | 16 | at Minnesota |
| | Fri. | 19 | Detroit |
| | Sun. | 21 | San Jose |
| | Tue. | 23 | Vancouver |
| | Fri. | 26 | Anaheim |
| | Sun. | 28 | at St. Louis* |
| | Tue. | 30 | at Detroit |
| **Apr.** | Fri. | 2 | at Dallas |
| | Sat. | 3 | at Phoenix |
| | Mon. | 5 | Minnesota |
| | Wed. | 7 | Colorado |
| | Sat. | 10 | at Los Angeles* |
| | Sun. | 11 | at Anaheim* |

* Denotes afternoon game.

*With his booming shot from the point, Sheldon Souray's 23 goals in 2008-09 tied him with Ales Hemsky for the Oilers' team lead. He was second behind Hemsky with 53 points.*

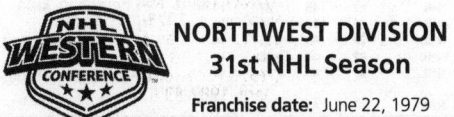

**NORTHWEST DIVISION**
**31st NHL Season**
**Franchise date:** June 22, 1979

# 2009-10 Player Personnel

| FORWARDS | HT | WT | S | Place of Birth | *Age | 2008-09 Club |
|---|---|---|---|---|---|---|
| BRULE, Gilbert | 5-10 | 180 | R | Edmonton, Alta. | 22 | Edmonton-Springfield |
| COGLIANO, Andrew | 5-10 | 184 | L | Toronto, Ont. | 22 | Edmonton |
| GAGNER, Sam | 5-11 | 191 | R | London, Ont. | 20 | Edmonton |
| HEMSKY, Ales | 6-0 | 192 | R | Pardubice, Czech. | 26 | Edmonton |
| HORCOFF, Shawn | 6-1 | 208 | L | Trail, B.C. | 31 | Edmonton |
| JACQUES, Jean-Francois | 6-4 | 217 | L | Montreal, Que. | 24 | Edmonton-Springfield |
| LERG, Bryan | 5-10 | 175 | L | Livonia, MI | 23 | Springfield-Stockton |
| MacINTYRE, Steve | 6-5 | 250 | L | Brock, Sask. | 29 | Edmonton |
| McDONALD, Colin | 6-3 | 205 | R | New Haven, CT | 25 | Stockton-Springfield |
| MINARD, Chris | 6-1 | 190 | L | Thompson, Man. | 27 | Pittsburgh-Wilkes-Barre |
| MOREAU, Ethan | 6-2 | 220 | L | Huntsville, Ont. | 34 | Edmonton |
| NILSSON, Robert | 5-11 | 185 | L | Calgary, Alta. | 24 | Edmonton |
| O'MARRA, Ryan | 6-2 | 207 | R | Tokyo, Japan | 22 | Springfield |
| O'SULLIVAN, Patrick | 5-11 | 190 | L | Toronto, Ont. | 24 | Los Angeles-Edmonton |
| PAUKOVICH, Geoff | 6-4 | 208 | L | Englewood, CO | 23 | Springfield-Stockton |
| PENNER, Dustin | 6-4 | 245 | L | Winkler, Man. | 27 | Edmonton |
| PISANI, Fernando | 6-1 | 205 | L | Edmonton, Alta. | 32 | Edmonton |
| POTULNY, Ryan | 6-0 | 190 | L | Grand Forks, ND | 25 | Edmonton-Springfield |
| POULIOT, Marc-Antoine | 6-1 | 195 | R | Quebec City, Que. | 24 | Edmonton |
| REDDOX, Liam | 5-10 | 180 | L | East York, Ont. | 23 | Edmonton-Springfield |
| SCHREMP, Rob | 5-11 | 200 | L | Syracuse, NY | 23 | Edmonton-Springfield |
| STONE, Ryan | 6-2 | 207 | L | Calgary, Alta. | 24 | Pit-Wilkes-Barre-Sprfld |
| STORTINI, Zack | 6-3 | 228 | R | Elliot Lake, Ont. | 24 | Edmonton |
| TRUKHNO, Vyacheslav | 6-1 | 197 | L | Khimki, USSR | 22 | Springfield |
| **DEFENSEMEN** | | | | | | |
| CHORNEY, Taylor | 5-11 | 182 | L | Thunder Bay, Ont. | 22 | Edmonton-Springfield |
| GILBERT, Tom | 6-3 | 206 | R | Minneapolis, MN | 26 | Edmonton |
| GREBESHKOV, Denis | 6-0 | 209 | L | Yaroslavl, USSR | 25 | Edmonton |
| MOTIN, Johan | 6-1 | 202 | R | Karlskoga, Sweden | 19 | Skare-Farjestad |
| NICKERSON, Matt | 6-4 | 230 | R | New London, CT | 24 | Ilves |
| PECKHAM, Theo | 6-2 | 223 | L | Richmond Hill, Ont. | 21 | Edmonton-Springfield |
| PLANTE, Alex | 6-4 | 225 | R | Brandon, Man. | 20 | Calgary (WHL) |
| SMID, Ladislav | 6-3 | 226 | L | Frydlant V Cechach, Czech. | 23 | Edmonton |
| SOURAY, Sheldon | 6-4 | 233 | L | Elk Point, Alta. | 33 | Edmonton |
| STAIOS, Steve | 6-1 | 200 | R | Hamilton, Ont. | 36 | Edmonton |
| STRUDWICK, Jason | 6-4 | 225 | L | Edmonton, Alta. | 34 | Edmonton |
| VISNOVSKY, Lubomir | 5-10 | 188 | L | Topolcany, Czech. | 33 | Edmonton |
| WILD, Cody | 6-1 | 185 | L | Limestone, ME | 22 | Stockton-Springfield |
| **GOALTENDERS** | **HT** | **WT** | **C** | **Place of Birth** | ***Age** | **2008-09 Club** |
| DESLAURIERS, Jeff | 6-4 | 200 | R | St-Jean-Richelieu, Que. | 25 | Edmonton-Springfield |
| DUBNYK, Devan | 6-5 | 194 | L | Regina, Sask. | 23 | Springfield |
| KHABIBULIN, Nikolai | 6-1 | 209 | L | Sverdlovsk, USSR | 36 | Chicago |
| PITTON, Bryan | 6-2 | 176 | L | Mississauga, Ont. | 21 | Stockton |

* – Age at start of 2009-10 season

## Coaching History

Glen Sather, 1979-80; Bryan Watson and Glen Sather, 1980-81; Glen Sather, 1981-82 to 1988-89; John Muckler, 1989-90, 1990-91; Ted Green, 1991-92, 1992-93; Ted Green and Glen Sather, 1993-94; George Burnett and Ron Low, 1994-95; Ron Low, 1995-96 to 1998-99; Kevin Lowe, 1999-2000; Craig MacTavish, 2000-01 to 2008-09; Pat Quinn, 2009-10.

# Pat Quinn

## Head Coach

*Born: Hamilton, Ont., January 29, 1943.*

The Edmonton Oilers announced the hiring of Pat Quinn as the ninth head coach in the franchise's NHL history on May 26, 2009. Quinn's extensive coaching career began with the Philadelphia Flyers in 1978-79. He has led his teams to two Stanley Cup Final appearances and won the Jack Adams Award as the NHL's coach of the year twice (1979-80 with the Philadelphia Flyers and 1991-92 with the Vancouver Canucks).

After four seasons with the Flyers, Quinn took time away from hockey to concentrate on earning a law degree from Widener University. In 1984-85, he joined the Los Angeles Kings and was head coach for three seasons. In 1987, he joined the Vancouver Canucks organization as president and general manager and took over as head coach in the 1990-91 season. He led the Canucks to the 1994 Stanley Cup Finals, losing to the New York Rangers in seven games. He left the Canucks after the 1997-98 season and became head coach of the Toronto Maple Leafs for seven seasons, including four seasons (1999 to 2003) where he also served as general manager. Quinn left the Leafs organization at the conclusion of the 2005-06 NHL season. He has enjoyed tremendous success on the international stage, guiding Team Canada to their first gold medal in 50 years at the 2002 Winter Olympic Games in Salt Lake City, Utah. He also led Canada to victory at the 2004 World Cup of Hockey, the 2008 World Under-18 Championship and at the 2009 World Junior Championship.

Over a nine-year NHL playing career (1968 to 1977), Quinn took part in 606 games, scoring 18 goals and 113 assists for 131 points, while collecting 950 penalty minutes. He also played 11 NHL playoff games recording one assist and 21 penalty minutes. In junior hockey, he was a member of the 1962-63 Memorial Cup champion Edmonton Oil Kings with former Oilers coach Glen Sather.

# 2008-09 Scoring

* – rookie

## Regular Season

| Pos | # | Player | Team | GP | G | A | Pts | TOI | +/– | PIM | PP | SH | GW | S | % |
|---|---|---|---|---|---|---|---|---|---|---|---|---|---|---|---|
| R | 83 | Ales Hemsky | EDM | 72 | 23 | 43 | 66 | 18:38 | 1 | 32 | 4 | 0 | 2 | 185 | 12.4 |
| D | 44 | Sheldon Souray | EDM | 81 | 23 | 30 | 53 | 24:50 | 1 | 98 | 12 | 1 | 5 | 268 | 8.6 |
| C | 10 | Shawn Horcoff | EDM | 80 | 17 | 36 | 53 | 21:21 | 7 | 39 | 8 | 0 | 2 | 178 | 9.6 |
| D | 77 | Tom Gilbert | EDM | 82 | 5 | 40 | 45 | 21:58 | 6 | 26 | 2 | 0 | 1 | 107 | 4.7 |
| R | 21 | Ales Kotalik | BUF | 56 | 13 | 19 | 32 | 15:14 | –7 | 28 | 8 | 0 | 1 | 153 | 8.5 |
| | | | EDM | 19 | 7 | 4 | 11 | 16:05 | 2 | 6 | 1 | 0 | 0 | 55 | 12.7 |
| | | | Total | 75 | 20 | 23 | 43 | 15:27 | –5 | 34 | 9 | 0 | 1 | 208 | 9.6 |
| C | 19 | Patrick O'Sullivan | L.A. | 62 | 14 | 23 | 37 | 19:25 | 1 | 16 | 2 | 1 | 1 | 200 | 7.0 |
| | | | EDM | 19 | 2 | 4 | 6 | 18:14 | –7 | 12 | 0 | 0 | 0 | 59 | 3.4 |
| | | | Total | 81 | 16 | 27 | 43 | 19:08 | –6 | 28 | 2 | 1 | 1 | 259 | 6.2 |
| C | 89 | Sam Gagner | EDM | 76 | 16 | 25 | 41 | 16:45 | –1 | 51 | 6 | 0 | 1 | 156 | 10.3 |
| D | 37 | Denis Grebeshkov | EDM | 72 | 7 | 32 | 39 | 21:10 | 12 | 38 | 2 | 0 | 0 | 62 | 11.3 |
| C | 13 | Andrew Cogliano | EDM | 82 | 18 | 20 | 38 | 14:24 | –6 | 22 | 4 | 0 | 4 | 116 | 15.5 |
| R | 27 | Dustin Penner | EDM | 78 | 17 | 20 | 37 | 15:22 | 7 | 61 | 5 | 0 | 5 | 137 | 12.4 |
| D | 71 | Lubomir Visnovsky | EDM | 50 | 8 | 23 | 31 | 23:00 | 6 | 30 | 5 | 0 | 1 | 86 | 9.3 |
| L | 12 | Robert Nilsson | EDM | 64 | 9 | 20 | 29 | 15:11 | 1 | 26 | 4 | 0 | 1 | 77 | 11.7 |
| C | 51 | Kyle Brodziak | EDM | 79 | 11 | 16 | 27 | 12:43 | 4 | 21 | 1 | 1 | 3 | 99 | 11.1 |
| L | 18 | Ethan Moreau | EDM | 77 | 14 | 12 | 26 | 15:21 | 0 | 133 | 0 | 1 | 2 | 159 | 8.8 |
| R | 78 | Marc-Antoine Pouliot | EDM | 63 | 8 | 12 | 20 | 11:30 | 1 | 23 | 0 | 0 | 2 | 94 | 8.5 |
| C | 34 | Fernando Pisani | EDM | 38 | 7 | 8 | 15 | 15:18 | –1 | 14 | 0 | 0 | 0 | 72 | 9.7 |
| D | 24 | Steve Staios | EDM | 80 | 2 | 12 | 14 | 19:48 | –5 | 92 | 0 | 0 | 0 | 78 | 2.6 |
| L | 85 * | Liam Reddox | EDM | 46 | 5 | 7 | 12 | 10:28 | –6 | 10 | 1 | 0 | 0 | 39 | 12.8 |
| R | 46 | Zach Stortini | EDM | 52 | 6 | 5 | 11 | 7:17 | –3 | 181 | 0 | 0 | 0 | 23 | 26.1 |
| D | 5 | Ladislav Smid | EDM | 60 | 0 | 11 | 11 | 14:57 | –6 | 57 | 0 | 0 | 0 | 33 | 0.0 |
| D | 43 | Jason Strudwick | EDM | 71 | 2 | 7 | 9 | 12:37 | –4 | 60 | 0 | 0 | 0 | 32 | 6.3 |
| C | 67 | Gilbert Brule | EDM | 11 | 2 | 1 | 3 | 9:52 | –3 | 12 | 0 | 0 | 1 | 13 | 15.4 |
| C | 88 * | Rob Schremp | EDM | 4 | 0 | 3 | 3 | 13:34 | 2 | 2 | 0 | 0 | 0 | 3 | 0.0 |
| C | 21 | Ryan Potulny | EDM | 8 | 0 | 3 | 3 | 10:29 | 2 | 0 | 0 | 0 | 0 | 9 | 0.0 |
| L | 33 | Steve MacIntyre | EDM | 22 | 2 | 0 | 2 | 3:54 | –2 | 40 | 0 | 0 | 1 | 6 | 33.3 |
| L | 22 | Jean-Francois Jacques | EDM | 7 | 1 | 0 | 1 | 7:22 | 0 | 9 | 0 | 0 | 0 | 3 | 33.3 |
| C | 62 * | Tim Sestito | EDM | 1 | 0 | 0 | 0 | 5:53 | 0 | 0 | 0 | 0 | 0 | 1 | 0.0 |
| R | 28 | Jesse Boulerice | EDM | 2 | 0 | 0 | 0 | 3:42 | 0 | 0 | 0 | 0 | 0 | 0 | 0.0 |
| D | 41 * | Taylor Chorney | EDM | 2 | 0 | 0 | 0 | 15:42 | –4 | 0 | 0 | 0 | 0 | 0 | 0.0 |
| D | 49 * | Theo Peckham | EDM | 15 | 0 | 0 | 0 | 11:37 | –1 | 59 | 0 | 0 | 0 | 8 | 0.0 |

## Goaltending

| No. | Goaltender | GPI | Mins | Avg | W | L | OT | EN | SO | GA | SA | S% | G | A | PIM |
|---|---|---|---|---|---|---|---|---|---|---|---|---|---|---|---|
| 35 | Dwayne Roloson | 63 | 3597 | 2.77 | 28 | 24 | 9 | 4 | 1 | 166 | 1953 | .915 | 0 | 1 | 10 |
| 32 | Mathieu Garon | 15 | 815 | 3.17 | 6 | 8 | 0 | 1 | 0 | 43 | 408 | .895 | 0 | 0 | 0 |
| 38 | * Jeff Deslauriers | 10 | 540 | 3.33 | 4 | 3 | 0 | 0 | 0 | 30 | 302 | .901 | 0 | 1 | 0 |
| | **Totals** | **82** | **4985** | **2.94** | **38** | **35** | **9** | **5** | **1** | **244** | **2668** | **.909** | | | |

## Coaching Record

| | | | Regular Season | | | | Playoffs | | | |
|---|---|---|---|---|---|---|---|---|---|---|
| **Season** | **Team** | **League** | **GC** | **W** | **L** | **O/T** | **GC** | **W** | **L** | **T** |
| **1978-79** | **Philadelphia** | **NHL** | **30** | **18** | **8** | **4** | **8** | **3** | **5** | .... |
| **1979-80** | **Philadelphia** | **NHL** | **80** | **48** | **12** | **20** | **19** | **13** | **6** | .... |
| **1980-81** | **Philadelphia** | **NHL** | **80** | **41** | **24** | **15** | **12** | **6** | **6** | .... |
| **1981-82** | **Philadelphia** | **NHL** | **72** | **34** | **29** | **9** | .... | .... | .... | .... |
| **1984-85** | **Los Angeles** | **NHL** | **80** | **34** | **32** | **14** | **3** | **0** | **3** | .... |
| **1985-86** | **Los Angeles** | **NHL** | **80** | **23** | **49** | **8** | .... | .... | .... | .... |
| **1986-87** | **Los Angeles** | **NHL** | **42** | **18** | **20** | **4** | .... | .... | .... | .... |
| **1990-91** | **Vancouver** | **NHL** | **26** | **9** | **13** | **4** | **6** | **2** | **4** | .... |
| **1991-92** | **Vancouver** | **NHL** | **80** | **42** | **26** | **12** | **13** | **6** | **7** | .... |
| **1992-93** | **Vancouver** | **NHL** | **84** | **46** | **29** | **9** | **12** | **6** | **6** | .... |
| **1993-94** | **Vancouver** | **NHL** | **84** | **41** | **40** | **3** | **24** | **15** | **9** | .... |
| **1995-96** | **Vancouver** | **NHL** | **6** | **3** | **3** | **0** | **6** | **2** | **4** | .... |
| **1998-99** | **Toronto** | **NHL** | **82** | **45** | **30** | **7** | **17** | **9** | **8** | .... |
| **99-2000** | **Toronto** | **NHL** | **82** | **45** | **27** | **10** | **12** | **6** | **6** | .... |
| **2000-01** | **Toronto** | **NHL** | **82** | **37** | **29** | **16** | **11** | **7** | **4** | .... |
| **2001-02** | **Toronto** | **NHL** | **82** | **43** | **25** | **14** | **20** | **10** | **10** | .... |
| **2002-03** | **Toronto** | **NHL** | **82** | **44** | **28** | **10** | **7** | **3** | **4** | .... |
| **2003-04** | **Toronto** | **NHL** | **82** | **45** | **24** | **13** | **13** | **6** | **7** | .... |
| **2004-05** | **Toronto** | | | | SEASON CANCELLED | | | | | |
| **2005-06** | **Toronto** | **NHL** | **82** | **41** | **33** | **8** | .... | .... | .... | .... |
| | **NHL Totals** | | **1318** | **657** | **481** | **180** | **183** | **94** | **89** | .... |

# Club Records

## Team

(Figures in brackets for season records are games played; records for fewest points, wins, ties, losses, goals, goals against are for 70 or more games)

**Most Points** ............... **119** 1983-84 (80), 1985-86 (80)
**Most Wins** ................. **57** 1983-84 (80)
**Most Ties** .................. **16** 1980-81 (80), 1999-2000 (82)
**Most Losses** ................ **50** 1992-93 (84)
**Most Goals** .............. ***446** 1983-84 (80)
**Most Goals Against** ......... **337** 1992-93 (84)
**Fewest Points** .............. **60** 1992-93 (84)
**Fewest Wins** ................ **25** 1993-94 (84)
**Fewest Ties** ................. **5** 1983-84 (80)
**Fewest Losses** .............. **17** 1981-82 (80), 1985-86 (80)
**Fewest Goals** .............. **195** 2006-07 (82)
**Fewest Goals Against** ....... **182** 2001-02 (82)
**Longest Winning Streak**
**Overall** .................... **9** Feb. 20-Mar. 13/01
**Home** ....................... **8** Jan. 19-Feb. 22/85, Feb. 24-Apr. 2/86
**Away** ....................... **8** Dec. 9/86-Jan. 17/87
**Longest Undefeated Streak**
**Overall** ................... **15** Oct. 11-Nov. 9/84 (12 wins, 3 ties)
**Home** ...................... **14** Nov. 15/89-Jan. 6/90 (11 wins, 3 ties)
**Away** ....................... **9** Jan. 17-Mar. 2/82 (6 wins, 3 ties), Nov. 23/82-Jan. 18/83 (7 wins, 2 ties)
**Longest Losing Streak**
**Overall** ................... **11** Oct. 16-Nov. 7/93
**Home** ....................... **9** Oct. 16-Nov. 24/93
**Away** ....................... **9** Nov. 25-Dec. 30/80, Feb. 25-Apr. 5/07
**Longest Winless Streak**
**Overall** ................... **14** Oct. 11-Nov. 7/93 (13 losses, 1 tie)
**Home** ....................... **9** Oct. 16-Nov. 24/93 (9 losses)
**Away** ...................... **11** Dec. 18/01-Feb. 8/02 (7 losses, 4 ties)
**Most Shutouts, Season** ........ **8** 1997-98 (82); 2000-01 (82); 2001-02 (82)
**Most PIM, Season** ......... **2,173** 1987-88 (80)
**Most Goals, Game** ........... **13** Nov. 19/83 (N.J. 4 at Edm. 13), Nov. 8/85 (Van. 0 at Edm. 13)

## Individual

**Most Seasons** ............... **15** Kevin Lowe
**Most Games** .............. **1,037** Kevin Lowe
**Most Goals, Career** ......... **583** Wayne Gretzky
**Most Assists, Career** ..... **1,086** Wayne Gretzky
**Most Points, Career** ...... **1,669** Wayne Gretzky (583G, 1,086A)
**Most PIM, Career** ......... **1,747** Kelly Buchberger
**Most Shutouts, Career** ....... **23** Tommy Salo
**Longest Consecutive Games Streak** ........... **518** Craig MacTavish (Oct. 12/86-Jan. 2/93)
**Most Goals, Season** ......... ***92** Wayne Gretzky (1981-82)
**Most Assists, Season** ...... ***163** Wayne Gretzky (1985-86)
**Most Points, Season** ....... ***215** Wayne Gretzky (1985-86; 52G, 163A)
**Most PIM, Season** .......... **286** Steve Smith (1987-88)
**Most Points, Defenseman, Season** ................ **138** Paul Coffey (1985-86; 48G, 90A)
**Most Points, Center, Season** ............... ***215** Wayne Gretzky (1985-86; 52G, 163A)
**Most Points, Right Wing, Season** ................ **135** Jari Kurri (1984-85; 71G, 64A)
**Most Points, Left Wing, Season** ................ **106** Mark Messier (1982-83; 48G, 58A)
**Most Points, Rookie, Season** ................. **75** Jari Kurri (1980-81; 32G, 43A)
**Most Shutouts, Season** ........ **8** Curtis Joseph (1997-98), Tommy Salo (2000-01)
**Most Goals, Game** ............ **5** Wayne Gretzky (Feb. 18/81), (Dec. 30/81), (Dec. 15/84), (Dec. 6/87); Jari Kurri (Nov. 19/83); Pat Hughes (Feb. 3/84)
**Most Assists, Game** ......... ***7** Wayne Gretzky (Feb. 15/80), (Dec. 11/85), (Feb. 14/86)
**Most Points, Game** ........... **8** Wayne Gretzky (Nov. 19/83; 3G, 5A), (Jan. 4/84; 4G, 4A); Paul Coffey (Mar. 14/86; 2G, 6A)

* NHL Record.

## Retired Numbers

| | | |
|---|---|---|
| 3 | Al Hamilton | 1972-1980 |
| 7 | Paul Coffey | 1980-1987 |
| 9 | Glenn Anderson | 1980-91, 1996 |
| 11 | Mark Messier | 1980-1991 |
| 17 | Jari Kurri | 1980-1990 |
| 31 | Grant Fuhr | 1981-1991 |
| 99 | Wayne Gretzky | 1979-1988 |

## Captains' History

Ron Chipperfield, 1979-80; Blair MacDonald and Lee Fogolin, Jr., 1980-81; Lee Fogolin, Jr., 1981-82, 1982-83; Wayne Gretzky, 1983-84 to 1987-88; Mark Messier, 1988-89 to 1990-91; Kevin Lowe, 1991-92; Craig MacTavish, 1992-93, 1993-94; Shayne Corson, 1994-95; Kelly Buchberger, 1995-96 to 1998-99; Doug Weight, 1999-2000, 2000-01; Jason Smith, 2001-02 to 2006-07; Ethan Moreau, 2007-08 to date.

# All-time Record vs. Other Clubs

## Regular Season

| | At Home | | | | | | | | On Road | | | | | | | | Total | | | | | | | |
|---|---|---|---|---|---|---|---|---|---|---|---|---|---|---|---|---|---|---|---|---|---|---|---|---|
| | GP | W | L | T | OL | GF | GA | PTS | GP | W | L | T | OL | GF | GA | PTS | GP | W | L | T | OL | GF | GA | PTS |
| Anaheim | 33 | 21 | 10 | 0 | 2 | 82 | 71 | 44 | 34 | 15 | 17 | 2 | 0 | 92 | 94 | 32 | 67 | 36 | 27 | 2 | 2 | 174 | 165 | 76 |
| Atlanta | 6 | 3 | 1 | 1 | 1 | 22 | 16 | 8 | 4 | 3 | 1 | 0 | 0 | 12 | 5 | 6 | 10 | 6 | 2 | 1 | 1 | 34 | 21 | 14 |
| Boston | 31 | 11 | 15 | 3 | 2 | 102 | 103 | 27 | 31 | 6 | 21 | 3 | 1 | 80 | 129 | 16 | 62 | 17 | 36 | 6 | 3 | 182 | 232 | 43 |
| Buffalo | 31 | 21 | 7 | 3 | 0 | 123 | 87 | 45 | 31 | 13 | 10 | 7 | 1 | 113 | 111 | 34 | 62 | 34 | 17 | 10 | 1 | 236 | 198 | 79 |
| Calgary | 96 | 50 | 34 | 10 | 2 | 343 | 301 | 112 | 96 | 34 | 53 | 9 | 0 | 307 | 372 | 77 | 192 | 84 | 87 | 19 | 2 | 650 | 673 | 189 |
| Carolina | 32 | 20 | 7 | 5 | 0 | 124 | 93 | 45 | 31 | 12 | 12 | 7 | 0 | 103 | 120 | 31 | 63 | 32 | 19 | 12 | 0 | 227 | 213 | 76 |
| Chicago | 53 | 27 | 21 | 5 | 0 | 190 | 168 | 59 | 52 | 19 | 26 | 7 | 0 | 172 | 194 | 45 | 105 | 46 | 47 | 12 | 0 | 362 | 362 | 104 |
| Colorado | 61 | 31 | 23 | 4 | 3 | 232 | 196 | 69 | 62 | 26 | 30 | 4 | 2 | 215 | 229 | 58 | 123 | 57 | 53 | 8 | 5 | 447 | 425 | 127 |
| Columbus | 16 | 12 | 3 | 0 | 1 | 53 | 34 | 25 | 16 | 9 | 3 | 3 | 1 | 56 | 38 | 22 | 32 | 21 | 6 | 3 | 2 | 109 | 72 | 47 |
| Dallas | 52 | 23 | 16 | 8 | 5 | 199 | 170 | 59 | 53 | 16 | 28 | 7 | 2 | 146 | 191 | 41 | 105 | 39 | 44 | 15 | 7 | 345 | 361 | 100 |
| Detroit | 52 | 24 | 17 | 10 | 1 | 194 | 180 | 59 | 52 | 19 | 28 | 3 | 2 | 163 | 202 | 43 | 104 | 43 | 45 | 13 | 3 | 357 | 382 | 102 |
| Florida | 9 | 5 | 3 | 1 | 0 | 28 | 19 | 11 | 10 | 3 | 5 | 2 | 0 | 28 | 27 | 8 | 19 | 8 | 8 | 3 | 0 | 56 | 46 | 19 |
| Los Angeles | 85 | 43 | 27 | 15 | 0 | 372 | 299 | 101 | 85 | 39 | 30 | 15 | 1 | 340 | 323 | 94 | 170 | 82 | 57 | 30 | 1 | 712 | 622 | 195 |
| Minnesota | 26 | 12 | 10 | 3 | 1 | 62 | 62 | 28 | 25 | 10 | 10 | 1 | 4 | 52 | 69 | 25 | 51 | 22 | 20 | 4 | 5 | 114 | 131 | 53 |
| Montreal | 37 | 20 | 17 | 0 | 0 | 129 | 118 | 40 | 32 | 10 | 16 | 4 | 2 | 100 | 112 | 26 | 69 | 30 | 33 | 4 | 2 | 229 | 230 | 66 |
| Nashville | 20 | 9 | 9 | 0 | 2 | 54 | 60 | 20 | 21 | 7 | 10 | 3 | 1 | 61 | 62 | 18 | 41 | 16 | 19 | 3 | 3 | 115 | 122 | 38 |
| New Jersey | 32 | 14 | 11 | 6 | 1 | 137 | 117 | 35 | 35 | 17 | 13 | 3 | 2 | 115 | 114 | 39 | 67 | 31 | 24 | 9 | 3 | 252 | 231 | 74 |
| NY Islanders | 31 | 18 | 8 | 5 | 0 | 114 | 89 | 41 | 32 | 7 | 15 | 9 | 1 | 112 | 131 | 24 | 63 | 25 | 23 | 14 | 1 | 226 | 220 | 65 |
| NY Rangers | 29 | 13 | 13 | 3 | 0 | 104 | 96 | 29 | 32 | 15 | 9 | 6 | 2 | 120 | 119 | 38 | 61 | 28 | 22 | 9 | 2 | 224 | 215 | 67 |
| Ottawa | 13 | 7 | 4 | 2 | 0 | 44 | 33 | 16 | 12 | 5 | 4 | 2 | 1 | 31 | 27 | 13 | 25 | 12 | 8 | 4 | 1 | 75 | 60 | 29 |
| Philadelphia | 29 | 15 | 8 | 6 | 0 | 103 | 86 | 36 | 33 | 11 | 20 | 2 | 0 | 93 | 134 | 24 | 62 | 26 | 28 | 8 | 0 | 196 | 220 | 60 |
| Phoenix | 80 | 52 | 21 | 6 | 1 | 351 | 255 | 111 | 79 | 42 | 28 | 5 | 4 | 340 | 307 | 93 | 159 | 94 | 49 | 11 | 5 | 691 | 562 | 204 |
| Pittsburgh | 31 | 22 | 8 | 1 | 0 | 150 | 102 | 45 | 32 | 13 | 15 | 3 | 1 | 134 | 123 | 30 | 63 | 35 | 23 | 4 | 1 | 284 | 225 | 75 |
| St. Louis | 52 | 27 | 19 | 4 | 2 | 186 | 167 | 60 | 52 | 21 | 23 | 7 | 1 | 180 | 180 | 50 | 104 | 48 | 42 | 11 | 3 | 366 | 347 | 110 |
| San Jose | 41 | 23 | 11 | 7 | 0 | 129 | 94 | 53 | 40 | 16 | 17 | 5 | 2 | 118 | 133 | 39 | 81 | 39 | 28 | 12 | 2 | 247 | 227 | 92 |
| Tampa Bay | 12 | 8 | 4 | 0 | 0 | 32 | 27 | 16 | 12 | 6 | 4 | 2 | 0 | 38 | 35 | 14 | 24 | 14 | 8 | 2 | 0 | 70 | 62 | 30 |
| Toronto | 45 | 23 | 15 | 6 | 1 | 182 | 146 | 53 | 39 | 16 | 21 | 2 | 0 | 161 | 159 | 34 | 84 | 39 | 36 | 8 | 1 | 343 | 305 | 87 |
| Vancouver | 96 | 57 | 29 | 7 | 3 | 396 | 302 | 124 | 97 | 45 | 36 | 12 | 4 | 362 | 342 | 106 | 193 | 102 | 65 | 19 | 7 | 758 | 644 | 230 |
| Washington | 30 | 16 | 10 | 4 | 0 | 124 | 91 | 36 | 31 | 10 | 18 | 2 | 1 | 102 | 125 | 23 | 61 | 26 | 28 | 6 | 1 | 226 | 216 | 59 |
| **Totals** | **1161** | **627** | **381** | **125** | **28** | **4361** | **3582** | **1407** | **1161** | **465** | **523** | **137** | **36** | **3946** | **4207** | **1103** | **2322** | **1092** | **904** | **262** | **64** | **8307** | **7789** | **2510** |

## Playoffs

| | Series | W | L | GP | W | L | T | GF | GA | Last Mtg. | Rnd. | Result |
|---|---|---|---|---|---|---|---|---|---|---|---|---|
| Anaheim | 1 | 1 | 0 | 5 | 4 | 1 | 0 | 16 | 13 | 2006 | CF | W 4-1 |
| Boston | 2 | 2 | 0 | 9 | 8 | 1 | 0 | 41 | 20 | 1990 | F | W 4-1 |
| Calgary | 5 | 4 | 1 | 30 | 19 | 11 | 0 | 132 | 96 | 1991 | DSF | W 4-3 |
| Carolina | 1 | 0 | 1 | 7 | 3 | 4 | 0 | 16 | 19 | 2006 | F | L 3-4 |
| Chicago | 4 | 3 | 1 | 20 | 12 | 8 | 0 | 102 | 77 | 1992 | CF | L 0-4 |
| Colorado | 2 | 1 | 1 | 12 | 5 | 7 | 0 | 30 | 35 | 1998 | CQF | W 4-3 |
| Dallas | 8 | 2 | 6 | 42 | 15 | 27 | 0 | 104 | 118 | 2003 | CQF | L 2-4 |
| Detroit | 3 | 3 | 0 | 16 | 12 | 4 | 0 | 58 | 43 | 2006 | CQF | W 4-2 |
| Los Angeles | 7 | 5 | 2 | 36 | 24 | 12 | 0 | 154 | 127 | 1992 | DSF | W 4-2 |
| Montreal | 1 | 1 | 0 | 3 | 3 | 0 | 0 | 15 | 6 | 1981 | PRE | W 3-0 |
| NY Islanders | 3 | 1 | 2 | 15 | 6 | 9 | 0 | 47 | 58 | 1984 | F | W 4-1 |
| Philadelphia | 3 | 2 | 1 | 15 | 8 | 7 | 0 | 49 | 44 | 1987 | F | W 4-3 |
| Phoenix | 6 | 6 | 0 | 26 | 22 | 4 | 0 | 120 | 75 | 1990 | DSF | W 4-3 |
| San Jose | 1 | 1 | 0 | 6 | 4 | 2 | 0 | 19 | 12 | 2006 | CSF | W 4-2 |
| Vancouver | 2 | 2 | 0 | 9 | 7 | 2 | 0 | 35 | 20 | 1992 | DF | W 4-2 |
| **Totals** | **49** | **34** | **15** | **251** | **152** | **99** | **0** | **938** | **763** | | | |

## Playoff Results 2009-2004

| Year | Round | Opponent | Result | GF | GA |
|---|---|---|---|---|---|
| 2006 | F | Carolina | L 3-4 | 16 | 19 |
| | CF | Anaheim | W 4-1 | 16 | 13 |
| | CSF | San Jose | W 4-2 | 19 | 12 |
| | CQF | Detroit | W 4-2 | 19 | 17 |

**Abbreviations: Round: F** - Final; **CF** - conference final; **CSF** - conference semi-final; **CQF** - conference quarter-final; **DF** - division final; **DSF** - division semi-final; **PRE** - preliminary round.

Calgary totals include Atlanta Flames, 1979-80.
Colorado totals include Quebec, 1979-80 to 1994-95.
New Jersey totals include Colorado Rockies, 1979-80 to 1981-82.
Carolina totals include Hartford, 1979-80 to 1996-97.
Dallas totals include Minnesota North Stars, 1979-80 to 1992-93.
Phoenix totals include Winnipeg, 1979-80 to 1995-96.

## 2008-09 Results

| | | | | | | | |
|---|---|---|---|---|---|---|---|
| **Oct.** | 12 | Colorado | 3-2 | | 13 | at Washington | 5-2 |
| | 15 | at Anaheim | 3-2 | | 15 | at Minnesota | 1-5 |
| | 17 | at Calgary | 4-3 | | 16 | at Colorado | 3-2 |
| | 18 | Calgary | 3-2 | | 18 | Phoenix | 6-3 |
| | 22 | at Chicago | 0-3 | | 20 | Columbus | 4-3 |
| | 23 | at Colorado | 1-4 | | 27 | Buffalo | 2-10 |
| | 25 | at Vancouver | 3-6 | | 30 | Minnesota | 3-1 |
| | 27 | Boston | 0-1* | **Feb.** | 1 | Nashville | 1-2 |
| | 30 | at Nashville | 1-3 | | 3 | Chicago | 1-3 |
| **Nov.** | 1 | at Carolina | 3-1 | | 5 | at St. Louis | 2-1† |
| | 2 | at Philadelphia | 5-4 | | 7 | at Detroit | 3-8 |
| | 5 | at Columbus | 4-5 | | 8 | at Minnesota | 2-3† |
| | 6 | at Pittsburgh | 4-5 | | 11 | Montreal | 7-2 |
| | 9 | at New Jersey | 2-1 | | 14 | at Los Angeles | 3-2† |
| | 10 | at NY Rangers | 3-2† | | 16 | at Phoenix | 3-1 |
| | 13 | Toronto | 2-5 | | 17 | at San Jose | 2-4 |
| | 15 | Colorado | 2-3† | | 19 | at Dallas | 2-4 |
| | 17 | at Detroit | 0-4 | | 21 | Calgary | 2-3† |
| | 18 | at Columbus | 7-2 | | 24 | Tampa Bay | 5-3 |
| | 20 | Detroit | 3-4 | | 26 | Columbus | 0-1 |
| | 26 | Los Angeles | 1-2 | | 28 | Minnesota | 3-2 |
| | 29 | at St. Louis | 4-2 | **Mar.** | 3 | at Nashville | 5-6* |
| | 30 | at Dallas | 3-4 | | 5 | at Ottawa | 2-4 |
| **Dec.** | 3 | Dallas | 5-2 | | 7 | at Toronto | 4-1 |
| | 5 | at Los Angeles | 5-4† | | 10 | at Montreal | 3-4* |
| | 6 | at San Jose | 3-2* | | 12 | Atlanta | 3-4* |
| | 11 | Florida | 0-2 | | 14 | Colorado | 2-3* |
| | 13 | Vancouver | 3-0 | | 17 | St. Louis | 2-1† |
| | 16 | Chicago | 2-9 | | 19 | at Colorado | 8-1 |
| | 17 | at Vancouver | 2-4 | | 20 | at Chicago | 5-4† |
| | 19 | Anaheim | 2-3† | | 22 | at Minnesota | 0-3 |
| | 22 | Phoenix | 4-2 | | 24 | Detroit | 2-3 |
| | 26 | at Vancouver | 3-2 | | 26 | at Phoenix | 2-3 |
| | 28 | Nashville | 5-2 | | 27 | at Anaheim | 5-3 |
| | 30 | Ottawa | 2-3 | | 29 | Minnesota | 2-3 |
| | 31 | at Calgary | 4-6 | | 31 | Anaheim | 3-5 |
| **Jan.** | 3 | Dallas | 4-1 | **Apr.** | 2 | San Jose | 1-2 |
| | 5 | NY Islanders | 3-2 | | 4 | Vancouver | 5-3 |
| | 7 | Vancouver | 2-4 | | 7 | Los Angeles | 1-2 |
| | 9 | San Jose | 1-4 | | 10 | Calgary | 5-1 |
| | 11 | St. Louis | 2-1 | | 11 | at Calgary | 1-4 |

* – Overtime † – Shootout

## Entry Draft Selections 2009-1995

Name in bold denotes played in NHL.

**2009**
Pick
10 Magnus Paajarvi-Svensson
40 Anton Lander
71 Troy Hesketh
82 Cameron Abney
99 Kyle Bigos
101 Toni Rajala
133 Olivier Roy

**2008**
Pick
22 Jordan Eberle
103 Johan Motin
133 Philippe Cornet
163 Teemu Hartikainen
193 Jordan Bendfeld

**2007**
Pick
6 **Sam Gagner**
15 Alex Plante
21 Riley Nash
97 Linus Omark
127 Milan Kytnar
157 William Quist

**2006**
Pick
45 Jeff Petry
75 **Theo Peckham**
133 Bryan Pitton
140 Cody Wild
170 Alexander Bumagin

**2005**
Pick
25 **Andrew Cogliano**
36 **Taylor Chorney**
81 **Danny Syvret**
86 Robby Dee
97 Chris Vande Velde
120 Vyacheslav Trukhno
157 Fredrik Pettersson
220 Matthew Glasser

**2004**
Pick
14 Devan Dubnyk
25 **Rob Schremp**
44 Roman Tesliuk
57 Geoff Paukovich
112 **Liam Reddox**
146 **Bryan Young**
177 Max Gordichuk
208 Stephane Goulet
242 Tyler Spurgeon
274 Bjorn Bjurling

**2003**
Pick
22 **Marc-Antoine Pouliot**
51 Colin McDonald
68 **Jean-Francois Jacques**
72 Mikhail Zhukov
94 **Zack Stortini**
147 Kalle Olsson
154 David Rohlfs
184 Dragan Umicevic
214 **Kyle Brodziak**
215 **Mathieu Roy**
248 Josef Hrabal
278 **Troy Bodie**

**2002**
Pick
15 Jesse Niinimaki
31 **Jeff Drouin-Deslauriers**
36 **Jarret Stoll**
44 **Matt Greene**
79 Brock Radunske
106 Ivan Koltsov
111 Jonas Almtorp
123 invalid pick
148 Glenn Fisher
181 **Mikko Luoma**
205 **J.F. Dufort**
211 Patrick Murphy
244 **Dwight Helminen**
245 Tomas Micka
274 Fredrik Johansson

**2001**
Pick
13 **Ales Hemsky**
43 **Doug Lynch**
52 Ed Caron
84 Kenny Smith
133 **Jussi Markkanen**
154 Jake Brenk
185 Mikael Svensk
215 Dan Baum
248 **Kari Haakana**
272 **Ales Pisa**
278 **Shay Stephenson**

**2000**
Pick
17 **Alexei Mikhnov**
35 **Brad Winchester**
83 Alexander Liubimov
113 Lou Dickenson
152 Paul Flache
184 Shaun Norrie
211 Joe Cullen
215 **Matthew Lombardi**
247 Jason Platt
274 Yevgeny Muratov

**1999**
Pick
13 **Jani Rita**
36 **Alexei Semenov**
41 **Tony Salmelainen**
81 **Adam Hauser**
91 **Mike Comrie**
139 Jonathan Fauteux
171 Chris Legg
199 Christian Chartier
256 Tamas Groschl

**1998**
Pick
13 Michael Henrich
67 **Alex Henry**
99 **Shawn Horcoff**
113 Kristian Antila
128 Paul Elliott
144 Oleg Smirnov
159 Trevor Ettinger
186 **Mike Morrison**
213 Christian Lefebvre
241 Maxim Spiridonov

**1997**
Pick
14 **Michel Riesen**
41 Patrick Dovigi
68 Sergei Yerkovich
94 Jonas Elofsson
121 **Jason Chimera**
141 **Peter Sarno**
176 Kevin Bolibruck
187 Chad Hinz
205 Chris Kerr
231 Alexander Fomichev

**1996**
Pick
6 **Boyd Devereaux**
19 **Matthieu Descoteaux**
32 **Chris Hajt**
59 **Tom Poti**
114 Brian Urick
141 Bryan Randall
168 David Bernier
170 Brandon Lafrance
195 **Fernando Pisani**
221 John Hultberg

**1995**
Pick
6 **Steve Kelly**
31 **Georges Laraque**
57 Lukas Zib
83 **Mike Minard**
109 Jan Snopek
161 Martin Cerven
187 Stephen Douglas
213 Jiri Antonin

### General Managers' History

Larry Gordon, 1979-80; Glen Sather, 1980-81 to 1999-2000; Kevin Lowe, 2000-01 to 2007-08; Steve Tambellini, 2008-09 to date.

## Steve Tambellini

### General Manager

*Born: Trail, B.C., May 14, 1958.*

Steve Tambellini joined the Edmonton Oilers as general manager on July 31, 2008 after 17 seasons as a member of the Vancouver Canucks management team. During his tenure with Vancouver, which began in 1990-91, Tambellini served in several positions. During his last three years with the club, he was vice president and assistant general manager. In that role, he was involved in all aspects of the team's hockey operations, including contract negotiations, scouting and minor league affiliates.

Tambellini took over in Edmonton from Kevin Lowe, who was promoted to the position of president of hockey operations. Tambellini and Lowe have previously worked together as members of Team Canada's management team, helping lead Canada to success on the international stage. As director of player personnel, Tambellini helped put together the roster that won the gold medal at the 2002 Winter Olympics in Salt Lake City and he was also a member of the management team for Team Canada's gold medal triumph at the 2004 World Cup of Hockey. He also served as the general manager of Team Canada at the 2003 and 2005 World Championships, winning gold in 2003 and silver in 2005.

Inducted into the B.C. Hockey Hall of Fame in 2004, Tambellini played 10 seasons in the NHL after being selected 15th overall in the 1978 NHL Amateur Draft by the New York Islanders. A member of the Islanders' 1980 Stanley Cup championship team, he played 553 career NHL games with five NHL teams between 1978-79 and 1987-88. He had 160 goals and 150 assists for 310 career points with 105 penalty minutes with the Islanders, Colorado Rockies, New Jersey Devils, Calgary Flames and Vancouver Canucks.

Besides his outstanding hockey resume, Tambellini has also been a contributor to the Canucks' off-ice activities. He served as the president of the Canucks for Kids Fund for 12 seasons and was awarded the B.C. Humanitarian of the Year Award by the B.C. Hockey Hall of Fame in 2006. He was also awarded the Jake Milford Plaque in 2004 for his significant and lasting contributions to hockey in his home province of British Columbia.

# Club Directory

**Rexall Place**

**Edmonton Oilers**
11230 – 110 Street
Edmonton, Alberta T5G 3H7
Phone **780/414-4000**
Press Box 780/409-3780
Ticketing 780/414-4625
Media Lounge 780/409-3778
FAX 780/409-5848
www.edmontonoilers.com
**Capacity:** 16,839

| | |
|---|---|
| Owner | Daryl A. Katz (Rexall Sports Corp) |
| Governor | Daryl A. Katz |
| Alternate Governors | Patrick LaForge, Kevin Lowe, Cal Nichols |
| President & Chief Executive Officer | Patrick LaForge |
| President of Hockey Operations | Kevin Lowe |
| Executive Assistant to the Hockey President | Connie Hadden |
| Executive Vice President, Commercial Operations | Stew MacDonald |
| Vice-President of Finance and CFO | Darryl Boessenkool |
| Executive Assistant to the President | Karen Berry |
| Executive Assistant to the CFO | Bobbie-Jo Dawe |
| Security | Michael Fluker |
| **Hockey Operations** | |
| General Manager | Steve Tambellini |
| Assistant G.M. & V.P., Hockey Operations | Kevin Prendergast |
| Assistant G.M. & Dir.of Hockey Ops/Legal Affairs | Ricky Olczyk |
| Head Coach | Pat Quinn |
| Associate Coach | Tom Renney |
| Assistant Coach | Kelly Buchberger |
| Goaltending Coach | Frederic Chabot |
| Video Coach | Myles Fee |
| Director of Player Development | TBD |
| Skating & Skills Coach | Steve Serdachny |
| Fitness Consultant | Simon Bennett |
| Dir. of Research, Analysis & Software Development | Sean Draper |
| Coordinator of Hockey Operations | James McGregor |
| Head Amateur Scout | Stu MacGregor |
| Head Pro Scout | Morey Gare |
| Amateur Scouts | Bob Brown, Bill Dandy, Brad Davis, Kent Hawley, Chris McCarthy, Mike Peluso |
| Pro Scouts | Michael Abbamont, Dave Semenko |
| European Scouts | Frank Musil, Kent Nilsson |
| Family Liaison | Jill Metz |
| **Medical and Training Staff** | |
| Head Medical Trainer | Ken Lowe |
| Head Equipment Manager | Barrie Stafford |
| Assistant Medical Trainer | Chris Davie |
| Equipment Managers | Lyle Kulchisky, Jeff Lang |
| Massage Therapist | Steve Lines |
| Medical Chief of Staff/Dir. Glen Sather Clinic | Dr. David C. Reid |
| Medical Staff | Drs. John Clarke, Dhiren Naidu, Don Groot, Ben Eastwood, Tony Sneazwell, Gordon Bell, Dave Magee, Brent Saik, Dr. John Dunn |
| **Finance and Administration** | |
| Senior Director, New Business Development | Jason Quilley |
| Controller | Zeina Charara |
| Human Resource Manager | Tandy Kustiak |
| Director of Administration & Legal Counsel | Keely Brown |
| Director, Facilities Operations & GM Telus Field | Craig Tkachuk |
| Payroll Manager / Accountant | Shawna Quigley / Christine Marceau |
| IT Director / Manager | Alfred Ng / Rod Pruden |
| **Communications and Broadcast** | |
| Vice President, Communications & Broadcast | Allan Watt |
| Director, Communications & Media Relations | J.J. Hebert |
| Manager, Communications & Team Services | Patrick Garland |
| Coordinator, Communications & Media Relations | Rob Thomas |
| Director of Broadcast | Don Metz |
| **Corporate Partnerships** | |
| Vice President, Corporate Partnerships | Brad MacGregor |
| Directors, Corporate Partnerships | Lisa Munro, Martha Henderson, Daryl Zelinski |
| Manager, Suites / Partnerships / Events | Bob Haromy / Abe Hajar / Kathy Grozic |
| Partner Activation Specialists | Angie Zander, Matt McPhee, David Reyner, Kendra Morton, Stephen Rausch, Sara Ripko, Greg Atkins |
| Business Analyst | Jason Lee |
| Event Coordinator | Jody Young, Dallas Fidierchuk |
| Manager, Digital Media Sales | Jessica Butts |
| **Ticket Sales and Customer Relationships** | |
| V.P., Ticket Sales and Customer Relationships | TBD |
| Manager, Ticket Operations | Gavin Morton |
| Manager, Customer Relationships | Carmen Day |
| Ticket Event Administrator | Lindsay Gilbert |
| Ticket Account Executives | John Sutherland, Ryan Fengstad, Brent Frew, Julian Solberg, Don Robinson, David Benson, Field Pieterse, Conrad Langier, Erik Hapke, Alex Shaw, Kevin Radomski |
| Customer Experience Representative | Dianne Kalita, Tyson Lazaruk, Michela Mantle, Brynn Tralnberg |
| Supervisor, Ticket Services | Curtis Griffith |
| Sr. Customer Services Representative | Paul Reid |
| **Marketing** | |
| V.P., Marketing – Oilers Brand | Pat McLaughlin |
| Senior Business Analyst | Sharon Lyseng |
| Manager, Marketing / Digital Media | Christine Dmytryshyn / Marc Ciampa |
| Digital Media Specialist / Producer | Jen Sharpe / Steve Taylor |
| Marketing Specialist / Coodinator | Debbie George / Avery Grbavac |
| Manager, Corporate Communications | Jessica McPhee |
| Game Night Supervisor / Director | Kristi Van Binsbergen / Derek Dawley |
| **Community** | |
| Exec. Director, Oilers Community Foundation | Natalie Minckler |
| Manager, Community & Fan Development | Trevor Murphy |
| Community & Fan Developmen Coordinator | Janine Forsey |
| Community Partnership Coordinator | Amanda Penner |
| Grant & Fund Development Coordinator | Lindsay Dvornik |
| ICE School Program Coordinator | Sandy VanRiper |
| Online Auction Coordinator | Dwain Tomkow |
| **Broadcast** | |
| Television Outlets | Sportsnet , CBXT TV & TSN |
| Radio Flagship Station | 630 CHED (AM); Rod Phillips (play-by-play) & Bob Stauffer (colour) |

# Florida Panthers

## 2008-09 Results: 41W-30L-3OTL-8SOL 93PTS.
## Third, Southeast Division

### Key Off-Season Signings/Acquisitions

**2009**

**June 19** • Acquired C **Steve Reinprecht** from Phoenix for C **Stefan Meyer.**

**27** • Acquired D **Jordan Leopold** and a 3rd-round pick in 2009 from Calgary for D **Jay Bouwmeester.**

**July 1** • Re-signed RW **Radek Dvorak** and LW **David Booth.**

**1** • Signed G **Scott Clemmensen** and D **Ville Koistinen.**

**6** • Signed C **Jeff Taffe.**

### Year-by-Year Record

| Season | GP | Home W | Home L | Home T | Home OL | Road W | Road L | Road T | Road OL | Overall W | Overall L | Overall T | Overall OL | GF | GA | Pts. | Finished | Playoff Result |
|---|---|---|---|---|---|---|---|---|---|---|---|---|---|---|---|---|---|---|
| 2008-09 | 82 | 22 | 12 | .... | 7 | 19 | 18 | .... | 4 | 41 | 30 | .... | 11 | 234 | 231 | 93 | 3rd, Southeast Div. | Out of Playoffs |
| 2007-08 | 82 | 18 | 15 | .... | 8 | 20 | 20 | .... | 1 | 38 | 35 | .... | 9 | 216 | 226 | 85 | 3rd, Southeast Div. | Out of Playoffs |
| 2006-07 | 82 | 23 | 12 | .... | 6 | 12 | 19 | .... | 10 | 35 | 31 | .... | 16 | 247 | 257 | 86 | 4th, Southeast Div. | Out of Playoffs |
| 2005-06 | 82 | 25 | 11 | .... | 5 | 12 | 23 | .... | 6 | 37 | 34 | .... | 11 | 240 | 257 | 85 | 4th, Southeast Div. | Out of Playoffs |
| 2004-05 | .... | .... | .... | .... | .... | .... | .... | .... | .... | .... | .... | .... | .... | .... | .... | .... | | |
| 2003-04 | 82 | 16 | 15 | 7 | 3 | 12 | 20 | 8 | 1 | 28 | 35 | 15 | 4 | 188 | 221 | 75 | 4th, Southeast Div. | Out of Playoffs |
| 2002-03 | 82 | 8 | 21 | 7 | 5 | 16 | 15 | 6 | 4 | 24 | 36 | 13 | 9 | 176 | 237 | 70 | 4th, Southeast Div. | Out of Playoffs |
| 2001-02 | 82 | 11 | 23 | 3 | 4 | 11 | 21 | 7 | 2 | 22 | 44 | 10 | 6 | 180 | 250 | 60 | 4th, Southeast Div. | Out of Playoffs |
| 2000-01 | 82 | 12 | 18 | 7 | 4 | 10 | 20 | 6 | 5 | 22 | 38 | 13 | 9 | 200 | 246 | 66 | 3rd, Southeast Div. | Out of Playoffs |
| 1999-2000 | 82 | 26 | 9 | 4 | 2 | 17 | 18 | 2 | 4 | 43 | 27 | 6 | 6 | 244 | 209 | 98 | 2nd, Southeast Div. | Lost Conf. Quarter-Final |
| 1998-99 | 82 | 17 | 17 | 7 | .... | 13 | 17 | 11 | .... | 30 | 34 | 18 | .... | 210 | 228 | 78 | 2nd, Southeast Div. | Out of Playoffs |
| 1997-98 | 82 | 11 | 24 | 6 | .... | 13 | 19 | 9 | .... | 24 | 43 | 15 | .... | 203 | 256 | 63 | 6th, Atlantic Div. | Out of Playoffs |
| 1996-97 | 82 | 21 | 12 | 8 | .... | 14 | 16 | 11 | .... | 35 | 28 | 19 | .... | 221 | 201 | 89 | 3rd, Atlantic Div. | Lost Conf. Quarter-Final |
| 1995-96 | 82 | 25 | 12 | 4 | .... | 16 | 19 | 6 | .... | 41 | 31 | 10 | .... | 254 | 234 | 92 | 3rd, Atlantic Div. | Lost Final |
| 1994-95 | 48 | 9 | 12 | 3 | .... | 11 | 10 | 3 | .... | 20 | 22 | 6 | .... | 115 | 127 | 46 | 5th, Atlantic Div. | Out of Playoffs |
| 1993-94 | 84 | 15 | 18 | 9 | .... | 18 | 16 | 8 | .... | 33 | 34 | 17 | .... | 233 | 233 | 83 | 5th, Atlantic Div. | Out of Playoffs |

### 2009-10 Schedule

| Month | Day | Date | Opponent |
|---|---|---|---|
| **Oct.** | Fri. | 2 | at Chicago† |
| | Sat. | 3 | Chicago† |
| | Fri. | 9 | at Carolina |
| | Sat. | 10 | New Jersey |
| | Mon. | 12 | at Tampa Bay |
| | Fri. | 16 | Philadelphia |
| | Wed. | 21 | Buffalo |
| | Fri. | 23 | at Pittsburgh |
| | Sat. | 24 | at Philadelphia |
| | Wed. | 28 | Ottawa |
| | Fri. | 30 | at Dallas |
| | Sat. | 31 | at St. Louis |
| **Nov.** | Wed. | 4 | Carolina |
| | Fri. | 6 | Washington |
| | Sat. | 7 | at Washington |
| | Thu. | 12 | at Boston |
| | Sat. | 14 | NY Islanders |
| | Mon. | 16 | Los Angeles |
| | Wed. | 18 | at Buffalo |
| | Fri. | 20 | at Detroit |
| | Sat. | 21 | at NY Rangers |
| | Mon. | 23 | Pittsburgh |
| | Wed. | 25 | NY Rangers |
| | Fri. | 27 | Toronto |
| | Sat. | 28 | at Nashville |
| | Mon. | 30 | at Atlanta |
| **Dec.** | Wed. | 2 | Colorado |
| | Thu. | 3 | at Washington |
| | Sat. | 5 | Atlanta |
| | Mon. | 7 | Edmonton |
| | Wed. | 9 | at Columbus |
| | Fri. | 11 | at New Jersey |
| | Sat. | 12 | at Pittsburgh |
| | Mon. | 14 | at NY Islanders |
| | Wed. | 16 | Atlanta |
| | Fri. | 18 | Carolina |
| | Sat. | 19 | at Carolina |
| | Mon. | 21 | at Philadelphia |
| | Wed. | 23 | at NY Rangers |
| | Sun. | 27 | Boston* |
| | Thu. | 31 | Montreal* |
| **Jan.** | Sun. | 3 | Pittsburgh* |
| | Tue. | 5 | at Toronto |
| | Thu. | 7 | at Montreal |
| | Sat. | 9 | at Ottawa |
| | Wed. | 13 | Washington |
| | Thu. | 14 | at Tampa Bay |
| | Sat. | 16 | Tampa Bay |
| | Mon. | 18 | Atlanta |
| | Wed. | 20 | at New Jersey |
| | Thu. | 21 | at NY Islanders |
| | Sat. | 23 | Toronto |
| | Tue. | 26 | Montreal |
| | Fri. | 29 | at Washington |
| | Sun. | 31 | NY Islanders* |
| **Feb.** | Mon. | 1 | Anaheim |
| | Fri. | 5 | Calgary |
| | Sat. | 6 | at Atlanta |
| | Tue. | 9 | at Carolina |
| | Thu. | 11 | Vancouver |
| | Sat. | 13 | Boston |
| **Mar.** | Tue. | 2 | at Atlanta |
| | Wed. | 3 | Philadelphia |
| | Sat. | 6 | Carolina |
| | Tue. | 9 | at Minnesota |
| | Thu. | 11 | at Colorado |
| | Sat. | 13 | at San Jose* |
| | Tue. | 16 | Washington |
| | Thu. | 18 | Phoenix |
| | Sat. | 20 | Buffalo |
| | Sun. | 21 | Tampa Bay* |
| | Tue. | 23 | at Toronto |
| | Thu. | 25 | at Montreal |
| | Sat. | 27 | at Ottawa |
| | Mon. | 29 | Nashville |
| | Wed. | 31 | at Buffalo |
| **Apr.** | Thu. | 1 | at Boston |
| | Sat. | 3 | NY Rangers |
| | Tue. | 6 | Ottawa |
| | Thu. | 8 | New Jersey |
| | Sat. | 10 | at Tampa Bay |
| | Sun. | 11 | Tampa Bay* |

* Denotes afternoon game. † Games played in Helsinki, FI.

*David Booth led the Panthers with 31 goals in 2008-09. In his three seasons in the NHL, Booth's scoring totals have jumped from three goals to 22 to 31. His points have gone from 10 to 40 to 60.*

**SOUTHEAST DIVISION**
**17th NHL Season**

**Franchise date:** June 14, 1993

# 2009-10 Player Personnel

| FORWARDS | HT | WT | S | Place of Birth | *Age | 2008-09 Club |
|---|---|---|---|---|---|---|
| BOOTH, David | 6-0 | 212 | L | Detroit, MI | 24 | Florida |
| BRINE, David | 6-1 | 201 | L | Truro, N.S. | 24 | Rochester |
| CAMPBELL, Gregory | 6-0 | 197 | L | London, Ont. | 25 | Florida |
| DVORAK, Radek | 6-2 | 200 | R | Tabor, Czech. | 32 | Florida |
| FROLIK, Michael | 6-1 | 185 | L | Kladno, Czech. | 21 | Florida |
| HORTON, Nathan | 6-2 | 229 | R | Welland, Ont. | 24 | Florida |
| JOHNSON, Jamie | 5-11 | 185 | R | Port Franks, Ont. | 27 | TPS |
| KREPS, Kamil | 6-2 | 194 | R | Litomerice, Czech. | 24 | Florida |
| MATTHIAS, Shawn | 6-3 | 211 | L | Mississauga, Ont. | 21 | Florida-Rochester |
| McARDLE, Kenndal | 5-11 | 190 | L | Toronto, Ont. | 22 | Florida-Rochester |
| MINK, Graham | 6-3 | 220 | R | Stowe, VT | 30 | Washington-Hershey |
| OLESZ, Rostislav | 6-1 | 214 | L | Bilovec, Czech. | 23 | Florida |
| REINPRECHT, Steve | 6-0 | 195 | L | Edmonton, Alta. | 33 | Phoenix |
| REPIK, Michal | 5-10 | 180 | R | Vlasim, Czech. | 20 | Florida-Rochester |
| STILLMAN, Cory | 6-0 | 200 | L | Peterborough, Ont. | 35 | Florida |
| TAFFE, Jeff | 6-3 | 207 | L | Hastings, MN | 28 | Pittsburgh-Wilkes-Barre |
| TARNASKY, Nick | 6-2 | 224 | L | Rocky Mtn. House, Alta. | 24 | Nashville-Florida |
| WEISS, Stephen | 5-11 | 185 | L | Toronto, Ont. | 26 | Florida |
| **DEFENSEMEN** | | | | | | |
| ALLEN, Bryan | 6-4 | 220 | L | Kingston, Ont. | 29 | Florida |
| BALLARD, Keith | 5-11 | 208 | L | Baudette, MN | 26 | Florida |
| ELLERBY, Keaton | 6-4 | 186 | L | Strathmore, Alta. | 20 | Rochester |
| FITZPATRICK, Rory | 6-2 | 208 | R | Rochester, NY | 34 | Rochester |
| GARRISON, Jason | 6-2 | 220 | L | White Rock, B.C. | 24 | Florida-Rochester |
| KOISTINEN, Ville | 5-11 | 187 | L | Oulu, Finland | 27 | Nashville |
| LEOPOLD, Jordan | 6-1 | 200 | L | Golden Valley, MN | 29 | Colorado-Calgary |
| McCABE, Bryan | 6-2 | 220 | L | St. Catharines, Ont. | 34 | Florida |
| WILSON, Clay | 6-0 | 195 | L | Sturgeon Lake, MN | 26 | CBJ-Syr-Atl-Chi (AHL) |

| GOALTENDERS | HT | WT | C | Place of Birth | *Age | 2008-09 Club |
|---|---|---|---|---|---|---|
| BECKFORD-TSEU, Chris | 6-2 | 201 | L | Toronto, Ont. | 25 | Roch-Fla (ECHL)-Phoenix |
| CLEMMENSEN, Scott | 6-3 | 205 | L | Des Moines, IA | 32 | New Jersey-Lowell |
| PLANTE, Tyler | 6-3 | 191 | L | Milwaukee, WI | 22 | Rochester-Dayton |
| SALAK, Alexander | 6-1 | 189 | L | Strakonice, Czech. | 22 | TPS |
| VOKOUN, Tomas | 6-0 | 195 | R | Karlovy Vary, Czech. | 33 | Florida |

* – Age at start of 2009-10 season

# 2008-09 Scoring

* – rookie

## Regular Season

| Pos | # | Player | Team | GP | G | A | Pts | TOI | +/– | PIM | PP | SH | GW | S | % |
|---|---|---|---|---|---|---|---|---|---|---|---|---|---|---|---|
| C | 9 | Stephen Weiss | FLA | 78 | 14 | 47 | 61 | 17:48 | 19 | 22 | 4 | 1 | 4 | 154 | 9.1 |
| L | 10 | David Booth | FLA | 72 | 31 | 29 | 60 | 17:05 | 10 | 38 | 11 | 0 | 5 | 246 | 12.6 |
| L | 61 | Cory Stillman | FLA | 63 | 17 | 32 | 49 | 16:35 | 1 | 37 | 8 | 0 | 2 | 115 | 14.8 |
| C | 16 | Nathan Horton | FLA | 67 | 22 | 23 | 45 | 17:51 | –5 | 48 | 5 | 1 | 5 | 131 | 16.8 |
| C | 67 * | Michael Frolik | FLA | 79 | 21 | 24 | 45 | 14:48 | 10 | 22 | 1 | 0 | 2 | 158 | 13.3 |
| D | 4 | Jay Bouwmeester | FLA | 82 | 15 | 27 | 42 | 26:59 | –2 | 68 | 9 | 0 | 2 | 182 | 8.2 |
| D | 24 | Bryan McCabe | FLA | 69 | 15 | 24 | 39 | 23:08 | –1 | 41 | 8 | 0 | 3 | 153 | 9.8 |
| R | 14 | Radek Dvorak | FLA | 81 | 15 | 21 | 36 | 16:26 | 0 | 42 | 0 | 4 | 3 | 136 | 11.0 |
| D | 2 | Keith Ballard | FLA | 82 | 6 | 28 | 34 | 22:23 | 14 | 72 | 1 | 0 | 1 | 106 | 5.7 |
| R | 20 | Richard Zednik | FLA | 70 | 17 | 16 | 33 | 15:35 | 2 | 46 | 3 | 0 | 4 | 153 | 11.1 |
| C | 11 | Gregory Campbell | FLA | 77 | 13 | 19 | 32 | 16:47 | 0 | 76 | 1 | 0 | 1 | 135 | 9.6 |
| L | 18 | Ville Peltonen | FLA | 79 | 12 | 19 | 31 | 15:15 | 6 | 31 | 0 | 0 | 1 | 121 | 9.9 |
| D | 55 | Steve Eminger | PHI | 12 | 0 | 2 | 2 | 17:52 | 0 | 8 | 0 | 0 | 0 | 9 | 0.0 |
| | | | T.B. | 50 | 4 | 19 | 23 | 23:33 | –4 | 36 | 2 | 0 | 0 | 63 | 6.3 |
| | | | FLA | 9 | 1 | 0 | 1 | 15:49 | 1 | 6 | 0 | 0 | 1 | 13 | 7.7 |
| | | | Total | 71 | 5 | 21 | 26 | 21:36 | –3 | 50 | 2 | 0 | 1 | 85 | 5.9 |
| D | 44 | Nick Boynton | FLA | 68 | 5 | 16 | 21 | 16:35 | 7 | 91 | 0 | 0 | 1 | 104 | 4.8 |
| C | 53 | Brett McLean | FLA | 80 | 7 | 12 | 19 | 12:25 | –12 | 29 | 0 | 0 | 2 | 114 | 6.1 |
| C | 28 | Kamil Kreps | FLA | 66 | 4 | 15 | 19 | 13:58 | 2 | 18 | 0 | 1 | 1 | 77 | 5.2 |
| D | 3 | Karlis Skrastins | FLA | 80 | 4 | 14 | 18 | 20:33 | 9 | 30 | 0 | 0 | 0 | 55 | 7.3 |
| D | 22 | Jassen Cullimore | FLA | 68 | 2 | 8 | 10 | 16:47 | –10 | 37 | 0 | 0 | 0 | 52 | 3.8 |
| L | 85 | Rostislav Olesz | FLA | 37 | 4 | 5 | 9 | 13:11 | –5 | 8 | 0 | 0 | 0 | 69 | 5.8 |
| C | 13 | Anthony Stewart | FLA | 59 | 2 | 5 | 7 | 7:38 | –6 | 34 | 0 | 0 | 0 | 56 | 3.6 |
| C | 74 | Nick Tarnasky | NSH | 11 | 0 | 1 | 1 | 5:38 | 1 | 17 | 0 | 0 | 0 | 6 | 0.0 |
| | | | FLA | 34 | 1 | 5 | 6 | 7:52 | –2 | 33 | 0 | 0 | 0 | 32 | 3.1 |
| | | | Total | 45 | 1 | 6 | 7 | 7:19 | –1 | 50 | 0 | 0 | 0 | 38 | 2.6 |
| R | 32 * | Michal Repik | FLA | 5 | 2 | 0 | 2 | 7:31 | 1 | 2 | 0 | 0 | 0 | 7 | 28.6 |
| C | 41 * | Shawn Matthias | FLA | 16 | 0 | 2 | 2 | 9:09 | –3 | 2 | 0 | 0 | 0 | 11 | 0.0 |
| D | 5 | Bryan Allen | FLA | 2 | 0 | 1 | 1 | 27:11 | 2 | 0 | 0 | 0 | 0 | 5 | 0.0 |
| C | 40 | Janis Sprukts | FLA | 1 | 0 | 0 | 0 | 12:19 | 0 | 0 | 0 | 0 | 0 | 1 | 0.0 |
| D | 52 * | Jason Garrison | FLA | 1 | 0 | 0 | 0 | 11:57 | 0 | 0 | 0 | 0 | 0 | 0 | 0.0 |
| L | 37 | Tanner Glass | FLA | 3 | 0 | 0 | 0 | 6:45 | 0 | 7 | 0 | 0 | 0 | 1 | 0.0 |
| L | 71 * | Kenndal McArdle | FLA | 3 | 0 | 0 | 0 | 7:30 | –1 | 2 | 0 | 0 | 0 | 1 | 0.0 |

## Goaltending

| No. | Goaltender | GPI | Mins | Avg | W | L | OT | EN | SO | GA | SA | S% | G | A | PIM |
|---|---|---|---|---|---|---|---|---|---|---|---|---|---|---|---|
| 29 | Tomas Vokoun | 59 | 3324 | 2.49 | 26 | 23 | 6 | 11 | 6 | 138 | 1856 | .926 | 0 | 1 | 2 |
| 31 | Craig Anderson | 31 | 1636 | 2.71 | 15 | 7 | 5 | 0 | 3 | 74 | 977 | .924 | 0 | 1 | 2 |
| | **Totals** | **82** | **4998** | **2.68** | **41** | **30** | **11** | **11** | **9** | **223** | **2844** | **.922** | | | |

*Stephen Weiss established career highs with 47 assists and 61 points in 2008-09 to lead the Panthers in both categories.*

# Peter DeBoer

## Head Coach

*Born: Dunnville, Ont., June 13, 1968.*

The Florida Panthers named Peter DeBoer the 10th head coach in the club's history on June 13, 2008. DeBoer joined the Panthers from the Kitchener Rangers of the Ontario Hockey League, after guiding the team to the 2008 OHL championship before falling to the Spokane Chiefs in the Memorial Cup finals.

During his seven-year tenure as both coach and general manager in Kitchener, DeBoer earned 297 wins for a .676 winning percentage, while guiding his club to the 2003 Memorial Cup title. DeBoer earned his 500th OHL coaching victory in 2007-08, joining only five other coaches to have reached this milestone. He amassed a total of 539 OHL wins while coaching the Detroit Whalers (1995 to 1997), Plymouth Whalers (1997 to 2001) and the Kitchener Rangers (2001 to 2008), earning OHL coach of the year honors in 1999 and 2000. DeBoer was also named the 2000 Canadian Hockey League coach of the year, and was also a member of the coaching staff on Team Canada's 2005 gold medal-winning World Junior team.

As a player, DeBoer won the 1988 Memorial Cup as a member of the Windsor Spitfires. He was a 12th-round selection of the Toronto Maple Leafs in the 1988 NHL Entry Draft and played two full seasons professionally with the Milwaukee Admirals of the International Hockey League. He holds a law degree from the University of Windsor/University of Detroit.

### Coaching Record

| | | | Regular Season | | | | Playoffs | | | |
|---|---|---|---|---|---|---|---|---|---|---|
| Season | Team | League | GC | W | L | O/T | GC | W | L | T |
| 1995-96 | Detroit | OHL | 66 | 40 | 22 | 4 | 17 | 9 | 8 | .... |
| 1996-97 | Detroit | OHL | 66 | 26 | 34 | 6 | 5 | 1 | 4 | .... |
| 1997-98 | Plymouth | OHL | 66 | 37 | 22 | 7 | 15 | 8 | 7 | .... |
| 1998-99 | Plymouth | OHL | 66 | 51 | 13 | 4 | 11 | 7 | 4 | .... |
| 99-2000 | Plymouth | OHL | 68 | 45 | 18 | 5 | 23 | 15 | 8 | .... |
| 2000-01 | Plymouth | OHL | 68 | 43 | 15 | 10 | 19 | 14 | 5 | .... |
| 2001-02 | Kitchener | OHL | 68 | 35 | 22 | 11 | 4 | 0 | 4 | .... |
| 2002-03 | Kitchener | OHL | 68 | 46 | 14 | 8 | 21 | 16 | 5 | .... |
| | Kitchener | M-Cup | .... | .... | .... | .... | 4 | 4 | 0 | .... |
| 2003-04 | Kitchener | OHL | 68 | 34 | 26 | 8 | 5 | 1 | 4 | .... |
| 2004-05 | Kitchener | OHL | 68 | 35 | 20 | 13 | 15 | 9 | 6 | .... |
| 2005-06 | Kitchener | OHL | 68 | 47 | 19 | 2 | 5 | 1 | 4 | .... |
| 2006-07 | Kitchener | OHL | 68 | 47 | 17 | 4 | 9 | 5 | 4 | .... |
| 2007-08 | Kitchener | OHL | 68 | 53 | 11 | 4 | 20 | 16 | 4 | .... |
| | Kitchener | M-Cup | .... | .... | .... | .... | 5 | 2 | 3 | .... |
| **2008-09** | **Florida** | **NHL** | **82** | **41** | **30** | **11** | .... | .... | .... | .... |
| | **NHL Totals** | | **82** | **41** | **30** | **11** | .... | .... | .... | .... |

## Coaching History

Roger Neilson, 1993-94, 1994-95; Doug MacLean, 1995-96, 1996-97; Doug MacLean and Bryan Murray, 1997-98; Terry Murray, 1998-99, 1999-2000; Terry Murray and Duane Sutter, 2000-01; Duane Sutter and Mike Keenan, 2001-02; Mike Keenan, 2002-03; Mike Keenan, Rick Dudley and John Torchetti, 2003-04; Jacques Martin, 2004-05 to 2007-08; Peter DeBoer, 2008-09 to date.

## General Managers' History

Bob Clarke, 1993-94; Bryan Murray, 1994-95 to 1999-2000; Bryan Murray and Bill Torrey, 2000-01; Bill Torrey and Chuck Fletcher, 2001-02; Rick Dudley, 2002-03, 2003-04; Mike Keenan, 2004-05, 2005-06; Jacques Martin, 2006-07 to 2008-09.

# Club Records

## Team

(Figures in brackets for season records are games played; records for fewest points, wins, ties, losses, goals, goals against are for 70 or more games)

| | | |
|---|---|---|
| **Most Points** | **98** | 1999-2000 (82) |
| **Most Wins** | **43** | 1999-2000 (82) |
| **Most Ties** | **19** | 1996-97 (82) |
| **Most Losses** | **44** | 2001-02 (82) |
| **Most Goals** | **254** | 1995-96 (82) |
| **Most Goals Against** | **257** | 2005-06 (82), 2006-07 (82) |
| **Fewest Points** | **60** | 2001-02 (82) |
| **Fewest Wins** | **22** | 2000-01 (82), 2001-02 (82) |
| **Fewest Ties** | **6** | 1999-2000 (82) |
| **Fewest Losses** | **27** | 1999-2000 (82) |
| **Fewest Goals** | **176** | 2002-03 (82) |
| **Fewest Goals Against** | **201** | 1996-97 (82) |
| **Longest Winning Streak** | | |
| **Overall** | **7** | Nov. 2-14/95, Mar. 17-29/06, Mar. 2-16/08 |
| **Home** | **5** | Nov. 5-14/95, Mar. 17-Apr. 1/06, Mar. 6-16/08, Jan. 27-Feb. 13/09 |
| **Away** | **5** | Nov. 30-Dec. 12/08 |
| **Longest Undefeated Streak** | | |
| **Overall** | **12** | Oct. 5-30/96 (8 wins, 4 ties) |
| **Home** | **8** | Nov. 5-26/95 (7 wins, 1 tie) |
| **Away** | **7** | Dec. 7-29/93 (5 wins, 2 ties), Oct. 5-29/96 (4 wins, 3 ties) |
| **Longest Losing Streak** | | |
| **Overall** | **13** | Feb. 7-Mar. 23/98 |
| **Home** | **6** | Feb. 25-Mar. 23/98 |
| **Away** | **13** | Oct. 27-Dec. 17/05 |
| **Longest Winless Streak** | | |
| **Overall** | **15** | Feb. 1-Mar. 23/98 (14 losses, 1 tie) |
| **Home** | **13** | Feb. 5-Mar. 24/03 (11 losses, 2 ties) |
| **Away** | **16** | Jan. 2-Mar. 21/98 (12 losses, 4 ties) |
| **Most Shutouts, Season** | **9** | 2008-09 (82) |
| **Most PIM, Season** | **1,994** | 2001-02 (82) |
| **Most Goals, Game** | **10** | Nov. 26/97 (Bos. 5 at Fla. 10) |

## Individual

| | | |
|---|---|---|
| **Most Seasons** | **9** | Paul Laus |
| **Most Games** | **573** | Robert Svehla |
| **Most Goals, Career** | **188** | Olli Jokinen |
| **Most Assists, Career** | **231** | Olli Jokinen |
| **Most Points, Career** | **419** | Olli Jokinen (188G, 231A) |
| **Most PIM, Career** | **1,702** | Paul Laus |
| **Most Shutouts, Career** | **26** | Roberto Luongo |
| **Longest Consecutive Games Streak** | **342** | Jay Bouwmeester (Feb. 27/04-Apr. 11/09) |
| **Most Goals, Season** | **59** | Pavel Bure (2000-01) |
| **Most Assists, Season** | **53** | Viktor Kozlov (1999-2000) |
| **Most Points, Season** | **94** | Pavel Bure (1999-2000; 58G, 36A) |
| **Most PIM, Season** | **354** | Peter Worrell (2001-02) |
| **Most Points, Defenseman, Season** | **57** | Robert Svehla (1995-96; 8G, 49A) |
| **Most Points, Center, Season** | **91** | Olli Jokinen (2006-07; 39G, 52A) |
| **Most Points, Right Wing, Season** | **94** | Pavel Bure (1999-2000; 58G, 36A) |
| **Most Points, Left Wing, Season** | **71** | Ray Whitney (1999-2000; 29G, 42A) |
| **Most Points, Rookie, Season** | **50** | Jesse Belanger (1993-94; 17G, 33A) |
| **Most Shutouts, Season** | **7** | Roberto Luongo (2003-04) |
| **Most Goals, Game** | **4** | Mark Parrish (Oct. 30/98) Pavel Bure (Jan. 1/00), (Feb. 10/01) |
| **Most Assists, Game** | **4** | Four times |
| **Most Points, Game** | **6** | Olli Jokinen (Mar. 17/07; 2G, 4A) |

## Captains' History

Brian Skrudland, 1993-94 to 1996-97; Scott Mellanby, 1997-98 to 2000-01; Pavel Bure, 2001-02; no captain, 2002-03; Olli Jokinen, 2003-04 to 2007-08; no captain, 2008-09.

# All-time Record vs. Other Clubs

## Regular Season

| | At Home | | | | | | | | On Road | | | | | | | | Total | | | | | | | |
|---|---|---|---|---|---|---|---|---|---|---|---|---|---|---|---|---|---|---|---|---|---|---|---|---|
| | GP | W | L | T | OL | GF | GA | PTS | GP | W | L | T | OL | GF | GA | PTS | GP | W | L | T | OL | GF | GA | PTS |
| Anaheim | 9 | 4 | 3 | 2 | 0 | 27 | 22 | 10 | 11 | 6 | 3 | 1 | 1 | 33 | 29 | 14 | 20 | 10 | 6 | 3 | 1 | 60 | 51 | 24 |
| Atlanta | 28 | 13 | 13 | 1 | 1 | 73 | 84 | 28 | 28 | 9 | 11 | 4 | 4 | 79 | 94 | 26 | 56 | 22 | 24 | 5 | 5 | 152 | 178 | 54 |
| Boston | 29 | 13 | 12 | 2 | 2 | 89 | 85 | 30 | 30 | 15 | 11 | 4 | 0 | 81 | 81 | 34 | 59 | 28 | 23 | 6 | 2 | 170 | 166 | 64 |
| Buffalo | 29 | 14 | 13 | 1 | 1 | 78 | 81 | 30 | 31 | 7 | 19 | 3 | 2 | 58 | 92 | 19 | 60 | 21 | 32 | 4 | 3 | 136 | 173 | 49 |
| Calgary | 10 | 3 | 3 | 2 | 2 | 22 | 24 | 10 | 10 | 4 | 4 | 1 | 1 | 27 | 28 | 10 | 20 | 7 | 7 | 3 | 3 | 49 | 52 | 20 |
| Carolina | 41 | 18 | 7 | 8 | 8 | 121 | 98 | 52 | 40 | 11 | 23 | 3 | 3 | 102 | 127 | 28 | 81 | 29 | 30 | 11 | 11 | 223 | 225 | 80 |
| Chicago | 10 | 3 | 6 | 1 | 0 | 22 | 37 | 7 | 11 | 4 | 5 | 2 | 0 | 33 | 35 | 10 | 21 | 7 | 11 | 3 | 0 | 55 | 72 | 17 |
| Colorado | 13 | 2 | 10 | 0 | 1 | 36 | 52 | 5 | 12 | 4 | 4 | 3 | 1 | 31 | 35 | 12 | 25 | 6 | 14 | 3 | 2 | 67 | 87 | 17 |
| Columbus | 5 | 2 | 1 | 0 | 2 | 14 | 15 | 6 | 3 | 2 | 1 | 0 | 0 | 9 | 6 | 4 | 8 | 4 | 2 | 0 | 2 | 23 | 21 | 10 |
| Dallas | 12 | 5 | 6 | 1 | 0 | 25 | 33 | 11 | 10 | 4 | 4 | 2 | 0 | 31 | 32 | 10 | 22 | 9 | 10 | 3 | 0 | 56 | 65 | 21 |
| Detroit | 11 | 2 | 5 | 2 | 2 | 22 | 32 | 8 | 9 | 1 | 5 | 3 | 0 | 23 | 35 | 5 | 20 | 3 | 10 | 5 | 2 | 45 | 67 | 13 |
| Edmonton | 10 | 5 | 2 | 2 | 1 | 27 | 28 | 13 | 9 | 3 | 5 | 1 | 0 | 19 | 28 | 7 | 19 | 8 | 7 | 3 | 1 | 46 | 56 | 20 |
| Los Angeles | 9 | 4 | 2 | 3 | 0 | 23 | 21 | 11 | 11 | 4 | 7 | 0 | 0 | 32 | 33 | 8 | 20 | 8 | 9 | 3 | 0 | 55 | 54 | 19 |
| Minnesota | 5 | 1 | 4 | 0 | 0 | 10 | 17 | 2 | 4 | 0 | 3 | 1 | 0 | 3 | 14 | 1 | 9 | 1 | 7 | 1 | 0 | 13 | 31 | 3 |
| Montreal | 30 | 15 | 11 | 3 | 1 | 87 | 78 | 34 | 29 | 13 | 8 | 3 | 5 | 68 | 76 | 34 | 59 | 28 | 19 | 6 | 6 | 155 | 154 | 68 |
| Nashville | 6 | 4 | 0 | 1 | 1 | 21 | 11 | 10 | 7 | 2 | 2 | 2 | 1 | 15 | 15 | 7 | 13 | 6 | 2 | 3 | 2 | 36 | 26 | 17 |
| New Jersey | 33 | 11 | 15 | 4 | 3 | 75 | 84 | 29 | 32 | 8 | 19 | 3 | 2 | 61 | 99 | 21 | 65 | 19 | 34 | 7 | 5 | 136 | 183 | 50 |
| NY Islanders | 33 | 17 | 10 | 6 | 0 | 104 | 94 | 40 | 33 | 14 | 13 | 2 | 4 | 86 | 88 | 34 | 66 | 31 | 23 | 8 | 4 | 190 | 182 | 74 |
| NY Rangers | 33 | 15 | 12 | 2 | 4 | 87 | 90 | 36 | 32 | 11 | 17 | 4 | 0 | 72 | 97 | 26 | 65 | 26 | 29 | 6 | 4 | 159 | 187 | 62 |
| Ottawa | 30 | 12 | 16 | 1 | 1 | 94 | 97 | 26 | 30 | 13 | 13 | 2 | 2 | 78 | 92 | 30 | 60 | 25 | 29 | 3 | 3 | 172 | 189 | 56 |
| Philadelphia | 32 | 9 | 19 | 1 | 3 | 74 | 107 | 22 | 33 | 13 | 13 | 6 | 1 | 84 | 87 | 33 | 65 | 22 | 32 | 7 | 4 | 158 | 194 | 55 |
| Phoenix | 9 | 4 | 5 | 0 | 0 | 28 | 23 | 8 | 12 | 4 | 4 | 3 | 1 | 35 | 35 | 12 | 21 | 8 | 9 | 3 | 1 | 63 | 58 | 20 |
| Pittsburgh | 30 | 17 | 11 | 1 | 1 | 88 | 73 | 36 | 31 | 12 | 13 | 3 | 3 | 91 | 94 | 30 | 61 | 29 | 24 | 4 | 4 | 179 | 167 | 66 |
| St. Louis | 11 | 4 | 4 | 2 | 1 | 25 | 24 | 11 | 11 | 2 | 8 | 1 | 0 | 13 | 29 | 5 | 22 | 6 | 12 | 3 | 1 | 38 | 53 | 16 |
| San Jose | 11 | 3 | 3 | 5 | 0 | 30 | 32 | 11 | 10 | 2 | 6 | 2 | 0 | 19 | 32 | 6 | 21 | 5 | 9 | 7 | 0 | 49 | 64 | 17 |
| Tampa Bay | 43 | 27 | 8 | 4 | 4 | 144 | 108 | 62 | 43 | 19 | 17 | 6 | 1 | 123 | 103 | 45 | 86 | 46 | 25 | 10 | 5 | 267 | 211 | 107 |
| Toronto | 25 | 8 | 10 | 5 | 2 | 69 | 73 | 23 | 23 | 8 | 11 | 2 | 2 | 66 | 74 | 20 | 48 | 16 | 21 | 7 | 4 | 135 | 147 | 43 |
| Vancouver | 9 | 4 | 3 | 1 | 1 | 25 | 30 | 10 | 11 | 1 | 4 | 5 | 1 | 25 | 34 | 8 | 20 | 5 | 7 | 6 | 2 | 50 | 64 | 18 |
| Washington | 43 | 20 | 17 | 4 | 2 | 113 | 110 | 46 | 43 | 18 | 18 | 5 | 2 | 111 | 126 | 43 | 86 | 38 | 35 | 9 | 4 | 224 | 236 | 89 |
| **Totals** | **599** | **259** | **231** | **65** | **44** | **1653** | **1663** | **627** | **599** | **214** | **271** | **77** | **37** | **1508** | **1750** | **542** | **1198** | **473** | **502** | **142** | **81** | **3161** | **3413** | **1169** |

## Playoffs

| | Series | W | L | GP | W | L | T | GF | GA | Last Mtg. | Rnd. | Result |
|---|---|---|---|---|---|---|---|---|---|---|---|---|
| Boston | 1 | 1 | 0 | 5 | 4 | 1 | 0 | 22 | 16 | 1996 | CQF | W 4-1 |
| Colorado | 1 | 0 | 1 | 4 | 0 | 4 | 0 | 4 | 15 | 1996 | F | L 0-4 |
| New Jersey | 1 | 0 | 1 | 4 | 0 | 4 | 0 | 6 | 12 | 2000 | CQF | L 0-4 |
| NY Rangers | 1 | 0 | 1 | 5 | 1 | 4 | 0 | 10 | 13 | 1997 | CQF | L 1-4 |
| Philadelphia | 1 | 1 | 0 | 6 | 4 | 2 | 0 | 15 | 11 | 1996 | CSF | W 4-2 |
| Pittsburgh | 1 | 1 | 0 | 7 | 4 | 3 | 0 | 20 | 15 | 1996 | CF | W 4-3 |
| **Totals** | **6** | **3** | **3** | **31** | **13** | **18** | **0** | **77** | **82** | | | |

Colorado totals include Quebec, 1993-94 to 1994-95.
Phoenix totals include Winnipeg, 1993-94 to 1995-96.

Carolina totals include Hartford, 1993-94 to 1996-97.

## Playoff Results 2009-2004

(Last playoff appearance: 2000)

**Abbreviations: Round: F** - Final; **CF** - conference final; **CSF** - conference semi-final; **CQF** - conference quarter-final.

## 2008-09 Results

| Month | Day | Opponent | Score |
|---|---|---|---|
| **Oct.** | 10 | at Carolina | 4-6 |
| | 11 | Atlanta | 3-2* |
| | 16 | Minnesota | 2-6 |
| | 18 | NY Islanders | 2-0 |
| | 20 | at Montreal | 1-3 |
| | 22 | at Ottawa | 3-1 |
| | 24 | San Jose | 4-3 |
| | 25 | at St. Louis | 0-4 |
| | 30 | Ottawa | 1-2 |
| **Nov.** | 1 | at Nashville | 2-3† |
| | 2 | at Atlanta | 3-5 |
| | 6 | at Los Angeles | 2-3 |
| | 8 | at Phoenix | 1-4 |
| | 9 | at Anaheim | 3-1 |
| | 12 | Tampa Bay | 4-0 |
| | 14 | Detroit | 2-3 |
| | 18 | at Tampa Bay | 4-3† |
| | 20 | at New Jersey | 1-3 |
| | 21 | at Boston | 2-4 |
| | 24 | Carolina | 3-2 |
| | 26 | New Jersey | 2-3* |
| | 28 | NY Rangers | 3-4† |
| | 30 | at NY Rangers | 4-0 |
| **Dec.** | 2 | at Washington | 5-3 |
| | 4 | Buffalo | 2-1 |
| | 6 | Boston | 0-4 |
| | 8 | at Ottawa | 4-3* |
| | 11 | at Edmonton | 2-0 |
| | 12 | at Calgary | 3-2† |
| | 14 | at Vancouver | 3-5 |
| | 18 | at Carolina | 1-2* |
| | 21 | Colorado | 3-0 |
| | 23 | Nashville | 3-0 |
| | 26 | Tampa Bay | 3-4† |
| | 27 | at Tampa Bay | 4-6 |
| | 29 | Montreal | 2-5 |
| | 31 | at NY Islanders | 2-4 |
| **Jan.** | 3 | at Pittsburgh | 6-1 |
| | 4 | at Montreal | 5-6† |
| | 6 | at Toronto | 4-2 |
| | 8 | Carolina | 4-2 |
| | 10 | Atlanta | 8-4 |
| | 16 | Philadelphia | 2-3† |
| | 17 | at Tampa Bay | 4-3 |
| | 19 | Buffalo | 2-3† |
| | 21 | Dallas | 1-4 |
| | 27 | Philadelphia | 3-2 |
| | 29 | Montreal | 5-1 |
| | 31 | at NY Islanders | 1-3 |
| **Feb.** | 3 | at Toronto | 4-3* |
| | 5 | NY Islanders | 3-2 |
| | 7 | at Washington | 1-3 |
| | 10 | Toronto | 5-4* |
| | 12 | at Carolina | 5-0 |
| | 13 | NY Rangers | 2-1† |
| | 15 | Washington | 2-4 |
| | 17 | New Jersey | 4-0 |
| | 19 | Chicago | 0-4 |
| | 21 | Boston | 2-0 |
| | 24 | at Boston | 1-6 |
| | 26 | at NY Rangers | 2-1 |
| | 28 | at New Jersey | 2-7 |
| **Mar.** | 1 | at Washington | 6-2 |
| | 3 | at Atlanta | 4-3 |
| | 5 | Pittsburgh | 1-4 |
| | 7 | St. Louis | 5-3 |
| | 10 | at Pittsburgh | 3-4† |
| | 12 | at Buffalo | 1-3 |
| | 14 | Tampa Bay | 3-4† |
| | 17 | Washington | 0-3 |
| | 19 | Toronto | 3-1 |
| | 21 | Columbus | 1-3 |
| | 23 | Carolina | 2-3* |
| | 25 | at Buffalo | 3-5 |
| | 26 | at Philadelphia | 4-2 |
| | 28 | at Dallas | 6-3 |
| | 31 | Ottawa | 5-2 |
| **Apr.** | 3 | Atlanta | 1-3 |
| | 5 | Pittsburgh | 4-2 |
| | 7 | at Philadelphia | 1-2 |
| | 9 | at Atlanta | 3-2 |
| | 11 | Washington | 7-4 |

* – Overtime † – Shootout

## Entry Draft Selections 2009-1995

Name in bold denotes played in NHL.

### 2009
**Pick**
- 14 Dmitri Kulikov
- 44 Drew Shore
- 67 Josh Birkholz
- 107 Garrett Wilson
- 135 Corban Knight
- 138 Wade Megan
- 165 Scott Timmins

### 2008
**Pick**
- 31 Jacob Markstrom
- 46 Colby Robak
- 80 Adam Comrie
- 100 A.J. Jenks
- 190 Matthew Bartkowski

### 2007
**Pick**
- 10 Keaton Ellerby
- 40 **Michal Repik**
- 71 Evgeni Dadonov
- 101 Matt Rust
- 131 John Lee
- 181 Corey Syvret
- 191 Ryan Watson
- 202 Sergei Gaiduchenko

### 2006
**Pick**
- 10 **Michael Frolik**
- 73 Brady Calla
- 103 Michael Caruso
- 116 Derrick Lapoint
- 155 Peter Aston
- 193 Marc Cheverie

### 2005
**Pick**
- 20 **Kenndal McArdle**
- 32 Tyler Plante
- 90 Dan Collins
- 93 Olivier Legault
- 104 Matt Duffy
- 161 Brian Foster
- 164 Roman Derlyuk
- 224 Zach Bearson

### 2004
**Pick**
- 7 **Rostislav Olesz**
- 37 David Shantz
- 53 **David Booth**
- 105 Evan Schafer
- 152 Bret Nasby
- 267 Spencer Dillon
- 283 Luke Beaverson

### 2003
**Pick**
- 3 **Nathan Horton**
- 25 **Anthony Stewart**
- 38 **Kamil Kreps**
- 55 **Stefan Meyer**
- 105 **Martin Lojek**
- 124 James Pemberton
- 141 Dan Travis
- 162 Martin Tuma
- 171 Denis Stasyuk
- 223 Dany Roussin
- 234 Petr Kadlec
- 264 John Hecimovic
- 265 **Tanner Glass**

### 2002
**Pick**
- 3 **Jay Bouwmeester**
- 9 **Petr Taticek**
- 40 **Rob Globke**
- 67 **Gregory Campbell**
- 134 Topi Jaakola
- 158 Vince Bellissimo
- 169 Jeremy Swanson
- 196 Mikael Vuorio
- 200 Denis Yachmenev
- 232 Peter Hafner

### 2001
**Pick**
- 4 **Stephen Weiss**
- 24 **Lukas Krajicek**
- 34 Greg Watson
- 64 **Tomas Malec**
- 68 **Grant McNeill**
- 117 Mike Woodford
- 136 Billy Thompson
- 169 Dustin Johner
- 200 Toni Koivisto
- 231 Kyle Bruce
- 263 Jan Blanar
- 267 **Ivan Majesky**

### 2000
**Pick**
- 58 Vladimir Sapozhnikov
- 77 Robert Fried
- 82 Sean O'Connor
- 115 Chris Eade
- 120 Davis Parley
- 190 **Josh Olson**
- 234 **Janis Sprukts**
- 253 Mathew Sommerfeld

### 1999
**Pick**
- 12 **Denis Shvidki**
- 40 **Alex Auld**
- 70 **Niklas Hagman**
- 80 Jean-Francois Laniel
- 103 Morgan McCormick
- 109 Rod Sarich
- 169 Brad Woods
- 198 Travis Eagles
- 227 Jonathon Charron

### 1998
**Pick**
- 30 **Kyle Rossiter**
- 61 **Joe DiPenta**
- 63 **Lance Ward**
- 89 **Ryan Jardine**
- 117 **Jaroslav Spacek**
- 148 Chris Ovington
- 176 B.J. Ketcheson
- 203 Ian Jacobs
- 231 Adrian Wichser

### 1997
**Pick**
- 20 **Mike Brown**
- 47 **Kristian Huselius**
- 56 Vratislav Cech
- 74 **Nick Smith**
- 95 **Ivan Novoseltsev**
- 127 Pat Parthenais
- 155 Keith Delaney
- 183 Tyler Palmer
- 211 Doug Schueller
- 237 Benoit Cote

### 1996
**Pick**
- 20 **Marcus Nilson**
- 60 **Chris Allen**
- 65 **Oleg Kvasha**
- 82 **Joey Tetarenko**
- 129 Andrew Long
- 156 Gaetan Poirier
- 183 Alexandre Couture
- 209 Denis Khloptonov
- 235 Russell Smith

### 1995
**Pick**
- 10 **Radek Dvorak**
- 36 Aaron MacDonald
- 62 Mike O'Grady
- 80 **Dave Duerden**
- 88 **Daniel Tjarnqvist**
- 114 Francois Cloutier
- 166 **Peter Worrell**
- 192 **Filip Kuba**
- 218 David Lemanowicz

## Randy Sexton
### Assistant General Manager
*Born: Brockville, Ont., July 24, 1959*

Randy Sexton joined the Florida Panthers as the team's assistant general manager on January 26, 2007. Since joining the club, Sexton has worked closely on all hockey-related matters and has been instrumental in re-signing the club's restricted free agents such as Stephen Weiss, Bryan Allen, Nathan Horton and Rostislav Olesz to long-term deals. He has also played an important role in acquiring players through trades and free agency.

Sexton joined the Panthers after spending three years as the executive director of Capital Sports Management Inc. (CSMI), a sister company to the Ottawa Senators Hockey Club. He spent eight years (1988 to 1996) with the Senators organization serving as the club's president, chief executive officer and general manager. During his tenure the Senators achieved enormous success and profitability in all areas of hockey and business operations and laid the foundation upon which the team's future success was built. Sexton directed the contract negotiations and signing of Alexei Yashin, the club's first pick in their first NHL Entry Draft in 1992. Under his tenure, he was also responsible for drafting and signing several other star NHL players that included Pavel Demitra, Daniel Alfredsson, Bryan Berrard, Martin Straka, Steve Duchesne and Jaroslav Modry.

Sexton completed his post-secondary education at St. Lawrence University, playing for the varsity hockey team from 1978 to 1982. He served as team captain during his final two seasons, earning numerous awards including All-American honors, Senior Male Athlete of the Year, Most Valuable Player and the Brian P. Doyle Leadership Award. From 1983 to 1985 he served as an assistant coach with St. Lawrence, while also handling scouting and recruiting responsibilities. He earned a Masters Degree in Business Administration from Clarkson University.

# Club Directory

**BankAtlantic Center**

**Florida Panthers**
BankAtlantic Center
One Panther Parkway
Sunrise, FL 33323
Phone **954/835-7000**
FAX 954/835-7700
www.floridapanthers.com
**Capacity:** 19,250

**Ownership**

| | |
|---|---|
| General Partner and Chairman of the Board/ Chief Executive Officer/Governor | Alan Cohen (Panthers Hockey LC) |
| Vice Chairman/Alternate Governor/Limited Partner | Cliff Viner (CGV Assets, LLC) |
| Managing Director/Limited Partner/ Chairman of Florida Panthers Foundation | Stu Siegel (Siegent S&E, LLC) |
| Limited Partners | Steve Cohen, David Epstein, Dr. Elliott Hahn (LABE Partners, LLC), H. Wayne Huizenga (HHI, LLC), Bernie Kosar (KHOC, LLC),Richard C. Lehman M.D. (RCL of Florida, LLC), Al E. Maroone, Michael E. Maroone, James L. Nederlander (Charley Dog, Inc.), Jordan Zimmerman (JRB Pelican Point, LLC) |

**Executive**

| | |
|---|---|
| President/Chief Operating Officer | Michael R. Yormark |
| Sr. VP, Corporate Marketing & New Business Development | Pedro Goncalves |
| Sr. VP, Sales & Marketing | Chad Johnson |
| Chief Financial Officer, V.P. Finance | Evelyn Lopez |
| General Manager, BankAtlantic Center/ VP, Operations | Brett Stefansson |
| General Manager/V.P. incredibleICE | Jeff Campol |
| Vice President, Human Resources/Payroll | Carol Duncanson |
| Vice President, Real Estate Development | Uri Man |
| Vice President, Corporate Development | RJ Martino |
| Vice President, Broadcasting & Panthers Alumni | Randy Moller |
| Vice President, Business Affairs | Ed Wildermuth |
| Vice President, Sales and Service | Ryan McCoy |
| Executive Assistant to the President/COO | Heidi Leigh |
| Executive Assistant to Chief Financial Officer | Cathy Stevenson |

**Hockey Operations**

| | |
|---|---|
| General Manager | TBD |
| Assistant General Manager | Randy Sexton |
| Alternate Governor | William A. Torrey |
| Director of Professional Scouting | Bill O'Flaherty |
| Director of Player Personnel/Pro Scout | Jack Birch |
| Pro Scout | Phil Myre |
| Director of Amateur Scouting | Scott Luce |
| Amateur Scouts | Fred Bandel, Craig Demetrick, Paul Gallagher, Erin Ginnell, Jari Kekalainen, Luke Williams, Mike Yandle |
| Executive Assistant to the General Manager | Giselle Seaone |
| Manager, Hockey Administration | Murray Cawker |
| Manager, Team Services | Mike Dixon |

**Coaching Staff**

| | |
|---|---|
| Head Coach | Peter DeBoer |
| Assistant Coach | Mike Kitchen |
| Assistant Coach | Jim Hulton |
| Strength & Conditioning Coach | Craig Slaunwhite |
| Video Coach | Jamie Pringle |
| Goaltending Coach | TBD |

**Training Staff**

| | |
|---|---|
| Head Athletic Trainer | David Zenobi |
| Assistant Athletic Trainer | Steve Dischiavi |
| Head Equipment Manager | Chris Scoppetto |
| Assistant Equipment Managers | Chris Moody, Jason MacDonald |

**Communications and Media Content**

| | |
|---|---|
| Director, Communications | Justin Copertino |
| Director, Public Relations/ Editor in Chief, Panthers Insider | Matthew F. Sacco |
| Director of Internet and Publication Content | Dave Joseph |
| Website Coordinator | Glenn Odebralski |
| Radio/TV Broadcasters | |
| Television | FSN FloridaTelevision |
| Play-By-Play | Steve Goldstein |
| Television Analyst | Bill Lindsay |
| Panthers Review Host | Craig Minervini |
| Radio | Sports Talk 790 The Ticket |
| Radio Play-By-Play | Randy Moller |

# Los Angeles Kings

## Key Off-Season Signings/Acquisitions

**2009**

**July 2** • Signed D **Rob Scuderi.**

**July 3** • Acquired LW **Ryan Smyth** from Colorado for D **Kyle Quincey**, D **Tom Preissing** and a 5th-round pick in 2010.

**July 17** • Re-signed D **Jack Johnson.**

**July 20** • Re-signed RW **Teddy Purcell.**

## 2008-09 Results: 34W-37L-3OTL-8SOL 79PTS.
## Fifth, Pacific Division

*Picked second overall in the 2008 Entry Draft, Drew Doughty played 81 games for the Kings in 2008-09 and led all NHL rookies with 23:50 of ice time per game.*

## 2009-10 Schedule

| | | | | | | | |
|---|---|---|---|---|---|---|---|
| **Oct.** | Sat. | 3 | Phoenix | **Jan.** | Sat. | 2 | Washington* |
| | Tue. | 6 | San Jose | | Mon. | 4 | at San Jose |
| | Thu. | 8 | Minnesota | | Thu. | 7 | Detroit |
| | Sat. | 10 | at St. Louis | | Sat. | 9 | St. Louis |
| | Mon. | 12 | at NY Islanders* | | Mon. | 11 | San Jose |
| | Wed. | 14 | at NY Rangers | | Thu. | 14 | Anaheim |
| | Thu. | 15 | at Detroit | | Sat. | 16 | Boston* |
| | Sat. | 17 | at Columbus | | Tue. | 19 | San Jose |
| | Mon. | 19 | at Dallas | | Thu. | 21 | Buffalo |
| | Thu. | 22 | Dallas | | Sat. | 23 | at Detroit |
| | Sat. | 24 | at Phoenix | | Tue. | 26 | at Toronto |
| | Sun. | 25 | Columbus | | Thu. | 28 | at Columbus |
| | Wed. | 28 | at San Jose | | Sat. | 30 | at Boston |
| | Thu. | 29 | Vancouver | | Sun. | 31 | at New Jersey* |
| **Nov.** | Mon. | 2 | at Phoenix | **Feb.** | Tue. | 2 | NY Rangers |
| | Thu. | 5 | Pittsburgh | | Thu. | 4 | Anaheim |
| | Sat. | 7 | Nashville* | | Sat. | 6 | Detroit* |
| | Mon. | 9 | at Chicago | | Mon. | 8 | at Anaheim |
| | Wed. | 11 | at Carolina | | Thu. | 11 | Edmonton |
| | Fri. | 13 | at Atlanta | | Sat. | 13 | Colorado |
| | Sat. | 14 | at Tampa Bay | **Mar.** | Tue. | 2 | at Dallas |
| | Mon. | 16 | at Florida | | Thu. | 4 | at Nashville |
| | Wed. | 18 | Philadelphia | | Sat. | 6 | Montreal |
| | Sat. | 21 | Calgary* | | Mon. | 8 | Columbus |
| | Wed. | 25 | at Edmonton | | Wed. | 10 | at Chicago |
| | Thu. | 26 | at Vancouver | | Fri. | 12 | at Dallas |
| | Sat. | 28 | Chicago | | Sun. | 14 | Nashville* |
| **Dec.** | Tue. | 1 | at Anaheim | | Thu. | 18 | Chicago |
| | Thu. | 3 | Ottawa | | Sat. | 20 | NY Islanders |
| | Sat. | 5 | St. Louis* | | Mon. | 22 | Colorado |
| | Mon. | 7 | Calgary | | Wed. | 24 | at Colorado |
| | Wed. | 9 | at San Jose | | Thu. | 25 | at St. Louis |
| | Thu. | 10 | Phoenix | | Sat. | 27 | Dallas |
| | Sat. | 12 | Dallas | | Mon. | 29 | at Minnesota |
| | Mon. | 14 | at Vancouver | | Tue. | 30 | at Nashville |
| | Tue. | 15 | at Edmonton | **Apr.** | Thu. | 1 | Vancouver |
| | Thu. | 17 | at Calgary | | Sat. | 3 | Anaheim |
| | Sat. | 26 | at Phoenix | | Tue. | 6 | at Anaheim |
| | Mon. | 28 | Minnesota | | Thu. | 8 | Phoenix |
| | Wed. | 30 | at Calgary | | Sat. | 10 | Edmonton* |
| | Thu. | 31 | at Minnesota | | Sun. | 11 | at Colorado* |

* Denotes afternoon game.

## Year-by-Year Record

| | | Home | | | | Road | | | | Overall | | | | | | | | |
|---|---|---|---|---|---|---|---|---|---|---|---|---|---|---|---|---|---|---|
| **Season** | **GP** | **W** | **L** | **T** | **OL** | **W** | **L** | **T** | **OL** | **W** | **L** | **T** | **OL** | **GF** | **GA** | **Pts.** | **Finished** | **Playoff Result** |
| 2008-09 | 82 | 18 | 15 | .... | 8 | 16 | 22 | .... | 3 | 34 | 37 | .... | 11 | 207 | 234 | 79 | 5th, Pacific Div. | Out of Playoffs |
| 2007-08 | 82 | 17 | 21 | .... | 3 | 15 | 22 | .... | 4 | 32 | 43 | .... | 7 | 231 | 266 | 71 | 5th, Pacific Div. | Out of Playoffs |
| 2006-07 | 82 | 16 | 16 | .... | 9 | 11 | 25 | .... | 5 | 27 | 41 | .... | 14 | 227 | 283 | 68 | 4th, Pacific Div. | Out of Playoffs |
| 2005-06 | 82 | 26 | 14 | .... | 1 | 16 | 21 | .... | 4 | 42 | 35 | .... | 5 | 249 | 270 | 89 | 4th, Pacific Div. | Out of Playoffs |
| 2004-05 | .... | .... | .... | .... | .... | .... | .... | .... | .... | .... | .... | .... | .... | .... | .... | .... | | |
| 2003-04 | 82 | 15 | 16 | 9 | 1 | 13 | 13 | 7 | 8 | 28 | 29 | 16 | 9 | 205 | 217 | 81 | 3rd, Pacific Div. | Out of Playoffs |
| 2002-03 | 82 | 19 | 19 | 2 | 1 | 14 | 18 | 4 | 5 | 33 | 37 | 6 | 6 | 203 | 221 | 78 | 3rd, Pacific Div. | Out of Playoffs |
| 2001-02 | 82 | 22 | 12 | 6 | 1 | 18 | 15 | 5 | 3 | 40 | 27 | 11 | 4 | 214 | 190 | 95 | 3rd, Pacific Div. | Lost Conf. Quarter-Final |
| 2000-01 | 82 | 20 | 12 | 8 | 1 | 18 | 16 | 5 | 2 | 38 | 28 | 13 | 3 | 252 | 228 | 92 | 3rd, Pacific Div. | Lost Conf. Semi-Final |
| 1999-2000 | 82 | 21 | 13 | 5 | 2 | 18 | 14 | 7 | 2 | 39 | 27 | 12 | 4 | 245 | 228 | 94 | 2nd, Pacific Div. | Lost Conf. Quater-Final |
| 1998-99 | 82 | 18 | 20 | 3 | .... | 14 | 25 | 2 | .... | 32 | 45 | 5 | .... | 189 | 222 | 69 | 5th, Pacific Div. | Out of Playoffs |
| 1997-98 | 82 | 22 | 16 | 3 | .... | 16 | 17 | 8 | .... | 38 | 33 | 11 | .... | 227 | 225 | 87 | 2nd, Pacific Div. | Lost Conf. Quater-Final |
| 1996-97 | 82 | 18 | 16 | 7 | .... | 10 | 27 | 4 | .... | 28 | 43 | 11 | .... | 214 | 268 | 67 | 6th, Pacific Div. | Out of Playoffs |
| 1995-96 | 82 | 16 | 16 | 9 | .... | 8 | 24 | 9 | .... | 24 | 40 | 18 | .... | 256 | 302 | 66 | 6th, Pacific Div. | Out of Playoffs |
| 1994-95 | 48 | 7 | 11 | 6 | .... | 9 | 12 | 3 | .... | 16 | 23 | 9 | .... | 142 | 174 | 41 | 4th, Pacific Div. | Out of Playoffs |
| 1993-94 | 84 | 18 | 19 | 5 | .... | 9 | 26 | 7 | .... | 27 | 45 | 12 | .... | 294 | 322 | 66 | 5th, Pacific Div. | Out of Playoffs |
| 1992-93 | 84 | 22 | 15 | 5 | .... | 17 | 20 | 5 | .... | 39 | 35 | 10 | .... | 338 | 340 | 88 | 3rd, Smythe Div. | Lost Final |
| 1991-92 | 80 | 20 | 11 | 9 | .... | 15 | 20 | 5 | .... | 35 | 31 | 14 | .... | 287 | 296 | 84 | 2nd, Smythe Div. | Lost Div. Semi-Final |
| 1990-91 | 80 | 26 | 9 | 5 | .... | 20 | 15 | 5 | .... | 46 | 24 | 10 | .... | 340 | 254 | 102 | 1st, Smythe Div. | Lost Div. Final |
| 1989-90 | 80 | 21 | 16 | 3 | .... | 13 | 23 | 4 | .... | 34 | 39 | 7 | .... | 338 | 337 | 75 | 4th, Smythe Div. | Lost Div. Final |
| 1988-89 | 80 | 25 | 12 | 3 | .... | 17 | 19 | 4 | .... | 42 | 31 | 7 | .... | 376 | 335 | 91 | 2nd, Smythe Div. | Lost Div. Final |
| 1987-88 | 80 | 19 | 18 | 3 | .... | 11 | 24 | 5 | .... | 30 | 42 | 8 | .... | 318 | 359 | 68 | 4th, Smythe Div. | Lost Div. Semi-Final |
| 1986-87 | 80 | 20 | 17 | 3 | .... | 11 | 24 | 5 | .... | 31 | 41 | 8 | .... | 318 | 341 | 70 | 4th, Smythe Div. | Lost Div. Semi-Final |
| 1985-86 | 80 | 9 | 27 | 4 | .... | 14 | 22 | 4 | .... | 23 | 49 | 8 | .... | 284 | 389 | 54 | 5th, Smythe Div. | Out of Playoffs |
| 1984-85 | 80 | 20 | 14 | 6 | .... | 14 | 18 | 8 | .... | 34 | 32 | 14 | .... | 339 | 326 | 82 | 4th, Smythe Div. | Lost Div. Semi-Final |
| 1983-84 | 80 | 13 | 19 | 8 | .... | 10 | 25 | 5 | .... | 23 | 44 | 13 | .... | 309 | 376 | 59 | 5th, Smythe Div. | Out of Playoffs |
| 1982-83 | 80 | 20 | 13 | 7 | .... | 7 | 28 | 5 | .... | 27 | 41 | 12 | .... | 308 | 365 | 66 | 5th, Smythe Div. | Out of Playoffs |
| 1981-82 | 80 | 19 | 15 | 6 | .... | 5 | 26 | 9 | .... | 24 | 41 | 15 | .... | 314 | 369 | 63 | 4th, Smythe Div. | Lost Div. Final |
| 1980-81 | 80 | 22 | 11 | 7 | .... | 21 | 13 | 6 | .... | 43 | 24 | 13 | .... | 337 | 290 | 99 | 2nd, Norris Div. | Lost Prelim. Round |
| 1979-80 | 80 | 18 | 13 | 9 | .... | 12 | 23 | 5 | .... | 30 | 36 | 14 | .... | 290 | 313 | 74 | 2nd, Norris Div. | Lost Prelim. Round |
| 1978-79 | 80 | 20 | 13 | 7 | .... | 14 | 21 | 5 | .... | 34 | 34 | 12 | .... | 292 | 286 | 80 | 3rd, Norris Div. | Lost Prelim. Round |
| 1977-78 | 80 | 18 | 16 | 6 | .... | 13 | 18 | 9 | .... | 31 | 34 | 15 | .... | 243 | 245 | 77 | 3rd, Norris Div. | Lost Prelim. Round |
| 1976-77 | 80 | 20 | 13 | 7 | .... | 14 | 18 | 8 | .... | 34 | 31 | 15 | .... | 271 | 241 | 83 | 2nd, Norris Div. | Lost Quarter-Final |
| 1975-76 | 80 | 22 | 13 | 5 | .... | 16 | 20 | 4 | .... | 38 | 33 | 9 | .... | 263 | 265 | 85 | 2nd, Norris Div. | Lost Quarter-Final |
| 1974-75 | 80 | 22 | 7 | 11 | .... | 20 | 10 | 10 | .... | 42 | 17 | 21 | .... | 269 | 185 | 105 | 2nd, Norris Div. | Lost Prelim. Round |
| 1973-74 | 78 | 22 | 13 | 4 | .... | 11 | 20 | 8 | .... | 33 | 33 | 12 | .... | 233 | 231 | 78 | 3rd, West Div. | Lost Quarter-Final |
| 1972-73 | 78 | 21 | 11 | 7 | .... | 10 | 25 | 4 | .... | 31 | 36 | 11 | .... | 232 | 245 | 73 | 6th, West Div. | Out of Playoffs |
| 1971-72 | 78 | 14 | 23 | 2 | .... | 6 | 26 | 7 | .... | 20 | 49 | 9 | .... | 206 | 305 | 49 | 7th, West Div. | Out of Playoffs |
| 1970-71 | 78 | 17 | 14 | 8 | .... | 8 | 26 | 5 | .... | 25 | 40 | 13 | .... | 239 | 303 | 63 | 5th, West Div. | Out of Playoffs |
| 1969-70 | 76 | 12 | 22 | 4 | .... | 2 | 30 | 6 | .... | 14 | 52 | 10 | .... | 168 | 290 | 38 | 6th, West Div. | Out of Playoffs |
| 1968-69 | 76 | 19 | 14 | 5 | .... | 5 | 28 | 5 | .... | 24 | 42 | 10 | .... | 185 | 260 | 58 | 4th, West Div. | Lost Semi-Final |
| 1967-68 | 74 | 20 | 13 | 4 | .... | 11 | 20 | 6 | .... | 31 | 33 | 10 | .... | 200 | 224 | 72 | 2nd, West Div. | Lost Quarter-Final |

**PACIFIC DIVISION**

**43rd NHL Season**

**Franchise date:** June 5, 1967

# 2009-10 Player Personnel

| FORWARDS | HT | WT | S | Place of Birth | *Age | 2008-09 Club |
|---|---|---|---|---|---|---|
| BROWN, Dustin | 6-0 | 207 | R | Ithaca, NY | 24 | Los Angeles |
| FROLOV, Alexander | 6-2 | 204 | R | Moscow, USSR | 27 | Los Angeles |
| HANDZUS, Michal | 6-4 | 218 | L | Banska Bystrica, Czech. | 32 | Los Angeles |
| IVANANS, Raitis | 6-4 | 256 | L | Riga, Latvia | 30 | Los Angeles |
| KOPITAR, Anze | 6-3 | 219 | L | Jesenice, Yugoslavia | 22 | Los Angeles |
| LEWIS, Trevor | 6-1 | 204 | R | Salt Lake City, UT | 22 | Los Angeles-Manchester |
| MOLLER, Oscar | 5-11 | 180 | R | Stockholm, Sweden | 20 | Los Angeles-Manchester |
| PURCELL, Teddy | 6-3 | 202 | R | St. Johns, Nfld. | 24 | Los Angeles-Manchester |
| RICHARDSON, Brad | 5-11 | 184 | L | Belleville, Ont. | 24 | Los Angeles-Manchester |
| SIMMONDS, Wayne | 6-2 | 181 | R | Scarborough, Ont. | 21 | Los Angeles |
| SMYTH, Ryan | 6-1 | 190 | L | Banff, Alta. | 33 | Colorado |
| STOLL, Jarret | 6-0 | 214 | R | Melville, Sask. | 27 | Los Angeles |
| WESTGARTH, Kevin | 6-5 | 241 | R | Amherstburg, Ont. | 25 | Los Angeles-Manchester |
| WILLIAMS, Justin | 6-1 | 195 | R | Cobourg, Ont. | 27 | Carolina-Los Angeles |
| ZEILER, John | 6-0 | 204 | R | Jefferson Hills, PA | 26 | Los Angeles-Manchester |
| **DEFENSEMEN** | | | | | | |
| DOUGHTY, Drew | 6-1 | 203 | R | London, Ont. | 19 | Los Angeles |
| DREWISKE, Davis | 6-2 | 215 | L | Hudson, WI | 24 | Los Angeles-Manchester |
| GREENE, Matt | 6-4 | 234 | R | Grand Ledge, MI | 26 | Los Angeles |
| HARROLD, Peter | 5-11 | 188 | R | Kirtland Hills, OH | 26 | Los Angeles |
| JOHNSON, Jack | 6-1 | 225 | L | Indianapolis, IN | 22 | Los Angeles |
| O'DONNELL, Sean | 6-2 | 230 | L | Ottawa, Ont. | 37 | Los Angeles |
| SCUDERI, Rob | 6-0 | 218 | L | Syosset, NY | 30 | Pittsburgh |

| GOALTENDERS | HT | WT | C | Place of Birth | *Age | 2008-09 Club |
|---|---|---|---|---|---|---|
| ERSBERG, Erik | 6-0 | 168 | L | Sala, Sweden | 27 | Los Angeles |
| QUICK, Jonathan | 6-1 | 216 | L | Milford, CT | 23 | Los Angeles-Manchester |

* – Age at start of 2009-10 season

# 2008-09 Scoring

* – rookie

## Regular Season

| Pos | # | Player | Team | GP | G | A | Pts | TOI | +/- | PIM | PP | SH | GW | S | % |
|---|---|---|---|---|---|---|---|---|---|---|---|---|---|---|---|
| C | 11 | Anze Kopitar | L.A. | 82 | 27 | 39 | 66 | 20:27 | –17 | 32 | 7 | 1 | 3 | 234 | 11.5 |
| R | 24 | Alexander Frolov | L.A. | 77 | 32 | 27 | 59 | 19:55 | –6 | 30 | 12 | 1 | 1 | 176 | 18.2 |
| R | 23 | Dustin Brown | L.A. | 80 | 24 | 29 | 53 | 19:24 | –15 | 64 | 7 | 0 | 6 | 292 | 8.2 |
| C | 26 | Michal Handzus | L.A. | 82 | 18 | 24 | 42 | 18:54 | –7 | 32 | 7 | 1 | 4 | 143 | 12.6 |
| C | 28 | Jarret Stoll | L.A. | 74 | 18 | 23 | 41 | 17:05 | –7 | 68 | 10 | 0 | 1 | 155 | 11.6 |
| D | 27 | Kyle Quincey | L.A. | 72 | 4 | 34 | 38 | 20:58 | –5 | 63 | 2 | 0 | 2 | 150 | 2.7 |
| L | 19 | Kyle Calder | L.A. | 74 | 8 | 19 | 27 | 13:09 | –1 | 41 | 2 | 0 | 1 | 93 | 8.6 |
| D | 8 | * Drew Doughty | L.A. | 81 | 6 | 21 | 27 | 23:50 | –17 | 56 | 3 | 0 | 1 | 126 | 4.8 |
| R | 17 | * Wayne Simmonds | L.A. | 82 | 9 | 14 | 23 | 13:50 | –8 | 73 | 2 | 0 | 2 | 127 | 7.1 |
| R | 54 | * Teddy Purcell | L.A. | 40 | 4 | 12 | 16 | 13:30 | –4 | 4 | 2 | 0 | 1 | 68 | 5.9 |
| C | 9 | * Oscar Moller | L.A. | 40 | 7 | 8 | 15 | 13:22 | –3 | 16 | 5 | 0 | 0 | 81 | 8.6 |
| R | 14 | Justin Williams | CAR | 32 | 3 | 7 | 10 | 15:08 | –9 | 9 | 2 | 0 | 0 | 80 | 3.8 |
| | | | L.A. | 12 | 1 | 3 | 4 | 17:50 | 1 | 8 | 1 | 0 | 0 | 28 | 3.6 |
| | | | Total | 44 | 4 | 10 | 14 | 15:52 | –8 | 17 | 3 | 0 | 0 | 108 | 3.7 |
| D | 2 | Matt Greene | L.A. | 82 | 2 | 12 | 14 | 19:44 | 1 | 111 | 0 | 0 | 0 | 76 | 2.6 |
| D | 5 | Peter Harrold | L.A. | 69 | 4 | 8 | 12 | 13:10 | –13 | 28 | 1 | 0 | 1 | 95 | 4.2 |
| D | 6 | Sean O'Donnell | L.A. | 82 | 0 | 12 | 12 | 20:29 | 2 | 71 | 0 | 0 | 0 | 32 | 0.0 |
| D | 3 | Jack Johnson | L.A. | 41 | 6 | 5 | 11 | 20:16 | –18 | 46 | 3 | 0 | 0 | 50 | 12.0 |
| C | 7 | Derek Armstrong | L.A. | 56 | 5 | 4 | 9 | 8:29 | –11 | 63 | 1 | 0 | 1 | 42 | 11.9 |
| D | 42 | Tom Preissing | L.A. | 22 | 3 | 4 | 7 | 16:44 | –7 | 6 | 2 | 0 | 0 | 40 | 7.5 |
| C | 22 | * Brian Boyle | L.A. | 28 | 4 | 1 | 5 | 10:08 | –9 | 42 | 0 | 0 | 1 | 36 | 11.1 |
| C | 15 | Brad Richardson | L.A. | 31 | 0 | 5 | 5 | 10:47 | –6 | 11 | 0 | 0 | 0 | 37 | 0.0 |
| D | 21 | Denis Gauthier | L.A. | 65 | 2 | 2 | 4 | 14:32 | –11 | 90 | 0 | 0 | 0 | 36 | 5.6 |
| C | 61 | * Trevor Lewis | L.A. | 6 | 1 | 2 | 3 | 11:35 | 0 | 0 | 0 | 0 | 0 | 10 | 10.0 |
| D | 44 | * Davis Drewiske | L.A. | 17 | 0 | 3 | 3 | 17:19 | 1 | 18 | 0 | 0 | 0 | 21 | 0.0 |
| L | 41 | Raitis Ivanans | L.A. | 76 | 2 | 0 | 2 | 6:22 | –8 | 145 | 0 | 0 | 2 | 25 | 8.0 |
| L | 25 | * Matt Moulson | L.A. | 7 | 1 | 0 | 1 | 14:29 | –4 | 2 | 0 | 0 | 1 | 6 | 16.7 |
| R | 13 | John Zeiler | L.A. | 27 | 0 | 1 | 1 | 6:33 | –2 | 42 | 0 | 0 | 0 | 3 | 0.0 |
| R | 33 | * Kevin Westgarth | L.A. | 9 | 0 | 0 | 0 | 5:02 | 1 | 9 | 0 | 0 | 0 | 1 | 0.0 |

## Goaltending

| No. | Goaltender | GPI | Mins | Avg | W | L | OT | EN | SO | GA | SA | S% | G | A | PIM |
|---|---|---|---|---|---|---|---|---|---|---|---|---|---|---|---|
| 32 | * Jonathan Quick | 44 | 2495 | 2.48 | 21 | 18 | 2 | 6 | 4 | 103 | 1200 | .914 | 0 | 1 | 0 |
| 31 | Erik Ersberg | 28 | 1477 | 2.64 | 8 | 11 | 5 | 4 | 0 | 65 | 651 | .900 | 0 | 0 | 2 |
| 30 | Jason LaBarbera | 19 | 995 | 2.83 | 5 | 8 | 4 | 1 | 2 | 47 | 439 | .893 | 0 | 0 | 2 |
| | **Totals** | **82** | **5002** | **2.71** | **34** | **37** | **11** | **11** | **6** | **226** | **2301** | **.902** | | | |

# Terry Murray

## Head Coach

*Born: Shawville, Que., July 20, 1950.*

The Los Angeles Kings named Terry Murray their head coach on July 17, 2008. Murray – formerly the head coach of the Washington Capitals, Florida Panthers and the Philadelphia Flyers, where he led that club to the 1997 Stanley Cup Finals –is the 22nd head coach in Kings history.

Murray spent the four seasons prior to being hired by the Kings as an assistant coach with the Flyers, an organization he had worked for as a head coach, assistant coach, pro scout and player. In 2007-08, he helped the Flyers record 95 points and advance to Eastern Conference Finals after earning just 56 points in 2006-07. Murray compiled a 118-64-30 record as head coach of the Flyers for three seasons from 1994-95 through 1996-97. In addition to the 1997 Stanley Cup Finals / Eastern Conference Championship, Murray coached the team to two Atlantic Division Championships (1995 and 1996).

Murray's NHL head coaching career began with Washington for five seasons (1989-90 through 1993-94), where he compiled a 163-134-28 record. In his first season he helped lead the Capitals to the Eastern Conference Finals. Murray also coached Florida for three seasons (1998-99 through 2000-01), which included a franchise-record 98-point season and a team-record 43 wins in 1999-2000. He has also worked as an assistant coach with the Capitals (1983-84 through 1987-88); as head coach with the Baltimore Skipjacks of the American Hockey League; and as head coach with the Cincinnati Cyclones of the International Hockey League (1993-94).

As an NHL defenseman, Murray played in 302 career NHL regular-season games over eight seasons with Washington, Philadelphia (two stints), the Detroit Red Wings and the California Golden Seals / California Seals, who originally drafted Murray in the seventh-round (88th overall) of the 1970 NHL Amateur Draft. He recorded 80 points (four goals, 76 assists) and 199 penalty minutes during his NHL career and he also played in 18 career NHL playoff games, recording two goals, two assists and 10 penalty minutes.

### Coaching Record

| | | | Regular Season | | | | Playoffs | | | |
|---|---|---|---|---|---|---|---|---|---|---|
| Season | Team | League | GC | W | L | O/T | GC | W | L | T |
| 1988-89 | Baltimore | AHL | 80 | 30 | 46 | 4 | .... | .... | .... | .... |
| 1989-90 | Baltimore | AHL | 45 | 26 | 17 | 2 | .... | .... | .... | .... |
| **1989-90** | **Washington** | **NHL** | **34** | **18** | **14** | **2** | **15** | **8** | **7** | .... |
| **1990-91** | **Washington** | **NHL** | **80** | **37** | **36** | **7** | **11** | **5** | **6** | .... |
| **1991-92** | **Washington** | **NHL** | **80** | **45** | **27** | **8** | **7** | **3** | **4** | .... |
| **1992-93** | **Washington** | **NHL** | **84** | **43** | **34** | **7** | **6** | **2** | **4** | .... |
| 1993-94 | Cincinnati | IHL | 28 | 17 | 7 | 4 | 11 | 6 | 5 | .... |
| **1993-94** | **Washington** | **NHL** | **47** | **20** | **23** | **4** | .... | .... | .... | .... |
| **1994-95** | **Philadelphia** | **NHL** | **48** | **28** | **16** | **4** | **15** | **10** | **5** | .... |
| **1995-96** | **Philadelphia** | **NHL** | **82** | **45** | **24** | **13** | **12** | **6** | **6** | .... |
| **1996-97** | **Philadelphia** | **NHL** | **82** | **45** | **24** | **13** | **19** | **12** | **7** | .... |
| **1998-99** | **Florida** | **NHL** | **82** | **30** | **34** | **18** | .... | .... | .... | .... |
| **99-2000** | **Florida** | **NHL** | **82** | **43** | **27** | **12** | **4** | **0** | **4** | .... |
| **2000-01** | **Florida** | **NHL** | **36** | **6** | **18** | **12** | .... | .... | .... | .... |
| **2008-09** | **Los Angeles** | **NHL** | **82** | **34** | **37** | **11** | .... | .... | .... | .... |
| | **NHL Totals** | | **819** | **394** | **314** | **111** | **89** | **46** | **43** | .... |

# Dean Lombardi

## President and General Manager

*Born: Holyoke, MA, March 5, 1958.*

The Los Angeles Kings named Dean Lombardi president and general manager on April 21, 2006. Lombardi, formerly a member of the San Jose Sharks front office for 13 years, including seven seasons as general manager, followed by three years as a pro scout for the Philadelphia Flyers from 2003 to 2006, is the eighth general manager in Kings history.

An executive in the San Jose front office since 1990, Lombardi first served as assistant general manager (a post he held the previous two seasons with the Minnesota North Stars) for the expansion Sharks before being elevated to vice president, director of hockey operations in 1992. Four years later, he was promoted to executive vice president and general manager and given the responsibility of turning around the young franchise. During his tenure as general manager in San Jose from 1996 to 2003, Lombardi helped build the Sharks into one of the premier teams in the NHL. Under Lombardi, San Jose reached the playoffs five times – highlighted by two trips to the Western Conference Semifinals – and one Pacific Division title in 2002. The Lombardi-led Sharks in 2002 also tied an NHL-record with six consecutive seasons of improved point totals under one g.m. (Bill Torrey/New York Islanders) while building a roster that became progressively younger in age each season.

During his time as general manager in San Jose, Lombardi made many key personnel and player moves, stocking the Sharks organization with a good mix of veteran stars and up-and-coming youngsters that helped make the Sharks legitimate Stanley Cup contenders.

From the NHL Entry Draft, Lombardi brought to San Jose players such as Patrick Marleau, Vesa Toskala, Jonathan Cheechoo, Brad Stuart, Scott Hannan, Marco Sturm, Marcel Goc and Christian Ehroff. *The Hockey News* ranked the Sharks' prospects (age 22 and under) as the best in the NHL in 1999-2000 and second best in 2000-01. Lombardi's history in San Jose as it relates to trades and free agency is impressive as well, having brought in such players as Owen Nolan, Teemu Selanne, Adam Graves, Vincent Damphousse, Mike Ricci, Kyle McLaren, Mike Vernon, Todd Harvey, Bryan Marchment and Scott Thornton.

Prior to joining the North Stars, Lombardi spent three seasons as a player representative, including the representation of five members of the 1988 United States Olympic team, and at the time he joined Minnesota's front office Lombardi was only the second former player agent to be employed in an NHL front office (Brian Burke/Vancouver Canucks was the other).

Born in Holyoke, Massachusetts, and raised in nearby Ludlow, Lombardi received his undergraduate degree from the University of New Haven where he finished third in his class. On the ice he was the hockey team's captain his final two seasons, and he received a full athletic scholarship and the school's student-athlete of the year award. In 1985, Lombardi earned his Law degree (with honors) from Tulane Law School where he specialized in Labor Law.

# Club Records

## Team

(Figures in brackets for season records are games played; records for fewest points, wins, ties, losses, goals, goals against are for 70 or more games)

**Most Points** ............... **105** 1974-75 (80)
**Most Wins** ............... **46** 1990-91 (80)
**Most Ties** ............... **21** 1974-75 (80)
**Most Losses** ............... **52** 1969-70 (76)
**Most Goals** ............... **376** 1988-89 (80)
**Most Goals Against** ......... **389** 1985-86 (80)
**Fewest Points** ............... **38** 1969-70 (76)
**Fewest Wins** ............... **14** 1969-70 (76)
**Fewest Ties** ............... **5** 1998-99 (82)
**Fewest Losses** ............... **17** 1974-75 (80)
**Fewest Goals** ............... **168** 1969-70 (76)
**Fewest Goals Against** ....... **185** 1974-75 (80)
**Longest Winning Streak**
**Overall** ............... **8** Oct. 21-Nov. 7/72, Feb. 23-Mar. 9/92
**Home** ............... **12** Oct. 10-Dec. 5/92
**Away** ............... **8** Dec. 18/74-Jan. 16/75
**Longest Undefeated Streak**
**Overall** ............... **11** Feb. 28-Mar. 24/74 (9 wins, 2 ties)
**Home** ............... **13** Oct. 10-Dec. 8/92 (12 wins, 1 tie)
**Away** ............... **11** Oct. 10-Dec. 11/74 (6 wins, 5 ties)
**Longest Losing Streak**
**Overall** ............... **11** Mar. 16-Apr. 4/04
**Home** ............... **9** Feb. 8-Mar. 12/86
**Away** ............... **11** Jan. 11-Feb. 15/70
**Longest Winless Streak**
**Overall** ............... **17** Jan. 29-Mar. 5/70 (13 losses, 4 ties)
**Home** ............... **9** Jan. 29-Mar. 5/70 (8 losses, 1 tie), Feb. 8-Mar. 12/86 (9 losses)
**Away** ............... **20** Jan. 11-Apr. 3/70 (16 losses, 4 ties)
**Most Shutouts, Season** ....... **10** 2000-01 (82)
**Most PIM, Season** ......... **2,247** 1992-93 (84)
**Most Goals, Game** ........... **12** Nov. 29/84 (Van. 1 at L.A. 12)

## Individual

**Most Seasons** ............... **17** Dave Taylor
**Most Games** ............. **1,111** Dave Taylor
**Most Goals, Career** ......... **557** Luc Robitaille
**Most Assists, Career** ........ **757** Marcel Dionne
**Most Points Career** ........ **1,307** Marcel Dionne (550G, 757A)
**Most PIM, Career** ......... **1,846** Marty McSorley
**Most Shutouts, Career** ....... **32** Rogie Vachon
**Longest Consecutive Games Streak** ........... **324** Marcel Dionne (Jan. 7/78-Jan. 9/82)
**Most Goals, Season** .......... **70** Bernie Nicholls (1988-89)
**Most Assists, Season** ........ **122** Wayne Gretzky (1990-91)
**Most Points, Season** ........ **168** Wayne Gretzky (1988-89; 54G, 114A)
**Most PIM, Season** .......... **399** Marty McSorley (1992-93)
**Most Points, Defenseman, Season** ................. **76** Larry Murphy (1980-81; 16G, 60A)
**Most Points, Center, Season** ................. **168** Wayne Gretzky (1988-89; 54G, 114A)
**Most Points, Right Wing, Season** ................. **112** Dave Taylor (1980-81; 47G, 65A)
**Most Points, Left Wing, Season** ................ ***125** Luc Robitaille (1992-93; 63G, 62A)
**Most Points, Rookie, Season** ................. **84** Luc Robitaille (1986-87; 45G, 39A)
**Most Shutouts, Season** ........ **8** Rogie Vachon (1976-77)
**Most Goals, Game** ........... **4** Seventeen times
**Most Assists, Game** ........... **6** Bernie Nicholls (Dec. 1/88), Tomas Sandstrom (Oct. 9/93)
**Most Points, Game** ............ **8** Bernie Nicholls (Dec. 1/88; 2G, 6A)

* NHL Record.

## Coaching History

Red Kelly, 1967-68, 1968-69; Hal Laycoe and Johnny Wilson, 1969-70; Larry Regan, 1970-71; Larry Regan and Fred Glover, 1971-72; Bob Pulford, 1972-73 to 1976-77; Ron Stewart, 1977-78; Bob Berry, 1978-79 to 1980-81; Parker MacDonald and Don Perry, 1981-82; Don Perry, 1982-83; Don Perry, Rogie Vachon and Roger Neilson, 1983-84; Pat Quinn, 1984-85, 1985-86; Pat Quinn and Mike Murphy 1986-87; Mike Murphy, Rogie Vachon and Robbie Ftorek, 1987-88; Robbie Ftorek, 1988-89; Tom Webster, 1989-90 to 1991-92; Barry Melrose, 1992-93, 1993-94; Barry Melrose and Rogie Vachon, 1994-95; Larry Robinson, 1995-96 to 1998-99; Andy Murray, 1999-2000 to 2004-05; Andy Murray and John Torchetti, 2005-06; Marc Crawford, 2006-07, 2007-08; Terry Murray, 2008-09 to date.

## Retired Numbers

| | | |
|---|---|---|
| **16** | Marcel Dionne | 1975-1987 |
| **18** | Dave Taylor | 1977-1994 |
| **20** | Luc Robitaille | 1986-94, 97-01, 03-06 |
| **30** | Rogie Vachon | 1971-1978 |
| **99** | Wayne Gretzky | 1988-1996 |

# All-time Record vs. Other Clubs

## Regular Season

| | At Home | | | | | | | | On Road | | | | | | | | Total | | | | | | | |
|---|---|---|---|---|---|---|---|---|---|---|---|---|---|---|---|---|---|---|---|---|---|---|---|---|
| | GP | W | L | T | OL | GF | GA | PTS | GP | W | L | T | OL | GF | GA | PTS | GP | W | L | T | OL | GF | GA | PTS |
| Anaheim | 45 | 24 | 14 | 4 | 3 | 133 | 117 | 55 | 45 | 15 | 20 | 7 | 3 | 118 | 152 | 40 | 90 | 39 | 34 | 11 | 6 | 251 | 269 | 95 |
| Atlanta | 6 | 4 | 0 | 0 | 2 | 32 | 22 | 10 | 5 | 3 | 1 | 0 | 1 | 18 | 13 | 7 | 11 | 7 | 1 | 0 | 3 | 50 | 35 | 17 |
| Boston | 62 | 21 | 33 | 7 | 1 | 216 | 232 | 50 | 63 | 13 | 44 | 6 | 0 | 178 | 289 | 32 | 125 | 34 | 77 | 13 | 1 | 394 | 521 | 82 |
| Buffalo | 55 | 23 | 23 | 9 | 0 | 193 | 189 | 55 | 55 | 16 | 30 | 9 | 0 | 158 | 232 | 41 | 110 | 39 | 53 | 18 | 0 | 351 | 421 | 96 |
| Calgary | 99 | 49 | 41 | 9 | 0 | 360 | 340 | 107 | 102 | 28 | 59 | 12 | 3 | 328 | 447 | 71 | 201 | 77 | 100 | 21 | 3 | 688 | 787 | 178 |
| Carolina | 32 | 18 | 11 | 3 | 0 | 135 | 119 | 39 | 32 | 11 | 14 | 5 | 2 | 116 | 116 | 29 | 64 | 29 | 25 | 8 | 2 | 251 | 235 | 68 |
| Chicago | 82 | 38 | 33 | 8 | 3 | 282 | 271 | 87 | 83 | 34 | 39 | 9 | 1 | 238 | 286 | 78 | 165 | 72 | 72 | 17 | 4 | 520 | 557 | 165 |
| Colorado | 51 | 28 | 17 | 5 | 1 | 201 | 171 | 62 | 50 | 21 | 26 | 3 | 0 | 169 | 204 | 45 | 101 | 49 | 43 | 8 | 1 | 370 | 375 | 107 |
| Columbus | 16 | 9 | 6 | 1 | 0 | 39 | 32 | 19 | 16 | 6 | 7 | 0 | 3 | 51 | 44 | 15 | 32 | 15 | 13 | 1 | 3 | 90 | 76 | 34 |
| Dallas | 97 | 43 | 34 | 19 | 1 | 319 | 286 | 106 | 99 | 25 | 57 | 13 | 4 | 259 | 369 | 67 | 196 | 68 | 91 | 32 | 5 | 578 | 655 | 173 |
| Detroit | 88 | 43 | 30 | 14 | 1 | 334 | 276 | 101 | 87 | 31 | 40 | 13 | 3 | 294 | 338 | 78 | 175 | 74 | 70 | 27 | 4 | 628 | 614 | 179 |
| Edmonton | 85 | 31 | 35 | 15 | 4 | 323 | 340 | 81 | 85 | 27 | 43 | 15 | 0 | 299 | 372 | 69 | 170 | 58 | 78 | 30 | 4 | 622 | 712 | 150 |
| Florida | 11 | 7 | 4 | 0 | 0 | 33 | 32 | 14 | 9 | 2 | 4 | 3 | 0 | 21 | 23 | 7 | 20 | 9 | 8 | 3 | 0 | 54 | 55 | 21 |
| Minnesota | 16 | 7 | 5 | 2 | 2 | 37 | 38 | 18 | 16 | 7 | 5 | 3 | 1 | 35 | 34 | 18 | 32 | 14 | 10 | 5 | 3 | 72 | 72 | 36 |
| Montreal | 66 | 19 | 38 | 9 | 0 | 201 | 261 | 47 | 66 | 8 | 47 | 11 | 0 | 165 | 296 | 27 | 132 | 27 | 85 | 20 | 0 | 366 | 557 | 74 |
| Nashville | 20 | 10 | 9 | 0 | 1 | 59 | 58 | 21 | 20 | 10 | 6 | 3 | 1 | 54 | 45 | 24 | 40 | 20 | 15 | 3 | 2 | 113 | 103 | 45 |
| New Jersey | 44 | 29 | 9 | 6 | 0 | 205 | 137 | 64 | 45 | 20 | 19 | 5 | 1 | 154 | 149 | 46 | 89 | 49 | 28 | 11 | 1 | 359 | 286 | 110 |
| NY Islanders | 46 | 22 | 17 | 7 | 0 | 167 | 145 | 51 | 46 | 17 | 24 | 5 | 0 | 130 | 160 | 39 | 92 | 39 | 41 | 12 | 0 | 297 | 305 | 90 |
| NY Rangers | 62 | 24 | 26 | 10 | 2 | 205 | 220 | 60 | 59 | 18 | 35 | 6 | 0 | 176 | 235 | 42 | 121 | 42 | 61 | 16 | 2 | 381 | 455 | 102 |
| Ottawa | 11 | 9 | 1 | 1 | 0 | 48 | 21 | 19 | 11 | 5 | 5 | 1 | 0 | 30 | 35 | 11 | 22 | 14 | 6 | 2 | 0 | 78 | 56 | 30 |
| Philadelphia | 68 | 22 | 38 | 8 | 0 | 198 | 228 | 52 | 65 | 16 | 41 | 7 | 1 | 158 | 249 | 40 | 133 | 38 | 79 | 15 | 1 | 356 | 477 | 92 |
| Phoenix | 89 | 36 | 38 | 14 | 1 | 337 | 326 | 87 | 91 | 30 | 47 | 11 | 3 | 288 | 355 | 74 | 180 | 66 | 85 | 25 | 4 | 625 | 681 | 161 |
| Pittsburgh | 70 | 44 | 17 | 8 | 1 | 268 | 187 | 97 | 75 | 25 | 40 | 10 | 0 | 236 | 273 | 60 | 145 | 69 | 57 | 18 | 1 | 504 | 460 | 157 |
| St. Louis | 86 | 41 | 33 | 12 | 0 | 293 | 244 | 94 | 86 | 21 | 54 | 10 | 1 | 218 | 317 | 53 | 172 | 62 | 87 | 22 | 1 | 511 | 561 | 147 |
| San Jose | 52 | 27 | 19 | 4 | 2 | 151 | 139 | 60 | 52 | 17 | 28 | 3 | 4 | 138 | 175 | 41 | 104 | 44 | 47 | 7 | 6 | 289 | 314 | 101 |
| Tampa Bay | 13 | 1 | 10 | 2 | 0 | 26 | 43 | 4 | 11 | 5 | 5 | 0 | 1 | 24 | 26 | 11 | 24 | 6 | 15 | 2 | 1 | 50 | 69 | 15 |
| Toronto | 67 | 35 | 22 | 10 | 0 | 240 | 196 | 80 | 69 | 23 | 34 | 11 | 1 | 225 | 267 | 58 | 136 | 58 | 56 | 21 | 1 | 465 | 463 | 138 |
| Vancouver | 107 | 55 | 35 | 16 | 1 | 411 | 331 | 127 | 105 | 35 | 53 | 16 | 1 | 323 | 391 | 87 | 212 | 90 | 88 | 32 | 2 | 734 | 722 | 214 |
| Washington | 49 | 28 | 14 | 6 | 1 | 194 | 149 | 63 | 48 | 22 | 18 | 7 | 1 | 179 | 193 | 52 | 97 | 50 | 32 | 13 | 2 | 373 | 342 | 115 |
| Defunct Clubs | 35 | 27 | 6 | 2 | 0 | 141 | 76 | 56 | 34 | 11 | 14 | 9 | 0 | 91 | 109 | 31 | 69 | 38 | 20 | 11 | 0 | 232 | 185 | 87 |
| **Totals** | **1630** | **774** | **618** | **211** | **27** | **5781** | **5226** | **1786** | **1630** | **522** | **859** | **213** | **36** | **4871** | **6194** | **1293** | **3260** | **1296** | **1477** | **424** | **63** | **10652** | **11420** | **3079** |

## Playoffs

| | Series | W | L | GP | W | L | T | GF | GA | Last Mtg. | Rnd. | Result |
|---|---|---|---|---|---|---|---|---|---|---|---|---|
| Boston | 2 | 0 | 2 | 13 | 5 | 8 | 0 | 38 | 56 | 1977 | QF | L 2-4 |
| Calgary | 6 | 4 | 2 | 26 | 13 | 13 | 0 | 105 | 112 | 1993 | DSF | W 4-2 |
| Chicago | 1 | 0 | 1 | 5 | 1 | 4 | 0 | 7 | 10 | 1974 | QF | L 1-4 |
| Colorado | 2 | 0 | 2 | 14 | 6 | 8 | 0 | 23 | 33 | 2002 | CQF | L 3-4 |
| Dallas | 1 | 0 | 1 | 7 | 3 | 4 | 0 | 21 | 26 | 1968 | QF | L 3-4 |
| Detroit | 2 | 1 | 1 | 10 | 4 | 6 | 0 | 21 | 32 | 2001 | CQF | W 4-2 |
| Edmonton | 7 | 2 | 5 | 36 | 12 | 24 | 0 | 127 | 154 | 1992 | DSF | L 2-4 |
| Montreal | 1 | 0 | 1 | 5 | 1 | 4 | 0 | 12 | 15 | 1993 | F | L 1-4 |
| NY Islanders | 1 | 0 | 1 | 4 | 1 | 3 | 0 | 10 | 21 | 1980 | PRE | L 1-3 |
| NY Rangers | 2 | 0 | 2 | 6 | 1 | 5 | 0 | 14 | 32 | 1981 | PRE | L 1-3 |
| St. Louis | 2 | 0 | 2 | 8 | 0 | 8 | 0 | 13 | 32 | 1998 | CQF | L 0-4 |
| Toronto | 3 | 1 | 2 | 12 | 5 | 7 | 0 | 31 | 41 | 1993 | CF | W 4-3 |
| Vancouver | 3 | 2 | 1 | 17 | 9 | 8 | 0 | 66 | 60 | 1993 | DF | W 4-2 |
| Defunct Clubs | 1 | 1 | 0 | 7 | 4 | 3 | 0 | 23 | 25 | | | |
| **Totals** | **34** | **11** | **23** | **170** | **65** | **105** | **0** | **511** | **649** | | | |

## Playoff Results 2009-2004

(Last playoff appearance: 2002)

**Abbreviations: Round: F** - Final; **CF** - conference final; **CQF** - conference quarter-final; **DF** - division final; **DSF** - division semi-final; **QF** - quarter-final; **PRE** - preliminary round.

Calgary totals include Atlanta Flames, 1972-73 to 1979-80.
Colorado totals include Quebec, 1979-80 to 1994-95.
New Jersey totals include Kansas City, 1974-75, 1975-76, and Colorado Rockies, 1976-77 to 1981-82.
Phoenix totals include Winnipeg, 1979-80 to 1995-96.
Carolina totals include Hartford, 1979-80 to 1996-97.
Dallas totals include Minnesota North Stars, 1967-68 to 1992-93.

## 2008-09 Results

| | | | | | | | |
|---|---|---|---|---|---|---|---|
| **Oct.** | 11 | at San Jose | 1-3 | | 12 | Tampa Bay | 1-3 |
| | 12 | San Jose | 0-1 | | 15 | Detroit | 0-4 |
| | 14 | Anaheim | 6-3 | | 17 | at Dallas | 2-3† |
| | 17 | Carolina | 4-3* | | 20 | at Minnesota | 5-2 |
| | 20 | Colorado | 3-4 | | 21 | at Colorado | 6-5 |
| | 24 | at St. Louis | 4-0 | | 29 | Chicago | 5-2 |
| | 25 | at Nashville | 4-5 | | 31 | at Montreal | 3-4 |
| | 27 | Detroit | 3-4† | **Feb.** | 3 | at Ottawa | 1-0 |
| | 30 | Vancouver | 0-4 | | 5 | at Washington | 5-4 |
| **Nov.** | 1 | Calgary | 2-3 | | 7 | at New Jersey | 3-1 |
| | 4 | Anaheim | 0-1* | | 10 | at NY Islanders | 4-3† |
| | 6 | Florida | 3-2 | | 12 | Calgary | 0-2 |
| | 8 | St. Louis | 5-3 | | 14 | Edmonton | 2-3† |
| | 11 | Dallas | 3-2† | | 16 | Atlanta | 6-7† |
| | 13 | at Dallas | 3-2 | | 18 | at Anaheim | 4-3 |
| | 15 | Nashville | 1-3 | | 19 | at San Jose | 2-4 |
| | 16 | at Anaheim | 0-2 | | 21 | Phoenix | 3-6 |
| | 20 | Washington | 5-2 | | 24 | at Minnesota | 2-1† |
| | 22 | Colorado | 3-4† | | 25 | at Philadelphia | 0-2 |
| | 25 | at Calgary | 2-6 | | 27 | at Detroit | 1-2 |
| | 26 | at Edmonton | 2-1 | **Mar.** | 1 | at Chicago | 2-4 |
| | 29 | Chicago | 5-2 | | 3 | at Columbus | 4-5 |
| **Dec.** | 1 | Toronto | 1-3 | | 5 | Dallas | 5-4* |
| | 2 | at Phoenix | 2-4 | | 7 | Minnesota | 4-3 |
| | 5 | Edmonton | 4-5† | | 9 | Vancouver | 3-2 |
| | 6 | Columbus | 3-0 | | 13 | at Vancouver | 2-4 |
| | 9 | at Colorado | 1-6 | | 14 | at San Jose | 1-2† |
| | 11 | St. Louis | 6-2 | | 16 | Nashville | 3-4 |
| | 13 | Minnesota | 3-1 | | 19 | at Boston | 3-2* |
| | 15 | San Jose | 2-3† | | 20 | at Pittsburgh | 1-4 |
| | 17 | NY Rangers | 2-3* | | 22 | at Chicago | 1-4 |
| | 19 | at Buffalo | 0-5 | | 24 | at St. Louis | 0-2 |
| | 20 | at Detroit | 4-6 | | 26 | at Dallas | 1-0† |
| | 23 | at Columbus | 3-0 | | 28 | at Nashville | 3-4* |
| | 26 | Phoenix | 1-2 | | 31 | Dallas | 2-3 |
| | 27 | at Phoenix | 4-0 | **Apr.** | 2 | at Phoenix | 1-2 |
| | 29 | Columbus | 0-2 | | 4 | Phoenix | 6-1 |
| **Jan.** | 3 | Philadelphia | 2-1† | | 6 | at Calgary | 1-4 |
| | 6 | at Anaheim | 1-3 | | 7 | at Edmonton | 2-1 |
| | 8 | Anaheim | 4-3 | | 9 | at Vancouver | 0-1 |
| | 10 | New Jersey | 1-5 | | 11 | San Jose | 4-3 |

* – Overtime † – Shootout

# Entry Draft Selections 2009-1995

Name in bold denotes played in NHL.

**2009**

| Pick | |
|---|---|
| 5 | Brayden Schenn |
| 35 | Kyle Clifford |
| 84 | Nicolas Deslauriers |
| 95 | Jean-Francois Berube |
| 96 | Linden Vey |
| 126 | David Kolomatis |
| 156 | Michael Pelech |
| 179 | Brandon Kozun |
| 186 | Jordan Nolan |
| 198 | Nic Dowd |

**2008**

| Pick | |
|---|---|
| 2 | **Drew Doughty** |
| 13 | Colten Teubert |
| 32 | Viatcheslav Voynov |
| 63 | Robert Czarnik |
| 74 | Andrew Campbell |
| 88 | Geordie Wudrick |
| 123 | Andrei Loktionov |
| 153 | Justin Azevedo |
| 183 | Garrett Roe |

**2007**

| Pick | |
|---|---|
| 4 | Thomas Hickey |
| 52 | **Oscar Moller** |
| 61 | **Wayne Simmonds** |
| 82 | Bryan Cameron |
| 95 | Alec Martinez |
| 109 | Dwight King |
| 124 | Linden Rowat |
| 137 | Joshua Turnbull |
| 184 | Josh Kidd |
| 188 | Matt Fillier |

**2006**

| Pick | |
|---|---|
| 11 | **Jonathan Bernier** |
| 17 | **Trevor Lewis** |
| 48 | Joe Ryan |
| 74 | Jeff Zatkoff |
| 86 | Bud Holloway |
| 114 | Niclas Andersen |
| 134 | David Meckler |
| 144 | Martin Nolet |
| 164 | Constantin Braun |

**2005**

| Pick | |
|---|---|
| 11 | **Anze Kopitar** |
| 50 | Dany Roussin |
| 60 | T.J. Fast |
| 72 | **Jonathan Quick** |
| 139 | Patrik Hersley |
| 184 | Ryan McGinnis |
| 206 | Josh Meyers |
| 226 | John Seymour |

**2004**

| Pick | |
|---|---|
| 11 | **Lauri Tukonen** |
| 95 | Paul Baier |
| 110 | Ned Lukacevic |
| 143 | Eric Neilson |
| 174 | Scott Parse |
| 205 | Mike Curry |
| 221 | **Daniel Taylor** |
| 238 | **Yutaka Fukufuji** |
| 264 | Valtteri Tenkanen |

**2003**

| Pick | |
|---|---|
| 13 | **Dustin Brown** |
| 26 | **Brian Boyle** |
| 27 | **Jeff Tambellini** |
| 44 | **Konstantin Pushkarev** |
| 82 | Ryan Munce |
| 152 | **Brady Murray** |
| 174 | **Esa Pirnes** |
| 231 | Matt Zaba |
| 244 | Mike Sullivan |
| 274 | Marty Guerin |

**2002**

| Pick | |
|---|---|
| 18 | **Denis Grebeshkov** |
| 50 | Sergei Anshakov |
| 66 | **Petr Kanko** |
| 104 | **Aaron Rome** |
| 115 | Mark Rooneem |
| 152 | Greg Hogeboom |
| 157 | Joel Andresen |
| 185 | Ryan Murphy |
| 215 | Mikhail Lyubushin |
| 248 | Tuukka Pulliainen |
| 279 | **Connor James** |

**2001**

| Pick | |
|---|---|
| 18 | Jens Karlsson |
| 30 | **David Steckel** |
| 49 | **Michael Cammalleri** |
| 51 | **Jaroslav Bednar** |
| 83 | Henrik Juntunen |
| 116 | **Richard Petiot** |
| 152 | Terry Denike |
| 153 | Tuukka Mantyla |
| 214 | **Cristobal Huet** |
| 237 | Mike Gabinet |
| 277 | Sebastien Laplante |

**2000**

| Pick | |
|---|---|
| 20 | **Alexander Frolov** |
| 54 | **Andreas Lilja** |
| 86 | **Yanick Lehoux** |
| 118 | **Lubomir Visnovsky** |
| 165 | Nathan Marsters |
| 201 | Yevgeny Fedorov |
| 206 | Tim Eriksson |
| 218 | Craig Olynick |
| 245 | Dan Welch |
| 250 | Flavien Conne |
| 282 | Carl Grahn |

**1999**

| Pick | |
|---|---|
| 43 | Andrei Shefer |
| 74 | Jason Crain |
| 76 | **Frantisek Kaberle** |
| 92 | Cory Campbell |
| 104 | **Brian McGrattan** |
| 125 | Daniel Johansson |
| 133 | Jean-Francois Nogues |
| 193 | Kevin Baker |
| 222 | **George Parros** |
| 250 | **Noah Clarke** |

**1998**

| Pick | |
|---|---|
| 21 | **Mathieu Biron** |
| 46 | **Justin Papineau** |
| 76 | Alexei Volkov |
| 103 | **Kip Brennan** |
| 133 | Joe Rullier |
| 163 | **Tomas Zizka** |
| 190 | Tommi Hannus |
| 217 | Jim Henkel |
| 248 | **Matthew Yeats** |

**1997**

| Pick | |
|---|---|
| 3 | **Olli Jokinen** |
| 15 | Matt Zultek |
| 29 | **Scott Barney** |
| 83 | **Joe Corvo** |
| 99 | Sean Blanchard |
| 137 | Richard Seeley |
| 150 | Jeff Katcher |
| 193 | Jay Kopischke |
| 220 | Konrad Brand |

**1996**

| Pick | |
|---|---|
| 30 | **Josh Green** |
| 37 | **Marian Cisar** |
| 57 | Greg Phillips |
| 84 | Mikael Simons |
| 96 | **Eric Belanger** |
| 120 | Jesse Black |
| 123 | Peter Hogan |
| 190 | **Steve Valiquette** |
| 193 | **Kai Nurminen** |
| 219 | Sebastien Simard |

**1995**

| Pick | |
|---|---|
| 3 | **Aki Berg** |
| 33 | **Don MacLean** |
| 50 | **Pavel Rosa** |
| 59 | **Vladimir Tsyplakov** |
| 118 | **Jason Morgan** |
| 137 | Igor Melyakov |
| 157 | Benoit Larose |
| 163 | Juha Vuorivirta |
| 215 | Brian Stewart |

*The team's first draft choice back in 2005, Anze Kopitar led the Kings in scoring for the second straight season in 2008-09.*

## General Managers' History

Larry Regan, 1967-68 to 1972-73; Larry Regan and Jake Milford, 1973-74; Jake Milford, 1974-75 to 1976-77; George Maguire, 1977-78 to 1982-83; George Maguire and Rogie Vachon, 1983-84; Rogie Vachon, 1984-85 to 1991-92; Nick Beverley, 1992-93, 1993-94; Sam McMaster, 1994-95 to 1996-97; Dave Taylor, 1997-98 to 2005-06; Dean Lombardi, 2006-07 to date.

## Captains' History

Bob Wall, 1967-68, 1968-69; Larry Cahan, 1969-70, 1970-71; Bob Pulford, 1971-72, 1972-73; Terry Harper, 1973-74, 1974-75; Mike Murphy, 1975-76 to 1980-81; Dave Lewis, 1981-82, 1982-83; Terry Ruskowski, 1983-84, 1984-85; Dave Taylor, 1985-86 to 1988-89; Wayne Gretzky, 1989-90 to 1991-92; Wayne Gretzky and Luc Robitaille, 1992-93; Wayne Gretzky, 1993-94, 1994-95; Wayne Gretzky and Rob Blake, 1995-96; Rob Blake, 1996-97 to 2000-01; Mattias Norstrom, 2001-02 to 2006-07; Rob Blake, 2007-08; Dustin Brown, 2008-09 to date.

# Club Directory

**STAPLES Center**

**Los Angeles Kings**
STAPLES Center
1111 South Figueroa Street
Los Angeles, CA 90015
Phone **213/742-7100**
GM FAX 310/535-4525
www.lakings.com
**Capacity:** 18,118

**Ownership**

| | |
|---|---|
| Owner | Philip F. Anschutz |
| Owner | Edward P. Roski, Jr. |
| Governor | Timothy J. Leiweke |
| Chief Operating Officer/Chief Financial Officer | Dan Beckerman |

**Kings Executive**

| | |
|---|---|
| President/General Manager, Alternate Governor | Dean Lombardi |
| President, Business Operations, Alternate Governor | Luc Robitaille |
| Chief Marketing Officer/Senior Vice President | Chris McGowan |
| Executive Administrative Assistant to the Governor | Carla Garcia |
| Executive Assistant to COO/CFO | Karen Zamora |
| Executive Assistant to President/General Manager | Tiffany Grommon |
| Executive Assistant to President, Business Operations | Kehly Sloane |
| Executive Assistant to Chief Marketing Officer | Alicia Gonzalez |

**Hockey Operations**

| | |
|---|---|
| Vice President/Assistant General Manager | Ron Hextall |
| Special Assistant to the General Manager | Jack Ferreira |
| Vice President/Hockey Operations and Legal Affairs | Jeff Solomon |
| Director of Team Operations | Marshall Dickerson |

**Coaches**

| | |
|---|---|
| Head Coach | Terry Murray |
| Assistant Coaches | Mark Hardy, Jamie Kompon |
| Goaltending Coach | Bill Ranford |
| Video Coordinator | Ryan Colville |

**Player Development**

| | |
|---|---|
| Player Development | Nelson Emerson |
| Pro Development and Special Assignments | Mike O'Connell |
| Goaltender Development | Kim Dillabaugh |

**Training Staff – Medical**

| | |
|---|---|
| Head Athletic Trainer | Chris Kingsley |
| Director of Rehabilitation/ Assistant Athletic Trainer | Joe Caligiuri |
| Strength and Conditioning Coach | Tim Adams |
| Assistant Athletic Trainer | Myles Hirayama |

**Training Staff – Equipment**

| | |
|---|---|
| Head Equipment Manager | Darren Granger |
| Assistant Equipment Managers | Corey Osmak, Dana Bryson |

**Medical**

| | |
|---|---|
| Team Physician / Internist | Dr. Ronald Kvitne / Dr. Michael Mellman |
| Team Dentist / Opthalmologist | Dr. Jeffrey Hoy / Dr. Howard Lazerson |

**Scouting/Hockey Operations**

| | |
|---|---|
| Scouting Operations Coordinator | Lee Callans |
| Pro Scouts | Rob Laird, Bob Berry, Oto Hascak, Steve Greeley, Alyn McCauley |
| Co-Directors of Amateur Scouting | Mark Yannetti, Michael Futa |
| Amateur Scouts | Brent McEwen, Tony Gasparini, Denis Fugere, Bob Crocker |
| Collegiate Scout | Mike Donnelly |
| Video Technicians | Bob Friedlander, Bill Gurney |

**Broadcasting**

| | |
|---|---|
| TV Play-by-Play / Color | Bob Miller / Jim Fox |
| Radio Play-by-Play Announcer | Nick Nickson / Daryl Evans |
| Television / Radio Flagship | FS West / KTLK AM 1150 |

**Communications**

| | |
|---|---|
| Vice President, Communications and Broadcasting | Michael Altieri |
| Senior Director, Communications | Jeff Moeller |
| Manager, Communications | Mike Kalinowski |
| Supervisor, Communications and Broadcasting | Jeremy Zager |
| Manager, Web Content | Thomas LaRocca |
| Manager, Production/Host – Kings Vision | Heidi Androl |
| Associate Producer/Editor | Aaron Brenner |

**Fan Development and Community Relations**

| | |
|---|---|
| Director, Fan Development/Community Relations | James Cefaly |

**Finance**

| | |
|---|---|
| Vice President, Finance | Peter Mazur |

**Global Partnerships**

| | |
|---|---|
| Senior Vice President, Corporate Partnerships | Bill Pedigo |
| Senior Vice President, Partnership Activation | Tracy Hartman |
| Vice President, Partnership Activation | Kelly Staley |

**Human Resources**

| | |
|---|---|
| Manager, Human Resources | LaShawnda Mikhael |

**Legal**

| | |
|---|---|
| Vice President and Senior Counsel | John Keenan |

**Marketing and Promotions**

| | |
|---|---|
| Senior Director, Marketing and Promotions | Jonathan Lowe |
| Director, Game Presentation and Events | Jon Adams |

**Merchandise**

| | |
|---|---|
| Vice President, Merchandising | Sean Ryan |

**Ticket Sales and Service**

| | |
|---|---|
| Vice President, Ticket Sales and Service | Kelly Cheeseman |
| Director, Ticket Sales and Service | Josh Bender |
| Director, Ticket Operations | Elizabeth Tockstein |

**Group Sales**

| | |
|---|---|
| Senior Vice President, Sales | Carola Ross |
| Vice President, Sales | Matt Rosenfeld |

# Minnesota Wild

## 2008-09 Results: 40W-33L-6OTL-3SOL 89PTS.
## Third, Northwest Division

### Key Off-Season Signings/Acquisitions

**2009**

**May 22** • Named **Chuck Fletcher** general manager.
**June 16** • Named **Todd Richards** head coach.
**27** • Acquired C **Kyle Brodziak** and a 6th-round pick in 2009 from Edmonton for a 4th- and 5th-round pick in 2009.
**July 1** • Signed RW **Martin Havlat** and D **Greg Zanon.**
**2** • Named **Mike Ramsey** and **Dave Barr** assistant coaches.
**3** • Signed D **Shane Hnidy.**
**15** • Re-signed LW **Benoit Pouliot.**
**17** • Signed G **Wade Dubielewicz.**
**29** • Re-signed G **Josh Harding.**

### Year-by-Year Record

| | | Home | | | | Road | | | | Overall | | | | | | | | |
|---|---|---|---|---|---|---|---|---|---|---|---|---|---|---|---|---|---|---|
| **Season** | **GP** | **W** | **L** | **T** | **OL** | **W** | **L** | **T** | **OL** | **W** | **L** | **T** | **OL** | **GF** | **GA** | **Pts.** | **Finished** | **Playoff Result** |
| 2008-09 | 82 | 23 | 11 | .... | 7 | 17 | 22 | .... | 2 | 40 | 33 | .... | 9 | 219 | 200 | 89 | 3rd, Northwest Div. | Out of Playoffs |
| 2007-08 | 82 | 25 | 11 | .... | 5 | 19 | 17 | .... | 5 | 44 | 28 | .... | 10 | 223 | 218 | 98 | 1st, Northwest Div. | Lost Conf. Quarter-Final |
| 2006-07 | 82 | 29 | 7 | .... | 5 | 19 | 19 | .... | 3 | 48 | 26 | .... | 8 | 235 | 191 | 104 | 2nd, Northwest Div. | Lost Conf. Quarter-Final |
| 2005-06 | 82 | 23 | 16 | .... | 2 | 15 | 20 | .... | 6 | 38 | 36 | .... | 8 | 231 | 215 | 84 | 5th, Northwest Div. | Out of Playoffs |
| 2004-05 | .... | .... | .... | .... | .... | .... | .... | .... | .... | .... | .... | .... | .... | .... | .... | .... | | |
| 2003-04 | 82 | 19 | 13 | 7 | 2 | 11 | 16 | 13 | 1 | 30 | 29 | 20 | 3 | 188 | 183 | 83 | 5th, Northwest Div. | Out of Playoffs |
| 2002-03 | 82 | 25 | 13 | 3 | 0 | 17 | 16 | 7 | 1 | 42 | 29 | 10 | 1 | 198 | 178 | 95 | 3rd, Northwest Div. | Lost Conf. Championship |
| 2001-02 | 82 | 14 | 14 | 8 | 5 | 12 | 21 | 4 | 4 | 26 | 35 | 12 | 9 | 195 | 238 | 73 | 5th, Northwest Div. | Out of Playoffs |
| 2000-01 | 82 | 14 | 13 | 10 | 4 | 11 | 26 | 3 | 1 | 25 | 39 | 13 | 5 | 168 | 210 | 68 | 5th, Northwest Div. | Out of Playoffs |

### 2009-10 Schedule

| | | | | | | | |
|---|---|---|---|---|---|---|---|
| **Oct.** | Sat. | 3 | at Columbus | **Jan.** | Sat. | 2 | New Jersey |
| | Tue. | 6 | Anaheim | | Tue. | 5 | at Chicago |
| | Thu. | 8 | at Los Angeles | | Wed. | 6 | Calgary |
| | Sat. | 10 | at San Jose | | Sat. | 9 | Chicago |
| | Wed. | 14 | at Anaheim | | Mon. | 11 | Pittsburgh |
| | Fri. | 16 | at Edmonton | | Wed. | 13 | Vancouver |
| | Sat. | 17 | at Vancouver | | Thu. | 14 | at St. Louis |
| | Wed. | 21 | Colorado | | Sat. | 16 | at Phoenix |
| | Fri. | 23 | at St. Louis | | Mon. | 18 | at Dallas |
| | Sat. | 24 | Carolina | | Thu. | 21 | Detroit |
| | Mon. | 26 | at Chicago | | Sat. | 23 | Columbus |
| | Wed. | 28 | Nashville | | Wed. | 27 | Detroit |
| | Fri. | 30 | NY Rangers | | Thu. | 28 | at Colorado |
| | Sat. | 31 | at Pittsburgh | | Sat. | 30 | at San Jose |
| **Nov.** | Thu. | 5 | Vancouver | **Feb.** | Tue. | 2 | at Dallas |
| | Sat. | 7 | Dallas | | Thu. | 4 | Edmonton |
| | Tue. | 10 | at Toronto | | Sat. | 6 | Philadelphia |
| | Thu. | 12 | at Tampa Bay | | Wed. | 10 | Phoenix |
| | Fri. | 13 | at Washington | | Fri. | 12 | Atlanta |
| | Sun. | 15 | at Carolina* | | Sun. | 14 | Vancouver* |
| | Wed. | 18 | Phoenix | **Mar.** | Wed. | 3 | at Calgary |
| | Fri. | 20 | NY Islanders | | Fri. | 5 | at Edmonton |
| | Wed. | 25 | Boston | | Sun. | 7 | Calgary* |
| | Fri. | 27 | Colorado* | | Tue. | 9 | Florida |
| | Sat. | 28 | at Colorado | | Thu. | 11 | at Detroit |
| **Dec.** | Wed. | 2 | Nashville | | Fri. | 12 | at Buffalo |
| | Fri. | 4 | Anaheim | | Sun. | 14 | St. Louis* |
| | Sat. | 5 | at Nashville | | Tue. | 16 | Edmonton |
| | Mon. | 7 | at Phoenix | | Thu. | 18 | at Nashville |
| | Wed. | 9 | at Colorado | | Fri. | 19 | at Columbus |
| | Fri. | 11 | at Calgary | | Sun. | 21 | Calgary* |
| | Sat. | 12 | at Vancouver | | Tue. | 23 | San Jose |
| | Tue. | 15 | Columbus | | Thu. | 25 | at Philadelphia |
| | Thu. | 17 | at Montreal | | Fri. | 26 | at Detroit |
| | Sat. | 19 | at Ottawa | | Mon. | 29 | Los Angeles |
| | Mon. | 21 | Colorado | | Wed. | 31 | Chicago |
| | Wed. | 23 | Edmonton | **Apr.** | Fri. | 2 | San Jose |
| | Sat. | 26 | St. Louis | | Sun. | 4 | at Vancouver |
| | Mon. | 28 | at Los Angeles | | Mon. | 5 | at Edmonton |
| | Tue. | 29 | at Anaheim | | Thu. | 8 | at Calgary |
| | Thu. | 31 | Los Angeles | | Sat. | 10 | Dallas |

* Denotes afternoon game.

*Niklas Backstrom had another big year for the Wild in 2008-09. His 71 games played was a far heavier workload than in his first two seasons and he also ranked among the NHL leaders in wins (37), average (2.33), save percentage (.923) and shutouts (8).*

**NORTHWEST DIVISION**
**10th NHL Season**

**Franchise date:** June 25, 1997

# 2009-10 Player Personnel

| FORWARDS | HT | WT | S | Place of Birth | *Age | 2008-09 Club |
|---|---|---|---|---|---|---|
| BELANGER, Eric | 5-11 | 187 | L | Sherbrooke, Que. | 31 | Minnesota |
| BOOGAARD, Derek | 6-8 | 257 | R | Saskatoon, Sask. | 27 | Minnesota |
| BOUCHARD, Pierre-Marc | 5-10 | 173 | L | Sherbrooke, Que. | 25 | Minnesota |
| BRODZIAK, Kyle | 6-2 | 209 | R | St. Paul, Alta. | 25 | Edmonton |
| BRUNETTE, Andrew | 6-1 | 210 | L | Sudbury, Ont. | 36 | Minnesota |
| CLUTTERBUCK, Cal | 5-11 | 213 | R | Welland, Ont. | 21 | Minnesota-Houston |
| DiSALVATORE, Jon | 6-1 | 200 | R | Bangor, ME | 28 | Lowell |
| GILLIES, Colton | 6-4 | 189 | L | White Rock, B.C. | 20 | Minnesota |
| HAVLAT, Martin | 6-2 | 217 | L | Mlada Boleslav, Czech. | 28 | Chicago |
| IRMEN, Danny | 6-0 | 190 | R | Fargo, ND | 25 | Houston |
| KALUS, Petr | 6-1 | 201 | L | Ostrava, Czech. | 22 | MVD-Houston |
| KASSIAN, Matt | 6-5 | 245 | L | Edmonton, Alta. | 22 | Houston |
| KOIVU, Mikko | 6-2 | 200 | L | Turku, Finland | 26 | Minnesota |
| MADSEN, Morten | 6-2 | 205 | L | Rodovre, Denmark | 22 | Houston |
| MIETTINEN, Antti | 6-0 | 190 | R | Hameenlinna, Finland | 29 | Minnesota |
| MILROY, Duncan | 6-0 | 195 | R | Edmonton, Alta. | 26 | Ingolstadt |
| NOLAN, Owen | 6-1 | 214 | R | Belfast, N.Ireland | 37 | Minnesota |
| POULIOT, Benoit | 6-3 | 199 | L | Alfred, Ont. | 23 | Minnesota-Houston |
| SHEPPARD, James | 6-2 | 210 | L | Halifax, N.S. | 21 | Minnesota |
| SMITH, Nathan | 6-2 | 206 | L | Edmonton, Alta. | 27 | Lake Erie |
| WELLER, Craig | 6-4 | 220 | R | Calgary, Alta. | 28 | Minnesota |
| **DEFENSEMEN** | | | | | | |
| BURNS, Brent | 6-5 | 219 | R | Ajax, Ont. | 24 | Minnesota |
| FRASER, Jamie | 6-1 | 200 | L | Sarnia, Ont. | 23 | NY Islanders-Bridgeport |
| HNIDY, Shane | 6-2 | 204 | R | Neepawa, Man. | 33 | Boston |
| JOHNSSON, Kim | 6-1 | 193 | L | Malmo, Sweden | 33 | Minnesota |
| LANNON, Ryan | 6-1 | 198 | L | Worcester, MA | 26 | San Antonio |
| ROGERS, Brandon | 6-1 | 195 | R | Rochester, NH | 27 | Houston |
| SCHULTZ, Nick | 6-1 | 200 | L | Strasbourg, Sask. | 27 | Minnesota |
| SCOTT, John | 6-8 | 258 | L | St. Catharines, Ont. | 27 | Minnesota-Houston |
| SIFERS, Jaime | 5-11 | 210 | R | Stratford, CT | 26 | Toronto-Toronto (AHL) |
| STONER, Clayton | 6-4 | 212 | L | Port McNeill, B.C. | 24 | Houston |
| ZANON, Greg | 5-11 | 201 | L | Burnaby, B.C. | 29 | Nashville |
| ZIDLICKY, Marek | 5-11 | 190 | R | Most, Czech. | 32 | Minnesota |

| GOALTENDERS | HT | WT | C | Place of Birth | *Age | 2008-09 Club |
|---|---|---|---|---|---|---|
| BACKSTROM, Niklas | 6-1 | 189 | L | Helsinki, Finland | 31 | Minnesota |
| BRUST, Barry | 6-2 | 235 | L | Swan River, Man. | 26 | Houston |
| DUBIELEWICZ, Wade | 5-10 | 185 | L | Invermere, B.C. | 30 | Kazan-Columbus |
| HARDING, Josh | 6-1 | 197 | R | Regina, Sask. | 25 | Minnesota |

* – Age at start of 2009-10 season

# 2008-09 Scoring

* – rookie

## Regular Season

| Pos | # | Player | Team | GP | G | A | Pts | TOI | +/– | PIM | PP | SH | GW | S | % |
|---|---|---|---|---|---|---|---|---|---|---|---|---|---|---|---|
| C | 9 | Mikko Koivu | MIN | 79 | 20 | 47 | 67 | 21:29 | 2 | 66 | 5 | 4 | 3 | 236 | 8.5 |
| L | 15 | Andrew Brunette | MIN | 80 | 22 | 28 | 50 | 16:56 | –5 | 18 | 9 | 0 | 3 | 118 | 18.6 |
| R | 96 | Pierre-Marc Bouchard | MIN | 71 | 16 | 30 | 46 | 16:58 | –5 | 20 | 2 | 0 | 1 | 142 | 11.3 |
| R | 11 | Owen Nolan | MIN | 59 | 25 | 20 | 45 | 16:23 | 5 | 26 | 12 | 0 | 5 | 148 | 16.9 |
| R | 20 | Antti Miettinen | MIN | 82 | 15 | 29 | 44 | 18:16 | –1 | 32 | 4 | 2 | 3 | 186 | 8.1 |
| D | 3 | Marek Zidlicky | MIN | 76 | 12 | 30 | 42 | 22:06 | –12 | 76 | 10 | 0 | 3 | 147 | 8.2 |
| C | 25 | Eric Belanger | MIN | 79 | 13 | 23 | 36 | 17:50 | –5 | 26 | 4 | 0 | 4 | 147 | 8.8 |
| D | 47 | Marc-Andre Bergeron | MIN | 72 | 14 | 18 | 32 | 16:54 | 5 | 30 | 7 | 0 | 3 | 140 | 10.0 |
| D | 8 | Brent Burns | MIN | 59 | 8 | 19 | 27 | 22:25 | –7 | 45 | 4 | 0 | 2 | 147 | 5.4 |
| C | 51 | James Sheppard | MIN | 82 | 5 | 19 | 24 | 15:10 | –14 | 41 | 0 | 0 | 1 | 88 | 5.7 |
| D | 5 | Kim Johnsson | MIN | 81 | 2 | 22 | 24 | 24:31 | –3 | 44 | 1 | 0 | 0 | 93 | 2.2 |
| R | 10 | Marian Gaborik | MIN | 17 | 13 | 10 | 23 | 19:59 | 3 | 2 | 2 | 1 | 2 | 68 | 19.1 |
| L | 19 | Stephane Veilleux | MIN | 81 | 13 | 10 | 23 | 15:47 | –17 | 40 | 0 | 1 | 1 | 146 | 8.9 |
| R | 22 * | Cal Clutterbuck | MIN | 78 | 11 | 7 | 18 | 13:00 | –5 | 76 | 1 | 0 | 1 | 136 | 8.1 |
| D | 41 | Martin Skoula | MIN | 81 | 4 | 12 | 16 | 19:57 | –12 | 10 | 0 | 0 | 0 | 55 | 7.3 |
| L | 49 | Dan Fritsche | NYR | 16 | 1 | 3 | 4 | 9:32 | –2 | 2 | 0 | 0 | 0 | 20 | 5.0 |
| | | | MIN | 34 | 4 | 5 | 9 | 11:09 | –3 | 10 | 1 | 1 | 0 | 34 | 11.8 |
| | | | Total | 50 | 5 | 8 | 13 | 10:38 | –5 | 12 | 1 | 1 | 0 | 54 | 9.3 |
| L | 67 * | Benoit Pouliot | MIN | 37 | 5 | 6 | 11 | 11:50 | 1 | 18 | 2 | 0 | 1 | 34 | 14.7 |
| D | 55 | Nick Schultz | MIN | 79 | 2 | 9 | 11 | 20:33 | –4 | 31 | 0 | 0 | 0 | 48 | 4.2 |
| L | 28 * | Peter Olvecky | MIN | 31 | 2 | 5 | 7 | 8:55 | 1 | 12 | 0 | 0 | 1 | 19 | 10.5 |
| L | 18 * | Colton Gillies | MIN | 45 | 2 | 5 | 7 | 8:13 | –2 | 18 | 0 | 0 | 1 | 22 | 9.1 |
| C | 39 | Krys Kolanos | MIN | 21 | 3 | 3 | 6 | 10:36 | 3 | 16 | 1 | 0 | 0 | 30 | 10.0 |
| D | 26 | Kurtis Foster | MIN | 10 | 1 | 5 | 6 | 13:35 | 7 | 6 | 0 | 0 | 0 | 10 | 10.0 |
| R | 12 | Craig Weller | MIN | 36 | 1 | 2 | 3 | 6:57 | –3 | 47 | 1 | 0 | 0 | 27 | 3.7 |
| L | 24 | Derek Boogaard | MIN | 51 | 0 | 3 | 3 | 4:59 | 3 | 87 | 0 | 0 | 0 | 13 | 0.0 |
| D | 6 | Tomas Mojzis | MIN | 4 | 0 | 1 | 1 | 7:14 | –1 | 2 | 0 | 0 | 0 | 2 | 0.0 |
| D | 36 * | John Scott | MIN | 20 | 0 | 1 | 1 | 9:14 | –1 | 21 | 0 | 0 | 0 | 6 | 0.0 |

## Goaltending

| No. | Goaltender | GPI | Mins | Avg | W | L | OT | EN | SO | GA | SA | S% | G | A | PIM |
|---|---|---|---|---|---|---|---|---|---|---|---|---|---|---|---|
| 29 | Josh Harding | 19 | 870 | 2.21 | 3 | 9 | 1 | 3 | 0 | 32 | 453 | .929 | 0 | 0 | 2 |
| 32 | Niklas Backstrom | 71 | 4088 | 2.33 | 37 | 24 | 8 | 3 | 8 | 159 | 2059 | .923 | 0 | 0 | 6 |
| | **Totals** | **82** | **4987** | **2.37** | **40** | **33** | **9** | **6** | **8** | **197** | **2518** | **.922** | | | |

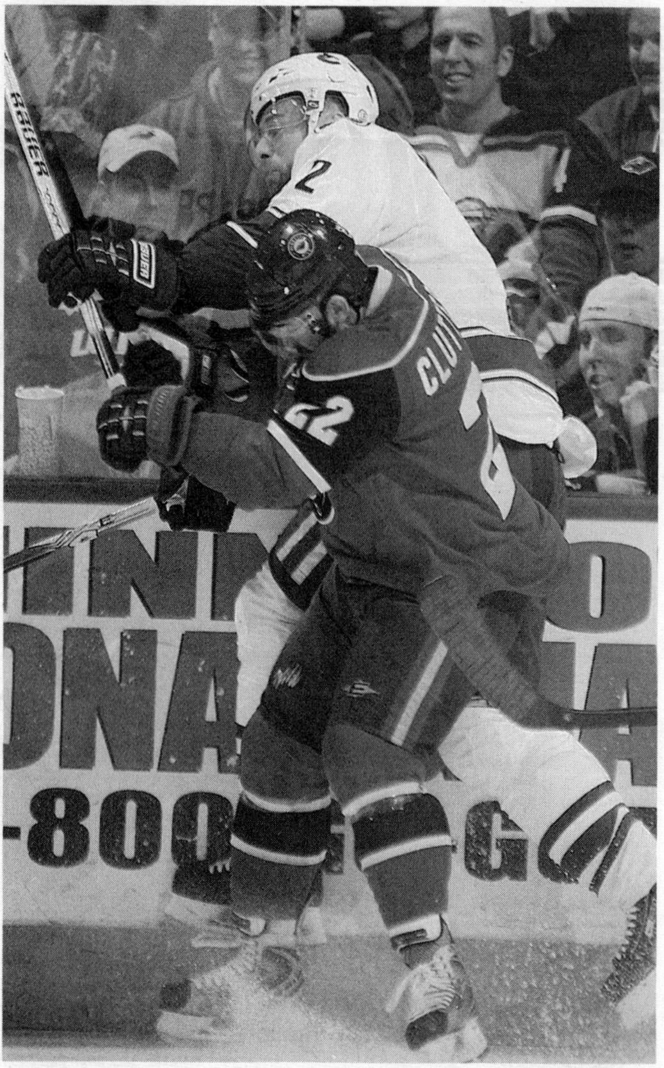

*Minnesota's Cal Clutterbuck (crunching Mattias Ohlund into the boards) set a single-season NHL record with 356 hits during the 2008-09 campaign.*

# Todd Richards

## Head Coach

*Born: Robbinsdale, MN, October 20, 1966.*

Minnesota Wild general manager Chuck Fletcher named Todd Richards as the second head coach in club history on June 16, 2009. Richards, who spent the 2008-09 season as an assistant coach with the San Jose Sharks, played collegiately at the University of Minnesota. He has made the playoffs in all 13 of his professional seasons as a player, and in all seven as a head coach or assistant coach. Richards helped the Sharks to an NHL-best 53-18-11 record and the Presidents' Trophy in 2008-09. He was responsible for the power-play, which ranked third in the NHL at 24.2 percent.

Richards spent two seasons (2006 to 2008) as head coach of the Wilkes-Barre/Scranton Penguins in the American Hockey League, where he led the team to a berth in the Calder Cup Finals in 2008. (Chuck Fletcher was the Baby Pens general manager during that time.) Before joining Wilkes-Barre/Scranton, Richards served as an assistant coach (2002 to 2006) with the Milwaukee Admirals. During his time in Milwaukee, the Admirals won two West Division titles (2003-04 and 2005-06) and made two trips to the Calder Cup Finals, winning the AHL title in 2003-04. A former defenseman, Richards captured several championships throughout his career, including a pair of Western Collegiate Hockey Association titles with the University of Minnesota (1988 and 1989), the 1991 Calder Cup with Springfield, the 2001 Turner Cup (International Hockey League) in Orlando and a Swiss-B League title with Servette Geneve in 2002.

Richards was drafted by the Montreal Canadiens in the second round (33rd overall) of the 1985 NHL Entry Draft and made his NHL debut with the Hartford Whalers in 1990-91. He played eight games over the next two seasons and posted four assists. He also appeared in 11 Stanley Cup playoff games with Hartford, totaling three assists. During his four seasons at the University of Minnesota, Richards was named a member of the WCHA Second All-Star Team for three consecutive seasons (1987 to 1989) and was team captain during his senior season. The Gophers lost to Harvard 4-3 in overtime in the NCAA championship game in 1989.

Following his stints in the Montreal and Hartford organizations, Richards joined the IHL's Las Vegas Thunder and was named the league's top defenseman in 1994-95. He spent the next six seasons with the Orlando Solar Bears, captaining the squad for four seasons and winning the IHL Championship in 2000-01, the league's final year of existence. Richards concluded his playing career with Servette Geneve of Switzerland in 2001-02, where he was he was also named the league's top defenseman.

### Coaching Record

| | | | Regular Season | | | | Playoffs | | | |
|---|---|---|---|---|---|---|---|---|---|---|
| Season | Team | League | GC | W | L | O/T | GC | W | L | T |
| 2006-07 | Wilkes-Barre | AHL | 80 | 51 | 23 | 6 | 11 | 5 | 6 | .... |
| 2007-08 | Wilkes-Barre | AHL | 80 | 47 | 26 | 6 | 23 | 14 | 9 | .... |

# Club Records

## Team

(Figures in brackets for season records are games played.)

**Most Points** .............. **104** 2006-07 (82)
**Most Wins** ................ **48** 2006-07 (82)
**Most Ties** ................ **20** 2003-04 (82)
**Most Losses** .............. **39** 2000-01 (82)
**Most Goals** ............... **235** 2006-07 (82)
**Most Goals Against** ....... **238** 2001-02 (82)
**Fewest Points** ............ **68** 2000-01 (82)
**Fewest Wins** .............. **25** 2000-01 (82)
**Fewest Ties** .............. **10** 2002-03 (82)
**Fewest Losses** ............ **26** 2006-07 (82)
**Fewest Goals** ............. **168** 2000-01 (82)
**Fewest Goals Against** ..... **178** 2002-03 (82)

**Longest Winning Streak**
**Overall** .................. **9** Mar. 8-24/07
**Home** ..................... **11** Apr. 4-Nov. 11/06
**Away** ..................... **5** Mar. 8-17/07

**Longest Undefeated Streak**
**Overall** .................. **9** Dec. 13-30/03 (4 wins, 5 ties) Mar. 8-24/07 (9 wins)
**Home** ..................... **9** Dec. 13/00-Jan. 10/01 (5 wins, 4 ties)
**Away** ..................... **7** Dec. 6-30/03 (2 wins, 5 ties)

**Longest Losing Streak**
**Overall** .................. **6** Dec. 5-17/08
**Home** ..................... **4** Oct. 29-Nov. 15/00
**Away** ..................... **11** Nov. 20/06-Jan. 9/07

**Longest Winless Streak**
**Overall** .................. **12** Mar. 11-Apr. 4/01 (9 losses, 3 ties)
**Home** ..................... **8** Feb. 26-Mar. 28/01 (5 losses, 3 ties)
**Away** ..................... **12** Dec. 18/03-Jan. 31/04 (5 losses, 7 ties)

**Most Shutouts, Season** ........ **8** 2006-07 (82), 2008-09 (82)
**Most PIM, Season** ......... **1,209** 2001-02 (82), 2005-06 (82)
**Most Goals, Game** ............ **8** Mar. 25/04 (Min. 8 at Chi. 2) Apr. 10/09 (Nsh. 2 at Min. 8)

## Individual

**Most Seasons** ............... **8** Marian Gaborik
**Most Games** ............... **527** Nick Schultz
**Most Goals, Career** ......... **219** Marian Gaborik
**Most Assists, Career** ....... **218** Marian Gaborik
**Most Points, Career** ........ **437** Marian Gaborik (219G, 218A)
**Most PIM, Career** ........... **698** Matt Johnson
**Most Shutouts, Career** ....... **17** Niklas Backstrom
**Longest Consecutive Games Streak** ........... **288** Antti Laaksonen (Oct. 6/00-Dec. 29/03)
**Most Goals, Season** .......... **42** Marian Gaborik (2007-08)
**Most Assists, Season** ......... **50** Pierre-Marc Bouchard (2007-08)
**Most Points, Season** ......... **83** Marian Gaborik (2007-08; 42G, 41A)
**Most PIM, Season** ........... **201** Matt Johnson (2002-03)
**Most Points, Defenseman, Season** .................. **43** Brent Burns (2007-08; 15G, 28A)
**Most Points, Center, Season** .................. **67** Mikko Koivu (2008-09; 20G, 47A)
**Most Points, Right Wing, Season** .................. **83** Marian Gaborik (2007-08; 42G, 41A)
**Most Points, Left Wing, Season** .................. **79** Brian Rolston (2005-06; 34G, 45A)
**Most Points, Rookie, Season** .................. **36** Marian Gaborik (2000-01; 18G, 18A)
**Most Shutouts, Season** ........ **8** Nicklas Backstrom (2008-09)
**Most Goals, Game** ............ **5** Marian Gaborik (Dec. 20/07)
**Most Assists, Game** ........... **4** Andrew Brunette (Mar. 10/02) Marian Gaborik (Oct. 26/02) Pascal Dupuis (Mar. 25/04) Eric Belanger (Nov. 15/07) Mikko Koivu (Oct. 16/08)
**Most Points, Game** ............ **6** Marian Gaborik (Oct. 26/02; 2G, 4A), (Dec. 20/07; 5G, 1A)

## Captains' History

Sean O'Donnell, Scott Pellerin, Wes Walz, Brad Bombardir, Darby Hendrickson, 2000-01; Jim Dowd, Filip Kuba, Brad Brown, Andrew Brunette, 2001-02; Brad Bombardir, Matt Johnson, Sergei Zholtok, 2002-03; Brad Brown, Andrew Brunette, Richard Park, Brad Bombardir, Jim Dowd, 2003-04; Alex Henry, Filip Kuba, Willie Mitchell, Brian Rolston, Wes Walz, 2005-06; Brian Rolston, Keith Carney, Mark Parrish, 2006-07; Pavol Demitra, Brian Rolston, Mark Parrish, Nick Schultz, Marian Gaborik, 2007-08; Mikko Koivu, Kim Johnsson, Andrew Brunette, 2008-09.

## General Managers' History

Doug Risebrough, 2000-01 to 2008-09; Chuck Fletcher, 2009-10.

## Coaching History

Jacques Lemaire, 2000-01 to 2008-09; Todd Richards, 2009-10.

# All-time Record vs. Other Clubs

## Regular Season

| | At Home | | | | | | | | On Road | | | | | | | | Total | | | | | | | |
|---|---|---|---|---|---|---|---|---|---|---|---|---|---|---|---|---|---|---|---|---|---|---|---|---|
| | GP | W | L | T | OL | GF | GA | PTS | GP | W | L | T | OL | GF | GA | PTS | GP | W | L | T | OL | GF | GA | PTS |
| Anaheim | 16 | 9 | 4 | 2 | 1 | 38 | 29 | 21 | 16 | 7 | 8 | 0 | 1 | 38 | 39 | 15 | 32 | 16 | 12 | 2 | 2 | 76 | 68 | 36 |
| Atlanta | 4 | 3 | 0 | 1 | 0 | 13 | 6 | 7 | 4 | 3 | 0 | 0 | 1 | 16 | 11 | 7 | 8 | 6 | 0 | 1 | 1 | 29 | 17 | 14 |
| Boston | 4 | 3 | 1 | 0 | 0 | 13 | 8 | 6 | 5 | 5 | 0 | 0 | 0 | 16 | 5 | 10 | 9 | 8 | 1 | 0 | 0 | 29 | 13 | 16 |
| Buffalo | 5 | 1 | 3 | 0 | 1 | 9 | 14 | 3 | 4 | 3 | 1 | 0 | 0 | 13 | 8 | 6 | 9 | 4 | 4 | 0 | 1 | 22 | 22 | 9 |
| Calgary | 26 | 12 | 8 | 1 | 5 | 61 | 52 | 30 | 25 | 3 | 18 | 3 | 1 | 47 | 71 | 10 | 51 | 15 | 26 | 4 | 6 | 108 | 123 | 40 |
| Carolina | 6 | 3 | 1 | 2 | 0 | 17 | 18 | 8 | 3 | 0 | 3 | 0 | 0 | 2 | 6 | 0 | 9 | 3 | 4 | 2 | 0 | 19 | 24 | 8 |
| Chicago | 16 | 12 | 4 | 0 | 0 | 49 | 37 | 24 | 16 | 10 | 5 | 1 | 0 | 48 | 33 | 21 | 32 | 22 | 9 | 1 | 0 | 97 | 70 | 45 |
| Colorado | 25 | 13 | 8 | 1 | 3 | 66 | 72 | 30 | 26 | 7 | 15 | 2 | 2 | 60 | 77 | 18 | 51 | 20 | 23 | 3 | 5 | 126 | 149 | 48 |
| Columbus | 16 | 12 | 3 | 0 | 1 | 47 | 32 | 25 | 15 | 4 | 8 | 1 | 2 | 30 | 42 | 11 | 31 | 16 | 11 | 1 | 3 | 77 | 74 | 36 |
| Dallas | 16 | 8 | 7 | 0 | 1 | 41 | 34 | 17 | 16 | 3 | 9 | 1 | 3 | 36 | 61 | 10 | 32 | 11 | 16 | 1 | 4 | 77 | 95 | 27 |
| Detroit | 16 | 4 | 7 | 2 | 3 | 37 | 46 | 13 | 16 | 4 | 11 | 1 | 0 | 37 | 60 | 9 | 32 | 8 | 18 | 3 | 3 | 74 | 106 | 22 |
| Edmonton | 25 | 14 | 9 | 1 | 1 | 69 | 52 | 30 | 26 | 11 | 9 | 3 | 3 | 62 | 62 | 28 | 51 | 25 | 18 | 4 | 4 | 131 | 114 | 58 |
| Florida | 4 | 3 | 0 | 1 | 0 | 14 | 3 | 7 | 5 | 4 | 1 | 0 | 0 | 17 | 10 | 8 | 9 | 7 | 1 | 1 | 0 | 31 | 13 | 15 |
| Los Angeles | 16 | 6 | 5 | 3 | 2 | 34 | 35 | 17 | 16 | 7 | 5 | 2 | 2 | 38 | 37 | 18 | 32 | 13 | 10 | 5 | 4 | 72 | 72 | 35 |
| Montreal | 4 | 2 | 1 | 0 | 1 | 11 | 10 | 5 | 4 | 1 | 2 | 1 | 0 | 10 | 13 | 3 | 8 | 3 | 3 | 1 | 1 | 21 | 23 | 8 |
| Nashville | 16 | 9 | 4 | 3 | 0 | 54 | 42 | 21 | 16 | 5 | 9 | 2 | 0 | 36 | 44 | 12 | 32 | 14 | 13 | 5 | 0 | 90 | 86 | 33 |
| New Jersey | 4 | 1 | 1 | 1 | 1 | 10 | 12 | 4 | 5 | 0 | 3 | 1 | 1 | 10 | 20 | 2 | 9 | 1 | 4 | 2 | 2 | 20 | 32 | 6 |
| NY Islanders | 5 | 4 | 1 | 0 | 0 | 17 | 13 | 8 | 5 | 3 | 2 | 0 | 0 | 16 | 11 | 6 | 10 | 7 | 3 | 0 | 0 | 33 | 24 | 14 |
| NY Rangers | 5 | 2 | 2 | 0 | 1 | 17 | 16 | 5 | 5 | 1 | 4 | 0 | 0 | 9 | 15 | 2 | 10 | 3 | 6 | 0 | 1 | 26 | 31 | 7 |
| Ottawa | 5 | 1 | 2 | 1 | 1 | 14 | 19 | 4 | 3 | 1 | 2 | 0 | 0 | 7 | 9 | 2 | 8 | 2 | 4 | 1 | 1 | 21 | 28 | 6 |
| Philadelphia | 3 | 1 | 1 | 1 | 0 | 6 | 6 | 3 | 6 | 1 | 5 | 0 | 0 | 6 | 17 | 2 | 9 | 2 | 6 | 1 | 0 | 12 | 23 | 5 |
| Phoenix | 16 | 9 | 4 | 2 | 1 | 44 | 30 | 21 | 16 | 7 | 7 | 1 | 1 | 37 | 42 | 16 | 32 | 16 | 11 | 3 | 2 | 81 | 72 | 37 |
| Pittsburgh | 4 | 2 | 1 | 1 | 0 | 11 | 9 | 5 | 5 | 4 | 1 | 0 | 0 | 19 | 7 | 8 | 9 | 6 | 2 | 1 | 0 | 30 | 16 | 13 |
| St. Louis | 16 | 9 | 3 | 2 | 2 | 49 | 29 | 22 | 16 | 6 | 6 | 3 | 1 | 33 | 37 | 16 | 32 | 15 | 9 | 5 | 3 | 82 | 66 | 38 |
| San Jose | 16 | 6 | 7 | 1 | 2 | 38 | 41 | 15 | 16 | 7 | 7 | 1 | 1 | 34 | 42 | 16 | 32 | 13 | 14 | 2 | 3 | 72 | 83 | 31 |
| Tampa Bay | 5 | 4 | 1 | 0 | 0 | 19 | 13 | 8 | 5 | 3 | 1 | 1 | 0 | 13 | 10 | 7 | 10 | 7 | 2 | 1 | 0 | 32 | 23 | 15 |
| Toronto | 3 | 2 | 1 | 0 | 0 | 11 | 5 | 4 | 4 | 0 | 4 | 0 | 0 | 6 | 15 | 0 | 7 | 2 | 5 | 0 | 0 | 17 | 20 | 4 |
| Vancouver | 26 | 12 | 9 | 2 | 3 | 69 | 61 | 29 | 25 | 10 | 8 | 3 | 4 | 63 | 68 | 27 | 51 | 22 | 17 | 5 | 7 | 132 | 129 | 56 |
| Washington | 5 | 5 | 0 | 0 | 0 | 13 | 6 | 10 | 4 | 1 | 3 | 0 | 0 | 7 | 11 | 2 | 9 | 6 | 3 | 0 | 0 | 20 | 17 | 12 |
| **Totals** | **328** | **172** | **98** | **28** | **30** | **891** | **750** | **402** | **328** | **121** | **157** | **27** | **23** | **766** | **883** | **292** | **656** | **293** | **255** | **55** | **53** | **1657** | **1633** | **694** |

## Playoffs

| | Series | W | L | GP | W | L | T | GF | GA | Last Mtg. | Rnd. | Result |
|---|---|---|---|---|---|---|---|---|---|---|---|---|
| Anaheim | 2 | 0 | 2 | 9 | 1 | 8 | 0 | 10 | 21 | 2007 | CQF | L 1-4 |
| Colorado | 2 | 1 | 1 | 13 | 6 | 7 | 0 | 28 | 34 | 2008 | CQF | L 2-4 |
| Vancouver | 1 | 1 | 0 | 7 | 4 | 3 | 0 | 26 | 17 | 2003 | CSF | W 4-3 |
| **Totals** | **5** | **2** | **3** | **29** | **11** | **18** | **0** | **64** | **72** | | | |

## Playoff Results 2009-2004

| Year | Round | Opponent | Result | GF | GA |
|---|---|---|---|---|---|
| 2008 | CQF | Colorado | L 2-4 | 12 | 17 |
| 2007 | CQF | Anaheim | L 1-4 | 9 | 12 |

**Abbreviations: Round: CF** – conference final; **CSF** – conference semi-final; **CQF** – conference quarter-final.

## 2008-09 Results

| | | | | | | | |
|---|---|---|---|---|---|---|---|
| **Oct.** | 11 | Boston | 4-3 | | 13 | Phoenix | 6-3 |
| | 14 | at Atlanta | 4-2 | | 15 | Edmonton | 5-1 |
| | 16 | at Florida | 6-2 | | 17 | Anaheim | 0-3 |
| | 18 | at Tampa Bay | 1-0† | | 19 | at Chicago | 4-1 |
| | 23 | Buffalo | 3-4* | | 20 | Los Angeles | 2-5 |
| | 25 | Columbus | 2-1 | | 27 | Toronto | 6-1 |
| | 27 | Chicago | 3-2 | | 30 | at Edmonton | 1-3 |
| | 29 | at Dallas | 2-4 | | 31 | at Vancouver | 4-3* |
| | 30 | Montreal | 1-2 | **Feb.** | 4 | Anaheim | 3-0 |
| **Nov.** | 1 | at Phoenix | 3-2 | | 6 | Nashville | 0-2 |
| | 4 | at San Jose | 1-3 | | 8 | Edmonton | 3-2† |
| | 6 | at Colorado | 3-1 | | 11 | Colorado | 3-2 |
| | 8 | at Vancouver | 0-2 | | 12 | at Detroit | 2-4 |
| | 13 | Phoenix | 4-0 | | 14 | Ottawa | 3-5 |
| | 15 | Columbus | 3-2† | | 19 | Calgary | 2-3* |
| | 18 | at Pittsburgh | 2-1† | | 21 | Detroit | 5-2 |
| | 20 | Vancouver | 2-3 | | 22 | at Chicago | 2-1 |
| | 22 | St. Louis | 1-2 | | 24 | Los Angeles | 1-2† |
| | 24 | Washington | 4-3 | | 27 | at Calgary | 1-4 |
| | 26 | Dallas | 3-4 | | 28 | at Edmonton | 2-3 |
| | 28 | Tampa Bay | 4-2 | **Mar.** | 3 | at Vancouver | 2-4 |
| | 29 | at Nashville | 6-2 | | 5 | at San Jose | 4-3* |
| **Dec.** | 1 | Colorado | 5-6 | | 7 | at Los Angeles | 3-4 |
| | 3 | St. Louis | 4-0 | | 8 | at Anaheim | 3-2 |
| | 5 | Vancouver | 1-2 | | 10 | San Jose | 4-5* |
| | 6 | at Nashville | 0-1 | | 12 | at Colorado | 1-2† |
| | 11 | at Phoenix | 1-3 | | 14 | at Dallas | 2-3* |
| | 13 | at Los Angeles | 1-3 | | 15 | at St. Louis | 3-5 |
| | 14 | at Anaheim | 2-4 | | 17 | Colorado | 3-2† |
| | 17 | Calgary | 2-3* | | 20 | at New Jersey | 0-4 |
| | 19 | NY Islanders | 4-1 | | 22 | Edmonton | 3-0 |
| | 20 | at St. Louis | 2-4 | | 24 | at NY Rangers | 1-2 |
| | 23 | Carolina | 3-2 | | 25 | at NY Islanders | 6-2 |
| | 28 | Chicago | 1-4 | | 28 | at Calgary | 2-3 |
| | 29 | at Calgary | 1-2 | | 29 | at Edmonton | 3-2 |
| | 31 | San Jose | 3-2* | | 31 | Vancouver | 1-2* |
| **Jan.** | 3 | Detroit | 2-3† | **Apr.** | 3 | Calgary | 4-0 |
| | 4 | at Colorado | 2-0 | | 5 | at Detroit | 2-3 |
| | 6 | at Boston | 1-0 | | 7 | Dallas | 3-1 |
| | 8 | at Philadelphia | 1-3 | | 10 | Nashville | 8-4 |
| | 10 | at Columbus | 2-4 | | 11 | at Columbus | 6-3 |

* – Overtime † – Shootout

## Entry Draft Selections 2009-2000

Name in bold denotes played in NHL.

### 2009

| Pick | |
|---|---|
| 16 | Nick Leddy |
| 77 | Matt Hackett |
| 103 | Kris Foucault |
| 116 | Alexander Fallstrom |
| 161 | Darcy Kuemper |
| 163 | Jere Sallinen |
| 182 | Erik Haula |
| 193 | Anthony Hamburg |

### 2008

| Pick | |
|---|---|
| 23 | Tyler Cuma |
| 55 | Marco Scandella |
| 115 | Sean Lorenz |
| 145 | Eero Elo |

### 2007

| Pick | |
|---|---|
| 16 | **Colton Gillies** |
| 110 | Justin Falk |
| 140 | Cody Almond |
| 170 | Harri Ilvonen |
| 200 | Carson McMillan |

### 2006

| Pick | |
|---|---|
| 9 | **James Sheppard** |
| 40 | Ondrej Fiala |
| 72 | **Cal Clutterbuck** |
| 102 | Kyle Medvec |
| 132 | Niko Hovinen |
| 162 | Julian Walker |
| 192 | Chris Hickey |

### 2005

| Pick | |
|---|---|
| 4 | **Benoit Pouliot** |
| 57 | Matt Kassian |
| 65 | Kristofer Westblom |
| 110 | Kyle Bailey |
| 122 | Morten Madsen |
| 129 | Anthony Aiello |
| 199 | Riley Emmerson |

### 2004

| Pick | |
|---|---|
| 12 | A.J. Thelen |
| 42 | Roman Voloshenko |
| 78 | **Peter Olvecky** |
| 79 | Clayton Stoner |
| 111 | **Ryan Jones** |
| 114 | Patrick Bordeleau |
| 117 | Julien Sprunger |
| 161 | Jean-Claude Sawyer |
| 175 | Aaron Boogaard |
| 195 | Jean-Michel Rizk |
| 206 | Anton Khudobin |
| 272 | Kyle Wilson |

### 2003

| Pick | |
|---|---|
| 20 | **Brent Burns** |
| 56 | **Patrick O'Sullivan** |
| 78 | Danny Irmen |
| 157 | Marcin Kolusz |
| 187 | Miroslav Kopriva |
| 207 | Georgy Misharin |
| 219 | Adam Courchaine |
| 251 | Mathieu Melanson |
| 281 | Jean-Michel Bolduc |

### 2002

| Pick | |
|---|---|
| 8 | **Pierre-Marc Bouchard** |
| 38 | **Josh Harding** |
| 72 | Mike Erickson |
| 73 | **Barry Brust** |
| 155 | Armands Berzins |
| 175 | **Matt Foy** |
| 204 | Niklas Eckerblom |
| 237 | **Christoph Brandner** |
| 268 | Mikhail Tyulyapkin |
| 269 | Mika Hannula |

### 2001

| Pick | |
|---|---|
| 6 | **Mikko Koivu** |
| 36 | **Kyle Wanvig** |
| 74 | Chris Heid |
| 93 | **Stephane Veilleux** |
| 103 | **Tony Virta** |
| 202 | **Derek Boogaard** |
| 239 | Jake Riddle |

### 2000

| Pick | |
|---|---|
| 3 | **Marian Gaborik** |
| 33 | **Nick Schultz** |
| 99 | Marc Cavosie |
| 132 | **Maxim Sushinsky** |
| 170 | **Erik Reitz** |
| 199 | Brian Passmore |
| 214 | **Peter Bartos** |
| 232 | **Lubomir Sekeras** |
| 255 | Eric Johansson |

## Chuck Fletcher

### General Manager

*Born: Montreal, Que., April 29, 1967.*

The Minnesota Wild announced the hiring of Chuck Fletcher as the second general manager in club history on May 22, 2009. Fletcher has been to the Stanley Cup finals in management with three different teams (Florida, Anaheim and Pittsburgh). With the Penguins from 2006 to 2009, he worked closely with general manager Ray Shero on all hockey-related matters, including scouting, overseeing the development of young prospects and contract negotiations. Fletcher also managed hockey operations for the club's American Hockey League affiliate, the Wilkes-Barre/Scranton Penguins. Under his leadership, Wilkes-Barre/Scranton reached the AHL's Calder Cup finals in 2007-08, and the division finals in 2008-09.

Fletcher, the son of Hockey Hall of Famer Cliff Fletcher, had extensive NHL management experience before he joined the Penguins in July 2006 – including a four-year stint with the Anaheim Ducks from 2002 to 2006 as director of hockey operations, assistant general manager, and vice president of amateur scouting and player development.

The Montreal native also spent nine years in the front office of the Florida Panthers from 1993 to 2002, working seven seasons as assistant general manager and part of one season (2001-02) as interim general manager. In 1996, the Panthers advanced to the Stanley Cup finals.

Fletcher graduated from Harvard in 1990 and spent one year as the sales and merchandising coordinator for Hockey Canada and two years as a player representative for Newport Sports Management before making the transition to the front office.

# Club Directory

Xcel Energy Center

**Minnesota Wild**
317 Washington Street
St. Paul, MN 55102
Phone **651/602-6000**
FAX 651/222-1055
Tickets 651/222-9453
www.wild.com
**Capacity:** 18,064

| | |
|---|---|
| **Executive Management** | |
| Owner/Governor | Craig Leipold |
| Minority Owner | Philip Falcone |
| Chief Operating Officer | Matt Majka |
| Chief Financial Officer | Jeff Pellegrom |
| Vice President, Brand Marketing | John Maher |
| Vice President, Customer Sales and Service/ Exec. V.P., Houston Aeros and AHL Governor | Jamie Spencer |
| Vice President, Facility Admin./G.M., RiverCentre | Jim Ibister |
| Vice President/General Manager, Xcel Energy Center | Jack Larson |
| Vice President, Communications and Broadcasting | Bill Robertson |
| Vice President, Corporate Partnerships | Carin Anderson |
| Executive Assistant | Stephanie Huseby |
| Executive Assistant, Hockey Operations | Laura Kinzel |
| Administrative Assistant, Sales and Service, Creative Services and Marketing | Tawnya Vidnovic |
| Administrative Assistant, Communications and Broadcasting, Corporate Sales & Service, Human Resource | Deb Hanson |
| **Hockey Operations** | |
| General Manager | Chuck Fletcher |
| Assistant General Managers | Brent Flahr, Tom Thompson |
| Assistant to the General Manager | Jim Mill |
| Head Coach | Todd Richards |
| Assistant Coaches | Mike Ramsey, Dave Barr |
| Goaltending Coach | Bob Mason |
| Strength and Conditioning Coach | Christopher Pietrzak-Wegner |
| Video Coordinator | P.J. DeLuca |
| Coordinator of Amateur Scouting | Guy Lapointe |
| Director of Professional Scouting | Blair Mackasey |
| Amateur Scouts | Marc Chamard, Paul Charles, Brian Fortin, Christopher Hamel, Brian Hunter, Marty Nanne, Ken Prost, Ernie Vargas |
| European Scouts | Pavel Routa, Branislav Gaborik, Jiri Koluch, Matti Vaisanen |
| Professional Scouts | Jamie Hislop, Chris Keller |
| Head Athletic Therapist | Don Fuller |
| Equipment Manager | Tony DaCosta |
| Assistant Athletic Trainer | Travis Green |
| Assistant Equipment Managers | Matt Benz, Brent Proulx |
| Director of Hockey Operations | Chris Snow |
| Director of Hockey Administration | Shep Harder |
| Hockey Operations Administrator | Cindy Sweiger |
| Medical Director | Dr. Sheldon Burns |
| Team Physician | Dr. Daniel Peterson |
| Orthopedic Surgeon | Dr. Joel Boyd |
| Assistant Team Orthopedic Surgeon | Dr. Brad Nelson |
| Oral Surgeon | David Hamlar |
| Team Dentists | Kyle Edlund, Mike Nanne, Mike Pelke |
| **Sales and Service** | |
| Director, Customer Sales | Matt Cords |
| Manager, Ticket Operations | Chris Turns |
| Account Manager, Group and Event Suites | Cory Effertz |
| New Business Development | Emily Iversen, Mike McDonough, Matt Sayer, Britny Holloway |
| Senior Manager, Customer Service | Maria Troje |
| Account Service Executives | Natalie Kaess, Joshua Simonson, Jennifer Watters |
| **Retail Operations** | |
| Director, Retail Operations | Matt Freiberg |
| Managers, Retail Operations / Warehouse | Scott Sarkis / Joe Ferens |
| **Corporate Partnerships** | |
| Senior Account Executive | Carl Levi |
| Account Executives | Bryan Bellows, Michelle Morgan |
| Interactive Account Executive | Brandon Latack |
| Senior Manager, Corporate Service | Kathleen Borschke |
| **Communications and Broadcasting** | |
| Manager, Media Relations and Team Services | Aaron Sickman |
| Coordinator, Media Relations and Team Services | Ryan Stanzel |
| Manager of Broadcasting | Maggie Kukar |
| Radio Operations Coordinator | Kevin Falness |
| Media Relations Apprentice | Carly Peters |
| Radio Play-By-Play / Analyst | Bob Kurtz / Tom Reid |
| Television Play-By-Play / Analyst | Dan Terhaar / Mike Greenlay |
| **Brand Marketing** | |
| Director, Events and Promotions | Wayne Petersen |
| Senior Manager, Digital & Interactive Group | Michael Brinkman |
| Manager, Game Presentation | Paul Loomis |
| Manager, Production Services | Hank Dolan |
| Manager, Marketing | Emily Gausman |
| Manager, E-mail and Database | Holly Doyle |
| Manager, Web and Creative Services | Dewayne Hankins |
| Team Curator | Roger Godin |
| **Community Giving** | |
| Director, Community Partnerships | Brad Bombardir |
| Manager, Community Giving | Amy Woog-Patnode |
| **Finance and Accounting** | |
| Controller | Molly Jungbauer |
| Director, Finance | Mitch Helgerson |
| Senior Manager, Accounting Services | Molly McArdle |
| **Human Resources** | |
| Senior Director, Human Resources | Delores Murphy |
| **Information Technology** | |
| Director, Information Technology | David Weisbrod |
| **Miscellaneous** | |
| Radio Network Flagship | WCCO (830 AM) |
| Television Networks | KSTC.TV Channel 45 (Over-the-Air), Fox Sports Net North (Cable) |
| Team Photographer | Bruce Kluckhohn |
| Public Address Announcer | Adam Abrams |

# Montreal Canadiens

## 2008-09 Results: 41W-30L-4OTL-7SOL 93PTS.

## Second, Northeast Division

### Key Off-Season Signings/Acquisitions

**2009**

**May 13** • Signed 2007 2nd-round pick (43rd overall) D **P.K. Subban.**

**June 1** • Named **Jacques Martin** head coach.

**30** • Acquired C **Scott Gomez**, C **Tom Pyatt** and D **Michael Busto** from NY Rangers for LW **Chris Higgins**, D **Ryan McDonagh**, D **Pavel Valentenko** and D **Doug Janik.**

**July 1** • Signed LW **Mike Cammalleri**, D **Jaroslav Spacek**, D **Hal Gill** and RW **Brian Gionta.**

**6** • Named Perry Pearn assistant coach.

**7** • Signed D **Paul Mara.**

**10** • Signed LW **Travis Moen.**

**11** • Re-signed C **Kyle Chipchura.**

**15** • Re-signed RW **Guillaume Latendresse.**

**20** • Signed G **Curtis Sanford.**

**21** • Re-signed C **Tomas Plekanec.**

### 2009-10 Schedule

|  |  |  |  |
|---|---|---|---|
| **Oct.** | Thu. | 1 | at Toronto |
| | Sat. | 3 | at Buffalo |
| | Tue. | 6 | at Calgary |
| | Wed. | 7 | at Vancouver |
| | Sat. | 10 | at Edmonton |
| | Thu. | 15 | Colorado |
| | Sat. | 17 | Ottawa |
| | Tue. | 20 | Atlanta |
| | Thu. | 22 | NY Islanders |
| | Sat. | 24 | NY Rangers |
| | Mon. | 26 | NY Islanders |
| | Wed. | 28 | at Pittsburgh |
| | Fri. | 30 | at Chicago |
| | Sat. | 31 | Toronto |
| **Nov.** | Tue. | 3 | Atlanta |
| | Thu. | 5 | at Boston |
| | Sat. | 7 | Tampa Bay |
| | Tue. | 10 | Calgary |
| | Thu. | 12 | at Phoenix |
| | Sat. | 14 | at Nashville |
| | Tue. | 17 | Carolina |
| | Fri. | 20 | at Washington |
| | Sat. | 21 | Detroit |
| | Tue. | 24 | Columbus |
| | Wed. | 25 | at Pittsburgh |
| | Sat. | 28 | Washington |
| **Dec.** | Tue. | 1 | Toronto |
| | Thu. | 3 | at Buffalo |
| | Fri. | 4 | Boston |
| | Mon. | 7 | Philadelphia |
| | Tue. | 8 | at Ottawa |
| | Thu. | 10 | Pittsburgh |
| | Sat. | 12 | at Atlanta |
| | Mon. | 14 | Buffalo |
| | Wed. | 16 | at New Jersey |
| | Thu. | 17 | Minnesota |
| | Sat. | 19 | at NY Islanders |
| | Mon. | 21 | at Atlanta |
| | Wed. | 23 | at Carolina |
| | Sat. | 26 | at Toronto |
| | Mon. | 28 | at Ottawa |
| | Wed. | 30 | at Tampa Bay |
| | Thu. | 31 | at Florida* |
| **Jan.** | Sun. | 3 | Buffalo* |
| | Tue. | 5 | at Washington |
| | Thu. | 7 | Florida |
| | Sat. | 9 | New Jersey |
| | Thu. | 14 | Dallas |
| | Sat. | 16 | Ottawa* |
| | Sun. | 17 | at NY Rangers |
| | Wed. | 20 | St. Louis |
| | Fri. | 22 | at New Jersey |
| | Sat. | 23 | NY Rangers |
| | Tue. | 26 | at Florida |
| | Wed. | 27 | at Tampa Bay |
| | Sat. | 30 | at Ottawa* |
| **Feb.** | Tue. | 2 | Vancouver |
| | Thu. | 4 | at Boston |
| | Sat. | 6 | Pittsburgh* |
| | Sun. | 7 | Boston* |
| | Wed. | 10 | Washington |
| | Fri. | 12 | at Philadelphia |
| | Sat. | 13 | Philadelphia |
| **Mar.** | Tue. | 2 | at Boston |
| | Thu. | 4 | at San Jose |
| | Sat. | 6 | at Los Angeles |
| | Sun. | 7 | at Anaheim* |
| | Tue. | 9 | Tampa Bay |
| | Thu. | 11 | Edmonton |
| | Sat. | 13 | Boston |
| | Tue. | 16 | at NY Rangers |
| | Sat. | 20 | at Toronto |
| | Mon. | 22 | Ottawa |
| | Wed. | 24 | at Buffalo |
| | Thu. | 25 | Florida |
| | Sat. | 27 | New Jersey |
| | Wed. | 31 | Carolina |
| **Apr.** | Fri. | 2 | at Philadelphia |
| | Sat. | 3 | Buffalo |
| | Tue. | 6 | at NY Islanders |
| | Thu. | 8 | at Carolina |
| | Sat. | 10 | Toronto |

* Denotes afternoon game.

### Year-by-Year Record

| Season | GP | Home W | Home L | Home T | Home OL | Road W | Road L | Road T | Road OL | Overall W | Overall L | Overall T | Overall OL | GF | GA | Pts. | Finished | Playoff Result |
|---|---|---|---|---|---|---|---|---|---|---|---|---|---|---|---|---|---|---|
| 2008-09 | 82 | 24 | 10 | .... | 7 | 17 | 20 | .... | 4 | 41 | 30 | .... | 11 | 249 | 247 | 93 | 2nd, Northeast Div. | Lost Conf. Quarter-Final |
| 2007-08 | 82 | 22 | 13 | .... | 6 | 25 | 12 | .... | 4 | 47 | 25 | .... | 10 | 262 | 222 | 104 | 1st, Northeast Div. | Lost Conf. Semi-Final |
| 2006-07 | 82 | 26 | 12 | .... | 3 | 16 | 22 | .... | 3 | 42 | 34 | .... | 6 | 245 | 256 | 90 | 4th, Northeast Div. | Out of Playoffs |
| 2005-06 | 82 | 24 | 13 | .... | 4 | 18 | 18 | .... | 5 | 42 | 31 | .... | 9 | 243 | 247 | 93 | 3rd, Northeast Div. | Lost Conf. Quarter-Final |
| 2004-05 | .... | .... | .... | .... | .... | .... | .... | .... | .... | .... | .... | .... | .... | .... | .... | .... | | |
| 2003-04 | 82 | 23 | 13 | 4 | 1 | 18 | 17 | 3 | 3 | 41 | 30 | 7 | 4 | 208 | 192 | 93 | 4th, Northeast Div. | Lost Conf. Semi-Final |
| 2002-03 | 82 | 16 | 16 | 5 | 4 | 14 | 19 | 3 | 5 | 30 | 35 | 8 | 9 | 206 | 234 | 77 | 4th, Northeast Div. | Out of Playoffs |
| 2001-02 | 82 | 21 | 13 | 6 | 1 | 15 | 18 | 6 | 2 | 36 | 31 | 12 | 3 | 207 | 209 | 87 | 4th, Northeast Div. | Lost Conf. Semi-Final |
| 2000-01 | 82 | 15 | 20 | 4 | 2 | 13 | 20 | 4 | 4 | 28 | 40 | 8 | 6 | 206 | 232 | 70 | 5th, Northeast Div. | Out of Playoffs |
| 1999-2000 | 82 | 18 | 17 | 5 | 1 | 17 | 17 | 4 | 3 | 35 | 34 | 9 | 4 | 196 | 194 | 83 | 4th, Northeast Div. | Out of Playoffs |
| 1998-99 | 82 | 21 | 15 | 5 | .... | 11 | 24 | 6 | .... | 32 | 39 | 11 | .... | 184 | 209 | 75 | 5th, Northeast Div. | Out of Playoffs |
| 1997-98 | 82 | 15 | 17 | 9 | .... | 22 | 15 | 4 | .... | 37 | 32 | 13 | .... | 235 | 208 | 87 | 4th, Northeast Div. | Lost Conf. Semi-Final |
| 1996-97 | 82 | 17 | 17 | 7 | .... | 14 | 19 | 8 | .... | 31 | 36 | 15 | .... | 249 | 276 | 77 | 4th, Northeast Div. | Lost Conf. Quarter-Final |
| 1995-96 | 82 | 23 | 12 | 6 | .... | 17 | 20 | 4 | .... | 40 | 32 | 10 | .... | 265 | 248 | 90 | 3rd, Northeast Div. | Lost Conf. Quarter-Final |
| 1994-95 | 48 | 15 | 5 | 4 | .... | 3 | 18 | 3 | .... | 18 | 23 | 7 | .... | 125 | 148 | 43 | 6th, Northeast Div. | Out of Playoffs |
| 1993-94 | 84 | 26 | 12 | 4 | .... | 15 | 17 | 10 | .... | 41 | 29 | 14 | .... | 283 | 248 | 96 | 3rd, Northeast Div. | Lost Conf. Quarter-Final |
| **1992-93** | **84** | **27** | **13** | **2** | .... | **21** | **17** | **4** | .... | **48** | **30** | **6** | .... | **326** | **280** | **102** | **3rd, Adams Div.** | **Won Stanley Cup** |
| 1991-92 | 80 | 27 | 8 | 5 | .... | 14 | 20 | 6 | .... | 41 | 28 | 11 | .... | 267 | 207 | 93 | 1st, Adams Div. | Lost Div. Final |
| 1990-91 | 80 | 23 | 12 | 5 | .... | 16 | 18 | 6 | .... | 39 | 30 | 11 | .... | 273 | 249 | 89 | 2nd, Adams Div. | Lost Div. Final |
| 1989-90 | 80 | 26 | 8 | 6 | .... | 15 | 20 | 5 | .... | 41 | 28 | 11 | .... | 288 | 234 | 93 | 3rd, Adams Div. | Lost Div. Final |
| 1988-89 | 80 | 30 | 6 | 4 | .... | 23 | 12 | 5 | .... | 53 | 18 | 9 | .... | 315 | 218 | 115 | 1st, Adams Div. | Lost Final |
| 1987-88 | 80 | 26 | 8 | 6 | .... | 19 | 14 | 7 | .... | 45 | 22 | 13 | .... | 298 | 238 | 103 | 1st, Adams Div. | Lost Div. Final |
| 1986-87 | 80 | 27 | 9 | 4 | .... | 14 | 20 | 6 | .... | 41 | 29 | 10 | .... | 277 | 241 | 92 | 2nd, Adams Div. | Lost Conf. Championship |
| **1985-86** | **80** | **25** | **11** | **4** | .... | **15** | **22** | **3** | .... | **40** | **33** | **7** | .... | **330** | **280** | **87** | **2nd, Adams Div.** | **Won Stanley Cup** |
| 1984-85 | 80 | 24 | 10 | 6 | .... | 17 | 17 | 6 | .... | 41 | 27 | 12 | .... | 309 | 262 | 94 | 1st, Adams Div. | Lost Div. Final |
| 1983-84 | 80 | 19 | 19 | 2 | .... | 16 | 21 | 3 | .... | 35 | 40 | 5 | .... | 286 | 295 | 75 | 4th, Adams Div. | Lost Conf. Championship |
| 1982-83 | 80 | 25 | 6 | 9 | .... | 17 | 18 | 5 | .... | 42 | 24 | 14 | .... | 350 | 286 | 98 | 2nd, Adams Div. | Lost Div. Semi-Final |
| 1981-82 | 80 | 25 | 6 | 9 | .... | 21 | 11 | 8 | .... | 46 | 17 | 17 | .... | 360 | 223 | 109 | 1st, Adams Div. | Lost Div. Semi-Final |
| 1980-81 | 80 | 31 | 7 | 2 | .... | 14 | 15 | 11 | .... | 45 | 22 | 13 | .... | 332 | 232 | 103 | 1st, Norris Div. | Lost Prelim. Round |
| 1979-80 | 80 | 30 | 7 | 3 | .... | 17 | 13 | 10 | .... | 47 | 20 | 13 | .... | 328 | 240 | 107 | 1st, Norris Div. | Lost Quarter-Final |
| **1978-79** | **80** | **29** | **6** | **5** | .... | **23** | **11** | **6** | .... | **52** | **17** | **11** | .... | **337** | **204** | **115** | **1st, Norris Div.** | **Won Stanley Cup** |
| **1977-78** | **80** | **32** | **4** | **4** | .... | **27** | **6** | **7** | .... | **59** | **10** | **11** | .... | **359** | **183** | **129** | **1st, Norris Div.** | **Won Stanley Cup** |
| **1976-77** | **80** | **33** | **1** | **6** | .... | **27** | **7** | **6** | .... | **60** | **8** | **12** | .... | **387** | **171** | **132** | **1st, Norris Div.** | **Won Stanley Cup** |
| **1975-76** | **80** | **32** | **3** | **5** | .... | **26** | **8** | **6** | .... | **58** | **11** | **11** | .... | **337** | **174** | **127** | **1st, Norris Div.** | **Won Stanley Cup** |
| 1974-75 | 80 | 27 | 8 | 5 | .... | 20 | 6 | 14 | .... | 47 | 14 | 19 | .... | 374 | 225 | 113 | 1st, Norris Div. | Lost Semi-Final |
| 1973-74 | 78 | 24 | 12 | 3 | .... | 21 | 12 | 6 | .... | 45 | 24 | 9 | .... | 293 | 240 | 99 | 2nd, East Div. | Lost Quarter-Final |
| **1972-73** | **78** | **29** | **4** | **6** | .... | **23** | **6** | **10** | .... | **52** | **10** | **16** | .... | **329** | **184** | **120** | **1st, East Div.** | **Won Stanley Cup** |
| 1971-72 | 78 | 29 | 3 | 7 | .... | 17 | 13 | 9 | .... | 46 | 16 | 16 | .... | 307 | 205 | 108 | 3rd, East Div. | Lost Quarter-Final |
| **1970-71** | **78** | **29** | **7** | **3** | .... | **13** | **16** | **10** | .... | **42** | **23** | **13** | .... | **291** | **216** | **97** | **3rd, East Div.** | **Won Stanley Cup** |
| 1969-70 | 76 | 21 | 9 | 8 | .... | 17 | 13 | 8 | .... | 38 | 22 | 16 | .... | 244 | 201 | 92 | 5th, East Div. | Out of Playoffs |
| **1968-69** | **76** | **26** | **7** | **5** | .... | **20** | **12** | **6** | .... | **46** | **19** | **11** | .... | **271** | **202** | **103** | **1st, East Div.** | **Won Stanley Cup** |
| **1967-68** | **74** | **26** | **5** | **6** | .... | **16** | **17** | **4** | .... | **42** | **22** | **10** | .... | **236** | **167** | **94** | **1st, East Div.** | **Won Stanley Cup** |
| 1966-67 | 70 | 19 | 9 | 7 | .... | 13 | 16 | 6 | .... | 32 | 25 | 13 | .... | 202 | 188 | 77 | 2nd, | Lost Final |
| **1965-66** | **70** | **23** | **11** | **1** | .... | **18** | **10** | **7** | .... | **41** | **21** | **8** | .... | **239** | **173** | **90** | **1st,** | **Won Stanley Cup** |
| **1964-65** | **70** | **20** | **8** | **7** | .... | **16** | **15** | **4** | .... | **36** | **23** | **11** | .... | **211** | **185** | **83** | **2nd,** | **Won Stanley Cup** |
| 1963-64 | 70 | 22 | 7 | 6 | .... | 14 | 14 | 7 | .... | 36 | 21 | 13 | .... | 209 | 167 | 85 | 1st, | Lost Semi-Final |
| 1962-63 | 70 | 15 | 10 | 10 | .... | 13 | 9 | 13 | .... | 28 | 19 | 23 | .... | 225 | 183 | 79 | 3rd, | Lost Semi-Final |
| 1961-62 | 70 | 26 | 2 | 7 | .... | 16 | 12 | 7 | .... | 42 | 14 | 14 | .... | 259 | 166 | 98 | 1st, | Lost Semi-Final |
| 1960-61 | 70 | 24 | 6 | 5 | .... | 17 | 13 | 5 | .... | 41 | 19 | 10 | .... | 254 | 188 | 92 | 1st, | Lost Semi-Final |
| **1959-60** | **70** | **23** | **4** | **8** | .... | **17** | **14** | **4** | .... | **40** | **18** | **12** | .... | **255** | **178** | **92** | **1st,** | **Won Stanley Cup** |
| **1958-59** | **70** | **21** | **8** | **6** | .... | **18** | **10** | **7** | .... | **39** | **18** | **13** | .... | **258** | **158** | **91** | **1st,** | **Won Stanley Cup** |
| **1957-58** | **70** | **23** | **8** | **4** | .... | **20** | **9** | **6** | .... | **43** | **17** | **10** | .... | **250** | **158** | **96** | **1st,** | **Won Stanley Cup** |
| **1956-57** | **70** | **23** | **6** | **6** | .... | **12** | **17** | **6** | .... | **35** | **23** | **12** | .... | **210** | **155** | **82** | **2nd,** | **Won Stanley Cup** |
| **1955-56** | **70** | **29** | **5** | **1** | .... | **16** | **10** | **9** | .... | **45** | **15** | **10** | .... | **222** | **131** | **100** | **1st,** | **Won Stanley Cup** |
| 1954-55 | 70 | 26 | 5 | 4 | .... | 15 | 13 | 7 | .... | 41 | 18 | 11 | .... | 228 | 157 | 93 | 2nd, | Lost Final |
| 1953-54 | 70 | 27 | 5 | 3 | .... | 8 | 19 | 8 | .... | 35 | 24 | 11 | .... | 195 | 141 | 81 | 2nd, | Lost Final |
| **1952-53** | **70** | **18** | **12** | **5** | .... | **10** | **11** | **14** | .... | **28** | **23** | **19** | .... | **155** | **148** | **75** | **2nd,** | **Won Stanley Cup** |
| 1951-52 | 70 | 22 | 8 | 5 | .... | 12 | 18 | 5 | .... | 34 | 26 | 10 | .... | 195 | 164 | 78 | 2nd, | Lost Final |
| 1950-51 | 70 | 17 | 10 | 8 | .... | 8 | 20 | 7 | .... | 25 | 30 | 15 | .... | 173 | 184 | 65 | 3rd, | Lost Final |
| 1949-50 | 70 | 17 | 8 | 10 | .... | 12 | 14 | 9 | .... | 29 | 22 | 19 | .... | 172 | 150 | 77 | 2nd, | Lost Semi-Final |
| 1948-49 | 60 | 19 | 8 | 3 | .... | 9 | 15 | 6 | .... | 28 | 23 | 9 | .... | 152 | 126 | 65 | 3rd, | Lost Semi-Final |
| 1947-48 | 60 | 13 | 13 | 4 | .... | 7 | 16 | 7 | .... | 20 | 29 | 11 | .... | 147 | 169 | 51 | 5th, | Out of Playoffs |
| 1946-47 | 60 | 19 | 6 | 5 | .... | 15 | 10 | 5 | .... | 34 | 16 | 10 | .... | 189 | 138 | 78 | 1st, | Lost Final |
| **1945-46** | **50** | **16** | **6** | **3** | .... | **12** | **11** | **2** | .... | **28** | **17** | **5** | .... | **172** | **134** | **61** | **1st,** | **Won Stanley Cup** |
| 1944-45 | 50 | 21 | 2 | 2 | .... | 17 | 6 | 2 | .... | 38 | 8 | 4 | .... | 228 | 121 | 80 | 1st, | Lost Semi-Final |
| **1943-44** | **50** | **22** | **0** | **3** | .... | **16** | **5** | **4** | .... | **38** | **5** | **7** | .... | **234** | **109** | **83** | **1st,** | **Won Stanley Cup** |
| 1942-43 | 50 | 14 | 4 | 7 | .... | 5 | 15 | 5 | .... | 19 | 19 | 12 | .... | 181 | 191 | 50 | 4th, | Lost Semi-Final |
| 1941-42 | 48 | 12 | 10 | 2 | .... | 6 | 17 | 1 | .... | 18 | 27 | 3 | .... | 134 | 173 | 39 | 6th, | Lost Quarter-Final |
| 1940-41 | 48 | 11 | 9 | 4 | .... | 5 | 17 | 2 | .... | 16 | 26 | 6 | .... | 121 | 147 | 38 | 6th, | Lost Quarter-Final |
| 1939-40 | 48 | 5 | 14 | 5 | .... | 5 | 19 | 0 | .... | 10 | 33 | 5 | .... | 90 | 168 | 25 | 7th, | Out of Playoffs |
| 1938-39 | 48 | 8 | 11 | 5 | .... | 7 | 13 | 4 | .... | 15 | 24 | 9 | .... | 115 | 146 | 39 | 6th, | Lost Quarter-Final |
| 1937-38 | 48 | 13 | 4 | 7 | .... | 5 | 13 | 6 | .... | 18 | 17 | 13 | .... | 123 | 128 | 49 | 3rd, Cdn. Div. | Lost Quarter-Final |
| 1936-37 | 48 | 16 | 8 | 0 | .... | 8 | 10 | 6 | .... | 24 | 18 | 6 | .... | 115 | 111 | 54 | 1st, Cdn. Div. | Lost Semi-Final |
| 1935-36 | 48 | 5 | 11 | 8 | .... | 6 | 15 | 3 | .... | 11 | 26 | 11 | .... | 82 | 123 | 33 | 4th, Cdn. Div. | Out of Playoffs |
| 1934-35 | 48 | 11 | 11 | 2 | .... | 8 | 12 | 4 | .... | 19 | 23 | 6 | .... | 110 | 145 | 44 | 3rd, Cdn. Div. | Lost Quarter-Final |
| 1933-34 | 48 | 16 | 6 | 2 | .... | 6 | 14 | 4 | .... | 22 | 20 | 6 | .... | 99 | 101 | 50 | 2nd, Cdn. Div. | Lost Quarter-Final |
| 1932-33 | 48 | 15 | 5 | 4 | .... | 3 | 20 | 1 | .... | 18 | 25 | 5 | .... | 92 | 115 | 41 | 3rd, Cdn. Div. | Lost Quarter-Final |
| 1931-32 | 48 | 18 | 3 | 3 | .... | 7 | 13 | 4 | .... | 25 | 16 | 7 | .... | 128 | 111 | 57 | 1st, Cdn. Div. | Lost Semi-Final |
| **1930-31** | **44** | **15** | **3** | **4** | .... | **11** | **7** | **4** | .... | **26** | **10** | **8** | .... | **129** | **89** | **60** | **1st, Cdn. Div.** | **Won Stanley Cup** |
| **1929-30** | **44** | **13** | **5** | **4** | .... | **8** | **9** | **5** | .... | **21** | **14** | **9** | .... | **142** | **114** | **51** | **2nd, Cdn. Div.** | **Won Stanley Cup** |
| 1928-29 | 44 | 12 | 4 | 6 | .... | 10 | 3 | 9 | .... | 22 | 7 | 15 | .... | 71 | 43 | 59 | 1st, Cdn. Div. | Lost Semi-Final |
| 1927-28 | 44 | 12 | 7 | 3 | .... | 14 | 4 | 4 | .... | 26 | 11 | 7 | .... | 116 | 48 | 59 | 1st, Cdn. Div. | Lost Semi-Final |
| 1926-27 | 44 | 15 | 5 | 2 | .... | 13 | 9 | 0 | .... | 28 | 14 | 2 | .... | 99 | 67 | 58 | 2nd, Cdn. Div. | Lost Semi-Final |
| 1925-26 | 36 | 5 | 12 | 1 | .... | 6 | 12 | 0 | .... | 11 | 24 | 1 | .... | 79 | 108 | 23 | 7th, | Out of Playoffs |
| 1924-25 | 30 | 10 | 5 | 0 | .... | 7 | 6 | 2 | .... | 17 | 11 | 2 | .... | 93 | 56 | 36 | 3rd, | Lost Final |
| **1923-24** | **24** | **10** | **2** | **0** | .... | **3** | **9** | **0** | .... | **13** | **11** | **0** | .... | **59** | **48** | **26** | **2nd,** | **Won Stanley Cup** |
| 1922-23 | 24 | 10 | 2 | 0 | .... | 3 | 7 | 2 | .... | 13 | 9 | 2 | .... | 73 | 61 | 28 | 2nd, | Lost NHL Final |
| 1921-22 | 24 | 8 | 3 | 1 | .... | 4 | 8 | 0 | .... | 12 | 11 | 1 | .... | 88 | 94 | 25 | 3rd, | Out of Playoffs |
| 1920-21 | 24 | 9 | 3 | 0 | .... | 4 | 8 | 0 | .... | 13 | 11 | 0 | .... | 112 | 99 | 26 | 3rd and 2nd* | Out of Playoffs |
| 1919-20 | 24 | 8 | 4 | 0 | .... | 5 | 7 | 0 | .... | 13 | 11 | 0 | .... | 129 | 113 | 26 | 2nd and 3rd* | Out of Playoffs |
| 1918-19 | 18 | 7 | 2 | 0 | .... | 3 | 6 | 0 | .... | 10 | 8 | 0 | .... | 88 | 78 | 20 | 1st and 2nd* | Cup Final but no Decision |
| 1917-18 | 22 | 8 | 3 | 0 | .... | 5 | 6 | 0 | .... | 13 | 9 | 0 | .... | 115 | 84 | 26 | 1st and 3rd* | Lost NHL Final |

* Season played in two halves with no combined standing at end.
From 1917-18 through 1925-26, NHL champions played against PCHA/WCHL champions for Stanley Cup.

**NORTHEAST DIVISION**
**93rd NHL Season**

**Franchise date:** November 22, 1917

# 2009-10 Player Personnel

| FORWARDS | HT | WT | S | Place of Birth | *Age | 2008-09 Club |
|---|---|---|---|---|---|---|
| CAMMALLERI, Michael | 5-9 | 185 | L | Richmond Hill, Ont. | 27 | Calgary |
| CHIPCHURA, Kyle | 6-2 | 204 | L | Westlock, Alta. | 23 | Montreal-Hamilton |
| D'AGOSTINI, Matt | 6-0 | 200 | R | Sault Ste. Marie, Ont. | 22 | Montreal-Hamilton |
| GIONTA, Brian | 5-7 | 175 | R | Rochester, NY | 30 | New Jersey |
| GOMEZ, Scott | 5-11 | 200 | L | Anchorage, AK | 29 | NY Rangers |
| KOSTITSYN, Andrei | 6-0 | 208 | L | Novopolotsk, USSR | 24 | Montreal |
| KOSTITSYN, Sergei | 6-0 | 204 | L | Novopolotsk, USSR | 22 | Montreal-Hamilton |
| LAPIERRE, Maxim | 6-2 | 207 | R | St. Leonard, Que. | 24 | Montreal |
| LARAQUE, Georges | 6-3 | 253 | R | Montreal, Que. | 32 | Montreal |
| LATENDRESSE, Guillaume | 6-2 | 230 | L | Ste-Catherine, Que. | 22 | Montreal |
| METROPOLIT, Glen | 5-10 | 195 | R | Toronto, Ont. | 35 | Philadelphia-Montreal |
| MOEN, Travis | 6-2 | 215 | L | Stewart Valley, Sask. | 27 | Anaheim-San Jose |
| PACIORETTY, Max | 6-2 | 192 | L | New Canaan, CT | 20 | Montreal-Hamilton |
| PLEKANEC, Tomas | 5-11 | 197 | L | Kladno, Czech. | 26 | Montreal |
| STEWART, Greg | 6-2 | 200 | L | Kitchener, Ont. | 23 | Montreal-Hamilton |
| **DEFENSEMEN** | | | | | | |
| GILL, Hal | 6-7 | 250 | L | Concord, MA | 34 | Pittsburgh |
| GORGES, Josh | 6-1 | 202 | L | Kelowna, B.C. | 25 | Montreal |
| HAMRLIK, Roman | 6-2 | 209 | L | Zlin, Czech. | 35 | Montreal |
| MARA, Paul | 6-4 | 212 | L | Ridgewood, NJ | 30 | NY Rangers |
| MARKOV, Andrei | 6-0 | 209 | L | Voskresensk, USSR | 30 | Montreal |
| O'BYRNE, Ryan | 6-5 | 228 | R | Victoria, B.C. | 25 | Montreal-Hamilton |
| SPACEK, Jaroslav | 5-11 | 204 | L | Rokycany, Czech. | 35 | Buffalo |
| WEBER, Yannick | 5-11 | 197 | R | Morges, Switz. | 21 | Montreal-Hamilton |

| GOALTENDERS | HT | WT | C | Place of Birth | *Age | 2008-09 Club |
|---|---|---|---|---|---|---|
| HALAK, Jaroslav | 5-11 | 182 | L | Bratislava, Czech. | 24 | Montreal |
| PRICE, Carey | 6-3 | 219 | L | Vancouver, B.C. | 22 | Montreal |

* – Age at start of 2009-10 season

## Captains' History

Jack Laviolette, 1909-10; Newsy Lalonde, 1910-11; Jack Laviolette, 1911-12; Newsy Lalonde, 1912-13; Jimmy Gardner, 1913-14, 1914-15; Howard McNamara, 1915-16; Newsy Lalonde, 1916-17 to 1921-22; Sprague Cleghorn, 1922-23 to 1924-25; Bill Coutu, 1925-26; Sylvio Mantha, 1926-27 to 1931-32; George Hainsworth, 1932-33; Sylvio Mantha, 1933-34 to 1935-36; Babe Siebert, 1936-37 to 1938-39; Walt Buswell, 1939-40; Toe Blake, 1940-41 to 1946-47; Toe Blake and Bill Durnan, 1947-48; Butch Bouchard, 1948-49 to 1955-56; Maurice Richard, 1956-57 to 1959-60; Doug Harvey, 1960-61; Jean Béliveau, 1961-62 to 1970-71; Henri Richard, 1971-72 to 1974-75; Yvan Cournoyer, 1975-76 to 1978-79; Serge Savard, 1979-80, 1980-81; Bob Gainey, 1981-82 to 1988-89; Guy Carbonneau and Chris Chelios, 1989-90; Guy Carbonneau, 1990-91 to 1993-94; Kirk Muller and Mike Keane, 1994-95; Mike Keane and Pierre Turgeon, 1995-96; Pierre Turgeon and Vincent Damphousse, 1996-97; Vincent Damphousse, 1997-98, 1998-99; Saku Koivu, 1999-2000 to 2008-09.

## General Managers' History

Jack Laviolette and Joseph Cattarinich, 1909-1910; George Kennedy, 1910-11 to 1920-21; Leo Dandurand, 1921-22 to 1934-35; Ernest Savard, 1935-36; Cecil Hart, 1936-37 to 1938-39; Jules Dugal, 1939-40; Tom P. Gorman, 1940-41 to 1945-46; Frank J. Selke, 1946-47 to 1963-64; Sam Pollock, 1964-65 to 1977-78; Irving Grundman, 1978-79 to 1982-83; Serge Savard, 1983-84 to 1994-95; Serge Savard and Réjean Houle, 1995-96; Réjean Houle, 1996-97 to 1999-2000; Réjean Houle and Andre Savard, 2000-01; Andre Savard, 2001-02, 2002-03; Bob Gainey, 2003-04 to date.

# Bob Gainey

## Vice President and General Manager

*Born: Peterborough, Ont., December 13, 1953.*

On June 2, 2003, the Montreal Canadiens announced the appointment of Bob Gainey as executive vice president and general manager, effective July 1, 2003. Twice during his tenure as general manager (in 2005-06 and 2008-09) Gainey has also taken over behind the bench. In 2007-08 the Canadiens finished first overall in the Eastern Conference.

As a player in Montreal, Gainey brought many elements to the Canadiens over his 16-year career. Described as the world's best all-around player by legendary Soviet national team coach Viktor Tikhonov, Gainey was a tenacious competitor, relentless checker and a respected team leader. His play helped the Canadiens win the Stanley Cup five times in the decade between 1976 and 1986. He won the Conn Smythe Trophy as playoff MVP in 1979 and was a four-time winner of the Selke Trophy as the NHL's best defensive forward. Gainey was captain of the Canadiens from 1981 until his retirement in 1989. He was elected to the Hockey Hall of Fame in 1992.

Gainey spent a year as a player-coach of the Epinal franchise in France before becoming head coach of the Minnesota North Stars in 1990-91. He was given the g.m.'s job in 1992 and was in the dual role when the Stars relocated to Dallas in 1993. Gainey stepped down as coach on January 8, 1996 to focus solely on the duties of general manager and built a powerhouse club that won five straight division titles from 1996-97 to 2000-01, the Presidents' Trophy in 1998 and 1999, and the Stanley Cup in 1999.

### Coaching Record

| | | | Regular Season | | | | Playoffs | | | |
|---|---|---|---|---|---|---|---|---|---|---|
| Season | Team | League | GC | W | L | O/T | GC | W | L | T |
| 1990-91 | Minnesota | NHL | 80 | 27 | 39 | 14 | 23 | 14 | 9 | .... |
| 1991-92 | Minnesota | NHL | 80 | 32 | 42 | 6 | 7 | 3 | 4 | .... |
| 1992-93 | Minnesota | NHL | 84 | 36 | 38 | 10 | .... | .... | .... | .... |
| 1993-94 | Dallas | NHL | 84 | 42 | 29 | 13 | 9 | 5 | 4 | .... |
| 1994-95 | Dallas | NHL | 48 | 17 | 23 | 8 | 5 | 1 | 4 | .... |
| 1995-96 | Dallas | NHL | 39 | 11 | 19 | 9 | .... | .... | .... | .... |
| 2005-06 | Montreal | NHL | 41 | 23 | 15 | 3 | 6 | 2 | 4 | .... |
| 2008-09 | Montreal | NHL | 16 | 6 | 6 | 4 | 4 | 0 | 4 | .... |
| | **NHL Totals** | | **472** | **194** | **211** | **67** | **54** | **25** | **29** | .... |

# 2008-09 Scoring

* – rookie

## Regular Season

| Pos | # | Player | Team | GP | G | A | Pts | TOI | +/- | PIM | PP | SH | GW | S | % |
|---|---|---|---|---|---|---|---|---|---|---|---|---|---|---|---|
| R | 27 | Alex Kovalev | MTL | 78 | 26 | 39 | 65 | 19:25 | –5 | 74 | 11 | 1 | 4 | 209 | 12.4 |
| D | 79 | Andrei Markov | MTL | 78 | 12 | 52 | 64 | 24:37 | –2 | 36 | 7 | 0 | 3 | 165 | 7.3 |
| C | 11 | Saku Koivu | MTL | 65 | 16 | 34 | 50 | 17:03 | 4 | 44 | 5 | 0 | 5 | 123 | 13.0 |
| L | 46 | Andrei Kostitsyn | MTL | 74 | 23 | 18 | 41 | 15:35 | –7 | 50 | 6 | 0 | 2 | 169 | 13.6 |
| L | 13 | Alex Tanguay | MTL | 50 | 16 | 25 | 41 | 16:05 | 13 | 34 | 5 | 0 | 3 | 76 | 21.1 |
| C | 14 | Tomas Plekanec | MTL | 80 | 20 | 19 | 39 | 17:15 | –9 | 54 | 6 | 3 | 2 | 202 | 9.9 |
| C | 20 | Robert Lang | MTL | 50 | 18 | 21 | 39 | 16:52 | 6 | 36 | 8 | 1 | 3 | 101 | 17.8 |
| D | 44 | Roman Hamrlik | MTL | 81 | 6 | 27 | 33 | 21:54 | 4 | 62 | 0 | 0 | 0 | 143 | 4.2 |
| D | 24 | Mathieu Schneider | ATL | 44 | 4 | 11 | 15 | 21:02 | –10 | 50 | 1 | 0 | 0 | 82 | 4.9 |
| | | | MTL | 23 | 5 | 12 | 17 | 20:56 | –2 | 14 | 5 | 0 | 2 | 46 | 10.9 |
| | | | Total | 67 | 9 | 23 | 32 | 21:00 | –12 | 64 | 6 | 0 | 2 | 128 | 7.0 |
| C | 40 | Maxim Lapierre | MTL | 79 | 15 | 13 | 28 | 14:47 | 9 | 76 | 1 | 2 | 2 | 165 | 9.1 |
| L | 84 | Guillaume Latendresse | MTL | 56 | 14 | 12 | 26 | 13:36 | 4 | 45 | 1 | 0 | 2 | 117 | 12.0 |
| L | 21 | Chris Higgins | MTL | 57 | 12 | 11 | 23 | 16:59 | –1 | 22 | 2 | 2 | 1 | 151 | 7.9 |
| L | 74 | Sergei Kostitsyn | MTL | 56 | 8 | 15 | 23 | 14:08 | –3 | 64 | 5 | 0 | 1 | 74 | 10.8 |
| D | 26 | Josh Gorges | MTL | 81 | 4 | 19 | 23 | 20:07 | 12 | 37 | 2 | 0 | 0 | 63 | 6.3 |
| R | 6 | Tom Kostopoulos | MTL | 78 | 8 | 14 | 22 | 14:08 | –1 | 106 | 0 | 1 | 0 | 121 | 6.6 |
| R | 36 * | Matt D'Agostini | MTL | 53 | 12 | 9 | 21 | 13:24 | –17 | 16 | 3 | 0 | 1 | 116 | 10.3 |
| D | 71 | Patrice Brisebois | MTL | 62 | 5 | 13 | 18 | 15:54 | –3 | 19 | 4 | 0 | 1 | 68 | 7.4 |
| C | 15 | Glen Metropolit | PHI | 55 | 4 | 10 | 14 | 12:58 | –1 | 15 | 1 | 0 | 0 | 63 | 6.3 |
| | | | MTL | 21 | 2 | 1 | 3 | 11:37 | –4 | 13 | 0 | 0 | 0 | 19 | 10.5 |
| | | | Total | 76 | 6 | 11 | 17 | 12:36 | –5 | 28 | 1 | 0 | 0 | 82 | 7.3 |
| R | 25 | Mathieu Dandenault | MTL | 41 | 4 | 8 | 12 | 11:45 | 7 | 17 | 0 | 0 | 0 | 46 | 8.7 |
| L | 67 * | Max Pacioretty | MTL | 34 | 3 | 8 | 11 | 12:37 | –3 | 27 | 1 | 0 | 0 | 57 | 5.3 |
| D | 8 | Mike Komisarek | MTL | 66 | 2 | 9 | 11 | 20:37 | 0 | 121 | 0 | 0 | 0 | 56 | 3.6 |
| D | 51 | Francis Bouillon | MTL | 54 | 5 | 4 | 9 | 16:29 | –7 | 53 | 0 | 0 | 1 | 51 | 9.8 |
| D | 3 | Ryan O'Byrne | MTL | 37 | 0 | 5 | 5 | 15:05 | –7 | 58 | 0 | 0 | 0 | 14 | 0.0 |
| C | 28 | Kyle Chipchura | MTL | 13 | 0 | 3 | 3 | 10:18 | –6 | 5 | 0 | 0 | 0 | 5 | 0.0 |
| R | 17 | Georges Laraque | MTL | 33 | 0 | 2 | 2 | 7:38 | –6 | 61 | 0 | 0 | 0 | 15 | 0.0 |
| D | 68 * | Yannick Weber | MTL | 3 | 0 | 1 | 1 | 15:05 | –1 | 2 | 0 | 0 | 0 | 6 | 0.0 |
| D | 53 | Doug Janik | DAL | 13 | 0 | 1 | 1 | 9:44 | –2 | 2 | 0 | 0 | 0 | 1 | 0.0 |
| | | | MTL | 2 | 0 | 0 | 0 | 13:53 | –1 | 2 | 0 | 0 | 0 | 0 | 0.0 |
| | | | Total | 15 | 0 | 1 | 1 | 10:17 | –3 | 4 | 0 | 0 | 0 | 1 | 0.0 |
| L | 70 * | Gregory Stewart | MTL | 20 | 0 | 1 | 1 | 8:36 | –4 | 32 | 0 | 0 | 0 | 16 | 0.0 |
| D | 24 | Alex Henry | MTL | 2 | 0 | 0 | 0 | 6:34 | –2 | 10 | 0 | 0 | 0 | 0 | 0.0 |
| C | 80 * | Ben Maxwell | MTL | 7 | 0 | 0 | 0 | 9:55 | –1 | 2 | 0 | 0 | 0 | 2 | 0.0 |

### Goaltending

| No. | Goaltender | GPI | Mins | Avg | W | L | OT | EN | SO | GA | SA | S% | G | A | PIM |
|---|---|---|---|---|---|---|---|---|---|---|---|---|---|---|---|
| 31 | Carey Price | 52 | 3036 | 2.83 | 23 | 16 | 10 | 4 | 1 | 143 | 1513 | .905 | 0 | 1 | 4 |
| 41 | Jaroslav Halak | 34 | 1931 | 2.86 | 18 | 14 | 1 | 0 | 1 | 92 | 1077 | .915 | 0 | 0 | 0 |
| 38 | Marc Denis | 1 | 20 | 3.00 | 0 | 0 | 0 | 0 | 0 | 1 | 7 | .857 | 0 | 0 | 0 |
| | **Totals** | **82** | **5007** | **2.88** | **41** | **30** | **11** | **4** | **2** | **240** | **2601** | **.908** | | | |

## Playoffs

| Pos | # | Player | Team | GP | G | A | Pts | TOI | +/- | PIM | PP | SH | GW | OT | S | % |
|---|---|---|---|---|---|---|---|---|---|---|---|---|---|---|---|---|
| R | 27 | Alex Kovalev | MTL | 4 | 2 | 1 | 3 | 19:53 | 0 | 2 | 0 | 0 | 0 | 0 | 12 | 16.7 |
| C | 11 | Saku Koivu | MTL | 4 | 0 | 3 | 3 | 17:45 | –1 | 2 | 0 | 0 | 0 | 0 | 6 | 0.0 |
| L | 21 | Chris Higgins | MTL | 4 | 2 | 0 | 2 | 17:34 | –1 | 2 | 0 | 0 | 0 | 0 | 8 | 25.0 |
| D | 68 * | Yannick Weber | MTL | 3 | 1 | 1 | 2 | 13:36 | 0 | 0 | 0 | 0 | 0 | 0 | 3 | 33.3 |
| C | 15 | Glen Metropolit | MTL | 4 | 0 | 2 | 2 | 16:04 | 0 | 2 | 0 | 0 | 0 | 0 | 5 | 0.0 |
| L | 46 | Andrei Kostitsyn | MTL | 4 | 1 | 0 | 1 | 14:14 | –2 | 2 | 0 | 0 | 0 | 0 | 9 | 11.1 |
| L | 13 | Alex Tanguay | MTL | 2 | 0 | 1 | 1 | 15:28 | 2 | 2 | 0 | 0 | 0 | 0 | 4 | 0.0 |
| R | 6 | Tom Kostopoulos | MTL | 4 | 0 | 1 | 1 | 14:01 | –1 | 4 | 0 | 0 | 0 | 0 | 5 | 0.0 |
| D | 26 | Josh Gorges | MTL | 4 | 0 | 1 | 1 | 23:45 | 0 | 7 | 0 | 0 | 0 | 0 | 2 | 0.0 |
| D | 71 | Patrice Brisebois | MTL | 1 | 0 | 0 | 0 | 16:07 | –1 | 0 | 0 | 0 | 0 | 0 | 1 | 0.0 |
| D | 51 | Francis Bouillon | MTL | 1 | 0 | 0 | 0 | 1:46 | 0 | 0 | 0 | 0 | 0 | 0 | 0 | 0.0 |
| L | 74 | Sergei Kostitsyn | MTL | 1 | 0 | 0 | 0 | 12:10 | 0 | 2 | 0 | 0 | 0 | 0 | 1 | 0.0 |
| D | 24 | Mathieu Schneider | MTL | 2 | 0 | 0 | 0 | 18:58 | –2 | 4 | 0 | 0 | 0 | 0 | 5 | 0.0 |
| D | 3 | Ryan O'Byrne | MTL | 2 | 0 | 0 | 0 | 13:04 | –1 | 2 | 0 | 0 | 0 | 0 | 0 | 0.0 |
| L | 70 * | Gregory Stewart | MTL | 2 | 0 | 0 | 0 | 8:30 | –3 | 2 | 0 | 0 | 0 | 0 | 2 | 0.0 |
| C | 14 | Tomas Plekanec | MTL | 3 | 0 | 0 | 0 | 13:35 | –5 | 4 | 0 | 0 | 0 | 0 | 1 | 0.0 |
| R | 36 * | Matt D'Agostini | MTL | 3 | 0 | 0 | 0 | 11:49 | –5 | 0 | 0 | 0 | 0 | 0 | 5 | 0.0 |
| D | 44 | Roman Hamrlik | MTL | 4 | 0 | 0 | 0 | 25:18 | –5 | 2 | 0 | 0 | 0 | 0 | 10 | 0.0 |
| R | 25 | Mathieu Dandenault | MTL | 4 | 0 | 0 | 0 | 21:04 | –2 | 0 | 0 | 0 | 0 | 0 | 8 | 0.0 |
| R | 17 | Georges Laraque | MTL | 4 | 0 | 0 | 0 | 10:57 | –1 | 4 | 0 | 0 | 0 | 0 | 5 | 0.0 |
| D | 8 | Mike Komisarek | MTL | 4 | 0 | 0 | 0 | 19:00 | –4 | 20 | 0 | 0 | 0 | 0 | 5 | 0.0 |
| C | 40 | Maxim Lapierre | MTL | 4 | 0 | 0 | 0 | 14:55 | –3 | 26 | 0 | 0 | 0 | 0 | 9 | 0.0 |
| L | 84 | Guillaume Latendresse | MTL | 4 | 0 | 0 | 0 | 11:44 | –2 | 12 | 0 | 0 | 0 | 0 | 5 | 0.0 |

### Goaltending

| No. | Goaltender | GPI | Mins | Avg | W | L | EN | SO | GA | SA | S% | G | A | PIM |
|---|---|---|---|---|---|---|---|---|---|---|---|---|---|---|
| 41 | Jaroslav Halak | 1 | 20 | 0.00 | 0 | 0 | 0 | 0 | 0 | 5 | 1.000 | 0 | 0 | 0 |
| 31 | Carey Price | 4 | 219 | 4.11 | 0 | 4 | 2 | 0 | 15 | 123 | .878 | 0 | 0 | 0 |
| | **Totals** | **4** | **240** | **4.25** | **0** | **4** | **2** | **0** | **17** | **130** | **.869** | | | |

## Coaching History

Jack Laviolette, 1909-10; Adolphe Lecours, 1910-11; Napoleon Dorval, 1911-12, 1912-13; Jimmy Gardner, 1913-14, 1914-15; Newsy Lalonde, 1915-16 to 1920-21; Newsy Lalonde and Léo Dandurand, 1921-22; Léo Dandurand, 1922-23 to 1925-26; Cecil Hart, 1926-27 to 1931-32; Newsy Lalonde, 1932-33, 1933-34; Newsy Lalonde and Léo Dandurand, 1934-35; Sylvio Mantha, 1935-36; Cecil Hart, 1936-37, 1937-38; Cecil Hart and Jules Dugal, 1938-39; Babe Siebert, 1939*; Pit Lepine, 1939-40; Dick Irvin 1940-41 to 1954-55; Toe Blake, 1955-56 to 1967-68; Claude Ruel, 1968-69, 1969-70; Claude Ruel and Al MacNeil, 1970-71; Scotty Bowman, 1971-72 to 1978-79; Bernie Geoffrion and Claude Ruel, 1979-80; Claude Ruel, 1980-81; Bob Berry, 1981-82, 1982-83; Bob Berry and Jacques Lemaire, 1983-84; Jacques Lemaire, 1984-85; Jean Perron, 1985-86 to 1987-88; Pat Burns, 1988-89 to 1991-92; Jacques Demers, 1992-93 to 1994-95; Jacques Demers, Jacques Laperriere, Mario Tremblay, 1995-96; Mario Tremblay, 1996-97; Alain Vigneault, 1997-98 to 1999-2000; Alain Vigneault and Michel Therrien, 2000-01; Michel Therrien, 2001-02; Michel Therrien and Claude Julien, 2002-03; Claude Julien, 2003-04, 2004-05; Claude Julien and Bob Gainey, 2005-06; Guy Carbonneau, 2006-07, 2007-08; Guy Carbonneau and Bob Gainey, 2008-09; Jacques Martin, 2009-10.

# Club Records

## Team

(Figures in brackets for season records are games played; records for fewest points, wins, ties, losses, goals, goals against are for 70 or more games)

| | | |
|---|---|---|
| **Most Points** | *132 | 1976-77 (80) |
| **Most Wins** | 60 | 1976-77 (80) |
| **Most Ties** | 23 | 1962-63 (70) |
| **Most Losses** | 40 | 1983-84 (80), 2000-01 (82) |
| **Most Goals** | 387 | 1976-77 (80) |
| **Most Goals Against** | 295 | 1983-84 (80) |
| **Fewest Points** | 65 | 1950-51 (70) |
| **Fewest Wins** | 25 | 1950-51 (70) |
| **Fewest Ties** | 5 | 1983-84 (80) |
| **Fewest Losses** | *8 | 1976-77 (80) |
| **Fewest Goals** | 155 | 1952-53 (70) |
| **Fewest Goals Against** | *131 | 1955-56 (70) |
| **Longest Winning Streak** | | |
| Overall | 12 | Jan. 6-Feb. 3/68 |
| Home | 13 | Nov. 2/43-Jan. 8/44, Jan. 30-Mar. 26/77 |
| Away | 8 | Dec. 18/77-Jan. 18/78, Jan. 21-Feb. 21/82 |
| **Longest Undefeated Streak** | | |
| Overall | 28 | Dec. 18/77-Feb. 23/78 (23 wins, 5 ties) |
| Home | *34 | Nov. 1/76-Apr. 2/77 (28 wins, 6 ties) |
| Away | *23 | Nov. 27/74-Mar. 12/75 (14 wins, 9 ties) |
| **Longest Losing Streak** | | |
| Overall | 12 | Feb. 13-Mar. 13/26 |
| Home | 7 | Dec. 16/39-Jan. 18/40, Oct. 28-Nov. 25/00 |
| Away | 10 | Jan. 16-Mar. 13/26 |
| **Longest Winless Streak** | | |
| Overall | 12 | Feb. 13-Mar. 13/26 (12 losses), Nov. 28-Dec. 29/35 (8 losses, 4 ties) |
| Home | 15 | Dec. 16/39-Mar. 7/40 (12 losses, 3 ties) |
| Away | 12 | Nov. 26/33-Jan. 28/34 (8 losses, 4 ties), Oct. 20-Dec. 13/51 (8 losses, 4 ties) |
| **Most Shutouts, Season** | *22 | 1928-29 (44) |
| **Most PIM, Season** | 1,847 | 1995-96 (82) |
| **Most Goals, Game** | *16 | Mar. 3/20 (Mtl. 16 at Que. 3) |

## Individual

| | | |
|---|---|---|
| **Most Seasons** | 20 | Henri Richard, Jean Béliveau |
| **Most Games** | 1,256 | Henri Richard |
| **Most Goals, Career** | 544 | Maurice Richard |
| **Most Assists, Career** | 728 | Guy Lafleur |
| **Most Points, Career** | 1,246 | Guy Lafleur (518G, 728A) |
| **Most PIM, Career** | 2,248 | Chris Nilan |
| **Most Shutouts, Career** | 75 | George Hainsworth |
| **Longest Consecutive Games Streak** | 560 | Doug Jarvis (Oct. 8/75-Apr. 4/82) |
| **Most Goals, Season** | 60 | Steve Shutt (1976-77) Guy Lafleur (1977-78) |
| **Most Assists, Season** | 82 | Pete Mahovlich (1974-75) |
| **Most Points, Season** | 136 | Guy Lafleur (1976-77; 56G, 80A) |
| **Most PIM, Season** | 358 | Chris Nilan (1984-85) |
| **Most Points, Defenseman, Season** | 85 | Larry Robinson (1976-77; 19G, 66A) |
| **Most Points, Center, Season** | 117 | Pete Mahovlich (1974-75; 35G, 82A) |
| **Most Points, Right Wing, Season** | 136 | Guy Lafleur (1976-77; 56G, 80A) |
| **Most Points, Left Wing, Season** | 110 | Mats Naslund (1985-86; 43G, 67A) |
| **Most Points, Rookie, Season** | 71 | Mats Naslund (1982-83; 26G, 45A) Kjell Dahlin (1985-86; 32G, 39A) |
| **Most Shutouts, Season** | *22 | George Hainsworth (1928-29) |
| **Most Goals, Game** | 6 | Newsy Lalonde (Jan. 10/20) |
| **Most Assists, Game** | 6 | Elmer Lach (Feb. 6/43) |
| **Most Points, Game** | 8 | Maurice Richard (Dec. 28/44; 5G, 3A) Bert Olmstead (Jan. 9/54; 4G, 4A) |

* NHL Record.

## Retired Numbers

| | | |
|---|---|---|
| 1 | Jacques Plante | 1952-1963 |
| 2 | Doug Harvey | 1947-1961 |
| 4 | Jean Béliveau | 1950-1971 |
| 5 | Bernard Geoffrion | 1950-1964 |
| 7 | Howie Morenz | 1923-1937 |
| 9 | Maurice Richard | 1942-1960 |
| 10 | Guy Lafleur | 1971-1984 |
| 12 | Dickie Moore | 1951-1963 |
| | Yvan Cournoyer | 1963-1979 |
| 16 | Henri Richard | 1955-1975 |
| 18 | Serge Savard | 1966-1981 |
| 19 | Larry Robinson | 1972-1989 |
| 23 | Bob Gainey | 1973-1989 |
| 29 | Ken Dryden | 1970-1979 |
| 33 | Patrick Roy | 1984-1996 |

# All-time Record vs. Other Clubs

## Regular Season

| | At Home | | | | | | | | On Road | | | | | | | | Total | | | | | | | |
|---|---|---|---|---|---|---|---|---|---|---|---|---|---|---|---|---|---|---|---|---|---|---|---|---|
| | GP | W | L | T | OL | GF | GA | PTS | GP | W | L | T | OL | GF | GA | PTS | GP | W | L | T | OL | GF | GA | PTS |
| Anaheim | 10 | 4 | 4 | 2 | 0 | 31 | 30 | 10 | 9 | 5 | 4 | 0 | 0 | 28 | 28 | 10 | 19 | 9 | 8 | 2 | 0 | 59 | 58 | 20 |
| Atlanta | 18 | 13 | 3 | 0 | 2 | 63 | 42 | 28 | 18 | 10 | 5 | 2 | 1 | 46 | 34 | 23 | 36 | 23 | 8 | 2 | 3 | 109 | 76 | 51 |
| Boston | 349 | 201 | 99 | 47 | 2 | 1176 | 823 | 451 | 350 | 133 | 157 | 56 | 4 | 947 | 1030 | 326 | 699 | 334 | 256 | 103 | 6 | 2123 | 1853 | 777 |
| Buffalo | 118 | 65 | 37 | 12 | 4 | 431 | 346 | 146 | 117 | 35 | 60 | 19 | 3 | 309 | 366 | 92 | 235 | 100 | 97 | 31 | 7 | 740 | 712 | 238 |
| Calgary | 48 | 28 | 12 | 8 | 0 | 172 | 117 | 64 | 51 | 26 | 17 | 7 | 1 | 168 | 155 | 60 | 99 | 54 | 29 | 15 | 1 | 340 | 272 | 124 |
| Carolina | 83 | 51 | 23 | 7 | 2 | 323 | 246 | 111 | 86 | 39 | 32 | 13 | 2 | 293 | 251 | 93 | 169 | 90 | 55 | 20 | 4 | 616 | 497 | 204 |
| Chicago | 278 | 176 | 54 | 48 | 0 | 1075 | 657 | 400 | 274 | 125 | 94 | 55 | 0 | 762 | 733 | 305 | 552 | 301 | 148 | 103 | 0 | 1837 | 1390 | 705 |
| Colorado | 65 | 39 | 15 | 10 | 1 | 269 | 203 | 89 | 65 | 27 | 32 | 5 | 1 | 227 | 220 | 60 | 130 | 66 | 47 | 15 | 2 | 496 | 423 | 149 |
| Columbus | 5 | 1 | 2 | 1 | 1 | 6 | 9 | 4 | 3 | 2 | 0 | 0 | 1 | 9 | 7 | 5 | 8 | 3 | 2 | 1 | 2 | 15 | 16 | 9 |
| Dallas | 59 | 38 | 12 | 9 | 0 | 254 | 146 | 85 | 61 | 31 | 18 | 12 | 0 | 207 | 158 | 74 | 120 | 69 | 30 | 21 | 0 | 461 | 304 | 159 |
| Detroit | 283 | 172 | 68 | 43 | 0 | 995 | 640 | 387 | 282 | 98 | 130 | 53 | 1 | 720 | 808 | 250 | 565 | 270 | 198 | 96 | 1 | 1715 | 1448 | 637 |
| Edmonton | 32 | 18 | 9 | 4 | 1 | 112 | 100 | 41 | 37 | 17 | 18 | 0 | 2 | 118 | 129 | 36 | 69 | 35 | 27 | 4 | 3 | 230 | 229 | 77 |
| Florida | 29 | 13 | 11 | 3 | 2 | 76 | 68 | 31 | 30 | 12 | 15 | 3 | 0 | 78 | 87 | 27 | 59 | 25 | 26 | 6 | 2 | 154 | 155 | 58 |
| Los Angeles | 66 | 47 | 8 | 11 | 0 | 296 | 165 | 105 | 66 | 38 | 19 | 9 | 0 | 261 | 201 | 85 | 132 | 85 | 27 | 20 | 0 | 557 | 366 | 190 |
| Minnesota | 4 | 2 | 1 | 1 | 0 | 13 | 10 | 5 | 4 | 2 | 1 | 0 | 1 | 10 | 11 | 5 | 8 | 4 | 2 | 1 | 1 | 23 | 21 | 10 |
| Nashville | 6 | 5 | 0 | 0 | 1 | 22 | 16 | 11 | 5 | 2 | 2 | 1 | 0 | 13 | 19 | 5 | 11 | 7 | 2 | 1 | 1 | 35 | 35 | 16 |
| New Jersey | 62 | 35 | 20 | 6 | 1 | 196 | 152 | 77 | 62 | 26 | 31 | 4 | 1 | 207 | 193 | 57 | 124 | 61 | 51 | 10 | 2 | 403 | 345 | 134 |
| NY Islanders | 68 | 41 | 16 | 9 | 2 | 242 | 186 | 93 | 68 | 30 | 30 | 6 | 2 | 196 | 205 | 68 | 136 | 71 | 46 | 15 | 4 | 438 | 391 | 161 |
| NY Rangers | 298 | 194 | 63 | 40 | 1 | 1155 | 698 | 429 | 298 | 121 | 121 | 54 | 2 | 864 | 860 | 298 | 596 | 315 | 184 | 94 | 3 | 2019 | 1558 | 727 |
| Ottawa | 48 | 26 | 17 | 4 | 1 | 146 | 137 | 57 | 46 | 20 | 23 | 1 | 2 | 127 | 148 | 43 | 94 | 46 | 40 | 5 | 3 | 273 | 285 | 100 |
| Philadelphia | 82 | 40 | 27 | 14 | 1 | 280 | 243 | 95 | 81 | 35 | 29 | 16 | 1 | 249 | 244 | 87 | 163 | 75 | 56 | 30 | 2 | 529 | 487 | 182 |
| Phoenix | 31 | 26 | 3 | 2 | 0 | 151 | 69 | 54 | 30 | 14 | 9 | 7 | 0 | 116 | 96 | 35 | 61 | 40 | 12 | 9 | 0 | 267 | 165 | 89 |
| Pittsburgh | 90 | 65 | 15 | 10 | 0 | 410 | 232 | 140 | 90 | 45 | 30 | 13 | 2 | 319 | 269 | 105 | 180 | 110 | 45 | 23 | 2 | 729 | 501 | 245 |
| St. Louis | 60 | 41 | 11 | 7 | 1 | 258 | 165 | 90 | 59 | 30 | 14 | 15 | 0 | 202 | 152 | 75 | 119 | 71 | 25 | 22 | 1 | 460 | 317 | 165 |
| San Jose | 13 | 9 | 2 | 2 | 0 | 45 | 24 | 20 | 12 | 4 | 5 | 2 | 1 | 32 | 39 | 11 | 25 | 13 | 7 | 4 | 1 | 77 | 63 | 31 |
| Tampa Bay | 30 | 16 | 12 | 1 | 1 | 84 | 72 | 34 | 31 | 14 | 12 | 5 | 0 | 87 | 75 | 33 | 61 | 30 | 24 | 6 | 1 | 171 | 147 | 67 |
| Toronto | 348 | 206 | 96 | 43 | 3 | 1216 | 873 | 458 | 348 | 123 | 178 | 45 | 2 | 918 | 1063 | 293 | 696 | 329 | 274 | 88 | 5 | 2134 | 1936 | 751 |
| Vancouver | 55 | 39 | 11 | 5 | 0 | 247 | 139 | 83 | 57 | 33 | 15 | 8 | 1 | 206 | 156 | 75 | 112 | 72 | 26 | 13 | 1 | 453 | 295 | 158 |
| Washington | 68 | 40 | 18 | 8 | 2 | 256 | 149 | 90 | 67 | 27 | 29 | 9 | 2 | 200 | 189 | 65 | 135 | 67 | 47 | 17 | 4 | 456 | 338 | 155 |
| Defunct Clubs | 231 | 148 | 58 | 25 | 0 | 779 | 469 | 321 | 230 | 98 | 97 | 35 | 0 | 586 | 606 | 231 | 461 | 246 | 155 | 60 | 0 | 1365 | 1075 | 552 |
| **Totals** | **2937** | **1799** | **727** | **382** | **29** | **10779** | **7226** | **4009** | **2937** | **1222** | **1227** | **455** | **33** | **8505** | **8532** | **2932** | **5874** | **3021** | **1954** | **837** | **62** | **19284** | **15758** | **6941** |

## Playoffs

| | Series | W | L | GP | W | L | T | GF | GA | Last Mtg. | Rnd. | Result |
|---|---|---|---|---|---|---|---|---|---|---|---|---|
| Boston | 32 | 24 | 8 | 163 | 99 | 64 | 0 | 494 | 403 | 2009 | CQF | L 0-4 |
| Buffalo | 7 | 4 | 3 | 35 | 18 | 17 | 0 | 124 | 111 | 1998 | CSF | L 0-4 |
| Calgary | 2 | 1 | 1 | 11 | 6 | 5 | 0 | 31 | 32 | 1989 | F | L 2-4 |
| Carolina | 7 | 5 | 2 | 39 | 23 | 16 | 0 | 125 | 106 | 2006 | CQF | L 2-4 |
| Chicago | 17 | 12 | 5 | 81 | 50 | 29 | 2 | 261 | 185 | 1976 | QF | W 4-0 |
| Colorado | 5 | 3 | 2 | 31 | 17 | 14 | 0 | 105 | 85 | 1993 | DSF | W 4-2 |
| Dallas | 2 | 1 | 1 | 13 | 7 | 6 | 0 | 48 | 37 | 1980 | QF | L 3-4 |
| Detroit | 12 | 5 | 7 | 62 | 33 | 29 | 0 | 161 | 149 | 1978 | QF | W 4-1 |
| Edmonton | 1 | 0 | 1 | 3 | 0 | 3 | 0 | 6 | 15 | 1981 | PRE | L 0-3 |
| Los Angeles | 1 | 1 | 0 | 5 | 4 | 1 | 0 | 15 | 12 | 1993 | F | W 4-1 |
| New Jersey | 1 | 0 | 1 | 5 | 1 | 4 | 0 | 11 | 22 | 1997 | CQF | L 1-4 |
| NY Islanders | 4 | 3 | 1 | 22 | 14 | 8 | 0 | 64 | 55 | 1993 | CF | W 4-1 |
| NY Rangers | 14 | 7 | 7 | 61 | 34 | 25 | 2 | 188 | 158 | 1996 | CQF | L 2-4 |
| Philadelphia | 5 | 3 | 2 | 26 | 15 | 11 | 0 | 86 | 72 | 2008 | CSF | L 1-4 |
| Pittsburgh | 1 | 1 | 0 | 6 | 4 | 2 | 0 | 18 | 15 | 1998 | CQF | W 4-2 |
| St. Louis | 3 | 3 | 0 | 12 | 12 | 0 | 0 | 42 | 14 | 1977 | QF | W 4-0 |
| Tampa Bay | 1 | 0 | 1 | 4 | 0 | 4 | 0 | 5 | 14 | 2004 | CSF | L 0-4 |
| Toronto | 15 | 8 | 7 | 71 | 42 | 29 | 0 | 215 | 160 | 1979 | QF | W 4-0 |
| Vancouver | 1 | 1 | 0 | 5 | 4 | 1 | 0 | 20 | 9 | 1975 | QF | W 4-1 |
| Defunct Clubs | 10* | 5 | 4 | 28 | 15 | 9 | 4 | 70 | 71 | | | |
| **Totals** | **141*** | **87** | **53** | **683** | **398** | **277** | **8** | **2089** | **1725** | | | |

* 1919 Final incomplete due to influenza epidemic.

## Playoff Results 2009-2004

| Year | Round | Opponent | Result | GF | GA |
|---|---|---|---|---|---|
| 2009 | CQF | Boston | L 0-4 | 6 | 17 |
| 2008 | CSF | Philadelphia | L 1-4 | 14 | 20 |
| | CQF | Boston | W 4-3 | 19 | 15 |
| 2006 | CQF | Carolina | L 2-4 | 17 | 15 |
| 2004 | CSF | Tampa Bay | L 0-4 | 5 | 14 |
| | CQF | Boston | W 4-3 | 19 | 14 |

**Abbreviations: Round: F** - Final; **CF** - conference final; **CSF** - conference semi-final; **CQF** - conference quarter-final; **DSF** - division semi-final; **QF** - quarter-final; **PRE** - preliminary round.

Calgary totals include Atlanta Flames, 1972-73 to 1979-80.
Carolina totals include Hartford, 1979-80 to 1996-97.
Colorado totals include Quebec, 1979-80 to 1994-95.
Dallas totals include Minnesota North Stars, 1967-68 to 1992-93.
New Jersey totals include Kansas City, 1974-75, 1975-76, and Colorado Rockies, 1976-77 to 1981-82.
Phoenix totals include Winnipeg, 1979-80 to 1995-96.

## 2008-09 Results

| | | | | | | | |
|---|---|---|---|---|---|---|---|
| **Oct.** | 10 | at Buffalo | 1-2† | | 13 | at Boston | 1-3 |
| | 11 | at Toronto | 6-1 | | 15 | Nashville | 3-2 |
| | 13 | at Philadelphia | 5-3 | | 17 | at Ottawa | 5-4† |
| | 15 | Boston | 4-3† | | 20 | at Atlanta | 2-4 |
| | 18 | Phoenix | 4-1 | | 21 | at New Jersey | 2-5 |
| | 20 | Florida | 3-1 | | 27 | at Tampa Bay | 3-5 |
| | 25 | Anaheim | 4-6 | | 29 | at Florida | 1-5 |
| | 28 | Carolina | 3-2† | | 31 | Los Angeles | 4-3 |
| | 30 | at Minnesota | 2-1 | **Feb.** | 1 | Boston | 1-3 |
| **Nov.** | 1 | at NY Islanders | 5-4 | | 3 | Pittsburgh | 4-2 |
| | 7 | at Columbus | 3-4† | | 6 | at Buffalo | 2-3 |
| | 8 | at Toronto | 3-6 | | 7 | Toronto | 2-5 |
| | 11 | Ottawa | 4-0 | | 9 | at Calgary | 2-6 |
| | 13 | at Boston | 1-6 | | 11 | at Edmonton | 2-7 |
| | 15 | Philadelphia | 1-2 | | 13 | at Colorado | 4-2 |
| | 16 | at St. Louis | 3-2† | | 15 | at Vancouver | 2-4 |
| | 18 | at Carolina | 1-2 | | 18 | at Washington | 3-4† |
| | 20 | at Ottawa | 3-2† | | 19 | at Pittsburgh | 4-5 |
| | 22 | Boston | 2-3† | | 21 | Ottawa | 5-3 |
| | 24 | NY Islanders | 3-4† | | 24 | Vancouver | 3-0 |
| | 26 | at Detroit | 3-1 | | 27 | at Philadelphia | 4-3* |
| | 28 | at Washington | 0-3 | | 28 | San Jose | 3-2 |
| | 29 | Buffalo | 3-2 | **Mar.** | 4 | at Buffalo | 1-5 |
| **Dec.** | 2 | Atlanta | 5-4 | | 6 | at Atlanta | 0-2 |
| | 4 | NY Rangers | 6-2 | | 8 | at Dallas | 3-1 |
| | 6 | New Jersey | 1-2* | | 10 | Edmonton | 4-3* |
| | 9 | Calgary | 4-1 | | 12 | NY Islanders | 2-3* |
| | 11 | Tampa Bay | 1-3 | | 14 | New Jersey | 1-3 |
| | 13 | Washington | 1-2 | | 17 | NY Rangers | 3-4† |
| | 16 | at Carolina | 2-3 | | 19 | at Ottawa | 4-5 |
| | 18 | Philadelphia | 5-2 | | 21 | Toronto | 2-5 |
| | 20 | Buffalo | 4-3* | | 24 | Atlanta | 6-3 |
| | 21 | Carolina | 2-3* | | 26 | Tampa Bay | 3-2* |
| | 27 | at Pittsburgh | 3-2 | | 28 | Buffalo | 3-4† |
| | 29 | at Florida | 5-2 | | 31 | Chicago | 4-1 |
| | 30 | at Tampa Bay | 2-1† | **Apr.** | 2 | at NY Islanders | 5-1 |
| **Jan.** | 2 | at New Jersey | 1-4 | | 4 | at Toronto | 6-2 |
| | 4 | Florida | 6-5† | | 6 | Ottawa | 2-3 |
| | 7 | at NY Rangers | 6-3 | | 7 | at NY Rangers | 1-3 |
| | 8 | Toronto | 6-2 | | 9 | at Boston | 4-5* |
| | 10 | Washington | 5-4 | | 11 | Pittsburgh | 1-3 |

* – Overtime † – Shootout

## Entry Draft Selections 2009-1995

Name in bold denotes played in NHL.

**2009**
Pick
18 Louis Leblanc
65 Joonas Nattinen
79 Mac Bennett
109 Alexander Avtsin
139 Gabriel Dumont
169 Dustin Walsh
199 Michael Cichy
211 Petteri Simila

**2008**
Pick
56 Danny Kristo
86 Steve Quailer
116 Jason Missiaen
138 Maxim Trunev
206 Patrick Johnson

**2007**
Pick
12 Ryan McDonagh
22 **Max Pacioretty**
43 P.K. Subban
65 Olivier Fortier
73 **Yannick Weber**
133 Joe Stejskal
142 Andrew Conboy
163 Nichlas Torp
192 Scott Kishel

**2006**
Pick
20 David Fischer
49 **Ben Maxwell**
53 Mathieu Carle
66 Ryan White
139 Pavel Valentenko
199 Cameron Cepek

**2005**
Pick
5 **Carey Price**
45 **Guillaume Latendresse**
121 Juraj Mikus
130 Mathieu Aubin
190 **Matt D'Agostini**
200 **Sergei Kostitsyn**
229 Philippe Paquet

**2004**
Pick
18 **Kyle Chipchura**
84 Alexei Yemelin
100 James Wyman
150 **Mikhail Grabovski**
181 Loic Lacasse
212 Jon Gleed
246 **Greg Stewart**
262 **Mark Streit**
278 Alex Dulac-Lemelin

**2003**
Pick
10 **Andrei Kostitsyn**
40 Cory Urquhart
61 **Maxim Lapierre**
79 **Ryan O'Byrne**
113 **Corey Locke**
123 Danny Stewart
177 Chris Heino-Lindberg
188 Mark Flood
217 Oskari Korpikari
241 Jimmy Bonneau
271 **Jaroslav Halak**

**2002**
Pick
14 **Christopher Higgins**
45 Tomas Linhart
99 Michael Lambert
182 **Andre Deveaux**
212 **Jonathan Ferland**
275 Konstantin Korneev

**2001**
Pick
7 **Mike Komisarek**
25 **Alexander Perezhogin**
37 **Duncan Milroy**
71 **Tomas Plekanec**
109 **Martti Jarventie**
171 Eric Himelfarb
203 Andrew Archer
266 Viktor Ujcik

**2000**
Pick
13 **Ron Hainsey**
16 **Marcel Hossa**
78 **Jozef Balej**
79 Tyler Hanchuck
109 Johan Eneqvist
114 Christian Larrivee
145 Ryan Glenn
172 Scott Selig
182 Petr Chvojka
243 Joni Puurula
275 Jonathan Gauthier

**1999**
Pick
39 Alexander Buturlin
58 **Matt Carkner**
97 Chris Dyment
107 Evan Lindsay
136 Dusty Jamieson
145 Marc-Andre Thinel
150 Matt Shasby
167 Sean Dixon
196 Vadim Tarasov
225 Mikko Hyytia
253 Jerome Marois

**1998**
Pick
16 **Eric Chouinard**
45 **Mike Ribeiro**
75 **Francois Beauchemin**
132 **Andrei Bashkirov**
152 **Gordie Dwyer**
162 **Andrei Markov**
189 Andrei Kruchinin
201 Craig Murray
216 **Michael Ryder**
247 Darcy Harris

**1997**
Pick
11 **Jason Ward**
37 Gregor Baumgartner
65 Ilkka Mikkola
91 Daniel Tetrault
118 Konstantin Sidulov
122 Gennady Razin
145 Jonathan Desroches
172 **Ben Guite**
197 Petr Kubos
202 Andrei Sidyakin
228 Jarl Espen Ygranes

**1996**
Pick
18 **Matt Higgins**
44 **Mathieu Garon**
71 **Arron Asham**
92 Kim Staal
99 Etienne Drapeau
127 Daniel Archambault
154 **Brett Clark**
181 Timo Vertala
207 Mattia Baldi
233 Michel Tremblay

**1995**
Pick
8 **Terry Ryan**
60 **Miloslav Guren**
74 Martin Hohenberger
86 **Jonathan Delisle**
112 Niklas Anger
138 Boyd Olson
164 **Stephane Robidas**
190 Greg Hart
216 **Eric Houde**

## Jacques Martin
### Head Coach

*Born: St. Pascal, Ont., October 1, 1952.*

The Montreal Canadiens announced the appointment of Jacques Martin as the club's new head coach on June 1, 2009. Martin was the Florida Panthers' general manager the previous three seasons (2006 to 2009).He had originally been hired as Panthers coach in 2004 and served in both capacities through the 2007-08 season.

Midway through the 1995-96 season, Martin was hired as head coach of the Ottawa Senators. In his nine-year tenure with the Senators, he led his team to three division titles and had four seasons of at least 100 points. Martin was nominated for the Jack Adams Trophy as NHL coach of the year four times (1997, 1999, 2001, 2003), winning the award in 1999.

In 1986-87, Martin entered the NHL as head coach of the St. Louis Blues. From 1988 to 1993, Martin worked as an assistant coach with the Chicago Blackhawks and associate coach with the Quebec Nordiques and, following a one-year stint as head coach of the American Hockey League's Cornwall Aces, with the Colorado Avalanche. Martin also has extensive experience on the international level serving as an associate coach on Team Canada for two Winter Olympics (Salt Lake City and Turin), earning a gold medal in 2002. He was also a member of the Canadian team coaching staff at the 2004 World Cup.

Martin began his coaching career in major junior hockey with the Ontario Hockey League's Peterborough Petes as an assistant to Dick Todd from 1982 to 1984. He then moved on to become Guelph's head coach in 1985-86 season leading the Platers to a Memorial Cup championship and winning the Matt Leyden Trophy as OHL coach of the year. As a player, Martin was a goaltender with the NCAA's St. Lawrence University from 1972 to 1974.

### Coaching Record

| | | | Regular Season | | | | Playoffs | | | |
|---|---|---|---|---|---|---|---|---|---|---|
| Season | Team | League | GC | W | L | O/T | GC | W | L | T |
| 1985-86 | Guelph | OHL | 66 | 41 | 23 | 2 | 20 | 15 | 3 | 2 |
| 1985-86 | Guelph | M-Cup | .... | .... | .... | .... | 4 | 3 | 1 | .... |
| **1986-87** | **St. Louis** | **NHL** | **80** | **32** | **33** | **15** | **6** | **2** | **4** | .... |
| **1987-88** | **St. Louis** | **NHL** | **80** | **34** | **38** | **8** | **10** | **5** | **5** | .... |
| 1993-94 | Cornwall | AHL | 80 | 33 | 36 | 22 | 13 | 8 | 5 | .... |
| **1995-96** | **Ottawa** | **NHL** | **38** | **10** | **24** | **4** | .... | .... | .... | .... |
| **1996-97** | **Ottawa** | **NHL** | **82** | **31** | **36** | **15** | **7** | **3** | **4** | .... |
| **1997-98** | **Ottawa** | **NHL** | **82** | **34** | **33** | **15** | **11** | **5** | **6** | .... |
| **1998-99** | **Ottawa** | **NHL** | **82** | **44** | **23** | **15** | **4** | **0** | **4** | .... |
| **99-2000** | **Ottawa** | **NHL** | **82** | **41** | **28** | **13** | **6** | **2** | **4** | .... |
| **2000-01** | **Ottawa** | **NHL** | **82** | **48** | **21** | **13** | **4** | **0** | **4** | .... |
| **2001-02** | **Ottawa** | **NHL** | **80** | **38** | **26** | **16** | **12** | **7** | **5** | .... |
| **2002-03** | **Ottawa** | **NHL** | **82** | **52** | **21** | **9** | **18** | **11** | **7** | .... |
| **2003-04** | **Ottawa** | **NHL** | **82** | **43** | **23** | **16** | **7** | **3** | **4** | .... |
| **2004-05** | **Florida** | | | | SEASON CANCELLED | | | | | |
| **2005-06** | **Florida** | **NHL** | **82** | **37** | **34** | **11** | .... | .... | .... | .... |
| **2006-07** | **Florida** | **NHL** | **82** | **35** | **31** | **16** | .... | .... | .... | .... |
| **2007-08** | **Florida** | **NHL** | **82** | **38** | **35** | **9** | .... | .... | .... | .... |
| | **NHL Totals** | | **1098** | **517** | **406** | **175** | **85** | **38** | **47** | .... |

# Club Directory

Bell Centre

**Club de Hockey Canadien**
1260 de La Gauchetière Street W.
Montréal, QC H3B 5E8
Phone: **514/932-2582**
Media Hotline: 514/989-2835
Fax Lines (all area code 514):
Communications 932-8285
Hockey 989-2717
Press Lounge 932-5258
Marketing 925-2145
Community Relations 925-2144
www.canadiens.com
**Capacity:** 21,273

**Executive Management**
Chairman and Governor .................... George N. Gillett Jr.
Vice-Chairman .................... Jeff Joyce
Managing Partner .................... Foster Gillett
President/CEO, Club de hockey Canadien & Bell Centre & Alternate Governor .......... Pierre Boivin
Exec. V.P., HockeyG.M./Alt. Gov. .......... Bob Gainey
Assistant General Manager .......... Pierre Gauthier
Vice President, Hockey Operations .......... Julien BriseBois
Chief Financial Officer & Alternate Governor...... Fred Steer
Vice President, Chief Sales and Marketing Officer .. Ray Lalonde
Vice President, Communications and Community Relations .......... Donald Beauchamp
Vice President, Building Operations .......... Alain Gauthier
Vice President & General Manager, Gillett Entertainment Group .......... Jacques Aubé
President, Effix – Advertising and Sponsorship Sales François Seigneur
President, Canadiens Alumni.......... Réjean Houle
Administrative Assistant to the President.......... Rolande Bernier

**Hockey**
Director of Player Recruitment and Development .. Trevor Timmins
Head Coach .......... Jacques Martin
Assistant Coaches.......... Perry Pearn, Kirk Muller
Goaltending Coach.......... Pierre Groulx
Professional Scouts .......... Gordie Roberts, Doug Gibson
Scouting Staff .......... Elmer Benning, Bill Berglund, Michel Boucher, Pelle Eklund, Frank Jay, Vaughn Karpan, Hannu Laine, Dave Mayville, Mike McCann, Denis Morel, Antonin Routa, Nikolai Vakourov, Pat Westrum
Team Services & Hockey Administration Manager .. Claudine Crépin
Administrative Assistant to the General Manager .. Suzanne Charlebois
Team Services Coordinator .......... Alain Gagnon

**Medical and Training Staff**
Club Physician and Chief Surgeon.......... Dr. David Mulder
Consultant, Orthopedic Surgeon.......... Dr. Eric Lenczner
Dentist.......... Dr. Jean-François Desjardins
Consultant, Ophthalmologist .......... Dr. John Little
Consultant, Sports Medicine .......... Dr. Vincent Lacroix
Consultant, Ostheopathy .......... Dave Campbell
Consultant, Physiotherapy .......... Donald Balmforth
Head Athletic Therapist.......... Graham Rynbend
Athletic Therapist .......... Nick Addey-Jibb
Strength & Conditioning Coordinator .......... Lorne Goldenberg
Video Coach.......... Mario Leblanc
Equipment Manager.......... Pierre Gervais
Assistants to the Equipment Manager.......... Richard Généreux, Patrick Langlois, Pierre Ouellette

**Communications**
Director of Media Relations.......... Dominick Saillant
Administrative Assistant to the VP Communications Sylvie Lambert
Manager, History and Archives .......... Carl Lavigne
Communications Coordinator.......... François Marchand

**Community Relations**
Director of Community Relations/ Exec. Dir, Children's Foundation .......... Geneviève Paquette
Manager, Events & Communications, Children's Foundation .......... Marie-Christine Boucher
Community Relations Coordinator .......... Anne-Marie Bégin
Coordinator, Donations & Administration, Children's Foundation.......... Sylvie Nadeau
Project Manager, Children's Foundation .......... Patrick Mahoney

**Marketing and Sales**
Director, Group Sales and Administration .......... Pierre Constant
Executive Director, Luxury Suites and Services ..... Richard Primeau
Director, Ticket Sales.......... Vincent Lucier
Director, Marketing and Broadcast .......... Jon Trzcienski
Director, Consumer Products .......... Matt Zalkowitz
Director, Publications and Creative Services.......... Jean Simard
Group Manager, Broadcast and Advertising ...... Jonathan Prunier
Group Manager, Game Production .......... Paul Gallant
Manager, Publications and Editorial .......... Manny Almela
Manager, Luxury Suites Services .......... Sabina D'Ascoli
Manager, Ticket Sales and Services .......... Andrea Geci
Manager, Digital Media .......... Alexandre Harvey
Manager, Event Planning and Logistics .......... David McGinnis
Manager, Youth Hockey.......... Stéphane Verret

**Building Operations**
Director of Ticket Office .......... Cathy D'Ascoli
Assistant Director of Ticket Office .......... Lucie Masse
Director of Building Operations.......... Xavier Luydlin
Director of Concessions .......... Alec Beaudry
Director of Customer Satisfaction .......... Caroline Hamel
Administrative Assistant to the VP Operations ..... Maryse Cartwright

**Finance**
Exec. Dir., Info. & Communication Technology .... Pierre-Éric Belzile
Controller.......... Dennis McKinley
Assistant Controller .......... Raymond Lamarche
Administrator, Human Resources .......... Susan Cryans
Administrative Assistant, Chief Financial Officer.... Christine Ouellette

**Broadcasting**
Play-by-play – Radio/TV .......... Pierre Houde (RDS), Martin McGuire (CKAC), Rick Moffat (CJAD)
Colormen – Radio/TV .......... Benoit Brunet (RDS), Dany Dubé (CKAC), Murray Wilson (CJAD)
Radio/television flagships .......... RDS (Cable 33), CKAC (730 AM), CJAD (800 AM)

# Nashville Predators

## Key Off-Season Signings/Acquisitions

**2009**

**Apr. 17** • Signed 2008 1st-round pick (seventh overall) C **Colin Wilson.**

**July 1** • Re-signed LW **Steve Sullivan** and RW **Joel Ward.**

**14** • Signed RW **Ben Guite.**

**16** • Signed LW **Peter Olvecky.**

## 2008-09 Results: 40W-34L-3OTL-5SOL 88PTS.
## Fifth, Central Division

### Year-by-Year Record

| | | Home | | | | Road | | | | Overall | | | | | | | | |
|---|---|---|---|---|---|---|---|---|---|---|---|---|---|---|---|---|---|---|
| Season | GP | W | L | T | OL | W | L | T | OL | W | L | T | OL | GF | GA | Pts. | Finished | Playoff Result |
| 2008-09 | 82 | 24 | 13 | .... | 4 | 16 | 21 | .... | 4 | 40 | 34 | .... | 8 | 213 | 233 | 88 | 5th, Central Div. | Out of Playoffs |
| 2007-08 | 82 | 23 | 14 | .... | 4 | 18 | 18 | .... | 5 | 41 | 32 | .... | 9 | 230 | 229 | 91 | 2nd, Central Div. | Lost Conf. Quarter-Final |
| 2006-07 | 82 | 28 | 8 | .... | 5 | 23 | 15 | .... | 3 | 51 | 23 | .... | 8 | 272 | 212 | 110 | 2nd, Central Div. | Lost Conf. Quarter-Final |
| 2005-06 | 82 | 32 | 8 | .... | 1 | 17 | 17 | .... | 7 | 49 | 25 | .... | 8 | 259 | 227 | 106 | 2nd, Central Div. | Lost Conf. Quarter-Final |
| 2004-05 | .... | .... | .... | .... | .... | .... | .... | .... | .... | .... | .... | .... | .... | .... | .... | .... | | |
| 2003-04 | 82 | 22 | 10 | 7 | 2 | 16 | 19 | 4 | 2 | 38 | 29 | 11 | 4 | 216 | 217 | 91 | 3rd, Central Div. | Lost Conf. Quarter-Final |
| 2002-03 | 82 | 18 | 17 | 5 | 1 | 9 | 18 | 8 | 6 | 27 | 35 | 13 | 7 | 183 | 206 | 74 | 4th, Central Div. | Out of Playoffs |
| 2001-02 | 82 | 17 | 16 | 8 | 0 | 11 | 25 | 5 | 0 | 28 | 41 | 13 | 0 | 196 | 230 | 69 | 4th, Central Div. | Out of Playoffs |
| 2000-01 | 82 | 16 | 18 | 7 | 0 | 18 | 18 | 2 | 3 | 34 | 36 | 9 | 3 | 186 | 200 | 80 | 3rd, Central Div. | Out of Playoffs |
| 1999-2000 | 82 | 15 | 21 | 3 | 2 | 13 | 19 | 4 | 5 | 28 | 40 | 7 | 7 | 199 | 240 | 70 | 4th, Central Div. | Out of Playoffs |
| 1998-99 | 82 | 15 | 22 | 4 | .... | 13 | 25 | 3 | .... | 28 | 47 | 7 | .... | 190 | 261 | 63 | 4th, Central Div. | Out of Playoffs |

## 2009-10 Schedule

| | | | | | | | |
|---|---|---|---|---|---|---|---|
| **Oct.** | Sat. | 3 | at Dallas | **Jan.** | Sat. | 2 | Anaheim |
| | Thu. | 8 | Colorado | | Tue. | 5 | Calgary |
| | Sat. | 10 | Buffalo | | Thu. | 7 | Carolina |
| | Mon. | 12 | Edmonton | | Sat. | 9 | Anaheim |
| | Wed. | 14 | at Dallas | | Mon. | 11 | at Vancouver |
| | Thu. | 15 | Chicago | | Tue. | 12 | at Edmonton |
| | Sat. | 17 | at Washington | | Fri. | 15 | at Calgary |
| | Wed. | 21 | at Boston | | Mon. | 18 | Toronto |
| | Thu. | 22 | at Ottawa | | Thu. | 21 | at Phoenix |
| | Sat. | 24 | at Chicago | | Fri. | 22 | at Colorado |
| | Wed. | 28 | at Minnesota | | Tue. | 26 | at Columbus |
| | Thu. | 29 | Chicago | | Fri. | 29 | at Detroit |
| | Sat. | 31 | Dallas | | Sat. | 30 | Atlanta |
| **Nov.** | Thu. | 5 | at Anaheim | **Feb.** | Tue. | 2 | Phoenix |
| | Sat. | 7 | at Los Angeles* | | Thu. | 4 | Colorado |
| | Tue. | 10 | at San Jose | | Sat. | 6 | San Jose |
| | Thu. | 12 | at St. Louis | | Tue. | 9 | at NY Islanders |
| | Sat. | 14 | Montreal | | Wed. | 10 | at NY Rangers |
| | Tue. | 17 | San Jose | | Fri. | 12 | at New Jersey |
| | Thu. | 19 | New Jersey | | Sun. | 14 | at Pittsburgh* |
| | Sat. | 21 | Columbus | **Mar.** | Tue. | 2 | Edmonton |
| | Mon. | 23 | Detroit | | Thu. | 4 | Los Angeles |
| | Wed. | 25 | at Colorado | | Fri. | 5 | at Detroit |
| | Fri. | 27 | St. Louis | | Sun. | 7 | Vancouver* |
| | Sat. | 28 | Florida | | Tue. | 9 | at Atlanta |
| | Mon. | 30 | Calgary | | Thu. | 11 | at San Jose |
| **Dec.** | Wed. | 2 | at Minnesota | | Fri. | 12 | at Anaheim |
| | Fri. | 4 | at Chicago | | Sun. | 14 | at Los Angeles* |
| | Sat. | 5 | Minnesota | | Tue. | 16 | Philadelphia |
| | Tue. | 8 | Vancouver | | Thu. | 18 | Minnesota |
| | Thu. | 10 | Columbus | | Sat. | 20 | Columbus |
| | Sat. | 12 | Detroit | | Sun. | 21 | at St. Louis* |
| | Mon. | 14 | at Columbus | | Tue. | 23 | Dallas |
| | Tue. | 15 | Tampa Bay | | Thu. | 25 | Phoenix |
| | Thu. | 17 | at Edmonton | | Sat. | 27 | Detroit |
| | Sat. | 19 | at Calgary* | | Mon. | 29 | at Florida |
| | Tue. | 22 | at Vancouver | | Tue. | 30 | Los Angeles |
| | Sat. | 26 | Chicago | **Apr.** | Thu. | 1 | St. Louis |
| | Sun. | 27 | at Chicago | | Sat. | 3 | at Detroit* |
| | Tue. | 29 | at St. Louis | | Wed. | 7 | at Phoenix |
| | Thu. | 31 | at Columbus | | Sat. | 10 | St. Louis |

* Denotes afternoon game.

*Nashville's Shea Weber set career highs (and ranked among the NHL's top defensemen) with 23 goals, 30 assists and 53 points in 2008-09. He was the NHL's only defenseman with more than 50 points and 175 hits.*

**CENTRAL DIVISION**
**12th NHL Season**

**Franchise date:** June 25, 1997

# 2009-10 Player Personnel

| FORWARDS | HT | WT | S | Place of Birth | *Age | 2008-09 Club |
|---|---|---|---|---|---|---|
| ARNOTT, Jason | 6-5 | 220 | R | Collingwood, Ont. | 34 | Nashville |
| BELAK, Wade | 6-5 | 225 | R | Saskatoon, Sask. | 33 | Florida-Nashville |
| DUMONT, J.P. | 6-1 | 219 | L | Montreal, Que. | 31 | Nashville |
| EAVES, Ben | 5-9 | 182 | R | Minneapolis, MN | 27 | Blues Espoo |
| ERAT, Martin | 6-0 | 203 | L | Trebic, Czech. | 28 | Nashville |
| GRANT, Triston | 6-1 | 210 | L | Neepawa, Man. | 25 | Milwaukee |
| GUITE, Ben | 6-1 | 211 | R | Montreal, Que. | 31 | Colorado |
| HORNQVIST, Patric | 5-11 | 186 | L | Sollentuna, Sweden | 22 | Nashville-Milwaukee |
| JESSIMAN, Hugh | 6-6 | 235 | R | New York, NY | 25 | Hartford-Milwaukee |
| JONES, Ryan | 6-1 | 206 | L | Chatham, Ont. | 25 | Nashville-Milwaukee |
| LEGWAND, David | 6-2 | 202 | L | Detroit, MI | 29 | Nashville |
| MAKI, Ryan | 6-2 | 210 | R | Medford, NJ | 24 | Milwaukee |
| OLVECKY, Peter | 6-2 | 195 | L | Trencin, Czech. | 23 | Minnesota-Houston |
| O'REILLY, Cal | 6-0 | 187 | L | Toronto, Ont. | 23 | Nashville-Milwaukee |
| PIHLSTROM, Antti | 5-11 | 190 | L | Vanntaa, Finland | 24 | Nashville-Milwaukee |
| RADULOV, Alexander | 6-1 | 188 | L | Nizhny Tagil, USSR | 23 | Ufa |
| SANTORELLI, Mike | 6-0 | 189 | R | Vancouver, B.C. | 23 | Nashville-Milwaukee |
| SMITHSON, Jerred | 6-3 | 204 | R | Vernon, B.C. | 30 | Nashville |
| SPALING, Nick | 6-1 | 190 | L | Palmerston, Ont. | 21 | Milwaukee |
| SULLIVAN, Steve | 5-9 | 173 | R | Timmins, Ont. | 35 | Nashville |
| THURESSON, Andreas | 6-1 | 204 | R | Kristianstad, Sweden | 21 | Milwaukee |
| TOOTOO, Jordin | 5-9 | 200 | R | Churchill, Man. | 26 | Nashville |
| WARD, Joel | 6-1 | 220 | R | Toronto, Ont. | 28 | Nashville |
| WILSON, Colin | 6-1 | 215 | L | Greenwich, CT | 19 | Boston University |
| **DEFENSEMEN** | | | | | | |
| BLUM, Jonathon | 6-1 | 183 | R | Long Beach, CA | 20 | Vancouver (WHL)-Milwaukee |
| FRANSON, Cody | 6-5 | 214 | R | Salmon Arm, B.C. | 22 | Milwaukee |
| HAMHUIS, Dan | 6-1 | 203 | L | Smithers, B.C. | 26 | Nashville |
| KLEIN, Kevin | 6-1 | 203 | R | Kitchener, Ont. | 24 | Nashville |
| LAAKSO, Teemu | 6-1 | 208 | R | Tuusula, Finland | 22 | Milwaukee |
| SULZER, Alexander | 6-1 | 196 | L | Kaufbeuren, West Germany | 25 | Nashville-Milwaukee |
| SUTER, Ryan | 6-1 | 194 | L | Madison, WI | 24 | Nashville |
| WEBER, Shea | 6-4 | 230 | R | Sicamous, B.C. | 24 | Nashville |

| GOALTENDERS | HT | WT | C | Place of Birth | *Age | 2008-09 Club |
|---|---|---|---|---|---|---|
| DEKANICH, Mark | 6-2 | 190 | L | N. Vancouver, B.C. | 23 | Milwaukee |
| ELLIS, Dan | 6-0 | 188 | L | Orangeville, Ont. | 29 | Nashville |
| RINNE, Pekka | 6-5 | 206 | L | Kempele, Finland | 26 | Nashville |

* – Age at start of 2009-10 season

## Captains' History

Tom Fitzgerald, 1998-99 to 2001-02; Greg Johnson, 2002-03 to 2005-06; Kimmo Timonen, 2006-07; Jason Arnott, 2007-08 to date.

## General Managers' History

David Poile, 1998-99 to date.

# David Poile

### Vice President and General Manager

*Born: Toronto, Ont., February 14, 1949.*

Hired as the first general manager in franchise history on July 9, 1997, David Poile has been committed to building the team through the NHL Draft. In 2003-04, Nashville reached the playoffs for the first time in franchise history. During the 2006-07 season, the team was in contention for first overall in the NHL, setting club records with 51 wins and 110 points. Though forced to rebuild the roster for 2007-08, the Predators reached the playoffs for the fourth year in a row. Poile has an impressive reputation as an NHL leader and in 2001 he received the Lester Patrick Trophy for his contributions to hockey in the United States. His father, Norman "Bud" Poile, had won the honor in 1989.

Prior to joining Nashville, Poile spent 15 seasons as vice president/general manager of the Washington Capitals. During his tenure in Washington, the Capitals made 14 postseason appearances, winning their only Patrick Division title in 1989 and advancing to the Conference Finals in 1990. During Poile's 15 years in Washington, the Capitals compiled a record of 594-454-132, finished second in the Patrick Division seven times and recorded 90-or-more points seven different seasons.

Poile started his professional hockey career as an administrative assistant for the Atlanta Flames in 1972, shortly after graduating from Northeastern University in Boston. At Northeastern, he was hockey team captain, leading scorer and most valuable player for two years.

In 1977, he was named assistant general manager of the Atlanta Flames (who moved to Calgary in 1980), serving as the manager and coordinator of the Flames farm club.

Poile was instrumental in the NHL's adoption of the instant replay rule in 1991. He was awarded *Inside Hockey*'s man of the year for his leadership on the issue. He has also been honored three times as *The Sporting News* NHL executive of the year in 1982-83, 1983-84 and 2006-07. Poile served as general manager of the 1998 and 1999 U.S. national teams for the World Championships.

# 2008-09 Scoring

* – rookie

## Regular Season

| Pos | # | Player | Team | GP | G | A | Pts | TOI | +/– | PIM | PP | SH | GW | S | % |
|---|---|---|---|---|---|---|---|---|---|---|---|---|---|---|---|
| R | 71 | J.P. Dumont | NSH | 82 | 16 | 49 | 65 | 17:29 | 1 | 20 | 5 | 0 | 4 | 176 | 9.1 |
| C | 19 | Jason Arnott | NSH | 65 | 33 | 24 | 57 | 18:54 | 2 | 49 | 9 | 0 | 5 | 196 | 16.8 |
| D | 6 | Shea Weber | NSH | 81 | 23 | 30 | 53 | 23:58 | 1 | 80 | 10 | 1 | 4 | 251 | 9.2 |
| R | 10 | Martin Erat | NSH | 71 | 17 | 33 | 50 | 18:33 | –7 | 48 | 3 | 0 | 3 | 149 | 11.4 |
| D | 20 | Ryan Suter | NSH | 82 | 7 | 38 | 45 | 24:15 | –16 | 73 | 3 | 0 | 3 | 143 | 4.9 |
| C | 11 | David Legwand | NSH | 73 | 20 | 22 | 42 | 19:26 | –3 | 32 | 1 | 3 | 1 | 175 | 11.4 |
| R | 29 | Joel Ward | NSH | 79 | 17 | 18 | 35 | 16:00 | 1 | 29 | 3 | 2 | 2 | 133 | 12.8 |
| L | 26 | Steve Sullivan | NSH | 41 | 11 | 21 | 32 | 18:29 | 2 | 30 | 3 | 0 | 2 | 83 | 13.3 |
| D | 2 | Dan Hamhuis | NSH | 82 | 3 | 23 | 26 | 22:50 | –4 | 67 | 1 | 1 | 1 | 135 | 2.2 |
| C | 14 | Radek Bonk | NSH | 66 | 9 | 16 | 25 | 15:26 | –12 | 34 | 6 | 0 | 2 | 102 | 8.8 |
| C | 38 | Vernon Fiddler | NSH | 78 | 11 | 6 | 17 | 13:57 | –13 | 24 | 1 | 2 | 2 | 114 | 9.6 |
| R | 28 * | Ryan Jones | NSH | 46 | 7 | 10 | 17 | 11:26 | 1 | 22 | 2 | 0 | 1 | 63 | 11.1 |
| R | 22 | Jordin Tootoo | NSH | 72 | 4 | 12 | 16 | 12:05 | –15 | 124 | 0 | 0 | 1 | 138 | 2.9 |
| C | 25 | Jerred Smithson | NSH | 82 | 4 | 9 | 13 | 13:50 | –6 | 49 | 0 | 0 | 0 | 74 | 5.4 |
| D | 8 * | Kevin Klein | NSH | 63 | 4 | 8 | 12 | 12:39 | –2 | 19 | 1 | 0 | 0 | 41 | 9.8 |
| D | 5 | Greg Zanon | NSH | 82 | 4 | 7 | 11 | 20:51 | 8 | 38 | 0 | 0 | 1 | 54 | 7.4 |
| D | 4 | Ville Koistinen | NSH | 38 | 3 | 8 | 11 | 14:42 | 0 | 14 | 1 | 0 | 2 | 42 | 7.1 |
| C | 12 | Scott Nichol | NSH | 43 | 4 | 6 | 10 | 11:04 | 0 | 41 | 0 | 0 | 0 | 42 | 9.5 |
| R | 27 * | Patric Hornqvist | NSH | 28 | 2 | 5 | 7 | 11:23 | –3 | 16 | 0 | 0 | 0 | 54 | 3.7 |
| L | 42 * | Antti Pihlstrom | NSH | 53 | 2 | 5 | 7 | 11:26 | –1 | 10 | 1 | 0 | 0 | 88 | 2.3 |
| C | 48 * | Cal O'Reilly | NSH | 11 | 3 | 2 | 5 | 12:36 | 2 | 2 | 0 | 0 | 0 | 6 | 50.0 |
| D | 7 | Greg de Vries | NSH | 71 | 1 | 4 | 5 | 15:07 | –15 | 65 | 0 | 0 | 0 | 38 | 2.6 |
| R | 3 | Wade Belak | FLA | 15 | 0 | 0 | 0 | 4:24 | 0 | 25 | 0 | 0 | 0 | 4 | 0.0 |
| | | | NSH | 38 | 0 | 2 | 2 | 5:35 | –1 | 54 | 0 | 0 | 0 | 15 | 0.0 |
| | | | Total | 53 | 0 | 2 | 2 | 5:15 | –1 | 79 | 0 | 0 | 0 | 19 | 0.0 |
| R | 41 | Jed Ortmeyer | NSH | 2 | 0 | 0 | 0 | 11:01 | 0 | 0 | 0 | 0 | 0 | 4 | 0.0 |
| D | 44 * | Alexander Sulzer | NSH | 2 | 0 | 0 | 0 | 6:33 | 0 | 0 | 0 | 0 | 0 | 0 | 0.0 |
| C | 53 * | Mike Santorelli | NSH | 7 | 0 | 0 | 0 | 12:15 | –5 | 2 | 0 | 0 | 0 | 11 | 0.0 |

## Goaltending

| No. | Goaltender | GPI | Mins | Avg | W | L | OT | EN | SO | GA | SA | S% | G | A | PIM |
|---|---|---|---|---|---|---|---|---|---|---|---|---|---|---|---|
| 35 | * Pekka Rinne | 52 | 2999 | 2.38 | 29 | 15 | 4 | 8 | 7 | 119 | 1435 | .917 | 0 | 1 | 6 |
| 39 | Dan Ellis | 35 | 1965 | 2.93 | 11 | 19 | 4 | 5 | 3 | 96 | 963 | .900 | 0 | 0 | 2 |
| | **Totals** | **82** | **4996** | **2.74** | **40** | **34** | **8** | **13** | **10** | **228** | **2411** | **.905** | | | |

## Coaching History

Barry Trotz, 1998-99 to date.

# Barry Trotz

### Head Coach

*Born: Winnipeg, Man., July 15, 1962.*

Barry Trotz became head coach of the Nashville Predators on August 6, 1997, after serving four seasons as head coach and director of hockey operations for the American Hockey League's Portland Pirates. He and assistant Paul Gardner spent the 1997-98 season scouting in preparation for the inaugural season of the Predators. In his sixth season behind the bench in 2003-04, Trotz led Nashville into the playoffs for the first time. During the 2006-07 season, Nashville was in contention for first overall in the NHL, setting club records with 51 wins and 110 points. In 2007-08, Trotz led a rebuilt Nashville roster back to the playoffs for the fourth consecutive season. Trotz has the second longest tenure among current NHL coaches behind only Buffalo's Lindy Ruff. He is the first and only head coach in Predators history.

Trotz began his coaching career in 1984 as assistant coach with the University of Manitoba for one season, before serving two seasons as the head coach and general manager of the Dauphin Kings Junior Hockey Club from 1985 to 1987. He became head coach of the University of Manitoba during the 1987 season and also served as a scout for the Spokane Chiefs of the Western Hockey League that season. Trotz joined the Washington Capitals organization as their chief western scout during the 1988 season. The Winnipeg, Manitoba native was appointed an assistant coach of the Capitals' American Hockey League affiliate in Baltimore prior to the 1991 season before being named head coach prior to the 1992 season. When the franchise relocated to Portland, he guided the Pirates to two AHL Calder Cup Final appearances in the club's first four seasons. He led the Pirates to a league-best 43-27-10 record, captured the Calder Cup championship and was named the American Hockey League coach of the year following the 1994-95 season.

In 1995, Trotz guided Portland to a new North American professional hockey league record 17-game unbeaten streak (14-0-3) to start the season. He was named head coach for the U.S. team at the American Hockey League All-Star Game in 1996.

Prior to his coaching career, Trotz played junior hockey for the Western Hockey League's Regina Pats from 1979-83. During that time, he recorded 39 goals, 121 assists for 160 points, along with 490 penalty minutes in 204 games.

### Coaching Record

| | | | Regular Season | | | | Playoffs | | | |
|---|---|---|---|---|---|---|---|---|---|---|
| Season | Team | League | GC | W | L | O/T | GC | W | L | T |
| 1992-93 | Baltimore | AHL | 80 | 28 | 40 | 12 | 7 | 3 | 4 | .... |
| 1993-94 | Portland | AHL | 80 | 43 | 27 | 10 | 8 | 6 | 2 | .... |
| 1994-95 | Portland | AHL | 80 | 46 | 22 | 12 | 7 | 3 | 4 | .... |
| 1995-96 | Portland | AHL | 80 | 32 | 34 | 14 | 24 | 14 | 10 | .... |
| 1996-97 | Portland | AHL | 80 | 37 | 26 | 17 | 5 | 2 | 3 | .... |
| **1998-99** | **Nashville** | **NHL** | **82** | **28** | **47** | **7** | .... | .... | .... | .... |
| **99-2000** | **Nashville** | **NHL** | **82** | **28** | **40** | **14** | .... | .... | .... | .... |
| **2000-01** | **Nashville** | **NHL** | **82** | **34** | **36** | **12** | .... | .... | .... | .... |
| **2001-02** | **Nashville** | **NHL** | **82** | **28** | **41** | **13** | .... | .... | .... | .... |
| **2002-03** | **Nashville** | **NHL** | **82** | **27** | **35** | **20** | .... | .... | .... | .... |
| **2003-04** | **Nashville** | **NHL** | **82** | **38** | **29** | **15** | **6** | **2** | **4** | .... |
| **2004-05** | **Nashville** | | | | SEASON CANCELLED | | | | | |
| **2005-06** | **Nashville** | **NHL** | **82** | **49** | **25** | **8** | **5** | **1** | **4** | .... |
| **2006-07** | **Nashville** | **NHL** | **82** | **51** | **23** | **8** | **5** | **1** | **4** | .... |
| **2007-08** | **Nashville** | **NHL** | **82** | **41** | **32** | **9** | **6** | **2** | **4** | .... |
| **2008-09** | **Nashville** | **NHL** | **82** | **40** | **34** | **8** | .... | .... | .... | .... |
| | **NHL Totals** | | **820** | **364** | **342** | **114** | **22** | **6** | **16** | .... |

# Club Records

## Team

(Figures in brackets for season records are games played; records for fewest points, wins, ties, losses, goals, goals against are for 70 or more games)

| | | |
|---|---|---|
| **Most Points** | **110** | 2006-07 (82) |
| **Most Wins** | **51** | 2006-07 (82) |
| **Most Ties** | **13** | 2001-02 (82), 2002-03 (82) |
| **Most Losses** | **47** | 1998-99 (82) |
| **Most Goals** | **272** | 2006-07 (82) |
| **Most Goals Against** | **261** | 1998-99 (82) |
| **Fewest Points** | **63** | 1998-99 (82) |
| **Fewest Wins** | **27** | 2002-03 (82) |
| **Fewest Ties** | **7** | 1998-99 (82)<br>1999-2000 (82) |
| **Fewest Losses** | **23** | 2006-07 (82) |
| **Fewest Goals** | **183** | 2002-03 (82) |
| **Fewest Goals Against** | **200** | 2000-01 (82) |
| **Longest Winning Streak** | | |
| **Overall** | **8** | Oct. 5-25/05 |
| **Home** | **8** | Jan. 6-Feb. 8/07 |
| **Away** | **7** | Oct. 16-Nov. 4/06 |
| **Longest Undefeated Streak** | | |
| **Overall** | **8** | Dec. 18/99-Jan. 1/00<br>(5 wins, 3 ties),<br>Oct. 5-25/05<br>(8 wins) |
| **Home** | **11** | Dec. 20/03-Jan. 31/04<br>(9 wins, 2 ties),<br>Nov. 3-Dec. 23/01<br>(8 wins, 3 ties) |
| **Away** | **7** | Oct. 16-Nov. 4/06<br>(7 wins) |
| **Longest Losing Streak** | | |
| **Overall** | **7** | Nov. 20-Dec. 2/99 |
| **Home** | **6** | Jan. 21-Feb. 15/99,<br>Feb. 26-Mar. 21/02,<br>Feb. 21-Mar. 20/08 |
| **Away** | **7** | Jan. 26-Mar. 5/06,<br>Dec. 8/08-Jan. 11/09 |
| **Longest Winless Streak** | | |
| **Overall** | **15** | Mar. 10-Apr. 6/03<br>(10 losses, 2 OT losses, 3 ties) |
| **Home** | **9** | Jan. 21-Mar. 2/99<br>(8 losses, 1 tie) |
| **Away** | **9** | Nov. 2-Dec. 2/01<br>(3 losses, 4 OT losses, 2 ties),<br>Oct. 11-Nov. 7/02<br>(3 losses, 4 OT losses, 2 ties),<br>Mar. 12-Apr. 6/03<br>(6 losses, 1 OT loss, 2 ties) |
| **Most Shutouts, Season** | **11** | 2006-07 (82) |
| **Most PIM, Season** | **1,533** | 2005-06 (82) |
| **Most Goals, Game** | **9** | Mar. 4/04<br>(Nsh. 9 at Pit. 4),<br>Mar. 18/06<br>(Cgy. 4 at Nsh. 9) |

## Individual

| | | |
|---|---|---|
| **Most Seasons** | **10** | David Legwand |
| **Most Games** | **622** | David Legwand |
| **Most Goals, Career** | **141** | David Legwand |
| **Most Assists, Career** | **228** | David Legwand |
| **Most Points, Career** | **369** | David Legwand<br>(141G, 228A) |
| **Most PIM, Career** | **544** | Scott Hartnell |
| **Most Shutouts, Career** | **21** | Tomas Vokoun |
| **Longest Consecutive Games Streak** | **269** | Karlis Skrastins<br>(Feb. 21/00-Apr. 6/03) |
| **Most Goals, Season** | **33** | Jason Arnott<br>(2008-09) |
| **Most Assists, Season** | **54** | Paul Kariya<br>(2005-06) |
| **Most Points, Season** | **85** | Paul Kariya<br>(2005-06; 31G, 54A) |
| **Most PIM, Season** | **242** | Patrick Cote<br>(1998-99) |
| **Most Points, Defenseman, Season** | **55** | Kimmo Timonen<br>(2006-07; 13G, 42A) |
| **Most Points, Center, Season** | **72** | Jason Arnott<br>(2007-08; 28G, 44A) |
| **Most Points, Right Wing, Season** | **72** | J.P. Dumont<br>(2007-08; 29G, 43A) |
| **Most Points, Left Wing, Season** | **85** | Paul Kariya<br>(2005-06; 31G, 54A) |
| **Most Points, Rookie, Season** | **37** | Alexander Radulov<br>(2006-07; 18G, 19A) |
| **Most Shutouts, Season** | **7** | Pekka Rinne<br>(2008-09) |
| **Most Goals, Game** | **3** | 16 times |
| **Most Assists, Game** | **5** | Marek Zidlicky<br>(Feb. 18/04) |
| **Most Points, Game** | **5** | Marek Zidlicky<br>(Feb. 18/04; 5A)<br>Dan Hamhuis<br>(Mar. 4/04; 1G, 4A) |

# All-time Record vs. Other Clubs

## Regular Season

| | At Home | | | | | | | | On Road | | | | | | | | Total | | | | | | | |
|---|---|---|---|---|---|---|---|---|---|---|---|---|---|---|---|---|---|---|---|---|---|---|---|---|
| | GP | W | L | T | OL | GF | GA | PTS | GP | W | L | T | OL | GF | GA | PTS | GP | W | L | T | OL | GF | GA | PTS |
| Anaheim | 20 | 10 | 6 | 2 | 2 | 47 | 46 | 24 | 20 | 4 | 13 | 0 | 3 | 36 | 65 | 11 | 40 | 14 | 19 | 2 | 5 | 83 | 111 | 35 |
| Atlanta | 5 | 3 | 2 | 0 | 0 | 17 | 13 | 6 | 6 | 2 | 2 | 1 | 1 | 17 | 19 | 6 | 11 | 5 | 4 | 1 | 1 | 34 | 32 | 12 |
| Boston | 8 | 4 | 4 | 0 | 0 | 21 | 18 | 8 | 6 | 2 | 3 | 1 | 0 | 10 | 17 | 5 | 14 | 6 | 7 | 1 | 0 | 31 | 35 | 13 |
| Buffalo | 6 | 2 | 3 | 0 | 1 | 12 | 16 | 5 | 6 | 4 | 1 | 1 | 0 | 22 | 17 | 9 | 12 | 6 | 4 | 1 | 1 | 34 | 33 | 14 |
| Calgary | 21 | 13 | 7 | 1 | 0 | 73 | 50 | 27 | 20 | 7 | 7 | 3 | 3 | 48 | 61 | 20 | 41 | 20 | 14 | 4 | 3 | 121 | 111 | 47 |
| Carolina | 5 | 4 | 1 | 0 | 0 | 10 | 7 | 8 | 7 | 3 | 2 | 1 | 1 | 22 | 21 | 8 | 12 | 7 | 3 | 1 | 1 | 32 | 28 | 16 |
| Chicago | 31 | 16 | 9 | 3 | 3 | 104 | 90 | 38 | 32 | 13 | 18 | 1 | 0 | 82 | 89 | 27 | 63 | 29 | 27 | 4 | 3 | 186 | 179 | 65 |
| Colorado | 20 | 8 | 9 | 3 | 0 | 56 | 61 | 19 | 20 | 7 | 10 | 2 | 1 | 42 | 54 | 17 | 40 | 15 | 19 | 5 | 1 | 98 | 115 | 36 |
| Columbus | 26 | 21 | 3 | 1 | 1 | 91 | 54 | 44 | 25 | 14 | 8 | 0 | 3 | 72 | 58 | 31 | 51 | 35 | 11 | 1 | 4 | 163 | 112 | 75 |
| Dallas | 20 | 11 | 8 | 1 | 0 | 53 | 43 | 23 | 20 | 4 | 15 | 0 | 1 | 27 | 58 | 9 | 40 | 15 | 23 | 1 | 1 | 80 | 101 | 32 |
| Detroit | 31 | 14 | 15 | 2 | 0 | 89 | 89 | 30 | 32 | 8 | 17 | 2 | 5 | 72 | 117 | 23 | 63 | 22 | 32 | 4 | 5 | 161 | 206 | 53 |
| Edmonton | 21 | 11 | 7 | 3 | 0 | 62 | 61 | 25 | 20 | 11 | 7 | 0 | 2 | 60 | 54 | 24 | 41 | 22 | 14 | 3 | 2 | 122 | 115 | 49 |
| Florida | 7 | 3 | 2 | 2 | 0 | 15 | 15 | 8 | 6 | 1 | 4 | 1 | 0 | 11 | 21 | 3 | 13 | 4 | 6 | 3 | 0 | 26 | 36 | 11 |
| Los Angeles | 20 | 7 | 10 | 3 | 0 | 45 | 54 | 17 | 20 | 10 | 7 | 0 | 3 | 58 | 59 | 23 | 40 | 17 | 17 | 3 | 3 | 103 | 113 | 40 |
| Minnesota | 16 | 9 | 4 | 2 | 1 | 44 | 36 | 21 | 16 | 4 | 8 | 3 | 1 | 42 | 54 | 12 | 32 | 13 | 12 | 5 | 2 | 86 | 90 | 33 |
| Montreal | 5 | 2 | 1 | 1 | 1 | 19 | 13 | 6 | 6 | 1 | 4 | 0 | 1 | 16 | 22 | 3 | 11 | 3 | 5 | 1 | 2 | 35 | 35 | 9 |
| New Jersey | 7 | 1 | 5 | 0 | 1 | 13 | 21 | 3 | 6 | 4 | 1 | 0 | 1 | 18 | 18 | 9 | 13 | 5 | 6 | 0 | 2 | 31 | 39 | 12 |
| NY Islanders | 7 | 5 | 2 | 0 | 0 | 17 | 17 | 10 | 5 | 3 | 1 | 0 | 1 | 14 | 12 | 7 | 12 | 8 | 3 | 0 | 1 | 31 | 29 | 17 |
| NY Rangers | 6 | 2 | 4 | 0 | 0 | 16 | 23 | 4 | 7 | 4 | 2 | 1 | 0 | 18 | 18 | 9 | 13 | 6 | 6 | 1 | 0 | 34 | 41 | 13 |
| Ottawa | 6 | 3 | 3 | 0 | 0 | 14 | 13 | 6 | 6 | 2 | 4 | 0 | 0 | 13 | 20 | 4 | 12 | 5 | 7 | 0 | 0 | 27 | 33 | 10 |
| Philadelphia | 5 | 1 | 2 | 2 | 0 | 8 | 10 | 4 | 7 | 3 | 3 | 1 | 0 | 13 | 23 | 7 | 12 | 4 | 5 | 3 | 0 | 21 | 33 | 11 |
| Phoenix | 20 | 12 | 6 | 2 | 0 | 59 | 47 | 26 | 20 | 8 | 10 | 0 | 2 | 59 | 57 | 18 | 40 | 20 | 16 | 2 | 2 | 118 | 104 | 44 |
| Pittsburgh | 8 | 6 | 2 | 0 | 0 | 31 | 17 | 12 | 6 | 2 | 2 | 2 | 0 | 18 | 18 | 6 | 14 | 8 | 4 | 2 | 0 | 49 | 35 | 18 |
| St. Louis | 32 | 17 | 9 | 3 | 3 | 78 | 74 | 40 | 31 | 13 | 15 | 1 | 2 | 66 | 88 | 29 | 63 | 30 | 24 | 4 | 5 | 144 | 162 | 69 |
| San Jose | 20 | 10 | 9 | 1 | 0 | 50 | 53 | 21 | 20 | 7 | 9 | 1 | 3 | 49 | 55 | 18 | 40 | 17 | 18 | 2 | 3 | 99 | 108 | 39 |
| Tampa Bay | 7 | 2 | 4 | 0 | 1 | 13 | 18 | 5 | 6 | 1 | 3 | 2 | 0 | 14 | 19 | 4 | 13 | 3 | 7 | 2 | 1 | 27 | 37 | 9 |
| Toronto | 2 | 2 | 0 | 0 | 0 | 7 | 4 | 4 | 8 | 4 | 3 | 1 | 0 | 21 | 16 | 9 | 10 | 6 | 3 | 1 | 0 | 28 | 20 | 13 |
| Vancouver | 21 | 8 | 8 | 1 | 4 | 58 | 58 | 21 | 20 | 6 | 13 | 1 | 0 | 47 | 71 | 13 | 41 | 14 | 21 | 2 | 4 | 105 | 129 | 34 |
| Washington | 7 | 3 | 2 | 1 | 1 | 19 | 17 | 8 | 6 | 2 | 3 | 0 | 1 | 16 | 16 | 5 | 13 | 5 | 5 | 1 | 2 | 35 | 33 | 13 |
| **Totals** | **410** | **210** | **147** | **34** | **19** | **1141** | **1038** | **473** | **410** | **154** | **195** | **26** | **35** | **1003** | **1217** | **369** | **820** | **364** | **342** | **60** | **54** | **2144** | **2255** | **842** |

## Playoffs

| | Series | W | L | GP | W | L | T | GF | GA | Last Mtg. | Rnd. | Result |
|---|---|---|---|---|---|---|---|---|---|---|---|---|
| Detroit | 2 | 0 | 2 | 12 | 4 | 8 | 0 | 21 | 29 | 2008 | CQF | L 2-4 |
| San Jose | 2 | 0 | 2 | 10 | 2 | 8 | 0 | 24 | 33 | 2007 | CQF | L 1-4 |
| **Totals** | **4** | **0** | **4** | **22** | **6** | **16** | **0** | **45** | **62** | | | |

## Playoff Results 2009-2004

| Year | Round | Opponent | Result | GF | GA |
|---|---|---|---|---|---|
| 2008 | CQF | Detroit | L 2-4 | 12 | 17 |
| 2007 | CQF | San Jose | L 1-4 | 14 | 16 |
| 2006 | CQF | San Jose | L 1-4 | 10 | 17 |
| 2004 | CQF | Detroit | L 2-4 | 9 | 12 |

**Abbreviations: Round: CQF** - conference quarter-final.

## 2008-09 Results

| | | | |
|---|---|---|---|
| **Oct.** | 10 | at St. Louis | 2-5 |
| | 11 | Dallas | 3-1 |
| | 13 | at Chicago | 3-2† |
| | 15 | at Dallas | 4-6 |
| | 17 | at Columbus | 3-5 |
| | 18 | Columbus | 6-3 |
| | 23 | Calgary | 3-5 |
| | 25 | Los Angeles | 5-4 |
| | 28 | at Washington | 3-4† |
| | 30 | Edmonton | 3-1 |
| **Nov.** | 1 | Florida | 3-2† |
| | 4 | at Vancouver | 0-4 |
| | 6 | at Calgary | 6-7 |
| | 8 | at Colorado | 0-1 |
| | 11 | at San Jose | 4-3* |
| | 14 | at Anaheim | 4-3* |
| | 15 | at Los Angeles | 3-1 |
| | 17 | San Jose | 1-4 |
| | 21 | at Tampa Bay | 1-4 |
| | 23 | at Carolina | 5-2 |
| | 25 | St. Louis | 0-1† |
| | 28 | at Atlanta | 4-3* |
| | 29 | Minnesota | 2-6 |
| **Dec.** | 1 | at Buffalo | 2-0 |
| | 4 | Colorado | 3-2 |
| | 6 | Minnesota | 1-0 |
| | 8 | at St. Louis | 3-6 |
| | 9 | Vancouver | 1-3 |
| | 11 | at Columbus | 1-2† |
| | 13 | Dallas | 3-0 |
| | 18 | at Phoenix | 1-2 |
| | 20 | NY Islanders | 1-0 |
| | 23 | at Florida | 0-3 |
| | 26 | Detroit | 3-2 |
| | 28 | at Edmonton | 2-5 |
| | 29 | at Colorado | 1-5 |
| **Jan.** | 1 | Vancouver | 1-2 |
| | 3 | Calgary | 2-3 |
| | 6 | Colorado | 1-2 |
| | 8 | Pittsburgh | 5-3 |
| | 10 | Chicago | 4-1 |
| | 11 | at Chicago | 1-3 |
| | 13 | at Toronto | 2-0 |
| | 15 | at Montreal | 2-3 |
| | 17 | Atlanta | 2-7 |
| | 19 | New Jersey | 1-3 |
| | 28 | at Vancouver | 5-3 |
| | 30 | at Calgary | 1-3 |
| **Feb.** | 1 | at Edmonton | 2-1 |
| | 3 | Phoenix | 2-1 |
| | 5 | Anaheim | 4-2 |
| | 6 | at Minnesota | 2-0 |
| | 8 | at Dallas | 1-4 |
| | 10 | Detroit | 3-5 |
| | 12 | St. Louis | 4-3† |
| | 14 | Boston | 3-2† |
| | 16 | Ottawa | 0-2 |
| | 18 | at Detroit | 2-6 |
| | 19 | St. Louis | 1-2* |
| | 21 | at St. Louis | 1-0* |
| | 24 | Chicago | 5-3 |
| | 26 | Phoenix | 4-1 |
| | 28 | Detroit | 8-0 |
| **Mar.** | 3 | Edmonton | 6-5* |
| | 5 | Columbus | 4-2 |
| | 7 | at Philadelphia | 1-4 |
| | 10 | Washington | 1-2* |
| | 12 | NY Rangers | 2-4 |
| | 14 | at Phoenix | 2-0 |
| | 16 | at Los Angeles | 4-3 |
| | 18 | at Anaheim | 3-4* |
| | 19 | at San Jose | 2-3† |
| | 24 | Anaheim | 1-2† |
| | 26 | San Jose | 3-2 |
| | 28 | Los Angeles | 4-3* |
| | 29 | at Detroit | 4-3 |
| | 31 | at Columbus | 1-2 |
| **Apr.** | 3 | at Chicago | 1-3 |
| | 4 | Columbus | 5-4† |
| | 7 | Chicago | 2-4 |
| | 9 | at Detroit | 4-3† |
| | 10 | at Minnesota | 4-8 |

* – Overtime † – Shootout

# Entry Draft Selections 2009-1998

Name in bold denotes played in NHL.

**2009**

| Pick | |
|---|---|
| 11 | Ryan Ellis |
| 41 | Zach Budish |
| 42 | Charles-Olivier Roussel |
| 70 | Taylor Beck |
| 72 | Michael Latta |
| 98 | Craig Smith |
| 102 | Mattias Ekholm |
| 110 | Nick Oliver |
| 132 | Gabriel Bourque |
| 192 | Cameron Reid |

**2008**

| Pick | |
|---|---|
| 7 | Colin Wilson |
| 18 | Chet Pickard |
| 38 | Roman Josi |
| 136 | Taylor Stefishen |
| 166 | Jeffrey Foss |
| 201 | Jani Lajunen |
| 207 | Anders Lindback |

**2007**

| Pick | |
|---|---|
| 23 | Jonathon Blum |
| 54 | Jeremy Smith |
| 58 | Nick Spaling |
| 81 | Ryan Thang |
| 114 | Ben Ryan |
| 119 | Mark Santorelli |
| 144 | Andreas Thuresson |
| 174 | Robert Dietrich |
| 204 | Atte Engren |

**2006**

| Pick | |
|---|---|
| 56 | Blake Geoffrion |
| 105 | Niko Snellman |
| 146 | Mark Dekanich |
| 176 | Ryan Flynn |
| 206 | Viktor Sjodin |

**2005**

| Pick | |
|---|---|
| 18 | **Ryan Parent** |
| 78 | Teemu Laakso |
| 79 | Cody Franson |
| 150 | **Cal O'Reilly** |
| 176 | Ryan Maki |
| 213 | Scott Todd |
| 230 | **Patric Hornqvist** |

**2004**

| Pick | |
|---|---|
| 15 | **Alexander Radulov** |
| 81 | Vaclav Meidl |
| 107 | Nick Fugere |
| 139 | Kyle Moir |
| 147 | **Janne Niskala** |
| 178 | **Mike Santorelli** |
| 193 | Kevin Schaeffer |
| 209 | Stanislav Balan |
| 243 | Denis Kulyash |
| 258 | **Pekka Rinne** |
| 275 | Craig Switzer |

**2003**

| Pick | |
|---|---|
| 7 | **Ryan Suter** |
| 35 | Konstantin Glazachev |
| 37 | **Kevin Klein** |
| 49 | **Shea Weber** |
| 76 | Richard Stehlik |
| 89 | Paul Brown |
| 92 | **Alexander Sulzer** |
| 98 | Grigory Shafigulin |
| 117 | Teemu Lassila |
| 133 | Rustam Sidikov |
| 210 | Andrei Mukhachev |
| 213 | Miroslav Hanuljak |
| 268 | Lauris Darzins |

**2002**

| Pick | |
|---|---|
| 6 | **Scottie Upshall** |
| 102 | **Brandon Segal** |
| 138 | Patrick Jarrett |
| 172 | **Mike McKenna** |
| 203 | Josh Morrow |
| 235 | Kaleb Betts |
| 264 | Matt Davis |
| 266 | Steven Spencer |

**2001**

| Pick | |
|---|---|
| 12 | **Dan Hamhuis** |
| 33 | **Timofei Shishkanov** |
| 42 | Tomas Slovak |
| 75 | Denis Platonov |
| 76 | Oliver Setzinger |
| 98 | **Jordin Tootoo** |
| 178 | Anton Lavrentiev |
| 240 | Gustav Grasberg |
| 271 | **Mikko Lehtonen** |

**2000**

| Pick | |
|---|---|
| 6 | **Scott Hartnell** |
| 36 | Daniel Widing |
| 72 | Mattias Nilsson |
| 89 | **Libor Pivko** |
| 131 | **Matt Hendricks** |
| 137 | **Mike Stuart** |
| 154 | **Matt Koalska** |
| 173 | Tomas Harant |
| 197 | Zbynek Irgl |
| 203 | Jure Penko |
| 236 | Mats Christeen |
| 284 | Martin Hohener |

**1999**

| Pick | |
|---|---|
| 6 | **Brian Finley** |
| 33 | **Jonas Andersson** |
| 52 | **Adam Hall** |
| 54 | **Andrew Hutchinson** |
| 61 | Ed Hill |
| 65 | **Jan Lasak** |
| 72 | Brett Angel |
| 121 | Yevgeny Pavlov |
| 124 | Alexandre Krevsun |
| 131 | Konstantin Panov |
| 162 | **Timo Helbling** |
| 191 | **Martin Erat** |
| 205 | Kyle Kettles |
| 220 | Miroslav Durak |
| 248 | **Darren Haydar** |

**1998**

| Pick | |
|---|---|
| 2 | **David Legwand** |
| 60 | **Denis Arkhipov** |
| 85 | Geoff Koch |
| 88 | Kent Sauer |
| 138 | Martin Beauchesne |
| 147 | Craig Brunel |
| 202 | Martin Bartek |
| 230 | **Karlis Skrastins** |

*Jason Arnott celebrates one of the 33 goals he scored during the 2008-09 season. Arnott was the Predators' top marksmen, tying a career-high he had established as a rookie back in 1993-94.*

# Club Directory

Sommet Center

**Nashville Predators**
Sommet Center
501 Broadway
Nashville, TN 37203
Phone **615/770-2300**
FAX 615/770-2309
Ticket Information 615/770-PUCK
www.nashvillepredators.com
**Capacity:** 17,113

| | |
|---|---|
| Owner | Predators Holdings LLC |
| Investor Group | Christopher Cigarran, Thomas Cigarran, Joel and Holly Dobberpuhl, David Freeman, Herbert Fritch, DeWitt Thompson V, John Thompson. |
| Chairman and Governor | David Freeman |
| Pres. Hockey Ops./G.M./Alt. Gov. | David Poile |
| Pres. Business Ops. & Alt. Gov. | Ed Lang |
| Exec. V.P./Chief Sales Officer | Chris Parker |
| Exec. V.P./Chief Marketing Officer | Derek Perez |
| Sr. V.P./Special Asst.to the Pres. | Gerry Helper |
| Sr. V.P./Chief Admin. Offficer and Corporate Counsel | Michelle Kennedy |
| **Hockey Operations** | |
| Assistant General Manager | Paul Fenton |
| Director of Hockey Operations | Michael Santos |
| Head Coach | Barry Trotz |
| Associate Coach | Brent Peterson |
| Assistant Coach | Peter Horachek |
| Goaltending Coach | Mitch Korn |
| Video Coach | Robert Bouchard |
| Strength and Conditioning Coach | David Good |
| Chief Amateur Scout | Jeff Kealty |
| Professional Scouts | Nick Beverley & Shawn Dineen |
| North American Amateur Scouts | Jason Bukala, Rick Knickle, Tom Nolan, Glen Sanders, David Westby |
| European Scouts | Martin Bakula, Lucas Bergman, Janne Kekalainen |
| Head Athletic Trainer / Assistant | Dan Redmond / Andy Hosler |
| Equipment Manger / Assistant | Pete Rogers / Jeff Camelio |
| Equip Asst. / Locker Room Attend. | Brad Peterson / Craig "Partner" Baugh |
| Manager of Hockey Operations | Brandon Walker |
| Executive Assistant | Connell Crow |
| **Team Doctors** | |
| Medical Staff | John E. Kuhn, M.D., Paul J. Rummo, D.O., James L. Carey, M.D., Charles L. Cox, M.D., Alex Diamond, D.O., Daniel S. Weikert, M.D., Kevin Hagan, M.D., Blair Summitt, M.D., Wesley Thayer, M.D., Jason Wendel, M.D., Cristin M. Wallace, D.D.S. |
| **Communications/Development** | |
| Director of Communications | Tim Darling |
| Communications Coordinator | Kevin Wilson |
| Corporate Communications Coordinator | Jessica Jones |
| Director of Community Relations | Rebecca Ward |
| Community Rel./Youth & Amateur Hockey Coord. | Erich Wilhelm |
| Community Relations Coordinator | Gina Maduri |
| Youth and Amateur Hockey Manager | Andee Boiman |
| Internet Development Manager | Jay Levin |
| Team Photographer | John Russell |
| **Corporate Partnerships** | |
| Sr. V.P./Corporate Development | Chris Junghans |
| Director of New Business Development | Bob Flynn |
| Director, Corporate Partnerships | Delmar Smith |
| Account Executives | Bradford Hollingsworth, Anne McElroy |
| Sr. Account Service Manager | Jennifer Maxwell |
| Account Service Managers | Kathryn Cloud, Emily Cutler |
| Sr. Manager, Admin. and Legal Affairs | Raquel Toombs |
| **Marketing** | |
| Vice President of Marketing | Randy Campbell |
| Entertainment Manager | Adam DeVault |
| Database Marketing Manager | Joe Wiese |
| **Premium Seats** | |
| Vice President of Premium Seat Service | Susie Masotti |
| Senior Manager of Premium Seat Sales | Tim Wilson |
| Director of Premium Seat Service | Britt Kincheloe |
| Premium Seat Manager | Chris Burton |
| **Finance/Administration/Human Resources** | |
| Vice President / Director of Finance | Beth Snider / Terry Crutcher |
| Dir. of Human Resources / Payroll Mgr. | Allison Simms / Susan Charnley |
| Sr. Manager, Admin. & Legal Affairs | Raquel Toombs |
| **Technical Operations** | |
| Director / Manager, Technical Ops. | Blake Grant / Patrick Abell |
| **Ticket Operations** | |
| V.P. / Director, Ticket Sales | Nat Harden / Marty Mulford |
| Inside Sales Manager | Brad Gillispie |
| Senior Account Executive | Dan Schaefer |
| Account Executives | Jack Burk, Chris Harrington, Travis Laufle, Mac Maddox, Charles Rand, Britni Sorbo |
| **Broadcast** | |
| Broadcasting Director | Bob Kohl |
| Play-by-Play / Color | Pete Weber / Terry Crisp |
| Radio Play-by-Play Announcer | Tom Callahan |
| Manager, Video Production | Mitch Jordan |
| Associate Producer | David White |
| Videographer/Editor | Brett Newkirk |
| Radio Flagships | WGFX 104.5-FM, WRQQ 97.1-FM |
| TV Flagship | FS Tennessee |

## Key Off-Season Signings/Acquisitions

**2009**

**June 1** • Re-signed LW **Pierre-Luc Letourneau-Leblond.**
**30** • Re-signed D **Johnny Oduya.**
**July 1** • Re-signed D **Andy Greene.**
**10** • Signed G **Yann Danis.**
**13** • Named **Jacques Lemaire** head coach and **Mario Tremblay** assistant coach.
**17** • Signed D **Cory Murphy.**
**22** • Re-signed C **Travis Zajac.**
**Aug. 5** • Re-signed LW **Brendan Shanahan.**

# New Jersey Devils

## 2008-09 Results: 51W-27L-2OTL-2SOL 106PTS.
## First, Atlantic Division

*New Jersey's Martin Brodeur trims the twine from his net to save as a souvenir after surpassing his boyhood idol Patrick Roy as the NHL's all-time win leader with his 552nd regular-season victory on March 17, 2009.*

## 2009-10 Schedule

| | | | |
|---|---|---|---|
| **Oct.** | Sat. | 3 | Philadelphia |
| | Mon. | 5 | NY Rangers |
| | Thu. | 8 | at Tampa Bay |
| | Sat. | 10 | at Florida |
| | Mon. | 12 | at Washington |
| | Fri. | 16 | Atlanta |
| | Sat. | 17 | Carolina |
| | Thu. | 22 | at NY Rangers |
| | Sat. | 24 | at Pittsburgh |
| | Wed. | 28 | Buffalo |
| | Thu. | 29 | at Boston |
| | Sat. | 31 | at Tampa Bay* |
| **Nov.** | Wed. | 4 | Washington |
| | Fri. | 6 | NY Islanders |
| | Sat. | 7 | at Ottawa |
| | Wed. | 11 | Anaheim |
| | Thu. | 12 | at Pittsburgh |
| | Sat. | 14 | Washington |
| | Mon. | 16 | at Philadelphia |
| | Thu. | 19 | at Nashville |
| | Sat. | 21 | at Dallas |
| | Wed. | 25 | Ottawa |
| | Fri. | 27 | at Boston |
| | Sat. | 28 | NY Islanders* |
| **Dec.** | Wed. | 2 | Vancouver |
| | Fri. | 4 | Tampa Bay |
| | Sat. | 5 | Detroit |
| | Mon. | 7 | at Buffalo |
| | Wed. | 9 | Carolina |
| | Fri. | 11 | Florida |
| | Sat. | 12 | Philadelphia |
| | Wed. | 16 | Montreal |
| | Fri. | 18 | Ottawa |
| | Sat. | 19 | at Atlanta |
| | Mon. | 21 | at Pittsburgh |
| | Sat. | 26 | at Washington |
| | Mon. | 28 | Atlanta |
| | Wed. | 30 | Pittsburgh |
| | Thu. | 31 | at Chicago |
| **Jan.** | Sat. | 2 | at Minnesota |
| | Tue. | 5 | Dallas |
| | Fri. | 8 | Tampa Bay |
| | Sat. | 9 | at Montreal |
| | Tue. | 12 | at NY Rangers |
| | Thu. | 14 | at Phoenix |
| | Sat. | 16 | at Colorado* |
| | Mon. | 18 | at NY Islanders* |
| | Wed. | 20 | Florida |
| | Fri. | 22 | Montreal |
| | Sat. | 23 | at NY Islanders |
| | Tue. | 26 | at Ottawa |
| | Wed. | 27 | at Buffalo |
| | Fri. | 29 | Toronto |
| | Sun. | 31 | Los Angeles* |
| **Feb.** | Tue. | 2 | at Toronto |
| | Fri. | 5 | Toronto |
| | Sat. | 6 | at NY Rangers |
| | Mon. | 8 | at Philadelphia |
| | Wed. | 10 | Philadelphia |
| | Fri. | 12 | Nashville |
| | Sat. | 13 | at Carolina |
| **Mar.** | Tue. | 2 | at San Jose |
| | Fri. | 5 | at Calgary |
| | Sun. | 7 | at Edmonton |
| | Wed. | 10 | NY Rangers |
| | Fri. | 12 | Pittsburgh |
| | Sat. | 13 | at NY Islanders |
| | Mon. | 15 | Boston |
| | Wed. | 17 | Pittsburgh |
| | Thu. | 18 | at Toronto |
| | Sat. | 20 | St. Louis |
| | Tue. | 23 | Columbus |
| | Thu. | 25 | NY Rangers |
| | Sat. | 27 | at Montreal |
| | Sun. | 28 | at Philadelphia |
| | Tue. | 30 | Boston |
| **Apr.** | Fri. | 2 | Chicago |
| | Sat. | 3 | at Carolina |
| | Tue. | 6 | at Atlanta |
| | Thu. | 8 | at Florida |
| | Sat. | 10 | NY Islanders |
| | Sun. | 11 | Buffalo* |

* Denotes afternoon game.

## Year-by-Year Record

| | | Home | | | | Road | | | | Overall | | | | | | | | |
|---|---|---|---|---|---|---|---|---|---|---|---|---|---|---|---|---|---|---|
| **Season** | **GP** | **W** | **L** | **T** | **OL** | **W** | **L** | **T** | **OL** | **W** | **L** | **T** | **OL** | **GF** | **GA** | **Pts.** | **Finished** | **Playoff Result** |
| 2008-09 | 82 | 28 | 12 | .... | 1 | 23 | 15 | .... | 3 | 51 | 27 | .... | 4 | 244 | 209 | 106 | 1st, Atlantic Div. | Lost Conf. Quarter-Final |
| 2007-08 | 82 | 25 | 14 | .... | 2 | 21 | 15 | .... | 5 | 46 | 29 | .... | 7 | 206 | 197 | 99 | 2nd, Atlantic Div. | Lost Conf. Quarter-Final |
| 2006-07 | 82 | 25 | 10 | .... | 6 | 24 | 14 | .... | 3 | 49 | 24 | .... | 9 | 216 | 201 | 107 | 1st, Atlantic Div. | Lost Conf. Semi-Final |
| 2005-06 | 82 | 27 | 11 | .... | 3 | 19 | 16 | .... | 6 | 46 | 27 | .... | 9 | 242 | 229 | 101 | 1st, Atlantic Div. | Lost Conf. Semi-Final |
| 2004-05 | .... | .... | .... | .... | .... | .... | .... | .... | .... | .... | .... | .... | .... | .... | .... | .... | | |
| 2003-04 | 82 | 22 | 13 | 5 | 1 | 21 | 12 | 7 | 1 | 43 | 25 | 12 | 2 | 213 | 164 | 100 | 2nd, Atlantic Div. | Lost Conf. Quarter-Final |
| **2002-03** | **82** | **25** | **11** | **3** | **2** | **21** | **9** | **7** | **4** | **46** | **20** | **10** | **6** | **216** | **166** | **108** | **1st, Atlantic Div.** | **Won Stanley Cup** |
| 2001-02 | 82 | 22 | 13 | 4 | 2 | 19 | 15 | 5 | 2 | 41 | 28 | 9 | 4 | 205 | 187 | 95 | 3rd, Atlantic Div. | Lost Conf. Quarter-Final |
| 2000-01 | 82 | 24 | 11 | 6 | 0 | 24 | 8 | 6 | 3 | 48 | 19 | 12 | 3 | 295 | 195 | 111 | 1st, Atlantic Div. | Lost Final |
| **1999-2000** | **82** | **28** | **9** | **3** | **1** | **17** | **15** | **5** | **4** | **45** | **24** | **8** | **5** | **251** | **203** | **103** | **2nd, Atlantic Div.** | **Won Stanley Cup** |
| 1998-99 | 82 | 19 | 14 | 8 | .... | 28 | 10 | 3 | .... | 47 | 24 | 11 | .... | 248 | 196 | 105 | 1st, Atlantic Div. | Lost Conf. Quarter-Final |
| 1997-98 | 82 | 29 | 10 | 2 | .... | 19 | 13 | 9 | .... | 48 | 23 | 11 | .... | 225 | 166 | 107 | 1st, Atlantic Div. | Lost Conf. Quarter-Final |
| 1996-97 | 82 | 23 | 9 | 9 | .... | 22 | 14 | 5 | .... | 45 | 23 | 14 | .... | 231 | 182 | 104 | 1st, Atlantic Div. | Lost Conf. Semi-Final |
| 1995-96 | 82 | 22 | 17 | 2 | .... | 15 | 16 | 10 | .... | 37 | 33 | 12 | .... | 215 | 202 | 86 | 6th, Atlantic Div. | Out of Playoffs |
| **1994-95** | **48** | **14** | **4** | **6** | .... | **8** | **14** | **2** | .... | **22** | **18** | **8** | .... | **136** | **121** | **52** | **2nd, Atlantic Div.** | **Won Stanley Cup** |
| 1993-94 | 84 | 29 | 11 | 2 | .... | 18 | 14 | 10 | .... | 47 | 25 | 12 | .... | 306 | 220 | 106 | 2nd, Atlantic Div. | Lost Conf. Championship |
| 1992-93 | 84 | 24 | 14 | 4 | .... | 16 | 23 | 3 | .... | 40 | 37 | 7 | .... | 308 | 299 | 87 | 4th, Patrick Div. | Lost Div. Semi-Final |
| 1991-92 | 80 | 24 | 12 | 4 | .... | 14 | 19 | 3 | .... | 38 | 31 | 11 | .... | 289 | 259 | 87 | 4th, Patrick Div. | Lost Div. Semi-Final |
| 1990-91 | 80 | 23 | 10 | 7 | .... | 9 | 23 | 8 | .... | 32 | 33 | 15 | .... | 272 | 264 | 79 | 4th, Patrick Div. | Lost Div. Semi-Final |
| 1989-90 | 80 | 22 | 15 | 3 | .... | 15 | 19 | 6 | .... | 37 | 34 | 9 | .... | 295 | 288 | 83 | 2nd, Patrick Div. | Lost Div. Semi-Final |
| 1988-89 | 80 | 17 | 18 | 5 | .... | 10 | 23 | 7 | .... | 27 | 41 | 12 | .... | 281 | 325 | 66 | 5th, Patrick Div. | Out of Playoffs |
| 1987-88 | 80 | 23 | 16 | 1 | .... | 15 | 20 | 5 | .... | 38 | 36 | 6 | .... | 295 | 296 | 82 | 4th, Patrick Div. | Lost Conf. Championship |
| 1986-87 | 80 | 20 | 17 | 3 | .... | 9 | 28 | 3 | .... | 29 | 45 | 6 | .... | 293 | 368 | 64 | 6th, Patrick Div. | Out of Playoffs |
| 1985-86 | 80 | 17 | 21 | 2 | .... | 11 | 28 | 1 | .... | 28 | 49 | 3 | .... | 300 | 374 | 59 | 6th, Patrick Div. | Out of Playoffs |
| 1984-85 | 80 | 13 | 21 | 6 | .... | 9 | 27 | 4 | .... | 22 | 48 | 10 | .... | 264 | 346 | 54 | 5th, Patrick Div. | Out of Playoffs |
| 1983-84 | 80 | 10 | 28 | 2 | .... | 7 | 28 | 5 | .... | 17 | 56 | 7 | .... | 231 | 350 | 41 | 5th, Patrick Div. | Out of Playoffs |
| 1982-83 | 80 | 11 | 20 | 9 | .... | 6 | 29 | 5 | .... | 17 | 49 | 14 | .... | 230 | 338 | 48 | 5th, Patrick Div. | Out of Playoffs |
| 1981-82** | 80 | 14 | 21 | 5 | .... | 4 | 28 | 8 | .... | 18 | 49 | 13 | .... | 241 | 362 | 49 | 5th, Smythe Div. | Out of Playoffs |
| 1980-81** | 80 | 15 | 16 | 9 | .... | 7 | 29 | 4 | .... | 22 | 45 | 13 | .... | 258 | 344 | 57 | 5th, Smythe Div. | Out of Playoffs |
| 1979-80** | 80 | 12 | 20 | 8 | .... | 7 | 28 | 5 | .... | 19 | 48 | 13 | .... | 234 | 308 | 51 | 6th, Smythe Div. | Out of Playoffs |
| 1978-79** | 80 | 8 | 24 | 8 | .... | 7 | 29 | 4 | .... | 15 | 53 | 12 | .... | 210 | 331 | 42 | 4th, Smythe Div. | Out of Playoffs |
| 1977-78** | 80 | 17 | 14 | 9 | .... | 2 | 26 | 12 | .... | 19 | 40 | 21 | .... | 257 | 305 | 59 | 2nd, Smythe Div. | Lost Prelim. Round |
| 1976-77** | 80 | 12 | 20 | 8 | .... | 8 | 26 | 6 | .... | 20 | 46 | 14 | .... | 226 | 307 | 54 | 5th, Smythe Div. | Out of Playoffs |
| 1975-76* | 80 | 8 | 24 | 8 | .... | 4 | 32 | 4 | .... | 12 | 56 | 12 | .... | 190 | 351 | 36 | 5th, Smythe Div. | Out of Playoffs |
| 1974-75* | 80 | 12 | 20 | 8 | .... | 3 | 34 | 3 | .... | 15 | 54 | 11 | .... | 184 | 328 | 41 | 5th, Smythe Div. | Out of Playoffs |

* Kansas City Scouts. ** Colorado Rockies.

**ATLANTIC DIVISION**
**36th NHL Season**

**Franchise date:** June 11, 1974

Transferred from Denver to New Jersey, June 30, 1982.
Transferred from Kansas City to Denver, August 25, 1976.

# 2009-10 Player Personnel

| FORWARDS | HT | WT | S | Place of Birth | *Age | 2008-09 Club |
|---|---|---|---|---|---|---|
| BERGFORS, Nicklas | 5-11 | 195 | R | Sodertalje, Sweden | 22 | New Jersey-Lowell |
| BERNARD, Ashton | 6-4 | 195 | L | Eskasoni, N.S. | 19 | Shawinigan |
| BERUBE, Jean-Sebastien | 6-3 | 195 | L | Matane, Que. | 19 | Rouyn-Noranda |
| CLARKSON, David | 6-1 | 200 | R | Toronto, Ont. | 25 | New Jersey |
| CORMIER, Kevin | 6-3 | 235 | L | Moncton, N.B. | 23 | Lowell-Trenton |
| CORMIER, Patrice | 6-2 | 200 | L | Moncton, N.B. | 19 | Rimouski |
| DAVIS, Patrick | 6-2 | 195 | R | Sterling, MI | 22 | New Jersey-Lowell |
| ELIAS, Patrik | 6-1 | 195 | L | Trebic, Czech. | 33 | New Jersey |
| HALISCHUK, Matt | 5-11 | 180 | R | Toronto, Ont. | 21 | New Jersey-Lowell |
| HENRIQUE, Adam | 5-11 | 190 | L | Brantford, Ont. | 19 | Windsor |
| LANGENBRUNNER, Jamie | 6-1 | 205 | R | Cloquet, MN | 34 | New Jersey |
| LETOURNEAU-LEBLOND, P-L | 6-2 | 210 | L | Levis, Que. | 24 | New Jersey-Lowell |
| MILLS, Brad | 6-0 | 195 | R | Terrace, B.C. | 26 | Lowell |
| NAGY, Kory | 5-11 | 195 | L | London, Ont. | 19 | Oshawa |
| PALMIERI, Nick | 6-3 | 215 | R | Utica, NY | 20 | Erie (OHL)-Belleville |
| PANDOLFO, Jay | 6-1 | 190 | L | Winchester, MA | 34 | New Jersey |
| PARISE, Zach | 5-11 | 190 | L | Minneapolis, MN | 25 | New Jersey |
| PELLEY, Rod | 5-11 | 195 | L | Kitimat, B.C. | 25 | Lowell |
| PERKOVICH, Nathan | 6-5 | 195 | R | Canton, MI | 23 | Lake Superior-Trenton |
| PIKKARAINEN, Ilkka | 6-2 | 220 | R | Sonkajarvi, Finland | 28 | HIFK |
| ROLSTON, Brian | 6-2 | 210 | L | Flint, MI | 36 | New Jersey |
| SESTITO, Tim | 6-0 | 195 | L | Rome, NY | 25 | Edmonton-Springfield |
| SHANAHAN, Brendan | 6-3 | 220 | R | Mimico, Ont. | 40 | New Jersey |
| SNETSINGER, Brad | 6-2 | 190 | L | Ajax, Ont. | 22 | Lowell-Trenton |
| STOESZ, Myles | 6-2 | 210 | R | Steinbach, Man. | 22 | Gwinnett-Trenton |
| SWIFT, Michael | 5-9 | 170 | L | Peterborough, Ont. | 22 | Lowell |
| VASYUNOV, Alexander | 6-0 | 190 | R | Yaroslavl, USSR | 21 | Lowell-Yaroslavl |
| WALTER, Ben | 6-1 | 195 | L | Beaconsfield, Que. | 25 | NY Islanders-Bridgeport |
| ZAJAC, Travis | 6-3 | 195 | R | Winnipeg, Man. | 24 | New Jersey |
| ZHARKOV, Vladimir | 6-1 | 195 | L | Elektrostal, USSR | 21 | Lowell |
| ZUBRUS, Dainius | 6-5 | 225 | L | Elektrenai, USSR | 31 | New Jersey |
| **DEFENSEMEN** | | | | | | |
| CORRENTE, Matthew | 6-0 | 200 | R | Mississauga, Ont. | 21 | Lowell |
| DAVISON, Rob | 6-3 | 220 | L | St. Catharines, Ont. | 29 | Vancouver |
| DELAHEY, Matt | 6-2 | 205 | L | Moose Jaw, Sask. | 20 | Regina |
| ECKFORD, Tyler | 6-1 | 200 | L | Vancouver, B.C. | 24 | Lowell |
| FRASER, Mark | 6-3 | 215 | L | Ottawa, Ont. | 23 | Lowell |
| GELINAS, Eric | 6-4 | 190 | L | Vanier, Ont. | 18 | Lewiston |
| GREENE, Andy | 5-11 | 190 | L | Trenton, MI | 26 | New Jersey |
| LEACH, Jay | 6-5 | 225 | L | Syracuse, NY | 30 | New Jersey-Lowell |
| MAGNAN-GRENIER, Olivier | 6-2 | 205 | L | Sherbrooke, Que. | 23 | Lowell |
| MARTIN, Paul | 6-1 | 200 | L | Minneapolis, MN | 28 | New Jersey |
| MOTTAU, Mike | 6-0 | 190 | L | Quincy, MA | 31 | New Jersey |
| MURPHY, Cory | 5-10 | 185 | L | Kanata, Ont. | 31 | Fla-Rochester-T.B. |
| ODUYA, Johnny | 6-0 | 200 | L | Stockholm, Sweden | 28 | New Jersey |
| SALVADOR, Bryce | 6-3 | 215 | L | Brandon, Man. | 33 | New Jersey |
| WHITE, Colin | 6-4 | 215 | L | New Glasgow, N.S. | 31 | New Jersey |
| YOUNG, Harry | 6-5 | 200 | L | Windsor, Ont. | 19 | Windsor |

| GOALTENDERS | HT | WT | C | Place of Birth | *Age | 2008-09 Club |
|---|---|---|---|---|---|---|
| BRODEUR, Martin | 6-2 | 215 | L | Montreal, Que. | 37 | New Jersey |
| DANIS, Yann | 6-0 | 180 | L | Lafontaine, Que. | 28 | NY Islanders-Bridgeport |
| FRAZEE, Jeff | 6-0 | 195 | L | Edina, MN | 22 | Lowell-Trenton |

* – Age at start of 2009-10 season

## Captains' History

Simon Nolet, 1974-75 to 1976-77; Wilf Paiement, 1977-78; Gary Croteau, 1978-79; Mike Christie, Rene Robert and Lanny McDonald, 1979-80; Lanny McDonald, 1980-81; Lanny McDonald and Rob Ramage, 1981-82; Don Lever, 1982-83; Don Lever and Mel Bridgman, 1983-84; Mel Bridgman, 1984-85 to 1986-87; Kirk Muller, 1987-88 to 1990-91; Bruce Driver, 1991-92; Scott Stevens, 1992-93 to 2002-03; Scott Stevens and Scott Neidermayer, 2003-04; no captain, 2005-06; Patrik Elias, 2006-07; Patrik Elias and Jamie Langenbrunner, 2007-08; Jamie Langenbrunner, 2008-09 to date.

# 2008-09 Scoring

* – rookie

## Regular Season

| Pos | # | Player | Team | GP | G | A | Pts | TOI | +/– | PIM | PP | SH | GW | S | % |
|---|---|---|---|---|---|---|---|---|---|---|---|---|---|---|---|
| L | 9 | Zach Parise | N.J. | 82 | 45 | 49 | 94 | 18:45 | 30 | 24 | 14 | 0 | 8 | 364 | 12.4 |
| L | 26 | Patrik Elias | N.J. | 77 | 31 | 47 | 78 | 18:34 | 18 | 32 | 12 | 2 | 6 | 247 | 12.6 |
| R | 15 | Jamie Langenbrunner | N.J. | 81 | 29 | 40 | 69 | 18:05 | 25 | 56 | 6 | 3 | 7 | 229 | 12.7 |
| C | 19 | Travis Zajac | N.J. | 82 | 20 | 42 | 62 | 18:38 | 33 | 29 | 5 | 1 | 2 | 185 | 10.8 |
| R | 14 | Brian Gionta | N.J. | 81 | 20 | 40 | 60 | 16:58 | 12 | 32 | 3 | 3 | 1 | 248 | 8.1 |
| R | 8 | Dainius Zubrus | N.J. | 82 | 15 | 25 | 40 | 15:15 | 6 | 69 | 1 | 0 | 3 | 130 | 11.5 |
| D | 7 | Paul Martin | N.J. | 73 | 5 | 28 | 33 | 24:22 | 21 | 36 | 2 | 0 | 1 | 107 | 4.7 |
| R | 23 | David Clarkson | N.J. | 82 | 17 | 15 | 32 | 12:03 | –1 | 164 | 4 | 0 | 3 | 158 | 10.8 |
| C | 12 | Brian Rolston | N.J. | 64 | 15 | 17 | 32 | 15:06 | 2 | 30 | 8 | 0 | 3 | 174 | 8.6 |
| D | 29 | Johnny Oduya | N.J. | 82 | 7 | 22 | 29 | 20:52 | 21 | 30 | 1 | 1 | 4 | 108 | 6.5 |
| C | 11 | John Madden | N.J. | 76 | 7 | 16 | 23 | 16:25 | –7 | 26 | 0 | 1 | 2 | 132 | 5.3 |
| D | 28 | Niclas Havelid | ATL | 63 | 2 | 13 | 15 | 20:54 | 4 | 42 | 0 | 1 | 0 | 41 | 4.9 |
| | | | N.J. | 15 | 0 | 4 | 4 | 19:43 | –2 | 6 | 0 | 0 | 0 | 15 | 0.0 |
| | | | Total | 78 | 2 | 17 | 19 | 20:40 | 2 | 48 | 0 | 1 | 0 | 56 | 3.6 |
| D | 5 | Colin White | N.J. | 71 | 1 | 17 | 18 | 19:01 | 18 | 46 | 0 | 0 | 0 | 68 | 1.5 |
| D | 24 | Bryce Salvador | N.J. | 76 | 3 | 13 | 16 | 19:28 | –1 | 78 | 0 | 0 | 2 | 68 | 4.4 |
| D | 27 | Mike Mottau | N.J. | 80 | 1 | 14 | 15 | 17:47 | 24 | 35 | 0 | 0 | 0 | 71 | 1.4 |
| R | 18 | Brendan Shanahan | N.J. | 34 | 6 | 8 | 14 | 14:53 | –2 | 29 | 2 | 0 | 1 | 77 | 7.8 |
| L | 20 | Jay Pandolfo | N.J. | 61 | 5 | 5 | 10 | 14:50 | –12 | 10 | 0 | 1 | 1 | 63 | 7.9 |
| C | 16 | Bobby Holik | N.J. | 62 | 4 | 5 | 9 | 10:11 | –2 | 66 | 0 | 0 | 1 | 79 | 5.1 |
| L | 17 | Mike Rupp | N.J. | 72 | 3 | 6 | 9 | 8:43 | –2 | 136 | 0 | 0 | 0 | 76 | 3.9 |
| D | 6 | Andy Greene | N.J. | 49 | 2 | 7 | 9 | 16:17 | 3 | 22 | 0 | 0 | 0 | 38 | 5.3 |
| R | 18 * | Niclas Bergfors | N.J. | 8 | 1 | 0 | 1 | 5:47 | –1 | 0 | 0 | 0 | 0 | 6 | 16.7 |
| C | 22 * | Petr Vrana | N.J. | 16 | 1 | 0 | 1 | 6:53 | –4 | 2 | 0 | 0 | 0 | 6 | 16.7 |
| R | 10 * | Matt Halischuk | N.J. | 1 | 0 | 1 | 1 | 9:47 | –1 | 0 | 0 | 0 | 0 | 0 | 0.0 |
| L | 25 * | P-L Letournea-Leblond | N.J. | 8 | 0 | 1 | 1 | 4:50 | 3 | 22 | 0 | 0 | 0 | 3 | 0.0 |
| D | 28 | Jay Leach | N.J. | 24 | 0 | 1 | 1 | 14:50 | 0 | 21 | 0 | 0 | 0 | 5 | 0.0 |
| C | 10 * | Patrick Davis | N.J. | 1 | 0 | 0 | 0 | 4:30 | 0 | 0 | 0 | 0 | 0 | 0 | 0.0 |
| R | 21 * | Barry Tallackson | N.J. | 4 | 0 | 0 | 0 | 4:29 | –1 | 0 | 0 | 0 | 0 | 2 | 0.0 |

### Goaltending

| No. | Goaltender | GPI | Mins | Avg | W | L | OT | EN | SO | GA | SA | S% | G | A | PIM |
|---|---|---|---|---|---|---|---|---|---|---|---|---|---|---|---|
| 35 | Scott Clemmensen | 40 | 2356 | 2.39 | 25 | 13 | 1 | 5 | 2 | 94 | 1138 | .917 | 0 | 0 | 2 |
| 30 | Martin Brodeur | 31 | 1814 | 2.41 | 19 | 9 | 3 | 2 | 5 | 73 | 870 | .916 | 0 | 0 | 4 |
| 1 | Kevin Weekes | 16 | 795 | 2.42 | 7 | 5 | 0 | 1 | 0 | 32 | 399 | .920 | 0 | 0 | 0 |
| | **Totals** | **82** | **4992** | **2.49** | **51** | **27** | **4** | **8** | **7** | **207** | **2415** | **.914** | | | |

## Playoffs

| Pos | # | Player | Team | GP | G | A | Pts | TOI | +/– | PIM | PP | SH | GW | OT | S | % |
|---|---|---|---|---|---|---|---|---|---|---|---|---|---|---|---|---|
| L | 9 | Zach Parise | N.J. | 7 | 3 | 3 | 6 | 19:01 | 2 | 2 | 1 | 0 | 1 | 0 | 29 | 10.3 |
| R | 14 | Brian Gionta | N.J. | 7 | 2 | 3 | 5 | 17:49 | 0 | 4 | 0 | 0 | 0 | 0 | 23 | 8.7 |
| C | 19 | Travis Zajac | N.J. | 7 | 1 | 3 | 4 | 17:51 | 0 | 6 | 0 | 0 | 1 | 1 | 11 | 9.1 |
| D | 7 | Paul Martin | N.J. | 7 | 0 | 4 | 4 | 26:19 | 0 | 2 | 0 | 0 | 0 | 0 | 9 | 0.0 |
| R | 15 | Jamie Langenbrunner | N.J. | 4 | 2 | 1 | 3 | 16:13 | 0 | 2 | 0 | 0 | 0 | 0 | 16 | 12.5 |
| R | 18 | Brendan Shanahan | N.J. | 7 | 1 | 2 | 3 | 16:46 | –1 | 2 | 0 | 0 | 0 | 0 | 25 | 4.0 |
| L | 26 | Patrik Elias | N.J. | 7 | 1 | 2 | 3 | 17:53 | –1 | 2 | 0 | 0 | 0 | 0 | 25 | 4.0 |
| R | 23 | David Clarkson | N.J. | 7 | 2 | 0 | 2 | 8:31 | –1 | 19 | 1 | 0 | 1 | 0 | 12 | 16.7 |
| C | 12 | Brian Rolston | N.J. | 7 | 1 | 1 | 2 | 14:09 | 2 | 4 | 1 | 0 | 0 | 0 | 18 | 5.6 |
| D | 27 | Mike Mottau | N.J. | 7 | 1 | 1 | 2 | 17:59 | –3 | 0 | 0 | 0 | 0 | 0 | 1 | 100.0 |
| L | 20 | Jay Pandolfo | N.J. | 7 | 1 | 0 | 1 | 16:35 | –2 | 0 | 0 | 0 | 0 | 0 | 8 | 12.5 |
| C | 16 | Bobby Holik | N.J. | 3 | 0 | 1 | 1 | 5:17 | 0 | 2 | 0 | 0 | 0 | 0 | 3 | 0.0 |
| D | 6 | Andy Greene | N.J. | 3 | 0 | 1 | 1 | 15:18 | –1 | 0 | 0 | 0 | 0 | 0 | 5 | 0.0 |
| R | 8 | Dainius Zubrus | N.J. | 7 | 0 | 1 | 1 | 13:56 | –2 | 10 | 0 | 0 | 0 | 0 | 14 | 0.0 |
| D | 5 | Colin White | N.J. | 7 | 0 | 1 | 1 | 19:46 | –3 | 6 | 0 | 0 | 0 | 0 | 3 | 0.0 |
| C | 11 | John Madden | N.J. | 7 | 0 | 1 | 1 | 18:24 | –3 | 4 | 0 | 0 | 0 | 0 | 18 | 0.0 |
| D | 28 | Niclas Havelid | N.J. | 7 | 0 | 1 | 1 | 17:31 | 0 | 2 | 0 | 0 | 0 | 0 | 3 | 0.0 |
| D | 24 | Bryce Salvador | N.J. | 4 | 0 | 0 | 0 | 15:29 | –3 | 4 | 0 | 0 | 0 | 0 | 4 | 0.0 |
| L | 17 | Mike Rupp | N.J. | 7 | 0 | 0 | 0 | 6:54 | –2 | 14 | 0 | 0 | 0 | 0 | 7 | 0.0 |
| D | 29 | Johnny Oduya | N.J. | 7 | 0 | 0 | 0 | 20:18 | 3 | 2 | 0 | 0 | 0 | 0 | 8 | 0.0 |

### Goaltending

| No. | Goaltender | GPI | Mins | Avg | W | L | EN | SO | GA | SA | S% | G | A | PIM |
|---|---|---|---|---|---|---|---|---|---|---|---|---|---|---|
| 30 | Martin Brodeur | 7 | 427 | 2.39 | 3 | 4 | 0 | 1 | 17 | 239 | .929 | 0 | 0 | 4 |
| | **Totals** | **7** | **428** | **2.38** | **3** | **4** | **0** | **1** | **17** | **239** | **.929** | | | |

# Jacques Lemaire

## Head Coach

*Born: LaSalle, Que., September 7, 1945.*

Jacques Lemaire, the coach with the most wins in Devils' history who led the team to its first Stanley Cup championship in 1995, was introduced on July 13, 2009 as the club's new head coach. Lemaire, re-joined the Devils after serving as head coach of the Minnesota Wild for nine seasons. As the only coach in franchise history through 2008-09, he compiled a 293-255-108 (.529) mark in 656 regular-season games. In 2002-03, he led the Wild to the Western Conference Finals while capturing his second career Jack Adams Award as the league's top coach.

As head coach of the Devils for five seasons from 1993-94 through 1997-98, Lemaire guided the squad to a 199-122-57 (.602) mark in 378 regular-season games, and a 34-22 (.607) record in 56 playoff contests until stepping down on May 8, 1998. Including the 1995 Stanley Cup championship, he led the team to four postseason appearances and guided it to the Eastern Conference's best record in both 1996-97 and 1997-98. In Lemaire's first season behind the team's bench, New Jersey advanced past the first round of the playoffs for the first time since 1988, while he won the Jack Adams Award for the first time. He was originally named the organization's eighth coach on June 28, 1993.

Prior to joining the Devils, Lemaire served the Montreal Canadiens' Hockey Operations department for eight seasons from 1985-86 through 1992-93. He was head coach of the Canadiens from 1983 to 1985. As a player, Lemaire won the Stanley Cup eight times in 12 years with the Canadiens between 1967 and 1979 and was elected to the Hockey Hall of Fame in 1984.

### Coaching Record

| | | | Regular Season | | | | Playoffs | | | |
|---|---|---|---|---|---|---|---|---|---|---|
| Season | Team | League | GC | W | L | O/T | GC | W | L | T |
| 1979-80 | Sierre | | STATISTICS UNAVAILABLE | | | | | | | |
| 1980-81 | Sierre | | STATISTICS UNAVAILABLE | | | | | | | |
| 1982-83 | Longueuil | QMJHL | 70 | 37 | 29 | 4 | 15 | 9 | 6 | .... |
| **1983-84** | **Montreal** | **NHL** | **17** | **7** | **10** | **0** | **15** | **9** | **6** | .... |
| **1984-85** | **Montreal** | **NHL** | **80** | **41** | **27** | **12** | **12** | **6** | **6** | .... |
| **1993-94** | **New Jersey** | **NHL** | **84** | **47** | **25** | **12** | **20** | **11** | **9** | .... |
| **1994-95♦** | **New Jersey** | **NHL** | **48** | **22** | **18** | **8** | **20** | **16** | **4** | .... |
| **1995-96** | **New Jersey** | **NHL** | **82** | **37** | **33** | **12** | .... | .... | .... | .... |
| **1996-97** | **New Jersey** | **NHL** | **82** | **45** | **23** | **14** | **10** | **5** | **5** | .... |
| **1997-98** | **New Jersey** | **NHL** | **82** | **48** | **23** | **11** | **6** | **2** | **4** | .... |
| **2000-01** | **Minnesota** | **NHL** | **82** | **25** | **39** | **18** | .... | .... | .... | .... |
| **2001-02** | **Minnesota** | **NHL** | **82** | **26** | **35** | **21** | .... | .... | .... | .... |
| **2002-03** | **Minnesota** | **NHL** | **82** | **42** | **29** | **11** | **18** | **8** | **10** | .... |
| **2003-04** | **Minnesota** | **NHL** | **82** | **30** | **29** | **23** | .... | .... | .... | .... |
| **2004-05** | **Minnesota** | | SEASON CANCELLED | | | | | | | |
| **2005-06** | **Minnesota** | **NHL** | **82** | **38** | **36** | **8** | .... | .... | .... | .... |
| **2006-07** | **Minnesota** | **NHL** | **82** | **48** | **26** | **8** | **5** | **1** | **4** | .... |
| **2007-08** | **Minnesota** | **NHL** | **82** | **44** | **28** | **10** | **6** | **2** | **4** | .... |
| **2008-09** | **Minnesota** | **NHL** | **82** | **40** | **33** | **9** | .... | .... | .... | .... |
| | **NHL Totals** | | **1131** | **540** | **414** | **177** | **112** | **60** | **52** | .... |

♦ Stanley Cup win.

# Club Records

## Team

(Figures in brackets for season records are games played; records for fewest points, wins, ties, losses, goals, goals against are for 70 or more games)

**Most Points** ............... **111** 2000-01 (82)
**Most Wins** ................. **51** 2008-09 (82)
**Most Ties** .................. **21** 1977-78 (80)
**Most Losses** ................ **56** 1975-76 (80), 1983-84 (80)
**Most Goals** ................ **308** 1992-93 (84)
**Most Goals Against** ......... **374** 1985-86 (80)
**Fewest Points** ............. ***36** 1975-76 (80)
**41** 1983-84 (80)
**Fewest Wins** ............. ***12** 1975-76 (80)
**17** 1982-83 (80), 1983-84 (80)
**Fewest Ties** ................. **3** 1985-86 (80)
**Fewest Losses** .............. **19** 2000-01 (82)
**Fewest Goals** ............ ***184** 1974-75 (80)
**205** 2001-02 (82)
**Fewest Goals Against** ....... **164** 2003-04 (82)
**Longest Winning Streak**
**Overall** .................. **13** Feb. 26-Mar. 23/01
**Home** .................... **11** Feb. 9-Mar. 20/09
**Away** .................. ****10** Feb. 27-Apr. 7/01
**Longest Undefeated Streak**
**Overall** .................. **13** Four times
**Home** .................... **15** Jan. 8-Mar. 15/97 (9 wins, 6 ties)
**Away** .................... **10** Feb. 27-Apr. 7/01 (10 wins)
**Longest Losing Streak**
**Overall** ................. ***14** Dec. 30/75-Jan. 29/76
**10** Oct. 14-Nov. 4/83
**Home** ..................... **9** Dec. 22/85-Feb. 6/86
**Away** .................... **12** Oct. 19-Dec. 1/83
**Longest Winless Streak**
**Overall** ................. ***27** Feb. 12-Apr. 4/76 (21 losses, 6 ties)
**18** Oct. 20-Nov. 26/82 (14 losses 4 ties)
**Home** .................... ***14** Feb. 12-Mar. 30/76 (10 losses, 4 ties), Feb. 4-Mar. 31/79 (12 losses, 2 ties)
**9** Dec. 22/85-Feb. 6/86 (9 losses)
**Away** .................... ***32** Nov. 12/77-Mar. 15/78 (22 losses, 10 ties)
**14** Dec. 26/82-Mar. 5/83 (13 losses, 1 tie)
**Most Shutouts, Season** ....... **14** 2003-04 (82)
**Most PIM, Season** ......... **2,494** 1988-89 (80)
**Most Goals, Game** ............ **9** Nine times

## Individual

**Most Seasons** ............... **20** Ken Daneyko
**Most Games** .............. **1,283** Ken Daneyko
**Most Goals, Career** ......... **347** John MacLean
**Most Assists, Career** ....... **411** Patrik Elias
**Most Points, Career** ......... **706** Patrik Elias (295G, 411A)
**Most PIM, Career** ......... **2,519** Ken Daneyko
**Most Shutouts, Career** ....... **101** Martin Brodeur
**Longest Consecutive Games Streak** ............ **388** Ken Daneyko (Nov. 4/89-Mar. 29/94)
**Most Goals, Season** .......... **48** Brian Gionta (2005-06)
**Most Assists, Season** ......... **60** Scott Stevens (1993-94)
**Most Points, Season** ......... **96** Patrik Elias (2000-01; 40G, 56A)
**Most PIM, Season** .......... **295** Krzysztof Oliwa (1997-98)
**Most Points, Defenseman, Season** .................. **78** Scott Stevens (1993-94; 18G, 60A)
**Most Points, Center, Season** .................. **94** Kirk Muller (1987-88; 37G, 57A)
**Most Points, Right Wing, Season** .................. **89** Brian Gionta (2005-06; 48G, 41A)
**Most Points, Left Wing, Season** .................. **96** Patrik Elias (2000-01; 40G, 56A)
**Most Points, Rookie, Season** .................. **70** Scott Gomez (1999-2000; 19G, 51A)
**Most Shutouts, Season** ....... **12** Martin Brodeur (2006-07)
**Most Goals, Game** ............ **4** Six times
**Most Assists, Game** ........... **5** Greg Adams (Oct. 10/85), Kirk Muller (Mar. 25/87), Tom Kurvers (Feb. 13/89), Scott Gomez (Mar. 30/03)
**Most Points, Game** ............ **6** Kirk Muller (Nov. 29/86; 3G, 3A)

* Records include Kansas City Scouts and Colorado Rockies, 1974-75 through 1981-82.
** NHL Record.

## General Managers' History

Sid Abel, 1974-75, 1975-76; Ray Miron, 1976-77 to 1980-81; Bill MacMillan, 1981-82, 1982-83; Bill MacMillan and Max McNab, 1983-84; Max McNab 1984-85 to 1986-87; Lou Lamoriello, 1987-88 to date.

## Retired Numbers

| | | |
|---|---|---|
| **3** | Ken Daneyko | 1982-2003 |
| **4** | Scott Stevens | 1991-2005 |

# All-time Record vs. Other Clubs

## Regular Season

| | At Home | | | | | | | | On Road | | | | | | | | Total | | | | | | | |
|---|---|---|---|---|---|---|---|---|---|---|---|---|---|---|---|---|---|---|---|---|---|---|---|---|
| | GP | W | L | T | OL | GF | GA | PTS | GP | W | L | T | OL | GF | GA | PTS | GP | W | L | T | OL | GF | GA | PTS |
| Anaheim | 9 | 7 | 2 | 0 | 0 | 32 | 16 | 14 | 12 | 5 | 6 | 1 | 0 | 31 | 34 | 11 | 21 | 12 | 8 | 1 | 0 | 63 | 50 | 25 |
| Atlanta | 18 | 9 | 5 | 1 | 3 | 52 | 40 | 22 | 18 | 11 | 3 | 2 | 2 | 65 | 39 | 26 | 36 | 20 | 8 | 3 | 5 | 117 | 79 | 48 |
| Boston | 61 | 21 | 29 | 11 | 0 | 158 | 188 | 53 | 64 | 22 | 32 | 8 | 2 | 198 | 242 | 54 | 125 | 43 | 61 | 19 | 2 | 356 | 430 | 107 |
| Buffalo | 62 | 24 | 29 | 9 | 0 | 179 | 193 | 57 | 62 | 20 | 33 | 8 | 1 | 188 | 235 | 49 | 124 | 44 | 62 | 17 | 1 | 367 | 428 | 106 |
| Calgary | 47 | 16 | 28 | 3 | 0 | 132 | 168 | 35 | 43 | 7 | 27 | 8 | 1 | 112 | 184 | 23 | 90 | 23 | 55 | 11 | 1 | 244 | 352 | 58 |
| Carolina | 53 | 30 | 19 | 4 | 0 | 182 | 161 | 64 | 52 | 22 | 20 | 8 | 2 | 153 | 156 | 54 | 105 | 52 | 39 | 12 | 2 | 335 | 317 | 118 |
| Chicago | 49 | 22 | 16 | 11 | 0 | 152 | 145 | 55 | 48 | 13 | 24 | 10 | 1 | 132 | 181 | 37 | 97 | 35 | 40 | 21 | 1 | 284 | 326 | 92 |
| Colorado | 38 | 20 | 13 | 4 | 1 | 154 | 125 | 45 | 36 | 14 | 18 | 4 | 0 | 102 | 126 | 32 | 74 | 34 | 31 | 8 | 1 | 256 | 251 | 77 |
| Columbus | 3 | 2 | 0 | 1 | 0 | 6 | 4 | 5 | 6 | 3 | 2 | 0 | 1 | 17 | 17 | 7 | 9 | 5 | 2 | 1 | 1 | 23 | 21 | 12 |
| Dallas | 45 | 23 | 19 | 3 | 0 | 155 | 134 | 49 | 47 | 13 | 27 | 6 | 1 | 120 | 171 | 33 | 92 | 36 | 46 | 9 | 1 | 275 | 305 | 82 |
| Detroit | 41 | 21 | 11 | 9 | 0 | 139 | 105 | 51 | 42 | 13 | 26 | 2 | 1 | 132 | 172 | 29 | 83 | 34 | 37 | 11 | 1 | 271 | 277 | 80 |
| Edmonton | 35 | 15 | 17 | 3 | 0 | 114 | 115 | 33 | 32 | 12 | 14 | 6 | 0 | 117 | 137 | 30 | 67 | 27 | 31 | 9 | 0 | 231 | 252 | 63 |
| Florida | 32 | 21 | 8 | 3 | 0 | 99 | 61 | 45 | 33 | 18 | 11 | 4 | 0 | 84 | 75 | 40 | 65 | 39 | 19 | 7 | 0 | 183 | 136 | 85 |
| Los Angeles | 45 | 20 | 20 | 5 | 0 | 149 | 154 | 45 | 44 | 9 | 27 | 6 | 2 | 137 | 205 | 26 | 89 | 29 | 47 | 11 | 2 | 286 | 359 | 71 |
| Minnesota | 5 | 4 | 0 | 1 | 0 | 20 | 10 | 9 | 4 | 2 | 1 | 1 | 0 | 12 | 10 | 5 | 9 | 6 | 1 | 2 | 0 | 32 | 20 | 14 |
| Montreal | 62 | 32 | 26 | 4 | 0 | 193 | 207 | 68 | 62 | 21 | 34 | 6 | 1 | 152 | 196 | 49 | 124 | 53 | 60 | 10 | 1 | 345 | 403 | 117 |
| Nashville | 6 | 2 | 3 | 0 | 1 | 18 | 18 | 5 | 7 | 6 | 1 | 0 | 0 | 21 | 13 | 12 | 13 | 8 | 4 | 0 | 1 | 39 | 31 | 17 |
| NY Islanders | 99 | 43 | 43 | 11 | 2 | 314 | 328 | 99 | 100 | 26 | 60 | 11 | 3 | 279 | 391 | 66 | 199 | 69 | 103 | 22 | 5 | 593 | 719 | 165 |
| NY Rangers | 101 | 54 | 38 | 7 | 2 | 339 | 316 | 117 | 99 | 28 | 47 | 20 | 4 | 283 | 361 | 80 | 200 | 82 | 85 | 27 | 6 | 622 | 677 | 197 |
| Ottawa | 31 | 19 | 10 | 2 | 0 | 89 | 74 | 40 | 32 | 20 | 8 | 3 | 1 | 83 | 73 | 44 | 63 | 39 | 18 | 5 | 1 | 172 | 147 | 84 |
| Philadelphia | 98 | 56 | 34 | 8 | 0 | 334 | 309 | 120 | 100 | 31 | 57 | 10 | 2 | 259 | 368 | 74 | 198 | 87 | 91 | 18 | 2 | 593 | 677 | 194 |
| Phoenix | 31 | 13 | 12 | 6 | 0 | 101 | 93 | 32 | 32 | 7 | 22 | 3 | 0 | 82 | 117 | 17 | 63 | 20 | 34 | 9 | 0 | 183 | 210 | 49 |
| Pittsburgh | 96 | 47 | 35 | 13 | 1 | 337 | 308 | 108 | 94 | 44 | 45 | 4 | 1 | 307 | 339 | 93 | 190 | 91 | 80 | 17 | 2 | 644 | 647 | 201 |
| St. Louis | 47 | 22 | 18 | 7 | 0 | 148 | 131 | 51 | 48 | 14 | 26 | 7 | 1 | 152 | 198 | 36 | 95 | 36 | 44 | 14 | 1 | 300 | 329 | 87 |
| San Jose | 14 | 9 | 4 | 1 | 0 | 53 | 31 | 19 | 11 | 6 | 3 | 1 | 1 | 32 | 26 | 14 | 25 | 15 | 7 | 2 | 1 | 85 | 57 | 33 |
| Tampa Bay | 34 | 23 | 7 | 2 | 2 | 123 | 70 | 50 | 33 | 17 | 9 | 5 | 2 | 100 | 75 | 41 | 67 | 40 | 16 | 7 | 4 | 223 | 145 | 91 |
| Toronto | 54 | 20 | 16 | 15 | 3 | 183 | 170 | 58 | 56 | 16 | 34 | 5 | 1 | 155 | 198 | 38 | 110 | 36 | 50 | 20 | 4 | 338 | 368 | 96 |
| Vancouver | 50 | 21 | 21 | 6 | 2 | 154 | 159 | 50 | 49 | 10 | 28 | 11 | 0 | 135 | 183 | 31 | 99 | 31 | 49 | 17 | 2 | 289 | 342 | 81 |
| Washington | 87 | 44 | 35 | 7 | 1 | 267 | 253 | 96 | 87 | 30 | 51 | 6 | 0 | 247 | 327 | 66 | 174 | 74 | 86 | 13 | 1 | 514 | 580 | 162 |
| Defunct Clubs | 8 | 4 | 2 | 2 | 0 | 25 | 19 | 10 | 8 | 2 | 3 | 3 | 0 | 19 | 27 | 7 | 16 | 6 | 5 | 5 | 0 | 44 | 46 | 17 |
| **Totals** | **1361** | **664** | **520** | **159** | **18** | **4401** | **4105** | **1505** | **1361** | **462** | **699** | **169** | **31** | **3906** | **4876** | **1124** | **2722** | **1126** | **1219** | **328** | **49** | **8307** | **8981** | **2629** |

## Playoffs

| | Series | W | L | GP | W | L | T | GF | GA | Last Mtg. | Rnd. | Result |
|---|---|---|---|---|---|---|---|---|---|---|---|---|
| Anaheim | 1 | 1 | 0 | 7 | 4 | 3 | 0 | 19 | 12 | 2003 | F | W 4-3 |
| Boston | 4 | 3 | 1 | 23 | 15 | 8 | 0 | 68 | 60 | 2003 | CQF | W 4-1 |
| Buffalo | 1 | 1 | 0 | 7 | 4 | 3 | 0 | 14 | 14 | 1994 | CQF | W 4-3 |
| Carolina | 4 | 1 | 3 | 24 | 10 | 14 | 0 | 56 | 51 | 2009 | CQF | L 3-4 |
| Colorado | 1 | 0 | 1 | 7 | 3 | 4 | 0 | 11 | 19 | 2001 | F | L 3-4 |
| Dallas | 1 | 1 | 0 | 6 | 4 | 2 | 0 | 15 | 9 | 2000 | F | W 4-2 |
| Detroit | 1 | 1 | 0 | 4 | 4 | 0 | 0 | 16 | 7 | 1995 | F | W 4-0 |
| Florida | 1 | 1 | 0 | 4 | 4 | 0 | 0 | 12 | 6 | 2000 | CQF | W 4-0 |
| Montreal | 1 | 1 | 0 | 5 | 4 | 1 | 0 | 22 | 11 | 1997 | CQF | W 4-1 |
| NY Islanders | 1 | 1 | 0 | 6 | 4 | 2 | 0 | 23 | 18 | 1988 | DSF | W 4-2 |
| NY Rangers | 5 | 1 | 4 | 28 | 12 | 16 | 0 | 75 | 79 | 2008 | CQF | L 1-4 |
| Ottawa | 3 | 1 | 2 | 18 | 7 | 11 | 0 | 40 | 41 | 2007 | CSF | L 1-4 |
| Philadelphia | 4 | 2 | 2 | 20 | 9 | 11 | 0 | 50 | 49 | 2004 | CQF | L 1-4 |
| Pittsburgh | 5 | 2 | 3 | 29 | 15 | 14 | 0 | 86 | 80 | 2001 | CF | W 4-1 |
| Tampa Bay | 2 | 2 | 0 | 11 | 8 | 3 | 0 | 33 | 22 | 2007 | CQF | W 4-2 |
| Toronto | 2 | 2 | 0 | 13 | 8 | 5 | 0 | 37 | 27 | 2001 | CSF | W 4-3 |
| Washington | 2 | 1 | 1 | 13 | 6 | 7 | 0 | 43 | 44 | 1990 | DSF | L 2-4 |
| **Totals** | **39** | **22** | **17** | **225** | **121** | **104** | **0** | **620** | **549** | | | |

Calgary totals include Atlanta Flames, 1974-75 to 1979-80.
Colorado totals include Quebec, 1979-80 to 1994-95.
Phoenix totals include Winnipeg, 1979-80 to 1995-96.
Carolina totals include Hartford, 1979-80 to 1996-97.
Dallas totals include Minnesota North Stars, 1974-75 to 1992-93.

## Playoff Results 2009-2004

| Year | Round | Opponent | Result | GF | GA |
|---|---|---|---|---|---|
| 2009 | CQF | Carolina | L 3-4 | 15 | 17 |
| 2008 | CQF | NY Rangers | L 1-4 | 12 | 19 |
| 2007 | CSF | Ottawa | L 1-4 | 11 | 15 |
| | CQF | Tampa Bay | W 4-2 | 19 | 14 |
| 2006 | CSF | Carolina | L 1-4 | 10 | 17 |
| | CQF | NY Rangers | W 4-0 | 17 | 4 |
| 2004 | CQF | Philadelphia | L 1-4 | 9 | 14 |

**Abbreviations: Round: F** – Final; **CF** – conference final; **CSF** – conference semi-final; **CQF** – conference quarter-final; **DSF** – division semi-final.

## 2008-09 Results

| | | | | | | | |
|---|---|---|---|---|---|---|---|
| **Oct.** | 10 | NY Islanders | 2-1 | | 11 | at Anaheim | 3-4 |
| | 11 | at Pittsburgh | 2-1* | | 13 | at Vancouver | 5-3 |
| | 13 | at NY Rangers | 1-4 | | 16 | at Columbus | 2-1 |
| | 16 | at Atlanta | 1-0 | | 17 | at NY Islanders | 3-1 |
| | 18 | at Washington | 4-3† | | 19 | at Nashville | 3-1 |
| | 22 | Dallas | 5-0 | | 21 | Montreal | 5-2 |
| | 24 | Philadelphia | 3-6 | | 27 | at Ottawa | 4-1 |
| | 25 | at Philadelphia | 2-3* | | 29 | at Boston | 4-3* |
| | 29 | Toronto | 5-6† | | 30 | Pittsburgh | 4-3* |
| **Nov.** | 1 | Atlanta | 6-1 | **Feb.** | 3 | Washington | 2-5 |
| | 3 | Buffalo | 0-2 | | 6 | at Atlanta | 5-1 |
| | 5 | Tampa Bay | 4-3† | | 7 | Los Angeles | 1-3 |
| | 8 | at Detroit | 1-3 | | 9 | NY Rangers | 3-0 |
| | 9 | Edmonton | 1-2 | | 11 | NY Islanders | 4-2 |
| | 12 | NY Rangers | 2-5 | | 13 | Boston | 1-0 |
| | 14 | at Washington | 1-3 | | 15 | San Jose | 6-5 |
| | 15 | Washington | 6-5† | | 17 | at Florida | 0-4 |
| | 20 | Florida | 3-1 | | 19 | at Tampa Bay | 3-2† |
| | 21 | NY Islanders | 5-2 | | 21 | at NY Islanders | 0-4 |
| | 23 | at Tampa Bay | 7-3 | | 26 | Colorado | 4-0 |
| | 26 | at Florida | 3-2* | | 28 | Florida | 7-2 |
| | 29 | at Pittsburgh | 1-4 | **Mar.** | 1 | Philadelphia | 3-0 |
| **Dec.** | 4 | at Philadelphia | 3-2* | | 3 | at Toronto | 3-2* |
| | 6 | at Montreal | 2-1* | | 7 | at NY Islanders | 3-7 |
| | 10 | Pittsburgh | 4-1 | | 10 | Calgary | 3-2 |
| | 12 | NY Rangers | 8-5 | | 12 | Phoenix | 5-2 |
| | 13 | Buffalo | 2-4 | | 14 | at Montreal | 3-1 |
| | 16 | at Toronto | 2-3† | | 17 | Chicago | 3-2 |
| | 17 | at Buffalo | 5-3 | | 18 | at Carolina | 2-4 |
| | 19 | Ottawa | 5-1 | | 20 | Minnesota | 4-0 |
| | 21 | Philadelphia | 3-2† | | 22 | at Boston | 1-4 |
| | 23 | Boston | 0-2 | | 23 | at Philadelphia | 2-4 |
| | 26 | Pittsburgh | 0-1 | | 27 | at Chicago | 2-3* |
| | 27 | at NY Rangers | 4-2 | | 28 | Carolina | 1-2 |
| | 30 | at St. Louis | 4-3 | | 30 | at NY Rangers | 0-3 |
| | 31 | at Dallas | 2-4 | **Apr.** | 1 | at Pittsburgh | 1-6 |
| **Jan.** | 2 | Montreal | 4-1 | | 3 | Tampa Bay | 5-4* |
| | 4 | Ottawa | 4-3* | | 4 | at Buffalo | 3-2 |
| | 6 | at Carolina | 2-3 | | 7 | Toronto | 1-4 |
| | 8 | Atlanta | 0-4 | | 9 | at Ottawa | 3-2† |
| | 10 | at Los Angeles | 5-1 | | 11 | Carolina | 3-2 |

* – Overtime † – Shootout

## Entry Draft Selections 2009-1995

Name in bold denotes played in NHL.

**2009**
Pick
20 Jacob Josefson
54 Eric Gelinas
73 Alexander Urbom
114 Seth Helgeson
144 Derek Rodwell
174 Ashton Bernard
204 Curtis Gedig

**2008**
Pick
24 Mattias Tedenby
52 Brandon Burlon
54 Patrice Cormier
82 Adam Henrique
112 Matt Delahey
142 Kory Nagy
172 David Wohlberg
202 Harry Young
205 Jean-Sebastien Berube

**2007**
Pick
57 Mike Hoeffel
79 Nick Palmieri
87 Corbin McPherson
117 **Matt Halischuk**
177 Vili Sopanen
207 Ryan Molle

**2006**
Pick
30 Matthew Corrente
58 Alexander Vasyunov
67 Kirill Tulupov
77 Vladimir Zharkov
107 Tyler Miller
148 Olivier Magnan-Grenier
178 Tony Romano
208 Kyell Henegan

**2005**
Pick
23 **Nicklas Bergfors**
38 Jeff Frazee
84 **Mark Fraser**
99 **Patrick Davis**
155 Mark Fayne
170 Sean Zimmerman
218 Alexander Sundstrom

**2004**
Pick
20 **Travis Zajac**
155 Alexander Mikhailishin
185 Josh Disher
216 **Pierre-Luc Letourneau-Leblond**
217 Tyler Eckford
250 Nathan Perkovich
282 Valeri Klimov

**2003**
Pick
17 **Zach Parise**
42 **Petr Vrana**
93 Ivan Khomutov
167 Zach Tarkir
197 Jason Smith
261 **Joey Tenute**
292 Arseny Bondarev

**2002**
Pick
51 Anton Kadeykin
53 **Barry Tallackson**
64 **Jason Ryznar**
84 Marek Chvatal
85 Ahren Nittel
117 **Cam Janssen**
154 Krisjanis Redlihs
187 Eric Johansson
218 Ilkka Pikkarainen
250 Dan Glover
281 Bill Kinkel

**2001**
Pick
28 Adrian Foster
44 Igor Pohanka
48 **Tuomas Pihlman**
60 Victor Uchevatov
67 Robin Leblanc
72 **Brandon Nolan**
128 Andrei Posnov
163 **Andreas Salomonsson**
194 James Massen
229 **Aaron Voros**
257 Yevgeny Gamalei

**2000**
Pick
22 **David Hale**
39 Teemu Laine
56 **Alexander Suglobov**
57 Matt DeMarchi
62 **Paul Martin**
67 Max Birbraer
76 **Mike Rupp**
125 Phil Cole
135 **Mike Danton**
164 Matus Kostur
194 Deryk Engelland
198 Ken Magowan
257 Warren McCutcheon

**1999**
Pick
27 Ari Ahonen
42 **Mike Commodore**
50 Brett Clouthier
95 Andre Lakos
100 Teemu Kesa
185 Scott Cameron
214 Chris Hartsburg
242 Justin Dziama

**1998**
Pick
26 **Mike Van Ryn**
27 **Scott Gomez**
37 **Christian Berglund**
82 **Brian Gionta**
96 **Mikko Jokela**
105 **Pierre Dagenais**
119 Anton But
143 **Ryan Flinn**
172 Jacques Lariviere
199 Erik Jensen
227 Marko Ahosilta
257 Ryan Held

**1997**
Pick
24 **Jean-Francois Damphousse**
38 **Stanislav Gron**
104 Lucas Nehrling
131 **Jiri Bicek**
159 **Sascha Goc**
188 Mathieu Benoit
215 **Scott Clemmensen**
241 Jan Srdinko

**1996**
Pick
10 **Lance Ward**
38 Wes Mason
41 Josh DeWolf
47 **Pierre Dagenais**
49 **Colin White**
63 **Scott Parker**
91 **Josef Boumedienne**
101 Josh MacNevin
118 Glenn Crawford
145 Sean Ritchlin
173 Daryl Andrews
199 **Willie Mitchell**
205 Jay Bertsch
225 Pasi Petrilainen

**1995**
Pick
18 **Petr Sykora**
44 **Nathan Perrott**
70 **Sergei Vyshedkevich**
78 **David Gosselin**
79 **Alyn McCauley**
96 Henrik Rehnberg
122 **Chris Mason**
148 Adam Young
174 Richard Rochefort
200 Frederic Henry
226 Colin O'Hara

## Coaching History

Bep Guidolin, 1974-75; Bep Guidolin, Sid Abel and Eddie Bush, 1975-76; Johnny Wilson, 1976-77; Pat Kelly, 1977-78; Pat Kelly and Aldo Guidolin, 1978-79; Don Cherry, 1979-80; Bill MacMillan, 1980-81; Bert Marshall and Marshall Johnston, 1981-82; Bill MacMillan, 1982-83; Bill MacMillan and Tom McVie, 1983-84; Doug Carpenter, 1984-85 to 1986-87; Doug Carpenter and Jim Schoenfeld, 1987-88; Jim Schoenfeld, 1988-89; Jim Schoenfeld and John Cunniff, 1989-90; John Cunniff and Tom McVie, 1990-91; Tom McVie, 1991-92; Herb Brooks, 1992-93; Jacques Lemaire, 1993-94 to 1997-98; Robbie Ftorek, 1998-99; Robbie Ftorek and Larry Robinson, 1999-2000; Larry Robinson, 2000-01; Larry Robinson and Kevin Constantine, 2001-02; Pat Burns, 2002-03 to 2004-05; Larry Robinson and Lou Lamoriello, 2005-06; Claude Julien and Lou Lamoriello, 2006-07; Brent Sutter, 2007-08, 2008-09; Jacques Lemaire, 2009-10.

# Lou Lamoriello

### President and General Manager

*Born: Providence, RI, October 21, 1942.*

Lou Lamoriello has been president and general manager of the Devils since 1987-88 following more than 20 years with Providence College as a player, coach and administrator. He will be inducted into the Hockey Hall of Fame's Builder category in November 2009. His trades, signings and draft choices helped lead the Devils to their first Stanley Cup Championship in 1995 and were followed by victories again in 2000 and 2003. During his tenure, the Devils have had 11 100-point seasons, four Eastern Conference titles and eight Atlantic Division regular-season championships. In 2005-06, Lamoriello took over behind the bench and coached the Devils to first place in the Atlantic Division.

While at Providence, Lamoriello served as hockey coach for 15 seasons, compiling an impressive .578 winning percentage (248-179-13), while guiding the Friars to 12 post-season tournaments in a row. During his last five seasons (1978-83) of coaching, the school compiled a record of 107-58-4 and had more players drafted by the National Hockey League after entering college than any other college team during those years. Lamoriello helped propel numerous players and administrators toward NHL careers during his tenure at Providence. He was hired as president of the Devils on April 30, 1987, and assumed the responsibility of general manager on September 10, 1987. Lamoriello was G.M. of Team USA for the first World Cup of Hockey in 1996 as the U.S. captured the championship. He was also the G.M. for the 1998 U.S. Olympic Team.

**Coaching Record**

| | | | Regular Season | | | | Playoffs | | | |
|---|---|---|---|---|---|---|---|---|---|---|
| Season | Team | League | GC | W | L | O/T | GC | W | L | T |
| 2005-06 | New Jersey | NHL | 50 | 32 | 14 | 4 | 9 | 5 | 4 | .... |
| 2006-07 | New Jersey | NHL | 3 | 2 | 0 | 1 | 11 | 5 | 6 | .... |
| | **NHL Totals** | | **53** | **34** | **14** | **5** | **20** | **10** | **10** | .... |

# Club Directory

Prudential Center

**New Jersey Devils**
Prudential Center
165 Mulberry Street
Newark, NJ 07102
Phone **973/757-6100**
FAX 973/757-6399
www.newjerseydevils.com
**Capacity:** 17,625

| | |
|---|---|
| Owners | Jeff Vanderbeek, Michael Gilfillan, Peter Simon |
| Chairman/Managing Partner | Jeff Vanderbeek |
| President/CEO/General Manager | Lou Lamoriello |
| Sr. Executive Vice President/Chief Operating Officer | Chris Modrzynski |
| Executive Vice President, Operations | Peter S. McMullen |
| Executive Vice President/Chief Financial Officer | Scott Struble |
| Executive Vice President, Administration | Gordon Lavalette |
| Senior Vice President, General Counsel | Joseph C. Benedetti |
| Senior Vice President, Ticket Operations | Terry Farmer |
| Senior Vice President, Facilities | Mark Gheduzzi |
| Senior Vice President, Communications | Mike Levine |
| Vice President, Ticket Sales/Customer Service | David S. Beck |
| Vice President, Marketing/Community Development | Jeff Longo |
| **Hockey Club Personnel** | |
| Exec. V.P., Hockey Operations/Director, Scouting | David Conte |
| Sr. V.P., Hockey Ops./GM, Lowell/Trenton & Scout | Chris Lamoriello |
| Vice President, Hockey Operations | Stephen Pellegrini |
| Head Coach | Jacques Lemaire |
| Assistant Coaches | Mario Tremblay, Tommy Albelin |
| Goaltending Coach | Jacques Caron |
| Special Assignment Coaches | Larry Robinson, Scott Stevens, Jacques Laperriere, Pat Burns |
| Assistant Director, Scouting | Claude Carrier |
| Scouting Staff | Timo Blomqvist, Glen Dirk, Milt Fisher, Ferny Flaman, Dan Labraaten, Scott Lachance, Pierre Mondou, Gates Orlando, Larry Perris, Marcel Pronovost, Lou Reycroft, Vaclav Slansky, Jr., Steve Smith, Geoff Stevens, Ed Thomlinson, Les Widdifield |
| Pro Scouting Staff | Bob Hoffmeyer, Jan Ludvig, Andre Boudrias |
| Hockey Ops. Video Coordinator/Asst. | Taran Singleton/Mike Ford |
| Scouting Staff Assistant | Callie A. Smith |
| Head Trainer | Richard Stinziano |
| Equipment Manager | Rich Matthews |
| Assistant Equipment Managers | Alex Abasto, Matthew Mitchell, Mike Thibault |
| Strength/Conditioning Coordinator | Michael Vasalani |
| Massage Therapist | Tommy Plasko |
| Team Orthopedists | Dr. Barry Fisher, Dr. Len Jaffe |
| Team Cardiologist | Dr. Joseph Niznik |
| Team Dentist/Team Optometrist | Dr. H. Hugh Gardy/Dr. Paul Berman |
| Fitness Consultant/Exercise Physiologist | Vladimir Bure/Dr. Garret Caffrey |
| **President's Office** | |
| Hockey Ops. Exec. Asst. to the Pres./CEO/G.M. | Marie Carnevale |
| Corp. Exec. Asst. to Pres./CEO/G.M. and Dir., Human Resources | Mary K. Morrison |
| Administrative Assistant | Christine DellaBarca |
| Senior Counsel | Christine Steinberg |
| Legal Assistant, Paralegal | Natalia Gonzalez |
| **Operations** | |
| Receptionist/Staff Assistant | Jelsa Belotta/Kyle Radzinski |
| Administrative Asst. to the Chief Operating Officer | Alessandra Weingartner |
| **Ticket Operations** | |
| Sr. Director/Asst. Director, Ticket Operations | Tom Bates/Frank Calandrillo |
| Director, Box Office Operations | Pat Shark |
| Ticket Service Manager | Kelly Baron |
| Senior Director, Group Sales | Neil Desormeaux |
| Group Sales Managers | John Tierney, Christine Myers |
| **Sales** | |
| Assistant Director, Ticket Sales | Brooke Alper |
| Account Managers | Jennifer Camp, Samantha Davis, Stephanie Fitzhenry, Doug Hine, William Lamont, John Picciuto, Isaac Satten, Glenn Sperber, Thomas Stocky |
| Manager, Inside Sales | Christopher Terwoord |
| Receptionist, Sales | Pat Maione |
| **Corporate Partnerships** | |
| Senior Director, Corporate Partnerships | Michael DeMartino |
| Director, Corporate Partner Services | Adam Manger |
| **Marketing/Community Development** | |
| Sr. Director, Merchandising | David Perricone |
| Sr. Dir., Premium Suites, Single Events/Grassroots | Michael Merolla |
| Coord., Premium Suites, Single Events/Grassroots | Jason Romano |
| Director, Game Entertainment | Gene Szucs |
| Manager, Game Entertainment | David Schwinger |
| Game Entertainment Assistant | Rob Peters |
| Coordinator, Game Entertainment Graphics | Daniel de Graaf |
| Manager, Web Ops./Creative Services | Greg Orlando |
| Coordinator, Web Ops./Creative Services | Scott Modrzynski |
| Marketing Manager/Assistant | Heather Hall/Bridgette Berra |
| **Communications** | |
| Senior Director, Communications | Jeff Altstadter |
| Assistant Director, Communications | Pete Albietz |
| Staff Writer/Coordinator, Communications | Eric Marin/Daniel Beam |
| **Finance** | |
| Contoller/Accounting Manager | Marc Weiss/Kristin Farina |
| Staff Accountants | Shanna Curlin, Skyler Daugherty, Stephen Musnikow, Shawn Santamaria, Michael Tonjes |
| Administrative Assistant | Kristen Gore |
| **Computer Operations** | |
| Sr. Director, Programming/Computer Operations | Jack Skelley |
| Programmer/Analyst | Joseph Wyks |
| Systems Administrator/Tech. Asst. | Mike Tukes/Antonio da Silva |
| Alumni Representatives | Ken Daneyko, Bruce Driver, Grant Marshall, Rob Skrlac |
| **Devils Arena Entertainment** | |
| Senior Vice President, Arena Operations | Jim Cima |
| Executive Asst. to the Chairman/Managing Partner | Debbie Hildebrant |
| Public Relations | Bob Sommer |
| Security Director/Asst. Security Director | Jim Crann/Angelo Damiano |
| Business Coordinator | Kim Rossi |
| Financial Analyst | David Steinfeld |
| Senior Staff Attorney | Tim Lamoriello |
| Manager, Practice Ice Rink | Jon Sorg |
| Sales/Marketing Coordinator | Dana Fabrikant |
| Marketing/Communications Coordinators | Tori D'Annunzio/Anne L. Sciano |
| Dock Manager | Sharnda Blackwell |
| Project Assistants | Amanda Brown, Javier Colon |
| **Television/Radio** | |
| Television | MSG Plus – Mike Emrick, play-by-play – Glenn Resch, color |
| Radio | SportsRadio 66 WFAN – Matt Loughlin, play-by-play – Sherry Ross, color |

# New York Islanders

## 2008-09 Results: 26W-47L-4OTL-5SOL 61PTS.
## Fifth, Atlantic Division

### Key Off-Season Signings/Acquisitions

**2009**

- **June 19** • Named Dean Chynoweth assistant coach.
- **26** • Selected C **John Tavares** (London, OHL) first overall in the 2009 Entry Draft.
- **July 1** • Signed G **Dwayne Roloson.**
- **21** • Named **Scott Allen** assistant coach.
- **22** • Signed G **Martin Biron.**
- **25** • Re-signed C **Nate Thompson.**
- **29** • Re-signed D **Jack Hillen.**
- **Aug. 3** • Re-signed RW **Blake Comeau.**

### 2009-10 Schedule

| | | | | | | | |
|---|---|---|---|---|---|---|---|
| **Oct.** | Sat. | 3 | Pittsburgh | | Thu. | 31 | at Ottawa |
| | Thu. | 8 | at Ottawa | **Jan.** | Sat. | 2 | Atlanta |
| | Sat. | 10 | at Boston | | Wed. | 6 | at Colorado |
| | Mon. | 12 | Los Angeles* | | Fri. | 8 | at Dallas |
| | Fri. | 16 | at Buffalo | | Sat. | 9 | at Phoenix |
| | Sat. | 17 | San Jose | | Tue. | 12 | Detroit |
| | Wed. | 21 | Carolina | | Sat. | 16 | Buffalo |
| | Thu. | 22 | at Montreal | | Mon. | 18 | New Jersey* |
| | Sat. | 24 | Washington | | Tue. | 19 | at Pittsburgh |
| | Mon. | 26 | at Montreal | | Thu. | 21 | Florida |
| | Wed. | 28 | NY Rangers | | Sat. | 23 | New Jersey |
| | Fri. | 30 | at Washington | | Tue. | 26 | Washington |
| | Sat. | 31 | Buffalo | | Thu. | 28 | at Carolina |
| **Nov.** | Mon. | 2 | Edmonton | | Sat. | 30 | at Philadelphia |
| | Wed. | 4 | at Buffalo | | Sun. | 31 | at Florida* |
| | Fri. | 6 | at New Jersey | **Feb.** | Thu. | 4 | at Tampa Bay |
| | Sat. | 7 | Atlanta | | Sat. | 6 | Carolina |
| | Wed. | 11 | at Washington | | Tue. | 9 | Nashville |
| | Fri. | 13 | at Carolina | | Wed. | 10 | at Pittsburgh |
| | Sat. | 14 | at Florida | | Sat. | 13 | Tampa Bay* |
| | Mon. | 16 | at Boston | | Sun. | 14 | Ottawa* |
| | Fri. | 20 | at Minnesota | **Mar.** | Tue. | 2 | Chicago |
| | Sat. | 21 | at St. Louis | | Thu. | 4 | at Atlanta |
| | Mon. | 23 | at Toronto | | Sat. | 6 | Boston* |
| | Wed. | 25 | Philadelphia | | Tue. | 9 | at Philadelphia |
| | Fri. | 27 | Pittsburgh* | | Thu. | 11 | St. Louis |
| | Sat. | 28 | at New Jersey* | | Sat. | 13 | New Jersey |
| **Dec.** | Thu. | 3 | at Atlanta | | Sun. | 14 | Toronto* |
| | Sat. | 5 | at Tampa Bay | | Tue. | 16 | at Vancouver |
| | Tue. | 8 | at Philadelphia | | Fri. | 19 | at Anaheim |
| | Wed. | 9 | at Toronto | | Sat. | 20 | at Los Angeles |
| | Sat. | 12 | Boston | | Wed. | 24 | at NY Rangers |
| | Mon. | 14 | Florida | | Thu. | 25 | Calgary |
| | Wed. | 16 | at NY Rangers | | Sat. | 27 | at Columbus |
| | Thu. | 17 | NY Rangers | | Tue. | 30 | NY Rangers |
| | Sat. | 19 | Montreal | **Apr.** | Thu. | 1 | Philadelphia |
| | Mon. | 21 | Tampa Bay | | Sat. | 3 | Ottawa* |
| | Wed. | 23 | Toronto | | Tue. | 6 | Montreal |
| | Sat. | 26 | at NY Rangers | | Thu. | 8 | at Pittsburgh |
| | Sun. | 27 | Philadelphia* | | Sat. | 10 | at New Jersey |
| | Tue. | 29 | Columbus | | Sun. | 11 | Pittsburgh* |

* Denotes afternoon game.

*In his first year with the club in 2008-09, defenseman Mark Streit led the Islanders in games played (74), assists (40), points (56), power-play goals (10), power-play assists (19), power-play points (29) and average time on ice (25:13).*

### Year-by-Year Record

| | | Home | | | | Road | | | | Overall | | | | | | | | |
|---|---|---|---|---|---|---|---|---|---|---|---|---|---|---|---|---|---|---|
| **Season** | **GP** | **W** | **L** | **T** | **OL** | **W** | **L** | **T** | **OL** | **W** | **L** | **T** | **OL** | **GF** | **GA** | **Pts.** | **Finished** | **Playoff Result** |
| 2008-09 | 82 | 17 | 18 | .... | 6 | 9 | 29 | .... | 3 | 26 | 47 | .... | 9 | 201 | 279 | 61 | 5th, Atlantic Div. | Out of Playoffs |
| 2007-08 | 82 | 18 | 18 | .... | 5 | 17 | 20 | .... | 4 | 35 | 38 | .... | 9 | 194 | 243 | 79 | 5th, Atlantic Div. | Out of Playoffs |
| 2006-07 | 82 | 22 | 13 | .... | 6 | 18 | 17 | .... | 6 | 40 | 30 | .... | 12 | 248 | 240 | 92 | 4th, Atlantic Div. | Lost Conf. Quarter-Final |
| 2005-06 | 82 | 20 | 18 | .... | 3 | 16 | 22 | .... | 3 | 36 | 40 | .... | 6 | 230 | 278 | 78 | 4th, Atlantic Div. | Out of Playoffs |
| 2004-05 | .... | .... | .... | .... | .... | .... | .... | .... | .... | .... | .... | .... | .... | .... | .... | .... | | |
| 2003-04 | 82 | 25 | 11 | 4 | 1 | 13 | 18 | 7 | 3 | 38 | 29 | 11 | 4 | 237 | 210 | 91 | 3rd, Atlantic Div. | Lost Conf. Quarter-Final |
| 2002-03 | 82 | 18 | 18 | 5 | 0 | 17 | 16 | 6 | 2 | 35 | 34 | 11 | 2 | 224 | 231 | 83 | 3rd, Atlantic Div. | Lost Conf. Quarter-Final |
| 2001-02 | 82 | 21 | 13 | 5 | 2 | 21 | 15 | 3 | 2 | 42 | 28 | 8 | 4 | 239 | 220 | 96 | 2nd, Atlantic Div. | Lost Conf. Quarter-Final |
| 2000-01 | 82 | 12 | 27 | 1 | 1 | 9 | 24 | 6 | 2 | 21 | 51 | 7 | 3 | 185 | 268 | 52 | 5th, Atlantic Div. | Out of Playoffs |
| 1999-2000 | 82 | 10 | 25 | 5 | 1 | 14 | 23 | 4 | 0 | 24 | 48 | 9 | 1 | 194 | 275 | 58 | 5th, Atlantic Div. | Out of Playoffs |
| 1998-99 | 82 | 11 | 23 | 7 | .... | 13 | 25 | 3 | .... | 24 | 48 | 10 | .... | 194 | 244 | 58 | 5th, Atlantic Div. | Out of Playoffs |
| 1997-98 | 82 | 17 | 20 | 4 | .... | 13 | 21 | 7 | .... | 30 | 41 | 11 | .... | 212 | 225 | 71 | 4th, Atlantic Div. | Out of Playoffs |
| 1996-97 | 82 | 19 | 18 | 4 | .... | 10 | 23 | 8 | .... | 29 | 41 | 12 | .... | 240 | 250 | 70 | 7th, Atlantic Div. | Out of Playoffs |
| 1995-96 | 82 | 14 | 21 | 6 | .... | 8 | 29 | 4 | .... | 22 | 50 | 10 | .... | 229 | 315 | 54 | 7th, Atlantic Div. | Out of Playoffs |
| 1994-95 | 48 | 10 | 11 | 3 | .... | 5 | 17 | 2 | .... | 15 | 28 | 5 | .... | 126 | 158 | 35 | 7th, Atlantic Div. | Out of Playoffs |
| 1993-94 | 84 | 23 | 15 | 4 | .... | 13 | 21 | 8 | .... | 36 | 36 | 12 | .... | 282 | 264 | 84 | 4th, Atlantic Div. | Lost Conf. Quarter-Final |
| 1992-93 | 84 | 20 | 19 | 3 | .... | 20 | 18 | 4 | .... | 40 | 37 | 7 | .... | 335 | 297 | 87 | 3rd, Patrick Div. | Lost Conf. Championship |
| 1991-92 | 80 | 20 | 15 | 5 | .... | 14 | 20 | 6 | .... | 34 | 35 | 11 | .... | 291 | 299 | 79 | 5th, Patrick Div. | Out of Playoffs |
| 1990-91 | 80 | 15 | 19 | 6 | .... | 10 | 26 | 4 | .... | 25 | 45 | 10 | .... | 223 | 290 | 60 | 6th, Patrick Div. | Out of Playoffs |
| 1989-90 | 80 | 15 | 17 | 8 | .... | 16 | 21 | 3 | .... | 31 | 38 | 11 | .... | 281 | 288 | 73 | 4th, Patrick Div. | Lost Div. Semi-Final |
| 1988-89 | 80 | 19 | 18 | 3 | .... | 9 | 29 | 2 | .... | 28 | 47 | 5 | .... | 265 | 325 | 61 | 6th, Patrick Div. | Out of Playoffs |
| 1987-88 | 80 | 24 | 10 | 6 | .... | 15 | 21 | 4 | .... | 39 | 31 | 10 | .... | 308 | 267 | 88 | 1st, Patrick Div. | Lost Div. Semi-Final |
| 1986-87 | 80 | 20 | 15 | 5 | .... | 15 | 18 | 7 | .... | 35 | 33 | 12 | .... | 279 | 281 | 82 | 3rd, Patrick Div. | Lost Div. Final |
| 1985-86 | 80 | 22 | 11 | 7 | .... | 17 | 18 | 5 | .... | 39 | 29 | 12 | .... | 327 | 284 | 90 | 3rd, Patrick Div. | Lost Div. Semi-Final |
| 1984-85 | 80 | 26 | 11 | 3 | .... | 14 | 23 | 3 | .... | 40 | 34 | 6 | .... | 345 | 312 | 86 | 3rd, Patrick Div. | Lost Div. Final |
| 1983-84 | 80 | 28 | 11 | 1 | .... | 22 | 15 | 3 | .... | 50 | 26 | 4 | .... | 357 | 269 | 104 | 1st, Patrick Div. | Lost Final |
| **1982-83** | **80** | **26** | **11** | **3** | .... | **16** | **15** | **9** | .... | **42** | **26** | **12** | .... | **302** | **226** | **96** | **2nd, Patrick Div.** | **Won Stanley Cup** |
| **1981-82** | **80** | **33** | **3** | **4** | .... | **21** | **13** | **6** | .... | **54** | **16** | **10** | .... | **385** | **250** | **118** | **1st, Patrick Div.** | **Won Stanley Cup** |
| **1980-81** | **80** | **23** | **6** | **11** | .... | **25** | **12** | **3** | .... | **48** | **18** | **14** | .... | **355** | **260** | **110** | **1st, Patrick Div.** | **Won Stanley Cup** |
| **1979-80** | **80** | **26** | **9** | **5** | .... | **13** | **19** | **8** | .... | **39** | **28** | **13** | .... | **281** | **247** | **91** | **2nd, Patrick Div.** | **Won Stanley Cup** |
| 1978-79 | 80 | 31 | 3 | 6 | .... | 20 | 12 | 8 | .... | 51 | 15 | 14 | .... | 358 | 214 | 116 | 1st, Patrick Div. | Lost Semi-Final |
| 1977-78 | 80 | 29 | 3 | 8 | .... | 19 | 14 | 7 | .... | 48 | 17 | 15 | .... | 334 | 210 | 111 | 1st, Patrick Div. | Lost Quarter-Final |
| 1976-77 | 80 | 24 | 11 | 5 | .... | 23 | 10 | 7 | .... | 47 | 21 | 12 | .... | 288 | 193 | 106 | 2nd, Patrick Div. | Lost Semi-Final |
| 1975-76 | 80 | 24 | 8 | 8 | .... | 18 | 13 | 9 | .... | 42 | 21 | 17 | .... | 297 | 190 | 101 | 2nd, Patrick Div. | Lost Semi-Final |
| 1974-75 | 80 | 22 | 6 | 12 | .... | 11 | 19 | 10 | .... | 33 | 25 | 22 | .... | 264 | 221 | 88 | 3rd, Patrick Div. | Lost Semi-Final |
| 1973-74 | 78 | 13 | 17 | 9 | .... | 6 | 24 | 9 | .... | 19 | 41 | 18 | .... | 182 | 247 | 56 | 8th, East Div. | Out of Playoffs |
| 1972-73 | 78 | 10 | 25 | 4 | .... | 2 | 35 | 2 | .... | 12 | 60 | 6 | .... | 170 | 347 | 30 | 8th, East Div. | Out of Playoffs |

**ATLANTIC DIVISION**
**38th NHL Season**

**Franchise date:** June 6, 1972

# 2009-10 Player Personnel

| FORWARDS | HT | WT | S | Place of Birth | *Age | 2008-09 Club |
|---|---|---|---|---|---|---|
| BAILEY, Joshua | 6-1 | 188 | L | Oshawa, Ont. | 19 | NY Islanders |
| BENTIVOGLIO, Sean | 5-10 | 190 | L | Thorold, Ont. | 23 | NY Islanders-Bridgeport |
| BERGENHEIM, Sean | 5-10 | 205 | L | Helsinki, Finland | 25 | NY Islanders |
| COMEAU, Blake | 6-1 | 207 | R | Meadow Lake, Sask. | 23 | NY Islanders-Bridgeport |
| HUNTER, Trent | 6-3 | 210 | R | Red Deer, Alta. | 29 | NY Islanders |
| JACKMAN, Tim | 6-4 | 210 | R | Minot, ND | 27 | NY Islanders-Bridgeport |
| JOENSUU, Jesse | 6-4 | 207 | L | Pori, Finland | 21 | NY Islanders-Bridgeport |
| MARCINKO, Tomas | 6-4 | 187 | R | Poprad, Czech. | 21 | Bridgeport |
| MAULDIN, Greg | 5-10 | 198 | R | Boston, MA | 27 | Binghamton |
| MOORE, Greg | 6-1 | 210 | R | Lisbon, ME | 25 | Hartford |
| MOULSON, Matt | 6-1 | 205 | L | North York, Ont. | 25 | Los Angeles-Manchester |
| NIELSEN, Frans | 5-11 | 172 | L | Herning, Denmark | 25 | NY Islanders |
| OKPOSO, Kyle | 6-1 | 200 | R | St. Paul, MN | 21 | NY Islanders-Bridgeport |
| PARK, Richard | 5-11 | 190 | R | Seoul, South Korea | 33 | NY Islanders |
| RECHLICZ, Joel | 6-4 | 220 | R | Brookfield, WI | 22 | NYI-Bridgeport-Utah |
| REICH, Jeremy | 6-1 | 203 | L | Craik, Sask. | 30 | Providence (AHL) |
| SIM, Jon | 5-10 | 195 | L | New Glasgow, N.S. | 32 | NY Islanders-Bridgeport |
| SMITH, Trevor | 6-1 | 195 | L | North Vancouver, B.C. | 24 | NY Islanders-Bridgeport |
| TAMBELLINI, Jeff | 5-11 | 186 | L | Calgary, Alta. | 25 | NY Islanders-Bridgeport |
| TAVARES, John | 6-0 | 195 | L | Mississauga, Ont. | 19 | Oshawa-London |
| THOMPSON, Nate | 6-0 | 207 | L | Anchorage, AK | 24 | NY Islanders |
| WEIGHT, Doug | 5-11 | 196 | L | Warren, MI | 38 | NY Islanders |
| **DEFENSEMEN** | | | | | | |
| FLOOD, Mark | 6-1 | 190 | R | Charlottetown, P.E.I. | 25 | Albany |
| GERVAIS, Bruno | 6-1 | 205 | R | Longueuil, Que. | 24 | NY Islanders |
| HILLEN, Jack | 5-11 | 200 | L | Minnetonka, MN | 23 | NY Islanders-Bridgeport |
| KOHN, Dustin | 6-2 | 182 | L | Edmonton, Alta. | 22 | Bridgeport |
| MacDONALD, Andrew | 6-1 | 188 | L | Judique, N.S. | 23 | NY Islanders-Bridgeport |
| MARTINEK, Radek | 6-1 | 203 | R | Havlickuv Brod, Czech. | 33 | NY Islanders |
| MEYER, Freddy | 5-10 | 192 | L | Sanbornville, NH | 28 | NY Islanders |
| STREIT, Mark | 6-0 | 197 | L | Englisberg, Switz. | 31 | NY Islanders |
| SUTTON, Andy | 6-6 | 245 | L | Kingston, Ont. | 34 | NY Islanders |
| WESTGARTH, Brett | 6-2 | 215 | R | Amherstburg, Ont. | 27 | Worcester |
| WITT, Brendan | 6-2 | 223 | L | Humboldt, Sask. | 34 | NY Islanders |

| GOALTENDERS | HT | WT | C | Place of Birth | *Age | 2008-09 Club |
|---|---|---|---|---|---|---|
| BIRON, Martin | 6-3 | 180 | L | Lac-St-Charles, Que. | 32 | Philadelphia |
| DiPIETRO, Rick | 6-1 | 210 | R | Winthrop, MA | 28 | NY Islanders |
| ROLOSON, Dwayne | 6-1 | 180 | L | Simcoe, Ont. | 39 | Edmonton |

* – Age at start of 2009-10 season

# 2008-09 Scoring

* – rookie

## Regular Season

| Pos | # | Player | Team | GP | G | A | Pts | TOI | +/– | PIM | PP | SH | GW | S | % |
|---|---|---|---|---|---|---|---|---|---|---|---|---|---|---|---|
| D | 2 | Mark Streit | NYI | 74 | 16 | 40 | 56 | 25:13 | 6 | 62 | 10 | 1 | 1 | 150 | 10.7 |
| R | 21 * | Kyle Okposo | NYI | 65 | 18 | 21 | 39 | 18:00 | –6 | 36 | 9 | 0 | 3 | 165 | 10.9 |
| C | 93 | Doug Weight | NYI | 53 | 10 | 28 | 38 | 18:17 | –15 | 55 | 5 | 0 | 0 | 96 | 10.4 |
| C | 51 | Frans Nielsen | NYI | 59 | 9 | 24 | 33 | 16:32 | –4 | 18 | 3 | 1 | 2 | 101 | 8.9 |
| R | 7 | Trent Hunter | NYI | 55 | 14 | 17 | 31 | 16:22 | –8 | 41 | 5 | 0 | 2 | 154 | 9.1 |
| R | 10 | Richard Park | NYI | 71 | 14 | 17 | 31 | 17:10 | –13 | 34 | 4 | 2 | 1 | 138 | 10.1 |
| L | 11 | Andy Hilbert | NYI | 67 | 11 | 16 | 27 | 16:09 | –3 | 22 | 1 | 1 | 0 | 167 | 6.6 |
| R | 57 | Blake Comeau | NYI | 53 | 7 | 18 | 25 | 16:16 | –17 | 32 | 2 | 0 | 0 | 78 | 9.0 |
| C | 12 * | Joshua Bailey | NYI | 68 | 7 | 18 | 25 | 15:28 | –14 | 16 | 3 | 0 | 0 | 74 | 9.5 |
| L | 20 | Sean Bergenheim | NYI | 59 | 15 | 9 | 24 | 14:14 | –2 | 64 | 0 | 4 | 5 | 152 | 9.9 |
| D | 8 | Bruno Gervais | NYI | 69 | 3 | 16 | 19 | 21:35 | –15 | 33 | 0 | 0 | 1 | 82 | 3.7 |
| C | 37 | Dean McAmmond | OTT | 44 | 3 | 4 | 7 | 9:40 | 2 | 16 | 0 | 1 | 2 | 40 | 7.5 |
| | | | NYI | 18 | 2 | 7 | 9 | 15:08 | 5 | 8 | 0 | 0 | 0 | 19 | 10.5 |
| | | | Total | 62 | 5 | 11 | 16 | 11:15 | 7 | 24 | 0 | 1 | 2 | 59 | 8.5 |
| L | 16 | Jon Sim | NYI | 49 | 9 | 6 | 15 | 12:10 | –12 | 42 | 3 | 0 | 0 | 90 | 10.0 |
| L | 15 | Jeff Tambellini | NYI | 65 | 7 | 8 | 15 | 13:06 | –20 | 32 | 0 | 0 | 0 | 98 | 7.1 |
| R | 28 | Tim Jackman | NYI | 69 | 5 | 7 | 12 | 11:44 | –17 | 155 | 0 | 1 | 0 | 99 | 5.1 |
| D | 24 | Radek Martinek | NYI | 51 | 6 | 4 | 10 | 21:33 | –16 | 28 | 1 | 0 | 1 | 54 | 11.1 |
| D | 25 | Andy Sutton | NYI | 23 | 2 | 8 | 10 | 20:14 | 3 | 40 | 0 | 0 | 0 | 19 | 10.5 |
| D | 44 | Freddy Meyer | NYI | 27 | 4 | 5 | 9 | 20:59 | –19 | 14 | 0 | 0 | 1 | 36 | 11.1 |
| D | 32 | Brendan Witt | NYI | 65 | 0 | 9 | 9 | 20:18 | –34 | 94 | 0 | 0 | 0 | 52 | 0.0 |
| D | 38 * | Jack Hillen | NYI | 40 | 1 | 5 | 6 | 15:12 | –9 | 16 | 0 | 0 | 0 | 47 | 2.1 |
| R | 36 * | Mike Iggulden | NYI | 11 | 1 | 4 | 5 | 12:07 | –3 | 4 | 0 | 0 | 0 | 16 | 6.3 |
| C | 45 * | Nate Thompson | NYI | 43 | 2 | 2 | 4 | 12:04 | –11 | 49 | 0 | 1 | 0 | 56 | 3.6 |
| L | 58 * | Jesse Joensuu | NYI | 7 | 1 | 2 | 3 | 12:05 | –1 | 4 | 0 | 0 | 0 | 9 | 11.1 |
| D | 17 | Thomas Pock | NYI | 59 | 1 | 2 | 3 | 12:42 | –17 | 35 | 0 | 0 | 0 | 51 | 2.0 |
| C | 18 | Mike Sillinger | NYI | 7 | 2 | 0 | 2 | 14:08 | –5 | 0 | 1 | 0 | 0 | 14 | 14.3 |
| D | 26 * | Joe Callahan | NYI | 18 | 0 | 2 | 2 | 14:59 | 5 | 4 | 0 | 0 | 0 | 6 | 0.0 |
| R | 54 | Kurtis McLean | NYI | 4 | 1 | 0 | 1 | 10:33 | 1 | 0 | 0 | 0 | 1 | 5 | 20.0 |
| L | 77 * | Trevor Smith | NYI | 7 | 1 | 0 | 1 | 11:48 | –3 | 0 | 0 | 0 | 0 | 7 | 14.3 |
| C | 27 | Jeremy Colliton | NYI | 6 | 0 | 1 | 1 | 11:03 | –2 | 2 | 0 | 0 | 0 | 4 | 0.0 |
| R | 40 * | Joel Rechlicz | NYI | 17 | 0 | 1 | 1 | 4:51 | –1 | 68 | 0 | 0 | 0 | 7 | 0.0 |
| D | 62 * | Jamie Fraser | NYI | 1 | 0 | 0 | 0 | 11:00 | 0 | 0 | 0 | 0 | 0 | 0 | 0.0 |
| L | 67 * | Sean Bentivoglio | NYI | 1 | 0 | 0 | 0 | 11:31 | 0 | 2 | 0 | 0 | 0 | 2 | 0.0 |
| D | 43 * | Andrew MacDonald | NYI | 3 | 0 | 0 | 0 | 10:10 | 2 | 2 | 0 | 0 | 0 | 1 | 0.0 |
| C | 29 | Ben Walter | NYI | 4 | 0 | 0 | 0 | 10:58 | –2 | 0 | 0 | 0 | 0 | 2 | 0.0 |
| D | 4 * | Brett Skinner | NYI | 11 | 0 | 0 | 0 | 11:42 | 2 | 4 | 0 | 0 | 0 | 5 | 0.0 |
| L | 49 | Mitchell Fritz | NYI | 20 | 0 | 0 | 0 | 2:40 | –4 | 42 | 0 | 0 | 0 | 2 | 0.0 |

## Goaltending

| No. | Goaltender | GPI | Mins | Avg | W | L | OT | EN | SO | GA | SA | S% | G | A | PIM |
|---|---|---|---|---|---|---|---|---|---|---|---|---|---|---|---|
| 34 | Yann Danis | 31 | 1760 | 2.86 | 10 | 17 | 3 | 1 | 2 | 84 | 933 | .910 | 0 | 0 | 0 |
| 35 | Joey MacDonald | 49 | 2792 | 3.37 | 14 | 26 | 6 | 7 | 1 | 157 | 1584 | .901 | 0 | 1 | 6 |
| 39 | Rick DiPietro | 5 | 256 | 3.52 | 1 | 3 | 0 | 0 | 0 | 15 | 139 | .892 | 0 | 2 | 2 |
| 1 | * Peter Mannino | 3 | 133 | 4.51 | 1 | 1 | 0 | 0 | 0 | 10 | 87 | .885 | 0 | 0 | 0 |
| | **Totals** | **82** | **4977** | **3.30** | **26** | **47** | **9** | **8** | **3** | **274** | **2751** | **.900** | | | |

*Selected ninth overall in the 2008 Entry Draft, Joshua Bailey missed the first 14 games of the 2008-09 NHL season due to injuries, but played in all 68 remaining after making his debut on November 11, 2008.*

# Scott Gordon

## Head Coach

*Born: Brockton, MA, February 6, 1963.*

The New York Islanders announced the hiring of Scott Gordon as their head coach on August 12, 2008. Gordon spent the previous eight seasons with the Providence Bruins, Boston's affiliate in the American Hockey League. He began as an assistant coach in Providence in 2000-01 and was hired as the head coach on July 25, 2003 after serving as interim head coach for part of the 2002-03 season. In 2007-08, he guided the Bruins to top spot in the AHL standings with a record of 55-18-7 and was named coach of the year.

Gordon began his coaching career with the International Hockey League's Atlanta Knights as an assistant coach in 1994-95. When he was named head coach on January 5, 1996, he became at age 32 the youngest head coach in the league's 53-year history. The team spent the next two seasons as the Quebec Rafales, with Gordon serving as an assistant. His next move came in 1998-99, when he was named head coach of the Roanoke Express of the East Coast Hockey League. He led the club to consecutive first-place finishes in the Northeast Division, setting franchise records for wins (44), points (94) and fewest goals against (181) in 1999-2000.

As a player, Gordon spent four years as a goaltender at Boston College from 1982 to 1986, posting a 64-35-3 record over that span. He backstopped the Eagles to a NCAA Final Four appearance in 1985 and was named a Hockey East First-Team All-Star in 1986. Following the completion of his collegiate career, Gordon began his professional playing career with the AHL's Frederiction Express in 1986-87. He made his NHL debut in 1989-90 playing 10 games with the Quebec Nordiques. He played 13 more games for Quebec in 1990-91. Gordon played on the 1992 United States Olympic team and was a member of the IHL's 1994 Turner Cup champions Atlanta Knights squad. Gordon played 150 AHL games with Fredericton, the Baltimore Skipjacks, the Halifax Citadels and the New Haven Nighthawks through 1993-94.

### Coaching Record

| | | | Regular Season | | | | Playoffs | | | |
|---|---|---|---|---|---|---|---|---|---|---|
| **Season** | **Team** | **League** | **GC** | **W** | **L** | **O/T** | **GC** | **W** | **L** | **T** |
| 1995-96 | Atlanta | IHL | 40 | 15 | 19 | 6 | 3 | 0 | 3 | .... |
| 1998-99 | Roanoke | ECHL | 70 | 38 | 22 | 10 | 12 | 6 | 6 | .... |
| 99-2000 | Roanoke | ECHL | 70 | 44 | 20 | 6 | 4 | 1 | 3 | .... |
| 2002-03 | Providence | AHL | 9 | 3 | 3 | 3 | 1 | 0 | 1 | .... |
| 2003-04 | Providence | AHL | 80 | 36 | 29 | 15 | 2 | 0 | 2 | .... |
| 2004-05 | Providence | AHL | 80 | 40 | 30 | 10 | 17 | 10 | 7 | .... |
| 2005-06 | Providence | AHL | 80 | 43 | 31 | 6 | 6 | 2 | 4 | .... |
| 2006-07 | Providence | AHL | 80 | 44 | 30 | 6 | 13 | 6 | 7 | .... |
| 2007-08 | Providence | AHL | 80 | 55 | 18 | 7 | 10 | 6 | 4 | .... |
| **2008-09** | **NY Islanders** | **NHL** | **82** | **26** | **47** | **9** | .... | .... | .... | .... |
| | **NHL Totals** | | **82** | **26** | **47** | **9** | .... | .... | .... | .... |

## Coaching History

Phil Goyette and Earl Ingarfield, 1972-73; Al Arbour, 1973-74 to 1985-86; Terry Simpson, 1986-87, 1987-88; Terry Simpson and Al Arbour, 1988-89; Al Arbour, 1989-90 to 1993-94; Lorne Henning, 1994-95; Mike Milbury, 1995-96; Mike Milbury and Rick Bowness, 1996-97; Rick Bowness and Mike Milbury, 1997-98; Mike Milbury and Bill Stewart, 1998-99; Butch Goring, 1999-2000; Butch Goring and Lorne Henning, 2000-01; Peter Laviolette, 2001-02, 2002-03; Steve Stirling, 2003-04, 2004-05; Steve Stirling and Brad Shaw, 2005-06; Ted Nolan, 2006-07, 2007-08; Scott Gordon, 2008-09 to date.

# Club Records

## Team

(Figures in brackets for season records are games played; records for fewest points, wins, ties, losses, goals, goals against are for 70 or more games)

| | | |
|---|---|---|
| **Most Points** | 118 | 1981-82 (80) |
| **Most Wins** | 54 | 1981-82 (80) |
| **Most Ties** | 22 | 1974-75 (80) |
| **Most Losses** | 60 | 1972-73 (78) |
| **Most Goals** | 385 | 1981-82 (80) |
| **Most Goals Against** | 347 | 1972-73 (78) |
| **Fewest Points** | 30 | 1972-73 (78) |
| **Fewest Wins** | 12 | 1972-73 (78) |
| **Fewest Ties** | 4 | 1983-84 (80) |
| **Fewest Losses** | 15 | 1978-79 (80) |
| **Fewest Goals** | 170 | 1972-73 (78) |
| **Fewest Goals Against** | 190 | 1975-76 (80) |
| **Longest Winning Streak** | | |
| Overall | 15 | Jan. 21-Feb. 20/82 |
| Home | 14 | Jan. 2-Feb. 25/82 |
| Away | 8 | Feb. 27-Mar. 29/81 |
| **Longest Undefeated Streak** | | |
| Overall | 15 | Three times |
| Home | 23 | Oct. 17/78-Jan. 20/79 (19 wins, 4 ties), Jan. 2-Apr. 3/82 (21 wins, 2 ties) |
| Away | 8 | Three times |
| **Longest Losing Streak** | | |
| Overall | 12 | Dec. 27/72-Jan. 16/73, Nov. 22-Dec. 15/88 |
| Home | 7 | Nov. 13-Dec. 14/99 |
| Away | 15 | Jan. 20-Mar. 31/73 |
| **Longest Winless Streak** | | |
| Overall | 15 | Nov. 22-Dec. 21/72 (12 losses, 3 ties) |
| Home | 9 | Mar. 2-Apr. 6/99 (7 losses, 2 ties) |
| Away | 20 | Nov. 3/72-Jan. 13/73 (19 losses, 1 tie) |
| **Most Shutouts, Season** | 10 | 1975-76 (80) |
| **Most PIM, Season** | 1,857 | 1986-87 (80) |
| **Most Goals, Game** | 11 | Dec. 20/83 (Pit. 3 at NYI 11), Mar. 3/84 (NYI 11 at Tor. 6) |

## Individual

| | | |
|---|---|---|
| **Most Seasons** | 17 | Billy Smith |
| **Most Games** | 1,123 | Bryan Trottier |
| **Most Goals, Career** | 573 | Mike Bossy |
| **Most Assists, Career** | 853 | Bryan Trottier |
| **Most Points, Career** | 1,353 | Bryan Trottier (500G, 853A) |
| **Most PIM, Career** | 1,879 | Mick Vukota |
| **Most Shutouts, Career** | 25 | Glenn Resch |
| **Longest Consecutive Games Streak** | 576 | Billy Harris (Oct. 7/72-Nov. 30/79) |
| **Most Goals, Season** | 69 | Mike Bossy (1978-79) |
| **Most Assists, Season** | 87 | Bryan Trottier (1978-79) |
| **Most Points, Season** | 147 | Mike Bossy (1981-82; 64G, 83A) |
| **Most PIM, Season** | 356 | Brian Curran (1986-87) |
| **Most Points, Defenseman, Season** | 101 | Denis Potvin (1978-79; 31G, 70A) |
| **Most Points, Center, Season** | 134 | Bryan Trottier (1978-79; 47G, 87A) |
| **Most Points, Right Wing, Season** | 147 | Mike Bossy (1981-82; 64G, 83A) |
| **Most Points, Left Wing, Season** | 100 | John Tonelli (1984-85; 42G, 58A) |
| **Most Points, Rookie, Season** | 95 | Bryan Trottier (1975-76; 32G, 63A) |
| **Most Shutouts, Season** | 7 | Glenn Resch (1975-76) |
| **Most Goals, Game** | 5 | Bryan Trottier (Dec. 23/78), (Feb. 13/82) John Tonelli (Jan. 6/81) |
| **Most Assists, Game** | 6 | Mike Bossy (Jan. 6/81) |
| **Most Points, Game** | 8 | Bryan Trottier (Dec. 23/78; 5G, 3A) |

## Captains' History

Ed Westfall, 1972-73 to 1975-76; Ed Westfall and Clark Gillies, 1976-77; Clark Gillies, 1977-78, 1978-79; Denis Potvin, 1979-80 to 1986-87; Brent Sutter, 1987-88 to 1990-91; Brent Sutter and Pat Flatley, 1991-92; Pat Flatley, 1992-93 to 1995-96; no captain, 1996-97; Bryan McCabe and Trevor Linden, 1997-98; Trevor Linden, 1998-99; Kenny Jonsson, 1999-2000, 2000-01; Michael Peca, 2001-02 to 2003-04; Alexei Yashin, 2005-06, 2006-07; Bill Guerin, 2007-08; Bill Guerin and no captain, 2008-09.

## Retired Numbers

| | | |
|---|---|---|
| **5** | Denis Potvin | 1973-1988 |
| **9** | Clark Gillies | 1974-1986 |
| **19** | Bryan Trottier | 1975-1990 |
| **22** | Mike Bossy | 1977-1987 |
| **23** | Bob Nystrom | 1972-1986 |
| **31** | Billy Smith | 1972-1989 |

# All-time Record vs. Other Clubs

## Regular Season

**At Home**

| | GP | W | L | T | OL | GF | GA | PTS |
|---|---|---|---|---|---|---|---|---|
| Anaheim | 10 | 5 | 4 | 1 | 0 | 26 | 27 | 11 |
| Atlanta | 18 | 9 | 9 | 0 | 0 | 59 | 47 | 18 |
| Boston | 69 | 29 | 30 | 10 | 0 | 225 | 218 | 68 |
| Buffalo | 69 | 30 | 29 | 9 | 1 | 191 | 193 | 70 |
| Calgary | 52 | 26 | 17 | 9 | 0 | 194 | 145 | 61 |
| Carolina | 52 | 23 | 24 | 4 | 1 | 153 | 152 | 51 |
| Chicago | 48 | 19 | 14 | 15 | 0 | 168 | 143 | 53 |
| Colorado | 34 | 20 | 13 | 1 | 0 | 138 | 115 | 41 |
| Columbus | 4 | 2 | 2 | 0 | 0 | 15 | 14 | 4 |
| Dallas | 50 | 26 | 15 | 8 | 1 | 181 | 142 | 61 |
| Detroit | 47 | 23 | 18 | 4 | 2 | 167 | 141 | 52 |
| Edmonton | 32 | 16 | 7 | 9 | 0 | 131 | 112 | 41 |
| Florida | 33 | 17 | 13 | 2 | 1 | 88 | 86 | 37 |
| Los Angeles | 46 | 24 | 16 | 5 | 1 | 160 | 130 | 54 |
| Minnesota | 5 | 2 | 3 | 0 | 0 | 11 | 16 | 4 |
| Montreal | 68 | 32 | 30 | 6 | 0 | 205 | 196 | 70 |
| Nashville | 5 | 2 | 2 | 0 | 1 | 12 | 14 | 5 |
| New Jersey | 100 | 63 | 24 | 11 | 2 | 391 | 279 | 139 |
| NY Rangers | 111 | 59 | 42 | 8 | 2 | 399 | 352 | 128 |
| Ottawa | 32 | 8 | 17 | 6 | 1 | 98 | 119 | 23 |
| Philadelphia | 113 | 54 | 42 | 15 | 2 | 394 | 340 | 125 |
| Phoenix | 32 | 15 | 9 | 8 | 0 | 119 | 95 | 38 |
| Pittsburgh | 101 | 54 | 35 | 8 | 4 | 393 | 333 | 120 |
| St. Louis | 51 | 26 | 13 | 11 | 1 | 190 | 136 | 64 |
| San Jose | 12 | 6 | 4 | 2 | 0 | 43 | 37 | 14 |
| Tampa Bay | 33 | 17 | 14 | 1 | 1 | 96 | 85 | 36 |
| Toronto | 61 | 35 | 21 | 3 | 2 | 234 | 176 | 75 |
| Vancouver | 49 | 27 | 12 | 10 | 0 | 177 | 138 | 64 |
| Washington | 89 | 47 | 38 | 2 | 2 | 326 | 272 | 98 |
| Defunct Clubs | 13 | 11 | 0 | 2 | 0 | 75 | 33 | 24 |
| **Totals** | **1439** | **727** | **517** | **170** | **25** | **5059** | **4286** | **1649** |

**On Road**

| | GP | W | L | T | OL | GF | GA | PTS |
|---|---|---|---|---|---|---|---|---|
| Anaheim | 10 | 5 | 2 | 3 | 0 | 29 | 22 | 13 |
| Atlanta | 18 | 10 | 4 | 2 | 2 | 71 | 57 | 24 |
| Boston | 67 | 19 | 35 | 11 | 2 | 184 | 247 | 51 |
| Buffalo | 69 | 22 | 36 | 9 | 2 | 192 | 233 | 55 |
| Calgary | 51 | 15 | 25 | 11 | 0 | 152 | 181 | 41 |
| Carolina | 53 | 21 | 27 | 5 | 0 | 169 | 187 | 47 |
| Chicago | 50 | 19 | 26 | 5 | 0 | 168 | 165 | 43 |
| Colorado | 35 | 11 | 20 | 3 | 1 | 98 | 125 | 26 |
| Columbus | 6 | 0 | 4 | 1 | 1 | 11 | 20 | 2 |
| Dallas | 48 | 22 | 18 | 8 | 0 | 173 | 139 | 52 |
| Detroit | 47 | 19 | 26 | 2 | 0 | 139 | 166 | 40 |
| Edmonton | 31 | 8 | 18 | 5 | 0 | 89 | 114 | 21 |
| Florida | 33 | 10 | 17 | 6 | 0 | 94 | 104 | 26 |
| Los Angeles | 46 | 17 | 22 | 7 | 0 | 145 | 167 | 41 |
| Minnesota | 5 | 1 | 3 | 0 | 1 | 13 | 17 | 3 |
| Montreal | 68 | 18 | 41 | 9 | 0 | 186 | 242 | 45 |
| Nashville | 7 | 2 | 5 | 0 | 0 | 17 | 17 | 4 |
| New Jersey | 99 | 45 | 40 | 11 | 3 | 328 | 314 | 104 |
| NY Rangers | 111 | 39 | 60 | 11 | 1 | 328 | 400 | 90 |
| Ottawa | 31 | 7 | 19 | 5 | 0 | 77 | 107 | 19 |
| Philadelphia | 110 | 34 | 64 | 11 | 1 | 303 | 389 | 80 |
| Phoenix | 32 | 15 | 13 | 4 | 0 | 112 | 107 | 34 |
| Pittsburgh | 103 | 38 | 49 | 14 | 2 | 348 | 391 | 92 |
| St. Louis | 48 | 21 | 17 | 9 | 1 | 159 | 169 | 52 |
| San Jose | 14 | 6 | 7 | 1 | 0 | 43 | 37 | 13 |
| Tampa Bay | 34 | 14 | 15 | 2 | 3 | 100 | 96 | 33 |
| Toronto | 63 | 25 | 32 | 4 | 2 | 207 | 226 | 56 |
| Vancouver | 48 | 21 | 23 | 3 | 1 | 155 | 158 | 46 |
| Washington | 89 | 34 | 42 | 11 | 2 | 278 | 293 | 81 |
| Defunct Clubs | 13 | 4 | 5 | 4 | 0 | 35 | 41 | 12 |
| **Totals** | **1439** | **522** | **715** | **177** | **25** | **4403** | **4931** | **1246** |

**Total**

| | GP | W | L | T | OL | GF | GA | PTS |
|---|---|---|---|---|---|---|---|---|
| Anaheim | 20 | 10 | 6 | 4 | 0 | 55 | 49 | 24 |
| Atlanta | 36 | 19 | 13 | 2 | 2 | 130 | 104 | 42 |
| Boston | 136 | 48 | 65 | 21 | 2 | 409 | 465 | 119 |
| Buffalo | 138 | 52 | 65 | 18 | 3 | 383 | 426 | 125 |
| Calgary | 103 | 41 | 42 | 20 | 0 | 346 | 326 | 102 |
| Carolina | 105 | 44 | 51 | 9 | 1 | 322 | 339 | 98 |
| Chicago | 98 | 38 | 40 | 20 | 0 | 336 | 308 | 96 |
| Colorado | 69 | 31 | 33 | 4 | 1 | 236 | 240 | 67 |
| Columbus | 10 | 2 | 6 | 1 | 1 | 26 | 34 | 6 |
| Dallas | 98 | 48 | 33 | 16 | 1 | 354 | 281 | 113 |
| Detroit | 94 | 42 | 44 | 6 | 2 | 306 | 307 | 92 |
| Edmonton | 63 | 24 | 25 | 14 | 0 | 220 | 226 | 62 |
| Florida | 66 | 27 | 30 | 8 | 1 | 182 | 190 | 63 |
| Los Angeles | 92 | 41 | 38 | 12 | 1 | 305 | 297 | 95 |
| Minnesota | 10 | 3 | 6 | 0 | 1 | 24 | 33 | 7 |
| Montreal | 136 | 50 | 71 | 15 | 0 | 391 | 438 | 115 |
| Nashville | 12 | 4 | 7 | 0 | 1 | 29 | 31 | 9 |
| New Jersey | 199 | 108 | 64 | 22 | 5 | 719 | 593 | 243 |
| NY Rangers | 222 | 98 | 102 | 19 | 3 | 727 | 752 | 218 |
| Ottawa | 63 | 15 | 36 | 11 | 1 | 175 | 226 | 42 |
| Philadelphia | 223 | 88 | 106 | 26 | 3 | 697 | 729 | 205 |
| Phoenix | 64 | 30 | 22 | 12 | 0 | 231 | 202 | 72 |
| Pittsburgh | 204 | 92 | 84 | 22 | 6 | 741 | 724 | 212 |
| St. Louis | 99 | 47 | 30 | 20 | 2 | 349 | 305 | 116 |
| San Jose | 26 | 12 | 11 | 3 | 0 | 86 | 74 | 27 |
| Tampa Bay | 67 | 31 | 29 | 3 | 4 | 196 | 181 | 69 |
| Toronto | 124 | 60 | 53 | 7 | 4 | 441 | 402 | 131 |
| Vancouver | 97 | 48 | 35 | 13 | 1 | 332 | 296 | 110 |
| Washington | 178 | 81 | 80 | 13 | 4 | 604 | 565 | 179 |
| Defunct Clubs | 26 | 15 | 5 | 6 | 0 | 110 | 74 | 36 |
| **Totals** | **2878** | **1249** | **1232** | **347** | **50** | **9462** | **9217** | **2895** |

## Playoffs

| | Series | W | L | GP | W | L | T | GF | GA | Last Mtg. | Rnd. | Result |
|---|---|---|---|---|---|---|---|---|---|---|---|---|
| Boston | 2 | 2 | 0 | 11 | 8 | 3 | 0 | 49 | 35 | 1983 | CF | W 4-2 |
| Buffalo | 4 | 3 | 1 | 21 | 13 | 8 | 0 | 70 | 62 | 2007 | CQF | L 1-4 |
| Chicago | 2 | 2 | 0 | 6 | 6 | 0 | 0 | 21 | 6 | 1979 | QF | W 4-0 |
| Colorado | 1 | 1 | 0 | 4 | 4 | 0 | 0 | 18 | 9 | 1982 | CF | W 4-0 |
| Dallas | 1 | 1 | 0 | 5 | 4 | 1 | 0 | 26 | 16 | 1981 | F | W 4-1 |
| Edmonton | 3 | 2 | 1 | 15 | 9 | 6 | 0 | 58 | 47 | 1984 | F | L 1-4 |
| Los Angeles | 1 | 1 | 0 | 4 | 3 | 1 | 0 | 21 | 10 | 1980 | PRE | W 3-1 |
| Montreal | 4 | 1 | 3 | 22 | 8 | 14 | 0 | 55 | 64 | 1993 | CF | L 1-4 |
| New Jersey | 1 | 0 | 1 | 6 | 2 | 4 | 0 | 18 | 23 | 1988 | DSF | L 2-4 |
| NY Rangers | 8 | 5 | 3 | 39 | 20 | 19 | 0 | 129 | 132 | 1994 | CQF | L 0-4 |
| Ottawa | 1 | 0 | 1 | 5 | 1 | 4 | 0 | 7 | 13 | 2003 | CQF | L 1-4 |
| Philadelphia | 4 | 1 | 3 | 25 | 11 | 14 | 0 | 69 | 83 | 1987 | DF | L 3-4 |
| Pittsburgh | 3 | 3 | 0 | 19 | 11 | 8 | 0 | 67 | 58 | 1993 | DF | W 4-3 |
| Tampa Bay | 1 | 0 | 1 | 5 | 1 | 4 | 0 | 5 | 12 | 2004 | CQF | L 1-4 |
| Toronto | 3 | 1 | 2 | 17 | 9 | 8 | 0 | 54 | 42 | 2002 | CQF | L 3-4 |
| Vancouver | 2 | 2 | 0 | 6 | 6 | 0 | 0 | 26 | 14 | 1982 | F | W 4-0 |
| Washington | 6 | 5 | 1 | 30 | 18 | 12 | 0 | 99 | 88 | 1993 | DSF | W 4-2 |
| **Totals** | **47** | **30** | **17** | **240** | **134** | **106** | **0** | **792** | **714** | | | |

Calgary totals include Atlanta Flames, 1972-73 to 1979-80.
Colorado totals include Quebec, 1979-80 to 1994-95.
New Jersey totals include Kansas City, 1974-75, 1975-76, and Colorado Rockies, 1976-77 to 1981-82.
Phoenix totals include Winnipeg, 1979-80 to 1995-96.
Carolina totals include Hartford, 1979-80 to 1996-97.
Dallas totals include Minnesota North Stars, 1972-73 to 1992-93.

## Playoff Results 2009-2004

| Year | Round | Opponent | Result | GF | GA |
|---|---|---|---|---|---|
| 2007 | CQF | Buffalo | L 1-4 | 11 | 17 |
| 2004 | CQF | Tampa Bay | L 1-4 | 5 | 12 |

**Abbreviations: Round: F** – Final; **CF** – conference final; **CQF** – conference quarter-final; **DF** – division final; **DSF** – division semi-final; **QF** – quarter-final; **PRE** – preliminary round.

## 2008-09 Results

| Month | Date | Opponent | Score |
|---|---|---|---|
| **Oct.** | 10 | at New Jersey | 1-2 |
| | 11 | St. Louis | 5-2 |
| | 13 | Buffalo | 1-7 |
| | 16 | at Tampa Bay | 4-3* |
| | 18 | at Florida | 0-2 |
| | 23 | Dallas | 3-5 |
| | 25 | Carolina | 3-4 |
| | 27 | NY Rangers | 2-4 |
| | 30 | at Philadelphia | 2-3* |
| **Nov.** | 1 | Montreal | 4-5 |
| | 3 | Columbus | 4-3* |
| | 4 | at NY Rangers | 2-1 |
| | 6 | at Atlanta | 3-4 |
| | 8 | Pittsburgh | 3-4† |
| | 11 | Philadelphia | 1-3 |
| | 13 | at Ottawa | 3-1 |
| | 15 | Ottawa | 3-2 |
| | 17 | Vancouver | 2-1† |
| | 21 | at New Jersey | 2-5 |
| | 22 | at Buffalo | 4-2 |
| | 24 | at Montreal | 4-3† |
| | 26 | Pittsburgh | 3-5 |
| | 28 | at Boston | 2-7 |
| | 29 | Ottawa | 4-2 |
| **Dec.** | 4 | at Washington | 2-5 |
| | 6 | Atlanta | 1-5 |
| | 8 | at Toronto | 2-4 |
| | 9 | at Philadelphia | 3-4 |
| | 11 | at Pittsburgh | 2-9 |
| | 13 | at Columbus | 1-3 |
| | 16 | Washington | 4-5* |
| | 19 | at Minnesota | 1-4 |
| | 20 | at Nashville | 0-1 |
| | 23 | Atlanta | 2-4 |
| | 26 | Toronto | 4-1 |
| | 27 | at Buffalo | 3-4† |
| | 29 | at NY Rangers | 4-5 |
| | 31 | Florida | 4-2 |
| **Jan.** | 2 | at Phoenix | 4-5 |
| | 3 | at San Jose | 3-5 |
| | 5 | at Edmonton | 2-3 |
| | 8 | at Calgary | 2-5 |
| | 13 | NY Rangers | 1-2 |
| | 15 | Boston | 1-2 |
| | 17 | New Jersey | 1-3 |
| | 19 | Washington | 1-2* |
| | 21 | Anaheim | 2-1 |
| | 29 | at Atlanta | 5-4 |
| | 31 | Florida | 3-1 |
| **Feb.** | 3 | Tampa Bay | 3-1 |
| | 5 | at Florida | 2-3 |
| | 7 | at Tampa Bay | 0-1 |
| | 10 | Los Angeles | 3-4† |
| | 11 | at New Jersey | 2-4 |
| | 14 | at Philadelphia | 1-5 |
| | 16 | Pittsburgh | 3-2† |
| | 18 | at NY Rangers | 1-3 |
| | 19 | Carolina | 2-6 |
| | 21 | New Jersey | 4-0 |
| | 25 | at Pittsburgh | 0-1 |
| | 26 | Toronto | 4-5† |
| | 28 | Buffalo | 2-0 |
| **Mar.** | 2 | Colorado | 4-2 |
| | 5 | NY Rangers | 2-4 |
| | 7 | New Jersey | 7-3 |
| | 8 | Phoenix | 3-2 |
| | 10 | at Toronto | 2-3* |
| | 12 | at Montreal | 3-2* |
| | 14 | at Boston | 1-2 |
| | 15 | at Chicago | 4-2 |
| | 20 | at Carolina | 4-5 |
| | 21 | at Ottawa | 2-5 |
| | 25 | Minnesota | 2-6 |
| | 27 | at Detroit | 2-0 |
| | 28 | Philadelphia | 3-4† |
| **Apr.** | 1 | at Washington | 3-5 |
| | 2 | Montreal | 1-5 |
| | 4 | Tampa Bay | 3-1 |
| | 7 | at Carolina | 0-9 |
| | 9 | at Pittsburgh | 1-6 |
| | 11 | Philadelphia | 2-3 |
| | 12 | Boston | 2-6 |

* – Overtime † – Shootout

# Entry Draft Selections 2009-1995

Name in bold denotes played in NHL.

**2009**
Pick
1 John Tavares
12 Calvin De Haan
31 Mikko Koskinen
62 Anders Nilsson
92 Casey Cizikas
122 Anton Klementjev
152 Anders Lee

**2008**
Pick
9 **Joshua Bailey**
36 Corey Trivino
40 Aaron Ness
53 Travis Hamonic
66 David Toews
72 Jyri Niemi
73 Kirill Petrov
96 Matt Donovan
102 David Ullstrom
126 Kevin Poulin
148 Matt Martin
156 Jared Spurgeon
175 Justin Dibenedetto

**2007**
Pick
62 Mark Katic
76 Jason Gregoire
106 Maxim Gratchev
166 Blake Kessel
196 Simon Lacroix

**2006**
Pick
7 **Kyle Okposo**
60 **Jesse Joensuu**
70 Robin Figren
100 Rhett Rakhshani
108 Jase Weslosky
115 Tomas Marcinko
119 Doug Rogers
126 Shane Sims
141 Kim Johansson
160 **Andrew Macdonald**
171 Brian Day
173 Stefan Ridderwall
190 Troy Mattila

**2005**
Pick
15 Ryan O'Marra
46 Dustin Kohn
76 Shea Guthrie
144 **Masi Marjamaki**
180 Tyrell Mason
196 Nicholas Tuzzolino
210 Luciano Aquino

**2004**
Pick
16 **Petteri Nokelainen**
47 **Blake Comeau**
82 Sergei Ogorodnikov
115 **Wes O'Neill**
148 **Steve Regier**
179 Jaroslav Mrazek
210 Emil Axelsson
227 **Chris Campoli**
244 Jason Pitton
276 Sylvain Michaud

**2003**
Pick
15 **Robert Nilsson**
48 Dmitri Chernykh
53 Evgeny Tunik
58 **Jeremy Colliton**
120 Stefan Blaho
182 **Bruno Gervais**
212 Denis Rehak
238 Cody Blanshan
246 Igor Volkov

**2002**
Pick
22 **Sean Bergenheim**
87 **Frans Nielsen**
149 Marcus Paulsson
189 Alexei Stonkus
220 Brad Topping
252 Martin Chabada
283 Per Braxenholm

**2001**
Pick
101 Cory Stillman
132 Dusan Salficky
166 **Andy Chiodo**
197 Jan Holub
228 Mike Bray
260 Bryan Perez
280 Roman Kuhtinov
287 Juha-Pekka Ketola

**2000**
Pick
1 **Rick DiPietro**
5 **Raffi Torres**
101 Arto Tukio
105 Vladimir Gorbunov
136 Dmitri Upper
148 Kristofer Ottosson
202 **Ryan Caldwell**
264 Dmitri Altarev
267 **Tomi Pettinen**

**1999**
Pick
5 **Tim Connolly**
8 **Taylor Pyatt**
10 **Branislav Mezei**
28 **Kristian Kudroc**
78 **Mattias Weinhandl**
87 Brian Collins
101 **Juraj Kolnik**
102 Johan Halvardsson
130 **Justin Mapletoft**
140 Adam Johnson
163 **Bjorn Melin**
228 **Radek Martinek**
255 Brett Henning
268 Tyler Scott

**1998**
Pick
9 **Mike Rupp**
36 **Chris Nielsen**
95 Andy Burnham
123 **Jiri Dopita**
155 Kevin Clauson
182 **Evgeny Korolev**
209 Frederik Brindamour
237 Ben Blais
242 Jason Doyle
250 Radek Matejovsky

**1997**
Pick
4 **Roberto Luongo**
5 **Eric Brewer**
31 **Jeff Zehr**
59 Jarrett Smith
79 **Robert Schnabel**
85 **Petr Mika**
115 Adam Edinger
139 Bobby Leavins
166 Kris Knoblauch
196 Jeremy Symington
222 Ryan Clark

**1996**
Pick
3 **J.P. Dumont**
29 **Dan LaCouture**
56 **Zdeno Chara**
83 **Tyrone Garner**
109 **Bubba Berenzweig**
128 Petr Sachl
138 Todd Miller
165 J.R. Prestifilippo
192 **Evgeny Korolev**
218 Mike Muzechka

**1995**
Pick
2 **Wade Redden**
28 **Jan Hlavac**
41 **D.J. Smith**
106 **Vladimir Orszagh**
158 Andrew Taylor
210 David MacDonald
211 Mike Broda

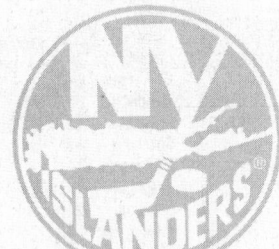

## General Managers' History

Bill Torrey, 1972-73 to 1991-92; Don Maloney, 1992-93 to 1994-95; Don Maloney and Mike Milbury, 1995-96; Mike Milbury, 1996-97 to 2005-06; Neil Smith and Garth Snow, 2006-07; Garth Snow, 2007-08 to date.

## Garth Snow

### General Manager

*Born: Wrentham, MA, June 28, 1969.*

Former Islanders' goaltender Garth Snow retired as a player on July 18, 2006 to become the fifth general manager of the New York Islanders. In his first season as general manager, Snow successfully bolstered the lineup with several key additions that helped to propel the Islanders into the postseason for the first time since the 2003–04 season and earned Snow the title of NHL Executive of the Year from *Sports Illustrated*.

Snow spent four seasons with the Islanders and 12 in the NHL. The goaltender was 135-147-44 with a 2.80 goals-against average and .901 save percentage over 368 games with Quebec, Philadelphia, Vancouver, Pittsburgh and the Islanders. Originally selected in the sixth round by Quebec in the 1987 NHL Entry Draft, the native of Wrentham, Massachusetts signed with the Islanders as a free agent on July 1, 2001.

# Club Directory

Nassau Veterans' Memorial Coliseum

**New York Islanders**
**Executive Office**
1535 Old Country Rd.
Plainview, NY 11803
Phone **516/501-6700**
FAX 516/501-6850
www.newyorkislanders.com
**Arena**
Nassau Veterans' Memorial Coliseum
Uniondale, NY 11553
**Capacity:** 16,234

| | |
|---|---|
| Owner & Governor | Charles B. Wang |
| President & Alternate Governor | Chris Dey |
| General Manager & Alternate Governor | Garth Snow |
| Alternate Governor | Art McCarthy |
| Alternate Governor | Michael Picker |
| Alternate Governor | Roy Reichbach |
| **Hockey Operations** | |
| Executive Director of Player Development | Bryan Trottier |
| Assistant G.M./Director of Amateur Scouting | Ryan Jankowski |
| Director of Pro Scouting | Ken Morrow |
| Assistant to the General Manager | Kerry Gwydir |
| Manager, Hockey Administration | Joanne Holewa |
| Head Coach | Scott Gordon |
| Assistant Coaches | Dean Chynoweth, Scott Allen |
| Goaltending Coach | Mike Dunham |
| Goaltending Consultant | Sudarshan Maharaj |
| Assistant Player Development | Eric Cairns |
| Equipment Manager | Scott Boggs |
| Assistant Equipment Manager | Richard Krouse |
| Equipment Assistant | Tom Kitz |
| Head Athletic Trainer | Garrett Timms |
| Assistant Athletic Trainer | Nates Goto |
| Strength and Conditioning Coach | Jesse Demers |
| Chief European Scout | Vellu-Pekka Kautonen |
| Pro Scouts | Anders Kallur, Mario Saraceno, Rob Cowie, Chris O'Sullivan, Toby O'Brien |
| Scouts | Brad Bowen, David Hymovitz, Joe Clark, Tim Maclean, Denny Scanlon, Tim Schurman |
| **Administration** | |
| Assistant to Charles B. Wang | Susie Schaefer |
| Executive Assistant to President | Denise Zimmermann |
| Director of Legal Affairs | Jaimie Wolf |
| Human Resources Coordinator | Michele Calabrese |
| IT Manager | Pawel Tauter |
| Receptionist | Bonnie Dreher |
| Office Attendant | Todd Aronovich |
| **Corporate Partnerships and Islanders Business Club** | |
| Exec. Director of Islanders Business Club | Mike Bossy |
| V.P.of Sales, Corporate Partnerships | Dave Decina |
| Asst. to V.P. of Sales, Corporate Partnerships | Lonnie Kussin |
| Sr. Director of Sales, Corporate Partnerships | Sean Argaman |
| Director of Sales, Corporate Partnerships | Chris Lombardo |
| Sales Executive, Corporate Partnerships | Kevin Waters |
| Director of Marketing Partnership | Larry Goldman |
| Marketing Partnerships Coordinator | Steven Olwell |
| **Ticket Sales and Operations** | |
| Vice President of Ticket Operations | Ralph Sellitti |
| General Sales Manager | Anthony Noto |
| Ticket Manager | Adam Ortiz |
| Assistant Ticket Manager | Karen Stepnowski |
| Ticket Services & Box Office Manager | Kerry Cornils |
| Director of Inside and Group Sales | Adam Jacobs |
| Senior Sales Executive, Group Tickets | Cliff Gault |
| Sales Executives, Group Tickets | Rose Barre, Jeffrey Picker |
| Sales Execs., Inside and Group Tickets | Brian Aiello, Tom Giulietti, Ariel Greenberg, Adam Wertheimer |
| Sr. Sales Executives, Integrated Sales | Steven Beisel, Bryan Davis, Marc Gersteim, Jeffrey Guida |
| Sales Executives, Integrated Sales | Chris Bukowski, Theresa Coscia, Sam Romanella |
| Sales Coordinators | Ed Flynn, Heather Tomko |
| **Marketing and Client Services** | |
| Director of Ticket Marketing and Services | Jessica Tuttle |
| Creative Service Manager | Thomas Rakoczy |
| Marketing Service Manager | Jeanne Borgia |
| Client Services & Suite Manager | Lori Ogden |
| Client Services Exec. & Graphic Designer | Paul Dippolito |
| Client Services Executives | David Dilello, Sara Pesserillo, Nicholas Tullo |
| **Media Relations / Communications** | |
| Director of Communications | Seth Sylvan |
| Communications Manager | Kimber Auerbach |
| **Game Operations** | |
| Vice President of Operations | Tim Beach |
| Asst. to V.P. of Operations | Alexa Conforti |
| Director of Operations | Ken Zore |
| Operations Manager | Ann Rina |
| Operations Coordinator | Andy Jacklin |
| Game Operations Manager | Mike Sciortino |
| Operations Production Coordinator | Brian Jones |
| Manager, Amateur Hockey Development | Michelle Winter |
| Amateur Hockey Coordinator | Ryan Maloney |
| Retail and Merchandise Operations | |
| Director of Retail Operations | Terry Goldstein |
| Retail Sales Executive | Colleen Carolan |
| Islanders Pro Shop Manager | Tim Murray |
| Team Store Manager | John Cornacchia |
| **Finance** | |
| Controller | Frank Romano |
| Accounting Manager | Chris Vardaro |
| Payroll Manager | Christine Bowler |
| Payroll Coordinator | Michele Finkelstein |
| Accounts Payable Coordinator | Janet Nelson |
| Staff Accountants | Laura Ferretti, Erica Palladino, Jennifer Penning |

# New York Rangers

## Key Off-Season Signings/Acquisitions

**2009**

**May 26** • Signed 2008 1st-round pick (20th overall) D **Michael Del Zotto.**

**June 30** • Acquired LW **Chris Higgins**, D **Ryan McDonagh**, D **Pavel Valentenko** and D **Doug Janik** from Montreal for C **Scott Gomez**, C **Tom Pyatt** and D **Michael Busto.**

**July 1** • Signed RW **Marian Gaborik** and LW **Donald Brashear.**

**July 3** • Signed C **Tyler Arnason.**

**July 9** • Signed RW **Ales Kotalik.**

**July 13** • Re-signed RW **Ryan Callahan.**

**July 13** • Acquired RW **Enver Lisin** from Phoenix for LW **Lauri Korpikoski.**

**July 16** • Named **Mike Sullivan** assistant coach.

## 2009-10 Schedule

| | | | |
|---|---|---|---|
| **Oct.** | Fri. | 2 | at Pittsburgh |
| | Sat. | 3 | Ottawa |
| | Mon. | 5 | at New Jersey |
| | Thu. | 8 | at Washington |
| | Sun. | 11 | Anaheim* |
| | Mon. | 12 | Toronto |
| | Wed. | 14 | Los Angeles |
| | Sat. | 17 | at Toronto |
| | Mon. | 19 | San Jose |
| | Thu. | 22 | New Jersey |
| | Sat. | 24 | at Montreal |
| | Mon. | 26 | Phoenix |
| | Wed. | 28 | at NY Islanders |
| | Fri. | 30 | at Minnesota |
| **Nov.** | Sun. | 1 | Boston* |
| | Tue. | 3 | at Vancouver |
| | Thu. | 5 | at Edmonton |
| | Sat. | 7 | at Calgary |
| | Thu. | 12 | Atlanta |
| | Sat. | 14 | at Ottawa |
| | Tue. | 17 | Washington |
| | Sat. | 21 | Florida |
| | Mon. | 23 | Columbus |
| | Wed. | 25 | at Florida |
| | Fri. | 27 | at Tampa Bay |
| | Sat. | 28 | at Pittsburgh |
| | Mon. | 30 | Pittsburgh |
| **Dec.** | Sat. | 5 | at Buffalo |
| | Sun. | 6 | Detroit |
| | Wed. | 9 | at Chicago |
| | Sat. | 12 | Buffalo |
| | Mon. | 14 | Atlanta |
| | Wed. | 16 | NY Islanders |
| | Thu. | 17 | at NY Islanders |
| | Sat. | 19 | at Philadelphia* |
| | Mon. | 21 | at Carolina |
| | Wed. | 23 | Florida |
| | Sat. | 26 | NY Islanders |
| | Wed. | 30 | Philadelphia |
| | Thu. | 31 | at Carolina |
| **Jan.** | Sat. | 2 | Carolina* |
| | Mon. | 4 | Boston |
| | Wed. | 6 | Dallas |
| | Thu. | 7 | at Atlanta |
| | Sat. | 9 | at Boston* |
| | Tue. | 12 | New Jersey |
| | Thu. | 14 | Ottawa |
| | Sat. | 16 | at St. Louis |
| | Sun. | 17 | Montreal |
| | Tue. | 19 | Tampa Bay |
| | Thu. | 21 | at Philadelphia |
| | Sat. | 23 | at Montreal |
| | Mon. | 25 | Pittsburgh |
| | Wed. | 27 | Carolina |
| | Sat. | 30 | at Phoenix |
| | Sun. | 31 | at Colorado |
| **Feb.** | Tue. | 2 | at Los Angeles |
| | Thu. | 4 | Washington |
| | Sat. | 6 | New Jersey |
| | Wed. | 10 | Nashville |
| | Fri. | 12 | at Pittsburgh |
| | Sun. | 14 | Tampa Bay* |
| **Mar.** | Tue. | 2 | at Ottawa |
| | Thu. | 4 | Pittsburgh |
| | Sat. | 6 | at Washington |
| | Sun. | 7 | Buffalo |
| | Wed. | 10 | at New Jersey |
| | Fri. | 12 | at Atlanta |
| | Sun. | 14 | Philadelphia* |
| | Tue. | 16 | Montreal |
| | Thu. | 18 | St. Louis |
| | Sun. | 21 | at Boston* |
| | Wed. | 24 | NY Islanders |
| | Thu. | 25 | at New Jersey |
| | Sat. | 27 | at Toronto |
| | Tue. | 30 | at NY Islanders |
| **Apr.** | Fri. | 2 | at Tampa Bay |
| | Sat. | 3 | at Florida |
| | Tue. | 6 | at Buffalo |
| | Wed. | 7 | Toronto |
| | Fri. | 9 | Philadelphia |
| | Sun. | 11 | at Philadelphia* |

* Denotes afternoon game.

## 2008-09 Results: 43W-30L-3OTL-6SOL 95PTS.
## Fourth, Atlantic Division

### Year-by-Year Record

| Season | GP | Home W | Home L | Home T | Home OL | Road W | Road L | Road T | Road OL | Overall W | Overall L | Overall T | Overall OL | GF | GA | Pts. | Finished | Playoff Result |
|---|---|---|---|---|---|---|---|---|---|---|---|---|---|---|---|---|---|---|
| 2008-09 | 82 | 26 | 11 | .... | 4 | 17 | 19 | .... | 5 | 43 | 30 | .... | 9 | 210 | 218 | 95 | 4th, Atlantic Div. | Lost Conf. Quarter-Final |
| 2007-08 | 82 | 25 | 13 | .... | 3 | 17 | 14 | .... | 10 | 42 | 27 | .... | 13 | 213 | 199 | 97 | 3rd, Atlantic Div. | Lost Conf. Semi-Final |
| 2006-07 | 82 | 21 | 15 | .... | 5 | 21 | 15 | .... | 5 | 42 | 30 | .... | 10 | 242 | 216 | 94 | 3rd, Atlantic Div. | Lost Conf. Semi-Final |
| 2005-06 | 82 | 25 | 10 | .... | 6 | 19 | 16 | .... | 6 | 44 | 26 | .... | 12 | 257 | 215 | 100 | 3rd, Atlantic Div. | Lost Conf. Quarter-Final |
| 2004-05 | .... | .... | .... | .... | .... | .... | .... | .... | .... | .... | .... | .... | .... | .... | .... | .... | | |
| 2003-04 | 82 | 13 | 21 | 3 | 4 | 14 | 19 | 4 | 4 | 27 | 40 | 7 | 8 | 206 | 250 | 69 | 4th, Atlantic Div. | Out of Playoffs |
| 2002-03 | 82 | 17 | 18 | 4 | 2 | 15 | 18 | 6 | 2 | 32 | 36 | 10 | 4 | 210 | 231 | 78 | 4th, Atlantic Div. | Out of Playoffs |
| 2001-02 | 82 | 19 | 19 | 2 | 1 | 17 | 19 | 2 | 3 | 36 | 38 | 4 | 4 | 227 | 258 | 80 | 4th, Atlantic Div. | Out of Playoffs |
| 2000-01 | 82 | 17 | 20 | 3 | 1 | 16 | 23 | 2 | 0 | 33 | 43 | 5 | 1 | 250 | 290 | 72 | 4th, Atlantic Div. | Out of Playoffs |
| 1999-2000 | 82 | 15 | 20 | 5 | 1 | 14 | 18 | 7 | 2 | 29 | 38 | 12 | 3 | 218 | 246 | 73 | 4th, Atlantic Div. | Out of Playoffs |
| 1998-99 | 82 | 17 | 19 | 5 | .... | 16 | 19 | 6 | .... | 33 | 38 | 11 | .... | 217 | 227 | 77 | 4th, Atlantic Div. | Out of Playoffs |
| 1997-98 | 82 | 14 | 18 | 9 | .... | 11 | 21 | 9 | .... | 25 | 39 | 18 | .... | 197 | 231 | 68 | 5th, Atlantic Div. | Out of Playoffs |
| 1996-97 | 82 | 21 | 14 | 6 | .... | 17 | 20 | 4 | .... | 38 | 34 | 10 | .... | 258 | 231 | 86 | 4th, Atlantic Div. | Lost Conf. Championship |
| 1995-96 | 82 | 22 | 10 | 9 | .... | 19 | 17 | 5 | .... | 41 | 27 | 14 | .... | 272 | 237 | 96 | 2nd, Atlantic Div. | Lost Conf. Semi-Final |
| 1994-95 | 48 | 11 | 10 | 3 | .... | 11 | 13 | 0 | .... | 22 | 23 | 3 | .... | 139 | 134 | 47 | 4th, Atlantic Div. | Lost Conf. Semi-Final |
| **1993-94** | **84** | **28** | **8** | **6** | .... | **24** | **16** | **2** | .... | **52** | **24** | **8** | .... | **299** | **231** | **112** | **1st, Atlantic Div.** | **Won Stanley Cup** |
| 1992-93 | 84 | 20 | 17 | 5 | .... | 14 | 22 | 6 | .... | 34 | 39 | 11 | .... | 304 | 308 | 79 | 6th, Patrick Div. | Out of Playoffs |
| 1991-92 | 80 | 28 | 8 | 4 | .... | 22 | 17 | 1 | .... | 50 | 25 | 5 | .... | 321 | 246 | 105 | 1st, Patrick Div. | Lost Div. Final |
| 1990-91 | 80 | 22 | 11 | 7 | .... | 14 | 20 | 6 | .... | 36 | 31 | 13 | .... | 297 | 265 | 85 | 2nd, Patrick Div. | Lost Div. Semi-Final |
| 1989-90 | 80 | 20 | 11 | 9 | .... | 16 | 20 | 4 | .... | 36 | 31 | 13 | .... | 279 | 267 | 85 | 1st, Patrick Div. | Lost Div. Final |
| 1988-89 | 80 | 21 | 17 | 2 | .... | 16 | 18 | 6 | .... | 37 | 35 | 8 | .... | 310 | 307 | 82 | 3rd, Patrick Div. | Lost Div. Semi-Final |
| 1987-88 | 80 | 22 | 13 | 5 | .... | 14 | 21 | 5 | .... | 36 | 34 | 10 | .... | 300 | 283 | 82 | 5th, Patrick Div. | Out of Playoffs |
| 1986-87 | 80 | 18 | 18 | 4 | .... | 16 | 20 | 4 | .... | 34 | 38 | 8 | .... | 307 | 323 | 76 | 4th, Patrick Div. | Lost Div. Semi-Final |
| 1985-86 | 80 | 20 | 18 | 2 | .... | 16 | 20 | 4 | .... | 36 | 38 | 6 | .... | 280 | 276 | 78 | 4th, Patick Div. | Lost Conf. Championship |
| 1984-85 | 80 | 16 | 18 | 6 | .... | 10 | 26 | 4 | .... | 26 | 44 | 10 | .... | 295 | 345 | 62 | 4th, Patrick Div. | Lost Div. Semi-Final |
| 1983-84 | 80 | 27 | 12 | 1 | .... | 15 | 17 | 8 | .... | 42 | 29 | 9 | .... | 314 | 304 | 93 | 4th, Patrick Div. | Lost Div. Semi-Final |
| 1982-83 | 80 | 24 | 13 | 3 | .... | 11 | 22 | 7 | .... | 35 | 35 | 10 | .... | 306 | 287 | 80 | 4th, Patrick Div. | Lost Div. Final |
| 1981-82 | 80 | 19 | 15 | 6 | .... | 20 | 12 | 8 | .... | 39 | 27 | 14 | .... | 316 | 306 | 92 | 2nd, Patrick Div. | Lost Div. Final |
| 1980-81 | 80 | 17 | 13 | 10 | .... | 13 | 23 | 4 | .... | 30 | 36 | 14 | .... | 312 | 317 | 74 | 4th, Patrick Div. | Lost Semi-Final |
| 1979-80 | 80 | 22 | 10 | 8 | .... | 16 | 22 | 2 | .... | 38 | 32 | 10 | .... | 308 | 284 | 86 | 3rd, Patrick Div. | Lost Quarter-Final |
| 1978-79 | 80 | 19 | 13 | 8 | .... | 21 | 16 | 3 | .... | 40 | 29 | 11 | .... | 316 | 292 | 91 | 3rd, Patrick Div. | Lost Final |
| 1977-78 | 80 | 18 | 15 | 7 | .... | 12 | 22 | 6 | .... | 30 | 37 | 13 | .... | 279 | 280 | 73 | 4th, Patrick Div. | Lost Prelim. Round |
| 1976-77 | 80 | 17 | 18 | 5 | .... | 12 | 19 | 9 | .... | 29 | 37 | 14 | .... | 272 | 310 | 72 | 4th, Patrick Div. | Out of Playoffs |
| 1975-76 | 80 | 16 | 16 | 8 | .... | 13 | 26 | 1 | .... | 29 | 42 | 9 | .... | 262 | 333 | 67 | 4th, Patrick Div. | Out of Playoffs |
| 1974-75 | 80 | 21 | 11 | 8 | .... | 16 | 18 | 6 | .... | 37 | 29 | 14 | .... | 319 | 276 | 88 | 2nd, Patrick Div. | Lost Prelim. Round |
| 1973-74 | 78 | 26 | 7 | 6 | .... | 14 | 17 | 8 | .... | 40 | 24 | 14 | .... | 300 | 251 | 94 | 3rd, East Div. | Lost Semi-Final |
| 1972-73 | 78 | 26 | 8 | 5 | .... | 21 | 15 | 3 | .... | 47 | 23 | 8 | .... | 297 | 208 | 102 | 3rd, East Div. | Lost Semi-Final |
| 1971-72 | 78 | 26 | 6 | 7 | .... | 22 | 11 | 6 | .... | 48 | 17 | 13 | .... | 317 | 192 | 109 | 2nd, East Div. | Lost Final |
| 1970-71 | 78 | 30 | 2 | 7 | .... | 19 | 16 | 4 | .... | 49 | 18 | 11 | .... | 259 | 177 | 109 | 2nd, East Div. | Lost Semi-Final |
| 1969-70 | 76 | 22 | 8 | 8 | .... | 16 | 14 | 8 | .... | 38 | 22 | 16 | .... | 246 | 189 | 92 | 4th, East Div. | Lost Quarter-Final |
| 1968-69 | 76 | 27 | 7 | 4 | .... | 14 | 19 | 5 | .... | 41 | 26 | 9 | .... | 231 | 196 | 91 | 3rd, East Div. | Lost Quarter-Final |
| 1967-68 | 74 | 22 | 8 | 7 | .... | 17 | 15 | 5 | .... | 39 | 23 | 12 | .... | 226 | 183 | 90 | 2nd, East Div. | Lost Quarter-Final |
| 1966-67 | 70 | 18 | 12 | 5 | .... | 12 | 16 | 7 | .... | 30 | 28 | 12 | .... | 188 | 189 | 72 | 4th, | Lost Semi-Final |
| 1965-66 | 70 | 12 | 16 | 7 | .... | 6 | 25 | 4 | .... | 18 | 41 | 11 | .... | 195 | 261 | 47 | 6th, | Out of Playoffs |
| 1964-65 | 70 | 8 | 19 | 8 | .... | 12 | 19 | 4 | .... | 20 | 38 | 12 | .... | 179 | 246 | 52 | 5th, | Out of Playoffs |
| 1963-64 | 70 | 14 | 13 | 8 | .... | 8 | 25 | 2 | .... | 22 | 38 | 10 | .... | 186 | 242 | 54 | 5th, | Out of Playoffs |
| 1962-63 | 70 | 12 | 17 | 6 | .... | 10 | 19 | 6 | .... | 22 | 36 | 12 | .... | 211 | 233 | 56 | 5th, | Out of Playoffs |
| 1961-62 | 70 | 16 | 11 | 8 | .... | 10 | 21 | 4 | .... | 26 | 32 | 12 | .... | 195 | 207 | 64 | 4th, | Lost Semi-Final |
| 1960-61 | 70 | 15 | 15 | 5 | .... | 7 | 23 | 5 | .... | 22 | 38 | 10 | .... | 204 | 248 | 54 | 5th, | Out of Playoffs |
| 1959-60 | 70 | 10 | 15 | 10 | .... | 7 | 23 | 5 | .... | 17 | 38 | 15 | .... | 187 | 247 | 49 | 6th, | Out of Playoffs |
| 1958-59 | 70 | 14 | 16 | 5 | .... | 12 | 16 | 7 | .... | 26 | 32 | 12 | .... | 201 | 217 | 64 | 5th, | Out of Playoffs |
| 1957-58 | 70 | 14 | 15 | 6 | .... | 18 | 10 | 7 | .... | 32 | 25 | 13 | .... | 195 | 188 | 77 | 2nd, | Lost Semi-Final |
| 1956-57 | 70 | 15 | 12 | 8 | .... | 11 | 18 | 6 | .... | 26 | 30 | 14 | .... | 184 | 227 | 66 | 4th, | Lost Semi-Final |
| 1955-56 | 70 | 20 | 7 | 8 | .... | 12 | 21 | 2 | .... | 32 | 28 | 10 | .... | 204 | 203 | 74 | 3rd, | Lost Semi-Final |
| 1954-55 | 70 | 10 | 12 | 13 | .... | 7 | 23 | 5 | .... | 17 | 35 | 18 | .... | 150 | 210 | 52 | 5th, | Out of Playoffs |
| 1953-54 | 70 | 18 | 12 | 5 | .... | 11 | 19 | 5 | .... | 29 | 31 | 10 | .... | 161 | 182 | 68 | 5th, | Out of Playoffs |
| 1952-53 | 70 | 11 | 14 | 10 | .... | 6 | 23 | 6 | .... | 17 | 37 | 16 | .... | 152 | 211 | 50 | 6th, | Out of Playoffs |
| 1951-52 | 70 | 16 | 13 | 6 | .... | 7 | 21 | 7 | .... | 23 | 34 | 13 | .... | 192 | 219 | 59 | 5th, | Out of Playoffs |
| 1950-51 | 70 | 14 | 11 | 10 | .... | 6 | 18 | 11 | .... | 20 | 29 | 21 | .... | 169 | 201 | 61 | 5th, | Out of Playoffs |
| 1949-50 | 70 | 19 | 12 | 4 | .... | 9 | 19 | 7 | .... | 28 | 31 | 11 | .... | 170 | 189 | 67 | 4th, | Lost Final |
| 1948-49 | 60 | 13 | 12 | 5 | .... | 5 | 19 | 6 | .... | 18 | 31 | 11 | .... | 133 | 172 | 47 | 6th, | Out of Playoffs |
| 1947-48 | 60 | 11 | 12 | 7 | .... | 10 | 14 | 6 | .... | 21 | 26 | 13 | .... | 176 | 201 | 55 | 4th, | Lost Semi-Final |
| 1946-47 | 60 | 11 | 14 | 5 | .... | 11 | 18 | 1 | .... | 22 | 32 | 6 | .... | 167 | 186 | 50 | 5th, | Out of Playoffs |
| 1945-46 | 50 | 8 | 12 | 5 | .... | 5 | 16 | 4 | .... | 13 | 28 | 9 | .... | 144 | 191 | 35 | 6th, | Out of Playoffs |
| 1944-45 | 50 | 7 | 11 | 7 | .... | 4 | 18 | 3 | .... | 11 | 29 | 10 | .... | 154 | 247 | 32 | 6th, | Out of Playoffs |
| 1943-44 | 50 | 4 | 17 | 4 | .... | 2 | 22 | 1 | .... | 6 | 39 | 5 | .... | 162 | 310 | 17 | 6th, | Out of Playoffs |
| 1942-43 | 50 | 7 | 13 | 5 | .... | 4 | 18 | 3 | .... | 11 | 31 | 8 | .... | 161 | 253 | 30 | 6th, | Out of Playoffs |
| 1941-42 | 48 | 15 | 8 | 1 | .... | 14 | 9 | 1 | .... | 29 | 17 | 2 | .... | 177 | 143 | 60 | 1st, | Lost Semi-Final |
| 1940-41 | 48 | 13 | 7 | 4 | .... | 8 | 12 | 4 | .... | 21 | 19 | 8 | .... | 143 | 125 | 50 | 4th, | Lost Quarter-Final |
| **1939-40** | **48** | **17** | **4** | **3** | .... | **10** | **7** | **7** | .... | **27** | **11** | **10** | .... | **136** | **77** | **64** | **2nd,** | **Won Stanley Cup** |
| 1938-39 | 48 | 13 | 8 | 3 | .... | 13 | 8 | 3 | .... | 26 | 16 | 6 | .... | 149 | 105 | 58 | 2nd, | Lost Semi-Final |
| 1937-38 | 48 | 15 | 5 | 4 | .... | 12 | 10 | 2 | .... | 27 | 15 | 6 | .... | 149 | 96 | 60 | 2nd, Amn. Div. | Lost Quarter-Final |
| 1936-37 | 48 | 9 | 7 | 8 | .... | 10 | 13 | 1 | .... | 19 | 20 | 9 | .... | 117 | 106 | 47 | 3rd, Amn. Div. | Lost Final |
| 1935-36 | 48 | 11 | 6 | 7 | .... | 8 | 11 | 5 | .... | 19 | 17 | 12 | .... | 91 | 96 | 50 | 4th, Amn. Div. | Out of Playoffs |
| 1934-35 | 48 | 11 | 8 | 5 | .... | 11 | 12 | 1 | .... | 22 | 20 | 6 | .... | 137 | 139 | 50 | 3rd, Amn. Div. | Lost Semi-Final |
| 1933-34 | 48 | 11 | 7 | 6 | .... | 10 | 12 | 2 | .... | 21 | 19 | 8 | .... | 120 | 113 | 50 | 3rd, Amn. Div. | Lost Quarter-Final |
| **1932-33** | **48** | **12** | **7** | **5** | .... | **11** | **10** | **3** | .... | **23** | **17** | **8** | .... | **135** | **107** | **54** | **3rd, Amn. Div.** | **Won Stanley Cup** |
| 1931-32 | 48 | 13 | 7 | 4 | .... | 10 | 10 | 4 | .... | 23 | 17 | 8 | .... | 134 | 112 | 54 | 1st, Amn. Div. | Lost Final |
| 1930-31 | 44 | 10 | 9 | 3 | .... | 9 | 7 | 6 | .... | 19 | 16 | 9 | .... | 106 | 87 | 47 | 3rd, Amn. Div. | Lost Semi-Final |
| 1929-30 | 44 | 11 | 5 | 6 | .... | 6 | 12 | 4 | .... | 17 | 17 | 10 | .... | 136 | 143 | 44 | 3rd, Amn. Div. | Lost Semi-Final |
| 1928-29 | 44 | 12 | 6 | 4 | .... | 9 | 7 | 6 | .... | 21 | 13 | 10 | .... | 72 | 65 | 52 | 2nd, Amn. Div. | Lost Final |
| **1927-28** | **44** | **10** | **8** | **4** | .... | **9** | **8** | **5** | .... | **19** | **16** | **9** | .... | **94** | **79** | **47** | **2nd, Amn. Div.** | **Won Stanley Cup** |
| 1926-27 | 44 | 13 | 5 | 4 | .... | 12 | 8 | 2 | .... | 25 | 13 | 6 | .... | 95 | 72 | 56 | 1st, Amn. Div. | Lost Quarter-Final |

**ATLANTIC DIVISION**
**84th NHL Season**

**Franchise date:** May 15, 1926

# 2009-10 Player Personnel

| FORWARDS | HT | WT | S | Place of Birth | *Age | 2008-09 Club |
|---|---|---|---|---|---|---|
| ANISIMOV, Artem | 6-4 | 194 | L | Yaroslavl, USSR | 21 | NY Rangers-Hartford |
| ARNASON, Tyler | 5-11 | 204 | L | Oklahoma City, OK | 30 | Colorado |
| AVERY, Sean | 5-10 | 195 | L | Pickering, Ont. | 29 | Dal-Hartford-NYR |
| BOYLE, Brian | 6-7 | 252 | L | Hingham, MA | 24 | Los Angeles-Manchester |
| BRASHEAR, Donald | 6-3 | 234 | L | Bedford, IN | 37 | Washington |
| CALLAHAN, Ryan | 5-11 | 188 | R | Rochester, NY | 24 | NY Rangers |
| DRURY, Chris | 5-10 | 190 | R | Trumbull, CT | 33 | NY Rangers |
| DUBINSKY, Brandon | 6-1 | 205 | L | Anchorage, AK | 23 | NY Rangers |
| GABORIK, Marian | 6-1 | 199 | L | Trencin, Czech. | 27 | Minnesota |
| HIGGINS, Christopher | 6-0 | 203 | L | Smithtown, NY | 26 | Montreal |
| KOTALIK, Ales | 6-1 | 227 | R | Jindrichuv Hradec, Czech. | 30 | Buffalo-Edmonton |
| LISIN, Enver | 6-1 | 190 | L | Moscow, USSR | 23 | Phoenix-San Antonio |
| PARENTEAU, P. A. | 5-11 | 195 | R | Hull, Que. | 26 | Hartford |
| RISSMILLER, Patrick | 6-4 | 220 | L | Belmont, MA | 30 | NY Rangers-Hartford |
| VOROS, Aaron | 6-3 | 215 | L | Vancouver, B.C. | 28 | NY Rangers |
| **DEFENSEMEN** | | | | | | |
| GILROY, Matt | 6-2 | 195 | R | North Bellmore, NY | 25 | Boston University |
| GIRARDI, Dan | 6-2 | 210 | R | Welland, Ont. | 25 | NY Rangers |
| HEIKKINEN, Ilkka | 6-2 | 191 | L | Rauma, Finland | 24 | HIFK |
| POTTER, Corey | 6-3 | 200 | R | Lansing, MI | 25 | NY Rangers-Hartford |
| REDDEN, Wade | 6-2 | 212 | L | Lloydminster, Sask. | 32 | NY Rangers |
| ROZSIVAL, Michal | 6-2 | 205 | R | Vlasim, Czech. | 31 | NY Rangers |
| SAUR, Michael | 6-3 | 215 | R | St. Cloud, MN | 22 | NY Rangers-Hartford |
| STAAL, Marc | 6-4 | 209 | L | Thunder Bay, Ont. | 22 | NY Rangers |

| GOALTENDERS | HT | WT | C | Place of Birth | *Age | 2008-09 Club |
|---|---|---|---|---|---|---|
| LUNDQVIST, Henrik | 6-1 | 195 | L | Are, Sweden | 27 | NY Rangers |
| VALIQUETTE, Steve | 6-6 | 210 | L | Etobicoke, Ont. | 32 | NY Rangers |

* – Age at start of 2009-10 season

## Captains' History

Bill Cook, 1926-27 to 1936-37; Art Coulter, 1937-38 to 1941-42; Ott Heller, 1942-43 to 1944-45; Neil Colville 1945-46 to 1948-49; Buddy O'Connor, 1949-50; Frank Eddolls, 1950-51; Frank Eddolls and Allan Stanley, 1951-52; Allan Stanley, 1952-53; Allan Stanley and Don Raleigh, 1953-54; Don Raleigh, 1954-55; Harry Howell, 1955-56, 1956-57; Red Sullivan, 1957-58 to 1960-61; Andy Bathgate, 1961-62, 1962-63; Andy Bathgate and Camille Henry, 1963-64; Camille Henry and Bob Nevin, 1964-65; Bob Nevin 1965-66 to 1970-71; Vic Hadfield, 1971-72 to 1973-74; Brad Park, 1974-75; Brad Park and Phil Esposito, 1975-76; Phil Esposito, 1976-77, 1977-78; Dave Maloney, 1978-79, 1979-80; Dave Maloney, Walt Tkaczuk and Barry Beck, 1980-81; Barry Beck, 1981-82 to 1985-86; Ron Greschner, 1986-87; Ron Greschner and Kelly Kisio, 1987-88; Kelly Kisio, 1988-89 to 1990-91; Mark Messier, 1991-92 to 1996-97; Brian Leetch, 1997-98 to 1999-2000; Mark Messier, 2000-01 to 2003-04; no captain, 2005-06; Jaromir Jagr, 2006-07, 2007-08; Chris Drury, 2008-09.

# John Tortorella

## Head Coach

*Born: Boston, MA, June 24, 1958.*

John Tortorella was named head coach of the New York Rangers on February 23, 2009. He returned to the organization after serving as head coach of the Tampa Bay Lightning for seven seasons. In 2003-04, Tortorella guided Tampa Bay to the club's first Stanley Cup championship and was awarded the Jack Adams Award as the NHL's coach of the year.

Tortorella joined Tampa Bay following a one-year stint with the Rangers in 1999-2000 where he was an assistant coach and served as head coach for the final four games of the season. Prior to joining the Rangers, he spent two seasons as an assistant coach with the Phoenix Coyotes. He joined Phoenix during the 1997-98 season, after spending the previous eight seasons with the Buffalo Sabres organization. Tortorella served as an assistant coach with the Sabres from 1989-90 to 1994-95 and as head coach with their American Hockey League affiliate, the Rochester Americans, during the 1995-96 and 1996-97 campaigns. He guided the club to the Calder Cup championship in 1995-96.

The Boston native spent two seasons as general manager and head coach of the Virginia Lancers of the Atlantic Coast Hockey League from 1986-87 to 1987-88, winning coach of the year honors both seasons and the league championship in 1986-87. Following the 1987-88 season, Tortorella joined the Fort Wayne Komets of the International Hockey League during their 1988 playoff run before serving as an assistant coach with the New Haven Nighthawks (AHL) in 1988-89.

Prior to joining the coaching ranks, Tortorella played at Salem State College before transferring to the University of Maine Black Bears of the East Coast Athletic Conference, where he skated for three seasons as a right winger and was twice named an ECAC All-Star. After playing in Sweden, he returned to North America to skate in the ACHL with the Hampton Roads Gulls, Erie Golden Blades and Virginia Lancers, recording 98 goals and 160 assists for 258 points, along with 302 penalty minutes in 200 games over four seasons.

### Coaching Record

| | | | Regular Season | | | | Playoffs | | | |
|---|---|---|---|---|---|---|---|---|---|---|
| **Season** | **Team** | **League** | **GC** | **W** | **L** | **O/T** | **GC** | **W** | **L** | **T** |
| 1995-96 | Rochester | AHL | 80 | 37 | 34 | 9 | 19 | 15 | 4 | .... |
| 1996-97 | Rochester | AHL | 80 | 40 | 30 | 10 | 10 | 6 | 4 | .... |
| **99-2000** | **NY Rangers** | **NHL** | **4** | **0** | **3** | **1** | .... | .... | .... | .... |
| **2000-01** | **Tampa Bay** | **NHL** | **43** | **12** | **27** | **4** | .... | .... | .... | .... |
| **2001-02** | **Tampa Bay** | **NHL** | **82** | **27** | **40** | **15** | .... | .... | .... | .... |
| **2002-03** | **Tampa Bay** | **NHL** | **82** | **36** | **25** | **21** | **11** | **5** | **6** | .... |
| **2003-04♦** | **Tampa Bay** | **NHL** | **82** | **46** | **22** | **14** | **23** | **16** | **7** | .... |
| **2004-05** | **Tampa Bay** | | | | SEASON CANCELLED | | | | | |
| **2005-06** | **Tampa Bay** | **NHL** | **82** | **43** | **33** | **6** | **5** | **1** | **4** | .... |
| **2006-07** | **Tampa Bay** | **NHL** | **82** | **44** | **33** | **5** | **6** | **2** | **4** | .... |
| **2007-08** | **Tampa Bay** | **NHL** | **82** | **31** | **42** | **9** | .... | .... | .... | .... |
| **2008-09** | **NY Rangers** | **NHL** | **21** | **12** | **7** | **2** | **7** | **3** | **4** | .... |
| | **NHL Totals** | | **560** | **251** | **232** | **77** | **52** | **27** | **25** | .... |

♦ Stanley Cup win.

# 2008-09 Scoring

* – rookie

## Regular Season

| Pos | # | Player | Team | GP | G | A | Pts | TOI | +/– | PIM | PP | SH | GW | S | % |
|---|---|---|---|---|---|---|---|---|---|---|---|---|---|---|---|
| R | 80 | Nik Antropov | TOR | 63 | 21 | 25 | 46 | 17:13 | –13 | 24 | 6 | 0 | 2 | 171 | 12.3 |
| | | | NYR | 18 | 7 | 6 | 13 | 17:05 | –1 | 6 | 2 | 0 | 2 | 53 | 13.2 |
| | | | Total | 81 | 28 | 31 | 59 | 17:11 | –14 | 30 | 8 | 0 | 4 | 224 | 12.5 |
| R | 13 | Nikolai Zherdev | NYR | 82 | 23 | 35 | 58 | 16:49 | 6 | 39 | 4 | 1 | 3 | 219 | 10.5 |
| C | 19 | Scott Gomez | NYR | 77 | 16 | 42 | 58 | 21:03 | –2 | 60 | 3 | 1 | 7 | 271 | 5.9 |
| C | 23 | Chris Drury | NYR | 81 | 22 | 34 | 56 | 20:14 | –8 | 32 | 10 | 1 | 2 | 219 | 10.0 |
| L | 91 | Markus Naslund | NYR | 82 | 24 | 22 | 46 | 17:10 | –10 | 57 | 8 | 0 | 0 | 215 | 11.2 |
| C | 17 | Brandon Dubinsky | NYR | 82 | 13 | 28 | 41 | 16:38 | –6 | 112 | 3 | 1 | 7 | 188 | 6.9 |
| R | 24 | Ryan Callahan | NYR | 81 | 22 | 18 | 40 | 17:03 | 7 | 45 | 2 | 1 | 1 | 237 | 9.3 |
| D | 33 | Michal Rozsival | NYR | 76 | 8 | 22 | 30 | 22:30 | –7 | 52 | 3 | 0 | 2 | 120 | 6.7 |
| D | 6 | Wade Redden | NYR | 81 | 3 | 23 | 26 | 22:20 | –5 | 51 | 2 | 0 | 0 | 161 | 1.9 |
| L | 16 | Sean Avery | DAL | 23 | 3 | 7 | 10 | 14:58 | 2 | 77 | 0 | 0 | 0 | 49 | 6.1 |
| | | | NYR | 18 | 5 | 7 | 12 | 16:44 | 4 | 34 | 2 | 0 | 0 | 50 | 10.0 |
| | | | Total | 41 | 8 | 14 | 22 | 15:45 | 6 | 111 | 2 | 0 | 0 | 99 | 8.1 |
| D | 5 | Dan Girardi | NYR | 82 | 4 | 18 | 22 | 21:31 | –14 | 53 | 2 | 0 | 1 | 122 | 3.3 |
| D | 27 | Paul Mara | NYR | 76 | 5 | 16 | 21 | 18:57 | 2 | 94 | 1 | 0 | 0 | 102 | 4.9 |
| D | 53 | Derek Morris | PHX | 57 | 5 | 7 | 12 | 21:16 | –13 | 24 | 0 | 1 | 0 | 89 | 5.6 |
| | | | NYR | 18 | 0 | 8 | 8 | 19:40 | 3 | 16 | 0 | 0 | 0 | 31 | 0.0 |
| | | | Total | 75 | 5 | 15 | 20 | 20:53 | –10 | 40 | 0 | 1 | 0 | 120 | 4.2 |
| L | 34 | Aaron Voros | NYR | 54 | 8 | 8 | 16 | 11:10 | –9 | 122 | 3 | 0 | 1 | 66 | 12.1 |
| D | 18 | Marc Staal | NYR | 82 | 3 | 12 | 15 | 21:07 | –7 | 64 | 0 | 0 | 1 | 96 | 3.1 |
| L | 29 * | Lauri Korpikoski | NYR | 68 | 6 | 8 | 14 | 10:54 | –10 | 14 | 0 | 0 | 1 | 63 | 9.5 |
| L | 20 | Fredrik Sjostrom | NYR | 79 | 7 | 6 | 13 | 12:10 | –11 | 30 | 0 | 2 | 0 | 95 | 7.4 |
| C | 15 | Blair Betts | NYR | 81 | 6 | 4 | 10 | 10:36 | –5 | 16 | 0 | 2 | 1 | 83 | 7.2 |
| R | 28 | Colton Orr | NYR | 82 | 1 | 4 | 5 | 6:29 | –15 | 193 | 0 | 0 | 0 | 40 | 2.5 |
| D | 38 * | Corey Potter | NYR | 5 | 1 | 1 | 2 | 13:14 | –1 | 0 | 0 | 0 | 0 | 4 | 25.0 |
| D | 4 | Erik Reitz | MIN | 31 | 1 | 1 | 2 | 9:51 | –2 | 41 | 0 | 0 | 0 | 15 | 6.7 |
| | | | NYR | 11 | 0 | 0 | 0 | 10:15 | –4 | 24 | 0 | 0 | 0 | 7 | 0.0 |
| | | | Total | 42 | 1 | 1 | 2 | 9:57 | –6 | 65 | 0 | 0 | 0 | 22 | 4.5 |
| C | 42 * | Artem Anisimov | NYR | 1 | 0 | 0 | 0 | 9:27 | 0 | 0 | 0 | 0 | 0 | 1 | 0.0 |
| L | 12 | Patrick Rissmiller | NYR | 2 | 0 | 0 | 0 | 9:12 | –2 | 0 | 0 | 0 | 0 | 2 | 0.0 |
| D | 56 * | Michael Sauer | NYR | 3 | 0 | 0 | 0 | 9:21 | –1 | 0 | 0 | 0 | 0 | 2 | 0.0 |

### Goaltending

| No. | Goaltender | GPI | Mins | Avg | W | L | OT | EN | SO | GA | SA | S% | G | A | PIM |
|---|---|---|---|---|---|---|---|---|---|---|---|---|---|---|---|
| 30 | Henrik Lundqvist | 70 | 4153 | 2.43 | 38 | 25 | 7 | 3 | 3 | 168 | 2007 | .916 | 0 | 2 | 0 |
| 40 | Steve Valiquette | 15 | 823 | 2.84 | 5 | 5 | 2 | 2 | 1 | 39 | 421 | .907 | 0 | 1 | 2 |
| | **Totals** | **82** | **5011** | **2.54** | **43** | **30** | **9** | **5** | **4** | **212** | **2433** | **.913** | | | |

## Playoffs

| Pos | # | Player | Team | GP | G | A | Pts | TOI | +/– | PIM | PP | SH | GW | OT | S | % |
|---|---|---|---|---|---|---|---|---|---|---|---|---|---|---|---|---|
| C | 19 | Scott Gomez | NYR | 7 | 2 | 3 | 5 | 19:58 | –4 | 4 | 1 | 0 | 0 | 0 | 15 | 13.3 |
| C | 17 | Brandon Dubinsky | NYR | 7 | 1 | 3 | 4 | 18:14 | 1 | 18 | 0 | 0 | 1 | 0 | 9 | 11.1 |
| R | 80 | Nik Antropov | NYR | 7 | 2 | 1 | 3 | 16:41 | –1 | 6 | 1 | 0 | 0 | 0 | 17 | 11.8 |
| L | 91 | Markus Naslund | NYR | 7 | 1 | 2 | 3 | 16:06 | 2 | 10 | 1 | 0 | 0 | 0 | 10 | 10.0 |
| R | 24 | Ryan Callahan | NYR | 7 | 2 | 0 | 2 | 19:43 | –1 | 4 | 1 | 0 | 1 | 0 | 19 | 10.5 |
| D | 27 | Paul Mara | NYR | 7 | 1 | 1 | 2 | 14:43 | –2 | 8 | 0 | 0 | 0 | 0 | 7 | 14.3 |
| L | 16 | Sean Avery | NYR | 6 | 0 | 2 | 2 | 17:38 | –3 | 24 | 0 | 0 | 0 | 0 | 15 | 0.0 |
| D | 6 | Wade Redden | NYR | 7 | 0 | 2 | 2 | 23:24 | –2 | 0 | 0 | 0 | 0 | 0 | 12 | 0.0 |
| D | 53 | Derek Morris | NYR | 7 | 0 | 2 | 2 | 16:23 | –2 | 0 | 0 | 0 | 0 | 0 | 6 | 0.0 |
| L | 29 * | Lauri Korpikoski | NYR | 7 | 0 | 2 | 2 | 13:09 | 0 | 0 | 0 | 0 | 0 | 0 | 5 | 0.0 |
| C | 23 | Chris Drury | NYR | 6 | 1 | 0 | 1 | 13:32 | –5 | 2 | 0 | 0 | 1 | 0 | 5 | 20.0 |
| D | 18 | Marc Staal | NYR | 7 | 1 | 0 | 1 | 21:32 | –3 | 0 | 0 | 0 | 0 | 0 | 4 | 25.0 |
| L | 20 | Fredrik Sjostrom | NYR | 7 | 0 | 1 | 1 | 11:45 | 0 | 0 | 0 | 0 | 0 | 0 | 9 | 0.0 |
| C | 42 * | Artem Anisimov | NYR | 1 | 0 | 0 | 0 | 5:35 | 0 | 0 | 0 | 0 | 0 | 0 | 0 | 0.0 |
| L | 34 | Aaron Voros | NYR | 4 | 0 | 0 | 0 | 6:51 | –2 | 14 | 0 | 0 | 0 | 0 | 3 | 0.0 |
| R | 28 | Colton Orr | NYR | 5 | 0 | 0 | 0 | 3:49 | –1 | 16 | 0 | 0 | 0 | 0 | 0 | 0.0 |
| C | 15 | Blair Betts | NYR | 6 | 0 | 0 | 0 | 9:08 | –1 | 0 | 0 | 0 | 0 | 0 | 1 | 0.0 |
| D | 33 | Michal Rozsival | NYR | 7 | 0 | 0 | 0 | 22:41 | 0 | 4 | 0 | 0 | 0 | 0 | 5 | 0.0 |
| R | 13 | Nikolai Zherdev | NYR | 7 | 0 | 0 | 0 | 12:32 | –3 | 2 | 0 | 0 | 0 | 0 | 12 | 0.0 |
| D | 5 | Dan Girardi | NYR | 7 | 0 | 0 | 0 | 21:04 | –3 | 6 | 0 | 0 | 0 | 0 | 12 | 0.0 |

### Goaltending

| No. | Goaltender | GPI | Mins | Avg | W | L | EN | SO | GA | SA | S% | G | A | PIM |
|---|---|---|---|---|---|---|---|---|---|---|---|---|---|---|
| 40 | Steve Valiquette | 2 | 40 | 0.00 | 0 | 0 | 0 | 0 | 0 | 9 | 1.000 | 0 | 0 | 0 |
| 30 | Henrik Lundqvist | 7 | 380 | 3.00 | 3 | 4 | 0 | 1 | 19 | 207 | .908 | 0 | 0 | 0 |
| | **Totals** | **7** | **420** | **2.71** | **3** | **4** | **0** | **1** | **19** | **216** | **.912** | | | |

## Coaching History

Lester Patrick, 1926-27 to 1938-39; Frank Boucher, 1939-40 to 1947-48; Frank Boucher and Lynn Patrick, 1948-49; Lynn Patrick, 1949-50; Neil Colville, 1950-51; Neil Colville and Bill Cook, 1951-52; Bill Cook, 1952-53; Frank Boucher and Muzz Patrick, 1953-54; Muzz Patrick, 1954-55; Phil Watson, 1955-56 to 1958-59; Phil Watson, Muzz Patrick and Alf Pike, 1959-60; Alf Pike, 1960-61; Doug Harvey, 1961-62; Muzz Patrick and Red Sullivan, 1962-63; Red Sullivan, 1963-64, 1964-65; Red Sullivan and Emile Francis, 1965-66; Emile Francis, 1966-67, 1967-68; Bernie Geoffrion and Emile Francis, 1968-69; Emile Francis, 1969-70 to 1972-73; Larry Popein and Emile Francis, 1973-74; Emile Francis, 1974-75; Ron Stewart and John Ferguson, 1975-76; John Ferguson, 1976-77; Jean-Guy Talbot, 1977-78; Fred Shero, 1978-79, 1979-80; Fred Shero and Craig Patrick, 1980-81; Herb Brooks, 1981-82 to 1983-84; Herb Brooks and Craig Patrick, 1984-85; Ted Sator, 1985-86; Ted Sator, Tom Webster and Phil Esposito, 1986-87; Michel Bergeron, 1987-88; Michel Bergeron and Phil Esposito, 1988-89; Roger Neilson, 1989-90 to 1991-92; Roger Neilson and Ron Smith, 1992-93; Mike Keenan, 1993-94; Colin Campbell, 1994-95 to 1996-97; Colin Campbell and John Muckler, 1997-98; John Muckler, 1998-99; John Muckler and John Tortorella, 1999-2000; Ron Low, 2000-01, 2001-02; Bryan Trottier and Glen Sather, 2002-03; Glen Sather and Tom Renney, 2003-04; Tom Renney, 2004-05 to 2007-08; Tom Renney and John Tortorella, 2008-09; John Tortorella, 2009-10.

# Club Records

## Team

(Figures in brackets for season records are games played; records for fewest points, wins, ties, losses, goals, goals against are for 70 or more games)

**Most Points** ............... **112** 1993-94 (84)
**Most Wins** ............... **52** 1993-94 (84)
**Most Ties** ............... **21** 1950-51 (70)
**Most Losses** ............... **44** 1984-85 (80)
**Most Goals** ............... **321** 1991-92 (80)
**Most Goals Against** ......... **345** 1984-85 (80)
**Fewest Points** ............... **47** 1965-66 (70)
**Fewest Wins** ............... **17** 1952-53 (70), 1954-55 (70), 1959-60 (70)
**Fewest Ties** ............... **4** 2001-02 (82)
**Fewest Losses** ............... **17** 1971-72 (78)
**Fewest Goals** ............... **150** 1954-55 (70)
**Fewest Goals Against** ....... **177** 1970-71 (78)

**Longest Winning Streak**
**Overall** ............... **10** Dec. 19/39-Jan. 13/40, Jan. 19-Feb. 10/73
**Home** ............... **14** Dec. 19/39-Feb. 25/40
**Away** ............... **7** Jan. 12-Feb. 12/35, Oct. 28-Nov. 29/78

**Longest Undefeated Streak**
**Overall** ............... **19** Nov. 23/39-Jan. 13/40 (14 wins, 5 ties)
**Home** ............... **24** Oct. 14/70-Jan. 31/71 (18 wins, 6 ties), Oct. 24/95-Feb.15/96 (18 wins, 6 ties)
**Away** ............... **11** Nov. 5/39-Jan. 13/40 (6 wins, 5 ties)

**Longest Losing Streak**
**Overall** ............... **11** Oct. 30-Nov. 27/43
**Home** ............... **7** Oct. 20-Nov. 14/76, Mar. 24-Apr. 14/93
**Away** ............... **10** Oct. 30-Dec. 23/43, Feb. 8-Mar. 15/61

**Longest Winless Streak**
**Overall** ............... **21** Jan. 23-Mar. 19/44 (17 losses, 4 ties)
**Home** ............... **10** Jan. 30-Mar. 19/44 (7 losses, 3 ties)
**Away** ............... **16** Oct. 9-Dec. 20/52 (12 losses, 4 ties)

**Most Shutouts, Season** ....... **13** 1928-29 (44)
**Most PIM, Season** ......... **2,018** 1989-90 (80)
**Most Goals, Game** ........... **12** Nov. 21/71 (Cal. 1 at NYR 12)

## Individual

**Most Seasons** ............... **18** Rod Gilbert
**Most Games** ............ **1,160** Harry Howell
**Most Goals, Career** ......... **406** Rod Gilbert
**Most Assists, Career** ........ **741** Brian Leetch
**Most Points, Career** ....... **1,021** Rod Gilbert (406G, 615A)
**Most PIM, Career** ......... **1,226** Ron Greschner
**Most Shutouts, Career** ........ **49** Ed Giacomin
**Longest Consecutive Games Streak** ........... **560** Andy Hebenton (Oct. 7/55-Mar. 24/63)
**Most Goals, Season** .......... **54** Jaromir Jagr (2005-06)
**Most Assists, Season** ......... **80** Brian Leetch (1991-92)
**Most Points, Season** ........ **123** Jaromir Jagr (2005-06; 54G, 69A)
**Most PIM, Season** .......... **305** Troy Mallette (1989-90)
**Most Points, Defenseman, Season** ............... **102** Brian Leetch (1991-92; 22G, 80A)
**Most Points, Center, Season** ............... **109** Jean Ratelle (1971-72; 46G, 63A)
**Most Points, Right Wing, Season** ............... **123** Jaromir Jagr (2005-06; 54G, 69A)
**Most Points, Left Wing, Season** ............... **106** Vic Hadfield (1971-72; 50G, 56A)
**Most Points, Rookie, Season** ............... **76** Mark Pavelich (1981-82; 33G, 43A)
**Most Shutouts, Season** ....... **13** John Ross Roach (1928-29)
**Most Goals, Game** ............ **5** Don Murdoch (Oct. 12/76), Mark Pavelich (Feb. 23/83)
**Most Assists, Game** ........... **5** Walt Tkaczuk (Feb. 12/72), Rod Gilbert (Mar. 2/75), (Mar. 30/75), (Oct. 8/76), Don Maloney (Jan. 3/87), Brian Leetch (Apr. 18/95), Wayne Gretzky (Feb. 15/99)
**Most Points, Game** ............ **7** Steve Vickers (Feb. 18/76; 3G, 4A)

## Retired Numbers

| | | |
|---|---|---|
| 1 | Ed Giacomin | 1965-1975 |
| 2 | Brian Leetch | 1987-2004 |
| 3 | Harry Howell | 1952-1969 |
| 7 | Rod Gilbert | 1960-1977 |
| 9 | Andy Bathgate | 1952-1964 |
| | Adam Graves | 1991-2001 |
| 11 | Mark Messier | 1991-97; 2000-04 |
| 35 | Mike Richter | 1989-2003 |

# All-time Record vs. Other Clubs

## Regular Season

| | At Home | | | | | | | | On Road | | | | | | | | Total | | | | | | | |
|---|---|---|---|---|---|---|---|---|---|---|---|---|---|---|---|---|---|---|---|---|---|---|---|---|
| | GP | W | L | T | OL | GF | GA | PTS | GP | W | L | T | OL | GF | GA | PTS | GP | W | L | T | OL | GF | GA | PTS |
| Anaheim | 11 | 4 | 6 | 1 | 0 | 28 | 32 | 9 | 10 | 4 | 6 | 0 | 0 | 32 | 36 | 8 | 21 | 8 | 12 | 1 | 0 | 60 | 68 | 17 |
| Atlanta | 18 | 7 | 6 | 1 | 4 | 50 | 51 | 19 | 18 | 10 | 5 | 0 | 3 | 60 | 54 | 23 | 36 | 17 | 11 | 1 | 7 | 110 | 105 | 42 |
| Boston | 310 | 138 | 117 | 55 | 0 | 948 | 866 | 331 | 306 | 100 | 162 | 42 | 2 | 852 | 1090 | 244 | 616 | 238 | 279 | 97 | 2 | 1800 | 1956 | 575 |
| Buffalo | 74 | 32 | 25 | 15 | 2 | 238 | 201 | 81 | 76 | 22 | 42 | 10 | 2 | 233 | 306 | 56 | 150 | 54 | 67 | 25 | 4 | 471 | 507 | 137 |
| Calgary | 54 | 25 | 24 | 5 | 0 | 182 | 189 | 55 | 50 | 12 | 28 | 10 | 0 | 151 | 220 | 34 | 104 | 37 | 52 | 15 | 0 | 333 | 409 | 89 |
| Carolina | 53 | 33 | 15 | 4 | 1 | 193 | 131 | 71 | 51 | 18 | 30 | 3 | 0 | 153 | 170 | 39 | 104 | 51 | 45 | 7 | 1 | 346 | 301 | 110 |
| Chicago | 287 | 119 | 113 | 55 | 0 | 847 | 810 | 293 | 288 | 116 | 128 | 43 | 1 | 796 | 874 | 276 | 575 | 235 | 241 | 98 | 1 | 1643 | 1684 | 569 |
| Colorado | 36 | 20 | 10 | 4 | 2 | 141 | 102 | 46 | 36 | 13 | 18 | 3 | 2 | 133 | 147 | 31 | 72 | 33 | 28 | 7 | 4 | 274 | 249 | 77 |
| Columbus | 3 | 1 | 1 | 1 | 0 | 9 | 8 | 3 | 6 | 2 | 4 | 0 | 0 | 13 | 21 | 4 | 9 | 3 | 5 | 1 | 0 | 22 | 29 | 7 |
| Dallas | 64 | 36 | 17 | 11 | 0 | 216 | 170 | 83 | 63 | 31 | 20 | 11 | 1 | 228 | 199 | 74 | 127 | 67 | 37 | 22 | 1 | 444 | 369 | 157 |
| Detroit | 285 | 134 | 93 | 58 | 0 | 871 | 742 | 326 | 287 | 76 | 165 | 45 | 1 | 706 | 1013 | 198 | 572 | 210 | 258 | 103 | 1 | 1577 | 1755 | 524 |
| Edmonton | 32 | 11 | 14 | 6 | 1 | 119 | 120 | 29 | 29 | 13 | 12 | 3 | 1 | 96 | 104 | 30 | 61 | 24 | 26 | 9 | 2 | 215 | 224 | 59 |
| Florida | 32 | 17 | 11 | 4 | 0 | 97 | 72 | 38 | 33 | 16 | 11 | 2 | 4 | 90 | 87 | 38 | 65 | 33 | 22 | 6 | 4 | 187 | 159 | 76 |
| Los Angeles | 59 | 35 | 18 | 6 | 0 | 235 | 176 | 76 | 62 | 28 | 24 | 10 | 0 | 220 | 205 | 66 | 121 | 63 | 42 | 16 | 0 | 455 | 381 | 142 |
| Minnesota | 5 | 4 | 1 | 0 | 0 | 15 | 9 | 8 | 5 | 3 | 2 | 0 | 0 | 16 | 17 | 6 | 10 | 7 | 3 | 0 | 0 | 31 | 26 | 14 |
| Montreal | 298 | 123 | 120 | 54 | 1 | 860 | 864 | 301 | 298 | 64 | 193 | 40 | 1 | 698 | 1155 | 169 | 596 | 187 | 313 | 94 | 2 | 1558 | 2019 | 470 |
| Nashville | 7 | 2 | 3 | 1 | 1 | 18 | 18 | 6 | 6 | 4 | 1 | 0 | 1 | 23 | 16 | 9 | 13 | 6 | 4 | 1 | 2 | 41 | 34 | 15 |
| New Jersey | 99 | 51 | 27 | 20 | 1 | 361 | 283 | 123 | 101 | 40 | 51 | 7 | 3 | 316 | 339 | 90 | 200 | 91 | 78 | 27 | 4 | 677 | 622 | 213 |
| NY Islanders | 111 | 61 | 36 | 11 | 3 | 400 | 328 | 136 | 111 | 44 | 58 | 8 | 1 | 352 | 399 | 97 | 222 | 105 | 94 | 19 | 4 | 752 | 727 | 233 |
| Ottawa | 31 | 13 | 18 | 0 | 0 | 91 | 94 | 26 | 31 | 14 | 13 | 3 | 1 | 79 | 89 | 32 | 62 | 27 | 31 | 3 | 1 | 170 | 183 | 58 |
| Philadelphia | 125 | 54 | 44 | 23 | 4 | 395 | 366 | 135 | 124 | 51 | 57 | 14 | 2 | 352 | 393 | 118 | 249 | 105 | 101 | 37 | 6 | 747 | 759 | 253 |
| Phoenix | 31 | 19 | 10 | 2 | 0 | 133 | 108 | 40 | 32 | 15 | 13 | 4 | 0 | 108 | 110 | 34 | 63 | 34 | 23 | 6 | 0 | 241 | 218 | 74 |
| Pittsburgh | 116 | 63 | 43 | 9 | 1 | 445 | 374 | 136 | 115 | 47 | 49 | 14 | 5 | 398 | 404 | 113 | 231 | 110 | 92 | 23 | 6 | 843 | 778 | 249 |
| St. Louis | 61 | 45 | 10 | 6 | 0 | 248 | 145 | 96 | 65 | 29 | 26 | 10 | 0 | 208 | 194 | 68 | 126 | 74 | 36 | 16 | 0 | 456 | 339 | 164 |
| San Jose | 11 | 8 | 2 | 1 | 0 | 43 | 30 | 17 | 15 | 10 | 3 | 2 | 0 | 54 | 35 | 22 | 26 | 18 | 5 | 3 | 0 | 97 | 65 | 39 |
| Tampa Bay | 35 | 19 | 12 | 2 | 2 | 113 | 98 | 42 | 33 | 15 | 14 | 3 | 1 | 103 | 106 | 34 | 68 | 34 | 26 | 5 | 3 | 216 | 204 | 76 |
| Toronto | 291 | 124 | 109 | 56 | 2 | 896 | 857 | 306 | 290 | 88 | 161 | 39 | 2 | 765 | 1001 | 217 | 581 | 212 | 270 | 95 | 4 | 1661 | 1858 | 523 |
| Vancouver | 56 | 38 | 13 | 5 | 0 | 242 | 148 | 81 | 52 | 33 | 16 | 3 | 0 | 204 | 166 | 69 | 108 | 71 | 29 | 8 | 0 | 446 | 314 | 150 |
| Washington | 90 | 45 | 34 | 9 | 2 | 335 | 300 | 101 | 92 | 34 | 46 | 9 | 3 | 290 | 341 | 80 | 182 | 79 | 80 | 18 | 5 | 625 | 641 | 181 |
| Defunct Clubs | 139 | 87 | 30 | 22 | 0 | 460 | 290 | 196 | 139 | 82 | 34 | 23 | 0 | 441 | 291 | 187 | 278 | 169 | 64 | 45 | 0 | 901 | 581 | 383 |
| **Totals** | **2824** | **1368** | **982** | **447** | **27** | **9229** | **7982** | **3210** | **2824** | **1034** | **1392** | **361** | **37** | **8170** | **9582** | **2466** | **5648** | **2402** | **2374** | **808** | **64** | **17399** | **17564** | **5676** |

## Playoffs

| | Series | W | L | GP | W | L | T | GF | GA | Last Mtg. | Rnd. | Result |
|---|---|---|---|---|---|---|---|---|---|---|---|---|
| Atlanta | 1 | 1 | 0 | 4 | 4 | 0 | 0 | 17 | 6 | 2007 | CQF | W 4-0 |
| Boston | 9 | 3 | 6 | 42 | 18 | 22 | 2 | 104 | 114 | 1973 | QF | W 4-1 |
| Buffalo | 2 | 0 | 2 | 9 | 3 | 6 | 0 | 19 | 28 | 2007 | CSF | L 2-4 |
| Calgary | 1 | 1 | 0 | 4 | 3 | 1 | 0 | 14 | 8 | 1980 | PRE | W 3-1 |
| Chicago | 5 | 1 | 4 | 24 | 10 | 14 | 0 | 54 | 66 | 1973 | SF | L 1-4 |
| Colorado | 1 | 1 | 0 | 6 | 4 | 2 | 0 | 25 | 19 | 1995 | CQF | W 4-2 |
| Detroit | 5 | 1 | 4 | 23 | 10 | 13 | 0 | 49 | 57 | 1950 | F | L 3-4 |
| Florida | 1 | 1 | 0 | 5 | 4 | 1 | 0 | 13 | 10 | 1997 | CQF | W 4-1 |
| Los Angeles | 2 | 2 | 0 | 6 | 5 | 1 | 0 | 32 | 14 | 1981 | PRE | W 3-1 |
| Montreal | 14 | 7 | 7 | 61 | 25 | 34 | 2 | 158 | 188 | 1996 | CQF | W 4-2 |
| New Jersey | 5 | 4 | 1 | 28 | 16 | 12 | 0 | 79 | 75 | 2008 | CQF | W 4-1 |
| NY Islanders | 8 | 3 | 5 | 39 | 19 | 20 | 0 | 132 | 129 | 1994 | CQF | W 4-0 |
| Philadelphia | 10 | 4 | 6 | 47 | 20 | 27 | 0 | 153 | 157 | 1997 | CF | L 1-4 |
| Pittsburgh | 4 | 0 | 4 | 20 | 4 | 16 | 0 | 57 | 79 | 2008 | CSF | L 1-4 |
| St. Louis | 1 | 1 | 0 | 6 | 4 | 2 | 0 | 29 | 22 | 1981 | QF | W 4-2 |
| Toronto | 8 | 5 | 3 | 35 | 19 | 16 | 0 | 86 | 86 | 1971 | QF | W 4-2 |
| Vancouver | 1 | 1 | 0 | 7 | 4 | 3 | 0 | 21 | 19 | 1994 | F | W 4-3 |
| Washington | 5 | 2 | 3 | 29 | 14 | 15 | 0 | 82 | 94 | 2009 | CQF | L 3-4 |
| Defunct Clubs | 9 | 6 | 3 | 22 | 11 | 7 | 4 | 43 | 29 | | | |
| **Totals** | **92** | **44** | **48** | **417** | **197** | **212** | **8** | **1167** | **1200** | | | |

Calgary totals include Atlanta Flames, 1972-73 to 1979-80.
Carolina totals include Hartford, 1979-80 to 1996-97.
Colorado totals include Quebec, 1979-80 to 1994-95.
Dallas totals include Minnesota North Stars, 1967-68 to 1992-93.
New Jersey totals include Kansas City, 1974-75, 1975-76, and Colorado Rockies, 1976-77 to 1981-82.
Phoenix totals include Winnipeg, 1979-80 to 1995-96.

## Playoff Results 2009-2004

| Year | Round | Opponent | Result | GF | GA |
|---|---|---|---|---|---|
| 2009 | CQF | Washington | L 3-4 | 11 | 19 |
| 2008 | CSF | Pittsburgh | L 1-4 | 12 | 15 |
| | CQF | New Jersey | W 4-1 | 19 | 12 |
| 2007 | CSF | Buffalo | L 2-4 | 13 | 17 |
| | CQF | Atlanta | W 4-0 | 17 | 6 |
| 2006 | CQF | New Jersey | L 0-4 | 4 | 17 |

**Abbreviations: Round: F** – Final; **CF** – conference final; **CSF** – conference semi-final; **CQF** – conference quarter-final; **SF** – semi-final; **QF** – quarter-final; **PRE** – preliminary round.

## 2008-09 Results

| | | | | | | | |
|---|---|---|---|---|---|---|---|
| **Oct.** | 4 | at Tampa Bay | 2-1 | | 7 | Montreal | 3-6 |
| | 5 | Tampa Bay | 2-1 | | 9 | at Buffalo | 1-2† |
| | 10 | Chicago | 4-2 | | 10 | at Ottawa | 2-0 |
| | 11 | at Philadelphia | 4-3 | | 13 | at NY Islanders | 2-1 |
| | 13 | New Jersey | 4-1 | | 16 | at Chicago | 3-2* |
| | 15 | Buffalo | 1-3 | | 18 | at Pittsburgh | 0-3 |
| | 17 | Toronto | 1-0† | | 20 | Anaheim | 4-2 |
| | 18 | at Detroit | 4-5* | | 27 | Carolina | 3-2 |
| | 20 | Dallas | 1-2 | | 28 | at Pittsburgh | 2-6 |
| | 24 | at Columbus | 3-1 | | 31 | at Boston | 0-1 |
| | 25 | Pittsburgh | 3-2† | **Feb.** | 3 | Atlanta | 1-2† |
| | 27 | at NY Islanders | 4-2 | | 6 | at Dallas | 2-10 |
| | 30 | Atlanta | 3-2 | | 9 | at New Jersey | 0-3 |
| **Nov.** | 1 | at Toronto | 2-5 | | 11 | Washington | 5-4† |
| | 4 | NY Islanders | 1-2 | | 13 | at Florida | 1-2† |
| | 6 | Tampa Bay | 5-2 | | 15 | Philadelphia | 2-5 |
| | 8 | at Washington | 1-3 | | 16 | at St. Louis | 1-2 |
| | 10 | Edmonton | 2-3† | | 18 | NY Islanders | 3-1 |
| | 12 | at New Jersey | 5-2 | | 21 | at Buffalo | 2-4 |
| | 15 | Boston | 3-2† | | 22 | Toronto | 2-3* |
| | 17 | Ottawa | 2-1† | | 25 | at Toronto | 1-2† |
| | 19 | Vancouver | 3-6 | | 26 | Florida | 1-2 |
| | 22 | at Ottawa | 1-4 | | 28 | Colorado | 6-1 |
| | 24 | Phoenix | 4-1 | **Mar.** | 5 | at NY Islanders | 4-2 |
| | 26 | at Tampa Bay | 3-2† | | 8 | Boston | 4-3 |
| | 28 | at Florida | 4-3† | | 9 | at Carolina | 0-3 |
| | 30 | Florida | 0-4 | | 12 | at Nashville | 4-2 |
| **Dec.** | 3 | Pittsburgh | 3-2† | | 14 | at Philadelphia | 2-4 |
| | 4 | at Montreal | 2-6 | | 15 | Philadelphia | 4-1 |
| | 7 | Calgary | 0-3 | | 17 | at Montreal | 4-3† |
| | 10 | at Atlanta | 3-2* | | 21 | Buffalo | 5-3 |
| | 12 | at New Jersey | 5-8 | | 22 | Ottawa | 1-2 |
| | 13 | Carolina | 3-2† | | 24 | Minnesota | 2-1 |
| | 16 | at Anaheim | 3-1 | | 26 | at Atlanta | 4-5† |
| | 17 | at Los Angeles | 3-2* | | 28 | at Pittsburgh | 3-4 |
| | 20 | at San Jose | 2-3 | | 30 | New Jersey | 3-0 |
| | 23 | Washington | 4-5* | **Apr.** | 2 | at Carolina | 2-4 |
| | 27 | New Jersey | 2-4 | | 4 | at Boston | 0-1 |
| | 29 | NY Islanders | 5-4 | | 7 | Montreal | 3-1 |
| **Jan.** | 3 | at Washington | 1-2 | | 9 | Philadelphia | 2-1 |
| | 5 | Pittsburgh | 4-0 | | 12 | at Philadelphia | 4-3 |

* – Overtime † – Shootout

## Entry Draft Selections 2009-1995

Name in bold denotes played in NHL.

**2009**
Pick
19 Chris Kreider
47 Ethan Werek
80 Ryan Bourque
127 Roman Horak
140 Scott Stajcer
170 Daniel Maggio
200 Mikhail Pashnin

**2008**
Pick
20 Michael Del Zotto
51 Derek Stepan
75 Yevgeny Grachev
90 Tomas Kundratek
111 Dale Weise
141 Chris Doyle
171 Mitch Gaulton

**2007**
Pick
17 Alexei Cherepanov
48 Antoine Lafleur
138 Max Campbell
168 Carl Hagelin
193 David Skokan
198 Danny Hobbs

**2006**
Pick
21 Bobby Sanguinetti
54 **Artem Anisimov**
84 Ryan Hillier
104 David Kveton
137 Tomas Zaborsky
174 Eric Hunter
204 Lukas Zeliska

**2005**
Pick
12 **Marc Staal**
40 **Michael Sauer**
56 Marc-Andre Cliche
66 Brodie Dupont
77 Dalyn Flatt
107 Tom Pyatt
147 Trevor Koverko
178 Greg Beller
211 Ryan Russell

**2004**
Pick
6 **Al Montoya**
19 **Lauri Korpikoski**
36 Darin Olver
48 **Dane Byers**
51 Bruce Graham
60 **Brandon Dubinsky**
73 Zdenek Bahensky
80 Billy Ryan
127 **Ryan Callahan**
135 Roman Psurny
169 Jordan Foote
247 Jonathan Paiement
266 **Jakub Petruzalek**

**2003**
Pick
12 Hugh Jessiman
50 **Ivan Baranka**
75 Ken Roche
122 **Corey Potter**
149 **Nigel Dawes**
176 Ivan Dornic
179 Philippe Furrer
180 **Chris Holt**
209 Dylan Reese
243 Jan Marek

**2002**
Pick
33 Lee Falardeau
81 Marcus Jonasen
127 **Nate Guenin**
143 Mike Walsh
177 Jake Taylor
194 Kim Hirschovits
226 **Joey Crabb**
240 **Petr Prucha**
270 Rob Flynn

**2001**
Pick
10 **Dan Blackburn**
40 **Fedor Tyutin**
79 **Garth Murray**
113 **Bryce Lampman**
139 Shawn Collymore
176 **Marek Zidlicky**
206 Petr Preucil
226 Pontus Petterstrom
230 Leonid Zhvachkin
238 **Ryan Hollweg**
269 Juris Stals

**2000**
Pick
64 **Filip Novak**
95 **Dominic Moore**
112 Premysl Duben
140 Nathan Martz
143 Brandon Snee
175 Sven Helfenstein
205 **Henrik Lundqvist**
238 Danny Eberly
269 Martin Richter

**1999**
Pick
4 **Pavel Brendl**
9 **Jamie Lundmark**
59 David Inman
79 Johan Asplund
90 Patrick Aufiero
137 Garrett Bembridge
177 Jay Dardis
197 Arto Laatikainen
226 Yevgeny Gusakov
251 Petter Henning
254 Alexei Bulatov

**1998**
Pick
7 **Manny Malhotra**
40 Randy Copley
66 **Jason LaBarbera**
114 **Boyd Kane**
122 **Patrick Leahy**
131 **Tomas Kloucek**
180 Stefan Lundqvist
207 **Johan Witehall**
235 **Jan Mertzig**

**1997**
Pick
19 Stefan Cherneski
46 Wes Jarvis
73 **Burke Henry**
93 Tomi Kallarsson
126 Jason McLean
134 **Johan Lindbom**
136 **Mike York**
154 Shawn Degagne
175 **Johan Holmqvist**
182 **Mike Mottau**
210 Andrew Proskurnicki
236 Richard Miller

**1996**
Pick
22 Jeff Brown
48 **Daniel Goneau**
76 Dmitri Subbotin
131 Colin Pepperall
158 Ola Sandberg
185 Jeff Dessner
211 Ryan McKie
237 **Ronnie Sundin**

**1995**
Pick
39 **Christian Dube**
65 Mike Martin
91 **Marc Savard**
110 **Alexei Vasiliev**
117 **Dale Purinton**
143 Peter Slamiar
169 Jeff Heil
195 Ilya Gorokhov
221 Bob Maudie

### General Managers' History

Lester Patrick, 1926-27 to 1945-46; Frank Boucher, 1946-47 to 1954-55; Muzz Patrick, 1955-56 to 1963-64; Emile Francis, 1964-65 to 1974-75; Emile Francis and John Ferguson, 1975-76; John Ferguson, 1976-77, 1977-78; Fred Shero, 1978-79, 1979-80; Fred Shero and Craig Patrick, 1980-81; Craig Patrick, 1981-82 to 1985-86; Phil Esposito, 1986-87 to 1988-89; Neil Smith, 1989-90 to 1999-2000; Glen Sather, 2000-01 to date.

## Glen Sather

### President and General Manager

*Born: High River, Alta., September 2, 1943.*

Glen Sather, who spent parts of four seasons with the New York Rangers as a player from 1970 to 1974, became the franchise's 12th president and tenth general manager on June 2, 2000. He also served as coach of the team from January 30, 2003, to February 25, 2004.

Sather joined the Rangers following a 24-year career with the Edmonton Oilers, where he was the architect of five Stanley Cup championships between 1984 and 1990. One of the most respected executives in the National Hockey League, Sather was honored for his tremendous achievements in 1997 by becoming the first member of the Oilers organization to be selected to the Hockey Hall of Fame.

Named coach and vice president of hockey operations for the Oilers when the franchise joined the NHL in June of 1979, Sather became general manager and club president in May of 1980. He coached through the 1988-89 season and also returned for 60 games behind the bench in 1993-94. Sather-coached teams won the Stanley Cup four times in the 1980s. As general manager, Sather was instrumental in the Oilers' fifth Cup triumph in 1990.

He played for six different teams during a 10-year NHL career. He scored 80 goals in 658 games.

#### Coaching Record

| | | | Regular Season | | | | Playoffs | | | |
|---|---|---|---|---|---|---|---|---|---|---|
| Season | Team | League | GC | W | L | O/T | GC | W | L | T |
| 1979-80 | Edmonton | NHL | 80 | 28 | 39 | 13 | 3 | 0 | 3 | .... |
| 1980-81 | Edmonton | NHL | 62 | 25 | 26 | 11 | 9 | 5 | 4 | .... |
| 1981-82 | Edmonton | NHL | 80 | 48 | 17 | 15 | 5 | 2 | 3 | .... |
| 1982-83 | Edmonton | NHL | 80 | 47 | 21 | 12 | 16 | 11 | 5 | .... |
| 1983-84♦ | Edmonton | NHL | 80 | 57 | 18 | 5 | 19 | 15 | 4 | .... |
| 1984-85♦ | Edmonton | NHL | 80 | 49 | 20 | 11 | 18 | 15 | 3 | .... |
| 1985-86 | Edmonton | NHL | 80 | 56 | 17 | 7 | 10 | 6 | 4 | .... |
| 1986-87♦ | Edmonton | NHL | 80 | 50 | 24 | 6 | 21 | 16 | 5 | .... |
| 1987-88♦* | Edmonton | NHL | 80 | 44 | 25 | 11 | 19 | 16 | 2 | 1 |
| 1988-89 | Edmonton | NHL | 80 | 38 | 34 | 8 | 7 | 3 | 4 | .... |
| 1993-94 | Edmonton | NHL | 60 | 22 | 27 | 11 | .... | .... | .... | .... |
| 2002-03 | NY Rangers | NHL | 28 | 11 | 10 | 7 | .... | .... | .... | .... |
| 2003-04 | NY Rangers | NHL | 62 | 22 | 29 | 11 | .... | .... | .... | .... |
| | NHL Totals | | 932 | 497 | 307 | 128 | 127 | 89 | 37 | 1 |

♦ Stanley Cup win.
* Playoff game May 24, 1988 suspended due to power failure. Score tied.

# Club Directory

Madison Square Garden

**New York Rangers**
14th Floor
2 Pennsylvania Plaza
New York, New York 10121
Phone **212/465-6486**
PR FAX 212/465-6494
www.newyorkrangers.com
**Capacity:** 18,200

**Team Executive Management**

| | |
|---|---|
| President and Chief Executive Officer, Cablevision Systems Corporation; Chairman, MSG and Governor | James L. Dolan |
| Vice Chairman, Cablevision Systems Corporation; Vice Chairman, MSG and Alternate Governor | Hank J. Ratner |
| President, G.M. and Alternate Governor | Glen Sather |
| President, MSG Sports and Alternate Governor | Scott O'Neil |
| Sr. V.P., Finance and Controller | John Cudmore |
| Sr. V.P., Marketing Partnerships | Greg Elliott |
| Sr. V.P., Sports Marketing – Teams | Howard Jacobs |
| Sr. V.P., Team Operations | Mark Piazza |
| Deputy General Counsel & Sr. V.P. – Teams | Marc Schoenfeld |
| V.P., Marketing | Jeanie Baumgartner |
| V.P., Comm. Rels & Field Marketing, MSG Teams | Karin Buchholz |
| V.P., Marketing Services | Janet Duch |
| V.P., Public Relations, MSG Sports | Stacey Escudero |
| V.P., Event Presentation | Ryan Halkett |
| V.P., Legal and Business Affairs – Teams | Jamaal Lesane |
| V.P., Finance | Jeanine McGrory |
| V.P., Suite Sales | Mike Ondrejko |
| V.P., Public Relations and Player Recruitment | John Rosasco |
| V.P., Team Sponsorships | Robert Scolaro |
| V.P., Publicity, Sports Teams | Sammy Steinlight |
| V.P., Community Relations, MSG Teams | Kerryann Tomlinson |
| V.P., Sports Team Operations | Jason Vogel |

**Hockey Club Personnel**

| | |
|---|---|
| Asst. G.M., Player Personnel & G.M., Hartford Wolf Pack | Jim Schoenfeld |
| Asst. G.M., Hockey Administration | Cameron Hope |
| Head Coach | John Tortorella |
| Assistant Coaches | Mike Sullivan, Benoit Allaire |
| Director, Player Personnel | Gordie Clark |
| Senior Advisor to the President and & G.M./ Director of U.S. Amateur Scouting | Mike Barnett |
| Hockey and Business Operations | Adam Graves |
| Director, Player Personnel – Europe | Christer Rockstrom |
| Assistant Director, Player Personnel | Jeff Gorton |
| Head Professional Scout, Europe | Anders Hedberg |
| European Scout | Jan Gajdosik |
| Amateur Scouting Staff | Larry Bernard, Rich Brown, Ray Clearwater, Daniel Dore, Ernie Gare, Vladimir Lutchenko, Shanon Sather |
| Professional Scouting Staff | Rick Kehoe, Gilles Leger, Kevin Maxwell, Peter Stephan |
| Head Athletic Trainer | Jim Ramsay |
| Equipment Manager | Acacio Marques |
| Assistant Equipment Manager | Jason Levy |
| Massage Therapist/Assistant Trainer | Bruce Lifrieri |
| Strength and Conditioning Coach | Reg Grant |
| Strength and Conditioning Consultant – Europe | Daniel Hedin |
| Video Coach | Jerry Dineen |
| Manager, MSG Training Center Operations | Alex Case |

**Operations**

| | |
|---|---|
| Manager of Scouting | Victor Saljanin |
| Manager of Hockey Administration | Sara Adamson |
| Administrator, Sports Team Operations | Tim Criscitelli |
| Administrative Assistant, Sports Team Operations | Caroline Giglio |
| Executive Assistant to the President, MSG Sports | Denise Schuler |

**Public Relations**

| | |
|---|---|
| Director, Public Relations | Brendan McIntyre |
| Manager, Public Relations | Lauren Buchman |
| Coordinator, Public Relations | Dino Ticinelli |

**Marketing**

| | |
|---|---|
| Manager, Marketing Partnerships | Nathan Finkel |
| Coordinator, Marketing Partnerships | Erica Diesel |
| Manager, Marketing | Leigh Anne Berte |
| Coordinator, Marketing | Rachel Wohl |
| Manager, Marketing Programs | Jayne Wise |
| Coordinator, Marketing Programs | Nicholas Brener |
| Administrative Assistant, Marketing | Keely Respass |
| Design Director | Joanecy Kagalingan |
| Art Director | Brei Smith |
| Manager, Event Presentation | Greg Kwizak |
| Music Director, MSG Sports | Ray Castoldi |
| Coordinating Producer, MSG Sports | Faith Astrada |
| Community Relations and Fan Development | |
| Director, Special Projects & Comm. Relations Rep. | Rod Gilbert |
| Director, Fan Development and Field Marketing | Dan Gladstone |
| Director, Fan Development | Rick Nadeau |
| Coordinator, Fan Development and Field Marketing | Devin Pacheco |
| Manager, Community Relations | David Martella |
| Coordinator, Community Relations | Anthony Zucconi |

**MSG Interactive**

| | |
|---|---|
| Vice President, MSG Interactive | Heather Pariseau |
| Director, Interactive Sports Programming | Chris Creed |
| Manager, MSG Interactive Websites – Teams | Dan David |

**Medical Staff**

| | |
|---|---|
| Team Physician and Orthopedic Surgeon | Dr. Andrew Feldman |
| Assistant Team Physician | Dr. Anthony Maddalo |
| Medical Consultants | Drs. Martin Posner, Ron Preston, Ronald Weissman |
| Team Dentists | Drs. Joe Esposito, Don Salomon |
| Additional Information | |
| Television Network | MSG Network |
| Radio Network | MSG Radio |

# Ottawa Senators

## 2008-09 Results: 36W-35L-5OTL-6SOL 83PTS.
## Fourth, Northeast Division

### Key Off-Season Signings/Acquisitions

**2009**

**Apr. 15** • Re-signed RW **Ryan Shannon.**
**May 7** • Signed 2008 1st-round pick (15th overall) D **Erik Karlsson.**
**July 1** • Re-signed RW **Chris Neil.**
**6** • Signed RW **Alex Kovalev.**
**23** • Named **Brad Lauer** assistant coach.
**Aug. 4** • Re-signed G **Brian Elliott.**

### Year-by-Year Record

| | | Home | | | | Road | | | | Overall | | | | | | | | |
|---|---|---|---|---|---|---|---|---|---|---|---|---|---|---|---|---|---|---|
| Season | GP | W | L | T | OL | W | L | T | OL | W | L | T | OL | GF | GA | Pts. | Finished | Playoff Result |
| 2008-09 | 82 | 22 | 12 | .... | 7 | 14 | 23 | .... | 4 | 36 | 35 | .... | 11 | 217 | 237 | 83 | 4th, Northeast Div. | Out of Playoffs |
| 2007-08 | 82 | 22 | 15 | .... | 4 | 21 | 16 | .... | 4 | 43 | 31 | .... | 8 | 261 | 247 | 94 | 2nd, Northeast Div. | Lost Conf. Quarter-Final |
| 2006-07 | 82 | 25 | 13 | .... | 3 | 23 | 12 | .... | 6 | 48 | 25 | .... | 9 | 288 | 222 | 105 | 2nd, Northeast Div. | Lost Final |
| 2005-06 | 82 | 29 | 9 | .... | 3 | 23 | 12 | .... | 6 | 52 | 21 | .... | 9 | 314 | 211 | 113 | 1st, Northeast Div. | Lost Conf. Semi-Final |
| 2004-05 | .... | .... | .... | .... | .... | .... | .... | .... | .... | .... | .... | .... | .... | .... | .... | .... | | |
| 2003-04 | 82 | 23 | 8 | 5 | 5 | 20 | 15 | 5 | 1 | 43 | 23 | 10 | 6 | 262 | 189 | 102 | 3rd, Northeast Div. | Lost Conf. Quarter-Final |
| 2002-03 | 82 | 28 | 9 | 3 | 1 | 24 | 12 | 5 | 0 | 52 | 21 | 8 | 1 | 263 | 182 | 113 | 1st, Northeast Div. | Lost Conf. Championship |
| 2001-02 | 82 | 21 | 13 | 3 | 4 | 18 | 14 | 6 | 3 | 39 | 27 | 9 | 7 | 243 | 208 | 94 | 3rd, Northeast Div. | Lost Conf. Semi-Final |
| 2000-01 | 82 | 26 | 7 | 5 | 3 | 22 | 14 | 4 | 1 | 48 | 21 | 9 | 4 | 274 | 205 | 109 | 1st, Northeast Div. | Lost Conf. Quarter-Final |
| 1999-2000 | 82 | 24 | 10 | 5 | 2 | 17 | 18 | 6 | 0 | 41 | 28 | 11 | 2 | 244 | 210 | 95 | 2nd, Northeast Div. | Lost Conf. Quarter-Final |
| 1998-99 | 82 | 22 | 11 | 8 | .... | 22 | 12 | 7 | .... | 44 | 23 | 15 | .... | 239 | 179 | 103 | 1st, Northeast Div. | Lost Conf. Quarter-Final |
| 1997-98 | 82 | 18 | 16 | 7 | .... | 16 | 17 | 8 | .... | 34 | 33 | 15 | .... | 193 | 200 | 83 | 5th, Northeast Div. | Lost Conf. Semi-Final |
| 1996-97 | 82 | 16 | 17 | 8 | .... | 15 | 19 | 7 | .... | 31 | 36 | 15 | .... | 226 | 234 | 77 | 3rd, Northeast Div. | Lost Conf. Quarter-Final |
| 1995-96 | 82 | 8 | 28 | 5 | .... | 10 | 31 | 0 | .... | 18 | 59 | 5 | .... | 191 | 291 | 41 | 6th, Northeast Div. | Out of Playoffs |
| 1994-95 | 48 | 5 | 16 | 3 | .... | 4 | 18 | 2 | .... | 9 | 34 | 5 | .... | 117 | 174 | 23 | 7th, Northeast Div. | Out of Playoffs |
| 1993-94 | 84 | 8 | 30 | 4 | .... | 6 | 31 | 5 | .... | 14 | 61 | 9 | .... | 201 | 397 | 37 | 7th, Northeast Div. | Out of Playoffs |
| 1992-93 | 84 | 9 | 29 | 4 | .... | 1 | 41 | 0 | .... | 10 | 70 | 4 | .... | 202 | 395 | 24 | 6th, Adams Div. | Out of Playoffs |

### 2009-10 Schedule

| | | | |
|---|---|---|---|
| **Oct.** | Sat. | 3 | at NY Rangers |
| | Tue. | 6 | at Toronto |
| | Thu. | 8 | NY Islanders |
| | Sat. | 10 | Atlanta |
| | Mon. | 12 | Pittsburgh |
| | Thu. | 15 | Tampa Bay |
| | Sat. | 17 | at Montreal |
| | Thu. | 22 | Nashville |
| | Sat. | 24 | Boston |
| | Wed. | 28 | at Florida |
| | Thu. | 29 | at Tampa Bay |
| | Sat. | 31 | Atlanta* |
| **Nov.** | Thu. | 5 | Tampa Bay |
| | Sat. | 7 | New Jersey |
| | Tue. | 10 | Edmonton |
| | Thu. | 12 | at Philadelphia |
| | Sat. | 14 | NY Rangers |
| | Tue. | 17 | Toronto |
| | Thu. | 19 | Pittsburgh |
| | Sat. | 21 | Buffalo |
| | Mon. | 23 | Washington |
| | Wed. | 25 | at New Jersey |
| | Thu. | 26 | Columbus |
| | Sat. | 28 | at Boston |
| **Dec.** | Tue. | 1 | at San Jose |
| | Thu. | 3 | at Los Angeles |
| | Sat. | 5 | at Phoenix |
| | Sun. | 6 | at Anaheim* |
| | Tue. | 8 | Montreal |
| | Thu. | 10 | at Philadelphia |
| | Sat. | 12 | Carolina |
| | Mon. | 14 | at Toronto |
| | Wed. | 16 | Buffalo |
| | Fri. | 18 | at New Jersey |
| | Sat. | 19 | Minnesota |
| | Mon. | 21 | Boston |
| | Wed. | 23 | at Pittsburgh |
| | Sat. | 26 | at Buffalo |
| | Mon. | 28 | Montreal |
| | Wed. | 30 | Colorado |
| | Thu. | 31 | NY Islanders |
| **Jan.** | Sun. | 3 | Philadelphia* |
| | Tue. | 5 | Boston |
| | Thu. | 7 | at Washington |
| | Sat. | 9 | Florida |
| | Sun. | 10 | at Carolina* |
| | Tue. | 12 | at Atlanta |
| | Thu. | 14 | at NY Rangers |
| | Sat. | 16 | at Montreal* |
| | Mon. | 18 | at Boston* |
| | Tue. | 19 | Chicago |
| | Thu. | 21 | St. Louis |
| | Sat. | 23 | at Boston* |
| | Tue. | 26 | New Jersey |
| | Thu. | 28 | at Pittsburgh |
| | Sat. | 30 | Montreal* |
| **Feb.** | Wed. | 3 | at Buffalo |
| | Thu. | 4 | Vancouver |
| | Sat. | 6 | at Toronto |
| | Tue. | 9 | Calgary |
| | Thu. | 11 | Washington |
| | Sat. | 13 | at Detroit |
| | Sun. | 14 | at NY Islanders* |
| **Mar.** | Tue. | 2 | NY Rangers |
| | Thu. | 4 | at Carolina |
| | Sat. | 6 | Toronto |
| | Tue. | 9 | at Edmonton |
| | Thu. | 11 | at Calgary |
| | Sat. | 13 | at Vancouver |
| | Tue. | 16 | Toronto |
| | Thu. | 18 | at Atlanta |
| | Sat. | 20 | at Dallas* |
| | Mon. | 22 | at Montreal |
| | Tue. | 23 | Philadelphia |
| | Fri. | 26 | at Buffalo |
| | Sat. | 27 | Florida |
| | Tue. | 30 | at Washington |
| **Apr.** | Thu. | 1 | Carolina |
| | Sat. | 3 | at NY Islanders* |
| | Tue. | 6 | at Florida |
| | Thu. | 8 | at Tampa Bay |
| | Sat. | 10 | Buffalo |

* Denotes afternoon game.

*Alexandre Picard, Daniel Alfredsson, Dany Heatley and Jason Spezza celebrate a Senators goal. Alfredsson was the team's top scorer with 74 points (24 goals, 50 assists) in 2008-09.*

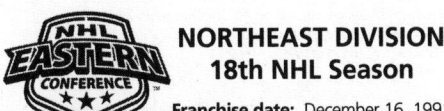

**NORTHEAST DIVISION**
**18th NHL Season**

**Franchise date:** December 16, 1991

# 2009-10 Player Personnel

| FORWARDS | HT | WT | S | Place of Birth | *Age | 2008-09 Club |
|---|---|---|---|---|---|---|
| ALFREDSSON, Daniel | 5-11 | 208 | R | Gothenburg, Sweden | 36 | Ottawa |
| BASS, Cody | 6-0 | 213 | R | Owen Sound, Ont. | 22 | Ottawa-Binghamton |
| DONOVAN, Shean | 6-3 | 218 | R | Timmins, Ont. | 34 | Ottawa |
| FISHER, Mike | 6-1 | 213 | R | Peterborough, Ont. | 29 | Ottawa |
| FOLIGNO, Nick | 6-0 | 205 | L | Buffalo, NY | 21 | Ottawa |
| HEATLEY, Dany | 6-4 | 221 | L | Freiburg, West Germany | 28 | Ottawa |
| HENNESSY, Josh | 6-0 | 192 | L | Brockton, MA | 24 | Ottawa-Binghamton |
| KELLER, Ryan | 5-10 | 186 | R | Saskatoon, Sask. | 25 | Blues |
| KELLY, Chris | 6-0 | 198 | L | Toronto, Ont. | 28 | Ottawa |
| KOVALEV, Alex | 6-1 | 215 | L | Togliatti, USSR | 36 | Montreal |
| NEIL, Chris | 6-1 | 212 | R | Markdale, Ont. | 30 | Ottawa |
| REGIN, Peter | 6-2 | 195 | L | Herning, Denmark | 23 | Ottawa-Binghamton |
| RUUTU, Jarkko | 6-1 | 207 | L | Vantaa, Finland | 34 | Ottawa |
| ST. PIERRE, Martin | 5-9 | 185 | L | Ottawa, Ont. | 26 | Boston-Providence (AHL) |
| SHANNON, Ryan | 5-9 | 171 | R | Darien, CT | 26 | Ottawa-Binghamton |
| SMITH, Zack | 6-2 | 209 | L | Medicine Hat, Alta. | 21 | Ottawa-Binghamton |
| SPEZZA, Jason | 6-3 | 215 | R | Mississauga, Ont. | 26 | Ottawa |
| WINCHESTER, Jesse | 6-1 | 204 | R | Long Sault, Ont. | 25 | Ottawa |
| YABLONSKI, Jeremy | 6-0 | 240 | R | Meadow Lake, Sask. | 29 | Binghamton |
| ZUBOV, Ilya | 6-0 | 200 | L | Chelyabinsk, USSR | 22 | Ottawa-Binghamton |
| **DEFENSEMEN** | | | | | | |
| CAMPOLI, Chris | 6-0 | 190 | L | North York, Ont. | 25 | NY Islanders-Ottawa |
| CARKNER, Matt | 6-4 | 226 | R | Winchester, Ont. | 28 | Ottawa-Binghamton |
| KINRADE, Geoff | 6-0 | 188 | L | Nelson, B.C. | 24 | Michigan Tech-T.B.-Norfolk |
| KUBA, Filip | 6-4 | 226 | L | Ostrava, Czech. | 32 | Ottawa |
| LEE, Brian | 6-2 | 202 | R | Fargo, ND | 22 | Ottawa-Binghamton |
| PHILLIPS, Chris | 6-3 | 217 | L | Calgary, Alta. | 31 | Ottawa |
| PICARD, Alexandre | 6-2 | 210 | L | Gatineau, Que. | 24 | Ottawa |
| SCHIRA, Craig | 6-0 | 196 | R | Spiritwood, Sask. | 21 | Vancouver (WHL) |
| SCHUBERT, Christoph | 6-3 | 230 | L | Munich, West Germany | 27 | Ottawa |
| SMITH, Derek | 6-1 | 200 | L | Belleville, Ont. | 24 | Binghamton |
| SMITH, Jason | 6-3 | 220 | R | Calgary, Alta. | 35 | Ottawa |
| VOLCHENKOV, Anton | 6-1 | 226 | L | Moscow, USSR | 27 | Ottawa |

| GOALTENDERS | HT | WT | C | Place of Birth | *Age | 2008-09 Club |
|---|---|---|---|---|---|---|
| BRODEUR, Mike | 6-2 | 171 | L | Calgary, Alta. | 26 | Rochester-Augusta |
| ELLIOTT, Brian | 6-2 | 199 | L | Newmarket, Ont. | 24 | Ottawa-Binghamton |
| LECLAIRE, Pascal | 6-2 | 200 | L | Repentigny, Que. | 26 | Columbus |

* – Age at start of 2009-10 season

# 2008-09 Scoring

* – rookie

## Regular Season

| Pos | # | Player | Team | GP | G | A | Pts | TOI | +/– | PIM | PP | SH | GW | S | % |
|---|---|---|---|---|---|---|---|---|---|---|---|---|---|---|---|
| R | 11 | Daniel Alfredsson | OTT | 79 | 24 | 50 | 74 | 20:52 | 7 | 24 | 8 | 1 | 3 | 204 | 11.8 |
| C | 19 | Jason Spezza | OTT | 82 | 32 | 41 | 73 | 19:41 | –14 | 79 | 13 | 1 | 3 | 246 | 13.0 |
| L | 15 | Dany Heatley | OTT | 82 | 39 | 33 | 72 | 20:06 | –11 | 88 | 15 | 0 | 6 | 258 | 15.1 |
| D | 17 | Filip Kuba | OTT | 71 | 3 | 37 | 40 | 23:16 | 4 | 28 | 2 | 0 | 0 | 111 | 2.7 |
| L | 71 | Nick Foligno | OTT | 81 | 17 | 15 | 32 | 13:40 | –10 | 59 | 7 | 0 | 2 | 145 | 11.7 |
| C | 12 | Mike Fisher | OTT | 78 | 13 | 19 | 32 | 18:29 | 0 | 66 | 1 | 2 | 3 | 182 | 7.1 |
| D | 14 | Chris Campoli | NYI | 51 | 6 | 11 | 17 | 19:49 | –20 | 43 | 0 | 1 | 2 | 53 | 11.3 |
| | | | OTT | 25 | 5 | 8 | 13 | 18:57 | 4 | 12 | 2 | 0 | 2 | 38 | 13.2 |
| | | | Total | 76 | 11 | 19 | 30 | 19:32 | –16 | 55 | 2 | 1 | 4 | 91 | 12.1 |
| C | 89 | Mike Comrie | NYI | 41 | 7 | 13 | 20 | 16:27 | –8 | 26 | 2 | 0 | 0 | 80 | 8.8 |
| | | | OTT | 22 | 3 | 4 | 7 | 14:17 | –7 | 6 | 0 | 0 | 1 | 41 | 7.3 |
| | | | Total | 63 | 10 | 17 | 27 | 15:42 | –15 | 32 | 2 | 0 | 1 | 121 | 8.3 |
| L | 22 | Chris Kelly | OTT | 82 | 12 | 11 | 23 | 15:36 | –10 | 38 | 0 | 1 | 1 | 118 | 10.2 |
| D | 4 | Chris Phillips | OTT | 82 | 6 | 16 | 22 | 21:52 | –14 | 66 | 0 | 1 | 0 | 88 | 6.8 |
| L | 73 | Jarkko Ruutu | OTT | 78 | 7 | 14 | 21 | 11:42 | 0 | 144 | 0 | 1 | 0 | 89 | 7.9 |
| D | 9 | Brendan Bell | OTT | 53 | 6 | 15 | 21 | 17:43 | –5 | 24 | 5 | 0 | 1 | 76 | 7.9 |
| R | 26 | Ryan Shannon | OTT | 35 | 8 | 12 | 20 | 15:04 | –1 | 2 | 3 | 0 | 1 | 61 | 13.1 |
| R | 18 * | Jesse Winchester | OTT | 76 | 3 | 15 | 18 | 10:35 | 0 | 33 | 0 | 0 | 1 | 115 | 2.6 |
| D | 45 | Alexandre Picard | OTT | 47 | 6 | 8 | 14 | 18:52 | –2 | 8 | 6 | 0 | 1 | 72 | 8.3 |
| D | 55 * | Brian Lee | OTT | 53 | 2 | 11 | 13 | 18:53 | –2 | 33 | 1 | 0 | 1 | 51 | 3.9 |
| R | 10 | Shean Donovan | OTT | 65 | 5 | 5 | 10 | 7:49 | –2 | 34 | 0 | 0 | 1 | 58 | 8.6 |
| R | 25 | Chris Neil | OTT | 60 | 3 | 7 | 10 | 10:58 | –13 | 146 | 0 | 0 | 0 | 59 | 5.1 |
| D | 24 | Anton Volchenkov | OTT | 68 | 2 | 8 | 10 | 20:08 | –10 | 36 | 0 | 0 | 1 | 79 | 2.5 |
| D | 5 | Christoph Schubert | OTT | 50 | 3 | 3 | 6 | 13:35 | –8 | 26 | 1 | 0 | 0 | 57 | 5.3 |
| C | 43 * | Peter Regin | OTT | 11 | 1 | 1 | 2 | 10:32 | 0 | 2 | 0 | 0 | 1 | 7 | 14.3 |
| C | 53 * | Ilya Zubov | OTT | 10 | 0 | 2 | 2 | 10:16 | –1 | 0 | 0 | 0 | 0 | 11 | 0.0 |
| D | 21 | Jason Smith | OTT | 63 | 1 | 0 | 1 | 17:32 | –3 | 47 | 0 | 0 | 1 | 53 | 1.9 |
| D | 39 | Matt Carkner | OTT | 1 | 0 | 0 | 0 | 4:08 | 0 | 0 | 0 | 0 | 0 | 0 | 0.0 |
| C | 36 * | Josh Hennessy | OTT | 1 | 0 | 0 | 0 | 13:40 | 0 | 0 | 0 | 0 | 0 | 0 | 0.0 |
| L | 47 * | Zack Smith | OTT | 1 | 0 | 0 | 0 | 7:01 | 0 | 0 | 0 | 0 | 0 | 0 | 0.0 |
| D | 2 | Luke Richardson | OTT | 2 | 0 | 0 | 0 | 12:45 | –3 | 2 | 0 | 0 | 0 | 0 | 0.0 |
| C | 58 * | Cody Bass | OTT | 12 | 0 | 0 | 0 | 5:40 | –2 | 15 | 0 | 0 | 0 | 5 | 0.0 |

## Goaltending

| No. | Goaltender | GPI | Mins | Avg | W | L | OT | EN | SO | GA | SA | S% | G | A | PIM |
|---|---|---|---|---|---|---|---|---|---|---|---|---|---|---|---|
| 31 | Alex Auld | 43 | 2449 | 2.47 | 16 | 18 | 7 | 7 | 1 | 101 | 1141 | .911 | 0 | 0 | 2 |
| 30 | * Brian Elliott | 31 | 1667 | 2.77 | 16 | 8 | 3 | 3 | 1 | 77 | 786 | .902 | 0 | 0 | 0 |
| 29 | Martin Gerber | 14 | 839 | 2.86 | 4 | 9 | 1 | 3 | 1 | 40 | 397 | .899 | 0 | 1 | 6 |
| | **Totals** | **82** | **4993** | **2.78** | **36** | **35** | **11** | **13** | **3** | **231** | **2337** | **.901** | | | |

# Cory Clouston

## Head Coach

*Born: Viking, Alta., September 19, 1969.*

Cory Clouston was in his second season with the Binghamton Senators of the American Hockey League when it was announced on February 2, 2009 that he would take over behind the bench in Ottawa. His first game as an NHL head coach came on February 3. On April 8, 2009, the Senators announced that Clouston had signed a two-year contract as the team's head coach.

Clouston was named head coach of the B-Sens on July 19, 2007 and completed his first professional season with Binghamton in 2007-08. Prior to joining the Senators' organization, Clouston spent five seasons as head of the Western Hockey League's Kootenay Ice, where he also served as assistant coach from 1999-2000 to 2001-02. Kootenay won the Memorial Cup in 2002.

A native of Viking, Alberta, Clouston had a career regular-season record of 209 wins, 110 losses, 24 overtime losses and 15 shootout defeats with Kootenay. Kootenay made the playoffs in each of his seasons behind the bench, advancing as far as the conference final in 2004-05. Clouston was named both the WHL and Canadian Hockey League coach of the year for the 2004-05 season, notching 47 wins, 15 losses, seven in overtime and another three by shootout, for a 104-point season. Clouston was also named WHL coach of the year in 2006-07.

Clouston served as general manager and head coach of the Grande Prairie Storm prior to coaching with Kootenay. In his first year with Grand Prairie in 1995-96, he led the team to a first-place finish and was named coach of the year in the Rocky Mountain Junior League. The team moved into the Alberta Junior Hockey League the following year, and Clouston remained behind the bench through the 1998-99 season. In all, his Grande Prairie teams compiled a .627 winning percentage (143-82-15). Clouston was also an assistant coach with the Powell River Paper Kings of the British Columbia Junior Hockey League in 1994-95.

In addition to his junior hockey experience, Clouston has participated in Hockey Canada's national team program, serving as assistant coach for the national under-18 2005 Junior World Cup gold medalists and head coach for the 2006 team that also took home gold. As a player, he spent four seasons with the Sherwood Park Rangers in the AJHL and four years at the University of Alberta.

### Coaching Record

| | | | Regular Season | | | | Playoffs | | | |
|---|---|---|---|---|---|---|---|---|---|---|
| Season | Team | League | GC | W | L | O/T | GC | W | L | T |
| 2002-03 | Kootenay | WHL | 72 | 36 | 25 | 11 | 11 | 5 | 6 | .... |
| 2003-04 | Kootenay | WHL | 72 | 32 | 30 | 10 | 4 | 0 | 4 | .... |
| 2004-05 | Kootenay | WHL | 72 | 47 | 15 | 10 | 10 | 10 | 6 | .... |
| 2005-06 | Kootenay | WHL | 72 | 45 | 23 | 4 | 6 | 2 | 4 | .... |
| 2006-07 | Kootenay | WHL | 72 | 49 | 17 | 6 | 7 | 3 | 4 | .... |
| 2007-08 | Binghamton | AHL | 80 | 34 | 32 | 14 | .... | .... | .... | .... |
| 2008-09 | Binghamton | AHL | 47 | 26 | 16 | 6 | .... | .... | .... | .... |
| **2008-09** | **Ottawa** | **NHL** | **34** | **19** | **11** | **4** | .... | .... | .... | .... |
| | **NHL Totals** | | **34** | **19** | **11** | **4** | .... | .... | .... | .... |

## General Managers' History

Mel Bridgman, 1992-93; Randy Sexton, 1993-94, 1994-95; Randy Sexton and Pierre Gauthier, 1995-96; Pierre Gauthier, 1996-97, 1997-98; Rick Dudley, 1998-99; Marshall Johnston, 1999-2000 to 2001-02; John Muckler, 2002-03 to 2006-07; Bryan Murray, 2007-08 to date.

*Filip Kuba established career highs with 37 assists and 40 points for Ottawa in 2008-09. Among Senators defensemen, he was the top scorer, tied for the lead in plus-minus and the leader in ice time at 23:16 per game.*

# Club Records

## Team

(Figures in brackets for season records are games played; records for fewest points, wins, ties, losses, goals, goals against are for 70 or more games)

| | | |
|---|---|---|
| **Most Points** | **113** | 2002-03 (82), 2005-06 (82) |
| **Most Wins** | **52** | 2002-03 (82), 2005-06 (82) |
| **Most Ties** | **15** | 1996-97 (82), 1997-98 (82), 1998-99 (82) |
| **Most Losses** | **70** | 1992-93 (84) |
| **Most Goals** | **312** | 2005-06 (82) |
| **Most Goals Against** | **397** | 1993-94 (84) |
| **Fewest Points** | **24** | 1992-93 (84) |
| **Fewest Wins** | **10** | 1992-93 (84) |
| **Fewest Ties** | **4** | 1992-93 (84) |
| **Fewest Losses** | **21** | 2000-01 (82), 2002-03 (82), 2005-06 (82) |
| **Fewest Goals** | **191** | 1995-96 (82) |
| **Fewest Goals Against** | **179** | 1998-99 (82) |
| **Longest Winning Streak** | | |
| **Overall** | **8** | Oct. 13-Nov. 6/07 |
| **Home** | **9** | Mar. 5-Apr. 7/09 |
| **Away** | **6** | Mar. 18-Apr. 5/03 |
| **Longest Undefeated Streak** | | |
| **Overall** | **11** | Three times |
| **Home** | **12** | Dec. 18/03-Jan. 24/04 (10 wins, 2 ties) |
| **Away** | **7** | Three times |
| **Longest Losing Streak** | | |
| **Overall** | **14** | Mar. 2-Apr. 7/93 |
| **Home** | ***11** | Oct. 27-Dec. 8/93 |
| **Away** | ***38** | Oct. 10/92-Apr. 3/93** |
| **Longest Winless Streak** | | |
| **Overall** | **21** | Oct. 10-Nov. 23/92 (20 losses, 1 tie) |
| **Home** | ***17** | Oct. 28/95-Jan. 27/96 (15 losses, 2 ties) |
| **Away** | ***38** | Oct. 10/92-Apr. 3/93 (38 losses) |
| **Most Shutouts, Season** | **10** | 2001-02 (82) |
| **Most PIM, Season** | **1,716** | 1992-93 (84) |
| **Most Goals, Game** | **11** | Nov. 13/01 (Ott. 11 at Wsh. 5) |

** NHL records do not include neutral site games

## Individual

| | | |
|---|---|---|
| **Most Seasons** | **13** | Daniel Alfredsson |
| **Most Games, Career** | **932** | Daniel Alfredsson |
| **Most Goals, Career** | **355** | Daniel Alfredsson |
| **Most Assists, Career** | **566** | Daniel Alfredsson |
| **Most Points, Career** | **921** | Daniel Alfredsson (355G, 566A) |
| **Most PIM, Career** | **1,298** | Chris Neil |
| **Most Shutouts, Career** | **30** | Patrick Lalime |
| **Longest Consecutive Games Streak** | **292** | Alexei Yashin (Dec. 31/95-Apr. 17/99) |
| **Most Goals, Season** | **50** | Dany Heatley (2005-06), (2006-07) |
| **Most Assists, Season** | **71** | Jason Spezza (2005-06) |
| **Most Points, Season** | **105** | Dany Heatley (2006-07; 50G, 55A) |
| **Most PIM, Season** | **318** | Mike Peluso (1992-93) |
| **Most Points, Defenseman, Season** | **63** | Norm Maciver (1992-93; 17G, 46A) |
| **Most Points, Center, Season** | **94** | Alexei Yashin (1998-99; 44G, 50A) |
| **Most Points, Right Wing, Season** | **103** | Daniel Alfredsson (2005-06; 43G, 60A) |
| **Most Points, Left Wing, Season** | **105** | Dany Heatley (2006-07; 50G, 55A) |
| **Most Points, Rookie, Season** | **79** | Alexei Yashin (1993-94; 30G, 49A) |
| **Most Shutouts, Season** | **8** | Patrick Lalime (2002-03) |
| **Most Goals, Game** | **4** | Marian Hossa (Jan. 2/03), Dany Heatley (Oct. 29/05), Daniel Alfredsson (Nov. 2/05), Martin Havlat (Nov. 2/05) |
| **Most Assists, Game** | **5** | Marian Hossa (Jan. 4/01) |
| **Most Points, Game** | **7** | Daniel Alfredsson (Jan. 24/08; 3G, 4A) |

* NHL Record.

## Coaching History

Rick Bowness, 1992-93 to 1994-95; Rick Bowness, Dave Allison and Jacques Martin, 1995-96; Jacques Martin, 1996-97 to 2000-01; Jacques Martin and Roger Neilson, 2001-02; Jacques Martin, 2002-03, 2003-04; Bryan Murray, 2004-05 to 2006-07; John Paddock and Bryan Murray, 2007-08; Craig Hartsburg and Cory Clouston, 2008-09; Cory Clouston, 2009-10.

## Retired Numbers

| | | |
|---|---|---|
| **8** | Frank Finnigan | 1924-1934 |

## Captains' History

Laurie Boschman, 1992-93; Brad Shaw, Mark Lamb and Gord Dineen, 1993-94; Randy Cunneyworth, 1994-95 to 1997-98; Alexei Yashin, 1998-99; Daniel Alfredsson, 1999-2000 to date.

# All-time Record vs. Other Clubs

## Regular Season

| | At Home | | | | | | | | On Road | | | | | | | | Total | | | | | | | |
|---|---|---|---|---|---|---|---|---|---|---|---|---|---|---|---|---|---|---|---|---|---|---|---|---|
| | GP | W | L | T | OL | GF | GA | PTS | GP | W | L | T | OL | GF | GA | PTS | GP | W | L | T | OL | GF | GA | PTS |
| Anaheim | 10 | 4 | 4 | 1 | 1 | 30 | 27 | 10 | 10 | 3 | 5 | 2 | 0 | 19 | 24 | 8 | 20 | 7 | 9 | 3 | 1 | 49 | 51 | 18 |
| Atlanta | 18 | 11 | 3 | 1 | 3 | 80 | 50 | 26 | 18 | 10 | 6 | 1 | 1 | 68 | 61 | 22 | 36 | 21 | 9 | 2 | 4 | 148 | 111 | 48 |
| Boston | 46 | 21 | 21 | 3 | 1 | 120 | 136 | 46 | 48 | 14 | 28 | 5 | 1 | 127 | 168 | 34 | 94 | 35 | 49 | 8 | 2 | 247 | 304 | 80 |
| Buffalo | 48 | 21 | 16 | 7 | 4 | 135 | 128 | 53 | 46 | 16 | 23 | 3 | 4 | 108 | 143 | 39 | 94 | 37 | 39 | 10 | 8 | 243 | 271 | 92 |
| Calgary | 12 | 5 | 3 | 3 | 1 | 30 | 31 | 14 | 13 | 4 | 7 | 1 | 1 | 29 | 46 | 10 | 25 | 9 | 10 | 4 | 2 | 59 | 77 | 24 |
| Carolina | 37 | 17 | 14 | 4 | 2 | 109 | 94 | 40 | 35 | 11 | 20 | 4 | 0 | 89 | 99 | 26 | 72 | 28 | 34 | 8 | 2 | 198 | 193 | 66 |
| Chicago | 11 | 4 | 5 | 0 | 2 | 34 | 34 | 10 | 10 | 2 | 5 | 2 | 1 | 21 | 24 | 7 | 21 | 6 | 10 | 2 | 3 | 55 | 58 | 17 |
| Colorado | 19 | 8 | 8 | 3 | 0 | 54 | 66 | 19 | 17 | 3 | 12 | 1 | 1 | 49 | 75 | 8 | 36 | 11 | 20 | 4 | 1 | 103 | 141 | 27 |
| Columbus | 4 | 2 | 0 | 1 | 1 | 14 | 9 | 6 | 4 | 1 | 2 | 1 | 0 | 11 | 14 | 3 | 8 | 3 | 2 | 2 | 1 | 25 | 23 | 9 |
| Dallas | 11 | 5 | 6 | 0 | 0 | 27 | 30 | 10 | 12 | 5 | 7 | 0 | 0 | 32 | 46 | 10 | 23 | 10 | 13 | 0 | 0 | 59 | 76 | 20 |
| Detroit | 12 | 4 | 6 | 1 | 1 | 33 | 34 | 10 | 10 | 4 | 5 | 0 | 1 | 22 | 35 | 9 | 22 | 8 | 11 | 1 | 2 | 55 | 69 | 19 |
| Edmonton | 12 | 5 | 5 | 2 | 0 | 27 | 31 | 12 | 13 | 4 | 7 | 2 | 0 | 33 | 44 | 10 | 25 | 9 | 12 | 4 | 0 | 60 | 75 | 22 |
| Florida | 30 | 15 | 11 | 2 | 2 | 92 | 78 | 34 | 30 | 17 | 12 | 1 | 0 | 97 | 94 | 35 | 60 | 32 | 23 | 3 | 2 | 189 | 172 | 69 |
| Los Angeles | 11 | 5 | 4 | 1 | 1 | 35 | 30 | 12 | 11 | 1 | 9 | 1 | 0 | 21 | 48 | 3 | 22 | 6 | 13 | 2 | 1 | 56 | 78 | 15 |
| Minnesota | 3 | 2 | 1 | 0 | 0 | 9 | 7 | 4 | 5 | 3 | 1 | 1 | 0 | 19 | 14 | 7 | 8 | 5 | 2 | 1 | 0 | 28 | 21 | 11 |
| Montreal | 46 | 25 | 18 | 1 | 2 | 148 | 127 | 53 | 48 | 18 | 25 | 4 | 1 | 137 | 146 | 41 | 94 | 43 | 43 | 5 | 3 | 285 | 273 | 94 |
| Nashville | 6 | 4 | 2 | 0 | 0 | 20 | 13 | 8 | 6 | 3 | 3 | 0 | 0 | 13 | 14 | 6 | 12 | 7 | 5 | 0 | 0 | 33 | 27 | 14 |
| New Jersey | 32 | 9 | 17 | 3 | 3 | 73 | 83 | 24 | 31 | 10 | 15 | 2 | 4 | 74 | 89 | 26 | 63 | 19 | 32 | 5 | 7 | 147 | 172 | 50 |
| NY Islanders | 31 | 19 | 7 | 5 | 0 | 107 | 77 | 43 | 32 | 18 | 7 | 6 | 1 | 119 | 98 | 43 | 63 | 37 | 14 | 11 | 1 | 226 | 175 | 86 |
| NY Rangers | 31 | 14 | 14 | 3 | 0 | 89 | 79 | 31 | 31 | 18 | 12 | 0 | 1 | 94 | 91 | 37 | 62 | 32 | 26 | 3 | 1 | 183 | 170 | 68 |
| Philadelphia | 32 | 14 | 12 | 6 | 0 | 94 | 92 | 34 | 31 | 11 | 18 | 2 | 0 | 89 | 105 | 24 | 63 | 25 | 30 | 8 | 0 | 183 | 197 | 58 |
| Phoenix | 13 | 6 | 6 | 1 | 0 | 42 | 39 | 13 | 11 | 6 | 4 | 1 | 0 | 42 | 36 | 13 | 24 | 12 | 10 | 2 | 0 | 84 | 75 | 26 |
| Pittsburgh | 35 | 12 | 15 | 5 | 3 | 102 | 115 | 32 | 35 | 13 | 16 | 4 | 2 | 99 | 117 | 32 | 70 | 25 | 31 | 9 | 5 | 201 | 232 | 64 |
| St. Louis | 11 | 5 | 6 | 0 | 0 | 26 | 38 | 10 | 11 | 5 | 4 | 2 | 0 | 32 | 30 | 12 | 22 | 10 | 10 | 2 | 0 | 58 | 68 | 22 |
| San Jose | 11 | 4 | 3 | 4 | 0 | 37 | 30 | 12 | 10 | 4 | 5 | 0 | 1 | 18 | 21 | 9 | 21 | 8 | 8 | 4 | 1 | 55 | 51 | 21 |
| Tampa Bay | 31 | 21 | 10 | 0 | 0 | 112 | 68 | 42 | 31 | 18 | 9 | 2 | 2 | 112 | 87 | 40 | 62 | 39 | 19 | 2 | 2 | 224 | 155 | 82 |
| Toronto | 35 | 22 | 9 | 1 | 3 | 114 | 94 | 48 | 37 | 18 | 16 | 2 | 1 | 111 | 100 | 39 | 72 | 40 | 25 | 3 | 4 | 225 | 194 | 87 |
| Vancouver | 12 | 5 | 5 | 1 | 1 | 27 | 31 | 12 | 13 | 5 | 6 | 1 | 1 | 28 | 39 | 12 | 25 | 10 | 11 | 2 | 2 | 55 | 70 | 24 |
| Washington | 31 | 17 | 12 | 1 | 1 | 111 | 91 | 36 | 32 | 11 | 16 | 4 | 1 | 91 | 111 | 27 | 63 | 28 | 28 | 5 | 2 | 202 | 202 | 63 |
| **Totals** | **641** | **306** | **243** | **60** | **32** | **1931** | **1762** | **704** | **641** | **256** | **305** | **55** | **25** | **1804** | **2019** | **592** | **1282** | **562** | **548** | **115** | **57** | **3735** | **3781** | **1296** |

## Playoffs

| | Series | W | L | GP | W | L | T | GF | GA | Last Mtg. | Rnd. | Result |
|---|---|---|---|---|---|---|---|---|---|---|---|---|
| Anaheim | 1 | 0 | 1 | 5 | 1 | 4 | 0 | 11 | 16 | 2007 | F | L 1-4 |
| Buffalo | 4 | 1 | 3 | 21 | 8 | 13 | 0 | 47 | 52 | 2007 | CF | W 4-1 |
| New Jersey | 3 | 2 | 1 | 18 | 11 | 7 | 0 | 41 | 40 | 2007 | CSF | W 4-1 |
| NY Islanders | 1 | 1 | 0 | 5 | 4 | 1 | 0 | 13 | 7 | 2003 | CQF | W 4-1 |
| Philadelphia | 2 | 2 | 0 | 11 | 8 | 3 | 0 | 28 | 12 | 2003 | CSF | W 4-2 |
| Pittsburgh | 2 | 1 | 1 | 9 | 4 | 5 | 0 | 23 | 26 | 2008 | CQF | L 0-4 |
| Tampa Bay | 1 | 1 | 0 | 5 | 4 | 1 | 0 | 23 | 13 | 2006 | CQF | W 4-1 |
| Toronto | 4 | 0 | 4 | 24 | 8 | 16 | 0 | 42 | 57 | 2004 | CQF | L 3-4 |
| Washington | 1 | 0 | 1 | 5 | 1 | 4 | 0 | 7 | 18 | 1998 | CSF | L 1-4 |
| **Totals** | **19** | **8** | **11** | **103** | **49** | **54** | **0** | **235** | **241** | | | |

## Playoff Results 2009-2004

| Year | Round | Opponent | Result | GF | GA |
|---|---|---|---|---|---|
| 2008 | CQF | Pittsburgh | L 0-4 | 5 | 16 |
| 2007 | F | Anaheim | L 1-4 | 11 | 16 |
| | CF | Buffalo | W 4-1 | 15 | 10 |
| | CSF | New Jersey | W 4-1 | 15 | 11 |
| | CQF | Pittsburgh | W 4-1 | 18 | 10 |
| 2006 | CSF | Buffalo | L 1-4 | 13 | 16 |
| | CQF | Tampa Bay | W 4-1 | 23 | 13 |
| 2004 | CQF | Toronto | L 3-4 | 11 | 14 |

**Abbreviations: Round: F** - Final; **CF** – conference final; **CSF** – conference semi-final; **CQF** – conference quarter-final.

Colorado totals include Quebec, 1992-93 to 1994-95.
Dallas totals include Minnesota North Stars, 1992-93.

Carolina totals include Hartford, 1992-93 to 1996-97.
Phoenix totals include Winnipeg, 1992-93 to 1995-96.

## 2008-09 Results

| | | | |
|---|---|---|---|
| **Oct.** | 4 | Pittsburgh | 3-4* |
| | 5 | at Pittsburgh | 3-1 |
| | 11 | Detroit | 2-3 |
| | 17 | Phoenix | 6-3 |
| | 18 | Boston | 2-4 |
| | 22 | Florida | 1-3 |
| | 24 | Anaheim | 3-4 |
| | 25 | at Toronto | 2-3 |
| | 27 | at Buffalo | 5-2 |
| | 30 | at Florida | 2-1 |
| **Nov.** | 1 | at Tampa Bay | 2-3† |
| | 4 | Washington | 2-1* |
| | 6 | Philadelphia | 4-1 |
| | 7 | at Carolina | 1-2 |
| | 11 | at Montreal | 0-4 |
| | 13 | NY Islanders | 1-3 |
| | 15 | at NY Islanders | 2-3 |
| | 17 | at NY Rangers | 1-2† |
| | 20 | Montreal | 2-3† |
| | 22 | NY Rangers | 4-1 |
| | 27 | Toronto | 2-1† |
| | 29 | at NY Islanders | 2-4 |
| **Dec.** | 3 | Atlanta | 5-1 |
| | 6 | Pittsburgh | 3-2 |
| | 8 | Florida | 3-4* |
| | 10 | at Chicago | 0-2 |
| | 12 | at Washington | 1-5 |
| | 13 | Tampa Bay | 2-0 |
| | 16 | Atlanta | 1-4 |
| | 19 | at New Jersey | 1-5 |
| | 20 | Dallas | 5-4* |
| | 23 | at Philadelphia | 4-6 |
| | 27 | at Calgary | 3-6 |
| | 28 | at Vancouver | 0-3 |
| | 30 | at Edmonton | 3-2 |
| **Jan.** | 3 | at Toronto | 1-3 |
| | 4 | at New Jersey | 3-4* |
| | 6 | at Buffalo | 2-4 |
| | 8 | at Boston | 4-6 |
| | 10 | NY Rangers | 0-2 |
| | 13 | Carolina | 5-1 |
| | 14 | at Atlanta | 3-2 |
| | 17 | Montreal | 4-5† |
| | 20 | Washington | 3-2 |
| | 27 | New Jersey | 1-4 |
| | 29 | at St. Louis | 3-1 |
| | 30 | at Columbus | 0-1 |
| **Feb.** | 1 | at Washington | 4-7 |
| | 3 | Los Angeles | 0-1 |
| | 5 | Boston | 3-4† |
| | 7 | Buffalo | 3-2† |
| | 11 | at Buffalo | 3-1 |
| | 12 | at Philadelphia | 5-2 |
| | 14 | at Minnesota | 5-3 |
| | 16 | at Nashville | 2-0 |
| | 17 | at Colorado | 2-3* |
| | 19 | Vancouver | 2-5 |
| | 21 | at Montreal | 3-5 |
| | 24 | Carolina | 4-2 |
| | 26 | San Jose | 1-2 |
| | 28 | Toronto | 3-4* |
| **Mar.** | 3 | Calgary | 3-6 |
| | 5 | Edmonton | 4-2 |
| | 7 | Buffalo | 6-3 |
| | 9 | Toronto | 2-1 |
| | 11 | Tampa Bay | 3-2* |
| | 12 | at Boston | 3-5 |
| | 14 | at Pittsburgh | 4-3† |
| | 17 | Buffalo | 4-2 |
| | 19 | Montreal | 5-4 |
| | 21 | NY Islanders | 5-2 |
| | 22 | at NY Rangers | 2-1 |
| | 25 | at Carolina | 1-2 |
| | 28 | at Atlanta | 3-6 |
| | 29 | at Tampa Bay | 3-0 |
| | 31 | at Florida | 2-5 |
| **Apr.** | 2 | at Boston | 1-2 |
| | 4 | Philadelphia | 4-3† |
| | 6 | at Montreal | 3-2 |
| | 7 | Boston | 3-2 |
| | 9 | New Jersey | 2-3† |
| | 11 | at Toronto | 2-5 |

* – Overtime † – Shootout

## Entry Draft Selections 2009-1995

Name in bold denotes played in NHL.

**2009**
**Pick**
9 Jared Cowen
39 Jakob Silfverberg
46 Robin Lehner
100 Chris Wideman
130 Mike Hoffman
146 Jeff Costello
160 Corey Cowick
190 Brad Peltz
191 Michael Sdao

**2008**
**Pick**
15 Erik Karlsson
42 Patrick Wiercioch
79 **Zack Smith**
109 Andre Petersson
119 Derek Grant
139 Mark Borowiecki
199 Emil Sandin

**2007**
**Pick**
29 James O'Brien
60 Ruslan Bashkirov
90 Louie Caporusso
120 Ben Blood

**2006**
**Pick**
28 **Nick Foligno**
68 Eric Gryba
91 Kaspars Daugavins
121 Pierre-Luc Lessard
151 Ryan Daniels
181 Kevin Koopman
211 Erik Condra

**2005**
**Pick**
9 **Brian Lee**
70 Vitali Anikeyenko
95 **Cody Bass**
98 **Ilya Zubov**
115 Janne Kolehmainen
136 Tomas Kudelka
186 Dmitri Megalinsky
204 Colin Greening

**2004**
**Pick**
23 **Andrej Meszaros**
58 Kirill Lyamin
77 Shawn Weller
87 **Peter Regin**
89 Jeff Glass
122 **Alexander Nikulin**
141 Jim McKenzie
156 Roman Wick
219 Joe Cooper
251 Matthew McIlvane
284 John Wikner

**2003**
**Pick**
29 **Patrick Eaves**
67 Igor Mirnov
100 Philippe Seydoux
135 Mattias Karlsson
142 Tim Cook
166 Sergei Gimayev
228 Will Colbert
260 Ossi Louhivaara
291 **Brian Elliott**

**2002**
**Pick**
16 **Jakub Klepis**
47 **Alexei Kaigorodov**
75 Arttu Luttinen
113 Scott Dobben
125 Johan Bjork
150 Brock Hooton
246 Josef Vavra
276 Vitali Atyushov

**2001**
**Pick**
2 **Jason Spezza**
23 **Tim Gleason**
81 Neil Komadoski
99 **Ray Emery**
127 **Christoph Schubert**
162 Stefan Schauer
193 **Brooks Laich**
218 Jan Platil
223 **Brandon Bochenski**
235 Neil Petruic
256 Gregg Johnson
286 **Toni Dahlman**

**2000**
**Pick**
21 **Anton Volchenkov**
45 **Mathieu Chouinard**
55 **Antoine Vermette**
87 Jan Bohac
122 Derrick Byfuglien
156 **Greg Zanon**
157 Grant Potulny
158 Sean Connolly
188 Jason Maleyko
283 James Demone

**1999**
**Pick**
26 **Martin Havlat**
48 **Simon Lajeunesse**
62 Teemu Sainomaa
94 **Chris Kelly**
154 Andrew Ianiero
164 **Martin Prusek**
201 Mikko Ruutu
209 **Layne Ulmer**
213 **Alexandre Giroux**
269 Konstantin Gorovikov

**1998**
**Pick**
15 **Mathieu Chouinard**
44 **Mike Fisher**
58 **Chris Bala**
74 **Julien Vauclair**
101 **Petr Schastlivy**
130 Gavin McLeod
161 **Chris Neil**
188 Michel Periard
223 Sergei Verenikin
246 Rastislav Pavlikovsky

**1997**
**Pick**
12 **Marian Hossa**
58 **Jani Hurme**
66 **Josh Langfeld**
119 **Magnus Arvedson**
146 Jeff Sullivan
173 Robin Bacul
203 Nick Gillis
229 **Karel Rachunek**

**1996**
**Pick**
1 **Chris Phillips**
81 **Antti-Jussi Niemi**
136 **Andreas Dackell**
163 Francois Hardy
212 **Erich Goldmann**
216 **Ivan Ciernik**
239 **Sami Salo**

**1995**
**Pick**
1 **Bryan Berard**
27 **Marc Moro**
53 **Brad Larsen**
89 Kevin Bolibruck
103 Kevin Boyd
131 David Hruska
183 Kaj Linna
184 **Ray Schultz**
231 Erik Kaminski

## Bryan Murray

### General Manager

*Born: Shawville, Que., December 5, 1942.*

On June 18, 2007, Bryan Murray was appointed as the seventh general manager of the Ottawa Senators. Murray had joined the organization on June 8, 2004, when he was named the club's head coach. Murray resigned as senior vice president and general manager of Anaheim to take the coaching position in Ottawa. As coach in Ottawa in 2006–07, Murray led the Senators to the Stanley Cup Finals for the first time in franchise history, only to lose to his former Anaheim team. He also has previous front office experience as vice president and general manager of the Florida Panthers from 1994 to 2001, assembling a team that reached the Stanley Cup Finals in just its third year of existence in 1996.

Murray, who was back behind the bench in Ottawa briefly in 2007-08, began his NHL career as head coach of the Washington Capials in 1981. He has served 16+ years behind the bench, coaching more than 1,300 regular-season and playoff games, including 672 wins. He earned the Jack Adams Award as coach of the year in 1983-84. Murray's regular-season coaching record in Ottawa is 107-55-20 and includes winning the 2007 Prince of Wales Trophy as the NHL's Eastern Conference champions.

**Coaching Record**

| | | | Regular Season | | | | Playoffs | | | |
|---|---|---|---|---|---|---|---|---|---|---|
| **Season** | **Team** | **League** | **GC** | **W** | **L** | **O/T** | **GC** | **W** | **L** | **T** |
| 1981-82 | Washington | NHL | 66 | 25 | 28 | 13 | .... | .... | .... | .... |
| 1982-83 | Washington | NHL | 80 | 39 | 25 | 16 | 4 | 1 | 3 | .... |
| 1983-84 | Washington | NHL | 80 | 48 | 27 | 5 | 8 | 4 | 4 | .... |
| 1984-85 | Washington | NHL | 80 | 46 | 25 | 9 | 5 | 2 | 3 | .... |
| 1985-86 | Washington | NHL | 80 | 50 | 23 | 7 | 9 | 5 | 4 | .... |
| 1986-87 | Washington | NHL | 80 | 38 | 32 | 10 | 7 | 3 | 4 | .... |
| 1987-88 | Washington | NHL | 80 | 38 | 33 | 9 | 14 | 7 | 7 | .... |
| 1988-89 | Washington | NHL | 80 | 41 | 29 | 10 | 6 | 2 | 4 | .... |
| 1989-90 | Washington | NHL | 46 | 18 | 24 | 4 | .... | .... | .... | .... |
| 1990-91 | Detroit | NHL | 80 | 34 | 38 | 8 | 7 | 3 | 4 | .... |
| 1991-92 | Detroit | NHL | 80 | 43 | 25 | 12 | 11 | 4 | 7 | .... |
| 1992-93 | Detroit | NHL | 84 | 47 | 28 | 9 | 7 | 3 | 4 | .... |
| 1997-98 | Florida | NHL | 59 | 17 | 31 | 11 | .... | .... | .... | .... |
| 2001-02 | Anaheim | NHL | 82 | 29 | 42 | 11 | .... | .... | .... | .... |
| 2004-05 | Ottawa | | | | SEASON CANCELLED | | | | | |
| 2005-06 | Ottawa | NHL | 82 | 52 | 21 | 9 | 10 | 5 | 5 | .... |
| 2006-07 | Ottawa | NHL | 82 | 48 | 25 | 9 | 20 | 13 | 7 | .... |
| 2007-08 | Ottawa | NHL | 18 | 7 | 9 | 2 | 4 | 0 | 4 | .... |
| | **NHL Totals** | | **1239** | **620** | **465** | **154** | **112** | **52** | **60** | .... |

# Club Directory

**Scotiabank Place**

**Ottawa Senators**
Scotiabank Place
1000 Palladium Drive
Ottawa, Ontario
K2V 1A5
Phone **613/599-0250**
FAX 613/599-0358
www.ottawasenators.com
**Capacity:** 19,153

**Executive**
Owner, Governor and Chairman .............. Eugene Melnyk
President and Alternate Governor .............. Cyril Leeder
Exec. V.P., CFO and Alternate Governor .............. Erin Crowe
Exec. V.P., G.M. and Alternate Governor .............. Bryan Murray
V.P. and Executive Director, Scotiabank Place ..... Tom Conroy
Exec. Assistant to the President .............. Kathy Downs
Exec. Assistant to the Exec. V.P. and CFO ........ Colette Hiscotte

**Hockey Operations**
Assistant General Manager .............. Tim Murray
Director of Player Personnel .............. Pierre Dorion
Director of Hockey Administration
and Player Development .............. Randy Lee
Assistant to the General Manager .............. Allison Vaughan
Head Coach .............. Cory Clouston
Assistant Coaches .............. Greg Carvel, Brad Lauer, Luke Richardson
Video Coach .............. Tim Pattyson
Conditioning Coach .............. Chris Schwarz
Director of Player Services .............. Chad Schella
Manager of Team Travel .............. Jordan Silmser
Head Athletic Therapist .............. Gerry Townend
Assistant Athletic Therapist .............. Dominic Nicoletta
Equipment Manager .............. Scott Allegrino
Assistant Equipment Manager .............. Chris Cook
Massage Therapist .............. Shawn Markwick

**Scouts**
Scouts .............. Vaclav Burda, George Fargher, Anders Forsberg, Bob Janecyk, Bob Lowes, Bill McCarthy, Lew Mongelluzzo, Greg Royce, Mikko Ruutu
Pro Scouts .............. Jim Clark, Archie Henderson, Nick Polano

**Communications and Publications**
Vice-President, Communications .............. Phil Legault
Director, Publications .............. Karen Ruttan
Director, Communications .............. Brian Morris
Communications Co-ordinator .............. Chris Moore
Writer/Edioria1 Manager .............. Rob Brodie
Translator .............. Eric Tremblay
Communications & Publications Assistant .............. Amanda Nigh

**Broadcasting**
Vice-President, Broadcast .............. Jim Steel

**Legal**
Senior Legal Council .............. Richard Stacey

**Corporate & Ticket Sales and Service**
Sr, V.P., Corporate & Ticketing Sales .............. Mark Bonneau
Exec. Ass't. to Sr. V.P., Corp. & Ticketing ........ Brooke Brown
Director, Corporate Sales .............. Bill Courchaine
Sr. Corporate Account Managers .............. Steve Chestnut, Mark Clatney, Francois Robert
Director, Business Development .............. Gina Hillcoat
Director, Ticket Sales .............. Jim Orban
Manager, Sales .............. Chris Atack
Manager, Group Sales .............. Devon Hogan
Manager, Premium Seating Sales .............. Joe Lowes
Director, Premium Services .............. Christine Clancy
Manager, Premium Client Services .............. Tracey Bonner

**Finance**
Controller .............. Derek Winch
Accounting Manager, Ottawa Senators .............. Morgan Cranley

**Information Technology**
Director, Information Technology .............. Sean Shrubsole
Systems Administrator, IT .............. Robin Zanichkowsky
Help Desk Supervisor, IT .............. Don Morin
Help Desk Support Technician, IT .............. Tom Spooner

**Marketing**
Vice-President, Marketing .............. Jeff Kyle
Executive Assistant, Marketing .............. Deborah Wilson
Director, Marketing .............. Isabelle Perrault-Lachapelle
Director, Merchandise .............. Kevin Lawton
Director, Game Entertainment .............. Glen Gower
Director, Fan and Community Development ...... Aaron Robinson
Art Director .............. Wendy Moenig
Manager, Marketing .............. Lisa Trevisanutto

**Operations and Events**
Assistant to the V.P. & Executive Director ........ Linda Julian
Director, Engineering & Operations .............. Ed Healy
Director, Scotiabank Place Marketing .............. Krista Galbraith

**People Department**
Director, People Department .............. Sandi Horner

**Sens Foundation**
President .............. Danielle Robinson

**Miscellaneous**
Radio .............. Team 1200 (English), 104,7 FM (French)
Television .............. Rogers Sportsnet and RDS
Team Photographer .............. Freestyle Photography (André Ringuette)
Anthem singer .............. Lyndon Slewidge
Mascot .............. Spartacat

# Philadelphia Flyers

## 2008-09 Results: 44W-27L-5OTL-6SOL 99PTS.
## Third, Atlantic Division

### Key Off-Season Signings/Acquisitions

**2009**

**June 10** • Signed G **Ray Emery.**

**26** • Acquired D **Chris Pronger** and C **Ryan Dingle** from Anaheim for RW **Joffrey Lupul**, D **Luca Sbisa**, Philadelphia's 1st-round picks in 2009 and 2010 and a conditional pick.

**July 1** • Signed RW **Ian Laperriere** and G **Brian Boucher.**

**30** • Signed D **Ole-Kristian Tollefsen.**

### 2009-10 Schedule

| Month | Day | Date | Opponent | Month | Day | Date | Opponent |
|---|---|---|---|---|---|---|---|
| **Oct.** | Fri. | 2 | at Carolina | | Wed. | 6 | Toronto |
| | Sat. | 3 | at New Jersey | | Thu. | 7 | at Pittsburgh |
| | Tue. | 6 | Washington | | Sat. | 9 | Tampa Bay |
| | Thu. | 8 | Pittsburgh | | Tue. | 12 | Dallas |
| | Sat. | 10 | Anaheim | | Thu. | 14 | at Toronto |
| | Fri. | 16 | at Florida | | Sun. | 17 | at Washington* |
| | Thu. | 22 | Boston | | Tue. | 19 | Columbus |
| | Sat. | 24 | Florida | | Thu. | 21 | NY Rangers |
| | Sun. | 25 | San Jose | | Sat. | 23 | Carolina* |
| | Tue. | 27 | at Washington | | Sun. | 24 | Pittsburgh* |
| | Sat. | 31 | Carolina* | | Thu. | 28 | Atlanta |
| **Nov.** | Mon. | 2 | Tampa Bay | | Sat. | 30 | NY Islanders |
| | Fri. | 6 | at Buffalo | **Feb.** | Mon. | 1 | at Calgary |
| | Sat. | 7 | St. Louis | | Wed. | 3 | at Edmonton |
| | Thu. | 12 | Ottawa | | Sat. | 6 | at Minnesota |
| | Sat. | 14 | Buffalo | | Mon. | 8 | New Jersey |
| | Mon. | 16 | New Jersey | | Wed. | 10 | at New Jersey |
| | Wed. | 18 | at Los Angeles | | Fri. | 12 | Montreal |
| | Fri. | 20 | at San Jose | | Sat. | 13 | at Montreal |
| | Sat. | 21 | at Phoenix | **Mar.** | Tue. | 2 | at Tampa Bay |
| | Mon. | 23 | at Colorado | | Wed. | 3 | at Florida |
| | Wed. | 25 | at NY Islanders | | Fri. | 5 | at Buffalo |
| | Fri. | 27 | Buffalo* | | Sun. | 7 | Toronto |
| | Sat. | 28 | at Atlanta | | Tue. | 9 | NY Islanders |
| **Dec.** | Thu. | 3 | Vancouver | | Thu. | 11 | Boston |
| | Sat. | 5 | Washington | | Sat. | 13 | Chicago* |
| | Mon. | 7 | at Montreal | | Sun. | 14 | at NY Rangers* |
| | Tue. | 8 | NY Islanders | | Tue. | 16 | at Nashville |
| | Thu. | 10 | Ottawa | | Thu. | 18 | at Dallas |
| | Sat. | 12 | at New Jersey | | Sat. | 20 | at Atlanta |
| | Mon. | 14 | at Boston | | Sun. | 21 | Atlanta |
| | Tue. | 15 | at Pittsburgh | | Tue. | 23 | at Ottawa |
| | Thu. | 17 | Pittsburgh | | Thu. | 25 | Minnesota |
| | Sat. | 19 | NY Rangers* | | Sat. | 27 | at Pittsburgh* |
| | Mon. | 21 | Florida | | Sun. | 28 | New Jersey |
| | Wed. | 23 | at Tampa Bay | **Apr.** | Thu. | 1 | at NY Islanders |
| | Sat. | 26 | at Carolina | | Fri. | 2 | Montreal |
| | Sun. | 27 | at NY Islanders* | | Sun. | 4 | Detroit* |
| | Wed. | 30 | at NY Rangers | | Tue. | 6 | at Toronto |
| **Jan.** | Fri. | 1 | at Boston* | | Fri. | 9 | at NY Rangers |
| | Sun. | 3 | at Ottawa* | | Sun. | 11 | NY Rangers* |

* Denotes afternoon game.

### Year-by-Year Record

| | | Home | | | | Road | | | | Overall | | | | | | | | |
|---|---|---|---|---|---|---|---|---|---|---|---|---|---|---|---|---|---|---|
| **Season** | **GP** | **W** | **L** | **T** | **OL** | **W** | **L** | **T** | **OL** | **W** | **L** | **T** | **OL** | **GF** | **GA** | **Pts.** | **Finished** | **Playoff Result** |
| 2008-09 | 82 | 24 | 13 | .... | 4 | 20 | 14 | .... | 7 | 44 | 27 | .... | 11 | 264 | 238 | 99 | 3rd, Atlantic Div. | Lost Conf. Quarter-Final |
| 2007-08 | 82 | 21 | 14 | .... | 6 | 21 | 15 | .... | 5 | 42 | 29 | .... | 11 | 248 | 233 | 95 | 4th, Atlantic Div. | Lost Conf. Championship |
| 2006-07 | 82 | 10 | 24 | .... | 7 | 12 | 24 | .... | 5 | 22 | 48 | .... | 12 | 214 | 303 | 56 | 5th, Atlantic Div. | Out of Playoffs |
| 2005-06 | 82 | 22 | 13 | .... | 6 | 23 | 13 | .... | 5 | 45 | 26 | .... | 11 | 267 | 259 | 101 | 2nd, Atlantic Div. | Lost Conf. Quarter-Final |
| 2004-05 | .... | .... | .... | .... | .... | .... | .... | .... | .... | .... | .... | .... | .... | .... | .... | .... | | |
| 2003-04 | 82 | 24 | 11 | 3 | 3 | 16 | 10 | 12 | 3 | 40 | 21 | 15 | 6 | 229 | 186 | 101 | 1st, Atlantic Div. | Lost Conf. Championship |
| 2002-03 | 82 | 21 | 10 | 8 | 2 | 24 | 10 | 5 | 2 | 45 | 20 | 13 | 4 | 211 | 166 | 107 | 2nd, Atlantic Div. | Lost Conf. Semi-Final |
| 2001-02 | 82 | 20 | 13 | 5 | 3 | 22 | 14 | 5 | 0 | 42 | 27 | 10 | 3 | 234 | 192 | 97 | 1st, Atlantic Div. | Lost Conf. Quarter-Final |
| 2000-01 | 82 | 26 | 11 | 4 | 0 | 17 | 14 | 7 | 3 | 43 | 25 | 11 | 3 | 240 | 207 | 100 | 2nd, Atlantic Div. | Lost Conf. Quarter-Final |
| 1999-2000 | 82 | 25 | 6 | 7 | 3 | 20 | 16 | 5 | 0 | 45 | 22 | 12 | 3 | 237 | 179 | 105 | 1st, Atlantic Div. | Lost Conf. Championship |
| 1998-99 | 82 | 21 | 9 | 11 | .... | 16 | 17 | 8 | .... | 37 | 26 | 19 | .... | 231 | 196 | 93 | 2nd, Atlantic Div. | Lost Conf. Quarter-Final |
| 1997-98 | 82 | 24 | 11 | 6 | .... | 18 | 18 | 5 | .... | 42 | 29 | 11 | .... | 242 | 193 | 95 | 2nd, Atlantic Div. | Lost Conf. Quarter-Final |
| 1996-97 | 82 | 23 | 12 | 6 | .... | 22 | 12 | 7 | .... | 45 | 24 | 13 | .... | 274 | 217 | 103 | 2nd, Atlantic Div. | Lost Final |
| 1995-96 | 82 | 27 | 9 | 5 | .... | 18 | 15 | 8 | .... | 45 | 24 | 13 | .... | 282 | 208 | 103 | 1st, Atlantic Div. | Lost Conf. Semi-Final |
| 1994-95 | 48 | 16 | 7 | 1 | .... | 12 | 9 | 3 | .... | 28 | 16 | 4 | .... | 150 | 132 | 60 | 1st, Atlantic Div. | Lost Conf. Championship |
| 1993-94 | 84 | 19 | 20 | 3 | .... | 16 | 19 | 7 | .... | 35 | 39 | 10 | .... | 294 | 314 | 80 | 6th, Atlantic Div. | Out of Playoffs |
| 1992-93 | 84 | 23 | 14 | 5 | .... | 13 | 23 | 6 | .... | 36 | 37 | 11 | .... | 319 | 319 | 83 | 5th, Patrick Div. | Out of Playoffs |
| 1991-92 | 80 | 22 | 11 | 7 | .... | 10 | 26 | 4 | .... | 32 | 37 | 11 | .... | 252 | 273 | 75 | 6th, Patrick Div. | Out of Playoffs |
| 1990-91 | 80 | 18 | 16 | 6 | .... | 15 | 21 | 4 | .... | 33 | 37 | 10 | .... | 252 | 267 | 76 | 5th, Patrick Div. | Out of Playoffs |
| 1989-90 | 80 | 17 | 19 | 4 | .... | 13 | 20 | 7 | .... | 30 | 39 | 11 | .... | 290 | 297 | 71 | 6th, Patrick Div. | Out of Playoffs |
| 1988-89 | 80 | 22 | 15 | 3 | .... | 14 | 21 | 5 | .... | 36 | 36 | 8 | .... | 307 | 285 | 80 | 4th, Patrick Div. | Lost Conf. Championship |
| 1987-88 | 80 | 20 | 14 | 6 | .... | 18 | 19 | 3 | .... | 38 | 33 | 9 | .... | 292 | 292 | 85 | 3rd, Patrick Div. | Lost Div. Semi-Final |
| 1986-87 | 80 | 29 | 9 | 2 | .... | 17 | 17 | 6 | .... | 46 | 26 | 8 | .... | 310 | 245 | 100 | 1st, Patrick Div. | Lost Final |
| 1985-86 | 80 | 33 | 6 | 1 | .... | 20 | 17 | 3 | .... | 53 | 23 | 4 | .... | 335 | 241 | 110 | 1st, Patrick Div. | Lost Div. Semi-Final |
| 1984-85 | 80 | 32 | 4 | 4 | .... | 21 | 16 | 3 | .... | 53 | 20 | 7 | .... | 348 | 241 | 113 | 1st, Patrick Div. | Lost Final |
| 1983-84 | 80 | 25 | 10 | 5 | .... | 19 | 16 | 5 | .... | 44 | 26 | 10 | .... | 350 | 290 | 98 | 3rd, Patrick Div. | Lost Div. Semi-Final |
| 1982-83 | 80 | 29 | 8 | 3 | .... | 20 | 15 | 5 | .... | 49 | 23 | 8 | .... | 326 | 240 | 106 | 1st, Patrick Div. | Lost Div. Semi-Final |
| 1981-82 | 80 | 25 | 10 | 5 | .... | 13 | 21 | 6 | .... | 38 | 31 | 11 | .... | 325 | 313 | 87 | 3rd. Patrick Div. | Lost Div. Semi-Final |
| 1980-81 | 80 | 23 | 9 | 8 | .... | 18 | 15 | 7 | .... | 41 | 24 | 15 | .... | 313 | 249 | 97 | 2nd, Patrick Div. | Lost Quarter-Final |
| 1979-80 | 80 | 27 | 5 | 8 | .... | 21 | 7 | 12 | .... | 48 | 12 | 20 | .... | 327 | 254 | 116 | 1st, Patrick Div. | Lost Final |
| 1978-79 | 80 | 26 | 10 | 4 | .... | 14 | 15 | 11 | .... | 40 | 25 | 15 | .... | 281 | 248 | 95 | 2nd, Patrick Div. | Lost Quarter-Final |
| 1977-78 | 80 | 29 | 6 | 5 | .... | 16 | 14 | 10 | .... | 45 | 20 | 15 | .... | 296 | 200 | 105 | 2nd, Patrick Div. | Lost Semi-Final |
| 1976-77 | 80 | 33 | 6 | 1 | .... | 15 | 10 | 15 | .... | 48 | 16 | 16 | .... | 323 | 213 | 112 | 1st, Patrick Div. | Lost Semi-Final |
| 1975-76 | 80 | 36 | 2 | 2 | .... | 15 | 11 | 14 | .... | 51 | 13 | 16 | .... | 348 | 209 | 118 | 1st, Patrick Div. | Lost Final |
| **1974-75** | **80** | **32** | **6** | **2** | .... | **19** | **12** | **9** | .... | **51** | **18** | **11** | .... | **293** | **181** | **113** | **1st, Patrick Div.** | **Won Stanley Cup** |
| **1973-74** | **78** | **28** | **6** | **5** | .... | **22** | **10** | **7** | .... | **50** | **16** | **12** | .... | **273** | **164** | **112** | **1st, West Div.** | **Won Stanley Cup** |
| 1972-73 | 78 | 27 | 8 | 4 | .... | 10 | 22 | 7 | .... | 37 | 30 | 11 | .... | 296 | 256 | 85 | 2nd, West Div. | Lost Semi-Final |
| 1971-72 | 78 | 19 | 13 | 7 | .... | 7 | 25 | 7 | .... | 26 | 38 | 14 | .... | 200 | 236 | 66 | 5th, West Div. | Out of Playoffs |
| 1970-71 | 78 | 20 | 10 | 9 | .... | 8 | 23 | 8 | .... | 28 | 33 | 17 | .... | 207 | 225 | 73 | 3rd, West Div. | Lost Quarter-Final |
| 1969-70 | 76 | 11 | 14 | 13 | .... | 6 | 21 | 11 | .... | 17 | 35 | 24 | .... | 197 | 225 | 58 | 5th, West Div. | Out of Playoffs |
| 1968-69 | 76 | 14 | 16 | 8 | .... | 6 | 19 | 13 | .... | 20 | 35 | 21 | .... | 174 | 225 | 61 | 3rd, West Div. | Lost Quarter-Final |
| 1967-68 | 74 | 17 | 13 | 7 | .... | 14 | 19 | 4 | .... | 31 | 32 | 11 | .... | 173 | 179 | 73 | 1st, West Div. | Lost Quarter-Final |

*Philadelphia's first draft pick back in 2003, Jeff Carter reached his full potential in 2008-09. He ranked second in the NHL with 46 goals and also topped the Flyers with 84 points.*

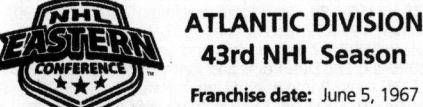

**ATLANTIC DIVISION**
**43rd NHL Season**

**Franchise date:** June 5, 1967

# 2009-10 Player Personnel

| FORWARDS | HT | WT | S | Place of Birth | *Age | 2008-09 Club |
|---|---|---|---|---|---|---|
| ASHAM, Arron | 5-11 | 205 | R | Portage La Prairie, Man. | 31 | Philadelphia |
| BRIERE, Daniel | 5-10 | 179 | R | Gatineau, Que. | 31 | Philadelphia |
| CARCILLO, Daniel | 6-0 | 205 | L | King City, Ont. | 24 | Phoenix-Philadelphia |
| CARTER, Jeff | 6-3 | 200 | R | London, Ont. | 24 | Philadelphia |
| COTE, Riley | 6-2 | 220 | L | Winnipeg, Man. | 27 | Philadelphia |
| GAGNE, Simon | 6-0 | 195 | L | Ste-Foy, Que. | 29 | Philadelphia |
| GIROUX, Claude | 5-11 | 172 | R | Hearst, Ont. | 21 | Phi-Phi (AHL) |
| HARTNELL, Scott | 6-2 | 210 | L | Regina, Sask. | 27 | Philadelphia |
| KALINSKI, Jon | 6-1 | 180 | L | Bonnyville , Alta. | 22 | Phi-Phi (AHL) |
| KASPAR, Lukas | 6-2 | 220 | L | Most, Czech. | 24 | San Jose-Worcester |
| KOLANOS, Krys | 6-3 | 206 | R | Calgary, Alta. | 28 | Minnesota-Houston |
| LAPERRIERE, Ian | 6-1 | 200 | R | Montreal, Que. | 35 | Colorado |
| NODL, Andreas | 6-1 | 190 | L | Vienna, Austria | 22 | Phi-Phi (AHL) |
| POWE, Darroll | 5-11 | 212 | L | Saskatoon, Sask. | 24 | Phi-Phi (AHL) |
| RICHARDS, Mike | 5-11 | 195 | L | Kenora, Ont. | 24 | Philadelphia |
| ROSS, Jared | 5-9 | 165 | L | Huntsville, AL | 27 | Phi-Phi (AHL) |
| WARD, Jason | 6-2 | 208 | R | Chapleau, Ont. | 30 | Tampa Bay-Norfolk |
| **DEFENSEMEN** | | | | | | |
| CARLE, Matt | 6-0 | 205 | L | Anchorage, AK | 25 | Tampa Bay-Philadelphia |
| COBURN, Braydon | 6-5 | 220 | L | Calgary, Alta. | 24 | Philadelphia |
| JONES, Randy | 6-2 | 200 | L | Quispamsis, N.B. | 28 | Phi-Phi (AHL) |
| MORMINA, Joey | 6-6 | 220 | L | Montreal, Que. | 27 | Wilkes-Barre |
| PARENT, Ryan | 6-3 | 183 | L | Prince Albert, Sask. | 22 | Phi-Phi (AHL) |
| PRONGER, Chris | 6-6 | 214 | L | Dryden, Ont. | 34 | Anaheim |
| TIMONEN, Kimmo | 5-10 | 194 | L | Kuopio, Finland | 34 | Philadelphia |
| TOLLEFSEN, Ole-Kristian | 6-2 | 211 | L | Oslo, Norway | 25 | Columbus |

| GOALTENDERS | HT | WT | C | Place of Birth | *Age | 2008-09 Club |
|---|---|---|---|---|---|---|
| BOUCHER, Brian | 6-2 | 200 | L | Woonsocket, RI | 32 | San Jose |
| EMERY, Ray | 6-2 | 196 | L | Cayuga, Ont. | 27 | Mytischi |

* – Age at start of 2009-10 season

## Coaching History

Keith Allen, 1967-68, 1968-69; Vic Stasiuk, 1969-70, 1970-71; Fred Shero, 1971-72 to 1977-78; Bob McCammon and Pat Quinn, 1978-79; Pat Quinn, 1979-80, 1980-81; Pat Quinn and Bob McCammon, 1981-82; Bob McCammon, 1982-83, 1983-84; Mike Keenan, 1984-85 to 1987-88; Paul Holmgren, 1988-89 to 1990-91; Paul Holmgren and Bill Dineen, 1991-92; Bill Dineen, 1992-93; Terry Simpson, 1993-94; Terry Murray, 1994-95 to 1996-97; Wayne Cashman and Roger Neilson, 1997-98; Roger Neilson, 1998-99, 1999-2000; Craig Ramsay and Bill Barber, 2000-01; Bill Barber, 2001-02; Ken Hitchcock, 2002-03 to 2005-06; Ken Hitchcock and John Stevens, 2006-07; John Stevens, 2007-08 to date.

# John Stevens

## Head Coach

*Born: Campbellton, N.B., December 30, 1965.*

John Stevens took over as head coach of the Philadelphia Flyers on October 22, 2006. In his first full season behind the bench in 2007-08, he led the Flyers back to the playoffs after finishing last overall in the NHL the year before. Stevens had been the head coach of the Flyers' American Hockey League affiliate, the Philadelphia Phantoms, for six seasons (2000-01 through 2005-06) and led the team to the Calder Cup championship in 2005. He was named assistant coach of the Flyers on June 5, 2006. Stevens joined the Phantoms coaching staff as an assistant on February 10, 1999 after announcing his retirement from hockey due to an eye injury. He became the second head coach in Phantoms history on June 8, 2000.

Stevens played 15 seasons of professional hockey as a defenseman (1984-85 to 1998-99), including 53 career NHL games with the Flyers and Hartford Whalers. Over parts of five seasons (1986-87 and 1987-88 with the Flyers and 1990-91, 1991-92 and 1993-94 with Hartford), Stevens recorded 10 assists and 48 penalty minutes in 53 games. He was a member of three Calder Cup championship teams as a player (Hershey,1988; Springfield, 1991; and Philadelphia, 1998) and won the Barry Ashbee Award as the Phantoms' top defenseman for the 1996-97 season. He was named the Phantoms' first captain on October 1, 1996. Stevens was originally drafted by the Flyers in the third round (47th overall) of the 1984 NHL Entry Draft.

### Coaching Record

| | | | Regular Season | | | | Playoffs | | | |
|---|---|---|---|---|---|---|---|---|---|---|
| Season | Team | League | GC | W | L | O/T | GC | W | L | T |
| 2000-01 | Philadelphia | AHL | 80 | 36 | 34 | 10 | 10 | 5 | 5 | .... |
| 2001-02 | Philadelphia | AHL | 80 | 33 | 27 | 20 | 5 | 2 | 3 | .... |
| 2002-03 | Philadelphia | AHL | 80 | 33 | 33 | 14 | .... | .... | .... | .... |
| 2003-04 | Philadelphia | AHL | 80 | 46 | 25 | 9 | 12 | 6 | 6 | .... |
| 2004-05 | Philadelphia | AHL | 80 | 48 | 25 | 7 | 21 | 16 | 5 | .... |
| **2006-07** | **Philadelphia** | **NHL** | **74** | **21** | **42** | **11** | .... | .... | .... | .... |
| **2007-08** | **Philadelphia** | **NHL** | **82** | **42** | **29** | **11** | **17** | **9** | **8** | .... |
| **2008-09** | **Philadelphia** | **NHL** | **82** | **44** | **27** | **11** | **6** | **2** | **4** | .... |
| | **NHL Totals** | | **238** | **107** | **98** | **33** | **23** | **11** | **12** | .... |

# 2008-09 Scoring

* – rookie

## Regular Season

| Pos | # | Player | Team | GP | G | A | Pts | TOI | +/- | PIM | PP | SH | GW | S | % |
|---|---|---|---|---|---|---|---|---|---|---|---|---|---|---|---|
| C | 17 | Jeff Carter | PHI | 82 | 46 | 38 | 84 | 20:57 | 23 | 68 | 13 | 4 | 12 | 342 | 13.5 |
| C | 18 | Mike Richards | PHI | 79 | 30 | 50 | 80 | 21:44 | 22 | 63 | 8 | 7 | 4 | 238 | 12.6 |
| L | 12 | Simon Gagne | PHI | 79 | 34 | 40 | 74 | 19:01 | 21 | 42 | 12 | 4 | 3 | 221 | 15.4 |
| L | 19 | Scott Hartnell | PHI | 82 | 30 | 30 | 60 | 17:48 | 14 | 143 | 6 | 1 | 5 | 210 | 14.3 |
| R | 15 | Joffrey Lupul | PHI | 79 | 25 | 25 | 50 | 15:41 | 1 | 58 | 6 | 0 | 4 | 194 | 12.9 |
| R | 22 | Mike Knuble | PHI | 82 | 27 | 20 | 47 | 18:10 | 5 | 62 | 11 | 0 | 6 | 173 | 15.6 |
| D | 44 | Kimmo Timonen | PHI | 77 | 3 | 40 | 43 | 24:31 | 19 | 54 | 2 | 0 | 0 | 104 | 2.9 |
| D | 5 | Braydon Coburn | PHI | 80 | 7 | 21 | 28 | 24:37 | 7 | 97 | 3 | 0 | 0 | 130 | 5.4 |
| R | 28 * | Claude Giroux | PHI | 42 | 9 | 18 | 27 | 15:09 | 10 | 14 | 2 | 0 | 0 | 67 | 13.4 |
| D | 25 | Matthew Carle | T.B. | 12 | 1 | 1 | 2 | 21:57 | 1 | 6 | 0 | 0 | 0 | 13 | 7.7 |
| | | | PHI | 64 | 4 | 20 | 24 | 21:17 | 2 | 16 | 0 | 0 | 2 | 72 | 5.6 |
| | | | Total | 76 | 5 | 21 | 26 | 21:23 | 3 | 22 | 0 | 0 | 2 | 85 | 5.9 |
| C | 48 | Daniel Briere | PHI | 29 | 11 | 14 | 25 | 15:39 | –1 | 26 | 4 | 0 | 0 | 54 | 20.4 |
| R | 45 | Arron Asham | PHI | 78 | 8 | 12 | 20 | 8:44 | 0 | 155 | 0 | 0 | 1 | 74 | 10.8 |
| L | 13 | Daniel Carcillo | PHX | 54 | 3 | 7 | 10 | 11:58 | –13 | 174 | 2 | 0 | 0 | 95 | 3.2 |
| | | | PHI | 20 | 0 | 4 | 4 | 10:16 | –2 | 80 | 0 | 0 | 0 | 35 | 0.0 |
| | | | Total | 74 | 3 | 11 | 14 | 11:31 | –15 | 254 | 2 | 0 | 0 | 130 | 2.3 |
| D | 41 | Andrew Alberts | PHI | 79 | 1 | 12 | 13 | 15:47 | 6 | 61 | 0 | 0 | 0 | 46 | 2.2 |
| C | 36 * | Darroll Powe | PHI | 60 | 6 | 5 | 11 | 10:32 | –8 | 35 | 0 | 0 | 0 | 72 | 8.3 |
| D | 6 | Randy Jones | PHI | 47 | 4 | 4 | 8 | 19:07 | 8 | 22 | 1 | 0 | 2 | 45 | 8.9 |
| D | 47 * | Luca Sbisa | PHI | 39 | 0 | 7 | 7 | 17:28 | –6 | 36 | 0 | 0 | 0 | 38 | 0.0 |
| R | 14 * | Andreas Nodl | PHI | 38 | 1 | 3 | 4 | 11:08 | –15 | 2 | 0 | 0 | 0 | 33 | 3.0 |
| D | 77 * | Ryan Parent | PHI | 31 | 0 | 4 | 4 | 18:12 | 3 | 10 | 0 | 0 | 0 | 9 | 0.0 |
| L | 46 * | Jon Kalinski | PHI | 12 | 1 | 2 | 3 | 7:36 | –2 | 0 | 0 | 0 | 1 | 7 | 14.3 |
| L | 24 | Josh Gratton | PHI | 19 | 1 | 2 | 3 | 6:14 | –2 | 57 | 0 | 0 | 0 | 14 | 7.1 |
| L | 32 | Riley Cote | PHI | 63 | 0 | 3 | 3 | 4:09 | –7 | 174 | 0 | 0 | 0 | 24 | 0.0 |
| D | 3 | Lasse Kukkonen | PHI | 22 | 0 | 2 | 2 | 10:42 | –2 | 10 | 0 | 0 | 0 | 10 | 0.0 |
| L | 11 | Boyd Kane | PHI | 1 | 0 | 0 | 0 | 8:12 | 0 | 0 | 0 | 0 | 0 | 0 | 0.0 |
| D | 29 | Nathan Guenin | PHI | 1 | 0 | 0 | 0 | 13:25 | 0 | 0 | 0 | 0 | 0 | 0 | 0.0 |
| R | 60 * | Nate Raduns | PHI | 1 | 0 | 0 | 0 | 6:02 | 0 | 0 | 0 | 0 | 0 | 0 | 0.0 |
| D | 40 * | David Sloane | PHI | 1 | 0 | 0 | 0 | 6:44 | 0 | 0 | 0 | 0 | 0 | 0 | 0.0 |
| D | 51 * | Jamie Fritsch | PHI | 1 | 0 | 0 | 0 | 4:34 | 1 | 0 | 0 | 0 | 0 | 0 | 0.0 |
| D | 26 | Danny Syvret | PHI | 2 | 0 | 0 | 0 | 9:25 | –1 | 0 | 0 | 0 | 0 | 0 | 0.0 |
| C | 42 * | Jared Ross | PHI | 10 | 0 | 0 | 0 | 7:44 | –4 | 2 | 0 | 0 | 0 | 12 | 0.0 |

### Goaltending

| No. | Goaltender | GPI | Mins | Avg | W | L | OT | EN | SO | GA | SA | S% | G | A | PIM |
|---|---|---|---|---|---|---|---|---|---|---|---|---|---|---|---|
| 30 | Antero Niittymaki | 32 | 1805 | 2.76 | 15 | 8 | 6 | 1 | 1 | 83 | 947 | .912 | 0 | 1 | 2 |
| 43 | Martin Biron | 55 | 3177 | 2.76 | 29 | 19 | 5 | 2 | 2 | 146 | 1718 | .915 | 0 | 4 | 0 |
| | **Totals** | **82** | **5005** | **2.78** | **44** | **27** | **11** | **3** | **3** | **232** | **2668** | **.913** | | | |

## Playoffs

| Pos | # | Player | Team | GP | G | A | Pts | TOI | +/- | PIM | PP | SH | GW | OT | S | % |
|---|---|---|---|---|---|---|---|---|---|---|---|---|---|---|---|---|
| R | 28 * | Claude Giroux | PHI | 6 | 2 | 3 | 5 | 15:56 | 2 | 6 | 0 | 0 | 0 | 0 | 9 | 22.2 |
| C | 18 | Mike Richards | PHI | 6 | 1 | 4 | 5 | 22:57 | –4 | 6 | 1 | 0 | 0 | 0 | 21 | 4.8 |
| L | 12 | Simon Gagne | PHI | 6 | 3 | 1 | 4 | 20:28 | –4 | 2 | 1 | 1 | 1 | 0 | 19 | 15.8 |
| C | 48 | Daniel Briere | PHI | 6 | 1 | 3 | 4 | 16:41 | –1 | 8 | 1 | 0 | 0 | 0 | 10 | 10.0 |
| R | 22 | Mike Knuble | PHI | 6 | 2 | 1 | 3 | 18:26 | –2 | 2 | 0 | 0 | 0 | 0 | 19 | 10.5 |
| C | 36 * | Darroll Powe | PHI | 6 | 1 | 2 | 3 | 14:01 | 0 | 7 | 0 | 0 | 0 | 0 | 10 | 10.0 |
| D | 5 | Braydon Coburn | PHI | 6 | 0 | 3 | 3 | 26:29 | 2 | 7 | 0 | 0 | 0 | 0 | 4 | 0.0 |
| D | 25 | Matthew Carle | PHI | 6 | 0 | 3 | 3 | 22:15 | 0 | 4 | 0 | 0 | 0 | 0 | 13 | 0.0 |
| L | 13 | Daniel Carcillo | PHI | 5 | 1 | 1 | 2 | 8:11 | 3 | 5 | 0 | 0 | 0 | 0 | 4 | 25.0 |
| R | 45 | Arron Asham | PHI | 6 | 1 | 1 | 2 | 7:54 | –1 | 6 | 0 | 0 | 1 | 0 | 4 | 25.0 |
| L | 19 | Scott Hartnell | PHI | 6 | 1 | 1 | 2 | 18:35 | –2 | 23 | 1 | 0 | 0 | 0 | 15 | 6.7 |
| R | 15 | Joffrey Lupul | PHI | 6 | 1 | 1 | 2 | 17:07 | 1 | 2 | 0 | 0 | 0 | 0 | 14 | 7.1 |
| C | 17 | Jeff Carter | PHI | 6 | 1 | 0 | 1 | 20:20 | –2 | 8 | 0 | 0 | 0 | 0 | 30 | 3.3 |
| C | 42 * | Jared Ross | PHI | 6 | 1 | 0 | 1 | 4:09 | 0 | 0 | 0 | 0 | 0 | 0 | 3 | 33.3 |
| D | 44 | Kimmo Timonen | PHI | 6 | 0 | 1 | 1 | 26:21 | –3 | 12 | 0 | 0 | 0 | 0 | 10 | 0.0 |
| D | 41 | Andrew Alberts | PHI | 6 | 0 | 1 | 1 | 13:39 | 1 | 10 | 0 | 0 | 0 | 0 | 2 | 0.0 |
| D | 6 | Randy Jones | PHI | 6 | 0 | 1 | 1 | 14:38 | 1 | 0 | 0 | 0 | 0 | 0 | 4 | 0.0 |
| D | 47 * | Luca Sbisa | PHI | 1 | 0 | 0 | 0 | 5:37 | 0 | 2 | 0 | 0 | 0 | 0 | 0 | 0.0 |
| D | 77 * | Ryan Parent | PHI | 6 | 0 | 0 | 0 | 18:52 | –3 | 6 | 0 | 0 | 0 | 0 | 3 | 0.0 |

### Goaltending

| No. | Goaltender | GPI | Mins | Avg | W | L | EN | SO | GA | SA | S% | G | A | PIM |
|---|---|---|---|---|---|---|---|---|---|---|---|---|---|---|
| 43 | Martin Biron | 6 | 375 | 2.56 | 2 | 4 | 2 | 1 | 16 | 198 | .919 | 0 | 0 | 0 |
| | **Totals** | **6** | **378** | **2.86** | **2** | **4** | **2** | **1** | **18** | **200** | **.910** | | | |

## Captains' History

Lou Angotti, 1967-68; Ed Van Impe, 1968-69 to 1971-72; Ed Van Impe and Bobby Clarke, 1972-73; Bobby Clarke, 1973-74 to 1978-79; Mel Bridgman, 1979-80, 1980-81; Bill Barber, 1981-82; Bill Barber and Bobby Clarke, 1982-83; Bobby Clarke, 1983-84; Dave Poulin, 1984-85 to 1988-89; Dave Poulin and Ron Sutter, 1989-90; Ron Sutter, 1990-91; Rick Tocchet, 1991-92; no captain, 1992-93; Kevin Dineen, 1993-94; Eric Lindros, 1994-95 to 1998-99; Eric Lindros and Eric Desjardins, 1999-2000; Eric Desjardins, 2000-01; Eric Desjardins and Keith Primeau, 2001-02; Keith Primeau, 2002-03, 2003-04; Keith Primeau and Derian Hatcher, 2005-06; Peter Forsberg, 2006-07; Jason Smith, 2007-08; Mike Richards, 2008-09 to date.

# Club Records

## Team

(Figures in brackets for season records are games played; records for fewest points, wins, ties, losses, goals, goals against are for 70 or more games)

| | | |
|---|---|---|
| **Most Points** | **118** | 1975-76 (80) |
| **Most Wins** | **53** | 1984-85 (80), 1985-86 (80) |
| **Most Ties** | ***24** | 1969-70 (76) |
| **Most Losses** | **48** | 2006-07 (82) |
| **Most Goals** | **350** | 1983-84 (80) |
| **Most Goals Against** | **319** | 1992-93 (84) |
| **Fewest Points** | **56** | 2006-07 (82) |
| **Fewest Wins** | **17** | 1969-70 (76) |
| **Fewest Ties** | **4** | 1985-86 (80) |
| **Fewest Losses** | **12** | 1979-80 (80) |
| **Fewest Goals** | **173** | 1967-68 (74) |
| **Fewest Goals Against** | **164** | 1973-74 (78) |
| **Longest Winning Streak** | | |
| **Overall** | **13** | Oct. 19-Nov. 17/85 |
| **Home** | ***20** | Jan. 4-Apr. 3/76 |
| **Away** | **8** | Dec. 22/82-Jan. 16/83 |
| **Longest Undefeated Streak** | | |
| **Overall** | ***35** | Oct. 14/79-Jan. 6/80 (25 wins, 10 ties) |
| **Home** | **26** | Oct. 11/79-Feb. 3/80 (19 wins, 7 ties) |
| **Away** | **16** | Oct. 20/79-Jan. 6/80 (11 wins, 5 ties) |
| **Longest Losing Streak** | | |
| **Overall** | **9** | Dec. 8-27/06 |
| **Home** | **13** | Nov. 29/06-Feb. 8/07 |
| **Away** | **8** | Oct. 25-Nov. 26/72, Mar. 3-29/88 |
| **Longest Winless Streak** | | |
| **Overall** | **12** | Feb. 24-Mar. 16/99 (8 losses, 4 ties) |
| **Home** | **13** | Nov. 29/06-Feb. 8/07 (13 losses) |
| **Away** | **19** | Oct. 23/71-Jan. 27/72 (15 losses, 4 ties) |
| **Most Shutouts, Season** | **13** | 1974-75 (80) |
| **Most PIM, Season** | **2,621** | 1980-81 (80) |
| **Most Goals, Game** | **13** | Mar. 22/84 (Pit. 4 at Phi. 13), Oct. 18/84 (Van. 2 at Phi. 13) |

## Individual

| | | |
|---|---|---|
| **Most Seasons** | **15** | Bobby Clarke |
| **Most Games** | **1,144** | Bobby Clarke |
| **Most Goals, Career** | **420** | Bill Barber |
| **Most Assists, Career** | **852** | Bobby Clarke |
| **Most Points, Career** | **1,210** | Bobby Clarke (358G, 852A) |
| **Most PIM, Career** | **1,817** | Rick Tocchet |
| **Most Shutouts, Career** | **50** | Bernie Parent |
| **Longest Consecutive Game Streak** | **484** | Rod Brind'Amour (Feb. 24/93-Apr. 18/99) |
| **Most Goals, Season** | **61** | Reggie Leach (1975-76) |
| **Most Assists, Season** | **89** | Bobby Clarke (1974-75), (1975-76) |
| **Most Points, Season** | **123** | Mark Recchi (1992-93; 53G, 70A) |
| **Most PIM, Season** | ***472** | Dave Schultz (1974-75) |
| **Most Points, Defenseman, Season** | **82** | Mark Howe (1985-86; 24G, 58A) |
| **Most Points, Center, Season** | **119** | Bobby Clarke (1975-76; 30G, 89A) |
| **Most Points, Right Wing, Season** | **123** | Mark Recchi (1992-93; 53G, 70A) |
| **Most Points, Left Wing, Season** | **112** | Bill Barber (1975-76; 50G, 62A) |
| **Most Points, Rookie, Season** | **82** | Mikael Renberg (1993-94; 38G, 44A) |
| **Most Shutouts, Season** | **12** | Bernie Parent (1973-74), (1974-75) |
| **Most Goals, Game** | **4** | Sixteen times |
| **Most Assists, Game** | **6** | Eric Lindros (Feb. 26/97) |
| **Most Points, Game** | **8** | Tom Bladon (Dec. 11/77; 4G, 4A) |

* NHL Record.

## Retired Numbers

| | | |
|---|---|---|
| 1 | Bernie Parent | 1967-1971, 1973-1979 |
| 4 | Barry Ashbee | 1970-1974 |
| 7 | Bill Barber | 1972-1985 |
| 16 | Bobby Clarke | 1969-1984 |

# All-time Record vs. Other Clubs

## Regular Season

| | At Home | | | | | | | | On Road | | | | | | | | Total | | | | | | | |
|---|---|---|---|---|---|---|---|---|---|---|---|---|---|---|---|---|---|---|---|---|---|---|---|---|
| | GP | W | L | T | OL | GF | GA | PTS | GP | W | L | T | OL | GF | GA | PTS | GP | W | L | T | OL | GF | GA | PTS |
| Anaheim | 9 | 4 | 2 | 3 | 0 | 25 | 17 | 11 | 11 | 5 | 3 | 2 | 1 | 40 | 38 | 13 | 20 | 9 | 5 | 5 | 1 | 65 | 55 | 24 |
| Atlanta | 18 | 14 | 1 | 2 | 1 | 77 | 49 | 31 | 18 | 15 | 2 | 1 | 0 | 66 | 37 | 31 | 36 | 29 | 3 | 3 | 1 | 143 | 86 | 62 |
| Boston | 81 | 34 | 35 | 10 | 2 | 264 | 243 | 80 | 84 | 25 | 45 | 11 | 3 | 236 | 302 | 64 | 165 | 59 | 80 | 21 | 5 | 500 | 545 | 144 |
| Buffalo | 75 | 43 | 17 | 12 | 3 | 260 | 194 | 101 | 71 | 27 | 36 | 8 | 0 | 201 | 240 | 62 | 146 | 70 | 53 | 20 | 3 | 461 | 434 | 163 |
| Calgary | 53 | 34 | 15 | 3 | 1 | 201 | 142 | 72 | 53 | 19 | 25 | 9 | 0 | 175 | 210 | 47 | 106 | 53 | 40 | 12 | 1 | 376 | 352 | 119 |
| Carolina | 51 | 33 | 10 | 5 | 3 | 190 | 132 | 74 | 52 | 28 | 14 | 9 | 1 | 189 | 162 | 66 | 103 | 61 | 24 | 14 | 4 | 379 | 294 | 140 |
| Chicago | 63 | 36 | 16 | 11 | 0 | 207 | 162 | 83 | 62 | 16 | 27 | 19 | 0 | 176 | 212 | 51 | 125 | 52 | 43 | 30 | 0 | 383 | 374 | 134 |
| Colorado | 36 | 23 | 9 | 2 | 2 | 130 | 97 | 50 | 37 | 11 | 13 | 12 | 1 | 125 | 131 | 35 | 73 | 34 | 22 | 14 | 3 | 255 | 228 | 85 |
| Columbus | 3 | 2 | 0 | 1 | 0 | 10 | 5 | 5 | 5 | 2 | 1 | 2 | 0 | 10 | 10 | 6 | 8 | 4 | 1 | 3 | 0 | 20 | 15 | 11 |
| Dallas | 69 | 43 | 10 | 16 | 0 | 260 | 157 | 102 | 67 | 23 | 28 | 16 | 0 | 214 | 219 | 62 | 136 | 66 | 38 | 32 | 0 | 474 | 376 | 164 |
| Detroit | 59 | 35 | 13 | 11 | 0 | 236 | 169 | 81 | 61 | 18 | 33 | 10 | 0 | 187 | 219 | 46 | 120 | 53 | 46 | 21 | 0 | 423 | 388 | 127 |
| Edmonton | 33 | 20 | 11 | 2 | 0 | 134 | 93 | 42 | 29 | 8 | 15 | 6 | 0 | 86 | 103 | 22 | 62 | 28 | 26 | 8 | 0 | 220 | 196 | 64 |
| Florida | 33 | 14 | 11 | 6 | 2 | 87 | 84 | 36 | 32 | 22 | 9 | 1 | 0 | 107 | 74 | 45 | 65 | 36 | 20 | 7 | 2 | 194 | 158 | 81 |
| Los Angeles | 65 | 42 | 15 | 7 | 1 | 249 | 158 | 92 | 68 | 38 | 21 | 8 | 1 | 228 | 198 | 85 | 133 | 80 | 36 | 15 | 2 | 477 | 356 | 177 |
| Minnesota | 6 | 5 | 1 | 0 | 0 | 17 | 6 | 10 | 3 | 1 | 1 | 1 | 0 | 6 | 6 | 3 | 9 | 6 | 2 | 1 | 0 | 23 | 12 | 13 |
| Montreal | 81 | 30 | 33 | 16 | 2 | 244 | 249 | 78 | 82 | 28 | 38 | 14 | 2 | 243 | 280 | 72 | 163 | 58 | 71 | 30 | 4 | 487 | 529 | 150 |
| Nashville | 7 | 3 | 2 | 1 | 1 | 23 | 13 | 8 | 5 | 2 | 0 | 2 | 1 | 10 | 8 | 7 | 12 | 5 | 2 | 3 | 2 | 33 | 21 | 15 |
| New Jersey | 100 | 59 | 27 | 10 | 4 | 368 | 259 | 132 | 98 | 34 | 52 | 8 | 4 | 309 | 334 | 80 | 198 | 93 | 79 | 18 | 8 | 677 | 593 | 212 |
| NY Islanders | 110 | 65 | 32 | 11 | 2 | 389 | 303 | 143 | 113 | 44 | 52 | 15 | 2 | 340 | 394 | 105 | 223 | 109 | 84 | 26 | 4 | 729 | 697 | 248 |
| NY Rangers | 124 | 59 | 48 | 14 | 3 | 393 | 352 | 135 | 125 | 48 | 51 | 23 | 3 | 366 | 395 | 122 | 249 | 107 | 99 | 37 | 6 | 759 | 747 | 257 |
| Ottawa | 31 | 18 | 10 | 2 | 1 | 105 | 89 | 39 | 32 | 12 | 12 | 6 | 2 | 92 | 94 | 32 | 63 | 30 | 22 | 8 | 3 | 197 | 183 | 71 |
| Phoenix | 33 | 24 | 9 | 0 | 0 | 140 | 89 | 48 | 32 | 16 | 14 | 2 | 0 | 106 | 103 | 34 | 65 | 40 | 23 | 2 | 0 | 246 | 192 | 82 |
| Pittsburgh | 121 | 89 | 22 | 8 | 2 | 505 | 312 | 188 | 121 | 43 | 53 | 22 | 3 | 386 | 427 | 111 | 242 | 132 | 75 | 30 | 5 | 891 | 739 | 299 |
| St. Louis | 68 | 46 | 12 | 10 | 0 | 268 | 156 | 102 | 70 | 36 | 27 | 7 | 0 | 224 | 200 | 79 | 138 | 82 | 39 | 17 | 0 | 492 | 356 | 181 |
| San Jose | 13 | 6 | 4 | 2 | 1 | 43 | 37 | 15 | 14 | 7 | 4 | 2 | 1 | 36 | 33 | 17 | 27 | 13 | 8 | 4 | 2 | 79 | 70 | 32 |
| Tampa Bay | 33 | 16 | 8 | 7 | 2 | 97 | 77 | 41 | 34 | 19 | 14 | 1 | 0 | 101 | 101 | 39 | 67 | 35 | 22 | 8 | 2 | 198 | 178 | 80 |
| Toronto | 75 | 46 | 21 | 8 | 0 | 280 | 181 | 100 | 75 | 32 | 27 | 14 | 2 | 245 | 236 | 80 | 150 | 78 | 48 | 22 | 2 | 525 | 417 | 180 |
| Vancouver | 55 | 37 | 17 | 1 | 0 | 238 | 164 | 75 | 53 | 31 | 10 | 12 | 0 | 214 | 148 | 74 | 108 | 68 | 27 | 13 | 0 | 452 | 312 | 149 |
| Washington | 91 | 56 | 28 | 6 | 1 | 345 | 245 | 119 | 88 | 38 | 34 | 13 | 3 | 282 | 286 | 92 | 179 | 94 | 62 | 19 | 4 | 627 | 531 | 211 |
| Defunct Clubs | 34 | 24 | 4 | 6 | 0 | 137 | 67 | 54 | 35 | 13 | 14 | 8 | 0 | 102 | 89 | 34 | 69 | 37 | 18 | 14 | 0 | 239 | 156 | 88 |
| **Totals** | **1630** | **960** | **443** | **193** | **34** | **5922** | **4301** | **2147** | **1630** | **661** | **675** | **264** | **30** | **5102** | **5289** | **1616** | **3260** | **1621** | **1118** | **457** | **64** | **11024** | **9590** | **3763** |

## Playoffs

| | Series | W | L | GP | W | L | T | GF | GA | Last Mtg. | Rnd. | Result |
|---|---|---|---|---|---|---|---|---|---|---|---|---|
| Boston | 4 | 2 | 2 | 20 | 9 | 11 | 0 | 57 | 60 | 1978 | SF | L 1-4 |
| Buffalo | 8 | 5 | 3 | 43 | 25 | 18 | 0 | 124 | 123 | 2006 | CQF | L 2-4 |
| Calgary | 2 | 1 | 1 | 11 | 7 | 4 | 0 | 43 | 28 | 1981 | QF | L 3-4 |
| Chicago | 1 | 0 | 1 | 4 | 0 | 4 | 0 | 8 | 20 | 1971 | QF | L 0-4 |
| Colorado | 2 | 2 | 0 | 11 | 7 | 4 | 0 | 39 | 29 | 1985 | CF | W 4-2 |
| Dallas | 2 | 2 | 0 | 11 | 8 | 3 | 0 | 41 | 26 | 1980 | SF | W 4-1 |
| Detroit | 1 | 0 | 1 | 4 | 0 | 4 | 0 | 6 | 16 | 1997 | F | L 0-4 |
| Edmonton | 3 | 1 | 2 | 15 | 7 | 8 | 0 | 44 | 49 | 1987 | F | L 3-4 |
| Florida | 1 | 0 | 1 | 6 | 2 | 4 | 0 | 11 | 15 | 1996 | CSF | L 2-4 |
| Montreal | 5 | 2 | 3 | 26 | 11 | 15 | 0 | 72 | 86 | 2008 | CSF | W 4-1 |
| New Jersey | 4 | 2 | 2 | 20 | 11 | 9 | 0 | 49 | 50 | 2004 | CQF | W 4-1 |
| NY Islanders | 4 | 3 | 1 | 25 | 14 | 11 | 0 | 83 | 69 | 1987 | DF | W 4-3 |
| NY Rangers | 10 | 6 | 4 | 47 | 27 | 20 | 0 | 157 | 153 | 1997 | CF | W 4-1 |
| Ottawa | 2 | 0 | 2 | 11 | 3 | 8 | 0 | 12 | 28 | 2003 | CSF | L 2-4 |
| Pittsburgh | 5 | 3 | 2 | 29 | 15 | 14 | 0 | 91 | 89 | 2009 | CQF | L 2-4 |
| St. Louis | 2 | 0 | 2 | 11 | 3 | 8 | 0 | 20 | 34 | 1969 | QF | L 0-4 |
| Tampa Bay | 2 | 1 | 1 | 13 | 7 | 6 | 0 | 45 | 34 | 2004 | CF | L 3-4 |
| Toronto | 6 | 5 | 1 | 36 | 22 | 14 | 0 | 119 | 85 | 2004 | CSF | W 4-2 |
| Vancouver | 1 | 1 | 0 | 3 | 2 | 1 | 0 | 15 | 9 | 1979 | PRE | W 2-1 |
| Washington | 4 | 2 | 2 | 23 | 11 | 12 | 0 | 78 | 85 | 2008 | CQF | W 4-3 |
| **Totals** | **69** | **38** | **31** | **369** | **191** | **178** | **0** | **1114** | **1088** | | | |

Calgary totals include Atlanta Flames, 1972-73 to 1979-80. Carolina totals include Hartford, 1979-80 to 1996-97.
Colorado totals include Quebec, 1979-80 to 1994-95. Dallas totals include Minnesota North Stars, 1967-68 to 1992-93.
New Jersey totals include Kansas City, 1974-75, 1975-76, and Colorado Rockies, 1976-77 to 1981-82.
Phoenix totals include Winnipeg, 1979-80 to 1995-96.

## Playoff Results 2009-2004

| Year | Round | Opponent | Result | GF | GA |
|---|---|---|---|---|---|
| 2009 | CQF | Pittsburgh | L 2-4 | 16 | 18 |
| 2008 | CF | Pittsburgh | L 1-4 | 9 | 20 |
| | CSF | Montreal | W 4-1 | 20 | 14 |
| | CQF | Washington | W 4-3 | 23 | 20 |
| 2006 | CQF | Buffalo | L 2-4 | 14 | 27 |
| 2004 | CF | Tampa Bay | L 3-4 | 19 | 21 |
| | CSF | Toronto | W 4-2 | 17 | 13 |
| | CQF | New Jersey | W 4-1 | 14 | 9 |

**Abbreviations: Round: F** – Final; **CF** – conference final; **CSF** – conference semi-final; **CQF** – conference quarter-final; **DF** – division final; **SF** – semi-final; **QF** – quarter-final; **PRE** – preliminary round.

## 2008-09 Results

| | | | | | | | |
|---|---|---|---|---|---|---|---|
| **Oct.** | 11 | NY Rangers | 3-4 | | 10 | Toronto | 4-1 |
| | 13 | Montreal | 3-5 | | 13 | Pittsburgh | 2-4 |
| | 14 | at Pittsburgh | 2-3* | | 15 | at Tampa Bay | 1-4 |
| | 16 | at Colorado | 2-5 | | 16 | at Florida | 3-2† |
| | 18 | at San Jose | 4-5* | | 21 | Atlanta | 5-3 |
| | 22 | San Jose | 6-7† | | 27 | at Florida | 2-3 |
| | 24 | at New Jersey | 6-3 | | 30 | at Tampa Bay | 6-1 |
| | 25 | New Jersey | 3-2* | | 31 | at St. Louis | 0-4 |
| | 28 | at Atlanta | 7-0 | **Feb.** | 4 | Boston | 1-3 |
| | 30 | NY Islanders | 3-2* | | 7 | at Boston | 4-3* |
| **Nov.** | 2 | Edmonton | 4-5 | | 8 | at Atlanta | 3-2 |
| | 6 | at Ottawa | 1-4 | | 12 | Ottawa | 2-5 |
| | 8 | Tampa Bay | 1-2 | | 14 | NY Islanders | 5-1 |
| | 11 | at NY Islanders | 3-1 | | 15 | at NY Rangers | 5-2 |
| | 13 | at Pittsburgh | 4-5† | | 19 | Buffalo | 6-3 |
| | 15 | at Montreal | 2-1 | | 21 | Pittsburgh | 4-5 |
| | 16 | Atlanta | 4-3 | | 24 | at Washington | 4-2 |
| | 21 | at Buffalo | 3-0 | | 25 | Los Angeles | 2-0 |
| | 22 | Phoenix | 4-3* | | 27 | Montreal | 3-4* |
| | 24 | Dallas | 4-3 | **Mar.** | 1 | at New Jersey | 0-3 |
| | 26 | at Carolina | 3-1 | | 3 | at Boston | 4-2 |
| | 28 | Carolina | 2-3* | | 5 | Calgary | 1-5 |
| | 29 | at Toronto | 2-4 | | 7 | Nashville | 4-1 |
| **Dec.** | 2 | Tampa Bay | 4-3* | | 10 | Buffalo | 5-2 |
| | 4 | New Jersey | 2-3* | | 12 | Washington | 1-2 |
| | 6 | at Carolina | 2-1* | | 14 | NY Rangers | 4-2 |
| | 9 | NY Islanders | 4-3 | | 15 | at NY Rangers | 1-4 |
| | 11 | Carolina | 6-5† | | 17 | at Detroit | 2-3 |
| | 13 | Pittsburgh | 6-3 | | 20 | at Buffalo | 6-4 |
| | 16 | Colorado | 5-2 | | 22 | at Pittsburgh | 3-1 |
| | 18 | at Montreal | 2-5 | | 23 | New Jersey | 4-2 |
| | 20 | Washington | 7-1 | | 26 | Florida | 2-4 |
| | 21 | at New Jersey | 2-3† | | 28 | at NY Islanders | 4-3† |
| | 23 | Ottawa | 6-4 | | 29 | Boston | 3-4 |
| | 26 | at Chicago | 1-5 | **Apr.** | 1 | at Toronto | 2-3 |
| | 27 | at Columbus | 0-3 | | 3 | Toronto | 8-5 |
| | 30 | at Vancouver | 3-2 | | 4 | at Ottawa | 3-4† |
| **Jan.** | 2 | at Anaheim | 5-4† | | 7 | Florida | 2-1 |
| | 3 | at Los Angeles | 1-2† | | 9 | at NY Rangers | 1-2 |
| | 6 | at Washington | 1-2† | | 11 | at NY Islanders | 3-2 |
| | 8 | Minnesota | 3-1 | | 12 | NY Rangers | 3-4 |

* – Overtime † – Shootout

## Entry Draft Selections 2009-1995

Name in bold denotes played in NHL.

**2009**
Pick
81 Adam Morrison
87 Simon Bertilsson
142 Nicola Riopel
153 Dave Labrecque
172 Eric Wellwood
196 Oliver Lauridsen

**2008**
Pick
19 **Luca Sbisa**
67 Marc-Andre Bourdon
84 Jacob Deserres
178 Zac Rinaldo
196 Joacim Eriksson

**2007**
Pick
2 James vanRiemsdyk
41 Kevin Marshall
66 Garrett Klotz
122 Mario Kempe
152 **Jonathon Kalinski**
161 Patrick Maroon
182 Brad Phillips

**2006**
Pick
22 **Claude Giroux**
39 **Andreas Nodl**
42 Michael Ratchuk
55 Denis Bodrov
79 Jonathan Matsumoto
101 Joonas Lehtivuori
109 Jakub Kovar
145 Jonathan Rheault
175 Michael Dupont
205 Andrei Popov

**2005**
Pick
29 **Steve Downie**
91 Oskars Bartulis
119 Jeremy Duchesne
152 Josh Beaulieu
174 John Flatters
215 Matt Clackson

**2004**
Pick
92 Rob Bellamy
101 R.J. Anderson
124 David Laliberte
144 Chris Zarb
149 Gino Pisellini
170 Ladislav Scurko
171 Frederik Cabana
232 **Martin Houle**
253 Travis Gawryletz
286 **Triston Grant**
291 John Carter

**2003**
Pick
11 **Jeff Carter**
24 **Mike Richards**
69 **Colin Fraser**
81 **Stefan Ruzicka**
85 **Alexandre Picard**
87 **Ryan Potulny**
95 Rick Kozak
108 Kevin Romy
140 David Tremblay
191 Rejean Beauchemin
193 Ville Hostikka

**2002**
Pick
4 **Joni Pitkanen**
105 Rosario Ruggeri
126 Konstantin Baranov
161 Dov Grumet-Morris
192 Nikita Korovkin
193 **Joey Mormina**
201 Mathieu Brunelle

**2001**
Pick
27 **Jeff Woywitka**
95 **Patrick Sharp**
146 **Jussi Timonen**
150 Bernd Bruckler
158 Roman Malek
172 **Dennis Seidenberg**
177 Andrei Razin
208 Thierry Douville
225 **David Printz**

**2000**
Pick
28 **Justin Williams**
94 Alexander Drozdetsky
171 **Roman Cechmanek**
195 Colin Shields
210 John Eichelberger
227 **Guillaume Lefebvre**
259 Regan Kelly
287 Milan Kopecky

**1999**
Pick
22 **Maxime Ouellet**
119 Jeff Feniak
160 Konstantin Rudenko
200 Pavel Kasparik
208 **Vaclav Pletka**
224 David Nystrom

**1998**
Pick
22 **Simon Gagne**
42 Jason Beckett
51 Ian Forbes
109 Jean-Philippe Morin
124 **Francis Belanger**
139 Garrett Prosofsky
168 **Antero Niittymaki**
175 Cam Ondrik
195 **Tomas Divisek**
222 Lubomir Pistek
243 **Petr Hubacek**
253 **Bruno St. Jacques**
258 Sergei Skrobot

**1997**
Pick
30 **Jean-Marc Pelletier**
50 **Pat Kavanagh**
62 Kris Mallette
103 Mikhail Chernov
158 Jordon Flodell
164 **Todd Fedoruk**
214 Marko Kauppinen
240 Par Styf

**1996**
Pick
15 **Dainius Zubrus**
64 Chester Gallant
124 Per-Ragna Bergqvist
133 **Jesse Boulerice**
187 Roman Malov
213 Jeff Milleker

**1995**
Pick
22 **Brian Boucher**
48 Shane Kenny
100 **Radovan Somik**
132 **Dmitri Tertyshny**
135 Jamie Sokolsky
152 **Martin Spanhel**
178 Martin Streit
204 Ruslan Shafikov
230 **Jeff Lank**

## General Managers' History

Bud Poile, 1967-68, 1968-69; Bud Poile and Keith Allen, 1969-70; Keith Allen, 1970-71 to 1982-83; Bob McCammon, 1983-84; Bob Clarke, 1984-85 to 1989-90; Russ Farwell, 1990-91 to 1993-94; Bob Clarke, 1994-95 to 2005-06; Bob Clarke and Paul Holmgren, 2006-07; Paul Holmgren, 2007-08 to date.

# Paul Holmgren

### General Manager

*Born: St. Paul, MN, December 2, 1955.*

Paul Holmgren was named interim general manager of the Philadelphia Flyers on November 11, 2006, replacing Bob Clarke who resigned on October 22. On March 14, 2007, Holmgren was officially announced as the club's new g.m. In his first full season on the job in 2007-08, the Flyers returned to the playoffs after finishing last overall in the NHL the year before. Prior to his promotion, Holmgren had served the previous seven seasons as the team's assistant general manager. He rejoined the Flyers organization as a scout after being replaced as the Hartford Whalers' head coach on November 6, 1995. He had served as a head coach with both the Whalers and the Flyers and also served as general manager in Hartford during the 1993–94 season.

Holmgren retired from playing after the 1984-85 season, having recorded 144 goals and 179 assists for 323 points and 1,684 penalty minutes in 527 career regular season NHL games with the Flyers and the Minnesota North Stars. He recorded 138 goals and 171 assists for 309 points and 1,600 penalty minutes in 500 games over parts of nine seasons with the Flyers (1975-76 to 1983-84). His 1,600 penalty minutes with the Flyers are second all-time in club history. Holmgren was drafted from the University of Minnesota by the Flyers in the sixth round (108th overall) of the 1975 NHL Entry Draft.

### Coaching Record

| | | | Regular Season | | | | Playoffs | | | |
|---|---|---|---|---|---|---|---|---|---|---|
| Season | Team | League | GC | W | L | O/T | GC | W | L | T |
| 1988-89 | Philadelphia | NHL | 80 | 36 | 36 | 8 | 19 | 10 | 9 | .... |
| 1989-90 | Philadelphia | NHL | 80 | 30 | 39 | 11 | .... | .... | .... | .... |
| 1990-91 | Philadelphia | NHL | 80 | 33 | 37 | 10 | .... | .... | .... | .... |
| 1991-92 | Philadelphia | NHL | 24 | 8 | 14 | 2 | .... | .... | .... | .... |
| 1992-93 | Hartford | NHL | 84 | 26 | 52 | 6 | .... | .... | .... | .... |
| 1993-94 | Hartford | NHL | 17 | 4 | 11 | 2 | .... | .... | .... | .... |
| 1994-95 | Hartford | NHL | 48 | 19 | 24 | 5 | .... | .... | .... | .... |
| 1995-96 | Hartford | NHL | 12 | 5 | 6 | 1 | .... | .... | .... | .... |
| | **NHL Totals** | | **425** | **161** | **219** | **45** | **19** | **10** | **9** | .... |

# Club Directory

Wachovia Center

**Philadelphia Flyers**
Wachovia Center
3601 South Broad Street
Philadelphia, PA 19148-5290
Phone **215/465-4500**
PR FAX 215/389-9403
www.philadelphiaflyers.com
**Capacity:** 19,537

**Executive Management**

| | |
|---|---|
| Chairman | Ed Snider |
| President and COO of Comcast-Spectacor | Peter A. Luukko |
| General Manager | Paul Holmgren |
| Senior Vice President | Bob Clarke |
| Executive Vice President | Keith Allen |
| Governor | Ed Snider |
| Alternate Governors | Paul Holmgren, Peter A. Luukko, Phil Weinberg |
| Senior Vice President, Business Operations | Shawn Tilger |

**Hockey Club Personnel**

| | |
|---|---|
| Assistant General Manager | Barry Hanrahan |
| Assistant General Manager | John Paddock |
| Director of Hockey Operations | Chris Pryor |
| Director of Player Development | Don Luce |
| Director of Player Personnel | Dave Brown |
| Head Coach | John Stevens |
| Assistant Coaches | Craig Berube, Jack McIlhargey, Joe Mullen |
| Goaltending Coach | Jeff Reese |
| Player Development Coach | Derian Hatcher |
| Video Coach | Adam Patterson |
| Pro Scouts | John Chapman, Al Hill |
| Scouting Staff | Andre Beaulieu, Patrick Burke, Wade Clarke, Ross Fitzpatrick, Mark Greig, Todd Hearty, Ken Hoodikoff, Matti Kautto, Simon Nolet, Dennis Patterson, John Riley, Ilkka Sinisalo, Vaclav Slansky, |
| Scouting Consultant | Bill Barber |
| Director, Team Services | Bryan Hardenbergh |
| Executive Assistant | Dianna Taylor |
| Administrative Assistant | Jody Clarke |

**Medical/Training Staff**

| | |
|---|---|
| Team Physicians | Peter DeLuca, M.D.; Gary Dorshimer, M.D.; Tom Graham, M.D.; John Gray, M.D; Guy Lanzi, D.M.D. |
| Athletic Trainer/ Strength and Conditioning Coach | Jim McCrossin |
| Assistant Athletic Trainer | Sal Raffa |
| Massage Therapist | Brad Smith |
| Head Equipment Manager | Derek Settlemyre |
| Equipment Managers | Harry Bricker, Anthony Oratorio, Luke Clarke |
| Training Center Maintenance | Mike Craytor |

**Communications**

| | |
|---|---|
| Senior Director, Communications | Zack Hill |
| Media Services and Publications Coordinator | Joe Siville |
| Public Relations Assistant | Brian Smith |

**Community Relations**

| | |
|---|---|
| Director, Community Relations & Special Events | Linda Mantai |
| Manager, Community Relations | Jason Tempesta |
| Ambassador of Hockey | Bob Kelly |
| Fan Relations Assistant | Jerry Callahan |
| Ambassadors | Gary Dornhoefer, Joe Kadlec, Bernie Parent |

**Customer Service**

| | |
|---|---|
| Vice President, Customer Solutions | Cindy Stutman |
| Director, Customer Service | Melissa Keeler |
| Customer Service Account Managers | Dan Fuchs, Vincent Galasso, Nadine Heeger, Lauren Pawlowski,Courtney Sams, Andrew Shanks |
| Customer Service Coordinator | Megan Bell |

**Game Presentation**

| | |
|---|---|
| Director, Game Presentation | Anthony Gioia |
| Game Operations Coordinator | Michaela Sweet |
| Producer/Director | Artie Halstead |
| Graphics Designer / Video Editor | Mike Cahill / Chris Shay |
| Public Address Announcer / Anthem Singer | Lou Nolan / Lauren Hart |

**Marketing**

| | |
|---|---|
| Director, Marketing | Lindsey Domers |
| Business Development Manager | Jeremy Bland |
| Marketing Manager | Rob Johnson |
| New Media Managers | Kevin Kurz, Lauren Cochran |
| Publicist | Shauna Adams |

**Ticket Sales**

| | |
|---|---|
| Vice President, Sales | Jim Willits |
| Ticket Sales Coordinator | Angela Prendergast |
| Senior Account Executive | Tim Gobs |
| Account Executives | Mike Andrews, Warren Avart, James Darlington, Erin Dunn, Steve Greenblatt, Steve Hanson, Lindsay Heck, Ilkka Kortesluoma, Travis Kraus, Sean Lacey, Dan Ryan, JT Stewart, Tony Sukanick |
| Sales Associates | Nate Cross, Austin Foley, Paul Haines-LaPenta, Greg Osborn, Brad Rinehart, Andrew Rowland, Josh Wentz |

**Ticketing**

| | |
|---|---|
| Vice President, Ticket Operations | Cecilia Baker |
| Ticket Office Manager / Asst.Manager | Linda Fleischer / Lisa Albertson |
| Ticket Operations and Processing Manager | Dan McGinnis |
| Ticket Office Administration | Joan Kadlec |

**Finance**

| | |
|---|---|
| Chief Financial Officer | Angelo Cardone |
| Controller / Staff Accountant | Judy Zdunkiewicz / Kim Chuba |
| Payroll Accountant / Accounting Clerk | Renee Eiler / Michele Dominic |
| Team Consultant | Ron Ryan |
| Executive Assistants | Sharon Allison, Cheri Arnao, Ann Marie Nasuti |

# Phoenix Coyotes

## Key Off-Season Signings/Acquisitions

**2009**

**June 19** • Acquired LW **Stefan Meyer** from Florida for C **Steve Reinprecht.**

**19** • Re-signed LW **Petr Prucha.**

**27** • Acquired D **Jim Vandermeer** from Calgary for RW **Brandon Prust.**

**27** • Acquired D **Sami Lepisto** from Washington for a 5th-round pick in 2010.

**July 1** • Signed C **Vernon Fiddler** and G **Jason LaBarbera.**

**2** • Signed D **Adrian Aucoin.**

**13** • Acquired LW **Lauri Korpikoski** from NY Rangers for RW **Enver Lisin.**

**16** • Re-signed D **Keith Yandle.**

**21** • Acquired RW **Radim Vrbata** from Tampa Bay for LW **Todd Fedoruk** and D **David Hale.**

**24** • LW **Daniel Winnik** awarded one-year contract in arbitration.

**29** • Re-signed LW **Scottie Upshall.**

## 2009-10 Schedule

|  |  |  |  |
|---|---|---|---|
| **Oct.** | Sat. | 3 | at Los Angeles |
| | Wed. | 7 | at Pittsburgh |
| | Thu. | 8 | at Buffalo |
| | Sat. | 10 | Columbus |
| | Mon. | 12 | at San Jose |
| | Thu. | 15 | St. Louis |
| | Sat. | 17 | Boston |
| | Thu. | 22 | Detroit |
| | Sat. | 24 | Los Angeles |
| | Mon. | 26 | at NY Rangers |
| | Wed. | 28 | at Columbus |
| | Thu. | 29 | at St. Louis |
| | Sat. | 31 | Anaheim |
| **Nov.** | Mon. | 2 | Los Angeles |
| | Wed. | 4 | at Colorado |
| | Thu. | 5 | Chicago |
| | Sat. | 7 | at Anaheim |
| | Thu. | 12 | Montreal |
| | Sat. | 14 | Dallas |
| | Mon. | 16 | Tampa Bay |
| | Wed. | 18 | at Minnesota |
| | Thu. | 19 | at St. Louis |
| | Sat. | 21 | Philadelphia |
| | Mon. | 23 | at Edmonton |
| | Wed. | 25 | at Calgary |
| | Fri. | 27 | Dallas |
| | Sun. | 29 | at Anaheim* |
| **Dec.** | Thu. | 3 | Calgary |
| | Sat. | 5 | Ottawa |
| | Mon. | 7 | Minnesota |
| | Thu. | 10 | at Los Angeles |
| | Sat. | 12 | San Jose |
| | Mon. | 14 | at Detroit |
| | Wed. | 16 | at Toronto |
| | Thu. | 17 | at Columbus |
| | Sat. | 19 | at Anaheim* |
| | Mon. | 21 | Columbus |
| | Wed. | 23 | Anaheim |
| | Sat. | 26 | Los Angeles |
| | Mon. | 28 | at San Jose |
| | Tue. | 29 | Vancouver |
| | Thu. | 31 | San Jose* |
| **Jan.** | Sat. | 2 | Detroit |
| | Tue. | 5 | at Edmonton |
| | Thu. | 7 | at Vancouver |
| | Sat. | 9 | NY Islanders |
| | Tue. | 12 | San Jose |
| | Thu. | 14 | New Jersey |
| | Sat. | 16 | Minnesota |
| | Mon. | 18 | Buffalo* |
| | Thu. | 21 | Nashville |
| | Sat. | 23 | at Washington |
| | Tue. | 26 | at Detroit |
| | Thu. | 28 | Calgary |
| | Sat. | 30 | NY Rangers |
| | Sun. | 31 | at Dallas* |
| **Feb.** | Tue. | 2 | at Nashville |
| | Fri. | 5 | at Chicago |
| | Sat. | 6 | at Dallas* |
| | Mon. | 8 | Edmonton |
| | Wed. | 10 | at Minnesota |
| | Fri. | 12 | at Colorado |
| | Sat. | 13 | Dallas |
| **Mar.** | Tue. | 2 | St. Louis |
| | Thu. | 4 | Colorado |
| | Sat. | 6 | Anaheim |
| | Wed. | 10 | Vancouver |
| | Sat. | 13 | at Carolina |
| | Sun. | 14 | at Atlanta* |
| | Tue. | 16 | at Tampa Bay |
| | Thu. | 18 | at Florida |
| | Sat. | 20 | Chicago |
| | Sun. | 21 | at Dallas |
| | Tue. | 23 | at Chicago |
| | Thu. | 25 | at Nashville |
| | Sat. | 27 | Colorado |
| | Tue. | 30 | at Vancouver |
| | Wed. | 31 | at Calgary |
| **Apr.** | Sat. | 3 | Edmonton |
| | Wed. | 7 | Nashville |
| | Thu. | 8 | at Los Angeles |
| | Sat. | 10 | at San Jose |

* Denotes afternoon game.

**PACIFIC DIVISION**
**31st NHL Season**

**Franchise date:** June 22, 1979

Transferred from Winnipeg to Phoenix, July 1, 1996.

## 2008-09 Results: 36W-39L-4OTL-3SOL 79PTS.
## Fourth, Pacific Division

### Year-by-Year Record

| | | Home | | | | Road | | | | Overall | | | | | | | | |
|---|---|---|---|---|---|---|---|---|---|---|---|---|---|---|---|---|---|---|
| **Season** | **GP** | **W** | **L** | **T** | **OL** | **W** | **L** | **T** | **OL** | **W** | **L** | **T** | **OL** | **GF** | **GA** | **Pts.** | **Finished** | **Playoff Result** |
| 2008-09 | 82 | 23 | 15 | .... | 3 | 13 | 24 | .... | 4 | 36 | 39 | .... | 7 | 208 | 252 | 79 | 4th, Pacific Div. | Out of Playoffs |
| 2007-08 | 82 | 17 | 20 | .... | 4 | 21 | 17 | .... | 3 | 38 | 37 | .... | 7 | 214 | 231 | 83 | 4th, Pacific Div. | Out of Playoffs |
| 2006-07 | 82 | 18 | 20 | .... | 3 | 13 | 26 | .... | 2 | 31 | 46 | .... | 5 | 216 | 284 | 67 | 5th, Pacific Div. | Out of Playoffs |
| 2005-06 | 82 | 19 | 18 | .... | 4 | 19 | 21 | .... | 1 | 38 | 39 | .... | 5 | 246 | 271 | 81 | 5th, Pacific Div. | Out of Playoffs |
| 2004-05 | .... | .... | .... | .... | .... | .... | .... | .... | .... | .... | .... | .... | .... | .... | .... | .... | | |
| 2003-04 | 82 | 11 | 19 | 7 | 4 | 11 | 17 | 11 | 2 | 22 | 36 | 18 | 6 | 188 | 245 | 68 | 5th, Pacific Div. | Out of Playoffs |
| 2002-03 | 82 | 17 | 16 | 6 | 2 | 14 | 19 | 5 | 3 | 31 | 35 | 11 | 5 | 204 | 230 | 78 | 4th, Pacific Div. | Out of Playoffs |
| 2001-02 | 82 | 27 | 8 | 3 | 3 | 13 | 19 | 6 | 3 | 40 | 27 | 9 | 6 | 228 | 210 | 95 | 2nd, Pacific Div. | Lost Conf. Quarter-Final |
| 2000-01 | 82 | 21 | 11 | 7 | 2 | 14 | 16 | 10 | 1 | 35 | 27 | 17 | 3 | 214 | 212 | 90 | 4th, Pacific Div. | Out of Playoffs |
| 1999-2000 | 82 | 22 | 16 | 2 | 1 | 17 | 15 | 6 | 3 | 39 | 31 | 8 | 4 | 232 | 228 | 90 | 3rd, Pacific Div. | Lost Conf. Quarter-Final |
| 1998-99 | 82 | 23 | 13 | 5 | .... | 16 | 18 | 7 | .... | 39 | 31 | 12 | .... | 205 | 197 | 90 | 2nd, Pacific Div. | Lost Conf. Quarter-Final |
| 1997-98 | 82 | 19 | 16 | 6 | .... | 16 | 19 | 6 | .... | 35 | 35 | 12 | .... | 224 | 227 | 82 | 4th, Central Div. | Lost Conf. Quarter-Final |
| 1996-97 | 82 | 15 | 19 | 7 | .... | 23 | 18 | 0 | .... | 38 | 37 | 7 | .... | 240 | 243 | 83 | 3rd, Central Div. | Lost Conf. Quarter-Final |
| 1995-96* | 82 | 22 | 16 | 3 | .... | 14 | 24 | 3 | .... | 36 | 40 | 6 | .... | 275 | 291 | 78 | 5th, Central Div. | Lost Conf. Quarter-Final |
| 1994-95* | 48 | 10 | 10 | 4 | .... | 6 | 15 | 3 | .... | 16 | 25 | 7 | .... | 157 | 177 | 39 | 6th, Central Div. | Out of Playoffs |
| 1993-94* | 84 | 15 | 23 | 4 | .... | 9 | 28 | 5 | .... | 24 | 51 | 9 | .... | 245 | 344 | 57 | 6th, Central Div. | Out of Playoffs |
| 1992-93* | 84 | 23 | 16 | 3 | .... | 17 | 21 | 4 | .... | 40 | 37 | 7 | .... | 322 | 320 | 87 | 4th, Smythe Div. | Lost Div. Semi-Final |
| 1991-92* | 80 | 20 | 14 | 6 | .... | 13 | 18 | 9 | .... | 33 | 32 | 15 | .... | 251 | 244 | 81 | 4th, Smythe Div. | Lost Div. Semi-Final |
| 1990-91* | 80 | 17 | 18 | 5 | .... | 9 | 25 | 6 | .... | 26 | 43 | 11 | .... | 260 | 288 | 63 | 5th, Smythe Div. | Out of Playoffs |
| 1989-90* | 80 | 22 | 13 | 5 | .... | 15 | 19 | 6 | .... | 37 | 32 | 11 | .... | 298 | 290 | 85 | 3rd, Smythe Div. | Lost Div. Semi-Final |
| 1988-89* | 80 | 17 | 18 | 5 | .... | 9 | 24 | 7 | .... | 26 | 42 | 12 | .... | 300 | 355 | 64 | 5th, Smythe Div. | Out of Playoffs |
| 1987-88* | 80 | 20 | 14 | 6 | .... | 13 | 22 | 5 | .... | 33 | 36 | 11 | .... | 292 | 310 | 77 | 3rd, Smythe Div. | Lost Div. Semi-Final |
| 1986-87* | 80 | 25 | 12 | 3 | .... | 15 | 20 | 5 | .... | 40 | 32 | 8 | .... | 279 | 271 | 88 | 3rd, Smythe Div. | Lost Div. Final |
| 1985-86* | 80 | 18 | 19 | 3 | .... | 8 | 28 | 4 | .... | 26 | 47 | 7 | .... | 295 | 372 | 59 | 3rd, Smythe Div. | Lost Div. Semi-Final |
| 1984-85* | 80 | 21 | 13 | 6 | .... | 22 | 14 | 4 | .... | 43 | 27 | 10 | .... | 358 | 332 | 96 | 2nd, Smythe Div. | Lost Div. Final |
| 1983-84* | 80 | 17 | 15 | 8 | .... | 14 | 23 | 3 | .... | 31 | 38 | 11 | .... | 340 | 374 | 73 | 4th, Smythe Div. | Lost Div. Semi-Final |
| 1982-83* | 80 | 22 | 16 | 2 | .... | 11 | 23 | 6 | .... | 33 | 39 | 8 | .... | 311 | 333 | 74 | 4th, Smythe Div. | Lost Div. Semi-Final |
| 1981-82* | 80 | 18 | 13 | 9 | .... | 15 | 20 | 5 | .... | 33 | 33 | 14 | .... | 319 | 332 | 80 | 2nd, Norris Div. | Lost Div. Semi-Final |
| 1980-81* | 80 | 7 | 25 | 8 | .... | 2 | 32 | 6 | .... | 9 | 57 | 14 | .... | 246 | 400 | 32 | 6th, Smythe Div. | Out of Playoffs |
| 1979-80* | 80 | 13 | 19 | 8 | .... | 7 | 30 | 3 | .... | 20 | 49 | 11 | .... | 214 | 314 | 51 | 5th, Smythe Div. | Out of Playoffs |

* Winnipeg Jets

*The Coyotes' Shane Doan scored 31 goals in 2008-09 to set a new career high. He also joined Dale Hawerchuk and Keith Tkachuk as the only players in franchise history to score 20 goals or more for nine straight seasons.*

# 2009-10 Player Personnel

| FORWARDS | HT | WT | S | Place of Birth | *Age | 2008-09 Club |
|---|---|---|---|---|---|---|
| BOEDKER, Mikkel | 5-11 | 195 | L | Brondby, Denmark | 19 | Phoenix |
| DOAN, Shane | 6-2 | 224 | R | Halkirk, Alta. | 32 | Phoenix |
| FIDDLER, Vernon | 5-11 | 201 | L | Edmonton, Alta. | 29 | Nashville |
| HANZAL, Martin | 6-5 | 218 | L | Pisek, Czech. | 22 | Phoenix |
| KOLARIK, Chad | 5-10 | 175 | R | Abington, PA | 23 | San Antonio |
| KORPIKOSKI, Lauri | 6-1 | 195 | L | Turku, Finland | 23 | NY Rangers-Hartford |
| LESSARD, Francis | 6-3 | 225 | R | Montreal, Que. | 30 | San Antonio |
| LOMBARDI, Matthew | 6-0 | 198 | L | Montreal, Que. | 27 | Calgary-Phoenix |
| LONG, Colin | 5-11 | 186 | R | Santa Ana, CA | 20 | Kelowna |
| MACLEAN, Brett | 6-2 | 197 | R | Port Elgin, Ont. | 20 | San Antonio |
| MEYER, Stefan | 6-2 | 194 | L | Medicine Hat, Alta. | 24 | Rochester |
| MUELLER, Peter | 6-2 | 205 | R | Bloomington, MN | 21 | Phoenix |
| PERRAULT, Joel | 6-1 | 197 | R | Montreal, Que. | 26 | Phoenix-San Antonio |
| PORTER, Kevin | 5-11 | 194 | L | Detroit, MI | 23 | Phoenix-San Antonio |
| PRUCHA, Petr | 6-0 | 175 | R | Chrudim, Czech. | 27 | NY Rangers-Phoenix |
| SPINA, David | 5-10 | 185 | L | Mesa, AZ | 26 | San Antonio |
| TIKHONOV, Viktor | 6-2 | 187 | R | Riga, Latvia | 21 | Phoenix-San Antonio |
| TURRIS, Kyle | 6-1 | 180 | R | New Westminster, B.C. | 20 | Phoenix-San Antonio |
| UPSHALL, Scottie | 6-0 | 197 | L | Fort McMurray, Alta. | 25 | Philadelphia-Phoenix |
| VRBATA, Radim | 6-1 | 190 | R | Mlada Boleslav, Czech. | 28 | T.B.-Ml. Boleslav-Liberec |
| WINNIK, Daniel | 6-2 | 210 | R | Toronto, Ont. | 24 | Phoenix-San Antonio |
| **DEFENSEMEN** | | | | | | |
| AHNELOV, Jonas | 6-3 | 205 | L | Huddinge, Sweden | 21 | San Antonio |
| AUCOIN, Adrian | 6-2 | 212 | R | Ottawa, Ont. | 36 | Calgary |
| HESHKA, Shaun | 6-1 | 198 | R | Melville, Sask. | 24 | Manitoba |
| JONES, Matt | 6-0 | 215 | L | Downers Grove, IL | 26 | San Antonio |
| JOVANOVSKI, Ed | 6-2 | 214 | L | Windsor, Ont. | 33 | Phoenix |
| LEPISTO, Sami | 6-1 | 195 | L | Espoo, Finland | 24 | Washington-Hershey |
| MICHALEK, Zbynek | 6-2 | 210 | R | Jindrichuv Hradec, Czech. | 26 | Phoenix |
| ROSS, Nick | 6-1 | 188 | L | Edmonton, Alta. | 20 | Kamloops-Vancouver (WHL) |
| SAUER, Kurt | 6-4 | 220 | L | St. Cloud, MN | 28 | Phoenix |
| SCHLEMKO, David | 6-1 | 195 | L | Edmonton, Alta. | 22 | Phoenix-San Antonio |
| VANDERMEER, Jim | 6-1 | 211 | L | Caroline, Alta. | 29 | Calgary |
| YANDLE, Keith | 6-2 | 195 | L | Boston, MA | 23 | Phoenix |
| ZIMMERMAN, Sean | 6-2 | 210 | R | Denver, CO | 22 | San Antonio-Arizona |

| GOALTENDERS | HT | WT | C | Place of Birth | *Age | 2008-09 Club |
|---|---|---|---|---|---|---|
| BRYZGALOV, Ilya | 6-3 | 199 | L | Togliatti, USSR | 29 | Phoenix |
| GISTEDT, Joel | 5-11 | 176 | L | Uddevalla, Sweden | 21 | Arizona-San Antonio |
| LaBARBERA, Jason | 6-3 | 225 | L | Burnaby, B.C. | 29 | Los Angeles-Vancouver |
| MONTOYA, Al | 6-2 | 185 | L | Chicago, IL | 24 | Phoenix-San Antonio |
| TORDJMAN, Josh | 6-1 | 155 | L | Montreal, Que. | 24 | Phoenix-San Antonio |

* – Age at start of 2009-10 season

# Wayne Gretzky

## Head Coach

*Born: Brantford, Ont., January 26, 1961.*

On August 8, 2005, Wayne Gretzky agreed to a multiyear contract to serve as head coach of the Phoenix Coyotes. In addition to serving as the Coyotes' head coach, Gretzky also continues as managing partner and alternate governor for the Coyotes, a role that he had performed for the previous four seasons. Gretzky officially joined the franchise on February 15, 2001, when the Steve Ellman and Jerry Moyes ownership group completed the purchase of the Coyotes.

Gretzky played 20 seasons in the National Hockey League with Edmonton, Los Angeles, St. Louis and the New York Rangers, dominating the game unlike any player in history. Gretzky helped win four Stanley Cup championships and three Canada Cup tournament titles during his illustrious playing career. He became the NHL's all-time leading goal, assist and point producer for a single season and career (both regular season and playoffs). Gretzky won the Art Ross Trophy as the NHL's leading scorer 10 times, the Hart Trophy as the League's MVP nine times (including eight consecutive seasons) and the Conn Smythe Trophy as playoff MVP twice. He earned the Lady Byng Trophy as the NHL's most gentlemanly player five times and made 18 consecutive All-Star Game appearances, securing three All-Star MVP Awards. Gretzky is an eight-time First All-Star Team member and seven-time Second All-Star Team member. He holds virtually every offensive record in the NHL and his tireless support of the game has contributed significantly to the popularity it enjoys today.

On November 22, 1999 – seven months after his retirement – Gretzky was inducted into the Hockey Hall of Fame in Toronto, becoming the tenth and final player in Hockey Hall of Fame history to have the mandatory three-year waiting period for enshrinement waived by the Hall's board of directors.

Gretzky's incredible success in hockey has continued past his playing career. In a managerial role with Team Canada, Gretzky served as executive director for Team Canada, responsible for assembling Canada's best hockey players at the 2002 Olympic Winter Games in Salt Lake City and again in 2004 at the World Cup of Hockey. Under Gretzky's leadership, Team Canada won the gold medal for the first time in 50 years at the 2002 Olympics. Two years later, Team Canada repeated the feat by winning the 2004 World Cup of Hockey championship. Gretzky also served as executive director again at the 2006 Olympics.

### Coaching Record

| | | | Regular Season | | | | Playoffs | | | |
|---|---|---|---|---|---|---|---|---|---|---|
| **Season** | **Team** | **League** | **GC** | **W** | **L** | **O/T** | **GC** | **W** | **L** | **T** |
| **2005-06** | **Phoenix** | **NHL** | 82 | 38 | 39 | 5 | .... | .... | .... | .... |
| **2006-07** | **Phoenix** | **NHL** | 82 | 31 | 46 | 5 | .... | .... | .... | .... |
| **2007-08** | **Phoenix** | **NHL** | 82 | 38 | 37 | 7 | .... | .... | .... | .... |
| **2008-09** | **Phoenix** | **NHL** | 82 | 36 | 39 | 7 | .... | .... | .... | .... |
| | **NHL Totals** | | **328** | **143** | **161** | **24** | .... | .... | .... | .... |

# 2008-09 Scoring

* – rookie

## Regular Season

| Pos | # | Player | Team | GP | G | A | Pts | TOI | +/– | PIM | PP | SH | GW | S | % |
|---|---|---|---|---|---|---|---|---|---|---|---|---|---|---|---|
| L | 19 | Shane Doan | PHX | 82 | 31 | 42 | 73 | 20:14 | 5 | 72 | 10 | 0 | 4 | 230 | 13.5 |
| C | 15 | Matthew Lombardi | CGY | 50 | 9 | 21 | 30 | 16:27 | 11 | 30 | 0 | 1 | 2 | 119 | 7.6 |
| | | | PHX | 19 | 5 | 11 | 16 | 20:54 | 2 | 14 | 1 | 0 | 0 | 58 | 8.6 |
| | | | Total | 69 | 14 | 32 | 46 | 17:40 | 13 | 44 | 1 | 1 | 2 | 177 | 7.9 |
| C | 28 | Steve Reinprecht | PHX | 73 | 14 | 27 | 41 | 15:54 | 0 | 20 | 3 | 0 | 3 | 95 | 14.7 |
| R | 88 | Peter Mueller | PHX | 72 | 13 | 23 | 36 | 16:04 | –7 | 24 | 5 | 0 | 4 | 138 | 9.4 |
| D | 55 | Ed Jovanovski | PHX | 82 | 9 | 27 | 36 | 22:09 | –15 | 106 | 6 | 0 | 3 | 194 | 4.6 |
| L | 8 | Scottie Upshall | PHI | 55 | 7 | 14 | 21 | 13:13 | 5 | 63 | 2 | 0 | 0 | 126 | 5.6 |
| | | | PHX | 19 | 8 | 5 | 13 | 18:35 | 2 | 26 | 3 | 0 | 1 | 66 | 12.1 |
| | | | Total | 74 | 15 | 19 | 34 | 14:35 | 7 | 89 | 5 | 0 | 1 | 192 | 7.8 |
| C | 11 | Martin Hanzal | PHX | 74 | 11 | 20 | 31 | 16:21 | –4 | 40 | 0 | 2 | 2 | 97 | 11.3 |
| D | 3 | Keith Yandle | PHX | 69 | 4 | 26 | 30 | 16:37 | –4 | 37 | 1 | 0 | 0 | 118 | 3.4 |
| R | 89 | * Mikkel Boedker | PHX | 78 | 11 | 17 | 28 | 15:32 | –6 | 18 | 2 | 0 | 3 | 116 | 9.5 |
| D | 4 | Zbynek Michalek | PHX | 82 | 6 | 21 | 27 | 22:42 | –13 | 28 | 0 | 0 | 0 | 106 | 5.7 |
| R | 18 | Enver Lisin | PHX | 48 | 13 | 8 | 21 | 14:49 | –13 | 24 | 1 | 0 | 2 | 105 | 12.4 |
| L | 14 | Nigel Dawes | NYR | 52 | 10 | 9 | 19 | 13:02 | –2 | 15 | 3 | 0 | 4 | 96 | 10.4 |
| | | | PHX | 12 | 0 | 2 | 2 | 14:09 | –4 | 0 | 0 | 0 | 0 | 19 | 0.0 |
| | | | Total | 64 | 10 | 11 | 21 | 13:15 | –6 | 15 | 3 | 0 | 4 | 115 | 8.7 |
| L | 36 | Joakim Lindstrom | PHX | 44 | 9 | 11 | 20 | 14:51 | –6 | 28 | 3 | 0 | 2 | 77 | 11.7 |
| C | 91 | * Kyle Turris | PHX | 63 | 8 | 12 | 20 | 12:55 | –15 | 21 | 3 | 0 | 3 | 91 | 8.8 |
| R | 16 | Petr Prucha | NYR | 28 | 4 | 5 | 9 | 12:08 | –2 | 16 | 0 | 0 | 0 | 44 | 9.1 |
| | | | PHX | 19 | 2 | 8 | 10 | 18:26 | 1 | 6 | 1 | 0 | 1 | 23 | 8.7 |
| | | | Total | 47 | 6 | 13 | 19 | 14:41 | –1 | 22 | 1 | 0 | 1 | 67 | 9.0 |
| D | 45 | Dmitri Kalinin | NYR | 58 | 1 | 12 | 13 | 17:01 | –7 | 26 | 0 | 0 | 0 | 51 | 2.0 |
| | | | PHX | 15 | 1 | 3 | 4 | 20:12 | –2 | 6 | 1 | 0 | 0 | 16 | 6.3 |
| | | | Total | 73 | 2 | 15 | 17 | 17:40 | –9 | 32 | 1 | 0 | 0 | 67 | 3.0 |
| R | 41 | * Viktor Tikhonov | PHX | 61 | 8 | 8 | 16 | 12:07 | –3 | 20 | 1 | 0 | 1 | 71 | 11.3 |
| L | 17 | Todd Fedoruk | PHX | 72 | 6 | 7 | 13 | 10:35 | –9 | 72 | 0 | 0 | 0 | 56 | 10.7 |
| D | 2 | Ken Klee | ANA | 3 | 0 | 0 | 0 | 16:57 | 0 | 4 | 0 | 0 | 0 | 4 | 0.0 |
| | | | PHX | 68 | 1 | 10 | 11 | 15:22 | 9 | 24 | 0 | 0 | 0 | 47 | 2.1 |
| | | | Total | 71 | 1 | 10 | 11 | 15:26 | 9 | 28 | 0 | 0 | 0 | 51 | 2.0 |
| C | 23 | * Kevin Porter | PHX | 34 | 5 | 5 | 10 | 13:37 | –2 | 4 | 1 | 0 | 2 | 39 | 12.8 |
| D | 21 | David Hale | PHX | 48 | 3 | 6 | 9 | 15:08 | –11 | 36 | 0 | 0 | 0 | 22 | 13.6 |
| L | 34 | Daniel Winnik | PHX | 49 | 3 | 4 | 7 | 13:04 | 1 | 63 | 0 | 0 | 0 | 66 | 4.5 |
| D | 44 | Kurt Sauer | PHX | 68 | 1 | 6 | 7 | 20:37 | –1 | 36 | 0 | 0 | 0 | 33 | 3.0 |
| R | 73 | Steven Goertzen | PHX | 16 | 2 | 2 | 4 | 9:42 | –2 | 24 | 0 | 0 | 0 | 18 | 11.1 |
| C | 26 | Joel Perrault | PHX | 7 | 2 | 1 | 3 | 12:52 | 2 | 4 | 0 | 0 | 0 | 15 | 13.3 |
| R | 29 | * Brandon Prust | CGY | 25 | 1 | 1 | 2 | 6:20 | –4 | 79 | 0 | 0 | 1 | 15 | 6.7 |
| | | | PHX | 11 | 0 | 1 | 1 | 9:58 | –4 | 29 | 0 | 0 | 0 | 8 | 0.0 |
| | | | Total | 36 | 1 | 2 | 3 | 7:27 | –8 | 108 | 0 | 0 | 1 | 23 | 4.3 |
| D | 6 | * David Schlemko | PHX | 3 | 0 | 1 | 1 | 19:16 | –2 | 0 | 0 | 0 | 0 | 3 | 0.0 |
| L | 15 | Jeff Hoggan | PHX | 4 | 0 | 1 | 1 | 12:00 | –1 | 7 | 0 | 0 | 0 | 7 | 0.0 |
| C | 14 | * Alexander Nikulin | PHX | 1 | 0 | 0 | 0 | 5:35 | –1 | 0 | 0 | 0 | 0 | 1 | 0.0 |
| R | 22 | Brian McGrattan | PHX | 5 | 0 | 0 | 0 | 5:31 | –2 | 22 | 0 | 0 | 0 | 2 | 0.0 |
| C | 39 | Garth Murray | PHX | 10 | 0 | 0 | 0 | 9:20 | –2 | 12 | 0 | 0 | 0 | 12 | 0.0 |

## Goaltending

| No. | Goaltender | GPI | Mins | Avg | W | L | OT | EN | SO | GA | SA | S% | G | A | PIM |
|---|---|---|---|---|---|---|---|---|---|---|---|---|---|---|---|
| 35 | * Al Montoya | 5 | 259 | 2.08 | 3 | 1 | 0 | 0 | 1 | 9 | 120 | .925 | 0 | 0 | 0 |
| 32 | Mikael Tellqvist | 15 | 798 | 2.86 | 7 | 5 | 1 | 2 | 0 | 38 | 408 | .907 | 0 | 0 | 0 |
| 30 | Ilja Bryzgalov | 65 | 3760 | 2.98 | 26 | 31 | 6 | 5 | 3 | 187 | 1994 | .906 | 0 | 2 | 4 |
| 42 | * Josh Tordjman | 2 | 118 | 4.07 | 0 | 2 | 0 | 0 | 0 | 8 | 62 | .871 | 0 | 0 | 0 |
| | **Totals** | **82** | **4962** | **3.01** | **36** | **39** | **7** | **7** | **4** | **249** | **2591** | **.904** | | | |

*After being dealt from Philadelphia to Phoenix at the 2009 trade deadline, Scottie Upshall scored eight goals in just 19 games for the Coyotes. He finished the 2008-09 season with a career-best 15 goals.*

## Coaching History

Tom McVie and Bill Sutherland, 1979-80; Tom McVie, Bill Sutherland and Mike Smith, 1980-81; Tom Watt, 1981-82, 1982-83; Tom Watt and Barry Long, 1983-84; Barry Long, 1984-85; Barry Long and John Ferguson, 1985-86; Dan Maloney, 1986-87, 1987-88; Dan Maloney and Rick Bowness, 1988-89; Bob Murdoch, 1989-90, 1990-91; John Paddock, 1991-92 to 1993-94; John Paddock and Terry Simpson, 1994-95; Terry Simpson, 1995-96; Don Hay, 1996-97; Jim Schoenfeld, 1997-98, 1998-99; Bob Francis, 1999-2000 to 2002-03; Bob Francis and Rick Bowness, 2003-04; Rick Bowness, 2004-05; Wayne Gretzky, 2005-06 to date.

# Club Records

## Team

(Figures in brackets for season records are games played; records for fewest points, wins, ties, losses, goals, goals against are for 70 or more games)

| | | |
|---|---|---|
| Most Points | 96 | 1984-85 (80) |
| Most Wins | 43 | 1984-85 (80) |
| Most Ties | 18 | 2003-04 (82) |
| Most Losses | 57 | 1980-81 (80) |
| Most Goals | 358 | 1984-85 (80) |
| Most Goals Against | 400 | 1980-81 (80) |
| Fewest Points | 32 | 1980-81 (80) |
| Fewest Wins | 9 | 1980-81 (80) |
| Fewest Ties | 6 | 1995-96 (82) |
| Fewest Losses | 27 | 1984-85 (80), 2000-01 (82), 2001-02 (82) |
| Fewest Goals | 188 | 2003-04 (82) |
| Fewest Goals Against | 197 | 1998-99 (82) |
| **Longest Winning Streak** | | |
| Overall | 9 | Mar. 8-27/85 |
| Home | 9 | Dec. 27/92-Jan. 23/93 |
| Away | 8 | Feb. 25-Apr. 6/85 |
| **Longest Undefeated Streak** | | |
| Overall | 14 | Oct. 25-Nov. 28/98 (12 wins, 2 ties) |
| Home | 11 | Dec. 23/83-Feb. 5/84 (6 wins, 5 ties), Oct. 15-Dec. 20/98 (10 wins, 1 tie) |
| Away | 9 | Feb. 25-Apr. 7/85 (8 wins, 1 tie), Dec. 7/03-Jan. 9/04 (5 wins, 4 ties) |
| **Longest Losing Streak** | | |
| Overall | 10 | Nov. 30-Dec. 20/80, Feb. 6-25/94 |
| Home | 6 | Oct. 6-Nov. 3/07, Jan. 27-Feb. 16/09 |
| Away | 13 | Jan. 26-Apr. 14/94 |
| **Longest Winless Streak** | | |
| Overall | *30 | Oct. 19-Dec. 20/80 (23 losses, 7 ties) |
| Home | 14 | Oct. 19-Dec. 14/80 (9 losses, 5 ties) |
| Away | 18 | Oct. 10-Dec. 20/80 (16 losses, 2 ties) |
| Most Shutouts, Season | 9 | 1998-99 (82) |
| Most PIM, Season | 2,278 | 1987-88 (80) |
| Most Goals, Game | 12 | Feb. 25/85 (Wpg. 12 at NYR 5) |

## Individual

| | | |
|---|---|---|
| Most Seasons | 15 | Teppo Numminen |
| Most Games | 1,098 | Teppo Numminen |
| Most Goals, Career | 379 | Dale Hawerchuk |
| Most Assists, Career | 553 | Thomas Steen |
| Most Points, Career | 929 | Dale Hawerchuk (379G, 550A) |
| Most PIM, Career | 1,508 | Keith Tkachuk |
| Most Shutouts, Career | 21 | Nikolai Khabibulin |
| Longest Consecutive Games Streak | 475 | Dale Hawerchuk (Dec. 19/82-Dec. 10/88) |
| Most Goals, Season | 76 | Teemu Selanne (1992-93) |
| Most Assists, Season | 79 | Phil Housley (1992-93) |
| Most Points, Season | 132 | Teemu Selanne (1992-93; 76G, 56A) |
| Most PIM, Season | 347 | Tie Domi (1993-94) |
| Most Points, Defenseman, Season | 97 | Phil Housley (1992-93; 18G, 79A) |
| Most Points, Center, Season | 130 | Dale Hawerchuk (1984-85; 53G, 77A) |
| Most Points, Right Wing, Season | 132 | Teemu Selanne (1992-93; 76G, 56A) |
| Most Points, Left Wing, Season | 98 | Keith Tkachuk (1995-96; 50G, 48A) |
| Most Points, Rookie, Season | *132 | Teemu Selanne (1992-93; 76G, 56A) |
| Most Shutouts, Season | 8 | Nikolai Khabibulin (1998-99) |
| Most Goals, Game | 5 | Willy Lindstrom (Mar. 2/82), Alexei Zhamnov (Apr. 1/95) |
| Most Assists, Game | 5 | Dale Hawerchuk (Mar. 6/84), (Mar. 18/89), (Mar. 4/90) Phil Housley (Jan. 18/93) Keith Tkachuk (Feb. 23/01) |
| Most Points, Game | 6 | Willy Lindstrom (Mar. 2/82; 5G, 1A) Dale Hawerchuk (Dec. 14/83; 3G, 3A), (Mar. 5/88; 2G, 4A), (Mar. 18/89; 1G, 5A) Thomas Steen (Oct. 24/84; 2G, 4A) Ed Olczyk (Dec. 21/91; 2G, 4A) |

* NHL Record.
Records include Winnipeg Jets, 1979-80 through 1995-96.

## Winnipeg Jets Retired Numbers

| | | |
|---|---|---|
| 9 | Bobby Hull | 1972-1980 |
| 10 | Dale Hawerchuk | 1981-1990 |
| 25 | Thomas Steen | 1981-1995 |

## Captains' History

Lars-Erik Sjoberg, 1979-80; Morris Lukowich and Scott Campbell, 1980-81; Dave Christian and Barry Long, 1981-82; Dave Christian and Lucien DeBlois, 1982-83; Lucien DeBlois, 1983-84; Dale Hawerchuk, 1984-85 to 1988-89; Randy Carlyle, Dale Hawerchuk and Thomas Steen (tri-captains), 1989-90; Randy Carlyle and Thomas Steen (co-captains), 1990-91; Troy Murray, 1991-92; Troy Murray and Dean Kennedy, 1992-93; Dean Kennedy and Keith Tkachuk, 1993-94; Keith Tkachuk, 1994-95; Kris King, 1995-96; Keith Tkachuk, 1996-97 to 2000-01; Teppo Numminen, 2001-02, 2002-03; Shane Doan, 2003-04 to date.

# All-time Record vs. Other Clubs

## Regular Season

| | At Home | | | | | | | | On Road | | | | | | | | Total | | | | | | | |
|---|---|---|---|---|---|---|---|---|---|---|---|---|---|---|---|---|---|---|---|---|---|---|---|---|
| | GP | W | L | T | OL | GF | GA | PTS | GP | W | L | T | OL | GF | GA | PTS | GP | W | L | T | OL | GF | GA | PTS |
| Anaheim | 41 | 17 | 17 | 2 | 5 | 111 | 123 | 41 | 42 | 13 | 23 | 3 | 3 | 102 | 130 | 32 | 83 | 30 | 40 | 5 | 8 | 213 | 253 | 73 |
| Atlanta | 7 | 6 | 0 | 1 | 0 | 25 | 12 | 13 | 5 | 4 | 1 | 0 | 0 | 17 | 10 | 8 | 12 | 10 | 1 | 1 | 0 | 42 | 22 | 21 |
| Boston | 31 | 13 | 15 | 3 | 0 | 102 | 105 | 29 | 32 | 6 | 22 | 4 | 0 | 96 | 138 | 16 | 63 | 19 | 37 | 7 | 0 | 198 | 243 | 45 |
| Buffalo | 31 | 14 | 15 | 2 | 0 | 93 | 96 | 30 | 33 | 7 | 21 | 5 | 0 | 83 | 133 | 19 | 64 | 21 | 36 | 7 | 0 | 176 | 229 | 49 |
| Calgary | 78 | 36 | 31 | 11 | 0 | 284 | 270 | 83 | 79 | 27 | 42 | 9 | 1 | 248 | 321 | 64 | 157 | 63 | 73 | 20 | 1 | 532 | 591 | 147 |
| Carolina | 33 | 15 | 15 | 2 | 1 | 120 | 123 | 33 | 32 | 11 | 14 | 6 | 1 | 93 | 108 | 29 | 65 | 26 | 29 | 8 | 2 | 213 | 231 | 62 |
| Chicago | 58 | 30 | 21 | 5 | 2 | 184 | 182 | 67 | 56 | 15 | 30 | 10 | 1 | 141 | 209 | 41 | 114 | 45 | 51 | 15 | 3 | 325 | 391 | 108 |
| Colorado | 48 | 19 | 21 | 7 | 1 | 164 | 168 | 46 | 49 | 19 | 22 | 5 | 3 | 165 | 173 | 46 | 97 | 38 | 43 | 12 | 4 | 329 | 341 | 92 |
| Columbus | 16 | 9 | 4 | 3 | 0 | 48 | 36 | 21 | 16 | 8 | 7 | 1 | 0 | 39 | 40 | 17 | 32 | 17 | 11 | 4 | 0 | 87 | 76 | 38 |
| Dallas | 69 | 28 | 34 | 4 | 3 | 212 | 231 | 63 | 70 | 27 | 32 | 9 | 2 | 204 | 235 | 65 | 139 | 55 | 66 | 13 | 5 | 416 | 466 | 128 |
| Detroit | 57 | 18 | 24 | 14 | 1 | 168 | 188 | 51 | 59 | 20 | 30 | 8 | 1 | 193 | 230 | 49 | 116 | 38 | 54 | 22 | 2 | 361 | 418 | 100 |
| Edmonton | 79 | 32 | 40 | 5 | 2 | 307 | 340 | 71 | 80 | 22 | 50 | 6 | 2 | 255 | 351 | 52 | 159 | 54 | 90 | 11 | 4 | 562 | 691 | 123 |
| Florida | 12 | 5 | 3 | 3 | 1 | 35 | 35 | 14 | 9 | 5 | 4 | 0 | 0 | 23 | 28 | 10 | 21 | 10 | 7 | 3 | 1 | 58 | 63 | 24 |
| Los Angeles | 91 | 50 | 28 | 11 | 2 | 355 | 288 | 113 | 89 | 39 | 34 | 14 | 2 | 326 | 337 | 94 | 180 | 89 | 62 | 25 | 4 | 681 | 625 | 207 |
| Minnesota | 16 | 8 | 7 | 1 | 0 | 42 | 37 | 17 | 16 | 5 | 9 | 2 | 0 | 30 | 44 | 12 | 32 | 13 | 16 | 3 | 0 | 72 | 81 | 29 |
| Montreal | 30 | 9 | 14 | 7 | 0 | 96 | 116 | 25 | 31 | 3 | 26 | 2 | 0 | 69 | 151 | 8 | 61 | 12 | 40 | 9 | 0 | 165 | 267 | 33 |
| Nashville | 20 | 12 | 6 | 0 | 2 | 57 | 59 | 26 | 20 | 6 | 9 | 2 | 3 | 47 | 59 | 17 | 40 | 18 | 15 | 2 | 5 | 104 | 118 | 43 |
| New Jersey | 32 | 22 | 7 | 3 | 0 | 117 | 82 | 47 | 31 | 12 | 13 | 6 | 0 | 93 | 101 | 30 | 63 | 34 | 20 | 9 | 0 | 210 | 183 | 77 |
| NY Islanders | 32 | 13 | 15 | 4 | 0 | 107 | 112 | 30 | 32 | 9 | 15 | 8 | 0 | 95 | 119 | 26 | 64 | 22 | 30 | 12 | 0 | 202 | 231 | 56 |
| NY Rangers | 32 | 13 | 14 | 4 | 1 | 110 | 108 | 31 | 31 | 10 | 18 | 2 | 1 | 108 | 133 | 23 | 63 | 23 | 32 | 6 | 2 | 218 | 241 | 54 |
| Ottawa | 11 | 4 | 6 | 1 | 0 | 36 | 42 | 9 | 13 | 6 | 6 | 1 | 0 | 39 | 42 | 13 | 24 | 10 | 12 | 2 | 0 | 75 | 84 | 22 |
| Philadelphia | 32 | 14 | 16 | 2 | 0 | 103 | 106 | 30 | 33 | 9 | 23 | 0 | 1 | 89 | 140 | 19 | 65 | 23 | 39 | 2 | 1 | 192 | 246 | 49 |
| Pittsburgh | 33 | 15 | 14 | 3 | 1 | 122 | 115 | 34 | 31 | 10 | 21 | 0 | 0 | 87 | 123 | 20 | 64 | 25 | 35 | 3 | 1 | 209 | 238 | 54 |
| St. Louis | 59 | 30 | 22 | 7 | 0 | 189 | 184 | 67 | 58 | 19 | 28 | 11 | 0 | 159 | 196 | 49 | 117 | 49 | 50 | 18 | 0 | 348 | 380 | 116 |
| San Jose | 50 | 25 | 19 | 3 | 3 | 153 | 143 | 56 | 47 | 20 | 23 | 4 | 0 | 135 | 157 | 44 | 97 | 45 | 42 | 7 | 3 | 288 | 300 | 100 |
| Tampa Bay | 13 | 7 | 6 | 0 | 0 | 32 | 31 | 14 | 11 | 5 | 6 | 0 | 0 | 36 | 38 | 10 | 24 | 12 | 12 | 0 | 0 | 68 | 69 | 24 |
| Toronto | 41 | 22 | 13 | 6 | 0 | 172 | 146 | 50 | 44 | 22 | 20 | 2 | 0 | 165 | 160 | 46 | 85 | 44 | 33 | 8 | 0 | 337 | 306 | 96 |
| Vancouver | 77 | 37 | 29 | 10 | 1 | 278 | 265 | 85 | 80 | 21 | 49 | 10 | 0 | 219 | 295 | 52 | 157 | 58 | 78 | 20 | 1 | 497 | 560 | 137 |
| Washington | 32 | 16 | 9 | 7 | 0 | 115 | 112 | 39 | 32 | 9 | 17 | 5 | 1 | 88 | 121 | 24 | 64 | 25 | 26 | 12 | 1 | 203 | 233 | 63 |
| **Totals** | **1161** | **539** | **465** | **131** | **26** | **3937** | **3855** | **1235** | **1161** | **389** | **615** | **135** | **22** | **3444** | **4322** | **935** | **2322** | **928** | **1080** | **266** | **48** | **7381** | **8177** | **2170** |

## Playoffs

| | Series | W | L | GP | W | L | T | GF | GA | Last Mtg. | Rnd. | Result |
|---|---|---|---|---|---|---|---|---|---|---|---|---|
| Anaheim | 1 | 0 | 1 | 7 | 3 | 4 | 0 | 17 | 17 | 1997 | CQF | L 3-4 |
| Calgary | 3 | 2 | 1 | 13 | 7 | 6 | 0 | 45 | 43 | 1987 | DSF | W 4-2 |
| Colorado | 1 | 0 | 1 | 5 | 1 | 4 | 0 | 10 | 17 | 2000 | CQF | L 1-4 |
| Detroit | 2 | 0 | 2 | 12 | 4 | 8 | 0 | 28 | 44 | 1998 | CQF | L 2-4 |
| Edmonton | 6 | 0 | 6 | 26 | 4 | 22 | 0 | 75 | 120 | 1990 | DSF | L 3-4 |
| St. Louis | 2 | 0 | 2 | 11 | 4 | 7 | 0 | 29 | 39 | 1999 | CQF | L 3-4 |
| San Jose | 1 | 0 | 1 | 5 | 1 | 4 | 0 | 7 | 13 | 2002 | CQF | L 1-4 |
| Vancouver | 2 | 0 | 2 | 13 | 5 | 8 | 0 | 34 | 50 | 1993 | DSF | L 2-4 |
| **Totals** | **18** | **2** | **16** | **92** | **29** | **63** | **0** | **245** | **343** | | | |

Calgary totals include Atlanta Flames, 1979-80.
Colorado totals include Quebec, 1979-80 to 1994-95.
New Jersey totals include Colorado Rockies, 1979-80 to 1981-82.
Carolina totals include Hartford, 1979-80 to 1996-97.
Dallas totals include Minnesota North Stars, 1979-80 to 1992-93.

## Playoff Results 2009-2004

(Last playoff appearance: 2002)

**Abbreviations: Round: CQF** – conference quarter-final; **DSF** – division semi-final.

## 2008-09 Results

| | | | |
|---|---|---|---|
| **Oct.** | 11 | Columbus | 3-1 |
| | 12 | at Anaheim | 4-2 |
| | 15 | at Chicago | 1-4 |
| | 17 | at Ottawa | 3-6 |
| | 18 | at Montreal | 1-4 |
| | 23 | Washington | 2-1 |
| | 25 | Calgary | 1-4 |
| | 30 | Pittsburgh | 4-1 |
| **Nov.** | 1 | Minnesota | 2-3 |
| | 4 | at Calgary | 4-2 |
| | 6 | at Vancouver | 0-1 |
| | 8 | Florida | 4-1 |
| | 9 | San Jose | 4-2 |
| | 12 | at Columbus | 5-2 |
| | 13 | at Minnesota | 0-4 |
| | 15 | Dallas | 2-3 |
| | 18 | Chicago | 2-3† |
| | 21 | at Carolina | 2-5 |
| | 22 | at Philadelphia | 3-4* |
| | 24 | at NY Rangers | 1-4 |
| | 26 | at Columbus | 3-2 |
| | 28 | Colorado | 2-1 |
| | 29 | San Jose | 2-3 |
| **Dec.** | 2 | Los Angeles | 4-2 |
| | 4 | Toronto | 6-3 |
| | 6 | at St. Louis | 3-4 |
| | 7 | at Chicago | 1-7 |
| | 10 | at Dallas | 5-3 |
| | 11 | Minnesota | 3-1 |
| | 13 | Detroit | 4-5† |
| | 16 | at Dallas | 1-2* |
| | 18 | Nashville | 2-1 |
| | 20 | Columbus | 2-0 |
| | 22 | at Edmonton | 2-4 |
| | 23 | at Colorado | 4-5* |
| | 26 | at Los Angeles | 2-1 |
| | 27 | Los Angeles | 0-4 |
| | 31 | Colorado | 3-1 |
| **Jan.** | 2 | NY Islanders | 5-4 |
| | 4 | at Anaheim | 0-2 |
| | 6 | Chicago | 0-6 |
| | 8 | Tampa Bay | 3-2 |
| | 10 | Dallas | 1-0† |
| | 13 | at Minnesota | 3-6 |
| | 15 | at Vancouver | 4-1 |
| | 17 | at Calgary | 4-3 |
| | 18 | at Edmonton | 3-6 |
| | 20 | Detroit | 6-3 |
| | 27 | Anaheim | 3-7 |
| | 29 | at San Jose | 0-2 |
| | 31 | Buffalo | 0-2 |
| **Feb.** | 3 | at Nashville | 1-2 |
| | 4 | at Detroit | 4-5 |
| | 7 | Carolina | 2-7 |
| | 11 | at Dallas | 1-0 |
| | 12 | Vancouver | 3-4 |
| | 14 | Calgary | 5-7 |
| | 16 | Edmonton | 1-3 |
| | 19 | Atlanta | 4-3† |
| | 21 | at Los Angeles | 6-3 |
| | 24 | at St. Louis | 1-2 |
| | 26 | at Nashville | 1-4 |
| | 28 | St. Louis | 1-3 |
| **Mar.** | 5 | at Boston | 2-1 |
| | 6 | at Buffalo | 1-5 |
| | 8 | at NY Islanders | 2-3 |
| | 10 | at Detroit | 2-3* |
| | 12 | at New Jersey | 2-5 |
| | 14 | Nashville | 0-2 |
| | 17 | San Jose | 4-3 |
| | 19 | Anaheim | 2-3† |
| | 21 | Vancouver | 5-1 |
| | 22 | at Anaheim | 2-6 |
| | 26 | Edmonton | 3-2 |
| | 28 | at San Jose | 2-3 |
| | 30 | Dallas | 6-5* |
| **Apr.** | 1 | at Colorado | 3-0 |
| | 2 | Los Angeles | 2-1 |
| | 4 | at Los Angeles | 1-6 |
| | 7 | St. Louis | 1-5 |
| | 9 | at San Jose | 4-1 |
| | 11 | Anaheim | 5-4† |

* – Overtime † – Shootout

## Entry Draft Selections 2009-1995

Name in bold denotes played in NHL.

**2009**
Pick
6 Oliver Ekman-Larsson
36 Chris Brown
91 Michael Lee
97 Jordan Szwarz
105 Justin Weller
157 Evan Bloodoff

**2008**
Pick
8 **Mikkel Boedker**
28 **Viktor Tikhonov**
49 Jared Staal
69 Michael Stone
76 Mathieu Brodeur
99 Colin Long
159 Brett Hextall
189 Tim Billingsley

**2007**
Pick
3 **Kyle Turris**
30 Nick Ross
32 Brett Maclean
36 Joel Gistedt
103 Vladimir Ruzicka
123 Maxim Goncharov
153 Scott Darling

**2006**
Pick
8 **Peter Mueller**
29 Chris Summers
88 Jonas Ahnelov
130 Brett Bennett
131 Martin Latal
152 Jordan Bendfeld
188 Chris Frank
196 Benn Ferriero

**2005**
Pick
17 **Martin Hanzal**
59 Pier-Olivier Pelletier
105 **Keith Yandle**
148 Anton Krysanov
212 Pat Brosnihan

**2004**
Pick
5 **Blake Wheeler**
35 Logan Stephenson
50 **Enver Lisin**
103 Roman Tomanek
119 **Kevin Porter**
168 Kevin Cormier
199 Chad Kolarik
240 Aaron Gagnon
261 Will Engasser
265 **Daniel Winnik**

**2003**
Pick
77 Tyler Redenbach
80 Dmitri Pestunov
115 Liam Lindstrom
178 Ryan Gibbons
208 Randall Gelech
242 Eduard Lewandowski
272 Sean Sullivan
290 Loic Burkhalter

**2002**
Pick
19 Jakub Koreis
23 **Ben Eager**
46 **David LeNeveu**
70 **Joe Callahan**
80 **Matt Jones**
97 Lance Monych
132 **John Zeiler**
186 Jeff Pietrasiak
216 Ladislav Kouba
249 Marcus Smith
280 Russell Spence

**2001**
Pick
11 **Fredrik Sjostrom**
31 **Matthew Spiller**
45 Martin Podlesak
78 Beat Forster
148 David Klema
180 Scott Polaski
210 Steve Belanger
243 Frantisek Lukes
273 Severin Blindenbacher

**2000**
Pick
19 **Krys Kolanos**
53 Alexander Tatarinov
85 **Ramzi Abid**
160 Nate Kiser
186 Brent Gauvreau
217 Igor Samoilov
249 Sami Venalainen
281 Peter Fabus

**1999**
Pick
15 Scott Kelman
19 **Kirill Safronov**
53 **Brad Ralph**
71 **Jason Jaspers**
116 Ryan Lauzon
123 Preston Mizzi
168 Erik Lewerstrom
234 **Goran Bezina**
262 Alexei Litvinenko

**1998**
Pick
14 **Patrick DesRochers**
43 **Ossi Vaananen**
73 Pat O'Leary
100 Ryan Vanbuskirk
115 **Jay Leach**
116 Josh Blackburn
129 **Robert Schnabel**
160 **Rickard Wallin**
187 **Erik Westrum**
214 Justin Hansen

**1997**
Pick
43 Juha Gustafsson
96 Scott McCallum
123 Curtis Suter
151 Robert Francz
207 Alexander Andreyev
233 **Wyatt Smith**

**1996**
Pick
11 **Dan Focht**
24 **Daniel Briere**
62 Per-Anton Lundstrom
119 **Richard Lintner**
139 **Robert Esche**
174 **Trevor Letowski**
200 Nicholas Lent
226 Marc-Etienne Hubert

**1995**
Pick
7 **Shane Doan**
32 **Marc Chouinard**
34 **Jason Doig**
67 **Brad Isbister**
84 **Justin Kurtz**
121 Brian Elder
136 Sylvain Daigle
162 Paul Traynor
188 **Jaroslav Obsut**
189 Fredrik Loven
214 Rob Deciantis

## General Managers' History

John Ferguson, 1979-80 to 1987-88; John Ferguson and Mike Smith, 1988-89; Mike Smith, 1989-90 to 1992-93; Mike Smith and John Paddock, 1993-94; John Paddock, 1994-95, 1995-96; John Paddock and Bobby Smith, 1996-97; Bobby Smith, 1997-98 to 1999-2000; Bobby Smith and Cliff Fletcher, 2000-01; Cliff Fletcher and Michael Barnett, 2001-02; Michael Barnett, 2002-03 to 2006-07; Don Maloney, 2007-08 to date.

# Don Maloney

## General Manager

*Born: Lindsay, Ont., September 5, 1958.*

Don Maloney was signed as general manager of the Phoenix Coyotes on May 30, 2007, joining the team from the New York Rangers for whom he served as vice president of player personnel and assistant general manager. He assisted Rangers' president and g.m. Glen Sather in all player transactions and contract negotiations and was involved with the team's professional and amateur scouting operations. Maloney spent 10 seasons in the Rangers' front office. He played a key role in the Rangers' development of several prospects into productive NHL players, including Henrik Lundqvist and Peter Prucha. Maloney also served as assistant general manager for Team Canada squads that won gold medals at the 2003 and 2004 World Championships.

Maloney's first front office position in the NHL was as assistant general manager of the New York Islanders following his retirement as a player with the club on January 17, 1991. Maloney later served as Islanders' general manager from August 17, 1992 to December 2, 1995. Among the players drafted by the Islanders during Maloney's tenure with the club were Todd Bertuzzi, Bryan McCabe, Ziggy Palffy, Tommy Salo and Darius Kasparaitis. Maloney then served as Eastern professional scout for the San Jose Sharks during the 1996-97 season prior to joining the Rangers' front office.

As a player, Maloney registered 214 goals, 350 assists, and 564 points as well as 815 penalty minutes in 765 regular-season games over 13 NHL campaigns with the Rangers, Hartford Whalers and Islanders. He also collected 22 goals, 35 assists, and 57 points in 94 career playoff games. Maloney spent 11 seasons with the Rangers after being selected by the club in the second round (26th overall) of the 1978 NHL Entry Draft. He helped lead the Rangers to the 1980 Stanley Cup Final by posting 20 points (7 goals, 13 assists) that postseason, a playoff record for rookies at the time. Maloney played in the NHL All-Star Game in 1983 and 1984. He was named MVP of the 1984 game.

# Club Directory

Jobing.com Arena

**Phoenix Coyotes**
6751 N. Sunset Blvd. #200
Glendale, AZ 85305
Phone **623/772-3200**
FAX 623/872-2000
Tickets 480/563-PUCK

**Jobing.com Arena**
9400 W. Maryland Avenue
Glendale, AZ 85305
Phone 623/772-3200
FAX 623/772-3201
**Capacity:** 17,125
www.PhoenixCoyotes.com

**Club Officers and Executives**

| | |
|---|---|
| Majority Investor | Jerry Moyes |
| Managing Partner, Alt. Gov. & Head Coach | Wayne Gretzky |
| President, Chief Operating Officer & Alt. Gov. | Douglas Moss |
| General Manager | Don Maloney |
| Assistant General Manager | Brad Treliving |
| Exec. V.P., Chief Marketing Officer | Michael Bucek |
| Exec. V.P., Chief Financial Officer | Michael Nealy |
| Exec. V.P., Chief Communications Officer | Jeff Holbrook |
| Executive Assistant to the President | Cheryl Taylor |
| Exec. Support/Legal & Risk Mgmt. Coordinator | Gail Avisar |

**Hockey Operations**

| | |
|---|---|
| Head Coach | Wayne Gretzky |
| Associate Coach | Ulf Samuelsson |
| Assistant Coach | Doug Sulliman |
| Goaltending Coach | Grant Fuhr |
| Video Coach | Steve Peters |
| Power Skating Coach | Mark Ciaccio |
| Director of Prospect Development | Sean Burke |
| Director of Hockey Administration | Chris O'Hearn |
| Manager of Hockey Operations | Kimberly Trichel |
| Head Athletic Trainer | Jason Serbus |
| Assistant Athletic Trainer | John Bernal |
| Strength & Conditioning Coordinator | Mike Bahn |
| Massage Therapist | Jukka Nieminen |
| Head Equipment Manager | Stan Wilson |
| Equipment Manager | Tony Silva |
| Assistant Equipment Manager | Jason Rudee |
| Team Travel Coordinator | Rick Braunstein |
| Director of Amateur Scouting | Keith Gretzky |
| Head Professional Scout | Frank Effinger |
| Assistant Director of Amateur Scouting | Steve Lyons |
| Head European Scout | Christian Ruuttu |
| Professional Scout | Derek MacKinnon |
| European & Amateur Scouts | Rob Murphy, Robert Nordmark, Barclay Parneta, Gord Pell, Keith Sullivan |
| Video Scout | David MacLean |
| Director of Team Security | Jim O'Neal |
| Team Internist | Robert Luberto, D.O. |
| Team Orthopedic Surgeons | Drs. Lawrence Emmott, Doug Freedberg, Gary Waslewski |
| Team Dentist | Dr. Ron Foeldi |
| San Antonio (AHL) Head Coach | Greg Ireland |
| San Antonio (AHL) Assistant Coach | Ray Edwards |
| San Antonio (AHL) Head Athletic Trainer | Mike Ermatinger |
| San Antonio (AHL) Equipment Manager | John Krouse |

**Broadcasting**

| | |
|---|---|
| TV Play-by-Play / Color | Dave Strader / TBD |
| TV/Radio Host | Todd Walsh |
| Radio Play-by-Play / Color | Bob Heethuis / Tyson Nash |
| Director of Broadcasting | Doug Cannon |
| Radio Host | Luke Lapinski |

**Communications**

| | |
|---|---|
| Director of Media Relations | Sergey Kocharov |
| Manager of Communications | Rob Crean |

**Community Relations**

| | |
|---|---|
| Director, Community Relations & Fan Development | Sarah Finecey |
| Manager of Hockey Development | Scott Storkan |

**News Content**

| | |
|---|---|
| Vice President of News Content | Dave Vest |

**Marketing**

| | |
|---|---|
| Vice President of Marketing | Stacey Cohen |
| Director of Advertising & Media | Ted Santiago |

**Corporate Sales & Service**

| | |
|---|---|
| Vice President of Corporate Partnerships | Judd Norris |

**Suite Sales**

| | |
|---|---|
| Director of Suite Sales | Mike Briody |

**Ticket Operations**

| | |
|---|---|
| Director of Ticket Operations | Douglas Vanderheyden |

**Ticket Sales & Services**

| | |
|---|---|
| Vice President of Ticket Sales | Flavil Hampsten |
| Sr. Director of Ticket Sales | David Burke |

**Finance & Accounting**

| | |
|---|---|
| Vice President of Finance and Controller | Joe Leibfried |
| Assistant Controller | Burlenti Shaban |

**Legal**

| | |
|---|---|
| Vice President, General Counsel | Steve Weinreich |

**Human Resources**

| | |
|---|---|
| Vice President of Human Resources | Julie Atherton |

**Technology**

| | |
|---|---|
| Senior Director of IT | Jay Gaskin |
| Senior IT Systems Engineer | Kevin Whitaker |

**Team Information**

| | |
|---|---|
| Broadcast Television Station | KAZT-TV |
| Regional Sports Network | FSN Arizona |
| Radio Station | XTRA Sports 910 |
| Team Photographer | Norm Hall |

# Pittsburgh Penguins

## Key Off-Season Signings/Acquisitions

**2009**

**June 17** • Re-signed D **Alex Goligoski.**
**29** • Re-signed RW **Craig Adams** and RW **Bill Guerin.**
**July 1** • Signed LW **Mike Rupp.**
**3** • Re-signed LW **Ruslan Fedotenko.**
**10** • Signed D **Jay McKee.**
**21** • Signed G **Brent Johnson.**
**Aug. 5** • Named **Tony Granato** assistant coach.

## 2008-09 Results: 45W-28L-3OTL-6SOL 99PTS.
## Second, Atlantic Division

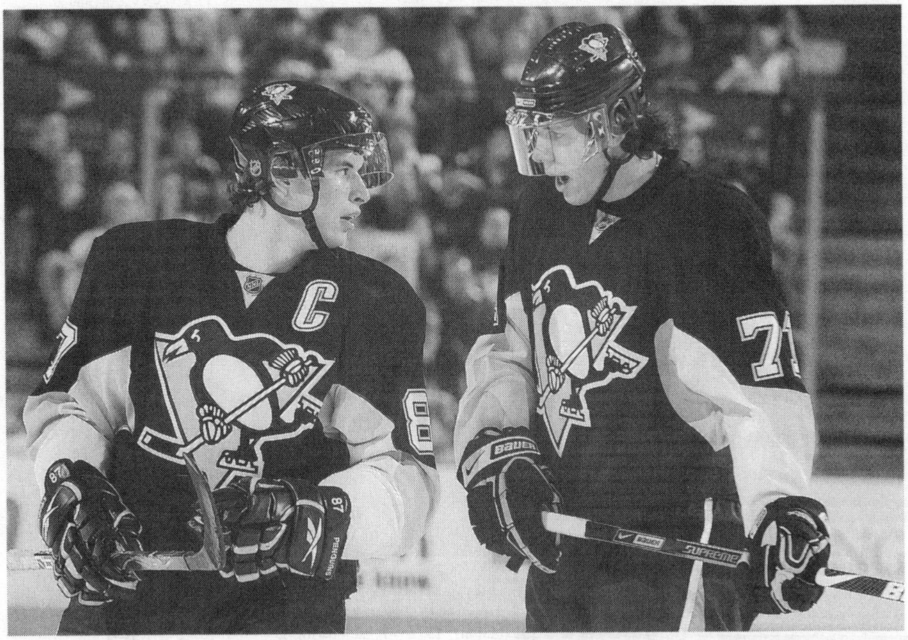

*Penguins superstars Evgeni Malkin and Sidney Crosby led their team to the Stanley Cup in 2009. Malkin also won the scoring title, putting his name with Crosby's among the eight different players who've led the NHL in scoring over the past eight seasons.*

## 2009-10 Schedule

| | | | | | | | |
|---|---|---|---|---|---|---|---|
| **Oct.** | Fri. | 2 | NY Rangers | **Jan.** | Sat. | 2 | at Tampa Bay* |
| | Sat. | 3 | at NY Islanders | | Sun. | 3 | at Florida* |
| | Wed. | 7 | Phoenix | | Tue. | 5 | Atlanta |
| | Thu. | 8 | at Philadelphia | | Thu. | 7 | Philadelphia |
| | Sat. | 10 | at Toronto | | Sat. | 9 | at Toronto |
| | Mon. | 12 | at Ottawa | | Mon. | 11 | at Minnesota |
| | Wed. | 14 | at Carolina | | Wed. | 13 | at Calgary |
| | Sat. | 17 | Tampa Bay | | Thu. | 14 | at Edmonton |
| | Tue. | 20 | St. Louis | | Sat. | 16 | at Vancouver |
| | Fri. | 23 | Florida | | Tue. | 19 | NY Islanders |
| | Sat. | 24 | New Jersey | | Thu. | 21 | Washington |
| | Wed. | 28 | Montreal | | Sun. | 24 | at Philadelphia* |
| | Fri. | 30 | at Columbus | | Mon. | 25 | at NY Rangers |
| | Sat. | 31 | Minnesota | | Thu. | 28 | Ottawa |
| **Nov.** | Tue. | 3 | at Anaheim | | Sun. | 31 | Detroit* |
| | Thu. | 5 | at Los Angeles | **Feb.** | Mon. | 1 | Buffalo |
| | Sat. | 7 | at San Jose | | Sat. | 6 | at Montreal* |
| | Tue. | 10 | at Boston | | Sun. | 7 | at Washington* |
| | Thu. | 12 | New Jersey | | Wed. | 10 | NY Islanders |
| | Sat. | 14 | Boston | | Fri. | 12 | NY Rangers |
| | Mon. | 16 | Anaheim | | Sun. | 14 | Nashville* |
| | Thu. | 19 | at Ottawa | **Mar.** | Tue. | 2 | Buffalo |
| | Sat. | 21 | at Atlanta | | Thu. | 4 | at NY Rangers |
| | Mon. | 23 | at Florida | | Sat. | 6 | Dallas* |
| | Wed. | 25 | Montreal | | Sun. | 7 | Boston* |
| | Fri. | 27 | at NY Islanders* | | Thu. | 11 | at Carolina |
| | Sat. | 28 | NY Rangers | | Fri. | 12 | at New Jersey |
| | Mon. | 30 | at NY Rangers | | Sun. | 14 | at Tampa Bay* |
| **Dec.** | Thu. | 3 | Colorado | | Wed. | 17 | at New Jersey |
| | Sat. | 5 | Chicago | | Thu. | 18 | at Boston |
| | Mon. | 7 | Carolina | | Sat. | 20 | Carolina* |
| | Thu. | 10 | at Montreal | | Mon. | 22 | at Detroit |
| | Sat. | 12 | Florida | | Wed. | 24 | at Washington |
| | Tue. | 15 | Philadelphia | | Sat. | 27 | Philadelphia* |
| | Thu. | 17 | at Philadelphia | | Sun. | 28 | Toronto* |
| | Sat. | 19 | at Buffalo | | Wed. | 31 | Tampa Bay |
| | Mon. | 21 | New Jersey | **Apr.** | Sat. | 3 | Atlanta* |
| | Wed. | 23 | Ottawa | | Tue. | 6 | Washington |
| | Sun. | 27 | Toronto | | Thu. | 8 | NY Islanders |
| | Tue. | 29 | at Buffalo | | Sat. | 10 | at Atlanta |
| | Wed. | 30 | at New Jersey | | Sun. | 11 | at NY Islanders* |

* Denotes afternoon game.

## Year-by-Year Record

| | | Home | | | | Road | | | | Overall | | | | | | | | |
|---|---|---|---|---|---|---|---|---|---|---|---|---|---|---|---|---|---|---|
| **Season** | **GP** | **W** | **L** | **T** | **OL** | **W** | **L** | **T** | **OL** | **W** | **L** | **T** | **OL** | **GF** | **GA** | **Pts.** | **Finished** | **Playoff Result** |
| **2008-09** | **82** | **25** | **13** | **....** | **3** | **20** | **15** | **....** | **6** | **45** | **28** | **....** | **9** | **264** | **239** | **99** | **2nd, Atlantic Div.** | **Won Stanley Cup** |
| 2007-08 | 82 | 26 | 10 | .... | 5 | 21 | 17 | .... | 3 | 47 | 27 | .... | 8 | 247 | 216 | 102 | 1st, Atlantic Div. | Lost Final |
| 2006-07 | 82 | 26 | 10 | .... | 5 | 21 | 14 | .... | 6 | 47 | 24 | .... | 11 | 277 | 246 | 105 | 2nd, Atlantic Div. | Lost Conf. Quarter-Final |
| 2005-06 | 82 | 12 | 21 | .... | 8 | 10 | 25 | .... | 6 | 22 | 46 | .... | 14 | 244 | 316 | 58 | 5th, Atlantic Div. | Out of Playoffs |
| 2004-05 | .... | .... | .... | .... | .... | .... | .... | .... | .... | .... | .... | .... | .... | .... | .... | .... | | |
| 2003-04 | 82 | 13 | 22 | 6 | 0 | 10 | 25 | 2 | 4 | 23 | 47 | 8 | 4 | 190 | 303 | 58 | 5th, Atlantic Div. | Out of Playoffs |
| 2002-03 | 82 | 15 | 22 | 2 | 2 | 12 | 22 | 4 | 3 | 27 | 44 | 6 | 5 | 189 | 255 | 65 | 5th, Atlantic Div. | Out of Playoffs |
| 2001-02 | 82 | 16 | 20 | 4 | 1 | 12 | 21 | 4 | 4 | 28 | 41 | 8 | 5 | 198 | 249 | 69 | 5th, Atlantic Div. | Out of Playoffs |
| 2000-01 | 82 | 24 | 15 | 2 | 0 | 18 | 13 | 7 | 3 | 42 | 28 | 9 | 3 | 281 | 256 | 96 | 3rd, Atlantic Div. | Lost Conf. Championship |
| 1999-2000 | 82 | 23 | 11 | 7 | 0 | 14 | 20 | 1 | 6 | 37 | 31 | 8 | 6 | 241 | 236 | 88 | 3rd, Atlantic Div. | Lost Conf. Semi-Final |
| 1998-99 | 82 | 21 | 10 | 10 | .... | 17 | 20 | 4 | .... | 38 | 30 | 14 | .... | 242 | 225 | 90 | 3rd, Atlantic Div. | Lost Conf. Semi-Final |
| 1997-98 | 82 | 21 | 10 | 10 | .... | 19 | 14 | 8 | .... | 40 | 24 | 18 | .... | 228 | 188 | 98 | 1st, Northeast Div. | Lost Conf. Quarter-Final |
| 1996-97 | 82 | 25 | 11 | 5 | .... | 13 | 25 | 3 | .... | 38 | 36 | 8 | .... | 285 | 280 | 84 | 2nd, Northeast Div. | Lost Conf. Quarter-Final |
| 1995-96 | 82 | 32 | 9 | 0 | .... | 17 | 20 | 4 | .... | 49 | 29 | 4 | .... | 362 | 284 | 102 | 1st, Northeast Div. | Lost Conf. Championship |
| 1994-95 | 48 | 18 | 5 | 1 | .... | 11 | 11 | 2 | .... | 29 | 16 | 3 | .... | 181 | 158 | 61 | 2nd, Northeast Div. | Lost Conf. Semi-Final |
| 1993-94 | 84 | 25 | 9 | 8 | .... | 19 | 18 | 5 | .... | 44 | 27 | 13 | .... | 299 | 285 | 101 | 1st, Northeast Div. | Lost Conf. Quarter-Final |
| 1992-93 | 84 | 32 | 6 | 4 | .... | 24 | 15 | 3 | .... | 56 | 21 | 7 | .... | 367 | 268 | 119 | 1st, Patrick Div. | Lost Div. Final |
| **1991-92** | **80** | **21** | **13** | **6** | **....** | **18** | **19** | **3** | **....** | **39** | **32** | **9** | **....** | **343** | **308** | **87** | **3rd, Patrick Div.** | **Won Stanley Cup** |
| **1990-91** | **80** | **25** | **12** | **3** | **....** | **16** | **21** | **3** | **....** | **41** | **33** | **6** | **....** | **342** | **305** | **88** | **1st, Patrick Div.** | **Won Stanley Cup** |
| 1989-90 | 80 | 22 | 15 | 3 | .... | 10 | 25 | 5 | .... | 32 | 40 | 8 | .... | 318 | 359 | 72 | 5th, Patrick Div. | Out of Playoffs |
| 1988-89 | 80 | 24 | 13 | 3 | .... | 16 | 20 | 4 | .... | 40 | 33 | 7 | .... | 347 | 349 | 87 | 2nd, Patrick Div. | Lost Div. Final |
| 1987-88 | 80 | 22 | 12 | 6 | .... | 14 | 23 | 3 | .... | 36 | 35 | 9 | .... | 319 | 316 | 81 | 6th, Patrick Div. | Out of Playoffs |
| 1986-87 | 80 | 19 | 15 | 6 | .... | 11 | 23 | 6 | .... | 30 | 38 | 12 | .... | 297 | 290 | 72 | 5th, Patrick Div. | Out of Playoffs |
| 1985-86 | 80 | 20 | 15 | 5 | .... | 14 | 23 | 3 | .... | 34 | 38 | 8 | .... | 313 | 305 | 76 | 5th, Patrick Div. | Out of Playoffs |
| 1984-85 | 80 | 17 | 20 | 3 | .... | 7 | 31 | 2 | .... | 24 | 51 | 5 | .... | 276 | 385 | 53 | 6th, Patrick Div. | Out of Playoffs |
| 1983-84 | 80 | 7 | 29 | 4 | .... | 9 | 29 | 2 | .... | 16 | 58 | 6 | .... | 254 | 390 | 38 | 6th, Patrick Div. | Out of Playoffs |
| 1982-83 | 80 | 14 | 22 | 4 | .... | 4 | 31 | 5 | .... | 18 | 53 | 9 | .... | 257 | 394 | 45 | 6th, Patrick Div. | Out of Playoffs |
| 1981-82 | 80 | 21 | 11 | 8 | .... | 10 | 25 | 5 | .... | 31 | 36 | 13 | .... | 310 | 337 | 75 | 4th, Patrick Div. | Lost Div. Semi-Final |
| 1980-81 | 80 | 21 | 16 | 3 | .... | 9 | 21 | 10 | .... | 30 | 37 | 13 | .... | 302 | 345 | 73 | 3rd, Norris Div. | Lost Prelim. Round |
| 1979-80 | 80 | 20 | 13 | 7 | .... | 10 | 24 | 6 | .... | 30 | 37 | 13 | .... | 251 | 303 | 73 | 3rd, Norris Div. | Lost Prelim. Round |
| 1978-79 | 80 | 23 | 12 | 5 | .... | 13 | 19 | 8 | .... | 36 | 31 | 13 | .... | 281 | 279 | 85 | 2nd, Norris Div. | Lost Quarter-Final |
| 1977-78 | 80 | 16 | 15 | 9 | .... | 9 | 22 | 9 | .... | 25 | 37 | 18 | .... | 254 | 321 | 68 | 4th, Norris Div. | Out of Playoffs |
| 1976-77 | 80 | 22 | 12 | 6 | .... | 12 | 21 | 7 | .... | 34 | 33 | 13 | .... | 240 | 252 | 81 | 3rd, Norris Div. | Lost Prelim. Round |
| 1975-76 | 80 | 23 | 11 | 6 | .... | 12 | 22 | 6 | .... | 35 | 33 | 12 | .... | 339 | 303 | 82 | 3rd, Norris Div. | Lost Prelim. Round |
| 1974-75 | 80 | 25 | 5 | 10 | .... | 12 | 23 | 5 | .... | 37 | 28 | 15 | .... | 326 | 289 | 89 | 3rd, Norris Div. | Lost Quarter-Final |
| 1973-74 | 78 | 15 | 18 | 6 | .... | 13 | 23 | 3 | .... | 28 | 41 | 9 | .... | 242 | 273 | 65 | 5th, West Div. | Out of Playoffs |
| 1972-73 | 78 | 24 | 11 | 4 | .... | 8 | 26 | 5 | .... | 32 | 37 | 9 | .... | 257 | 265 | 73 | 5th, West Div. | Out of Playoffs |
| 1971-72 | 78 | 18 | 15 | 6 | .... | 8 | 23 | 8 | .... | 26 | 38 | 14 | .... | 220 | 258 | 66 | 4th, West Div. | Lost Quarter-Final |
| 1970-71 | 78 | 18 | 12 | 9 | .... | 3 | 25 | 11 | .... | 21 | 37 | 20 | .... | 221 | 240 | 62 | 6th, West Div. | Out of Playoffs |
| 1969-70 | 76 | 17 | 13 | 8 | .... | 9 | 25 | 4 | .... | 26 | 38 | 12 | .... | 182 | 238 | 64 | 2nd, West Div. | Lost Semi-Final |
| 1968-69 | 76 | 12 | 20 | 6 | .... | 8 | 25 | 5 | .... | 20 | 45 | 11 | .... | 189 | 252 | 51 | 5th, West Div. | Out of Playoffs |
| 1967-68 | 74 | 15 | 12 | 10 | .... | 12 | 22 | 3 | .... | 27 | 34 | 13 | .... | 195 | 216 | 67 | 5th, West Div. | Out of Playoffs |

**ATLANTIC DIVISION**
**43rd NHL Season**

**Franchise date:** June 5, 1967

# 2009-10 Player Personnel

| FORWARDS | HT | WT | S | Place of Birth | *Age | 2008-09 Club |
|---|---|---|---|---|---|---|
| ADAMS, Craig | 6-0 | 197 | R | Seria, Brunei | 32 | Chicago-Pittsburgh |
| BOOGAARD, Aaron | 6-3 | 220 | R | Newmarket, Ont. | 23 | Wilkes-Barre |
| BROOKBANK, Wade | 6-4 | 225 | L | Lanigan, Sask. | 32 | Carolina-Norfolk |
| CAPUTI, Luca | 6-2 | 184 | L | Toronto, Ont. | 21 | Pit-Wilkes-Barre-Whlng |
| CONNER, Chris | 5-8 | 180 | L | Westland, MI | 25 | Dallas-Peoria |
| COOKE, Matt | 5-11 | 205 | L | Belleville, Ont. | 31 | Pittsburgh |
| CROSBY, Sidney | 5-11 | 200 | L | Cole Harbour, N.S. | 22 | Pittsburgh |
| DUPUIS, Pascal | 6-1 | 205 | L | Laval, Que. | 30 | Pittsburgh |
| FEDOTENKO, Ruslan | 6-2 | 195 | L | Kiev, USSR | 30 | Pittsburgh |
| GODARD, Eric | 6-4 | 214 | R | Vernon, B.C. | 29 | Pittsburgh |
| GUERIN, Bill | 6-2 | 220 | R | Worcester, MA | 38 | NY Islanders-Pittsburgh |
| JEFFREY, Dustin | 6-1 | 205 | L | Sarnia, Ont. | 21 | Pittsburgh-Wilkes-Barre |
| JOHNSON, Nick | 6-1 | 183 | R | Calgary, Alta. | 23 | Wheeling-Wilkes-Barre |
| KENNEDY, Tyler | 5-11 | 183 | R | Sault Ste. Marie, Ont. | 23 | Pittsburgh |
| KUNITZ, Chris | 6-0 | 193 | L | Regina, Sask. | 30 | Anaheim-Pittsburgh |
| LETESTU, Mark | 5-11 | 195 | R | Elk Point, Alta. | 24 | Wilkes-Barre |
| MALKIN, Evgeni | 6-3 | 195 | L | Magnitogorsk, USSR | 23 | Pittsburgh |
| RUPP, Mike | 6-5 | 230 | L | Cleveland, OH | 29 | New Jersey |
| SMITH, Wyatt | 5-11 | 205 | L | Thief River Falls, MN | 32 | Norfolk-San Antonio |
| STAAL, Jordan | 6-4 | 220 | L | Thunder Bay, Ont. | 21 | Pittsburgh |
| TALBOT, Maxime | 5-11 | 190 | L | Lemoyne, Que. | 25 | Pittsburgh |
| WALLACE, Tim | 6-1 | 207 | R | Anchorage, AK | 25 | Pittsburgh-Wilkes-Barre |
| **DEFENSEMEN** | | | | | | |
| BISSONNETTE, Paul | 6-2 | 211 | L | Welland, Ont. | 24 | Pittsburgh-Wilkes-Barre |
| D'AVERSA, Jonathan | 6-2 | 200 | R | Richmond Hill, Ont. | 23 | Wilkes-Barre-Wheeling |
| EATON, Mark | 6-2 | 204 | L | Wilmington, DE | 32 | Pittsburgh |
| FERNHOLM, Daniel | 6-4 | 218 | L | Stockholm, Sweden | 25 | Linkoping |
| GOLIGOSKI, Alex | 5-11 | 180 | L | Grand Rapids, MN | 24 | Pittsburgh-Wilkes-Barre |
| GONCHAR, Sergei | 6-2 | 211 | L | Chelyabinsk, USSR | 35 | Pittsburgh |
| GUENIN, Nate | 6-2 | 210 | R | Sewickley, PA | 26 | Phi-Phi (AHL) |
| LEE, Chris | 6-0 | 185 | L | MacTier, Ont. | 28 | Bridgeport |
| LETANG, Kris | 6-0 | 201 | R | Montreal, Que. | 22 | Pittsburgh |
| LOVEJOY, Ben | 6-2 | 215 | R | Concord, NH | 25 | Pittsburgh-Wilkes-Barre |
| McKEE, Jay | 6-4 | 203 | L | Kingston, Ont. | 32 | St. Louis |
| ORPIK, Brooks | 6-2 | 219 | L | San Francisco, CA | 29 | Pittsburgh |

| GOALTENDERS | HT | WT | C | Place of Birth | *Age | 2008-09 Club |
|---|---|---|---|---|---|---|
| CURRY, John | 5-11 | 185 | L | Shorewood, MN | 25 | Pittsburgh-Wilkes-Barre |
| FLEURY, Marc-Andre | 6-2 | 180 | L | Sorel, Que. | 24 | Pittsburgh |
| JOHNSON, Brent | 6-3 | 199 | L | Farmington, MI | 32 | Washington |

* – Age at start of 2009-10 season

## General Managers' History

Jack Riley, 1967-68 to 1969-70; Red Kelly, 1970-71; Red Kelly and Jack Riley, 1971-72; Jack Riley, 1972-73; Jack Riley and Jack Button, 1973-74; Jack Button, 1974-75; Wren Blair, 1975-76; Wren Blair and Baz Bastien, 1976-77; Baz Bastien, 1977-78 to 1982-83; Eddie Johnston, 1983-84 to 1987-88; Tony Esposito, 1988-89; Tony Esposito and Craig Patrick, 1989-90; Craig Patrick, 1990-91 to 2005-06; Ray Shero, 2006-07 to date.

# Dan Bylsma

### Head Coach

*Born: Grand Haven, MI, September 19, 1970.*

Dan Bylsma was named interim head coach of the Pittsburgh Penguins on February 15, 2009. He had the interim tag removed on April 28. Bylsma had been serving as head coach of the team's American Hockey League affiliate in Wilkes-Barre/Scranton when he was promoted to Pittsburgh. He took over a slumping Penguins team that was six points out of a playoff spot with 25 games to go and guided them to the Stanley Cup. Bylsma is the 14th rookie head coach, and just the fourth in the past 50 years, to win the Stanley Cup. Of these, only Montreal's Al MacNeil (1970-71) took over in midseason.

Bylsma played nine NHL seasons as a right winger with Los Angeles and Anaheim from 1995 to 2004. A role player who excelled at killing penalties and blocking shots, he played 429 NHL regular-season games and also played in the 2003 Stanley Cup Final with Anaheim. He retired as a player following the 2003-04 season. The native of Grand Haven, Michigan began his coaching career as an assistant with the Cincinnati Mighty Ducks of the AHL in 2004-05. He made his NHL coaching debut as an assistant with the New York Islanders in 2005-06.

Bylsma joined the Penguins organization as an assistant to Todd Richards in Wilkes-Barre/Scranton in 2006-07. The Baby Penguins won the AHL East Division and Eastern Conference championships in 2007-08 and advanced to the Calder Cup Final. When Richards accepted the job as an assistant coach with the NHL's San Jose Sharks in the offseason, Bylsma was elevated to head coach at Wilkes-Barre/Scranton.

Bylsma was an outstanding athlete at West Michigan Christian High School, winning a state individual golf championship and starting in left field on a state championship baseball team. He played Junior B hockey for St. Mary's of the Ontario Hockey Association before playing four years of college hockey at Bowling Green. He was twice selected to the Central Collegiate Hockey Association (CCHA) All-Academic Team. Dan and his father, Jay, also have written four books about sports for kids and families, including "So Your Son Wants to Play in the NHL" and "So You Want to Play in the NHL." He operates Dan Bylsma's Western Michigan Hockey Camp and has established the Dan Bylsma Charitable Trust Fund, which provides a means to assist children with the high cost of participating in youth sports, especially hockey.

# 2008-09 Scoring

* – rookie

## Regular Season

| Pos | # | Player | Team | GP | G | A | Pts | TOI | +/– | PIM | PP | SH | GW | S | % |
|---|---|---|---|---|---|---|---|---|---|---|---|---|---|---|---|
| C | 71 | Evgeni Malkin | PIT | 82 | 35 | 78 | 113 | 22:31 | 17 | 80 | 14 | 2 | 4 | 290 | 12.1 |
| C | 87 | Sidney Crosby | PIT | 77 | 33 | 70 | 103 | 21:56 | 3 | 76 | 7 | 0 | 3 | 238 | 13.9 |
| L | 14 | Chris Kunitz | ANA | 62 | 16 | 19 | 35 | 16:29 | 9 | 55 | 3 | 0 | 2 | 139 | 11.5 |
| | | | PIT | 20 | 7 | 11 | 18 | 16:16 | 3 | 16 | 3 | 0 | 1 | 39 | 17.9 |
| | | | Total | 82 | 23 | 30 | 53 | 16:26 | 12 | 71 | 6 | 0 | 3 | 178 | 12.9 |
| C | 11 | Jordan Staal | PIT | 82 | 22 | 27 | 49 | 19:50 | 5 | 37 | 2 | 1 | 3 | 166 | 13.3 |
| R | 13 | Bill Guerin | NYI | 61 | 16 | 20 | 36 | 17:12 | –15 | 63 | 5 | 0 | 3 | 181 | 8.8 |
| | | | PIT | 17 | 5 | 7 | 12 | 14:43 | 3 | 18 | 0 | 0 | 1 | 45 | 11.1 |
| | | | Total | 78 | 21 | 27 | 48 | 16:40 | –12 | 81 | 5 | 0 | 4 | 226 | 9.3 |
| R | 17 | Petr Sykora | PIT | 76 | 25 | 21 | 46 | 16:17 | 3 | 36 | 13 | 0 | 10 | 180 | 13.9 |
| L | 26 | Ruslan Fedotenko | PIT | 65 | 16 | 23 | 39 | 14:06 | 18 | 44 | 1 | 0 | 3 | 117 | 13.7 |
| R | 81 | Miroslav Satan | PIT | 65 | 17 | 19 | 36 | 15:45 | 3 | 36 | 6 | 0 | 2 | 120 | 14.2 |
| C | 48 | Tyler Kennedy | PIT | 67 | 15 | 20 | 35 | 13:46 | 15 | 30 | 0 | 0 | 3 | 171 | 8.8 |
| D | 58 | Kris Letang | PIT | 74 | 10 | 23 | 33 | 21:08 | –7 | 24 | 4 | 1 | 3 | 138 | 7.2 |
| L | 24 | Matt Cooke | PIT | 76 | 13 | 18 | 31 | 14:12 | 0 | 101 | 0 | 0 | 1 | 86 | 15.1 |
| R | 9 | Pascal Dupuis | PIT | 71 | 12 | 16 | 28 | 14:13 | 1 | 30 | 0 | 0 | 2 | 145 | 8.3 |
| C | 25 | Maxime Talbot | PIT | 75 | 12 | 10 | 22 | 14:08 | –9 | 63 | 0 | 2 | 1 | 102 | 11.8 |
| D | 3 * | Alex Goligoski | PIT | 45 | 6 | 14 | 20 | 18:18 | 5 | 16 | 4 | 0 | 0 | 61 | 9.8 |
| D | 55 | Sergei Gonchar | PIT | 25 | 6 | 13 | 19 | 25:11 | 6 | 26 | 5 | 0 | 1 | 71 | 8.5 |
| D | 44 | Brooks Orpik | PIT | 79 | 2 | 17 | 19 | 20:19 | 10 | 73 | 1 | 0 | 0 | 39 | 5.1 |
| D | 4 | Rob Scuderi | PIT | 81 | 1 | 15 | 16 | 19:09 | 23 | 18 | 0 | 0 | 0 | 51 | 2.0 |
| D | 2 | Hal Gill | PIT | 62 | 2 | 8 | 10 | 17:53 | 11 | 53 | 0 | 0 | 0 | 40 | 5.0 |
| D | 7 | Mark Eaton | PIT | 68 | 4 | 5 | 9 | 17:46 | 3 | 36 | 1 | 0 | 0 | 34 | 11.8 |
| D | 43 | Philippe Boucher | DAL | 16 | 0 | 3 | 3 | 21:43 | –4 | 15 | 0 | 0 | 0 | 29 | 0.0 |
| | | | PIT | 25 | 3 | 3 | 6 | 19:04 | 10 | 24 | 0 | 0 | 0 | 37 | 8.1 |
| | | | Total | 41 | 3 | 6 | 9 | 20:06 | 6 | 39 | 0 | 0 | 0 | 66 | 4.5 |
| R | 27 | Craig Adams | CHI | 36 | 2 | 4 | 6 | 8:43 | –3 | 22 | 1 | 0 | 0 | 38 | 5.3 |
| | | | PIT | 9 | 0 | 1 | 1 | 8:33 | 0 | 0 | 0 | 0 | 0 | 9 | 0.0 |
| | | | Total | 45 | 2 | 5 | 7 | 8:41 | –3 | 22 | 1 | 0 | 0 | 47 | 4.3 |
| C | 15 | Mike Zigomanis | PIT | 22 | 2 | 4 | 6 | 11:25 | –2 | 27 | 0 | 0 | 0 | 23 | 8.7 |
| R | 28 | Eric Godard | PIT | 71 | 2 | 2 | 4 | 4:04 | –3 | 171 | 0 | 0 | 0 | 20 | 10.0 |
| R | 37 | Bill Thomas | PIT | 16 | 2 | 1 | 3 | 9:31 | –4 | 2 | 0 | 1 | 0 | 17 | 11.8 |
| C | 42 * | Dustin Jeffrey | PIT | 14 | 1 | 2 | 3 | 10:47 | 4 | 0 | 0 | 0 | 0 | 18 | 5.6 |
| L | 14 | Chris Minard | PIT | 20 | 1 | 2 | 3 | 9:24 | 0 | 4 | 0 | 0 | 1 | 33 | 3.0 |
| L | 22 | Jeff Taffe | PIT | 8 | 0 | 2 | 2 | 8:30 | –4 | 2 | 0 | 0 | 0 | 5 | 0.0 |
| R | 63 * | Tim Wallace | PIT | 16 | 0 | 2 | 2 | 8:07 | 2 | 7 | 0 | 0 | 0 | 17 | 0.0 |
| L | 61 * | Luca Caputi | PIT | 5 | 1 | 0 | 1 | 10:16 | –1 | 4 | 0 | 0 | 0 | 7 | 14.3 |
| L | 16 * | Paul Bissonnette | PIT | 15 | 0 | 1 | 1 | 3:31 | –1 | 22 | 0 | 0 | 0 | 4 | 0.0 |
| L | 36 | Connor James | PIT | 1 | 0 | 0 | 0 | 8:15 | 0 | 0 | 0 | 0 | 0 | 0 | 0.0 |
| C | 33 * | Ryan Stone | PIT | 2 | 0 | 0 | 0 | 10:20 | 1 | 2 | 0 | 0 | 0 | 5 | 0.0 |
| D | 65 * | Ben Lovejoy | PIT | 2 | 0 | 0 | 0 | 11:53 | 0 | 0 | 0 | 0 | 0 | 1 | 0.0 |
| L | 20 | Janne Pesonen | PIT | 7 | 0 | 0 | 0 | 7:27 | –3 | 0 | 0 | 0 | 0 | 3 | 0.0 |

### Goaltending

| No. | Goaltender | GPI | Mins | Avg | W | L | OT | EN | SO | GA | SA | S% | G | A | PIM |
|---|---|---|---|---|---|---|---|---|---|---|---|---|---|---|---|
| 1 | * John Curry | 3 | 150 | 2.40 | 2 | 1 | 0 | 0 | 0 | 6 | 69 | .913 | 0 | 0 | 0 |
| 29 | Marc-Andre Fleury | 62 | 3641 | 2.67 | 35 | 18 | 7 | 5 | 4 | 162 | 1850 | .912 | 0 | 1 | 8 |
| 30 | Dany Sabourin | 19 | 989 | 2.85 | 6 | 8 | 2 | 3 | 0 | 47 | 463 | .898 | 0 | 0 | 2 |
| 32 | Mathieu Garon | 4 | 206 | 2.91 | 2 | 1 | 0 | 0 | 0 | 10 | 94 | .894 | 0 | 0 | 0 |
| | **Totals** | **82** | **5010** | **2.79** | **45** | **28** | **9** | **8** | **4** | **233** | **2484** | **.906** | | | |

## Playoffs

| Pos | # | Player | Team | GP | G | A | Pts | TOI | +/– | PIM | PP | SH | GW | OT | S | % |
|---|---|---|---|---|---|---|---|---|---|---|---|---|---|---|---|---|
| C | 71 | Evgeni Malkin | PIT | 24 | 14 | 22 | 36 | 20:57 | 3 | 51 | 7 | 0 | 3 | 1 | 104 | 13.5 |
| C | 87 | Sidney Crosby | PIT | 24 | 15 | 16 | 31 | 20:48 | 9 | 14 | 5 | 0 | 2 | 0 | 79 | 19.0 |
| R | 13 | Bill Guerin | PIT | 24 | 7 | 8 | 15 | 17:01 | 8 | 15 | 2 | 0 | 2 | 1 | 70 | 10.0 |
| L | 26 | Ruslan Fedotenko | PIT | 24 | 7 | 7 | 14 | 14:31 | 9 | 4 | 0 | 0 | 0 | 0 | 58 | 12.1 |
| D | 55 | Sergei Gonchar | PIT | 22 | 3 | 11 | 14 | 23:02 | 3 | 12 | 2 | 0 | 2 | 0 | 41 | 7.3 |
| L | 14 | Chris Kunitz | PIT | 24 | 1 | 13 | 14 | 16:54 | 3 | 19 | 0 | 0 | 0 | 0 | 46 | 2.2 |
| C | 25 | Maxime Talbot | PIT | 24 | 8 | 5 | 13 | 15:13 | 8 | 19 | 0 | 0 | 2 | 0 | 37 | 21.6 |
| D | 58 | Kris Letang | PIT | 23 | 4 | 9 | 13 | 19:18 | 1 | 26 | 2 | 0 | 1 | 1 | 54 | 7.4 |
| C | 48 | Tyler Kennedy | PIT | 24 | 5 | 4 | 9 | 13:39 | –1 | 4 | 0 | 0 | 3 | 0 | 68 | 7.4 |
| C | 11 | Jordan Staal | PIT | 24 | 4 | 5 | 9 | 19:13 | –5 | 8 | 0 | 1 | 0 | 0 | 58 | 6.9 |
| D | 7 | Mark Eaton | PIT | 24 | 4 | 3 | 7 | 18:07 | 4 | 10 | 1 | 0 | 0 | 0 | 16 | 25.0 |
| L | 24 | Matt Cooke | PIT | 24 | 1 | 6 | 7 | 15:09 | –2 | 22 | 0 | 0 | 0 | 0 | 31 | 3.2 |
| R | 81 | Miroslav Satan | PIT | 17 | 1 | 5 | 6 | 9:54 | 1 | 11 | 0 | 0 | 0 | 0 | 21 | 4.8 |
| R | 27 | Craig Adams | PIT | 24 | 3 | 2 | 5 | 9:44 | –1 | 16 | 0 | 0 | 0 | 0 | 26 | 11.5 |
| D | 4 | Rob Scuderi | PIT | 24 | 1 | 4 | 5 | 20:29 | 5 | 6 | 0 | 0 | 0 | 0 | 8 | 12.5 |
| D | 43 | Philippe Boucher | PIT | 9 | 1 | 3 | 4 | 11:23 | –2 | 4 | 1 | 0 | 1 | 0 | 10 | 10.0 |
| D | 44 | Brooks Orpik | PIT | 24 | 0 | 4 | 4 | 20:04 | –1 | 22 | 0 | 0 | 0 | 0 | 12 | 0.0 |
| D | 2 | Hal Gill | PIT | 24 | 0 | 2 | 2 | 19:25 | 8 | 6 | 0 | 0 | 0 | 0 | 17 | 0.0 |
| D | 3 * | Alex Goligoski | PIT | 2 | 0 | 1 | 1 | 10:21 | –1 | 0 | 0 | 0 | 0 | 0 | 1 | 0.0 |
| R | 17 | Petr Sykora | PIT | 7 | 0 | 1 | 1 | 11:55 | –3 | 0 | 0 | 0 | 0 | 0 | 7 | 0.0 |
| R | 9 | Pascal Dupuis | PIT | 16 | 0 | 0 | 0 | 8:23 | –5 | 8 | 0 | 0 | 0 | 0 | 17 | 0.0 |

### Goaltending

| No. | Goaltender | GPI | Mins | Avg | W | L | EN | SO | GA | SA | S% | G | A | PIM |
|---|---|---|---|---|---|---|---|---|---|---|---|---|---|---|
| 32 | Mathieu Garon | 1 | 24 | 0.00 | 0 | 0 | 0 | 0 | 0 | 8 | 1.000 | 0 | 0 | 0 |
| 29 | Marc-Andre Fleury | 24 | 1447 | 2.61 | 16 | 8 | 1 | 0 | 63 | 686 | .908 | 0 | 0 | 2 |
| | **Totals** | **24** | **1480** | **2.59** | **16** | **8** | **1** | **0** | **64** | **695** | **.908** | | | |

### Coaching Record

| | | | Regular Season | | | | Playoffs | | | |
|---|---|---|---|---|---|---|---|---|---|---|
| Season | Team | League | GC | W | L | O/T | GC | W | L | T |
| 2008-09 | Wilkes-Barre | AHL | 55 | 36 | 16 | 3 | .... | .... | .... | .... |
| **2008-09♦** | **Pittsburgh** | **NHL** | **25** | **18** | **3** | **4** | **24** | **16** | **8** | .... |
| | **NHL Totals** | | **25** | **18** | **3** | **4** | **24** | **16** | **8** | .... |

♦ Stanley Cup win.

# Club Records

## Team

(Figures in brackets for season records are games played; records for fewest points, wins, ties, losses, goals, goals against are for 70 or more games)

**Most Points** ............... **119** 1992-93 (84)
**Most Wins** ................ **56** 1992-93 (84)
**Most Ties** ................. **20** 1970-71 (78)
**Most Losses** ............... **58** 1983-84 (80)
**Most Goals** ............... **367** 1992-93 (84)
**Most Goals Against** ........ **394** 1982-83 (80)
**Fewest Points** .............. **38** 1983-84 (80)
**Fewest Wins** ............... **16** 1983-84 (80)
**Fewest Ties** ................. **4** 1995-96 (82)
**Fewest Losses** .............. **21** 1992-93 (84)
**Fewest Goals** .............. **182** 1969-70 (76)
**Fewest Goals Against** ....... **188** 1997-98 (82)

**Longest Winning Streak**
**Overall** ................. ***17** Mar. 9-Apr. 10/93
**Home** .................... **11** Jan. 5-Mar. 7/91
**Away** ..................... **7** Mar. 14-Apr. 9/93

**Longest Undefeated Streak**
**Overall** .................. **18** Mar. 9-Apr. 14/93 (17 wins, 1 tie)
**Home** .................... **20** Nov. 30/74-Feb. 22/75 (12 wins, 8 ties)
**Away** ..................... **8** Mar. 14-Apr. 14/93 (7 wins, 1 tie)

**Longest Losing Streak**
**Overall** .................. **18** Jan. 13-Feb. 22/04
**Home** .................... **14** Dec. 31/03-Feb. 22/04
**Away** .................... **18** Dec. 23/82-Mar. 4/83

**Longest Winless Streak**
**Overall** .................. **18** Jan. 2-Feb. 10/83 (17 losses, 1 tie), Jan. 13-Feb. 22/04 (18 losses)
**Home** .................... **16** Dec. 31/03-Mar. 4/04 (15 losses, 1 tie)
**Away** .................... **18** Oct. 25/70-Jan. 14/71 (11 losses, 7 ties), Dec. 23/82-Mar. 4/83 (18 losses)

**Most Shutouts, Season** ........ **9** 1998-99 (82)
**Most PIM, Season** ......... **2,670** 1988-89 (80)
**Most Goals, Game** ........... **12** Mar. 15/75 (Wsh. 1 at Pit. 12), Dec. 26/91 (Tor. 1 at Pit. 12)

## Individual

**Most Seasons** ............... **17** Mario Lemieux
**Most Games** ............... **915** Mario Lemieux
**Most Goals, Career** ......... **690** Mario Lemieux
**Most Assists, Career** ....... **1,033** Mario Lemieux
**Most Points, Career** ....... **1,723** Mario Lemieux (690G, 1,033A)
**Most PIM, Career** ......... **1,048** Kevin Stevens
**Most Shutouts, Career** ........ **22** Tom Barrasso
**Longest Consecutive Games Streak** ........... **313** Ron Schock (Oct. 24/73-Apr. 3/77)
**Most Goals, Season** .......... **85** Mario Lemieux (1988-89)
**Most Assists, Season** ........ **114** Mario Lemieux (1988-89)
**Most Points, Season** ........ **199** Mario Lemieux (1988-89; 85G, 114A)
**Most PIM, Season** .......... **409** Paul Baxter (1981-82)
**Most Points, Defenseman, Season** ................. **113** Paul Coffey (1988-89; 30G, 83A)
**Most Points, Center, Season** ................. **199** Mario Lemieux (1988-89; 85G, 114A)
**Most Points, Right Wing, Season** ................ ***149** Jaromir Jagr (1995-96; 62G, 87A)
**Most Points, Left Wing, Season** ................. **123** Kevin Stevens (1991-92; 54G, 69A)
**Most Points, Rookie, Season** ................. **102** Sidney Crosby (2005-06; 39G, 63A)
**Most Shutouts, Season** ........ **7** Tom Barrasso (1997-98)
**Most Goals, Game** ............ **5** Mario Lemieux (Dec. 31/88), (Apr. 9/93), (Mar. 26/96)
**Most Assists, Game** ........... **6** Ron Stackhouse (Mar. 8/75) Greg Malone (Nov. 28/79) Mario Lemieux (Oct. 15/88), (Dec. 5/92), (Nov. 1/95)
**Most Points, Game** ............ **8** Mario Lemieux (Oct. 15/88; 2G, 6A), (Dec. 31/88; 5G, 3A)

* NHL Record.

## Captains' History

Ab McDonald, 1967-68; Earl Ingarfield, 1968-69; no captain, 1968-69 to 1972-73; Ron Schock, 1973-74 to 1976-77; Jean Pronovost, 1977-78; Orest Kindrachuk, 1978-79 to 1980-81; Randy Carlyle, 1981-82 to 1983-84; Mike Bullard, 1984-85, 1985-86; Mike Bullard and Terry Ruskowski, 1986-87; Dan Frawley and Mario Lemieux, 1987-88; Mario Lemieux, 1988-89 to 1993-94; Ron Francis, 1994-95; Mario Lemieux, 1995-96, 1996-97; Ron Francis, 1997-98; Jaromir Jagr, 1998-99 to 2000-01; Mario Lemieux, 2001-02 to 2004-05; Mario Lemieux and no captain, 2005-06; no captain, 2006-07; Sidney Crosby, 2007-08 to date.

## Retired Numbers

| | | |
|---|---|---|
| **21** | Michel Brière | 1969-1970 |
| **66** | Mario Lemieux | 1984-2006 |

# All-time Record vs. Other Clubs

## Regular Season

| | At Home | | | | | | | | On Road | | | | | | | | Total | | | | | | | |
|---|---|---|---|---|---|---|---|---|---|---|---|---|---|---|---|---|---|---|---|---|---|---|---|---|
| | GP | W | L | T | OL | GF | GA | PTS | GP | W | L | T | OL | GF | GA | PTS | GP | W | L | T | OL | GF | GA | PTS |
| Anaheim | 11 | 7 | 2 | 2 | 0 | 37 | 32 | 16 | 9 | 3 | 4 | 0 | 2 | 26 | 32 | 8 | 20 | 10 | 6 | 2 | 2 | 63 | 64 | 24 |
| Atlanta | 18 | 14 | 3 | 0 | 1 | 70 | 44 | 29 | 18 | 12 | 4 | 0 | 2 | 62 | 54 | 26 | 36 | 26 | 7 | 0 | 3 | 132 | 98 | 55 |
| Boston | 88 | 35 | 36 | 15 | 2 | 301 | 313 | 87 | 86 | 19 | 60 | 6 | 1 | 242 | 376 | 45 | 174 | 54 | 96 | 21 | 3 | 543 | 689 | 132 |
| Buffalo | 79 | 40 | 20 | 18 | 1 | 294 | 241 | 99 | 79 | 24 | 37 | 17 | 1 | 214 | 296 | 66 | 158 | 64 | 57 | 35 | 2 | 508 | 537 | 165 |
| Calgary | 46 | 25 | 11 | 10 | 0 | 171 | 136 | 60 | 47 | 12 | 27 | 8 | 0 | 143 | 206 | 32 | 93 | 37 | 38 | 18 | 0 | 314 | 342 | 92 |
| Carolina | 54 | 27 | 21 | 6 | 0 | 210 | 194 | 60 | 56 | 23 | 25 | 5 | 3 | 197 | 206 | 54 | 110 | 50 | 46 | 11 | 3 | 407 | 400 | 114 |
| Chicago | 60 | 30 | 23 | 7 | 0 | 215 | 194 | 67 | 62 | 12 | 40 | 10 | 0 | 163 | 244 | 34 | 122 | 42 | 63 | 17 | 0 | 378 | 438 | 101 |
| Colorado | 38 | 16 | 17 | 5 | 0 | 149 | 155 | 37 | 34 | 13 | 18 | 2 | 1 | 127 | 150 | 29 | 72 | 29 | 35 | 7 | 1 | 276 | 305 | 66 |
| Columbus | 5 | 4 | 1 | 0 | 0 | 21 | 13 | 8 | 5 | 2 | 2 | 0 | 1 | 13 | 20 | 5 | 10 | 6 | 3 | 0 | 1 | 34 | 33 | 13 |
| Dallas | 64 | 39 | 19 | 6 | 0 | 240 | 179 | 84 | 66 | 23 | 36 | 6 | 1 | 221 | 250 | 53 | 130 | 62 | 55 | 12 | 1 | 461 | 429 | 137 |
| Detroit | 67 | 44 | 19 | 4 | 0 | 281 | 200 | 92 | 67 | 14 | 40 | 12 | 1 | 186 | 262 | 41 | 134 | 58 | 59 | 16 | 1 | 467 | 462 | 133 |
| Edmonton | 32 | 16 | 13 | 3 | 0 | 123 | 134 | 35 | 31 | 8 | 22 | 1 | 0 | 102 | 150 | 17 | 63 | 24 | 35 | 4 | 0 | 225 | 284 | 52 |
| Florida | 31 | 16 | 11 | 3 | 1 | 94 | 91 | 36 | 30 | 12 | 15 | 1 | 2 | 73 | 88 | 27 | 61 | 28 | 26 | 4 | 3 | 167 | 179 | 63 |
| Los Angeles | 75 | 40 | 25 | 10 | 0 | 273 | 236 | 90 | 70 | 18 | 43 | 8 | 1 | 187 | 268 | 45 | 145 | 58 | 68 | 18 | 1 | 460 | 504 | 135 |
| Minnesota | 5 | 1 | 3 | 0 | 1 | 7 | 19 | 3 | 4 | 1 | 2 | 1 | 0 | 9 | 11 | 3 | 9 | 2 | 5 | 1 | 1 | 16 | 30 | 6 |
| Montreal | 90 | 32 | 43 | 13 | 2 | 269 | 319 | 79 | 90 | 15 | 62 | 10 | 3 | 232 | 410 | 43 | 180 | 47 | 105 | 23 | 5 | 501 | 729 | 122 |
| Nashville | 6 | 2 | 2 | 2 | 0 | 18 | 18 | 6 | 8 | 2 | 6 | 0 | 0 | 17 | 31 | 4 | 14 | 4 | 8 | 2 | 0 | 35 | 49 | 10 |
| New Jersey | 94 | 46 | 40 | 4 | 4 | 339 | 307 | 100 | 96 | 36 | 44 | 13 | 3 | 308 | 337 | 88 | 190 | 82 | 84 | 17 | 7 | 647 | 644 | 188 |
| NY Islanders | 103 | 51 | 36 | 14 | 2 | 391 | 348 | 118 | 101 | 39 | 51 | 8 | 3 | 333 | 393 | 89 | 204 | 90 | 87 | 22 | 5 | 724 | 741 | 207 |
| NY Rangers | 115 | 54 | 45 | 14 | 2 | 404 | 398 | 124 | 116 | 44 | 59 | 9 | 4 | 374 | 445 | 101 | 231 | 98 | 104 | 23 | 6 | 778 | 843 | 225 |
| Ottawa | 35 | 18 | 11 | 4 | 2 | 117 | 99 | 42 | 35 | 18 | 12 | 5 | 0 | 115 | 102 | 41 | 70 | 36 | 23 | 9 | 2 | 232 | 201 | 83 |
| Philadelphia | 121 | 56 | 43 | 22 | 0 | 427 | 386 | 134 | 121 | 24 | 85 | 8 | 4 | 312 | 505 | 60 | 242 | 80 | 128 | 30 | 4 | 739 | 891 | 194 |
| Phoenix | 31 | 21 | 10 | 0 | 0 | 123 | 87 | 42 | 33 | 15 | 15 | 3 | 0 | 115 | 122 | 33 | 64 | 36 | 25 | 3 | 0 | 238 | 209 | 75 |
| St. Louis | 65 | 32 | 21 | 12 | 0 | 239 | 194 | 76 | 66 | 16 | 42 | 6 | 2 | 177 | 253 | 40 | 131 | 48 | 63 | 18 | 2 | 416 | 447 | 116 |
| San Jose | 11 | 5 | 4 | 1 | 1 | 44 | 35 | 12 | 15 | 6 | 7 | 2 | 0 | 57 | 39 | 14 | 26 | 11 | 11 | 3 | 1 | 101 | 74 | 26 |
| Tampa Bay | 31 | 17 | 8 | 3 | 3 | 108 | 84 | 40 | 31 | 13 | 15 | 2 | 1 | 79 | 94 | 29 | 62 | 30 | 23 | 5 | 4 | 187 | 178 | 69 |
| Toronto | 77 | 40 | 30 | 6 | 1 | 307 | 250 | 87 | 75 | 26 | 35 | 11 | 3 | 242 | 301 | 66 | 152 | 66 | 65 | 17 | 4 | 549 | 551 | 153 |
| Vancouver | 52 | 33 | 12 | 7 | 0 | 230 | 178 | 73 | 51 | 24 | 22 | 4 | 1 | 189 | 181 | 53 | 103 | 57 | 34 | 11 | 1 | 419 | 359 | 126 |
| Washington | 91 | 52 | 31 | 7 | 1 | 355 | 287 | 112 | 94 | 38 | 46 | 9 | 1 | 342 | 385 | 86 | 185 | 90 | 77 | 16 | 2 | 697 | 672 | 198 |
| Defunct Clubs | 35 | 22 | 6 | 7 | 0 | 148 | 93 | 51 | 34 | 13 | 10 | 11 | 0 | 108 | 101 | 37 | 69 | 35 | 16 | 18 | 0 | 256 | 194 | 88 |
| **Totals** | **1630** | **835** | **566** | **205** | **24** | **6005** | **5264** | **1899** | **1630** | **525** | **886** | **178** | **41** | **4965** | **6312** | **1269** | **3260** | **1360** | **1452** | **383** | **65** | **10970** | **11576** | **3168** |

## Playoffs

| | Series | W | L | GP | W | L | T | GF | GA | Last Mtg. | Rnd. | Result |
|---|---|---|---|---|---|---|---|---|---|---|---|---|
| Boston | 4 | 2 | 2 | 19 | 10 | 9 | 0 | 67 | 62 | 1992 | CF | W 4-0 |
| Buffalo | 2 | 2 | 0 | 10 | 6 | 4 | 0 | 26 | 26 | 2001 | CSF | W 4-3 |
| Carolina | 1 | 1 | 0 | 4 | 4 | 0 | 0 | 20 | 9 | 2009 | CF | W 4-0 |
| Chicago | 2 | 1 | 1 | 8 | 4 | 4 | 0 | 23 | 24 | 1992 | F | W 4-0 |
| Dallas | 1 | 1 | 0 | 6 | 4 | 2 | 0 | 28 | 16 | 1991 | F | W 4-2 |
| Detroit | 2 | 1 | 1 | 13 | 6 | 7 | 0 | 24 | 34 | 2009 | F | W 4-3 |
| Florida | 1 | 0 | 1 | 7 | 3 | 4 | 0 | 15 | 20 | 1996 | CF | L 3-4 |
| Montreal | 1 | 0 | 1 | 6 | 2 | 4 | 0 | 15 | 18 | 1998 | CQF | L 2-4 |
| New Jersey | 5 | 3 | 2 | 29 | 14 | 15 | 0 | 80 | 86 | 2001 | CF | L 1-4 |
| NY Islanders | 3 | 0 | 3 | 19 | 8 | 11 | 0 | 58 | 67 | 1993 | DF | L 3-4 |
| NY Rangers | 4 | 4 | 0 | 20 | 16 | 4 | 0 | 79 | 57 | 2008 | CSF | W 4-1 |
| Ottawa | 2 | 1 | 1 | 9 | 5 | 4 | 0 | 26 | 23 | 2008 | CQF | W 4-0 |
| Philadelphia | 5 | 2 | 3 | 29 | 14 | 15 | 0 | 89 | 91 | 2009 | CQF | W 4-2 |
| St. Louis | 3 | 1 | 2 | 13 | 6 | 7 | 0 | 40 | 45 | 1981 | PRE | L 2-3 |
| Toronto | 3 | 0 | 3 | 12 | 4 | 8 | 0 | 27 | 39 | 1999 | CSF | L 2-4 |
| Washington | 8 | 7 | 1 | 49 | 30 | 19 | 0 | 164 | 143 | 2009 | CSF | W 4-3 |
| Defunct Clubs | 1 | 1 | 0 | 4 | 4 | 0 | 0 | 13 | 6 | | | |
| **Totals** | **48** | **27** | **21** | **257** | **140** | **117** | **0** | **794** | **766** | | | |

Calgary totals include Atlanta Flames, 1972-73 to 1979-80. Carolina totals include Hartford, 1979-80 to 1996-97.
Colorado totals include Quebec, 1979-80 to 1994-95. Dallas totals include Minnesota North Stars, 1967-68 to 1992-93.
New Jersey totals include Kansas City, 1974-75, 1975-76, and Colorado Rockies, 1976-77 to 1981-82.
Phoenix totals include Winnipeg, 1979-80 to 1995-96.

## Playoff Results 2009-2004

| Year | Round | Opponent | Result | GF | GA |
|---|---|---|---|---|---|
| **2009** | **F** | **Detroit** | **W 4-3** | **14** | **17** |
| | CF | Carolina | W 4-0 | 20 | 9 |
| | CSF | Washington | W 4-3 | 27 | 22 |
| | CQF | Philadelphia | W 4-2 | 18 | 16 |
| 2008 | F | Detroit | L 2-4 | 10 | 17 |
| | CF | Philadelphia | W 4-1 | 20 | 9 |
| | CSF | NY Rangers | W 4-1 | 15 | 12 |
| | CQF | Ottawa | W 4-0 | 16 | 5 |
| 2007 | CQF | Ottawa | L 1-4 | 10 | 18 |

**Abbreviations: Round: F** – Final; **CF** – conference final; **CSF** – conference semi-final; **CQF** – conference quarter-final; **DF** – division final; **PRE** – preliminary round.

## 2008-09 Results

| | | | | | | | |
|---|---|---|---|---|---|---|---|
| **Oct.** | 4 | at Ottawa | 4-3* | | 8 | at Nashville | 3-5 |
| | 5 | Ottawa | 1-3 | | 10 | at Colorado | 3-5 |
| | 11 | New Jersey | 1-2* | | 13 | at Philadelphia | 4-2 |
| | 14 | Philadelphia | 3-2* | | 14 | Washington | 3-6 |
| | 16 | Washington | 3-4 | | 16 | Anaheim | 3-1 |
| | 18 | Toronto | 4-1 | | 18 | NY Rangers | 3-0 |
| | 20 | at Boston | 2-1† | | 20 | Carolina | 1-2 |
| | 23 | Carolina | 4-1 | | 28 | NY Rangers | 6-2 |
| | 25 | at NY Rangers | 2-3† | | 30 | at New Jersey | 3-4* |
| | 28 | at San Jose | 1-2 | | 31 | at Toronto | 4-5 |
| | 30 | at Phoenix | 1-4 | **Feb.** | 3 | at Montreal | 2-4 |
| **Nov.** | 1 | at St. Louis | 6-3 | | 4 | Tampa Bay | 4-3* |
| | 6 | Edmonton | 5-4 | | 6 | Columbus | 4-1 |
| | 8 | at NY Islanders | 4-3† | | 8 | Detroit | 0-3 |
| | 11 | at Detroit | 7-6* | | 11 | San Jose | 2-1† |
| | 13 | Philadelphia | 5-4† | | 14 | at Toronto | 2-6 |
| | 15 | Buffalo | 5-2 | | 16 | at NY Islanders | 2-3† |
| | 18 | Minnesota | 1-2† | | 19 | Montreal | 5-4 |
| | 20 | at Atlanta | 3-2 | | 21 | at Philadelphia | 5-4 |
| | 22 | Vancouver | 1-3 | | 22 | at Washington | 2-5 |
| | 26 | at NY Islanders | 5-3 | | 25 | NY Islanders | 1-0 |
| | 28 | at Buffalo | 3-4 | | 27 | at Chicago | 5-4* |
| | 29 | New Jersey | 4-1 | **Mar.** | 1 | at Dallas | 4-1 |
| **Dec.** | 3 | at NY Rangers | 2-3† | | 3 | at Tampa Bay | 3-1 |
| | 4 | at Carolina | 5-2 | | 5 | at Florida | 4-1 |
| | 6 | at Ottawa | 2-3 | | 8 | at Washington | 4-3† |
| | 8 | Buffalo | 3-4 | | 10 | Florida | 4-3† |
| | 10 | at New Jersey | 1-4 | | 12 | at Columbus | 3-4† |
| | 11 | NY Islanders | 9-2 | | 14 | Ottawa | 3-4† |
| | 13 | at Philadelphia | 3-6 | | 15 | Boston | 6-4 |
| | 18 | at Atlanta | 6-3 | | 17 | Atlanta | 6-2 |
| | 20 | Toronto | 3-7 | | 20 | Los Angeles | 4-1 |
| | 22 | at Buffalo | 4-3* | | 22 | Philadelphia | 1-3 |
| | 23 | Tampa Bay | 0-2 | | 25 | Calgary | 2-0 |
| | 26 | at New Jersey | 1-0 | | 28 | NY Rangers | 4-3 |
| | 27 | Montreal | 2-3 | **Apr.** | 1 | New Jersey | 6-1 |
| | 30 | Boston | 2-5 | | 4 | at Carolina | 2-3* |
| **Jan.** | 1 | at Boston | 2-4 | | 5 | at Florida | 2-4 |
| | 3 | Florida | 1-6 | | 7 | at Tampa Bay | 6-4 |
| | 5 | at NY Rangers | 0-4 | | 9 | NY Islanders | 6-1 |
| | 6 | Atlanta | 3-1 | | 11 | at Montreal | 3-1 |

* – Overtime † – Shootout

## Entry Draft Selections 2009-1995

Name in bold denotes played in NHL.

**2009**
Pick
30 Simon Despres
61 Philip Samuelsson
63 Ben Hanowski
121 Nick Petersen
123 Alex Velischek
151 Andy Bathgate
181 Viktor Ekbom

**2008**
Pick
120 Nathan Moon
150 Alexander Pechursky
180 Patrick Killeen
210 Nicholas D'Agostino

**2007**
Pick
20 Angelo Esposito
51 Keven Veilleux
78 Robert Bortuzzo
80 Casey Pierro-Zabotel
111 **Luca Caputi**
118 Alex Grant
141 Jake Muzzin
171 **Dustin Jeffrey**

**2006**
Pick
2 **Jordan Staal**
32 Carl Sneep
65 Brian Strait
125 Chad Johnson
185 Timo Seppanen

**2005**
Pick
1 **Sidney Crosby**
61 Michael Gergen
62 **Kris Letang**
125 Tommi Leinonen
126 Tim Crowder
194 Jean-Philippe Paquet
195 Joe Vitale

**2004**
Pick
2 **Evgeni Malkin**
31 Johannes Salmonsson
61 **Alex Goligoski**
67 Nick Johnson
85 Brian Gifford
99 **Tyler Kennedy**
130 Michal Sersen
164 Moises Gutierrez
194 Chris Peluso
222 Jordan Morrison
228 David Brown
259 Brian Ihnacak

**2003**
Pick
1 **Marc-Andre Fleury**
32 **Ryan Stone**
70 **Jonathan Filewich**
73 **Daniel Carcillo**
121 **Paul Bissonnette**
161 Evgeni Isakov
169 Lukas Bolf
199 **Andy Chiodo**
229 Stephen Dixon
232 **Joe Jensen**
263 **Matt Moulson**

**2002**
Pick
5 **Ryan Whitney**
35 Ondrej Nemec
69 **Erik Christensen**
101 Daniel Fernholm
136 Andrew Sertich
137 **Cam Paddock**
171 Robert Goepfert
202 Patrik Bartschi
234 **Maxime Talbot**
239 Ryan Lannon
265 Dwight Labrosse

**2001**
Pick
21 **Colby Armstrong**
54 **Noah Welch**
86 **Drew Fata**
96 Alexandre Rouleau
120 **Tomas Surovy**
131 Ben Eaves
156 Andy Schneider
217 Tomas Duba
250 Brandon Crawford-West

**2000**
Pick
18 **Brooks Orpik**
52 **Shane Endicott**
84 Peter Hamerlik
124 **Michel Ouellet**
146 **David Koci**
185 Patrick Foley
216 Jim Abbott
248 Steve Crampton
273 **Roman Simicek**
280 Nick Boucher

**1999**
Pick
18 **Konstantin Koltsov**
51 **Matt Murley**
57 Jeremy Van Hoof
86 **Sebastien Caron**
115 **Ryan Malone**
144 Tomas Skvaridlo
157 Vladimir Malenkykh
176 Doug Meyer
204 **Tom Kostopoulos**
233 Darcy Robinson
261 Andrew McPherson

**1998**
Pick
23 **Milan Kraft**
54 Alexander Zevakhin
80 David Cameron
110 Scott Myers
134 **Rob Scuderi**
169 Jan Fadrny
196 Joel Scherban
224 Mika Lehto
244 **Toby Petersen**
254 **Matt Hussey**

**1997**
Pick
17 **Robert Dome**
44 Brian Gaffaney
71 **Josef Melichar**
97 Alexandre Mathieu
124 Harlan Pratt
152 Petr Havelka
179 Mark Moore
208 **Andrew Ference**
234 Eric Lind

**1996**
Pick
23 Craig Hillier
28 **Pavel Skrbek**
72 **Boyd Kane**
77 Boris Protsenko
105 **Michal Rozsival**
150 Peter Bergman
186 **Eric Meloche**
238 Timo Seikkula

**1995**
Pick
24 **Aleksey Morozov**
76 **Jean-Sebastien Aubin**
102 Oleg Belov
128 **Jan Hrdina**
154 Alexei Kolkunov
180 Derrick Pyke
206 Sergei Voronov
232 Frank Ivankovic

## Coaching History

Red Sullivan, 1967-68, 1968-69; Red Kelly, 1969-70 to 1971-72; Red Kelly and Ken Schinkel, 1972-73; Ken Schinkel and Marc Boileau, 1973-74; Marc Boileau, 1974-75; Marc Boileau and Ken Schinkel, 1975-76; Ken Schinkel, 1976-77; Johnny Wilson, 1977-78 to 1979-80; Eddie Johnston, 1980-81 to 1982-83; Lou Angotti, 1983-84; Bob Berry, 1984-85 to 1986-87; Pierre Creamer, 1987-88; Gene Ubriaco, 1988-89; Gene Ubriaco and Craig Patrick, 1989-90; Bob Johnson, 1990-91; Scotty Bowman, 1991-92, 1992-93; Eddie Johnston, 1993-94 to 1995-96; Eddie Johnston and Craig Patrick, 1996-97; Kevin Constantine, 1997-98, 1998-99; Kevin Constantine and Herb Brooks, 1999-2000; Ivan Hlinka, 2000-01; Ivan Hlinka and Rick Kehoe, 2001-02; Rick Kehoe, 2002-03; Ed Olczyk, 2003-04, 2004-05; Ed Olczyk and Michel Therrien, 2005-06; Michel Therrien, 2006-07, 2007-08; Michel Therrien and Dan Bylsma, 2008-09; Dan Bylsma, 2009-10.

# Ray Shero

### General Manager

*Born: St. Paul, MN, July 28, 1962.*

The Pittsburgh Penguins signed Ray Shero to a five-year contract as their new general manager on May 25, 2006. His fresh ideas and calm but firm management style helped transform the Penguins organization in his first year on the job as the team made the playoffs in 2006-07 for the first time since 2000-01. In 2007-08 the team posted the second-best record in the Eastern Conference and advanced to the Stanley Cup Final. They won the Stanley Cup in 2009. Shero is the son of the late Fred Shero, who coached the Philadelphia Flyers for seven years and led them to back-to-back Stanley Cup championships in 1973-74 and 1974-75. Fred Shero also was g.m. and coach of the New York Rangers from 1978 to 1980. Ray Shero played college hockey at St. Lawrence University, serving twice as team captain, and was drafted by the Los Angeles Kings in 1982. He worked as a player agent for seven years before entering NHL management.

Before joining the Penguins, Shero had been assistant general manager of the Nashville Predators for eight seasons, working closely with Predators g.m. David Poile on all aspects of the club's hockey operations. His specific responsibilities included scouting at the amateur and professional levels, contract negotiations, and personnel matters such as arbitration, in addition to overseeing operations of the Predators top minor-league affiliate, the Milwaukee Admirals of the American Hockey League. Before joining the Predators organization, Shero spent six seasons as assistant general manager of the Ottawa Senators – joining the club in its second year of existence as an expansion team.

Both Ottawa and Nashville made significant improvement during Shero's tenure as assistant g.m., building with youth while adhering to a budget and business plan. The Predators went 49-25-8 and established a club record with 106 points in 2005-06, qualifying for the Stanley Cup playoffs for the second straight season. They had the third-best record in the Western Conference and fifth-best in the NHL.

Shero also played an important role in the success of the Milwaukee Admirals, Nashville's top affiliate in the American Hockey League. In 2003-04, the Admirals led the AHL in wins (43) and points (102) and won the Calder Cup by defeating the Wilkes-Barre/Scranton Penguins in the league final. Milwaukee reached the Calder Cup Final again in 2005-06.

# Club Directory

Mellon Arena

**Pittsburgh Penguins**
Mellon Arena
66 Mario Lemieux Place
Pittsburgh, PA 15219
Phone **412/642-1300**
FAX 412/642-1859
Media Relations FAX 412/642-1322
www.pittsburghpenguins.com
**Capacity:** 16,940

Ownership . . . . . . . . Pittsburgh Penguins LP

**Executive Operations**
Co-owner/Chairman . . . . . . . . Mario Lemieux
Co-owner . . . . . . . . Ron Burkle
CEO . . . . . . . . Ken Sawyer
President . . . . . . . . David Morehouse
Executive VP/General Manager . . . . . . . . Ray Shero
Vice President, Business & Legal Affairs . . . . . . . . Travis Williams
Vice President & Controller . . . . . . . . Kevin Hart
Vice President of Business Partnerships . . . . . . . . David Peart
Sr. Vice President, Sales . . . . . . . . David Soltesz
Vice President, Marketing . . . . . . . . James Santilli
Vice President, Communications . . . . . . . . Tom McMillan
Senior Consultant . . . . . . . . Ron Porter
Director, Consol Energy Center Project . . . . . . . . Brian Magness
Director of Goverment Affairs . . . . . . . . Abass B. Kamara
Executive Assistants . . . . . . . . Fay McNamara, Kim Wood
Receptionist . . . . . . . . Kelly Hart
Mailroom Supervisor . . . . . . . . Brett Hart

**Hockey Operations**
Assistant General Manager . . . . . . . . Jason Botterill
Senior Advisor, Hockey Operations . . . . . . . . Ed Johnston
Head Coach . . . . . . . . Dan Bylsma
Assistant Coaches . . . . . . . . Tom Fitzgerald, Mike Yeo, Tony Granato
Goaltending Coach . . . . . . . . Gilles Meloche
Strength & Conditioning Coach . . . . . . . . Mike Kadar
Sr. Director of Team Operations/Communications . . . . . . . . Frank Buonomo
Executive Assistant . . . . . . . . Kristen Yunn
Video Coach . . . . . . . . Travis Ramsay

**Scouting**
Director of Professional Scouting . . . . . . . . Dan MacKinnon
Professional Scouts . . . . . . . . Derek Clancey, Kevin Stevens
Director of Amateur Scouting . . . . . . . . Jay Heinbuck
Amateur Scouts . . . . . . . . Brian Fitzgerald, Luc Gauthier, Chuck Grillo, Jim Madigan, David McNamara, Wayne Meier, Ron Pyette
European Scouts . . . . . . . . Patrik Allvin, Robert Neuhauser

**Training Staff**
Equipment Manager . . . . . . . . Dana Heinze
Assistant Equipment Managers . . . . . . . . Paul DeFazio, Danny Kroll
Team Physician . . . . . . . . Dr. Charles Burke
Head Athletic Trainer . . . . . . . . Chris Stewart
Assistant Athletic Trainer . . . . . . . . Scott Adams
Physical Therapist . . . . . . . . Mark Mortland

**Communications**
Director of Communications . . . . . . . . Jennifer Bullano
Communications Coordinator . . . . . . . . Erik Heasley
Editor/Online Content . . . . . . . . Sam Kasan
Executive Producer, Penguins Radio Network . . . . . . . . Ray Walker
Radio Broadcasters . . . . . . . . Mike Lange, Phil Bourque

**Marketing**
Director of Marketing . . . . . . . . Ross Miller
Marketing Coordinator . . . . . . . . Sarah Swartz
Creative Director . . . . . . . . Barb Pilarski
Graphic Designer . . . . . . . . Erin Halley
Director of Fan Development & Special Events . . . . . . . . Jill Shipley
Director of Community/Alumni Relations . . . . . . . . Cindy Himes
Community Relations Coordinator . . . . . . . . Kathleen Unger
Director of Amateur Hockey . . . . . . . . Mark Shuttleworth
Director of New Media . . . . . . . . Jeremy Zimmer
New Media Coordinator . . . . . . . . Jon Meck

**Game Entertainment**
Director of Game Ops/Video Production . . . . . . . . Chris DeVivo
Director Video Prod./Exec. Producer Pens TV . . . . . . . . Drew Warren
Game Night Producer . . . . . . . . Billy Wareham
Manager of Arts & Graphics . . . . . . . . Dori Minnis
Editors . . . . . . . . James Archer, Mike Davenport, Steve Finerty, Aaron Spiegel
Pens TV Host . . . . . . . . Katie O'Malley

**Corporate Sales**
Senior Director of Corporate Sales . . . . . . . . Kimberly Bogesdorfer
Managers of Corporate Sales . . . . . . . . Beth Folcik, Robbie Hofmann, David Schleter,Danny Smith
Senior Account Service Manager . . . . . . . . Lori Wineland
Account Service Managers . . . . . . . . Jamie Greenwald, Ronald Hay
Account Service Coordinator . . . . . . . . Jeffrey Harshman
Corporate Sales Liaison . . . . . . . . Pierre Larouche
Corporate Sales Media Director . . . . . . . . Mark Turley

**Finance**
Assistant Controller . . . . . . . . Mark R. Kuczinski
Senior Accountant . . . . . . . . Troy Ussack
Payroll Manager . . . . . . . . Andrea Winschel
Accounts Payable . . . . . . . . Tawni Love

**Ticketing**
Senior Director of Ticketing . . . . . . . . Chad Slencak
Manager of Ticket Sales . . . . . . . . George Murphy
Director of Premium Seating/Group Sales . . . . . . . . Mike Guiffre
Coordinator of Premium Services . . . . . . . . Lydia Tobiasz
Group Sales Account Executive . . . . . . . . Mike Zatchey
Ticket Sales Account Executives . . . . . . . . George Birman, Jeff Blizman, Bonnie Golinski, Nicole Kyslinger, Chuck Pukansky
Box Office Manager . . . . . . . . Carol Coulson
Manager of Box Office Operations . . . . . . . . Jason Onufer
Box Office Assistant . . . . . . . . Kelly Gabany
Director of Customer Service . . . . . . . . Kathy Davis
Customer Service Representatives . . . . . . . . Cori Shrader, Amanda Rameas, Amber Shaak
Director of Database Marketing . . . . . . . . Erin Exley
Database Marketing Coordinator . . . . . . . . Dana Cammer

# St. Louis Blues

## Key Off-Season Signings/Acquisitions

**2009**

**May 26** • Re-signed C **Jay McClement.**
**June 19** • Re-signed LW **Keith Tkachuk.**
**29** • Re-signed D **Mike Weaver** and LW **Brad Winchester.**
**July 1** • Signed G **Ty Conklin.**
**6** • Re-signed RW **B.J. Crombeen.**
**9** • Re-signed G **Hannu Toivonen.**
**21** • Re-signed D **Steve Wagner.**
**25** • Re-signed D **Roman Polak.**
**31** • Signed D **Brendan Bell.**

## 2008-09 Results: 41W-31L-4OTL-6SOL 92PTS.
## Third, Central Division

*David Backes scored 23 goals combined in his first two seasons with St. Louis. He scored 31 times in 2008-09. Backes, Eric Staal and Dainius Zubrus were the only NHL players to score four goals in a game last season.*

## 2009-10 Schedule

| | | | | | | | |
|---|---|---|---|---|---|---|---|
| **Oct.** | Fri. | 2 | Detroit† | | Wed. | 6 | at San Jose |
| | Sat. | 3 | at Detroit† | | Thu. | 7 | at Anaheim |
| | Thu. | 8 | Atlanta | | Sat. | 9 | at Los Angeles |
| | Sat. | 10 | Los Angeles | | Tue. | 12 | Columbus |
| | Thu. | 15 | at Phoenix | | Thu. | 14 | Minnesota |
| | Sat. | 17 | at Anaheim | | Sat. | 16 | NY Rangers |
| | Tue. | 20 | at Pittsburgh | | Mon. | 18 | at Columbus |
| | Fri. | 23 | Minnesota | | Wed. | 20 | at Montreal |
| | Sat. | 24 | Dallas | | Thu. | 21 | at Ottawa |
| | Wed. | 28 | at Carolina | | Sat. | 23 | Anaheim |
| | Thu. | 29 | Phoenix | | Mon. | 25 | at Calgary |
| | Sat. | 31 | Florida | | Wed. | 27 | at Vancouver |
| **Nov.** | Thu. | 5 | Calgary | | Thu. | 28 | at Edmonton |
| | Sat. | 7 | at Philadelphia | | Sat. | 30 | Columbus |
| | Sun. | 8 | at Atlanta* | **Feb.** | Wed. | 3 | at Chicago |
| | Tue. | 10 | Vancouver | | Thu. | 4 | San Jose |
| | Thu. | 12 | Nashville | | Sat. | 6 | Chicago |
| | Sat. | 14 | San Jose | | Mon. | 8 | at Colorado |
| | Thu. | 19 | Phoenix | | Tue. | 9 | Detroit |
| | Sat. | 21 | NY Islanders | | Fri. | 12 | Toronto |
| | Mon. | 23 | Boston | | Sat. | 13 | Washington |
| | Wed. | 25 | at Dallas | **Mar.** | Tue. | 2 | at Phoenix |
| | Fri. | 27 | at Nashville | | Thu. | 4 | at Dallas |
| | Sat. | 28 | Detroit | | Sat. | 6 | at Colorado |
| | Mon. | 30 | at Columbus | | Thu. | 11 | at NY Islanders |
| **Dec.** | Thu. | 3 | at San Jose | | Sat. | 13 | at Columbus |
| | Sat. | 5 | at Los Angeles* | | Sun. | 14 | at Minnesota* |
| | Mon. | 7 | Colorado | | Tue. | 16 | Colorado |
| | Wed. | 9 | at Detroit | | Thu. | 18 | at NY Rangers |
| | Fri. | 11 | Edmonton | | Sat. | 20 | at New Jersey |
| | Tue. | 15 | Calgary | | Sun. | 21 | Nashville* |
| | Wed. | 16 | at Chicago | | Wed. | 24 | at Detroit |
| | Fri. | 18 | Tampa Bay | | Thu. | 25 | Los Angeles |
| | Sun. | 20 | at Vancouver | | Sun. | 28 | Edmonton* |
| | Mon. | 21 | at Edmonton | | Tue. | 30 | Chicago |
| | Wed. | 23 | at Calgary | **Apr.** | Thu. | 1 | at Nashville |
| | Sat. | 26 | at Minnesota | | Sat. | 3 | Dallas |
| | Sun. | 27 | Buffalo* | | Mon. | 5 | Columbus |
| | Tue. | 29 | Nashville | | Wed. | 7 | at Chicago |
| | Thu. | 31 | Vancouver | | Fri. | 9 | Anaheim |
| **Jan.** | Sat. | 2 | Chicago | | Sat. | 10 | at Nashville |

* Denotes afternoon game. † Games played in Stockholm, SE.

**CENTRAL DIVISION**
**43rd NHL Season**

**Franchise date:** June 5, 1967

## Year-by-Year Record

| | | Home | | | | Road | | | | Overall | | | | | | | | |
|---|---|---|---|---|---|---|---|---|---|---|---|---|---|---|---|---|---|---|
| **Season** | **GP** | **W** | **L** | **T** | **OL** | **W** | **L** | **T** | **OL** | **W** | **L** | **T** | **OL** | **GF** | **GA** | **Pts.** | **Finished** | **Playoff Result** |
| 2008-09 | 82 | 23 | 13 | .... | 5 | 18 | 18 | .... | 5 | 41 | 31 | .... | 10 | 233 | 233 | 92 | 3rd, Central Div. | Lost Conf. Quarter-Final |
| 2007-08 | 82 | 20 | 15 | .... | 6 | 13 | 21 | .... | 7 | 33 | 36 | .... | 13 | 205 | 237 | 79 | 5th, Central Div. | Out of Playoffs |
| 2006-07 | 82 | 18 | 19 | .... | 4 | 16 | 16 | .... | 9 | 34 | 35 | .... | 13 | 214 | 254 | 81 | 3rd, Central Div. | Out of Playoffs |
| 2005-06 | 82 | 12 | 23 | .... | 6 | 9 | 23 | .... | 9 | 21 | 46 | .... | 15 | 197 | 292 | 57 | 5th, Central Div. | Out of Playoffs |
| 2004-05 | .... | .... | .... | .... | .... | .... | .... | .... | .... | .... | .... | .... | .... | .... | .... | .... | | |
| 2003-04 | 82 | 23 | 11 | 7 | 0 | 16 | 19 | 4 | 2 | 39 | 30 | 11 | 2 | 191 | 198 | 91 | 2nd, Central Div. | Lost Conf. Quarter-Final |
| 2002-03 | 82 | 23 | 11 | 4 | 3 | 18 | 13 | 7 | 3 | 41 | 24 | 11 | 6 | 253 | 222 | 99 | 2nd, Central Div. | Lost Conf. Quarter-Final |
| 2001-02 | 82 | 27 | 12 | 1 | 1 | 16 | 15 | 7 | 3 | 43 | 27 | 8 | 4 | 227 | 188 | 98 | 2nd, Central Div. | Lost Conf. Semi-Final |
| 2000-01 | 82 | 28 | 5 | 5 | 3 | 15 | 17 | 7 | 2 | 43 | 22 | 12 | 5 | 249 | 195 | 103 | 2nd, Central Div. | Lost Conf. Championship |
| 1999-2000 | 82 | 24 | 9 | 7 | 1 | 27 | 10 | 4 | 0 | 51 | 19 | 11 | 1 | 248 | 165 | 114 | 1st, Central Div. | Lost Conf. Quarter-Final |
| 1998-99 | 82 | 18 | 17 | 6 | .... | 19 | 15 | 7 | .... | 37 | 32 | 13 | .... | 237 | 209 | 87 | 2nd, Central Div. | Lost Conf. Semi-Final |
| 1997-98 | 82 | 26 | 10 | 5 | .... | 19 | 19 | 3 | .... | 45 | 29 | 8 | .... | 256 | 204 | 98 | 3rd, Central Div. | Lost Conf. Semi-Final |
| 1996-97 | 82 | 17 | 20 | 4 | .... | 19 | 15 | 7 | .... | 36 | 35 | 11 | .... | 236 | 239 | 83 | 4th, Central Div. | Lost Conf. Quarter-Final |
| 1995-96 | 82 | 15 | 17 | 9 | .... | 17 | 17 | 7 | .... | 32 | 34 | 16 | .... | 219 | 248 | 80 | 4th, Central Div. | Lost Conf. Semi-Final |
| 1994-95 | 48 | 16 | 6 | 2 | .... | 12 | 9 | 3 | .... | 28 | 15 | 5 | .... | 178 | 135 | 61 | 2nd, Central Div. | Lost Conf. Quarter-Final |
| 1993-94 | 84 | 23 | 11 | 8 | .... | 17 | 22 | 3 | .... | 40 | 33 | 11 | .... | 270 | 283 | 91 | 4th, Central Div. | Lost Conf. Quarter-Final |
| 1992-93 | 84 | 22 | 13 | 7 | .... | 15 | 23 | 4 | .... | 37 | 36 | 11 | .... | 282 | 278 | 85 | 4th, Norris Div. | Lost Div. Final |
| 1991-92 | 80 | 25 | 12 | 3 | .... | 11 | 21 | 8 | .... | 36 | 33 | 11 | .... | 279 | 266 | 83 | 3rd, Norris Div. | Lost Div. Semi-Final |
| 1990-91 | 80 | 24 | 9 | 7 | .... | 23 | 13 | 4 | .... | 47 | 22 | 11 | .... | 310 | 250 | 105 | 2nd, Norris Div. | Lost Div. Final |
| 1989-90 | 80 | 20 | 15 | 5 | .... | 17 | 19 | 4 | .... | 37 | 34 | 9 | .... | 295 | 279 | 83 | 2nd, Norris Div. | Lost Div. Final |
| 1988-89 | 80 | 22 | 11 | 7 | .... | 11 | 24 | 5 | .... | 33 | 35 | 12 | .... | 275 | 285 | 78 | 2nd, Norris Div. | Lost Div. Final |
| 1987-88 | 80 | 18 | 17 | 5 | .... | 16 | 21 | 3 | .... | 34 | 38 | 8 | .... | 278 | 294 | 76 | 2nd, Norris Div. | Lost Div. Final |
| 1986-87 | 80 | 21 | 12 | 7 | .... | 11 | 21 | 8 | .... | 32 | 33 | 15 | .... | 281 | 293 | 79 | 1st, Norris Div. | Lost Div. Semi-Final |
| 1985-86 | 80 | 23 | 11 | 6 | .... | 14 | 23 | 3 | .... | 37 | 34 | 9 | .... | 302 | 291 | 83 | 3rd, Norris Div. | Lost Conf. Championship |
| 1984-85 | 80 | 21 | 12 | 7 | .... | 16 | 19 | 5 | .... | 37 | 31 | 12 | .... | 299 | 288 | 86 | 1st, Norris Div. | Lost Div. Semi-Final |
| 1983-84 | 80 | 23 | 14 | 3 | .... | 9 | 27 | 4 | .... | 32 | 41 | 7 | .... | 293 | 316 | 71 | 2nd, Norris Div. | Lost Div. Final |
| 1982-83 | 80 | 16 | 16 | 8 | .... | 9 | 24 | 7 | .... | 25 | 40 | 15 | .... | 285 | 316 | 65 | 4th, Norris Div. | Lost Div. Semi-Final |
| 1981-82 | 80 | 22 | 14 | 4 | .... | 10 | 26 | 4 | .... | 32 | 40 | 8 | .... | 315 | 349 | 72 | 3rd Norris Div. | Lost Div. Final |
| 1980-81 | 80 | 29 | 7 | 4 | .... | 16 | 11 | 13 | .... | 45 | 18 | 17 | .... | 352 | 281 | 107 | 1st, Smythe Div. | Lost Quarter-Final |
| 1979-80 | 80 | 20 | 13 | 7 | .... | 14 | 21 | 5 | .... | 34 | 34 | 12 | .... | 266 | 278 | 80 | 2nd, Smythe Div. | Lost Prelim. Round |
| 1978-79 | 80 | 14 | 20 | 6 | .... | 4 | 30 | 6 | .... | 18 | 50 | 12 | .... | 249 | 348 | 48 | 3rd, Smythe Div. | Out of Playoffs |
| 1977-78 | 80 | 12 | 20 | 8 | .... | 8 | 27 | 5 | .... | 20 | 47 | 13 | .... | 195 | 304 | 53 | 4th, Smythe Div. | Out of Playoffs |
| 1976-77 | 80 | 22 | 13 | 5 | .... | 10 | 26 | 4 | .... | 32 | 39 | 9 | .... | 239 | 276 | 73 | 1st, Smythe Div. | Lost Quarter-Final |
| 1975-76 | 80 | 20 | 12 | 8 | .... | 9 | 25 | 6 | .... | 29 | 37 | 14 | .... | 249 | 290 | 72 | 3rd, Smythe Div. | Lost Prelim. Round |
| 1974-75 | 80 | 23 | 13 | 4 | .... | 12 | 18 | 10 | .... | 35 | 31 | 14 | .... | 269 | 267 | 84 | 2nd, Smythe Div. | Lost Prelim. Round |
| 1973-74 | 78 | 16 | 16 | 7 | .... | 10 | 24 | 5 | .... | 26 | 40 | 12 | .... | 206 | 248 | 64 | 6th, West Div. | Out of Playoffs |
| 1972-73 | 78 | 21 | 11 | 7 | .... | 11 | 23 | 5 | .... | 32 | 34 | 12 | .... | 233 | 251 | 76 | 4th, West Div. | Lost Quarter-Final |
| 1971-72 | 78 | 17 | 17 | 5 | .... | 11 | 22 | 6 | .... | 28 | 39 | 11 | .... | 208 | 247 | 67 | 3rd, West Div. | Lost Semi-Final |
| 1970-71 | 78 | 23 | 7 | 9 | .... | 11 | 18 | 10 | .... | 34 | 25 | 19 | .... | 223 | 208 | 87 | 2nd, West Div. | Lost Quarter-Final |
| 1969-70 | 76 | 24 | 9 | 5 | .... | 13 | 18 | 7 | .... | 37 | 27 | 12 | .... | 224 | 179 | 86 | 1st, West Div. | Lost Final |
| 1968-69 | 76 | 21 | 8 | 9 | .... | 16 | 17 | 5 | .... | 37 | 25 | 14 | .... | 204 | 157 | 88 | 1st, West Div. | Lost Final |
| 1967-68 | 74 | 18 | 12 | 7 | .... | 9 | 19 | 9 | .... | 27 | 31 | 16 | .... | 177 | 191 | 70 | 3rd, West Div. | Lost Final |

# 2009-10 Player Personnel

| FORWARDS | HT | WT | S | Place of Birth | *Age | 2008-09 Club |
|---|---|---|---|---|---|---|
| BACKES, David | 6-3 | 220 | R | Blaine, MN | 25 | St. Louis |
| BERGLUND, Patrik | 6-3 | 211 | L | Vasteras, Sweden | 21 | St. Louis |
| BOYES, Brad | 6-0 | 200 | R | Mississauga, Ont. | 27 | St. Louis |
| CRACKNELL, Adam | 6-1 | 191 | R | Prince Albert, Sask. | 24 | Quad City |
| CROMBEEN, B.J. | 6-2 | 212 | R | Denver, CO | 24 | Dallas-St. Louis |
| DRAZENOVIC, Nicholas | 6-0 | 185 | L | Prince George, B.C. | 22 | Peoria |
| ELLER, Lars | 6-1 | 192 | L | Herlev, Denmark | 20 | Frolunda |
| FILEWICH, Jonathan | 6-2 | 208 | R | Kelowna, B.C. | 24 | Wilkes-Barre-Peoria |
| JANSSEN, Cam | 6-0 | 218 | R | St. Louis, MO | 25 | St. Louis |
| KANA, Tomas | 6-0 | 208 | R | Opava, Czech. | 21 | Peoria-Alaska |
| KARIYA, Paul | 5-10 | 185 | L | Vancouver, B.C. | 34 | St. Louis |
| KING, D.J. | 6-3 | 229 | L | Meadow Lake, Sask. | 25 | St. Louis |
| LEMTYUGOV, Nikolai | 6-0 | 200 | L | Miass, USSR | 23 | Cherepovets |
| McCLEMENT, Jay | 6-1 | 201 | L | Kingston, Ont. | 26 | St. Louis |
| McDONALD, Andy | 5-10 | 190 | L | Strathroy, Ont. | 32 | St. Louis |
| OSHIE, T.J. | 5-11 | 189 | R | Mt. Vernon, WA | 22 | St. Louis |
| PADDOCK, Cam | 6-1 | 191 | R | Vancouver, B.C. | 26 | St. Louis-Peoria |
| PALUSHAJ, Aaron | 5-11 | 187 | R | Livonia, MI | 20 | U. of Michigan-Peoria |
| PERRON, David | 5-11 | 192 | R | Sherbrooke, Que. | 21 | St. Louis |
| PORTER, Chris | 6-1 | 205 | L | Toronto, Ont. | 25 | St. Louis-Peoria |
| REAVES, Ryan | 6-1 | 220 | R | Winnipeg, Man. | 22 | Peoria |
| STASTNY, Yan | 5-10 | 191 | L | Quebec City, Que. | 27 | St. Louis-Peoria |
| STEEN, Alex | 6-1 | 205 | L | Winnipeg, Man. | 25 | Toronto-St. Louis |
| TALBOT, Julian | 5-11 | 181 | L | Wahnapitae, Ont. | 24 | Peoria |
| TALLACKSON, Barry | 6-5 | 215 | R | Grafton, ND | 26 | New Jersey-Lowell |
| TKACHUK, Keith | 6-2 | 232 | L | Melrose, MA | 37 | St. Louis |
| TUREK, Ryan | 6-0 | 188 | R | Southfield, MI | 22 | Alaska-Michigan State |
| WINCHESTER, Brad | 6-5 | 228 | L | Madison, WI | 28 | St. Louis-Peoria |
| **DEFENSEMEN** | | | | | | |
| BELL, Brendan | 6-2 | 211 | L | Ottawa, Ont. | 26 | Ottawa-Binghamton |
| BREWER, Eric | 6-3 | 220 | L | Vernon, B.C. | 30 | St. Louis |
| COLAIACOVO, Carlo | 6-1 | 200 | L | Toronto, Ont. | 26 | Toronto-St. Louis |
| FAST, T.J. | 6-1 | 190 | L | Calgary, Alta. | 22 | Peoria-Alaska |
| FLETCHER, Justin | 5-11 | 190 | L | Maryville, IL | 26 | Peoria |
| HELLSTROM, Alexander | 6-3 | 210 | L | Falun, Sweden | 22 | Peoria-Alaska |
| JACKMAN, Barret | 6-0 | 203 | L | Trail, B.C. | 28 | St. Louis |
| JOHNSON, Erik | 6-4 | 225 | R | Bloomington, MN | 21 | St. Louis |
| JUNLAND, Jonas | 6-2 | 198 | L | Linkoping, Sweden | 21 | St. Louis-Peoria |
| LAMPMAN, Bryce | 6-1 | 199 | L | Rochester, MN | 27 | Khabarovsk |
| PELUSO, Anthony | 6-3 | 230 | R | North York, Ont. | 20 | Sault Ste. Marie-Brampton |
| PIETRANGELO, Alex | 6-3 | 204 | R | King City, Ont. | 19 | St. Louis-Niagara-Peoria |
| POLAK, Roman | 6-0 | 232 | R | Ostrava, Czech. | 23 | St. Louis |
| RICHMOND, Danny | 6-0 | 192 | L | Chicago, IL | 25 | Wilkes-Barre-Peoria |
| STRACHAN, Tyson | 6-1 | 212 | R | Melfort, Sask. | 24 | St. Louis-Peoria |
| WAGNER, Steve | 6-2 | 203 | L | Grand Rapids, MN | 25 | St. Louis-Peoria |
| WEAVER, Mike | 5-9 | 188 | R | Bramalea, Ont. | 31 | St. Louis |

| GOALTENDERS | HT | WT | C | Place of Birth | *Age | 2008-09 Club |
|---|---|---|---|---|---|---|
| BISHOP, Ben | 6-7 | 210 | L | Denver, CO | 22 | St. Louis-Peoria |
| CONKLIN, Ty | 6-0 | 184 | L | Anchorage, AK | 33 | Detroit |
| HOLT, Chris | 6-3 | 221 | L | Vancouver, B.C. | 24 | St. Louis-Peoria-Alaska |
| MASON, Chris | 6-0 | 195 | L | Red Deer, Alta. | 33 | St. Louis |
| TOIVONEN, Hannu | 6-2 | 200 | L | Kalvola, Finland | 25 | Ilves |

* – Age at start of 2009-10 season

## General Managers' History

Lynn Patrick, 1967-68; Scotty Bowman, 1968-69 to 1970-71; Lynn Patrick, 1971-72; Sid Abel, 1972-73; Charles Catto, 1973-74; Gerry Ehman, 1974-75; Dennis Ball, 1975-76; Emile Francis, 1976-77 to 1982-83; Ron Caron, 1983-84 to 1993-94; Mike Keenan, 1994-95, 1995-96; Mike Keenan and Ron Caron, 1996-97; Larry Pleau, 1997-98 to date.

# Andy Murray

### Head Coach

*Born: Gladstone, Man., March 3, 1951.*

Andy Murray was named the head coach of the St. Louis Blues on December 11, 2006. In 2008-09 he guided the team to the playoffs for the first time since the 2003-04 season. Previously, Murray coached the Los Angeles Kings from 1999 to 2006 and is the all-time franchise leader in wins (215) and games coached (480). Prior to joining the Kings, Murray was the head coach of the Canadian national team from 1996 to 1998. During the 1998-99 season, Murray coached Shattuck-St. Mary's in Faribault, Minnesota, where he led the prep school to a 70-9-2 record and the Midget Triple A USA Hockey national championship.

Murray's coaching career began in 1976 with the Brandon Travelers of the Manitoba Junior A Hockey League. He moved on to become head coach for Brandon University from 1978 to 1981 and led the Bobcats to a league championship and the number-one ranking in Canadian University hockey during his final year. His lengthy coaching experience also includes seven seasons as an NHL assistant or associate coach with the Winnipeg Jets (1993 to 1995), Minnesota North Stars (1990 to 1992) and Philadelphia Flyers (1988 to 1990). He has also coached in Europe and guided Canada to gold medals at the World Championship in 1997, 2003 and 2007.

### Coaching Record

| | | | Regular Season | | | | Playoffs | | | |
|---|---|---|---|---|---|---|---|---|---|---|
| **Season** | **Team** | **League** | **GC** | **W** | **L** | **O/T** | **GC** | **W** | **L** | **T** |
| **99-2000** | **Los Angeles** | **NHL** | **82** | **39** | **27** | **16** | **4** | **0** | **4** | .... |
| **2000-01** | **Los Angeles** | **NHL** | **82** | **38** | **28** | **16** | **13** | **7** | **6** | .... |
| **2001-02** | **Los Angeles** | **NHL** | **82** | **40** | **27** | **15** | **7** | **3** | **4** | .... |
| **2002-03** | **Los Angeles** | **NHL** | **82** | **33** | **37** | **12** | .... | .... | .... | .... |
| **2003-04** | **Los Angeles** | **NHL** | **82** | **28** | **29** | **25** | .... | .... | .... | .... |
| **2004-05** | **Los Angeles** | | | | SEASON CANCELLED | | | | | |
| **2005-06** | **Los Angeles** | **NHL** | **70** | **37** | **28** | **5** | .... | .... | .... | .... |
| **2006-07** | **St. Louis** | **NHL** | **54** | **27** | **18** | **9** | .... | .... | .... | .... |
| **2007-08** | **St. Louis** | **NHL** | **82** | **33** | **36** | **13** | .... | .... | .... | .... |
| **2008-09** | **St. Louis** | **NHL** | **82** | **41** | **31** | **10** | **4** | **0** | **4** | .... |
| | **NHL Totals** | | **698** | **316** | **261** | **121** | **28** | **10** | **18** | .... |

# 2008-09 Scoring

* – rookie

## Regular Season

| Pos | # | Player | Team | GP | G | A | Pts | TOI | +/– | PIM | PP | SH | GW | S | % |
|---|---|---|---|---|---|---|---|---|---|---|---|---|---|---|---|
| C | 22 | Brad Boyes | STL | 82 | 33 | 39 | 72 | 19:08 | –20 | 26 | 16 | 0 | 11 | 220 | 15.0 |
| C | 42 | David Backes | STL | 82 | 31 | 23 | 54 | 17:41 | –3 | 165 | 6 | 2 | 1 | 208 | 14.9 |
| L | 57 | David Perron | STL | 81 | 15 | 35 | 50 | 14:31 | 13 | 50 | 4 | 0 | 3 | 161 | 9.3 |
| C | 7 | Keith Tkachuk | STL | 79 | 25 | 24 | 49 | 16:57 | –11 | 61 | 14 | 0 | 4 | 185 | 13.5 |
| C | 21 | * Patrik Berglund | STL | 76 | 21 | 26 | 47 | 14:43 | 19 | 16 | 7 | 0 | 1 | 143 | 14.7 |
| C | 10 | Andy McDonald | STL | 46 | 15 | 29 | 44 | 19:04 | –13 | 24 | 6 | 1 | 1 | 128 | 11.7 |
| C | 74 | * T.J. Oshie | STL | 57 | 14 | 25 | 39 | 16:34 | 16 | 30 | 6 | 1 | 1 | 101 | 13.9 |
| D | 28 | Carlo Colaiacovo | TOR | 10 | 0 | 1 | 1 | 16:52 | –2 | 6 | 0 | 0 | 0 | 9 | 0.0 |
| | | | STL | 63 | 3 | 26 | 29 | 18:28 | 2 | 29 | 0 | 0 | 0 | 78 | 3.8 |
| | | | Total | 73 | 3 | 27 | 30 | 18:15 | 0 | 35 | 0 | 0 | 0 | 87 | 3.4 |
| C | 20 | Alex Steen | TOR | 20 | 2 | 2 | 4 | 15:37 | –4 | 6 | 1 | 0 | 0 | 31 | 6.5 |
| | | | STL | 61 | 6 | 18 | 24 | 16:34 | –6 | 24 | 2 | 1 | 0 | 117 | 5.1 |
| | | | Total | 81 | 8 | 20 | 28 | 16:20 | –10 | 30 | 3 | 1 | 0 | 148 | 5.4 |
| C | 18 | Jay McClement | STL | 82 | 12 | 14 | 26 | 16:36 | –10 | 29 | 0 | 3 | 3 | 137 | 8.8 |
| R | 26 | * Brandon Crombeen | DAL | 15 | 1 | 4 | 5 | 8:14 | –1 | 26 | 0 | 0 | 0 | 12 | 8.3 |
| | | | STL | 66 | 11 | 6 | 17 | 13:44 | –8 | 122 | 0 | 1 | 3 | 112 | 9.8 |
| | | | Total | 81 | 12 | 10 | 22 | 12:43 | –9 | 148 | 0 | 1 | 3 | 124 | 9.7 |
| L | 15 | Brad Winchester | STL | 64 | 13 | 8 | 21 | 12:09 | –1 | 89 | 5 | 0 | 3 | 82 | 15.9 |
| D | 5 | Barret Jackman | STL | 82 | 4 | 17 | 21 | 23:26 | –17 | 86 | 1 | 1 | 0 | 89 | 4.5 |
| D | 29 | Jeff Woywitka | STL | 65 | 3 | 15 | 18 | 18:28 | 8 | 57 | 2 | 0 | 1 | 71 | 4.2 |
| L | 9 | Paul Kariya | STL | 11 | 2 | 13 | 15 | 18:06 | 1 | 2 | 0 | 0 | 0 | 31 | 6.5 |
| D | 46 | Roman Polak | STL | 69 | 1 | 14 | 15 | 21:32 | –15 | 45 | 0 | 0 | 1 | 73 | 1.4 |
| D | 77 | Jay McKee | STL | 69 | 1 | 7 | 8 | 17:18 | 11 | 44 | 0 | 0 | 1 | 43 | 2.3 |
| C | 25 | Yan Stastny | STL | 34 | 3 | 4 | 7 | 12:44 | –14 | 20 | 0 | 0 | 0 | 30 | 10.0 |
| D | 43 | Mike Weaver | STL | 58 | 0 | 7 | 7 | 17:15 | –3 | 12 | 0 | 0 | 0 | 36 | 0.0 |
| D | 4 | Eric Brewer | STL | 28 | 1 | 5 | 6 | 25:07 | –14 | 24 | 1 | 0 | 0 | 49 | 2.0 |
| R | 13 | Dan Hinote | STL | 51 | 1 | 4 | 5 | 10:54 | –7 | 64 | 0 | 0 | 0 | 24 | 4.2 |
| L | 41 | Steve Regier | STL | 8 | 3 | 1 | 4 | 10:59 | –1 | 4 | 2 | 0 | 0 | 11 | 27.3 |
| D | 49 | * Steve Wagner | STL | 22 | 2 | 2 | 4 | 15:37 | –5 | 18 | 0 | 0 | 0 | 16 | 12.5 |
| R | 55 | Cam Janssen | STL | 56 | 1 | 3 | 4 | 5:01 | –5 | 131 | 0 | 0 | 0 | 22 | 4.5 |
| C | 65 | * Cam Paddock | STL | 16 | 2 | 1 | 3 | 10:40 | –4 | 0 | 0 | 0 | 0 | 17 | 11.8 |
| D | 62 | * Tyson Strachan | STL | 30 | 0 | 3 | 3 | 13:26 | 8 | 39 | 0 | 0 | 0 | 21 | 0.0 |
| C | 32 | * Chris Porter | STL | 6 | 1 | 1 | 2 | 10:31 | –1 | 0 | 0 | 0 | 0 | 7 | 14.3 |
| L | 19 | D.J. King | STL | 1 | 0 | 1 | 1 | 8:20 | 0 | 0 | 0 | 0 | 0 | 0 | 0.0 |
| C | 23 | Trent Whitfield | STL | 3 | 0 | 1 | 1 | 11:02 | 2 | 0 | 0 | 0 | 0 | 4 | 0.0 |
| D | 27 | * Alex Pietrangelo | STL | 8 | 0 | 1 | 1 | 16:30 | 0 | 2 | 0 | 0 | 0 | 7 | 0.0 |
| D | 33 | Andy Wozniewski | STL | 1 | 0 | 0 | 0 | 6:44 | 0 | 0 | 0 | 0 | 0 | 0 | 0.0 |
| D | 53 | * Jonas Junland | STL | 1 | 0 | 0 | 0 | 12:28 | 0 | 2 | 0 | 0 | 0 | 0 | 0.0 |

### Goaltending

| No. | Goaltender | GPI | Mins | Avg | W | L | OT | EN | SO | GA | SA | S% | G | A | PIM |
|---|---|---|---|---|---|---|---|---|---|---|---|---|---|---|---|
| 35 | * Chris Holt | 1 | 19 | 0.00 | 0 | 0 | 0 | 0 | 0 | 0 | 3 | 1.000 | 0 | 0 | 0 |
| 40 | * Marek Schwarz | 2 | 15 | 0.00 | 0 | 0 | 0 | 0 | 0 | 0 | 5 | 1.000 | 0 | 0 | 0 |
| 50 | Chris Mason | 57 | 3215 | 2.41 | 27 | 21 | 7 | 7 | 6 | 129 | 1544 | .916 | 0 | 1 | 0 |
| 30 | * Ben Bishop | 6 | 245 | 2.94 | 1 | 1 | 1 | 1 | 0 | 12 | 112 | .893 | 0 | 0 | 0 |
| 34 | Manny Legace | 29 | 1452 | 3.18 | 13 | 9 | 2 | 1 | 0 | 77 | 669 | .885 | 0 | 0 | 0 |
| | **Totals** | **82** | **4995** | **2.73** | **41** | **31** | **10** | **9** | **7** | **227** | **2342** | **.903** | | | |

## Playoffs

| Pos | # | Player | Team | GP | G | A | Pts | TOI | +/– | PIM | PP | SH | GW | OT | S | % |
|---|---|---|---|---|---|---|---|---|---|---|---|---|---|---|---|---|
| C | 10 | Andy McDonald | STL | 4 | 1 | 3 | 4 | 23:34 | 1 | 0 | 0 | 0 | 0 | 0 | 19 | 5.3 |
| C | 22 | Brad Boyes | STL | 4 | 2 | 1 | 3 | 21:34 | –1 | 0 | 1 | 0 | 0 | 0 | 13 | 15.4 |
| C | 42 | David Backes | STL | 4 | 1 | 2 | 3 | 22:55 | 1 | 10 | 0 | 0 | 0 | 0 | 11 | 9.1 |
| L | 57 | David Perron | STL | 4 | 1 | 1 | 2 | 17:12 | 3 | 4 | 0 | 0 | 0 | 0 | 12 | 8.3 |
| D | 5 | Barret Jackman | STL | 4 | 0 | 1 | 1 | 25:18 | –2 | 5 | 0 | 0 | 0 | 0 | 4 | 0.0 |
| C | 20 | Alex Steen | STL | 4 | 0 | 1 | 1 | 17:46 | –3 | 0 | 0 | 0 | 0 | 0 | 19 | 0.0 |
| R | 55 | Cam Janssen | STL | 1 | 0 | 0 | 0 | 3:59 | 0 | 0 | 0 | 0 | 0 | 0 | 0 | 0.0 |
| R | 13 | Dan Hinote | STL | 3 | 0 | 0 | 0 | 8:50 | –1 | 4 | 0 | 0 | 0 | 0 | 1 | 0.0 |
| C | 7 | Keith Tkachuk | STL | 4 | 0 | 0 | 0 | 18:27 | –1 | 2 | 0 | 0 | 0 | 0 | 7 | 0.0 |
| D | 77 | Jay McKee | STL | 4 | 0 | 0 | 0 | 14:56 | 0 | 4 | 0 | 0 | 0 | 0 | 1 | 0.0 |
| D | 43 | Mike Weaver | STL | 4 | 0 | 0 | 0 | 17:02 | 1 | 0 | 0 | 0 | 0 | 0 | 2 | 0.0 |
| L | 15 | Brad Winchester | STL | 4 | 0 | 0 | 0 | 11:41 | –4 | 10 | 0 | 0 | 0 | 0 | 4 | 0.0 |
| D | 28 | Carlo Colaiacovo | STL | 4 | 0 | 0 | 0 | 22:19 | 0 | 2 | 0 | 0 | 0 | 0 | 11 | 0.0 |
| D | 29 | Jeff Woywitka | STL | 4 | 0 | 0 | 0 | 18:47 | –1 | 0 | 0 | 0 | 0 | 0 | 3 | 0.0 |
| C | 18 | Jay McClement | STL | 4 | 0 | 0 | 0 | 16:28 | –4 | 4 | 0 | 0 | 0 | 0 | 8 | 0.0 |
| R | 26 | * Brandon Crombeen | STL | 4 | 0 | 0 | 0 | 9:45 | –2 | 12 | 0 | 0 | 0 | 0 | 3 | 0.0 |
| D | 46 | Roman Polak | STL | 4 | 0 | 0 | 0 | 21:48 | –3 | 0 | 0 | 0 | 0 | 0 | 4 | 0.0 |
| C | 74 | * T.J. Oshie | STL | 4 | 0 | 0 | 0 | 19:01 | 0 | 2 | 0 | 0 | 0 | 0 | 6 | 0.0 |
| C | 21 | * Patrik Berglund | STL | 4 | 0 | 0 | 0 | 10:11 | 0 | 2 | 0 | 0 | 0 | 0 | 3 | 0.0 |

### Goaltending

| No. | Goaltender | GPI | Mins | Avg | W | L | EN | SO | GA | SA | S% | G | A | PIM |
|---|---|---|---|---|---|---|---|---|---|---|---|---|---|---|
| 50 | Chris Mason | 4 | 256 | 2.34 | 0 | 4 | 1 | 0 | 10 | 119 | .916 | 0 | 0 | 0 |
| | **Totals** | **4** | **260** | **2.54** | **0** | **4** | **1** | **0** | **11** | **120** | **.908** | | | |

## Coaching History

Lynn Patrick and Scotty Bowman, 1967-68; Scotty Bowman, 1968-69, 1969-70; Al Arbour and Scotty Bowman, 1970-71; Sid Abel, Bill McCreary and Al Arbour, 1971-72; Al Arbour and Jean-Guy Talbot, 1972-73; Jean-Guy Talbot and Lou Angotti, 1973-74; Lou Angotti, Lynn Patrick and Garry Young, 1974-75; Garry Young, Lynn Patrick and Leo Boivin, 1975-76; Emile Francis, 1976-77; Leo Boivin and Barclay Plager, 1977-78; Barclay Plager, 1978-79; Barclay Plager and Red Berenson, 1979-80; Red Berenson, 1980-81; Red Berenson and Emile Francis, 1981-82; Emile Francis and Barclay Plager, 1982-83; Jacques Demers, 1983-84 to 1985-86; Jacques Martin, 1986-87, 1987-88; Brian Sutter, 1988-89 to 1991-92; Bob Plager and Bob Berry, 1992-93; Bob Berry, 1993-94; Mike Keenan, 1994-95, 1995-96; Mike Keenan, Jim Roberts and Joel Quenneville, 1996-97; Joel Quenneville, 1997-98 to 2002-03; Joel Quenneville and Mike Kitchen, 2003-04; Mike Kitchen, 2004-05, 2005-06; Mike Kitchen and Andy Murray, 2006-07; Andy Murray, 2007-08 to date.

# Club Records

## Team

(Figures in brackets for season records are games played; records for fewest points, wins, ties, losses, goals, goals against are for 70 or more games)

| Record | | |
|---|---|---|
| Most Points | 114 | 1999-2000 (82) |
| Most Wins | 51 | 1999-2000 (82) |
| Most Ties | 19 | 1970-71 (78) |
| Most Losses | 50 | 1978-79 (80) |
| Most Goals | 352 | 1980-81 (80) |
| Most Goals Against | 349 | 1981-82 (80) |
| Fewest Points | 48 | 1978-79 (80) |
| Fewest Wins | 18 | 1978-79 (80) |
| Fewest Ties | 7 | 1983-84 (80) |
| Fewest Losses | 18 | 1980-81 (80) |
| Fewest Goals | 177 | 1967-68 (74) |
| Fewest Goals Against | 157 | 1968-69 (76) |
| **Longest Winning Streak** | | |
| Overall | 10 | Jan. 3-23/02 |
| Home | 9 | Jan. 26-Feb. 26/91 |
| Away | *10 | Jan. 21-Mar. 2/00 |
| **Longest Undefeated Streak** | | |
| Overall | 12 | Nov. 10-Dec. 8/68 (5 wins, 7 ties), Nov. 24-Dec. 26/00 (11 wins, 1 tie) |
| Home | 11 | Four times |
| Away | 11 | Jan. 21-Mar. 4/00 (10 wins, 1 tie) |
| **Longest Losing Streak** | | |
| Overall | 13 | Mar. 16-Apr. 8/06 |
| Home | 7 | Oct. 22-Nov. 26/05, Nov. 25-Dec. 17/06 |
| Away | 10 | Jan. 20-Mar. 8/82, Dec. 29/05-Feb. 1/06, Feb. 16-Mar. 15/08 |
| **Longest Winless Streak** | | |
| Overall | 13 | Mar. 16-Apr. 8/06 (13 losses) |
| Home | 7 | Dec. 28/82-Jan. 25/83 (5 losses, 2 ties), Oct. 22-Nov. 26/05 (7 losses) |
| Away | 17 | Jan. 23-Apr. 7/74 (14 losses, 3 ties) |
| Most Shutouts, Season | 13 | 1968-69 (76) |
| Most PIM, Season | 2,041 | 1990-91 (80) |
| Most Goals, Game | 11 | Feb. 26/94 (St.L. 11 at Ott. 1) |

## Individual

|  | | |
|---|---|---|
| Most Seasons | 13 | Bernie Federko |
| Most Games | 927 | Bernie Federko |
| Most Goals, Career | 527 | Brett Hull |
| Most Assists, Career | 721 | Bernie Federko |
| Most Points, Career | 1,073 | Bernie Federko (352G, 721A) |
| Most PIM, Career | 1,786 | Brian Sutter |
| Most Shutouts, Career | 16 | Glenn Hall |
| Longest Consecutive Games Streak | 662 | Garry Unger (Feb. 7/71-Apr. 8/79) |
| Most Goals, Season | 86 | Brett Hull (1990-91) |
| Most Assists, Season | 90 | Adam Oates (1990-91) |
| Most Points, Season | 131 | Brett Hull (1990-91; 86G, 45A) |
| Most PIM, Season | 306 | Bob Gassoff (1975-76) |
| Most Points, Defenseman, Season | 78 | Jeff Brown (1992-93; 25G, 53A) |
| Most Points, Center, Season | 115 | Adam Oates (1990-91; 25G, 90A) |
| Most Points, Right Wing, Season | 131 | Brett Hull (1990-91; 86G, 45A) |
| Most Points, Left Wing, Season | 102 | Brendan Shanahan (1993-94; 52G, 50A) |
| Most Points, Rookie, Season | 73 | Jorgen Pettersson (1980-81; 37G, 36A) |
| Most Shutouts, Season | 8 | Glenn Hall (1968-69) |
| Most Goals, Game | 6 | Red Berenson (Nov. 7/68) |
| Most Assists, Game | 5 | Brian Sutter (Nov. 22/83), Bernie Federko (Feb. 27/88), Adam Oates (Jan. 26/91), Dallas Drake (Oct. 29/03) |
| Most Points, Game | 7 | Red Berenson (Nov. 7/68; 6G, 1A), Garry Unger (Mar. 13/71; 3G, 4A) |

* NHL Record.

## Retired Numbers

| | | |
|---|---|---|
| 2 | Al MacInnis | 1994-2004 |
| 3 | Bob Gassoff | 1973-1977 |
| 8 | Barclay Plager | 1967-1977 |
| 11 | Brian Sutter | 1976-1988 |
| 16 | Brett Hull | 1987-1998 |
| 24 | Bernie Federko | 1976-1989 |

# All-time Record vs. Other Clubs

## Regular Season

| | At Home | | | | | | | | On Road | | | | | | | | Total | | | | | | | |
|---|---|---|---|---|---|---|---|---|---|---|---|---|---|---|---|---|---|---|---|---|---|---|---|---|
| | GP | W | L | T | OL | GF | GA | PTS | GP | W | L | T | OL | GF | GA | PTS | GP | W | L | T | OL | GF | GA | PTS |
| Anaheim | 30 | 16 | 8 | 3 | 3 | 92 | 80 | 38 | 30 | 14 | 13 | 2 | 1 | 85 | 86 | 31 | 60 | 30 | 21 | 5 | 4 | 177 | 166 | 69 |
| Atlanta | 4 | 3 | 0 | 0 | 1 | 13 | 4 | 7 | 6 | 3 | 2 | 1 | 0 | 20 | 18 | 7 | 10 | 6 | 2 | 1 | 1 | 33 | 22 | 14 |
| Boston | 61 | 28 | 24 | 9 | 0 | 194 | 206 | 65 | 61 | 17 | 35 | 9 | 0 | 170 | 252 | 43 | 122 | 45 | 59 | 18 | 0 | 364 | 458 | 108 |
| Buffalo | 51 | 30 | 14 | 7 | 0 | 183 | 127 | 67 | 54 | 18 | 30 | 6 | 0 | 171 | 207 | 42 | 105 | 48 | 44 | 13 | 0 | 354 | 334 | 109 |
| Calgary | 72 | 33 | 29 | 9 | 1 | 250 | 226 | 76 | 70 | 29 | 33 | 5 | 3 | 195 | 230 | 66 | 142 | 62 | 62 | 14 | 4 | 445 | 456 | 142 |
| Carolina | 33 | 20 | 10 | 3 | 0 | 120 | 95 | 43 | 33 | 17 | 14 | 2 | 0 | 100 | 98 | 36 | 66 | 37 | 24 | 5 | 0 | 220 | 193 | 79 |
| Chicago | 130 | 65 | 45 | 17 | 3 | 433 | 396 | 150 | 133 | 40 | 70 | 18 | 5 | 379 | 482 | 103 | 263 | 105 | 115 | 35 | 8 | 812 | 878 | 253 |
| Colorado | 48 | 27 | 15 | 4 | 2 | 174 | 140 | 60 | 49 | 17 | 25 | 7 | 0 | 130 | 167 | 41 | 97 | 44 | 40 | 11 | 2 | 304 | 307 | 101 |
| Columbus | 26 | 19 | 6 | 1 | 0 | 95 | 61 | 39 | 25 | 11 | 10 | 2 | 2 | 66 | 66 | 26 | 51 | 30 | 16 | 3 | 2 | 161 | 127 | 65 |
| Dallas | 125 | 70 | 34 | 21 | 0 | 452 | 350 | 161 | 123 | 42 | 56 | 22 | 3 | 355 | 413 | 109 | 248 | 112 | 90 | 43 | 3 | 807 | 763 | 270 |
| Detroit | 125 | 60 | 45 | 20 | 0 | 401 | 358 | 140 | 125 | 47 | 58 | 17 | 3 | 370 | 452 | 114 | 250 | 107 | 103 | 37 | 3 | 771 | 810 | 254 |
| Edmonton | 52 | 24 | 18 | 7 | 3 | 180 | 180 | 58 | 52 | 21 | 25 | 4 | 2 | 167 | 186 | 48 | 104 | 45 | 43 | 11 | 5 | 347 | 366 | 106 |
| Florida | 11 | 8 | 2 | 1 | 0 | 29 | 13 | 17 | 11 | 5 | 4 | 2 | 0 | 24 | 25 | 12 | 22 | 13 | 6 | 3 | 0 | 53 | 38 | 29 |
| Los Angeles | 86 | 55 | 20 | 10 | 1 | 317 | 218 | 121 | 86 | 33 | 41 | 12 | 0 | 244 | 293 | 78 | 172 | 88 | 61 | 22 | 1 | 561 | 511 | 199 |
| Minnesota | 16 | 7 | 5 | 3 | 1 | 37 | 33 | 18 | 16 | 5 | 7 | 2 | 2 | 29 | 49 | 14 | 32 | 12 | 12 | 5 | 3 | 66 | 82 | 32 |
| Montreal | 59 | 14 | 29 | 15 | 1 | 152 | 202 | 44 | 60 | 12 | 41 | 7 | 0 | 165 | 258 | 31 | 119 | 26 | 70 | 22 | 1 | 317 | 460 | 75 |
| Nashville | 31 | 17 | 10 | 1 | 3 | 88 | 66 | 38 | 32 | 12 | 11 | 3 | 6 | 74 | 78 | 33 | 63 | 29 | 21 | 4 | 9 | 162 | 144 | 71 |
| New Jersey | 48 | 27 | 13 | 7 | 1 | 198 | 152 | 62 | 47 | 18 | 22 | 7 | 0 | 131 | 148 | 43 | 95 | 45 | 35 | 14 | 1 | 329 | 300 | 105 |
| NY Islanders | 48 | 18 | 19 | 9 | 2 | 169 | 159 | 47 | 51 | 14 | 26 | 11 | 0 | 136 | 190 | 39 | 99 | 32 | 45 | 20 | 2 | 305 | 349 | 86 |
| NY Rangers | 65 | 26 | 28 | 10 | 1 | 194 | 208 | 63 | 61 | 10 | 44 | 6 | 1 | 145 | 248 | 27 | 126 | 36 | 72 | 16 | 2 | 339 | 456 | 90 |
| Ottawa | 11 | 4 | 5 | 2 | 0 | 30 | 32 | 10 | 11 | 6 | 5 | 0 | 0 | 38 | 26 | 12 | 22 | 10 | 10 | 2 | 0 | 68 | 58 | 22 |
| Philadelphia | 70 | 27 | 34 | 7 | 2 | 200 | 224 | 63 | 68 | 12 | 45 | 10 | 1 | 156 | 268 | 35 | 138 | 39 | 79 | 17 | 3 | 356 | 492 | 98 |
| Phoenix | 58 | 28 | 19 | 11 | 0 | 196 | 159 | 67 | 59 | 22 | 27 | 7 | 3 | 184 | 189 | 54 | 117 | 50 | 46 | 18 | 3 | 380 | 348 | 121 |
| Pittsburgh | 66 | 44 | 16 | 6 | 0 | 253 | 177 | 94 | 65 | 21 | 31 | 12 | 1 | 194 | 239 | 55 | 131 | 65 | 47 | 18 | 1 | 447 | 416 | 149 |
| San Jose | 36 | 20 | 14 | 1 | 1 | 110 | 92 | 42 | 32 | 21 | 8 | 1 | 2 | 104 | 80 | 45 | 68 | 41 | 22 | 2 | 3 | 214 | 172 | 87 |
| Tampa Bay | 12 | 10 | 2 | 0 | 0 | 48 | 29 | 20 | 15 | 6 | 5 | 3 | 1 | 50 | 46 | 16 | 27 | 16 | 7 | 3 | 1 | 98 | 75 | 36 |
| Toronto | 103 | 58 | 30 | 14 | 1 | 349 | 285 | 131 | 101 | 32 | 58 | 11 | 0 | 300 | 375 | 75 | 204 | 90 | 88 | 25 | 1 | 649 | 660 | 206 |
| Vancouver | 79 | 46 | 22 | 9 | 2 | 292 | 223 | 103 | 80 | 36 | 32 | 9 | 3 | 252 | 238 | 84 | 159 | 82 | 54 | 18 | 5 | 544 | 461 | 187 |
| Washington | 42 | 21 | 13 | 8 | 0 | 169 | 130 | 50 | 41 | 15 | 21 | 4 | 1 | 123 | 145 | 35 | 83 | 36 | 34 | 12 | 1 | 292 | 275 | 85 |
| Defunct Clubs | 32 | 25 | 4 | 3 | 0 | 131 | 55 | 53 | 33 | 11 | 10 | 12 | 0 | 95 | 100 | 34 | 65 | 36 | 14 | 15 | 0 | 226 | 155 | 87 |
| **Totals** | **1630** | **850** | **533** | **218** | **29** | **5549** | **4680** | **1947** | **1630** | **567** | **809** | **214** | **40** | **4652** | **5652** | **1388** | **3260** | **1417** | **1342** | **432** | **69** | **10201** | **10332** | **3335** |

## Playoffs

| | Series | W | L | GP | W | L | T | GF | GA | Last Mtg. | Rnd. | Result |
|---|---|---|---|---|---|---|---|---|---|---|---|---|
| Boston | 2 | 0 | 2 | 8 | 0 | 8 | 0 | 15 | 48 | 1972 | SF | L 0-4 |
| Buffalo | 1 | 0 | 1 | 3 | 1 | 2 | 0 | 8 | 7 | 1976 | PRE | L 1-2 |
| Calgary | 1 | 0 | 1 | 7 | 3 | 4 | 0 | 22 | 28 | 1986 | CF | L 3-4 |
| Chicago | 10 | 3 | 7 | 50 | 22 | 28 | 0 | 142 | 171 | 2002 | CQF | W 4-1 |
| Colorado | 1 | 0 | 1 | 5 | 1 | 4 | 0 | 11 | 17 | 2001 | CF | L 1-4 |
| Dallas | 12 | 6 | 6 | 66 | 32 | 34 | 0 | 187 | 197 | 2001 | CSF | W 4-0 |
| Detroit | 7 | 2 | 5 | 40 | 16 | 24 | 0 | 103 | 125 | 2002 | CSF | L 1-4 |
| Los Angeles | 2 | 2 | 0 | 8 | 8 | 0 | 0 | 32 | 13 | 1998 | CQF | W 4-0 |
| Montreal | 3 | 0 | 3 | 12 | 0 | 12 | 0 | 14 | 42 | 1977 | QF | L 0-4 |
| NY Rangers | 1 | 0 | 1 | 6 | 2 | 4 | 0 | 22 | 29 | 1981 | QF | L 2-4 |
| Philadelphia | 2 | 2 | 0 | 11 | 8 | 3 | 0 | 34 | 20 | 1969 | QF | W 4-0 |
| Phoenix | 2 | 2 | 0 | 11 | 7 | 4 | 0 | 39 | 29 | 1999 | CQF | W 4-3 |
| Pittsburgh | 3 | 2 | 1 | 13 | 7 | 6 | 0 | 45 | 40 | 1981 | PRE | W 3-2 |
| San Jose | 3 | 1 | 2 | 18 | 8 | 10 | 0 | 47 | 43 | 2004 | CQF | L 1-4 |
| Toronto | 5 | 3 | 2 | 31 | 17 | 14 | 0 | 88 | 90 | 1996 | CQF | W 4-2 |
| Vancouver | 3 | 0 | 3 | 18 | 6 | 12 | 0 | 53 | 55 | 2009 | CQF | L 0-4 |
| **Totals** | **58** | **23** | **35** | **307** | **138** | **169** | **0** | **862** | **954** | | | |

Calgary totals include Atlanta Flames, 1972-73 to 1979-80.
Carolina totals include Hartford, 1979-80 to 1996-97.
Colorado totals include Quebec, 1979-80 to 1994-95.
Dallas totals include Minnesota North Stars, 1967-68 to 1992-93.
New Jersey totals include Kansas City, 1974-75, 1975-76, and Colorado Rockies, 1976-77 to 1981-82.
Phoenix totals include Winnipeg, 1979-80 to 1995-96.

## Playoff Results 2009-2004

| Year | Round | Opponent | Result | GF | GA |
|---|---|---|---|---|---|
| 2009 | CQF | Vancouver | L 0-4 | 5 | 11 |
| 2004 | CQF | San Jose | L 1-4 | 9 | 12 |

**Abbreviations: Round: CF** – conference final; **CSF** – conference semi-final; **CQF** – conference quarter-final; **SF** – semi-final; **QF** – quarter-final; **PRE** – preliminary round.

## 2008-09 Results

| | | | |
|---|---|---|---|
| **Oct.** | 10 | Nashville | 5-2 |
| | 11 | at NY Islanders | 2-5 |
| | 13 | at Toronto | 5-4† |
| | 16 | Dallas | 6-1 |
| | 18 | Chicago | 4-3† |
| | 22 | Detroit | 3-4 |
| | 24 | Los Angeles | 0-4 |
| | 25 | Florida | 4-0 |
| | 30 | Carolina | 0-1 |
| **Nov.** | 1 | Pittsburgh | 3-6 |
| | 5 | at Anaheim | 2-5 |
| | 6 | at San Jose | 4-5† |
| | 8 | at Los Angeles | 3-5 |
| | 12 | at Buffalo | 3-4 |
| | 14 | at Chicago | 4-3* |
| | 16 | Montreal | 2-3† |
| | 21 | Anaheim | 3-2* |
| | 22 | at Minnesota | 2-1 |
| | 25 | at Nashville | 1-0† |
| | 26 | at Colorado | 1-3 |
| | 29 | Edmonton | 2-4 |
| | 30 | at Atlanta | 4-2 |
| **Dec.** | 3 | at Minnesota | 0-4 |
| | 5 | Calgary | 3-4* |
| | 6 | Phoenix | 4-3 |
| | 8 | Nashville | 6-3 |
| | 10 | at Anaheim | 2-4 |
| | 11 | at Los Angeles | 2-6 |
| | 13 | at San Jose | 4-5 |
| | 16 | Calgary | 3-6 |
| | 18 | at Washington | 2-4 |
| | 20 | Minnesota | 4-2 |
| | 21 | Boston | 3-6 |
| | 23 | at Detroit | 1-4 |
| | 27 | San Jose | 3-2† |
| | 28 | Anaheim | 3-4 |
| | 30 | New Jersey | 3-4 |
| **Jan.** | 2 | at Carolina | 1-2 |
| | 3 | Columbus | 5-2 |
| | 9 | at Vancouver | 6-4 |
| | 11 | at Edmonton | 1-2 |
| | 13 | at Calgary | 1-3 |
| | 15 | Colorado | 5-2 |
| | 17 | Chicago | 1-2* |
| | 19 | at Boston | 5-4† |
| | 21 | at Chicago | 2-0 |
| | 29 | Ottawa | 1-3 |
| | 31 | Philadelphia | 4-0 |
| **Feb.** | 2 | at Detroit | 3-4† |
| | 3 | at Columbus | 4-2 |
| | 5 | Edmonton | 1-2† |
| | 7 | Colorado | 4-1 |
| | 10 | Vancouver | 4-6 |
| | 12 | at Nashville | 3-4† |
| | 13 | Chicago | 1-0 |
| | 16 | NY Rangers | 2-1 |
| | 18 | at Columbus | 3-4 |
| | 19 | at Nashville | 2-1* |
| | 21 | Nashville | 0-1* |
| | 24 | Phoenix | 2-1 |
| | 26 | at Dallas | 3-1 |
| | 28 | at Phoenix | 3-1 |
| **Mar.** | 3 | Detroit | 0-5 |
| | 6 | at Tampa Bay | 4-3* |
| | 7 | at Florida | 3-5 |
| | 10 | Dallas | 5-2 |
| | 12 | San Jose | 3-1 |
| | 14 | Detroit | 2-5 |
| | 15 | Minnesota | 5-3 |
| | 17 | at Edmonton | 1-2† |
| | 19 | at Vancouver | 0-3 |
| | 20 | at Calgary | 3-2 |
| | 24 | Los Angeles | 2-0 |
| | 26 | Vancouver | 4-2 |
| | 28 | Columbus | 4-3† |
| | 29 | at Columbus | 5-2 |
| **Apr.** | 1 | at Chicago | 1-3 |
| | 2 | at Detroit | 5-4 |
| | 4 | at Dallas | 4-5* |
| | 7 | at Phoenix | 5-1 |
| | 10 | Columbus | 3-1 |
| | 12 | at Colorado | 1-0 |

* – Overtime † – Shootout

## Entry Draft Selections 2009-1995

Name in bold denotes played in NHL.

**2009**
Pick
17 David Rundblad
48 Brett Ponich
78 Sergei Andronov
108 Tyler Shattock
168 David Shields
202 Maxwell Tardy

**2008**
Pick
4 **Alex Pietrangelo**
33 Philip McRae
34 Jake Allen
65 Jori Lehtera
70 James Livingston
87 Ian Schultz
95 David Warsofsky
125 Kristofer Berglund
155 Anthony Nigro
185 Paul Karpowich

**2007**
Pick
13 Lars Eller
18 Ian Cole
26 **David Perron**
39 Simon Hjalmarsson
44 Aaron Palushaj
85 Brett Sonne
96 Cade Fairchild
100 Travis Erstad
160 Anthony Peluso
190 Trevor Nill

**2006**
Pick
1 **Erik Johnson**
25 **Patrik Berglund**
31 Tomas Kana
64 **Jonas Junland**
94 Ryan Turek
106 Reto Berra
124 Andy Sackrison
154 Matthew McCollem
184 Alexander Hellstrom

**2005**
Pick
24 **T.J. Oshie**
37 Scott Jackson
85 **Ben Bishop**
156 Ryan Reaves
169 Mike Gauthier
171 Nicholas Drazenovic
219 Nikolai Lemtyugov

**2004**
Pick
17 **Marek Schwarz**
49 Carl Soderberg
83 Viktor Alexandrov
116 Michal Birner
136 Nikita Nikitin
180 **Roman Polak**
211 David Fredriksson
277 Jonathan Michel Boutin

**2003**
Pick
30 **Shawn Belle**
62 **David Backes**
84 Konstantin Barulin
88 **Zach Fitzgerald**
101 Konstantin Zakharov
127 **Alexandre Bolduc**
148 **Lee Stempniak**
159 **Chris Beckford-Tseu**
189 Jonathan Lehun
221 Evgeny Skachkov
253 Andrei Pervyshin
284 Juhamatti Aaltonen

**2002**
Pick
48 Alexei Shkotov
62 Andrei Mikhnov
89 Tomas Troliga
120 Robin Jonsson
165 Justin Maiser
191 **D.J. King**
221 Jonas Johnson
253 **Tom Koivisto**
284 Ryan MacMurchy

**2001**
Pick
57 **Jay McClement**
89 Tuomas Nissinen
122 Igor Valeev
159 Dmitri Semin
190 Brett Scheffelmaier
253 **Petr Cajanek**
270 Grant Jacobsen
283 Simon Skoog

**2000**
Pick
30 **Jeff Taffe**
65 **Dave Morisset**
75 **Justin Papineau**
96 Antoine Bergeron
129 Troy Riddle
167 **Craig Weller**
229 Brett Lutes
261 **Reinhard Divis**
293 Lauri Kinos

**1999**
Pick
17 **Barret Jackman**
85 **Peter Smrek**
114 Chad Starling
143 Trevor Byrne
180 Tore Vikingstad
203 Phil Osaer
221 **Colin Hemingway**
232 **Alexander Khavanov**
260 Brian McMeekin
270 James Desmarais

**1998**
Pick
24 **Christian Backman**
41 Maxim Linnik
83 **Matt Walker**
157 Brad Voth
170 Andrei Troschinsky
197 Brad Twordik
225 Yevgeny Pastukh
255 **John Pohl**

**1997**
Pick
40 Tyler Rennette
86 Didier Tremblay
98 Jan Horacek
106 **Jame Pollock**
149 Nicholas Bilotto
177 **Ladislav Nagy**
206 Bobby Haglund
232 Dmitri Plekhanov
244 Marek Ivan

**1996**
Pick
14 **Marty Reasoner**
67 **Gordie Dwyer**
95 Jonathan Zukiwsky
97 Andrei Petrakov
159 Stephen Wagner
169 **Daniel Corso**
177 **Reed Low**
196 **Andrej Podkonicky**
203 Tony Hutchins
229 **Konstantin Shafranov**

**1995**
Pick
49 **Jochen Hecht**
75 Scott Roche
101 **Michal Handzus**
127 Jeff Ambrosio
153 **Denis Hamel**
179 **Jean-Luc Grand-Pierre**
205 **Derek Bekar**
209 **Libor Zabransky**

## Captains' History

Al Arbour, 1967-68 to 1969-70; Red Berenson and Barclay Plager, 1970-71; Barclay Plager, 1971-72 to 1975-76; no captain, 1976-77; Red Berenson, 1977-78; Barry Gibbs, 1978-79; Brian Sutter, 1979-80 to 1987-88; Bernie Federko, 1988-89; Rick Meagher, 1989-90; Scott Stevens, 1990-91; Garth Butcher, 1991-92; Brett Hull, 1992-93 to 1994-95; Brett Hull, Shayne Corson and Wayne Gretzky, 1995-96; no captain, 1996-97; Chris Pronger, 1997-98 to 2001-02; Al MacInnis, 2002-03, 2003-04; Dallas Drake, 2005-06, 2006-07; Eric Brewer, 2007-08 to date.

## Larry Pleau

### Senior Vice President and General Manager

*Born: Lynn, MA, June 29, 1947.*

Larry Pleau was named general manager on June 9, 1997, becoming the tenth person to hold that position in team history. Under his leadership the Blues won the President's Trophy in 1999-2000 and reached the Western Conference Finals in 2000-01. In international hockey, he served as associate general manager of the silver medal-winning 2002 U.S. Olympic team and as general manager of Team USA at the World Championships in 2003 and 2004 (bronze medal) and at the 2004 World Cup.

Pleau joined the Blues after spending eight seasons with the New York Rangers organization, reaching the position of vice president of player personnel. He joined the Rangers in 1989 as assistant general manager of player development. During Pleau's tenure in New York, the Rangers drafted NHL stars Sergei Zubov, Doug Weight, Alex Kovalev and Niklas Sundstrom. Prior to joining the Rangers, Pleau spent 17 seasons with the Hartford Whalers organization as a player, assistant coach, head coach, general manager and minor league general manager and head coach. He was also instrumental in drafting Ray Ferraro, Ron Francis, Kevin Dineen and Ulf Samuelsson while a member of the Whalers organization.

Pleau played three seasons with the Montreal Canadiens (1969-1972) in the National Hockey League before being the first player signed by the Hartford Whalers of the World Hockey Association. He was a center/left wing for the Whalers from 1972 until his retirement in 1979. He played in 468 regular season games for Hartford, accumulating 157 goals and 215 assists for 372 points. He also played for the 1968 United States Olympic team, the 1969 U.S. national team and went to training camp with Team USA for the 1976 Canada Cup tournament.

### Coaching Record

| | | | Regular Season | | | | Playoffs | | | |
|---|---|---|---|---|---|---|---|---|---|---|
| Season | Team | League | GC | W | L | O/T | GC | W | L | T |
| 1980-81 | Hartford | NHL | 20 | 6 | 12 | 2 | .... | .... | .... | .... |
| 1981-82 | Hartford | NHL | 80 | 21 | 41 | 18 | .... | .... | .... | .... |
| 1982-83 | Hartford | NHL | 18 | 4 | 13 | 1 | .... | .... | .... | .... |
| 1987-88 | Hartford | NHL | 26 | 13 | 13 | 0 | 6 | 2 | 4 | .... |
| 1988-89 | Hartford | NHL | 80 | 37 | 38 | 5 | 4 | 0 | 4 | .... |
| | NHL Totals | | 224 | 81 | 117 | 26 | 10 | 2 | 8 | .... |

# Club Directory

Scottrade Center

**St. Louis Blues**
Scottrade Center
1401 Clark Avenue
St. Louis, MO 63103
Phone **314/622-2500**
FAX 314/622-2582
www.stlouisblues.com
**Capacity:** 19,150

**SCP Worldwide**

| | |
|---|---|
| Principal Owner and Chairman/Governor/ Chairman, SCP Worldwide | David W. Checketts |
| Vice Chairman/Alternate Governor/Partner, SCP Worldwide | Michael McCarthy |
| Alternate Governor/Partner, SCP Worldwide | Kenneth Munoz |
| Partner, SCP Worldwide | Dean Howes |
| Partner, SCP Worldwide | Steven Potter |
| Partner, SCP Worldwide | Carl Vogel |
| Minority Owner | Tom Stillman |

**Executive**

| | |
|---|---|
| President of Hockey Operations/Alt. Gov. | John Davidson |
| CEO of St. Louis Blues Enterprises/Alt. Gov. | Peter McLoughlin |
| Sr. V.P. and General Manager | Larry Pleau |
| Vice President, Player Personnel | Doug Armstrong |
| Vice President, Hockey Operations | Al MacInnis |
| Exec. V.P., G.M., Scottrade Center | Marty Brooks |
| Exec. V.P., Chief Marketing Officer | David Bullock |
| Exec. V.P., Corporate and Sponsorship Sales | Mark Toffolo |
| Sr. V.P., Sales | Todd Lambert |
| Sr. V.P., Finance and Administration | Phil Siddle |
| Sr. V.P., Business Development | Eric Stisser |
| Sr. V.P., Marketing | Karrie Yager |
| Vice President, Public Relations | Mike Caruso |
| Vice President, Suite Sales | Chris Diiorio |
| Vice President, Radio Sales | Jim Goessling |
| Vice President, Corporate and Sponsorship Sales | Bryan Lucas |
| Vice President, Entertainment and Event Marketing | Mark Tamar |
| Exec. Asst. to the President and GM | Donna Lembke |
| Exec. Asst. to the CEO, St. Louis Blues Enterprises | Amber Daniels |

**Hockey Operations**

| | |
|---|---|
| Assistant G.M./Director, Amateur Scouting | Jarmo Kekalainen |
| Assistant G.M./Director, Pro Scouting/Peoria G.M. | Kevin McDonald |
| Head Coach | Andy Murray |
| Assistant Coach/Goaltending Coach | Rick Wamsley |
| Assistant Coaches | Ray Bennett, Brad Shaw |
| Strength and Conditioning Coach | Nelson Ayotte |
| Video Coach | Scott Masters |
| Goaltending Consultant | Ed Belfour |
| Asst. Director, Public Relations/Team Services | Rich Jankowski |

**Scouting**

| | |
|---|---|
| Professional Scouts | Rob DiMaio, Tony Feltrin, Wayne Mundey, Jan Vopat |
| Amateur Scouts | Mike Antonovich, Bill Armstrong, Dan Ginnell, Basil McRae, Ville Siren |
| Part-Time Amateur Scouts | Thomas Carlsson, Marshall Davidson, Vladimir Havluj Jr., Rick Meagher, J Niemiec, Michel Picard, Georgi Zhuravlev |

**Training**

| | |
|---|---|
| Athletic Trainer / Asst. Trainer | Ray Barile / Mike Hannegan |
| Equipment Manager / Asst. Manager | Bert Godin / Joel Farnsworth |
| Equipment Assistant | Ray Halle |
| Massage Therapist | Jeff Wright |

**Medical**

| | |
|---|---|
| Orthopedic Surgeons | Drs. Jerome Gilden, Matt Matava, Dr. Rick Wright |
| Internists | Drs. Aaron Birenbaum, William Birenbaum |
| Neurosurgeon | Dr. Ralph Dacey |
| General Surgery / Plastic Surgery | Dr. Michael Brunt / Dr. Tom Francel |
| Dentist / Oral Surgeon | Dr. Glenn Edwards / Dr. Ken Kram |
| Ophthalmologist | Dr. Rex Ghormley |

**Broadcasting**

| | |
|---|---|
| Exec. Director, Broadcasting and Blues Alumni | Bruce Affleck |
| Radio / Television Stations | KMOX, 1120 AM / FS?Midwest |
| Radio Play-by-Play | Chris Kerber |
| Radio Color Analyst/Community Relations | Kelly Chase |
| Community Relations and KMOX Radio | Bob Plager |
| Television Play-by-Play / Color | John Kelly / Darren Pang, Bernie Federko |
| FS Midwest Analyst | Dan McLaughlin |

**Marketing**

| | |
|---|---|
| Senior Director, Advertising/Promotions | Lisa Kampeter |
| Senior Director, Digital Media | Beth Schwartz |
| Director, Event Presentation | Chris Frome |
| Director, Community Relations/14 Fund | Renah Jones |
| Team Photographer | Mark Buckner |

**Sponsorship**

| | |
|---|---|
| Director, Sponsorship Sales | Deni Allen |
| Corporate Sales Executive | Matt Poling |
| Director, Corporate Sponsorship Services | Julie Drochelman |

**Ticket Sales**

| | |
|---|---|
| Director, Client Services | Abby Jones |
| Managers, Ticket Sales | Yancey Jones, Nick Wierciak |

**Group Ticket Sales**

| | |
|---|---|
| Senior Director, Group Sales | Jennifer Nevins |
| Manager, Group Sales | Kari Takmajian |

**Finance**

| | |
|---|---|
| Finance Controller | Keith Hegger |
| Managers, Accounting | Craig Bryant, Kristal Edwards, Kristy Horner |
| Managers, Payroll | Pam Di Rie, Crystal Strasburg |
| Manager, IT | Tony Kostansek |

**Retail**

| | |
|---|---|
| Director, Retail | George Pavlik |
| Manager, Retail | Barry Smith |

**Box Office**

| | |
|---|---|
| Senior Director, Ticket Operations | Rob Fasoldt |

# San Jose Sharks

## 2008-09 Results: 53W-18L-6OTL-5SOL 117PTS.
## First, Pacific Division

## Key Off-Season Signings/Acquisitions

**2009**

**July 6** • Re-signed LW **Ryane Clowe.**
**9** • Re-signed D **Rob Blake** and D **Kent Huskins.**
**15** • Signed C **Scott Nichol.**
**16** • Signed C **Dwight Helminen** and RW **Jed Ortmeyer.**
**16** • Re-signed RW **Ryan Vesce.**
**17** • Named **Matt Shaw** assistant coach.

## Year-by-Year Record

| | | Home | | | | Road | | | | Overall | | | | | | | | |
|---|---|---|---|---|---|---|---|---|---|---|---|---|---|---|---|---|---|---|
| **Season** | **GP** | **W** | **L** | **T** | **OL** | **W** | **L** | **T** | **OL** | **W** | **L** | **T** | **OL** | **GF** | **GA** | **Pts.** | **Finished** | **Playoff Result** |
| 2008-09 | 82 | 32 | 5 | .... | 4 | 21 | 13 | .... | 7 | 53 | 18 | .... | 11 | 257 | 204 | 117 | 1st, Pacific Div. | Lost Conf. Quarter-Final |
| 2007-08 | 82 | 22 | 13 | .... | 6 | 27 | 10 | .... | 4 | 49 | 23 | .... | 10 | 222 | 193 | 108 | 1st, Pacific Div. | Lost Conf. Semi-Final |
| 2006-07 | 82 | 25 | 12 | .... | 4 | 26 | 14 | .... | 1 | 51 | 26 | .... | 5 | 258 | 199 | 107 | 2nd, Pacific Div. | Lost Conf. Semi-Final |
| 2005-06 | 82 | 25 | 9 | .... | 7 | 19 | 18 | .... | 4 | 44 | 27 | .... | 11 | 266 | 242 | 99 | 2nd, Pacific Div. | Lost Conf. Semi-Final |
| 2004-05 | .... | .... | .... | .... | .... | .... | .... | .... | .... | .... | .... | .... | .... | .... | .... | .... | | |
| 2003-04 | 82 | 24 | 8 | 7 | 2 | 19 | 13 | 5 | 4 | 43 | 21 | 12 | 6 | 219 | 183 | 104 | 1st, Pacific Div. | Lost Conf. Championship |
| 2002-03 | 82 | 17 | 16 | 5 | 3 | 11 | 21 | 4 | 5 | 28 | 37 | 9 | 8 | 214 | 239 | 73 | 5th, Pacific Div. | Out of Playoffs |
| 2001-02 | 82 | 25 | 11 | 3 | 2 | 19 | 16 | 5 | 1 | 44 | 27 | 8 | 3 | 248 | 199 | 99 | 1st, Pacific Div. | Lost Conf. Semi-Final |
| 2000-01 | 82 | 22 | 14 | 4 | 1 | 18 | 13 | 8 | 2 | 40 | 27 | 12 | 3 | 217 | 192 | 95 | 2nd, Pacific Div. | Lost Conf. Quarter-Final |
| 1999-2000 | 82 | 21 | 14 | 3 | 3 | 14 | 16 | 7 | 4 | 35 | 30 | 10 | 7 | 225 | 214 | 87 | 4th, Pacific Div. | Lost Conf. Semi-Final |
| 1998-99 | 82 | 17 | 15 | 9 | .... | 14 | 18 | 9 | .... | 31 | 33 | 18 | .... | 196 | 191 | 80 | 4th, Pacific Div. | Lost Conf. Quarter-Final |
| 1997-98 | 82 | 17 | 19 | 5 | .... | 17 | 19 | 5 | .... | 34 | 38 | 10 | .... | 210 | 216 | 78 | 4th, Pacific Div. | Lost Conf. Quarter-Final |
| 1996-97 | 82 | 14 | 23 | 4 | .... | 13 | 24 | 4 | .... | 27 | 47 | 8 | .... | 211 | 278 | 62 | 7th, Pacific Div. | Out of Playoffs |
| 1995-96 | 82 | 12 | 26 | 3 | .... | 8 | 29 | 4 | .... | 20 | 55 | 7 | .... | 252 | 357 | 47 | 7th, Pacific Div. | Out of Playoffs |
| 1994-95 | 48 | 10 | 13 | 1 | .... | 9 | 12 | 3 | .... | 19 | 25 | 4 | .... | 129 | 161 | 42 | 3rd, Pacific Div. | Lost Conf. Semi-Final |
| 1993-94 | 84 | 19 | 13 | 10 | .... | 14 | 22 | 6 | .... | 33 | 35 | 16 | .... | 252 | 265 | 82 | 3rd, Pacific Div. | Lost Conf. Semi-Final |
| 1992-93 | 84 | 8 | 33 | 1 | .... | 3 | 38 | 1 | .... | 11 | 71 | 2 | .... | 218 | 414 | 24 | 6th, Smythe Div. | Out of Playoffs |
| 1991-92 | 80 | 14 | 23 | 3 | .... | 3 | 35 | 2 | .... | 17 | 58 | 5 | .... | 219 | 359 | 39 | 6th, Smythe Div. | Out of Playoffs |

## 2009-10 Schedule

| | | | |
|---|---|---|---|
| **Oct.** Thu. | 1 at Colorado | **Jan.** Sat. | 2 Edmonton |
| Sat. | 3 at Anaheim | Mon. | 4 Los Angeles |
| Tue. | 6 at Los Angeles | Wed. | 6 St. Louis |
| Thu. | 8 Columbus | Sat. | 9 Detroit |
| Sat. | 10 Minnesota | Mon. | 11 at Los Angeles |
| Mon. | 12 Phoenix | Tue. | 12 at Phoenix |
| Thu. | 15 at Washington | Thu. | 14 Boston |
| Sat. | 17 at NY Islanders | Sat. | 16 Edmonton* |
| Mon. | 19 at NY Rangers | Mon. | 18 Calgary |
| Thu. | 22 at Tampa Bay | Tue. | 19 at Los Angeles |
| Sat. | 24 at Atlanta | Thu. | 21 Anaheim |
| Sun. | 25 at Philadelphia | Sat. | 23 Buffalo |
| Wed. | 28 Los Angeles | Thu. | 28 Chicago |
| Fri. | 30 Colorado | Sat. | 30 Minnesota |
| **Nov.** Sun. | 1 at Carolina* | **Feb.** Tue. | 2 Detroit |
| Wed. | 4 at Columbus | Thu. | 4 at St. Louis |
| Thu. | 5 at Detroit | Sat. | 6 at Nashville |
| Sat. | 7 Pittsburgh | Mon. | 8 at Toronto |
| Tue. | 10 Nashville | Wed. | 10 at Columbus |
| Thu. | 12 Dallas | Thu. | 11 at Detroit |
| Sat. | 14 at St. Louis | Sat. | 13 at Buffalo |
| Sun. | 15 at Chicago | **Mar.** Tue. | 2 New Jersey |
| Tue. | 17 at Nashville | Thu. | 4 Montreal |
| Fri. | 20 Philadelphia | Sat. | 6 Columbus |
| Sat. | 21 at Anaheim | Thu. | 11 Nashville |
| Wed. | 25 Chicago | Sat. | 13 Florida* |
| Fri. | 27 at Edmonton | Sun. | 14 at Anaheim* |
| Sun. | 29 at Vancouver | Tue. | 16 at Dallas |
| **Dec.** Tue. | 1 Ottawa | Thu. | 18 at Vancouver |
| Thu. | 3 St. Louis | Fri. | 19 at Calgary |
| Sat. | 5 Calgary | Sun. | 21 at Edmonton |
| Wed. | 9 Los Angeles | Tue. | 23 at Minnesota |
| Fri. | 11 Dallas | Thu. | 25 Dallas |
| Sat. | 12 at Phoenix | Sat. | 27 Vancouver |
| Thu. | 17 Anaheim | Sun. | 28 Colorado* |
| Mon. | 21 at Dallas | Wed. | 31 at Dallas |
| Tue. | 22 at Chicago | **Apr.** Fri. | 2 at Minnesota |
| Sat. | 26 Anaheim | Sun. | 4 at Colorado |
| Mon. | 28 Phoenix | Tue. | 6 at Calgary |
| Wed. | 30 Washington | Thu. | 8 Vancouver |
| Thu. | 31 at Phoenix* | Sat. | 10 Phoenix |

* Denotes afternoon game.

*Sharks captain Patrick Marleau bounced back from a poor performance with a big season in 2008-09. He scored a career-high 38 goals to help San Jose win the Presidents' Trophy for the first time.*

**PACIFIC DIVISION**
**19th NHL Season**

**Franchise date:** May 9, 1990

# 2009-10 Player Personnel

| FORWARDS | HT | WT | S | Place of Birth | *Age | 2008-09 Club |
|---|---|---|---|---|---|---|
| CHEECHOO, Jonathan | 6-1 | 200 | R | Moose Factory, Ont. | 29 | San Jose |
| CLOWE, Ryane | 6-2 | 225 | L | St. John's, Nfld. | 27 | San Jose |
| COUTURE, Logan | 6-1 | 195 | L | Guelph, Ont. | 20 | Ottawa (OHL)-Worcester |
| HELMINEN, Dwight | 5-10 | 190 | L | Hancock, MI | 26 | Carolina-Albany |
| JONES, Matt | 6-4 | 210 | R | Kentwood, MI | 23 | Worcester-Phoenix |
| MARLEAU, Patrick | 6-2 | 220 | L | Aneroid, Sask. | 30 | San Jose |
| MASHINTER, Brandon | 6-4 | 235 | L | Bradford, Ont. | 21 | Kitchener-Belleville |
| McCARTHY, John | 6-1 | 200 | L | Boston, MA | 23 | Boston University |
| McGINN, Jamie | 6-0 | 200 | L | Fergus, Ont. | 21 | San Jose-Worcester |
| McLAREN, Frazer | 6-5 | 235 | L | Winnipeg, Man. | 21 | Worcester |
| MICHALEK, Milan | 6-2 | 225 | L | Jindrichuv Hradec, Czech. | 24 | San Jose |
| MITCHELL, Torrey | 5-11 | 190 | R | Montreal, Que. | 24 | Worcester-San Jose |
| NICHOL, Scott | 5-9 | 180 | R | Edmonton, Alta. | 34 | Nashville |
| ORTMEYER, Jed | 6-0 | 200 | R | Omaha, NE | 31 | Nashville-Milwaukee |
| PAVELSKI, Joe | 5-11 | 195 | L | Plover, WI | 25 | San Jose |
| SETOGUCHI, Devin | 6-0 | 200 | R | Taber, Alta. | 22 | San Jose |
| SHELLEY, Jody | 6-3 | 225 | L | Thompson, Man. | 33 | San Jose |
| STAUBITZ, Brad | 6-1 | 215 | R | Bright's Grove, Ont. | 25 | San Jose-Worcester |
| THORNTON, Joe | 6-4 | 235 | L | London, Ont. | 30 | San Jose |
| VESCE, Ryan | 5-8 | 175 | R | Lloyd Harbor, NY | 27 | San Jose-Worcester |
| ZALEWSKI, Steven | 6-0 | 195 | L | Utica, NY | 23 | Worcester |
| **DEFENSEMEN** | | | | | | |
| BLAKE, Rob | 6-4 | 225 | R | Simcoe, Ont. | 39 | San Jose |
| BOYLE, Dan | 5-11 | 190 | R | Ottawa, Ont. | 33 | San Jose |
| CALLAHAN, Joe | 6-3 | 220 | R | Brockton, MA | 26 | NY Islanders-Bridgeport |
| DEMERS, Jason | 6-1 | 195 | R | Dorval, Que. | 21 | Worcester |
| EHRHOFF, Christian | 6-2 | 205 | L | Moers, West Germany | 27 | San Jose |
| GROULX, Danny | 6-0 | 205 | L | LaSalle, Que. | 28 | Rockford |
| HUSKINS, Kent | 6-4 | 205 | L | Ottawa, Ont. | 30 | Anaheim |
| JOSLIN, Derek | 6-1 | 205 | L | Richmond Hill, Ont. | 22 | San Jose-Worcester |
| LOPRIENO, Joe | 6-3 | 225 | R | Bloomingdale, IL | 22 | Merrimack |
| LUKOWICH, Brad | 6-1 | 200 | L | Cranbrook, B.C. | 33 | San Jose |
| MOORE, Mike | 6-1 | 200 | L | Calgary, Alta. | 24 | Worcester |
| MURRAY, Douglas | 6-3 | 240 | L | Bromma, Sweden | 29 | San Jose |
| PETRECKI, Nicholas | 6-3 | 215 | L | Schenectady, NY | 20 | Boston College |
| VLASIC, Marc-Edouard | 6-1 | 200 | L | Montreal, Que. | 22 | San Jose |

| GOALTENDERS | HT | WT | C | Place of Birth | *Age | 2008-09 Club |
|---|---|---|---|---|---|---|
| GREISS, Thomas | 6-1 | 210 | L | Straubing, West Germany | 23 | Worcester |
| NABOKOV, Evgeni | 6-0 | 205 | L | Ust-Kamenogorsk, USSR | 34 | San Jose |
| SEXSMITH, Tyson | 5-11 | 210 | L | Calgary, Alta. | 20 | Vancouver (WHL) |
| STALOCK, Alex | 5-11 | 170 | L | St. Paul, MN | 22 | U. Minn-Duluth |

* – Age at start of 2009-10 season

# Todd McLellan

## Head Coach

*Born: Melville, Sask., October 3, 1967.*

Named to his post as the seventh head coach in San Jose Sharks history on June 12, 2008, Todd McLellan produced one of the most remarkable debuts in league history in 2008-09. Named as a finalist for the Jack Adams Award, McLellan became just the sixth NHL coach (and first since 1990) to lead his team to the Presidents' Trophy for the best overall regular-season record (53-18-11) in his first season behind the bench. Only Tom Johnson's 1970-71 Boston Bruins won more home games (33) than McLellan's Sharks (32) and the team's 53 wins tied him for second behind Johnson (57 wins) for most overall coaching wins by a rookie head coach.

Prior to joining the Sharks, McLellan had captured the 2008 Stanley Cup in his third season as an assistant coach under Mike Babcock with the Detroit Red Wings. Over the course of those three seasons, the Red Wings won the Presidents' Trophy as the NHL's top regular season team twice (2005-06 and 2007-08) and finished second in 2006-07, tying the Buffalo Sabres for first in points (113) but having three fewer wins. One of McLellan's key responsibilities was working with the Detroit power play, which finished third in the NHL in 2007-08 (20.7%) and first in 2005-06 (22.1%).

Before being hired in Detroit, McLellan spent four seasons as head coach of the Houston Aeros in the American Hockey League, including capturing the 2003 AHL Calder Cup championship. He also was selected to coach in two AHL All-Star Games during his tenure with Houston. In 2000-01, he served as the head coach of the Cleveland Lumberjacks of the International Hockey League.

From 1994-95 through 1999-2000, McLellan coached the Swift Current Broncos of the Western Hockey League, where he also served as general manager in his final four WHL seasons. He was named WHL coach of the year in 2000 and WHL executive of the year in 1997. In his 14 years of serving as a head and assistant coach prior to arriving in San Jose, McLellan?s teams never missed the postseason.

McLellan played his junior hockey with Saskatoon (WHL) and was drafted by the New York Islanders in the fifth round (104th overall) in the 1986 NHL Entry Draft. He played parts of two seasons with Springfield in the American Hockey League and played in five games with the Islanders in 1987-88, posting two points (one goal, one assist) before a shoulder injury ended his NHL career.

### Coaching Record

| | | | Regular Season | | | | Playoffs | | | |
|---|---|---|---|---|---|---|---|---|---|---|
| Season | Team | League | GC | W | L | O/T | GC | W | L | T |
| 1994-95 | Swift Current | WHL | 72 | 31 | 34 | 7 | 6 | 2 | 4 | .... |
| 1995-96 | Swift Current | WHL | 72 | 36 | 31 | 5 | 6 | 2 | 4 | .... |
| 1996-97 | Swift Current | WHL | 72 | 44 | 23 | 5 | 10 | 4 | 4 | .... |
| 1997-98 | Swift Current | WHL | 72 | 44 | 19 | 9 | 12 | 7 | 5 | .... |
| 1998-99 | Swift Current | WHL | 72 | 34 | 32 | 6 | 6 | 2 | 4 | .... |
| 99-2000 | Swift Current | WHL | 72 | 47 | 18 | 7 | 12 | 6 | 6 | .... |
| 2000-01 | Cleveland | IHL | 82 | 43 | 32 | 7 | 4 | 0 | 4 | .... |
| 2001-02 | Houston | AHL | 80 | 39 | 26 | 15 | 14 | 8 | 6 | .... |
| 2002-03 | Houston | AHL | 80 | 47 | 23 | 10 | 23 | 15 | 8 | .... |
| 2003-04 | Houston | AHL | 80 | 28 | 34 | 18 | 2 | 0 | 2 | .... |
| 2004-05 | Houston | AHL | 80 | 40 | 28 | 12 | 5 | 1 | 4 | .... |
| **2008-09** | **San Jose** | **NHL** | **82** | **53** | **18** | **11** | **6** | **2** | **4** | .... |
| | **NHL Totals** | | **82** | **53** | **18** | **11** | **6** | **2** | **4** | .... |

# 2008-09 Scoring

* – rookie

## Regular Season

| Pos | # | Player | Team | GP | G | A | Pts | TOI | +/– | PIM | PP | SH | GW | S | % |
|---|---|---|---|---|---|---|---|---|---|---|---|---|---|---|---|
| C | 19 | Joe Thornton | S.J. | 82 | 25 | 61 | 86 | 19:27 | 16 | 56 | 11 | 0 | 3 | 139 | 18.0 |
| C | 12 | Patrick Marleau | S.J. | 76 | 38 | 33 | 71 | 21:21 | 16 | 18 | 11 | 5 | 10 | 251 | 15.1 |
| R | 16 | Devin Setoguchi | S.J. | 81 | 31 | 34 | 65 | 16:12 | 16 | 25 | 11 | 0 | 3 | 246 | 12.6 |
| C | 8 | Joe Pavelski | S.J. | 80 | 25 | 34 | 59 | 18:57 | 5 | 46 | 8 | 3 | 3 | 266 | 9.4 |
| L | 9 | Milan Michalek | S.J. | 77 | 23 | 34 | 57 | 18:27 | 11 | 52 | 6 | 0 | 6 | 179 | 12.8 |
| D | 22 | Dan Boyle | S.J. | 77 | 16 | 41 | 57 | 24:46 | 6 | 52 | 8 | 0 | 4 | 213 | 7.5 |
| L | 29 | Ryane Clowe | S.J. | 71 | 22 | 30 | 52 | 17:46 | 8 | 51 | 11 | 0 | 1 | 161 | 13.7 |
| D | 4 | Rob Blake | S.J. | 73 | 10 | 35 | 45 | 21:16 | 15 | 110 | 6 | 0 | 1 | 198 | 5.1 |
| D | 10 | Christian Ehrhoff | S.J. | 77 | 8 | 34 | 42 | 21:14 | –12 | 63 | 5 | 0 | 2 | 165 | 4.8 |
| D | 44 | Marc-Edouard Vlasic | S.J. | 82 | 6 | 30 | 36 | 23:54 | 15 | 42 | 3 | 0 | 1 | 104 | 5.8 |
| R | 14 | Jonathan Cheechoo | S.J. | 66 | 12 | 17 | 29 | 15:19 | –3 | 59 | 5 | 1 | 4 | 152 | 7.9 |
| R | 25 | Mike Grier | S.J. | 62 | 10 | 13 | 23 | 15:00 | 8 | 25 | 0 | 1 | 2 | 108 | 9.3 |
| L | 24 | Travis Moen | ANA | 63 | 4 | 7 | 11 | 14:52 | –17 | 77 | 0 | 2 | 1 | 77 | 5.2 |
| | | | S.J. | 19 | 3 | 2 | 5 | 15:21 | –1 | 14 | 0 | 1 | 1 | 24 | 12.5 |
| | | | Total | 82 | 7 | 9 | 16 | 14:59 | –18 | 91 | 0 | 3 | 2 | 101 | 6.9 |
| C | 39 * | Tomas Plihal | S.J. | 64 | 5 | 8 | 13 | 10:08 | –4 | 22 | 0 | 1 | 1 | 79 | 6.3 |
| C | 27 | Jeremy Roenick | S.J. | 42 | 4 | 9 | 13 | 11:38 | –1 | 24 | 1 | 0 | 0 | 50 | 8.0 |
| C | 11 | Marcel Goc | S.J. | 55 | 2 | 9 | 11 | 13:55 | –6 | 18 | 0 | 0 | 1 | 104 | 1.9 |
| D | 21 | Alexei Semenov | S.J. | 47 | 1 | 7 | 8 | 13:02 | 3 | 57 | 0 | 0 | 0 | 28 | 3.6 |
| D | 37 | Brad Lukowich | S.J. | 58 | 0 | 8 | 8 | 16:12 | 5 | 12 | 0 | 0 | 0 | 43 | 0.0 |
| D | 3 | Doug Murray | S.J. | 75 | 0 | 7 | 7 | 16:38 | 6 | 38 | 0 | 0 | 0 | 56 | 0.0 |
| L | 64 * | Jamie McGinn | S.J. | 35 | 4 | 2 | 6 | 8:55 | –6 | 2 | 1 | 0 | 1 | 27 | 14.8 |
| L | 43 * | Lukas Kaspar | S.J. | 13 | 2 | 2 | 4 | 9:08 | 0 | 8 | 0 | 0 | 1 | 14 | 14.3 |
| L | 45 | Jody Shelley | S.J. | 70 | 2 | 2 | 4 | 6:11 | –6 | 116 | 0 | 0 | 1 | 44 | 4.5 |
| R | 59 * | Brad Staubitz | S.J. | 35 | 1 | 2 | 3 | 6:13 | 0 | 76 | 0 | 0 | 1 | 22 | 4.5 |
| R | 47 | Tom Cavanagh | S.J. | 17 | 1 | 1 | 2 | 7:43 | –2 | 4 | 0 | 0 | 0 | 9 | 11.1 |
| R | 32 | Claude Lemieux | S.J. | 18 | 0 | 1 | 1 | 7:39 | –5 | 21 | 0 | 0 | 0 | 17 | 0.0 |
| C | 40 * | Riley Armstrong | S.J. | 2 | 0 | 0 | 0 | 7:26 | –1 | 2 | 0 | 0 | 0 | 1 | 0.0 |
| R | 53 | Ryan Vesce | S.J. | 10 | 0 | 0 | 0 | 9:44 | –2 | 4 | 0 | 0 | 0 | 11 | 0.0 |
| D | 65 * | Derek Joslin | S.J. | 12 | 0 | 0 | 0 | 11:21 | –3 | 6 | 0 | 0 | 0 | 9 | 0.0 |

### Goaltending

| No. | Goaltender | GPI | Mins | Avg | W | L | OT | EN | SO | GA | SA | S% | G | A | PIM |
|---|---|---|---|---|---|---|---|---|---|---|---|---|---|---|---|
| 33 | Brian Boucher | 22 | 1291 | 2.18 | 12 | 6 | 3 | 2 | 2 | 47 | 563 | .917 | 0 | 0 | 2 |
| 20 | Evgeni Nabokov | 62 | 3686 | 2.44 | 41 | 12 | 8 | 0 | 7 | 150 | 1663 | .910 | 0 | 1 | 12 |
| | **Totals** | **82** | **5000** | **2.39** | **53** | **18** | **11** | **2** | **9** | **199** | **2228** | **.911** | | | |

## Playoffs

| Pos | # | Player | Team | GP | G | A | Pts | TOI | +/– | PIM | PP | SH | GW | OT | S | % |
|---|---|---|---|---|---|---|---|---|---|---|---|---|---|---|---|---|
| C | 19 | Joe Thornton | S.J. | 6 | 1 | 4 | 5 | 19:14 | –3 | 5 | 1 | 0 | 0 | 0 | 17 | 5.9 |
| D | 22 | Dan Boyle | S.J. | 6 | 2 | 2 | 4 | 23:16 | –1 | 8 | 1 | 0 | 0 | 0 | 18 | 11.1 |
| D | 4 | Rob Blake | S.J. | 6 | 1 | 3 | 4 | 21:50 | –5 | 4 | 0 | 0 | 0 | 0 | 26 | 3.8 |
| C | 12 | Patrick Marleau | S.J. | 6 | 2 | 1 | 3 | 20:28 | 0 | 8 | 1 | 0 | 2 | 1 | 12 | 16.7 |
| R | 16 | Devin Setoguchi | S.J. | 6 | 1 | 2 | 3 | 16:20 | –1 | 2 | 0 | 0 | 0 | 0 | 17 | 5.9 |
| R | 14 | Jonathan Cheechoo | S.J. | 6 | 1 | 1 | 2 | 10:10 | 1 | 4 | 0 | 0 | 0 | 0 | 17 | 5.9 |
| L | 29 | Ryane Clowe | S.J. | 6 | 1 | 1 | 2 | 18:22 | –4 | 8 | 0 | 0 | 0 | 0 | 11 | 9.1 |
| L | 9 | Milan Michalek | S.J. | 6 | 1 | 0 | 1 | 19:22 | –3 | 2 | 1 | 0 | 0 | 0 | 20 | 5.0 |
| C | 27 | Jeremy Roenick | S.J. | 6 | 0 | 1 | 1 | 12:14 | –1 | 12 | 0 | 0 | 0 | 0 | 11 | 0.0 |
| C | 8 | Joe Pavelski | S.J. | 6 | 0 | 1 | 1 | 19:21 | –3 | 9 | 0 | 0 | 0 | 0 | 18 | 0.0 |
| D | 44 | Marc-Edouard Vlasic | S.J. | 6 | 0 | 1 | 1 | 20:39 | –6 | 0 | 0 | 0 | 0 | 0 | 5 | 0.0 |
| R | 32 | Claude Lemieux | S.J. | 1 | 0 | 0 | 0 | 5:07 | 0 | 0 | 0 | 0 | 0 | 0 | 1 | 0.0 |
| L | 45 | Jody Shelley | S.J. | 1 | 0 | 0 | 0 | 2:02 | 0 | 0 | 0 | 0 | 0 | 0 | 0 | 0.0 |
| C | 17 | Torrey Mitchell | S.J. | 4 | 0 | 0 | 0 | 9:38 | –1 | 2 | 0 | 0 | 0 | 0 | 9 | 0.0 |
| R | 25 | Mike Grier | S.J. | 6 | 0 | 0 | 0 | 10:32 | –2 | 6 | 0 | 0 | 0 | 0 | 8 | 0.0 |
| D | 37 | Brad Lukowich | S.J. | 6 | 0 | 0 | 0 | 14:30 | 1 | 0 | 0 | 0 | 0 | 0 | 6 | 0.0 |
| D | 3 | Doug Murray | S.J. | 6 | 0 | 0 | 0 | 16:51 | –1 | 9 | 0 | 0 | 0 | 0 | 3 | 0.0 |
| L | 24 | Travis Moen | S.J. | 6 | 0 | 0 | 0 | 12:53 | –4 | 2 | 0 | 0 | 0 | 0 | 4 | 0.0 |
| C | 11 | Marcel Goc | S.J. | 6 | 0 | 0 | 0 | 10:32 | –2 | 2 | 0 | 0 | 0 | 0 | 7 | 0.0 |
| D | 10 | Christian Ehrhoff | S.J. | 6 | 0 | 0 | 0 | 24:47 | –2 | 2 | 0 | 0 | 0 | 0 | 20 | 0.0 |

### Goaltending

| No. | Goaltender | GPI | Mins | Avg | W | L | EN | SO | GA | SA | S% | G | A | PIM |
|---|---|---|---|---|---|---|---|---|---|---|---|---|---|---|
| 20 | Evgeni Nabokov | 6 | 362 | 2.82 | 2 | 4 | 1 | 0 | 17 | 155 | .890 | 0 | 0 | 0 |
| | **Totals** | **6** | **366** | **2.95** | **2** | **4** | **1** | **0** | **18** | **156** | **.885** | | | |

## General Managers' History

Jack Ferreira, 1991-92; Chuck Grillo (V.P. Director of Player Personnel), 1992-93 to 1995-96; Dean Lombardi, 1996-97 to 2002-03; Doug Wilson, 2003-04 to date.

## Coaching History

George Kingston, 1991-92, 1992-93; Kevin Constantine, 1993-94, 1994-95; Kevin Constantine and Jim Wiley, 1995-96; Al Sims, 1996-97; Darryl Sutter, 1997-98 to 2001-02; Darryl Sutter, Cap Raeder and Ron Wilson, 2002-03; Ron Wilson, 2003-04 to 2007-08; Todd McLellan, 2008-09 to date.

# Club Records

## Team

(Figures in brackets for season records are games played; records for fewest points, wins, ties, losses, goals, goals against are for 70 or more games)

| | | |
|---|---|---|
| **Most Points** | **117** | 2008-09 (82) |
| **Most Wins** | **53** | 2008-09 (82) |
| **Most Ties** | **18** | 1998-99 (82) |
| **Most Losses** | ***71** | 1992-93 (84) |
| **Most Goals** | **266** | 2005-06 (82) |
| **Most Goals Against** | **414** | 1992-93 (84) |
| **Fewest Points** | **24** | 1992-93 (84) |
| **Fewest Wins** | **11** | 1992-93 (84) |
| **Fewest Ties** | ***2** | 1992-93 (84) |
| **Fewest Losses** | **18** | 2008-09 (82) |
| **Fewest Goals** | **196** | 1998-99 (82) |
| **Fewest Goals Against** | **183** | 2003-04 (82) |
| **Longest Winning Streak** | | |
| **Overall** | **11** | Feb. 21-Mar. 14/08 |
| **Home** | **9** | Oct. 9-Nov. 8/08 |
| **Away** | **10** | Nov. 14-Dec. 31/07 |
| **Longest Undefeated Streak** | | |
| **Overall** | **10** | Nov. 27-Dec. 19/01 (9 wins, 1 tie) |
| **Home** | **11** | Nov. 15-Dec. 29/03 (8 wins, 3 ties) |
| **Away** | **10** | Dec. 26/00-Feb. 16/01 (6 wins, 4 ties) |
| **Longest Losing Streak** | | |
| **Overall** | ***17** | Jan. 4-Feb. 12/93 |
| **Home** | **9** | Nov. 19-Dec. 19/92 |
| **Away** | **19** | Nov. 27/92-Feb. 12/93 |
| **Longest Winless Streak** | | |
| **Overall** | **20** | Dec. 29/92-Feb. 12/93 (19 losses, 1 tie) |
| **Home** | **9** | Nov. 19-Dec. 19/92 (9 losses), Oct. 16-Nov. 18/03 (4 losses, 5 ties) |
| **Away** | **19** | Nov. 27/92-Feb. 12/93 (19 losses) |
| **Most Shutouts, Season** | **11** | 2003-04 (82), 2006-07 (82) |
| **Most PIM, Season** | **2,134** | 1992-93 (84) |
| **Most Goals, Game** | **10** | Jan. 13/96 (S.J. 10 at Pit. 8), Mar. 30/02 (CBJ 2 at S.J. 10) |

## Individual

| | | |
|---|---|---|
| **Most Seasons** | **11** | Mike Rathje, Patrick Marleau |
| **Most Games, Career** | **871** | Patrick Marleau |
| **Most Goals, Career** | **276** | Patrick Marleau |
| **Most Assists, Career** | **334** | Patrick Marleau |
| **Most Points, Career** | **610** | Patrick Marleau (276G, 334A) |
| **Most PIM, Career** | **1,001** | Jeff Odgers |
| **Most Shutouts, Career** | **47** | Evgeni Nabokov |
| **Longest Consecutive Games Streak** | **304** | Joe Thornton (Dec. 1/05-to date) |
| **Most Goals, Season** | **56** | Jonathan Cheechoo (2005-06) |
| **Most Assists, Season** | **92** | Joe Thornton (2006-07) |
| **Most Points, Season** | **114** | Joe Thornton (2006-07; 22G, 92A) |
| **Most PIM, Season** | **326** | Link Gaetz (1991-92) |
| **Most Points, Defenseman, Season** | **64** | Sandis Ozolinsh (1993-94; 26G, 38A) |
| **Most Points, Center, Season** | **114** | Joe Thornton (2006-07; 22G, 92A) |
| **Most Points, Right Wing, Season** | **93** | Jonathan Cheechoo (2005-06; 56G, 37A) |
| **Most Points, Left Wing, Season** | **66** | Johan Garpenlov (1992-93; 22G, 44A), Milan Michalek (2006-07; 26G, 40A) |
| **Most Points, Rookie, Season** | **59** | Pat Falloon (1991-92; 25G, 34A) |
| **Most Shutouts, Season** | **9** | Evgeni Nabokov (2003-04) |
| **Most Goals, Game** | **4** | Owen Nolan (Dec. 19/95) |
| **Most Assists, Game** | **4** | Sixteen times |
| **Most Points, Game** | **6** | Owen Nolan (Oct. 4/99; 3G, 3A) |

* NHL Record.

## Captains' History

Doug Wilson, 1991-92, 1992-93; Bob Errey, 1993-94; Bob Errey and Jeff Odgers, 1994-95; Jeff Odgers, 1995-96; Todd Gill, 1996-97, 1997-98; Owen Nolan, 1998-99 to 2002-03; Mike Ricci, Vincent Damphousse, Alyn McCauley, Patrick Marleau, 2003-04; Patrick Marleau, 2005-06 to date.

# All-time Record vs. Other Clubs

## Regular Season

| | At Home | | | | | | | | On Road | | | | | | | | Total | | | | | | | |
|---|---|---|---|---|---|---|---|---|---|---|---|---|---|---|---|---|---|---|---|---|---|---|---|---|
| | GP | W | L | T | OL | GF | GA | PTS | GP | W | L | T | OL | GF | GA | PTS | GP | W | L | T | OL | GF | GA | PTS |
| Anaheim | 45 | 20 | 21 | 2 | 2 | 120 | 122 | 44 | 45 | 25 | 14 | 2 | 4 | 135 | 119 | 56 | 90 | 45 | 35 | 4 | 6 | 255 | 241 | 100 |
| Atlanta | 6 | 5 | 0 | 1 | 0 | 24 | 11 | 11 | 5 | 3 | 0 | 1 | 1 | 16 | 8 | 8 | 11 | 8 | 0 | 2 | 1 | 40 | 19 | 19 |
| Boston | 12 | 4 | 6 | 2 | 0 | 31 | 40 | 10 | 12 | 2 | 7 | 3 | 0 | 37 | 43 | 7 | 24 | 6 | 13 | 5 | 0 | 68 | 83 | 17 |
| Buffalo | 11 | 5 | 2 | 4 | 0 | 37 | 40 | 14 | 13 | 1 | 11 | 0 | 1 | 37 | 58 | 3 | 24 | 6 | 13 | 4 | 1 | 74 | 98 | 17 |
| Calgary | 42 | 17 | 19 | 4 | 2 | 127 | 123 | 40 | 40 | 13 | 22 | 4 | 1 | 109 | 141 | 31 | 82 | 30 | 41 | 8 | 3 | 236 | 264 | 71 |
| Carolina | 13 | 8 | 4 | 0 | 1 | 57 | 38 | 17 | 12 | 5 | 7 | 0 | 0 | 27 | 40 | 10 | 25 | 13 | 11 | 0 | 1 | 84 | 78 | 27 |
| Chicago | 34 | 20 | 10 | 3 | 1 | 100 | 87 | 44 | 33 | 16 | 12 | 2 | 3 | 107 | 101 | 37 | 67 | 36 | 22 | 5 | 4 | 207 | 188 | 81 |
| Colorado | 32 | 13 | 18 | 1 | 0 | 89 | 108 | 27 | 31 | 10 | 16 | 4 | 1 | 66 | 106 | 25 | 63 | 23 | 34 | 5 | 1 | 155 | 214 | 52 |
| Columbus | 16 | 15 | 0 | 0 | 1 | 63 | 25 | 31 | 16 | 7 | 7 | 0 | 2 | 33 | 41 | 16 | 32 | 22 | 7 | 0 | 3 | 96 | 66 | 47 |
| Dallas | 45 | 17 | 22 | 1 | 5 | 105 | 126 | 40 | 44 | 20 | 19 | 4 | 1 | 108 | 116 | 45 | 89 | 37 | 41 | 5 | 6 | 213 | 242 | 85 |
| Detroit | 34 | 14 | 16 | 3 | 1 | 123 | 130 | 32 | 33 | 4 | 26 | 1 | 2 | 56 | 132 | 11 | 67 | 18 | 42 | 4 | 3 | 179 | 262 | 43 |
| Edmonton | 40 | 19 | 13 | 5 | 3 | 133 | 118 | 46 | 41 | 11 | 21 | 7 | 2 | 94 | 129 | 31 | 81 | 30 | 34 | 12 | 5 | 227 | 247 | 77 |
| Florida | 10 | 6 | 2 | 2 | 0 | 32 | 19 | 14 | 11 | 3 | 3 | 5 | 0 | 32 | 30 | 11 | 21 | 9 | 5 | 7 | 0 | 64 | 49 | 25 |
| Los Angeles | 52 | 32 | 16 | 3 | 1 | 175 | 138 | 68 | 52 | 21 | 25 | 4 | 2 | 139 | 151 | 48 | 104 | 53 | 41 | 7 | 3 | 314 | 289 | 116 |
| Minnesota | 16 | 8 | 5 | 1 | 2 | 42 | 34 | 19 | 16 | 9 | 4 | 1 | 2 | 41 | 38 | 21 | 32 | 17 | 9 | 2 | 4 | 83 | 72 | 40 |
| Montreal | 12 | 6 | 3 | 2 | 1 | 39 | 32 | 15 | 13 | 2 | 9 | 2 | 0 | 24 | 45 | 6 | 25 | 8 | 12 | 4 | 1 | 63 | 77 | 21 |
| Nashville | 20 | 12 | 5 | 1 | 2 | 55 | 49 | 27 | 20 | 9 | 9 | 1 | 1 | 53 | 50 | 20 | 40 | 21 | 14 | 2 | 3 | 108 | 99 | 47 |
| New Jersey | 11 | 4 | 5 | 1 | 1 | 26 | 32 | 10 | 14 | 4 | 8 | 1 | 1 | 31 | 53 | 10 | 25 | 8 | 13 | 2 | 2 | 57 | 85 | 20 |
| NY Islanders | 14 | 7 | 5 | 1 | 1 | 37 | 43 | 16 | 12 | 4 | 6 | 2 | 0 | 37 | 43 | 10 | 26 | 11 | 11 | 3 | 1 | 74 | 86 | 26 |
| NY Rangers | 15 | 3 | 10 | 2 | 0 | 35 | 54 | 8 | 11 | 2 | 7 | 1 | 1 | 30 | 43 | 6 | 26 | 5 | 17 | 3 | 1 | 65 | 97 | 14 |
| Ottawa | 10 | 6 | 4 | 0 | 0 | 21 | 18 | 12 | 11 | 3 | 4 | 4 | 0 | 30 | 37 | 10 | 21 | 9 | 8 | 4 | 0 | 51 | 55 | 22 |
| Philadelphia | 14 | 5 | 7 | 2 | 0 | 33 | 36 | 12 | 13 | 5 | 6 | 2 | 0 | 37 | 43 | 12 | 27 | 10 | 13 | 4 | 0 | 70 | 79 | 24 |
| Phoenix | 47 | 23 | 16 | 4 | 4 | 157 | 135 | 54 | 50 | 22 | 23 | 3 | 2 | 143 | 153 | 49 | 97 | 45 | 39 | 7 | 6 | 300 | 288 | 103 |
| Pittsburgh | 15 | 7 | 6 | 2 | 0 | 39 | 57 | 16 | 11 | 5 | 4 | 1 | 1 | 35 | 44 | 12 | 26 | 12 | 10 | 3 | 1 | 74 | 101 | 28 |
| St. Louis | 32 | 10 | 19 | 1 | 2 | 80 | 104 | 23 | 36 | 15 | 18 | 1 | 2 | 92 | 110 | 33 | 68 | 25 | 37 | 2 | 4 | 172 | 214 | 56 |
| Tampa Bay | 12 | 5 | 6 | 1 | 0 | 42 | 38 | 11 | 14 | 6 | 6 | 1 | 1 | 38 | 34 | 14 | 26 | 11 | 12 | 2 | 1 | 80 | 72 | 25 |
| Toronto | 17 | 7 | 7 | 3 | 0 | 40 | 44 | 17 | 19 | 5 | 12 | 2 | 0 | 52 | 73 | 12 | 36 | 12 | 19 | 5 | 0 | 92 | 117 | 29 |
| Vancouver | 42 | 18 | 17 | 5 | 2 | 123 | 122 | 43 | 40 | 15 | 20 | 4 | 1 | 110 | 137 | 35 | 82 | 33 | 37 | 9 | 3 | 233 | 259 | 78 |
| Washington | 12 | 8 | 3 | 1 | 0 | 40 | 29 | 17 | 13 | 8 | 5 | 0 | 0 | 39 | 36 | 16 | 25 | 16 | 8 | 1 | 0 | 79 | 65 | 33 |
| **Totals** | **681** | **324** | **267** | **58** | **32** | **2025** | **1952** | **738** | **681** | **255** | **331** | **63** | **32** | **1788** | **2154** | **605** | **1362** | **579** | **598** | **121** | **64** | **3813** | **4106** | **1343** |

## Playoffs

| | Series | W | L | GP | W | L | T | GF | GA | Last Mtg. | Rnd. | Result |
|---|---|---|---|---|---|---|---|---|---|---|---|---|
| Anaheim | 1 | 0 | 1 | 6 | 2 | 4 | 0 | 10 | 18 | 2009 | CQF | L 2-4 |
| Calgary | 3 | 2 | 1 | 20 | 10 | 10 | 0 | 57 | 68 | 2008 | CQF | W 4-3 |
| Colorado | 3 | 1 | 2 | 19 | 9 | 10 | 0 | 52 | 51 | 2004 | CSF | W 4-2 |
| Dallas | 3 | 0 | 3 | 17 | 5 | 12 | 0 | 30 | 46 | 2008 | CSF | L 2-4 |
| Detroit | 3 | 1 | 2 | 17 | 6 | 11 | 0 | 36 | 64 | 2007 | CSF | L 2-4 |
| Edmonton | 1 | 0 | 1 | 6 | 2 | 4 | 0 | 12 | 19 | 2006 | CSF | L 2-4 |
| Nashville | 2 | 2 | 0 | 10 | 8 | 2 | 0 | 33 | 24 | 2007 | CQF | W 4-1 |
| Phoenix | 1 | 1 | 0 | 5 | 4 | 1 | 0 | 13 | 7 | 2002 | CQF | W 4-1 |
| St. Louis | 3 | 2 | 1 | 18 | 10 | 8 | 0 | 43 | 47 | 2004 | CQF | W 4-1 |
| Toronto | 1 | 0 | 1 | 7 | 3 | 4 | 0 | 21 | 26 | 1994 | CSF | L 3-4 |
| **Totals** | **21** | **9** | **12** | **125** | **59** | **66** | **0** | **307** | **370** | | | |

Carolina totals include Hartford, 1991-92 to 1996-97.
Dallas totals include Minnesota North Stars, 1991-92 to 1992-93.

## Playoff Results 2009-2004

| Year | Round | Opponent | Result | GF | GA |
|---|---|---|---|---|---|
| 2009 | CQF | Anaheim | L 2-4 | 10 | 18 |
| 2008 | CSF | Dallas | L 2-4 | 11 | 15 |
| | CQF | Calgary | W 4-3 | 19 | 17 |
| 2007 | CSF | Detroit | L 2-4 | 9 | 13 |
| | CQF | Nashville | W 4-1 | 16 | 14 |
| 2006 | CSF | Edmonton | L 2-4 | 12 | 19 |
| | CQF | Nashville | W 4-1 | 17 | 10 |
| 2004 | CF | Calgary | L 2-4 | 12 | 16 |
| | CSF | Colorado | W 4-2 | 14 | 7 |
| | CQF | St. Louis | W 4-1 | 12 | 9 |

**Abbreviations: Round: CF** – conference final; **CSF** – conference semi-final; **CQF** – conference quarter-final.

Colorado totals include Quebec, 1991-92 to 1994-95.
Phoenix totals include Winnipeg, 1991-92 to 1995-96.

## 2008-09 Results

| | | | |
|---|---|---|---|
| **Oct.** | 9 | Anaheim | 4-1 |
| | 11 | Los Angeles | 3-1 |
| | 12 | at Los Angeles | 1-0 |
| | 14 | Columbus | 5-2 |
| | 17 | at Anaheim | 0-4 |
| | 18 | Philadelphia | 5-4* |
| | 22 | at Philadelphia | 7-6† |
| | 24 | at Florida | 3-4 |
| | 25 | at Tampa Bay | 3-0 |
| | 28 | Pittsburgh | 2-1 |
| | 30 | Detroit | 4-2 |
| **Nov.** | 2 | at Colorado | 5-3 |
| | 4 | Minnesota | 3-1 |
| | 6 | St. Louis | 5-4† |
| | 8 | Dallas | 2-1 |
| | 9 | at Phoenix | 2-4 |
| | 11 | Nashville | 3-4* |
| | 13 | Calgary | 6-1 |
| | 16 | at Chicago | 6-5 |
| | 17 | at Nashville | 4-1 |
| | 22 | Washington | 7-2 |
| | 26 | Chicago | 3-2* |
| | 28 | at Dallas | 6-2 |
| | 29 | at Phoenix | 3-2 |
| **Dec.** | 2 | Toronto | 5-2 |
| | 4 | Columbus | 3-2 |
| | 6 | Edmonton | 2-3* |
| | 11 | Anaheim | 2-0 |
| | 13 | St. Louis | 5-4 |
| | 15 | at Los Angeles | 3-2† |
| | 17 | at Columbus | 1-2* |
| | 18 | at Detroit | 0-6 |
| | 20 | NY Rangers | 3-2 |
| | 23 | Vancouver | 5-0 |
| | 27 | at St. Louis | 2-3† |
| | 29 | at Dallas | 3-1 |
| | 31 | at Minnesota | 2-3* |
| **Jan.** | 3 | NY Islanders | 5-3 |
| | 6 | at Calgary | 2-5 |
| | 9 | at Edmonton | 4-1 |
| | 10 | at Vancouver | 4-2 |
| | 13 | Tampa Bay | 7-1 |
| | 15 | Calgary | 2-3 |
| | 17 | Detroit | 6-5 |
| | 20 | Vancouver | 2-1* |
| | 27 | at Colorado | 3-0 |
| | 29 | Phoenix | 2-0 |
| | 31 | Chicago | 2-4 |
| **Feb.** | 5 | Carolina | 3-4† |
| | 7 | at Columbus | 2-3* |
| | 10 | at Boston | 5-2 |
| | 11 | at Pittsburgh | 1-2† |
| | 13 | at Buffalo | 5-6† |
| | 15 | at New Jersey | 5-6 |
| | 17 | Edmonton | 4-2 |
| | 19 | Los Angeles | 4-2 |
| | 21 | Atlanta | 3-1 |
| | 23 | at Dallas | 1-0 |
| | 25 | at Detroit | 1-4 |
| | 26 | at Ottawa | 2-1 |
| | 28 | at Montreal | 2-3 |
| **Mar.** | 3 | Dallas | 1-4 |
| | 5 | Minnesota | 3-4* |
| | 7 | at Vancouver | 1-3 |
| | 10 | at Minnesota | 5-4* |
| | 12 | at St. Louis | 1-3 |
| | 14 | Los Angeles | 2-1† |
| | 15 | at Anaheim | 1-0 |
| | 17 | at Phoenix | 3-4 |
| | 19 | Nashville | 3-2† |
| | 21 | Dallas | 5-2 |
| | 22 | Colorado | 3-1 |
| | 25 | at Chicago | 5-6† |
| | 26 | at Nashville | 2-3 |
| | 28 | Phoenix | 3-2 |
| | 30 | at Calgary | 2-1 |
| **Apr.** | 2 | at Edmonton | 2-1 |
| | 4 | Anaheim | 2-5 |
| | 5 | at Anaheim | 3-2 |
| | 7 | Colorado | 1-0† |
| | 9 | Phoenix | 1-4 |
| | 11 | at Los Angeles | 3-4 |

* – Overtime † – Shootout

# Entry Draft Selections 2009-1995

Name in bold denotes played in NHL.

### 2009

| Pick | |
|---|---|
| 43 | William Wrenn |
| 57 | Taylor Doherty |
| 147 | Philip Varone |
| 189 | Marek Viedensky |
| 207 | Dominik Bielke |

### 2008

| Pick | |
|---|---|
| 62 | Justin Daniels |
| 92 | Samuel Groulx |
| 106 | Harri Sateri |
| 146 | Julien Demers |
| 177 | Tommy Wingels |
| 186 | Jason Demers |
| 194 | Drew Daniels |

### 2007

| Pick | |
|---|---|
| 9 | Logan Couture |
| 28 | Nicholas Petrecki |
| 83 | Timo Pielmeier |
| 91 | Tyson Sexsmith |
| 165 | Patrik Zackrisson |
| 173 | Nick Bonino |
| 201 | Justin Braun |
| 203 | Frazer McLaren |

### 2006

| Pick | |
|---|---|
| 16 | **Ty Wishart** |
| 36 | **Jamie McGinn** |
| 98 | James Delory |
| 143 | Ashton Rome |
| 202 | John McCarthy |
| 203 | Jay Barriball |

### 2005

| Pick | |
|---|---|
| 8 | **Devin Setoguchi** |
| 35 | **Marc-Edouard Vlasic** |
| 112 | Alex Stalock |
| 140 | Taylor Dakers |
| 149 | **Derek Joslin** |
| 162 | P.J. Fenton |
| 183 | Will Colbert |
| 193 | Tony Lucia |

### 2004

| Pick | |
|---|---|
| 22 | **Lukas Kaspar** |
| 94 | **Thomas Greiss** |
| 126 | **Torrey Mitchell** |
| 129 | Jason Churchill |
| 153 | Steven Zalewski |
| 201 | **Michael Vernace** |
| 225 | David MacDonald |
| 234 | Derek MacIntyre |
| 288 | Brian Mahoney-Wilson |
| 289 | Christian Jensen |

### 2003

| Pick | |
|---|---|
| 6 | **Milan Michalek** |
| 16 | **Steve Bernier** |
| 43 | **Josh Hennessy** |
| 47 | **Matt Carle** |
| 139 | Patrick Ehelechner |
| 201 | Jonathan Tremblay |
| 205 | **Joe Pavelski** |
| 216 | Kai Hospelt |
| 236 | Alexander Hult |
| 267 | Brian O'Hanley |
| 276 | Carter Lee |

### 2002

| Pick | |
|---|---|
| 27 | Mike Morris |
| 52 | Dan Spang |
| 86 | Jonas Fiedler |
| 139 | **Kris Newbury** |
| 163 | Tom Walsh |
| 217 | **Tim Conboy** |
| 288 | Michael Hutchins |

### 2001

| Pick | |
|---|---|
| 20 | **Marcel Goc** |
| 106 | **Christian Ehrhoff** |
| 107 | **Dimitri Patzold** |
| 140 | **Tomas Plihal** |
| 175 | **Ryane Clowe** |
| 182 | **Tom Cavanagh** |

### 2000

| Pick | |
|---|---|
| 41 | Tero Maatta |
| 104 | **Jon DiSalvatore** |
| 142 | Michal Pinc |
| 166 | **Nolan Schaefer** |
| 183 | Michal Macho |
| 246 | **Chad Wiseman** |
| 256 | Pasi Saarinen |

### 1999

| Pick | |
|---|---|
| 14 | **Jeff Jillson** |
| 82 | Mark Concannon |
| 111 | Willie Levesque |
| 155 | **Niko Dimitrakos** |
| 229 | Eric Betournay |
| 241 | **Douglas Murray** |
| 257 | **Hannes Hyvonen** |

### 1998

| Pick | |
|---|---|
| 3 | **Brad Stuart** |
| 29 | **Jonathan Cheechoo** |
| 65 | Eric Laplante |
| 98 | **Rob Davison** |
| 104 | **Miroslav Zalesak** |
| 127 | Brandon Coalter |
| 145 | **Mikael Samuelsson** |
| 185 | Robert Mulick |
| 212 | **Jim Fahey** |

### 1997

| Pick | |
|---|---|
| 2 | **Patrick Marleau** |
| 23 | **Scott Hannan** |
| 82 | Adam Colagiacomo |
| 107 | Adam Nittel |
| 163 | Joe Dusbabek |
| 192 | **Cam Severson** |
| 219 | **Mark Smith** |

### 1996

| Pick | |
|---|---|
| 2 | **Andrei Zyuzin** |
| 21 | **Marco Sturm** |
| 55 | Terry Friesen |
| 102 | **Matt Bradley** |
| 137 | **Michel Larocque** |
| 164 | Jake Deadmarsh |
| 191 | Cory Cyrenne |
| 217 | David Thibeault |

### 1995

| Pick | |
|---|---|
| 12 | Teemu Riihijarvi |
| 38 | Peter Roed |
| 64 | Marko Makinen |
| 90 | **Vesa Toskala** |
| 116 | **Miikka Kiprusoff** |
| 130 | Michal Bros |
| 140 | Timo Hakanen |
| 142 | Jaroslav Kudrna |
| 167 | Brad Mehalko |
| 168 | Robert Jindrich |
| 194 | **Ryan Kraft** |
| 220 | Mikko Markkanen |

# Doug Wilson

## Vice President and General Manager

*Born: Ottawa, Ont., July 5, 1957.*

Hired as executive vice president and general manager on May 13, 2003, Doug Wilson has led the San Jose Sharks to its most successful era since the team's inception. In 2003-04, the Sharks rebounded from missing the playoffs to capture the Pacific Division title and advance to the Western Conference Final. Since then, the Sharks have continually ranked among the top teams during the regular season. In 2008-09, they set new club records with 53 wins and 117 points and won the Presidents' Trophy for the first time.

In his role with the Sharks, Wilson has overall authority regarding all hockey-related operations. He oversees all player personnel decisions, negotiates player contracts, coordinates the efforts of the team's scouting department, leads the team in its draft-day preparations and administers the club's player evaluation process at all professional, minor and junior levels.

In his previous role as the team's director of pro development (1997 to 2003), the 16-year NHL veteran's primary responsibilities included evaluating talent at all professional and minor league levels and continuous assessment of the Sharks roster and reserve list. In addition, he provided valuable input assisting the club's player development programs and consulting with the hockey department on all major personnel issues, special assignments and contract negotiations.

A first-round choice (sixth overall) of the Blackhawks in 1977 after a stellar junior career with the Ottawa 67s, Wilson played 14 seasons in Chicago and still ranks as the club's highest scoring defenseman in goals (225), assists (554) and points (779). In addition, he led all Blackhawks defensemen in scoring for 10 consecutive seasons (1981-82 through 1990-91) and captured the 1982 Norris Trophy, symbolic of the NHL's top defenseman, when he tallied 39 goals and 85 points – still Blackhawks single-season records for goals and points by a defenseman.

# Club Directory

HP Pavilion at San Jose

**San Jose Sharks**
HP Pavilion at San Jose
525 West Santa Clara Street
San Jose, CA 95113
Phone **408/287-7070**
FAX 408/999-5797
www.sjsharks.com
**Capacity:** 17,496

**San Jose Sports & Entertainment Enterprises Ownership Group**
Kevin Compton, Hasso Plattner, Stratton Sclavos, Gary Valenzuela, Gordon Russell, Rudy Staedler, Floyd Kvamme, Greg Jamison, Harvey Armstrong, Tom McEnery, George Gund III

**Executive**
President & Chief Executive Officer/ NHL Executive Committee . . . . . Greg Jamison
Executive V.P. of Business Operations . . . . . Malcolm Bordelon
Executive V.P. & G.M. (HP Pavilion at San Jose) . . . . Jim Goddard
Executive V.P. & General Counsel . . . . . Don Gralnek
Executive V.P. & G.M. (Sharks) . . . . . Doug Wilson
Executive V.P. & Chief Financial Officer . . . . . Charlie Faas
President, Sharks Minor Holdings . . . . . Michael T. Lehr
Vice President of Finance . . . . . Ken Caveney
Vice President of Corporate Partnerships . . . . . Eric Mastalir
Vice President of Sales & Marketing . . . . . Kent Russell
Vice President of Building Operations . . . . . Rich Sotelo
Vice President and Assistant G.M. (Sharks) . . . . . Wayne Thomas
Executive Assistants . . . . . Tricia Sullivan-Minsky, Michelle Simmons
Sr. Administrative Assistant . . . . . Misty Macias

**Hockey Operations**
Director of Hockey Operations . . . . . Joe Will
Head Coach . . . . . Todd McLellan
Assistant Coaches . . . . . Trent Yawney, Matt Shaw, Jay Woodcroft
Goaltending Development Coach . . . . . Corey Schwab
Development Coach . . . . . Mike Ricci
Director of Scouting . . . . . Tim Burke
Director of Pro Scouting . . . . . John Ferguson
Scouts . . . . . Gilles Cote, Pat Funk, Jack Gardiner, Dirk Graham, Rob Grillo, Brian Gross, Shin Larsson, Bryan Marchment, Karel Masopust, Jason Rowe
Director of Hockey Administratio . . . . . Rosemary Tebaldi
Manager of Hockey Technology . . . . . Paul Fink
Video Assistant . . . . . Brett Heimlich
Head Athletic Trainer . . . . . Ray Tufts, ATC
Assistant Athletic Trainer . . . . . Wes Howard, ATC
Strength & Conditioning Coordinator . . . . . Mike Potenza
Massage Therapist . . . . . Arnulfo Aguirre, CMT
Equipment Manager . . . . . Mike Aldrich
Assistant Equipment Manager . . . . . Rick Bronwell
Equipment Assistant & Transportation . . . . . Roy Sneesby
Cleaning Specialist . . . . . Norma Hernandez
Team Physician . . . . . Arthur J. Ting, M.D.
Team Internists . . . . . Greg Whitley M.D., John Chiu, M.D.
Team Dentists . . . . . Don Goudy, D.D.S., Robert Bonahoom, D.D.S.
Team Vision Specialists . . . . . Vincent S. Zuccaro, O.D., F.A.A.O.
Medical Staff . . . . . Steve Franzino, M.D., Robert Millard, M.D., Mark Sontag, M.D.
Chiropractic Consultant . . . . . Mike McMurray, D. C.
Manual Therapy Consultant . . . . . Tobe Hanson"

**SVS&E/Business Operations**
Senior Director of Communications . . . . . Ken Arnold
Director of Broadcasting . . . . . Frank Albin
Director of Marketing . . . . . Doug Bentz
Director of Ticket Sales . . . . . John Castro
Director of Media Relations . . . . . Scott Emmert
Director of Event Presentation . . . . . Steve Maroni
Director of Suite Sales & Service . . . . . Bruce Ross
Director of Communications & Internet Services . . . Roger Ross
Director of Public Relations . . . . . Jim Sparaco
Senior Sales Managers, Corporate Partnerships . . . . Jennifer Birmingham, Bryan Deierling
Senior Ticket Operations Manager . . . . . Scott Fitzsimmons
Senior Service Manager, Corporate Partnerships . . . Heather Hunter
Sales Managers, Corporate Partnerships . . . . . Darren O'Donnell, Kevin Hilton
Account Sales Managers . . . . . Ted Chuba, Mike Hollywood, Patrick Frost, Adam King
Account Service Managers . . . . . Sharon Holman, Sarah Bauerle, Julie Kennedy
Marketing Manager . . . . . Deanna Miller
Internet Services Manager . . . . . Alex Aragon
Fan Development Managers . . . . . Erin Buchanan, Jeff Cafuir
Creative Services Manager . . . . . Derik Green
Media Relations Manager . . . . . Tom Holy
Suite Sales and Service Managers . . . . . Chris Hutchins, Kathy Payne-Tovar
Sharks Foundation Manager . . . . . Laura Johnston
Mascot Operations Manager . . . . . Tim Patnode
Service Managers, Corporate Partnerships . . . . . Jennifer De Carlo, Kristin Toth
Media Relations and Team Services Coordinator . . . Ryan Stenn
Executive Assistant . . . . . Mary Grace Miller

**Finance**
Director of Human Resources . . . . . Cathy Chandler
Director of Information Technology . . . . . Uy Ut
Controller . . . . . Stephanie Reitz

**Building Operations**
Director of Ticket Operations . . . . . Daniel DeBoer
Director of Booking & Events . . . . . Steve Kirsner, James Hamnett
Director of Guest Services . . . . . David Cahill
Director of Building Services . . . . . Monte Chavez
Facilities Technical Director . . . . . Greg Carrolan

**Miscellaneous**
Television Station . . . . . Comcast SportsNet California
Radio Network Flagship . . . . . 98.5 K-FOX (KUFX FM)
Television Play-By-Play / Color . . . . . Randy Hahn / Drew Remenda
Radio Play-By-Play Broadcaster / Color / Reporter . . . Dan Rusanowsky / Jamie Baker / David Maley
P.A. Announcer . . . . . Danny Miller
Mascot . . . . . S.J. Sharkie

# Tampa Bay Lightning

## Key Off-Season Signings/Acquisitions

**2009**

**June 26** • Selected D **Victor Hedman** (MoDo, Sweden) second overall in the 2009 Entry Draft.

**July 1** • Signed D **Mattias Ohlund** and D **Matt Walker.**

**1** • Re-signed D **Lukas Krajicek.**

**7** • Signed LW **Stephane Veilleux.**

**8** • Signed D **Kurtis Foster.**

**10** • Signed G **Antero Niittymaki.**

**21** • Acquired LW **Todd Fedoruk** and D **David Hale** from Phoenix for RW **Radim Vrbata.**

**26** • Re-signed D **Matt Smaby.**

**29** • Named **Rick Wilson** associate coach.

## 2008-09 Results: 24W-40L-8OTL-10SOL 66PTS.
## Fifth, Southeast Division

### Year-by-Year Record

| | | Home | | | | Road | | | | Overall | | | | | | | | |
|---|---|---|---|---|---|---|---|---|---|---|---|---|---|---|---|---|---|---|
| **Season** | **GP** | **W** | **L** | **T** | **OL** | **W** | **L** | **T** | **OL** | **W** | **L** | **T** | **OL** | **GF** | **GA** | **Pts.** | **Finished** | **Playoff Result** |
| 2008-09 | 82 | 12 | 18 | .... | 11 | 12 | 22 | .... | 7 | 24 | 40 | .... | 18 | 210 | 279 | 66 | 5th, Southeast Div. | Out of Playoffs |
| 2007-08 | 82 | 20 | 18 | .... | 3 | 11 | 24 | .... | 6 | 31 | 42 | .... | 9 | 223 | 267 | 71 | 5th, Southeast Div. | Out of Playoffs |
| 2006-07 | 82 | 22 | 18 | .... | 1 | 22 | 15 | .... | 4 | 44 | 33 | .... | 5 | 253 | 261 | 93 | 2nd, Southeast Div. | Lost Conf. Quarter-Final |
| 2005-06 | 82 | 25 | 14 | .... | 2 | 18 | 19 | .... | 4 | 43 | 33 | .... | 6 | 252 | 260 | 92 | 2nd, Southeast Div. | Lost Conf. Quarter-Final |
| 2004-05 | .... | .... | .... | .... | .... | .... | .... | .... | .... | .... | .... | .... | .... | .... | .... | .... | | |
| **2003-04** | **82** | **24** | **10** | **4** | **3** | **22** | **12** | **4** | **3** | **46** | **22** | **8** | **6** | **245** | **192** | **106** | **1st, Southeast Div.** | **Won Stanley Cup** |
| 2002-03 | 82 | 22 | 9 | 7 | 3 | 14 | 16 | 9 | 2 | 36 | 25 | 16 | 5 | 219 | 210 | 93 | 1st, Southeast Div. | Lost Conf. Semi-Final |
| 2001-02 | 82 | 16 | 17 | 5 | 3 | 11 | 23 | 6 | 1 | 27 | 40 | 11 | 4 | 178 | 219 | 69 | 3rd, Southeast Div. | Out of Playoffs |
| 2000-01 | 82 | 17 | 19 | 3 | 2 | 7 | 28 | 3 | 3 | 24 | 47 | 6 | 5 | 201 | 280 | 59 | 5th, Southeast Div. | Out of Playoffs |
| 1999-2000 | 82 | 13 | 20 | 4 | 4 | 6 | 27 | 5 | 3 | 19 | 47 | 9 | 7 | 204 | 310 | 54 | 4th, Southeast Div. | Out of Playoffs |
| 1998-99 | 82 | 12 | 25 | 4 | .... | 7 | 29 | 5 | .... | 19 | 54 | 9 | .... | 179 | 292 | 47 | 4th, Southeast Div. | Out of Playoffs |
| 1997-98 | 82 | 11 | 23 | 7 | .... | 6 | 32 | 3 | .... | 17 | 55 | 10 | .... | 151 | 269 | 44 | 7th, Atlantic Div. | Out of Playoffs |
| 1996-97 | 82 | 15 | 18 | 8 | .... | 17 | 22 | 2 | .... | 32 | 40 | 10 | .... | 217 | 247 | 74 | 6th, Atlantic Div. | Out of Playoffs |
| 1995-96 | 82 | 22 | 14 | 5 | .... | 16 | 18 | 7 | .... | 38 | 32 | 12 | .... | 238 | 248 | 88 | 5th, Atlantic Div. | Lost Conf. Quarter-Final |
| 1994-95 | 48 | 10 | 14 | 0 | .... | 7 | 14 | 3 | .... | 17 | 28 | 3 | .... | 120 | 144 | 37 | 6th, Atlantic Div. | Out of Playoffs |
| 1993-94 | 84 | 14 | 22 | 6 | .... | 16 | 21 | 5 | .... | 30 | 43 | 11 | .... | 224 | 251 | 71 | 7th, Atlantic Div. | Out of Playoffs |
| 1992-93 | 84 | 12 | 27 | 3 | .... | 11 | 27 | 4 | .... | 23 | 54 | 7 | .... | 245 | 332 | 53 | 6th, Norris Div. | Out of Playoffs |

## 2009-10 Schedule

| | | | |
|---|---|---|---|
| **Oct.** | Sat. | 3 | at Atlanta |
| | Tue. | 6 | at Carolina |
| | Thu. | 8 | New Jersey |
| | Sat. | 10 | Carolina |
| | Mon. | 12 | Florida |
| | Thu. | 15 | at Ottawa |
| | Sat. | 17 | at Pittsburgh |
| | Thu. | 22 | San Jose |
| | Sat. | 24 | Buffalo |
| | Thu. | 29 | Ottawa |
| | Sat. | 31 | New Jersey* |
| **Nov.** | Mon. | 2 | at Philadelphia |
| | Tue. | 3 | at Toronto |
| | Thu. | 5 | at Ottawa |
| | Sat. | 7 | at Montreal |
| | Thu. | 12 | Minnesota |
| | Sat. | 14 | Los Angeles |
| | Mon. | 16 | at Phoenix |
| | Thu. | 19 | at Anaheim |
| | Sat. | 21 | at Carolina |
| | Sun. | 22 | at Atlanta* |
| | Wed. | 25 | Toronto |
| | Fri. | 27 | NY Rangers |
| | Sat. | 28 | at Dallas |
| | Mon. | 30 | Colorado |
| **Dec.** | Wed. | 2 | at Boston |
| | Fri. | 4 | at New Jersey |
| | Sat. | 5 | NY Islanders |
| | Mon. | 7 | Washington |
| | Wed. | 9 | Edmonton |
| | Fri. | 11 | at Colorado |
| | Sun. | 13 | at Chicago |
| | Tue. | 15 | at Nashville |
| | Thu. | 17 | at Detroit |
| | Fri. | 18 | at St. Louis |
| | Mon. | 21 | at NY Islanders |
| | Wed. | 23 | Philadelphia |
| | Sat. | 26 | Atlanta |
| | Mon. | 28 | Boston |
| | Wed. | 30 | Montreal |
| **Jan.** | Sat. | 2 | Pittsburgh* |
| | Wed. | 6 | at Buffalo |
| | Fri. | 8 | at New Jersey |
| | Sat. | 9 | at Philadelphia |
| | Tue. | 12 | Washington |
| | Thu. | 14 | Florida |
| | Sat. | 16 | at Florida |
| | Mon. | 18 | at Carolina |
| | Tue. | 19 | at NY Rangers |
| | Thu. | 21 | Toronto |
| | Sat. | 23 | Atlanta |
| | Wed. | 27 | Montreal |
| | Fri. | 29 | Anaheim |
| | Sun. | 31 | at Washington* |
| **Feb.** | Tue. | 2 | at Atlanta |
| | Thu. | 4 | NY Islanders |
| | Sat. | 6 | Calgary |
| | Tue. | 9 | Vancouver |
| | Thu. | 11 | Boston |
| | Sat. | 13 | at NY Islanders* |
| | Sun. | 14 | at NY Rangers* |
| **Mar.** | Tue. | 2 | Philadelphia |
| | Thu. | 4 | at Washington |
| | Sat. | 6 | Atlanta |
| | Tue. | 9 | at Montreal |
| | Thu. | 11 | at Toronto |
| | Fri. | 12 | at Washington |
| | Sun. | 14 | Pittsburgh* |
| | Tue. | 16 | Phoenix |
| | Thu. | 18 | Buffalo |
| | Sat. | 20 | Washington |
| | Sun. | 21 | at Florida* |
| | Tue. | 23 | Carolina |
| | Thu. | 25 | at Boston |
| | Sat. | 27 | at Buffalo |
| | Tue. | 30 | at Columbus |
| | Wed. | 31 | at Pittsburgh |
| **Apr.** | Fri. | 2 | NY Rangers |
| | Tue. | 6 | Carolina |
| | Thu. | 8 | Ottawa |
| | Sat. | 10 | Florida |
| | Sun. | 11 | at Florida* |

* Denotes afternoon game.

**SOUTHEAST DIVISION**
**18th NHL Season**

**Franchise date:** December 16, 1991

*Martin St. Louis led the Lightning in goals (30), assists (50) and points (80) during the 2008-09 season. His 30 goals marked the fifth time in the past six NHL seasons that he has scored at least that many.*

# 2009-10 Player Personnel

| FORWARDS | HT | WT | S | Place of Birth | *Age | 2008-09 Club |
|---|---|---|---|---|---|---|
| ARTYUKHIN, Evgeny | 6-5 | 254 | L | Moscow, USSR | 26 | Tampa Bay |
| BOCHENSKI, Brandon | 6-1 | 187 | R | Blaine, MN | 27 | Tampa Bay-Norfolk |
| CRAIG, Ryan | 6-2 | 212 | L | Abbotsford, B.C. | 27 | Tampa Bay |
| DOWNIE, Steve | 5-11 | 200 | R | Newmarket, Ont. | 22 | Phi-Phi (AHL)-T.B.-Norfolk |
| FEDORUK, Todd | 6-2 | 240 | L | Redwater, Alta. | 30 | Phoenix |
| HALL, Adam | 6-3 | 206 | R | Kalamazoo, MI | 29 | Tampa Bay |
| HALPERN, Jeff | 6-0 | 203 | R | Potomac, MD | 33 | Tampa Bay |
| JONES, Blair | 6-3 | 210 | R | Central Butte, Sask. | 23 | Norfolk |
| KARSUMS, Martins | 5-10 | 198 | R | Riga, Latvia | 23 | Bos-Prov (AHL)-T.B. |
| KONOPKA, Zenon | 6-1 | 213 | L | Niagara Falls, Ont. | 28 | Tampa Bay-Norfolk |
| LECAVALIER, Vincent | 6-4 | 219 | L | Ile Bizard, Que. | 29 | Tampa Bay |
| MALONE, Ryan | 6-4 | 224 | L | Pittsburgh, PA | 29 | Tampa Bay |
| ST. LOUIS, Martin | 5-9 | 177 | L | Laval, Que. | 34 | Tampa Bay |
| STAMKOS, Steven | 6-1 | 196 | R | Markham, Ont. | 19 | Tampa Bay |
| SZCZECHURA, Paul | 5-11 | 190 | R | Brantford, Ont. | 23 | Tampa Bay-Norfolk |
| VEILLEUX, Stephane | 6-0 | 190 | L | Beauceville, Que. | 27 | Minnesota |
| **DEFENSEMEN** | | | | | | |
| FOSTER, Kurtis | 6-5 | 220 | R | Carp, Ont. | 27 | Minnesota-Houston |
| HALE, David | 6-2 | 213 | L | Colorado Springs, CO | 28 | Phoenix |
| HEDMAN, Victor | 6-6 | 220 | L | Ornskoldsvik, Sweden | 18 | MODO Jr.-MODO |
| KRAJICEK, Lukas | 6-2 | 196 | L | Prostejov, Czech. | 26 | Tampa Bay |
| LASHOFF, Matt | 6-2 | 204 | L | Albany, NY | 23 | Bos-Prov (AHL)-T.B.-Norfolk |
| LUNDIN, Mike | 6-2 | 188 | L | Burnsville, MN | 25 | Tampa Bay-Norfolk |
| MESZAROS, Andrej | 6-2 | 218 | L | Povazska Bystrica, Czech. | 23 | Tampa Bay |
| OHLUND, Mattias | 6-3 | 220 | L | Pitea, Sweden | 33 | Vancouver |
| RANGER, Paul | 6-3 | 208 | L | Whitby, Ont. | 25 | Tampa Bay |
| SMABY, Matt | 6-5 | 222 | L | Minneapolis, MN | 24 | Tampa Bay-Norfolk |
| WALKER, Matt | 6-3 | 214 | R | Beaverlodge, Alta. | 29 | Chicago |

| GOALTENDERS | HT | WT | C | Place of Birth | *Age | 2008-09 Club |
|---|---|---|---|---|---|---|
| NIITTYMAKI, Antero | 6-1 | 195 | L | Turku, Finland | 29 | Philadelphia |
| SMITH, Mike | 6-4 | 218 | L | Kingston, Ont. | 27 | Tampa Bay |

* – Age at start of 2009-10 season

## Coaching History

Terry Crisp, 1992-93 to 1996-97; Terry Crisp, Rick Paterson and Jacques Demers, 1997-98; Jacques Demers, 1998-99; Steve Ludzik, 1999-2000; Steve Ludzik and John Tortorella, 2000-01; John Tortorella, 2001-02 to 2007-08; Barry Melrose and Rick Tocchet, 2008-09; Rick Tocchet, 2009-10.

## Rick Tocchet

### Head Coach

*Born: Scarborough, Ont., April 9, 1964.*

Rick Tocchet was named as associate coach of the Tampa Bay Lightning on July 9, 2008. He was moved up to interim head coach on November 14, 2008 and was given the job on a permanent basis on May 11, 2009.

Tocchet has been in the NHL, first as a player, and then as a coach, since 1984. He played 18 seasons with Philadelphia, Pittsburgh, Los Angeles, Boston, Washington and Phoenix. During his career he amassed 1,144 career games and he recorded 440 goals, 952 points and 2,972 penalty minutes. He also appeared in 145 playoff games and netted 52 goals with 112 points and 471 penalty minutes. Tocchet won the Stanley Cup with the Pittsburgh Penguins in 1992 and appeared in the Stanley Cup Finals with Philadelphia in 1987. He played in four NHL All-Star teams (1989, 1990, 1991, 1993).

Tocchet is one of three players in the history of the NHL to record 400 goals or more and at least 2,500 penalty minutes. He was an 11-time 20-goal scorer, and a two-time 30-goal scorer. He also recorded three 40-goal campaigns. In 1992-93 he set career highs for goals with 48, assists with 61 and points with 109 in 80 games with the Penguins. Internationally, Tocchet represented Canada at the 1990 and 1991 World Championships as well as in the 1987 and 1991 Canada Cup Tournaments.

He was originally drafted by Philadelphia in the sixth-round, 125th overall, at the 1983 NHL Entry Draft. Tocchet began his career with the Flyers in 1984-85 and retired midway through the 2001-02 season, also with Philadelphia. Shortly after retiring he joined the Colorado Avalanche as an assistant coach. He spent a season and a half on the bench with the Avalanche before joining former teammate Wayne Gretzky as an assistant coach with the Phoenix Coyotes in 2005.

### Coaching Record

| | | | Regular Season | | | | Playoffs | | | |
|---|---|---|---|---|---|---|---|---|---|---|
| Season | Team | League | GC | W | L | O/T | GC | W | L | T |
| 2008-09 | Tampa Bay | NHL | 66 | 19 | 33 | 14 | .... | .... | .... | .... |
| | NHL Totals | | 66 | 19 | 33 | 14 | .... | .... | .... | .... |

# 2008-09 Scoring

* – rookie

## Regular Season

| Pos | # | Player | Team | GP | G | A | Pts | TOI | +/- | PIM | PP | SH | GW | S | % |
|---|---|---|---|---|---|---|---|---|---|---|---|---|---|---|---|
| R | 26 | Martin St. Louis | T.B. | 82 | 30 | 50 | 80 | 21:17 | 4 | 14 | 7 | 2 | 3 | 262 | 11.5 |
| C | 4 | Vincent Lecavalier | T.B. | 77 | 29 | 38 | 67 | 20:15 | –9 | 54 | 10 | 1 | 6 | 291 | 10.0 |
| C | 91 | * Steven Stamkos | T.B. | 79 | 23 | 23 | 46 | 14:56 | –13 | 39 | 9 | 0 | 1 | 181 | 12.7 |
| L | 12 | Ryan Malone | T.B. | 70 | 26 | 19 | 45 | 17:45 | 4 | 98 | 7 | 0 | 3 | 124 | 21.0 |
| L | 20 | Vaclav Prospal | T.B. | 82 | 19 | 26 | 45 | 17:40 | –20 | 52 | 7 | 0 | 2 | 194 | 9.8 |
| D | 2 | Lukas Krajicek | T.B. | 71 | 2 | 17 | 19 | 19:37 | –8 | 48 | 0 | 0 | 0 | 66 | 3.0 |
| C | 11 | Jeff Halpern | T.B. | 52 | 7 | 9 | 16 | 17:01 | –13 | 32 | 1 | 1 | 1 | 60 | 11.7 |
| R | 76 | Evgeny Artyukhin | T.B. | 73 | 6 | 10 | 16 | 10:40 | 1 | 151 | 1 | 0 | 0 | 100 | 6.0 |
| D | 21 | Cory Murphy | FLA | 7 | 0 | 1 | 1 | 10:10 | –1 | 2 | 0 | 0 | 0 | 8 | 0.0 |
| | | | T.B. | 25 | 5 | 10 | 15 | 20:08 | –3 | 12 | 4 | 0 | 0 | 47 | 10.6 |
| | | | Total | 32 | 5 | 11 | 16 | 17:57 | –4 | 14 | 4 | 0 | 0 | 55 | 9.1 |
| D | 14 | Andrej Meszaros | T.B. | 52 | 2 | 14 | 16 | 24:10 | –4 | 36 | 1 | 0 | 1 | 87 | 2.3 |
| L | 24 | Matt Pettinger | T.B. | 59 | 8 | 7 | 15 | 12:18 | –14 | 24 | 2 | 0 | 1 | 82 | 9.8 |
| D | 54 | Paul Ranger | T.B. | 42 | 2 | 11 | 13 | 24:30 | –5 | 56 | 0 | 0 | 0 | 69 | 2.9 |
| R | 18 | Adam Hall | T.B. | 74 | 5 | 5 | 10 | 11:11 | –9 | 29 | 1 | 0 | 0 | 90 | 5.6 |
| C | 38 | * Paul Szczechura | T.B. | 31 | 4 | 5 | 9 | 13:33 | –1 | 12 | 1 | 0 | 0 | 51 | 7.8 |
| D | 6 | Josef Melichar | CAR | 15 | 0 | 4 | 4 | 8:39 | –1 | 8 | 0 | 0 | 0 | 3 | 0.0 |
| | | | T.B. | 24 | 0 | 5 | 5 | 16:58 | 1 | 29 | 0 | 0 | 0 | 16 | 0.0 |
| | | | Total | 39 | 0 | 9 | 9 | 13:46 | 0 | 37 | 0 | 0 | 0 | 19 | 0.0 |
| D | 55 | Matt Lashoff | BOS | 16 | 0 | 1 | 1 | 13:06 | 1 | 10 | 0 | 0 | 0 | 6 | 0.0 |
| | | | T.B. | 12 | 0 | 7 | 7 | 23:46 | –7 | 10 | 0 | 0 | 0 | 19 | 0.0 |
| | | | Total | 28 | 0 | 8 | 8 | 17:40 | –6 | 20 | 0 | 0 | 0 | 25 | 0.0 |
| L | 10 | Gary Roberts | T.B. | 30 | 4 | 3 | 7 | 11:38 | –11 | 27 | 2 | 0 | 1 | 32 | 12.5 |
| R | 17 | Radim Vrbata | T.B. | 18 | 3 | 3 | 6 | 14:13 | –1 | 8 | 1 | 0 | 0 | 41 | 7.3 |
| R | 9 | Steve Downie | PHI | 6 | 0 | 0 | 0 | 5:56 | –4 | 11 | 0 | 0 | 0 | 1 | 0.0 |
| | | | T.B. | 23 | 3 | 3 | 6 | 9:04 | 2 | 54 | 0 | 0 | 1 | 25 | 12.0 |
| | | | Total | 29 | 3 | 3 | 6 | 8:25 | –2 | 65 | 0 | 0 | 1 | 26 | 11.5 |
| C | 34 | Ryan Craig | T.B. | 54 | 2 | 4 | 6 | 10:16 | –7 | 60 | 0 | 0 | 0 | 64 | 3.1 |
| R | 44 | * Martins Karsums | BOS | 6 | 0 | 1 | 1 | 9:44 | –3 | 0 | 0 | 0 | 0 | 6 | 0.0 |
| | | | T.B. | 18 | 1 | 4 | 5 | 11:40 | –5 | 6 | 0 | 0 | 0 | 22 | 4.5 |
| | | | Total | 24 | 1 | 5 | 6 | 11:11 | –8 | 6 | 0 | 0 | 0 | 28 | 3.6 |
| D | 22 | Marek Malik | T.B. | 42 | 0 | 5 | 5 | 19:09 | –3 | 36 | 0 | 0 | 0 | 22 | 0.0 |
| D | 32 | * Matt Smaby | T.B. | 43 | 0 | 4 | 4 | 19:05 | –11 | 50 | 0 | 0 | 0 | 28 | 0.0 |
| D | 29 | Janne Niskala | T.B. | 6 | 1 | 2 | 3 | 13:42 | 0 | 6 | 1 | 0 | 0 | 10 | 10.0 |
| D | 50 | Richard Petiot | T.B. | 11 | 0 | 3 | 3 | 20:36 | 5 | 21 | 0 | 0 | 0 | 10 | 0.0 |
| D | 56 | * Vladimir Mihalik | T.B. | 11 | 0 | 3 | 3 | 13:23 | –3 | 6 | 0 | 0 | 0 | 7 | 0.0 |
| L | 33 | David Koci | T.B. | 1 | 0 | 0 | 0 | :41 | 0 | 4 | 0 | 0 | 0 | 0 | 0.0 |
| | | | STL | 4 | 0 | 0 | 0 | 3:36 | –2 | 9 | 0 | 0 | 0 | 5 | 0.0 |
| | | | T.B. | 32 | 1 | 1 | 2 | 6:24 | 3 | 128 | 0 | 0 | 0 | 8 | 12.5 |
| | | | Total | 37 | 1 | 1 | 2 | 5:57 | 1 | 141 | 0 | 0 | 0 | 13 | 7.7 |
| D | 7 | Noah Welch | FLA | 23 | 1 | 1 | 2 | 6:38 | –5 | 11 | 0 | 0 | 0 | 11 | 9.1 |
| | | | T.B. | 17 | 0 | 0 | 0 | 16:45 | –4 | 14 | 0 | 0 | 0 | 11 | 0.0 |
| | | | Total | 40 | 1 | 1 | 2 | 10:56 | –9 | 25 | 0 | 0 | 0 | 22 | 4.5 |
| D | 23 | Jamie Heward | T.B. | 13 | 0 | 2 | 2 | 11:48 | –1 | 4 | 0 | 0 | 0 | 11 | 0.0 |
| D | 39 | Mike Lundin | T.B. | 25 | 0 | 2 | 2 | 16:38 | –4 | 4 | 0 | 0 | 0 | 8 | 0.0 |
| D | 3 | * Ty Wishart | T.B. | 5 | 0 | 1 | 1 | 10:07 | 0 | 0 | 0 | 0 | 0 | 2 | 0.0 |
| L | 52 | * Radek Smolenak | T.B. | 6 | 0 | 1 | 1 | 8:20 | 1 | 10 | 0 | 0 | 0 | 14 | 0.0 |
| D | 51 | * Kevin Quick | T.B. | 6 | 0 | 1 | 1 | 13:23 | 0 | 0 | 0 | 0 | 0 | 7 | 0.0 |
| R | 27 | Brandon Bochenski | T.B. | 7 | 0 | 1 | 1 | 10:47 | –3 | 2 | 0 | 0 | 0 | 11 | 0.0 |
| C | 28 | Zenon Konopka | T.B. | 7 | 0 | 1 | 1 | 7:00 | –1 | 29 | 0 | 0 | 0 | 6 | 0.0 |
| R | 16 | Jason Ward | T.B. | 1 | 0 | 0 | 0 | 9:31 | 0 | 2 | 0 | 0 | 0 | 1 | 0.0 |
| D | 71 | * Geoff Kinrade | T.B. | 1 | 0 | 0 | 0 | 17:32 | –1 | 0 | 0 | 0 | 0 | 1 | 0.0 |
| R | 53 | * Brandon Segal | T.B. | 2 | 0 | 0 | 0 | 13:47 | 0 | 0 | 0 | 0 | 0 | 2 | 0.0 |

## Goaltending

| No. | Goaltender | GPI | Mins | Avg | W | L | OT | EN | SO | GA | SA | S% | G | A | PIM |
|---|---|---|---|---|---|---|---|---|---|---|---|---|---|---|---|
| 35 | * Riku Helenius | 1 | 7 | 0.00 | 0 | 0 | 0 | 0 | 0 | 0 | 2 | 1.000 | 0 | 0 | 0 |
| 41 | Mike Smith | 41 | 2471 | 2.62 | 14 | 18 | 9 | 5 | 2 | 108 | 1282 | .916 | 0 | 1 | 23 |
| 30 | * Mike McKenna | 15 | 776 | 3.56 | 4 | 8 | 1 | 2 | 1 | 46 | 406 | .887 | 0 | 1 | 0 |
| 37 | Olaf Kolzig | 8 | 410 | 3.66 | 2 | 4 | 1 | 0 | 0 | 25 | 245 | .898 | 0 | 0 | 0 |
| 31 | * Karri Ramo | 24 | 1312 | 3.66 | 4 | 10 | 7 | 3 | 0 | 80 | 756 | .894 | 0 | 1 | 2 |
| | **Totals** | **82** | **5008** | **3.22** | **24** | **40** | **18** | **10** | **3** | **269** | **2701** | **.900** | | | |

*Ryan Malone and Steven Stamkos celebrate a goal. Malone scored 26 times for the Lightning and led the NHL with a 21.0 shooting percentage. Top draft pick Stamkos scored 23 goals and added 23 assists as a rookie.*

# Club Records

## Team

(Figures in brackets for season records are games played; records for fewest points, wins, ties, losses, goals, goals against are for 70 or more games)

**Most Points** ............... **106** 2003-04 (82)
**Most Wins** ................. **46** 2003-04 (82)
**Most Ties** .................. **16** 2002-03 (82)
**Most Losses** ............... **55** 1997-98 (82)
**Most Goals** ................ **253** 2006-07 (82)
**Most Goals Against** ......... **332** 1992-93 (84)
**Fewest Points** .............. **44** 1997-98 (82)
**Fewest Wins** ................ **17** 1997-98 (82)
**Fewest Ties** ................. **6** 2000-01 (82)
**Fewest Losses** ............... **22** 2003-04 (82)
**Fewest Goals** ............. **151** 1997-98 (82)
**Fewest Goals Against** ....... **192** 2003-04 (82)
**Longest Winning Streak**
**Overall** .................... **8** Feb. 23-Mar. 6/04
**Home** ...................... **8** Mar. 17-Apr. 8/06
**Away** ...................... **7** Jan. 7-Feb. 1/07
**Longest Undefeated Streak**
**Overall** ................... **13** Mar. 7-Apr. 2/03 (7 wins, 6 ties)
**Home** ..................... **10** Jan. 29-Mar. 12/04 (9 wins, 1 tie)
**Away** ...................... **7** Feb. 23-Mar. 10/04 (6 wins, 1 tie), Jan. 7-Feb. 1/07 (7 wins)
**Longest Losing Streak**
**Overall** ................... **13** Jan. 3-Feb. 2/98
**Home** ..................... **10** Jan. 3-Feb. 26/98
**Away** ..................... **11** Oct. 24-Dec. 10/97
**Longest Winless Streak**
**Overall** ................... **16** Oct. 10-Nov. 17/97 (15 losses, 1 tie), Jan. 2-Feb. 5/98 (14 losses, 2 ties)
**Home** ..................... **11** Jan. 2-Feb. 26/98 (10 losses, 1 tie)
**Away** ..................... **17** Dec. 2/99-Feb. 19/00 (14 losses, 3 ties)
**Most Shutouts, Season** ........ **9** 2001-02 (82)
**Most PIM, Season** ......... **1,823** 1997-98 (82)
**Most Goals, Game** ............ **9** Nov. 8/03 (Pit. 0 at T.B. 9)

## Individual

**Most Seasons** .............. **10** Vincent Lecavalier
**Most Games, Career** ........ **787** Vincent Lecavalier
**Most Goals, Career** ......... **302** Vincent Lecavalier
**Most Assists, Career** ........ **367** Vincent Lecavalier
**Most Points, Career** ......... **669** Vincent Lecavalier (302G, 367A)
**Most PIM, Career** ........... **828** Chris Gratton
**Most Shutouts, Career** ........ **14** Nikolai Khabibulin
**Longest Consecutive Games Streak** ........... **388** Cory Sarich (Nov. 27/01-Apr. 7/07)
**Most Goals, Season** .......... **52** Vincent Lecavalier (2006-07)
**Most Assists, Season** ......... **68** Brad Richards (2005-06)
**Most Points, Season** ........ **108** Vincent Lecavalier (2006-07; 52G, 56A)
**Most PIM, Season** .......... **258** Enrico Ciccone (1995-96)
**Most Points, Defenseman, Season** .................. **65** Roman Hamrlik (1995-96; 16G, 49A)
**Most Points, Center, Season** ................. **108** Vincent Lecavalier (2006-07; 52G, 56A)
**Most Points, Right Wing, Season** ................. **102** Martin St. Louis (2006-07; 43G, 59A)
**Most Points, Left Wing, Season** .................. **80** Cory Stillman (2003-04; 25G, 55A), Vaclav Prospal (2005-06; 25G, 55A)
**Most Points, Rookie, Season** .................. **62** Brad Richards (2000-01; 21G, 41A)
**Most Shutouts, Season** ........ **7** Nikolai Khabibulin (2001-02)
**Most Goals, Game** ............ **4** Chris Kontos (Oct. 7/92)
**Most Assists, Game** ........... **5** Mark Recchi (Mar. 1/09)
**Most Points, Game** ............ **6** Doug Crossman (Nov. 7/92; 3G, 3A)

## Captains' History

No captain, 1992-93 to 1994-95; Paul Ysebaert, 1995-96, 1996-97; Paul Ysebaert and Mikael Renberg, 1997-98; Rob Zamuner, 1998-99; Bill Houlder, Chris Gratton and Vincent Lecavalier, 1999-2000; Vincent Lecavalier, 2000-01; no captain, 2001-02; Dave Andreychuk, 2002-03 to 2004-05; Dave Andreychuk and no captain, 2005-06; Tim Taylor, 2006-07, 2007-08; Vincent Lecavalier, 2008-09 to date.

# All-time Record vs. Other Clubs

## Regular Season

| | At Home | | | | | | | | On Road | | | | | | | | Total | | | | | | | |
|---|---|---|---|---|---|---|---|---|---|---|---|---|---|---|---|---|---|---|---|---|---|---|---|---|
| | GP | W | L | T | OL | GF | GA | PTS | GP | W | L | T | OL | GF | GA | PTS | GP | W | L | T | OL | GF | GA | PTS |
| Anaheim | 10 | 4 | 6 | 0 | 0 | 20 | 27 | 8 | 10 | 4 | 5 | 1 | 0 | 26 | 31 | 9 | 20 | 8 | 11 | 1 | 0 | 46 | 58 | 17 |
| Atlanta | 28 | 17 | 8 | 1 | 2 | 100 | 73 | 37 | 28 | 8 | 14 | 3 | 3 | 74 | 93 | 22 | 56 | 25 | 22 | 4 | 5 | 174 | 166 | 59 |
| Boston | 31 | 12 | 14 | 3 | 2 | 89 | 93 | 29 | 31 | 3 | 19 | 6 | 3 | 74 | 118 | 15 | 62 | 15 | 33 | 9 | 5 | 163 | 211 | 44 |
| Buffalo | 31 | 7 | 18 | 3 | 3 | 69 | 100 | 20 | 31 | 10 | 17 | 2 | 2 | 88 | 100 | 24 | 62 | 17 | 35 | 5 | 5 | 157 | 200 | 44 |
| Calgary | 11 | 5 | 5 | 1 | 0 | 37 | 41 | 11 | 12 | 6 | 5 | 0 | 1 | 35 | 40 | 13 | 23 | 11 | 10 | 1 | 1 | 72 | 81 | 24 |
| Carolina | 41 | 23 | 14 | 3 | 1 | 121 | 112 | 50 | 42 | 10 | 22 | 7 | 3 | 113 | 135 | 30 | 83 | 33 | 36 | 10 | 4 | 234 | 247 | 80 |
| Chicago | 13 | 5 | 4 | 3 | 1 | 32 | 35 | 14 | 15 | 4 | 9 | 2 | 0 | 36 | 50 | 10 | 28 | 9 | 13 | 5 | 1 | 68 | 85 | 24 |
| Colorado | 14 | 8 | 3 | 1 | 2 | 40 | 37 | 19 | 15 | 3 | 10 | 2 | 0 | 33 | 58 | 8 | 29 | 11 | 13 | 3 | 2 | 73 | 95 | 27 |
| Columbus | 5 | 4 | 1 | 0 | 0 | 11 | 6 | 8 | 4 | 1 | 2 | 1 | 0 | 7 | 10 | 3 | 9 | 5 | 3 | 1 | 0 | 18 | 16 | 11 |
| Dallas | 15 | 2 | 10 | 2 | 1 | 25 | 41 | 7 | 12 | 4 | 7 | 1 | 0 | 33 | 42 | 9 | 27 | 6 | 17 | 3 | 1 | 58 | 83 | 16 |
| Detroit | 16 | 4 | 10 | 1 | 1 | 49 | 71 | 10 | 13 | 1 | 11 | 1 | 0 | 23 | 51 | 3 | 29 | 5 | 21 | 2 | 1 | 72 | 122 | 13 |
| Edmonton | 12 | 4 | 5 | 2 | 1 | 35 | 38 | 11 | 12 | 4 | 8 | 0 | 0 | 27 | 32 | 8 | 24 | 8 | 13 | 2 | 1 | 62 | 70 | 19 |
| Florida | 43 | 18 | 17 | 6 | 2 | 103 | 123 | 44 | 43 | 12 | 23 | 4 | 4 | 108 | 144 | 32 | 86 | 30 | 40 | 10 | 6 | 211 | 267 | 76 |
| Los Angeles | 11 | 6 | 4 | 0 | 1 | 26 | 24 | 13 | 13 | 10 | 1 | 2 | 0 | 43 | 26 | 22 | 24 | 16 | 5 | 2 | 1 | 69 | 50 | 35 |
| Minnesota | 5 | 1 | 2 | 1 | 1 | 10 | 13 | 4 | 5 | 1 | 4 | 0 | 0 | 13 | 19 | 2 | 10 | 2 | 6 | 1 | 1 | 23 | 32 | 6 |
| Montreal | 31 | 12 | 12 | 5 | 2 | 75 | 87 | 31 | 30 | 13 | 15 | 1 | 1 | 72 | 84 | 28 | 61 | 25 | 27 | 6 | 3 | 147 | 171 | 59 |
| Nashville | 6 | 3 | 1 | 2 | 0 | 19 | 14 | 8 | 7 | 5 | 2 | 0 | 0 | 18 | 13 | 10 | 13 | 8 | 3 | 2 | 0 | 37 | 27 | 18 |
| New Jersey | 33 | 11 | 16 | 5 | 1 | 75 | 100 | 28 | 34 | 9 | 20 | 2 | 3 | 70 | 123 | 23 | 67 | 20 | 36 | 7 | 4 | 145 | 223 | 51 |
| NY Islanders | 34 | 18 | 12 | 2 | 2 | 96 | 100 | 40 | 33 | 15 | 16 | 1 | 1 | 85 | 96 | 32 | 67 | 33 | 28 | 3 | 3 | 181 | 196 | 72 |
| NY Rangers | 33 | 15 | 13 | 3 | 2 | 106 | 103 | 35 | 35 | 14 | 18 | 2 | 1 | 98 | 113 | 31 | 68 | 29 | 31 | 5 | 3 | 204 | 216 | 66 |
| Ottawa | 31 | 11 | 17 | 2 | 1 | 87 | 112 | 25 | 31 | 10 | 19 | 0 | 2 | 68 | 112 | 22 | 62 | 21 | 36 | 2 | 3 | 155 | 224 | 47 |
| Philadelphia | 34 | 14 | 18 | 1 | 1 | 101 | 101 | 30 | 33 | 10 | 15 | 7 | 1 | 77 | 97 | 28 | 67 | 24 | 33 | 8 | 2 | 178 | 198 | 58 |
| Phoenix | 11 | 6 | 5 | 0 | 0 | 38 | 36 | 12 | 13 | 6 | 7 | 0 | 0 | 31 | 32 | 12 | 24 | 12 | 12 | 0 | 0 | 69 | 68 | 24 |
| Pittsburgh | 31 | 16 | 13 | 2 | 0 | 94 | 79 | 34 | 31 | 11 | 15 | 3 | 2 | 84 | 108 | 27 | 62 | 27 | 28 | 5 | 2 | 178 | 187 | 61 |
| St. Louis | 15 | 6 | 5 | 3 | 1 | 46 | 50 | 16 | 12 | 2 | 9 | 0 | 1 | 29 | 48 | 5 | 27 | 8 | 14 | 3 | 2 | 75 | 98 | 21 |
| San Jose | 14 | 7 | 6 | 1 | 0 | 34 | 38 | 15 | 12 | 6 | 5 | 1 | 0 | 38 | 42 | 13 | 26 | 13 | 11 | 2 | 0 | 72 | 80 | 28 |
| Toronto | 28 | 8 | 17 | 1 | 2 | 65 | 93 | 19 | 29 | 9 | 17 | 1 | 2 | 76 | 107 | 21 | 57 | 17 | 34 | 2 | 4 | 141 | 200 | 40 |
| Vancouver | 10 | 4 | 5 | 0 | 1 | 35 | 40 | 9 | 11 | 0 | 8 | 2 | 1 | 19 | 47 | 3 | 21 | 4 | 13 | 2 | 2 | 54 | 87 | 12 |
| Washington | 44 | 16 | 25 | 2 | 1 | 111 | 141 | 35 | 44 | 12 | 26 | 4 | 2 | 112 | 162 | 30 | 88 | 28 | 51 | 6 | 3 | 223 | 303 | 65 |
| **Totals** | **641** | **267** | **286** | **56** | **32** | **1749** | **1928** | **622** | **641** | **203** | **349** | **56** | **33** | **1610** | **2133** | **495** | **1282** | **470** | **635** | **112** | **65** | **3359** | **4061** | **1117** |

## Playoffs

| | Series | W | L | GP | W | L | T | GF | GA | Last Mtg. | Rnd. | Result |
|---|---|---|---|---|---|---|---|---|---|---|---|---|
| Calgary | 1 | 1 | 0 | 7 | 4 | 3 | 0 | 13 | 14 | 2004 | F | W 4-3 |
| Montreal | 1 | 1 | 0 | 4 | 4 | 0 | 0 | 14 | 5 | 2004 | CSF | W 4-0 |
| New Jersey | 2 | 0 | 2 | 11 | 3 | 8 | 0 | 22 | 33 | 2007 | CQF | L 2-4 |
| NY Islanders | 1 | 1 | 0 | 5 | 4 | 1 | 0 | 12 | 5 | 2004 | CQF | W 4-1 |
| Ottawa | 1 | 0 | 1 | 5 | 1 | 4 | 0 | 13 | 23 | 2006 | CQF | L 1-4 |
| Philadelphia | 2 | 1 | 1 | 13 | 6 | 7 | 0 | 34 | 45 | 2004 | CF | W 4-3 |
| Washington | 1 | 1 | 0 | 6 | 4 | 2 | 0 | 14 | 15 | 2003 | CQF | W 4-2 |
| **Totals** | **9** | **5** | **4** | **51** | **26** | **25** | **0** | **122** | **140** | | | |

## Playoff Results 2009-2004

| Year | Round | Opponent | Result | GF | GA |
|---|---|---|---|---|---|
| 2007 | CQF | New Jersey | L 2-4 | 14 | 19 |
| 2006 | CQF | Ottawa | L 1-4 | 13 | 23 |
| **2004** | **F** | **Calgary** | **W 4-3** | **13** | **14** |
| | CF | Philadelphia | W 4-3 | 21 | 19 |
| | CSF | Montreal | W 4-0 | 14 | 5 |
| | CQF | NY Islanders | W 4-1 | 12 | 5 |

**Abbreviations: Round: F** – Final; **CF** – conference final; **CSF** – conference semi-final; **CQF** – conference quarter-final.

Carolina totals include Hartford, 1992-93 to 1996-97.
Dallas totals include Minnesota North Stars, 1992-93.
Colorado totals include Quebec, 1992-93 to 1994-95.
Phoenix totals include Winnipeg, 1992-93 to 1995-96.

## 2008-09 Results

| | | | |
|---|---|---|---|
| **Oct.** | 4 | NY Rangers | 1-2 |
| | 5 | at NY Rangers | 1-2 |
| | 11 | Carolina | 3-4* |
| | 16 | NY Islanders | 3-4* |
| | 18 | Minnesota | 0-1† |
| | 21 | Atlanta | 3-2* |
| | 25 | San Jose | 0-3 |
| | 28 | at Toronto | 3-2 |
| | 30 | at Buffalo | 5-2 |
| **Nov.** | 1 | Ottawa | 3-2† |
| | 5 | at New Jersey | 3-4† |
| | 6 | at NY Rangers | 2-5 |
| | 8 | at Philadelphia | 2-1 |
| | 10 | at Washington | 2-4 |
| | 12 | at Florida | 0-4 |
| | 13 | Detroit | 3-4 |
| | 16 | at Carolina | 2-3† |
| | 18 | Florida | 3-4† |
| | 21 | Nashville | 4-1 |
| | 23 | New Jersey | 3-7 |
| | 26 | NY Rangers | 2-3† |
| | 28 | at Minnesota | 2-4 |
| | 29 | at Colorado | 3-4 |
| **Dec.** | 2 | at Philadelphia | 3-4* |
| | 4 | Boston | 1-3 |
| | 6 | Buffalo | 3-4 |
| | 8 | at Boston | 3-5 |
| | 10 | at Buffalo | 2-4 |
| | 11 | at Montreal | 3-1 |
| | 13 | at Ottawa | 0-2 |
| | 18 | Colorado | 1-2† |
| | 20 | at Atlanta | 3-4 |
| | 23 | at Pittsburgh | 2-0 |
| | 26 | at Florida | 4-3† |
| | 27 | Florida | 6-4 |
| | 30 | Montreal | 1-2† |
| **Jan.** | 1 | at Washington | 4-7 |
| | 3 | Carolina | 2-3 |
| | 4 | at Atlanta | 4-1 |
| | 8 | at Phoenix | 2-3 |
| | 9 | at Anaheim | 4-3 |
| | 12 | at Los Angeles | 3-1 |
| | 13 | at San Jose | 1-7 |
| | 15 | Philadelphia | 4-1 |
| | 17 | Florida | 3-4 |
| | 19 | Dallas | 4-2 |
| | 21 | Buffalo | 5-3 |
| | 27 | Montreal | 5-3 |
| | 29 | at Carolina | 2-3 |
| | 30 | Philadelphia | 1-6 |
| **Feb.** | 3 | at NY Islanders | 1-3 |
| | 4 | at Pittsburgh | 3-4* |
| | 7 | NY Islanders | 1-0 |
| | 10 | Atlanta | 1-3 |
| | 12 | Toronto | 6-4 |
| | 14 | Washington | 1-5 |
| | 17 | Chicago | 3-5 |
| | 19 | New Jersey | 2-3† |
| | 20 | at Carolina | 1-4 |
| | 22 | Boston | 4-3 |
| | 24 | at Edmonton | 3-5 |
| | 27 | at Vancouver | 1-2 |
| **Mar.** | 1 | at Calgary | 8-6 |
| | 3 | Pittsburgh | 1-3 |
| | 6 | St. Louis | 3-4* |
| | 7 | Carolina | 3-9 |
| | 11 | at Ottawa | 2-3* |
| | 12 | at Toronto | 4-1 |
| | 14 | at Florida | 4-3† |
| | 17 | Toronto | 3-4† |
| | 19 | Washington | 2-5 |
| | 21 | Atlanta | 3-4† |
| | 24 | Columbus | 2-1* |
| | 26 | at Montreal | 2-3* |
| | 27 | at Washington | 3-5 |
| | 29 | Ottawa | 0-3 |
| | 31 | at Boston | 1-3 |
| **Apr.** | 3 | at New Jersey | 4-5* |
| | 4 | at NY Islanders | 1-3 |
| | 7 | Pittsburgh | 4-6 |
| | 9 | Washington | 2-4 |
| | 11 | at Atlanta | 2-6 |

* – Overtime † – Shootout

## Entry Draft Selections 2009-1995

Name in bold denotes played in NHL.

**2009**

| Pick | |
|---|---|
| 2 | Victor Hedman |
| 29 | Carter Ashton |
| 52 | Richard Panik |
| 93 | Alex Hutchings |
| 148 | Michael Zador |
| 162 | Jaroslav Janus |
| 183 | Kirill Gotovets |

**2008**

| Pick | |
|---|---|
| 1 | **Steven Stamkos** |
| 117 | James Wright |
| 122 | Dustin Tokarski |
| 147 | Kyle De Coste |
| 152 | Mark Barberio |
| 160 | Luke Witkowski |
| 182 | Matias Sointu |
| 203 | David Carle |

**2007**

| Pick | |
|---|---|
| 47 | Dana Tyrell |
| 75 | Luca Cunti |
| 77 | Alexander Killorn |
| 107 | Mitch Fadden |
| 150 | Matt Marshall |
| 167 | Johan Harju |
| 183 | Torrie Jung |
| 197 | Michael Ward |
| 210 | Justin Courtnall |

**2006**

| Pick | |
|---|---|
| 15 | **Riku Helenius** |
| 78 | **Kevin Quick** |
| 168 | Dane Crowley |
| 198 | Denis Kazionov |

**2005**

| Pick | |
|---|---|
| 30 | **Vladimir Mihalik** |
| 73 | **Radek Smolenak** |
| 89 | Chris Lawrence |
| 92 | Marek Bartanus |
| 102 | **Blair Jones** |
| 133 | Stanislav Lascek |
| 163 | Marek Kvapil |
| 165 | Kevin Beech |
| 225 | John Wessbecker |

**2004**

| Pick | |
|---|---|
| 30 | Andy Rogers |
| 65 | Mark Tobin |
| 102 | **Mike Lundin** |
| 158 | Brandon Elliott |
| 163 | Dusty Collins |
| 188 | Jan Zapletal |
| 191 | **Karri Ramo** |
| 245 | Justin Keller |

**2003**

| Pick | |
|---|---|
| 34 | Mike Egener |
| 41 | **Matt Smaby** |
| 96 | Jonathan Boutin |
| 192 | **Doug O'Brien** |
| 224 | **Gerald Coleman** |
| 227 | Jay Rosehill |
| 255 | Raimonds Danilics |
| 256 | Brady Greco |
| 273 | Albert Vishnyakov |
| 286 | Zbynek Hrdel |
| 287 | **Nick Tarnasky** |

**2002**

| Pick | |
|---|---|
| 60 | Adam Henrich |
| 100 | Dmitri Kazionov |
| 135 | Joe Pearce |
| 162 | Gerard Dicaire |
| 170 | P.J. Atherton |
| 174 | Karri Akkanen |
| 183 | **Paul Ranger** |
| 213 | **Fredrik Norrena** |
| 233 | Vasily Koshechkin |
| 255 | **Ryan Craig** |
| 256 | **Darren Reid** |
| 286 | Alexei Glukhov |
| 287 | John Toffey |

**2001**

| Pick | |
|---|---|
| 3 | **Alexander Svitov** |
| 47 | Alexander Polushin |
| 61 | Andreas Holmqvist |
| 94 | **Evgeny Artyukhin** |
| 123 | Aaron Lobb |
| 138 | Paul Lynch |
| 188 | Art Femenella |
| 219 | Dennis Packard |
| 222 | Jeremy Van Hoof |
| 252 | J.F. Soucy |
| 259 | Dmitri Bezrukov |
| 261 | Vitali Smolyaninov |
| 281 | Ilja Solarev |
| 289 | Henrik Bergfors |

**2000**

| Pick | |
|---|---|
| 8 | **Nikita Alexeev** |
| 34 | Ruslan Zainullin |
| 81 | **Alexander Kharitonov** |
| 126 | Johan Hagglund |
| 161 | Pavel Sedov |
| 191 | Aaron Gionet |
| 222 | Marek Priechodsky |
| 226 | **Brian Eklund** |
| 233 | Alexander Polukeyev |
| 263 | **Thomas Ziegler** |

**1999**

| Pick | |
|---|---|
| 47 | **Sheldon Keefe** |
| 67 | **Evgeny Konstantinov** |
| 75 | Brett Scheffelmaier |
| 88 | **Jimmie Olvestad** |
| 127 | **Kaspars Astashenko** |
| 148 | Michal Lanicek |
| 182 | **Fedor Fedorov** |
| 187 | Ivan Rachunek |
| 216 | Erkki Rajamaki |
| 244 | Mikko Kuparinen |

**1998**

| Pick | |
|---|---|
| 1 | **Vincent Lecavalier** |
| 64 | **Brad Richards** |
| 72 | **Dmitry Afanasenkov** |
| 92 | **Eric Beaudoin** |
| 121 | Curtis Rich |
| 146 | Sergei Kuznetsov |
| 174 | Brett Allan |
| 194 | Oak Hewer |
| 221 | Daniel Hulak |
| 229 | Chris Lyness |
| 252 | **Martin Cibak** |

**1997**

| Pick | |
|---|---|
| 7 | **Paul Mara** |
| 33 | Kyle Kos |
| 61 | **Matt Elich** |
| 108 | Mark Thompson |
| 109 | Jan Sulc |
| 112 | **Karel Betik** |
| 153 | **Andrei Skopintsev** |
| 168 | Justin Jack |
| 170 | Eero Somervuori |
| 185 | Samuel St-Pierre |
| 198 | Shawn Skolney |
| 224 | **Paul Comrie** |

**1996**

| Pick | |
|---|---|
| 16 | **Mario Larocque** |
| 69 | Curtis Tipler |
| 125 | Jason Robinson |
| 152 | Nikolai Ignatov |
| 157 | **Xavier Delisle** |
| 179 | **Pavel Kubina** |

**1995**

| Pick | |
|---|---|
| 5 | **Daymond Langkow** |
| 30 | **Mike McBain** |
| 56 | **Shane Willis** |
| 108 | Konstantin Golokhvastov |
| 134 | Eduard Pershin |
| 160 | Cory Murphy |
| 186 | Joe Cardarelli |
| 212 | **Zac Bierk** |

## General Managers' History

Phil Esposito, 1992-93 to 1997-98; Jacques Demers, 1998-99; Rick Dudley, 1999-2000, 2000-01; Rick Dudley and Jay Feaster, 2001-02; Jay Feaster, 2002-03 to 2007-08; Brian Lawton, 2008-09 to date.

## Brian Lawton

### Executive Vice President and General Manager

*Born: New Brunswick, NJ, June 29, 1965.*

Brian Lawton was elevated to the position of executive vice president and general manager of the Tampa Bay Lightning on October 21, 2009 after being hired as the team's vice president of hockey operations on June 25, 2008. He oversees all aspects of the team's hockey operations department, including player procurement and development and minor league affiliate relations.

Before joining the Lightning, Lawton spent the previous 14 years as a player agent, representing prominent NHLers such as Mike Modano, Mark Parrish and the Lightning's Jeff Halpern, to name a few. A native of New Jersey who grew up in Rhode Island, Lawton was drafted first overall by the Minnesota North Stars in 1983, becoming the first player ever selected first overall directly out of a U.S. high school. He went on to play 483 NHL games for Minnesota, the New York Rangers, Hartford, Quebec, Boston and San Jose between 1983-84 and 1992-93.

Having served four seasons as his team's player representative for the NHL Players Association, Lawton put that knowledge to use when he retired by becoming a player agent. He started his own firm, Lawton Sport and Financial, in 1994, and became a prominent agent, negotiating more than $300 million in player contracts.

Named three times to The Hockey News' list of the "100 Most Powerful People in Hockey," Lawton eventually sold his business in 1998 to Octagon Athlete Representation, one of the largest sports agencies in the United States. Based out of Minneapolis, Lawton became Managing Director of Octagon's Hockey Division. With Octagon Lawton built the second largest hockey agency in the NHL, with clients that included Bret Hedican, Keith Carney, Ryan Miller, Ryan Malone and Kari Lehtonen.

A graduate of Mount Saint Charles Academy in Woonsocket, Rhode Island, Lawton represented the U.S. on several occasions, including the 1982 World Junior Championship, the 1983 World Championship, the 1984 Canada Cup, the 1987 World Championship and the 1988 Canada Cup.

# Club Directory

St. Pete Times Forum

**Tampa Bay Lightning**
St. Pete Times Forum
401 Channelside Drive
Tampa, FL 33602
Phone **813/301-6500**
FAX 813/301-1480
Ticket Info. 813/301-6600
www.tampabaylightning.com
**Capacity:** 19,758

**Executive**

| | |
|---|---|
| Ownership Group | OK Hockey |
| Owner, Governor | Oren Koules |
| Owner, Alternate Governor, President | Len Barrie |
| Owners | Mark Burg, Russell Belinsky, Dr. Richards C. Lehman, Irwin Novack, Craig Sher, Jordan Zimmerman |
| Exec. V.P., General Manager | Brian Lawton |
| Exec. V.P., Finance/CFO | Joe Fada |
| Exec. V.P., Business Operations | Brian Rogers |
| Exec. V.P., Corporate Sales & Mktg. Partnerships | Steven Thomas |
| Exec. V.P., Communications | Bill Wickett |
| Vice President, I.T. and Telecommunications | David Everett |
| Sr. Vice President, Sales and Marketing | Brad Lott |
| Vice President and General Counsel | Paul Davis |
| Vice President, Human Resources | Keith Harris |
| Vice President, Strategic Planning | Imran Khan |
| Vice President, Corporate Communications | Angelina Lawton |
| Vice President, Ticket Operations | Jim Mannino |
| Vice President, Operations | Mary Milne |
| Vice President, Client Services | Courtney Simons |
| Vice President, Event Booking | Elmer Straub |
| Director of Govt. Relations/Community Affairs | Ron Pierce |
| Executive Assistant | Michele Rooney |

**Hockey Operations**

| | |
|---|---|
| Assistant General Managers | Tom Kurvers, Claude Loiselle |
| Hockey Operations Executive Assistant | Liz Sylvia |
| Director of Player Personnel | Jim Hammett |
| Head Coach | Rick Tocchet |
| Associate Coach | Rick Wilson |
| Assistant Coaches | Cap Raeder, Wes Walz |
| Video Coach | Nigel Kirwan |
| Strength and Conditioning Coach | Chuck Lobe |
| Player Development/Defense Coach | Jim Johnson |
| Chief Scout | Greg Malone |
| Head Amateur Scout | Darryl Plandowski |
| Scouting Staff | Mikael Andersson, Micah Aivazoff, Stephen Baker, Len Barrie Sr., Angelo Bumbacco, Dave Heitz, Charlie Hodge, Kari Kettunen, Gerry O'Flaherty, Chris Snell |
| Director of Team Services | Ryan Belec |
| Medical Director | Dr. Ira Guttentag |
| Head Athletic Trainer | Thomas Mulligan |
| Assistant Athletic Trainer | Mike Poirier |
| Massage Therapist | Mike Griebel |
| Equipment Manager | Ray Thill |
| Assistant Equipment Managers | Rob Kennedy, Clay Roffer |
| Head Coach, Norfolk Admirals | Darren Rumble |
| Assistant Coach, Norfolk Admirals | Alan May |
| Head Athletic Trainer, Norfolk Admirals | Brad Chavis |
| Head Equipment Manager, Norfolk Admirals | TBD |

**Client Services**

| | |
|---|---|
| Director of Client Services | Amanda Graul |
| Director of Client Sales and Retention | Paul Wallace |

**Finance**

| | |
|---|---|
| Controller | Doug Riefler |
| Accounts Payable Coordinators | Donna Clark, Angie Edwards |
| Staff Accountants | Kathleen Cook, Krystal Mihopoulos, Jill Harper |

**Internal Support Staff**

| | |
|---|---|
| Human Resources & Legal Coordinator | Sabrina Odria |
| Office Services Coordinator | Ryan Messier |

**Box Office**

| | |
|---|---|
| Box Office Manager | Helen Junker |
| Box Office Supervisors | Missy Davis, Chrissy Hitchman, Bobby Loman, Liz Mulhearn |
| Assistant Box Office Coordinator | Brendan Shaughnessy |

**Ticket Sales**

| | |
|---|---|
| Director of Sales | Ryan West |
| Director of Suite Sales | Matt Hill |

**Corporate Sales and Marketing Partnerships**

| | |
|---|---|
| V.P.s, Corporate Sales & Mktg. Partnerships | Kyle Draper, Rob Keith |
| Sr. V.P., Corporate Sales & Mktg. Partnerships | Patrick Duffy |

**Communications**

| | |
|---|---|
| Media Relations Manager | Brian Breseman |
| Manager of Web Services | Justen Fox |
| Audio Manager | Tom Gilbert |

**Community Relations and Lightning Foundation**

| | |
|---|---|
| Interim Exec. Director, Lightning Foundation | Arlynn Haarer |
| Lightning Foundation Coordinator | Nina Lopez |
| Director, Community Relations/Youth | Mark Sofia |

**Event Production and Entertainment**

| | |
|---|---|
| V.P., Event Production and Entertainment | John Franzone |
| Director of Production | Jim Ciotoli |

**Broadcast Information**

| | |
|---|---|
| Television / Radio | Sun Sports Network / WDAE 620 AM |
| Television Play by Play / Color | Rick Peckham / Bobby "the Chief" Taylor |
| Television Host | Paul Kennedy |
| Manager of Radio Programming/Radio Host | Matt Sammon |
| Radio Play by Play / Color | David Mishkin / Phil Esposito |

# Toronto Maple Leafs

## 2008-09 Results: 34W-35L-6OTL-7SOL 81PTS.
## Fifth, Northeast Division

### Key Off-Season Signings/Acquisitions

**2009**

**July**
- **1** • Signed D **Mike Komisarek** and RW **Colton Orr.**
- **1** • Acquired D **Garnet Exelby** and LW **Colin Stuart** from Atlanta for D **Pavel Kubina** and RW **Tim Stapleton.**
- **2** • Re-signed C **Mikhail Grabovski.**
- **6** • Signed D **Francois Beauchemin.**
- **7** • Signed G **Jonas Gustavsson.**
- **10** • Signed C **Rickard Wallin.**
- **23** • Named **Dave Poulin** vice president of hockey operations.
- **27** • Acquired C **Wayne Primeau** and Calgary's 2nd-round pick in 2011 from Calgary for D **Anton Stralman**, LW **Colin Stuart** and Toronto's 7th-round pick in 2012.

### 2009-10 Schedule

|  |  |  |  |
|---|---|---|---|
| **Oct.** | Thu. | 1 | Montreal |
| | Sat. | 3 | at Washington |
| | Tue. | 6 | Ottawa |
| | Sat. | 10 | Pittsburgh |
| | Mon. | 12 | at NY Rangers |
| | Tue. | 13 | Colorado |
| | Sat. | 17 | NY Rangers |
| | Sat. | 24 | at Vancouver* |
| | Mon. | 26 | at Anaheim |
| | Wed. | 28 | at Dallas |
| | Fri. | 30 | at Buffalo |
| | Sat. | 31 | at Montreal |
| **Nov.** | Tue. | 3 | Tampa Bay |
| | Fri. | 6 | at Carolina |
| | Sat. | 7 | Detroit |
| | Tue. | 10 | Minnesota |
| | Fri. | 13 | at Chicago |
| | Sat. | 14 | Calgary |
| | Tue. | 17 | at Ottawa |
| | Thu. | 19 | at Carolina |
| | Sat. | 21 | Washington |
| | Mon. | 23 | NY Islanders |
| | Wed. | 25 | at Tampa Bay |
| | Fri. | 27 | at Florida |
| | Mon. | 30 | Buffalo |
| **Dec.** | Tue. | 1 | at Montreal |
| | Thu. | 3 | at Columbus |
| | Sat. | 5 | at Boston |
| | Mon. | 7 | Atlanta |
| | Wed. | 9 | NY Islanders |
| | Thu. | 10 | at Boston |
| | Sat. | 12 | Washington |
| | Mon. | 14 | Ottawa |
| | Wed. | 16 | Phoenix |
| | Fri. | 18 | at Buffalo |
| | Sat. | 19 | Boston |
| | Mon. | 21 | Buffalo |
| | Wed. | 23 | at NY Islanders |
| | Sat. | 26 | Montreal |
| | Sun. | 27 | at Pittsburgh |
| | Wed. | 30 | at Edmonton |
| **Jan.** | Sat. | 2 | at Calgary* |
| | Tue. | 5 | Florida |
| | Wed. | 6 | at Philadelphia |
| | Fri. | 8 | at Buffalo |
| | Sat. | 9 | Pittsburgh |
| | Tue. | 12 | Carolina |
| | Thu. | 14 | Philadelphia |
| | Fri. | 15 | at Washington |
| | Mon. | 18 | at Nashville |
| | Tue. | 19 | at Atlanta |
| | Thu. | 21 | at Tampa Bay |
| | Sat. | 23 | at Florida |
| | Tue. | 26 | Los Angeles |
| | Fri. | 29 | at New Jersey |
| | Sat. | 30 | Vancouver |
| **Feb.** | Tue. | 2 | New Jersey |
| | Fri. | 5 | at New Jersey |
| | Sat. | 6 | Ottawa |
| | Mon. | 8 | San Jose |
| | Fri. | 12 | at St. Louis |
| **Mar.** | Tue. | 2 | Carolina |
| | Thu. | 4 | at Boston |
| | Sat. | 6 | at Ottawa |
| | Sun. | 7 | at Philadelphia |
| | Tue. | 9 | Boston |
| | Thu. | 11 | Tampa Bay |
| | Sat. | 13 | Edmonton |
| | Sun. | 14 | at NY Islanders* |
| | Tue. | 16 | at Ottawa |
| | Thu. | 18 | New Jersey |
| | Sat. | 20 | Montreal |
| | Tue. | 23 | Florida |
| | Thu. | 25 | at Atlanta |
| | Sat. | 27 | NY Rangers |
| | Sun. | 28 | at Pittsburgh* |
| | Tue. | 30 | Atlanta |
| **Apr.** | Thu. | 1 | Buffalo |
| | Sat. | 3 | Boston |
| | Tue. | 6 | Philadelphia |
| | Wed. | 7 | at NY Rangers |
| | Sat. | 10 | at Montreal |

* Denotes afternoon game.

### Year-by-Year Record

| | | Home | | | | Road | | | | Overall | | | | | | | | |
|---|---|---|---|---|---|---|---|---|---|---|---|---|---|---|---|---|---|---|
| Season | GP | W | L | T | OL | W | L | T | OL | W | L | T | OL | GF | GA | Pts. | Finished | Playoff Result |
| 2008-09 | 82 | 16 | 16 | .... | 9 | 18 | 19 | .... | 4 | 34 | 35 | .... | 13 | 250 | 293 | 81 | 5th, Northeast Div. | Out of Playoffs |
| 2007-08 | 82 | 18 | 17 | .... | 6 | 18 | 18 | .... | 5 | 36 | 35 | .... | 11 | 231 | 260 | 83 | 5th, Northeast Div. | Out of Playoffs |
| 2006-07 | 82 | 21 | 15 | .... | 5 | 19 | 16 | .... | 6 | 40 | 31 | .... | 11 | 258 | 269 | 91 | 3rd, Northeast Div. | Out of Playoffs |
| 2005-06 | 82 | 26 | 12 | .... | 3 | 15 | 21 | .... | 5 | 41 | 33 | .... | 8 | 257 | 270 | 90 | 4th, Northeast Div. | Out of Playoffs |
| 2004-05 | .... | .... | .... | .... | .... | .... | .... | .... | .... | .... | .... | .... | .... | .... | .... | .... | | |
| 2003-04 | 82 | 22 | 14 | 3 | 2 | 23 | 10 | 7 | 1 | 45 | 24 | 10 | 3 | 242 | 204 | 103 | 2nd, Northeast Div. | Lost Conf. Semi-Final |
| 2002-03 | 82 | 24 | 13 | 4 | 0 | 20 | 15 | 3 | 3 | 44 | 28 | 7 | 3 | 236 | 208 | 98 | 2nd, Northeast Div. | Lost Conf. Quarter-Final |
| 2001-02 | 82 | 24 | 11 | 6 | 0 | 19 | 14 | 4 | 4 | 43 | 25 | 10 | 4 | 249 | 207 | 100 | 2nd, Northeast Div. | Lost Conf. Championship |
| 2000-01 | 82 | 19 | 11 | 7 | 4 | 18 | 18 | 4 | 1 | 37 | 29 | 11 | 5 | 232 | 207 | 90 | 3rd, Northeast Div. | Lost Conf. Semi-Final |
| 1999-2000 | 82 | 24 | 12 | 5 | 0 | 21 | 15 | 2 | 3 | 45 | 27 | 7 | 3 | 246 | 222 | 100 | 1st, Northeast Div. | Lost Conf. Semi-Final |
| 1998-99 | 82 | 23 | 13 | 5 | .... | 22 | 17 | 2 | .... | 45 | 30 | 7 | .... | 268 | 231 | 97 | 2nd, Northeast Div. | Lost Conf. Championship |
| 1997-98 | 82 | 16 | 20 | 5 | .... | 14 | 23 | 4 | .... | 30 | 43 | 9 | .... | 194 | 237 | 69 | 6th, Central Div. | Out of Playoffs |
| 1996-97 | 82 | 18 | 20 | 3 | .... | 12 | 24 | 5 | .... | 30 | 44 | 8 | .... | 230 | 273 | 68 | 6th, Central Div. | Out of Playoffs |
| 1995-96 | 82 | 19 | 15 | 7 | .... | 15 | 21 | 5 | .... | 34 | 36 | 12 | .... | 247 | 252 | 80 | 3rd, Central Div. | Lost Conf. Quarter-Final |
| 1994-95 | 48 | 15 | 7 | 2 | .... | 6 | 12 | 6 | .... | 21 | 19 | 8 | .... | 135 | 146 | 50 | 4th, Central Div. | Lost Conf. Quarter-Final |
| 1993-94 | 84 | 23 | 15 | 4 | .... | 20 | 14 | 8 | .... | 43 | 29 | 12 | .... | 280 | 243 | 98 | 2nd, Central Div. | Lost Conf. Championship |
| 1992-93 | 84 | 25 | 11 | 6 | .... | 19 | 18 | 5 | .... | 44 | 29 | 11 | .... | 288 | 241 | 99 | 3rd, Norris Div. | Lost Conf. Championship |
| 1991-92 | 80 | 21 | 16 | 3 | .... | 9 | 27 | 4 | .... | 30 | 43 | 7 | .... | 234 | 294 | 67 | 5th, Norris Div. | Out of Playoffs |
| 1990-91 | 80 | 15 | 21 | 4 | .... | 8 | 25 | 7 | .... | 23 | 46 | 11 | .... | 241 | 318 | 57 | 5th, Norris Div. | Out of Playoffs |
| 1989-90 | 80 | 24 | 14 | 2 | .... | 14 | 24 | 2 | .... | 38 | 38 | 4 | .... | 337 | 358 | 80 | 3rd, Norris Div. | Lost Div. Semi-Final |
| 1988-89 | 80 | 15 | 20 | 5 | .... | 13 | 26 | 1 | .... | 28 | 46 | 6 | .... | 259 | 342 | 62 | 5th, Norris Div. | Out of Playoffs |
| 1987-88 | 80 | 14 | 20 | 6 | .... | 7 | 29 | 4 | .... | 21 | 49 | 10 | .... | 273 | 345 | 52 | 4th, Norris Div. | Lost Div. Semi-Final |
| 1986-87 | 80 | 22 | 14 | 4 | .... | 10 | 28 | 2 | .... | 32 | 42 | 6 | .... | 286 | 319 | 70 | 4th, Norris Div. | Lost Div. Final |
| 1985-86 | 80 | 16 | 21 | 3 | .... | 9 | 27 | 4 | .... | 25 | 48 | 7 | .... | 311 | 386 | 57 | 4th, Norris Div. | Lost Div. Final |
| 1984-85 | 80 | 10 | 28 | 2 | .... | 10 | 24 | 6 | .... | 20 | 52 | 8 | .... | 253 | 358 | 48 | 5th, Norris Div. | Out of Playoffs |
| 1983-84 | 80 | 17 | 16 | 7 | .... | 9 | 29 | 2 | .... | 26 | 45 | 9 | .... | 303 | 387 | 61 | 5th, Norris Div. | Out of Playoffs |
| 1982-83 | 80 | 20 | 15 | 5 | .... | 8 | 25 | 7 | .... | 28 | 40 | 12 | .... | 293 | 330 | 68 | 3rd, Norris Div. | Lost Div. Semi-Final |
| 1981-82 | 80 | 12 | 20 | 8 | .... | 8 | 24 | 8 | .... | 20 | 44 | 16 | .... | 298 | 380 | 56 | 5th, Norris Div. | Out of Playoffs |
| 1980-81 | 80 | 14 | 21 | 5 | .... | 14 | 16 | 10 | .... | 28 | 37 | 15 | .... | 322 | 367 | 71 | 5th, Adams Div. | Lost Prelim. Round |
| 1979-80 | 80 | 17 | 19 | 4 | .... | 18 | 21 | 1 | .... | 35 | 40 | 5 | .... | 304 | 327 | 75 | 4th, Adams Div. | Lost Prelim. Round |
| 1978-79 | 80 | 20 | 12 | 8 | .... | 14 | 21 | 5 | .... | 34 | 33 | 13 | .... | 267 | 252 | 81 | 3rd, Adams Div. | Lost Quarter-Final |
| 1977-78 | 80 | 21 | 13 | 6 | .... | 20 | 16 | 4 | .... | 41 | 29 | 10 | .... | 271 | 237 | 92 | 3rd, Adams Div. | Lost Semi-Final |
| 1976-77 | 80 | 18 | 13 | 9 | .... | 15 | 19 | 6 | .... | 33 | 32 | 15 | .... | 301 | 285 | 81 | 3rd, Adams Div. | Lost Quarter-Final |
| 1975-76 | 80 | 23 | 12 | 5 | .... | 11 | 19 | 10 | .... | 34 | 31 | 15 | .... | 294 | 276 | 83 | 3rd, Adams Div. | Lost Quarter-Final |
| 1974-75 | 80 | 19 | 12 | 9 | .... | 12 | 21 | 7 | .... | 31 | 33 | 16 | .... | 280 | 309 | 78 | 3rd, Adams Div. | Lost Quarter-Final |
| 1973-74 | 78 | 21 | 11 | 7 | .... | 14 | 16 | 9 | .... | 35 | 27 | 16 | .... | 274 | 230 | 86 | 4th, East Div. | Lost Quarter-Final |
| 1972-73 | 78 | 20 | 12 | 7 | .... | 7 | 29 | 3 | .... | 27 | 41 | 10 | .... | 247 | 279 | 64 | 6th, East Div. | Out of Playoffs |
| 1971-72 | 78 | 21 | 11 | 7 | .... | 12 | 20 | 7 | .... | 33 | 31 | 14 | .... | 209 | 208 | 80 | 4th, East Div. | Lost Quarter-Final |
| 1970-71 | 78 | 24 | 9 | 6 | .... | 13 | 24 | 2 | .... | 37 | 33 | 8 | .... | 248 | 211 | 82 | 4th, East Div. | Lost Quarter-Final |
| 1969-70 | 76 | 18 | 13 | 7 | .... | 11 | 21 | 6 | .... | 29 | 34 | 13 | .... | 222 | 242 | 71 | 6th, East Div. | Out of Playoffs |
| 1968-69 | 76 | 20 | 8 | 10 | .... | 15 | 18 | 5 | .... | 35 | 26 | 15 | .... | 234 | 217 | 85 | 4th, East Div. | Lost Quarter-Final |
| 1967-68 | 74 | 24 | 9 | 4 | .... | 9 | 22 | 6 | .... | 33 | 31 | 10 | .... | 209 | 176 | 76 | 5th, East Div. | Out of Playoffs |
| **1966-67** | **70** | **21** | **8** | **6** | .... | **11** | **19** | **5** | .... | **32** | **27** | **11** | .... | **204** | **211** | **75** | **3rd,** | **Won Stanley Cup** |
| 1965-66 | 70 | 22 | 9 | 4 | .... | 12 | 16 | 7 | .... | 34 | 25 | 11 | .... | 208 | 187 | 79 | 3rd, | Lost Semi-Final |
| 1964-65 | 70 | 17 | 15 | 3 | .... | 13 | 11 | 11 | .... | 30 | 26 | 14 | .... | 204 | 173 | 74 | 4th, | Lost Semi-Final |
| **1963-64** | **70** | **22** | **7** | **6** | .... | **11** | **18** | **6** | .... | **33** | **25** | **12** | .... | **192** | **172** | **78** | **3rd,** | **Won Stanley Cup** |
| **1962-63** | **70** | **21** | **8** | **6** | .... | **14** | **15** | **6** | .... | **35** | **23** | **12** | .... | **221** | **180** | **82** | **1st,** | **Won Stanley Cup** |
| **1961-62** | **70** | **25** | **5** | **5** | .... | **12** | **17** | **6** | .... | **37** | **22** | **11** | .... | **232** | **180** | **85** | **2nd,** | **Won Stanley Cup** |
| 1960-61 | 70 | 21 | 6 | 8 | .... | 18 | 13 | 4 | .... | 39 | 19 | 12 | .... | 234 | 176 | 90 | 2nd, | Lost Semi-Final |
| 1959-60 | 70 | 20 | 9 | 6 | .... | 15 | 17 | 3 | .... | 35 | 26 | 9 | .... | 199 | 195 | 79 | 2nd, | Lost Final |
| 1958-59 | 70 | 17 | 13 | 5 | .... | 10 | 19 | 6 | .... | 27 | 32 | 11 | .... | 189 | 201 | 65 | 4th, | Lost Final |
| 1957-58 | 70 | 12 | 16 | 7 | .... | 9 | 22 | 4 | .... | 21 | 38 | 11 | .... | 192 | 226 | 53 | 6th, | Out of Playoffs |
| 1956-57 | 70 | 12 | 16 | 7 | .... | 9 | 18 | 8 | .... | 21 | 34 | 15 | .... | 174 | 192 | 57 | 5th, | Out of Playoffs |
| 1955-56 | 70 | 19 | 10 | 6 | .... | 5 | 23 | 7 | .... | 24 | 33 | 13 | .... | 153 | 181 | 61 | 4th, | Lost Semi-Final |
| 1954-55 | 70 | 14 | 10 | 11 | .... | 10 | 14 | 11 | .... | 24 | 24 | 22 | .... | 147 | 135 | 70 | 3rd, | Lost Semi-Final |
| 1953-54 | 70 | 22 | 6 | 7 | .... | 10 | 18 | 7 | .... | 32 | 24 | 14 | .... | 152 | 131 | 78 | 3rd, | Lost Semi-Final |
| 1952-53 | 70 | 17 | 12 | 6 | .... | 10 | 18 | 7 | .... | 27 | 30 | 13 | .... | 156 | 167 | 67 | 5th, | Out of Playoffs |
| 1951-52 | 70 | 17 | 10 | 8 | .... | 12 | 15 | 8 | .... | 29 | 25 | 16 | .... | 168 | 157 | 74 | 3rd, | Lost Semi-Final |
| **1950-51** | **70** | **22** | **8** | **5** | .... | **19** | **8** | **8** | .... | **41** | **16** | **13** | .... | **212** | **138** | **95** | **2nd,** | **Won Stanley Cup** |
| 1949-50 | 70 | 18 | 9 | 8 | .... | 13 | 18 | 4 | .... | 31 | 27 | 12 | .... | 176 | 173 | 74 | 3rd, | Lost Semi-Final |
| **1948-49** | **60** | **12** | **8** | **10** | .... | **10** | **17** | **3** | .... | **22** | **25** | **13** | .... | **147** | **161** | **57** | **4th,** | **Won Stanley Cup** |
| **1947-48** | **60** | **22** | **3** | **5** | .... | **10** | **12** | **8** | .... | **32** | **15** | **13** | .... | **182** | **143** | **77** | **1st,** | **Won Stanley Cup** |
| **1946-47** | **60** | **20** | **8** | **2** | .... | **11** | **11** | **8** | .... | **31** | **19** | **10** | .... | **209** | **172** | **72** | **2nd,** | **Won Stanley Cup** |
| 1945-46 | 50 | 10 | 13 | 2 | .... | 9 | 11 | 5 | .... | 19 | 24 | 7 | .... | 174 | 185 | 45 | 5th, | Out of Playoffs |
| **1944-45** | **50** | **13** | **9** | **3** | .... | **11** | **13** | **1** | .... | **24** | **22** | **4** | .... | **183** | **161** | **52** | **3rd,** | **Won Stanley Cup** |
| 1943-44 | 50 | 13 | 11 | 1 | .... | 10 | 12 | 3 | .... | 23 | 23 | 4 | .... | 214 | 174 | 50 | 3rd, | Lost Semi-Final |
| 1942-43 | 50 | 17 | 6 | 2 | .... | 5 | 13 | 7 | .... | 22 | 19 | 9 | .... | 198 | 159 | 53 | 3rd, | Lost Semi-Final |
| **1941-42** | **48** | **18** | **6** | **0** | .... | **9** | **12** | **3** | .... | **27** | **18** | **3** | .... | **158** | **136** | **57** | **2nd,** | **Won Stanley Cup** |
| 1940-41 | 48 | 16 | 5 | 3 | .... | 12 | 9 | 3 | .... | 28 | 14 | 6 | .... | 145 | 99 | 62 | 2nd, | Lost Semi-Final |
| 1939-40 | 48 | 15 | 3 | 6 | .... | 10 | 14 | 0 | .... | 25 | 17 | 6 | .... | 134 | 110 | 56 | 3rd, | Lost Final |
| 1938-39 | 48 | 13 | 8 | 3 | .... | 6 | 12 | 6 | .... | 19 | 20 | 9 | .... | 114 | 107 | 47 | 3rd, | Lost Final |
| 1937-38 | 48 | 13 | 6 | 5 | .... | 11 | 9 | 4 | .... | 24 | 15 | 9 | .... | 151 | 127 | 57 | 1st, Cdn. Div. | Lost Final |
| 1936-37 | 48 | 14 | 9 | 1 | .... | 8 | 12 | 4 | .... | 22 | 21 | 5 | .... | 119 | 115 | 49 | 3rd, Cdn. Div. | Lost Quarter-Final |
| 1935-36 | 48 | 15 | 4 | 5 | .... | 8 | 15 | 1 | .... | 23 | 19 | 6 | .... | 126 | 106 | 52 | 2nd, Cdn. Div. | Lost Final |
| 1934-35 | 48 | 16 | 6 | 2 | .... | 14 | 8 | 2 | .... | 30 | 14 | 4 | .... | 157 | 111 | 64 | 1st, Cdn. Div. | Lost Final |
| 1933-34 | 48 | 19 | 2 | 3 | .... | 7 | 11 | 6 | .... | 26 | 13 | 9 | .... | 174 | 119 | 61 | 1st, Cdn. Div. | Lost Semi-Final |
| 1932-33 | 48 | 16 | 4 | 4 | .... | 8 | 14 | 2 | .... | 24 | 18 | 6 | .... | 119 | 111 | 54 | 1st, Cdn. Div. | Lost Final |
| **1931-32** | **48** | **17** | **4** | **3** | .... | **6** | **14** | **4** | .... | **23** | **18** | **7** | .... | **155** | **127** | **53** | **2nd, Cdn. Div.** | **Won Stanley Cup** |
| 1930-31 | 44 | 15 | 4 | 3 | .... | 7 | 9 | 6 | .... | 22 | 13 | 9 | .... | 118 | 99 | 53 | 2nd, Cdn. Div. | Lost Quarter-Final |
| 1929-30 | 44 | 10 | 8 | 4 | .... | 7 | 13 | 2 | .... | 17 | 21 | 6 | .... | 116 | 124 | 40 | 4th, Cdn. Div. | Out of Playoffs |
| 1928-29 | 44 | 15 | 5 | 2 | .... | 6 | 13 | 3 | .... | 21 | 18 | 5 | .... | 85 | 69 | 47 | 3rd, Cdn. Div. | Lost Semi-Final |
| 1927-28 | 44 | 9 | 8 | 5 | .... | 9 | 10 | 3 | .... | 18 | 18 | 8 | .... | 89 | 88 | 44 | 4th, Cdn. Div. | Out of Playoffs |
| 1926-27* | 44 | 10 | 10 | 2 | .... | 5 | 14 | 3 | .... | 15 | 24 | 5 | .... | 79 | 94 | 35 | 5th, Cdn. Div. | Out of Playoffs |
| 1925-26 | 36 | 11 | 5 | 2 | .... | 1 | 16 | 1 | .... | 12 | 21 | 3 | .... | 92 | 114 | 27 | 6th, | Out of Playoffs |
| 1924-25 | 30 | 10 | 5 | 0 | .... | 9 | 6 | 0 | .... | 19 | 11 | 0 | .... | 90 | 84 | 38 | 2nd, | Lost NHL S-Final |
| 1923-24 | 24 | 7 | 5 | 0 | .... | 3 | 9 | 0 | .... | 10 | 14 | 0 | .... | 59 | 85 | 20 | 3rd, | Out of Playoffs |
| 1922-23 | 24 | 10 | 1 | 1 | .... | 3 | 9 | 0 | .... | 13 | 10 | 1 | .... | 82 | 88 | 27 | 3rd, | Out of Playoffs |
| **1921-22** | **24** | **8** | **4** | **0** | .... | **5** | **6** | **1** | .... | **13** | **10** | **1** | .... | **98** | **97** | **27** | **2nd,** | **Won Stanley Cup** |
| 1920-21 | 24 | 9 | 3 | 0 | .... | 6 | 6 | 0 | .... | 15 | 9 | 0 | .... | 105 | 100 | 30 | 2nd and 1st*** | Lost NHL Final |
| 1919-20** | 24 | 8 | 4 | 0 | .... | 4 | 8 | 0 | .... | 12 | 12 | 0 | .... | 119 | 106 | 24 | 3rd and 2nd*** | Out of Playoffs |
| 1918-19 | 18 | 5 | 4 | 0 | .... | 0 | 9 | 0 | .... | 5 | 13 | 0 | .... | 64 | 92 | 10 | 3rd and 3rd*** | Out of Playoffs |
| **1917-18** | **22** | **10** | **1** | **0** | .... | **3** | **8** | **0** | .... | **13** | **9** | **0** | .... | **108** | **109** | **26** | **2nd and 1st*** ** | **Won Stanley Cup** |

* Name changed from St. Patricks to Maple Leafs (February, 1927). ** Name changed from Arenas to St. Patricks.
*** Season played in two halves with no combined standing at end.
From 1917-18 through 1925-26, NHL champions played against PCHA/WCHL champions for Stanley Cup.

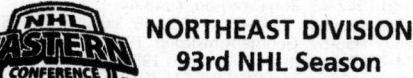

**NORTHEAST DIVISION**
**93rd NHL Season**

**Franchise date:** November 22, 1917

# 2009-10 Player Personnel

| FORWARDS | HT | WT | S | Place of Birth | *Age | 2008-09 Club |
|---|---|---|---|---|---|---|
| BLAKE, Jason | 5-10 | 180 | L | Moorhead, MN | 36 | Toronto |
| BOZAK, Tyler | 6-0 | 165 | R | Regina, Sask. | 23 | U. of Denver |
| BRENT, Tim | 6-0 | 197 | R | Cambridge, Ont. | 25 | Chicago-Rockford |
| GRABOVSKI, Mikhail | 5-11 | 179 | L | Potsdam, East Germany | 25 | Toronto |
| HAGMAN, Niklas | 6-0 | 205 | L | Espoo, Finland | 29 | Toronto |
| HANSON, Christian | 6-3 | 202 | R | Glens Falls, NY | 23 | U. of Notre Dame-Toronto |
| KADRI, Nazem | 6-0 | 167 | L | London, Ont. | 18 | London |
| KULEMIN, Nikolai | 6-1 | 183 | L | Magnitogorsk, USSR | 23 | Toronto-Toronto (AHL) |
| MAYERS, Jamal | 6-1 | 214 | R | Toronto, Ont. | 34 | Toronto |
| MITCHELL, John | 6-1 | 182 | L | Waterloo, Ont. | 24 | Toronto |
| ORR, Colton | 6-3 | 222 | R | Winnipeg, Man. | 27 | NY Rangers |
| PONIKAROVSKY, Alexei | 6-4 | 220 | L | Kiev, USSR | 29 | Toronto |
| PRIMEAU, Wayne | 6-4 | 225 | L | Scarborough, Ont. | 33 | Calgary |
| SLANEY, Robert | 6-2 | 203 | L | Upper Island Cove, Nfld. | 20 | Cape Breton |
| STAJAN, Matt | 6-1 | 200 | L | Mississauga, Ont. | 25 | Toronto |
| STEMPNIAK, Lee | 6-0 | 195 | R | Buffalo, NY | 26 | St. Louis-Toronto |
| TLUSTY, Jiri | 6-0 | 209 | L | Slany, Czech. | 21 | Toronto-Toronto (AHL) |
| WALLIN, Rickard | 6-2 | 185 | L | Stockholm, Sweden | 29 | Farjestad |
| **DEFENSEMEN** | | | | | | |
| BEAUCHEMIN, Francois | 6-0 | 207 | L | Sorel, Que. | 29 | Anaheim |
| EXELBY, Garnet | 6-1 | 215 | L | Ste. Anne, Man. | 28 | Atlanta |
| FINGER, Jeff | 6-1 | 205 | R | Hancock, MI | 29 | Toronto |
| FROGREN, Jonas | 6-2 | 194 | L | Falun, Sweden | 29 | Toronto-Toronto (AHL) |
| KABERLE, Tomas | 6-1 | 198 | L | Rakovnik, Czech. | 31 | Toronto |
| KOMISAREK, Mike | 6-4 | 243 | R | West Islip, NY | 27 | Montreal |
| SCHENN, Luke | 6-2 | 216 | R | Saskatoon, Sask. | 19 | Toronto |
| VAN RYN, Mike | 6-1 | 198 | R | London, Ont. | 30 | Toronto |
| WHITE, Ian | 5-10 | 185 | R | Steinbach, Man. | 25 | Toronto |

| GOALTENDERS | HT | WT | C | Place of Birth | *Age | 2008-09 Club |
|---|---|---|---|---|---|---|
| GUSTAVSSON, Jonas | 6-3 | 192 | L | Stockholm, Sweden | 24 | Farjestad |
| TOSKALA, Vesa | 5-10 | 195 | L | Tampere, Finland | 32 | Toronto |

* – Age at start of 2009-10 season

# 2008-09 Scoring

* – rookie

## Regular Season

| Pos | # | Player | Team | GP | G | A | Pts | TOI | +/- | PIM | PP | SH | GW | S | % |
|---|---|---|---|---|---|---|---|---|---|---|---|---|---|---|---|
| L | 55 | Jason Blake | TOR | 78 | 25 | 38 | 63 | 18:20 | –2 | 40 | 5 | 1 | 5 | 302 | 8.3 |
| L | 23 | Alexei Ponikarovsky | TOR | 82 | 23 | 38 | 61 | 15:47 | 6 | 38 | 5 | 0 | 3 | 185 | 12.4 |
| C | 14 | Matt Stajan | TOR | 76 | 15 | 40 | 55 | 16:55 | –4 | 54 | 5 | 1 | 1 | 114 | 13.2 |
| C | 84 * | Mikhail Grabovski | TOR | 78 | 20 | 28 | 48 | 16:13 | –8 | 92 | 6 | 0 | 2 | 120 | 16.7 |
| R | 12 | Lee Stempniak | STL | 14 | 3 | 10 | 13 | 19:28 | –3 | 2 | 0 | 0 | 1 | 43 | 7.0 |
| | | | TOR | 61 | 11 | 20 | 31 | 15:52 | –9 | 31 | 3 | 0 | 0 | 128 | 8.6 |
| | | | Total | 75 | 14 | 30 | 44 | 16:32 | –12 | 33 | 3 | 0 | 1 | 171 | 8.2 |
| R | 9 | Niklas Hagman | TOR | 65 | 22 | 20 | 42 | 17:04 | –5 | 4 | 6 | 0 | 3 | 168 | 13.1 |
| D | 77 | Pavel Kubina | TOR | 82 | 14 | 26 | 40 | 22:03 | –15 | 94 | 9 | 0 | 4 | 184 | 7.6 |
| L | 41 * | Nikolai Kulemin | TOR | 73 | 15 | 16 | 31 | 13:48 | –8 | 18 | 2 | 0 | 1 | 129 | 11.6 |
| D | 15 | Tomas Kaberle | TOR | 57 | 4 | 27 | 31 | 23:27 | –8 | 8 | 3 | 0 | 1 | 93 | 4.3 |
| C | 39 * | John Mitchell | TOR | 76 | 12 | 17 | 29 | 13:48 | –16 | 33 | 2 | 0 | 0 | 98 | 12.2 |
| D | 7 | Ian White | TOR | 71 | 10 | 16 | 26 | 22:50 | 6 | 57 | 2 | 0 | 2 | 158 | 6.3 |
| D | 4 | Jeff Finger | TOR | 66 | 6 | 17 | 23 | 20:29 | –7 | 43 | 0 | 0 | 0 | 68 | 8.8 |
| R | 21 | Jamal Mayers | TOR | 71 | 7 | 9 | 16 | 10:32 | –7 | 82 | 0 | 0 | 1 | 72 | 9.7 |
| D | 2 * | Luke Schenn | TOR | 70 | 2 | 12 | 14 | 21:32 | –12 | 71 | 1 | 0 | 0 | 102 | 2.0 |
| D | 36 | Anton Stralman | TOR | 38 | 1 | 12 | 13 | 15:34 | –2 | 20 | 0 | 0 | 1 | 43 | 2.3 |
| C | 22 | Boyd Devereaux | TOR | 23 | 6 | 5 | 11 | 13:41 | 3 | 2 | 0 | 3 | 0 | 41 | 14.6 |
| D | 26 | Mike Van Ryn | TOR | 27 | 3 | 8 | 11 | 19:37 | 2 | 14 | 2 | 0 | 0 | 53 | 5.7 |
| R | 18 * | Jeremy Williams | TOR | 11 | 5 | 2 | 7 | 13:26 | 2 | 2 | 0 | 0 | 0 | 21 | 23.8 |
| D | 24 | Jonas Frogren | TOR | 41 | 1 | 6 | 7 | 13:26 | 0 | 28 | 0 | 0 | 0 | 12 | 8.3 |
| L | 10 | Brad May | ANA | 20 | 0 | 5 | 5 | 6:21 | 5 | 28 | 0 | 0 | 0 | 5 | 0.0 |
| | | | TOR | 38 | 1 | 1 | 2 | 7:43 | –5 | 61 | 0 | 0 | 0 | 27 | 3.7 |
| | | | Total | 58 | 1 | 6 | 7 | 7:15 | 0 | 89 | 0 | 0 | 0 | 32 | 3.1 |
| R | 51 | Jeff Hamilton | TOR | 15 | 3 | 3 | 6 | 12:57 | 2 | 4 | 0 | 0 | 1 | 30 | 10.0 |
| L | 11 | Jiri Tlusty | TOR | 14 | 0 | 4 | 4 | 12:42 | 0 | 0 | 0 | 0 | 0 | 22 | 0.0 |
| C | 20 * | Christian Hanson | TOR | 5 | 1 | 1 | 2 | 16:19 | –1 | 2 | 0 | 0 | 0 | 9 | 11.1 |
| D | 40 * | Phil Oreskovic | TOR | 10 | 1 | 1 | 2 | 16:13 | –2 | 21 | 0 | 0 | 0 | 12 | 8.3 |
| D | 59 * | Jaime Sifers | TOR | 23 | 0 | 2 | 2 | 12:49 | –4 | 18 | 0 | 0 | 0 | 25 | 0.0 |
| L | 44 | Ryan Hollweg | TOR | 25 | 0 | 2 | 2 | 6:27 | –7 | 38 | 0 | 0 | 0 | 12 | 0.0 |
| C | 42 | Tim Stapleton | TOR | 4 | 1 | 0 | 1 | 15:05 | –3 | 0 | 0 | 0 | 0 | 9 | 11.1 |
| D | 43 * | Jay Harrison | TOR | 7 | 0 | 1 | 1 | 17:15 | –2 | 10 | 0 | 0 | 0 | 6 | 0.0 |
| R | 56 * | Andre Deveaux | TOR | 21 | 0 | 1 | 1 | 7:14 | –3 | 75 | 0 | 0 | 0 | 15 | 0.0 |
| C | 54 | Kris Newbury | TOR | 1 | 0 | 0 | 0 | 4:55 | 0 | 2 | 0 | 0 | 0 | 0 | 0.0 |
| R | 25 | Ben Ondrus | TOR | 11 | 0 | 0 | 0 | 9:27 | –4 | 34 | 0 | 0 | 0 | 2 | 0.0 |

## Goaltending

| No. | Goaltender | GPI | Mins | Avg | W | L | OT | EN | SO | GA | SA | S% | G | A | PIM |
|---|---|---|---|---|---|---|---|---|---|---|---|---|---|---|---|
| 29 | Martin Gerber | 12 | 706 | 3.23 | 6 | 5 | 0 | 1 | 0 | 38 | 402 | .905 | 0 | 0 | 10 |
| 35 | Vesa Toskala | 53 | 3056 | 3.26 | 22 | 17 | 11 | 3 | 1 | 166 | 1518 | .891 | 0 | 0 | 2 |
| 31 | Curtis Joseph | 21 | 841 | 3.57 | 5 | 9 | 1 | 1 | 0 | 50 | 383 | .869 | 0 | 0 | 0 |
| 1 * | Justin Pogge | 7 | 372 | 4.35 | 1 | 4 | 1 | 0 | 0 | 27 | 173 | .844 | 0 | 0 | 0 |
| | **Totals** | **82** | **5006** | **3.43** | **34** | **35** | **13** | **5** | **1** | **286** | **2481** | **.885** | | | |

# Ron Wilson

### Head Coach

*Born: Windsor, Ont., May 28, 1955.*

The Toronto Maple Leafs announced on June 10, 2008 that Ron Wilson had been named the 27th head coach in the club's history. Wilson previously held NHL head coaching duties with Anaheim, Washington, and the San Jose Sharks.

Under Wilson's guidance the Sharks were the only NHL team to have won at least one playoff round in each season from 2003-04 through 2007-08. In his four full seasons behind the Sharks bench, the team advanced to the Western Conference Final for the first time ever in 2004, and reached the Conference semifinals in 2006, 2007 and 2008. His Sharks teams garnered two Pacific Division championships (2004 and 2008); twice finished second in their division, and twice posted the second-best point total in the conference. With 206 victories in San Jose, Wilson surpassed Darryl Sutter as the Sharks' all-time wins leader on March 1, 2008.

Wilson coached the Washington Capitals from 1997 until 2002, with his tenure in the United State's capital highlighted by the team's only trip to the Stanley Cup Final in 1998. Prior to spending five seasons with the Capitals, Wilson had served as the first head coach of the expansion Mighty Ducks of Anaheim in 1993, and he led the team to the postseason for the very first time in 1996-97.

Throughout his professional and amateur career, Wilson has enjoyed a long-standing relationship with USA Hockey. He led Team USA to the gold medal in 1996 at the inaugural World Cup of Hockey and he coached the team again at the 2004 tournament. Wilson coached the U.S. team at the World Championship in 1994, 1996 and again in 2009. He also served as head coach for Team USA at the 1998 Nagano Olympics and will do again at the 2010 Vancouver Games.

Wilson was a seventh-round selection of the Toronto Maple Leafs (132nd overall) in the 1975 NHL Amateur Draft. He made his NHL debut by playing in 13 games for Toronto in 1977-78, followed by 46 games in 1978-79 and five games in 1979-80. In 177 career NHL games as a player with Toronto and Minnesota, Wilson recorded 26 goals and 67 assists for 93 points. He is one of 15 individuals that have both played for the Maple Leafs and then went on to coach at least one game for the Original Six franchise. He is the son of Larry Wilson and the nephew of Johnny Wilson, both former players on Stanley Cup winning teams from Detroit.

### Coaching Record

| | | | Regular Season | | | | Playoffs | | | |
|---|---|---|---|---|---|---|---|---|---|---|
| Season | Team | League | GC | W | L | O/T | GC | W | L | T |
| 1993-94 | Anaheim | NHL | 84 | 33 | 46 | 5 | .... | .... | .... | .... |
| 1994-95 | Anaheim | NHL | 48 | 16 | 27 | 5 | .... | .... | .... | .... |
| 1995-96 | Anaheim | NHL | 82 | 35 | 39 | 8 | .... | .... | .... | .... |
| 1996-97 | Anaheim | NHL | 82 | 36 | 33 | 13 | 11 | 4 | 7 | .... |
| 1997-98 | Washington | NHL | 82 | 40 | 30 | 12 | 21 | 12 | 9 | .... |
| 1998-99 | Washington | NHL | 82 | 31 | 45 | 6 | .... | .... | .... | .... |
| 99-2000 | Washington | NHL | 82 | 44 | 24 | 14 | 5 | 1 | 4 | .... |
| 2000-01 | Washington | NHL | 82 | 41 | 27 | 14 | 6 | 2 | 4 | .... |
| 2001-02 | Washington | NHL | 82 | 36 | 33 | 13 | .... | .... | .... | .... |
| 2002-03 | San Jose | NHL | 57 | 19 | 25 | 13 | .... | .... | .... | .... |
| 2003-04 | San Jose | NHL | 82 | 43 | 21 | 18 | 17 | 10 | 7 | .... |
| 2004-05 | San Jose | | | | SEASON CANCELLED | | | | | |
| 2005-06 | San Jose | NHL | 82 | 44 | 27 | 11 | 11 | 6 | 5 | .... |
| 2006-07 | San Jose | NHL | 82 | 51 | 26 | 5 | 11 | 6 | 5 | .... |
| 2007-08 | San Jose | NHL | 82 | 49 | 23 | 10 | 13 | 6 | 7 | .... |
| 2008-09 | Toronto | NHL | 82 | 34 | 35 | 13 | .... | .... | .... | .... |
| | NHL Totals | | 1173 | 552 | 461 | 160 | 95 | 47 | 48 | .... |

## Coaching History

Dick Carroll, 1917-18, 1918-19; Frank Heffernan and Harry Sproule, 1919-20; Frank Carroll, 1920-21; George O'Donohue, 1921-22; George O'Donohue and Charles Querrie, 1922-23; Charles Querrie, 1923-24; Eddie Powers, 1924-25, 1925-26; Charles Querrie, Mike Rodden and Alex Romeril, 1926-27; Conn Smythe, 1927-28 to 1929-30; Conn Smythe and Art Duncan, 1930-31; Art Duncan and Dick Irvin, 1931-32; Dick Irvin, 1932-33 to 1939-40; Hap Day, 1940-41 to 1949-50; Joe Primeau, 1950-51 to 1952-53; King Clancy, 1953-54 to 1955-56; Howie Meeker, 1956-57; Billy Reay, 1957-58; Billy Reay and Punch Imlach, 1958-59; Punch Imlach, 1959-60 to 1968-69; John McLellan, 1969-70 to 1972-73; Red Kelly, 1973-74 to 1976-77; Roger Neilson, 1977-78, 1978-79; Floyd Smith, Dick Duff and Punch Imlach, 1979-80; Joe Crozier and Mike Nykoluk, 1980-81; Mike Nykoluk, 1981-82 to 1983-84; Dan Maloney, 1984-85, 1985-86; John Brophy, 1986-87, 1987-88; John Brophy and George Armstrong, 1988-89; Doug Carpenter, 1989-90; Doug Carpenter and Tom Watt, 1990-91; Tom Watt, 1991-92; Pat Burns, 1992-93 to 1994-95; Pat Burns and Nick Beverley, 1995-96; Mike Murphy, 1996-97, 1997-98; Pat Quinn, 1998-99 to 2005-06; Paul Maurice, 2006-07, 2007-08; Ron Wilson, 2008-09 to date.

## Captains' History

Hap Day, 1927-28 to 1936-37; Charlie Conacher, 1937-38; Red Horner, 1938-39, 1939-40; Syl Apps, 1940-41 to 1942-43; Bob Davidson, 1943-44, 1944-45; Syl Apps, 1945-46 to 1947-48; Ted Kennedy, 1948-49 to 1954-55; Sid Smith, 1955-56; Jimmy Thomson, Ted Kennedy, 1956-57; George Armstrong, 1957-58 to 1968-69; Dave Keon, 1969-70 to 1974-75; Darryl Sittler, 1975-76 to 1980-81; Rick Vaive, 1981-82 to 1985-86; no captain, 1986-87 to 1988-89; Rob Ramage, 1989-90, 1990-91; Wendel Clark, 1991-92 to 1993-94; Doug Gilmour, 1994-95 to 1996-97; Mats Sundin, 1997-98 to 2007-08; no captain, 2008-09 to date.

# Club Records

## Team

(Figures in brackets for season records are games played; records for fewest points, wins, ties, losses, goals, goals against are for 70 or more games)

**Most Points** .............. **103** 2003-04 (82)
**Most Wins** ................ **45** 1998-99 (82), 1999-2000 (82), 2003-04 (82)
**Most Ties** ................. **22** 1954-55 (70)
**Most Losses** ............... **52** 1984-85 (80)
**Most Goals** ................ **337** 1989-90 (80)
**Most Goals Against** ......... **387** 1983-84 (80)
**Fewest Points** .............. **48** 1984-85 (80)
**Fewest Wins** ................ **20** 1981-82 (80), 1984-85 (80)
**Fewest Ties** ................. **4** 1989-90 (80)
**Fewest Losses** ............... **16** 1950-51 (70)
**Fewest Goals** ................ **147** 1954-55 (70)
**Fewest Goals Against** ...... ***131** 1953-54 (70)
**Longest Winning Streak**
**Overall** .................... **10** Oct. 7-28/93
**Home** ...................... **9** Nov. 11-Dec. 26/53, Mar. 6-Apr. 7/07
**Away** ...................... **7** Three times
**Longest Undefeated Streak**
**Overall** .................... **11** Oct. 15-Nov. 8/50 (8 wins, 3 ties), Jan. 6-Feb. 1/94 (7 wins, 4 ties)
**Home** ...................... **18** Nov. 28/33-Mar. 10/34 (15 wins, 3 ties), Oct. 31/53-Jan. 23/54 (16 wins, 2 ties)
**Away** ...................... **9** Nov. 30/47-Jan. 11/48 (4 wins, 5 ties)
**Longest Losing Streak**
**Overall** .................... **10** Jan. 15-Feb. 8/67
**Home** ...................... **7** Nov. 11-Dec. 5/84
**Away** ...................... **11** Feb. 20-Apr. 1/88
**Longest Winless Streak**
**Overall** .................... **15** Dec. 26/87-Jan. 25/88 (11 losses, 4 ties)
**Home** ...................... **11** Dec. 19/87-Jan. 25/88 (7 losses, 4 ties)
**Away** ...................... **18** Oct. 6/82-Jan. 5/83 (13 losses, 5 ties)
**Most Shutouts, Season** ....... **13** 1953-54 (70)
**Most PIM, Season** ......... **2,419** 1989-90 (80)
**Most Goals, Game** ........... **14** Mar. 16/57 (NYR 1 at Tor. 14)

## Individual

**Most Seasons** ............... **21** George Armstrong
**Most Games** ............. **1,187** George Armstrong
**Most Goals, Career** ......... **420** Mats Sundin
**Most Assists, Career** ........ **620** Borje Salming
**Most Points, Career** ......... **987** Mats Sundin (420G, 567A)
**Most PIM, Career** ......... **2,265** Tie Domi
**Most Shutouts, Career** ........ **62** Turk Broda
**Longest Consecutive Games Streak** ........... **486** Tim Horton (Feb. 11/61-Feb. 4/68)
**Most Goals, Season** .......... **54** Rick Vaive (1981-82)
**Most Assists, Season** ......... **95** Doug Gilmour (1992-93)
**Most Points, Season** ........ **127** Doug Gilmour (1992-93; 32G, 95A)
**Most PIM, Season** .......... **365** Tie Domi (1997-98)
**Most Points, Defenseman, Season** .................. **79** Ian Turnbull (1976-77; 22G, 57A)
**Most Points, Center, Season** .................. **127** Doug Gilmour (1992-93; 32G, 95A)
**Most Points, Right Wing, Season** .................. **97** Wilf Paiement (1980-81; 40G, 57A)
**Most Points, Left Wing, Season** .................. **99** Dave Andreychuk (1993-94; 53G, 46A)
**Most Points, Rookie, Season** .................. **66** Peter Ihnacak (1982-83; 28G, 38A)
**Most Shutouts, Season** ....... **13** Harry Lumley (1953-54)
**Most Goals, Game** ............ **6** Corb Denneny (Jan. 26/21), Darryl Sittler (Feb. 7/76)
**Most Assists, Game** ........... **6** Babe Pratt (Jan. 8/44), Doug Gilmour (Feb. 13/93)
**Most Points, Game** .......... ***10** Darryl Sittler (Feb. 7/76; 6G, 4A)

* NHL Record.

### Retired Numbers

| | | |
|---|---|---|
| **5** | Bill Barilko | 1946-1951 |
| **6** | Ace Bailey | 1926-1934 |

### Honored Numbers

| | | |
|---|---|---|
| **1** | Turk Broda | 1936-43, 45-52 |
| | Johnny Bower | 1958-1970 |
| **4** | Hap Day | 1926-1937 |
| | Red Kelly | 1959-1967 |
| **7** | King Clancy | 1930-1937 |
| | Tim Horton | 1949-50, 51-70 |
| **9** | Charlie Conacher | 1929-1938 |
| | Ted Kennedy | 1942-55, 56-57 |
| **10** | Syl Apps | 1936-43, 45-48 |
| | George Armstrong | 1949-50, 51-71 |
| **17** | Wendel Clark | 1985-94, 96-98, 2000 |
| **21** | Borje Salming | 1973-1989 |
| **27** | Frank Mahovlich | 1956-1968 |
| | Darryl Sittler | 1970-1982 |
| **93** | Doug Gilmour | 1992-97, 2003 |

# All-time Record vs. Other Clubs

## Regular Season

| | At Home | | | | | | | | On Road | | | | | | | | Total | | | | | | | |
|---|---|---|---|---|---|---|---|---|---|---|---|---|---|---|---|---|---|---|---|---|---|---|---|---|
| | GP | W | L | T | OL | GF | GA | PTS | GP | W | L | T | OL | GF | GA | PTS | GP | W | L | T | OL | GF | GA | PTS |
| Anaheim | 17 | 10 | 2 | 4 | 1 | 55 | 35 | 25 | 12 | 5 | 6 | 1 | 0 | 28 | 39 | 11 | 29 | 15 | 8 | 5 | 1 | 83 | 74 | 36 |
| Atlanta | 17 | 10 | 4 | 1 | 2 | 62 | 45 | 23 | 17 | 11 | 4 | 0 | 2 | 63 | 33 | 24 | 34 | 21 | 8 | 1 | 4 | 125 | 78 | 47 |
| Boston | 314 | 161 | 101 | 51 | 1 | 1044 | 823 | 374 | 313 | 96 | 166 | 47 | 4 | 838 | 1016 | 243 | 627 | 257 | 267 | 98 | 5 | 1882 | 1839 | 617 |
| Buffalo | 82 | 32 | 36 | 12 | 2 | 242 | 284 | 78 | 84 | 25 | 52 | 6 | 1 | 221 | 332 | 57 | 166 | 57 | 88 | 18 | 3 | 463 | 616 | 135 |
| Calgary | 55 | 30 | 17 | 7 | 1 | 215 | 199 | 68 | 63 | 22 | 34 | 5 | 2 | 198 | 244 | 51 | 118 | 52 | 51 | 12 | 3 | 413 | 443 | 119 |
| Carolina | 44 | 17 | 21 | 5 | 1 | 145 | 155 | 40 | 45 | 16 | 20 | 6 | 3 | 147 | 172 | 41 | 89 | 33 | 41 | 11 | 4 | 292 | 327 | 81 |
| Chicago | 317 | 164 | 98 | 54 | 1 | 1079 | 832 | 383 | 319 | 120 | 157 | 42 | 0 | 832 | 971 | 282 | 636 | 284 | 255 | 96 | 1 | 1911 | 1803 | 665 |
| Colorado | 36 | 16 | 16 | 4 | 0 | 119 | 137 | 36 | 31 | 8 | 18 | 5 | 0 | 97 | 120 | 21 | 67 | 24 | 34 | 9 | 0 | 216 | 257 | 57 |
| Columbus | 5 | 3 | 0 | 1 | 1 | 16 | 9 | 8 | 2 | 1 | 0 | 0 | 1 | 7 | 6 | 3 | 7 | 4 | 0 | 1 | 2 | 23 | 15 | 11 |
| Dallas | 103 | 49 | 37 | 17 | 0 | 359 | 329 | 115 | 98 | 36 | 51 | 11 | 0 | 307 | 368 | 83 | 201 | 85 | 88 | 28 | 0 | 666 | 697 | 198 |
| Detroit | 317 | 165 | 105 | 47 | 0 | 1048 | 848 | 377 | 324 | 109 | 169 | 46 | 0 | 796 | 975 | 264 | 641 | 274 | 274 | 93 | 0 | 1844 | 1823 | 641 |
| Edmonton | 39 | 21 | 16 | 2 | 0 | 159 | 161 | 44 | 45 | 16 | 22 | 6 | 1 | 146 | 182 | 39 | 84 | 37 | 38 | 8 | 1 | 305 | 343 | 83 |
| Florida | 23 | 13 | 7 | 2 | 1 | 74 | 66 | 29 | 25 | 12 | 7 | 5 | 1 | 73 | 69 | 30 | 48 | 25 | 14 | 7 | 2 | 147 | 135 | 59 |
| Los Angeles | 69 | 35 | 23 | 11 | 0 | 267 | 225 | 81 | 67 | 22 | 35 | 10 | 0 | 196 | 240 | 54 | 136 | 57 | 58 | 21 | 0 | 463 | 465 | 135 |
| Minnesota | 4 | 4 | 0 | 0 | 0 | 15 | 6 | 8 | 3 | 1 | 2 | 0 | 0 | 5 | 11 | 2 | 7 | 5 | 2 | 0 | 0 | 20 | 17 | 10 |
| Montreal | 348 | 180 | 119 | 45 | 4 | 1063 | 918 | 409 | 348 | 99 | 204 | 43 | 2 | 873 | 1216 | 243 | 696 | 279 | 323 | 88 | 6 | 1936 | 2134 | 652 |
| Nashville | 8 | 3 | 4 | 1 | 0 | 16 | 21 | 7 | 2 | 0 | 1 | 0 | 1 | 4 | 7 | 1 | 10 | 3 | 5 | 1 | 1 | 20 | 28 | 8 |
| New Jersey | 56 | 35 | 15 | 5 | 1 | 198 | 155 | 76 | 54 | 19 | 18 | 15 | 2 | 170 | 183 | 55 | 110 | 54 | 33 | 20 | 3 | 368 | 338 | 131 |
| NY Islanders | 63 | 34 | 24 | 4 | 1 | 226 | 207 | 73 | 61 | 23 | 32 | 3 | 3 | 176 | 234 | 52 | 124 | 57 | 56 | 7 | 4 | 402 | 441 | 125 |
| NY Rangers | 290 | 163 | 86 | 39 | 2 | 1001 | 765 | 367 | 291 | 111 | 121 | 56 | 3 | 857 | 896 | 281 | 581 | 274 | 207 | 95 | 5 | 1858 | 1661 | 648 |
| Ottawa | 37 | 17 | 14 | 2 | 4 | 100 | 111 | 40 | 35 | 12 | 19 | 1 | 3 | 94 | 114 | 28 | 72 | 29 | 33 | 3 | 7 | 194 | 225 | 68 |
| Philadelphia | 75 | 29 | 31 | 14 | 1 | 236 | 245 | 73 | 75 | 21 | 45 | 8 | 1 | 181 | 280 | 51 | 150 | 50 | 76 | 22 | 2 | 417 | 525 | 124 |
| Phoenix | 44 | 20 | 22 | 2 | 0 | 160 | 165 | 42 | 41 | 13 | 22 | 6 | 0 | 146 | 172 | 32 | 85 | 33 | 44 | 8 | 0 | 306 | 337 | 74 |
| Pittsburgh | 75 | 38 | 25 | 11 | 1 | 301 | 242 | 88 | 77 | 31 | 40 | 6 | 0 | 250 | 307 | 68 | 152 | 69 | 65 | 17 | 1 | 551 | 549 | 156 |
| St. Louis | 101 | 58 | 29 | 11 | 3 | 375 | 300 | 130 | 103 | 31 | 58 | 14 | 0 | 285 | 349 | 76 | 204 | 89 | 87 | 25 | 3 | 660 | 649 | 206 |
| San Jose | 19 | 12 | 5 | 2 | 0 | 73 | 52 | 26 | 17 | 7 | 7 | 3 | 0 | 44 | 40 | 17 | 36 | 19 | 12 | 5 | 0 | 117 | 92 | 43 |
| Tampa Bay | 29 | 19 | 9 | 1 | 0 | 107 | 76 | 39 | 28 | 19 | 6 | 1 | 2 | 93 | 65 | 41 | 57 | 38 | 15 | 2 | 2 | 200 | 141 | 80 |
| Vancouver | 62 | 28 | 22 | 11 | 1 | 222 | 204 | 68 | 66 | 24 | 31 | 11 | 0 | 221 | 233 | 59 | 128 | 52 | 53 | 22 | 1 | 443 | 437 | 127 |
| Washington | 56 | 30 | 20 | 6 | 0 | 233 | 188 | 66 | 58 | 21 | 33 | 4 | 0 | 164 | 206 | 46 | 114 | 51 | 53 | 10 | 0 | 397 | 394 | 112 |
| Defunct Clubs | 232 | 158 | 53 | 21 | 0 | 860 | 515 | 337 | 233 | 84 | 120 | 29 | 0 | 607 | 745 | 197 | 465 | 242 | 173 | 50 | 0 | 1467 | 1260 | 534 |
| **Totals** | **2937** | **1554** | **961** | **393** | **29** | **10070** | **8318** | **3530** | **2937** | **1015** | **1500** | **390** | **32** | **8119** | **9825** | **2452** | **5874** | **2569** | **2461** | **783** | **61** | **18189** | **18143** | **5982** |

## Playoffs

| | Series | W | L | GP | W | L | T | GF | GA | Last Mtg. | Rnd. | Result |
|---|---|---|---|---|---|---|---|---|---|---|---|---|
| Boston | 13 | 8 | 5 | 62 | 31 | 30 | 1 | 150 | 153 | 1974 | QF | L 0-4 |
| Buffalo | 1 | 0 | 1 | 5 | 1 | 4 | 0 | 16 | 21 | 1999 | CF | L 1-4 |
| Calgary | 1 | 1 | 0 | 2 | 2 | 0 | 0 | 9 | 5 | 1979 | PRE | W 2-0 |
| Carolina | 1 | 0 | 1 | 6 | 2 | 4 | 0 | 6 | 10 | 2002 | CF | L 2-4 |
| Chicago | 9 | 6 | 3 | 38 | 22 | 15 | 1 | 111 | 89 | 1995 | CQF | L 3-4 |
| Dallas | 2 | 0 | 2 | 7 | 1 | 6 | 0 | 26 | 35 | 1983 | DSF | L 1-3 |
| Detroit | 23 | 12 | 11 | 117 | 58 | 59 | 0 | 311 | 321 | 1993 | DSF | W 4-3 |
| Los Angeles | 3 | 2 | 1 | 12 | 7 | 5 | 0 | 41 | 31 | 1993 | CF | L 3-4 |
| Montreal | 15 | 7 | 8 | 71 | 29 | 42 | 0 | 160 | 215 | 1979 | QF | L 0-4 |
| New Jersey | 2 | 0 | 2 | 13 | 5 | 8 | 0 | 27 | 37 | 2001 | CSF | L 3-4 |
| NY Islanders | 3 | 2 | 1 | 17 | 8 | 9 | 0 | 42 | 54 | 2002 | CQF | W 4-3 |
| NY Rangers | 8 | 3 | 5 | 35 | 16 | 19 | 0 | 86 | 86 | 1971 | QF | L 2-4 |
| Ottawa | 4 | 4 | 0 | 24 | 16 | 8 | 0 | 57 | 42 | 2004 | CQF | W 4-3 |
| Philadelphia | 6 | 1 | 5 | 36 | 14 | 22 | 0 | 85 | 119 | 2004 | CSF | L 2-4 |
| Pittsburgh | 3 | 3 | 0 | 12 | 8 | 4 | 0 | 39 | 27 | 1999 | CSF | W 4-2 |
| St. Louis | 5 | 2 | 3 | 31 | 14 | 17 | 0 | 90 | 88 | 1996 | CQF | L 2-4 |
| San Jose | 1 | 1 | 0 | 7 | 4 | 3 | 0 | 26 | 21 | 1994 | CSF | W 4-3 |
| Vancouver | 1 | 0 | 1 | 5 | 1 | 4 | 0 | 9 | 16 | 1994 | CF | L 1-4 |
| Defunct Clubs | 8 | 6 | 2 | 24 | 12 | 10 | 2 | 59 | 57 | | | |
| **Totals** | **109** | **58** | **51** | **524** | **251** | **269** | **4** | **1350** | **1427** | | | |

## Playoff Results 2009-2004

| Year | Round | Opponent | Result | GF | GA |
|---|---|---|---|---|---|
| 2004 | CSF | Philadelphia | L 2-4 | 13 | 17 |
| | CQF | Ottawa | W 4-3 | 14 | 11 |

**Abbreviations: Round: CF** – conference final; **CSF** – conference semi-final; **CQF** – conference quarter-final; **DSF** – division semi-final; **QF** – quarter-final; **PRE** – preliminary round.

Calgary totals include Atlanta Flames, 1972-73 to 1979-80.
Carolina totals include Hartford, 1979-80 to 1996-97.
Colorado totals include Quebec, 1979-80 to 1994-95.
Dallas totals include Minnesota North Stars, 1967-68 to 1992-93.
New Jersey totals include Kansas City, 1974-75, 1975-76, and Colorado Rockies, 1976-77 to 1981-82.
Phoenix totals include Winnipeg, 1979-80 to 1995-96.

## 2008-09 Results

| | | | | | | | |
|---|---|---|---|---|---|---|---|
| **Oct.** | 9 | at Detroit | 3-2 | | 10 | at Philadelphia | 1-4 |
| | 11 | Montreal | 1-6 | | 13 | Nashville | 0-2 |
| | 13 | St. Louis | 4-5† | | 15 | at Carolina | 6-4 |
| | 17 | at NY Rangers | 0-1† | | 16 | at Atlanta | 3-4* |
| | 18 | at Pittsburgh | 1-4 | | 19 | Carolina | 0-2 |
| | 21 | Anaheim | 2-3† | | 21 | Boston | 3-4† |
| | 23 | at Boston | 4-2 | | 27 | at Minnesota | 1-6 |
| | 25 | Ottawa | 3-2 | | 29 | at Colorado | 7-4 |
| | 28 | Tampa Bay | 2-3 | | 31 | Pittsburgh | 5-4 |
| | 29 | at New Jersey | 6-5† | **Feb.** | 3 | Florida | 3-4* |
| **Nov.** | 1 | NY Rangers | 5-2 | | 4 | at Buffalo | 0-5 |
| | 2 | at Carolina | 4-6 | | 7 | at Montreal | 5-2 |
| | 4 | Carolina | 4-5* | | 10 | at Florida | 4-5* |
| | 6 | at Boston | 2-5 | | 12 | at Tampa Bay | 4-6 |
| | 8 | Montreal | 6-3 | | 14 | Pittsburgh | 6-2 |
| | 11 | at Calgary | 3-4 | | 17 | Buffalo | 1-4 |
| | 13 | at Edmonton | 5-2 | | 19 | Columbus | 3-4† |
| | 15 | at Vancouver | 2-4 | | 21 | Vancouver | 2-3† |
| | 17 | Boston | 2-3 | | 22 | at NY Rangers | 3-2* |
| | 22 | Chicago | 4-5* | | 25 | NY Rangers | 2-1† |
| | 25 | Atlanta | 3-6 | | 26 | at NY Islanders | 5-4† |
| | 27 | at Ottawa | 1-2† | | 28 | at Ottawa | 4-3* |
| | 29 | Philadelphia | 4-2 | **Mar.** | 3 | New Jersey | 2-3* |
| **Dec.** | 1 | at Los Angeles | 3-1 | | 5 | at Washington | 2-1 |
| | 2 | at San Jose | 2-5 | | 7 | Edmonton | 1-4 |
| | 4 | at Phoenix | 3-6 | | 9 | at Ottawa | 1-2 |
| | 6 | Washington | 1-2 | | 10 | NY Islanders | 3-2* |
| | 8 | NY Islanders | 4-2 | | 12 | Tampa Bay | 1-4 |
| | 12 | at Buffalo | 2-1 | | 14 | Calgary | 8-6 |
| | 16 | New Jersey | 3-2† | | 17 | at Tampa Bay | 4-3† |
| | 18 | at Boston | 5-8 | | 19 | at Florida | 1-3 |
| | 20 | at Pittsburgh | 7-3 | | 21 | at Montreal | 5-2 |
| | 22 | at Atlanta | 6-2 | | 24 | Washington | 3-2† |
| | 23 | Dallas | 2-8 | | 27 | at Buffalo | 3-5 |
| | 26 | at NY Islanders | 1-4 | | 28 | Boston | 5-7 |
| | 28 | at Washington | 1-4 | **Apr.** | 1 | Philadelphia | 3-2 |
| | 30 | Atlanta | 4-3* | | 3 | at Philadelphia | 5-8 |
| **Jan.** | 1 | Buffalo | 1-4 | | 4 | Montreal | 2-6 |
| | 3 | Ottawa | 3-1 | | 7 | at New Jersey | 4-1 |
| | 6 | Florida | 2-4 | | 8 | Buffalo | 1-3 |
| | 8 | at Montreal | 2-6 | | 11 | Ottawa | 5-2 |

* – Overtime † – Shootout

## Entry Draft Selections 2009-1995

Name in bold denotes played in NHL.

**2009**
Pick
7 Nazem Kadri
50 Kenny Ryan
58 Jesse Blacker
68 Jamie Devane
128 Eric Knodel
158 Jerry D'Amigo
188 Barron Smith

**2008**
Pick
5 **Luke Schenn**
60 Jimmy Hayes
98 Mikhail Stefanovich
128 Greg Pateryn
129 Joel Champagne
130 Jerome Flaake
158 Grant Rollheiser
188 Andrew MacWilliam

**2007**
Pick
74 Dale Mitchell
99 Matt Frattin
104 Ben Winnett
134 Juraj Mikus
164 Christopher Didomenico
194 Carl Gunnarsson

**2006**
Pick
13 **Jiri Tlusty**
44 **Nikolai Kulemin**
99 James Reimer
111 Korbinian Holzer
161 Viktor Stahlberg
166 Tyler Ruegsegger
180 Leo Komarov

**2005**
Pick
21 **Tuukka Rask**
82 **Phil Oreskovic**
153 Alex Berry
173 Johan Dahlberg
216 **Anton Stralman**
228 Chad Rau

**2004**
Pick
90 **Justin Pogge**
113 Roman Kukumberg
157 Dmitri Vorobiev
187 **Robbie Earl**
220 Maxim Semenov
252 Jan Steber
285 Pierce Norton

**2003**
Pick
57 John Doherty
91 Martin Sagat
125 Konstantin Volkov
158 **John Mitchell**
220 **Jeremy Williams**
237 Shaun Landolt

**2002**
Pick
24 **Alex Steen**
57 **Matt Stajan**
74 Todd Ford
88 Dominic D'Amour
122 David Turon
191 **Ian White**
222 Scott May
254 **Jarkko Immonen**
285 **Staffan Kronwall**

**2001**
Pick
17 **Carlo Colaiacovo**
39 **Karel Pilar**
65 **Brendan Bell**
82 **Jay Harrison**
88 Nicolas Corbeil
134 **Kyle Wellwood**
168 **Maxim Kondratiev**
183 Jaroslav Sklenar
198 Ivan Kolozvary
213 Jan Chovan
246 **Tomas Mojzis**
276 Mike Knoepfli

**2000**
Pick
24 **Brad Boyes**
51 **Kris Vernarsky**
70 **Mikael Tellqvist**
90 Jean-Francois Racine
100 Miguel Delisle
179 Vadim Sozinov
209 Markus Seikola
223 Lubos Velebny
254 Alexander Shinkar
265 **Jean-Philippe Cote**

**1999**
Pick
24 Luca Cereda
60 Peter Reynolds
108 Mirko Murovic
110 Jon Zion
151 Vaclav Zavoral
161 Jan Sochor
211 Vladimir Kulikov
239 **Pierre Hedin**
267 Peter Metcalf

**1998**
Pick
10 **Nik Antropov**
35 **Petr Svoboda**
69 Jamie Hodson
87 **Alexei Ponikarovsky**
126 Morgan Warren
154 **Allan Rourke**
181 Jonathan Gagnon
215 Dwight Wolfe
228 Michal Travnicek
236 Sergei Rostov

**1997**
Pick
57 **Jeff Farkas**
84 **Adam Mair**
111 Frantisek Mrazek
138 Eric Gooldy
165 Hugo Marchand
190 **Shawn Thornton**
194 Russ Bartlett
221 **Jonathan Hedstrom**

**1996**
Pick
36 **Marek Posmyk**
50 Francis Larivee
66 Mike Lankshear
68 Konstantin Kalmikov
86 Jason Sessa
103 Vladimir Antipov
110 Peter Cava
111 Brandon Sugden
140 **Dmitri Yakushin**
148 Chris Bogas
151 Lucio DeMartinis
178 Reggie Berg
204 **Tomas Kaberle**
230 Jared Hope

**1995**
Pick
15 **Jeff Ware**
54 Ryan Pepperall
139 Doug Bonner
145 **Yannick Tremblay**
171 Marek Melenovsky
197 Mark Murphy
223 **Danny Markov**

### General Managers' History

Charles Querrie, 1917-18 to 1926-27; Conn Smythe, 1927-28 to 1956-57; Hap Day, 1957-58; Punch Imlach, 1958-59 to 1968-69; Jim Gregory, 1969-70 to 1978-79; Punch Imlach, 1979-80, 1980-81; Punch Imlach and Gerry McNamara, 1981-82; Gerry McNamara, 1982-83 to 1987-88; Gord Stellick, 1988-89; Floyd Smith, 1989-90, 1990-91; Cliff Fletcher, 1991-92 to 1996-97; Ken Dryden, 1997-98, 1998-99; Pat Quinn, 1999-2000 to 2002-03; John Ferguson, 2003-04 to 2006-07; John Ferguson and Cliff Fletcher, 2007-08; Cliff Fletcher and Brian Burke, 2008-09; Brian Burke, 2009-10.

## Brian Burke

### President and General Manager

*Born: Providence, RI, June 30, 1955.*

Brian Burke was named president and general manager of the Toronto Maple Leafs on November 29, 2008, bringing over 20 years of National Hockey League experience in various roles to the franchise. Most recently, Burke had served as executive vice president and general manager of the Anaheim Ducks from 2005 to 2008. In just over three seasons in Anaheim, Burke guided the Ducks to their first Stanley Cup (2007), first Pacific Division title (2007), and first-two 100+ point seasons (2006-07 and 2007-08).

Burke received two outstanding honours in the summer of 2008. On June 6, he was chosen by USA Hockey as general manager of the 2010 U.S. Olympic hockey team, and on August 7, he was named a recipient of the 2008 Lester Patrick Award for outstanding service to hockey in the United States. Burke was also ranked number one by The Hockey News in the magazine's Annual GM rankings in March of 2008, and was a finalist for The Hockey News Executive of the Year in 2006. He was named The Sporting News Executive of the Year in 2001, and was a runner-up for the same award following the 2005-06 season.

Burke joined the Ducks after a six-year stint (1998 to 2004) as president and general manager of the Vancouver Canucks where he revitalized the team en route to consecutive 100+ point seasons and the 2004 Northwest Division title. Under Burke's leadership, the Canucks improved their point total in four consecutive years from 1999-2003.

Born in Providence, Rhode Island and raised in Edina, Minnesota, Burke was named the vice president and director of hockey operations by the Vancouver Canucks in June of 1987. Burke left Vancouver to serve as general manager of the Hartford Whalers for one season in 1992, before joining the NHL front office as senior vice president and director of hockey operations in September of 1993.

After earning his Bachelor of Arts in history from Providence College in 1977, Burke signed with the Philadelphia Flyers prior to the 1977-78 season and won a Calder Cup championship with the Flyers' American Hockey League affiliate the Maine Mariners. He then returned to school and graduated from Harvard Law in 1981. Burke practiced law in Boston for the next six years, representing professional hockey players until joining the Canucks in 1987.

# Club Directory

Air Canada Centre

**Toronto Maple Leafs**
Air Canada Centre
40 Bay St., Suite 400
Toronto, Ontario M5J 2X2
Phone **416/815-5700**
FAX 416/359-9331
www.mapleleafs.com
**Capacity:** 18,819

**Board of Directors**
Lawrence M. Tanenbaum (Chairman of the Board), Robert G. Bertram, Erol Uzumeri, Dean Metcalf, Glen Silvestri, Ivan Fecan, Robert MacLellan, Dale H. Lastman, Richard Peddie

**Maple Leaf Sports & Entertainment**

| | |
|---|---|
| Chairman, NHL Governor | Lawrence M. Tanenbaum |
| President, Chief Executive Officer and Alternate NHL Governor | Richard Peddie |
| Alternate NHL Governor | Erol Uzumeri |
| Alternate NHL Governor | Dale H. Lastman |
| Executive Vice-President, Chief Operating Officer | Tom Anselmi |
| Executive V.P., CFO & Business Development | Ian Clarke |
| Executive Vice-President, Venues and Entertainment | Bob Hunter |
| Sr. V.P., General Counsel and Corporate Secretary | Robin Brudner |
| Senior Vice-President, People | Mardi Walker |
| Senior Vice-President, Broadcast and Content | Chris Hebb |
| Sr. V.P., Corporate and Community Partnerships | Dave Hopkinson |
| Senior Vice-President, Finance | Kevin Nonomura |
| Senior Vice-President, Ticket Sales and Service | Beth Robertson |
| Vice-President, Live Entertainment | Patti-Anne Tarlton |
| Vice-President, Food & Beverage | Michael Doyle |
| President, General Manager, Toronto Raptors | Bryan Colangelo |

**Management**

| | |
|---|---|
| President, G.M. and Alt. Governor | Brian Burke |
| Senior Vice-President of Hockey Operations | David Nonis |
| Vice-President of Hockey Operations | Dave Poulin |
| Assit. G.M. and Director of Hockey Operations | Jeff Jackson |
| Senior Advisor | Cliff Fletcher |
| Head Coach | Ron Wilson |
| Assistant Coaches | Keith Acton, Tim Hunter, Rob Zettler |
| Goaltending Consultant | Francois Allaire |
| Goaltending Coach | Corey Hirsch |
| Skating Coach | Graeme Townshend |
| Head Coach, Toronto Marlies AHL | Dallas Eakins |
| Player Development Coach | Paul Dennis |
| Director, Hockey and Scouting Administration | Reid Mitchell |
| Strength and Conditioning Coordinator | Anthony Belza |
| Manager, Team Services | Dave Griffiths |
| Video Analyst | Chris Dennis |
| Director of Pro Scouting | Mike Penny |
| Director of Amateur Scouting | Dave Morrison |
| Pro Scout | Tom Watt |
| Amateur Scouts | Gary Harker, John Lilley, Garth Malarchuk, Mike Palmateer, Allan Power, George Armstrong |
| European Scouts | Thommie Bergman, Peter Ihnacak, Nikolai Ladygin, Jari Gronstrand |
| Community Representatives | Wendel Clark, Darryl Sittler |
| Assistant to the General Manager's Office | Brad Lynn |

**Medical and Training Staff**

| | |
|---|---|
| Head Athletic Therapist | Andy Playter |
| Equipment Manager | Brian Papineau |
| Assistant Equipment Managers | Tom Blatchford, Bobby Hastings |
| Medical Director, Maple Leafs and Marlies | Dr. Noah Forman |
| Orthopedic Consultant | Dr. John Theodoropoulos |
| Team Dentists | Dr. Marvin Lean, Dr. Charles Goldberg |

**Communications**

| | |
|---|---|
| Director, Media Relations | Pat Park |
| Coordinators, Media Relations | Craig Downey, Aaron Gogishvili |

**Television and Radio Broadcast Information**

| | |
|---|---|
| Senior Vice-President, Broadcast and Content | Chris Hebb |
| Senior Networks Producer | Mark Askin |
| Game Director | Jacques Primeau |
| Talent, Leafs TV | Joe Bowen, Paul Hendrick, Bob McGill, Greg Millen, Andi Petrillo, Marc Moro |
| AM 640 Toronto Radio, Play-By-Play | Joe Bowen, Dennis Beyak (mid-week) |
| AM 640 Toronto Radio, Analyst | Jim Ralph |
| Television Play-By-Play | Joe Bowen (mid-week) |
| Television Analysts | Bob McGill, Greg Millen |

# Vancouver Canucks

## 2008-09 Results: 45W-27L-3OTL-7SOL 100PTS.
## First, Northwest Division

### Key Off-Season Signings/Acquisitions

**2009**

**May 14** • Re-signed RW **Steve Bernier.**
**27** • Re-signed C **Rick Rypien.**
**July 1** • Re-signed LW **Daniel Sedin** and C **Henrik Sedin.**
**3** • Signed RW **Mikael Samuelsson.**
**6** • Re-signed D **Shane O'Brien.**
**6** • Signed G **Andrew Raycroft.**
**31** • C **Kyle Wellwood** awarded one-year contract in arbitration.
**Aug. 5** • Re-signed RW **Jannik Hansen.**

*Ryan Kesler was the Canucks' top scorer in 2008-09 not named Sedin, reaching career highs in goals (26), assists (33) and points (59). Alexandre Burrows scored 28 times after scoring just 22 goals during his first three NHL seasons.*

### 2009-10 Schedule

| Month | Day | Date | Opponent |
|---|---|---|---|
| **Oct.** | Thu. | 1 | at Calgary |
| | Sat. | 3 | at Colorado* |
| | Mon. | 5 | Columbus |
| | Wed. | 7 | Montreal |
| | Sun. | 11 | Dallas |
| | Fri. | 16 | at Calgary |
| | Sat. | 17 | Minnesota |
| | Mon. | 19 | at Edmonton |
| | Wed. | 21 | at Chicago |
| | Sat. | 24 | Toronto* |
| | Sun. | 25 | Edmonton |
| | Tue. | 27 | Detroit |
| | Thu. | 29 | at Los Angeles |
| | Fri. | 30 | at Anaheim |
| **Nov.** | Sun. | 1 | Colorado |
| | Tue. | 3 | NY Rangers |
| | Thu. | 5 | at Minnesota |
| | Fri. | 6 | at Dallas |
| | Tue. | 10 | at St. Louis |
| | Thu. | 12 | at Detroit |
| | Sat. | 14 | at Colorado |
| | Fri. | 20 | Colorado |
| | Sun. | 22 | Chicago |
| | Thu. | 26 | Los Angeles |
| | Sat. | 28 | Edmonton |
| | Sun. | 29 | San Jose |
| **Dec.** | Wed. | 2 | at New Jersey |
| | Thu. | 3 | at Philadelphia |
| | Sat. | 5 | at Carolina* |
| | Tue. | 8 | at Nashville |
| | Thu. | 10 | Atlanta |
| | Sat. | 12 | Minnesota |
| | Mon. | 14 | Los Angeles |
| | Wed. | 16 | Anaheim |
| | Fri. | 18 | Washington |
| | Sun. | 20 | St. Louis |
| | Tue. | 22 | Nashville |
| | Sat. | 26 | Edmonton |
| | Sun. | 27 | at Calgary |
| | Tue. | 29 | at Phoenix |
| | Thu. | 31 | at St. Louis |
| **Jan.** | Sat. | 2 | at Dallas* |
| | Tue. | 5 | Columbus |
| | Thu. | 7 | Phoenix |
| | Sat. | 9 | Calgary |
| | Mon. | 11 | Nashville |
| | Wed. | 13 | at Minnesota |
| | Sat. | 16 | Pittsburgh |
| | Wed. | 20 | at Edmonton |
| | Thu. | 21 | Dallas |
| | Sat. | 23 | Chicago |
| | Mon. | 25 | Buffalo |
| | Wed. | 27 | St. Louis |
| | Sat. | 30 | at Toronto |
| **Feb.** | Tue. | 2 | at Montreal |
| | Thu. | 4 | at Ottawa |
| | Sat. | 6 | at Boston* |
| | Tue. | 9 | at Tampa Bay |
| | Thu. | 11 | at Florida |
| | Fri. | 12 | at Columbus |
| | Sun. | 14 | at Minnesota* |
| **Mar.** | Tue. | 2 | at Columbus |
| | Wed. | 3 | at Detroit |
| | Fri. | 5 | at Chicago |
| | Sun. | 7 | at Nashville* |
| | Tue. | 9 | at Colorado |
| | Wed. | 10 | at Phoenix |
| | Sat. | 13 | Ottawa |
| | Sun. | 14 | Calgary |
| | Tue. | 16 | NY Islanders |
| | Thu. | 18 | San Jose |
| | Sat. | 20 | Detroit |
| | Tue. | 23 | at Edmonton |
| | Wed. | 24 | Anaheim |
| | Sat. | 27 | at San Jose |
| | Tue. | 30 | Phoenix |
| **Apr.** | Thu. | 1 | at Los Angeles |
| | Fri. | 2 | at Anaheim |
| | Sun. | 4 | Minnesota |
| | Tue. | 6 | Colorado |
| | Thu. | 8 | at San Jose |
| | Sat. | 10 | Calgary |

* Denotes afternoon game.

### Year-by-Year Record

| | | Home | | | | Road | | | | Overall | | | | | | | | |
|---|---|---|---|---|---|---|---|---|---|---|---|---|---|---|---|---|---|---|
| Season | GP | W | L | T | OL | W | L | T | OL | W | L | T | OL | GF | GA | Pts. | Finished | Playoff Result |
| 2008-09 | 82 | 24 | 12 | .... | 5 | 21 | 15 | .... | 5 | 45 | 27 | .... | 10 | 246 | 220 | 100 | 1st, Northwest Div. | Lost Conf. Semi-Final |
| 2007-08 | 82 | 21 | 15 | .... | 5 | 18 | 18 | .... | 5 | 39 | 33 | .... | 10 | 213 | 215 | 88 | 5th, Northwest Div. | Out of Playoffs |
| 2006-07 | 82 | 26 | 11 | .... | 4 | 23 | 15 | .... | 3 | 49 | 26 | .... | 7 | 222 | 201 | 105 | 1st, Northwest Div. | Lost Conf. Semi-Final |
| 2005-06 | 82 | 25 | 10 | .... | 6 | 17 | 22 | .... | 2 | 42 | 32 | .... | 8 | 256 | 255 | 92 | 4th, Northwest Div. | Out of Playoffs |
| 2004-05 | .... | .... | .... | .... | .... | .... | .... | .... | .... | .... | .... | .... | .... | .... | .... | .... | | |
| 2003-04 | 82 | 21 | 13 | 7 | 0 | 22 | 11 | 3 | 5 | 43 | 24 | 10 | 5 | 235 | 194 | 101 | 1st, Northwest Div. | Lost Conf. Quarter-Final |
| 2002-03 | 82 | 22 | 13 | 6 | 0 | 23 | 10 | 7 | 1 | 45 | 23 | 13 | 1 | 264 | 208 | 104 | 2nd, Northwest Div. | Lost Conf. Semi-Final |
| 2001-02 | 82 | 23 | 11 | 5 | 2 | 19 | 19 | 2 | 1 | 42 | 30 | 7 | 3 | 254 | 211 | 94 | 2nd, Northwest Div. | Lost Conf. Quarter-Final |
| 2000-01 | 82 | 21 | 12 | 5 | 3 | 15 | 16 | 6 | 4 | 36 | 28 | 11 | 7 | 239 | 238 | 90 | 3rd, Northwest Div. | Lost Conf. Quarter-Final |
| 1999-2000 | 82 | 16 | 14 | 5 | 6 | 14 | 15 | 10 | 2 | 30 | 29 | 15 | 8 | 227 | 237 | 83 | 3rd, Northwest Div. | Out of Playoffs |
| 1998-99 | 82 | 14 | 21 | 6 | .... | 9 | 26 | 6 | .... | 23 | 47 | 12 | .... | 192 | 258 | 58 | 4th, Northwest Div. | Out of Playoffs |
| 1997-98 | 82 | 15 | 22 | 4 | .... | 10 | 21 | 10 | .... | 25 | 43 | 14 | .... | 224 | 273 | 64 | 7th, Pacific Div. | Out of Playoffs |
| 1996-97 | 82 | 20 | 17 | 4 | .... | 15 | 23 | 3 | .... | 35 | 40 | 7 | .... | 257 | 273 | 77 | 4th, Pacific Div. | Out of Playoffs |
| 1995-96 | 82 | 15 | 19 | 7 | .... | 17 | 16 | 8 | .... | 32 | 35 | 15 | .... | 278 | 278 | 79 | 3rd, Pacific Div. | Lost Conf. Quarter-Final |
| 1994-95 | 48 | 10 | 8 | 6 | .... | 8 | 10 | 6 | .... | 18 | 18 | 12 | .... | 153 | 148 | 48 | 2nd, Pacific Div. | Lost Conf. Semi-Final |
| 1993-94 | 84 | 20 | 19 | 3 | .... | 21 | 21 | 0 | .... | 41 | 40 | 3 | .... | 279 | 276 | 85 | 2nd, Pacific Div. | Lost Final |
| 1992-93 | 84 | 27 | 11 | 4 | .... | 19 | 18 | 5 | .... | 46 | 29 | 9 | .... | 346 | 278 | 101 | 1st, Smythe Div. | Lost Div. Final |
| 1991-92 | 80 | 23 | 10 | 7 | .... | 19 | 16 | 5 | .... | 42 | 26 | 12 | .... | 285 | 250 | 96 | 1st, Smythe Div. | Lost Div. Final |
| 1990-91 | 80 | 18 | 17 | 5 | .... | 10 | 26 | 4 | .... | 28 | 43 | 9 | .... | 243 | 315 | 65 | 4th, Smythe Div. | Lost Div. Semi-Final |
| 1989-90 | 80 | 13 | 16 | 11 | .... | 12 | 25 | 3 | .... | 25 | 41 | 14 | .... | 245 | 306 | 64 | 5th, Smythe Div. | Out of Playoffs |
| 1988-89 | 80 | 19 | 15 | 6 | .... | 14 | 24 | 2 | .... | 33 | 39 | 8 | .... | 251 | 253 | 74 | 4th, Smythe Div. | Lost Div. Semi-Final |
| 1987-88 | 80 | 15 | 20 | 5 | .... | 10 | 26 | 4 | .... | 25 | 46 | 9 | .... | 272 | 320 | 59 | 5th, Smythe Div. | Out of Playoffs |
| 1986-87 | 80 | 17 | 19 | 4 | .... | 12 | 24 | 4 | .... | 29 | 43 | 8 | .... | 282 | 314 | 66 | 5th, Smythe Div. | Out of Playoffs |
| 1985-86 | 80 | 17 | 18 | 5 | .... | 6 | 26 | 8 | .... | 23 | 44 | 13 | .... | 282 | 333 | 59 | 4th, Smythe Div. | Lost Div. Semi-Final |
| 1984-85 | 80 | 15 | 21 | 4 | .... | 10 | 25 | 5 | .... | 25 | 46 | 9 | .... | 284 | 401 | 59 | 5th, Smythe Div. | Out of Playoffs |
| 1983-84 | 80 | 20 | 16 | 4 | .... | 12 | 23 | 5 | .... | 32 | 39 | 9 | .... | 306 | 328 | 73 | 3rd, Smythe Div. | Lost Div. Semi-Final |
| 1982-83 | 80 | 20 | 12 | 8 | .... | 10 | 23 | 7 | .... | 30 | 35 | 15 | .... | 303 | 309 | 75 | 3rd, Smythe Div. | Lost Div. Semi-Final |
| 1981-82 | 80 | 20 | 8 | 12 | .... | 10 | 25 | 5 | .... | 30 | 33 | 17 | .... | 290 | 286 | 77 | 2nd, Smythe Div. | Lost Final |
| 1980-81 | 80 | 17 | 12 | 11 | .... | 11 | 20 | 9 | .... | 28 | 32 | 20 | .... | 289 | 301 | 76 | 3rd, Smythe Div. | Lost Prelim. Round |
| 1979-80 | 80 | 14 | 17 | 9 | .... | 13 | 20 | 7 | .... | 27 | 37 | 16 | .... | 256 | 281 | 70 | 3rd, Smythe Div. | Lost Prelim. Round |
| 1978-79 | 80 | 15 | 18 | 7 | .... | 10 | 24 | 6 | .... | 25 | 42 | 13 | .... | 217 | 291 | 63 | 2nd, Smythe Div. | Lost Prelim. Round |
| 1977-78 | 80 | 13 | 15 | 12 | .... | 7 | 28 | 5 | .... | 20 | 43 | 17 | .... | 239 | 320 | 57 | 3rd, Smythe Div. | Out of Playoffs |
| 1976-77 | 80 | 13 | 21 | 6 | .... | 12 | 21 | 7 | .... | 25 | 42 | 13 | .... | 235 | 294 | 63 | 4th, Smythe Div. | Out of Playoffs |
| 1975-76 | 80 | 22 | 11 | 7 | .... | 11 | 21 | 8 | .... | 33 | 32 | 15 | .... | 271 | 272 | 81 | 2nd, Smythe Div. | Lost Prelim. Round |
| 1974-75 | 80 | 23 | 12 | 5 | .... | 15 | 20 | 5 | .... | 38 | 32 | 10 | .... | 271 | 254 | 86 | 1st, Smythe Div. | Lost Quarter-Final |
| 1973-74 | 78 | 14 | 18 | 7 | .... | 10 | 25 | 4 | .... | 24 | 43 | 11 | .... | 224 | 296 | 59 | 7th, East Div. | Out of Playoffs |
| 1972-73 | 78 | 17 | 18 | 4 | .... | 5 | 29 | 5 | .... | 22 | 47 | 9 | .... | 233 | 339 | 53 | 7th, East Div. | Out of Playoffs |
| 1971-72 | 78 | 14 | 20 | 5 | .... | 6 | 30 | 3 | .... | 20 | 50 | 8 | .... | 203 | 297 | 48 | 7th, East Div. | Out of Playoffs |
| 1970-71 | 78 | 17 | 18 | 4 | .... | 7 | 28 | 4 | .... | 24 | 46 | 8 | .... | 229 | 296 | 56 | 6th, East Div. | Out of Playoffs |

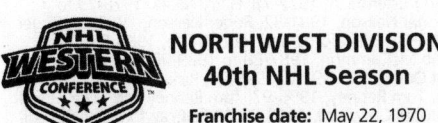

**NORTHWEST DIVISION**
**40th NHL Season**
**Franchise date:** May 22, 1970

# 2009-10 Player Personnel

| FORWARDS | HT | WT | S | Place of Birth | *Age | 2008-09 Club |
|---|---|---|---|---|---|---|
| BERNIER, Steve | 6-2 | 225 | R | Quebec City, Que. | 24 | Vancouver |
| BURROWS, Alexandre | 6-1 | 190 | L | Pincourt, Que. | 28 | Vancouver |
| DEMITRA, Pavol | 6-0 | 200 | L | Dubnica, Czech. | 34 | Vancouver |
| GLASS, Tanner | 6-0 | 196 | L | Regina, Sask. | 25 | Florida-Rochester |
| GRABNER, Michael | 6-0 | 187 | L | Villach, Austria | 21 | Manitoba |
| HANSEN, Jannik | 6-1 | 201 | R | Herlev, Denmark | 23 | Vancouver-Manitoba |
| HODGSON, Cody | 6-0 | 185 | R | Toronto, Ont. | 19 | Brampton-Manitoba |
| HORDICHUK, Darcy | 6-1 | 215 | L | Kamsack, Sask. | 29 | Vancouver |
| JOHNSON, Ryan | 6-1 | 202 | L | Thunder Bay, Ont. | 33 | Vancouver |
| KESLER, Ryan | 6-2 | 205 | R | Livonia, MI | 25 | Vancouver |
| RAYMOND, Mason | 6-0 | 182 | L | Cochrane, Alta. | 24 | Vancouver |
| RYPIEN, Rick | 5-11 | 170 | R | Coleman, Alta. | 25 | Vancouver |
| SAMUELSSON, Mikael | 6-2 | 213 | R | Mariefred, Sweden | 32 | Detroit |
| SEDIN, Daniel | 6-1 | 185 | L | Ornskoldsvik, Sweden | 29 | Vancouver |
| SEDIN, Henrik | 6-2 | 190 | L | Ornskoldsvik, Sweden | 29 | Vancouver |
| WALSKY, Eric | 5-11 | 196 | R | Anchorage, AK | 25 | Colorado College-Manitoba |
| WELLWOOD, Kyle | 5-10 | 180 | R | Windsor, Ont. | 26 | Vancouver |
| **DEFENSEMEN** | | | | | | |
| BAUMGARTNER, Nolan | 6-2 | 205 | R | Calgary, Alta. | 33 | Manitoba |
| BIEKSA, Kevin | 6-0 | 205 | R | Grimsby, Ont. | 28 | Vancouver |
| EDLER, Alexander | 6-3 | 220 | L | Ostersund, Sweden | 23 | Vancouver |
| McIVER, Nathan | 6-2 | 206 | L | Kinkora, P.E.I. | 24 | Anaheim-Manitoba |
| MITCHELL, Willie | 6-3 | 210 | L | Port McNeill, B.C. | 32 | Vancouver |
| NYCHOLAT, Lawrence | 6-0 | 200 | L | Calgary, Alta. | 30 | Van-Manitoba-Col |
| O'BRIEN, Shane | 6-3 | 224 | L | Port Hope, Ont. | 26 | Tampa Bay-Vancouver |
| ROME, Aaron | 6-1 | 223 | L | Nesbitt, Man. | 26 | Columbus-Syracuse |
| SALO, Sami | 6-3 | 215 | R | Turku, Finland | 35 | Vancouver |

| GOALTENDERS | HT | WT | C | Place of Birth | *Age | 2008-09 Club |
|---|---|---|---|---|---|---|
| LUONGO, Roberto | 6-3 | 205 | L | Montreal, Que. | 30 | Vancouver |
| RAYCROFT, Andrew | 6-0 | 185 | L | Belleville, Ont. | 29 | Colorado |

* – Age at start of 2009-10 season

# Alain Vigneault

## Head Coach

*Born: Quebec City, Que., May 14, 1961.*

On June 20, 2006, Alain Vigneault became the 16th head coach in Vancouver Canucks history. He previously served in the NHL as head coach of the Montreal Canadiens from 1997 to 2001, becoming the second youngest coach in club history at the age of 36. Vigneault was nominated for the Jack Adams Award as NHL coach of the year following the 1999-2000 season. In 2006-07, he led the Canucks to first place in the Northwest Division by setting new club records with 49 wins and 105 points after the club had missed the playoffs the previous season. Vigneault was rewarded with the Jack Adams Award as NHL coach of the year. In 2008-09, the Canucks won the Northwest Division title again.

Vigneault joined the Canucks from the club's AHL affiliate, the Manitoba Moose, where he led the team to within one game of the conference finals in 2005-06. Prior to joining the Moose, Vigneault spent many years as a head coach in the QMJHL with Trois-Rivieres, Hull, Beauport and PEI. In 1988, Vigneault led the Hull Olympiques into the Memorial Cup and was subsequently named CHL coach of the year. He has also been honoured as coach of the QMJHL's Second All-Star team on three separate occasions. Vigneault has also achieved success on the international stage. He served as an assistant coach with Canada's national junior team in 1989 and 1991, winning a gold medal at the 1991 World Junior Championships in Saskatoon.

As a player, Vigneault was a member of the St. Louis Blues from 1981 to 1983. Drafted by the Blues in the eighth round, 167th overall, in the 1981 Entry Draft, the defenceman recorded two goals, five assists and 82 penalty minutes in his NHL career. Vigneault went on to serve as a scout for the Blues for two seasons and as an assistant coach for the Ottawa Senators from 1992 to 1996.

### Coaching Record

| | | | Regular Season | | | | Playoffs | | | |
|---|---|---|---|---|---|---|---|---|---|---|
| Season | Team | League | GC | W | L | O/T | GC | W | L | T |
| 1986-87 | Trois-Rivieres | QMJHL | 70 | 28 | 40 | 2 | .... | .... | .... | .... |
| 1987-88 | Hull | QMJHL | 70 | 43 | 23 | 4 | 19 | 12 | 7 | .... |
| | Hull | M-Cup | .... | .... | .... | .... | 4 | 1 | 3 | .... |
| 1988-89 | Hull | QMJHL | 70 | 40 | 25 | 5 | 9 | 5 | 4 | .... |
| 1989-90 | Hull | QMJHL | 70 | 36 | 29 | 5 | 11 | 4 | 7 | .... |
| 1990-91 | Hull | QMJHL | 70 | 36 | 27 | 7 | 6 | 2 | 4 | .... |
| 1991-92 | Hull | QMJHL | 70 | 41 | 24 | 5 | 6 | 2 | 4 | .... |
| 1995-96 | Beauport | QMJHL | 31 | 19 | 7 | 5 | 20 | 13 | 7 | .... |
| 1996-97 | Beauport | QMJHL | 70 | 24 | 44 | 2 | 4 | 1 | 3 | .... |
| **1997-98** | **Montreal** | **NHL** | **82** | **37** | **32** | **13** | **10** | **4** | **6** | .... |
| **1998-99** | **Montreal** | **NHL** | **82** | **32** | **39** | **11** | .... | .... | .... | .... |
| **99-2000** | **Montreal** | **NHL** | **82** | **35** | **34** | **13** | .... | .... | .... | .... |
| **2000-01** | **Montreal** | **NHL** | **20** | **5** | **13** | **2** | .... | .... | .... | .... |
| 2003-04 | PEI | QMJHL | 70 | 40 | 19 | 11 | 11 | 6 | 5 | .... |
| 2004-05 | PEI | QMJHL | 70 | 24 | 39 | 7 | .... | .... | .... | .... |
| 2005-06 | Manitoba | AHL | 80 | 44 | 24 | 12 | 13 | 7 | 6 | .... |
| **2006-07** | **Vancouver** | **NHL** | **82** | **49** | **26** | **7** | **12** | **5** | **7** | .... |
| **2007-08** | **Vancouver** | **NHL** | **82** | **39** | **33** | **10** | .... | .... | .... | .... |
| **2008-09** | **Vancouver** | **NHL** | **82** | **45** | **27** | **10** | **10** | **6** | **4** | .... |
| | **NHL Totals** | | **512** | **242** | **204** | **66** | **32** | **15** | **17** | .... |

# 2008-09 Scoring

* – rookie

## Regular Season

| Pos | # | Player | Team | GP | G | A | Pts | TOI | +/– | PIM | PP | SH | GW | S | % |
|---|---|---|---|---|---|---|---|---|---|---|---|---|---|---|---|
| L | 22 | Daniel Sedin | VAN | 82 | 31 | 51 | 82 | 18:47 | 24 | 36 | 9 | 0 | 7 | 285 | 10.9 |
| C | 33 | Henrik Sedin | VAN | 82 | 22 | 60 | 82 | 19:31 | 22 | 48 | 4 | 0 | 8 | 143 | 15.4 |
| C | 17 | Ryan Kesler | VAN | 82 | 26 | 33 | 59 | 19:27 | 8 | 61 | 10 | 2 | 2 | 179 | 14.5 |
| R | 38 | Pavol Demitra | VAN | 69 | 20 | 33 | 53 | 17:28 | 6 | 20 | 4 | 0 | 1 | 143 | 14.0 |
| L | 14 | Alexandre Burrows | VAN | 82 | 28 | 23 | 51 | 16:50 | 23 | 150 | 0 | 4 | 3 | 175 | 16.0 |
| D | 3 | Kevin Bieksa | VAN | 72 | 11 | 32 | 43 | 23:29 | –4 | 97 | 5 | 0 | 2 | 153 | 7.2 |
| D | 23 | Alexander Edler | VAN | 80 | 10 | 27 | 37 | 21:07 | 11 | 54 | 5 | 0 | 1 | 145 | 6.9 |
| R | 18 | Steve Bernier | VAN | 81 | 15 | 17 | 32 | 13:50 | 4 | 27 | 2 | 0 | 4 | 137 | 10.9 |
| C | 13 | Mats Sundin | VAN | 41 | 9 | 19 | 28 | 16:50 | –5 | 28 | 5 | 0 | 2 | 84 | 10.7 |
| C | 42 | Kyle Wellwood | VAN | 74 | 18 | 9 | 27 | 13:47 | 2 | 4 | 10 | 0 | 3 | 94 | 19.1 |
| D | 2 | Mattias Ohlund | VAN | 82 | 6 | 19 | 25 | 21:34 | 14 | 105 | 3 | 0 | 1 | 131 | 4.6 |
| D | 6 | Sami Salo | VAN | 60 | 5 | 20 | 25 | 20:10 | 5 | 26 | 5 | 0 | 2 | 110 | 4.5 |
| L | 21 | Mason Raymond | VAN | 72 | 11 | 12 | 23 | 13:42 | 2 | 24 | 4 | 0 | 0 | 145 | 7.6 |
| D | 8 | Willie Mitchell | VAN | 82 | 3 | 20 | 23 | 22:54 | 29 | 59 | 0 | 0 | 1 | 88 | 3.4 |
| R | 36 * | Jannik Hansen | VAN | 55 | 6 | 15 | 21 | 12:30 | 5 | 37 | 0 | 0 | 1 | 64 | 9.4 |
| L | 9 | Taylor Pyatt | VAN | 69 | 10 | 9 | 19 | 14:42 | 0 | 43 | 0 | 0 | 1 | 99 | 10.1 |
| D | 5 | Ossi Vaananen | PHI | 46 | 1 | 9 | 10 | 18:27 | 7 | 22 | 0 | 0 | 0 | 18 | 5.6 |
| | | | VAN | 3 | 0 | 1 | 1 | 9:28 | 1 | 0 | 0 | 0 | 0 | 2 | 0.0 |
| | | | Total | 49 | 1 | 10 | 11 | 17:54 | 8 | 22 | 0 | 0 | 0 | 20 | 5.0 |
| D | 55 | Shane O'Brien | T.B. | 1 | 0 | 0 | 0 | 14:04 | –1 | 0 | 0 | 0 | 0 | 0 | 0.0 |
| | | | VAN | 76 | 0 | 10 | 10 | 14:55 | 6 | 196 | 0 | 0 | 0 | 39 | 0.0 |
| | | | Total | 77 | 0 | 10 | 10 | 14:55 | 5 | 196 | 0 | 0 | 0 | 39 | 0.0 |
| C | 10 | Ryan Johnson | VAN | 62 | 2 | 7 | 9 | 11:01 | 1 | 12 | 0 | 0 | 1 | 22 | 9.1 |
| L | 24 | Darcy Hordichuk | VAN | 73 | 4 | 1 | 5 | 5:31 | 1 | 109 | 0 | 0 | 0 | 26 | 15.4 |
| L | 29 | Jason Jaffray | VAN | 14 | 2 | 2 | 4 | 9:03 | –2 | 14 | 0 | 0 | 2 | 11 | 18.2 |
| C | 37 * | Rick Rypien | VAN | 12 | 3 | 0 | 3 | 9:19 | –3 | 19 | 0 | 1 | 0 | 16 | 18.8 |
| D | 4 | Rob Davison | VAN | 23 | 0 | 2 | 2 | 10:05 | –4 | 51 | 0 | 0 | 0 | 15 | 0.0 |
| C | 27 | Jason Krog | VAN | 4 | 1 | 0 | 1 | 10:14 | 0 | 2 | 1 | 0 | 0 | 5 | 20.0 |
| C | 49 * | Alexandre Bolduc | VAN | 7 | 0 | 1 | 1 | 7:20 | 1 | 4 | 0 | 0 | 0 | 7 | 0.0 |
| R | 25 | Michel Ouellet | VAN | 3 | 0 | 0 | 0 | 9:38 | 1 | 0 | 0 | 0 | 0 | 3 | 0.0 |

### Goaltending

| No. | Goaltender | GPI | Mins | Avg | W | L | OT | EN | SO | GA | SA | S% | G | A | PIM |
|---|---|---|---|---|---|---|---|---|---|---|---|---|---|---|---|
| 1 | Roberto Luongo | 54 | 3181 | 2.34 | 33 | 13 | 7 | 5 | 9 | 124 | 1542 | .920 | 0 | 1 | 4 |
| 41 | Curtis Sanford | 19 | 973 | 2.59 | 7 | 8 | 0 | 2 | 1 | 42 | 448 | .906 | 0 | 0 | 2 |
| 30 | Jason LaBarbera | 9 | 451 | 2.66 | 3 | 2 | 2 | 0 | 0 | 20 | 235 | .915 | 0 | 0 | 0 |
| 35 | * Cory Schneider | 8 | 355 | 3.38 | 2 | 4 | 1 | 0 | 0 | 20 | 162 | .877 | 0 | 0 | 0 |
| | **Totals** | **82** | **4990** | **2.56** | **45** | **27** | **10** | **7** | **10** | **213** | **2394** | **.911** | | | |

## Playoffs

| Pos | # | Player | Team | GP | G | A | Pts | TOI | +/– | PIM | PP | SH | GW | OT | S | % |
|---|---|---|---|---|---|---|---|---|---|---|---|---|---|---|---|---|
| L | 22 | Daniel Sedin | VAN | 10 | 4 | 6 | 10 | 18:36 | 4 | 8 | 2 | 0 | 0 | 0 | 36 | 11.1 |
| C | 33 | Henrik Sedin | VAN | 10 | 4 | 6 | 10 | 20:06 | 2 | 2 | 1 | 0 | 0 | 0 | 19 | 21.1 |
| C | 13 | Mats Sundin | VAN | 8 | 3 | 5 | 8 | 15:54 | –1 | 2 | 0 | 0 | 1 | 0 | 15 | 20.0 |
| D | 23 | Alexander Edler | VAN | 10 | 1 | 7 | 8 | 22:08 | –2 | 6 | 1 | 0 | 0 | 0 | 14 | 7.1 |
| D | 6 | Sami Salo | VAN | 7 | 3 | 4 | 7 | 18:36 | 0 | 2 | 2 | 0 | 2 | 0 | 12 | 25.0 |
| C | 42 | Kyle Wellwood | VAN | 10 | 1 | 5 | 6 | 15:04 | –1 | 0 | 0 | 0 | 0 | 0 | 7 | 14.3 |
| D | 3 | Kevin Bieksa | VAN | 10 | 0 | 5 | 5 | 24:07 | 3 | 14 | 0 | 0 | 0 | 0 | 18 | 0.0 |
| L | 14 | Alexandre Burrows | VAN | 10 | 3 | 1 | 4 | 18:47 | 3 | 20 | 0 | 0 | 1 | 1 | 22 | 13.6 |
| R | 18 | Steve Bernier | VAN | 10 | 2 | 2 | 4 | 15:00 | –1 | 7 | 2 | 0 | 2 | 0 | 15 | 13.3 |
| C | 17 | Ryan Kesler | VAN | 10 | 2 | 2 | 4 | 20:29 | –2 | 14 | 1 | 0 | 0 | 0 | 28 | 7.1 |
| L | 21 | Mason Raymond | VAN | 10 | 2 | 1 | 3 | 15:12 | –2 | 2 | 0 | 0 | 0 | 0 | 17 | 11.8 |
| R | 38 | Pavol Demitra | VAN | 6 | 1 | 2 | 3 | 17:37 | –2 | 2 | 1 | 0 | 0 | 0 | 13 | 7.7 |
| D | 2 | Mattias Ohlund | VAN | 10 | 1 | 2 | 3 | 23:53 | 5 | 6 | 1 | 0 | 0 | 0 | 15 | 6.7 |
| C | 10 | Ryan Johnson | VAN | 10 | 1 | 1 | 2 | 11:51 | 0 | 2 | 0 | 0 | 0 | 0 | 4 | 25.0 |
| D | 55 | Shane O'Brien | VAN | 10 | 1 | 1 | 2 | 12:05 | –3 | 24 | 0 | 0 | 0 | 0 | 9 | 11.1 |
| D | 8 | Willie Mitchell | VAN | 10 | 0 | 2 | 2 | 24:12 | –2 | 22 | 0 | 0 | 0 | 0 | 1 | 0.0 |
| C | 37 * | Rick Rypien | VAN | 10 | 0 | 2 | 2 | 7:29 | –1 | 40 | 0 | 0 | 0 | 0 | 6 | 0.0 |
| L | 24 | Darcy Hordichuk | VAN | 10 | 1 | 0 | 1 | 5:19 | 1 | 14 | 0 | 0 | 0 | 0 | 4 | 25.0 |
| R | 36 * | Jannik Hansen | VAN | 2 | 0 | 0 | 0 | 10:16 | 0 | 0 | 0 | 0 | 0 | 0 | 0 | 0.0 |
| D | 5 | Ossi Vaananen | VAN | 3 | 0 | 0 | 0 | 9:13 | 0 | 2 | 0 | 0 | 0 | 0 | 0 | 0.0 |
| L | 9 | Taylor Pyatt | VAN | 4 | 0 | 0 | 0 | 14:12 | –3 | 2 | 0 | 0 | 0 | 0 | 8 | 0.0 |

### Goaltending

| No. | Goaltender | GPI | Mins | Avg | W | L | EN | SO | GA | SA | S% | G | A | PIM |
|---|---|---|---|---|---|---|---|---|---|---|---|---|---|---|
| 1 | Roberto Luongo | 10 | 618 | 2.52 | 6 | 4 | 2 | 1 | 26 | 304 | .914 | 0 | 0 | 0 |
| | **Totals** | **10** | **623** | **2.70** | **6** | **4** | **2** | **1** | **28** | **306** | **.908** | | | |

# Captains' History

Orland Kurtenbach, 1970-71 to 1973-74; no captain, 1974-75; Andre Boudrias, 1975-76; Chris Oddleifson, 1976-77; Don Lever, 1977-78; Don Lever and Kevin McCarthy, 1978-79; Kevin McCarthy, 1979-80 to 1981-82; Stan Smyl, 1982-83 to 1989-90; Dan Quinn, Doug Lidster and Trevor Linden, 1990-91; Trevor Linden, 1991-92 to 1996-97; Mark Messier, 1997-98 to 1999-2000; Markus Naslund, 2000-01 to 2007-08; Roberto Luongo, 2008-09 to date.

# Coaching History

Hal Laycoe, 1970-71, 1971-72; Vic Stasiuk, 1972-73; Bill McCreary and Phil Maloney, 1973-74; Phil Maloney, 1974-75, 1975-76; Phil Maloney and Orland Kurtenbach, 1976-77; Orland Kurtenbach, 1977-78; Harry Neale, 1978-79 to 1980-81; Harry Neale and Roger Neilson, 1981-82; Roger Neilson, 1982-83; Roger Neilson and Harry Neale, 1983-84; Bill Laforge and Harry Neale, 1984-85; Tom Watt, 1985-86, 1986-87; Bob McCammon, 1987-88 to 1989-90; Bob McCammon and Pat Quinn, 1990-91; Pat Quinn, 1991-92 to 1993-94; Rick Ley, 1994-95; Rick Ley and Pat Quinn, 1995-96; Tom Renney, 1996-97; Tom Renney and Mike Keenan, 1997-98; Mike Keenan and Marc Crawford, 1998-99; Marc Crawford, 1999-2000 to 2005-06; Alain Vigneault, 2006-07 to date.

# Club Records

## Team

(Figures in brackets for season records are games played; records for fewest points, wins, ties, losses, goals, goals against are for 70 or more games)

| | | |
|---|---|---|
| **Most Points** | **105** | 2006-07 (82) |
| **Most Wins** | **49** | 2006-07 (82) |
| **Most Ties** | **20** | 1980-81 (80) |
| **Most Losses** | **50** | 1971-72 (78) |
| **Most Goals** | **346** | 1992-93 (84) |
| **Most Goals Against** | **401** | 1984-85 (80) |
| **Fewest Points** | **48** | 1971-72 (78) |
| **Fewest Wins** | **20** | 1971-72 (78), 1977-78 (80) |
| **Fewest Ties** | **3** | 1993-94 (84) |
| **Fewest Losses** | **24** | 2002-03 (82) |
| **Fewest Goals** | **192** | 1998-99 (82) |
| **Fewest Goals Against** | **194** | 2003-04 (82) |
| **Longest Winning Streak** | | |
| **Overall** | **10** | Nov. 9-30/02 |
| **Home** | **11** | Feb. 3-Mar. 19/09 |
| **Away** | **8** | Dec. 20/03-Jan. 13/04 |
| **Longest Undefeated Streak** | | |
| **Overall** | **14** | Jan.26-Feb. 25/03 (10 wins, 4 ties) |
| **Home** | **18** | Nov. 4/92-Jan. 16/93 (16 wins, 2 ties) |
| **Away** | **9** | Feb. 4-Mar. 3/03 (6 wins, 3 ties) |
| **Longest Losing Streak** | | |
| **Overall** | **10** | Oct. 23-Nov. 11/97 |
| **Home** | **6** | Dec. 18/70-Jan. 20/71 |
| **Away** | **12** | Nov. 28/81-Feb. 6/82 |
| **Longest Winless Streak** | | |
| **Overall** | **13** | Nov. 9-Dec. 7/73 (10 losses, 3 ties) |
| **Home** | **11** | Dec. 18/70-Feb. 6/71 (10 losses, 1 tie) |
| **Away** | **20** | Jan. 2-Apr. 2/86 (14 losses, 6 ties) |
| **Most Shutouts, Season** | **10** | 2008-09 (82) |
| **Most PIM, Season** | **2,326** | 1992-93 (84) |
| **Most Goals, Game** | **11** | Mar. 28/71 (Cal. 5 at Van. 11), Nov. 25/86 (L.A. 5 at Van. 11), Mar. 1/92 (Cgy. 0 at Van. 11) |

## Individual

| | | |
|---|---|---|
| **Most Seasons** | **16** | Trevor Linden |
| **Most Games** | **1,140** | Trevor Linden |
| **Most Goals, Career** | **346** | Markus Naslund |
| **Most Assists, Career** | **415** | Trevor Linden |
| **Most Points, Career** | **756** | Markus Naslund (346G, 410A) |
| **Most PIM, Career** | **2,127** | Gino Odjick |
| **Most Shutouts, Career** | **20** | Kirk McLean, Roberto Luongo |
| **Longest Consecutive Games Streak** | **534** | Brendan Morrison (Mar. 16/00-Dec. 10/07) |
| **Most Goals, Season** | **60** | Pavel Bure (1992-93), (1993-94) |
| **Most Assists, Season** | **71** | Henrik Sedin (2006-07) |
| **Most Points, Season** | **110** | Pavel Bure (1992-93; 60G, 50A) |
| **Most PIM, Season** | **372** | Donald Brashear (1997-98) |
| **Most Points, Defenseman, Season** | **63** | Doug Lidster (1986-87; 12G, 51A) |
| **Most Points, Center, Season** | **91** | Patrik Sundstrom (1983-84; 38G, 53A) |
| **Most Points, Right Wing, Season** | **110** | Pavel Bure (1992-93; 60G, 50A) |
| **Most Points, Left Wing, Season** | **104** | Markus Naslund (2002-03; 48G, 56A) |
| **Most Points, Rookie, Season** | **60** | Ivan Hlinka (1981-82; 23G, 37A), Pavel Bure (1991-92; 34G, 26A) |
| **Most Shutouts, Season** | **9** | Roberto Luongo (2008-09) |
| **Most Goals, Game** | **4** | Twelve times |
| **Most Assists, Game** | **6** | Patrik Sundstrom (Feb. 29/84) |
| **Most Points, Game** | **7** | Patrik Sundstrom (Feb. 29/84; 1G, 6A) |

## General Managers' History

Bud Poile, 1970-71 to 1972-73; Hal Laycoe, 1973-74; Phil Maloney, 1974-75 to 1976-77; Jake Milford, 1977-78 to 1981-82; Harry Neale, 1982-83 to 1984-85; Jack Gordon, 1985-86, 1986-87; Pat Quinn, 1987-88 to 1997-98; Brian Burke, 1998-99 to 2003-04; David Nonis, 2004-05 to 2007-08; Mike Gillis, 2008-09 to date.

## Retired Numbers

| | | |
|---|---|---|
| 12 | Stan Smyl | 1978-1991 |
| 16 | Trevor Linden | 1988-98; 2001-08 |

# All-time Record vs. Other Clubs

## Regular Season

| | At Home | | | | | | | | On Road | | | | | | | | Total | | | | | | | |
|---|---|---|---|---|---|---|---|---|---|---|---|---|---|---|---|---|---|---|---|---|---|---|---|---|
| | GP | W | L | T | OL | GF | GA | PTS | GP | W | L | T | OL | GF | GA | PTS | GP | W | L | T | OL | GF | GA | PTS |
| Anaheim | 34 | 19 | 12 | 2 | 1 | 110 | 84 | 41 | 33 | 15 | 10 | 7 | 1 | 98 | 89 | 38 | 67 | 34 | 22 | 9 | 2 | 208 | 173 | 79 |
| Atlanta | 4 | 2 | 1 | 1 | 0 | 13 | 7 | 5 | 5 | 3 | 1 | 0 | 1 | 17 | 16 | 7 | 9 | 5 | 2 | 1 | 1 | 30 | 23 | 12 |
| Boston | 53 | 17 | 27 | 8 | 1 | 171 | 212 | 43 | 53 | 7 | 38 | 7 | 1 | 124 | 219 | 22 | 106 | 24 | 65 | 15 | 2 | 295 | 431 | 65 |
| Buffalo | 53 | 26 | 16 | 11 | 0 | 197 | 163 | 63 | 54 | 18 | 27 | 8 | 1 | 157 | 195 | 45 | 107 | 44 | 43 | 19 | 1 | 354 | 358 | 108 |
| Calgary | 114 | 45 | 49 | 18 | 2 | 390 | 370 | 110 | 113 | 34 | 64 | 15 | 0 | 323 | 431 | 83 | 227 | 79 | 113 | 33 | 2 | 713 | 801 | 193 |
| Carolina | 32 | 16 | 10 | 6 | 0 | 113 | 87 | 38 | 30 | 12 | 13 | 5 | 0 | 101 | 97 | 29 | 62 | 28 | 23 | 11 | 0 | 214 | 184 | 67 |
| Chicago | 80 | 41 | 24 | 15 | 0 | 242 | 225 | 97 | 79 | 23 | 47 | 7 | 2 | 189 | 284 | 55 | 159 | 64 | 71 | 22 | 2 | 431 | 509 | 152 |
| Colorado | 62 | 24 | 27 | 7 | 4 | 197 | 230 | 59 | 62 | 22 | 29 | 8 | 3 | 170 | 206 | 55 | 124 | 46 | 56 | 15 | 7 | 367 | 436 | 114 |
| Columbus | 16 | 11 | 2 | 0 | 3 | 61 | 43 | 25 | 16 | 7 | 6 | 2 | 1 | 52 | 41 | 17 | 32 | 18 | 8 | 2 | 4 | 113 | 84 | 42 |
| Dallas | 79 | 36 | 31 | 10 | 2 | 274 | 235 | 84 | 79 | 24 | 41 | 12 | 2 | 228 | 280 | 62 | 158 | 60 | 72 | 22 | 4 | 502 | 515 | 146 |
| Detroit | 73 | 33 | 30 | 10 | 0 | 259 | 231 | 76 | 74 | 21 | 43 | 8 | 2 | 213 | 298 | 52 | 147 | 54 | 73 | 18 | 2 | 472 | 529 | 128 |
| Edmonton | 97 | 40 | 42 | 12 | 3 | 342 | 362 | 95 | 96 | 32 | 52 | 7 | 5 | 302 | 396 | 76 | 193 | 72 | 94 | 19 | 8 | 644 | 758 | 171 |
| Florida | 11 | 5 | 1 | 5 | 0 | 34 | 25 | 15 | 9 | 4 | 3 | 1 | 1 | 30 | 25 | 10 | 20 | 9 | 4 | 6 | 1 | 64 | 50 | 25 |
| Los Angeles | 105 | 54 | 33 | 16 | 2 | 391 | 323 | 126 | 107 | 36 | 54 | 16 | 1 | 331 | 411 | 89 | 212 | 90 | 87 | 32 | 3 | 722 | 734 | 215 |
| Minnesota | 25 | 12 | 5 | 3 | 5 | 68 | 63 | 32 | 26 | 12 | 11 | 2 | 1 | 61 | 69 | 27 | 51 | 24 | 16 | 5 | 6 | 129 | 132 | 59 |
| Montreal | 57 | 16 | 33 | 8 | 0 | 156 | 206 | 40 | 55 | 11 | 39 | 5 | 0 | 139 | 247 | 27 | 112 | 27 | 72 | 13 | 0 | 295 | 453 | 67 |
| Nashville | 20 | 13 | 5 | 1 | 1 | 71 | 47 | 28 | 21 | 12 | 8 | 1 | 0 | 58 | 58 | 25 | 41 | 25 | 13 | 2 | 1 | 129 | 105 | 53 |
| New Jersey | 49 | 28 | 10 | 11 | 0 | 183 | 135 | 67 | 50 | 23 | 21 | 6 | 0 | 159 | 154 | 52 | 99 | 51 | 31 | 17 | 0 | 342 | 289 | 119 |
| NY Islanders | 48 | 24 | 21 | 3 | 0 | 158 | 155 | 51 | 49 | 12 | 25 | 10 | 2 | 138 | 177 | 36 | 97 | 36 | 46 | 13 | 2 | 296 | 332 | 87 |
| NY Rangers | 52 | 16 | 33 | 3 | 0 | 166 | 204 | 35 | 56 | 13 | 38 | 5 | 0 | 148 | 242 | 31 | 108 | 29 | 71 | 8 | 0 | 314 | 446 | 66 |
| Ottawa | 13 | 7 | 5 | 1 | 0 | 39 | 28 | 15 | 12 | 6 | 5 | 1 | 0 | 31 | 27 | 13 | 25 | 13 | 10 | 2 | 0 | 70 | 55 | 28 |
| Philadelphia | 53 | 10 | 30 | 12 | 1 | 148 | 214 | 33 | 55 | 17 | 36 | 1 | 1 | 164 | 238 | 36 | 108 | 27 | 66 | 13 | 2 | 312 | 452 | 69 |
| Phoenix | 80 | 49 | 20 | 10 | 1 | 295 | 219 | 109 | 77 | 30 | 36 | 10 | 1 | 265 | 278 | 71 | 157 | 79 | 56 | 20 | 2 | 560 | 497 | 180 |
| Pittsburgh | 51 | 23 | 23 | 4 | 1 | 181 | 189 | 51 | 52 | 12 | 33 | 7 | 0 | 178 | 230 | 31 | 103 | 35 | 56 | 11 | 1 | 359 | 419 | 82 |
| St. Louis | 80 | 35 | 36 | 9 | 0 | 238 | 252 | 79 | 79 | 24 | 46 | 9 | 0 | 223 | 292 | 57 | 159 | 59 | 82 | 18 | 0 | 461 | 544 | 136 |
| San Jose | 40 | 21 | 14 | 4 | 1 | 137 | 110 | 47 | 42 | 19 | 17 | 5 | 1 | 122 | 123 | 44 | 82 | 40 | 31 | 9 | 2 | 259 | 233 | 91 |
| Tampa Bay | 11 | 9 | 0 | 2 | 0 | 47 | 19 | 20 | 10 | 6 | 4 | 0 | 0 | 40 | 35 | 12 | 21 | 15 | 4 | 2 | 0 | 87 | 54 | 32 |
| Toronto | 66 | 31 | 22 | 11 | 2 | 233 | 221 | 75 | 62 | 23 | 28 | 11 | 0 | 204 | 222 | 57 | 128 | 54 | 50 | 22 | 2 | 437 | 443 | 132 |
| Washington | 40 | 19 | 15 | 5 | 1 | 139 | 125 | 44 | 42 | 15 | 22 | 4 | 1 | 124 | 139 | 35 | 82 | 34 | 37 | 9 | 2 | 263 | 264 | 79 |
| Defunct Clubs | 19 | 14 | 3 | 2 | 0 | 82 | 48 | 30 | 19 | 10 | 8 | 1 | 0 | 71 | 68 | 21 | 38 | 24 | 11 | 3 | 0 | 153 | 116 | 51 |
| **Totals** | **1517** | **696** | **580** | **210** | **31** | **5135** | **4832** | **1633** | **1517** | **503** | **805** | **181** | **28** | **4460** | **5587** | **1215** | **3034** | **1199** | **1385** | **391** | **59** | **9595** | **10419** | **2848** |

## Playoffs

| | Series | W | L | GP | W | L | T | GF | GA | Last Mtg. | Rnd. | Result |
|---|---|---|---|---|---|---|---|---|---|---|---|---|
| Anaheim | 1 | 0 | 1 | 5 | 1 | 4 | 0 | 8 | 14 | 2007 | CSF | L 1-4 |
| Buffalo | 2 | 0 | 2 | 7 | 1 | 6 | 0 | 14 | 28 | 1981 | PRE | L 0-3 |
| Calgary | 6 | 2 | 4 | 32 | 15 | 17 | 0 | 96 | 101 | 2004 | CQF | L 3-4 |
| Chicago | 3 | 1 | 2 | 15 | 6 | 9 | 0 | 43 | 47 | 2009 | CSF | L 2-4 |
| Colorado | 2 | 0 | 2 | 10 | 2 | 8 | 0 | 26 | 40 | 2001 | CQF | L 0-4 |
| Dallas | 2 | 2 | 0 | 12 | 8 | 4 | 0 | 31 | 23 | 2007 | CQF | W 4-3 |
| Detroit | 1 | 0 | 1 | 6 | 2 | 4 | 0 | 16 | 22 | 2002 | CQF | L 2-4 |
| Edmonton | 2 | 0 | 2 | 9 | 2 | 7 | 0 | 20 | 35 | 1992 | DF | L 2-4 |
| Los Angeles | 3 | 1 | 2 | 17 | 8 | 9 | 0 | 60 | 66 | 1993 | DF | L 2-4 |
| Minnesota | 1 | 0 | 1 | 7 | 3 | 4 | 0 | 17 | 26 | 2003 | CSF | L 3-4 |
| Montreal | 1 | 0 | 1 | 5 | 1 | 4 | 0 | 9 | 20 | 1975 | QF | L 1-4 |
| NY Islanders | 2 | 0 | 2 | 6 | 0 | 6 | 0 | 14 | 26 | 1982 | F | L 0-4 |
| NY Rangers | 1 | 0 | 1 | 7 | 3 | 4 | 0 | 19 | 21 | 1994 | F | L 3-4 |
| Philadelphia | 1 | 0 | 1 | 3 | 1 | 2 | 0 | 9 | 15 | 1979 | PRE | L 1-2 |
| Phoenix | 2 | 2 | 0 | 13 | 8 | 5 | 0 | 50 | 34 | 1993 | DSF | W 4-2 |
| St. Louis | 3 | 3 | 0 | 18 | 12 | 6 | 0 | 55 | 53 | 2009 | CQF | W 4-0 |
| Toronto | 1 | 1 | 0 | 5 | 4 | 1 | 0 | 16 | 9 | 1994 | CF | W 4-1 |
| **Totals** | **34** | **12** | **22** | **177** | **77** | **100** | **0** | **503** | **580** | | | |

## Playoff Results 2009-2004

| Year | Round | Opponent | Result | GF | GA |
|---|---|---|---|---|---|
| 2009 | CSF | Chicago | L 2-4 | 19 | 23 |
| | CQF | St. Louis | W 4-0 | 11 | 5 |
| 2007 | CSF | Anaheim | L 1-4 | 8 | 14 |
| | CQF | Dallas | W 4-3 | 13 | 12 |
| 2004 | CQF | Calgary | L 3-4 | 16 | 19 |
| 2003 | CSF | Minnesota | L 3-4 | 17 | 26 |
| | CQF | St. Louis | W 4-3 | 17 | 21 |

**Abbreviations: Round: F** – Final; **CF** – conference final; **CSF** – conference semi-final; **CQF** – conference quarter-final; **DF** – division final; **DSF** – division semi-final; **QF** – quarter-final; **PRE** – preliminary round.

Calgary totals include Atlanta Flames, 1972-73 to 1979-80.
Colorado totals include Quebec, 1979-80 to 1994-95.
New Jersey totals include Kansas City, 1974-75, 1975-76, and Colorado Rockies, 1976-77 to 1981-82.
Phoenix totals include Winnipeg, 1979-80 to 1995-96.
Carolina totals include Hartford, 1979-80 to 1996-97.
Dallas totals include Minnesota North Stars, 1970-71 to 1992-93.

## 2008-09 Results

| | | | | | | | |
|---|---|---|---|---|---|---|---|
| **Oct.** | 9 | Calgary | 6-0 | | 7 | at Edmonton | 4-2 |
| | 11 | at Calgary | 5-4* | | 9 | St. Louis | 4-6 |
| | 13 | at Washington | 1-5 | | 10 | San Jose | 2-4 |
| | 16 | at Detroit | 4-3* | | 13 | New Jersey | 3-5 |
| | 17 | at Buffalo | 2-5 | | 15 | Phoenix | 1-4 |
| | 19 | at Chicago | 2-4 | | 18 | Columbus | 5-6† |
| | 21 | at Columbus | 2-4 | | 20 | at San Jose | 1-2* |
| | 25 | Edmonton | 6-3 | | 28 | Nashville | 3-5 |
| | 28 | Boston | 0-1 | | 31 | Minnesota | 3-4* |
| | 30 | at Los Angeles | 4-0 | **Feb.** | 3 | Carolina | 4-3 |
| | 31 | at Anaheim | 7-6† | | 7 | Chicago | 7-3 |
| **Nov.** | 2 | Detroit | 2-3 | | 10 | at St. Louis | 6-4 |
| | 4 | Nashville | 4-0 | | 12 | at Phoenix | 4-3 |
| | 6 | Phoenix | 1-0 | | 13 | at Dallas | 1-2 |
| | 8 | Minnesota | 2-0 | | 15 | Montreal | 4-2 |
| | 12 | Colorado | 1-2† | | 17 | at Calgary | 4-3† |
| | 15 | Toronto | 4-2 | | 19 | at Ottawa | 5-2 |
| | 17 | at NY Islanders | 1-2† | | 21 | at Toronto | 3-2† |
| | 19 | at NY Rangers | 6-3 | | 24 | at Montreal | 0-3 |
| | 20 | at Minnesota | 3-2 | | 27 | Tampa Bay | 2-1 |
| | 22 | at Pittsburgh | 3-1 | **Mar.** | 1 | Columbus | 3-1 |
| | 24 | Detroit | 3-2* | | 3 | Minnesota | 4-2 |
| | 27 | Calgary | 3-4 | | 7 | San Jose | 3-1 |
| | 29 | at Calgary | 1-3 | | 9 | at Los Angeles | 2-3 |
| **Dec.** | 1 | at Columbus | 2-3 | | 11 | at Anaheim | 3-4* |
| | 4 | at Detroit | 5-6 | | 13 | Los Angeles | 4-2 |
| | 5 | at Minnesota | 2-1 | | 15 | Colorado | 4-2 |
| | 7 | at Colorado | 4-5† | | 17 | Dallas | 4-2 |
| | 9 | at Nashville | 3-1 | | 19 | St. Louis | 3-0 |
| | 13 | at Edmonton | 0-3 | | 21 | at Phoenix | 1-5 |
| | 14 | Florida | 5-3 | | 24 | at Dallas | 5-2 |
| | 17 | Edmonton | 4-2 | | 26 | at St. Louis | 2-4 |
| | 20 | Chicago | 1-3 | | 27 | at Colorado | 4-1 |
| | 22 | Anaheim | 4-3 | | 29 | at Chicago | 4-0 |
| | 23 | at San Jose | 0-5 | | 31 | at Minnesota | 2-1* |
| | 26 | Edmonton | 2-3 | **Apr.** | 2 | Anaheim | 5-6† |
| | 28 | Ottawa | 3-0 | | 4 | at Edmonton | 3-5 |
| | 30 | Philadelphia | 2-3 | | 5 | Colorado | 1-4 |
| **Jan.** | 1 | at Nashville | 2-1 | | 7 | Calgary | 4-1 |
| | 2 | at Atlanta | 3-4† | | 9 | Los Angeles | 1-0 |
| | 4 | Dallas | 2-3† | | 11 | at Colorado | 1-0* |

## Entry Draft Selections 2009-1995

Name in bold denotes played in NHL.

**2009**
Pick
22 Jordan Schroeder
53 Anton Rodin
83 Kevin Connauton
113 Jeremy Price
143 Peter Andersson
173 Joe Cannata
187 Steven Anthony

**2008**
Pick
10 Cody Hodgson
41 Yann Sauve
131 Prab Rai
161 Mats Froshaug
191 Morgan Clark

**2007**
Pick
25 Patrick White
33 Taylor Ellington
145 Charles-Antoine Messier
146 Ilja Kablukov
176 Taylor Matson
206 Dan Gendur

**2006**
Pick
14 Michael Grabner
82 Daniel Rahimi
163 Sergei Shirokov
167 Juraj Simek
197 Evan Fuller

**2005**
Pick
10 **Luc Bourdon**
51 **Mason Raymond**
114 Alexandre Vincent
138 Matt Butcher
185 Kris Fredheim
205 Mario Bliznak

**2004**
Pick
26 **Cory Schneider**
91 **Alexander Edler**
125 Andrew Sarauer
159 **Mike Brown**
189 Julien Ellis
254 David Schulz
287 **Jannik Hansen**

**2003**
Pick
23 **Ryan Kesler**
60 Marc-Andre Bernier
111 **Brandon Nolan**
128 Ty Morris
160 Nicklas Danielsson
190 Chad Brownlee
222 Francois-Pierre Guenette
252 Sergei Topol
254 **Nathan McIver**
285 Matthew Hansen

**2002**
Pick
49 Kirill Koltsov
55 Denis Grot
68 **Brett Skinner**
83 Lukas Mensator
114 John Laliberte
151 **Rob McVicar**
214 Marc-Andre Roy
223 Ilia Krikunov
247 Matt Violin
277 Thomas Nussli
278 Matt Gens

**2001**
Pick
16 **R.J. Umberger**
66 **Fedor Fedorov**
114 Evgeny Gladskikh
151 **Kevin Bieksa**
212 **Jason King**
245 Konstantin Mikhailov

**2000**
Pick
23 **Nathan Smith**
71 Thatcher Bell
93 Tim Branham
144 Pavel Duma
208 **Brandon Reid**
241 Nathan Barrett
272 Tim Smith

**1999**
Pick
2 **Daniel Sedin**
3 **Henrik Sedin**
69 Rene Vydareny
129 Ryan Thorpe
172 Josh Reed
189 Kevin Swanson
218 Markus Kankaanpera
271 Darrell Hay

**1998**
Pick
4 **Bryan Allen**
31 **Artem Chubarov**
68 **Jarkko Ruutu**
81 Justin Morrison
90 Regan Darby
136 David Ytfeldt
140 Rick Bertran
149 Paul Cabana
177 Vincent Malts
204 Greg Mischler
219 Curtis Valentine
232 Jason Metcalfe

**1997**
Pick
10 **Brad Ference**
34 **Ryan Bonni**
36 **Harold Druken**
64 **Kyle Freadrich**
90 Chris Stanley
114 David Darguzas
117 Matt Cockell
144 **Matt Cooke**
148 Larry Shapley
171 Rod Leroux
201 Denis Martynyuk
227 Peter Brady

**1996**
Pick
12 **Josh Holden**
75 **Zenith Komarniski**
93 Jonas Soling
121 Tyler Prosofsky
147 Nolan McDonald
175 Clint Cabana
201 Jeff Scissons
227 **Lubomir Vaic**

**1995**
Pick
40 **Chris McAllister**
61 **Larry Courville**
66 **Peter Schaefer**
92 Lloyd Shaw
120 Todd Norman
144 **Brent Sopel**
170 Stewart Bodtker
196 Tyler Willis
222 Jason Cugnet

## Mike Gillis

### President and General Manager

*Born: Sudbury, Ont., December 1, 1958.*

The Vancouver Canucks announced on April 23, 2008, that Mike Gillis had been named the tenth general manager in club history. Gillis joined the Canucks organization after spending the previous 16 years as a player representative. In his first year with the club in 2008-09, the Canucks won the Northwest Division title.

Gillis began his NHL career in 1978 as a member of the Colorado Rockies. In 246 NHL regular season games, Gillis recorded 76 points (33 goals, 43 assists) and 186 penalty minutes with Colorado and Boston before a leg injury forced him to retire in 1985. He then returned to Kingston, Ontario, where he had grown up, to obtain his law degree from Queen's University in 1990. Gillis began his career as a NHL player representative in 1992 and became one of the most successful in his industry. His ability to evaluate players, negotiate contracts and his extensive knowledge of the Collective Bargaining Agreement, provided him the opportunity to work with a number of the NHL's most elite players.

# Club Directory

General Motors Place

**Vancouver Canucks**
General Motors Place
800 Griffiths Way
Vancouver, B.C. V6B 6G1
Phone **604/899-4600**
FAX 604/899-4640
www.canucks.com
**Capacity:** 18,630

**Executive**

| | |
|---|---|
| Chairman & Governor, NHL | Francesco Aquilini |
| Alternate Governor, NHL | Paolo Aquilini |
| Alternate Governor, NHL | Roberto Aquilini |
| Executive Office Manager | Cheryl Loveseth |
| President & General Manager & Alternate Governor, NHL | Mike Gillis |
| Chief Operating Officer | Victor De Bonis |
| Executive Vice President, Business & General Counsel | Jon Festinger |
| Vice President, Business Development | Gord Forbes |
| Vice President, Hockey Ops & Asst. G.M. | Laurence Gilman |
| Vice President, People Development | TBD |
| Vice President, Player Personnel & Asst. G.M. | Lorne Henning |
| Vice President & G.M., Arena Operations | Harvey Jones |
| Vice President, Finance & CFO | Todd Kobus |

**Hockey Operations**

| | |
|---|---|
| General Manager & Alternate Governor, NHL | Mike Gillis |
| Executive Assistants | Michelle Di Tomaso, Joan Stobbs |
| Vice President, Player Personnel & Asst. G.M. | Lorne Henning |
| Vice President, Hockey Ops & Asst. G.M. | Laurence Gilman |
| Senior Advisor to the General Manager | Stan Smyl |
| Head Coach | Alain Vigneault |
| Associate Coach | Rick Bowness |
| Assistant Coach | Ryan Walter |
| Assistant Coach, Video | Darryl Williams |
| Goaltending Consultant | Ian Clark |
| Strength & Conditioning Coach | Roger Takahashi |
| Director, Player Development | Dave Gagner |
| Head Coach, Manitoba Moose | Scott Arniel |
| Assistant Coaches, Manitoba Moose | Keith McCambridge, Rick St. Croix |
| Director, Media Relations & Team Operations | TC Carling |
| Manager, Media Relations & Team Operations | Ben Brown |
| Coordinator, Media Relations & Publications | Stephanie Maniago |
| Assistant, Media Relations | Jen Herrington |
| Director, Community Partnerships | Debbie Butt |
| Director of Charitable, Corporate & On-Ice Events | Karen Christiansen |
| Coordinator, Community Partnerships & Education | Jessica Danylchuk |
| Coordinator, Community Partnerships | Tara Clarke |
| Manager, Hockey Development & Alumni Liaison | Rod Brathwaite |
| Coord., Community Partnerships & Mascot Liaison | Paul Buckley |

**Scouting Staff**

| | |
|---|---|
| Chief Amateur Scout | Ron Delorme |
| Associate Head Scout | Thomas Gradin |
| Amateur Scouts | Brian Chapman, Sergei Chibisov, Frank Kollar, Tim Lenardon, Harold Snepsts, Darrell Young, Jonathan Bates, Brad Berry, Judd Brackett, Mark Jooris, Inge Hammarstrom |
| Director of Professional Scouting | Eric Crawford |
| Professional Scouts | Lucien DeBlois, Lars Lindgren, Scott Mellanby |
| Director of Hockey Administration | Jonathan Wall |
| Hockey Operations Assistant | Mike Brown |

**Medical & Training Staff**

| | |
|---|---|
| Head Athletic Trainer / Asst. Trainers | Mike Burnstein / Jon Sanderson, Marty Dudgeon |
| Equipment Manager / Asst. Manager | Pat O'Neill / Jamie Hendricks |
| Equipment Assistant | Brian Hamilton |
| Game Dressing Room Attendants | John Jukich, Ron Shute, Brian Brumwell |
| Team Physicians | Dr. Bill Regan, Dr. Mike Wilkinson |
| Team Dentist | Dr. Jeffrey Norden |
| Team Chiropractor | Dr. Sid Sheard |
| Team Optometrist | Dr. Alan R. Boyco |

**Broadcast**

| | |
|---|---|
| Director, Facilities & In-House Productions | Paul Brettell |
| Director, Production Services | Mike Hall |
| Senior Broadcast Technician | Greg Story |
| Multimedia Senior Producer / Producer | Jason Steensma / Gayla Anderson |
| Broadcast Business Manager | Shannon Baker |
| Production Assistant & Editor | Rory McGarry |

**Game Entertainment & Events**

| | |
|---|---|
| Coordinator, Animation & Display Services | Art Green |
| Manager / Coordinator | Cam Goudreau, Rebecca Grant |

**Event Services**

| | |
|---|---|
| Director, Event Services | Indira Fisher |

**Business Development**

| | |
|---|---|
| Directors | David Altman, James Douglas, Sean Monahan, Darren Moscovitch |

**Client Service & Ticket Operations**

| | |
|---|---|
| Director, Client Service & Ticket Operations | Mary Nagy |

**Engineering**

| | |
|---|---|
| Director, Engineering | Al Hutchings |

**Finance & Administration**

| | |
|---|---|
| Director, Finance | Aaron Wilson |
| Controller, Hockey Operations | Patricia Bigonzi |

**Information Technology**

| | |
|---|---|
| Manager, Information Technology | William Cheng |

**Marketing, Creative Services**

| | |
|---|---|
| Director, Brand Management | Paul Dal Monte |
| Marketing Manager | Bianca Bujan |
| Manager, Creative Services | Ryan Castle |

**People Development**

| | |
|---|---|
| Manager, People Development | Dana Clark |

**Canucks Team Store**

| | |
|---|---|
| Director, Retail & Consumer Product Marketing | Janeil Mackay |

**Travel**

| | |
|---|---|
| Travel Manager | Cathie Moroney |

**Web Development**

| | |
|---|---|
| Director, Website & New Media | Kevin Kinghorn |

**Legal**

| | |
|---|---|
| Paralegal | Perry Bahniwal |

## Key Off-Season Signings/Acquisitions

**2009**

**June 22** • Named **Bob Woods** assistant coach.
**July 1** • Signed RW **Mike Knuble.**
**10** • Signed C **Brendan Morrison.**
**13** • Re-signed C **Boyd Gordon.**
**15** • Re-signed D **Shaone Morrisonn**, RW **Eric Fehr** and LW **Chris Bourque.**
**16** • Re-signed D **Jeff Schultz.**
**31** • D **Milan Jurcina** awarded one-year contract in arbitration.

# Washington Capitals

## 2008-09 Results: 50W-24L-3OTL-5SOL 108PTS.
## First, Southeast Division

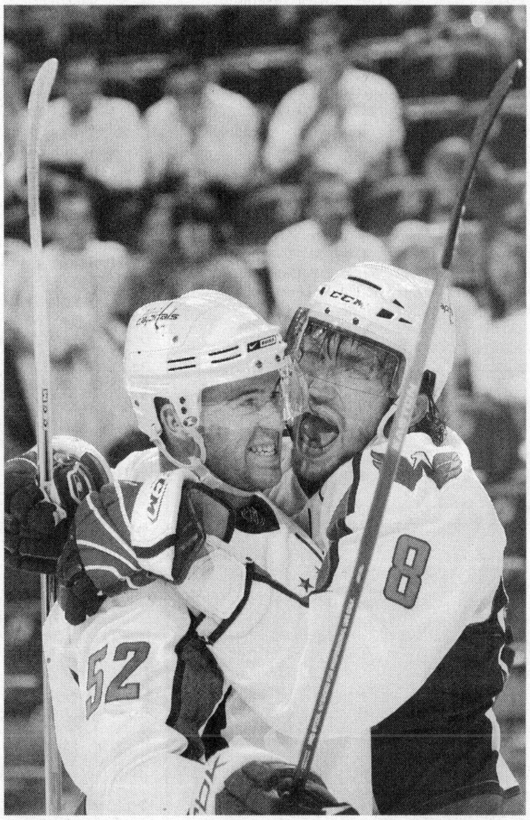

*Mike Green and Alex Ovechkin celebrate a Washington goal. Between them, they combined for 87 goals in 2008-09, with Green leading all defenseman with 31 and Ovechkin topping the league with 56.*

## 2009-10 Schedule

|  |  |  |  |
|---|---|---|---|
| **Oct.** | Thu. | 1 | at Boston |
| | Sat. | 3 | Toronto |
| | Tue. | 6 | at Philadelphia |
| | Thu. | 8 | NY Rangers |
| | Sat. | 10 | at Detroit |
| | Mon. | 12 | New Jersey |
| | Thu. | 15 | San Jose |
| | Sat. | 17 | Nashville |
| | Thu. | 22 | at Atlanta |
| | Sat. | 24 | at NY Islanders |
| | Tue. | 27 | Philadelphia |
| | Thu. | 29 | at Atlanta |
| | Fri. | 30 | NY Islanders |
| **Nov.** | Sun. | 1 | Columbus* |
| | Wed. | 4 | at New Jersey |
| | Fri. | 6 | at Florida |
| | Sat. | 7 | Florida |
| | Wed. | 11 | NY Islanders |
| | Fri. | 13 | Minnesota |
| | Sat. | 14 | at New Jersey |
| | Tue. | 17 | at NY Rangers |
| | Fri. | 20 | Montreal |
| | Sat. | 21 | at Toronto |
| | Mon. | 23 | at Ottawa |
| | Wed. | 25 | Buffalo |
| | Sat. | 28 | at Montreal |
| | Mon. | 30 | at Carolina |
| **Dec.** | Thu. | 3 | Florida |
| | Sat. | 5 | at Philadelphia |
| | Mon. | 7 | at Tampa Bay |
| | Wed. | 9 | at Buffalo |
| | Fri. | 11 | Carolina |
| | Sat. | 12 | at Toronto |
| | Tue. | 15 | at Colorado |
| | Fri. | 18 | at Vancouver |
| | Sat. | 19 | at Edmonton |
| | Wed. | 23 | Buffalo |
| | Sat. | 26 | New Jersey |
| | Mon. | 28 | Carolina |
| | Wed. | 30 | at San Jose |
| **Jan.** | Sat. | 2 | at Los Angeles* |
| | Tue. | 5 | Montreal |
| | Thu. | 7 | Ottawa |
| | Sat. | 9 | at Atlanta |
| | Tue. | 12 | at Tampa Bay |
| | Wed. | 13 | at Florida |
| | Fri. | 15 | Toronto |
| | Sun. | 17 | Philadelphia* |
| | Tue. | 19 | Detroit |
| | Thu. | 21 | at Pittsburgh |
| | Sat. | 23 | Phoenix |
| | Tue. | 26 | at NY Islanders |
| | Wed. | 27 | Anaheim |
| | Fri. | 29 | Florida |
| | Sun. | 31 | Tampa Bay* |
| **Feb.** | Tue. | 2 | at Boston |
| | Thu. | 4 | at NY Rangers |
| | Fri. | 5 | Atlanta |
| | Sun. | 7 | Pittsburgh* |
| | Wed. | 10 | at Montreal |
| | Thu. | 11 | at Ottawa |
| | Sat. | 13 | at St. Louis |
| **Mar.** | Wed. | 3 | at Buffalo |
| | Thu. | 4 | Tampa Bay |
| | Sat. | 6 | NY Rangers |
| | Mon. | 8 | Dallas |
| | Wed. | 10 | Carolina |
| | Fri. | 12 | Tampa Bay |
| | Sun. | 14 | at Chicago |
| | Tue. | 16 | at Florida |
| | Thu. | 18 | at Carolina |
| | Sat. | 20 | at Tampa Bay |
| | Wed. | 24 | Pittsburgh |
| | Thu. | 25 | at Carolina |
| | Sun. | 28 | Calgary* |
| | Tue. | 30 | Ottawa |
| **Apr.** | Thu. | 1 | Atlanta |
| | Sat. | 3 | at Columbus |
| | Mon. | 5 | Boston |
| | Tue. | 6 | at Pittsburgh |
| | Fri. | 9 | Atlanta |
| | Sun. | 11 | Boston* |

* Denotes afternoon game.

### Year-by-Year Record

| | | Home | | | | Road | | | | Overall | | | | | | | | |
|---|---|---|---|---|---|---|---|---|---|---|---|---|---|---|---|---|---|---|
| **Season** | **GP** | **W** | **L** | **T** | **OL** | **W** | **L** | **T** | **OL** | **W** | **L** | **T** | **OL** | **GF** | **GA** | **Pts.** | **Finished** | **Playoff Result** |
| 2008-09 | 82 | 29 | 9 | .... | 3 | 21 | 15 | .... | 5 | 50 | 24 | .... | 8 | 272 | 245 | 108 | 1st, Southeast Div. | Lost Conf. Semi-Final |
| 2007-08 | 82 | 23 | 15 | .... | 3 | 20 | 16 | .... | 5 | 43 | 31 | .... | 8 | 242 | 231 | 94 | 1st, Southeast Div. | Lost Conf. Quarter-Final |
| 2006-07 | 82 | 17 | 17 | .... | 7 | 11 | 23 | .... | 7 | 28 | 40 | .... | 14 | 235 | 286 | 70 | 5th, Southeast Div. | Out of Playoffs |
| 2005-06 | 82 | 16 | 18 | .... | 7 | 13 | 23 | .... | 5 | 29 | 41 | .... | 12 | 237 | 306 | 70 | 5th, Southeast Div. | Out of Playoffs |
| 2004-05 | .... | .... | .... | .... | .... | .... | .... | .... | .... | .... | .... | .... | .... | .... | .... | .... | | |
| 2003-04 | 82 | 13 | 20 | 6 | 2 | 10 | 26 | 4 | 1 | 23 | 46 | 10 | 3 | 186 | 253 | 59 | 5th, Southeast Div. | Out of Playoffs |
| 2002-03 | 82 | 24 | 13 | 2 | 2 | 15 | 16 | 6 | 4 | 39 | 29 | 8 | 6 | 224 | 220 | 92 | 2nd, Southeast Div. | Lost Conf. Quarter-Final |
| 2001-02 | 82 | 21 | 12 | 6 | 2 | 15 | 21 | 5 | 0 | 36 | 33 | 11 | 2 | 228 | 240 | 85 | 2nd, Southeast Div. | Out of Playoffs |
| 2000-01 | 82 | 24 | 9 | 6 | 2 | 17 | 18 | 4 | 2 | 41 | 27 | 10 | 4 | 233 | 211 | 96 | 1st, Southeast Div. | Lost Conf. Quarter-Final |
| 1999-2000 | 82 | 26 | 5 | 8 | 2 | 18 | 19 | 4 | 0 | 44 | 24 | 12 | 2 | 227 | 194 | 102 | 1st, Southeast Div. | Lost Conf. Quarter-Final |
| 1998-99 | 82 | 16 | 23 | 2 | .... | 15 | 22 | 4 | .... | 31 | 45 | 6 | .... | 200 | 218 | 68 | 3rd, Southeast Div. | Out of Playoffs |
| 1997-98 | 82 | 23 | 12 | 6 | .... | 17 | 18 | 6 | .... | 40 | 30 | 12 | .... | 219 | 202 | 92 | 3rd, Atlantic Div. | Lost Final |
| 1996-97 | 82 | 19 | 17 | 5 | .... | 14 | 23 | 4 | .... | 33 | 40 | 9 | .... | 214 | 231 | 75 | 5th, Atlantic Div. | Out of Playoffs |
| 1995-96 | 82 | 21 | 15 | 5 | .... | 18 | 17 | 6 | .... | 39 | 32 | 11 | .... | 234 | 204 | 89 | 4th, Atlantic Div. | Lost Conf. Quarter-Final |
| 1994-95 | 48 | 15 | 6 | 3 | .... | 7 | 12 | 5 | .... | 22 | 18 | 8 | .... | 136 | 120 | 52 | 3rd, Atlantic Div. | Lost Conf. Quarter-Final |
| 1993-94 | 84 | 17 | 16 | 9 | .... | 22 | 19 | 1 | .... | 39 | 35 | 10 | .... | 277 | 263 | 88 | 3rd, Atlantic Div. | Lost Conf. Semi-Final |
| 1992-93 | 84 | 21 | 15 | 6 | .... | 22 | 19 | 1 | .... | 43 | 34 | 7 | .... | 325 | 286 | 93 | 2nd, Patrick Div. | Lost Div. Semi-Final |
| 1991-92 | 80 | 25 | 12 | 3 | .... | 20 | 15 | 5 | .... | 45 | 27 | 8 | .... | 330 | 275 | 98 | 2nd, Patrick Div. | Lost Div. Semi-Final |
| 1990-91 | 80 | 21 | 14 | 5 | .... | 16 | 22 | 2 | .... | 37 | 36 | 7 | .... | 258 | 258 | 81 | 3rd, Patrick Div. | Lost Div. Final |
| 1989-90 | 80 | 19 | 18 | 3 | .... | 17 | 20 | 3 | .... | 36 | 38 | 6 | .... | 284 | 275 | 78 | 3rd, Patrick Div. | Lost Conf. Championship |
| 1988-89 | 80 | 25 | 12 | 3 | .... | 16 | 17 | 7 | .... | 41 | 29 | 10 | .... | 305 | 259 | 92 | 1st, Patrick Div. | Lost Div. Semi-Final |
| 1987-88 | 80 | 22 | 14 | 4 | .... | 16 | 19 | 5 | .... | 38 | 33 | 9 | .... | 281 | 249 | 85 | 2nd, Patrick Div. | Lost Div. Final |
| 1986-87 | 80 | 22 | 15 | 3 | .... | 16 | 17 | 7 | .... | 38 | 32 | 10 | .... | 285 | 278 | 86 | 2nd, Patrick Div. | Lost Div. Semi-Final |
| 1985-86 | 80 | 30 | 8 | 2 | .... | 20 | 15 | 5 | .... | 50 | 23 | 7 | .... | 315 | 272 | 107 | 2nd, Patrick Div. | Lost Div. Final |
| 1984-85 | 80 | 27 | 11 | 2 | .... | 19 | 14 | 7 | .... | 46 | 25 | 9 | .... | 322 | 240 | 101 | 2nd, Patrick Div. | Lost Div. Semi-Final |
| 1983-84 | 80 | 26 | 11 | 3 | .... | 22 | 16 | 2 | .... | 48 | 27 | 5 | .... | 308 | 226 | 101 | 2nd, Patrick Div. | Lost Div. Final |
| 1982-83 | 80 | 22 | 12 | 6 | .... | 17 | 13 | 10 | .... | 39 | 25 | 16 | .... | 306 | 283 | 94 | 3rd, Patrick Div. | Lost Div. Semi-Final |
| 1981-82 | 80 | 16 | 16 | 8 | .... | 10 | 25 | 5 | .... | 26 | 41 | 13 | .... | 319 | 338 | 65 | 5th, Patrick Div. | Out of Playoffs |
| 1980-81 | 80 | 16 | 17 | 7 | .... | 10 | 19 | 11 | .... | 26 | 36 | 18 | .... | 286 | 317 | 70 | 5th, Patrick Div. | Out of Playoffs |
| 1979-80 | 80 | 20 | 14 | 6 | .... | 7 | 26 | 7 | .... | 27 | 40 | 13 | .... | 261 | 293 | 67 | 5th, Patrick Div. | Out of Playoffs |
| 1978-79 | 80 | 15 | 19 | 6 | .... | 9 | 22 | 9 | .... | 24 | 41 | 15 | .... | 273 | 338 | 63 | 4th, Norris Div. | Out of Playoffs |
| 1977-78 | 80 | 10 | 23 | 7 | .... | 7 | 26 | 7 | .... | 17 | 49 | 14 | .... | 195 | 321 | 48 | 5th, Norris Div. | Out of Playoffs |
| 1976-77 | 80 | 17 | 15 | 8 | .... | 7 | 27 | 6 | .... | 24 | 42 | 14 | .... | 221 | 307 | 62 | 4th, Norris Div. | Out of Playoffs |
| 1975-76 | 80 | 6 | 26 | 8 | .... | 5 | 33 | 2 | .... | 11 | 59 | 10 | .... | 224 | 394 | 32 | 5th, Norris Div. | Out of Playoffs |
| 1974-75 | 80 | 7 | 28 | 5 | .... | 1 | 39 | 0 | .... | 8 | 67 | 5 | .... | 181 | 446 | 21 | 5th, Norris Div. | Out of Playoffs |

**SOUTHEAST DIVISION**
**36th NHL Season**

**Franchise date:** June 11, 1974

# 2009-10 Player Personnel

| FORWARDS | HT | WT | S | Place of Birth | *Age | 2008-09 Club |
|---|---|---|---|---|---|---|
| AUCOIN, Keith | 5-8 | 165 | R | Waltham, MA | 30 | Washington-Hershey |
| BACKSTROM, Nicklas | 6-1 | 210 | L | Gavle, Sweden | 21 | Washington |
| BEAGLE, Jay | 6-3 | 208 | R | Calgary, Alta. | 23 | Washington-Hershey |
| BOUCHARD, Francois | 6-1 | 195 | L | Sherbrooke, Que. | 21 | Hershey |
| BOURQUE, Chris | 5-10 | 177 | L | Boston, MA | 23 | Washington-Hershey |
| BRADLEY, Matt | 6-3 | 200 | R | Stittsville, Ont. | 31 | Washington |
| BRUESS, Trevor | 6-0 | 209 | R | Minneapolis, MN | 23 | Minnesota State |
| CLARK, Chris | 6-0 | 196 | R | South Windsor, CT | 33 | Washington |
| FEHR, Eric | 6-4 | 212 | R | Winkler, Man. | 24 | Washington |
| FLEISCHMANN, Tomas | 6-1 | 190 | L | Koprivnice, Czech. | 25 | Washington |
| GORDON, Andrew | 6-0 | 198 | R | Halifax, N.S. | 23 | Washington-Hershey |
| GORDON, Boyd | 6-1 | 200 | R | Unity, Sask. | 25 | Washington |
| GUSTAFSSON, Anton | 6-2 | 194 | L | Karlskoga, Sweden | 19 | Bofors-Frolunda Jr. |
| HAUSWIRTH, Jake | 6-5 | 200 | L | Merrill, WI | 21 | Omaha |
| KANE, Boyd | 6-2 | 220 | L | Swift Current, Sask. | 31 | Phi-Phi (AHL) |
| KNUBLE, Mike | 6-3 | 230 | R | Toronto, Ont. | 37 | Philadelphia |
| LAICH, Brooks | 6-2 | 200 | L | Wawota, Sask. | 26 | Washington |
| LAING, Quintin | 6-2 | 200 | L | Rosetown, Sask. | 30 | Washington-Hershey |
| MORRISON, Brendan | 5-11 | 181 | L | Pitt Meadows, B.C. | 34 | Anaheim-Dallas |
| NYLANDER, Michael | 6-1 | 195 | L | Stockholm, Sweden | 36 | Washington |
| OSALA, Oskar | 6-4 | 225 | L | Vaasa, Finland | 21 | Washington-Hershey |
| OVECHKIN, Alex | 6-2 | 225 | R | Moscow, USSR | 24 | Washington |
| PERREAULT, Mathieu | 5-10 | 175 | L | Drummondville, Que. | 21 | Hershey |
| PINIZZOTTO, Steve | 6-1 | 200 | R | Mississauga, Ont. | 25 | Hershey-South Carolina |
| SEMIN, Alexander | 6-2 | 205 | L | Krasnoyarsk, USSR | 25 | Washington |
| STECKEL, David | 6-5 | 222 | L | Westbend, WI | 27 | Washington |
| WILSON, Kyle | 6-1 | 200 | R | Oakville, Ont. | 24 | Hershey |

| DEFENSEMEN | HT | WT | S | Place of Birth | *Age | 2008-09 Club |
|---|---|---|---|---|---|---|
| ALZNER, Karl | 6-2 | 205 | L | Burnaby, B.C. | 21 | Washington-Hershey |
| CARLSON, John | 6-3 | 211 | R | Natick, MA | 19 | London-Hershey |
| COLLINS, Sean | 6-1 | 212 | R | Troy, MI | 25 | Washington-Hershey |
| ERSKINE, John | 6-4 | 216 | L | Kingston, Ont. | 29 | Washington |
| FINLEY, Joe | 6-7 | 245 | L | Edina, MN | 22 | North Dakota-Hershey |
| GODFREY, Josh | 6-1 | 202 | R | Collingwood, Ont. | 21 | Hershey-South Carolina |
| GREEN, Mike | 6-1 | 208 | R | Calgary, Alta. | 23 | Washington |
| JURCINA, Milan | 6-4 | 240 | R | Liptovsky Mikulas, Czech. | 26 | Washington |
| McNEILL, Patrick | 6-0 | 198 | L | Strathroy, Ont. | 22 | Hershey |
| MISKOVIC, Zach | 6-1 | 195 | R | River Forest, IL | 24 | St. Lawrence |
| MORRISONN, Shaone | 6-4 | 215 | L | Vancouver, B.C. | 26 | Washington |
| POTHIER, Brian | 6-0 | 200 | R | New Bedford, MA | 32 | Washington-Hershey |
| POTI, Tom | 6-3 | 200 | L | Worcester, MA | 32 | Washington |
| SCHULTZ, Jeff | 6-6 | 227 | L | Calgary, Alta. | 23 | Washington |
| SLOAN, Tyler | 6-4 | 203 | L | Calgary, Alta. | 28 | Washington-Hershey |

| GOALTENDERS | HT | WT | C | Place of Birth | *Age | 2008-09 Club |
|---|---|---|---|---|---|---|
| NEUVIRTH, Michal | 6-1 | 199 | L | Usti nad Labem, Czech. | 21 | Wsh-Her-South Carolina |
| THEODORE, Jose | 5-11 | 182 | R | Laval, Que. | 33 | Washington |
| VARLAMOV, Semyon | 6-1 | 201 | L | Kuybyshev, USSR | 21 | Washington-Hershey |

* – Age at start of 2009-10 season

## General Managers' History

Milt Schmidt, 1974-75; Milt Schmidt and Max McNab, 1975-76; Max McNab, 1976-77 to 1980-81; Max McNab and Roger Crozier, 1981-82; David Poile, 1982-83 to 1996-97; George McPhee, 1997-98 to date.

# George McPhee

### Vice President and General Manager

*Born: Wallaceburg, Ont., July 2, 1958.*

On June 9, 1997, George McPhee became the fifth general manager of the Washington Capitals. In his first year on the job, McPhee led the Caps to the Stanley Cup Finals for the first time in franchise history. He has begun rebuilding the Capitals with younger players and used the first overall choice at the 2004 NHL Entry Draft to select Alex Ovechkin. In 2007-08 and 2008-09, the Capitals won the Southeast Division. They tied a franchise record with 50 wins in 2008-09 and set a new one with 108 points.

Prior to joining the Capitals, McPhee spent five years in the front office of the Vancouver Canucks where he served as vice president of hockey operations and alternate governor. He has earned degrees in both law and business and, while attending law school at Rutgers University, interned at the United States Court of International Trade in 1991.

A back injury forced McPhee to retire as an active player at the conclusion of the 1988-89 season, after a seven year playing career with the New York Rangers and New Jersey Devils. McPhee originally signed as a free agent with the Rangers in July, 1982, after graduating from Bowling Green State University with a business degree. McPhee did not waste any time in college, tallying 40 goals and 48 assists in his freshman season and easily winning CCHA rookie of the year honors. His outstanding collegiate hockey career was capped off when he was named the recipient of the Hobey Baker Award as the top U.S. collegiate player in his senior season. McPhee also earned All-America honors as a senior and finished his career at Bowling Green as the CCHA's all-time leading scorer with 114-153-267. He was the first player in CCHA history to make the Conference's all-academic team three straight seasons.

# 2008-09 Scoring

* – rookie

## Regular Season

| Pos | # | Player | Team | GP | G | A | Pts | TOI | +/– | PIM | PP | SH | GW | S | % |
|---|---|---|---|---|---|---|---|---|---|---|---|---|---|---|---|
| L | 8 | Alex Ovechkin | WSH | 79 | 56 | 54 | 110 | 23:00 | 8 | 72 | 19 | 1 | 10 | 528 | 10.6 |
| C | 19 | Nicklas Backstrom | WSH | 82 | 22 | 66 | 88 | 19:56 | 16 | 46 | 14 | 0 | 1 | 174 | 12.6 |
| L | 28 | Alexander Semin | WSH | 62 | 34 | 45 | 79 | 19:14 | 25 | 77 | 8 | 0 | 8 | 223 | 15.2 |
| D | 52 | Mike Green | WSH | 68 | 31 | 42 | 73 | 25:45 | 24 | 68 | 18 | 1 | 4 | 243 | 12.8 |
| C | 21 | Brooks Laich | WSH | 82 | 23 | 30 | 53 | 17:16 | –1 | 31 | 9 | 1 | 3 | 185 | 12.4 |
| C | 25 | Viktor Kozlov | WSH | 67 | 13 | 28 | 41 | 15:39 | –9 | 16 | 2 | 0 | 0 | 153 | 8.5 |
| L | 14 | Tomas Fleischmann | WSH | 73 | 19 | 18 | 37 | 15:04 | –3 | 20 | 7 | 0 | 4 | 131 | 14.5 |
| C | 91 | Sergei Fedorov | WSH | 52 | 11 | 22 | 33 | 16:30 | 4 | 50 | 2 | 0 | 2 | 118 | 9.3 |
| C | 92 | Michael Nylander | WSH | 72 | 9 | 24 | 33 | 14:02 | 0 | 32 | 4 | 0 | 2 | 87 | 10.3 |
| R | 16 | Eric Fehr | WSH | 61 | 12 | 13 | 25 | 11:14 | 8 | 22 | 1 | 0 | 2 | 134 | 9.0 |
| C | 39 | David Steckel | WSH | 76 | 8 | 11 | 19 | 13:48 | 2 | 34 | 0 | 2 | 1 | 103 | 7.8 |
| C | 15 | Boyd Gordon | WSH | 63 | 5 | 9 | 14 | 13:27 | –4 | 16 | 0 | 1 | 2 | 69 | 7.2 |
| D | 23 | Milan Jurcina | WSH | 79 | 3 | 11 | 14 | 16:09 | 1 | 68 | 0 | 0 | 1 | 95 | 3.2 |
| D | 3 | Tom Poti | WSH | 52 | 3 | 10 | 13 | 21:08 | 3 | 28 | 0 | 0 | 1 | 48 | 6.3 |
| D | 26 | Shaone Morrisonn | WSH | 72 | 3 | 10 | 13 | 17:59 | 4 | 77 | 0 | 0 | 1 | 50 | 6.0 |
| D | 55 | Jeff Schultz | WSH | 64 | 1 | 11 | 12 | 19:45 | 13 | 21 | 0 | 1 | 0 | 40 | 2.5 |
| R | 10 | Matt Bradley | WSH | 81 | 5 | 6 | 11 | 10:36 | –1 | 59 | 0 | 0 | 1 | 98 | 5.1 |
| C | 20 | Keith Aucoin | WSH | 12 | 2 | 4 | 6 | 10:19 | 5 | 4 | 1 | 0 | 0 | 15 | 13.3 |
| R | 17 | Chris Clark | WSH | 32 | 1 | 5 | 6 | 11:34 | –3 | 32 | 0 | 0 | 0 | 36 | 2.8 |
| D | 89 | Tyler Sloan | WSH | 26 | 1 | 4 | 5 | 16:38 | 4 | 14 | 0 | 0 | 0 | 8 | 12.5 |
| D | 27 * | Karl Alzner | WSH | 30 | 1 | 4 | 5 | 19:25 | –1 | 2 | 0 | 0 | 0 | 31 | 3.2 |
| L | 87 | Donald Brashear | WSH | 63 | 1 | 3 | 4 | 8:14 | –6 | 121 | 0 | 0 | 1 | 43 | 2.3 |
| D | 42 * | Sami Lepisto | WSH | 7 | 0 | 4 | 4 | 19:36 | –3 | 6 | 0 | 0 | 0 | 7 | 0.0 |
| D | 4 | John Erskine | WSH | 52 | 0 | 4 | 4 | 16:47 | 1 | 63 | 0 | 0 | 0 | 50 | 0.0 |
| D | 2 | Brian Pothier | WSH | 9 | 1 | 2 | 3 | 16:34 | 0 | 4 | 0 | 0 | 1 | 8 | 12.5 |
| D | 43 | Bryan Helmer | WSH | 12 | 0 | 3 | 3 | 16:36 | –1 | 2 | 0 | 0 | 0 | 8 | 0.0 |
| C | 33 | Alexandre Giroux | WSH | 12 | 1 | 1 | 2 | 10:34 | 4 | 10 | 0 | 0 | 1 | 20 | 5.0 |
| D | 62 * | Sean Collins | WSH | 15 | 1 | 1 | 2 | 14:32 | 1 | 12 | 0 | 0 | 0 | 14 | 7.1 |
| L | 56 * | Chris Bourque | WSH | 8 | 1 | 0 | 1 | 9:46 | 0 | 0 | 0 | 0 | 0 | 11 | 9.1 |
| L | 53 | Quintin Laing | WSH | 1 | 0 | 0 | 0 | 10:19 | 1 | 0 | 0 | 0 | 0 | 2 | 0.0 |
| R | 63 * | Andrew Gordon | WSH | 1 | 0 | 0 | 0 | 7:12 | 0 | 0 | 0 | 0 | 0 | 1 | 0.0 |
| L | 38 | Graham Mink | WSH | 2 | 0 | 0 | 0 | 8:03 | 0 | 0 | 0 | 0 | 0 | 4 | 0.0 |
| L | 48 * | Oskar Osala | WSH | 2 | 0 | 0 | 0 | 8:43 | –1 | 0 | 0 | 0 | 0 | 1 | 0.0 |
| D | 44 | Staffan Kronwall | WSH | 3 | 0 | 0 | 0 | 13:13 | –1 | 0 | 0 | 0 | 0 | 4 | 0.0 |
| C | 83 * | Jay Beagle | WSH | 3 | 0 | 0 | 0 | 7:36 | –3 | 2 | 0 | 0 | 0 | 5 | 0.0 |

### Goaltending

| No. | Goaltender | GPI | Mins | Avg | W | L | OT | EN | SO | GA | SA | S% | G | A | PIM |
|---|---|---|---|---|---|---|---|---|---|---|---|---|---|---|---|
| 40 | * Semyon Varlamov | 6 | 329 | 2.37 | 4 | 0 | 1 | 0 | 0 | 13 | 159 | .918 | 0 | 0 | 2 |
| 1 | Brent Johnson | 21 | 1131 | 2.81 | 12 | 6 | 2 | 2 | 0 | 53 | 579 | .908 | 0 | 1 | 4 |
| 60 | Jose Theodore | 57 | 3287 | 2.87 | 32 | 17 | 5 | 4 | 2 | 157 | 1572 | .900 | 0 | 3 | 6 |
| 30 | * Michal Neuvirth | 5 | 220 | 3.00 | 2 | 1 | 0 | 0 | 0 | 11 | 102 | .892 | 0 | 0 | 0 |
| | **Totals** | **82** | **4986** | **2.89** | **50** | **24** | **8** | **6** | **2** | **240** | **2418** | **.901** | | | |

## Playoffs

| Pos | # | Player | Team | GP | G | A | Pts | TOI | +/– | PIM | PP | SH | GW | OT | S | % |
|---|---|---|---|---|---|---|---|---|---|---|---|---|---|---|---|---|
| L | 8 | Alex Ovechkin | WSH | 14 | 11 | 10 | 21 | 23:21 | 10 | 8 | 3 | 0 | 1 | 0 | 90 | 12.2 |
| C | 19 | Nicklas Backstrom | WSH | 14 | 3 | 12 | 15 | 21:39 | 3 | 8 | 2 | 0 | 0 | 0 | 33 | 9.1 |
| L | 28 | Alexander Semin | WSH | 14 | 5 | 9 | 14 | 19:58 | –1 | 16 | 1 | 0 | 1 | 0 | 42 | 11.9 |
| D | 52 | Mike Green | WSH | 14 | 1 | 8 | 9 | 24:59 | –5 | 12 | 1 | 0 | 0 | 0 | 24 | 4.2 |
| C | 91 | Sergei Fedorov | WSH | 14 | 1 | 7 | 8 | 16:39 | 1 | 12 | 0 | 0 | 1 | 0 | 24 | 4.2 |
| C | 21 | Brooks Laich | WSH | 14 | 3 | 4 | 7 | 17:27 | 0 | 10 | 2 | 0 | 0 | 0 | 24 | 12.5 |
| D | 3 | Tom Poti | WSH | 14 | 2 | 5 | 7 | 21:36 | 8 | 4 | 1 | 0 | 0 | 0 | 13 | 15.4 |
| C | 25 | Viktor Kozlov | WSH | 14 | 4 | 2 | 6 | 15:54 | 5 | 6 | 0 | 0 | 1 | 0 | 23 | 17.4 |
| R | 10 | Matt Bradley | WSH | 14 | 2 | 4 | 6 | 12:44 | 3 | 0 | 0 | 1 | 1 | 0 | 15 | 13.3 |
| C | 39 | David Steckel | WSH | 14 | 3 | 2 | 5 | 16:03 | 0 | 4 | 0 | 0 | 1 | 1 | 19 | 15.8 |
| L | 14 | Tomas Fleischmann | WSH | 14 | 3 | 1 | 4 | 14:19 | 0 | 4 | 1 | 0 | 1 | 0 | 22 | 13.6 |
| C | 15 | Boyd Gordon | WSH | 14 | 0 | 3 | 3 | 11:16 | –1 | 4 | 0 | 0 | 0 | 0 | 10 | 0.0 |
| D | 23 | Milan Jurcina | WSH | 14 | 2 | 0 | 2 | 16:46 | 6 | 12 | 0 | 1 | 0 | 0 | 10 | 20.0 |
| D | 2 | Brian Pothier | WSH | 13 | 0 | 2 | 2 | 16:48 | 1 | 8 | 0 | 0 | 0 | 0 | 11 | 0.0 |
| R | 17 | Chris Clark | WSH | 8 | 1 | 0 | 1 | 6:31 | –2 | 8 | 0 | 0 | 0 | 0 | 7 | 14.3 |
| D | 89 | Tyler Sloan | WSH | 2 | 0 | 1 | 1 | 18:23 | 1 | 0 | 0 | 0 | 0 | 0 | 1 | 0.0 |
| D | 4 | John Erskine | WSH | 12 | 0 | 1 | 1 | 19:06 | 1 | 16 | 0 | 0 | 0 | 0 | 8 | 0.0 |
| D | 26 | Shaone Morrisonn | WSH | 14 | 0 | 1 | 1 | 18:03 | 1 | 8 | 0 | 0 | 0 | 0 | 6 | 0.0 |
| D | 55 | Jeff Schultz | WSH | 1 | 0 | 0 | 0 | 12:26 | –1 | 0 | 0 | 0 | 0 | 0 | 1 | 0.0 |
| C | 92 | Michael Nylander | WSH | 3 | 0 | 0 | 0 | 8:47 | –1 | 2 | 0 | 0 | 0 | 0 | 0 | 0.0 |
| L | 87 | Donald Brashear | WSH | 4 | 0 | 0 | 0 | 3:25 | 0 | 18 | 0 | 0 | 0 | 0 | 2 | 0.0 |
| C | 83 * | Jay Beagle | WSH | 4 | 0 | 0 | 0 | 3:32 | –1 | 0 | 0 | 0 | 0 | 0 | 1 | 0.0 |
| R | 16 | Eric Fehr | WSH | 9 | 0 | 0 | 0 | 7:22 | –3 | 0 | 0 | 0 | 0 | 0 | 10 | 0.0 |

### Goaltending

| No. | Goaltender | GPI | Mins | Avg | W | L | EN | SO | GA | SA | S% | G | A | PIM |
|---|---|---|---|---|---|---|---|---|---|---|---|---|---|---|
| 40 | * Semyon Varlamov | 13 | 759 | 2.53 | 7 | 6 | 0 | 2 | 32 | 389 | .918 | 0 | 0 | 2 |
| 60 | Jose Theodore | 2 | 97 | 3.71 | 0 | 1 | 0 | 0 | 6 | 33 | .818 | 0 | 0 | 0 |
| | **Totals** | **14** | **861** | **2.65** | **7** | **7** | **0** | **2** | **38** | **422** | **.910** | | | |

## Coaching History

Jim Anderson, Red Sullivan and Milt Schmidt, 1974-75; Milt Schmidt and Tom McVie, 1975-76; Tom McVie, 1976-77, 1977-78; Danny Belisle, 1978-79; Danny Belisle and Gary Green, 1979-80; Gary Green, 1980-81; Gary Green, Roger Crozier and Bryan Murray, 1981-82; Bryan Murray, 1982-83 to 1988-89; Bryan Murray and Terry Murray, 1989-90; Terry Murray, 1990-91 to 1992-93; Terry Murray and Jim Schoenfeld, 1993-94; Jim Schoenfeld, 1994-95 to 1996-97; Ron Wilson, 1997-98 to 2001-02; Bruce Cassidy, 2002-03; Bruce Cassidy and Glen Hanlon, 2003-04; Glen Hanlon, 2004-05 to 2006-07; Glen Hanlon and Bruce Boudreau, 2007-08; Bruce Boudreau, 2008-09 to date.

# Club Records

## Team

(Figures in brackets for season records are games played; records for fewest points, wins, ties, losses, goals, goals against are for 70 or more games)

| | | |
|---|---|---|
| **Most Points** | **108** | 2008-09 (82) |
| **Most Wins** | **50** | 1985-86 (80), 2008-09 (82) |
| **Most Ties** | **18** | 1980-81 (80) |
| **Most Losses** | **67** | 1974-75 (80) |
| **Most Goals** | **330** | 1991-92 (80) |
| **Most Goals Against** | ***446** | 1974-75 (80) |
| **Fewest Points** | ***21** | 1974-75 (80) |
| **Fewest Wins** | ***8** | 1974-75 (80) |
| **Fewest Ties** | **5** | 1974-75 (80), 1983-84 (80) |
| **Fewest Losses** | **23** | 1985-86 (80) |
| **Fewest Goals** | **181** | 1974-75 (80) |
| **Fewest Goals Against** | **194** | 1999-00 (82) |
| **Longest Winning Streak** | | |
| **Overall** | **10** | Jan. 27-Feb. 18/84 |
| **Home** | **10** | Jan. 4-Feb. 23/00 |
| **Away** | **6** | Feb. 26-Apr. 1/84 |
| **Longest Undefeated Streak** | | |
| **Overall** | **14** | Nov. 24-Dec. 23/82 (9 wins, 5 ties), Jan. 17-Feb. 18/84 (13 wins, 1 tie) |
| **Home** | **13** | Nov. 25/92-Jan. 31/93 (9 wins, 4 ties), Dec. 27/99-Feb. 23/00 (11 wins, 2 ties) |
| **Away** | **10** | Nov. 24/82-Jan. 8/83 (6 wins, 4 ties) |
| **Longest Losing Streak** | | |
| **Overall** | ***17** | Feb. 18-Mar. 26/75 |
| **Home** | ***11** | Feb. 18-Mar. 30/75 |
| **Away** | **37** | Oct. 9/74-Mar. 26/75 |
| **Longest Winless Streak** | | |
| **Overall** | **25** | Nov. 29/75-Jan. 21/76 (22 losses, 3 ties) |
| **Home** | **14** | Dec. 3/75-Jan. 21/76 (11 losses, 3 ties) |
| **Away** | **37** | Oct. 9/74-Mar. 26/75 (37 losses) |
| **Most Shutouts, Season** | **9** | 1995-96 (82) |
| **Most PIM, Season** | **2,204** | 1989-90 (80) |
| **Most Goals, Game** | **12** | Feb. 6/90 (Que. 2 at Wsh. 12), Jan. 11/03 (Fla. 2 at Wsh. 12) |

## Individual

| | | |
|---|---|---|
| **Most Seasons** | **16** | Olaf Kolzig |
| **Most Games** | **983** | Calle Johansson |
| **Most Goals, Career** | **472** | Peter Bondra |
| **Most Assists, Career** | **418** | Michal Pivonka |
| **Most Points, Career** | **825** | Peter Bondra (472G, 353A) |
| **Most PIM, Career** | **2,003** | Dale Hunter |
| **Most Shutouts, Career** | **35** | Olaf Kolzig |
| **Longest Consecutive Games Streak** | **422** | Bob Carpenter (Oct. 7/81-Nov. 22/86) |
| **Most Goals, Season** | **65** | Alex Ovechkin (2007-08) |
| **Most Assists, Season** | **76** | Dennis Maruk (1981-82) |
| **Most Points, Season** | **136** | Dennis Maruk (1981-82; 60G, 76A) |
| **Most PIM, Season** | **339** | Alan May (1989-90) |
| **Most Points, Defenseman, Season** | **81** | Larry Murphy (1986-87; 23G, 58A) |
| **Most Points, Center, Season** | **136** | Dennis Maruk (1981-82; 60G, 76A) |
| **Most Points, Right Wing, Season** | **102** | Mike Gartner (1984-85; 50G, 52A) |
| **Most Points, Left Wing, Season** | **112** | Alex Ovechkin (2007-08; 65G, 47A) |
| **Most Points, Rookie, Season** | **106** | Alex Ovechkin (2005-06; 52G, 54A) |
| **Most Shutouts, Season** | **9** | Jim Carey (1995-96) |
| **Most Goals, Game** | **5** | Bengt Gustafsson (Jan. 8/84), Peter Bondra (Feb. 5/94) |
| **Most Assists, Game** | **6** | Mike Ridley (Jan. 7/89) |
| **Most Points, Game** | **7** | Dino Ciccarelli (Mar. 18/89; 4G, 3A), Jaromir Jagr (Jan. 11/03; 3G, 4A) |

* NHL Record.

## Retired Numbers

| | | |
|---|---|---|
| **5** | Rod Langway | 1982-1993 |
| **7** | Yvon Labre | 1974-1981 |
| **11** | Mike Gartner | 1979-1989 |
| **32** | Dale Hunter | 1987-1999 |

## Captains' History

Doug Mohns, 1974-75; Bill Clement and Yvon Labre, 1975-76; Yvon Labre, 1976-77, 1977-78; Guy Charron, 1978-79; Ryan Walter, 1979-80 to 1981-82; Rod Langway, 1982-83 to 1991-92; Rod Langway and Kevin Hatcher, 1992-93; Kevin Hatcher, 1993-94; Dale Hunter, 1994-95 to 1998-99; Adam Oates, 1999-2000, 2000-01; Brendan Witt and Steve Konowalchuk, 2001-02; Steve Konowalchuk, 2002-03; Steve Konowalchuk and no captain, 2003-04; Jeff Halpern, 2005-06; Chris Clark, 2006-07 to date.

# All-time Record vs. Other Clubs

## Regular Season

| | At Home | | | | | | | | On Road | | | | | | | | Total | | | | | | | |
|---|---|---|---|---|---|---|---|---|---|---|---|---|---|---|---|---|---|---|---|---|---|---|---|---|
| | GP | W | L | T | OL | GF | GA | PTS | GP | W | L | T | OL | GF | GA | PTS | GP | W | L | T | OL | GF | GA | PTS |
| Anaheim | 10 | 4 | 6 | 0 | 0 | 17 | 28 | 8 | 11 | 4 | 6 | 1 | 0 | 31 | 35 | 9 | 21 | 8 | 12 | 1 | 0 | 48 | 63 | 17 |
| Atlanta | 28 | 17 | 7 | 3 | 1 | 101 | 82 | 38 | 28 | 11 | 11 | 2 | 4 | 81 | 84 | 28 | 56 | 28 | 18 | 5 | 5 | 182 | 166 | 66 |
| Boston | 63 | 21 | 27 | 12 | 3 | 181 | 209 | 57 | 64 | 17 | 34 | 9 | 4 | 167 | 230 | 47 | 127 | 38 | 61 | 21 | 7 | 348 | 439 | 104 |
| Buffalo | 64 | 17 | 36 | 9 | 2 | 164 | 226 | 45 | 64 | 18 | 40 | 6 | 0 | 169 | 252 | 42 | 128 | 35 | 76 | 15 | 2 | 333 | 478 | 87 |
| Calgary | 42 | 22 | 14 | 6 | 0 | 156 | 141 | 50 | 40 | 8 | 25 | 7 | 0 | 98 | 161 | 23 | 82 | 30 | 39 | 13 | 0 | 254 | 302 | 73 |
| Carolina | 62 | 37 | 20 | 4 | 1 | 209 | 160 | 79 | 64 | 29 | 23 | 10 | 2 | 193 | 185 | 70 | 126 | 66 | 43 | 14 | 3 | 402 | 345 | 149 |
| Chicago | 43 | 22 | 15 | 5 | 1 | 152 | 133 | 50 | 41 | 12 | 23 | 6 | 0 | 120 | 156 | 30 | 84 | 34 | 38 | 11 | 1 | 272 | 289 | 80 |
| Colorado | 35 | 19 | 11 | 4 | 1 | 134 | 110 | 43 | 35 | 15 | 15 | 5 | 0 | 121 | 108 | 35 | 70 | 34 | 26 | 9 | 1 | 255 | 218 | 78 |
| Columbus | 4 | 2 | 1 | 1 | 0 | 11 | 10 | 5 | 6 | 4 | 2 | 0 | 0 | 19 | 17 | 8 | 10 | 6 | 3 | 1 | 0 | 30 | 27 | 13 |
| Dallas | 41 | 16 | 17 | 8 | 0 | 124 | 132 | 40 | 43 | 13 | 22 | 8 | 0 | 117 | 161 | 34 | 84 | 29 | 39 | 16 | 0 | 241 | 293 | 74 |
| Detroit | 48 | 22 | 21 | 5 | 0 | 175 | 153 | 49 | 48 | 15 | 20 | 11 | 2 | 138 | 165 | 43 | 96 | 37 | 41 | 16 | 2 | 313 | 318 | 92 |
| Edmonton | 31 | 19 | 10 | 2 | 0 | 125 | 102 | 40 | 30 | 10 | 16 | 4 | 0 | 91 | 124 | 24 | 61 | 29 | 26 | 6 | 0 | 216 | 226 | 64 |
| Florida | 43 | 20 | 13 | 5 | 5 | 126 | 111 | 50 | 43 | 19 | 19 | 4 | 1 | 110 | 113 | 43 | 86 | 39 | 32 | 9 | 6 | 236 | 224 | 93 |
| Los Angeles | 48 | 19 | 22 | 7 | 0 | 193 | 179 | 45 | 49 | 15 | 28 | 6 | 0 | 149 | 194 | 36 | 97 | 34 | 50 | 13 | 0 | 342 | 373 | 81 |
| Minnesota | 4 | 3 | 1 | 0 | 0 | 11 | 7 | 6 | 5 | 0 | 4 | 0 | 1 | 6 | 13 | 1 | 9 | 3 | 5 | 0 | 1 | 17 | 20 | 7 |
| Montreal | 67 | 31 | 27 | 9 | 0 | 189 | 200 | 71 | 68 | 20 | 39 | 8 | 1 | 149 | 256 | 49 | 135 | 51 | 66 | 17 | 1 | 338 | 456 | 120 |
| Nashville | 6 | 4 | 2 | 0 | 0 | 16 | 16 | 8 | 7 | 3 | 3 | 1 | 0 | 17 | 19 | 7 | 13 | 7 | 5 | 1 | 0 | 33 | 35 | 15 |
| New Jersey | 87 | 51 | 26 | 6 | 4 | 327 | 247 | 112 | 87 | 36 | 40 | 7 | 4 | 253 | 267 | 83 | 174 | 87 | 66 | 13 | 8 | 580 | 514 | 195 |
| NY Islanders | 89 | 44 | 33 | 11 | 1 | 293 | 278 | 100 | 89 | 40 | 46 | 2 | 1 | 272 | 326 | 83 | 178 | 84 | 79 | 13 | 2 | 565 | 604 | 183 |
| NY Rangers | 92 | 49 | 31 | 9 | 3 | 341 | 290 | 110 | 90 | 36 | 43 | 9 | 2 | 300 | 335 | 83 | 182 | 85 | 74 | 18 | 5 | 641 | 625 | 193 |
| Ottawa | 32 | 17 | 11 | 4 | 0 | 111 | 91 | 38 | 31 | 13 | 16 | 1 | 1 | 91 | 111 | 28 | 63 | 30 | 27 | 5 | 1 | 202 | 202 | 66 |
| Philadelphia | 88 | 37 | 38 | 13 | 0 | 286 | 282 | 87 | 91 | 29 | 56 | 6 | 0 | 245 | 345 | 64 | 179 | 66 | 94 | 19 | 0 | 531 | 627 | 151 |
| Phoenix | 32 | 18 | 8 | 5 | 1 | 121 | 88 | 42 | 32 | 9 | 16 | 7 | 0 | 112 | 115 | 25 | 64 | 27 | 24 | 12 | 1 | 233 | 203 | 67 |
| Pittsburgh | 94 | 47 | 35 | 9 | 3 | 385 | 342 | 106 | 91 | 32 | 51 | 7 | 1 | 287 | 355 | 72 | 185 | 79 | 86 | 16 | 4 | 672 | 697 | 178 |
| St. Louis | 41 | 22 | 15 | 4 | 0 | 145 | 123 | 48 | 42 | 13 | 21 | 8 | 0 | 130 | 169 | 34 | 83 | 35 | 36 | 12 | 0 | 275 | 292 | 82 |
| San Jose | 13 | 5 | 7 | 0 | 1 | 36 | 39 | 11 | 12 | 3 | 8 | 1 | 0 | 29 | 40 | 7 | 25 | 8 | 15 | 1 | 1 | 65 | 79 | 18 |
| Tampa Bay | 44 | 28 | 10 | 4 | 2 | 162 | 112 | 62 | 44 | 26 | 14 | 2 | 2 | 141 | 111 | 56 | 88 | 54 | 24 | 6 | 4 | 303 | 223 | 118 |
| Toronto | 58 | 33 | 20 | 4 | 1 | 206 | 164 | 71 | 56 | 20 | 28 | 6 | 2 | 188 | 233 | 48 | 114 | 53 | 48 | 10 | 3 | 394 | 397 | 119 |
| Vancouver | 42 | 23 | 15 | 4 | 0 | 139 | 124 | 50 | 40 | 16 | 18 | 5 | 1 | 125 | 139 | 38 | 82 | 39 | 33 | 9 | 1 | 264 | 263 | 88 |
| Defunct Clubs | 10 | 2 | 8 | 0 | 0 | 28 | 42 | 4 | 10 | 4 | 5 | 1 | 0 | 30 | 39 | 9 | 20 | 6 | 13 | 1 | 0 | 58 | 81 | 13 |
| **Totals** | **1361** | **671** | **507** | **153** | **30** | **4664** | **4221** | **1525** | **1361** | **490** | **692** | **150** | **29** | **3979** | **4858** | **1159** | **2722** | **1161** | **1199** | **303** | **59** | **8643** | **9079** | **2684** |

## Playoffs

| | Series | W | L | GP | W | L | T | GF | GA | Last Mtg. | Rnd. | Result |
|---|---|---|---|---|---|---|---|---|---|---|---|---|
| Boston | 2 | 1 | 1 | 10 | 4 | 6 | 0 | 21 | 28 | 1998 | CQF | W 4-2 |
| Buffalo | 1 | 1 | 0 | 6 | 4 | 2 | 0 | 13 | 11 | 1998 | CF | W 4-2 |
| Detroit | 1 | 0 | 1 | 4 | 0 | 4 | 0 | 7 | 13 | 1998 | F | L 0-4 |
| New Jersey | 2 | 1 | 1 | 13 | 7 | 6 | 0 | 44 | 43 | 1990 | DSF | W 4-2 |
| NY Islanders | 6 | 1 | 5 | 30 | 12 | 18 | 0 | 88 | 99 | 1993 | DSF | L 2-4 |
| NY Rangers | 5 | 3 | 2 | 29 | 15 | 14 | 0 | 94 | 82 | 2009 | CQF | W 4-3 |
| Ottawa | 1 | 1 | 0 | 5 | 4 | 1 | 0 | 18 | 7 | 1998 | CSF | W 4-1 |
| Philadelphia | 4 | 2 | 2 | 23 | 12 | 11 | 0 | 85 | 78 | 2008 | CQF | L 3-4 |
| Pittsburgh | 8 | 1 | 7 | 49 | 19 | 30 | 0 | 143 | 164 | 2009 | CSF | L 3-4 |
| Tampa Bay | 1 | 0 | 1 | 6 | 2 | 4 | 0 | 15 | 14 | 2003 | CQF | L 2-4 |
| **Totals** | **31** | **11** | **20** | **175** | **79** | **96** | **0** | **528** | **539** | | | |

## Playoff Results 2009-2004

| Year | Round | Opponent | Result | GF | GA |
|---|---|---|---|---|---|
| 2009 | CSF | Pittsburgh | L 3-4 | 22 | 27 |
| | CQF | NY Rangers | W 4-3 | 19 | 11 |
| 2008 | CQF | Philadelphia | L 3-4 | 20 | 23 |

**Abbreviations: Round: F** – Final; **CF** – conference final; **CSF** – conference semi-final; **CQF** – conference quarter-final; **DSF** – division semi-final.

Calgary totals include Atlanta Flames, 1974-75 to 1979-80. Carolina totals include Hartford, 1979-80 to 1996-97.
Colorado totals include Quebec, 1979-80 to 1994-95. Dallas totals include Minnesota North Stars, 1974-75 to 1992-93.
New Jersey totals include Kansas City, 1974-75, 1975-76, and Colorado Rockies, 1976-77 to 1981-82.
Phoenix totals include Winnipeg, 1979-80 to 1995-96.

## 2008-09 Results

| | | | |
|---|---|---|---|
| **Oct.** | 10 | at Atlanta | 4-7 |
| | 11 | Chicago | 4-2 |
| | 13 | Vancouver | 5-1 |
| | 16 | at Pittsburgh | 4-3 |
| | 18 | New Jersey | 3-4† |
| | 21 | at Calgary | 1-2 |
| | 23 | at Phoenix | 1-2 |
| | 25 | at Dallas | 6-5* |
| | 28 | Nashville | 4-3† |
| **Nov.** | 1 | at Buffalo | 0-5 |
| | 4 | at Ottawa | 1-2* |
| | 6 | Carolina | 3-2 |
| | 8 | NY Rangers | 3-1 |
| | 10 | Tampa Bay | 4-2 |
| | 12 | at Carolina | 5-1 |
| | 14 | New Jersey | 3-1 |
| | 15 | at New Jersey | 5-6† |
| | 19 | at Anaheim | 6-4 |
| | 20 | at Los Angeles | 2-5 |
| | 22 | at San Jose | 2-7 |
| | 24 | at Minnesota | 3-4 |
| | 26 | Atlanta | 5-3 |
| | 28 | Montreal | 3-0 |
| | 29 | at Columbus | 0-3 |
| **Dec.** | 2 | Florida | 3-5 |
| | 4 | NY Islanders | 5-2 |
| | 6 | at Toronto | 2-1 |
| | 7 | at Carolina | 1-3 |
| | 10 | Boston | 3-1 |
| | 12 | Ottawa | 5-1 |
| | 13 | at Montreal | 2-1 |
| | 16 | at NY Islanders | 5-4* |
| | 18 | St. Louis | 4-2 |
| | 20 | at Philadelphia | 1-7 |
| | 23 | at NY Rangers | 5-4* |
| | 26 | Buffalo | 3-2 |
| | 28 | Toronto | 4-1 |
| | 30 | at Buffalo | 4-2 |
| **Jan.** | 1 | Tampa Bay | 7-4 |
| | 3 | NY Rangers | 2-1 |
| | 6 | Philadelphia | 2-1† |
| | 9 | Columbus | 0-3 |
| | 10 | at Montreal | 4-5 |
| | 13 | Edmonton | 2-5 |
| | 14 | at Pittsburgh | 6-3 |
| | 17 | Boston | 2-1 |
| | 19 | at NY Islanders | 2-1* |
| | 20 | at Ottawa | 2-3 |
| | 27 | at Boston | 2-3* |
| | 31 | Detroit | 4-2 |
| **Feb.** | 1 | Ottawa | 7-4 |
| | 3 | at New Jersey | 5-2 |
| | 5 | Los Angeles | 4-5 |
| | 7 | Florida | 3-1 |
| | 11 | at NY Rangers | 4-5† |
| | 14 | at Tampa Bay | 5-1 |
| | 15 | at Florida | 4-2 |
| | 18 | Montreal | 4-3† |
| | 20 | Colorado | 1-4 |
| | 22 | Pittsburgh | 5-2 |
| | 24 | Philadelphia | 2-4 |
| | 26 | Atlanta | 4-3 |
| | 28 | at Boston | 4-3* |
| **Mar.** | 1 | Florida | 2-6 |
| | 3 | Carolina | 2-5 |
| | 5 | Toronto | 1-2 |
| | 8 | Pittsburgh | 3-4† |
| | 10 | at Nashville | 2-1* |
| | 12 | at Philadelphia | 2-1 |
| | 14 | Carolina | 5-4† |
| | 16 | at Atlanta | 1-5 |
| | 17 | at Florida | 3-0 |
| | 19 | at Tampa Bay | 5-2 |
| | 21 | at Carolina | 1-4 |
| | 24 | at Toronto | 2-3† |
| | 27 | Tampa Bay | 5-3 |
| **Apr.** | 1 | NY Islanders | 5-3 |
| | 3 | Buffalo | 4-5* |
| | 5 | Atlanta | 6-4 |
| | 7 | at Atlanta | 4-2 |
| | 9 | at Tampa Bay | 4-2 |
| | 11 | at Florida | 4-7 |

* – Overtime † – Shootout

# Entry Draft Selections 2009-1995

Name in bold denotes played in NHL.

**2009**
Pick
24 Marcus Johansson
55 Dmitri Orlov
85 Cody Eakin
115 Patrick Wey
145 Brett Flemming
175 Garrett Mitchell
205 Benjamin Casavant

**2008**
Pick
21 Anton Gustafsson
27 John Carlson
57 Eric Mestery
58 Dmitry Kugryshev
93 Braden Holtby
144 Joel Broda
174 Greg Burke
204 Stefan Della Rovere

**2007**
Pick
5 **Karl Alzner**
34 Josh Godfrey
46 Theo Ruth
84 Phil Desimone
108 Brett Bruneteau
125 Brett Leffler
154 Dan Dunn
180 Justin Taylor
185 Nick Larson
199 Andrew Glass

**2006**
Pick
4 **Nicklas Backstrom**
23 **Semyon Varlamov**
34 **Michal Neuvirth**
35 Francois Bouchard
52 Keith Seabrook
97 **Oskar Osala**
122 Luke Lynes
127 Maxime Lacroix
157 Brent Gwidt
177 Mathieu Perreault

**2005**
Pick
14 Sasha Pokulok
27 Joe Finley
109 Andrew Thomas
118 Patrick McNeill
143 Daren Machesney
181 **Tim Kennedy**
209 Viktor Dovgan

**2004**
Pick
1 **Alex Ovechkin**
27 **Jeff Schultz**
29 **Mike Green**
33 **Chris Bourque**
62 Mikhail Yunkov
66 **Sami Lepisto**
88 Clayton Barthel
132 Oscar Hedman
138 Pasi Salonen
166 Peter Guggisberg
197 **Andrew Gordon**
230 Justin Mrazek
263 Travis Morin

**2003**
Pick
18 **Eric Fehr**
83 Steve Werner
109 Andreas Valdix
155 Josh Robertson
249 Andrew Joudrey
279 Mark Olafson

**2002**
Pick
12 **Steve Eminger**
13 **Alexander Semin**
17 **Boyd Gordon**
59 Maxime Daigneault
77 Patrick Wellar
92 Derek Krestanovich
109 Jevon Desautels
118 Petr Dvorak
145 Rob Gherson
179 Marian Havel
209 Joni Lindlof
242 Igor Ignatushkin
272 Patric Blomdahl

**2001**
Pick
58 **Nathan Paetsch**
90 **Owen Fussey**
125 Jeff Lucky
160 Artem Ternavsky
191 Zbynek Novak
221 **Johnny Oduya**
249 Matt Maglione
254 Peter Polcik
275 Robert Muller
284 Viktor Hubl

**2000**
Pick
26 **Brian Sutherby**
43 **Matt Pettinger**
61 **Jakub Cutta**
121 Ryan Vanbuskirk
163 Ivan Nepryayev
289 Bjorn Nord

**1999**
Pick
7 **Kris Beech**
29 **Michal Sivek**
31 **Charlie Stephens**
34 **Ross Lupaschuk**
37 **Nolan Yonkman**
132 **Roman Tvrdon**
175 Kyle Clark
192 David Bornhammar
219 Maxim Orlov
249 Igor Shadilov

**1998**
Pick
49 Jomar Cruz
59 Todd Hornung
106 **Krys Barch**
107 **Chris Corrinet**
118 **Mike Siklenka**
125 Erik Wendell
179 Nate Forster
193 **Rastislav Stana**
220 **Mike Farrell**
251 Blake Evans

**1997**
Pick
9 **Nick Boynton**
35 **Jean-Francois Fortin**
89 Curtis Cruickshank
116 Kevin Caulfield
143 Henrik Petre
200 Pierre-Luc Therrien
226 Matt Oikawa

**1996**
Pick
4 **Alexandre Volchkov**
17 **Jaroslav Svejkovsky**
43 **Jan Bulis**
58 Sergei Zimakov
74 Dave Weninger
78 Shawn McNeil
85 Justin Davis
126 Matthew Lahey
153 Andrew Van Bruggen
180 Michael Anderson
206 Oleg Orekhovsky
232 Chad Cavanagh

**1995**
Pick
17 **Brad Church**
23 **Miika Elomo**
43 **Dwayne Hay**
93 **Sebastien Charpentier**
95 Joel Theriault
105 **Benoit Gratton**
124 Joel Cort
147 Frederick Jobin
199 Vasili Turkovsky
225 Scott Swanson

# Bruce Boudreau

## Head Coach

*Born: Toronto, Ont., January 9, 1955.*

Bruce Boudreau became the 14th head coach in Washington Capitals history when he was named to the position on an interim basis on November 22, 2007. He had the interim tag removed on December 26. His tremendously successful first season behind the bench in Washington landed the Capitals a playoff berth and earned Boudreau the Jack Adams Award as the NHL's coach of the year. Boudreau led the Capitals on a remarkable comeback from 30th in the NHL when he took over the team to the Southeast Division championship. He was the first coach in NHL history to lead his team from 14th place at midseason to a playoff berth. The Capitals won a second consecutive Southeast Division title in 2008-09, tying a franchise record with 50 wins and setting a new record with 108 points.

Boudreau spent nine seasons as a head coach in the American Hockey League, compiling a record of 340-216-99. He won the Calder Cup with the Hershey Bears in 2006 and won the Kelly Cup as head coach and director of hockey operations for the Mississippi Sea Wolves (ECHL) in 1999. He was named coach of the year in the International Hockey League in 1994 after leading the Fort Wayne Komets to the Turner Cup finals.

Boudreau played parts of eight seasons in the NHL with the Toronto Maple Leafs and Chicago Blackhawks, recording 70 points in 141 games. He enjoyed one of the best seasons ever by a Canadian junior player during 1974-75, collecting 165 points for the Toronto Marlboros, a Canadian Hockey League record until Wayne Gretzky surpassed the mark during the 1977-78 season. An outstanding minor league scorer, no AHL player in the 1980s notched more points than Boudreau.

### Coaching Record

| | | | Regular Season | | | | Playoffs | | | |
|---|---|---|---|---|---|---|---|---|---|---|
| Season | Team | League | GC | W | L | O/T | GC | W | L | T |
| 1992-93 | Muskegon | CoHL | 60 | 28 | 27 | 5 | 7 | 3 | 4 | .... |
| 1993-94 | Fort Wayne | IHL | 81 | 41 | 29 | 11 | 18 | 10 | 8 | .... |
| 1994-95 | Fort Wayne | IHL | 39 | 15 | 21 | 3 | .... | .... | .... | .... |
| 1996-97 | Mississippi | ECHL | 70 | 34 | 26 | 10 | 3 | 0 | 3 | .... |
| 1997-98 | Mississippi | ECHL | 70 | 34 | 27 | 9 | .... | .... | .... | .... |
| 1998-99 | Mississippi | ECHL | 70 | 41 | 22 | 7 | 18 | 14 | 4 | .... |
| 99-2000 | Lowell | AHL | 80 | 33 | 36 | 11 | 7 | 3 | 4 | .... |
| 2000-01 | Lowell | AHL | 80 | 35 | 35 | 10 | 4 | 1 | 3 | .... |
| 2001-02 | Manchester | AHL | 80 | 38 | 28 | 14 | 5 | 2 | 3 | .... |
| 2002-03 | Manchester | AHL | 80 | 40 | 23 | 17 | 3 | 0 | 3 | .... |
| 2003-04 | Manchester | AHL | 80 | 40 | 28 | 12 | 6 | 2 | 4 | .... |
| 2004-05 | Manchester | AHL | 80 | 51 | 21 | 8 | 6 | 2 | 4 | .... |
| 2005-06 | Hershey | AHL | 80 | 44 | 21 | 15 | 21 | 16 | 5 | .... |
| 2006-07 | Hershey | AHL | 80 | 51 | 17 | 12 | 19 | 13 | 6 | .... |
| 2007-08 | Hershey | AHL | 15 | 8 | 7 | 0 | .... | .... | .... | .... |
| **2007-08** | **Washington** | **NHL** | **61** | **37** | **17** | **7** | **7** | **3** | **4** | .... |
| **2008-09** | **Washington** | **NHL** | **82** | **50** | **24** | **8** | **14** | **7** | **7** | .... |
| | **NHL Totals** | | **143** | **87** | **41** | **15** | **21** | **10** | **11** | .... |

# Club Directory

**Verizon Center**

**Washington Capitals**
627 N. Glebe Road, Suite 850
Arlington, VA 22203
Phone **202/266-2200**
PR FAX 202/266-2360
www.washingtoncaps.com
**Capacity:** 18,277

**Ownership (Lincoln Holdings LLC)**
Chairman & Majority Owner .................... Ted Leonsis
President & Owner .................... Dick Patrick
Owners .................... Jack Davies, Richard Fairbank, Raul Fernandez, Michelle D. Freeman, Sheila Johnson, Richard Kay, Jeong Kim, Mark D. Lerner, George Stamas
Senior Director of Office Administration .................... Michelle Trostle

**Hockey Operations**
Vice President & General Manager .................... George McPhee
Assistant General Manager, Dir. of Legal Affairs .................... Don Fishman
Head Coach .................... Bruce Boudreau
Assistant Coaches .................... Dean Evason, Blaine Forsythe, Bob Woods
Goaltending Coach .................... Arturs Irbe
Strength and Conditioning Coach .................... Mark Nemish
Physiologist .................... Jack Blatherwick
Director, Team Operations .................... Katy Headman
Hockey Operations Assistants .................... Eric Garvey, Evan Gold
Manager, Team Services .................... Ian Anderson
Head Coach / Asst. Coach, Hershey Bears .................... Mark French, Troy Mann

**Scouting Staff**
Assistant General Manager, Player Personnel .................... Brian MacLellan
Pro Scouts .................... Larry Carriere, Jason Fitzsimmons
Player Development .................... Steve Richmond
Director, Amateur Scouting .................... Ross Mahoney
Amateur Scouts .................... Darroll Baumgartner, Steve Bowman, Ed McColgan, Martin Pouliot, Tony Richardson
European Scouts .................... Gleb Chistyakov, Vojtech Kucera, Petri Skriko, Mats Weiderstal
Director, Scouting Operations .................... Kris Wagner

**Medical Staff**
Head Athletic Trainer .................... Greg Smith
Assistant Athletic Trainer .................... Ben Reisz
Massage Therapist .................... Shawn Reid
Team Physician / Internist .................... Ben Shaffer, MD / Chris Walsh, MD
Team Ophthalmologist / Dentist .................... Thomas Clinch, MD / Thomas Lenz, DDS, PC

**Equipment Staff**
Head Equipment Manager .................... Brock Myles
Assistant Equipment Manager .................... Craig Leydig
Equipment Assistant .................... Jeff Lewis

**Business Operations**
Director, Information Technology .................... Brian McPartland
Office Assistant .................... Valerie Garrett
Receptionist .................... Chuquita Pettus
Building Engineer .................... Edwin Hernandez

**Marketing and Communications**
Senior Vice President, Chief Marketing Officer .................... Tim McDermott
Vice President, Communications, CCO .................... Kurt Kehl
Senior Director, Media Relations .................... Nate Ewell
Assistant Director, Media Relations .................... Paul Rovnak
Communications Coordinator .................... Kelly Murray
Director, Community Relations .................... Elizabeth Wodatch
Community Relations Coordinator .................... Jennifer Vassil
Director, New Media .................... Sean Parker
Senior Writer .................... Mike Vogel
Graphic Designer .................... Andrew Mattice
Website Producer .................... Brett Leonhardt
Senior Director, Marketing .................... Joe Dupriest
Game Entertainment Coordinator .................... Rachel Becker
Senior Manager, Fan Development & Promotions .................... Kim Frank
Senior Manager, Marketing .................... Mike Chan
Amateur Hockey & Fan Development Coordinator .................... Peter Robinson
Promotions Coordinator .................... Lauren Gilmore
Mascot Coordinator .................... Kevin Giambi

**Finance**
Vice President, Finance .................... Keith Burrows
Accounting Manager .................... Jill Ruehle
Accounts Payable Manager .................... Adam Porcelli
Staff Accountant .................... Marta Sokol

**Sales**
Vice President, Ticket Sales .................... Jim Van Stone
Director, Season Ticket Sales .................... Anthony Aspaas
Director, Amateur Hockey Sales .................... Tim Bronaugh
Director, Inside Sales .................... Bill Hanni
Director, Group Sales .................... Darren Montgomery
Assistant Director, Group Sales .................... Jeff Keeney
Senior Regional Sales Managers .................... Nova Ackerman, David Boettinger
Regional Sales Managers, Groups .................... Jimm Bonk, Pat Jeffries, Pete Sekulow
Regional Sales Manager .................... Travis Gendron, Sean Goodman, Kirk Madsen, Sara Plietz,
Account Executives .................... Joshua Gains, Scott Haberle, Jim Minichiello, Michelle Mooney, Greg Roberts, Rob Van Der Eijk

**Corporate Sponsorships**
Vice President, Corporate Sponsorships .................... John Greeley
Directors, Corporate Sponsorships .................... Marco Gentile, Bruce Zalbe
Senior Account Manager, Corporate Sponsorships .................... Joe LaBue
Senior Sponsorship Activation Manager .................... Letitia Petrillo
Sponsorship Activation Manager .................... Graham Dunn

**Ticket Operations**
Director, Ticket Operations .................... Chris Sheap
Manager, Ticket Operations .................... Jordan Cookler
Assistant Manager, Ticket Operations .................... Stephen Kaufman
Coordinator, Ticket Operations .................... Jill Salisbury

**Guest Services**
Director, Guest Services .................... Greg Monares
Specialists, Guest Services .................... Julie Bohling, Christi Carson, Justin Fenlon, Ryan Kronebusch, Rick Olivieri

**Broadcasting**
Radio Play-by-Play / Analyst / Host .................... Steve Kolbe / Ken Sabourin / Jonathan Warner
Television Rightsholder .................... Comcast SportsNet
Television Play-by-Play / Analyst .................... Joe Beninati / Craig Laughlin
Television Reporters .................... Al Koken, Lisa Hillary

# 2008-2009 Final Statistics

## Standings

**Abbreviations: GP** – games played; **W** – wins; **L** – losses; **OT** – overtime and shootout losses; **GF** – goals for; **GA** – goals against; **PTS** – points.

### EASTERN CONFERENCE

#### Northeast Division

| | GP | W | L | OT | GF | GA | PTS |
|---|---|---|---|---|---|---|---|
| Boston | 82 | 53 | 19 | 10 | 274 | 196 | 116 |
| Montreal | 82 | 41 | 30 | 11 | 249 | 247 | 93 |
| Buffalo | 82 | 41 | 32 | 9 | 250 | 234 | 91 |
| Ottawa | 82 | 36 | 35 | 11 | 217 | 237 | 83 |
| Toronto | 82 | 34 | 35 | 13 | 250 | 293 | 81 |

#### Atlantic Division

| | GP | W | L | OT | GF | GA | PTS |
|---|---|---|---|---|---|---|---|
| New Jersey | 82 | 51 | 27 | 4 | 244 | 209 | 106 |
| Pittsburgh | 82 | 45 | 28 | 9 | 264 | 239 | 99 |
| Philadelphia | 82 | 44 | 27 | 11 | 264 | 238 | 99 |
| NY Rangers | 82 | 43 | 30 | 9 | 210 | 218 | 95 |
| NY Islanders | 82 | 26 | 47 | 9 | 201 | 279 | 61 |

#### Southeast Division

| | GP | W | L | OT | GF | GA | PTS |
|---|---|---|---|---|---|---|---|
| Washington | 82 | 50 | 24 | 8 | 272 | 245 | 108 |
| Carolina | 82 | 45 | 30 | 7 | 239 | 226 | 97 |
| Florida | 82 | 41 | 30 | 11 | 234 | 231 | 93 |
| Atlanta | 82 | 35 | 41 | 6 | 257 | 280 | 76 |
| Tampa Bay | 82 | 24 | 40 | 18 | 210 | 279 | 66 |

### WESTERN CONFERENCE

#### Central Division

| | GP | W | L | OT | GF | GA | PTS |
|---|---|---|---|---|---|---|---|
| Detroit | 82 | 51 | 21 | 10 | 295 | 244 | 112 |
| Chicago | 82 | 46 | 24 | 12 | 264 | 216 | 104 |
| St. Louis | 82 | 41 | 31 | 10 | 233 | 233 | 92 |
| Columbus | 82 | 41 | 31 | 10 | 226 | 230 | 92 |
| Nashville | 82 | 40 | 34 | 8 | 213 | 233 | 88 |

#### Pacific Division

| | GP | W | L | OT | GF | GA | PTS |
|---|---|---|---|---|---|---|---|
| San Jose | 82 | 53 | 18 | 11 | 257 | 204 | 117 |
| Anaheim | 82 | 42 | 33 | 7 | 245 | 238 | 91 |
| Dallas | 82 | 36 | 35 | 11 | 230 | 257 | 83 |
| Phoenix | 82 | 36 | 39 | 7 | 208 | 252 | 79 |
| Los Angeles | 82 | 34 | 37 | 11 | 207 | 234 | 79 |

#### Northwest Division

| | GP | W | L | OT | GF | GA | PTS |
|---|---|---|---|---|---|---|---|
| Vancouver | 82 | 45 | 27 | 10 | 246 | 220 | 100 |
| Calgary | 82 | 46 | 30 | 6 | 254 | 248 | 98 |
| Minnesota | 82 | 40 | 33 | 9 | 219 | 200 | 89 |
| Edmonton | 82 | 38 | 35 | 9 | 234 | 248 | 85 |
| Colorado | 82 | 32 | 45 | 5 | 199 | 257 | 69 |

*Washington's Alex Ovechkin crosses into the Tampa Bay zone en route to his 50th goal of the 2008-09 season. Ovechkin enjoyed the third 50-goal campaign of his career and won the Maurice Richard Trophy as the NHL's top goal-scorer for the second straight season.*

## INDIVIDUAL LEADERS

### Goal Scoring

| Player | Team | GP | G |
|---|---|---|---|
| Alex Ovechkin | Washington | 79 | 56 |
| Jeff Carter | Philadelphia | 82 | 46 |
| Zach Parise | New Jersey | 82 | 45 |
| Ilya Kovalchuk | Atlanta | 79 | 43 |
| Thomas Vanek | Buffalo | 73 | 40 |
| Marian Hossa | Detroit | 74 | 40 |
| Rick Nash | Columbus | 78 | 40 |
| Eric Staal | Carolina | 82 | 40 |
| Mike Cammalleri | Calgary | 81 | 39 |
| Dany Heatley | Ottawa | 82 | 39 |

### Assists

| Player | Team | GP | A |
|---|---|---|---|
| Evgeni Malkin | Pittsburgh | 82 | 78 |
| Sidney Crosby | Pittsburgh | 77 | 70 |
| Ryan Getzlaf | Anaheim | 81 | 66 |
| Nicklas Backstrom | Washington | 82 | 66 |
| Pavel Datsyuk | Detroit | 81 | 65 |
| Marc Savard | Boston | 82 | 63 |
| Joe Thornton | San Jose | 82 | 61 |
| Henrik Sedin | Vancouver | 82 | 60 |
| Mike Ribeiro | Dallas | 82 | 56 |
| Alex Ovechkin | Washington | 79 | 54 |
| Jarome Iginla | Calgary | 82 | 54 |

### Power-play Goals

| Player | Team | GP | PP |
|---|---|---|---|
| Thomas Vanek | Buffalo | 73 | 20 |
| Alex Ovechkin | Washington | 79 | 19 |
| Mike Cammalleri | Calgary | 81 | 19 |
| Mike Green | Washington | 68 | 18 |
| Teemu Selanne | Anaheim | 65 | 16 |
| Brad Boyes | St. Louis | 82 | 16 |
| Dany Heatley | Ottawa | 82 | 15 |
| Keith Tkachuk | St. Louis | 79 | 14 |
| Eric Staal | Carolina | 82 | 14 |
| Zach Parise | New Jersey | 82 | 14 |
| Evgeni Malkin | Pittsburgh | 82 | 14 |
| Nicklas Backstrom | Washington | 82 | 14 |

### Shorthand Goals

| Player | Team | GP | SH |
|---|---|---|---|
| Mike Richards | Philadelphia | 79 | 7 |
| Patrick Marleau | San Jose | 76 | 5 |
| Rick Nash | Columbus | 78 | 5 |
| Sean Bergenheim | NY Islanders | 59 | 4 |
| *Kris Versteeg | Chicago | 78 | 4 |
| Simon Gagne | Philadelphia | 79 | 4 |
| Mikko Koivu | Minnesota | 79 | 4 |
| Radek Dvorak | Florida | 81 | 4 |
| Alexandre Burrows | Vancouver | 82 | 4 |
| Jeff Carter | Philadelphia | 82 | 4 |

### Game-winning Goals

| Player | Team | GP | GW |
|---|---|---|---|
| Jeff Carter | Philadelphia | 82 | 12 |
| Brad Boyes | St. Louis | 82 | 11 |
| Petr Sykora | Pittsburgh | 76 | 10 |
| Patrick Marleau | San Jose | 76 | 10 |
| Alex Ovechkin | Washington | 79 | 10 |

### Shots

| Player | Team | GP | S |
|---|---|---|---|
| Alex Ovechkin | Washington | 79 | 528 |
| Eric Staal | Carolina | 82 | 372 |
| Zach Parise | New Jersey | 82 | 364 |
| Jeff Carter | Philadelphia | 82 | 342 |
| Henrik Zetterberg | Detroit | 77 | 309 |

### Shooting Percentage

(minimum 82 shots)

| Player | Team | GP | G | S | % |
|---|---|---|---|---|---|
| Ryan Malone | Tampa Bay | 70 | 26 | 124 | 21.0 |
| Loui Eriksson | Dallas | 82 | 36 | 178 | 20.2 |
| Kyle Wellwood | Vancouver | 74 | 18 | 94 | 19.1 |
| Thomas Vanek | Buffalo | 73 | 40 | 211 | 19.0 |
| Andrew Brunette | Minnesota | 80 | 22 | 118 | 18.6 |

### Penalty Minutes

| Player | Team | GP | PIM |
|---|---|---|---|
| Daniel Carcillo | Phx-Phi | 74 | 254 |
| Shane O'Brien | T.B-Van | 77 | 196 |
| Colton Orr | NY Rangers | 82 | 193 |
| Zach Stortini | Edmonton | 52 | 181 |
| Jared Boll | Columbus | 75 | 180 |

### Plus/Minus

| Player | Team | GP | +/– |
|---|---|---|---|
| David Krejci | Boston | 82 | 37 |
| *Blake Wheeler | Boston | 81 | 36 |
| Pavel Datsyuk | Detroit | 81 | 34 |
| Duncan Keith | Chicago | 77 | 33 |
| Travis Zajac | New Jersey | 82 | 33 |

# Individual Leaders

**Abbreviations: GP** – games played; **G** – goals; **A** – assists; **Pts** – points; **+/–** – difference between Goals For (**GF**) scored when a player is on the ice with his team at even strength or shorthanded and Goals Against (**GA**) scored when the same player is on the ice with his team at even strength or on a power play; **PIM** – penalties in minutes; **PP** – power play goals; **SH** – shorthanded goals; **GW** – game-winning goals; **S** – shots on goal; **%** – percentage of shots on goal resulting in goals.

## Individual Scoring Leaders for Art Ross Trophy

| Player | Team | GP | G | A | Pts | +/– | PIM | PP | SH | GW | S | % |
|---|---|---|---|---|---|---|---|---|---|---|---|---|
| Evgeni Malkin | Pittsburgh | 82 | 35 | 78 | 113 | 17 | 80 | 14 | 2 | 4 | 290 | 12.1 |
| Alex Ovechkin | Washington | 79 | 56 | 54 | 110 | 8 | 72 | 19 | 1 | 10 | 528 | 10.6 |
| Sidney Crosby | Pittsburgh | 77 | 33 | 70 | 103 | 3 | 76 | 7 | 0 | 3 | 238 | 13.9 |
| Pavel Datsyuk | Detroit | 81 | 32 | 65 | 97 | 34 | 22 | 11 | 1 | 3 | 248 | 12.9 |
| Zach Parise | New Jersey | 82 | 45 | 49 | 94 | 30 | 24 | 14 | 0 | 8 | 364 | 12.4 |
| Ilya Kovalchuk | Atlanta | 79 | 43 | 48 | 91 | –12 | 50 | 12 | 0 | 6 | 275 | 15.6 |
| Ryan Getzlaf | Anaheim | 81 | 25 | 66 | 91 | 5 | 121 | 9 | 0 | 2 | 227 | 11.0 |
| Jarome Iginla | Calgary | 82 | 35 | 54 | 89 | –2 | 37 | 10 | 0 | 4 | 289 | 12.1 |
| Marc Savard | Boston | 82 | 25 | 63 | 88 | 25 | 70 | 9 | 0 | 5 | 213 | 11.7 |
| Nicklas Backstrom | Washington | 82 | 22 | 66 | 88 | 16 | 46 | 14 | 0 | 1 | 174 | 12.6 |
| Joe Thornton | San Jose | 82 | 25 | 61 | 86 | 16 | 56 | 11 | 0 | 3 | 139 | 18.0 |
| Jeff Carter | Philadelphia | 82 | 46 | 38 | 84 | 23 | 68 | 13 | 4 | 12 | 342 | 13.5 |
| Mike Cammalleri | Calgary | 81 | 39 | 43 | 82 | –2 | 44 | 19 | 0 | 6 | 255 | 15.3 |
| Daniel Sedin | Vancouver | 82 | 31 | 51 | 82 | 24 | 36 | 9 | 0 | 7 | 285 | 10.9 |
| Henrik Sedin | Vancouver | 82 | 22 | 60 | 82 | 22 | 48 | 4 | 0 | 8 | 143 | 15.4 |
| Mike Richards | Philadelphia | 79 | 30 | 50 | 80 | 22 | 63 | 8 | 7 | 4 | 238 | 12.6 |
| Martin St. Louis | Tampa Bay | 82 | 30 | 50 | 80 | 4 | 14 | 7 | 2 | 3 | 262 | 11.5 |
| Rick Nash | Columbus | 78 | 40 | 39 | 79 | 11 | 52 | 6 | 5 | 5 | 263 | 15.2 |
| Alexander Semin | Washington | 62 | 34 | 45 | 79 | 25 | 77 | 8 | 0 | 8 | 223 | 15.2 |
| Patrik Elias | New Jersey | 77 | 31 | 47 | 78 | 18 | 32 | 12 | 2 | 6 | 247 | 12.6 |
| Mike Ribeiro | Dallas | 82 | 22 | 56 | 78 | –4 | 52 | 7 | 0 | 1 | 163 | 13.5 |
| Martin Havlat | Chicago | 81 | 29 | 48 | 77 | 29 | 30 | 5 | 0 | 5 | 249 | 11.6 |
| Ray Whitney | Carolina | 82 | 24 | 53 | 77 | 2 | 32 | 7 | 0 | 2 | 219 | 11.0 |
| Vyacheslav Kozlov | Atlanta | 82 | 26 | 50 | 76 | –14 | 44 | 12 | 0 | 3 | 165 | 15.8 |
| Eric Staal | Carolina | 82 | 40 | 35 | 75 | 15 | 50 | 14 | 1 | 8 | 372 | 10.8 |
| Simon Gagne | Philadelphia | 79 | 34 | 40 | 74 | 21 | 42 | 12 | 4 | 3 | 221 | 15.4 |

## Defencemen Scoring Leaders

| Player | Team | GP | G | A | Pts | +/– | PIM | PP | SH | GW | S | % |
|---|---|---|---|---|---|---|---|---|---|---|---|---|
| Mike Green | Washington | 68 | 31 | 42 | 73 | 24 | 68 | 18 | 1 | 4 | 243 | 12.8 |
| Andrei Markov | Montreal | 78 | 12 | 52 | 64 | –2 | 36 | 7 | 0 | 3 | 165 | 7.3 |
| Nicklas Lidstrom | Detroit | 78 | 16 | 43 | 59 | 31 | 30 | 10 | 0 | 4 | 180 | 8.9 |
| Scott Niedermayer | Anaheim | 82 | 14 | 45 | 59 | –8 | 70 | 9 | 0 | 2 | 178 | 7.9 |
| Brian Rafalski | Detroit | 78 | 10 | 49 | 59 | 17 | 20 | 5 | 0 | 1 | 141 | 7.1 |
| Dan Boyle | San Jose | 77 | 16 | 41 | 57 | 6 | 52 | 8 | 0 | 4 | 213 | 7.5 |
| Mark Streit | NY Islanders | 74 | 16 | 40 | 56 | 6 | 62 | 10 | 1 | 1 | 150 | 10.7 |
| Sheldon Souray | Edmonton | 81 | 23 | 30 | 53 | 1 | 98 | 12 | 1 | 5 | 268 | 8.6 |
| Shea Weber | Nashville | 81 | 23 | 30 | 53 | 1 | 80 | 10 | 1 | 4 | 251 | 9.2 |
| Brian Campbell | Chicago | 82 | 7 | 45 | 52 | 5 | 22 | 4 | 0 | 1 | 108 | 6.5 |
| Niklas Kronvall | Detroit | 80 | 6 | 45 | 51 | 2 | 50 | 4 | 0 | 1 | 121 | 5.0 |
| Zdeno Chara | Boston | 80 | 19 | 31 | 50 | 23 | 95 | 11 | 0 | 3 | 216 | 8.8 |
| Dennis Wideman | Boston | 79 | 13 | 37 | 50 | 32 | 34 | 6 | 1 | 2 | 169 | 7.7 |
| Chris Pronger | Anaheim | 82 | 11 | 37 | 48 | 0 | 88 | 4 | 0 | 2 | 196 | 5.6 |
| Dion Phaneuf | Calgary | 80 | 11 | 36 | 47 | –11 | 100 | 4 | 0 | 4 | 277 | 4.0 |
| Rob Blake | San Jose | 73 | 10 | 35 | 45 | 15 | 110 | 6 | 0 | 1 | 198 | 5.1 |
| Jaroslav Spacek | Buffalo | 80 | 8 | 37 | 45 | 2 | 38 | 4 | 0 | 0 | 130 | 6.2 |
| Ryan Suter | Nashville | 82 | 7 | 38 | 45 | –16 | 73 | 3 | 0 | 3 | 143 | 4.9 |
| Tom Gilbert | Edmonton | 82 | 5 | 40 | 45 | 6 | 26 | 2 | 0 | 1 | 107 | 4.7 |
| Duncan Keith | Chicago | 77 | 8 | 36 | 44 | 33 | 60 | 2 | 1 | 1 | 173 | 4.6 |
| Kevin Bieksa | Vancouver | 72 | 11 | 32 | 43 | –4 | 97 | 5 | 0 | 2 | 153 | 7.2 |
| Kimmo Timonen | Philadelphia | 77 | 3 | 40 | 43 | 19 | 54 | 2 | 0 | 0 | 104 | 2.9 |
| Jay Bouwmeester | Florida | 82 | 15 | 27 | 42 | –2 | 68 | 9 | 0 | 2 | 182 | 8.2 |
| Marek Zidlicky | Minnesota | 76 | 12 | 30 | 42 | –12 | 76 | 10 | 0 | 3 | 147 | 8.2 |
| Christian Ehrhoff | San Jose | 77 | 8 | 34 | 42 | –12 | 63 | 5 | 0 | 2 | 165 | 4.8 |
| Pavel Kubina | Toronto | 82 | 14 | 26 | 40 | –15 | 94 | 9 | 0 | 4 | 184 | 7.6 |

## CONSECUTIVE SCORING STREAKS

### Goals

| Games | Player | Team | G |
|---|---|---|---|
| 8 | Mike Green | Washington | 10 |
| 6 | Ilya Kovalchuk | Atlanta | 9 |
| 6 | Keith Tkachuk | St. Louis | 7 |
| 6 | Zach Parise | New Jersey | 7 |
| 6 | Phil Kessel | Boston | 7 |
| 6 | Alexander Semin | Washington | 6 |

### Assists

| Games | Player | Team | A |
|---|---|---|---|
| 13 | Evgeni Malkin | Pittsburgh | 21 |
| 9 | Evgeni Malkin | Pittsburgh | 14 |
| 9 | Andrei Markov | Montreal | 9 |
| 8 | Ryan Getzlaf | Anaheim | 12 |
| 8 | Filip Kuba | Ottawa | 11 |
| 8 | Jason Pominville | Buffalo | 10 |
| 7 | Corey Perry | Anaheim | 11 |
| 7 | Andrei Markov | Montreal | 10 |
| 7 | Alex Ovechkin | Washington | 10 |
| 7 | Joe Thornton | San Jose | 9 |
| 7 | Ryan Getzlaf | Anaheim | 9 |
| 7 | Phil Kessel | Boston | 9 |
| 7 | Todd White | Atlanta | 8 |
| 7 | Devin Setoguchi | San Jose | 8 |

### Points

| Games | Player | Team | G | A | PTS |
|---|---|---|---|---|---|
| 18 | Phil Kessel | Boston | 14 | 14 | 28 |
| 13 | Evgeni Malkin | Pittsburgh | 6 | 21 | 27 |
| 12 | Sidney Crosby | Pittsburgh | 7 | 13 | 20 |
| 10 | Alex Ovechkin | Washington | 11 | 11 | 22 |
| 10 | Patrik Elias | New Jersey | 8 | 9 | 17 |
| 10 | David Krejci | Boston | 6 | 11 | 17 |
| 10 | Alex Ovechkin | Washington | 11 | 5 | 16 |
| 10 | Ryan Getzlaf | Anaheim | 3 | 11 | 14 |
| 10 | Evgeni Malkin | Pittsburgh | 5 | 9 | 14 |
| 10 | Nicklas Backstrom | Washington | 4 | 9 | 13 |

*Evgeni Malkin celebrates a goal with his Penguins teammates. After finishing second in the NHL scoring race in 2007-08, Malkin won the Art Ross Trophy in 2008-09. He joined Mario Lemieux, Jaromir Jagr and Sidney Crosby as Pittsburgh players who led the NHL in scoring.*

# Individual Rookie Scoring Leaders

| Rookie | Team | GP | G | A | Pts | +/– | PIM | PP | SH | GW | S | % |
|---|---|---|---|---|---|---|---|---|---|---|---|---|
| Bobby Ryan | Anaheim | 64 | 31 | 26 | 57 | 13 | 33 | 12 | 0 | 3 | 174 | 17.8 |
| Kris Versteeg | Chicago | 78 | 22 | 31 | 53 | 15 | 55 | 6 | 4 | 3 | 139 | 15.8 |
| Mikhail Grabovski | Toronto | 78 | 20 | 28 | 48 | –8 | 92 | 6 | 0 | 2 | 120 | 16.7 |
| Patrik Berglund | St. Louis | 76 | 21 | 26 | 47 | 19 | 16 | 7 | 0 | 1 | 143 | 14.7 |
| Steven Stamkos | Tampa Bay | 79 | 23 | 23 | 46 | –13 | 39 | 9 | 0 | 1 | 181 | 12.7 |
| Michael Frolik | Florida | 79 | 21 | 24 | 45 | 10 | 22 | 1 | 0 | 2 | 158 | 13.3 |
| Blake Wheeler | Boston | 81 | 21 | 24 | 45 | 36 | 46 | 3 | 2 | 3 | 150 | 14.0 |
| Kyle Okposo | Ny Islanders | 65 | 18 | 21 | 39 | –6 | 36 | 9 | 0 | 3 | 165 | 10.9 |
| T.J. Oshie | St. Louis | 57 | 14 | 25 | 39 | 16 | 30 | 6 | 1 | 1 | 101 | 13.9 |
| Jakub Voracek | Columbus | 80 | 9 | 29 | 38 | 11 | 44 | 0 | 0 | 1 | 101 | 8.9 |
| James Neal | Dallas | 77 | 24 | 13 | 37 | –11 | 51 | 9 | 0 | 2 | 171 | 14.0 |
| Andrew Ebbett | Anaheim | 48 | 8 | 24 | 32 | 8 | 24 | 6 | 0 | 0 | 100 | 8.0 |
| Nikolai Kulemin | Toronto | 73 | 15 | 16 | 31 | –8 | 18 | 2 | 0 | 1 | 129 | 11.6 |
| Fabian Brunnstrom | Dallas | 55 | 17 | 12 | 29 | –8 | 8 | 4 | 0 | 5 | 81 | 21.0 |
| John Mitchell | Toronto | 76 | 12 | 17 | 29 | –16 | 33 | 2 | 0 | 0 | 98 | 12.2 |
| Mikkel Boedker | Phoenix | 78 | 11 | 17 | 28 | –6 | 18 | 2 | 0 | 3 | 116 | 9.5 |
| Claude Giroux | Philadelphia | 42 | 9 | 18 | 27 | 10 | 14 | 2 | 0 | 0 | 67 | 13.4 |
| Matt Hunwick | Boston | 53 | 6 | 21 | 27 | 15 | 31 | 0 | 0 | 1 | 58 | 10.3 |
| Drew Doughty | Los Angeles | 81 | 6 | 21 | 27 | –17 | 56 | 3 | 0 | 1 | 126 | 4.8 |
| Troy Brouwer | Chicago | 69 | 10 | 16 | 26 | 7 | 50 | 4 | 1 | 0 | 126 | 7.9 |
| Derick Brassard | Columbus | 31 | 10 | 15 | 25 | 12 | 17 | 3 | 0 | 1 | 59 | 16.9 |
| Josh Bailey | NY Islanders | 68 | 7 | 18 | 25 | –14 | 16 | 3 | 0 | 0 | 74 | 9.5 |
| Wayne Simmonds | Los Angeles | 82 | 9 | 14 | 23 | –8 | 73 | 2 | 0 | 2 | 127 | 7.1 |
| Brandon Crombeen | Dal-St.L. | 81 | 12 | 10 | 22 | –9 | 148 | 0 | 1 | 3 | 124 | 9.7 |
| Matt D'Agostini | Montreal | 53 | 12 | 9 | 21 | –17 | 16 | 3 | 0 | 1 | 116 | 10.3 |
| Jannik Hansen | Vancouver | 55 | 6 | 15 | 21 | 5 | 37 | 0 | 0 | 1 | 64 | 9.4 |

## Goal Scoring

| Name | Team | GP | G |
|---|---|---|---|
| Bobby Ryan | Anaheim | 64 | 31 |
| James Neal | Dallas | 77 | 24 |
| Steven Stamkos | Tampa Bay | 79 | 23 |
| Kris Versteeg | Chicago | 78 | 22 |
| Patrik Berglund | St. Louis | 76 | 21 |
| Michael Frolik | Florida | 79 | 21 |
| Blake Wheeler | Boston | 81 | 21 |
| Mikhail Grabovski | Toronto | 78 | 20 |
| Kyle Okposo | NY Islanders | 65 | 18 |
| Fabian Brunnstrom | Dallas | 55 | 17 |
| Nikolai Kulemin | Toronto | 73 | 15 |

## Assists

| Name | Team | GP | A |
|---|---|---|---|
| Kris Versteeg | Chicago | 78 | 31 |
| Jakub Voracek | Columbus | 80 | 29 |
| Mikhail Grabovski | Toronto | 78 | 28 |
| Bobby Ryan | Anaheim | 64 | 26 |
| Patrik Berglund | St. Louis | 76 | 26 |
| T.J. Oshie | St. Louis | 57 | 25 |
| Andrew Ebbett | Anaheim | 48 | 24 |

## Power-play Goals

| Name | Team | GP | PP |
|---|---|---|---|
| Bobby Ryan | Anaheim | 64 | 12 |
| Kyle Okposo | NY Islanders | 65 | 9 |
| James Neal | Dallas | 77 | 9 |
| Steven Stamkos | Tampa Bay | 79 | 9 |
| Patrik Berglund | St. Louis | 76 | 7 |
| Andrew Ebbett | Anaheim | 48 | 6 |
| T.J. Oshie | St. Louis | 57 | 6 |
| Kris Versteeg | Chicago | 78 | 6 |
| Mikhail Grabovski | Toronto | 78 | 6 |

## Shorthand Goals

| Name | Team | GP | SH |
|---|---|---|---|
| Kris Versteeg | Chicago | 78 | 4 |
| Blake Wheeler | Boston | 81 | 2 |
| Rick Rypien | Vancouver | 12 | 1 |
| Martin St. Pierre | Boston | 14 | 1 |
| Joey Crabb | Atlanta | 29 | 1 |
| Nate Thompson | NY Islanders | 43 | 1 |
| Zach Bogosian | Atlanta | 47 | 1 |
| Chris Stewart | Colorado | 53 | 1 |
| T.J. Oshie | St. Louis | 57 | 1 |
| Tomas Plihal | San Jose | 64 | 1 |
| Troyb Rouwer | Chicago | 69 | 1 |
| Brandon Crombeen | Dal-St.L. | 81 | 1 |
| Colin Fraser | Chicago | 81 | 1 |

## Game-winning Goals

| Name | Team | GP | GW |
|---|---|---|---|
| Fabian Brunnstrom | Dallas | 55 | 5 |
| Kyle Turris | Phoenix | 63 | 3 |
| Bobby Ryan | Anaheim | 64 | 3 |
| Kyle Okposo | NY Islanders | 65 | 3 |
| Kris Versteeg | Chicago | 78 | 3 |
| Mikkel Boedker | Phoenix | 78 | 3 |
| Brandon Crombeen | Dal-St.L. | 81 | 3 |
| Blake Wheeler | Boston | 81 | 3 |

## Shots

| Name | Team | GP | S |
|---|---|---|---|
| Steven Stamkos | Tampa Bay | 79 | 181 |
| Bobby Ryan | Anaheim | 64 | 174 |
| James Neal | Dallas | 77 | 171 |
| Kyle Okposo | Ny Islanders | 65 | 165 |
| Michael Frolik | Florida | 79 | 158 |
| Blake Wheeler | Boston | 81 | 150 |
| Patrik Berglund | St. Louis | 76 | 143 |

## Shooting Percentage

(minimum 82 shots)

| Name | Team | GP | G | S | % |
|---|---|---|---|---|---|
| Bobby Ryan | Anaheim | 64 | 31 | 174 | 17.8 |
| Mikhail Grabovski | Toronto | 78 | 20 | 120 | 16.7 |
| Kris Versteeg | Chicago | 78 | 22 | 139 | 15.8 |
| Patrik Berglund | St. Louis | 76 | 21 | 143 | 14.7 |
| James Neal | Dallas | 77 | 24 | 171 | 14.0 |
| Blake Wheeler | Boston | 81 | 21 | 150 | 14.0 |
| T.J. Oshie | St. Louis | 57 | 14 | 101 | 13.9 |
| Michael Frolik | Florida | 79 | 21 | 158 | 13.3 |
| Steven Stamkos | Tampa Bay | 79 | 23 | 181 | 12.7 |
| John Mitchell | Toronto | 76 | 12 | 98 | 12.2 |

## Penalty Minutes

| Name | Team | GP | PIM |
|---|---|---|---|
| Derek Dorsett | Columbus | 52 | 150 |
| Brandon Crombeen | Dal-St.L. | 81 | 148 |
| Mike Brown | Van-Ana | 48 | 145 |
| Boris Valabik | Atlanta | 50 | 132 |
| Brandon Prust | Cgy-Phx | 36 | 108 |
| Mikhail Grabovski | Toronto | 78 | 92 |

## Plus/Minus

| Name | Team | GP | +/– |
|---|---|---|---|
| Blake Wheeler | Boston | 81 | 36 |
| Patrik Berglund | St. Louis | 76 | 19 |
| T.J. Oshie | St. Louis | 57 | 16 |
| Matt Hunwick | Boston | 53 | 15 |
| Kris Versteeg | Chicago | 78 | 15 |
| Bobby Ryan | Anaheim | 64 | 13 |
| Derick Brassard | Columbus | 31 | 12 |
| Chris Butler | Buffalo | 47 | 11 |
| Zach Bogosian | Atlanta | 47 | 11 |
| Jakub Voracek | Columbus | 80 | 11 |

# Three-or-More-Goal Games

| Player | Team | Date | Final Score | G |
|---|---|---|---|---|
| Jason Arnott | Nashville | Feb. 28 | Det 0 Nsh 8 | 3 |
| David Backes | St. Louis | Apr. 02 | St.L. 5 Det 4 | 4 |
| Sean Bergenheim | NY Islanders | Mar. 07 | N.J 3 NYI 7 | 3 |
| Jason Blake | Toronto | Jan. 15 | Tor 6 Car 4 | 3 |
| David Booth | Florida | Nov. 09 | Fla 3 Ana 1 | 3 |
| David Booth | Florida | Mar. 07 | St.L. 3 Fla 5 | 3 |
| Rene Bourque | Calgary | Dec. 27 | Ott 3 Cgy 6 | 3 |
| Dustin Brown | Los Angeles | Dec. 11 | St.L. 2 L.A 6 | 3 |
| *Fabian Brunnstrom | Dallas | Oct. 15 | Nsh 4 Dal 6 | 3 |
| Mike Cammalleri | Calgary | Nov. 27 | Cgy 4 Van 3 | 3 |
| Mike Cammalleri | Calgary | Jan. 28 | Buf 2 Cgy 5 | 3 |
| Jeff Carter | Philadelphia | Apr. 03 | Tor 5 Phi 8 | 3 |
| Erik Cole | Edmonton | Jan. 13 | Edm 5 Wsh 2 | 3 |
| *Brandon Crombeen | St. Louis | Dec. 08 | Nsh 3 St.L. 6 | 3 |
| Sidney Crosby | Pittsburgh | Nov. 29 | N.J 1 Pit 4 | 3 |
| Matt Cullen | Carolina | Feb. 22 | Col 2 Car 5 | 3 |
| Boyd Devereaux | Toronto | Apr. 11 | Ott 2 Tor 5 | 3 |
| Chris Drury | NY Rangers | Nov. 06 | T.B 2 NYR 5 | 3 |
| Pascal Dupuis | Pittsburgh | Dec. 11 | NYI 2 Pit 9 | 3 |
| Loui Eriksson | Dallas | Dec. 18 | CBJ 5 Dal 6 | 3 |
| *Nikita Filatov | Columbus | Jan. 10 | Min 2 CBJ 4 | 3 |
| Sam Gagner | Edmonton | Mar. 19 | Edm 8 Col 1 | 3 |
| Michal Handzus | Los Angeles | Mar. 05 | Dal 4 L.A 5 | 3 |
| Martin Hanzal | Phoenix | Dec. 04 | Tor 3 Phx 6 | 3 |
| Scott Hartnell | Philadelphia | Dec. 11 | Car 5 Phi 6 | 3 |
| Scott Hartnell | Philadelphia | Dec. 20 | Wsh 1 Phi 7 | 3 |
| Chris Higgins | Montreal | Nov. 11 | Ott 0 Mtl 4 | 3 |
| Jarome Iginla | Calgary | Oct. 23 | Cgy 5 Nsh 3 | 3 |
| Olli Jokinen | Phoenix | Feb. 21 | Phx 6 L.A 3 | 3 |
| Olli Jokinen | Calgary | Mar. 14 | Cgy 6 Tor 8 | 3 |
| Andrei Kostitsyn | Montreal | Dec. 27 | Mtl 3 Pit 2 | 3 |
| Phil Kessel | Boston | Apr. 12 | Bos 6 NYI 2 | 3 |
| Ilya Kovalchuk | Atlanta | Feb. 15 | Atl 8 Ana 4 | 3 |
| David Krejci | Boston | Dec. 18 | Tor 5 Bos 8 | 3 |
| Robert Lang | Montreal | Jan. 07 | Mtl 6 NYR 3 | 3 |
| Maxim Lapierre | Montreal | Dec. 29 | Mtl 5 Fla 2 | 3 |
| Bryan Little | Atlanta | Dec. 26 | Car 5 Atl 4 | 3 |
| Milan Lucic | Boston | Oct. 25 | Atl 4 Bos 5 | 3 |
| Evgeni Malkin | Pittsburgh | Nov. 26 | Pit 5 NYI 3 | 3 |
| Ethan Moreau | Edmonton | Jan. 18 | Phx 3 Edm 6 | 3 |
| David Moss | Calgary | Mar. 03 | Cgy 6 Ott 3 | 3 |
| Rick Nash | Columbus | Jan. 27 | Det 2 CBJ 3 | 3 |
| Rick Nash | Columbus | Mar. 07 | CBJ 8 Det 2 | 3 |
| *James Neal | Dallas | Dec. 23 | Dal 8 Tor 2 | 3 |
| Alex Ovechkin | Washington | Nov. 26 | Atl 3 Wsh 5 | 3 |
| Alex Ovechkin | Washington | Feb. 01 | Ott 4 Wsh 7 | 3 |
| Alex Ovechkin | Washington | Feb. 15 | Wsh 4 Fla 2 | 3 |
| Mark Parrish | Dallas | Nov. 07 | Dal 5 Ana 2 | 3 |
| Mike Ribeiro | Dallas | Jan. 21 | Dal 4 Fla 1 | 3 |
| *Bobby Ryan | Anaheim | Jan. 08 | Ana 3 L.A 4 | 3 |
| Teemu Selanne | Anaheim | Oct. 29 | Det 4 Ana 5 | 3 |
| Jason Spezza | Ottawa | Dec. 06 | Pit 2 Ott 3 | 3 |
| Eric Staal | Carolina | Nov. 21 | Phx 2 Car 5 | 3 |
| Eric Staal | Carolina | Dec. 26 | Car 5 Atl 4 | 3 |
| Eric Staal | Carolina | Mar. 07 | Car 9 T.B 3 | 4 |
| Eric Staal | Carolina | Apr. 07 | NYI 0 Car 9 | 3 |
| Jordan Staal | Pittsburgh | Nov. 11 | Pit 7 Det 6 | 3 |
| Drew Stafford | Buffalo | Jan. 27 | Buf 10 Edm 2 | 3 |
| *Steven Stamkos | Tampa Bay | Feb. 17 | Chi 5 T.B 3 | 3 |
| Petr Sykora | Pittsburgh | Dec. 11 | NYI 2 Pit 9 | 3 |
| Jonathan Toews | Chicago | Feb. 27 | Pit 5 Chi 4 | 3 |
| Thomas Vanek | Buffalo | Feb. 04 | Tor 0 Buf 5 | 3 |
| *Blake Wheeler | Boston | Nov. 06 | Tor 2 Bos 5 | 3 |
| Ray Whitney | Carolina | Mar. 06 | Cgy 1 Car 6 | 3 |
| Dainius Zubrus | New Jersey | Nov. 23 | N.J 7 T.B 3 | 4 |

# 2008-09 Penalty Shots

*(For shootout statistics, see page 149.)*

## Scored

**Milan Hejduk** (Col.) scored against Mathieu Garon (Edm.)
Oct. 12. Final Score: Col. 2 at Edm. 3

**Michael Nylander** (Wsh.) scored against Roberto Luongo (Van.)
Oct. 13. Final Score: Van. 1 at Wsh. 5

**Simon Gagne** (Phi.) scored against Andrew Raycroft (Col.)
Oct. 16. Final Score: Phi. 2 at Col. 5

**Alex Tanguay** (Mtl.) scored against Cam Ward (Car.)
Oct. 28. Final Score: Car. 2 at Mtl. 3

**Vernon Fiddler** (Nsh.) scored against Miikka Kiprusoff (Cgy.)
Nov. 6. Final Score: Nsh. 6 at Cgy. 7

**Taylor Pyatt** (Van.) scored against Peter Budaj (Col.)
Nov. 12. Final Score: Col. 2 at Van. 1

**Ryan Malone** (T.B.) scored against Scott Clemmensen (N.J.)
Nov. 23. Final Score: N.J. 7 at T.B. 3

**Jordan Leopold** (Col.) scored against Chris Osgood (Det.)
Dec. 15. Final Score: Col 3 at Det. 2

**Guillaume Latendresse** (Mtl.) scored against Cam Ward (Car.)
Dec. 16. Final Score: Mtl. 2 at Car. 3

**Michal Rozsival** (NYR) scored against Jason LaBarbera (L.A.)
Dec. 17. Final Score: NYR 3 at L.A. 2

**Rick Nash** (CBJ) scored against Peter Budaj (Col.)
Jan. 2. Final Score: CBJ 6 at Col. 1

**Michael Frolik** (Fla.) scored against Kari Lehtonen (Atl.)
Jan. 10. Final Score: Atl. 4 at Fla. 8

**Vincent Lecavalier** (T.B.) scored against Martin Biron (Phi.)
Jan. 15. Final Score: Phi. 1 at T.B. 4

**David Booth** (Fla.) scored against Ryan Miller (Buf.)
Jan. 19. Final Score: Buf. 3 at Fla. 2

**Radek Dvorak** (Fla.) scored against Carey Price (Mtl.)
Jan. 29. Final Score: Mtl. 1 at Fla. 5

**Matt Cullen** (Car.) scored against Evgeni Nabokov (S.J.)
Feb. 5. Final Score: Car. 4 at S.J. 3

**Patrick O'Sullivan** (L.A.) scored against Scott Clemmensen (N.J.)
Feb. 7. Final Score: L.A. 3 at N.J. 1

**Simon Gagne** (Phi.) scored against Yann Danis (NYI)
Feb. 14. Final Score: NYI 1 at Phi. 5

**Eric Staal** (Car.) scored against Michal Neuvirth (Wsh.)
Mar. 3. Final Score: Car. 5 at Wsh. 2

**Brendan Shanahan** (N.J.) scored against Karri Ramo (T.B.)
Apr. 3. Final Score: T.B. 4 at N.J. 5

**Darroll Powe** (Phi.) scored against Alex Auld (Ott.)
Apr. 4. Final Score: Phi. 3 at Ott. 4

**Derek Roy** (Buf.) scored against Michael Leighton (Car.)
Apr. 9. Final Score: Buf. 5 at Car. 1

**Dustin Byfuglien** (Chi.) scored against Ty Conklin (Det.)
Apr. 11. Final Score: Chi. 4 at Det. 2

## Stopped

**Kyle Okposo** (NYI) unsuccessful against Martin Brodeur (N.J.)
Oct. 10. Final Score: NYI 1 at N.J. 2

**Alex Ovechkin** (Wsh.) unsuccessful against Kari Lehtonen (Atl.)
Oct. 10. Final Score: Wsh. 4 at Atl. 7

**Corey Perry** (Ana.) unsuccessful against Carey Price (Mtl.)
Oct. 25. Final Score: Ana. 6 at Mtl. 4

**Doug Weight** (NYI) unsuccessful against Cam Ward (Car.)
Oct. 25. Final Score: Car. 4 at NYI 3

**Sam Gagner** (Edm.) unsuccessful against Roberto Luongo (Van.)
Oct. 25. Final Score: Edm. 3 at Van. 6

**Mike Richards** (Phi.) unsuccessful against Kari Lehtonen (Atl.)
Oct. 28. Final Score: Phi. 7 at Atl. 0

**Alexander Frolov** (L.A.) unsuccessful against Roberto Luongo (Van.)
Oct. 30. Final Score: Van. 4 at L.A. 0

**Chris Drury** (NYR) unsuccessful against Brent Johnson (Wsh.)
Nov. 8. Final Score: NYR 1 at Wsh. 3

**Patrick Sharp** (Chi.) unsuccessful against Tim Thomas (Bos.)
Nov. 12. Final Score: Bos. 2 at Chi. 1

**Matt Stajan** (Tor.) unsuccessful against Nikolai Khabibulin (Chi.)
Nov. 22. Final Score: Chi. 5 at Tor. 4

**Ryan Malone** (T.B.) unsuccessful against Martin Biron (Phi.)
Dec. 2. Final Score: T.B. 3 at PHI 4

**Patrick O'Sullivan** (L.A.) unsuccessful against Steve Mason (CBJ)
Dec. 6. Final Score: CBJ 0 at L.A. 3

**Alex Ovechkin** (Wsh.) unsuccessful against Michael Leighton (Car.)
Dec. 7. Final Score: Wsh. 1 at Car. 3

**P.J. Axelsson** (Bos.) unsuccessful against Mike Smith (T.B.)
Dec. 8. Final Score: T.B. 3 at Bos. 5

**Alexandre Giroux** (Wsh.) unsuccessful against Manny Fernandez (Bos.) Dec. 10. Final Score: Bos. 1 at Wsh. 3

**Patrick Marleau** (S.J.) unsuccessful against Marty Turco (Dal.)
Dec. 29. Final Score: S.J. 3 at Dal. 1

**Niklas Hagman** (Tor.) unsuccessful against Ryan Miller (Buf.)
Jan. 1. Final Score: Buf. 4 at Tor. 1

**Adam Hall** (T.B.) unsuccessful against Brent Johnson (Wsh.)
Jan. 1. Final Score: T.B. 4 at Wsh. 7

**Scott Hartnell** (Phi.) unsuccessful against Jonathan Quick (L.A.)
Jan. 3. Final Score: Phi. 1 at L.A. 2

**Sidney Crosby** (Pit.) unsuccessful against Henrik Lundqvist (NYR)
Jan. 18. Final Score: NYR 0 at Pit. 3

**Mark Recchi** (T.B.) unsuccessful against Carey Price (Mtl.)
Jan. 27. Final Score: Mtl. 3 at T.B. 5

**Martin St. Louis** (T.B.) unsuccessful against Antero Niittymaki (Phi.)
Jan. 30. Final Score: Phi. 6 at T.B. 1

**Steven Stamkos** (T.B.) unsuccessful against Kari Lehtonen (Atl.)
Feb. 10. Final Score: Atl. 3 at T.B. 1

**Sean Bergenheim** (NYI) unsuccessful against Vesa Toskala (Tor.)
Feb. 26. Final Score: Tor. 5 at NYI 4

**David Booth** (Fla.) unsuccessful against Jose Theodore (Wsh.)
Mar. 1. Final Score: Fla. 6 at Wsh. 2

**Evgeni Malkin** (Pit.) unsuccessful against Johan Hedberg (Atl.)
Mar. 17. Final Score: Atl. 2 at Pit. 6

**Mike Richards** (Phi.) unsuccessful against Patrick Lalime (Buf.)
Mar. 20. Final Score: Phi. 6 at Buf. 4

**Jonathan Toews** (Chi.) unsuccessful against Dwayne Roloson (Edm.)
Mar. 20. Final Score: Edm. 5 at Chi. 4

**Lauri Korpikoski** (NYR) unsuccessful against Patrick Lalime (Buf.)
Mar. 21. Final Score: Buf. 3 at NYR 5

**Pavol Demitra** (Van.) unsuccessful against Andrew Raycroft (Col.)
Mar. 27. Final Score: Van. 4 at Col. 1

**Patrick Sharp** (Chi.) unsuccessful against Roberto Luongo (Van.)
Mar. 29. Final Score: Van. 4 at Chi. 0

**Tom Kostopoulos** (Mtl.) unsuccessful against Yann Danis (NYI)
Apr. 2. Final Score: Mtl. 5 at NYI 1

**Guillaume Latendresse** (Mtl.) unsuccessful against Martin Gerber (Tor.) Apr. 4. Final Score: Mtl. 6 at Tor. 2

**Evgeni Malkin** (Pit.) unsuccessful against Cam Ward (Car.)
Apr. 4. Final Score: Pit. 2 at Car. 3

**Chris Higgins** (Mtl.) unsuccessful against Alex Auld (Ott.)
Apr. 6. Final Score: Ott. 3 at Mtl. 2

**Rick Nash** (CBJ) unsuccessful against Nikolai Khabibulin (Chi.)
Apr. 8. Final Score: CBJ 4 at Chi. 3

Total Shots: 59

Total Goals: 23

Total Saves: 36

*Philadelphia's Simon Gagne was the only NHL player to score two goals on penalty shots in 2008-09. Here he gets his first of the season against Colorado's Andrew Raycroft on October 16, 2008.*

# Goaltending Leaders

Minimum 25 games

## Goals Against Average

| Goaltender | Team | GPI | MINS | GA | Avg |
|---|---|---|---|---|---|
| Tim Thomas | Boston | 54 | 3259 | 114 | 2.10 |
| *Steve Mason | Columbus | 61 | 3664 | 140 | 2.29 |
| Niklas Backstrom | Minnesota | 71 | 4088 | 159 | 2.33 |
| Nikolai Khabibulin | Chicago | 42 | 2467 | 96 | 2.33 |
| Roberto Luongo | Vancouver | 54 | 3181 | 124 | 2.34 |
| *Pekka Rinne | Nashville | 52 | 2999 | 119 | 2.38 |
| Jonas Hiller | Anaheim | 46 | 2486 | 99 | 2.39 |
| Scott Clemmensen | New Jersey | 40 | 2356 | 94 | 2.39 |

## Save Percentage

| Goaltender | Team | GPI | MINS | GA | SA | S% | W | L |
|---|---|---|---|---|---|---|---|---|
| Tim Thomas | Boston | 54 | 3259 | 114 | 1694 | .933 | 36 | 11 |
| Tomas Vokoun | Florida | 59 | 3324 | 138 | 1856 | .926 | 26 | 23 |
| Craig Anderson | Florida | 31 | 1636 | 74 | 977 | .924 | 15 | 7 |
| Niklas Backstrom | Minnesota | 71 | 4088 | 159 | 2059 | .923 | 37 | 24 |
| Roberto Luongo | Vancouver | 54 | 3181 | 124 | 1542 | .920 | 33 | 13 |
| Jonas Hiller | Anaheim | 46 | 2486 | 99 | 1217 | .919 | 23 | 15 |
| Nikolai Khabibulin | Chicago | 42 | 2467 | 96 | 1192 | .919 | 25 | 8 |

## Wins

| Goaltender | Team | GPI | MINS | W | L | OT |
|---|---|---|---|---|---|---|
| Miikka Kiprusoff | Calgary | 76 | 4418 | 45 | 24 | 5 |
| Evgeni Nabokov | San Jose | 62 | 3686 | 41 | 12 | 8 |
| Cam Ward | Carolina | 68 | 3928 | 39 | 23 | 5 |
| Henrik Lundqvist | NY Rangers | 70 | 4153 | 38 | 25 | 7 |
| Niklas Backstrom | Minnesota | 71 | 4088 | 37 | 24 | 8 |
| Tim Thomas | Boston | 54 | 3259 | 36 | 11 | 7 |
| Marc-Andre Fleury | Pittsburgh | 62 | 3641 | 35 | 18 | 7 |

## Shutouts

| Goaltender | Team | GPI | MINS | SO | W | L | OT |
|---|---|---|---|---|---|---|---|
| *Steve Mason | Columbus | 61 | 3664 | 10 | 33 | 20 | 7 |
| Roberto Luongo | Vancouver | 54 | 3181 | 9 | 33 | 13 | 7 |
| Niklas Backstrom | Minnesota | 71 | 4088 | 8 | 37 | 24 | 8 |
| *Pekka Rinne | Nashville | 52 | 2999 | 7 | 29 | 15 | 4 |
| Evgeni Nabokov | San Jose | 62 | 3686 | 7 | 41 | 12 | 8 |

# Team-by-Team Point Totals

## 2003-04 to 2008-09

(Ranked by five-year point %)

| Team | 08-09 | 07-08 | 06-07 | 05-06 | 03-04 | Pts% |
|---|---|---|---|---|---|---|
| Detroit | 112 | 115 | 113 | 124 | 109 | .699 |
| San Jose | 117 | 108 | 107 | 99 | 104 | .652 |
| New Jersey | 106 | 99 | 107 | 101 | 100 | .626 |
| Ottawa | 83 | 94 | 105 | 113 | 102 | .606 |
| Dallas | 83 | 97 | 107 | 112 | 97 | .605 |
| Buffalo | 91 | 90 | 113 | 110 | 85 | .596 |
| Vancouver | 100 | 88 | 105 | 92 | 101 | .593 |
| Nashville | 88 | 91 | 110 | 106 | 91 | .593 |
| Calgary | 98 | 94 | 96 | 103 | 94 | .591 |
| Anaheim | 91 | 102 | 110 | 98 | 76 | .582 |
| Montreal | 93 | 104 | 90 | 93 | 93 | .557 |
| Carolina | 97 | 92 | 88 | 112 | 76 | .567 |
| Boston | 116 | 94 | 76 | 74 | 104 | .566 |
| Minnesota | 89 | 98 | 104 | 84 | 83 | .559 |
| NY Rangers | 95 | 97 | 94 | 100 | 69 | .555 |
| Colorado | 69 | 95 | 95 | 95 | 100 | .554 |
| Philadelphia | 99 | 95 | 56 | 101 | 101 | .551 |
| Toronto | 81 | 83 | 91 | 90 | 103 | .546 |
| Edmonton | 85 | 88 | 71 | 95 | 89 | .522 |
| Tampa Bay | 66 | 71 | 93 | 92 | 106 | .522 |
| Florida | 93 | 85 | 86 | 85 | 75 | .517 |
| Pittsburgh | 99 | 102 | 105 | 58 | 58 | .515 |
| Atlanta | 76 | 76 | 97 | 90 | 78 | .509 |
| Washington | 108 | 94 | 70 | 70 | 60 | .490 |
| NY Islanders | 61 | 79 | 92 | 78 | 91 | .489 |
| St. Louis | 92 | 79 | 81 | 57 | 91 | .488 |
| Los Angeles | 79 | 71 | 68 | 89 | 81 | .473 |
| Chicago | 104 | 88 | 71 | 65 | 59 | .472 |
| Columbus | 92 | 80 | 73 | 74 | 62 | .465 |
| Phoenix | 79 | 83 | 67 | 81 | 68 | .461 |

# Team Record When Scoring First Goal of a Game

| Team | FG | W | L | OT |
|---|---|---|---|---|
| Anaheim | 43 | 34 | 6 | 3 |
| Atlanta | 39 | 26 | 10 | 3 |
| Boston | 47 | 34 | 8 | 5 |
| Buffalo | 44 | 29 | 10 | 5 |
| Calgary | 37 | 26 | 6 | 5 |
| Carolina | 39 | 25 | 10 | 4 |
| Chicago | 43 | 33 | 5 | 5 |
| Colorado | 31 | 18 | 11 | 2 |
| Columbus | 41 | 28 | 9 | 4 |
| Dallas | 38 | 23 | 11 | 4 |
| Detroit | 46 | 37 | 4 | 5 |
| Edmonton | 39 | 28 | 7 | 4 |
| Florida | 39 | 24 | 11 | 4 |
| Los Angeles | 39 | 26 | 9 | 4 |
| Minnesota | 39 | 27 | 10 | 2 |
| Montreal | 38 | 27 | 6 | 5 |
| Nashville | 41 | 29 | 9 | 3 |
| New Jersey | 44 | 37 | 5 | 2 |
| NY Islanders | 37 | 20 | 15 | 2 |
| NY Rangers | 42 | 28 | 9 | 5 |
| Ottawa | 46 | 27 | 12 | 7 |
| Philadelphia | 43 | 29 | 8 | 6 |
| Phoenix | 36 | 21 | 14 | 1 |
| Pittsburgh | 46 | 30 | 10 | 6 |
| San Jose | 46 | 36 | 6 | 4 |
| St. Louis | 35 | 24 | 7 | 4 |
| Tampa Bay | 34 | 15 | 10 | 9 |
| Toronto | 40 | 22 | 10 | 8 |
| Vancouver | 47 | 33 | 8 | 6 |
| Washington | 45 | 34 | 8 | 3 |

# Team Plus/Minus Differential

| Team | GF | PPGF | Net GF | GA | PPGA | Net GA | Goal Differential |
|---|---|---|---|---|---|---|---|
| Boston | 274 | 74 | 200 | 196 | 54 | 142 | +58 |
| Chicago | 264 | 70 | 194 | 216 | 64 | 152 | +42 |
| New Jersey | 244 | 58 | 186 | 209 | 65 | 144 | +42 |
| Detroit | 295 | 90 | 205 | 244 | 71 | 173 | +32 |
| Vancouver | 246 | 67 | 179 | 220 | 69 | 151 | +28 |
| Pittsburgh | 264 | 62 | 202 | 239 | 60 | 179 | +23 |
| Philadelphia | 264 | 71 | 193 | 238 | 67 | 171 | +22 |
| Washington | 272 | 85 | 187 | 245 | 75 | 170 | +17 |
| Columbus | 226 | 41 | 185 | 230 | 62 | 168 | +17 |
| San Jose | 257 | 87 | 170 | 204 | 51 | 153 | +17 |
| Anaheim | 245 | 73 | 172 | 238 | 78 | 160 | +12 |
| Florida | 234 | 51 | 183 | 231 | 54 | 177 | +6 |
| Calgary | 254 | 61 | 193 | 248 | 58 | 190 | +3 |
| Buffalo | 250 | 75 | 175 | 234 | 61 | 173 | +2 |
| Edmonton | 234 | 60 | 174 | 248 | 76 | 172 | +2 |
| Carolina | 239 | 70 | 169 | 226 | 59 | 167 | +2 |
| Atlanta | 257 | 69 | 188 | 280 | 88 | 192 | –4 |
| Montreal | 249 | 72 | 177 | 247 | 65 | 182 | –5 |
| Dallas | 230 | 54 | 176 | 257 | 70 | 187 | –11 |
| Nashville | 213 | 50 | 163 | 233 | 59 | 174 | –11 |
| Minnesota | 219 | 66 | 153 | 200 | 36 | 164 | –11 |
| St. Louis | 233 | 72 | 161 | 233 | 58 | 175 | –14 |
| NY Rangers | 210 | 48 | 162 | 218 | 40 | 178 | –16 |
| Ottawa | 217 | 66 | 151 | 237 | 64 | 173 | –22 |
| Phoenix | 208 | 50 | 158 | 252 | 68 | 184 | –26 |
| Toronto | 250 | 62 | 188 | 293 | 78 | 215 | –27 |
| Los Angeles | 207 | 69 | 138 | 234 | 62 | 172 | –34 |
| Tampa Bay | 210 | 61 | 149 | 279 | 89 | 190 | –41 |
| Colorado | 199 | 50 | 149 | 257 | 64 | 193 | –44 |
| NY Islanders | 201 | 54 | 147 | 279 | 73 | 206 | –59 |

# Team Record When Leading, Trailing, Tied

| Team | Leading after 1 period | | | Leading after 2 periods | | | Trailing after 1 period | | | Trailing after 2 periods | | | Tied after 1 period | | | Tied after 2 periods | | |
|---|---|---|---|---|---|---|---|---|---|---|---|---|---|---|---|---|---|---|
| | W | L | OT | W | L | OT | W | L | OT | W | L | OT | W | L | OT | W | L | OT |
| Anaheim | 19 | 4 | 2 | 26 | 1 | 0 | 2 | 20 | 3 | 3 | 23 | 2 | 21 | 9 | 2 | 13 | 9 | 5 |
| Atlanta | 20 | 5 | 1 | 22 | 2 | 0 | 4 | 26 | 1 | 6 | 30 | 3 | 11 | 10 | 4 | 7 | 9 | 3 |
| Boston | 27 | 4 | 3 | 38 | 2 | 3 | 10 | 5 | 4 | 2 | 11 | 4 | 16 | 10 | 3 | 13 | 6 | 3 |
| Buffalo | 26 | 7 | 3 | 27 | 1 | 6 | 8 | 15 | 2 | 7 | 23 | 2 | 7 | 10 | 4 | 7 | 8 | 1 |
| Calgary | 17 | 2 | 4 | 28 | 1 | 3 | 10 | 19 | 0 | 4 | 29 | 0 | 19 | 9 | 2 | 14 | 0 | 3 |
| Carolina | 19 | 8 | 2 | 31 | 3 | 2 | 8 | 18 | 5 | 8 | 21 | 3 | 18 | 4 | 0 | 6 | 6 | 2 |
| Chicago | 25 | 3 | 4 | 35 | 2 | 4 | 10 | 13 | 4 | 3 | 17 | 4 | 11 | 8 | 4 | 8 | 5 | 4 |
| Colorado | 15 | 8 | 0 | 20 | 0 | 2 | 3 | 24 | 0 | 5 | 34 | 1 | 14 | 13 | 5 | 7 | 11 | 2 |
| Columbus | 20 | 6 | 2 | 21 | 3 | 0 | 5 | 13 | 2 | 4 | 25 | 4 | 16 | 12 | 6 | 16 | 3 | 6 |
| Dallas | 19 | 3 | 1 | 26 | 1 | 3 | 10 | 22 | 5 | 3 | 27 | 2 | 7 | 10 | 5 | 7 | 7 | 6 |
| Detroit | 26 | 1 | 6 | 34 | 2 | 6 | 10 | 11 | 3 | 8 | 16 | 0 | 15 | 9 | 1 | 9 | 3 | 4 |
| Edmonton | 21 | 4 | 1 | 25 | 1 | 2 | 5 | 19 | 3 | 2 | 29 | 2 | 12 | 12 | 5 | 11 | 5 | 5 |
| Florida | 17 | 6 | 3 | 29 | 3 | 3 | 9 | 14 | 5 | 3 | 22 | 5 | 15 | 10 | 3 | 9 | 5 | 3 |
| Los Angeles | 18 | 3 | 1 | 24 | 4 | 2 | 3 | 18 | 5 | 4 | 28 | 4 | 13 | 16 | 5 | 6 | 5 | 5 |
| Minnesota | 21 | 5 | 1 | 28 | 1 | 1 | 4 | 13 | 5 | 3 | 24 | 4 | 15 | 15 | 3 | 9 | 8 | 4 |
| Montreal | 24 | 2 | 2 | 29 | 2 | 3 | 7 | 19 | 3 | 7 | 25 | 1 | 10 | 9 | 6 | 5 | 3 | 7 |
| Nashville | 15 | 2 | 2 | 22 | 2 | 0 | 6 | 17 | 1 | 7 | 27 | 1 | 19 | 15 | 5 | 11 | 5 | 7 |
| New Jersey | 27 | 4 | 3 | 39 | 1 | 1 | 10 | 16 | 1 | 6 | 22 | 0 | 14 | 7 | 0 | 6 | 4 | 3 |
| NY Islanders | 9 | 9 | 3 | 21 | 5 | 4 | 4 | 23 | 5 | 1 | 35 | 5 | 13 | 15 | 1 | 4 | 7 | 0 |
| NY Rangers | 14 | 5 | 4 | 27 | 2 | 3 | 10 | 13 | 2 | 6 | 20 | 2 | 19 | 12 | 3 | 10 | 8 | 4 |
| Ottawa | 16 | 3 | 1 | 22 | 2 | 3 | 5 | 20 | 3 | 3 | 27 | 3 | 15 | 12 | 7 | 11 | 6 | 5 |
| Philadelphia | 23 | 3 | 2 | 27 | 3 | 2 | 9 | 16 | 5 | 4 | 22 | 3 | 12 | 8 | 4 | 13 | 2 | 6 |
| Phoenix | 16 | 5 | 0 | 27 | 1 | 1 | 4 | 17 | 2 | 3 | 33 | 4 | 16 | 17 | 5 | 6 | 5 | 2 |
| Pittsburgh | 19 | 6 | 4 | 25 | 3 | 5 | 9 | 11 | 1 | 11 | 21 | 2 | 17 | 11 | 4 | 9 | 4 | 2 |
| San Jose | 24 | 2 | 3 | 33 | 1 | 4 | 11 | 12 | 5 | 5 | 16 | 4 | 18 | 4 | 3 | 15 | 1 | 3 |
| St. Louis | 17 | 5 | 4 | 28 | 2 | 3 | 8 | 16 | 3 | 4 | 22 | 3 | 16 | 10 | 3 | 9 | 7 | 4 |
| Tampa Bay | 11 | 6 | 8 | 17 | 3 | 5 | 4 | 21 | 5 | 3 | 32 | 7 | 9 | 13 | 5 | 4 | 5 | 6 |
| Toronto | 12 | 5 | 6 | 18 | 0 | 8 | 12 | 20 | 3 | 7 | 32 | 3 | 10 | 10 | 4 | 9 | 3 | 2 |
| Vancouver | 25 | 5 | 4 | 30 | 0 | 3 | 9 | 18 | 2 | 5 | 21 | 2 | 11 | 4 | 4 | 10 | 6 | 5 |
| Washington | 30 | 3 | 3 | 33 | 3 | 2 | 8 | 14 | 1 | 4 | 17 | 1 | 12 | 7 | 4 | 13 | 4 | 5 |

*Boston's Tim Thomas led the NHL with a 2.10 goals-against average and .933 save percentage en route to winning the Vezina Trophy.*

# Team Statistics

## TEAMS' HOME AND ROAD RECORD

### Eastern Conference

| | Home | | | | | | | Road | | | | | | |
|---|---|---|---|---|---|---|---|---|---|---|---|---|---|---|
| Team | GP | W | L | OT | GF | GA | PTS | GP | W | L | OT | GF | GA | PTS |
| BOS | 41 | 29 | 6 | 6 | 153 | 97 | 64 | 41 | 24 | 13 | 4 | 121 | 99 | 52 |
| WSH | 41 | 29 | 9 | 3 | 146 | 112 | 61 | 41 | 21 | 15 | 5 | 126 | 133 | 47 |
| N.J. | 41 | 28 | 12 | 1 | 137 | 98 | 57 | 41 | 23 | 15 | 3 | 107 | 111 | 49 |
| PIT. | 41 | 25 | 13 | 3 | 134 | 104 | 53 | 41 | 20 | 15 | 6 | 130 | 135 | 46 |
| PHI. | 41 | 24 | 13 | 4 | 151 | 125 | 52 | 41 | 20 | 14 | 7 | 113 | 113 | 47 |
| CAR. | 41 | 26 | 14 | 1 | 117 | 106 | 53 | 41 | 19 | 16 | 6 | 122 | 120 | 44 |
| NYR | 41 | 26 | 11 | 4 | 114 | 94 | 56 | 41 | 17 | 19 | 5 | 96 | 124 | 39 |
| MTL | 41 | 24 | 10 | 7 | 133 | 111 | 55 | 41 | 17 | 20 | 4 | 116 | 136 | 38 |
| FLA | 41 | 22 | 12 | 7 | 114 | 105 | 51 | 41 | 19 | 18 | 4 | 120 | 126 | 42 |
| BUF | 41 | 23 | 15 | 3 | 128 | 112 | 49 | 41 | 18 | 17 | 6 | 122 | 122 | 42 |
| OTT | 41 | 22 | 12 | 7 | 121 | 110 | 51 | 41 | 14 | 23 | 4 | 96 | 127 | 32 |
| TOR | 41 | 16 | 16 | 9 | 119 | 142 | 41 | 41 | 18 | 19 | 4 | 131 | 151 | 40 |
| ATL | 41 | 18 | 21 | 2 | 124 | 139 | 38 | 41 | 17 | 20 | 4 | 133 | 141 | 38 |
| T.B. | 41 | 12 | 18 | 11 | 105 | 140 | 35 | 41 | 12 | 22 | 7 | 105 | 139 | 31 |
| NYI | 41 | 17 | 18 | 6 | 112 | 129 | 40 | 41 | 9 | 29 | 3 | 89 | 150 | 21 |
| **Total** | **615** | **341** | **200** | **74** | **1908** | **1724** | **756** | **615** | **268** | **275** | **72** | **1727** | **1927** | **608** |

### Western Conference

| | | | | | | | | | | | | | | |
|---|---|---|---|---|---|---|---|---|---|---|---|---|---|---|
| S.J. | 41 | 32 | 5 | 4 | 141 | 90 | 68 | 41 | 21 | 13 | 7 | 116 | 114 | 49 |
| DET | 41 | 27 | 9 | 5 | 158 | 118 | 59 | 41 | 24 | 12 | 5 | 137 | 126 | 53 |
| CHI | 41 | 24 | 9 | 8 | 140 | 105 | 56 | 41 | 22 | 15 | 4 | 124 | 111 | 48 |
| VAN | 41 | 24 | 12 | 5 | 129 | 101 | 53 | 41 | 21 | 15 | 5 | 117 | 119 | 47 |
| CGY | 41 | 27 | 10 | 4 | 147 | 110 | 58 | 41 | 19 | 20 | 2 | 107 | 138 | 40 |
| ST.L. | 41 | 23 | 13 | 5 | 122 | 107 | 51 | 41 | 18 | 18 | 5 | 111 | 126 | 41 |
| CBJ | 41 | 25 | 13 | 3 | 111 | 108 | 53 | 41 | 16 | 18 | 7 | 115 | 122 | 39 |
| ANA | 41 | 20 | 18 | 3 | 124 | 119 | 43 | 41 | 22 | 15 | 4 | 121 | 119 | 48 |
| MIN | 41 | 23 | 11 | 7 | 124 | 96 | 53 | 41 | 17 | 22 | 2 | 95 | 104 | 36 |
| NSH | 41 | 24 | 13 | 4 | 116 | 104 | 52 | 41 | 16 | 21 | 4 | 97 | 129 | 36 |
| EDM | 41 | 18 | 17 | 6 | 109 | 114 | 42 | 41 | 20 | 18 | 3 | 125 | 134 | 43 |
| DAL | 41 | 20 | 16 | 5 | 121 | 122 | 45 | 41 | 16 | 19 | 6 | 109 | 135 | 38 |
| PHX | 41 | 23 | 15 | 3 | 114 | 117 | 49 | 41 | 13 | 24 | 4 | 94 | 135 | 30 |
| L.A. | 41 | 18 | 15 | 8 | 116 | 118 | 44 | 41 | 16 | 22 | 3 | 91 | 116 | 35 |
| COL | 41 | 18 | 21 | 2 | 107 | 125 | 38 | 41 | 14 | 24 | 3 | 92 | 132 | 31 |
| **Total** | **615** | **346** | **197** | **72** | **1879** | **1654** | **764** | **615** | **275** | **276** | **64** | **1651** | **1860** | **614** |
| | **1230** | **687** | **397** | **146** | **3787** | **3378** | **1520** | **1230** | **543** | **551** | **136** | **3378** | **3787** | **1222** |

*Philadelphia's Mike Richards led the NHL with seven shorthand goals in 2008-09. As a team, the Flyers led the NHL with 16 shorthand goals*

## TEAMS' DIVISIONAL RECORD

### Northeast Division

| | Against Own Division | | | | | | | Against Other Divisions | | | | | | |
|---|---|---|---|---|---|---|---|---|---|---|---|---|---|---|
| Team | GP | W | L | OT | GF | GA | PTS | GP | W | L | OT | GF | GA | PTS |
| BOS | 24 | 17 | 5 | 2 | 92 | 71 | 36 | 58 | 36 | 14 | 8 | 182 | 125 | 80 |
| MTL | 24 | 10 | 10 | 4 | 75 | 80 | 24 | 58 | 31 | 20 | 7 | 174 | 167 | 69 |
| BUF | 24 | 14 | 8 | 2 | 76 | 62 | 30 | 58 | 27 | 24 | 7 | 174 | 172 | 61 |
| OTT | 24 | 10 | 10 | 4 | 68 | 77 | 24 | 58 | 26 | 25 | 7 | 149 | 160 | 59 |
| TOR | 24 | 9 | 13 | 2 | 67 | 88 | 20 | 58 | 25 | 22 | 11 | 183 | 205 | 61 |
| **Total** | **120** | **60** | **46** | **14** | **378** | **378** | **134** | **290** | **145** | **105** | **40** | **862** | **829** | **330** |

### Atlantic Division

| | | | | | | | | | | | | | | |
|---|---|---|---|---|---|---|---|---|---|---|---|---|---|---|
| N.J. | 24 | 13 | 10 | 1 | 63 | 69 | 27 | 58 | 38 | 17 | 3 | 181 | 140 | 79 |
| PIT | 24 | 15 | 4 | 5 | 81 | 60 | 35 | 58 | 30 | 24 | 4 | 183 | 179 | 64 |
| PHI | 24 | 13 | 7 | 4 | 77 | 67 | 30 | 58 | 31 | 20 | 7 | 187 | 171 | 69 |
| NYR | 24 | 15 | 9 | 0 | 71 | 64 | 30 | 58 | 28 | 21 | 9 | 139 | 154 | 65 |
| NYI | 24 | 4 | 17 | 3 | 53 | 85 | 11 | 58 | 22 | 30 | 6 | 148 | 194 | 50 |
| **Total** | **120** | **60** | **47** | **13** | **345** | **345** | **133** | **290** | **149** | **112** | **29** | **838** | **838** | **327** |

### Southeast Division

| | | | | | | | | | | | | | | |
|---|---|---|---|---|---|---|---|---|---|---|---|---|---|---|
| WSH | 24 | 16 | 8 | 0 | 90 | 78 | 32 | 58 | 34 | 16 | 8 | 182 | 167 | 76 |
| CAR | 24 | 15 | 8 | 1 | 77 | 67 | 31 | 58 | 30 | 22 | 6 | 162 | 159 | 66 |
| FLA | 24 | 13 | 7 | 4 | 84 | 73 | 30 | 58 | 28 | 23 | 7 | 150 | 158 | 63 |
| ATL | 24 | 11 | 11 | 2 | 81 | 79 | 24 | 58 | 24 | 30 | 4 | 176 | 201 | 52 |
| T.B. | 24 | 5 | 15 | 4 | 63 | 98 | 14 | 58 | 19 | 25 | 14 | 147 | 181 | 52 |
| **Total** | **120** | **60** | **49** | **11** | **395** | **395** | **131** | **290** | **135** | **116** | **39** | **817** | **866** | **309** |

### Central Division

| | | | | | | | | | | | | | | |
|---|---|---|---|---|---|---|---|---|---|---|---|---|---|---|
| DET | 24 | 14 | 8 | 2 | 86 | 75 | 30 | 58 | 37 | 13 | 8 | 209 | 169 | 82 |
| CHI | 24 | 10 | 7 | 7 | 64 | 69 | 27 | 58 | 36 | 17 | 5 | 200 | 147 | 77 |
| ST.L. | 24 | 14 | 6 | 4 | 68 | 62 | 32 | 58 | 27 | 25 | 6 | 165 | 171 | 60 |
| CBJ | 24 | 10 | 10 | 4 | 66 | 79 | 24 | 58 | 31 | 21 | 6 | 160 | 151 | 68 |
| NSH | 24 | 12 | 9 | 3 | 71 | 70 | 27 | 58 | 28 | 25 | 5 | 142 | 163 | 61 |
| **Total** | **120** | **60** | **40** | **20** | **355** | **355** | **140** | **290** | **159** | **101** | **30** | **876** | **801** | **348** |

### Pacific Division

| | | | | | | | | | | | | | | |
|---|---|---|---|---|---|---|---|---|---|---|---|---|---|---|
| S.J. | 24 | 17 | 7 | 0 | 60 | 48 | 34 | 58 | 36 | 11 | 11 | 197 | 156 | 83 |
| ANA | 24 | 12 | 10 | 2 | 68 | 62 | 26 | 58 | 30 | 23 | 5 | 177 | 176 | 65 |
| DAL | 24 | 8 | 9 | 7 | 56 | 67 | 23 | 58 | 28 | 26 | 4 | 174 | 190 | 60 |
| PHX | 24 | 13 | 9 | 2 | 63 | 68 | 28 | 58 | 23 | 30 | 5 | 145 | 184 | 51 |
| L.A. | 24 | 10 | 10 | 4 | 58 | 60 | 24 | 58 | 24 | 27 | 7 | 149 | 174 | 55 |
| **Total** | **120** | **60** | **45** | **15** | **305** | **305** | **135** | **290** | **141** | **117** | **32** | **842** | **880** | **314** |

### Northwest Division

| | | | | | | | | | | | | | | |
|---|---|---|---|---|---|---|---|---|---|---|---|---|---|---|
| VAN | 24 | 15 | 6 | 3 | 73 | 57 | 33 | 58 | 30 | 21 | 7 | 173 | 163 | 67 |
| CGY | 24 | 14 | 8 | 2 | 67 | 69 | 30 | 58 | 32 | 22 | 4 | 187 | 179 | 68 |
| MIN | 24 | 10 | 10 | 4 | 56 | 55 | 24 | 58 | 30 | 23 | 5 | 163 | 145 | 65 |
| EDM | 24 | 11 | 9 | 4 | 67 | 70 | 26 | 58 | 27 | 26 | 5 | 167 | 178 | 59 |
| COL | 24 | 10 | 12 | 2 | 57 | 69 | 22 | 58 | 22 | 33 | 3 | 142 | 188 | 47 |
| **Total** | **120** | **60** | **45** | **15** | **320** | **320** | **135** | **290** | **141** | **125** | **24** | **832** | **853** | **306** |

## TEAM STREAKS

### Consecutive Wins

| Games | Team | From | To |
|---|---|---|---|
| 10 | Boston | Dec. 12 | Jan. 1 |
| 9 | San Jose | Nov. 13 | Dec. 4 |
| 9 | Chicago | Dec. 7 | Dec. 28 |
| 9 | Carolina | Mar. 18 | Apr. 7 |
| 8 | New Jersey | Jan. 13 | Jan. 30 |
| 7 | San Jose | Oct. 25 | Nov. 8 |
| 7 | Washington | Dec. 23 | Jan. 6 |
| 7 | Pittsburgh | Feb. 25 | Mar. 10 |

### Consecutive Home Wins

| Games | Team | From | To |
|---|---|---|---|
| 14 | Boston | Oct. 25 | Jan. 1 |
| 12 | Carolina | Feb. 20 | Apr. 7 |
| 11 | Vancouver | Feb. 3 | Mar. 19 |
| 11 | New Jersey | Feb. 9 | Mar. 20 |
| 9 | San Jose | Oct. 9 | Nov. 8 |
| 9 | Washington | Dec. 4 | Jan. 6 |
| 9 | Ottawa | Mar. 5 | Apr. 7 |

### Consecutive Road Wins

| Games | Team | From | To |
|---|---|---|---|
| 7 | Boston | Dec. 12 | Jan. 15 |
| 7 | New Jersey | Jan. 13 | Feb. 6 |
| 6 | Calgary | Feb. 12 | Mar. 5 |
| 6 | Anaheim | Mar. 19 | Apr. 4 |
| 5 | Detroit | Oct. 11 | Oct. 27 |
| 5 | Anaheim | Oct. 21 | Nov. 4 |
| 5 | Pittsburgh | Nov. 1 | Nov. 26 |
| 5 | Detroit | Nov. 2 | Nov. 22 |
| 5 | San Jose | Nov. 16 | Dec. 15 |
| 5 | Florida | Nov. 30 | Dec. 12 |
| 5 | Chicago | Dec. 12 | Dec. 28 |
| 5 | Los Angeles | Feb. 3 | Feb. 18 |
| 5 | Washington | Feb. 14 | Mar. 12 |
| 5 | Pittsburgh | Feb. 27 | Mar. 8 |
| 5 | Detroit | Mar. 3 | Mar. 20 |

## TEAM PENALTIES

**Abbreviations: GP** – games played; **PEN** – total penalty minutes including bench minutes; **BMI** – total bench minor minutes; **AVG** – average penalty minutes/game calculated by dividing total penalty minutes by games played

| Team | GP | PEN | BMI | AVG | Team | GP | PEN | BMI | AVG |
|---|---|---|---|---|---|---|---|---|---|
| CAR | 82 | 802 | 16 | 9.8 | DAL | 82 | 1144 | 10 | 14.0 |
| DET | 82 | 824 | 14 | 10.0 | CHI | 82 | 1157 | 28 | 14.1 |
| MIN | 82 | 889 | 20 | 10.8 | NYR | 82 | 1199 | 24 | 14.6 |
| FLA | 82 | 900 | 16 | 11.0 | L.A | 82 | 1207 | 16 | 14.7 |
| NSH | 82 | 994 | 12 | 12.1 | NYI | 82 | 1216 | 18 | 14.8 |
| BOS | 82 | 1028 | 12 | 12.5 | CBJ | 82 | 1227 | 20 | 15.0 |
| WSH | 82 | 1041 | 20 | 12.7 | MTL | 82 | 1229 | 6 | 15.0 |
| S.J | 82 | 1053 | 16 | 12.8 | EDM | 82 | 1247 | 20 | 15.2 |
| N.J | 82 | 1058 | 20 | 12.9 | STL | 82 | 1248 | 22 | 15.2 |
| COL | 82 | 1062 | 18 | 13.0 | ATL | 82 | 1256 | 12 | 15.3 |
| PHX | 82 | 1092 | 18 | 13.3 | CGY | 82 | 1299 | 18 | 15.8 |
| OTT | 82 | 1098 | 14 | 13.4 | T.B | 82 | 1306 | 26 | 15.9 |
| PIT | 82 | 1114 | 8 | 13.6 | VAN | 82 | 1351 | 28 | 16.5 |
| BUF | 82 | 1121 | 16 | 13.7 | ANA | 82 | 1426 | 8 | 17.4 |
| TOR | 82 | 1125 | 12 | 13.7 | PHI | 82 | 1434 | 26 | 17.5 |
| | | | | | **Total** | **1230** | **34147** | **514** | **27.8** |

*Detroit led the NHL with 90 power-play goals and a 25.5 percentage in 2008-09. Henrik Zetterberg led the Red Wings with 12 power-play goals.*

## TEAMS' POWER-PLAY RECORD

**Abbreviations: ADV** – total advantages; **PPGF** – power-play goals for; **%** – calculated by dividing number of power-play goals by total advantages.

| | Home | | | | | Road | | | | | Overall | | | | |
|---|---|---|---|---|---|---|---|---|---|---|---|---|---|---|---|
| | Team | GP | ADV | PPGF | % | Team | GP | ADV | PPGF | % | Team | GP | ADV | PPGF | % |
| 1 | WSH | 41 | 177 | 50 | 28.2 | S.J | 41 | 163 | 46 | 28.2 | DET | 82 | 353 | 90 | 25.5 |
| 2 | BOS | 41 | 157 | 44 | 28.0 | DET | 41 | 167 | 44 | 26.3 | WSH | 82 | 337 | 85 | 25.2 |
| 3 | PHI | 41 | 159 | 43 | 27.0 | ANA | 41 | 139 | 34 | 24.5 | S.J | 82 | 360 | 87 | 24.2 |
| 4 | DET | 41 | 186 | 46 | 24.7 | BUF | 41 | 164 | 39 | 23.8 | BOS | 82 | 313 | 74 | 23.6 |
| 5 | STL | 41 | 187 | 44 | 23.5 | WSH | 41 | 160 | 35 | 21.9 | ANA | 82 | 309 | 73 | 23.6 |
| 6 | ANA | 41 | 170 | 39 | 22.9 | CHI | 41 | 150 | 32 | 21.3 | PHI | 82 | 316 | 71 | 22.5 |
| 7 | OTT | 41 | 173 | 39 | 22.5 | ATL | 41 | 170 | 36 | 21.2 | BUF | 82 | 358 | 75 | 20.9 |
| 8 | L.A | 41 | 200 | 43 | 21.5 | TOR | 41 | 168 | 35 | 20.8 | STL | 82 | 351 | 72 | 20.5 |
| 9 | MIN | 41 | 160 | 34 | 21.3 | MTL | 41 | 176 | 36 | 20.5 | MIN | 82 | 328 | 66 | 20.1 |
| 10 | S.J | 41 | 197 | 41 | 20.8 | CAR | 41 | 173 | 34 | 19.7 | OTT | 82 | 339 | 66 | 19.5 |
| 11 | VAN | 41 | 193 | 39 | 20.2 | N.J | 41 | 148 | 29 | 19.6 | CHI | 82 | 363 | 70 | 19.3 |
| 12 | CGY | 41 | 181 | 35 | 19.3 | T.B | 41 | 164 | 32 | 19.5 | MTL | 82 | 374 | 72 | 19.3 |
| 13 | PIT | 41 | 199 | 38 | 19.1 | BOS | 41 | 156 | 30 | 19.2 | ATL | 82 | 357 | 69 | 19.3 |
| 14 | BUF | 41 | 194 | 36 | 18.6 | EDM | 41 | 172 | 33 | 19.2 | L.A | 82 | 360 | 69 | 19.2 |
| 15 | N.J | 41 | 159 | 29 | 18.2 | MIN | 41 | 168 | 32 | 19.0 | N.J | 82 | 307 | 58 | 18.9 |
| 16 | MTL | 41 | 198 | 36 | 18.2 | NYI | 41 | 157 | 29 | 18.5 | TOR | 82 | 330 | 62 | 18.8 |
| 17 | COL | 41 | 162 | 29 | 17.9 | PHI | 41 | 157 | 28 | 17.8 | VAN | 82 | 357 | 67 | 18.8 |
| 18 | CAR | 41 | 201 | 36 | 17.9 | FLA | 41 | 158 | 28 | 17.7 | CAR | 82 | 374 | 70 | 18.7 |
| 19 | CHI | 41 | 213 | 38 | 17.8 | STL | 41 | 164 | 28 | 17.1 | T.B | 82 | 343 | 61 | 17.8 |
| 20 | ATL | 41 | 187 | 33 | 17.6 | VAN | 41 | 164 | 28 | 17.1 | PIT | 82 | 360 | 62 | 17.2 |
| 21 | TOR | 41 | 162 | 27 | 16.7 | OTT | 41 | 166 | 27 | 16.3 | CGY | 82 | 358 | 61 | 17.0 |
| 22 | T.B | 41 | 179 | 29 | 16.2 | L.A | 41 | 160 | 26 | 16.3 | NYI | 82 | 320 | 54 | 16.9 |
| 23 | NSH | 41 | 167 | 27 | 16.2 | NSH | 41 | 151 | 23 | 15.2 | EDM | 82 | 354 | 60 | 16.9 |
| 24 | DAL | 41 | 188 | 30 | 16.0 | PIT | 41 | 161 | 24 | 14.9 | FLA | 82 | 308 | 51 | 16.6 |
| 25 | NYI | 41 | 163 | 25 | 15.3 | CGY | 41 | 177 | 26 | 14.7 | COL | 82 | 318 | 50 | 15.7 |
| 26 | FLA | 41 | 150 | 23 | 15.3 | DAL | 41 | 163 | 24 | 14.7 | NSH | 82 | 318 | 50 | 15.7 |
| 27 | PHX | 41 | 189 | 29 | 15.3 | NYR | 41 | 166 | 23 | 13.9 | DAL | 82 | 351 | 54 | 15.4 |
| 28 | EDM | 41 | 182 | 27 | 14.8 | COL | 41 | 156 | 21 | 13.5 | PHX | 82 | 344 | 50 | 14.5 |
| 29 | NYR | 41 | 180 | 25 | 13.9 | PHX | 41 | 155 | 21 | 13.5 | NYR | 82 | 346 | 48 | 13.9 |
| 30 | CBJ | 41 | 188 | 23 | 12.2 | CBJ | 41 | 134 | 18 | 13.4 | CBJ | 82 | 322 | 41 | 12.7 |
| **TOTAL** | | **1230** | **5401** | **1037** | **19.2** | | **1230** | **4827** | **901** | **18.7** | | **1230** | **10228** | **1938** | **18.9** |

## TEAMS' PENALTY KILLING RECORD

**Abbreviations: TSH** – total times shorthanded; **PPGA** – power-play goals against; **%** – calculated by dividing times short minus power-play goals against by times short.

| | Home | | | | | Road | | | | | Overall | | | | |
|---|---|---|---|---|---|---|---|---|---|---|---|---|---|---|---|
| | Team | GP | TSH | PPGA | % | Team | GP | TSH | PPGA | % | Team | GP | TSH | PPGA | % |
| 1 | NYR | 41 | 147 | 16 | 89.1 | MIN | 41 | 156 | 17 | 89.1 | NYR | 82 | 329 | 40 | 87.8 |
| 2 | NSH | 41 | 150 | 17 | 88.7 | NYR | 41 | 182 | 24 | 86.8 | MIN | 82 | 291 | 36 | 87.6 |
| 3 | STL | 41 | 181 | 23 | 87.3 | L.A | 41 | 193 | 30 | 84.5 | STL | 82 | 357 | 58 | 83.8 |
| 4 | CGY | 41 | 146 | 20 | 86.3 | BOS | 41 | 158 | 25 | 84.2 | CGY | 82 | 349 | 58 | 83.4 |
| 5 | MIN | 41 | 135 | 19 | 85.9 | FLA | 41 | 165 | 28 | 83.0 | S.J | 82 | 306 | 51 | 83.3 |
| 6 | S.J | 41 | 135 | 20 | 85.2 | OTT | 41 | 188 | 33 | 82.4 | PHI | 82 | 393 | 67 | 83.0 |
| 7 | PIT | 41 | 180 | 27 | 85.0 | BUF | 41 | 187 | 33 | 82.4 | L.A | 82 | 362 | 62 | 82.9 |
| 8 | CBJ | 41 | 174 | 27 | 84.5 | PHI | 41 | 216 | 38 | 82.4 | PIT | 82 | 347 | 60 | 82.7 |
| 9 | PHI | 41 | 177 | 29 | 83.6 | VAN | 41 | 204 | 37 | 81.9 | FLA | 82 | 311 | 54 | 82.6 |
| 10 | MTL | 41 | 169 | 28 | 83.4 | S.J | 41 | 171 | 31 | 81.9 | NSH | 82 | 338 | 59 | 82.5 |
| 11 | FLA | 41 | 146 | 26 | 82.2 | N.J | 41 | 165 | 30 | 81.8 | BOS | 82 | 306 | 54 | 82.4 |
| 12 | WSH | 41 | 184 | 34 | 81.5 | MTL | 41 | 201 | 37 | 81.6 | MTL | 82 | 370 | 65 | 82.4 |
| 13 | BUF | 41 | 149 | 28 | 81.2 | CGY | 41 | 203 | 38 | 81.3 | CBJ | 82 | 346 | 62 | 82.1 |
| 14 | L.A | 41 | 169 | 32 | 81.1 | COL | 41 | 164 | 31 | 81.1 | BUF | 82 | 336 | 61 | 81.8 |
| 15 | NYI | 41 | 184 | 35 | 81.0 | CHI | 41 | 165 | 32 | 80.6 | OTT | 82 | 346 | 64 | 81.5 |
| 16 | CAR | 41 | 141 | 27 | 80.9 | PIT | 41 | 167 | 33 | 80.2 | VAN | 82 | 371 | 69 | 81.4 |
| 17 | VAN | 41 | 167 | 32 | 80.8 | STL | 41 | 176 | 35 | 80.1 | CHI | 82 | 330 | 64 | 80.6 |
| 18 | CHI | 41 | 165 | 32 | 80.6 | ANA | 41 | 200 | 40 | 80.0 | WSH | 82 | 387 | 75 | 80.6 |
| 19 | OTT | 41 | 158 | 31 | 80.4 | CAR | 41 | 160 | 32 | 80.0 | CAR | 82 | 301 | 59 | 80.4 |
| 20 | DET | 41 | 153 | 30 | 80.4 | WSH | 41 | 203 | 41 | 79.8 | COL | 82 | 318 | 64 | 79.9 |
| 21 | BOS | 41 | 148 | 29 | 80.4 | CBJ | 41 | 172 | 35 | 79.7 | N.J | 82 | 324 | 65 | 79.9 |
| 22 | T.B | 41 | 199 | 40 | 79.9 | TOR | 41 | 164 | 34 | 79.3 | NYI | 82 | 361 | 73 | 79.8 |
| 23 | ANA | 41 | 185 | 38 | 79.5 | EDM | 41 | 185 | 39 | 78.9 | ANA | 82 | 385 | 78 | 79.7 |
| 24 | DAL | 41 | 162 | 34 | 79.0 | NYI | 41 | 177 | 38 | 78.5 | DAL | 82 | 327 | 70 | 78.6 |
| 25 | COL | 41 | 154 | 33 | 78.6 | PHX | 41 | 162 | 35 | 78.4 | DET | 82 | 327 | 71 | 78.3 |
| 26 | N.J | 41 | 159 | 35 | 78.0 | DAL | 41 | 165 | 36 | 78.2 | T.B | 82 | 405 | 89 | 78.0 |
| 27 | EDM | 41 | 153 | 37 | 75.8 | NSH | 41 | 188 | 42 | 77.7 | EDM | 82 | 338 | 76 | 77.5 |
| 28 | ATL | 41 | 182 | 45 | 75.3 | ATL | 41 | 184 | 43 | 76.6 | PHX | 82 | 293 | 68 | 76.8 |
| 29 | PHX | 41 | 131 | 33 | 74.8 | DET | 41 | 174 | 41 | 76.4 | ATL | 82 | 366 | 88 | 76.0 |
| 30 | TOR | 41 | 144 | 44 | 69.4 | T.B | 41 | 206 | 49 | 76.2 | TOR | 82 | 308 | 78 | 74.7 |
| **TOTAL** | | **1230** | **4827** | **901** | **81.3** | | **1230** | **5401** | **1037** | **80.8** | | **1230** | **10228** | **1938** | **81.1** |

## SHORTHAND GOALS FOR

| | Home | | | Road | | | Overall | | |
|---|---|---|---|---|---|---|---|---|---|
| | Team | GP | SHGF | Team | GP | SHGF | Team | GP | SHGF |
| 1 | S.J | 41 | 7 | PHI | 41 | 9 | PHI | 82 | 16 |
| 2 | N.J | 41 | 7 | ATL | 41 | 8 | ATL | 82 | 13 |
| 3 | STL | 41 | 7 | BOS | 41 | 7 | S.J | 82 | 12 |
| 4 | NYI | 41 | 7 | PIT | 41 | 6 | N.J | 82 | 12 |
| 5 | PHI | 41 | 7 | OTT | 41 | 5 | NYI | 82 | 12 |
| 6 | MIN | 41 | 6 | NYI | 41 | 5 | CHI | 82 | 10 |
| 7 | NYR | 41 | 5 | CHI | 41 | 5 | MTL | 82 | 10 |
| 8 | ATL | 41 | 5 | MTL | 41 | 5 | STL | 82 | 10 |
| 9 | NSH | 41 | 5 | N.J | 41 | 5 | NYR | 82 | 9 |
| 10 | CHI | 41 | 5 | CAR | 41 | 5 | NSH | 82 | 9 |
| 11 | MTL | 41 | 5 | S.J | 41 | 5 | MIN | 82 | 9 |
| 12 | DET | 41 | 4 | NYR | 41 | 4 | OTT | 82 | 8 |
| 13 | VAN | 41 | 4 | FLA | 41 | 4 | BOS | 82 | 8 |
| 14 | TOR | 41 | 4 | WSH | 41 | 4 | CAR | 82 | 8 |
| 15 | CGY | 41 | 4 | NSH | 41 | 4 | CBJ | 82 | 8 |
| 16 | CBJ | 41 | 4 | CBJ | 41 | 4 | PIT | 82 | 7 |
| 17 | OTT | 41 | 3 | BUF | 41 | 4 | VAN | 82 | 7 |
| 18 | COL | 41 | 3 | ANA | 41 | 3 | FLA | 82 | 7 |
| 19 | CAR | 41 | 3 | STL | 41 | 3 | BUF | 82 | 7 |
| 20 | BUF | 41 | 3 | VAN | 41 | 3 | WSH | 82 | 7 |
| 21 | WSH | 41 | 3 | PHX | 41 | 3 | DET | 82 | 6 |
| 22 | FLA | 41 | 3 | MIN | 41 | 3 | TOR | 82 | 6 |
| 23 | ANA | 41 | 3 | T.B | 41 | 2 | CGY | 82 | 6 |
| 24 | T.B | 41 | 2 | TOR | 41 | 2 | ANA | 82 | 6 |
| 25 | DAL | 41 | 2 | CGY | 41 | 2 | PHX | 82 | 5 |
| 26 | PHX | 41 | 2 | DET | 41 | 2 | T.B | 82 | 4 |
| 27 | L.A | 41 | 2 | L.A | 41 | 2 | COL | 82 | 4 |
| 28 | PIT | 41 | 1 | EDM | 41 | 2 | L.A | 82 | 4 |
| 29 | EDM | 41 | 1 | COL | 41 | 1 | EDM | 82 | 3 |
| 30 | BOS | 41 | 1 | DAL | 41 | 0 | DAL | 82 | 2 |
| **TOTAL** | | **1230** | **118** | | **1230** | **117** | | **1230** | **235** |

## SHORTHAND GOALS AGAINST

| | Home | | | Road | | | Overall | | |
|---|---|---|---|---|---|---|---|---|---|
| | Team | GP | SHGA | Team | GP | SHGA | Team | GP | SHGA |
| 1 | VAN | 41 | 1 | PHI | 41 | 0 | PHI | 82 | 1 |
| 2 | PHI | 41 | 1 | NYI | 41 | 1 | DET | 82 | 4 |
| 3 | BOS | 41 | 1 | DET | 41 | 1 | N.J | 82 | 4 |
| 4 | OTT | 41 | 2 | PHX | 41 | 1 | DAL | 82 | 4 |
| 5 | N.J | 41 | 2 | BUF | 41 | 1 | PHX | 82 | 4 |
| 6 | DAL | 41 | 2 | N.J | 41 | 2 | OTT | 82 | 5 |
| 7 | CHI | 41 | 2 | DAL | 41 | 2 | VAN | 82 | 5 |
| 8 | T.B | 41 | 3 | OTT | 41 | 3 | NYI | 82 | 5 |
| 9 | DET | 41 | 3 | ATL | 41 | 3 | BUF | 82 | 5 |
| 10 | COL | 41 | 3 | MIN | 41 | 3 | CHI | 82 | 6 |
| 11 | TOR | 41 | 3 | TOR | 41 | 4 | MIN | 82 | 6 |
| 12 | NSH | 41 | 3 | ANA | 41 | 4 | TOR | 82 | 7 |
| 13 | MIN | 41 | 3 | CHI | 41 | 4 | BOS | 82 | 7 |
| 14 | PHX | 41 | 3 | STL | 41 | 4 | COL | 82 | 8 |
| 15 | EDM | 41 | 3 | CAR | 41 | 4 | ANA | 82 | 8 |
| 16 | BUF | 41 | 4 | VAN | 41 | 4 | STL | 82 | 8 |
| 17 | STL | 41 | 4 | L.A | 41 | 4 | NSH | 82 | 8 |
| 18 | NYI | 41 | 4 | NYR | 41 | 5 | L.A | 82 | 8 |
| 19 | FLA | 41 | 4 | CGY | 41 | 5 | EDM | 82 | 8 |
| 20 | ANA | 41 | 4 | FLA | 41 | 5 | T.B | 82 | 9 |
| 21 | L.A | 41 | 4 | NSH | 41 | 5 | CAR | 82 | 9 |
| 22 | S.J | 41 | 5 | COL | 41 | 5 | FLA | 82 | 9 |
| 23 | CAR | 41 | 5 | EDM | 41 | 5 | ATL | 82 | 10 |
| 24 | WSH | 41 | 5 | T.B | 41 | 6 | S.J | 82 | 11 |
| 25 | MTL | 41 | 5 | BOS | 41 | 6 | MTL | 82 | 11 |
| 26 | PIT | 41 | 6 | MTL | 41 | 6 | WSH | 82 | 11 |
| 27 | CBJ | 41 | 6 | WSH | 41 | 6 | CBJ | 82 | 12 |
| 28 | ATL | 41 | 7 | CBJ | 41 | 6 | PIT | 82 | 13 |
| 29 | NYR | 41 | 9 | S.J | 41 | 6 | NYR | 82 | 14 |
| 30 | CGY | 41 | 10 | PIT | 41 | 7 | CGY | 82 | 15 |
| **TOTAL** | | **1230** | **117** | | **1230** | **118** | | **1230** | **235** |

# Regular-Season Overtime Results

## 2008-09 to 1988-89

| | 2008-09 | | | | 2007-08 | | | | 2006-07 | | | | 2005-06 | | | | 2003-04 | | | |
|---|---|---|---|---|---|---|---|---|---|---|---|---|---|---|---|---|---|---|---|---|
| Team | GP | W | L | SO | GP | W | L | SO | GP | W | L | SO | GP | W | L | SO | GP | W | L | T |
| ANA | 19 | 5 | 4 | 10 | 20 | 4 | 1 | 15 | 23 | 5 | 4 | 14 | 18 | 3 | 5 | 10 | 22 | 4 | 8 | 10 |
| ATL | 17 | 4 | 5 | 8 | 23 | 6 | 2 | 15 | 25 | 7 | 7 | 11 | 18 | 5 | 3 | 10 | 18 | 6 | 4 | 8 |
| BOS | 17 | 3 | 4 | 10 | 21 | 3 | 5 | 13 | 19 | 4 | 2 | 13 | 22 | 4 | 8 | 10 | 30 | 8 | 7 | 15 |
| BUF | 19 | 2 | 4 | 13 | 21 | 5 | 3 | 13 | 22 | 5 | 3 | 14 | 17 | 6 | 1 | 10 | 13 | 2 | 4 | 7 |
| CGY | 12 | 3 | 4 | 5 | 16 | 3 | 7 | 6 | 15 | 2 | 5 | 8 | 15 | 2 | 4 | 9 | 13 | 3 | 3 | 7 |
| CAR/HFD | 17 | 7 | 2 | 8 | 13 | 5 | 3 | 5 | 14 | 6 | 3 | 5 | 20 | 4 | 6 | 10 | 25 | 5 | 6 | 14 |
| CHI | 22 | 6 | 5 | 11 | 17 | 4 | 4 | 9 | 18 | 3 | 2 | 13 | 22 | 7 | 7 | 8 | 23 | 4 | 8 | 11 |
| COL/QUE | 17 | 3 | 1 | 13 | 18 | 4 | 4 | 10 | 15 | 3 | 3 | 9 | 15 | 3 | 3 | 9 | 28 | 8 | 7 | 13 |
| CBJ | 21 | 5 | 3 | 13 | 17 | 2 | 4 | 11 | 16 | 4 | 2 | 10 | 18 | 6 | 1 | 11 | 18 | 6 | 4 | 8 |
| DAL/MIN | 22 | 5 | 5 | 12 | 15 | 3 | 4 | 8 | 22 | 6 | 3 | 13 | 21 | 3 | 5 | 13 | 18 | 3 | 2 | 13 |
| DET | 19 | 3 | 6 | 10 | 14 | 2 | 2 | 10 | 18 | 3 | 5 | 10 | 15 | 3 | 5 | 7 | 20 | 7 | 2 | 11 |
| EDM | 16 | 1 | 5 | 10 | 25 | 4 | 2 | 19 | 11 | 1 | 4 | 6 | 26 | 6 | 4 | 16 | 23 | 6 | 5 | 12 |
| FLA | 18 | 4 | 3 | 11 | 18 | 4 | 3 | 11 | 21 | 3 | 8 | 10 | 23 | 8 | 6 | 9 | 24 | 5 | 4 | 15 |
| L.A. | 19 | 3 | 3 | 13 | 14 | 2 | 4 | 8 | 20 | 2 | 8 | 10 | 15 | 4 | 4 | 7 | 27 | 2 | 9 | 16 |
| MIN | 17 | 3 | 6 | 8 | 19 | 6 | 2 | 11 | 25 | 7 | 1 | 17 | 14 | 1 | 5 | 8 | 24 | 1 | 3 | 20 |
| MTL | 22 | 4 | 4 | 14 | 20 | 5 | 4 | 11 | 14 | 2 | 1 | 11 | 18 | 7 | 6 | 5 | 16 | 5 | 4 | 7 |
| NSH | 20 | 6 | 3 | 11 | 17 | 5 | 4 | 8 | 17 | 3 | 3 | 11 | 17 | 3 | 5 | 9 | 22 | 7 | 4 | 11 |
| N.J. | 19 | 9 | 2 | 8 | 22 | 7 | 3 | 12 | 22 | 3 | 1 | 18 | 22 | 4 | 5 | 13 | 21 | 7 | 2 | 12 |
| NYI | 15 | 3 | 4 | 8 | 19 | 5 | 6 | 8 | 22 | 2 | 7 | 13 | 18 | 3 | 3 | 12 | 17 | 2 | 4 | 11 |
| NYR | 22 | 3 | 3 | 16 | 25 | 4 | 4 | 17 | 22 | 3 | 5 | 14 | 23 | 4 | 8 | 11 | 18 | 3 | 8 | 7 |
| OTT | 18 | 3 | 5 | 10 | 14 | 3 | 3 | 8 | 13 | 2 | 3 | 8 | 13 | 2 | 3 | 8 | 19 | 3 | 6 | 10 |
| PHI | 21 | 6 | 5 | 10 | 17 | 3 | 5 | 9 | 16 | 3 | 6 | 7 | 22 | 7 | 5 | 10 | 23 | 2 | 6 | 15 |
| PHX/WPG | 11 | 1 | 4 | 6 | 16 | 4 | 1 | 11 | 12 | 2 | 3 | 7 | 15 | 6 | 2 | 7 | 29 | 5 | 6 | 18 |
| PIT | 21 | 6 | 3 | 12 | 16 | 1 | 4 | 11 | 27 | 6 | 5 | 16 | 19 | 4 | 8 | 7 | 19 | 7 | 4 | 8 |
| ST.L. | 20 | 4 | 4 | 12 | 17 | 1 | 8 | 8 | 23 | 4 | 7 | 12 | 22 | 3 | 7 | 12 | 24 | 11 | 2 | 11 |
| S.J. | 21 | 4 | 6 | 11 | 19 | 3 | 4 | 12 | 8 | 1 | 3 | 4 | 21 | 9 | 4 | 8 | 21 | 3 | 6 | 12 |
| T.B. | 23 | 2 | 8 | 13 | 13 | 2 | 8 | 3 | 20 | 5 | 3 | 12 | 18 | 6 | 2 | 10 | 18 | 4 | 6 | 8 |
| TOR | 23 | 4 | 6 | 13 | 19 | 5 | 7 | 7 | 19 | 4 | 4 | 11 | 18 | 7 | 1 | 10 | 17 | 4 | 3 | 10 |
| VAN | 18 | 5 | 3 | 10 | 20 | 4 | 1 | 15 | 24 | 12 | 3 | 9 | 16 | 4 | 4 | 8 | 26 | 11 | 5 | 10 |
| WSH | 18 | 6 | 3 | 9 | 19 | 7 | 4 | 8 | 19 | 4 | 3 | 12 | 21 | 2 | 6 | 13 | 14 | 1 | 3 | 10 |
| **Totals** | **282** | **123** | | **159** | **272** | **116** | | **156** | **281** | **117** | | **164** | **281** | **136** | | **145** | **315** | **145** | | **170** |

| | 2002-03 | | | | 2001-02 | | | | 2000-01 | | | | 1999-2000 | | | | 1998-99 | | | |
|---|---|---|---|---|---|---|---|---|---|---|---|---|---|---|---|---|---|---|---|---|
| Team | GP | W | L | T | GP | W | L | T | GP | W | L | T | GP | W | L | T | GP | W | L | T |
| ANA | 21 | 6 | 6 | 9 | 14 | 3 | 3 | 8 | 20 | 4 | 5 | 11 | 18 | 3 | 3 | 12 | 17 | 1 | 3 | 13 |
| ATL | 19 | 7 | 5 | 7 | 19 | 3 | 5 | 11 | 16 | 2 | 2 | 12 | 11 | 0 | 4 | 7 | ... | ... | ... | ... |
| BOS | 21 | 6 | 4 | 11 | 24 | 9 | 9 | 6 | 20 | 4 | 8 | 8 | 26 | 1 | 6 | 19 | 17 | 2 | 2 | 13 |
| BUF | 21 | 3 | 8 | 10 | 16 | 4 | 1 | 11 | 10 | 4 | 1 | 5 | 20 | 5 | 4 | 11 | 23 | 3 | 3 | 17 |
| CGY | 19 | 2 | 6 | 11 | 17 | 2 | 3 | 12 | 22 | 3 | 4 | 15 | 26 | 11 | 5 | 10 | 16 | 3 | 1 | 12 |
| CAR/HFD | 15 | 4 | 3 | 8 | 27 | 6 | 5 | 16 | 18 | 6 | 3 | 9 | 14 | 4 | 0 | 10 | 24 | 1 | 5 | 18 |
| CHI | 23 | 6 | 4 | 13 | 17 | 3 | 1 | 13 | 15 | 2 | 5 | 8 | 17 | 5 | 2 | 10 | 15 | 1 | 2 | 12 |
| COL/QUE | 23 | 4 | 6 | 13 | 13 | 4 | 1 | 8 | 20 | 6 | 4 | 10 | 17 | 5 | 1 | 11 | 12 | 2 | 0 | 10 |
| CBJ | 28 | 7 | 8 | 13 | 15 | 2 | 5 | 8 | 18 | 3 | 6 | 9 | ... | ... | ... | ... | ... | ... | ... | ... |
| DAL/MIN | 24 | 5 | 4 | 15 | 21 | 3 | 5 | 13 | 16 | 6 | 2 | 8 | 19 | 3 | 6 | 10 | 16 | 3 | 1 | 12 |
| DET | 21 | 7 | 4 | 10 | 24 | 10 | 4 | 10 | 23 | 10 | 4 | 9 | 16 | 4 | 2 | 10 | 10 | 2 | 1 | 7 |
| EDM | 27 | 7 | 9 | 11 | 19 | 3 | 4 | 12 | 20 | 5 | 3 | 12 | 27 | 3 | 8 | 16 | 20 | 3 | 5 | 12 |
| FLA | 26 | 4 | 9 | 13 | 16 | 0 | 6 | 10 | 24 | 2 | 9 | 13 | 15 | 3 | 6 | 6 | 21 | 1 | 2 | 18 |
| L.A. | 19 | 6 | 7 | 6 | 18 | 3 | 4 | 11 | 19 | 3 | 3 | 13 | 21 | 5 | 4 | 12 | 12 | 5 | 2 | 5 |
| MIN | 19 | 8 | 1 | 10 | 21 | 0 | 9 | 12 | 22 | 4 | 5 | 13 | ... | ... | ... | ... | ... | ... | ... | ... |
| MTL | 19 | 2 | 9 | 8 | 17 | 2 | 3 | 12 | 16 | 2 | 6 | 8 | 17 | 4 | 4 | 9 | 15 | 0 | 4 | 11 |
| NSH | 24 | 8 | 6 | 10 | 18 | 5 | 0 | 13 | 17 | 5 | 3 | 9 | 18 | 4 | 7 | 7 | 10 | 1 | 2 | 7 |
| N.J. | 25 | 5 | 7 | 13 | 19 | 6 | 4 | 9 | 20 | 5 | 3 | 12 | 16 | 3 | 5 | 8 | 15 | 3 | 1 | 11 |
| NYI | 18 | 5 | 2 | 11 | 18 | 6 | 4 | 8 | 12 | 2 | 3 | 7 | 15 | 5 | 1 | 9 | 17 | 1 | 6 | 10 |
| NYR | 20 | 6 | 4 | 10 | 13 | 5 | 4 | 4 | 11 | 5 | 1 | 5 | 21 | 6 | 3 | 12 | 19 | 5 | 3 | 11 |
| OTT | 16 | 7 | 1 | 8 | 19 | 3 | 7 | 9 | 16 | 3 | 4 | 9 | 15 | 2 | 2 | 11 | 18 | 1 | 2 | 15 |
| PHI | 23 | 6 | 4 | 13 | 16 | 3 | 3 | 10 | 19 | 5 | 3 | 11 | 21 | 6 | 3 | 12 | 24 | 2 | 3 | 19 |
| PHX/WPG | 20 | 4 | 5 | 11 | 19 | 4 | 6 | 9 | 23 | 3 | 3 | 17 | 16 | 4 | 4 | 8 | 15 | 2 | 1 | 12 |
| PIT | 14 | 3 | 5 | 6 | 20 | 7 | 5 | 8 | 15 | 3 | 3 | 9 | 17 | 3 | 6 | 8 | 22 | 7 | 1 | 14 |
| ST.L. | 19 | 2 | 8 | 9 | 18 | 6 | 4 | 8 | 23 | 6 | 5 | 12 | 17 | 5 | 1 | 11 | 15 | 1 | 1 | 13 |
| S.J. | 23 | 6 | 6 | 11 | 13 | 2 | 3 | 8 | 22 | 7 | 3 | 12 | 21 | 4 | 7 | 10 | 21 | 1 | 2 | 18 |
| T.B. | 23 | 2 | 5 | 16 | 19 | 4 | 4 | 11 | 13 | 2 | 5 | 6 | 16 | 0 | 7 | 9 | 12 | 1 | 2 | 9 |
| TOR | 17 | 7 | 3 | 7 | 17 | 3 | 4 | 10 | 19 | 3 | 5 | 11 | 17 | 7 | 3 | 7 | 14 | 6 | 1 | 7 |
| VAN | 19 | 5 | 1 | 13 | 14 | 4 | 3 | 7 | 23 | 5 | 7 | 11 | 27 | 4 | 8 | 15 | 13 | 0 | 1 | 12 |
| WSH | 20 | 6 | 6 | 8 | 19 | 6 | 2 | 11 | 16 | 2 | 4 | 10 | 19 | 5 | 2 | 12 | 11 | 2 | 3 | 6 |
| **Totals** | **313** | **156** | | **157** | **270** | **121** | | **149** | **274** | **122** | | **152** | **260** | **114** | | **146** | **222** | **60** | | **162** |

| | 1997-98 | | | | 1996-97 | | | | 1995-96 | | | | 1994-95 | | | | 1993-94 | | | |
|---|---|---|---|---|---|---|---|---|---|---|---|---|---|---|---|---|---|---|---|---|
| Team | GP | W | L | T | GP | W | L | T | GP | W | L | T | GP | W | L | T | GP | W | L | T |
| ANA | 20 | 3 | 4 | 13 | 16 | 3 | 0 | 13 | 16 | 6 | 2 | 8 | 7 | 2 | 0 | 5 | 12 | 2 | 5 | 5 |
| ATL | ... | ... | ... | ... | ... | ... | ... | ... | ... | ... | ... | ... | ... | ... | ... | ... | ... | ... | ... | ... |
| BOS | 17 | 3 | 1 | 13 | 15 | 3 | 3 | 9 | 19 | 2 | 6 | 11 | 8 | 2 | 3 | 3 | 17 | 2 | 2 | 13 |
| BUF | 21 | 3 | 1 | 17 | 21 | 5 | 4 | 12 | 15 | 2 | 6 | 7 | 9 | 1 | 1 | 7 | 13 | 0 | 4 | 9 |
| CGY | 22 | 4 | 3 | 15 | 16 | 3 | 4 | 9 | 16 | 2 | 3 | 11 | 9 | 1 | 1 | 7 | 18 | 3 | 2 | 13 |
| CAR/HFD | 12 | 2 | 2 | 8 | 18 | 3 | 4 | 11 | 14 | 2 | 3 | 9 | 9 | 1 | 1 | 7 | 14 | 4 | 1 | 9 |
| CHI | 18 | 1 | 4 | 13 | 19 | 1 | 5 | 13 | 19 | 1 | 4 | 14 | 7 | 2 | 0 | 5 | 16 | 2 | 5 | 9 |
| COL/QUE | 22 | 2 | 3 | 17 | 15 | 2 | 3 | 10 | 6 | 1 | 0 | 5 | 8 | 0 | 0 | 8 | 15 | 3 | 3 | 9 |
| CBJ | ... | ... | ... | ... | ... | ... | ... | ... | ... | ... | ... | ... | ... | ... | ... | ... | ... | ... | ... | ... |
| DAL/MIN | 17 | 5 | 1 | 11 | 15 | 4 | 3 | 8 | 15 | 1 | 0 | 14 | 9 | 0 | 1 | 8 | 22 | 6 | 3 | 13 |
| DET | 15 | 0 | 0 | 15 | 27 | 7 | 2 | 18 | 11 | 3 | 1 | 7 | 4 | 0 | 0 | 4 | 15 | 5 | 2 | 8 |
| EDM | 15 | 3 | 2 | 10 | 16 | 1 | 6 | 9 | 14 | 4 | 2 | 8 | 7 | 1 | 2 | 4 | 21 | 1 | 6 | 14 |
| FLA | 20 | 3 | 2 | 15 | 26 | 3 | 4 | 19 | 13 | 0 | 3 | 10 | 9 | 0 | 3 | 6 | 24 | 2 | 5 | 17 |
| L.A. | 16 | 3 | 2 | 11 | 14 | 0 | 3 | 11 | 23 | 3 | 2 | 18 | 9 | 0 | 0 | 9 | 18 | 3 | 3 | 12 |
| MIN | ... | ... | ... | ... | ... | ... | ... | ... | ... | ... | ... | ... | ... | ... | ... | ... | ... | ... | ... | ... |
| MTL | 20 | 3 | 4 | 13 | 21 | 2 | 4 | 15 | 15 | 2 | 3 | 10 | 10 | 1 | 2 | 7 | 19 | 3 | 2 | 14 |
| NSH | ... | ... | ... | ... | ... | ... | ... | ... | ... | ... | ... | ... | ... | ... | ... | ... | ... | ... | ... | ... |
| N.J. | 16 | 2 | 3 | 11 | 17 | 1 | 2 | 14 | 19 | 7 | 0 | 12 | 11 | 1 | 2 | 8 | 14 | 1 | 1 | 12 |
| NYI | 13 | 0 | 2 | 11 | 17 | 3 | 2 | 12 | 17 | 2 | 5 | 10 | 7 | 1 | 1 | 5 | 19 | 5 | 2 | 12 |
| NYR | 24 | 2 | 4 | 18 | 13 | 3 | 0 | 10 | 17 | 2 | 1 | 14 | 3 | 0 | 0 | 3 | 12 | 3 | 1 | 8 |
| OTT | 17 | 2 | 0 | 15 | 17 | 0 | 2 | 15 | 8 | 0 | 3 | 5 | 7 | 1 | 1 | 5 | 17 | 4 | 4 | 9 |
| PHI | 15 | 3 | 1 | 11 | 18 | 3 | 2 | 13 | 20 | 4 | 3 | 13 | 8 | 3 | 1 | 4 | 18 | 3 | 5 | 10 |
| PHX/WPG | 14 | 0 | 2 | 12 | 16 | 5 | 4 | 7 | 8 | 2 | 0 | 6 | 9 | 0 | 2 | 7 | 15 | 1 | 5 | 9 |
| PIT | 23 | 3 | 2 | 18 | 13 | 1 | 4 | 8 | 9 | 3 | 2 | 4 | 5 | 1 | 1 | 3 | 19 | 4 | 2 | 13 |
| ST.L. | 12 | 2 | 2 | 8 | 13 | 1 | 1 | 11 | 18 | 1 | 1 | 16 | 7 | 1 | 1 | 5 | 17 | 4 | 2 | 11 |
| S.J. | 12 | 0 | 2 | 10 | 12 | 3 | 1 | 8 | 9 | 1 | 1 | 7 | 5 | 1 | 0 | 4 | 19 | 2 | 1 | 16 |
| T.B. | 13 | 0 | 3 | 10 | 16 | 4 | 2 | 10 | 18 | 3 | 3 | 12 | 7 | 2 | 2 | 3 | 18 | 3 | 4 | 11 |
| TOR | 10 | 1 | 0 | 9 | 10 | 1 | 1 | 8 | 18 | 4 | 2 | 12 | 8 | 0 | 0 | 8 | 17 | 4 | 1 | 12 |
| VAN | 17 | 0 | 3 | 14 | 14 | 5 | 2 | 7 | 20 | 1 | 4 | 15 | 13 | 0 | 1 | 12 | 12 | 5 | 4 | 3 |
| WSH | 17 | 4 | 1 | 12 | 13 | 2 | 2 | 9 | 16 | 4 | 1 | 11 | 9 | 0 | 1 | 8 | 14 | 2 | 2 | 10 |
| **Totals** | **219** | **54** | | **165** | **214** | **70** | | **144** | **201** | **64** | | **137** | **101** | **26** | | **75** | **214** | **74** | | **140** |

| | 1992-93 | | | | 1991-92 | | | | 1990-91 | | | | 1989-90 | | | | 1988-89 | | | |
|---|---|---|---|---|---|---|---|---|---|---|---|---|---|---|---|---|---|---|---|---|
| Team | GP | W | L | T | GP | W | L | T | GP | W | L | T | GP | W | L | T | GP | W | L | T |
| ANA | ... | ... | ... | ... | ... | ... | ... | ... | ... | ... | ... | ... | ... | ... | ... | ... | ... | ... | ... | ... |
| ATL | ... | ... | ... | ... | ... | ... | ... | ... | ... | ... | ... | ... | ... | ... | ... | ... | ... | ... | ... | ... |
| BOS | 15 | 5 | 3 | 7 | 20 | 6 | 2 | 12 | 17 | 5 | 0 | 12 | 14 | 3 | 2 | 9 | 19 | 3 | 2 | 14 |
| BUF | 18 | 4 | 4 | 10 | 16 | 2 | 2 | 12 | 24 | 3 | 2 | 19 | 15 | 4 | 3 | 8 | 13 | 2 | 4 | 7 |
| CGY | 19 | 4 | 4 | 11 | 19 | 2 | 5 | 12 | 15 | 3 | 4 | 8 | 21 | 3 | 3 | 15 | 17 | 5 | 3 | 9 |
| CAR/HFD | 18 | 3 | 9 | 6 | 18 | 2 | 3 | 13 | 9 | 1 | 1 | 7 | 9 | 0 | 0 | 9 | 10 | 1 | 4 | 5 |
| CHI | 16 | 1 | 3 | 12 | 19 | 2 | 2 | 15 | 12 | 3 | 1 | 8 | 10 | 2 | 2 | 6 | 17 | 2 | 3 | 12 |
| COL/QUE | 15 | 4 | 1 | 10 | 17 | 0 | 5 | 12 | 18 | 1 | 3 | 14 | 8 | 0 | 1 | 7 | 10 | 2 | 1 | 7 |
| CBJ | ... | ... | ... | ... | ... | ... | ... | ... | ... | ... | ... | ... | ... | ... | ... | ... | ... | ... | ... | ... |
| DAL/MIN | 10 | 0 | 0 | 10 | 8 | 0 | 2 | 6 | 17 | 0 | 3 | 14 | 11 | 3 | 4 | 4 | 17 | 0 | 1 | 16 |
| DET | 11 | 2 | 0 | 9 | 16 | 3 | 1 | 12 | 14 | 2 | 4 | 8 | 17 | 2 | 1 | 14 | 16 | 3 | 1 | 12 |
| EDM | 17 | 5 | 4 | 8 | 12 | 0 | 2 | 10 | 15 | 4 | 5 | 6 | 20 | 5 | 1 | 14 | 15 | 4 | 3 | 8 |
| FLA | ... | ... | ... | ... | ... | ... | ... | ... | ... | ... | ... | ... | ... | ... | ... | ... | ... | ... | ... | ... |
| L.A. | 13 | 2 | 1 | 10 | 16 | 1 | 1 | 14 | 16 | 4 | 2 | 10 | 12 | 3 | 2 | 7 | 14 | 6 | 1 | 7 |
| MIN | ... | ... | ... | ... | ... | ... | ... | ... | ... | ... | ... | ... | ... | ... | ... | ... | ... | ... | ... | ... |
| MTL | 14 | 5 | 3 | 6 | 20 | 6 | 3 | 11 | 17 | 3 | 3 | 11 | 17 | 4 | 2 | 11 | 11 | 2 | 0 | 9 |
| NSH | ... | ... | ... | ... | ... | ... | ... | ... | ... | ... | ... | ... | ... | ... | ... | ... | ... | ... | ... | ... |
| N.J. | 11 | 4 | 0 | 7 | 17 | 2 | 4 | 11 | 17 | 1 | 1 | 15 | 16 | 3 | 4 | 9 | 17 | 1 | 4 | 12 |
| NYI | 13 | 3 | 3 | 7 | 16 | 3 | 2 | 11 | 15 | 2 | 3 | 10 | 16 | 3 | 2 | 11 | 11 | 3 | 3 | 5 |
| NYR | 17 | 2 | 4 | 11 | 11 | 5 | 1 | 5 | 16 | 1 | 2 | 13 | 17 | 2 | 2 | 13 | 10 | 1 | 1 | 8 |
| OTT | 10 | 0 | 6 | 4 | ... | ... | ... | ... | ... | ... | ... | ... | ... | ... | ... | ... | ... | ... | ... | ... |
| PHI | 17 | 4 | 2 | 11 | 17 | 2 | 4 | 11 | 11 | 1 | 0 | 10 | 18 | 2 | 5 | 11 | 14 | 1 | 5 | 8 |
| PHX/WPG | 11 | 2 | 2 | 7 | 20 | 1 | 4 | 15 | 14 | 1 | 2 | 11 | 19 | 4 | 4 | 11 | 20 | 6 | 2 | 12 |
| PIT | 10 | 3 | 0 | 7 | 12 | 2 | 1 | 9 | 12 | 4 | 2 | 6 | 14 | 3 | 3 | 8 | 10 | 2 | 1 | 7 |
| ST.L. | 17 | 2 | 4 | 11 | 15 | 2 | 2 | 11 | 18 | 3 | 4 | 11 | 15 | 2 | 4 | 9 | 16 | 3 | 1 | 12 |
| S.J. | 10 | 3 | 5 | 2 | 9 | 1 | 3 | 5 | ... | ... | ... | ... | ... | ... | ... | ... | ... | ... | ... | ... |
| T.B. | 14 | 3 | 4 | 7 | ... | ... | ... | ... | ... | ... | ... | ... | ... | ... | ... | ... | ... | ... | ... | ... |
| TOR | 13 | 1 | 1 | 11 | 11 | 4 | 0 | 7 | 17 | 4 | 2 | 11 | 11 | 3 | 4 | 4 | 11 | 1 | 4 | 6 |
| VAN | 10 | 1 | 0 | 9 | 17 | 4 | 1 | 12 | 15 | 3 | 3 | 9 | 21 | 2 | 5 | 14 | 14 | 2 | 4 | 8 |
| WSH | 11 | 2 | 2 | 7 | 12 | 2 | 2 | 8 | 14 | 4 | 3 | 7 | 9 | 2 | 1 | 6 | 16 | 2 | 4 | 10 |
| **Totals** | **165** | **65** | | **100** | **169** | **52** | | **117** | **166** | **54** | | **112** | **155** | **55** | | **100** | **149** | **52** | | **97** |

**Abbreviations: GP** – games played; **W** – overtime win; **L** – overtime loss;
**SO** – game tied after overtime. Game decided in shootout. (2005-06 to date); See page 143.
**T** – game tied after overtime. (Up to and including 2003-04.)

# 2008-09 Shootout Summary

## Team Shootout Statistics

| | OVERALL | | | | | | | | | HOME | | | | | | | | ROAD | | | | | | | |
|---|---|---|---|---|---|---|---|---|---|---|---|---|---|---|---|---|---|---|---|---|---|---|---|---|---|
| Team | GP | W | L | G | S | S% | SA | GA | Sv% | W | L | G | S | S% | SA | GA | Sv% | W | L | G | S | S% | SA | GA | Sv% |
| ANA | 10 | 7 | 3 | 14 | 43 | 32.6 | 43 | 9 | .791 | 1 | 2 | 3 | 20 | 15.0 | 19 | 4 | .789 | 6 | 1 | 11 | 23 | 47.8 | 24 | 5 | .792 |
| ATL | 8 | 7 | 1 | 12 | 33 | 36.4 | 35 | 6 | .829 | 3 | 0 | 5 | 13 | 38.5 | 13 | 2 | .846 | 4 | 1 | 7 | 20 | 35.0 | 22 | 4 | .818 |
| BOS | 10 | 4 | 6 | 10 | 38 | 26.3 | 37 | 13 | .649 | 0 | 2 | 1 | 7 | 14.3 | 7 | 4 | .429 | 4 | 4 | 9 | 31 | 29.0 | 30 | 9 | .700 |
| BUF | 13 | 8 | 5 | 19 | 50 | 38.0 | 50 | 13 | .740 | 5 | 1 | 9 | 21 | 42.9 | 21 | 3 | .857 | 3 | 4 | 10 | 29 | 34.5 | 29 | 10 | .655 |
| CAR | 8 | 3 | 5 | 7 | 24 | 29.2 | 24 | 10 | .583 | 2 | 0 | 3 | 5 | 60.0 | 5 | 0 | 1.000 | 1 | 5 | 4 | 19 | 21.0 | 19 | 10 | .474 |
| CBJ | 13 | 6 | 7 | 11 | 34 | 32.4 | 36 | 12 | .667 | 3 | 2 | 5 | 14 | 35.7 | 12 | 3 | .750 | 3 | 5 | 6 | 20 | 30.0 | 24 | 9 | .625 |
| CGY | 5 | 3 | 2 | 4 | 15 | 26.7 | 14 | 3 | .786 | 1 | 2 | 1 | 9 | 11.1 | 8 | 2 | .750 | 2 | 0 | 3 | 6 | 50.0 | 6 | 1 | .833 |
| CHI | 11 | 4 | 7 | 11 | 31 | 35.5 | 31 | 14 | .548 | 2 | 5 | 7 | 20 | 35.0 | 19 | 11 | .421 | 2 | 2 | 4 | 11 | 36.4 | 12 | 3 | .750 |
| COL | 13 | 9 | 4 | 22 | 43 | 51.2 | 43 | 14 | .674 | 4 | 1 | 11 | 16 | 68.8 | 15 | 6 | .600 | 5 | 3 | 11 | 27 | 40.7 | 28 | 8 | .714 |
| DAL | 12 | 6 | 6 | 19 | 45 | 42.2 | 46 | 18 | .609 | 3 | 3 | 8 | 21 | 38.1 | 21 | 7 | .667 | 3 | 3 | 11 | 24 | 45.8 | 25 | 11 | .560 |
| DET | 10 | 6 | 4 | 13 | 33 | 39.4 | 34 | 10 | .706 | 2 | 3 | 6 | 18 | 33.3 | 18 | 7 | .611 | 4 | 1 | 7 | 15 | 46.7 | 16 | 3 | .813 |
| EDM | 10 | 6 | 4 | 11 | 29 | 37.9 | 30 | 6 | .800 | 1 | 3 | 2 | 14 | 14.3 | 14 | 4 | .714 | 5 | 1 | 9 | 15 | 60.0 | 16 | 2 | .875 |
| FLA | 11 | 3 | 8 | 6 | 32 | 18.8 | 30 | 13 | .567 | 1 | 5 | 4 | 19 | 21.0 | 16 | 9 | .438 | 2 | 3 | 2 | 13 | 15.4 | 14 | 4 | .714 |
| L.A. | 13 | 5 | 8 | 13 | 44 | 29.6 | 41 | 18 | .561 | 2 | 6 | 7 | 24 | 29.2 | 22 | 13 | .409 | 3 | 2 | 6 | 20 | 30.0 | 19 | 5 | .737 |
| MIN | 8 | 5 | 3 | 8 | 23 | 34.8 | 23 | 6 | .739 | 3 | 2 | 6 | 17 | 35.3 | 15 | 4 | .733 | 2 | 1 | 2 | 6 | 33.3 | 8 | 2 | .750 |
| MTL | 14 | 7 | 7 | 12 | 38 | 31.6 | 42 | 15 | .643 | 3 | 4 | 5 | 21 | 23.8 | 24 | 7 | .708 | 4 | 3 | 7 | 17 | 41.2 | 18 | 8 | .556 |
| N.J. | 8 | 6 | 2 | 12 | 25 | 48.0 | 28 | 8 | .714 | 3 | 1 | 6 | 14 | 42.9 | 15 | 4 | .733 | 3 | 1 | 6 | 11 | 54.6 | 13 | 4 | .692 |
| NSH | 11 | 6 | 5 | 12 | 33 | 36.4 | 35 | 11 | .686 | 4 | 2 | 5 | 17 | 29.4 | 19 | 4 | .789 | 2 | 3 | 7 | 16 | 43.8 | 16 | 7 | .563 |
| NYI | 8 | 3 | 5 | 7 | 23 | 30.4 | 20 | 9 | .550 | 2 | 4 | 5 | 18 | 27.8 | 16 | 7 | .563 | 1 | 1 | 2 | 5 | 40.0 | 4 | 2 | .500 |
| NYR | 16 | 10 | 6 | 19 | 54 | 35.2 | 52 | 13 | .750 | 7 | 2 | 12 | 31 | 38.7 | 28 | 6 | .786 | 3 | 4 | 7 | 23 | 30.4 | 24 | 7 | .708 |
| OTT | 10 | 4 | 6 | 13 | 42 | 31.0 | 41 | 15 | .634 | 3 | 4 | 9 | 26 | 34.6 | 25 | 10 | .600 | 1 | 2 | 4 | 16 | 25.0 | 16 | 5 | .688 |
| PHI | 10 | 4 | 6 | 8 | 31 | 25.8 | 35 | 11 | .686 | 1 | 1 | 2 | 4 | 50.0 | 4 | 2 | .500 | 3 | 5 | 6 | 27 | 22.2 | 31 | 9 | .710 |
| PHX | 6 | 3 | 3 | 10 | 28 | 35.7 | 28 | 11 | .607 | 3 | 3 | 10 | 28 | 35.7 | 28 | 11 | .607 | 0 | 0 | 0 | 0 | 0.0 | 0 | 0 | .000 |
| PIT | 12 | 6 | 6 | 11 | 40 | 27.5 | 41 | 11 | .732 | 3 | 2 | 5 | 20 | 25.0 | 18 | 3 | .833 | 3 | 4 | 6 | 20 | 30.0 | 23 | 8 | .652 |
| S.J. | 11 | 6 | 5 | 14 | 37 | 37.8 | 38 | 13 | .658 | 4 | 1 | 8 | 20 | 40.0 | 20 | 5 | .750 | 2 | 4 | 6 | 17 | 35.3 | 18 | 8 | .556 |
| ST.L. | 12 | 6 | 6 | 14 | 35 | 40.0 | 35 | 13 | .629 | 3 | 2 | 6 | 16 | 37.5 | 16 | 6 | .625 | 3 | 4 | 8 | 19 | 42.1 | 19 | 7 | .632 |
| T.B. | 13 | 3 | 10 | 11 | 45 | 24.4 | 40 | 20 | .500 | 1 | 8 | 6 | 34 | 17.6 | 28 | 14 | .500 | 2 | 2 | 5 | 11 | 45.4 | 12 | 6 | .500 |
| TOR | 13 | 6 | 7 | 16 | 43 | 37.2 | 42 | 19 | .548 | 3 | 5 | 9 | 25 | 36.0 | 23 | 12 | .478 | 3 | 2 | 7 | 18 | 38.9 | 19 | 7 | .632 |
| VAN | 10 | 3 | 7 | 10 | 40 | 25.0 | 41 | 16 | .610 | 0 | 4 | 3 | 13 | 23.1 | 12 | 8 | .333 | 3 | 3 | 7 | 27 | 25.9 | 29 | 8 | .724 |
| WSH | 9 | 4 | 5 | 8 | 28 | 28.6 | 24 | 7 | .708 | 4 | 2 | 7 | 18 | 38.9 | 15 | 3 | .800 | 0 | 3 | 1 | 10 | 10.0 | 9 | 4 | .556 |

## Team Shootout Leaders

### Wins

| | W | L | Win% |
|---|---|---|---|
| NYR | **10** | 6 | .625 |
| COL | **9** | 4 | .692 |
| BUF | **8** | 5 | .615 |
| ATL | **7** | 1 | .875 |
| ANA | **7** | 3 | .700 |
| MTL | **7** | 7 | .500 |
| 10 teams tied with | **6** | | |

### Goals Scored

| | G | S | S% |
|---|---|---|---|
| COL | **22** | 43 | .512 |
| DAL | **19** | 45 | .422 |
| BUF | **19** | 50 | .380 |
| NYR | **19** | 54 | .352 |
| TOR | **16** | 43 | .372 |
| ST.L. | **14** | 35 | .400 |
| S.J. | **14** | 37 | .378 |
| ANA | **14** | 43 | .326 |
| DET | **13** | 33 | .394 |
| OTT | **13** | 42 | .310 |
| L.A. | **13** | 44 | .296 |

### Fewest Goals Against

| | GA | SA | Sv% |
|---|---|---|---|
| CGY | **3** | 14 | .786 |
| MIN | **6** | 23 | .739 |
| ATL | **6** | 35 | .829 |
| EDM | **6** | 30 | .800 |
| WSH | **7** | 24 | .708 |
| N.J. | **8** | 28 | .714 |
| NYI | **9** | 20 | .550 |
| ANA | **9** | 43 | .791 |
| DET | **10** | 34 | .706 |
| CAR | **10** | 24 | .583 |

### Winning Percentage

| | Win% | W | L |
|---|---|---|---|
| ATL | **.875** | 7 | 1 |
| N.J. | **.750** | 6 | 2 |
| ANA | **.700** | 7 | 3 |
| COL | **.692** | 9 | 4 |
| NYR | **.625** | 10 | 6 |
| MIN | **.625** | 5 | 3 |
| BUF | **.615** | 8 | 5 |
| CGY | **.600** | 3 | 2 |
| DET | **.600** | 6 | 4 |
| EDM | **.600** | 6 | 4 |

### Shootout Abbreviations

G........Goals Scored
GA......Goals Against
GDG ...Game Deciding Goal
S.........Shots Taken
SA ......Shots Against
S% ....Goal Scoring %
Sv%....Save %

## Individual Shootout Leaders – Goaltenders

### Goaltender Shootout Wins

| | Team | W | L |
|---|---|---|---|
| Lundqvist, Henrik | NYR | **9** | 4 |
| Miller, Ryan | BUF | **8** | 2 |
| Budaj, Peter | COL | **7** | 4 |
| Mason, Steve | CBJ | **6** | 5 |
| Hiller, Jonas | ANA | **5** | 1 |
| Backstrom, Niklas | MIN | **5** | 2 |
| Rinne, Pekka | NSH | **5** | 2 |
| Nabokov, Evgeni | S.J. | **5** | 4 |
| Price, Carey | MTL | **5** | 6 |
| Turco, Marty | DAL | **5** | 6 |

### Goaltender Shootout Shots Against

| | Team | SA | GA | Sv% |
|---|---|---|---|---|
| Turco, Marty | DAL | **43** | 16 | .628 |
| Miller, Ryan | BUF | **40** | 9 | .775 |
| Lundqvist, Henrik | NYR | **40** | 10 | .750 |
| Budaj, Peter | COL | **35** | 13 | .629 |
| Price, Carey | MTL | **35** | 13 | .629 |
| Nabokov, Evgeni | S.J. | **32** | 11 | .656 |
| Hiller, Jonas | ANA | **31** | 5 | .839 |
| Mason, Steve | CBJ | **31** | 9 | 710 |
| Luongo, Roberto | VAN | **29** | 8 | .724 |
| Toskala, Vesa | TOR | **29** | 14 | .517 |
| Thomas, Tim | BOS | **28** | 9 | .679 |

### Goaltender Shootout Save Percentage

| *(min. 10 shots faced)* | Team | Sv% | SA | GA |
|---|---|---|---|---|
| Hedberg, Johan | ATL | **.923** | 13 | 1 |
| Hiller, Jonas | ANA | **.839** | 31 | 5 |
| Rinne, Pekka | NSH | **.792** | 24 | 5 |
| Roloson, Dwayne | EDM | **.792** | 24 | 5 |
| Kiprusoff, Miikka | CGY | **.786** | 14 | 3 |
| Miller, Ryan | BUF | **.775** | 40 | 9 |
| Lehtonen, Kari | ATL | **.773** | 22 | 5 |
| Backstrom, Niklas | MIN | **.762** | 21 | 5 |
| Lundqvist, Henrik | NYR | **.750** | 40 | 10 |
| Clemmensen, Scott | N.J. | **.750** | 12 | 3 |
| Valiquette, Stephen | NYR | **.750** | 12 | 3 |

*Colorado's Wojtek Wolski tied Jussi Jokinen's NHL record by scoring 10 shootout goals in 2008-09. With 17 goals on 26 shots in his career, Wolski's .654 shootout scoring percentage is the best in the NHL entering the 2009-10 season.*

## Individual Shootout Leaders – Skaters

### Shootout Goals Scored

| | Team | G | S | S% |
|---|---|---|---|---|
| Wolski, Wojtek | COL | **10** | 12 | 83.3 |
| Kotalik, Ales | EDM | **8** | 13 | 61.5 |
| Kozlov, Vyacheslav | ATL | **6** | 8 | 75.0 |
| Toews, Jonathan | CHI | **6** | 10 | 60.0 |
| Ribeiro, Mike | DAL | **6** | 11 | 54.6 |
| Boyes, Brad | ST.L. | **6** | 12 | 50.0 |
| Hejduk, Milan | COL | **6** | 13 | 46.2 |
| Eight players tied with | | **5** | | |

### Shootout Shots Taken

| | Team | S | G | S% |
|---|---|---|---|---|
| Zherdev, Nikolai | NYR | **14** | 5 | 35.7 |
| Kotalik, Ales | EDM | **13** | 8 | 61.5 |
| Hejduk, Milan | COL | **13** | 6 | 46.2 |
| Wolski, Wojtek | COL | **12** | 10 | 83.3 |
| Boyes, Brad | ST.L. | **12** | 6 | 50.0 |
| Jokinen, Jussi | CAR | **12** | 5 | 41.7 |
| Naslund, Markus | NYR | **12** | 5 | 41.7 |

### Shootout Scoring Percentage

| *(min. 5 shots taken)* | Team | S% | S | G |
|---|---|---|---|---|
| Wolski, Wojtek | COL | **83.3** | 12 | 10 |
| Kozlov, Vyacheslav | ATL | **75.0** | 8 | 6 |
| Neal, James | DAL | **71.4** | 7 | 5 |
| Kotalik, Ales | EDM | **61.5** | 13 | 8 |
| Toews, Jonathan | CHI | **60.0** | 10 | 6 |
| Getzlaf, Ryan | ANA | **55.6** | 9 | 5 |
| Alfredsson, Daniel | OTT | **55.6** | 9 | 5 |
| Ribeiro, Mike | DAL | **54.6** | 11 | 6 |
| Datsyuk, Pavel | DET | **50.0** | 10 | 5 |
| Boyes, Brad | ST.L. | **50.0** | 12 | 6 |

### Shootout Game-Deciding Goals

| | Team | GDG | S | G |
|---|---|---|---|---|
| Kotalik, Ales | EDM | **5** | 13 | 8 |
| Selanne, Teemu | ANA | **3** | 7 | 3 |
| Zidlicky, Marek | MIN | **3** | 5 | 3 |
| Drury, Chris | NYR | **3** | 7 | 3 |
| Svatos, Marek | COL | **3** | 9 | 3 |
| Datsyuk, Pavel | DET | **3** | 10 | 5 |
| Zherdev, Nikolai | NYR | **3** | 14 | 5 |
| Kozlov, Vyacheslav | ATL | **3** | 8 | 6 |

# Shootout Register, 2008-09

## Skaters

| Player | Team | S | G | S% | GDG |
|---|---|---|---|---|---|
| Alfredsson, Daniel | OTT | 9 | 5 | 55.6 | 0 |
| Antropov, Nik | NYR | 3 | 1 | 33.3 | 0 |
| Armstrong, Colby | ATL | 1 | 0 | 0.0 | 0 |
| Arnott, Jason | NSH | 1 | 1 | 100.0 | 1 |
| Artyukhin, Evgeny | T.B. | 3 | 1 | 33.3 | 1 |
| Axelsson, P.J. | BOS | 5 | 2 | 40.0 | 2 |
| Backes, David | ST.L. | 1 | 0 | 0.0 | 0 |
| Backstrom, Nicklas | WSH | 3 | 1 | 33.3 | 0 |
| Bailey, Josh | NYI | 2 | 0 | 0.0 | 0 |
| Beauchemin, Francois | ANA | 1 | 0 | 0.0 | 0 |
| Bell, Brendan | OTT | 1 | 0 | 0.0 | 0 |
| Bergeron, Patrice | BOS | 7 | 0 | 0.0 | 0 |
| Berglund, Patrik | ST.L. | 1 | 0 | 0.0 | 0 |
| Bernier, Steve | VAN | 1 | 0 | 0.0 | 0 |
| Bertuzzi, Todd | CGY | 3 | 2 | 66.7 | 2 |
| Bieksa, Kevin | VAN | 1 | 0 | 0.0 | 0 |
| Blake, Jason | TOR | 8 | 4 | 50.0 | 1 |
| Boedker, Mikkel | PHX | 1 | 0 | 0.0 | 0 |
| Bolland, Dave | CHI | 3 | 0 | 0.0 | 0 |
| Bonk, Radek | NSH | 2 | 0 | 0.0 | 0 |
| Bouchard, Pierre-Marc | MIN | 1 | 0 | 0.0 | 0 |
| Boyes, Brad | ST.L. | 12 | 6 | 50.0 | 1 |
| Boyle, Dan | S.J. | 7 | 2 | 28.6 | 0 |
| Brassard, Derick | CBJ | 2 | 1 | 50.0 | 0 |
| Briere, Danny | PHI | 3 | 2 | 66.7 | 0 |
| Brind'Amour, Rod | CAR | 2 | 1 | 50.0 | 0 |
| Brown, Dustin | L.A. | 6 | 1 | 16.7 | 0 |
| Brunette, Andrew | MIN | 1 | 0 | 0.0 | 0 |
| Brunnstrom, Fabian | DAL | 4 | 1 | 25.0 | 0 |
| Burns, Brent | MIN | 3 | 0 | 0.0 | 0 |
| Burrows, Alexandre | VAN | 6 | 1 | 16.7 | 0 |
| Callahan, Ryan | NYR | 3 | 1 | 33.3 | 1 |
| Cammalleri, Michael | CGY | 5 | 1 | 20.0 | 0 |
| Carcillo, Daniel | PHI | 1 | 1 | 100.0 | 1 |
| Carter, Jeff | PHI | 5 | 0 | 0.0 | 0 |
| Chara, Zdeno | BOS | 1 | 0 | 0.0 | 0 |
| Cheechoo, Jonathan | S.J. | 3 | 2 | 66.7 | 2 |
| Christensen, Erik | ANA | 5 | 2 | 40.0 | 2 |
| Cleary, Dan | DET | 2 | 0 | 0.0 | 0 |
| Clowe, Ryane | S.J. | 5 | 3 | 60.0 | 2 |
| Comrie, Mike | OTT | 2 | 1 | 50.0 | 1 |
| Connolly, Tim | BUF | 6 | 1 | 16.7 | 0 |
| Crosby, Sidney | PIT | 10 | 3 | 30.0 | 2 |
| Cullen, Matt | CAR | 5 | 0 | 0.0 | 0 |
| Datsyuk, Pavel | DET | 10 | 5 | 50.0 | 3 |
| Dawes, Nigel | PHX | 5 | 1 | 20.0 | 0 |
| Demitra, Pavol | VAN | 7 | 3 | 42.9 | 1 |
| Doan, Shane | PHX | 4 | 2 | 50.0 | 0 |
| Doughty, Drew | L.A. | 3 | 1 | 33.3 | 1 |
| Drury, Chris | NYR | 7 | 3 | 42.9 | 3 |
| Dumont, J.P. | NSH | 2 | 1 | 50.0 | 0 |
| Edler, Alexander | VAN | 2 | 0 | 0.0 | 0 |
| Elias, Patrik | N.J. | 7 | 3 | 42.9 | 1 |
| Erat, Martin | NSH | 5 | 2 | 40.0 | 1 |
| Eriksson, Loui | DAL | 5 | 1 | 20.0 | 0 |
| Fedorov, Sergei | WSH | 1 | 0 | 0.0 | 0 |
| Fiddler, Vernon | NSH | 6 | 2 | 33.3 | 0 |
| Fisher, Mike | OTT | 5 | 2 | 40.0 | 2 |
| Foligno, Nick | OTT | 2 | 0 | 0.0 | 0 |
| Franzen, Johan | DET | 1 | 0 | 0.0 | 0 |
| Frolik, Michael | FLA | 6 | 0 | 0.0 | 0 |
| Frolov, Alexander | L.A. | 6 | 1 | 16.7 | 1 |
| Gagne, Simon | PHI | 6 | 2 | 33.3 | 2 |
| Gagner, Sam | EDM | 8 | 3 | 37.5 | 1 |
| Getzlaf, Ryan | ANA | 9 | 5 | 55.6 | 1 |
| Gionta, Brian | N.J. | 2 | 0 | 0.0 | 0 |
| Giroux, Claude | PHI | 2 | 0 | 0.0 | 0 |
| Goligoski, Alex | PIT | 2 | 1 | 50.0 | 1 |
| Gomez, Scott | NYR | 2 | 0 | 0.0 | 0 |
| Grabovski, Mikhail | TOR | 3 | 1 | 33.3 | 0 |
| Guerin, Bill | PIT | 2 | 1 | 50.0 | 0 |
| Hall, Adam | T.B. | 1 | 1 | 100.0 | 0 |
| Hamilton, Jeff | TOR | 2 | 2 | 100.0 | 1 |
| Handzus, Michal | L.A. | 1 | 0 | 0.0 | 0 |
| Hartnell, Scott | PHI | 1 | 0 | 0.0 | 0 |
| Havlat, Martin | CHI | 3 | 0 | 0.0 | 0 |
| Heatley, Dany | OTT | 3 | 0 | 0.0 | 0 |
| Hejduk, Milan | COL | 13 | 6 | 46.2 | 1 |
| Hemsky, Ales | EDM | 6 | 2 | 33.3 | 2 |
| Horcoff, Shawn | EDM | 1 | 0 | 0.0 | 0 |
| Horton, Nathan | FLA | 7 | 2 | 28.6 | 1 |
| Hossa, Marian | DET | 4 | 2 | 50.0 | 2 |
| Hudler, Jiri | DET | 7 | 3 | 42.9 | 1 |
| Hunter, Trent | NYI | 3 | 0 | 0.0 | 0 |
| Huselius, Kristian | CBJ | 8 | 2 | 25.0 | 2 |
| Iginla, Jarome | CGY | 5 | 0 | 0.0 | 0 |
| Johnson, Jack | L.A. | 6 | 3 | 50.0 | 1 |
| Johnson, Ryan | VAN | 1 | 0 | 0.0 | 0 |
| Jokinen, Jussi | CAR | 12 | 5 | 41.7 | 1 |
| Jokinen, Olli | CGY | 3 | 1 | 33.3 | 1 |
| Kaberle, Tomas | TOR | 3 | 1 | 33.3 | 0 |
| Kane, Patrick | CHI | 9 | 3 | 33.3 | 1 |
| Kariya, Paul | ST.L. | 1 | 0 | 0.0 | 0 |
| Kesler, Ryan | VAN | 3 | 1 | 33.3 | 0 |
| Kessel, Philip | BOS | 8 | 1 | 12.5 | 0 |
| Koistinen, Ville | NSH | 4 | 3 | 75.0 | 1 |
| Koivu, Mikko | MIN | 6 | 2 | 33.3 | 1 |
| Koivu, Saku | MTL | 6 | 1 | 16.7 | 1 |
| Kolanos, Krystofer | MIN | 1 | 0 | 0.0 | 0 |
| Kopitar, Anze | L.A. | 7 | 2 | 28.6 | 0 |
| Kostitsyn, Andrei | MTL | 5 | 0 | 0.0 | 0 |
| Kotalik, Ales | EDM | 13 | 8 | 61.5 | 5 |
| Kovalchuk, Ilya | ATL | 5 | 1 | 20.0 | 0 |
| Kovalev, Alexei | MTL | 8 | 4 | 50.0 | 2 |
| Kozlov, Viktor | WSH | 5 | 1 | 20.0 | 1 |
| Kozlov, Vyacheslav | ATL | 8 | 6 | 75.0 | 3 |
| Krejci, David | BOS | 3 | 1 | 33.3 | 0 |
| Kreps, Kamil | FLA | 1 | 0 | 0.0 | 0 |
| Kubina, Pavel | TOR | 1 | 0 | 0.0 | 0 |
| Kulemin, Nikolai | TOR | 9 | 3 | 33.3 | 1 |
| Kunitz, Chris | PIT | 2 | 0 | 0.0 | 0 |
| Langenbrunner, Jamie | N.J. | 5 | 3 | 60.0 | 1 |
| Lapierre, Maxim | MTL | 3 | 2 | 66.7 | 1 |
| Lecavalier, Vincent | T.B. | 11 | 3 | 27.3 | 0 |
| Legwand, David | NSH | 3 | 1 | 33.3 | 1 |
| Leopold, Jordan | CGY | 1 | 1 | 100.0 | 1 |
| Letang, Kris | PIT | 8 | 2 | 25.0 | 1 |
| Lindstrom, Joakim | PHX | 3 | 0 | 0.0 | 0 |
| Little, Bryan | ATL | 7 | 1 | 14.3 | 0 |
| Lombardi, Matthew | PHX | 1 | 0 | 0.0 | 0 |
| Lydman, Toni | BUF | 1 | 1 | 100.0 | 1 |
| MacArthur, Clarke | BUF | 1 | 0 | 0.0 | 0 |
| Malkin, Evgeni | PIT | 7 | 2 | 28.6 | 0 |
| Malone, Ryan | T.B. | 4 | 1 | 25.0 | 1 |
| Markov, Andrei | MTL | 7 | 3 | 42.9 | 1 |
| Marleau, Patrick | S.J. | 2 | 1 | 50.0 | 0 |
| McAmmond, Dean | NYI | 1 | 0 | 0.0 | 0 |
| McDonald, Andy | ST.L. | 6 | 2 | 33.3 | 0 |
| Michalek, Milan | S.J. | 4 | 1 | 25.0 | 0 |
| Miettinen, Antti | MIN | 5 | 3 | 60.0 | 1 |
| Mitchell, John | TOR | 2 | 1 | 50.0 | 1 |
| Modano, Mike | DAL | 5 | 2 | 40.0 | 1 |
| Montador, Steve | BOS | 1 | 0 | 0.0 | 0 |
| Morrison, Brendan | DAL | 1 | 0 | 0.0 | 0 |
| Mueller, Peter | PHX | 6 | 3 | 50.0 | 0 |
| Nash, Rick | CBJ | 11 | 4 | 36.4 | 1 |
| Naslund, Markus | NYR | 12 | 5 | 41.7 | 1 |
| Neal, James | DAL | 7 | 5 | 71.4 | 2 |
| Nielsen, Frans | NYI | 5 | 3 | 60.0 | 1 |
| Nilsson, Robert | EDM | 5 | 2 | 40.0 | 1 |
| Nolan, Owen | MIN | 1 | 0 | 0.0 | 0 |
| Novotny, Jiri | CBJ | 1 | 0 | 0.0 | 0 |
| Nylander, Michael | WSH | 3 | 1 | 33.3 | 1 |
| O'Sullivan, Patrick | EDM | 11 | 4 | 36.4 | 2 |
| Ohlund, Mattias | VAN | 1 | 1 | 100.0 | 1 |
| Okposo, Kyle | NYI | 4 | 0 | 0.0 | 0 |
| Olesz, Rostislav | FLA | 2 | 1 | 50.0 | 0 |
| Oshie, T.J. | ST.L. | 6 | 2 | 33.3 | 2 |
| Ovechkin, Alex | WSH | 7 | 2 | 28.6 | 0 |
| Pahlsson, Sammy | CHI | 1 | 0 | 0.0 | 0 |
| Parise, Zach | N.J. | 8 | 4 | 50.0 | 2 |
| Park, Richard | NYI | 2 | 1 | 50.0 | 1 |
| Parrish, Mark | DAL | 1 | 0 | 0.0 | 0 |
| Pavelski, Joe | S.J. | 10 | 4 | 40.0 | 2 |
| Peltonen, Ville | FLA | 1 | 0 | 0.0 | 0 |
| Perrin, Eric | ATL | 2 | 0 | 0.0 | 0 |
| Perron, David | ST.L. | 6 | 3 | 50.0 | 2 |
| Perry, Corey | ANA | 10 | 5 | 50.0 | 2 |
| Peverley, Rich | ATL | 7 | 1 | 14.3 | 1 |
| Plekanec, Tomas | MTL | 3 | 0 | 0.0 | 0 |
| Pominville, Jason | BUF | 5 | 2 | 40.0 | 1 |
| Pronger, Chris | ANA | 1 | 0 | 0.0 | 0 |
| Prospal, Vaclav | T.B. | 5 | 0 | 0.0 | 0 |
| Prucha, Petr | PHX | 1 | 0 | 0.0 | 0 |
| Purcell, Teddy | L.A. | 2 | 0 | 0.0 | 0 |
| Pyatt, Taylor | VAN | 2 | 0 | 0.0 | 0 |
| Raymond, Mason | VAN | 1 | 0 | 0.0 | 0 |
| Recchi, Mark | BOS | 1 | 0 | 0.0 | 0 |
| Reinprecht, Steven | PHX | 3 | 2 | 66.7 | 0 |
| Ribeiro, Mike | DAL | 11 | 6 | 54.6 | 2 |
| Richards, Brad | DAL | 7 | 2 | 28.6 | 1 |
| Richards, Mike | PHI | 10 | 4 | 40.0 | 2 |
| Roenick, Jeremy | S.J. | 4 | 1 | 25.0 | 0 |
| Rolston, Brian | N.J. | 1 | 0 | 0.0 | 0 |
| Roy, Derek | BUF | 9 | 4 | 44.4 | 1 |
| Ruutu, Jarkko | OTT | 5 | 2 | 40.0 | 0 |
| Ruutu, Tuomo | CAR | 6 | 3 | 50.0 | 1 |
| Ryan, Bobby | ANA | 6 | 1 | 16.7 | 1 |
| Ryder, Michael | BOS | 3 | 1 | 33.3 | 1 |
| St. Louis, Martin | T.B. | 5 | 1 | 20.0 | 0 |
| St. Pierre, Martin | BOS | 1 | 1 | 100.0 | 0 |
| Salo, Sami | VAN | 1 | 0 | 0.0 | 0 |
| Samsonov, Sergei | CAR | 3 | 1 | 33.3 | 1 |
| Satan, Miroslav | PIT | 4 | 0 | 0.0 | 0 |
| Savard, Marc | BOS | 3 | 0 | 0.0 | 0 |
| Schremp, Rob | EDM | 1 | 0 | 0.0 | 0 |
| Sedin, Henrik | VAN | 1 | 0 | 0.0 | 0 |
| Selanne, Teemu | ANA | 7 | 3 | 42.9 | 3 |
| Semin, Alexander | WSH | 7 | 3 | 42.9 | 2 |
| Setoguchi, Devin | S.J. | 2 | 0 | 0.0 | 0 |
| Shanahan, Brendan | N.J. | 1 | 1 | 100.0 | 1 |
| Sharp, Patrick | CHI | 4 | 1 | 25.0 | 0 |
| Simmonds, Wayne | L.A. | 2 | 1 | 50.0 | 0 |
| Sjostrom, Fredrik | NYR | 9 | 3 | 33.3 | 2 |
| Smyth, Ryan | COL | 4 | 1 | 25.0 | 1 |
| Spezza, Jason | OTT | 10 | 3 | 30.0 | 1 |
| Staal, Eric | CAR | 2 | 0 | 0.0 | 0 |
| Stafford, Drew | BUF | 11 | 4 | 36.4 | 0 |
| Stajan, Matt | TOR | 1 | 0 | 0.0 | 0 |
| Stamkos, Steven | T.B. | 5 | 1 | 20.0 | 1 |
| Stapleton, Tim | TOR | 1 | 1 | 100.0 | 1 |
| Steen, Alex | ST.L. | 1 | 0 | 0.0 | 0 |
| Stewart, Chris | COL | 1 | 0 | 0.0 | 0 |
| Stillman, Cory | FLA | 5 | 1 | 20.0 | 0 |
| Sullivan, Steve | NSH | 6 | 1 | 16.7 | 1 |
| Sundin, Mats | VAN | 2 | 1 | 50.0 | 1 |
| Svatos, Marek | COL | 9 | 3 | 33.3 | 3 |
| Sykora, Petr | PIT | 8 | 3 | 37.5 | 1 |
| Tambellini, Jeff | NYI | 2 | 2 | 100.0 | 1 |
| Tanguay, Alex | MTL | 5 | 2 | 40.0 | 2 |
| Tikhonov, Viktor | PHX | 2 | 1 | 50.0 | 1 |
| Timonen, Kimmo | PHI | 2 | 0 | 0.0 | 0 |
| Tkachuk, Keith | ST.L. | 1 | 0 | 0.0 | 0 |
| Toews, Jonathan | CHI | 10 | 6 | 60.0 | 2 |
| Tucker, Darcy | COL | 1 | 1 | 100.0 | 1 |
| Turris, Kyle | PHX | 4 | 1 | 25.0 | 1 |
| Vanek, Thomas | BUF | 6 | 1 | 16.7 | 1 |
| Vermette, Antoine | CBJ | 5 | 0 | 0.0 | 0 |
| Versteeg, Kris | CHI | 2 | 1 | 50.0 | 1 |
| Voracek, Jakub | CBJ | 3 | 1 | 33.3 | 1 |
| Vrbata, Radim | T.B. | 1 | 0 | 0.0 | 0 |
| Weight, Doug | NYI | 1 | 0 | 0.0 | 0 |
| Weiss, Stephen | FLA | 6 | 1 | 16.7 | 1 |
| Wellwood, Kyle | VAN | 9 | 3 | 33.3 | 0 |
| Wheeler, Blake | BOS | 7 | 4 | 57.1 | 1 |
| White, Todd | ATL | 2 | 1 | 50.0 | 1 |
| Whitney, Ray | CAR | 2 | 0 | 0.0 | 0 |
| Williams, Jason | CBJ | 7 | 2 | 28.6 | 1 |
| Williams, Jeremy | TOR | 1 | 1 | 100.0 | 0 |
| Williams, Justin | L.A. | 2 | 1 | 50.0 | 1 |
| Winchester, Brad | ST.L. | 1 | 1 | 100.0 | 1 |
| Witt, Brendan | NYI | 1 | 0 | 0.0 | 0 |
| Wolski, Wojtek | COL | 12 | 10 | 83.3 | 2 |
| Zednik, Richard | FLA | 2 | 1 | 50.0 | 1 |
| Zetterberg, Henrik | DET | 9 | 3 | 33.3 | 0 |
| Zherdev, Nikolai | NYR | 14 | 5 | 35.7 | 3 |
| Zidlicky, Marek | MIN | 5 | 3 | 60.0 | 3 |
| Zubov, Sergei | DAL | 2 | 0 | 0.0 | 0 |

## Goaltenders

| Goaltender | Team | W | L | SA | GA | Sv % |
|---|---|---|---|---|---|---|
| Anderson, Craig | FLA | 0 | 4 | 11 | 7 | .364 |
| Auld, Alex | OTT | 2 | 4 | 25 | 9 | .640 |
| Backstrom, Niklas | MIN | 5 | 2 | 21 | 5 | .762 |
| Biron, Martin | PHI | 2 | 3 | 17 | 5 | .706 |
| Bishop, Ben | ST.L. | 0 | 1 | 4 | 2 | .500 |
| Boucher, Brian | S.J. | 1 | 1 | 6 | 2 | .667 |
| Brodeur, Martin | N.J. | 2 | 1 | 10 | 3 | .700 |
| Bryzgalov, Ilya | PHX | 2 | 3 | 20 | 10 | .500 |
| Budaj, Peter | COL | 7 | 4 | 35 | 13 | .629 |
| Clemmensen, Scott | N.J. | 2 | 1 | 12 | 3 | .750 |
| Climie, Matt | DAL | 1 | 0 | 3 | 2 | .333 |
| Conklin, Ty | DET | 2 | 2 | 13 | 4 | .692 |
| Danis, Yann | NYI | 0 | 2 | 5 | 3 | .400 |
| Deslauriers, Jeff | EDM | 1 | 0 | 3 | 0 | 1.000 |
| Elliott, Brian | OTT | 2 | 2 | 16 | 6 | .625 |
| Ellis, Dan | NSH | 1 | 3 | 11 | 6 | .454 |
| Ersberg, Erik | L.A. | 1 | 4 | 20 | 8 | .600 |
| Fernandez, Manny | BOS | 0 | 2 | 9 | 4 | .556 |
| Fleury, Marc-Andre | PIT | 3 | 4 | 22 | 6 | .727 |
| Garon, Mathieu | PIT | 1 | 0 | 3 | 1 | .667 |
| Giguere, J-S | ANA | 2 | 2 | 12 | 4 | .667 |
| Halak, Jaroslav | MTL | 2 | 1 | 7 | 2 | .714 |
| Harding, Josh | MIN | 0 | 1 | 2 | 1 | .500 |
| Hedberg, Johan | ATL | 3 | 0 | 13 | 1 | .923 |
| Hiller, Jonas | ANA | 5 | 1 | 31 | 5 | .839 |
| Huet, Cristobal | CHI | 2 | 2 | 12 | 5 | .583 |
| Johnson, Brent | WSH | 0 | 1 | 2 | 1 | .500 |
| Joseph, Curtis | TOR | 2 | 1 | 11 | 3 | .727 |
| Khabibulin, Nikolai | CHI | 2 | 5 | 19 | 9 | .526 |
| Kiprusoff, Miikka | CGY | 3 | 2 | 14 | 3 | .786 |
| LaBarbera, Jason | VAN | 0 | 5 | 16 | 11 | .312 |
| Lalime, Patrick | BUF | 0 | 3 | 10 | 4 | .600 |
| Leclaire, Pascal | OTT | 0 | 1 | 3 | 2 | .330 |
| Legace, Manny | ST.L. | 3 | 1 | 13 | 4 | .692 |
| Lehtonen, Kari | ATL | 4 | 1 | 22 | 5 | .773 |
| Leighton, Michael | CAR | 1 | 1 | 5 | 3 | .400 |
| Lundqvist, Henrik | NYR | 9 | 4 | 40 | 10 | .750 |
| Luongo, Roberto | VAN | 3 | 4 | 29 | 8 | .724 |
| MacDonald, Joey | NYI | 3 | 3 | 15 | 6 | .600 |
| Mason, Chris | ST.L. | 3 | 4 | 18 | 7 | .611 |
| Mason, Steve | CBJ | 6 | 5 | 31 | 9 | .710 |
| Miller, Ryan | BUF | 8 | 2 | 40 | 9 | .775 |
| Nabokov, Evgeni | S.J. | 5 | 4 | 32 | 11 | .656 |
| Niittymaki, Antero | PHI | 2 | 3 | 18 | 6 | .667 |
| Norrena, Fredrik | CBJ | 0 | 1 | 2 | 1 | .500 |
| Osgood, Chris | DET | 4 | 2 | 21 | 6 | .714 |
| Pogge, Justin | TOR | 0 | 1 | 2 | 2 | .000 |
| Price, Carey | MTL | 5 | 6 | 35 | 13 | .629 |
| Quick, Jonathan | L.A. | 4 | 1 | 14 | 4 | .714 |
| Ramo, Karri | T.B. | 1 | 3 | 13 | 5 | .615 |
| Raycroft, Andrew | COL | 2 | 0 | 8 | 1 | .875 |
| Rinne, Pekka | NSH | 5 | 2 | 24 | 5 | .792 |
| Roloson, Dwayne | EDM | 4 | 4 | 24 | 5 | .792 |
| Sabourin, Dany | EDM | 3 | 2 | 19 | 5 | .737 |
| Schneider, Cory | VAN | 0 | 1 | 3 | 3 | .000 |
| Smith, Mike | T.B. | 2 | 7 | 27 | 15 | .444 |
| Tellqvist, Mikael | BUF | 1 | 0 | 8 | 1 | .875 |
| Theodore, Jose | WSH | 4 | 4 | 22 | 6 | .727 |
| Thomas, Tim | BOS | 4 | 4 | 28 | 9 | .679 |
| Toskala, Vesa | TOR | 4 | 5 | 29 | 14 | .517 |
| Turco, Marty | DAL | 5 | 6 | 43 | 16 | .628 |
| Valiquette, Stephen | NYR | 1 | 2 | 12 | 3 | .750 |
| Vokoun, Tomas | FLA | 3 | 4 | 19 | 6 | .684 |
| Ward, Cam | CAR | 2 | 4 | 19 | 7 | .632 |
| Weekes, Kevin | N.J. | 2 | 0 | 6 | 2 | .667 |

# NHL Record Book

## Year-By-Year Final Standings & Leading Scorers

*Stanley Cup winner

### 1917-18

**First Half**

| Team | GP | W | L | T | GF | GA | PTS |
|---|---|---|---|---|---|---|---|
| Montreal | 14 | 10 | 4 | 0 | 81 | 47 | 20 |
| Toronto | 14 | 8 | 6 | 0 | 71 | 75 | 16 |
| Ottawa | 14 | 5 | 9 | 0 | 67 | 79 | 10 |
| **Mtl. Wanderers | 6 | 1 | 5 | 0 | 17 | 35 | 2 |

**Montreal Arena burned down and Wanderers forced to withdraw from League. Montreal Canadiens and Toronto each counted a win for defaulted games with Wanderers.

**Second Half**

| Team | GP | W | L | T | GF | GA | PTS |
|---|---|---|---|---|---|---|---|
| *Toronto | 8 | 5 | 3 | 0 | 37 | 34 | 10 |
| Ottawa | 8 | 4 | 4 | 0 | 35 | 35 | 8 |
| Montreal | 8 | 3 | 5 | 0 | 34 | 37 | 6 |

**Leading Scorers**

| Player | Team | GP | G | A | PTS | PIM |
|---|---|---|---|---|---|---|
| Joe Malone | Montreal | 20 | 44 | 4 | 48 | 30 |
| Cy Denneny | Ottawa | 20 | 36 | 10 | 46 | 80 |
| Reg Noble | Toronto | 20 | 30 | 10 | 40 | 35 |
| Newsy Lalonde | Montreal | 14 | 23 | 7 | 30 | 51 |
| Corb Denneny | Toronto | 21 | 20 | 9 | 29 | 14 |
| Harry Cameron | Toronto | 21 | 17 | 10 | 27 | 28 |
| Didier Pitre | Montreal | 20 | 17 | 6 | 23 | 29 |
| Eddie Gerard | Ottawa | 20 | 13 | 7 | 20 | 26 |
| Jack Darragh | Ottawa | 18 | 14 | 5 | 19 | 26 |
| Frank Nighbor | Ottawa | 10 | 11 | 8 | 19 | 6 |
| Harry Meeking | Toronto | 21 | 10 | 9 | 19 | 28 |

### 1918-19

**First Half**

| Team | GP | W | L | T | GF | GA | PTS |
|---|---|---|---|---|---|---|---|
| • Montreal | 10 | 7 | 3 | 0 | 57 | 50 | 14 |
| Ottawa | 10 | 5 | 5 | 0 | 39 | 39 | 10 |
| Toronto | 10 | 3 | 7 | 0 | 42 | 49 | 6 |

**Second Half**

| Team | GP | W | L | T | GF | GA | PTS |
|---|---|---|---|---|---|---|---|
| Ottawa | 8 | 7 | 1 | 0 | 32 | 14 | 14 |
| Montreal | 8 | 3 | 5 | 0 | 31 | 28 | 6 |
| Toronto | 8 | 2 | 6 | 0 | 22 | 43 | 4 |

• NHL Champion. Stanley Cup not awarded due to influenza epidemic.

**Leading Scorers**

| Player | Team | GP | G | A | PTS | PIM |
|---|---|---|---|---|---|---|
| Newsy Lalonde | Montreal | 17 | 22 | 10 | 32 | 40 |
| Odie Cleghorn | Montreal | 17 | 22 | 6 | 28 | 22 |
| Frank Nighbor | Ottawa | 18 | 19 | 9 | 28 | 27 |
| Cy Denneny | Ottawa | 18 | 18 | 4 | 22 | 58 |
| Didier Pitre | Montreal | 17 | 14 | 5 | 19 | 12 |
| Alf Skinner | Toronto | 17 | 12 | 4 | 16 | 26 |
| Harry Cameron | Tor., Ott. | 14 | 11 | 3 | 14 | 35 |
| Jack Darragh | Ottawa | 14 | 11 | 3 | 14 | 33 |
| Ken Randall | Toronto | 15 | 8 | 6 | 14 | 27 |
| Sprague Cleghorn | Ottawa | 18 | 7 | 6 | 13 | 27 |

## All-Time Standings of NHL Teams

(ranked by percentage)

**Active Clubs**

| Team | Games | Wins | Losses | Ties | OT Losses | SO Losses | Goals For | Goals Against | Points | Pts % | First Season |
|---|---|---|---|---|---|---|---|---|---|---|---|
| Montreal | 5874 | 3021 | 1954 | 837 | 41 | 21 | 19284 | 15758 | 6941 | .591 | 1917-18 |
| Philadelphia | 3260 | 1621 | 1118 | 457 | 40 | 24 | 11024 | 9590 | 3763 | .577 | 1967-68 |
| Boston | 5714 | 2722 | 2123 | 791 | 53 | 25 | 18388 | 16862 | 6313 | .552 | 1924-25 |
| Buffalo | 3034 | 1442 | 1131 | 409 | 29 | 23 | 10170 | 9209 | 3345 | .551 | 1970-71 |
| Edmonton | 2322 | 1092 | 904 | 262 | 44 | 20 | 8307 | 7789 | 2510 | .540 | 1979-80 |
| Calgary | 2878 | 1319 | 1124 | 379 | 39 | 17 | 9750 | 9212 | 3073 | .534 | 1972-73 |
| Detroit | 5648 | 2572 | 2207 | 815 | 34 | 20 | 17647 | 16810 | 6013 | .532 | 1926-27 |
| Minnesota | 656 | 293 | 255 | 55 | 32 | 21 | 1657 | 1633 | 694 | .529 | 2000-01 |
| Colorado | 2322 | 1060 | 952 | 261 | 32 | 17 | 7885 | 7676 | 2430 | .523 | 1979-80 |
| Nashville | 820 | 364 | 342 | 60 | 36 | 18 | 2144 | 2255 | 842 | .513 | 1998-99 |
| St. Louis | 3260 | 1417 | 1342 | 432 | 44 | 25 | 10201 | 10332 | 3335 | .512 | 1967-68 |
| Toronto | 5874 | 2569 | 2461 | 783 | 36 | 25 | 18189 | 18143 | 5982 | .509 | 1917-18 |
| Ottawa | 1282 | 562 | 548 | 115 | 34 | 23 | 3735 | 3781 | 1296 | .505 | 1992-93 |
| Anaheim | 1198 | 518 | 507 | 107 | 39 | 27 | 3182 | 3304 | 1209 | .505 | 1993-94 |
| Dallas | 3260 | 1389 | 1362 | 459 | 36 | 14 | 10138 | 10393 | 3287 | .504 | 1967-68 |
| NY Islanders | 2878 | 1249 | 1232 | 347 | 34 | 16 | 9462 | 9217 | 2895 | .503 | 1972-73 |
| NY Rangers | 5648 | 2402 | 2374 | 808 | 40 | 24 | 17399 | 17564 | 5676 | .502 | 1926-27 |
| San Jose | 1362 | 579 | 598 | 121 | 44 | 20 | 3813 | 4106 | 1343 | .493 | 1991-92 |
| Washington | 2722 | 1161 | 1199 | 303 | 33 | 26 | 8643 | 9079 | 2684 | .493 | 1974-75 |
| Chicago | 5648 | 2319 | 2451 | 814 | 40 | 24 | 16758 | 17130 | 5516 | .488 | 1926-27 |
| Florida | 1198 | 473 | 502 | 142 | 54 | 27 | 3161 | 3413 | 1169 | .488 | 1993-94 |
| Pittsburgh | 3260 | 1360 | 1452 | 383 | 43 | 22 | 10970 | 11576 | 3168 | .486 | 1967-68 |
| New Jersey | 2722 | 1126 | 1219 | 328 | 31 | 18 | 8307 | 8981 | 2629 | .483 | 1974-75 |
| Carolina | 2322 | 941 | 1069 | 263 | 34 | 15 | 7129 | 7861 | 2194 | .472 | 1979-80 |
| Los Angeles | 3260 | 1296 | 1477 | 424 | 45 | 18 | 10652 | 11420 | 3079 | .472 | 1967-68 |
| Vancouver | 3034 | 1199 | 1385 | 391 | 35 | 24 | 9595 | 10419 | 2848 | .469 | 1970-71 |
| Phoenix | 2322 | 928 | 1080 | 266 | 34 | 14 | 7381 | 8177 | 2170 | .467 | 1979-80 |
| Columbus | 656 | 247 | 325 | 33 | 28 | 23 | 1587 | 1965 | 578 | .441 | 2000-01 |
| Atlanta | 738 | 273 | 367 | 45 | 37 | 16 | 2008 | 2489 | 644 | .436 | 1999-2000 |
| Tampa Bay | 1282 | 470 | 635 | 112 | 48 | 17 | 3359 | 4061 | 1117 | .436 | 1992-93 |

**Defunct Clubs**

| Team | Games | Wins | Losses | Ties | Goals For | Goals Against | Points | Pts % | First Season | Last Season |
|---|---|---|---|---|---|---|---|---|---|---|
| Ottawa Senators | 542 | 258 | 221 | 63 | 1458 | 1333 | 579 | .534 | 1917-18 | 1933-34 |
| Montreal Maroons | 622 | 271 | 260 | 91 | 1474 | 1405 | 633 | .509 | 1924-25 | 1937-38 |
| NY/Brooklyn Americans | 784 | 255 | 402 | 127 | 1643 | 2182 | 637 | .406 | 1925-26 | 1941-42 |
| Hamilton Tigers | 126 | 47 | 78 | 1 | 414 | 475 | 95 | .377 | 1920-21 | 1924-25 |
| Cleveland Barons | 160 | 47 | 87 | 26 | 470 | 617 | 120 | .375 | 1976-77 | 1977-78 |
| Pittsburgh Pirates | 212 | 67 | 122 | 23 | 376 | 519 | 157 | .370 | 1925-26 | 1929-30 |
| Calif./Oakland Seals | 698 | 182 | 401 | 115 | 1826 | 2580 | 479 | .343 | 1967-68 | 1975-76 |
| St. Louis Eagles | 48 | 11 | 31 | 6 | 86 | 144 | 28 | .292 | 1934-35 | 1934-35 |
| Quebec Bulldogs | 24 | 4 | 20 | 0 | 91 | 177 | 8 | .167 | 1919-20 | 1919-20 |
| Montreal Wanderers | 6 | 1 | 5 | 0 | 17 | 35 | 2 | .167 | 1917-18 | 1917-18 |
| Philadelphia Quakers | 44 | 4 | 36 | 4 | 76 | 184 | 12 | .136 | 1930-31 | 1930-31 |

Calgary totals include Atlanta Flames, 1972-73 to 1979-80.
Carolina totals include Hartford, 1979-80 to 1996-97.
Colorado totals include Quebec, 1979-80 to 1994-95.
Dallas totals include Minnesota North Stars, 1967-68 to 1992-93.
Detroit totals include Cougars, 1926-27 to 1929-30, and Falcons, 1930-31 to 1931-32.
New Jersey totals include Kansas City, 1974-75 to 1975-76, and Colorado Rockies, 1976-77 to 1981-82.
Phoenix totals include Winnipeg, 1979-80 to 1995-96.
Toronto totals include Arenas, 1917-18 to 1918-19, and St. Patricks, 1919-20 to 1925-26.

### 1919-20

**First Half**

| Team | GP | W | L | T | GF | GA | PTS |
|---|---|---|---|---|---|---|---|
| Ottawa | 12 | 9 | 3 | 0 | 59 | 23 | 18 |
| Montreal | 12 | 8 | 4 | 0 | 62 | 51 | 16 |
| Toronto | 12 | 5 | 7 | 0 | 52 | 62 | 10 |
| Quebec | 12 | 2 | 10 | 0 | 44 | 81 | 4 |

**Second Half**

| Team | GP | W | L | T | GF | GA | PTS |
|---|---|---|---|---|---|---|---|
| *Ottawa | 12 | 10 | 2 | 0 | 62 | 41 | 20 |
| Toronto | 12 | 7 | 5 | 0 | 67 | 44 | 14 |
| Montreal | 12 | 5 | 7 | 0 | 67 | 62 | 10 |
| Quebec | 12 | 2 | 10 | 0 | 47 | 96 | 4 |

**Leading Scorers**

| Player | Team | GP | G | A | PTS | PIM |
|---|---|---|---|---|---|---|
| Joe Malone | Quebec | 24 | 39 | 10 | 49 | 12 |
| Newsy Lalonde | Montreal | 23 | 37 | 9 | 46 | 34 |
| Frank Nighbor | Ottawa | 23 | 26 | 15 | 41 | 18 |
| Corb Denneny | Toronto | 24 | 24 | 12 | 36 | 20 |
| Jack Darragh | Ottawa | 23 | 22 | 14 | 36 | 22 |
| Reg Noble | Toronto | 24 | 24 | 9 | 33 | 52 |
| Amos Arbour | Montreal | 22 | 21 | 5 | 26 | 13 |
| Cully Wilson | Toronto | 23 | 20 | 6 | 26 | 86 |
| Didier Pitre | Montreal | 22 | 14 | 12 | 26 | 6 |
| Punch Broadbent | Ottawa | 21 | 19 | 6 | 25 | 40 |

### 1920-21

**First Half**

| Team | GP | W | L | T | GF | GA | PTS |
|---|---|---|---|---|---|---|---|
| *Ottawa | 10 | 8 | 2 | 0 | 49 | 23 | 16 |
| Toronto | 10 | 5 | 5 | 0 | 39 | 47 | 10 |
| Montreal | 10 | 4 | 6 | 0 | 37 | 51 | 8 |
| Hamilton | 10 | 3 | 7 | 0 | 34 | 38 | 6 |

**Second Half**

| Team | GP | W | L | T | GF | GA | PTS |
|---|---|---|---|---|---|---|---|
| Toronto | 14 | 10 | 4 | 0 | 66 | 53 | 20 |
| Montreal | 14 | 9 | 5 | 0 | 75 | 48 | 18 |
| Ottawa | 14 | 6 | 8 | 0 | 48 | 52 | 12 |
| Hamilton | 14 | 3 | 11 | 0 | 58 | 94 | 6 |

**Leading Scorers**

| Player | Team | GP | G | A | PTS | PIM |
|---|---|---|---|---|---|---|
| Newsy Lalonde | Montreal | 24 | 33 | 10 | 43 | 36 |
| Babe Dye | Ham., Tor. | 24 | 35 | 5 | 40 | 32 |
| Cy Denneny | Ottawa | 24 | 34 | 5 | 39 | 10 |
| Joe Malone | Hamilton | 20 | 28 | 9 | 37 | 6 |
| Frank Nighbor | Ottawa | 24 | 19 | 10 | 29 | 10 |
| Reg Noble | Toronto | 24 | 19 | 8 | 27 | 54 |
| Harry Cameron | Toronto | 24 | 18 | 9 | 27 | 35 |
| Goldie Prodgers | Hamilton | 24 | 18 | 9 | 27 | 8 |
| Corb Denneny | Toronto | 20 | 19 | 7 | 26 | 29 |
| Jack Darragh | Ottawa | 24 | 11 | 15 | 26 | 20 |

## 1921-22

| Team | GP | W | L | T | GF | GA | PTS |
|---|---|---|---|---|---|---|---|
| Ottawa | 24 | 14 | 8 | 2 | 106 | 84 | 30 |
| *Toronto | 24 | 13 | 10 | 1 | 98 | 97 | 27 |
| Montreal | 24 | 12 | 11 | 1 | 88 | 94 | 25 |
| Hamilton | 24 | 7 | 17 | 0 | 88 | 105 | 14 |

### Leading Scorers

| Player | Team | GP | G | A | PTS | PIM |
|---|---|---|---|---|---|---|
| Punch Broadbent | Ottawa | 24 | 32 | 14 | 46 | 28 |
| Cy Denneny | Ottawa | 22 | 27 | 12 | 39 | 20 |
| Babe Dye | Toronto | 24 | 31 | 7 | 38 | 39 |
| Harry Cameron | Toronto | 24 | 18 | 17 | 35 | 22 |
| Joe Malone | Hamilton | 24 | 24 | 7 | 31 | 4 |
| Corb Denneny | Toronto | 24 | 19 | 9 | 28 | 28 |
| Reg Noble | Toronto | 24 | 17 | 11 | 28 | 19 |
| Sprague Cleghorn | Montreal | 24 | 17 | 9 | 26 | 80 |
| Georges Boucher | Ottawa | 23 | 13 | 12 | 25 | 12 |
| Odie Cleghorn | Montreal | 23 | 21 | 3 | 24 | 26 |

## 1922-23

| Team | GP | W | L | T | GF | GA | PTS |
|---|---|---|---|---|---|---|---|
| *Ottawa | 24 | 14 | 9 | 1 | 77 | 54 | 29 |
| Montreal | 24 | 13 | 9 | 2 | 73 | 61 | 28 |
| Toronto | 24 | 13 | 10 | 1 | 82 | 88 | 27 |
| Hamilton | 24 | 6 | 18 | 0 | 81 | 110 | 12 |

### Leading Scorers

| Player | Team | GP | G | A | PTS | PIM |
|---|---|---|---|---|---|---|
| Babe Dye | Toronto | 22 | 26 | 11 | 37 | 19 |
| Cy Denneny | Ottawa | 24 | 23 | 11 | 34 | 28 |
| Billy Boucher | Montreal | 24 | 24 | 7 | 31 | 55 |
| Jack Adams | Toronto | 23 | 19 | 9 | 28 | 42 |
| Mickey Roach | Hamilton | 24 | 17 | 10 | 27 | 8 |
| Odie Cleghorn | Montreal | 24 | 19 | 6 | 25 | 18 |
| Georges Boucher | Ottawa | 24 | 14 | 9 | 23 | 58 |
| Reg Noble | Toronto | 24 | 12 | 11 | 23 | 47 |
| Cully Wilson | Hamilton | 23 | 16 | 5 | 21 | 46 |
| Aurel Joliat | Montreal | 24 | 12 | 9 | 21 | 37 |

## 1923-24

| Team | GP | W | L | T | GF | GA | PTS |
|---|---|---|---|---|---|---|---|
| Ottawa | 24 | 16 | 8 | 0 | 74 | 54 | 32 |
| *Montreal | 24 | 13 | 11 | 0 | 59 | 48 | 26 |
| Toronto | 24 | 10 | 14 | 0 | 59 | 85 | 20 |
| Hamilton | 24 | 9 | 15 | 0 | 63 | 68 | 18 |

### Leading Scorers

| Player | Team | GP | G | A | PTS | PIM |
|---|---|---|---|---|---|---|
| Cy Denneny | Ottawa | 22 | 22 | 2 | 24 | 10 |
| Georges Boucher | Ottawa | 21 | 13 | 10 | 23 | 38 |
| Billy Boucher | Montreal | 23 | 16 | 6 | 22 | 48 |
| Billy Burch | Hamilton | 24 | 16 | 6 | 22 | 6 |
| Aurel Joliat | Montreal | 24 | 15 | 5 | 20 | 27 |
| Babe Dye | Toronto | 19 | 16 | 3 | 19 | 23 |
| Jack Adams | Toronto | 22 | 14 | 4 | 18 | 51 |
| Reg Noble | Toronto | 24 | 12 | 5 | 17 | 79 |
| Frank Nighbor | Ottawa | 20 | 11 | 6 | 17 | 16 |
| Howie Morenz | Montreal | 24 | 13 | 3 | 16 | 20 |
| King Clancy | Ottawa | 24 | 8 | 8 | 16 | 26 |

## 1924-25

| Team | GP | W | L | T | GF | GA | PTS |
|---|---|---|---|---|---|---|---|
| Hamilton | 30 | 19 | 10 | 1 | 90 | 60 | 39 |
| Toronto | 30 | 19 | 11 | 0 | 90 | 84 | 38 |
| • Montreal | 30 | 17 | 11 | 2 | 93 | 56 | 36 |
| Ottawa | 30 | 17 | 12 | 1 | 83 | 66 | 35 |
| Mtl. Maroons | 30 | 9 | 19 | 2 | 45 | 65 | 20 |
| Boston | 30 | 6 | 24 | 0 | 49 | 119 | 12 |

• NHL Champion (Stanley Cup won by Victoria Cougars, WCHL)

### Leading Scorers

| Player | Team | GP | G | A | PTS | PIM |
|---|---|---|---|---|---|---|
| Babe Dye | Toronto | 29 | 38 | 8 | 46 | 41 |
| Cy Denneny | Ottawa | 29 | 27 | 15 | 42 | 16 |
| Aurel Joliat | Montreal | 25 | 30 | 11 | 41 | 85 |
| Howie Morenz | Montreal | 30 | 28 | 11 | 39 | 46 |
| Red Green | Hamilton | 30 | 19 | 15 | 34 | 81 |
| Jack Adams | Toronto | 27 | 21 | 10 | 31 | 67 |
| Billy Boucher | Montreal | 30 | 17 | 13 | 30 | 92 |
| Billy Burch | Hamilton | 27 | 20 | 7 | 27 | 10 |
| Jimmy Herberts | Boston | 30 | 17 | 7 | 24 | 55 |
| Hooley Smith | Ottawa | 30 | 10 | 13 | 23 | 81 |

## 1925-26

| Team | GP | W | L | T | GF | GA | PTS |
|---|---|---|---|---|---|---|---|
| Ottawa | 36 | 24 | 8 | 4 | 77 | 42 | 52 |
| *Mtl. Maroons | 36 | 20 | 11 | 5 | 91 | 73 | 45 |
| Pittsburgh | 36 | 19 | 16 | 1 | 82 | 70 | 39 |
| Boston | 36 | 17 | 15 | 4 | 92 | 85 | 38 |
| NY Americans | 36 | 12 | 20 | 4 | 68 | 89 | 28 |
| Toronto | 36 | 12 | 21 | 3 | 92 | 114 | 27 |
| Montreal | 36 | 11 | 24 | 1 | 79 | 108 | 23 |

### Leading Scorers

| Player | Team | GP | G | A | PTS | PIM |
|---|---|---|---|---|---|---|
| Nels Stewart | Mtl. Maroons | 36 | 34 | 8 | 42 | 119 |
| Cy Denneny | Ottawa | 36 | 24 | 12 | 36 | 18 |
| Carson Cooper | Boston | 36 | 28 | 3 | 31 | 10 |
| Jimmy Herberts | Boston | 36 | 26 | 5 | 31 | 47 |
| Howie Morenz | Montreal | 31 | 23 | 3 | 26 | 39 |
| Jack Adams | Toronto | 36 | 21 | 5 | 26 | 52 |
| Aurel Joliat | Montreal | 35 | 17 | 9 | 26 | 52 |
| Billy Burch | NY Americans | 36 | 22 | 3 | 25 | 33 |
| Hooley Smith | Ottawa | 28 | 16 | 9 | 25 | 53 |
| Frank Nighbor | Ottawa | 35 | 12 | 13 | 25 | 40 |

## 1926-27

### Canadian Division

| Team | GP | W | L | T | GF | GA | PTS |
|---|---|---|---|---|---|---|---|
| *Ottawa | 44 | 30 | 10 | 4 | 86 | 69 | 64 |
| Montreal | 44 | 28 | 14 | 2 | 99 | 67 | 58 |
| Mtl. Maroons | 44 | 20 | 20 | 4 | 71 | 68 | 44 |
| NY Americans | 44 | 17 | 25 | 2 | 82 | 91 | 36 |
| Toronto | 44 | 15 | 24 | 5 | 79 | 94 | 35 |

### American Division

| Team | GP | W | L | T | GF | GA | PTS |
|---|---|---|---|---|---|---|---|
| NY Rangers | 44 | 25 | 13 | 6 | 95 | 72 | 56 |
| Boston | 44 | 21 | 20 | 3 | 97 | 89 | 45 |
| Chicago | 44 | 19 | 22 | 3 | 115 | 116 | 41 |
| Pittsburgh | 44 | 15 | 26 | 3 | 79 | 108 | 33 |
| Detroit | 44 | 12 | 28 | 4 | 76 | 105 | 28 |

### Leading Scorers

| Player | Team | GP | G | A | PTS | PIM |
|---|---|---|---|---|---|---|
| Bill Cook | NY Rangers | 44 | 33 | 4 | 37 | 58 |
| Dick Irvin | Chicago | 43 | 18 | 18 | 36 | 34 |
| Howie Morenz | Montreal | 44 | 25 | 7 | 32 | 49 |
| Frank Fredrickson | Det., Bos. | 41 | 18 | 13 | 31 | 46 |
| Babe Dye | Chicago | 41 | 25 | 5 | 30 | 14 |
| Ace Bailey | Toronto | 42 | 15 | 13 | 28 | 82 |
| Frank Boucher | NY Rangers | 44 | 13 | 15 | 28 | 17 |
| Billy Burch | NY Americans | 43 | 19 | 8 | 27 | 40 |
| Harry Oliver | Boston | 42 | 18 | 6 | 24 | 17 |
| Duke Keats | Bos., Det. | 42 | 16 | 8 | 24 | 52 |

## 1927-28

### Canadian Division

| Team | GP | W | L | T | GF | GA | PTS |
|---|---|---|---|---|---|---|---|
| Montreal | 44 | 26 | 11 | 7 | 116 | 48 | 59 |
| Mtl. Maroons | 44 | 24 | 14 | 6 | 96 | 77 | 54 |
| Ottawa | 44 | 20 | 14 | 10 | 78 | 57 | 50 |
| Toronto | 44 | 18 | 18 | 8 | 89 | 88 | 44 |
| NY Americans | 44 | 11 | 27 | 6 | 63 | 128 | 28 |

### American Division

| Team | GP | W | L | T | GF | GA | PTS |
|---|---|---|---|---|---|---|---|
| Boston | 44 | 20 | 13 | 11 | 77 | 70 | 51 |
| *NY Rangers | 44 | 19 | 16 | 9 | 94 | 79 | 47 |
| Pittsburgh | 44 | 19 | 17 | 8 | 67 | 76 | 46 |
| Detroit | 44 | 19 | 19 | 6 | 88 | 79 | 44 |
| Chicago | 44 | 7 | 34 | 3 | 68 | 134 | 17 |

### Leading Scorers

| Player | Team | GP | G | A | PTS | PIM |
|---|---|---|---|---|---|---|
| Howie Morenz | Montreal | 43 | 33 | 18 | 51 | 66 |
| Aurel Joliat | Montreal | 44 | 28 | 11 | 39 | 105 |
| Frank Boucher | NY Rangers | 44 | 23 | 12 | 35 | 15 |
| George Hay | Detroit | 42 | 22 | 13 | 35 | 20 |
| Nels Stewart | Mtl. Maroons | 41 | 27 | 7 | 34 | 104 |
| Art Gagne | Montreal | 44 | 20 | 10 | 30 | 75 |
| Bun Cook | NY Rangers | 44 | 14 | 14 | 28 | 45 |
| Bill Carson | Toronto | 32 | 20 | 6 | 26 | 36 |
| Frank Finnigan | Ottawa | 38 | 20 | 5 | 25 | 34 |
| Bill Cook | NY Rangers | 43 | 18 | 6 | 24 | 42 |
| Duke Keats | Det., Chi. | 38 | 14 | 10 | 24 | 60 |

## 1928-29

### Canadian Division

| Team | GP | W | L | T | GF | GA | PTS |
|---|---|---|---|---|---|---|---|
| Montreal | 44 | 22 | 7 | 15 | 71 | 43 | 59 |
| NY Americans | 44 | 19 | 13 | 12 | 53 | 53 | 50 |
| Toronto | 44 | 21 | 18 | 5 | 85 | 69 | 47 |
| Ottawa | 44 | 14 | 17 | 13 | 54 | 67 | 41 |
| Mtl. Maroons | 44 | 15 | 20 | 9 | 67 | 65 | 39 |

### American Division

| Team | GP | W | L | T | GF | GA | PTS |
|---|---|---|---|---|---|---|---|
| *Boston | 44 | 26 | 13 | 5 | 89 | 52 | 57 |
| NY Rangers | 44 | 21 | 13 | 10 | 72 | 65 | 52 |
| Detroit | 44 | 19 | 16 | 9 | 72 | 63 | 47 |
| Pittsburgh | 44 | 9 | 27 | 8 | 46 | 80 | 26 |
| Chicago | 44 | 7 | 29 | 8 | 33 | 85 | 22 |

### Leading Scorers

| Player | Team | GP | G | A | PTS | PIM |
|---|---|---|---|---|---|---|
| Ace Bailey | Toronto | 44 | 22 | 10 | 32 | 78 |
| Nels Stewart | Mtl. Maroons | 44 | 21 | 8 | 29 | 74 |
| Carson Cooper | Detroit | 43 | 18 | 9 | 27 | 14 |
| Howie Morenz | Montreal | 42 | 17 | 10 | 27 | 47 |
| Andy Blair | Toronto | 44 | 12 | 15 | 27 | 41 |
| Frank Boucher | NY Rangers | 44 | 10 | 16 | 26 | 8 |
| Harry Oliver | Boston | 43 | 17 | 6 | 23 | 24 |
| Bill Cook | NY Rangers | 43 | 15 | 8 | 23 | 41 |
| Jimmy Ward | Mtl. Maroons | 43 | 14 | 8 | 22 | 46 |

Seven players tied with 19 points

## 1929-30

### Canadian Division

| Team | GP | W | L | T | GF | GA | PTS |
|---|---|---|---|---|---|---|---|
| Mtl. Maroons | 44 | 23 | 16 | 5 | 141 | 114 | 51 |
| *Montreal | 44 | 21 | 14 | 9 | 142 | 114 | 51 |
| Ottawa | 44 | 21 | 15 | 8 | 138 | 118 | 50 |
| Toronto | 44 | 17 | 21 | 6 | 116 | 124 | 40 |
| NY Americans | 44 | 14 | 25 | 5 | 113 | 161 | 33 |

### American Division

| Team | GP | W | L | T | GF | GA | PTS |
|---|---|---|---|---|---|---|---|
| Boston | 44 | 38 | 5 | 1 | 179 | 98 | 77 |
| Chicago | 44 | 21 | 18 | 5 | 117 | 111 | 47 |
| NY Rangers | 44 | 17 | 17 | 10 | 136 | 143 | 44 |
| Detroit | 44 | 14 | 24 | 6 | 117 | 133 | 34 |
| Pittsburgh | 44 | 5 | 36 | 3 | 102 | 185 | 13 |

### Leading Scorers

| Player | Team | GP | G | A | PTS | PIM |
|---|---|---|---|---|---|---|
| Cooney Weiland | Boston | 44 | 43 | 30 | 73 | 27 |
| Frank Boucher | NY Rangers | 42 | 26 | 36 | 62 | 16 |
| Dit Clapper | Boston | 44 | 41 | 20 | 61 | 48 |
| Bill Cook | NY Rangers | 44 | 29 | 30 | 59 | 56 |
| Hec Kilrea | Ottawa | 44 | 36 | 22 | 58 | 72 |
| Nels Stewart | Mtl. Maroons | 44 | 39 | 16 | 55 | 81 |
| Howie Morenz | Montreal | 44 | 40 | 10 | 50 | 72 |
| Normie Himes | NY Americans | 44 | 28 | 22 | 50 | 15 |
| Joe Lamb | Ottawa | 44 | 29 | 20 | 49 | 119 |
| Dutch Gainor | Boston | 42 | 18 | 31 | 49 | 39 |

## 1930-31

### Canadian Division

| Team | GP | W | L | T | GF | GA | PTS |
|---|---|---|---|---|---|---|---|
| *Montreal | 44 | 26 | 10 | 8 | 129 | 89 | 60 |
| Toronto | 44 | 22 | 13 | 9 | 118 | 99 | 53 |
| Mtl. Maroons | 44 | 20 | 18 | 6 | 105 | 106 | 46 |
| NY Americans | 44 | 18 | 16 | 10 | 76 | 74 | 46 |
| Ottawa | 44 | 10 | 30 | 4 | 91 | 142 | 24 |

### American Division

| Team | GP | W | L | T | GF | GA | PTS |
|---|---|---|---|---|---|---|---|
| Boston | 44 | 28 | 10 | 6 | 143 | 90 | 62 |
| Chicago | 44 | 24 | 17 | 3 | 108 | 78 | 51 |
| NY Rangers | 44 | 19 | 16 | 9 | 106 | 87 | 47 |
| Detroit | 44 | 16 | 21 | 7 | 102 | 105 | 39 |
| Philadelphia | 44 | 4 | 36 | 4 | 76 | 184 | 12 |

### Leading Scorers

| Player | Team | GP | G | A | PTS | PIM |
|---|---|---|---|---|---|---|
| Howie Morenz | Montreal | 39 | 28 | 23 | 51 | 49 |
| Ebbie Goodfellow | Detroit | 44 | 25 | 23 | 48 | 32 |
| Charlie Conacher | Toronto | 37 | 31 | 12 | 43 | 78 |
| Bill Cook | NY Rangers | 43 | 30 | 12 | 42 | 39 |
| Ace Bailey | Toronto | 40 | 23 | 19 | 42 | 46 |
| Joe Primeau | Toronto | 38 | 9 | 32 | 41 | 18 |
| Nels Stewart | Mtl. Maroons | 42 | 25 | 14 | 39 | 75 |
| Frank Boucher | NY Rangers | 44 | 12 | 27 | 39 | 20 |
| Cooney Weiland | Boston | 44 | 25 | 13 | 38 | 14 |
| Bun Cook | NY Rangers | 44 | 18 | 17 | 35 | 72 |
| Aurel Joliat | Montreal | 43 | 13 | 22 | 35 | 73 |

## 1931-32

### Canadian Division

| Team | GP | W | L | T | GF | GA | PTS |
|---|---|---|---|---|---|---|---|
| Montreal | 48 | 25 | 16 | 7 | 128 | 111 | 57 |
| *Toronto | 48 | 23 | 18 | 7 | 155 | 127 | 53 |
| Mtl. Maroons | 48 | 19 | 22 | 7 | 142 | 139 | 45 |
| NY Americans | 48 | 16 | 24 | 8 | 95 | 142 | 40 |

### American Division

| Team | GP | W | L | T | GF | GA | PTS |
|---|---|---|---|---|---|---|---|
| NY Rangers | 48 | 23 | 17 | 8 | 134 | 112 | 54 |
| Chicago | 48 | 18 | 19 | 11 | 86 | 101 | 47 |
| Detroit | 48 | 18 | 20 | 10 | 95 | 108 | 46 |
| Boston | 48 | 15 | 21 | 12 | 122 | 117 | 42 |

### Leading Scorers

| Player | Team | GP | G | A | PTS | PIM |
|---|---|---|---|---|---|---|
| Busher Jackson | Toronto | 48 | 28 | 25 | 53 | 63 |
| Joe Primeau | Toronto | 46 | 13 | 37 | 50 | 25 |
| Howie Morenz | Montreal | 48 | 24 | 25 | 49 | 46 |
| Charlie Conacher | Toronto | 44 | 34 | 14 | 48 | 66 |
| Bill Cook | NY Rangers | 48 | 34 | 14 | 48 | 33 |
| Dave Trottier | Mtl. Maroons | 48 | 26 | 18 | 44 | 94 |
| Hooley Smith | Mtl. Maroons | 43 | 11 | 33 | 44 | 49 |
| Babe Siebert | Mtl. Maroons | 48 | 21 | 18 | 39 | 64 |
| Dit Clapper | Boston | 48 | 17 | 22 | 39 | 21 |
| Aurel Joliat | Montreal | 48 | 15 | 24 | 39 | 46 |

## 1932-33

### Canadian Division

| Team | GP | W | L | T | GF | GA | PTS |
|---|---|---|---|---|---|---|---|
| Toronto | 48 | 24 | 18 | 6 | 119 | 111 | 54 |
| Mtl. Maroons | 48 | 22 | 20 | 6 | 135 | 119 | 50 |
| Montreal | 48 | 18 | 25 | 5 | 92 | 115 | 41 |
| NY Americans | 48 | 15 | 22 | 11 | 91 | 118 | 41 |
| Ottawa | 48 | 11 | 27 | 10 | 88 | 131 | 32 |

### American Division

| Team | GP | W | L | T | GF | GA | PTS |
|---|---|---|---|---|---|---|---|
| Boston | 48 | 25 | 15 | 8 | 124 | 88 | 58 |
| Detroit | 48 | 25 | 15 | 8 | 111 | 93 | 58 |
| *NY Rangers | 48 | 23 | 17 | 8 | 135 | 107 | 54 |
| Chicago | 48 | 16 | 20 | 12 | 88 | 101 | 44 |

### Leading Scorers

| Player | Team | GP | G | A | PTS | PIM |
|---|---|---|---|---|---|---|
| Bill Cook | NY Rangers | 48 | 28 | 22 | 50 | 51 |
| Busher Jackson | Toronto | 48 | 27 | 17 | 44 | 43 |
| Baldy Northcott | Mtl. Maroons | 48 | 22 | 21 | 43 | 30 |
| Hooley Smith | Mtl. Maroons | 48 | 20 | 21 | 41 | 66 |
| Paul Haynes | Mtl. Maroons | 48 | 16 | 25 | 41 | 18 |
| Aurel Joliat | Montreal | 48 | 18 | 21 | 39 | 53 |
| Marty Barry | Boston | 48 | 24 | 13 | 37 | 40 |
| Bun Cook | NY Rangers | 48 | 22 | 15 | 37 | 35 |
| Nels Stewart | Boston | 47 | 18 | 18 | 36 | 62 |
| Howie Morenz | Montreal | 46 | 14 | 21 | 35 | 32 |
| Johnny Gagnon | Montreal | 48 | 12 | 23 | 35 | 64 |
| Eddie Shore | Boston | 48 | 8 | 27 | 35 | 102 |
| Frank Boucher | NY Rangers | 46 | 7 | 28 | 35 | 4 |

## 1933-34

### Canadian Division

| Team | GP | W | L | T | GF | GA | PTS |
|---|---|---|---|---|---|---|---|
| Toronto | 48 | 26 | 13 | 9 | 174 | 119 | 61 |
| Montreal | 48 | 22 | 20 | 6 | 99 | 101 | 50 |
| Mtl. Maroons | 48 | 19 | 18 | 11 | 117 | 122 | 49 |
| NY Americans | 48 | 15 | 23 | 10 | 104 | 132 | 40 |
| Ottawa | 48 | 13 | 29 | 6 | 115 | 143 | 32 |

### American Division

| Team | GP | W | L | T | GF | GA | PTS |
|---|---|---|---|---|---|---|---|
| Detroit | 48 | 24 | 14 | 10 | 113 | 98 | 58 |
| *Chicago | 48 | 20 | 17 | 11 | 88 | 83 | 51 |
| NY Rangers | 48 | 21 | 19 | 8 | 120 | 113 | 50 |
| Boston | 48 | 18 | 25 | 5 | 111 | 130 | 41 |

### Leading Scorers

| Player | Team | GP | G | A | PTS | PIM |
|---|---|---|---|---|---|---|
| Charlie Conacher | Toronto | 42 | 32 | 20 | 52 | 38 |
| Joe Primeau | Toronto | 45 | 14 | 32 | 46 | 8 |
| Frank Boucher | NY Rangers | 48 | 14 | 30 | 44 | 4 |
| Marty Barry | Boston | 48 | 27 | 12 | 39 | 12 |
| Cecil Dillon | NY Rangers | 48 | 13 | 26 | 39 | 10 |
| Nels Stewart | Boston | 48 | 21 | 17 | 38 | 68 |
| Busher Jackson | Toronto | 38 | 20 | 18 | 38 | 38 |
| Aurel Joliat | Montreal | 48 | 22 | 15 | 37 | 27 |
| Hooley Smith | Mtl. Maroons | 47 | 18 | 19 | 37 | 58 |
| Paul Thompson | Chicago | 48 | 20 | 16 | 36 | 17 |

## 1934-35

### Canadian Division

| Team | GP | W | L | T | GF | GA | PTS |
|---|---|---|---|---|---|---|---|
| Toronto | 48 | 30 | 14 | 4 | 157 | 111 | 64 |
| *Mtl. Maroons | 48 | 24 | 19 | 5 | 123 | 92 | 53 |
| Montreal | 48 | 19 | 23 | 6 | 110 | 145 | 44 |
| NY Americans | 48 | 12 | 27 | 9 | 100 | 142 | 33 |
| St. Louis | 48 | 11 | 31 | 6 | 86 | 144 | 28 |

### American Division

| Team | GP | W | L | T | GF | GA | PTS |
|---|---|---|---|---|---|---|---|
| Boston | 48 | 26 | 16 | 6 | 129 | 112 | 58 |
| Chicago | 48 | 26 | 17 | 5 | 118 | 88 | 57 |
| NY Rangers | 48 | 22 | 20 | 6 | 137 | 139 | 50 |
| Detroit | 48 | 19 | 22 | 7 | 127 | 114 | 45 |

### Leading Scorers

| Player | Team | GP | G | A | PTS | PIM |
|---|---|---|---|---|---|---|
| Charlie Conacher | Toronto | 47 | 36 | 21 | 57 | 24 |
| Syd Howe | St.L., Det. | 50 | 22 | 25 | 47 | 34 |
| Larry Aurie | Detroit | 48 | 17 | 29 | 46 | 24 |
| Frank Boucher | NY Rangers | 48 | 13 | 32 | 45 | 2 |
| Busher Jackson | Toronto | 42 | 22 | 22 | 44 | 27 |
| Herbie Lewis | Detroit | 47 | 16 | 27 | 43 | 26 |
| Art Chapman | NY Americans | 47 | 9 | 34 | 43 | 4 |
| Marty Barry | Boston | 48 | 20 | 20 | 40 | 33 |
| Sweeney Schriner | NY Americans | 48 | 18 | 22 | 40 | 6 |
| Nels Stewart | Boston | 47 | 21 | 18 | 39 | 45 |
| Paul Thompson | Chicago | 48 | 16 | 23 | 39 | 20 |

## 1935-36

### Canadian Division

| Team | GP | W | L | T | GF | GA | PTS |
|---|---|---|---|---|---|---|---|
| Mtl. Maroons | 48 | 22 | 16 | 10 | 114 | 106 | 54 |
| Toronto | 48 | 23 | 19 | 6 | 126 | 106 | 52 |
| NY Americans | 48 | 16 | 25 | 7 | 109 | 122 | 39 |
| Montreal | 48 | 11 | 26 | 11 | 82 | 123 | 33 |

### American Division

| Team | GP | W | L | T | GF | GA | PTS |
|---|---|---|---|---|---|---|---|
| *Detroit | 48 | 24 | 16 | 8 | 124 | 103 | 56 |
| Boston | 48 | 22 | 20 | 6 | 92 | 83 | 50 |
| Chicago | 48 | 21 | 19 | 8 | 93 | 92 | 50 |
| NY Rangers | 48 | 19 | 17 | 12 | 91 | 96 | 50 |

### Leading Scorers

| Player | Team | GP | G | A | PTS | PIM |
|---|---|---|---|---|---|---|
| Sweeney Schriner | NY Americans | 48 | 19 | 26 | 45 | 8 |
| Marty Barry | Detroit | 48 | 21 | 19 | 40 | 16 |
| Paul Thompson | Chicago | 45 | 17 | 23 | 40 | 19 |
| Bill Thoms | Toronto | 48 | 23 | 15 | 38 | 29 |
| Charlie Conacher | Toronto | 44 | 23 | 15 | 38 | 74 |
| Hooley Smith | Mtl. Maroons | 47 | 19 | 19 | 38 | 75 |
| Doc Romnes | Chicago | 48 | 13 | 25 | 38 | 6 |
| Art Chapman | NY Americans | 47 | 10 | 28 | 38 | 14 |
| Herbie Lewis | Detroit | 45 | 14 | 23 | 37 | 25 |
| Baldy Northcott | Mtl. Maroons | 48 | 15 | 21 | 36 | 41 |

## 1936-37

### Canadian Division

| Team | GP | W | L | T | GF | GA | PTS |
|---|---|---|---|---|---|---|---|
| Montreal | 48 | 24 | 18 | 6 | 115 | 111 | 54 |
| Mtl. Maroons | 48 | 22 | 17 | 9 | 126 | 110 | 53 |
| Toronto | 48 | 22 | 21 | 5 | 119 | 115 | 49 |
| NY Americans | 48 | 15 | 29 | 4 | 122 | 161 | 34 |

### American Division

| Team | GP | W | L | T | GF | GA | PTS |
|---|---|---|---|---|---|---|---|
| *Detroit | 48 | 25 | 14 | 9 | 128 | 102 | 59 |
| Boston | 48 | 23 | 18 | 7 | 120 | 110 | 53 |
| NY Rangers | 48 | 19 | 20 | 9 | 117 | 106 | 47 |
| Chicago | 48 | 14 | 27 | 7 | 99 | 131 | 35 |

### Leading Scorers

| Player | Team | GP | G | A | PTS | PIM |
|---|---|---|---|---|---|---|
| Sweeney Schriner | NY Americans | 48 | 21 | 25 | 46 | 17 |
| Syl Apps | Toronto | 48 | 16 | 29 | 45 | 10 |
| Marty Barry | Detroit | 48 | 17 | 27 | 44 | 6 |
| Larry Aurie | Detroit | 45 | 23 | 20 | 43 | 20 |
| Busher Jackson | Toronto | 46 | 21 | 19 | 40 | 12 |
| Johnny Gagnon | Montreal | 48 | 20 | 16 | 36 | 38 |
| Bob Gracie | Mtl. Maroons | 47 | 11 | 25 | 36 | 18 |
| Nels Stewart | Bos., NYA | 43 | 23 | 12 | 35 | 37 |
| Paul Thompson | Chicago | 47 | 17 | 18 | 35 | 28 |
| Bill Cowley | Boston | 46 | 13 | 22 | 35 | 4 |

## 1937-38

### Canadian Division

| Team | GP | W | L | T | GF | GA | PTS |
|---|---|---|---|---|---|---|---|
| Toronto | 48 | 24 | 15 | 9 | 151 | 127 | 57 |
| NY Americans | 48 | 19 | 18 | 11 | 110 | 111 | 49 |
| Montreal | 48 | 18 | 17 | 13 | 123 | 128 | 49 |
| Mtl. Maroons | 48 | 12 | 30 | 6 | 101 | 149 | 30 |

### American Division

| Team | GP | W | L | T | GF | GA | PTS |
|---|---|---|---|---|---|---|---|
| Boston | 48 | 30 | 11 | 7 | 142 | 89 | 67 |
| NY Rangers | 48 | 27 | 15 | 6 | 149 | 96 | 60 |
| *Chicago | 48 | 14 | 25 | 9 | 97 | 139 | 37 |
| Detroit | 48 | 12 | 25 | 11 | 99 | 133 | 35 |

### Leading Scorers

| Player | Team | GP | G | A | PTS | PIM |
|---|---|---|---|---|---|---|
| Gordie Drillon | Toronto | 48 | 26 | 26 | 52 | 4 |
| Syl Apps | Toronto | 47 | 21 | 29 | 50 | 9 |
| Paul Thompson | Chicago | 48 | 22 | 22 | 44 | 14 |
| Georges Mantha | Montreal | 47 | 23 | 19 | 42 | 12 |
| Cecil Dillon | NY Rangers | 48 | 21 | 18 | 39 | 6 |
| Bill Cowley | Boston | 48 | 17 | 22 | 39 | 8 |
| Sweeney Schriner | NY Americans | 49 | 21 | 17 | 38 | 22 |
| Bill Thoms | Toronto | 48 | 14 | 24 | 38 | 14 |
| Clint Smith | NY Rangers | 48 | 14 | 23 | 37 | 0 |
| Nels Stewart | NY Americans | 48 | 19 | 17 | 36 | 29 |
| Neil Colville | NY Rangers | 45 | 17 | 19 | 36 | 11 |

## 1938-39

| Team | GP | W | L | T | GF | GA | PTS |
|---|---|---|---|---|---|---|---|
| *Boston | 48 | 36 | 10 | 2 | 156 | 76 | 74 |
| NY Rangers | 48 | 26 | 16 | 6 | 149 | 105 | 58 |
| Toronto | 48 | 19 | 20 | 9 | 114 | 107 | 47 |
| NY Americans | 48 | 17 | 21 | 10 | 119 | 157 | 44 |
| Detroit | 48 | 18 | 24 | 6 | 107 | 128 | 42 |
| Montreal | 48 | 15 | 24 | 9 | 115 | 146 | 39 |
| Chicago | 48 | 12 | 28 | 8 | 91 | 132 | 32 |

### Leading Scorers

| Player | Team | GP | G | A | PTS | PIM |
|---|---|---|---|---|---|---|
| Toe Blake | Montreal | 48 | 24 | 23 | 47 | 10 |
| Sweeney Schriner | NY Americans | 48 | 13 | 31 | 44 | 20 |
| Bill Cowley | Boston | 34 | 8 | 34 | 42 | 2 |
| Clint Smith | NY Rangers | 48 | 21 | 20 | 41 | 2 |
| Marty Barry | Detroit | 48 | 13 | 28 | 41 | 4 |
| Syl Apps | Toronto | 44 | 15 | 25 | 40 | 4 |
| Tom Anderson | NY Americans | 48 | 13 | 27 | 40 | 14 |
| Johnny Gottselig | Chicago | 48 | 16 | 23 | 39 | 15 |
| Paul Haynes | Montreal | 47 | 5 | 33 | 38 | 27 |
| Roy Conacher | Boston | 47 | 26 | 11 | 37 | 12 |
| Lorne Carr | NY Americans | 46 | 19 | 18 | 37 | 16 |
| Neil Colville | NY Rangers | 48 | 18 | 19 | 37 | 12 |
| Phil Watson | NY Rangers | 48 | 15 | 22 | 37 | 42 |

## 1939-40

| Team | GP | W | L | T | GF | GA | PTS |
|---|---|---|---|---|---|---|---|
| Boston | 48 | 31 | 12 | 5 | 170 | 98 | 67 |
| *NY Rangers | 48 | 27 | 11 | 10 | 136 | 77 | 64 |
| Toronto | 48 | 25 | 17 | 6 | 134 | 110 | 56 |
| Chicago | 48 | 23 | 19 | 6 | 112 | 120 | 52 |
| Detroit | 48 | 16 | 26 | 6 | 91 | 126 | 38 |
| NY Americans | 48 | 15 | 29 | 4 | 106 | 140 | 34 |
| Montreal | 48 | 10 | 33 | 5 | 90 | 168 | 25 |

### Leading Scorers

| Player | Team | GP | G | A | PTS | PIM |
|---|---|---|---|---|---|---|
| Milt Schmidt | Boston | 48 | 22 | 30 | 52 | 37 |
| Woody Dumart | Boston | 48 | 22 | 21 | 43 | 16 |
| Bobby Bauer | Boston | 48 | 17 | 26 | 43 | 2 |
| Gordie Drillon | Toronto | 43 | 21 | 19 | 40 | 13 |
| Bill Cowley | Boston | 48 | 13 | 27 | 40 | 24 |
| Bryan Hextall | NY Rangers | 48 | 24 | 15 | 39 | 52 |
| Neil Colville | NY Rangers | 48 | 19 | 19 | 38 | 22 |
| Syd Howe | Detroit | 46 | 14 | 23 | 37 | 17 |
| Toe Blake | Montreal | 48 | 17 | 19 | 36 | 48 |
| Murray Armstrong | NY Americans | 48 | 16 | 20 | 36 | 12 |

## 1940-41

| Team | GP | W | L | T | GF | GA | PTS |
|---|---|---|---|---|---|---|---|
| *Boston | 48 | 27 | 8 | 13 | 168 | 102 | 67 |
| Toronto | 48 | 28 | 14 | 6 | 145 | 99 | 62 |
| Detroit | 48 | 21 | 16 | 11 | 112 | 102 | 53 |
| NY Rangers | 48 | 21 | 19 | 8 | 143 | 125 | 50 |
| Chicago | 48 | 16 | 25 | 7 | 112 | 139 | 39 |
| Montreal | 48 | 16 | 26 | 6 | 121 | 147 | 38 |
| NY Americans | 48 | 8 | 29 | 11 | 99 | 186 | 27 |

### Leading Scorers

| Player | Team | GP | G | A | PTS | PIM |
|---|---|---|---|---|---|---|
| Bill Cowley | Boston | 46 | 17 | 45 | 62 | 16 |
| Bryan Hextall | NY Rangers | 48 | 26 | 18 | 44 | 16 |
| Gordie Drillon | Toronto | 42 | 23 | 21 | 44 | 2 |
| Syl Apps | Toronto | 41 | 20 | 24 | 44 | 6 |
| Lynn Patrick | NY Rangers | 48 | 20 | 24 | 44 | 12 |
| Syd Howe | Detroit | 48 | 20 | 24 | 44 | 8 |
| Neil Colville | NY Rangers | 48 | 14 | 28 | 42 | 28 |
| Eddie Wiseman | Boston | 48 | 16 | 24 | 40 | 10 |
| Bobby Bauer | Boston | 48 | 17 | 22 | 39 | 2 |
| Sweeney Schriner | Toronto | 48 | 24 | 14 | 38 | 6 |
| Roy Conacher | Boston | 40 | 24 | 14 | 38 | 7 |
| Milt Schmidt | Boston | 44 | 13 | 25 | 38 | 23 |

## 1941-42

| Team | GP | W | L | T | GF | GA | PTS |
|---|---|---|---|---|---|---|---|
| NY Rangers | 48 | 29 | 17 | 2 | 177 | 143 | 60 |
| *Toronto | 48 | 27 | 18 | 3 | 158 | 136 | 57 |
| Boston | 48 | 25 | 17 | 6 | 160 | 118 | 56 |
| Chicago | 48 | 22 | 23 | 3 | 145 | 155 | 47 |
| Detroit | 48 | 19 | 25 | 4 | 140 | 147 | 42 |
| Montreal | 48 | 18 | 27 | 3 | 134 | 173 | 39 |
| Brooklyn | 48 | 16 | 29 | 3 | 133 | 175 | 35 |

### Leading Scorers

| Player | Team | GP | G | A | PTS | PIM |
|---|---|---|---|---|---|---|
| Bryan Hextall | NY Rangers | 48 | 24 | 32 | 56 | 30 |
| Lynn Patrick | NY Rangers | 47 | 32 | 22 | 54 | 18 |
| Don Grosso | Detroit | 48 | 23 | 30 | 53 | 13 |
| Phil Watson | NY Rangers | 48 | 15 | 37 | 52 | 48 |
| Sid Abel | Detroit | 48 | 18 | 31 | 49 | 45 |
| Toe Blake | Montreal | 47 | 17 | 28 | 45 | 19 |
| Bill Thoms | Chicago | 47 | 15 | 30 | 45 | 8 |
| Gordie Drillon | Toronto | 48 | 23 | 18 | 41 | 6 |
| Syl Apps | Toronto | 38 | 18 | 23 | 41 | 0 |
| Tom Anderson | Brooklyn | 48 | 12 | 29 | 41 | 54 |

## 1942-43

| Team | GP | W | L | T | GF | GA | PTS |
|---|---|---|---|---|---|---|---|
| *Detroit | 50 | 25 | 14 | 11 | 169 | 124 | 61 |
| Boston | 50 | 24 | 17 | 9 | 195 | 176 | 57 |
| Toronto | 50 | 22 | 19 | 9 | 198 | 159 | 53 |
| Montreal | 50 | 19 | 19 | 12 | 181 | 191 | 50 |
| Chicago | 50 | 17 | 18 | 15 | 179 | 180 | 49 |
| NY Rangers | 50 | 11 | 31 | 8 | 161 | 253 | 30 |

### Leading Scorers

| Player | Team | GP | G | A | PTS | PIM |
|---|---|---|---|---|---|---|
| Doug Bentley | Chicago | 50 | 33 | 40 | 73 | 18 |
| Bill Cowley | Boston | 48 | 27 | 45 | 72 | 10 |
| Max Bentley | Chicago | 47 | 26 | 44 | 70 | 2 |
| Lynn Patrick | NY Rangers | 50 | 22 | 39 | 61 | 28 |
| Lorne Carr | Toronto | 50 | 27 | 33 | 60 | 15 |
| Billy Taylor | Toronto | 50 | 18 | 42 | 60 | 2 |
| Bryan Hextall | NY Rangers | 50 | 27 | 32 | 59 | 28 |
| Toe Blake | Montreal | 48 | 23 | 36 | 59 | 28 |
| Elmer Lach | Montreal | 45 | 18 | 40 | 58 | 14 |
| Buddy O'Connor | Montreal | 50 | 15 | 43 | 58 | 2 |

## 1943-44

| Team | GP | W | L | T | GF | GA | PTS |
|---|---|---|---|---|---|---|---|
| *Montreal | 50 | 38 | 5 | 7 | 234 | 109 | 83 |
| Detroit | 50 | 26 | 18 | 6 | 214 | 177 | 58 |
| Toronto | 50 | 23 | 23 | 4 | 214 | 174 | 50 |
| Chicago | 50 | 22 | 23 | 5 | 178 | 187 | 49 |
| Boston | 50 | 19 | 26 | 5 | 223 | 268 | 43 |
| NY Rangers | 50 | 6 | 39 | 5 | 162 | 310 | 17 |

### Leading Scorers

| Player | Team | GP | G | A | PTS | PIM |
|---|---|---|---|---|---|---|
| Herb Cain | Boston | 48 | 36 | 46 | 82 | 4 |
| Doug Bentley | Chicago | 50 | 38 | 39 | 77 | 22 |
| Lorne Carr | Toronto | 50 | 36 | 38 | 74 | 9 |
| Carl Liscombe | Detroit | 50 | 36 | 37 | 73 | 17 |
| Elmer Lach | Montreal | 48 | 24 | 48 | 72 | 23 |
| Clint Smith | Chicago | 50 | 23 | 49 | 72 | 4 |
| Bill Cowley | Boston | 36 | 30 | 41 | 71 | 12 |
| Bill Mosienko | Chicago | 50 | 32 | 38 | 70 | 10 |
| Art Jackson | Boston | 49 | 28 | 41 | 69 | 8 |
| Gus Bodnar | Toronto | 50 | 22 | 40 | 62 | 18 |

## 1944-45

| Team | GP | W | L | T | GF | GA | PTS |
|---|---|---|---|---|---|---|---|
| Montreal | 50 | 38 | 8 | 4 | 228 | 121 | 80 |
| Detroit | 50 | 31 | 14 | 5 | 218 | 161 | 67 |
| *Toronto | 50 | 24 | 22 | 4 | 183 | 161 | 52 |
| Boston | 50 | 16 | 30 | 4 | 179 | 219 | 36 |
| Chicago | 50 | 13 | 30 | 7 | 141 | 194 | 33 |
| NY Rangers | 50 | 11 | 29 | 10 | 154 | 247 | 32 |

### Leading Scorers

| Player | Team | GP | G | A | PTS | PIM |
|---|---|---|---|---|---|---|
| Elmer Lach | Montreal | 50 | 26 | 54 | 80 | 37 |
| Maurice Richard | Montreal | 50 | 50 | 23 | 73 | 36 |
| Toe Blake | Montreal | 49 | 29 | 38 | 67 | 15 |
| Bill Cowley | Boston | 49 | 25 | 40 | 65 | 2 |
| Ted Kennedy | Toronto | 49 | 29 | 25 | 54 | 14 |
| Bill Mosienko | Chicago | 50 | 28 | 26 | 54 | 0 |
| Joe Carveth | Detroit | 50 | 26 | 28 | 54 | 6 |
| Ab DeMarco | NY Rangers | 50 | 24 | 30 | 54 | 10 |
| Clint Smith | Chicago | 50 | 23 | 31 | 54 | 0 |
| Syd Howe | Detroit | 46 | 17 | 36 | 53 | 6 |

## 1945-46

| Team | GP | W | L | T | GF | GA | PTS |
|---|---|---|---|---|---|---|---|
| *Montreal | 50 | 28 | 17 | 5 | 172 | 134 | 61 |
| Boston | 50 | 24 | 18 | 8 | 167 | 156 | 56 |
| Chicago | 50 | 23 | 20 | 7 | 200 | 178 | 53 |
| Detroit | 50 | 20 | 20 | 10 | 146 | 159 | 50 |
| Toronto | 50 | 19 | 24 | 7 | 174 | 185 | 45 |
| NY Rangers | 50 | 13 | 28 | 9 | 144 | 191 | 35 |

### Leading Scorers

| Player | Team | GP | G | A | PTS | PIM |
|---|---|---|---|---|---|---|
| Max Bentley | Chicago | 47 | 31 | 30 | 61 | 6 |
| Gaye Stewart | Toronto | 50 | 37 | 15 | 52 | 8 |
| Toe Blake | Montreal | 50 | 29 | 21 | 50 | 2 |
| Clint Smith | Chicago | 50 | 26 | 24 | 50 | 2 |
| Maurice Richard | Montreal | 50 | 27 | 21 | 48 | 50 |
| Bill Mosienko | Chicago | 40 | 18 | 30 | 48 | 12 |
| Ab DeMarco | NY Rangers | 50 | 20 | 27 | 47 | 20 |
| Elmer Lach | Montreal | 50 | 13 | 34 | 47 | 34 |
| Alex Kaleta | Chicago | 49 | 19 | 27 | 46 | 17 |
| Billy Taylor | Toronto | 48 | 23 | 18 | 41 | 14 |
| Pete Horeck | Chicago | 50 | 20 | 21 | 41 | 34 |

## 1946-47

| Team | GP | W | L | T | GF | GA | PTS |
|---|---|---|---|---|---|---|---|
| Montreal | 60 | 34 | 16 | 10 | 189 | 138 | 78 |
| *Toronto | 60 | 31 | 19 | 10 | 209 | 172 | 72 |
| Boston | 60 | 26 | 23 | 11 | 190 | 175 | 63 |
| Detroit | 60 | 22 | 27 | 11 | 190 | 193 | 55 |
| NY Rangers | 60 | 22 | 32 | 6 | 167 | 186 | 50 |
| Chicago | 60 | 19 | 37 | 4 | 193 | 274 | 42 |

### Leading Scorers

| Player | Team | GP | G | A | PTS | PIM |
|---|---|---|---|---|---|---|
| Max Bentley | Chicago | 60 | 29 | 43 | 72 | 12 |
| Maurice Richard | Montreal | 60 | 45 | 26 | 71 | 69 |
| Billy Taylor | Detroit | 60 | 17 | 46 | 63 | 35 |
| Milt Schmidt | Boston | 59 | 27 | 35 | 62 | 40 |
| Ted Kennedy | Toronto | 60 | 28 | 32 | 60 | 27 |
| Doug Bentley | Chicago | 52 | 21 | 34 | 55 | 18 |
| Bobby Bauer | Boston | 58 | 30 | 24 | 54 | 4 |
| Roy Conacher | Detroit | 60 | 30 | 24 | 54 | 6 |
| Bill Mosienko | Chicago | 59 | 25 | 27 | 52 | 2 |
| Woody Dumart | Boston | 60 | 24 | 28 | 52 | 12 |

## 1947-48

| Team | GP | W | L | T | GF | GA | PTS |
|---|---|---|---|---|---|---|---|
| *Toronto | 60 | 32 | 15 | 13 | 182 | 143 | 77 |
| Detroit | 60 | 30 | 18 | 12 | 187 | 148 | 72 |
| Boston | 60 | 23 | 24 | 13 | 167 | 168 | 59 |
| NY Rangers | 60 | 21 | 26 | 13 | 176 | 201 | 55 |
| Montreal | 60 | 20 | 29 | 11 | 147 | 169 | 51 |
| Chicago | 60 | 20 | 34 | 6 | 195 | 225 | 46 |

### Leading Scorers

| Player | Team | GP | G | A | PTS | PIM |
|---|---|---|---|---|---|---|
| Elmer Lach | Montreal | 60 | 30 | 31 | 61 | 72 |
| Buddy O'Connor | NY Rangers | 60 | 24 | 36 | 60 | 8 |
| Doug Bentley | Chicago | 60 | 20 | 37 | 57 | 16 |
| Gaye Stewart | Tor., Chi. | 61 | 27 | 29 | 56 | 83 |
| Max Bentley | Chi., Tor. | 59 | 26 | 28 | 54 | 14 |
| Bud Poile | Tor., Chi. | 58 | 25 | 29 | 54 | 17 |
| Maurice Richard | Montreal | 53 | 28 | 25 | 53 | 89 |
| Syl Apps | Toronto | 55 | 26 | 27 | 53 | 12 |
| Ted Lindsay | Detroit | 60 | 33 | 19 | 52 | 95 |
| Roy Conacher | Chicago | 52 | 22 | 27 | 49 | 4 |

## 1948-49

| Team | GP | W | L | T | GF | GA | PTS |
|---|---|---|---|---|---|---|---|
| Detroit | 60 | 34 | 19 | 7 | 195 | 145 | 75 |
| Boston | 60 | 29 | 23 | 8 | 178 | 163 | 66 |
| Montreal | 60 | 28 | 23 | 9 | 152 | 126 | 65 |
| *Toronto | 60 | 22 | 25 | 13 | 147 | 161 | 57 |
| Chicago | 60 | 21 | 31 | 8 | 173 | 211 | 50 |
| NY Rangers | 60 | 18 | 31 | 11 | 133 | 172 | 47 |

### Leading Scorers

| Player | Team | GP | G | A | PTS | PIM |
|---|---|---|---|---|---|---|
| Roy Conacher | Chicago | 60 | 26 | 42 | 68 | 8 |
| Doug Bentley | Chicago | 58 | 23 | 43 | 66 | 38 |
| Sid Abel | Detroit | 60 | 28 | 26 | 54 | 49 |
| Ted Lindsay | Detroit | 50 | 26 | 28 | 54 | 97 |
| Jim Conacher | Det., Chi. | 59 | 26 | 23 | 49 | 43 |
| Paul Ronty | Boston | 60 | 20 | 29 | 49 | 11 |
| Harry Watson | Toronto | 60 | 26 | 19 | 45 | 0 |
| Billy Reay | Montreal | 60 | 22 | 23 | 45 | 33 |
| Gus Bodnar | Chicago | 59 | 19 | 26 | 45 | 14 |
| Johnny Peirson | Boston | 59 | 22 | 21 | 43 | 45 |

## 1949-50

| Team | GP | W | L | T | GF | GA | PTS |
|---|---|---|---|---|---|---|---|
| *Detroit | 70 | 37 | 19 | 14 | 229 | 164 | 88 |
| Montreal | 70 | 29 | 22 | 19 | 172 | 150 | 77 |
| Toronto | 70 | 31 | 27 | 12 | 176 | 173 | 74 |
| NY Rangers | 70 | 28 | 31 | 11 | 170 | 189 | 67 |
| Boston | 70 | 22 | 32 | 16 | 198 | 228 | 60 |
| Chicago | 70 | 22 | 38 | 10 | 203 | 244 | 54 |

### Leading Scorers

| Player | Team | GP | G | A | PTS | PIM |
|---|---|---|---|---|---|---|
| Ted Lindsay | Detroit | 69 | 23 | 55 | 78 | 141 |
| Sid Abel | Detroit | 69 | 34 | 35 | 69 | 46 |
| Gordie Howe | Detroit | 70 | 35 | 33 | 68 | 69 |
| Maurice Richard | Montreal | 70 | 43 | 22 | 65 | 114 |
| Paul Ronty | Boston | 70 | 23 | 36 | 59 | 8 |
| Roy Conacher | Chicago | 70 | 25 | 31 | 56 | 16 |
| Doug Bentley | Chicago | 64 | 20 | 33 | 53 | 28 |
| Johnny Peirson | Boston | 57 | 27 | 25 | 52 | 49 |
| Metro Prystai | Chicago | 65 | 29 | 22 | 51 | 31 |
| Bep Guidolin | Chicago | 70 | 17 | 34 | 51 | 42 |

## 1950-51

| Team | GP | W | L | T | GF | GA | PTS |
|---|---|---|---|---|---|---|---|
| Detroit | 70 | 44 | 13 | 13 | 236 | 139 | 101 |
| *Toronto | 70 | 41 | 16 | 13 | 212 | 138 | 95 |
| Montreal | 70 | 25 | 30 | 15 | 173 | 184 | 65 |
| Boston | 70 | 22 | 30 | 18 | 178 | 197 | 62 |
| NY Rangers | 70 | 20 | 29 | 21 | 169 | 201 | 61 |
| Chicago | 70 | 13 | 47 | 10 | 171 | 280 | 36 |

### Leading Scorers

| Player | Team | GP | G | A | PTS | PIM |
|---|---|---|---|---|---|---|
| Gordie Howe | Detroit | 70 | 43 | 43 | 86 | 74 |
| Maurice Richard | Montreal | 65 | 42 | 24 | 66 | 97 |
| Max Bentley | Toronto | 67 | 21 | 41 | 62 | 34 |
| Sid Abel | Detroit | 69 | 23 | 38 | 61 | 30 |
| Milt Schmidt | Boston | 62 | 22 | 39 | 61 | 33 |
| Ted Kennedy | Toronto | 63 | 18 | 43 | 61 | 32 |
| Ted Lindsay | Detroit | 67 | 24 | 35 | 59 | 110 |
| Tod Sloan | Toronto | 70 | 31 | 25 | 56 | 105 |
| Red Kelly | Detroit | 70 | 17 | 37 | 54 | 24 |
| Sid Smith | Toronto | 70 | 30 | 21 | 51 | 10 |
| Cal Gardner | Toronto | 66 | 23 | 28 | 51 | 42 |

## 1951-52

| Team | GP | W | L | T | GF | GA | PTS |
|---|---|---|---|---|---|---|---|
| *Detroit | 70 | 44 | 14 | 12 | 215 | 133 | 100 |
| Montreal | 70 | 34 | 26 | 10 | 195 | 164 | 78 |
| Toronto | 70 | 29 | 25 | 16 | 168 | 157 | 74 |
| Boston | 70 | 25 | 29 | 16 | 162 | 176 | 66 |
| NY Rangers | 70 | 23 | 34 | 13 | 192 | 219 | 59 |
| Chicago | 70 | 17 | 44 | 9 | 158 | 241 | 43 |

### Leading Scorers

| Player | Team | GP | G | A | PTS | PIM |
|---|---|---|---|---|---|---|
| Gordie Howe | Detroit | 70 | 47 | 39 | 86 | 78 |
| Ted Lindsay | Detroit | 70 | 30 | 39 | 69 | 123 |
| Elmer Lach | Montreal | 70 | 15 | 50 | 65 | 36 |
| Don Raleigh | NY Rangers | 70 | 19 | 42 | 61 | 14 |
| Sid Smith | Toronto | 70 | 27 | 30 | 57 | 6 |
| Bernie Geoffrion | Montreal | 67 | 30 | 24 | 54 | 66 |
| Bill Mosienko | Chicago | 70 | 31 | 22 | 53 | 10 |
| Sid Abel | Detroit | 62 | 17 | 36 | 53 | 32 |
| Ted Kennedy | Toronto | 70 | 19 | 33 | 52 | 33 |
| Milt Schmidt | Boston | 69 | 21 | 29 | 50 | 57 |
| Johnny Peirson | Boston | 68 | 20 | 30 | 50 | 30 |

## 1952-53

| Team | GP | W | L | T | GF | GA | PTS |
|---|---|---|---|---|---|---|---|
| Detroit | 70 | 36 | 16 | 18 | 222 | 133 | 90 |
| *Montreal | 70 | 28 | 23 | 19 | 155 | 148 | 75 |
| Boston | 70 | 28 | 29 | 13 | 152 | 172 | 69 |
| Chicago | 70 | 27 | 28 | 15 | 169 | 175 | 69 |
| Toronto | 70 | 27 | 30 | 13 | 156 | 167 | 67 |
| NY Rangers | 70 | 17 | 37 | 16 | 152 | 211 | 50 |

### Leading Scorers

| Player | Team | GP | G | A | PTS | PIM |
|---|---|---|---|---|---|---|
| Gordie Howe | Detroit | 70 | 49 | 46 | 95 | 57 |
| Ted Lindsay | Detroit | 70 | 32 | 39 | 71 | 111 |
| Maurice Richard | Montreal | 70 | 28 | 33 | 61 | 112 |
| Wally Hergesheimer | NY Rangers | 70 | 30 | 29 | 59 | 10 |
| Alex Delvecchio | Detroit | 70 | 16 | 43 | 59 | 28 |
| Paul Ronty | NY Rangers | 70 | 16 | 38 | 54 | 20 |
| Metro Prystai | Detroit | 70 | 16 | 34 | 50 | 12 |
| Red Kelly | Detroit | 70 | 19 | 27 | 46 | 8 |
| Bert Olmstead | Montreal | 69 | 17 | 28 | 45 | 83 |
| Fleming Mackell | Boston | 65 | 27 | 17 | 44 | 63 |
| Jim McFadden | Chicago | 70 | 23 | 21 | 44 | 29 |

## 1953-54

| Team | GP | W | L | T | GF | GA | PTS |
|---|---|---|---|---|---|---|---|
| *Detroit | 70 | 37 | 19 | 14 | 191 | 132 | 88 |
| Montreal | 70 | 35 | 24 | 11 | 195 | 141 | 81 |
| Toronto | 70 | 32 | 24 | 14 | 152 | 131 | 78 |
| Boston | 70 | 32 | 28 | 10 | 177 | 181 | 74 |
| NY Rangers | 70 | 29 | 31 | 10 | 161 | 182 | 68 |
| Chicago | 70 | 12 | 51 | 7 | 133 | 242 | 31 |

### Leading Scorers

| Player | Team | GP | G | A | PTS | PIM |
|---|---|---|---|---|---|---|
| Gordie Howe | Detroit | 70 | 33 | 48 | 81 | 109 |
| Maurice Richard | Montreal | 70 | 37 | 30 | 67 | 112 |
| Ted Lindsay | Detroit | 70 | 26 | 36 | 62 | 110 |
| Bernie Geoffrion | Montreal | 54 | 29 | 25 | 54 | 87 |
| Bert Olmstead | Montreal | 70 | 15 | 37 | 52 | 85 |
| Red Kelly | Detroit | 62 | 16 | 33 | 49 | 18 |
| Dutch Reibel | Detroit | 69 | 15 | 33 | 48 | 18 |
| Ed Sandford | Boston | 70 | 16 | 31 | 47 | 42 |
| Fleming Mackell | Boston | 67 | 15 | 32 | 47 | 60 |
| Ken Mosdell | Montreal | 67 | 22 | 24 | 46 | 64 |
| Paul Ronty | NY Rangers | 70 | 13 | 33 | 46 | 18 |

## 1954-55

| Team | GP | W | L | T | GF | GA | PTS |
|---|---|---|---|---|---|---|---|
| *Detroit | 70 | 42 | 17 | 11 | 204 | 134 | 95 |
| Montreal | 70 | 41 | 18 | 11 | 228 | 157 | 93 |
| Toronto | 70 | 24 | 24 | 22 | 147 | 135 | 70 |
| Boston | 70 | 23 | 26 | 21 | 169 | 188 | 67 |
| NY Rangers | 70 | 17 | 35 | 18 | 150 | 210 | 52 |
| Chicago | 70 | 13 | 40 | 17 | 161 | 235 | 43 |

### Leading Scorers

| Player | Team | GP | G | A | PTS | PIM |
|---|---|---|---|---|---|---|
| Bernie Geoffrion | Montreal | 70 | 38 | 37 | 75 | 57 |
| Maurice Richard | Montreal | 67 | 38 | 36 | 74 | 125 |
| Jean Béliveau | Montreal | 70 | 37 | 36 | 73 | 58 |
| Dutch Reibel | Detroit | 70 | 25 | 41 | 66 | 15 |
| Gordie Howe | Detroit | 64 | 29 | 33 | 62 | 68 |
| Red Sullivan | Chicago | 69 | 19 | 42 | 61 | 51 |
| Bert Olmstead | Montreal | 70 | 10 | 48 | 58 | 103 |
| Sid Smith | Toronto | 70 | 33 | 21 | 54 | 14 |
| Ken Mosdell | Montreal | 70 | 22 | 32 | 54 | 82 |
| Danny Lewicki | NY Rangers | 70 | 29 | 24 | 53 | 8 |

## 1955-56

| Team | GP | W | L | T | GF | GA | PTS |
|---|---|---|---|---|---|---|---|
| *Montreal | 70 | 45 | 15 | 10 | 222 | 131 | 100 |
| Detroit | 70 | 30 | 24 | 16 | 183 | 148 | 76 |
| NY Rangers | 70 | 32 | 28 | 10 | 204 | 203 | 74 |
| Toronto | 70 | 24 | 33 | 13 | 153 | 181 | 61 |
| Boston | 70 | 23 | 34 | 13 | 147 | 185 | 59 |
| Chicago | 70 | 19 | 39 | 12 | 155 | 216 | 50 |

### Leading Scorers

| Player | Team | GP | G | A | PTS | PIM |
|---|---|---|---|---|---|---|
| Jean Béliveau | Montreal | 70 | 47 | 41 | 88 | 143 |
| Gordie Howe | Detroit | 70 | 38 | 41 | 79 | 100 |
| Maurice Richard | Montreal | 70 | 38 | 33 | 71 | 89 |
| Bert Olmstead | Montreal | 70 | 14 | 56 | 70 | 94 |
| Tod Sloan | Toronto | 70 | 37 | 29 | 66 | 100 |
| Andy Bathgate | NY Rangers | 70 | 19 | 47 | 66 | 59 |
| Bernie Geoffrion | Montreal | 59 | 29 | 33 | 62 | 66 |
| Dutch Reibel | Detroit | 68 | 17 | 39 | 56 | 10 |
| Alex Delvecchio | Detroit | 70 | 25 | 26 | 51 | 24 |
| Dave Creighton | NY Rangers | 70 | 20 | 31 | 51 | 43 |
| Bill Gadsby | NY Rangers | 70 | 9 | 42 | 51 | 84 |

## 1956-57

| Team | GP | W | L | T | GF | GA | PTS |
|---|---|---|---|---|---|---|---|
| Detroit | 70 | 38 | 20 | 12 | 198 | 157 | 88 |
| *Montreal | 70 | 35 | 23 | 12 | 210 | 155 | 82 |
| Boston | 70 | 34 | 24 | 12 | 195 | 174 | 80 |
| NY Rangers | 70 | 26 | 30 | 14 | 184 | 227 | 66 |
| Toronto | 70 | 21 | 34 | 15 | 174 | 192 | 57 |
| Chicago | 70 | 16 | 39 | 15 | 169 | 225 | 47 |

### Leading Scorers

| Player | Team | GP | G | A | PTS | PIM |
|---|---|---|---|---|---|---|
| Gordie Howe | Detroit | 70 | 44 | 45 | 89 | 72 |
| Ted Lindsay | Detroit | 70 | 30 | 55 | 85 | 103 |
| Jean Béliveau | Montreal | 69 | 33 | 51 | 84 | 105 |
| Andy Bathgate | NY Rangers | 70 | 27 | 50 | 77 | 60 |
| Ed Litzenberger | Chicago | 70 | 32 | 32 | 64 | 48 |
| Maurice Richard | Montreal | 63 | 33 | 29 | 62 | 74 |
| Don McKenney | Boston | 69 | 21 | 39 | 60 | 31 |
| Dickie Moore | Montreal | 70 | 29 | 29 | 58 | 56 |
| Henri Richard | Montreal | 63 | 18 | 36 | 54 | 71 |
| Norm Ullman | Detroit | 64 | 16 | 36 | 52 | 47 |

## 1957-58

| Team | GP | W | L | T | GF | GA | PTS |
|---|---|---|---|---|---|---|---|
| *Montreal | 70 | 43 | 17 | 10 | 250 | 158 | 96 |
| NY Rangers | 70 | 32 | 25 | 13 | 195 | 188 | 77 |
| Detroit | 70 | 29 | 29 | 12 | 176 | 207 | 70 |
| Boston | 70 | 27 | 28 | 15 | 199 | 194 | 69 |
| Chicago | 70 | 24 | 39 | 7 | 163 | 202 | 55 |
| Toronto | 70 | 21 | 38 | 11 | 192 | 226 | 53 |

### Leading Scorers

| Player | Team | GP | G | A | PTS | PIM |
|---|---|---|---|---|---|---|
| Dickie Moore | Montreal | 70 | 36 | 48 | 84 | 65 |
| Henri Richard | Montreal | 67 | 28 | 52 | 80 | 56 |
| Andy Bathgate | NY Rangers | 65 | 30 | 48 | 78 | 42 |
| Gordie Howe | Detroit | 64 | 33 | 44 | 77 | 40 |
| Bronco Horvath | Boston | 67 | 30 | 36 | 66 | 71 |
| Ed Litzenberger | Chicago | 70 | 32 | 30 | 62 | 63 |
| Fleming Mackell | Boston | 70 | 20 | 40 | 60 | 72 |
| Jean Béliveau | Montreal | 55 | 27 | 32 | 59 | 93 |
| Alex Delvecchio | Detroit | 70 | 21 | 38 | 59 | 22 |
| Don McKenney | Boston | 70 | 28 | 30 | 58 | 22 |

## 1958-59

| Team | GP | W | L | T | GF | GA | PTS |
|---|---|---|---|---|---|---|---|
| *Montreal | 70 | 39 | 18 | 13 | 258 | 158 | 91 |
| Boston | 70 | 32 | 29 | 9 | 205 | 215 | 73 |
| Chicago | 70 | 28 | 29 | 13 | 197 | 208 | 69 |
| Toronto | 70 | 27 | 32 | 11 | 189 | 201 | 65 |
| NY Rangers | 70 | 26 | 32 | 12 | 201 | 217 | 64 |
| Detroit | 70 | 25 | 37 | 8 | 167 | 218 | 58 |

### Leading Scorers

| Player | Team | GP | G | A | PTS | PIM |
|---|---|---|---|---|---|---|
| Dickie Moore | Montreal | 70 | 41 | 55 | 96 | 61 |
| Jean Béliveau | Montreal | 64 | 45 | 46 | 91 | 67 |
| Andy Bathgate | NY Rangers | 70 | 40 | 48 | 88 | 48 |
| Gordie Howe | Detroit | 70 | 32 | 46 | 78 | 57 |
| Ed Litzenberger | Chicago | 70 | 33 | 44 | 77 | 37 |
| Bernie Geoffrion | Montreal | 59 | 22 | 44 | 66 | 30 |
| Red Sullivan | NY Rangers | 70 | 21 | 42 | 63 | 56 |
| Andy Hebenton | NY Rangers | 70 | 33 | 29 | 62 | 8 |
| Don McKenney | Boston | 70 | 32 | 30 | 62 | 20 |
| Tod Sloan | Chicago | 59 | 27 | 35 | 62 | 79 |

## 1959-60

| Team | GP | W | L | T | GF | GA | PTS |
|---|---|---|---|---|---|---|---|
| *Montreal | 70 | 40 | 18 | 12 | 255 | 178 | 92 |
| Toronto | 70 | 35 | 26 | 9 | 199 | 195 | 79 |
| Chicago | 70 | 28 | 29 | 13 | 191 | 180 | 69 |
| Detroit | 70 | 26 | 29 | 15 | 186 | 197 | 67 |
| Boston | 70 | 28 | 34 | 8 | 220 | 241 | 64 |
| NY Rangers | 70 | 17 | 38 | 15 | 187 | 247 | 49 |

### Leading Scorers

| Player | Team | GP | G | A | PTS | PIM |
|---|---|---|---|---|---|---|
| Bobby Hull | Chicago | 70 | 39 | 42 | 81 | 68 |
| Bronco Horvath | Boston | 68 | 39 | 41 | 80 | 60 |
| Jean Béliveau | Montreal | 60 | 34 | 40 | 74 | 57 |
| Andy Bathgate | NY Rangers | 70 | 26 | 48 | 74 | 28 |
| Henri Richard | Montreal | 70 | 30 | 43 | 73 | 66 |
| Gordie Howe | Detroit | 70 | 28 | 45 | 73 | 46 |
| Bernie Geoffrion | Montreal | 59 | 30 | 41 | 71 | 36 |
| Don McKenney | Boston | 70 | 20 | 49 | 69 | 28 |
| Vic Stasiuk | Boston | 69 | 29 | 39 | 68 | 121 |
| Dean Prentice | NY Rangers | 70 | 32 | 34 | 66 | 43 |

## 1960-61

| Team | GP | W | L | T | GF | GA | PTS |
|---|---|---|---|---|---|---|---|
| Montreal | 70 | 41 | 19 | 10 | 254 | 188 | 92 |
| Toronto | 70 | 39 | 19 | 12 | 234 | 176 | 90 |
| *Chicago | 70 | 29 | 24 | 17 | 198 | 180 | 75 |
| Detroit | 70 | 25 | 29 | 16 | 195 | 215 | 66 |
| NY Rangers | 70 | 22 | 38 | 10 | 204 | 248 | 54 |
| Boston | 70 | 15 | 42 | 13 | 176 | 254 | 43 |

### Leading Scorers

| Player | Team | GP | G | A | PTS | PIM |
|---|---|---|---|---|---|---|
| Bernie Geoffrion | Montreal | 64 | 50 | 45 | 95 | 29 |
| Jean Béliveau | Montreal | 69 | 32 | 58 | 90 | 57 |
| Frank Mahovlich | Toronto | 70 | 48 | 36 | 84 | 131 |
| Andy Bathgate | NY Rangers | 70 | 29 | 48 | 77 | 22 |
| Gordie Howe | Detroit | 64 | 23 | 49 | 72 | 30 |
| Norm Ullman | Detroit | 70 | 28 | 42 | 70 | 34 |
| Red Kelly | Toronto | 64 | 20 | 50 | 70 | 12 |
| Dickie Moore | Montreal | 57 | 35 | 34 | 69 | 62 |
| Henri Richard | Montreal | 70 | 24 | 44 | 68 | 91 |
| Alex Delvecchio | Detroit | 70 | 27 | 35 | 62 | 26 |

## 1961-62

| Team | GP | W | L | T | GF | GA | PTS |
|---|---|---|---|---|---|---|---|
| Montreal | 70 | 42 | 14 | 14 | 259 | 166 | 98 |
| *Toronto | 70 | 37 | 22 | 11 | 232 | 180 | 85 |
| Chicago | 70 | 31 | 26 | 13 | 217 | 186 | 75 |
| NY Rangers | 70 | 26 | 32 | 12 | 195 | 207 | 64 |
| Detroit | 70 | 23 | 33 | 14 | 184 | 219 | 60 |
| Boston | 70 | 15 | 47 | 8 | 177 | 306 | 38 |

### Leading Scorers

| Player | Team | GP | G | A | PTS | PIM |
|---|---|---|---|---|---|---|
| Bobby Hull | Chicago | 70 | 50 | 34 | 84 | 35 |
| Andy Bathgate | NY Rangers | 70 | 28 | 56 | 84 | 44 |
| Gordie Howe | Detroit | 70 | 33 | 44 | 77 | 54 |
| Stan Mikita | Chicago | 70 | 25 | 52 | 77 | 97 |
| Frank Mahovlich | Toronto | 70 | 33 | 38 | 71 | 87 |
| Alex Delvecchio | Detroit | 70 | 26 | 43 | 69 | 18 |
| Ralph Backstrom | Montreal | 66 | 27 | 38 | 65 | 29 |
| Norm Ullman | Detroit | 70 | 26 | 38 | 64 | 54 |
| Bill Hay | Chicago | 60 | 11 | 52 | 63 | 34 |
| Claude Provost | Montreal | 70 | 33 | 29 | 62 | 22 |

## 1962-63

| Team | GP | W | L | T | GF | GA | PTS |
|---|---|---|---|---|---|---|---|
| *Toronto | 70 | 35 | 23 | 12 | 221 | 180 | 82 |
| Chicago | 70 | 32 | 21 | 17 | 194 | 178 | 81 |
| Montreal | 70 | 28 | 19 | 23 | 225 | 183 | 79 |
| Detroit | 70 | 32 | 25 | 13 | 200 | 194 | 77 |
| NY Rangers | 70 | 22 | 36 | 12 | 211 | 233 | 56 |
| Boston | 70 | 14 | 39 | 17 | 198 | 281 | 45 |

### Leading Scorers

| Player | Team | GP | G | A | PTS | PIM |
|---|---|---|---|---|---|---|
| Gordie Howe | Detroit | 70 | 38 | 48 | 86 | 100 |
| Andy Bathgate | NY Rangers | 70 | 35 | 46 | 81 | 54 |
| Stan Mikita | Chicago | 65 | 31 | 45 | 76 | 69 |
| Frank Mahovlich | Toronto | 67 | 36 | 37 | 73 | 56 |
| Henri Richard | Montreal | 67 | 23 | 50 | 73 | 57 |
| Jean Béliveau | Montreal | 69 | 18 | 49 | 67 | 68 |
| John Bucyk | Boston | 69 | 27 | 39 | 66 | 36 |
| Alex Delvecchio | Detroit | 70 | 20 | 44 | 64 | 8 |
| Bobby Hull | Chicago | 65 | 31 | 31 | 62 | 27 |
| Murray Oliver | Boston | 65 | 22 | 40 | 62 | 38 |

## 1963-64

| Team | GP | W | L | T | GF | GA | PTS |
|---|---|---|---|---|---|---|---|
| Montreal | 70 | 36 | 21 | 13 | 209 | 167 | 85 |
| Chicago | 70 | 36 | 22 | 12 | 218 | 169 | 84 |
| *Toronto | 70 | 33 | 25 | 12 | 192 | 172 | 78 |
| Detroit | 70 | 30 | 29 | 11 | 191 | 204 | 71 |
| NY Rangers | 70 | 22 | 38 | 10 | 186 | 242 | 54 |
| Boston | 70 | 18 | 40 | 12 | 170 | 212 | 48 |

### Leading Scorers

| Player | Team | GP | G | A | PTS | PIM |
|---|---|---|---|---|---|---|
| Stan Mikita | Chicago | 70 | 39 | 50 | 89 | 146 |
| Bobby Hull | Chicago | 70 | 43 | 44 | 87 | 50 |
| Jean Béliveau | Montreal | 68 | 28 | 50 | 78 | 42 |
| Andy Bathgate | NYR, Tor. | 71 | 19 | 58 | 77 | 34 |
| Gordie Howe | Detroit | 69 | 26 | 47 | 73 | 70 |
| Kenny Wharram | Chicago | 70 | 39 | 32 | 71 | 18 |
| Murray Oliver | Boston | 70 | 24 | 44 | 68 | 41 |
| Phil Goyette | NY Rangers | 67 | 24 | 41 | 65 | 15 |
| Rod Gilbert | NY Rangers | 70 | 24 | 40 | 64 | 62 |
| Dave Keon | Toronto | 70 | 23 | 37 | 60 | 6 |

## 1964-65

| Team | GP | W | L | T | GF | GA | PTS |
|---|---|---|---|---|---|---|---|
| Detroit | 70 | 40 | 23 | 7 | 224 | 175 | 87 |
| *Montreal | 70 | 36 | 23 | 11 | 211 | 185 | 83 |
| Chicago | 70 | 34 | 28 | 8 | 224 | 176 | 76 |
| Toronto | 70 | 30 | 26 | 14 | 204 | 173 | 74 |
| NY Rangers | 70 | 20 | 38 | 12 | 179 | 246 | 52 |
| Boston | 70 | 21 | 43 | 6 | 166 | 253 | 48 |

### Leading Scorers

| Player | Team | GP | G | A | PTS | PIM |
|---|---|---|---|---|---|---|
| Stan Mikita | Chicago | 70 | 28 | 59 | 87 | 154 |
| Norm Ullman | Detroit | 70 | 42 | 41 | 83 | 70 |
| Gordie Howe | Detroit | 70 | 29 | 47 | 76 | 104 |
| Bobby Hull | Chicago | 61 | 39 | 32 | 71 | 32 |
| Alex Delvecchio | Detroit | 68 | 25 | 42 | 67 | 16 |
| Claude Provost | Montreal | 70 | 27 | 37 | 64 | 28 |
| Rod Gilbert | NY Rangers | 70 | 25 | 36 | 61 | 52 |
| Pierre Pilote | Chicago | 68 | 14 | 45 | 59 | 162 |
| John Bucyk | Boston | 68 | 26 | 29 | 55 | 24 |
| Ralph Backstrom | Montreal | 70 | 25 | 30 | 55 | 41 |
| Phil Esposito | Chicago | 70 | 23 | 32 | 55 | 44 |

## 1965-66

| Team | GP | W | L | T | GF | GA | PTS |
|---|---|---|---|---|---|---|---|
| *Montreal | 70 | 41 | 21 | 8 | 239 | 173 | 90 |
| Chicago | 70 | 37 | 25 | 8 | 240 | 187 | 82 |
| Toronto | 70 | 34 | 25 | 11 | 208 | 187 | 79 |
| Detroit | 70 | 31 | 27 | 12 | 221 | 194 | 74 |
| Boston | 70 | 21 | 43 | 6 | 174 | 275 | 48 |
| NY Rangers | 70 | 18 | 41 | 11 | 195 | 261 | 47 |

### Leading Scorers

| Player | Team | GP | G | A | PTS | PIM |
|---|---|---|---|---|---|---|
| Bobby Hull | Chicago | 65 | 54 | 43 | 97 | 70 |
| Stan Mikita | Chicago | 68 | 30 | 48 | 78 | 58 |
| Bobby Rousseau | Montreal | 70 | 30 | 48 | 78 | 20 |
| Jean Béliveau | Montreal | 67 | 29 | 48 | 77 | 50 |
| Gordie Howe | Detroit | 70 | 29 | 46 | 75 | 83 |
| Norm Ullman | Detroit | 70 | 31 | 41 | 72 | 35 |
| Alex Delvecchio | Detroit | 70 | 31 | 38 | 69 | 16 |
| Bob Nevin | NY Rangers | 69 | 29 | 33 | 62 | 10 |
| Henri Richard | Montreal | 62 | 22 | 39 | 61 | 47 |
| Murray Oliver | Boston | 70 | 18 | 42 | 60 | 30 |

## 1966-67

| Team | GP | W | L | T | GF | GA | PTS |
|---|---|---|---|---|---|---|---|
| Chicago | 70 | 41 | 17 | 12 | 264 | 170 | 94 |
| Montreal | 70 | 32 | 25 | 13 | 202 | 188 | 77 |
| *Toronto | 70 | 32 | 27 | 11 | 204 | 211 | 75 |
| NY Rangers | 70 | 30 | 28 | 12 | 188 | 189 | 72 |
| Detroit | 70 | 27 | 39 | 4 | 212 | 241 | 58 |
| Boston | 70 | 17 | 43 | 10 | 182 | 253 | 44 |

### Leading Scorers

| Player | Team | GP | G | A | PTS | PIM |
|---|---|---|---|---|---|---|
| Stan Mikita | Chicago | 70 | 35 | 62 | 97 | 12 |
| Bobby Hull | Chicago | 66 | 52 | 28 | 80 | 52 |
| Norm Ullman | Detroit | 68 | 26 | 44 | 70 | 26 |
| Kenny Wharram | Chicago | 70 | 31 | 34 | 65 | 21 |
| Gordie Howe | Detroit | 69 | 25 | 40 | 65 | 53 |
| Bobby Rousseau | Montreal | 68 | 19 | 44 | 63 | 58 |
| Phil Esposito | Chicago | 69 | 21 | 40 | 61 | 40 |
| Phil Goyette | NY Rangers | 70 | 12 | 49 | 61 | 6 |
| Doug Mohns | Chicago | 61 | 25 | 35 | 60 | 58 |
| Henri Richard | Montreal | 65 | 21 | 34 | 55 | 28 |
| Alex Delvecchio | Detroit | 70 | 17 | 38 | 55 | 10 |

## 1967-68

### East Division

| Team | GP | W | L | T | GF | GA | PTS |
|---|---|---|---|---|---|---|---|
| *Montreal | 74 | 42 | 22 | 10 | 236 | 167 | 94 |
| NY Rangers | 74 | 39 | 23 | 12 | 226 | 183 | 90 |
| Boston | 74 | 37 | 27 | 10 | 259 | 216 | 84 |
| Chicago | 74 | 32 | 26 | 16 | 212 | 222 | 80 |
| Toronto | 74 | 33 | 31 | 10 | 209 | 176 | 76 |
| Detroit | 74 | 27 | 35 | 12 | 245 | 257 | 66 |

### West Division

| Team | GP | W | L | T | GF | GA | PTS |
|---|---|---|---|---|---|---|---|
| Philadelphia | 74 | 31 | 32 | 11 | 173 | 179 | 73 |
| Los Angeles | 74 | 31 | 33 | 10 | 200 | 224 | 72 |
| St. Louis | 74 | 27 | 31 | 16 | 177 | 191 | 70 |
| Minnesota | 74 | 27 | 32 | 15 | 191 | 226 | 69 |
| Pittsburgh | 74 | 27 | 34 | 13 | 195 | 216 | 67 |
| Oakland | 74 | 15 | 42 | 17 | 153 | 219 | 47 |

### Leading Scorers

| Player | Team | GP | G | A | PTS | PIM |
|---|---|---|---|---|---|---|
| Stan Mikita | Chicago | 72 | 40 | 47 | 87 | 14 |
| Phil Esposito | Boston | 74 | 35 | 49 | 84 | 21 |
| Gordie Howe | Detroit | 74 | 39 | 43 | 82 | 53 |
| Jean Ratelle | NY Rangers | 74 | 32 | 46 | 78 | 18 |
| Rod Gilbert | NY Rangers | 73 | 29 | 48 | 77 | 12 |
| Bobby Hull | Chicago | 71 | 44 | 31 | 75 | 39 |
| Norm Ullman | Det., Tor. | 71 | 35 | 37 | 72 | 28 |
| Alex Delvecchio | Detroit | 74 | 22 | 48 | 70 | 14 |
| John Bucyk | Boston | 72 | 30 | 39 | 69 | 8 |
| Kenny Wharram | Chicago | 74 | 27 | 42 | 69 | 18 |

## 1968-69

### East Division

| Team | GP | W | L | T | GF | GA | PTS |
|---|---|---|---|---|---|---|---|
| *Montreal | 76 | 46 | 19 | 11 | 271 | 202 | 103 |
| Boston | 76 | 42 | 18 | 16 | 303 | 221 | 100 |
| NY Rangers | 76 | 41 | 26 | 9 | 231 | 196 | 91 |
| Toronto | 76 | 35 | 26 | 15 | 234 | 217 | 85 |
| Detroit | 76 | 33 | 31 | 12 | 239 | 221 | 78 |
| Chicago | 76 | 34 | 33 | 9 | 280 | 246 | 77 |

### West Division

| Team | GP | W | L | T | GF | GA | PTS |
|---|---|---|---|---|---|---|---|
| St. Louis | 76 | 37 | 25 | 14 | 204 | 157 | 88 |
| Oakland | 76 | 29 | 36 | 11 | 219 | 251 | 69 |
| Philadelphia | 76 | 20 | 35 | 21 | 174 | 225 | 61 |
| Los Angeles | 76 | 24 | 42 | 10 | 185 | 260 | 58 |
| Pittsburgh | 76 | 20 | 45 | 11 | 189 | 252 | 51 |
| Minnesota | 76 | 18 | 43 | 15 | 189 | 270 | 51 |

### Leading Scorers

| Player | Team | GP | G | A | PTS | PIM |
|---|---|---|---|---|---|---|
| Phil Esposito | Boston | 74 | 49 | 77 | 126 | 79 |
| Bobby Hull | Chicago | 74 | 58 | 49 | 107 | 48 |
| Gordie Howe | Detroit | 76 | 44 | 59 | 103 | 58 |
| Stan Mikita | Chicago | 74 | 30 | 67 | 97 | 52 |
| Ken Hodge | Boston | 75 | 45 | 45 | 90 | 75 |
| Yvan Cournoyer | Montreal | 76 | 43 | 44 | 87 | 31 |
| Alex Delvecchio | Detroit | 72 | 25 | 58 | 83 | 8 |
| Red Berenson | St. Louis | 76 | 35 | 47 | 82 | 43 |
| Jean Béliveau | Montreal | 69 | 33 | 49 | 82 | 55 |
| Frank Mahovlich | Detroit | 76 | 49 | 29 | 78 | 38 |
| Jean Ratelle | NY Rangers | 75 | 32 | 46 | 78 | 26 |

## 1969-70

### East Division

| Team | GP | W | L | T | GF | GA | PTS |
|---|---|---|---|---|---|---|---|
| Chicago | 76 | 45 | 22 | 9 | 250 | 170 | 99 |
| *Boston | 76 | 40 | 17 | 19 | 277 | 216 | 99 |
| Detroit | 76 | 40 | 21 | 15 | 246 | 199 | 95 |
| NY Rangers | 76 | 38 | 22 | 16 | 246 | 189 | 92 |
| Montreal | 76 | 38 | 22 | 16 | 244 | 201 | 92 |
| Toronto | 76 | 29 | 34 | 13 | 222 | 242 | 71 |

### West Division

| Team | GP | W | L | T | GF | GA | PTS |
|---|---|---|---|---|---|---|---|
| St. Louis | 76 | 37 | 27 | 12 | 224 | 179 | 86 |
| Pittsburgh | 76 | 26 | 38 | 12 | 182 | 238 | 64 |
| Minnesota | 76 | 19 | 35 | 22 | 224 | 257 | 60 |
| Oakland | 76 | 22 | 40 | 14 | 169 | 243 | 58 |
| Philadelphia | 76 | 17 | 35 | 24 | 197 | 225 | 58 |
| Los Angeles | 76 | 14 | 52 | 10 | 168 | 290 | 38 |

### Leading Scorers

| Player | Team | GP | G | A | PTS | PIM |
|---|---|---|---|---|---|---|
| Bobby Orr | Boston | 76 | 33 | 87 | 120 | 125 |
| Phil Esposito | Boston | 76 | 43 | 56 | 99 | 50 |
| Stan Mikita | Chicago | 76 | 39 | 47 | 86 | 50 |
| Phil Goyette | St. Louis | 72 | 29 | 49 | 78 | 16 |
| Walt Tkaczuk | NY Rangers | 76 | 27 | 50 | 77 | 38 |
| Jean Ratelle | NY Rangers | 75 | 32 | 42 | 74 | 28 |
| Red Berenson | St. Louis | 67 | 33 | 39 | 72 | 38 |
| Jean-Paul Parise | Minnesota | 74 | 24 | 48 | 72 | 72 |
| Gordie Howe | Detroit | 76 | 31 | 40 | 71 | 58 |
| Frank Mahovlich | Detroit | 74 | 38 | 32 | 70 | 59 |
| Dave Balon | NY Rangers | 76 | 33 | 37 | 70 | 100 |
| John McKenzie | Boston | 72 | 29 | 41 | 70 | 114 |

## 1970-71

### East Division

| Team | GP | W | L | T | GF | GA | PTS |
|---|---|---|---|---|---|---|---|
| Boston | 78 | 57 | 14 | 7 | 399 | 207 | 121 |
| NY Rangers | 78 | 49 | 18 | 11 | 259 | 177 | 109 |
| *Montreal | 78 | 42 | 23 | 13 | 291 | 216 | 97 |
| Toronto | 78 | 37 | 33 | 8 | 248 | 211 | 82 |
| Buffalo | 78 | 24 | 39 | 15 | 217 | 291 | 63 |
| Vancouver | 78 | 24 | 46 | 8 | 229 | 296 | 56 |
| Detroit | 78 | 22 | 45 | 11 | 209 | 308 | 55 |

### West Division

| Team | GP | W | L | T | GF | GA | PTS |
|---|---|---|---|---|---|---|---|
| Chicago | 78 | 49 | 20 | 9 | 277 | 184 | 107 |
| St. Louis | 78 | 34 | 25 | 19 | 223 | 208 | 87 |
| Philadelphia | 78 | 28 | 33 | 17 | 207 | 225 | 73 |
| Minnesota | 78 | 28 | 34 | 16 | 191 | 223 | 72 |
| Los Angeles | 78 | 25 | 40 | 13 | 239 | 303 | 63 |
| Pittsburgh | 78 | 21 | 37 | 20 | 221 | 240 | 62 |
| California | 78 | 20 | 53 | 5 | 199 | 320 | 45 |

### Leading Scorers

| Player | Team | GP | G | A | PTS | PIM |
|---|---|---|---|---|---|---|
| Phil Esposito | Boston | 78 | 76 | 76 | 152 | 71 |
| Bobby Orr | Boston | 78 | 37 | 102 | 139 | 91 |
| John Bucyk | Boston | 78 | 51 | 65 | 116 | 8 |
| Ken Hodge | Boston | 78 | 43 | 62 | 105 | 113 |
| Bobby Hull | Chicago | 78 | 44 | 52 | 96 | 32 |
| Norm Ullman | Toronto | 73 | 34 | 51 | 85 | 24 |
| Wayne Cashman | Boston | 77 | 21 | 58 | 79 | 100 |
| John McKenzie | Boston | 65 | 31 | 46 | 77 | 120 |
| Dave Keon | Toronto | 76 | 38 | 38 | 76 | 4 |
| Jean Béliveau | Montreal | 70 | 25 | 51 | 76 | 40 |
| Fred Stanfield | Boston | 75 | 24 | 52 | 76 | 12 |

## 1971-72

### East Division

| Team | GP | W | L | T | GF | GA | PTS |
|---|---|---|---|---|---|---|---|
| *Boston | 78 | 54 | 13 | 11 | 330 | 204 | 119 |
| NY Rangers | 78 | 48 | 17 | 13 | 317 | 192 | 109 |
| Montreal | 78 | 46 | 16 | 16 | 307 | 205 | 108 |
| Toronto | 78 | 33 | 31 | 14 | 209 | 208 | 80 |
| Detroit | 78 | 33 | 35 | 10 | 261 | 262 | 76 |
| Buffalo | 78 | 16 | 43 | 19 | 203 | 289 | 51 |
| Vancouver | 78 | 20 | 50 | 8 | 203 | 297 | 48 |

### West Division

| Team | GP | W | L | T | GF | GA | PTS |
|---|---|---|---|---|---|---|---|
| Chicago | 78 | 46 | 17 | 15 | 256 | 166 | 107 |
| Minnesota | 78 | 37 | 29 | 12 | 212 | 191 | 86 |
| St. Louis | 78 | 28 | 39 | 11 | 208 | 247 | 67 |
| Pittsburgh | 78 | 26 | 38 | 14 | 220 | 258 | 66 |
| Philadelphia | 78 | 26 | 38 | 14 | 200 | 236 | 66 |
| California | 78 | 21 | 39 | 18 | 216 | 288 | 60 |
| Los Angeles | 78 | 20 | 49 | 9 | 206 | 305 | 49 |

### Leading Scorers

| Player | Team | GP | G | A | PTS | PIM |
|---|---|---|---|---|---|---|
| Phil Esposito | Boston | 76 | 66 | 67 | 133 | 76 |
| Bobby Orr | Boston | 76 | 37 | 80 | 117 | 106 |
| Jean Ratelle | NY Rangers | 63 | 46 | 63 | 109 | 4 |
| Vic Hadfield | NY Rangers | 78 | 50 | 56 | 106 | 142 |
| Rod Gilbert | NY Rangers | 73 | 43 | 54 | 97 | 64 |
| Frank Mahovlich | Montreal | 76 | 43 | 53 | 96 | 36 |
| Bobby Hull | Chicago | 78 | 50 | 43 | 93 | 24 |
| Yvan Cournoyer | Montreal | 73 | 47 | 36 | 83 | 15 |
| John Bucyk | Boston | 78 | 32 | 51 | 83 | 4 |
| Bobby Clarke | Philadelphia | 78 | 35 | 46 | 81 | 87 |
| Jacques Lemaire | Montreal | 77 | 32 | 49 | 81 | 26 |

## 1972-73

### East Division

| Team | GP | W | L | T | GF | GA | PTS |
|---|---|---|---|---|---|---|---|
| *Montreal | 78 | 52 | 10 | 16 | 329 | 184 | 120 |
| Boston | 78 | 51 | 22 | 5 | 330 | 235 | 107 |
| NY Rangers | 78 | 47 | 23 | 8 | 297 | 208 | 102 |
| Buffalo | 78 | 37 | 27 | 14 | 257 | 219 | 88 |
| Detroit | 78 | 37 | 29 | 12 | 265 | 243 | 86 |
| Toronto | 78 | 27 | 41 | 10 | 247 | 279 | 64 |
| Vancouver | 78 | 22 | 47 | 9 | 233 | 339 | 53 |
| NY Islanders | 78 | 12 | 60 | 6 | 170 | 347 | 30 |

### West Division

| Team | GP | W | L | T | GF | GA | PTS |
|---|---|---|---|---|---|---|---|
| Chicago | 78 | 42 | 27 | 9 | 284 | 225 | 93 |
| Philadelphia | 78 | 37 | 30 | 11 | 296 | 256 | 85 |
| Minnesota | 78 | 37 | 30 | 11 | 254 | 230 | 85 |
| St. Louis | 78 | 32 | 34 | 12 | 233 | 251 | 76 |
| Pittsburgh | 78 | 32 | 37 | 9 | 257 | 265 | 73 |
| Los Angeles | 78 | 31 | 36 | 11 | 232 | 245 | 73 |
| Atlanta | 78 | 25 | 38 | 15 | 191 | 239 | 65 |
| California | 78 | 16 | 46 | 16 | 213 | 323 | 48 |

### Leading Scorers

| Player | Team | GP | G | A | PTS | PIM |
|---|---|---|---|---|---|---|
| Phil Esposito | Boston | 78 | 55 | 75 | 130 | 87 |
| Bobby Clarke | Philadelphia | 78 | 37 | 67 | 104 | 80 |
| Bobby Orr | Boston | 63 | 29 | 72 | 101 | 99 |
| Rick MacLeish | Philadelphia | 78 | 50 | 50 | 100 | 69 |
| Jacques Lemaire | Montreal | 77 | 44 | 51 | 95 | 16 |
| Jean Ratelle | NY Rangers | 78 | 41 | 53 | 94 | 12 |
| Mickey Redmond | Detroit | 76 | 52 | 41 | 93 | 24 |
| John Bucyk | Boston | 78 | 40 | 53 | 93 | 12 |
| Frank Mahovlich | Montreal | 78 | 38 | 55 | 93 | 51 |
| Jim Pappin | Chicago | 76 | 41 | 51 | 92 | 82 |

*Tim Young of the Minnesota North Stars cracked the top 10 in scoring for the only time during his second NHL season with 95 points in 1976-77.*

## 1973-74

**East Division**

| Team | GP | W | L | T | GF | GA | PTS |
|---|---|---|---|---|---|---|---|
| Boston | 78 | 52 | 17 | 9 | 349 | 221 | 113 |
| Montreal | 78 | 45 | 24 | 9 | 293 | 240 | 99 |
| NY Rangers | 78 | 40 | 24 | 14 | 300 | 251 | 94 |
| Toronto | 78 | 35 | 27 | 16 | 274 | 230 | 86 |
| Buffalo | 78 | 32 | 34 | 12 | 242 | 250 | 76 |
| Detroit | 78 | 29 | 39 | 10 | 255 | 319 | 68 |
| Vancouver | 78 | 24 | 43 | 11 | 224 | 296 | 59 |
| NY Islanders | 78 | 19 | 41 | 18 | 182 | 247 | 56 |

**West Division**

| Team | GP | W | L | T | GF | GA | PTS |
|---|---|---|---|---|---|---|---|
| *Philadelphia | 78 | 50 | 16 | 12 | 273 | 164 | 112 |
| Chicago | 78 | 41 | 14 | 23 | 272 | 164 | 105 |
| Los Angeles | 78 | 33 | 33 | 12 | 233 | 231 | 78 |
| Atlanta | 78 | 30 | 34 | 14 | 214 | 238 | 74 |
| Pittsburgh | 78 | 28 | 41 | 9 | 242 | 273 | 65 |
| St. Louis | 78 | 26 | 40 | 12 | 206 | 248 | 64 |
| Minnesota | 78 | 23 | 38 | 17 | 235 | 275 | 63 |
| California | 78 | 13 | 55 | 10 | 195 | 342 | 36 |

### Leading Scorers

| Player | Team | GP | G | A | PTS | PIM |
|---|---|---|---|---|---|---|
| Phil Esposito | Boston | 78 | 68 | 77 | 145 | 58 |
| Bobby Orr | Boston | 74 | 32 | 90 | 122 | 82 |
| Ken Hodge | Boston | 76 | 50 | 55 | 105 | 43 |
| Wayne Cashman | Boston | 78 | 30 | 59 | 89 | 111 |
| Bobby Clarke | Philadelphia | 77 | 35 | 52 | 87 | 113 |
| Rick Martin | Buffalo | 78 | 52 | 34 | 86 | 38 |
| Syl Apps Jr. | Pittsburgh | 75 | 24 | 61 | 85 | 37 |
| Darryl Sittler | Toronto | 78 | 38 | 46 | 84 | 55 |
| Lowell MacDonald | Pittsburgh | 78 | 43 | 39 | 82 | 14 |
| Brad Park | NY Rangers | 78 | 25 | 57 | 82 | 148 |
| Dennis Hextall | Minnesota | 78 | 20 | 62 | 82 | 138 |

## 1974-75

**PRINCE OF WALES CONFERENCE**

**Norris Division**

| Team | GP | W | L | T | GF | GA | PTS |
|---|---|---|---|---|---|---|---|
| Montreal | 80 | 47 | 14 | 19 | 374 | 225 | 113 |
| Los Angeles | 80 | 42 | 17 | 21 | 269 | 185 | 105 |
| Pittsburgh | 80 | 37 | 28 | 15 | 326 | 289 | 89 |
| Detroit | 80 | 23 | 45 | 12 | 259 | 335 | 58 |
| Washington | 80 | 8 | 67 | 5 | 181 | 446 | 21 |

**Adams Division**

| Team | GP | W | L | T | GF | GA | PTS |
|---|---|---|---|---|---|---|---|
| Buffalo | 80 | 49 | 16 | 15 | 354 | 240 | 113 |
| Boston | 80 | 40 | 26 | 14 | 345 | 245 | 94 |
| Toronto | 80 | 31 | 33 | 16 | 280 | 309 | 78 |
| California | 80 | 19 | 48 | 13 | 212 | 316 | 51 |

**CLARENCE CAMPBELL CONFERENCE**

**Patrick Division**

| Team | GP | W | L | T | GF | GA | PTS |
|---|---|---|---|---|---|---|---|
| *Philadelphia | 80 | 51 | 18 | 11 | 293 | 181 | 113 |
| NY Rangers | 80 | 37 | 29 | 14 | 319 | 276 | 88 |
| NY Islanders | 80 | 33 | 25 | 22 | 264 | 221 | 88 |
| Atlanta | 80 | 34 | 31 | 15 | 243 | 233 | 83 |

**Smythe Division**

| Team | GP | W | L | T | GF | GA | PTS |
|---|---|---|---|---|---|---|---|
| Vancouver | 80 | 38 | 32 | 10 | 271 | 254 | 86 |
| St. Louis | 80 | 35 | 31 | 14 | 269 | 267 | 84 |
| Chicago | 80 | 37 | 35 | 8 | 268 | 241 | 82 |
| Minnesota | 80 | 23 | 50 | 7 | 221 | 341 | 53 |
| Kansas City | 80 | 15 | 54 | 11 | 184 | 328 | 41 |

### Leading Scorers

| Player | Team | GP | G | A | PTS | PIM |
|---|---|---|---|---|---|---|
| Bobby Orr | Boston | 80 | 46 | 89 | 135 | 101 |
| Phil Esposito | Boston | 79 | 61 | 66 | 127 | 62 |
| Marcel Dionne | Detroit | 80 | 47 | 74 | 121 | 14 |
| Guy Lafleur | Montreal | 70 | 53 | 66 | 119 | 37 |
| Pete Mahovlich | Montreal | 80 | 35 | 82 | 117 | 64 |
| Bobby Clarke | Philadelphia | 80 | 27 | 89 | 116 | 125 |
| Rene Robert | Buffalo | 74 | 40 | 60 | 100 | 75 |
| Rod Gilbert | NY Rangers | 76 | 36 | 61 | 97 | 22 |
| Gilbert Perreault | Buffalo | 68 | 39 | 57 | 96 | 36 |
| Rick Martin | Buffalo | 68 | 52 | 43 | 95 | 72 |

## 1975-76

**PRINCE OF WALES CONFERENCE**

**Norris Division**

| Team | GP | W | L | T | GF | GA | PTS |
|---|---|---|---|---|---|---|---|
| *Montreal | 80 | 58 | 11 | 11 | 337 | 174 | 127 |
| Los Angeles | 80 | 38 | 33 | 9 | 263 | 265 | 85 |
| Pittsburgh | 80 | 35 | 33 | 12 | 339 | 303 | 82 |
| Detroit | 80 | 26 | 44 | 10 | 226 | 300 | 62 |
| Washington | 80 | 11 | 59 | 10 | 224 | 394 | 32 |

**Adams Division**

| Team | GP | W | L | T | GF | GA | PTS |
|---|---|---|---|---|---|---|---|
| Boston | 80 | 48 | 15 | 17 | 313 | 237 | 113 |
| Buffalo | 80 | 46 | 21 | 13 | 339 | 240 | 105 |
| Toronto | 80 | 34 | 31 | 15 | 294 | 276 | 83 |
| California | 80 | 27 | 42 | 11 | 250 | 278 | 65 |

**CLARENCE CAMPBELL CONFERENCE**

**Patrick Division**

| Team | GP | W | L | T | GF | GA | PTS |
|---|---|---|---|---|---|---|---|
| Philadelphia | 80 | 51 | 13 | 16 | 348 | 209 | 118 |
| NY Islanders | 80 | 42 | 21 | 17 | 297 | 190 | 101 |
| Atlanta | 80 | 35 | 33 | 12 | 262 | 237 | 82 |
| NY Rangers | 80 | 29 | 42 | 9 | 262 | 333 | 67 |

**Smythe Division**

| Team | GP | W | L | T | GF | GA | PTS |
|---|---|---|---|---|---|---|---|
| Chicago | 80 | 32 | 30 | 18 | 254 | 261 | 82 |
| Vancouver | 80 | 33 | 32 | 15 | 271 | 272 | 81 |
| St. Louis | 80 | 29 | 37 | 14 | 249 | 290 | 72 |
| Minnesota | 80 | 20 | 53 | 7 | 195 | 303 | 47 |
| Kansas City | 80 | 12 | 56 | 12 | 190 | 351 | 36 |

### Leading Scorers

| Player | Team | GP | G | A | PTS | PIM |
|---|---|---|---|---|---|---|
| Guy Lafleur | Montreal | 80 | 56 | 69 | 125 | 36 |
| Bobby Clarke | Philadelphia | 76 | 30 | 89 | 119 | 136 |
| Gilbert Perreault | Buffalo | 80 | 44 | 69 | 113 | 36 |
| Bill Barber | Philadelphia | 80 | 50 | 62 | 112 | 104 |
| Pierre Larouche | Pittsburgh | 76 | 53 | 58 | 111 | 33 |
| Jean Ratelle | Bos., NYR | 80 | 36 | 69 | 105 | 18 |
| Pete Mahovlich | Montreal | 80 | 34 | 71 | 105 | 76 |
| Jean Pronovost | Pittsburgh | 80 | 52 | 52 | 104 | 24 |
| Darryl Sittler | Toronto | 79 | 41 | 59 | 100 | 90 |
| Syl Apps Jr. | Pittsburgh | 80 | 32 | 67 | 99 | 24 |

## 1976-77

**PRINCE OF WALES CONFERENCE**

**Norris Division**

| Team | GP | W | L | T | GF | GA | PTS |
|---|---|---|---|---|---|---|---|
| *Montreal | 80 | 60 | 8 | 12 | 387 | 171 | 132 |
| Los Angeles | 80 | 34 | 31 | 15 | 271 | 241 | 83 |
| Pittsburgh | 80 | 34 | 33 | 13 | 240 | 252 | 81 |
| Washington | 80 | 24 | 42 | 14 | 221 | 307 | 62 |
| Detroit | 80 | 16 | 55 | 9 | 183 | 309 | 41 |

**Adams Division**

| Team | GP | W | L | T | GF | GA | PTS |
|---|---|---|---|---|---|---|---|
| Boston | 80 | 49 | 23 | 8 | 312 | 240 | 106 |
| Buffalo | 80 | 48 | 24 | 8 | 301 | 220 | 104 |
| Toronto | 80 | 33 | 32 | 15 | 301 | 285 | 81 |
| Cleveland | 80 | 25 | 42 | 13 | 240 | 292 | 63 |

**CLARENCE CAMPBELL CONFERENCE**

**Patrick Division**

| Team | GP | W | L | T | GF | GA | PTS |
|---|---|---|---|---|---|---|---|
| Philadelphia | 80 | 48 | 16 | 16 | 323 | 213 | 112 |
| NY Islanders | 80 | 47 | 21 | 12 | 288 | 193 | 106 |
| Atlanta | 80 | 34 | 34 | 12 | 264 | 265 | 80 |
| NY Rangers | 80 | 29 | 37 | 14 | 272 | 310 | 72 |

**Smythe Division**

| Team | GP | W | L | T | GF | GA | PTS |
|---|---|---|---|---|---|---|---|
| St. Louis | 80 | 32 | 39 | 9 | 239 | 276 | 73 |
| Minnesota | 80 | 23 | 39 | 18 | 240 | 310 | 64 |
| Chicago | 80 | 26 | 43 | 11 | 240 | 298 | 63 |
| Vancouver | 80 | 25 | 42 | 13 | 235 | 294 | 63 |
| Colorado | 80 | 20 | 46 | 14 | 226 | 307 | 54 |

### Leading Scorers

| Player | Team | GP | G | A | PTS | PIM |
|---|---|---|---|---|---|---|
| Guy Lafleur | Montreal | 80 | 56 | 80 | 136 | 20 |
| Marcel Dionne | Los Angeles | 80 | 53 | 69 | 122 | 12 |
| Steve Shutt | Montreal | 80 | 60 | 45 | 105 | 28 |
| Rick MacLeish | Philadelphia | 79 | 49 | 48 | 97 | 42 |
| Gilbert Perreault | Buffalo | 80 | 39 | 56 | 95 | 30 |
| Tim Young | Minnesota | 80 | 29 | 66 | 95 | 58 |
| Jean Ratelle | Boston | 78 | 33 | 61 | 94 | 22 |
| Lanny McDonald | Toronto | 80 | 46 | 44 | 90 | 77 |
| Darryl Sittler | Toronto | 73 | 38 | 52 | 90 | 89 |
| Bobby Clarke | Philadelphia | 80 | 27 | 63 | 90 | 71 |

## 1977-78

**PRINCE OF WALES CONFERENCE**

**Norris Division**

| Team | GP | W | L | T | GF | GA | PTS |
|---|---|---|---|---|---|---|---|
| *Montreal | 80 | 59 | 10 | 11 | 359 | 183 | 129 |
| Detroit | 80 | 32 | 34 | 14 | 252 | 266 | 78 |
| Los Angeles | 80 | 31 | 34 | 15 | 243 | 245 | 77 |
| Pittsburgh | 80 | 25 | 37 | 18 | 254 | 321 | 68 |
| Washington | 80 | 17 | 49 | 14 | 195 | 321 | 48 |

**Adams Division**

| Team | GP | W | L | T | GF | GA | PTS |
|---|---|---|---|---|---|---|---|
| Boston | 80 | 51 | 18 | 11 | 333 | 218 | 113 |
| Buffalo | 80 | 44 | 19 | 17 | 288 | 215 | 105 |
| Toronto | 80 | 41 | 29 | 10 | 271 | 237 | 92 |
| Cleveland | 80 | 22 | 45 | 13 | 230 | 325 | 57 |

**CLARENCE CAMPBELL CONFERENCE**

**Patrick Division**

| Team | GP | W | L | T | GF | GA | PTS |
|---|---|---|---|---|---|---|---|
| NY Islanders | 80 | 48 | 17 | 15 | 334 | 210 | 111 |
| Philadelphia | 80 | 45 | 20 | 15 | 296 | 200 | 105 |
| Atlanta | 80 | 34 | 27 | 19 | 274 | 252 | 87 |
| NY Rangers | 80 | 30 | 37 | 13 | 279 | 280 | 73 |

**Smythe Division**

| Team | GP | W | L | T | GF | GA | PTS |
|---|---|---|---|---|---|---|---|
| Chicago | 80 | 32 | 29 | 19 | 230 | 220 | 83 |
| Colorado | 80 | 19 | 40 | 21 | 257 | 305 | 59 |
| Vancouver | 80 | 20 | 43 | 17 | 239 | 320 | 57 |
| St. Louis | 80 | 20 | 47 | 13 | 195 | 304 | 53 |
| Minnesota | 80 | 18 | 53 | 9 | 218 | 325 | 45 |

### Leading Scorers

| Player | Team | GP | G | A | PTS | PIM |
|---|---|---|---|---|---|---|
| Guy Lafleur | Montreal | 78 | 60 | 72 | 132 | 26 |
| Bryan Trottier | NY Islanders | 77 | 46 | 77 | 123 | 46 |
| Darryl Sittler | Toronto | 80 | 45 | 72 | 117 | 100 |
| Jacques Lemaire | Montreal | 76 | 36 | 61 | 97 | 14 |
| Denis Potvin | NY Islanders | 80 | 30 | 64 | 94 | 81 |
| Mike Bossy | NY Islanders | 73 | 53 | 38 | 91 | 6 |
| Terry O'Reilly | Boston | 77 | 29 | 61 | 90 | 211 |
| Gilbert Perreault | Buffalo | 79 | 41 | 48 | 89 | 20 |
| Bobby Clarke | Philadelphia | 71 | 21 | 68 | 89 | 83 |
| Lanny McDonald | Toronto | 74 | 47 | 40 | 87 | 54 |
| Wilf Paiement | Colorado | 80 | 31 | 56 | 87 | 114 |

## 1978-79

**PRINCE OF WALES CONFERENCE**

**Norris Division**

| Team | GP | W | L | T | GF | GA | PTS |
|---|---|---|---|---|---|---|---|
| *Montreal | 80 | 52 | 17 | 11 | 337 | 204 | 115 |
| Pittsburgh | 80 | 36 | 31 | 13 | 281 | 279 | 85 |
| Los Angeles | 80 | 34 | 34 | 12 | 292 | 286 | 80 |
| Washington | 80 | 24 | 41 | 15 | 273 | 338 | 63 |
| Detroit | 80 | 23 | 41 | 16 | 252 | 295 | 62 |

**Adams Division**

| Team | GP | W | L | T | GF | GA | PTS |
|---|---|---|---|---|---|---|---|
| Boston | 80 | 43 | 23 | 14 | 316 | 270 | 100 |
| Buffalo | 80 | 36 | 28 | 16 | 280 | 263 | 88 |
| Toronto | 80 | 34 | 33 | 13 | 267 | 252 | 81 |
| Minnesota | 80 | 28 | 40 | 12 | 257 | 289 | 68 |

**CLARENCE CAMPBELL CONFERENCE**

**Patrick Division**

| Team | GP | W | L | T | GF | GA | PTS |
|---|---|---|---|---|---|---|---|
| NY Islanders | 80 | 51 | 15 | 14 | 358 | 214 | 116 |
| Philadelphia | 80 | 40 | 25 | 15 | 281 | 248 | 95 |
| NY Rangers | 80 | 40 | 29 | 11 | 316 | 292 | 91 |
| Atlanta | 80 | 41 | 31 | 8 | 327 | 280 | 90 |

**Smythe Division**

| Team | GP | W | L | T | GF | GA | PTS |
|---|---|---|---|---|---|---|---|
| Chicago | 80 | 29 | 36 | 15 | 244 | 277 | 73 |
| Vancouver | 80 | 25 | 42 | 13 | 217 | 291 | 63 |
| St. Louis | 80 | 18 | 50 | 12 | 249 | 348 | 48 |
| Colorado | 80 | 15 | 53 | 12 | 210 | 331 | 42 |

### Leading Scorers

| Player | Team | GP | G | A | PTS | PIM |
|---|---|---|---|---|---|---|
| Bryan Trottier | NY Islanders | 76 | 47 | 87 | 134 | 50 |
| Marcel Dionne | Los Angeles | 80 | 59 | 71 | 130 | 30 |
| Guy Lafleur | Montreal | 80 | 52 | 77 | 129 | 28 |
| Mike Bossy | NY Islanders | 80 | 69 | 57 | 126 | 25 |
| Bob MacMillan | Atlanta | 79 | 37 | 71 | 108 | 14 |
| Guy Chouinard | Atlanta | 80 | 50 | 57 | 107 | 14 |
| Denis Potvin | NY Islanders | 73 | 31 | 70 | 101 | 58 |
| Bernie Federko | St. Louis | 74 | 31 | 64 | 95 | 14 |
| Dave Taylor | Los Angeles | 78 | 43 | 48 | 91 | 124 |
| Clark Gillies | NY Islanders | 75 | 35 | 56 | 91 | 68 |

## 1979-80

### PRINCE OF WALES CONFERENCE

**Norris Division**

| Team | GP | W | L | T | GF | GA | PTS |
|---|---|---|---|---|---|---|---|
| Montreal | 80 | 47 | 20 | 13 | 328 | 240 | 107 |
| Los Angeles | 80 | 30 | 36 | 14 | 290 | 313 | 74 |
| Pittsburgh | 80 | 30 | 37 | 13 | 251 | 303 | 73 |
| Hartford | 80 | 27 | 34 | 19 | 303 | 312 | 73 |
| Detroit | 80 | 26 | 43 | 11 | 268 | 306 | 63 |

**Adams Division**

| Team | GP | W | L | T | GF | GA | PTS |
|---|---|---|---|---|---|---|---|
| Buffalo | 80 | 47 | 17 | 16 | 318 | 201 | 110 |
| Boston | 80 | 46 | 21 | 13 | 310 | 234 | 105 |
| Minnesota | 80 | 36 | 28 | 16 | 311 | 253 | 88 |
| Toronto | 80 | 35 | 40 | 5 | 304 | 327 | 75 |
| Quebec | 80 | 25 | 44 | 11 | 248 | 313 | 61 |

### CLARENCE CAMPBELL CONFERENCE

**Patrick Division**

| Team | GP | W | L | T | GF | GA | PTS |
|---|---|---|---|---|---|---|---|
| Philadelphia | 80 | 48 | 12 | 20 | 327 | 254 | 116 |
| *NY Islanders | 80 | 39 | 28 | 13 | 281 | 247 | 91 |
| NY Rangers | 80 | 38 | 32 | 10 | 308 | 284 | 86 |
| Atlanta | 80 | 35 | 32 | 13 | 282 | 269 | 83 |
| Washington | 80 | 27 | 40 | 13 | 261 | 293 | 67 |

**Smythe Division**

| Team | GP | W | L | T | GF | GA | PTS |
|---|---|---|---|---|---|---|---|
| Chicago | 80 | 34 | 27 | 19 | 241 | 250 | 87 |
| St. Louis | 80 | 34 | 34 | 12 | 266 | 278 | 80 |
| Vancouver | 80 | 27 | 37 | 16 | 256 | 281 | 70 |
| Edmonton | 80 | 28 | 39 | 13 | 301 | 322 | 69 |
| Winnipeg | 80 | 20 | 49 | 11 | 214 | 314 | 51 |
| Colorado | 80 | 19 | 48 | 13 | 234 | 308 | 51 |

**Leading Scorers**

| Player | Team | GP | G | A | PTS | PIM |
|---|---|---|---|---|---|---|
| Marcel Dionne | Los Angeles | 80 | 53 | 84 | 137 | 32 |
| Wayne Gretzky | Edmonton | 79 | 51 | 86 | 137 | 21 |
| Guy Lafleur | Montreal | 74 | 50 | 75 | 125 | 12 |
| Gilbert Perreault | Buffalo | 80 | 40 | 66 | 106 | 57 |
| Mike Rogers | Hartford | 80 | 44 | 61 | 105 | 10 |
| Bryan Trottier | NY Islanders | 78 | 42 | 62 | 104 | 68 |
| Charlie Simmer | Los Angeles | 64 | 56 | 45 | 101 | 65 |
| Blaine Stoughton | Hartford | 80 | 56 | 44 | 100 | 16 |
| Darryl Sittler | Toronto | 73 | 40 | 57 | 97 | 62 |
| Blair MacDonald | Edmonton | 80 | 46 | 48 | 94 | 6 |
| Bernie Federko | St. Louis | 79 | 38 | 56 | 94 | 24 |

## 1980-81

### PRINCE OF WALES CONFERENCE

**Norris Division**

| Team | GP | W | L | T | GF | GA | PTS |
|---|---|---|---|---|---|---|---|
| Montreal | 80 | 45 | 22 | 13 | 332 | 232 | 103 |
| Los Angeles | 80 | 43 | 24 | 13 | 337 | 290 | 99 |
| Pittsburgh | 80 | 30 | 37 | 13 | 302 | 345 | 73 |
| Hartford | 80 | 21 | 41 | 18 | 292 | 372 | 60 |
| Detroit | 80 | 19 | 43 | 18 | 252 | 339 | 56 |

**Adams Division**

| Team | GP | W | L | T | GF | GA | PTS |
|---|---|---|---|---|---|---|---|
| Buffalo | 80 | 39 | 20 | 21 | 327 | 250 | 99 |
| Boston | 80 | 37 | 30 | 13 | 316 | 272 | 87 |
| Minnesota | 80 | 35 | 28 | 17 | 291 | 263 | 87 |
| Quebec | 80 | 30 | 32 | 18 | 314 | 318 | 78 |
| Toronto | 80 | 28 | 37 | 15 | 322 | 367 | 71 |

### CLARENCE CAMPBELL CONFERENCE

**Patrick Division**

| Team | GP | W | L | T | GF | GA | PTS |
|---|---|---|---|---|---|---|---|
| *NY Islanders | 80 | 48 | 18 | 14 | 355 | 260 | 110 |
| Philadelphia | 80 | 41 | 24 | 15 | 313 | 249 | 97 |
| Calgary | 80 | 39 | 27 | 14 | 329 | 298 | 92 |
| NY Rangers | 80 | 30 | 36 | 14 | 312 | 317 | 74 |
| Washington | 80 | 26 | 36 | 18 | 286 | 317 | 70 |

**Smythe Division**

| Team | GP | W | L | T | GF | GA | PTS |
|---|---|---|---|---|---|---|---|
| St. Louis | 80 | 45 | 18 | 17 | 352 | 281 | 107 |
| Chicago | 80 | 31 | 33 | 16 | 304 | 315 | 78 |
| Vancouver | 80 | 28 | 32 | 20 | 289 | 301 | 76 |
| Edmonton | 80 | 29 | 35 | 16 | 328 | 327 | 74 |
| Colorado | 80 | 22 | 45 | 13 | 258 | 344 | 57 |
| Winnipeg | 80 | 9 | 57 | 14 | 246 | 400 | 32 |

**Leading Scorers**

| Player | Team | GP | G | A | PTS | PIM |
|---|---|---|---|---|---|---|
| Wayne Gretzky | Edmonton | 80 | 55 | 109 | 164 | 28 |
| Marcel Dionne | Los Angeles | 80 | 58 | 77 | 135 | 70 |
| Kent Nilsson | Calgary | 80 | 49 | 82 | 131 | 26 |
| Mike Bossy | NY Islanders | 79 | 68 | 51 | 119 | 32 |
| Dave Taylor | Los Angeles | 72 | 47 | 65 | 112 | 130 |
| Peter Stastny | Quebec | 77 | 39 | 70 | 109 | 37 |
| Charlie Simmer | Los Angeles | 65 | 56 | 49 | 105 | 62 |
| Mike Rogers | Hartford | 80 | 40 | 65 | 105 | 32 |
| Bernie Federko | St. Louis | 78 | 31 | 73 | 104 | 47 |
| Jacques Richard | Quebec | 78 | 52 | 51 | 103 | 39 |
| Rick Middleton | Boston | 80 | 44 | 59 | 103 | 16 |
| Bryan Trottier | NY Islanders | 73 | 31 | 72 | 103 | 74 |

## 1981-82

### CLARENCE CAMPBELL CONFERENCE

**Norris Division**

| Team | GP | W | L | T | GF | GA | PTS |
|---|---|---|---|---|---|---|---|
| Minnesota | 80 | 37 | 23 | 20 | 346 | 288 | 94 |
| Winnipeg | 80 | 33 | 33 | 14 | 319 | 332 | 80 |
| St. Louis | 80 | 32 | 40 | 8 | 315 | 349 | 72 |
| Chicago | 80 | 30 | 38 | 12 | 332 | 363 | 72 |
| Toronto | 80 | 20 | 44 | 16 | 298 | 380 | 56 |
| Detroit | 80 | 21 | 47 | 12 | 270 | 351 | 54 |

**Smythe Division**

| Team | GP | W | L | T | GF | GA | PTS |
|---|---|---|---|---|---|---|---|
| Edmonton | 80 | 48 | 17 | 15 | 417 | 295 | 111 |
| Vancouver | 80 | 30 | 33 | 17 | 290 | 286 | 77 |
| Calgary | 80 | 29 | 34 | 17 | 334 | 345 | 75 |
| Los Angeles | 80 | 24 | 41 | 15 | 314 | 369 | 63 |
| Colorado | 80 | 18 | 49 | 13 | 241 | 362 | 49 |

### PRINCE OF WALES CONFERENCE

**Adams Division**

| Team | GP | W | L | T | GF | GA | PTS |
|---|---|---|---|---|---|---|---|
| Montreal | 80 | 46 | 17 | 17 | 360 | 223 | 109 |
| Boston | 80 | 43 | 27 | 10 | 323 | 285 | 96 |
| Buffalo | 80 | 39 | 26 | 15 | 307 | 273 | 93 |
| Quebec | 80 | 33 | 31 | 16 | 356 | 345 | 82 |
| Hartford | 80 | 21 | 41 | 18 | 264 | 351 | 60 |

**Patrick Division**

| Team | GP | W | L | T | GF | GA | PTS |
|---|---|---|---|---|---|---|---|
| *NY Islanders | 80 | 54 | 16 | 10 | 385 | 250 | 118 |
| NY Rangers | 80 | 39 | 27 | 14 | 316 | 306 | 92 |
| Philadelphia | 80 | 38 | 31 | 11 | 325 | 313 | 87 |
| Pittsburgh | 80 | 31 | 36 | 13 | 310 | 337 | 75 |
| Washington | 80 | 26 | 41 | 13 | 319 | 338 | 65 |

**Leading Scorers**

| Player | Team | GP | G | A | PTS | PIM |
|---|---|---|---|---|---|---|
| Wayne Gretzky | Edmonton | 80 | 92 | 120 | 212 | 26 |
| Mike Bossy | NY Islanders | 80 | 64 | 83 | 147 | 22 |
| Peter Stastny | Quebec | 80 | 46 | 93 | 139 | 91 |
| Dennis Maruk | Washington | 80 | 60 | 76 | 136 | 128 |
| Bryan Trottier | NY Islanders | 80 | 50 | 79 | 129 | 88 |
| Denis Savard | Chicago | 80 | 32 | 87 | 119 | 82 |
| Marcel Dionne | Los Angeles | 78 | 50 | 67 | 117 | 50 |
| Bobby Smith | Minnesota | 80 | 43 | 71 | 114 | 82 |
| Dino Ciccarelli | Minnesota | 76 | 55 | 51 | 106 | 138 |
| Dave Taylor | Los Angeles | 78 | 39 | 67 | 106 | 130 |

## 1982-83

### CLARENCE CAMPBELL CONFERENCE

**Norris Division**

| Team | GP | W | L | T | GF | GA | PTS |
|---|---|---|---|---|---|---|---|
| Chicago | 80 | 47 | 23 | 10 | 338 | 268 | 104 |
| Minnesota | 80 | 40 | 24 | 16 | 321 | 290 | 96 |
| Toronto | 80 | 28 | 40 | 12 | 293 | 330 | 68 |
| St. Louis | 80 | 25 | 40 | 15 | 285 | 316 | 65 |
| Detroit | 80 | 21 | 44 | 15 | 263 | 344 | 57 |

**Smythe Division**

| Team | GP | W | L | T | GF | GA | PTS |
|---|---|---|---|---|---|---|---|
| Edmonton | 80 | 47 | 21 | 12 | 424 | 315 | 106 |
| Calgary | 80 | 32 | 34 | 14 | 321 | 317 | 78 |
| Vancouver | 80 | 30 | 35 | 15 | 303 | 309 | 75 |
| Winnipeg | 80 | 33 | 39 | 8 | 311 | 333 | 74 |
| Los Angeles | 80 | 27 | 41 | 12 | 308 | 365 | 66 |

### PRINCE OF WALES CONFERENCE

**Adams Division**

| Team | GP | W | L | T | GF | GA | PTS |
|---|---|---|---|---|---|---|---|
| Boston | 80 | 50 | 20 | 10 | 327 | 228 | 110 |
| Montreal | 80 | 42 | 24 | 14 | 350 | 286 | 98 |
| Buffalo | 80 | 38 | 29 | 13 | 318 | 285 | 89 |
| Quebec | 80 | 34 | 34 | 12 | 343 | 336 | 80 |
| Hartford | 80 | 19 | 54 | 7 | 261 | 403 | 45 |

**Patrick Division**

| Team | GP | W | L | T | GF | GA | PTS |
|---|---|---|---|---|---|---|---|
| Philadelphia | 80 | 49 | 23 | 8 | 326 | 240 | 106 |
| *NY Islanders | 80 | 42 | 26 | 12 | 302 | 226 | 96 |
| Washington | 80 | 39 | 25 | 16 | 306 | 283 | 94 |
| NY Rangers | 80 | 35 | 35 | 10 | 306 | 287 | 80 |
| New Jersey | 80 | 17 | 49 | 14 | 230 | 338 | 48 |
| Pittsburgh | 80 | 18 | 53 | 9 | 257 | 394 | 45 |

**Leading Scorers**

| Player | Team | GP | G | A | PTS | PIM |
|---|---|---|---|---|---|---|
| Wayne Gretzky | Edmonton | 80 | 71 | 125 | 196 | 59 |
| Peter Stastny | Quebec | 75 | 47 | 77 | 124 | 78 |
| Denis Savard | Chicago | 78 | 35 | 86 | 121 | 99 |
| Mike Bossy | NY Islanders | 79 | 60 | 58 | 118 | 20 |
| Marcel Dionne | Los Angeles | 80 | 56 | 51 | 107 | 22 |
| Barry Pederson | Boston | 77 | 46 | 61 | 107 | 47 |
| Mark Messier | Edmonton | 77 | 48 | 58 | 106 | 72 |
| Michel Goulet | Quebec | 80 | 57 | 48 | 105 | 51 |
| Glenn Anderson | Edmonton | 72 | 48 | 56 | 104 | 70 |
| Kent Nilsson | Calgary | 80 | 46 | 58 | 104 | 10 |
| Jari Kurri | Edmonton | 80 | 45 | 59 | 104 | 22 |

## 1983-84

### CLARENCE CAMPBELL CONFERENCE

**Norris Division**

| Team | GP | W | L | T | GF | GA | PTS |
|---|---|---|---|---|---|---|---|
| Minnesota | 80 | 39 | 31 | 10 | 345 | 344 | 88 |
| St. Louis | 80 | 32 | 41 | 7 | 293 | 316 | 71 |
| Detroit | 80 | 31 | 42 | 7 | 298 | 323 | 69 |
| Chicago | 80 | 30 | 42 | 8 | 277 | 311 | 68 |
| Toronto | 80 | 26 | 45 | 9 | 303 | 387 | 61 |

**Smythe Division**

| Team | GP | W | L | T | GF | GA | PTS |
|---|---|---|---|---|---|---|---|
| *Edmonton | 80 | 57 | 18 | 5 | 446 | 314 | 119 |
| Calgary | 80 | 34 | 32 | 14 | 311 | 314 | 82 |
| Vancouver | 80 | 32 | 39 | 9 | 306 | 328 | 73 |
| Winnipeg | 80 | 31 | 38 | 11 | 340 | 374 | 73 |
| Los Angeles | 80 | 23 | 44 | 13 | 309 | 376 | 59 |

### PRINCE OF WALES CONFERENCE

**Adams Division**

| Team | GP | W | L | T | GF | GA | PTS |
|---|---|---|---|---|---|---|---|
| Boston | 80 | 49 | 25 | 6 | 336 | 261 | 104 |
| Buffalo | 80 | 48 | 25 | 7 | 315 | 257 | 103 |
| Quebec | 80 | 42 | 28 | 10 | 360 | 278 | 94 |
| Montreal | 80 | 35 | 40 | 5 | 286 | 295 | 75 |
| Hartford | 80 | 28 | 42 | 10 | 288 | 320 | 66 |

**Patrick Division**

| Team | GP | W | L | T | GF | GA | PTS |
|---|---|---|---|---|---|---|---|
| NY Islanders | 80 | 50 | 26 | 4 | 357 | 269 | 104 |
| Washington | 80 | 48 | 27 | 5 | 308 | 226 | 101 |
| Philadelphia | 80 | 44 | 26 | 10 | 350 | 290 | 98 |
| NY Rangers | 80 | 42 | 29 | 9 | 314 | 304 | 93 |
| New Jersey | 80 | 17 | 56 | 7 | 231 | 350 | 41 |
| Pittsburgh | 80 | 16 | 58 | 6 | 254 | 390 | 38 |

**Leading Scorers**

| Player | Team | GP | G | A | PTS | PIM |
|---|---|---|---|---|---|---|
| Wayne Gretzky | Edmonton | 74 | 87 | 118 | 205 | 39 |
| Paul Coffey | Edmonton | 80 | 40 | 86 | 126 | 104 |
| Michel Goulet | Quebec | 75 | 56 | 65 | 121 | 76 |
| Peter Stastny | Quebec | 80 | 46 | 73 | 119 | 73 |
| Mike Bossy | NY Islanders | 67 | 51 | 67 | 118 | 8 |
| Barry Pederson | Boston | 80 | 39 | 77 | 116 | 64 |
| Jari Kurri | Edmonton | 64 | 52 | 61 | 113 | 14 |
| Bryan Trottier | NY Islanders | 68 | 40 | 71 | 111 | 59 |
| Bernie Federko | St. Louis | 79 | 41 | 66 | 107 | 43 |
| Rick Middleton | Boston | 80 | 47 | 58 | 105 | 14 |

## 1984-85

### CLARENCE CAMPBELL CONFERENCE

**Norris Division**

| Team | GP | W | L | T | GF | GA | PTS |
|---|---|---|---|---|---|---|---|
| St. Louis | 80 | 37 | 31 | 12 | 299 | 288 | 86 |
| Chicago | 80 | 38 | 35 | 7 | 309 | 299 | 83 |
| Detroit | 80 | 27 | 41 | 12 | 313 | 357 | 66 |
| Minnesota | 80 | 25 | 43 | 12 | 268 | 321 | 62 |
| Toronto | 80 | 20 | 52 | 8 | 253 | 358 | 48 |

**Smythe Division**

| Team | GP | W | L | T | GF | GA | PTS |
|---|---|---|---|---|---|---|---|
| *Edmonton | 80 | 49 | 20 | 11 | 401 | 298 | 109 |
| Winnipeg | 80 | 43 | 27 | 10 | 358 | 332 | 96 |
| Calgary | 80 | 41 | 27 | 12 | 363 | 302 | 94 |
| Los Angeles | 80 | 34 | 32 | 14 | 339 | 326 | 82 |
| Vancouver | 80 | 25 | 46 | 9 | 284 | 401 | 59 |

### PRINCE OF WALES CONFERENCE

**Adams Division**

| Team | GP | W | L | T | GF | GA | PTS |
|---|---|---|---|---|---|---|---|
| Montreal | 80 | 41 | 27 | 12 | 309 | 262 | 94 |
| Quebec | 80 | 41 | 30 | 9 | 323 | 275 | 91 |
| Buffalo | 80 | 38 | 28 | 14 | 290 | 237 | 90 |
| Boston | 80 | 36 | 34 | 10 | 303 | 287 | 82 |
| Hartford | 80 | 30 | 41 | 9 | 268 | 318 | 69 |

**Patrick Division**

| Team | GP | W | L | T | GF | GA | PTS |
|---|---|---|---|---|---|---|---|
| Philadelphia | 80 | 53 | 20 | 7 | 348 | 241 | 113 |
| Washington | 80 | 46 | 25 | 9 | 322 | 240 | 101 |
| NY Islanders | 80 | 40 | 34 | 6 | 345 | 312 | 86 |
| NY Rangers | 80 | 26 | 44 | 10 | 295 | 345 | 62 |
| New Jersey | 80 | 22 | 48 | 10 | 264 | 346 | 54 |
| Pittsburgh | 80 | 24 | 51 | 5 | 276 | 385 | 53 |

**Leading Scorers**

| Player | Team | GP | G | A | PTS | PIM |
|---|---|---|---|---|---|---|
| Wayne Gretzky | Edmonton | 80 | 73 | 135 | 208 | 52 |
| Jari Kurri | Edmonton | 73 | 71 | 64 | 135 | 30 |
| Dale Hawerchuk | Winnipeg | 80 | 53 | 77 | 130 | 74 |
| Marcel Dionne | Los Angeles | 80 | 46 | 80 | 126 | 46 |
| Paul Coffey | Edmonton | 80 | 37 | 84 | 121 | 97 |
| Mike Bossy | NY Islanders | 76 | 58 | 59 | 117 | 38 |
| John Ogrodnick | Detroit | 79 | 55 | 50 | 105 | 30 |
| Denis Savard | Chicago | 79 | 38 | 67 | 105 | 56 |
| Bernie Federko | St. Louis | 76 | 30 | 73 | 103 | 27 |
| Mike Gartner | Washington | 80 | 50 | 52 | 102 | 71 |

## 1985-86

### CLARENCE CAMPBELL CONFERENCE

#### Norris Division

| Team | GP | W | L | T | GF | GA | PTS |
|---|---|---|---|---|---|---|---|
| Chicago | 80 | 39 | 33 | 8 | 351 | 349 | 86 |
| Minnesota | 80 | 38 | 33 | 9 | 327 | 305 | 85 |
| St. Louis | 80 | 37 | 34 | 9 | 302 | 291 | 83 |
| Toronto | 80 | 25 | 48 | 7 | 311 | 386 | 57 |
| Detroit | 80 | 17 | 57 | 6 | 266 | 415 | 40 |

#### Smythe Division

| Team | GP | W | L | T | GF | GA | PTS |
|---|---|---|---|---|---|---|---|
| Edmonton | 80 | 56 | 17 | 7 | 426 | 310 | 119 |
| Calgary | 80 | 40 | 31 | 9 | 354 | 315 | 89 |
| Winnipeg | 80 | 26 | 47 | 7 | 295 | 372 | 59 |
| Vancouver | 80 | 23 | 44 | 13 | 282 | 333 | 59 |
| Los Angeles | 80 | 23 | 49 | 8 | 284 | 389 | 54 |

### PRINCE OF WALES CONFERENCE

#### Adams Division

| Team | GP | W | L | T | GF | GA | PTS |
|---|---|---|---|---|---|---|---|
| Quebec | 80 | 43 | 31 | 6 | 330 | 289 | 92 |
| *Montreal | 80 | 40 | 33 | 7 | 330 | 280 | 87 |
| Boston | 80 | 37 | 31 | 12 | 311 | 288 | 86 |
| Hartford | 80 | 40 | 36 | 4 | 332 | 302 | 84 |
| Buffalo | 80 | 37 | 37 | 6 | 296 | 291 | 80 |

#### Patrick Division

| Team | GP | W | L | T | GF | GA | PTS |
|---|---|---|---|---|---|---|---|
| Philadelphia | 80 | 53 | 23 | 4 | 335 | 241 | 110 |
| Washington | 80 | 50 | 23 | 7 | 315 | 272 | 107 |
| NY Islanders | 80 | 39 | 29 | 12 | 327 | 284 | 90 |
| NY Rangers | 80 | 36 | 38 | 6 | 280 | 276 | 78 |
| Pittsburgh | 80 | 34 | 38 | 8 | 313 | 305 | 76 |
| New Jersey | 80 | 28 | 49 | 3 | 300 | 374 | 59 |

#### Leading Scorers

| Player | Team | GP | G | A | PTS | PIM |
|---|---|---|---|---|---|---|
| Wayne Gretzky | Edmonton | 80 | 52 | 163 | 215 | 52 |
| Mario Lemieux | Pittsburgh | 79 | 48 | 93 | 141 | 43 |
| Paul Coffey | Edmonton | 79 | 48 | 90 | 138 | 120 |
| Jari Kurri | Edmonton | 78 | 68 | 63 | 131 | 22 |
| Mike Bossy | NY Islanders | 80 | 61 | 62 | 123 | 14 |
| Peter Stastny | Quebec | 76 | 41 | 81 | 122 | 60 |
| Denis Savard | Chicago | 80 | 47 | 69 | 116 | 111 |
| Mats Naslund | Montreal | 80 | 43 | 67 | 110 | 16 |
| Dale Hawerchuk | Winnipeg | 80 | 46 | 59 | 105 | 44 |
| Neal Broten | Minnesota | 80 | 29 | 76 | 105 | 47 |

## 1986-87

### CLARENCE CAMPBELL CONFERENCE

#### Norris Division

| Team | GP | W | L | T | GF | GA | PTS |
|---|---|---|---|---|---|---|---|
| St. Louis | 80 | 32 | 33 | 15 | 281 | 293 | 79 |
| Detroit | 80 | 34 | 36 | 10 | 260 | 274 | 78 |
| Chicago | 80 | 29 | 37 | 14 | 290 | 310 | 72 |
| Toronto | 80 | 32 | 42 | 6 | 286 | 319 | 70 |
| Minnesota | 80 | 30 | 40 | 10 | 296 | 314 | 70 |

#### Smythe Division

| Team | GP | W | L | T | GF | GA | PTS |
|---|---|---|---|---|---|---|---|
| *Edmonton | 80 | 50 | 24 | 6 | 372 | 284 | 106 |
| Calgary | 80 | 46 | 31 | 3 | 318 | 289 | 95 |
| Winnipeg | 80 | 40 | 32 | 8 | 279 | 271 | 88 |
| Los Angeles | 80 | 31 | 41 | 8 | 318 | 341 | 70 |
| Vancouver | 80 | 29 | 43 | 8 | 282 | 314 | 66 |

### PRINCE OF WALES CONFERENCE

#### Adams Division

| Team | GP | W | L | T | GF | GA | PTS |
|---|---|---|---|---|---|---|---|
| Hartford | 80 | 43 | 30 | 7 | 287 | 270 | 93 |
| Montreal | 80 | 41 | 29 | 10 | 277 | 241 | 92 |
| Boston | 80 | 39 | 34 | 7 | 301 | 276 | 85 |
| Quebec | 80 | 31 | 39 | 10 | 267 | 276 | 72 |
| Buffalo | 80 | 28 | 44 | 8 | 280 | 308 | 64 |

#### Patrick Division

| Team | GP | W | L | T | GF | GA | PTS |
|---|---|---|---|---|---|---|---|
| Philadelphia | 80 | 46 | 26 | 8 | 310 | 245 | 100 |
| Washington | 80 | 38 | 32 | 10 | 285 | 278 | 86 |
| NY Islanders | 80 | 35 | 33 | 12 | 279 | 281 | 82 |
| NY Rangers | 80 | 34 | 38 | 8 | 307 | 323 | 76 |
| Pittsburgh | 80 | 30 | 38 | 12 | 297 | 290 | 72 |
| New Jersey | 80 | 29 | 45 | 6 | 293 | 368 | 64 |

#### Leading Scorers

| Player | Team | GP | G | A | PTS | PIM |
|---|---|---|---|---|---|---|
| Wayne Gretzky | Edmonton | 79 | 62 | 121 | 183 | 28 |
| Jari Kurri | Edmonton | 79 | 54 | 54 | 108 | 41 |
| Mario Lemieux | Pittsburgh | 63 | 54 | 53 | 107 | 57 |
| Mark Messier | Edmonton | 77 | 37 | 70 | 107 | 73 |
| Doug Gilmour | St. Louis | 80 | 42 | 63 | 105 | 58 |
| Dino Ciccarelli | Minnesota | 80 | 52 | 51 | 103 | 92 |
| Dale Hawerchuk | Winnipeg | 80 | 47 | 53 | 100 | 54 |
| Michel Goulet | Quebec | 75 | 49 | 47 | 96 | 61 |
| Tim Kerr | Philadelphia | 75 | 58 | 37 | 95 | 57 |
| Raymond Bourque | Boston | 78 | 23 | 72 | 95 | 36 |

## 1987-88

### CLARENCE CAMPBELL CONFERENCE

#### Norris Division

| Team | GP | W | L | T | GF | GA | PTS |
|---|---|---|---|---|---|---|---|
| Detroit | 80 | 41 | 28 | 11 | 322 | 269 | 93 |
| St. Louis | 80 | 34 | 38 | 8 | 278 | 294 | 76 |
| Chicago | 80 | 30 | 41 | 9 | 284 | 328 | 69 |
| Toronto | 80 | 21 | 49 | 10 | 273 | 345 | 52 |
| Minnesota | 80 | 19 | 48 | 13 | 242 | 349 | 51 |

#### Smythe Division

| Team | GP | W | L | T | GF | GA | PTS |
|---|---|---|---|---|---|---|---|
| Calgary | 80 | 48 | 23 | 9 | 397 | 305 | 105 |
| *Edmonton | 80 | 44 | 25 | 11 | 363 | 288 | 99 |
| Winnipeg | 80 | 33 | 36 | 11 | 292 | 310 | 77 |
| Los Angeles | 80 | 30 | 42 | 8 | 318 | 359 | 68 |
| Vancouver | 80 | 25 | 46 | 9 | 272 | 320 | 59 |

### PRINCE OF WALES CONFERENCE

#### Adams Division

| Team | GP | W | L | T | GF | GA | PTS |
|---|---|---|---|---|---|---|---|
| Montreal | 80 | 45 | 22 | 13 | 298 | 238 | 103 |
| Boston | 80 | 44 | 30 | 6 | 300 | 251 | 94 |
| Buffalo | 80 | 37 | 32 | 11 | 283 | 305 | 85 |
| Hartford | 80 | 35 | 38 | 7 | 249 | 267 | 77 |
| Quebec | 80 | 32 | 43 | 5 | 271 | 306 | 69 |

#### Patrick Division

| Team | GP | W | L | T | GF | GA | PTS |
|---|---|---|---|---|---|---|---|
| NY Islanders | 80 | 39 | 31 | 10 | 308 | 267 | 88 |
| Washington | 80 | 38 | 33 | 9 | 281 | 249 | 85 |
| Philadelphia | 80 | 38 | 33 | 9 | 292 | 292 | 85 |
| New Jersey | 80 | 38 | 36 | 6 | 295 | 296 | 82 |
| NY Rangers | 80 | 36 | 34 | 10 | 300 | 283 | 82 |
| Pittsburgh | 80 | 36 | 35 | 9 | 319 | 316 | 81 |

#### Leading Scorers

| Player | Team | GP | G | A | PTS | PIM |
|---|---|---|---|---|---|---|
| Mario Lemieux | Pittsburgh | 77 | 70 | 98 | 168 | 92 |
| Wayne Gretzky | Edmonton | 64 | 40 | 109 | 149 | 24 |
| Denis Savard | Chicago | 80 | 44 | 87 | 131 | 95 |
| Dale Hawerchuk | Winnipeg | 80 | 44 | 77 | 121 | 59 |
| Luc Robitaille | Los Angeles | 80 | 53 | 58 | 111 | 82 |
| Peter Stastny | Quebec | 76 | 46 | 65 | 111 | 69 |
| Mark Messier | Edmonton | 77 | 37 | 74 | 111 | 103 |
| Jimmy Carson | Los Angeles | 80 | 55 | 52 | 107 | 45 |
| Hakan Loob | Calgary | 80 | 50 | 56 | 106 | 47 |
| Michel Goulet | Quebec | 80 | 48 | 58 | 106 | 56 |

## 1988-89

### CLARENCE CAMPBELL CONFERENCE

#### Norris Division

| Team | GP | W | L | T | GF | GA | PTS |
|---|---|---|---|---|---|---|---|
| Detroit | 80 | 34 | 34 | 12 | 313 | 316 | 80 |
| St. Louis | 80 | 33 | 35 | 12 | 275 | 285 | 78 |
| Minnesota | 80 | 27 | 37 | 16 | 258 | 278 | 70 |
| Chicago | 80 | 27 | 41 | 12 | 297 | 335 | 66 |
| Toronto | 80 | 28 | 46 | 6 | 259 | 342 | 62 |

#### Smythe Division

| Team | GP | W | L | T | GF | GA | PTS |
|---|---|---|---|---|---|---|---|
| *Calgary | 80 | 54 | 17 | 9 | 354 | 226 | 117 |
| Los Angeles | 80 | 42 | 31 | 7 | 376 | 335 | 91 |
| Edmonton | 80 | 38 | 34 | 8 | 325 | 306 | 84 |
| Vancouver | 80 | 33 | 39 | 8 | 251 | 253 | 74 |
| Winnipeg | 80 | 26 | 42 | 12 | 300 | 355 | 64 |

### PRINCE OF WALES CONFERENCE

#### Adams Division

| Team | GP | W | L | T | GF | GA | PTS |
|---|---|---|---|---|---|---|---|
| Montreal | 80 | 53 | 18 | 9 | 315 | 218 | 115 |
| Boston | 80 | 37 | 29 | 14 | 289 | 256 | 88 |
| Buffalo | 80 | 38 | 35 | 7 | 291 | 299 | 83 |
| Hartford | 80 | 37 | 38 | 5 | 299 | 290 | 79 |
| Quebec | 80 | 27 | 46 | 7 | 269 | 342 | 61 |

#### Patrick Division

| Team | GP | W | L | T | GF | GA | PTS |
|---|---|---|---|---|---|---|---|
| Washington | 80 | 41 | 29 | 10 | 305 | 259 | 92 |
| Pittsburgh | 80 | 40 | 33 | 7 | 347 | 349 | 87 |
| NY Rangers | 80 | 37 | 35 | 8 | 310 | 307 | 82 |
| Philadelphia | 80 | 36 | 36 | 8 | 307 | 285 | 80 |
| New Jersey | 80 | 27 | 41 | 12 | 281 | 325 | 66 |
| NY Islanders | 80 | 28 | 47 | 5 | 265 | 325 | 61 |

#### Leading Scorers

| Player | Team | GP | G | A | PTS | PIM |
|---|---|---|---|---|---|---|
| Mario Lemieux | Pittsburgh | 76 | 85 | 114 | 199 | 100 |
| Wayne Gretzky | Los Angeles | 78 | 54 | 114 | 168 | 26 |
| Steve Yzerman | Detroit | 80 | 65 | 90 | 155 | 61 |
| Bernie Nicholls | Los Angeles | 79 | 70 | 80 | 150 | 96 |
| Rob Brown | Pittsburgh | 68 | 49 | 66 | 115 | 118 |
| Paul Coffey | Pittsburgh | 75 | 30 | 83 | 113 | 193 |
| Joe Mullen | Calgary | 79 | 51 | 59 | 110 | 16 |
| Jari Kurri | Edmonton | 76 | 44 | 58 | 102 | 69 |
| Jimmy Carson | Edmonton | 80 | 49 | 51 | 100 | 36 |
| Luc Robitaille | Los Angeles | 78 | 46 | 52 | 98 | 65 |

## 1989-90

### CLARENCE CAMPBELL CONFERENCE

#### Norris Division

| Team | GP | W | L | T | GF | GA | PTS |
|---|---|---|---|---|---|---|---|
| Chicago | 80 | 41 | 33 | 6 | 316 | 294 | 88 |
| St. Louis | 80 | 37 | 34 | 9 | 295 | 279 | 83 |
| Toronto | 80 | 38 | 38 | 4 | 337 | 358 | 80 |
| Minnesota | 80 | 36 | 40 | 4 | 284 | 291 | 76 |
| Detroit | 80 | 28 | 38 | 14 | 288 | 323 | 70 |

#### Smythe Division

| Team | GP | W | L | T | GF | GA | PTS |
|---|---|---|---|---|---|---|---|
| Calgary | 80 | 42 | 23 | 15 | 348 | 265 | 99 |
| *Edmonton | 80 | 38 | 28 | 14 | 315 | 283 | 90 |
| Winnipeg | 80 | 37 | 32 | 11 | 298 | 290 | 85 |
| Los Angeles | 80 | 34 | 39 | 7 | 338 | 337 | 75 |
| Vancouver | 80 | 25 | 41 | 14 | 245 | 306 | 64 |

### PRINCE OF WALES CONFERENCE

#### Adams Division

| Team | GP | W | L | T | GF | GA | PTS |
|---|---|---|---|---|---|---|---|
| Boston | 80 | 46 | 25 | 9 | 289 | 232 | 101 |
| Buffalo | 80 | 45 | 27 | 8 | 286 | 248 | 98 |
| Montreal | 80 | 41 | 28 | 11 | 288 | 234 | 93 |
| Hartford | 80 | 38 | 33 | 9 | 275 | 268 | 85 |
| Quebec | 80 | 12 | 61 | 7 | 240 | 407 | 31 |

#### Patrick Division

| Team | GP | W | L | T | GF | GA | PTS |
|---|---|---|---|---|---|---|---|
| NY Rangers | 80 | 36 | 31 | 13 | 279 | 267 | 85 |
| New Jersey | 80 | 37 | 34 | 9 | 295 | 288 | 83 |
| Washington | 80 | 36 | 38 | 6 | 284 | 275 | 78 |
| NY Islanders | 80 | 31 | 38 | 11 | 281 | 288 | 73 |
| Pittsburgh | 80 | 32 | 40 | 8 | 318 | 359 | 72 |
| Philadelphia | 80 | 30 | 39 | 11 | 290 | 297 | 71 |

#### Leading Scorers

| Player | Team | GP | G | A | PTS | PIM |
|---|---|---|---|---|---|---|
| Wayne Gretzky | Los Angeles | 73 | 40 | 102 | 142 | 42 |
| Mark Messier | Edmonton | 79 | 45 | 84 | 129 | 79 |
| Steve Yzerman | Detroit | 79 | 62 | 65 | 127 | 79 |
| Mario Lemieux | Pittsburgh | 59 | 45 | 78 | 123 | 78 |
| Brett Hull | St. Louis | 80 | 72 | 41 | 113 | 24 |
| Bernie Nicholls | L.A., NYR | 79 | 39 | 73 | 112 | 86 |
| Pierre Turgeon | Buffalo | 80 | 40 | 66 | 106 | 29 |
| Pat LaFontaine | NY Islanders | 74 | 54 | 51 | 105 | 38 |
| Paul Coffey | Pittsburgh | 80 | 29 | 74 | 103 | 95 |
| Joe Sakic | Quebec | 80 | 39 | 63 | 102 | 27 |
| Adam Oates | St. Louis | 80 | 23 | 79 | 102 | 30 |

## 1990-91

### CLARENCE CAMPBELL CONFERENCE

#### Norris Division

| Team | GP | W | L | T | GF | GA | PTS |
|---|---|---|---|---|---|---|---|
| Chicago | 80 | 49 | 23 | 8 | 284 | 211 | 106 |
| St. Louis | 80 | 47 | 22 | 11 | 310 | 250 | 105 |
| Detroit | 80 | 34 | 38 | 8 | 273 | 298 | 76 |
| Minnesota | 80 | 27 | 39 | 14 | 256 | 266 | 68 |
| Toronto | 80 | 23 | 46 | 11 | 241 | 318 | 57 |

#### Smythe Division

| Team | GP | W | L | T | GF | GA | PTS |
|---|---|---|---|---|---|---|---|
| Los Angeles | 80 | 46 | 24 | 10 | 340 | 254 | 102 |
| Calgary | 80 | 46 | 26 | 8 | 344 | 263 | 100 |
| Edmonton | 80 | 37 | 37 | 6 | 272 | 272 | 80 |
| Vancouver | 80 | 28 | 43 | 9 | 243 | 315 | 65 |
| Winnipeg | 80 | 26 | 43 | 11 | 260 | 288 | 63 |

### PRINCE OF WALES CONFERENCE

#### Adams Division

| Team | GP | W | L | T | GF | GA | PTS |
|---|---|---|---|---|---|---|---|
| Boston | 80 | 44 | 24 | 12 | 299 | 264 | 100 |
| Montreal | 80 | 39 | 30 | 11 | 273 | 249 | 89 |
| Buffalo | 80 | 31 | 30 | 19 | 292 | 278 | 81 |
| Hartford | 80 | 31 | 38 | 11 | 238 | 276 | 73 |
| Quebec | 80 | 16 | 50 | 14 | 236 | 354 | 46 |

#### Patrick Division

| Team | GP | W | L | T | GF | GA | PTS |
|---|---|---|---|---|---|---|---|
| *Pittsburgh | 80 | 41 | 33 | 6 | 342 | 305 | 88 |
| NY Rangers | 80 | 36 | 31 | 13 | 297 | 265 | 85 |
| Washington | 80 | 37 | 36 | 7 | 258 | 258 | 81 |
| New Jersey | 80 | 32 | 33 | 15 | 272 | 264 | 79 |
| Philadelphia | 80 | 33 | 37 | 10 | 252 | 267 | 76 |
| NY Islanders | 80 | 25 | 45 | 10 | 223 | 290 | 60 |

#### Leading Scorers

| Player | Team | GP | G | A | PTS | PIM |
|---|---|---|---|---|---|---|
| Wayne Gretzky | Los Angeles | 78 | 41 | 122 | 163 | 16 |
| Brett Hull | St. Louis | 78 | 86 | 45 | 131 | 22 |
| Adam Oates | St. Louis | 61 | 25 | 90 | 115 | 29 |
| Mark Recchi | Pittsburgh | 78 | 40 | 73 | 113 | 48 |
| John Cullen | Pit., Hfd. | 78 | 39 | 71 | 110 | 101 |
| Joe Sakic | Quebec | 80 | 48 | 61 | 109 | 24 |
| Steve Yzerman | Detroit | 80 | 51 | 57 | 108 | 34 |
| Theoren Fleury | Calgary | 79 | 51 | 53 | 104 | 136 |
| Al MacInnis | Calgary | 78 | 28 | 75 | 103 | 90 |
| Steve Larmer | Chicago | 80 | 44 | 57 | 101 | 79 |

## 1991-92

### CLARENCE CAMPBELL CONFERENCE

#### Norris Division

| Team | GP | W | L | T | GF | GA | PTS |
|---|---|---|---|---|---|---|---|
| Detroit | 80 | 43 | 25 | 12 | 320 | 256 | 98 |
| Chicago | 80 | 36 | 29 | 15 | 257 | 236 | 87 |
| St. Louis | 80 | 36 | 33 | 11 | 279 | 266 | 83 |
| Minnesota | 80 | 32 | 42 | 6 | 246 | 278 | 70 |
| Toronto | 80 | 30 | 43 | 7 | 234 | 294 | 67 |

#### Smythe Division

| Team | GP | W | L | T | GF | GA | PTS |
|---|---|---|---|---|---|---|---|
| Vancouver | 80 | 42 | 26 | 12 | 285 | 250 | 96 |
| Los Angeles | 80 | 35 | 31 | 14 | 287 | 296 | 84 |
| Edmonton | 80 | 36 | 34 | 10 | 295 | 297 | 82 |
| Winnipeg | 80 | 33 | 32 | 15 | 251 | 244 | 81 |
| Calgary | 80 | 31 | 37 | 12 | 296 | 305 | 74 |
| San Jose | 80 | 17 | 58 | 5 | 219 | 359 | 39 |

### PRINCE OF WALES CONFERENCE

#### Adams Division

| Team | GP | W | L | T | GF | GA | PTS |
|---|---|---|---|---|---|---|---|
| Montreal | 80 | 41 | 28 | 11 | 267 | 207 | 93 |
| Boston | 80 | 36 | 32 | 12 | 270 | 275 | 84 |
| Buffalo | 80 | 31 | 37 | 12 | 289 | 299 | 74 |
| Hartford | 80 | 26 | 41 | 13 | 247 | 283 | 65 |
| Quebec | 80 | 20 | 48 | 12 | 255 | 318 | 52 |

#### Patrick Division

| Team | GP | W | L | T | GF | GA | PTS |
|---|---|---|---|---|---|---|---|
| NY Rangers | 80 | 50 | 25 | 5 | 321 | 246 | 105 |
| Washington | 80 | 45 | 27 | 8 | 330 | 275 | 98 |
| *Pittsburgh | 80 | 39 | 32 | 9 | 343 | 308 | 87 |
| New Jersey | 80 | 38 | 31 | 11 | 289 | 259 | 87 |
| NY Islanders | 80 | 34 | 35 | 11 | 291 | 299 | 79 |
| Philadelphia | 80 | 32 | 37 | 11 | 252 | 273 | 75 |

#### Leading Scorers

| Player | Team | GP | G | A | PTS | PIM |
|---|---|---|---|---|---|---|
| Mario Lemieux | Pittsburgh | 64 | 44 | 87 | 131 | 94 |
| Kevin Stevens | Pittsburgh | 80 | 54 | 69 | 123 | 254 |
| Wayne Gretzky | Los Angeles | 74 | 31 | 90 | 121 | 34 |
| Brett Hull | St. Louis | 73 | 70 | 39 | 109 | 48 |
| Luc Robitaille | Los Angeles | 80 | 44 | 63 | 107 | 95 |
| Mark Messier | NY Rangers | 79 | 35 | 72 | 107 | 76 |
| Jeremy Roenick | Chicago | 80 | 53 | 50 | 103 | 23 |
| Steve Yzerman | Detroit | 79 | 45 | 58 | 103 | 64 |
| Brian Leetch | NY Rangers | 80 | 22 | 80 | 102 | 26 |
| Adam Oates | St.L., Bos. | 80 | 20 | 79 | 99 | 22 |

## 1992-93

### CLARENCE CAMPBELL CONFERENCE

#### Norris Division

| Team | GP | W | L | T | GF | GA | PTS |
|---|---|---|---|---|---|---|---|
| Chicago | 84 | 47 | 25 | 12 | 279 | 230 | 106 |
| Detroit | 84 | 47 | 28 | 9 | 369 | 280 | 103 |
| Toronto | 84 | 44 | 29 | 11 | 288 | 241 | 99 |
| St. Louis | 84 | 37 | 36 | 11 | 282 | 278 | 85 |
| Minnesota | 84 | 36 | 38 | 10 | 272 | 293 | 82 |
| Tampa Bay | 84 | 23 | 54 | 7 | 245 | 332 | 53 |

#### Smythe Division

| Team | GP | W | L | T | GF | GA | PTS |
|---|---|---|---|---|---|---|---|
| Vancouver | 84 | 46 | 29 | 9 | 346 | 278 | 101 |
| Calgary | 84 | 43 | 30 | 11 | 322 | 282 | 97 |
| Los Angeles | 84 | 39 | 35 | 10 | 338 | 340 | 88 |
| Winnipeg | 84 | 40 | 37 | 7 | 322 | 320 | 87 |
| Edmonton | 84 | 26 | 50 | 8 | 242 | 337 | 60 |
| San Jose | 84 | 11 | 71 | 2 | 218 | 414 | 24 |

### PRINCE OF WALES CONFERENCE

#### Adams Division

| Team | GP | W | L | T | GF | GA | PTS |
|---|---|---|---|---|---|---|---|
| Boston | 84 | 51 | 26 | 7 | 332 | 268 | 109 |
| Quebec | 84 | 47 | 27 | 10 | 351 | 300 | 104 |
| *Montreal | 84 | 48 | 30 | 6 | 326 | 280 | 102 |
| Buffalo | 84 | 38 | 36 | 10 | 335 | 297 | 86 |
| Hartford | 84 | 26 | 52 | 6 | 284 | 369 | 58 |
| Ottawa | 84 | 10 | 70 | 4 | 202 | 395 | 24 |

#### Patrick Division

| Team | GP | W | L | T | GF | GA | PTS |
|---|---|---|---|---|---|---|---|
| Pittsburgh | 84 | 56 | 21 | 7 | 367 | 268 | 119 |
| Washington | 84 | 43 | 34 | 7 | 325 | 286 | 93 |
| NY Islanders | 84 | 40 | 37 | 7 | 335 | 297 | 87 |
| New Jersey | 84 | 40 | 37 | 7 | 308 | 299 | 87 |
| Philadelphia | 84 | 36 | 37 | 11 | 319 | 319 | 83 |
| NY Rangers | 84 | 34 | 39 | 11 | 304 | 308 | 79 |

#### Leading Scorers

| Player | Team | GP | G | A | PTS | PIM |
|---|---|---|---|---|---|---|
| Mario Lemieux | Pittsburgh | 60 | 69 | 91 | 160 | 38 |
| Pat LaFontaine | Buffalo | 84 | 53 | 95 | 148 | 63 |
| Adam Oates | Boston | 84 | 45 | 97 | 142 | 32 |
| Steve Yzerman | Detroit | 84 | 58 | 79 | 137 | 44 |
| Teemu Selanne | Winnipeg | 84 | 76 | 56 | 132 | 45 |
| Pierre Turgeon | NY Islanders | 83 | 58 | 74 | 132 | 26 |
| Alexander Mogilny | Buffalo | 77 | 76 | 51 | 127 | 40 |
| Doug Gilmour | Toronto | 83 | 32 | 95 | 127 | 100 |
| Luc Robitaille | Los Angeles | 84 | 63 | 62 | 125 | 100 |
| Mark Recchi | Philadelphia | 84 | 53 | 70 | 123 | 95 |

## 1993-94

### EASTERN CONFERENCE

#### Northeast Division

| Team | GP | W | L | T | GF | GA | PTS |
|---|---|---|---|---|---|---|---|
| Pittsburgh | 84 | 44 | 27 | 13 | 299 | 285 | 101 |
| Boston | 84 | 42 | 29 | 13 | 289 | 252 | 97 |
| Montreal | 84 | 41 | 29 | 14 | 283 | 248 | 96 |
| Buffalo | 84 | 43 | 32 | 9 | 282 | 218 | 95 |
| Quebec | 84 | 34 | 42 | 8 | 277 | 292 | 76 |
| Hartford | 84 | 27 | 48 | 9 | 227 | 288 | 63 |
| Ottawa | 84 | 14 | 61 | 9 | 201 | 397 | 37 |

#### Atlantic Division

| Team | GP | W | L | T | GF | GA | PTS |
|---|---|---|---|---|---|---|---|
| *NY Rangers | 84 | 52 | 24 | 8 | 299 | 231 | 112 |
| New Jersey | 84 | 47 | 25 | 12 | 306 | 220 | 106 |
| Washington | 84 | 39 | 35 | 10 | 277 | 263 | 88 |
| NY Islanders | 84 | 36 | 36 | 12 | 282 | 264 | 84 |
| Florida | 84 | 33 | 34 | 17 | 233 | 233 | 83 |
| Philadelphia | 84 | 35 | 39 | 10 | 294 | 314 | 80 |
| Tampa Bay | 84 | 30 | 43 | 11 | 224 | 251 | 71 |

### WESTERN CONFERENCE

#### Central Division

| Team | GP | W | L | T | GF | GA | PTS |
|---|---|---|---|---|---|---|---|
| Detroit | 84 | 46 | 30 | 8 | 356 | 275 | 100 |
| Toronto | 84 | 43 | 29 | 12 | 280 | 243 | 98 |
| Dallas | 84 | 42 | 29 | 13 | 286 | 265 | 97 |
| St. Louis | 84 | 40 | 33 | 11 | 270 | 283 | 91 |
| Chicago | 84 | 39 | 36 | 9 | 254 | 240 | 87 |
| Winnipeg | 84 | 24 | 51 | 9 | 245 | 344 | 57 |

#### Pacific Division

| Team | GP | W | L | T | GF | GA | PTS |
|---|---|---|---|---|---|---|---|
| Calgary | 84 | 42 | 29 | 13 | 302 | 256 | 97 |
| Vancouver | 84 | 41 | 40 | 3 | 279 | 276 | 85 |
| San Jose | 84 | 33 | 35 | 16 | 252 | 265 | 82 |
| Anaheim | 84 | 33 | 46 | 5 | 229 | 251 | 71 |
| Los Angeles | 84 | 27 | 45 | 12 | 294 | 322 | 66 |
| Edmonton | 84 | 25 | 45 | 14 | 261 | 305 | 64 |

#### Leading Scorers

| Player | Team | GP | G | A | PTS | PIM |
|---|---|---|---|---|---|---|
| Wayne Gretzky | Los Angeles | 81 | 38 | 92 | 130 | 20 |
| Sergei Fedorov | Detroit | 82 | 56 | 64 | 120 | 34 |
| Adam Oates | Boston | 77 | 32 | 80 | 112 | 45 |
| Doug Gilmour | Toronto | 83 | 27 | 84 | 111 | 105 |
| Pavel Bure | Vancouver | 76 | 60 | 47 | 107 | 86 |
| Jeremy Roenick | Chicago | 84 | 46 | 61 | 107 | 125 |
| Mark Recchi | Philadelphia | 84 | 40 | 67 | 107 | 46 |
| Brendan Shanahan | St. Louis | 81 | 52 | 50 | 102 | 211 |
| Dave Andreychuk | Toronto | 83 | 53 | 46 | 99 | 98 |
| Jaromir Jagr | Pittsburgh | 80 | 32 | 67 | 99 | 61 |

## 1994-95

### EASTERN CONFERENCE

#### Northeast Division

| Team | GP | W | L | T | GF | GA | PTS |
|---|---|---|---|---|---|---|---|
| Quebec | 48 | 30 | 13 | 5 | 185 | 134 | 65 |
| Pittsburgh | 48 | 29 | 16 | 3 | 181 | 158 | 61 |
| Boston | 48 | 27 | 18 | 3 | 150 | 127 | 57 |
| Buffalo | 48 | 22 | 19 | 7 | 130 | 119 | 51 |
| Hartford | 48 | 19 | 24 | 5 | 127 | 141 | 43 |
| Montreal | 48 | 18 | 23 | 7 | 125 | 148 | 43 |
| Ottawa | 48 | 9 | 34 | 5 | 117 | 174 | 23 |

#### Atlantic Division

| Team | GP | W | L | T | GF | GA | PTS |
|---|---|---|---|---|---|---|---|
| Philadelphia | 48 | 28 | 16 | 4 | 150 | 132 | 60 |
| *New Jersey | 48 | 22 | 18 | 8 | 136 | 121 | 52 |
| Washington | 48 | 22 | 18 | 8 | 136 | 120 | 52 |
| NY Rangers | 48 | 22 | 23 | 3 | 139 | 134 | 47 |
| Florida | 48 | 20 | 22 | 6 | 115 | 127 | 46 |
| Tampa Bay | 48 | 17 | 28 | 3 | 120 | 144 | 37 |
| NY Islanders | 48 | 15 | 28 | 5 | 126 | 158 | 35 |

### WESTERN CONFERENCE

#### Central Division

| Team | GP | W | L | T | GF | GA | PTS |
|---|---|---|---|---|---|---|---|
| Detroit | 48 | 33 | 11 | 4 | 180 | 117 | 70 |
| St. Louis | 48 | 28 | 15 | 5 | 178 | 135 | 61 |
| Chicago | 48 | 24 | 19 | 5 | 156 | 115 | 53 |
| Toronto | 48 | 21 | 19 | 8 | 135 | 146 | 50 |
| Dallas | 48 | 17 | 23 | 8 | 136 | 135 | 42 |
| Winnipeg | 48 | 16 | 25 | 7 | 157 | 177 | 39 |

#### Pacific Division

| Team | GP | W | L | T | GF | GA | PTS |
|---|---|---|---|---|---|---|---|
| Calgary | 48 | 24 | 17 | 7 | 163 | 135 | 55 |
| Vancouver | 48 | 18 | 18 | 12 | 153 | 148 | 48 |
| San Jose | 48 | 19 | 25 | 4 | 129 | 161 | 42 |
| Los Angeles | 48 | 16 | 23 | 9 | 142 | 174 | 41 |
| Edmonton | 48 | 17 | 27 | 4 | 136 | 183 | 38 |
| Anaheim | 48 | 16 | 27 | 5 | 125 | 164 | 37 |

#### Leading Scorers

| Player | Team | GP | G | A | PTS | PIM |
|---|---|---|---|---|---|---|
| Jaromir Jagr | Pittsburgh | 48 | 32 | 38 | 70 | 37 |
| Eric Lindros | Philadelphia | 46 | 29 | 41 | 70 | 60 |
| Alex Zhamnov | Winnipeg | 48 | 30 | 35 | 65 | 20 |
| Joe Sakic | Quebec | 47 | 19 | 43 | 62 | 30 |
| Ron Francis | Pittsburgh | 44 | 11 | 48 | 59 | 18 |
| Theoren Fleury | Calgary | 47 | 29 | 29 | 58 | 112 |
| Paul Coffey | Detroit | 45 | 14 | 44 | 58 | 72 |
| Mikael Renberg | Philadelphia | 47 | 26 | 31 | 57 | 20 |
| John LeClair | Mtl., Phi. | 46 | 26 | 28 | 54 | 30 |
| Mark Messier | NY Rangers | 46 | 14 | 39 | 53 | 40 |
| Adam Oates | Boston | 48 | 12 | 41 | 53 | 8 |

## 1995-96

### EASTERN CONFERENCE

#### Northeast Division

| Team | GP | W | L | T | GF | GA | PTS |
|---|---|---|---|---|---|---|---|
| Pittsburgh | 82 | 49 | 29 | 4 | 362 | 284 | 102 |
| Boston | 82 | 40 | 31 | 11 | 282 | 269 | 91 |
| Montreal | 82 | 40 | 32 | 10 | 265 | 248 | 90 |
| Hartford | 82 | 34 | 39 | 9 | 237 | 259 | 77 |
| Buffalo | 82 | 33 | 42 | 7 | 247 | 262 | 73 |
| Ottawa | 82 | 18 | 59 | 5 | 191 | 291 | 41 |

#### Atlantic Division

| Team | GP | W | L | T | GF | GA | PTS |
|---|---|---|---|---|---|---|---|
| Philadelphia | 82 | 45 | 24 | 13 | 282 | 208 | 103 |
| NY Rangers | 82 | 41 | 27 | 14 | 272 | 237 | 96 |
| Florida | 82 | 41 | 31 | 10 | 254 | 234 | 92 |
| Washington | 82 | 39 | 32 | 11 | 234 | 204 | 89 |
| Tampa Bay | 82 | 38 | 32 | 12 | 238 | 248 | 88 |
| New Jersey | 82 | 37 | 33 | 12 | 215 | 202 | 86 |
| NY Islanders | 82 | 22 | 50 | 10 | 229 | 315 | 54 |

### WESTERN CONFERENCE

#### Central Division

| Team | GP | W | L | T | GF | GA | PTS |
|---|---|---|---|---|---|---|---|
| Detroit | 82 | 62 | 13 | 7 | 325 | 181 | 131 |
| Chicago | 82 | 40 | 28 | 14 | 273 | 220 | 94 |
| Toronto | 82 | 34 | 36 | 12 | 247 | 252 | 80 |
| St. Louis | 82 | 32 | 34 | 16 | 219 | 248 | 80 |
| Winnipeg | 82 | 36 | 40 | 6 | 275 | 291 | 78 |
| Dallas | 82 | 26 | 42 | 14 | 227 | 280 | 66 |

#### Pacific Division

| Team | GP | W | L | T | GF | GA | PTS |
|---|---|---|---|---|---|---|---|
| *Colorado | 82 | 47 | 25 | 10 | 326 | 240 | 104 |
| Calgary | 82 | 34 | 37 | 11 | 241 | 240 | 79 |
| Vancouver | 82 | 32 | 35 | 15 | 278 | 278 | 79 |
| Anaheim | 82 | 35 | 39 | 8 | 234 | 247 | 78 |
| Edmonton | 82 | 30 | 44 | 8 | 240 | 304 | 68 |
| Los Angeles | 82 | 24 | 40 | 18 | 256 | 302 | 66 |
| San Jose | 82 | 20 | 55 | 7 | 252 | 357 | 47 |

#### Leading Scorers

| Player | Team | GP | G | A | PTS | PIM |
|---|---|---|---|---|---|---|
| Mario Lemieux | Pittsburgh | 70 | 69 | 92 | 161 | 54 |
| Jaromir Jagr | Pittsburgh | 82 | 62 | 87 | 149 | 96 |
| Joe Sakic | Colorado | 82 | 51 | 69 | 120 | 44 |
| Ron Francis | Pittsburgh | 77 | 27 | 92 | 119 | 56 |
| Peter Forsberg | Colorado | 82 | 30 | 86 | 116 | 47 |
| Eric Lindros | Philadelphia | 73 | 47 | 68 | 115 | 163 |
| Paul Kariya | Anaheim | 82 | 50 | 58 | 108 | 20 |
| Teemu Selanne | Wpg., Ana. | 79 | 40 | 68 | 108 | 22 |
| Alexander Mogilny | Vancouver | 79 | 55 | 52 | 107 | 16 |
| Sergei Fedorov | Detroit | 78 | 39 | 68 | 107 | 48 |

## 1996-97

### EASTERN CONFERENCE

#### Northeast Division

| Team | GP | W | L | T | GF | GA | PTS |
|---|---|---|---|---|---|---|---|
| Buffalo | 82 | 40 | 30 | 12 | 237 | 208 | 92 |
| Pittsburgh | 82 | 38 | 36 | 8 | 285 | 280 | 84 |
| Ottawa | 82 | 31 | 36 | 15 | 226 | 234 | 77 |
| Montreal | 82 | 31 | 36 | 15 | 249 | 276 | 77 |
| Hartford | 82 | 32 | 39 | 11 | 226 | 256 | 75 |
| Boston | 82 | 26 | 47 | 9 | 234 | 300 | 61 |

#### Atlantic Division

| Team | GP | W | L | T | GF | GA | PTS |
|---|---|---|---|---|---|---|---|
| New Jersey | 82 | 45 | 23 | 14 | 231 | 182 | 104 |
| Philadelphia | 82 | 45 | 24 | 13 | 274 | 217 | 103 |
| Florida | 82 | 35 | 28 | 19 | 221 | 201 | 89 |
| NY Rangers | 82 | 38 | 34 | 10 | 258 | 231 | 86 |
| Washington | 82 | 33 | 40 | 9 | 214 | 231 | 75 |
| Tampa Bay | 82 | 32 | 40 | 10 | 217 | 247 | 74 |
| NY Islanders | 82 | 29 | 41 | 12 | 240 | 250 | 70 |

### WESTERN CONFERENCE

#### Central Division

| Team | GP | W | L | T | GF | GA | PTS |
|---|---|---|---|---|---|---|---|
| Dallas | 82 | 48 | 26 | 8 | 252 | 198 | 104 |
| *Detroit | 82 | 38 | 26 | 18 | 253 | 197 | 94 |
| Phoenix | 82 | 38 | 37 | 7 | 240 | 243 | 83 |
| St. Louis | 82 | 36 | 35 | 11 | 236 | 239 | 83 |
| Chicago | 82 | 34 | 35 | 13 | 223 | 210 | 81 |
| Toronto | 82 | 30 | 44 | 8 | 230 | 273 | 68 |

#### Pacific Division

| Team | GP | W | L | T | GF | GA | PTS |
|---|---|---|---|---|---|---|---|
| Colorado | 82 | 49 | 24 | 9 | 277 | 205 | 107 |
| Anaheim | 82 | 36 | 33 | 13 | 245 | 233 | 85 |
| Edmonton | 82 | 36 | 37 | 9 | 252 | 247 | 81 |
| Vancouver | 82 | 35 | 40 | 7 | 257 | 273 | 77 |
| Calgary | 82 | 32 | 41 | 9 | 214 | 239 | 73 |
| Los Angeles | 82 | 28 | 43 | 11 | 214 | 268 | 67 |
| San Jose | 82 | 27 | 47 | 8 | 211 | 278 | 62 |

#### Leading Scorers

| Player | Team | GP | G | A | PTS | PIM |
|---|---|---|---|---|---|---|
| Mario Lemieux | Pittsburgh | 76 | 50 | 72 | 122 | 65 |
| Teemu Selanne | Anaheim | 78 | 51 | 58 | 109 | 34 |
| Paul Kariya | Anaheim | 69 | 44 | 55 | 99 | 6 |
| John LeClair | Philadelphia | 82 | 50 | 47 | 97 | 58 |
| Wayne Gretzky | NY Rangers | 82 | 25 | 72 | 97 | 28 |
| Jaromir Jagr | Pittsburgh | 63 | 47 | 48 | 95 | 40 |
| Mats Sundin | Toronto | 82 | 41 | 53 | 94 | 59 |
| Ziggy Palffy | NY Islanders | 80 | 48 | 42 | 90 | 43 |
| Ron Francis | Pittsburgh | 81 | 27 | 63 | 90 | 20 |
| Brendan Shanahan | Hfd., Det. | 81 | 47 | 41 | 88 | 131 |

## 1997-98

### EASTERN CONFERENCE

#### Northeast Division

| Team | GP | W | L | T | GF | GA | PTS |
|---|---|---|---|---|---|---|---|
| Pittsburgh | 82 | 40 | 24 | 18 | 228 | 188 | 98 |
| Boston | 82 | 39 | 30 | 13 | 221 | 194 | 91 |
| Buffalo | 82 | 36 | 29 | 17 | 211 | 187 | 89 |
| Montreal | 82 | 37 | 32 | 13 | 235 | 208 | 87 |
| Ottawa | 82 | 34 | 33 | 15 | 193 | 200 | 83 |
| Carolina | 82 | 33 | 41 | 8 | 200 | 219 | 74 |

#### Atlantic Division

| | | | | | | | |
|---|---|---|---|---|---|---|---|
| New Jersey | 82 | 48 | 23 | 11 | 225 | 166 | 107 |
| Philadelphia | 82 | 42 | 29 | 11 | 242 | 193 | 95 |
| Washington | 82 | 40 | 30 | 12 | 219 | 202 | 92 |
| NY Islanders | 82 | 30 | 41 | 11 | 212 | 225 | 71 |
| NY Rangers | 82 | 25 | 39 | 18 | 197 | 231 | 68 |
| Florida | 82 | 24 | 43 | 15 | 203 | 256 | 63 |
| Tampa Bay | 82 | 17 | 55 | 10 | 151 | 269 | 44 |

### WESTERN CONFERENCE

#### Central Division

| | | | | | | | |
|---|---|---|---|---|---|---|---|
| Dallas | 82 | 49 | 22 | 11 | 242 | 167 | 109 |
| *Detroit | 82 | 44 | 23 | 15 | 250 | 196 | 103 |
| St. Louis | 82 | 45 | 29 | 8 | 256 | 204 | 98 |
| Phoenix | 82 | 35 | 35 | 12 | 224 | 227 | 82 |
| Chicago | 82 | 30 | 39 | 13 | 192 | 199 | 73 |
| Toronto | 82 | 30 | 43 | 9 | 194 | 237 | 69 |

#### Pacific Division

| | | | | | | | |
|---|---|---|---|---|---|---|---|
| Colorado | 82 | 39 | 26 | 17 | 231 | 205 | 95 |
| Los Angeles | 82 | 38 | 33 | 11 | 227 | 225 | 87 |
| Edmonton | 82 | 35 | 37 | 10 | 215 | 224 | 80 |
| San Jose | 82 | 34 | 38 | 10 | 210 | 216 | 78 |
| Calgary | 82 | 26 | 41 | 15 | 217 | 252 | 67 |
| Anaheim | 82 | 26 | 43 | 13 | 205 | 261 | 65 |
| Vancouver | 82 | 25 | 43 | 14 | 224 | 273 | 64 |

#### Leading Scorers

| Player | Team | GP | G | A | PTS | PIM |
|---|---|---|---|---|---|---|
| Jaromir Jagr | Pittsburgh | 77 | 35 | 67 | 102 | 64 |
| Peter Forsberg | Colorado | 72 | 25 | 66 | 91 | 94 |
| Pavel Bure | Vancouver | 82 | 51 | 39 | 90 | 48 |
| Wayne Gretzky | NY Rangers | 82 | 23 | 67 | 90 | 28 |
| John LeClair | Philadelphia | 82 | 51 | 36 | 87 | 32 |
| Ziggy Palffy | NY Islanders | 82 | 45 | 42 | 87 | 34 |
| Ron Francis | Pittsburgh | 81 | 25 | 62 | 87 | 20 |
| Teemu Selanne | Anaheim | 73 | 52 | 34 | 86 | 30 |
| Jason Allison | Boston | 81 | 33 | 50 | 83 | 60 |
| Jozef Stumpel | Los Angeles | 77 | 21 | 58 | 79 | 53 |

## 1998-99

### EASTERN CONFERENCE

#### Northeast Division

| Team | GP | W | L | T | GF | GA | PTS |
|---|---|---|---|---|---|---|---|
| Ottawa | 82 | 44 | 23 | 15 | 239 | 179 | 103 |
| Toronto | 82 | 45 | 30 | 7 | 268 | 231 | 97 |
| Boston | 82 | 39 | 30 | 13 | 214 | 181 | 91 |
| Buffalo | 82 | 37 | 28 | 17 | 207 | 175 | 91 |
| Montreal | 82 | 32 | 39 | 11 | 184 | 209 | 75 |

#### Atlantic Division

| | | | | | | | |
|---|---|---|---|---|---|---|---|
| New Jersey | 82 | 47 | 24 | 11 | 248 | 196 | 105 |
| Philadelphia | 82 | 37 | 26 | 19 | 231 | 196 | 93 |
| Pittsburgh | 82 | 38 | 30 | 14 | 242 | 225 | 90 |
| NY Rangers | 82 | 33 | 38 | 11 | 217 | 227 | 77 |
| NY Islanders | 82 | 24 | 48 | 10 | 194 | 244 | 58 |

#### Southeast Division

| | | | | | | | |
|---|---|---|---|---|---|---|---|
| Carolina | 82 | 34 | 30 | 18 | 210 | 202 | 86 |
| Florida | 82 | 30 | 34 | 18 | 210 | 228 | 78 |
| Washington | 82 | 31 | 45 | 6 | 200 | 218 | 68 |
| Tampa Bay | 82 | 19 | 54 | 9 | 179 | 292 | 47 |

### WESTERN CONFERENCE

#### Central Division

| | | | | | | | |
|---|---|---|---|---|---|---|---|
| Detroit | 82 | 43 | 32 | 7 | 245 | 202 | 93 |
| St Louis | 82 | 37 | 32 | 13 | 237 | 209 | 87 |
| Chicago | 82 | 29 | 41 | 12 | 202 | 248 | 70 |
| Nashville | 82 | 28 | 47 | 7 | 190 | 261 | 63 |

#### Pacific Division

| | | | | | | | |
|---|---|---|---|---|---|---|---|
| *Dallas | 82 | 51 | 19 | 12 | 236 | 168 | 114 |
| Phoenix | 82 | 39 | 31 | 12 | 205 | 197 | 90 |
| Anaheim | 82 | 35 | 34 | 13 | 215 | 206 | 83 |
| San Jose | 82 | 31 | 33 | 18 | 196 | 191 | 80 |
| Los Angeles | 82 | 32 | 45 | 5 | 189 | 222 | 69 |

#### Northwest Division

| | | | | | | | |
|---|---|---|---|---|---|---|---|
| Colorado | 82 | 44 | 28 | 10 | 239 | 205 | 98 |
| Edmonton | 82 | 33 | 37 | 12 | 230 | 226 | 78 |
| Calgary | 82 | 30 | 40 | 12 | 211 | 234 | 72 |
| Vancouver | 82 | 23 | 47 | 12 | 192 | 258 | 58 |

#### Leading Scorers

| Player | Team | GP | G | A | PTS | PIM |
|---|---|---|---|---|---|---|
| Jaromir Jagr | Pittsburgh | 81 | 44 | 83 | 127 | 66 |
| Teemu Selanne | Anaheim | 75 | 47 | 60 | 107 | 30 |
| Paul Kariya | Anaheim | 82 | 39 | 62 | 101 | 40 |
| Peter Forsberg | Colorado | 78 | 30 | 67 | 97 | 108 |
| Joe Sakic | Colorado | 73 | 41 | 55 | 96 | 29 |
| Alexei Yashin | Ottawa | 82 | 44 | 50 | 94 | 54 |
| Eric Lindros | Philadelphia | 71 | 40 | 53 | 93 | 120 |
| Theoren Fleury | Cgy., Col. | 75 | 40 | 53 | 93 | 86 |
| John LeClair | Philadelphia | 76 | 43 | 47 | 90 | 30 |
| Pavol Demitra | St Louis | 82 | 37 | 52 | 89 | 16 |

## 1999-2000

### EASTERN CONFERENCE

#### Northeast Division

| Team | GP | W | L | T | OTL | GF | GA | PTS |
|---|---|---|---|---|---|---|---|---|
| Toronto | 82 | 45 | 27 | 7 | 3 | 246 | 222 | 100 |
| Ottawa | 82 | 41 | 28 | 11 | 2 | 244 | 210 | 95 |
| Buffalo | 82 | 35 | 32 | 11 | 4 | 213 | 204 | 85 |
| Montreal | 82 | 35 | 34 | 9 | 4 | 196 | 194 | 83 |
| Boston | 82 | 24 | 33 | 19 | 6 | 210 | 248 | 73 |

#### Atlantic Division

| | | | | | | | | |
|---|---|---|---|---|---|---|---|---|
| Philadelphia | 82 | 45 | 22 | 12 | 3 | 237 | 179 | 105 |
| *New Jersey | 82 | 45 | 24 | 8 | 5 | 251 | 203 | 103 |
| Pittsburgh | 82 | 37 | 31 | 8 | 6 | 241 | 236 | 88 |
| NY Rangers | 82 | 29 | 38 | 12 | 3 | 218 | 246 | 73 |
| NY Islanders | 82 | 24 | 48 | 9 | 1 | 194 | 275 | 58 |

#### Southeast Division

| | | | | | | | | |
|---|---|---|---|---|---|---|---|---|
| Washington | 82 | 44 | 24 | 12 | 2 | 227 | 194 | 102 |
| Florida | 82 | 43 | 27 | 6 | 6 | 244 | 209 | 98 |
| Carolina | 82 | 37 | 35 | 10 | 0 | 217 | 216 | 84 |
| Tampa Bay | 82 | 19 | 47 | 9 | 7 | 204 | 310 | 54 |
| Atlanta | 82 | 14 | 57 | 7 | 4 | 170 | 313 | 39 |

### WESTERN CONFERENCE

#### Central Division

| | | | | | | | | |
|---|---|---|---|---|---|---|---|---|
| St. Louis | 82 | 51 | 19 | 11 | 1 | 248 | 165 | 114 |
| Detroit | 82 | 48 | 22 | 10 | 2 | 278 | 210 | 108 |
| Chicago | 82 | 33 | 37 | 10 | 2 | 242 | 245 | 78 |
| Nashville | 82 | 28 | 40 | 7 | 7 | 199 | 240 | 70 |

#### Pacific Division

| | | | | | | | | |
|---|---|---|---|---|---|---|---|---|
| Dallas | 82 | 43 | 23 | 10 | 6 | 211 | 184 | 102 |
| Los Angeles | 82 | 39 | 27 | 12 | 4 | 245 | 228 | 94 |
| Phoenix | 82 | 39 | 31 | 8 | 4 | 232 | 228 | 90 |
| San Jose | 82 | 35 | 30 | 10 | 7 | 225 | 214 | 87 |
| Anaheim | 82 | 34 | 33 | 12 | 3 | 217 | 227 | 83 |

#### Northwest Division

| | | | | | | | | |
|---|---|---|---|---|---|---|---|---|
| Colorado | 82 | 42 | 28 | 11 | 1 | 233 | 201 | 96 |
| Edmonton | 82 | 32 | 26 | 16 | 8 | 226 | 212 | 88 |
| Vancouver | 82 | 30 | 29 | 15 | 8 | 227 | 237 | 83 |
| Calgary | 82 | 31 | 36 | 10 | 5 | 211 | 256 | 77 |

#### Leading Scorers

| Player | Team | GP | G | A | PTS | PIM |
|---|---|---|---|---|---|---|
| Jaromir Jagr | Pittsburgh | 63 | 42 | 54 | 96 | 50 |
| Pavel Bure | Florida | 74 | 58 | 36 | 94 | 16 |
| Mark Recchi | Philadelphia | 82 | 28 | 63 | 91 | 50 |
| Paul Kariya | Anaheim | 74 | 42 | 44 | 86 | 24 |
| Teemu Selanne | Anaheim | 79 | 33 | 52 | 85 | 12 |
| Owen Nolan | San Jose | 78 | 44 | 40 | 84 | 110 |
| Tony Amonte | Chicago | 82 | 43 | 41 | 84 | 48 |
| Mike Modano | Dallas | 77 | 38 | 43 | 81 | 48 |
| Joe Sakic | Colorado | 60 | 28 | 53 | 81 | 28 |
| Steve Yzerman | Detroit | 78 | 35 | 44 | 79 | 34 |

## 2000-01

### EASTERN CONFERENCE

#### Northeast Division

| Team | GP | W | L | T | OTL | GF | GA | PTS |
|---|---|---|---|---|---|---|---|---|
| Ottawa | 82 | 48 | 21 | 9 | 4 | 274 | 205 | 109 |
| Buffalo | 82 | 46 | 30 | 5 | 1 | 218 | 184 | 98 |
| Toronto | 82 | 37 | 29 | 11 | 5 | 232 | 207 | 90 |
| Boston | 82 | 36 | 30 | 8 | 8 | 227 | 249 | 88 |
| Montreal | 82 | 28 | 40 | 8 | 6 | 206 | 232 | 70 |

#### Atlantic Division

| | | | | | | | | |
|---|---|---|---|---|---|---|---|---|
| New Jersey | 82 | 48 | 19 | 12 | 3 | 295 | 195 | 111 |
| Philadelphia | 82 | 43 | 25 | 11 | 3 | 240 | 207 | 100 |
| Pittsburgh | 82 | 42 | 28 | 9 | 3 | 281 | 256 | 96 |
| NY Rangers | 82 | 33 | 43 | 5 | 1 | 250 | 290 | 72 |
| NY Islanders | 82 | 21 | 51 | 7 | 3 | 185 | 268 | 52 |

#### Southeast Division

| | | | | | | | | |
|---|---|---|---|---|---|---|---|---|
| Washington | 82 | 41 | 27 | 10 | 4 | 233 | 211 | 96 |
| Carolina | 82 | 38 | 32 | 9 | 3 | 212 | 225 | 88 |
| Florida | 82 | 22 | 38 | 13 | 9 | 200 | 246 | 66 |
| Atlanta | 82 | 23 | 45 | 12 | 2 | 211 | 289 | 60 |
| Tampa Bay | 82 | 24 | 47 | 6 | 5 | 201 | 280 | 59 |

### WESTERN CONFERENCE

#### Central Division

| | | | | | | | | |
|---|---|---|---|---|---|---|---|---|
| Detroit | 82 | 49 | 20 | 9 | 4 | 253 | 202 | 111 |
| St. Louis | 82 | 43 | 22 | 12 | 5 | 249 | 195 | 103 |
| Nashville | 82 | 34 | 36 | 9 | 3 | 186 | 200 | 80 |
| Chicago | 82 | 29 | 40 | 8 | 5 | 210 | 246 | 71 |
| Columbus | 82 | 28 | 39 | 9 | 6 | 190 | 233 | 71 |

#### Pacific Division

| | | | | | | | | |
|---|---|---|---|---|---|---|---|---|
| Dallas | 82 | 48 | 24 | 8 | 2 | 241 | 187 | 106 |
| San Jose | 82 | 40 | 27 | 12 | 3 | 217 | 192 | 95 |
| Los Angeles | 82 | 38 | 28 | 13 | 3 | 252 | 228 | 92 |
| Phoenix | 82 | 35 | 27 | 17 | 3 | 214 | 212 | 90 |
| Anaheim | 82 | 25 | 41 | 11 | 5 | 188 | 245 | 66 |

#### Northwest Division

| | | | | | | | | |
|---|---|---|---|---|---|---|---|---|
| *Colorado | 82 | 52 | 16 | 10 | 4 | 270 | 192 | 118 |
| Edmonton | 82 | 39 | 28 | 12 | 3 | 243 | 222 | 93 |
| Vancouver | 82 | 36 | 28 | 11 | 7 | 239 | 238 | 90 |
| Calgary | 82 | 27 | 36 | 15 | 4 | 197 | 236 | 73 |
| Minnesota | 82 | 25 | 39 | 13 | 5 | 168 | 210 | 68 |

#### Leading Scorers

| Player | Team | GP | G | A | PTS | PIM |
|---|---|---|---|---|---|---|
| Jaromir Jagr | Pittsburgh | 81 | 52 | 69 | 121 | 42 |
| Joe Sakic | Colorado | 82 | 54 | 64 | 118 | 30 |
| Patrik Elias | New Jersey | 82 | 40 | 56 | 96 | 51 |
| Alex Kovalev | Pittsburgh | 79 | 44 | 51 | 95 | 96 |
| Jason Allison | Boston | 82 | 36 | 59 | 95 | 85 |
| Martin Straka | Pittsburgh | 82 | 27 | 68 | 95 | 38 |
| Pavel Bure | Florida | 82 | 59 | 33 | 92 | 58 |
| Doug Weight | Edmonton | 82 | 25 | 65 | 90 | 91 |
| Ziggy Palffy | Los Angeles | 73 | 38 | 51 | 89 | 20 |
| Peter Forsberg | Colorado | 73 | 27 | 62 | 89 | 54 |

## 2001-02

### EASTERN CONFERENCE

#### Northeast Division

| Team | GP | W | L | T | OTL | GF | GA | PTS |
|---|---|---|---|---|---|---|---|---|
| Boston | 82 | 43 | 24 | 6 | 9 | 236 | 201 | 101 |
| Toronto | 82 | 43 | 25 | 10 | 4 | 249 | 207 | 100 |
| Ottawa | 82 | 39 | 27 | 9 | 7 | 243 | 208 | 94 |
| Montreal | 82 | 36 | 31 | 12 | 3 | 207 | 209 | 87 |
| Buffalo | 82 | 35 | 35 | 11 | 1 | 213 | 200 | 82 |

#### Atlantic Division

| | | | | | | | | |
|---|---|---|---|---|---|---|---|---|
| Philadelphia | 82 | 42 | 27 | 10 | 3 | 234 | 192 | 97 |
| NY Islanders | 82 | 42 | 28 | 8 | 4 | 239 | 220 | 96 |
| New Jersey | 82 | 41 | 28 | 9 | 4 | 205 | 187 | 95 |
| NY Rangers | 82 | 36 | 38 | 4 | 4 | 227 | 258 | 80 |
| Pittsburgh | 82 | 28 | 41 | 8 | 5 | 198 | 249 | 69 |

#### Southeast Division

| | | | | | | | | |
|---|---|---|---|---|---|---|---|---|
| Carolina | 82 | 35 | 26 | 16 | 5 | 217 | 217 | 91 |
| Washington | 82 | 36 | 33 | 11 | 2 | 228 | 240 | 85 |
| Tampa Bay | 82 | 27 | 40 | 11 | 4 | 178 | 219 | 69 |
| Florida | 82 | 22 | 44 | 10 | 6 | 180 | 250 | 60 |
| Atlanta | 82 | 19 | 47 | 11 | 5 | 187 | 288 | 54 |

### WESTERN CONFERENCE

#### Central Division

| | | | | | | | | |
|---|---|---|---|---|---|---|---|---|
| *Detroit | 82 | 51 | 17 | 10 | 4 | 251 | 187 | 116 |
| St. Louis | 82 | 43 | 27 | 8 | 4 | 227 | 188 | 98 |
| Chicago | 82 | 41 | 27 | 13 | 1 | 216 | 207 | 96 |
| Nashville | 82 | 28 | 41 | 13 | 0 | 196 | 230 | 69 |
| Columbus | 82 | 22 | 47 | 8 | 5 | 164 | 255 | 57 |

#### Pacific Division

| | | | | | | | | |
|---|---|---|---|---|---|---|---|---|
| San Jose | 82 | 44 | 27 | 8 | 3 | 248 | 199 | 99 |
| Phoenix | 82 | 40 | 27 | 9 | 6 | 228 | 210 | 95 |
| Los Angeles | 82 | 40 | 27 | 11 | 4 | 214 | 190 | 95 |
| Dallas | 82 | 36 | 28 | 13 | 5 | 215 | 213 | 90 |
| Anaheim | 82 | 29 | 42 | 8 | 3 | 175 | 198 | 69 |

#### Northwest Division

| | | | | | | | | |
|---|---|---|---|---|---|---|---|---|
| Colorado | 82 | 45 | 28 | 8 | 1 | 212 | 169 | 99 |
| Vancouver | 82 | 42 | 30 | 7 | 3 | 254 | 211 | 94 |
| Edmonton | 82 | 38 | 28 | 12 | 4 | 205 | 182 | 92 |
| Calgary | 82 | 32 | 35 | 12 | 3 | 201 | 220 | 79 |
| Minnesota | 82 | 26 | 35 | 12 | 9 | 195 | 238 | 73 |

#### Leading Scorers

| Player | Team | GP | G | A | PTS | PIM |
|---|---|---|---|---|---|---|
| Jarome Iginla | Calgary | 82 | 52 | 44 | 96 | 77 |
| Markus Naslund | Vancouver | 81 | 40 | 50 | 90 | 50 |
| Todd Bertuzzi | Vancouver | 72 | 36 | 49 | 85 | 110 |
| Mats Sundin | Toronto | 82 | 41 | 39 | 80 | 94 |
| Jaromir Jagr | Washington | 69 | 31 | 48 | 79 | 30 |
| Joe Sakic | Colorado | 82 | 26 | 53 | 79 | 18 |
| Pavol Demitra | St. Louis | 82 | 35 | 43 | 78 | 46 |
| Adam Oates | Wsh., Phi. | 80 | 14 | 64 | 78 | 28 |
| Mike Modano | Dallas | 78 | 34 | 43 | 77 | 38 |
| Ron Francis | Carolina | 80 | 27 | 50 | 77 | 18 |

## 2002-03

### EASTERN CONFERENCE

#### Northeast Division

| Team | GP | W | L | T | OTL | GF | GA | PTS |
|---|---|---|---|---|---|---|---|---|
| Ottawa | 82 | 52 | 21 | 8 | 1 | 263 | 182 | 113 |
| Toronto | 82 | 44 | 28 | 7 | 3 | 236 | 208 | 98 |
| Boston | 82 | 36 | 31 | 11 | 4 | 245 | 237 | 87 |
| Montreal | 82 | 30 | 35 | 8 | 9 | 206 | 234 | 77 |
| Buffalo | 82 | 27 | 37 | 10 | 8 | 190 | 219 | 72 |

#### Atlantic Division

| Team | GP | W | L | T | OTL | GF | GA | PTS |
|---|---|---|---|---|---|---|---|---|
| *New Jersey | 82 | 46 | 20 | 10 | 6 | 216 | 166 | 108 |
| Philadelphia | 82 | 45 | 20 | 13 | 4 | 211 | 166 | 107 |
| NY Islanders | 82 | 35 | 34 | 11 | 2 | 224 | 231 | 83 |
| NY Rangers | 82 | 32 | 36 | 10 | 4 | 210 | 231 | 78 |
| Pittsburgh | 82 | 27 | 44 | 6 | 5 | 189 | 255 | 65 |

#### Southeast Division

| Team | GP | W | L | T | OTL | GF | GA | PTS |
|---|---|---|---|---|---|---|---|---|
| Tampa Bay | 82 | 36 | 25 | 16 | 5 | 219 | 210 | 93 |
| Washington | 82 | 39 | 29 | 8 | 6 | 224 | 220 | 92 |
| Atlanta | 82 | 31 | 39 | 7 | 5 | 226 | 284 | 74 |
| Florida | 82 | 24 | 36 | 13 | 9 | 176 | 237 | 70 |
| Carolina | 82 | 22 | 43 | 11 | 6 | 171 | 240 | 61 |

### WESTERN CONFERENCE

#### Central Division

| Team | GP | W | L | T | OTL | GF | GA | PTS |
|---|---|---|---|---|---|---|---|---|
| Detroit | 82 | 48 | 20 | 10 | 4 | 269 | 203 | 110 |
| St. Louis | 82 | 41 | 24 | 11 | 6 | 253 | 222 | 99 |
| Chicago | 82 | 30 | 33 | 13 | 6 | 207 | 226 | 79 |
| Nashville | 82 | 27 | 35 | 13 | 7 | 183 | 206 | 74 |
| Columbus | 82 | 29 | 42 | 8 | 3 | 213 | 263 | 69 |

#### Pacific Division

| Team | GP | W | L | T | OTL | GF | GA | PTS |
|---|---|---|---|---|---|---|---|---|
| Dallas | 82 | 46 | 17 | 15 | 4 | 245 | 169 | 111 |
| Anaheim | 82 | 40 | 27 | 9 | 6 | 203 | 193 | 95 |
| Los Angeles | 82 | 33 | 37 | 6 | 6 | 203 | 221 | 78 |
| Phoenix | 82 | 31 | 35 | 11 | 5 | 204 | 230 | 78 |
| San Jose | 82 | 28 | 37 | 9 | 8 | 214 | 239 | 73 |

#### Northwest Division

| Team | GP | W | L | T | OTL | GF | GA | PTS |
|---|---|---|---|---|---|---|---|---|
| Colorado | 82 | 42 | 19 | 13 | 8 | 251 | 194 | 105 |
| Vancouver | 82 | 45 | 23 | 13 | 1 | 264 | 208 | 104 |
| Minnesota | 82 | 42 | 29 | 10 | 1 | 198 | 178 | 95 |
| Edmonton | 82 | 36 | 26 | 11 | 9 | 231 | 230 | 92 |
| Calgary | 82 | 29 | 36 | 13 | 4 | 186 | 228 | 75 |

### Leading Scorers

| Player | Team | GP | G | A | PTS | PIM |
|---|---|---|---|---|---|---|
| Peter Forsberg | Colorado | 75 | 29 | 77 | 106 | 70 |
| Markus Naslund | Vancouver | 82 | 48 | 56 | 104 | 52 |
| Joe Thornton | Boston | 77 | 36 | 65 | 101 | 109 |
| Milan Hejduk | Colorado | 82 | 50 | 48 | 98 | 52 |
| Todd Bertuzzi | Vancouver | 82 | 46 | 51 | 97 | 144 |
| Pavol Demitra | St. Louis | 78 | 36 | 57 | 93 | 32 |
| Glen Murray | Boston | 82 | 44 | 48 | 92 | 64 |
| Mario Lemieux | Pittsburgh | 67 | 28 | 63 | 91 | 43 |
| Dany Heatley | Atlanta | 77 | 41 | 48 | 89 | 58 |
| Ziggy Palffy | Los Angeles | 76 | 37 | 48 | 85 | 47 |
| Mike Modano | Dallas | 79 | 28 | 57 | 85 | 30 |

## 2003-04

### EASTERN CONFERENCE

#### Northeast Division

| Team | GP | W | L | T | OTL | GF | GA | PTS |
|---|---|---|---|---|---|---|---|---|
| Boston | 82 | 41 | 19 | 15 | 7 | 209 | 188 | 104 |
| Toronto | 82 | 45 | 24 | 10 | 3 | 242 | 204 | 103 |
| Ottawa | 82 | 43 | 23 | 10 | 6 | 262 | 189 | 102 |
| Montreal | 82 | 41 | 30 | 7 | 4 | 208 | 192 | 93 |
| Buffalo | 82 | 37 | 34 | 7 | 4 | 220 | 221 | 85 |

#### Atlantic Division

| Team | GP | W | L | T | OTL | GF | GA | PTS |
|---|---|---|---|---|---|---|---|---|
| Philadelphia | 82 | 40 | 21 | 15 | 6 | 229 | 186 | 101 |
| New Jersey | 82 | 43 | 25 | 12 | 2 | 213 | 164 | 100 |
| NY Islanders | 82 | 38 | 29 | 11 | 4 | 237 | 210 | 91 |
| NY Rangers | 82 | 27 | 40 | 7 | 8 | 206 | 250 | 69 |
| Pittsburgh | 82 | 23 | 47 | 8 | 4 | 190 | 303 | 58 |

#### Southeast Division

| Team | GP | W | L | T | OTL | GF | GA | PTS |
|---|---|---|---|---|---|---|---|---|
| *Tampa Bay | 82 | 46 | 22 | 8 | 6 | 245 | 192 | 106 |
| Atlanta | 82 | 33 | 37 | 8 | 4 | 214 | 243 | 78 |
| Carolina | 82 | 28 | 34 | 14 | 6 | 172 | 209 | 76 |
| Florida | 82 | 28 | 35 | 15 | 4 | 188 | 221 | 75 |
| Washington | 82 | 23 | 46 | 10 | 3 | 186 | 253 | 59 |

### WESTERN CONFERENCE

#### Central Division

| Team | GP | W | L | T | OTL | GF | GA | PTS |
|---|---|---|---|---|---|---|---|---|
| Detroit | 82 | 48 | 21 | 11 | 2 | 255 | 189 | 109 |
| St. Louis | 82 | 39 | 30 | 11 | 2 | 191 | 198 | 91 |
| Nashville | 82 | 38 | 29 | 11 | 4 | 216 | 217 | 91 |
| Columbus | 82 | 25 | 45 | 8 | 4 | 177 | 238 | 62 |
| Chicago | 82 | 20 | 43 | 11 | 8 | 188 | 259 | 59 |

#### Pacific Division

| Team | GP | W | L | T | OTL | GF | GA | PTS |
|---|---|---|---|---|---|---|---|---|
| San Jose | 82 | 43 | 21 | 12 | 6 | 219 | 183 | 104 |
| Dallas | 82 | 41 | 26 | 13 | 2 | 194 | 175 | 97 |
| Los Angeles | 82 | 28 | 29 | 16 | 9 | 205 | 217 | 81 |
| Anaheim | 82 | 29 | 35 | 10 | 8 | 184 | 213 | 76 |
| Phoenix | 82 | 22 | 36 | 18 | 6 | 188 | 245 | 68 |

#### Northwest Division

| Team | GP | W | L | T | OTL | GF | GA | PTS |
|---|---|---|---|---|---|---|---|---|
| Vancouver | 82 | 43 | 24 | 10 | 5 | 235 | 194 | 101 |
| Colorado | 82 | 40 | 22 | 13 | 7 | 236 | 198 | 100 |
| Calgary | 82 | 42 | 30 | 7 | 3 | 200 | 176 | 94 |
| Edmonton | 82 | 36 | 29 | 12 | 5 | 221 | 208 | 89 |
| Minnesota | 82 | 30 | 29 | 20 | 3 | 188 | 183 | 83 |

### Leading Scorers

| Player | Team | GP | G | A | PTS | PIM |
|---|---|---|---|---|---|---|
| Martin St. Louis | Tampa Bay | 82 | 38 | 56 | 94 | 24 |
| Ilya Kovalchuk | Atlanta | 81 | 41 | 46 | 87 | 63 |
| Joe Sakic | Colorado | 81 | 33 | 54 | 87 | 42 |
| Markus Naslund | Vancouver | 78 | 35 | 49 | 84 | 58 |
| Marian Hossa | Ottawa | 81 | 36 | 46 | 82 | 46 |
| Patrik Elias | New Jersey | 82 | 38 | 43 | 81 | 44 |
| Daniel Alfredsson | Ottawa | 77 | 32 | 48 | 80 | 24 |
| Cory Stillman | Tampa Bay | 81 | 25 | 55 | 80 | 36 |
| Robert Lang | Wsh., Det. | 69 | 30 | 49 | 79 | 24 |
| Brad Richards | Tampa Bay | 82 | 26 | 53 | 79 | 12 |
| Alex Tanguay | Colorado | 69 | 25 | 54 | 79 | 42 |

## 2004-05

SEASON CANCELLED

## 2005-06

### EASTERN CONFERENCE

#### Northeast Division

| Team | GP | W | L | OL | GF | GA | PTS |
|---|---|---|---|---|---|---|---|
| Ottawa | 82 | 52 | 21 | 9 | 314 | 211 | 113 |
| Buffalo | 82 | 52 | 24 | 6 | 281 | 239 | 110 |
| Montreal | 82 | 42 | 31 | 9 | 243 | 247 | 93 |
| Toronto | 82 | 41 | 33 | 8 | 257 | 270 | 90 |
| Boston | 82 | 29 | 37 | 16 | 230 | 266 | 74 |

#### Atlantic Division

| Team | GP | W | L | OL | GF | GA | PTS |
|---|---|---|---|---|---|---|---|
| New Jersey | 82 | 46 | 27 | 9 | 242 | 229 | 101 |
| Philadelphia | 82 | 45 | 26 | 11 | 267 | 259 | 101 |
| NY Rangers | 82 | 44 | 26 | 12 | 257 | 215 | 100 |
| NY Islanders | 82 | 36 | 40 | 6 | 230 | 278 | 78 |
| Pittsburgh | 82 | 22 | 46 | 14 | 244 | 316 | 58 |

#### Southeast Division

| Team | GP | W | L | OL | GF | GA | PTS |
|---|---|---|---|---|---|---|---|
| *Carolina | 82 | 52 | 22 | 8 | 294 | 260 | 112 |
| Tampa Bay | 82 | 43 | 33 | 6 | 252 | 260 | 92 |
| Atlanta | 82 | 41 | 33 | 8 | 281 | 275 | 90 |
| Florida | 82 | 37 | 34 | 11 | 240 | 257 | 85 |
| Washington | 82 | 29 | 41 | 12 | 237 | 306 | 70 |

### WESTERN CONFERENCE

#### Central Division

| Team | GP | W | L | OL | GF | GA | PTS |
|---|---|---|---|---|---|---|---|
| Detroit | 82 | 58 | 16 | 8 | 305 | 209 | 124 |
| Nashville | 82 | 49 | 25 | 8 | 259 | 227 | 106 |
| Columbus | 82 | 35 | 43 | 4 | 223 | 279 | 74 |
| Chicago | 82 | 26 | 43 | 13 | 211 | 285 | 65 |
| St. Louis | 82 | 21 | 46 | 15 | 197 | 292 | 57 |

#### Pacific Division

| Team | GP | W | L | OL | GF | GA | PTS |
|---|---|---|---|---|---|---|---|
| Dallas | 82 | 53 | 23 | 6 | 265 | 218 | 112 |
| San Jose | 82 | 44 | 27 | 11 | 266 | 242 | 99 |
| Anaheim | 82 | 43 | 27 | 12 | 254 | 229 | 98 |
| Los Angeles | 82 | 42 | 35 | 5 | 249 | 270 | 89 |
| Phoenix | 82 | 38 | 39 | 5 | 246 | 271 | 81 |

#### Northwest Division

| Team | GP | W | L | OL | GF | GA | PTS |
|---|---|---|---|---|---|---|---|
| Calgary | 82 | 46 | 25 | 11 | 218 | 200 | 103 |
| Colorado | 82 | 43 | 30 | 9 | 283 | 257 | 95 |
| Edmonton | 82 | 41 | 28 | 13 | 256 | 251 | 95 |
| Vancouver | 82 | 42 | 32 | 8 | 256 | 255 | 92 |
| Minnesota | 82 | 38 | 36 | 8 | 231 | 215 | 84 |

### Leading Scorers

| Player | Team | GP | G | A | PTS | PIM |
|---|---|---|---|---|---|---|
| Joe Thornton | Bos., S.J. | 81 | 29 | 96 | 125 | 61 |
| Jaromir Jagr | NY Rangers | 82 | 54 | 69 | 123 | 72 |
| Alex Ovechkin | Washington | 81 | 52 | 54 | 106 | 52 |
| Dany Heatley | Ottawa | 82 | 50 | 53 | 103 | 86 |
| Daniel Alfredsson | Ottawa | 77 | 43 | 60 | 103 | 50 |
| Sidney Crosby | Pittsburgh | 81 | 39 | 63 | 102 | 110 |
| Eric Staal | Carolina | 82 | 45 | 55 | 100 | 81 |
| Ilya Kovalchuk | Atlanta | 78 | 52 | 46 | 98 | 68 |
| Marc Savard | Atlanta | 82 | 28 | 69 | 97 | 100 |
| Jonathan Cheechoo | San Jose | 82 | 56 | 37 | 93 | 58 |

*Atlanta's Ilya Kovalchuk (right) made his first appearance among the NHL's top 10 in scoring when he finished second to Tampa Bay's Martin St. Louis in 2003-04. Since then, Kovalchuk has cracked the top 10 again in 2005-06, 2007-08 and 2008-09.*

## 2006-07

### EASTERN CONFERENCE

#### Northeast Division

| Team | GP | W | L | OL | GF | GA | PTS |
|---|---|---|---|---|---|---|---|
| Buffalo | 82 | 53 | 22 | 7 | 308 | 242 | 113 |
| Ottawa | 82 | 48 | 25 | 9 | 288 | 222 | 105 |
| Toronto | 82 | 40 | 31 | 11 | 258 | 269 | 91 |
| Montreal | 82 | 42 | 34 | 6 | 245 | 256 | 90 |
| Boston | 82 | 35 | 41 | 6 | 219 | 289 | 76 |

#### Atlantic Division

| Team | GP | W | L | OL | GF | GA | PTS |
|---|---|---|---|---|---|---|---|
| New Jersey | 82 | 49 | 24 | 9 | 216 | 201 | 107 |
| Pittsburgh | 82 | 47 | 24 | 11 | 277 | 246 | 105 |
| NY Rangers | 82 | 42 | 30 | 10 | 242 | 216 | 94 |
| NY Islanders | 82 | 40 | 30 | 12 | 248 | 240 | 92 |
| Philadelphia | 82 | 22 | 48 | 12 | 214 | 303 | 56 |

#### Southeast Division

| Team | GP | W | L | OL | GF | GA | PTS |
|---|---|---|---|---|---|---|---|
| Atlanta | 82 | 43 | 28 | 11 | 246 | 245 | 97 |
| Tampa Bay | 82 | 44 | 33 | 5 | 253 | 261 | 93 |
| Carolina | 82 | 40 | 34 | 8 | 241 | 253 | 88 |
| Florida | 82 | 35 | 31 | 16 | 247 | 257 | 86 |
| Washington | 82 | 28 | 40 | 14 | 235 | 286 | 70 |

### WESTERN CONFERENCE

#### Central Division

| Team | GP | W | L | OL | GF | GA | PTS |
|---|---|---|---|---|---|---|---|
| Detroit | 82 | 50 | 19 | 13 | 254 | 199 | 113 |
| Nashville | 82 | 51 | 23 | 8 | 272 | 212 | 110 |
| St. Louis | 82 | 34 | 35 | 13 | 214 | 254 | 81 |
| Columbus | 82 | 33 | 42 | 7 | 201 | 249 | 73 |
| Chicago | 82 | 31 | 42 | 9 | 201 | 258 | 71 |

#### Pacific Division

| Team | GP | W | L | OL | GF | GA | PTS |
|---|---|---|---|---|---|---|---|
| *Anaheim | 82 | 48 | 20 | 14 | 258 | 208 | 110 |
| San Jose | 82 | 51 | 26 | 5 | 258 | 199 | 107 |
| Dallas | 82 | 50 | 25 | 7 | 226 | 197 | 107 |
| Los Angeles | 82 | 27 | 41 | 14 | 227 | 283 | 68 |
| Phoenix | 82 | 31 | 46 | 5 | 216 | 284 | 67 |

#### Northwest Division

| Team | GP | W | L | OL | GF | GA | PTS |
|---|---|---|---|---|---|---|---|
| Vancouver | 82 | 49 | 26 | 7 | 222 | 201 | 105 |
| Minnesota | 82 | 48 | 26 | 8 | 235 | 191 | 104 |
| Calgary | 82 | 43 | 29 | 10 | 258 | 226 | 96 |
| Colorado | 82 | 44 | 31 | 7 | 272 | 251 | 95 |
| Edmonton | 82 | 32 | 43 | 7 | 195 | 248 | 71 |

### Leading Scorers

| Player | Team | GP | G | A | PTS | PIM |
|---|---|---|---|---|---|---|
| Sidney Crosby | Pittsburgh | 79 | 36 | 84 | 120 | 60 |
| Joe Thornton | San Jose | 82 | 22 | 92 | 114 | 44 |
| Vincent Lecavalier | Tampa Bay | 82 | 52 | 56 | 108 | 44 |
| Dany Heatley | Ottawa | 82 | 50 | 55 | 105 | 74 |
| Martin St. Louis | Tampa Bay | 82 | 43 | 59 | 102 | 28 |
| Marian Hossa | Atlanta | 82 | 43 | 57 | 100 | 49 |
| Joe Sakic | Colorado | 82 | 36 | 64 | 100 | 46 |
| Jaromir Jagr | NY Rangers | 82 | 30 | 66 | 96 | 78 |
| Marc Savard | Boston | 82 | 22 | 74 | 96 | 96 |
| Daniel Briere | Buffalo | 81 | 32 | 63 | 95 | 89 |

## 2007-08

### EASTERN CONFERENCE

#### Northeast Division

| Team | GP | W | L | OL | GF | GA | PTS |
|---|---|---|---|---|---|---|---|
| Montreal | 82 | 47 | 25 | 10 | 262 | 222 | 104 |
| Ottawa | 82 | 43 | 31 | 8 | 261 | 247 | 94 |
| Boston | 82 | 41 | 29 | 12 | 212 | 222 | 94 |
| Buffalo | 82 | 39 | 31 | 12 | 255 | 242 | 90 |
| Toronto | 82 | 36 | 35 | 11 | 231 | 260 | 83 |

#### Atlantic Division

| Team | GP | W | L | OL | GF | GA | PTS |
|---|---|---|---|---|---|---|---|
| Pittsburgh | 82 | 47 | 27 | 8 | 247 | 216 | 102 |
| New Jersey | 82 | 46 | 29 | 7 | 206 | 197 | 99 |
| NY Rangers | 82 | 42 | 27 | 13 | 213 | 199 | 97 |
| Philadelphia | 82 | 42 | 29 | 11 | 248 | 233 | 95 |
| NY Islanders | 82 | 35 | 38 | 9 | 194 | 243 | 79 |

#### Southeast Division

| Team | GP | W | L | OL | GF | GA | PTS |
|---|---|---|---|---|---|---|---|
| Washington | 82 | 43 | 31 | 8 | 242 | 231 | 94 |
| Carolina | 82 | 43 | 33 | 6 | 252 | 249 | 92 |
| Florida | 82 | 38 | 35 | 9 | 216 | 226 | 85 |
| Atlanta | 82 | 34 | 40 | 8 | 216 | 272 | 76 |
| Tampa Bay | 82 | 31 | 42 | 9 | 223 | 267 | 71 |

### WESTERN CONFERENCE

#### Central Division

| Team | GP | W | L | OL | GF | GA | PTS |
|---|---|---|---|---|---|---|---|
| *Detroit | 82 | 54 | 21 | 7 | 257 | 184 | 115 |
| Nashville | 82 | 41 | 32 | 9 | 230 | 229 | 91 |
| Chicago | 82 | 40 | 34 | 8 | 239 | 235 | 88 |
| Columbus | 82 | 34 | 36 | 12 | 193 | 218 | 80 |
| St. Louis | 82 | 33 | 36 | 13 | 205 | 237 | 79 |

#### Pacific Division

| Team | GP | W | L | OL | GF | GA | PTS |
|---|---|---|---|---|---|---|---|
| San Jose | 82 | 49 | 23 | 10 | 222 | 193 | 108 |
| Anaheim | 82 | 47 | 27 | 8 | 205 | 191 | 102 |
| Dallas | 82 | 45 | 30 | 7 | 242 | 207 | 97 |
| Phoenix | 82 | 38 | 37 | 7 | 214 | 231 | 83 |
| Los Angeles | 82 | 32 | 43 | 7 | 231 | 266 | 71 |

#### Northwest Division

| Team | GP | W | L | OL | GF | GA | PTS |
|---|---|---|---|---|---|---|---|
| Minnesota | 82 | 44 | 28 | 10 | 223 | 218 | 98 |
| Colorado | 82 | 44 | 31 | 7 | 231 | 219 | 95 |
| Calgary | 82 | 42 | 30 | 10 | 229 | 227 | 94 |
| Edmonton | 82 | 41 | 35 | 6 | 235 | 251 | 88 |
| Vancouver | 82 | 39 | 33 | 10 | 213 | 215 | 88 |

### Leading Scorers

| Player | Team | GP | G | A | PTS | PIM |
|---|---|---|---|---|---|---|
| Alex Ovechkin | Washington | 82 | 65 | 47 | 112 | 40 |
| Evgeni Malkin | Pittsburgh | 82 | 47 | 59 | 106 | 78 |
| Jarome Iginla | Calgary | 82 | 50 | 48 | 98 | 83 |
| Pavel Datsyuk | Detroit | 82 | 31 | 66 | 97 | 20 |
| Joe Thornton | San Jose | 82 | 29 | 67 | 96 | 59 |
| Henrik Zetterberg | Detroit | 75 | 43 | 49 | 92 | 34 |
| Vincent Lecavalier | Tampa Bay | 81 | 40 | 52 | 92 | 89 |
| Jason Spezza | Ottawa | 76 | 34 | 58 | 92 | 66 |
| Daniel Alfredsson | Ottawa | 70 | 40 | 49 | 89 | 34 |
| Ilya Kovalchuk | Atlanta | 79 | 52 | 35 | 87 | 52 |

## 2008-09

### EASTERN CONFERENCE

#### Northeast Division

| Team | GP | W | L | OL | GF | GA | PTS |
|---|---|---|---|---|---|---|---|
| Boston | 82 | 53 | 19 | 10 | 274 | 196 | 116 |
| Montreal | 82 | 41 | 30 | 11 | 249 | 247 | 93 |
| Buffalo | 82 | 41 | 32 | 9 | 250 | 234 | 91 |
| Ottawa | 82 | 36 | 35 | 11 | 217 | 237 | 83 |
| Toronto | 82 | 34 | 35 | 13 | 250 | 293 | 81 |

#### Atlantic Division

| Team | GP | W | L | OL | GF | GA | PTS |
|---|---|---|---|---|---|---|---|
| New Jersey | 82 | 51 | 27 | 4 | 244 | 209 | 106 |
| *Pittsburgh | 82 | 45 | 28 | 9 | 264 | 239 | 99 |
| Philadelphia | 82 | 44 | 27 | 11 | 264 | 238 | 99 |
| NY Rangers | 82 | 43 | 30 | 9 | 210 | 218 | 95 |
| NY Islanders | 82 | 26 | 47 | 9 | 201 | 279 | 61 |

#### Southeast Division

| Team | GP | W | L | OL | GF | GA | PTS |
|---|---|---|---|---|---|---|---|
| Washington | 82 | 50 | 24 | 8 | 272 | 245 | 108 |
| Carolina | 82 | 45 | 30 | 7 | 239 | 226 | 97 |
| Florida | 82 | 41 | 30 | 11 | 234 | 231 | 93 |
| Atlanta | 82 | 35 | 41 | 6 | 257 | 280 | 76 |
| Tampa Bay | 82 | 24 | 40 | 18 | 210 | 279 | 66 |

### WESTERN CONFERENCE

#### Central Division

| Team | GP | W | L | OL | GF | GA | PTS |
|---|---|---|---|---|---|---|---|
| Detroit | 82 | 51 | 21 | 10 | 295 | 244 | 112 |
| Chicago | 82 | 46 | 24 | 12 | 264 | 216 | 104 |
| St. Louis | 82 | 41 | 31 | 10 | 233 | 233 | 92 |
| Columbus | 82 | 41 | 31 | 10 | 226 | 230 | 92 |
| Nashville | 82 | 40 | 34 | 8 | 213 | 233 | 88 |

#### Pacific Division

| Team | GP | W | L | OL | GF | GA | PTS |
|---|---|---|---|---|---|---|---|
| San Jose | 82 | 53 | 18 | 11 | 257 | 204 | 117 |
| Anaheim | 82 | 42 | 33 | 7 | 245 | 238 | 91 |
| Dallas | 82 | 36 | 35 | 11 | 230 | 257 | 83 |
| Phoenix | 82 | 36 | 39 | 7 | 208 | 252 | 79 |
| Los Angeles | 82 | 34 | 37 | 11 | 207 | 234 | 79 |

#### Northwest Division

| Team | GP | W | L | OL | GF | GA | PTS |
|---|---|---|---|---|---|---|---|
| Vancouver | 82 | 45 | 27 | 10 | 246 | 220 | 100 |
| Calgary | 82 | 46 | 30 | 6 | 254 | 248 | 98 |
| Minnesota | 82 | 40 | 33 | 9 | 219 | 200 | 89 |
| Edmonton | 82 | 38 | 35 | 9 | 234 | 248 | 85 |
| Colorado | 82 | 32 | 45 | 5 | 199 | 257 | 69 |

### Leading Scorers

| Player | Team | GP | G | A | PTS | PIM |
|---|---|---|---|---|---|---|
| Evgeni Malkin | Pittsburgh | 82 | 35 | 78 | 113 | 80 |
| Alex Ovechkin | Washington | 79 | 56 | 54 | 110 | 72 |
| Sidney Crosby | Pittsburgh | 77 | 33 | 70 | 103 | 76 |
| Pavel Datsyuk | Detroit | 81 | 32 | 65 | 97 | 34 |
| Zach Parise | New Jersey | 82 | 45 | 49 | 94 | 24 |
| Ilya Kovalchuk | Atlanta | 79 | 43 | 48 | 91 | 50 |
| Ryan Getzlaf | Anaheim | 81 | 25 | 66 | 91 | 121 |
| Jarome Iginla | Calgary | 82 | 35 | 54 | 89 | 37 |
| Marc Savard | Boston | 82 | 25 | 63 | 88 | 70 |
| Nicklas Backstrom | Washington | 82 | 22 | 66 | 88 | 46 |

**Note:** Detailed statistics for 2008-09 are listed in the Final Statistics, 2008-09 section of the *NHL Guide & Record Book.* **See page 141.**

*Ryan Getzlaf set a new Ducks record with 66 assists in 2008-09. He finished tied for third in the NHL in that category and also ranked among the top 10 with 91 points.*

*Zach Parise finished third in the NHL with 45 goals in 2008-09. He also established a new career high with 49 assists to rank fifth in scoring with 94 points.*

# Team Records

## Regular Season

### FINAL STANDINGS

**MOST POINTS, ONE SEASON:**
**132 – Montreal Canadiens**, 1976-77. 60W-8L-12T. 80GP
131 – Detroit Red Wings, 1995-96. 62W-13L-7T. 82GP
129 – Montreal Canadiens, 1977-78. 59W-10L-11T. 80GP

**BEST POINTS PERCENTAGE, ONE SEASON:**
**.875 – Boston Bruins**, 1929-30. 38W-5L-1T. 77PTS in 44GP
.830 – Montreal Canadiens, 1943-44. 38W-5L-7T. 83PTS in 50GP
.825 – Montreal Canadiens, 1976-77. 60W-8L-12T. 132PTS in 80GP
.806 – Montreal Canadiens, 1977-78. 59W-10L-11T. 129PTS in 80GP
.800 – Montreal Canadiens, 1944-45. 38W-8L-4T. 80PTS in 50GP

**FEWEST POINTS, ONE SEASON:**
**8 – Quebec Bulldogs**, 1919-20. 4W-20L-0T. 24GP
10 – Toronto Arenas, 1918-19. 5W-13L-0T. 18GP
12 – Hamilton Tigers, 1920-21. 6W-18L-0T. 24GP
– Hamilton Tigers, 1922-23. 6W-18L-0T. 24GP
– Boston Bruins, 1924-25. 6W-24L-0T. 30GP
– Philadelphia Quakers, 1930-31. 4W-36L-4T. 44GP

**FEWEST POINTS, ONE SEASON (MINIMUM 70-GAME SCHEDULE):**
**21 – Washington Capitals**, 1974-75. 8W-67L-5T. 80GP
24 – Ottawa Senators, 1992-93. 10W-70L-4T. 84GP
– San Jose Sharks, 1992-93. 11W-71L-2T. 84GP
30 – New York Islanders, 1972-73. 12W-60L-6T. 78GP

**WORST POINTS PERCENTAGE, ONE SEASON:**
**.131 – Washington Capitals**, 1974-75. 8W-67L-5T. 21PTS in 80GP
.136 – Philadelphia Quakers, 1930-31. 4W-36L-4T. 12PTS in 44GP
.143 – Ottawa Senators, 1992-93. 10W-70L-4T. 24PTS in 84GP
– San Jose Sharks, 1992-93. 11W-71L-2T. 24PTS in 84GP
.148 – Pittsburgh Pirates, 1929-30. 5W-36L-3T. 13PTS in 44GP

### TEAM WINS

#### Most Wins

**MOST WINS, ONE SEASON:**
**62 – Detroit Red Wings**, 1995-96. 82GP
60 – Montreal Canadiens, 1976-77. 80GP
59 – Montreal Canadiens, 1977-78. 80GP

**MOST HOME WINS, ONE SEASON:**
**36 – Philadelphia Flyers**, 1975-76. 40GP
**– Detroit Red Wings**, 1995-96. 41GP
33 – Boston Bruins, 1970-71. 39GP
– Boston Bruins, 1973-74. 39GP
– Montreal Canadiens, 1976-77. 40GP
– Philadelphia Flyers, 1976-77. 40GP
– New York Islanders, 1981-82. 40GP
– Philadelphia Flyers, 1985-86. 40GP

**MOST ROAD WINS, ONE SEASON:**
**31 – Detroit Red Wings**, 2005-06. 41GP
28 – New Jersey Devils, 1998-99. 41GP
27 – Montreal Canadiens, 1976-77. 40GP
– Montreal Canadiens, 1977-78. 40GP
– St. Louis Blues, 1999-2000. 41GP
– San Jose Sharks, 2007-08. 41GP
26 – Boston Bruins, 1971-72. 39GP
– Montreal Canadiens, 1975-76. 40GP
– Edmonton Oilers, 1983-84. 40GP
– Detroit Red Wings, 1995-96. 41GP
– San Jose Sharks, 2006-07. 41GP

#### Fewest Wins

**FEWEST WINS, ONE SEASON:**
**4 – Quebec Bulldogs**, 1919-20. 24GP
**– Philadelphia Quakers**, 1930-31. 44GP
5 – Toronto Arenas, 1918-19. 18GP
Pittsburgh Pirates, 1929-30. 44GP

**FEWEST WINS, ONE SEASON (MINIMUM 70-GAME SCHEDULE):**
**8 – Washington Capitals**, 1974-75. 80GP
9 – Winnipeg Jets, 1980-81. 80GP
10 – Ottawa Senators, 1992-93. 84GP

**FEWEST HOME WINS, ONE SEASON:**
**2 – Chicago Blackhawks**, 1927-28. 22GP
3 – Boston Bruins, 1924-25. 15GP
– Chicago Blackhawks, 1928-29. 22GP
– Philadelphia Quakers, 1930-31. 22GP

**FEWEST HOME WINS, ONE SEASON (MINIMUM 70-GAME SCHEDULE):**
**6 – Chicago Blackhawks**, 1954-55. 35GP
**– Washington Capitals**, 1975-76. 40GP
7 – Boston Bruins, 1962-63. 35GP
– Washington Capitals, 1974-75. 40GP
– Winnipeg Jets, 1980-81. 40GP
– Pittsburgh Penguins, 1983-84. 40GP

**FEWEST ROAD WINS, ONE SEASON:**
**0 – Toronto Arenas**, 1918-19. 9GP
**– Quebec Bulldogs**, 1919-20. 12GP
**– Pittsburgh Pirates**, 1929-30. 22GP
1 – Hamilton Tigers, 1921-22. 12GP
– Toronto St. Patricks, 1925-26. 18GP
– Philadelphia Quakers, 1930-31. 22GP
– New York Americans, 1940-41. 24GP
– Washington Capitals, 1974-75. 40GP
* – Ottawa Senators, 1992-93. 41GP

**FEWEST ROAD WINS, ONE SEASON (MINIMUM 70-GAME SCHEDULE):**
**1 – Washington Capitals**, 1974-75. 40GP
*** – Ottawa Senators**, 1992-93. 41GP
2 – Boston Bruins, 1960-61. 35GP
– Los Angeles Kings, 1969-70. 38GP
– New York Islanders, 1972-73. 39GP
– California Golden Seals, 1973-74. 39GP
– Colorado Rockies, 1977-78. 40GP
– Winnipeg Jets, 1980-81. 40GP
– Quebec Nordiques, 1991-92. 40GP

### TEAM LOSSES

#### Fewest Losses

**FEWEST LOSSES, ONE SEASON:**
**5 – Ottawa Senators**, 1919-20. 24GP
**– Boston Bruins**, 1929-30. 44GP
**– Montreal Canadiens**, 1943-44. 50GP

**FEWEST HOME LOSSES, ONE SEASON:**
**0 – Ottawa Senators**, 1922-23. 12GP
**– Montreal Canadiens**, 1943-44. 25GP
1 – Toronto Arenas, 1917-18. 11GP
– Ottawa Senators, 1918-19. 9GP
– Ottawa Senators, 1919-20. 12GP
– Toronto St. Patricks, 1922-23. 12GP
– Boston Bruins, 1929-30. 22GP
– Boston Bruins, 1930-31. 22GP
– Montreal Canadiens, 1976-77. 40GP
– Quebec Nordiques, 1994-95. 24GP

**FEWEST ROAD LOSSES, ONE SEASON:**
**3 – Montreal Canadiens**, 1928-29. 22GP
4 – Ottawa Senators, 1919-20. 12GP
– Montreal Canadiens, 1927-28. 22GP
– Boston Bruins, 1929-30. 20GP
– Boston Bruins, 1940-41. 24GP

**FEWEST LOSSES, ONE SEASON (MINIMUM 70-GAME SCHEDULE):**
**8 – Montreal Canadiens**, 1976-77. 80GP
10 – Montreal Canadiens, 1972-73. 78GP
– Montreal Canadiens, 1977-78. 80GP
11 – Montreal Canadiens, 1975-76. 80GP

**FEWEST HOME LOSSES, ONE SEASON (MINIMUM 70-GAME SCHEDULE):**
**1 – Montreal Canadiens**, 1976-77. 40GP
2 – Montreal Canadiens, 1961-62. 35GP
– New York Rangers, 1970-71. 39GP
– Philadelphia Flyers, 1975-76. 40GP

**FEWEST ROAD LOSSES, ONE SEASON (MINIMUM 70-GAME SCHEDULE):**
**6 – Montreal Canadiens**, 1972-73. 39GP
**– Montreal Canadiens**, 1974-75. 40GP
**– Montreal Canadiens**, 1977-78. 40GP
7 – Detroit Red Wings, 1951-52. 35GP
– Montreal Canadiens, 1976-77. 40GP
– Philadelphia Flyers, 1979-80. 40GP
– Boston Bruins, 2003-04. 41GP
– Detroit Red Wings, 2005-06. 41GP

#### Most Losses

**MOST LOSSES, ONE SEASON:**
**71 – San Jose Sharks**, 1992-93. 84GP
70 – Ottawa Senators, 1992-93. 84GP
67 – Washington Capitals, 1974-75. 80GP
61 – Quebec Nordiques, 1989-90. 80GP
– Ottawa Senators, 1993-94. 84GP

**MOST HOME LOSSES, ONE SEASON:**
***32 – San Jose Sharks**, 1992-93. 41GP
29 – Pittsburgh Penguins, 1983-84. 40GP
* – Ottawa Senators, 1993-94. 41GP

**MOST ROAD LOSSES, ONE SEASON:**
***40 – Ottawa Senators**, 1992-93. 41GP
39 – Washington Capitals, 1974-75. 40GP
37 – California Golden Seals, 1973-74. 39GP
* – San Jose Sharks, 1992-93. 41GP

* – Does not include neutral site games

## TEAM TIES

### Most Ties

**MOST TIES, ONE SEASON:**
**24 – Philadelphia Flyers**, 1969-70. 76GP
23 – Montreal Canadiens, 1962-63. 70GP
– Chicago Blackhawks, 1973-74. 78GP

**MOST HOME TIES, ONE SEASON:**
**13 – New York Rangers**, 1954-55. 35GP
**– Philadelphia Flyers**, 1969-70. 38GP
**– California Golden Seals**, 1971-72. 39GP
**– California Golden Seals**, 1972-73. 39GP
**– Chicago Blackhawks**, 1973-74. 39GP

**MOST ROAD TIES, ONE SEASON:**
**15 – Philadelphia Flyers**, 1976-77. 40GP
14 – Montreal Canadiens, 1952-53. 35GP
– Montreal Canadiens, 1974-75. 40GP
– Philadelphia Flyers, 1975-76. 40GP

### Fewest Ties

**FEWEST TIES, ONE SEASON (Since 1926-27):**
**1 – Boston Bruins**, 1929-30. 44GP
2 – Montreal Canadiens, 1926-27. 44GP
– New York Americans, 1926-27. 44GP
– Boston Bruins, 1938-39. 48GP
– New York Rangers, 1941-42. 48GP
– San Jose Sharks, 1992-93. 84GP

**FEWEST TIES, ONE SEASON (MINIMUM 70-GAME SCHEDULE):**
**2 – San Jose Sharks**, 1992-93. 84GP
3 – New Jersey Devils, 1985-86. 80GP
– Calgary Flames, 1986-87. 80GP
– Vancouver Canucks, 1993-94. 84GP

## WINNING STREAKS

**LONGEST WINNING STREAK, ONE SEASON:**
**17 Games – Pittsburgh Penguins**, Mar. 9 – Apr. 10, 1993.
15 Games – New York Islanders, Jan. 21 – Feb. 20, 1982.
14 Games – Boston Bruins, Dec. 3, 1929 – Jan. 9, 1930.

**LONGEST HOME WINNING STREAK, ONE SEASON:**
**20 Games – Boston Bruins**, Dec. 3, 1929 – Mar. 18, 1930.
**– Philadelphia Flyers**, Jan. 4 – Apr. 3, 1976.

**LONGEST ROAD WINNING STREAK, ONE SEASON:**
**12 Games – Detroit Red Wings**, Mar. 1 – Apr. 15, 2006.
10 Games – Buffalo Sabres, Dec. 10, 1983 – Jan. 23, 1984.
– St. Louis Blues, Jan. 21 – Mar. 2, 2000.
– New Jersey Devils, Feb. 27 – Apr. 7, 2001.
– Buffalo Sabres, Oct. 4 – Nov. 13, 2006.
– San Jose Sharks, Nov. 14 – Dec. 31, 2007.

**LONGEST WINNING STREAK FROM START OF SEASON:**
**10 Games – Toronto Maple Leafs**, 1993-94.
**– Buffalo Sabres**, 2006-07.
8 Games – Toronto Maple Leafs, 1934-35.
– Buffalo Sabres, 1975-76.
– Nashville Predators, 2005-06.
7 Games – Edmonton Oilers, 1983-84.
– Quebec Nordiques, 1985-86.
– Pittsburgh Penguins, 1986-87.
– Pittsburgh Penguins, 1994-95.

**LONGEST HOME WINNING STREAK FROM START OF SEASON:**
**11 Games – Chicago Blackhawks**, 1963-64.
10 Games – Ottawa Senators, 1925-26.
9 Games – Montreal Canadiens, 1953-54.
– Chicago Blackhawks, 1971-72.
– San Jose Sharks, 2008-09.

**LONGEST ROAD WINNING STREAK FROM START OF SEASON:**
**7 Games – Toronto Maple Leafs**, Nov. 14 – Dec. 15, 1940.
**– Philadelphia Flyers**, Oct. 12 – Nov. 16, 1985.
**– Detroit Red Wings**, Oct. 6 – Nov. 6, 2005.

**LONGEST WINNING STREAK, INCLUDING PLAYOFFS:**
**15 Games – Detroit Red Wings**, Feb. 27 – Apr. 5, 1955.
(9 regular-season games, 6 playoff games)
**– New Jersey Devils**, Mar. 28 – Apr. 29, 2006.
(11 regular-season games, 4 playoff games)

**LONGEST HOME WINNING STREAK, INCLUDING PLAYOFFS:**
**24 Games – Philadelphia Flyers**, Jan. 4 – Apr. 25, 1976.
(20 regular-season games, 4 playoff games)

**LONGEST ROAD WINNING STREAK, INCLUDING PLAYOFFS:**
**11 Games – New Jersey Devils**, Feb. 27 – Apr. 17, 2001.
(10 regular-season games, 1 playoff game)

## UNDEFEATED STREAKS

**LONGEST UNDEFEATED STREAK, ONE SEASON:**
**35 Games – Philadelphia Flyers**, Oct. 14, 1979 – Jan. 6, 1980. 25W-10T
28 Games – Montreal Canadiens, Dec. 18, 1977 – Feb. 23, 1978. 23W-5T

**LONGEST HOME UNDEFEATED STREAK, ONE SEASON:**
**34 Games – Montreal Canadiens**, Nov. 1, 1976 – Apr. 2, 1977. 28W-6T
27 Games – Boston Bruins, Nov. 22, 1970 – Mar. 20, 1971. 26W-1T

**LONGEST ROAD UNDEFEATED STREAK, ONE SEASON:**
**23 Games – Montreal Canadiens**, Nov. 27, 1974 – Mar. 12, 1975. 14W-9T
17 Games – Montreal Canadiens, Dec. 18, 1977 – Mar. 1, 1978. 14W-3T

**LONGEST UNDEFEATED STREAK FROM START OF SEASON:**
**15 Games – Edmonton Oilers**, 1984-85. 12W-3T
14 Games – Montreal Canadiens, 1943-44. 11W-3T

**LONGEST HOME UNDEFEATED STREAK FROM START OF SEASON:**
**26 Games – Philadelphia Flyers**, Oct. 11, 1979 – Feb. 3, 1980. 19W-7T

**LONGEST ROAD UNDEFEATED STREAK FROM START OF SEASON:**
**15 Games – Detroit Red Wings**, Oct. 18 – Dec. 20, 1951. 10W-5T

**LONGEST UNDEFEATED STREAK, INCLUDING PLAYOFFS:**
**24 Games – Montreal Canadiens**, Feb. 21 – Apr. 11, 1980.
15W-6T in regular season and 3W in playoffs.
21 Games – Philadelphia Flyers, Mar. 9 – May 4, 1975.
13W-1T in regular season and 7W in playoffs.
– Pittsburgh Penguins, Mar. 9 – Apr. 22, 1993.
17W-1T in regular season and 3W in playoffs.

**LONGEST HOME UNDEFEATED STREAK, INCLUDING PLAYOFFS:**
**38 Games – Montreal Canadiens**, Nov. 1, 1976 – Apr. 26, 1977.
28W-6T in regular season and 4W in playoffs.

**LONGEST ROAD UNDEFEATED STREAK, INCLUDING PLAYOFFS:**
**13 Games – Philadelphia Flyers**, Feb. 26 – Apr. 21, 1977. 6W-4T in regular season and 3W in playoffs.
**– Montreal Canadiens**, Feb. 26 – Apr. 20, 1980. 6W-4T in regular season and 3W in playoffs.
**– New York Islanders**, Mar. 16 – May 1, 1980. 3W-3T in regular season and 7W in playoffs.

## LOSING STREAKS

**LONGEST LOSING STREAK, ONE SEASON:**
**17 Games – Washington Capitals**, Feb. 18 – Mar. 26, 1975.
**– San Jose Sharks**, Jan. 4 – Feb. 12, 1993.
15 Games – Philadelphia Quakers, Nov. 29, 1930 – Jan. 8, 1931.

**LONGEST HOME LOSING STREAK, ONE SEASON:**
**14 Games – Pittsburgh Penguins**, Dec. 31, 2003 – Feb. 22, 2004.
11 Games – Boston Bruins, Dec. 8, 1924 – Feb. 17, 1925.
– Washington Capitals, Feb. 18 – Mar. 30, 1975.
– Ottawa Senators, Oct. 27 – Dec. 8, 1993.

**LONGEST ROAD LOSING STREAK, ONE SEASON:**
***38 Games – Ottawa Senators**, Oct. 10, 1992 – Apr. 3, 1993.
37 Games – Washington Capitals, Oct. 9, 1974 – Mar. 26, 1975.

**LONGEST LOSING STREAK FROM START OF SEASON:**
**11 Games – New York Rangers**, 1943-44.
7 Games – Montreal Canadiens, 1938-39.
– Chicago Blackhawks, 1947-48.
– Washington Capitals, 1983-84.
– Chicago Blackhawks, 1997-98.

**LONGEST HOME LOSING STREAK FROM START OF SEASON:**
**8 Games – Los Angeles Kings**, Oct. 13 – Nov. 6, 1971.

**LONGEST ROAD LOSING STREAK FROM START OF SEASON:**
***38 Games – Ottawa Senators**, Oct. 10, 1992 – Apr. 3, 1993.

## WINLESS STREAKS

**LONGEST WINLESS STREAK, ONE SEASON:**
**30 Games – Winnipeg Jets**, Oct. 19 – Dec. 20, 1980. 23L-7T
27 Games – Kansas City Scouts, Feb. 12 – Apr. 4, 1976. 21L-6T
25 Games – Washington Capitals, Nov. 29, 1975 – Jan. 21, 1976. 22L-3T

**LONGEST HOME WINLESS STREAK, ONE SEASON:**
**17 Games – Ottawa Senators**, Oct. 28, 1995 – Jan. 27, 1996. 15L-2T
**– Atlanta Thrashers**, Jan. 19 – Mar. 29, 2000. 15L-2T
16 Games – Pittsburgh Penguins, Dec. 31, 2003 – Mar. 4, 2004. 15L-1T

**LONGEST ROAD WINLESS STREAK, ONE SEASON:**
***38 Games – Ottawa Senators**, Oct. 10, 1992 – Apr. 3, 1993. 38L
37 Games – Washington Capitals, Oct. 9, 1974 – Mar. 26, 1975. 37L

**LONGEST WINLESS STREAK FROM START OF SEASON:**
**15 Games – New York Rangers**, 1943-44. 14L-1T
11 Games – Pittsburgh Pirates, 1927-28. 8L-3T
– Minnesota North Stars, 1973-74. 5L-6T
– San Jose Sharks, 1995-96. 7L-4T

**LONGEST HOME WINLESS STREAK FROM START OF SEASON:**
**11 Games – Pittsburgh Penguins**, Oct. 8 – Nov. 19, 1983. 9L-2T

**LONGEST ROAD WINLESS STREAK FROM START OF SEASON:**
***38 Games – Ottawa Senators**, Oct. 10, 1992 – Apr. 3, 1993. 38L

## NON-SHUTOUT STREAKS

**LONGEST NON-SHUTOUT STREAK:**
**264 Games – Calgary Flames**, Nov. 12, 1981 – Jan. 9, 1985.
261 Games – Los Angeles Kings, Mar. 15, 1986 – Oct. 22, 1989.
244 Games – Washington Capitals, Oct. 31, 1989 – Nov. 11, 1993.
236 Games – New York Rangers, Dec. 20, 1989 – Dec. 13, 1992.
230 Games – Quebec Nordiques, Feb. 10, 1980 – Jan. 12, 1983.

**LONGEST NON-SHUTOUT STREAK, INCLUDING PLAYOFFS:**
**264 Games – Los Angeles Kings**, Mar. 15, 1986 – Apr. 6, 1989.
(5 playoff games in 1987; 5 in 1988; 2 in 1989).
262 Games – Chicago Blackhawks, Mar. 14, 1970 – Feb. 21, 1973.
(8 playoff games in 1970; 18 in 1971; 8 in 1972).
251 Games – Quebec Nordiques, Feb. 10, 1980 – Jan. 12, 1983.
(5 playoff games in 1981; 16 in 1982).
246 Games – Pittsburgh Penguins, Jan. 7, 1989 – Oct. 26, 1991.
(11 playoff games in 1989; 24 in 1991).

* – Does not include neutral site games

# TEAM GOALS

## Most Goals

**MOST GOALS, ONE SEASON:**
**446 – Edmonton Oilers**, 1983-84. 80GP
426 – Edmonton Oilers, 1985-86. 80GP
424 – Edmonton Oilers, 1982-83. 80GP
417 – Edmonton Oilers, 1981-82. 80GP
401 – Edmonton Oilers, 1984-85. 80GP

**MOST GOALS, ONE TEAM, ONE GAME:**
**16 – Montreal Canadiens**, Mar. 3, 1920, at Quebec. Montreal won 16-3.

**MOST GOALS, BOTH TEAMS, ONE GAME:**
**21 – Montreal Canadiens (14), Toronto St. Patricks (7)**, Jan. 10, 1920, at Montreal.
**– Edmonton Oilers (12), Chicago Blackhawks (9)**, Dec. 11, 1985, at Chicago.
20 – Edmonton Oilers (12), Minnesota North Stars (8), Jan. 4, 1984, at Edmonton.
– Toronto Maple Leafs (11), Edmonton Oilers (9), Jan. 8, 1986, at Toronto.
19 – Montreal Wanderers (10), Toronto Arenas (9), Dec. 19, 1917, at Montreal.
– Montreal Canadiens (16), Quebec Bulldogs (3), Mar. 3, 1920, at Quebec.
– Montreal Canadiens (13), Hamilton Tigers (6), Feb. 26, 1921, at Montreal.
– Boston Bruins (10), New York Rangers (9), Mar. 4, 1944, at Boston.
– Detroit Red Wings (10), Boston Bruins (9), Mar. 16, 1944, at Detroit.
– Vancouver Canucks (10), Minnesota North Stars (9), Oct. 7, 1983, at Vancouver.

**MOST GOALS, ONE TEAM, ONE PERIOD:**
**9 – Buffalo Sabres**, Mar. 19, 1981, at Buffalo, second period during 14-4 win over Toronto.
8 – Detroit Red Wings, Jan. 23, 1944, at Detroit, third period during 15-0 win over NY Rangers.
– Boston Bruins, Mar. 16, 1969, at Boston, second period during 11-3 win over Toronto.
– New York Rangers, Nov. 21, 1971, at NY Rangers, third period during 12-1 win over California.
– Philadelphia Flyers, Mar. 31, 1973, at Philadelphia, second period during 10-2 win over NY Islanders.
– Buffalo Sabres, Dec. 21, 1975, at Buffalo, third period during 14-2 win over Washington.
– Minnesota North Stars, Nov. 11, 1981, at Minnesota, second period during 15-2 win over Winnipeg.
– Pittsburgh Penguins, Dec. 17, 1991, at Pittsburgh, second period during 10-2 win over San Jose.
– Washington Capitals, Feb. 3, 1999, at Washington, second period during 10-1 win over Tampa Bay.

**MOST GOALS, BOTH TEAMS, ONE PERIOD:**
**12 – Buffalo Sabres (9), Toronto Maple Leafs (3)**, Mar. 19, 1981, at Buffalo, second period. Buffalo won 14-4.
**– Edmonton Oilers (6), Chicago Blackhawks (6)**, Dec. 11, 1985, at Chicago, second period. Edmonton won 12-9.
10 – New York Rangers (7), New York Americans (3), Mar. 16, 1939, at NY Americans, third period. NY Rangers won 11-5.
– Toronto Maple Leafs (6), Detroit Red Wings (4), Mar. 17, 1946, at Detroit, third period. Toronto won 11-7.
– Buffalo Sabres (6), Vancouver Canucks (4), Jan. 8, 1976, at Buffalo, third period. Buffalo won 8-5.
– Buffalo Sabres (5), Montreal Canadiens (5), Oct. 26, 1982, at Montreal, first period. Teams tied 7-7.
– Quebec Nordiques (6), Boston Bruins (4), Dec. 7, 1982, at Quebec, second period. Quebec won 10-5.
– Vancouver Canucks (6), Calgary Flames (4), Jan. 16, 1987, at Vancouver, first period. Vancouver won 9-5.
– Detroit Red Wings (7), Winnipeg Jets (3), Nov. 25, 1987, at Detroit, third period. Detroit won 10-8.
– Chicago Blackhawks (5), St. Louis Blues (5), Mar. 15, 1988, at St. Louis, third period. Teams tied 7-7.

**MOST CONSECUTIVE GOALS, ONE TEAM, ONE GAME:**
**15 – Detroit Red Wings**, Jan. 23, 1944, at Detroit during 15-0 win over NY Rangers.

## Fewest Goals

**FEWEST GOALS, ONE SEASON:**
**33 – Chicago Blackhawks**, 1928-29. 44GP
45 – Montreal Maroons, 1924-25. 30GP
46 – Pittsburgh Pirates, 1928-29. 44GP

**FEWEST GOALS, ONE SEASON (MINIMUM 70-GAME SCHEDULE):**
**133 – Chicago Blackhawks**, 1953-54. 70GP
147 – Toronto Maple Leafs, 1954-55. 70GP
– Boston Bruins, 1955-56. 70GP
150 – New York Rangers, 1954-55. 70GP

# TEAM POWER-PLAY GOALS

**MOST POWER-PLAY GOALS, ONE SEASON:**
**119 – Pittsburgh Penguins**, 1988-89. 80GP
113 – Detroit Red Wings, 1992-93. 84GP
111 – New York Rangers, 1987-88. 80GP
110 – Pittsburgh Penguins, 1987-88. 80GP
– Winnipeg Jets, 1987-88. 80GP

# TEAM SHORTHAND GOALS

**MOST SHORTHAND GOALS, ONE SEASON:**
**36 – Edmonton Oilers**, 1983-84. 80GP
28 – Edmonton Oilers, 1986-87. 80GP
27 – Edmonton Oilers, 1985-86. 80GP
– Edmonton Oilers, 1988-89. 80GP

# TEAM GOALS-PER-GAME

**HIGHEST GOALS-PER-GAME AVERAGE, ONE SEASON:**
**5.58 – Edmonton Oilers**, 1983-84. 446G in 80GP.
5.38 – Montreal Canadiens, 1919-20. 129G in 24GP.
5.33 – Edmonton Oilers, 1985-86. 426G in 80GP.
5.30 – Edmonton Oilers, 1982-83. 424G in 80GP.
5.23 – Montreal Canadiens, 1917-18. 115G in 22GP.

**LOWEST GOALS-PER-GAME AVERAGE, ONE SEASON:**
**0.75 – Chicago Blackhawks**, 1928-29. 33G in 44GP.
1.05 – Pittsburgh Pirates, 1928-29. 46G in 44GP.
1.20 – New York Americans, 1928-29. 53G in 44GP.

# TEAM ASSISTS

**MOST ASSISTS, ONE SEASON:**
**737 – Edmonton Oilers**, 1985-86. 80GP
736 – Edmonton Oilers, 1983-84. 80GP
706 – Edmonton Oilers, 1981-82. 80GP

**FEWEST ASSISTS, ONE SEASON (Since 1926-27):**
**45 – New York Rangers**, 1926-27. 44GP

**FEWEST ASSISTS, ONE SEASON (MINIMUM 70-GAME SCHEDULE):**
**206 – Chicago Blackhawks**, 1953-54. 70GP

# TEAM TOTAL POINTS

**MOST SCORING POINTS, ONE SEASON:**
**1,182 – Edmonton Oilers**, 1983-84. (446G-736A) 80GP
1,163 – Edmonton Oilers, 1985-86. (426G-737A) 80GP
1,123 – Edmonton Oilers, 1981-82. (417G-706A) 80GP

**MOST SCORING POINTS, ONE TEAM, ONE GAME:**
**40 – Buffalo Sabres**, Dec. 21, 1975, at Buffalo. Buffalo defeated Washington 14-2, and had 26A.
39 – Minnesota North Stars, Nov. 11, 1981, at Minnesota. Minnesota defeated Winnipeg 15-2, and had 24A.
37 – Detroit Red Wings, Jan. 23, 1944, at Detroit. Detroit defeated NY Rangers 15-0, and had 22A.
– Toronto Maple Leafs, Mar. 16, 1957, at Toronto. Toronto defeated NY Rangers 14-1, and had 23A.
– Buffalo Sabres, Feb. 25, 1978, at Cleveland. Buffalo defeated Cleveland 13-3, and had 24A.
– Calgary Flames, Feb. 10, 1993, at Calgary. Calgary defeated San Jose 13-1, and had 24A.

**MOST SCORING POINTS, BOTH TEAMS, ONE GAME:**
**62 – Edmonton Oilers, Chicago Blackhawks**, Dec. 11, 1985, at Chicago. Edmonton won 12-9. Edmonton had 24A, Chicago, 17A.
53 – Quebec Nordiques, Washington Capitals, Feb. 22, 1981, at Washington. Quebec won 11-7. Quebec had 22A, Washington, 13A.
– Edmonton Oilers, Minnesota North Stars, Jan. 4, 1984, at Edmonton. Edmonton won 12-8. Edmonton had 20A, Minnesota, 13A.
– Minnesota North Stars, St. Louis Blues, Jan. 27, 1984, at St. Louis. Minnesota won 10-8. Minnesota had 19A, St. Louis, 16A.
– Toronto Maple Leafs, Edmonton Oilers, Jan. 8, 1986, at Toronto. Toronto won 11-9. Toronto had 17A, Edmonton, 16A.
52 – Montreal Maroons, New York Americans, Feb. 18, 1936, at NY Americans. Teams tied 8-8. NY Americans had 20A, Montreal, 16A. (3A allowed for each goal.)
– Vancouver Canucks, Minnesota North Stars, Oct. 7, 1983, at Vancouver. Vancouver won 10-9. Vancouver had 16A, Minnesota, 17A.

**MOST SCORING POINTS, ONE TEAM, ONE PERIOD:**
**23 – New York Rangers**, Nov. 21, 1971, at NY Rangers, third period during 12-1 win over California. NY Rangers had 8G, 15A.
**– Buffalo Sabres**, Dec. 21, 1975, at Buffalo, third period during 14-2 win over Washington. Buffalo had 8G, 15A.
**– Buffalo Sabres**, Mar. 19, 1981, at Buffalo, second period during 14-4 win over Toronto. Buffalo had 9G, 14A.
22 – Detroit Red Wings, Jan. 23, 1944, at Detroit, third period during 15-0 win over NY Rangers. Detroit had 8G, 14A.
– Boston Bruins, Mar. 16, 1969, at Boston, second period during 11-3 win over Toronto. Boston had 8G, 14A.
– Minnesota North Stars, Nov. 11, 1981, at Minnesota, second period during 15-2 win over Winnipeg. Minnesota had 8G, 14A.
– Pittsburgh Penguins, Dec. 17, 1991, at Pittsburgh, second period during 10-2 win over San Jose. Pittsburgh had 8G, 14A.
– Washington Capitals, Feb. 3, 1999, at Washington, second period during 10-1 win over Tampa Bay. Washington had 8G, 14A.

**MOST SCORING POINTS, BOTH TEAMS, ONE PERIOD:**
**35 – Edmonton, Oilers, Chicago Blackhawks**, Dec. 11, 1985, at Chicago, second period. Edmonton won 12-9. Edmonton had 6G, 12A; Chicago, 6G, 11A.
31 – Buffalo Sabres, Toronto Maple Leafs, Mar. 19, 1981, at Buffalo, second period. Buffalo won 14-4. Buffalo had 9G, 14A; Toronto, 3G, 5A.
29 – Winnipeg Jets, Detroit Red Wings, Nov. 25, 1987, at Detroit, third period. Detroit won 10-8. Detroit had 7G, 13A; Winnipeg, 3G, 6A.
– Chicago Blackhawks, St. Louis Blues, Mar. 15, 1988, at St. Louis, third period. Teams tied 7-7. St. Louis had 5G, 10A; Chicago, 5G, 9A.

## FASTEST GOALS

**FASTEST SIX GOALS, BOTH TEAMS:**

**3:00 – Quebec Nordiques, Washington Capitals**, Feb. 22, 1981, at Washington. Scorers: Peter Stastny, Quebec, 18:51; Pierre Lacroix, Quebec, 19:57 (first period); Anton Stastny, Quebec, 0:34; Jacques Richard, Quebec, 1:07 and 1:37; Rick Green, Washington, 1:51 (second period). Quebec won 11-7.

3:15 – Montreal Canadiens, Toronto Maple Leafs, Jan. 4, 1944, at Montreal, first period. Scorers: Maurice Richard, Montreal, 14:10; Don Webster, Toronto, 15:13; Fern Majeau, Montreal, 15:41; Phil Watson, Montreal, 15:52; Lorne Carr, Toronto, 16:55; Butch Bouchard, Montreal, 17:25. Montreal won 6-3.

**FASTEST FIVE GOALS, BOTH TEAMS:**

**1:24 – Chicago Blackhawks, Toronto Maple Leafs**, Oct. 15, 1983, at Toronto, second period. Scorers: Gaston Gingras, Toronto, 16:49; Denis Savard, Chicago, 17:12; Steve Larmer, Chicago, 17:27; Denis Savard, Chicago, 17:42; John Anderson, Toronto, 18:13. Toronto won 10-8.

1:39 – Detroit Red Wings, Toronto Maple Leafs, Nov. 15, 1944, at Toronto, third period. Scorers: Ted Kennedy, Toronto, 10:36 and 10:55; Harold Jackson, Detroit, 11:48; Steve Wojciechowski, Detroit, 12:02; Don Grosso, Detroit, 12:15. Detroit won 8-4.

**FASTEST FIVE GOALS, ONE TEAM:**

**2:07 – Pittsburgh Penguins**, Nov. 22, 1972, at Pittsburgh, third period. Scorers: Bryan Hextall, Jr., 12:00; Jean Pronovost, 12:18; Al McDonough, 13:40; Ken Schinkel, 13:49; Ron Schock, 14:07. Pittsburgh defeated St. Louis 10-4.

2:37 – New York Islanders, Jan. 26, 1982, at NY Islanders, first period. Scorers: Duane Sutter, 1:31; John Tonelli, 2:30; Bryan Trottier, 2:46 and 3:31; Duane Sutter, 4:08. NY Islanders defeated Pittsburgh 9-2.

2:55 – Boston Bruins, Dec. 19, 1974, at Boston. Scorers: Bobby Schmautz, 19:13 (first period); Ken Hodge, 0:18; Phil Esposito, 0:43; Don Marcotte, 0:58; John Bucyk, 2:08 (second period). Boston defeated NY Rangers 11-3.

**FASTEST FOUR GOALS, BOTH TEAMS:**

**0:53 – Chicago Blackhawks, Toronto Maple Leafs**, Oct. 15, 1983, at Toronto, second period. Scorers: Gaston Gingras, Toronto, 16:49; Denis Savard, Chicago, 17:12; Steve Larmer, Chicago, 17:27; Denis Savard, Chicago, 17:42. Toronto won 10-8.

0:57 – Quebec Nordiques, Detroit Red Wings, Jan. 27, 1990, at Quebec, first period. Scorers: Paul Gillis, Quebec, 18:01; Claude Loiselle, Quebec, 18:12; Joe Sakic, Quebec, 18:27; Jimmy Carson, Detroit, 18:58. Detroit won 8-6.

1:01 – Colorado Rockies, New York Rangers, Jan. 15, 1980, at NY Rangers, first period. Scorers: Doug Sulliman, NY Rangers, 7:52; Eddie Johnstone, NY Rangers, 7:57; Warren Miller, NY Rangers, 8:20; Rob Ramage, Colorado, 8:53. Teams tied 6-6.

– Chicago Blackhawks, Toronto Maple Leafs, Oct. 15, 1983, at Toronto, second period. Scorers: Denis Savard, Chicago, 17:12; Steve Larmer, Chicago, 17:27; Denis Savard, Chicago, 17:42; John Anderson, Toronto, 18:13. Toronto won 10-8.

**FASTEST FOUR GOALS, ONE TEAM:**

**1:20 – Boston Bruins**, Jan. 21, 1945, at Boston, second period. Scorers: Bill Thoms, 6:34; Frank Mario, 7:08 and 7:27; Ken Smith, 7:54. Boston defeated NY Rangers 14-3.

**FASTEST THREE GOALS, BOTH TEAMS:**

**0:15 – Minnesota North Stars, New York Rangers**, Feb. 10, 1983, at Minnesota, second period. Scorers: Mark Pavelich, NY Rangers, 19:18; Ron Greschner, NY Rangers, 19:27; Willi Plett, Minnesota, 19:33. Minnesota won 7-5.

0:18 – Montreal Canadiens, New York Rangers, Dec. 12, 1963, at Montreal, first period. Scorers: Dave Balon, Montreal, 0:58; Gilles Tremblay, Montreal, 1:04; Camille Henry, NY Rangers, 1:16. Montreal won 6-4.

– California Golden Seals, Buffalo Sabres, Feb. 1, 1976, at California, third period. Scorers: Jim Moxey, California, 19:38; Wayne Merrick, California, 19:45; Danny Gare, Buffalo, 19:56. Buffalo won 9-5.

**FASTEST THREE GOALS, ONE TEAM:**

**0:20 – Boston Bruins**, Feb. 25, 1971, at Boston, third period. Scorers: John Bucyk, 4:50; Ed Westfall, 5:02; Ted Green, 5:10. Boston defeated Vancouver 8-3.

0:21 – Chicago Blackhawks, Mar. 23, 1952, at NY Rangers, third period. Bill Mosienko scored all three goals, at 6:09, 6:20 and 6:30. Chicago defeated NY Rangers 7-6.

– Washington Capitals, Nov. 23, 1990, at Washington, first period. Scorers: Michal Pivonka, 16:18; Stephen Leach, 16:29 and 16:39. Washington defeated Pittsburgh 7-3.

**FASTEST THREE GOALS FROM START OF PERIOD, BOTH TEAMS:**

**1:05 – Hartford Whalers, Montreal Canadiens**, Mar. 11, 1989, at Montreal, second period. Scorers: Kevin Dineen, Hartford, 0:11; Guy Carbonneau, Montreal, 0:36; Petr Svoboda, Montreal, 1:05. Montreal won 5-3.

**FASTEST THREE GOALS FROM START OF PERIOD, ONE TEAM:**

**0:53 – Calgary Flames**, Feb. 10, 1993, at Calgary, third period. Scorers: Gary Suter, 0:17; Chris Lindberg, 0:40; Ron Stern, 0:53. Calgary defeated San Jose 13-1.

**FASTEST TWO GOALS, BOTH TEAMS:**

**0:02 – St. Louis Blues, Boston Bruins**, Dec. 19, 1987, at Boston, third period. Scorers: Ken Linseman, Boston, 19:50; Doug Gilmour, St. Louis, 19:52. St. Louis won 7-5.

0:03 – Chicago Blackhawks, Minnesota North Stars, Nov. 5, 1988, at Minnesota, third period. Scorers: Steve Thomas, Chicago, 6:03; Dave Gagner, Minnesota, 6:06. Teams tied 5-5.

**FASTEST TWO GOALS, ONE TEAM:**

**0:03 – Minnesota Wild**, Jan. 21, 2004, at Minnesota, third period. Scorers: Jim Dowd, 19:44; Richard Park, 19:47. Minnesota defeated Chicago 4-2.

0:04 – Montreal Maroons, Jan. 3, 1931, at Montreal, third period. Nels Stewart scored both goals, at 8:24 and 8:28. Mtl. Maroons defeated Boston 5-3.

– Buffalo Sabres, Oct. 17, 1974, at Buffalo, third period. Scorers: Lee Fogolin, Jr., 14:55; Don Luce, 14:59. Buffalo defeated California 6-1.

– Toronto Maple Leafs, Dec. 29, 1988, at Quebec, third period. Scorers: Ed Olczyk, 5:24; Gary Leeman, 5:28. Toronto defeated Quebec 6-5.

– Calgary Flames, Oct. 17, 1989, at Quebec, third period. Scorers: Doug Gilmour, 19:45; Paul Ranheim, 19:49. Teams tied 8-8.

– Winnipeg Jets, Dec. 15, 1995, at Winnipeg, second period. Deron Quint scored both goals, at 7:51 and 7:55. Winnipeg defeated Edmonton 9-4.

**FASTEST TWO GOALS FROM START OF GAME, ONE TEAM:**

**0:24 – Edmonton Oilers**, Mar. 28, 1982, at Los Angeles. Scorers: Mark Messier, 0:14; Dave Lumley, 0:24. Edmonton defeated Los Angeles 6-2.

0:27 – Boston Bruins, Feb. 14, 2003, at Florida. Mike Knuble scored both goals, at 0:10 and 0:27. Boston defeated Florida 6-5.

0:29 – Pittsburgh Penguins, Dec. 6, 1980, at Pittsburgh. Scorers: George Ferguson, 0:17; Greg Malone, 0:29. Pittsburgh defeated Chicago 6-4.

**FASTEST TWO GOALS FROM START OF PERIOD, BOTH TEAMS:**

**0:14 – New York Rangers, Quebec Nordiques**, Nov. 5, 1983, at Quebec, third period. Scorers: Andre Savard, Quebec, 0:08; Pierre Larouche, NY Rangers, 0:14. Teams tied 4-4.

0:25 – St. Louis Blues, Chicago Blackhawks, Feb. 2, 2006, at St. Louis, second period. Scorers: Peter Cajanek, St. Louis, 0:10; Tyler Arnason, Chicago, 0:25. St. Louis won 6-5.

0:28 – Boston Bruins, Montreal Canadiens, Oct. 11, 1989, at Montreal, third period. Scorers: Jim Wiemer, Boston 0:10; Tom Chorske, Montreal 0:28. Montreal won 4-2.

**FASTEST TWO GOALS FROM START OF PERIOD, ONE TEAM:**

**0:21 – Chicago Blackhawks**, Nov. 5, 1983, at Minnesota, second period. Scorers: Ken Yaremchuk, 0:12; Darryl Sutter, 0:21. Minnesota defeated Chicago 10-5.

0:24 – Edmonton Oilers, Mar. 28, 1982, at Los Angeles, first period. Scorers: Mark Messier, 0:14; Dave Lumley, 0:24. Edmonton defeated Los Angeles 6-2.

0:27 – Boston Bruins, Feb. 14, 2003, at Florida. Mike Knuble scored both goals, at 0:10 and 0:27. Boston defeated Florida 6-5.

## 50, 40, 30, 20-GOAL SCORERS

**MOST 50-OR-MORE GOAL SCORERS, ONE SEASON:**

**3 – Edmonton Oilers**, 1983-84. 80GP. Wayne Gretzky, 87; Glenn Anderson, 54; Jari Kurri, 52.

**– Edmonton Oilers**, 1985-86. 80GP. Jari Kurri, 68; Glenn Anderson, 54; Wayne Gretzky, 52.

2 – Boston Bruins, 1970-71. 78GP. Phil Esposito, 76; John Bucyk, 51.

– Boston Bruins, 1973-74. 78GP. Phil Esposito, 68; Ken Hodge, 50.

– Philadelphia Flyers, 1975-76. 80GP. Reggie Leach, 61; Bill Barber, 50.

– Pittsburgh Penguins, 1975-76. 80GP. Pierre Larouche, 53; Jean Pronovost, 52.

– Montreal Canadiens, 1976-77. 80GP. Steve Shutt, 60; Guy Lafleur, 56.

– Los Angeles Kings, 1979-80. 80GP. Charlie Simmer, 56; Marcel Dionne, 53.

– Montreal Canadiens, 1979-80. 80GP. Pierre Larouche, 50; Guy Lafleur, 50.

– Los Angeles Kings, 1980-81. 80GP. Marcel Dionne, 58; Charlie Simmer, 56.

– Edmonton Oilers, 1981-82. 80GP. Wayne Gretzky, 92; Mark Messier, 50.

– New York Islanders, 1981-82. 80GP. Mike Bossy, 64; Bryan Trottier, 50.

– Edmonton Oilers, 1984-85. 80GP. Wayne Gretzky, 73; Jari Kurri, 71.

– Washington Capitals, 1984-85. 80GP. Bob Carpenter, 53; Mike Gartner, 50.

– Edmonton Oilers, 1986-87. 80GP. Wayne Gretzky, 62; Jari Kurri, 54.

– Calgary Flames, 1987-88. 80GP. Joe Nieuwendyk, 51; Hakan Loob, 50.

– Los Angeles Kings, 1987-88. 80GP. Jimmy Carson, 55; Luc Robitaille, 53.

– Calgary Flames, 1988-89. 80GP. Joe Nieuwendyk, 51; Joe Mullen, 51.

– Los Angeles Kings, 1988-89. 80GP. Bernie Nicholls, 70; Wayne Gretzky, 54.

– Buffalo Sabres, 1992-93. 84GP. Alexander Mogilny, 76; Pat LaFontaine, 53.

– Pittsburgh Penguins, 1992-93. 84GP. Mario Lemieux, 69; Kevin Stevens, 55.

– St. Louis Blues, 1992-93. 84GP. Brett Hull, 54; Brendan Shanahan, 51.

– Detroit Red Wings, 1993-94. 84GP. Sergei Fedorov, 56; Ray Sheppard, 52.

– St. Louis Blues, 1993-94. 84GP. Brett Hull, 57; Brendan Shanahan, 52.

– Pittsburgh Penguins, 1995-96. 82GP. Mario Lemieux, 69; Jaromir Jagr, 62.

**MOST 40-OR-MORE GOAL SCORERS, ONE SEASON:**

**4 – Edmonton Oilers**, 1982-83. 80GP. Wayne Gretzky, 71; Glenn Anderson, 48; Mark Messier, 48; Jari Kurri, 45.

**– Edmonton Oilers**, 1983-84. 80GP. Wayne Gretzky, 87; Glenn Anderson, 54; Jari Kurri, 52; Paul Coffey, 40.

**– Edmonton Oilers**, 1984-85. 80GP. Wayne Gretzky, 73; Jari Kurri, 71; Mike Krushelnyski, 43; Glenn Anderson, 42.

**– Edmonton Oilers**, 1985-86. 80GP. Jari Kurri, 68; Glenn Anderson, 54; Wayne Gretzky, 52; Paul Coffey, 48.

**– Calgary Flames**, 1987-88. 80GP. Joe Nieuwendyk, 51; Hakan Loob, 50; Mike Bullard, 48; Joe Mullen, 40.

3 – Boston Bruins, 1970-71. 78GP. Phil Esposito, 76; John Bucyk, 51; Ken Hodge, 43.

– New York Rangers, 1971-72. 78GP. Vic Hadfield, 50; Jean Ratelle, 46; Rod Gilbert, 43.

– Buffalo Sabres, 1975-76. 80GP. Danny Gare, 50; Rick Martin, 49; Gilbert Perreault, 44.

– Montreal Canadiens, 1979-80. 80GP. Guy Lafleur, 50; Pierre Larouche, 50; Steve Shutt, 47.

– Buffalo Sabres, 1979-80. 80GP. Danny Gare, 56; Rick Martin, 45; Gilbert Perreault, 40.

– Los Angeles Kings, 1980-81. 80GP. Marcel Dionne, 58; Charlie Simmer, 56; Dave Taylor, 47.

– Los Angeles Kings, 1984-85. 80GP. Marcel Dionne, 46; Bernie Nicholls, 46; Dave Taylor, 41.

– New York Islanders, 1984-85. 80GP. Mike Bossy, 58; Brent Sutter, 42; John Tonelli, 42.

– Chicago Blackhawks, 1985-86. 80GP. Denis Savard, 47; Troy Murray, 45; Al Secord, 40.

– Chicago Blackhawks, 1987-88. 80GP. Denis Savard, 44; Rick Vaive, 43; Steve Larmer, 41.
– Edmonton Oilers, 1987-88. 80GP. Craig Simpson, 43; Jari Kurri, 43; Wayne Gretzky, 40.
– Los Angeles Kings, 1988-89. 80GP. Bernie Nicholls, 70; Wayne Gretzky, 54; Luc Robitaille, 46.
– Los Angeles Kings, 1990-91. 80GP. Luc Robitaille, 45; Tomas Sandstrom, 45; Wayne Gretzky, 41.
– Pittsburgh Penguins, 1991-92. 80GP. Kevin Stevens, 54; Mario Lemieux, 44; Joe Mullen, 42.
– Pittsburgh Penguins, 1992-93. 84GP. Mario Lemieux, 69; Kevin Stevens, 55; Rick Tocchet, 48.
– Calgary Flames, 1993-94. 84GP. Gary Roberts, 41; Robert Reichel, 40; Theoren Fleury, 40.
– Pittsburgh Penguins, 1995-96. 82GP. Mario Lemieux, 69; Jaromir Jagr, 62; Petr Nedved, 45.

**MOST 30-OR-MORE GOAL SCORERS, ONE SEASON:**
**6 – Buffalo Sabres**, 1974-75. 80GP. Rick Martin, 52; Rene Robert, 40; Gilbert Perreault, 39; Don Luce, 33; Rick Dudley, 31; Danny Gare, 31.
**– New York Islanders**, 1977-78. 80GP. Mike Bossy, 53; Bryan Trottier, 46; Clark Gillies, 35; Denis Potvin, 30; Bob Nystrom, 30; Bob Bourne, 30.
**– Winnipeg Jets**, 1984-85. 80GP. Dale Hawerchuk, 53; Paul MacLean, 41; Laurie Boschman, 32; Brian Mullen, 32; Doug Smail, 31; Thomas Steen, 30.
5 – Chicago Blackhawks, 1968-69. 76GP
– Boston Bruins, 1970-71. 78GP
– Montreal Canadiens, 1971-72. 78GP
– Philadelphia Flyers, 1972-73. 78GP
– Boston Bruins, 1973-74. 78GP
– Montreal Canadiens, 1974-75. 80GP
– Montreal Canadiens, 1975-76. 80GP
– Pittsburgh Penguins, 1975-76. 80GP
– New York Islanders, 1978-79. 80GP
– Detroit Red Wings, 1979-80. 80GP
– Philadelphia Flyers, 1979-80. 80GP
– New York Islanders, 1980-81. 80GP
– St. Louis Blues, 1980-81. 80GP
– Chicago Blackhawks, 1981-82. 80GP
– Edmonton Oilers, 1981-82. 80GP
– Montreal Canadiens, 1981-82. 80GP
– Quebec Nordiques, 1981-82. 80GP
– Washington Capitals, 1981-82. 80GP
– Edmonton Oilers, 1982-83. 80GP
– Edmonton Oilers, 1983-84. 80GP
– Edmonton Oilers, 1984-85. 80GP
– Los Angeles Kings, 1984-85. 80GP
– Edmonton Oilers, 1985-86. 80GP
– Edmonton Oilers, 1986-87. 80GP
– Edmonton Oilers, 1987-88. 80GP
– Edmonton Oilers, 1988-89. 80GP
– Detroit Red Wings, 1991-92. 80GP
– New York Rangers, 1991-92. 80GP
– Pittsburgh Penguins, 1991-92. 80GP
– Detroit Red Wings, 1992-93. 84GP
– Pittsburgh Penguins, 1992-93. 84GP

**MOST 20-OR-MORE GOAL SCORERS, ONE SEASON:**
**11 – Boston Bruins**, 1977-78. 80GP. Peter McNab, 41; Terry O'Reilly, 29; Bobby Schmautz, 27; Stan Jonathan, 27; Jean Ratelle, 25; Rick Middleton, 25; Wayne Cashman, 24; Gregg Sheppard, 23; Brad Park, 22; Don Marcotte, 20; Bob Miller, 20.
10 – Boston Bruins, 1970-71. 78GP
– Montreal Canadiens, 1974-75. 80GP
– St. Louis Blues, 1980-81. 80GP

## 100-POINT SCORERS

**MOST 100 OR-MORE-POINT SCORERS, ONE SEASON:**
**4 – Boston Bruins**, 1970-71. 78GP. Phil Esposito, 76G-76A-152PTS; Bobby Orr, 37G-102A-139PTS; John Bucyk, 51G-65A-116PTS; Ken Hodge, 43G-62A-105PTS.
**– Edmonton Oilers**, 1982-83. 80GP. Wayne Gretzky, 71G-125A-196PTS; Mark Messier, 48G-58A-106PTS; Glenn Anderson, 48G-56A-104PTS; Jari Kurri, 45G-59A-104PTS.
**– Edmonton Oilers**, 1983-84. 80GP. Wayne Gretzky, 87G-118A-205PTS; Paul Coffey, 40G-86A-126PTS; Jari Kurri, 52G-61A-113PTS; Mark Messier, 37G-64A-101PTS.
**– Edmonton Oilers**,1985-86. 80GP. Wayne Gretzky, 52G-163A-215PTS; Paul Coffey, 48G-90A-138PTS; Jari Kurri, 68G-63A-131PTS; Glenn Anderson, 54G-48A-102PTS.
**– Pittsburgh Penguins**,1992-93. 84GP. Mario Lemieux, 69G-91A-160PTS; Kevin Stevens, 55G-56A-111PTS; Rick Tocchet, 48G-61A-109PTS; Ron Francis, 24G-76A-100PTS.
3 – Boston Bruins, 1973-74. 78GP. Phil Esposito, 68G-77A-145PTS; Bobby Orr, 32G-90A-122PTS; Ken Hodge, 50G-55A-105PTS.
– New York Islanders, 1978-79. 80GP. Bryan Trottier, 47G-87A-134PTS; Mike Bossy, 69G-57A-126PTS; Denis Potvin, 31G-70A-101PTS.
– Los Angeles Kings, 1980-81. 80GP. Marcel Dionne, 58G-77A-135PTS; Dave Taylor, 47G-65A-112PTS; Charlie Simmer, 56G-49A-105PTS.
– Edmonton Oilers, 1984-85. 80GP. Wayne Gretzky, 73G-135A-208PTS; Jari Kurri, 71G-64A-135PTS; Paul Coffey, 37G-84A-121PTS.
– New York Islanders, 1984-85. 80GP. Mike Bossy, 58G-59A-117PTS; Brent Sutter, 42G-60A-102PTS; John Tonelli, 42G-58A-100PTS.
– Edmonton Oilers, 1986-87. 80GP. Wayne Gretzky, 62G-121A-183PTS; Jari Kurri, 54G-54A-108PTS; Mark Messier, 37G-70A-107PTS.
– Pittsburgh Penguins, 1988-89. 80GP. Mario Lemieux, 85G-114A-199PTS; Rob Brown, 49G-66A-115PTS; Paul Coffey, 30G-83A-113PTS.
– Pittsburgh Penguins, 1995-96. 82GP. Mario Lemieux, 69G-92A-161PTS; Jaromir Jagr, 62G-87A-149PTS; Ron Francis, 27G-92A-119PTS.

## SHOTS ON GOAL

**MOST SHOTS, BOTH TEAMS, ONE GAME:**
**141 – New York Americans, Pittsburgh Pirates**, Dec. 26, 1925, at NY Americans. NY Americans won 3-1 with 73 shots; Pittsburgh had 68 shots.

**MOST SHOTS, ONE TEAM, ONE GAME:**
**83 – Boston Bruins**, Mar. 4, 1941, at Boston. Boston defeated Chicago 3-2.
73 – New York Americans, Dec. 26, 1925, at NY Americans. NY Americans defeated Pittsburgh 3-1.
– Boston Bruins, Mar. 21, 1991, at Boston. Boston tied Quebec 3-3.
72 – Boston Bruins, Dec. 10, 1970, at Boston. Boston defeated Buffalo 8-2.

**MOST SHOTS, ONE TEAM, ONE PERIOD:**
**33 – Boston Bruins**, Mar. 4, 1941, at Boston, second period. Boston defeated Chicago 3-2.

## TEAM GOALS AGAINST

### Fewest Goals Against

**FEWEST GOALS AGAINST, ONE SEASON:**
**42 – Ottawa Senators**, 1925-26. 36GP
43 – Montreal Canadiens, 1928-29. 44GP
48 – Montreal Canadiens, 1923-24. 24GP
– Montreal Canadiens, 1927-28. 44GP

**FEWEST GOALS AGAINST, ONE SEASON (MINIMUM 70-GAME SCHEDULE):**
**131 – Toronto Maple Leafs**, 1953-54. 70GP
**– Montreal Canadiens**, 1955-56. 70GP
132 – Detroit Red Wings, 1953-54. 70GP
133 – Detroit Red Wings, 1951-52. 70GP
– Detroit Red Wings, 1952-53. 70GP

**LOWEST GOALS-AGAINST-PER-GAME AVERAGE, ONE SEASON:**
**0.98 – Montreal Canadiens**, 1928-29. 43GA in 44GP.
1.09 – Montreal Canadiens, 1927-28. 48GA in 44GP.
1.17 – Ottawa Senators, 1925-26. 42GA in 36GP.

### Most Goals Against

**MOST GOALS AGAINST, ONE SEASON:**
**446 – Washington Capitals**, 1974-75. 80GP
415 – Detroit Red Wings, 1985-86. 80GP
414 – San Jose Sharks, 1992-93. 84GP
407 – Quebec Nordiques, 1989-90. 80GP
403 – Hartford Whalers, 1982-83. 80GP

**HIGHEST GOALS-AGAINST-PER-GAME AVERAGE, ONE SEASON:**
**7.38 – Quebec Bulldogs**, 1919-20. 177GA in 24GP.
6.20 – New York Rangers, 1943-44. 310GA in 50GP.
5.58 – Washington Capitals, 1974-75. 446GA in 80GP.

**MOST POWER-PLAY GOALS AGAINST, ONE SEASON:**
**122 – Chicago Blackhawks**, 1988-89. 80GP
120 – Pittsburgh Penguins, 1987-88. 80GP
116 – Washington Capitals, 2005-06. 82GP
115 – New Jersey Devils, 1988-89. 80GP
– Ottawa Senators, 1992-93. 84GP
114 – Los Angeles Kings, 1992-93. 84GP

**MOST SHORTHAND GOALS AGAINST, ONE SEASON:**
**22 – Pittsburgh Penguins**, 1984-85. 80GP
**– Minnesota North Stars**, 1991-92. 80GP
**– Colorado Avalanche**, 1995-96. 82GP
21 – Calgary Flames, 1984-85. 80GP
– Pittsburgh Penguins, 1989-90. 80GP

## SHUTOUTS

**MOST SHUTOUTS, ONE SEASON:**
**22 – Montreal Canadiens**, 1928-29. All by George Hainsworth. 44GP
16 – New York Americans, 1928-29. Roy Worters 13, Flat Walsh 3. 44GP
15 – Ottawa Senators, 1925-26. All by Alex Connell. 36GP
– Ottawa Senators, 1927-28. All by Alex Connell. 44GP
– Boston Bruins, 1927-28. All by Hal Winkler. 44GP
– Chicago Blackhawks, 1969-70. All by Tony Esposito. 76GP

**MOST CONSECUTIVE SHUTOUTS, ONE SEASON:**
**6 – Ottawa Senators**, Jan. 31 – Feb. 18, 1928. All by Alex Connell.

**MOST CONSECUTIVE SHUTOUTS TO START SEASON:**
**5 – Toronto Maple Leafs**, Nov. 13 – 22, 1930. Lorne Chabot 3, Benny Grant 2.

**MOST GAMES SHUTOUT, ONE SEASON:**
**20 – Chicago Blackhawks**, 1928-29. 44GP

**MOST CONSECUTIVE GAMES SHUTOUT:**
**8 – Chicago Blackhawks**, Feb. 7 – 28, 1929.

**MOST CONSECUTIVE GAMES SHUTOUT TO START SEASON:**
**3 – Montreal Maroons**, Nov. 11 – 18, 1930.

## TEAM SHOOTOUT RECORDS

**MOST SHOOTOUT GAMES, ONE SEASON:**
**19 – Edmonton Oilers**, 2007-08
18 – New Jersey Devils, 2006-07
17 – Minnesota Wild, 2006-07
– New York Rangers, 2007-08

**MOST SHOOTOUT GAMES, ALL-TIME:**
**58 – New York Rangers**
51 – Edmonton Oilers
– New Jersey Devils

**MOST SHOOTOUT WINS, ONE SEASON:**
**15 – Edmonton Oilers**, 2007-08, 19GP
12 – Dallas Stars, 2005-06, 13GP
10 – Tampa Bay Lightning, 2006-07, 12GP
– Buffalo Sabres, 2006-07, 14GP
– Pittsburgh Penguins, 2006-07, 16GP
– New York Rangers, 2008-09, 16GP
– Minnesota Wild, 2006-07, 17GP
– New Jersey Devils, 2006-07, 18GP

**MOST SHOOTOUT WINS, ALL-TIME:**
**34 – New York Rangers**, 58GP
33 – New Jersey Devils, 51GP
32 – Dallas Stars, 46GP

**MOST SHOOTOUT HOME WINS, ONE SEASON:**
**8 – Edmonton Oilers**, 2007-08, 9GP
7 – New York Rangers, 2008-09, 9GP
– Anaheim Ducks, 2007-08, 10GP
– Minnesota Wild, 2006-07, 11GP

**MOST SHOOTOUT HOME WINS, ALL-TIME:**
**19 – New York Rangers**, 26GP
**– New Jersey Devils**, 29GP
16 – Atlanta Thrashers, 22GP

**MOST SHOOTOUT ROAD WINS, ONE SEASON:**
**7 – Dallas Stars**, 2005-06, 8GP
**– Dallas Stars**, 2006-07, 9GP
**– Edmonton Oilers**, 2007-08, 10GP

**MOST SHOOTOUT ROAD WINS, ALL-TIME:**
**20 – Dallas Stars**, 28GP
17 – Edmonton Oilers, 28GP
15 – Buffalo Sabres, 28GP
– New York Rangers, 32GP

**MOST SHOOTOUT SHOTS TAKEN, ONE SEASON:**
**65 – Edmonton Oilers**, 2007-08, 19GP
62 – Minnesota Wild, 2006-07, 17GP
– New Jersey Devils, 2006-07, 18GP

**MOST SHOOTOUT SHOTS TAKEN, ALL-TIME:**
**213 – New York Rangers**, 58GP
177 – Anaheim Ducks, 49GP
174 – New Jersey Devils, 51GP

**MOST SHOOTOUT GOALS SCORED, ONE SEASON:**
**27 – Minnesota Wild**, 2006-07, 17GP
25 – New Jersey Devils, 2006-07, 18GP
24 – Dallas Stars, 2005-06, 13GP
– Edmonton Oilers, 2007-08, 19GP

**MOST SHOOTOUT GOALS SCORED, ALL-TIME:**
**71 – Dallas Stars**, 46GP
70 – New Jersey Devils, 51GP
69 – New York Rangers, 58GP

**BEST SHOOTOUT SCORING PERCENTAGE, ONE SEASON:**
**.583 – San Jose Sharks**, 2006-07, 4GP (7G, 12S)
.571 – Dallas Stars, 2005-06, 13GP (24G, 42S)
.517 – Atlanta Thrashers, 2006-07, 11GP (15G, 29S)

**BEST SHOOTOUT SCORING PERCENTAGE, ALL-TIME:**
**.428 – Dallas Stars**, 46GP (71G, 166S)
.402 – New Jersey Devils, 51GP (70G, 174S)
.389 – Nashville Predators, 39GP (44G, 113S)

**FEWEST SHOOTOUT GOALS AGAINST, ONE SEASON:**
**3 – Tampa Bay Lightning**, 2007-08, 3GP (9SA)
**– Calgary Flames**, 2008-09, 5GP (14SA)
**– Los Angeles Kings**, 2005-06, 7GP (21SA)

**FEWEST SHOOTOUT GOALS AGAINST, ALL-TIME:**
**32 – Calgary Flames**, 28GP (84SA)
36 – Carolina Hurricanes, 28GP (91SA)
– Phoenix Coyotes, 31GP (124SA)

**BEST SHOOTOUT WINNING PERCENTAGE, ONE SEASON:**
**.923 – Dallas Stars**, 2005-06, 13GP (12W)
.875 – Atlanta Thrashers, 2008-09, 8GP (7W)
.857 – Los Angeles Kings, 2005-06, 7GP (6W)

**BEST SHOOTOUT WINNING PERCENTAGE, ALL-TIME:**
**.696 – Dallas Stars**, 46GP (32W)
.647 – New Jersey Devils, 51GP (33W)
.636 – Atlanta Thrashers, 44GP (28W)

## TEAM PENALTIES

**MOST PENALTY MINUTES, ONE SEASON:**
**2,713 – Buffalo Sabres**, 1991-92. 80GP
2,670 – Pittsburgh Penguins, 1988-89. 80GP
2,663 – Chicago Blackhawks, 1991-92. 80GP
2,643 – Calgary Flames, 1991-92. 80GP
2,621 – Philadelphia Flyers, 1980-81. 80GP

**MOST PENALTIES, BOTH TEAMS, ONE GAME:**
**85 – Edmonton Oilers (44), Los Angeles Kings (41),** Feb. 28, 1990, at Los Angeles. Edmonton received 26 minors, 7 majors, 6 10-minute misconducts, 4 game misconducts and 1 match penalty; Los Angeles received 26 minors, 9 majors, 3 10-minute misconducts and 3 game misconducts.

**MOST PENALTY MINUTES, BOTH TEAMS, ONE GAME:**
**419 – Ottawa Senators (206), Philadelphia Flyers (213),** Mar. 5, 2004, at Philadelphia. Ottawa received 8 minors, 10 majors, 4 10-minute misconducts and 10 game misconducts. Philadelphia received 9 minors, 11 majors, 4 10-minute misconducts and 10 game misconducts.

**MOST PENALTIES, ONE TEAM, ONE GAME:**
**44 – Edmonton Oilers**, Feb. 28, 1990, at Los Angeles. Edmonton received 26 minors, 7 majors, 6 10-minute misconducts, 4 game misconducts and 1 match penalty.
42 – Minnesota North Stars, Feb. 26, 1981, at Boston. Minnesota received 18 minors, 13 majors, 4 10-minute misconducts and 7 game misconducts.
– Boston Bruins, Feb. 26, 1981, at Boston vs. Minnesota. Boston received 20 minors, 13 majors, 3 10-minute misconducts and 6 game misconducts.

**MOST PENALTY MINUTES, ONE TEAM, ONE GAME:**
**213 – Philadelphia Flyers**, Mar. 5, 2004, at Philadelphia. Philadelphia received 9 minors, 11 majors, 4 10-minute misconducts and 10 game misconducts.

**MOST PENALTIES, BOTH TEAMS, ONE PERIOD:**
**67 – Minnesota North Stars (34), Boston Bruins (33),** Feb. 26, 1981, at Boston, first period. Minnesota received 15 minors, 8 majors, 4 10-minute misconducts and 7 game misconducts. Boston had 16 minors, 8 majors, 3 10-minute misconducts and 6 game misconducts.

**MOST PENALTY MINUTES, BOTH TEAMS, ONE PERIOD:**
**409 – Ottawa Senators (200), Philadelphia Flyers (209),** Mar. 5, 2004, at Philadelphia, third period. Ottawa received 5 minors, 10 majors, 4 10-minute misconducts and 10 game misconducts. Philadelphia received 7 minors, 11 majors, 4 10-minute misconducts and 10 game misconducts.

**MOST PENALTIES, ONE TEAM, ONE PERIOD:**
**34 – Minnesota North Stars**, Feb. 26, 1981, at Boston, first period. Minnesota received 15 minors, 8 majors, 4 10-minute misconducts and 7 game misconducts.

**MOST PENALTY MINUTES, ONE TEAM, ONE PERIOD:**
**209 – Philadelphia Flyers**, Mar. 5, 2004, at Philadelphia vs. Ottawa, third period. Philadelphia received 7 minors, 11 majors, 4 10-minute misconducts and 10 game misconducts.
200 – Ottawa Senators, Mar. 5, 2004, at Philadelphia, third period. Ottawa received 5 minors, 10 majors, 4 10-minute misconducts and 10 game misconducts.

# NHL Individual Scoring Records – History

Six individual scoring records stand as benchmarks in the history of the game: most goals, single-season and career; most assists, single-season and career; and most points, single-season and career. The evolution of these six records is traced here, beginning with 1917-18, the NHL's first season. New research has resulted in changes to scoring records in the NHL's first nine seasons.

## MOST GOALS, ONE SEASON

44 —Joe Malone, Montreal, 1917-18.
Scored goal #44 against Toronto's Harry Holmes on March 2, 1918 and finished the season with 44 goals.
50 —Maurice Richard, Montreal, 1944-45.
Scored goal #45 against Toronto's Frank McCool on February 25, 1945 and finished the season with 50 goals.
50 —Bernie Geoffrion, Montreal, 1960-61.
Scored goal #50 against Toronto's Cesare Maniago on March 16, 1961 and finished the season with 50 goals.
50 —Bobby Hull, Chicago, 1961-62.
Scored goal #50 against NY Rangers' Gump Worsley on March 25, 1962 and finished the season with 50 goals.
54 —Bobby Hull, Chicago, 1965-66.
Scored goal #51 against NY Rangers' Cesare Maniago on March 12, 1966 and finished the season with 54 goals.
58 —Bobby Hull, Chicago, 1968-69.
Scored goal #55 against Boston's Gerry Cheevers on March 20, 1969 and finished the season with 58 goals.
76 —Phil Esposito, Boston, 1970-71.
Scored goal #59 against Los Angeles' Denis DeJordy on March 11, 1971 and finished the season with 76 goals.
92 —Wayne Gretzky, Edmonton, 1981-82.
Scored goal #77 against Buffalo's Don Edwards on February 24, 1982 and finished the season with 92 goals.

## MOST ASSISTS, ONE SEASON

10 —Cy Denneny, Ottawa, 1917-18.
—Reg Noble, Toronto, 1917-18.
—Harry Cameron, Toronto, 1917-18.
—Newsy Lalonde, Montreal, 1918-19.
15 —Frank Nighbor, Ottawa, 1919-20.
—Jack Darragh, Ottawa, 1920-21.
17 —Harry Cameron, Toronto, 1921-22.
18 —Dick Irvin, Chicago, 1926-27.
—Howie Morenz, Montreal, 1927-28.
36 —Frank Boucher, NY Rangers, 1929-30.
37 —Joe Primeau, Toronto, 1931-32.
45 —Bill Cowley, Boston, 1940-41.
—Bill Cowley, Boston, 1942-43.
49 —Clint Smith, Chicago, 1943-44.
54 —Elmer Lach, Montreal, 1944-45.
55 —Ted Lindsay, Detroit, 1949-50.
56 —Bert Olmstead, Montreal, 1955-56.
58 —Jean Beliveau, Montreal, 1960-61.
—Andy Bathgate, NY Rangers/Toronto, 1963-64.
59 —Stan Mikita, Chicago, 1964-65.
62 —Stan Mikita, Chicago, 1966-67.
77 —Phil Esposito, Boston, 1968-69.
87 —Bobby Orr, Boston, 1969-70.
102 —Bobby Orr, Boston, 1970-71.
109 —Wayne Gretzky, Edmonton, 1980-81.
120 —Wayne Gretzky, Edmonton, 1981-82.
125 —Wayne Gretzky, Edmonton, 1982-83.
135 —Wayne Gretzky, Edmonton, 1984-85.
163 —Wayne Gretzky, Edmonton, 1985-86.

## MOST POINTS, ONE SEASON

48 —Joe Malone, Montreal, 1917-18.
49 —Joe Malone, Montreal, 1919-20.
51 —Howie Morenz, Montreal, 1927-28.
73 —Cooney Weiland, Boston, 1929-30.
—Doug Bentley, Chicago, 1942-43.
82 —Herb Cain, Boston, 1943-44.
86 —Gordie Howe, Detroit, 1950-51.
95 —Gordie Howe, Detroit, 1952-53.
96 —Dickie Moore, Montreal, 1958-59.
97 —Bobby Hull, Chicago, 1965-66.
—Stan Mikita, Chicago, 1966-67.
126 —Phil Esposito, Boston, 1968-69.
152 —Phil Esposito, Boston, 1970-71.
164 —Wayne Gretzky, Edmonton, 1980-81.
212 —Wayne Gretzky, Edmonton, 1981-82.
215 —Wayne Gretzky, Edmonton, 1985-86.

## MOST REGULAR-SEASON GOALS, CAREER

44 —Joe Malone, Montreal.
Malone led the NHL in goals in the league's first season with 44 goals in 20 games in 1917-18.
54 —Cy Denneny, Ottawa.
Denneny passed Malone during the 1918-19 season, and led the NHL in goals with 54 after two seasons.
143 —Joe Malone, Montreal, Quebec Bulldogs, Hamilton.
Malone passed Denneny during the 1919-20 season and finished his career with 143 goals.
248 —Cy Denneny, Ottawa, Boston.
Denneny passed Malone with goal #144 during the 1922-23 season and finished his career with 248 goals.
271 —Howie Morenz, Montreal, Chicago, NY Rangers.
Morenz passed Denneny with goal #249 during the 1933-34 season and finished his career with 271 goals.
324 —Nels Stewart, Montreal Maroons, Boston, NY Americans.
Stewart passed Morenz with goal #272 during the 1936-37 season and finished his career with 324 goals.
544 —Maurice Richard, Montreal.
Richard passed Stewart with goal #325 on Nov. 8, 1952 and finished his career with 544 goals.
801 —Gordie Howe, Detroit, Hartford.
Howe passed Richard with goal #545 on Nov. 10, 1963 and finished his career with 801 goals.
894 —Wayne Gretzky, Edmonton, Los Angeles, St. Louis, NY Rangers.
Gretzky passed Howe with goal #802 on March 23, 1994 and finished his career with 894 goals.

*Dickie Moore, above, first joined the Montreal Canadiens midway through the 1951-52 NHL season. An excellent stickhandler and skater with a hard, accurate shot, Moore became one of the NHL's top offensive stars. Although plagued by injuries throughout his career, Moore managed to lead the NHL in scoring twice. In 1958-59, he established career highs with 41 goals and 55 assists, breaking Gordie Howe's single-season record of 95 points set six years before. Reg Noble, right, played in Toronto from 1916 (in the National Hockey Association) through 1924. He scored a career-high 30 goals in just 20 games played during the first NHL season of 1917-18 and was one of four players to tie for the league lead with 10 assists.*

## MOST REGULAR-SEASON ASSISTS, CAREER

(minimum 100 assists)

100 —Frank Boucher, Ottawa, NY Rangers.
In 1930-31, Boucher became the first NHL player to reach the 100-assist milestone.

263 —Frank Boucher, Ottawa, NY Rangers.
Boucher retired as the NHL's career assist leader in 1938 with 253. He returned to the NHL in 1943-44 and remained the NHL's career assist leader until he was overtaken by Bill Cowley in 1943-44. He finished his career with 263 assists.

353 —Bill Cowley, St. Louis Eagles, Boston.
Cowley passed Boucher with assist #264 in 1943-44. He retired as the NHL's career assist leader in 1947 with 353.

408 —Elmer Lach, Montreal.
Lach passed Cowley with assist #354 in 1951-52. He retired as the NHL's career assist leader in 1954 with 408.

1,049 —Gordie Howe, Detroit, Hartford.
Howe passed Lach with assist #409 in 1957-58. He retired as the NHL's career assist leader in 1980 with 1,049.

1,963 —Wayne Gretzky, Edmonton, Los Angeles, St. Louis, NY Rangers.
Gretzky passed Howe with assist #1,050 in 1987-88. He retired as the NHL's current career assist leader with 1,963.

## MOST REGULAR-SEASON POINTS, CAREER

(minimum 100 points)

100 —Joe Malone, Montreal, Quebec Bulldogs, Hamilton.
In 1919-20, Malone became the first player in NHL history to record 100 points.

200 —Cy Denneny, Ottawa.
In 1923-24, Denneny became the first player in NHL history to record 200 points.

300 —Cy Denneny, Ottawa.
In 1926-27, Denneny became the first player in NHL history to record 300 points.

333 —Cy Denneny, Ottawa, Boston.
Denneny retired as the NHL's career point-scoring leader in 1929 with 333 points.

472 —Howie Morenz, Montreal, Chicago, NY Rangers.
Morenz passed Cy Denneny with point #334 in 1931-32. At the time his career ended in 1937, he was the NHL's career point- scoring leader with 472 points.

515 —Nels Stewart, Montreal Maroons, Boston, NY Americans.
Stewart passed Morenz with point #473 in 1938-39. He retired as the NHL's career point-scoring leader in 1940 with 515 points.

528 —Syd Howe, Ottawa, Philadelphia Quakers, Toronto, St. Louis Eagles, Detroit.
Howe passed Nels Stewart with point #516 on March 8, 1945. He retired as the NHL's career point-scoring leader in 1946 with 528 points.

548 —Bill Cowley, St. Louis Eagles, Boston.
Cowley passed Syd Howe with point #529 on Feb. 12, 1947. He retired as the NHL's career point-scoring leader in 1947 with 548 points.

610 —Elmer Lach, Montreal.
Lach passed Bill Cowley with point #549 on Feb. 23, 1952. He remained the NHL's career point-scoring leader until he was overtaken by Maurice Richard in 1953-54. He finished his career with 623 points.

946 —Maurice Richard, Montreal.
Richard passed teammate Elmer Lach with point #611 on Dec. 12, 1953. He remained the NHL's career point-scoring leader until he was overtaken by Gordie Howe in 1959-60. He finished his career with 965 points.

1,850 —Gordie Howe, Detroit, Hartford.
Howe passed Richard with point #947 on Jan. 16, 1960. He retired as the NHL's career point-scoring leader in 1980 with 1,850 points.

2,857 —Wayne Gretzky, Edmonton, Los Angeles, St. Louis, NY Rangers.
Gretzky passed Howe with point #1,851 on Oct. 15, 1989. He retired as the NHL's current career points leader with 2,857.

# Individual Records

## Regular Season

### SEASONS

**MOST SEASONS:**
**26 – Gordie Howe**, Detroit, 1946-47 – 1970-71; Hartford, 1979-80.
25 – Mark Messier, Edmonton, NY Rangers, Vancouver, 1979-80 – 2003-04.
– Chris Chelios, Montreal, Chicago, Detroit, 1983-84 – 2003-04, 2005-06 – 2008-09.
24 – Alex Delvecchio, Detroit, 1950-51 – 1973-74.
– Tim Horton, Toronto, NY Rangers, Pittsburgh, Buffalo, 1949-50, 1951-52 – 1973-74.
23 – John Bucyk, Detroit, Boston, 1955-56 – 1977-78.
– Ron Francis, Hartford, Pittsburgh, Carolina, Toronto, 1981-82 – 2003-04.
– Al MacInnis, Calgary, St. Louis, 1981-82 – 2003-04.
– Dave Andreychuk, Buffalo, Toronto, New Jersey, Boston, Colorado, Tampa Bay, 1982-83 – 2003-04, 2005-06.

### GAMES

**MOST GAMES:**
**1,767 – Gordie Howe**, Detroit, 1946-47 – 1970-71; Hartford, 1979-80.
1,756 – Mark Messier, Edmonton, NY Rangers, Vancouver, 1979-80 – 2003-04.
1,731 – Ron Francis, Hartford, Pittsburgh, Carolina, Toronto, 1981-82 – 2003-04.
1,644 – Chris Chelios, Montreal, Chicago, Detroit, 1983-84 – 2003-04, 2005-06 – 2008-09.
1,639 – Dave Andreychuk, Buffalo, Toronto, New Jersey, Boston, Colorado, Tampa Bay, 1982-83 – 2003-04, 2005-06.
1,635 – Scott Stevens, Washington, St. Louis, New Jersey, 1982-83 – 2003-04.

**MOST GAMES, INCLUDING PLAYOFFS:**
**1,992 – Mark Messier**, Edmonton, NY Rangers, Vancouver, 1,756 regular-season games, 236 playoff games.
1,924 – Gordie Howe, Detroit, Hartford, 1,767 regular-season games, 157 playoff games.
1,910 – Chris Chelios, Montreal, Chicago, Detroit, 1,644 regular-season games, 266 playoff games.
1,902 – Ron Francis, Hartford, Pittsburgh, Carolina, Toronto, 1,731 regular-season games, 171 playoff games.
1,868 – Scott Stevens, Washington, St. Louis, New Jersey, 1,635 regular-season games, 233 playoff games.

**MOST CONSECUTIVE GAMES:**
**964 – Doug Jarvis**, Montreal, Washington, Hartford, Oct. 8, 1975 – Oct. 10, 1987.
914 – Garry Unger, Toronto, Detroit, St. Louis, Atlanta, Feb. 24, 1968 – Dec. 21, 1979.
884 – Steve Larmer, Chicago, Oct. 6, 1982 – Apr. 15, 1993.
776 – Craig Ramsay, Buffalo, Mar. 27, 1973 – Feb. 10, 1983.
630 – Andy Hebenton, NY Rangers, Boston, Oct. 7, 1955 – Mar. 22, 1964.

### GOALS

**MOST GOALS:**
**894 – Wayne Gretzky**, Edmonton, Los Angeles, St. Louis, NY Rangers, in 20 seasons. 1,487GP
801 – Gordie Howe, Detroit, Hartford, in 26 seasons. 1,767GP
741 – Brett Hull, Calgary, St. Louis, Dallas, Detroit, Phoenix, in 19 seasons. 1,269GP
731 – Marcel Dionne, Detroit, Los Angeles, NY Rangers, in 18 seasons. 1,348GP
717 – Phil Esposito, Chicago, Boston, NY Rangers, in 18 seasons. 1,282GP

**MOST GOALS, INCLUDING PLAYOFFS:**
**1,016 – Wayne Gretzky**, Edmonton, Los Angeles, St. Louis, NY Rangers, 894G in 1,487 regular-season games, 122G in 208 playoff games.
869 – Gordie Howe, Detroit, Hartford, 801G in 1,767 regular-season games, 68G in 157 playoff games.
844 – Brett Hull, Calgary, St. Louis, Dallas, Detroit, Phoenix, 741G in 1,269 regular-season games, 103G in 202 playoff games.
803 – Mark Messier, Edmonton, NY Rangers, Vancouver, 694G in 1,756 regular-season games, 109G in 236 playoff games.
778 – Phil Esposito, Chicago, Boston, NY Rangers, 717G in 1,282 regular-season games, 61G in 130 playoff games.

**MOST GOALS, ONE SEASON:**
**92 – Wayne Gretzky**, Edmonton, 1981-82. 80GP – 80 game schedule.
87 – Wayne Gretzky, Edmonton, 1983-84. 74GP – 80 game schedule.
86 – Brett Hull, St. Louis, 1990-91. 78GP – 80 game schedule.
85 – Mario Lemieux, Pittsburgh, 1988-89. 76GP – 80 game schedule.
76 – Phil Esposito, Boston, 1970-71. 78GP – 78 game schedule.
– Alexander Mogilny, Buffalo, 1992-93. 77GP – 84 game schedule.
– Teemu Selanne, Winnipeg, 1992-93. 84GP – 84 game schedule.
73 – Wayne Gretzky, Edmonton, 1984-85. 80GP – 80 game schedule.
72 – Brett Hull, St. Louis, 1989-90. 80GP – 80 game schedule.
71 – Wayne Gretzky, Edmonton, 1982-83. 80GP – 80 game schedule.
– Jari Kurri, Edmonton, 1984-85. 73GP – 80 game schedule.
70 – Mario Lemieux, Pittsburgh, 1987-88. 77GP – 80 game schedule.
– Bernie Nicholls, Los Angeles, 1988-89. 79GP – 80 game schedule.
– Brett Hull, St. Louis, 1991-92. 73GP – 80 game schedule.

**MOST GOALS, ONE SEASON, INCLUDING PLAYOFFS:**
**100 – Wayne Gretzky**, Edmonton, 1983-84, 87G in 74 regular-season games, 13G in 19 playoff games.
97 – Wayne Gretzky, Edmonton, 1981-82, 92G in 80 regular-season games, 5G in 5 playoff games.
– Mario Lemieux, Pittsburgh, 1988-89, 85G in 76 regular-season games, 12G in 11 playoff games.
– Brett Hull, St. Louis, 1990-91, 86G in 78 regular-season games, 11G in 13 playoff games.
90 – Wayne Gretzky, Edmonton, 1984-85, 73G in 80 regular-season games, 17G in 18 playoff games.
– Jari Kurri, Edmonton, 1984-85, 71G in 80 regular-season games, 19G in 18 playoff games.
85 – Mike Bossy, NY Islanders, 1980-81, 68G in 79 regular-season games, 17G in 18 playoff games.
– Brett Hull, St. Louis, 1989-90, 72G in 80 regular-season games, 13G in 12 playoff games.
83 – Wayne Gretzky, Edmonton, 1982-83, 71G in 73 regular-season games, 12G in 16 playoff games.
– Alexander Mogilny, Buffalo, 1992-93, 76G in 77 regular-season games, 7G in 7 playoff games.

**MOST GOALS, 50 GAMES FROM START OF SEASON:**
**61 – Wayne Gretzky**, Edmonton, 1981-82. Oct. 7, 1981 – Jan. 22, 1982. (80-game schedule)
**– Wayne Gretzky**, Edmonton, 1983-84. Oct. 5, 1983 – Jan. 25, 1984. (80-game schedule)
54 – Mario Lemieux, Pittsburgh, 1988-89. Oct. 7, 1988 – Jan. 31, 1989. (80-game schedule)
53 – Wayne Gretzky, Edmonton, 1984-85. Oct. 11, 1984 – Jan. 28, 1985. (80-game schedule)
52 – Brett Hull, St. Louis, 1990-91. Oct. 4, 1990 – Jan. 26, 1991. (80-game schedule)
50 – Maurice Richard, Montreal, 1944-45. Oct. 28, 1944 – Mar. 18, 1945. (50-game schedule)
– Mike Bossy, NY Islanders, 1980-81. Oct. 11, 1980 – Jan. 24, 1981. (80-game schedule)
– Brett Hull, St. Louis, 1991-92. Oct. 5, 1991 – Jan. 28, 1992. (80-game schedule)

**MOST GOALS, ONE GAME:**
**7 – Joe Malone**, Quebec, Jan. 31, 1920, at Quebec. Quebec 10, Toronto 6.
6 – Newsy Lalonde, Montreal, Jan. 10, 1920, at Montreal. Montreal 14, Toronto 7.
– Joe Malone, Quebec, Mar. 10, 1920, at Quebec. Quebec 10, Ottawa 4.
– Corb Denneny, Toronto, Jan. 26, 1921, at Toronto. Toronto 10, Hamilton 3.
– Cy Denneny, Ottawa, Mar. 7, 1921, at Ottawa. Ottawa 12, Hamilton 5.
– Syd Howe, Detroit, Feb. 3, 1944, at Detroit. Detroit 12, NY Rangers 2.
– Red Berenson, St. Louis, Nov. 7, 1968, at Philadelphia. St. Louis 8, Philadelphia 0.
– Darryl Sittler, Toronto, Feb. 7, 1976, at Toronto. Toronto 11, Boston 4.

*No relation to Gordie, Detroit star Sid Howe scored six goals for the Red Wings in a 12-2 win over the New York Rangers on February 3, 1944. He was the first player in 23 seasons to accomplish the feat. Only two others have managed it since.*

*Alexei Zhamnov of the Winnipeg Jets, seen here putting the moves on Tommy Soderstrom of the New York Islanders, scored five goals against the Kings in a 7-7 tie at Los Angeles on April 1, 1995. No NHL player has scored five goals in a road game since that day.*

**MOST GOALS, ONE ROAD GAME:**

**6 – Red Berenson**, St. Louis, Nov. 7, 1968, at Philadelphia. St. Louis 8, Philadelphia 0.
5 – Joe Malone, Montreal, Dec. 19, 1917, at Ottawa. Montreal 7, Ottawa 4.
– Red Green, Hamilton, Dec. 5, 1924, at Toronto. Hamilton 10, Toronto 3.
– Babe Dye, Toronto, Dec. 22, 1924, at Boston. Toronto 10, Boston 1.
– Punch Broadbent, Mtl. Maroons, Jan. 7, 1925, at Hamilton. Mtl. Maroons 6, Hamilton 2.
– Don Murdoch, NY Rangers, Oct. 12, 1976, at Minnesota. NY Rangers 10, Minnesota 4.
– Tim Young, Minnesota, Jan. 15, 1979, at NY Rangers. Minnesota 8, NY Rangers 1.
– Willy Lindstrom, Winnipeg, Mar. 2, 1982, at Philadelphia. Winnipeg 7, Philadelphia 6.
– Bengt Gustafsson, Washington, Jan. 8, 1984, at Philadelphia. Washington 7, Philadelphia 1.
– Wayne Gretzky, Edmonton, Dec. 15, 1984, at St. Louis. Edmonton 8, St. Louis 2.
– Dave Andreychuk, Buffalo, Feb. 6, 1986, at Boston. Buffalo 8, Boston 6.
– Mats Sundin, Quebec, Mar. 5, 1992, at Hartford. Quebec 10, Hartford 4.
– Mario Lemieux, Pittsburgh, Apr. 9, 1993, at NY Rangers. Pittsburgh 10, NY Rangers 4.
– Mike Ricci, Quebec, Feb. 17, 1994, at San Jose. Quebec 8, San Jose 2.
– Alex Zhamnov, Winnipeg, Apr. 1, 1995, at Los Angeles. Winnipeg 7, Los Angeles 7.

**MOST GOALS, ONE PERIOD:**

**4 – Busher Jackson**, Toronto, Nov. 20, 1934, at St. Louis, third period. Toronto 5, St. Louis 2.
**– Max Bentley**, Chicago, Jan. 28, 1943, at Chicago, third period. Chicago 10, NY Rangers 1.
**– Clint Smith**, Chicago, Mar. 4, 1945, at Chicago, third period. Chicago 6, Montreal 4.
**– Red Berenson**, St. Louis, Nov. 7, 1968, at Philadelphia, second period. St. Louis 8, Philadelphia 0.
**– Wayne Gretzky**, Edmonton, Feb. 18, 1981, at Edmonton, third period. Edmonton 9, St. Louis 2.
**– Grant Mulvey**, Chicago, Feb. 3, 1982, at Chicago, first period. Chicago 9, St. Louis 5.
**– Bryan Trottier**, NY Islanders, Feb. 13, 1982, at NY Islanders, second period. NY Islanders 8, Philadelphia 2.
**– Al Secord**, Chicago, Jan. 7, 1987, at Chicago, second period. Chicago 6, Toronto 4.
**– Joe Nieuwendyk**, Calgary, Jan. 11, 1989, at Calgary, second period. Calgary 8, Winnipeg 3.
**– Peter Bondra**, Washington, Feb. 5, 1994, at Washington, first period. Washington 6, Tampa Bay 3.
**– Mario Lemieux**, Pittsburgh, Jan. 26, 1997, at Montreal, third period. Pittsburgh 5, Montreal 2.

## ASSISTS

**MOST ASSISTS:**

**1,963 – Wayne Gretzky,** Edmonton, Los Angeles, St. Louis, NY Rangers, in 20 seasons. 1,487GP
1,249 – Ron Francis, Hartford, Pittsburgh, Carolina, Toronto, in 23 seasons. 1,731GP
1,193 – Mark Messier, Edmonton, NY Rangers, Vancouver, in 25 seasons. 1,756GP
1,169 – Raymond Bourque, Boston, Colorado, in 22 seasons. 1,612GP
1,135 – Paul Coffey, Edmonton, Pittsburgh, Los Angeles, Detroit, Hartford, Philadelphia, Chicago, Carolina, Boston, in 21 seasons. 1,409GP

**MOST ASSISTS, INCLUDING PLAYOFFS:**

**2,223 – Wayne Gretzky**, Edmonton, Los Angeles, St. Louis, NY Rangers, 1,963A in 1,487 regular-season games, 260A in 208 playoff games.
1,379 – Mark Messier, Edmonton, NY Rangers, Vancouver, 1,193A in 1,756 regular-season games, 186A in 236 playoff games.
1,346 – Ron Francis, Hartford, Pittsburgh, Carolina, Toronto, 1,249A in 1,731 regular-season games, 97A in 171 playoff games.
1,308 – Raymond Bourque, Boston, Colorado, 1,169A in 1,612 regular-season games, 139A in 214 playoff games.
1,272 – Paul Coffey, Edmonton, Pittsburgh, Los Angeles, Detroit, Hartford, Philadelphia, Chicago, Carolina, Boston, 1,135A in 1,409 regular-season games, 137A in 194 playoff games.

**MOST ASSISTS, ONE SEASON:**

**163 – Wayne Gretzky**, Edmonton, 1985-86. 80GP – 80 game schedule.
135 – Wayne Gretzky, Edmonton, 1984-85. 80GP – 80 game schedule.
125 – Wayne Gretzky, Edmonton, 1982-83. 80GP – 80 game schedule.
122 – Wayne Gretzky, Los Angeles, 1990-91. 78GP – 80 game schedule.
121 – Wayne Gretzky, Edmonton, 1986-87. 79GP – 80 game schedule.
120 – Wayne Gretzky, Edmonton, 1981-82. 80GP – 80 game schedule.
118 – Wayne Gretzky, Edmonton, 1983-84. 74GP – 80 game schedule.
114 – Mario Lemieux, Pittsburgh, 1988-89. 76GP – 80 game schedule.
– Wayne Gretzky, Los Angeles, 1988-89. 78GP – 80 game schedule.
109 – Wayne Gretzky, Edmonton, 1980-81. 80GP – 80 game schedule.
– Wayne Gretzky, Edmonton, 1987-88. 64GP – 80 game schedule.
102 – Bobby Orr, Boston, 1970-71. 78GP – 78 game schedule.
– Wayne Gretzky, Los Angeles, 1989-90. 73GP – 80 game schedule.

**MOST ASSISTS, ONE SEASON, INCLUDING PLAYOFFS:**
**174 – Wayne Gretzky**, Edmonton, 1985-86,
163A in 80 regular-season games, 11A in 10 playoff games.
165 – Wayne Gretzky, Edmonton, 1984-85,
135A in 80 regular-season games, 30A in 18 playoff games.
151 – Wayne Gretzky, Edmonton, 1982-83,
125A in 80 regular-season games, 26A in 16 playoff games.
150 – Wayne Gretzky, Edmonton, 1986-87,
121A in 79 regular-season games, 29A in 21 playoff games.
140 – Wayne Gretzky, Edmonton, 1983-84,
118A in 74 regular-season games, 22A in 19 playoff games.
– Wayne Gretzky, Edmonton, 1987-88,
109A in 64 regular-season games, 31A in 19 playoff games.
133 – Wayne Gretzky, Los Angeles, 1990-91,
122A in 78 regular-season games, 11A in 12 playoff games.
131 – Wayne Gretzky, Los Angeles, 1988-89,
114A in 78 regular-season games, 17A in 11 playoff games.
127 – Wayne Gretzky, Edmonton, 1981-82,
120A in 80 regular-season games, 7A in 5 playoff games.
123 – Wayne Gretzky, Edmonton, 1980-81,
109A in 80 regular-season games, 14A in 9 playoff games.
121 – Mario Lemieux, Pittsburgh, 1988-89,
114A in 76 regular-season games, 7A in 11 playoff games.

**MOST ASSISTS, ONE GAME:**
**7 – Billy Taylor**, Detroit, Mar. 16, 1947, at Chicago. Detroit 10, Chicago 6.
**– Wayne Gretzky**, Edmonton, Feb. 15, 1980, at Edmonton. Edmonton 8, Washington 2.
**– Wayne Gretzky**, Edmonton, Dec. 11, 1985, at Chicago. Edmonton 12, Chicago 9.
**– Wayne Gretzky**, Edmonton, Feb. 14, 1986, at Edmonton. Edmonton 8, Quebec 2.
6 – Six assists have been recorded in one game on 24 occasions since Elmer Lach of Montreal first accomplished the feat vs. Boston on Feb. 6, 1943. The most recent player is Eric Lindros of Philadelphia on Feb. 26, 1997 at Ottawa.

**MOST ASSISTS, ONE ROAD GAME:**
**7 – Billy Taylor**, Detroit, Mar. 16, 1947, at Chicago. Detroit 10, Chicago 6.
**– Wayne Gretzky**, Edmonton, Dec. 11, 1985, at Chicago. Edmonton 12, Chicago 9.
6 – Bobby Orr, Boston, Jan. 1, 1973, at Vancouver. Boston 8, Vancouver 2.
– Patrik Sundstrom, Vancouver, Feb. 29, 1984, at Pittsburgh. Vancouver 9, Pittsburgh 5.
– Mario Lemieux, Pittsburgh, Dec. 5, 1992, at San Jose. Pittsburgh 9, San Jose 4.
– Eric Lindros, Philadelphia, Feb. 26, 1997, at Ottawa. Philadelphia 8, Ottawa 5.

**MOST ASSISTS, ONE PERIOD:**
**5 – Dale Hawerchuk**, Winnipeg, Mar. 6, 1984, at Los Angeles, second period. Winnipeg 7, Los Angeles 3.
4 – Four assists have been recorded in one period on 67 occasions since Mickey Roach of Hamilton first accomplished the feat vs. Toronto on Feb. 23, 1921. The most recent player is Joe Thornton of San Jose on Apr. 1, 2007 vs. Los Angeles.

## POINTS

**MOST POINTS:**
**2,857 – Wayne Gretzky**, Edmonton, Los Angeles, St. Louis, NY Rangers, in 20 seasons. 1,487GP (894G-1,963A)
1,887 – Mark Messier, Edmonton, NY Rangers, Vancouver, in 25 seasons. 1,756GP (694G-1,193A)
1,850 – Gordie Howe, Detroit, Hartford, in 26 seasons. 1,767GP (801G-1,049A)
1,798 – Ron Francis, Hartford, Pittsburgh, Carolina, Toronto, in 23 seasons. 1,731GP (549G-1,249A)
1,771 – Marcel Dionne, Detroit, Los Angeles, NY Rangers, in 18 seasons. 1,348GP (731G-1,040A)

**MOST POINTS, INCLUDING PLAYOFFS:**
**3,239 – Wayne Gretzky**, Edmonton, Los Angeles, St. Louis, NY Rangers,
2,857PTS in 1,487 regular-season games, 382PTS in 208 playoff games.
2,182 – Mark Messier, Edmonton, NY Rangers, Vancouver,
1,887PTS in 1,756 regular-season games, 295PTS in 236 playoff games.
2,010 – Gordie Howe, Detroit, Hartford,
1,850PTS in 1,767 regular-season games, 160PTS in 157 playoff games.
1,941 – Ron Francis, Hartford, Pittsburgh, Carolina, Toronto,
1,798PTS in 1,731 regular-season games, 143PTS in 171 playoff games
1,940 – Steve Yzerman, Detroit,
1,755PTS in 1,514 regular-season games, 185PTS in 196 playoff games.

**MOST POINTS, ONE SEASON:**
**215 – Wayne Gretzky**, Edmonton, 1985-86. 80GP – 80 game schedule.
212 – Wayne Gretzky, Edmonton, 1981-82. 80GP – 80 game schedule.
208 – Wayne Gretzky, Edmonton, 1984-85. 80GP – 80 game schedule.
205 – Wayne Gretzky, Edmonton, 1983-84. 74GP – 80 game schedule.
199 – Mario Lemieux, Pittsburgh, 1988-89. 76GP – 80 game schedule.
196 – Wayne Gretzky, Edmonton, 1982-83. 80GP – 80 game schedule.
183 – Wayne Gretzky, Edmonton, 1986-87. 79GP – 80 game schedule.
168 – Mario Lemieux, Pittsburgh, 1987-88, 77GP – 80 game schedule.
– Wayne Gretzky, Los Angeles, 1988-89. 78GP – 80 game schedule.
164 – Wayne Gretzky, Edmonton, 1980-81. 80GP – 80 game schedule.
163 – Wayne Gretzky, Los Angeles, 1990-91. 78GP – 80 game schedule.
161 – Mario Lemieux, Pittsburgh, 1995-96. 70GP – 82 game schedule.
160 – Mario Lemieux, Pittsburgh, 1992-93. 60GP – 84 game schedule.

**MOST POINTS, ONE SEASON, INCLUDING PLAYOFFS:**
**255 – Wayne Gretzky**, Edmonton, 1984-85,
208PTS in 80 regular-season games, 47PTS in 18 playoff games.
240 – Wayne Gretzky, Edmonton, 1983-84,
205PTS in 74 regular-season games, 35PTS in 19 playoff games.
234 – Wayne Gretzky, Edmonton, 1982-83,
196PTS in 80 regular-season games, 38PTS in 16 playoff games.
– Wayne Gretzky, Edmonton, 1985-86,
215PTS in 80 regular-season games, 19PTS in 10 playoff games.
224 – Wayne Gretzky, Edmonton, 1981-82,
212PTS in 80 regular-season games, 12PTS in 5 playoff games.
218 – Mario Lemieux, Pittsburgh, 1988-89,
199PTS in 76 regular-season games, 19PTS in 11 playoff games.
217 – Wayne Gretzky, Edmonton, 1986-87,
183PTS in 79 regular-season games, 34PTS in 21 playoff games.
192 – Wayne Gretzky, Edmonton, 1987-88,
149PTS in 64 regular-season games, 43PTS in 19 playoff games.
190 – Wayne Gretzky, Los Angeles, 1988-89,
168PTS in 78 regular-season games, 22PTS in 11 playoff games.
188 – Mario Lemieux, Pittsburgh, 1995-96,
161PTS in 70 regular-season games, 27PTS in 18 playoff games.
185 – Wayne Gretzky, Edmonton, 1980-81,
164PTS in 80 regular-season games, 21PTS in 9 playoff games.

**MOST POINTS, ONE GAME:**
**10 – Darryl Sittler**, Toronto, Feb. 7, 1976, at Toronto, 6G-4A. Toronto 11, Boston 4.
8 – Maurice Richard, Montreal, Dec. 28, 1944, at Montreal, 5G-3A. Montreal 9, Detroit 1.
– Bert Olmstead, Montreal, Jan. 9, 1954, at Montreal, 4G-4A. Montreal 12, Chicago 1.
– Tom Bladon, Philadelphia, Dec. 11, 1977, at Philadelphia, 4G-4A. Philadelphia 11, Cleveland 1.
– Bryan Trottier, NY Islanders, Dec. 23, 1978, at NY Islanders, 5G-3A. NY Islanders 9, NY Rangers 4.
– Peter Stastny, Quebec, Feb. 22, 1981, at Washington, 4G-4A. Quebec 11, Washington 7.
– Anton Stastny, Quebec, Feb. 22, 1981, at Washington, 3G-5A. Quebec 11, Washington 7.
– Wayne Gretzky, Edmonton, Nov. 19, 1983, at Edmonton, 3G-5A. Edmonton 13, New Jersey 4.
– Wayne Gretzky, Edmonton, Jan. 4, 1984, at Edmonton, 4G-4A. Edmonton 12, Minnesota 8.
– Paul Coffey, Edmonton, Mar. 14, 1986, at Edmonton, 2G-6A. Edmonton 12, Detroit 3.
– Mario Lemieux, Pittsburgh, Oct. 15, 1988, at Pittsburgh, 2G-6A. Pittsburgh 9, St. Louis 2.
– Bernie Nicholls, Los Angeles, Dec. 1, 1988, at Los Angeles, 2G-6A. Los Angeles 9, Toronto 3.
– Mario Lemieux, Pittsburgh, Dec. 31, 1988, at Pittsburgh, 5G-3A. Pittsburgh 8, New Jersey 6.

**MOST POINTS, ONE ROAD GAME:**
**8 – Peter Stastny**, Quebec, Feb. 22, 1981, at Washington. 4G-4A. Quebec 11, Washington 7.
**– Anton Stastny**, Quebec, Feb. 22, 1981, at Washington. 3G-5A. Quebec 11, Washington 7.
7 – Red Green, Hamilton, Dec. 5, 1924, at Toronto. 5G-2A. Hamilton 10, Toronto 3.
– Billy Taylor, Detroit, Mar. 16, 1947, at Chicago. 7A. Detroit 10, Chicago 6.
– Red Berenson, St. Louis, Nov. 7, 1968, at Philadelphia. 6G-1A. St. Louis 8, Philadelphia 0.
– Gilbert Perreault, Buffalo, Feb. 1, 1976, at California. 2G-5A. Buffalo 9, California 5.
– Peter Stastny, Quebec, Apr. 1, 1982, at Boston. 3G-4A. Quebec 8, Boston 5.
– Wayne Gretzky, Edmonton, Nov. 6, 1983, at Winnipeg. 4G-3A. Edmonton 8, Winnipeg 5.
– Patrik Sundstrom, Vancouver, Feb. 29, 1984, at Pittsburgh. 1G-6A. Vancouver 9, Pittsburgh 5.
– Wayne Gretzky, Edmonton, Dec. 11, 1985, at Chicago. 7A. Edmonton 12, Chicago 9.
– Cam Neely, Boston, Oct. 16, 1988, at Chicago. 3G-4A. Boston 10, Chicago 3.
– Mario Lemieux, Pittsburgh, Jan. 21, 1989, at Edmonton. 2G-5A. Pittsburgh 7, Edmonton 4.
– Dino Ciccarelli, Washington, Mar. 18, 1989, at Hartford. 4G-3A. Washington 8, Hartford 2.
– Mats Sundin, Quebec, Mar. 5, 1992, at Hartford. 5G-2A. Quebec 10, Hartford 4.
– Mario Lemieux, Pittsburgh, Dec. 5, 1992, at San Jose. 1G-6A. Pittsburgh 9, San Jose 4.
– Eric Lindros, Philadelphia, Feb. 26, 1997, at Ottawa. 1G-6A. Philadelphia 8, Ottawa 5.
– Daniel Alfredsson, Ottawa, Jan. 24, 2008, at Tampa Bay. 3G-4A. Ottawa 8, Tampa Bay 4.

**MOST POINTS, ONE PERIOD:**
**6 – Bryan Trottier**, NY Islanders, Dec. 23, 1978, at NY Islanders, second period. 3G-3A. NY Islanders 9, NY Rangers 4.
5 – Bill Cook, NY Rangers, Mar. 12, 1933, at NY Americans, third period. 3G-2A. NY Rangers 8, NY Americans 2.
– Les Cunningham, Chicago, Jan. 28, 1940, at Chicago, third period. 2G-3A. Chicago 8, Montreal 1.
– Max Bentley, Chicago, Jan. 28, 1943, at Chicago, third period. 4G-1A. Chicago 10, NY Rangers 1.
– Leo Labine, Boston, Nov. 28, 1954, at Boston, second period. 3G-2A. Boston 6, Detroit 2.
– Darryl Sittler, Toronto, Feb. 7, 1976, at Toronto, second period. 3G-2A. Toronto 11, Boston 4.
– Grant Mulvey, Chicago, Feb. 3, 1982, at Chicago, first period. 4G-1A. Chicago 9, St. Louis 5.
– Dale Hawerchuk, Winnipeg, Mar. 6, 1984, at Los Angeles, second period. 5A. Winnipeg 7, Los Angeles 3.
– Jari Kurri, Edmonton, Oct. 26, 1984, at Edmonton, second period. 2G-3A. Edmonton 8, Los Angeles 2.
– Pat Elynuik, Winnipeg, Jan. 20, 1989, at Winnipeg, second period. 2G-3A. Winnipeg 7, Pittsburgh 3.
– Ray Ferraro, Hartford, Dec. 9, 1989, at Hartford, first period. 3G-2A. Hartford 7, New Jersey 3.
– Stephane Richer, Montreal, Feb. 14, 1990, at Montreal, first period. 2G-3A. Montreal 10, Vancouver 1.
– Cliff Ronning, Vancouver, Apr. 15, 1993, at Los Angeles, third period. 3G-2A. Vancouver 8, Los Angeles 6.
– Peter Forsberg, Colorado, Mar. 3, 1999, at Florida, third period. 2G-3A. Colorado 7, Florida 5.

## POWER-PLAY AND SHORTHAND GOALS

**MOST POWER-PLAY GOALS, CAREER:**
**274 – Dave Andreychuk**, Buffalo, Toronto, New Jersey, Boston, Colorado, Tampa Bay, in 23 seasons. 1,639GP
265 – Brett Hull, Calgary, St. Louis, Dallas, Detroit, Phoenix, in 19 seasons. 1,269GP
249 – Phil Esposito, Chicago, Boston, NY Rangers, in 18 seasons. 1,282GP

**MOST POWER-PLAY GOALS, ONE SEASON:**
**34 – Tim Kerr**, Philadelphia, 1985-86. 76GP – 80 game schedule.
32 – Dave Andreychuk, Buffalo, Toronto, 1992-93. 83GP – 84 game schedule.
31 – Joe Nieuwendyk, Calgary, 1987-88. 75GP – 80 game schedule.
– Mario Lemieux, Pittsburgh, 1988-89. 76GP – 80 game schedule.
– Mario Lemieux, Pittsburgh, 1995-96. 70GP – 82 game schedule.
29 – Michel Goulet, Quebec, 1987-88. 80GP – 80 game schedule.
– Brett Hull, St. Louis, 1990-91. 78GP – 80 game schedule.
– Brett Hull, St. Louis, 1992-93. 80GP – 84 game schedule.

**MOST POWER-PLAY GOALS, ONE GAME**
**4 – Camille Henry,** NY Rangers, Mar. 13, 1954, at Detroit. NY Rangers 5, Detroit 2.
**– Bernie Geoffrion**, Montreal, Feb. 19, 1955, at Montreal. Montreal 10, NY Rangers 2.
**– Bryan Trottier**, NY Islanders, Feb. 13, 1982, at NY Islanders. NY Islanders 8, Philadephia 2.
**– Chris Valentine**, Washington, Feb. 27, 1982, at Washington. Washington 7, Hartford 1.
**– Dave Andreychuk**, Buffalo, Mar. 19, 1992, at Los Angeles. Buffalo 8, Los Angeles 2.
**– Mario Lemieux**, Pittsburgh, Mar. 20, 1993, at Pittsburgh. Pittsburgh 9, Philadephia 3.
**– Luc Robitaille**, Los Angeles, Nov. 25, 1993, at Quebec. Quebec 8, Los Angeles 6.
**– Scott Mellanby**, St. Louis, Mar. 6, 2003, at St. Louis. St. Louis 6, Phoenix 3.

**MOST SHORTHAND GOALS, ONE SEASON:**
**13 – Mario Lemieux**, Pittsburgh, 1988-89. 76GP – 80 game schedule.
12 – Wayne Gretzky, Edmonton, 1983-84. 74GP – 80 game schedule.
11 – Wayne Gretzky, Edmonton, 1984-85. 80GP – 80 game schedule.
10 – Marcel Dionne, Detroit, 1974-75. 80GP – 80 game schedule.
– Mario Lemieux, Pittsburgh, 1987-88. 77GP – 80 game schedule.
– Dirk Graham, Chicago, 1988-89. 80GP – 80 game schedule.

**MOST SHORTHAND GOALS, ONE GAME:**
**3 – Theoren Fleury**, Calgary, Mar. 9, 1991, at St. Louis. Calgary 8, St. Louis 4.

## OVERTIME SCORING

**MOST OVERTIME GOALS, CAREER:**
**15 – Mats Sundin**, Quebec, Toronto.
**– Jaromir Jagr**, Pittsburgh, Washington, NY Rangers.
**– Sergei Fedorov,** Detroit, Anaheim, Columbus, Washington.
**– Patrik Elias**, New Jersey.
13 – Steve Thomas, Toronto, Chicago, NY Islanders, New Jersey, Anaheim.
12 – Nels Stewart, Mtl. Maroons, Boston, NY Americans.
– Brett Hull, Calgary, St. Louis, Dallas, Detroit, Phoenix.
– Brendan Shanahan, New Jersey, St. Louis, Hartford, Detroit, NY Rangers.
– Olli Jokinen, Los Angeles, NY Islanders, Florida.
– Scott Niedermayer, New Jersey, Anaheim.

**MOST OVERTIME ASSISTS, CAREER:**
**18 – Mark Messier**, Edmonton, NY Rangers, Vancouver.
**– Nicklas Lidstrom**, Detroit.
**– Pavol Demitra**, Ottawa, St. Louis, Los Angeles, Minnesota, Vancouver.
17 – Adam Oates, Detroit, St. Louis, Boston, Washington, Philadelphia, Anaheim.
16 – Sergei Fedorov, Detroit, Anaheim, Columbus, Washington.
– Tomas Kaberle, Toronto.

**MOST OVERTIME POINTS, CAREER:**
**31 – Sergei Fedorov**, Detroit, Anaheim, Columbus, Washington. 15G-16A
28 – Mats Sundin, Quebec, Toronto. 15G-13A
27 – Jaromir Jagr, Pittsburgh, Washington, NY Rangers. 15G-12A
– Patrik Elias, New Jersey. 15G-12A
– Pavol Demitra, Ottawa, St. Louis, Los Angeles, Minnesota, Vancouver. 9G-18A
26 – Mark Messier, Edmonton, NY Rangers, Vancouver. 8G-18A
– Jaromir Jagr, Pittsburgh, Washington, NY Rangers. 15G-11A
23 – Steve Thomas, Toronto, Chicago, NY Islanders, New Jersey, Anaheim. 13G-10A
– Tomas Kaberle, Toronto. 7G-16A

**MOST OVERTIME GOALS, ONE SEASON:**
**4 – Howie Morenz**, Montreal, 1929-30.
**– Frank Finnigan**, Ottawa, 1929-30.
**– Johnny Gagnon**, Montreal 1936-37.
**– Mats Sundin,** Toronto, 1999-2000.
**– Scott Niedermayer**, New Jersey, 2001-02.
**– Patrik Elias**, New Jersey, 2003-04.
**– Markus Naslund**, Vancouver, 2003-04.
**– Olli Jokinen**, Florida, 2005-06.
**– Daniel Sedin**, Vancouver 2006-07.

## SHOOTOUT GOALS

**MOST SHOOTOUT GOALS, ONE SEASON:**
**10 – Wojtek Wolski**, Colorado, 2008-09, (12s)
**– Jussi Jokinen**, Dallas, 2005-06, (13s)
8 – Viktor Kozlov, New Jersey, 2005-06, (12s)
– Ales Kotalik, Buffalo, Edmonton, 2008-09, (13s)
– Erik Christensen, Pittsburgh, 2006-07, (14s)
– Mikko Koivu, Minnesota, 2006-07, (15s)

**MOST SHOOTOUT GOALS, ALL-TIME:**
**23 – Vyacheslav Kozlov**, Atlanta (40s)
22 – Jussi Jokinen, Dallas, Tampa Bay, Carolina (41s)
20 – Ales Kotalik, Buffalo, Edmonton (38s)
17 – Wojtek Wolski, Colorado (26s)
– Erik Christensen, Pittsburgh, Atlanta, Anaheim (31s)
– Pavel Datsyuk, Detroit (36s)
– Viktor Kozlov, New Jersey, NY Islanders, Washington (37s)

**MOST SHOOTOUT SHOTS TAKEN, ONE SEASON:**
**17 – Sam Gagner**, Edmonton, 2007-08, (5G)
16 – Ales Hemsky, Edmonton, 2007-08, (6G)
15 – Mikko Koivu, Minnesota, 2006-07, (8G)
– Sidney Crosby, Pittsburgh, 2006-07, (5G)
– Brendan Shanahan, NY Rangers, 2007-08, (5G)

**MOST SHOOTOUT SHOTS TAKEN, ALL-TIME:**
**42 – Ales Hemsky**, Edmonton, (14G)
41 – Jussi Jokinen, Dallas, Tampa Bay, Carolina, (22G)
40 – Vyacheslav Kozlov, Atlanta, (23G)
38 – Ales Kotalik, Buffalo, Edmonton, (20G)
– Sidney Crosby, Pittsburgh, (12G)
– Alex Ovechkin, Washington, (11G)

**BEST SHOOTOUT SCORING PERCENTAGE, ONE SEASON:** *(minimum 5 shots)*
**.857 – Petteri Nummelin**, Minnesota, 2006-07 (6G, 7s)
.833 – Wojtek Wolski, Colorado, 2008-09 (10G, 12s)
– Patrik Elias, New Jersey, 2007-08, (5G, 6s)
.800 – Ray Whitney, Carolina, 2005-06 (4G, 5s)
– Kristian Huselius, Calgary, 2007-08 (4G, 5s)
– Patrick O'Sullivan, Los Angeles, 2007-08 (4G, 5s)
– Jeremy Roenick, San Jose, 2007-08 (4G, 5s)

**BEST SHOOTOUT SCORING PERCENTAGE, ALL-TIME:** *(minimum 10 shots)*
**.800 – Petteri Nummelin**, Minnesota (8G, 10s)
.654 – Wojtek Wolski, Colorado (17G, 26s)
.583 – Joe Pavelski, San Jose (14G, 24s)
– Trevor Linden, Vancouver (7G, 12s)

**GAME DECIDING SHOOTOUT GOALS, ONE SEASON:**
**5 – Miroslav Satan**, NY Islanders, 2005-06, (10s)
**– Viktor Kozlov**, New Jersey, 2005-06, (12s)
**– Vyacheslav Kozlov**, Atlanta, 2006-07, (11s)
**– Phil Kessel**, Boston, 2007-08, (12s)
**– Ales Kotalik**, Buffalo, Edmonton, 2008-09, (13s)

**GAME DECIDING SHOOTOUT GOALS, ALL-TIME:**
**11 – Ales Kotalik**, Buffalo, Edmonton (38s)
**– Vyacheslav Kozlov**, Atlanta (40s)
9 – Phil Kessel, Boston (28s)
– Viktor Kozlov, New Jersey, NY Islanders, Washington (37s)
– Sidney Crosby, Pittsburgh (38s)

## SCORING BY A CENTER

**MOST GOALS BY A CENTER, CAREER:**
**894 – Wayne Gretzky**, Edmonton, Los Angeles, St. Louis, NY Rangers, in 20 seasons. 1,487GP
731 – Marcel Dionne, Detroit, Los Angeles, NY Rangers, in 18 seasons. 1,348GP
717 – Phil Esposito, Chicago, Boston, NY Rangers, in 18 seasons. 1,282GP
694 – Mark Messier, Edmonton, NY Rangers, Vancouver, in 25 seasons. 1,756GP
692 – Steve Yzerman, Detroit, in 22 seasons. 1,514GP

**MOST GOALS BY A CENTER, ONE SEASON:**
**92 – Wayne Gretzky**, Edmonton, 1981-82. 80GP – 80 game schedule.
87 – Wayne Gretzky, Edmonton, 1983-84. 74GP – 80 game schedule.
85 – Mario Lemieux, Pittsburgh, 1988-89. 76GP – 80 game schedule.
76 – Phil Esposito, Boston, 1970-71. 78GP – 78 game schedule.
73 – Wayne Gretzky, Edmonton, 1984-85. 80GP – 80 game schedule.

**MOST ASSISTS BY A CENTER, CAREER:**
**1,963 – Wayne Gretzky**, Edmonton, Los Angeles, St. Louis, NY Rangers, in 20 seasons. 1,487GP
1,249 – Ron Francis, Hartford, Pittsburgh, Carolina, Toronto, in 23 seasons. 1,731GP
1,193 – Mark Messier, Edmonton, NY Rangers, Vancouver, in 25 seasons. 1,756GP
1,079 – Adam Oates, Detroit, St. Louis, Boston, Washington, Philadelphia, Anaheim, Edmonton, in 19 seasons. 1,337GP
1,063 – Steve Yzerman, Detroit, in 22 seasons. 1,514GP

**MOST ASSISTS BY A CENTER, ONE SEASON:**
**163 – Wayne Gretzky**, Edmonton, 1985-86. 80GP – 80 game schedule.
135 – Wayne Gretzky, Edmonton, 1984-85. 80GP – 80 game schedule.
125 – Wayne Gretzky, Edmonton, 1982-83. 80GP – 80 game schedule.
122 – Wayne Gretzky, Los Angeles, 1990-91. 78GP – 80 game schedule.
121 – Wayne Gretzky, Edmonton, 1986-87. 79GP – 80 game schedule.

**MOST POINTS BY A CENTER, CAREER:**
**2,857 – Wayne Gretzky**, Edmonton, Los Angeles, St. Louis, NY Rangers, in 20 seasons. 1,487GP (894G-1,963A)
1,887 – Mark Messier, Edmonton, NY Rangers, Vancouver, in 25 seasons. 1,756GP (694G-1,193A)
1,798 – Ron Francis, Hartford, Pittsburgh, Carolina, Toronto, in 23 seasons. 1,731GP (549G-1,249A)
1,771 – Marcel Dionne, Detroit, Los Angeles, NY Rangers, in 18 seasons. 1,348GP (731G-1,040A)
1,755 – Steve Yzerman, Detroit, in 22 seasons. 1,514GP (692G-1,063A)

**MOST POINTS BY A CENTER, ONE SEASON:**
**215 – Wayne Gretzky**, Edmonton, 1985-86. 80GP – 80 game schedule.
212 – Wayne Gretzky, Edmonton, 1981-82. 80GP – 80 game schedule.
208 – Wayne Gretzky, Edmonton, 1984-85. 80GP – 80 game schedule.
205 – Wayne Gretzky, Edmonton, 1983-84. 74GP – 80 game schedule.
199 – Mario Lemieux, Pittsburgh, 1988-89. 76GP – 80 game schedule.

## SCORING BY A LEFT WING

**MOST GOALS BY A LEFT WING, CAREER:**
**668 – Luc Robitaille**, Los Angeles, Pittsburgh, NY Rangers, Detroit, in 19 seasons. 1,431GP
656 – Brendan Shanahan, New Jersey, St. Louis, Hartford, Detroit, NY Rangers, in 21 seasons. 1,524GP
640 – Dave Andreychuk, Buffalo, Toronto, New Jersey, Boston, Colorado, Tampa Bay, in 23 seasons. 1,639GP
610 – Bobby Hull, Chicago, Winnipeg, Hartford, in 16 seasons. 1,063GP
556 – John Bucyk, Detroit, Boston, in 23 seasons. 1,540GP

*Though remembered more as a scorer who topped 50 goals for six straight seasons in the 1970s, Montreal Canadiens great Guy Lafleur ranks among the all-time and single-season leaders in assists by a right winger.*

**MOST GOALS BY A LEFT WING, ONE SEASON:**
**65 – Alex Ovechkin**, Washington, 2007-08. 82GP – 82 game schedule.
63 – Luc Robitaille, Los Angeles, 1992-93. 84GP – 84 game schedule.
60 – Steve Shutt, Montreal, 1976-77. 80GP – 80 game schedule.
58 – Bobby Hull, Chicago, 1968-69. 74GP – 76 game schedule.
57 – Michel Goulet, Quebec, 1982-83. 80GP – 80 game schedule.

**MOST ASSISTS BY A LEFT WING, CAREER:**
**813 – John Bucyk**, Detroit, Boston, in 23 seasons. 1,540GP
726 – Luc Robitaille, Los Angeles, Pittsburgh, NY Rangers, Detroit, in 19 seasons. 1,431GP
698 – Dave Andreychuk, Buffalo, Toronto, New Jersey, Boston, Colorado, Tampa Bay, in 23 seasons. 1,639GP
– Brendan Shanahan, New Jersey, St. Louis, Hartford, Detroit, NY Rangers, in 21 seasons. 1,524GP
604 – Michel Goulet, Quebec, Chicago, in 15 seasons. 1,089GP

**MOST ASSISTS BY A LEFT WING, ONE SEASON:**
**70 – Joe Juneau**, Boston, 1992-93. 84GP – 84 game schedule.
69 – Kevin Stevens, Pittsburgh, 1991-92. 80GP – 80 game schedule.
67 – Mats Naslund, Montreal, 1985-86. 80GP – 80 game schedule.
65 – John Bucyk, Boston, 1970-71. 78GP – 78 game schedule.
– Michel Goulet, Quebec, 1983-84. 75GP – 80 game schedule.
64 – Mark Messier, Edmonton, 1983-84. 73GP – 80 game schedule.

**MOST POINTS BY A LEFT WING, CAREER:**
**1,394 – Luc Robitaille**, Los Angeles, Pittsburgh, NY Rangers, Detroit, in 19 seasons. 1,431GP (668G-726A)
1,369 – John Bucyk, Detroit, Boston, in 23 seasons. 1,540GP (556G-813A)
1,354 – Brendan Shanahan, New Jersey, St. Louis, Hartford, Detroit, NY Rangers, in 21 seasons. 1,524GP (656G-698A)
1,338 – Dave Andreychuk, Buffalo, Toronto, New Jersey, Boston, Colorado, Tampa Bay, in 23 seasons. 1,639GP (640G-698A)
1,170 – Bobby Hull, Chicago, Winnipeg, Hartford, in 16 seasons. 1,063GP (610G-560A)

**MOST POINTS BY A LEFT WING, ONE SEASON:**
**125 – Luc Robitaille**, Los Angeles, 1992-93. 84GP – 84 game schedule.
123 – Kevin Stevens, Pittsburgh, 1991-92. 80GP – 80 game schedule.
121 – Michel Goulet, Quebec, 1983-84. 75GP – 80 game schedule.
116 – John Bucyk, Boston, 1970-71. 78GP – 78 game schedule.
112 – Bill Barber, Philadelphia, 1975-76. 80GP – 80 game schedule.
– Alex Ovechkin, Washington, 2007-08. 82GP – 82 game schedule.

## SCORING BY A RIGHT WING

**MOST GOALS BY A RIGHT WING, CAREER:**
**801 – Gordie Howe**, Detroit, Hartford, in 26 seasons. 1,767GP
741 – Brett Hull, Calgary, St. Louis, Dallas, Detroit, Phoenix, in 19 seasons. 1,269GP
708 – Mike Gartner, Washington, Minnesota, NY Rangers, Toronto, Phoenix, in 19 seasons. 1,432GP
646 – Jaromir Jagr, Pittsburgh, Washington, NY Rangers, in 17 seasons. 1,273GP
608 – Dino Ciccarelli, Minnesota, Washington, Detroit, Tampa Bay, Florida, in 19 seasons. 1,232GP

**MOST GOALS BY A RIGHT WING, ONE SEASON:**
**86 – Brett Hull**, St. Louis, 1990-91. 78GP – 80 game schedule.
76 – Alexander Mogilny, Buffalo, 1992-93. 77GP – 84 game schedule.
– Teemu Selanne, Winnipeg, 1992-93. 84GP – 84 game schedule.
72 – Brett Hull, St. Louis, 1989-90. 80GP – 80 game schedule.
71 – Jari Kurri, Edmonton, 1984-85. 73GP – 80 game schedule.
70 – Brett Hull, St. Louis, 1991-92. 73GP – 80 game schedule.

**MOST ASSISTS BY A RIGHT WING, CAREER:**
**1,049 – Gordie Howe**, Detroit, Hartford, in 26 seasons. 1,767GP
953 – Jaromir Jagr, Pittsburgh, Washington, NY Rangers, in 17 seasons. 1,273GP
897 – Mark Recchi, Pittsburgh, Philadelphia, Montreal, Carolina, Atlanta, Boston, in 20 seasons. 1,490GP
797 – Jari Kurri, Edmonton, Los Angeles, NY Rangers, Anaheim, Colorado, in 17 seasons. 1,251GP
793 – Guy Lafleur, Montreal, NY Rangers, Quebec, in 17 seasons. 1,126GP

**MOST ASSISTS BY A RIGHT WING, ONE SEASON:**
**87 – Jaromir Jagr**, Pittsburgh, 1995-96. 82GP – 82 game schedule.
83 – Mike Bossy, NY Islanders, 1981-82. 80GP – 80 game schedule.
– Jaromir Jagr, Pittsburgh, 1998-99. 81GP – 82 game schedule.
80 – Guy Lafleur, Montreal, 1976-77. 80GP – 80 game schedule.
77 – Guy Lafleur, Montreal, 1978-79. 80GP – 80 game schedule.

**MOST POINTS BY A RIGHT WING, CAREER:**
**1,850 – Gordie Howe**, Detroit, Hartford, in 26 seasons. 1,767GP (801G-1,049A)
1,599 – Jaromir Jagr, Pittsburgh, Washington, NY Rangers, in 17 seasons. 1,273GP (646G-953A)
1,442 – Mark Recchi, Pittsburgh, Philadelphia, Montreal, Carolina, Atlanta, Boston, in 20 seasons. 1,490GP (545G-897A)
1,398 – Jari Kurri, Edmonton, Los Angeles, NY Rangers, Anaheim, Colorado, in 17 seasons. 1,251GP (601G-797A)
1,391 – Brett Hull, Calgary, St. Louis, Dallas, Detroit, Phoenix, in 19 seasons. 1,269GP (741G-650A)

**MOST POINTS BY A RIGHT WING, ONE SEASON:**
**149 – Jaromir Jagr**, Pittsburgh, 1995-96. 82GP – 82 game schedule.
147 – Mike Bossy, NY Islanders, 1981-82. 80GP – 80 game schedule.
136 – Guy Lafleur, Montreal, 1976-77. 80GP – 80 game schedule.
135 – Jari Kurri, Edmonton, 1984-85. 73GP – 80 game schedule.
132 – Guy Lafleur, Montreal, 1977-78. 78GP – 80 game schedule.
– Teemu Selanne, Winnipeg, 1992-93. 84GP – 84 game schedule.

## SCORING BY A DEFENSEMAN

**MOST GOALS BY A DEFENSEMAN, CAREER:**
**410 – Raymond Bourque**, Boston, Colorado, in 22 seasons. 1,612GP
396 – Paul Coffey, Edmonton, Pittsburgh, Los Angeles, Detroit, Hartford, Philadelphia, Chicago, Carolina, Boston, in 21 seasons. 1,409GP
340 – Al MacInnis, Calgary, St. Louis, in 23 seasons. 1,416GP
338 – Phil Housley, Buffalo, Winnipeg, St. Louis, Calgary, New Jersey, Washington, Chicago, Toronto, in 21 seasons. 1,495GP
310 – Denis Potvin, NY Islanders, in 15 seasons. 1,060GP

**MOST GOALS BY A DEFENSEMAN, ONE SEASON:**
**48 – Paul Coffey**, Edmonton, 1985-86. 79GP – 80 game schedule.
46 – Bobby Orr, Boston, 1974-75. 80GP – 80 game schedule.
40 – Paul Coffey, Edmonton, 1983-84. 80GP – 80 game schedule.
39 – Doug Wilson, Chicago, 1981-82. 76GP – 80 game schedule.
37 – Bobby Orr, Boston, 1970-71. 78GP – 78 game schedule.
– Bobby Orr, Boston, 1971-72. 76GP – 78 game schedule.
– Paul Coffey, Edmonton, 1984-85. 80GP – 80 game schedule.

**MOST GOALS BY A DEFENSEMAN, ONE GAME:**
**5 – Ian Turnbull**, Toronto, Feb. 2, 1977, at Toronto. Toronto 9, Detroit 1.
4 – Harry Cameron, Toronto, Dec. 26, 1917, at Toronto. Toronto 7, Montreal 5.
– Harry Cameron, Montreal, Mar. 3, 1920, at Quebec. Montreal 16, Quebec 3.
– Sprague Cleghorn, Montreal, Jan. 14, 1922, at Montreal. Montreal 10, Hamilton 6.
– John McKinnon, Pittsburgh, Nov. 19, 1929, at Pittsburgh. Pittsburgh 10, Toronto 5.
– Hap Day, Toronto, Nov. 19, 1929, at Pittsburgh. Pittsburgh 10, Toronto 5.
– Tom Bladon, Philadelphia, Dec. 11, 1977, at Philadelphia. Philadelphia 11, Cleveland 1.
– Ian Turnbull, Los Angeles, Dec. 12, 1981, at Los Angeles. Los Angeles 7, Vancouver 5.
– Paul Coffey, Edmonton, Oct. 26, 1984, at Calgary. Edmonton 6, Calgary 5.

**MOST ASSISTS BY A DEFENSEMAN, CAREER:**
**1,169 – Raymond Bourque**, Boston, Colorado, in 22 seasons. 1,612GP
1,135 – Paul Coffey, Edmonton, Pittsburgh, Los Angeles, Detroit, Hartford, Philadelphia, Chicago, Carolina, Boston, in 21 seasons. 1,409GP
934 – Al MacInnis, Calgary, St. Louis, in 23 seasons. 1,416GP
929 – Larry Murphy, Los Angeles, Washington, Minnesota, Pittsburgh, Toronto, Detroit, in 21 seasons. 1,615GP
894 – Phil Housley, Buffalo, Winnipeg, St. Louis, Calgary, New Jersey, Washington, Chicago, Toronto, in 21 seasons. 1,495GP

**MOST ASSISTS BY A DEFENSEMAN, ONE SEASON:**
**102 – Bobby Orr**, Boston, 1970-71. 78GP – 78 game schedule.
90 – Bobby Orr, Boston, 1973-74. 74GP – 78 game schedule.
– Paul Coffey, Edmonton, 1985-86. 79GP – 80 game schedule.
89 – Bobby Orr, Boston, 1974-75. 80GP – 80 game schedule.
87 – Bobby Orr, Boston, 1969-70. 76GP – 78 game schedule.

**MOST ASSISTS BY A DEFENSEMAN, ONE GAME:**
**6 – Babe Pratt**, Toronto, Jan. 8, 1944, at Toronto. Toronto 12, Boston 3.
**– Pat Stapleton**, Chicago, Mar. 30, 1969, at Chicago. Chicago 9, Detroit 5.
**– Bobby Orr**, Boston, Jan. 1, 1973, at Vancouver. Boston 8, Vancouver 2.
**– Ron Stackhouse**, Pittsburgh, Mar. 8, 1975, at Pittsburgh. Pittsburgh 8, Philadelphia 2.
**– Paul Coffey**, Edmonton, Mar. 14, 1986, at Edmonton. Edmonton 12, Detroit 3.
**– Gary Suter**, Calgary, Apr. 4, 1986, at Calgary. Calgary 9, Edmonton 3.

**MOST POINTS BY A DEFENSEMAN, CAREER:**
**1,579 – Raymond Bourque**, Boston, Colorado, in 22 seasons. 1,612GP (410G-1,169A)
1,531 – Paul Coffey, Edmonton, Pittsburgh, Los Angeles, Detroit, Hartford, Philadelphia, Chicago, Carolina, Boston, in 21 seasons. 1,409GP (396G-1,135A)
1,274 – Al MacInnis, Calgary, St. Louis, in 23 seasons. 1,416GP (340G-934A)
1,232 – Phil Housley, Buffalo, Winnipeg, St. Louis, Calgary, New Jersey, Washington, Chicago, Toronto, in 21 seasons. 1,495GP (338G-894A)
1,216 – Larry Murphy, Los Angeles, Washington, Minnesota, Pittsburgh, Toronto, Detroit, in 21 seasons. 1,615GP (287G-929A)

**MOST POINTS BY A DEFENSEMAN, ONE SEASON:**
**139 – Bobby Orr**, Boston, 1970-71. 78GP – 78 game schedule.
138 – Paul Coffey, Edmonton, 1985-86. 79GP – 80 game schedule.
135 – Bobby Orr, Boston, 1974-75. 80GP – 80 game schedule.
126 – Paul Coffey, Edmonton, 1983-84. 80GP – 80 game schedule.
122 – Bobby Orr, Boston, 1973-74. 74GP – 78 game schedule.

**MOST POINTS BY A DEFENSEMAN, ONE GAME:**
**8 – Tom Bladon**, Philadelphia, Dec. 11, 1977, at Philadelphia. 4G-4A. Philadelphia 11, Cleveland 1.
**– Paul Coffey**, Edmonton, Mar. 14, 1986, at Edmonton. 2G-6A. Edmonton 12, Detroit 3.
7 – Bobby Orr, Boston, Nov. 15, 1973, at Boston. 3G-4A. Boston 10, NY Rangers 2.

## SCORING BY A GOALTENDER

**MOST POINTS BY A GOALTENDER, CAREER:**
**48 – Tom Barrasso**, Buffalo, Pittsburgh, Ottawa, Carolina, Toronto, St. Louis, in 19 seasons. 777GP
46 – Grant Fuhr, Edmonton, Toronto, Buffalo, Los Angeles, St. Louis, Calgary, in 19 seasons. 868GP

**MOST POINTS BY A GOALTENDER, ONE SEASON:**
**14 – Grant Fuhr**, Edmonton, 1983-84. 45GP – 80 game schedule.
9 – Curtis Joseph, St. Louis, 1991-92. 60GP – 80 game schedule.
8 – Mike Palmateer, Washington, 1980-81. 49GP – 80 game schedule.
– Grant Fuhr, Edmonton, 1987-88. 75GP – 80 game schedule.
– Ron Hextall, Philadelphia, 1988-89. 64GP – 80 game schedule.
– Tom Barrasso, Pittsburgh, 1992-93. 63GP – 84 game schedule.

**MOST POINTS BY A GOALTENDER, ONE GAME:**
**3 – Jeff Reese**, Calgary, Feb. 10, 1993, at Calgary. Calgary 13, San Jose 1.

*Though he's slipped into third place on the NHL's all-time scoring list, Gordie Howe's 1,850 points still rank far ahead of any other right winger in NHL history. In fact, only Jaromir Jagr comes within 450 points of his total.*

## SCORING BY A ROOKIE

**MOST GOALS BY A ROOKIE, ONE SEASON:**
**76 – Teemu Selanne**, Winnipeg, 1992-93. 84GP – 84 game schedule.
53 – Mike Bossy, NY Islanders, 1977-78. 73GP – 80 game schedule.
52 – Alex Ovechkin, Washington, 2005-06. 81GP – 82 game schedule.
51 – Joe Nieuwendyk, Calgary, 1987-88. 75GP – 80 game schedule.
45 – Dale Hawerchuk, Winnipeg, 1981-82. 80GP – 80 game schedule.
– Luc Robitaille, Los Angeles, 1986-87. 79GP – 80 game schedule.

**MOST GOALS BY A PLAYER IN HIS FIRST NHL SEASON, ONE GAME:**
**5 – Howie Meeker**, Toronto, Jan. 8, 1947, at Toronto. Toronto 10, Chicago 4.
**– Don Murdoch**, NY Rangers, Oct. 12, 1976, at Minnesota. NY Rangers 10, Minnesota 4.

**MOST GOALS BY A PLAYER IN HIS FIRST NHL GAME:**
**3 – Alex Smart**, Montreal, Jan. 14, 1943, at Montreal. Montreal 5, Chicago 1.
**– Real Cloutier**, Quebec, Oct. 10, 1979, at Quebec. Atlanta 5, Quebec 3.
**– Fabian Brunnstrom**, Dallas, Oct. 15, 2008, at Dallas. Dallas 6, Nashville 4.

**MOST ASSISTS BY A ROOKIE, ONE SEASON:**
**70 – Peter Stastny**, Quebec, 1980-81. 77GP – 80 game schedule.
**– Joe Juneau**, Boston, 1992-93. 84GP – 84 game schedule.
63 – Bryan Trottier, NY Islanders, 1975-76. 80GP – 80 game schedule.
– Sidney Crosby, Pittsburgh, 2005–06. 81GP – 82 game schedule.
62 – Sergei Makarov, Calgary, 1989-90. 80GP – 80 game schedule.
60 – Larry Murphy, Los Angeles, 1980-81. 80GP – 80 game schedule.

**MOST ASSISTS BY A PLAYER IN HIS FIRST NHL SEASON, ONE GAME:**
**7 – Wayne Gretzky**, Edmonton, Feb. 15, 1980, at Edmonton. Edmonton 8, Washington 2.
6 – Gary Suter, Calgary, Apr. 4, 1986, at Calgary. Calgary 9, Edmonton 3.

**MOST ASSISTS BY A PLAYER IN HIS FIRST NHL GAME:**
**4 – Dutch Reibel**, Detroit, Oct. 8, 1953, at Detroit. Detroit 4, NY Rangers 1.
**– Roland Eriksson**, Minnesota, Oct. 6, 1976, at NY Rangers. NY Rangers 6, Minnesota 5.
3 – Al Hill, Philadelphia, Feb. 14, 1977, at Philadelphia. Philadelphia 6, St. Louis 4.
– Jarno Kultanen, Boston, Oct. 5, 2000, at Boston. Boston 4, Ottawa 4.
– Stanislav Chistov, Anaheim, Oct. 10, 2002, at St. Louis. Anaheim 4, St. Louis 3.
– Dominic Moore, NY Rangers, Nov. 1, 2003, at Montreal. NY Rangers 5, Montreal 1.

**MOST POINTS BY A ROOKIE, ONE SEASON:**
**132 – Teemu Selanne**, Winnipeg, 1992-93. 84GP – 84 game schedule.
109 – Peter Stastny, Quebec, 1980-81. 77GP – 80 game schedule.
106 – Alex Ovechkin, Washington, 2005-06. 81GP – 82 game schedule.
103 – Dale Hawerchuk, Winnipeg, 1981-82. 80GP – 80 game schedule.
102 – Joe Juneau, Boston, 1992-93. 84GP – 84 game schedule.
– Sidney Crosby, Pittsburgh, 2005–06. 81GP – 82 game schedule.
100 – Mario Lemieux, Pittsburgh, 1984-85. 73GP – 80 game schedule.

**MOST POINTS BY A PLAYER IN HIS FIRST NHL SEASON, ONE GAME:**
**8 – Peter Stastny**, Quebec, Feb. 22, 1981, at Washington. 4G-4A. Quebec 11, Washington 7.
**– Anton Stastny**, Quebec, Feb. 22, 1981, at Washington. 3G-5A. Quebec 11, Washington 7.
7 – Wayne Gretzky, Edmonton, Feb. 15, 1980, at Edmonton. 7A. Edmonton 8, Washington 2.
– Sergei Makarov, Calgary, Feb. 25, 1990, at Calgary. 2G-5A. Calgary 10, Edmonton 4.
6 – Wayne Gretzky, Edmonton, Mar. 29, 1980, at Toronto. 2G-4A. Edmonton 8, Toronto 5.
– Gary Suter, Calgary, Apr. 4, 1986, at Calgary. 6A. Calgary 9, Edmonton 3.

**MOST POINTS BY A PLAYER IN HIS FIRST NHL GAME:**
**5 – Al Hill**, Philadelphia, Feb. 14, 1977, at Philadelphia. 2G-3A. Philadelphia 6, St. Louis 4.
4 – Alex Smart, Montreal, Jan. 14, 1943, at Montreal. 3G-1A. Montreal 5, Chicago 1.
– Dutch Reibel, Detroit, Oct. 8, 1953, at Detroit. 4A. Detroit 4, NY Rangers 1.
– Roland Eriksson, Minnesota, Oct. 6, 1976, at NY Rangers. 4A. NY Rangers 6, Minnesota 5.
– Stanislav Chistov, Anaheim, Oct. 10, 2002, at St. Louis. 1G-3A. Anaheim 4, St. Louis 3.

## SCORING BY A ROOKIE DEFENSEMAN

**MOST GOALS BY A ROOKIE DEFENSEMAN, ONE SEASON:**
**23 – Brian Leetch**, NY Rangers, 1988-89. 68GP – 80 game schedule.
22 – Barry Beck, Colorado, 1977-78. 75GP – 80 game schedule.
20 – Dion Phaneuf, 2005-06. 82GP – 82 game schedule.

**MOST ASSISTS BY A ROOKIE DEFENSEMAN, ONE SEASON:**
**60 – Larry Murphy**, Los Angeles, 1980-81. 80GP – 80 game schedule.
55 – Chris Chelios, Montreal, 1984-85. 74GP – 80 game schedule.
50 – Stefan Persson, NY Islanders, 1977-78. 66GP – 80 game schedule.
– Gary Suter, Calgary, 1985-86. 80GP – 80 game schedule.
49 – Nicklas Lidstrom, Detroit, 1991-92. 80GP – 80 game schedule.

**MOST POINTS BY A ROOKIE DEFENSEMAN, ONE SEASON:**
**76 – Larry Murphy**, Los Angeles, 1980-81. 80GP – 80 game schedule.
71 – Brian Leetch, NY Rangers, 1988-89. 68GP – 80 game schedule.
68 – Gary Suter, Calgary, 1985-86. 80GP – 80 game schedule.
66 – Phil Housley, Buffalo, 1982-83. 77GP – 80 game schedule.
65 – Raymond Bourque, Boston, 1979-80. 80GP – 80 game schedule.

*Only six players who are considered rookies have scored 100 points or more in their debut season in the NHL. Mario Lemieux, left, had exactly 100 in 1984-85. Sidney Crosby, right, broke his Penguins rookie record with 102 points in 2005-06. At 18 years and 8 months old, Crosby is the youngest player in history to score 100 points in a season.*

## PER-GAME SCORING AVERAGES

**HIGHEST GOALS-PER-GAME AVERAGE, CAREER (AMONG PLAYERS WITH 200-OR-MORE GOALS):**

**.762 – Mike Bossy**, NY Islanders, 1977-78 – 1986-87, with 573G in 752GP.
.756 – Cy Denneny, Ottawa, Boston, 1917-18 – 1928-29, with 248G in 328GP.
.754 – Mario Lemieux, Pittsburgh, 1984-85 – 1996-97, 2000-01 – 2003-04, 2005-06, with 690G in 915GP.
.742 – Babe Dye, Toronto, Hamilton, Chicago, NY Americans, 1919-20 – 1930-31, with 201G in 271GP.
.676 – Alex Ovechkin, Washington, 2005-06 – 2008-09, with 219G in 324GP.

**HIGHEST GOALS-PER-GAME AVERAGE, ONE SEASON (AMONG PLAYERS WITH 20-OR-MORE GOALS):**

**2.20 – Joe Malone**, Montreal, 1917-18, with 44G in 20GP.
1.80 – Cy Denneny, Ottawa, 1917-18, with 36G in 20GP.
1.64 – Newsy Lalonde, Montreal, 1917-18, with 23G in 14GP.
1.63 – Joe Malone, Quebec, 1919-20, with 39G in 24GP.
1.61 – Newsy Lalonde, Montreal, 1919-20, with 37G in 23GP.

**HIGHEST GOALS-PER-GAME AVERAGE, ONE SEASON (AMONG PLAYERS WITH 50-OR-MORE GOALS):**

**1.18 – Wayne Gretzky**, Edmonton, 1983-84, with 87G in 74GP.
1.15 – Wayne Gretzky, Edmonton, 1981-82, with 92G in 80GP.
– Mario Lemieux, Pittsburgh, 1992-93, with 69G in 60GP.
1.12 – Mario Lemieux, Pittsburgh, 1988-89, with 85G in 76GP.
1.10 – Brett Hull, St. Louis, 1990-91, with 86G in 78GP.
1.02 – Cam Neely, Boston, 1993-94, with 50G in 49GP.
1.00 – Maurice Richard, Montreal, 1944-45, with 50G in 50GP.

**HIGHEST ASSISTS-PER-GAME AVERAGE, CAREER (AMONG PLAYERS WITH 300-OR-MORE ASSISTS):**

**1.320 – Wayne Gretzky**, Edmonton, Los Angeles, St. Louis, NY Rangers, 1979-80 – 1998-99, with 1,963A in 1,487GP.
1.129 – Mario Lemieux, Pittsburgh, 1984-85 – 1996-97, 2000-01 – 2003-04, 2005-06, with 1,033A in 915GP.
.982 – Bobby Orr, Boston, Chicago, 1966-67 – 1978-79, with 645A in 657GP.
.901 – Peter Forsberg, Quebec, Colorado, Philadelphia, Nashville, 1994-95 – 2000-01, 2002-03, 2003-04, 2005-06 – 2007-08 with 636A in 706GP.
.808 – Peter Stastny, Quebec, New Jersey, St. Louis, 1980-81 – 1994-95, with 789A in 977GP.

**HIGHEST ASSISTS-PER-GAME AVERAGE, ONE SEASON (AMONG PLAYERS WITH 35-OR-MORE ASSISTS):**

**2.04 – Wayne Gretzky, Edmonton**, 1985-86, with 163A in 80GP.
1.70 – Wayne Gretzky, Edmonton, 1987-88, with 109A in 64GP.
1.69 – Wayne Gretzky, Edmonton, 1984-85, with 135A in 80GP.
1.59 – Wayne Gretzky, Edmonton, 1983-84, with 118A in 74GP.
1.56 – Wayne Gretzky, Edmonton, 1982-83, with 125A in 80GP.
– Wayne Gretzky, Los Angeles, 1990-91, with 122A in 78GP.
1.53 – Wayne Gretzky, Edmonton, 1986-87, with 121A in 79GP.
1.52 – Mario Lemieux, Pittsburgh, 1992-93, with 91A in 60GP.
1.50 – Wayne Gretzky, Edmonton, 1981-82, with 120A in 80GP.
– Mario Lemieux, Pittsburgh, 1988-89, with 114A in 76GP.

**HIGHEST POINTS-PER-GAME AVERAGE, CAREER (AMONG PLAYERS WITH 500-OR-MORE POINTS):**

**1.921 – Wayne Gretzky**, Edmonton, Los Angeles, St. Louis, NY Rangers, 1979-80 – 1998-99, with 2,857PTS (894G-1,963A) in 1,487GP.
1.883 – Mario Lemieux, Pittsburgh, 1984-85 – 1996-97, 2000-01 – 2003-04, 2005-06, with 1,723PTS (690G-1,033A) in 915GP.
1.497 – Mike Bossy, NY Islanders, 1977-78 – 1986-87, with 1,126PTS (573G-553A) in 752GP.
1.393 – Bobby Orr, Boston, Chicago, 1966-67 – 1978-79, with 915PTS (270G-645A) in 657GP.
1.314 – Marcel Dionne, Detroit, Los Angeles, NY Rangers, 1971-72 – 1988-89, with 1,771PTS (731G-1,040A) in 1,348GP.

**HIGHEST POINTS-PER-GAME AVERAGE, ONE SEASON (AMONG PLAYERS WITH 50-OR-MORE POINTS):**

**2.77 – Wayne Gretzky**, Edmonton, 1983-84, with 205PTS in 74GP.
2.69 – Wayne Gretzky, Edmonton, 1985-86, with 215PTS in 80GP.
2.67 – Mario Lemieux, Pittsburgh, 1992-93, with 160PTS in 60GP.
2.65 – Wayne Gretzky, Edmonton, 1981-82, with 212PTS in 80GP.
2.62 – Mario Lemieux, Pittsburgh, 1988-89, with 199PTS in 76GP.
2.60 – Wayne Gretzky, Edmonton, 1984-85, with 208PTS in 80GP.
2.45 – Wayne Gretzky, Edmonton, 1982-83, with 196PTS in 80GP.
2.33 – Wayne Gretzky, Edmonton, 1987-88, with 149PTS in 64GP.
2.32 – Wayne Gretzky, Edmonton, 1986-87, with 183PTS in 79GP.
2.30 – Mario Lemieux, Pittsburgh, 1995-96, with 161PTS in 70GP.
2.18 – Mario Lemieux, Pittsburgh, 1987-88, with 168PTS in 77GP.
2.15 – Wayne Gretzky, Los Angeles, 1988-89, with 168PTS in 78GP.
2.09 – Wayne Gretzky, Los Angeles, 1990-91, with 163PTS in 78GP.
2.08 – Mario Lemieux, Pittsburgh, 1989-90, with 123PTS in 59GP.

## SCORING PLATEAUS

**MOST 20-OR-MORE GOAL SEASONS:**

**22 – Gordie Howe**, Detroit, Hartford, in 26 seasons.
20 – Ron Francis, Hartford, Pittsburgh, Carolina, Toronto, in 23 seasons.
19 – Dave Andreychuk, Buffalo, Toronto, New Jersey, Boston, Colorado, Tampa Bay, in 23 seasons.
– Brendan Shanahan, New Jersey, St. Louis, Hartford, Detroit, NY Rangers, in 21 seasons.
17 – Marcel Dionne, Detroit, Los Angeles, NY Rangers, in 18 seasons.
– Mike Gartner, Washington, Minnesota, NY Rangers, Toronto, Phoenix, in 19 seasons.
– Wayne Gretzky, Edmonton, Los Angeles, St. Louis, NY Rangers, in 20 seasons.
– Mark Messier, Edmonton, NY Rangers, Vancouver, in 25 seasons.
– Brett Hull, Calgary, St. Louis, Dallas, Detroit, Phoenix, in 19 seasons.
– Joe Sakic, Quebec, Colorado, in 20 seasons.
– Mats Sundin, Quebec, Toronto, Vancouver, in 18 seasons.
– Jaromir Jagr, Pittsburgh, Washington, NY Rangers, in 17 seasons.

**MOST CONSECUTIVE 20-OR-MORE GOAL SEASONS:**

**22 – Gordie Howe**, Detroit, 1949-50 – 1970-71.
19 – Brendan Shanahan, New Jersey, St. Louis, Hartford, Detroit, NY Rangers, 1988-89 – 2007-08.
17 – Marcel Dionne, Detroit, Los Angeles, NY Rangers, 1971-72 – 1987-88.
– Brett Hull, Calgary, St. Louis, Dallas, Detroit, 1987-88 – 2003-04.
– Jaromir Jagr, Pittsburgh, Washington, NY Rangers, 1990-91 – 2007-08.
– Mats Sundin, Quebec, Toronto, 1990-91 – 2007-08.

*Only Gordie Howe reached the 20-goal plateau more times than Ron Francis, who scored 20 or more 20 times in 23 NHL seasons. Francis scored 549 goals in his career, and his 1,249 assists rank him second all-time behind Wayne Gretzky.*

**MOST 30-OR-MORE GOAL SEASONS:**
**17 – Mike Gartner**, Washington, Minnesota, NY Rangers, Toronto, Phoenix, in 19 seasons.
15 – Jaromir Jagr, Pittsburgh, Washington, NY Rangers, in 17 seasons.
14 – Gordie Howe, Detroit, Hartford, in 26 seasons.
– Marcel Dionne, Detroit, Los Angeles, NY Rangers, in 18 seasons.
– Wayne Gretzky, Edmonton, Los Angeles, St. Louis, NY Rangers, in 20 seasons.
13 – Bobby Hull, Chicago, Winnipeg, Hartford, in 16 seasons.
– Phil Esposito, Chicago, Boston, NY Rangers, in 18 seasons.
– Brett Hull, Calgary, St. Louis, Dallas, Detroit, Phoenix, in 19 seasons.
– Mats Sundin, Quebec, Toronto, Vancouver, in 18 seasons.

**MOST CONSECUTIVE 30-OR-MORE GOAL SEASONS:**
**15 – Mike Gartner**, Washington, Minnesota, NY Rangers, Toronto, 1979-80 – 1993-94.
**– Jaromir Jagr**, Pittsburgh, Washington, NY Rangers, 1991-92 – 2006-07.
13 – Bobby Hull, Chicago, 1959-60 – 1971-72.
– Phil Esposito, Boston, NY Rangers, 1967-68 – 1979-80.
– Wayne Gretzky, Edmonton, Los Angeles, 1979-80 – 1991-92.

**MOST 40-OR-MORE GOAL SEASONS:**
**12 – Wayne Gretzky**, Edmonton, Los Angeles, St. Louis, NY Rangers, in 20 seasons.
10 – Marcel Dionne, Detroit, Los Angeles, NY Rangers, in 18 seasons.
– Mario Lemieux, Pittsburgh, in 17 seasons.
9 – Mike Bossy, NY Islanders, in 10 seasons.
– Mike Gartner, Washington, Minnesota, NY Rangers, Toronto, Phoenix, in 19 seasons.

**MOST CONSECUTIVE 40-OR-MORE GOAL SEASONS:**
**12 – Wayne Gretzky**, Edmonton, Los Angeles, 1979-80 – 1990-91.
9 – Mike Bossy, NY Islanders, 1977-78 – 1985-86.
8 – Luc Robitaille, Los Angeles, 1986-87 – 1993-94.
7 – Phil Esposito, Boston, 1968-69 – 1974-75.
– Michel Goulet, Quebec, 1981-82 – 1987-88.
– Jari Kurri, Edmonton, 1982-83 – 1988-89.

**MOST 50-OR-MORE GOAL SEASONS:**
**9 – Mike Bossy**, NY Islanders, in 10 seasons.
**– Wayne Gretzky**, Edmonton, Los Angeles, St. Louis, NY Rangers, in 20 seasons.
6 – Guy Lafleur, Montreal, NY Rangers, Quebec, in 17 seasons.
– Marcel Dionne, Detroit, Los Angeles, NY Rangers, in 18 seasons.
– Mario Lemieux, Pittsburgh, in 17 seasons.
5 – Bobby Hull, Chicago, Winnipeg, Hartford, in 16 seasons.
– Phil Esposito, Chicago, Boston, NY Rangers, in 18 seasons.
– Brett Hull, Calgary, St. Louis, Dallas, Detroit, Phoenix, in 19 seasons.
– Steve Yzerman, Detroit, in 22 seasons.
– Pavel Bure, Vancouver, Florida, NY Rangers, in 12 seasons.

**MOST CONSECUTIVE 50-OR-MORE GOAL SEASONS:**
**9 – Mike Bossy**, NY Islanders, 1977-78 – 1985-86.
8 – Wayne Gretzky, Edmonton, 1979-80 – 1986-87.
6 – Guy Lafleur, Montreal, 1974-75 – 1979-80.
5 – Phil Esposito, Boston, 1970-71 – 1974-75.
– Marcel Dionne, Los Angeles, 1978-79 – 1982-83.
– Brett Hull, St. Louis, 1989-90 – 1993-94.

**MOST 60-OR-MORE GOAL SEASONS:**
**5 – Mike Bossy**, NY Islanders, in 10 seasons.
**– Wayne Gretzky**, Edmonton, Los Angeles, St. Louis, NY Rangers, in 20 seasons.
4 – Phil Esposito, Chicago, Boston, NY Rangers, in 18 seasons.
– Mario Lemieux, Pittsburgh, in 17 seasons.

**MOST CONSECUTIVE 60-OR-MORE GOAL SEASONS:**
**4 – Wayne Gretzky**, Edmonton, 1981-82 – 1984-85.
3 – Mike Bossy, NY Islanders, 1980-81 – 1982-83.
– Brett Hull, St. Louis, 1989-90 – 1991-92.
2 – Phil Esposito, Boston, 1970-71 – 1971-72, 1973-74 – 1974-75.
– Jari Kurri, Edmonton, 1984-85 – 1985-86.
– Mario Lemieux, Pittsburgh, 1987-88 – 1988-89.
– Steve Yzerman, Detroit, 1988-89 – 1989-90.
– Pavel Bure, Vancouver, 1992-93 – 1993-94.

**MOST 100-OR-MORE POINT SEASONS:**
**15 – Wayne Gretzky**, Edmonton, Los Angeles, St. Louis, NY Rangers, in 20 seasons.
10 – Mario Lemieux, Pittsburgh, in 17 seasons.
8 – Marcel Dionne, Detroit, Los Angeles, NY Rangers, in 18 seasons.
7 – Mike Bossy, NY Islanders, in 10 seasons.
– Peter Stastny, Quebec, New Jersey, St. Louis, in 15 seasons.

**MOST CONSECUTIVE 100-OR-MORE POINT SEASONS:**
**13 – Wayne Gretzky**, Edmonton, Los Angeles, 1979-80 – 1991-92.
6 – Bobby Orr, Boston, 1969-70 – 1974-75.
– Guy Lafleur, Montreal, 1974-75 – 1979-80.
– Mike Bossy, NY Islanders,1980-81 – 1985-86.
– Peter Stastny, Quebec, 1980-81 – 1985-86.
– Mario Lemieux, Pittsburgh, 1984-85 – 1989-90.
– Steve Yzerman, Detroit, 1987-88 – 1992-93.

## THREE-OR-MORE-GOAL GAMES

**MOST THREE-OR-MORE GOAL GAMES, CAREER:**
**50 – Wayne Gretzky**, Edmonton, Los Angeles, St. Louis, NY Rangers, in 20 seasons, 37 three-goal games, 9 four-goal games, 4 five-goal games.
40 – Mario Lemieux, Pittsburgh, in 17 seasons, 27 three-goal games, 10 four-goal games, 3 five-goal games.
39 – Mike Bossy, NY Islanders, in 10 seasons, 30 three-goal games, 9 four-goal games.
33 – Brett Hull, Calgary, St. Louis, Dallas, Detroit, Phoenix, in 19 seasons, 30 three-goal games, 3 four-goal games.
32 – Phil Esposito, Chicago, Boston, NY Rangers, in 18 seasons, 27 three-goal games, 5 four-goal games.

**MOST THREE-OR-MORE GOAL GAMES, ONE SEASON:**
**10 – Wayne Gretzky**, Edmonton, 1981-82. 6 three-goal games, 3 four-goal games, 1 five-goal game.
**– Wayne Gretzky**, Edmonton, 1983-84. 6 three-goal games, 4 four-goal games.
9 – Mike Bossy, NY Islanders, 1980-81. 6 three-goal games, 3 four-goal games.
– Mario Lemieux, Pittsburgh, 1988-89. 7 three-goal games, 1 four-goal game, 1 five-goal game.
8 – Brett Hull, St. Louis, 1991-92. 8 three-goal games.
7 – Joe Malone, Montreal, 1917-18. 2 three-goal games, 2 four-goal games, 3 five-goal games.
– Phil Esposito, Boston, 1970-71. 7 three-goal games.
– Rick Martin, Buffalo, 1975-76. 6 three-goal games, 1 four-goal game.
– Alexander Mogilny, Buffalo, 1992-93. 5 three-goal games, 2 four-goal games.

## SCORING STREAKS

**LONGEST CONSECUTIVE GOAL-SCORING STREAK:**
**16 Games – Punch Broadbent**, Ottawa, 1921-22. 27G
14 Games – Joe Malone, Montreal, 1917-18. 35G
13 Games – Newsy Lalonde, Montreal, 1920-21. 24G
– Charlie Simmer, Los Angeles, 1979-80. 17G
12 Games – Cy Denneny, Ottawa, 1917-18. 23G
– Dave Lumley, Edmonton, 1981-82. 15G
– Mario Lemieux, Pittsburgh, 1992-93. 18G

**LONGEST CONSECUTIVE ASSIST-SCORING STREAK:**
**23 Games – Wayne Gretzky**, Los Angeles, 1990-91. 48A
18 Games – Adam Oates, Boston, 1992-93. 28A
17 Games – Wayne Gretzky, Edmonton, 1983-84. 38A
– Paul Coffey, Edmonton, 1985-86. 27A
– Wayne Gretzky, Los Angeles, 1989-90. 35A
16 Games – Jaromir Jagr, Pittsburgh, 2000-01. 24A

**LONGEST CONSECUTIVE POINT-SCORING STREAK:**
**51 Games – Wayne Gretzky**, Edmonton, 1983-84. 61G-92A-153PTS
46 Games – Mario Lemieux, Pittsburgh, 1989-90. 39G-64A-103PTS
39 Games – Wayne Gretzky, Edmonton, 1985-86. 33G-75A-108PTS
30 Games – Wayne Gretzky, Edmonton, 1982-83. 24G-52A-76PTS
– Mats Sundin, Quebec, 1992-93. 21G-25A-46PTS

*Punch Broadbent starred with the original Ottawa Senators both before and after they entered the NHL in 1917. He holds one of the oldest records in hockey history, scoring at least one goal in 16 consecutive games during the 1921-22 season.*

**LONGEST CONSECUTIVE POINT-SCORING STREAK FROM START OF SEASON:**

**51 Games – Wayne Gretzky**, Edmonton, 1983-84. 61G-92A-153PTS. Streak ended by Los Angeles and goaltender Markus Mattsson on Jan. 28, 1984.

**LONGEST CONSECUTIVE POINT-SCORING STREAK BY A DEFENSEMAN:**

**28 Games – Paul Coffey**, Edmonton, 1985-86. 16G-39A-55PTS
19 Games – Raymond Bourque, Boston, 1987-88. 6G-21A-27PTS
17 Games – Raymond Bourque, Boston, 1984-85. 4G-24A-28PTS
– Brian Leetch, NY Rangers, 1991-92. 5G-24A-29PTS
16 Games – Gary Suter, Calgary, 1987-88. 8G-17A-25PTS
15 Games – Bobby Orr, Boston, 1970-71. 10G-23A-33PTS
– Bobby Orr, Boston, 1973-74. 8G-15A-23PTS
– Steve Duchesne, Quebec, 1992-93. 4G-17A-21PTS
– Chris Chelios, Chicago, 1995-96. 4G-16A-20PTS

**LONGEST CONSECUTIVE POINT-SCORING STREAK BY A ROOKIE:**

**20 Games –Paul Stastny**, Colorado, 2006-07. 11G-18A-29PTS
17 Games –Teemu Selanne, Winnipeg, 1992-93. 20G-14A-34PTS
16 Games –Peter Stastny, Quebec, 1980-81
15 Games –Jude Drouin, Minnesota North Stars, 1970-71

## FASTEST GOALS AND ASSISTS

**FASTEST GOAL FROM START OF A GAME:**

**0:05 – Doug Smail**, Winnipeg, Dec. 20, 1981, at Winnipeg. Winnipeg 5, St. Louis 4.
**– Bryan Trottier**, NY Islanders, Mar. 22, 1984, at Boston. NY Islanders 3, Boston 3.
**– Alexander Mogilny**, Buffalo, Dec. 21, 1991, at Toronto. Buffalo 4, Toronto 1.
0:06 – Henry Boucha, Detroit, Jan. 28, 1973, at Montreal. Detroit 4, Montreal 2.
– Jean Pronovost, Pittsburgh, Mar. 25, 1976, at St. Louis. St. Louis 5, Pittsburgh 2.
0:07 – Charlie Conacher, Toronto, Feb. 6, 1932, at Toronto. Toronto 6, Boston 0.
– Danny Gare, Buffalo, Dec. 17, 1978, at Buffalo. Buffalo 6, Vancouver 3.
– Tiger Williams, Los Angeles, Feb. 14, 1987, at Los Angeles. Los Angeles 5, Harford 2.
0:08 – Ron Martin, NY Americans, Dec. 4, 1932, at NY Americans. NY Americans 4, Montreal 2.
– Chuck Arnason, Colorado, Jan. 28, 1977, at Atlanta. Colorado 3, Atlanta 3.
– Wayne Gretzky, Edmonton, Dec. 14, 1983, at NY Rangers. Edmonton 9, NY Rangers 4.
– Gaetan Duchesne, Washington, Mar. 14, 1987, at St. Louis. Washington 3, St. Louis 3.
– Tim Kerr, Philadelphia, Mar. 7, 1989, at Philadelphia. Philadelphia 4, Edmonton 4.
– Grant Ledyard, Buffalo, Dec. 4, 1991, at Winnipeg. Buffalo 4, Winnipeg 4.
– Brent Sutter, Chicago, Feb. 5, 1995, at Vancouver. Chicago 9, Vancouver 4.
– Paul Kariya, Anaheim, Mar. 9, 1997, at Colorado. Anaheim 2, Colorado 2.
– Tony Hrkac, Dallas, Nov. 7, 1998, at Los Angeles. Dallas 4, Los Angeles 3.
– Sergei Fedorov, Detroit, Nov. 21, 1998, at Vancouver. Detroit 4, Vancouver 2.
– Ronald Petrovicky, Atlanta, Dec. 20, 2003, at Pittsburgh. Atlanta 7, Pittsburgh 4.
– Mike Modano, Dallas, Dec. 27, 2003, at Columbus. Dallas 4, Columbus 3.
– Antti Laaksonen, Colorado, Feb. 10, 2006, at Columbus. Colorado 4, Columbus 1.

**FASTEST GOAL FROM START OF A PERIOD:**

**0:04 – Claude Provost**, Montreal, Nov. 9, 1957, at Montreal, second period. Montreal 4, Boston 2.
**– Denis Savard**, Chicago, Jan. 12, 1986, at Chicago, third period. Chicago 4, Hartford 2.

**FASTEST GOAL BY A PLAYER IN HIS FIRST NHL GAME:**

**0:15 – Gus Bodnar**, Toronto, Oct. 30, 1943, at Toronto. Toronto 5, NY Rangers 2.
0:18 – Danny Gare, Buffalo, Oct. 10, 1974, at Buffalo. Buffalo 9, Boston 5.
0:20 – Alexander Mogilny, Buffalo, Oct. 5, 1989, at Buffalo. Buffalo 4, Quebec 3.

**FASTEST TWO GOALS FROM START OF A GAME:**

**0:27 – Mike Knuble**, Boston, Feb. 14, 2003, at Florida. 0:10 and 0:27. Boston 6, Florida 5.

**FASTEST TWO GOALS:**

**0:04 – Nels Stewart**, Mtl. Maroons, Jan. 3, 1931, at Mtl. Maroons. 8:24 and 8:28, third period. Mtl. Maroons 5, Boston 3.
**– Deron Quint**, Winnipeg, Dec. 15, 1995, at Winnipeg. 7:51 and 7:55, second period. Winnipeg 9, Edmonton 4.
0:05 – Pete Mahovlich, Montreal, Feb. 20, 1971, at Montreal. 12:16 and 12:21, third period. Montreal 7, Chicago 1.
0:06 – Jim Pappin, Chicago, Feb. 16, 1972, at Chicago. 2:57 and 3:03, third period. Chicago 3, Philadelphia 3.
– Ralph Backstrom, Los Angeles, Nov. 2, 1972, at Los Angeles. 8:30 and 8:36, third period. Los Angeles 5, Boston 2.
– Lanny McDonald, Calgary, Mar. 22, 1984, at Calgary. 16:23 and 16:29, first period. Detroit 6, Calgary 4.
– Sylvain Turgeon, Hartford, Mar. 28, 1987, at Hartford. 13:59 and 14:05, second period. Hartford 5, Pittsburgh 4.

**FASTEST THREE GOALS:**

**0:21 – Bill Mosienko**, Chicago, Mar. 23, 1952, at NY Rangers, against goaltender Lorne Anderson. Mosienko scored at 6:09, 6:20 and 6:30 of third period, all with both teams at full strength. Chicago 7, NY Rangers 6.
0:44 – Jean Béliveau, Montreal, Nov. 5, 1955, at Montreal, against goaltender Terry Sawchuk. Béliveau scored at 0:42, 1:08 and 1:26 of second period, all with Montreal holding a 6-4 man advantage. Montreal 4, Boston 2.

**FASTEST THREE ASSISTS:**

**0:21 – Gus Bodnar**, Chicago, Mar. 23, 1952, at NY Rangers, Bodnar assisted on Bill Mosienko's three goals at 6:09, 6:20 and 6:30 of third period. Chicago 7, NY Rangers 6.
0:44 – Bert Olmstead, Montreal, Nov. 5, 1955, at Montreal, Olmstead assisted on Jean Béliveau's three goals at 0:42, 1:08 and 1:26 of second period. Montreal 4, Boston 2.

## SHOTS ON GOAL

**MOST SHOTS ON GOAL, ONE SEASON:**

**550 – Phil Esposito**, Boston, 1970-71. 78GP – 78 game schedule.
528 – Alex Ovechkin, Washington, 2008-09. 79GP – 82 game schedule.
446 – Alex Ovechkin, Washington, 2007-08. 82GP – 82 game schedule.
429 – Paul Kariya, Anaheim, 1998-99. 82GP – 82 game schedule.
426 – Phil Esposito, Boston, 1971-72. 76GP – 78 game schedule.

## PENALTIES

**MOST PENALTY MINUTES, CAREER:**

**3,966 – Tiger Williams,** Toronto, Vancouver, Detroit, Los Angeles, Hartford, in 14 seasons. 962GP
3,565 – Dale Hunter, Quebec, Washington, Colorado, in 19 seasons. 1,407GP
3,515 – Tie Domi, Toronto, NY Rangers, Winnipeg, in 16 seasons. 1,020GP
3,381 – Marty McSorley, Pittsburgh, Edmonton, Los Angeles, NY Rangers, San Jose, Boston, in 17 seasons. 961GP
3,300 – Bob Probert, Detroit, Chicago, in 17 seasons. 935GP

**MOST PENALTY MINUTES, CAREER, INCLUDING PLAYOFFS:**

**4,421 – Tiger Williams**, Toronto, Vancouver, Detroit, Los Angeles, Hartford, 3,966 in 962 regular-season games; 455 in 83 playoff games.
4,294 – Dale Hunter, Quebec, Washington, Colorado, 3,565 in 1,407 regular-season games; 729 in 186 playoff games.
3,755 – Marty McSorley, Pittsburgh, Edmonton, Los Angeles, NY Rangers, San Jose, Boston, 3,381 in 961 regular-season games; 374 in 115 playoff games.
3,753 – Tie Domi, Toronto, NY Rangers, Winnipeg, 3,515 in 1,020 regular-season games; 238 in 98 playoff games.
3,584 – Chris Nilan, Montreal, NY Rangers, Boston, 3,043 in 688 regular-season games; 541 in 111 playoff games.

**MOST PENALTY MINUTES, ONE SEASON:**

**472 – Dave Schultz**, Philadelphia, 1974-75.
409 – Paul Baxter, Pittsburgh, 1981-82.
408 – Mike Peluso, Chicago, 1991-92.
405 – Dave Schultz, Los Angeles, Pittsburgh, 1977-78.

**MOST PENALTIES, ONE GAME:**

**10 – Chris Nilan**, Boston, Mar. 31, 1991, at Boston vs. Hartford. 6 minors, 2 majors, 1 10-minute misconduct, 1 game misconduct.
9 – Jim Dorey, Toronto, Oct. 16, 1968, at Toronto vs. Pittsburgh. 4 minors, 2 majors, 2 10-minute misconducts, 1 game misconduct.
– Dave Schultz, Pittsburgh, Apr. 6, 1978, at Detroit. 5 minors, 2 majors, 2 10-minute misconducts.
– Randy Holt, Los Angeles, Mar. 11, 1979, at Philadelphia. 1 minor, 3 majors, 2 10-minute misconducts, 3 game misconducts.
– Russ Anderson, Pittsburgh, Jan. 19, 1980, at Pittsburgh vs. Edmonton. 3 minors, 3 majors, 3 game misconducts.
– Kim Clackson, Quebec, Mar. 8, 1981, at Quebec vs. Chicago. 4 minors, 3 majors, 2 game misconducts.
– Terry O'Reilly, Boston, Dec. 19, 1984, at Hartford. 5 minors, 3 majors, 1 game misconduct.
– Larry Playfair, Los Angeles, Dec. 9, 1986, at NY Islanders. 6 minors, 2 majors, 1 10-minute misconduct.
– Marty McSorley, Los Angeles, Apr. 14, 1992, at Vancouver. 5 minors, 2 majors, 1 10-minute misconduct, 1 game misconduct.
– Reed Low, St. Louis, Dec. 31, 2002, at Detroit. 4 minors, 1 major, 1 10-minute misconduct, 3 game misconducts.

**MOST PENALTY MINUTES, ONE GAME:**

**67 – Randy Holt**, Los Angeles, Mar. 11, 1979, at Philadelphia. 1 minor, 3 majors, 2 10-minute misconducts, 3 game misconducts.
57 – Brad Smith, Toronto, Nov. 15, 1986, at Toronto vs. Detroit. 1 minor, 3 majors, 2 10-minute misconducts, 2 game misconducts.
– Reed Low, St. Louis, Feb. 28, 2002, at St. Louis vs. Calgary. 1 minor, 3 majors, 1 10-minute misconduct, 3 game misconducts.

**MOST PENALTIES, ONE PERIOD:**

**9 – Randy Holt**, Los Angeles, Mar. 11, 1979, at Philadelphia, first period. 1 minor, 3 majors, 2 10-minute misconducts, 3 game misconducts.

**MOST PENALTY MINUTES, ONE PERIOD:**

**67 – Randy Holt**, Los Angeles, Mar. 11, 1979, at Philadelphia, first period. 1 minor, 3 majors, 2 10-minute misconducts, 3 game misconducts.

## GOALTENDING

### MOST GAMES APPEARED IN BY A GOALTENDER, CAREER:
**1,029 – Patrick Roy**, Montreal, Colorado, 1984-85 – 2002-03.
999 – Martin Brodeur, New Jersey, 1991-92 – 2003-04, 2005-06 – 2008-09.
971 – Terry Sawchuk, Detroit, Boston, Toronto, Los Angeles, NY Rangers, 1949-50 – 1969-70.
963 – Ed Belfour, Chicago, San Jose, Dallas, Toronto, Florida, 1988-89 – 2003-04, 2005-06, 2006-07.
943 – Curtis Joseph, St. Louis, Edmonton, Toronto, Detroit, Phoenix, Calgary, 1989-90 – 2003-04, 2005-06 – 2008-09.

### MOST CONSECUTIVE COMPLETE GAMES BY A GOALTENDER:
**502 – Glenn Hall**, Detroit, Chicago. Played 502 games from beginning of 1955-56 season through first 12 games of 1962-63 season. In his 503rd straight game, Nov. 7, 1962, at Chicago, Hall was removed from the game against Boston with a back injury in the first period.

### MOST GAMES APPEARED IN BY A GOALTENDER, ONE SEASON:
**79 – Grant Fuhr**, St. Louis, 1995-96.
78 – Martin Brodeur, New Jersey, 2006-07.
77 – Martin Brodeur, New Jersey, 1995-96.
– Bill Ranford, Edmonton, Boston, 1995-96.
– Arturs Irbe, Carolina, 2000-01.
– Marc Denis, Columbus, 2002-03.
– Martin Brodeur, New Jersey, 2007-08
– Evgeni Nabokov, San Jose, 2007-08.

### MOST MINUTES PLAYED BY A GOALTENDER, CAREER:
**60,235 – Patrick Roy**, Montreal, Colorado, 1984-85 – 2002-03.
59,022 – Martin Brodeur, New Jersey, 1991-92 – 2003-04, 2005-06 – 2008-09.
57,194 – Terry Sawchuk, Detroit, Boston, Toronto, Los Angeles, NY Rangers, 1949-50 – 1969-70.

### MOST MINUTES PLAYED BY A GOALTENDER, ONE SEASON:
**4,697 – Martin Brodeur**, New Jersey, 2006-07.
4,635 – Martin Brodeur, New Jersey, 2007-08.
4,561 – Evgeni Nabokov, San Jose, 2007-08.
4,555 – Martin Brodeur, New Jersey, 2003-04.
4,511 – Marc Denis, Columbus, 2002-03.

### MOST SHUTOUTS, CAREER:
**103 – Terry Sawchuk**, Detroit, Boston, Toronto, Los Angeles, NY Rangers, in 21 seasons. (1949-50 – 1969-70)
101 – Martin Brodeur, New Jersey, in 16 seasons. (1991-92, 1993-94 – 2003-04, 2005-06 – 2008-09)
94 – George Hainsworth, Montreal, Toronto, in 11 seasons. (1926-27 – 1936-37)

### MOST SHUTOUTS, ONE SEASON:
**22 – George Hainsworth**, Montreal, 1928-29. 44GP
15 – Alec Connell, Ottawa, 1925-26. 36GP
– Alec Connell, Ottawa, 1927-28. 44GP
– Hal Winkler, Boston, 1927-28. 44GP
– Tony Esposito, Chicago, 1969-70. 63GP
14 – George Hainsworth, Montreal, 1926-27. 44GP

### LONGEST SHUTOUT SEQUENCE BY A GOALTENDER:
**461:29 – Alec Connell**, Ottawa, 1927-28, six consecutive shutouts.
(Forward passing not permitted in attacking zones in 1927-28.)
343:05 – George Hainsworth, Montreal, 1928-29, four consecutive shutouts.
(Forward passing not permitted in attacking zones in 1928-29.)
332:01 – Brian Boucher, Phoenix, 2003-04, five consecutive shutouts.
324:40 – Roy Worters, NY Americans, 1930-31, four consecutive shutouts.
309:21 – Bill Durnan, Montreal, 1948-49, four consecutive shutouts.

### MOST WINS BY A GOALTENDER, CAREER:
**557 – Martin Brodeur**, New Jersey, in 16 seasons. 999GP
551 – Patrick Roy, Montreal, Colorado, in 19 seasons. 1,029GP
484 – Ed Belfour, Chicago, San Jose, Dallas, Toronto, Florida, in 17 seasons. 963GP
454 – Curtis Joseph, St. Louis, Edmonton, Toronto, Detroit, Phoenix, Calgary, in 19 seasons. 943GP
447 – Terry Sawchuk, Detroit, Boston, Toronto, Los Angeles, NY Rangers, in 21 seasons. 971GP

### MOST WINS BY A GOALTENDER, ONE SEASON:
**48 – Martin Brodeur**, New Jersey, 2006-07. 78GP
47 – Bernie Parent, Philadelphia, 1973-74. 73GP
– Roberto Luongo, Vancouver, 2006-07. 76GP
46 – Evgeni Nabokov, San Jose, 2007-08. 77GP
45 – Miikka Kiprusoff, Calgary, 2008-09. 76GP

### LONGEST WINNING STREAK BY A GOALTENDER, ONE SEASON:
**17 – Gilles Gilbert**, Boston, 1975-76.
14 – Tiny Thompson, Boston, 1929-30.
– Ross Brooks, Boston, 1973-74.
– Don Beaupre, Minnesota, 1985-86.
– Tom Barrasso, Pittsburgh, 1992-93.

### LONGEST UNDEFEATED STREAK BY A GOALTENDER, ONE SEASON:
**32 Games – Gerry Cheevers,** Boston, 1971-72. 24W-8T
31 Games – Pete Peeters, Boston, 1982-83. 26W-5T
27 Games – Pete Peeters, Philadelphia, 1979-80. 22W-5T

### LONGEST UNDEFEATED STREAK BY A GOALTENDER IN HIS FIRST NHL SEASON:
**23 Games – Grant Fuhr**, Edmonton, 1981-82. 15W-8T

### LONGEST UNDEFEATED STREAK BY A GOALTENDER FROM START OF CAREER:
**16 Games – Patrick Lalime**, Pittsburgh, 1996-97. 14W-2T

### MOST 30-OR-MORE WIN SEASONS BY A GOALTENDER:
**13 – Patrick Roy**, Montreal, Colorado, in 19 seasons.
12 – Martin Brodeur, New Jersey, in 16 seasons.
9 – Ed Belfour, Chicago, San Jose, Dallas, Toronto, Florida, in 17 seasons.
8 – Tony Esposito, Montreal, Chicago, in 16 seasons.
7 – Jacques Plante, Montreal, NY Rangers, St. Louis, Toronto, Boston, in 18 seasons.
– Ken Dryden, Montreal, in 8 seasons.
– Curtis Joseph, St. Louis, Edmonton, Toronto, Detroit, Phoenix, Calgary, in 19 seasons.
– Dominik Hasek, Chicago, Buffalo, Detroit, Ottawa, in 16 seasons.

### MOST CONSECUTIVE 30-OR-MORE WIN SEASONS BY A GOALTENDER:
**12 – Martin Brodeur**, New Jersey, 1995-96 – 2003-04, 2005-06 – 2007-08.
8 – Patrick Roy, Montreal, Colorado, 1995-96 – 2002-03.
7 – Tony Esposito, Chicago, 1969-70 – 1975-76.
6 – Jacques Plante, Montreal, 1954-55 – 1959-60.
– Marty Turco, Dallas, 2002-03, 2003-04, 2005-06 – 2008-09.
5 – Terry Sawchuk, Detroit, 1950-51 – 1954-55.
– Ken Dryden, Montreal, 1974-75 – 1978-79.

### MOST 40-OR-MORE WIN SEASONS BY A GOALTENDER:
**7 – Martin Brodeur**, New Jersey, in 16 seasons.
3 – Terry Sawchuk, Detroit, Boston, Toronto, Los Angeles, NY Rangers, in 21 seasons.
– Jacques Plante, Montreal, NY Rangers, St. Louis, Toronto, Boston, in 18 seasons.
– Miikka Kiprusoff, San Jose, Calgary, in 8 seasons.
2 – Bernie Parent, Boston, Philadelphia, Toronto, in 13 seasons.
– Ken Dryden, Montreal, in 8 seasons.
– Ed Belfour, Chicago, San Jose, Dallas, Toronto, Florida, in 17 seasons.

### MOST CONSECUTIVE 40-OR-MORE WIN SEASONS BY A GOALTENDER:
**3 – Martin Brodeur**, New Jersey, 2005-06 – 2007-08.
2 – Terry Sawchuk, Detroit, 1950-51 – 1951-52.
– Bernie Parent, Philadelphia, 1973-74 – 1974-75.
– Ken Dryden, Montreal, 1975-76 – 1976-77.
– Martin Brodeur, New Jersey, 1999-2000 – 2000-01.
– Miikka Kiprusoff, Calgary, 2005-06 – 2006-07.
– Evgeni Nabokov, San Jose, 2007-08 – 2008-09.

### MOST LOSSES BY A GOALTENDER, CAREER:
**352 – Gump Worsley**, NY Rangers, Montreal, Minnesota, in 21 seasons. 861GP
**– Curtis Joseph**, St. Louis, Edmonton, Toronto, Detroit, Phoenix, in 19 seasons. 943GP
351 – Gilles Meloche, Chicago, California, Cleveland, Minnesota, Pittsburgh, in 18 seasons. 788GP
346 – John Vanbiesbrouck, NY Rangers, Florida, Philadelphia, NY Islanders, New Jersey, in 20 seasons. 882GP
341 – Sean Burke, New Jersey, Hartford, Carolina, Vancouver, Philadelphia, Florida, Phoenix, Tampa Bay, Los Angeles, in 18 seasons. 820GP

### MOST LOSSES BY A GOALTENDER, ONE SEASON:
**48 – Gary Smith**, California, 1970-71. 71GP
47 – Al Rollins, Chicago, 1953-54. 66GP
46 – Peter Sidorkiewicz, Ottawa, 1992-93. 64GP

## GOALTENDER SHOOTOUT RECORDS

### MOST SHOOTOUT WINS, ONE SEASON:
**10 – Mathieu Garon**, Edmonton, 2007-08, (10GP)
**– Ryan Miller**, Buffalo, 2006-07, (14GP)
**– Martin Brodeur**, New Jersey, 2006-07, (16GP)
9 – Henrik Lundqvist, NY Rangers, 2008-09, (13GP)
– Marc-Andre Fleury, Pittsburgh, 2006-07, (14GP)

### MOST SHOOTOUT WINS, CAREER:
**28 – Martin Brodeur**, New Jersey, (42GP)
27 – Henrik Lundqvist, NY Rangers (45GP)
25 – Ryan Miller, Buffalo (40GP)
24 – Marty Turco, Dallas, (38GP)

### MOST SHOOTOUT SHOTS AGAINST, ONE SEASON:
**60 – Martin Brodeur**, New Jersey, 2006-07, (20GA)
54 – Roberto Luongo, Vancouver, 2007-08, (15GA)
50 – Henrik Lundqvist, NY Rangers, 2006-07, (9GA)
46 – Tim Thomas, Boston, 2006-07, (8GA)
– Ryan Miller, Buffalo, 2006-07, (9GA)
– Marty Turco, Dallas, 2006-07, (11GA)

### MOST SHOOTOUT SHOTS AGAINST, CAREER:
**169 – Henrik Lundqvist**, NY Rangers, (41GA)
151 – Martin Brodeur, New Jersey, (43GA)
141 – Roberto Luongo, Florida, Vancouver, (40GA)
136 – Ryan Miller, Buffalo, (37GA)
– Marty Turco, Dallas, (42GA)

### BEST SHOOTOUT SAVE PERCENTAGE, ONE SEASON: *(minimum 20 shots)*
**.938 – Mathieu Garon**, Edmonton, 2007-08, (32S, 2GA)
.900 – Marc Denis, Tampa Bay, 2006-07, (20S, 2GA)
.879 – Johan Holmqvist, Tampa Bay, 2006-07, (33S, 4GA)
.850 – Kari Lehtonen, Atlanta, 2005-06, (20S, 3GA)

### BEST SHOOTOUT SAVE PERCENTAGE, CAREER: *(minimum 40 shots)*
**.854 – Marc Denis**, Columbus, Tampa Bay, Montreal, (41S, 6GA)
.820 – Johan Hedberg, Dallas, Atlanta, (61S, 11GA)
.812 – Mathieu Garon, Los Angeles, Edmonton, Pittsburgh, (69S, 13GA)
.790 – Jose Theodore, Colorado, Washington, (62S, 13GA)

# Active NHL Players' Three-or-More-Goal Games

## Regular Season

Teams named are the ones the players were with at the time of their multiple-scoring games. Players listed alphabetically.

| Player | Team(s) | 3-Goals | 4-Goals | 5-Goals |
|---|---|---|---|---|
| Alfredsson, Daniel | Ottawa | 5 | 1 | — |
| Antropov, Nik | Toronto | 2 | — | — |
| Armstrong, Derek | Los Angeles | 1 | — | — |
| Arnason, Tyler | Chicago | 1 | — | — |
| Arnott, Jason | Edm., N.J., Dal., Nsh. | 8 | — | — |
| Backes, David | St. Louis | 1 | — | — |
| Battaglia, Bates | Carolina | 1 | — | — |
| Belanger, Eric | Los Angeles | 1 | — | — |
| Bergenheim, Sean | NY Islanders | 1 | — | — |
| Bergeron, Marc-Andre | Edmonton | 1 | — | — |
| Bertuzzi, Todd | Vancouver | 5 | — | — |
| Blake, Jason | NYI, Tor. | 6 | — | — |
| Blake, Rob | Los Angeles | 1 | — | — |
| Bochenski, Brandon | Ottawa | 1 | — | — |
| Bonk, Radek | Ottawa | 1 | — | — |
| Booth, David | Florida | 2 | — | — |
| Boucher, Philippe | Dallas | 1 | — | — |
| Bourque, Rene | Calgary | 1 | — | — |
| Boyes, Brad | Boston | 1 | — | — |
| Boyle, Dan | Tampa Bay | 1 | — | — |
| Briere, Daniel | Buf., Phi. | 3 | — | — |
| Brind'Amour, Rod | Phi., Car. | 3 | — | — |
| Brown, Curtis | Buffalo | 1 | — | — |
| Brown, Dustin | Los Angeles | 1 | — | — |
| Brunette, Andrew | Colorado | 1 | — | — |
| Brunnstrom, Fabian | Dallas | 1 | — | — |
| Burrows, Alexandre | Vancouver | 1 | — | — |
| Byfuglien, Dustin | Chicago | 1 | — | — |
| Cammalleri, Mike | Calgary | 2 | — | — |
| Carcillo, Daniel | Phoenix | 1 | — | — |
| Carter, Jeff | Philadelphia | 1 | — | — |
| Cheechoo, Jonathan | San Jose | 9 | — | — |
| Chouinard, Marc | Minnesota | 1 | — | — |
| Clark, Chris | Washington | 2 | — | — |
| Cleary, Daniel | Detroit | 1 | — | — |
| Clowe, Ryane | San Jose | 1 | — | — |
| Cole, Erik | Car., Edm. | 5 | — | — |
| Conroy, Craig | St.L., L.A. | 2 | — | — |
| Corvo, Joe | Carolina | 1 | — | — |
| Crombeen, Brandon | St. Louis | 1 | — | — |
| Crosby, Sidney | Pittsburgh | 2 | — | — |
| Cullen, Matt | Carolina | 1 | — | — |
| Demitra, Pavol | St.L., L.A. | 4 | — | — |
| Devereaux, Boyd | Edm., Tor. | 2 | — | — |
| Donovan, Shean | Atlanta | 1 | — | — |
| Drury, Chris | Buf., NYR | 2 | — | — |
| Dumont, J.P. | Chi., Buf. | 3 | — | — |
| Dupuis, Pascal | Pittsburgh | 1 | — | — |
| Dvorak, Radek | NY Rangers | 1 | 1 | — |
| Ekman, Nils | Pittsburgh | 1 | — | — |
| Elias, Patrik | New Jersey | 6 | 1 | — |
| Erat, Martin | Nashville | 1 | — | — |
| Eriksson, Loui | Dallas | 1 | — | — |
| Filatov, Nikita | Columbus | 1 | — | — |
| Fisher, Mike | Ottawa | 1 | — | — |
| Frolov, Alexander | Los Angeles | 3 | — | — |
| Gaborik, Marian | Minnesota | 6 | — | 1 |
| Gagne, Simon | Philadelphia | 2 | — | — |
| Gagner, Sam | Edmonton | 1 | — | — |
| Gionta, Brian | New Jersey | 1 | — | — |
| Gomez, Scott | New Jersey | 2 | — | — |
| Gonchar, Sergei | Washington | 1 | — | — |
| Gratton, Chris | Tampa Bay | 1 | — | — |
| Grier, Mike | Edmonton | 1 | — | — |
| Guerin, Bill | N.J., Bos., Dal., St.L., S.J., NYI | 9 | — | — |
| Hagman, Niklas | Dallas | 1 | — | — |
| Hamilton, Jeff | Chicago | 2 | — | — |
| Handzus, Michal | St.L., L.A. | 2 | — | — |
| Hanzal, Martin | Phoenix | 1 | — | — |
| Hartnell, Scott | Nsh., Phi. | 5 | — | — |
| Havlat, Martin | Ottawa | 3 | 1 | — |
| Heatley, Dany | Atl., Ott. | 6 | 1 | — |
| Hecht, Jochen | Buffalo | 1 | — | — |
| Hejduk, Milan | Colorado | 4 | — | — |
| Higgins, Chris | Montreal | 1 | — | — |
| Holmstrom, Tomas | Detroit | 3 | — | — |
| Horcoff, Shawn | Edmonton | 1 | — | — |
| Horton, Nathan | Florida | 1 | — | — |
| Hossa, Marian | Ott., Atl. | 6 | 1 | — |
| Huselius, Kristian | Calgary | 1 | — | — |
| Iginla, Jarome | Calgary | 7 | 1 | — |
| Jagr, Jaromir | Pit., NYR | 13 | 1 | — |
| Jokinen, Jussi | Dallas | — | 1 | — |
| Jokinen, Olli | Fla., Phx., Cgy., | 6 | — | — |
| Kaberle, Tomas | Toronto | 1 | — | — |
| Kapanen, Niko | Dallas | 1 | — | — |

*Eric Staal celebrates with teammates after scoring his league-leading fourth hat trick of the season versus the New York Islanders on April 7, 2009.*

| Player | Team(s) | 3-Goals | 4-Goals | 5-Goals |
|---|---|---|---|---|
| Kariya, Paul | Ana., Nsh., St.L. | 10 | — | — |
| Kessel, Phil | Boston | 2 | — | — |
| Knuble, Mike | Philadelphia | 1 | — | — |
| Kobasew, Chuck | Calgary | 1 | — | — |
| Koivu, Saku | Montreal | 1 | — | — |
| Kostitsyn, Andrei | Montreal | 1 | — | — |
| Kovalchuk, Ilya | Atlanta | 10 | 1 | — |
| Kovalev, Alex | NYR, Pit. | 10 | — | — |
| Kozlov, Viktor | Fla., NYI | 1 | 1 | — |
| Kozlov, Vyacheslav | Det., Atl. | 4 | 1 | — |
| Krejci, David | Boston | 1 | — | — |
| Kunitz, Chris | Anaheim | 1 | — | — |
| Laaksonen, Antti | Minnesota | 1 | — | — |
| Lang, Robert | Wsh., Mtl. | 2 | — | — |
| Langkow, Daymond | Phx., Cgy. | 3 | — | — |
| Laperriere, Ian | Los Angeles | 1 | — | — |
| Lapierre, Maxim | Montreal | 1 | — | — |
| Laraque, Georges | Edmonton | 1 | — | — |
| Larose, Chad | Carolina | 1 | — | — |
| Lecavalier, Vincent | Tampa Bay | 6 | — | — |
| Legwand, David | Nashville | 2 | — | — |
| Lehtinen, Jere | Dallas | 2 | — | — |
| Little, Bryan | Atlanta | 1 | — | — |
| Lombardi, Matthew | Calgary | 1 | — | — |
| Lucic, Milan | Boston | 1 | — | — |
| Lupul, Joffrey | Philadelphia | 2 | — | — |
| Madden, John | New Jersey | 1 | 1 | — |
| Malkin, Evgeni | Pittsburgh | 3 | — | — |
| Malone, Ryan | Pittsburgh | 2 | — | — |
| Maltby, Kirk | Detroit | 1 | — | — |
| Marleau, Patrick | San Jose | 2 | — | — |
| Modano, Mike | Min., Dal. | 6 | 1 | — |
| Modin, Fredrik | Tampa Bay | 3 | — | — |
| Moreau, Ethan | Edmonton | 1 | — | — |
| Morrison, Brendan | Vancouver | 1 | — | — |
| Morrow, Brenden | Dallas | 1 | — | — |
| Moss, Dave | Calgary | 1 | — | — |
| Mueller, Peter | Phoenix | 2 | — | — |
| Nagy, Ladislav | Phx., L.A. | 3 | — | — |
| Nash, Rick | Columbus | 4 | — | — |
| Neal, James | Dallas | 1 | — | — |
| Nolan, Owen | Que., S.J., Cgy. | 10 | 1 | — |
| Nylander, Michael | Hfd., Chi. | 1 | 1 | — |
| Orszagh, Vladimir | Nashville | 1 | — | — |
| Ovechkin, Alex | Washington | 6 | 2 | — |
| Pandolfo, Jay | New Jersey | 1 | — | — |
| Parise, Zach | New Jersey | 1 | — | — |
| Parrish, Mark | Fla., NYI, Min., Dal. | 5 | 1 | — |
| Peca, Michael | Buffalo | 1 | — | — |
| Petersen, Toby | Pittsburgh | 1 | — | — |
| Petrovicky, Ronald | Atlanta | 1 | — | — |
| Pisani, Fernando | Edmonton | 1 | — | — |
| Plekanec, Thomas | Montreal | 1 | — | — |
| Pominville, Jason | Buffalo | 1 | — | — |
| Prospal, Vaclav | Ana., T.B. | 2 | — | — |
| Pyatt, Taylor | Buffalo | 2 | — | — |
| Recchi, Mark | Pit., Mtl., Phi. | 7 | — | — |
| Reinprecht, Steve | Col., Phx. | 3 | — | — |
| Ribeiro, Mike | Dallas | 1 | — | — |

| Player | Team(s) | 3-Goals | 4-Goals | 5-Goals |
|---|---|---|---|---|
| Richards, Mike | Philadelphia | 1 | — | — |
| Rolston, Brian | N.J., Min. | 2 | — | — |
| Roy, Derek | Buffalo | 3 | — | — |
| Ryan, Bobby | Anaheim | 1 | — | — |
| Ryder, Michael | Montreal | 2 | — | — |
| Salo, Sami | Ottawa | 1 | — | — |
| Samsonov, Sergei | Boston | 1 | — | — |
| Satan, Miroslav | Buf., NYI | 6 | 1 | — |
| Savard, Marc | Calgary | 1 | 1 | — |
| Schneider, Mathieu | Detroit | 2 | — | — |
| Sedin, Daniel | Vancouver | 1 | 1 | — |
| Selanne, Teemu | Wpg., Ana., S.J. | 19 | 2 | — |
| Semin, Alexander | Washington | 2 | — | — |
| Shanahan, Brendan | N.J., St.L., Hfd., Det., NYR | 17 | 1 | — |
| Sharp, Patrick | Chicago | 1 | — | — |
| Sim, Jon | Florida | 1 | — | — |
| Sjostrom, Fredrik | Phoenix | 1 | — | — |
| Smyth, Ryan | Edmonton | 5 | — | — |
| Souray, Sheldon | Montreal | 1 | — | — |
| Spezza, Jason | Ottawa | 2 | — | — |
| St. Louis, Martin | Tampa Bay | 4 | — | — |
| Staal, Eric | Carolina | 7 | — | — |
| Staal, Jordan | Pittsburgh | 2 | — | — |
| Stafford, Drew | Buffalo | 2 | — | — |
| Stamkos, Steven | Tampa Bay | 1 | — | — |
| Stastny, Paul | Colorado | 1 | — | — |
| Steen, Alex | Toronto | 1 | — | — |
| Stillman, Cory | Cgy., St.L., Car. | 4 | — | — |
| Sturm, Marco | S.J., Bos. | 2 | — | — |
| Sullivan, Steve | Tor., Chi., Nsh. | 5 | 1 | — |
| Sundin, Mats | Que., Tor. | 6 | 1 | 1 |
| Svatos, Marek | Colorado | 2 | — | — |
| Sydor, Darryl | Dallas | 1 | — | — |
| Sykora, Petr | Pittsburgh | 1 | — | — |
| Tanguay, Alex | Colorado | 2 | — | — |
| Tenkrat, Petr | Nashville | 1 | — | — |
| Thornton, Joe | Bos., S.J. | 3 | — | — |
| Tkachuk, Keith | Phoenix | 7 | 2 | — |
| Toews, Jonathan | Chicago | 1 | — | — |
| Umberger, R.J. | Philadelphia | 1 | — | — |
| Vanek, Thomas | Buffalo | 5 | — | — |
| Vasicek, Josef | Carolina | 1 | — | — |
| Vermette, Antoine | Ottawa | 1 | — | — |
| Visnovsky, Lubomir | Los Angeles | 1 | — | — |
| Vrbata, Radim | Col., Car., Phx. | 3 | — | — |
| Vyborny, David | Columbus | 1 | — | — |
| Walker, Scott | Nashville | 2 | — | — |
| Weight, Doug | Edm., St.L. | 2 | — | — |
| Weiss, Stephen | Florida | 1 | — | — |
| Wellwood, Kyle | Toronto | 1 | — | — |
| Wheeler, Blake | Boston | 1 | — | — |
| Whitney, Ray | CBJ, Car. | 3 | — | — |
| Williams, Jason | Detroit | 1 | — | — |
| Williams, Justin | Carolina | 1 | — | — |
| Zednik, Richard | Wsh., Fla. | 2 | — | — |
| Zetterberg, Henrik | Detroit | 3 | — | — |
| Zubrus, Dainus | Mtl., N.J. | 1 | 1 | — |

# Top 100 All-Time Goal-Scoring Leaders

* active player

*Owen Nolan enjoyed his first 20-goal season since 2002-03, scoring 25 times for the Minnesota Wild in 2008-09. He scored his 400th career goal on March 10, 2009.*

| | Player | Seasons | Games | Goals | Goals per game |
|---|---|---|---|---|---|
| 1. | **Wayne Gretzky**, Edm., L.A., St.L., NYR | 20 | 1487 | **894** | .601 |
| 2. | **Gordie Howe**, Det., Hfd. | 26 | 1767 | **801** | .453 |
| 3. | **Brett Hull**, Cgy., St.L., Dal., Det., Phx. | 20 | 1269 | **741** | .584 |
| 4. | **Marcel Dionne**, Det., L.A., NYR | 18 | 1348 | **731** | .542 |
| 5. | **Phil Esposito**, Chi., Bos., NYR | 18 | 1282 | **717** | .559 |
| 6. | **Mike Gartner**, Wsh., Min., NYR, Tor., Phx. | 19 | 1432 | **708** | .494 |
| 7. | **Mark Messier**, Edm., NYR, Van. | 25 | 1756 | **694** | .395 |
| 8. | **Steve Yzerman**, Det. | 22 | 1514 | **692** | .457 |
| 9. | **Mario Lemieux**, Pit. | 18 | 915 | **690** | .754 |
| 10. | **Luc Robitaille**, L.A., Pit., NYR, Det. | 19 | 1431 | **668** | .467 |
| * 11. | **Brendan Shanahan**, N.J., St.L., Hfd., Det., NYR | 21 | 1524 | **656** | .430 |
| 12. | **Jaromir Jagr**, Pit., Wsh., NYR | 17 | 1273 | **646** | .507 |
| 13. | **Dave Andreychuk**, Buf., Tor., N.J., Bos., Col., T.B. | 23 | 1639 | **640** | .390 |
| 14. | **Joe Sakic**, Que., Col. | 20 | 1378 | **625** | .454 |
| 15. | **Bobby Hull**, Chi., Wpg., Hfd. | 16 | 1063 | **610** | .574 |
| 16. | **Dino Ciccarelli**, Min., Wsh., Det., T.B., Fla. | 19 | 1232 | **608** | .494 |
| 17. | **Jari Kurri**, Edm., L.A., NYR, Ana., Col. | 17 | 1251 | **601** | .480 |
| * 18. | **Teemu Selanne**, Wpg., Ana., S.J., Col. | 16 | 1132 | **579** | .511 |
| 19. | **Mike Bossy**, NYI | 10 | 752 | **573** | .762 |
| 20. | **Joe Nieuwendyk**, Cgy., Dal., N.J., Tor., Fla. | 20 | 1257 | **564** | .449 |
| * 21. | **Mats Sundin**, Que., Tor., Van. | 18 | 1346 | **564** | .419 |
| 22. | **Guy Lafleur**, Mtl., NYR, Que. | 17 | 1126 | **560** | .497 |
| 23. | **John Bucyk**, Det., Bos. | 23 | 1540 | **556** | .361 |
| 24. | **Ron Francis**, Hfd., Pit., Car., Tor. | 23 | 1731 | **549** | .317 |
| 25. | **Michel Goulet**, Que., Chi. | 15 | 1089 | **548** | .503 |
| * 26. | **Mark Recchi**, Pit., Phi., Mtl., Car., Atl., T.B., Bos. | 20 | 1490 | **545** | .366 |
| 27. | **Maurice Richard**, Mtl. | 18 | 978 | **544** | .556 |
| * 28. | **Mike Modano**, Min., Dal. | 20 | 1400 | **543** | .388 |
| 29. | **Stan Mikita**, Chi. | 22 | 1394 | **541** | .388 |
| 30. | **Frank Mahovlich**, Tor., Det., Mtl. | 18 | 1181 | **533** | .451 |
| * 31. | **Keith Tkachuk**, Wpg., Phx., St.L., Atl. | 17 | 1134 | **525** | .463 |
| 32. | **Bryan Trottier**, NYI, Pit. | 18 | 1279 | **524** | .410 |
| 33. | **Pat Verbeek**, N.J., Hfd., NYR, Dal., Det. | 20 | 1424 | **522** | .367 |
| 34. | **Dale Hawerchuk**, Wpg., Buf., St.L., Phi. | 16 | 1188 | **518** | .436 |
| 35. | **Pierre Turgeon**, Buf., NYI, Mtl., St.L., Dal., Col. | 19 | 1294 | **515** | .398 |
| 36. | **Jeremy Roenick**, Chi., Phx., Phi., L.A., S.J. | 20 | 1363 | **513** | .376 |
| 37. | **Gilbert Perreault**, Buf. | 17 | 1191 | **512** | .430 |
| 38. | **Jean Beliveau**, Mtl. | 20 | 1125 | **507** | .451 |
| 39. | **Peter Bondra**, Wsh., Ott., Atl., Chi. | 16 | 1081 | **503** | .465 |
| 40. | **Joe Mullen**, St.L., Cgy., Pit., Bos. | 17 | 1062 | **502** | .473 |
| 41. | **Lanny McDonald**, Tor., Col., Cgy. | 16 | 1111 | **500** | .450 |
| 42. | **Glenn Anderson**, Edm., Tor., NYR, St.L. | 16 | 1129 | **498** | .441 |
| 43. | **Jean Ratelle**, NYR, Bos. | 21 | 1281 | **491** | .383 |
| 44. | **Norm Ullman**, Det., Tor. | 20 | 1410 | **490** | .348 |
| 45. | **Brian Bellows**, Min., Mtl., T.B., Ana., Wsh. | 17 | 1188 | **485** | .408 |
| 46. | **Darryl Sittler**, Tor., Phi., Det. | 15 | 1096 | **484** | .442 |
| 47. | **Sergei Fedorov**, Det., Ana., CBJ, Wsh. | 18 | 1248 | **483** | .387 |
| 48. | **Bernie Nicholls**, L.A., NYR, Edm., N.J., Chi., S.J. | 18 | 1127 | **475** | .421 |
| 49. | **Alexander Mogilny**, Buf., Van., N.J., Tor. | 16 | 990 | **473** | .478 |
| 50. | **Denis Savard**, Chi., Mtl., T.B. | 17 | 1196 | **473** | .395 |
| 51. | **Pat LaFontaine**, NYI, Buf., NYR | 15 | 865 | **468** | .541 |
| 52. | **Alex Delvecchio**, Det. | 24 | 1549 | **456** | .294 |
| 53. | **Theoren Fleury**, Cgy., Col., NYR, Chi. | 15 | 1084 | **455** | .420 |
| 54. | **Peter Stastny**, Que., N.J., St.L. | 15 | 977 | **450** | .461 |
| 55. | **Doug Gilmour**, St.L., Cgy., Tor., N.J., Chi., Buf., Mtl. | 20 | 1474 | **450** | .305 |
| 56. | **Rick Middleton**, NYR, Bos. | 14 | 1005 | **448** | .446 |
| * 57. | **Rod Brind'Amour**, St.L., Phi., Car. | 20 | 1404 | **443** | .316 |
| 58. | **Rick Vaive**, Van., Tor., Chi., Buf. | 13 | 876 | **441** | .503 |
| 59. | **Steve Larmer**, Chi., NYR | 15 | 1006 | **441** | .438 |
| 60. | **Rick Tocchet**, Phi., Pit., L.A., Bos., Wsh., Phx. | 18 | 1144 | **440** | .385 |
| 61. | **Gary Roberts**, Cgy., Car., Tor., Fla., Pit., T.B. | 22 | 1224 | **438** | .358 |
| 62. | **Pavel Bure**, Van., Fla., NYR | 12 | 702 | **437** | .623 |
| 63. | **Vincent Damphousse**, Tor., Edm., Mtl., S.J. | 18 | 1378 | **432** | .313 |
| 64. | **Dave Taylor**, L.A. | 17 | 1111 | **431** | .388 |
| 65. | **Yvan Cournoyer**, Mtl. | 16 | 968 | **428** | .442 |
| 66. | **Brian Propp**, Phi., Bos., Min., Hfd. | 15 | 1016 | **425** | .418 |
| 67. | **Steve Shutt**, Mtl., L.A. | 13 | 930 | **424** | .456 |
| 68. | **Stephane Richer**, Mtl., N.J., T.B., St.L., Pit. | 17 | 1054 | **421** | .399 |
| 69. | **Steve Thomas**, Tor., Chi., NYI, N.J., Ana., Det. | 20 | 1235 | **421** | .341 |
| 70. | **Bill Barber**, Phi. | 14 | 903 | **420** | .465 |
| 71. | **Tony Amonte**, NYR, Chi., Phx., Phi., Cgy. | 16 | 1174 | **416** | .354 |
| 72. | **Garry Unger**, Tor., Det., St.L., Atl., L.A., Edm. | 16 | 1105 | **413** | .374 |
| 73. | **John MacLean**, N.J., S.J., NYR, Dal. | 18 | 1194 | **413** | .346 |
| 74. | **Raymond Bourque**, Bos., Col. | 22 | 1612 | **410** | .254 |
| * 75. | **Jarome Iginla**, Cgy. | 13 | 942 | **409** | .434 |
| * 76. | **Bill Guerin**, N.J., Edm., Bos., Dal., St.L., S.J., NYI, Pit. | 17 | 1185 | **408** | .344 |
| 77. | **Ray Ferraro**, Hfd., NYI, NYR, L.A., Atl., St.L. | 18 | 1258 | **408** | .324 |
| 78. | **John LeClair**, Mtl., Phi., Pit. | 16 | 967 | **406** | .420 |
| 79. | **Rod Gilbert**, NYR | 18 | 1065 | **406** | .381 |
| * 80. | **Owen Nolan**, Que., Col., S.J., Tor., Phx., Cgy., Min. | 17 | 1127 | **406** | .360 |
| 81. | **John Ogrodnick**, Det., Que., NYR | 14 | 928 | **402** | .433 |
| 82. | **Dave Keon**, Tor., Hfd. | 18 | 1296 | **396** | .306 |
| 83. | **Paul Coffey**, Edm., Pit., L.A., Det., Hfd., Phi., Chi., Car., Bos. | 21 | 1409 | **396** | .281 |
| 84. | **Pierre Larouche**, Pit., Mtl., Hfd., NYR | 14 | 812 | **395** | .486 |
| 85. | **Cam Neely**, Van., Bos. | 13 | 726 | **395** | .544 |
| 86. | **Markus Naslund**, Pit., Van., NYR | 15 | 1117 | **395** | .354 |
| 87. | **Tomas Sandstrom**, NYR, L.A., Pit., Det., Ana. | 15 | 983 | **394** | .401 |
| * 88. | **Alex Kovalev**, NYR, Pit., Mtl. | 16 | 1151 | **394** | .342 |
| 89. | **Bernie Geoffrion**, Mtl., NYR | 16 | 883 | **393** | .445 |
| 90. | **Jean Pronovost**, Pit., Atl., Wsh. | 14 | 998 | **391** | .392 |
| 91. | **Dean Prentice**, NYR, Bos., Det., Pit., Min. | 22 | 1378 | **391** | .284 |
| 92. | **Rick Martin**, Buf., L.A. | 11 | 685 | **384** | .561 |
| * 93. | **Paul Kariya**, Ana., Col., Nsh., St.L. | 14 | 914 | **384** | .420 |
| 94. | **Reggie Leach**, Bos., Cal., Phi., Det. | 13 | 934 | **381** | .408 |
| 95. | **Ted Lindsay**, Det., Chi. | 17 | 1068 | **379** | .355 |
| 96. | **Claude Lemieux**, Mtl., N.J., Col., Phx., Dal., S.J. | 21 | 1215 | **379** | .312 |
| 97. | **Butch Goring**, L.A., NYI, Bos. | 16 | 1107 | **375** | .339 |
| 98. | **Trevor Linden**, Van., NYI, Mtl., Wsh. | 19 | 1382 | **375** | .271 |
| 99. | **Eric Lindros**, Phi., NYR, Tor., Dal. | 14 | 760 | **372** | .489 |
| 100. | **Rick Kehoe**, Tor., Pit. | 14 | 906 | **371** | .409 |

# Top 100 Active Goal-Scoring Leaders

| Player | Seasons | Games | Goals | Goals per game |
|---|---|---|---|---|
| 1. **Brendan Shanahan**, N.J., St.L., Hfd., Det., NYR | 21 | 1524 | **656** | .430 |
| 2. **Teemu Selanne**, Wpg., Ana., S.J., Col. | 16 | 1132 | **579** | .511 |
| 3. **Mats Sundin**, Que., Tor., Van. | 18 | 1346 | **564** | .419 |
| 4. **Mark Recchi**, Pit., Phi., Mtl., Car., Atl., T.B., Bos. | 20 | 1490 | **545** | .366 |
| 5. **Mike Modano**, Min., Dal. | 20 | 1400 | **543** | .388 |
| 6. **Keith Tkachuk**, Wpg., Phx., St.L., Atl. | 17 | 1134 | **525** | .463 |
| 7. **Rod Brind'Amour**, St.L., Phi., Car. | 20 | 1404 | **443** | .316 |
| 8. **Jarome Iginla**, Cgy. | 13 | 942 | **409** | .434 |
| 9. **Bill Guerin**, N.J., Edm., Bos., Dal., St.L., S.J., NYI, Pit. | 17 | 1185 | **408** | .344 |
| 10. **Owen Nolan**, Que., Col., S.J., Tor., Phx., Cgy., Min. | 17 | 1127 | **406** | .360 |
| 11. **Alex Kovalev**, NYR, Pit., Mtl. | 16 | 1151 | **394** | .342 |
| 12. **Paul Kariya**, Ana., Col., Nsh., St.L. | 14 | 914 | **384** | .420 |
| 13. **Jason Arnott**, Edm., N.J., Dal., Nsh. | 15 | 1036 | **364** | .351 |
| 14. **Daniel Alfredsson**, Ott. | 13 | 932 | **355** | .381 |
| 15. **Miroslav Satan**, Edm., Buf., NYI, Pit. | 13 | 1012 | **354** | .350 |
| 16. **Vyacheslav Kozlov**, Det., Buf., Atl. | 17 | 1127 | **348** | .309 |
| 17. **Marian Hossa**, Ott., Atl., Pit., Det. | 11 | 775 | **339** | .437 |
| 18. **Milan Hejduk**, Col. | 10 | 783 | **312** | .398 |
| 19. **Ryan Smyth**, Edm., NYI, Col. | 14 | 920 | **310** | .337 |
| 20. **Ray Whitney**, S.J., Edm., Fla., CBJ, Det., Car. | 17 | 992 | **303** | .305 |
| 21. **Vincent Lecavalier**, T.B. | 10 | 787 | **302** | .384 |
| 22. **Pavol Demitra**, Ott., St.L., L.A., Min., Van. | 15 | 819 | **301** | .368 |
| 23. **Brian Rolston**, N.J., Col., Bos., Min. | 14 | 1041 | **301** | .289 |
| 24. **Petr Sykora**, N.J., Ana., NYR, Edm., Pit. | 11 | 921 | **300** | .326 |
| 25. **Ilya Kovalchuk**, Atl. | 7 | 545 | **297** | .545 |
| 26. **Patrik Elias**, N.J. | 13 | 822 | **295** | .359 |
| 27. **Patrick Marleau**, S.J. | 11 | 871 | **276** | .317 |
| 28. **Doug Weight**, NYR, Edm., St.L., Car., Ana., NYI | 18 | 1184 | **275** | .232 |
| 29. **Joe Thornton**, Bos., S.J. | 11 | 836 | **265** | .317 |
| 30. **Dany Heatley**, Atl., Ott. | 7 | 507 | **260** | .513 |
| 31. **Shane Doan**, Wpg., Phx. | 13 | 965 | **258** | .267 |
| 32. **Todd Bertuzzi**, NYI, Van., Fla., Det., Ana., Cgy. | 13 | 859 | **255** | .297 |
| 33. **Robert Lang**, L.A., Bos., Pit., Wsh., Det., Chi., Mtl. | 15 | 925 | **252** | .272 |
| 34. **Cory Stillman**, Cgy., St.L., T.B., Car., Ott., Fla. | 10 | 902 | **251** | .278 |
| 35. **Daymond Langkow**, T.B., Phi., Phx., Cgy. | 13 | 941 | **245** | .260 |
| 36. **Simon Gagne**, Phi. | 8 | 606 | **242** | .399 |
| 37. **Chris Drury**, Col., Cgy., Buf., NYR | 10 | 791 | **240** | .303 |
| 38. **Mike Sillinger**, Det., Ana., Van., Phi., T.B., Fla., Ott., CBJ, Phx., St.L. | 18 | 1049 | **240** | .229 |
| 39. **Steve Sullivan**, N.J., Tor., Chi., Nsh. | 12 | 764 | **239** | .313 |
| 40. **Jere Lehtinen**, Dal. | 13 | 817 | **239** | .293 |
| 41. **Martin St. Louis**, Cgy., T.B. | 10 | 690 | **238** | .345 |
| 42. **Olli Jokinen**, L.A., NYI, Fla., Phx., Cgy. | 11 | 799 | **237** | .297 |
| 43. **Rob Blake**, L.A., Col., S.J. | 19 | 1200 | **233** | .194 |
| 44. **Nicklas Lidstrom**, Det. | 17 | 1330 | **228** | .171 |
| 45. **Mathieu Schneider**, Mtl., NYI, Tor., NYR, L.A., Det., Ana., Atl. | 20 | 1264 | **221** | .175 |
| 46. **Fredrik Modin**, Tor., T.B., CBJ | 12 | 814 | **220** | .270 |
| 47. **Alex Ovechkin**, Wsh. | 4 | 324 | **219** | .676 |
| 48. **Marian Gaborik**, Min. | 8 | 502 | **219** | .436 |
| 49. **Mark Parrish**, Fla., NYI, L.A., Min., Dal. | 10 | 704 | **216** | .307 |
| 50. **Mike Knuble**, Det., NYR, Bos., Phi. | 12 | 820 | **215** | .262 |
| 51. **Chris Gratton**, T.B., Phi., Buf., Phx., Col., Fla., CBJ | 15 | 1092 | **214** | .196 |
| 52. **Andrew Brunette**, Wsh., Nsh., Atl., Min., Col. | 13 | 868 | **213** | .245 |
| 53. **Marco Sturm**, S.J., Bos. | 11 | 779 | **212** | .272 |
| 54. **Jamie Langenbrunner**, Dal., N.J. | 14 | 884 | **209** | .236 |
| 55. **Michael Nylander**, Hfd., Cgy., T.B., Chi., Wsh., Bos., NYR | 15 | 920 | **209** | .227 |
| 56. **Sergei Samsonov**, Bos., Edm., Mtl., Chi., Car. | 11 | 738 | **208** | .282 |
| 57. **Darcy Tucker**, Mtl., T.B., Tor., Col. | 13 | 876 | **205** | .234 |
| 58. **Daniel Briere**, Phx., Buf., Phi. | 11 | 591 | **204** | .345 |
| 59. **Richard Zednik**, Wsh., Mtl., NYI, Fla. | 13 | 745 | **200** | .268 |
| 60. **Vaclav Prospal**, Phi., Ott., Fla., T.B., Ana. | 12 | 874 | **198** | .227 |
| 61. **Viktor Kozlov**, S.J., Fla., N.J., NYI, Wsh. | 14 | 897 | **198** | .221 |
| 62. **Marc Savard**, NYR, Cgy., Atl., Bos. | 11 | 741 | **195** | .263 |
| 63. **Rick Nash**, CBJ | 6 | 441 | **194** | .440 |
| 64. **Radek Bonk**, Ott., Mtl., Nsh. | 14 | 969 | **194** | .200 |
| 65. **Radek Dvorak**, Fla., NYR, Edm., St.L. | 13 | 976 | **194** | .199 |
| 66. **Alex Tanguay**, Col., Cgy., Mtl. | 9 | 659 | **193** | .293 |
| 67. **Saku Koivu**, Mtl. | 13 | 792 | **191** | .241 |
| 68. **Sergei Gonchar**, Wsh., Bos., Pit. | 14 | 929 | **191** | .206 |
| 69. **Tomas Holmstrom**, Det. | 12 | 811 | **189** | .233 |

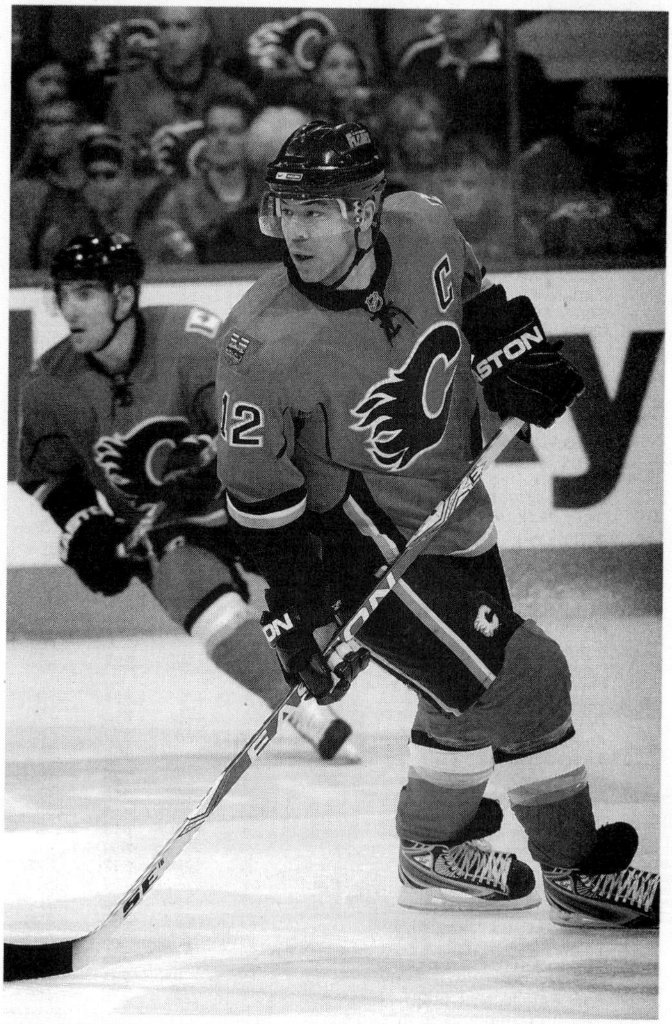

*Calgary's Jarome Iginla recorded both his 400th career goal and 400th career assist during the 2008-09 season. The milestone goal came on March 1, 2009.*

| Player | Seasons | Games | Goals | Goals per game |
|---|---|---|---|---|
| 70. **J.P. Dumont**, Chi., Buf., Nsh. | 10 | 678 | **187** | .276 |
| 71. **Chris Chelios**, Mtl., Chi., Det. | 25 | 1644 | **185** | .113 |
| 72. **Henrik Zetterberg**, Det. | 6 | 432 | **183** | .424 |
| 73. **Daniel Sedin**, Van. | 8 | 642 | **179** | .279 |
| 74. **Dean McAmmond**, Chi., Edm., Phi., Cgy., Col., St.L., Ott., NYI | 16 | 934 | **178** | .191 |
| 75. **Craig Conroy**, Mtl., St.L., Cgy., L.A. | 14 | 928 | **177** | .191 |
| 76. **Michael Peca**, Van., Buf., NYI, Edm., Tor., CBJ | 14 | 864 | **176** | .204 |
| 77. **Todd Marchant**, NYR, Edm., CBJ, Ana. | 15 | 1038 | **176** | .170 |
| 78. **Brendan Morrison**, N.J., Van., Ana., Dal. | 11 | 755 | **175** | .232 |
| 79. **Jason Blake**, L.A., NYI, Tor. | 10 | 668 | **174** | .260 |
| 80. **Brenden Morrow**, Dal. | 9 | 591 | **173** | .293 |
| 81. **Pavel Datsyuk**, Det. | 7 | 526 | **171** | .325 |
| 82. **Rob Niedermayer**, Fla., Cgy., Ana. | 15 | 1011 | **171** | .169 |
| 83. **Martin Havlat**, Ott., Chi. | 8 | 470 | **169** | .360 |
| 84. **Brad Richards**, T.B., Dal. | 8 | 620 | **168** | .271 |
| 85. **Dainius Zubrus**, Phi., Mtl., Wsh., Buf., N.J. | 12 | 853 | **166** | .195 |
| 86. **Jonathan Cheechoo**, S.J. | 6 | 440 | **165** | .375 |
| 87. **Eric Staal**, Car. | 5 | 409 | **164** | .401 |
| 88. **Scott Niedermayer**, N.J., Ana. | 17 | 1183 | **162** | .137 |
| 89. **Mike Comrie**, Edm., Phi., Phx., Ott., NYI | 8 | 525 | **154** | .293 |
| 90. **Kristian Huselius**, Fla., Cgy., CBJ | 7 | 547 | **153** | .280 |
| 91. **Matt Cullen**, Ana., Fla., Car., NYR | 11 | 799 | **153** | .191 |
| 92. **Brian Gionta**, N.J. | 7 | 473 | **152** | .321 |
| 93. **Sergei Zubov**, NYR, Pit., Dal. | 16 | 1068 | **152** | .142 |
| 94. **Alexander Frolov**, L.A. | 6 | 455 | **149** | .327 |
| 95. **Jason Spezza**, Ott. | 6 | 404 | **148** | .366 |
| 96. **Scott Gomez**, N.J., NYR | 9 | 706 | **148** | .210 |
| 97. **Kris Draper**, Wpg., Det. | 18 | 1029 | **148** | .144 |
| 98. **Erik Cole**, Car., Edm. | 7 | 498 | **147** | .295 |
| 99. **Scott Hartnell**, Nsh., Phi. | 8 | 598 | **147** | .246 |
| 100. **Mike Grier**, Edm., Wsh., Buf., S.J. | 12 | 914 | **147** | .161 |

# Top 100 All-Time Assist Leaders

* active player

| | Player | Seasons | Games | Assists | Assists per game |
|---|---|---|---|---|---|
| 1. | **Wayne Gretzky**, Edm., L.A., St.L., NYR | 20 | 1487 | **1963** | 1.320 |
| 2. | **Ron Francis**, Hfd., Pit., Car., Tor. | 23 | 1731 | **1249** | .722 |
| 3. | **Mark Messier**, Edm., NYR, Van. | 25 | 1756 | **1193** | .679 |
| 4. | **Raymond Bourque**, Bos., Col. | 22 | 1612 | **1169** | .725 |
| 5. | **Paul Coffey**, Edm., Pit., L.A., Det., Hfd., Phi., Chi., Car., Bos. | 21 | 1409 | **1135** | .806 |
| 6. | **Adam Oates**, Det., St.L., Bos., Wsh., Phi., Ana., Edm. | 19 | 1337 | **1079** | .807 |
| 7. | **Steve Yzerman**, Det. | 22 | 1514 | **1063** | .702 |
| 8. | **Gordie Howe**, Det., Hfd. | 26 | 1767 | **1049** | .594 |
| 9. | **Marcel Dionne**, Det., L.A., NYR | 18 | 1348 | **1040** | .772 |
| 10. | **Mario Lemieux**, Pit. | 18 | 915 | **1033** | 1.129 |
| 11. | **Joe Sakic**, Que., Col. | 20 | 1378 | **1016** | .737 |
| 12. | **Doug Gilmour**, St.L., Cgy., Tor., N.J., Chi., Buf., Mtl. | 20 | 1474 | **964** | .654 |
| 13. | **Jaromir Jagr**, Pit., Wsh., NYR | 17 | 1273 | **953** | .749 |
| 14. | **Al MacInnis**, Cgy., St.L. | 23 | 1416 | **934** | .660 |
| 15. | **Larry Murphy**, L.A., Wsh., Min., Pit., Tor., Det. | 21 | 1615 | **929** | .575 |
| 16. | **Stan Mikita**, Chi. | 22 | 1394 | **926** | .664 |
| 17. | **Bryan Trottier**, NYI, Pit. | 18 | 1279 | **901** | .704 |
| * 18. | **Mark Recchi**, Pit., Phi., Mtl., Car., Atl., T.B., Bos. | 20 | 1490 | **897** | .602 |
| 19. | **Phil Housley**, Buf., Wpg., St.L., Cgy., N.J., Wsh., Chi., Tor. | 21 | 1495 | **894** | .598 |
| 20. | **Dale Hawerchuk**, Wpg., Buf., St.L., Phi. | 16 | 1188 | **891** | .750 |
| 21. | **Phil Esposito**, Chi., Bos., NYR | 18 | 1282 | **873** | .681 |
| 22. | **Denis Savard**, Chi., Mtl., T.B. | 17 | 1196 | **865** | .723 |
| 23. | **Bobby Clarke**, Phi. | 15 | 1144 | **852** | .745 |
| 24. | **Alex Delvecchio**, Det. | 24 | 1549 | **825** | .533 |
| 25. | **Gilbert Perreault**, Buf. | 17 | 1191 | **814** | .683 |
| 26. | **John Bucyk**, Det., Bos. | 23 | 1540 | **813** | .528 |
| 27. | **Pierre Turgeon**, Buf., NYI, Mtl., St.L., Dal., Col. | 19 | 1294 | **812** | .628 |
| 28. | **Jari Kurri**, Edm., L.A., NYR, Ana., Col. | 17 | 1251 | **797** | .637 |
| 29. | **Guy Lafleur**, Mtl., NYR, Que. | 17 | 1126 | **793** | .704 |
| 30. | **Peter Stastny**, Que., N.J., St.L. | 15 | 977 | **789** | .808 |
| * 31. | **Mike Modano**, Min., Dal. | 20 | 1400 | **786** | .561 |
| * 32. | **Mats Sundin**, Que., Tor., Van. | 18 | 1346 | **785** | .583 |
| 33. | **Brian Leetch**, NYR, Tor., Bos. | 18 | 1205 | **781** | .648 |
| 34. | **Jean Ratelle**, NYR, Bos. | 21 | 1281 | **776** | .606 |
| 35. | **Vincent Damphousse**, Tor., Edm., Mtl., S.J. | 18 | 1378 | **773** | .561 |
| * 36. | **Nicklas Lidstrom**, Det. | 17 | 1330 | **769** | .578 |
| * 37. | **Chris Chelios**, Mtl., Chi., Det. | 25 | 1644 | **763** | .464 |
| 38. | **Bernie Federko**, St.L., Det. | 14 | 1000 | **761** | .761 |
| 39. | **Larry Robinson**, Mtl., L.A. | 20 | 1384 | **750** | .542 |
| 40. | **Denis Potvin**, NYI | 15 | 1060 | **742** | .700 |
| 41. | **Norm Ullman**, Det., Tor. | 20 | 1410 | **739** | .524 |
| 42. | **Bernie Nicholls**, L.A., NYR, Edm., N.J., Chi., S.J. | 18 | 1127 | **734** | .651 |
| * 43. | **Doug Weight**, NYR, Edm., St.L., Car., Ana., NYI | 18 | 1184 | **732** | .618 |
| 44. | **Luc Robitaille**, L.A., Pit., NYR, Det. | 19 | 1431 | **726** | .507 |
| * 45. | **Rod Brind'Amour**, St.L., Phi., Car. | 20 | 1404 | **722** | .514 |
| 46. | **Jean Beliveau**, Mtl. | 20 | 1125 | **712** | .633 |
| 47. | **Scott Stevens**, Wsh., St.L., N.J. | 22 | 1635 | **712** | .435 |
| 48. | **Jeremy Roenick**, Chi., Phx., Phi., L.A., S.J. | 20 | 1363 | **703** | .516 |
| * 49. | **Brendan Shanahan**, N.J., St.L., Hfd., Det., NYR | 21 | 1524 | **698** | .458 |
| 50. | **Dave Andreychuk**, Buf., Tor., N.J., Bos., Col., T.B. | 23 | 1639 | **698** | .426 |
| 51. | **Dale Hunter**, Que., Wsh., Col. | 19 | 1407 | **697** | .495 |
| 52. | **Sergei Fedorov**, Det., Ana., CBJ, Wsh. | 18 | 1248 | **696** | .558 |
| 53. | **Henri Richard**, Mtl. | 20 | 1256 | **688** | .548 |
| 54. | **Brad Park**, NYR, Bos., Det. | 17 | 1113 | **683** | .614 |
| 55. | **Bobby Smith**, Min., Mtl. | 15 | 1077 | **679** | .630 |
| 56. | **Brett Hull**, Cgy., St.L., Dal., Det., Phx. | 20 | 1269 | **650** | .512 |
| 57. | **Bobby Orr**, Bos., Chi. | 12 | 657 | **645** | .982 |
| 58. | **Gary Suter**, Cgy., Chi., S.J. | 17 | 1145 | **641** | .560 |
| 59. | **Dave Taylor**, L.A. | 17 | 1111 | **638** | .574 |
| 60. | **Darryl Sittler**, Tor., Phi., Det. | 15 | 1096 | **637** | .581 |
| 61. | **Borje Salming**, Tor., Det. | 17 | 1148 | **637** | .555 |
| 62. | **Peter Forsberg**, Que., Col., Phi., Nsh. | 13 | 706 | **636** | .901 |
| 63. | **Neal Broten**, Min., Dal., N.J., L.A. | 17 | 1099 | **634** | .577 |
| 64. | **Theoren Fleury**, Cgy., Col., NYR, Chi. | 15 | 1084 | **633** | .584 |
| * 65. | **Teemu Selanne**, Wpg., Ana., S.J., Col. | 16 | 1132 | **633** | .559 |
| 66. | **Mike Gartner**, Wsh., Min., NYR, Tor., Phx. | 19 | 1432 | **627** | .438 |
| 67. | **Andy Bathgate**, NYR, Tor., Det., Pit. | 17 | 1069 | **624** | .584 |
| * 68. | **Sergei Zubov**, NYR, Pit., Dal. | 16 | 1068 | **619** | .580 |
| 69. | **Rod Gilbert**, NYR | 18 | 1065 | **615** | .577 |
| 70. | **Michel Goulet**, Que., Chi. | 15 | 1089 | **604** | .555 |
| 71. | **Kirk Muller**, N.J., Mtl., NYI, Tor., Fla., Dal. | 19 | 1349 | **602** | .446 |
| 72. | **Glenn Anderson**, Edm., Tor., NYR, St.L. | 16 | 1129 | **601** | .532 |

*Anaheim's Scott Niedermayer recorded his 500th career assist on January 2, 2009. Niedermayer led all NHL players with 16 assists that month.*

| | Player | Seasons | Games | Assists | Assists per game |
|---|---|---|---|---|---|
| 73. | **Dino Ciccarelli**, Min., Wsh., Det., T.B., Fla. | 19 | 1232 | **592** | .481 |
| 74. | **Doug Wilson**, Chi., S.J. | 16 | 1024 | **590** | .576 |
| 75. | **Dave Keon**, Tor., Hfd. | 18 | 1296 | **590** | .455 |
| 76. | **Dave Babych**, Wpg., Hfd., Van., Phi., L.A. | 19 | 1195 | **581** | .486 |
| 77. | **Brian Propp**, Phi., Bos., Min., Hfd. | 15 | 1016 | **579** | .570 |
| * 78. | **Joe Thornton**, Bos., S.J. | 11 | 836 | **577** | .690 |
| 79. | **Steve Larmer**, Chi., NYR | 15 | 1006 | **571** | .568 |
| 80. | **Frank Mahovlich**, Tor., Det., Mtl. | 18 | 1181 | **570** | .483 |
| * 81. | **Daniel Alfredsson**, Ott. | 13 | 932 | **566** | .607 |
| 82. | **Craig Janney**, Bos., St.L., S.J., Wpg., Phx., T.B., NYI | 12 | 760 | **563** | .741 |
| 83. | **Cliff Ronning**, St.L., Van., Phx., Nsh., L.A., Min., NYI | 18 | 1137 | **563** | .495 |
| * 84. | **Paul Kariya**, Ana., Col., Nsh., St.L. | 14 | 914 | **562** | .615 |
| 85. | **Joe Nieuwendyk**, Cgy., Dal., N.J., Tor., Fla. | 20 | 1257 | **562** | .447 |
| 86. | **Joe Mullen**, St.L., Cgy., Pit., Bos. | 17 | 1062 | **561** | .528 |
| 87. | **Bobby Hull**, Chi., Wpg., Hfd. | 16 | 1063 | **560** | .527 |
| 88. | **Alexander Mogilny**, Buf., Van., N.J., Tor. | 16 | 990 | **559** | .565 |
| 89. | **Mike Bossy**, NYI | 10 | 752 | **553** | .735 |
| 90. | **Thomas Steen**, Wpg. | 14 | 950 | **553** | .582 |
| 91. | **Ken Linseman**, Phi., Edm., Bos., Tor. | 14 | 860 | **551** | .641 |
| 92. | **Tom Lysiak**, Atl., Chi. | 13 | 919 | **551** | .600 |
| * 93. | **Alex Kovalev**, NYR, Pit., Mtl. | 16 | 1151 | **547** | .475 |
| 94. | **Pat LaFontaine**, NYI, Buf., NYR | 15 | 865 | **545** | .630 |
| 95. | **Mark Howe**, Hfd., Phi., Det. | 16 | 929 | **545** | .587 |
| 96. | **Red Kelly**, Det., Tor. | 20 | 1316 | **542** | .412 |
| 97. | **Pat Verbeek**, N.J., Hfd., NYR, Dal., Det. | 20 | 1424 | **541** | .380 |
| 98. | **Rick Middleton**, NYR, Bos. | 14 | 1005 | **540** | .537 |
| 99. | **Brian Bellows**, Min., Mtl., T.B., Ana., Wsh. | 17 | 1188 | **537** | .452 |
| *100. | **Scott Niedermayer**, N.J., Ana. | 17 | 1183 | **530** | .448 |

# Top 100 Active Assist Leaders

| | Player | Seasons | Games | Assists | Assists per game |
|---|---|---|---|---|---|
| 1. | **Mark Recchi**, Pit., Phi., Mtl., Car., Atl., T.B., Bos. | 20 | 1490 | **897** | .602 |
| 2. | **Mike Modano**, Min., Dal. | 20 | 1400 | **786** | .561 |
| 3. | **Mats Sundin**, Que., Tor., Van. | 18 | 1346 | **785** | .583 |
| 4. | **Nicklas Lidstrom**, Det. | 17 | 1330 | **769** | .578 |
| 5. | **Chris Chelios**, Mtl., Chi., Det. | 25 | 1644 | **763** | .464 |
| 6. | **Doug Weight**, NYR, Edm., St.L., Car., Ana., NYI | 18 | 1184 | **732** | .618 |
| 7. | **Rod Brind'Amour**, St.L., Phi., Car. | 20 | 1404 | **722** | .514 |
| 8. | **Brendan Shanahan**, N.J., St.L., Hfd., Det., NYR | 21 | 1524 | **698** | .458 |
| 9. | **Teemu Selanne**, Wpg., Ana., S.J., Col. | 16 | 1132 | **633** | .559 |
| 10. | **Sergei Zubov**, NYR, Pit., Dal. | 16 | 1068 | **619** | .580 |
| 11. | **Joe Thornton**, Bos., S.J. | 11 | 836 | **577** | .690 |
| 12. | **Daniel Alfredsson**, Ott. | 13 | 932 | **566** | .607 |
| 13. | **Paul Kariya**, Ana., Col., Nsh., St.L. | 14 | 914 | **562** | .615 |
| 14. | **Alex Kovalev**, NYR, Pit., Mtl. | 16 | 1151 | **547** | .475 |
| 15. | **Scott Niedermayer**, N.J., Ana. | 17 | 1183 | **530** | .448 |
| 16. | **Rob Blake**, L.A., Col., S.J. | 19 | 1200 | **514** | .428 |
| 17. | **Mathieu Schneider**, Mtl., NYI, Tor., NYR, L.A., Det., Ana., Atl. | 20 | 1264 | **513** | .406 |
| 18. | **Ray Whitney**, S.J., Edm., Fla., CBJ, Det., Car. | 17 | 992 | **508** | .512 |
| 19. | **Keith Tkachuk**, Wpg., Phx., St.L., Atl. | 17 | 1134 | **508** | .448 |
| 20. | **Vyacheslav Kozlov**, Det., Buf., Atl. | 17 | 1127 | **479** | .425 |
| 21. | **Gary Roberts**, Cgy., Car., Tor., Fla., Pit., T.B. | 22 | 1224 | **472** | .386 |
| 22. | **Michael Nylander**, Hfd., Cgy., T.B., Chi., Wsh., Bos., NYR | 15 | 920 | **470** | .511 |
| 23. | **Marc Savard**, NYR, Cgy., Atl., Bos. | 11 | 741 | **468** | .632 |
| 24. | **Chris Pronger**, Hfd., St.L., Edm., Ana. | 15 | 1022 | **464** | .454 |
| 25. | **Jason Arnott**, Edm., N.J., Dal., Nsh. | 15 | 1036 | **463** | .447 |
| 26. | **Pavol Demitra**, Ott., St.L., L.A., Min., Van. | 15 | 819 | **451** | .551 |
| 27. | **Saku Koivu**, Mtl. | 13 | 792 | **450** | .568 |
| 28. | **Owen Nolan**, Que., Col., S.J., Tor., Phx., Cgy., Min. | 17 | 1127 | **446** | .396 |
| 29. | **Sergei Gonchar**, Wsh., Bos., Pit. | 14 | 929 | **443** | .477 |
| 30. | **Jarome Iginla**, Cgy. | 13 | 942 | **442** | .469 |
| 31. | **Scott Gomez**, N.J., NYR | 9 | 706 | **430** | .609 |
| 32. | **Robert Lang**, L.A., Bos., Pit., Wsh., Det., Chi., Mtl. | 15 | 925 | **422** | .456 |
| 33. | **Roman Hamrlik**, T.B., Edm., NYI, Cgy., Mtl. | 16 | 1157 | **422** | .365 |
| 34. | **Patrik Elias**, N.J. | 13 | 822 | **411** | .500 |
| 35. | **Bill Guerin**, N.J., Edm., Bos., Dal., St.L., S.J., NYI, Pit. | 17 | 1185 | **403** | .340 |
| 36. | **Vaclav Prospal**, Phi., Ott., Fla., T.B., Ana. | 12 | 874 | **401** | .459 |
| 37. | **Darryl Sydor**, L.A., Dal., CBJ, T.B., Pit. | 17 | 1244 | **401** | .322 |
| 38. | **Cory Stillman**, Cgy., St.L., T.B., Car., Ott., Fla. | 10 | 902 | **400** | .443 |
| 39. | **Alex Tanguay**, Col., Cgy., Mtl. | 9 | 659 | **387** | .587 |
| 40. | **Andrew Brunette**, Wsh., Nsh., Atl., Min., Col. | 13 | 868 | **386** | .445 |
| 41. | **Brad Richards**, T.B., Dal. | 8 | 620 | **380** | .613 |
| 42. | **Marian Hossa**, Ott., Atl., Pit., Det. | 11 | 775 | **380** | .490 |
| 43. | **Petr Sykora**, N.J., Ana., NYR, Edm., Pit. | 11 | 921 | **374** | .406 |
| 44. | **Steve Sullivan**, N.J., Tor., Chi., Nsh. | 12 | 764 | **370** | .484 |
| 45. | **Todd Bertuzzi**, NYI, Van., Fla., Det., Ana., Cgy. | 13 | 859 | **369** | .430 |
| 46. | **Vincent Lecavalier**, T.B. | 10 | 787 | **367** | .466 |
| 47. | **Miroslav Satan**, Edm., Buf., NYI, Pit. | 13 | 1012 | **367** | .363 |
| 48. | **Shane Doan**, Wpg., Phx. | 13 | 965 | **365** | .378 |
| 49. | **Brian Rolston**, N.J., Col., Bos., Min. | 14 | 1041 | **365** | .351 |
| 50. | **Tomas Kaberle**, Tor. | 10 | 738 | **360** | .488 |
| 51. | **Daymond Langkow**, T.B., Phi., Phx., Cgy. | 13 | 941 | **359** | .382 |
| 52. | **Brian Rafalski**, N.J., Det. | 9 | 692 | **358** | .517 |
| 53. | **Chris Gratton**, T.B., Phi., Buf., Phx., Col., Fla., CBJ | 15 | 1092 | **354** | .324 |
| 54. | **Pavel Datsyuk**, Det. | 7 | 526 | **351** | .667 |
| 55. | **Henrik Sedin**, Van. | 8 | 646 | **351** | .543 |
| 56. | **Ryan Smyth**, Edm., NYI, Col. | 14 | 920 | **350** | .380 |
| 57. | **Craig Conroy**, Mtl., St.L., Cgy., L.A. | 14 | 928 | **348** | .375 |
| 58. | **Martin St. Louis**, Cgy., T.B. | 10 | 690 | **347** | .503 |
| 59. | **Milan Hejduk**, Col. | 10 | 783 | **345** | .441 |
| 60. | **Viktor Kozlov**, S.J., Fla., N.J., NYI, Wsh. | 14 | 897 | **339** | .378 |
| 61. | **Chris Drury**, Col., Cgy., Buf., NYR | 10 | 791 | **338** | .427 |
| 62. | **Jamie Langenbrunner**, Dal., N.J. | 14 | 884 | **336** | .380 |
| 63. | **Patrick Marleau**, S.J. | 11 | 871 | **334** | .383 |
| 64. | **Wade Redden**, Ott., NYR | 12 | 919 | **332** | .361 |
| 65. | **Brendan Morrison**, N.J., Van., Ana., Dal. | 11 | 755 | **330** | .437 |
| 66. | **Bryan McCabe**, NYI, Van., Chi., Tor., Fla. | 13 | 986 | **327** | .332 |
| 67. | **Patrice Brisebois**, Mtl., Col. | 18 | 1009 | **322** | .319 |
| 68. | **Ed Jovanovski**, Fla., Van., Phx. | 13 | 903 | **315** | .349 |
| 69. | **Radek Dvorak**, Fla., NYR, Edm., St.L. | 13 | 976 | **308** | .316 |

*Detroit's Pavel Datsyuk ranked fifth in the NHL with 65 assists in 2008-09. He collected the 300th of his career on November 28, 2008.*

| | Player | Seasons | Games | Assists | Assists per game |
|---|---|---|---|---|---|
| 70. | **Mike Sillinger**, Det., Ana., Van., Phi., T.B., Fla., Ott., CBJ, Phx., St.L. | 18 | 1049 | **308** | .294 |
| 71. | **Radek Bonk**, Ott., Mtl., Nsh. | 14 | 969 | **303** | .313 |
| 72. | **Kimmo Timonen**, Nsh., Phi. | 10 | 730 | **298** | .408 |
| 73. | **Sergei Samsonov**, Bos., Edm., Mtl., Chi., Car. | 11 | 738 | **294** | .398 |
| 74. | **Todd Marchant**, NYR, Edm., CBJ, Ana. | 15 | 1038 | **292** | .281 |
| 75. | **Michael Peca**, Van., Buf., NYI, Edm., Tor., CBJ | 14 | 864 | **289** | .334 |
| 76. | **Dany Heatley**, Atl., Ott. | 7 | 507 | **283** | .558 |
| 77. | **Daniel Sedin**, Van. | 8 | 642 | **283** | .441 |
| 78. | **Olli Jokinen**, L.A., NYI, Fla., Phx., Cgy. | 11 | 799 | **281** | .352 |
| 79. | **J.P. Dumont**, Chi., Buf., Nsh. | 10 | 678 | **272** | .401 |
| 80. | **Dainius Zubrus**, Phi., Mtl., Wsh., Buf., N.J. | 12 | 853 | **272** | .319 |
| 81. | **Jason Spezza**, Ott. | 6 | 404 | **270** | .668 |
| 82. | **Daniel Briere**, Phx., Buf., Phi. | 11 | 591 | **269** | .455 |
| 83. | **Sidney Crosby**, Pit. | 4 | 290 | **265** | .914 |
| 84. | **Derek Morris**, Cgy., Col., Phx., NYR | 11 | 793 | **264** | .333 |
| 85. | **Ilya Kovalchuk**, Atl. | 7 | 545 | **260** | .477 |
| 86. | **Matt Cullen**, Ana., Fla., Car., NYR | 11 | 799 | **260** | .325 |
| 87. | **Jere Lehtinen**, Dal. | 13 | 817 | **258** | .316 |
| 88. | **Dan Boyle**, Fla., T.B., S.J. | 10 | 600 | **257** | .428 |
| 89. | **Rob Niedermayer**, Fla., Cgy., Ana. | 15 | 1011 | **257** | .254 |
| 90. | **Mike Ribeiro**, Mtl., Dal. | 9 | 515 | **256** | .497 |
| 91. | **Andrei Markov**, Mtl. | 8 | 571 | **255** | .447 |
| 92. | **Dean McAmmond**, Chi., Edm., Phi., Cgy., Col., St.L., Ott., NYI | 16 | 934 | **253** | .271 |
| 93. | **Darcy Tucker**, Mtl., T.B., Tor., Col. | 13 | 876 | **247** | .282 |
| 94. | **Scott Walker**, Van., Nsh., Car. | 14 | 787 | **243** | .309 |
| 95. | **Simon Gagne**, Phi. | 8 | 606 | **242** | .399 |
| 96. | **Bret Hedican**, St.L., Van., Fla., Car., Ana. | 17 | 1039 | **239** | .230 |
| 97. | **Ales Hemsky**, Edm. | 6 | 421 | **238** | .565 |
| 98. | **Tomas Holmstrom**, Det. | 12 | 811 | **235** | .290 |
| 99. | **Lubomir Visnovsky**, L.A., Edm. | 8 | 549 | **232** | .423 |
| 100. | **Mattias Ohlund**, Van. | 11 | 770 | **232** | .301 |

# Top 100 All-Time Point Leaders

* active player

| Player | Seasons | Games | Goals | Assists | Points | Points per game |
|---|---|---|---|---|---|---|
| 1. **Wayne Gretzky**, Edm., L.A., St.L., NYR | 20 | 1487 | 894 | 1963 | **2857** | 1.921 |
| 2. **Mark Messier**, Edm., NYR, Van. | 25 | 1756 | 694 | 1193 | **1887** | 1.075 |
| 3. **Gordie Howe**, Det., Hfd. | 26 | 1767 | 801 | 1049 | **1850** | 1.047 |
| 4. **Ron Francis**, Hfd., Pit., Car., Tor. | 23 | 1731 | 549 | 1249 | **1798** | 1.039 |
| 5. **Marcel Dionne**, Det., L.A., NYR | 18 | 1348 | 731 | 1040 | **1771** | 1.314 |
| 6. **Steve Yzerman**, Det. | 22 | 1514 | 692 | 1063 | **1755** | 1.159 |
| 7. **Mario Lemieux**, Pit. | 18 | 915 | 690 | 1033 | **1723** | 1.883 |
| 8. **Joe Sakic**, Que., Col. | 20 | 1378 | 625 | 1016 | **1641** | 1.191 |
| 9. **Jaromir Jagr**, Pit., Wsh., NYR | 17 | 1273 | 646 | 953 | **1599** | 1.256 |
| 10. **Phil Esposito**, Chi., Bos., NYR | 18 | 1282 | 717 | 873 | **1590** | 1.240 |
| 11. **Raymond Bourque**, Bos., Col. | 22 | 1612 | 410 | 1169 | **1579** | .980 |
| 12. **Paul Coffey**, Edm., Pit., L.A., Det., Hfd., Phi., Chi., Car., Bos. | 21 | 1409 | 396 | 1135 | **1531** | 1.087 |
| 13. **Stan Mikita**, Chi. | 22 | 1394 | 541 | 926 | **1467** | 1.052 |
| * 14. **Mark Recchi**, Pit., Phi., Mtl., Car., Atl., T.B., Bos. | 20 | 1490 | 545 | 897 | **1442** | .968 |
| 15. **Bryan Trottier**, NYI, Pit. | 18 | 1279 | 524 | 901 | **1425** | 1.114 |
| 16. **Adam Oates**, Det., St.L., Bos., Wsh., Phi., Ana., Edm. | 19 | 1337 | 341 | 1079 | **1420** | 1.062 |
| 17. **Doug Gilmour**, St.L., Cgy., Tor., N.J., Chi., Buf., Mtl. | 20 | 1474 | 450 | 964 | **1414** | .959 |
| 18. **Dale Hawerchuk**, Wpg., Buf., St.L., Phi. | 16 | 1188 | 518 | 891 | **1409** | 1.186 |
| 19. **Jari Kurri**, Edm., L.A., NYR, Ana., Col. | 17 | 1251 | 601 | 797 | **1398** | 1.118 |
| 20. **Luc Robitaille**, L.A., Pit., NYR, Det. | 19 | 1431 | 668 | 726 | **1394** | .974 |
| 21. **Brett Hull**, Cgy., St.L., Dal., Det., Phx. | 20 | 1269 | 741 | 650 | **1391** | 1.096 |
| 22. **John Bucyk**, Det., Bos. | 23 | 1540 | 556 | 813 | **1369** | .889 |
| * 23. **Brendan Shanahan**, N.J., St.L., Hfd., Det., NYR | 21 | 1524 | 656 | 698 | **1354** | .888 |
| 24. **Guy Lafleur**, Mtl., NYR, Que. | 17 | 1126 | 560 | 793 | **1353** | 1.202 |
| * 25. **Mats Sundin**, Que., Tor., Van. | 18 | 1346 | 564 | 785 | **1349** | 1.002 |
| 26. **Denis Savard**, Chi., Mtl., T.B. | 17 | 1196 | 473 | 865 | **1338** | 1.119 |
| 27. **Dave Andreychuk**, Buf., Tor., N.J., Bos., Col., T.B. | 23 | 1639 | 640 | 698 | **1338** | .816 |
| 28. **Mike Gartner**, Wsh., Min., NYR, Tor., Phx. | 19 | 1432 | 708 | 627 | **1335** | .932 |
| * 29. **Mike Modano**, Min., Dal. | 20 | 1400 | 543 | 786 | **1329** | .949 |
| 30. **Pierre Turgeon**, Buf., NYI, Mtl., St.L., Dal., Col. | 19 | 1294 | 515 | 812 | **1327** | 1.026 |
| 31. **Gilbert Perreault**, Buf. | 17 | 1191 | 512 | 814 | **1326** | 1.113 |
| 32. **Alex Delvecchio**, Det. | 24 | 1549 | 456 | 825 | **1281** | .827 |
| 33. **Al MacInnis**, Cgy., St.L. | 23 | 1416 | 340 | 934 | **1274** | .900 |
| 34. **Jean Ratelle**, NYR, Bos. | 21 | 1281 | 491 | 776 | **1267** | .989 |
| 35. **Peter Stastny**, Que., N.J., St.L. | 15 | 977 | 450 | 789 | **1239** | 1.268 |
| 36. **Phil Housley**, Buf., Wpg., St.L., Cgy., N.J., Wsh., Chi., Tor. | 21 | 1495 | 338 | 894 | **1232** | .824 |
| 37. **Norm Ullman**, Det., Tor. | 20 | 1410 | 490 | 739 | **1229** | .872 |
| 38. **Jean Beliveau**, Mtl. | 20 | 1125 | 507 | 712 | **1219** | 1.084 |
| 39. **Jeremy Roenick**, Chi., Phx., Phi., L.A., S.J. | 20 | 1363 | 513 | 703 | **1216** | .892 |
| 40. **Larry Murphy**, L.A., Wsh., Min., Pit., Tor., Det. | 21 | 1615 | 287 | 929 | **1216** | .753 |
| * 41. **Teemu Selanne**, Wpg., Ana., S.J., Col. | 16 | 1132 | 579 | 633 | **1212** | 1.071 |
| 42. **Bobby Clarke**, Phi. | 15 | 1144 | 358 | 852 | **1210** | 1.058 |
| 43. **Bernie Nicholls**, L.A., NYR, Edm., N.J., Chi., S.J. | 18 | 1127 | 475 | 734 | **1209** | 1.073 |
| 44. **Vincent Damphousse**, Tor., Edm., Mtl., S.J. | 18 | 1378 | 432 | 773 | **1205** | .874 |
| 45. **Dino Ciccarelli**, Min., Wsh., Det., T.B., Fla. | 19 | 1232 | 608 | 592 | **1200** | .974 |
| 46. **Sergei Fedorov**, Det., Ana., CBJ, Wsh. | 18 | 1248 | 483 | 696 | **1179** | .945 |
| 47. **Bobby Hull**, Chi., Wpg., Hfd. | 16 | 1063 | 610 | 560 | **1170** | 1.101 |
| * 48. **Rod Brind'Amour**, St.L., Phi., Car. | 20 | 1404 | 443 | 722 | **1165** | .830 |
| 49. **Michel Goulet**, Que., Chi. | 15 | 1089 | 548 | 604 | **1152** | 1.058 |
| 50. **Bernie Federko**, St.L., Det. | 14 | 1000 | 369 | 761 | **1130** | 1.130 |
| 51. **Mike Bossy**, NYI | 10 | 752 | 573 | 553 | **1126** | 1.497 |
| 52. **Joe Nieuwendyk**, Cgy., Dal., N.J., Tor., Fla. | 20 | 1257 | 564 | 562 | **1126** | .896 |
| 53. **Darryl Sittler**, Tor., Phi., Det. | 15 | 1096 | 484 | 637 | **1121** | 1.023 |
| 54. **Frank Mahovlich**, Tor., Det., Mtl. | 18 | 1181 | 533 | 570 | **1103** | .934 |
| 55. **Glenn Anderson**, Edm., Tor., NYR, St.L. | 16 | 1129 | 498 | 601 | **1099** | .973 |
| 56. **Theoren Fleury**, Cgy., Col., NYR, Chi. | 15 | 1084 | 455 | 633 | **1088** | 1.004 |
| 57. **Dave Taylor**, L.A. | 17 | 1111 | 431 | 638 | **1069** | .962 |

*Mark Recchi of the Bruins (camped in front of Chicago's Cristobal Huet) moved himself into 14th place on the NHL's all-time scoring list in 2008-09.*

| Player | Seasons | Games | Goals | Assists | Points | Points per game |
|---|---|---|---|---|---|---|
| 58. **Joe Mullen**, St.L., Cgy., Pit., Bos. | 17 | 1062 | 502 | 561 | **1063** | 1.001 |
| 59. **Pat Verbeek**, N.J., Hfd., NYR, Dal., Det. | 20 | 1424 | 522 | 541 | **1063** | .746 |
| 60. **Denis Potvin**, NYI | 15 | 1060 | 310 | 742 | **1052** | .992 |
| 61. **Henri Richard**, Mtl. | 20 | 1256 | 358 | 688 | **1046** | .833 |
| 62. **Bobby Smith**, Min., Mtl. | 15 | 1077 | 357 | 679 | **1036** | .962 |
| * 63. **Keith Tkachuk**, Wpg., Phx., St.L., Atl. | 17 | 1134 | 525 | 508 | **1033** | .911 |
| 64. **Alexander Mogilny**, Buf., Van., N.J., Tor. | 16 | 990 | 473 | 559 | **1032** | 1.042 |
| 65. **Brian Leetch**, NYR, Tor., Bos. | 18 | 1205 | 247 | 781 | **1028** | .853 |
| 66. **Brian Bellows**, Min., Mtl., T.B., Ana., Wsh. | 17 | 1188 | 485 | 537 | **1022** | .860 |
| 67. **Rod Gilbert**, NYR | 18 | 1065 | 406 | 615 | **1021** | .959 |
| 68. **Dale Hunter**, Que., Wsh., Col. | 19 | 1407 | 323 | 697 | **1020** | .725 |
| 69. **Pat LaFontaine**, NYI, Buf., NYR | 15 | 865 | 468 | 545 | **1013** | 1.171 |
| 70. **Steve Larmer**, Chi., NYR | 15 | 1006 | 441 | 571 | **1012** | 1.006 |
| * 71. **Doug Weight**, NYR, Edm., St.L., Car., Ana., NYI | 18 | 1184 | 275 | 732 | **1007** | .851 |
| 72. **Lanny McDonald**, Tor., Col., Cgy. | 16 | 1111 | 500 | 506 | **1006** | .905 |
| 73. **Brian Propp**, Phi., Bos., Min., Hfd. | 15 | 1016 | 425 | 579 | **1004** | .988 |
| * 74. **Nicklas Lidstrom**, Det. | 17 | 1330 | 228 | 769 | **997** | .750 |
| 75. **Rick Middleton**, NYR, Bos. | 14 | 1005 | 448 | 540 | **988** | .983 |
| 76. **Dave Keon**, Tor., Hfd. | 18 | 1296 | 396 | 590 | **986** | .761 |
| 77. **Andy Bathgate**, NYR, Tor., Det., Pit. | 17 | 1069 | 349 | 624 | **973** | .910 |
| 78. **Maurice Richard**, Mtl. | 18 | 978 | 544 | 421 | **965** | .987 |
| 79. **Kirk Muller**, N.J., Mtl., NYI, Tor., Fla., Dal. | 19 | 1349 | 357 | 602 | **959** | .711 |
| 80. **Larry Robinson**, Mtl., L.A. | 20 | 1384 | 208 | 750 | **958** | .692 |
| 81. **Rick Tocchet**, Phi., Pit., L.A., Bos., Wsh., Phx. | 18 | 1144 | 440 | 512 | **952** | .832 |
| * 82. **Chris Chelios**, Mtl., Chi., Det. | 25 | 1644 | 185 | 763 | **948** | .577 |
| * 83. **Paul Kariya**, Ana., Col., Nsh., St.L. | 14 | 914 | 384 | 562 | **946** | 1.035 |
| * 84. **Alex Kovalev**, NYR, Pit., Mtl. | 16 | 1151 | 394 | 547 | **941** | .818 |
| 85. **Steve Thomas**, Tor., Chi., NYI, N.J., Ana., Det. | 20 | 1235 | 421 | 512 | **933** | .755 |
| 86. **Neal Broten**, Min., Dal., N.J., L.A. | 17 | 1099 | 289 | 634 | **923** | .840 |
| * 87. **Daniel Alfredsson**, Ott. | 13 | 932 | 355 | 566 | **921** | .988 |
| 88. **Bobby Orr**, Bos., Chi. | 12 | 657 | 270 | 645 | **915** | 1.393 |
| 89. **Gary Roberts**, Cgy., Car., Tor., Fla., Pit., T.B. | 22 | 1224 | 438 | 472 | **910** | .743 |
| 90. **Scott Stevens**, Wsh., St.L., N.J. | 22 | 1635 | 196 | 712 | **908** | .555 |
| 91. **Tony Amonte**, NYR, Chi., Phx., Phi., Cgy. | 16 | 1174 | 416 | 484 | **900** | .767 |
| 92. **Ray Ferraro**, Hfd., NYI, NYR, L.A., Atl., St.L. | 18 | 1258 | 408 | 490 | **898** | .714 |
| 93. **Brad Park**, NYR, Bos., Det. | 17 | 1113 | 213 | 683 | **896** | .805 |
| 94. **Peter Bondra**, Wsh., Ott., Atl., Chi. | 16 | 1081 | 503 | 389 | **892** | .825 |
| 95. **Butch Goring**, L.A., NYI, Bos. | 16 | 1107 | 375 | 513 | **888** | .802 |
| 96. **Peter Forsberg**, Que., Col., Phi., Nsh. | 13 | 706 | 249 | 636 | **885** | 1.254 |
| 97. **Bill Barber**, Phi. | 14 | 903 | 420 | 463 | **883** | .978 |
| 98. **Dennis Maruk**, Cal., Cle., Min., Wsh. | 14 | 888 | 356 | 522 | **878** | .989 |
| 99. **Markus Naslund**, Pit., Van., NYR | 15 | 1117 | 395 | 474 | **869** | .778 |
| 100. **Cliff Ronning**, St.L., Van., Phx., Nsh., L.A., Min., NYI | 18 | 1137 | 306 | 563 | **869** | .764 |

# Top 100 Active Points Leaders

*With 16 goals and 43 assists in 2008-09, Nicklas Lidstrom ranked among the NHL's top-scoring defenseman and pushed his career total to 997 points.*

| | Player | Seasons | Games | Goals | Assists | Points | Points per game |
|---|---|---|---|---|---|---|---|
| 1. | **Mark Recchi**, Pit., Phi., Mtl., Car., Atl., T.B., Bos. | 20 | 1490 | 545 | 897 | **1442** | .968 |
| 2. | **Brendan Shanahan**, N.J., St.L., Hfd., Det., NYR | 21 | 1524 | 656 | 698 | **1354** | .888 |
| 3. | **Mats Sundin**, Que., Tor., Van. | 18 | 1346 | 564 | 785 | **1349** | 1.002 |
| 4. | **Mike Modano**, Min., Dal. | 20 | 1400 | 543 | 786 | **1329** | .949 |
| 5. | **Teemu Selanne**, Wpg., Ana., S.J., Col. | 16 | 1132 | 579 | 633 | **1212** | 1.071 |
| 6. | **Rod Brind'Amour**, St.L., Phi., Car. | 20 | 1404 | 443 | 722 | **1165** | .830 |
| 7. | **Keith Tkachuk**, Wpg., Phx., St.L., Atl. | 17 | 1134 | 525 | 508 | **1033** | .911 |
| 8. | **Doug Weight**, NYR, Edm., St.L., Car., Ana., NYI | 18 | 1184 | 275 | 732 | **1007** | .851 |
| 9. | **Nicklas Lidstrom**, Det. | 17 | 1330 | 228 | 769 | **997** | .750 |
| 10. | **Chris Chelios**, Mtl., Chi., Det. | 25 | 1644 | 185 | 763 | **948** | .577 |
| 11. | **Paul Kariya**, Ana., Col., Nsh., St.L. | 14 | 914 | 384 | 562 | **946** | 1.035 |
| 12. | **Alex Kovalev**, NYR, Pit., Mtl. | 16 | 1151 | 394 | 547 | **941** | .818 |
| 13. | **Daniel Alfredsson**, Ott. | 13 | 932 | 355 | 566 | **921** | .988 |
| 14. | **Owen Nolan**, Que., Col., S.J., Tor., Phx., Cgy., Min. | 17 | 1127 | 406 | 446 | **852** | .756 |
| 15. | **Jarome Iginla**, Cgy. | 13 | 942 | 409 | 442 | **851** | .903 |
| 16. | **Joe Thornton**, Bos., S.J. | 11 | 836 | 265 | 577 | **842** | 1.007 |
| 17. | **Jason Arnott**, Edm., N.J., Dal., Nsh. | 15 | 1036 | 364 | 463 | **827** | .798 |
| 18. | **Vyacheslav Kozlov**, Det., Buf., Atl. | 17 | 1127 | 348 | 479 | **827** | .734 |
| 19. | **Ray Whitney**, S.J., Edm., Fla., CBJ, Det., Car. | 17 | 992 | 303 | 508 | **811** | .818 |
| 20. | **Bill Guerin**, N.J., Edm., Bos., Dal., St.L., S.J., NYI, Pit. | 17 | 1185 | 408 | 403 | **811** | .684 |
| 21. | **Sergei Zubov**, NYR, Pit., Dal. | 16 | 1068 | 152 | 619 | **771** | .722 |
| 22. | **Pavol Demitra**, Ott., St.L., L.A., Min., Van. | 15 | 819 | 301 | 451 | **752** | .918 |
| 23. | **Rob Blake**, L.A., Col., S.J. | 19 | 1200 | 233 | 514 | **747** | .623 |
| 24. | **Mathieu Schneider**, Mtl., NYI, Tor., NYR, L.A., Det., Ana., Atl. | 20 | 1264 | 221 | 513 | **734** | .581 |
| 25. | **Miroslav Satan**, Edm., Buf., NYI, Pit. | 13 | 1012 | 354 | 367 | **721** | .712 |
| 26. | **Marian Hossa**, Ott., Atl., Pit., Det. | 11 | 775 | 339 | 380 | **719** | .928 |
| 27. | **Patrik Elias**, N.J. | 13 | 822 | 295 | 411 | **706** | .859 |
| 28. | **Scott Niedermayer**, N.J., Ana. | 17 | 1183 | 162 | 530 | **692** | .585 |
| 29. | **Michael Nylander**, Hfd., Cgy., T.B., Chi., Wsh., Bos., NYR | 15 | 920 | 209 | 470 | **679** | .738 |
| 30. | **Petr Sykora**, N.J., Ana., NYR, Edm., Pit. | 11 | 921 | 300 | 374 | **674** | .732 |
| 31. | **Robert Lang**, L.A., Bos., Pit., Wsh., Det., Chi., Mtl. | 15 | 925 | 252 | 422 | **674** | .729 |
| 32. | **Vincent Lecavalier**, T.B. | 10 | 787 | 302 | 367 | **669** | .850 |
| 33. | **Brian Rolston**, N.J., Col., Bos., Min. | 14 | 1041 | 301 | 365 | **666** | .640 |
| 34. | **Marc Savard**, NYR, Cgy., Atl., Bos. | 11 | 741 | 195 | 468 | **663** | .895 |
| 35. | **Ryan Smyth**, Edm., NYI, Col. | 14 | 920 | 310 | 350 | **660** | .717 |
| 36. | **Milan Hejduk**, Col. | 10 | 783 | 312 | 345 | **657** | .839 |
| 37. | **Cory Stillman**, Cgy., St.L., T.B., Car., Ott., Fla. | 10 | 902 | 251 | 400 | **651** | .722 |
| 38. | **Saku Koivu**, Mtl. | 13 | 792 | 191 | 450 | **641** | .809 |
| 39. | **Sergei Gonchar**, Wsh., Bos., Pit. | 14 | 929 | 191 | 443 | **634** | .682 |
| 40. | **Todd Bertuzzi**, NYI, Van., Fla., Det., Ana., Cgy. | 13 | 859 | 255 | 369 | **624** | .726 |
| 41. | **Shane Doan**, Wpg., Phx. | 13 | 965 | 258 | 365 | **623** | .646 |
| 42. | **Patrick Marleau**, S.J. | 11 | 871 | 276 | 334 | **610** | .700 |
| 43. | **Steve Sullivan**, N.J., Tor., Chi., Nsh. | 12 | 764 | 239 | 370 | **609** | .797 |
| 44. | **Chris Pronger**, Hfd., St.L., Edm., Ana. | 15 | 1022 | 142 | 464 | **606** | .593 |
| 45. | **Daymond Langkow**, T.B., Phi., Phx., Cgy. | 13 | 941 | 245 | 359 | **604** | .642 |
| 46. | **Andrew Brunette**, Wsh., Nsh., Atl., Min., Col. | 13 | 868 | 213 | 386 | **599** | .690 |
| 47. | **Vaclav Prospal**, Phi., Ott., Fla., T.B., Ana. | 12 | 874 | 198 | 401 | **599** | .685 |
| 48. | **Martin St. Louis**, Cgy., T.B. | 10 | 690 | 238 | 347 | **585** | .848 |
| 49. | **Alex Tanguay**, Col., Cgy., Mtl. | 9 | 659 | 193 | 387 | **580** | .880 |
| 50. | **Scott Gomez**, N.J., NYR | 9 | 706 | 148 | 430 | **578** | .819 |
| 51. | **Chris Drury**, Col., Cgy., Buf., NYR | 10 | 791 | 240 | 338 | **578** | .731 |
| 52. | **Chris Gratton**, T.B., Phi., Buf., Phx., Col., Fla., CBJ | 15 | 1092 | 214 | 354 | **568** | .520 |
| 53. | **Roman Hamrlik**, T.B., Edm., NYI, Cgy., Mtl. | 16 | 1157 | 142 | 422 | **564** | .487 |
| 54. | **Ilya Kovalchuk**, Atl. | 7 | 545 | 297 | 260 | **557** | 1.022 |
| 55. | **Brad Richards**, T.B., Dal. | 8 | 620 | 168 | 380 | **548** | .884 |
| 56. | **Mike Sillinger**, Det., Ana., Van., Phi., T.B., Fla., Ott., CBJ, Phx., St.L. | 18 | 1049 | 240 | 308 | **548** | .522 |
| 57. | **Jamie Langenbrunner**, Dal., N.J. | 14 | 884 | 209 | 336 | **545** | .617 |
| 58. | **Dany Heatley**, Atl., Ott. | 7 | 507 | 260 | 283 | **543** | 1.071 |
| 59. | **Viktor Kozlov**, S.J., Fla., N.J., NYI, Wsh. | 14 | 897 | 198 | 339 | **537** | .599 |
| 60. | **Craig Conroy**, Mtl., St.L., Cgy., L.A. | 14 | 928 | 177 | 348 | **525** | .566 |
| 61. | **Pavel Datsyuk**, Det. | 7 | 526 | 171 | 351 | **522** | .992 |
| 62. | **Olli Jokinen**, L.A., NYI, Fla., Phx., Cgy. | 11 | 799 | 237 | 281 | **518** | .648 |
| 63. | **Brendan Morrison**, N.J., Van., Ana., Dal. | 11 | 755 | 175 | 330 | **505** | .669 |
| 64. | **Sergei Samsonov**, Bos., Edm., Mtl., Chi., Car. | 11 | 738 | 208 | 294 | **502** | .680 |
| 65. | **Radek Dvorak**, Fla., NYR, Edm., St.L. | 13 | 976 | 194 | 308 | **502** | .514 |
| 66. | **Darryl Sydor**, L.A., Dal., CBJ, T.B., Pit. | 17 | 1244 | 98 | 401 | **499** | .401 |
| 67. | **Jere Lehtinen**, Dal. | 13 | 817 | 239 | 258 | **497** | .608 |
| 68. | **Radek Bonk**, Ott., Mtl., Nsh. | 14 | 969 | 194 | 303 | **497** | .513 |
| 69. | **Simon Gagne**, Phi. | 8 | 606 | 242 | 242 | **484** | .799 |
| 70. | **Daniel Briere**, Phx., Buf., Phi. | 11 | 591 | 204 | 269 | **473** | .800 |
| 71. | **Todd Marchant**, NYR, Edm., CBJ, Ana. | 15 | 1038 | 176 | 292 | **468** | .451 |
| 72. | **Michael Peca**, Van., Buf., NYI, Edm., Tor., CBJ | 14 | 864 | 176 | 289 | **465** | .538 |
| 73. | **Daniel Sedin**, Van. | 8 | 642 | 179 | 283 | **462** | .720 |
| 74. | **Henrik Sedin**, Van. | 8 | 646 | 109 | 351 | **460** | .712 |
| 75. | **J.P. Dumont**, Chi., Buf., Nsh. | 10 | 678 | 187 | 272 | **459** | .677 |
| 76. | **Bryan McCabe**, NYI, Van., Chi., Tor., Fla. | 13 | 986 | 130 | 327 | **457** | .463 |
| 77. | **Darcy Tucker**, Mtl., T.B., Tor., Col. | 13 | 876 | 205 | 247 | **452** | .516 |
| 78. | **Fredrik Modin**, Tor., T.B., CBJ | 12 | 814 | 220 | 221 | **441** | .542 |
| 79. | **Dainius Zubrus**, Phi., Mtl., Wsh., Buf., N.J. | 12 | 853 | 166 | 272 | **438** | .513 |
| 80. | **Marian Gaborik**, Min. | 8 | 502 | 219 | 218 | **437** | .871 |
| 81. | **Wade Redden**, Ott., NYR | 12 | 919 | 104 | 332 | **436** | .474 |
| 82. | **Tomas Kaberle**, Tor. | 10 | 738 | 73 | 360 | **433** | .587 |
| 83. | **Ed Jovanovski**, Fla., Van., Phx. | 13 | 903 | 118 | 315 | **433** | .480 |
| 84. | **Dean McAmmond**, Chi., Edm., Phi., Cgy., Col., St.L., Ott., NYI | 16 | 934 | 178 | 253 | **431** | .461 |
| 85. | **Marco Sturm**, S.J., Bos. | 11 | 779 | 212 | 217 | **429** | .551 |
| 86. | **Mike Knuble**, Det., NYR, Bos., Phi. | 12 | 820 | 215 | 214 | **429** | .523 |
| 87. | **Rob Niedermayer**, Fla., Cgy., Ana. | 15 | 1011 | 171 | 257 | **428** | .423 |
| 88. | **Brian Rafalski**, N.J., Det. | 9 | 692 | 67 | 358 | **425** | .614 |
| 89. | **Tomas Holmstrom**, Det. | 12 | 811 | 189 | 235 | **424** | .523 |
| 90. | **Alex Ovechkin**, Wsh. | 4 | 324 | 219 | 201 | **420** | 1.296 |
| 91. | **Patrice Brisebois**, Mtl., Col. | 18 | 1009 | 98 | 322 | **420** | .416 |
| 92. | **Jason Spezza**, Ott. | 6 | 404 | 148 | 270 | **418** | 1.035 |
| 93. | **Matt Cullen**, Ana., Fla., Car., NYR | 11 | 799 | 153 | 260 | **413** | .517 |
| 94. | **Henrik Zetterberg**, Det. | 6 | 432 | 183 | 222 | **405** | .938 |
| 95. | **Jason Blake**, L.A., NYI, Tor. | 10 | 668 | 174 | 227 | **401** | .600 |
| 96. | **Sidney Crosby**, Pit. | 4 | 290 | 132 | 265 | **397** | 1.369 |
| 97. | **Martin Havlat**, Ott., Chi. | 8 | 470 | 169 | 227 | **396** | .843 |
| 98. | **Brenden Morrow**, Dal. | 9 | 591 | 173 | 216 | **389** | .658 |
| 99. | **Scott Walker**, Van., Nsh., Car. | 14 | 787 | 146 | 243 | **389** | .494 |
| 100. | **Kimmo Timonen**, Nsh., Phi. | 10 | 730 | 90 | 298 | **388** | .532 |

# Top 100 All-Time Games Played Leaders

* active player

| | Player | Seasons | Games Played |
|---|---|---|---|
| 1. | **Gordie Howe**, Det., Hfd. | 26 | **1767** |
| 2. | **Mark Messier**, Edm., NYR, Van. | 25 | **1756** |
| 3. | **Ron Francis**, Hfd., Pit., Car., Tor. | 23 | **1731** |
| * 4. | **Chris Chelios**, Mtl., Chi., Det. | 25 | **1644** |
| 5. | **Dave Andreychuk**, Buf., Tor., N.J., Bos., Col., T.B. | 23 | **1639** |
| 6. | **Scott Stevens**, Wsh., St.L., N.J. | 22 | **1635** |
| 7. | **Larry Murphy**, L.A., Wsh., Min., Pit., Tor., Det. | 21 | **1615** |
| 8. | **Raymond Bourque**, Bos., Col. | 22 | **1612** |
| 9. | **Alex Delvecchio**, Det. | 24 | **1549** |
| 10. | **John Bucyk**, Det., Bos. | 23 | **1540** |
| * 11. | **Brendan Shanahan**, N.J., St.L., Hfd., Det., NYR | 21 | **1524** |
| 12. | **Steve Yzerman**, Det. | 22 | **1514** |
| 13. | **Phil Housley**, Buf., Wpg., St.L., Cgy., N.J., Wsh., Chi., Tor. | 21 | **1495** |
| * 14. | **Mark Recchi**, Pit., Phi., Mtl., Car., Atl., T.B., Bos. | 20 | **1490** |
| 15. | **Wayne Gretzky**, Edm., L.A., St.L., NYR | 20 | **1487** |
| 16. | **Doug Gilmour**, St.L., Cgy., Tor., N.J., Chi., Buf., Mtl. | 20 | **1474** |
| 17. | **Glen Wesley**, Bos., Hfd., Car., Tor. | 20 | **1457** |
| 18. | **Tim Horton**, Tor., NYR, Pit., Buf. | 24 | **1446** |
| 19. | **Mike Gartner**, Wsh., Min., NYR, Tor., Phx. | 19 | **1432** |
| 20. | **Luc Robitaille**, L.A., Pit., NYR, Det. | 19 | **1431** |
| | **Scott Mellanby**, Phi., Edm., Fla., St.L., Atl. | 21 | **1431** |
| 22. | **Pat Verbeek**, N.J., Hfd., NYR, Dal., Det. | 20 | **1424** |
| 23. | **Luke Richardson**, Tor., Edm., Phi., CBJ, T.B., Ott. | 21 | **1417** |
| 24. | **Al MacInnis**, Cgy., St.L. | 23 | **1416** |
| 25. | **Harry Howell**, NYR, Oak., Cal., L.A. | 21 | **1411** |
| 26. | **Norm Ullman**, Det., Tor. | 20 | **1410** |
| 27. | **Paul Coffey**, Edm., Pit., L.A., Det., Hfd., Phi., Chi., Car., Bos. | 21 | **1409** |
| 28. | **Dale Hunter**, Que., Wsh., Col. | 19 | **1407** |
| * 29. | **Rod Brind'Amour**, St.L., Phi., Car. | 20 | **1404** |
| * 30. | **Mike Modano**, Min., Dal. | 20 | **1400** |
| 31. | **Stan Mikita**, Chi. | 22 | **1394** |
| 32. | **Doug Mohns**, Bos., Chi., Min., Atl., Wsh. | 22 | **1390** |
| 33. | **Larry Robinson**, Mtl., L.A. | 20 | **1384** |
| 34. | **Trevor Linden**, Van., NYI, Mtl., Wsh. | 19 | **1382** |
| 35. | **Vincent Damphousse**, Tor., Edm., Mtl., S.J. | 18 | **1378** |
| | **Joe Sakic**, Que., Col. | 20 | **1378** |
| | **Dean Prentice**, NYR, Bos., Det., Pit., Min. | 22 | **1378** |
| 38. | **Teppo Numminen**, Wpg., Phx., Dal., Buf. | 20 | **1372** |
| 39. | **Jeremy Roenick**, Chi., Phx., Phi., L.A., S.J. | 20 | **1363** |
| 40. | **Ron Stewart**, Tor., Bos., St.L., NYR, Van., NYI | 21 | **1353** |
| 41. | **Kirk Muller**, N.J., Mtl., NYI, Tor., Fla., Dal. | 19 | **1349** |
| 42. | **Marcel Dionne**, Det., L.A., NYR | 18 | **1348** |
| * 43. | **Mats Sundin**, Que., Tor., Van. | 18 | **1346** |
| 44. | **Adam Oates**, Det., St.L., Bos., Wsh., Phi., Ana., Edm. | 19 | **1337** |
| * 45. | **Nicklas Lidstrom**, Det. | 17 | **1330** |
| 46. | **Guy Carbonneau**, Mtl., St.L., Dal. | 19 | **1318** |
| 47. | **Red Kelly**, Det., Tor. | 20 | **1316** |
| 48. | **Bobby Holik**, Hfd., N.J., NYR, Atl. | 18 | **1314** |
| 49. | **Dave Keon**, Tor., Hfd. | 18 | **1296** |
| 50. | **Pierre Turgeon**, Buf., NYI, Mtl., St.L., Dal., Col. | 19 | **1294** |
| 51. | **Ken Daneyko**, N.J. | 20 | **1283** |
| 52. | **Phil Esposito**, Chi., Bos., NYR | 18 | **1282** |
| 53. | **Jean Ratelle**, NYR, Bos. | 21 | **1281** |
| 54. | **James Patrick**, NYR, Hfd., Cgy., Buf. | 21 | **1280** |
| 55. | **Bryan Trottier**, NYI, Pit. | 18 | **1279** |
| 56. | **Jaromir Jagr**, Pit., Wsh., NYR | 17 | **1273** |
| | **Martin Gelinas**, Edm., Que., Van., Car., Cgy., Fla., Nsh. | 19 | **1273** |
| 58. | **Brett Hull**, Cgy., St.L., Dal., Det., Phx. | 20 | **1269** |
| * 59. | **Mathieu Schneider**, Mtl., NYI, Tor., NYR, L.A., Det., Ana., Atl. | 20 | **1264** |
| 60. | **Ray Ferraro**, Hfd., NYI, NYR, L.A., Atl., St.L. | 18 | **1258** |
| 61. | **Joe Nieuwendyk**, Cgy., Dal., N.J., Tor., Fla. | 20 | **1257** |
| 62. | **Craig Ludwig**, Mtl., NYI, Min., Dal. | 17 | **1256** |
| | **Henri Richard**, Mtl. | 20 | **1256** |
| 64. | **Kevin Lowe**, Edm., NYR. | 19 | **1254** |
| 65. | **Jari Kurri**, Edm., L.A., NYR, Ana., Col. | 17 | **1251** |
| 66. | **Sergei Fedorov**, Det., Ana., CBJ, Wsh. | 18 | **1248** |
| | **Bill Gadsby**, Chi., NYR, Det. | 20 | **1248** |
| * 68. | **Darryl Sydor**, L.A., Dal., CBJ, T.B., Pit. | 17 | **1244** |
| | **Allan Stanley**, NYR, Chi., Bos., Tor., Phi. | 21 | **1244** |
| 70. | **Steve Thomas**, Tor., Chi., NYI, N.J., Ana., Det. | 20 | **1235** |
| 71. | **Dino Ciccarelli**, Min., Wsh., Det., T.B., Fla. | 19 | **1232** |
| 72. | **Ed Westfall**, Bos., NYI | 18 | **1226** |
| 73. | **Gary Roberts**, Cgy., Car., Tor., Fla., Pit., T.B. | 22 | **1224** |
| 74. | **Brad McCrimmon**, Bos., Phi., Cgy., Det., Hfd., Phx. | 18 | **1222** |
| 75. | **Eric Nesterenko**, Tor., Chi. | 21 | **1219** |
| 76. | **Claude Lemieux**, Mtl., N.J., Col., Phx., Dal., S.J. | 21 | **1215** |
| 77. | **Marcel Pronovost**, Det., Tor. | 21 | **1206** |
| 78. | **Brian Leetch**, NYR, Tor., Bos. | 18 | **1205** |
| * 79. | **Rob Blake**, L.A., Col., S.J. | 19 | **1200** |
| 80. | **Denis Savard**, Chi., Mtl., T.B. | 17 | **1196** |

*Mike Modano played 80 games in 2008-09, upping his career total to 1,400. Among players who have spent their entire career with one franchise, only Alex Delvecchio and Steve Yzerman have played more games.*

| | Player | Seasons | Games Played |
|---|---|---|---|
| 81. | **Dave Babych**, Wpg., Hfd., Van., Phi., L.A. | 19 | **1195** |
| 82. | **John MacLean**, N.J., S.J., NYR, Dal. | 18 | **1194** |
| 83. | **Gilbert Perreault**, Buf. | 17 | **1191** |
| | **Marc Bergevin**, Chi., NYI, Hfd., T.B., Det., St.L., Pit., Van. | 20 | **1191** |
| 85. | **Dale Hawerchuk**, Wpg., Buf., St.L., Phi. | 16 | **1188** |
| | **Brian Bellows**, Min., Mtl., T.B., Ana., Wsh. | 17 | **1188** |
| | **Kevin Dineen**, Hfd., Phi., Car., Ott., CBJ | 19 | **1188** |
| 88. | **George Armstrong**, Tor. | 21 | **1187** |
| * 89. | **Bill Guerin**, N.J., Edm., Bos., Dal., St.L., S.J., NYI, Pit. | 17 | **1185** |
| * 90. | **Doug Weight**, NYR, Edm., St.L., Car., Ana., NYI. | 18 | **1184** |
| * 91. | **Scott Niedermayer**, N.J., Ana. | 17 | **1183** |
| 92. | **Kelly Buchberger**, Edm., Atl., L.A., Phx., Pit. | 18 | **1182** |
| 93. | **Scott Young**, Hfd., Pit., Que., Col., Ana., St.L., Dal. | 17 | **1181** |
| | **Frank Mahovlich**, Tor., Det., Mtl. | 18 | **1181** |
| 95. | **Bob Carpenter**, Wsh., NYR, L.A., Bos., N.J. | 19 | **1178** |
| 96. | **Don Marshall**, Mtl., NYR, Buf., Tor. | 19 | **1176** |
| 97. | **Tony Amonte**, NYR, Chi., Phx., Phi., Cgy. | 16 | **1174** |
| 98. | **Sylvain Cote**, Hfd., Wsh., Tor., Chi., Dal. | 19 | **1171** |
| 99. | **Mike Keane**, Mtl., Col., NYR, Dal., St.L., Van. | 16 | **1161** |
| 100. | **Bob Gainey**, Mtl. | 16 | **1160** |

# Top 100 Active Games Played Leaders

| | Player | Seasons | Games Played |
|---|---|---|---|
| 1. | **Chris Chelios**, Mtl., Chi., Det. | 25 | **1644** |
| 2. | **Brendan Shanahan**, N.J., St.L., Hfd., Det., NYR | 21 | **1524** |
| 3. | **Mark Recchi**, Pit., Phi., Mtl., Car., Atl., T.B., Bos. | 20 | **1490** |
| 4. | **Rod Brind'Amour**, St.L., Phi., Car. | 20 | **1404** |
| 5. | **Mike Modano**, Min., Dal. | 20 | **1400** |
| 6. | **Mats Sundin**, Que., Tor., Van. | 18 | **1346** |
| 7. | **Nicklas Lidstrom**, Det. | 17 | **1330** |
| 8. | **Mathieu Schneider**, Mtl., NYI, Tor., NYR, L.A., Det., Ana., Atl. | 20 | **1264** |
| 9. | **Darryl Sydor**, L.A., Dal., CBJ, T.B., Pit. | 17 | **1244** |
| 10. | **Rob Blake**, L.A., Col., S.J. | 19 | **1200** |
| 11. | **Bill Guerin**, N.J., Edm., Bos., Dal., St.L., S.J., NYI, Pit. | 17 | **1185** |
| 12. | **Doug Weight**, NYR, Edm., St.L., Car., Ana., NYI | 18 | **1184** |
| 13. | **Scott Niedermayer**, N.J., Ana. | 17 | **1183** |
| 14. | **Roman Hamrlik**, T.B., Edm., NYI, Cgy., Mtl. | 16 | **1157** |
| 15. | **Alex Kovalev**, NYR, Pit., Mtl. | 16 | **1151** |
| 16. | **Keith Tkachuk**, Wpg., Phx., St.L., Atl. | 17 | **1134** |
| 17. | **Teemu Selanne**, Wpg., Ana., S.J., Col. | 16 | **1132** |
| 18. | **Owen Nolan**, Que., Col., S.J., Tor., Phx., Cgy., Min. | 17 | **1127** |
| | **Vyacheslav Kozlov**, Det., Buf., Atl. | 17 | **1127** |
| 20. | **Chris Gratton**, T.B., Phi., Buf., Phx., Col., Fla., CBJ | 15 | **1092** |
| 21. | **Mike Sillinger**, Det., Ana., Van., Phi., T.B., Fla., Ott., CBJ, Phx., St.L. | 18 | **1049** |
| 22. | **Brian Rolston**, N.J., Col., Bos., Min. | 14 | **1041** |
| 23. | **Adam Foote**, Que., Col., CBJ | 17 | **1040** |
| 24. | **Bret Hedican**, St.L., Van., Fla., Car., Ana. | 17 | **1039** |
| 25. | **Todd Marchant**, NYR, Edm., CBJ, Ana. | 15 | **1038** |
| 26. | **Jason Arnott**, Edm., N.J., Dal., Nsh. | 15 | **1036** |
| 27. | **Kris Draper**, Wpg., Det. | 18 | **1029** |
| 28. | **Chris Pronger**, Hfd., St.L., Edm., Ana. | 15 | **1022** |
| 29. | **Kirk Maltby**, Edm., Det. | 15 | **1020** |
| 30. | **Sean O'Donnell**, L.A., Min., N.J., Bos., Phx., Ana. | 14 | **1014** |
| 31. | **Miroslav Satan**, Edm., Buf., NYI, Pit. | 13 | **1012** |
| 32. | **Rob Niedermayer**, Fla., Cgy., Ana. | 15 | **1011** |
| 33. | **Patrice Brisebois**, Mtl., Col. | 18 | **1009** |
| 34. | **Jason Smith**, N.J., Tor., Edm., Phi., Ott. | 14 | **1008** |
| 35. | **Ian Laperriere**, St.L., NYR, L.A., Col. | 15 | **1001** |
| | **Brad May**, Buf., Van., Phx., Col., Ana., Tor. | 17 | **1001** |
| 37. | **Martin Brodeur**, N.J. | 16 | **999** |
| 38. | **Ray Whitney**, S.J., Edm., Fla., CBJ, Det., Car. | 17 | **992** |
| 39. | **Donald Brashear**, Mtl., Van., Phi., Wsh. | 15 | **989** |
| 40. | **Bryan McCabe**, NYI, Van., Chi., Tor., Fla. | 13 | **986** |
| 41. | **Radek Dvorak**, Fla., NYR, Edm., St.L. | 13 | **976** |
| 42. | **Radek Bonk**, Ott., Mtl., Nsh. | 14 | **969** |
| 43. | **Shane Doan**, Wpg., Phx. | 13 | **965** |
| 44. | **Curtis Joseph**, Edm., Tor., Det., Phx., Cgy. | 19 | **943** |
| 45. | **Jarome Iginla**, Cgy. | 13 | **942** |
| 46. | **Daymond Langkow**, T.B., Phi., Phx., Cgy. | 13 | **941** |
| 47. | **Ken Klee**, Wsh., Tor., N.J., Col., Atl., Ana., Phx. | 14 | **934** |
| | **Dean McAmmond**, Chi., Edm., Phi., Cgy., Col., St.L., Ott., NYI | 16 | **934** |
| 49. | **Daniel Alfredsson**, Ott. | 13 | **932** |
| 50. | **Sergei Gonchar**, Wsh., Bos., Pit. | 14 | **929** |
| 51. | **Craig Conroy**, Mtl., St.L., Cgy., L.A. | 14 | **928** |
| 52. | **Robert Lang**, L.A., Bos., Pit., Wsh., Det., Chi., Mtl. | 15 | **925** |
| 53. | **Petr Sykora**, N.J., Ana., NYR, Edm., Pit. | 11 | **921** |
| | **Stephane Yelle**, Col., Cgy., Bos. | 13 | **921** |
| | **Shean Donovan**, S.J., Col., Atl., Pit., Cgy., Bos., Ott. | 14 | **921** |
| 56. | **Ryan Smyth**, Edm., NYI, Col. | 14 | **920** |
| | **Michael Nylander**, Hfd., Cgy., T.B., Chi., Wsh., Bos., NYR | 15 | **920** |
| 58. | **Wade Redden**, Ott., NYR | 12 | **919** |
| 59. | **Mike Grier**, Edm., Wsh., Buf., S.J. | 12 | **914** |
| | **Paul Kariya**, Ana., Col., Nsh., St.L. | 14 | **914** |
| 61. | **Ed Jovanovski**, Fla., Van., Phx. | 13 | **903** |
| 62. | **Cory Stillman**, Cgy., St.L., T.B., Car., Ott., Fla. | 10 | **902** |
| 63. | **Viktor Kozlov**, S.J., Fla., N.J., NYI, Wsh. | 14 | **897** |
| 64. | **Jamie Langenbrunner**, Dal., N.J. | 14 | **884** |
| 65. | **Greg de Vries**, Edm., Nsh., Col., NYR, Ott., Atl. | 13 | **878** |
| 66. | **Darcy Tucker**, Mtl., T.B., Tor., Col. | 13 | **876** |
| 67. | **Vaclav Prospal**, Phi., Ott., Fla., T.B., Ana. | 12 | **874** |
| 68. | **Patrick Marleau**, S.J. | 11 | **871** |
| 69. | **Andrew Brunette**, Wsh., Nsh., Atl., Min., Col. | 13 | **868** |
| | **Mathieu Dandenault**, Det., Mtl. | 13 | **868** |
| 71. | **Michael Peca**, Van., Buf., NYI, Edm., Tor., CBJ | 14 | **864** |
| 72. | **Todd Bertuzzi**, NYI, Van., Fla., Det., Ana., Cgy. | 13 | **859** |
| 73. | **Dainius Zubrus**, Phi., Mtl., Wsh., Buf., N.J. | 12 | **853** |
| 74. | **Hal Gill**, Bos., Tor., Pit. | 11 | **851** |
| | **Adrian Aucoin**, Van., T.B., NYI, Chi., Cgy. | 14 | **851** |
| 76. | **Brendan Witt**, Wsh., Nsh., NYI | 13 | **848** |
| 77. | **Steve Staios**, Bos., Van., Atl., Edm. | 13 | **839** |
| 78. | **Joe Thornton**, Bos., S.J. | 11 | **836** |
| 79. | **Ruslan Salei**, Ana., Fla., Col. | 12 | **828** |
| 80. | **Patrik Elias**, N.J. | 13 | **822** |
| 81. | **Mike Knuble**, Det., NYR, Bos., Phi. | 12 | **820** |
| 82. | **Pavol Demitra**, Ott., St.L., L.A., Min., Van. | 15 | **819** |
| 83. | **Jere Lehtinen**, Dal. | 13 | **817** |
| 84. | **Fredrik Modin**, Tor., T.B., CBJ | 12 | **814** |
| 85. | **Tomas Holmstrom**, Det. | 12 | **811** |
| 86. | **Craig Rivet**, Mtl., S.J., Buf. | 14 | **808** |
| 87. | **Olli Jokinen**, L.A., NYI, Fla., Phx., Cgy. | 11 | **799** |
| | **Matt Cullen**, Ana., Fla., Car., NYR | 11 | **799** |
| 89. | **P.J. Axelsson**, Bos. | 11 | **797** |
| 90. | **Derek Morris**, Cgy., Col., Phx., NYR | 11 | **793** |
| 91. | **Saku Koivu**, Mtl. | 13 | **792** |
| 92. | **Chris Drury**, Col., Cgy., Buf., NYR | 10 | **791** |
| 93. | **Vincent Lecavalier**, T.B. | 10 | **787** |
| | **Ethan Moreau**, Chi., Edm. | 13 | **787** |
| | **Scott Walker**, Van., Nsh., Car. | 14 | **787** |
| 96. | **Milan Hejduk**, Col. | 10 | **783** |
| 97. | **Chris Phillips**, Ott. | 11 | **781** |
| 98. | **Marco Sturm**, S.J., Bos. | 11 | **779** |
| 99. | **Jassen Cullimore**, Van., Mtl., T.B., Chi., Fla. | 14 | **776** |
| 100. | **Marian Hossa**, Ott., Atl., Pit., Det. | 11 | **775** |

*Chris Pronger appeared in his 1,000th career game when the Anaheim Ducks visited Detroit on February 20, 2009. Now a member of the Philadelphia Flyers, Pronger was one of 15 players to reach that milestone during the 2008-09 season.*

# Goaltending Records

## All-Time Shutout Leaders (Minimum 50 Shutouts)

| | Goaltender | Team | Shutouts | Games | Seasons |
|---|---|---|---|---|---|
| 1. | **Terry Sawchuk** (1949-1970) | Detroit | 85 | 734 | 14 |
| | | Boston | 11 | 102 | 2 |
| | | Toronto | 4 | 91 | 3 |
| | | Los Angeles | 2 | 36 | 1 |
| | | NY Rangers | 1 | 8 | 1 |
| | | **Total** | **103** | 971 | 21 |
| 2. | ***Martin Brodeur** (1991-2009) | New Jersey | **101** | 999 | 16 |
| 3. | **George Hainsworth** (1926-1937) | Montreal | 75 | 318 | 7½ |
| | | Toronto | 19 | 147 | 3½ |
| | | **Total** | **94** | 465 | 11 |
| 4. | **Glenn Hall** (1952-1971) | Detroit | 17 | 148 | 4 |
| | | Chicago | 51 | 618 | 10 |
| | | St. Louis | 16 | 140 | 4 |
| | | **Total** | **84** | 906 | 18 |
| 5. | **Jacques Plante** (1952-1973) | Montreal | 58 | 556 | 11 |
| | | NY Rangers | 5 | 98 | 2 |
| | | St. Louis | 10 | 69 | 2 |
| | | Toronto | 7 | 106 | 2¾ |
| | | Boston | 2 | 8 | ¼ |
| | | **Total** | **82** | 837 | 18 |
| 6. | **Alec Connell** (1924-1937) | Ottawa | 64 | 293 | 8 |
| | | Detroit | 6 | 48 | 1 |
| | | NY Americans | 0 | 1 | 1 |
| | | Mtl. Maroons | 11 | 75 | 2 |
| | | **Total** | **81** | 417 | 12 |
| 7. | **Tiny Thompson** (1928-1940) | Boston | 74 | 468 | 10¼ |
| | | Detroit | 7 | 85 | 1¾ |
| | | **Total** | **81** | 553 | 12 |
| 8. | **Dominik Hasek** (1990-2008) | Chicago | 1 | 25 | 2 |
| | | Buffalo | 55 | 491 | 9 |
| | | Detroit | 20 | 176 | 4 |
| | | Ottawa | 5 | 43 | 1 |
| | | **Total** | **81** | 735 | 16 |
| 9. | **Tony Esposito** (1968-1984) | Montreal | 2 | 13 | 1 |
| | | Chicago | 74 | 873 | 15 |
| | | **Total** | **76** | 886 | 16 |
| 10. | **Ed Belfour** (1988-2007) | Chicago | 30 | 415 | 7⅔ |
| | | San Jose | 1 | 13 | ⅓ |
| | | Dallas | 27 | 307 | 5 |
| | | Toronto | 17 | 170 | 3 |
| | | Florida | 1 | 58 | 1 |
| | | **Total** | **76** | 963 | 17 |
| 11. | **Lorne Chabot** (1926-1937) | NY Rangers | 21 | 80 | 2 |
| | | Toronto | 31 | 214 | 5 |
| | | Montreal | 8 | 47 | 1 |
| | | Chicago | 8 | 48 | 1 |
| | | Mtl. Maroons | 2 | 16 | 1 |
| | | NY Americans | 1 | 6 | 1 |
| | | **Total** | **71** | 411 | 11 |
| 12. | **Harry Lumley** (1943-1960) | Detroit | 26 | 324 | 6½ |
| | | NY Rangers | 0 | 1 | ½ |
| | | Chicago | 5 | 134 | 2 |
| | | Toronto | 34 | 267 | 4 |
| | | Boston | 6 | 78 | 3 |
| | | **Total** | **71** | 804 | 16 |
| 13. | **Roy Worters** (1925-1937) | Pittsburgh Pirates | 22 | 123 | 3 |
| | | NY Americans | 45 | 360 | 9 |
| | | **Montreal | 0 | 1 | |
| | | **Total** | **67** | 484 | 12 |
| 14. | **Patrick Roy** (1984-2003) | Montreal | 29 | 551 | 11½ |
| | | Colorado | 37 | 478 | 7½ |
| | | **Total** | **66** | 1,029 | 19 |
| 15. | **Turk Broda** (1936-1952) | Toronto | **62** | 629 | 14 |
| 16. | **John Ross Roach** (1921-1935) | Toronto | 13 | 222 | 7 |
| | | NY Rangers | 30 | 89 | 4 |
| | | Detroit | 15 | 180 | 3 |
| | | **Total** | **58** | 491 | 14 |
| 17. | **Clint Benedict** (1917-1930) | Ottawa | 19 | 158 | 7 |
| | | Mtl. Maroons | 38 | 204 | 6 |
| | | **Total** | **57** | 362 | 13 |
| 18. | **Bernie Parent** (1965-1979) | Boston | 1 | 57 | 2 |
| | | Philadelphia | 50 | 486 | 9½ |
| | | Toronto | 3 | 65 | 1½ |
| | | **Total** | **54** | 608 | 13 |
| 19. | **Ed Giacomin** (1965-1978) | NY Rangers | 49 | 539 | 10¼ |
| | | Detroit | 5 | 71 | 2¾ |
| | | **Total** | **54** | 610 | 13 |
| 20. | **Dave Kerr** (1930-1941) | Mtl. Maroons | 11 | 101 | 3 |
| | | NY Americans | 0 | 1 | 1 |
| | | NY Rangers | 40 | 324 | 7 |
| | | **Total** | **51** | 426 | 11 |
| 21. | **Rogie Vachon** (1966-1982) | Montreal | 13 | 206 | 5¼ |
| | | Los Angeles | 32 | 389 | 6¾ |
| | | Detroit | 4 | 109 | 2 |
| | | Boston | 2 | 91 | 2 |
| | | **Total** | **51** | 795 | 16 |
| 22. | ***Curtis Joseph** (1989-2009) | St. Louis | 5 | 280 | 6 |
| | | Edmonton | 14 | 177 | 3 |
| | | Toronto | 17 | 270 | 5 |
| | | Detroit | 7 | 92 | 2 |
| | | Phoenix | 8 | 115 | 2 |
| | | Calgary | 0 | 9 | 1 |
| | | **Total** | **51** | 943 | 19 |

* Active goalie
** Played 1 game for Montreal in 1929-30.

## Ten or More Shutouts, One Season

| Number of Shutouts | Goaltender | Team | Season | Length of Schedule |
|---|---|---|---|---|
| 22 | George Hainsworth | Montreal | 1928-29 | 44 |
| 15 | Alec Connell | Ottawa | 1925-26 | 36 |
| | Alec Connell | Ottawa | 1927-28 | 44 |
| | Hal Winkler | Boston | 1927-28 | 44 |
| | Tony Esposito | Chicago | 1969-70 | 76 |
| 14 | George Hainsworth | Montreal | 1926-27 | 44 |
| 13 | Clint Benedict | Mtl. Maroons | 1926-27 | 44 |
| | Alec Connell | Ottawa | 1926-27 | 44 |
| | George Hainsworth | Montreal | 1927-28 | 44 |
| | John Ross Roach | NY Rangers | 1928-29 | 44 |
| | Roy Worters | NY Americans | 1928-29 | 44 |
| | Harry Lumley | Toronto | 1953-54 | 70 |
| | Dominik Hasek | Buffalo | 1997-98 | 82 |
| 12 | Tiny Thompson | Boston | 1928-29 | 44 |
| | Charlie Gardiner | Chicago | 1930-31 | 44 |
| | Terry Sawchuk | Detroit | 1951-52 | 70 |
| | Terry Sawchuk | Detroit | 1953-54 | 70 |
| | Terry Sawchuk | Detroit | 1954-55 | 70 |
| | Glenn Hall | Detroit | 1955-56 | 70 |
| | Bernie Parent | Philadelphia | 1973-74 | 78 |
| | Bernie Parent | Philadelphia | 1974-75 | 80 |
| | Martin Brodeur | New Jersey | 2006-07 | 82 |
| 11 | Lorne Chabot | NY Rangers | 1927-28 | 44 |
| | Hap Holmes | Detroit | 1927-28 | 44 |
| | Roy Worters | Pittsburgh Pirates | 1927-28 | 44 |
| | Clint Benedict | Mtl. Maroons | 1928-29 | 44 |
| | Joe Miller | Pittsburgh Pirates | 1928-29 | 44 |
| | Tiny Thompson | Boston | 1932-33 | 48 |
| | Terry Sawchuk | Detroit | 1950-51 | 70 |
| | Dominik Hasek | Buffalo | 2000-01 | 82 |
| | Martin Brodeur | New Jersey | 2003-04 | 82 |
| 10 | Lorne Chabot | NY Rangers | 1926-27 | 44 |
| | Lorne Chabot | Toronto | 1928-29 | 44 |
| | Dolly Dolson | Detroit | 1928-29 | 44 |
| | John Ross Roach | Detroit | 1932-33 | 48 |
| | Charlie Gardiner | Chicago | 1933-34 | 48 |
| | Tiny Thompson | Boston | 1935-36 | 48 |
| | Frank Brimsek | Boston | 1938-39 | 48 |
| | Bill Durnan | Montreal | 1948-49 | 60 |
| | Harry Lumley | Toronto | 1952-53 | 70 |
| | Gerry McNeil | Montreal | 1952-53 | 70 |
| | Tony Esposito | Chicago | 1973-74 | 78 |
| | Ken Dryden | Montreal | 1976-77 | 80 |
| | Martin Brodeur | New Jersey | 1996-97 | 82 |
| | Martin Brodeur | New Jersey | 1997-98 | 82 |
| | Byron Dafoe | Boston | 1998-99 | 82 |
| | Roman Cechmanek | Philadelphia | 2000-01 | 82 |
| | Ed Belfour | Toronto | 2003-04 | 82 |
| | Miikka Kiprusoff | Calgary | 2005-06 | 82 |
| | Henrik Lundqvist | NY Rangers | 2007-08 | 82 |
| | Steve Mason | Columbus | **2008-09** | 82 |

## All-Time Win Leaders

### (Minimum 250 Wins)

| Goaltender | Wins | GP | Dec. | Losses | OT/Ties |
|---|---|---|---|---|---|
| 1. * Martin Brodeur | **557** | 999 | 984 | 299 | 128 |
| 2. Patrick Roy | **551** | 1029 | 997 | 315 | 131 |
| 3. Ed Belfour | **484** | 963 | 929 | 320 | 125 |
| 4. * Curtis Joseph | **454** | 943 | 902 | 352 | 96 |
| 5. Terry Sawchuk | **447** | 971 | 949 | 330 | 172 |
| 6. Jacques Plante | **437** | 837 | 829 | 247 | 145 |
| 7. Tony Esposito | **423** | 886 | 880 | 306 | 151 |
| 8. Glenn Hall | **407** | 906 | 896 | 326 | 163 |
| 9. Grant Fuhr | **403** | 868 | 812 | 295 | 114 |
| 10. * Chris Osgood | **389** | 710 | 682 | 204 | 89 |
| 11. Dominik Hasek | **389** | 735 | 707 | 223 | 95 |
| 12. Mike Vernon | **385** | 781 | 750 | 273 | 92 |
| 13. John Vanbiesbrouck | **374** | 882 | 839 | 346 | 119 |
| 14. Andy Moog | **372** | 713 | 669 | 209 | 88 |
| 15. Tom Barrasso | **369** | 777 | 732 | 277 | 86 |
| 16. Rogie Vachon | **355** | 795 | 773 | 291 | 127 |
| 17. Gump Worsley | **335** | 861 | 837 | 352 | 150 |
| 18. Harry Lumley | **330** | 803 | 801 | 329 | 142 |
| 19. Sean Burke | **324** | 820 | 775 | 341 | 110 |
| 20. Billy Smith | **305** | 680 | 643 | 233 | 105 |
| 21. * Olaf Kolzig | **303** | 719 | 687 | 297 | 87 |
| 22. Turk Broda | **302** | 629 | 627 | 224 | 101 |
| 23. Mike Richter | **301** | 666 | 632 | 258 | 73 |
| 24. * Nikolai Khabibulin | **299** | 678 | 648 | 267 | 82 |
| 25. Ron Hextall | **296** | 608 | 579 | 214 | 69 |
| 26. Mike Liut | **294** | 664 | 639 | 271 | 74 |
| 27. Ed Giacomin | **289** | 609 | 594 | 208 | 97 |
| 28. Dan Bouchard | **286** | 655 | 631 | 232 | 113 |
| 29. Tiny Thompson | **284** | 553 | 553 | 194 | 75 |
| 30. Bernie Parent | **271** | 608 | 590 | 198 | 121 |
| 31. Kelly Hrudey | **271** | 677 | 624 | 265 | 88 |
| 32. Gilles Meloche | **270** | 788 | 752 | 351 | 131 |
| 33. Don Beaupre | **268** | 667 | 620 | 277 | 75 |
| 34. Felix Potvin | **266** | 635 | 611 | 260 | 85 |
| 35. Ken Dryden | **258** | 397 | 389 | 57 | 74 |
| 36. Frank Brimsek | **252** | 514 | 514 | 182 | 80 |
| 37. Johnny Bower | **250** | 552 | 535 | 195 | 90 |

* active player

## Active Shutout Leaders

### (Minimum 25 Shutouts)

| Goaltender | Teams | Shutouts | Games | Seasons |
|---|---|---|---|---|
| 1. Martin Brodeur | New Jersey | **101** | 999 | 16 |
| 2. Curtis Joseph | St.L., Edm., Tor., Det., Phx., Cgy. | **51** | 943 | 19 |
| 3. Chris Osgood | Det., NYI, St.L. | **49** | 710 | 15 |
| 4. Evgeni Nabokov | San Jose | **47** | 492 | 9 |
| 5. Roberto Luongo | NYI, Fla., Van. | **47** | 544 | 9 |
| 6. Nikolai Khabibulin | Wpg., Phx., T.B., Chi. | **41** | 678 | 13 |
| 7. Marty Turco | Dallas | **36** | 456 | 8 |
| 8. Patrick Lalime | Pit., Ott., St.L., Chi., Buf. | **35** | 421 | 10 |
| 9. Olaf Kolzig | Washington, Tampa Bay | **35** | 719 | 17 |
| 10. Jean-Sebastien Giguere | Hfd., Cgy., Ana. | **31** | 457 | 11 |
| 11. Tomas Vokoun | Mtl., Nas., Fla. | **31** | 512 | 11 |
| 12. Miikka Kiprusoff | San Jose, Calgary | **30** | 385 | 8 |
| 13. Jose Theodore | Mtl., Col., Wsh. | **28** | 501 | 12 |
| 14. Martin Biron | Buffalo, Philadelphia | **25** | 433 | 11 |

## All-Time Penalty-Minute Leaders

* active player

| Player | Seasons | Games | Penalty Mins. | Mins. per game |
|---|---|---|---|---|
| 1. **Tiger Williams**, Tor., Van., Det., L.A., Hfd. | 14 | 962 | **3966** | 4.12 |
| 2. **Dale Hunter**, Que., Wsh., Col. | 19 | 1407 | **3565** | 2.53 |
| 3. **Tie Domi**, Tor., NYR, Wpg. | 16 | 1020 | **3515** | 3.45 |
| 4. **Marty McSorley**, Pit., Edm., L.A., NYR, S.J., Bos. | 17 | 961 | **3381** | 3.52 |
| 5. **Bob Probert**, Det., Chi. | 16 | 935 | **3300** | 3.53 |
| 6. **Rob Ray**, Buf., Ott. | 15 | 900 | **3207** | 3.56 |
| 7. **Craig Berube**, Phi., Tor., Cgy., Wsh., NYI | 17 | 1054 | **3149** | 2.99 |
| 8. **Tim Hunter**, Cgy., Que., Van., S.J. | 16 | 815 | **3146** | 3.86 |
| 9. **Chris Nilan**, Mtl., NYR, Bos. | 13 | 688 | **3043** | 4.42 |
| 10. **Rick Tocchet**, Phi., Pit., L.A., Bos., Wsh., Phx. | 18 | 1144 | **2972** | 2.60 |
| 11. **Pat Verbeek**, N.J., Hfd., NYR, Dal., Det. | 20 | 1424 | **2905** | 2.04 |
| * 12. **Chris Chelios**, Mtl., Chi., Det. | 25 | 1644 | **2891** | 1.76 |
| 13. **Dave Manson**, Chi., Edm., Wpg., Phx., Mtl., Dal., Tor. | 16 | 1103 | **2792** | 2.53 |
| 14. **Scott Stevens**, Wsh., St.L., N.J. | 22 | 1635 | **2785** | 1.70 |
| 15. **Willi Plett**, Atl., Cgy., Min., Bos. | 13 | 834 | **2572** | 3.08 |

## Goals-Against Average Leaders (Minimum 25 games played)

(Exceptions: Minimum 13 games played, 1994-95; minimum 26 games played, 1992-93 to 1993-94; minimum 15 games played, 1917-18 to 1925-26)

| Season | Goaltender, Team | GP | Mins. | GA | SO | AVG. |
|---|---|---|---|---|---|---|
| 2008-09 | Tim Thomas, Boston | 54 | 3,259 | 114 | 5 | 2.10 |
| 2007-08 | Chris Osgood, Detroit | 43 | 2,409 | 84 | 4 | 2.09 |
| 2006-07 | Niklas Backstrom, Minnesota | 41 | 2,227 | 73 | 5 | 1.97 |
| 2005-06 | Miikka Kiprusoff, Calgary | 74 | 4,380 | 151 | 10 | 2.07 |
| 2003-04 | Miikka Kiprusoff, Calgary | 38 | 2,301 | 65 | 4 | 1.69 |
| 2002-03 | Marty Turco, Dallas | 55 | 3,203 | 92 | 7 | 1.72 |
| 2001-02 | Patrick Roy, Colorado | 63 | 3,773 | 122 | 9 | 1.94 |
| 2000-01 | Marty Turco, Dallas | 26 | 1,266 | 40 | 3 | 1.90 |
| 99-2000 | Brian Boucher, Philadelphia | 35 | 2,038 | 65 | 4 | 1.91 |
| 1998-99 | Ron Tugnutt, Ottawa | 43 | 2,508 | 75 | 3 | 1.79 |
| 1997-98 | Ed Belfour, Dallas | 61 | 3,581 | 112 | 9 | 1.88 |
| 1996-97 | Martin Brodeur, New Jersey | 67 | 3,838 | 120 | 10 | 1.88 |
| 1995-96 | Ron Hextall, Philadelphia | 53 | 3,102 | 112 | 4 | 2.17 |
| 1994-95 | Dominik Hasek, Buffalo | 41 | 2,416 | 85 | 5 | 2.11 |
| 1993-94 | Dominik Hasek, Buffalo | 58 | 3,358 | 109 | 7 | 1.95 |
| 1992-93 | Felix Potvin, Toronto | 48 | 2,781 | 116 | 2 | 2.50 |
| 1991-92 | Patrick Roy, Montreal | 67 | 3,935 | 155 | 5 | 2.36 |
| 1990-91 | Ed Belfour, Chicago | 74 | 4,127 | 170 | 4 | 2.47 |
| 1989-90 | Mike Liut, Hartford, Washington | 37 | 2,161 | 91 | 4 | 2.53 |
| 1988-89 | Patrick Roy, Montreal | 48 | 2,744 | 113 | 4 | 2.47 |
| 1987-88 | Pete Peeters, Washington | 35 | 1,896 | 88 | 2 | 2.78 |
| 1986-87 | Brian Hayward, Montreal | 37 | 2,178 | 102 | 1 | 2.81 |
| 1985-86 | Bob Froese, Philadelphia | 51 | 2,728 | 116 | 5 | 2.55 |
| 1984-85 | Tom Barrasso, Buffalo | 54 | 3,248 | 144 | 5 | 2.66 |
| 1983-84 | Pat Riggin, Washington | 41 | 2,299 | 102 | 4 | 2.66 |
| 1982-83 | Pete Peeters, Boston | 62 | 3,611 | 142 | 8 | 2.36 |
| 1981-82 | Denis Herron, Montreal | 27 | 1,547 | 68 | 3 | 2.64 |
| 1980-81 | Richard Sevigny, Montreal | 33 | 1,777 | 71 | 2 | 2.40 |
| 1979-80 | Bob Sauve, Buffalo | 32 | 1,880 | 74 | 4 | 2.36 |
| 1978-79 | Ken Dryden, Montreal | 47 | 2,814 | 108 | 5 | 2.30 |
| 1977-78 | Ken Dryden, Montreal | 52 | 3,071 | 105 | 5 | 2.05 |
| 1976-77 | Michel Larocque, Montreal | 26 | 1,525 | 53 | 4 | 2.09 |
| 1975-76 | Ken Dryden, Montreal | 62 | 3,580 | 121 | 8 | 2.03 |
| 1974-75 | Bernie Parent, Philadelphia | 68 | 4,041 | 137 | 12 | 2.03 |
| 1973-74 | Bernie Parent, Philadelphia | 73 | 4,314 | 136 | 12 | 1.89 |
| 1972-73 | Ken Dryden, Montreal | 54 | 3,165 | 119 | 6 | 2.26 |
| 1971-72 | Tony Esposito, Chicago | 48 | 2,780 | 82 | 9 | 1.77 |
| 1970-71 | Jacques Plante, Toronto | 40 | 2,329 | 73 | 4 | 1.88 |
| 1969-70 | Ernie Wakely, St. Louis | 30 | 1,651 | 58 | 4 | 2.11 |
| 1968-69 | Jacques Plante, St. Louis | 37 | 2,139 | 70 | 5 | 1.96 |
| 1967-68 | Gump Worsley, Montreal | 40 | 2,213 | 73 | 6 | 1.98 |
| 1966-67 | Glenn Hall, Chicago | 32 | 1,664 | 66 | 2 | 2.38 |
| 1965-66 | Johnny Bower, Toronto | 35 | 1,998 | 75 | 3 | 2.25 |
| 1964-65 | Johnny Bower, Toronto | 34 | 2,040 | 81 | 3 | 2.38 |
| 1963-64 | Johnny Bower, Toronto | 51 | 3,009 | 106 | 5 | 2.11 |
| 1962-63 | Don Simmons, Toronto | 28 | 1,680 | 69 | 1 | 2.46 |
| 1961-62 | Jacques Plante, Montreal | 70 | 4,200 | 166 | 4 | 2.37 |
| 1960-61 | Charlie Hodge, Montreal | 30 | 1,800 | 74 | 4 | 2.47 |
| 1959-60 | Jacques Plante, Montreal | 69 | 4,140 | 175 | 3 | 2.54 |
| 1958-59 | Jacques Plante, Montreal | 67 | 4,000 | 144 | 9 | 2.16 |
| 1957-58 | Jacques Plante, Montreal | 57 | 3,386 | 119 | 9 | 2.11 |
| 1956-57 | Jacques Plante, Montreal | 61 | 3,660 | 122 | 9 | 2.00 |
| 1955-56 | Jacques Plante, Montreal | 64 | 3,840 | 119 | 7 | 1.86 |
| 1954-55 | Harry Lumley, Toronto | 69 | 4,140 | 134 | 8 | 1.94 |
| 1953-54 | Harry Lumley, Toronto | 69 | 4,140 | 128 | 13 | 1.86 |
| 1952-53 | Terry Sawchuk, Detroit | 63 | 3,780 | 120 | 9 | 1.90 |
| 1951-52 | Terry Sawchuk, Detroit | 70 | 4,200 | 133 | 12 | 1.90 |
| 1950-51 | Al Rollins, Toronto | 40 | 2,367 | 70 | 5 | 1.77 |
| 1949-50 | Bill Durnan, Montreal | 64 | 3,840 | 141 | 8 | 2.20 |
| 1948-49 | Bill Durnan, Montreal | 60 | 3,600 | 126 | 10 | 2.10 |
| 1947-48 | Turk Broda, Toronto | 60 | 3,600 | 143 | 5 | 2.38 |
| 1946-47 | Bill Durnan, Montreal | 60 | 3,600 | 138 | 4 | 2.30 |
| 1945-46 | Bill Durnan, Montreal | 40 | 2,400 | 104 | 4 | 2.60 |
| 1944-45 | Bill Durnan, Montreal | 50 | 3,000 | 121 | 1 | 2.42 |
| 1943-44 | Bill Durnan, Montreal | 50 | 3,000 | 109 | 2 | 2.18 |
| 1942-43 | Johnny Mowers, Detroit | 50 | 3,010 | 124 | 6 | 2.47 |
| 1941-42 | Frank Brimsek, Boston | 47 | 2,930 | 115 | 3 | 2.35 |
| 1940-41 | Turk Broda, Toronto | 48 | 2,970 | 99 | 5 | 2.00 |
| 1939-40 | Dave Kerr, NY Rangers | 48 | 3,000 | 77 | 8 | 1.54 |
| 1938-39 | Frank Brimsek, Boston | 43 | 2,610 | 68 | 10 | 1.56 |
| 1937-38 | Tiny Thompson, Boston | 48 | 2,970 | 89 | 7 | 1.80 |
| 1936-37 | Normie Smith, Detroit | 48 | 2,980 | 102 | 6 | 2.05 |
| 1935-36 | Tiny Thompson, Boston | 48 | 2,930 | 82 | 10 | 1.68 |
| 1934-35 | Lorne Chabot, Chicago | 48 | 2,940 | 88 | 8 | 1.80 |
| 1933-34 | Wilf Cude, Detroit, Montreal | 30 | 1,920 | 47 | 5 | 1.47 |
| 1932-33 | Tiny Thompson, Boston | 48 | 3,000 | 88 | 11 | 1.76 |
| 1931-32 | Charlie Gardiner, Chicago | 48 | 2,989 | 92 | 4 | 1.85 |
| 1930-31 | Roy Worters, NY Americans | 44 | 2,760 | 74 | 8 | 1.61 |
| 1929-30 | Tiny Thompson, Boston | 44 | 2,680 | 98 | 3 | 2.19 |
| 1928-29 | George Hainsworth, Montreal | 44 | 2,800 | 43 | 22 | 0.92 |
| 1927-28 | George Hainsworth, Montreal | 44 | 2,730 | 48 | 13 | 1.05 |
| 1926-27 | Clint Benedict, Mtl. Maroons | 43 | 2,748 | 65 | 13 | 1.42 |
| 1925-26 | Alec Connell, Ottawa | 36 | 2,251 | 42 | 15 | 1.12 |
| 1924-25 | Georges Vezina, Montreal | 30 | 1,860 | 56 | 5 | 1.81 |
| 1923-24 | Georges Vezina, Montreal | 24 | 1,459 | 48 | 3 | 1.97 |
| 1922-23 | Clint Benedict, Ottawa | 24 | 1,478 | 54 | 4 | 2.18 |
| 1921-22 | Clint Benedict, Ottawa | 24 | 1,508 | 84 | 2 | 3.34 |
| 1920-21 | Clint Benedict, Ottawa | 24 | 1,457 | 75 | 2 | 3.09 |
| 1919-20 | Clint Benedict, Ottawa | 24 | 1,444 | 64 | 5 | 2.66 |
| 1918-19 | Clint Benedict, Ottawa | 18 | 1,113 | 53 | 2 | 2.86 |
| 1917-18 | Georges Vezina, Montreal | 21 | 1,282 | 84 | 1 | 3.93 |

# All-Time Regular-Season NHL Coaching Register

## Regular Season, 1917-2009

| Coach | Team | Games Coached | Wins | Losses | O/T | Years | Cup Wins | Career |
|---|---|---|---|---|---|---|---|---|
| Abel, Sid | Chicago | 140 | 39 | 79 | 22 | 2 | | |
| | Detroit | 811 | 340 | 339 | 132 | 12 | | |
| | St. Louis | 10 | 3 | 6 | 1 | 1 | | |
| | Kansas City | 3 | 0 | 3 | 0 | 1 | | |
| | Totals | 964 | 382 | 427 | 155 | 16 | | 1952-76 |
| Adams, Jack | Detroit | 964 | 413 | 390 | 161 | 20 | 3 | 1927-47 |
| Agnew, Gary | Columbus | 5 | 0 | 4 | 1 | 1 | | 2006-07 |
| Allen, Keith | Philadelphia | 150 | 51 | 67 | 32 | 2 | | 1967-69 |
| Allison, Dave | Ottawa | 25 | 2 | 22 | 1 | 1 | | 1995-96 |
| Anderson, Jim | Washington | 54 | 4 | 45 | 5 | 1 | | 1974-75 |
| Anderson, John | Atlanta | 82 | 35 | 41 | 6 | 1 | | 2008-09 |
| Angotti, Lou | St. Louis | 32 | 6 | 20 | 6 | 2 | | |
| | Pittsburgh | 80 | 16 | 58 | 6 | 1 | | |
| | Totals | 112 | 22 | 78 | 12 | 3 | | 1973-84 |
| Arbour, Al | St. Louis | 107 | 42 | 40 | 25 | 3 | | |
| | NY Islanders | 1500 | 740 | 537 | 223 | 20 | 4 | |
| | Totals | 1607 | 782 | 577 | 248 | 23 | 4 | 1970-08 |
| Armstrong, George | Toronto | 47 | 17 | 26 | 4 | 1 | | 1988-89 |
| Babcock, Mike | Anaheim | 164 | 69 | 62 | 33 | 3 | | |
| | Detroit | 328 | 213 | 77 | 38 | 4 | 1 | |
| | Totals | 492 | 282 | 139 | 71 | 7 | 1 | 2002-09 |
| Barber, Bill | Philadelphia | 136 | 73 | 40 | 23 | 2 | | 2000-02 |
| Barkley, Doug | Detroit | 77 | 20 | 46 | 11 | 3 | | 1970-76 |
| Beaulieu, Andre | Minnesota | 32 | 6 | 23 | 3 | 1 | | 1977-78 |
| Belisle, Danny | Washington | 96 | 28 | 51 | 17 | 2 | | 1978-80 |
| Berenson, Red | St. Louis | 204 | 100 | 72 | 32 | 3 | | 1979-82 |
| Bergeron, Michel | Quebec | 634 | 265 | 283 | 86 | 8 | | |
| | NY Rangers | 158 | 73 | 67 | 18 | 2 | | |
| | Totals | 792 | 338 | 350 | 104 | 10 | | 1980-90 |
| Berry, Bob | Los Angeles | 240 | 107 | 94 | 39 | 3 | | |
| | Montreal | 223 | 116 | 71 | 36 | 3 | | |
| | Pittsburgh | 240 | 88 | 127 | 25 | 3 | | |
| | St. Louis | 157 | 73 | 63 | 21 | 2 | | |
| | Totals | 860 | 384 | 355 | 121 | 11 | | 1978-94 |
| Beverley, Nick | Toronto | 17 | 9 | 6 | 2 | 1 | | 1995-96 |
| Blackburn, Don | Hartford | 140 | 42 | 63 | 35 | 2 | | 1979-81 |
| Blair, Wren | Minnesota | 147 | 48 | 65 | 34 | 3 | | 1967-70 |
| Blake, Toe | Montreal | 914 | 500 | 255 | 159 | 13 | 8 | 1955-68 |
| Boileau, Marc | Pittsburgh | 151 | 66 | 61 | 24 | 3 | | 1973-76 |
| Boivin, Leo | St. Louis | 97 | 28 | 53 | 16 | 2 | | 1975-78 |
| Boucher, Frank | NY Rangers | 527 | 181 | 263 | 83 | 11 | 1 | 1939-54 |
| Boucher, Georges | Mtl. Maroons | 12 | 6 | 5 | 1 | 1 | | |
| | Ottawa | 48 | 13 | 29 | 6 | 1 | | |
| | St. Louis | 35 | 9 | 20 | 6 | 1 | | |
| | Boston | 70 | 22 | 32 | 16 | 1 | | |
| | Totals | 165 | 50 | 86 | 29 | 4 | | 1930-50 |
| Boudreau, Bruce | Washington | 143 | 87 | 41 | 15 | 2 | | 2007-09 |
| Bowman, Scotty | St. Louis | 238 | 110 | 83 | 45 | 4 | | |
| | Montreal | 634 | 419 | 110 | 105 | 8 | 5 | |
| | Buffalo | 404 | 210 | 134 | 60 | 7 | | |
| | Pittsburgh | 164 | 95 | 53 | 16 | 2 | 1 | |
| | Detroit | 701 | 410 | 193 | 98 | 9 | 3 | |
| | Totals | 2141 | 1244 | 573 | 324 | 30 | 9 | 1967-02 |
| Bowness, Rick | Winnipeg | 28 | 8 | 17 | 3 | 1 | | |
| | Boston | 80 | 36 | 32 | 12 | 1 | | |
| | Ottawa | 235 | 39 | 178 | 18 | 4 | | |
| | NY Islanders | 100 | 38 | 50 | 12 | 2 | | |
| | Phoenix | 20 | 2 | 12 | 6 | 2 | | |
| | Totals | 463 | 123 | 289 | 51 | 10 | | 1988-05 |
| Brooks, Herb | NY Rangers | 285 | 131 | 113 | 41 | 4 | | |
| | Minnesota | 80 | 19 | 48 | 13 | 1 | | |
| | New Jersey | 84 | 40 | 37 | 7 | 1 | | |
| | Pittsburgh | 57 | 29 | 21 | 7 | 1 | | |
| | Totals | 506 | 219 | 219 | 68 | 7 | | 1981-00 |
| Brophy, John | Toronto | 193 | 64 | 111 | 18 | 3 | | 1986-89 |
| Burnett, George | Edmonton | 35 | 12 | 20 | 3 | 1 | | 1994-95 |
| Burns, Charlie | Minnesota | 86 | 22 | 50 | 14 | 2 | | 1969-75 |
| Burns, Pat | Montreal | 320 | 174 | 104 | 42 | 4 | | |
| | Toronto | 281 | 133 | 107 | 41 | 4 | | |
| | Boston | 254 | 105 | 97 | 52 | 4 | | |
| | New Jersey | 164 | 89 | 45 | 30 | 3 | 1 | |
| | Totals | 1019 | 501 | 353 | 165 | 15 | 1 | 1988-05 |
| Bush, Eddie | Kansas City | 32 | 1 | 23 | 8 | 1 | | 1975-76 |
| Bylsma, Dan | Pittsburgh | 25 | 18 | 3 | 4 | 1 | 1 | 2008-09 |
| Campbell, Colin | NY Rangers | 269 | 118 | 108 | 43 | 4 | | 1994-98 |
| Carbonneau, Guy | Montreal | 230 | 124 | 83 | 23 | 3 | | 2006-09 |
| Carlyle, Randy | Anaheim | 328 | 180 | 107 | 41 | 4 | 1 | 2005-09 |
| Carpenter, Doug | New Jersey | 290 | 100 | 166 | 24 | 4 | | |
| | Toronto | 91 | 39 | 47 | 5 | 2 | | |
| | Totals | 381 | 139 | 213 | 29 | 6 | | 1984-91 |
| Carroll, Dick | Toronto | 40 | 18 | 22 | 0 | 2 | 1 | 1917-19 |
| Carroll, Frank | Toronto | 24 | 15 | 9 | 0 | 1 | | 1920-21 |
| Cashman, Wayne | Philadelphia | 61 | 32 | 20 | 9 | 1 | | 1997-98 |
| Cassidy, Bruce | Washington | 110 | 47 | 47 | 16 | 2 | | 2002-04 |
| Chambers, Dave | Quebec | 98 | 19 | 64 | 15 | 2 | | 1990-92 |
| Chapman, Art | NY Americans | 48 | 8 | 29 | 11 | 1 | | |
| | Brooklyn | 48 | 16 | 29 | 3 | 1 | | |
| | Totals | 96 | 24 | 58 | 14 | 2 | | 1940-42 |
| Charron, Guy | Calgary | 16 | 6 | 7 | 3 | 1 | | |
| | Anaheim | 49 | 14 | 26 | 9 | 1 | | |
| | Totals | 65 | 20 | 33 | 12 | 2 | | 1991-01 |
| Cheevers, Gerry | Boston | 376 | 204 | 126 | 46 | 5 | | 1980-85 |
| Cherry, Don | Boston | 400 | 231 | 105 | 64 | 5 | | |
| | Colorado | 80 | 19 | 48 | 13 | 1 | | |
| | Totals | 480 | 250 | 153 | 77 | 6 | | 1974-80 |
| Clancy, King | Mtl. Maroons | 18 | 6 | 11 | 1 | 1 | | |
| | Toronto | 210 | 80 | 81 | 49 | 3 | | |
| | Totals | 228 | 86 | 92 | 50 | 4 | | 1937-56 |
| Clapper, Dit | Boston | 230 | 102 | 88 | 40 | 4 | | 1945-49 |
| Cleghorn, Odie | Pittsburgh | 168 | 62 | 86 | 20 | 4 | | 1925-29 |
| Cleghorn, Sprague | Mtl. Maroons | 48 | 19 | 22 | 7 | 1 | | 1931-32 |
| Clouston, Cory | Ottawa | 34 | 19 | 11 | 4 | 1 | | 2008-09 |
| Colville, Neil | NY Rangers | 93 | 26 | 41 | 26 | 2 | | 1950-52 |
| Conacher, Charlie | Chicago | 162 | 56 | 84 | 22 | 3 | | 1947-50 |
| Conacher, Lionel | NY Americans | 44 | 14 | 25 | 5 | 1 | | 1929-30 |
| Constantine, Kevin | San Jose | 157 | 55 | 78 | 24 | 3 | | |
| | Pittsburgh | 189 | 86 | 64 | 39 | 3 | | |
| | New Jersey | 31 | 20 | 8 | 3 | 1 | | |
| | Totals | 377 | 161 | 150 | 66 | 7 | | 1993-02 |
| Cook, Bill | NY Rangers | 117 | 34 | 59 | 24 | 2 | | 1951-53 |
| Crawford, Marc | Quebec | 48 | 30 | 13 | 5 | 1 | | |
| | Colorado | 246 | 135 | 75 | 36 | 3 | 1 | |
| | Vancouver | 529 | 246 | 189 | 94 | 8 | | |
| | Los Angeles | 164 | 59 | 84 | 21 | 2 | | |
| | Totals | 987 | 470 | 361 | 156 | 14 | 1 | 1994-08 |
| Creamer, Pierre | Pittsburgh | 80 | 36 | 35 | 9 | 1 | | 1987-88 |
| Creighton, Fred | Atlanta | 348 | 156 | 136 | 56 | 5 | | |
| | Boston | 73 | 40 | 20 | 13 | 1 | | |
| | Totals | 421 | 196 | 156 | 69 | 6 | | 1974-80 |
| Crisp, Terry | Calgary | 240 | 144 | 63 | 33 | 3 | 1 | |
| | Tampa Bay | 391 | 142 | 204 | 45 | 6 | | |
| | Totals | 631 | 286 | 267 | 78 | 9 | 1 | 1987-98 |
| Crozier, Joe | Buffalo | 192 | 77 | 80 | 35 | 3 | | |
| | Toronto | 40 | 13 | 22 | 5 | 1 | | |
| | Totals | 232 | 90 | 102 | 40 | 4 | | 1971-81 |
| Crozier, Roger | Washington | 1 | 0 | 1 | 0 | 1 | | 1981-82 |
| Cunniff, John | Hartford | 13 | 3 | 9 | 1 | 1 | | |
| | New Jersey | 133 | 59 | 56 | 18 | 2 | | |
| | Totals | 146 | 62 | 65 | 19 | 3 | | 1982-91 |
| Curry, Alex | Ottawa | 36 | 24 | 8 | 4 | 1 | | 1925-26 |
| Dandurand, Leo | Montreal | 163 | 78 | 76 | 9 | 6 | 1 | 1921-35 |
| Day, Hap | Toronto | 546 | 259 | 206 | 81 | 10 | 5 | 1940-50 |
| Dea, Billy | Detroit | 11 | 3 | 8 | 0 | 1 | | 1981-82 |
| DeBoer, Peter | Florida | 82 | 41 | 30 | 11 | 1 | | 2008-09 |
| Delvecchio, Alex | Detroit | 245 | 82 | 131 | 32 | 4 | | 1973-77 |
| Demers, Jacques | Quebec | 80 | 25 | 44 | 11 | 1 | | |
| | St. Louis | 240 | 106 | 106 | 28 | 3 | | |
| | Detroit | 320 | 137 | 136 | 47 | 4 | | |
| | Montreal | 220 | 107 | 86 | 27 | 4 | 1 | |
| | Tampa Bay | 147 | 34 | 96 | 17 | 2 | | |
| | Totals | 1007 | 409 | 468 | 130 | 14 | 1 | 1979-99 |
| Denneny, Cy | Boston | 44 | 26 | 13 | 5 | 1 | 1 | |
| | Ottawa | 48 | 11 | 27 | 10 | 1 | | |
| | Totals | 92 | 37 | 40 | 15 | 2 | 1 | 1928-33 |
| Dineen, Bill | Philadelphia | 140 | 60 | 60 | 20 | 2 | | 1991-93 |
| Dudley, Rick | Buffalo | 188 | 85 | 72 | 31 | 3 | | |
| | Florida | 40 | 13 | 15 | 12 | 1 | | |
| | Totals | 228 | 98 | 87 | 43 | 4 | | 1989-04 |
| Duff, Dick | Toronto | 2 | 0 | 2 | 0 | 1 | | 1979-80 |
| Dugal, Jules | Montreal | 18 | 9 | 6 | 3 | 1 | | 1938-39 |
| Duncan, Art | Detroit | 33 | 10 | 21 | 2 | 1 | | |
| | Toronto | 47 | 21 | 16 | 10 | 2 | | |
| | Totals | 80 | 31 | 37 | 12 | 3 | | 1926-32 |
| Dutton, Red | NY Americans | 192 | 66 | 97 | 29 | 4 | | 1936-40 |
| Eddolls, Frank | Chicago | 70 | 13 | 40 | 17 | 1 | | 1954-55 |
| Esposito, Phil | NY Rangers | 45 | 24 | 21 | 0 | 2 | | 1986-89 |
| Evans, Jack | California | 80 | 27 | 42 | 11 | 1 | | |
| | Cleveland | 160 | 47 | 87 | 26 | 2 | | |
| | Hartford | 374 | 163 | 174 | 37 | 5 | | |
| | Totals | 614 | 237 | 303 | 74 | 8 | | 1975-88 |
| Fashoway, Gordie | Oakland | 10 | 4 | 5 | 1 | 1 | | 1967-68 |
| Ferguson, John | NY Rangers | 121 | 43 | 59 | 19 | 2 | | |
| | Winnipeg | 14 | 7 | 6 | 1 | 1 | | |
| | Totals | 135 | 50 | 65 | 20 | 3 | | 1975-86 |
| Filion, Maurice | Quebec | 6 | 1 | 3 | 2 | 1 | | 1980-81 |
| Francis, Bob | Phoenix | 390 | 165 | 144 | 81 | 5 | | 1999-04 |
| Francis, Emile | NY Rangers | 654 | 342 | 209 | 103 | 10 | | |
| | St. Louis | 124 | 46 | 64 | 14 | 3 | | |
| | Totals | 778 | 388 | 273 | 117 | 13 | | 1965-83 |
| Fraser, Curt | Atlanta | 279 | 64 | 169 | 46 | 4 | | 1999-03 |
| Fredrickson, Frank | Pittsburgh | 44 | 5 | 36 | 3 | 1 | | 1929-30 |
| Ftorek, Robbie | Los Angeles | 132 | 65 | 56 | 11 | 2 | | |
| | New Jersey | 156 | 88 | 44 | 24 | 2 | | |
| | Boston | 155 | 76 | 52 | 27 | 2 | | |
| | Totals | 443 | 229 | 152 | 62 | 6 | | 1987-03 |
| Gadsby, Bill | Detroit | 78 | 35 | 31 | 12 | 2 | | 1968-70 |

| Coach | Team | Games Coached | Wins | Losses | O/T | Years | Cup Wins | Career |
|---|---|---|---|---|---|---|---|---|
| Gainey, Bob | Minnesota | 244 | 95 | 119 | 30 | 3 | | |
| | Dallas | 171 | 70 | 71 | 30 | 3 | | |
| | Montreal | 57 | 29 | 21 | 7 | 2 | | |
| | **Totals** | **472** | **194** | **211** | **67** | **8** | | **1990-09** |
| Gallant, Gerard | Columbus | 142 | 56 | 76 | 10 | 4 | | 2003-07 |
| Gardiner, Herb | Chicago | 32 | 5 | 23 | 4 | 1 | | 1928-29 |
| Gardner, Jimmy | Hamilton | 30 | 19 | 10 | 1 | 1 | | 1924-25 |
| Garvin, Ted | Detroit | 11 | 2 | 8 | 1 | 1 | | 1973-74 |
| Geoffrion, Bernie | NY Rangers | 43 | 22 | 18 | 3 | 1 | | |
| | Atlanta | 208 | 77 | 92 | 39 | 3 | | |
| | Montreal | 30 | 15 | 9 | 6 | 1 | | |
| | **Totals** | **281** | **114** | **119** | **48** | **5** | | **1968-80** |
| Gerard, Eddie | Ottawa | 22 | 9 | 13 | 0 | 1 | | |
| | Mtl. Maroons | 294 | 129 | 122 | 43 | 7 | 1 | |
| | NY Americans | 92 | 34 | 40 | 18 | 2 | | |
| | St. Louis | 13 | 2 | 11 | 0 | 1 | | |
| | **Totals** | **421** | **174** | **186** | **61** | **11** | **1** | **1917-35** |
| Gilbert, Greg | Calgary | 121 | 42 | 56 | 23 | 3 | | 2000-03 |
| Gill, David | Ottawa | 132 | 64 | 41 | 27 | 3 | 1 | 1926-29 |
| Glover, Fred | Oakland | 152 | 51 | 76 | 25 | 2 | | |
| | California | 204 | 45 | 131 | 28 | 4 | | |
| | Los Angeles | 68 | 18 | 42 | 8 | 1 | | |
| | **Totals** | **424** | **114** | **249** | **61** | **6** | | **1968-74** |
| Goodfellow, Ebbie | Chicago | 140 | 30 | 91 | 19 | 2 | | 1950-52 |
| Gordon, Jackie | Minnesota | 289 | 116 | 123 | 50 | 5 | | 1970-75 |
| Gordon, Scott | NY Islanders | 82 | 26 | 47 | 9 | 1 | | 2008-09 |
| Goring, Butch | Boston | 93 | 42 | 38 | 13 | 2 | | |
| | NY Islanders | 147 | 41 | 88 | 18 | 2 | | |
| | **Totals** | **240** | **83** | **126** | **31** | **4** | | **1985-01** |
| Gorman, Tommy | NY Americans | 80 | 31 | 33 | 16 | 2 | | |
| | Chicago | 73 | 28 | 28 | 17 | 2 | 1 | |
| | Mtl. Maroons | 174 | 74 | 71 | 29 | 4 | 1 | |
| | **Totals** | **327** | **133** | **132** | **62** | **8** | **2** | **1925-38** |
| Gottselig, Johnny | Chicago | 187 | 62 | 105 | 20 | 4 | | 1944-48 |
| Goyette, Phil | NY Islanders | 48 | 6 | 38 | 4 | 1 | | 1972-73 |
| Graham, Dirk | Chicago | 59 | 16 | 35 | 8 | 1 | | 1998-99 |
| Granato, Tony | Colorado | 215 | 104 | 78 | 33 | 3 | | 2002-09 |
| Green, Gary | Washington | 157 | 50 | 78 | 29 | 3 | | 1979-82 |
| Green, Pete | Ottawa | 150 | 94 | 52 | 4 | 6 | 3 | 1919-25 |
| Green, Shorty | NY Americans | 44 | 11 | 27 | 6 | 1 | | 1927-28 |
| Green, Ted | Edmonton | 188 | 65 | 102 | 21 | 3 | | 1991-94 |
| Gretzky, Wayne | Phoenix | 328 | 143 | 161 | 24 | 4 | | 2005-09 |
| Guidolin, Aldo | Colorado | 59 | 12 | 39 | 8 | 1 | | 1978-79 |
| Guidolin, Bep | Boston | 104 | 72 | 23 | 9 | 2 | | |
| | Kansas City | 125 | 26 | 84 | 15 | 2 | | |
| | **Totals** | **229** | **98** | **107** | **24** | **4** | | **1972-76** |
| Hanlon, Glen | Washington | 239 | 78 | 122 | 39 | 5 | | 2003-08 |
| Harkness, Ned | Detroit | 38 | 12 | 22 | 4 | 1 | | 1970-71 |
| Harris, Ted | Minnesota | 179 | 48 | 104 | 27 | 3 | | 1975-78 |
| Hart, Cecil | Montreal | 394 | 196 | 125 | 73 | 9 | 2 | 1926-39 |
| Hartley, Bob | Colorado | 359 | 193 | 108 | 58 | 5 | 1 | |
| | Atlanta | 291 | 136 | 118 | 37 | 6 | | |
| | **Totals** | **650** | **329** | **226** | **95** | **10** | **1** | **1998-08** |
| Hartsburg, Craig | Chicago | 246 | 104 | 102 | 40 | 3 | | |
| | Anaheim | 197 | 80 | 82 | 35 | 3 | | |
| | Ottawa | 48 | 17 | 24 | 7 | 1 | | |
| | **Totals** | **491** | **201** | **208** | **82** | **7** | | **1995-09** |
| Harvey, Doug | NY Rangers | 70 | 26 | 32 | 12 | 1 | | 1961-62 |
| Hay, Don | Phoenix | 82 | 38 | 37 | 7 | 1 | | |
| | Calgary | 68 | 23 | 28 | 17 | 1 | | |
| | **Totals** | **150** | **61** | **65** | **24** | **2** | | **1996-01** |
| Heffernan, Frank | Toronto | 12 | 5 | 7 | 0 | 1 | | 1919-20 |
| Helmer, Rosie | NY Americans | 48 | 16 | 25 | 7 | 1 | | 1935-36 |
| Henning, Lorne | Minnesota | 158 | 68 | 72 | 18 | 2 | | |
| | NY Islanders | 65 | 19 | 39 | 7 | 2 | | |
| | **Totals** | **223** | **87** | **111** | **25** | **4** | | **1985-01** |
| Hitchcock, Ken | Dallas | 503 | 277 | 154 | 72 | 7 | 1 | |
| | Philadelphia | 254 | 131 | 73 | 50 | 5 | | |
| | Columbus | 226 | 103 | 96 | 27 | 3 | | |
| | **Totals** | **983** | **511** | **323** | **149** | **14** | **1** | **1995-09** |
| Hlinka, Ivan | Pittsburgh | 86 | 42 | 32 | 12 | 2 | | 2000-02 |
| Holmgren, Paul | Philadelphia | 264 | 107 | 126 | 31 | 4 | | |
| | Hartford | 161 | 54 | 93 | 14 | 4 | | |
| | **Totals** | **425** | **161** | **219** | **45** | **8** | | **1988-96** |
| Howell, Harry | Minnesota | 11 | 3 | 6 | 2 | 1 | | 1978-79 |
| Imlach, Punch | Toronto | 770 | 370 | 275 | 125 | 12 | 4 | |
| | Buffalo | 119 | 32 | 62 | 25 | 2 | | |
| | **Totals** | **889** | **402** | **337** | **150** | **14** | **4** | **1958-80** |
| Ingarfield, Earl | NY Islanders | 30 | 6 | 22 | 2 | 1 | | 1972-73 |
| Inglis, Bill | Buffalo | 56 | 28 | 18 | 10 | 1 | | 1978-79 |
| Irvin, Dick | Chicago | 126 | 45 | 62 | 19 | 3 | | |
| | Toronto | 427 | 216 | 152 | 59 | 9 | 1 | |
| | Montreal | 896 | 431 | 313 | 152 | 15 | 3 | |
| | **Totals** | **1449** | **692** | **527** | **230** | **27** | **4** | **1928-56** |
| Ivan, Tommy | Detroit | 470 | 262 | 118 | 90 | 7 | 3 | |
| | Chicago | 103 | 26 | 56 | 21 | 2 | | |
| | **Totals** | **573** | **288** | **174** | **111** | **9** | **3** | **1947-58** |
| Iverson, Emil | Chicago | 21 | 8 | 7 | 6 | 1 | | 1932-33 |
| Johnson, Bob | Calgary | 400 | 193 | 155 | 52 | 5 | | |
| | Pittsburgh | 80 | 41 | 33 | 6 | 1 | 1 | |
| | **Totals** | **480** | **234** | **188** | **58** | **6** | **1** | **1982-91** |
| Johnson, Tom | Boston | 208 | 142 | 43 | 23 | 3 | 1 | 1970-73 |
| Johnston, Eddie | Chicago | 80 | 34 | 27 | 19 | 1 | | |
| | Pittsburgh | 516 | 232 | 224 | 60 | 7 | | |
| | **Totals** | **596** | **266** | **251** | **79** | **8** | | **1979-97** |

| Coach | Team | Games Coached | Wins | Losses | O/T | Years | Cup Wins | Career |
|---|---|---|---|---|---|---|---|---|
| Johnston, Marshall | California | 69 | 13 | 45 | 11 | 2 | | |
| | Colorado | 56 | 15 | 32 | 9 | 1 | | |
| | **Totals** | **125** | **28** | **77** | **20** | **3** | | **1973-82** |
| Julien, Claude | Montreal | 159 | 72 | 62 | 25 | 4 | | |
| | New Jersey | 79 | 47 | 24 | 8 | 1 | | |
| | Boston | 164 | 94 | 48 | 31 | 2 | | |
| | **Totals** | **402** | **213** | **134** | **64** | **7** | | **2002-09** |
| Kasper, Steve | Boston | 164 | 66 | 78 | 20 | 2 | | 1995-97 |
| Keats, Duke | Detroit | 11 | 2 | 7 | 2 | 1 | | 1926-27 |
| Keenan, Mike | Philadelphia | 320 | 190 | 102 | 28 | 4 | | |
| | Chicago | 320 | 153 | 126 | 41 | 4 | | |
| | NY Rangers | 84 | 52 | 24 | 8 | 1 | 1 | |
| | St. Louis | 163 | 75 | 66 | 22 | 3 | | |
| | Vancouver | 108 | 36 | 54 | 18 | 2 | | |
| | Boston | 74 | 33 | 26 | 15 | 1 | | |
| | Florida | 153 | 45 | 73 | 35 | 3 | | |
| | Calgary | 164 | 88 | 60 | 16 | 2 | | |
| | **Totals** | **1386** | **672** | **531** | **183** | **20** | **1** | **1984-09** |
| Kehoe, Rick | Pittsburgh | 160 | 55 | 81 | 22 | 2 | | 2001-03 |
| Kelly, Pat | Colorado | 101 | 22 | 54 | 25 | 2 | | 1977-79 |
| Kelly, Red | Los Angeles | 150 | 55 | 75 | 20 | 2 | | |
| | Pittsburgh | 274 | 90 | 132 | 52 | 4 | | |
| | Toronto | 318 | 133 | 123 | 62 | 4 | | |
| | **Totals** | **742** | **278** | **330** | **134** | **10** | | **1967-77** |
| King, Dave | Calgary | 216 | 109 | 76 | 31 | 3 | | |
| | Columbus | 204 | 64 | 106 | 34 | 3 | | |
| | **Totals** | **420** | **173** | **182** | **65** | **6** | | **1992-03** |
| Kingston, George | San Jose | 164 | 28 | 129 | 7 | 2 | | 1991-93 |
| Kish, Larry | Hartford | 49 | 12 | 32 | 5 | 1 | | 1982-83 |
| Kitchen, Mike | St. Louis | 131 | 38 | 70 | 23 | 4 | | 2003-07 |
| Kromm, Bobby | Detroit | 231 | 79 | 111 | 41 | 3 | | 1977-80 |
| Kurtenbach, Orland | Vancouver | 125 | 36 | 62 | 27 | 2 | | 1976-78 |
| LaForge, Bill | Vancouver | 20 | 4 | 14 | 2 | 1 | | 1984-85 |
| Lalonde, Newsy | Montreal | 207 | 96 | 97 | 14 | 8 | | |
| | NY Americans | 44 | 17 | 25 | 2 | 1 | | |
| | Ottawa | 88 | 31 | 45 | 12 | 2 | | |
| | **Totals** | **339** | **144** | **167** | **28** | **11** | | **1917-35** |
| Lamoriello, Lou | New Jersey | 53 | 34 | 14 | 5 | 2 | | 2005-07 |
| Laperriere, Jacques | Montreal | 1 | 0 | 1 | 0 | 1 | | 1995-96 |
| Lapointe, Ron | Quebec | 89 | 33 | 50 | 6 | 2 | | 1987-89 |
| Laviolette, Peter | NY Islanders | 164 | 77 | 62 | 25 | 2 | | |
| | Carolina | 323 | 167 | 122 | 34 | 6 | 1 | |
| | **Totals** | **487** | **244** | **184** | **59** | **7** | **1** | **2001-08** |
| Laycoe, Hal | Los Angeles | 24 | 5 | 18 | 1 | 1 | | |
| | Vancouver | 156 | 44 | 96 | 16 | 2 | | |
| | **Totals** | **180** | **49** | **114** | **17** | **3** | | **1969-72** |
| Lehman, Hugh | Chicago | 21 | 3 | 17 | 1 | 1 | | 1927-28 |
| Lemaire, Jacques | Montreal | 97 | 48 | 37 | 12 | 2 | | |
| | New Jersey | 378 | 199 | 122 | 57 | 5 | 1 | |
| | Minnesota | 656 | 293 | 255 | 108 | 9 | | |
| | **Totals** | **1131** | **540** | **414** | **177** | **16** | **1** | **1983-09** |
| Lepine, Pit | Montreal | 48 | 10 | 33 | 5 | 1 | | 1939-40 |
| LeSueur, Percy | Hamilton | 10 | 3 | 7 | 0 | 1 | | 1923-24 |
| Lewis, Dave | Detroit * | 169 | 100 | 42 | 27 | 4 | | |
| | Boston | 82 | 35 | 41 | 6 | 1 | | |
| | **Totals** | **251** | **135** | **83** | **33** | **5** | | **1998-07** |

* Shared a record of 4-1-0 with co-coach Barry Smith in 1998-99

| Coach | Team | Games Coached | Wins | Losses | O/T | Years | Cup Wins | Career |
|---|---|---|---|---|---|---|---|---|
| Ley, Rick | Hartford | 160 | 69 | 71 | 20 | 2 | | |
| | Vancouver | 124 | 47 | 50 | 27 | 2 | | |
| | **Totals** | **284** | **116** | **121** | **47** | **4** | | **1989-96** |
| Lindsay, Ted | Detroit | 29 | 5 | 21 | 3 | 2 | | 1979-81 |
| Long, Barry | Winnipeg | 205 | 87 | 93 | 25 | 3 | | 1983-86 |
| Loughlin, Clem | Chicago | 144 | 61 | 63 | 20 | 3 | | 1934-37 |
| Low, Ron | Edmonton | 341 | 139 | 162 | 40 | 5 | | |
| | NY Rangers | 164 | 69 | 81 | 14 | 2 | | |
| | **Totals** | **505** | **208** | **243** | **54** | **7** | | **1994-02** |
| Lowe, Kevin | Edmonton | 82 | 32 | 26 | 24 | 1 | | 1999-00 |
| Ludzik, Steve | Tampa Bay | 121 | 31 | 67 | 23 | 2 | | 1999-01 |
| MacDonald, Parker | Minnesota | 61 | 20 | 30 | 11 | 1 | | |
| | Los Angeles | 42 | 13 | 24 | 5 | 1 | | |
| | **Totals** | **103** | **33** | **54** | **16** | **2** | | **1973-82** |
| MacLean, Doug | Florida | 187 | 83 | 71 | 33 | 3 | | |
| | Columbus | 79 | 24 | 43 | 12 | 2 | | |
| | **Totals** | **266** | **107** | **114** | **45** | **5** | | **1995-04** |
| MacMillan, Bill | Colorado | 80 | 22 | 45 | 13 | 1 | | |
| | New Jersey | 100 | 19 | 67 | 14 | 2 | | |
| | **Totals** | **180** | **41** | **112** | **27** | **3** | | **1980-84** |
| MacNeil, Al | Montreal | 55 | 31 | 15 | 9 | 1 | 1 | |
| | Atlanta | 80 | 35 | 32 | 13 | 1 | | |
| | Calgary | 171 | 72 | 66 | 33 | 3 | | |
| | **Totals** | **306** | **138** | **113** | **55** | **5** | **1** | **1970-03** |
| MacTavish, Craig | Edmonton | 656 | 301 | 252 | 103 | 9 | | 2000-09 |
| Magnuson, Keith | Chicago | 132 | 49 | 57 | 26 | 2 | | 1980-82 |
| Mahoney, Bill | Minnesota | 93 | 42 | 39 | 12 | 2 | | 1983-85 |
| Maloney, Dan | Toronto | 160 | 45 | 100 | 15 | 2 | | |
| | Winnipeg | 212 | 91 | 93 | 28 | 3 | | |
| | **Totals** | **372** | **136** | **193** | **43** | **5** | | **1984-89** |
| Maloney, Phil | Vancouver | 232 | 95 | 105 | 32 | 4 | | 1973-77 |
| Mantha, Sylvio | Montreal | 48 | 11 | 26 | 11 | 1 | | 1935-36 |
| Marshall, Bert | Colorado | 24 | 3 | 17 | 4 | 1 | | 1981-82 |
| Martin, Jacques | St. Louis | 160 | 66 | 71 | 23 | 2 | | |
| | Ottawa | 692 | 341 | 235 | 116 | 9 | | |
| | Florida | 246 | 110 | 100 | 36 | 4 | | |
| | **Totals** | **1098** | **517** | **406** | **175** | **15** | | **1986-08** |
| Matheson, Godfrey | Chicago | 2 | 0 | 2 | 0 | 1 | | 1932-33 |

| Coach | Team | Games Coached | Wins | Losses | O/T | Years | Cup Wins | Career |
|---|---|---|---|---|---|---|---|---|
| Maurice, Paul | Hartford | 152 | 61 | 72 | 19 | 2 | | |
| | Carolina | 579 | 240 | 238 | 101 | 8 | | |
| | Toronto | 164 | 76 | 66 | 22 | 2 | | |
| | **Totals** | **895** | **377** | **376** | **142** | **12** | | **1995-09** |
| Maxner, Wayne | Detroit | 129 | 34 | 68 | 27 | 2 | | 1980-82 |
| McCammon, Bob | Philadelphia | 218 | 119 | 68 | 31 | 4 | | |
| | Vancouver | 294 | 102 | 156 | 36 | 4 | | |
| | **Totals** | **512** | **221** | **224** | **67** | **8** | | **1978-91** |
| McCreary, Bill | St. Louis | 24 | 6 | 14 | 4 | 1 | | |
| | Vancouver | 41 | 9 | 25 | 7 | 1 | | |
| | California | 32 | 8 | 20 | 4 | 1 | | |
| | **Totals** | **97** | **23** | **59** | **15** | **3** | | **1971-75** |
| McGuire, Pierre | Hartford | 67 | 23 | 37 | 7 | 1 | | 1993-94 |
| McLellan, John | Toronto | 310 | 126 | 139 | 45 | 4 | | 1969-73 |
| McLellan, Todd | San Jose | 82 | 53 | 18 | 11 | 1 | | 2008-09 |
| McVie, Tom | Washington | 204 | 49 | 122 | 33 | 3 | | |
| | Winnipeg | 105 | 20 | 67 | 18 | 2 | | |
| | New Jersey | 153 | 57 | 74 | 22 | 3 | | |
| | **Totals** | **462** | **126** | **263** | **73** | **8** | | **1975-92** |
| Meeker, Howie | Toronto | 70 | 21 | 34 | 15 | 1 | | 1956-57 |
| Melrose, Barry | Los Angeles | 209 | 79 | 101 | 29 | 3 | | |
| | Tampa Bay | 16 | 5 | 7 | 4 | 1 | | |
| | **Totals** | **225** | **84** | **108** | **33** | **4** | | **1992-09** |
| Milbury, Mike | Boston | 160 | 90 | 49 | 21 | 2 | | |
| | NY Islanders | 191 | 56 | 111 | 24 | 4 | | |
| | **Totals** | **351** | **146** | **160** | **45** | **6** | | **1989-99** |
| Molleken, Lorne | Chicago | 47 | 18 | 19 | 10 | 2 | | 1998-00 |
| Muckler, John | Minnesota | 35 | 6 | 23 | 6 | 1 | | |
| | Edmonton | 160 | 75 | 65 | 20 | 2 | 1 | |
| | Buffalo | 268 | 125 | 109 | 34 | 4 | | |
| | NY Rangers | 185 | 70 | 88 | 27 | 3 | | |
| | **Totals** | **648** | **276** | **285** | **87** | **10** | **1** | **1968-00** |
| Muldoon, Pete | Chicago | 44 | 19 | 22 | 3 | 1 | | 1926-27 |
| Munro, Dunc | Mtl. Maroons | 76 | 37 | 29 | 10 | 2 | | 1929-31 |
| Murdoch, Bob | Chicago | 80 | 30 | 41 | 9 | 1 | | |
| | Winnipeg | 160 | 63 | 75 | 22 | 2 | | |
| | **Totals** | **240** | **93** | **116** | **31** | **3** | | **1987-91** |
| Murphy, Mike | Los Angeles | 65 | 20 | 37 | 8 | 2 | | |
| | Toronto | 164 | 60 | 87 | 17 | 2 | | |
| | **Totals** | **229** | **80** | **124** | **25** | **4** | | **1986-98** |
| Murray, Andy | Los Angeles | 480 | 215 | 176 | 89 | 7 | | |
| | St. Louis | 218 | 101 | 85 | 32 | 3 | | |
| | **Totals** | **698** | **316** | **261** | **121** | **10** | | **1999-09** |
| Murray, Bryan | Washington | 672 | 343 | 246 | 83 | 9 | | |
| | Detroit | 244 | 124 | 91 | 29 | 3 | | |
| | Florida | 59 | 17 | 31 | 11 | 1 | | |
| | Anaheim | 82 | 29 | 42 | 11 | 1 | | |
| | Ottawa | 182 | 107 | 55 | 20 | 4 | | |
| | **Totals** | **1239** | **620** | **465** | **154** | **18** | | **1981-08** |
| Murray, Terry | Washington | 325 | 163 | 134 | 28 | 5 | | |
| | Philadelphia | 212 | 118 | 64 | 30 | 3 | | |
| | Florida | 200 | 79 | 79 | 42 | 3 | | |
| | Los Angeles | 82 | 34 | 37 | 11 | 1 | | |
| | **Totals** | **819** | **394** | **314** | **111** | **12** | | **1989-09** |
| Nanne, Lou | Minnesota | 29 | 7 | 18 | 4 | 1 | | 1977-78 |
| Neale, Harry | Vancouver | 407 | 142 | 189 | 76 | 6 | | |
| | Detroit | 35 | 8 | 23 | 4 | 1 | | |
| | **Totals** | **442** | **150** | **212** | **80** | **7** | | **1978-86** |
| Neilson, Roger | Toronto | 160 | 75 | 62 | 23 | 2 | | |
| | Buffalo | 80 | 39 | 20 | 21 | 1 | | |
| | Vancouver | 133 | 51 | 61 | 21 | 3 | | |
| | Los Angeles | 28 | 8 | 17 | 3 | 1 | | |
| | NY Rangers | 280 | 141 | 104 | 35 | 4 | | |
| | Florida | 132 | 53 | 56 | 23 | 2 | | |
| | Philadelphia | 185 | 92 | 57 | 36 | 3 | | |
| | Ottawa | 2 | 1 | 1 | 0 | 1 | | |
| | **Totals** | **1000** | **460** | **378** | **162** | **16** | | **1977-02** |
| Nolan, Ted | Buffalo | 164 | 73 | 72 | 19 | 2 | | |
| | NY Islanders | 163 | 74 | 68 | 21 | 2 | | |
| | **Totals** | **327** | **147** | **140** | **40** | **4** | | **1995-08** |
| Nykoluk, Mike | Toronto | 280 | 89 | 144 | 47 | 4 | | 1980-84 |
| O'Connell, Mike | Boston | 9 | 3 | 3 | 3 | 1 | | 2002-03 |
| O'Donoghue, George | Toronto | 29 | 15 | 13 | 1 | 2 | 1 | 1921-23 |
| Olczyk, Ed | Pittsburgh | 113 | 31 | 64 | 18 | 3 | | 2003-06 |
| Oliver, Murray | Minnesota | 37 | 18 | 12 | 7 | 1 | | 1982-83 |
| Olmstead, Bert | Oakland | 64 | 11 | 37 | 16 | 1 | | 1967-68 |
| O'Reilly, Terry | Oakland | 227 | 115 | 86 | 26 | 3 | | 1986-89 |
| Paddock, John | Winnipeg | 281 | 106 | 138 | 37 | 4 | | |
| | Ottawa | 64 | 36 | 22 | 6 | 1 | | |
| | **Totals** | **345** | **142** | **160** | **43** | **5** | | **1991-08** |
| Page, Pierre | Minnesota | 160 | 63 | 77 | 20 | 2 | | |
| | Quebec | 230 | 98 | 103 | 29 | 3 | | |
| | Calgary | 164 | 66 | 78 | 20 | 2 | | |
| | Anaheim | 82 | 26 | 43 | 13 | 1 | | |
| | **Totals** | **636** | **253** | **301** | **82** | **8** | | **1988-98** |
| Park, Brad | Detroit | 45 | 9 | 34 | 2 | 1 | | 1985-86 |
| Paterson, Rick | Tampa Bay | 6 | 0 | 6 | 0 | 1 | | 1997-98 |
| Patrick, Craig | NY Rangers | 95 | 37 | 45 | 13 | 2 | | |
| | Pittsburgh | 74 | 29 | 36 | 9 | 2 | | |
| | **Totals** | **169** | **66** | **81** | **22** | **4** | | **1980-97** |
| Patrick, Frank | Boston | 96 | 48 | 36 | 12 | 2 | | 1934-36 |
| Patrick, Lester | NY Rangers | 604 | 281 | 216 | 107 | 13 | 2 | 1926-39 |

| Coach | Team | Games Coached | Wins | Losses | O/T | Years | Cup Wins | Career |
|---|---|---|---|---|---|---|---|---|
| Patrick, Lynn | NY Rangers | 107 | 40 | 51 | 16 | 2 | | |
| | NY Rangers | 310 | 117 | 130 | 63 | 5 | | |
| | St. Louis | 26 | 8 | 15 | 3 | 3 | | |
| | **Totals** | **443** | **165** | **196** | **82** | **10** | | **1948-76** |
| Patrick, Muzz | NY Rangers | 136 | 43 | 66 | 27 | 4 | | 1953-63 |
| Perron, Jean | Montreal | 240 | 126 | 84 | 30 | 3 | 1 | |
| | Quebec | 47 | 16 | 26 | 5 | 1 | | |
| | **Totals** | **287** | **142** | **110** | **35** | **4** | **1** | **1985-89** |
| Perry, Don | Los Angeles | 168 | 52 | 85 | 31 | 3 | | 1981-84 |
| Pike, Alf | NY Rangers | 123 | 36 | 66 | 21 | 2 | | 1959-61 |
| Pilous, Rudy | Chicago | 387 | 162 | 151 | 74 | 6 | 1 | 1957-63 |
| Plager, Barclay | St. Louis | 178 | 49 | 96 | 33 | 4 | | 1977-83 |
| Plager, Bob | St. Louis | 11 | 4 | 6 | 1 | 1 | | 1992-93 |
| Playfair, Jim | Calgary | 82 | 43 | 29 | 10 | 1 | | 2006-07 |
| Pleau, Larry | Hartford | 224 | 81 | 117 | 26 | 5 | | 1980-89 |
| Polano, Nick | Detroit | 240 | 79 | 127 | 34 | 3 | | 1982-85 |
| Popein, Larry | NY Rangers | 41 | 18 | 14 | 9 | 1 | | 1973-74 |
| Powers, Eddie | Toronto | 66 | 31 | 32 | 3 | 2 | | 1924-26 |
| Primeau, Joe | Toronto | 210 | 97 | 71 | 42 | 3 | 1 | 1950-53 |
| Pronovost, Marcel | Buffalo | 104 | 52 | 29 | 23 | 2 | | 1977-79 |
| Pulford, Bob | Los Angeles | 396 | 178 | 150 | 68 | 5 | | |
| | Chicago | 433 | 185 | 180 | 68 | 7 | | |
| | **Totals** | **829** | **363** | **330** | **136** | **12** | | **1972-00** |
| Quenneville, Joel | St. Louis | 593 | 307 | 191 | 95 | 8 | | |
| | Colorado | 246 | 131 | 92 | 23 | 4 | | |
| | Chicago | 78 | 45 | 22 | 11 | 1 | | |
| | **Totals** | **917** | **483** | **305** | **129** | **13** | | **1996-09** |
| Querrie, Charles | Toronto | 72 | 29 | 38 | 5 | 3 | | 1922-27 |
| Quinn, Mike | Quebec | 24 | 4 | 20 | 0 | 1 | | 1919-20 |
| Quinn, Pat | Philadelphia | 262 | 141 | 73 | 48 | 4 | | |
| | Los Angeles | 202 | 75 | 101 | 26 | 3 | | |
| | Vancouver | 280 | 141 | 111 | 28 | 5 | | |
| | Toronto | 574 | 300 | 196 | 78 | 8 | | |
| | **Totals** | **1318** | **657** | **481** | **180** | **20** | | **1978-06** |
| Raeder, Cap | San Jose | 1 | 1 | 0 | 0 | 1 | | 2002-03 |
| Ramsay, Craig | Buffalo | 21 | 4 | 15 | 2 | 1 | | |
| | Philadelphia | 28 | 12 | 12 | 4 | 1 | | |
| | **Totals** | **49** | **16** | **27** | **6** | **2** | | **1986-01** |
| Randall, Ken | Hamilton | 14 | 6 | 8 | 0 | 1 | | 1923-24 |
| Reay, Billy | Toronto | 90 | 26 | 50 | 14 | 2 | | |
| | Chicago | 1012 | 516 | 335 | 161 | 14 | | |
| | **Totals** | **1102** | **542** | **385** | **175** | **16** | | **1957-77** |
| Regan, Larry | Los Angeles | 88 | 27 | 47 | 14 | 2 | | 1970-72 |
| Renney, Tom | Vancouver | 101 | 39 | 53 | 9 | 2 | | |
| | NY Rangers | 327 | 164 | 117 | 46 | 6 | | |
| | **Totals** | **428** | **203** | **170** | **55** | **8** | | **1996-09** |
| Risebrough, Doug | Calgary | 144 | 71 | 56 | 17 | 2 | | 1990-92 |
| Roberts, Jim | Buffalo | 45 | 21 | 16 | 8 | 1 | | |
| | Hartford | 80 | 26 | 41 | 13 | 1 | | |
| | St. Louis | 9 | 3 | 3 | 3 | 1 | | |
| | **Totals** | **134** | **50** | **60** | **24** | **3** | | **1981-97** |
| Robinson, Larry | Los Angeles | 328 | 122 | 161 | 45 | 4 | | |
| | New Jersey | 173 | 87 | 56 | 30 | 4 | 1 | |
| | **Totals** | **501** | **209** | **217** | **75** | **8** | **1** | **1995-06** |
| Rodden, Mike | Toronto | 2 | 0 | 2 | 0 | 1 | | 1926-27 |
| Romeril, Alex | Toronto | 13 | 7 | 5 | 1 | 1 | | 1926-27 |
| Ross, Art | Mtl. Wanderers | 6 | 1 | 5 | 0 | 1 | | |
| | Hamilton | 24 | 6 | 18 | 0 | 1 | | |
| | Boston | 728 | 361 | 277 | 90 | 16 | 1 | |
| | **Totals** | **758** | **368** | **300** | **90** | **18** | **1** | **1917-45** |
| Ruel, Claude | Montreal | 305 | 172 | 82 | 51 | 5 | 1 | 1968-81 |
| Ruff, Lindy | Buffalo | 902 | 438 | 334 | 130 | 12 | | 1997-09 |
| Sather, Glen | Buffalo | 842 | 464 | 268 | 110 | 11 | 4 | |
| | NY Rangers | 90 | 33 | 39 | 18 | 2 | | |
| | **Totals** | **932** | **497** | **307** | **128** | **13** | **4** | **1979-04** |
| Sator, Ted | NY Rangers | 99 | 41 | 48 | 10 | 2 | | |
| | Buffalo | 207 | 96 | 89 | 22 | 3 | | |
| | **Totals** | **306** | **137** | **137** | **32** | **4** | | **1985-89** |
| Savard, Andre | Quebec | 24 | 10 | 13 | 1 | 1 | | 1987-88 |
| Savard, Denis | Chicago | 147 | 65 | 66 | 16 | 3 | | 2006-09 |
| Schinkel, Ken | Pittsburgh | 203 | 83 | 92 | 28 | 4 | | 1972-77 |
| Schmidt, Milt | Boston | 726 | 245 | 360 | 121 | 11 | | |
| | Washington | 44 | 5 | 34 | 5 | 2 | | |
| | **Totals** | **770** | **250** | **394** | **126** | **13** | | **1954-76** |
| Schoenfeld, Jim | Buffalo | 43 | 19 | 19 | 5 | 1 | | |
| | New Jersey | 124 | 50 | 59 | 15 | 3 | | |
| | Washington | 249 | 113 | 102 | 34 | 4 | | |
| | Phoenix | 164 | 74 | 66 | 24 | 2 | | |
| | **Totals** | **580** | **256** | **246** | **78** | **10** | | **1985-99** |
| Shaughnessy, Tom | Chicago | 21 | 10 | 8 | 3 | 1 | | 1929-30 |
| Shaw, Brad | NY Islanders | 40 | 18 | 18 | 4 | 1 | | 2005-06 |
| Shero, Fred | Philadelphia | 554 | 308 | 151 | 95 | 7 | 2 | |
| | NY Rangers | 180 | 82 | 74 | 24 | 3 | | |
| | **Totals** | **734** | **390** | **225** | **119** | **10** | **2** | **1971-81** |
| Simpson, Joe | NY Americans | 144 | 42 | 72 | 30 | 3 | | 1932-35 |
| Simpson, Terry | NY Islanders | 187 | 81 | 82 | 24 | 3 | | |
| | Philadelphia | 84 | 35 | 39 | 10 | 1 | | |
| | Winnipeg | 97 | 43 | 47 | 7 | 2 | | |
| | **Totals** | **368** | **159** | **168** | **41** | **6** | | **1986-96** |
| Sims, Al | San Jose | 82 | 27 | 47 | 8 | 1 | | 1996-97 |
| Sinden, Harry | Boston | 327 | 153 | 116 | 58 | 6 | 1 | 1966-85 |
| Skinner, Jimmy | Detroit | 247 | 123 | 78 | 46 | 4 | 1 | 1954-58 |
| Smeaton, Cooper | Philadelphia | 44 | 4 | 36 | 4 | 1 | | 1930-31 |
| Smith, Alf | Ottawa | 18 | 12 | 6 | 0 | 1 | | 1918-19 |

| Coach | Team | Games Coached | Wins | Losses | O/T | Years | Cup Wins | Career |
|---|---|---|---|---|---|---|---|---|
| Smith, Barry | Detroit * | 5 | 4 | 1 | 0 | 1 | | 1998-99 |
| | * Results Shared with co-coach Dave Lewis | | | | | | | |
| Smith, Floyd | Buffalo | 241 | 143 | 62 | 36 | 4 | | |
| | Toronto | 68 | 30 | 33 | 5 | 1 | | |
| | Totals | 309 | 173 | 95 | 41 | 5 | | 1971-80 |
| Smith, Mike | Winnipeg | 23 | 2 | 17 | 4 | 1 | | 1980-81 |
| Smith, Ron | NY Rangers | 44 | 15 | 22 | 7 | 1 | | 1992-93 |
| Smythe, Conn | Toronto | 134 | 57 | 57 | 20 | 4 | | 1927-31 |
| Sonmor, Glen | Minnesota | 421 | 177 | 161 | 83 | 7 | | 1978-87 |
| Sproule, Harvey | Toronto | 12 | 7 | 5 | 0 | 1 | | 1919-20 |
| Stanley, Barney | Chicago | 23 | 4 | 17 | 2 | 1 | | 1927-28 |
| Stasiuk, Vic | Philadelphia | 154 | 45 | 68 | 41 | 2 | | |
| | California | 75 | 21 | 38 | 16 | 1 | | |
| | Vancouver | 78 | 22 | 47 | 9 | 1 | | |
| | Totals | 307 | 88 | 153 | 66 | 4 | | 1969-73 |
| Stevens, John | Philadelphia | 238 | 107 | 98 | 33 | 3 | | 2006-09 |
| Stewart, Bill | NY Islanders | 37 | 11 | 19 | 7 | 1 | | 1998-99 |
| Stewart, Bill | Chicago | 69 | 22 | 35 | 12 | 2 | 1 | 1937-39 |
| Stewart, Ron | NY Rangers | 39 | 15 | 20 | 4 | 1 | | |
| | Los Angeles | 80 | 31 | 34 | 15 | 1 | | |
| | Totals | 119 | 46 | 54 | 19 | 2 | | 1975-78 |
| Stirling, Steve | NY Islanders | 124 | 56 | 51 | 17 | 3 | | 2003-06 |
| Suhonen, Alpo | Chicago | 82 | 29 | 41 | 12 | 1 | | 2000-01 |
| Sullivan, Mike | Boston | 164 | 70 | 56 | 38 | 3 | | 2003-06 |
| Sullivan, Red | NY Rangers | 196 | 58 | 103 | 35 | 4 | | |
| | Pittsburgh | 150 | 47 | 79 | 24 | 2 | | |
| | Washington | 18 | 2 | 16 | 0 | 1 | | |
| | Totals | 364 | 107 | 198 | 59 | 7 | | 1962-75 |
| Sutherland, Bill | Winnipeg | 32 | 7 | 22 | 3 | 2 | | 1979-81 |
| Sutter, Brent | New Jersey | 164 | 97 | 56 | 11 | 2 | | 2007-09 |
| Sutter, Brian | St. Louis | 320 | 153 | 124 | 43 | 4 | | |
| | Boston | 216 | 120 | 73 | 23 | 3 | | |
| | Calgary | 246 | 87 | 117 | 42 | 3 | | |
| | Chicago | 246 | 91 | 103 | 52 | 4 | | |
| | Totals | 1028 | 451 | 417 | 160 | 14 | | 1988-05 |
| Sutter, Darryl | Chicago | 216 | 110 | 80 | 26 | 3 | | |
| | San Jose | 434 | 192 | 167 | 75 | 6 | | |
| | Calgary | 210 | 107 | 73 | 30 | 4 | | |
| | Totals | 860 | 409 | 320 | 131 | 12 | | 1992-06 |
| Sutter, Duane | Florida | 72 | 22 | 35 | 15 | 2 | | 2000-02 |
| Talbot, Jean-Guy | St. Louis | 120 | 52 | 53 | 15 | 2 | | |
| | NY Rangers | 80 | 30 | 37 | 13 | 1 | | |
| | Totals | 200 | 82 | 90 | 28 | 3 | | 1972-78 |
| Tessier, Orval | Chicago | 213 | 99 | 93 | 21 | 3 | | 1982-85 |
| Therrien, Michel | Montreal | 190 | 77 | 77 | 36 | 3 | | |
| | Pittsburgh | 272 | 135 | 105 | 32 | 4 | | |
| | Totals | 462 | 212 | 182 | 68 | 7 | | 2000-09 |
| Thompson, Paul | Chicago | 272 | 104 | 127 | 41 | 7 | | 1938-45 |
| Thompson, Percy | Hamilton | 48 | 13 | 35 | 0 | 2 | | 1920-22 |
| Tippett, Dave | Dallas | 492 | 271 | 156 | 65 | 7 | | 2002-09 |
| Tobin, Bill | Chicago | 71 | 29 | 29 | 13 | 2 | | 1929-32 |
| Tocchet, Rick | Tampa Bay | 66 | 19 | 33 | 14 | 1 | | 2008-09 |
| Torchetti, John | Florida | 27 | 10 | 12 | 5 | 1 | | |
| | Los Angeles | 12 | 5 | 7 | 0 | 1 | | |
| | Totals | 39 | 15 | 19 | 5 | 2 | | 2003-06 |
| Tortorella, John | NY Rangers | 25 | 12 | 10 | 3 | 2 | | |
| | Tampa Bay | 535 | 239 | 222 | 74 | 8 | 1 | |
| | Totals | 560 | 251 | 232 | 77 | 10 | 1 | 1999-09 |
| Tremblay, Mario | Montreal | 159 | 71 | 63 | 25 | 2 | | 1995-97 |
| Trottier, Bryan | NY Rangers | 54 | 21 | 26 | 7 | 1 | | 2002-03 |
| Trotz, Barry | Nashville | 820 | 364 | 342 | 114 | 11 | | 1998-09 |
| Ubriaco, Gene | Pittsburgh | 106 | 50 | 47 | 9 | 2 | | 1988-90 |
| Vachon, Rogie | Los Angeles | 10 | 4 | 3 | 3 | 3 | | 1983-95 |
| Vigneault, Alain | Montreal | 266 | 109 | 118 | 39 | 4 | | |
| | Vancouver | 246 | 133 | 86 | 27 | 3 | | |
| | Totals | 512 | 242 | 204 | 66 | 7 | | 1997-09 |
| Waddell, Don | Atlanta | 86 | 38 | 39 | 9 | 2 | | 2002-08 |
| Watson, Bryan | Edmonton | 18 | 4 | 9 | 5 | 1 | | 1980-81 |
| Watson, Phil | NY Rangers | 295 | 119 | 124 | 52 | 5 | | |
| | Boston | 84 | 16 | 55 | 13 | 2 | | |
| | Totals | 379 | 135 | 179 | 65 | 7 | | 1955-63 |
| Watt, Tom | Winnipeg | 181 | 72 | 85 | 24 | 3 | | |
| | Vancouver | 160 | 52 | 87 | 21 | 2 | | |
| | Toronto | 149 | 52 | 80 | 17 | 2 | | |
| | Totals | 490 | 176 | 252 | 62 | 7 | | 1981-92 |
| Webster, Tom | NY Rangers | 18 | 5 | 9 | 4 | 1 | | |
| | Los Angeles | 240 | 115 | 94 | 31 | 3 | | |
| | Totals | 258 | 120 | 103 | 35 | 4 | | 1986-92 |
| Weiland, Cooney | Boston | 96 | 58 | 20 | 18 | 2 | 1 | 1939-41 |
| White, Bill | Chicago | 46 | 16 | 24 | 6 | 1 | | 1976-77 |
| Wiley, Jim | San Jose | 57 | 17 | 37 | 3 | 1 | | 1995-96 |
| Wilson, Johnny | Los Angeles | 52 | 9 | 34 | 9 | 1 | | |
| | Detroit | 145 | 67 | 56 | 22 | 2 | | |
| | Colorado | 80 | 20 | 46 | 14 | 1 | | |
| | Pittsburgh | 240 | 91 | 105 | 44 | 3 | | |
| | Totals | 517 | 187 | 241 | 89 | 7 | | 1969-80 |
| Wilson, Larry | Detroit | 36 | 3 | 29 | 4 | 1 | | 1976-77 |
| Wilson, Rick | Dallas | 32 | 13 | 11 | 8 | 1 | | 2001-02 |
| Wilson, Ron | Anaheim | 296 | 120 | 145 | 31 | 4 | | |
| | Washington | 410 | 192 | 159 | 59 | 5 | | |
| | San Jose | 385 | 206 | 122 | 57 | 6 | | |
| | Toronto | 82 | 34 | 35 | 13 | 1 | | |
| | Totals | 1173 | 552 | 461 | 160 | 16 | | 1993-09 |
| Yawney, Trent | Chicago | 103 | 33 | 55 | 15 | 2 | | 2005-07 |
| Young, Garry | California | 12 | 2 | 7 | 3 | 1 | | |
| | St. Louis | 98 | 41 | 41 | 16 | 2 | | |
| | Totals | 110 | 43 | 48 | 19 | 3 | | 1972-76 |

*Claude Julien (left) won the Jack Adams Award as coach of the year after leading the Boston Bruins to the best record in the Eastern Conference at 53-19-10 and 116 points. Andy Murray (center) finished as runner-up after leading St. Louis to a second-half surge that saw the Blues reach the postseason for the first time since 2003-04. Todd McLellan (right) finished third in voting after leading the San Jose Sharks to the best record in the NHL in his rookie season as an NHL head coach.*

# Year-by-Year Individual Regular-Season Leaders

| Season | Goals | G | Assists | A | Points | Pts. | Penalty Minutes | PIM |
|---|---|---|---|---|---|---|---|---|
| 1917-18 | Joe Malone | 44 | Cy Denneny, Reg Noble, Harry Cameron | 10 | Joe Malone | 48 | Joe Hall | 100 |
| 1918-19 | Newsy Lalonde | 22 | Newsy Lalonde | 10 | Newsy Lalonde | 32 | Joe Hall | 135 |
| 1919-20 | Joe Malone | 39 | Frank Nighbor | 15 | Joe Malone | 49 | Cully Wilson | 86 |
| 1920-21 | Babe Dye | 35 | Jack Darragh | 15 | Newsy Lalonde | 43 | Bert Corbeau | 86 |
| 1921-22 | Punch Broadbent | 32 | Harry Cameron | 17 | Punch Broadbent | 46 | Sprague Cleghorn | 63 |
| 1922-23 | Babe Dye | 26 | Eddie Gerard | 13 | Babe Dye | 37 | Georges Boucher | 58 |
| 1923-24 | Cy Denneny | 22 | Georges Boucher | 10 | Cy Denneny | 24 | Reg Noble | 79 |
| 1924-25 | Babe Dye | 38 | Cy Denneny, Red Green | 15 | Babe Dye | 46 | Georges Boucher | 95 |
| 1925-26 | Nels Stewart | 34 | Frank Nighbor | 13 | Nels Stewart | 42 | Bert Corbeau | 121 |
| 1926-27 | Bill Cook | 33 | Dick Irvin | 18 | Bill Cook | 37 | Nels Stewart | 133 |
| 1927-28 | Howie Morenz | 33 | Howie Morenz | 18 | Howie Morenz | 51 | Eddie Shore | 165 |
| 1928-29 | Ace Bailey | 22 | Frank Boucher | 16 | Ace Bailey | 32 | Red Dutton | 139 |
| 1929-30 | Cooney Weiland | 43 | Frank Boucher | 36 | Cooney Weiland | 73 | Joe Lamb | 119 |
| 1930-31 | Charlie Conacher | 31 | Joe Primeau | 32 | Howie Morenz | 51 | Harvey Rockburn | 118 |
| 1931-32 | Charlie Conacher, Bill Cook | 34 | Joe Primeau | 37 | Busher Jackson | 53 | Red Dutton | 107 |
| 1932-33 | Bill Cook | 28 | Frank Boucher | 28 | Bill Cook | 50 | Red Horner | 144 |
| 1933-34 | Charlie Conacher | 32 | Joe Primeau | 32 | Charlie Conacher | 52 | Red Horner | 126 * |
| 1934-35 | Charlie Conacher | 36 | Art Chapman | 34 | Charlie Conacher | 57 | Red Horner | 125 |
| 1935-36 | Charlie Conacher, Bill Thoms | 23 | Art Chapman | 28 | Sweeney Schriner | 45 | Red Horner | 167 |
| 1936-37 | Larry Aurie, Nels Stewart | 23 | Syl Apps | 29 | Sweeney Schriner | 46 | Red Horner | 124 |
| 1937-38 | Gordie Drillon | 26 | Syl Apps | 29 | Gordie Drillon | 52 | Art Coulter | 90 |
| 1938-39 | Roy Conacher | 26 | Bill Cowley | 34 | Toe Blake | 47 | Red Horner | 85 |
| 1939-40 | Bryan Hextall | 24 | Milt Schmidt | 30 | Milt Schmidt | 52 | Red Horner | 87 |
| 1940-41 | Bryan Hextall | 26 | Bill Cowley | 45 | Bill Cowley | 62 | Jimmy Orlando | 99 |
| 1941-42 | Lynn Patrick | 32 | Phil Watson | 37 | Bryan Hextall | 56 | Pat Egan | 124 |
| 1942-43 | Doug Bentley | 33 | Bill Cowley | 45 | Doug Bentley | 73 | Jimmy Orlando | 89 * |
| 1943-44 | Doug Bentley | 38 | Clint Smith | 49 | Herb Cain | 82 | Mike McMahon | 98 |
| 1944-45 | Maurice Richard | 50 | Elmer Lach | 54 | Elmer Lach | 80 | Pat Egan | 86 |
| 1945-46 | Gaye Stewart | 37 | Elmer Lach | 34 | Max Bentley | 61 | Jack Stewart | 73 |
| 1946-47 | Maurice Richard | 45 | Billy Taylor | 46 | Max Bentley | 72 | Gus Mortson | 133 |
| 1947-48 | Ted Lindsay | 33 | Doug Bentley | 37 | Elmer Lach | 61 | Bill Barilko | 147 |
| 1948-49 | Sid Abel | 28 | Doug Bentley | 43 | Roy Conacher | 68 | Bill Ezinicki | 145 |
| 1949-50 | Maurice Richard | 43 | Ted Lindsay | 55 | Ted Lindsay | 78 | Bill Ezinicki | 144 |
| 1950-51 | Gordie Howe | 43 | Gordie Howe, Ted Kennedy | 43 | Gordie Howe | 86 | Gus Mortson | 142 |
| 1951-52 | Gordie Howe | 47 | Elmer Lach | 50 | Gordie Howe | 86 | Gus Kyle | 127 |
| 1952-53 | Gordie Howe | 49 | Gordie Howe | 46 | Gordie Howe | 95 | Maurice Richard | 112 |
| 1953-54 | Maurice Richard | 37 | Gordie Howe | 48 | Gordie Howe | 81 | Gus Mortson | 132 |
| 1954-55 | Maurice Richard, Bernie Geoffrion | 38 | Bert Olmstead | 48 | Bernie Geoffrion | 75 | Fern Flaman | 150 |
| 1955-56 | Jean Beliveau | 47 | Bert Olmstead | 56 | Jean Beliveau | 88 | Lou Fontinato | 202 |
| 1956-57 | Gordie Howe | 44 | Ted Lindsay | 55 | Gordie Howe | 89 | Gus Mortson | 147 |
| 1957-58 | Dickie Moore | 36 | Henri Richard | 52 | Dickie Moore | 84 | Lou Fontinato | 152 |
| 1958-59 | Jean Beliveau | 45 | Dickie Moore | 55 | Dickie Moore | 96 | Ted Lindsay | 184 |
| 1959-60 | Bobby Hull, Bronco Horvath | 39 | Don McKenney | 49 | Bobby Hull | 81 | Carl Brewer | 150 |
| 1960-61 | Bernie Geoffrion | 50 | Jean Beliveau | 58 | Bernie Geoffrion | 95 | Pierre Pilote | 165 |
| 1961-62 | Bobby Hull | 50 | Andy Bathgate | 56 | Bobby Hull, Andy Bathgate | 84 | Lou Fontinato | 167 |
| 1962-63 | Gordie Howe | 38 | Henri Richard | 50 | Gordie Howe | 86 | Howie Young | 273 |
| 1963-64 | Bobby Hull | 43 | Andy Bathgate | 58 | Stan Mikita | 89 | Vic Hadfield | 151 |
| 1964-65 | Norm Ullman | 42 | Stan Mikita | 59 | Stan Mikita | 87 | Carl Brewer | 177 |
| 1965-66 | Bobby Hull | 54 | Stan Mikita, Bobby Rousseau, Jean Beliveau | 48 | Bobby Hull | 97 | Reggie Fleming | 166 |
| 1966-67 | Bobby Hull | 52 | Stan Mikita | 62 | Stan Mikita | 97 | John Ferguson | 177 |
| 1967-68 | Bobby Hull | 44 | Phil Esposito | 49 | Stan Mikita | 87 | Barclay Plager | 153 |
| 1968-69 | Bobby Hull | 58 | Phil Esposito | 77 | Phil Esposito | 126 | Forbes Kennedy | 219 |
| 1969-70 | Phil Esposito | 43 | Bobby Orr | 87 | Bobby Orr | 120 | Keith Magnuson | 213 |
| 1970-71 | Phil Esposito | 76 | Bobby Orr | 102 | Phil Esposito | 152 | Keith Magnuson | 291 |
| 1971-72 | Phil Esposito | 66 | Bobby Orr | 80 | Phil Esposito | 133 | Bryan Watson | 212 |
| 1972-73 | Phil Esposito | 55 | Phil Esposito | 75 | Phil Esposito | 130 | Dave Schultz | 259 |
| 1973-74 | Phil Esposito | 68 | Bobby Orr | 90 | Phil Esposito | 145 | Dave Schultz | 348 |
| 1974-75 | Phil Esposito | 61 | Bobby Orr, Bobby Clarke | 89 | Bobby Orr | 135 | Dave Schultz | 472 |
| 1975-76 | Reggie Leach | 61 | Bobby Clarke | 89 | Guy Lafleur | 125 | Steve Durbano | 370 |
| 1976-77 | Steve Shutt | 60 | Guy Lafleur | 80 | Guy Lafleur | 136 | Tiger Williams | 338 |
| 1977-78 | Guy Lafleur | 60 | Bryan Trottier | 77 | Guy Lafleur | 132 | Dave Schultz | 405 |
| 1978-79 | Mike Bossy | 69 | Bryan Trottier | 87 | Bryan Trottier | 134 | Tiger Williams | 298 |
| 1979-80 | Charlie Simmer, Danny Gare, Blaine Stoughton | 56 | Wayne Gretzky | 86 | Marcel Dionne, Wayne Gretzky | 137 | Jimmy Mann | 287 |
| 1980-81 | Mike Bossy | 68 | Wayne Gretzky | 109 | Wayne Gretzky | 164 | Tiger Williams | 343 |
| 1981-82 | Wayne Gretzky | 92 | Wayne Gretzky | 120 | Wayne Gretzky | 212 | Paul Baxter | 409 |
| 1982-83 | Wayne Gretzky | 71 | Wayne Gretzky | 125 | Wayne Gretzky | 196 | Randy Holt | 275 |
| 1983-84 | Wayne Gretzky | 87 | Wayne Gretzky | 118 | Wayne Gretzky | 205 | Chris Nilan | 338 |
| 1984-85 | Wayne Gretzky | 73 | Wayne Gretzky | 135 | Wayne Gretzky | 208 | Chris Nilan | 358 |
| 1985-86 | Jari Kurri | 68 | Wayne Gretzky | 163 | Wayne Gretzky | 215 | Joe Kocur | 377 |
| 1986-87 | Wayne Gretzky | 62 | Wayne Gretzky | 121 | Wayne Gretzky | 183 | Tim Hunter | 361 |
| 1987-88 | Mario Lemieux | 70 | Wayne Gretzky | 109 | Mario Lemieux | 168 | Bob Probert | 398 |
| 1988-89 | Mario Lemieux | 85 | Mario Lemieux, Wayne Gretzky | 114 | Mario Lemieux | 199 | Tim Hunter | 375 |
| 1989-90 | Brett Hull | 72 | Wayne Gretzky | 102 | Wayne Gretzky | 142 | Basil McRae | 351 |
| 1990-91 | Brett Hull | 86 | Wayne Gretzky | 122 | Wayne Gretzky | 163 | Rob Ray | 350 |
| 1991-92 | Brett Hull | 70 | Wayne Gretzky | 90 | Mario Lemieux | 131 | Mike Peluso | 408 |
| 1992-93 | Teemu Selanne, Alexander Mogilny | 76 | Adam Oates | 97 | Mario Lemieux | 160 | Marty McSorley | 399 |
| 1993-94 | Pavel Bure | 60 | Wayne Gretzky | 92 | Wayne Gretzky | 130 | Tie Domi | 347 |
| 1994-95 | Peter Bondra | 34 | Ron Francis | 48 | Jaromir Jagr, Eric Lindros | 70 | Enrico Ciccone | 225 |
| 1995-96 | Mario Lemieux | 69 | Mario Lemieux, Ron Francis | 92 | Mario Lemieux | 161 | Matthew Barnaby | 335 |
| 1996-97 | Keith Tkachuk | 52 | Mario Lemieux, Wayne Gretzky | 72 | Mario Lemieux | 122 | Gino Odjick | 371 |
| 1997-98 | Teemu Selanne, Peter Bondra | 52 | Jaromir Jagr, Wayne Gretzky | 67 | Jaromir Jagr | 102 | Donald Brashear | 372 |
| 1998-99 | Teemu Selanne | 47 | Jaromir Jagr | 83 | Jaromir Jagr | 127 | Rob Ray | 261 |
| 99-2000 | Pavel Bure | 58 | Mark Recchi | 63 | Jaromir Jagr | 96 | Denny Lambert | 219 |
| 2000-01 | Pavel Bure | 59 | Jaromir Jagr, Adam Oates | 69 | Jaromir Jagr | 121 | Matthew Barnaby | 265 |
| 2001-02 | Jarome Iginla | 52 | Adam Oates | 64 | Jarome Iginla | 96 | Peter Worell | 354 |
| 2002-03 | Milan Hejduk | 50 | Peter Forsberg | 77 | Peter Forsberg | 106 | Jody Shelley | 249 |
| 2003-04 | Rick Nash, Jarome Iginla, Ilya Kovalchuk | 41 | Scott Gomez, Martin St. Louis | 56 | Martin St. Louis | 94 | Sean Avery | 261 |
| 2004-05 | .... | .... | .... | .... | .... | .... | .... | .... |
| 2005-06 | Jonathan Cheechoo | 56 | Joe Thornton | 96 | Joe Thornton | 125 | Sean Avery | 257 |
| 2006-07 | Vincent Lecavalier | 52 | Joe Thornton | 92 | Sidney Crosby | 120 | Ben Eager | 233 |
| 2007-08 | Alex Ovechkin | 65 | Joe Thornton | 67 | Alex Ovechkin | 112 | Daniel Carcillo | 324 |
| 2008-09 | Alex Ovechkin | 56 | Evgeni Malkin | 78 | Evgeni Malkin | 113 | Daniel Carcillo | 254 |

* Match Misconduct penalty not included in total penalty minutes.
1946-47 was the first season that a Match penalty was automaticaly written into the player's total penalty minutes as 20 minutes.
Beginning in 1947-48 all penalties, Match, Game Misconduct, and Misconduct, are written as 10 minutes.

# One Season Scoring Records

## Goals-Per-Game Leaders, One Season

**(Among players with 20 goals or more in one season)**

| Player | Team | Season | Games | Goals | Goals per game average |
|---|---|---|---|---|---|
| Joe Malone | Montreal | 1917-18 | 20 | 44 | 2.20 |
| Cy Denneny | Ottawa | 1917-18 | 20 | 36 | 1.80 |
| Newsy Lalonde | Montreal | 1917-18 | 14 | 23 | 1.64 |
| Joe Malone | Quebec | 1919-20 | 24 | 39 | 1.63 |
| Newsy Lalonde | Montreal | 1919-20 | 23 | 37 | 1.61 |
| Reg Noble | Toronto | 1917-18 | 20 | 30 | 1.50 |
| Babe Dye | Ham., Tor. | 1920-21 | 24 | 35 | 1.46 |
| Cy Denneny | Ottawa | 1920-21 | 24 | 34 | 1.42 |
| Joe Malone | Hamilton | 1920-21 | 20 | 28 | 1.40 |
| Newsy Lalonde | Montreal | 1920-21 | 24 | 33 | 1.38 |
| Punch Broadbent | Ottawa | 1921-22 | 24 | 32 | 1.33 |
| Babe Dye | Toronto | 1924-25 | 29 | 38 | 1.31 |
| Babe Dye | Toronto | 1921-22 | 24 | 31 | 1.29 |
| Newsy Lalonde | Montreal | 1918-19 | 17 | 22 | 1.29 |
| Odie Cleghorn | Montreal | 1918-19 | 17 | 22 | 1.29 |
| Cy Denneny | Ottawa | 1921-22 | 22 | 27 | 1.23 |
| Aurel Joliat | Montreal | 1924-25 | 25 | 30 | 1.20 |
| Wayne Gretzky | Edmonton | 1983-84 | 74 | 87 | 1.18 |
| Babe Dye | Toronto | 1922-23 | 22 | 26 | 1.18 |
| Wayne Gretzky | Edmonton | 1981-82 | 80 | 92 | 1.15 |
| Mario Lemieux | Pittsburgh | 1992-93 | 60 | 69 | 1.15 |
| Frank Nighbor | Ottawa | 1919-20 | 23 | 26 | 1.13 |
| Mario Lemieux | Pittsburgh | 1988-89 | 76 | 85 | 1.12 |
| Brett Hull | St. Louis | 1990-91 | 78 | 86 | 1.10 |
| Cam Neely | Boston | 1993-94 | 49 | 50 | 1.02 |
| Maurice Richard | Montreal | 1944-45 | 50 | 50 | 1.00 |
| Reg Noble | Toronto | 1919-20 | 24 | 24 | 1.00 |
| Corb Denneny | Toronto | 1919-20 | 24 | 24 | 1.00 |
| Joe Malone | Hamilton | 1921-22 | 24 | 24 | 1.00 |
| Billy Boucher | Montreal | 1922-23 | 24 | 24 | 1.00 |
| Cy Denneny | Ottawa | 1923-24 | 22 | 22 | 1.00 |
| Alexander Mogilny | Buffalo | 1992-93 | 77 | 76 | 0.99 |
| Mario Lemieux | Pittsburgh | 1995-96 | 70 | 69 | 0.99 |
| Cooney Weiland | Boston | 1929-30 | 44 | 43 | 0.98 |
| Phil Esposito | Boston | 1970-71 | 78 | 76 | 0.97 |
| Jari Kurri | Edmonton | 1984-85 | 73 | 71 | 0.97 |

*One of the prettiest playmakers of his era, Chicago Blackhawks' future Hall of Famer Denis Savard averaged better than an assist per game over the course of an entire season four times in the 1980s.*

## Assists-Per-Game Leaders, One Season

**(Among players with 35 assists or more in one season)**

| Player | Team | Season | Games | Assists | Assists per game average |
|---|---|---|---|---|---|
| Wayne Gretzky | Edmonton | 1985-86 | 80 | 163 | 2.04 |
| Wayne Gretzky | Edmonton | 1987-88 | 64 | 109 | 1.70 |
| Wayne Gretzky | Edmonton | 1984-85 | 80 | 135 | 1.69 |
| Wayne Gretzky | Edmonton | 1983-84 | 74 | 118 | 1.59 |
| Wayne Gretzky | Edmonton | 1982-83 | 80 | 125 | 1.56 |
| Wayne Gretzky | Los Angeles | 1990-91 | 78 | 122 | 1.56 |
| Wayne Gretzky | Edmonton | 1986-87 | 79 | 121 | 1.53 |
| Mario Lemieux | Pittsburgh | 1992-93 | 60 | 91 | 1.52 |
| Wayne Gretzky | Edmonton | 1981-82 | 80 | 120 | 1.50 |
| Mario Lemieux | Pittsburgh | 1988-89 | 76 | 114 | 1.50 |
| Adam Oates | St. Louis | 1990-91 | 61 | 90 | 1.48 |
| Wayne Gretzky | Los Angeles | 1988-89 | 78 | 114 | 1.46 |
| Wayne Gretzky | Los Angeles | 1989-90 | 73 | 102 | 1.40 |
| Wayne Gretzky | Edmonton | 1980-81 | 80 | 109 | 1.36 |
| Mario Lemieux | Pittsburgh | 1991-92 | 64 | 87 | 1.36 |
| Mario Lemieux | Pittsburgh | 1989-90 | 59 | 78 | 1.32 |
| Bobby Orr | Boston | 1970-71 | 78 | 102 | 1.31 |
| Mario Lemieux | Pittsburgh | 1995-96 | 70 | 92 | 1.31 |
| Mario Lemieux | Pittsburgh | 1987-88 | 77 | 98 | 1.27 |
| Bobby Orr | Boston | 1973-74 | 74 | 90 | 1.22 |
| Wayne Gretzky | Los Angeles | 1991-92 | 74 | 90 | 1.22 |
| Joe Thornton | Bos., S.J. | 2005-06 | 81 | 96 | 1.19 |
| Ron Francis | Pittsburgh | 1995-96 | 77 | 92 | 1.19 |
| Mario Lemieux | Pittsburgh | 1985-86 | 79 | 93 | 1.18 |
| Bobby Clarke | Philadelphia | 1975-76 | 76 | 89 | 1.17 |
| Peter Stastny | Quebec | 1981-82 | 80 | 93 | 1.16 |
| Adam Oates | Boston | 1992-93 | 84 | 97 | 1.15 |
| Doug Gilmour | Toronto | 1992-93 | 83 | 95 | 1.14 |
| Wayne Gretzky | Los Angeles | 1993-94 | 81 | 92 | 1.14 |
| Paul Coffey | Edmonton | 1985-86 | 79 | 90 | 1.14 |
| Bobby Orr | Boston | 1969-70 | 76 | 87 | 1.14 |
| Bryan Trottier | NY Islanders | 1978-79 | 76 | 87 | 1.14 |
| Bobby Orr | Boston | 1972-73 | 63 | 72 | 1.14 |
| Bill Cowley | Boston | 1943-44 | 36 | 41 | 1.14 |
| Pat LaFontaine | Buffalo | 1992-93 | 84 | 95 | 1.13 |
| Steve Yzerman | Detroit | 1988-89 | 80 | 90 | 1.13 |
| Paul Coffey | Pittsburgh | 1987-88 | 46 | 52 | 1.13 |
| Joe Thornton | San Jose | 2006-07 | 82 | 92 | 1.12 |
| Bobby Orr | Boston | 1974-75 | 80 | 89 | 1.11 |
| Bobby Clarke | Philadelphia | 1974-75 | 80 | 89 | 1.11 |
| Paul Coffey | Pittsburgh | 1988-89 | 75 | 83 | 1.11 |
| Wayne Gretzky | Los Angeles | 1992-93 | 45 | 49 | 1.11 |
| Denis Savard | Chicago | 1982-83 | 78 | 86 | 1.10 |
| Denis Savard | Chicago | 1981-82 | 80 | 87 | 1.09 |
| Denis Savard | Chicago | 1987-88 | 80 | 87 | 1.09 |
| Wayne Gretzky | Edmonton | 1979-80 | 79 | 86 | 1.09 |
| Ron Francis | Pittsburgh | 1994-95 | 44 | 48 | 1.09 |
| Paul Coffey | Edmonton | 1983-84 | 80 | 86 | 1.08 |
| Elmer Lach | Montreal | 1944-45 | 50 | 54 | 1.08 |
| Peter Stastny | Quebec | 1985-86 | 76 | 81 | 1.07 |
| Jaromir Jagr | Pittsburgh | 1995-96 | 82 | 87 | 1.06 |
| Mark Messier | Edmonton | 1989-90 | 79 | 84 | 1.06 |
| Sidney Crosby | Pittsburgh | 2006-07 | 79 | 84 | 1.06 |
| Peter Forsberg | Colorado | 1995-96 | 82 | 86 | 1.05 |
| Paul Coffey | Edmonton | 1984-85 | 80 | 84 | 1.05 |
| Marcel Dionne | Los Angeles | 1979-80 | 80 | 84 | 1.05 |
| Bobby Orr | Boston | 1971-72 | 76 | 80 | 1.05 |
| Mike Bossy | NY Islanders | 1981-82 | 80 | 83 | 1.04 |
| Adam Oates | Boston | 1993-94 | 77 | 80 | 1.04 |
| Phil Esposito | Boston | 1968-69 | 74 | 77 | 1.04 |
| Bryan Trottier | NY Islanders | 1983-84 | 68 | 71 | 1.04 |
| Jason Spezza | Ottawa | 2005-06 | 68 | 71 | 1.04 |
| Pete Mahovlich | Montreal | 1974-75 | 80 | 82 | 1.03 |
| Kent Nilsson | Calgary | 1980-81 | 80 | 82 | 1.03 |
| Peter Stastny | Quebec | 1982-83 | 75 | 77 | 1.03 |
| Peter Forsberg | Colorado | 2002-03 | 75 | 77 | 1.03 |
| Denis Savard | Chicago | 1988-89 | 58 | 59 | 1.02 |
| Jaromir Jagr | Pittsburgh | 1998-99 | 81 | 83 | 1.02 |
| Doug Gilmour | Toronto | 1993-94 | 83 | 84 | 1.01 |
| Bernie Nicholls | Los Angeles | 1988-89 | 79 | 80 | 1.01 |
| Guy Lafleur | Montreal | 1979-80 | 74 | 75 | 1.01 |
| Guy Lafleur | Montreal | 1976-77 | 80 | 80 | 1.00 |
| Marcel Dionne | Los Angeles | 1984-85 | 80 | 80 | 1.00 |
| Brian Leetch | NY Rangers | 1991-92 | 80 | 80 | 1.00 |
| Bryan Trottier | NY Islanders | 1977-78 | 77 | 77 | 1.00 |
| Mike Bossy | NY Islanders | 1983-84 | 67 | 67 | 1.00 |
| Jean Ratelle | NY Rangers | 1971-72 | 63 | 63 | 1.00 |
| Steve Yzerman | Detroit | 1993-94 | 58 | 58 | 1.00 |
| Ron Francis | Hartford | 1985-86 | 53 | 53 | 1.00 |
| Guy Chouinard | Calgary | 1980-81 | 52 | 52 | 1.00 |
| Elmer Lach | Montreal | 1943-44 | 48 | 48 | 1.00 |

## Points-Per-Game Leaders, One Season

**(Among players with 50 points or more in one season)**

| Player | Team | Season | Games | Points | Points per game average |
|---|---|---|---|---|---|
| Wayne Gretzky | Edmonton | 1983-84 | 74 | 205 | 2.77 |
| Wayne Gretzky | Edmonton | 1985-86 | 80 | 215 | 2.69 |
| Mario Lemieux | Pittsburgh | 1992-93 | 60 | 160 | 2.67 |
| Wayne Gretzky | Edmonton | 1981-82 | 80 | 212 | 2.65 |
| Mario Lemieux | Pittsburgh | 1988-89 | 76 | 199 | 2.62 |
| Wayne Gretzky | Edmonton | 1984-85 | 80 | 208 | 2.60 |
| Wayne Gretzky | Edmonton | 1982-83 | 80 | 196 | 2.45 |
| Wayne Gretzky | Edmonton | 1987-88 | 64 | 149 | 2.33 |
| Wayne Gretzky | Edmonton | 1986-87 | 79 | 183 | 2.32 |
| Mario Lemieux | Pittsburgh | 1995-96 | 70 | 161 | 2.30 |
| Mario Lemieux | Pittsburgh | 1987-88 | 77 | 168 | 2.18 |
| Wayne Gretzky | Los Angeles | 1988-89 | 78 | 168 | 2.15 |
| Wayne Gretzky | Los Angeles | 1990-91 | 78 | 163 | 2.09 |
| Mario Lemieux | Pittsburgh | 1989-90 | 59 | 123 | 2.08 |
| Wayne Gretzky | Edmonton | 1980-81 | 80 | 164 | 2.05 |
| Mario Lemieux | Pittsburgh | 1991-92 | 64 | 131 | 2.05 |
| Bill Cowley | Boston | 1943-44 | 36 | 71 | 1.97 |
| Phil Esposito | Boston | 1970-71 | 78 | 152 | 1.95 |
| Wayne Gretzky | Los Angeles | 1989-90 | 73 | 142 | 1.95 |
| Steve Yzerman | Detroit | 1988-89 | 80 | 155 | 1.94 |
| Bernie Nicholls | Los Angeles | 1988-89 | 79 | 150 | 1.90 |
| Adam Oates | St. Louis | 1990-91 | 61 | 115 | 1.89 |
| Phil Esposito | Boston | 1973-74 | 78 | 145 | 1.86 |
| Jari Kurri | Edmonton | 1984-85 | 73 | 135 | 1.85 |
| Mike Bossy | NY Islanders | 1981-82 | 80 | 147 | 1.84 |
| Jaromir Jagr | Pittsburgh | 1995-96 | 82 | 149 | 1.82 |
| Mario Lemieux | Pittsburgh | 1985-86 | 79 | 141 | 1.78 |
| Bobby Orr | Boston | 1970-71 | 78 | 139 | 1.78 |
| Jari Kurri | Edmonton | 1983-84 | 64 | 113 | 1.77 |
| Mario Lemieux | Pittsburgh | 2000-01 | 43 | 76 | 1.77 |
| Pat LaFontaine | Buffalo | 1992-93 | 84 | 148 | 1.76 |
| Bryan Trottier | NY Islanders | 1978-79 | 76 | 134 | 1.76 |
| Mike Bossy | NY Islanders | 1983-84 | 67 | 118 | 1.76 |
| Paul Coffey | Edmonton | 1985-86 | 79 | 138 | 1.75 |
| Phil Esposito | Boston | 1971-72 | 76 | 133 | 1.75 |
| Peter Stastny | Quebec | 1981-82 | 80 | 139 | 1.74 |
| Wayne Gretzky | Edmonton | 1979-80 | 79 | 137 | 1.73 |
| Jean Ratelle | NY Rangers | 1971-72 | 63 | 109 | 1.73 |
| Marcel Dionne | Los Angeles | 1979-80 | 80 | 137 | 1.71 |
| Herb Cain | Boston | 1943-44 | 48 | 82 | 1.71 |
| Guy Lafleur | Montreal | 1976-77 | 80 | 136 | 1.70 |
| Dennis Maruk | Washington | 1981-82 | 80 | 136 | 1.70 |
| Phil Esposito | Boston | 1968-69 | 74 | 126 | 1.70 |
| Guy Lafleur | Montreal | 1974-75 | 70 | 119 | 1.70 |
| Mario Lemieux | Pittsburgh | 1986-87 | 63 | 107 | 1.70 |
| Adam Oates | Boston | 1992-93 | 84 | 142 | 1.69 |
| Bobby Orr | Boston | 1974-75 | 80 | 135 | 1.69 |
| Marcel Dionne | Los Angeles | 1980-81 | 80 | 135 | 1.69 |
| Guy Lafleur | Montreal | 1977-78 | 78 | 132 | 1.69 |
| Guy Lafleur | Montreal | 1979-80 | 74 | 125 | 1.69 |
| Rob Brown | Pittsburgh | 1988-89 | 68 | 115 | 1.69 |
| Jari Kurri | Edmonton | 1985-86 | 78 | 131 | 1.68 |
| Brett Hull | St. Louis | 1990-91 | 78 | 131 | 1.68 |
| Phil Esposito | Boston | 1972-73 | 78 | 130 | 1.67 |
| Cooney Weiland | Boston | 1929-30 | 44 | 73 | 1.66 |
| Alexander Mogilny | Buffalo | 1992-93 | 77 | 127 | 1.65 |
| Peter Stastny | Quebec | 1982-83 | 75 | 124 | 1.65 |
| Bobby Orr | Boston | 1973-74 | 74 | 122 | 1.65 |
| Kent Nilsson | Calgary | 1980-81 | 80 | 131 | 1.64 |
| Denis Savard | Chicago | 1987-88 | 80 | 131 | 1.64 |
| Wayne Gretzky | Los Angeles | 1991-92 | 74 | 121 | 1.64 |
| Steve Yzerman | Detroit | 1992-93 | 84 | 137 | 1.63 |
| Marcel Dionne | Los Angeles | 1978-79 | 80 | 130 | 1.63 |
| Dale Hawerchuk | Winnipeg | 1984-85 | 80 | 130 | 1.63 |
| Mark Messier | Edmonton | 1989-90 | 79 | 129 | 1.63 |
| Bryan Trottier | NY Islanders | 1983-84 | 68 | 111 | 1.63 |
| Pat LaFontaine | Buffalo | 1991-92 | 57 | 93 | 1.63 |
| Charlie Simmer | Los Angeles | 1980-81 | 65 | 105 | 1.62 |
| Guy Lafleur | Montreal | 1978-79 | 80 | 129 | 1.61 |
| Bryan Trottier | NY Islanders | 1981-82 | 80 | 129 | 1.61 |
| Phil Esposito | Boston | 1974-75 | 79 | 127 | 1.61 |
| Steve Yzerman | Detroit | 1989-90 | 79 | 127 | 1.61 |
| Peter Stastny | Quebec | 1985-86 | 76 | 122 | 1.61 |
| Mario Lemieux | Pittsburgh | 1996-97 | 76 | 122 | 1.61 |
| Michel Goulet | Quebec | 1983-84 | 75 | 121 | 1.61 |
| Wayne Gretzky | Los Angeles | 1993-94 | 81 | 130 | 1.60 |
| Bryan Trottier | NY Islanders | 1977-78 | 77 | 123 | 1.60 |
| Bobby Orr | Boston | 1972-73 | 63 | 101 | 1.60 |
| Guy Chouinard | Calgary | 1980-81 | 52 | 83 | 1.60 |
| Elmer Lach | Montreal | 1944-45 | 50 | 80 | 1.60 |
| Pierre Turgeon | NY Islanders | 1992-93 | 83 | 132 | 1.59 |
| Steve Yzerman | Detroit | 1987-88 | 64 | 102 | 1.59 |
| Mike Bossy | NY Islanders | 1978-79 | 80 | 126 | 1.58 |
| Paul Coffey | Edmonton | 1983-84 | 80 | 126 | 1.58 |
| Marcel Dionne | Los Angeles | 1984-85 | 80 | 126 | 1.58 |
| Bobby Orr | Boston | 1969-70 | 76 | 120 | 1.58 |
| Eric Lindros | Philadelphia | 1995-96 | 73 | 115 | 1.58 |
| Charlie Simmer | Los Angeles | 1979-80 | 64 | 101 | 1.58 |
| Teemu Selanne | Winnipeg | 1992-93 | 84 | 132 | 1.57 |
| Jaromir Jagr | Pittsburgh | 1998-99 | 81 | 127 | 1.57 |
| Bobby Clarke | Philadelphia | 1975-76 | 76 | 119 | 1.57 |
| Guy Lafleur | Montreal | 1975-76 | 80 | 125 | 1.56 |
| Dave Taylor | Los Angeles | 1980-81 | 72 | 112 | 1.56 |
| Denis Savard | Chicago | 1982-83 | 78 | 121 | 1.55 |
| Ron Francis | Pittsburgh | 1995-96 | 77 | 119 | 1.55 |
| Joe Thornton | Bos., S.J. | 2005-06 | 81 | 125 | 1.54 |
| Mike Bossy | NY Islanders | 1985-86 | 80 | 123 | 1.54 |
| Kevin Stevens | Pittsburgh | 1991-92 | 80 | 123 | 1.54 |
| Bobby Orr | Boston | 1971-72 | 76 | 117 | 1.54 |
| Mike Bossy | NY Islanders | 1984-85 | 76 | 117 | 1.54 |
| Kevin Stevens | Pittsburgh | 1992-93 | 72 | 111 | 1.54 |
| Doug Bentley | Chicago | 1943-44 | 50 | 77 | 1.54 |
| Doug Gilmour | Toronto | 1992-93 | 83 | 127 | 1.53 |
| Marcel Dionne | Los Angeles | 1976-77 | 80 | 122 | 1.53 |
| Sidney Crosby | Pittsburgh | 2006-07 | 79 | 120 | 1.52 |
| Jaromir Jagr | Pittsburgh | 99-2000 | 63 | 96 | 1.52 |
| Eric Lindros | Philadelphia | 1996-97 | 52 | 79 | 1.52 |
| Eric Lindros | Philadelphia | 1994-95 | 46 | 70 | 1.52 |
| Marcel Dionne | Detroit | 1974-75 | 80 | 121 | 1.51 |
| Mike Bossy | NY Islanders | 1980-81 | 79 | 119 | 1.51 |
| Paul Coffey | Edmonton | 1984-85 | 80 | 121 | 1.51 |
| Dale Hawerchuk | Winnipeg | 1987-88 | 80 | 121 | 1.51 |
| Paul Coffey | Pittsburgh | 1988-89 | 75 | 113 | 1.51 |
| Jaromir Jagr | Pittsburgh | 1996-97 | 63 | 95 | 1.51 |
| Cam Neely | Boston | 1993-94 | 49 | 74 | 1.51 |

*Montreal's Elmer Lach, surrounded by Murray Henderson (#8), Fern Flaman and Woody Dumart (#14) in front of Bruins goalie Frank Brimsek, set an NHL record with 54 assists in 1944-45. His 80 points in 50 games that season gave him a scoring average of 1.60 points per game.*

*Anaheim's Bobby Ryan led all NHL rookies with 31 goals and 57 points in just 64 games in 2008-09. Ryan outscored veteran Ducks teammate Teemu Selanne (27 goals, 54 points) during the season, but was a long way off the rookie scoring records Selanne set with the Winnipeg Jets back in 1992-93.*

# Rookie Scoring Records

## All-Time Top 50 Goal-Scoring Rookies

| | Rookie | Team | Position | Season | GP | G | A | PTS |
|---|---|---|---|---|---|---|---|---|
| 1. | * Teemu Selanne | Winnipeg | Right wing | 1992-93 | 84 | **76** | 56 | 132 |
| 2. | * Mike Bossy | NY Islanders | Right wing | 1977-78 | 73 | **53** | 38 | 91 |
| 3. | * Alex Ovechkin | Washington | Left wing | 2005-06 | 81 | **52** | 54 | 106 |
| 4. | * Joe Nieuwendyk | Calgary | Center | 1987-88 | 75 | **51** | 41 | 92 |
| 5. | * Dale Hawerchuk | Winnipeg | Center | 1981-82 | 80 | **45** | 58 | 103 |
| | * Luc Robitaille | Los Angeles | Left wing | 1986-87 | 79 | **45** | 39 | 84 |
| 7. | Rick Martin | Buffalo | Left wing | 1971-72 | 73 | **44** | 30 | 74 |
| | Barry Pederson | Boston | Center | 1981-82 | 80 | **44** | 48 | 92 |
| 9. | * Steve Larmer | Chicago | Right wing | 1982-83 | 80 | **43** | 47 | 90 |
| | * Mario Lemieux | Pittsburgh | Center | 1984-85 | 73 | **43** | 57 | 100 |
| 11. | Eric Lindros | Philadelphia | Center | 1992-93 | 61 | **41** | 34 | 75 |
| 12. | Darryl Sutter | Chicago | Left wing | 1980-81 | 76 | **40** | 22 | 62 |
| | Sylvain Turgeon | Hartford | Left wing | 1983-84 | 76 | **40** | 32 | 72 |
| | Warren Young | Pittsburgh | Left wing | 1984-85 | 80 | **40** | 32 | 72 |
| 15. | * Eric Vail | Atlanta | Left wing | 1974-75 | 72 | **39** | 21 | 60 |
| | * Peter Stastny | Quebec | Center | 1980-81 | 77 | **39** | 70 | 109 |
| | Anton Stastny | Quebec | Left wing | 1980-81 | 80 | **39** | 46 | 85 |
| | Steve Yzerman | Detroit | Center | 1983-84 | 80 | **39** | 48 | 87 |
| | Sidney Crosby | Pittsburgh | Center | 2005-06 | 81 | **39** | 63 | 102 |
| 20. | * Gilbert Perreault | Buffalo | Center | 1970-71 | 78 | **38** | 34 | 72 |
| | Neal Broten | Minnesota | Center | 1981-82 | 73 | **38** | 60 | 98 |
| | Ray Sheppard | Buffalo | Right wing | 1987-88 | 74 | **38** | 27 | 65 |
| | Mikael Renberg | Philadelphia | Left wing | 1993-94 | 83 | **38** | 44 | 82 |
| 24. | Jorgen Pettersson | St. Louis | Left wing | 1980-81 | 62 | **37** | 36 | 73 |
| | Jimmy Carson | Los Angeles | Center | 1986-87 | 80 | **37** | 42 | 79 |
| 26. | Mike Foligno | Detroit | Right wing | 1979-80 | 80 | **36** | 35 | 71 |
| | Paul MacLean | Winnipeg | Right wing | 1981-82 | 74 | **36** | 25 | 61 |
| | Mike Bullard | Pittsburgh | Center | 1981-82 | 75 | **36** | 27 | 63 |
| | Tony Granato | NY Rangers | Right wing | 1988-89 | 78 | **36** | 27 | 63 |
| 30. | Marian Stastny | Quebec | Right wing | 1981-82 | 74 | **35** | 54 | 89 |
| | Brian Bellows | Minnesota | Right wing | 1982-83 | 78 | **35** | 30 | 65 |
| | Tony Amonte | NY Rangers | Right wing | 1991-92 | 79 | **35** | 34 | 69 |
| 33. | Nels Stewart | Mtl. Maroons | Center | 1925-26 | 36 | **34** | 8 | 42 |
| | * Danny Grant | Minnesota | Left wing | 1968-69 | 75 | **34** | 31 | 65 |
| | Norm Ferguson | Oakland | Right wing | 1968-69 | 76 | **34** | 20 | 54 |
| | Brian Propp | Philadelphia | Left wing | 1979-80 | 80 | **34** | 41 | 75 |
| | Wendel Clark | Toronto | Left wing | 1985-86 | 66 | **34** | 11 | 45 |
| | * Pavel Bure | Vancouver | Right wing | 1991-92 | 65 | **34** | 26 | 60 |
| 39. | * Willi Plett | Atlanta | Right wing | 1976-77 | 64 | **33** | 23 | 56 |
| | Dale McCourt | Detroit | Center | 1977-78 | 76 | **33** | 39 | 72 |
| | Steve Bozek | Los Angeles | Center | 1981-82 | 71 | **33** | 23 | 56 |
| | Ron Flockhart | Philadelphia | Center | 1981-82 | 72 | **33** | 39 | 72 |
| | Mark Pavelich | NY Rangers | Center | 1981-82 | 79 | **33** | 43 | 76 |
| | Jason Arnott | Edmonton | Center | 1993-94 | 78 | **33** | 35 | 68 |
| | * Evgeni Malkin | Pittsburgh | Center | 2006-07 | 78 | **33** | 52 | 85 |
| 46. | Bill Mosienko | Chicago | Right wing | 1943-44 | 50 | **32** | 38 | 70 |
| | Michel Bergeron | Detroit | Right wing | 1975-76 | 72 | **32** | 27 | 59 |
| | * Bryan Trottier | NY Islanders | Center | 1975-76 | 80 | **32** | 63 | 95 |
| | Don Murdoch | NY Rangers | Right wing | 1976-77 | 59 | **32** | 24 | 56 |
| | Jari Kurri | Edmonton | Left wing | 1980-81 | 75 | **32** | 43 | 75 |
| | Bobby Carpenter | Washington | Center | 1981-82 | 80 | **32** | 35 | 67 |
| | Petr Klima | Detroit | Left wing | 1985-86 | 74 | **32** | 24 | 56 |
| | Kjell Dahlin | Montreal | Right wing | 1985-86 | 77 | **32** | 39 | 71 |
| | Darren Turcotte | NY Rangers | Right wing | 1989-90 | 76 | **32** | 34 | 66 |
| | Joe Juneau | Boston | Center | 1992-93 | 84 | **32** | 70 | 102 |
| | Marek Svatos | Colorado | Right wing | 2005-06 | 61 | **32** | 18 | 50 |

* Calder Trophy Winner

## All-Time Top 50 Point-Scoring Rookies

| | Rookie | Team | Position | Season | GP | G | A | PTS |
|---|---|---|---|---|---|---|---|---|
| 1. | * Teemu Selanne | Winnipeg | Right wing | 1992-93 | 84 | 76 | 56 | **132** |
| 2. | * Peter Stastny | Quebec | Center | 1980-81 | 77 | 39 | 70 | **109** |
| 3. | * Alex Ovechkin | Washington | Left wing | 2005-06 | 81 | 52 | 54 | **106** |
| 4. | * Dale Hawerchuk | Winnipeg | Center | 1981-82 | 80 | 45 | 58 | **103** |
| 5. | Joe Juneau | Boston | Center | 1992-93 | 84 | 32 | 70 | **102** |
| | Sidney Crosby | Pittsburgh | Center | 2005-06 | 81 | 39 | 63 | **102** |
| 7. | * Mario Lemieux | Pittsburgh | Center | 1984-85 | 73 | 43 | 57 | **100** |
| 8. | Neal Broten | Minnesota | Center | 1981-82 | 73 | 38 | 60 | **98** |
| 9. | * Bryan Trottier | NY Islanders | Center | 1975-76 | 80 | 32 | 63 | **95** |
| 10. | Barry Pederson | Boston | Center | 1981-82 | 80 | 44 | 48 | **92** |
| | * Joe Nieuwendyk | Calgary | Center | 1987-88 | 75 | 51 | 41 | **92** |
| 12. | * Mike Bossy | NY Islanders | Right wing | 1977-78 | 73 | 53 | 38 | **91** |
| 13. | * Steve Larmer | Chicago | Right wing | 1982-83 | 80 | 43 | 47 | **90** |
| 14. | Marian Stastny | Quebec | Right wing | 1981-82 | 74 | 35 | 54 | **89** |
| 15. | Steve Yzerman | Detroit | Center | 1983-84 | 80 | 39 | 48 | **87** |
| 16. | * Sergei Makarov | Calgary | Right wing | 1989-90 | 80 | 24 | 62 | **86** |
| 17. | Anton Stastny | Quebec | Left wing | 1980-81 | 80 | 39 | 46 | **85** |
| 18. | * Evgeni Malkin | Pittsburgh | Center | 2006-07 | 78 | 33 | 52 | **85** |
| 19. | * Luc Robitaille | Los Angeles | Left wing | 1986-87 | 79 | 45 | 39 | **84** |
| 20. | Mikael Renberg | Philadelphia | Left wing | 1993-94 | 83 | 38 | 44 | **82** |
| 21. | Jimmy Carson | Los Angeles | Center | 1986-87 | 80 | 37 | 42 | **79** |
| | Sergei Fedorov | Detroit | Center | 1990-91 | 77 | 31 | 48 | **79** |
| | Alexei Yashin | Ottawa | Center | 1993-94 | 83 | 30 | 49 | **79** |
| 24. | Paul Stastny | Colorado | Center | 2006-07 | 82 | 28 | 50 | **78** |
| 25. | Marcel Dionne | Detroit | Center | 1971-72 | 78 | 28 | 49 | **77** |
| 26. | Larry Murphy | Los Angeles | Defense | 1980-81 | 80 | 16 | 60 | **76** |
| | Mark Pavelich | NY Rangers | Center | 1981-82 | 79 | 33 | 43 | **76** |
| | Dave Poulin | Philadelphia | Center | 1983-84 | 73 | 31 | 45 | **76** |
| 29. | Brian Propp | Philadelphia | Left wing | 1979-80 | 80 | 34 | 41 | **75** |
| | Jari Kurri | Edmonton | Left wing | 1980-81 | 75 | 32 | 43 | **75** |
| | Denis Savard | Chicago | Center | 1980-81 | 76 | 28 | 47 | **75** |
| | Mike Modano | Minnesota | Center | 1989-90 | 80 | 29 | 46 | **75** |
| | Eric Lindros | Philadelphia | Center | 1992-93 | 61 | 41 | 34 | **75** |
| 34. | Rick Martin | Buffalo | Left wing | 1971-72 | 73 | 44 | 30 | **74** |
| | * Bobby Smith | Minnesota | Center | 1978-79 | 80 | 30 | 44 | **74** |
| 36. | Jorgen Pettersson | St. Louis | Left wing | 1980-81 | 62 | 37 | 36 | **73** |
| 37. | * Gilbert Perreault | Buffalo | Center | 1970-71 | 78 | 38 | 34 | **72** |
| | Dale McCourt | Detroit | Center | 1977-78 | 76 | 33 | 39 | **72** |
| | Ron Flockhart | Philadelphia | Center | 1981-82 | 72 | 33 | 39 | **72** |
| | Sylvain Turgeon | Hartford | Left wing | 1983-84 | 76 | 40 | 32 | **72** |
| | Carey Wilson | Calgary | Center | 1984-85 | 74 | 24 | 48 | **72** |
| | Warren Young | Pittsburgh | Left wing | 1984-85 | 80 | 40 | 32 | **72** |
| | Alex Zhamnov | Winnipeg | Center | 1992-93 | 68 | 25 | 47 | **72** |
| | * Patrick Kane | Chicago | Right Wing | 2007-08 | 82 | 21 | 51 | **72** |
| 45. | Mike Foligno | Detroit | Right wing | 1979-80 | 80 | 36 | 35 | **71** |
| | Dave Christian | Winnipeg | Center | 1980-81 | 80 | 28 | 43 | **71** |
| | Mats Naslund | Montreal | Left wing | 1982-83 | 74 | 26 | 45 | **71** |
| | Kjell Dahlin | Montreal | Right wing | 1985-86 | 77 | 32 | 39 | **71** |
| | * Brian Leetch | NY Rangers | Defense | 1988-89 | 68 | 23 | 48 | **71** |
| 50. | Bill Mosienko | Chicago | Right wing | 1943-44 | 50 | 32 | 38 | **70** |
| | * Scott Gomez | New Jersey | Center | 99-2000 | 82 | 19 | 51 | **70** |

* Calder Trophy Winner

# 50-Goal Seasons

*Bernie Geoffrion*

*Rick MacLeish*

*Danny Gare*

| Player | Team | Date of 50th Goal | Score | Goaltender | Player's Game No. | Team Game No. | Total Goals | Total Games | Age When First 50th Scored (Yrs. & Mos.) |
|---|---|---|---|---|---|---|---|---|---|
| Maurice Richard | Mtl. | Mar. 18/45 | Mtl. 4 at Bos. 2 | Harvey Bennett | 50 | 50 | 50 | 50 | 23.7 |
| Bernie Geoffrion | Mtl. | Mar. 16/61 | Tor. 2 at Mtl. 5 | Cesare Maniago | 62 | 68 | 50 | 64 | 30.1 |
| Bobby Hull | Chi. | Mar. 25/62 | Chi. 1 at NYR 4 | Gump Worsley | 70 | 70 | 50 | 70 | 23.2 |
| Bobby Hull | Chi. | Mar. 2/66 | Det. 4 at Chi. 5 | Hank Bassen | 52 | 57 | 54 | 65 | |
| Bobby Hull | Chi. | Mar. 18/67 | Chi. 5 at Tor. 9 | Bruce Gamble | 63 | 66 | 52 | 66 | |
| Bobby Hull | Chi. | Mar. 5/69 | NYR 4 at Chi. 4 | Ed Giacomin | 64 | 66 | 58 | 74 | |
| Phil Esposito | Bos. | Feb. 20/71 | Bos. 4 at L.A. 5 | Denis DeJordy | 58 | 58 | 76 | 78 | 29.0 |
| John Bucyk | Bos. | Mar. 16/71 | Bos. 11 at Det. 4 | Roy Edwards | 69 | 69 | 51 | 78 | 35.10 |
| Phil Esposito | Bos. | Feb. 20/72 | Bos. 3 at Chi. 1 | Tony Esposito | 60 | 60 | 66 | 76 | |
| Bobby Hull | Chi. | Apr. 2/72 | Det. 1 at Chi. 6 | Andy Brown | 78 | 78 | 50 | 78 | |
| Vic Hadfield | NYR | Apr. 2/72 | Mtl. 6 at NYR 5 | Denis DeJordy | 78 | 78 | 50 | 78 | 31.6 |
| Phil Esposito | Bos. | Mar. 25/73 | Buf. 1 at Bos. 6 | Roger Crozier | 75 | 75 | 55 | 78 | |
| Mickey Redmond | Det. | Mar. 27/73 | Det. 8 at Tor. 1 | Ron Low | 73 | 75 | 52 | 76 | 25.3 |
| Rick MacLeish | Phi. | Apr. 1/73 | Phi. 4 at Pit. 5 | Cam Newton | 78 | 78 | 50 | 78 | 23.2 |
| Phil Esposito | Bos. | Feb. 20/74 | Bos. 5 at Min. 5 | Cesare Maniago | 56 | 56 | 68 | 78 | |
| Mickey Redmond | Det. | Mar. 23/74 | NYR 3 at Det. 5 | Ed Giacomin | 69 | 71 | 51 | 76 | |
| Ken Hodge | Bos. | Apr. 6/74 | Bos. 2 at Mtl. 6 | Michel Larocque | 75 | 77 | 50 | 76 | 29.10 |
| Rick Martin | Buf. | Apr. 7/74 | St.L. 2 at Buf. 5 | Wayne Stephenson | 78 | 78 | 52 | 78 | 22.9 |
| Phil Esposito | Bos. | Feb. 8/75 | Bos. 8 at Det. 5 | Jim Rutherford | 54 | 54 | 61 | 79 | |
| Guy Lafleur | Mtl. | Mar. 29/75 | K.C. 1 at Mtl. 4 | Denis Herron | 66 | 76 | 53 | 70 | 23.6 |
| Danny Grant | Det. | Apr. 2/75 | Wsh. 3 at Det. 8 | John Adams | 78 | 78 | 50 | 80 | 29.2 |
| Rick Martin | Buf. | Apr. 3/75 | Bos. 2 at Buf. 4 | Ken Broderick | 67 | 79 | 52 | 68 | |
| Reggie Leach | Phi. | Mar. 14/76 | Atl. 1 at Phi. 6 | Dan Bouchard | 69 | 69 | 61 | 80 | 25.11 |
| Jean Pronovost | Pit. | Mar. 24/76 | Bos. 5 at Pit. 5 | Gilles Gilbert | 74 | 74 | 52 | 80 | 30.3 |
| Guy Lafleur | Mtl. | Mar. 27/76 | K.C. 2 at Mtl. 8 | Denis Herron | 76 | 76 | 56 | 80 | |
| Bill Barber | Phi. | Apr. 3/76 | Buf. 2 at Phi. 5 | Al Smith | 79 | 79 | 50 | 80 | 23.9 |
| Pierre Larouche | Pit. | Apr. 3/76 | Wsh. 5 at Pit. 4 | Ron Low | 75 | 79 | 53 | 76 | 20.5 |
| Danny Gare | Buf. | Apr. 4/76 | Tor. 2 at Buf. 5 | Gord McRae | 79 | 80 | 50 | 79 | 21.11 |
| Steve Shutt | Mtl. | Mar. 1/77 | Mtl. 5 at NYI 4 | Glenn Resch | 65 | 65 | 60 | 80 | 24.8 |
| Guy Lafleur | Mtl. | Mar. 6/77 | Mtl. 1 at Buf. 4 | Don Edwards | 68 | 68 | 56 | 80 | |
| Marcel Dionne | L.A. | Apr. 2/77 | Min. 2 at L.A. 7 | Pete LoPresti | 79 | 79 | 53 | 80 | 25.8 |
| Guy Lafleur | Mtl. | Mar. 8/78 | Wsh. 3 at Mtl. 4 | Jim Bedard | 63 | 65 | 60 | 78 | |
| Mike Bossy | NYI | Apr. 1/78 | Wsh. 2 at NYI 3 | Bernie Wolfe | 69 | 76 | 53 | 73 | 21.2 |
| Mike Bossy | NYI | Feb. 24/79 | Det. 1 at NYI 3 | Rogie Vachon | 58 | 58 | 69 | 80 | |
| Marcel Dionne | L.A. | Mar. 11/79 | L.A. 3 at Phi. 6 | Wayne Stephenson | 68 | 68 | 59 | 80 | |
| Guy Lafleur | Mtl. | Mar. 31/79 | Pit. 3 at Mtl. 5 | Denis Herron | 76 | 76 | 52 | 80 | |
| Guy Chouinard | Atl. | Apr. 6/79 | NYR 2 at Atl. 9 | John Davidson | 79 | 79 | 50 | 80 | 22.5 |
| Marcel Dionne | L.A. | Mar. 12/80 | L.A. 2 at Pit. 4 | Nick Ricci | 70 | 70 | 53 | 80 | |
| Mike Bossy | NYI | Mar. 16/80 | NYI 6 at Chi. 1 | Tony Esposito | 68 | 71 | 51 | 75 | |
| Charlie Simmer | L.A. | Mar. 19/80 | Det. 3 at L.A. 4 | Jim Rutherford | 57 | 73 | 56 | 64 | 26.0 |
| Pierre Larouche | Mtl. | Mar. 25/80 | Chi. 4 at Mtl. 8 | Tony Esposito | 72 | 75 | 50 | 73 | |
| Danny Gare | Buf. | Mar. 27/80 | Det. 1 at Buf. 10 | Jim Rutherford | 71 | 75 | 56 | 76 | |
| Blaine Stoughton | Hfd. | Mar. 28/80 | Hfd. 4 at Van. 4 | Glen Hanlon | 75 | 75 | 56 | 80 | 27.0 |
| Guy Lafleur | Mtl. | Apr. 2/80 | Mtl. 7 at Det. 2 | Rogie Vachon | 72 | 78 | 50 | 74 | |
| Wayne Gretzky | Edm. | Apr. 2/80 | Min. 1 at Edm. 1 | Gary Edwards | 78 | 79 | 51 | 79 | 19.2 |
| Reggie Leach | Phi. | Apr. 3/80 | Wsh. 2 at Phi. 4 | empty net | 75 | 79 | 50 | 76 | |
| Mike Bossy | NYI | Jan. 24/81 | Que. 3 at NYI 7 | Ron Grahame | 50 | 50 | 68 | 79 | |
| Charlie Simmer | L.A. | Jan. 26/81 | L.A. 7 at Que. 5 | Michel Dion | 51 | 51 | 56 | 65 | |
| Marcel Dionne | L.A. | Mar. 8/81 | L.A. 4 at Wpg. 1 | Markus Mattsson | 68 | 68 | 58 | 80 | |
| Wayne Babych | St.L. | Mar. 12/81 | St.L. 3 at Mtl. 4 | Richard Sevigny | 70 | 68 | 54 | 78 | 22.9 |
| Wayne Gretzky | Edm. | Mar. 15/81 | Edm. 3 at Cgy. 3 | Pat Riggin | 69 | 69 | 55 | 80 | |
| Rick Kehoe | Pit. | Mar. 16/81 | Pit. 7 at Edm. 6 | Eddie Mio | 70 | 70 | 55 | 80 | 29.7 |
| Jacques Richard | Que. | Mar. 29/81 | Mtl. 0 at Que. 4 | Richard Sevigny | 76 | 75 | 52 | 78 | 28.6 |
| Dennis Maruk | Wsh. | Apr. 5/81 | Det. 2 at Wsh. 7 | Larry Lozinski | 80 | 80 | 50 | 80 | 25.3 |
| Wayne Gretzky | Edm. | Dec. 30/81 | Phi. 5 at Edm. 7 | empty net | 39 | 39 | 92 | 80 | |
| Dennis Maruk | Wsh. | Feb. 21/82 | Wpg. 3 at Wsh. 6 | Doug Soetaert | 61 | 61 | 60 | 80 | |
| Mike Bossy | NYI | Mar. 4/82 | Tor. 1 at NYI 10 | Michel Larocque | 66 | 66 | 64 | 80 | |
| Dino Ciccarelli | Min. | Mar. 8/82 | St.L. 1 at Min. 8 | Mike Liut | 67 | 68 | 55 | 76 | 22.1 |
| Rick Vaive | Tor. | Mar. 24/82 | St.L. 3 at Tor. 4 | Mike Liut | 72 | 75 | 54 | 77 | 22.10 |
| Blaine Stoughton | Hfd. | Mar. 28/82 | Min. 5 at Hfd. 2 | Gilles Meloche | 76 | 76 | 52 | 80 | |
| Rick Middleton | Bos. | Mar. 28/82 | Bos. 5 at Buf. 9 | Paul Harrison | 72 | 77 | 51 | 75 | 28.11 |
| Marcel Dionne | L.A. | Mar. 30/82 | Cgy. 7 at L.A. 5 | Pat Riggin | 75 | 77 | 50 | 78 | |
| Mark Messier | Edm. | Mar. 31/82 | L.A. 3 at Edm. 7 | Mario Lessard | 78 | 79 | 50 | 78 | 21.3 |
| Bryan Trottier | NYI | Apr. 3/82 | Phi. 3 at NYI 6 | Pete Peeters | 79 | 79 | 50 | 80 | 25.9 |
| Lanny McDonald | Cgy. | Feb. 18/83 | Cgy. 1 at Buf. 5 | Bob Sauve | 60 | 60 | 66 | 80 | 30.0 |
| Wayne Gretzky | Edm. | Feb. 19/83 | Edm. 10 at Pit. 7 | Nick Ricci | 60 | 60 | 71 | 80 | |
| Michel Goulet | Que. | Mar. 5/83 | Hfd. 3 at Que. 10 | Mike Veisor | 67 | 67 | 57 | 80 | 22.11 |
| Mike Bossy | NYI | Mar. 12/83 | Wsh. 2 at NYI 6 | Al Jensen | 70 | 71 | 60 | 79 | |
| Marcel Dionne | L.A. | Mar. 17/83 | Que. 3 at L.A. 4 | Dan Bouchard | 71 | 71 | 56 | 80 | |
| Al Secord | Chi. | Mar. 20/83 | Tor. 3 at Chi. 7 | Mike Palmateer | 73 | 73 | 54 | 80 | 25.0 |
| Rick Vaive | Tor. | Mar. 30/83 | Tor. 4 at Det. 2 | Gilles Gilbert | 76 | 78 | 51 | 78 | |
| Wayne Gretzky | Edm. | Jan. 7/84 | Hfd. 3 at Edm. 5 | Greg Millen | 42 | 42 | 87 | 74 | |
| Michel Goulet | Que. | Mar. 8/84 | Que. 8 at Pit. 6 | Denis Herron | 63 | 69 | 56 | 75 | |
| Rick Vaive | Tor. | Mar. 14/84 | Min. 3 at Tor. 3 | Gilles Meloche | 69 | 72 | 52 | 76 | |
| Mike Bullard | Pit. | Mar. 14/84 | Pit. 6 at L.A. 7 | Markus Mattsson | 71 | 72 | 51 | 76 | 23.0 |
| Jari Kurri | Edm. | Mar. 15/84 | Edm. 2 at Mtl. 3 | Rick Wamsley | 57 | 73 | 52 | 64 | 23.10 |
| Glenn Anderson | Edm. | Mar. 21/84 | Hfd. 3 at Edm. 5 | Greg Millen | 76 | 76 | 54 | 80 | 23.6 |
| Tim Kerr | Phi. | Mar. 22/84 | Pit. 4 at Phi. 13 | Denis Herron | 74 | 75 | 54 | 79 | 24.3 |

| Player | Team | Date of 50th Goal | Score | | Goaltender | Player's Game No. | Team Game No. | Total Goals | Total Games | Age When First 50th Scored (Yrs. & Mos.) |
|---|---|---|---|---|---|---|---|---|---|---|
| Mike Bossy | NYI | Mar. 31/84 | NYI 3 | at Wsh. 1 | Pat Riggin | 67 | 79 | 51 | 67 | |
| Wayne Gretzky | Edm. | Jan. 26/85 | Pit. 3 | at Edm. 6 | Denis Herron | 49 | 49 | 73 | 80 | |
| Jari Kurri | Edm. | Feb. 3/85 | Hfd. 3 | at Edm. 6 | Greg Millen | 50 | 53 | 71 | 73 | |
| Mike Bossy | NYI | Mar. 5/85 | Phi. 5 | at NYI 4 | Bob Froese | 61 | 65 | 58 | 76 | |
| Michel Goulet | Que. | Mar. 6/85 | Buf. 3 | at Que. 4 | Tom Barrasso | 62 | 73 | 55 | 69 | |
| Tim Kerr | Phi. | Mar. 7/85 | Wsh. 6 | at Phi. 9 | Pat Riggin | 63 | 65 | 54 | 74 | |
| John Ogrodnick | Det. | Mar. 13/85 | Det. 6 | at Edm. 7 | Grant Fuhr | 69 | 69 | 55 | 79 | 25.9 |
| Bob Carpenter | Wsh. | Mar. 21/85 | Wsh. 2 | at Mtl. 3 | Steve Penney | 72 | 72 | 53 | 80 | 21.9 |
| Dale Hawerchuk | Wpg. | Mar. 29/85 | Chi. 5 | at Wpg. 5 | W. Skorodenski | 77 | 77 | 53 | 80 | 21.11 |
| Mike Gartner | Wsh. | Apr. 7/85 | Pit. 3 | at Wsh. 7 | Brian Ford | 80 | 80 | 50 | 80 | 25.5 |
| Jari Kurri | Edm. | Mar. 4/86 | Edm. 6 | at Van. 2 | Richard Brodeur | 63 | 65 | 68 | 78 | |
| Mike Bossy | NYI | Mar. 11/86 | Cgy. 4 | at NYI 8 | Reggie Lemelin | 67 | 67 | 61 | 80 | |
| Glenn Anderson | Edm. | Mar. 14/86 | Det. 3 | at Edm. 12 | Greg Stefan | 63 | 71 | 54 | 72 | |
| Michel Goulet | Que. | Mar. 17/86 | Que. 8 | at Mtl. 6 | Patrick Roy | 67 | 72 | 53 | 75 | |
| Wayne Gretzky | Edm. | Mar. 18/86 | Wpg. 2 | at Edm. 6 | Brian Hayward | 72 | 72 | 52 | 80 | |
| Tim Kerr | Phi. | Mar. 20/86 | Pit. 1 | at Phi. 5 | Roberto Romano | 68 | 72 | 58 | 76 | |
| Wayne Gretzky | Edm. | Feb. 4/87 | Edm. 6 | at Min. 5 | Don Beaupre | 55 | 55 | 62 | 79 | |
| Dino Ciccarelli | Min. | Mar. 7/87 | Pit. 7 | at Min. 3 | Gilles Meloche | 66 | 66 | 52 | 80 | |
| Mario Lemieux | Pit. | Mar. 12/87 | Que. 3 | at Pit. 6 | Mario Gosselin | 53 | 70 | 54 | 63 | 21.5 |
| Tim Kerr | Phi. | Mar. 17/87 | NYR 1 | at Phi. 4 | J. Vanbiesbrouck | 67 | 71 | 58 | 75 | |
| Jari Kurri | Edm. | Mar. 17/87 | N.J. 4 | at Edm. 7 | Craig Billington | 69 | 70 | 54 | 79 | |
| Mario Lemieux | Pit. | Feb. 2/88 | Wsh. 2 | at Pit. 3 | Pete Peeters | 51 | 54 | 70 | 77 | |
| Steve Yzerman | Det. | Mar. 1/88 | Buf. 0 | at Det. 4 | Tom Barrasso | 64 | 64 | 50 | 64 | 22.10 |
| Joe Nieuwendyk | Cgy. | Mar. 12/88 | Buf. 4 | at Cgy. 10 | Tom Barrasso | 66 | 70 | 51 | 75 | 21.5 |
| Craig Simpson | Edm. | Mar. 15/88 | Buf. 4 | at Edm. 6 | Jacques Cloutier | 71 | 71 | 56 | 80 | 21.1 |
| Jimmy Carson | L.A. | Mar. 26/88 | Chi. 5 | at L.A. 9 | Darren Pang | 77 | 77 | 55 | 88 | 19.8 |
| Luc Robitaille | L.A. | Apr. 1/88 | L.A. 6 | at Cgy. 3 | Mike Vernon | 79 | 79 | 53 | 80 | 21.10 |
| Hakan Loob | Cgy. | Apr. 3/88 | Min. 1 | at Cgy. 4 | Don Beaupre | 80 | 80 | 50 | 80 | 27.9 |
| Stephane Richer | Mtl. | Apr. 3/88 | Mtl. 4 | at Buf. 4 | Tom Barrasso | 72 | 80 | 50 | 72 | 21.10 |
| Mario Lemieux | Pit. | Jan. 20/89 | Pit. 3 | at Wpg. 7 | Pokey Reddick | 44 | 46 | 85 | 76 | |
| Bernie Nicholls | L.A. | Jan. 28/89 | Edm. 7 | at L.A. 6 | Grant Fuhr | 51 | 51 | 70 | 79 | 27.7 |
| Steve Yzerman | Det. | Feb. 5/89 | Det. 6 | at Wpg. 2 | Pokey Reddick | 55 | 55 | 65 | 80 | |
| Wayne Gretzky | L.A. | Mar. 4/89 | Phi. 2 | at L.A. 6 | Ron Hextall | 66 | 67 | 54 | 78 | |
| Joe Nieuwendyk | Cgy. | Mar. 21/89 | NYI 1 | at Cgy. 4 | Mark Fitzpatrick | 72 | 74 | 51 | 77 | |
| Joe Mullen | Cgy. | Mar. 31/89 | Wpg. 1 | at Cgy. 4 | Bob Essensa | 78 | 79 | 51 | 79 | 32.1 |
| Brett Hull | St.L. | Feb. 6/90 | Tor. 4 | at St.L. 6 | Jeff Reese | 54 | 54 | 72 | 80 | 25.6 |
| Steve Yzerman | Det. | Feb. 24/90 | Det. 3 | at NYI 3 | Glenn Healy | 63 | 63 | 62 | 79 | |
| Cam Neely | Bos. | Mar. 10/90 | Bos. 3 | at NYI 3 | Mark Fitzpatrick | 69 | 71 | 55 | 76 | 24.9 |
| Brian Bellows | Min. | Mar. 22/90 | Min. 5 | at Det. 1 | Tim Cheveldae | 75 | 75 | 55 | 80 | 25.6 |
| Pat LaFontaine | NYI | Mar. 24/90 | NYI 5 | at Edm. 5 | Bill Ranford | 71 | 77 | 54 | 74 | 25.1 |
| Stephane Richer | Mtl. | Mar. 24/90 | Mtl. 4 | at Hfd. 7 | Peter Sidorkiewicz | 75 | 77 | 51 | 75 | |
| Gary Leeman | Tor. | Mar. 28/90 | NYI 6 | at Tor. 3 | Mark Fitzpatrick | 78 | 78 | 51 | 80 | 26.1 |
| Luc Robitaille | L.A. | Mar. 31/90 | L.A. 3 | at Van. 6 | Kirk McLean | 79 | 79 | 52 | 80 | |
| Brett Hull | St.L. | Jan. 25/91 | St.L. 9 | at Det. 4 | David Gagnon | 49 | 49 | 86 | 78 | |
| Cam Neely | Bos. | Mar. 26/91 | Bos. 7 | at Que. 4 | empty net | 67 | 78 | 51 | 69 | |
| Theoren Fleury | Cgy. | Mar. 26/91 | Van. 2 | at Cgy. 7 | Bob Mason | 77 | 77 | 51 | 79 | 22.9 |
| Steve Yzerman | Det. | Mar. 30/91 | NYR 5 | at Det. 6 | Mike Richter | 79 | 79 | 51 | 80 | |
| Brett Hull | St.L. | Jan. 28/92 | St.L. 3 | at L.A. 3 | Kelly Hrudey | 50 | 50 | 70 | 73 | |
| Jeremy Roenick | Chi. | Mar. 7/92 | Chi. 2 | at Bos. 1 | Daniel Berthiaume | 67 | 67 | 53 | 80 | 22.2 |
| Kevin Stevens | Pit. | Mar. 24/92 | Pit. 3 | at Det. 4 | Tim Cheveldae | 74 | 74 | 54 | 80 | 26.11 |
| Gary Roberts | Cgy. | Mar. 31/92 | Edm. 2 | at Cgy. 5 | Bill Ranford | 73 | 77 | 53 | 76 | 25.10 |
| Alexander Mogilny | Buf. | Feb. 3/93 | Hfd. 2 | at Buf. 3 | Sean Burke | 46 | 53 | 76 | 77 | 23.11 |
| Teemu Selanne | Wpg. | Feb. 28/93 | Min. 6 | at Wpg. 7 | Darcy Wakaluk | 63 | 63 | 76 | 84 | 22.6 |
| Pavel Bure | Van. | Mar. 1/93 | Van. 5 | at Buf. 2* | Grant Fuhr | 63 | 63 | 60 | 83 | 21.11 |
| Steve Yzerman | Det. | Mar. 10/93 | Det. 6 | at Edm. 3 | Bill Ranford | 70 | 70 | 58 | 84 | |
| Luc Robitaille | L.A. | Mar. 15/93 | L.A. 4 | at Buf. 2 | Grant Fuhr | 69 | 69 | 63 | 84 | |
| Brett Hull | St.L. | Mar. 20/93 | St.L. 2 | at L.A. 3 | Robb Stauber | 73 | 73 | 54 | 80 | |
| Mario Lemieux | Pit. | Mar. 21/93 | Pit. 6 | at Edm. 4** | Ron Tugnutt | 48 | 72 | 69 | 60 | |
| Kevin Stevens | Pit. | Mar. 21/93 | Pit. 6 | at Edm. 4** | Ron Tugnutt | 62 | 72 | 55 | 72 | |
| Dave Andreychuk | Tor. | Mar. 23/93 | Tor. 5 | at Wpg. 4 | Bob Essensa | 72 | 73 | 54 | 83 | 29.6 |
| Pat LaFontaine | Buf. | Mar. 28/93 | Ott. 1 | at Buf. 3 | Peter Sidorkiewicz | 75 | 75 | 53 | 84 | |
| Pierre Turgeon | NYI | Apr. 2/93 | NYI 3 | at NYR 2 | Mike Richter | 75 | 76 | 58 | 83 | 23.8 |
| Mark Recchi | Phi. | Apr. 3/93 | T.B. 2 | at Phi. 6 | J-C Bergeron | 77 | 77 | 53 | 84 | 25.2 |
| Brendan Shanahan | St.L. | Apr. 15/93 | T.B. 5 | at St.L. 6 | Pat Jablonski | 71 | 84 | 51 | 71 | 24.3 |
| Jeremy Roenick | Chi. | Apr. 15/93 | Tor. 2 | at Chi. 3 | Felix Potvin | 84 | 84 | 50 | 84 | |
| Cam Neely | Bos. | Mar. 7/94 | Wsh. 3 | at Bos. 6 | Don Beaupre | 44 | 66 | 50 | 49 | |
| Sergei Fedorov | Det. | Mar. 15/94 | Van. 2 | at Det. 5 | Kirk McLean | 67 | 69 | 56 | 82 | 24.3 |
| Pavel Bure | Van. | Mar. 23/94 | Van. 6 | at L.A. 3 | empty net | 65 | 73 | 60 | 76 | |
| Adam Graves | NYR | Mar. 23/94 | NYR 5 | at Edm. 3 | Bill Ranford | 74 | 74 | 51 | 84 | 25.11 |
| Dave Andreychuk | Tor. | Mar. 24/94 | S.J. 2 | at Tor. 1 | Arturs Irbe | 73 | 74 | 53 | 83 | |
| Brett Hull | St.L. | Mar. 25/94 | Dal. 3 | at St.L. 5 | Andy Moog | 71 | 74 | 52 | 81 | |
| Ray Sheppard | Det. | Mar. 29/94 | Hfd. 2 | at Det. 6 | Sean Burke | 74 | 76 | 52 | 82 | 27.10 |
| Brendan Shanahan | St.L. | Apr. 12/94 | St.L. 5 | at Dal. 9 | Andy Moog | 80 | 83 | 52 | 81 | |
| Mike Modano | Dal. | Apr. 12/94 | St.L. 5 | at Dal. 9 | Curtis Joseph | 75 | 83 | 50 | 76 | 23.11 |
| Mario Lemieux | Pit. | Feb. 23/96 | Hfd. 4 | at Pit. 5 | Sean Burke | 50 | 59 | 69 | 70 | |
| Jaromir Jagr | Pit. | Feb. 23/96 | Hfd. 4 | at Pit. 5 | Sean Burke | 59 | 59 | 62 | 82 | 24.0 |
| Alexander Mogilny | Van. | Feb. 29/96 | St.L. 2 | at Van. 2 | Grant Fuhr | 60 | 63 | 55 | 79 | |
| Peter Bondra | Wsh. | Apr. 3/96 | Wsh. 5 | at Buf. 1 | Andrei Trefilov | 62 | 77 | 52 | 67 | 28.1 |
| Joe Sakic | Col. | Apr. 7/96 | Col. 4 | at Dal. 1 | empty net | 79 | 79 | 51 | 82 | 26.7 |
| John LeClair | Phi. | Apr. 10/96 | Phi. 5 | at N.J. 1 | Corey Schwab | 80 | 80 | 51 | 82 | 26.7 |
| Keith Tkachuk | Wpg. | Apr. 12/96 | L.A. 3 | at Wpg. 5 | empty net | 75 | 81 | 50 | 76 | 24.0 |
| Paul Kariya | Ana. | Apr. 14/96 | Wpg. 2 | at Ana. 5 | N. Khabibulin | 82 | 82 | 50 | 82 | 21.5 |
| Keith Tkachuk | Phx. | Apr. 6/97 | Phx. 1 | at Col. 2 | Patrick Roy | 78 | 79 | 52 | 81 | |
| Teemu Selanne | Ana. | Apr. 9/97 | L.A. 1 | at Ana. 4 | empty net | 77 | 81 | 51 | 78 | |
| Mario Lemieux | Pit. | Apr. 11/97 | Pit. 2 | at Fla. 4 | J. Vanbiesbrouck | 75 | 81 | 50 | 76 | |

*Mike Bossy*

*Brett Hull*

*Adam Graves*

Alex Ovechkin

| Player | Team | Date of 50th Goal | Score | | Goaltender | Player's Game No. | Team Game No. | Total Goals | Total Games | Age When First 50th Scored (Yrs. & Mos.) |
|---|---|---|---|---|---|---|---|---|---|---|
| John LeClair | Phi. | Apr. 13/97 | N.J. 4 | at Phi. 5 | Mike Dunham | 82 | 82 | 50 | 82 | |
| Teemu Selanne | Ana. | Mar. 25/98 | Ana. 3 | at Chi. 2 | Jeff Hackett | 66 | 71 | 52 | 73 | |
| John LeClair | Phi. | Apr. 13/98 | Phi. 1 | at Buf. 2 | Dominik Hasek | 79 | 79 | 51 | 82 | |
| Pavel Bure | Van. | Apr. 17/98 | Cgy. 4 | at Van. 2 | Dwayne Roloson | 81 | 81 | 51 | 82 | |
| Peter Bondra | Wsh. | Apr. 18/98 | Wsh. 4 | at Car. 3 | Mike Fountain | 75 | 80 | 52 | 76 | |
| Pavel Bure | Fla. | Mar. 18/00 | Fla. 4 | at NYI 2 | empty net | 63 | 71 | 58 | 74 | |
| Pavel Bure | Fla. | Mar. 16/01 | Pit. 6 | at Fla. 3 | Johan Hedberg | 72 | 72 | 59 | 82 | |
| Joe Sakic | Col. | Apr. 4/01 | Ana. 1 | at Col. 1 | J-S Giguere | 80 | 80 | 54 | 82 | |
| Jaromir Jagr | Pit. | Apr. 4/01 | T.B. 2 | at Pit. 4 | Kevin Weekes | 80 | 80 | 52 | 81 | |
| Jarome Iginla | Cgy. | Apr. 7/02 | Cgy. 2 | at Chi. 3 | Jocelyn Thibault | 79 | 79 | 52 | 82 | 24.9 |
| Milan Hejduk | Col. | Apr. 6/03 | St. L. 2 | at Col. 5 | Brent Johnson | 82 | 82 | 50 | 82 | 27.1 |
| Jaromir Jagr | NYR | Mar. 24/06 | NYR 2 | at Fla. 3 | Roberto Luongo | 70 | 70 | 54 | 82 | |
| Ilya Kovalchuk | Atl. | Apr. 6/06 | Atl. 2 | at T.B. 3 | Sean Burke | 72 | 76 | 52 | 78 | 22.11 |
| Jonathan Cheechoo | S.J. | Apr. 10/06 | S.J. 3 | at Phx. 2 | David LeNeveu | 78 | 78 | 56 | 82 | 25.8 |
| Alex Ovechkin | Wsh. | Apr. 13/06 | Wsh. 3 | at Atl. 5 | Mike Dunham | 78 | 79 | 52 | 81 | 20.6 |
| Dany Heatley | Ott. | Apr. 18/06 | Ott. 5 | at NYR 1 | Henrik Lundqvist | 82 | 82 | 50 | 82 | 25.2 |
| Vincent Lecavalier | T.B. | Mar. 30/07 | T.B. 4 | at Car. 2 | Cam Ward | 78 | 78 | 52 | 82 | 26.11 |
| Dany Heatley | Ott. | Apr. 7/07 | Ott. 6 | at Bos. 3 | Tim Thomas | 82 | 82 | 50 | 82 | |
| Alex Ovechkin | Wsh. | Mar. 3/08 | Bos. 2 | at Wsh. 10 | Tim Thomas | 67 | 67 | 65 | 82 | |
| Ilya Kovalchuk | Atl. | Mar. 18/08 | Atl. 2 | at Phi. 3 | Antero Niittymaki | 72 | 75 | 52 | 79 | |
| Jarome Iginla | Cgy. | Apr. 5/08 | Cgy. 7 | at Van. 1 | Curtis Sanford | 82 | 82 | 50 | 82 | |
| Alex Ovechkin | Wsh. | Mar. 19/09 | Wsh. 5 | at T.B. 2 | Mike McKenna | 70 | 73 | 56 | 79 | |

* neutral site game played at Hamilton; ** neutral site game played at Cleveland

# 100-Point Seasons

Marcel Dionne

Pete Mahovlich

| Player | Team | Date of 100th Point | G or A | Score | | Player's Game No. | Team Game No. | G - A — PTS | Total Games | Age when first 100th point scored (Yrs. & Mos.) |
|---|---|---|---|---|---|---|---|---|---|---|
| Phil Esposito | Bos. | Mar. 2/69 | (G) | Pit. 0 | at Bos. 4 | 60 | 62 | 49-77 — 126 | 74 | 27.1 |
| Bobby Hull | Chi. | Mar. 20/69 | (G) | Chi. 5 | at Bos. 5 | 71 | 71 | 58-49 — 107 | 76 | 30.2 |
| Gordie Howe | Det. | Mar. 30/69 | (G) | Det. 5 | at Chi. 9 | 76 | 76 | 44-59 — 103 | 76 | 41.0 |
| Bobby Orr | Bos. | Mar. 15/70 | (G) | Det. 5 | at Bos. 5 | 67 | 67 | 33-87 — 120 | 76 | 22.11 |
| Phil Esposito | Bos. | Feb. 6/71 | (A) | Buf. 3 | at Bos. 4 | 51 | 51 | 76-76 — 152 | 78 | |
| Bobby Orr | Bos. | Feb. 20/71 | (A) | Bos. 4 | at L.A. 5 | 58 | 58 | 37-102 — 139 | 78 | |
| John Bucyk | Bos. | Mar. 13/71 | (G) | Bos. 6 | at Van. 3 | 68 | 68 | 51-65 — 116 | 78 | 35.10 |
| Ken Hodge | Bos. | Mar. 21/71 | (A) | Buf. 7 | at Bos. 5 | 72 | 72 | 43-62 — 105 | 78 | 26.9 |
| Jean Ratelle | NYR | Feb. 18/72 | (A) | NYR 2 | at Cal. 2 | 58 | 58 | 46-63 — 109 | 63 | 31.4 |
| Phil Esposito | Bos. | Feb. 19/72 | (A) | Bos. 6 | at Min. 4 | 59 | 59 | 66-67 — 133 | 76 | |
| Bobby Orr | Bos. | Mar. 2/72 | (A) | Van. 3 | at Bos. 7 | 64 | 64 | 37-80 — 117 | 76 | |
| Vic Hadfield | NYR | Mar. 25/72 | (A) | NYR 3 | at Mtl. 3 | 74 | 74 | 50-56 — 106 | 78 | 31.5 |
| Phil Esposito | Bos. | Mar. 3/73 | (A) | Bos. 1 | at Mtl. 5 | 64 | 64 | 55-75 — 130 | 78 | |
| Bobby Clarke | Phi. | Mar. 29/73 | (G) | Atl. 2 | at Phi. 4 | 76 | 76 | 37-67 — 104 | 78 | 23.7 |
| Bobby Orr | Bos. | Mar. 31/73 | (G) | Bos. 3 | at Tor. 7 | 62 | 77 | 29-72 — 101 | 63 | |
| Rick MacLeish | Phi. | Apr. 1/73 | (G) | Phi. 4 | at Pit. 5 | 78 | 78 | 50-50 — 100 | 78 | 23.3 |
| Phil Esposito | Bos. | Feb. 13/74 | (A) | Bos. 9 | at Cal. 6 | 53 | 53 | 68-77 — 145 | 78 | |
| Bobby Orr | Bos. | Mar. 12/74 | (A) | Buf. 0 | at Bos. 4 | 62 | 66 | 32-90 — 122 | 74 | |
| Ken Hodge | Bos. | Mar. 24/74 | (A) | Mtl. 3 | at Bos. 6 | 72 | 72 | 50-55 — 105 | 76 | |
| Phil Esposito | Bos. | Feb. 8/75 | (A) | Bos. 8 | at Det. 5 | 54 | 54 | 61-66 — 127 | 79 | |
| Bobby Orr | Bos. | Feb. 13/75 | (A) | Bos. 1 | at Buf. 3 | 57 | 57 | 46-89 — 135 | 80 | |
| Guy Lafleur | Mtl. | Mar. 7/75 | (G) | Wsh. 4 | at Mtl. 8 | 56 | 66 | 53-66 — 119 | 70 | 24.6 |
| Marcel Dionne | Det. | Mar. 9/75 | (A) | Det. 5 | at Phi. 8 | 67 | 67 | 47-74 — 121 | 80 | 23.7 |
| Pete Mahovlich | Mtl. | Mar. 9/75 | (G) | Mtl. 5 | at NYR 3 | 67 | 67 | 35-82 — 117 | 80 | 29.5 |
| Bobby Clarke | Phi. | Mar. 22/75 | (A) | Min. 0 | at Phi. 4 | 72 | 72 | 27-89 — 116 | 80 | |
| Rene Robert | Buf. | Apr. 5/75 | (A) | Buf. 4 | at Tor. 2 | 74 | 80 | 40-60 — 100 | 74 | 26.4 |
| Guy Lafleur | Mtl. | Mar. 10/76 | (G) | Mtl. 5 | at Chi. 1 | 69 | 69 | 56-69 — 125 | 80 | |
| Bobby Clarke | Phi. | Mar. 11/76 | (A) | Buf. 1 | at Phi. 6 | 64 | 68 | 30-89 — 119 | 76 | |
| Bill Barber | Phi. | Mar. 18/76 | (A) | Van. 2 | at Phi. 3 | 71 | 71 | 50-62 — 112 | 80 | 23.8 |
| Gilbert Perreault | Buf. | Mar. 21/76 | (A) | K.C. 1 | at Buf. 3 | 73 | 73 | 44-69 — 113 | 80 | 25.4 |
| Pierre Larouche | Pit. | Mar. 24/76 | (G) | Bos. 5 | at Pit. 5 | 70 | 74 | 53-58 — 111 | 76 | 20.4 |
| Pete Mahovlich | Mtl. | Mar. 28/76 | (A) | Mtl. 2 | at Bos. 2 | 77 | 77 | 34-71 — 105 | 80 | |
| Jean Ratelle | Bos. | Mar. 30/76 | (G) | Buf. 4 | at Bos. 4 | 77 | 77 | 36-69 — 105 | 80 | |
| Jean Pronovost | Pit. | Apr. 3/76 | (A) | Wsh. 5 | at Pit. 4 | 79 | 79 | 52-52 — 104 | 80 | 30.4 |
| Darryl Sittler | Tor. | Apr. 3/76 | (A) | Bos. 4 | at Tor. 2 | 78 | 79 | 41-59 — 100 | 79 | 25.7 |
| Guy Lafleur | Mtl. | Feb. 26/77 | (A) | Cle. 3 | at Mtl. 5 | 63 | 63 | 56-80 — 136 | 80 | |
| Marcel Dionne | L.A. | Mar. 5/77 | (G) | Pit. 3 | at L.A. 3 | 67 | 67 | 53-69 — 122 | 80 | |
| Steve Shutt | Mtl. | Mar. 27/77 | (A) | Mtl. 6 | at Det. 0 | 77 | 77 | 60-45 — 105 | 80 | 24.9 |
| Bryan Trottier | NYI | Feb. 25/78 | (A) | Chi. 1 | at NYI 7 | 59 | 60 | 46-77 — 123 | 77 | 21.7 |
| Guy Lafleur | Mtl. | Feb. 28/78 | (G) | Det. 3 | at Mtl. 9 | 69 | 61 | 60-72 — 132 | 78 | |
| Darryl Sittler | Tor. | Mar. 12/78 | (A) | Tor. 7 | at Pit. 1 | 67 | 67 | 45-72 — 117 | 80 | |
| Guy Lafleur | Mtl. | Feb. 27/79 | (A) | Mtl. 3 | at NYI 7 | 61 | 61 | 52-77 — 129 | 80 | |
| Bryan Trottier | NYI | Mar. 6/79 | (A) | Buf. 3 | at NYI 2 | 59 | 63 | 47-87 — 134 | 76 | |
| Marcel Dionne | L.A. | Mar. 8/79 | (G) | L.A. 4 | at Buf. 6 | 66 | 66 | 59-71 — 130 | 80 | |
| Mike Bossy | NYI | Mar. 11/79 | (G) | NYI 4 | at Bos. 4 | 66 | 66 | 69-57 — 126 | 80 | 22.2 |

| Player | Team | Date of 100th Point | G or A | Score | Player's Game No. | Team Game No. | G - A PTS | Total Games | Age when first 100th point scored (Yrs. & Mos.) |
|---|---|---|---|---|---|---|---|---|---|
| Bob MacMillan | Atl. | Mar. 15/79 | (A) | Atl. 4 at Phi. 5 | 68 | 69 | 37-71 — 108 | 79 | 26.6 |
| Guy Chouinard | Atl. | Mar. 30/79 | (G) | L.A. 3 at Atl. 5 | 75 | 75 | 50-57 — 107 | 80 | 22.5 |
| Denis Potvin | NYI | Apr. 8/79 | (A) | NYI 5 at NYR 2 | 73 | 80 | 31-70 — 101 | 73 | 25.5 |
| | | | | | | | | | |
| Marcel Dionne | L.A. | Feb. 6/80 | (A) | L.A. 3 at Hfd. 7 | 53 | 53 | 53-84 — 137 | 80 | |
| Guy Lafleur | Mtl. | Feb. 10/80 | (A) | Mtl. 3 at Bos. 2 | 55 | 55 | 50-75 — 125 | 74 | |
| Wayne Gretzky | Edm. | Feb. 24/80 | (A) | Bos. 4 at Edm. 2 | 61 | 62 | 51-86 — 137 | 79 | 19.2 |
| Bryan Trottier | NYI | Mar. 30/80 | (A) | NYI 9 at Que. 6 | 75 | 77 | 42-62 — 104 | 78 | |
| Gilbert Perreault | Buf. | Apr. 1/80 | (A) | Buf. 5 at Atl. 2 | 77 | 77 | 40-66 — 106 | 80 | |
| Mike Rogers | Hfd. | Apr. 4/80 | (A) | Que. 2 at Hfd. 9 | 79 | 79 | 44-61 — 105 | 80 | 25.5 |
| Charlie Simmer | L.A. | Apr. 5/80 | (G) | Van. 5 at L.A. 3 | 64 | 80 | 56-45 — 101 | 64 | 26.0 |
| Blaine Stoughton | Hfd. | Apr. 6/80 | (A) | Det. 3 at Hfd. 5 | 80 | 80 | 56-44 — 100 | 80 | 27.0 |
| | | | | | | | | | |
| Wayne Gretzky | Edm. | Feb. 6/81 | (G) | Wpg. 4 at Edm. 10 | 53 | 53 | 55-109 — 164 | 80 | |
| Marcel Dionne | L.A. | Feb. 12/81 | (A) | L.A. 5 at Chi. 5 | 58 | 58 | 58-77 — 135 | 80 | |
| Charlie Simmer | L.A. | Feb. 14/81 | (A) | Bos. 5 at L.A. 4 | 59 | 59 | 56-49 — 105 | 65 | |
| Kent Nilsson | Cgy. | Feb. 27/81 | (G) | Hfd. 1 at Cgy. 5 | 64 | 64 | 49-82 — 131 | 80 | 24.6 |
| Mike Bossy | NYI | Mar. 3/81 | (G) | Edm. 8 at NYI 8 | 65 | 66 | 68-51 — 119 | 79 | |
| Dave Taylor | L.A. | Mar. 14/81 | (G) | Min. 4 at L.A. 10 | 63 | 70 | 47-65 — 112 | 72 | 25.3 |
| Mike Rogers | Hfd. | Mar. 22/81 | (G) | Tor. 3 at Hfd. 3 | 74 | 74 | 40-65 — 105 | 80 | |
| Bernie Federko | St.L. | Mar. 28/81 | (A) | Buf. 4 at St.L. 7 | 74 | 76 | 31-73 — 104 | 78 | 24.10 |
| Rick Middleton | Bos. | Mar. 28/81 | (A) | Chi. 2 at Bos. 5 | 76 | 76 | 44-59 — 103 | 80 | 27.4 |
| Bryan Trottier | NYI | Mar. 29/81 | (G) | NYI 5 at Wsh. 4 | 69 | 76 | 31-72 — 103 | 73 | |
| Jacques Richard | Que. | Mar. 29/81 | (G) | Mtl. 0 at Que. 4 | 75 | 76 | 52-51 — 103 | 78 | 28.6 |
| Peter Stastny | Que. | Mar. 29/81 | (A) | Mtl. 0 at Que. 4 | 73 | 76 | 39-70 — 109 | 77 | 24.6 |
| | | | | | | | | | |
| Wayne Gretzky | Edm. | Dec. 27/81 | (G) | L.A. 3 at Edm. 10 | 38 | 38 | 92-120 — 212 | 80 | |
| Mike Bossy | NYI | Feb. 13/82 | (A) | Phi. 2 at NYI 8 | 55 | 55 | 64-83 — 147 | 80 | |
| Peter Stastny | Que. | Feb. 16/82 | (A) | Wpg. 3 at Que. 7 | 60 | 60 | 46-93 — 139 | 80 | |
| Dennis Maruk | Wsh. | Feb. 20/82 | (G) | Wsh. 3 at Min. 7 | 60 | 60 | 60-76 — 136 | 80 | 26.3 |
| Bryan Trottier | NYI | Feb. 23/82 | (G) | Chi. 1 at NYI 5 | 61 | 61 | 50-79 — 129 | 80 | |
| Denis Savard | Chi. | Feb. 27/82 | (A) | Chi. 5 at L.A. 3 | 64 | 64 | 32-87 — 119 | 80 | 21.1 |
| Bobby Smith | Min. | Mar. 3/82 | (A) | Det. 4 at Min. 6 | 66 | 66 | 43-71 — 114 | 80 | 24.1 |
| Marcel Dionne | L.A. | Mar. 6/82 | (G) | L.A. 6 at Hfd. 7 | 64 | 66 | 50-67 — 117 | 78 | |
| Dave Taylor | L.A. | Mar. 20/82 | (A) | Pit. 5 at L.A. 7 | 71 | 72 | 39-67 — 106 | 78 | |
| Dale Hawerchuk | Wpg. | Mar. 24/82 | (G) | L.A. 3 at Wpg. 5 | 74 | 74 | 45-58 — 103 | 80 | 18.11 |
| Dino Ciccarelli | Min. | Mar. 27/82 | (A) | Min. 6 at Bos. 5 | 72 | 76 | 55-52 — 107 | 76 | 21.8 |
| Glenn Anderson | Edm. | Mar. 28/82 | (G) | Edm. 6 at L.A. 2 | 78 | 78 | 38-67 — 105 | 80 | 21.7 |
| Mike Rogers | NYR | Apr. 2/82 | (G) | Pit. 7 at NYR 5 | 79 | 79 | 38-65 — 103 | 80 | |
| | | | | | | | | | |
| Wayne Gretzky | Edm. | Jan. 5/83 | (A) | Edm. 8 at Wpg. 3 | 42 | 42 | 71-125 — 196 | 80 | |
| Mike Bossy | NYI | Mar. 3/83 | (A) | Tor. 1 at NYI 5 | 66 | 67 | 60-58 — 118 | 79 | |
| Peter Stastny | Que. | Mar. 5/83 | (A) | Hfd. 3 at Que. 10 | 62 | 67 | 47-77 — 124 | 75 | |
| Denis Savard | Chi. | Mar. 6/83 | (G) | Mtl. 4 at Chi. 5 | 65 | 67 | 35-86 — 121 | 78 | |
| Mark Messier | Edm. | Mar. 23/83 | (G) | Edm. 4 at Wpg. 7 | 73 | 76 | 48-58 — 106 | 77 | 22.2 |
| Barry Pederson | Bos. | Mar. 26/83 | (A) | Hfd. 4 at Bos. 7 | 73 | 76 | 46-61 — 107 | 77 | 22.0 |
| Marcel Dionne | L.A. | Mar. 26/83 | (A) | Edm. 9 at L.A. 3 | 75 | 75 | 56-51 — 107 | 80 | |
| Michel Goulet | Que. | Mar. 27/83 | (A) | Que. 6 at Buf. 6 | 77 | 77 | 57-48 — 105 | 80 | 22.11 |
| Glenn Anderson | Edm. | Mar. 29/83 | (A) | Edm. 7 at Van. 4 | 70 | 78 | 48-56 — 104 | 72 | |
| Jari Kurri | Edm. | Mar. 29/83 | (A) | Edm. 7 at Van. 4 | 78 | 78 | 45-59 — 104 | 80 | 22.10 |
| Kent Nilsson | Cgy. | Mar. 29/83 | (G) | L.A. 3 at Cgy. 5 | 78 | 78 | 46-58 — 104 | 80 | |
| | | | | | | | | | |
| Wayne Gretzky | Edm. | Dec. 18/83 | (G) | Edm. 7 at Wpg. 5 | 34 | 34 | 87-118 — 205 | 74 | |
| Paul Coffey | Edm. | Mar. 4/84 | (A) | Mtl. 1 at Edm. 6 | 68 | 68 | 40-86 — 126 | 80 | 22.9 |
| Michel Goulet | Que. | Mar. 4/84 | (A) | Que. 1 at Buf. 1 | 62 | 67 | 56-65 — 121 | 75 | |
| Jari Kurri | Edm. | Mar. 7/84 | (G) | Chi. 4 at Edm. 7 | 53 | 69 | 52-61 — 113 | 64 | |
| Peter Stastny | Que. | Mar. 8/84 | (A) | Que. 8 at Pit. 6 | 69 | 69 | 46-73 — 119 | 80 | |
| Mike Bossy | NYI | Mar. 8/84 | (G) | Tor. 5 at NYI 9 | 56 | 68 | 51-67 — 118 | 67 | |
| Barry Pederson | Bos. | Mar. 14/84 | (A) | Bos. 4 at Det. 2 | 71 | 71 | 39-77 — 116 | 80 | |
| Bryan Trottier | NYI | Mar. 18/84 | (G) | NYI 4 at Hfd. 5 | 62 | 73 | 40-71 — 111 | 68 | |
| Bernie Federko | St.L. | Mar. 20/84 | (A) | Wpg. 3 at St.L. 9 | 75 | 76 | 41-66 — 107 | 79 | |
| Rick Middleton | Bos. | Mar. 27/84 | (G) | Bos. 6 at Que. 4 | 77 | 77 | 47-58 — 105 | 80 | |
| Dale Hawerchuk | Wpg. | Mar. 27/84 | (G) | Wpg. 3 at L.A. 3 | 77 | 77 | 37-65 — 102 | 80 | |
| Mark Messier | Edm. | Mar. 27/84 | (G) | Edm. 9 at Cgy. 2 | 72 | 79 | 37-64 — 101 | 73 | |
| | | | | | | | | | |
| Wayne Gretzky | Edm. | Dec. 29/84 | (A) | Det. 3 at Edm. 6 | 35 | 35 | 73-135 — 208 | 80 | |
| Jari Kurri | Edm. | Jan. 29/85 | (G) | Edm. 4 at Cgy. 2 | 48 | 51 | 71-64 — 135 | 73 | |
| Mike Bossy | NYI | Feb. 23/85 | (G) | Bos. 1 at NYI 7 | 56 | 60 | 58-59 — 117 | 76 | |
| Dale Hawerchuk | Wpg. | Feb. 25/85 | (A) | Wpg. 12 at NYR 5 | 64 | 64 | 53-77 — 130 | 80 | |
| Marcel Dionne | L.A. | Mar. 5/85 | (A) | Pit. 0 at L.A. 6 | 66 | 66 | 46-80 — 126 | 80 | |
| Brent Sutter | NYI | Mar. 12/85 | (A) | NYI 6 at St.L. 5 | 68 | 68 | 42-60 — 102 | 72 | 22.10 |
| John Ogrodnick | Det. | Mar. 22/85 | (A) | NYR 3 at Det. 5 | 73 | 73 | 55-50 — 105 | 79 | 25.9 |
| Paul Coffey | Edm. | Mar. 26/85 | (G) | Edm. 7 at NYI 5 | 74 | 74 | 37-84 — 121 | 80 | |
| Denis Savard | Chi. | Mar. 29/85 | (A) | Chi. 5 at Wpg. 5 | 75 | 76 | 38-67 — 105 | 79 | |
| Peter Stastny | Que. | Apr. 2/85 | (A) | Bos. 4 at Que. 6 | 74 | 77 | 32-68 — 100 | 75 | |
| Bernie Federko | St.L. | Apr. 4/85 | (A) | NYR 5 at St.L. 4 | 74 | 78 | 30-73 — 103 | 76 | |
| Paul MacLean | Wpg. | Apr. 6/85 | (A) | Wpg. 6 at Edm. 5 | 78 | 79 | 41-60 — 101 | 79 | 27.1 |
| Bernie Nicholls | L.A. | Apr. 6/85 | (A) | Van. 4 at L.A. 4 | 80 | 80 | 46-54 — 100 | 80 | 22.9 |
| John Tonelli | NYI | Apr. 6/85 | (G) | N.J. 5 at NYI 5 | 80 | 80 | 42-58 — 100 | 80 | 28.1 |
| Mike Gartner | Wsh. | Apr. 7/85 | (G) | Pit. 3 at Wsh. 7 | 80 | 80 | 50-52 — 102 | 80 | 25.6 |
| Mario Lemieux | Pit. | Apr. 7/85 | (G) | Pit. 3 at Wsh. 7 | 73 | 80 | 43-57 — 100 | 73 | 19.6 |
| | | | | | | | | | |
| Wayne Gretzky | Edm. | Jan. 4/86 | (A) | Hfd. 3 at Edm. 4 | 39 | 39 | 52-163 — 215 | 80 | |
| Mario Lemieux | Pit. | Feb. 15/86 | (G) | Van. 4 at Pit. 9 | 55 | 56 | 48-93 — 141 | 79 | |
| Paul Coffey | Edm. | Feb. 19/86 | (A) | Tor. 5 at Edm. 9 | 59 | 60 | 48-90 — 138 | 79 | |
| Peter Stastny | Que. | Mar. 1/86 | (A) | Buf. 8 at Que. 4 | 66 | 68 | 41-81 — 122 | 76 | |
| Jari Kurri | Edm. | Mar. 2/86 | (G) | Phi. 1 at Edm. 2 | 62 | 64 | 68-63 — 131 | 78 | |
| Mike Bossy | NYI | Mar. 8/86 | (G) | Wsh. 6 at NYI 2 | 65 | 65 | 61-62 — 123 | 80 | |
| Denis Savard | Chi. | Mar. 12/86 | (A) | Buf. 7 at Chi. 6 | 69 | 69 | 47-69 — 116 | 80 | |
| Mats Naslund | Mtl. | Mar. 13/86 | (A) | Mtl. 2 at Bos. 3 | 70 | 70 | 43-67 — 110 | 80 | 26.4 |
| Michel Goulet | Que. | Mar. 24/86 | (A) | Que. 1 at Min. 0 | 70 | 75 | 53-50 — 103 | 75 | |

*Dennis Maruk*

*Peter Stastny*

*Mats Naslund*

*Wayne Gretzky*

*Brian Leetch*

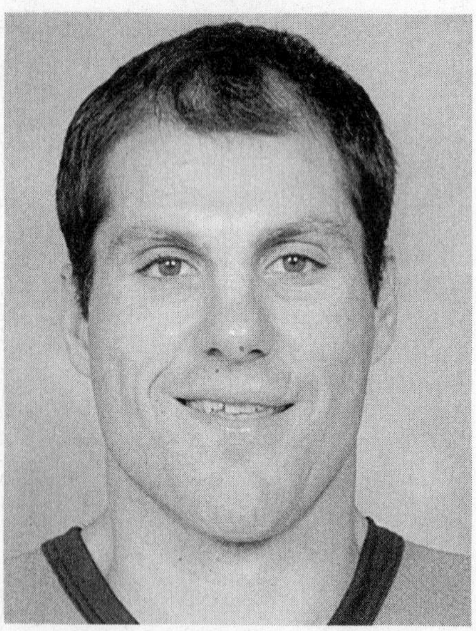

*Rick Tocchet*

| Player | Team | Date of 100th Point | G or A | Score | | Player's Game No. | Team Game No. | G - A PTS | Total Games | Age when first 100th point scored (Yrs. & Mos.) |
|---|---|---|---|---|---|---|---|---|---|---|
| Glenn Anderson | Edm. | Mar. 25/86 | (G) | Edm. 7 | at Det. 2 | 66 | 74 | 54-48 — 102 | 72 | |
| Neal Broten | Min. | Mar. 26/86 | (A) | Min. 6 | at Tor. 1 | 76 | 76 | 29-76 — 105 | 80 | 26.4 |
| Dale Hawerchuk | Wpg. | Mar. 31/86 | (A) | Wpg. 5 | at L.A. 2 | 78 | 78 | 46-59 — 105 | 80 | |
| Bernie Federko | St.L. | Apr. 5/86 | (G) | Chi. 5 | at St.L. 7 | 79 | 79 | 34-68 — 102 | 80 | |
| Wayne Gretzky | Edm. | Jan. 11/87 | (A) | Cgy. 3 | at Edm. 5 | 42 | 42 | 62-121 — 183 | 79 | |
| Jari Kurri | Edm. | Mar. 14/87 | (A) | Buf. 3 | at Edm. 5 | 67 | 68 | 54-54 — 108 | 79 | |
| Mario Lemieux | Pit. | Mar. 18/87 | (A) | St.L. 4 | at Pit. 5 | 55 | 72 | 54-53 — 107 | 63 | |
| Mark Messier | Edm. | Mar. 19/87 | (A) | Edm. 4 | at Cgy. 5 | 71 | 71 | 37-70 — 107 | 77 | |
| Dino Ciccarelli | Min. | Mar. 30/87 | (A) | NYR 6 | at Min. 5 | 78 | 78 | 52-51 — 103 | 80 | |
| Doug Gilmour | St.L. | Apr. 2/87 | (A) | Buf. 3 | at St.L. 5 | 78 | 78 | 42-63 — 105 | 80 | 23.10 |
| Dale Hawerchuk | Wpg. | Apr. 5/87 | (A) | Wpg. 3 | at Cgy. 1 | 80 | 80 | 47-53 — 100 | 80 | |
| Mario Lemieux | Pit. | Jan. 20/88 | (G) | Pit. 8 | at Chi. 3 | 45 | 48 | 70-98 — 168 | 77 | |
| Wayne Gretzky | Edm. | Feb. 11/88 | (A) | Edm. 7 | at Van. 2 | 43 | 56 | 40-109 — 149 | 64 | |
| Denis Savard | Chi. | Feb. 12/88 | (A) | St.L. 3 | at Chi. 4 | 57 | 57 | 44-87 — 131 | 80 | |
| Dale Hawerchuk | Wpg. | Feb. 23/88 | (G) | Wpg. 4 | at Pit. 3 | 61 | 61 | 44-77 — 121 | 80 | |
| Steve Yzerman | Det. | Feb. 27/88 | (A) | Det. 4 | at Que. 5 | 63 | 63 | 50-52 — 102 | 64 | 22.10 |
| Peter Stastny | Que. | Mar. 8/88 | (A) | Hfd. 4 | at Que. 6 | 63 | 67 | 46-65 — 111 | 76 | |
| Mark Messier | Edm. | Mar. 15/88 | (A) | Buf. 4 | at Edm. 6 | 68 | 71 | 37-74 — 111 | 77 | |
| Jimmy Carson | L.A. | Mar. 26/88 | (A) | Chi. 5 | at L.A. 9 | 77 | 77 | 55-52 — 107 | 80 | 19.8 |
| Hakan Loob | Cgy. | Mar. 26/88 | (A) | Van. 1 | at Cgy. 6 | 76 | 76 | 50-56 — 106 | 80 | 27.9 |
| Mike Bullard | Cgy. | Mar. 26/88 | (A) | Van. 1 | at Cgy. 6 | 76 | 76 | 48-55 — 103 | 79 | 27.1 |
| Michel Goulet | Que. | Mar. 27/88 | (A) | Pit. 6 | at Que. 3 | 76 | 76 | 48-58 — 106 | 80 | |
| Luc Robitaille | L.A. | Mar. 30/88 | (G) | Cgy. 7 | at L.A. 9 | 78 | 78 | 53-58 — 111 | 80 | 22.1 |
| Mario Lemieux | Pit. | Dec. 31/88 | (A) | N.J. 6 | at Pit. 8 | 36 | 38 | 85-114 — 199 | 76 | |
| Wayne Gretzky | L.A. | Jan. 21/89 | (A) | L.A. 4 | at Hfd. 5 | 47 | 48 | 54-114 — 168 | 78 | |
| Bernie Nicholls | L.A. | Jan. 21/89 | (A) | L.A. 4 | at Hfd. 5 | 48 | 48 | 70-80 — 150 | 79 | |
| Steve Yzerman | Det. | Jan. 27/89 | (G) | Tor. 1 | at Det. 8 | 50 | 50 | 65-90 — 155 | 80 | |
| Rob Brown | Pit. | Mar. 16/89 | (A) | Pit. 2 | at N.J. 1 | 60 | 72 | 49-66 — 115 | 68 | 20.11 |
| Paul Coffey | Pit. | Mar. 20/89 | (A) | Pit. 2 | at Min. 7 | 69 | 74 | 30-83 — 113 | 75 | |
| Joe Mullen | Cgy. | Mar. 23/89 | (A) | L.A. 2 | at Cgy. 4 | 74 | 75 | 51-59 — 110 | 79 | 32.1 |
| Jari Kurri | Edm. | Mar. 29/89 | (A) | Edm. 5 | at Van. 2 | 75 | 79 | 44-58 — 102 | 76 | |
| Jimmy Carson | Edm. | Apr. 2/89 | (A) | Edm. 2 | at Cgy. 4 | 80 | 80 | 49-51 — 100 | 80 | |
| Mario Lemieux | Pit. | Jan. 28/90 | (G) | Pit. 2 | at Buf. 7 | 50 | 50 | 45-78 — 123 | 59 | |
| Wayne Gretzky | L.A. | Jan. 30/90 | (A) | N.J. 2 | at L.A. 5 | 51 | 51 | 40-102 — 142 | 73 | |
| Steve Yzerman | Det. | Feb. 19/90 | (A) | Mtl. 5 | at Det. 5 | 61 | 61 | 62-65 — 127 | 79 | |
| Mark Messier | Edm. | Feb. 20/90 | (A) | Edm. 4 | at Van. 2 | 62 | 62 | 45-84 — 129 | 79 | |
| Brett Hull | St.L. | Mar. 3/90 | (A) | NYI 4 | at St.L. 5 | 67 | 67 | 72-41 — 113 | 80 | 25.7 |
| Bernie Nicholls | NYR | Mar. 12/90 | (A) | L.A. 6 | at NYR 2 | 70 | 71 | 39-73 — 112 | 79 | |
| Pierre Turgeon | Buf. | Mar. 25/90 | (G) | N.J. 4 | at Buf. 3 | 76 | 76 | 40-66 — 106 | 80 | 20.7 |
| Paul Coffey | Pit. | Mar. 25/90 | (A) | Pit. 2 | at Hfd. 4 | 77 | 77 | 29-74 — 103 | 80 | |
| Pat LaFontaine | NYI | Mar. 27/90 | (G) | Cgy. 4 | at NYI 2 | 72 | 78 | 54-51 — 105 | 74 | 25.1 |
| Adam Oates | St.L. | Mar. 29/90 | (G) | Pit. 4 | at St.L. 5 | 79 | 79 | 23-79 — 102 | 80 | 27.7 |
| Joe Sakic | Que. | Mar. 31/90 | (G) | Hfd. 3 | at Que. 2 | 79 | 79 | 39-63 — 102 | 80 | 20.8 |
| Ron Francis | Hfd. | Mar. 31/90 | (G) | Hfd. 3 | at Que. 2 | 79 | 79 | 32-69 — 101 | 80 | 27.0 |
| Luc Robitaille | L.A. | Apr. 1/90 | (A) | L.A. 4 | at Cgy. 8 | 80 | 80 | 52-49 — 101 | 80 | |
| Wayne Gretzky | L.A. | Jan. 30/91 | (A) | N.J. 4 | at L.A. 2 | 50 | 51 | 41-122 — 163 | 78 | |
| Brett Hull | St.L. | Feb. 23/91 | (G) | Bos. 2 | at St.L. 9 | 60 | 62 | 86-45 — 131 | 78 | |
| Mark Recchi | Pit. | Mar. 5/91 | (G) | Van. 1 | at Pit. 4 | 66 | 67 | 40-73 — 113 | 78 | 23.1 |
| Steve Yzerman | Det. | Mar. 10/91 | (G) | Det. 4 | at St.L. 1 | 72 | 72 | 51-57 — 108 | 80 | |
| John Cullen | Hfd. | Mar. 16/91 | (G) | N.J. 2 | at Hfd. 6 | 71 | 71 | 39-71 — 110 | 78 | 26.7 |
| Adam Oates | St.L. | Mar. 17/91 | (A) | St.L. 4 | at Chi. 6 | 54 | 73 | 25-90 — 115 | 61 | |
| Joe Sakic | Que. | Mar. 19/91 | (G) | Edm. 7 | at Que. 6 | 74 | 74 | 48-61 — 109 | 80 | |
| Steve Larmer | Chi. | Mar. 24/91 | (A) | Min. 4 | at Chi. 5 | 76 | 76 | 44-57 — 101 | 80 | 29.9 |
| Theoren Fleury | Cgy. | Mar. 26/91 | (G) | Van. 2 | at Cgy. 7 | 77 | 77 | 51-53 — 104 | 79 | 22.9 |
| Al MacInnis | Cgy. | Mar. 28/91 | (A) | Edm. 4 | at Cgy. 4 | 78 | 78 | 28-75 — 103 | 78 | 27.8 |
| Brett Hull | St.L. | Mar. 2/92 | (G) | St.L. 5 | at Van. 3 | 66 | 66 | 70-39 — 109 | 73 | |
| Wayne Gretzky | L.A. | Mar. 3/92 | (A) | Phi. 1 | at L.A. 4 | 60 | 66 | 31-90 — 121 | 74 | |
| Kevin Stevens | Pit. | Mar. 7/92 | (A) | Pit. 3 | at L.A. 5 | 66 | 66 | 54-69 — 123 | 80 | 26.11 |
| Mario Lemieux | Pit. | Mar. 10/92 | (A) | Cgy. 2 | at Pit. 5 | 53 | 67 | 44-87 — 131 | 64 | |
| Luc Robitaille | L.A. | Mar. 17/92 | (A) | Wpg. 4 | at L.A. 5 | 73 | 73 | 44-63 — 107 | 80 | |
| Mark Messier | NYR | Mar. 22/92 | (G) | N.J. 3 | at NYR 6 | 74 | 75 | 35-72 — 107 | 79 | |
| Jeremy Roenick | Chi. | Mar. 29/92 | (A) | Tor. 1 | at Chi. 5 | 77 | 77 | 53-50 — 103 | 80 | 22.2 |
| Steve Yzerman | Det. | Apr. 14/92 | (G) | Det. 7 | at Min. 4 | 79 | 80 | 45-58 — 103 | 79 | |
| Brian Leetch | NYR | Apr. 16/92 | (G) | Pit. 1 | at NYR 7 | 80 | 80 | 22-80 — 102 | 80 | 24.1 |
| Mario Lemieux | Pit. | Dec. 31/92 | (G) | Tor. 3 | at Pit. 3 | 38 | 39 | 69-91 — 160 | 60 | |
| Pat LaFontaine | Buf. | Feb. 10/93 | (A) | Buf. 6 | at Wpg. 2 | 55 | 55 | 53-95 — 148 | 84 | |
| Adam Oates | Bos. | Feb. 14/93 | (A) | Bos. 3 | at T.B. 3 | 58 | 58 | 45-97 — 142 | 84 | |
| Steve Yzerman | Det. | Feb. 24/93 | (A) | Det. 7 | at Buf. 10 | 64 | 64 | 58-79 — 137 | 84 | |
| Pierre Turgeon | NYI | Feb. 28/93 | (G) | NYI 7 | at Hfd. 6 | 62 | 63 | 58-74 — 132 | 83 | |
| Doug Gilmour | Tor. | Mar. 3/93 | (A) | Min. 1 | at Tor. 3 | 64 | 64 | 32-95 — 127 | 83 | |
| Alexander Mogilny | Buf. | Mar. 5/93 | (A) | Hfd. 4 | at Buf. 2 | 58 | 65 | 76-51 — 127 | 77 | 24.1 |
| Mark Recchi | Phi. | Mar. 7/93 | (G) | Phi. 3 | at N.J. 7 | 66 | 66 | 53-70 — 123 | 84 | |
| Teemu Selanne | Wpg. | Mar. 9/93 | (G) | Wpg. 4 | at T.B. 2 | 68 | 68 | 76-56 — 132 | 84 | 22.7 |
| Luc Robitaille | L.A. | Mar. 15/93 | (A) | L.A. 4 | at Buf. 2 | 69 | 69 | 63-62 — 125 | 84 | |
| Kevin Stevens | Pit. | Mar. 23/93 | (A) | S.J. 2 | at Pit. 7 | 63 | 73 | 55-56 — 111 | 72 | |
| Mats Sundin | Que. | Mar. 27/93 | (G) | Phi. 3 | at Que. 8 | 71 | 75 | 47-67 — 114 | 80 | 22.1 |
| Pavel Bure | Van. | Apr. 1/93 | (G) | Van. 5 | at T.B. 3 | 77 | 77 | 60-50 — 110 | 83 | 22.0 |
| Jeremy Roenick | Chi. | Apr. 4/93 | (G) | St.L. 4 | at Chi. 5 | 79 | 79 | 50-57 — 107 | 84 | |
| Craig Janney | St.L. | Apr. 4/93 | (G) | St.L. 4 | at Chi. 5 | 79 | 79 | 24-82 — 106 | 84 | 25.7 |
| Rick Tocchet | Pit. | Apr. 7/93 | (G) | Mtl. 3 | at Pit. 4 | 77 | 81 | 48-61 — 109 | 80 | 28.11 |
| Joe Sakic | Que. | Apr. 8/93 | (A) | Que. 2 | at Bos. 6 | 75 | 81 | 48-57 — 105 | 78 | |
| Ron Francis | Pit. | Apr. 9/93 | (A) | Pit. 10 | at NYR 4 | 82 | 82 | 24-76 — 100 | 84 | |
| Brett Hull | St.L. | Apr. 11/93 | (G) | Min. 1 | at St.L. 5 | 78 | 82 | 54-47 — 101 | 80 | |

| Player | Team | Date of 100th Point | G or A | Score | Player's Game No. | Team Game No. | G - A PTS | Total Games | Age when first 100th point scored (Yrs. & Mos.) |
|---|---|---|---|---|---|---|---|---|---|
| Theoren Fleury | Cgy. | Apr. 11/93 | (G) | Cgy. 3 at Van. 6 | 82 | 82 | 34-66 — 100 | 83 | |
| Joe Juneau | Bos. | Apr. 14/93 | (A) | Bos. 4 at Ott. 2 | 84 | 84 | 32-70 — 102 | 84 | 25.3 |
| Wayne Gretzky | L.A. | Feb. 14/94 | (A) | Bos. 3 at L.A. 2 | 56 | 56 | 38-92 — 130 | 81 | |
| Sergei Fedorov | Det. | Mar. 1/94 | (A) | Cgy. 2 at Det. 5 | 63 | 63 | 56-64 — 120 | 82 | 24.2 |
| Doug Gilmour | Tor. | Mar. 23/94 | (G) | Tor. 1 at Fla. 1 | 74 | 74 | 27-84 — 111 | 83 | |
| Adam Oates | Bos. | Mar. 26/94 | (A) | Mtl. 3 at Bos. 6 | 68 | 75 | 32-80 — 112 | 77 | |
| Mark Recchi | Phi. | Mar. 27/94 | (A) | Ana. 3 at Phi. 2 | 76 | 76 | 40-67 — 107 | 84 | |
| Pavel Bure | Van. | Mar. 28/94 | (A) | Tor. 2 at Van. 3 | 68 | 76 | 60-47 — 107 | 76 | |
| Jeremy Roenick | Chi. | Mar. 31/94 | (G) | Chi. 3 at Wsh. 6 | 78 | 78 | 46-61 — 107 | 84 | |
| Brendan Shanahan | St.L. | Apr. 12/94 | (G) | St.L. 5 at Dal. 9 | 80 | 83 | 52-50 — 102 | 81 | 25.2 |
| Mario Lemieux | Pit. | Jan. 16/96 | (G) | Col. 5 at Pit. 2 | 38 | 44 | 69-92 — 161 | 70 | |
| Jaromir Jagr | Pit. | Feb. 6/96 | (G) | Bos. 5 at Pit. 6 | 52 | 52 | 62-87 — 149 | 82 | 23.11 |
| Ron Francis | Pit. | Mar. 9/96 | (A) | N.J. 4 at Pit. 3 | 61 | 66 | 27-92 — 119 | 77 | |
| Peter Forsberg | Col. | Mar. 9/96 | (A) | Col. 7 at Van. 5 | 68 | 68 | 30-86 — 116 | 82 | 22.7 |
| Joe Sakic | Col. | Mar. 17/96 | (A) | Edm. 1 at Col. 8 | 70 | 70 | 51-69 — 120 | 82 | |
| Eric Lindros | Phi. | Mar. 25/96 | (A) | Hfd. 0 at Phi. 3 | 65 | 73 | 47-68 — 115 | 73 | 23 |
| Teemu Selanne | Ana. | Mar. 25/96 | (A) | Ana. 1 at Det. 5 | 70 | 73 | 40-68 — 108 | 79 | |
| Alexander Mogilny | Van. | Mar. 25/96 | (A) | L.A. 1 at Van. 4 | 72 | 75 | 55-52 — 107 | 79 | |
| Wayne Gretzky | St.L. | Mar. 28/96 | (A) | N.J. 4 at St.L. 4 | 76 | 75 | 23-79 — 102 | 80 | |
| Doug Weight | Edm. | Mar. 30/96 | (G) | Tor. 4 at Edm. 3 | 76 | 76 | 25-79 — 104 | 82 | 25.3 |
| Sergei Fedorov | Det. | Apr. 2/96 | (A) | Det. 3 at S.J. 6 | 72 | 76 | 39-68 — 107 | 78 | |
| Paul Kariya | Ana. | Apr. 7/96 | (G) | Ana. 5 at S.J. 3 | 78 | 78 | 50-58 — 108 | 82 | 21.5 |
| Mario Lemieux | Pit. | Mar. 8/97 | (A) | Phi. 2 at Pit. 3 | 61 | 65 | 50-72 — 122 | 76 | |
| Teemu Selanne | Ana. | Apr. 1/97 | (A) | Chi. 3 at Ana. 3 | 74 | 78 | 51-58 — 109 | 78 | |
| Jaromir Jagr | Pit. | Apr. 15/98 | (G) | T.B. 1 at Pit. 5 | 76 | 80 | 35-67 — 102 | 77 | |
| Jaromir Jagr | Pit. | Mar. 13/99 | (G) | Phi. 0 at Pit. 4 | 65 | 65 | 44-83 — 127 | 81 | |
| Teemu Selanne | Ana. | Apr. 5/99 | (A) | Ana. 2 at Det. 3 | 69 | 76 | 47-60 — 107 | 75 | |
| Paul Kariya | Ana. | Apr. 17/99 | (G) | Ana. 3 at S.J. 3 | 82 | 82 | 39-62 — 101 | 82 | |
| Jaromir Jagr | Pit. | Mar. 10/01 | (G) | Cgy. 3 at Pit. 6 | 68 | 68 | 52-69 — 121 | 81 | |
| Joe Sakic | Col. | Mar. 18/01 | (G) | Min. 3 at Col. 4 | 72 | 72 | 54-64 — 118 | 82 | |
| Markus Naslund | Van. | Mar. 27/03 | (A) | Phx. 1 at Van. 5 | 78 | 78 | 48-56 — 104 | 82 | 29.8 |
| Peter Forsberg | Col. | Mar. 31/03 | (A) | S.J. 1 at Col. 3 | 72 | 79 | 29-77 — 106 | 79 | |
| Joe Thornton | Bos. | Apr. 4/03 | (A) | Buf. 5 at Bos. 8 | 77 | 82 | 36-65 — 101 | 77 | 23.9 |
| Jaromir Jagr | NYR | Mar. 18/06 | A | Tor. 2 at NYR 5 | 67 | 67 | 54-69 — 123 | 82 | |
| Joe Thornton | S.J. | Mar. 21/06 | A | S.J. 6 at St.L. 0 | 66 | 67 | 29-96 — 125 | 81 | |
| Alex Ovechkin | Wsh. | Apr. 10/06 | G | Wsh. 2 at Bos. 1 | 77 | 78 | 52-54 — 106 | 81 | 20.6 |
| Dany Heatley | Ott. | Apr. 13/06 | A | Fla. 5 at Ott. 4 | 80 | 80 | 50-53 — 103 | 82 | 25.2 |
| Daniel Alfredsson | Ott. | Apr. 15/06 | A | Fla. 5 at Ott. 4 | 76 | 81 | 43-60 — 103 | 77 | 33.4 |
| Eric Staal | Car. | Apr. 15/06 | A | Car. 2 at T.B. 3 | 81 | 81 | 45-55 — 100 | 82 | 21.5 |
| Sidney Crosby | Pit. | Apr. 17/06 | A | NYI 1 at Pit. 6 | 80 | 81 | 39-63 — 102 | 81 | 18.8 |
| Sidney Crosby | Pit. | Mar. 10/07 | G | NYR 2 at Pit. 3 | 65 | 68 | 36-84 — 120 | 79 | |
| Joe Thornton | S.J. | Mar. 22/07 | A | S.J. 5 at Atl. 1 | 75 | 75 | 22-92 — 114 | 82 | |
| Vincent Lecavalier | T.B. | Mar. 24/07 | A | Ott. 7 at T.B. 2 | 76 | 76 | 52-56 — 108 | 82 | 26.11 |
| Dany Heatley | Ott. | Mar. 31/07 | G | Ott. 5 at NYI 2 | 79 | 79 | 50-55 — 105 | 82 | |
| Martin St. Louis | T.B. | Mar. 31/07 | A | Wsh. 2 at T.B. 5 | 79 | 79 | 43-59 — 102 | 82 | 31.10 |
| Marian Hossa | Atl. | Apr. 7/07 | A | T.B. 2 at Atl. 3 | 82 | 82 | 43-57 — 100 | 82 | 28.3 |
| Joe Sakic | Col. | Apr. 8/07 | G | Cgy. 3 at Col. 6 | 82 | 82 | 36-64 — 100 | 82 | |
| Alex Ovechkin | Wsh. | Mar. 18/08 | A | Wsh. 4 at Nsh. 2 | 74 | 74 | 65-47 — 112 | 82 | |
| Evgeni Malkin | Pit. | Mar. 22/08 | G | N.J. 1 at Pit. 7 | 75 | 75 | 47-59 — 106 | 82 | 21.8 |
| Evgeni Malkin | Pit. | Mar. 17/09 | G | Atl. 2 at Pit. 6 | 72 | 72 | 35-78 — 113 | 82 | |
| Alex Ovechkin | Wsh. | Mar. 27/09 | G | T.B. 3 at Wsh. 5 | 73 | 76 | 56-54 — 110 | 79 | |
| Sidney Crosby | Pit. | Apr. 7/09 | G | Pit. 6 at T.B. 4 | 75 | 80 | 33-70 — 103 | 77 | |

*Alexander Mogilny*

*Sidney Crosby*

*Evgeni Malkin*

# Five-or-more-Goal Games

| Player | Team | Date | Score | Opposing Goaltender |
|---|---|---|---|---|
| **SEVEN GOALS** | | | | |
| Joe Malone | Quebec Bulldogs | Jan. 31/20 | Tor. 6 at Que. 10 | Ivan Mitchell |
| **SIX GOALS** | | | | |
| Newsy Lalonde | Montreal | Jan. 10/20 | Tor. 7 at Mtl. 14 | Ivan Mitchell |
| Joe Malone | Quebec Bulldogs | Mar. 10/20 | Ott. 4 at Que. 10 | Clint Benedict |
| Corb Denneny | Toronto St. Pats | Jan. 26/21 | Ham. 3 at Tor. 10 | Howard Lockhart |
| Cy Denneny | Ottawa Senators | Mar. 7/21 | Ham. 5 at Ott. 12 | Howard Lockhart |
| Syd Howe | Detroit | Feb. 3/44 | NYR 2 at Det. 12 | Ken McAuley |
| Red Berenson | St. Louis | Nov. 7/68 | St.L. 8 at Phi. 0 | Doug Favell |
| Darryl Sittler | Toronto | Feb. 7/76 | Bos. 4 at Tor. 11 | Dave Reece |
| **FIVE GOALS** | | | | |
| Joe Malone | Montreal | Dec. 19/17 | Mtl. 7 at Ott. 4 | Clint Benedict |
| Harry Hyland | Mtl. Wanderers | Dec. 19/17 | Tor. 9 at Mtl. W. 10 | Art Brooks,<br>Sammy Hebert |
| Joe Malone | Montreal | Jan. 12/18 | Ott. 4 at Mtl. 9 | Clint Benedict |
| Joe Malone | Montreal | Feb. 2/18 | Tor. 2 at Mtl. 11 | Hap Holmes |
| Mickey Roach | Toronto St. Pats | Mar. 6/20 | Que. 2 at Tor. 11 | Howard Lockhart |
| Newsy Lalonde | Montreal | Feb. 16/21 | Ham. 5 at Mtl. 10 | Howard Lockhart |
| Babe Dye | Toronto St. Pats | Dec. 16/22 | Mtl. 2 at Tor. 7 | Georges Vezina |
| Red Green | Hamilton Tigers | Dec. 5/24 | Ham. 10 at Tor. 3 | John Ross Roach |
| Babe Dye | Toronto St. Pats | Dec. 22/24 | Tor. 10 at Bos. 1 | Hec Fowler |
| Punch Broadbent | Mtl. Maroons | Jan. 7/25 | Mtl. 6 at Ham. 2 | Jake Forbes |
| Pit Lepine | Montreal | Dec. 14/29 | Ott. 4 at Mtl. 6 | Alex Connell |
| Howie Morenz | Montreal | Mar. 18/30 | NYA 3 at Mtl. 8 | Roy Worters |
| Charlie Conacher | Toronto | Jan. 19/32 | NYA 3 at Tor. 11 | Roy Worters (3)<br>Al Shields (2) |
| Ray Getliffe | Montreal | Feb. 6/43 | Bos. 3 at Mtl. 8 | Frank Brimsek |
| Maurice Richard | Montreal | Dec. 28/44 | Det. 1 at Mtl. 9 | Harry Lumley |
| Howie Meeker | Toronto | Jan. 8/47 | Chi. 4 at Tor. 10 | Paul Bibeault |
| Bernie Geoffrion | Montreal | Feb. 19/55 | NYR 2 at Mtl. 10 | Gump Worsley |
| Bobby Rousseau | Montreal | Feb. 1/64 | Det. 3 at Mtl. 9 | Roger Crozier |
| Yvan Cournoyer | Montreal | Feb. 15/75 | Chi. 3 at Mtl. 12 | Mike Veisor |
| Don Murdoch | NY Rangers | Oct. 12/76 | NYR 10 at Min. 4 | Gary Smith |
| Ian Turnbull | Toronto | Feb. 2/77 | Det. 1 at Tor. 9 | Ed Giacomin (2)<br>Jim Rutherford (3) |
| Bryan Trottier | NY Islanders | Dec. 23/78 | NYR 4 at NYI 9 | Wayne Thomas (4)<br>John Davidson (1) |
| Tim Young | Minnesota | Jan. 15/79 | Min. 8 at NYR 1 | Doug Soetaert (3)<br>Wayne Thomas (2) |
| John Tonelli | NY Islanders | Jan. 6/81 | Tor. 3 at NYI 6 | Jiri Crha (4)<br>empty net (1) |
| Wayne Gretzky | Edmonton | Feb. 18/81 | St.L. 2 at Edm. 9 | Mike Liut (3)<br>Ed Staniowski (2) |
| Wayne Gretzky | Edmonton | Dec. 30/81 | Phi. 5 at Edm. 7 | Pete Peeters (4)<br>empty net (1) |
| Grant Mulvey | Chicago | Feb. 3/82 | St.L. 5 at Chi. 9 | Mike Liut (4)<br>Gary Edwards (1) |
| Bryan Trottier | NY Islanders | Feb. 13/82 | Phi. 2 at NYI 8 | Pete Peeters |
| Willy Lindstrom | Winnipeg | Mar. 2/82 | Wpg. 7 at Phi. 6 | Pete Peeters |
| Mark Pavelich | NY Rangers | Feb. 23/83 | Hfd. 3 at NYR 11 | Greg Millen |
| Jari Kurri | Edmonton | Nov. 19/83 | N.J. 4 at Edm. 13 | Glenn Resch (3)<br>Ron Low (2) |
| Bengt Gustafsson | Washington | Jan. 8/84 | Wsh. 7 at Phi. 1 | Pelle Lindbergh |
| Pat Hughes | Edmonton | Feb. 3/84 | Cgy. 5 at Edm. 10 | Don Edwards (3)<br>Reggie Lemelin (2) |
| Wayne Gretzky | Edmonton | Dec. 15/84 | Edm. 8 at St.L. 2 | Rick Wamsley (4)<br>Mike Liut(1) |
| Dave Andreychuk | Buffalo | Feb. 6/86 | Buf. 8 at Bos. 6 | Pat Riggin (1)<br>Doug Keans (4) |
| Wayne Gretzky | Edmonton | Dec. 6/87 | Min. 4 at Edm. 10 | Don Beaupre (4)<br>Kari Takko (1) |
| Mario Lemieux | Pittsburgh | Dec. 31/88 | N.J. 6 at Pit. 8 | Bob Sauve (3)<br>Chris Terreri (2) |
| Joe Nieuwendyk | Calgary | Jan. 11/89 | Wpg. 3 at Cgy. 8 | Daniel Berthiaume |
| Mats Sundin | Quebec | Mar. 5/92 | Que. 10 at Hfd. 4 | Peter Sidorkiewicz (3)<br>Kay Whitmore (2) |
| Mario Lemieux | Pittsburgh | Apr. 9/93 | Pit. 10 at NYR 4 | Corey Hirsch (3)<br>Mike Richter (2) |
| Peter Bondra | Washington | Feb. 5/94 | T.B. 3 at Wsh. 6 | Daren Puppa (4)<br>Pat Jablonski (1) |
| Mike Ricci | Quebec | Feb. 17/94 | Que. 8 at S.J. 2 | Arturs Irbe (3)<br>Jimmy Waite (2) |
| Alex Zhamnov | Winnipeg | Apr. 1/95 | Wpg. 7 at L.A. 7 | Kelly Hrudey (3)<br>Grant Fuhr (2) |
| Mario Lemieux | Pittsburgh | Mar. 26/96 | St.L. 4 at Pit. 8 | Grant Fuhr (1)<br>Jon Casey (4) |
| Sergei Fedorov | Detroit | Dec. 26/96 | Wsh. 4 at Det. 5 | Jim Carey |
| Marian Gaborik | Minnesota | Dec. 20/07 | NYR 3 at Min. 6 | Henrik Lundqvist |

# Players' 500th Goals

## Regular Season

| Player | Team | Date | Game No. | Score | Opposing Goaltender | Total Goals | Total Games |
|---|---|---|---|---|---|---|---|
| Maurice Richard | Montreal | Oct. 19/57 | 863 | Chi. 1 at Mtl. 3 | Glenn Hall | 544 | 978 |
| Gordie Howe | Detroit | Mar. 14/62 | 1,045 | Det. 2 at NYR 3 | Gump Worsley | 801 | 1,767 |
| Bobby Hull | Chicago | Feb. 21/70 | 861 | NYR. 2 at Chi. 4 | Ed Giacomin | 610 | 1,063 |
| Jean Béliveau | Montreal | Feb. 11/71 | 1,101 | Min. 2 at Mtl. 6 | Gilles Gilbert | 507 | 1,125 |
| Frank Mahovlich | Montreal | Mar. 21/73 | 1,105 | Van. 2 at Mtl. 3 | Dunc Wilson | 533 | 1,181 |
| Phil Esposito | Boston | Dec. 22/74 | 803 | Det. 4 at Bos. 5 | Jim Rutherford | 717 | 1,282 |
| John Bucyk | Boston | Oct. 30/75 | 1,370 | St.L. 2 at Bos. 3 | Yves Bélanger | 556 | 1,540 |
| Stan Mikita | Chicago | Feb. 27/77 | 1,221 | Van. 4 at Chi. 3 | Cesare Maniago | 541 | 1,394 |
| Marcel Dionne | Los Angeles | Dec. 14/82 | 887 | L.A. 2 at Wsh. 7 | Al Jensen | 731 | 1,348 |
| Guy Lafleur | Montreal | Dec. 20/83 | 918 | Mtl. 6 at N.J. 0 | Glenn Resch | 560 | 1,126 |
| Mike Bossy | NY Islanders | Jan. 2/86 | 647 | Bos. 5 at NYI 7 | empty net | 573 | 752 |
| Gilbert Perreault | Buffalo | Mar. 9/86 | 1,159 | N.J. 3 at Buf. 4 | Alain Chevrier | 512 | 1,191 |
| Wayne Gretzky | Edmonton | Nov. 22/86 | 575 | Van. 2 at Edm. 5 | empty net | 894 | 1,487 |
| Lanny McDonald | Calgary | Mar. 21/89 | 1,107 | NYI 1 at Cgy. 4 | Mark Fitzpatrick | 500 | 1,111 |
| Bryan Trottier | NY Islanders | Feb. 13/90 | 1,104 | Cgy. 4 at NYI 2 | Rick Wamsley | 524 | 1,279 |
| Mike Gartner | NY Rangers | Oct. 14/91 | 936 | Wsh. 5 at NYR 3 | Mike Liut | 708 | 1,432 |
| Michel Goulet | Chicago | Feb. 16/92 | 951 | Cgy. 5 at Chi. 5 | Jeff Reese | 548 | 1,089 |
| Jari Kurri | Los Angeles | Oct. 17/92 | 833 | Bos. 6 at L.A. 8 | empty net | 601 | 1,251 |
| Dino Ciccarelli | Detroit | Jan. 8/94 | 946 | Det. 6 at L.A. 3 | Kelly Hrudey | 608 | 1,232 |
| Mario Lemieux | Pittsburgh | Oct. 26/95 | 605 | Pit. 7 at NYI 5 | Tommy Soderstrom | 690 | 915 |
| Mark Messier | NY Rangers | Nov. 6/95 | 1,141 | Cgy. 2 at NYR 4 | Rick Tabaracci | 694 | 1,756 |
| Steve Yzerman | Detroit | Jan. 17/96 | 906 | Col. 2 at Det. 3 | Patrick Roy | 692 | 1,514 |
| Dale Hawerchuk | St. Louis | Jan. 31/96 | 1,103 | St.L. 4 at Tor. 0 | Felix Potvin | 518 | 1,188 |
| Brett Hull | St. Louis | Dec. 22/96 | 693 | L.A. 4 at St.L. 7 | Stephane Fiset | 741 | 1,269 |
| Joe Mullen | Pittsburgh | Mar. 14/97 | 1,052 | Pit. 3 at Col. 6 | Patrick Roy | 502 | 1,062 |
| Dave Andreychuk | New Jersey | Mar. 15/97 | 1,070 | Wsh. 2 at N.J. 3 | Bill Ranford | 640 | 1,639 |
| Luc Robitaille | Los Angeles | Jan. 7/99 | 928 | Buf. 2 at L.A. 4 | Dwayne Roloson | 668 | 1,431 |
| Pat Verbeek | Detroit | Mar. 22/00 | 1,285 | Cgy. 2 at Det. 2 | Fred Brathwaite | 522 | 1,424 |
| Ron Francis | Carolina | Jan. 2/02 | 1,533 | Bos. 6 at Car. 3 | Byron Dafoe | 549 | 1,731 |
| *Brendan Shanahan | Detroit | Mar. 23/02 | 1,100 | Det. 2 at Col. 0 | Patrick Roy | 656 | 1,524 |
| Joe Sakic | Colorado | Dec. 11/02 | 1,044 | Col. 1 at Van. 3 | Dan Cloutier | 625 | 1,378 |
| Joe Nieuwendyk | New Jersey | Jan. 17/03 | 1,094 | N.J. 2 at Car. 1 | Kevin Weekes | 564 | 1,257 |
| Jaromir Jagr | Washington | Feb. 4/03 | 928 | Wsh. 5 at T.B. 1 | John Grahame | 646 | 1,273 |
| Pierre Turgeon | Colorado | Nov. 8/05 | 1,229 | S.J. 2 at Col. 5 | Vesa Toskala | 515 | 1,294 |
| *Mats Sundin | Toronto | Oct. 14/06 | 1,162 | Cgy. 4 at Tor. 5 | Miikka Kiprusoff | 564 | 1,346 |
| *Teemu Selanne | Anaheim | Nov. 22/06 | 982 | Ana. 2 at Col. 3 | Jose Theodore | 579 | 1,132 |
| Peter Bondra | Chicago | Dec. 22/06 | 1,050 | Tor. 1 at Chi. 3 | J.S. Aubin | 503 | 1,081 |
| *Mark Recchi | Pittsburgh | Jan. 26/07 | 1,303 | Pit. 4 at Dal. 3 | Marty Turco | 545 | 1,490 |
| *Mike Modano | Dallas | Mar. 13/07 | 1,225 | Phi. 2 at Dal. 3 | Antero Niittymaki | 543 | 1,400 |
| Jeremy Roenick | San Jose | Nov. 10/07 | 1,267 | Phx. 1 at S.J. 4 | Alex Auld | 513 | 1,363 |
| *Keith Tkachuk | St. Louis | Apr. 6/08 | 1,055 | St.L. 4 at CBJ 1 | empty net | 525 | 1,134 |

*Active

*Bobby Hull became just the third player in NHL history to reach the 500-goal plateau back on February 21, 1970. When Brett Hull scored his 500th 26 years later, they became the first (and only) father-son duo to each reach this milestone.*

# Players' 1,000th Points

## Regular Season

| Player | Team | Date | Game No. | G or A | Score | Total Points G A PTS | Total Games |
|---|---|---|---|---|---|---|---|
| Gordie Howe | Detroit | Nov. 27/60 | 938 | (A) | Tor. 0 at Det. 2 | 801-1,049–1,850 | 1,767 |
| Jean Béliveau | Montreal | Mar. 3/68 | 911 | (G) | Mtl. 2 at Det. 5 | 507-712–1,219 | 1,125 |
| Alex Delvecchio | Detroit | Feb. 16/69 | 1,143 | (A) | L.A. 3 at Det. 6 | 456-825–1,281 | 1,549 |
| Bobby Hull | Chicago | Dec. 13/70 | 909 | (A) | Min. 2 at Chi. 5 | 610-560–1,170 | 1,063 |
| Norm Ullman | Toronto | Oct. 16/71 | 1,113 | (A) | NYR 5 at Tor. 3 | 490-739–1,229 | 1,410 |
| Stan Mikita | Chicago | Oct. 15/72 | 924 | (A) | St.L. 3 at Chi. 1 | 541-926–1,467 | 1,394 |
| John Bucyk | Boston | Nov. 9/72 | 1,144 | (G) | Det. 3 at Bos. 8 | 556-813–1,369 | 1,540 |
| Frank Mahovlich | Montreal | Feb. 17/73 | 1,090 | (A) | Phi. 7 at Mtl. 6 | 533-570–1,103 | 1,181 |
| Henri Richard | Montreal | Dec. 20/73 | 1,194 | (A) | Mtl. 2 at Buf. 2 | 358-688–1,046 | 1,256 |
| Phil Esposito | Boston | Feb. 15/74 | 745 | (A) | Bos. 4 at Van. 2 | 717-873–1,590 | 1,282 |
| Rod Gilbert | NY Rangers | Feb. 19/77 | 1,027 | (G) | NYR 2 at NYI 5 | 406-615–1,021 | 1,065 |
| Jean Ratelle | Boston | Apr. 3/77 | 1,007 | (A) | Tor. 4 at Bos. 7 | 491-776–1,267 | 1,281 |
| Marcel Dionne | Los Angeles | Jan. 7/81 | 740 | (G) | L.A. 5 at Hfd. 3 | 731-1,040–1,771 | 1,348 |
| Guy Lafleur | Montreal | Mar. 4/81 | 720 | (G) | Wpg. 3 at Mtl. 9 | 560-793–1,353 | 1,126 |
| Bobby Clarke | Philadelphia | Mar. 19/81 | 922 | (G) | Bos. 3 at Phi. 5 | 358-852–1,210 | 1,144 |
| Gilbert Perreault | Buffalo | Apr. 3/82 | 871 | (A) | Buf. 5 at Mtl. 4 | 512-814–1,326 | 1,191 |
| Darryl Sittler | Philadelphia | Jan. 20/83 | 927 | (G) | Cgy. 2 at Phi. 5 | 484-637–1,121 | 1,096 |
| Wayne Gretzky | Edmonton | Dec. 19/84 | 424 | (A) | L.A. 3 at Edm. 7 | 894-1,963–2,875 | 1,487 |
| Bryan Trottier | NY Islanders | Jan. 29/85 | 726 | (G) | Min. 4 at NYI 4 | 524-901–1,425 | 1,279 |
| Mike Bossy | NY Islanders | Jan. 24/86 | 656 | (A) | NYI 7 at Wsh. 5 | 573-553–1,126 | 752 |
| Denis Potvin | NY Islanders | Apr. 4/87 | 987 | (G) | Buf. 6 at NYI 6 | 310-742–1,052 | 1,060 |
| Bernie Federko | St. Louis | Mar. 19/88 | 855 | (A) | Hfd. 5 at St.L. 3 | 369-761–1,130 | 1,000 |
| Lanny McDonald | Calgary | Mar. 7/89 | 1,101 | (G) | Wpg. 5 at Cgy. 9 | 500-506–1,006 | 1,111 |
| Peter Stastny | Quebec | Oct. 19/89 | 682 | (G) | Que. 5 at Chi. 3 | 450-789–1,239 | 977 |
| Jari Kurri | Edmonton | Jan. 2/90 | 716 | (A) | Edm. 6 at St.L. 4 | 601-797–1,398 | 1,251 |
| Denis Savard | Chicago | Mar. 11/90 | 727 | (A) | St.L. 6 at Chi. 4 | 473-865–1,338 | 1,196 |
| Paul Coffey | Pittsburgh | Dec. 22/90 | 770 | (A) | Pit. 4 at NYI 3 | 396-1,135–1,531 | 1,409 |
| Mark Messier | Edmonton | Jan. 13/91 | 822 | (A) | Edm. 5 at Phi. 3 | 694-1,193–1,887 | 1,756 |
| Dave Taylor | Los Angeles | Feb. 5/91 | 930 | (A) | L.A. 3 at Phi. 2 | 431-638–1,069 | 1,111 |
| Michel Goulet | Chicago | Feb. 23/91 | 878 | (G) | Chi. 3 at Min. 3 | 548-604–1,152 | 1,089 |
| Dale Hawerchuk | Buffalo | Mar. 8/91 | 781 | (G) | Chi. 5 at Buf. 3 | 518-891–1,409 | 1,188 |
| Bobby Smith | Minnesota | Nov. 30/91 | 986 | (A) | Min. 4 at Tor. 3 | 357-679–1,036 | 1,077 |
| Mike Gartner | NY Rangers | Jan. 4/92 | 971 | (G) | NYR 4 at N.J. 6 | 708-627–1,335 | 1,432 |
| Raymond Bourque | Boston | Feb. 29/92 | 933 | (A) | Wsh. 5 at Bos. 5 | 410-1,169–1,579 | 1,612 |
| Mario Lemieux | Pittsburgh | Mar. 24/92 | 513 | (A) | Pit. 3 at Det. 4 | 690-1,033–1,723 | 915 |
| Glenn Anderson | Toronto | Feb. 22/93 | 954 | (G) | Tor. 8 at Van. 1 | 498-601–1,099 | 1,129 |
| Steve Yzerman | Detroit | Feb. 24/93 | 737 | (A) | Det. 7 at Buf. 10 | 692-1,063–1,755 | 1,514 |
| Ron Francis | Pittsburgh | Oct. 28/93 | 893 | (G) | Que. 7 at Pit. 3 | 549-1,249–1,798 | 1,731 |
| Bernie Nicholls | New Jersey | Feb. 13/94 | 858 | (G) | N.J. 3 at T.B. 3 | 475-734–1,209 | 1,127 |
| Dino Ciccarelli | Detroit | Mar. 9/94 | 957 | (G) | Det. 5 at Cgy. 1 | 608-592–1,200 | 1,232 |
| Brian Propp | Hartford | Mar. 19/94 | 1,008 | (G) | Hfd. 5 at Phi. 3 | 425-579–1,004 | 1,016 |
| Joe Mullen | Pittsburgh | Feb. 7/95 | 935 | (A) | Fla. 3 at Pit. 7 | 502-561–1,063 | 1,062 |
| Steve Larmer | NY Rangers | Mar. 8/95 | 983 | (A) | N.J. 4 at NYR 6 | 441-571–1,012 | 1,006 |
| Doug Gilmour | Toronto | Dec. 23/95 | 935 | (A) | Edm. 1 at Tor. 6 | 450-964–1,414 | 1,474 |
| Larry Murphy | Toronto | Mar. 27/96 | 1,228 | (G) | Tor. 6 at Van. 2 | 287-929–1,216 | 1,615 |
| Dave Andreychuk | New Jersey | Apr. 7/96 | 998 | (G) | NYR 2 at N.J. 4 | 640-698–1,338 | 1,639 |
| Adam Oates | Washington | Oct. 8/97 | 830 | (G) | Wsh. 6 at NYI 3 | 341-1,079–1,420 | 1,337 |
| Phil Housley | Washington | Nov. 8/97 | 1,081 | (A) | Edm. 1 at Wsh. 2 | 338-894–1,232 | 1,495 |
| Dale Hunter | Washington | Jan. 9/98 | 1,308 | (A) | Phi. 1 at Wsh. 4 | 323-697–1,020 | 1,407 |
| Pat LaFontaine | NY Rangers | Jan. 22/98 | 847 | (G) | Phi. 4 at NYR 3 | 468-545–1,013 | 865 |
| Luc Robitaille | Los Angeles | Jan. 29/98 | 882 | (A) | Cgy. 3 at L.A. 5 | 668-726–1,394 | 1,431 |
| Al MacInnis | St. Louis | Apr. 7/98 | 1,056 | (A) | St.L. 3 at Det. 5 | 340-934–1,274 | 1,416 |
| Brett Hull | Dallas | Nov. 14/98 | 815 | (A) | Dal. 3 at Bos. 1 | 741-650–1,391 | 1,269 |
| Brian Bellows | Washington | Jan. 2/99 | 1,147 | (A) | Tor. 2 at Wsh. 5 | 485-537–1,022 | 1,188 |
| Pierre Turgeon | St. Louis | Oct. 9/99 | 881 | (G) | St.L. 4 at Edm. 3 | 515-812–1,327 | 1,294 |
| Joe Sakic | Colorado | Dec. 27/99 | 810 | (A) | St.L. 1 at Col. 5 | 625-1,016–1,641 | 1,378 |
| Pat Verbeek | Detroit | Feb. 27/00 | 1,275 | (A) | T.B. 1 at Det. 3 | 522-541–1,063 | 1,424 |
| V. Damphousse | San Jose | Oct. 14/00 | 1,090 | (A) | Bos. 2 at S.J. 5 | 432-773–1,205 | 1,378 |
| Jaromir Jagr | Pittsburgh | Dec. 30/00 | 763 | (G) | Ott. 3 at Pit. 5 | 646-953–1,599 | 1,273 |
| *Mark Recchi | Philadelphia | Mar. 13/01 | 920 | (A) | St.L. 2 at Phi. 5 | 545-897–1,442 | 1,490 |
| Theoren Fleury | NY Rangers | Oct. 29/01 | 960 | (A) | Dal. 2 at NYR 4 | 455-633–1,088 | 1,084 |
| *B. Shanahan | Detroit | Jan. 12/02 | 1,073 | (G) | Dal. 2 at Det. 5 | 656-698–1,354 | 1,524 |
| Jeremy Roenick | Philadelphia | Jan. 30/02 | 961 | (G) | Phi. 1 at Ott. 3 | 513-703–1,216 | 1,363 |
| *Mike Modano | Dallas | Nov. 15/02 | 965 | (A) | Col. 2 at Dal. 4 | 543-786–1,329 | 1,400 |
| Joe Nieuwendyk | New Jersey | Feb. 23/03 | 1,094 | (G) | N.J. 4 at Pit. 3 | 564-562–1,126 | 1,257 |
| *Mats Sundin | Toronto | Mar. 10/03 | 994 | (G) | Tor. 3 at Edm. 2 | 564-785–1,349 | 1,346 |
| Sergei Fedorov | Anaheim | Feb. 14/04 | 965 | (A) | Ana. 2 at Van. 1 | 483-696–1,179 | 1,248 |
| Alexander Mogilny | Toronto | Mar. 15/04 | 946 | (A) | Tor. 6 at Buf. 5 | 473-559–1,032 | 990 |
| Brian Leetch | Boston | Oct. 18/05 | 1,151 | (A) | Bos. 3 at Mtl. 4 | 247-781–1,028 | 1,205 |
| *Teemu Selanne | Anaheim | Jan. 30/06 | 928 | (G) | L.A. 3 at Ana. 4 | 579-633–1,212 | 1,132 |
| *Rod Brind'Amour | Carolina | Nov. 4/06 | 1,202 | (A) | Car. 3 at Ott. 2 | 443-722–1,165 | 1,404 |
| *Keith Tkachuk | St. Louis | Nov. 30/08 | 1,077 | (G) | St.L. 4 at Atl. 2 | 525-508–1,033 | 1,134 |
| *Doug Weight | NY Islanders | Jan. 2/09 | 1,167 | (A) | NYI 4 at Phx. 5 | 275-732–1,007 | 1,184 |

*Active

*The Blues' Keith Tkachuk (above) and Doug Weight of the Islanders (top) became the seventh and eighth American-born players in NHL history to reach the 1,000-point plateau during the 2008-09 season.*

# Individual Awards

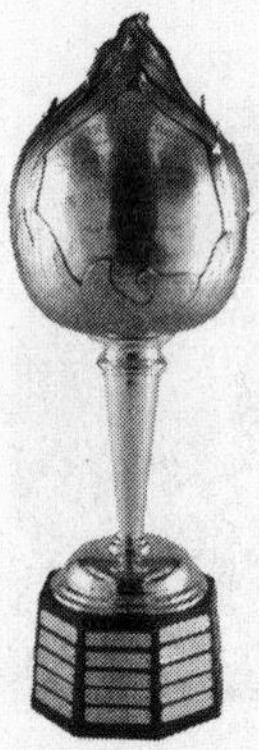

*Hart Memorial Trophy*

*Art Ross Trophy*

*Calder Memorial Trophy*

*James Norris Memorial Trophy*

## HART MEMORIAL TROPHY

An annual award "to the player adjudged to be the most valuable to his team." Winner selected in a poll by the Professional Hockey Writers' Association in the 30 NHL cities at the end of the regular schedule.

History: The Hart Memorial Trophy was presented by the National Hockey League in 1960 after the original Hart Trophy was retired to the Hockey Hall of Fame. The original Hart Trophy was donated to the NHL in 1924 by Dr. David A. Hart, father of Cecil Hart, former manager-coach of the Montreal Canadiens.

**2008-09 Winner:** **Alex Ovechkin, Washington Capitals**
**Runners-up:** **Evgeni Malkin, Pittsburgh Penguins**
**Pavel Datsyuk, Detroit Red Wings**

Alex Ovechkin of the Washington Capitals captured the Hart Memorial Trophy for the second year in a row. Ovechkin is the first repeat winner since Dominik Hasek in 1997 and 1998 and the 11th player in NHL history to win in consecutive years. Ovechkin received 115 first-place votes among the 133 ballots cast and accumulated 1,264 points to finish ahead of second-place Evgeni Malkin of the Pittsburgh Penguins, who was the top selection on 12 ballots and earned 787 points. Detroit's Pavel Datsyuk received four first-place votes and 404 points. Zdeno Chara received the other two first place votes but finished eighth with 79 points behind Steve Mason (266), Zach Parise (257), Sidney Crosby (103) and Tim Thomas (100). Ovechkin won the Maurice Rocket Richard Trophy for the second straight season for leading the NHL with 56 goals the third time in his four NHL seasons that he's eclipsed 50 goals and his 110 points left him three points shy of becoming the NHL's first repeat scoring titlist since Jaromir Jagr in 2000 and 2001. Ovechkin's 528 shots on goal were the second highest single-season total in NHL history behind Phil Esposito's 550 in 1970-71. His 19 power-play goals ranked him second in the league and his 10 game-winning goals ranked third.

## ART ROSS TROPHY

An annual award "to the player who leads the league in scoring points at the end of the regular season."

History: Arthur Howey Ross, former manager-coach of the Boston Bruins, presented the trophy to the National Hockey League in 1947. If two players finish the schedule with the same number of points, the trophy is awarded in the following manner: 1. Player with most goals. 2. Player with fewer games played. 3. Player scoring first goal of the season.

**2008-09 Winner:** **Evgeni Malkin, Pittsburgh Penguins**
**Runners-up:** **Alex Ovechkin, Washington Capitals**
**Sidney Crosby, Pittsburgh Penguins**

Center Evgeni Malkin of the Pittsburgh Penguins received the Art Ross Trophy for the first time, finishing the 2008-09 regular season with a league-leading and career-high 113 points (35 goals, 78 assists) to edge Washington Capitals left winger Alex Ovechkin, last year's Art Ross champion (56-54-110). Like Ovechkin, Malkin won the award in just his third season in the NHL. Malkin, who also led the league with 78 assists, becomes the eighth player in the past eight seasons to capture the Art Ross, joining Jaromir Jagr in 2001, Jarome Iginla in 2002, Peter Forsberg in 2003, Martin St. Louis in 2004, Joe Thornton in 2006, Sidney Crosby in 2007 and Ovechkin in 2008. Crosby finished third in this years scoring race with 103 points (33 goals, 70 assists).

## CALDER MEMORIAL TROPHY

An annual award "to the player selected as the most proficient in his first year of competition in the National Hockey League." Winner selected in a poll by the Professional Hockey Writers' Association at the end of the regular schedule.

History: From 1936-37 until his death in 1943, Frank Calder, NHL President, bought a trophy each year to be given permanently to the outstanding rookie. After Calder's death, the NHL presented the Calder Memorial Trophy in his memory and the trophy is to be kept in perpetuity. To be eligible for the award, a player cannot have played more than 25 games in any single preceding season nor in six or more games in each of any two preceding seasons in any major professional league. Beginning in 1990-91, to be eligible for this award a player must not have attained his twenty-sixth birthday by September 15th of the season in which he is eligible.

**2008-09 Winner:** **Steve Mason, Columbus Blue Jackets**
**Runners-up:** **Bobby Ryan, Anaheim Ducks**
**Kris Versteeg, Chicago Blackhawks**

Goaltender Steve Mason of the Columbus Blue Jackets won the Calder Memorial Trophy. Mason received 121 of 132 first-place votes and 1,268 points, outdistancing Anaheim Ducks' forward Bobby Ryan, who polled nine first-place votes and 829 points. Kris Versteeg of Chicago received one first-place votes and 323 points. Blake Wheeler of Boston received the final first-place vote, and finished sixth in the standings with 157 points. Pekka Rinne of Nashville (319 points) and Drew Doughty of Los Angeles (303) ranked fourth and fifth in the balloting. Mason's career soared ahead of schedule when he won his first three NHL starts on November 5, 7 and 8 to seize the Blue Jackets net. Named the NHL's Rookie of the Month for both November and December, he posted a franchise-record three straight shutouts in late December during a four-game winning streak in which he stopped 94 of 95 shots. Mason finished strong, going 8-2-4 from March 7 to April 8 as Columbus captured the first playoff berth in franchise history. His 10 shutouts led the NHL and his 2.29 goals against average ranked second to Tim Thomas' 2.10 for Boston.

## JAMES NORRIS MEMORIAL TROPHY

An annual award "to the defense player who demonstrates throughout the season the greatest all-round ability in the position." Winner selected in a poll by the Professional Hockey Writers' Association at the end of the regular schedule.

History: The James Norris Memorial Trophy was presented in 1953 by the four children of the late James Norris in memory of the former owner-president of the Detroit Red Wings.

**2008-09 Winner:** **Zdeno Chara, Boston Bruins**
**Runners-up:** **Mike Green, Washington Capitals**
**Nicklas Lidstrom, Detroit Red Wings**

Zdeno Chara of the Boston Bruins has won the James Norris Memorial Trophy for the first time. Chara received 68 of 133 first-place votes and 1,034 points to edge Mike Green of the Washington Capitals, who garnered 50 first-place votes and 982 points. Six-time winner Nicklas Lidstrom of Detroit finished third in the balloting with 14 first-place votes and 733 points. Teammate Brian Rafalski received the final first-place vote, but finished ninth in points with 27 behind Nashville's Shea Weber (186), San Jose's Dan Boyle (173), Chicago's Keith Duncan (95), Andrei Markov of the Canadiens (95) and Mark Streit of the Islanders (29).

Chara captured his first career Norris Trophy in his third season as a finalist; he finished second with the Ottawa Senators in 2004 and was third as a Bruin in 2008. Chara was the cornerstone of a Bruins' defense that helped the club post the NHL's lowest goals-per-game figure in 2008-09 (2.29). He ranked sixth in the NHL in average ice time (26:04), was 12th among all defensemen in scoring with 50 points (19 goals, 31 assists) and posted a +23 rating.

Vezina Trophy

Lady Byng Memorial Trophy

Frank J. Selke Trophy

Conn Smythe Trophy

## VEZINA TROPHY

An annual award "to the goalkeeper adjudged to be the best at his position" as voted by the general managers of each of the 30 clubs.

History: Leo Dandurand, Louis Letourneau and Joe Cattarinich, former owners of the Montreal Canadiens, presented the trophy to the National Hockey League in 1926-27 in memory of Georges Vezina, outstanding goalkeeper of the Canadiens who collapsed during an NHL game on November 28, 1925, and died of tuberculosis a few months later. Until the 1981-82 season, the goalkeeper(s) of the team allowing the fewest number of goals during the regular season were awarded the Vezina Trophy.

**2008-09 Winner:** **Tim Thomas, Boston Bruins**
**Runners-up:** **Steve Mason, Columbus Blue Jackets**
**Niklas Backstrom, Minnesota Wild**

Tim Thomas of the Boston Bruins captured the Vezina Trophy for the first time in his career. Thomas was named on 29 of 30 ballots, including 22 first-place selections, and collected 127 points. Rookie Steve Mason of the Columbus Blue Jackets, with three first-place votes and 33 points, edged Niklas Backstrom of the Minnesota Wild (one and 31) and Roberto Luongo (two and 30) of the Vancouver Canucks in a close three-way race for second place. Evgeni Nabokov of San Jose (20 points) and Henrik Lundqvist of the Rangers (14) also received first-place votes.

Thomas took his game to a different level this season while backstopping the Bruins to their highest victory (53) and points (116) totals since 1971-72. He led the NHL in goals-against average (2.10) and save percentage (.933) while posting a career-high 36 wins. He won a career-best seven straight decisions from December 4 to December 30 and closed the regular season by winning his last six starts. Thomas and Boston teammate Manny Fernandez are also winners of the William Jennings Trophy as the Bruins allowed an NHL-low 196 goals this season.

## LADY BYNG MEMORIAL TROPHY

An annual award "to the player adjudged to have exhibited the best type of sportsmanship and gentlemanly conduct combined with a high standard of playing ability." Winner selected in a poll by the Professional Hockey Writers' Association at the end of the regular schedule.

History: Lady Byng, wife of Canada's Governor-General at the time, presented the Lady Byng Trophy in the 1924-25 season. After Frank Boucher of the New York Rangers won the award seven times in eight seasons, he was given the trophy to keep and Lady Byng donated another trophy in 1936. After Lady Byng's death in 1949, the National Hockey League presented a new trophy, changing the name to Lady Byng Memorial Trophy.

**2008-09 Winner:** **Pavel Datsyuk, Detroit Red Wings**
**Runners-up:** **Martin St. Louis, Tampa Bay Lightning**
**Zach Parise, New Jersey Devils**

Detroit Red Wings' center Pavel Datsyuk won the Lady Byng Memorial Trophy for the fourth consecutive time. Datsyuk received 64 first-place votes and 933 points to finish ahead of Martin St. Louis of the Tampa Bay Lightning (30 first-place votes, 662 points), who finished as Lady Byng runner-up for the third consecutive season. New Jersey's Zach Parise garnered 15 first-place votes and 521 points. In all, 13 players received at least one first-place vote, with San Jose's Patrick Marleau (203 points), Detroit's Nicklas Lidstrom (116) and Ottawa's Daniel Alfredsson (113) all topping 100 points.

Datsyuk finished fourth in the NHL scoring race with 97 points (32 goals, 65 assists), equaling his career high set in 2007-08. He ranked second among NHL players in takeaways with 89, placed third in plus-minus with a +34 rating and was whistled for just 11 minor penalties totaling 22 minutes. Datsyuk joins Hockey Hall of Fame forward Frank Boucher as the only players in NHL history to capture the Lady Byng Trophy for four consecutive seasons. Boucher claimed the trophy from 1928 through 1931 with the New York Rangers.

## FRANK J. SELKE TROPHY

An annual award "to the forward who best excels in the defensive aspects of the game." Winner selected in a poll by the Professional Hockey Writers' Association at the end of the regular schedule.

History: Presented to the National Hockey League in 1977 by the Board of Governors of the NHL in honor of Frank J. Selke, one of the great architects of Montreal and Toronto championship teams.

**2008-09 Winner:** **Pavel Datsyuk, Detroit Red Wings**
**Runners-up:** **Mike Richards, Philadelphia Flyers**
**Ryan Kesler, Vancouver Canucks**

Detroit Red Wings' center Pavel Datsyuk captured the Frank Selke Trophy for the second year in a row. Datsyuk edged Philadelphia Flyers' center Mike Richards 945-942 in the closest Selke vote since the trophy was introduced in 1978. Richards actually received 61 first-place votes to Datsyuk's 55, but Datsyuk was named on more total ballots. Vancouver's Ryan Kesler received one first-place vote and 290 points. Nine other players had at least one first-place vote, including Detroit's Henrik Zetterberg, who had three and 154 points and Minnesota's Mikko Koivu, who had one but also finished with 154 points.

Datsyuk ranked second among NHL players in takeaways with 89, placed third in plus-minus with a +34 rating and won 56 percent of his face-offs (636 of 1,135). He is the fifth player to win the award in consecutive seasons, joining Montreal's Bob Gainey (1978 through 1981), Montreal's Guy Carbonneau (1988 and 1989), Jere Lehtinen of Dallas (1998 and 1999) and Carolina's Rod Brind'Amour (2006 and 2007).

## WILLIAM M. JENNINGS TROPHY

An annual award "to the goalkeeper(s) having played a minimum of 25 games for the team with the fewest goals scored against it." Winners selected on regular-season play.

History: The Jennings Trophy was presented in 1981-82 by the National Hockey League's Board of Governors to honor the late William M. Jennings, longtime governor and president of the New York Rangers and one of the great builders of hockey in the United States.

**2008-09 Winners:** **Tim Thomas/Manny Fernandez, Boston Bruins**
**Runners-up:** **Niklas Backstrom, Minnesota Wild**
**Evgeni Nabokov, San Jose Sharks**

Tim Thomas and Manny Fernandez, who shared time in the Boston Bruins net with 54 and 28 appearances, respectively, backstopped the club to the NHL's top defensive record with 190 team goals against, plus six in shootout losses for a total of 196. Thomas, who led the NHL with a 2.10 goals-against average and .933 save percentage while posting a career-high 36 wins, won the Jennings Trophy for the first time. Fernandez had shared it with Niklas Backstrom in Minnesota in 2006-07. Backstrom was the runner-up this year, playing in 71 of 82 games for the Wild, who allowed 197 goals, plus three in shootout losses. Evgeni Nabokov played in 62 of 82 games for San Jose, which allowed 199 goals, plus four in shootout losses.

## CONN SMYTHE TROPHY

An annual award "to the most valuable player for his team in the playoffs." Winner selected by the Professional Hockey Writers' Association at the conclusion of the final game in the Stanley Cup Finals.

History: Presented by Maple Leaf Gardens Limited in 1964 to honor Conn Smythe, the former coach, manager, president and owner-governor of the Toronto Maple Leafs.

**2008-09 Winner:** **Evgeni Malkin, Pittsburgh Penguins**

Pittsburgh Penguins' center Evgeni Malkin won the Conn Smythe Trophy after leading the playoffs in scoring with 14 goals and 22 assists for 36 points in 24 games. Malkin (22 years, 10 months) is the third-youngest player to capture the award behind goaltender Patrick Roy, who won the Conn Smythe Trophy for the first of a record three times as a 20-year-old with the Montreal Canadiens in 1986, and goaltender Cam Ward (22 years, three months), who backstopped the Carolina Hurricanes to the Stanley Cup in 2006. Malkin led all scorers in the Stanley Cup Final with eight points (two goals, six assists) in seven games and his 36 points in total marked the best single-playoff performance since Wayne Gretzky had 40 points (15 goals, 25 assists) in 24 games for the Los Angeles Kings in 1992-93. Malkin joins Gretzky, Mario Lemieux, Guy Lafleur and Phil Esposito as players in the expansion era (since 1968) who swept regular-season and playoff scoring titles in the same season. Malkin captured the 2008-09 Art Ross Trophy as the NHL's regular-season points leader with 113 (35 goals, 78 assists) in 82 games.

William M. Jennings Trophy

Jack Adams Award

Bill Masterton Trophy

Lester Patrick Trophy

## JACK ADAMS AWARD

An annual award presented by the National Hockey League Broadcasters' Association to "the NHL coach adjudged to have contributed the most to his team's success." Winner selected by a poll among members of the NHL Broadcasters' Association at the end of the regular season.

History: The award was presented by the NHL Broadcasters' Association in 1974 to commemorate the late Jack Adams, coach and general manager of the Detroit Red Wings, whose lifetime dedication to hockey serves as an inspiration to all who aspire to further the game.

**2008-09 Winner:** **Claude Julien, Boston Bruins**
**Runners-up:** **Andy Murray, St. Louis Blues**
**Todd McLellan, San Jose Sharks**

Boston Bruins' head coach Claude Julien captured the Jack Adams Award. Julien was named on 56 of 71 ballots, received 35 first-place votes and collected 224 points. Second-place Andy Murray of the St. Louis Blues garnered 15 first-place votes and 135 points. Todd McLellan of San Jose had nine-first place votes and 98 points. Four other coaches received at least one first-place vote. Ken Hitchcock of Columbus had five and 69 points, while Brent Sutter of New Jersey had three and 36 points and Mike Babcock received three and 20 points. Chicago's Joel Quenneville had one first-place vote and 15 points. Julien guided the Bruins to the best record in the Eastern Conference, finishing 53-19-10 for 116 points the third-highest total in franchise history, a 22-point increase over 2007-08 and 40 points more than 2006-07. The Bruins ranked second in the NHL in offense with 274 goals, a dramatic turnaround from their #25 ranking in 2007-08 when they tallied 212. They hit the 30-win mark in their 41st game of the season (30-7-4) on January 8 versus Ottawa, the fastest they have reached 30 wins since 1929-30 (30-4-1).

## BILL MASTERTON MEMORIAL TROPHY

An annual award under the trusteeship of the Professional Hockey Writers' Association to "the National Hockey League player who best exemplifies the qualities of perseverance, sportsmanship and dedication to hockey." Winner selected by a poll among the 30 chapters of the PHWA at the end of the regular season. A $2,500 grant from the PHWA is awarded annually to the Bill Masterton Scholarship Fund, based in Bloomington, MN, in the name of the Masterton Trophy winner.

History: The trophy was presented by the NHL Writers' Association in 1968 to commemorate the late Bill Masterton, a player with the Minnesota North Stars, who exhibited to a high degree the qualities of perseverance, sportsmanship and dedication to hockey, and who died January 15, 1968.

**2008-09 Winner:** **Steve Sullivan, Nashville Predators**
**Runners-up:** **Chris Chelios, Detroit Red Wings**
**Richard Zednik, Florida Panthers**

Nashville Predators right winger Steve Sullivan is the 2008-09 recipient of the Bill Masterton Memorial Trophy. Sullivan's perseverance was measured in months, not weeks or days. He missed almost two full years - 687 days, to be precise - following a back injury suffered in February of 2007. Sullivan underwent two back surgeries in attempts to repair a fragmented disc and tried a myriad of cures. But it wasn't until he began an intensive workout regimen with strength and conditioning coach Dave Good that he finally began to heal. When Sullivan returned to the Nashville lineup on January 10, 2009, he became just the third player since World War II (Mario Lemieux and Jim Peplinski are the others) to play 150 games with a team, then miss at least 600 consecutive days before returning to the same team.

## LESTER PATRICK TROPHY

An annual award "for outstanding service to hockey in the United States." Eligible recipients are players, officials, coaches, executives and referees. Winners are selected by an award committee consisting of the commissioner of the NHL, an NHL governor, a representative of the New York Rangers, a member of the Hockey Hall of Fame builder's section, a member of the Hockey Hall of Fame player's section, a member of the U.S. Hockey Hall of Fame, a member of the NHL Broadcasters' Association and a member of the Professional Hockey Writers' Association. Each except the League Commissioner is rotated annually. The winner receives a miniature of the trophy.

History: Presented by the New York Rangers in 1966 to honor the late Lester Patrick, longtime general manager and coach of the New York Rangers, whose teams finished out of the playoffs only once in his first 16 years with the club.

**2009 Winners:** **Mark Messier**
**Mike Richter**
**Jim Devellano**

Mark Messier's combination of power, speed and skill made him one of the great leaders in the NHL. He was a six-time Stanley Cup champion and had played more playoff games than anyone in history at the time of his retirement. Only Gordie Howe played more regular-season games than Messier's 1,756 and only Wayne Gretzky tops his 1,887 career points. Messier entered the NHL with the Edmonton Oilers in 1979-80 and quickly became a star. When the Oilers won their first Stanley Cup title in 1984, Messier earned the Conn Smythe Trophy as playoff MVP. When Wayne Gretzky was traded in 1988, Messier responded to the challenge of becoming captain. He established career highs with 84 assists and 129 points in 1989-90, won the Hart Trophy as NHL MVP and led the Oilers to a fifth Stanley Cup title. As captain of the New York Rangers, Messier won the Hart Trophy again in 1992. A Stanley Cup title came two years later. Messier's inspirational words and play in the Eastern Conference final against the New Jersey Devils that spring went a long way toward bringing the Rangers their first championship in 54 years.

Mike Richter played 666 games during his 14-year NHL career, all with the New York Rangers. His 301 wins are a club record and in 1994 he helped the Rangers win the Stanley Cup for the first time since 1940. Playing full-time for the Rangers beginning in 1990-91, Richter was a finalist for the Vezina Trophy as the league's top goalie in just his second full season in the NHL. In 1993-94, Richter was selected as the MVP of the All-Star Game and went on to set a club single-season record with 42 wins in leading the team to the Presidents' Trophy and the Stanley Cup. Richter was also an integral part of the U.S. hockey program and is one of just 10 Americans to compete in at least three Olympic Games, including in 2002 when the team won a silver medal. In addition, he led Team USA to the World Cup of Hockey championship in 1996 and was named tournament MVP. He also played in two World Junior Championships (1985 and 1986), three World Championships (1986, 1987 and 1993) and the 1991 Canada Cup.

Jim Devellano's career as a hockey scout and executive began in his native Toronto. He entered the NHL as a scout with the St. Louis Blues when the league expanded in 1967, then joined the New York Islanders in 1972. It was Devellano who recommended the Islanders hire Al Arbour to coach the team and his scouting contributed to the four consecutive Stanley Cup titles the Islanders won from 1980 and 1983. Devellano was the first person hired by owners Mike and Marian Ilitch after purchasing the Detroit Red Wings in 1982. He was the team's general manager for eight seasons before becoming senior vice president in 1990. Devellano selected Steve Yzerman as the club's first draft choice in 1983 and built a strong European scouting staff. The result was Stanley Cup victories in 1997, 1998, 2002 and 2008. Still working in the Red Wings' front office, Devellano's lengthy tenure as head of hockey operations in Detroit is second only to the 35 years served by the legendary Jack Adams.

*King Clancy Memorial Trophy*

*Presidents' Trophy*

*Maurice "Rocket" Richard Trophy*

*Lester B. Pearson Award*

## KING CLANCY MEMORIAL TROPHY

An annual award "to the player who best exemplifies leadership qualities on and off the ice and has made a noteworthy humanitarian contribution in his community."

History: The King Clancy Memorial Trophy was presented to the National Hockey League by the Board of Governors in 1988 to honor the late Frank "King" Clancy.

**2008-09 Winner: Ethan Moreau, Edmonton Oilers**

Edmonton Oilers' left winger Ethan Moreau is the 2008-09 recipient of the King Clancy Memorial Trophy. The main focus of Moreau's work in the community has been Edmonton's Inner City High School. Last year, the Edmonton Oilers Community Foundation announced plans for a major community project that would leave a lasting legacy in the city, the redevelopment of a new Inner City High. The school, which offers troubled youth an academic and arts-based alternative to the traditional school setting, is in need of an upgraded facility. With Moreau taking on a leadership role, the Oilers, through the Foundation, have taken on the daunting task of building a new $20 million facility that will accommodate 150 students, a 125% increase over the current building. It will provide a top-quality educational environment and a residence capable of accommodating a portion of the student population.

As Oilers' captain, Moreau has led the charge in the dressing room for two of the Foundation's annual fundraisers. Caps for Cancer gives fans the opportunity to purchase an autographed pink or blue Oilers ball cap in support of the battle against cancer. This season, Ethan encouraged each of his teammates to sign 400 hats, which helped raise $250,000 for the Canadian Breast Cancer Foundation and Kids with Cancer Society. For Puck Surprise, Oilers fans purchased 1,500 signed pucks in support of the Make-A-Wish Foundation and The Rainbow Society of Alberta. Combined with an online auction, Moreau helped the Oilers raise over $70,000.

Moreau assists with a number of other charities, including the Cystic Fybrosis Foundation, Canadian Cancer Foundation and United Way Coats For Kids Campaign, and makes a number of visits and contributions throughout the year to the Youth Emergency Shelter. Moreau also makes regular visits to the Stollery Children's Hospital. In 2008, he and his family accepted the role of Ambassador Family, representing the Stollery Children's Hospital Foundation at numerous fundraising and community events throughout the year.

## PRESIDENTS' TROPHY

An annual award to the club finishing the regular-season with the best overall record.

History: Presented to the National Hockey League in 1985-86 by the NHL Board of Governors to recognize the team compiling the top regular-season record.

**2008-09 Winner: San Jose Sharks**
**Runners-up: Boston Bruins**
**Detroit Red Wings**

The San Jose Sharks captured the Presidents' Trophy for the first time in franchise history, leading the NHL with 117 points by posting a record of 53-18-11. Both their 53 wins and 117 points set new club records. The Sharks won the Pacific Division title for the second year in a row and the fourth time in club history. The Boston Bruins posted a record of 53-19-10 and finished just one point back of San Jose in the overall standings. The Bruins won the Northeast Division for the first time since 2003-04 and finished atop the Eastern Conference standings for the first time since 2001-02. The Detroit Red Wings won the Central Division title for the seventh year in a row with a record of 51-21-10 and 112 points.

## MAURICE "ROCKET" RICHARD TROPHY

An annual award "presented to the player finishing the regular season as the League's goal-scoring leader."

History: A gift to the NHL from the Montreal Canadiens in 1999, the Maurice "Rocket" Richard Trophy honors one of the game's greatest stars. During his 18-year career with the Canadiens from 1942-43 through 1959-60, Richard was the first player in NHL history to score 50 goals in a season and 500 in his career. He played on eight Stanley Cup champions and led the League in goal scoring five times.

**2008-09 Winner: Alex Ovechkin, Washington Capitals**
**Runners-up: Jeff Carter, Philadelphia Flyers**
**Zach Parise, New Jersey Devils**

Left winger Alex Ovechkin of the Washington Capitals is the winner of the Maurice Rocket Richard Trophy for the second year in a row. Ovechkin followed up on his 65-goal performance of 2007-08 with 56 goals in 2008-09 and becoming the first NHL goal-scoring leader in consecutive seasons since Pavel Bure of the Florida Panthers in 2000 and 2001. Ovechkin reached the 50-goal milestone for the third time in his career and became the second active player to record three 50-goal seasons (joining Teemu Selanne). Ovechkin also became the third player all-time to post three 50-goal seasons in his first four years in the NHL (joining Mike Bossy and Wayne Gretzky). Ovechkin's 528 shots on goal in 2008-09 were the second highest single-season total in NHL history behind Phil Esposito's 550 in 1970-71. His 19 power-play goals ranked him second in the league and his 10 game-winning goals ranked third. Ovechkin tallied 10 more goals than second-place scorer Jeff Carter of Philadelphia, who had 46 goals. New Jersey's Zach Parise ranked third in the NHL with 45.

## LESTER B. PEARSON AWARD

The Lester B. Pearson Award is presented annually to the "most outstanding player" in the NHL as voted by fellow members of the National Hockey League Players' Association. The winner receives $20,000, and the two finalists receive $10,000 each to donate to the grassroots hockey program of their choice, through the NHLPA's Goals & Dreams Fund.

History: The award was first presented in 1970-71 by the NHLPA in honor of the late Lester B. Pearson, former Prime Minister of Canada.

**2008-09 Winner: Alex Ovechkin, Washington Capitals**
**Runners-up: Pavel Datsyuk, Detroit Red Wings**
**Evgeni Malkin, Pittsburgh Penguins**

Alex Ovechkin of the Washington Capitals was the recipient of the Lester B. Pearson Award for the second year in a row. Ovechkin appeared in 79 games for the Washington Capitals in 2008-09, finishing second in league points (110) and leading the NHL with 56 goals to win his second Maurice "Rocket" Richard Trophy. He also led the Capitals to their second-consecutive Southeast Division title in 2008-09. Ovechkin has quickly gained the admiration of his fellow players and is regarded as one of the most exciting athletes in all of professional sports. Ovechkin becomes just the sixth player to win the Lester B. Pearson Award in consecutive seasons. The Capitals star was also a finalist for the Pearson Award in 2005-06. Sergei Fedorov (1993-94) is the only other Russian born player to receive the Lester B. Pearson Award. In honour of the Lester B. Pearson nominees outstanding seasons, the NHLPA Goals & Dreams fund will be allocating a total of $20,000 to the grassroots hockey programs of the Pearson Finalists choice. Ovechkin will designate a youth hockey program as the beneficiary of the $10,000 that accompanies the Pearson Award, while Datsyuk and Malkin will each allocate $5,000 to their selected grassroots hockey programs.

*Calgary's Jarome Iginla (left) won the Mark Messier Leadership Award in 2009, an award named after his childhood hero. Rick Nash of Columbus (center) won the NHL Foundation Player Award for his many charitable contributions on behalf of young people in Ohio. Vancouver's Roberto Luongo (right) was chosen as the inaugural recipient of the Scotiabank/NHL Fan Fav Award, the first award to be bestowed by a vote of NHL fans.*

## NHL LIFETIME ACHIEVEMENT AWARD

An annual award presented to an individual "whose long-term contributions to hockey have been representative of all that is outstanding about the National Hockey League and the game, both on and off the ice."

History: This award was first presented in 2008.

**2008-09 Winner: Jean Béliveau**

Jean Béliveau is the 2009 recipient of the NHL Lifetime Achievement Award. Béliveau was a young hockey prodigy who went on to realize his potential and much more. He played his entire 20-season professional career with the Montreal Canadiens, the last 10 as team captain, and retired in 1971 as a 10-time Stanley Cup winner. He finished his NHL career with 507 goals and 712 assists for 1,219 points in 1,125 regular-season games and added 79 goals and 97 assists for 176 points in 162 playoff games. Upon his retirement, Béliveau was the Canadiens' all-time scoring leader and the NHL's all-time leading playoffs scorer.

Beyond these impressive statistics, Béliveau is acknowledged as one of hockey's classiest individuals. He was a gifted skater and natural leader who played a poised and stylish game. Béliveau won the Hart Trophy as NHL Most Valuable Player in 1956 and 1964 and was voted the first winner of the Conn Smythe Trophy as playoffs MVP in 1965. As an executive with the Canadiens, he contributed to another seven Stanley Cup championships and remains a great asset to the club as a goodwill ambassador. His Jean Béliveau Foundation accomplished a great deal for young people and became part of the Quebec Society for Disabled Children in 1993.

Béliveau holds several honorary doctorates from Canadian universities, is an Officer of the National Order of Quebec and a Companion of the Order of Canada. He has been portrayed on a Canadian postage stamp and, in 2008, saw a railway station named in his honor. In 1972, his # 4 jersey was retired by the Canadiens and he was inducted into the Hockey Hall of Fame.

## MARK MESSIER NHL LEADERSHIP AWARD
### presented by Bridgestone

An annual award presented "to the player who exemplifies great leadership qualitites to his team, on and off the ice during the regular season." Suggestions for nominees are solicited from fans, clubs and NHL personnel, but the selection of the three finalists and the ultimate winner is made by Mark Messier himself.

History: Presented by Bridgestone in honor of one of hockey's great leaders, this award was first handed out in 2007.

**2008-09 Winner: Jarome Iginla, Calgary Flames**
**Runners-up: Zdeno Chara, Boston Bruins**
**Sidney Crosby, Pittsburgh Penguins**

Right winger Jarome Iginla of the Calgary Flames is the recipient of the Mark Messier NHL Leadership Award. Growing up in Edmonton and idolizing Messier, Iginla has spent his 12 seasons in the NHL following in the Hall of Famer's leadership footsteps. Like Messier, Iginla plays with a combination of superior skill and fierce toughness. Like Messier, he leads his team both with motivational words and fearless deeds. A five-time NHL All-Star and two-time Canadian Olympian, Iginla is a pillar of the Calgary community. Since 2000, he has been an ambassador for KidSport Calgary, which purchases equipment and pays registration fees for disadvantaged families, and donates $2,000 for every goal he scores. He supports the Juvenile Diabetes and Doctors Without Borders foundations and is a member of the Garth Brooks Teammates for Kids Foundation. Iginla is generous and tireless in donating his money and time to a variety of other causes, including literacy programs, hockey diversity initiatives and youth hockey programs. He was awarded the 2004 NHL Foundation Award for community service and the 2004 King Clancy Memorial Trophy for his humanitarian contributions.

## NHL FOUNDATION PLAYER AWARD

An annual award presented to "an NHL player who applies the core values of hockey – commitment, perseverance and teamwork – to enrich the lives of people in his community." In recognition of this dedication, the NHL Foundation annually awards $25,000 to a current player's charity.

History: NHL players have a long-standing tradition of supporting charities and other important causes in their communities. NHL member clubs are constant in their quest to help local schools, hospitals and charitable organizations. Clubs submit nominations for the NHL Foundation Player Award and the finalists are selected by a judging panel. This award was first presented in 1998.

**2008-09 Winner: Rick Nash, Columbus Blue Jackets**
**Runners-up: Dustin Brown, Los Angeles Kings**
**Alex Kovalev, Montreal Canadiens**

Left winger Rick Nash of the Columbus Blue Jackets is the recipient of the 2009 NHL Foundation Player Award. Nash has become one of the most active Blue Jackets in the community, giving his time, money and support to improve the lives of people throughout Central Ohio. He established the #61 Club to encourage students to make healthy choices and rewards those who do. Through the #61 Club Good Health Challenge, Nash provides more than 30 tickets to every Blue Jackets home game to students who make 61 healthy choices in a month.

Nash donated $100,000 to the Ohio State University Athletics Department to endow a scholarship for a student-athlete and gave $25,000 as a founding donor of the John H. McConnell Scholarship Fund in memory of the Blue Jackets founder and majority owner. He made a $5,000 contribution to the 2009 Quebec Pee Wee Major team that represented Columbus, to pay for travel expenses so families would be able to attend with their children. For the past four years, Nash has donated $15,000 annually to Santa's Silent Helpers, which helps families with children, single mothers and the elderly in Central Ohio who are experiencing financial hardships. He also developed the "Rick Bands" program to promote leadership and character among local youths and has allocated the sales of the wristbands to benefit the Columbus Blue Jackets Foundation in support of fighting pediatric cancer and promoting education and children's health and safety.

Nash serves as the spokesperson for several Blue Jackets' charitable initiatives, including the Columbus Dispatch Newspapers in Education program, which educates students in history, sportsmanship and health; the Jackets For Jackets program, which collected more than 1,200 coats during the holiday season; and the Time Warner Cable Adult Literacy Campaign, which educates the public about the importance of adult literacy.

## SCOTIABANK/NHL FAN FAV AWARD

The Scotiabank/NHL Fan Fav Award is presented to the player judged to be the best overall regular-season performer as selected by fans of the National Hockey League.

History: This award was first presented in 2009.

**2008-09 Winner: Roberto Luongo, Vancouver Canucks**
**Runners-up: Martin Brodeur, New Jersey Devils;**
**Sidney Crosby, Pittsburgh Penguins;**
**Mike Green, Washington Capitals;**
**Jarome Iginla, Calgary Flames;**
**Miikka Kiprusoff, Calgary Flames;**
**Steve Mason, Columbus Blue Jackets;**
**Evgeni Nabokov, San Jose Sharks;**
**Alex Ovechkin, Washington Capitals;**
**Eric Staal, Carolina Hurricanes**

Supported by the National Hockey League, the National Hockey League Players' Association and Scotiabank in Canada, this is the NHL's first fan-driven award. More than one million votes were cast each week as fans selected those players who demonstrated the best skills and strongest overall performance. All of the weekly Scotiabank/NHL Fan Fav Award nominees from the regular season were evaluated by a panel of NHL experts to determine the ten finalists.

Vancouver Canucks' goaltender Roberto Luongo was the recipient of the 2008-09 Scotiabank/NHL Fan Fav Award. Luongo finished the season with 33 wins, a 2.34 goals-against average and nine shutouts. He was the first goaltender since Montreal's Bill Durnan in 1947-48 to be named team captain.

# NATIONAL HOCKEY LEAGUE INDIVIDUAL AWARD WINNERS

## ART ROSS TROPHY

| | Winner | Runner-up |
|---|---|---|
| 2009 | Evgeni Malkin, Pit. | Alex Ovechkin, Wsh. |
| 2008 | Alex Ovechkin, Wsh. | Evgeni Malkin, Pit. |
| 2007 | Sidney Crosby, Pit. | Joe Thornton, S.J. |
| 2006 | Joe Thornton, Bos., S.J. | Jaromir Jagr, NYR |
| 2005 | .... | .... |
| 2004 | Martin St. Louis, T.B. | Ilya Kovalchuk, Atl. |
| 2003 | Peter Forsberg, Col. | Markus Naslund, Van. |
| 2002 | Jarome Iginla, Cgy. | Markus Naslund, Van. |
| 2001 | Jaromir Jagr, Pit. | Joe Sakic, Col. |
| 2000 | Jaromir Jagr, Pit. | Pavel Bure, Fla. |
| 1999 | Jaromir Jagr, Pit. | Teemu Selanne, Ana. |
| 1998 | Jaromir Jagr, Pit. | Peter Forsberg, Col. |
| 1997 | Mario Lemieux, Pit. | Teemu Selanne, Ana. |
| 1996 | Mario Lemieux, Pit. | Jaromir Jagr, Pit. |
| 1995 | Jaromir Jagr, Pit. | Eric Lindros, Phi. |
| 1994 | Wayne Gretzky, L.A. | Sergei Fedorov, Det. |
| 1993 | Mario Lemieux, Pit. | Pat LaFontaine, Buf. |
| 1992 | Mario Lemieux, Pit. | Kevin Stevens, Pit. |
| 1991 | Wayne Gretzky, L.A. | Brett Hull, St.L. |
| 1990 | Wayne Gretzky, L.A. | Mark Messier, Edm. |
| 1989 | Mario Lemieux, Pit. | Wayne Gretzky, L.A. |
| 1988 | Mario Lemieux, Pit. | Wayne Gretzky, Edm. |
| 1987 | Wayne Gretzky, Edm. | Jari Kurri, Edm. |
| 1986 | Wayne Gretzky, Edm. | Mario Lemieux, Pit. |
| 1985 | Wayne Gretzky, Edm. | Jari Kurri, Edm. |
| 1984 | Wayne Gretzky, Edm. | Paul Coffey, Edm. |
| 1983 | Wayne Gretzky, Edm. | Peter Stastny, Que. |
| 1982 | Wayne Gretzky, Edm. | Mike Bossy, NYI |
| 1981 | Wayne Gretzky, Edm. | Marcel Dionne, L.A. |
| 1980 | Marcel Dionne, L.A. | Wayne Gretzky, Edm. |
| 1979 | Bryan Trottier, NYI | Marcel Dionne, L.A. |
| 1978 | Guy Lafleur, Mtl. | Bryan Trottier, NYI |
| 1977 | Guy Lafleur, Mtl. | Marcel Dionne, L.A. |
| 1976 | Guy Lafleur, Mtl. | Bobby Clarke, Phi. |
| 1975 | Bobby Orr, Bos. | Phil Esposito, Bos. |
| 1974 | Phil Esposito, Bos. | Bobby Orr, Bos. |
| 1973 | Phil Esposito, Bos. | Bobby Clarke, Phi. |
| 1972 | Phil Esposito, Bos. | Bobby Orr, Bos. |
| 1971 | Phil Esposito, Bos. | Bobby Orr, Bos. |
| 1970 | Bobby Orr, Bos. | Phil Esposito, Bos. |
| 1969 | Phil Esposito, Bos. | Bobby Hull, Chi. |
| 1968 | Stan Mikita, Chi. | Phil Esposito, Bos. |
| 1967 | Stan Mikita, Chi. | Bobby Hull, Chi. |
| 1966 | Bobby Hull, Chi. | Stan Mikita, Chi. |
| 1965 | Stan Mikita, Chi. | Norm Ullman, Det. |
| 1964 | Stan Mikita, Chi. | Bobby Hull, Chi. |
| 1963 | Gordie Howe, Det. | Andy Bathgate, NYR |
| 1962 | Bobby Hull, Chi. | Andy Bathgate, NYR |
| 1961 | Bernie Geoffrion, Mtl. | Jean Beliveau, Mtl. |
| 1960 | Bobby Hull, Chi. | Bronco Horvath, Bos. |
| 1959 | Dickie Moore, Mtl. | Jean Beliveau, Mtl. |
| 1958 | Dickie Moore, Mtl. | Henri Richard, Mtl. |
| 1957 | Gordie Howe, Det. | Ted Lindsay, Det. |
| 1956 | Jean Beliveau, Mtl. | Gordie Howe, Det. |
| 1955 | Bernie Geoffrion, Mtl. | Maurice Richard, Mtl. |
| 1954 | Gordie Howe, Det. | Maurice Richard, Mtl. |
| 1953 | Gordie Howe, Det. | Ted Lindsay, Det. |
| 1952 | Gordie Howe, Det. | Ted Lindsay, Det. |
| 1951 | Gordie Howe, Det. | Maurice Richard, Mtl. |
| 1950 | Ted Lindsay, Det. | Sid Abel, Det. |
| 1949 | Roy Conacher, Chi. | Doug Bentley, Chi. |
| 1948* | Elmer Lach, Mtl. | Buddy O'Connor, NYR |
| 1947 | Max Bentley, Chi. | Maurice Richard, Mtl. |
| 1946 | Max Bentley, Chi. | Gaye Stewart, Tor. |
| 1945 | Elmer Lach, Mtl. | Maurice Richard, Mtl. |
| 1944 | Herb Cain, Bos. | Doug Bentley, Chi. |
| 1943 | Doug Bentley, Chi. | Bill Cowley, Bos. |
| 1942 | Bryan Hextall, NYR | Lynn Patrick, NYR |
| 1941 | Bill Cowley, Bos. | Bryan Hextall, NYR |
| 1940 | Milt Schmidt, Bos. | Woody Dumart, Bos. |
| 1939 | Toe Blake, Mtl. | Sweeney Schriner, NYA |
| 1938 | Gordie Drillon, Tor. | Syl Apps, Tor. |
| 1937 | Sweeney Schriner, NYA | Syl Apps, Tor. |
| 1936 | Sweeney Schriner, NYA | Marty Barry, Det. |
| 1935 | Charlie Conacher, Tor. | Syd Howe, St.L., Det. |
| 1934 | Charlie Conacher, Tor. | Joe Primeau, Tor |
| 1933 | Bill Cook, NYR | Busher Jackson, Tor. |
| 1932 | Busher Jackson, Tor. | Joe Primeau, Tor. |
| 1931 | Howie Morenz, Mtl. | Ebbie Goodfellow, Det. |
| 1930 | Cooney Weiland, Bos. | Frank Boucher, NYR |
| 1929 | Ace Bailey, Tor. | Nels Stewart, Mtl.M |
| 1928 | Howie Morenz, Mtl. | Aurel Joliat, Mtl. |
| 1927 | Bill Cook, NYR | Dick Irvin, Chi. |
| 1926 | Nels Stewart, Mtl.M. | Cy Denneny, Ott. |
| 1925 | Babe Dye, Tor. | Cy Denneny, Ott. |
| 1924 | Cy Denneny, Ott. | Billy Boucher, Mtl. |
| 1923 | Babe Dye, Tor. | Cy Denneny, Ott. |
| 1922 | Punch Broadbent, Ott. | Cy Denneny, Ott. |
| 1921 | Newsy Lalonde, Mtl. | Babe Dye, Ham., Tor. |
| 1920 | Joe Malone, Que. | Newsy Lalonde, Mtl. |
| 1919 | Newsy Lalonde, Mtl. | Odie Cleghorn, Mtl. |
| 1918 | Joe Malone, Mtl. | Cy Denneny, Ott. |

## HART MEMORIAL TROPHY

| | Winner | Runner-up |
|---|---|---|
| 2009 | Alex Ovechkin, Wsh. | Evgeni Malkin, Pit. |
| 2008 | Alex Ovechkin, Wsh. | Evgeni Malkin, Pit. |
| 2007 | Sidney Crosby, Pit. | Roberto Luongo, Van. |
| 2006 | Joe Thornton, Bos., S.J. | Jaromir Jagr, NYR |
| 2005 | .... | .... |
| 2004 | Martin St. Louis, T.B. | Jarome Iginla, Cgy. |
| 2003 | Peter Forsberg, Col. | Markus Naslund, Van. |
| 2002 | Jose Theodore, Mtl. | Jarome Iginla, Cgy. |
| 2001 | Joe Sakic, Col. | Mario Lemieux, Pit. |
| 2000 | Chris Pronger, St.L. | Jaromir Jagr, Pit. |
| 1999 | Jaromir Jagr, Pit. | Alexei Yashin, Ott. |
| 1998 | Dominik Hasek, Buf. | Jaromir Jagr, Pit. |
| 1997 | Dominik Hasek, Buf. | Paul Kariya, Ana. |
| 1996 | Mario Lemieux, Pit. | Mark Messier, NYR |
| 1995 | Eric Lindros, Phi. | Jaromir Jagr, Pit. |
| 1994 | Sergei Fedorov, Det. | Dominik Hasek, Buf. |
| 1993 | Mario Lemieux, Pit. | Doug Gilmour, Tor. |
| 1992 | Mark Messier, NYR | Patrick Roy, Mtl. |
| 1991 | Brett Hull, St.L. | Wayne Gretzky, L.A. |
| 1990 | Mark Messier, Edm. | Raymond Bourque, Bos. |
| 1989 | Wayne Gretzky, L.A. | Mario Lemieux, Pit. |
| 1988 | Mario Lemieux, Pit. | Grant Fuhr, Edm. |
| 1987 | Wayne Gretzky, Edm. | Raymond Bourque, Bos. |
| 1986 | Wayne Gretzky, Edm. | Mario Lemieux, Pit. |
| 1985 | Wayne Gretzky, Edm. | Dale Hawerchuk, Wpg. |
| 1984 | Wayne Gretzky, Edm. | Rod Langway, Wsh. |
| 1983 | Wayne Gretzky, Edm. | Pete Peeters, Bos. |
| 1982 | Wayne Gretzky, Edm. | Bryan Trottier, NYI |
| 1981 | Wayne Gretzky, Edm. | Mike Liut, St.L. |
| 1980 | Wayne Gretzky, Edm. | Marcel Dionne, L.A. |
| 1979 | Bryan Trottier, NYI | Guy Lafleur, Mtl |
| 1978 | Guy Lafleur, Mtl. | Bryan Trottier, NYI |
| 1977 | Guy Lafleur, Mtl. | Bobby Clarke, Phi. |
| 1976 | Bobby Clarke, Phi. | Denis Potvin, NYI |
| 1975 | Bobby Clarke, Phi. | Rogie Vachon, L.A. |
| 1974 | Phil Esposito, Bos. | Bernie Parent, Phi. |
| 1973 | Bobby Clarke, Phi. | Phil Esposito, Bos. |
| 1972 | Bobby Orr, Bos. | Ken Dryden, Mtl. |
| 1971 | Bobby Orr, Bos. | Phil Esposito, Bos. |
| 1970 | Bobby Orr, Bos. | Tony Esposito, Chi. |
| 1969 | Phil Esposito, Bos. | Jean Beliveau, Mtl. |
| 1968 | Stan Mikita, Chi. | Jean Beliveau, Mtl. |
| 1967 | Stan Mikita, Chi. | Ed Giacomin, NYR |
| 1966 | Bobby Hull, Chi. | Jean Beliveau, Mtl. |
| 1965 | Bobby Hull, Chi. | Norm Ullman, Det. |
| 1964 | Jean Beliveau, Mtl. | Bobby Hull, Chi. |
| 1963 | Gordie Howe, Det. | Stan Mikita, Chi. |
| 1962 | Jacques Plante, Mtl. | Doug Harvey, NYR |
| 1961 | Bernie Geoffrion, Mtl. | Johnny Bower, Tor. |
| 1960 | Gordie Howe, Det. | Bobby Hull, Chi. |
| 1959 | Andy Bathgate, NYR | Gordie Howe, Det. |
| 1958 | Gordie Howe, Det. | Andy Bathgate, NYR |
| 1957 | Gordie Howe, Det. | Jean Beliveau, Mtl. |
| 1956 | Jean Beliveau, Mtl. | Tod Sloan, Tor. |
| 1955 | Ted Kennedy, Tor. | Harry Lumley, Tor. |
| 1954 | Al Rollins, Chi. | Red Kelly, Det. |
| 1953 | Gordie Howe, Det. | Al Rollins, Chi. |
| 1952 | Gordie Howe, Det. | Elmer Lach, Mtl. |
| 1951 | Milt Schmidt, Bos. | Maurice Richard, Mtl. |
| 1950 | Chuck Rayner, NYR | Ted Kennedy, Tor. |
| 1949 | Sid Abel, Det. | Bill Durnan, Mtl. |
| 1948 | Buddy O'Connor, NYR | Frank Brimsek, Bos. |
| 1947 | Maurice Richard, Mtl. | Milt Schmidt, Bos. |
| 1946 | Max Bentley, Chi. | Gaye Stewart, Tor. |
| 1945 | Elmer Lach, Mtl. | Maurice Richard, Mtl. |
| 1944 | Babe Pratt, Tor. | Bill Cowley, Bos. |
| 1943 | Bill Cowley, Bos. | Doug Bentley, Chi. |
| 1942 | Tom Anderson, Bro. | Syl Apps, Tor. |
| 1941 | Bill Cowley, Bos. | Dit Clapper, Bos. |
| 1940 | Ebbie Goodfellow, Det. | Syl Apps, Tor. |
| 1939 | Toe Blake, Mtl. | Syl Apps, Tor. |
| 1938 | Eddie Shore, Bos. | Paul Thompson, Chi. |
| 1937 | Babe Siebert, Mtl. | Lionel Conacher, Mtl.M |
| 1936 | Eddie Shore, Bos. | Hooley Smith, Mtl.M |
| 1935 | Eddie Shore, Bos. | Charlie Conacher, Tor. |
| 1934 | Aurel Joliat, Mtl. | Lionel Conacher, Chi. |
| 1933 | Eddie Shore, Bos. | Bill Cook, NYR |
| 1932 | Howie Morenz, Mtl. | Ching Johnson, NYR |
| 1931 | Howie Morenz, Mtl. | Eddie Shore, Bos. |
| 1930 | Nels Stewart, Mtl.M. | Lionel Hitchman, Bos. |
| 1929 | Roy Worters, NYA | Ace Bailey, Tor. |
| 1928 | Howie Morenz, Mtl. | Roy Worters, Pit. |
| 1927 | Herb Gardiner, Mtl. | Bill Cook, NYR |
| 1926 | Nels Stewart, Mtl.M. | Sprague Cleghorn, Bos. |
| 1925 | Billy Burch, Ham. | Howie Morenz, Mtl. |
| 1924 | Frank Nighbor, Ott. | Sprague Cleghorn, Mtl. |

## MAURICE "ROCKET" RICHARD TROPHY

| | | |
|---|---|---|
| 2009 | Alex Ovechkin | Washington |
| 2008 | Alex Ovechkin | Washington |
| 2007 | Vincent Lecavalier | Tampa Bay |
| 2006 | Jonathan Cheechoo | San Jose |
| 2005 | .... | .... |
| 2004 | Rick Nash | Columbus |
| | Jarome Iginla | Calgary |
| | Ilya Kovalchuk | Atlanta |
| 2003 | Milan Hejduk | Colorado |
| 2002 | Jarome Iginla | Calgary |
| 2001 | Pavel Bure | Florida |
| 2000 | Pavel Bure | Florida |
| 1999 | Teemu Selanne | Anaheim |

## WILLIAM M. JENNINGS TROPHY

| | Winner | Runner-up |
|---|---|---|
| 2009 | Tim Thomas, Bos. | Niklas Backstrom, Min. |
| | Manny Fernandez, Bos. | |
| 2008 | Chris Osgood, Det. | Jean-Sebastien Giguere, Ana. |
| | Dominik Hasek, Det. | |
| 2007 | Niklas Backstrom, Min. | Dominik Hasek, Det. |
| | Manny Fernandez, Min. | |
| 2006 | Miikka Kiprusoff, Cgy. | Manny Legace, Det. |
| | | Chris Osgood, Det. |
| 2005 | .... | .... |
| 2004 | Martin Brodeur, N.J. | Marty Turco, Dal. |
| 2003 | Martin Brodeur, N.J. | Marty Turco, Dal. |
| | Roman Cechmanek, Phi. | Ron Tugnutt, Dal. |
| | Robert Esche, Phi. | |
| 2002 | Patrick Roy, Col. | Tommy Salo, Edm. |
| 2001 | Dominik Hasek, Buf. | Ed Belfour, Dal. |
| | | Marty Turco, Dal. |
| 2000 | Roman Turek, St.L. | John Vanbiesbrouck, Phi. |
| | | Brian Boucher, Phi. |
| 1999 | Ed Belfour, Dal. | Dominik Hasek, Buf. |
| | Roman Turek, Dal. | |
| 1998 | Martin Brodeur, N.J. | Ed Belfour, Dal. |
| 1997 | Martin Brodeur, N.J. | Chris Osgood, Det. |
| | Mike Dunham, N.J. | Mike Vernon, Det. |
| 1996 | Chris Osgood, Det. | Martin Brodeur, N.J. |
| | Mike Vernon, Det. | |
| 1995 | Ed Belfour, Chi. | Mike Vernon, Det. |
| | | Chris Osgood, Det. |
| 1994 | Dominik Hasek, Buf. | Martin Brodeur, N.J. |
| | Grant Fuhr, Buf. | Chris Terreri, N.J. |
| 1993 | Ed Belfour, Chi. | Felix Potvin, Tor. |
| | | Grant Fuhr, Tor. |
| 1992 | Patrick Roy, Mtl. | Ed Belfour, Chi. |
| 1991 | Ed Belfour, Chi. | Patrick Roy, Mtl. |
| 1990 | Andy Moog, Bos. | Patrick Roy, Mtl. |
| | Reggie Lemelin, Bos. | Brian Hayward, Mtl. |
| 1989 | Patrick Roy, Mtl. | Mike Vernon, Cgy. |
| | Brian Hayward, Mtl. | Rick Wamsley, Cgy. |
| 1988 | Patrick Roy, Mtl. | Clint Malarchuk, Wsh. |
| | Brian Hayward, Mtl. | Pete Peeters, Wsh. |
| 1987 | Patrick Roy, Mtl. | Ron Hextall, Phi. |
| | Brian Hayward, Mtl. | |
| 1986 | Bob Froese, Phi. | Al Jensen, Wsh. |
| | Darren Jensen, Phi. | Pete Peeters, Wsh. |
| 1985 | Tom Barrasso, Buf. | Pat Riggin, Wsh. |
| | Bob Sauve, Buf. | |
| 1984 | Al Jensen, Wsh. | Tom Barrasso, Buf. |
| | Pat Riggin, Wsh. | Bob Sauve, Buf. |
| 1983 | Roland Melanson, NYI | Pete Peeters, Bos. |
| | Billy Smith, NYI | |
| 1982 | Rick Wamsley, Mtl. | Billy Smith, NYI |
| | Denis Herron, Mtl. | Roland Melanson, NYI |

## BILL MASTERTON MEMORIAL TROPHY

| | | |
|---|---|---|
| 2009 | Steve Sullivan | Nashville |
| 2008 | Jason Blake | Toronto |
| 2007 | Phil Kessel | Boston |
| 2006 | Teemu Selanne | Anaheim |
| 2005 | .... | .... |
| 2004 | Bryan Berard | Chicago |
| 2003 | Steve Yzerman | Detroit |
| 2002 | Saku Koivu | Montreal |
| 2001 | Adam Graves | NY Rangers |
| 2000 | Ken Daneyko | New Jersey |
| 1999 | John Cullen | Tampa Bay |
| 1998 | Jamie McLennan | St. Louis |
| 1997 | Tony Granato | San Jose |
| 1996 | Gary Roberts | Calgary |
| 1995 | Pat LaFontaine | Buffalo |
| 1994 | Cam Neely | Boston |
| 1993 | Mario Lemieux | Pittsburgh |
| 1992 | Mark Fitzpatrick | NY Islanders |
| 1991 | Dave Taylor | Los Angeles |
| 1990 | Gord Kluzak | Boston |
| 1989 | Tim Kerr | Philadelphia |
| 1988 | Bob Bourne | Los Angeles |
| 1987 | Doug Jarvis | Hartford |
| 1986 | Charlie Simmer | Boston |
| 1985 | Anders Hedberg | NY Rangers |
| 1984 | Brad Park | Detroit |
| 1983 | Lanny McDonald | Calgary |
| 1982 | Glenn Resch | Colorado |
| 1981 | Blake Dunlop | St. Louis |
| 1980 | Al MacAdam | Minnesota |
| 1979 | Serge Savard | Montreal |
| 1978 | Butch Goring | Los Angeles |
| 1977 | Ed Westfall | NY Islanders |
| 1976 | Rod Gilbert | NY Rangers |
| 1975 | Don Luce | Buffalo |
| 1974 | Henri Richard | Montreal |
| 1973 | Lowell MacDonald | Pittsburgh |
| 1972 | Bobby Clarke | Philadelphia |
| 1971 | Jean Ratelle | NY Rangers |
| 1970 | Pit Martin | Chicago |
| 1969 | Ted Hampson | Oakland |
| 1968 | Claude Provost | Montreal |

## SCOTIABANK/NHL FAN FAV AWARD

| | | |
|---|---|---|
| 2009 | Roberto Luongo | Vancouver |

## LADY BYNG MEMORIAL TROPHY

| | Winner | Runner-up |
|---|---|---|
| 2009 | Pavel Datsyuk, Det. | Martin St. Louis, T.B. |
| 2008 | Pavel Datsyuk, Det. | Martin St. Louis, T.B. |
| 2007 | Pavel Datsyuk, Det. | Martin St. Louis, T.B. |
| 2006 | Pavel Datsyuk, Det. | Brad Richards, T.B. |
| 2005 | .... | .... |
| 2004 | Brad Richards, T.B. | Daniel Alfredsson, Ott. |
| 2003 | Alexander Mogilny, Tor. | Nicklas Lidstrom, Det. |
| 2002 | Ron Francis, Car. | Joe Sakic, Col. |
| 2001 | Joe Sakic, Col. | Nicklas Lidstrom, Det. |
| 2000 | Pavol Demitra, St.L. | Nicklas Lidstrom, Det. |
| 1999 | Wayne Gretzky, NYR. | Nicklas Lidstrom, Det. |
| 1998 | Ron Francis, Pit. | Teemu Selanne, Ana. |
| 1997 | Paul Kariya, Ana. | Teemu Selanne, Ana. |
| 1996 | Paul Kariya, Ana. | Adam Oates, Bos. |
| 1995 | Ron Francis, Pit. | Adam Oates, Bos. |
| 1994 | Wayne Gretzky, L.A. | Adam Oates, Bos. |
| 1993 | Pierre Turgeon, NYI | Adam Oates, Bos. |
| 1992 | Wayne Gretzky, L.A. | Joe Sakic, Que. |
| 1991 | Wayne Gretzky, L.A. | Brett Hull, St.L. |
| 1990 | Brett Hull, St.L. | Wayne Gretzky, L.A. |
| 1989 | Joe Mullen, Cgy. | Wayne Gretzky, L.A. |
| 1988 | Mats Naslund, Mtl. | Wayne Gretzky, Edm. |
| 1987 | Joe Mullen, Cgy. | Wayne Gretzky, Edm. |
| 1986 | Mike Bossy, NYI | Jari Kurri, Edm. |
| 1985 | Jari Kurri, Edm. | Joe Mullen, St.L. |
| 1984 | Mike Bossy, NYI | Rick Middleton, Bos. |
| 1983 | Mike Bossy, NYI | Rick Middleton, Bos. |
| 1982 | Rick Middleton, Bos. | Mike Bossy, NYI |
| 1981 | Rick Kehoe, Pit. | Wayne Gretzky, Edm. |
| 1980 | Wayne Gretzky, Edm. | Marcel Dionne, L.A. |
| 1979 | Bob MacMillan, Atl. | Marcel Dionne, L.A. |
| 1978 | Butch Goring, L.A. | Peter McNab, Bos. |
| 1977 | Marcel Dionne, L.A. | Jean Ratelle, Bos. |
| 1976 | Jean Ratelle, NYR-Bos. | Jean Pronovost, Pit. |
| 1975 | Marcel Dionne, Det. | John Bucyk, Bos. |
| 1974 | John Bucyk, Bos. | Lowell MacDonald, Pit. |
| 1973 | Gilbert Perreault, Buf. | Jean Ratelle, NYR |
| 1972 | Jean Ratelle, NYR | John Bucyk, Bos. |
| 1971 | John Bucyk, Bos. | Dave Keon, Tor. |
| 1970 | Phil Goyette, St.L. | John Bucyk, Bos. |
| 1969 | Alex Delvecchio, Det. | Ted Hampson, Oak. |
| 1968 | Stan Mikita, Chi. | John Bucyk, Bos. |
| 1967 | Stan Mikita, Chi. | Dave Keon, Tor. |
| 1966 | Alex Delvecchio, Det. | Bobby Rousseau, Mtl. |
| 1965 | Bobby Hull, Chi. | Alex Delvecchio, Det. |
| 1964 | Kenny Wharram, Chi. | Dave Keon, Tor. |
| 1963 | Dave Keon, Tor. | Camille Henry, NYR |
| 1962 | Dave Keon, Tor. | Claude Provost, Mtl. |
| 1961 | Red Kelly, Tor. | Norm Ullman, Det. |
| 1960 | Don McKenney, Bos. | Andy Hebenton, NYR |
| 1959 | Alex Delvecchio, Det. | Andy Hebenton, NYR |
| 1958 | Camille Henry, NYR | Don Marshall, Mtl. |
| 1957 | Andy Hebenton, NYR | Dutch Reibel, Det. |
| 1956 | Dutch Reibel, Det. | Floyd Curry, Mtl. |
| 1955 | Sid Smith, Tor. | Danny Lewicki, NYR |
| 1954 | Red Kelly, Det. | Don Raleigh, NYR |
| 1953 | Red Kelly, Det. | Wally Hergesheimer, NYR |
| 1952 | Sid Smith, Tor. | Red Kelly, Det. |
| 1951 | Red Kelly, Det. | Woody Dumart, Bos. |
| 1950 | Edgar Laprade, NYR | Red Kelly, Det. |
| 1949 | Bill Quackenbush, Det. | Harry Watson, Tor. |
| 1948 | Bobby O'Connor, NYR | Syl Apps, Tor. |
| 1947 | Bobby Bauer, Bos. | Syl Apps, Tor. |
| 1946 | Toe Blake, Mtl. | Clint Smith, Chi. |
| 1945 | Bill Mosienko, Chi. | Syd Howe, Det. |
| 1944 | Clint Smith, Chi. | Herb Cain, Bos. |
| 1943 | Max Bentley, Chi. | Buddy O'Connor, Mtl. |
| 1942 | Syl Apps, Tor. | Gordie Drillon, Tor. |
| 1941 | Bobby Bauer, Bos. | Gordie Drillon, Tor. |
| 1940 | Bobby Bauer, Bos. | Clint Smith, NYR |
| 1939 | Clint Smith, NYR | Marty Barry, Det. |
| 1938 | Gordie Drillon, Tor. | Clint Smith, NYR |
| 1937 | Marty Barry, Det. | Gordie Drillon, Tor. |
| 1936 | Doc Romnes, Chi. | Sweeney Schriner, NYA |
| 1935 | Frank Boucher, NYR | Russ Blinco, Mtl.M |
| 1934 | Frank Boucher, NYR | Joe Primeau, Tor. |
| 1933 | Frank Boucher, NYR | Joe Primeau, Tor. |
| 1932 | Joe Primeau, Tor. | Frank Boucher, NYR |
| 1931 | Frank Boucher, NYR | Normie Himes, NYA |
| 1930 | Frank Boucher, NYR | Normie Himes, NYA |
| 1929 | Frank Boucher, NYR | Harold Darragh, Pit. |
| 1928 | Frank Boucher, NYR | George Hay, Det. |
| 1927 | Billy Burch, NYA | Dick Irvin, Chi. |
| 1926 | Frank Nighbor, Ott. | Billy Burch, NYA |
| 1925 | Frank Nighbor, Ott. | none |

## KING CLANCY MEMORIAL TROPHY

| | | |
|---|---|---|
| 2009 | Ethan Moreau | Edmonton |
| 2008 | Vincent Lecavalier | Tampa Bay |
| 2007 | Saku Koivu | Montreal |
| 2006 | Olaf Kolzig | Washington |
| 2005 | .... | .... |
| 2004 | Jarome Iginla | Calgary |
| 2003 | Brendan Shanahan | Detroit |
| 2002 | Ron Francis | Carolina |
| 2001 | Shjon Podein | Colorado |
| 2000 | Curtis Joseph | Toronto |
| 1999 | Rob Ray | Buffalo |
| 1998 | Kelly Chase | St. Louis |
| 1997 | Trevor Linden | Vancouver |
| 1996 | Kris King | Winnipeg |
| 1995 | Joe Nieuwendyk | Calgary |
| 1994 | Adam Graves | NY Rangers |
| 1993 | Dave Poulin | Boston |
| 1992 | Raymond Bourque | Boston |
| 1991 | Dave Taylor | Los Angeles |
| 1990 | Kevin Lowe | Edmonton |
| 1989 | Bryan Trottier | NY Islanders |
| 1988 | Lanny McDonald | Calgary |

## VEZINA TROPHY

| | Winner | Runner-up |
|---|---|---|
| 2009 | Tim Thomas, Bos. | Steve Mason, CBJ |
| 2008 | Martin Brodeur, N.J. | Evgeni Nabokov, S.J. |
| 2007 | Martin Brodeur, N.J. | Roberto Luongo, Van. |
| 2006 | Miikka Kiprusoff, Cgy. | Martin Brodeur, N.J. |
| 2005 | .... | .... |
| 2004 | Martin Brodeur, N.J. | Miikka Kiprusoff, Cgy. |
| 2003 | Martin Brodeur, N.J. | Marty Turco, Dal. |
| 2002 | Jose Theodore, Mtl. | Patrick Roy, Col. |
| 2001 | Dominik Hasek, Buf. | Roman Cechmanek, Phi. |
| 2000 | Olaf Kolzig, Wsh. | Roman Turek, St.L. |
| 1999 | Dominik Hasek, Buf. | Curtis Joseph, Tor. |
| 1998 | Dominik Hasek, Buf. | Martin Brodeur, N.J. |
| 1997 | Dominik Hasek, Buf. | Martin Brodeur, N.J. |
| 1996 | Jim Carey, Wsh. | Chris Osgood, Det. |
| 1995 | Dominik Hasek, Buf. | Ed Belfour, Chi. |
| 1994 | Dominik Hasek, Buf. | John Vanbiesbrouck, Fla. |
| 1993 | Ed Belfour, Chi. | Tom Barrasso, Pit. |
| 1992 | Patrick Roy, Mtl. | Kirk McLean, Van. |
| 1991 | Ed Belfour, Chi. | Patrick Roy, Mtl. |
| 1990 | Patrick Roy, Mtl. | Daren Puppa, Buf. |
| 1989 | Patrick Roy, Mtl. | Mike Vernon, Cgy. |
| 1988 | Grant Fuhr, Edm. | Tom Barrasso, Buf. |
| 1987 | Ron Hextall, Phi. | Mike Liut, Hfd. |
| 1986 | John Vanbiesbrouck, NYR | Bob Froese, Phi. |
| 1985 | Pelle Lindbergh, Phi. | Tom Barrasso, Buf. |
| 1984 | Tom Barrasso, Buf. | Reggie Lemelin, Cgy. |
| 1983 | Pete Peeters, Bos. | Roland Melanson, NYI |
| 1982 | Billy Smith, NYI | Grant Fuhr, Edm. |
| 1981 | Richard Sevigny, Mtl. | Pete Peeters, Phi. |
| | Denis Herron, Mtl. | Rick St. Croix, Phi. |
| | Michel Larocque, Mtl. | |
| 1980 | Bob Sauve, Buf. | Gerry Cheevers, Bos. |
| | Don Edwards, Buf. | Gilles Gilbert, Bos. |
| 1979 | Ken Dryden, Mtl. | Glenn Resch, NYI |
| | Michel Larocque, Mtl. | Billy Smith, NYI |
| 1978 | Ken Dryden, Mtl. | Bernie Parent, Phi. |
| | Michel Larocque, Mtl. | Wayne Stephenson, Phi. |
| 1977 | Ken Dryden, Mtl. | Glenn Resch, NYI |
| | Michel Larocque, Mtl. | Billy Smith, NYI |
| 1976 | Ken Dryden, Mtl. | Glenn Resch, NYI |
| | | Billy Smith, NYI |
| 1975 | Bernie Parent, Phi. | Rogie Vachon, L.A. |
| | | Gary Edwards, L.A. |
| 1974 | Bernie Parent, Phi. (tie) | Gilles Gilbert, Bos. |
| | Tony Esposito, Chi. (tie) | |
| 1973 | Ken Dryden, Mtl. | Ed Giacomin, NYR |
| | | Gilles Villemure, NYR |
| 1972 | Tony Esposito, Chi. | Cesare Maniago, Min. |
| | Gary Smith, Chi. | Gump Worsley, Min. |
| 1971 | Ed Giacomin, NYR | Tony Esposito, Chi. |
| | Gilles Villemure, NYR | |
| 1970 | Tony Esposito, Chi. | Jacques Plante, St.L. |
| | | Ernie Wakely, St.L. |
| 1969 | Jacques Plante, St.L. | Ed Giacomin, NYR |
| | Glenn Hall, St.L. | |
| 1968 | Gump Worsley, Mtl. | Johnny Bower, Tor. |
| | Rogie Vachon, Mtl. | Bruce Gamble, Tor. |
| 1967 | Glenn Hall, Chi. | Charlie Hodge, Mtl. |
| | Denis DeJordy, Chi. | |
| 1966 | Gump Worsley, Mtl. | Glenn Hall, Chi. |
| | Charlie Hodge, Mtl. | |
| 1965 | Terry Sawchuk, Tor. | Roger Crozier, Det. |
| | Johnny Bower, Tor. | |
| 1964 | Charlie Hodge, Mtl. | Glenn Hall, Chi. |
| 1963 | Glenn Hall, Chi. | Johnny Bower, Tor. |
| | | Don Simmons, Tor. |
| 1962 | Jacques Plante, Mtl. | Johnny Bower, Tor. |
| 1961 | Johnny Bower, Tor. | Glenn Hall, Chi. |
| 1960 | Jacques Plante, Mtl. | Glenn Hall, Chi. |
| 1959 | Jacques Plante, Mtl. | Johnny Bower, Tor. |
| | | Ed Chadwick, Tor. |
| 1958 | Jacques Plante, Mtl. | Gump Worsley, NYR |
| | | Marcel Paille, NYR |
| 1957 | Jacques Plante, Mtl. | Glenn Hall, Det. |
| 1956 | Jacques Plante, Mtl. | Glenn Hall, Det. |
| 1955 | Terry Sawchuk, Det. | Harry Lumley, Tor. |
| 1954 | Harry Lumley, Tor. | Terry Sawchuk, Det. |
| 1953 | Terry Sawchuk, Det. | Gerry McNeil, Mtl. |
| 1952 | Terry Sawchuk, Det. | Al Rollins, Tor. |
| 1951 | Al Rollins, Tor. | Terry Sawchuk, Det. |
| 1950 | Bill Durnan, Mtl. | Harry Lumley, Det. |
| 1949 | Bill Durnan, Mtl. | Harry Lumley, Det. |
| 1948 | Turk Broda, Tor. | Harry Lumley, Det. |
| 1947 | Bill Durnan, Mtl. | Turk Broda, Tor. |
| 1946 | Bill Durnan, Mtl. | Frank Brimsek, Bos. |
| 1945 | Bill Durnan, Mtl. | Frank McCool, Tor. (tie) |
| | | Harry Lumley, Det. (tie) |
| 1944 | Bill Durnan, Mtl. | Paul Bibeault, Tor. |
| 1943 | Johnny Mowers, Det. | Turk Broda, Tor. |
| 1942 | Frank Brimsek, Bos. | Turk Broda, Tor. |
| 1941 | Turk Broda, Tor. | Frank Brimsek, Bos. (tie) |
| | | Johnny Mowers, Det. (tie) |
| 1940 | Dave Kerr, NYR | Frank Brimsek, Bos. |
| 1939 | Frank Brimsek, Bos. | Dave Kerr, NYR |
| 1938 | Tiny Thompson, Bos. | Dave Kerr, NYR |
| 1937 | Normie Smith, Det. | Dave Kerr, NYR |
| 1936 | Tiny Thompson, Bos. | Mike Karakas, Chi. |
| 1935 | Lorne Chabot, Chi. | Alex Connell, Mtl.M |
| 1934 | Charlie Gardiner, Chi. | Wilf Cude, Det. |
| 1933 | Tiny Thompson, Bos. | John Ross Roach, Det. |
| 1932 | Charlie Gardiner, Chi. | Alex Connell, Det. |
| 1931 | Roy Worters, NYA | Charlie Gardiner, Chi. |
| 1930 | Tiny Thompson, Bos. | Charlie Gardiner, Chi. |
| 1929 | George Hainsworth, Mtl. | Tiny Thompson, Bos. |
| 1928 | George Hainsworth, Mtl. | Alex Connell, Ott. |
| 1927 | George Hainsworth, Mtl. | Clint Benedict, Mtl.M |

## CALDER MEMORIAL TROPHY

| | Winner | Runner-up |
|---|---|---|
| 2009 | Steve Mason, CBJ | Bobby Ryan, Ana. |
| 2008 | Patrick Kane, Chi. | Nicklas Backstrom, Wsh. |
| 2007 | Evgeni Malkin, Pit. | Paul Stastny, Col. |
| 2006 | Alex Ovechkin, Wsh. | Sidney Crosby, Pit. |
| 2005 | .... | .... |
| 2004 | Andrew Raycroft, Bos. | Michael Ryder, Mtl. |
| 2003 | Barret Jackman, St.L. | Henrik Zetterberg, Det. |
| 2002 | Dany Heatley, Atl. | Ilya Kovalchuk, Atl. |
| 2001 | Evgeni Nabokov, S.J. | Brad Richards, T.B. |
| 2000 | Scott Gomez, N.J. | Brad Stuart, S.J. |
| 1999 | Chris Drury, Col. | Marian Hossa, Ott. |
| 1998 | Sergei Samsonov, Bos. | Mattias Ohlund, Van. |
| 1997 | Bryan Berard, NYI | Jarome Iginla, Cgy. |
| 1996 | Daniel Alfredsson, Ott. | Eric Daze, Chi. |
| 1995 | Peter Forsberg, Que. | Jim Carey, Wsh. |
| 1994 | Martin Brodeur, N.J. | Jason Arnott, Edm. |
| 1993 | Teemu Selanne, Wpg. | Joe Juneau, Bos. |
| 1992 | Pavel Bure, Van. | Nicklas Lidstrom, Det |
| 1991 | Ed Belfour, Chi. | Sergei Fedorov, Det. |
| 1990 | Sergei Makarov, Cgy. | Mike Modano, Min. |
| 1989 | Brian Leetch, NYR | Trevor Linden, Van. |
| 1988 | Joe Nieuwendyk, Cgy. | Ray Sheppard, Buf. |
| 1987 | Luc Robitaille, L.A. | Ron Hextall, Phi. |
| 1986 | Gary Suter, Cgy. | Wendel Clark, Tor. |
| 1985 | Mario Lemieux, Pit. | Chris Chelios, Mtl. |
| 1984 | Tom Barrasso, Buf. | Steve Yzerman, Det. |
| 1983 | Steve Larmer, Chi. | Phil Housley, Buf. |
| 1982 | Dale Hawerchuk, Wpg. | Barry Pederson, Bos. |
| 1981 | Peter Stastny, Que. | Larry Murphy, L.A. |
| 1980 | Raymond Bourque, Bos. | Mike Foligno, Det. |
| 1979 | Bobby Smith, Min | Ryan Walter, Wsh. |
| 1978 | Mike Bossy, NYI | Barry Beck, Col. |
| 1977 | Willi Plett, Atl. | Don Murdoch, NYR |
| 1976 | Bryan Trottier, NYI | Glenn Resch, NYI |
| 1975 | Eric Vail, Atl. | Pierre Larouche, Pit. |
| 1974 | Denis Potvin, NYI | Tom Lysiak, Atl. |
| 1973 | Steve Vickers, NYR | Bill Barber, Phi. |
| 1972 | Ken Dryden, Mtl. | Rick Martin, Buf. |
| 1971 | Gilbert Perreault, Buf. | Jude Drouin, Min. |
| 1970 | Tony Esposito, Chi. | Bill Fairbairn, NYR |
| 1969 | Danny Grant, Min. | Norm Ferguson, Oak. |
| 1968 | Derek Sanderson, Bos. | Jacques Lemaire, Mtl. |
| 1967 | Bobby Orr, Bos. | Ed Van Impe, Chi. |
| 1966 | Brit Selby, Tor. | Bert Marshall, Det. |
| 1965 | Roger Crozier, Det. | Ron Ellis, Tor. |
| 1964 | Jacques Laperriere, Mtl. | John Ferguson, Mtl. |
| 1963 | Kent Douglas, Tor. | Doug Barkley, Det. |
| 1962 | Bobby Rousseau, Mtl. | Cliff Pennington, Bos. |
| 1961 | Dave Keon, Tor. | Bob Nevin, Tor. |
| 1960 | Bill Hay, Chi. | Murray Oliver, Det. |
| 1959 | Ralph Backstrom, Mtl. | Carl Brewer, Tor. |
| 1958 | Frank Mahovlich, Tor. | Bobby Hull, Chi. |
| 1957 | Larry Regan, Bos. | Ed Chadwick, Tor. |
| 1956 | Glenn Hall, Det. | Andy Hebenton, NYR |
| 1955 | Ed Litzenberger, Chi. | Don McKenney, Bos. |
| 1954 | Camille Henry, NYR | Dutch Reibel, Det. |
| 1953 | Gump Worsley, NYR | Gord Hannigan, Tor. |
| 1952 | Bernie Geoffrion, Mtl. | Hy Buller, NYR |
| 1951 | Terry Sawchuk, Det. | Al Rollins, Tor. |
| 1950 | Jack Gelineau, Bos. | Phil Maloney, Bos. |
| 1949 | Pentti Lund, NYR | Allan Stanley, NYR |
| 1948 | Jim McFadden, Det. | Pete Babando, Bos. |
| 1947 | Howie Meeker, Tor. | Jim Conacher, Det. |
| 1946 | Edgar Laprade, NYR | George Gee, Chi. |
| 1945 | Frank McCool, Tor. | Ken Smith, Bos. |
| 1944 | Gus Bodnar, Tor. | Bill Durnan, Mtl. |
| 1943 | Gaye Stewart, Tor. | Glen Harmon, Mtl. |
| 1942 | Grant Warwick, NYR | Buddy O'Connor, Mtl. |
| 1941 | John Quilty, Mtl. | Johnny Mowers, Det. |
| 1940 | Kilby MacDonald, NYR | Wally Stanowski, Tor. |
| 1939 | Frank Brimsek, Bos. | Roy Conacher, Bos. |
| 1938 | Cully Dahlstrom, Chi. | Murph Chamberlain, Tor. |
| 1937 | Syl Apps, Tor. | Gordie Drillon, Tor. |
| 1936 | Mike Karakas, Chi. | Bucko McDonald, Det. |
| 1935 | Sweeney Schriner, NYA | Bert Connelly, NYR |
| 1934 | Russ Blinco, Mtl.M. | none |
| 1933 | Carl Voss, Det. | none |

## NHL LIFETIME ACHEIVEMENT AWARD

| | Winner |
|---|---|
| 2009 | Jean Beliveau |
| 2008 | Gordie Howe |

## MARK MESSIER NHL LEADERSHIP AWARD

| | Winner | |
|---|---|---|
| 2009 | Jarome Iginla | Calgary |
| 2008 | Mats Sundin | Toronto |
| 2007 | Chris Chelios | Detroit |

## NHL FOUNDATION AWARD

| | Winner | |
|---|---|---|
| 2009 | Rick Nash | Columbus |
| 2008 | Trevor Linden | Vancouver |
| | Vincent Lecavalier | Tampa Bay |
| 2007 | Joe Sakic | Colorado |
| 2006 | Marty Turco | Dallas |
| 2004 | Jarome Iginla | Calgary |
| 2003 | Darren McCarty | Detroit |
| 2002 | Ron Francis | Carolina |
| 2001 | Olaf Kolzig | Washington |
| 2000 | Adam Graves | NY Rangers |
| 1999 | Rob Ray | Buffalo |
| 1998 | Kelly Chase | St. Louis |

## CONN SMYTHE TROPHY

| | | |
|---|---|---|
| 2009 | Evgeni Malkin | Pittsburgh |
| 2008 | Henrik Zetterberg | Detroit |
| 2007 | Scott Niedermayer | Anaheim |
| 2006 | Cam Ward | Carolina |
| 2005 | .... | .... |
| 2004 | Brad Richards | Tampa Bay |
| 2003 | Jean-Sebastien Giguere | Anaheim |
| 2002 | Nicklas Lidstrom | Detroit |
| 2001 | Patrick Roy | Colorado |
| 2000 | Scott Stevens | New Jersey |
| 1999 | Joe Nieuwendyk | Dallas |
| 1998 | Steve Yzerman | Detroit |
| 1997 | Mike Vernon | Detroit |
| 1996 | Joe Sakic | Colorado |
| 1995 | Claude Lemieux | New Jersey |
| 1994 | Brian Leetch | NY Rangers |
| 1993 | Patrick Roy | Montreal |
| 1992 | Mario Lemieux | Pittsburgh |
| 1991 | Mario Lemieux | Pittsburgh |
| 1990 | Bill Ranford | Edmonton |
| 1989 | Al MacInnis | Calgary |
| 1988 | Wayne Gretzky | Edmonton |
| 1987 | Ron Hextall | Philadelphia |
| 1986 | Patrick Roy | Montreal |
| 1985 | Wayne Gretzky | Edmonton |
| 1984 | Mark Messier | Edmonton |
| 1983 | Billy Smith | NY Islanders |
| 1982 | Mike Bossy | NY Islanders |
| 1981 | Butch Goring | NY Islanders |
| 1980 | Bryan Trottier | NY Islanders |
| 1979 | Bob Gainey | Montreal |
| 1978 | Larry Robinson | Montreal |
| 1977 | Guy Lafleur | Montreal |
| 1976 | Reggie Leach | Philadelphia |
| 1975 | Bernie Parent | Philadelphia |
| 1974 | Bernie Parent | Philadelphia |
| 1973 | Yvan Cournoyer | Montreal |
| 1972 | Bobby Orr | Boston |
| 1971 | Ken Dryden | Montreal |
| 1970 | Bobby Orr | Boston |
| 1969 | Serge Savard | Montreal |
| 1968 | Glenn Hall | St. Louis |
| 1967 | Dave Keon | Toronto |
| 1966 | Roger Crozier | Detroit |
| 1965 | Jean Beliveau | Montreal |

## JAMES NORRIS MEMORIAL TROPHY

| | Winner | Runner-up |
|---|---|---|
| 2009 | Zdeno Chara, Bos. | Mike Green, Wsh. |
| 2008 | Nicklas Lidstrom, Det. | Dion Phaneuf, Cgy. |
| 2007 | Nicklas Lidstrom, Det. | Scott Niedermayer, Ana. |
| 2006 | Nicklas Lidstrom, Det. | Scott Niedermayer, Ana. |
| 2005 | .... | .... |
| 2004 | Scott Niedermayer, N.J. | Zdeno Chara, Ott. |
| 2003 | Nicklas Lidstrom, Det. | Al MacInnis, St.L. |
| 2002 | Nicklas Lidstrom, Det. | Chris Chelios, Det. |
| 2001 | Nicklas Lidstrom, Det. | Raymond Bourque, Col. |
| 2000 | Chris Pronger, St.L. | Nicklas Lidstrom, Det. |
| 1999 | Al MacInnis, St.L. | Nicklas Lidstrom, Det. |
| 1998 | Rob Blake, L.A. | Nicklas Lidstrom, Det. |
| 1997 | Brian Leetch, NYR | V. Konstantinov, Det. |
| 1996 | Chris Chelios, Chi. | Raymond Bourque, Bos. |
| 1995 | Paul Coffey, Det. | Chris Chelios, Chi. |
| 1994 | Raymond Bourque, Bos. | Scott Stevens, N.J. |
| 1993 | Chris Chelios, Chi. | Raymond Bourque, Bos. |
| 1992 | Brian Leetch, NYR | Raymond Bourque, Bos. |
| 1991 | Raymond Bourque, Bos. | Al MacInnis, Cgy. |
| 1990 | Raymond Bourque, Bos. | Al MacInnis, Cgy. |
| 1989 | Chris Chelios, Mtl | Paul Coffey, Pit. |
| 1988 | Raymond Bourque, Bos. | Scott Stevens, Wsh. |
| 1987 | Raymond Bourque, Bos. | Mark Howe, Phi. |
| 1986 | Paul Coffey, Edm. | Mark Howe, Phi. |
| 1985 | Paul Coffey, Edm. | Raymond Bourque, Bos. |
| 1984 | Rod Langway, Wsh. | Paul Coffey, Edm. |
| 1983 | Rod Langway, Wsh. | Mark Howe, Phi. |
| 1982 | Doug Wilson, Chi. | Raymond Bourque, Bos. |
| 1981 | Randy Carlyle, Pit. | Denis Potvin, NYI |
| 1980 | Larry Robinson, Mtl. | Borje Salming, Tor. |
| 1979 | Denis Potvin, NYI | Larry Robinson, Mtl. |
| 1978 | Denis Potvin, NYI | Brad Park, Bos. |
| 1977 | Larry Robinson, Mtl. | Borje Salming, Tor. |
| 1976 | Denis Potvin, NYI | Brad Park, NYR-Bos. |
| 1975 | Bobby Orr, Bos. | Denis Potvin, NYI |
| 1974 | Bobby Orr, Bos. | Brad Park, NYR |
| 1973 | Bobby Orr, Bos. | Guy Lapointe, Mtl. |
| 1972 | Bobby Orr, Bos. | Brad Park, NYR |
| 1971 | Bobby Orr, Bos. | Brad Park, NYR |
| 1970 | Bobby Orr, Bos. | Brad Park, NYR |
| 1969 | Bobby Orr, Bos. | Tim Horton, Tor. |
| 1968 | Bobby Orr, Bos. | J.C. Tremblay, Mtl |
| 1967 | Harry Howell, NYR | Pierre Pilote, Chi. |
| 1966 | Jacques Laperriere, Mtl. | Pierre Pilote, Chi. |
| 1965 | Pierre Pilote, Chi. | Jacques Laperriere, Mtl. |
| 1964 | Pierre Pilote, Chi. | Tim Horton, Tor. |
| 1963 | Pierre Pilote, Chi. | Carl Brewer, Tor. |
| 1962 | Doug Harvey, NYR | Pierre Pilote, Chi. |
| 1961 | Doug Harvey, Mtl. | Marcel Pronovost, Det. |
| 1960 | Doug Harvey, Mtl. | Allan Stanley, Tor. |
| 1959 | Tom Johnson, Mtl. | Bill Gadsby, NYR |
| 1958 | Doug Harvey, Mtl. | Bill Gadsby, NYR |
| 1957 | Doug Harvey, Mtl. | Red Kelly, Det. |
| 1956 | Doug Harvey, Mtl. | Bill Gadsby, NYR |
| 1955 | Doug Harvey, Mtl. | Red Kelly, Det. |
| 1954 | Red Kelly, Det. | Doug Harvey, Mtl. |

## LESTER PATRICK TROPHY

| | | |
|---|---|---|
| 2009 | Mark Messier | Jim Devellano |
| | Mike Richter | |
| 2008 | Brian Burke | Phil Housley |
| | Ted Lindsay | Bob Naegele, Jr. |
| 2007 | Brian Leetch | Cammi Granato |
| | Stan Fischler | John Halligan |
| 2006 | Red Berenson | Marcel Dionne |
| | Reed Larson | Glen Sonmor |
| | Steve Yzerman | |
| 2005 | .... | |
| 2004 | John Davidson | Mike Emrick |
| | Ray Miron | |
| 2003 | Raymond Bourque | Ron DeGregorio |
| | Willie O'Ree | |
| 2002 | Herb Brooks | Larry Pleau |
| | 1960 U.S. Olympic Team | |
| 2001 | Gary Bettman | Scotty Bowman |
| | David Poile | |
| 2000 | Mario Lemieux | Craig Patrick |
| | Lou Vairo | |
| 1999 | Harry Sinden | |
| | 1998 U.S. Olympic Women's Team | |
| 1998 | Neal Broten | Peter Karmanos |
| | John Mayasich | Max McNab |
| 1997 | Bill Cleary | * Seymour H. Knox III |
| | Pat LaFontaine | |
| 1996 | George Gund | Ken Morrow |
| | Milt Schmidt | |
| 1995 | Bob Fleming | Brian Mullen |
| | Joe Mullen | |
| 1994 | Wayne Gretzky | Robert Ridder |
| 1993 | *Frank Boucher | * Mervyn "Red" Dutton |
| | Bruce McNall | Gil Stein |
| 1992 | Al Arbour | Art Berglund |
| | Lou Lamoriello | |
| 1991 | Rod Gilbert | Mike Ilitch |
| 1990 | Len Ceglarski | |
| 1989 | Dan Kelly | Lou Nanne |
| | *Lynn Patrick | Bud Poile |
| 1988 | Keith Allen | Fred Cusick |
| | Bob Johnson | |
| 1987 | *Hobey Baker | Frank Mathers |
| 1986 | John MacInnes | Jack Riley |
| 1985 | Jack Butterfield | Arthur M. Wirtz |
| 1984 | *Arthur Howey Ross | John A. Ziegler, Jr. |
| 1983 | Bill Torrey | |
| 1982 | Emile P. Francis | |
| 1981 | Charles M. Schulz | |
| 1980 | Bobby Clarke | Frederick A. Shero |
| | Edward M. Snider | 1980 U.S. Olympic Team |
| 1979 | Bobby Orr | |
| 1978 | Phil Esposito | Tom Fitzgerald |
| | William T. Tutt | William W. Wirtz |
| 1977 | Murray A. Armstrong | John P. Bucyk |
| | John Mariucci | |
| 1976 | George A. Leader | Stanley Mikita |
| | Bruce A. Norris | |
| 1975 | William L. Chadwick | Donald M. Clark |
| | Thomas N. Ivan | |
| 1974 | *Weston W. Adams, Sr. | * Charles L. Crovat |
| | Alex Delvecchio | Murray Murdoch |
| 1973 | Walter L. Bush, Jr. | |
| 1972 | Clarence S. Campbell | John A. "Snooks" Kelly |
| | *James D. Norris | Ralph "Cooney" Weiland |
| 1971 | William M. Jennings | * Terrance G. Sawchuk |
| | *John B. Sollenberger | |
| 1970 | *James C. V. Hendy | Edward W. Shore |
| 1969 | Robert M. Hull | * Edward J. Jeremiah |
| 1968 | *Walter A. Brown | * Gen. John R. Kilpatrick |
| | Thomas F. Lockhart | |
| 1967 | *Charles F. Adams | Gordon Howe |
| | *James Norris, Sr. | |
| 1966 | J.J. "Jack" Adams | |

* awarded posthumously

## FRANK J. SELKE TROPHY

| | Winner | Runner-up |
|---|---|---|
| 2009 | Pavel Datsyuk, Det. | Mike Richards, Wsh. |
| 2008 | Pavel Datsyuk, Det. | John Madden, N.J. |
| 2007 | Rod Brind'Amour, Car. | Samuel Pahlsson, Ana. |
| 2006 | Rod Brind'Amour, Car. | Jere Lehtinen, Dal. |
| 2005 | .... | .... |
| 2004 | Kris Draper, Det. | John Madden, N.J. |
| 2003 | Jere Lehtinen, Dal. | John Madden, N.J. |
| 2002 | Michael Peca, NYI | Craig Conroy, Cgy. |
| 2001 | John Madden, N.J. | Joe Sakic, Col. |
| 2000 | Steve Yzerman, Det. | Michal Handzus, St.L. |
| 1999 | Jere Lehtinen, Dal. | Magnus Arvedson, Ott. |
| 1998 | Jere Lehtinen, Dal. | Michael Peca, Buf. |
| 1997 | Michael Peca, Buf. | Peter Forsberg, Col. |
| 1996 | Sergei Fedorov, Det. | Ron Francis, Pit. |
| 1995 | Ron Francis, Pit. | Esa Tikkanen, St.L. |
| 1994 | Sergei Fedorov, Det. | Doug Gilmour, Tor. |
| 1993 | Doug Gilmour, Tor. | Dave Poulin, Bos. |
| 1992 | Guy Carbonneau, Mtl. | Sergei Fedorov, Det. |
| 1991 | Dirk Graham, Chi. | Esa Tikkanen, Edm. |
| 1990 | Rick Meagher, St.L. | Guy Carbonneau, Mtl. |
| 1989 | Guy Carbonneau, Mtl. | Esa Tikkanen, Edm. |
| 1988 | Guy Carbonneau, Mtl. | Steve Kasper, Bos. |
| 1987 | Dave Poulin, Phi. | Guy Carbonneau, Mtl. |
| 1986 | Troy Murray, Chi. | Ron Sutter, Phi. |
| 1985 | Craig Ramsay, Buf. | Doug Jarvis, Wsh. |
| 1984 | Doug Jarvis, Wsh. | Bryan Trottier, NYI |
| 1983 | Bobby Clarke, Phi. | Jari Kurri, Edm. |
| 1982 | Steve Kasper, Bos. | Bob Gainey, Mtl. |
| 1981 | Bob Gainey, Mtl. | Craig Ramsay, Buf. |
| 1980 | Bob Gainey, Mtl. | Craig Ramsay, Buf. |
| 1979 | Bob Gainey, Mtl. | Don Marcotte, Bos. |
| 1978 | Bob Gainey, Mtl. | Craig Ramsay, Buf. |

## PRESIDENTS' TROPHY

| | Winner | Runner-up |
|---|---|---|
| 2009 | San Jose Sharks | Boston Bruins |
| 2008 | Detroit Red Wings | San Jose Sharks |
| 2007 | Buffalo Sabres | Detroit Red Wings |
| 2006 | Detroit Red Wings | Ottawa Senators |
| 2005 | .... | .... |
| 2004 | Detroit Red Wings | Tampa Bay Lightning |
| 2003 | Ottawa Senators | Dallas Stars |
| 2002 | Detroit Red Wings | Boston Bruins |
| 2001 | Colorado Avalanche | Detroit Red Wings |
| 2000 | St. Louis Blues | Detroit Red Wings |
| 1999 | Dallas Stars | New Jersey Devils |
| 1998 | Dallas Stars | New Jersey Devils |
| 1997 | Colorado Avalanche | Dallas Stars |
| 1996 | Detroit Red Wings | Colorado Avalanche |
| 1995 | Detroit Red Wings | Quebec Nordiques |
| 1994 | New York Rangers | New Jersey Devils |
| 1993 | Pittsburgh Penguins | Boston Bruins |
| 1992 | New York Rangers | Washington Capitals |
| 1991 | Chicago Blackhawks | St. Louis Blues |
| 1990 | Boston Bruins | Calgary Flames |
| 1989 | Calgary Flames | Montreal Canadiens |
| 1988 | Calgary Flames | Montreal Canadiens |
| 1987 | Edmonton Oilers | Philadelphia Flyers |
| 1986 | Edmonton Oilers | Philadelphia Flyers |

## LESTER B. PEARSON AWARD

| | | |
|---|---|---|
| 2009 | Alex Ovechkin | Washington |
| 2008 | Alex Ovechkin | Washington |
| 2007 | Sidney Crosby | Pittsburgh |
| 2006 | Jaromir Jagr | NY Rangers |
| 2005 | .... | .... |
| 2004 | Martin St. Louis | Tampa Bay |
| 2003 | Markus Naslund | Vancouver |
| 2002 | Jarome Iginla | Calgary |
| 2001 | Joe Sakic | Colorado |
| 2000 | Jaromir Jagr | Pittsburgh |
| 1999 | Jaromir Jagr | Pittsburgh |
| 1998 | Dominik Hasek | Buffalo |
| 1997 | Dominik Hasek | Buffalo |
| 1996 | Mario Lemieux | Pittsburgh |
| 1995 | Eric Lindros | Philadelphia |
| 1994 | Sergei Fedorov | Detroit |
| 1993 | Mario Lemieux | Pittsburgh |
| 1992 | Mark Messier | NY Rangers |
| 1991 | Brett Hull | St. Louis |
| 1990 | Mark Messier | Edmonton |
| 1989 | Steve Yzerman | Detroit |
| 1988 | Mario Lemieux | Pittsburgh |
| 1987 | Wayne Gretzky | Edmonton |
| 1986 | Mario Lemieux | Pittsburgh |
| 1985 | Wayne Gretzky | Edmonton |
| 1984 | Wayne Gretzky | Edmonton |
| 1983 | Wayne Gretzky | Edmonton |
| 1982 | Wayne Gretzky | Edmonton |
| 1981 | Mike Liut | St. Louis |
| 1980 | Marcel Dionne | Los Angeles |
| 1979 | Marcel Dionne | Los Angeles |
| 1978 | Guy Lafleur | Montreal |
| 1977 | Guy Lafleur | Montreal |
| 1976 | Guy Lafleur | Montreal |
| 1975 | Bobby Orr | Boston |
| 1974 | Phil Esposito | Boston |
| 1973 | Bobby Clarke | Philadelphia |
| 1972 | Jean Ratelle | NY Rangers |
| 1971 | Phil Esposito | Boston |

## JACK ADAMS AWARD

| | Winner | Runner-up |
|---|---|---|
| 2009 | Claude Julien, Bos. | Andy Murray, St.L. |
| 2008 | Bruce Boudreau, Wsh. | Guy Carbonneau, Mtl. |
| 2007 | Alain Vigneault, Van. | Lindy Ruff, Buf. |
| 2006 | Lindy Ruff, Buf. | Peter Laviolette, Car. |
| 2005 | .... | .... |
| 2004 | John Tortorella, T.B. | Ron Wilson, S.J. |
| 2003 | Jacques Lemaire, Min. | John Tortorella, T.B. |
| 2002 | Bob Francis, Phx. | Brian Sutter, Chi. |
| 2001 | Bill Barber, Phi. | Scotty Bowman, Det. |
| 2000 | Joel Quenneville, St.L. | Alain Vigneault, Mtl. |
| 1999 | Jacques Martin, Ott. | Pat Quinn, Tor. |
| 1998 | Pat Burns, Bos. | Larry Robinson, L.A. |
| 1997 | Ted Nolan, Buf. | Ken Hitchcock, Dal. |
| 1996 | Scotty Bowman, Det. | Doug MacLean, Fla. |
| 1995 | Marc Crawford, Que. | Scotty Bowman, Det. |
| 1994 | Jacques Lemaire, N.J. | Kevin Constantine, S.J. |
| 1993 | Pat Burns, Tor. | Brian Sutter, Bos. |
| 1992 | Pat Quinn, Van. | Roger Neilson, NYR |
| 1991 | Brian Sutter, St.L. | Tom Webster, L.A. |
| 1990 | Bob Murdoch, Wpg. | Mike Milbury, Bos. |
| 1989 | Pat Burns, Mtl. | Bob McCammon, Van. |
| 1988 | Jacques Demers, Det. | Terry Crisp, Cgy. |
| 1987 | Jacques Demers, Det. | Jack Evans, Hfd. |
| 1986 | Glen Sather, Edm. | Jacques Demers, St.L. |
| 1985 | Mike Keenan, Phi. | Barry Long, Wpg. |
| 1984 | Bryan Murray, Wsh. | Scotty Bowman, Buf. |
| 1983 | Orval Tessier, Chi. | |
| 1982 | Tom Watt, Wpg. | |
| 1981 | Red Berenson, St.L. | Bob Berry, L.A. |
| 1980 | Pat Quinn, Phi. | |
| 1979 | Al Arbour, NYI | Fred Shero, NYR |
| 1978 | Bobby Kromm, Det. | Don Cherry, Bos. |
| 1977 | Scotty Bowman, Mtl. | Tom McVie, Wsh. |
| 1976 | Don Cherry, Bos. | |
| 1975 | Bob Pulford, L.A. | |
| 1974 | Fred Shero, Phi. | |

# NHL Entry Draft

## Draft Summary

Following is a summary of the players drafted from the Ontario Hockey League (OHL), Quebec Major Junior Hockey League (QMJHL), Western Hockey League (WHL), United States colleges, United States high schools, European leagues and other North American leagues since 1969. "Other" may include Canadian and U.S. Jr. A and Jr. B, minor professional leagues (AHL, IHL), midget and other teams playing in leagues not listed above.

| Year | Total | OHL | | QMJHL | | WHL | | College | | Hi School | | Int'l | | Other | |
|---|---|---|---|---|---|---|---|---|---|---|---|---|---|---|---|
| | Picks | Picks | % | Picks | % | Picks | % | Picks | % | Picks | % | Picks | % | Picks | % |
| 1969 | 84 | 36 | 42.9 | 11 | 13.1 | 20 | 23.8 | 7 | 8.3 | - | - | 1 | 1.2 | 9 | 10.7 |
| 1970 | 115 | 51 | 44.3 | 13 | 11.3 | 22 | 19.1 | 16 | 13.9 | - | - | - | - | 13 | 11.3 |
| 1971 | 117 | 41 | 35.0 | 13 | 11.1 | 28 | 23.9 | 22 | 18.8 | - | - | - | - | 13 | 11.1 |
| 1972 | 152 | 46 | 30.3 | 30 | 19.7 | 44 | 28.9 | 21 | 13.8 | - | - | - | - | 11 | 7.2 |
| 1973 | 168 | 56 | 33.3 | 24 | 14.3 | 49 | 29.2 | 25 | 14.9 | - | - | - | - | 14 | 8.3 |
| 1974 | 247 | 69 | 27.9 | 40 | 16.2 | 66 | 26.7 | 41 | 16.6 | - | - | 6 | 2.4 | 25 | 10.1 |
| 1975 | 217 | 55 | 25.3 | 28 | 12.9 | 57 | 26.3 | 59 | 27.2 | - | - | 6 | 2.8 | 12 | 5.5 |
| 1976 | 135 | 47 | 34.8 | 18 | 13.3 | 33 | 24.4 | 26 | 19.3 | - | - | 8 | 5.9 | 3 | 2.2 |
| 1977 | 185 | 42 | 22.7 | 40 | 21.6 | 44 | 23.8 | 49 | 26.5 | - | - | 5 | 2.7 | 5 | 2.7 |
| 1978 | 234 | 59 | 25.2 | 22 | 9.4 | 48 | 20.5 | 73 | 31.2 | - | - | 16 | 6.8 | 16 | 6.8 |
| 1979 | 126 | 48 | 38.1 | 19 | 15.1 | 37 | 29.4 | 15 | 11.9 | - | - | 6 | 4.8 | 1 | 0.8 |
| 1980 | 210 | 73 | 34.8 | 24 | 11.4 | 41 | 19.5 | 42 | 20.0 | 7 | 3.3 | 13 | 6.2 | 10 | 4.8 |
| 1981 | 211 | 59 | 28.0 | 28 | 13.3 | 37 | 17.5 | 21 | 10.0 | 17 | 8.1 | 32 | 15.2 | 17 | 8.1 |
| 1982 | 252 | 60 | 23.8 | 17 | 6.7 | 55 | 21.8 | 20 | 7.9 | 47 | 18.7 | 35 | 13.9 | 18 | 7.1 |
| 1983 | 242 | 57 | 23.6 | 24 | 9.9 | 41 | 16.9 | 14 | 5.8 | 35 | 14.5 | 34 | 14.0 | 37 | 15.3 |
| 1984 | 250 | 55 | 22.0 | 16 | 6.4 | 37 | 14.8 | 22 | 8.8 | 44 | 17.6 | 40 | 16.0 | 36 | 14.4 |
| 1985 | 252 | 59 | 23.4 | 15 | 6.0 | 48 | 19.0 | 20 | 7.9 | 48 | 19.0 | 31 | 12.3 | 31 | 12.3 |
| 1986 | 252 | 66 | 26.2 | 22 | 8.7 | 32 | 12.7 | 22 | 8.7 | 40 | 15.9 | 28 | 11.1 | 42 | 16.7 |
| 1987 | 252 | 32 | 12.7 | 17 | 6.7 | 36 | 14.3 | 40 | 15.9 | 69 | 27.4 | 38 | 15.1 | 20 | 7.9 |
| 1988 | 252 | 32 | 12.7 | 22 | 8.7 | 30 | 11.9 | 48 | 19.0 | 56 | 22.2 | 39 | 15.5 | 25 | 9.9 |
| 1989 | 252 | 39 | 15.5 | 16 | 6.3 | 44 | 17.5 | 48 | 19.0 | 47 | 18.7 | 38 | 15.1 | 20 | 7.9 |
| 1990 | 250 | 39 | 15.6 | 14 | 5.6 | 33 | 13.2 | 38 | 15.2 | 57 | 22.8 | 53 | 21.2 | 16 | 6.4 |
| 1991 | 264 | 43 | 16.3 | 25 | 9.5 | 40 | 15.2 | 43 | 16.3 | 37 | 14.0 | 55 | 20.8 | 21 | 8.0 |
| 1992 | 264 | 57 | 21.6 | 22 | 8.3 | 45 | 17.0 | 9 | 3.4 | 25 | 9.5 | 84 | 31.8 | 22 | 8.3 |
| 1993 | 286 | 60 | 21.0 | 23 | 8.0 | 44 | 15.4 | 17 | 5.9 | 33 | 11.5 | 78 | 27.3 | 31 | 10.8 |
| 1994 | 286 | 45 | 15.7 | 28 | 9.8 | 66 | 23.1 | 6 | 2.1 | 28 | 9.8 | 80 | 28.0 | 33 | 11.5 |
| 1995 | 234 | 54 | 23.1 | 35 | 15.0 | 55 | 23.5 | 5 | 2.1 | 2 | 0.9 | 69 | 29.5 | 14 | 6.0 |
| 1996 | 241 | 51 | 21.2 | 31 | 12.9 | 54 | 22.4 | 25 | 10.4 | 6 | 2.5 | 58 | 24.1 | 16 | 6.6 |
| 1997 | 246 | 52 | 21.1 | 19 | 7.7 | 63 | 25.6 | 26 | 10.6 | 4 | 1.6 | 63 | 25.6 | 19 | 7.7 |
| 1998 | 258 | 50 | 19.4 | 41 | 15.9 | 44 | 17.1 | 27 | 10.5 | 7 | 2.7 | 75 | 29.1 | 14 | 5.4 |
| 1999 | 272 | 52 | 19.1 | 20 | 7.4 | 40 | 14.7 | 36 | 13.2 | 9 | 3.3 | 94 | 34.6 | 21 | 7.7 |
| 2000 | 293 | 39 | 13.3 | 21 | 7.2 | 41 | 14.0 | 35 | 11.9 | 7 | 2.4 | 123 | 42.0 | 27 | 9.2 |
| 2001 | 289 | 41 | 14.2 | 26 | 9.0 | 45 | 15.6 | 24 | 8.3 | 8 | 2.8 | 119 | 41.2 | 26 | 9.0 |
| 2002 | 290 | 35 | 12.1 | 23 | 7.9 | 43 | 14.8 | 41 | 14.1 | 6 | 2.1 | 110 | 37.9 | 32 | 11.0 |
| 2003 | 292 | 44 | 15.1 | 38 | 13.0 | 41 | 14.0 | 23 | 7.9 | 10 | 3.4 | 93 | 31.8 | 43 | 14.7 |
| 2004 | 291 | 42 | 14.4 | 27 | 9.3 | 44 | 15.1 | 28 | 9.6 | 18 | 6.2 | 88 | 30.2 | 44 | 15.1 |
| 2005 | 230 | 43 | 18.7 | 23 | 10.0 | 43 | 18.7 | 13 | 5.6 | 18 | 7.8 | 50 | 21.7 | 40 | 17.4 |
| 2006 | 213 | 29 | 13.6 | 25 | 11.7 | 24 | 11.2 | 18 | 8.4 | 19 | 8.9 | 63 | 29.5 | 35 | 16.4 |
| 2007 | 211 | 35 | 16.6 | 25 | 11.8 | 37 | 17.5 | 8 | 3.8 | 14 | 6.6 | 36 | 17.0 | 56 | 56.5 |
| 2008 | 211 | 46 | 21.8 | 27 | 12.8 | 37 | 17.5 | 9 | 4.2 | 15 | 7.1 | 39 | 18.5 | 38 | 18.0 |
| 2009 | 210 | 45 | 21.4 | 23 | 11.0 | 31 | 14.8 | 7 | 3.3 | 19 | 9.0 | 41 | 19.5 | 44 | 21.0 |
| **Total** | | **1984** | **21.3** | **975** | **10.4** | **1719** | **18.4** | **1089** | **11.7** | **752** | **8.1** | **1847** | **19.8** | **970** | **10.4** |

### Total Players Drafted (1969-2009): 9,336

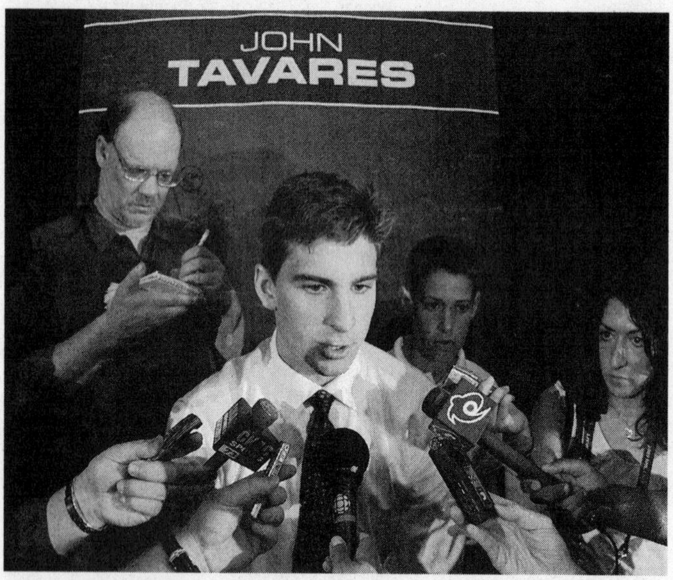


*Reporters and microphones surround John Tavares the day before the 2009 NHL Entry Draft in Montreal. Tavares had been touted as a future #1 pick since he was 14 years old, but the New York Islanders managed to keep their intentions to themselves despite all the media attention. On draft day, Islanders general manager Garth Snow confirmed Tavares as the top pick.*

## History

| Year | Location | Date | Players Drafted |
|---|---|---|---|
| 1963–1968 | Montreal | — | 122 |
| 1969 | Queen Elizabeth Hotel, Montreal | June 12 | 84 |
| 1970 | Queen Elizabeth Hotel, Montreal | June 11 | 115 |
| 1971 | Queen Elizabeth Hotel, Montreal | June 10 | 117 |
| 1972 | Queen Elizabeth Hotel, Montreal | June 8 | 152 |
| 1973 | Mount Royal Hotel, Montreal | May 15 | 168 |
| 1974 | NHL Montreal Office | May 28 | 247 |
| 1975 | NHL Montreal Office | June 3 | 217 |
| 1976 | NHL Montreal Office | June 1 | 135 |
| 1977 | NHL Montreal Office | June 14 | 185 |
| 1978 | Queen Elizabeth Hotel, Montreal | June 15 | 234 |
| 1979 | Queen Elizabeth Hotel, Montreal | August 9 | 126 |
| 1980 | Montreal Forum | June 11 | 210 |
| 1981 | Montreal Forum | June 10 | 211 |
| 1982 | Montreal Forum | June 9 | 252 |
| 1983 | Montreal Forum | June 8 | 242 |
| 1984 | Montreal Forum | June 9 | 250 |
| 1985 | Toronto Convention Centre | June 15 | 252 |
| 1986 | Montreal Forum | June 21 | 252 |
| 1987 | Joe Louis Arena, Detroit | June 13 | 252 |
| 1988 | Montreal Forum | June 11 | 252 |
| 1989 | Met Sports Center, Minnesota | June 17 | 252 |
| 1990 | B.C. Place, Vancouver | June 16 | 250 |
| 1991 | Memorial Auditorium, Buffalo | June 22 | 264 |
| 1992 | Montreal Forum | June 20 | 264 |
| 1993 | Le Colisée, Quebec | June 26 | 286 |
| 1994 | Hartford Civic Center | June 28-29 | 286 |
| 1995 | Edmonton Coliseum | July 8 | 234 |
| 1996 | Kiel Center, St. Louis | June 22 | 241 |
| 1997 | Civic Arena, Pittsburgh | June 21 | 246 |
| 1998 | Marine Midland Arena, Buffalo | June 27 | 258 |
| 1999 | FleetCenter, Boston | June 26 | 272 |
| 2000 | Saddledome, Calgary | June 24-25 | 293 |
| 2001 | National Car Rental Center, Florida | June 23-24 | 289 |
| 2002 | Air Canada Centre, Toronto | June 22-23 | 290 |
| 2003 | Gaylord Entertainment Center, Nashville | June 21-22 | 292 |
| 2004 | RBC Center, Carolina | June 26-27 | 291 |
| 2005 | Sheraton Hotel and Towers, Ottawa | July 30 | 230 |
| 2006 | General Motors Place, Vancouver | June 24 | 213 |
| 2007 | Nationwide Arena, Columbus | June 22-23 | 211 |
| 2008 | Scotiabank Place, Ottawa | June 20-21 | 211 |
| 2009 | Bell Centre, Montreal | June 26-27 | 210 |

## First Selections

| Year | Player | Pos | Team | Drafted From | Age |
|---|---|---|---|---|---|
| 1963 | Garry Monahan | LW | Montreal | St. Michael's Juveniles | 16.7 |
| 1964 | Claude Gauthier | | Detroit | Comite des jeunes (Rosemont) | |
| 1965 | Andre Veilleux | RW | NY Rangers | Montreal Ranger Jr. B | |
| 1966 | Barry Gibbs | D | Boston | Estevan Bruins | 17.7 |
| 1967 | Rick Pagnutti | D | Los Angeles | Garson Native Sons | 20.6 |
| 1968 | Michel Plasse | G | Montreal | Drummondville Rangers | 20.0 |
| 1969 | Rejean Houle | LW | Montreal | Montreal Jr. Canadiens | 19.8 |
| 1970 | Gilbert Perreault | C | Buffalo | Montreal Jr. Canadiens | 19.7 |
| 1971 | Guy Lafleur | RW | Montreal | Quebec Remparts | 19.9 |
| 1972 | Billy Harris | RW | NY Islanders | Toronto Marlboros | 20.4 |
| 1973 | Denis Potvin | D | NY Islanders | Ottawa 67's | 19.7 |
| 1974 | Greg Joly | D | Washington | Regina Pats | 20.0 |
| 1975 | Mel Bridgman | C | Philadelphia | Victoria Cougars | 20.1 |
| 1976 | Rick Green | D | Washington | London Knights | 20.3 |
| 1977 | Dale McCourt | C | Detroit | St. Catharines Fincups | 20.4 |
| 1978 | Bobby Smith | C | Minnesota | Ottawa 67's | 20.4 |
| 1979 | Rob Ramage | D | Colorado | London Knights | 20.5 |
| 1980 | Doug Wickenheiser | C | Montreal | Regina Pats | 19.2 |
| 1981 | Dale Hawerchuk | C | Winnipeg | Cornwall Royals | 18.2 |
| 1982 | Gord Kluzak | D | Boston | Nanaimo Islanders | 18.3 |
| 1983 | Brian Lawton | C | Minnesota | Mount St. Charles HS | 18.11 |
| 1984 | Mario Lemieux | C | Pittsburgh | Laval Voisins | 18.8 |
| 1985 | Wendel Clark | LW/D | Toronto | Saskatoon Blades | 18.7 |
| 1986 | Joe Murphy | C | Detroit | Michigan State Spartans | 18.8 |
| 1987 | Pierre Turgeon | C | Buffalo | Granby Bisons | 17.10 |
| 1988 | Mike Modano | C | Minnesota | Prince Albert Raiders | 18.0 |
| 1989 | Mats Sundin | RW | Quebec | Nacka (Sweden) | 18.4 |
| 1990 | Owen Nolan | RW | Quebec | Cornwall Royals | 18.4 |
| 1991 | Eric Lindros | C | Quebec | Oshawa Generals | 18.3 |
| 1992 | Roman Hamrlik | D | Tampa Bay | ZPS Zlin (Czech.) | 18.2 |
| 1993 | Alexandre Daigle | C | Ottawa | Victoriaville Tigres | 18.5 |
| 1994 | Ed Jovanovski | D | Florida | Windsor Spitfires | 18.0 |
| 1995 | Bryan Berard | D | Ottawa | Detroit Jr. Red Wings | 18.4 |
| 1996 | Chris Phillips | D | Ottawa | Prince Albert Raiders | 18.3 |
| 1997 | Joe Thornton | C | Boston | Sault Ste. Marie Greyhounds | 17.11 |
| 1998 | Vincent Lecavalier | C | Tampa Bay | Rimouski Oceanic | 18.2 |
| 1999 | Patrik Stefan | C | Atlanta | Long Beach Ice Dogs (IHL) | 18.9 |
| 2000 | Rick DiPietro | G | NY Islanders | Boston University Terriers | 18.9 |
| 2001 | Ilya Kovalchuk | LW | Atlanta | Spartak (Russia) | 18.2 |
| 2002 | Rick Nash | LW | Columbus | London Knights | 18.0 |
| 2003 | Marc-Andre Fleury | G | Pittsburgh | Cape Breton Screaming Eagles | 18.0 |
| 2004 | Alex Ovechkin | LW | Washington | Dynamo Moscow (Russia) | 18.9 |
| 2005 | Sidney Crosby | C | Pittsburgh | Rimouski Oceanic | 17.11 |
| 2006 | Erik Johnson | D | St. Louis | U.S. National U-18 | 18.3 |
| 2007 | Patrick Kane | RW | Chicago | London Knights | 18.7 |
| 2008 | Steven Stamkos | C | Tampa Bay | Sarnia Sting | 18.4 |
| 2009 | John Tavares | C | NY Islanders | London Knights | 18.9 |

## Ontario Hockey League Draft Selections by Club

| Total | Club | '09 | '08 | '07 | '06 | '05 | '04 | '03 | '02 | '01 | '00 | '99 | '98 | '97 | '96 | '95 | '94 | '93 | '92 | '91 | '90 | '89 | '88 | '87 | '86 | '85 | '84 | '83 | '82 | '81 | '80 | '79 | '69 to '78 |
|---|---|---|---|---|---|---|---|---|---|---|---|---|---|---|---|---|---|---|---|---|---|---|---|---|---|---|---|---|---|---|---|---|---|
| 26 | Barrie | 2 | 2 | – | 1 | – | – | 1 | 1 | 1 | 3 | 6 | 3 | 4 | 2 | – | – | – | – | – | – | – | – | – | – | – | – | – | – | – | – | – | – |
| 65 | Belleville | 1 | 3 | 4 | 2 | 2 | – | – | 2 | 3 | 1 | 5 | 2 | 5 | – | 3 | 3 | – | 4 | 1 | 2 | 4 | – | 2 | 5 | 4 | 4 | 3 | – | – | – | – | – |
| 33 | Brampton | 2 | 3 | – | 4 | 4 | 2 | 4 | 3 | 3 | 6 | 2 | – | – | – | – | – | – | – | – | – | – | – | – | – | – | – | – | – | – | – | – | – |
| 26 | Erie | 3 | 1 | 5 | – | 2 | 2 | – | 2 | 2 | 3 | 2 | 1 | 3 | – | – | – | – | – | – | – | – | – | – | – | – | – | – | – | – | – | – | – |
| 76 | Guelph | 5 | 3 | 1 | 1 | 2 | 2 | 1 | 2 | 4 | 1 | 3 | 5 | 1 | 6 | 5 | 7 | 2 | 2 | – | – | 4 | – | 2 | 8 | 3 | 5 | 1 | – | – | – | – | – |
| 101 | Kingston | 2 | 2 | – | 4 | 2 | – | 1 | 1 | 2 | – | 4 | 1 | 4 | 4 | 3 | 2 | 5 | 3 | 2 | 2 | – | 1 | 1 | 4 | 3 | 3 | 1 | 2 | 5 | 8 | 2 | 27 |
| 143 | Kitchener | 1 | 2 | 4 | – | 4 | 2 | 1 | 4 | 1 | 1 | – | 5 | 3 | 2 | 4 | 2 | 4 | 1 | 3 | 5 | 7 | 1 | 2 | 3 | 6 | 4 | 8 | 5 | 5 | 4 | 4 | 45 |
| 145 | London | 3 | 1 | 3 | 1 | 3 | 6 | 4 | 2 | 2 | 1 | 4 | 8 | 1 | 4 | 1 | 1 | 4 | 3 | 1 | 3 | 3 | 6 | 2 | 3 | 1 | 7 | 3 | 5 | 5 | 2 | 6 | 46 |
| 13 | Niagara/Mississauga | – | 1 | 3 | 1 | 1 | 3 | 2 | – | – | 2 | – | – | – | – | – | – | – | – | – | – | – | – | – | – | – | – | – | – | – | – | – | – |
| 153 | Oshawa | 3 | 2 | 2 | 2 | – | 3 | 3 | 3 | 1 | 2 | 3 | 4 | 3 | 1 | 10 | 1 | 4 | 4 | 4 | 2 | 4 | 2 | 3 | 6 | 6 | 6 | 5 | 5 | 9 | 2 | 3 | 45 |
| 136 | Ottawa | 1 | 2 | 1 | 1 | 2 | 3 | 2 | – | 3 | 2 | 6 | 2 | 5 | 2 | 1 | 1 | 4 | 6 | 5 | 5 | – | 1 | 2 | 3 | 3 | 2 | 2 | 9 | 4 | 8 | 3 | 45 |
| 32 | Owen Sound | 3 | 1 | 1 | 2 | 2 | 1 | 1 | 1 | – | 1 | – | 1 | 2 | 3 | 2 | 3 | 4 | 2 | 1 | 1 | – | – | – | – | – | – | – | – | – | – | – | 0 |
| 166 | Peterborough | 2 | 2 | 1 | 1 | 2 | 5 | 5 | 1 | 2 | 1 | 4 | 1 | 5 | 4 | 5 | 2 | 4 | 4 | 3 | 4 | 2 | 2 | 5 | 2 | 9 | 3 | 7 | 5 | 3 | 10 | 9 | 51 |
| 60 | Plymouth | 2 | 2 | 3 | 2 | 3 | 3 | 3 | 3 | 3 | 6 | 2 | 2 | 4 | 3 | 6 | 2 | 7 | 2 | 2 | – | – | – | – | – | – | – | – | – | – | – | – | – |
| 70 | Saginaw/North Bay | 3 | 3 | – | 2 | 3 | 1 | 2 | 2 | 3 | 2 | 2 | 2 | 1 | 1 | 2 | 7 | 2 | 5 | 2 | 4 | 1 | 3 | 3 | 3 | 3 | 4 | 4 | – | – | – | – | – |
| 34 | Sarnia | – | 4 | 1 | 1 | 3 | – | 5 | 2 | 1 | 3 | 1 | 3 | 2 | 7 | 1 | – | – | – | – | – | – | – | – | – | – | – | – | – | – | – | – | – |
| 110 | Sault Ste. Marie | 1 | 2 | 3 | – | 1 | 3 | 1 | 2 | 1 | 1 | 1 | 4 | 1 | 4 | 3 | 4 | 3 | 7 | 2 | 1 | 3 | 2 | 1 | 7 | 5 | 4 | 6 | 1 | 8 | 3 | 3 | 22 |
| 24 | St. Michael's | 4 | 4 | – | – | – | 4 | 5 | 1 | 5 | 1 | – | – | – | – | – | – | – | – | – | – | – | – | – | – | – | – | – | – | – | – | – | – |
| 112 | Sudbury | 2 | 2 | 1 | 2 | 4 | – | 1 | 1 | 2 | – | 5 | 5 | 3 | 1 | 2 | 2 | 10 | 2 | 8 | 2 | 1 | – | 1 | 3 | 5 | 2 | – | 4 | 2 | 7 | 3 | 29 |
| 87 | Windsor | 5 | 4 | 2 | 2 | 3 | 2 | 2 | 2 | 2 | 2 | 2 | 1 | 5 | 1 | 4 | 3 | – | 3 | – | 1 | 2 | 5 | – | 7 | 3 | 2 | 2 | 3 | 5 | 3 | 2 | 7 |

### Teams no longer operating

| Total | Club | '09 | '08 | '07 | '06 | '05 | '04 | '03 | '02 | '01 | '00 | '99 | '98 | '97 | '96 | '95 | '94 | '93 | '92 | '91 | '90 | '89 | '88 | '87 | '86 | '85 | '84 | '83 | '82 | '81 | '80 | '79 | '69 to '78 |
|---|---|---|---|---|---|---|---|---|---|---|---|---|---|---|---|---|---|---|---|---|---|---|---|---|---|---|---|---|---|---|---|---|---|
| 27 | Brantford | – | – | – | – | – | – | – | – | – | – | – | – | – | – | – | – | – | – | – | – | – | – | – | – | – | 2 | 7 | 2 | 5 | 8 | 3 | 0 |
| 37 | Cornwall | – | – | – | – | – | – | – | – | – | – | – | – | – | – | – | – | – | 5 | 3 | 3 | 2 | 3 | 3 | 2 | 2 | 3 | 4 | 7 | – | – | – | – |
| 62 | Hamilton | – | – | – | – | – | – | – | – | – | – | – | – | – | – | – | – | – | – | 2 | – | – | 4 | 4 | 6 | 3 | – | – | – | – | – | 1 | 42 |
| 20 | Montreal | – | – | – | – | – | – | – | – | – | – | – | – | – | – | – | – | – | – | – | – | – | – | – | – | – | – | – | – | – | – | – | 20 |
| 5 | Newmarket | – | – | – | – | – | – | – | – | – | – | – | – | – | – | – | 2 | 3 | – | – | – | – | – | – | – | – | – | – | – | – | – | – | – |
| 72 | Niagara Falls | – | – | – | – | – | – | – | – | – | – | – | – | – | 6 | 2 | 3 | 4 | 4 | 4 | 4 | 4 | – | – | – | – | – | – | 6 | 6 | 8 | 5 | 16 |
| 52 | St. Catharines | – | – | – | – | – | – | – | – | – | – | – | – | – | – | – | – | – | – | – | – | – | – | – | – | – | – | – | – | – | – | – | 52 |
| 97 | Toronto | – | – | – | – | – | – | – | – | – | – | – | – | – | – | – | – | – | – | – | – | 2 | 2 | 1 | 4 | 3 | 4 | 4 | 6 | 2 | 10 | 4 | 55 |

## Quebec Major Junior Hockey League Draft Selections by Club

| Total | Club | '09 | '08 | '07 | '06 | '05 | '04 | '03 | '02 | '01 | '00 | '99 | '98 | '97 | '96 | '95 | '94 | '93 | '92 | '91 | '90 | '89 | '88 | '87 | '86 | '85 | '84 | '83 | '82 | '81 | '80 | '79 | '69 to '78 |
|---|---|---|---|---|---|---|---|---|---|---|---|---|---|---|---|---|---|---|---|---|---|---|---|---|---|---|---|---|---|---|---|---|---|
| 9 | Acadie-Bathurst | – | – | – | 2 | – | – | 3 | 2 | – | – | 2 | – | – | – | – | – | – | – | – | – | – | – | – | – | – | – | – | – | – | – | – | – |
| 21 | Baie-Comeau | 1 | 2 | 1 | 3 | – | 3 | 2 | 1 | 3 | 2 | – | 3 | – | – | – | – | – | – | – | – | – | – | – | – | – | – | – | – | – | – | – | – |
| 15 | Cape Breton | 1 | 1 | – | 1 | – | 3 | 2 | 2 | 1 | 1 | – | 3 | – | – | – | – | – | – | – | – | – | – | – | – | – | – | – | – | – | – | – | – |
| 54 | Chicoutimi | – | 3 | – | – | 4 | – | 1 | 3 | 1 | 1 | – | 1 | 2 | – | 2 | 3 | 1 | 1 | – | 1 | 1 | 2 | 2 | 1 | 3 | – | 3 | 1 | 6 | 3 | 1 | 7 |
| 57 | Drummondville | 3 | – | – | 2 | 2 | 1 | 1 | – | 1 | 1 | – | 2 | 2 | 3 | 4 | 1 | 2 | 2 | 4 | – | 1 | 4 | 2 | 2 | 2 | 1 | – | – | – | – | – | 14 |
| 74 | Gatineau/Hull | – | 1 | 1 | 2 | – | 4 | 4 | 5 | 2 | – | 4 | 3 | – | 3 | 3 | 1 | 3 | 3 | 3 | 3 | 2 | 2 | 3 | 4 | – | 1 | 3 | – | 1 | 3 | – | 10 |
| 30 | Halifax | – | – | 2 | 3 | 1 | 3 | 6 | – | 3 | 2 | – | 3 | 3 | 1 | 3 | – | – | – | – | – | – | – | – | – | – | – | – | – | – | – | – | – |
| 78 | Lewiston/Sher. | 1 | 2 | 3 | 2 | 5 | 2 | 1 | – | 3 | – | – | 5 | 1 | – | 4 | 2 | 3 | – | – | – | – | – | – | – | – | – | – | 2 | 5 | 1 | 4 | 32 |
| 21 | Moncton | 2 | 1 | 1 | 3 | 1 | 2 | 3 | 2 | – | – | 2 | 2 | 1 | 1 | – | – | – | – | – | – | – | – | – | – | – | – | – | – | – | – | – | – |
| 23 | PEI/Mtl. Rocket | 1 | 2 | 2 | – | 2 | 8 | 1 | 3 | 1 | 1 | 2 | – | – | – | – | – | – | – | – | – | – | – | – | – | – | – | – | – | – | – | – | – |
| 25 | Quebec | 1 | 3 | 2 | 2 | 2 | 1 | 3 | 1 | 3 | – | 3 | 4 | – | – | – | – | – | – | – | – | – | – | – | – | – | – | – | – | – | – | – | – |
| 30 | Rimouski | 2 | 2 | 4 | – | 2 | 3 | 4 | – | 4 | 2 | 2 | 5 | – | – | – | – | – | – | – | – | – | – | – | – | – | – | – | – | – | – | – | – |
| 18 | Rouyn-Noranda | 1 | 2 | 1 | 3 | 1 | – | 2 | – | – | 4 | 1 | 3 | – | – | – | – | – | – | – | – | – | – | – | – | – | – | – | – | – | – | – | – |
| 6 | Saint John | 2 | 1 | 2 | 1 | – | – | – | – | – | – | – | – | – | – | – | – | – | – | – | – | – | – | – | – | – | – | – | – | – | – | – | – |
| 7 | Montreal/St. John's | 1 | 2 | 4 | – | – | – | – | – | – | – | – | – | – | – | – | – | – | – | – | – | – | – | – | – | – | – | – | – | – | – | – | – |
| 81 | Shawinigan | 6 | – | 1 | 1 | 1 | 3 | 2 | 2 | 1 | 1 | 1 | 3 | 1 | 4 | 2 | 1 | 1 | 3 | 2 | – | 2 | – | 1 | 2 | – | 2 | 5 | 5 | 2 | 2 | – | 24 |
| 23 | Val-d'Or | – | 2 | – | – | 2 | 1 | 1 | 1 | 2 | 2 | 3 | – | 2 | 4 | 2 | 1 | – | – | – | – | – | – | – | – | – | – | – | – | – | – | – | – |
| 35 | Victoriaville | 1 | 3 | 1 | – | – | – | – | 3 | 1 | 3 | 2 | 1 | 2 | 3 | 1 | 1 | 6 | 2 | – | 1 | – | 4 | – | – | – | – | – | – | – | – | – | – |

### Teams no longer operating

| Total | Club | '09 | '08 | '07 | '06 | '05 | '04 | '03 | '02 | '01 | '00 | '99 | '98 | '97 | '96 | '95 | '94 | '93 | '92 | '91 | '90 | '89 | '88 | '87 | '86 | '85 | '84 | '83 | '82 | '81 | '80 | '79 | '69 to '78 |
|---|---|---|---|---|---|---|---|---|---|---|---|---|---|---|---|---|---|---|---|---|---|---|---|---|---|---|---|---|---|---|---|---|---|
| 21 | Beauport | – | – | – | – | – | – | – | – | – | – | – | – | 3 | 3 | 7 | 3 | 1 | 3 | 1 | – | – | – | – | – | – | – | – | – | – | – | – | – |
| 45 | Cornwall | – | – | – | – | – | – | – | – | – | – | – | – | – | – | – | – | – | – | – | – | – | – | – | – | – | – | – | – | 5 | 5 | 1 | 34 |
| 30 | Granby | – | – | – | – | – | – | – | – | – | – | – | – | 1 | 3 | 2 | 5 | 1 | – | 2 | – | 2 | – | 4 | 2 | 2 | 3 | 1 | 2 | – | – | – | – |
| 54 | Laval | – | – | – | – | – | – | – | – | – | – | – | 3 | 1 | 2 | 4 | 5 | 2 | 1 | 4 | 3 | 3 | 1 | 3 | 5 | – | 2 | 1 | 2 | – | – | 1 | 11 |
| 12 | Longueuil | – | – | – | – | – | – | – | – | – | – | – | – | – | – | – | – | – | – | 3 | 2 | – | – | 1 | 2 | 1 | 2 | 1 | – | – | – | – | – |
| 32 | Montreal | – | – | – | – | – | – | – | – | – | – | – | – | – | – | – | – | – | – | – | – | – | – | – | – | – | – | – | 3 | – | 3 | 4 | 22 |
| 47 | Quebec | – | – | – | – | – | – | – | – | – | – | – | – | – | – | – | – | – | – | – | – | – | – | – | – | 3 | 2 | 2 | 1 | 2 | 2 | 3 | 32 |
| 15 | St. Hyacinthe | – | – | – | – | – | – | – | – | – | – | – | – | – | 4 | – | 4 | 1 | 2 | 1 | 3 | – | – | – | – | – | – | – | – | – | – | – | – |
| 16 | St. Jean | – | – | – | – | – | – | – | – | – | – | – | – | – | – | 1 | 1 | 2 | 1 | 3 | – | 1 | 3 | 0 | 1 | 1 | – | 2 | – | – | – | – | – |
| 2 | St. Jerome | – | – | – | – | – | – | – | – | – | – | – | – | – | – | – | – | – | – | – | – | – | – | – | – | – | – | – | – | – | – | – | 2 |
| 28 | Sorel | – | – | – | – | – | – | – | – | – | – | – | – | – | – | – | – | – | – | – | – | – | – | – | – | – | – | – | – | 5 | – | – | 23 |
| 47 | Trois Rivieres | – | – | – | – | – | – | – | – | – | – | – | – | – | – | – | – | – | 1 | 2 | 1 | 3 | 3 | 1 | – | 3 | – | 3 | 1 | 2 | 2 | 2 | 23 |
| 27 | Verdun | – | – | – | – | – | – | – | – | – | – | – | – | – | – | – | – | – | 3 | – | – | 1 | 3 | 0 | 3 | – | 3 | 3 | – | – | 3 | 3 | 5 |

## 2009 NHL Entry Draft Order of Selection

The first 14 picks of the 2009 Entry Draft were determined by the NHL's annual Draft Drawing, a weighted lottery system used to determine the order of selection.

The 14 teams that did not qualify for the 2009 Stanley Cup Playoffs, or clubs that acquired those clubs' 2009 first-round draft picks, participated in the drawing.

The club selected in the drawing may not move up more than four positions in the draft order, thus only the five clubs with the fewest regular-season points have the opportunity to select first overall. No club can move down more than one position as a result of the Draft Drawing. For 2009, the NY Islanders won the right to the first overall pick.

**In the first round** of the 2009 Entry Draft, the order of selection was as follows:

a) The winner of the Draft Drawing followed by the remaining non-playoff teams, in inverse order of points. (Note that the original holder of each selection is listed followed by the club that acquired and used that selection in the first round of the 2009 Entry Draft.)

| | |
|---|---|
| 1. NY Islanders | 8. Dallas |
| 2. Tampa Bay | 9. Ottawa |
| 3. Colorado | 10. Edmonton |
| 4. Atlanta | 11. Nashville |
| 5. Los Angeles | 12. Min. – NYI |
| 6. Phoenix | 13. Buffalo |
| 7. Toronto | 14. Florida |

b) Clubs eliminated in the first two rounds of the 2009 Stanley Cup Playoffs, regular-season division winners excluded, in inverse order of points;

| | |
|---|---|
| 15. Anaheim | 19. NY Rangers |
| 16. CBJ – Min. | 20. Cgy. – N.J. |
| 17. St. Louis | 21. Phi. – CBJ |
| 18. Montreal | |

c) Regular-season division winning clubs eliminated in the first two rounds of the 2009 Stanley Cup Playoffs, in inverse order of points;

| | |
|---|---|
| 22. Vancouver | 24. Washington |
| 23. N.J. – Cgy. | 25. Boston |
| 26. S.J. – Ana. | |

d) Clubs eliminated in the 2009 Conference Finals, in inverse order of points;

| | |
|---|---|
| 27. Carolina | 28. Chicago |

e) Loser of Stanley Cup Final
29. Det. – T.B.

f) Stanley Cup champion
30. Pittsburgh

Because NY Islanders were both the winner of the Draft Drawing and the Club with the fewest regular-season points, the order of selection in the second and subsequent rounds was identical to that used in the first round.

*Tampa Bay's Steven Stamkos (top) was selected first overall in 2008 from the Sarnia Sting of the OHL. He had 23 goals and 23 assists as an NHL rookie in 2008-09. Luke Schenn played 70 games for the Toronto Maple Leafs after being picked fifth overall from Kelowna in the WHL.*

## Western Hockey League Draft Selections by Club

| Total | Club | '09 | '08 | '07 | '06 | '05 | '04 | '03 | '02 | '01 | '00 | '99 | '98 | '97 | '96 | '95 | '94 | '93 | '92 | '91 | '90 | '89 | '88 | '87 | '86 | '85 | '84 | '83 | '82 | '81 | '80 | '79 | '69 to '78 |
|---|---|---|---|---|---|---|---|---|---|---|---|---|---|---|---|---|---|---|---|---|---|---|---|---|---|---|---|---|---|---|---|---|---|
| 102 | Brandon | 2 | 2 | 1 | 1 | 2 | – | 3 | 4 | 2 | – | – | 4 | 5 | 2 | 6 | 5 | 2 | 1 | 1 | 1 | – | 3 | 3 | 1 | 2 | 3 | 1 | 2 | 2 | 5 | 10 | 26 |
| 38 | Calgary | 2 | 2 | 4 | 1 | 2 | 5 | 3 | 2 | 1 | 4 | 6 | 3 | – | 3 | – | – | – | – | – | – | – | – | – | – | – | – | – | – | – | – | – | – |
| 3 | Chilliwack | 1 | – | 2 | – | – | – | – | – | – | – | – | – | – | – | – | – | – | – | – | – | – | – | – | – | – | – | – | – | – | – | – | – |
| 1 | Edmonton | 1 | – | – | – | – | – | – | – | – | – | – | – | – | – | – | – | – | – | – | – | – | – | – | – | – | – | – | – | – | – | – | – |
| 10 | Everett | 2 | 1 | 3 | 4 | – | – | – | – | – | – | – | – | – | – | – | – | – | – | – | – | – | – | – | – | – | – | – | – | – | – | – | – |
| 108 | Kamloops | 2 | – | 1 | 1 | 2 | 5 | 2 | 5 | 2 | 4 | 4 | 1 | 3 | 4 | 5 | 9 | 2 | 3 | 6 | 4 | 5 | 1 | 3 | 4 | 4 | 4 | 4 | 2 | – | – | – | 16 |
| 37 | Kelowna | 3 | 4 | 2 | – | 2 | 4 | 4 | 1 | 1 | 1 | 2 | 2 | 7 | 4 | – | – | – | – | – | – | – | – | – | – | – | – | – | – | – | – | – | – |
| 17 | Kootenay | 1 | – | 1 | 1 | 3 | 2 | 1 | 3 | 2 | 1 | 2 | – | – | – | – | – | – | – | – | – | – | – | – | – | – | – | – | – | – | – | – | – |
| 91 | Lethbridge | 1 | 2 | 2 | 1 | – | 2 | 2 | 2 | 1 | 3 | – | 1 | 5 | 1 | 3 | 3 | 4 | 3 | 7 | 4 | 3 | 3 | – | 1 | 5 | 1 | 2 | 7 | 4 | 1 | 4 | 13 |
| 108 | Medicine Hat | 1 | 2 | – | 2 | 4 | 2 | 3 | 3 | 2 | – | 1 | 4 | 2 | 7 | 2 | 6 | 1 | 3 | 3 | 1 | 4 | 1 | 5 | 2 | 6 | 1 | 2 | 1 | 2 | 4 | – | 31 |
| 62 | Moose Jaw | – | 3 | 1 | 1 | 3 | 3 | 3 | 3 | 3 | 5 | 1 | 2 | 4 | 4 | 4 | 3 | 2 | 3 | 2 | 1 | 3 | – | 3 | 1 | 4 | – | – | – | – | – | – | – |
| 107 | Portland | 1 | – | 2 | 1 | 3 | 2 | 1 | 2 | – | 6 | 1 | 3 | 3 | 1 | 2 | 3 | 4 | 4 | 1 | 1 | 4 | 1 | 3 | 4 | 2 | 5 | 7 | 7 | 6 | 8 | 7 | 12 |
| 81 | Prince Albert | 1 | – | – | – | 2 | 4 | 2 | 1 | 4 | 2 | 3 | 3 | 5 | 3 | 4 | 3 | 5 | 2 | 6 | 4 | 3 | 3 | 1 | 6 | 6 | 2 | 2 | 4 | – | – | – | – |
| 27 | Prince George | 1 | – | 1 | 4 | 1 | 2 | 2 | – | 4 | – | 2 | 4 | 2 | 2 | 2 | – | – | – | – | – | – | – | – | – | – | – | – | – | – | – | – | – |
| 47 | Red Deer | 4 | 1 | 1 | 1 | 1 | 1 | 4 | 4 | 6 | 1 | 1 | 5 | 3 | 4 | 2 | 5 | 3 | – | – | – | – | – | – | – | – | – | – | – | – | – | – | – |
| 112 | Regina | 1 | 3 | 3 | 1 | 1 | – | 2 | 1 | 2 | 2 | 4 | 2 | 3 | 4 | 2 | 3 | – | 4 | – | 1 | 5 | – | 2 | 3 | 4 | 4 | 8 | 6 | 5 | 3 | 1 | 32 |
| 111 | Saskatoon | 3 | 3 | 3 | – | 4 | 1 | – | – | 4 | 1 | 4 | 2 | 2 | 2 | 2 | 4 | 2 | 3 | 2 | 2 | 3 | 4 | 4 | 5 | 1 | 3 | 5 | 5 | 3 | 2 | 2 | 30 |
| 94 | Seattle | – | 2 | 1 | 1 | 3 | 2 | 5 | 1 | 5 | 4 | 6 | 2 | 8 | 1 | 5 | 5 | 4 | 2 | 3 | 6 | 2 | 4 | 2 | 1 | 3 | 1 | – | 6 | – | 3 | 2 | 4 |
| 65 | Spokane | 2 | 3 | 3 | 1 | 4 | 1 | – | 3 | 3 | 2 | 1 | 1 | 4 | 5 | 4 | 4 | 4 | 7 | 5 | 1 | 2 | 3 | 1 | – | – | – | – | – | 1 | – | – | – |
| 65 | Swift Current | 1 | 4 | 2 | 2 | 1 | 2 | 2 | 4 | 1 | 3 | 1 | 2 | 2 | 1 | 4 | 4 | 5 | 1 | 1 | 2 | 2 | 2 | 5 | – | – | – | – | – | – | – | – | 11 |
| 53 | Tri-City | – | 2 | – | – | 2 | 4 | 1 | 3 | 2 | 2 | 1 | 4 | 1 | 6 | 6 | 2 | 2 | 5 | 3 | 3 | 4 | – | – | – | – | – | – | – | – | – | – | – |
| 16 | Vancouver | 1 | 3 | 4 | 1 | 3 | 2 | 1 | 1 | – | – | – | – | – | – | – | – | – | – | – | – | – | – | – | – | – | – | – | – | – | – | – | – |
| **Teams no longer operating** | | | | | | | | | | | | | | | | | | | | | | | | | | | | | | | | | |
| 13 | Billings | – | – | – | – | – | – | – | – | – | – | – | – | – | – | – | – | – | – | – | – | – | – | – | – | – | – | – | – | 2 | 4 | 3 | 4 |
| 66 | Calgary | – | – | – | – | – | – | – | – | – | – | – | – | – | – | – | – | – | – | – | – | – | – | – | 2 | 3 | 3 | 3 | 4 | 5 | 2 | – | 44 |
| 38 | Edmonton | – | – | – | – | – | – | – | – | – | – | – | – | 4 | – | – | – | – | – | – | – | – | – | – | – | – | – | – | – | – | – | 2 | 32 |
| 12 | Estevan | – | – | – | – | – | – | – | – | – | – | – | – | – | – | – | – | – | – | – | – | – | – | – | – | – | – | – | – | – | – | – | 12 |
| 39 | Flin Flon | – | – | – | – | – | – | – | – | – | – | – | – | – | – | – | – | – | – | – | – | – | – | – | – | – | – | – | – | – | – | – | 39 |
| 11 | Kelowna | – | – | – | – | – | – | – | – | – | – | – | – | – | – | – | – | – | – | – | – | – | – | – | – | 5 | 4 | 2 | – | – | – | – | – |
| 6 | Nanaimo | – | – | – | – | – | – | – | – | – | – | – | – | – | – | – | – | – | – | – | – | – | – | – | – | – | – | 1 | 5 | – | – | – | – |
| 62 | New Westm'r | – | – | – | – | – | – | – | – | – | – | – | – | – | – | – | – | – | – | – | – | – | 1 | 2 | 1 | 1 | 2 | – | – | – | 1 | 5 | 49 |
| 12 | Tacoma | – | – | – | – | – | – | – | – | – | – | – | – | – | – | 2 | 5 | 2 | 3 | – | – | – | – | – | – | – | – | – | – | – | – | – | – |
| 2 | Vancouver | – | – | – | – | – | – | – | – | – | – | – | – | – | – | – | – | – | – | – | – | – | – | – | – | – | – | – | – | – | – | – | 2 |
| 70 | Victoria | – | – | – | – | – | – | – | – | – | – | – | – | – | – | – | 2 | 2 | 1 | – | 2 | 4 | 4 | 2 | 1 | 2 | 4 | 3 | 2 | 6 | 8 | 1 | 35 |
| 34 | Winnipeg | – | – | – | – | – | – | – | – | – | – | – | – | – | – | – | – | – | – | – | – | – | – | – | – | – | – | 1 | 4 | 1 | – | – | 28 |

## U.S. College Hockey Draft Selections by School

| Total | School | '09 | '08 | '07 | '06 | '05 | '04 | '03 | '02 | '01 | '00 | '99 | '98 | '97 | '96 | '95 | '94 | '93 | '92 | '91 | '90 | '89 | '88 | '87 | '86 | '85 | '84 | '83 | '82 | '81 | '80 | '79 | '69 to '78 |
|---|---|---|---|---|---|---|---|---|---|---|---|---|---|---|---|---|---|---|---|---|---|---|---|---|---|---|---|---|---|---|---|---|---|
| 38 | Boston College | – | 1 | – | 1 | 1 | 1 | 1 | 3 | 2 | 3 | – | 3 | 3 | 2 | – | – | – | – | – | – | 2 | – | 2 | 1 | – | – | – | 1 | 1 | 2 | – | 8 |
| 53 | Boston U. | 1 | 1 | – | 1 | – | 1 | – | 3 | 2 | 1 | 3 | 2 | 1 | 1 | 1 | – | 1 | 1 | 2 | 2 | 1 | 3 | 2 | 2 | 1 | 1 | – | – | 1 | – | 1 | 17 |
| 28 | Bowling Green | – | – | – | 1 | 1 | – | – | 1 | 1 | – | 1 | 1 | 1 | – | – | – | – | 1 | 3 | 1 | 2 | 3 | – | – | – | – | 1 | – | – | 1 | 1 | 8 |
| 13 | Brown | – | – | – | – | – | 1 | – | – | – | 1 | – | – | – | – | – | – | – | – | 1 | – | – | – | – | – | – | – | – | 1 | – | – | – | 9 |
| 33 | Clarkson | – | – | – | 1 | – | – | – | – | – | 1 | 1 | 3 | – | – | – | – | 1 | 1 | 2 | 3 | 1 | 1 | 1 | – | – | 1 | 1 | 1 | 1 | 1 | 1 | 11 |
| 13 | Colgate | – | – | – | 1 | – | 1 | – | 1 | – | – | – | – | – | – | – | – | – | – | 2 | 2 | 1 | 1 | – | – | – | – | – | – | – | – | 1 | 3 |
| 33 | Colorado | – | – | 1 | – | 1 | – | 2 | 1 | 1 | 2 | 1 | 3 | – | – | 1 | – | – | – | – | 2 | – | 1 | – | 1 | – | 3 | – | – | – | 1 | – | 12 |
| 34 | Cornell | – | – | – | – | 1 | 2 | 2 | 1 | – | 2 | 2 | – | 1 | – | – | – | – | – | – | 2 | 5 | 2 | 1 | – | 2 | 1 | – | 1 | 1 | 1 | – | 7 |
| 10 | Dartmouth | – | – | 1 | – | – | 1 | 2 | – | – | 1 | – | – | – | – | – | – | – | – | 1 | – | – | – | 1 | – | – | – | – | – | – | 1 | – | 2 |
| 43 | Denver | – | – | – | – | 2 | 1 | – | 1 | – | – | 1 | – | 3 | – | – | – | – | – | – | – | 1 | 1 | 4 | 2 | 1 | – | – | 1 | – | 1 | 2 | 22 |
| 34 | Harvard | – | – | – | – | 1 | – | – | 3 | 2 | 2 | 1 | 2 | 1 | 3 | – | 1 | 2 | – | – | – | 2 | 1 | 1 | – | 2 | – | 1 | 1 | – | – | – | 8 |
| 24 | Lake Superior | – | – | – | – | – | – | – | 1 | – | – | 1 | – | 1 | 1 | – | – | 1 | – | 1 | 3 | 2 | 3 | – | 3 | – | 1 | – | – | – | – | – | 6 |
| 22 | Maine | – | – | – | 1 | – | 1 | 2 | – | – | 1 | 4 | 1 | 1 | 1 | – | – | 1 | – | – | 1 | 2 | 3 | – | 1 | – | – | 1 | 1 | – | – | – | – |
| 24 | Miami U. | 2 | 1 | 1 | 1 | 1 | 2 | – | 1 | 1 | – | – | 1 | – | – | – | – | 1 | 1 | 2 | – | 2 | 4 | 2 | – | 1 | – | – | – | – | – | – | – |
| 67 | Michigan | – | – | 1 | 2 | 1 | 3 | 2 | 3 | 2 | 1 | 2 | 3 | 1 | 3 | – | 1 | 1 | 2 | 4 | 5 | 3 | 2 | 1 | – | 1 | 1 | – | – | – | 4 | – | 18 |
| 48 | Michigan State | – | – | – | 1 | – | 2 | 1 | 4 | – | 2 | 2 | 1 | 1 | 1 | – | 1 | 1 | 1 | 4 | 5 | 4 | 4 | 1 | 1 | – | 2 | – | 2 | – | 2 | – | 5 |
| 46 | Michigan Tech | – | – | – | – | – | – | – | – | 1 | – | – | – | – | 1 | – | 2 | 1 | – | 2 | 1 | 2 | 1 | 1 | 2 | 2 | 2 | – | 1 | – | 4 | 1 | 22 |
| 69 | Minnesota | 1 | – | 1 | 1 | 1 | – | 2 | 3 | – | 3 | 3 | 1 | 2 | 3 | 2 | – | – | – | – | – | 1 | 1 | 1 | 2 | – | – | 1 | 1 | 1 | 3 | 2 | 33 |
| 13 | Minn.-Duluth | – | – | – | – | – | – | – | – | – | – | – | 1 | – | – | – | – | – | – | 1 | 2 | 1 | 2 | – | – | – | – | – | – | 1 | – | – | 5 |
| 31 | New Hampshire | – | – | – | – | – | 1 | – | 1 | – | 2 | 1 | – | 1 | – | – | – | – | – | – | – | – | 1 | – | – | – | 2 | 1 | 1 | 1 | 2 | 1 | 16 |
| 39 | North Dakota | – | – | – | 1 | – | 1 | 1 | 1 | – | 1 | 1 | – | 2 | – | – | – | – | – | 1 | 1 | 2 | – | – | – | – | 1 | – | – | 1 | 3 | 3 | 19 |
| 10 | Northeastern | – | – | – | – | – | – | – | – | – | – | 1 | 1 | – | – | – | – | – | – | – | 1 | 1 | – | – | 1 | 1 | – | 1 | – | – | 1 | – | 21 |
| 23 | Northern Mich. | – | 1 | – | – | – | 2 | 2 | – | – | 1 | – | – | – | 1 | – | – | – | – | 1 | – | 2 | 1 | 4 | – | – | – | – | 1 | 2 | 1 | – | 4 |
| 32 | Notre Dame | – | – | 1 | 1 | – | 2 | – | 2 | 1 | 1 | 2 | – | 2 | 1 | – | – | – | – | – | – | – | – | – | – | – | – | – | – | – | 1 | 1 | 17 |
| 21 | Ohio State | – | – | – | – | 1 | – | 1 | 2 | 2 | – | 1 | – | 1 | 1 | – | – | 1 | 1 | 1 | 1 | – | 2 | 2 | – | – | 1 | – | – | – | – | – | 3 |
| 10 | Princeton | – | – | – | – | – | – | – | – | 1 | – | – | 1 | – | – | – | – | 1 | – | – | – | 1 | – | 1 | – | – | – | 1 | – | 1 | 1 | – | 2 |
| 36 | Providence | – | – | – | 2 | – | – | 1 | 1 | – | 2 | – | 2 | 1 | – | – | – | – | – | – | 1 | – | – | – | 1 | 1 | – | 2 | 1 | 4 | 5 | – | 12 |
| 26 | RPI | – | 1 | – | – | – | – | – | – | 1 | 2 | 2 | – | 1 | – | – | – | – | 1 | 3 | – | – | 2 | 2 | – | 1 | – | 1 | 1 | 2 | 1 | – | 5 |
| 23 | St. Lawrence | – | – | – | – | – | – | – | 1 | – | – | 1 | – | 1 | 1 | – | – | 1 | – | 2 | 1 | 1 | 1 | 1 | 1 | 1 | 1 | – | 3 | – | – | – | 6 |
| 20 | Vermont | – | – | – | – | 1 | – | – | – | 2 | – | – | – | – | 1 | – | 1 | – | – | 1 | – | – | 1 | – | – | 2 | 1 | 1 | – | 1 | 1 | – | 7 |
| 25 | W. Michigan | 1 | – | – | 1 | – | – | – | 1 | – | – | – | 1 | 1 | – | – | – | 2 | – | 4 | 1 | 1 | 1 | 1 | 2 | – | 2 | 2 | – | – | 2 | – | 2 |
| 45 | Wisconsin | – | 2 | – | – | – | 2 | – | – | – | 3 | 2 | – | – | – | – | – | – | – | 1 | – | 1 | – | 1 | – | 1 | 1 | – | 2 | 3 | – | 1 | 25 |
| 16 | Yale | – | – | 1 | – | 2 | – | 3 | – | – | – | – | – | – | – | – | 1 | – | – | – | 1 | – | 2 | 1 | – | – | – | – | – | 1 | – | 4 | |

**Colleges with fewer than 10 players selected:** 9 - Ferris State, Merrimack, St.Cloud State; 7 - Mass.-Lowell; 6 - Illinois-Chicago, St. Louis; 5 - Pennsylvania, Union College, Mass.-Amherst; 4 - Alaska-Anchorage, Nebraska-Omaha; 3 - Babson College, Alaska (Fairbanks), Minnesota State (Mankato); 1 - Air Force, American International College, Army, Bemidji State, Greenway, Hamilton, St. Anselm College, St. Thomas, Salem State, San Diego U., Wisconsin-River Falls.

## U.S. High and Prep Schools Draft Selections by School (10 or more players drafted)

| Total | School (State) | '09 | '08 | '07 | '06 | '05 | '04 | '03 | '02 | '01 | '00 | '99 | '98 | '97 | '96 | '95 | '94 | '93 | '92 | '91 | '90 | '89 | '88 | '87 | '86 | '85 | '84 | '83 | '82 | '81 | '80 |
|---|---|---|---|---|---|---|---|---|---|---|---|---|---|---|---|---|---|---|---|---|---|---|---|---|---|---|---|---|---|---|---|
| 12 | Avon Old Farms (CT) | 1 | – | 1 | – | – | – | – | – | – | – | – | 1 | 1 | – | – | – | – | – | – | 3 | 3 | – | – | 1 | 1 | – | – | – | – | – |
| 17 | Belmont Hill (MA) | – | – | – | 1 | – | – | – | – | – | – | – | – | – | – | – | 1 | – | 2 | 1 | 2 | 3 | 1 | 2 | 1 | 2 | – | 1 | – | – | – |
| 11 | Canterbury (CT) | – | – | – | – | – | – | 1 | – | – | – | – | – | – | – | – | – | 1 | 2 | – | 2 | – | 3 | – | 2 | – | – | – | – | – | – |
| 14 | Catholic Memorial (MA) | – | – | – | – | – | 2 | – | – | – | – | – | 1 | – | – | – | 2 | 1 | 2 | – | – | 2 | 1 | 1 | – | 2 | – | – | – | – | – |
| 10 | Choate-Rosemary (CT) | – | – | – | – | – | – | – | – | – | 1 | – | – | – | – | – | – | – | 1 | 1 | 1 | – | 3 | 2 | – | 1 | – | – | – | – | – |
| 12 | Culver Mil. Acad. (IN) | – | – | – | – | – | – | – | – | – | – | – | – | – | – | – | – | 2 | 2 | 1 | 2 | 2 | 1 | 2 | – | – | – | – | – | – | – |
| 21 | Cushing Acad. (MA) | – | – | – | 1 | 1 | 2 | – | – | 1 | – | – | – | 1 | 1 | – | 2 | 2 | – | 1 | 3 | 2 | 3 | – | – | – | 1 | – | – | – | – |
| 14 | Deerfield (IL) | – | – | 1 | – | – | 1 | 1 | 1 | – | 2 | 1 | – | – | – | – | – | – | – | 1 | – | 2 | 1 | 1 | – | 1 | 1 | – | – | – | – |
| 17 | Edina (MN) | 2 | – | – | – | – | – | – | – | – | – | – | – | – | – | – | – | – | 1 | – | 1 | 2 | 2 | 1 | – | – | 2 | 2 | 4 | – | – |
| 15 | Hill-Murray (MN) | – | – | – | – | – | – | – | – | – | – | – | – | – | – | – | 1 | – | – | – | 3 | 2 | – | 3 | 3 | – | 3 | – | – | – | – |
| 12 | Hotchkiss (CT) | 1 | – | – | – | – | 1 | – | – | 1 | – | – | – | – | 2 | 1 | 3 | – | – | – | 1 | – | 1 | – | – | 1 | – | – | – | – | – |
| 10 | Lawrence Acad. (MA) | – | – | – | – | – | – | – | – | – | – | – | – | – | 1 | – | 1 | 1 | – | 1 | 1 | – | 2 | – | – | 2 | – | 1 | – | – | – |
| 10 | Matignon (MA) | – | – | – | – | – | – | – | – | – | – | – | – | – | – | – | – | – | – | 1 | – | – | – | 3 | – | – | 3 | – | 1 | 1 | 1 |
| 11 | Minnetonka (MN) | 1 | 1 | – | – | – | – | – | – | – | – | – | – | – | – | – | – | – | – | 1 | – | 2 | – | 2 | – | 2 | 1 | 1 | – | – | – |
| 13 | Mount St. Charles (RI) | – | – | – | – | – | – | – | – | – | – | – | – | – | – | – | – | – | – | – | 1 | 1 | 3 | 1 | 2 | – | 1 | 3 | – | 1 | – |
| 20 | Northwood Prep (NY) | – | 1 | – | – | – | 1 | – | – | – | 1 | – | – | – | – | – | 1 | 1 | – | – | 3 | 1 | 1 | 3 | 2 | 2 | – | 1 | 2 | – | – |
| 12 | Roseau (MN) | 2 | – | – | – | – | – | – | – | – | – | – | – | – | – | – | – | – | – | 1 | 3 | 1 | – | – | 1 | – | 1 | 1 | 1 | – | 1 |
| 13 | St. Sebastian's (MA) | – | – | – | 1 | – | – | 4 | 1 | 1 | – | – | 1 | – | – | – | 1 | 2 | 2 | – | – | – | – | – | – | – | – | – | – | – | – |
| 12 | Shattuck St. Mary's (MN) | 3 | 3 | 1 | 1 | 2 | – | 1 | – | – | – | – | – | – | 1 | – | – | – | – | – | – | – | – | – | – | – | – | – | – | – | – |
| 10 | Thayer Acad. (MA) | – | – | – | – | 2 | 1 | – | – | – | – | 2 | | – | – | – | – | – | 2 | – | – | – | 2 | – | 1 | – | – | – | – | – | – |

### U.S. College and High School Firsts

*Michigan Tech's Al Karlander played 212 games over four seasons with the Detroit Red Wings.*

**1967 – First U.S. College Player Drafted •** Michigan Tech center Al Karlander was selected 17th overall by the Detroit Red Wings.

**1979 – First U.S. College First- Round Selection •** Minnesota-born defenseman Mike Ramsey (currently an assistant coach with the Minnesota Wild) was selected 11th overall by the Buffalo Sabres.

**1980 – First U.S. High School Player Drafted •** Center Jay North of Bloomington-Jefferson H.S. was taken 62nd overall by the Buffalo Sabres in 1980.

**1981 – First U.S. High School First- Round Selection •** Center Bob Carpenter of St. John's prep school was selected third overall by Washington in 1981.

**1983 – First U.S. High School Player Drafted First Overall •** Minnesota North Stars selected left winger Brian Lawton from Mount St. Charles H.S. first overall in 1983.

**1986 – First U.S. College Player Drafted First Overall •** Detroit selected right winger Joe Murphy from Michigan State first overall in 1986.

**2005 – Most U.S. College Players Selected in the First Round •** The 2005 draft saw eight U.S. college players selected in the first round, the most in Entry Draft history. Seven were selected in the first round in 2003 and 1986, six in 2000, five in 2002, four in 2001 and three in each of the 1986 and 1999 Entry Drafts.

## International

*Ranked by total number of players drafted*

| Total | Country | '09 | '08 | '07 | '06 | '05 | '04 | '03 | '02 | '01 | '00 | '99 | '98 | '97 | '96 | '95 | '94 | '93 | '92 | '91 | '90 | '89 | '88 | '87 | '86 | '85 | '84 | '83 | '82 | '81 | '80 | '79 | '69 to '78 |
|---|---|---|---|---|---|---|---|---|---|---|---|---|---|---|---|---|---|---|---|---|---|---|---|---|---|---|---|---|---|---|---|---|---|
| 525 | Russia/CIS/USSR | 6 | 9 | 7 | 16 | 11 | 24 | 32 | 33 | 36 | 44 | 29 | 22 | 16 | 17 | 27 | 35 | 31 | 45 | 25 | 14 | 18 | 11 | 2 | 1 | 2 | 1 | 5 | 3 | – | – | – | 3 |
| 486 | Sweden | 23 | 19 | 16 | 18 | 15 | 18 | 19 | 24 | 14 | 24 | 24 | 19 | 14 | 16 | 8 | 17 | 18 | 11 | 11 | 7 | 9 | 14 | 15 | 9 | 16 | 14 | 10 | 14 | 14 | 9 | 5 | 22 |
| 408 | CzRep/Slovakia | 3 | 2 | 4 | 11 | 15 | 24 | 20 | 21 | 28 | 28 | 20 | 20 | 17 | 14 | 21 | 18 | 15 | 17 | 9 | 21 | 8 | 5 | 11 | 6 | 8 | 13 | 9 | 13 | 4 | – | 1 | 2 |
| 320 | Finland | 8 | 6 | 4 | 13 | 8 | 14 | 12 | 26 | 29 | 19 | 17 | 12 | 11 | 7 | 12 | 8 | 9 | 8 | 6 | 9 | 3 | 7 | 6 | 10 | 4 | 10 | 9 | 5 | 12 | 4 | – | 12 |
| 46 | Germany | 1 | 1 | 4 | 2 | 1 | 1 | 4 | 1 | 7 | 1 | – | – | 1 | 3 | 1 | 1 | 3 | 2 | 1 | – | – | 2 | 1 | – | 1 | 2 | 1 | – | 2 | – | – | 2 |
| 44 | Switzerland | – | 1 | 1 | 3 | – | 4 | 5 | 4 | 5 | 7 | 3 | 2 | 3 | 1 | – | 1 | 2 | – | 1 | – | – | – | – | – | – | – | – | – | – | – | – | 1 |
| 8 | Norway | – | 1 | – | – | – | – | – | 1 | – | – | – | – | 1 | – | – | – | – | – | 1 | 2 | – | – | 2 | – | – | – | – | – | – | – | – | – |
| 4 | Denmark | – | – | – | – | – | 2 | – | – | – | – | – | – | – | – | – | – | – | – | – | – | – | – | 1 | 1 | – | – | – | – | – | – | – | – |
| 2 | Japan | – | – | – | – | – | 1 | – | – | – | – | – | – | – | – | – | – | – | 1 | – | – | – | – | – | – | – | – | – | – | – | – | – | – |
| 2 | Poland | – | – | – | – | – | – | 1 | – | – | – | – | – | – | – | – | – | – | – | 1 | – | – | – | – | – | – | – | – | – | – | – | – | – |
| 1 | Hungary | – | – | – | – | – | – | – | – | – | – | 1 | – | – | – | – | – | – | – | – | – | – | – | – | – | – | – | – | – | – | – | – | – |
| 1 | Scotland | – | – | – | – | – | – | – | – | – | – | – | – | – | – | – | – | – | – | – | – | – | – | – | 1 | – | – | – | – | – | – | – | – |

## Czech Republic and Slovakia

| Total | Club | '09 | '08 | '07 | '06 | '05 | '04 | '03 | '02 | '01 | '00 | '99 | '98 | '97 | '96 | '95 | '94 | '93 | '92 | '91 | '90 | '89 | '88 | '87 | '86 | '85 | '84 | '83 | '82 | '81 | '80 | '79 | '69 to '78 |
|---|---|---|---|---|---|---|---|---|---|---|---|---|---|---|---|---|---|---|---|---|---|---|---|---|---|---|---|---|---|---|---|---|---|
| 8 | Brno | – | – | – | – | – | – | – | – | – | – | – | 1 | – | – | – | – | – | 1 | – | 2 | – | – | 3 | – | 1 | – | – | – | – | – | – | – |
| 32 | Ceske Budejovice | 1 | – | – | 2 | 2 | 1 | 2 | – | 2 | 3 | 1 | 1 | 2 | 1 | 3 | 2 | 1 | – | – | 2 | 1 | – | 1 | – | – | 1 | 1 | 2 | – | – | – | – |
| 3 | Havirov | – | – | – | – | – | – | – | 2 | – | 1 | – | – | – | – | – | – | – | – | – | – | – | – | – | – | – | – | – | – | – | – | – | – |
| 28 | Jihlava | – | – | – | – | – | - | – | – | – | 1 | – | – | – | 2 | 2 | 1 | 1 | 1 | 2 | 3 | 1 | 1 | 3 | – | 1 | 3 | 4 | 2 | – | – | – | – |
| 4 | Karlovy Vary | – | – | – | – | – | – | 1 | 1 | 1 | 1 | – | – | – | – | – | – | – | – | – | – | – | – | – | – | – | – | – | – | – | – | – | – |
| 23 | Kladno | – | – | – | 3 | 1 | 1 | 1 | – | 1 | 1 | 2 | – | – | 2 | – | 2 | 1 | – | 2 | 1 | – | – | – | 1 | – | 1 | – | 1 | 2 | – | – | – |
| 15 | Kosice | – | – | – | 1 | 1 | – | – | – | 1 | – | 1 | 1 | 1 | 1 | – | – | – | – | – | 2 | – | – | – | 1 | – | 2 | – | 2 | 1 | – | – | – |
| 4 | Liberec | – | – | – | – | 1 | 1 | – | – | 2 | – | – | – | – | – | – | – | – | – | – | – | – | – | – | – | – | – | – | – | – | – | – | – |
| 34 | Litvinov | – | – | – | – | – | 3 | 2 | – | 1 | – | 1 | 1 | 2 | 2 | 2 | 4 | 2 | 3 | 1 | 2 | 2 | – | – | – | – | 2 | 1 | 3 | – | – | – | – |
| 6 | Martin | – | – | – | – | – | 1 | – | – | 1 | 1 | – | – | – | – | 2 | – | – | – | – | – | – | 1 | – | – | – | – | – | – | – | – | – | – |
| 7 | Nitra | – | – | – | – | – | – | 1 | – | 1 | – | – | 1 | – | 1 | – | – | 1 | – | 2 | – | – | – | – | – | – | – | – | – | – | – | – | – |
| 7 | Olomouc | – | – | – | – | – | – | – | – | – | – | – | 1 | – | – | 2 | 1 | – | 2 | – | – | 1 | – | – | – | – | – | – | – | – | – | – | – |
| 13 | Pardubice | – | – | – | – | – | – | – | 3 | 1 | – | – | – | 1 | – | 1 | 2 | – | – | – | – | – | – | 1 | – | 2 | – | 2 | – | – | – | – | – |
| 14 | Plzen | – | 1 | – | – | – | – | – | 2 | 1 | 1 | – | 1 | – | – | 1 | 1 | – | 3 | – | 1 | 1 | – | – | 1 | – | – | – | – | – | – | – | – |
| 3 | Presov | – | – | – | – | 1 | – | – | – | – | – | – | – | 1 | – | – | – | 1 | – | – | – | – | – | – | – | – | – | – | – | – | – | – | – |
| 28 | Slavia Praha | – | – | 1 | – | 1 | 1 | 2 | 2 | 5 | 3 | 2 | 5 | 4 | – | – | – | 1 | – | – | – | – | – | – | – | – | 1 | – | – | – | – | – | – |
| 22 | Slovan Bratis. | – | – | – | – | – | – | 3 | 1 | – | 2 | 2 | 1 | 1 | 1 | – | 3 | – | – | – | 1 | – | – | 1 | 1 | 1 | – | – | 2 | – | – | 1 | 1 |
| 28 | Sparta Praha | – | – | – | 1 | 2 | 4 | 1 | 1 | 2 | 1 | – | 1 | 1 | – | 1 | – | 1 | 1 | – | 2 | 1 | 2 | 1 | 1 | 1 | 2 | – | 1 | – | – | – | – |
| 30 | Trencin | – | – | 1 | 1 | 1 | 4 | 3 | – | 2 | 3 | 2 | – | 1 | 2 | 1 | – | 2 | 2 | – | 2 | 1 | 1 | – | – | – | 1 | – | – | – | – | – | – |
| 10 | Trinec | 1 | 1 | – | 1 | 1 | – | 1 | 1 | 1 | 1 | 2 | – | – | – | – | – | – | – | – | – | – | – | – | – | – | – | – | – | – | – | – | – |
| 19 | Vitkovice | – | – | – | 1 | 1 | 2 | – | 2 | – | 1 | 1 | 1 | – | 1 | 1 | 1 | 3 | 1 | – | 1 | – | – | – | – | – | – | – | – | 1 | – | – | 1 |
| 14 | Vsetin | – | – | 1 | 1 | – | 1 | 1 | 3 | 2 | 2 | – | 1 | 2 | – | – | – | – | – | – | – | – | – | – | – | – | – | – | – | – | – | – | – |
| 21 | Zlin[1] | – | – | – | – | 1 | 2 | – | – | 2 | – | 2 | 2 | 1 | – | 2 | – | 1 | 2 | 2 | – | – | – | 1 | 1 | 1 | – | 1 | – | – | – | – | – |
| 8 | Zvolen | 1 | – | – | – | – | – | – | – | – | 2 | 2 | – | – | 1 | 1 | – | – | 1 | – | – | – | – | – | – | – | – | – | – | – | – | – | – |

**Former club names:** [1]–Gottwaldov. **Teams with two players selected:** Ingstav Brno, IS Banska Bystrica, Dubnica, Michalovce, Partizan Liptovsky Mikulas, VTJ Pisek, Skalica, Spisska Nova Ves, Topolcany. **Teams with one player selected:** Banik Sokolov, KLH Chomutov, Havlickuv Brod, Ostrava, KC SKP Poprad, Povazska Bystrica, HK Trnava, KHM Zvolen.

## Finland

| Total | Club | '09 | '08 | '07 | '06 | '05 | '04 | '03 | '02 | '01 | '00 | '99 | '98 | '97 | '96 | '95 | '94 | '93 | '92 | '91 | '90 | '89 | '88 | '87 | '86 | '85 | '84 | '83 | '82 | '81 | '80 | '79 | '69 to '78 |
|---|---|---|---|---|---|---|---|---|---|---|---|---|---|---|---|---|---|---|---|---|---|---|---|---|---|---|---|---|---|---|---|---|---|
| 16 | Assat | – | – | – | 2 | – | – | – | 1 | – | – | – | 1 | – | – | 1 | 1 | 1 | – | – | 1 | – | 1 | – | – | – | 2 | 2 | – | 1 | – | – | 2 |
| 20 | Blues Espoo | 3 | 1 | – | – | 1 | 1 | – | 1 | 2 | – | 2 | – | 1 | – | 1 | 2 | – | 2 | 1 | 1 | – | 1 | – | – | – | – | – | – | – | – | – | – |
| 39 | HIFK Helsinki | – | – | – | 4 | 1 | 2 | – | 5 | 2 | 2 | 4 | 2 | 1 | – | 1 | – | 2 | – | – | – | 1 | 2 | – | – | 1 | 2 | 2 | 1 | 1 | – | – | 3 |
| 12 | HPK | – | – | – | 1 | – | – | – | 1 | 1 | 3 | 1 | 1 | 1 | – | – | – | – | 2 | – | – | 1 | – | – | – | – | – | – | – | – | – | – | – |
| 35 | Ilves | 1 | 1 | – | 3 | 3 | – | – | 2 | 4 | 3 | 1 | 2 | – | – | 2 | – | – | – | 1 | 1 | – | 1 | – | 1 | – | 2 | 2 | – | 2 | – | – | 3 |
| 36 | Jokerit | – | – | – | 2 | – | 1 | 2 | 6 | 4 | 3 | 3 | 1 | 1 | 1 | – | 1 | – | 3 | – | 2 | – | 1 | 1 | – | – | 1 | – | – | 1 | 2 | – | – |
| 12 | JyP Jyvaskyla | 1 | – | – | – | – | 1 | – | 2 | 1 | – | 3 | – | 1 | 2 | – | – | – | – | – | – | – | – | 1 | – | – | – | – | – | – | – | – | – |
| 12 | KalPa | 1 | 1 | – | 1 | – | – | 1 | – | 2 | 1 | – | 1 | – | – | – | 2 | 1 | – | – | – | – | – | 1 | – | – | – | – | – | – | – | – | – |
| 25 | Karpat | 1 | – | – | – | 2 | 2 | 3 | 3 | 3 | – | – | 1 | 1 | – | – | – | 1 | – | 1 | – | – | – | 2 | 2 | – | 1 | – | 1 | – | 1 | – | – |
| 3 | Kiekoo-67 | – | – | – | – | – | – | – | – | – | – | – | – | – | – | 3 | – | – | – | – | – | – | – | – | – | – | – | – | – | – | – | – | – |
| 20 | Lukko | – | 1 | 1 | – | – | 1 | 1 | 1 | 3 | 1 | 2 | – | – | – | – | – | – | 1 | – | 1 | – | – | 1 | – | 1 | – | 2 | – | – | – | – | 3 |
| 9 | Pelicans | – | – | 1 | – | – | 1 | – | – | – | – | – | – | – | 1 | – | – | 1 | – | 2 | – | – | – | – | – | – | 1 | 1 | 1 | – | – | – | – |
| 7 | SaiPa | – | – | – | – | 1 | 1 | 1 | – | 1 | 1 | – | – | – | – | – | – | – | – | – | 1 | – | – | – | – | – | – | – | – | 1 | – | – | – |
| 24 | Tappara | – | 2 | 2 | – | – | 1 | 2 | 2 | 2 | 1 | – | – | 2 | 1 | 1 | – | – | – | – | 1 | – | 1 | – | 4 | – | – | – | 2 | – | – | – | 1 |
| 35 | TPS Turku | 2 | – | – | – | – | 1 | 1 | 1 | 3 | 3 | 1 | 3 | 3 | 1 | 3 | 2 | 3 | – | – | – | – | – | – | 1 | 1 | – | – | – | 6 | 1 | – | – |

**Teams with two players selected:** KooKoo Kouvola, Sapko Savonlinna, Sport Vaasa, TuTo.
**Teams with one player selected:** Ahmat Hyvinkaa, Hermes Kokkola, Junkkarit Kalajoki, GrIFK Kauniainen, LeKi, S-Kiekko Seinajoki.

*Born in the old Soviet Union but raised in California, Viktor Tikhonov (top) played in Russia before making his NHL debut with Phoenix in 2008-09. He was selected 28th overall in the 2008 Entry Draft. David Krejci (right) of the Czech Republic played his first full NHL season in 2008-09 after being Boston's first choice (63rd overall) in 2004.*

**Note:** International draft selections played outside North America in their draft year.

European-born players drafted from the OHL, QMJHL, WHL, U.S. colleges or other North American leagues are not counted as International players.

For analysis by birthplace, see the following page.

## Russia/CIS/USSR

| Total | Club | '09 | '08 | '07 | '06 | '05 | '04 | '03 | '02 | '01 | '00 | '99 | '98 | '97 | '96 | '95 | '94 | '93 | '92 | '91 | '90 | '89 | '88 | '87 | '86 | '85 | '84 | '83 | '82 | '81 | '80 | '79 | '69 to '78 |
|---|---|---|---|---|---|---|---|---|---|---|---|---|---|---|---|---|---|---|---|---|---|---|---|---|---|---|---|---|---|---|---|---|---|
| 6 | Ak Bars Kazan | – | 1 | – | – | – | – | 1 | – | 1 | 1 | – | 1 | – | – | – | 1 | – | – | – | – | – | – | – | – | – | – | – | – | – | – | – | – |
| 3 | Ak Bars Kazan 2 | – | – | – | – | – | – | 1 | – | 1 | – | 1 | – | – | – | – | – | – | – | – | – | – | – | – | – | – | – | – | – | – | – | – | – |
| 9 | Avangard Omsk | – | – | – | – | – | – | – | 1 | 3 | 1 | – | – | – | 1 | – | 3 | – | – | – | – | – | – | – | – | – | – | – | – | – | – | – | – |
| 5 | Avangard Omsk 2 | – | – | – | – | – | 1 | 1 | – | 3 | – | – | – | – | – | – | – | – | – | – | – | – | – | – | – | – | – | – | – | – | – | – | – |
| 5 | CSK VVS Samara | – | – | – | – | – | 1 | 1 | – | 1 | – | 1 | – | – | – | 1 | – | – | – | – | – | – | – | – | – | – | – | – | – | – | – | – | – |
| 64 | CSKA Moscow | – | – | 2 | 1 | 1 | 3 | 3 | – | – | – | 3 | 1 | – | 3 | 2 | 5 | 3 | 7 | 4 | 3 | 8 | 5 | 1 | 1 | 1 | – | 4 | 1 | – | – | – | 2 |
| 13 | CSKA Moscow 2 | – | 2 | – | 2 | 1 | 1 | 2 | – | – | – | – | – | 2 | 2 | – | 1 | – | – | – | – | – | – | – | – | – | – | – | – | – | – | – | – |
| 46 | Dynamo Moscow | – | – | 1 | – | – | 1 | 1 | – | – | 2 | 2 | 1 | 1 | 1 | 7 | 1 | 2 | 10 | 7 | 4 | 3 | 2 | – | – | – | – | – | – | – | – | – | – |
| 17 | Dyn'o Moscow 2 | 1 | – | – | – | – | – | 1 | – | – | 4 | – | 3 | 3 | – | – | 2 | 1 | 2 | – | – | – | – | – | – | – | – | – | – | – | – | – | – |
| 4 | Dyn-Energ. Yekat.[1] | – | – | – | – | – | – | 1 | – | – | – | 1 | 1 | – | 1 | – | – | – | – | – | – | – | – | – | – | – | – | – | – | – | – | – | – |
| 16 | Elektrostal | – | – | – | – | – | – | 2 | 9 | 1 | – | – | – | 1 | – | – | – | – | 3 | – | – | – | – | – | – | – | – | – | – | – | – | – | – |
| 11 | HC CSKA | – | – | – | – | – | – | – | 4 | – | 5 | 2 | – | – | – | – | – | – | – | – | – | – | – | – | – | – | – | – | – | – | – | – | – |
| 3 | Kristall Saratov | – | – | – | – | – | 1 | – | – | 1 | – | – | – | – | – | – | – | 1 | – | – | – | – | – | – | – | – | – | – | – | – | – | – | – |
| 33 | Krylja Sovetov | – | – | – | 1 | 1 | 2 | – | 1 | 1 | 1 | 2 | 1 | 1 | 2 | 3 | 5 | 1 | 3 | 4 | 2 | 1 | 1 | – | – | – | – | – | – | – | – | – | – |
| 4 | Krylja Sovetov 2 | – | – | – | – | – | – | – | 3 | – | – | – | – | – | – | – | – | 1 | – | – | – | – | – | – | – | – | – | – | – | – | – | – | – |
| 19 | Lada Togliatti | 1 | – | – | 2 | – | 2 | – | 2 | – | 2 | 2 | 1 | 3 | 1 | – | – | 2 | 1 | – | – | – | – | – | – | – | – | – | – | – | – | – | – |
| 6 | Lada Togliatti 2 | – | – | – | – | 1 | – | – | – | 2 | 2 | 1 | – | – | – | – | – | – | – | – | – | – | – | – | – | – | – | – | – | – | – | – | – |
| 22 | Lokomotiv Yaro.[2] | – | – | – | – | – | – | 4 | 2 | – | 1 | 1 | 3 | 1 | 1 | 5 | 1 | – | – | 2 | 1 | – | – | – | – | – | – | – | – | – | – | – | – |
| 32 | Lokomotiv Yaro.2 | 1 | 2 | 1 | 3 | 2 | – | 3 | 1 | 1 | 9 | – | 4 | 2 | 2 | 1 | – | – | – | – | – | – | – | – | – | – | – | – | – | – | – | – | – |
| 7 | Magnitogorsk | – | – | – | 1 | – | 1 | 1 | 1 | 3 | – | – | – | – | – | – | – | – | – | – | – | – | – | – | – | – | – | – | – | – | – | – | – |
| 3 | Magnitogorsk 2 | 1 | 1 | – | – | – | 1 | – | – | – | – | – | – | – | – | – | – | – | – | – | – | – | – | – | – | – | – | – | – | – | – | – | – |
| 6 | Nizhnekamsk | – | – | – | – | – | 1 | – | – | 2 | 2 | – | – | 1 | – | – | – | – | – | – | – | – | – | – | – | – | – | – | – | – | – | – | – |
| 4 | Nizhny Novgorod[3] | – | – | – | – | – | – | – | – | – | 1 | – | – | – | – | – | – | – | 2 | – | 1 | – | – | – | – | – | – | – | – | – | – | – | – |
| 8 | Novokuznetsk | 1 | – | – | – | – | 1 | 1 | – | 1 | 2 | 2 | – | – | – | – | – | – | – | – | – | – | – | – | – | – | – | – | – | – | – | – | – |
| 9 | Pardaugava Riga[4] | – | – | – | – | – | – | – | – | – | – | – | – | – | – | – | – | 1 | 4 | 1 | – | 2 | 1 | – | – | – | – | – | – | – | – | – | – |
| 5 | Perm | – | – | – | – | – | – | – | 1 | 1 | 1 | – | – | – | – | 1 | 1 | – | – | – | – | – | – | – | – | – | – | – | – | – | – | – | – |
| 14 | Severstal Cher.[5] | – | 1 | – | 1 | – | – | 2 | – | – | 1 | 5 | – | – | 1 | 1 | – | 1 | 1 | – | – | – | – | – | – | – | – | – | – | – | – | – | – |
| 4 | Severstal Cher. 2 | – | 1 | – | – | – | – | – | 1 | – | 1 | 1 | – | – | – | – | – | – | – | – | – | – | – | – | – | – | – | – | – | – | – | – | – |
| 12 | SKA St. Pete.[6] | – | – | – | – | – | – | – | – | 2 | 1 | 2 | – | – | – | – | 1 | – | 1 | 2 | – | – | – | – | – | – | – | – | 1 | – | – | – | 2 |
| 11 | Sokol Kiev | – | – | – | – | – | – | – | – | – | – | – | – | – | – | 2 | – | 1 | 3 | 2 | 1 | – | 1 | – | – | – | 1 | – | – | – | – | – | – |
| 22 | Spartak Moscow | – | – | – | – | – | – | – | – | 6 | – | 1 | – | – | – | 1 | 6 | – | 4 | 1 | – | – | – | 1 | – | 1 | – | – | 1 | – | – | – | – |
| 9 | THC Tver | – | – | – | – | – | 3 | 3 | – | 1 | 2 | – | – | – | – | – | – | – | – | – | – | – | – | – | – | – | – | – | – | – | – | – | – |
| 5 | Tivali Minsk[7] | – | – | – | – | – | 1 | – | – | – | – | – | – | – | – | – | 1 | 2 | – | – | – | – | 1 | – | – | – | – | – | – | – | – | – | – |
| 21 | Traktor Chelyabinsk | – | 1 | 1 | 1 | 2 | – | – | 1 | – | – | – | 1 | 1 | – | 1 | 1 | 7 | 2 | – | – | 2 | – | – | – | – | – | – | – | – | – | – | – |
| 9 | Ufa | – | – | – | – | – | – | 1 | – | – | 1 | – | – | 1 | 1 | 1 | 2 | 2 | – | – | – | – | – | – | – | – | – | – | – | – | – | – | – |
| 9 | Ust-Kamenogorsk | – | – | – | – | – | – | 1 | – | – | – | 1 | 2 | – | – | 1 | 2 | 1 | 1 | – | – | – | – | – | – | – | – | – | – | – | – | – | – |
| 14 | Voskresensk | – | – | – | – | – | – | 1 | – | 1 | 1 | – | 2 | – | – | – | 1 | – | 2 | 1 | 3 | 1 | – | – | – | – | – | 1 | – | – | – | – | – |

**Former club names:** 1–Avtomobilist Yekaterinburg, 2–Torpedo Yaroslavl, 3–Torpedo Gorky, 4–Dynamo Riga,HC Riga, 5–Metallurg Cherepovets, 6–SKA Leningrad, 7–Dynamo Minsk. **Teams with two players selected:** Dizelist Penza, Mechel Chelyabinsk, Metallurg Magnitogorsk 2, Metallurg Novokuznetsk 2, Salavat Yulayev Ufa 2, Spartak Moscow 2, Torpedo Nizhny Novgorod 2, Yunost Minsk. **Teams with one player selected:** Amur Khabarovsk, Argus Moscow, Avangard Omsk, HC CSKA Moscow 2, Dynamo Khazov, Dynamo-81 Riga, Gazovik Tyumen, HK Gomel, Izohets St. Petersburg, Kapitan Stupino, Khimik Novopolotsk, Khimik Voskresensk 2, Metalurgs Liepaja, Mostovik Kurgan, Neftekhimik Nizhnekamsk 2, Neftyanik Almetjevsk, SKA St. Petersburg 2, Spartak St. Petersburg, Sibir Novosibirsk 2, Stalkers-Juniors, Torpedo Nizhny Novgorod 2, THC Tver, Vityaz Podolsk, Vityaz Podolsk 2.

## Sweden

| Total | Club | '09 | '08 | '07 | '06 | '05 | '04 | '03 | '02 | '01 | '00 | '99 | '98 | '97 | '96 | '95 | '94 | '93 | '92 | '91 | '90 | '89 | '88 | '87 | '86 | '85 | '84 | '83 | '82 | '81 | '80 | '79 | '69 to '78 |
|---|---|---|---|---|---|---|---|---|---|---|---|---|---|---|---|---|---|---|---|---|---|---|---|---|---|---|---|---|---|---|---|---|---|
| 24 | AIK Solna | – | – | – | – | – | – | – | 1 | 1 | – | 3 | 1 | 1 | – | – | 1 | – | 1 | 1 | 1 | – | – | – | – | 4 | – | 1 | 3 | 2 | – | 1 | 2 |
| 9 | Bjorkloven | – | 1 | – | 2 | 1 | – | – | – | – | – | – | – | – | – | – | – | – | – | – | – | – | 1 | – | – | 1 | – | – | – | 1 | 2 | – | – |
| 3 | Boden | – | – | – | – | – | – | – | – | – | – | – | – | – | – | – | 1 | – | – | – | – | – | – | – | 1 | – | – | – | – | – | – | – | 1 |
| 32 | Brynas Gavle | 3 | 4 | 1 | 1 | – | – | 2 | – | 2 | 1 | 1 | 2 | 1 | 1 | – | – | 1 | – | – | – | – | – | 4 | – | – | 2 | 1 | – | 1 | 1 | 1 | 2 |
| 42 | Djurgarden | 3 | 1 | – | 1 | 1 | 2 | – | 2 | 1 | 4 | 1 | – | 2 | 2 | 3 | – | 1 | 1 | 2 | 1 | 1 | – | 2 | 1 | – | 1 | 2 | 1 | – | 2 | 1 | 3 |
| 3 | Falun | – | – | – | – | – | – | – | – | – | – | – | – | – | – | – | – | – | – | 1 | – | – | 1 | – | – | – | – | – | – | 1 | – | – | – |
| 34 | Farjestad | 1 | – | – | 1 | – | – | – | 2 | 1 | – | 1 | 6 | 3 | – | 2 | – | 1 | 2 | 1 | – | 1 | – | – | – | 2 | 1 | 1 | 1 | 2 | 1 | – | 4 |
| 49 | Frolunda | 3 | 4 | 5 | 3 | 3 | 4 | 2 | 3 | 3 | 4 | 2 | 1 | – | 1 | 1 | 3 | – | 1 | – | – | 1 | 1 | 1 | – | 1 | 2 | – | – | – | – | – | – |
| 3 | Grums | – | – | – | – | – | – | – | – | – | 1 | 1 | – | – | – | – | 1 | – | – | – | – | – | – | – | – | – | – | – | – | – | – | – | – |
| 10 | Hammarby | – | – | – | 1 | – | – | – | 3 | – | 1 | – | – | 1 | – | – | – | 1 | 1 | – | – | – | – | – | – | – | – | – | – | – | 1 | 1 | – |
| 7 | Huddinge | – | – | – | 1 | – | – | – | 1 | 1 | – | 1 | – | – | 2 | – | – | – | – | 1 | – | – | – | – | – | – | – | – | – | – | – | – | – |
| 27 | HV 71 | 1 | 3 | 1 | – | 1 | 2 | 1 | 1 | – | 1 | 3 | 4 | 1 | 2 | – | 2 | – | – | – | 1 | – | 1 | 1 | – | – | – | – | – | 1 | – | – | – |
| 31 | Leksand | 1 | – | – | 1 | 1 | – | 2 | – | – | 5 | – | 2 | – | 1 | – | 2 | 2 | – | 2 | – | 1 | 2 | 1 | 1 | 2 | 2 | – | 1 | – | – | 1 | 1 |
| 6 | Linkoping | 1 | 1 | 1 | 1 | 1 | 1 | – | – | – | – | – | – | – | – | – | – | – | – | – | – | – | – | – | – | – | – | – | – | – | – | – | – |
| 15 | Lulea | 1 | – | 3 | – | – | 1 | – | – | – | 2 | – | 1 | 1 | – | – | – | – | 1 | – | – | – | 1 | 1 | 1 | – | – | – | – | 1 | 1 | – | – |
| 19 | Malmo | 1 | 1 | 1 | 1 | 1 | 1 | 1 | 4 | – | 1 | 1 | – | – | 2 | – | 1 | 1 | 1 | – | – | – | 1 | – | – | – | – | – | – | – | – | – | – |
| 37 | MODO | 1 | – | – | – | 1 | 1 | – | 3 | – | 3 | 7 | – | 3 | 3 | – | – | 5 | 2 | 2 | – | – | – | 1 | – | – | 2 | – | 1 | – | – | 1 | 1 |
| 7 | Mora | 1 | – | – | – | – | – | 1 | – | 1 | – | – | – | 1 | 1 | – | – | – | – | – | – | – | – | – | 1 | – | – | 1 | – | – | – | – | – |
| 3 | Morrum | – | – | – | – | – | – | – | 2 | 1 | – | – | – | – | – | – | – | – | – | – | – | – | – | – | – | – | – | – | – | – | – | – | – |
| 4 | Nacka | – | – | – | – | – | – | – | – | – | – | – | – | – | – | – | – | – | 2 | – | – | 1 | – | – | 1 | – | – | – | – | – | – | – | – |
| 6 | Orebro | – | – | – | – | – | 1 | – | – | – | – | – | – | – | – | – | – | – | – | – | – | – | – | 1 | – | 1 | – | 1 | – | – | – | – | 2 |
| 3 | Pitea | – | – | – | – | – | – | – | – | – | – | – | – | – | – | – | 1 | – | – | – | 1 | – | – | – | – | – | – | – | 1 | – | – | – | – |
| 10 | Rogle | – | – | 1 | – | – | – | – | – | – | – | 1 | – | – | – | 1 | 2 | 2 | – | – | – | – | 2 | 1 | – | – | – | – | – | – | – | – | – |
| 13 | Skelleftea | 3 | – | – | – | – | – | – | – | – | – | – | – | 1 | – | – | – | 1 | – | – | – | – | 1 | – | – | – | 1 | 2 | 1 | 1 | – | – | 2 |
| 25 | Sodertalje | – | – | 1 | 2 | 3 | 1 | 2 | – | 1 | 1 | – | 1 | – | – | – | – | 1 | – | – | – | 2 | – | – | 2 | 2 | 2 | 1 | 1 | 1 | – | – | 1 |
| 3 | Stocksund | – | – | – | – | – | 2 | – | – | – | – | – | – | – | – | – | – | – | – | – | – | – | – | – | – | – | – | – | 1 | – | – | – | – |
| 3 | Team Kiruna | – | – | – | – | – | – | – | – | – | – | – | – | – | – | – | – | 1 | – | – | – | – | – | – | – | – | – | – | 1 | – | – | – | 1 |
| 10 | Timra | 2 | – | – | – | – | – | – | 1 | – | – | 1 | – | – | – | – | 1 | – | – | – | – | – | – | – | 1 | 1 | – | – | – | 2 | 1 | – | – |
| 4 | Troja/Ljungby | – | – | – | – | – | – | 1 | – | – | – | 1 | – | – | – | – | – | – | – | – | – | – | 1 | – | – | 1 | – | – | – | – | – | – | – |
| 16 | Vasteras | – | 1 | 1 | 3 | – | 1 | – | 1 | – | 1 | – | – | – | – | – | 1 | 1 | – | 1 | 1 | 2 | 2 | – | – | – | – | – | – | – | – | – | – |
| 3 | Vita Hasten | – | 1 | – | – | – | – | – | – | 1 | – | – | – | – | 1 | – | – | – | – | – | – | – | – | – | – | – | – | – | – | – | – | – | – |

**Teams with two players selected:** Almtuna, Bofors, Ostersund, Tingsryd. **Teams with one player selected:** Arboga, Arvika, Danderyd Hockey, Fagersta, Jamtland, Karskoga, Kumla, Stocksund, S/G Hockey 83 Gavle, Skovde, Sunne, Talje, Tunabro, Uppsala, Vallentuna, Vasby. Karskoga, Kumla, Skare, Stocksund, S/G Hockey 83 Gavle, Skovde, Sunne, Talje, Tunabro, Uppsala, Vallentuna, Vasby.

## European Draft Firsts

**1969 – First European (and Finn)** • LW Tommi Salmelainen, 66th overall by St. Louis.

**1974 – First Swede** • C Per Alexandersson, 49th overall by Toronto. Four other Swedish-born players were selected that year, including defenseman Stefan Persson, 214th overall by the NY Islanders, who became the first European-trained player to be part of a Stanley Cup winner with the Islanders in 1980.

**1975 – First Russian** • C Viktor Khatulev, 160th overall by Philadelphia.

**1976 – First European Taken in the First Round** • Swedish D Bjorn Johansson, 5th overall by the California Seals.

**1976 – First Swiss** • C Jacques Soguel, 121st overall by St. Louis.

**1978 – First Czechoslovak** • LW Ladislav Svozil, 194th overall by Detroit.

**1978 – First Germans** • G Bernard Englbrecht, 196th overall by Atlanta and F Gerd Truntschka, 200th overall by St. Louis.

**1989 – First European Taken First Overall** • Swedish C Mats Sundin, first overall by Quebec in 1989.

## 2009 Entry Draft Analysis

### BY BIRTHPLACE

#### Country of Origin

| Country | Players Drafted |
|---|---|
| Canada | 102 |
| USA | 55 |
| Sweden | 24 |
| Finland | 10 |
| Russia | 7 |
| Slovakia | 5 |
| Czech Republic | 3 |
| Belarus | 1 |
| Denmark | 1 |
| England | 1 |
| Germany | 1 |
| **Total** | **210** |

#### Canadian-Born Players

| Province | Players Drafted |
|---|---|
| Ontario | 46 |
| Quebec | 20 |
| British Columbia | 13 |
| Alberta | 9 |
| Saskatchewan | 9 |
| Manitoba | 3 |
| Nova Scotia | 2 |
| **Total** | **102** |

#### U.S.-Born Players

| State | Players Drafted |
|---|---|
| Minnesota | 12 |
| New York | 9 |
| Massachusetts | 5 |
| California | 3 |
| Connecticut | 3 |
| Illinois | 3 |
| Colorado | 2 |
| Michigan | 2 |
| North Dakota | 2 |
| Pennsylvania | 2 |
| Texas | 2 |
| Wisconsin | 2 |
| Alaska | 1 |
| Alabama | 1 |
| Florida | 1 |
| Maine | 1 |
| Missouri | 1 |
| New Jersey | 1 |
| Rhode Island | 1 |
| Utah | 1 |
| **Total** | **55** |

### BY BIRTH YEAR

| Year | Players Drafted |
|---|---|
| 1991 | 119 |
| 1990 | 68 |
| 1989 | 22 |
| 1988 | 1 |

### BY POSITION

| Position | Players Drafted |
|---|---|
| Defense | 70 |
| Center | 58 |
| Right Wing | 31 |
| Left Wing | 30 |
| Goaltender | 21 |

# Notes on 2009 First-Round Selections

**1.** NY ISLANDERS • **JOHN TAVARES** • C • Projected as a future #1 draft pick from the time he was 14, John Tavares is a proven goal-scorer with the ability to raise his game when the pressure is on. He entered the OHL as a 15-year-old and broke Wayne Gretzky's record for goals at age 16 with 72 in 2006-07 to earn CHL player of the year honors. He ended his four-year junior career with an OHL-record 215 goals in 247 games and won back-to-back gold medals with Team Canada at the World Junior Championship in 2008 and 2009.

**2.** TAMPA BAY • **VICTOR HEDMAN** • D • A 6'6" defenseman who is mobile and strong, Victor Hedman brings to his game unsurpassed combinations of size, explosiveness in his skating, quickness and offensive ability. Hedman, who patterns his game on Nicklas Lidstrom, has spent two seasons in the Swedish Elite League. He has also represented Sweden in several major international tournaments, including the World Junior Championship in 2008 and 2009.

**3.** COLORADO • **MATT DUCHENE** • C • An excellent all-round skater with great speed, Matt Duchene's ability to see the ice and move the puck through traffic is outstanding. His above average hockey sense allows him to play well in both ends of the ice. Duchene led Brampton to the OHL Finals in 2008-09. During an eight-month span in 2008, he won gold medals at the World Under-17 challenge, the Under-18 Ivan Hlinka tournament and the World Under-18 Championship.

**4.** ATLANTA • **EVANDER KANE** • C • Named after boxer Evander Holyfield, Evander Kane is an offensive threat who is not afraid to go into the corners or to fight his way to the front of the net. After a nomination for WHL rookie of the year in 2007-08, Kane doubled his production from 24 goals to 48 in 2008-09. He was the last player cut from Canada's 2009 World Junior team, but was then added to the team as an injury replacement and had six points in six games played.

**5.** LOS ANGELES • **BRAYDEN SCHENN** • C • The younger brother of Toronto's Luke Schenn, who was picked fifth overall in 2008, Brayden Schenn is a two-way player who has been compared to Philadelphia's Mike Richards. Schenn was named WHL rookie of the year in 2007-08 and has led the Brandon Wheat Kings in scoring for two straight seasons. He won gold medals for Team Canada at the 2008 World Under-18 Championship and at the Ivan Hlinka tournament.

**6.** PHOENIX • **OLIVER EKMAN-LARSSON** • D • A smooth skater, Oliver Ekman-Larsson is an offensive defenseman who can handle the puck at top speed. He has a hard shot from the blue line and can quarterback the power-play. Ekman-Larsson played in the Swedish second division in 2008-09 and ranked first in the league with a plus-44 rating and was first in points (39) among under-18 players.

**7.** TORONTO • **NAZEM KADRI** • C • A fast skater with skill and grit, Nazem Kadri patterns his game on Vincent Lecavalier. Kadri helped the Kitchener Rangers reach the Memorial Cup final in 2008 before being traded to his hometown London Knights. Despite being slowed by a broken jaw in 2008-09, he led the OHL with 10 shorthanded points and finished ninth in the league with 53 assists in just 56 games.

**8.** DALLAS • **SCOTT GLENNIE** • RW • A gifted offensive player, Scott Glennie is a strong skater and an excellent puck handler who uses his speed to his advantage. A linemate of Brayden Schenn with Brandon, he had an excellent rookie season in 2007-08 and recovered from injuries to have another fine season in 2008-09, collecting 70 points in just 55 games and ranking among the WHL leaders in playoff scoring.

**9.** OTTAWA • **JARED COWEN** • D • A 6'5" defenseman who is big, strong and rangy, Jared Cowen has good speed and plays well at both ends of the ice. In his first year with Spokane in 2007-08, Cowen led all WHL rookie defensemen with a plus-28 rating and helped the Chiefs win the Memorial Cup. He also won a gold medal at the Under-18 Ivan Hlinka tournament. A knee injury cut short his 2008-09 season.

**10.** EDMONTON • **MAGNUS PAAJARVI-SVENSSON** • LW • A player with extraordinary outside speed and skill, Magnus Paajarvi-Svensson has the ability to freeze defenders. As a 16-year-old in 2008, he became the youngest Swede to play in the World Junior Championship and the youngest since Sidney Crosby debuted at the 2004 tourney. He won a silver medal at the event in 2008 and again in 2009.

**11.** NASHVILLE • **RYAN ELLIS** • D • Though small for a defenseman at 5'9", Ryan Ellis has a great shot and his puck movement is excellent. He is a high-end offensive player who can get his shot through to the net, but is also not afraid to take the body defensively. Ellis helped Windsor win the Memorial Cup in 2009, and led all defensemen in scoring while finishing seventh overall in the OHL with 89 points (22 goals, 67 assists) in 57 games. His plus-minus rating was +52.

**12.** NY ISLANDERS • **CALVIN DE HAAN** • D • A poised and patient defenseman, Calvin De Haan sees the ice very well and moves the puck through traffic. He also has a hard and accurate shot, but his biggest asset is his hockey sense. In his first season in the OHL with Oshawa, De Haan finished second in the league among rookie defensemen with 63 points (eight goals, 55 assists) in 68 games. He also played for Team Canada at the 2009 World Under-18 Championship.

**13.** BUFFALO • **ZACK KASSIAN** • RW • A physical player who can fight and is tough along the boards, Zack Kassian protects the puck very well and battles through checks. He also has very good playmaking and puck-handling abilities. Kassian is often compared to Boston's Milan Lucic. He finished second in scoring with 63 points in 61 games for Peterborough in 2008-09 and finished in the top 20 in the OHL with 136 penalty minutes.

**14.** FLORIDA • **DMITRY KULIKOV** • D • A great skater who can carry the puck and shoot it well, Dmitry Kulikov is a defensive defenseman first, but knows when to join the rush. Kulikov had 62 points in 57 games for Drummondville in 2008-09 and was both rookie of the year and defenseman of the year in the QMJHL. He won a bronze medal for Russia at the 2009 World Junior Championship and has won silver (2008) and gold (2007) at the Under-18 Championship.

**15.** ANAHEIM • **PETER HOLLAND** • D • A smart player who skates very well and generates good speed, Peter Holland is a two-way player who can be good offensively and defensively responsible as well. Holland represented the OHL in the 2008 Canada/Russia Challenge and was selected to the 2009 OHL All-Star Classic. He also played for Team Canada at the 2009 World Under-18 Championship. He had 67 points (28 goals, 39 assists) in 68 games for Guelph in 2008-09.

**16.** MINNESOTA • **NICK LEDDY** • D • An explosive skater who plays a reliable two-way game, Nick Leddy also has a great shot and makes good decisions with the puck. Leddy was named Minnesota high school's "Mr. Hockey" in 2009 after leading Eden Prairie to the first Class 2A State Championship in school history. In 2008, he represented the United States at the Under-18 Ivan Hlinka tournament. He will attend the University of Minnesota beginning in 2009-10.

**17.** ST. LOUIS • **DAVID RUNDBLAD** • D • A defenseman with very good puck skills and speed, David Rundblad is a smart player who is learning to be more physical. Rundblad was a 17-year-old rookie in the Swedish Elite League for most of the 2008-09 season. He had 15 points (eight goals, seven assists) in just 10 games in the Swedish junior league. He also won a silver medal at the 2009 World Junior Championship.

**18.** MONTREAL • **LOUIS LEBLANC** • C • A player with good hands who's evasive on the ice, Louis Leblanc left Quebec for the USHL in 2008-09 and will attend Harvard for the 2009-10 season. He had 59 points in 60 games to lead Omaha in scoring and was tied for tenth overall in the league. Leblanc was named rookie of the year. In 2008, he helped Canada win gold at the Under-18 Ivan Hlinka tournament.

**19.** NY RANGERS • **CHRIS KREIDER** • C • Considered by some scouts to be the best skater in the draft, Chris Kreider has explosive speed and acceleration. His short-distance speed is exceptional and he is an excellent passer and playmaker. Kreider was a grade 11 student who had 33 goals and 23 assists for 56 points in just 26 games for Andover Academy in 2008-09 and plans to attend Boston College in 2010-11.

**20.** NEW JERSEY • **JACOB JOSEFSON** • C • A smart, two-way player, Jacob Josefson is a playmaker who sees the ice well and is responsible in his own end. Josefson spent most of the 2008-09 season as a 17-year-old playing against men in the Swedish Elite League. He played at both the World Junior Championship and the World Under-18 Championship in 2009, winning a silver medal at the WJC despite the flu.

**21.** COLUMBUS • **JOHN MOORE** • D • A gifted skater who has been compared to Hall of Famer Paul Coffey and patterns his game on Scott Niedermayer, John Moore is poised with the puck and gets his shots through to the net. Moore needs to improve his defensive zone play, put is a team leader with Chicago in the USHL and was named the league's defenseman of the year in 2008-09. A lifelong native of Chicago, Illinois, Moore will attend Colorado College in 2009-10.

**22.** VANCOUVER • **JORDAN SCHROEDER** • C • Just 5'8" but stocky and strong, Jordan Schroeder is a dynamic player who's tough to knock off the puck. He has a hard wrist shot and the skill to go around defenders or freeze goaltenders and pass to his wingers. Schroeder played for the U.S. National Team Development Program and went on to be named WCHA rookie of the year at Minnesota in 2008-09. He led U.S. scorers at the 2009 World Junior Championship.

**23.** CALGARY • **TIM ERIXON** • D • The son of former NHL player Jan Erixon, Tim Erixon is a smart defenseman who can either lead a rush or support the rush from behind. Born in the U.S. while his father played for the Rangers but raised in Sweden, Erixon spent most of the 2008-09 season playing against much older competition in the Swedish Elite League. He won a silver medal at the World Junior Championship in 2009 and was an all-star at the World Under-18 event.

**24.** WASHINGTON • **MARCUS JOHANSSON** • LW • A player with good offensive instincts and a fine understanding of his defensive duties, Marcus Johansson's overall skill level and stickhandling give him room to move the puck and shoot. He has a good selection of shots with a quick, precise wrist shot. Johansson played with Swedish Elite League champions Farjestad in 2008-09 and also won a silver medal at the 2009 World Junior Championship.

**25.** BOSTON • **JORDAN CARON** • RW • A very steady, dependable player who works hard, Jordan Caron has put up good numbers playing junior hockey in Quebec despite battling injuries. Caron is not a flashy player, but he plays his position well. He had 36 goals in 2008-09 despite playing just 56 games to lead Rimouski and rank 11th in the QMJHL. He has soft hands and good size at 6'3" and 202 pounds. Caron played for the QMJHL at the 2008 Canada/Russia Challenge.

**26.** ANAHEIM • **KYLE PALMIERI** • C/RW • A player with good speed who knows where he needs to be to score goals, Kyle Palmieri has passion, natural skills and tenaciousness. Palmieri is a product of the U.S. National Team Development Program who participated in the 2008 World Under-18 Championships, helping the U.S. win a bronze medal. At the 2008 Five Nations Tournament, Palmieri scored a hat trick to lead the U.S. to a gold medal in a 5-3 victory over Finland.

**27.** CAROLINA • **PHILIPPE PARADIS** • C • A good skater who can shoot the puck and goes to the net well, Philippe Paradis also pays attention to the defensive aspects of the game. Paradis helped lead the Shawinigan Cataractes to the Quebec Major Junior Hockey League Final in 2008-09. At the 2009 CHL Top Prospects event, Paradis blasted a 95.7 miles-per-hour shot in the hardest shot competition.

**28.** CHICAGO • **DYLAN OLSEN** • D • A strong puck-moving defenseman with good offensive instincts, Dylan Olsen was the only Junior A player on Canada's 2009 World Under-18 Championship team. As a rookie with the Camrose Kodiaks in 2007-08, he helped the Alberta Junior Hockey League team reach the finals of the Royal Bank Cup. In 2008-09 he was the team's top-scoring defenseman with 10 goals.

**29.** TAMPA BAY • **CARTER ASHTON** • RW • The son of former NHLer Brent Ashton, Carter Ashton is a 6'3", 205-pound power forward. He is a smart player who knows the offensive and defensive side of his game. Ashton scored 30 goals for Lethbridge in the WHL in 2008-09 after injuries cut short his 2007-08 season. He scored the gold medal-winning goal for Canada at the 2008 Under-18 Ivan Hlinka tournament.

**30.** PITTSBURGH • **SIMON DESPRES** • D • Standing 6'4" and weighing 205 pounds, Simon Despres has size and mobility. He is a good skater who plays well without the puck. Despres led a poor Saint John team in plus-minus at +16 in 2008-09 and was an assistant captain for Team Canada at the 2009 World Under-18 Championship. He was also a member of Canada's gold medal team at the 2008 Ivan Hlinka event.

1: John Tavares
C – NY Islanders

2: Victor Hedman
D – Tampa Bay

3: Matt Duchene
C – Colorado

4: Evander Kane
C – Atlanta

5: Brayden Schenn
C – Los Angeles

6: Oliver Ekman-Larsson
D – Phoenix

7: Nazem Kadri
C – Toronto

8: Scott Glennie
RW – Dallas

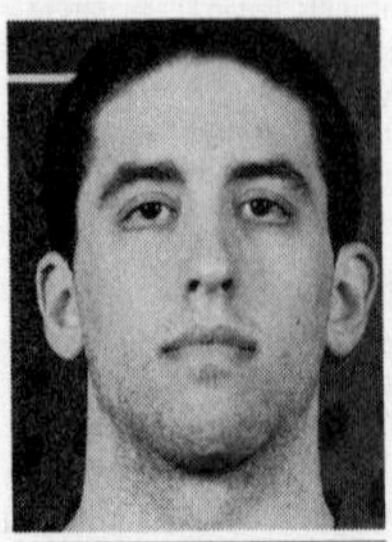

9: Jared Cowen
D – Ottawa

10: Magnus Paajarvi-Svensson
LW – Edmonton

*Players selected first through tenth in the 2009 NHL Entry Draft.*

# 2009 NHL ENTRY DRAFT

## FIRST ROUND

| Pick | Claimed by | | Amateur Club | Position |
|---|---|---|---|---|
| 1 | NYI | John Tavares | London | C |
| 2 | T.B. | Victor Hedman | MODO | D |
| 3 | COL | Matt Duchene | Brampton | C |
| 4 | ATL | Evander Kane | Vancouver | C |
| 5 | L.A. | Brayden Schenn | Brandon | C |
| 6 | PHX | Oliver Ekman-Larsson | Leksand | D |
| 7 | TOR | Nazem Kadri | London | C |
| 8 | DAL | Scott Glennie | Brandon | RW |
| 9 | OTT | Jared Cowen | Spokane | D |
| 10 | EDM | Magnus Paajarvi-Svensson | Timra | LW |
| 11 | NSH | Ryan Ellis | Windsor | D |
| 12 | NYI | Calvin De Haan | Oshawa | D |
| 13 | BUF | Zack Kassian | Peterborough | RW |
| 14 | FLA | Dmitry Kulikov | Drummondville | D |
| 15 | ANA | Peter Holland | Guelph | C |
| 16 | MIN | Nick Leddy | Eden Prairie | D |
| 17 | STL | David Rundblad | Skelleftea | D |
| 18 | MTL | Louis Leblanc | Omaha | C |
| 19 | NYR | Chris Kreider | Andover | C |
| 20 | N.J. | Jacob Josefson | Djurgarden | C |
| 21 | CBJ | John Moore | Chicago | D |
| 22 | VAN | Jordan Schroeder | U of Minnesota | C |
| 23 | CGY | Tim Erixon | Skelleftea | D |
| 24 | WSH | Marcus Johansson | Farjestad | C |
| 25 | BOS | Jordan Caron | Rimouski | RW |
| 26 | ANA | Kyle Palmieri | USA U-18 | C/RW |
| 27 | CAR | Philippe Paradis | Shawinigan | C |
| 28 | CHI | Dylan Olsen | Camrose | D |
| 29 | T.B. | Carter Ashton | Lethbridge | RW |
| 30 | PIT | Simon Despres | Saint John | D |

## SECOND ROUND

| Pick | Claimed by | | Amateur Club | Position |
|---|---|---|---|---|
| 31 | NYI | Mikko Koskinen | Blues | G |
| 32 | DET | Landon Ferraro | Red Deer | C |
| 33 | COL | Ryan O'Reilly | Erie | C |
| 34 | ATL | Carl Klingberg | Frolunda Jr. | LW |
| 35 | L.A. | Kyle Clifford | Barrie | LW |
| 36 | PHX | Chris Brown | USA U-18 | C |
| 37 | ANA | Matt Clark | Brampton | D |
| 38 | DAL | Alex Chiasson | Des Moines | RW |
| 39 | OTT | Jakob Silfverberg | Brynas | LW |
| 40 | EDM | Anton Lander | Timra | C |
| 41 | NSH | Zach Budish | Edina High | RW |
| 42 | NSH | Charles-Olivier Roussel | Shawinigan | D |
| 43 | S.J. | William Wrenn | USA U-18 | D |
| 44 | FLA | Drew Shore | USA U-18 | C |
| 45 | ATL | Jeremy Morin | USA U-18 | LW |
| 46 | OTT | Robin Lehner | Frolunda Jr. | G |
| 47 | NYR | Ethan Werek | Kingston | C |
| 48 | STL | Brett Ponich | Portland | D |
| 49 | COL | Stefan Elliott | Saskatoon | D |
| 50 | TOR | Kenny Ryan | USA U-18 | RW |
| 51 | CAR | Brian Dumoulin | Jr. Monarchs | D |
| 52 | T.B. | Richard Panik | Trinec | RW |
| 53 | VAN | Anton Rodin | Brynas Jr. | RW |
| 54 | N.J. | Eric Gelinas | Lewiston | D |
| 55 | WSH | Dmitri Orlov | Novokuznetsk | D |
| 56 | CBJ | Kevin Lynch | USA U-18 | C |
| 57 | S.J. | Taylor Doherty | Kingston | D |
| 58 | TOR | Jesse Blacker | Windsor | D |
| 59 | CHI | Brandon Pirri | Georgetown | C |
| 60 | DET | Tomas Tatar | Zvolen | C |
| 61 | PIT | Philip Samuelsson | Chicago | D |

## THIRD ROUND

| Pick | Claimed by | | Amateur Club | Position |
|---|---|---|---|---|
| 62 | NYI | Anders Nilsson | Lulea Jr. | G |
| 63 | PIT | Ben Hanowski | Little Falls H.S. | W |
| 64 | COL | Tyson Barrie | Kelowna | D |
| 65 | MTL | Joonas Nattinen | Blues Jr. | C |
| 66 | BUF | Brayden McNabb | Kootenay | D |
| 67 | FLA | Josh Birkholz | Fargo | RW |
| 68 | TOR | Jamie Devane | Plymouth | LW |
| 69 | DAL | Reilly Smith | St. Michaels | RW |
| 70 | NSH | Taylor Beck | Guelph | LW |
| 71 | EDM | Troy Hesketh | Minnetonka | D |
| 72 | NSH | Michael Latta | Guelph | C |
| 73 | N.J. | Alexander Urbom | Djurgarden | D |
| 74 | CGY | Ryan Howse | Chilliwack | LW |
| 75 | DET | Andrej Nestrasil | Victoriaville | RW |
| 76 | ANA | Igor Bobkov | Magnitogorsk 2 | G |
| 77 | MIN | Matthew Hackett | Plymouth | G |
| 78 | STL | Sergei Andronov | Togliatti | RW |
| 79 | MTL | Mac Bennett | Hotchkiss School | D |
| 80 | NYR | Ryan Bourque | USA U-18 | C |
| 81 | PHI | Adam Morrison | Saskatoon | G |
| 82 | EDM | Cameron Abney | Everett | RW |
| 83 | VAN | Kevin Connauton | Western Michigan | D |
| 84 | L.A. | Nicolas Deslauriers | Rouyn-Noranda | D |
| 85 | WSH | Cody Eakin | Swift Current | C |
| 86 | BOS | Ryan Button | Prince Albert | D |
| 87 | PHI | Simon Bertilsson | Brynas | D |
| 88 | CAR | Mattias Lindstrom | Skelleftea Jr. | LW |
| 89 | CHI | Daniel Delisle | Totino Grace | C/LW |
| 90 | DET | Gleason Fournier | Rimouski | D |
| 91 | PHX | Michael Lee | Fargo | G |

## FOURTH ROUND

| Pick | Claimed by | | Amateur Club | Position |
|---|---|---|---|---|
| 92 | NYI | Casey Cizikas | St. Michael's | C |
| 93 | T.B. | Alex Hutchings | Barrie | LW |
| 94 | CBJ | David Savard | Moncton | D |
| 95 | L.A. | Jean-Francois Berube | Montreal | G |
| 96 | L.A. | Linden Vey | Medicine Hat | RW |
| 97 | PHX | Jordan Szwarz | Saginaw | RW |
| 98 | NSH | Craig Smith | Waterloo | C |
| 99 | EDM | Kyle Bigos | Vernon | D |
| 100 | OTT | Chris Wideman | Miami U. | D |
| 101 | EDM | Toni Rajala | Ilves | RW |
| 102 | NSH | Mattias Ekholm | Mora | D |
| 103 | MIN | Kristopher Foucault | Calgary | LW |
| 104 | BUF | Marcus Foligno | Sudbury | LW |
| 105 | PHX | Justin Weller | Red Deer | D |
| 106 | ANA | Sami Vatanen | JYP Jr. | D |
| 107 | FLA | Garrett Wilson | Owen Sound | LW |
| 108 | STL | Tyler Shattock | Kamloops | RW |
| 109 | MTL | Alexander Avtsin | Dynamo Moscow 2 | RW |
| 110 | NSH | Nick Oliver | Roseau High | C/LW |
| 111 | CGY | Henrik Bjorklund | Skare | RW |
| 112 | BOS | Lane MacDermid | Windsor | LW |
| 113 | VAN | Jeremy Price | Nepean | D |
| 114 | N.J. | Seth Helgeson | Sioux City | D |
| 115 | WSH | Patrick Wey | Waterloo | D |
| 116 | MIN | Alexander Fallstrom | Shattuck St. Mary's | RW |
| 117 | ATL | Edward Pasquale | Saginaw | G |
| 118 | CAR | – forfeited selection – | | |
| 119 | CHI | Byron Froese | Everett | C |
| 120 | ATL | Ben Chiarot | Guelph | D |
| 121 | PIT | Nick Petersen | Shawinigan | RW |

## FIFTH ROUND

| Pick | Claimed by | | Amateur Club | Position |
|---|---|---|---|---|
| 122 | NYI | Anton Klementjev | Yaroslavl 2 | D |
| 123 | PIT | Alex Velischek | Delbarton | D |
| 124 | COL | Kieran Millan | Boston University | G |
| 125 | ATL | Cody Sol | Saginaw | D |
| 126 | L.A. | David Kolomatis | Owen Sound | D |
| 127 | NYR | Roman Horak | Ceske Budejovice | C |
| 128 | TOR | Eric Knodel | Philadelphia Jr. Flyers | D |
| 129 | DAL | Tomas Vincour | Edmonton | C |
| 130 | OTT | Mike Hoffman | Drummondville | C/LW |
| 131 | CAR | Matt Kennedy | Guelph | RW |
| 132 | NSH | Gabriel Bourque | Baie-Comeau | LW |
| 133 | EDM | Olivier Roy | Cape Breton | G |
| 134 | BUF | Mark Adams | Malden Catholic | D |
| 135 | FLA | Corban Knight | Okotoks | C |
| 136 | ANA | Radoslav Illo | Tri-City | C |
| 137 | CBJ | Thomas Larkin | Exeter | D |
| 138 | FLA | Wade Megan | South Kent School | C |
| 139 | MTL | Gabriel Dumont | Drummondville | C |
| 140 | NYR | Scott Stajcer | Owen Sound | G |
| 141 | CGY | Spencer Bennett | Surrey | LW |
| 142 | PHI | Nicola Riopel | Moncton | G |
| 143 | VAN | Peter Andersson | Frolunda Jr. | D |
| 144 | N.J. | Derek Rodwell | Okotoks | LW |
| 145 | WSH | Brett Flemming | St. Michael's | D |
| 146 | OTT | Jeff Costello | Cedar Rapids | LW |
| 147 | S.J. | Philip Varone | London | C |
| 148 | T.B. | Michael Zador | Oshawa | G |
| 149 | CHI | Marcus Kruger | Djurgarden | C |
| 150 | DET | Nick Jensen | Green Bay | D |
| 151 | PIT | Andy Bathgate | Belleville | C |

## SIXTH ROUND

| Pick | Claimed by | | Amateur Club | Position |
|---|---|---|---|---|
| 152 | NYI | Anders Lee | Edina High | C |
| 153 | PHI | Dave Labrecque | Shawinigan | C |
| 154 | COL | Brandon Maxwell | USA U-18 | G |
| 155 | ATL | Jimmy Bubnick | Kamloops | C |
| 156 | L.A. | Michael Pelech | St. Michael's | C/LW |
| 157 | PHX | Evan Bloodoff | Kelowna | LW |
| 158 | TOR | Jerry D'Amigo | USA U-18 | RW |
| 159 | DAL | Curtis McKenzie | Penticton | LW |
| 160 | OTT | Corey Cowick | Ottawa | LW |
| 161 | MIN | Darcy Kuemper | Red Deer | G |
| 162 | T.B. | Jaroslav Janus | Erie | G |
| 163 | MIN | Jere Sallinen | Blues Jr. | RW |
| 164 | BUF | Connor Knapp | Miami U. | G |
| 165 | FLA | Scott Timmins | Windsor | C |
| 166 | ANA | Scott Valentine | Oshawa | D |
| 167 | CBJ | Anton Blomqvist | Malmo Jr. | D |
| 168 | STL | David Shields | Erie | D |
| 169 | MTL | Dustin Walsh | Kingston | C |
| 170 | NYI | Daniel Maggio | Sudbury | D |
| 171 | CGY | Joni Ortio | TPS Jr. | G |
| 172 | PHI | Eric Wellwood | Windsor | LW |
| 173 | VAN | Joe Cannata | Merrimack | G |
| 174 | N.J. | Ashton Bernard | Shawinigan | LW |
| 175 | WSH | Garrett Mitchell | Regina | RW |
| 176 | BOS | Tyler Randell | Kitchener | RW |
| 177 | CHI | David Pacan | Cumberland | C |
| 178 | CAR | Rasmus Rissanen | KalPa Jr. | D |
| 179 | L.A. | Brandon Kozun | Calgary | RW |
| 180 | DET | Mitchell Callahan | Kelowna | RW |
| 181 | PIT | Viktor Ekbom | Linkoping | D |

SEVENTH ROUND

| Pick | Claimed by | | Amateur Club | Position |
|---|---|---|---|---|
| 182 | MIN | Erik Haula | Shattuck St. Mary's | LW |
| 183 | T.B. | Kirill Gotovets | Shattuck St. Mary's | D |
| 184 | COL | Gus Young | Nobles | D |
| 185 | ATL | Levko Koper | Spokane | LW |
| 186 | L.A. | Jordan Nolan | Sault Ste. Marie | C |
| 187 | VAN | Steven Anthony | Saint John | LW |
| 188 | TOR | Barron Smith | Peterborough | D |
| 189 | S.J. | Marek Viedensky | Prince George | C |
| 190 | OTT | Brad Peltz | Avon Old Farms | LW |
| 191 | OTT | Michael Sdao | Lincoln | D |
| 192 | NSH | Cameron Reid | Westside | C |
| 193 | MIN | Anthony Hamburg | Dallas Stars AAA | C |
| 194 | BUF | Maxime Legault | Shawinigan | RW |
| 195 | CHI | Paul Phillips | Cedar Rapids | D |
| 196 | PHI | Oliver Lauridsen | St. Cloud State | D |
| 197 | CBJ | Kyle Neuber | St. Michael's | RW |
| 198 | L.A. | Nic Dowd | Wenatchee | C |
| 199 | MTL | Michael Cichy | Indiana | C |
| 200 | NYI | Mihail Pashnin | Mechel | D |
| 201 | CGY | Gaelan Patterson | Saskatoon | C |
| 202 | STL | Maxwell Tardy | Duluth East | C |
| 203 | ATL | Jordan Samuels-Thomas | Waterloo | LW |
| 204 | N.J. | Curtis Gedig | Cowichan Valley | D |
| 205 | WSH | Benjamin Casavant | PEI | LW |
| 206 | BOS | Ben Sexton | Nepean | C |
| 207 | S.J. | Dominik Bielke | Eisbaren Jrs. Berlin | D |
| 208 | CAR | Tommi Kivisto | Red Deer | D |
| 209 | CHI | David Gilbert | Quebec | C |
| 210 | DET | Adam Almqvist | HV 71 Jr. | D |
| 211 | MTL | Petteri Simila | Karpat Jr. | G |

# First Two Rounds 2008–2006

FIRST ROUND

| Pick | Claimed by | | Amateur Club | Position |
|---|---|---|---|---|
| 1 | T.B. | Steven Stamkos | Sarnia | C |
| 2 | L.A. | Drew Doughty | Guelph | D |
| 3 | ATL | Zach Bogosian | Peterborough | D |
| 4 | STL | Alex Pietrangelo | Niagara | D |
| 5 | TOR | Luke Schenn | Kelowna | D |
| 6 | CBJ | Nikita Filatov | CSKA 2 | LW |
| 7 | NSH | Colin Wilson | Boston University | C |
| 8 | PHX | Mikkel Boedker | Kitchener | LW |
| 9 | NYI | Joshua Bailey | Windsor | C |
| 10 | VAN | Cody Hodgson | Brampton | C |
| 11 | CHI | Kyle Beach | Everett | C |
| 12 | BUF | Tyler Myers | Kelowna | D |
| 13 | L.A. | Colten Teubert | Regina | D |
| 14 | CAR | Zach Boychuk | Lethbridge | C |
| 15 | OTT | Erik Karlsson | Frolunda Jr. | D |
| 16 | BOS | Joe Colborne | Camrose | C |
| 17 | ANA | Jake Gardiner | Minnetonka | D |
| 18 | NSH | Chet Pickard | Tri-City | G |
| 19 | PHI | Luca Sbisa | Lethbridge | D |
| 20 | NYR | Michael Del Zotto | Oshawa | D |
| 21 | WSH | Anton Gustafsson | Frolunda Jr. | C |
| 22 | EDM | Jordan Eberle | Regina | C |
| 23 | MIN | Tyler Cuma | Ottawa | D |
| 24 | N.J. | Mattias Tedenby | HV 71 | LW |
| 25 | CGY | Greg Nemisz | Windsor | C |
| 26 | BUF | Tyler Ennis | Medicine Hat | C |
| 27 | WSH | John Carlson | Indiana | D |
| 28 | PHX | Viktor Tikhonov | Cherepovets | W |
| 29 | ATL | Daultan Leveille | St. Catharines | C |
| 30 | DET | Thomas McCollum | Guelph | G |

SECOND ROUND

| Pick | Claimed by | | Amateur Club | Position |
|---|---|---|---|---|
| 31 | FLA | Jacob Markstrom | Brynas Jr. | G |
| 32 | L.A. | Vjateslav Voinov | Chelyabinsk | D |
| 33 | STL | Philip McRae | London | C |
| 34 | STL | Jake Allen | St. John's | G |
| 35 | ANA | Nicolas Deschamps | Chicoutimi | C |
| 36 | NYI | Corey Trivino | Stouffville | C |
| 37 | CBJ | Cody Goloubef | U. of Wisconsin | D |
| 38 | NSH | Roman Josi | Bern | D |
| 39 | ANA | Eric O'Dell | Sudbury | C |
| 40 | NYI | Aaron Ness | Roseau High | D |
| 41 | VAN | Yann Sauve | Saint John | D |
| 42 | OTT | Patrick Wiercioch | Omaha | D |
| 43 | ANA | Justin Schultz | Westside | D |
| 44 | BUF | Luke Adam | St. John's | C |
| 45 | CAR | Zac Dalpe | Penticton | C/RW |
| 46 | FLA | Colby Robak | Brandon | D |
| 47 | BOS | Maxime Sauve | Val d'Or | C |
| 48 | CGY | Mitch Wahl | Spokane | C |
| 49 | PHX | Jared Staal | Sudbury | RW |
| 50 | COL | Cameron Gaunce | St. Michael's | D |
| 51 | NYR | Derek Stepan | Shattuck St.Mary's | C |
| 52 | N.J. | Brandon Burlon | St. Michael's | D |
| 53 | NYI | Travis Hamonic | Moose Jaw | D |
| 54 | N.J. | Patrice Cormier | Rimouski | C |
| 55 | MIN | Marco Scandella | Val d'Or | D |
| 56 | MTL | Danny Kristo | U-18 | RW |
| 57 | WSH | Eric Mestery | Tri-City | D |
| 58 | WSH | Dmitri Kugryshev | CSKA 2 | RW |
| 59 | DAL | Tyler Beskorowany | Owen Sound | G |
| 60 | TOR | Jimmy Hayes | Lincoln | RW |
| 61 | COL | Peter Delmas | Lewiston | G |

## 2007

FIRST ROUND

| Pick | Claimed by | | Amateur Club | Position |
|---|---|---|---|---|
| 1 | CHI | Patrick Kane | London | RW |
| 2 | PHI | James vanRiemsdyk | USA U-18 | LW |
| 3 | PHX | Kyle Turris | Burnaby | C |
| 4 | LA | Thomas Hickey | Seattle | D |
| 5 | WSH | Karl Alzner | Calgary | D |
| 6 | EDM | Sam Gagner | London | C/W |
| 7 | CBJ | Jakub Voracek | Halifax | RW |
| 8 | BOS | Zach Hamill | Everett | C |
| 9 | SJ | Logan Couture | Ottawa | C |
| 10 | FLA | Keaton Ellerby | Kamloops | D |
| 11 | CAR | Brandon Sutter | Red Deer | C/RW |
| 12 | MTL | Ryan McDonagh | Cretin-Derham | D |
| 13 | STL | Lars Eller | Frolunda Jr. | C |
| 14 | COL | Kevin Shattenkirk | USA U-18 | D |
| 15 | EDM | Alex Plante | Calgary | D |
| 16 | MIN | Colton Gillies | Saskatoon | C |
| 17 | NYR | Alexei Cherepanov | Omsk | RW |
| 18 | STL | Ian Cole | USA U-18 | D |
| 19 | ANA | Logan MacMillan | Halifax | C |
| 20 | PIT | Angelo Esposito | Quebec | C |
| 21 | EDM | Riley Nash | Salmon Arm | C |
| 22 | MTL | Max Pacioretty | Sioux City | LW |
| 23 | NSH | Jonathon Blum | Vancouver | D |
| 24 | CGY | Mikael Backlund | Vasteras | C |
| 25 | VAN | Patrick White | Tri-City | C |
| 26 | STL | David Perron | Lewiston | LW |
| 27 | DET | Brendan Smith | St. Michael's | D |
| 28 | SJ | Nicholas Petrecki | Omaha | D |
| 29 | OTT | James O'Brien | U of Minnesota | C |
| 30 | PHX | Nick Ross | Regina | D |

SECOND ROUND

| Pick | Claimed by | | Amateur Club | Position |
|---|---|---|---|---|
| 31 | BUF | T.J. Brennan | St. John's | D |
| 32 | PHX | Brett MacLean | Oshawa | LW |
| 33 | VAN | Taylor Ellington | Everett | D |
| 34 | WSH | Josh Godfrey | Sault Ste. Marie | D |
| 35 | BOS | Tommy Cross | Westminster | D |
| 36 | PHX | Joel Gistedt | Frolunda | G |
| 37 | CBJ | Stefan Legein | Mississauga | RW |
| 38 | CHI | William Sweatt | Colorado College | LW |
| 39 | STL | Simon Hjalmarsson | Frolunda Jr. | RW |
| 40 | FLA | Michal Repik | Vancouver | RW |
| 41 | PHI | Kevin Marshall | Lewiston | D |
| 42 | ANA | Eric Tangradi | Belleville | C |
| 43 | MTL | P.K. Subban | Belleville | D |
| 44 | STL | Aaron Palushaj | Des Moines | RW |
| 45 | COL | Colby Cohen | Lincoln | D |
| 46 | WSH | Theo Ruth | USA U-18 | D |
| 47 | TB | Dana Tyrell | Prince George | C/RW |
| 48 | NYR | Antoine Lafleur | PEI | G |
| 49 | COL | Trevor Cann | Peterborough | G |
| 50 | LA | Nico Sacchetti | Virginia High | C |
| 51 | PIT | Keven Veilleux | Victoriaville | C |
| 52 | LA | Oscar Moller | Chilliwack | RW |
| 53 | CBJ | Will Weber | Gaylord High | D |
| 54 | NSH | Jeremy Smith | Plymouth | G |
| 55 | COL | T.J. Galiardi | Dartmouth | W |
| 56 | CHI | Akim Aliu | Sudbury | C/RW |
| 57 | NJ | Mike Hoeffel | USA U-18 | W |
| 58 | NSH | Nick Spaling | Kitchener | C |
| 59 | BUF | Drew Schiestel | Mississauga | D |
| 60 | OTT | Ruslan Bashkirov | Quebec | LW |
| 61 | LA | Wayne Simmonds | Owen Sound | RW |

## 2006

FIRST ROUND

| Pick | Claimed by | | Amateur Club | Position |
|---|---|---|---|---|
| 1 | STL | Erik Johnson | USA U-18 | D |
| 2 | PIT | Jordan Staal | Peterborough | C |
| 3 | CHI | Jonathan Toews | U. of North Dakota | C |
| 4 | WSH | Nicklas Backstrom | Brynas | C |
| 5 | BOS | Phil Kessel | U. of Minnesota | C |
| 6 | CBJ | Derick Brassard | Drummondville | C |
| 7 | NYI | Kyle Okposo | Des Moines | RW |
| 8 | PHX | Peter Mueller | Everett | C |
| 9 | MIN | James Sheppard | Cape Breton | C |
| 10 | FLA | Michael Frolik | Kladno | C |
| 11 | L.A. | Jonathan Bernier | Lewiston | G |
| 12 | ATL | Bryan Little | Barrie | C |
| 13 | TOR | Jiri Tlusty | Kladno | C |
| 14 | VAN | Michael Grabner | Spokane | RW |
| 15 | T.B. | Riku Helenius | Ilves | G |
| 16 | S.J. | Ty Wishart | Prince George | D |
| 17 | L.A. | Trevor Lewis | Des Moines | C |
| 18 | COL | Chris Stewart | Kingston | RW |
| 19 | ANA | Mark Mitera | U. of Michigan | D |
| 20 | MTL | David Fischer | Apple Valley | D |
| 21 | NYR | Bobby Sanguinetti | Owen Sound | D |
| 22 | PHI | Claude Giroux | Gatineau | RW |
| 23 | WSH | Simeon Varlamov | Yaroslavl 2 | G |
| 24 | BUF | Dennis Persson | Vasteras | D |
| 25 | STL | Patrik Berglund | Vasteras | C |
| 26 | CGY | Leland Irving | Everett | G |
| 27 | DAL | Ivan Vishnevskiy | Rouyn Noranda | D |
| 28 | OTT | Nick Foligno | Sudbury | LW |
| 29 | PHX | Chris Summers | USA U-18 | D |
| 30 | N.J. | Matthew Corrente | Saginaw | D |

SECOND ROUND

| Pick | Claimed by | | Amateur Club | Position |
|---|---|---|---|---|
| 31 | STL | Tomas Kana | Vitkovice | C |
| 32 | PIT | Carl Sneep | Brainerd | D |
| 33 | CHI | Igor Makarov | Krylja | RW |
| 34 | WSH | Michal Neuvirth | Sparta Jr. | G |
| 35 | WSH | Francois Bouchard | Baie Comeau | RW |
| 36 | S.J. | Jamie McGinn | Ottawa | LW |
| 37 | BOS | Yuri Alexandrov | Cherepovets | D |
| 38 | ANA | Bryce Swan | Halifax | RW |
| 39 | PHI | Andreas Nodl | Sioux Falls | RW |
| 40 | MIN | Ondrej Fiala | Everett | C |
| 41 | DET | Cory Emmerton | Kingston | C |
| 42 | PHI | Michael Ratchuk | USA U-18 | D |
| 43 | ATL | Riley Holzapfel | Moose Jaw | C |
| 44 | TOR | Nikolai Kulemin | Magnitogorsk | W |
| 45 | EDM | Jeff Petry | Des Moines | D |
| 46 | BUF | Jhonas Enroth | Sodertalje | G |
| 47 | DET | Shawn Matthias | Belleville | C |
| 48 | L.A. | Joe Ryan | Quebec | D |
| 49 | MTL | Ben Maxwell | Kootenay | C |
| 50 | BOS | Milan Lucic | Vancouver | LW |
| 51 | COL | Nigel Williams | USA U-18 | D |
| 52 | WSH | Keith Seabrook | Burnaby | D |
| 53 | MTL | Mathieu Carle | Acadie-Bathurst | D |
| 54 | NYR | Artem Anisimov | Yaroslavl | C |
| 55 | PHI | Denis Bodrov | Togliatti | D |
| 56 | NSH | Blake Geoffrion | USA U-18 | LW |
| 57 | BUF | Mike Weber | Windsor | D |
| 58 | N.J. | Alexander Vasyunov | Yaroslavl 2 | LW |
| 59 | COL | Codey Burki | Brandon | C |
| 60 | NYI | Jesse Joensuu | Assat | W |
| 61 | CHI | Simon Danis-Pepin | U. of Maine | D |
| 62 | DET | Dick Axelsson | Huddinge | W |
| 63 | CAR | Jamie McBain | USA U-18 | D |

# First Round and Other Notable Selections 2005–1969

## 2005

FIRST ROUND

| Pick | Claimed by | | Amateur Club | Position |
|---|---|---|---|---|
| 1 | PIT | Sidney Crosby | Rimouski | C |
| 2 | ANA | Bobby Ryan | Owen Sound | RW |
| 3 | CAR | Jack Johnson | USA U-18 | D |
| 4 | MIN | Benoit Pouliot | Sudbury | LW |
| 5 | MTL | Carey Price | Tri-City | G |
| 6 | CBJ | Gilbert Brule | Vancouver | C |
| 7 | CHI | Jack Skille | USA U-18 | RW |
| 8 | S.J. | Devin Setoguchi | Saskatoon | RW |
| 9 | OTT | Brian Lee | Moorhead | D |
| 10 | VAN | Luc Bourdon | Val D'or | D |
| 11 | L.A. | Anze Kopitar | Sodertalje Jr. | C |
| 12 | NYR | Marc Staal | Sudbury | D |
| 13 | BUF | Marek Zagrapan | Chicoutimi | C |
| 14 | WSH | Sasha Pokulok | Cornell | D |
| 15 | NYI | Ryan O'Marra | Erie | C |
| 16 | ATL | Alex Bourret | Lewiston | RW |
| 17 | PHX | Martin Hanzal | C. Budejovice | C |
| 18 | NSH | Ryan Parent | Guelph | D |
| 19 | DET | Jakub Kindl | Kitchener | D |
| 20 | FLA | Kenndal McArdle | Moose Jaw | LW |
| 21 | TOR | Tuukka Rask | Ilves Jr. | G |
| 22 | BOS | Matt Lashoff | Kitchener | D |
| 23 | N.J. | Nicklas Bergfors | Sodertalje | RW |
| 24 | STL | T.J. Oshie | Warroad | C |
| 25 | EDM | Andrew Cogliano | St. Mike's B's | C |
| 26 | CGY | Matt Pelech | Sarnia | D |
| 27 | WSH | Joe Finley | Sioux Falls | D |
| 28 | DAL | Matt Niskanen | Virginia | D |
| 29 | PHI | Steve Downie | Windsor | RW |
| 30 | T.B. | Vladimir Mihalik | Presov | D |

OTHER NOTABLE SELECTIONS

| Pick | Claimed by | | Amateur Club | Position |
|---|---|---|---|---|
| 35 | S.J. | Marc-Edouard Vlasic | Quebec | D |
| 42 | DET | Justin Abdelkader | Cedar Rapids | LW |
| 43 | CHI | Michael Blunden | Erie | RW |
| 44 | COL | Paul Stastny | U. of Denver | C |
| 45 | MTL | Guillaume Latendresse | Drummondville | RW |
| 51 | VAN | Mason Raymond | Camrose | LW |
| 132 | DET | Darren Helm | Medicine Hat | C/LW |
| 200 | MTL | Sergei Kostitsyn | Gomel | LW |

## 2004

FIRST ROUND

| Pick | Claimed by | | Amateur Club | Position |
|---|---|---|---|---|
| 1 | WSH | Alex Ovechkin | Dynamo | LW |
| 2 | PIT | Evgeni Malkin | Magnitogorsk | C |
| 3 | CHI | Cam Barker | Medicine Hat | D |
| 4 | CAR | Andrew Ladd | Calgary | LW |
| 5 | PHX | Blake Wheeler | Breck | RW |
| 6 | NYR | Al Montoya | U. of Michigan | G |
| 7 | FLA | Rostislav Olesz | Vitkovice | C |
| 8 | CBJ | Alexandre Picard | Lewiston | LW |
| 9 | ANA | Ladislav Smid | Liberec | D |

| Pick | Claimed by | | Amateur Club | Position |
|---|---|---|---|---|
| 10 | ATL | Boris Valabik | Kitchener | D |
| 11 | L.A. | Lauri Tukonen | Blues Espoo | RW |
| 12 | MIN | A.J. Thelen | Michigan State | D |
| 13 | BUF | Drew Stafford | U. of North Dakota | RW |
| 14 | EDM | Devan Dubnyk | Kamloops | G |
| 15 | NSH | Alexander Radulov | Tver | LW |
| 16 | NYI | Petteri Nokelainen | SaiPa | C |
| 17 | STL | Marek Schwarz | Sparta Praha | G |
| 18 | MTL | Kyle Chipchura | Prince Albert | C |
| 19 | NYR | Lauri Korpikoski | TPS Turku Jr. | LW |
| 20 | N.J. | Travis Zajac | Salmon Arm | C |
| 21 | COL | Wojtek Wolski | Brampton | LW |
| 22 | S.J. | Lukas Kaspar | Litvinov | RW |
| 23 | OTT | Andrej Meszaros | Trencin | D |
| 24 | CGY | Kris Chucko | Salmon Arm | LW |
| 25 | EDM | Rob Schremp | London | C |
| 26 | VAN | Cory Schneider | Phillips-Andover | G |
| 27 | WSH | Jeff Schultz | Calgary | D |
| 28 | DAL | Mark Fistric | Vancouver | D |
| 29 | WSH | Mike Green | Saskatoon | D |
| 30 | T.B. | Andy Rogers | Calgary | D |

### OTHER NOTABLE SELECTIONS

| Pick | Claimed by | | Amateur Club | Position |
|---|---|---|---|---|
| 53 | FLA | David Booth | Michigan State | LW |
| 60 | NYR | Brandon Dubinsky | Portland | C |
| 63 | BOS | David Krejci | Kladno Jr. | C |
| 91 | VAN | Alexander Edler | Jamtland | D |
| 97 | DET | Johan Franzen | Linkoping | C |
| 99 | PIT | Tyler Kennedy | Sault Ste. Marie | C |
| 127 | NYR | Ryan Callahan | Guelph | RW |
| 134 | BOS | Kris Versteeg | Lethbridge | RW |
| 150 | MTL | Mikhail Grabovski | Nizhnekamsk | C |
| 191 | T.B. | Karri Ramo | Pelicans Jr. | G |
| 224 | BOS | Matt Hunwick | U. of Michigan | D |
| 227 | NYI | Chris Campoli | Erie | D |
| 258 | NSH | Pekka Rinne | Karpat | G |
| 262 | MTL | Mark Streit | Zurich | D |

## 2003

### FIRST ROUND

| Pick | Claimed by | | Amateur Club | Position |
|---|---|---|---|---|
| 1 | PIT | Marc-Andre Fleury | Cape Breton | G |
| 2 | CAR | Eric Staal | Peterborough | C |
| 3 | FLA | Nathan Horton | Oshawa | C |
| 4 | CBJ | Nikolai Zherdev | CSKA Moscow | W |
| 5 | BUF | Thomas Vanek | U. of Minnesota | LW |
| 6 | S.J. | Milan Michalek | Budejovice | RW |
| 7 | NSH | Ryan Suter | U.S. National U-18 | D |
| 8 | ATL | Braydon Coburn | Portland | D |
| 9 | CGY | Dion Phaneuf | Red Deer | D |
| 10 | MTL | Andrei Kostitsyn | CSKA Moscow 2 | RW |
| 11 | PHI | Jeff Carter | Sault Ste. Marie | C |
| 12 | NYR | Hugh Jessiman | Dartmouth | RW |
| 13 | L.A. | Dustin Brown | Guelph | RW |
| 14 | CHI | Brent Seabrook | Lethbridge | D |
| 15 | NYI | Robert Nilsson | Leksand | RW |
| 16 | S.J. | Steve Bernier | Moncton | RW |
| 17 | N.J. | Zach Parise | North Dakota | C |
| 18 | WSH | Eric Fehr | Brandon | RW |
| 19 | ANA | Ryan Getzlaf | Calgary | C |
| 20 | MIN | Brent Burns | Brampton | RW |
| 21 | BOS | Mark Stuart | Colorado College | D |
| 22 | EDM | Marc-Antoine Pouliot | Rimouski | C |
| 23 | VAN | Ryan Kesler | Ohio State | C |
| 24 | PHI | Mike Richards | Kitchener | C |
| 25 | FLA | Anthony Stewart | Kingston | C |
| 26 | L.A. | Brian Boyle | St. Sebastian's H.S. | C |
| 27 | L.A. | Jeff Tambellini | U. of Michigan | LW |
| 28 | ANA | Corey Perry | London | RW |
| 29 | OTT | Patrick Eaves | Boston College | RW |
| 30 | STL | Shawn Belle | Tri-City | D |

### OTHER NOTABLE SELECTIONS

| Pick | Claimed by | | Amateur Club | Position |
|---|---|---|---|---|
| 45 | BOS | Patrice Bergeron | Acadie-Bathurst | C |
| 47 | S.J. | Matt Carle | River City | D |
| 49 | NSH | Shea Weber | Kelowna | D |
| 61 | MTL | Maxim Lapierre | Montreal | C |
| 62 | ST.L. | David Backes | Lincoln | C |
| 73 | PHX | Daniel Carcillo | Sarnia | LW |
| 106 | BUF | Jan Hejda | Slavia Praha | D |
| 205 | S.J. | Joe Pavelski | Waterloo Jr. A | C |
| 239 | ATL | Tobias Enstrom | MoDo | D |
| 245 | CHI | Dustin Byfuglien | Prince George | RW |
| 250 | ANA | Shane O'Brien | St. Michael's | D |
| 271 | MTL | Jaroslav Halak | Bratislava Jr. | G |

## 2002

### FIRST ROUND

| Pick | Claimed by | | Amateur Club | Position |
|---|---|---|---|---|
| 1 | CBJ | Rick Nash | London | LW |
| 2 | ATL | Kari Lehtonen | Jokerit | G |
| 3 | FLA | Jay Bouwmeester | Medicine Hat | D |
| 4 | PHI | Joni Pitkanen | Karpat | D |
| 5 | PIT | Ryan Whitney | Boston U. | D |
| 6 | NSH | Scottie Upshall | Kamloops | RW |
| 7 | ANA | Joffrey Lupul | Medicine Hat | C |
| 8 | MIN | Pierre-Marc Bouchard | Chicoutimi | C |
| 9 | FLA | Petr Taticek | Sault Ste. Marie | C |
| 10 | CGY | Eric Nystrom | U. of Michigan | LW |
| 11 | BUF | Keith Ballard | U. of Minnesota | D |
| 12 | WSH | Steve Eminger | Kitchener | D |
| 13 | WSH | Alexander Semin | Chelyabinsk | LW |
| 14 | MTL | Christopher Higgins | Yale | C |
| 15 | EDM | Jesse Niinimaki | Ilves Tampere | C |
| 16 | OTT | Jakub Klepis | Portland | C |
| 17 | WSH | Boyd Gordon | Red Deer | RW |
| 18 | L.A. | Denis Grebeshkov | Yaroslavl | D |
| 19 | PHX | Jakub Koreis | Plzen | C |
| 20 | BUF | Dan Paille | Guelph | LW |
| 21 | CHI | Anton Babchuk | Elektrostal | D |
| 22 | NYI | Sean Bergenheim | Jokerit | C |
| 23 | PHX | Ben Eager | Oshawa | LW |
| 24 | TOR | Alexander Steen | Vastra Frolunda | C |
| 25 | CAR | Cam Ward | Red Deer | G |
| 26 | DAL | Martin Vagner | Hull | D |
| 27 | S.J. | Mike Morris | St. Sebastian's H.S. | RW |
| 28 | COL | Jonas Johansson | HV 71 Jonkoping Jr. | RW |
| 29 | BOS | Hannu Toivonen | HPK Jr. | G |
| 30 | ATL | Jim Slater | Michigan State | C |

### OTHER NOTABLE SELECTIONS

| Pick | Claimed by | | Amateur Club | Position |
|---|---|---|---|---|
| 36 | EDM | Jarret Stoll | Kootenay | C |
| 43 | DAL | Trevor Daley | Sault Ste. Marie | D |
| 44 | EDM | Matt Greene | Green Bay | D |
| 54 | CHI | Duncan Keith | Michigan State | D |
| 57 | TOR | Matt Stajan | Belleville | C |
| 58 | DET | Jiri Hudler | Vsetin | C |
| 90 | CGY | Matthew Lomardi | Victoriaville | C |
| 95 | DET | Valtteri Filppula | Jokerit Jr. | C |
| 156 | CHI | James Wisniewski | Plymouth | D |
| 183 | TB | Paul Ranger | Oshawa | D |
| 234 | PIT | Maxime Talbot | Hull | C |
| 240 | NYR | Petr Prucha | Pardubice | RW |
| 241 | BUF | Dennis Wideman | London | D |
| 282 | CHI | Adam Burish | Green Bay | RW |
| 291 | DET | Jonathan Ericsson | Hasten Jr. | D |

## 2001

### FIRST ROUND

| Pick | Claimed by | | Amateur Club | Position |
|---|---|---|---|---|
| 1 | ATL | Ilya Kovalchuk | Spartak | LW |
| 2 | OTT | Jason Spezza | Windsor | C |
| 3 | T.B. | Alexander Svitov | Avangard Omsk | C |
| 4 | FLA | Stephen Weiss | Plymouth | C |
| 5 | ANA | Stanislav Chistov | Avangard Omsk | LW |
| 6 | MIN | Mikko Koivu | TPS Turku | C |
| 7 | MTL | Mike Komisarek | U. of Michigan | D |
| 8 | CBJ | Pascal Leclaire | Halifax | G |
| 9 | CHI | Tuomo Ruutu | Jokerit | C/LW |
| 10 | NYR | Dan Blackburn | Kootenay | G |
| 11 | PHX | Fredrik Sjostrom | Vastra Frolunda | RW |
| 12 | NSH | Dan Hamhuis | Prince George | D |
| 13 | EDM | Ales Hemsky | Hull | RW |
| 14 | CGY | Chuck Kobasew | Boston College | C |
| 15 | CAR | Igor Knyazev | Spartak | D |
| 16 | VAN | R.J. Umberger | Ohio State | C |
| 17 | TOR | Carlo Colaiacovo | Erie | D |
| 18 | L.A. | Jens Karlsson | Vastra Frolunda | RW |
| 19 | BOS | Shaone Morrisonn | Kamloops | D |
| 20 | S.J. | Marcel Goc | Schwenningen | C |
| 21 | PIT | Colby Armstrong | Red Deer | RW |
| 22 | BUF | Jiri Novotny | Budejovice | C |
| 23 | OTT | Tim Gleason | Windsor | D |
| 24 | FLA | Lukas Krajicek | Peterborough | D |
| 25 | MTL | Alexander Perezhogin | Avangard Omsk | C |
| 26 | DAL | Jason Bacashihua | Chicago (NAHL) | G |
| 27 | PHI | Jeff Woywitka | Red Deer | D |
| 28 | N.J. | Adrian Foster | Saskatoon | C |
| 29 | CHI | Adam Munro | Erie | G |
| 30 | L.A. | Dave Steckel | Ohio State | C |

### OTHER NOTABLE SELECTIONS

| Pick | Claimed by | | Amateur Club | Position |
|---|---|---|---|---|
| 32 | BUF | Derek Roy | Kitchener | C |
| 49 | L.A. | Mike Cammalleri | U. of Michigan | C |
| 55 | BUF | Jason Pominville | Shawinigan | RW |
| 71 | MTL | Tomas Plekanec | Kladno | LW |
| 95 | PHI | Patrick Sharp | U. of Vermont | C |
| 98 | NSH | Jordin Tootoo | Brandon | RW |
| 99 | OTT | Ray Emery | S.S. Marie | G |
| 106 | S.J. | Christoph Ehrhoff | Krefeld | D |
| 134 | TOR | Kyle Wellwood | Belleville | C |
| 151 | VAN | Kevin Bieksa | Bowling Green | D |
| 172 | PHI | Dennis Seidenberg | Mannheim | D |
| 175 | SJ | Ryan Clowe | Rimouski | RW |
| 176 | NSH | Marek Zidlicky | HIFK | D |
| 192 | DAL | Jussi Jokinen | Karpat Jr. | F |
| 193 | OTT | Brooks Laich | Moose Jaw | C |
| 232 | ANA | Martin Gerber | Langnau | G |

## 2000

### FIRST ROUND

| Pick | Claimed by | | Amateur Club | Position |
|---|---|---|---|---|
| 1 | NYI | Rick DiPietro | Boston U. | G |
| 2 | ATL | Dany Heatley | U. of Wisconsin | RW |
| 3 | MIN | Marian Gaborik | Dukla Trencin | RW |
| 4 | CBJ | Rostislav Klesla | Brampton | D |
| 5 | NYI | Raffi Torres | Brampton | LW |
| 6 | NSH | Scott Hartnell | Prince Albert | LW |
| 7 | BOS | Lars Jonsson | Leksand | D |
| 8 | T.B. | Nikita Alexeev | Erie | RW |
| 9 | CGY | Brent Krahn | Calgary | G |
| 10 | CHI | Mikhail Yakubov | Lada Togliatti | C |
| 11 | CHI | Pavel Vorobiev | Yaroslavl | RW |
| 12 | ANA | Alexei Smirnov | Tver | LW |
| 13 | MTL | Ron Hainsey | U. of Mass-Lowell | D |
| 14 | COL | Vaclav Nedorost | Budejovice | C |
| 15 | BUF | Artem Kryukov | Yaroslavl | C |
| 16 | MTL | Marcel Hossa | Portland | LW |
| 17 | EDM | Alexei Mikhnov | Yaroslavl | LW |
| 18 | PIT | Brooks Orpik | Boston College | D |
| 19 | PHX | Krys Kolanos | Boston College | C |
| 20 | L.A. | Alexander Frolov | Yaroslavl 2 | LW |
| 21 | OTT | Anton Volchenkov | HC Moscow | D |
| 22 | N.J. | David Hale | Sioux City | D |
| 23 | VAN | Nathan Smith | Swift Current | C |
| 24 | TOR | Brad Boyes | Erie | C |
| 25 | DAL | Steve Ott | Windsor | C |
| 26 | WSH | Brian Sutherby | Moose Jaw | C |
| 27 | BOS | Martin Samuelsson | MoDo Ornskoldsvik | RW |
| 28 | PHI | Justin Williams | Plymouth | RW |
| 29 | DET | Niklas Kronwall | Djurgarden | D |
| 30 | STL | Jeff Taffe | U. of Minnesota | C |

### OTHER NOTABLE SELECTIONS

| Pick | Claimed by | | Amateur Club | Position |
|---|---|---|---|---|
| 33 | MIN | Nick Schultz | Prince Albert | D |
| 44 | ANA | Ilya Bryzgalov | Lada Togliatti | G |
| 46 | CGY | Jarret Stoll | Kootenay | C |
| 54 | L.A. | Andreas Lilja | Malmo | D |
| 55 | OTT | Antoine Vermette | Victoriaville | D |
| 60 | DAL | Dan Ellis | Omaha | G |
| 62 | COL | Paul Martin | Elk River H.S. | D |
| 76 | N.J. | Michael Rupp | Erie | LW |
| 97 | CAR | Niclas Wallin | Brynas | D |
| 118 | L.A. | Lubomir Visnovsky | Bratislava | D |
| 155 | CGY | Travis Moen | Kelowna | LW |
| 159 | COL | John-Michael Liles | Michigan State | D |
| 171 | PHI | Roman Cechmanek | Vsetin | G |
| 205 | NYR | Henrik Lundqvist | Vastre Frolunda Jr. | G |
| 215 | BUF | Matthew Lombardi | Victoriaville | C |
| 220 | BUF | Paul Gaustad | Portland | C |
| 224 | DAL | Antti Miettinen | HPK Jr. | RW |

## 1999

### FIRST ROUND

| Pick | Claimed by | | Amateur Club | Position |
|---|---|---|---|---|
| 1 | ATL | Patrik Stefan | Long Beach | C |
| 2 | VAN | Daniel Sedin | MoDo Ornskoldsvik | LW |
| 3 | VAN | Henrik Sedin | MoDo Ornskoldsvik | C |
| 4 | NYR | Pavel Brendl | Calgary | RW |
| 5 | NYI | Tim Connolly | Erie | C |
| 6 | NSH | Brian Finley | Barrie | G |
| 7 | WSH | Kris Beech | Calgary | C |
| 8 | NYI | Taylor Pyatt | Sudbury | LW |
| 9 | NYR | Jamie Lundmark | Moose Jaw | C |
| 10 | NYI | Branislav Mezei | Belleville | D |
| 11 | CGY | Oleg Saprykin | Seattle | LW |
| 12 | FLA | Denis Shvidki | Barrie | RW |
| 13 | EDM | Jani Rita | Jokerit | LW |
| 14 | S.J. | Jeff Jillson | U. of Michigan | D |
| 15 | PHX | Scott Kelman | Seattle | C |
| 16 | CAR | David Tanabe | U. of Wisconsin | D |
| 17 | STL | Barret Jackman | Regina | D |
| 18 | PIT | Konstantin Koltsov | Cherepovets | RW |
| 19 | PHX | Kirill Safronov | St. Petersburg | D |
| 20 | BUF | Barrett Heisten | U. of Maine | LW |
| 21 | BOS | Nick Boynton | Ottawa | D |
| 22 | PHI | Maxime Ouellet | Quebec | G |
| 23 | CHI | Steve McCarthy | Kootenay | D |
| 24 | TOR | Luca Cereda | Ambri | C |
| 25 | COL | Mikhail Kuleshov | Cherepovets | LW |
| 26 | OTT | Martin Havlat | Trinec | LW |
| 27 | N.J. | Ari Ahonen | JyP HT Jr. | G |
| 28 | NYI | Kristian Kudroc | Michalovce | D |

### OTHER NOTABLE SELECTIONS

| Pick | Claimed by | | Amateur Club | Position |
|---|---|---|---|---|
| 40 | FLA | Alex Auld | North Bay | G |
| 42 | N.J. | Mike Commodore | North Dakota | D |
| 44 | ANA | Jordan Leopold | U. of Minnesota | D |
| 70 | FLA | Niklas Hagman | HIFK Helsinki | LW |
| 76 | L.A. | Frantisek Kaberle | MoDo Ornskoldsvik | D |
| 83 | ANA | Niclas Havelid | Malmo | D |
| 91 | EDM | Mike Comrie | U. of Michigan | C |
| 115 | PIT | Ryan Malone | Omaha | LW |
| 138 | BUF | Ryan Miller | Soo | G |
| 191 | NSH | Martin Erat | ZPS Zlin Jr. | LW |
| 210 | DET | Henrik Zetterberg | Timra | LW |
| 222 | L.A. | George Parros | Chicago Freeze | RW |
| 240 | COL | Jeff Finger | Green Bay | D |
| 247 | BOS | Mikko Eloranta | TPS Turku | LW |

## 1998

### FIRST ROUND

| Pick | Claimed by | | Amateur Club | Position |
|---|---|---|---|---|
| 1 | T.B. | Vincent Lecavalier | Rimouski | C |
| 2 | NSH | David Legwand | Plymouth | C |
| 3 | S.J. | Brad Stuart | Regina | D |
| 4 | VAN | Bryan Allen | Oshawa | D |
| 5 | ANA | Vitaly Vishnevski | Yaroslavl 2 | D |

| Pick | Claimed by | Player | Amateur Club | Position |
|---|---|---|---|---|
| 6 | CGY | Rico Fata | London | RW |
| 7 | NYR | Manny Malhotra | Guelph | C |
| 8 | CHI | Mark Bell | Ottawa | C |
| 9 | NYI | Mike Rupp | Erie | RW |
| 10 | TOR | Nik Antropov | Ust-Kamenogorsk | C |
| 11 | CAR | Jeff Heerema | Sarnia | RW |
| 12 | COL | Alex Tanguay | Halifax | LW |
| 13 | EDM | Michael Henrich | Barrie | RW |
| 14 | PHX | Patrick DesRochers | Sarnia | G |
| 15 | OTT | Mathieu Chouinard | Shawinigan | G |
| 16 | MTL | Eric Chouinard | Quebec | LW |
| 17 | COL | Martin Skoula | Barrie | D |
| 18 | BUF | Dmitri Kalinin | Chelyabinsk | D |
| 19 | COL | Robyn Regehr | Kamloops | D |
| 20 | COL | Scott Parker | Kelowna | RW |
| 21 | L.A. | Mathieu Biron | Shawinigan | D |
| 22 | PHI | Simon Gagne | Quebec | LW |
| 23 | PIT | Milan Kraft | Keramika Plzen Jr. | C |
| 24 | STL | Christian Backman | Vastra Frolunda Jr. | D |
| 25 | DET | Jiri Fischer | Hull | D |
| 26 | N.J. | Mike Van Ryn | U. of Michigan | D |
| 27 | N.J. | Scott Gomez | Tri-City | C |

### OTHER NOTABLE SELECTIONS

| Pick | Claimed by | Player | Amateur Club | Position |
|---|---|---|---|---|
| 29 | S.J. | Jonathan Cheechoo | Belleville | RW |
| 43 | PHX | Ossi Vaananen | Jokerit Jr. | D |
| 44 | OTT | Mike Fisher | Sudbury | C |
| 64 | T.B. | Brad Richards | Rimouski | C |
| 68 | VAN | Jarkko Ruutu | HIFK Helsinki | RW |
| 71 | CAR | Erik Cole | Clarkson | LW |
| 75 | MTL | Francois Beauchemin | Laval | D |
| 82 | NJ | Brian Gionta | Boston College | RW |
| 87 | TOR | Alexei Ponikarovsky | Dyn-2 Moscow | LW |
| 91 | CAR | Josef Vasicek | Slavia Praha Jr. | C |
| 99 | EDM | Shawn Horcoff | Michigan State | C |
| 117 | FLA | Jaroslav Spacek | Farjestad Karlstad | D |
| 135 | BOS | Andrew Raycroft | Sudbury | G |
| 145 | SJ | Mikael Samuelsson | Sodertalje | LW |
| 150 | ANA | Trent Hunter | Prince George | RW |
| 161 | OTT | Chris Neil | North Bay | RW |
| 162 | MTL | Andrei Markov | Khimik | D |
| 164 | BUF | Ales Kotalik | Ceske Budejovice Jr. | RW |
| 168 | PHI | Antero Niittymaki | TPS Turku Jr. | G |
| 171 | DET | Pavel Datsyuk | Yekateringburg | C |
| 216 | MTL | Michael Ryder | Hull | RW |
| 230 | NSH | Karlis Skrastins | TPS Turku | D |

## 1997

### FIRST ROUND

| Pick | Claimed by | Player | Amateur Club | Position |
|---|---|---|---|---|
| 1 | BOS | Joe Thornton | Sault Ste. Marie | C |
| 2 | S.J. | Patrick Marleau | Seattle | C |
| 3 | L.A. | Olli Jokinen | HIFK Helsinki | C |
| 4 | NYI | Roberto Luongo | Val-d'Or | G |
| 5 | NYI | Eric Brewer | Prince George | D |
| 6 | CGY | Daniel Tkaczuk | Barrie | C |
| 7 | T.B. | Paul Mara | Sudbury | D |
| 8 | BOS | Sergei Samsonov | Detroit | LW |
| 9 | WSH | Nick Boynton | Ottawa | D |
| 10 | VAN | Brad Ference | Spokane | D |
| 11 | MTL | Jason Ward | Erie | RW |
| 12 | OTT | Marian Hossa | Dukla Trencin | RW |
| 13 | CHI | Daniel Cleary | Belleville | RW |
| 14 | EDM | Michel Riesen | Biel-Bienne | RW |
| 15 | L.A. | Matt Zultek | Ottawa | LW |
| 16 | CHI | Ty Jones | Spokane | RW |
| 17 | PIT | Robert Dome | Las Vegas (IHL) | RW |
| 18 | ANA | Mikael Holmqvist | Djurgarden | C |
| 19 | NYR | Stefan Cherneski | Brandon | RW |
| 20 | FLA | Mike Brown | Red Deer | LW |
| 21 | BUF | Mika Noronen | Tappara Tampere | G |
| 22 | CAR | Nikos Tselios | Belleville | D |
| 23 | S.J. | Scott Hannan | Kelowna | D |
| 24 | N.J. | J-F Damphousse | Moncton | G |
| 25 | DAL | Brenden Morrow | Portland | LW |
| 26 | COL | Kevin Grimes | Kingston | D |

### OTHER NOTABLE SELECTIONS

| Pick | Claimed by | Player | Amateur Club | Position |
|---|---|---|---|---|
| 47 | FLA | Kristian Huselius | Farjestad Karlstad | LW |
| 48 | BUF | Henrik Tallinder | AIK Solna | D |
| 69 | BUF | Maxim Afinogenov | Dynamo Moscow | RW |
| 78 | COL | Ville Nieminen | Tappara Tampere | RW |
| 83 | L.A. | Joe Corvo | U. of Western Michigan | D |
| 119 | OTT | Magnus Arvedson | Farjestad Karlstad | LW |
| 130 | CHI | Kyle Calder | Regina | LW |
| 136 | NYR | Mike York | Michigan State | LW |
| 144 | VAN | Matt Cooke | Windsor | C |
| 156 | BUF | Brian Campbell | Ottawa | D |
| 161 | COL | David Aebischer | Fribourg-Gotteron | G |
| 177 | STL | Ladislav Nagy | Dragon Presov | LW |
| 191 | BOS | Antti Laaksonen | U. of Denver | LW |
| 208 | PIT | Andrew Ference | Portland | D |
| 215 | N.J. | Scott Clemmensen | Des Moines Jr. A | G |
| 229 | OTT | Karel Rachunek | ZPS Zlin Jr. | D |
| 242 | CHI | Brett McLean | Kelowna | C |

## 1996

### FIRST ROUND

| Pick | Claimed by | Player | Amateur Club | Position |
|---|---|---|---|---|
| 1 | OTT | Chris Phillips | Prince Albert | D |
| 2 | S.J. | Andrei Zyuzin | Salavat Yulayev Ufa | D |
| 3 | NYI | J.P. Dumont | Val-d'Or | RW |
| 4 | WSH | Alexandre Volchkov | Barrie | C |
| 5 | DAL | Ric Jackman | Sault Ste. Marie | D |
| 6 | EDM | Boyd Devereaux | Kitchener | C |
| 7 | BUF | Erik Rasmussen | U. of Minnesota | LW/C |
| 8 | BOS | Johnathan Aitken | Medicine Hat | D |
| 9 | ANA | Ruslan Salei | Las Vegas (IHL) | D |
| 10 | N.J. | Lance Ward | Red Deer | D |
| 11 | PHX | Dan Focht | Tri-City | D |
| 12 | VAN | Josh Holden | Regina | C |
| 13 | CGY | Derek Morris | Regina | D |
| 14 | STL | Marty Reasoner | Boston College | C |
| 15 | PHI | Dainius Zubrus | Pembroke Jr. A | RW |
| 16 | T.B. | Mario Larocque | Hull | D |
| 17 | WSH | Jaroslav Svejkovsky | Tri-City | RW |
| 18 | MTL | Matt Higgins | Moose Jaw | C |
| 19 | EDM | Matthieu Descoteaux | Shawinigan | D |
| 20 | FLA | Marcus Nilson | Djurgarden | LW |
| 21 | S.J. | Marco Sturm | Landshut | LW |
| 22 | NYR | Jeff Brown | Sarnia | D |
| 23 | PIT | Craig Hillier | Ottawa | G |
| 24 | PHX | Daniel Briere | Drummondville | C |
| 25 | COL | Peter Ratchuk | Shattuck St. Mary's H.S. | D |
| 26 | DET | Jesse Wallin | Red Deer | D |

### OTHER NOTABLE SELECTIONS

| Pick | Claimed by | Player | Amateur Club | Position |
|---|---|---|---|---|
| 27 | BUF | Cory Sarich | Saskatoon | D |
| 35 | ANA | Matt Cullen | St. Cloud State | C |
| 44 | MTL | Mathieu Garon | Victoriaville | G |
| 49 | N.J. | Colin White | Hull | D |
| 56 | NYI | Zdeno Chara | Dukla Trencin | D |
| 59 | EDM | Tom Poti | Cushing Academy | D |
| 79 | COL | Mark Parrish | St. Cloud State | RW |
| 89 | CGY | Toni Lydman | Reipas Lahti | D |
| 96 | L.A. | Eric Belanger | Beauport | C |
| 102 | S.J. | Matt Bradley | Kingston | RW |
| 105 | PIT | Michal Rozsival | Dukla Jihlava | D |
| 139 | PHX | Robert Esche | Detroit | G |
| 154 | MTL | Brett Clark | U. of Maine | D |
| 167 | COL | Dan Hinote | Army | RW |
| 174 | PHX | Trevor Letowski | Sarnia | RW |
| 176 | COL | Samuel Pahlsson | MoDo | C |
| 179 | T.B. | Pavel Kubina | Vitkovice | D |
| 199 | N.J. | Willie Mitchell | Melfort Jr. A | D |
| 204 | TOR | Tomas Kaberle | Kladno | D |
| 239 | OTT | Sami Salo | TPS Turku | D |

## 1995

### FIRST ROUND

| Pick | Claimed by | Player | Amateur Club | Position |
|---|---|---|---|---|
| 1 | OTT | Bryan Berard | Detroit | D |
| 2 | NYI | Wade Redden | Brandon | D |
| 3 | L.A. | Aki Berg | Kiekko-67 Turku | D |
| 4 | ANA | Chad Kilger | Kingston | C |
| 5 | T.B. | Daymond Langkow | Tri-City | C |
| 6 | EDM | Steve Kelly | Prince Albert | C |
| 7 | WPG | Shane Doan | Kamloops | RW |
| 8 | MTL | Terry Ryan | Tri-City | LW |
| 9 | BOS | Kyle McLaren | Tacoma | D |
| 10 | FLA | Radek Dvorak | HC Ceske Budejovice | RW |
| 11 | DAL | Jarome Iginla | Kamloops | RW |
| 12 | S.J. | Teemu Riihijarvi | Kiekko-Espoo | LW |
| 13 | HFD | Jean-Sebastien Giguere | Halifax | G |
| 14 | BUF | Jay McKee | Niagara Falls | D |
| 15 | TOR | Jeff Ware | Oshawa | D |
| 16 | BUF | Martin Biron | Beauport | G |
| 17 | WSH | Brad Church | Prince Albert | LW |
| 18 | N.J. | Petr Sykora | Detroit | RW |
| 19 | CHI | Dmitri Nabokov | Krylja Sovetov | C/LW |
| 20 | CGY | Denis Gauthier | Drummondville | D |
| 21 | BOS | Sean Brown | Belleville | D |
| 22 | PHI | Brian Boucher | Tri-City | G |
| 23 | WSH | Miika Elomo | Kiekko-67 Turku | LW |
| 24 | PIT | Aleksey Morozov | Krylja Sovetov | RW |
| 25 | COL | Marc Denis | Chicoutimi | G |
| 26 | DET | Maxim Kuznetsov | Dynamo | D |

### OTHER NOTABLE SELECTIONS

| Pick | Claimed by | Player | Amateur Club | Position |
|---|---|---|---|---|
| 31 | EDM | Georges Laraque | St-Jean | RW |
| 49 | STL | Jochen Hecht | Mannheim | C |
| 66 | VAN | Peter Schaefer | Brandon | LW |
| 67 | WPG | Brad Isbister | Portland | LW |
| 76 | PIT | Jean-Sebastien Aubin | Sherbrooke | G |
| 79 | N.J. | Alyn McCauley | Ottawa | C |
| 87 | HFD | Sami Kapanen | HIFK Helsinki | RW |
| 90 | S.J. | Vesa Toskala | Ilves Tampere | G |
| 91 | NYR | Marc Savard | Oshawa | C |
| 101 | STL | Michal Handzus | IS Banska Bystrica | C |
| 116 | S.J. | Miikka Kiprusoff | TPS Turku Jr. | G |
| 122 | N.J. | Chris Mason | Prince George | G |
| 128 | PIT | Jan Hrdina | Seattle | C |
| 129 | COL | Brent Johnson | Owen Sound | G |
| 144 | VAN | Brent Sopel | Swift Current | D |
| 164 | MTL | Stephane Robidas | Shawinigan | D |
| 177 | BOS | P.J. Axelsson | Vastra Frolunda | LW |
| 192 | FLA | Filip Kuba | HC Vitkovice Jr. | D |
| 223 | TOR | Danny Markov | Spartak | D |

## 1994

### FIRST ROUND

| Pick | Claimed by | Player | Amateur Club | Position |
|---|---|---|---|---|
| 1 | FLA | Ed Jovanovski | Windsor | D |
| 2 | ANA | Oleg Tverdovsky | Krylja Sovetov | D |
| 3 | OTT | Radek Bonk | Las Vegas (IHL) | C |
| 4 | EDM | Jason Bonsignore | Niagara Falls | C |
| 5 | HFD | Jeff O'Neill | Guelph | RW |
| 6 | EDM | Ryan Smyth | Moose Jaw | LW |
| 7 | L.A. | Jamie Storr | Owen Sound | G |
| 8 | T.B. | Jason Wiemer | Portland | C |
| 9 | NYI | Brett Lindros | Kingston | RW |
| 10 | WSH | Nolan Baumgartner | Kamloops | D |
| 11 | S.J. | Jeff Friesen | Regina | LW |
| 12 | QUE | Wade Belak | Saskatoon | D/RW |
| 13 | VAN | Mattias Ohlund | Pitea | D |
| 14 | CHI | Ethan Moreau | Niagara Falls | LW |
| 15 | WSH | Alexander Kharlamov | CSKA Moscow | C |
| 16 | TOR | Eric Fichaud | Chictoutimi | G |
| 17 | BUF | Wayne Primeau | Owen Sound | C |
| 18 | MTL | Brad Brown | North Bay | D |
| 19 | CGY | Chris Dingman | Brandon | LW |
| 20 | DAL | Jason Botterill | U. of Michigan | LW |
| 21 | BOS | Evgeni Ryabchikov | Molot Perm | G |
| 22 | QUE | Jeffrey Kealty | Catholic Memorial H.S. | D |
| 23 | DET | Yan Golubovsky | Dynamo 2 | D |
| 24 | PIT | Chris Wells | Seattle | C |
| 25 | N.J. | Vadim Sharifijanov | Salavat Yulayev Ufa | LW |
| 26 | NYR | Dan Cloutier | Sault Ste. Marie | G |

### OTHER NOTABLE SELECTIONS

| Pick | Claimed by | Player | Amateur Club | Position |
|---|---|---|---|---|
| 43 | BUF | Curtis Brown | Moose Jaw | C/LW |
| 44 | MTL | Jose Theodore | St-Jean | G |
| 49 | DET | Mathieu Dandenault | Sherbrooke | RW/D |
| 51 | N.J. | Patrik Elias | Kladno | C |
| 64 | TOR | Fredrik Modin | Timra | LW |
| 71 | N.J. | Sheldon Souray | Tri-City | D |
| 72 | QUE | Chris Drury | Fairfield Prep | C |
| 87 | QUE | Milan Hejduk | Pardubice | RW |
| 90 | NYI | Brad Lukowich | Kamloops | D |
| 124 | DAL | Marty Turco | Cambridge Jr. A | G |
| 133 | OTT | Daniel Alfredsson | Vastra Frolunda | RW |
| 151 | BOS | Andre Roy | Chicoutimi | RW |
| 217 | QUE | Tim Thomas | U. of Vermont | G |
| 218 | PHI | Johan Hedberg | Leksand | G |
| 219 | S.J. | Evgeni Nabokov | Ust-Kamengorsk | G |
| 226 | MTL | Tomas Vokoun | HC Kladno | G |
| 233 | N.J. | Steve Sullivan | Sault Ste. Marie | RW |
| 249 | WSH | Richard Zednik | IS Banka Bystricia | RW |
| 257 | DET | Tomas Holmstrom | Bodens IK | LW |
| 272 | NYI | Dick Tarnstrom | AIK Solna | D |

## 1993

### FIRST ROUND

| Pick | Claimed by | Player | Amateur Club | Position |
|---|---|---|---|---|
| 1 | OTT | Alexandre Daigle | Victoriaville | C |
| 2 | HFD | Chris Pronger | Peterborough | D |
| 3 | T.B. | Chris Gratton | Kingston | C |
| 4 | ANA | Paul Kariya | U. of Maine | LW |
| 5 | FLA | Rob Niedermayer | Medicine Hat | C |
| 6 | S.J. | Viktor Kozlov | Dynamo | C |
| 7 | EDM | Jason Arnott | Oshawa | C |
| 8 | NYR | Niklas Sundstrom | MoDo Ornskoldsvik | RW |
| 9 | DAL | Todd Harvey | Detroit | RW/C |
| 10 | QUE | Jocelyn Thibault | Sherbrooke | G |
| 11 | WSH | Brendan Witt | Seattle | D |
| 12 | TOR | Kenny Jonsson | Rogle Angelholm | D |
| 13 | N.J. | Denis Pederson | Prince Albert | C/RW |
| 14 | QUE | Adam Deadmarsh | Portland | RW |
| 15 | WPG | Mats Lindgren | Skelleftea | C/LW |
| 16 | EDM | Nick Stajduhar | London | D |
| 17 | WSH | Jason Allison | London | C |
| 18 | CGY | Jesper Mattsson | Malmo | C |
| 19 | TOR | Landon Wilson | Dubuque Jr. A | RW |
| 20 | VAN | Mike Wilson | Sudbury | D |
| 21 | MTL | Saku Koivu | TPS Turku | C |
| 22 | DET | Anders Eriksson | MoDo Ornskoldsvik | D |
| 23 | NYI | Todd Bertuzzi | Guelph | RW |
| 24 | CHI | Eric Lecompte | Hull | LW |
| 25 | BOS | Kevyn Adams | Miami of Ohio | C |
| 26 | PIT | Stefan Bergkvist | Leksand | D |

### OTHER NOTABLE SELECTIONS

| Pick | Claimed by | Player | Amateur Club | Position |
|---|---|---|---|---|
| 28 | S.J. | Shean Donovan | Ottawa | RW |
| 32 | N.J. | Jay Pandolfo | Boston University | LW |
| 35 | DAL | Jamie Langenbrunner | Cloquet | C |
| 36 | PHI | Janne Niinimaa | Karpat Oulu | D |
| 39 | NJ | Brendan Morrison | Spokane | C |
| 40 | NYI | Bryan McCabe | Spokane | D |
| 41 | FLA | Kevin Weekes | Owen Sound | G |
| 71 | PHI | Vaclav Prospal | Motor Ceske Budejovice | C |
| 72 | HFD | Marek Malik | Vitkovice | D |
| 90 | CHI | Eric Daze | Beauport | RW |
| 111 | EDM | Miroslav Satan | Dukla Trencin | LW |
| 118 | NYI | Tommy Salo | Vasteras | G |
| 124 | VAN | Scott Walker | Owen Sound | RW |
| 164 | NYR | Todd Marchant | Clarkson | C |
| 188 | HFD | Manny Legace | Niagara Falls | G |
| 207 | BOS | Hal Gill | Nashoba H.S. | D |
| 227 | OTT | Pavol Demitra | Dukla Trencin | LW |
| 250 | LA | Kimmo Timonen | KalPa Kuopio | D |

## 1992

### FIRST ROUND

| Pick | Claimed by | | Amateur Club | Position |
|---|---|---|---|---|
| 1 | T.B. | Roman Hamrlik | ZPS Zlin | D |
| 2 | OTT | Alexei Yashin | Dynamo | C |
| 3 | S.J. | Mike Rathje | Medicine Hat | D |
| 4 | QUE | Todd Warriner | Windsor | LW |
| 5 | NYI | Darius Kasparaitis | Dynamo | D |
| 6 | CGY | Cory Stillman | Windsor | LW |
| 7 | PHI | Ryan Sittler | Nichols H.S. | LW |
| 8 | TOR | Brandon Convery | Sudbury | C |
| 9 | HFD | Robert Petrovicky | Dukla Trencin | C |
| 10 | S.J. | Andrei Nazarov | Dynamo | LW |
| 11 | BUF | David Cooper | Medicine Hat | D |
| 12 | CHI | Sergei Krivokrasov | CSKA Moscow | RW |
| 13 | EDM | Joe Hulbig | St. Sebastian's H.S. | LW |
| 14 | WSH | Sergei Gonchar | Chelyabinsk | D |
| 15 | PHI | Jason Bowen | Tri-City | D |
| 16 | BOS | Dmitri Kvartalnov | San Diego (IHL) | LW |
| 17 | WPG | Sergei Bautin | Dynamo | D |
| 18 | N.J. | Jason Smith | Regina | D |
| 19 | PIT | Martin Straka | HC Skoda Plzen | C |
| 20 | MTL | David Wilkie | Kamloops | D |
| 21 | VAN | Libor Polasek | Vitkovice | C |
| 22 | DET | Curtis Bowen | Ottawa | LW |
| 23 | TOR | Grant Marshall | Ottawa | RW |
| 24 | NYR | Peter Ferraro | Waterloo Jr. A | LW |

### OTHER NOTABLE SELECTIONS

| Pick | Claimed by | | Amateur Club | Position |
|---|---|---|---|---|
| 27 | WPG | Boris Mironov | CSKA Moscow | D |
| 33 | MTL | Valeri Bure | Spokane | RW |
| 38 | STL | Igor Korolev | Dynamo | C |
| 40 | VAN | Michael Peca | Ottawa | C |
| 42 | N.J. | Sergei Brylin | CSKA Moscow | C |
| 46 | DET | Darren McCarty | Bellevile | RW |
| 48 | NYR | Mattias Norstrom | AIK Solna | D |
| 52 | QUE | Manny Fernandez | Laval | G |
| 65 | EDM | Kirk Maltby | Owen Sound | RW |
| 68 | MTL | Craig Rivet | Kingston | D |
| 88 | MIN | Jere Lehtinen | Kiekko-Espoo | RW |
| 117 | VAN | Adrian Aucoin | Boston University | D |
| 158 | STL | Ian Laperriere | Drummondville | C/RW |
| 186 | N.J. | Stephane Yelle | Oshawa | C |
| 204 | WPG | Nikolai Khabibulin | CSKA Moscow | G |
| 220 | QUE | Anson Carter | Wexford Jr. A | C |

## 1991

### FIRST ROUND

| Pick | Claimed by | | Amateur Club | Position |
|---|---|---|---|---|
| 1 | QUE | Eric Lindros | Oshawa | C |
| 2 | S.J. | Pat Falloon | Spokane | RW |
| 3 | N.J. | Scott Niedermayer | Kamloops | D |
| 4 | NYI | Scott Lachance | Boston U. | D |
| 5 | WPG | Aaron Ward | U. of Michigan | D |
| 6 | PHI | Peter Forsberg | MoDo Ornskoldsvik | C |
| 7 | VAN | Alek Stojanov | Hamilton | RW |
| 8 | MIN | Richard Matvichuk | Saskatoon | D |
| 9 | HFD | Patrick Poulin | St-Hyacinthe | C |
| 10 | DET | Martin Lapointe | Laval | RW |
| 11 | N.J. | Brian Rolston | Detroit Compuware Jr. A | C/RW |
| 12 | EDM | Tyler Wright | Swift Current | C |
| 13 | BUF | Philippe Boucher | Granby | D |
| 14 | WSH | Pat Peake | Detroit | C |
| 15 | NYR | Alex Kovalev | Dynamo | RW |
| 16 | PIT | Markus Naslund | MoDo Ornskoldsvik | LW |
| 17 | MTL | Brent Bilodeau | Seattle | D |
| 18 | BOS | Glen Murray | Sudbury | RW |
| 19 | CGY | Niklas Sundblad | AIK Solna | RW |
| 20 | EDM | Martin Rucinsky | CHZ Litvinov | LW |
| 21 | WSH | Trevor Halverson | North Bay | LW |
| 22 | CHI | Dean McAmmond | Prince Albert | LW |

### OTHER NOTABLE SELECTIONS

| Pick | Claimed by | | Amateur Club | Position |
|---|---|---|---|---|
| 23 | S.J. | Ray Whitney | Spokane | LW |
| 26 | NYI | Ziggy Palffy | AC Nitra | RW |
| 30 | S.J. | Sandis Ozolinsh | Dynamo Riga | D |
| 40 | BOS | Jozef Stumpel | AC Nitra | C |
| 47 | TOR | Yanic Perreault | Trois-Rivieres | C |
| 52 | CGY | Sandy McCarthy | Laval | RW |
| 54 | DET | Chris Osgood | Medicine Hat | G |
| 59 | HFD | Michael Nylander | Huddinge | C |
| 76 | DET | Mike Knuble | Kalamazoo Jr. A | RW |
| 81 | L.A. | Alexei Zhitnik | Sokol Kiev | D |
| 106 | BOS | Mariusz Czerkawski | GKS Tychy | RW |
| 122 | PHI | Dmitry Yushkevich | Yaroslavl | D |
| 123 | BUF | Sean O'Donnell | Sudbury | D |
| 171 | MTL | Brian Savage | Miami of Ohio | LW |
| 203 | WPG | Igor Ulanov | Khimik Voskresensk | D |

## 1990

### FIRST ROUND

| Pick | Claimed by | | Amateur Club | Position |
|---|---|---|---|---|
| 1 | QUE | Owen Nolan | Cornwall | RW |
| 2 | VAN | Petr Nedved | Seattle | C |
| 3 | DET | Keith Primeau | Niagara Falls | C |
| 4 | PHI | Mike Ricci | Peterborough | C |
| 5 | PIT | Jaromir Jagr | Kladno | RW |
| 6 | NYI | Scott Scissons | Saskatoon | C |
| 7 | L.A. | Darryl Sydor | Kamloops | D |
| 8 | MIN | Derian Hatcher | North Bay | D |
| 9 | WSH | John Slaney | Cornwall | D |
| 10 | TOR | Drake Berehowsky | Kingston | D |
| 11 | CGY | Trevor Kidd | Brandon | G |
| 12 | MTL | Turner Stevenson | Seattle | RW |
| 13 | NYR | Michael Stewart | Michigan State | D |
| 14 | BUF | Brad May | Niagara Falls | LW |
| 15 | HFD | Mark Greig | Lethbridge | RW |
| 16 | CHI | Karl Dykhuis | Hull | D |
| 17 | EDM | Scott Allison | Prince Albert | C |
| 18 | VAN | Shawn Antoski | North Bay | LW |
| 19 | WPG | Keith Tkachuk | Malden Catholic H.S. | LW |
| 20 | N.J. | Martin Brodeur | St-Hyacinthe | G |
| 21 | BOS | Bryan Smolinski | Michigan State | C |

### OTHER NOTABLE SELECTIONS

| Pick | Claimed by | | Amateur Club | Position |
|---|---|---|---|---|
| 25 | PHI | Chris Simon | Ottawa | LW |
| 31 | TOR | Felix Potvin | Chicoutimi | G |
| 34 | NYR | Doug Weight | Lake Superior State | C |
| 36 | HFD | Geoff Sanderson | Swift Current | LW |
| 45 | DET | Vyacheslav Kozlov | Khimik Voskresensk | RW |
| 47 | PHI | Chris Therien | Northwood Prep | D |
| 77 | WPG | Alexei Zhamnov | Dynamo Moscow | C |
| 85 | NYR | Sergei Zubov | CSKA Moscow | D |
| 86 | VAN | Gino Odjick | Laval | RW |
| 113 | MIN | Roman Turek | Plzen | G |
| 123 | MTL | Craig Conroy | Northwood Prep | C |
| 133 | L.A. | Robert Lang | CHZ Litvinov | C |
| 156 | WSH | Peter Bondra | Kosice | RW |
| 158 | QUE | Alexander Karpovtsev | VSZ Dynamo | D |
| 179 | N.J. | Jaroslav Modry | Budejovice | D |
| 244 | NYR | Sergei Nemchinov | Krylja Sovetov | LW |

## 1989

### FIRST ROUND

| Pick | Claimed by | | Amateur Club | Position |
|---|---|---|---|---|
| 1 | QUE | Mats Sundin | Nacka | C |
| 2 | NYI | Dave Chyzowski | Kamloops | LW |
| 3 | TOR | Scott Thornton | Belleville | LW |
| 4 | WPG | Stu Barnes | Tri-City | C |
| 5 | N.J. | Bill Guerin | Springfield Jr. B. | RW |
| 6 | CHI | Adam Bennett | Sudbury | D |
| 7 | MIN | Doug Zmolek | John Marshall H.S. | D |
| 8 | VAN | Jason Herter | North Dakota | D |
| 9 | STL | Jason Marshall | Vernon Jr. A | D |
| 10 | HFD | Bobby Holik | Dukla Jihlava | C |
| 11 | DET | Mike Sillinger | Regina | C |
| 12 | TOR | Rob Pearson | Belleville | RW |
| 13 | MTL | Lindsay Vallis | Seattle | D |
| 14 | BUF | Kevin Haller | Regina | D |
| 15 | EDM | Jason Soules | Niagara Falls | D |
| 16 | PIT | Jamie Heward | Regina | D |
| 17 | BOS | Shayne Stevenson | Kitchener | RW |
| 18 | N.J. | Jason Miller | Medicine Hat | LW |
| 19 | WSH | Olaf Kolzig | Tri-City | G |
| 20 | NYR | Steven Rice | Kitchener | RW |
| 21 | TOR | Steve Bancroft | Belleville | D |

### OTHER NOTABLE SELECTIONS

| Pick | Claimed by | | Amateur Club | Position |
|---|---|---|---|---|
| 22 | QUE | Adam Foote | Sault Ste. Marie | D |
| 30 | MTL | Patrice Brisebois | Laval | D |
| 53 | DET | Nicklas Lidstrom | Vasteras | D |
| 62 | WPG | Kris Draper | Canadian National | C |
| 70 | CGY | Robert Reichel | Litvinov | C |
| 73 | HFD | Jim McKenzie | Victoria | LW |
| 74 | DET | Sergei Fedorov | CSKA Moscow | C |
| 113 | VAN | Pavel Bure | CSKA Moscow | RW |
| 116 | DET | Dallas Drake | Northern Michigan | RW |
| 183 | BUF | Donald Audette | Laval | RW |
| 191 | NYI | Vladimir Malakhov | CSKA Moscow | D |
| 196 | MIN | Arturs Irbe | Dynamo Riga | G |
| 221 | DET | Vladimir Konstantinov | CSKA Moscow | D |

## 1988

### FIRST ROUND

| Pick | Claimed by | | Amateur Club | Position |
|---|---|---|---|---|
| 1 | MIN | Mike Modano | Prince Albert | C |
| 2 | VAN | Trevor Linden | Medicine Hat | RW |
| 3 | QUE | Curtis Leschyshyn | Saskatoon | D |
| 4 | PIT | Darrin Shannon | Windsor | LW |
| 5 | QUE | Daniel Dore | Drummondville | RW |
| 6 | TOR | Scott Pearson | Kingston | LW |
| 7 | L.A. | Martin Gelinas | Hull | LW |
| 8 | CHI | Jeremy Roenick | Thayer Academy | C |
| 9 | STL | Rod Brind'Amour | Notre Dame Jr. A | C |
| 10 | WPG | Teemu Selanne | Jokerit | RW |
| 11 | HFD | Chris Govedaris | Toronto | LW |
| 12 | N.J. | Corey Foster | Peterborough | D |
| 13 | BUF | Joel Savage | Victoria | RW |
| 14 | PHI | Claude Boivin | Drummondville | LW |
| 15 | WSH | Reggie Savage | Victoriaville | C |
| 16 | NYI | Kevin Cheveldayoff | Brandon | D |
| 17 | DET | Kory Kocur | Saskatoon | RW |
| 18 | BOS | Rob Cimetta | Toronto | W |
| 19 | EDM | Francois Leroux | St-Jean | D |
| 20 | MTL | Eric Charron | Trois-Rivieres | D |
| 21 | CGY | Jason Muzzatti | Michigan State | G |

### OTHER NOTABLE SELECTIONS

| Pick | Claimed by | | Amateur Club | Position |
|---|---|---|---|---|
| 27 | TOR | Tie Domi | Peterborough | RW |
| 67 | PIT | Mark Recchi | Kamloops | RW |
| 68 | NYR | Tony Amonte | Thayer Academy | RW |
| 70 | L.A. | Rob Blake | Bowling Green | D |
| 76 | BUF | Keith Carney | Mount St. Charles | D |
| 81 | BOS | Joe Juneau | R.P.I. | C |
| 89 | BUF | Alexander Mogilny | CSKA Moscow | RW |
| 97 | BUF | Rob Ray | Cornwall | RW |
| 129 | QUE | Valeri Kamensky | CSKA Moscow | D |
| 198 | STL | Bret Hedican | North St. Paul H.S. | D |
| 234 | QUE | Claude Lapointe | Laval | LW/C |

## 1987

### FIRST ROUND

| Pick | Claimed by | | Amateur Club | Position |
|---|---|---|---|---|
| 1 | BUF | Pierre Turgeon | Granby | C |
| 2 | N.J. | Brendan Shanahan | London | LW |
| 3 | BOS | Glen Wesley | Portland | D |
| 4 | L.A. | Wayne McBean | Medicine Hat | D |
| 5 | PIT | Chris Joseph | Seattle | D |
| 6 | MIN | Dave Archibald | Portland | C/LW |
| 7 | TOR | Luke Richardson | Peterborough | D |
| 8 | CHI | Jimmy Waite | Chicoutimi | G |
| 9 | QUE | Bryan Fogarty | Kingston | D |
| 10 | NYR | Jay More | New Westminster | D |
| 11 | DET | Yves Racine | Longueuil | D |
| 12 | STL | Keith Osborne | North Bay | RW |
| 13 | NYI | Dean Chynoweth | Medicine Hat | D |
| 14 | BOS | Stephane Quintal | Granby | D |
| 15 | QUE | Joe Sakic | Swift Current | C |
| 16 | WPG | Bryan Marchment | Belleville | D |
| 17 | MTL | Andrew Cassels | Ottawa | C |
| 18 | HFD | Jody Hull | Peterborough | RW |
| 19 | CGY | Bryan Deasley | U. of Michigan | LW |
| 20 | PHI | Darren Rumble | Kitchener | D |
| 21 | EDM | Peter Soberlak | Swift Current | LW |

### OTHER NOTABLE SELECTIONS

| Pick | Claimed by | | Amateur Club | Position |
|---|---|---|---|---|
| 33 | MTL | John LeClair | Bellows Academy | LW |
| 38 | MTL | Eric Desjardins | Granby | D |
| 44 | MTL | Mathieu Schneider | Cornwall | D |
| 71 | TOR | Joe Sacco | Medford H.S. | RW |
| 110 | PIT | Shawn McEachern | Matignon H.S. | RW |
| 114 | QUE | Garth Snow | Mount St. Charles H.S. | G |
| 118 | NYI | Rob DiMaio | Medicine Hat | RW |
| 149 | N.J. | Jim Dowd | Brick H.S. | C |
| 166 | CGY | Theoren Fleury | Moose Jaw | RW |

## 1986

### FIRST ROUND

| Pick | Claimed by | | Amateur Club | Position |
|---|---|---|---|---|
| 1 | DET | Joe Murphy | Michigan State | RW |
| 2 | L.A. | Jimmy Carson | Verdun | C |
| 3 | N.J. | Neil Brady | Medicine Hat | C |
| 4 | PIT | Zarley Zalapski | Canadian National | D |
| 5 | BUF | Shawn Anderson | Canadian National | D |
| 6 | TOR | Vincent Damphousse | Laval | C |
| 7 | VAN | Dan Woodley | Portland | RW |
| 8 | WPG | Pat Elynuik | Prince Albert | RW |
| 9 | NYR | Brian Leetch | Avon Old Farms H.S. | D |
| 10 | STL | Jocelyn Lemieux | Laval | RW |
| 11 | HFD | Scott Young | Boston U. | RW |
| 12 | MIN | Warren Babe | Lethbridge | LW |
| 13 | BOS | Craig Janney | Boston College | C |
| 14 | CHI | Everett Sanipass | Verdun | LW |
| 15 | MTL | Mark Pederson | Medicine Hat | LW |
| 16 | CGY | George Pelawa | Bemidji H.S. | RW |
| 17 | NYI | Tom Fitzgerald | Austin Prep | RW |
| 18 | QUE | Ken McRae | Sudbury | C |
| 19 | WSH | Jeff Greenlaw | Canadian National | LW |
| 20 | PHI | Kerry Huffman | Guelph | D |
| 21 | EDM | Kim Issel | Prince Albert | RW |

### OTHER NOTABLE SELECTIONS

| Pick | Claimed by | | Amateur Club | Position |
|---|---|---|---|---|
| 22 | DET | Adam Graves | Windsor | LW |
| 29 | WPG | Teppo Numminen | Tappara Tampere | D |
| 67 | PIT | Rob Brown | Kamloops | RW |
| 72 | NYR | Mark Janssens | Regina | C |
| 81 | QUE | Ron Tugnutt | Peterborough | G |
| 85 | DET | Johan Garpenlov | Nacka | LW |
| 114 | NYR | Darren Turcotte | North Bay | C |
| 141 | MTL | Lyle Odelein | Moose Jaw | D |
| 143 | NYI | Rich Pilon | Prince Albert AAA | D |
| 202 | BOS | Greg Hawgood | Kamloops | D |

## 1985

### FIRST ROUND

| Pick | Claimed by | | Amateur Club | Position |
|---|---|---|---|---|
| 1 | TOR | Wendel Clark | Saskatoon | LW/D |
| 2 | PIT | Craig Simpson | Michigan State | LW |
| 3 | N.J. | Craig Wolanin | Kitchener | D |
| 4 | VAN | Jim Sandlak | London | RW |
| 5 | HFD | Dana Murzyn | Calgary | D |
| 6 | NYI | Brad Dalgarno | Hamilton | RW |
| 7 | NYR | Ulf Dahlen | Ostersund | LW |
| 8 | DET | Brent Fedyk | Regina | LW |
| 9 | L.A. | Craig Duncanson | Sudbury | LW |
| 10 | L.A. | Dan Gratton | Oshawa | C |

| Pick | Claimed by | | Amateur Club | Position |
|---|---|---|---|---|
| 11 | CHI | Dave Manson | Prince Albert | D |
| 12 | MTL | Jose Charbonneau | Drummondville | RW |
| 13 | NYI | Derek King | Sault Ste. Marie | LW |
| 14 | BUF | Calle Johansson | Vastra Frolunda | D |
| 15 | QUE | David Latta | Kitchener | LW |
| 16 | MTL | Tom Chorske | Minneapolis SW H.S. | LW |
| 17 | CGY | Chris Biotti | Belmont Hill H.S. | D |
| 18 | WPG | Ryan Stewart | Kamloops | C |
| 19 | WSH | Yvon Corriveau | Toronto | LW |
| 20 | EDM | Scott Metcalfe | Kingston | LW |
| 21 | PHI | Glen Seabrooke | Peterborough | C |

### OTHER NOTABLE SELECTIONS

| Pick | Claimed by | | Amateur Club | Position |
|---|---|---|---|---|
| 24 | N.J. | Sean Burke | Toronto | G |
| 27 | CGY | Joe Nieuwendyk | Cornell | C |
| 28 | NYR | Mike Richter | Northwood Prep | G |
| 32 | N.J. | Eric Weinrich | North Yarmouth Academy | D |
| 35 | BUF | Benoit Hogue | St-Jean | C |
| 50 | DET | Steve Chiasson | Guelph | D |
| 52 | BOS | Bill Ranford | New Westminster | G |
| 81 | WPG | Fredrik Olausson | Farjestad Karlstad | D |
| 113 | DET | Randy McKay | Michigan Tech | RW |
| 157 | BOS | Randy Burridge | Peterborough | LW |
| 188 | EDM | Kelly Buchberger | Moose Jaw | RW |
| 189 | PHI | Gord Murphy | Oshawa | D |
| 214 | VAN | Igor Larionov | CSKA Moscow | C |
| 245 | BUF | Ken Baumgartner | Prince Albert | D |

## 1984

### FIRST ROUND

| Pick | Claimed by | | Amateur Club | Position |
|---|---|---|---|---|
| 1 | PIT | Mario Lemieux | Laval | C |
| 2 | N.J. | Kirk Muller | Guelph | LW |
| 3 | CHI | Eddie Olczyk | Team USA | C |
| 4 | TOR | Al Iafrate | Belleville | D |
| 5 | MTL | Petr Svoboda | CHZ Litvinov | D |
| 6 | L.A. | Craig Redmond | U. of Denver | D |
| 7 | DET | Shawn Burr | Kitchener | LW/C |
| 8 | MTL | Shayne Corson | Brantford | LW |
| 9 | PIT | Doug Bodger | Kamloops | D |
| 10 | VAN | J.J. Daigneault | Longueuil | D |
| 11 | HFD | Sylvain Cote | Quebec | D |
| 12 | CGY | Gary Roberts | Ottawa | LW |
| 13 | MIN | David Quinn | Kent H.S. | D |
| 14 | NYR | Terry Carkner | Peterborough | D |
| 15 | QUE | Trevor Stienburg | Guelph | RW |
| 16 | PIT | Roger Belanger | Kingston | C |
| 17 | WSH | Kevin Hatcher | North Bay | D |
| 18 | BUF | Mikael Andersson | Vastra Frolunda | LW |
| 19 | BOS | Dave Pasin | Prince Albert | RW |
| 20 | NYI | Duncan MacPherson | Saskatoon | D |
| 21 | EDM | Selmar Odelein | Regina | D |

### OTHER NOTABLE SELECTIONS

| Pick | Claimed by | | Amateur Club | Position |
|---|---|---|---|---|
| 25 | TOR | Todd Gill | Windsor | D |
| 27 | PHI | Scott Mellanby | Henry Carr Jr. B | RW |
| 29 | MTL | Stephane Richer | Granby | RW |
| 36 | QUE | Jeff Brown | Sudbury | D |
| 51 | MTL | Patrick Roy | Granby | G |
| 107 | N.J. | Kirk McLean | Oshawa | G |
| 117 | CGY | Brett Hull | Penticton Jr. A | RW |
| 119 | NYR | Kjell Samuelsson | Leksand | D |
| 166 | BOS | Don Sweeney | St. Paul's H.S. | D |
| 171 | L.A. | Luc Robitaille | Hull | LW |
| 180 | CGY | Gary Suter | U. of Wisconsin | D |

## 1983

### FIRST ROUND

| Pick | Claimed by | | Amateur Club | Position |
|---|---|---|---|---|
| 1 | MIN | Brian Lawton | Mount St. Charles H.S. | LW |
| 2 | HFD | Sylvain Turgeon | Hull | LW |
| 3 | NYI | Pat LaFontaine | Verdun | C |
| 4 | DET | Steve Yzerman | Peterborough | C |
| 5 | BUF | Tom Barrasso | Acton-Boxborough | G |
| 6 | N.J. | John MacLean | Oshawa | RW |
| 7 | TOR | Russ Courtnall | Victoria | RW |
| 8 | WPG | Andrew McBain | North Bay | RW |
| 9 | VAN | Cam Neely | Portland | RW |
| 10 | BUF | Normand Lacombe | New Hampshire | RW |
| 11 | BUF | Adam Creighton | Ottawa | C |
| 12 | NYR | Dave Gagner | Brantford | C |
| 13 | CGY | Dan Quinn | Belleville | C |
| 14 | WPG | Bobby Dollas | Laval | D |
| 15 | PIT | Bob Errey | Peterborough | LW |
| 16 | NYI | Gerald Diduck | Lethbridge | D |
| 17 | MTL | Alfie Turcotte | Portland | C |
| 18 | CHI | Bruce Cassidy | Ottawa | D |
| 19 | EDM | Jeff Beukeboom | Sault Ste. Marie | D |
| 20 | HFD | David Jensen | Lawrence Academy | C |
| 21 | BOS | Nevin Markwart | Regina | LW |

### OTHER NOTABLE SELECTIONS

| Pick | Claimed by | | Amateur Club | Position |
|---|---|---|---|---|
| 26 | MTL | Claude Lemieux | Trois-Rivieres | RW |
| 27 | MTL | Sergio Momesso | Shawinigan | LW |
| 41 | PHI | Peter Zezel | Toronto | C |
| 82 | EDM | Esa Tikkanen | HIFK Helsinki | LW |
| 88 | DET | Petr Klima | Dukla Jihlava | W |
| 91 | DET | Joe Kocur | Saskatoon | RW |
| 112 | L.A. | Kevin Stevens | Silvere Lake H.S. | LW |
| 125 | PHI | Rick Tocchet | Sault Ste. Marie | RW |

| Pick | Claimed by | | Amateur Club | Position |
|---|---|---|---|---|
| 139 | BUF | Christian Ruuttu | Assat Pori | C |
| 150 | N.J. | Viacheslav Fetisov | CSKA Moscow | D |
| 207 | CHI | Dominik Hasek | Pardubice | G |
| 223 | BUF | Uwe Krupp | Koln | D |
| 241 | CGY | Sergei Makarov | CSKA Moscow | RW |

## 1982

### FIRST ROUND

| Pick | Claimed by | | Amateur Club | Position |
|---|---|---|---|---|
| 1 | BOS | Gord Kluzak | Billings | D |
| 2 | MIN | Brian Bellows | Kitchener | LW |
| 3 | TOR | Gary Nylund | Portland | D |
| 4 | PHI | Ron Sutter | Lethbridge | C |
| 5 | WSH | Scott Stevens | Kitchener | D |
| 6 | BUF | Phil Housley | South St. Paul H.S. | D |
| 7 | CHI | Ken Yaremchuk | Portland | C |
| 8 | N.J. | Rocky Trottier | Nanaimo | RW |
| 9 | BUF | Paul Cyr | Victoria | LW |
| 10 | PIT | Rich Sutter | Lethbridge | RW |
| 11 | VAN | Michel Petit | Sherbrooke | D |
| 12 | WPG | Jim Kyte | Cornwall | D |
| 13 | QUE | David Shaw | Kitchener | D |
| 14 | HFD | Paul Lawless | Windsor | LW |
| 15 | NYR | Chris Kontos | Toronto | LW/C |
| 16 | BUF | Dave Andreychuk | Oshawa | LW |
| 17 | DET | Murray Craven | Medicine Hat | LW |
| 18 | N.J. | Ken Daneyko | Seattle | D |
| 19 | MTL | Alain Heroux | Chicoutimi | LW |
| 20 | EDM | Jim Playfair | Portland | D |
| 21 | NYI | Pat Flatley | U. of Wisconsin | RW |

### OTHER NOTABLE SELECTIONS

| Pick | Claimed by | | Amateur Club | Position |
|---|---|---|---|---|
| 36 | NYR | Tomas Sandstrom | Farjestad Karlstad | RW |
| 43 | N.J. | Pat Verbeek | Sudbury | RW |
| 45 | TOR | Ken Wregget | Lethbridge | G |
| 56 | HFD | Kevin Dineen | U. of Denver | RW |
| 67 | HFD | Ulf Samuelsson | Leksand | D |
| 75 | WPG | Dave Ellett | Ottawa Jr. A | D |
| 80 | MIN | Bob Rouse | Nanaimo | D |
| 88 | HFD | Ray Ferraro | Penticton Jr. A | C |
| 119 | PHI | Ron Hextall | Brandon | G |
| 120 | NYR | Tony Granato | Northwood Prep | RW |
| 134 | STL | Doug Gilmour | Cornwall | C |
| 140 | PHI | Dave Brown | Saskatoon | RW |

## 1981

### FIRST ROUND

| Pick | Claimed by | | Amateur Club | Position |
|---|---|---|---|---|
| 1 | WPG | Dale Hawerchuk | Cornwall | C |
| 2 | L.A. | Doug Smith | Ottawa | C |
| 3 | WSH | Bob Carpenter | St. John's Prep | C |
| 4 | HFD | Ron Francis | Sault Ste. Marie | C |
| 5 | COL | Joe Cirella | Oshawa | D |
| 6 | TOR | Jim Benning | Portland | D |
| 7 | MTL | Mark Hunter | Brantford | RW |
| 8 | EDM | Grant Fuhr | Victoria | G |
| 9 | NYR | James Patrick | Prince Albert | D |
| 10 | VAN | Garth Butcher | Regina | D |
| 11 | QUE | Randy Moller | Lethbridge | D |
| 12 | CHI | Tony Tanti | Oshawa | RW |
| 13 | MIN | Ron Meighan | Niagara Falls | D |
| 14 | BOS | Normand Leveille | Chicoutimi | LW |
| 15 | CGY | Al MacInnis | Kitchener | D |
| 16 | PHI | Steve Smith | Sault Ste. Marie | D |
| 17 | BUF | Jiri Dudacek | Kladno | RW |
| 18 | MTL | Gilbert Delorme | Chicoutimi | D |
| 19 | MTL | Jan Ingman | Farjestad Karlstad | LW |
| 20 | STL | Marty Ruff | Lethbridge | D |
| 21 | NYI | Paul Boutilier | Sherbrooke | D |

### OTHER NOTABLE SELECTIONS

| Pick | Claimed by | | Amateur Club | Position |
|---|---|---|---|---|
| 22 | WPG | Scott Arniel | Cornwall | LW |
| 40 | MTL | Chris Chelios | Moose Jaw | D |
| 56 | CGY | Mike Vernon | Calgary | G |
| 72 | NYR | John Vanbiesbrouck | Sault Ste. Marie | G |
| 107 | DET | Gerard Gallant | Sherbrooke | LW |
| 108 | COL | Bruce Driver | U. of Wisconsin | D |
| 111 | EDM | Steve Smith | London | D |
| 145 | MTL | Tom Kurvers | Minnesota-Duluth | D |
| 152 | WSH | Gaetan Duchesne | Quebec | LW |

## 1980

### FIRST ROUND

| Pick | Claimed by | | Amateur Club | Position |
|---|---|---|---|---|
| 1 | MTL | Doug Wickenheiser | Regina | C |
| 2 | WPG | Dave Babych | Portland | D |
| 3 | CHI | Denis Savard | Montreal | C |
| 4 | L.A. | Larry Murphy | Peterborough | D |
| 5 | WSH | Darren Veitch | Regina | D |
| 6 | EDM | Paul Coffey | Kitchener | D |
| 7 | VAN | Rick Lanz | Oshawa | D |
| 8 | HFD | Fred Arthur | Cornwall | D |
| 9 | PIT | Mike Bullard | Brantford | C |
| 10 | L.A. | Jim Fox | Ottawa | RW |
| 11 | DET | Mike Blaisdell | Regina | RW |
| 12 | STL | Rik Wilson | Kingston | D |
| 13 | CGY | Denis Cyr | Montreal | RW |
| 14 | NYR | Jim Malone | Toronto | C |
| 15 | CHI | Jerome Dupont | Toronto | D |

| Pick | Claimed by | | Amateur Club | Position |
|---|---|---|---|---|
| 16 | MIN | Brad Palmer | Victoria | LW |
| 17 | NYI | Brent Sutter | Red Deer Jr. A | C |
| 18 | BOS | Barry Pederson | Victoria | C |
| 19 | COL | Paul Gagne | Windsor | LW |
| 20 | BUF | Steve Patrick | Brandon | RW |
| 21 | PHI | Mike Stothers | Kingston | D |

### OTHER NOTABLE SELECTIONS

| Pick | Claimed by | | Amateur Club | Position |
|---|---|---|---|---|
| 37 | MIN | Don Beaupre | Sudbury | G |
| 38 | NYI | Kelly Hrudey | Medicine Hat | G |
| 57 | CHI | Troy Murray | St. Albert Jr. A | C |
| 61 | MTL | Craig Ludwig | North Dakota | D |
| 69 | EDM | Jari Kurri | Jokerit | RW |
| 73 | L.A. | Bernie Nicholls | Kingston | C |
| 80 | NYI | Greg Gilbert | Toronto | LW |
| 81 | BOS | Steve Kasper | Verdun | C |
| 106 | COL | Aaron Broten | Minnesota-Duluth | LW/C |
| 120 | CHI | Steve Larmer | Niagara Falls | RW |
| 124 | MTL | Mike McPhee | RPI | LW |
| 128 | WPG | Brian Mullen | U.S. Jr. National | RW |
| 132 | EDM | Andy Moog | Billings | G |
| 181 | CGY | Hakan Loob | Farjestad Karlstad | RW |

## 1979

### FIRST ROUND

| Pick | Claimed by | | Amateur Club | Position |
|---|---|---|---|---|
| 1 | COL | Rob Ramage | London | D |
| 2 | STL | Perry Turnbull | Portland | C |
| 3 | DET | Mike Foligno | Sudbury | RW |
| 4 | WSH | Mike Gartner | Niagara Falls | RW |
| 5 | VAN | Rick Vaive | Sherbrooke | RW |
| 6 | MIN | Craig Hartsburg | Sault Ste. Marie | D |
| 7 | CHI | Keith Brown | Portland | D |
| 8 | BOS | Raymond Bourque | Verdun | D |
| 9 | TOR | Laurie Boschman | Brandon | C |
| 10 | MIN | Tom McCarthy | Oshawa | LW |
| 11 | BUF | Mike Ramsey | U. of Minnesota | D |
| 12 | ATL | Paul Reinhart | Kitchener | D |
| 13 | NYR | Doug Sulliman | Kitchener | RW |
| 14 | PHI | Brian Propp | Brandon | LW |
| 15 | BOS | Brad McCrimmon | Brandon | D |
| 16 | L.A. | Jay Wells | Kingston | D |
| 17 | NYI | Duane Sutter | Lethbridge | RW |
| 18 | HFD | Ray Allison | Brandon | RW |
| 19 | WPG | Jimmy Mann | Sherbrooke | RW |
| 20 | QUE | Michel Goulet | Quebec | LW |
| 21 | EDM | Kevin Lowe | Quebec | D |

### OTHER NOTABLE SELECTIONS

| Pick | Claimed by | | Amateur Club | Position |
|---|---|---|---|---|
| 32 | BUF | Lindy Ruff | Lethbridge | D/LW |
| 37 | MTL | Mats Naslund | Brynas Gavle | LW |
| 40 | WPG | Dave Christian | North Dakota | RW |
| 41 | QUE | Dale Hunter | Sudbury | C |
| 42 | MIN | Neal Broten | Minnesota-Duluth | C |
| 44 | MTL | Guy Carbonneau | Chicoutimi | C |
| 48 | EDM | Mark Messier | St. Albert Jr. A | C |
| 54 | ATL | Tim Hunter | Seattle | RW |
| 57 | BOS | Keith Crowder | Peterborough | RW |
| 58 | MTL | Rick Wamsley | Brantford | G |
| 66 | DET | John Ogrodnick | New Westminster | LW |
| 69 | EDM | Glenn Anderson | U. of Denver | RW |
| 75 | ATL | Jim Peplinski | Toronto | RW |
| 83 | QUE | Anton Stastny | Slovan Bratislava | LW |
| 89 | VAN | Dirk Graham | Regina | RW/LW |
| 103 | WPG | Thomas Steen | Leksand | C |
| 120 | BOS | Mike Krushelnyski | Montreal | LW/C |

## 1978

### FIRST ROUND

| Pick | Claimed by | | Amateur Club | Position |
|---|---|---|---|---|
| 1 | MIN | Bobby Smith | Ottawa | C |
| 2 | WSH | Ryan Walter | Seattle | C/LW |
| 3 | STL | Wayne Babych | Portland | RW |
| 4 | VAN | Bill Derlago | Brandon | C |
| 5 | COL | Mike Gillis | Kingston | LW |
| 6 | PHI | Behn Wilson | Kingston | D |
| 7 | PHI | Ken Linseman | Kingston | C |
| 8 | MTL | Danny Geoffrion | Cornwall | RW |
| 9 | DET | Willie Huber | Hamilton | D |
| 10 | CHI | Tim Higgins | Ottawa | RW |
| 11 | ATL | Brad Marsh | London | D |
| 12 | DET | Brent Peterson | Portland | C |
| 13 | BUF | Larry Playfair | Portland | D |
| 14 | PHI | Danny Lucas | Sault Ste. Marie | RW |
| 15 | NYI | Steve Tambellini | Lethbridge | C |
| 16 | BOS | Al Secord | Hamilton | LW |
| 17 | MTL | Dave Hunter | Sudbury | LW |
| 18 | WSH | Tim Coulis | Hamilton | LW |

### OTHER NOTABLE SELECTIONS

| Pick | Claimed by | | Amateur Club | Position |
|---|---|---|---|---|
| 19 | MIN | Steve Payne | Ottawa | LW |
| 21 | TOR | Joel Quenneville | Windsor | D |
| 22 | VAN | Curt Fraser | Victoria | LW |
| 26 | NYR | Don Maloney | Kitchener | LW |
| 32 | BUF | Tony McKegney | Kingston | LW |
| 40 | VAN | Stan Smyl | New Westminster | RW |
| 54 | MIN | Curt Giles | Minnesota-Duluth | D |
| 55 | WSH | Bengt Gustafsson | Farjestad Karlstad | RW |
| 93 | NYR | Tom Laidlaw | Northern Michigan | D |
| 103 | MTL | Keith Acton | Peterborough | C |

| Pick | Claimed by | | Amateur Club | Position |
|---|---|---|---|---|
| 109 | STL | Paul MacLean | Hull | RW |
| 153 | BOS | Craig MacTavish | University of Lowell | C |
| 173 | STL | Risto Siltanen | Ilves Tampere | D |
| 179 | CHI | Darryl Sutter | Lethbridge | LW |
| 231 | MTL | Chris Nilan | Northeastern | RW |

# 1977

### FIRST ROUND

| Pick | Claimed by | | Amateur Club | Position |
|---|---|---|---|---|
| 1 | DET | Dale McCourt | St. Catharines | C |
| 2 | COL | Barry Beck | New Westminster | D |
| 3 | WSH | Robert Picard | Montreal | D |
| 4 | VAN | Jere Gillis | Sherbrooke | LW |
| 5 | Cle. | Mike Crombeen | Kingston | RW |
| 6 | CHI | Doug Wilson | Ottawa | D |
| 7 | MIN | Brad Maxwell | New Westminster | D |
| 8 | NYR | Lucien DeBlois | Sorel | C |
| 9 | STL | Scott Campbell | London | D |
| 10 | MTL | Mark Napier | Toronto | RW |
| 11 | TOR | John Anderson | Toronto | RW |
| 12 | TOR | Trevor Johansen | Toronto | D |
| 13 | NYR | Ron Duguay | Sudbury | C/RW |
| 14 | BUF | Ric Seiling | St. Catharines | RW/C |
| 15 | NYI | Mike Bossy | Laval | RW |
| 16 | BOS | Dwight Foster | Kitchener | RW |
| 17 | PHI | Kevin McCarthy | Winnipeg | D |
| 18 | MTL | Norm Dupont | Montreal | LW |

### OTHER NOTABLE SELECTIONS

| Pick | Claimed by | | Amateur Club | Position |
|---|---|---|---|---|
| 25 | MIN | Dave Semenko | Brandon | LW |
| 33 | NYI | John Tonelli | Toronto | LW |
| 36 | MTL | Rod Langway | New Hampshire | D |
| 40 | VAN | Glen Hanlon | Brandon | G |
| 54 | MTL | Gordie Roberts | Victoria | D |
| 66 | PIT | Mark Johnson | U. of Wisconsin | C |
| 102 | PIT | Greg Millen | Peterborough | G |
| 135 | PHI | Pete Peeters | Medicine Hat | G |
| 162 | MTL | Craig Laughlin | Clarkson | RW |

# 1976

### FIRST ROUND

| Pick | Claimed by | | Amateur Club | Position |
|---|---|---|---|---|
| 1 | WSH | Rick Green | London | D |
| 2 | PIT | Blair Chapman | Saskatoon | RW |
| 3 | MIN | Glen Sharpley | Hull | C |
| 4 | DET | Fred Williams | Saskatoon | C |
| 5 | CAL | Bjorn Johansson | Orebro | D |
| 6 | NYR | Don Murdoch | Medicine Hat | RW |
| 7 | STL | Bernie Federko | Saskatoon | C |
| 8 | ATL | Dave Shand | Peterborough | D |
| 9 | CHI | Real Cloutier | Quebec | RW |
| 10 | ATL | Harold Phillipoff | New Westminster | LW |
| 11 | K.C. | Paul Gardner | Oshawa | C |
| 12 | MTL | Peter Lee | Ottawa | RW |
| 13 | MTL | Rod Schutt | Sudbury | LW |
| 14 | NYI | Alex McKendry | Sudbury | W |
| 15 | WSH | Greg Carroll | Medicine Hat | C |
| 16 | BOS | Clayton Pachal | New Westminster | C/LW |
| 17 | PHI | Mark Suzor | Kingston | D |
| 18 | MTL | Bruce Baker | Ottawa | RW |

### OTHER NOTABLE SELECTIONS

| Pick | Claimed by | | Amateur Club | Position |
|---|---|---|---|---|
| 19 | PIT | Greg Malone | Oshawa | C |
| 20 | STL | Brian Sutter | Lethbridge | LW |
| 22 | DET | Reed Larson | Minnesota-Duluth | D |
| 30 | TOR | Randy Carlyle | Sudbury | D |
| 45 | CHI | Thomas Gradin | MoDo Ornskoldsvik | C |
| 47 | PIT | Morris Lukowich | Medicine Hat | LW |
| 56 | STL | Mike Liut | Bowling Green | G |
| 64 | ATL | Kent Nilsson | Djurgarden | C |
| 68 | NYI | Ken Morrow | Bowling Green | D |
| 133 | MTL | Ron Wilson | St. Catharines | C |

# 1975

### FIRST ROUND

| Pick | Claimed by | | Amateur Club | Position |
|---|---|---|---|---|
| 1 | PHI | Mel Bridgman | Victoria | C |
| 2 | K.C. | Barry Dean | Medicine Hat | LW |
| 3 | CAL | Ralph Klassen | Saskatoon | C |
| 4 | MIN | Bryan Maxwell | Medicine Hat | D |
| 5 | DET | Rick Lapointe | Victoria | D |
| 6 | TOR | Don Ashby | Calgary | C |
| 7 | CHI | Greg Vaydik | Medicine Hat | C |
| 8 | ATL | Richard Mulhern | Sherbrooke | D |
| 9 | MTL | Robin Sadler | Edmonton | D |
| 10 | VAN | Rick Blight | Brandon | RW |
| 11 | NYI | Pat Price | Saskatoon | D |
| 12 | NYR | Wayne Dillon | Toronto | C |
| 13 | PIT | Gord Laxton | New Westminster | G |
| 14 | BOS | Doug Halward | Peterborough | D |
| 15 | MTL | Pierre Mondou | Montreal | C |
| 16 | L.A. | Tim Young | Ottawa | C |

### OTHER NOTABLE SELECTIONS

| Pick | Claimed by | | Amateur Club | Position |
|---|---|---|---|---|
| 17 | BUF | Bob Sauve | Laval | G |
| 21 | CAL | Dennis Maruk | London | C |
| 22 | MTL | Brian Engblom | Wisconsin | D |
| 24 | TOR | Doug Jarvis | Peterborough | C |
| 43 | CHI | Mike O'Connell | Kingston | D |
| 57 | CAL | Greg Smith | Colorado College | D |
| 80 | ATL | Willi Plett | St. Catharines | RW |
| 108 | PHI | Paul Holmgren | U. of Minnesota | RW |
| 210 | L.A. | Dave Taylor | Clarkson | RW |

# 1974

### FIRST ROUND

| Pick | Claimed by | | Amateur Club | Position |
|---|---|---|---|---|
| 1 | WSH | Greg Joly | Regina | D |
| 2 | K.C. | Wilf Paiement | St. Catharines | RW |
| 3 | CAL | Rick Hampton | St. Catharines | LW/D |
| 4 | NYI | Clark Gillies | Regina | LW |
| 5 | MTL | Cam Connor | Flin Flon | RW |
| 6 | MIN | Doug Hicks | Flin Flon | D |
| 7 | MTL | Doug Risebrough | Kitchener | C |
| 8 | PIT | Pierre Larouche | Sorel | C |
| 9 | DET | Bill Lochead | Oshawa | LW |
| 10 | MTL | Rick Chartraw | Kitchener | D/RW |
| 11 | BUF | Lee Fogolin Jr. | Oshawa | D |
| 12 | MTL | Mario Tremblay | Montreal | RW |
| 13 | TOR | Jack Valiquette | Sault Ste. Marie | C |
| 14 | NYR | Dave Maloney | Kitchener | D |
| 15 | MTL | Gord McTavish | Sudbury | C |
| 16 | CHI | Grant Mulvey | Calgary | RW |
| 17 | CAL | Ron Chipperfield | Brandon | C |
| 18 | BOS | Don Larway | Swift Current | RW |

### OTHER NOTABLE SELECTIONS

| Pick | Claimed by | | Amateur Club | Position |
|---|---|---|---|---|
| 22 | NYI | Bryan Trottier | Swift Current | C |
| 25 | BOS | Mark Howe | Toronto | D |
| 29 | BUF | Danny Gare | Calgary | RW |
| 31 | TOR | Tiger Williams | Swift Current | LW |
| 32 | NYR | Ron Greschner | New Westminster | D |
| 38 | K.C. | Bob Bourne | Saskatoon | C |
| 39 | CAL | Charlie Simmer | Sault Ste. Marie | LW |
| 52 | CHI | Bob Murray | Cornwall | D |
| 70 | CHI | Terry Ruskowski | Swift Current | C |
| 77 | VAN | Mike Rogers | Calgary | C |
| 85 | TOR | Mike Palmateer | Toronto | G |
| 125 | PHI | Reggie Lemelin | Sherbrooke | G |
| 199 | MTL | Dave Lumley | New Hampshire | RW |
| 214 | NYI | Stefan Persson | Brynas Gavle | D |

# 1973

### FIRST ROUND

| Pick | Claimed by | | Amateur Club | Position |
|---|---|---|---|---|
| 1 | NYI | Denis Potvin | Ottawa | D |
| 2 | ATL | Tom Lysiak | Medicine Hat | C |
| 3 | VAN | Dennis Ververgaert | London | RW |
| 4 | TOR | Lanny McDonald | Medicine Hat | RW |
| 5 | STL | John Davidson | Calgary | G |
| 6 | BOS | Andre Savard | Quebec | C |
| 7 | PIT | Blaine Stoughton | Flin Flon | RW |
| 8 | MTL | Bob Gainey | Peterborough | LW |
| 9 | VAN | Bob Dailey | Toronto | D |
| 10 | TOR | Bob Neely | Peterborough | LW |
| 11 | DET | Terry Richardson | New Westminster | G |
| 12 | BUF | Morris Titanic | Sudbury | LW |
| 13 | CHI | Darcy Rota | Edmonton | LW |
| 14 | NYR | Rick Middleton | Oshawa | RW |
| 15 | TOR | Ian Turnbull | Ottawa | D |
| 16 | ATL | Vic Mercredi | New Westminster | C |

### OTHER NOTABLE SELECTIONS

| Pick | Claimed by | | Amateur Club | Position |
|---|---|---|---|---|
| 21 | ATL | Eric Vail | Sudbury | LW |
| 27 | PIT | Colin Campbell | Peterborough | D |
| 30 | NYR | Pat Hickey | Hamilton | LW |
| 33 | NYI | Dave Lewis | Saskatoon | D |
| 49 | NYI | Andre St. Laurent | Montreal | C |
| 85 | ATL | Ken Houston | Chatham Jr. B | RW |
| 130 | CAL | Larry Patey | Braintree H.S. | C |
| 134 | PIT | Gord Lane | New Westminster | D |
| 162 | ATL | Greg Fox | U. of Michigan | D |

# 1972

### FIRST ROUND

| Pick | Claimed by | | Amateur Club | Position |
|---|---|---|---|---|
| 1 | NYI | Billy Harris | Toronto | RW |
| 2 | ATL | Jacques Richard | Quebec | LW |
| 3 | VAN | Don Lever | Niagara Falls | LW |
| 4 | MTL | Steve Shutt | Toronto | LW |
| 5 | BUF | Jim Schoenfeld | Niagara Falls | D |
| 6 | MTL | Michel Larocque | Ottawa | G |
| 7 | PHI | Bill Barber | Kitchener | LW |
| 8 | MTL | Dave Gardner | Toronto | C |
| 9 | STL | Wayne Merrick | Ottawa | C |
| 10 | NYR | Al Blanchard | Kitchener | LW |
| 11 | TOR | George Ferguson | Toronto | C |
| 12 | MIN | Jerry Byers | Kitchener | LW |
| 13 | CHI | Phil Russell | Edmonton | D |
| 14 | MTL | John Van Boxmeer | Guelph | D |
| 15 | NYR | Bob MacMillan | St. Catharines | RW |
| 16 | BOS | Mike Bloom | St. Catharines | LW |

### OTHER NOTABLE SELECTIONS

| Pick | Claimed by | | Amateur Club | Position |
|---|---|---|---|---|
| 17 | NYI | Lorne Henning | New Westminster | C |
| 23 | PHI | Tom Bladon | Edmonton | D |
| 33 | NYI | Bob Nystrom | Calgary | RW |
| 39 | PHI | Jimmy Watson | Calgary | D |
| 55 | PHI | Al MacAdam | University of PEI | RW |
| 85 | BUF | Peter McNab | U. of Denver | C |
| 97 | NYI | Richard Brodeur | Cornwall | G |
| 139 | TOR | Pat Boutette | Minnesota-Duluth | C/RW |
| 144 | NYI | Garry Howatt | Flin Flon | LW |

# 1971

### FIRST ROUND

| Pick | Claimed by | | Amateur Club | Position |
|---|---|---|---|---|
| 1 | MTL | Guy Lafleur | Quebec | RW |
| 2 | DET | Marcel Dionne | St. Catharines | C |
| 3 | VAN | Jocelyn Guevremont | Montreal | D |
| 4 | STL | Gene Carr | Flin Flon | C |
| 5 | BUF | Rick Martin | Montreal | LW |
| 6 | BOS | Ron Jones | Edmonton | D |
| 7 | MTL | Chuck Arnason | Flin Flon | RW |
| 8 | PHI | Larry Wright | Regina | C |
| 9 | PHI | Pierre Plante | Drummondville | RW |
| 10 | NYR | Steve Vickers | Toronto | LW |
| 11 | MTL | Murray Wilson | Ottawa | LW |
| 12 | CHI | Dan Spring | Edmonton | C |
| 13 | NYR | Steve Durbano | Toronto | D |
| 14 | BOS | Terry O'Reilly | Oshawa | RW |

### OTHER NOTABLE SELECTIONS

| Pick | Claimed by | | Amateur Club | Position |
|---|---|---|---|---|
| 17 | VAN | Bobby Lalonde | Montreal | C |
| 19 | BUF | Craig Ramsay | Peterborough | LW |
| 20 | MTL | Larry Robinson | Kitchener | D |
| 22 | TOR | Rick Kehoe | Hamilton | RW |
| 33 | BUF | Bill Hajt | Saskatoon | D |
| 48 | L.A. | Neil Komadoski | Winnipeg | D |
| 55 | NYR | Jerry Butler | Hamilton | RW |

# 1970

### FIRST ROUND

| Pick | Claimed by | | Amateur Club | Position |
|---|---|---|---|---|
| 1 | BUF | Gilbert Perreault | Montreal | C |
| 2 | VAN | Dale Tallon | Toronto | D |
| 3 | BOS | Reggie Leach | Flin Flon | RW |
| 4 | BOS | Rick MacLeish | Peterborough | C |
| 5 | MTL | Ray Martyniuk | Flin Flon | G |
| 6 | MTL | Chuck Lefley | Canadian National | LW |
| 7 | PIT | Greg Polis | Estevan | LW |
| 8 | TOR | Darryl Sittler | London | C |
| 9 | BOS | Ron Plumb | Peterborough | D |
| 10 | CAL | Chris Oddleifson | Winnipeg | C |
| 11 | NYR | Norm Gratton | Montreal | LW |
| 12 | DET | Serge Lajeunesse | Montreal | D/RW |
| 13 | BOS | Bob Stewart | Oshawa | D |
| 14 | CHI | Dan Maloney | London | LW |

### OTHER NOTABLE SELECTIONS

| Pick | Claimed by | | Amateur Club | Position |
|---|---|---|---|---|
| 18 | PHI | Bill Clement | Ottawa | C |
| 20 | MIN | Fred Barrett | Toronto | D |
| 22 | TOR | Errol Thompson | Charlottetown Sr. | LW |
| 25 | NYR | Mike Murphy | Toronto | RW |
| 27 | BOS | Dan Bouchard | London | G |
| 32 | PHI | Bob Kelly | Oshawa | LW |
| 40 | DET | Yvon Lambert | Drummondville | LW |
| 59 | L.A. | Billy Smith | Cornwall | G |
| 70 | CHI | Gilles Meloche | Verdun | G |
| 88 | OAK | Terry Murray | Ottawa | D |
| 103 | TOR | Ron Low | Dauphin Jr. A | G |

# 1969

### FIRST ROUND

| Pick | Claimed by | | Amateur Club | Position |
|---|---|---|---|---|
| 1 | MTL | Rejean Houle | Montreal | W |
| 2 | MTL | Marc Tardif | Montreal | LW |
| 3 | BOS | Don Tannahill | Niagara Falls | LW |
| 4 | BOS | Frank Spring | Edmonton | RW |
| 5 | MIN | Dick Redmond | St. Catharines | D |
| 6 | PHI | Bob Currier | Cornwall | C |
| 7 | OAK | Tony Featherstone | Peterborough | RW |
| 8 | NYR | Andre Dupont | Montreal | D |
| 9 | TOR | Ernie Moser | Estevan | RW |
| 10 | DET | Jim Rutherford | Hamilton | G |
| 11 | BOS | Ivan Boldirev | Oshawa | C |
| 12 | NYR | Pierre Jarry | Ottawa | LW |

### OTHER NOTABLE SELECTIONS

| Pick | Claimed by | | Amateur Club | Position |
|---|---|---|---|---|
| 13 | CHI | J.P. Bordeleau | Montreal | RW |
| 17 | PHI | Bobby Clarke | Flin Flon | C |
| 18 | OAK | Ron Stackhouse | Peterborough | D |
| 25 | MIN | Gilles Gilbert | London | G |
| 26 | PIT | Michel Briere | Shawinigan | C |
| 51 | L.A. | Butch Goring | Dauphin Jr. A | C |
| 52 | PHI | Dave Schultz | Sorel | LW |
| 55 | TOR | Brian Spencer | Swift Current | LW |
| 64 | PHI | Don Saleski | Regina | RW |

# NHL All-Stars

## Active Players' All-Star Selection Records

| | Total | | First Team Selections | | Second Team Selections |
|---|---|---|---|---|---|
| **GOALTENDER** | | | | | |
| Martin Brodeur | **7** | (3) | 2002-03; 2003-04; 2006-07. | (4) | 1996-97; 1997-98; 2005-06; 2007-08. |
| Roberto Luongo | **2** | (0) | | (2) | 2003-04; 2006-07. |
| Olaf Kolzig | **1** | (1) | 99-2000. | (0) | |
| Miikka Kiprusoff | **1** | (1) | 2005-06. | (0) | |
| Evgeni Nabokov | **1** | (1) | 2007-08. | (0) | |
| Tim Thomas | **1** | (1) | 2008-09. | (0) | |
| Chris Osgood | **1** | (0) | | (1) | 1995-96. |
| Jose Theodore | **1** | (0) | | (1) | 2001-02. |
| Marty Turco | **1** | (0) | | (1) | 2002-03. |
| Steve Mason | **1** | (0) | | (1) | 2008-09. |
| **DEFENSE** | | | | | |
| Nicklas Lidstrom | **10** | (9) | 1997-98; 1998-99; 99-2000; 2000-01; 2001-02; 2002-03; 2005-06; 2006-07; 2007-08. | (1) | 2008-09. |
| Chris Chelios | **7** | (5) | 1988-89; 1992-93; 1994-95; 1995-96; 2001-02. | (2) | 1990-91; 1996-97. |
| Scott Niedermayer | **4** | (3) | 2003-04; 2005-06; 2006-07. | (1) | 2002-03. |
| Zdeno Chara | **4** | (2) | 2003-04; 2008-09. | (2) | 2005-06; 2007-08. |
| Rob Blake | **4** | (1) | 1997-98. | (3) | 99-2000; 2000-01; 2001-02. |
| Chris Pronger | **4** | (1) | 99-2000. | (3) | 1997-98; 2003-04; 2006-07. |
| Sergei Gonchar | **2** | (0) | | (2) | 2001-02; 2002-03. |
| Dan Boyle | **2** | (0) | | (2) | 2006-07; 2008-09. |
| Dion Phaneuf | **1** | (1) | 2007-08. | (0) | |
| Mike Green | **1** | (1) | 2008-09. | (0) | |
| Bryan McCabe | **1** | (0) | | (1) | 2003-04. |
| Sergei Zubov | **1** | (0) | | (1) | 2005-06. |
| Brian Campbell | **1** | (0) | | (1) | 2007-08. |
| **CENTER** | | | | | |
| Joe Thornton | **3** | (1) | 2005-06. | (2) | 2002-03; 2007-08. |
| Evgeni Malkin | **2** | (2) | 2007-08; 2008-09 | (0) | |
| Mats Sundin | **2** | (0) | | (2) | 2001-02; 2003-04. |
| Sidney Crosby | **1** | (1) | 2006-07. | (0) | |
| Mike Modano | **1** | (0) | | (1) | 99-2000. |
| Eric Staal | **1** | (0) | | (1) | 2005-06. |
| Vincent Lecavalier | **1** | (0) | | (1) | 2006-07. |
| Pavel Datsyuk | **1** | (0) | | (1) | 2008-09. |
| **RIGHT WING** | | | | | |
| Jarome Iginla | **4** | (3) | 2001-02; 2007-08; 2008-09. | (1) | 2003-04. |
| Teemu Selanne | **4** | (2) | 1992-93; 1996-97. | (2) | 1997-98; 1998-99. |
| Martin St. Louis | **2** | (1) | 2003-04. | (1) | 2006-07. |
| Todd Bertuzzi | **1** | (1) | 2002-03. | (0) | |
| Dany Heatley | **1** | (1) | 2006-07. | (0) | |
| Mark Recchi | **1** | (0) | | (1) | 1991-92. |
| Bill Guerin | **1** | (0) | | (1) | 2001-02. |
| Milan Hejduk | **1** | (0) | | (1) | 2002-03. |
| Daniel Alfredsson | **1** | (0) | | (1) | 2005-06. |
| Alex Kovalev | **1** | (0) | | (1) | 2007-08. |
| Marian Hossa | **1** | (0) | | (1) | 2008-09. |
| **LEFT WING** | | | | | |
| Paul Kariya | **5** | (3) | 1995-96; 1996-97; 1998-99. | (2) | 99-2000; 2002-03. |
| Alex Ovechkin | **4** | (4) | 2005-06; 2006-07; 2007-08; 2008-09. | (0) | |
| Brendan Shanahan | **3** | (2) | 1993-94; 99-2000. | (1) | 2001-02. |
| Keith Tkachuk | **2** | (0) | | (2) | 1994-95; 1997-98. |
| Patrik Elias | **1** | (1) | 2000-01. | (0) | |
| Ilya Kovalchuk | **1** | (0) | | (1) | 2003-04. |
| Dany Heatley | **1** | (0) | | (1) | 2005-06. |
| Thomas Vanek | **1** | (0) | | (1) | 2006-07. |
| Henrik Zetterberg | **1** | (0) | | (1) | 2007-08. |
| Zach Parise | **1** | (0) | | (1) | 2008-09. |

## Leading NHL All-Stars 1930-31 to 2008-09

| Player | Pos. | Team(s) | Total Selections | First Team Selections | Second Team Selections | NHL Seasons |
|---|---|---|---|---|---|---|
| Gordie Howe | RW | Detroit | **21** | 12 | 9 | 26 |
| Raymond Bourque | D | Bos., Col. | **19** | 13 | 6 | 22 |
| Wayne Gretzky | C | Edm., L.A., NYR | **15** | 8 | 7 | 20 |
| Maurice Richard | RW | Montreal | **14** | 8 | 6 | 18 |
| Bobby Hull | LW | Chicago | **12** | 10 | 2 | 16 |
| Doug Harvey | D | Mtl., NYR | **11** | 10 | 1 | 19 |
| Glenn Hall | G | Det., Chi., St.L. | **11** | 7 | 4 | 18 |
| * Nicklas Lidstrom | D | Detroit | **10** | 9 | 1 | 17 |
| Jean Beliveau | C | Montreal | **10** | 6 | 4 | 20 |
| Earl Seibert | D | NYR, Chi. | **10** | 4 | 6 | 15 |
| Bobby Orr | D | Boston | **9** | 8 | 1 | 12 |
| Ted Lindsay | LW | Detroit | **9** | 8 | 1 | 17 |
| Mario Lemieux | C | Pittsburgh | **9** | 5 | 4 | 17 |
| Frank Mahovlich | LW | Tor., Det., Mtl. | **9** | 3 | 6 | 18 |
| Eddie Shore | D | Boston | **8** | 7 | 1 | 14 |
| Jaromir Jagr | RW | Pit., NYR | **8** | 7 | 1 | 17 |
| Phil Esposito | C | Boston | **8** | 6 | 2 | 18 |
| Red Kelly | D | Detroit | **8** | 6 | 2 | 20 |
| Stan Mikita | C | Chicago | **8** | 6 | 2 | 22 |
| Mike Bossy | RW | NY Islanders | **8** | 5 | 3 | 10 |
| Pierre Pilote | D | Chicago | **8** | 5 | 3 | 14 |
| Luc Robitaille | LW | Los Angeles | **8** | 5 | 3 | 19 |
| Paul Coffey | D | Edm., Pit., Det. | **8** | 4 | 4 | 21 |
| Frank Brimsek | G | Boston | **8** | 2 | 6 | 10 |
| Denis Potvin | D | NY Islanders | **7** | 5 | 2 | 15 |
| Brad Park | D | NYR, Bos. | **7** | 5 | 2 | 17 |
| * Chris Chelios | D | Mtl., Chi., Det. | **7** | 5 | 2 | 25 |
| Al MacInnis | D | Cgy., St.L. | **7** | 4 | 3 | 23 |
| Jacques Plante | G | Mtl., Tor. | **7** | 3 | 4 | 18 |
| Bill Gadsby | D | Chi., NYR, Det. | **7** | 3 | 4 | 20 |
| Terry Sawchuk | G | Detroit | **7** | 3 | 4 | 21 |
| * Martin Brodeur | G | New Jersey | **7** | 3 | 4 | 16 |
| Bill Durnan | G | Montreal | **6** | 6 | 0 | 7 |
| Dominik Hasek | G | Buffalo | **6** | 6 | 0 | 15 |
| Guy Lafleur | RW | Montreal | **6** | 6 | 0 | 17 |
| Ken Dryden | G | Montreal | **6** | 5 | 1 | 8 |
| Patrick Roy | G | Mtl., Col. | **6** | 4 | 2 | 19 |
| Dit Clapper | RW/D | Boston | **6** | 3 | 3 | 20 |
| Larry Robinson | D | Montreal | **6** | 3 | 3 | 20 |
| Tim Horton | D | Toronto | **6** | 3 | 3 | 24 |
| Borje Salming | D | Toronto | **6** | 1 | 5 | 17 |
| Bill Cowley | C | Boston | **5** | 4 | 1 | 13 |
| Busher Jackson | LW | Toronto | **5** | 4 | 1 | 15 |
| Mark Messier | LW/C | Edm., NYR | **5** | 4 | 1 | 25 |
| * Paul Kariya | LW | Anaheim | **5** | 3 | 2 | 14 |
| Charlie Conacher | RW | Toronto | **5** | 3 | 2 | 12 |
| Jack Stewart | D | Detroit | **5** | 3 | 2 | 12 |
| Toe Blake | LW | Montreal | **5** | 3 | 2 | 14 |
| Elmer Lach | C | Montreal | **5** | 3 | 2 | 14 |
| Bill Quackenbush | D | Det., Bos. | **5** | 3 | 2 | 14 |
| Michel Goulet | LW | Quebec | **5** | 3 | 2 | 15 |
| Tony Esposito | G | Chicago | **5** | 3 | 2 | 16 |
| Ken Reardon | D | Montreal | **5** | 2 | 3 | 7 |
| Syl Apps | C | Toronto | **5** | 2 | 3 | 10 |
| John LeClair | LW | Mtl., Phi. | **5** | 2 | 3 | 16 |
| Ed Giacomin | G | NY Rangers | **5** | 2 | 3 | 13 |
| Brian Leetch | D | NY Rangers | **5** | 2 | 3 | 17 |
| Jari Kurri | RW | Edmonton | **5** | 2 | 3 | 17 |
| Scott Stevens | D | Wsh., N.J. | **5** | 2 | 3 | 21 |

* Active

## Position Leaders in All-Star Selections

| Position | Player | Total | First Team | Second Team | NHL Seasons | Career |
|---|---|---|---|---|---|---|
| **GOALTENDER** | Glenn Hall | **11** | 7 | 4 | 18 | 1952-53 to 1970-71 |
| | Frank Brimsek | **8** | 2 | 6 | 10 | 1938-39 to 1949-50 |
| | * Martin Brodeur | **7** | 3 | 4 | 16 | 1991-92 to 2008-09 |
| | Jacques Plante | **7** | 3 | 4 | 18 | 1952-53 to 1972-73 |
| | Terry Sawchuk | **7** | 3 | 4 | 21 | 1949-50 to 1969-70 |
| | Bill Durnan | **6** | 6 | 0 | 7 | 1943-44 to 1949-50 |
| | Dominik Hasek | **6** | 6 | 0 | 15 | 1990-91 to 2007-08 |
| | Ken Dryden | **6** | 5 | 1 | 8 | 1970-71 to 1978-79 |
| | Patrick Roy | **6** | 4 | 2 | 19 | 1984-85 to 2002-03 |
| **DEFENSE** | Raymond Bourque | **19** | 13 | 6 | 22 | 1979-80 to 2000-01 |
| | Doug Harvey | **11** | 10 | 1 | 20 | 1947-48 to 1968-69 |
| | * Nicklas Lidstrom | **10** | 9 | 1 | 17 | 1991-92 to 2008-09 |
| | Earl Seibert | **10** | 4 | 6 | 15 | 1931-32 to 1945-46 |
| | Bobby Orr | **9** | 8 | 1 | 12 | 1966-67 to 1978-79 |
| | Eddie Shore | **8** | 7 | 1 | 14 | 1926-27 to 1939-40 |
| | Red Kelly | **8** | 6 | 2 | 20 | 1947-48 to 1966-67 |
| | Pierre Pilote | **8** | 5 | 3 | 14 | 1955-56 to 1968-69 |
| | Paul Coffey | **8** | 4 | 4 | 21 | 1980-81 to 2000-01 |

| Position | Player | Total | First Team | Second Team | NHL Seasons | Career |
|---|---|---|---|---|---|---|
| **CENTER** | Wayne Gretzky | **15** | 8 | 7 | 20 | 1979-80 to 1998-99 |
| | Jean Beliveau | **10** | 6 | 4 | 20 | 1950-51 to 1970-71 |
| | Mario Lemieux | **9** | 5 | 4 | 18 | 1984-85 to 2005-06 |
| | Phil Esposito | **8** | 6 | 2 | 18 | 1963-64 to 1980-81 |
| | Stan Mikita | **8** | 6 | 2 | 22 | 1958-59 to 1979-80 |
| **RIGHT WING** | Gordie Howe | **21** | 12 | 9 | 26 | 1946-47 to 1979-80 |
| | Maurice Richard | **14** | 8 | 6 | 18 | 1942-43 to 1959-60 |
| | Jaromir Jagr | **8** | 7 | 1 | 17 | 1990-91 to 2007-08 |
| | Mike Bossy | **8** | 5 | 3 | 10 | 1977-78 to 1986-87 |
| | Guy Lafleur | **6** | 6 | 0 | 17 | 1971-72 to 1990-91 |
| **LEFT WING** | Bobby Hull | **12** | 10 | 2 | 16 | 1957-58 to 1979-80 |
| | Ted Lindsay | **9** | 8 | 1 | 17 | 1944-45 to 1964-65 |
| | Frank Mahovlich | **9** | 3 | 6 | 18 | 1956-57 to 1973-74 |
| | Luc Robitaille | **8** | 5 | 3 | 19 | 1986-87 to 2005-06 |

* active player

# All-Star Teams

## 1930-2009

Voting for the NHL All-Star Team is conducted among the representatives of the Professional Hockey Writers' Association at the end of the season.

Following is a list of the First and Second All-Star Teams since their inception in 1930-31.

### 2008-09

| First Team | | Second Team |
|---|---|---|
| Tim Thomas, Bos. | G | Steve Mason, CBJ |
| Zdeno Chara, Bos | D | Nicklas Lidstrom, Det. |
| Mike Green, Wsh. | D | Dan Boyle, S.J. |
| Evgeni Malkin, Pit. | C | Pavel Datsyuk, Det. |
| Jarome Iginla, Cgy. | RW | Marian Hossa, Det. |
| Alex Ovechkin, Wsh. | LW | Zach Parise, N.J. |

### 2007-08

| First Team | | Second Team |
|---|---|---|
| Evgeni Nabokov, S.J. | G | Martin Brodeur, N.J. |
| Nicklas Lidstrom, Det. | D | Brian Campbell, Buf., S.J. |
| Dion Phaneuf, Cgy. | D | Zdeno Chara, Bos. |
| Evgeni Malkin, Pit. | C | Joe Thornton, S.J. |
| Jarome Iginla, Cgy. | RW | Alex Kovalev, Mtl. |
| Alex Ovechkin, Wsh. | LW | Henrik Zetterberg, Det. |

### 2006-07

| First Team | | Second Team |
|---|---|---|
| Martin Brodeur, N.J. | G | Roberto Luongo, Van. |
| Nicklas Lidstrom, Det. | D | Chris Pronger, Ana. |
| Scott Niedermayer, Ana. | D | Dan Boyle, T.B. |
| Sidney Crosby, Pit. | C | Vincent Lecavalier, T.B. |
| Dany Heatley, Ott. | RW | Martin St. Louis, T.B. |
| Alex Ovechkin, Wsh. | LW | Thomas Vanek, Buf. |

### 2005-06

| First Team | | Second Team |
|---|---|---|
| Miikka Kiprusoff, Cgy. | G | Martin Brodeur, N.J. |
| Nicklas Lidstrom, Det. | D | Zdeno Chara, Ott. |
| Scott Niedermayer, Ana. | D | Sergei Zubov, Dal. |
| Joe Thornton, Bos., S.J. | C | Eric Staal, Car. |
| Jaromir Jagr, NYR | RW | Daniel Alfredsson, Ott. |
| Alex Ovechkin, Wsh. | LW | Dany Heatley, Ott. |

### 2004-05

*Season Cancelled*

### 2003-04

| First Team | | Second Team |
|---|---|---|
| Martin Brodeur, N.J. | G | Roberto Luongo, Fla. |
| Scott Niedermayer, N.J. | D | Chris Pronger, St.L. |
| Zdeno Chara, Ott. | D | Bryan McCabe, Tor. |
| Joe Sakic, Col. | C | Mats Sundin, Tor. |
| Martin St. Louis, T.B. | RW | Jarome Iginla, Cgy. |
| Markus Naslund, Van. | LW | Ilya Kovalchuk, Atl. |

### 2002-03

| First Team | | Second Team |
|---|---|---|
| Martin Brodeur, N.J. | G | Marty Turco, Dal. |
| Al MacInnis, St.L. | D | Sergei Gonchar, Wsh. |
| Nicklas Lidstrom, Det. | D | Derian Hatcher, Dal. |
| Peter Forsberg, Col. | C | Joe Thornton, Bos. |
| Todd Bertuzzi, Van. | RW | Milan Hejduk, Col. |
| Markus Naslund, Van. | LW | Paul Kariya, Ana. |

### 2001-02

| First Team | | Second Team |
|---|---|---|
| Patrick Roy, Col. | G | Jose Theodore, Mtl. |
| Nicklas Lidstrom, Det. | D | Rob Blake, Col. |
| Chris Chelios, Det. | D | Sergei Gonchar, Wsh. |
| Joe Sakic, Col. | C | Mats Sundin, Tor. |
| Jarome Iginla, Cgy. | RW | Bill Guerin, Bos. |
| Markus Naslund, Van. | LW | Brendan Shanahan, Det. |

### 2000-01

| First Team | | Second Team |
|---|---|---|
| Dominik Hasek, Buf. | G | Roman Cechmanek, Phi. |
| Nicklas Lidstrom, Det. | D | Rob Blake, L.A., Col. |
| Raymond Bourque, Col. | D | Scott Stevens, N.J. |
| Joe Sakic, Col. | C | Mario Lemieux, Pit. |
| Jaromir Jagr, Pit. | RW | Pavel Bure, Fla. |
| Patrik Elias, N.J. | LW | Luc Robitaille, L.A. |

### 1999-2000

| First Team | | Second Team |
|---|---|---|
| Olaf Kolzig, Wsh. | G | Roman Turek, St.L. |
| Chris Pronger, St.L. | D | Rob Blake, L.A. |
| Nicklas Lidstrom, Det. | D | Eric Desjardins, Phi. |
| Steve Yzerman, Det. | C | Mike Modano, Dal. |
| Jaromir Jagr, Pit. | RW | Pavel Bure, Fla. |
| Brendan Shanahan, Det. | LW | Paul Kariya, Ana. |

### 1998-99

| First Team | | Second Team |
|---|---|---|
| Dominik Hasek, Buf. | G | Byron Dafoe, Bos. |
| Al MacInnis, St.L. | D | Raymond Bourque, Bos. |
| Nicklas Lidstrom, Det. | D | Eric Desjardins, Phi. |
| Peter Forsberg, Col. | C | Alexei Yashin, Ott. |
| Jaromir Jagr, Pit. | RW | Teemu Selanne, Ana. |
| Paul Kariya, Ana. | LW | John LeClair, Phi. |

### 1997-98

| First Team | | Second Team |
|---|---|---|
| Dominik Hasek, Buf. | G | Martin Brodeur, N.J. |
| Nicklas Lidstrom, Det. | D | Chris Pronger, St.L. |
| Rob Blake, L.A. | D | Scott Niedermayer, N.J. |
| Peter Forsberg, Col. | C | Wayne Gretzky, NYR |
| Jaromir Jagr, Pit. | RW | Teemu Selanne, Ana. |
| John LeClair, Phi. | LW | Keith Tkachuk, Phx. |

### 1996-97

| First Team | | Second Team |
|---|---|---|
| Dominik Hasek, Buf. | G | Martin Brodeur, N.J. |
| Brian Leetch, NYR | D | Chris Chelios, Chi. |
| Sandis Ozolinsh, Col. | D | Scott Stevens, N.J. |
| Mario Lemieux, Pit. | C | Wayne Gretzky, NYR |
| Teemu Selanne, Ana. | RW | Jaromir Jagr, Pit. |
| Paul Kariya, Ana. | LW | John LeClair, Phi. |

### 1995-96

| First Team | | Second Team |
|---|---|---|
| Jim Carey, Wsh. | G | Chris Osgood, Det. |
| Chris Chelios, Chi. | D | V. Konstantinov, Det. |
| Raymond Bourque, Bos. | D | Brian Leetch, NYR |
| Mario Lemieux, Pit. | C | Eric Lindros, Phi. |
| Jaromir Jagr, Pit. | RW | Alexander Mogilny, Van. |
| Paul Kariya, Ana. | LW | John LeClair, Phi. |

### 1994-95

| First Team | | Second Team |
|---|---|---|
| Dominik Hasek, Buf. | G | Ed Belfour, Chi. |
| Paul Coffey, Det. | D | Raymond Bourque, Bos. |
| Chris Chelios, Chi. | D | Larry Murphy, Pit. |
| Eric Lindros, Phi. | C | Alexei Zhamnov, Wpg. |
| Jaromir Jagr, Pit. | RW | Theoren Fleury, Cgy. |
| John LeClair, Mtl., Phi. | LW | Keith Tkachuk, Wpg. |

### 1993-94

| First Team | | Second Team |
|---|---|---|
| Dominik Hasek, Buf. | G | John Vanbiesbrouck, Fla. |
| Raymond Bourque, Bos. | D | Al MacInnis, Cgy. |
| Scott Stevens, N.J. | D | Brian Leetch, NYR |
| Sergei Fedorov, Det. | C | Wayne Gretzky, L.A. |
| Pavel Bure, Van. | RW | Cam Neely, Bos. |
| Brendan Shanahan, St.L. | LW | Adam Graves, NYR |

### 1992-93

| First Team | | Second Team |
|---|---|---|
| Ed Belfour, Chi. | G | Tom Barrasso, Pit. |
| Chris Chelios, Chi. | D | Larry Murphy, Pit. |
| Raymond Bourque, Bos. | D | Al Iafrate, Wsh. |
| Mario Lemieux, Pit. | C | Pat LaFontaine, Buf. |
| Teemu Selanne, Wpg. | RW | Alexander Mogilny, Buf. |
| Luc Robitaille, L.A. | LW | Kevin Stevens, Pit. |

### 1991-92

| First Team | | Second Team |
|---|---|---|
| Patrick Roy, Mtl. | G | Kirk McLean, Van. |
| Brian Leetch, NYR | D | Phil Housley, Wpg. |
| Raymond Bourque, Bos. | D | Scott Stevens, N.J. |
| Mark Messier, NYR | C | Mario Lemieux, Pit. |
| Brett Hull, St.L. | RW | Mark Recchi, Pit., Phi. |
| Kevin Stevens, Pit. | LW | Luc Robitaille, L.A. |

### 1990-91

| First Team | | Second Team |
|---|---|---|
| Ed Belfour, Chi. | G | Patrick Roy, Mtl. |
| Raymond Bourque, Bos. | D | Chris Chelios, Chi. |
| Al MacInnis, Cgy. | D | Brian Leetch, NYR |
| Wayne Gretzky, L.A. | C | Adam Oates, St.L. |
| Brett Hull, St.L. | RW | Cam Neely, Bos. |
| Luc Robitaille, L.A. | LW | Kevin Stevens, Pit. |

### 1989-90

| First Team | | Second Team |
|---|---|---|
| Patrick Roy, Mtl. | G | Daren Puppa, Buf. |
| Raymond Bourque, Bos. | D | Paul Coffey, Pit. |
| Al MacInnis, Cgy. | D | Doug Wilson, Chi. |
| Mark Messier, Edm. | C | Wayne Gretzky, L.A. |
| Brett Hull, St.L. | RW | Cam Neely, Bos. |
| Luc Robitaille, L.A. | LW | Brian Bellows, Min. |

### 1988-89

| First Team | | Second Team |
|---|---|---|
| Patrick Roy, Mtl. | G | Mike Vernon, Cgy. |
| Chris Chelios, Mtl. | D | Al MacInnis, Cgy. |
| Paul Coffey, Pit. | D | Raymond Bourque, Bos. |
| Mario Lemieux, Pit. | C | Wayne Gretzky, L.A. |
| Joe Mullen, Cgy. | RW | Jari Kurri, Edm. |
| Luc Robitaille, L.A. | LW | Gerard Gallant, Det. |

### 1987-88

| First Team | | Second Team |
|---|---|---|
| Grant Fuhr, Edm. | G | Patrick Roy, Mtl. |
| Raymond Bourque, Bos. | D | Gary Suter, Cgy. |
| Scott Stevens, Wsh. | D | Brad McCrimmon, Cgy. |
| Mario Lemieux, Pit. | C | Wayne Gretzky, Edm. |
| Hakan Loob, Cgy. | RW | Cam Neely, Bos. |
| Luc Robitaille, L.A. | LW | Michel Goulet, Que. |

### 1986-87

| First Team | | Second Team |
|---|---|---|
| Ron Hextall, Phi. | G | Mike Liut, Hfd. |
| Raymond Bourque, Bos. | D | Larry Murphy, Wsh. |
| Mark Howe, Phi. | D | Al MacInnis, Cgy. |
| Wayne Gretzky, Edm. | C | Mario Lemieux, Pit. |
| Jari Kurri, Edm. | RW | Tim Kerr, Phi. |
| Michel Goulet, Que. | LW | Luc Robitaille, L.A. |

### 1985-86

| First Team | | Second Team |
|---|---|---|
| John Vanbiesbrouck, NYR | G | Bob Froese, Phi. |
| Paul Coffey, Edm. | D | Larry Robinson, Mtl. |
| Mark Howe, Phi. | D | Raymond Bourque, Bos. |
| Wayne Gretzky, Edm. | C | Mario Lemieux, Pit. |
| Mike Bossy, NYI | RW | Jari Kurri, Edm. |
| Michel Goulet, Que. | LW | Mats Naslund, Mtl. |

### 1984-85

| First Team | | Second Team |
|---|---|---|
| Pelle Lindbergh, Phi. | G | Tom Barrasso, Buf. |
| Paul Coffey, Edm. | D | Rod Langway, Wsh. |
| Raymond Bourque, Bos. | D | Doug Wilson, Chi. |
| Wayne Gretzky, Edm. | C | Dale Hawerchuk, Wpg. |
| Jari Kurri, Edm. | RW | Mike Bossy, NYI |
| John Ogrodnick, Det. | LW | John Tonelli, NYI |

### 1983-84

| First Team | | Second Team |
|---|---|---|
| Tom Barrasso, Buf. | G | Pat Riggin, Wsh. |
| Rod Langway, Wsh. | D | Paul Coffey, Edm. |
| Raymond Bourque, Bos. | D | Denis Potvin, NYI |
| Wayne Gretzky, Edm. | C | Bryan Trottier, NYI |
| Mike Bossy, NYI | RW | Jari Kurri, Edm. |
| Michel Goulet, Que. | LW | Mark Messier, Edm. |

### 1982-83

| First Team | | Second Team |
|---|---|---|
| Pete Peeters, Bos. | G | Roland Melanson, NYI |
| Mark Howe, Phi. | D | Raymond Bourque, Bos. |
| Rod Langway, Wsh. | D | Paul Coffey, Edm. |
| Wayne Gretzky, Edm. | C | Denis Savard, Chi. |
| Mike Bossy, NYI | RW | Lanny McDonald, Cgy. |
| Mark Messier, Edm. | LW | Michel Goulet, Que. |

### 1981-82

| First Team | | Second Team |
|---|---|---|
| Billy Smith, NYI | G | Grant Fuhr, Edm. |
| Doug Wilson, Chi. | D | Paul Coffey, Edm. |
| Raymond Bourque, Bos. | D | Brian Engblom, Mtl. |
| Wayne Gretzky, Edm. | C | Bryan Trottier, NYI |
| Mike Bossy, NYI | RW | Rick Middleton, Bos. |
| Mark Messier, Edm. | LW | John Tonelli, NYI |

### 1980-81

| First Team | | Second Team |
|---|---|---|
| Mike Liut, St.L. | G | Mario Lessard, L.A. |
| Denis Potvin, NYI | D | Larry Robinson, Mtl. |
| Randy Carlyle, Pit. | D | Raymond Bourque, Bos. |
| Wayne Gretzky, Edm. | C | Marcel Dionne, L.A. |
| Mike Bossy, NYI | RW | Dave Taylor, L.A. |
| Charlie Simmer, L.A. | LW | Bill Barber, Phi. |

### 1979-80

| First Team | | Second Team |
|---|---|---|
| Tony Esposito, Chi. | G | Don Edwards, Buf. |
| Larry Robinson, Mtl. | D | Borje Salming, Tor. |
| Raymond Bourque, Bos. | D | Jim Schoenfeld, Buf. |
| Marcel Dionne, L.A. | C | Wayne Gretzky, Edm. |
| Guy Lafleur, Mtl. | RW | Danny Gare, Buf. |
| Charlie Simmer, L.A. | LW | Steve Shutt, Mtl. |

### 1978-79

| First Team | | Second Team |
|---|---|---|
| Ken Dryden, Mtl. | G | Glenn Resch, NYI |
| Denis Potvin, NYI | D | Borje Salming, Tor. |
| Larry Robinson, Mtl. | D | Serge Savard, Mtl. |
| Bryan Trottier, NYI | C | Marcel Dionne, L.A. |
| Guy Lafleur, Mtl. | RW | Mike Bossy, NYI |
| Clark Gillies, NYI | LW | Bill Barber, Phi. |

### 1977-78

| First Team | | Second Team |
|---|---|---|
| Ken Dryden, Mtl. | G | Don Edwards, Buf. |
| Denis Potvin, NYI | D | Larry Robinson, Mtl. |
| Brad Park, Bos. | D | Borje Salming, Tor. |
| Bryan Trottier, NYI | C | Darryl Sittler, Tor. |
| Guy Lafleur, Mtl. | RW | Mike Bossy, NYI |
| Clark Gillies, NYI | LW | Steve Shutt, Mtl. |

### 1976-77

| First Team | | Second Team |
|---|---|---|
| Ken Dryden, Mtl. | G | Rogie Vachon, L.A. |
| Larry Robinson, Mtl. | D | Denis Potvin, NYI |
| Borje Salming, Tor. | D | Guy Lapointe, Mtl. |
| Marcel Dionne, L.A. | C | Gilbert Perreault, Buf. |
| Guy Lafleur, Mtl. | RW | Lanny McDonald, Tor. |
| Steve Shutt, Mtl. | LW | Rick Martin, Buf. |

### 1975-76

| First Team | | Second Team |
|---|---|---|
| Ken Dryden, Mtl. | G | Glenn Resch, NYI |
| Denis Potvin, NYI | D | Borje Salming, Tor. |
| Brad Park, Bos. | D | Guy Lapointe, Mtl. |
| Bobby Clarke, Phi. | C | Gilbert Perreault, Buf. |
| Guy Lafleur, Mtl. | RW | Reggie Leach, Phi. |
| Bill Barber, Phi. | LW | Rick Martin, Buf. |

### 1974-75

| First Team | | Second Team |
|---|---|---|
| Bernie Parent, Phi. | G | Rogie Vachon, L.A. |
| Bobby Orr, Bos. | D | Guy Lapointe, Mtl. |
| Denis Potvin, NYI | D | Borje Salming, Tor. |
| Bobby Clarke, Phi. | C | Phil Esposito, Bos. |
| Guy Lafleur, Mtl. | RW | René Robert, Buf. |
| Rick Martin, Buf. | LW | Steve Vickers, NYR |

### 1973-74

| First Team | | Second Team |
|---|---|---|
| Bernie Parent, Phi. | G | Tony Esposito, Chi. |
| Bobby Orr, Bos. | D | Bill White, Chi. |
| Brad Park, NYR | D | Barry Ashbee, Phi. |
| Phil Esposito, Bos. | C | Bobby Clarke, Phi. |
| Ken Hodge, Bos. | RW | Mickey Redmond, Det. |
| Rick Martin, Buf. | LW | Wayne Cashman, Bos. |

### 1972-73

| First Team | | Second Team |
|---|---|---|
| Ken Dryden, Mtl. | G | Tony Esposito, Chi. |
| Bobby Orr, Bos. | D | Brad Park, NYR |
| Guy Lapointe, Mtl. | D | Bill White, Chi. |
| Phil Esposito, Bos. | C | Bobby Clarke, Phi. |
| Mickey Redmond, Det. | RW | Yvan Cournoyer, Mtl. |
| Frank Mahovlich, Mtl. | LW | Dennis Hull, Chi. |

### 1971-72

| First Team | | Second Team |
|---|---|---|
| Tony Esposito, Chi. | G | Ken Dryden, Mtl. |
| Bobby Orr, Bos. | D | Bill White, Chi. |
| Brad Park, NYR | D | Pat Stapleton, Chi. |
| Phil Esposito, Bos. | C | Jean Ratelle, NYR |
| Rod Gilbert, NYR | RW | Yvan Cournoyer, Mtl. |
| Bobby Hull, Chi. | LW | Vic Hadfield, NYR |

### 1970-71

| First Team | | Second Team |
|---|---|---|
| Ed Giacomin, NYR | G | Jacques Plante, Tor. |
| Bobby Orr, Bos. | D | Brad Park, NYR |
| J.C. Tremblay, Mtl. | D | Pat Stapleton, Chi. |
| Phil Esposito, Bos. | C | Dave Keon, Tor. |
| Ken Hodge, Bos. | RW | Yvan Cournoyer, Mtl. |
| John Bucyk, Bos. | LW | Bobby Hull, Chi. |

### 1969-70

| First Team | | Second Team |
|---|---|---|
| Tony Esposito, Chi. | G | Ed Giacomin, NYR |
| Bobby Orr, Bos. | D | Carl Brewer, Det. |
| Brad Park, NYR | D | Jacques Laperriere, Mtl. |
| Phil Esposito, Bos. | C | Stan Mikita, Chi. |
| Gordie Howe, Det. | RW | John McKenzie, Bos. |
| Bobby Hull, Chi. | LW | Frank Mahovlich, Det. |

### 1968-69

| First Team | | Second Team |
|---|---|---|
| Glenn Hall, St.L. | G | Ed Giacomin, NYR |
| Bobby Orr, Bos. | D | Ted Green, Bos. |
| Tim Horton, Tor. | D | Ted Harris, Mtl. |
| Phil Esposito, Bos. | C | Jean Béliveau, Mtl. |
| Gordie Howe, Det. | RW | Yvan Cournoyer, Mtl. |
| Bobby Hull, Chi. | LW | Frank Mahovlich, Det. |

### 1967-68

| First Team | | Second Team |
|---|---|---|
| Gump Worsley, Mtl. | G | Ed Giacomin, NYR |
| Bobby Orr, Bos. | D | J.C. Tremblay, Mtl. |
| Tim Horton, Tor. | D | Jim Neilson, NYR |
| Stan Mikita, Chi. | C | Phil Esposito, Bos. |
| Gordie Howe, Det. | RW | Rod Gilbert, NYR |
| Bobby Hull, Chi. | LW | John Bucyk, Bos. |

### 1966-67

| First Team | | Second Team |
|---|---|---|
| Ed Giacomin, NYR | G | Glenn Hall, Chi. |
| Pierre Pilote, Chi. | D | Tim Horton, Tor. |
| Harry Howell, NYR | D | Bobby Orr, Bos. |
| Stan Mikita, Chi. | C | Norm Ullman, Det. |
| Kenny Wharram, Chi. | RW | Gordie Howe, Det. |
| Bobby Hull, Chi. | LW | Don Marshall, NYR |

### 1965-66

| First Team | | Second Team |
|---|---|---|
| Glenn Hall, Chi. | G | Gump Worsley, Mtl. |
| Jacques Laperriere, Mtl. | D | Allan Stanley, Tor. |
| Pierre Pilote, Chi. | D | Pat Stapleton, Chi. |
| Stan Mikita, Chi. | C | Jean Béliveau, Mtl. |
| Gordie Howe, Det. | RW | Bobby Rousseau, Mtl. |
| Bobby Hull, Chi. | LW | Frank Mahovlich, Tor. |

### 1964-65

| First Team | | Second Team |
|---|---|---|
| Roger Crozier, Det. | G | Charlie Hodge, Mtl. |
| Pierre Pilote, Chi. | D | Bill Gadsby, Det. |
| Jacques Laperriere, Mtl. | D | Carl Brewer, Tor. |
| Norm Ullman, Det. | C | Stan Mikita, Chi. |
| Claude Provost, Mtl. | RW | Gordie Howe, Det. |
| Bobby Hull, Chi. | LW | Frank Mahovlich, Tor. |

### 1963-64

| First Team | | Second Team |
|---|---|---|
| Glenn Hall, Chi. | G | Charlie Hodge, Mtl. |
| Pierre Pilote, Chi. | D | Moose Vasko, Chi. |
| Tim Horton, Tor. | D | Jacques Laperriere, Mtl. |
| Stan Mikita, Chi. | C | Jean Béliveau, Mtl. |
| Kenny Wharram, Chi. | RW | Gordie Howe, Det. |
| Bobby Hull, Chi. | LW | Frank Mahovlich, Tor. |

### 1962-63

| First Team | | Second Team |
|---|---|---|
| Glenn Hall, Chi. | G | Terry Sawchuk, Det. |
| Pierre Pilote, Chi. | D | Tim Horton, Tor. |
| Carl Brewer, Tor. | D | Moose Vasko, Chi. |
| Stan Mikita, Chi. | C | Henri Richard, Mtl. |
| Gordie Howe, Det. | RW | Andy Bathgate, NYR |
| Frank Mahovlich, Tor. | LW | Bobby Hull, Chi. |

### 1961-62

| First Team | | Second Team |
|---|---|---|
| Jacques Plante, Mtl. | G | Glenn Hall, Chi. |
| Doug Harvey, NYR | D | Carl Brewer, Tor. |
| Jean-Guy Talbot, Mtl. | D | Pierre Pilote, Chi. |
| Stan Mikita, Chi. | C | Dave Keon, Tor. |
| Andy Bathgate, NYR | RW | Gordie Howe, Det. |
| Bobby Hull, Chi. | LW | Frank Mahovlich, Tor. |

### 1960-61

| First Team | | Second Team |
|---|---|---|
| Johnny Bower, Tor. | G | Glenn Hall, Chi. |
| Doug Harvey, Mtl. | D | Allan Stanley, Tor. |
| Marcel Pronovost, Det. | D | Pierre Pilote, Chi. |
| Jean Béliveau, Mtl. | C | Henri Richard, Mtl. |
| Bernie Geoffrion, Mtl. | RW | Gordie Howe, Det. |
| Frank Mahovlich, Tor. | LW | Dickie Moore, Mtl. |

### 1959-60

| First Team | | Second Team |
|---|---|---|
| Glenn Hall, Chi. | G | Jacques Plante, Mtl. |
| Doug Harvey, Mtl. | D | Allan Stanley, Tor. |
| Marcel Pronovost, Det. | D | Pierre Pilote, Chi. |
| Jean Béliveau, Mtl. | C | Bronco Horvath, Bos. |
| Gordie Howe, Det. | RW | Bernie Geoffrion, Mtl. |
| Bobby Hull, Chi. | LW | Dean Prentice, NYR |

### 1958-59

| First Team | | Second Team |
|---|---|---|
| Jacques Plante, Mtl. | G | Terry Sawchuk, Det. |
| Tom Johnson, Mtl. | D | Marcel Pronovost, Det. |
| Bill Gadsby, NYR | D | Doug Harvey, Mtl. |
| Jean Béliveau, Mtl. | C | Henri Richard, Mtl. |
| Andy Bathgate, NYR | RW | Gordie Howe, Det. |
| Dickie Moore, Mtl. | LW | Alex Delvecchio, Det. |

### 1957-58

| First Team | | Second Team |
|---|---|---|
| Glenn Hall, Chi. | G | Jacques Plante, Mtl. |
| Doug Harvey, Mtl. | D | Fern Flaman, Bos. |
| Bill Gadsby, NYR | D | Marcel Pronovost, Det. |
| Henri Richard, Mtl. | C | Jean Béliveau, Mtl. |
| Gordie Howe, Det. | RW | Andy Bathgate, NYR |
| Dickie Moore, Mtl. | LW | Camille Henry, NYR |

### 1956-57

| First Team | | Second Team |
|---|---|---|
| Glenn Hall, Det. | G | Jacques Plante, Mtl. |
| Doug Harvey, Mtl. | D | Fern Flaman, Bos. |
| Red Kelly, Det. | D | Bill Gadsby, NYR |
| Jean Béliveau, Mtl. | C | Ed Litzenberger, Chi. |
| Gordie Howe, Det. | RW | Maurice Richard, Mtl. |
| Ted Lindsay, Det. | LW | Real Chevrefils, Bos. |

### 1955-56

| First Team | | Second Team |
|---|---|---|
| Jacques Plante, Mtl. | G | Glenn Hall, Det. |
| Doug Harvey, Mtl. | D | Red Kelly, Det. |
| Bill Gadsby, NYR | D | Tom Johnson, Mtl. |
| Jean Béliveau, Mtl. | C | Tod Sloan, Tor. |
| Maurice Richard, Mtl. | RW | Gordie Howe, Det. |
| Ted Lindsay, Det. | LW | Bert Olmstead, Mtl. |

### 1954-55

| First Team | | Second Team |
|---|---|---|
| Harry Lumley, Tor. | G | Terry Sawchuk, Det. |
| Doug Harvey, Mtl. | D | Bob Goldham, Det. |
| Red Kelly, Det. | D | Fern Flaman, Bos. |
| Jean Béliveau, Mtl. | C | Ken Mosdell, Mtl. |
| Maurice Richard, Mtl. | RW | Bernie Geoffrion, Mtl. |
| Sid Smith, Tor. | LW | Danny Lewicki, NYR |

### 1953-54

| First Team | | Second Team |
|---|---|---|
| Harry Lumley, Tor. | G | Terry Sawchuk, Det. |
| Red Kelly, Det. | D | Bill Gadsby, Chi. |
| Doug Harvey, Mtl. | D | Tim Horton, Tor. |
| Ken Mosdell, Mtl. | C | Ted Kennedy, Tor. |
| Gordie Howe, Det. | RW | Maurice Richard, Mtl. |
| Ted Lindsay, Det. | LW | Ed Sandford, Bos. |

### 1952-53

| First Team | | Second Team |
|---|---|---|
| Terry Sawchuk, Det. | G | Gerry McNeil, Mtl. |
| Red Kelly, Det. | D | Bill Quackenbush, Bos. |
| Doug Harvey, Mtl. | D | Bill Gadsby, Chi. |
| Fleming MacKell, Bos. | C | Alex Delvecchio, Det. |
| Gordie Howe, Det. | RW | Maurice Richard, Mtl. |
| Ted Lindsay, Det. | LW | Bert Olmstead, Mtl. |

### 1951-52

| First Team | | Second Team |
|---|---|---|
| Terry Sawchuk, Det. | G | Jim Henry, Bos. |
| Red Kelly, Det. | D | Hy Buller, NYR |
| Doug Harvey, Mtl. | D | Jimmy Thomson, Tor. |
| Elmer Lach, Mtl. | C | Milt Schmidt, Bos. |
| Gordie Howe, Det. | RW | Maurice Richard, Mtl. |
| Ted Lindsay, Det. | LW | Sid Smith, Tor. |

### 1950-51

| First Team | | Second Team |
|---|---|---|
| Terry Sawchuk, Det. | G | Chuck Rayner, NYR |
| Red Kelly, Det. | D | Jimmy Thomson, Tor. |
| Bill Quackenbush, Bos. | D | Leo Reise Jr., Det. |
| Milt Schmidt, Bos. | C | Sid Abel, Det.<br>Ted Kennedy, Tor. (tied) |
| Gordie Howe, Det. | RW | Maurice Richard, Mtl. |
| Ted Lindsay, Det. | LW | Sid Smith, Tor. |

### 1949-50

| First Team | | Second Team |
|---|---|---|
| Bill Durnan, Mtl. | G | Chuck Rayner, NYR |
| Gus Mortson, Tor. | D | Leo Reise Jr., Det. |
| Ken Reardon, Mtl. | D | Red Kelly, Det. |
| Sid Abel, Det. | C | Ted Kennedy, Tor. |
| Maurice Richard, Mtl. | RW | Gordie Howe, Det. |
| Ted Lindsay, Det. | LW | Tony Leswick, NYR |

### 1948-49

| First Team | | Second Team |
|---|---|---|
| Bill Durnan, Mtl. | G | Chuck Rayner, NYR |
| Bill Quackenbush, Det. | D | Glen Harmon, Mtl. |
| Jack Stewart, Det. | D | Ken Reardon, Mtl. |
| Sid Abel, Det. | C | Doug Bentley, Chi. |
| Maurice Richard, Mtl. | RW | Gordie Howe, Det. |
| Roy Conacher, Chi. | LW | Ted Lindsay, Det. |

### 1947-48

| First Team | | Second Team |
|---|---|---|
| Turk Broda, Tor. | G | Frank Brimsek, Bos. |
| Bill Quackenbush, Det. | D | Ken Reardon, Mtl. |
| Jack Stewart, Det. | D | Neil Colville, NYR |
| Elmer Lach, Mtl. | C | Buddy O'Connor, NYR |
| Maurice Richard, Mtl. | RW | Bud Poile, Chi. |
| Ted Lindsay, Det. | LW | Gaye Stewart, Chi. |

### 1946-47

| First Team | | Second Team |
|---|---|---|
| Bill Durnan, Mtl. | G | Frank Brimsek, Bos. |
| Ken Reardon, Mtl. | D | Jack Stewart, Det. |
| Butch Bouchard, Mtl. | D | Bill Quackenbush, Det. |
| Milt Schmidt, Bos. | C | Max Bentley, Chi. |
| Maurice Richard, Mtl. | RW | Bobby Bauer, Bos. |
| Doug Bentley, Chi. | LW | Woody Dumart, Bos. |

### 1945-46

| First Team | | Second Team |
|---|---|---|
| Bill Durnan, Mtl. | G | Frank Brimsek, Bos. |
| Jack Crawford, Bos. | D | Ken Reardon, Mtl. |
| Butch Bouchard, Mtl. | D | Jack Stewart, Det. |
| Max Bentley, Chi. | C | Elmer Lach, Mtl. |
| Maurice Richard, Mtl. | RW | Bill Mosienko, Chi. |
| Gaye Stewart, Tor. | LW | Toe Blake, Mtl. |
| Dick Irvin, Mtl. | Coach | Johnny Gottselig, Chi. |

### 1944-45

| First Team | | Second Team |
|---|---|---|
| Bill Durnan, Mtl. | G | Mike Karakas, Chi. |
| Butch Bouchard, Mtl. | D | Glen Harmon, Mtl. |
| Flash Hollett, Det. | D | Babe Pratt, Tor. |
| Elmer Lach, Mtl. | C | Bill Cowley, Bos. |
| Maurice Richard, Mtl. | RW | Bill Mosienko, Chi. |
| Toe Blake, Mtl. | LW | Syd Howe, Det. |
| Dick Irvin, Mtl. | Coach | Jack Adams, Det. |

### 1943-44

| First Team | | Second Team |
|---|---|---|
| Bill Durnan, Mtl. | G | Paul Bibeault, Tor. |
| Earl Seibert, Chi. | D | Butch Bouchard, Mtl. |
| Babe Pratt, Tor. | D | Dit Clapper, Bos. |
| Bill Cowley, Bos. | C | Elmer Lach, Mtl. |
| Lorne Carr, Tor. | RW | Maurice Richard, Mtl. |
| Doug Bentley, Chi. | LW | Herb Cain, Bos. |
| Dick Irvin, Mtl. | Coach | Hap Day, Tor. |

### 1942-43

| First Team | | Second Team |
|---|---|---|
| Johnny Mowers, Det. | G | Frank Brimsek, Bos. |
| Earl Seibert, Chi. | D | Jack Crawford, Bos. |
| Jack Stewart, Det. | D | Flash Hollett, Bos. |
| Bill Cowley, Bos. | C | Syl Apps, Tor. |
| Lorne Carr, Tor. | RW | Bryan Hextall, NYR |
| Doug Bentley, Chi. | LW | Lynn Patrick, NYR |
| Jack Adams, Det. | Coach | Art Ross, Bos. |

### 1941-42

| First Team | | Second Team |
|---|---|---|
| Frank Brimsek, Bos. | G | Turk Broda, Tor. |
| Earl Seibert, Chi. | D | Pat Egan, Bro. |
| Tom Anderson, Bro. | D | Bucko McDonald, Tor. |
| Syl Apps, Tor. | C | Phil Watson, NYR |
| Bryan Hextall, NYR | RW | Gordie Drillon, Tor. |
| Lynn Patrick, NYR | LW | Sid Abel, Det. |
| Frank Boucher, NYR | Coach | Paul Thompson, Chi. |

### 1940-41

| First Team | | Second Team |
|---|---|---|
| Turk Broda, Tor. | G | Frank Brimsek, Bos. |
| Dit Clapper, Bos. | D | Earl Seibert, Chi. |
| Wally Stanowski, Tor. | D | Ott Heller, NYR |
| Bill Cowley, Bos. | C | Syl Apps, Tor. |
| Bryan Hextall, NYR | RW | Bobby Bauer, Bos. |
| Sweeney Schriner, Tor. | LW | Woody Dumart, Bos. |
| Cooney Weiland, Bos. | Coach | Dick Irvin, Mtl. |

### 1939-40

| First Team | | Second Team |
|---|---|---|
| Dave Kerr, NYR | G | Frank Brimsek, Bos. |
| Dit Clapper, Bos. | D | Art Coulter, NYR |
| Ebbie Goodfellow, Det. | D | Earl Seibert, Chi. |
| Milt Schmidt, Bos. | C | Neil Colville, NYR |
| Bryan Hextall, NYR | RW | Bobby Bauer, Bos. |
| Toe Blake, Mtl. | LW | Woody Dumart, Bos. |
| Paul Thompson, Chi. | Coach | Frank Boucher, NYR |

### 1938-39

| First Team | | Second Team |
|---|---|---|
| Frank Brimsek, Bos. | G | Earl Robertson, NYA |
| Eddie Shore, Bos. | D | Earl Seibert, Chi. |
| Dit Clapper, Bos. | D | Art Coulter, NYR |
| Syl Apps, Tor. | C | Neil Colville, NYR |
| Gordie Drillon, Tor. | RW | Bobby Bauer, Bos. |
| Toe Blake, Mtl. | LW | Johnny Gottselig, Chi. |
| Art Ross, Bos. | Coach | Red Dutton, NYA |

### 1937-38

| First Team | | Second Team |
|---|---|---|
| Tiny Thompson, Bos. | G | Dave Kerr, NYR |
| Eddie Shore, Bos. | D | Art Coulter, NYR |
| Babe Siebert, Mtl. | D | Earl Seibert, Chi. |
| Bill Cowley, Bos. | C | Syl Apps, Tor. |
| Cecil Dillon, NYR<br>Gordie Drillon, Tor. *(tied)* | RW | |
| Paul Thompson, Chi. | LW | Toe Blake, Mtl. |
| Lester Patrick, NYR | Coach | Art Ross, Bos. |

### 1936-37

| First Team | | Second Team |
|---|---|---|
| Normie Smith, Det. | G | Wilf Cude, Mtl. |
| Babe Siebert, Mtl. | D | Earl Seibert, Chi. |
| Ebbie Goodfellow, Det. | D | Lionel Conacher, Mtl. M. |
| Marty Barry, Det. | C | Art Chapman, NYA |
| Larry Aurie, Det. | RW | Cecil Dillon, NYR |
| Busher Jackson, Tor. | LW | Sweeney Schriner, NYA |
| Jack Adams, Det. | Coach | Cecil Hart, Mtl. |

### 1935-36

| First Team | | Second Team |
|---|---|---|
| Tiny Thompson, Bos. | G | Wilf Cude, Mtl. |
| Eddie Shore, Bos. | D | Earl Seibert, Chi. |
| Babe Siebert, Bos. | D | Ebbie Goodfellow, Det. |
| Hooley Smith, Mtl. M. | C | Bill Thoms, Tor. |
| Charlie Conacher, Tor. | RW | Cecil Dillon, NYR |
| Sweeney Schriner, NYA | LW | Paul Thompson, Chi. |
| Lester Patrick, NYR | Coach | Tommy Gorman, Mtl. M. |

### 1934-35

| First Team | | Second Team |
|---|---|---|
| Lorne Chabot, Chi. | G | Tiny Thompson, Bos. |
| Eddie Shore, Bos. | D | Cy Wentworth, Mtl. M. |
| Earl Seibert, NYR | D | Art Coulter, Chi. |
| Frank Boucher, NYR | C | Cooney Weiland, Det. |
| Charlie Conacher, Tor. | RW | Dit Clapper, Bos. |
| Busher Jackson, Tor. | LW | Aurel Joliat, Mtl. |
| Lester Patrick, NYR | Coach | Dick Irvin, Tor. |

### 1933-34

| First Team | | Second Team |
|---|---|---|
| Charlie Gardiner, Chi. | G | Roy Worters, NYA |
| King Clancy, Tor. | D | Eddie Shore, Bos. |
| Lionel Conacher, Chi. | D | Ching Johnson, NYR |
| Frank Boucher, NYR | C | Joe Primeau, Tor. |
| Charlie Conacher, Tor. | RW | Bill Cook, NYR |
| Busher Jackson, Tor. | LW | Aurel Joliat, Mtl. |
| Lester Patrick, NYR | Coach | Dick Irvin, Tor. |

### 1932-33

| First Team | | Second Team |
|---|---|---|
| John Ross Roach, Det. | G | Charlie Gardiner, Chi. |
| Eddie Shore, Bos. | D | King Clancy, Tor. |
| Ching Johnson, NYR | D | Lionel Conacher, Mtl. M. |
| Frank Boucher, NYR | C | Howie Morenz, Mtl. |
| Bill Cook, NYR | RW | Charlie Conacher, Tor. |
| Baldy Northcott, Mtl. M. | LW | Busher Jackson, Tor. |
| Lester Patrick, NYR | Coach | Dick Irvin, Tor. |

### 1931-32

| First Team | | Second Team |
|---|---|---|
| Charlie Gardiner, Chi. | G | Roy Worters, NYA |
| Eddie Shore, Bos. | D | Sylvio Mantha, Mtl. |
| Ching Johnson, NYR | D | King Clancy, Tor. |
| Howie Morenz, Mtl. | C | Hooley Smith, Mtl. M. |
| Bill Cook, NYR | RW | Charlie Conacher, Tor. |
| Busher Jackson, Tor. | LW | Aurel Joliat, Mtl. |
| Lester Patrick, NYR | Coach | Dick Irvin, Tor. |

### 1930-31

| First Team | | Second Team |
|---|---|---|
| Charlie Gardiner, Chi. | G | Tiny Thompson, Bos. |
| Eddie Shore, Bos. | D | Sylvio Mantha, Mtl. |
| King Clancy, Tor. | D | Ching Johnson, NYR |
| Howie Morenz, Mtl. | C | Frank Boucher, NYR |
| Bill Cook, NYR | RW | Dit Clapper, Bos. |
| Aurel Joliat, Mtl. | LW | Bun Cook, NYR |
| Lester Patrick, NYR | Coach | Dick Irvin, Chi. |

## NHL ALL-ROOKIE TEAM

Voting for the NHL All-Rookie Team is conducted among the representatives of the Professional Hockey Writers' Association at the end of the season. The rookie all-star team was first selected for the 1982-83 season.

| | **2008-09** |
|---|---|
| *Goal* | Steve Mason, Columbus |
| *Defense* | Drew Doughty, Los Angeles |
| *Defense* | Luke Schenn, Toronto |
| *Forward* | Patrik Berglund, St. Louis |
| *Forward* | Bobby Ryan, Anaheim |
| *Forward* | Kris Versteeg, Chicago |
| | **2007-08** |
| *Goal* | Carey Price, Montreal |
| *Defense* | Tobias Enstrom, Atlanta |
| *Defense* | Tom Gilbert, Edmonton |
| *Forward* | Nicklas Backstrom, Washington |
| *Forward* | Patrick Kane, Chicago |
| *Forward* | Jonathan Toews, Chicago |
| | **2006-07** |
| *Goal* | Mike Smith, Dallas |
| *Defense* | Matt Carle, San Jose |
| *Defense* | Marc-Edouard Vlasic, San Jose |
| *Forward* | Evgeni Malkin, Pittsburgh |
| *Forward* | Jordan Staal, Pittsburgh |
| *Forward* | Paul Stastny, Colorado |
| | **2005-06** |
| *Goal* | Henrik Lundqvist, NY Rangers |
| *Defense* | Andrej Meszaros, Ottawa |
| *Defense* | Dion Phaneuf, Calgary |
| *Forward* | Brad Boyes, Boston |
| *Forward* | Sidney Crosby, Pittsburgh |
| *Forward* | Alex Ovechkin, Washington |
| | **2004-05** |
| *Goal* | |
| *Defense* | |
| *Defense* | *Season Cancelled* |
| *Forward* | |
| *Forward* | |
| *Forward* | |
| | **2003-04** |
| *Goal* | Andrew Raycroft, Boston |
| *Defense* | John-Michael Liles, Colorado |
| *Defense* | Joni Pitkanen, Philadelphia |
| *Forward* | Trent Hunter, NY Islanders |
| *Forward* | Ryan Malone, Pittsburgh |
| *Forward* | Michael Ryder, Montreal |

**2002-03**
Sebastien Caron, Pittsburgh
Jay Bouwmeester, Florida
Barret Jackman, St. Louis
Tyler Arnason, Chicago
Rick Nash, Columbus
Henrik Zetterberg, Detroit

**2001-02**
Dan Blackburn, NY Rangers
Nick Boynton, Boston
Rostislav Klesla, Columbus
Dany Heatley, Atlanta
Ilya Kovalchuk, Atlanta
Kristian Huselius, Florida

**2000-01**
Evgeni Nabokov, San Jose
Lubomir Visnovsky, Los Angeles
Colin White, New Jersey
Martin Havlat, Ottawa
Brad Richards, Tampa Bay
Shane Willis, Carolina

**1999-2000**
Brian Boucher, Philadelphia
Brian Rafalski, New Jersey
Brad Stuart, San Jose
Simon Gagne, Philadelphia
Scott Gomez, New Jersey
Michael York, NY Rangers

**1998-99**
Jamie Storr, Los Angeles
Tom Poti, Edmonton
Sami Salo, Ottawa
Chris Drury, Colorado
Milan Hejduk, Colorado
Marian Hossa, Ottawa

**1997-98**
Jamie Storr, Los Angeles
Mattias Ohlund, Vancouver
Derek Morris, Calgary
Sergei Samsonov, Boston
Patrick Elias, New Jersey
Mike Johnson, Toronto

**1996-97**
Patrick Lalime, Pittsburgh
Bryan Berard, NY Islanders
Janne Niinimaa, Philadelphia
Jarome Iginla, Calgary
Jim Campbell, St. Louis
Sergei Berezin, Toronto

**1995-96**
Corey Hirsch, Vancouver
Ed Jovanovski, Florida
Kyle McLaren, Boston
Daniel Alfredsson, Ottawa
Eric Daze, Chicago
Petr Sykora, New Jersey

**1994-95**
Jim Carey, Washington
Chris Therien, Philadelphia
Kenny Jonsson, Toronto
Peter Forsberg, Quebec
Jeff Friesen, San Jose
Paul Kariya, Anaheim

**1993-94**
Martin Brodeur, New Jersey
Chris Pronger, Hartford
Boris Mironov, Wpg./Edm.
Jason Arnott, Edmonton
Mikael Renberg, Philadelphia
Oleg Petrov, Montreal

**1992-93**
Felix Potvin, Toronto
Vladimir Malakhov, NY Islanders
Scott Niedermayer, New Jersey
Eric Lindros, Philadelphia
Teemu Selanne, Winnipeg
Joe Juneau, Boston

**1991-92**
Dominik Hasek, Chicago
Nicklas Lidstrom, Detroit
Vladimir Konstantinov, Detroit
Kevin Todd, New Jersey
Tony Amonte, NY Rangers
Gilbert Dionne, Montreal

**1990-91**
Ed Belfour, Chicago
Eric Weinrich, New Jersey
Rob Blake, Los Angeles
Sergei Fedorov, Detroit
Ken Hodge, Boston
Jaromir Jagr, Pittsburgh

**1989-90**
Bob Essensa, Winnipeg
Brad Shaw, Hartford
Geoff Smith, Edmonton
Mike Modano, Minnesota
Sergei Makarov, Calgary
Rod Brind'Amour, St. Louis

**1988-89**
Peter Sidorkiewicz, Hartford
Brian Leetch, NY Rangers
Zarley Zalapski, Pittsburgh
Trevor Linden, Vancouver
Tony Granato, NY Rangers
David Volek, NY Islanders

**1987-88**
Darren Pang, Chicago
Glen Wesley, Boston
Calle Johansson, Buffalo
Joe Nieuwendyk, Calgary
Ray Sheppard, Buffalo
Iain Duncan, Winnipeg

**1986-87**
Ron Hextall, Philadelphia
Steve Duchesne, Los Angeles
Brian Benning, St. Louis
Jimmy Carson, Los Angeles
Jim Sandlak, Vancouver
Luc Robitaille, Los Angeles

**1985-86**
Patrick Roy, Montreal
Gary Suter, Calgary
Dana Murzyn, Hartford
Mike Ridley, NY Rangers
Kjell Dahlin, Montreal
Wendel Clark, Toronto

**1984-85**
Steve Penney, Montreal
Chris Chelios, Montreal
Bruce Bell, Quebec
Mario Lemieux, Pittsburgh
Tomas Sandstrom, NY Rangers
Warren Young, Pittsburgh

**1983-84**
Tom Barrasso, Buffalo
Thomas Eriksson, Philadelphia
Jamie Macoun, Calgary
Steve Yzerman, Detroit
Hakan Loob, Calgary
Sylvain Turgeon, Hartford

**1982-83**
Pelle Lindbergh, Philadelphia
Scott Stevens, Washington
Phil Housley, Buffalo
Dan Daoust, Mtl./Tor.
Steve Larmer, Chicago
Mats Naslund, Montreal

## 2009 All-Star Game Summary

### JANUARY 25, 2009 at Montreal, Quebec East 12, West 11

PLAYERS ON ICE: **East** — C. Price, H. Lundqvist, T. Thomas, Bouwmeester, J. Carter, Chara, Heatley, T. Kaberle, Komisarek, Kovalchuk, Kovalev, Lecavalier, Malkin, Markov, Ovechkin, Parise, St. Louis, Savard, E. Staal, Streit, Vanek.

**West** — Giguere, N. Backstrom, Luongo, Boyle, D. Brown, B. Campbell, Doan, Getzlaf, Hejduk, Iginla, Kane, Marleau, Modano, Nash, S. Niedermayer, Robidas, Souray, J. Thornton, Tkachuk, Toews, Weber.

**SUMMARY**

**First Period**

| | | | | |
|---|---|---|---|---|
| 1. | West | Tkachuk | (Nash, Hejduk) | 1:16 |
| 2. | East | Ovechkin | (Savard) | 6:26 |
| 3. | East | E. Staal | (Bouwmeester, Kovalev) | 9:30 |
| 4. | East | Kovalev | (Kaberle) | 16:34 |
| 5. | East | Markov | (Ovechkin, Savard) | 19:23 |
| 6. | West | Marleau | (Thornton, S. Niedermayer) | 19:48 |

PENALTIES: None

**Second Period**

| | | | | |
|---|---|---|---|---|
| 7. | East | St. Louis | (T. Kaberle) | 1:21 |
| 8. | East | Parise | (St. Louis, Streit) | 2:11 |
| 9. | West | Souray | (Hejduk) | 3:29 |
| 10. | West | Boyle | (Doan, B. Campbell) | 5:14 |
| 11. | East | Malkin | (unassisted). | 7:45 |
| 12. | West | Nash | (unassisted) | 8:27 |
| 13. | West | Hejduk | (Boyle, Nash) | 9:02 |
| 14. | West | Souray | (Thornton, Marleau) | 10:34 |
| 15. | East | Kovalev | (unassisted) | 13:35 |
| 16. | West | Iginla | (Thornton, Marleau) | 16:46 |

PENALTIES: None

**Third Period**

| | | | | |
|---|---|---|---|---|
| 17. | West | Doan | (Modano, D. Brown) | :32 |
| 18. | East | Heatley | (Savard) | 2:17 |
| 19. | West | Toews | (Kane, Souray) | 2:32 |
| 20. | East | St. Louis | (Streit, Bouwmeester) | 13:19 |
| 21. | West | Kane | (Getzlaf) | 15:19 |
| 22. | East | Bouwmeester | (Ovechkin) | 16:21 |

PENALTIES: None

**Overtime**

No scoring
PENALTIES: East: Komisarek, hooking, 2:22

Shootout Goaltenders: East - T. Thomas; West - Luongo
Round 1 Lecavalier (East) and Doan (West) did not score.
Round 2 Kovalev (East) scored. Nash (West) did not score.
Round 3 Ovechkin (East) scored.

SHOTS ON GOAL BY:

| | | | | | |
|---|---|---|---|---|---|
| East | 11 | 21 | 13 | 3 | 48 |
| West | 11 | 21 | 19 | 3 | 54 |

*Kris Versteeg of Chicago and Patrik Berglund of St. Louis were both named to the NHL All-Rookie Team for 2008-09. Versteeg led all NHL rookies with 31 assists and was second to Anaheim's Bobby Ryan with 53 points. Berglund ranked among the rookie leaders with 21 goals, 26 assists and 47 points.*

| | Goaltenders: | Time | SA | GA | ENG | Dec |
|---|---|---|---|---|---|---|
| East | Price | 20:00 | 11 | 2 | 0 | |
| East | Lundqvist | 20:00 | 21 | 6 | 0 | |
| East | T. Thomas | 25:00 | 22 | 3 | 0 | W |
| West | Giguere | 20:00 | 11 | 4 | 0 | |
| West | N. Backstrom | 20:00 | 21 | 4 | 0 | |
| West | Luongo | 25:00 | 16 | 3 | 0 | L |

PP Conversions: East 0/0; West 0/1.
Referees: Brad Meier, Marc Joannette; Linesmen: Greg Devorski, Pierre Racicot
Attendance: 21,273

# All-Star Game Results

| Year | Venue | Score | Coaches | Attendance |
|---|---|---|---|---|
| 2009 | Montreal | East 12, West 11 | Claude Julien, Todd McLellan | 21,273 |
| 2008 | Atlanta | East 8, West 7 | John Paddock, Mike Babcock | 18,644 |
| 2007 | Dallas | West 12, East 9 | Lindy Ruff, Randy Carlyle | 18,532 |
| 2004 | Minnesota | East 6, West 4 | Pat Quinn, Dave Lewis | 19,434 |
| 2003 | Florida | West 6, East 5 | Marc Crawford, Jacques Martin | 19,250 |
| 2002 | Los Angeles | World 8, North America 5 | Scotty Bowman, Pat Quinn | 18,118 |
| 2001 | Colorado | North America 14, World 12 | Joel Quenneville, Jacques Martin | 18,646 |
| 2000 | Toronto | World 9, North America 4 | Scotty Bowman, Pat Quinn | 19,300 |
| 1999 | Tampa Bay | North America 8, World 6 | Lindy Ruff, Ken Hitchcock | 19,758 |
| 1998 | Vancouver | North America 8, World 7 | Jacques Lemaire, Ken Hitchcock | 18,422 |
| 1997 | San Jose | East 11, West 7 | Doug MacLean, Ken Hitchcock | 17,422 |
| 1996 | Boston | East 5, West 4 | Doug MacLean, Scotty Bowman | 17,565 |
| 1994 | NY Rangers | East 9, West 8 | Jacques Demers, Barry Melrose | 18,200 |
| 1993 | Montreal | Wales 16, Campbell 6 | Scotty Bowman, Mike Keenan | 17,137 |
| 1992 | Philadelphia | Campbell 10, Wales 6 | Bob Gainey, Scotty Bowman | 17,380 |
| 1991 | Chicago | Campbell 11, Wales 5 | John Muckler, Mike Milbury | 18,472 |
| 1990 | Pittsburgh | Wales 12, Campbell 7 | Pat Burns, Terry Crisp | 16,236 |
| 1989 | Edmonton | Campbell 9, Wales 5 | Glen Sather, Terry O'Reilly | 17,503 |
| 1988 | St. Louis | Wales 6, Campbell 5 OT | Mike Keenan, Glen Sather | 17,878 |
| 1986 | Hartford | Wales 4, Campbell 3 OT | Mike Keenan, Glen Sather | 15,100 |
| 1985 | Calgary | Wales 6, Campbell 4 | Al Arbour, Glen Sather | 16,825 |
| 1984 | New Jersey | Wales 7, Campbell 6 | Al Arbour, Glen Sather | 18,939 |
| 1983 | NY Islanders | Campbell 9, Wales 3 | Roger Neilson, Al Arbour | 15,230 |
| 1982 | Washington | Wales 4, Campbell 2 | Al Arbour, Glen Sonmor | 18,130 |
| 1981 | Los Angeles | Campbell 4, Wales 1 | Pat Quinn, Scotty Bowman | 15,761 |
| 1980 | Detroit | Wales 6, Campbell 3 | Scotty Bowman, Al Arbour | 21,002 |
| 1978 | Buffalo | Wales 3, Campbell 2 OT | Scotty Bowman, Fred Shero | 16,433 |
| 1977 | Vancouver | Wales 4, Campbell 3 | Scotty Bowman, Fred Shero | 15,607 |
| 1976 | Philadelphia | Wales 7, Campbell 5 | Floyd Smith, Fred Shero | 16,436 |
| 1975 | Montreal | Wales 7, Campbell 1 | Bep Guidolin, Fred Shero | 16,080 |
| 1974 | Chicago | West 6, East 4 | Billy Reay, Scotty Bowman | 16,426 |
| 1973 | NY Rangers | East 5, West 4 | Tom Johnson, Billy Reay | 16,986 |
| 1972 | Minnesota | East 3, West 2 | Al MacNeil, Billy Reay | 15,423 |
| 1971 | Boston | West 2, East 1 | Scotty Bowman, Harry Sinden | 14,790 |
| 1970 | St. Louis | East 4, West 1 | Claude Ruel, Scotty Bowman | 16,587 |
| 1969 | Montreal | East 3, West 3 | Toe Blake, Scotty Bowman | 16,260 |
| 1968 | Toronto | Toronto 4, All-Stars 3 | Punch Imlach, Toe Blake | 15,753 |
| 1967 | Montreal | Montreal 3, All-Stars 0 | Toe Blake, Sid Abel | 14,284 |
| 1965 | Montreal | All-Stars 5, Montreal 2 | Billy Reay, Toe Blake | 13,529 |
| 1964 | Toronto | All-Stars 3, Toronto 2 | Sid Abel, Punch Imlach | 14,232 |
| 1963 | Toronto | All-Stars 3, Toronto 3 | Sid Abel, Punch Imlach | 14,034 |
| 1962 | Toronto | Toronto 4, All-Stars 1 | Punch Imlach, Rudy Pilous | 14,236 |
| 1961 | Chicago | All-Stars 3, Chicago 1 | Sid Abel, Rudy Pilous | 14,534 |
| 1960 | Montreal | All-Stars 2, Montreal 1 | Punch Imlach, Toe Blake | 13,949 |
| 1959 | Montreal | Montreal 6, All-Stars 1 | Toe Blake, Punch Imlach | 13,818 |
| 1958 | Montreal | Montreal 6, All-Stars 3 | Toe Blake, Milt Schmidt | 13,989 |
| 1957 | Montreal | All-Stars 5, Montreal 3 | Milt Schmidt, Toe Blake | 13,003 |
| 1956 | Montreal | All-Stars 1, Montreal 1 | Jim Skinner, Toe Blake | 13,095 |
| 1955 | Detroit | Detroit 3, All-Stars 1 | Jim Skinner, Dick Irvin | 10,111 |
| 1954 | Detroit | All-Stars 2, Detroit 2 | King Clancy, Jim Skinner | 10,689 |
| 1953 | Montreal | All-Stars 3, Montreal 1 | Lynn Patrick, Dick Irvin | 14,153 |
| 1952 | Detroit | 1st Team 1, 2nd Team 1 | Tommy Ivan, Dick Irvin | 10,680 |
| 1951 | Toronto | 1st Team 2, 2nd Team 2 | Joe Primeau, Dick Irvin | 11,469 |
| 1950 | Detroit | Detroit 7, All-Stars 1 | Tommy Ivan, Lynn Patrick | 9,166 |
| 1949 | Toronto | All-Stars 3, Toronto 1 | Tommy Ivan, Hap Day | 13,541 |
| 1948 | Chicago | All-Stars 3, Toronto 1 | Tommy Ivan, Hap Day | 12,794 |
| 1947 | Toronto | All-Stars 4, Toronto 3 | Dick Irvin, Hap Day | 14,169 |

There was no All-Star contest during the calendar year of 1966 because the game was moved from the start of season to mid-season. In 1979, the Challenge Cup series between the Soviet Union and Team NHL replaced the All-Star Game. In 1987, Rendez-Vous '87, two games between the Soviet Union and Team NHL replaced the All-Star Game.

## NHL ALL-STAR GAME MVP

| | |
|---|---|
| 2009 | Alex Kovalev, Mtl. |
| 2008 | Eric Staal, Car. |
| 2007 | Daniel Briere, Buf. |
| 2004 | Joe Sakic, Col.. |
| 2003 | Dany Heatley, Atl. |
| 2002 | Eric Daze, Chi. |
| 2001 | Bill Guerin, Bos. |
| 2000 | Pavel Bure, Fla. |
| 1999 | Wayne Gretzky, NYR |
| 1998 | Teemu Selanne, Ana. |
| 1997 | Mark Recchi, Mtl. |
| 1996 | Raymond Bourque, Bos. |
| 1994 | Mike Richter, NYR |
| 1993 | Mike Gartner, NYR |
| 1992 | Brett Hull, St.L. |
| 1991 | Vincent Damphousse, Tor. |
| 1990 | Mario Lemieux, Pit. |
| 1989 | Wayne Gretzky, L.A. |
| 1988 | Mario Lemieux, Pit. |
| 1986 | Grant Fuhr, Edm. |
| 1985 | Mario Lemieux, Pit. |
| 1984 | Don Maloney, NYR |
| 1983 | Wayne Gretzky, Edm. |
| 1982 | Mike Bossy, NYI |
| 1981 | Mike Liut, St.L. |
| 1980 | Reggie Leach, Phi. |
| 1978 | Billy Smith, NYI |
| 1977 | Rick Martin, Buf. |
| 1976 | Pete Mahovlich, Mtl. |
| 1975 | Syl Apps Jr., Pit. |
| 1974 | Garry Unger, St.L. |
| 1973 | Greg Polis, Pit. |
| 1972 | Bobby Orr, Bos. |
| 1971 | Bobby Hull, Chi. |
| 1970 | Bobby Hull, Chi. |
| 1969 | Frank Mahovlich, Det. |
| 1968 | Bruce Gamble, Tor. |
| 1967 | Henri Richard, Mtl. |
| 1965 | Gordie Howe, Det. |
| 1964 | Jean Beliveau, Mtl. |
| 1963 | Frank Mahovlich, Tor. |
| 1962 | Eddie Shack, Tor. |

# All-Star Game Records 1947 through 2009

## TEAM RECORDS

### MOST GOALS, BOTH TEAMS, ONE GAME:
**26** — North America 14, World 12, 2001 at Colorado
23 — East 12, West 11, 2009 at Montreal
22 — Wales 16, Campbell 6, 1993 at Montreal
21 — West 12, East 9, 2007 at Dallas
19 — Wales 12, Campbell 7, 1990 at Pittsburgh
18 — East 11, West 7, 1997 at San Jose
17 — East 9, West 8, 1994 at NY Rangers

### FEWEST GOALS, BOTH TEAMS, ONE GAME:
**2** — First Team All-Stars 1, Second Team All-Stars 1, 1952 at Detroit
— NHL All-Stars 1, Montreal Canadiens 1, 1956 at Montreal
3 — NHL All-Stars 2, Montreal Canadiens 1, 1960 at Montreal
— Montreal Canadiens 3, NHL All-Stars 0, 1967 at Montreal
— West 2, East 1, 1971 at Boston

### MOST GOALS, ONE TEAM, ONE GAME:
**16** — Wales 16, Campbell 6, 1993 at Montreal
14 — North America 14, World 12, 2001 at Colorado
12 — Wales 12, Campbell 7, 1990 at Pittsburgh
— World 12, North America 14, 2001 at Colorado
— West 12, East 9, 2007 at Dallas
— East 12, West 11, 2009 at Montreal

### FEWEST GOALS, ONE TEAM, ONE GAME:
**0** — NHL All-Stars 0, Montreal Canadiens 3, 1967 at Montreal
1 — 17 times (1981, 1975, 1971, 1970, 1962, 1961, 1960, 1959, both teams 1956, 1955, 1953, both teams 1952, 1950, 1949, 1948)

### MOST SHOTS, BOTH TEAMS, ONE GAME (SINCE 1955):
**102** — 1994 at NY Rangers — East 9 (56 shots), West 8 (46 shots)
2009 at Montreal — East 12 (48 shots) — West 11 (54 shots)
98 — 2001 at Denver — North America 14 (53 shots), World 12 (45 shots)
90 — 1993 at Montreal — Wales 16 (49 shots), Campbell 6 (41 shots)

### FEWEST SHOTS, BOTH TEAMS, ONE GAME (SINCE 1955):
**52** — 1978 at Buffalo — Campbell 2 (12 shots) Wales 3 (40 shots)
53 — 1960 at Montreal — NHL All-Stars 2 (27 shots) Montreal Canadiens 1 (26 shots)
55 — 1956 at Montreal — NHL All-Stars 1 (28 shots) Montreal Canadiens 1 (27 shots)
— 1971 at Boston — West 2 (28 shots) East 1 (27 shots)

### MOST SHOTS, ONE TEAM, ONE GAME (SINCE 1955):
**56** — 1994 at NY Rangers — East (9-8 vs. West)
54 — 2009 at Montreal — East (12-11 vs. West)
53 — 2001 at Colorado — North America (14-12 vs. World)
51 — 2008 at Atlanta — West (7-8 vs. East)

### FEWEST SHOTS, ONE TEAM, ONE GAME (SINCE 1955):
**12** — 1978 at Buffalo — Campbell (2-3 vs. Wales)
17 — 1970 at St. Louis — West (1-4 vs. East)
23 — 1961 at Chicago — Chicago Black Hawks (1-3 vs. NHL All-Stars)
24 — 1976 at Philadelphia — Campbell (5-7 vs. Wales)

### MOST POWER-PLAY GOALS, BOTH TEAMS, ONE GAME (SINCE 1950):
**3** — 1953 at Montreal — NHL All-Stars 3 (2 power-play goals), Montreal Canadiens 1 (1 power-play goal)
— 1954 at Detroit — NHL All-Stars 2 (1 power-play goal) Detroit Red Wings 2 (2 power-play goals)
— 1958 at Montreal — NHL All-Stars 3 (1 power-play goal) Montreal Canadiens 6 (2 power-play goals)

### FEWEST POWER-PLAY GOALS, BOTH TEAMS, ONE GAME (SINCE 1950):
**0** — 25 times (1952, 1959, 1960, 1967, 1968, 1969, 1972, 1973, 1976, 1980, 1981, 1984, 1985, 1992, 1994, 1996, 1999, 2000, 2001, 2002, 2003, 2004, 2007, 2008, 2009)

### FASTEST TWO GOALS, BOTH TEAMS, FROM START OF GAME:
**0:37** — 1970 at St. Louis — Jacques Laperriere of East scored at 0:20 and Dean Prentice of West scored at 0:37. Final score: East 4, West 1.

1:20 — 2008 at Atlanta — Rick Nash of West scored at 0:12 and Eric Staal of East scored at 1:20. Final score: East 8, West 7.

2:15 — 1998 at Vancouver — Teemu Selanne scored at 0:53 and Jaromir Jagr scored at 2:15 for World. Final score: North America 8, World 7.

### FASTEST TWO GOALS, BOTH TEAMS:
**0:08** — 1997 at San Jose — Owen Nolan scored at 18:54 and 19:02 of second period for West. Final Score: East 11, West 7.

0:10 — 1976 at Philadelphia — Dennis Ververgaert scored at 4:33 and at 4:43 of third period for Campbell. Final score: Wales 7, Campbell 5.

0:13 — 1998 at Vancouver — Teemu Selanne scored at 4:00 of first period for World and John LeClair scored at 4:13 for North America. Final score: North America 8, World 7.

**FASTEST THREE GOALS, BOTH TEAMS:**
**0:48** — 2007 at Dallas — Martin Havlat scored at 19:00 of third period for West; Sheldon Souray scored at 19:25 for East; Dion Phaneuf scored at 19:48 for West. Final score: West 12, East 9.

1:08 — 1993 at Montreal — all by Wales — Mike Gartner scored at 3:15 and at 3:37 of first period; Peter Bondra scored at 4:23. Final score: Wales 16, Campbell 6.

1:14 — 1994 at NY Rangers — Bob Kudelski scored at 9:46 of first period for East; Sergei Fedorov scored at 10:20 for West; Eric Lindros scored at 11:00 for East. Final score: East 9, West 8.

**FASTEST FOUR GOALS, BOTH TEAMS:**
**2:24** — 1997 at San Jose — Brendan Shanahan scored at 16:38 of second period for West; Dale Hawerchuk scored at 17:28 for East; Owen Nolan scored at 18:54 and 19:02 for West. Final score: East 11, West 7.

2:49 — 2009 at Montreal — Evgeni Malkin scored at 7:45 of second period for East; Rick Nash scored at 8:27 for West; Milan Hejduk scored at 9:02 for West; Sheldon Souray scored at 10:34 for West.

2:52 — 2007 at Dallas — Rick Nash scored at 10:40 of second period for West; Martin Havlat scored at 11:34 for West; Yanic Perreault scored at 12:47 for West; Alex Ovechkin scored at 13:32 for East. Final score: West 12, East 9.

**FASTEST TWO GOALS, ONE TEAM, FROM START OF GAME:**
**2:15** — 1998 at Vancouver — World — Teemu Selanne scored at 0:53 and Jaromir Jagr scored at 2:15. Final score: North America 8, World 7.

3:37 — 1993 at Montreal — Wales — Mike Gartner scored at 3:15 and at 3:37. Final score: Wales 16, Campbell 6.

4:19 — 1980 at Detroit — Wales — Larry Robinson scored at 3:58 and Steve Payne scored at 4:19. Final score: Wales 6, Campbell 3.

**FASTEST TWO GOALS, ONE TEAM:**
**0:08** — 1997 at San Jose — West — Owen Nolan scored at 18:54 and at 19:02 of second period. Final score: East 11, West 7.

0:10 — 1976 at Philadelphia — Campbell — Dennis Ververgaert scored at 4:33 and at 4:43 of third period. Final score: Wales 7, Campbell 5.

0:14 — 1989 at Edmonton — Campbell — Steve Yzerman and Gary Leeman scored at 17:21 and 17:35 of second period. Final score: Campbell 9, Wales 5.

**FASTEST THREE GOALS, ONE TEAM:**
**1:08** — 1993 at Montreal — Wales — Mike Gartner scored at 3:15 and 3:37 of first period; Peter Bondra scored at 4:23. Final score: Wales 16, Campbell 6.

1:32 — 1980 at Detroit — Wales — Ron Stackhouse scored at 11:40 of third period; Craig Hartsburg scored at 12:40; Reed Larson scored at 13:12. Final score: Wales 6, Campbell 3.

1:39 — 2002 at Los Angeles — Markus Naslund scored at 18:17 of third period; Alex Zhamnov scored at 19:12; Sami Kapanen scored at 19:56. Final score: World 8, North America 5.

**FASTEST FOUR GOALS, ONE TEAM:**
**2:57** — 2002 at Los Angeles — World — Sergei Fedorov scored at 16:59 of third period; Markus Naslund scored at 18:17; Alex Zhamnov scored at 19:12; Sami Kapanen scored at 19:56. Final score: World 8, North America 5.

4:17 — 2007 at Dallas — Brian Rolston scored at 8:30 of second period; Rick Nash scored at 10:40; Martin Havlat scored at 11:34; Yanic Perreault scored at 12:47. Final score: West 12, East 9.

4:19 — 1992 at Philadelphia — Campbell — Brian Bellows scored at 7:40 of second period; Jeremy Roenick scored at 8:13; Theoren Fleury scored at 11:06, Brett Hull scored at 11:59. Final score: Campbell 10, Wales 6.

**MOST GOALS, BOTH TEAMS, ONE PERIOD:**
**10** — 1997 at San Jose — Second period — East (6), West (4).
Final score: East 11, West 7.

— 2001 at Colorado — Second period — North America (6), World (4).
Final score: North America 14, World 12.

— 2001 at Colorado — Third period — North America (5), World (5).
Final score: North America 14, World 12.

— 2009 at Montreal — Second period — West (6), East (4).
Final Score: East 12, West 11.

9 — 1990 at Pittsburgh — First period — Wales (7), Campbell (2).
Final score: Wales 12, Campbell 7.

— 2007 at Dallas — Second period — West (6), East (3).
Final score: West 12, East 9.

**MOST GOALS, ONE TEAM, ONE PERIOD:**
**7** — 1990 at Pittsburgh — First period — Wales. Final score: Wales 12, Campbell 7.

6 — 1983 at NY Islanders — Third period — Campbell.
Final score: Campbell 9, Wales 3.

— 1992 at Philadelphia — Second period — Campbell.
Final score: Campbell 10, Wales 6.

— 1993 at Montreal — First period — Wales.
Final score: Wales 16, Campbell 6.

— 1993 at Montreal — Second period — Wales.
Final score: Wales 16, Campbell 6.

— 1997 at San Jose — Second period — East.
Final score: East 11, West 7.

— 2001 at Colorado — Second period — North America.
Final score: North America 14, World 12.

— 2007 at Dallas — Second period — West.
Final score: West 12, East 9.

— 2009 at Montreal — Second period — West.
Final score: East 12, West 11.

**MOST SHOTS, BOTH TEAMS, ONE PERIOD:**
**42** — 2009 at Montreal — Second period — West (21), East (21).
Final score: East 12, West 11.

39 — 1994 at NY Rangers — Second period — West (21), East (18).
Final score: East 9, West 8.

— 2001 at Colorado — Third period — World (23), North America (16).
Final score: North America 14, World 12.

36 — 1990 at Pittsburgh — Third period — Campbell (22), Wales (14).
Final score: Wales 12, Campbell 7.

— 1994 at NY Rangers — First period — East (19), West (17).
Final score: East 9, West 8.

— 2002 at Los Angeles — Third period — North America (20), World (16).
Final score: World 8, North America 5.

**MOST SHOTS, ONE TEAM, ONE PERIOD:**
**23** — 2001 at Colorado — Third period — World.
Final score: North America 14, World 12.

22 — 1990 at Pittsburgh — Third period — Campbell.
Final score: Wales 12, Campbell 7.

— 1991 at Chicago — Third period — Wales.
Final score: Campbell 11, Wales 5.

— 1993 at Montreal — First period — Wales.
Final score: Wales 16, Campbell 6.

**FEWEST SHOTS, BOTH TEAMS, ONE PERIOD:**
**9** — 1971 at Boston — Third period — East (2), West (7).
Final score: West 2, East 1.

— 1980 at Detroit — Second period — Campbell (4), Wales (5).
Final score: Wales 6, Campbell 3.

13 — 1982 at Washington — Third period — Campbell (6), Wales (7).
Final score: Wales 4, Campbell 2.

14 — 1978 at Buffalo — First period — Campbell (7), Wales (7).
Final score: Wales 3, Campbell 2.

— 1986 at Hartford — First period — Campbell (6), Wales (8).
Final score: Wales 4, Campbell 3.

**FEWEST SHOTS, ONE TEAM, ONE PERIOD:**
**2** — 1971 at Boston — Third period — East.
Final score: West 2, East 1.

— 1978 at Buffalo — Second period — Campbell.
Final score: Wales 3, Campbell 2.

3 — 1978 at Buffalo — Third period — Campbell.
Final score: Wales 3, Campbell 2.

4 — 1955 at Detroit — First period — NHL All-Stars.
Final score: Detroit Red Wings 3, NHL All-Stars 1.

— 1980 at Detroit — Second period — Campbell.
Final score: Wales 6, Campbell 3.

*Alex Kovalev, then a member of the hometown Canadiens, celebrates with his Eastern Conference teammates after scoring a shootout goal in the 2009 NHL All-Star Game in Montreal. Kovalev (who had already scored two breakaway goals) was named MVP of the East's 12-11 victory.*

# INDIVIDUAL RECORDS

## Games

**MOST GAMES PLAYED:**
**23 — Gordie Howe**, 1948 through 1980
19 — Raymond Bourque, 1981 through 2001
18 — Wayne Gretzky, 1980 through 1999
15 — Frank Mahovlich, 1959 through 1974
— Mark Messier, 1982 through 2004

## Goals

**MOST GOALS, CAREER:**
**13 — Wayne Gretzky** in 18GP
**— Mario Lemieux** in 10GP
10 — Gordie Howe in 23GP
9 — Teemu Selanne in 10GP
8 — Frank Mahovlich in 15GP
— Luc Robitaille in 8GP

**MOST GOALS, ONE GAME:**
**4 — Wayne Gretzky,** Campbell, 1983
**— Mario Lemieux,** Wales, 1990
**— Vince Damphousse,** Campbell, 1991
**— Mike Gartner,** Wales, 1993
**— Dany Heatley,** East, 2003
3 — Ted Lindsay, Detroit, 1950
— Mario Lemieux, Wales, 1988
— Pierre Turgeon, Wales, 1993
— Mark Recchi, East, 1997
— Owen Nolan, West, 1997
— Teemu Selanne, World, 1998
— Pavel Bure, World, 2000
— Bill Guerin, North America, 2001
— Joe Sakic, West, 2004
— Rick Nash, West, 2008

**MOST GOALS, ONE PERIOD:**
**4 — Wayne Gretzky,** Campbell, Third period, 1983
3 — Mario Lemieux, Wales, First period, 1990
— Vincent Damphousse, Campbell, Third period, 1991
— Mike Gartner, Wales, First period, 1993

## Assists

**MOST ASSISTS, CAREER:**
**16 — Joe Sakic** in 12GP
14 — Mark Messier in 15GP
13 — Raymond Bourque in 19GP
12 — Adam Oates in 5GP
— Mats Sundin in 8GP
— Wayne Gretzky in 18GP

**MOST ASSISTS, ONE GAME:**
**5 — Mats Naslund,** Wales, 1988
4 — Raymond Bourque, Wales, 1985
— Adam Oates, Campbell, 1991
— Adam Oates, Wales, 1993
— Mark Recchi, Wales, 1993
— Pierre Turgeon, East, 1994
— Fredrik Modin, World, 2001
— Joe Sakic, West, 2007
— Daniel Briere, East, 2007
— Marian Hossa, East, 2007

**MOST ASSISTS, ONE PERIOD:**
**4 — Adam Oates,** Wales, First period, 1993
3 — Mark Messier, Campbell, Third period, 1983
3 — Marian Hossa, East, Third period, 2007

## Points

**MOST POINTS, CAREER:**
**25 — Wayne Gretzky** (13G-12A in 18GP)
23 — Mario Lemieux (13G-10A in 10GP)
22 — Joe Sakic (6G-16A in 12GP)
20 — Mark Messier (6G-14A in 15GP)
19 — Gordie Howe (10G-9A in 23GP)

**MOST POINTS, ONE GAME:**
**6 — Mario Lemieux,** Wales, 1988 (3G-3A)
5 — Mats Naslund, Wales, 1988 (5A)
— Adam Oates, Campbell, 1991 (1G-4A)
— Mike Gartner, Wales, 1993 (4G-1A)
— Mark Recchi, Wales, 1993 (1G-4A)
— Pierre Turgeon, Wales, 1993 (3G-2A)
— Bill Guerin, North America, 2001 (3G-2A)
— Dany Heatley, East, 2003 (4G-1A)
— Daniel Briere, East, 2007 (1G-4A)

**MOST POINTS, ONE PERIOD:**
**4 — Wayne Gretzky,** Campbell, Third period, 1983 (4G)
**— Mike Gartner,** Wales, First period, 1993 (3G-1A)
**— Adam Oates,** Wales, First period, 1993 (4A)
3 — Gordie Howe, NHL All-Stars, Second period, 1965 (1G-2A)
— Pete Mahovlich, Wales, First period, 1976 (1G-2A)
— Mark Messier, Campbell, Third period, 1983 (3A)
— Mario Lemieux, Wales, Second period, 1988 (1G-2A)
— Mario Lemieux, Wales, First period, 1990 (3G)
— Vince Damphousse, Campbell, Third period, 1991 (3G)
— Mark Recchi, Wales, Second period, 1993 (1G-2A)
— Tony Amonte, North America, Second period, 2001 (2G-1A)
— Daniel Alfredsson, East, Second period, 2004 (2G-1A)
— Marian Hossa, East, Third period, 2007 (3A)

## Power-Play Goals

**MOST POWER-PLAY GOALS, CAREER:**
**6 — Gordie Howe** in 23GP
3 — Bobby Hull in 12GP
— Maurice Richard in 13GP

## Fastest Goals

**FASTEST GOAL FROM START OF GAME:**
**0:12 — Rick Nash,** West, 2008
0:19 — Ted Lindsay, Detroit, 1950
0:20 — Jacques Laperriere, East, 1970
0:21 — Mario Lemieux, Wales, 1990
0:35 — Vincent Damphousse, North America, 2002

**FASTEST GOAL FROM START OF A PERIOD:**
**0:12 — Rick Nash,** West, 2008 (first period)
0:17 — Raymond Bourque, North America, 1999 (second period)
0:19 — Ted Lindsay, Detroit, 1950 (first period)
— Rick Tocchet, Wales, 1993 (second period)
0:20 — Jacques Laperriere, East, 1970 (first period)

**FASTEST TWO GOALS, ONE PLAYER, FROM START OF GAME:**
**3:37 — Mike Gartner,** Wales, 1993, at 3:15 and 3:37.
4:00 — Teemu Selanne, World, 1998, at 0:53 and 4:00
5:25 — Wally Hergesheimer, NHL All-Stars, 1953, at 4:06 and 5:25.

**FASTEST TWO GOALS, ONE PLAYER, FROM START OF A PERIOD:**
**3:37 — Mike Gartner,** Wales, 1993, at 3:15 and 3:37 of first period.
4:00 — Teemu Selanne, World, 1998, at 0:53 and 4:00 of first period.
4:43 — Dennis Ververgaert, Campbell, 1976, at 4:33 and 4:43 of third period.

**FASTEST TWO GOALS, ONE PLAYER:**
**0:08 — Owen Nolan,** West, 1997. Scored at 18:54 and 19:02 of second period.
0:10 — Dennis Ververgaert, Campbell, 1976. Scored at 4:33 and 4:43 of third period.
0:22 — Mike Gartner, Wales, 1993. Scored at 3:15 and 3:37 of first period.

## Penalties

**MOST PENALTY MINUTES:**
**25 — Gordie Howe** in 23GP
21 — Gus Mortson in 9GP
16 — Harry Howell in 7GP

## Goaltenders

**MOST GAMES PLAYED:**
**13 — Glenn Hall** from 1955 through 1969
11 — Terry Sawchuk from 1950 through 1968
— Patrick Roy from 1988 through 2003
9 — Martin Brodeur from 1996 through 2007
8 — Jacques Plante from 1956 through 1970

**MOST MINUTES PLAYED:**
**540 — Glenn Hall** in 13GP
467 — Terry Sawchuk in 11GP
370 — Jacques Plante in 8GP
250 — Patrick Roy in 11GP
209 — Turk Broda in 4GP

**MOST GOALS AGAINST:**
**31 — Patrick Roy** in 11GP
22 — Martin Brodeur in 9GP
— Glenn Hall in 13GP
21 — Mike Vernon in 5GP
19 — Terry Sawchuk in 11GP

**BEST GOALS-AGAINST-AVERAGE AMONG THOSE WITH AT LEAST TWO GAMES PLAYED:**
**0.68 — Gilles Villemure** in 3GP
1.49 — Gerry McNeil in 3GP
1.50 — Johnny Bower in 4GP
1.51 — Frank Brimsek in 3GP
1.64 — Gump Worsley in 4GP

# Hockey Hall of Fame

(Year of induction is listed after each Honoured Members name)

**Location:** Brookfield Place, at the corner of Front and Yonge Streets in the heart of downtown Toronto. Easy access from all major highways running into Toronto. Close to TTC subway and Union Station.

**Telephone:** administration (416) 360-7735; information (416) 360-7765.

**Public Hours of Operation:** Open every day except Christmas Day, New Year's Day and Induction Day (November 9, 2009). Please call our information number (above) or visit our website (below) for times.

The Hockey Hall of Fame can be booked for private functions after hours.

Website address: www.hhof.com

**History:** The Hockey Hall of Fame was established in 1943. Members were first honoured in 1945. On August 26, 1961, the Hockey Hall of Fame opened its doors to the public in a building located on the grounds of the Canadian National Exhibition in Toronto. The Hockey Hall of Fame relocated to its current location and welcomed the hockey world on June 18, 1993.

**Honour Roll:** There are 357 Honoured Members in the Hockey Hall of Fame. 244 have been inducted as players, 98 as builders and 15 as Referees/Linesmen. In addition, there are 82 media honourees.

**Founding/Premiere Sponsors:** Imperial Oil, International Ice Hockey Federation, Molson Canada, National Hockey League, National Hockey League Players' Association, Panasonic Canada, Pepsi-Cola Canada, RBC Financial Group, The Toronto Sun, The Sports Network (TSN/RDS), Verizon.

*Steve Yzerman captained the Detroit Red Wings to their first Stanley Cup victory in 42 years in 1997. He would raise the Cup again in 1998 and 2002. A scoring star who later became an outstanding defensive forward, Yzerman had 692 goals and 1,063 assists for 1,755 points in his Hall of Fame career.*

## PLAYERS

* Abel, Sidney Gerald 1969
* Adams, John James "Jack" 1959
Anderson, Glenn 2008
* Apps, Charles Joseph Sylvanus "Syl" 1961
Armstrong, George Edward 1975
* Bailey, Irvine Wallace "Ace" 1975
* Bain, Donald H. "Dan" 1949
* Baker, Hobart "Hobey" 1945
Barber, William Charles "Bill" 1990
* Barry, Martin J. "Marty" 1965
Bathgate, Andrew James "Andy" 1978
* Bauer, Robert Theodore "Bobby" 1996
Béliveau, Jean Arthur 1972
* Benedict, Clinton S. 1965
* Bentley, Douglas Wagner 1964
* Bentley, Maxwell H. L. 1966
* Blake, Hector "Toe" 1966
Boivin, Leo Joseph 1986
* Boon, Richard R. "Dickie" 1952
Bossy, Michael 1991
Bouchard, Emile Joseph "Butch" 1966
* Boucher, Frank 1958
* Boucher, Georges "Buck" 1960
Bourque, Raymond 2004
Bower, John William 1976
* Bowie, Russell 1947
* Brimsek, Francis Charles 1966
* Broadbent, Harry L. "Punch" 1962
* Broda, Walter Edward "Turk" 1967
Bucyk, John Paul 1981
* Burch, Billy 1974
* Cameron, Harold Hugh "Harry" 1962
Cheevers, Gerald Michael "Gerry" 1985
* Clancy, Francis Michael "King" 1958
* Clapper, Aubrey "Dit" 1947
Clarke, Robert "Bobby" 1987
* Cleghorn, Sprague 1958
Coffey, Paul 2004
* Colville, Neil MacNeil 1967
* Conacher, Charles W. 1961
* Conacher, Lionel Pretoria 1994
* Conacher, Roy Gordon 1998
* Connell, Alex 1958
* Cook, Fred "Bun" 1995
* Cook, William Osser 1952
* Coulter, Arthur Edmund 1974
Cournoyer, Yvan Serge 1982
* Cowley, William Mailes 1968
* Crawford, Samuel Russell "Rusty" 1962
* Darragh, John Proctor "Jack" 1962
* Davidson, Allan M. "Scotty" 1950
* Day, Clarence Henry "Hap" 1961
Delvecchio, Alex 1977
* Denneny, Cyril "Cy" 1959
Dionne, Marcel 1992
* Drillon, Gordon Arthur 1975
* Drinkwater, Charles Graham 1950
Dryden, Kenneth Wayne 1983
Duff, Dick 2006
* Dumart, Woodrow "Woody" 1992
* Dunderdale, Thomas 1974
* Durnan, William Ronald 1964
* Dutton, Mervyn A. "Red" 1958
* Dye, Cecil Henry "Babe" 1970
Esposito, Anthony James "Tony" 1988
Esposito, Philip Anthony 1984
* Farrell, Arthur F. 1965
Federko, Bernie 2002
Fetisov, Viacheslav 2001
Flaman, Ferdinand Charles "Fern" 1990
* Foyston, Frank 1958
Francis, Ron 2007
* Fredrickson, Frank 1958
Fuhr, Grant 2003
Gadsby, William Alexander 1970
Gainey, Bob 1992
* Gardiner, Charles Robert "Chuck" 1945
* Gardiner, Herbert Martin "Herb" 1958
* Gardner, James Henry "Jimmy" 1962
Gartner, Michael Alfred 2001
* Geoffrion, Jos. A. Bernard "Boom Boom" 1972
* Gerard, Eddie 1945
Giacomin, Edward "Eddie" 1987
Gilbert, Rodrigue Gabriel "Rod" 1982
Gillies, Clark 2002
* Gilmour, Hamilton Livingstone "Billy" 1962
* Goheen, Frank Xavier "Moose" 1952
* Goodfellow, Ebenezer R. "Ebbie" 1963
Goulet, Michel 1998
* Grant, Michael "Mike" 1950
* Green, Wilfred "Shorty" 1962
Gretzky, Wayne Douglas 1999
* Griffis, Silas Seth "Si" 1950
* Hainsworth, George 1961
Hall, Glenn Henry 1975
* Hall, Joseph Henry 1961
* Harvey, Douglas Norman 1973
Hawerchuk, Dale Martin 2001
* Hay, George 1958
* Hern, William Milton "Riley" 1962
* Hextall, Bryan Aldwyn 1969
* Holmes, Harry "Hap" 1972
* Hooper, Charles Thomas "Tom" 1962
* Horner, George Reginald "Red" 1965
* Horton, Miles Gilbert "Tim" 1977
Howe, Gordon 1972
* Howe, Sydney Harris 1965
Howell, Henry Vernon "Harry" 1979
**Hull, Brett 2009**
Hull, Robert Marvin 1983
* Hutton, John Bower "Bouse" 1962
* Hyland, Harry M. 1962
* Irvin, James Dickenson "Dick" 1958
* Jackson, Harvey "Busher" 1971
* Johnson, Ernest "Moose" 1952
* Johnson, Ivan "Ching" 1958
* Johnson, Thomas Christian 1970
* Joliat, Aurel 1947
* Keats, Gordon "Duke" 1958
Kelly, Leonard Patrick "Red" 1969
Kennedy, Theodore Samuel "Teeder" 1966
Keon, David Michael 1986
* Kharlamov, Valeri 2005
Kurri, Jari 2001
Lach, Elmer James 1966
Lafleur, Guy Damien 1988
LaFontaine, Pat 2003
* Lalonde, Edouard Charles "Newsy" 1950
Langway, Rod Corry 2002
Laperriere, Jacques 1987
Lapointe, Guy 1993
Laprade, Edgar 1993
Larionov, Igor 2008
* Laviolette, Jean Baptiste "Jack" 1962
* Lehman, Hugh 1958
Lemaire, Jacques Gerard 1984
Lemieux, Mario 1997
* LeSueur, Percy 1961
**Leetch, Brian 2009**
* Lewis, Herbert A. 1989
Lindsay, Robert Blake Theodore "Ted" 1966
* Lumley, Harry 1980
MacInnis, Al 2007
* MacKay, Duncan "Mickey" 1952
Mahovlich, Frank William 1981
* Malone, Joseph "Joe" 1950
* Mantha, Sylvio 1960
* Marshall, John "Jack" 1965
* Maxwell, Fred G. "Steamer" 1962
McDonald, Lanny 1992
* McGee, Frank 1945
* McGimsie, William George "Billy" 1962
* McNamara, George 1958
Messier, Mark 2007
Mikita, Stanley 1983
Moore, Richard Winston "Dickie" 1974
* Moran, Patrick Joseph "Paddy" 1958
* Morenz, Howie 1945
* Mosienko, William "Billy" 1965
Mullen, Joseph P. 2000
Murphy, Larry 2004
Neely, Cam 2005
* Nighbor, Frank 1947
* Noble, Edward Reginald "Reg" 1962
* O'Connor, Herbert William "Buddy" 1988
* Oliver, Harry 1967
Olmstead, Murray Bert "Bert" 1985
Orr, Robert Gordon 1979
Parent, Bernard Marcel 1984
Park, Douglas Bradford "Brad" 1988
* Patrick, Joseph Lynn 1980
* Patrick, Lester 1947
Perreault, Gilbert 1990
* Phillips, Tommy 1945
Pilote, Joseph Albert Pierre Paul 1975
* Pitre, Didier "Pit" 1962
* Plante, Joseph Jacques Omer 1978
Potvin, Denis 1991
* Pratt, Walter "Babe" 1966
* Primeau, A. Joseph 1963
Pronovost, Joseph René Marcel 1978
Pulford, Bob 1991
* Pulford, Harvey 1945
* Quackenbush, Hubert George "Bill" 1976
* Rankin, Frank 1961
Ratelle, Joseph Gilbert Yvan Jean "Jean" 1985
* Rayner, Claude Earl "Chuck" 1973
* Reardon, Kenneth Joseph 1966
Richard, Joseph Henri 1979
* Richard, Joseph Henri Maurice "Rocket" 1961
* Richardson, George Taylor 1950
* Roberts, Gordon 1971
Robinson, Larry 1995
**Robitaille, Luc 2009**
* Ross, Arthur Howey 1949
Roy, Patrick 2006
* Russel, Blair 1965
* Russell, Ernest 1965
* Ruttan, J.D. "Jack" 1962
Salming, Borje Anders 1996
Savard, Denis Joseph 2000
Savard, Serge 1986
* Sawchuk, Terrance Gordon "Terry" 1971
* Scanlan, Fred 1965

Schmidt, Milton Conrad "Milt" 1961
* Schriner, David "Sweeney" 1962
* Seibert, Earl Walter 1963
* Seibert, Oliver Levi 1961
* Shore, Edward W. "Eddie" 1947
Shutt, Stephen 1993
* Siebert, Albert C. "Babe" 1964
* Simpson, Harold Edward "Bullet Joe" 1962
Sittler, Darryl Glen 1989
* Smith, Alfred E. 1962
* Smith, Clint 1991
* Smith, Reginald "Hooley" 1972
* Smith, Thomas James 1973
Smith, William John "Billy" 1993
Stanley, Allan Herbert 1981
* Stanley, Russell "Barney" 1962
Stastny, Peter 1998
Stevens, Scott 2007
* Stewart, John Sherratt "Black Jack" 1964
* Stewart, Nelson "Nels" 1952
* Stuart, Bruce 1961
* Stuart, Hod 1945
* Taylor, Frederick "Cyclone" (O.B.E.) 1947
* Thompson, Cecil R. "Tiny" 1959
Tretiak, Vladislav 1989
* Trihey, Col. Harry J. 1950
Trottier, Bryan 1997
Ullman, Norman V. Alexander "Norm" 1982
* Vezina, Georges 1945
* Walker, John Phillip "Jack" 1960
* Walsh, Martin "Marty" 1962
* Watson, Harry E. 1962
* Watson, Harry 1994
* Weiland, Ralph "Cooney" 1971
* Westwick, Harry 1962
* Whitcroft, Fred 1962
* Wilson, Gordon Allan "Phat" 1962
* Worsley, Lorne John "Gump" 1980
* Worters, Roy 1969
**Yzerman, Steve 2009**

## BUILDERS

* Adams, Charles 1960
* Adams, Weston W. 1972
* Ahearn, Thomas Franklin "Frank" 1962
* Ahearne, John Francis "Bunny" 1977
* Allan, Sir Montagu (C.V.O.) 1945
Allen, Keith 1992
Arbour, Alger Joseph "Al" 1996
* Ballard, Harold Edwin 1977
* Bauer, Father David 1989
* Bickell, John Paris 1978
Bowman, Scotty 1991
* Brooks, Herb 2006
* Brown, George V. 1961
* Brown, Walter A. 1962
* Buckland, Frank 1975
Bush, Walter 2000
Butterfield, Jack Arlington 1980
* Calder, Frank 1947
* Campbell, Angus D. 1964
* Campbell, Clarence Sutherland 1966
* Cattarinich, Joseph 1977
* Chynoweth, Ed 2008
Costello, Murray 2005
* Dandurand, Joseph Viateur "Leo" 1963
* Dilio, Francis Paul 1964
* Dudley, George S. 1958
* Dunn, James A. 1968
Fletcher, Cliff 2004
Francis, Emile 1982
* Gibson, Dr. John L. "Jack" 1976
* Gorman, Thomas Patrick "Tommy" 1963
Gregory, Jim 2007
* Griffiths, Frank A. 1993
* Hanley, William 1986
* Hay, Charles 1974
* Hendy, James C. 1968
* Hewitt, Foster 1965
* Hewitt, William Abraham 1947
Hotchkiss, Harley 2006
* Hume, Fred J. 1962
Illitch, Mike 2003
* Imlach, George "Punch" 1984
* Ivan, Thomas N. 1974
* Jennings, William M. 1975
* Johnson, Bob 1992
* Juckes, Gordon W. 1979
* Kilpatrick, Gen. John Reed 1960
Kilrea, Brian Blair 2003
* Knox, Seymour H. III 1993
**Lamoriello, Lou 2009**
* Leader, George Alfred 1969
* LeBel, Robert 1970
* Lockhart, Thomas F. 1965
* Loicq, Paul 1961
* Mariucci, John 1985
* Mathers, Frank 1992
* McLaughlin, Major Frederic 1963
* Milford, John "Jake" 1984
* Molson, Hon. Hartland de Montarville 1973
Morrison, Ian "Scotty" 1999
* Murray, Monsignor Athol 1998
* Neilson, Roger 2002
* Nelson, Francis 1947
* Norris, Bruce A. 1969
* Norris, Sr., James 1958
* Norris, James Dougan 1962
* Northey, William M. 1947
* O'Brien, John Ambrose 1962
O'Neill, Brian 1994
* Page, Fred 1993
Patrick, Craig 2001
* Patrick, Frank 1950
* Pickard, Allan W. 1958
* Pilous, Rudy 1985
* Poile, Norman "Bud" 1990
* Pollock, Samuel Patterson Smyth 1978
* Raymond, Sen. Donat 1958
* Robertson, John Ross 1947
* Robinson, Claude C. 1947
* Ross, Philip D. 1976
* Sabetzki, Dr. Gunther 1995
Sather, Glen 1997
* Selke, Frank J. 1960
Sinden, Harry James 1983
* Smith, Frank D. 1962
* Smythe, Conn 1958
Snider, Edward M. 1988
* Stanley of Preston, Lord (G.C.B.) 1945
* Sutherland, Cap. James T. 1947
* Tarasov, Anatoli V. 1974
Torrey, Bill 1995
* Turner, Lloyd 1958
* Tutt, William Thayer 1978
* Voss, Carl Potter 1974
* Waghorne, Fred 1961
* Wirtz, Arthur Michael 1971
* Wirtz, William W. "Bill" 1976
Ziegler, John A. Jr. 1987

## REFEREES/LINESMEN

Armstrong, Neil 1991
* Ashley, John George 1981
Chadwick, William L. 1964
* D'Amico, John 1993
* Elliott, Chaucer 1961
* Hayes, George William 1988
* Hewitson, Robert W. 1963
* Ion, Fred J. "Mickey" 1961
Pavelich, Matt 1987
* Rodden, Michael J. "Mike" 1962
Scapinello, Ray 2008
* Smeaton, J. Cooper 1961
* Storey, Roy Alvin "Red" 1967
Udvari, Frank Joseph 1973
Van Hellemond, Andy 1999

*Luc Robitaille spent 14 seasons with the Kings during three different stints with Los Angeles over the course of his 19-year career. His career-best 63 goals in 1992-93 set a record for left wingers that was broken by Alex Ovechkin in 2007-08, but his lifetime totals of 668 goals and 1,394 points remain the best for anyone at that position through the 2008-09 season.*

## Foster Hewitt Memorial Award Winners

In recognition of members of the radio and television industry who made outstanding contributions to their profession and the game during their career in hockey broadcasting. Selected by the NHL Broadcasters' Association.

Cole, Bob, Hockey Night in Canada 1996
Cusick, Fred, Boston 1984
* Darling, Ted, Buffalo 1994
Emrick, Mike, New Jersey, U.S. networks, 2008
**Davidson, John, MSG Network/HNIC 2009**
* Gallivan, Danny, Montreal 1984
Garneau, Richard, Montreal 1999
* Hart, Gene, Philadelphia 1997
* Hewitt, Bill, Hockey Night in Canada 2007
* Hewitt, Foster, Toronto 1984
Irvin, Dick, Montreal 1988
Kaiton, Chuck, Hartford/Carolina 2004
* Kelly, Dan, St. Louis 1989
Lange, Mike, Pittsburgh 2001
* Lecavelier, René, Montreal 1984
Lynch, Budd, Detroit 1985
Maher, Peter, Calgary 2006
Martyn, Bruce, Detroit 1991
McDonald, Jiggs, Los Angeles, Atlanta, NY Islanders 1990
McFarlane, Brian, Hockey Night in Canada 1995
* McKnight, Wes, Toronto 1986
Meeker, Howie, Hockey Night in Canada 1998
Messina, Sal, New York 2005
Miller, Bob, Los Angeles 2000
Pettit, Lloyd, Chicago 1986
Phillips, Rod, Edmonton 2003
Robson, Jim, Vancouver 1992
Shaver, Al, Minnesota 1993
* Smith, Doug, Montreal 1985
Tremblay, Gilles, La Soirée du Hockey 2002
Wilson, Bob, Boston 1987

* Deceased

### Elmer Ferguson Memorial Award Winners

In recognition of distinguished members of the newspaper profession whose words have brought honor to journalism and to hockey. Selected by the Professional Hockey Writers' Association.

* Barton, Charlie, Buffalo-Courier Express 1985
* Beauchamp, Jacques, Montreal Matin/Journal de Montréal 1984
* Brennan, Bill, Detroit News 1987
* Burchard, Jim, New York World Telegram 1984
* Burnett, Red, Toronto Star 1984
* Carroll, Dink, Montreal Gazette 1984
* Coleman, Jim, Southam Newspapers 1984
Conway, Russ, Eagle-Tribune 1999
* Damata, Ted, Chicago Tribune 1984
Delano, Hugh, New York Post 1991
Desjardins, Marcel, Montréal La Presse 1984
Duhatschek, Eric, Calgary Herald/Globe and Mail 2001
* Dulmage, Jack, Windsor Star 1984
* Dunnell, Milt, Toronto Star 1984
Dupont, Kevin Paul, Boston Globe 2002
Elliott, Helene, Los Angeles Times 2005
Farber, Michael, Montreal Gazette/Sports Illustrated 2003
Fay, Dave, Washington Times 2007
* Ferguson, Elmer, Montreal Herald/Star 1984
* Fitzgerald, Tom, Boston Globe 1984
Frayne, Trent, Toronto Telegram/Globe and Mail/Sun 1984
Gatecliff, Jack, St. Catharines Standard 1995
Gross, George, Toronto Telegram/Sun 1985
Johnston, Dick, Buffalo News 1986
Kelley, Jim, Buffalo News 2004
* Laney, Al, New York Herald-Tribune 1984
* Larochelle, Claude, Le Soleil 1989
L'Esperance, Zotique, Journal de Montréal/ le Petit Journal 1985
* MacLeod, Rex, Toronto Globe and Mail/Star 1987
Matheson, Jim, Edmonton Journal 2000
* Mayer, Charles, Journal de Montréal/la Patrie 1985
* McKenzie, Ken, The Hockey News 1997
**Molinari, Dave Pittsburgh Post-Gazette 2009**
Monahan, Leo, Boston Daily Record/Record-American/ Herald American 1986
Moriarty, Tim, UPI/Newsday 1986
Morrison, Scott, Toronto Sun/Rogers Sportsnet 2006
* Nichols, Joe, New York Times 1984
* O'Brien, Andy, Weekend Magazine 1985
Orr, Frank, Toronto Star 1989
Olan, Ben, New York Associated Press 1987
* O'Meara, Basil, Montreal Star 1984
Pedneault, Yvon, La Presse/Journal de Montréal 1998
* Proudfoot, Jim, Toronto Star 1988
Raymond, Bertrand, Journal de Montréal 1990
Rosa, Fran, Boston Globe 1987
Stevens, Neil, Canadian Press 2008
Strachan, Al, Globe and Mail/Toronto Sun 1993
* Vipond, Jim, Toronto Globe and Mail 1984
Walter, Lewis, Detroit Times 1984
* Young, Scott, Toronto Globe and Mail/Telegram 1988

# United States Hockey Hall of Fame

On May 11, 2007, the U.S. Hockey Hall of Fame and USA Hockey came to a historic agreement that transferred rights to the selection process and induction event associated with the Hall, including the Wayne Gretzky International Award, to USA Hockey. As part of the agreement, the U.S. Hockey Hall of Fame Museum, located in Eveleth, Minn., formed a separate Board of Directors to govern the national shrine for American Hockey.

There are 143 enshrined members in the U.S. Hockey Hall of Fame (www.ushockeyhalloffame.com). New members are inducted annually and must have made a significant contribution to hockey in the United States during the course of their career. A special Wayne Gretzky International Award pays tribute to international individuals who have made major contributions to hockey in the USA.

The United States Hockey Hall of Fame Museum was opened on June 21, 1973. It is dedicated to honoring the sport of ice hockey in the United States by preserving those previous memories and legends of the game. It is located in Eveleth, Minn., 60 miles north of Duluth on Highway 53. The facility is open Memorial Day through Labor Day, Monday to Saturday, 9 a.m. to 5 p.m. and Sundays from 10 a.m. to 3 p.m. After Labor Day, it is open Friday through Sunday. Admission is $8.00 for adults, $7.00 for seniors and youths (13-17) and $6.00 for children (6-12). Children under 6 are free. For further information, call 800-443-7825 or 218-744-5167, or visit www.ushockeyhall.com.

## INDIVIDUALS

* Abel, Clarence "Taffy" 1973
* Almquist, Oscar 1983
**Amonte, Tony 2009**
* Baker, Hobart "Hobey" 1973
**Barrasso, Tom 2009**
* Bartholome, Earl 1977
Bessone, Amo 1992
* Bessone, Peter 1978
* Blake, Robert 1985
Boucha, Henry 1995
* Brimsek, Frank 1973
Brink, Milton "Curly" 2006
* Brooks, Herb 1990
Broten, Aaron 2007
Broten, Neal 2000
Brown, George V. 1973
Brown, Walter A. 1973
Bush, Walter 1980
Carpenter, Bobby 2007
Cavanagh, Joe 1994
Ceglarski, Len 1992
Chadwick, William 1974
* Chaisson, Ray 1974
* Chase, John P. 1973
Christian, Dave 2001
Christian, Roger 1989
Christian, William "Bill" 1984
Christiansen, Keith 2005
* Clark, Donald 1978
Claypool, James 1995
Cleary, Robert 1981
Cleary, William 1976
* Conroy, Anthony 1975
Coppo, Paul 2004
* Cunniff, John 2003
Curran, Mike 1998
* Dahlstrom, Carl "Cully" 1973
* Desjardins, Victor 1974
* Desmond, Richard 1988
* Dill, Robert 1979
Dougherty, Richard "Dick" 2003
* Everett, Doug 1974
Ftorek, Robbie 1991
* Fullerton, James 1992
Fusco, Mark 2002
Fusco, Scott 2002
Gambucci, Gary 2006
Gambucci, Sergio 1996
* Garrison, John B. 1973
Garrity, Jack 1986
* Gibson, J.C. "Doc" 1973
* Goheen, Frank "Moose" 1973
* Gordon, Malcolm K. 1973
Granato, Cammi 2008
Grant, Wally 1994
* Harding, Francis "Austie" 1975
* Harkness, Nevin D. "Ned" 1994
* Heyliger, Victor 1974
* Holt, Jr. Charles E. 1997
Housley, Phil 2004
Howe, Mark 2003
Hull, Brett 2008
* Iglehart, Stewart 1975
Ikola, Willard 1990
Ilitch, Mike 2004
* Jennings, William M. 1981
* Jeremiah, Edward J. 1973
* Johnson, Bob 1991
Johnson, Mark 2004
Johnson, Paul 2001
* Johnson, Virgil 1974
* Kahler, Nick 1980
* Karakas, Mike 1973
* Kelley, John "Snooks" 1974
Kelley, John H. "Jack" 1993
Kirrane, Jack 1987
LaFontaine, Pat 2003
* Lane, Myles J. 1973
Langevin, David R. 1993
Langway, Rod 1999
Larson, Reed 1996
**LeClair, John 2009**
Leetch, Brian 2008
* Linder, Joseph 1975
* Lockhart, Thomas F. 1973
* LoPresti, Sam L. 1973
MacDonald, Lane 2005
MacInnes, John 2007
* Mariucci, John 1973
* Marvin, Cal 1982
Matchefts, John 1991
* Mather, Bruce 1998
Mayasich, John 1976
McCartan, Jack 1983
Milbury, Mike 2006
* Moe, William 1974
Morrow, Ken 1995
* Moseley, Fred 1975
Mullen, Joe 1998
* Murray, Sr. Hugh "Muzz" 1987
Nanne, Lou 1998
* Nelson, Hubert "Hub" 1978
* Nyrop, William D. 1997
* Olson, Eddie 1977
* Owen, Jr. George 1973
Palazzari, Doug 2000
* Palmer, Winthrop 1973
Paradise, Robert 1989
Patrick, Craig 1996
Pleau, Larry 2000
* Pleban, Jon "Connie" 1990
* Purpur, Clifford "Fido" 1974
Ramsey, Mike 2001
Richter, Mike 2008
* Ridder, Robert 1976
Riley, Jack 1979
* Riley, Joe 2002
* Riley, William 1977
Roberts, Gordie 1999
* Roberts, Moe 2005
* Romnes, Elwin "Doc" 1973
* Rondeau, Richard 1985
* Ross, Larry 1988
* Schulz, Charles M. 1993
Sheehy, Timothy K. 1997
* Stewart, William 1982
* Thompson, Clifford R. 1973
Trumble, Harold 1985
* Tutt, William Thayer 1973
Vanbiesbrouck, John 2007
* Watson, Sid 1999
* Williams, Thomas 1981
Williamson, Murray 2005
Winsor, Alfred "Ralph" 1973
* Winters, Frank "Coddy" 1973
Wirtz, William W. "Bill" 1984
Woog, Doug 2002
* Wright, Lyle Z. 1973
* Yackel, Ken 1986
**Zamboni, Frank 2009**

## TEAMS

1960 Olympic Men's Team 2000
1980 Olympic Men's Team 2003
**1998 Olympic Women's Team 2009**

## WAYNE GRETZKY AWARD

Wayne Gretzky 1999
The Howe family 2000
Scotty Morrison 2001
Scotty Bowman 2002
Bobby Hull 2003
* Herb Brooks 2004
* Anatoli Tarasov 2008

* Deceased

# International Ice Hockey Federation Hall of Fame

The IIHF Hall of Fame was founded in 1997.

Candidates for election as Honoured Members in the player category shall be chosen on the basis of their playing ability, sportsmanship, character and their contribution to their team or teams and to the game of ice hockey in general.

Candidates for election as Honoured Members in the builder category shall be chosen on the basis of their coaching, managerial or executive ability, where applicable, their sportsmanship and character, and their contribution to their organization or organizations and to the game of ice hockey in general.

Candidates for election as Honoured Members in the referee or linesman category shall be chosen on the basis of their officiating ability, sportsmanship, character and their contribution to the game of ice hockey in general. The Paul Loicq Award, named for the longtime former IIHF president, is presented to honor a person for his service to the international hockey community.

Inductees' names are followed by their country and year of induction.

## PLAYERS

Alexandrov, Veniamin, RUS, 2007
Balderis, Helmut, LAT, 1998
Ball, Rudi, GER, 2004
Bergqvist, Sven, SWE, 1999
Bjorn, Lars, SWE, 1998
Bobrov, Vsevolod, RUS, 1997
Bourbonnais, Roger, CAN, 1999
Bouzek, Vladimir, CzRep, 2007
Bozon, Phillippe, FRA 2008
Bubnik, Vlastimil, CzRep, 1997
Cattini, Ferdinand, SUI, 1998
Cattini, Hans, SUI, 1998
Cerny, Josef, CzRep, 2007
Christian, Bill, USA, 1998
Cleary, Bill, USA, 1997
Cosby, Gerry, USA, 1997
Craig, Jim, USA, 1999
Curran, Mike, USA, 1999
Davydov, Vitaly, RUS, 2004
Drobny, Jaroslav, CzRep, 1997
Dzurilla, Vladimir, SVK, 1998
Erhardt, Carl, G.B., 1998
Fetisov, Viacheslav, RUS, 2005
Firsov, Anatoli, RUS, 1998
Golonka, Josef, SVK, 1998
Granato, Cammi, USA 2008
Gretzky, Wayne, CAN, 2000
Gruth, Henryk, POL, 2006
Gustafsson, Bengt-Ake, SWE, 2003
Gut, Karel, CzRep, 1998
Heaney, Geraldine, CAN 2008
Hedberg, Anders, SWE, 1997
**Hiti, Rudi, SLO, 2009**
Hlinka, Ivan, CzRep, 2002
Holecek, Jiri, CzRep, 1998
Holik, Jiri, CzRep, 1999
Holmqvist, Leif, SWE, 1999
Huck, Fran, CAN, 1999
Jaenecke, Gustav, GER, 1998
James, Angela, CAN 2008
Johnson, Mark, USA, 1999
Johnston, Marshall, CAN, 1998
Jonsson, Tomas, SWE, 2000
Jutila, Timo, FIN, 2003
**Kasatonov, Alexei, RUS, 2009**
Keinonen, Matti, FIN, 2002
Kharlamov, Valeri, RUS, 1998
Kiessling, Udo, GER, 2000
Kolliker, Jakob, SUI, 2007
Konovalenko, Viktor, RUS, 2007
Kuhnhackl, Erich, GER, 1997
Kurri, Jari, FIN, 2000
Kuzkin, Viktor, RUS, 2005
Lacarriere, Jacques, FRA, 1998
Larionov, Igor RUS 2008
Lemieux, Mario CAN 2008
Loktev, Konstantin, RUS, 2007
Loob, Hakan, SWE, 1998
Lundquist, Vic, CAN, 1997
Machac, Oldrich, CzRep, 1999
MacKenzie, Barry, CAN, 1999
Makarov, Sergei, RUS, 2001
Malecek, Josef, CzRep, 2003
Maltsev, Alexander, RUS, 1999
Marjamaki, Pekka, FIN, 1998
Martin, Seth, CAN, 1997
Martinec, Vladimir, CzRep, 2001
Mayasich, John, USA, 1997
Mayorov, Boris, RUS, 1999
McCartan, Jack, USA, 1998
McLeod, Jackie, CAN, 1999
Mikhailov, Boris, RUS, 2000
Nanne, Lou, USA, 2004
Naslund, Mats, SWE, 2005
Nedomansky, Vaclav, CzRep, 1997
Nilsson, Kent, SWE, 2006
Nilsson, Nisse, SWE, 2002
O'Malley, Terry, CAN, 1998
Oksanen, Lasse, FIN, 1999
Pana, Eduard, ROM, 1998
Patton, Peter, G.B., 2002
Peltonen, Esa, FIN, 2007
Petrov, Vladimir, RUS, 2006
Pettersson, Ronald, SWE, 2004
Pospisil, Frantisek, CzRep, 1999
Puschnig, Josef, AUT, 1999
Ragulin, Alexander, RUS, 1997
Rampf, Hans, GER, 2001
Rundqvist, Thomas, SWE, 2007
Salming, Borje, SWE, 1998
Schloder, Alois, GER, 2005
Sinden, Harry, CAN, 1997
Sologubov, Nikolai, RUS, 2004
Starshinov, Vyacheslav, RUS, 2007
Stastny, Peter, SVK, 2000
Sterner, Ulf, SWE, 2001
Stoltz, Roland, SWE, 1999
**Suchy, Jan, CzRep, 2009**
Tikal, Frantisek, CzRep, 2004
Torriani, Bibi, SUI, 1997
Tretiak, Vladislav, RUS, 1997
Tumba, Sven, SWE, 1997
Valtonen, Jorma, FIN, 1999
Vasiliev, Valeri, RUS, 1998
Wahlsten, Vladimir, FIN, 2006
Watson, Harry, CAN, 1998
Yakushev, Alexander, RUS, 2003
Ylonen, Urpo, FIN, 1997
Zabrodsky, Vladimir, CzRep, 1997
Ziesche, Joachim, GER, 1999
Tikhonov, Viktor, RUS, 1998
Tomita, Shoichi, JPN, 2006
Trumble, Hal, USA, 1999
Tsutsumi, Yoshiaki, JPN, 1999
Tutt, Thayer, USA, 2002
Unsinn, Xaver, GER, 1998
Wasservogel, Walter, AUT, 1997
Yurzinov, Vladimir, RUS, 2002

## BUILDERS

Ahearne, Bunny, G.B., 1997
Aljancic Sr., Ernest, SLO, 2002
Bauer, Father David, CAN, 1997
Berglund, Art USA 2008
Berglund, Curt, SWE, 2003
Bokac, Ludek, CzRep, 2007
Brooks, Herb, USA, 1999
Brown, Walter, USA, 1997
Buckna, Mike, CAN, 2004
**Bush, Walter Jr. USA, 2009**
Calcaterra, Enrico, ITA, 1999
Chernyshev, Arkady, RUS, 1999
Dimitriev, Igor, RUS, 2007
Dobida, Hans, AUT, 2007
Eklow, Rudolf, SWE, 1999
Grunander, Arne, SWE, 1997
Henschel, Heinz, GER, 2003
Hewitt, William, CAN, 1998
Holmes, Derek, CAN, 1999
Horsky, Ladislav, SVK, 2004
Hviid, Jorgen, DEN, 2005
Johannessen, Tore, NOR, 1999
Juckes, Gordon, CAN, 1997
Kawabuchi, Tsutomu, JPN, 2004
Khorozov, Anatoli, UKR, 2006
King, Dave, CAN, 2001
Kostka, Vladimir, CzRep, 1997
LeBel, Bob, CAN, 1997
Lindblad, Harry, FIN, 1999
Loicq, Paul, BEL, 1997
Luhti, Cesar W., SUI, 1998
Magnus, Louis, FRA, 1997
Pasztor, Gyorgy, HUN, 2001
Renwick, Gordon, CAN, 2002
Ridder, Bob, USA, 1998
Riley, Jack, USA, 1998
Sabetzki, Dr. Gunther, GER, 1997
Starovoitov, Andrei, RUS, 1997
Starsi, Jan, SVK, 1999
Stromberg, Arne, SWE, 1998
Stubb, Goran, FIN, 2000
Subrt, Miroslav, CzRep, 2004
Tarasov, Anatoli, RUS, 1997

## REFEREES

Adamec, Quido, CzRep, 2005
Dahlberg, Ove, SWE, 2004
Karandin, Yuri, RUS, 2004
Kompalla, Josef, GER, 2003
**Schell, Laszlo, HUN, 2009**
Wiitala, Unto, FIN, 2003

## PAUL LOICQ AWARD

Montag, Wolf-Dieter, GER, 1998
Neumayer, Roman, GER, 1999
Kukushkin, Vsevolod, RUS, 2000
Kataoka, Isao, JPN, 2001
Marsh, Pat, G.B., 2002
Nagobads, George, USA, 2003
Kukulowicz, Aggie, CAN, 2004
Hrabcek, Rita, AUS, 2005
Tovland, Bo, SWE, 2006
Nadin, Bob, CAN, 2007
Okolicany, Juraj, SVK 2008
**Griebel, Harald, GER, 2009**

## CENTENNIAL ALL-STAR TEAM (1908-2008)

Goaltender: Vladislav Tretiak, RUS
Defenseman: Viacheslav Fetisov, RUS
Defenseman: Borje Salming, SWE
Winger: Valeri Kharlamov, RUS
Winger: Sergei Makarov, RUS
Center: Wayne Gretzky, CAN

*Alexei Kasatonov began his hockey career with SKA Leningrad (1976 to 1978) and later played for CSKA Moscow (Central Red Army) from 1978 to 1989. His teams won the Soviet national title 11 times. Kasatonov joined the New Jersey Devils in 1989-90 and played seven seasons in the NHL with New Jersey, Anaheim, St. Louis and Boston. Internationally, he participated at the 1980, 1984 and 1988 Olympics and at eight World and European Championships. He won Olympic gold in Sarajevo in 1984 and Calgary in 1988 and won the World Championship five times.*

*Walter Bush Jr. has been involved with International hockey since he managed the U.S. national team in 1959. He has been the chairman of the board of USA Hockey since June of 2003 after serving as president of USA Hockey for nearly two decades. His interest in hockey began at the Breck School in Minneapolis, and he was responsible for bringing NHL hockey to Minnesota in 1967.*

# 2009 Stanley Cup Playoffs

# Results

## CONFERENCE QUARTER-FINALS

(Best-of-seven series)

### Eastern Conference

**Series 'A'**

| | | | |
|---|---|---|---|
| Thu. Apr. 16 | Montreal 2 | at | Boston 4 |
| Sat. Apr. 18 | Montreal 1 | at | Boston 5 |
| Mon. Apr. 20 | Boston 4 | at | Montreal 2 |
| Wed. Apr. 22 | Boston 4 | at | Montreal 1 |

**(Boston won series 4-0)**

**Series 'B'**

| | | | |
|---|---|---|---|
| Wed. Apr. 15 | NY Rangers 4 | at | Washington 3 |
| Sat. Apr. 18 | NY Rangers 1 | at | Washington 0 |
| Mon. Apr. 20 | Washington 4 | at | NY Rangers 0 |
| Wed. Apr. 22 | Washington 1 | at | NY Rangers 2 |
| Fri. Apr. 24 | NY Rangers 0 | at | Washington 4 |
| Sun. Apr. 26 | Washington 5 | at | NY Rangers 3 |
| Tue. Apr. 28 | NY Rangers 1 | at | Washington 2 |

**(Washington won series 4-3)**

**Series 'C'**

| | | | |
|---|---|---|---|
| Wed. Apr. 15 | Carolina 1 | at | New Jersey 4 |
| Fri. Apr. 17 | Carolina 2 | at | New Jersey 1* |
| Sun. Apr. 19 | New Jersey 3 | at | Carolina 2** |
| Tue. Apr. 21 | New Jersey 3 | at | Carolina 4 |
| Thu. Apr. 23 | Carolina 0 | at | New Jersey 1 |
| Sun. Apr. 26 | New Jersey 0 | at | Carolina 4 |
| Tue. Apr. 28 | Carolina 4 | at | New Jersey 3 |

*Tim Gleason scored at 2:40 of overtime
**Travis Zajac scored at 4:58 of overtime

**(Carolina won series 4-3)**

**Series 'D'**

| | | | |
|---|---|---|---|
| Wed. Apr. 15 | Philadelphia 1 | at | Pittsburgh 4 |
| Fri. Apr. 17 | Philadelphia 2 | at | Pittsburgh 3* |
| Sun. Apr. 19 | Pittsburgh 3 | at | Philadelphia 6 |
| Tue. Apr. 21 | Pittsburgh 3 | at | Philadelphia 1 |
| Thu. Apr. 23 | Philadelphia 3 | at | Pittsburgh 0 |
| Sat. Apr. 25 | Pittsburgh 5 | at | Philadelphia 3 |

*Bill Guerin scored at 18:29 of overtime

**(Pittsburgh won series 4-2)**

### Western Conference

**Series 'E'**

| | | | |
|---|---|---|---|
| Thu. Apr. 16 | Anaheim 2 | at | San Jose 0 |
| Sun. Apr. 19 | Anaheim 3 | at | San Jose 2 |
| Tue. Apr. 21 | San Jose 4 | at | Anaheim 3 |
| Thu. Apr. 23 | San Jose 0 | at | Anaheim 4 |
| Sat. Apr. 25 | Anaheim 2 | at | San Jose 3* |
| Mon. Apr. 27 | San Jose 1 | at | Anaheim 4 |

*Patrick Marleau scored at 6:02 of overtime

**(Anaheim won series 4-2)**

**Series 'F'**

| | | | |
|---|---|---|---|
| Thu. Apr. 16 | Columbus 1 | at | Detroit 4 |
| Sat. Apr. 18 | Columbus 0 | at | Detroit 4 |
| Tue. Apr. 21 | Detroit 4 | at | Columbus 1 |
| Thu. Apr. 23 | Detroit 6 | at | Columbus 5 |

**(Detroit won series 4-0)**

**Series 'G'**

| | | | |
|---|---|---|---|
| Wed. Apr. 15 | St. Louis 1 | at | Vancouver 2 |
| Fri. Apr. 17 | St. Louis 0 | at | Vancouver 3 |
| Sun. Apr. 19 | Vancouver 3 | at | St. Louis 2 |
| Tue. Apr. 21 | Vancouver 3 | at | St. Louis 2* |

*Alexandre Burrows scored at 19:41 of overtime

**(Vancouver won series 4-0)**

**Series 'H'**

| | | | |
|---|---|---|---|
| Thu. Apr. 16 | Calgary 2 | at | Chicago 3* |
| Sat. Apr. 18 | Calgary 2 | at | Chicago 3 |
| Mon. Apr. 20 | Chicago 2 | at | Calgary 4 |
| Wed. Apr. 22 | Chicago 4 | at | Calgary 6 |
| Sat. Apr. 25 | Calgary 1 | at | Chicago 5 |
| Mon. Apr. 27 | Chicago 4 | at | Calgary 1 |

*Martin Havlat scored at 0:12 of overtime

**(Chicago won series 4-2)**

## CONFERENCE SEMI-FINALS

(Best-of-seven series)

### Eastern Conference

**Series 'I'**

| | | | |
|---|---|---|---|
| Fri. May 1 | Carolina 1 | at | Boston 4 |
| Sun. May 3 | Carolina 3 | at | Boston 0 |
| Wed. May 6 | Boston 2 | at | Carolina 3* |
| Fri. May 8 | Boston 1 | at | Carolina 4 |
| Sun. May 10 | Carolina 0 | at | Boston 4 |
| Tue. May 12 | Boston 4 | at | Carolina 2 |
| Thu. May 14 | Carolina 3 | at | Boston 2** |

*Jussi Jokinen scored at 2:48 of overtime
**Scott Walker scored at 18:46 of overtime

**(Carolina won series 4-3)**

**Series 'J'**

| | | | |
|---|---|---|---|
| Sat. May 2 | Pittsburgh 2 | at | Washington 3 |
| Mon. May 4 | Pittsburgh 3 | at | Washington 4 |
| Wed. May 6 | Washington 2 | at | Pittsburgh 3* |
| Fri. May 8 | Washington 3 | at | Pittsburgh 5 |
| Sat. May 9 | Pittsburgh 4 | at | Washington 3** |
| Mon. May 11 | Washington 5 | at | Pittsburgh 4*** |
| Wed. May 13 | Pittsburgh 6 | at | Washington 2 |

*Kris Letang scored at 11:23 of overtime
**Evgeni Malkin scored at 3:28 of overtime
***David Steckel scored at 6:22 of overtime

**(Pittsburgh won series 4-3)**

### Western Conference

**Series 'K'**

| | | | |
|---|---|---|---|
| Fri. May 1 | Anaheim 2 | at | Detroit 3 |
| Sun. May 3 | Anaheim 4 | at | Detroit 3* |
| Tue. May 5 | Detroit 1 | at | Anaheim 2 |
| Thu. May 7 | Detroit 6 | at | Anaheim 3 |
| Sun. May 10 | Anaheim 1 | at | Detroit 4 |
| Tue. May 12 | Detroit 1 | at | Anaheim 2 |
| Thu. May 14 | Anaheim 3 | at | Detroit 4 |

*Todd Marchant scored at 41:15 of overtime

**(Detroit won series 4-3)**

**Series 'L'**

| | | | |
|---|---|---|---|
| Thu. Apr. 30 | Chicago 3 | at | Vancouver 5 |
| Sat. May 2 | Chicago 6 | at | Vancouver 3 |
| Tue. May 5 | Vancouver 3 | at | Chicago 1 |
| Thu. May 7 | Vancouver 1 | at | Chicago 2* |
| Sat. May 9 | Chicago 4 | at | Vancouver 2 |
| Mon. May 11 | Vancouver 5 | at | Chicago 7 |

*Andrew Ladd scored at 2:52 of overtime

**(Chicago won series 4-2)**

## CONFERENCE FINALS

(Best-of-seven series)

### Eastern Conference

**Series 'M'**

| | | | |
|---|---|---|---|
| Mon. May 18 | Carolina 2 | at | Pittsburgh 3 |
| Thu. May 21 | Carolina 4 | at | Pittsburgh 7 |
| Sat. May 23 | Pittsburgh 6 | at | Carolina 2 |
| Tue. May 26 | Pittsburgh 4 | at | Carolina 1 |

**(Pittsburgh won series 4-0)**

### Western Conference

**Series 'N'**

| | | | |
|---|---|---|---|
| Sun. May 17 | Chicago 2 | at | Detroit 5 |
| Tue. May 19 | Chicago 2 | at | Detroit 3* |
| Fri. May 22 | Detroit 3 | at | Chicago 4** |
| Sun. May 24 | Detroit 6 | at | Chicago 1 |
| Wed. May 27 | Chicago 1 | at | Detroit 2*** |

*Mikael Samuelsson scored at 5:14 of overtime
**Patrick Sharp scored at 1:52 of overtime
***Darren Helm scored at 3:58 of overtime

**(Detroit won series 4-1)**

## STANLEY CUP FINAL

(Best-of-seven series)

**Series 'O'**

| | | | |
|---|---|---|---|
| Sat. May 30 | Pittsburgh 1 | at | Detroit 3 |
| Sun. May 31 | Pittsburgh 1 | at | Detroit 3 |
| Tue. June 2 | Detroit 2 | at | Pittsburgh 4 |
| Thu. June 4 | Detroit 2 | at | Pittsburgh 4 |
| Sat. June 6 | Pittsburgh 0 | at | Detroit 5 |
| Tue. June 9 | Detroit 1 | at | Pittsburgh 2 |
| Fri. June 12 | Pittsburgh 2 | at | Detroit 1 |

**(Pittsburgh won series 4-3)**

## Team Playoff Records

| | GP | W | L | GF | GA | % |
|---|---|---|---|---|---|---|
| Pittsburgh | 24 | 16 | 8 | 79 | 64 | .667 |
| Detroit | 23 | 15 | 8 | 76 | 48 | .652 |
| Chicago | 17 | 9 | 8 | 54 | 54 | .529 |
| Carolina | 18 | 8 | 10 | 42 | 52 | .444 |
| Boston | 11 | 7 | 4 | 34 | 22 | .636 |
| Anaheim | 13 | 7 | 6 | 35 | 32 | .538 |
| Washington | 14 | 7 | 7 | 41 | 38 | .500 |
| Vancouver | 10 | 6 | 4 | 30 | 28 | .600 |
| New Jersey | 7 | 3 | 4 | 15 | 17 | .429 |
| Ny Rangers | 7 | 3 | 4 | 11 | 19 | .429 |
| Philadelphia | 6 | 2 | 4 | 16 | 18 | .333 |
| Calgary | 6 | 2 | 4 | 16 | 21 | .333 |
| San Jose | 6 | 2 | 4 | 10 | 18 | .333 |
| St. Louis | 4 | 0 | 4 | 5 | 11 | .000 |
| Columbus | 4 | 0 | 4 | 7 | 18 | .000 |
| Montreal | 4 | 0 | 4 | 6 | 17 | .000 |

# Individual Leaders

**Abbreviations: GP** – games played; **G** – goals; **A** – assists; **PTS** – points; **+/–** – difference between Goals For (**GF**) scored when a player is on the ice with his team at even strength or shorthanded and Goals Against (**GA**) scored when the same player is on the ice with his team at even strength or on a power play; **PIM** – penalties in minutes; **PP** – power play goals; **SH** – shorthanded goals; **GW** – game-winning goals; **OT** – overtime goals; **S** – shots on goal; **%** – percentage of shots resulting in goals.

## Playoff Scoring Leaders

| Player | Team | GP | G | A | PTS | +/– | PIM | PP | SH | GW | OT | S | % |
|---|---|---|---|---|---|---|---|---|---|---|---|---|---|
| Evgeni Malkin | Pittsburgh | 24 | 14 | 22 | 36 | 3 | 51 | 7 | 0 | 3 | 1 | 104 | 13.5 |
| Sidney Crosby | Pittsburgh | 24 | 15 | 16 | 31 | 9 | 14 | 5 | 0 | 2 | 0 | 79 | 19.0 |
| Henrik Zetterberg | Detroit | 23 | 11 | 13 | 24 | 13 | 13 | 4 | 0 | 0 | 0 | 82 | 13.4 |
| Johan Franzen | Detroit | 23 | 12 | 11 | 23 | 8 | 12 | 4 | 0 | 3 | 0 | 72 | 16.7 |
| Alex Ovechkin | Washington | 14 | 11 | 10 | 21 | 10 | 8 | 3 | 0 | 1 | 0 | 90 | 12.2 |
| Ryan Getzlaf | Anaheim | 13 | 4 | 14 | 18 | 3 | 25 | 1 | 0 | 0 | 0 | 25 | 16.0 |
| Nicklas Lidstrom | Detroit | 21 | 4 | 12 | 16 | 11 | 6 | 3 | 0 | 1 | 0 | 59 | 6.8 |
| Valtteri Filppula | Detroit | 23 | 3 | 13 | 16 | 8 | 8 | 1 | 0 | 1 | 0 | 35 | 8.6 |
| Eric Staal | Carolina | 18 | 10 | 5 | 15 | 3- | 4 | 3 | 0 | 1 | 0 | 73 | 13.7 |
| Daniel Cleary | Detroit | 23 | 9 | 6 | 15 | 17 | 12 | 0 | 0 | 3 | 0 | 57 | 15.8 |
| Bill Guerin | Pittsburgh | 24 | 7 | 8 | 15 | 8 | 15 | 2 | 0 | 2 | 1 | 70 | 10.0 |
| Marian Hossa | Detroit | 23 | 6 | 9 | 15 | 5 | 10 | 2 | 1 | 1 | 0 | 100 | 6.0 |
| Martin Havlat | Chicago | 16 | 5 | 10 | 15 | 0 | 8 | 0 | 0 | 1 | 1 | 35 | 14.3 |
| Nicklas Backstrom | Washington | 14 | 3 | 12 | 15 | 3 | 8 | 2 | 0 | 0 | 0 | 33 | 9.1 |
| Patrick Kane | Chicago | 16 | 9 | 5 | 14 | 9- | 12 | 2 | 0 | 0 | 0 | 34 | 26.5 |
| Corey Perry | Anaheim | 13 | 8 | 6 | 14 | 2 | 36 | 2 | 0 | 1 | 0 | 41 | 19.5 |
| Ruslan Fedotenko | Pittsburgh | 24 | 7 | 7 | 14 | 9 | 4 | 0 | 0 | 0 | 0 | 58 | 12.1 |
| Alexander Semin | Washington | 14 | 5 | 9 | 14 | 1- | 16 | 1 | 0 | 1 | 0 | 42 | 11.9 |
| Sergei Gonchar | Pittsburgh | 22 | 3 | 11 | 14 | 3 | 12 | 2 | 0 | 2 | 0 | 41 | 7.3 |
| Chris Kunitz | Pittsburgh | 24 | 1 | 13 | 14 | 3 | 19 | 0 | 0 | 0 | 0 | 46 | 2.2 |
| Maxime Talbot | Pittsburgh | 24 | 8 | 5 | 13 | 8 | 19 | 0 | 0 | 2 | 0 | 37 | 21.6 |
| Jonathan Toews | Chicago | 17 | 7 | 6 | 13 | 1- | 26 | 5 | 0 | 2 | 0 | 43 | 16.3 |
| Marc Savard | Boston | 11 | 6 | 7 | 13 | 2 | 4 | 3 | 0 | 2 | 0 | 17 | 35.3 |
| Michael Ryder | Boston | 11 | 5 | 8 | 13 | 4 | 8 | 1 | 0 | 1 | 0 | 25 | 20.0 |
| Kris Letang | Pittsburgh | 23 | 4 | 9 | 13 | 1 | 26 | 2 | 0 | 1 | 1 | 54 | 7.4 |

## Playoff Defencemen Scoring Leaders

| Player | Team | GP | G | A | PTS | +/– | PIM | PP | SH | GW | OT | S | % |
|---|---|---|---|---|---|---|---|---|---|---|---|---|---|
| Nicklas Lidstrom | Detroit | 21 | 4 | 12 | 16 | 11 | 6 | 3 | 0 | 1 | 0 | 59 | 6.8 |
| Sergei Gonchar | Pittsburgh | 22 | 3 | 11 | 14 | 3 | 12 | 2 | 0 | 2 | 0 | 41 | 7.3 |
| Kris Letang | Pittsburgh | 23 | 4 | 9 | 13 | 1 | 26 | 2 | 0 | 1 | 1 | 54 | 7.4 |
| Brian Rafalski | Detroit | 18 | 3 | 9 | 12 | 11 | 11 | 3 | 0 | 1 | 0 | 24 | 12.5 |
| Brent Seabrook | Chicago | 17 | 1 | 11 | 12 | 0 | 14 | 1 | 0 | 0 | 0 | 36 | 2.8 |
| Scott Niedermayer | Anaheim | 13 | 3 | 7 | 10 | 0 | 11 | 3 | 0 | 2 | 0 | 32 | 9.4 |
| Chris Pronger | Anaheim | 13 | 2 | 8 | 10 | 4 | 12 | 1 | 0 | 0 | 0 | 27 | 7.4 |
| Brian Campbell | Chicago | 17 | 2 | 8 | 10 | 0 | 0 | 2 | 0 | 0 | 0 | 27 | 7.4 |
| Cam Barker | Chicago | 17 | 3 | 6 | 9 | 3- | 2 | 0 | 0 | 0 | 0 | 32 | 9.4 |
| Brad Stuart | Detroit | 23 | 3 | 6 | 9 | 5 | 12 | 1 | 0 | 0 | 0 | 34 | 8.8 |
| Niklas Kronvall | Detroit | 23 | 2 | 7 | 9 | 4 | 33 | 2 | 0 | 0 | 0 | 32 | 6.3 |
| Mike Green | Washington | 14 | 1 | 8 | 9 | 5- | 12 | 1 | 0 | 0 | 0 | 24 | 4.2 |
| *Jonathan Ericsson | Detroit | 22 | 4 | 4 | 8 | 9 | 25 | 0 | 0 | 1 | 0 | 33 | 12.1 |
| Alexander Edler | Vancouver | 10 | 1 | 7 | 8 | 2- | 6 | 1 | 0 | 0 | 0 | 14 | 7.1 |

# GOALTENDING LEADERS

## Goals Against Average

| Goaltender | Team | GP | Mins | GA | Avg. |
|---|---|---|---|---|---|
| Tim Thomas | Boston | 11 | 680 | 21 | 1.85 |
| Chris Osgood | Detroit | 23 | 1406 | 47 | 2.01 |
| Jonas Hiller | Anaheim | 13 | 807 | 30 | 2.23 |
| Martin Brodeur | New Jersey | 7 | 427 | 17 | 2.39 |
| Roberto Luongo | Vancouver | 10 | 618 | 26 | 2.52 |
| *Semyon Varlamov | Washington | 13 | 759 | 32 | 2.53 |
| Marc-Andre Fleury | Pittsburgh | 24 | 1447 | 63 | 2.61 |
| Cam Ward | Carolina | 18 | 1101 | 49 | 2.67 |
| Nikolai Khabibulin | Chicago | 15 | 881 | 43 | 2.93 |

## Wins

| Goaltender | Team | GP | Mins | W | L |
|---|---|---|---|---|---|
| Marc-Andre Fleury | Pittsburgh | 24 | 1447 | 16 | 8 |
| Chris Osgood | Detroit | 23 | 1406 | 15 | 8 |
| Nikolai Khabibulin | Chicago | 15 | 881 | 8 | 6 |
| Cam Ward | Carolina | 18 | 1101 | 8 | 10 |
| Tim Thomas | Boston | 11 | 680 | 7 | 4 |
| *Semyon Varlamov | Washington | 13 | 759 | 7 | 6 |
| Jonas Hiller | Anaheim | 13 | 807 | 7 | 6 |

## Save Percentage

| Goaltender | Team | GP | Mins | GA | SA | S% | W | L |
|---|---|---|---|---|---|---|---|---|
| Jonas Hiller | Anaheim | 13 | 807 | 30 | 524 | .943 | 7 | 6 |
| Tim Thomas | Boston | 11 | 680 | 21 | 323 | .935 | 7 | 4 |
| Martin Brodeur | New Jersey | 7 | 427 | 17 | 239 | .929 | 3 | 4 |
| Chris Osgood | Detroit | 23 | 1406 | 47 | 637 | .926 | 15 | 8 |
| *Semyon Varlamov | Washington | 13 | 759 | 32 | 389 | .918 | 7 | 6 |

## Shutouts

| Goaltender | Team | GP | Mins | SO |
|---|---|---|---|---|
| *Semyon Varlamov | Washington | 13 | 759 | 2 |
| Jonas Hiller | Anaheim | 13 | 807 | 2 |
| Cam Ward | Carolina | 18 | 1101 | 2 |
| Chris Osgood | Detroit | 23 | 1406 | 2 |
| Martin Biron | Philadelphia | 6 | 375 | 1 |
| Henrik Lundqvist | Ny Rangers | 7 | 380 | 1 |
| Martin Brodeur | New Jersey | 7 | 427 | 1 |
| Roberto Luongo | Vancouver | 10 | 618 | 1 |
| Tim Thomas | Boston | 11 | 680 | 1 |

* Rookie

## Goals

| Name | Team | GP | G |
|---|---|---|---|
| Sidney Crosby | Pittsburgh | 24 | 15 |
| Evgeni Malkin | Pittsburgh | 24 | 14 |
| Johan Franzen | Detroit | 23 | 12 |
| Alex Ovechkin | Washington | 14 | 11 |
| Henrik Zetterberg | Detroit | 23 | 11 |
| Eric Staal | Carolina | 18 | 10 |
| Patrick Kane | Chicago | 16 | 9 |
| Daniel Cleary | Detroit | 23 | 9 |
| Corey Perry | Anaheim | 13 | 8 |
| Maxime Talbot | Pittsburgh | 24 | 8 |
| Patrick Sharp | Chicago | 17 | 7 |
| Jonathan Toews | Chicago | 17 | 7 |
| Jussi Jokinen | Carolina | 18 | 7 |
| Bill Guerin | Pittsburgh | 24 | 7 |
| Ruslan Fedotenko | Pittsburgh | 24 | 7 |

## Assists

| Name | Team | GP | A |
|---|---|---|---|
| Evgeni Malkin | Pittsburgh | 24 | 22 |
| Sidney Crosby | Pittsburgh | 24 | 16 |
| Ryan Getzlaf | Anaheim | 13 | 14 |
| Henrik Zetterberg | Detroit | 23 | 13 |
| Valtteri Filppula | Detroit | 23 | 13 |
| Chris Kunitz | Pittsburgh | 24 | 13 |
| Nicklas Backstrom | Washington | 14 | 12 |
| Nicklas Lidstrom | Detroit | 21 | 12 |
| Brent Seabrook | Chicago | 17 | 11 |
| Sergei Gonchar | Pittsburgh | 22 | 11 |
| Johan Franzen | Detroit | 23 | 11 |
| Alex Ovechkin | Washington | 14 | 10 |
| Martin Havlat | Chicago | 16 | 10 |

## Power-play Goals

| Name | Team | GP | PP |
|---|---|---|---|
| Evgeni Malkin | Pittsburgh | 24 | 7 |
| Jonathan Toews | Chicago | 17 | 5 |
| Sidney Crosby | Pittsburgh | 24 | 5 |
| Henrik Zetterberg | Detroit | 23 | 4 |
| Johan Franzen | Detroit | 23 | 4 |

## Game-winning Goals

| Name | Team | GP | GW |
|---|---|---|---|
| Jussi Jokinen | Carolina | 18 | 3 |
| Daniel Cleary | Detroit | 23 | 3 |
| Johan Franzen | Detroit | 23 | 3 |
| Evgeni Malkin | Pittsburgh | 24 | 3 |
| Tyler Kennedy | Pittsburgh | 24 | 3 |

## Shorthanded Goals

| Name | Team | GP | SH |
|---|---|---|---|
| Simon Gagne | Philadelphia | 6 | 1 |
| Matt Bradley | Washington | 14 | 1 |
| Milan Jurcina | Washington | 14 | 1 |
| Dave Bolland | Chicago | 17 | 1 |
| Matt Cullen | Carolina | 18 | 1 |
| Marian Hossa | Detroit | 23 | 1 |
| Jordan Staal | Pittsburgh | 24 | 1 |

## Overtime Goals

| Name | Team | GP | OT |
|---|---|---|---|
| Patrick Marleau | San Jose | 6 | 1 |
| Travis Zajac | New Jersey | 7 | 1 |
| Alexandre Burrows | Vancouver | 10 | 1 |
| Todd Marchant | Anaheim | 13 | 1 |
| David Steckel | Washington | 14 | 1 |
| Martin Havlat | Chicago | 16 | 1 |
| Patrick Sharp | Chicago | 17 | 1 |
| Andrew Ladd | Chicago | 17 | 1 |
| Scott Walker | Carolina | 18 | 1 |
| Tim Gleason | Carolina | 18 | 1 |
| Jussi Jokinen | Carolina | 18 | 1 |
| Mikael Samuelsson | Detroit | 23 | 1 |
| Kris Letang | Pittsburgh | 23 | 1 |
| *Darren Helm | Detroit | 23 | 1 |
| Bill Guerin | Pittsburgh | 24 | 1 |
| Evgeni Malkin | Pittsburgh | 24 | 1 |

## Shots

| Name | Team | GP | S |
|---|---|---|---|
| Evgeni Malkin | Pittsburgh | 24 | 104 |
| Marian Hossa | Detroit | 23 | 100 |
| Alex Ovechkin | Washington | 14 | 90 |
| Henrik Zetterberg | Detroit | 23 | 82 |
| Mikael Samuelsson | Detroit | 23 | 79 |
| Sidney Crosby | Pittsburgh | 24 | 79 |

## Plus/Minus

| Name | Team | GP | +/– |
|---|---|---|---|
| Daniel Cleary | Detroit | 23 | 17 |
| Henrik Zetterberg | Detroit | 23 | 13 |
| Milan Lucic | Boston | 10 | 12 |
| Brian Rafalski | Detroit | 18 | 11 |
| Nicklas Lidstrom | Detroit | 21 | 11 |

## TEAMS' PLAYOFF HOME/ROAD RECORD

| | HOME | | | | | | ROAD | | | | | |
|---|---|---|---|---|---|---|---|---|---|---|---|---|
| Team | GP | W | L | GF | GA | Win % | GP | W | L | GF | GA | Win % |
| PIT | 11 | 9 | 2 | 39 | 27 | .818 | 13 | 7 | 6 | 40 | 37 | .538 |
| DET | 13 | 11 | 2 | 44 | 20 | .846 | 10 | 4 | 6 | 32 | 28 | .400 |
| CHI | 8 | 6 | 2 | 26 | 23 | .750 | 9 | 3 | 6 | 28 | 31 | .333 |
| CAR | 8 | 4 | 4 | 22 | 23 | .500 | 10 | 4 | 6 | 20 | 29 | .400 |
| BOS | 6 | 4 | 2 | 19 | 10 | .667 | 5 | 3 | 2 | 15 | 12 | .600 |
| ANA | 6 | 4 | 2 | 18 | 13 | .667 | 7 | 3 | 4 | 17 | 19 | .429 |
| WSH | 8 | 4 | 4 | 21 | 21 | .500 | 6 | 3 | 3 | 20 | 17 | .500 |
| VAN | 5 | 3 | 2 | 15 | 14 | .600 | 5 | 3 | 2 | 15 | 14 | .600 |
| N.J. | 4 | 2 | 2 | 9 | 7 | .500 | 3 | 1 | 2 | 6 | 10 | .333 |
| NYR | 3 | 1 | 2 | 5 | 10 | .333 | 4 | 2 | 2 | 6 | 9 | .500 |
| PHI | 3 | 1 | 2 | 10 | 11 | .333 | 3 | 1 | 2 | 6 | 7 | .333 |
| CGY | 3 | 2 | 1 | 11 | 10 | .667 | 3 | 0 | 3 | 5 | 11 | .000 |
| S.J. | 3 | 1 | 2 | 5 | 7 | .333 | 3 | 1 | 2 | 5 | 11 | .333 |
| ST.L. | 2 | 0 | 2 | 4 | 6 | .000 | 2 | 0 | 2 | 1 | 5 | .000 |
| CBJ | 2 | 0 | 2 | 6 | 10 | .000 | 2 | 0 | 2 | 1 | 8 | .000 |
| MTL | 2 | 0 | 2 | 3 | 8 | .000 | 2 | 0 | 2 | 3 | 9 | .000 |
| **Total** | **87** | **52** | **35** | **257** | **220** | **.598** | **87** | **35** | **52** | **220** | **257** | **.402** |

## TEAMS' POWER-PLAY RECORD

**Abbreviations: ADV**-total advantages; **PPGF**-power play goals for; **%** arrived by dividing number of power-play goals by total advantages.

| HOME | | | | | | ROAD | | | | | OVERALL | | | | |
|---|---|---|---|---|---|---|---|---|---|---|---|---|---|---|---|
| | Team | GP | ADV | PPGF | % | Team | GP | ADV | PPGF | % | Team | GP | ADV | PPGF | % |
| 1 | CBJ | 2 | 6 | 3 | 50.0 | S.J | 3 | 9 | 3 | 33.3 | CHI | 17 | 68 | 19 | 27.9 |
| 2 | CHI | 8 | 30 | 8 | 26.7 | ANA | 7 | 24 | 7 | 29.2 | ANA | 13 | 50 | 13 | 26.0 |
| 3 | VAN | 5 | 26 | 6 | 23.1 | CHI | 9 | 38 | 11 | 28.9 | VAN | 10 | 44 | 11 | 25.0 |
| 4 | ANA | 6 | 26 | 6 | 23.1 | VAN | 5 | 18 | 5 | 27.8 | DET | 23 | 97 | 23 | 23.7 |
| 5 | PIT | 11 | 51 | 11 | 21.6 | DET | 10 | 41 | 11 | 26.8 | CBJ | 4 | 13 | 3 | 23.1 |
| 6 | DET | 13 | 56 | 12 | 21.4 | WSH | 6 | 24 | 6 | 25.0 | WSH | 14 | 52 | 11 | 21.2 |
| 7 | WSH | 8 | 28 | 5 | 17.9 | PIT | 13 | 46 | 9 | 19.6 | PIT | 24 | 97 | 20 | 20.6 |
| 8 | BOS | 6 | 29 | 5 | 17.2 | PHI | 3 | 13 | 2 | 15.4 | S.J | 6 | 24 | 4 | 16.7 |
| 9 | N.J | 4 | 18 | 3 | 16.7 | NYR | 4 | 14 | 2 | 14.3 | BOS | 11 | 43 | 6 | 14.0 |
| 10 | CGY | 3 | 7 | 1 | 14.3 | STL | 2 | 11 | 1 | 9.1 | PHI | 6 | 30 | 4 | 13.3 |
| 11 | CAR | 8 | 32 | 4 | 12.5 | CGY | 3 | 11 | 1 | 9.1 | NYR | 7 | 31 | 4 | 12.9 |
| 12 | NYR | 3 | 17 | 2 | 11.8 | BOS | 5 | 14 | 1 | 7.1 | CGY | 6 | 18 | 2 | 11.1 |
| 13 | PHI | 3 | 17 | 2 | 11.8 | CAR | 10 | 28 | 2 | 7.1 | N.J | 7 | 27 | 3 | 11.1 |
| 14 | S.J | 3 | 15 | 1 | 6.7 | MTL | 2 | 3 | 0 | 0.0 | CAR | 18 | 60 | 6 | 10.0 |
| 15 | MTL | 2 | 5 | 0 | 0.0 | CBJ | 2 | 7 | 0 | 0.0 | STL | 4 | 24 | 1 | 4.2 |
| 16 | STL | 2 | 13 | 0 | 0.0 | N.J | 3 | 9 | 0 | 0.0 | MTL | 4 | 8 | 0 | 0.0 |
| **Total** | | **87** | **376** | **69** | **18.4** | | **87** | **310** | **61** | **19.7** | | **87** | **686** | **130** | **19.0** |

## TEAMS' PENALTY KILLING RECORD

**Abbreviations: TSH** – Total times shorthanded; **PPGA** – power-play goals against; **%** arrived by dividing times shorthanded minus power-play goals against by times short.

| HOME | | | | | | ROAD | | | | | OVERALL | | | | |
|---|---|---|---|---|---|---|---|---|---|---|---|---|---|---|---|
| | Team | GP | TSH | PPGA | % | Team | GP | TSH | PPGA | % | Team | GP | TSH | PPGA | % |
| 1 | MTL | 2 | 7 | 0 | 100.0 | N.J | 3 | 15 | 1 | 93.3 | N.J | 7 | 29 | 2 | 93.1 |
| 2 | BOS | 6 | 12 | 0 | 100.0 | STL | 2 | 10 | 1 | 90.0 | BOS | 11 | 27 | 3 | 88.9 |
| 3 | PHI | 3 | 15 | 1 | 93.3 | NYR | 4 | 19 | 2 | 89.5 | CAR | 18 | 71 | 8 | 88.7 |
| 4 | N.J | 4 | 14 | 1 | 92.9 | CAR | 10 | 46 | 5 | 89.1 | PHI | 6 | 32 | 4 | 87.5 |
| 5 | CAR | 8 | 25 | 3 | 88.0 | ANA | 7 | 32 | 5 | 84.4 | PIT | 24 | 84 | 14 | 83.3 |
| 6 | PIT | 11 | 36 | 6 | 83.3 | VAN | 5 | 24 | 4 | 83.3 | VAN | 10 | 51 | 9 | 82.4 |
| 7 | VAN | 5 | 27 | 5 | 81.5 | PIT | 13 | 48 | 8 | 83.3 | NYR | 7 | 33 | 6 | 81.8 |
| 8 | DET | 13 | 37 | 8 | 78.4 | WSH | 6 | 35 | 6 | 82.9 | ANA | 13 | 55 | 11 | 80.0 |
| 9 | CHI | 8 | 32 | 7 | 78.1 | PHI | 3 | 17 | 3 | 82.4 | WSH | 14 | 65 | 13 | 80.0 |
| 10 | S.J | 3 | 9 | 2 | 77.8 | CGY | 3 | 11 | 2 | 81.8 | CHI | 17 | 65 | 14 | 78.5 |
| 11 | WSH | 8 | 30 | 7 | 76.7 | BOS | 5 | 15 | 3 | 80.0 | S.J | 6 | 23 | 5 | 78.3 |
| 12 | ANA | 6 | 23 | 6 | 73.9 | CHI | 9 | 33 | 7 | 78.8 | STL | 4 | 18 | 4 | 77.8 |
| 13 | NYR | 3 | 14 | 4 | 71.4 | S.J | 3 | 14 | 3 | 78.6 | MTL | 4 | 16 | 4 | 75.0 |
| 14 | CBJ | 2 | 8 | 3 | 62.5 | CBJ | 2 | 14 | 4 | 71.4 | DET | 23 | 71 | 19 | 73.2 |
| 15 | STL | 2 | 8 | 3 | 62.5 | DET | 10 | 34 | 11 | 67.6 | CGY | 6 | 24 | 7 | 70.8 |
| 16 | CGY | 3 | 13 | 5 | 61.5 | MTL | 2 | 9 | 4 | 55.6 | CBJ | 4 | 22 | 7 | 68.2 |
| **Total** | | **87** | **310** | **61** | **80.3** | | **87** | **376** | **69** | **81.6** | | **87** | **686** | **130** | **81.0** |

## SHORTHAND GOALS

| GOALS FOR | | | GOALS AGAINST | | |
|---|---|---|---|---|---|
| Team | GP | GF | Team | GP | GA |
| WSH | 14 | 2 | CAR | 18 | 0 |
| PHI | 6 | 1 | WSH | 14 | 0 |
| CHI | 17 | 1 | ANA | 13 | 0 |
| CAR | 18 | 1 | N.J | 7 | 0 |
| DET | 23 | 1 | PHI | 6 | 0 |
| PIT | 24 | 1 | S.J | 6 | 0 |
| MTL | 4 | 0 | CGY | 6 | 0 |
| CBJ | 4 | 0 | MTL | 4 | 0 |
| STL | 4 | 0 | CBJ | 4 | 0 |
| S.J | 6 | 0 | STL | 4 | 0 |
| CGY | 6 | 0 | DET | 23 | 1 |
| NYR | 7 | 0 | CHI | 17 | 1 |
| N.J | 7 | 0 | BOS | 11 | 1 |
| VAN | 10 | 0 | VAN | 10 | 1 |
| BOS | 11 | 0 | NYR | 7 | 1 |
| ANA | 13 | 0 | PIT | 24 | 2 |
| **Total** | **87** | **7** | | **87** | **7** |

## TEAM PENALTIES

**Abbreviations: GP** – games played; **PEN** – total penalty minutes, including bench penalties; **BMI** – total bench minor minutes; **AVG** – average penalty minutes/game arrived by dividing total penalty minutes by games played

| Team | GP | PEN | BMI | AVG |
|---|---|---|---|---|
| DET | 23 | 226 | 2 | 9.8 |
| WSH | 14 | 162 | 0 | 11.6 |
| PIT | 24 | 283 | 4 | 11.8 |
| CAR | 18 | 231 | 4 | 12.8 |
| N.J | 7 | 91 | 0 | 13.0 |
| BOS | 11 | 147 | 0 | 13.4 |
| CGY | 6 | 83 | 4 | 13.8 |
| S.J | 6 | 85 | 0 | 14.2 |
| CBJ | 4 | 60 | 2 | 15.0 |
| STL | 4 | 63 | 2 | 15.8 |
| ANA | 13 | 220 | 6 | 16.9 |
| NYR | 7 | 120 | 2 | 17.1 |
| CHI | 17 | 297 | 6 | 17.5 |
| VAN | 10 | 191 | 0 | 19.1 |
| PHI | 6 | 116 | 0 | 19.3 |
| MTL | 4 | 103 | 2 | 25.8 |
| **Total** | **87** | **2478** | **34** | **28.5** |

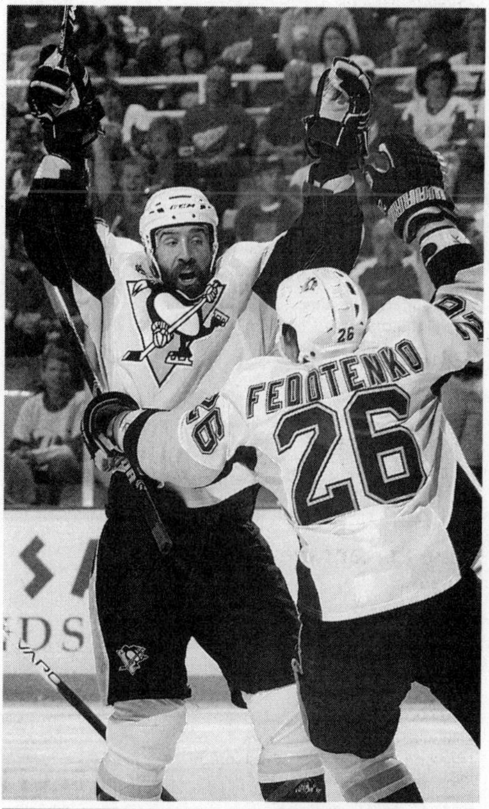

*Maxime Talbot and Ruslan Fedotenko celebrate after the first of Talbot's two goals in Pittsburgh's 2-1 win over Detroit in game seven of the Stanley Cup Finals. When Fedotenko played for Tampa Bay back in 2004, he scored both goals for the Lightning in a 2-1 win over Calgary in game seven.*

# Stanley Cup Record Book

**History:** The Stanley Cup, the oldest trophy competed for by professional athletes in North America, was donated by Frederick Arthur, Lord Stanley of Preston and son of the Earl of Derby, in 1893. Lord Stanley purchased the trophy for 10 guineas ($50 at that time) for presentation to the amateur hockey champions of Canada. Since 1906, when Canadian teams began to pay their players openly, the Stanley Cup has been the symbol of professional hockey supremacy. It has been competed for only by NHL teams since 1926-27 and has been under the exclusive control of the NHL since 1947.

## Stanley Cup Standings

### 1918-2009

(ranked by Cup wins)

| Teams | Cup Wins | Yrs. | Series | Wins | Losses | Games | Wins | Losses | Ties | Goals For | Goals Against | Winning % |
|---|---|---|---|---|---|---|---|---|---|---|---|---|
| **Montreal**[1,2] | 23 | 77 | 141 | 87 | 53 | 683 | 398 | 277 | 8 | 2089 | 1725 | .589 |
| **Toronto**[3] | 13 | 64 | 109 | 58 | 51 | 524 | 251 | 269 | 4 | 1350 | 1427 | .483 |
| **Detroit** | 11 | 57 | 111 | 65 | 46 | 563 | 300 | 262 | 1 | 1598 | 1421 | .534 |
| **Boston** | 5 | 64 | 107 | 48 | 59 | 530 | 252 | 272 | 6 | 1537 | 1557 | .481 |
| **Edmonton** | 5 | 20 | 49 | 34 | 15 | 251 | 152 | 99 | 0 | 938 | 763 | .606 |
| **NY Rangers** | 4 | 52 | 92 | 44 | 48 | 417 | 197 | 212 | 8 | 1167 | 1200 | .482 |
| **NY Islanders** | 4 | 21 | 47 | 30 | 17 | 240 | 134 | 106 | 0 | 792 | 714 | .558 |
| **Chicago** | 3 | 54 | 93 | 42 | 51 | 428 | 197 | 226 | 5 | 1213 | 1349 | .466 |
| **Pittsburgh** | 3 | 24 | 48 | 27 | 21 | 257 | 140 | 117 | 0 | 794 | 766 | .545 |
| **New Jersey**[4] | 3 | 20 | 39 | 22 | 17 | 225 | 121 | 104 | 0 | 620 | 549 | .538 |
| **Philadelphia** | 2 | 33 | 69 | 38 | 31 | 369 | 191 | 178 | 0 | 1114 | 1088 | .518 |
| **Colorado**[5] | 2 | 20 | 43 | 25 | 18 | 243 | 130 | 113 | 0 | 715 | 684 | .535 |
| **Dallas**[6] | 1 | 29 | 56 | 28 | 28 | 307 | 154 | 153 | 0 | 897 | 910 | .502 |
| **Calgary**[7] | 1 | 26 | 40 | 15 | 25 | 208 | 94 | 114 | 0 | 648 | 701 | .452 |
| **Carolina**[8] | 1 | 13 | 22 | 10 | 12 | 127 | 59 | 68 | 0 | 323 | 368 | .465 |
| **Anaheim** | 1 | 7 | 17 | 11 | 6 | 92 | 53 | 39 | 0 | 228 | 220 | .576 |
| **Tampa Bay** | 1 | 5 | 9 | 5 | 4 | 51 | 26 | 25 | 0 | 122 | 140 | .510 |
| **St. Louis** | 0 | 35 | 58 | 23 | 35 | 307 | 138 | 169 | 0 | 862 | 954 | .450 |
| **Buffalo** | 0 | 27 | 48 | 21 | 27 | 243 | 119 | 124 | 0 | 730 | 727 | .490 |
| **Los Angeles** | 0 | 23 | 34 | 11 | 23 | 170 | 65 | 105 | 0 | 511 | 649 | .382 |
| **Vancouver** | 0 | 22 | 34 | 12 | 22 | 177 | 77 | 100 | 0 | 503 | 580 | .435 |
| **Washington** | 0 | 20 | 31 | 11 | 20 | 175 | 79 | 96 | 0 | 528 | 539 | .451 |
| **Phoenix**[9] | 0 | 16 | 18 | 2 | 16 | 92 | 29 | 63 | 0 | 245 | 343 | .315 |
| **San Jose** | 0 | 12 | 21 | 9 | 12 | 125 | 59 | 66 | 0 | 307 | 370 | .472 |
| **Ottawa**[10] | 0 | 11 | 19 | 8 | 11 | 103 | 49 | 54 | 0 | 235 | 241 | .476 |
| **Nashville** | 0 | 4 | 4 | 0 | 4 | 22 | 6 | 16 | 0 | 45 | 62 | .273 |
| **Florida** | 0 | 3 | 6 | 3 | 3 | 31 | 13 | 18 | 0 | 77 | 82 | .419 |
| **Minnesota** | 0 | 3 | 5 | 2 | 3 | 29 | 11 | 18 | 0 | 64 | 72 | .379 |
| **Atlanta** | 0 | 1 | 1 | 0 | 1 | 4 | 0 | 4 | 0 | 6 | 17 | .000 |
| **Columbus** | 0 | 1 | 1 | 0 | 1 | 4 | 0 | 4 | 0 | 7 | 18 | .000 |

1 Montreal also won the Stanley Cup in 1916.
2 1919 final incomplete due to influenza epidemic.
3 Toronto Blueshirts also won the Stanley Cup in 1914.
4 Includes totals of Colorado Rockies 1976-82.
5 Includes totals of Quebec Nordiques 1979-95.
6 Includes totals of Minnesota North Stars 1967-93.
7 Includes totals of Atlanta Flames 1972-80.
8 Includes totals of Hartford Whalers 1979-97.
9 Includes totals of Winnipeg Jets 1979-96.
10 Modern Ottawa Senators franchise only, 1992 to date.

## Stanley Cup Winners Prior to Formation of NHL in 1917

| Season | Champions | Manager | Coach |
|---|---|---|---|
| 1916-17 | Seattle Metropolitans | Pete Muldoon | Pete Muldoon |
| 1915-16 | Montreal Canadiens | George Kennedy | George Kennedy |
| 1914-15 | Vancouver Millionaires | Frank Patrick | Frank Patrick |
| 1913-14 | Toronto Blueshirts | Jack Marshall | Scotty Davidson* |
| 1912-13** | Quebec Bulldogs | M.J. Quinn | Joe Malone* |
| 1911-12 | Quebec Bulldogs | M.J. Quinn | Charley Nolan |
| 1910-11 | Ottawa Senators | | Percy LeSueur |
| 1909-10 | Montreal Wanderers (Mar. 1910) | Dickie Boon | Pud Glass* |
| 1909-10 | Ottawa Senators (Jan. 1910) | | Bruce Stuart* |
| 1908-09 | Ottawa Senators | | Bruce Stuart* |
| 1907-08 | Montreal Wanderers | Dickie Boon | Cecil Blachford |
| 1906-07 | Montreal Wanderers (Mar. 25, 1907) | Dickie Boon | Cecil Blachford |
| 1906-07 | Kenora Thistles (Jan./Mar. 18, 1907) | F.A. Hudson | Tom Phillips* |
| 1905-06 | Montreal Wanderers (Mar. 1906) | Cecil Blachford* | |
| 1905-06 | Ottawa Silver Seven (Feb. 1906) | | Alf Smith |
| 1904-05 | Ottawa Silver Seven | | Alf Smith |
| 1903-04 | Ottawa Silver Seven | | Alf Smith |
| 1902-03 | Ottawa Silver Seven (Mar. 1903) | | Alf Smith |
| 1902-03 | Montreal A.A.A. (Feb. 1903) | | C. McKerrow |
| 1901-02 | Montreal A.A.A. (Mar. 1902) | | C. McKerrow |
| 1901-02 | Winnipeg Victorias (Jan. 1902) | | |
| 1900-01 | Winnipeg Victorias | | Dan Bain* |
| 1899-1900 | Montreal Shamrocks | | Harry Trihey* |
| 1898-99 | Montreal Shamrocks (Mar. 1899) | | Harry Trihey* |
| 1898-99 | Montreal Victorias (Feb. 1899) | | Mike Grant* |
| 1897-98 | Montreal Victorias | | Frank Richardson |
| 1896-97 | Montreal Victorias | | Mike Grant* |
| 1895-96 | Montreal Victorias (Dec. 1896) | | Mike Grant* |
| 1895-96 | Winnipeg Victorias (Feb. 1896) | | Jack Armitage |
| 1894-95 | Montreal Victorias | | Mike Grant* |
| 1893-94 | Montreal A.A.A. | | |
| 1892-93 | Montreal A.A.A. | | |

* In the early years the teams were frequently run by the Captain. *Indicates Captain
** Victoria defeated Quebec in challenge series. No official recognition.

## Stanley Cup Winners

| Year | W-L-T in Finals | Winner | Coach | Finalist | Coach |
|---|---|---|---|---|---|
| 2009 | 4-3 | Pittsburgh | Dan Bylsma | Detroit | Mike Babcock |
| 2008 | 4-2 | Detroit | Mike Babcock | Pittsburgh | Michel Therrien |
| 2007 | 4-1 | Anaheim | Randy Carlyle | Ottawa | Bryan Murray |
| 2006 | 4-3 | Carolina | Peter Laviolette | Edmonton | Craig MacTavish |
| 2005 | .... | .... | .... | .... | .... |
| 2004 | 4-3 | Tampa Bay | John Tortorella | Calgary | Darryl Sutter |
| 2003 | 4-3 | New Jersey | Pat Burns | Anaheim | Mike Babcock |
| 2002 | 4-1 | Detroit | Scotty Bowman | Carolina | Paul Maurice |
| 2001 | 4-3 | Colorado | Bob Hartley | New Jersey | Larry Robinson |
| 2000 | 4-2 | New Jersey | Larry Robinson | Dallas | Ken Hitchcock |
| 1999 | 4-2 | Dallas | Ken Hitchcock | Buffalo | Lindy Ruff |
| 1998 | 4-0 | Detroit | Scotty Bowman | Washington | Ron Wilson |
| 1997 | 4-0 | Detroit | Scotty Bowman | Philadelphia | Terry Murray |
| 1996 | 4-0 | Colorado | Marc Crawford | Florida | Doug MacLean |
| 1995 | 4-0 | New Jersey | Jacques Lemaire | Detroit | Scotty Bowman |
| 1994 | 4-3 | NY Rangers | Mike Keenan | Vancouver | Pat Quinn |
| 1993 | 4-1 | Montreal | Jacques Demers | Los Angeles | Barry Melrose |
| 1992 | 4-0 | Pittsburgh | Scotty Bowman | Chicago | Mike Keenan |
| 1991 | 4-2 | Pittsburgh | Bob Johnson | Minnesota | Bob Gainey |
| 1990 | 4-1 | Edmonton | John Muckler | Boston | Mike Milbury |
| 1989 | 4-2 | Calgary | Terry Crisp | Montreal | Pat Burns |
| 1988 | 4-0 | Edmonton | Glen Sather | Boston | Terry O'Reilly |
| 1987 | 4-3 | Edmonton | Glen Sather | Philadelphia | Mike Keenan |
| 1986 | 4-1 | Montreal | Jean Perron | Calgary | Bob Johnson |
| 1985 | 4-1 | Edmonton | Glen Sather | Philadelphia | Mike Keenan |
| 1984 | 4-1 | Edmonton | Glen Sather | NY Islanders | Al Arbour |
| 1983 | 4-0 | NY Islanders | Al Arbour | Edmonton | Glen Sather |
| 1982 | 4-0 | NY Islanders | Al Arbour | Vancouver | Roger Neilson |
| 1981 | 4-1 | NY Islanders | Al Arbour | Minnesota | Glen Sonmor |
| 1980 | 4-2 | NY Islanders | Al Arbour | Philadelphia | Pat Quinn |
| 1979 | 4-1 | Montreal | Scotty Bowman | NY Rangers | Fred Shero |
| 1978 | 4-2 | Montreal | Scotty Bowman | Boston | Don Cherry |
| 1977 | 4-0 | Montreal | Scotty Bowman | Boston | Don Cherry |
| 1976 | 4-0 | Montreal | Scotty Bowman | Philadelphia | Fred Shero |
| 1975 | 4-2 | Philadelphia | Fred Shero | Buffalo | Floyd Smith |
| 1974 | 4-2 | Philadelphia | Fred Shero | Boston | Bep Guidolin |
| 1973 | 4-2 | Montreal | Scotty Bowman | Chicago | Billy Reay |
| 1972 | 4-2 | Boston | Tom Johnson | NY Rangers | Emile Francis |
| 1971 | 4-3 | Montreal | Al MacNeil | Chicago | Billy Reay |
| 1970 | 4-0 | Boston | Harry Sinden | St. Louis | Scotty Bowman |
| 1969 | 4-0 | Montreal | Claude Ruel | St. Louis | Scotty Bowman |
| 1968 | 4-0 | Montreal | Toe Blake | St. Louis | Scotty Bowman |
| 1967 | 4-2 | Toronto | Punch Imlach | Montreal | Toe Blake |
| 1966 | 4-2 | Montreal | Toe Blake | Detroit | Sid Abel |
| 1965 | 4-3 | Montreal | Toe Blake | Chicago | Billy Reay |
| 1964 | 4-3 | Toronto | Punch Imlach | Detroit | Sid Abel |
| 1963 | 4-1 | Toronto | Punch Imlach | Detroit | Sid Abel |
| 1962 | 4-2 | Toronto | Punch Imlach | Chicago | Rudy Pilous |
| 1961 | 4-2 | Chicago | Rudy Pilous | Detroit | Sid Abel |
| 1960 | 4-0 | Montreal | Toe Blake | Toronto | Punch Imlach |
| 1959 | 4-1 | Montreal | Toe Blake | Toronto | Punch Imlach |
| 1958 | 4-2 | Montreal | Toe Blake | Boston | Milt Schmidt |
| 1957 | 4-1 | Montreal | Toe Blake | Boston | Milt Schmidt |
| 1956 | 4-1 | Montreal | Toe Blake | Detroit | Jimmy Skinner |
| 1955 | 4-3 | Detroit | Jimmy Skinner | Montreal | Dick Irvin |
| 1954 | 4-3 | Detroit | Tommy Ivan | Montreal | Dick Irvin |
| 1953 | 4-1 | Montreal | Dick Irvin | Boston | Lynn Patrick |
| 1952 | 4-0 | Detroit | Tommy Ivan | Montreal | Dick Irvin |
| 1951 | 4-1 | Toronto | Joe Primeau | Montreal | Dick Irvin |
| 1950 | 4-3 | Detroit | Tommy Ivan | NY Rangers | Lynn Patrick |
| 1949 | 4-0 | Toronto | Hap Day | Detroit | Tommy Ivan |
| 1948 | 4-0 | Toronto | Hap Day | Detroit | Tommy Ivan |
| 1947 | 4-2 | Toronto | Hap Day | Montreal | Dick Irvin |
| 1946 | 4-1 | Montreal | Dick Irvin | Boston | Dit Clapper |
| 1945 | 4-3 | Toronto | Hap Day | Detroit | Jack Adams |
| 1944 | 4-0 | Montreal | Dick Irvin | Chicago | Paul Thompson |
| 1943 | 4-0 | Detroit | Jack Adams | Boston | Art Ross |
| 1942 | 4-3 | Toronto | Hap Day | Detroit | Jack Adams |
| 1941 | 4-0 | Boston | Cooney Weiland | Detroit | Ebbie Goodfellow |
| 1940 | 4-2 | NY Rangers | Frank Boucher | Toronto | Dick Irvin |
| 1939 | 4-1 | Boston | Art Ross | Toronto | Dick Irvin |
| 1938 | 3-1 | Chicago | Bill Stewart | Toronto | Dick Irvin |
| 1937 | 3-2 | Detroit | Jack Adams | NY Rangers | Lester Patrick |
| 1936 | 3-1 | Detroit | Jack Adams | Toronto | Dick Irvin |
| 1935 | 3-0 | Mtl. Maroons | Tommy Gorman | Toronto | Dick Irvin |
| 1934 | 3-1 | Chicago | Tommy Gorman | Detroit | Herbie Lewis |
| 1933 | 3-1 | NY Rangers | Lester Patrick | Toronto | Dick Irvin |
| 1932 | 3-0 | Toronto | Dick Irvin | NY Rangers | Lester Patrick |
| 1931 | 3-2 | Montreal | Cecil Hart | Chicago | Dick Irvin |
| 1930 | 2-0 | Montreal | Cecil Hart | Boston | Art Ross |
| 1929 | 2-0 | Boston | Cy Denneny | NY Rangers | Lester Patrick |
| 1928 | 3-2 | NY Rangers | Lester Patrick | Mtl. Maroons | Eddie Gerard |
| 1927 | 2-0-2 | Ottawa | Dave Gill | Boston | Art Ross |
| | | **The National Hockey League assumed control of Stanley Cup competition after 1926** | | | |
| 1926 | 3-1 | Mtl. Maroons | Eddie Gerard | Victoria | Lester Patrick |
| 1925 | 3-1 | Victoria | Lester Patrick | Montreal | Leo Dandurand |
| 1924 | 2-0 | Montreal | Leo Dandurand | Cgy. Tigers | Eddie Oatman |
| 1923 | 2-0 | Ottawa | Pete Green | Edm. Eskimos | Ken McKenzie |
| 1922 | 3-2 | Tor. St. Pats | George O'Donoghue | Van. Millionaires | Lloyd Cook/Frank Patrick |
| 1921 | 3-2 | Ottawa | Pete Green | Van. Millionaires | Lloyd Cook/Frank Patrick |
| 1920 | 3-2 | Ottawa | Pete Green | Seattle | Pete Muldoon |
| 1919 | 2-2-1 | No decision - series between Montreal and Seattle cancelled due to influenza epidemic | | | |
| 1918 | 3-2 | Tor. Arenas | Dick Carroll | Van. Millionaires | Frank Patrick |

# Championship Trophies

## PRINCE OF WALES TROPHY

**Beginning with the 1993-94 season, the club which advances to the Stanley Cup Finals as the winner of the Eastern Conference Championship is presented with the Prince of Wales Trophy.**

**History:** His Royal Highness, the Prince of Wales, donated the trophy to the National Hockey League in 1925. It was originally awarded to the winner of the first game played in Madison Square Garden, December 15, 1925 (Montreal Canadiens 3 at NY Americans 1). It was then awarded to the NHL playoff champion in 1925-26 and 1926-27. From 1927-28 through 1937-38, the award was presented to the regular-season champion of the American Division of the NHL. (The team finishing first in the Canadian Division received the O'Brien Trophy during these years.) From 1938-39, when the NHL reverted to one section, to 1966-67, it was presented to the team winning the NHL regular-season championship. With expansion in 1967-68, it again became a divisional trophy, awarded to the regular-season champions of the East Division through to the end of the 1973-74 season. Beginning in 1974-75, it was awarded to the regular-season winner of the conference bearing the name of the trophy. From 1981-82 to 1992-93 the trophy was presented to the playoff champion in the Wales Conference. Since 1993-94, the trophy has been presented to the playoff champion in the Eastern Conference.

**2008-09 Winner: Pittsburgh Penguins**

The Pittsburgh Penguins won the Prince of Wales Trophy on May 26, 2009 after defeating the Carolina Hurricanes 4-1 in game 4 of the Eastern Conference Finals. Before defeating the Hurricanes, Pittsburgh had series wins over the Philadelphia Flyers and the Washington Capitals.

**PRINCE OF WALES TROPHY WINNERS**

| | | | | | |
|---|---|---|---|---|---|
| 2008-09 | Pittsburgh | 1978-79 | Montreal | 1949-50 | Detroit |
| 2007-08 | Pittsburgh | 1977-78 | Montreal | 1948-49 | Detroit |
| 2006-07 | Ottawa | 1976-77 | Montreal | 1947-48 | Toronto |
| 2005-06 | Carolina | 1975-76 | Montreal | 1946-47 | Montreal |
| 2003-04 | Tampa Bay | 1974-75 | Buffalo | 1945-46 | Montreal |
| 2002-03 | New Jersey | 1973-74 | Boston | 1944-45 | Montreal |
| 2001-02 | Carolina | 1972-73 | Montreal | 1943-44 | Montreal |
| 2000-01 | New Jersey | 1971-72 | Boston | 1942-43 | Detroit |
| 99-2000 | New Jersey | 1970-71 | Boston | 1941-42 | NY Rangers |
| 1998-99 | Buffalo | 1969-70 | Chicago | 1940-41 | Boston |
| 1997-98 | Washington | 1968-69 | Montreal | 1939-40 | Boston |
| 1996-97 | Philadelphia | 1967-68 | Montreal | 1938-39 | Boston |
| 1995-96 | Florida | 1966-67 | Chicago | 1937-38 | Boston |
| 1994-95 | New Jersey | 1965-66 | Montreal | 1936-37 | Detroit |
| 1993-94 | NY Rangers | 1964-65 | Detroit | 1935-36 | Detroit |
| 1992-93 | Montreal | 1963-64 | Montreal | 1934-35 | Boston |
| 1991-92 | Pittsburgh | 1962-63 | Toronto | 1933-34 | Detroit |
| 1990-91 | Pittsburgh | 1961-62 | Montreal | 1932-33 | Boston |
| 1989-90 | Boston | 1960-61 | Montreal | 1931-32 | NY Rangers |
| 1988-89 | Montreal | 1959-60 | Montreal | 1930-31 | Boston |
| 1987-88 | Boston | 1958-59 | Montreal | 1929-30 | Boston |
| 1986-87 | Philadelphia | 1957-58 | Montreal | 1928-29 | Boston |
| 1985-86 | Montreal | 1956-57 | Detroit | 1927-28 | Boston |
| 1984-85 | Philadelphia | 1955-56 | Montreal | 1926-27 | Ottawa |
| 1983-84 | NY Islanders | 1954-55 | Detroit | 1925-26 | Mtl. Maroons |
| 1982-83 | NY Islanders | 1953-54 | Detroit | Dec. 15/25 | Montreal |
| 1981-82 | NY Islanders | 1952-53 | Detroit | 1923-24 | Montreal* |
| 1980-81 | Montreal | 1951-52 | Detroit | | |
| 1979-80 | Buffalo | 1950-51 | Detroit | | |

* Engraved by Montreal Canadiens in 1925-26.

## CLARENCE S. CAMPBELL BOWL

**Beginning with the 1993-94 season, the club which advances to the Stanley Cup Finals as the winner of the Western Conference Championship is presented with the Clarence S. Campbell Bowl.**

**History:** Presented by the member clubs in 1968 for perpetual competition by the National Hockey League in recognition of the services of Clarence S. Campbell, President of the NHL from 1946 to 1977. From 1967-68 through 1973-74, the trophy was awarded to the regular-season champions of the West Division. Beginning in 1974-75, it was awarded to the regular-season winner of the conference bearing the name of the trophy. From 1981-82 to 1992-93 the trophy was presented to the playoff champion in the Campbell Conference. Since 1993-94, the trophy has been presented to the playoff champion in the Western Conference. The trophy itself is a hallmark piece made of sterling silver and was crafted by a British silversmith in 1878.

**2008-09 Winner: Detroit Red Wings**

The Detroit Red Wings won the Clarence Campbell Bowl on May 27, 2009 after defeating the Chicago Blackhawks 2-1 in game 5 of the Western Conference Finals. Before defeating the Blackhawks, Detroit had series wins over the Columbus Blue Jackets and the Anaheim Ducks.

**CLARENCE S. CAMPBELL BOWL WINNERS**

| | | | | | |
|---|---|---|---|---|---|
| 2008-09 | Detroit | 1993-94 | Vancouver | 1979-80 | Philadelphia |
| 2007-08 | Detroit | 1992-93 | Los Angeles | 1978-79 | NY Islanders |
| 2006-07 | Anaheim | 1991-92 | Chicago | 1977-78 | NY Islanders |
| 2005-06 | Edmonton | 1990-91 | Minnesota | 1976-77 | Philadelphia |
| 2003-04 | Calgary | 1989-90 | Edmonton | 1975-76 | Philadelphia |
| 2002-03 | Anaheim | 1988-89 | Calgary | 1974-75 | Philadelphia |
| 2001-02 | Detroit | 1987-88 | Edmonton | 1973-74 | Philadelphia |
| 2000-01 | Colorado | 1986-87 | Edmonton | 1972-73 | Chicago |
| 99-2000 | Dallas | 1985-86 | Calgary | 1971-72 | Chicago |
| 1998-99 | Dallas | 1984-85 | Edmonton | 1970-71 | Chicago |
| 1997-98 | Detroit | 1983-84 | Edmonton | 1969-70 | St. Louis |
| 1996-97 | Detroit | 1982-83 | Edmonton | 1968-69 | St. Louis |
| 1995-96 | Colorado | 1981-82 | Vancouver | 1967-68 | Philadelphia |
| 1994-95 | Detroit | 1980-81 | NY Islanders | | |

*Prince of Wales Trophy*

*Clarence S. Campbell Bowl*

*Stanley Cup*

# Stanley Cup Winners

## Rosters and Final Series Scores

**2008-09 — Pittsburgh Penguins —** Sidney Crosby (Captain), Craig Adams, Philippe Boucher, Matt Cooke, Pascal Dupuis, Mark Eaton, Ruslan Fedotenko, Marc-Andre Fleury, Mathieu Garon, Hal Gill, Eric Godard, Alex Goligoski, Sergei Gonchar, Bill Guerin, Tyler Kennedy, Chris Kunitz, Kris Letang, Evgeni Malkin, Brooks Orpik, Miroslav Satan, Rob Scuderi, Jordan Staal, Petr Sykora, Maxime Talbot, Mike Zigomanis, Mario Lemieux (Co-owner/Chairman), Ron Burkle (Co-owner), Bill Kassling, Tom Grealish, Tony Liberati (Directors), Ken Sawyer (Chief Executive Officer), David Morehouse (President), Ray Shero (Executive Vice President amd General Manager), Chuck Fletcher (Assistant General Manager), Ed Johnston (Senior Advisor, Hockey Operations), Jason Botterill (Director of Hockey Administration), Dan Bylsma (Head Coach), Mike Yeo (Assistant Coach), Tom Fitzgerald (Director of Player Development), Gilles Meloche (Goaltending Coach), Mike Kadar (Strength and Conditioning Coach), Travis Ramsay (Video Coordinator), Chris Stewart (Head Athletic Trainer), Scott Adams (Assistant Athletic Trainer), Mark Mortland (Physical Therapist), Dana Heinze (Equipment Manager), Paul DeFazio, Danny Kroll (Assistant Equipment Managers), Frank Buonomo (Senior Director of Team Services and Communications), Tom McMillan (Vice President, Communications), Dan MacKinnon (Director of Professional Scouting), Jay Heinbuck (Director of Amateur Scouting).

**Scores:** May 30, at Detroit — Detroit 3, Pittsburgh 1; May 31 at Detroit — Detroit 3, Pittsburgh 1; June 2, at Pittsburgh — Pittsburgh 4, Detroit 2; June 4, at Pittsburgh — Pittsburgh 4, Detroit 2; June 6 at Detroit — Detroit 5, Pittsburgh 0; June 9, at Pittsburgh — Pittsburgh 2, Detroit 1; June 12, at Detroit — Pittsburgh 2, Detroit 1.

**2007-08 — Detroit Red Wings —** Nicklas Lidstrom (Captain), Chris Chelios, Daniel Cleary, Pavel Datsyuk, Aaron Downey, Dallas Drake, Kris Draper, Valtteri Filppula, Johan Franzen, Dominik Hasek, Darren Helm, Tomas Holmstrom, Jiri Hudler, Tomas Kopecky, Niklas Kronwall, Brett Lebda, Andreas Lilja, Kirk Maltby, Darren McCarty, Derek Meech, Chris Osgood, Brian Rafalski, Mikael Samuelsson, Brad Stuart, Henrik Zetterberg, Michael Ilitch (Owner/Governor), Marian Ilitch (Owner/Secretary-Treasurer), Christopher Ilitch (Vice President/Alternate Governor), Denise Ilitch, Ronald Ilitch, Michael Ilitch Jr., Lisa Ilitch Murray, Atanas Ilitch, Carole Ilitch. Jim Devellano (Senior Vice President/Alternate Governor), Ken Holland (General Manager/Alternate Governor), Steve Yzerman (Vice President/Alternate Governor), Jim Nill (Assistant General Manager), Ryan Martin (Director, Hockey Operations), Scotty Bowman (Consultant), Mike Babcock (Head Coach), Todd McLellan (Associate Coach), Paul MacLean (Assistant Coach), Jim Bedard (Goaltending Consultant), Jay Woodcroft (Video Coordinator), Mark Howe (Director, Pro Scouting), Joe McDonnell (Director, Amateur Scouting), Hakan Andersson (Director, Amateur Scouting Europe), Piet Van Zant (Athletic Trainer), Paul Boyer (Equipment Manager), Russ Baumann, Christopher Scoppetto (Assistant Athletic Trainers).

**Scores:** May 24, at Detroit — Detroit 4, Pittsburgh 0; May 26, at Detroit — Detroit 3, Pittsburgh 0; May 28, at Pittsburgh — Pittsburgh 3, Detroit 2; May 31, at Pittsburgh — Detroit 2, Pittsburgh 1; June 2, at Detroit — Pittsburgh 4, Detroit 3; June 4, at Pittsburgh — Detroit 3, Pittsburgh 2.

**2006-07 — Anaheim Ducks** — Scott Niedermayer (Captain), Rob Niedermayer, Chris Pronger, Teemu Selanne, Sean O'Donnell, Brad May, Todd Marchant, Jean-Sebastien Giguere, Andy McDonald, Samuel Pahlsson, Shawn Thornton, Ric Jackman, Joe DiPenta, Kent Huskins, Chris Kunitz, George Parros, Joe Motzko, Ilya Bryzgalov, Francois Beauchemin, Travis Moen, Ryan Carter, Drew Miller, Ryan Shannon, Dustin Penner, Ryan Getzlaf, Corey Perry; Henry Samueli, Susan Samueli (Owners), Michael Schulman (CEO), Brian Burke (Executive Vice President/General Manager), Tim Ryan (Executive Vice President/COO), Bob Wagner (Senior Vice President/Chief Marketing Officer), Bob Murray (Senior Vice President-Hockey Operations), David McNab (Assistant General Manager), Al Coates (Senior Advisor to GM), Randy Carlyle (Head Coach), Dave Farrish, Newell Brown (Assistant Coaches), Francois Allaire (Goaltending Consultant), Sean Skahan (Strength and Conditioning Coach), Joe Trotta (Video Coordinator), Tim Clark (Head Trainer), Mark O'Neill (Equipment Manager), John Allaway (Assistant Equipment Manager), James Partida (Massage Therapist), Rick Paterson (Director of Professional Scouting), Alain Chainey (Director of Amateur Scouting).

**Scores:** May 28, at Anaheim - Anaheim 3, Ottawa 2; May 30, at Anaheim - Anaheim 1, Ottawa 0; June 2, at Ottawa - Ottawa 5, Anaheim 3; June 4, at Ottawa - Anaheim 3, Ottawa 2; June 6, at Anaheim - Anaheim 6, Ottawa 2.

**2005-06 — Carolina Hurricanes** — Rod Brind'Amour (Captain), Glen Wesley, Cory Stillman, Kevyn Adams, Craig Adams, Anton Babchuk, Erik Cole, Mike Commodore, Matt Cullen, Martin Gerber, Bret Hedican, Andrew Hutchinson, Frantisek Kaberle, Andrew Ladd, Chad LaRose, Mark Recchi, Eric Staal, Oleg Tverdovsky, Josef Vasicek, Niclas Wallin, Aaron Ward, Cam Ward, Doug Weight, Ray Whitney, Justin Williams; Peter Karmanos Jr., Thomas Thewes (Owners), Jim Rutherford (President/General Manager), Jason Karmanos (Vice President/Assistant General Manager), Mike Amendola (Chief Financial Officer), Peter Laviolette (Head Coach), Kevin McCarthy, Jeff Daniels (Assistant Coaches), Greg Stefan (Goaltending Coach), Chris Huffine (Video Coordinator), Skip Cunningham, Wally Tatomir, Bob Gorman (Equipment Managers), Peter Friesen (Head Athletic Therapist/Strength and Conditioning Coach), Chris Stewart (Associate Athletic Trainer), Brian Tatum (Team Services Manager), Kelly Kirwin (Event Coordinator-Hockey Operations), Mike Sundheim (Director of Media Relations), Kyle Hanlin (Manager of Media Relations), Sheldon Ferguson (Director of Amateur Scouting), Marshall Johnston (Director of Professional Scouting), Claude Larose, Ron Smith (Professional Scouts), Bert Marshall, Tony MacDonald, Martin Madden (Amateur Scouts), Tom Rowe (Lowell (AHL) - Coach).

**Scores:** June 5, at Carolina - Carolina 5, Edmonton 4; June 7, at Carolina - Carolina 5, Edmonton 0; June 10, at Edmonton - Edmonton 2, Carolina 1; June 12, at Edmonton - Carolina 2, Edmonton 1; June 14, at Carolina - Edmonton 4, Carolina 3; June 17, at Edmonton - Edmonton 4, Carolina 0; June 19, at Carolina - Carolina 3, Edmonton 1.

**2003-04 — Tampa Bay Lightning** — Dave Andreychuk (Captain), Fredrik Modin, Vincent Lecavalier, Martin St. Louis, Brad Richards, Nikolai Khabibulin, Pavel Kubina, Dan Boyle, Ruslan Fedotenko, Darryl Sydor, Cory Sarich, Tim Taylor, Cory Stillman, Jassen Cullimore, John Grahame, Chris Dingman, Nolan Pratt, Brad Lukowich, Andre Roy, Dmitry Afanasenkov, Martin Cibak, Ben Clymer, Darren Rumble, Stan Neckar, Eric Perrin; William Davidson (Owner), Tom Wilson (Governor), Ron Campbell (President), Jay Feaster (General Manager), John Tortorella (Head Coach), Craig Ramsay (Associate Coach), Jeff Reese (Assistant Coach), Nigel Kirwan (Video Coach), Eric Lawson (Strength and Conditioning Coach), Tom Mulligan (Trainer), Adam Rambo (Assistant Trainer), Ray Thill (Equipment Manager), Dana Heinze, Jim Pickard (Assistant Equipment Managers), Mike Griebel (Massage Therapist), Bill Barber (Director of Player Personnel), Jake Goertzen (Head Scout), Phil Thibodeau (Director of Team Services), Ryan Belec (Assistant to the GM), Rick Paterson (Chief Pro Scout), Kari Kettunen, Glen Zacharias, Steve Baker, Dave Heitz, Yuri Yanchenkov, (Scouts), Bill Wickett (Senior Vice President - Communications), Sean Henry (Executive Vice President/COO).

**Scores:** May 25, at Tampa Bay - Calgary 4, Tampa Bay 1; May 27, at Tampa Bay - Tampa Bay 4, Calgary 1; May 29, at Calgary - Calgary 3, Tampa Bay 0; May 31, at Calgary - Tampa Bay 1, Calgary 0; June 3, at Tampa Bay - Calgary 3, Tampa Bay 2; June 5, at Calgary - Tampa Bay 3, Calgary 2; June 7, at Tampa Bay - Tampa Bay 2, Calgary 1.

**2002-03 — New Jersey Devils** — Tommy Albelin, Jiri Bicek, Martin Brodeur, Sergei Brylin, Ken Daneyko, Patrik Elias, Jeff Friesen, Brian Gionta, Scott Gomez, Jamie Langenbrunner, John Madden, Grant Marshall, Jim McKenzie, Scott Niedermayer, Joe Nieuwendyk, Jay Pandolfo, Brian Rafalski, Pascal Rheaume, Mike Rupp, Corey Schwab, Richard Smehlik, Scott Stevens (Captain), Turner Stevenson, Oleg Tverdovsky, Colin White; Raymond Chambers, Lewis Catz (Owners), Peter Simon (Chairman), Lou Lamoriello (CEO/President/General Manager), Pat Burns (Head Coach), Bob Carpenter, John MacLean (Assistant Coaches), Jacques Caron (Goaltending Coach), Larry Robinson (Special Assignment Coach), David Conte (Director - Scouting), Claude Carrier (Assistant Director - Scouting), Chris Lamoriello (Scout/Albany (AHL) - General Manager), Milt Fisher, Dan Labraaten, Marcel Pronovost (Scouts), Bob Hoffmeyer, Jan Ludvig (Pro Scouts), Dr. Barry Fisher (Orthopedist), Chris Modrzynski (Executive Vice President), Terry Farmer (Vice President - Ticket Operations), Vladimir Bure (Fitness Consultant), Taran Singleton (Hockey Operations), Bill Murray (Medical Trainer), Michael Vasalani (Strength and Conditioning Coordinator), Rick Matthews (Equipment Manager), Juergen Merz (Massage Therapist), Alex Abasto (Assistant Equipment Manager).

**Scores:** May 27, at New Jersey - New Jersey 3, Anaheim 0; May 29, at New Jersey - New Jersey 3, Anaheim 0; May 31, at Anaheim - Anaheim 3, New Jersey 2; June 2, at Anaheim - Anaheim 1, New Jersey 0; June 5, at New Jersey - New Jersey 6, Anaheim 3; June 7, at Anaheim - Anaheim 5, New Jersey 2; June 9, at New Jersey - New Jersey 3, Anaheim 0.

**2001-02 — Detroit Red Wings** — Steve Yzerman (Captain), Dominik Hasek, Manny Legace, Chris Chelios, Mathieu Dandenault, Steve Duchesne, Jiri Fischer, Nicklas Lidstrom, Fredrik Olausson, Jiri Slegr, Pavel Datsyuk, Boyd Devereaux, Kris Draper, Sergei Fedorov, Tomas Holmstrom, Brett Hull, Igor Larionov, Kirk Maltby, Darren McCarty, Luc Robitaille, Brendan Shanahan, Jason Williams; Michael Ilitch (Owner/Governor), Marian Ilitch (Owner/Secretary Treasurer), Christoper Ilitch (Vice President), Denise Ilitch (Alternate Governor), Ronald Ilitch, Michael Ilitch Jr., Lisa Ilitch Murray, Atanas Ilitch, Carole Ilitch, Jim Devellano (Senior Vice President), Ken Holland (General Manager), Jim Nill (Assistant General Manager), Scotty Bowman (Head Coach), Dave Lewis, Barry Smith (Associate Coaches), Jim Bedard (Goaltending Consultant), Joe Kocur (Video Coordinator), John Wharton (Athletic Trainer), Piet Van Zant (Assistant Athletic Trainer), Paul Boyer (Equipment Manager), Paul MacDonald (Senior Director of Finance), Nancy Beard (Executive Assistant), Dan Belisle, Mark Howe, Bob McCammon (Pro Scouts), Hakan Andersson (Director of European Scouting), Bruce Haralson, Mark Leach, Joe McDonnell, Glenn Merkosky (Scouts).

**Scores:** June 4, at Detroit - Carolina 3, Detroit 2; June 6, at Detroit - Detroit 3, Carolina 1; June 8, at Carolina - Detroit 3, Carolina 2; June 10, at Carolina - Detroit 3, Carolina 0; June 13, at Detroit - Detroit 3, Carolina 1.

**2000-01 — Colorado Avalanche** — David Aebischer, Rob Blake, Raymond Bourque, Greg de Vries, Chris Dingman, Chris Drury, Adam Foote, Peter Forsberg, Milan Hejduk, Dan Hinote, Jon Klemm, Eric Messier, Bryan Muir, Ville Nieminen, Scott Parker, Shjon Podein, Nolan Pratt, Dave Reid, Steve Reinprecht, Patrick Roy, Joe Sakic (Captain), Martin Skoula, Alex Tanguay, Stephane Yelle; E. Stanley Kroenke (Owner/Governor), Pierre Lacroix (President/ General Manager), Bob Hartley (Head Coach), Jacques Cloutier, Bryan Trottier (Assistant Coaches), Paul Fixter (Video Coach), Francois Giguere (Vice President - Hockey Operations), Brian MacDonald (Assistant General Manager), Michel Goulet (Vice President - Player Personnel), Jean Martineau (Vice President - Communications and Team Services), Pat Karns (Head Athletic Trainer), Matthew Sokolowski (Assistant Athletic Trainer), Wayne Flemming, Mark Miller (Equipment Managers), Dave Randolph (Assistant Equipment Manager), Paul Goldberg (Strength and Conditioning Coach), Gregorio Pradera (Massage Therapist), Brad Smith (Pro Scout), Jim Hammett (Chief Scout), Garth Joy, Steve Lyons, Joni Lehto, Orval Tessier (Scouts), Charlotte Grahame (Director of Hockey Administration).

**Scores:** May 26, at Colorado - Colorado 5, New Jersey 0; May 29, at Colorado - New Jersey 2, Colorado 1; May 31, at New Jersey - Colorado 3, New Jersey 1; June 2, at New Jersey - New Jersey 3, Colorado 2; June 4, at Colorado - New Jersey 4, Colorado 1; June 7, at New Jersey - Colorado 4, New Jersey 0; June 9, at Colorado - Colorado 3, New Jersey 1.

**1999-2000 — New Jersey Devils** — Jason Arnott, Brad Bombardir, Martin Brodeur, Steve Brule, Sergei Brylin, Ken Daneyko, Patrik Elias, Scott Gomez, Bobby Holik, Steve Kelly, Claude Lemieux, John Madden, Vladimir Malakhov, Randy McKay, Alexander Mogilny, Sergei Nemchinov, Scott Niedermayer, Krzysztof Oliwa, Jay Pandolfo, Brian Rafalski, Ken Sutton, Scott Stevens (Captain), Petr Sykora, Chris Terreri, Colin White; Dr. John J. McMullen (Owner/Chairman), Peter S. McMullen (Owner), Lou Lamoriello (President/General Manager), Larry Robinson (Head Coach), Viacheslav Fetisov (Assistant Coach), Jacques Caron (Goaltending Coach), Bob Carpenter (Assistant Coach), John Cuniff (Albany (AHL) - Coach), David Conte (Director of Scouting), Claude Carrier (Assistant Director of Scouting), Milt Fisher, Dan Labraaten, Marcel Pronovost (Scouts), Bob Hoffmeyer (Pro Scout), Dr. Barry Fisher (Orthopedist), Dennis Gendron (Albany (AHL) - Assistant Coach), Robbie Ftorek (Coach), Vladimir Bure (Consultant), Taran Singleton, Marie Carnevale, Callie Smith (Hockey Operations), Bill Murray (Medical Trainer), Michael Vasalani (Strength and Conditioning Coordinator), Dana McGuane (Equipment Manager), Juergen Merz (Massage Therapist), Harry Bricker, Lou Centanni Jr. (Assistant Equipment Managers).

**Scores:** May 30, at New Jersey - New Jersey 7, Dallas 3; June 1, at New Jersey - Dallas 2, New Jersey 1; June 3, at Dallas - New Jersey 2, Dallas 1; June 5, at Dallas - New Jersey 3, Dallas 1; June 8, at New Jersey - Dallas 1 - New Jersey 0; June 10, at Dallas, New Jersey 2 - Dallas 1.

**1998-99 — Dallas Stars** — Derian Hatcher (Captain), Mike Modano, Joe Nieuwendyk, Craig Ludwig, Sergei Zubov, Ed Belfour, Guy Carbonneau, Shawn Chambers, Benoit Hogue, Tony Hrkac, Brett Hull, Mike Keane, Jamie Langenbrunner, Jere Lehtinen, Grant Marshall, Richard Matvichuk, Derek Plante, Dave Reid, Brent Severyn, Jon Sim, Brian Skrudland, Blake Sloan, Darryl Sydor, Roman Turek, Pat Verbeek; Thomas Hicks (Chairman/Owner), Jim Lites (President), Bob Gainey (Vice President - Hockey Operations/General Manager), Doug Armstrong (Assistant General Manager), Craig Button (Director of Player Personnel), Ken Hitchcock (Head Coach), Doug Jarvis, Rick Wilson (Assistant Coaches), Rick McLaughlin (Vice President/Chief Financial Officer), Jeff Cogen (Vice President - Marketing and Promotion), Bill Strong (Vice President - Marketing and Broadcasting), Tim Bernhardt (Director of Amateur Scouting), Doug Overton (Director of Pro Scouting), Bob Gernander (Chief Scout), Stu MacGregor (Western Scout), Dave Suprenant (Medical Trainer), Dave Smith, Rich Matthews (Equipment Managers), J.J. McQueen (Strength and Conditioning Coach), Rick St. Croix (Goaltending Consultant), Dan Stuchal (Director of Team Services), Larry Kelly (Director of Public Relations).

**Scores:** June 8, at Dallas - Buffalo 3, Dallas 2; June 10, at Dallas - Dallas 4, Buffalo 2; June 12, at Buffalo - Dallas 2, Buffalo 1; June 15, at Buffalo - Buffalo 2, Dallas 1; June 17, at Dallas - Dallas 2, Buffalo 0; June 19, at Buffalo - Dallas 2, Buffalo 1.

**1997-98 — Detroit Red Wings** — Steve Yzerman (Captain), Doug Brown, Mathieu Dandenault, Kris Draper, Anders Eriksson, Sergei Fedorov, Viacheslav Fetisov, Brent Gilchrist, Kevin Hodson, Tomas Holmstrom, Mike Knuble, Joe Kocur, Vladimir Konstantinov, Vyacheslav Kozlov, Martin Lapointe, Igor Larionov, Nicklas Lidstrom, Jamie Macoun, Kirk Maltby, Darren McCarty, Dmitri Mironov, Larry Murphy, Chris Osgood, Bob Rouse, Brendan Shanahan, Aaron Ward; Mike Ilitch, (Owner/Chairman), Marian Ilitch (Owner), Atanas Ilitch, Christopher Ilitch (Vice Presidents), Denise Ilitch, Ronald Ilitch, Michael Ilitch Jr., Lisa Ilitch Murray, Carole Ilitch Trepeck, Jim Devellano (Senior Vice President), Ken Holland (General Manager), Don Waddell (Assistant General Manager), Scotty Bowman (Head Coach), Barry Smith, Dave Lewis (Associate Coaches), Jim Nill (Director of Player Development), Dan Belisle, Mark Howe (Pro Scouts), Jim Bedard (Goaltending Consultant), Hakan Andersson (Director of European Scouting), Mark Leach (USA Scout), Joe McDonnell (Eastern Scout), Bruce Haralson (Western Scout), John Wharton (Athletic Trainer), Paul Boyer (Equipment Manager), Tim Abbott (Assistant Equipment Manager), Bob Huddleston (Masseur), Sergei Mnatsakanov, Wally Crossman (Dressing Room Assistant).

**Scores:** June 9, at Detroit — Detroit 2, Washington 1; June 11, at Detroit — Detroit 5, Washington 4; June 13, at Washington — Detroit 2, Washington 1; June 16, at Washington — Detroit 4, Washington 1.

**1996-97 — Detroit Red Wings** — Steve Yzerman (Captain), Doug Brown, Mathieu Dandenault, Kris Draper, Sergei Fedorov, Viacheslav Fetisov, Kevin Hodson, Tomas Holmstrom, Joe Kocur, Vladimir Konstantinov, Vyacheslav Kozlov, Martin Lapointe, Igor Larionov, Nicklas Lidstrom, Kirk Maltby, Darren McCarty, Larry Murphy, Chris Osgood, Jamie Pushor, Bob Rouse, Tomas Sandstrom, Brendan Shanahan, Tim Taylor, Mike Vernon, Aaron Ward; Mike Ilitch (Owner/Chairman), Marian Ilitch (Owner), Atanas Ilitch, Christopher Ilitch (Vice Presidents), Denise Ilitch Lites, Ronald Ilitch, Michael Ilitch Jr., Lisa Ilitch Murray, Carole Ilitch Trepeck, Jim Devellano (Senior Vice President), Scotty Bowman (Head Coach/Director of Player Personnel), Ken Holland (Assistant General Manager), Barry Smith, Dave Lewis (Associate Coaches), Mike Krushelnyski (Assistant Coach), Jim Nill (Director of Player Development), Dan Belisle, Bruce Haralson, Mark Howe (Scouts), Hakan Andersson (Director of European Scouting), John Wharton (Athletic Trainer), Wally Crossman (Dressing Room Assistant), Mark Leach (Scout), Paul Boyer (Equipment Manager), Tim Abbott (Assistant Equipment Manager), Sergei Mnatsakanov (Masseur), Joe McDonnell (Scout).

**Scores:** May 31, at Philadelphia — Detroit 4, Philadelphia 2; June 3, at Philadelphia — Detroit 4, Philadelphia 2; June 5, at Detroit — Detroit 6, Philadelphia 1; June 7, at Detroit — Detroit 2, Philadelphia 1.

**1995-96 — Colorado Avalanche —** Rene Corbet, Adam Deadmarsh, Stephane Fiset, Adam Foote, Peter Forsberg, Alexei Gusarov, Dave Hannan, Valeri Kamensky, Mike Keane, Jon Klemm, Uwe Krupp, Sylvain Lefebvre, Claude Lemieux, Curtis Leschyshyn, Troy Murray, Sandis Ozolinsh, Mike Ricci, Patrick Roy, Warren Rychel, Joe Sakic (Captain), Chris Simon, Craig Wolanin, Stephane Yelle, Scott Young; Charlie Lyons (Chairman/CEO), Pierre Lacroix (Executive Vice President/General Manager), Marc Crawford (Head Coach), Joel Quenneville, Jacques Cloutier (Assistant Coaches), Francois Giguere (Assistant General Manager), Michel Goulet (Director of Player Personnel), Dave Draper (Chief Scout), Jean Martineau (Director of Public Relations), Pat Karns (Trainer), Matthew Sokolowski (Assistant Trainer), Rob McLean (Equipment Manager), Mike Kramer, Brock Gibbins (Assistant Equipment Managers), Skip Allen (Strength and Conditioning Coach), Paul Fixter (Video Coordinator), Leo Vyssokov (Massage Therapist).
**Scores:** June 4, at Colorado — Colorado 3, Florida 1; June 6, at Colorado — Colorado 8, Florida 1; June 8, at Florida — Colorado 3, Florida 2; June 10, at Florida — Colorado 1, Florida 0.

**1994-95 — New Jersey Devils —** Tommy Albelin, Martin Brodeur, Neal Broten, Sergei Brylin, Bob Carpenter, Shawn Chambers, Tom Chorske, Danton Cole, Ken Daneyko, Kevin Dean, Jim Dowd, Bruce Driver, Bill Guerin, Bobby Holik, Claude Lemieux, John MacLean, Chris McAlpine, Randy McKay, Scott Niedermayer, Mike Peluso, Stephane Richer, Brian Rolston, Scott Stevens (Captain), Chris Terreri, Valeri Zelepukin; Dr. John J. McMullen (Owner/Chairman), Peter S. McMullen (Owner), Lou Lamoriello (President/General Manager), Jacques Lemaire (Head Coach), Jacques Caron (Goaltender Coach), Dennis Gendron, Larry Robinson (Assistant Coaches), Robbie Ftorek (Albany (AHL) - Coach), Alex Abasto (Assistant Equipment Manager), Bob Huddleston (Massage Therapist), David Nichols (Equipment Manager), Ted Schuch (Medical Trainer), Michael Vasalani (Strength and Conditioning Coach), David Conte (Director of Scouting), Milt Fisher, Claude Carrier, Dan Labraaten, Marcel Pronovost (Scouts).
**Scores:** June 17, at Detroit — New Jersey 2, Detroit 1; June 20, at Detroit — New Jersey 4, Detroit 2; June 22, at New Jersey — New Jersey 5, Detroit 2; June 24, at New Jersey — New Jersey 5, Detroit 2.

**1993-94 — New York Rangers —** Mark Messier (Captain), Brian Leetch, Kevin Lowe, Adam Graves, Steve Larmer, Glenn Anderson, Jeff Beukeboom, Greg Gilbert, Glenn Healy, Mike Hudson, Alexander Karpovtsev, Joe Kocur, Alex Kovalev, Nick Kypreos, Doug Lidster, Stephane Matteau, Craig MacTavish, Sergei Nemchinov, Brian Noonan, Esa Tikkanen, Mike Richter, Jay Wells, Sergei Zubov, Ed Olczyk, Mike Hartman; Neil Smith (President/General Manager/Governor), Robert Gutkowski, Stanley Jaffe, Kenneth Munoz (Governors), Larry Pleau (Assistant General Manager), Mike Keenan (Head Coach), Colin Campbell (Associate Coach), Dick Todd (Assistant Coach), Matthew Loughren (Manager - Team Operations), Barry Watkins (Director - Communications), Christer Rockstrom, Tony Feltrin, Martin Madden, Herb Hammond, Darwin Bennett (Scouts), Dave Smith, Joe Murphy, Mike Folga, Bruce Lifrieri (Trainers).
**Scores:** May 31, at New York — Vancouver 3, NY Rangers 2; June 2, at New York — NY Rangers 3, Vancouver 1; June 4, at Vancouver — NY Rangers 5, Vancouver 1; June 7, at Vancouver — NY Rangers 4, Vancouver 2; June 9, at New York — Vancouver 6, at NY Rangers 3; June 11, at Vancouver — Vancouver 4, NY Rangers 1; June 14, at New York — NY Rangers 3, Vancouver 2.

**1992-93 — Montreal Canadiens —** Guy Carbonneau (Captain), Patrick Roy, Andre Racicot, Rob Ramage, Kirk Muller, Mike Keane, Kevin Haller, Paul DiPietro, John LeClair, Denis Savard, Benoit Brunet, Brian Bellows, Lyle Odelein, Vincent Damphousse, Gary Leeman, Mathieu Schneider, Eric Desjardins, Jesse Belanger, Ed Ronan, Mario Roberge, Donald Dufresne, Todd Ewen, Sean Hill, Patrice Brisebois, Gilbert Dionne, Stephan Lebeau, J.J. Daigneault; Ronald Corey (President), Serge Savard (Managing Director/Vice President - Hockey), Jacques Demers (Head Coach), Jacques Laperriere, Charles Thiffault (Assistant Coaches), Francois Allaire (Goaltending Instructor), Jean Béliveau (Senior Vice President - Corporate Affairs), Jacques Lemaire (Assistant to the Managing Director), André Boudrias (Assistant to the Managing Director/Director of Scouting), Gaeten Lefebvre (Athletic Trainer), John Shipman (Assistant to the Athletic Trainer), Eddy Palchak (Equipment Manager), Pierre Gervais, Robert Boulanger (Assistants to the Equipment Manager).
**Scores:** June 1, at Montreal — Los Angeles 4, Montreal 1; June 2, at Montreal — Montreal 3, Los Angeles 2; June 5, at Los Angeles — Montreal 4, Los Angeles 3; June 7, at Los Angeles — Montreal 3, Los Angeles 2; June 9, at Montreal — Montreal 4, Los Angeles 1.

**1991-92 — Pittsburgh Penguins —** Mario Lemieux (Captain), Ron Francis, Bryan Trottier, Kevin Stevens, Bob Errey, Phil Bourque, Troy Loney, Rick Tocchet, Joe Mullen, Jaromir Jagr, Jiri Hrdina, Shawn McEachern, Ulf Samuelsson, Kjell Samuelsson, Larry Murphy, Gordie Roberts, Jim Paek, Paul Stanton, Tom Barrasso, Ken Wregget, Jay Caufield, Jamie Leach, Wendell Young, Grant Jennings, Peter Taglianetti, Jock Callander, Dave Michayluk, Mike Needham, Jeff Chychrun, Ken Priestlay, Jeff Daniels; Morris Belzberg, Howard Baldwin, Thomas Ruta (Owners), Donn Patton (Executive Vice President/Chief Financial Officer), Paul Martha (Executive Vice President/General Counsel), Craig Patrick (Executive Vice President/General Manager), Bob Johnson (Head Coach), Scotty Bowman (Director of Player Development/Coach), Barry Smith, Rick Kehoe, Pierre McGuire, Gilles Meloche, Rick Paterson (Assistant Coaches), Steve Latin (Equipment Manager), Skip Thayer (Trainer), John Welday (Strength and Conditioning Coach), Greg Malone, Les Binkley, Charlie Hodge, John Gill, Ralph Cox (Scouts).
**Scores:** May 26, at Pittsburgh — Pittsburgh 5, Chicago 4; May 28, at Pittsburgh — Pittsburgh 3, Chicago 1; May 30, at Chicago — Pittsburgh 1, Chicago 0; June 1, at Chicago — Pittsburgh 6, Chicago 5.

**1990-91 — Pittsburgh Penguins —** Mario Lemieux (Captain), Paul Coffey, Randy Hillier, Bob Errey, Tom Barrasso, Phil Bourque, Jay Caufield, Ron Francis, Randy Gilhen, Jiri Hrdina, Jaromir Jagr, Grant Jennings, Troy Loney, Joe Mullen, Larry Murphy, Jim Paek, Frank Pietrangelo, Barry Pederson, Mark Recchi, Gordie Roberts, Ulf Samuelsson, Paul Stanton, Kevin Stevens, Peter Taglianetti, Bryan Trottier, Scott Young, Wendell Young; Edward J. DeBartolo Sr. (Owner), Marie D. DeBartolo York (President), Paul Martha (Vice President/General Counsel), Craig Patrick (General Manager), Scotty Bowman (Director of Player Development and Recruitment), Bob Johnson (Head Coach), Rick Kehoe, Rick Paterson, Barry Smith (Assistant Coaches), Gilles Meloche (Goaltending Coach/Scout), Steve Latin (Equipment Manager), Skip Thayer (Trainer), John Welday (Strength and Conditioning Coach), Greg Malone (Scout).

**Scores:** May 15, at Pittsburgh — Minnesota 5, Pittsburgh 4; May 17, at Pittsburgh — Pittsburgh 4, Minnesota 1; May 19, at Minnesota — Minnesota 3, Pittsburgh 1; May 21, at Minnesota — Pittsburgh 5, Minnesota 3; May 23, at Pittsburgh — Pittsburgh 6, Minnesota 4; May 25, at Minnesota — Pittsburgh 8, Minnesota 0.

**1989-90 — Edmonton Oilers —** Mark Messier (Captain), Jari Kurri, Kevin Lowe, Steve Smith, Jeff Beukeboom, Mark Lamb, Joe Murphy, Glenn Anderson, Adam Graves, Craig MacTavish, Kelly Buchberger, Craig Simpson, Martin Gelinas, Randy Gregg, Charlie Huddy, Geoff Smith, Reijo Ruotsalainen, Craig Muni, Bill Ranford, Dave Brown, Pokey Reddick, Petr Klima, Esa Tikkanen, Grant Fuhr; Peter Pocklington (Owner), Glen Sather (President/General Manager), John Muckler (Head Coach), Ted Green (Co-Coach), Ron Low (Assistant Coach), Bruce MacGregor (Assistant General Manager), Barry Fraser (Director of Player Personnel), Bill Tuele (Director of Public Relations), Werner Baum (Vice President), Dr. Gordon Cameron (Medical Chief of Staff), Dr. David Reid (Team Physician), Ken Lowe (Athletic Therapist), Barrie Stafford (Athletic Trainer), Stuart Poirier (Massage Therapist), Lyle Kulchisky (Assistant Trainer), John Blackwell (Cape Breton (AHL) - Director of Operations), Ace Bailey, Ed Chadwick, Lorne Davis, Harry Howell, Albert Reeves, Matti Vaisanen (Scouts).
**Scores:** May 15, at Boston — Edmonton 3, Boston 2; May 18, at Boston — Edmonton 7, Boston 2; May 20, at Edmonton — Boston 2, Edmonton 1; May 22, at Edmonton — Edmonton 5, Boston 1; May 24, at Boston — Edmonton 4, Boston 1.

**1988-89 — Calgary Flames —** Lanny McDonald (Co- Captain), Jim Peplinski (Co-Captain), Tim Hunter, Mike Vernon, Rick Wamsley, Al MacInnis, Brad McCrimmon, Dana Murzyn, Ric Nattress, Joe Mullen, Gary Roberts, Colin Patterson, Hakan Loob, Theoren Fleury, Jiri Hrdina, Gary Suter, Mark Hunter, Joe Nieuwendyk, Brian MacLellan, Joel Otto, Jamie Macoun, Doug Gilmour, Rob Ramage; Norman Green, Harley Hotchkiss, Norman Kwong, Sonia Scurfield, B.J. Seaman, D.K. Seaman (Owners), Cliff Fletcher (President/General Manager), Al MacNeil (Assistant General Manager), Al Coates (Assistant to the President), Terry Crisp (Head Coach), Doug Risebrough, Tom Watt (Assistant Coaches), Glenn Hall (Goaltending Consultant), Jim Murray (Trainer), Al Murray (Assistant Trainer), Bob Stewart (Equipment Manager).
**Scores:** May 14, at Calgary — Calgary 3, Montreal 2; May 17, at Calgary— Montreal 4, Calgary 2; May 19, at Montreal — Montreal 4, Calgary 3; May 21, at Montreal — Calgary 4, Montreal 2; May 23, at Calgary — Calgary 3, Montreal 2; May 25, at Montreal — Calgary 4, Montreal 2.

**1987-88 — Edmonton Oilers —** Wayne Gretzky (Captain), Keith Acton, Glenn Anderson, Jeff Beukeboom, Geoff Courtnall, Grant Fuhr, Randy Gregg, Dave Hannan, Charlie Huddy, Mike Krushelnyski, Jari Kurri, Normand Lacombe, Kevin Lowe, Craig MacTavish, Kevin McClelland, Marty McSorley, Mark Messier, Craig Muni, Bill Ranford, Craig Simpson, Steve Smith, Esa Tikkanen; Peter Pocklington (Owner), Glen Sather (General Manager/Coach), John Muckler (Co-Coach), Ted Green (Assistant Coach), Bruce MacGregor (Assistant General Manager), Barry Fraser (Director of Player Personnel), Bill Tuele (Director of Public Relations), Dr. Gordon Cameron (Team Doctor), Peter Millar (Athletic Therapist), Juergen Merz (Massage Therapist), Barrie Stafford (Trainer), Lyle Kulchisky (Assistant Trainer).
**Scores:** May 18, at Edmonton — Edmonton 2, Boston 1; May 20, at Edmonton — Edmonton 4, Boston 2; May 22, at Boston — Edmonton 6, Boston 3; May 24, at Boston — Boston 3, Edmonton 3 (suspended due to power failure); May 26, at Edmonton — Edmonton 6, Boston 3.

**1986-87 — Edmonton Oilers —** Wayne Gretzky (Captain), Glenn Anderson, Jeff Beukeboom, Kelly Buchberger, Paul Coffey, Grant Fuhr, Randy Gregg, Charlie Huddy, Dave Hunter, Mike Krushelnyski, Jari Kurri, Moe Lemay, Kevin Lowe, Craig MacTavish, Kevin McClelland, Marty McSorley, Mark Messier, Andy Moog, Craig Muni, Kent Nilsson, Jaroslav Pouzar, Reijo Ruotsalainen, Steve Smith, Esa Tikkanen; Peter Pocklington (Owner), Glen Sather (General Manager/Coach), Bruce MacGregor (Assistant General Manager), John Muckler (Co-Coach), Ted Green, Ron Low (Assistant Coaches), Barry Fraser (Director of Player Personnel), Garnet Bailey, Ed Chadwick, Lorne Davis, Matti Vaisanen (Scouts), Peter Millar (Athletic Therapist), Juergen Merz (Massage Therapist), Dr. Gordon Cameron (Team Doctor), Barrie Stafford (Trainer), Lyle Kulchisky (Assistant Trainer).
**Scores:** May 17, at Edmonton — Edmonton 4, Philadelphia 2; May 20, at Edmonton — Edmonton 3, Philadelphia 2; May 22, at Philadelphia — Philadelphia 5, Edmonton 3; May 24, at Philadelphia — Edmonton 4, Philadelphia 1; May 26, at Edmonton — Philadelphia 4, Edmonton 3; May 28, at Philadelphia — Philadelphia 3, Edmonton 2; May 31, at Edmonton — Edmonton 3, Philadelphia 1.

**1985-86 — Montreal Canadiens —** Bob Gainey (Captain), Doug Soetaert, Patrick Roy, Rick Green, David Maley, Ryan Walter, Serge Boisvert, Mario Tremblay, Bobby Smith, Craig Ludwig, Tom Kurvers, Kjell Dahlin, Larry Robinson, Guy Carbonneau, Chris Chelios, Petr Svoboda, Mats Naslund, Lucien DeBlois, Steve Rooney, Gaston Gingras, Mike Lalor, Chris Nilan, John Kordic, Claude Lemieux, Mike McPhee, Brian Skrudland, Stephane Richer; Ronald Corey (President), Serge Savard (General Manager), Jean Perron (Coach), Jacques Laperrière (Assistant Coach), Jean Béliveau, Francois-Xavier Seigneur, Fred Steer (Vice Presidents), Jacques Lemaire, André Boudrias (Assistant General Managers), Claude Ruel (Player Development), Yves Belanger (Athletic Therapist), Gaetan Lefebvre (Assistant Athletic Therapist), Eddy Palchak (Trainer), Sylvain Toupin (Assistant Trainer).
**Scores:** May 16, at Calgary — Calgary 5, Montreal 2; May 18, at Calgary — Montreal 3, Calgary 2; May 20, at Montreal — Montreal 5, Calgary 3; May 22, at Montreal — Montreal 1, Calgary 0; May 24, at Calgary — Montreal 4, Calgary 3.

**1984-85 — Edmonton Oilers —** Wayne Gretzky (Captain), Glenn Anderson, Billy Carroll, Paul Coffey, Lee Fogolin Jr., Grant Fuhr, Randy Gregg, Charlie Huddy, Pat Hughes, Dave Hunter, Don Jackson, Mike Krushelnyski, Jari Kurri, Willy Lindstrom, Kevin Lowe, Dave Lumley, Kevin McClelland, Larry Melnyk, Mark Messier, Andy Moog, Mark Napier, Jaroslav Pouzar, Dave Semenko, Esa Tikkanen; Peter Pocklington (Owner), Glen Sather (General Manager/Coach), Bruce MacGregor (Assistant General Manager), John Muckler, Ted Green (Assistant Coaches), Barry Fraser (Director of Player Personnel/Chief Scout), Garnet Bailey, Ed Chadwick, Lorne Davis, Matti Vaisanen (Scouts), Peter Millar (Athletic Therapist), Dr. Gordon Cameron (Team Doctor), Barrie Stafford (Trainer), Lyle Kulchisky (Assistant Trainer).
**Scores:** May 21, at Philadelphia — Philadelphia 4, Edmonton 1; May 23, at Philadelphia — Edmonton 3, Philadelphia 1; May 25, at Edmonton — Edmonton 4, Philadelphia 3; May 28, at Edmonton — Edmonton 5, Philadelphia 3; May 30, at Edmonton — Edmonton 8, Philadelphia 3.

**1983-84 — Edmonton Oilers —** Wayne Gretzky (Captain), Glenn Anderson, Paul Coffey, Pat Conacher, Lee Fogolin Jr., Grant Fuhr, Randy Gregg, Charlie Huddy, Pat Hughes, Dave Hunter, Don Jackson, Jari Kurri, Willy Lindstrom, Ken Linseman, Kevin Lowe, Dave Lumley, Kevin McClelland, Mark Messier, Andy Moog, Jaroslav Pouzar, Dave Semenko; Peter Pocklington (Owner), Glen Sather (General Manager/Coach), Bruce MacGregor (Assistant General Manager), John Muckler, Ted Green (Assistant Coaches), Barry Fraser (Director of Player Personnel/Chief Scout), Pete Millar (Athletic Therapist), Barrie Stafford (Trainer), Lyle Kulchisky (Assistant Trainer).
**Scores:** May 10, at New York — Edmonton 1, NY Islanders 0; May 12, at New York — NY Islanders 6, Edmonton 1; May 15, at Edmonton — Edmonton 7, NY Islanders 2; May 17, at Edmonton — Edmonton 7, NY Islanders 2; May 19, at Edmonton — Edmonton 5, NY Islanders 2.

**1982-83 — New York Islanders —** Denis Potvin (Captain), Mike Bossy, Bob Bourne, Paul Boutilier, Billy Carroll, Greg Gilbert, Clark Gillies, Butch Goring, Mats Hallin, Tomas Jonsson, Anders Kallur, Gord Lane, Dave Langevin, Mike McEwen, Roland Melanson, Wayne Merrick, Ken Morrow, Bob Nystrom, Stefan Persson, Billy Smith, Brent Sutter, Duane Sutter, John Tonelli, Bryan Trottier; Bill Torrey (President/General Manager), John Pickett Jr. (Chairman), Gerry Ehman (Assistant General Manager/Director of Scouting), Al Arbour (Coach), Lorne Henning (Assistant Coach), Ron Waske (Trainer), Jim Pickard (Assistant Trainer).
**Scores:** May 10, at Edmonton — NY Islanders 2, Edmonton 0; May 12, at Edmonton — NY Islanders 6, Edmonton 3; May 14, at New York — NY Islanders 5, Edmonton 1; May 17, at New York — NY Islanders 4, Edmonton 2

**1981-82 — New York Islanders —** Denis Potvin (Captain), Mike Bossy, Bob Bourne, Billy Carroll, Greg Gilbert, Clark Gillies, Butch Goring, Tomas Jonsson, Anders Kallur, Gord Lane, Dave Langevin, Hector Marini, Mike McEwen, Roland Melanson, Wayne Merrick, Ken Morrow, Bob Nystrom, Stefan Persson, Billy Smith, Brent Sutter, Duane Sutter, John Tonelli, Bryan Trottier; Bill Torrey (President/General Manager), John Pickett Jr. (Chairman), Jim Devellano (Assistant General Manager/Director of Scouting), Al Arbour (Coach), Lorne Henning (Assistant Coach), Gerry Ehman (Head Scout), Ron Waske (Trainer), Jim Pickard (Assistant Trainer).
**Scores:** May 8, at New York — NY Islanders 6, Vancouver 5; May 11, at New York — NY Islanders 6, Vancouver 4; May 13, at Vancouver — NY Islanders 3, Vancouver 0; May 16, at Vancouver — NY Islanders 3, Vancouver 1

**1980-81 — New York Islanders —** Denis Potvin (Captain), Mike Bossy, Bob Bourne, Billy Carroll, Clark Gillies, Butch Goring, Garry Howatt, Anders Kallur, Gord Lane, Dave Langevin, Bob Lorimer, Hector Marini, Mike McEwen, Roland Melanson, Wayne Merrick, Ken Morrow, Bob Nystrom, Stefan Persson, Jean Potvin, Billy Smith, Duane Sutter, John Tonelli, Bryan Trottier; Bill Torrey (President/General Manager), John Pickett Jr. (Chairman), Al Arbour (Coach), Lorne Henning (Player/Assistant Coach), Jim Devellano (Chief Scout), Gerry Ehman, Mario Saraceno, Harry Boyd (Scouts), Ron Waske (Trainer), Jim Pickard (Assistant Trainer).
**Scores:** May 12, at New York — NY Islanders 6, Minnesota 3; May 14, at New York — NY Islanders 6, Minnesota 3; May 17, at Minnesota — NY Islanders 7, Minnesota 5; May 19, at Minnesota— Minnesota 4, NY Islanders 2; May 21, at New York — NY Islanders 5, Minnesota 1.

**1979-80 — New York Islanders —** Denis Potvin (Captain), Mike Bossy, Bob Bourne, Clark Gillies, Butch Goring, Lorne Henning, Garry Howatt, Anders Kallur, Gord Lane, Dave Langevin, Bob Lorimer, Alex McKendry, Wayne Merrick, Ken Morrow, Bob Nystrom, Stefan Persson, Jean Potvin, Glenn Resch, Billy Smith, Duane Sutter, Steve Tambellini, John Tonelli, Bryan Trottier; Bill Torrey (President/General Manager), John Pickett Jr. (Chairman), Al Arbour (Coach), Billy MacMillan (Assistant Coach), Jim Devellano (Chief Scout), Gerry Ehman, Mario Saraceno, Harry Boyd (Scouts), Ron Waske (Trainer), Jim Pickard (Assistant Trainer).
**Scores:** May 13, at Philadelphia — NY Islanders 4, Philadelphia 3; May 15, at Philadelphia — Philadelphia 8, NY Islanders 3; May 17, at New York — NY Islanders 6, Philadelphia 2; May 19, at New York — NY Islanders 5, Philadelphia 2; May 22, at Philadelphia — Philadelphia 6, NY Islanders 3; May 24, at New York — NY Islanders 5, Philadelphia 4.

**1978-79 — Montreal Canadiens —** Yvan Cournoyer (Captain), Guy Lafleur, Ken Dryden, Rick Chartraw, Brian Engblom, Bob Gainey, Mario Tremblay, Guy Lapointe, Doug Risebrough, Réjean Houle, Pat Hughes, Michel Larocque, Doug Jarvis, Yvon Lambert, Pierre Larouche, Gilles Lupien, Rod Langway, Jacques Lemaire, Pierre Mondou, Larry Robinson, Mark Napier, Serge Savard, Steve Shutt, Cam Connor, Richard Sévigny; Jacques Courtois (President), Sam Pollock (Director), Irving Grundman (Vice President/Managing Director), Jean Beliveau (Vice President - Corporate Affairs), Scotty Bowman (Coach), Claude Ruel (Director of Player Development), Al MacNeil (Director of Player Personnel), Morgan McCammon (Director), Ron Caron (Director of Recruitment), Eddy Palchak (Trainer), Pierre Meilleur (Assistant Trainer).
**Scores:** May 13, at Montreal — NY Rangers 4, Montreal 1; May 15, at Montreal — Montreal 6, NY Rangers 2; May 17, at New York — Montreal 4, NY Rangers 1; May 19, at New York — Montreal 4, NY Rangers 3; May 21, at Montreal — Montreal 4, NY Rangers 1.

**1977-78 — Montreal Canadiens —** Yvan Cournoyer (Captain), Guy Lafleur, Ken Dryden, Michel Larocque, Rick Chartraw, Réjean Houle, Pierre Larouche, Brian Engblom, Yvon Lambert, Jacques Lemaire, Bob Gainey, Guy Lapointe, Doug Jarvis, Gilles Lupien, Pierre Mondou, Larry Robinson, Bill Nyrop, Murray Wilson, Serge Savard, Steve Shutt, Mario Tremblay, Pierre Bouchard, Doug Risebrough; Jacques Courtois (President), Sam Pollock (Vice President/General Manager), Jean Beliveau (Vice President/Director of Corporate Relations), Scotty Bowman (Coach), Peter Bronfman, Edward Bronfman (Directors), Al MacNeil (Director of Player Development), Eddy Palchak (Trainer), Pierre Meilleur (Assistant Trainer), Claude Ruel (Director of Player Development), Floyd Curry, Ron Caron (Assistant General Managers).
**Scores:** May 13, at Montreal — Montreal 4, Boston 1; May 16, at Montreal — Montreal 3, Boston 2; May 18, at Boston — Boston 4, Montreal 0; May 21, at Boston — Boston 4, Montreal 3; May 23, at Montreal — Montreal 4, Boston 1; May 25, at Boston — Montreal 4, Boston 1.

**1976-77 — Montreal Canadiens —** Yvan Cournoyer (Captain), Larry Robinson, Guy Lafleur, Pierre Bouchard, Rejean Houle, Yvon Lambert, Bob Gainey, Jacques Lemaire, Guy Lapointe, Ken Dryden, Rick Chartraw, Bill Nyrop, Michel Larocque, Pierre Mondou, Serge Savard, Steve Shutt, Mario Tremblay, Murray Wilson, Doug Jarvis, Mike Polich, Jimmy Roberts, Pete Mahovlich, Doug Risebrough, Jacques Courtois (President), Sam Pollock (Vice President/General Manager), Jean Beliveau (Vice President/Director of Corporate Relations), Scotty Bowman (Coach), Peter Bronfman, Edward Bronfman (Directors), Claude Ruel (Director of Player Development), Floyd Curry, Ron Caron (Assistant General Managers), Pierre Meilleur (Assistant Trainer), Eddy Palchak (Trainer).
**Scores:** May 7, at Montreal — Montreal 7, Boston 3; May 10, at Montreal — Montreal 3, Boston 0; May 12, at Boston — Montreal 4, Boston 2; May 14, at Boston — Montreal 2, Boston 1.

**1975-76 — Montreal Canadiens —** Yvan Cournoyer (Captain), Bob Gainey, Larry Robinson, Pierre Bouchard, Rick Chartraw, Ken Dryden, Pete Mahovlich, Guy Lafleur, Yvon Lambert, Michel Larocque, Serge Savard, Doug Jarvis, Jacques Lemaire, Guy Lapointe, Jimmy Roberts, Doug Risebrough, Steve Shutt, Murray Wilson, Mario Tremblay, Bill Nyrop; Jacques Courtois (President), Jean Beliveau (Vice President), Peter Bronfman (Chairman), Edward Bronfman (Director), Sam Pollock (Vice President/General Manager), Scotty Bowman (Coach), Eddy Palchak (Trainer), Pierre Meilleur (Assistant Trainer), Claude Ruel (Director of Player Development).
**Scores:** May 9, at Montreal — Montreal 4, Philadelphia 3; May 11, at Montreal — Montreal 2, Philadelphia 1; May 13, at Philadelphia — Montreal 3, Philadelphia 2; May 16, at Philadelphia — Montreal 5, Philadelphia 3.

**1974-75 — Philadelphia Flyers —** Bobby Clarke (Captain), Bernie Parent, Bobby Taylor, Wayne Stephenson, Ed Van Impe, Don Saleski, Tom Bladon, Larry Goodenough, Bill Barber, Gary Dornhoefer, Dave Schultz, Joe Watson, Ross Lonsberry, André Dupont, Terry Crisp, Orest Kindrachuk, Bill Clement, Bob Kelly, Rick MacLeish, Jimmy Watson, Reggie Leach, Ted Harris; Ed Snider (Chairman), Joe Scott (President), Eugene Dixon Jr. (Vice Chairman), Fred Shero (Coach), Keith Allen (Vice President/General Manager), Lou Scheinfeld (Vice President), Mike Nykoluk (Assistant Coach), Marcel Pelletier (Player Personnel Director), Barry Ashbee (Assistant Coach), Frank Lewis (Trainer), Jim McKenzie (Assistant Trainer).
**Scores:** May 15, at Philadelphia — Philadelphia 4, Buffalo 1; May 18, at Philadelphia — Philadelphia 2, Buffalo 1; May 20, at Buffalo — Buffalo 5, Philadelphia 4; May 22, at Buffalo — Buffalo 4, Philadelphia 2; May 25, at Philadelphia — Philadelphia 5, Buffalo 1; May 27, at Buffalo — Philadelphia 2, Buffalo 0.

**1973-74 — Philadelphia Flyers —** Bobby Clarke (Captain), Bernie Parent, Bobby Taylor, Bill Clement, Ross Lonsberry, Bill Barber, Orest Kindrachuk, Ed Van Impe, Don Saleski, Gary Dornhoefer, Barry Ashbee, Jimmy Watson, Dave Schultz, André Dupont, Bruce Cowick, Rick MacLeish, Terry Crisp, Bill Flett, Simon Nolet, Joe Watson, Bob Kelly, Tom Bladon; Ed Snider (Chairman), Joe Scott (President), Eugene Dixon Jr. (Vice Chairman), Fred Shero (Coach), Keith Allen (Vice President/General Manager), Mike Nykoluk (Assistant Coach), Marcel Pelletier (Player Personnel Director), Frank Lewis (Trainer), Jim McKenzie (Assistant Trainer).
**Scores:** May 7, at Boston — Boston 3, Philadelphia 2; May 9, at Boston — Philadelphia 3, Boston 2; May 12, at Philadelphia — Philadelphia 4, Boston 1; May 14, at Philadelphia — Philadelphia 4, Boston 2; May 16, at Boston — Boston 5, Philadelphia 1; May 19, at Philadelphia — Philadelphia 1, Boston 0.

**1972-73 — Montreal Canadiens —** Henri Richard (Captain), Jacques Laperrière, Ken Dryden, Yvan Cournoyer, Jacques Lemaire, Marc Tardif, Serge Savard, Pete Mahovlich, Guy Lapointe, Réjean Houle, Claude Larose, Pierre Bouchard, Frank Mahovlich, Jimmy Roberts, Chuck Lefley, Guy Lafleur, Bob Murdoch, Michel Plasse, Murray Wilson, Larry Robinson, Steve Shutt; Jacques Courtois (President), Jean Beliveau (Vice President), Peter Bronfman (Chairman), Sam Pollock (Vice President/General Manager), Edward Bronfman (Executive Director), Scotty Bowman (Coach), Bob Williams (Trainer).
**Scores:** April 29, at Montreal — Montreal 8, Chicago 3; May 1, at Montreal — Montreal 4, Chicago 1; May 3, at Chicago — Chicago 7, Montreal 4; May 6, at Chicago — Montreal 4, Chicago 0; May 8, at Montreal — Chicago 8, Montreal 7; May 10, at Chicago — Montreal 6, Chicago 4.

**1971-72 — Boston Bruins —** Bobby Orr, Gerry Cheevers, Eddie Johnston, Dallas Smith, Derek Sanderson, Carol Vadnais, Phil Esposito, Fred Stanfield, Don Awrey, Ted Green, Ken Hodge, John Bucyk, Wayne Cashman, John McKenzie, Ed Westfall, Mike Walton, Garnet Bailey, Don Marcotte; Weston Adams (Chairman), Weston Adams Jr. (President), Shelby Davis (Vice President), Charles Mulcahy (Junior Vice President/General Counsel), Eddie Powers (Vice President/Treasurer), Milt Schmidt (General Manager), Tom Johnson (Coach), Dan Canney (Trainer), John Forristall (Assistant Trainer).
**Scores:** April 30, at Boston — Boston 6, NY Rangers 5; May 2, at Boston — Boston 2, NY Rangers 1; May 4, at New York — NY Rangers 5, Boston 2; May 7, at New York — Boston 3, NY Rangers 2; May 9, at Boston — NY Rangers 3, Boston 2; May 11, at New York — Boston 3, NY Rangers 0.

**1970-71 — Montreal Canadiens —** Jean Béliveau (Captain), Pierre Bouchard, Yvan Cournoyer, John Ferguson, Jacques Laperrière, Terry Harper, Réjean Houle, Guy Lapointe, Claude Larose, Marc Tardif, Chuck Lefley, Jacques Lemaire, Frank Mahovlich, Henri Richard, Phil Roberto, Pete Mahovlich, Bob Murdoch, Serge Savard (37GP – injured), Bobby Sheehan, Leon Rochefort, J.C. Tremblay, Ken Dryden, Rogie Vachon; David Molson (President), William Molson, Peter Molson (Vice Presidents), Sam Pollock (Vice President/General Manager), Ron Caron (Assistant General Manager), Al MacNeil (Coach), Yves Belanger (Trainer), Phil Langlois, Eddie Palchak (Assistant Trainers).
**Scores:** May 4, at Chicago — Chicago 2, Montreal 1; May 6, at Chicago — Chicago 5, Montreal 3; May 9, at Montreal — Montreal 4, Chicago 2; May 11, at Montreal — Montreal 5, Chicago 2; May 13, at Chicago — Chicago 2, Montreal 0; May 16, at Montreal — Montreal 4, Chicago 3; May 18, at Chicago — Montreal 3, Chicago 2.

**1969-70 — Boston Bruins —** Don Awrey, John Bucyk, Garnet Bailey, Wayne Carleton, Wayne Cashman, Gary Doak, Phil Esposito, Ted Green, Ken Hodge, Bobby Orr, Don Marcotte, John McKenzie, Derek Sanderson, Dallas Smith, Rick Smith, Bill Speer, Fred Stanfield, Ed Westfall, Gerry Cheevers, Eddie Johnston, John Adams, Jim Lorentz, Ron Murphy, Bill Lesuk, Ivan Boldirev, Danny Schock; Weston Adams Sr. (Chairman), Weston Adams Jr. (President), Charles Mulcahy, Eddie Powers, Shelby Davis (Vice Presidents), Harry Sinden (Coach), Milt Schmidt (General Manager), Tom Johnson (Assistant General Manager), Dan Canney (Trainer), John Forristall (Assistant Trainer).
**Scores:** May 3, at St. Louis — Boston 6, St. Louis 1; May 5, at St. Louis — Boston 6, St. Louis 2; May 7, at Boston — Boston 4, St. Louis 1; May 10, at Boston — Boston 4, St. Louis 3.

**1968-69 — Montreal Canadiens —** Jean Béliveau (Captain), Ralph Backstrom, Jacques Lemaire, Dick Duff, Christian Bordeleau, Mickey Redmond, Yvan Cournoyer, Henri Richard, Bobby Rousseau, John Ferguson, Serge Savard, Terry Harper, Gilles Tremblay, Ted Harris, J.C. Tremblay, Larry Hillman, Jacques Laperrière, Claude Provost, Tony Esposito, Rogie Vachon, Gump Worsley; David Molson (President), William Molson, Peter Molson (Vice Presidents), Sam Pollock (Vice President/General Manager), Claude Ruel (Coach), Larry Aubut (Trainer), Eddie Palchak (Assistant Trainer).
**Scores:** April 27, at Montreal — Montreal 3, St. Louis 1; April 29, at Montreal — Montreal 3, St. Louis 1; May 1, at St. Louis — Montreal 4, St. Louis 0; May 4, at St. Louis — Montreal 2, St. Louis 1.

**1967-68 — Montreal Canadiens** — Jean Béliveau (Captain), Ralph Backstrom, Yvan Cournoyer, Dick Duff, John Ferguson, Danny Grant, Terry Harper, Ted Harris, Serge Savard, Jacques Laperrière, Claude Larose, Jacques Lemaire, Claude Provost, Mickey Redmond, Henri Richard, Bobby Rousseau, Gilles Tremblay, J.C. Tremblay, Carol Vadnais, Rogie Vachon, Ernie Wakely, Gump Worsley; Hartland Molson (Chairman), David Molson (President), Sam Pollock (Vice President/General Manager), Toe Blake (Coach), Larry Aubut (Trainer), Eddie Palchak (Assistant Trainer).
**Scores:** May 5, at St. Louis — Montreal 3, St. Louis 2; May 7, at St. Louis — Montreal 1, St. Louis 0; May 9, at Montreal — Montreal 4, St. Louis 3; May 11, at Montreal — Montreal 3, St. Louis 2.

**1966-67 — Toronto Maple Leafs** — George Armstrong (Captain), Bob Baun, Johnny Bower, Brian Conacher, Ron Ellis, Aut Erickson, Larry Hillman, Tim Horton, Red Kelly, Larry Jeffrey, Dave Keon, Frank Mahovlich, Milan Marcetta, Jim Pappin, Marcel Pronovost, Bob Pulford, Terry Sawchuk, Eddie Shack, Allan Stanley, Pete Stemkowski, Mike Walton; Stafford Smythe (President), Harold Ballard (Executive Vice President), John Bassett (Chairman), Punch Imlach (General Manager/Coach), King Clancy (Assistant Coach/Assistant General Manager), Bob Davidson (Chief Scout), John Anderson (Business Manager), Bob Haggert (Trainer), Tom Nayler (Assistant Trainer), Karl Elieff (Physiotherapist), Richard Smythe (Mascot).
**Scores:** April 20, at Montreal — Toronto 2, Montreal 6; April 22, at Montreal — Toronto 3, Montreal 0; April 25, at Toronto — Toronto 3, Montreal 2; April 27, at Toronto — Toronto 2, Montreal 6; April 29, at Montreal — Toronto 4, Montreal 1; May 2, at Toronto — Toronto 3, Montreal 1.

**1965-66 — Montreal Canadiens** — Jean Béliveau (Captain), Ralph Backstrom, Dave Balon, Yvan Cournoyer, Bobby Rousseau, Dick Duff, John Ferguson, Terry Harper, Ted Harris, Charlie Hodge, Jacques Laperrière, Claude Larose, Noel Price, Claude Provost, Henri Richard, Jimmy Roberts, Leon Rochefort, Jean-Guy Talbot, Gilles Tremblay, J.C. Tremblay, Gump Worsley; Hartland Molson (Chairman), David Molson (President), Sam Pollock (General Manager), Toe Blake (Coach), Andy Galley (Trainer), Larry Aubut (Assistant Trainer).
**Scores:** April 24, at Montreal — Detroit 3, Montreal 2; April 26, at Montreal — Detroit 5, Montreal 2; April 28, at Detroit — Montreal 4, Detroit 2; May 1, at Detroit — Montreal 2, Detroit 1; May 3, at Montreal — Montreal 5, Detroit 1; May 5, at Detroit — Montreal 3, Detroit 2.

**1964-65 — Montreal Canadiens** — Jean Béliveau (Captain), Ralph Backstrom, Dave Balon, Red Berenson, Yvan Cournoyer, Dick Duff, John Ferguson, Jean Gauthier, Charlie Hodge, Terry Harper, Ted Harris, Jacques Laperrière, Claude Larose, Garry Peters, Noel Picard, Claude Provost, Henri Richard, Jimmy Roberts, Bobby Rousseau, Jean-Guy Talbot, Gilles Tremblay, J.C. Tremblay, Ernie Wakely, Bryan Watson, Gump Worsley; Hartland Molson (Chairman), David Molson (President), Maurice Richard (Assistant to the President), Sam Pollock (General Manager), Toe Blake (Coach), Andy Galley (Trainer), Larry Aubut (Assistant Trainer).
**Scores:** April 17, at Montreal — Montreal 3, Chicago 2; April 20, at Montreal — Montreal 2, Chicago 0; April 22, at Chicago — Montreal 1, Chicago 3; April 25, at Chicago — Montreal 1, Chicago 5; April 7, at Montreal — Montreal 6, Chicago 0; April 29, at Chicago — Montreal 1, Chicago 2; May 1, at Montreal — Montreal 4, Chicago 0.

**1963-64 — Toronto Maple Leafs** — George Armstrong (Captain), Andy Bathgate, Bob Baun, Johnny Bower, Carl Brewer, Gerry Ehman, Billy Harris, Larry Hillman, Dave Keon, Tim Horton, Red Kelly, Frank Mahovlich, Don McKenney, Jim Pappin, Bob Pulford, Eddie Shack, Don Simmons, Allan Stanley, Ron Stewart, Al Arbour, Ed Litzenberger; Stafford Smythe (President), Harold Ballard (Executive Vice President), John Bassett (Chairman), Punch Imlach (Coach/General Manager), King Clancy (Assistant Coach/Assistant General Manager), Bob Haggert (Trainer), Tom Nayler (Assistant Trainer), Hugh Hoult (Stick Boy).
**Scores** April 11, at Toronto — Toronto 3, Detroit 2; April 14, at Toronto — Toronto 3, Detroit 4; April 16, at Detroit — Toronto 3, Detroit 4; April 18, at Detroit — Toronto 4, Detroit 2; April 21, at Toronto — Toronto 1, Detroit 2; April 23, at Detroit — Toronto 4, Detroit 3; April 25, at Toronto — Toronto 4, Detroit 0.

**1962-63 — Toronto Maple Leafs** — George Armstrong (Captain), Bob Baun, Johnny Bower, Carl Brewer, Kent Douglas, Dick Duff, Billy Harris, Larry Hillman, Tim Horton, Red Kelly, Dave Keon, Ed Litzenberger, John MacMillan, Frank Mahovlich, Bob Nevin, Bob Pulford, Eddie Shack, Don Simmons, Allan Stanley, Ron Stewart; Stafford Smythe (President), Harold Ballard (Executive Vice President), John Bassett (Chairman), Punch Imlach (Coach/General Manager), King Clancy (Assistant Coach/Assistant General Manager), Bob Haggert (Trainer), Tom Nayler (Assistant Trainer), Hugh Hoult (Stick Boy).
**Scores:** April 9, at Toronto — Toronto 4, Detroit 2; April 11, at Toronto — Toronto 4, Detroit 2; April 14, at Detroit — Toronto 2, Detroit 3; April 16, at Detroit — Toronto 4, Detroit 2; April 18, at Toronto — Toronto 3, Detroit 1.

*The Detroit Red Wings defeated the Montreal Canadiens in a seven-game Stanley Cup Final in both 1954 and 1955.*

**1961-62 — Toronto Maple Leafs** — George Armstrong (Captain), Al Arbour, Bob Baun, Johnny Bower, Carl Brewer, Dick Duff, Billy Harris, Larry Hillman, Dave Keon, Tim Horton, Red Kelly, Ed Litzenberger, John MacMillan, Frank Mahovlich, Bob Nevin, Bert Olmstead, Bob Pulford, Eddie Shack, Allan Stanley, Don Simmons, Ron Stewart; Stafford Smythe (President), Harold Ballard (Executive Vice President), John Bassett (Vice President), Conn Smythe (Chairman), Punch Imlach (Coach/General Manager), King Clancy (Assistant Coach), Bob Davidson (Chief Scout), Bob Haggert (Trainer), Tom Nayler (Assistant Trainer), Hugh Hoult (Stick Boy).
**Scores:** April 10, at Toronto — Toronto 4, Chicago 1; April 12, at Toronto — Toronto 3, Chicago 2; April 15, at Chicago — Toronto 0, Chicago 3; April 17, at Chicago — Toronto 1, Chicago 4; April 19, at Toronto —Toronto 8, Chicago 4; April 22, at Chicago — Toronto 2, Chicago 1.

**1960-61 — Chicago Black Hawks** — Ed Litzenberger (Captain), Al Arbour, Earl Balfour, Murray Balfour, Glenn Hall, Jack Evans, Roy Edwards, Denis DeJordy, Bill Hay, Wayne Hicks, Reggie Fleming, Wayne Hillman, Bobby Hull, Chico Maki, Ab McDonald, Moose Vasko, Stan Mikita, Ron Murphy, Eric Nesterenko, Pierre Pilote, Tod Sloan, Dollard St. Laurent, Kenny Wharram; Arthur Wirtz (President), Arthur Wirtz Jr. (Vice President), James Norris (Chairman), Tommy Ivan (General Manager), Rudy Pilous (Coach), Nick Garen, Walter Humeniuk (Trainers).
**Scores:** April 6, at Chicago — Chicago 3, Detroit 2; April 8, at Detroit — Detroit 3, Chicago 1; April 10, at Chicago — Chicago 3, Detroit 1; April 12, at Detroit — Detroit 2, Chicago 1; April 14, at Chicago — Chicago 6, Detroit 3; April 16, at Detroit — Chicago 5, Detroit 1.

**1959-60 — Montreal Canadiens** — Maurice Richard (Captain), Ralph Backstrom, Marcel Bonin, Jean Béliveau, Bernie Geoffrion, Phil Goyette, Doug Harvey, Bill Hicke, Charlie Hodge, Tom Johnson, Albert Langlois, Don Marshall, Dickie Moore, Ab McDonald, Jacques Plante, Henri Richard, André Pronovost, Claude Provost, Bob Turner, Jean-Guy Talbot; Senator Hartland Molson (President), Frank Selke (Managing Director), Ken Reardon (Vice President), Sam Pollock (Personnel Director), Toe Blake (Coach), Hector Dubois, Larry Aubut (Trainers).
**Scores:** April 7, at Montreal — Montreal 4, Toronto 2; April 9, at Montreal — Montreal 2, Toronto 1; April 12, at Toronto — Montreal 5, Toronto 2; April 14, at Toronto — Montreal 4, Toronto 0.

**1958-59 — Montreal Canadiens** — Maurice Richard (Captain), Ralph Backstrom, Marcel Bonin, Jean Béliveau, Ian Cushenan, Bernie Geoffrion, Charlie Hodge, Phil Goyette, Doug Harvey, Bill Hicke, Tom Johnson, Albert Langlois, Don Marshall, Ab McDonald, Dickie Moore, Jacques Plante, Ken Mosdell, André Pronovost, Claude Provost, Henri Richard, Jean-Guy Talbot, Bob Turner; Senator Hartland Molson (President), Frank Selke (Managing Director), Ken Reardon (Vice President), Sam Pollock (Personnel Director), Toe Blake (Coach), Hector Dubois, Larry Aubut (Trainers).
**Scores:** April 9, at Montreal — Montreal 5, Toronto 3; April 11, at Montreal — Montreal 3, Toronto 1; April 14, at Toronto — Toronto 3, Montreal 2; April 16, at Toronto — Montreal 3, Toronto 2; April 18, at Montreal — Montreal 5, Toronto 3.

**1957-58 — Montreal Canadiens** — Maurice Richard (Captain), Jean Béliveau, Marcel Bonin, Floyd Curry, Connie Broden, Bernie Geoffrion, Phil Goyette, Doug Harvey, Charlie Hodge, Tom Johnson, Albert Langlois, Don Marshall, Ab McDonald, Gerry McNeil, Dickie Moore, Bert Olmstead, Jacques Plante, André Pronovost, Henri Richard, Claude Provost, Dollard St. Laurent, Jean-Guy Talbot, Bob Turner; Senator Hartland Molson (President), Frank Selke (Managing Director), Ken Reardon (Vice President), Toe Blake (Coach), Hector Dubois, Larry Aubut (Trainers).
**Scores:** April 8, at Montreal —Montreal 2, Boston 1; April 10, at Montreal — Boston 5, Montreal 2; April 13, at Boston — Montreal 3, Boston 0; April 15, at Boston — Boston 3, Montreal 1; April 17, at Montreal — Montreal 3, Boston 2; April 20, at Boston — Montreal 5, Boston 3.

**1956-57 — Montreal Canadiens** — Maurice Richard (Captain), Jean Béliveau, Connie Broden, Floyd Curry, Bernie Geoffrion, Phil Goyette, Doug Harvey, Tom Johnson, Don Marshall, Gerry McNeil, Dickie Moore, Bert Olmstead, Jacques Plante, André Pronovost, Claude Provost, Henri Richard, Dollard St. Laurent, Jean-Guy Talbot, Bob Turner; William Northey (President), Donat Raymond (Chairman), Ken Reardon (Vice President), Frank Selke (Managing Director), Toe Blake (Coach), Hector Dubois, Larry Aubut (Trainers).
**Scores:** April 6, at Montreal — Montreal 5, Boston 1; April 9, at Montreal — Montreal 1, Boston 0; April 11, at Boston — Montreal 4, Boston 2; April 14, at Boston — Boston 2, Montreal 0; April 16, at Montreal — Montreal 5, Boston 1.

**1955-56 — Montreal Canadiens** — Butch Bouchard (Captain), Bob Turner, Jean Béliveau, Bert Olmstead, Floyd Curry, Bernie Geoffrion, Jacques Plante, Doug Harvey, Claude Provost, Charlie Hodge, Henri Richard, Tom Johnson, Maurice Richard, Jackie LeClair, Dollard St. Laurent, Don Marshall, Jean-Guy Talbot, Dickie Moore, Ken Mosdell; Donat Raymond (President), Frank Selke (Managing Director), D'Alton Coleman, William Northey (Vice Presidents), Ken Reardon (Assistant Manager), Toe Blake (Coach), Hector Dubois, Gaston Bettez (Trainers).
**Scores:** March 31, at Montreal — Montreal 6, Detroit 4; April 3, at Montreal — Montreal 5, Detroit 1; April 5, at Detroit — Detroit 3, Montreal 1; April 8, at Detroit — Montreal 3, Detroit 0; April 10, at Montreal — Montreal 3, Detroit 1.

**1954-55 — Detroit Red Wings** — Dutch Reibel, Terry Sawchuk, Jim Hay, Vic Stasiuk, Johnny Wilson, Gordie Howe, Red Kelly, Tony Leswick, Ted Lindsay (Captain), Marty Pavelich, Marcel Pronovost, Marcel Bonin, Alex Delvecchio, Bill Dineen, Bob Goldham, Benny Woit, Larry Hillman, Glen Skov; Bruce Norris (President), Marguerite Norris (President), Jack Adams (Manager), Jimmy Skinner (Coach), John Mitchell (Chief Scout), Fred Huber (Publicity Director), Carl Mattson, Lefty Wilson (Trainers).
**Scores:** April 3, at Detroit — Detroit 4, Montreal 2; April 5, at Detroit — Detroit 7, Montreal; April 7, at Montreal — Montreal 4, Detroit 2; April 9, at Montreal — Montreal 5, Detroit 3; April 10, at Detroit — Detroit 5, Montreal 1; April 12, at Montreal — Montreal 6, Detroit 3; April 14, at Detroit — Detroit 3, Montreal 1.

**1953-54 — Detroit Red Wings** — Marty Pavelich, Jimmy Peters, Marcel Pronovost, Metro Prystai, Dutch Reibel, Terry Sawchuk, Bob Goldham, Gordie Howe, Earl Johnson, Red Kelly, Tony Leswick, Ted Lindsay (Captain), Keith Allen, Al Arbour, Alex Delvecchio, Bill Dineen, Gilles Dube, Dave Gatherum, Glen Skov, Johnny Wilson, Benny Woit; Bruce Norris (Owner), Marguerite Norris (President), Jack Adams (Manager), Tommy Ivan (Coach), John Mitchell (Chief Scout), Fred Huber (Publicity Director), Carl Mattson, Lefty Wilson (Trainers), Wally Crossman (Assistant Trainer).
**Scores:** April 4, at Detroit — Detroit 3, Montreal 1; April 6, at Detroit — Montreal 3, Detroit 1; April 8, at Montreal — Detroit 5, Montreal 2; April 10, at Montreal — Detroit 2, Montreal 0; April 11, at Detroit — Montreal 1, Detroit 0; April 13, at Montreal — Montreal 4, Detroit 1; April 16, at Detroit — Detroit 2, Montreal 1.

**1952-53 — Montreal Canadiens** — Floyd Curry, Bernie Geoffrion, Bert Olmstead, Paul Meger, Dick Gamble, Dickie Moore, Tom Johnson, Bud MacPherson, Billy Reay, Ken Mosdell, Paul Masnick, John McCormack, Butch Bouchard (Captain), Maurice Richard, Elmer Lach, Gerry McNeil, Doug Harvey, Dollard St. Laurent, Jacques Plante, Lorne Davis, Calum MacKay, Eddie Mazur, Donat Raymond (President), Dalton Coleman (Director), William Northey (Special Advisor), Frank Selke (Manager), Dick Irvin (Coach), Hector Dubois, Gaston Bettez (Trainers).
**Scores:** April 9, at Montreal — Montreal 4, Boston 2; April 11, at Montreal — Boston 4, Montreal 1; April 12, at Boston — Montreal 3, Boston 0; April 14, at Boston — Montreal 7, Boston 3; April 16, at Montreal — Montreal 1, Boston 0.

**1951-52 — Detroit Red Wings** — Metro Prystai, Leo Reise Jr., Terry Sawchuk, Enio Sclisizzi, Glen Skov, Vic Stasiuk, Gordie Howe, Red Kelly, Tony Leswick, Ted Lindsay, Marty Pavelich, Marcel Pronovost, Sid Abel (Captain), Alex Delvecchio, Fred Glover, Bob Goldham, Glenn Hall, Benny Woit, Johnny Wilson, Larry Zeidel; James Norris (President), Bruce Norris (Owner), Jack Adams (Manager), Tommy Ivan (Coach), Fred Huber (Publicity Director), Carson Cooper (Scout), Carl Mattson, Lefty Wilson (Trainers), Wally Crossman (Assistant Trainer).
**Scores:** April 10, at Montreal — Detroit 3, Montreal 1; April 12, at Montreal — Detroit 2, Montreal 1; April 13, at Detroit — Detroit 3, Montreal 0; April 15, at Detroit — Detroit 3, Montreal 0.

**1950-51 — Toronto Maple Leafs** — Bill Barilko, Max Bentley, Hugh Bolton, Turk Broda, Fern Flaman, Cal Gardner, Bob Hassard, Bill Juzda, Ted Kennedy (Captain), Joe Klukay, Danny Lewicki, Fleming MacKell, Howie Meeker, Gus Mortson, John McCormack, Al Rollins, Tod Sloan, Sid Smith, Jimmy Thomson, Ray Timgren, Harry Watson; Joe Primeau (Coach), Bill MacBrien (Chairman), Conn Smythe (President/Manager), Hap Day (Assistant Manager), George McCullagh, J.Y. Murdoch (Vice Presidents), J.P. Bickell, Ed Bickle (Directors), Tim Daly (Trainer), Archie Campbell, Tommy Naylor (Assistant Trainers), Dr. Norman Delarue, Dr. James Murray, Dr. Horace MacIntyre (Club Doctors), Ed Fitkin (Publicity Director), Squib Walker (Chief Scout).
**Scores:** April 11, at Toronto — Toronto 3, Montreal 2; April 14, at Toronto — Montreal 3, Toronto 2; April 17, at Montreal — Toronto 2, Montreal 1; April 19, at Montreal — Toronto 3, Montreal 2; April 21, at Toronto — Toronto 3, Montreal 2.

**1949-50 — Detroit Red Wings** — Sid Abel (Captain), Pete Babando, Steve Black, Joe Carveth, Gerry Couture, Al Dewsbury, Lee Fogolin, George Gee, Gordie Howe, Red Kelly, Ted Lindsay, Harry Lumley, Clare Martin, Jim McFadden, Max McNab, Marty Pavelich, Jimmy Peters, Marcel Pronovost, Leo Reise Jr., Jack Stewart, Johnny Wilson, Larry Wilson, Doug McKay; James Norris (President), James Norris Jr. (Vice President), Arthur Wirtz (Secretary Treasurer), Jack Adams (Manager), Tommy Ivan (Coach), Fred Huber Jr. (Publicity Director), Carson Cooper (Head Scout), Carl Mattson (Trainer), Walter Humeniuk (Assistant Trainer).
**Scores:** April 11, at Detroit — Detroit 4, NY Rangers 1; April 13, at Toronto* — NY Rangers 3, Detroit 1; April 15, at Toronto* — Detroit 4, NY Rangers 0; April 18, at Detroit — NY Rangers 4, Detroit 3; April 20, at Detroit — NY Rangers 2, Detroit 1; April 22, at Detroit — Detroit 5, NY Rangers 4; April 23, at Detroit — Detroit 4, NY Rangers 3.
*Ice was unavailable in Madison Square Garden and NY Rangers elected to play second and third games on Toronto ice.

**1948-49 — Toronto Maple Leafs** — Bill Barilko, Max Bentley, Garth Boesch, Turk Broda, Bob Dawes, Bill Ezinicki, Cal Gardner, Bill Juzda, Ted Kennedy (Captain), Joe Klukay, Vic Lynn, Howie Meeker, Don Metz, Fleming MacKell, Gus Mortson, Sid Smith, Harry Taylor, Ray Timgren, Jimmy Thomson, Harry Watson; Hap Day (Coach), Bill MacBrien (Chairman), Conn Smythe (President/Manager), George McCullagh, J.Y. Murdoch (Vice Presidents), J.P. Bickell, Ed Bickle (Directors), Tim Daly (Trainer), Archie Campbell (Assistant Trainer), Dr. Norman Delarue, Dr. James Murray, Dr. Horace MacIntyre (Club Doctors), Ed Fitkin (Publicity Director), Squib Walker (Chief Scout), Kerry Day (Mascot).
**Scores:** April 8, at Detroit — Toronto 3, Detroit 2; April 10, at Detroit — Toronto 3, Detroit 1; April 13, at Toronto — Toronto 3, Detroit 1; April 16, at Toronto — Toronto 3, Detroit 1.

**1947-48 — Toronto Maple Leafs** — Syl Apps (Captain), Bill Barilko, Max Bentley, Garth Boesch, Turk Broda, Les Costello, Bill Ezinicki, Ted Kennedy, Joe Klukay, Vic Lynn, Howie Meeker, Nick Metz, Don Metz, Gus Mortson, Phil Samis, Sid Smith, Wally Stanowski, Jimmy Thomson, Harry Watson; Hap Day (Coach), Conn Smythe (Manager), Tim Daly (Trainer).
**Scores:** April 7, at Toronto — Toronto 5, Detroit 3; April 10, at Toronto — Toronto 4, Detroit 2; April 11, at Detroit — Toronto 2, Detroit 0; April 14, at Detroit — Toronto 7, Detroit 2.

**1946-47 — Toronto Maple Leafs** — Turk Broda, Garth Boesch, Gus Mortson, Jimmy Thomson, Wally Stanowski, Bill Barilko, Harry Watson, Bud Poile, Ted Kennedy, Syl Apps (Captain), Don Metz, Nick Metz, Bill Ezinicki, Vic Lynn, Howie Meeker, Gaye Stewart, Joe Klukay, Gus Bodnar, Bob Goldham; Conn Smythe (Manager), Hap Day (Coach), Tim Daly (Trainer).
**Scores:** April 8, at Montreal — Montreal 6, Toronto 0; April 10, at Montreal — Toronto 4, Montreal 0; April 12, at Toronto — Toronto 4, Montreal 2; April 15, at Toronto — Toronto 2, Montreal 1; April 17, at Montreal — Montreal 3, Toronto 1; April 19, at Toronto — Toronto 2, Montreal 1.

**1945-46 — Montreal Canadiens** — Elmer Lach, Toe Blake (Captain), Maurice Richard, Bob Fillion, Dutch Hiller, Murph Chamberlain, Ken Mosdell, Buddy O'Connor, Glen Harmon, Jimmy Peters, Butch Bouchard, Billy Reay, Ken Reardon, Leo Lamoureux, Frank Eddolls, Gerry Plamondon, Joe Benoit, Bill Durnan; Tommy Gorman (Manager), Dick Irvin (Coach), Ernie Cook (Trainer).
**Scores:** March 30, at Montreal — Montreal 4, Boston 3; April 2, at Montreal — Montreal 3, Boston 2; April 4, at Boston — Montreal 4, Boston 2; April 7, at Boston — Boston 3, Montreal 2; April 9, at Montreal — Montreal 6, Boston 3.

**1944-45 — Toronto Maple Leafs** — Don Metz, Frank McCool, Wally Stanowski, Reg Hamilton, Moe Morris, John McCreedy, Tom O'Neill, Ted Kennedy, Babe Pratt, Gus Bodnar, Art Jackson, Jack McLean, Mel Hill, Nick Metz, Bob Davidson (Captain), Sweeney Schriner, Lorne Carr, Pete Backor, Ross Johnstone; Conn Smythe (Manager), Frank Selke (Business Manager), Hap Day (Coach), Tim Daly (Trainer).
**Scores:** April 6, at Detroit — Toronto 1, Detroit 0; April 8, at Detroit — Toronto 2, Detroit 0; April 12, at Toronto — Toronto 1, Detroit 0; April 14, at Toronto — Detroit 5, Toronto 3; April 19, at Detroit — Detroit 2, Toronto 0; April 21, at Toronto — Detroit 1, Toronto 0; April 22, at Detroit — Toronto 2, Detroit 1.

**1943-44 — Montreal Canadiens** — Toe Blake (Captain), Maurice Richard, Elmer Lach, Ray Getliffe, Murph Chamberlain, Phil Watson, Butch Bouchard, Glen Harmon, Buddy O'Connor, Gerry Heffernan, Mike McMahon, Leo Lamoureux, Fern Majeau, Bob Fillion, Bill Durnan; Tommy Gorman (Manager), Dick Irvin (Coach), Ernie Cook (Trainer).
**Scores:** April 4, at Montreal — Montreal 5, Chicago 1; April 6, at Chicago — Montreal 3, Chicago 1; April 9, at Chicago — Montreal 3, Chicago 2; April 13, at Montreal — Montreal 5, Chicago 4.

**1942-43 — Detroit Red Wings** — Jack Stewart, Jimmy Orlando, Sid Abel (captain), Alex Motter, Harry Watson, Joe Carveth, Mud Bruneteau, Eddie Wares, Johnny Mowers, Cully Simon, Don Grosso, Carl Liscombe, Connie Brown, Syd Howe, Les Douglas, Harold Jackson, Joe Fisher, Adam Brown; Jack Adams (Manager), Ebbie Goodfellow (Playing Coach), Honey Walker (Trainer).
**Scores:** April 1, at Detroit — Detroit 6, Boston 2; April 4, at Detroit — Detroit 4, Boston 3; April 7, at Boston — Detroit 4, Boston 0; April 8, at Boston — Detroit 2, Boston 0.

**1941-42 — Toronto Maple Leafs** — Wally Stanowski, Syl Apps (Captain), Bob Goldham, Gordie Drillon, Hank Goldup, Ernie Dickens, Sweeney Schriner, Bucko McDonald, Bob Davidson, Nick Metz, Bingo Kampman, Don Metz, Gaye Stewart, Turk Broda, John McCreedy, Lorne Carr, Pete Langelle, Billy Taylor, Reg Hamilton; Conn Smythe (Manager), Hap Day (Coach), Frank Selke (Business Manager), Tim Daly (Trainer).
**Scores:** April 4, at Toronto — Detroit 3, Toronto 2; April 7, at Toronto — Detroit 4, Toronto 2; April 9, at Detroit — Detroit 5, Toronto 2; April 12, at Detroit — Toronto 4, Detroit 3; April 14, at Toronto — Toronto 9, Detroit 3; April 16, at Detroit — Toronto 3, Detroit 0; April 18, at Toronto — Toronto 3, Detroit 1.

**1940-41 — Boston Bruins** — Bill Cowley, Des Smith, Dit Clapper (Captain), Frank Brimsek, Flash Hollett, Jack Crawford, Bobby Bauer, Pat McReavy, Herb Cain, Mel Hill, Milt Schmidt, Woody Dumart, Roy Conacher, Terry Reardon, Art Jackson, Eddie Wiseman, Jack Shewchuck; Art Ross (Manager), Cooney Weiland (Coach), Win Green (Trainer).
**Scores:** April 6, at Boston — Detroit 2, Boston 3; April 8, at Boston — Detroit 1, Boston 2; April 10, at Detroit — Boston 4, Detroit 2; April 12, at Detroit — Boston 3, Detroit 1.

**1939-40 — New York Rangers** — Dave Kerr, Art Coulter (Captain), Ott Heller, Alex Shibicky, Mac Colville, Neil Colville, Phil Watson, Lynn Patrick, Clint Smith, Muzz Patrick, Babe Pratt, Bryan Hextall, Kilby MacDonald, Dutch Hiller, Alf Pike, Stan Smith; Lester Patrick (Manager), Frank Boucher (Coach), Harry Westerby (Trainer).
**Scores:** April 2, at New York — NY Rangers 2, Toronto 1; April 3, at New York — NY Rangers 6, Toronto 2; April 6, at Toronto — NY Rangers 1, Toronto 2; April 9, at Toronto — NY Rangers 0, Toronto 3; April 11, at Toronto — NY Rangers 2, Toronto 1; April 13, at Toronto — NY Rangers 3, Toronto 2.

**1938-39 — Boston Bruins** — Bobby Bauer, Mel Hill, Flash Hollett, Roy Conacher, Gord Pettinger, Charlie Sands, Milt Schmidt, Woody Dumart, Jack Crawford, Ray Getliffe, Frank Brimsek, Eddie Shore, Dit Clapper, Bill Cowley, Jack Portland, Red Hamill, Harry Frost, Cooney Weiland (Captain); Art Ross (Manager/Coach), Win Green (Trainer).
**Scores:** April 6, at Boston — Toronto 1, Boston 2; April 9, at Boston — Toronto 3, Boston 2; April 11, at Toronto — Toronto 1, Boston 3; April 13, at Toronto — Toronto 0, Boston 2; April 16, at Boston — Toronto 1, Boston 3.

**1937-38 — Chicago Black Hawks** — Art Wiebe, Carl Voss, Harold Jackson, Mike Karakas, Mush March, Jack Shill, Earl Seibert, Cully Dahlstrom, Alex Levinsky, Johnny Gottselig (Captain), Lou Trudel, Pete Palangio, Bill MacKenzie, Doc Romnes, Paul Thompson, Roger Jenkins, Alfie Moore, Bert Connelly, Virgil Johnson, Paul Goodman; Bill Stewart (Manager/Coach), Eddie Froelich (Trainer).
**Scores:** April 5, at Toronto — Chicago 3, Toronto 1; April 7, at Toronto — Chicago 1, Toronto 5; April 10, at Chicago — Chicago 2, Toronto 1; April 12, at Chicago — Chicago 4, Toronto 1.

**1936-37 — Detroit Red Wings** — Normie Smith, Pete Kelly, Larry Aurie, Herbie Lewis, Hec Kilrea, Mud Bruneteau, Syd Howe, Wally Kilrea, Jimmy Franks, Bucko McDonald, Gord Pettinger, Ebbie Goodfellow, John Gallagher, Ralph Bowman, John Sorrell, Marty Barry, Earl Robertson, John Sherf, Howie Mackie, Rolly Roulston, Doug Young (Captain); Jack Adams (Manager/Coach), Honey Walker (Trainer).
**Scores:** April 6, at New York — Detroit 1, NY Rangers 5; April 8, at Detroit — Detroit 4, NY Rangers 2; April 11, at Detroit — Detroit 0, NY Rangers 1; April 13, at Detroit — Detroit 1, NY Rangers 0; April 15, at Detroit — Detroit 3, NY Rangers 0.

**1935-36 — Detroit Red Wings** — John Sorrell, Syd Howe, Marty Barry, Herbie Lewis, Mud Bruneteau, Wally Kilrea, Hec Kilrea, Gord Pettinger, Bucko McDonald, Ralph Bowman, Pete Kelly, Doug Young (Captain), Ebbie Goodfellow, Normie Smith, Larry Aurie; Jack Adams (Manager/Coach), Honey Walker (Trainer).
**Scores:** April 5, at Detroit — Detroit 3, Toronto 1; April 7, at Detroit — Detroit 9, Toronto 4; April 9, at Toronto — Detroit 3, Toronto 4; April 11, at Toronto — Detroit 3, Toronto 2.

**1934-35 — Montreal Maroons** — Lionel Conacher, Cy Wentworth, Alec Connell, Toe Blake, Stewart Evans, Earl Robinson, Bill Miller, Dave Trottier, Jimmy Ward, Baldy Northcott, Hooley Smith (Captain), Russ Blinco, Al Shields, Sammy McManus, Gus Marker, Bob Gracie, Herb Cain, Dutch Gainor; Tommy Gorman (Manager/Coach), Bill O'Brien (Trainer).
**Scores:** April 4, at Toronto — Mtl. Maroons 3, Toronto 2; April 6, at Toronto — Mtl. Maroons 3, Toronto 1; April 9, at Montreal — Mtl. Maroons 4, Toronto 1.

**1933-34 — Chicago Black Hawks** — Clarence Abel, Rosie Couture, Lou Trudel, Lionel Conacher, Paul Thompson, Leroy Goldsworthy, Art Coulter, Roger Jenkins, Don McFadyen, Tom Cook, Doc Romnes, Johnny Gottselig, Mush March, Johnny Sheppard, Charlie Gardiner (Captain), Bill Kendall, Jack Leswick; Tommy Gorman (Manager/Coach), Eddie Froelich (Trainer).
**Scores:** April 3, at Detroit — Chicago 2, Detroit 1; April 5, at Detroit — Chicago 4, Detroit 1; April 8, at Chicago — Detroit 5, Chicago 2; April 10, at Chicago — Chicago 1, Detroit 0.

**1932-33 — New York Rangers** — Ching Johnson, Butch Keeling, Frank Boucher, Art Somers, Babe Siebert, Bun Cook, Andy Aitkenhead, Ott Heller, Oscar Asmundson, Gord Pettinger, Doug Brennan, Cecil Dillon, Bill Cook (Captain), Murray Murdoch, Earl Seibert; Lester Patrick (Manager/Coach), Harry Westerby (Trainer).
**Scores:** April 4, at New York — NY Rangers 5, Toronto 1; April 8, at Toronto — NY Rangers 3, Toronto 1; April 11, at Toronto — Toronto 3, NY Rangers 2; April 13, at Toronto — NY Rangers 1, Toronto 0.

**1931-32 — Toronto Maple Leafs** — Charlie Conacher, Busher Jackson, King Clancy, Andy Blair, Red Horner, Lorne Chabot, Alex Levinsky, Joe Primeau, Harold Darragh, Baldy Cotton, Frank Finnigan, Hap Day (Captain), Ace Bailey, Bob Gracie, Fred Robertson, Earl Miller; Conn Smythe (Manager), Dick Irvin (Coach), Tim Daly (Trainer).
**Scores:** April 5, at New York — Toronto 6, NY Rangers 4; April 7, at Boston* — Toronto 6, NY Rangers 2; April 9, at Toronto — Toronto 6, NY Rangers 4.

*Seventy-five years ago this season, the 1934-35 Montreal Maroons won their second (and final) Stanley Cup championship. Coach and g.m. Tom Gorman had guided Chicago to a Stanley Cup title the year before. The Maroons are the last Stanley Cup champions who no longer exist in the NHL.*

**1930-31 — Montreal Canadiens** — George Hainsworth, Wildor Larochelle, Marty Burke, Sylvio Mantha (Captain), Howie Morenz, Johnny Gagnon, Aurel Joliat, Armand Mondou, Pit Lepine, Albert Leduc, Georges Mantha, Art Lesieur, Nick Wasnie, Gus Rivers, Jean Pusie; Léo Dandurand (Manager), Cecil Hart (Coach), Ed Dufour (Trainer).
**Scores:** April 3, at Chicago — Montreal 2, Chicago 1; April 5, at Chicago — Chicago 2, Montreal 1; April 9, at Montreal — Chicago 3, Montreal 2; April 11, at Montreal — Montreal 4, Chicago 2; April 14, at Montreal — Montreal 2, Chicago 0.

**1929-30 — Montreal Canadiens** — George Hainsworth, Marty Burke, Sylvio Mantha (Captain), Howie Morenz, Bert McCaffrey, Aurel Joliat, Albert Leduc, Pit Lepine, Wildor Larochelle, Nick Wasnie, Gerry Carson, Armand Mondou, Georges Mantha, Gus Rivers; Léo Dandurand (Manager), Cecil Hart (Coach), Ed Dufour (Trainer).
**Scores:** April 1, at Boston — Montreal 3, Boston 0; April 3, at Montreal — Montreal 4, Boston 3.

**1928-29 — Boston Bruins** — Tiny Thompson, Eddie Shore, Lionel Hitchman (Captain), Percy Galbraith, Mickey MacKay, Red Green, Dutch Gainor, Harry Oliver, Eddie Rodden, Dit Clapper, Cooney Weiland, Lloyd Klein, Cy Denneny, Bill Carson, George Owen, Myles Lane; Art Ross (Manager/Coach), Win Green (Trainer).
**Scores:** March 28, at Boston — Boston 2, NY Rangers 0; March 29, at New York — Boston 2, NY Rangers 1.

**1927-28 — New York Rangers** — Lorne Chabot, Clarence Abel, Leo Bourgeault, Ching Johnson, Bill Cook (Captain), Bun Cook, Frank Boucher, Bill Boyd, Murray Murdoch, Paul Thompson, Alex Gray, Joe Miller, Patsy Callighen; Lester Patrick (Manager/Coach), Harry Westerby (Trainer).
**Scores:** April 5, at Montreal — Mtl. Maroons 2, NY Rangers 0; April 7, at Montreal — NY Rangers 2, Mtl. Maroons 1; April 10, at Montreal — Mtl. Maroons 2, NY Rangers 0; April 12, at Montreal — NY Rangers 1, Mtl. Maroons 0; April 14, at Montreal — NY Rangers 2, Mtl. Maroons 1.

**1926-27 — Ottawa Senators** — Alec Connell, King Clancy, Georges Boucher (Captain), Ed Gorman, Frank Finnigan, Alex Smith, Hec Kilrea, Hooley Smith, Cy Denneny, Frank Nighbor, Jack Adams, Milt Halliday; Dave Gill (Manager/Coach).
**Scores:** April 7, at Boston — Ottawa 0, Boston 0; April 9, at Boston — Ottawa 3, Boston 1; April 11, at Ottawa — Boston 1, Ottawa 1; April 13, at Ottawa — Ottawa 3, Boston 1.

**1925-26 — Montreal Maroons** — Clint Benedict, Reg Noble, Frank Carson, Dunc Munro (Captain), Nels Stewart, Punch Broadbent, Babe Siebert, Chuck Dinsmore, Merlyn Phillips, Hobie Kitchen, Sam Rothschild, Albert Holway, George Horne, Bernie Brophy; Eddie Gerard (Manager/Coach), Bill O'Brien (Trainer).
**Scores:** March 30, at Montreal — Mtl. Maroons 3, Victoria 0; April 1, at Montreal — Mtl. Maroons 3, Victoria 0; April 3, at Montreal — Victoria 3, Mtl. Maroons 2; April 6, at Montreal — Mtl. Maroons 2, Victoria 0.

The series in the spring of 1926 ended the annual playoffs between the champions of the East and the champions of the West. Since 1926-27 the annual playoffs in the National Hockey League have decided the Stanley Cup champions.

**1924-25 — Victoria Cougars** — Hap Holmes, Clem Loughlin (Captain), Gord Fraser, Frank Fredrickson, Jack Walker, Gizzy Hart, Harold Halderson, Frank Foyston, Wally Elmer, Harry Meeking, Jocko Anderson; Lester Patrick (Manager/Coach).
**Scores:** March 21, at Victoria — Victoria 5, Montreal 2; March 23, at Vancouver — Victoria 3, Montreal 1; March 27, at Victoria — Montreal 4, Victoria 2; March 30, at Victoria — Victoria 6, Montreal 1.

**1923-24 — Montreal Canadiens** — Georges Vezina, Sprague Cleghorn (Captain), Billy Coutu, Howie Morenz, Aurel Joliat, Billy Boucher, Odie Cleghorn, Sylvio Mantha, Bobby Boucher, Billy Bell, Billy Cameron, Joe Malone, Charles Fortier; Leo Dandurand (Manager/Coach).
**Scores:** March 22, at Montreal — Montreal 6, Cgy. Tigers 1; March 25, at Ottawa* — Montreal 3, Cgy. Tigers 0.

* Game transferred to Ottawa to benefit from artificial ice surface.

**1922-23 — Ottawa Senators** — Georges Boucher, Lionel Hitchman, Frank Nighbor, King Clancy, Harry Helman, Clint Benedict, Jack Darragh, Eddie Gerard (Captain), Cy Denneny, Punch Broadbent; Tommy Gorman (Manager), Pete Green (Coach), F. Dolan (Trainer).
**Scores:** March 29, at Vancouver — Ottawa 2, Edm. Eskimos 1; March 31, at Vancouver — Ottawa 1, Edm. Eskimos 0.

**1921-22 — Toronto St. Patricks** — Ted Stackhouse, Corb Denneny, Rod Smylie, Lloyd Andrews, John Ross Roach, Harry Cameron, Billy Stuart, Babe Dye, Ken Randall, Reg Noble (Captain), Eddie Gerard (borrowed for one game from Ottawa), Stan Jackson, Ivan Mitchell; Charlie Querrie (Manager), George O'Donoghue (Coach).
**Scores:** March 17, at Toronto — Van. Millionaires 4, Toronto 3; March 20, at Toronto — Toronto 2, Van. Millionaires 1; March 23, at Toronto — Van. Millionaires 3, Toronto 0; March 25, at Toronto — Toronto 6, Van. Millionaires 0; March 28, at Toronto — Toronto 5, Van. Millionaires 1.

**1920-21 — Ottawa Senators** — Jack MacKell, Jack Darragh, Morley Bruce, Georges Boucher, Eddie Gerard (Captain), Clint Benedict, Sprague Cleghorn, Frank Nighbor, Punch Broadbent, Cy Denneny, Leth Graham; Tommy Gorman (Manager), Pete Green (Coach), F. Dolan (Trainer).
**Scores:** March 21, at Vancouver — Van. Millionaires 2, Ottawa 1; March 24, at Vancouver — Ottawa 4, Van. Millionaires 3; March 28, at Vancouver — Ottawa 3, Van. Millionaires 2; March 31, at Vancouver — Van. Millionaires 3, Ottawa 2; April 4, at Vancouver — Ottawa 2, Van. Millionaires 1

**1919-20 — Ottawa Senators** — Jack MacKell, Jack Darragh, Morley Bruce, Horace Merrill, Georges Boucher, Eddie Gerard (Captain), Clint Benedict, Sprague Cleghorn, Frank Nighbor, Punch Broadbent, Cy Denneny, Tommy Gorman (Manager), Pete Green (Coach).
**Scores:** March 22, at Ottawa — Ottawa 3, Seattle 2; March 24, at Ottawa — Ottawa 3, Seattle 0; March 27, at Ottawa — Seattle 3, Ottawa 1; March 30, at Toronto* — Seattle 5, Ottawa 2; April 1, at Toronto* — Ottawa 6, Seattle 1.

* Games transferred to Toronto to benefit from artificial ice surface.

**1918-19** — No decision, Series halted by Spanish influenza epidemic, illness of several players and death of Joe Hall of Montreal Canadiens from the flu. Five games had been played when the series was halted, each team having won two and tied one. Final scores are listed below.
**Scores:** March 19, at Seattle — Seattle 7, Montreal 0; March 22, at Seattle — Montreal 4, Seattle 2; March 24, at Seattle — Seattle 7, Montreal 2; March 26, at Seattle — Montreal 0, Seattle 0; March 30, at Seattle — Montreal 4, Seattle 3.

**1917-18 — Toronto Arenas** — Rusty Crawford, Harry Meeking, Ken Randall (Captain), Corb Denneny, Harry Cameron, Jack Adams, Alf Skinner, Harry Mummery, Hap Holmes, Reg Noble, Sammy Hebert, Jack Marks, Jack Coughlin; Charlie Querrie (Manager), Dick Carroll (Coach), Frank Carroll (Trainer).
**Scores:** March 20, at Toronto — Toronto 5, Van. Millionaires 3; March 23, at Toronto — Van. Millionaires 6, Toronto 4; March 26, at Toronto — Toronto 6, Van. Millionaires 3; March 28, at Toronto — Van. Millionaires 8, Toronto 1; March 30, at Toronto — Toronto 2, Van. Millionaires 1.

**1916-17 — Seattle Metropolitans** — Hap Holmes, Ed Carpenter, Cully Wilson, Jack Walker, Bernie Morris, Frank Foyston, Roy Rickey, Jim Riley, Bobby Rowe (Captain); Peter Muldoon (Manager).
**Scores:** March 17, at Seattle — Montreal 8, Seattle 4; March 20, at Seattle — Seattle 6, Montreal 1; March 23, at Seattle — Seattle 4, Montreal 1; March 26, at Seattle — Seattle 9, Montreal 1.

**1915-16 — Montreal Canadiens** — Georges Vezina, Bert Corbeau, Jack Laviolette, Newsy Lalonde, Louis Berlinquette, Goldie Prodger, Howard McNamara (Captain), Didier Pitre, Skene Ronan, Amos Arbour, Skinner Poulin, Jack Fournier; George Kennedy (Manager).
**Scores:** March 20, at Montreal — Portland 2, Montreal 0; March 22, at Montreal — Montreal 2, Portland 1; March 25, at Montreal — Montreal 6, Portland 3; March 28, at Montreal — Portland 6, Montreal 5; March 30, at Montreal — Montreal 2, Portland 1.

**1914-15 — Vancouver Millionaires —** Ken Mallen, Frank Nighbor, Cyclone Taylor, Hugh Lehman, Lloyd Cook, Mickey MacKay, Barney Stanley, Jim Seaborn, Si Griffis (Captain), Johnny Matz; Frank Patrick (Playing Manager).
**Scores:** March 22, at Vancouver — Van. Millionaires 6, Ottawa 2; March 24, at Vancouver — Van. Millionaires 8, Ottawa 3; March 26, at Vancouver — Van. Millionaires 12, Ottawa 3.

**1913-14 — Toronto Blueshirts —** Con Corbeau, Roy McGiffen, Jack Walker, George McNamara, Cully Wilson, Frank Foyston, Harry Cameron, Hap Holmes, Scotty Davidson (Captain), Harriston; Jack Marshall (Playing Manager), Frank Carroll, Dick Carroll (Trainers).
**Scores:** March 14, at Toronto — Toronto 5, Victoria 2; March 17, at Toronto — Toronto 6, Victoria 5; March 19, at Toronto — Toronto 2, Victoria 1.

Prior to 1914, teams could challenge the Stanley Cup champions for the title, thus there was more than one Championship Series played in most of the seasons between 1894 and 1913.

**1912-13 — Quebec Bulldogs —** Joe Malone (Captain), Joe Hall, Paddy Moran, Harry Mummery, Tommy Smith, Jack Marks, Rusty Crawford, Billy Creighton, Jeff Malone, Rocket Power; M.J. Quinn (Manager), D. Beland (Trainer).
**Scores:** March 8, at Quebec — Que. Bulldogs 14, Sydney 3; March 10, at Quebec — Que. Bulldogs 6, Sydney 2.

Victoria challenged Quebec but the Bulldogs refused to put the Stanley Cup in competition so the two teams played an exhibition series with Victoria winning two games to one by scores of 7-5, 3-6, 6-1. It was the first meeting between the Eastern champions and the Western champions. The following year, and until the Western Hockey League disbanded after the 1926 playoffs, the Cup went to the winner of the series between East and West.

**1911-12 — Quebec Bulldogs —** Goldie Prodger, Joe Hall, Walter Rooney, Paddy Moran, Jack Marks, Jack McDonald, Eddie Oatman, George Leonard, Joe Malone (Captain); Charley Nolan (Coach), M.J. Quinn (Manager), D. Beland (Trainer).
**Scores:** March 11, at Quebec — Que. Bulldogs 9, Moncton 3; March 13, at Quebec — Que. Bulldogs 8, Moncton 0.

**1910-11 — Ottawa Senators —** Hamby Shore, Percy LeSueur (Captain), Jack Darragh, Bruce Stuart, Marty Walsh, Bruce Ridpath, Fred Lake, Dubbie Kerr, Alex Currie, Horace Gaul.
**Scores:** March 13, at Ottawa — Ottawa 7, Galt 4; March 16, at Ottawa — Ottawa 13, Port Arthur 4.

**1909-10 —** (March) **— Montreal Wanderers —** Cecil Blachford, Moose Johnson, Ernie Russell, Riley Hern, Harry Hyland, Jack Marshall, Pud Glass (Captain), Jimmy Gardner; Dickie Boon (Manager).
**Scores:** March 12, at Montreal — Mtl. Wanderers 7, Berlin (Kitchener) 3.

By winning the 1910 NHA title, the Montreal Wanderers took possession of the Stanley Cup from Ottawa and accepted a challenge from Berlin, 1910 champions of the OPHL

**1909-10 —** (January) **— Ottawa Senators —** Dubbie Kerr, Fred Lake, Percy LeSueur, Ken Mallen, Bruce Ridpath, Gord Roberts, Hamby Shore, Bruce Stuart (Captain), Marty Walsh.

The Senators accepted two challenges as defending Cup champions. The first was against Galt in a 2-game, total-goals series, and the second was against Edmonton, also a 2-game, total-goals series.
**Scores:** January 5, at Ottawa — Ottawa 12, Galt 3; January 7, at Ottawa — Ottawa 3, Galt 1; January 18, at Ottawa — Ottawa 8, Edm. Eskimos 4; January 20, at Ottawa — Ottawa 13, Edm. Eskimos 7.

**1908-09 — Ottawa Senators —** Fred Lake, Percy LeSueur, Cyclone Taylor, Billy Gilmour, Dubbie Kerr, Edgar Dey, Marty Walsh, Bruce Stuart (Captain).

Ottawa, as champions of the Eastern Canada Hockey Association took over the Stanley Cup in 1909 and, although a challenge was accepted by the Cup trustees from Winnipeg Shamrocks, games could not be arranged because of the lateness of the season. No other challenges were made in 1909.

**1907-08 — Montreal Wanderers —** Riley Hern, Art Ross, Walter Smaill, Pud Glass, Bruce Stuart, Ernie Russell, Moose Johnson, Cecil Blachford (Captain), Tom Hooper, Larry Gilmour, Ernie Liffiton; Dickie Boon (Manager).
**Scores:** Wanderers accepted four challenges for the Cup: January 9, at Montreal — Mtl. Wanderers 9, Ott. Victorias 3; January 13, at Montreal — Mtl. Wanderers 13, Ott. Victorias 1; March 10, at Montreal — Mtl. Wanderers 11, Wpg. Maple Leafs 5; March 12, at Montreal — Mtl. Wanderers 9, Wpg. Maple Leafs 3; March 14, at Montreal — Mtl. Wanderers 6, Toronto (OPHL) 4. At start of following season, 1908-09, Wanderers were challenged by Edmonton. Results: December 28, at Montreal — Mtl. Wanderers 7, Edm. Eskimos 3; December 30, at Montreal — Edm. Eskimos 7, Mtl. Wanderers 6. Total goals: Mtl. Wanderers 13, Edm. Eskimos 10.

**1906-07 —** (March 25) **— Montreal Wanderers —** Billy Strachan, Riley Hern, Lester Patrick, Hod Stuart, Pud Glass, Ernie Russell, Cecil Blachford (Captain), Moose Johnson, Rod Kennedy, Jack Marshall; Dickie Boon (Manager).

**1906-07 —** (March 18) **— Kenora Thistles —** Eddie Giroux, Si Griffis, Tom Hooper, Fred Whitcroft, Alf Smith, Harry Westwick, Roxy Beaudro, Tommy Phillips (Captain), Russell Phillips.
**Scores:** March 16, at Winnipeg — Kenora 8, Brandon 6; March 18, at Winnipeg — Kenora 4, Brandon 1; March 23, at Winnipeg — Mtl. Wanderers 7, Kenora 2; March 25, at Winnipeg — Kenora 6, Mtl. Wanderers 5. Total goals: Mtl. Wanderers 12, Kenora 8.

**1906-07 —** (January) **— Kenora Thistles —** Eddie Giroux, Art Ross, Si Griffis, Tom Hooper, Billy McGimsie, Roxy Beaudro, Tommy Phillips (Captain), Joe Hall, Russell Phillips.
**Scores:** January 17, at Montreal — Kenora 4, Mtl. Wanderers 2; Jan. 21, at Montreal — Kenora 8, Mtl. Wanderers 6.

**1906-07 —** (December) **— Montreal Wanderers —** Riley Hern, Billy Strachan, Rod Kennedy, Lester Patrick, Pud Glass, Ernie Russell, Moose Johnson, Cecil Blachford (Captain), Dickie Boon (Manager).

**1905-06 —** (March) **— Montreal Wanderers —** Henri Menard, Billy Strachan, Rod Kennedy, Lester Patrick, Pud Glass, Ernie Russell, Moose Johnson, Cecil Blachford (Captain), Josh Arnold; Dickie Boon (Manager).
**Scores:** March 14, at Montreal — Mtl. Wanderers 9, Ottawa 1; March 17, at Ottawa — Ottawa 9, Mtl. Wanderers 3. Total goals: Mtl. Wanderers 12, Ottawa 10. Wanderers accepted a challenge from New Glasgow, N.S., prior to the start of the 1906-07 season. Results: December 27, at Montreal — Mtl. Wanderers 10, New Glasgow 3; December 29, at Montreal — Mtl. Wanderers 7, New Glasgow 2.

**1905-06 —** (February) **— Ottawa Silver Seven —** Harvey Pulford (Captain), Arthur Moore, Harry Westwick, Frank McGee, Alf Smith (Playing Coach), Billy Gilmour, Billy Hague, Percy LeSueur, Harry Smith, Tommy Smith, Dion, Ebbs.
**Scores:** February 27, at Ottawa — Ottawa 16, Queen's University 7; February 28, at Ottawa — Ottawa 12, Queen's University 7; March 6, at Ottawa — Ottawa 6, Smiths Falls 5; March 8, at Ottawa — Ottawa 8, Smiths Falls 2.

**1904-05 —** Ottawa Silver Seven — Dave Finnie, Harvey Pulford (Captain), Arthur Moore, Harry Westwick, Frank McGee, Alf Smith (Playing Coach), Billy Gilmour, Frank White, Horace Gaul, Hamby Shore, Bones Allen.
**Scores:** January 13, at Ottawa — Ottawa 9, Dawson City 2; January 16, at Ottawa — Ottawa 23, Dawson City 2; March 7, at Ottawa — Rat Portage 9, Ottawa 3; March 9, at Ottawa — Ottawa 4, Rat Portage 2; March 11, at Ottawa — Ottawa 5, Rat Portage 4.

**1903-04 — Ottawa Silver Seven —** Suddy Gilmour, Arthur Moore, Frank McGee, Bouse Hutton, Billy Gilmour, Jim McGee, Harry Westwick, Harvey Pulford (Captain), Scott, Alf Smith (Playing Coach).
**Scores:** December 30, at Ottawa — Ottawa 9, Wpg. Rowing Club 1; January 1, at Ottawa — Wpg. Rowing Club 6, Ottawa 2; January 4, at Ottawa — Ottawa 2, Wpg. Rowing Club 0. February 23, at Ottawa — Ottawa 6, Tor. Marlboros 3; February 25, at Ottawa — Ottawa 11, Tor. Marlboros 2; March 2, at Montreal — Ottawa 5, Mtl. Wanderers 5. Following the tie game, a new two-game series was ordered to be played in Ottawa but the Wanderers refused unless the tie game was replayed in Montreal. When no settlement could be reached, the series was abandoned and Ottawa retained the Cup and accepted a two-game challenge from Brandon. Results: (both games at Ottawa), March 9, Ottawa 6, Brandon 3; March 11, Ottawa 9, Brandon 3.

**1902-03 — (March) — Ottawa Silver Seven —** Suddy Gilmour, Percy Sims, Bouse Hutton, Dave Gilmour, Billy Gilmour, Harry Westwick, Frank McGee, F.H. Wood, A.A. Fraser, Charles Spittal, Harvey Pulford (Captain), Arthur Moore; Alf Smith (Coach).
**Scores:** March 7, at Montreal — Ottawa 1, Mtl. Victorias 1; March 10, at Ottawa — Ottawa 8, Mtl. Victorias 0. Total goals: Ottawa 9, Mtl. Victorias 1; March 12, at Ottawa — Ottawa 6, Rat Portage 2; March 14, at Ottawa — Ottawa 4, Rat Portage 2.

**1902-03 — (February) — Montreal AAA —** Tom Hodge, Dickie Boon, Billy Nicholson, Tommy Phillips, Art Hooper, Billy Bellingham, Charles Liffiton, Jack Marshall, Jimmy Gardner, Cecil Blachford, George Smith.
**Scores:** January 29, at Montreal — Mtl. AAA 8, Wpg. Victorias 1; January 31, at Montreal — Wpg. Victorias 2, Mtl. AAA 2; February 2, at Montreal — Wpg. Victorias 4, Mtl. AAA 2; February 4, at Montreal — Mtl. AAA 5, Wpg. Victorias 1.

**1901-02 — (March) — Montreal AAA —** Tom Hodge, Dickie Boon, Billy Nicholson, Art Hooper, Billy Bellingham, Charles Liffiton, Jack Marshall, Roland Elliot, Jimmy Gardner.
**Scores:** March 13, at Winnipeg — Wpg. Victorias 1, Mtl. AAA 0; March 15, at Winnipeg — Mtl. AAA 5, Wpg. Victorias 0; March 17, at Winnipeg — Mtl. AAA 2, Wpg. Victorias 1.

**1901-02 — (January) — Winnipeg Victorias —** Burke Wood, Tony Gingras, Charles Johnstone, Rod Flett, Magnus Flett, Dan Bain (Captain), Fred Scanlon, F. Cadham, Art Brown.
**Scores:** January 21, at Winnipeg — Wpg. Victorias 5, Tor Wellingtons 3; January 23, at Winnipeg — Wpg. Victorias 5, Tor. Wellingtons 3.

**1900-01 — Winnipeg Victorias —** Burke Wood, Jack Marshall, Tony Gingras, Charles Johnstone, Rod Flett, Magnus Flett, Dan Bain (Captain), Art Brown, George Carruthers.
**Scores:** January 29, at Montreal — Wpg. Victorias 4, Mtl. Shamrocks 3; January 31, at Montreal — Wpg. Victorias 2, Mtl. Shamrocks 1.

**1899-1900 — Montreal Shamrocks —** oe McKenna, Frank Tansey, Frank Wall, Art Farrell, Fred Scanlon, Harry Trihey (Captain), Jack Brannen.
**Scores:** February 12, at Montreal — Mtl. Shamrocks 4, Wpg. Victorias 3; February 14, at Montreal — Wpg. Victorias 3, Mtl. Shamrocks 2; February 16, at Montreal — Mtl. Shamrocks 5, Wpg. Victorias 4; March 5, at Montreal — Mtl. Shamrocks 10, Halifax 2; March 7, at Montreal — Mtl. Shamrocks 11, Halifax 0.

**1898-99 — (March) — Montreal Shamrocks —** Joe McKenna, Frank Tansey, Frank Wall, Harry Trihey (Captain), Art Farrell, Fred Scanlon, Jack Brannen, John Dobby, Charles Hoerner.
**Scores:** March 14, at Montreal — Mtl. Shamrocks 6, Queen's University 2.

**1898-99 — (February) — Montreal Victorias —** Gordon Lewis, Mike Grant (Captain), Graham Drinkwater, Cam Davidson, Bob McDougall, Ernie McLea, Frank Richardson, Jack Ewing, Russell Bowie, Douglas Acer, Fred McRobie.
**Scores:** February 15, at Montreal — Mtl. Victorias 2, Wpg. Victorias 1; February 18, at Montreal — Mtl. Victorias 3, Wpg. Victorias 2.

**1897-98 — Montreal Victorias —** Gordon Lewis, Hartland McDougall, Mike Grant, Graham Drinkwater, Cam Davidson, Bob McDougall, Ernie McLea, Frank Richardson (Captain), Jack Ewing.

**1896-97 — Montreal Victorias —** Gordon Lewis, Harold Henderson, Mike Grant (Captain), Cam Davidson, Graham Drinkwater, Bob McDougall, Ernie McLea, Shirley Davidson, Hartland McDougall, Jack Ewing, Percy Molson, David Gillilan, McLellan.
**Scores:** December 27, at Montreal — Mtl. Victorias 15, Ott. Capitals 2.

**1895-96 — (December) — Montreal Victorias —** Harold Henderson, Mike Grant (Captain), Bob McDougall, Graham Drinkwater, Shirley Davidson, Hartland McDougall, Ernie McLea, Cam Davidson, David Gillilan, Stanley Willett, Gordon Lewis, W. Wallace.
**Scores:** December 30, at Winnipeg — Mtl. Victorias 6, Wpg. Victorias 5.

**1895-96 — (February) — Winnipeg Victorias —** Whitey Merritt, Rod Flett, Fred Higginbotham, Jack Armitage (Captain), Tote Campbell, Dan Bain, Charles Johnstone, Attie Howard.
**Scores:** February 14, at Montreal — Wpg. Victorias 2, Mtl. Victorias 0.

**1894-95 — Montreal Victorias —** Robert Jones, Harold Henderson, Mike Grant (Captain), Shirley Davidson, Hartland McDougall, Bob McDougall, Norman Rankin, Graham Drinkwater, Roland Elliot, William Pullan, Arthur Fenwick, A. McDougall.

**1893-94 — Montreal AAA —** Herb Collins, Allan Cameron, George James, Billy Barlow, Clare Mussen, Archie Hodgson, Haviland Routh, Alex Irving, James Stewart, E. O'Brien, Toad Wand, Alex Kingan.
**Scores:** March 17, at Mtl. Victorias — Mtl. AAA 3, Mtl. Victorias 2; March 22, at Montreal — Mtl. AAA 3, Ott. Capitals 1.

**1892-93 — Montreal AAA —** Tom Paton, James Stewart, Allan Cameron, Haviland Routh, Archie Hodgson, Billy Barlow, Alex Irving, Alex Kingan, G.S. Low.

# All-Time NHL Playoff Formats

**1917-18** — The regular-season was split into two halves. The winners of both halves faced each other in a two-game, total-goals series for the NHL championship and the right to meet the PCHA champion in the best-of-five Stanley Cup Finals.

**1918-19** — Same as 1917-18, except that the Stanley Cup Finals was extended to a best-of-seven series.

**1919-20** — Same as 1917-1918, except that Ottawa won both halves of the split regular-season schedule to earn an automatic berth into the best-of-five Stanley Cup Finals against the PCHA champions.

**1921-22** — The top two teams at the conclusion of the regular-season faced each other in a two-game, total-goals series for the NHL championship. The NHL champion then moved on to play the winner of the PCHA-WCHL playoff series in the best-of-five Stanley Cup Finals.

**1922-23** — The top two teams at the conclusion of the regular-season faced each other in a two-game, total-goals series for the NHL championship. The NHL champion then moved on to play the PCHA champion in the best-of-three Stanley Cup Semi-Finals, and the winner of the Semi-Finals played the WCHL champion, which had been given a bye, in the best-of-three Stanley Cup Finals.

**1923-24** — The top two teams at the conclusion of the regular-season faced each other in a two-game, total-goals series for the NHL championship. The NHL champion then moved on to play the loser of the PCHA-WCHL playoff (the winner of the PCHA-WCHL playoff earned a bye into the Stanley Cup Finals) in the best-of-three Stanley Cup Semi-Finals. The winner of this series met the PCHA-WCHL playoff winner in the best-of-three Stanley Cup Finals.

**1924-25** — The first place team (Hamilton) at the conclusion of the regular-season was supposed to play the winner of a two-game, total-goals series between the second (Toronto) and third (Montreal) place clubs. However, Hamilton refused to abide by this new format, demanding greater compensation than offered by the League. Thus, Toronto and Montreal played their two-game, total-goals series, and the winner (Montreal) earned the NHL title and then played the WCHL champion (Victoria) in the best-of-five Stanley Cup Finals.

**1925-26** — The format which was intended for 1924-25 went into effect. The winner of the two-game, total-goals series between the second and third place teams squared off against the first place team in the two-game, total-goals NHL championship series. The NHL champion then moved on to play the WHL champion in the best-of-five Stanley Cup Finals.

After the 1925-26 season, the NHL was the only major professional hockey league still in existence and consequently took over sole control of the Stanley Cup competition.

**1926-27** — The 10-team league was divided into two divisions — Canadian and American — of five teams apiece. In each division, the winner of the two-game, total-goals series between the second and third place teams faced the first place team in a two-game, total-goals series for the division title. The two division title winners then met in the best-of-five Stanley Cup Finals.

**1928-29** — Both first place teams in the two divisions played each other in a best-of-five series. Both second place teams in the two divisions played each other in a two-game, total-goals series as did the two third place teams. The winners of these latter two series then played each other in a best-of-three series for the right to meet the winner of the series between the two first place clubs. This Stanley Cup Final was a best-of-three.

Series A: First in Canadian Division vs. first in American (best-of-five)
Series B: Second in Canadian Division vs. second in American (two-game, total-goals)
Series C: Third in Canadian Division vs. third in American (two-game, total-goals)
Series D: Winner of Series B vs. winner of Series C (best-of-three)
Series E: Winner of Series A vs. winner of Series D (best-of-three) for Stanley Cup

**1931-32** — Same as 1928-29, except that Series D was changed to a two-game, total-goals format and Series E was changed to best-of-five.

**1936-37** — Same as 1931-32, except that Series B, C, and D were each best-of-three.

**1938-39** — With the NHL reduced to seven teams, the two-division system was replaced by one seven-team league. Based on final regular-season standings, the following playoff format was adopted:

Series A: First vs. Second (best-of-seven)
Series B: Third vs. Fourth (best-of-three)
Series C: Fifth vs. Sixth (best-of-three)
Series D: Winner of Series B vs. winner of Series C (best-of-three)
Series E: Winner of Series A vs. winner of Series D (best-of-seven)

**1942-43** — With the NHL reduced to six teams (the "original six"), only the top four finishers qualified for playoff action. The best-of-seven Semi-Finals pitted Team #1 vs. Team #3 and Team #2 vs. Team #4. The winners of each Semi-Final series met in the best-of-seven Stanley Cup Finals.

**1967-68** — When it doubled in size from 6 to 12 teams, the NHL once again was divided into two divisions — East and West — of six teams apiece. The top four clubs in each division qualified for the playoffs (all series were best-of-seven):

Series A: Team #1 (East) vs. Team #3 (East)
Series B: Team #2 (East) vs. Team #4 (East)
Series C: Team #1 (West) vs. Team #3 (West)
Series D: Team #2 (West) vs. Team #4 (West)
Series E: Winner of Series A vs. winner of Series B
Series F: Winner of Series C vs. winner of Series D
Series G: Winner of Series E vs. Winner of Series F

**1970-71** — Same as 1967-68 except that Series E matched the winners of Series A and D, and Series F matched the winners of Series B and C.

**1971-72** — Same as 1970-71, except that Series A and C matched Team #1 vs. Team #4, and Series B and D matched Team #2 vs. Team #3.

**1974-75** — With the League now expanded to 18 teams in four divisions, a completely new playoff format was introduced. First, the #2 and #3 teams in each of the four divisions were pooled together in the Preliminary round. These eight (#2 and #3) clubs were ranked #1 to #8 based on regular-season record:

Series A: Team #1 vs. Team #8 (best-of-three)
Series B: Team #2 vs. Team #7 (best-of-three)
Series C: Team #3 vs. Team #6 (best-of-three)
Series D: Team #4 vs. Team #5 (best-of-three)
The winners of this Preliminary round then pooled together with the four division winners, which had received byes into this Quarter-Final round. These eight teams were again ranked #1 to #8 based on regular-season record:
Series E: Team #1 vs. Team #8 (best-of-seven)
Series F: Team #2 vs. Team #7 (best-of-seven)
Series G: Team #3 vs. Team #6 (best-of-seven)
Series H: Team #4 vs. Team #5 (best-of-seven)
The four Quarter-Finals winners, which moved on to the Semi-Finals, were then ranked #1 to #4 based on regular season record:
Series I: Team #1 vs. Team #4 (best-of-seven)
Series J: Team #2 vs. Team #3 (best-of-seven)
Series K: Winner of Series I vs. winner of Series J (best-of-seven)

**1977-78** — Same as 1974-75, except that the Preliminary round consisted of the #2 teams in the four divisions and the next four teams based on regular-season record (not their standings within their divisions).

**1979-80** — With the addition of four WHA franchises, the League expanded its playoff structure to include 16 of its 21 teams. The four first place teams in the four divisions automatically earned playoff berths. Among the 17 other clubs, the top 12, according to regular-season record, also earned berths. All 16 teams were then pooled together and ranked #1 to #16 based on regular-season record:

Series A: Team #1 vs. Team #16 (best-of-five)
Series B: Team #2 vs. Team #15 (best-of-five)
Series C: Team #3 vs. Team #14 (best-of-five)
Series D: Team #4 vs. Team #13 (best-of-five)
Series E: Team #5 vs. Team #12 (best-of-five)
Series F: Team #6 vs. Team #11 (best-of-five)
Series G: Team #7 vs. Team #10 (best-of-five)
Series H: Team #8 vs. Team # 9 (best-of-five)
The eight Preliminary round winners, ranked #1 to #8 based on regular-season record, moved on to the Quarter-Finals:
Series I: Team #1 vs. Team #8 (best-of-seven)
Series J: Team #2 vs. Team #7 (best-of-seven)
Series K: Team #3 vs. Team #6 (best-of-seven)
Series L: Team #4 vs. Team #5 (best-of-seven)
The four Quarter-Finals winners, ranked #1 to #4 based on regular-season record, moved on to the semi-finals:
Series M: Team #1 vs. Team #4 (best-of-seven)
Series N: Team #2 vs. Team #3 (best-of-seven)
Series O: Winner of Series M vs. winner of Series N (best-of-seven)

**1981-82** — The first four teams in each division earned playoff berths. In each division, the first-place team opposed the fourth-place team and the second-place team opposed the third-place team in a best-of-five Division Semi-Final series (DSF). In each division, the two winners of the DSF met in a best-of-seven Division Final series (DF). The two DF winners in each conference met in a best-of-seven Conference Final series (CF). In the Prince of Wales Conference, the Adams Division winner opposed the Patrick Division winner; in the Clarence Campbell Conference, the Smythe Division winner opposed the Norris Division winner. The two CF winners met in a best-of-seven Stanley Cup Final (F) series.

**1986-87** — Division Semi-Final series changed from best-of-five to best-of-seven.

**1993-94** — The NHL's playoff draw is conference-based rather than division-based. At the conclusion of the regular season, the top eight teams in each of the Eastern and Western Conferences qualify for the playoffs. The teams that finish in first place in each of the League's divisions are seeded first and second in each conference's playoff draw and are assured of home ice advantage in the first two playoff rounds. The remaining teams are seeded based on their regular-season point totals. In each conference, the team seeded #1 plays #8; #2 vs. #7; #3 vs. #6; and #4 vs. #5. All series are best-of-seven with home ice rotating on a 2-2-1-1-1 basis, with the exception of matchups between Central and Pacific Division teams. These matchups will be played on a 2-3-2 basis to reduce travel. In a 2-3-2 series, the team with the most points will have its choice to start the series at home or on the road. The Eastern Conference champion will face the Western Conference champion in the Stanley Cup Final.

**1994-95** — Same as 1993-94, except that in first, second or third-round playoff series involving Central and Pacific Division teams, the team with the better record has the choice of using either a 2-3-2 or a 2-2-1-1-1 format. When a 2-3-2 format is selected, the higher-ranked team also has the choice of playing games 1, 2, 6 and 7 at home or playing games 3, 4 and 5 at home. The format for the Stanley Cup Final remains 2-2-1-1-1.

**1998-99** — The NHL's clubs are re-aligned into two conferences each consisting of three divisions. The number of teams qualifying for the Stanley Cup Playoffs remains unchanged at 16.

First-round playoff berths will be awarded to the first-place team in each division as well as to the next five best teams based on regular-season point totals in each conference. The three division winners in each conference will be seeded first through third, in order of points, for the playoffs and the next five best teams, in order of points, will be seeded fourth through eighth. In each conference, the team seeded #1 will play #8; #2 vs. #7; #3 vs. #6; and #4 vs. #5 in the quarterfinal round. Home-ice in the Conference Quarter-Finals is granted to those teams seeded first through fourth in each conference.

In the Conference Semi-Finals and Conference Finals, teams will be re-seeded according to the same criteria as the Conference Quarter-Finals. Higher seeded teams will have home-ice advantage.

Home-ice advantage for the Stanley Cup Finals will be determined by points.

All series remain best-of-seven.

*Jean Beliveau prepares a celebratory drink in the Montreal dressing room in 1965. Beliveau had already won the Stanley Cup five times before, but this was the first of five more wins as captain of the Canadiens. He later won the Cup seven more times while working in the club's front office.*

# Team Records

**1918-2009**

## GAMES PLAYED

**MOST GAMES PLAYED BY ALL TEAMS, ONE PLAYOFF YEAR:**
**92 — 1991.** There were 51 DSF, 24 DF, 11 CF and 6 F games.
90 — 1994. There were 48 CQF, 23 CSF, 12 CF and 7 F games.
— 2002. There were 47 CQF, 25 CSF, 13 CF and 5 F games.

**MOST GAMES PLAYED, ONE TEAM, ONE PLAYOFF YEAR:**
**26 — Philadelphia Flyers,** 1987. Won DSF 4-2 vs. NY Rangers, DF 4-3 vs. NY Islanders, CF 4-2 vs. Montreal, and lost F 4-3 vs. Edmonton.
— **Calgary Flames,** 2004. Won DSF 4-3 vs. Vancouver, DF 4-2 vs. Detroit, CF 4-2 vs. San Jose, and lost F 4-3 vs. Tampa Bay.
25 — New Jersey Devils, 2001. Won CQF 4-2 vs. Carolina, CSF 4-3 vs. Toronto, CF 4-1 vs. Pittsburgh, and lost F 4-3 vs. Colorado.
— Carolina Hurricanes, 2006. Won CQF 4-2 vs. Montreal, CSF 4-1 vs. New Jersey, CF 4-3 vs. Buffalo, and F 4-3 vs. Edmonton

## PLAYOFF APPEARANCES

**MOST STANLEY CUP CHAMPIONSHIPS:**
**23 — Montreal Canadiens** (1924-30-31-44-46-53-56-57-58-59-60-65-66-68-69-71-73-76-77-78-79-86-93)
13 — Toronto Maple Leafs (1918-22-32-42-45-47-48-49-51-62-63-64-67)
11 — Detroit Red Wings (1936-37-43-50-52-54-55-97-98-2002-08)

**MOST CONSECUTIVE STANLEY CUP CHAMPIONSHIPS:**
**5 — Montreal Canadiens** (1956-57-58-59-60)
4 — Montreal Canadiens (1976-77-78-79)
— NY Islanders (1980-81-82-83)

**MOST FINAL SERIES APPEARANCES:**
**32 — Montreal Canadiens** in 92-year history.
24 — Detroit Red Wings in 83-year history.
21 — Toronto Maple Leafs in 92-year history.

**MOST CONSECUTIVE FINAL SERIES APPEARANCES:**
**10 — Montreal Canadiens,** (1951-60, inclusive)
5 — Montreal Canadiens, (1965-69, inclusive)
— NY Islanders, (1980-84, inclusive)

**MOST YEARS IN PLAYOFFS:**
**76 — Montreal Canadiens** in 92-year history.
64 — Toronto Maple Leafs in 92-year history.
63 — Boston Bruins in 85-year history.

**MOST CONSECUTIVE PLAYOFF APPEARANCES:**
**29 — Boston Bruins** (1968-96, inclusive)
28 — Chicago Blackhawks (1970-97, inclusive)
25 — St. Louis Blues (1980-2004, inclusive)
24 — Montreal Canadiens (1971-94, inclusive)
21 — Montreal Canadiens (1949-69, inclusive)

## TEAM WINS

**MOST HOME WINS, ONE TEAM, ONE PLAYOFF YEAR:**
**12 — New Jersey Devils,** 2003 in 13 home games.
11 — Edmonton Oilers, 1988 in 11 home games.
— Detroit Red Wings, 2009 in 13 home games.
10 — Edmonton Oilers, 1985 in 10 home games.
— Montreal Canadiens, 1986 in 11 home games.
— Montreal Canadiens, 1993 in 11 home games.
— Carolina Hurricanes, 2006 in 14 home games.
— Anaheim Ducks, 2007 in 12 home games.

**MOST HOME WINS, ALL TEAMS, ONE PLAYOFF YEAR:**
**57 — 1991.** Of 92 games played, home teams won 57 (29 DSF, 17 DF, 8 CF and 3 in F).

**MOST ROAD WINS, ONE TEAM, ONE PLAYOFF YEAR:**
**10 — New Jersey Devils,** 1995. Won three at Boston in CQF; two at Pittsburgh in CSF; three at Philadelphia in CF; and two at Detroit in F.
— **New Jersey Devils,** 2000. Won two at Florida in CQF; two at Toronto in CSF; three at Philadelphia in CF; and three at Dallas in F.
— **Calgary Flames,** 2004. Won three at Vancouver in DSF; two at Detroit in DF; three at San Jose in CF; and two at Tampa Bay in F.
8 — NY Islanders, 1980. Won two at Los Angeles in PR; three at Boston in QF; two at Buffalo in SF; and one at Philadelphia in F.
— Philadelphia Flyers, 1987. Won two at NY Rangers in DSF; two at NY Islanders in DF; three at Montreal in CF; and one at Edmonton in F.
— Edmonton Oilers, 1990. Won one at Winnipeg in DSF; two at Los Angeles in DF; two at Chicago in CF and three at Boston in F.
— Pittsburgh Penguins, 1992. Won two at Washington in DSF; two at NY Rangers in DF; two at Boston in CF; and two at Chicago in F.
— Vancouver Canucks, 1994. Won three at Calgary in CQF; two at Dallas in CSF; one at Toronto in CF and two at NY Rangers in F.
— Colorado Avalanche, 1996. Won two at Vancouver in CQF; two at Chicago in CSF; two at Detroit in CF; and two at Florida in F.
— Detroit Red Wings, 1998. Won two at Phoenix in CQF; three at St. Louis in CSF; one at Dallas in CF; and two at Washington in F.
— Colorado Avalanche, 1999. Won three at San Jose in CQF; three at Detroit in CSF; and two at Dallas in CF.
— New Jersey Devils, 2001. Won two at Carolina in CQF; two at Toronto in CSF; two at Pittsburgh in CF; and two at Colorado in F.
— Detroit Red Wings, 2002. Won three at Vancouver in CQF; one at St. Louis in CSF; two at Colorado in CF; and two at Carolina in F.

**MOST ROAD WINS, ALL TEAMS, ONE PLAYOFF YEAR:**
**46 — 1987.** Of 87 games played, road teams won 46 (22 DSF, 14 DF, 8 CF and 2 in F).

**MOST OVERTIME WINS, ONE TEAM, ONE PLAYOFF YEAR:**
**10 — Montreal Canadiens, 1993.** Won two vs. Quebec in DSF; three vs. Buffalo in DF; two vs. NY Islanders in CF; and three vs. Los Angeles in F.
7 — Carolina Hurricanes, 2002. Won two vs. New Jersey in CQF; one vs. Montreal in CSF; three vs. Toronto in CF; and one vs. Detroit in F.
— Anaheim Mighty Ducks, 2003. Won two vs. Detroit in CQF; two vs. Dallas in CSF; one vs. Minnestoa in CF; and two vs. New Jersey in F.

**MOST OVERTIME WINS AT HOME, ONE TEAM, ONE PLAYOFF YEAR:**
**4 — St. Louis Blues, 1968.** Won one vs. Philadelphia in QF; three vs. Minnesota in SF.

— **Montreal Canadiens, 1993.** Won one vs. Quebec in DSF; one vs. Buffalo in DF, one vs. NY Islanders in CF; one vs. Los Angeles in F.

**MOST OVERTIME WINS ON THE ROAD, ONE TEAM, ONE PLAYOFF YEAR:**

**6 — Montreal Canadiens, 1993.** Won one vs. Quebec in DSF; two vs. Buffalo in DF; one vs. NY Islanders in CF; two vs. Los Angeles in F.

## TEAM LOSSES

**MOST LOSSES, ONE TEAM, ONE PLAYOFF YEAR:**

**11 — Philadelphia Flyers, 1987.** Lost two vs. NY Rangers in DSF; three vs. NY Islanders in DF; two vs. Montreal in CF; four vs. Edmonton in F.

— **Calgary Flames, 2004.** Lost three vs. Vancouver in CQF; two vs. Detroit in CSF; two vs. San Jose in CF; four vs. Tampa Bay in F

**MOST HOME LOSSES, ONE TEAM, ONE PLAYOFF YEAR:**

**7 — Calgary Flames, 2004.** Lost two vs. Vancouver in CQF; one vs. Detroit in CSF; two vs. San Jose in CF; two vs. Tampa Bay in F.

6 — Philadelphia Flyers, 1987. Lost one vs. NY Rangers in DSF; two vs. NY Islanders in DF; two vs. Montreal in CF; one vs. Edmonton in F.

— Washington Capitals, 1998. Lost two vs. Boston in CQF; two vs. Buffalo in CF; two vs. Detroit in F.

— Colorado Avalanche, 1999. Lost two vs. San Jose in CQF; two vs. Detroit in CSF; two vs. Dallas in CF.

— New Jersey Devils, 2001. Lost one vs. Carolina in CQF; two vs. Toronto in CSF; one vs. Pittsburgh in CF; two vs Colorado in F.

— Minnesota Wild, 2003. Lost two vs. Colorado in CQF; two vs. Vancouver in CSF; two vs. Anaheim in CF.

**MOST ROAD LOSSES, ONE TEAM, ONE PLAYOFF YEAR:**

**7 — New Jersey Devils, 2003.** Lost one at Boston in CQF; one at Tampa Bay in CSF; two at Ottawa in CF; three at Anaheim in F.

**MOST OVERTIME LOSSES, ONE TEAM, ONE PLAYOFF YEAR:**

**4 — Montreal Canadiens, 1951.** Lost four vs. Toronto in F.

— **St. Louis Blues, 1968.** Lost one vs. Philadelphia in QF; one vs. Minnesota in SF; two vs. Montreal in F.

— **New York Rangers, 1979.** Lost one vs. Philadelphia in QF; two vs. NY Islanders in SF; one vs. Montreal in F.

— **Los Angeles Kings, 1991.** Lost one vs. Vancouver in DSF; three vs. Edmonton in DF.

— **Los Angeles Kings, 1993.** Lost one vs. Toronto in CF; three vs. Montreal in F.

— **New Jersey Devils, 1994.** Lost one vs. Buffalo in CQF; one vs. Boston in CSF; two vs. NY Rangers in CF.

— **Chicago Blackhawks, 1995.** Lost one vs. Toronto in CQF; three vs. Detroit in CF.

— **Philadelphia Flyers, 1996.** Lost two vs. Tampa Bay in CQF; two vs. Florida in CSF.

— **Dallas Stars, 1999.** Lost two vs. St. Louis in CSF; one vs. Colorado in CF; one vs. Buffalo in F.

— **Detroit Red Wings, 2002.** Lost one vs. Vancouver in CQF; two vs. Colorado in CF; one vs. Carolina in F.

— **New Jersey Devils, 2003.** Lost two vs. Ottawa in CF; two vs. Anaheim in F.

**MOST OVERTIME LOSSES AT HOME, ONE TEAM, ONE PLAYOFF YEAR:**

**4 — Detroit Red Wings, 2002.** Lost one vs. Vancouver in CQF; two vs. Colorado in CF; one vs. Carolina in F.

**MOST OVERTIME LOSSES ON THE ROAD, ONE TEAM, ONE PLAYOFF YEAR:**

**3 — Los Angeles Kings, 1991.** Lost one at Vancouver in DSF; two at Edmonton in DF.

— **Chicago Blackhawks, 1995.** Lost one at Toronto in CQF; two at Detroit in CF.

— **St. Louis Blues, 1996.** Lost two at Toronto in CQF; one at Detroit in CSF.

— **Dallas Stars, 1999.** Lost two at St. Louis in CSF; one at Colorado in CF.

— **New Jersey Devils, 2003.** Lost one at Ottawa in CF; two at Anaheim in F.

## PLAYOFF WINNING STREAKS

**LONGEST PLAYOFF WINNING STREAK:**

**14 — Pittsburgh Penguins.** Streak started May 9, 1992 as Pittsburgh won the first of three straight games in DF vs. NY Rangers. Continued with four wins vs. Boston in 1992 CF and four wins vs. Chicago in 1992 F. Pittsburgh then won the first three games of 1993 DSF vs. New Jersey. New Jersey ended the streak April 25, 1993, at New Jersey with a 4-1 win vs. Pittsburgh in the fourth game of 1993 DSF.

12 — Edmonton Oilers. Streak started May 15, 1984 as Edmonton won the first of three straight games in F vs. NY Islanders. Continued with three wins vs. Los Angeles in 1985 DSF and four wins vs. Winnipeg in 1985 DF. Edmonton then won the first two games of 1985 CF vs. Chicago. Chicago ended the streak May 9, 1985, at Chicago with a 5-2 win vs. Edmonton in the third game of 1985 CF.

**MOST CONSECUTIVE WINS, ONE TEAM, ONE PLAYOFF YEAR:**

**11 — Chicago Blackhawks** in 1992. Chicago won last three games of DSF vs. St. Louis to win series 4-2, defeated Detroit 4-0 in DF and Edmonton 4-0 in CF.

— **Pittsburgh Penguins** in 1992. Pittsburgh won last three games of DF vs. NY Rangers to win series 4-2, defeated Boston 4-0 in CF and Chicago 4-0 in F.

— **Montreal Canadiens** in 1993. Montreal won last four games of DSF vs. Quebec to win series 4-2, defeated Buffalo 4-0 in DF and won first three games of CF vs. NY Islanders.

## PLAYOFF LOSING STREAKS

**LONGEST PLAYOFF LOSING STREAK:**

**16 — Chicago Black Hawks.** Streak started April 20, 1975 at Chicago with a 6-2 loss in fourth game of QF vs. Buffalo, won by Buffalo 4-1. Continued with four consecutive losses vs. Montreal, in 1976 QF and two straight losses vs. NY Islanders in 1977 best-of-three PRE. Chicago then lost four games vs. Boston in 1978 QF and four games vs. NY Islanders in 1979 QF. Chicago ended the streak April 8, 1980, at Chicago with a 3-2 win vs. St. Louis in the opening game of 1980 PRE.

14 — Los Angeles Kings. Streak started June 3, 1993 at Montreal with a 3-2 loss in second game of F vs. Montreal, won by Montreal 4-1. Los Angeles failed to qualify for the playoffs for the next four years. Then Los Angeles lost four games vs. St. Louis in 1998 CQF; missed the 1999 playoffs and lost four games vs. Detroit in 2000 CQF. Los Angeles then lost the first two games of 2001 CQF vs. Detroit. Los Angeles ended the streak April 15, 2001, at Los Angeles with a 2-1 win vs. Detroit in the third game of 2001 CQF.

*Team owner Mario Lemieux and captain Sidney Crosby share a moment with the Stanley Cup. When Lemieux captained Pittsburgh to its last championship in 1992, the Penguins would close out the playoffs with 11 straight victories. They ran their streak to 14 straight games to open the playoffs in 1993.*

## MOST GOALS IN A SERIES, ONE TEAM

**MOST GOALS, ONE TEAM, ONE PLAYOFF SERIES:**
**44 — Edmonton Oilers** in 1985. Edmonton won best-of-seven CF 4-2, outscoring Chicago 44-25.
35 — Edmonton Oilers in 1983. Edmonton won best-of-seven DF 4-1, outscoring Calgary 35-13.
— Calgary Flames in 1995. Calgary lost best-of-seven CQF 4-3, outscoring San Jose 35-26.

**MOST GOALS, ONE TEAM, TWO-GAME SERIES:**
**11 — Buffalo Sabres** in 1977. Buffalo won best-of-three PRE 2-0, outscoring Minnesota 11-3.
**— Toronto Maple Leafs** in 1978. Toronto won best-of-three PRE 2-0, outscoring Los Angeles 11-3.

**MOST GOALS, ONE TEAM, THREE-GAME SERIES:**
**23 — Chicago Blackhawks** in 1985. Chicago won best-of-five DSF 3-0, outscoring Detroit 23-8.
20 — Minnesota North Stars in 1981. Minnesota won best-of-five PRE 3-0, outscoring Boston 20-13.
— NY Islanders in 1981. NY Islanders won best-of-five PRE 3-0, outscoring Toronto 20-4.

**MOST GOALS, ONE TEAM, FOUR-GAME SERIES:**
**28 — Boston Bruins** in 1972. Boston won best-of-seven SF 4-0, outscoring St. Louis 28-8.

**MOST GOALS, ONE TEAM, FIVE-GAME SERIES:**
**35 — Edmonton Oilers** in 1983. Edmonton won best-of-seven DF 4-1, outscoring Calgary 35-13.
32 — Edmonton Oilers in 1987. Edmonton won best-of-seven DSF 4-1, outscoring Los Angeles 32-20.
30 — Calgary Flames in 1988. Calgary won best-of-seven DSF 4-1, outscoring Los Angeles 30-18.

**MOST GOALS, ONE TEAM, SIX-GAME SERIES:**
**44 — Edmonton Oilers** in 1985. Edmonton won best-of-seven CF 4-2, outscoring Chicago 44-25.
33 — Montreal Canadiens in 1973. Montreal won best-of-seven F 4-2, outscoring Chicago 33-23.
— Chicago Blackhawks in 1985. Chicago won best-of-seven DF 4-2, outscoring Minnesota 33-29.
— Los Angeles Kings in 1993. Los Angeles won best-of-seven DSF 4-2, outscoring Calgary 33-28.

**MOST GOALS, ONE TEAM, SEVEN-GAME SERIES:**
**35 — Calgary Flames** in 1995. Calgary lost best-of-seven CQF 4-3, outscoring San Jose 35-26.
33 — Philadelphia Flyers in 1976. Philadelphia won best-of-seven QF 4-3, outscoring Toronto 33-23.
— Boston Bruins in 1983. Boston won best-of-seven DF 4-3, outscoring Buffalo 33-23.
— Edmonton Oilers in 1984. Edmonton won best-of-seven DF 4-3, outscoring Calgary 33-27.

*Though his career was short, Charlie Gardiner was one of the greatest goalies in NHL history. In 1931, he blanked the New York Rangers in both games of a total-goals series to lead Chicago to the Stanley Cup Finals.*

## FEWEST GOALS IN A SERIES, ONE TEAM

**FEWEST GOALS, ONE TEAM, TWO-GAME SERIES:**
**0 — Toronto St. Patricks** in 1921. Toronto lost two-game, total-goals NHL F 7-0 vs. Ottawa.
**— New York Americans** in 1929. NY Americans lost two-game, total-goals QF 1-0 vs. NY Rangers.
**— New York Rangers** in 1931. NY Rangers lost two-game, total-goals SF 3-0 vs. Chicago.
**— Chicago Black Hawks** in 1935. Chicago lost two-game, total-goals SF 1-0 vs. Mtl. Maroons.
**— Montreal Maroons** in 1937. Mtl. Maroons lost best-of-three SF 2-0, outscored by NY Rangers 5-0.
**— New York Americans** in 1939. NY Americans lost best-of-three QF 2-0, outscored by Toronto 5-0.

**FEWEST GOALS, ONE TEAM, THREE-GAME SERIES:**
**1 — Montreal Maroons** in 1936. Mtl. Maroons lost best-of-five SF 3-0, outscored by Detroit 6-1.

**FEWEST GOALS, ONE TEAM, FOUR-GAME SERIES:**
**1 — Minnesota Wild** in 2003. Minnesota lost best-of-seven CF 4-0, outscored by Anaheim 9-1.

**FEWEST GOALS, ONE TEAM, FIVE-GAME SERIES:**
**2 — Philadelphia Flyers** in 2002. Ottawa won best-of-seven CQF 4-1, while outscoring Philadelphia 11-2.

**FEWEST GOALS, ONE TEAM, SIX-GAME SERIES:**
**5 — Boston Bruins** in 1951. Toronto won best-of-seven SF 4-1 with 1 tie, outscoring Boston 17-5.

**FEWEST GOALS, ONE TEAM, SEVEN-GAME SERIES:**
**9 — Toronto Maple Leafs,** in 1945. Toronto won best-of- seven F 4-3; teams tied in scoring 9-9.
**— Detroit Red Wings,** in 1945. Toronto won best-of-seven F 4-3; teams tied in scoring 9-9.

## MOST GOALS IN A SERIES, BOTH TEAMS

**MOST GOALS, BOTH TEAMS, ONE PLAYOFF SERIES:**
**69 — Edmonton Oilers (44), Chicago Black Hawks (25)** in 1985. Edmonton won best-of-seven CF 4-2.
62 — Chicago Black Hawks (33), Minnesota North Stars (29) in 1985. Chicago won best-of-seven DF 4-2.
61 — Los Angeles Kings (33), Calgary Flames (28) in 1993. Los Angeles won best-of-seven DSF 4-2.
— Calgary Flames (35), San Jose Sharks (26) in 1995. San Jose won best-of-seven CQF 4-3.

**MOST GOALS, BOTH TEAMS, TWO-GAME SERIES:**
**17 — Toronto St. Patricks (10), Montreal Canadiens (7)** in 1918. Toronto won two-game total-goals NHL F.
15 — Boston Bruins (10), Chicago Black Hawks (5) in 1927. Boston won two-game total-goals QF.
— Pittsburgh Penguins (9), St. Louis Blues (6) in 1975. Pittsburgh won best-of-three PRE 2-0.

**MOST GOALS, BOTH TEAMS, THREE-GAME SERIES:**
**33 — Minnesota North Stars (20), Boston Bruins (13)** in 1981. Minnesota won best-of-five PRE 3-0.
31 — Chicago Black Hawks (23), Detroit Red Wings (8) in 1985. Chicago won best-of-five DSF 3-0.
28 — Toronto Maple Leafs (18), New York Rangers (10) in 1932. Toronto won best-of-five F 3-0.

**MOST GOALS, BOTH TEAMS, FOUR-GAME SERIES:**
**36 — Boston Bruins (28), St. Louis Blues (8)** in 1972. Boston won best-of-seven SF 4-0.
**— Minnesota North Stars (18), Toronto Maple Leafs (18)** in 1983. Minnesota won best-of-five DSF 3-1.
**— Edmonton Oilers (25), Chicago Black Hawks (11)** in 1983. Edmonton won best-of-seven CF 4-0.
35 — New York Rangers (23), Los Angeles Kings (12) in 1981. NY Rangers won best-of-five PRE 3-1.

**MOST GOALS, BOTH TEAMS, FIVE-GAME SERIES:**
**52 — Edmonton Oilers (32), Los Angeles Kings (20)** in 1987. Edmonton won best-of-seven DSF 4-1.
50 — Los Angeles Kings (27), Edmonton Oilers (23) in 1982. Los Angeles won best-of-five DSF 3-2.
48 — Edmonton Oilers (35), Calgary Flames (13) in 1983. Edmonton won best-of-seven DF 4-1.
— Calgary Flames (30), Los Angeles Kings (18) in 1988. Calgary won best-of-seven DSF 4-1.

**MOST GOALS, BOTH TEAMS, SIX-GAME SERIES:**
**69 — Edmonton Oilers (44), Chicago Black Hawks (25)** in 1985. Edmonton won best-of-seven CF 4-2.
62 — Chicago Black Hawks (33), Minnesota North Stars (29) in 1985. Chicago won best-of-seven DF 4-2.
61 — Los Angeles Kings (33), Calgary Flames (28) in 1993. Los Angeles won best-of-seven DSF 4-2.

**MOST GOALS, BOTH TEAMS, SEVEN-GAME SERIES:**
**61 — Calgary Flames (35), San Jose Sharks (26)** in 1995. San Jose won best-of-seven CQF 4-3.
60 — Edmonton Oilers (33), Calgary Flames (27) in 1984. Edmonton won best-of-seven DF 4-3.

## FEWEST GOALS IN A SERIES, BOTH TEAMS

**FEWEST GOALS, BOTH TEAMS, TWO-GAME SERIES:**
**1 — New York Rangers (1), New York Americans (0)** in 1929. NY Rangers won two-game total-goals QF.
**— Montreal Maroons (1), Chicago Black Hawks (0)** in 1935. Mtl. Maroons won two-game total-goals SF.

**FEWEST GOALS, BOTH TEAMS, THREE-GAME SERIES:**
**7 — Boston Bruins (5), Montreal Canadiens (2)** in 1929. Boston won best-of-five SF 3-0.
**— Detroit Red Wings (6), Montreal Maroons (1)** in 1936. Detroit won best-of-five SF 3-0.

**FEWEST GOALS, BOTH TEAMS, FOUR-GAME SERIES:**
**9 — Toronto Maple Leafs (7), Boston Bruins (2)** in 1935. Toronto won best-of-five SF 3-1.

**FEWEST GOALS, BOTH TEAMS, FIVE-GAME SERIES:**
**11 — Montreal Maroons (6), New York Rangers (5)** in 1928. NY Rangers won best-of-five F 3-2.

**FEWEST GOALS, BOTH TEAMS, SIX-GAME SERIES:**
**16 — Carolina Hurricanes (10), Toronto Maple Leafs (6)** in 2002. Carolina won best-of-seven CF 4-2.

**FEWEST GOALS, BOTH TEAMS, SEVEN-GAME SERIES:**
**18 — Toronto Maple Leafs (9), Detroit Red Wings (9)** in 1945. Toronto won best-of-seven F 4-3.

## MOST GOALS IN A GAME OR PERIOD

**MOST GOALS, ONE TEAM, ONE GAME:**
**13 — Edmonton Oilers** April 9, 1987, vs. Los Angeles at Edmonton. Edmonton won 13-3.
12 — Los Angeles Kings, April 10, 1990, vs. Calgary at Los Angeles. Los Angeles won 12-4.
11 — Montreal Canadiens, March 30, 1944, vs. Toronto at Montreal. Montreal won 11-0.
— Edmonton Oilers, May 4, 1985, vs. Chicago at Edmonton. Edmonton won 11-2.

**MOST GOALS, ONE TEAM, ONE PERIOD:**
**7 — Montreal Canadiens,** March 30, 1944, vs. Toronto at Montreal, third period. Montreal won 11-0.

**MOST GOALS, BOTH TEAMS, ONE GAME:**
**18 — Los Angeles Kings (10), Edmonton Oilers (8)**, April 7, 1982, at Edmonton. Los Angeles won best-of-five DSF 3-2.
17 — Pittsburgh Penguins (10), Philadelphia Flyers (7), April 25, 1989, at Pittsburgh. Pittsburgh won best-of-seven DF 4-3.
16 — Edmonton Oilers (13), Los Angeles Kings (3), April 9, 1987, at Edmonton. Edmonton won best-of-seven DSF 4-1.
— Los Angeles Kings (12), Calgary Flames (4), April 10, 1990, at Los Angeles. Los Angeles won best-of-seven DF 4-2.

**MOST GOALS, BOTH TEAMS, ONE PERIOD:**
**9 — New York Rangers (6), Philadelphia Flyers (3),** April 24, 1979, third period, at Philadelphia. NY Rangers won 8-3.
**— Los Angeles Kings (5), Calgary Flames (4)**, April 10, 1990, second period, at Los Angeles. Los Angeles won 12-4.
8 — Chicago Black Hawks (5), Montreal Canadiens (3), May 8, 1973, second period, at Montreal. Chicago won 8-7.
— Chicago Black Hawks (5), Edmonton Oilers (3), May 12, 1985, first period, at Chicago. Chicago won 8-6.
— Edmonton Oilers (6), Winnipeg Jets (2), April 6, 1988, third period, at Edmonton. Edmonton won 7-4.
— Hartford Whalers (5), Montreal Canadiens (3), April 10, 1988, third period, at Montreal. Hartford won 7-5.
— Vancouver Canucks (5), New York Rangers (3), June 9, 1994, third period, at NY Rangers. Vancouver won 6-3.

## TEAM POWER-PLAY GOALS

**MOST POWER-PLAY GOALS BY ALL TEAMS, ONE PLAYOFF YEAR:**
**199 — 1988** in 83 games.

**MOST POWER-PLAY GOALS, ONE TEAM, ONE PLAYOFF YEAR:**
**35 — Minnesota North Stars,** 1991 in 23 games.
32 — Edmonton Oilers, 1988 in 18 games.
31 — New York Islanders, 1981 in 18 games.

**MOST POWER-PLAY GOALS, ONE TEAM, ONE SERIES:**
**15 — New York Islanders** in 1980 F vs. Philadelphia. NY Islanders won series 4-2.
**— Minnesota North Stars** in 1991 DSF vs. Chicago. Minnesota won series 4-2.
13 — New York Islanders in 1981 QF vs. Edmonton. NY Islanders won series 4-2.
— Calgary Flames in 1986 CF vs. St. Louis. Calgary won series 4-3.
12 — Toronto Maple Leafs in 1976 QF vs. Philadelphia. Philadelphia won series 4-3.

**MOST POWER-PLAY GOALS, BOTH TEAMS, ONE SERIES:**
**21 — New York Islanders (15), Philadelphia Flyers (6)** in 1980 best-of-seven F won by NY Islanders 4-2.
**— New York Islanders (13), Edmonton Oilers (8)** in 1981 best-of-seven QF won by NY Islanders 4-2.
**— Philadelphia Flyers (11), Pittsburgh Penguins (10)** in 1989 best-of-seven DF won by Philadelphia 4-3.
**— Minnesota North Stars (15), Chicago Black Hawks (6)** in 1991 best-of-seven DSF won by Minnesota 4-2.
20 — Toronto Maple Leafs (12), Philadelphia Flyers (8) in 1976 best-of-seven QF won by Philadelphia 4-3.

**MOST POWER-PLAY GOALS, ONE TEAM, ONE GAME:**
**6 — Boston Bruins,** April 2, 1969, at Boston vs. Toronto. Boston won 10-0.

**MOST POWER-PLAY GOALS, BOTH TEAMS, ONE GAME:**
**8 — Minnesota North Stars (4), St. Louis Blues (4),** April 24, 1991, at Minnesota. Minnesota won 8-4.
7 — Minnesota North Stars (4), Edmonton Oilers (3), April 28, 1984, at Minnesota. Edmonton won 8-5.
— Philadelphia Flyers (4), New York Rangers (3), April 13, 1985, at NY Rangers. Philadelphia won 6-5.
— Chicago Black Hawks (5), Edmonton Oilers (2), May 14, 1985, at Edmonton. Edmonton won 10-5.
— Edmonton Oilers (5), Los Angeles Kings (2), April 9, 1987, at Edmonton. Edmonton won 13-3.
— Vancouver Canucks (4), Calgary Flames (3), April 9, 1989, at Vancouver. Vancouver won 5-3.

**MOST POWER-PLAY GOALS, ONE TEAM, ONE PERIOD:**
**4 — Toronto Maple Leafs,** March 26, 1936, second period vs. Boston at Toronto. Toronto won 8-3.
**— Minnesota North Stars,** April 28, 1984, second period vs. Edmonton at Minnesota. Edmonton won 8-5.
**— Boston Bruins,** April 11, 1991, third period vs. Hartford at Boston. Boston won 6-1.
**— Minnesota North Stars,** April 24, 1991, second period vs. St. Louis at Minnesota. Minnesota won 8-4.
**— St. Louis Blues,** April 27, 1998, third period at Los Angeles. St. Louis won 4-3.

**MOST POWER-PLAY GOALS, BOTH TEAMS, ONE PERIOD:**
**5 — Minnesota North Stars (4), Edmonton Oilers (1),** April 28, 1984, at Minnesota. Edmonton won 8-5.
**— Vancouver Canucks (3), Calgary Flames (2),** April 9, 1989, at Vancouver. Vancouver won 5-3.
**— Minnesota North Stars (4), St. Louis Blues (1),** April 24, 1991, at Minnesota. Minnesota won 8-4.

## TEAM SHORTHAND GOALS

**MOST SHORTHAND GOALS BY ALL TEAMS, ONE PLAYOFF YEAR:**
**33 — 1988,** in 83 games.

**MOST SHORTHAND GOALS, ONE TEAM, ONE PLAYOFF YEAR:**
**10 — Edmonton Oilers,** 1983, in 16 games.
9 — New York Islanders, 1981, in 19 games.
8 — Philadelphia Flyers, 1989, in 19 games.

**MOST SHORTHAND GOALS, ONE TEAM, ONE SERIES:**
**6 — Calgary Flames** in 1995 vs. San Jose in best-of-seven CQF won by San Jose 4-3.
**— Vancouver Canucks** in 1995 vs. St. Louis in best-of-seven CQF won by Vancouver 4-3.
5 — New York Rangers in 1979 vs. Philadelphia in best-of-seven QF won by NY Rangers 4-1.
— Edmonton Oilers in 1983 vs. Calgary in best-of-seven DF won by Edmonton 4-1.

**MOST SHORTHAND GOALS, BOTH TEAMS, ONE SERIES:**
**7 — Boston Bruins (4), New York Rangers (3),** in 1958 SF won by Boston 4-2.
**— Edmonton Oilers (5), Calgary Flames (2),** in 1983 DF won by Edmonton 4-1.
**— Vancouver Canucks (6), St. Louis Blues (1),** in 1995 CQF won by Vancouver 4-3.

**MOST SHORTHAND GOALS, ONE TEAM, ONE GAME:**
**3 — Boston Bruins,** April 11, 1981, at Minnesota North Stars. Minnesota won 6-3.
**— New York Islanders,** April 17, 1983, at NY Rangers. NY Rangers won 7-6.
**— Toronto Maple Leafs,** May 8, 1994, at San Jose Sharks. Toronto won 8-3.

**MOST SHORTHAND GOALS, BOTH TEAMS, ONE GAME:**

4 — **Boston Bruins (3), Minnesota North Stars (1),** April 11, 1981, at Minnesota. Minnesota won 6-3.
— **New York Islanders (3), New York Rangers (1),** April 17, 1983, at NY Rangers. NY Rangers won 7-6.
— **Toronto Maple Leafs (3), San Jose Sharks (1),** May 8, 1994, at San Jose. Toronto won 8-3.

3 — Toronto Maple Leafs (2), Detroit Red Wings (1), April 5, 1947, at Toronto. Toronto won 6-1.
— New York Rangers (2), Boston Bruins (1), April 1, 1958, at Boston. NY Rangers won 5-2.
— Minnesota North Stars (2), Philadelphia Flyers (1), May 4, 1980, at Minnesota. Philadelphia won 5-3.
— Winnipeg Jets (2), Edmonton Oilers (1), April 9, 1988, at Winnipeg. Winnipeg won 6-4.
— New York Islanders (2), New Jersey Devils (1), April 14, 1988, at New Jersey. New Jersey won 6-5.
— Montreal Canadiens (2), New Jersey Devils (1), April 17, 1997, at New Jersey. New Jersey won 5-2.
— Dallas Stars (2), San Jose Sharks (1), May 5, 2000, at San Jose. Dallas won 5-4.
— Detroit Red Wings (2), Calgary Flames (1), April 21, 2007, at Detroit. Detroit won 5-1.

**MOST SHORTHAND GOALS, ONE TEAM, ONE PERIOD:**

2 — **Toronto Maple Leafs,** April 5, 1947, first period vs. Detroit at Toronto. Toronto won 6-1.
— **Toronto Maple Leafs,** April 13, 1965, first period vs. Montreal at Toronto. Montreal won 4-3.
— **Boston Bruins,** April 20, 1969, first period vs. Montreal at Boston. Boston won 3-2.
— **Boston Bruins,** April 8, 1970, second period vs. NY Rangers at Boston. Boston won 8-2.
— **Boston Bruins,** April 30, 1972, first period vs. NY Rangers at Boston. Boston won 6-5.
— **Chicago Black Hawks,** May 3, 1973, first period vs. Montreal at Chicago. Chicago won 7-4.
— **Montreal Canadiens,** April 23, 1978, first period at Detroit. Montreal won 8-0.
— **New York Islanders,** April 8, 1980, second period vs. Los Angeles at NY Islanders. NY Islanders won 8-1.
— **Los Angeles Kings,** April 9, 1980, first period at NY Islanders. Los Angeles won 6-3.
— **Boston Bruins,** April 13, 1980, second period at Pittsburgh. Boston won 8-3.
— **Minnesota North Stars,** May 4, 1980, second period vs. Philadelphia at Minnesota. Philadelphia won 5-3.
— **Boston Bruins,** April 11, 1981, third period at Minnesota North Stars. Minnesota won 6-3.
— **New York Islanders,** May 12, 1981, first period vs. Minnesota North Stars at NY Islanders. NY Islanders won 6-3.
— **Montreal Canadiens,** April 7, 1982, third period vs. Quebec at Montreal. Montreal won 5-1.
— **Edmonton Oilers,** April 24, 1983, third period vs. Chicago at Edmonton. Edmonton won 8-4.
— **Winnipeg Jets,** April 14, 1985, second period at Calgary. Winnipeg won 5-3.
— **Boston Bruins,** April 6, 1988, first period vs. Buffalo at Boston. Boston won 7-3.
— **New York Islanders,** April 14, 1988, third period at New Jersey. New Jersey won 6-5.
— **Detroit Red Wings,** April 29, 1993, second period at Toronto. Detroit won 7-3.
— **Toronto Maple Leafs,** May 8, 1994, third period at San Jose. Toronto won 8-3.
— **Calgary Flames,** May 11, 1995, first period at San Jose. Calgary won 9-2.
— **Vancouver Canucks,** May 15, 1995, second period at St. Louis. Vancouver won 6-5.
— **Montreal Canadiens,** April 17, 1997, second period at New Jersey. New Jersey won 5-2.
— **Philadelphia Flyers,** April 26, 1997, first period vs. Pittsburgh at Philadelphia. Philadelphia won 6-3.
— **Phoenix Coyotes,** April 24, 1998, second period at Detroit. Phoenix won 7-4.
— **Buffalo Sabres,** April 27, 1998, second period vs. Philadelphia at Buffalo. Buffalo won 6-1.
— **San Jose Sharks,** April 30, 1999, third period at Colorado. San Jose won 7-3.
— **Detroit Red Wings,** April 27, 2002, second period at Vancouver. Detroit won 6-4.
— **Detroit Red Wings,** April 21, 2007, second period at Detroit. Detroit won 5-1.

**MOST SHORTHAND GOALS, BOTH TEAMS, ONE PERIOD:**

3 — **Toronto Maple Leafs (2), Detroit Red Wings (1),** April 5, 1947, first period at Toronto. Toronto won 6-1.
— **Toronto Maple Leafs (2), San Jose Sharks (1),** May 8, 1994, third period at San Jose. Toronto won 8-3.

## FASTEST GOALS

**FASTEST FIVE GOALS, BOTH TEAMS:**

**3:06 — Minnesota North Stars, Chicago Black Hawks,** April 21, 1985, at Chicago. Keith Brown scored for Chicago at 1:12 of the second period; Ken Yaremchuk, Chicago, 1:27; Dino Ciccarelli, Minnesota, 2:48; Tony McKegney, Minnesota, 4:07; and Curt Fraser, Chicago, 4:18. Chicago won 6-2 and won best-of-seven DF 4-2.

3:20 — Minnesota North Stars, Philadelphia Flyers, April 29, 1980, at Philadelphia. Paul Shmyr scored for Minnesota at 13:20 of the first period; Steve Christoff, Minnesota, 13:59; Ken Linseman, Philadelphia, 14:54; Tom Gorence, Philadelphia, 15:36; and Ken Linseman, Philadelphia, 16:40. Minnesota won 6-5. Philadelphia won best-of-seven SF 4-1.

4:00 — Los Angeles Kings, Detroit Red Wings, April 15, 2000, at Detroit. Brendan Shanahan scored for Detroit at 0:55 of the first period; Martin Lapointe, Detroit, 1:33; Luc Robitaille, Los Angeles, 2:04; Kris Draper, Detroit, 3:32; and Ziggy Palffy, Los Angeles, 4:55. Detroit won 8-5 and won best-of-seven CQF 4-0.

**FASTEST FIVE GOALS, ONE TEAM:**

**3:36 — Montreal Canadiens,** March 30, 1944, at Montreal vs. Toronto. Toe Blake scored at 7:58 and 8:37 of the third period; Maurice Richard, 9:17; Ray Getliffe, 10:33; and Buddy O'Connor, 11:34. Canadiens won 11-0 and won best-of-seven SF 4-1.

**FASTEST FOUR GOALS, BOTH TEAMS:**

**1:33 — Toronto Maple Leafs, Philadelphia Flyers,** April 20, 1976, at Philadelphia. Don Saleski scored for Philadelphia at 10:04 of the second period; Bob Neely, Toronto, 10:42; Gary Dornhoefer, Philadelphia, 11:24; and Don Saleski, Philadelphia, 11:37. Philadelphia won 7-1 and won best-of-seven SF 4-3.

1:34 — Calgary Flames, Montreal Canadiens, May 20, 1986, at Montreal. Joel Otto scored for Calgary at 17:59 of the first period; Bobby Smith, Montreal, 18:25; Mats Naslund, Montreal, 19:17; and Bob Gainey, Montreal, 19:33. Montreal won 5-3 and won best-of-seven F 4-1.

1:38 — Boston Bruins, Philadelphia Flyers, April 26, 1977, at Philadelphia. Gregg Sheppard scored for Boston at 14:01 of the second period; Mike Milbury, Boston, 15:01; Gary Dornhoefer, Philadelphia, 15:16; and Jean Ratelle, Boston, 15:39. Boston won 5-4 and won best-of-seven SF 4-0.

**FASTEST FOUR GOALS, ONE TEAM:**

**2:35 — Montreal Canadiens,** March 30, 1944, at Montreal. Toe Blake scored at 7:58 and 8:37 of the third period; Maurice Richard, 9:17; and Ray Getliffe, 10:33. Montreal won 11-0 and won best-of-seven SF 4-1.

**FASTEST THREE GOALS, BOTH TEAMS:**

**0:21 — Chicago Black Hawks, Edmonton Oilers,** May 7, 1985, at Edmonton. Behn Wilson scored for Chicago at 19:22 of the third period; Jari Kurri, Edmonton, 19:36; and Glenn Anderson, Edmonton, 19:43. Edmonton won 7-3 and won best-of-seven CF 4-2.

0:27 — Phoenix Coyotes, Detroit Red Wings, April 24, 1998, at Detroit. Jeremy Roenick scored for Phoenix at 13:24 of the second period; Mathieu Dandenault, Detroit, 13:32; and Keith Tkachuk, Phoenix, 13:51. Phoenix won 7-4. Detroit won best-of-seven CQF 4-2.

0:30 — Pittsburgh Penguins, Chicago Blackhawks, June 1, 1992, at Chicago. Dirk Graham scored for Chicago at 6:21 of the first period; Kevin Stevens, Pittsburgh, 6:33; and Dirk Graham, Chicago, 6:51. Pittsburgh won 6-5 and won best-of-seven F 4-0.

**FASTEST THREE GOALS, ONE TEAM:**

**0:23 — Toronto Maple Leafs,** April 12, 1979, at Toronto vs. Atlanta Flames. Darryl Sittler scored at 4:04 and 4:16 of the first period; and Ron Ellis, 4:27. Toronto won 7-4 and won best-of-three PRE 2-0.

0:38 — New York Rangers, April 12, 1986, at NY Rangers vs. Philadelphia. Jim Weimer scored at 12:29 of the third period; Bob Brooke, 12:43; and Ron Greschner, 13:07. NY Rangers won 5-2 and won best-of-five DSF 3-2.
— Colorado Avalanche, April 18, 2001, at Vancouver. Peter Forsberg scored at 9:11 of the third period; Joe Sakic, 9:28; and Eric Messier, 9:49. Colorado won 5-1 and won best-of-seven CQF 4-0.

**FASTEST TWO GOALS, BOTH TEAMS:**

**0:05 — Pittsburgh Penguins, Buffalo Sabres,** April 14, 1979, at Buffalo. Gilbert Perreault scored for Buffalo at 12:59 of the first period; and Jim Hamilton, Pittsburgh, 13:04. Pittsburgh won 4-3 and won best-of-three PRE 2-1.

0:08 — St. Louis Blues, Minnesota North Stars, April 9, 1989, at Minnesota. Bernie Federko scored for St. Louis at 2:28 of the third period; and Perry Berezan, Minnesota, 2:36. Minnesota won 5-4. St. Louis won best-of-seven DSF 4-1.
— Phoenix Coyotes, Detroit Red Wings, April 24, 1998, at Detroit. Jeremy Roenick scored for Phoenix at 13:24 of the second period; and Mathieu Dandenault, Detroit, 13:32. Phoenix won 7-4. Detroit won best-of-seven CQF 4-2.

**FASTEST TWO GOALS, ONE TEAM:**

**0:05 — Detroit Red Wings,** April 11, 1965, at Detroit vs. Chicago. Norm Ullman scored at 17:35 and 17:40 of the second period. Detroit won 4-2. Chicago won best-of-seven SF 4-3.

*Detroit's Norm Ullman scored a hat trick against Chicago's Glenn Hall on April 11, 1965 ... including a playoff record two goals in five seconds.*

*After playing just six games during the 2008-09 season, Semyon Varlamov led the Washington Capitals to game seven of the Eastern Conference semi-finals. He was one of four goalies to tie for the playoff lead with two shutouts.*

## OVERTIME

**SHORTEST OVERTIME:**

**0:09 — Montreal Canadiens, Calgary Flames,** May 18, 1986, at Calgary. Montreal won 3-2 on Brian Skrudland's goal at 0:09 of the first overtime period. Montreal won best-of-seven F 4-1.

0:11 — New York Islanders, New York Rangers, April 11, 1975, at NY Rangers. NY Islanders won 4-3 on J.P. Parise's goal at 0:11 of the first overtime period. NY Islanders won best-of-three PRE 2-1.

**LONGEST OVERTIME:**

**116:30 — Detroit Red Wings, Montreal Maroons,** March 24, 1936, at Montreal. Mtl. Maroons won 1-0 on Mud Bruneteau's goal at 16:30 of the sixth overtime period. Detroit won best-of-five SF 3-0.

**MOST OVERTIME GAMES, ONE PLAYOFF YEAR:**

**28 — 1993.** Of 85 games played, 28 went into overtime.
26 — 2001. Of 86 games played, 26 went into overtime.
22 — 2003. Of 89 games played, 22 went into overtime.

**FEWEST OVERTIME GAMES, ONE PLAYOFF YEAR:**

**0 — 1963.** None of the 16 games went into overtime, the only year since 1926 that no overtime was required in any playoff series.

**MOST OVERTIME GAMES, ONE SERIES:**

**5 — Toronto Maple Leafs, Montreal Canadiens** in 1951. Toronto won best-of-seven F 4-1.
4 — Toronto Maple Leafs, Boston Bruins in 1933. Toronto won best-of-five SF 3-2.
— Boston Bruins, NY Rangers in 1939. Boston won best-of-seven SF 4-3.
— St. Louis Blues, Minnesota North Stars in 1968. St. Louis won best-of-seven SF 4-3.
— Dallas Stars, St. Louis Blues in 1999. Dallas won best-of-seven CSF 4-2.
— Dallas Stars, Edmonton Oilers in 2001. Dallas won best-of-seven CQF 4-2.
— Dallas Stars, San Jose Sharks in 2008. Dallas won best-of-seven CSF 4-2

## TEAM HAT-TRICKS

**MOST HAT-TRICKS, BY ALL TEAMS, ONE PLAYOFF YEAR:**

**12 — 1983** in 66 games.
**— 1988** in 83 games.
11 — 1985 in 70 games.
— 1992 in 86 games.

**MOST HAT-TRICKS, ONE TEAM, ONE PLAYOFF YEAR:**

**6 — Edmonton Oilers** in 16 games, 1983.
**— Edmonton Oilers** in 18 games, 1985.

## SHUTOUTS

**MOST SHUTOUTS, ONE PLAYOFF YEAR, ALL TEAMS:**

**25 — 2002.** Of 90 games played, Detroit had 6; Ottawa had 4; Carolina, Colorado, St. Louis and Toronto had 3 each; while Los Angeles, New Jersey and Philadelphia had 1 each.
23 — 2004. Of 89 games played, Tampa Bay and Calgary had 5 each; Toronto and San Jose had 3 each; while Boston, Colorado, Detroit, Montreal, Nashville, NY Islanders and Philadelphia had 1 each.
19 — 2001. Of 86 games played, Colorado and New Jersey had 4 each, Toronto had 3, Pittsburgh and Los Angeles had 2 each, while Buffalo, Washington, Detroit and San Jose had 1 each.

**FEWEST SHUTOUTS, ONE PLAYOFF YEAR, ALL TEAMS:**

**0 — 1959.** 18 games played.

**MOST SHUTOUTS, BOTH TEAMS, ONE SERIES:**

**5 — Toronto Maple Leafs (3), Detroit Red Wings (2),** in 1945. Toronto won best-of-seven F 4-3.
**— Toronto Maple Leafs (3), Detroit Red Wings (2),** in 1950. Detroit won best-of-seven SF 4-3.

## TEAM PENALTIES

**FEWEST PENALTIES, BOTH TEAMS, BEST-OF-SEVEN SERIES:**

**19 — Detroit Red Wings, Toronto Maple Leafs** in 1945. Detroit received 10 minors, Toronto received 9 minors. Detroit won best-of-seven F 4-3.

**FEWEST PENALTIES, ONE TEAM, BEST-OF-SEVEN SERIES:**

**9 — Toronto Maple Leafs** in 1945 vs. Detroit. Toronto received 9 minors. Detroit won best-of-seven F 4-3.

**MOST PENALTIES, BOTH TEAMS, ONE SERIES:**

**218 — New Jersey Devils, Washington Capitals** in 1988. New Jersey received 97 minors, 11 majors, 9 misconducts and 1 match penalty. Washington received 80 minors, 11 majors, 8 misconducts and 1 match penalty. New Jersey won best-of-seven DF 4-3.

**MOST PENALTY MINUTES, BOTH TEAMS, ONE SERIES:**

**654 — New Jersey Devils (349), Washington Capitals (305)** in 1988. New Jersey won best-of-seven DF 4-3.

**MOST PENALTIES, ONE TEAM, ONE SERIES:**

**118 — New Jersey Devils** in 1988 vs. Washington. New Jersey received 97 minors, 11 majors, 9 misconducts and 1 match penalty. New Jersey won best-of-seven DF 4-3.

**MOST PENALTY MINUTES, ONE TEAM, ONE SERIES:**

**349 — New Jersey Devils** in 1988 vs. Washington. New Jersey won best-of-seven DF 4-3.

**MOST PENALTIES, BOTH TEAMS, ONE GAME:**

**66 — Detroit Red Wings (33), St. Louis Blues (33),** April 12, 1991, at St. Louis. St. Louis won 6-1.
63 — Minnesota North Stars (34), Chicago Blackhawks (29), April 6, 1990, at Chicago. Chicago won 5-3.
62 — New Jersey Devils (32), Washington Capitals (30), April 22, 1988, at New Jersey. New Jersey won 10-4.

**MOST PENALTY MINUTES, BOTH TEAMS, ONE GAME:**

**298 — Detroit Red Wings (152), St. Louis Blues (146),** April 12, 1991, at St. Louis. Detroit received 33 penalties; St. Louis received 33 penalties. St. Louis won 6-1.
267 — New York Rangers (142), Los Angeles Kings (125), April 9, 1981, at Los Angeles. NY Rangers received 31 penalties; Los Angeles received 28 penalties. Los Angeles won 5-4.

**MOST PENALTIES, ONE TEAM, ONE GAME:**

**34 — Minnesota North Stars,** April 6, 1990, at Chicago. Chicago won 5-3.
33 — Detroit Red Wings, April 12, 1991, at St. Louis. St. Louis won 6-1.
— St. Louis Blues, April 12, 1991, at St. Louis vs. Detroit. St. Louis won 6-1.

**MOST PENALTY MINUTES, ONE TEAM, ONE GAME:**

**152 — Detroit Red Wings,** April 12, 1991, at St. Louis. St. Louis won 6-1.
146 — St. Louis Blues, April 12, 1991, at St. Louis vs. Detroit. St. Louis won 6-1.
142 — New York Rangers, April 9, 1981, at Los Angeles. Los Angeles won 5-4.

**MOST PENALTIES, BOTH TEAMS, ONE PERIOD:**

**43 — New York Rangers (24), Los Angeles Kings (19),** April 9, 1981, first period at Los Angeles. Los Angeles won 5-4.

**MOST PENALTY MINUTES, BOTH TEAMS, ONE PERIOD:**

**248 — New York Islanders (124), Boston Bruins (124),** April 17, 1980, first period at Boston. NY Islanders won 5-4.

**MOST PENALTIES, ONE TEAM, ONE PERIOD:**

**24 — New York Rangers,** April 9, 1981, first period at Los Angeles. Los Angeles won 5-4.

**MOST PENALTY MINUTES, ONE TEAM, ONE PERIOD:**

**125 — New York Rangers,** April 9, 1981, first period at Los Angeles. Los Angeles won 5-4.

# Individual Records

## GAMES PLAYED

### MOST YEARS IN PLAYOFFS:
**24 — Chris Chelios, Montreal, Chicago, Detroit** (1984-97 inclusive; 1999-2004 inclusive, 2006-2009 inclusive)
21 — Raymond Bourque, Boston, Colorado (1980-96 inclusive; 98-2001 inclusive)
20 — Gordie Howe, Detroit, Hartford
— Larry Robinson, Montreal, Los Angeles
— Larry Murphy, Los Angeles, Washington, Minnesota, Pittsburgh, Toronto, Detroit
— Scott Stevens, Washington, St. Louis, New Jersey
— Steve Yzerman, Detroit

### MOST CONSECUTIVE YEARS IN PLAYOFFS:
**20 — Larry Robinson, Montreal, Los Angeles** (1973-92, inclusive).
19 — Brett Hull, Calgary, St. Louis, Dallas, Detroit (1986-2004, inclusive).
18 — Larry Murphy, Los Angeles, Washington, Minnesota, Pittsburgh, Toronto, Detroit (1984-2001, inclusive).
17 — Brad Park, NY Rangers, Boston, Detroit (1969-85, inclusive).
— Raymond Bourque, Boston (1980-96, inclusive).
— Nicklas Lidstrom, Detroit (1992-2004 inclusive; 2006-2009 inclusive)

### MOST PLAYOFF GAMES:
**266 — Chris Chelios**, Montreal, Chicago, Detroit
247 — Patrick Roy, Montreal, Colorado
236 — Mark Messier, Edmonton, NY Rangers
235 — Nicklas Lidstrom, Detroit
234 — Claude Lemieux, Montreal, New Jersey, Colorado, Phoenix, Dallas, San Jose

## GOALS

### MOST GOALS IN PLAYOFFS, CAREER:
**122 — Wayne Gretzky, Edmonton, Los Angeles, St. Louis, NY Rangers**
109 — Mark Messier, Edmonton, NY Rangers
106 — Jari Kurri, Edmonton, Los Angeles, NY Rangers, Anaheim
103 — Brett Hull, Calgary, St. Louis, Dallas, Detroit
93 — Glenn Anderson, Edmonton, Toronto, NY Rangers, St. Louis

### MOST GOALS, ONE PLAYOFF YEAR:
**19 — Reggie Leach, Philadelphia,** 1976. 16 games.
**— Jari Kurri, Edmonton,** 1985. 18 games.
18 — Joe Sakic, Colorado, 1996. 22 games.
17 — Newsy Lalonde, Montreal, 1919. 10 games.
— Mike Bossy, NY Islanders, 1981. 18 games.
— Steve Payne, Minnesota, 1981. 19 games.
— Mike Bossy, NY Islanders, 1982. 19 games.
— Mike Bossy, NY Islanders, 1983. 19 games
— Wayne Gretzky, Edmonton, 1985. 18 games.
— Kevin Stevens, Pittsburgh, 1991. 24 games.

### MOST GOALS IN ONE SERIES (OTHER THAN FINAL):
**12 — Jari Kurri, Edmonton,** in 1985 CF, 6 games vs. Chicago.
11 — Newsy Lalonde, Montreal, in 1919 NHL F, 5 games vs. Ottawa.
10 — Tim Kerr, Philadelphia, in 1989 DF, 7 games vs. Pittsburgh.
9 — Reggie Leach, Philadelphia, in 1976 SF, 5 games vs. Boston.
— Bill Barber, Philadelphia, in 1980 SF, 5 games vs. Minnesota.
— Mike Bossy, NY Islanders, in 1983 CF, 6 games vs. Boston.
— Mario Lemieux, Pittsburgh, in 1989 DF, 7 games vs. Philadelphia.
— John Druce, Washington, in 1990 DF, 5 games vs. NY Rangers.
— Johan Franzen, Detroit, in 2008 CSF, 4 games vs. Colorado.

### MOST GOALS IN FINAL SERIES (NHL PLAYERS ONLY):
**9 — Babe Dye, Toronto,** in 1922, 5 games vs. Van. Millionaires.
8 — Alf Skinner, Toronto, in 1918, 5 games vs. Van. Millionaires.
7 — Jean Beliveau, Montreal, in 1956, 5 games vs. Detroit.
— Mike Bossy, NY Islanders, in 1982, 4 games vs. Vancouver.
— Wayne Gretzky, Edmonton, in 1985, 5 games vs. Philadelphia.

### MOST GOALS, ONE GAME:
**5 — Newsy Lalonde, Montreal,** March 1, 1919, at Montreal. Final score: Montreal 6, Ottawa 3.
**— Maurice Richard, Montreal,** March 23, 1944, at Montreal. Final score: Montreal 5, Toronto 1.
**— Darryl Sittler, Toronto,** April 22, 1976, at Toronto. Final score: Toronto 8, Philadelphia 5.
**— Reggie Leach, Philadelphia,** May 6, 1976, at Philadelphia. Final score: Philadelphia 6, Boston 3.
**— Mario Lemieux, Pittsburgh,** April 25, 1989, at Pittsburgh. Final score: Pittsburgh 10, Philadelphia 7.

### MOST GOALS, ONE PERIOD:
**4 — Tim Kerr, Philadelphia,** April 13, 1985, at NY Rangers, second period. Final score: Philadelphia 6, NY Rangers 5.
**— Mario Lemieux, Pittsburgh,** April 25, 1989, at Pittsburgh vs. Philadelphia, first period. Final score: Pittsburgh 10, Philadelphia 7.

## ASSISTS

### MOST ASSISTS IN PLAYOFFS, CAREER:
**260 — Wayne Gretzky, Edmonton, Los Angeles, St. Louis, NY Rangers**
186 — Mark Messier, Edmonton, NY Rangers
139 — Raymond Bourque, Boston, Colorado
137 — Paul Coffey, Edmonton, Pittsburgh, Los Angeles, Detroit, Philadelphia, Carolina
128 — Doug Gilmour, St. Louis, Calgary, Toronto, New Jersey, Buffalo, Montreal

### MOST ASSISTS, ONE PLAYOFF YEAR:
**31 — Wayne Gretzky, Edmonton,** 1988. 19 games.
30 — Wayne Gretzky, Edmonton, 1985. 18 games.
29 — Wayne Gretzky, Edmonton, 1987. 21 games.
28 — Mario Lemieux, Pittsburgh, 1991. 23 games.
26 — Wayne Gretzky, Edmonton, 1983. 16 games.

### MOST ASSISTS IN ONE SERIES (OTHER THAN FINAL):
**14 — Rick Middleton, Boston,** in 1983 DF, 7 games vs. Buffalo.
**— Wayne Gretzky, Edmonton,** in 1985 CF, 6 games vs. Chicago.
13 — Wayne Gretzky, Edmonton, in 1987 DSF, 5 games vs. Los Angeles.
— Doug Gilmour, Toronto, in 1994 CSF, 7 games vs. San Jose.
11 — Al MacInnis, Calgary, in 1984 DF, 7 games vs. Edmonton.
— Mark Messier, Edmonton, in 1989 DSF, 7 games vs. Los Angeles.
— Mike Ridley, Washington, in 1992 DSF, 7 games vs. Pittsburgh.
— Ron Francis, Pittsburgh, in 1995 CQF, 7 games vs. Washington.
10 — Fleming Mackell, Boston, in 1958 SF, 6 games vs. NY Rangers.
— Stan Mikita, Chicago, in 1962 SF, 6 games vs. Montreal.
— Bob Bourne, NY Islanders, in 1983 DF, 6 games vs. NY Rangers.
— Wayne Gretzky, Edmonton, in 1988 DSF, 5 games vs. Winnipeg.
— Mario Lemieux, Pittsburgh, in 1992 DSF, 6 games vs. Washington.

### MOST ASSISTS IN FINAL SERIES:
**10 — Wayne Gretzky, Edmonton,** in 1988, 4 games plus suspended game vs. Boston.
9 — Jacques Lemaire, Montreal, in 1973, 6 games vs. Chicago.
— Wayne Gretzky, Edmonton, in 1987, 7 games vs. Philadelphia.
— Larry Murphy, Pittsburgh, in 1991, 6 games vs. Minnesota.

### MOST ASSISTS, ONE GAME:
**6 — Mikko Leinonen, NY Rangers,** April 8, 1982, at NY Rangers. Final score: NY Rangers 7, Philadelphia 3.
**— Wayne Gretzky, Edmonton,** April 9, 1987, at Edmonton. Final score: Edmonton 13, Los Angeles 3.
5 — Toe Blake, Montreal, March 23, 1944, at Montreal. Final score: Montreal 5, Toronto 1.
— Maurice Richard, Montreal, March 27, 1956, at Montreal. Final score: Montreal 7, NY Rangers 0.
— Bert Olmstead, Montreal, March 30, 1957, at Montreal. Final score: Montreal 8, NY Rangers 3.
— Don McKenney, Boston, April 5, 1958, at Boston. Final score: Boston 8, NY Rangers 2.
— Stan Mikita, Chicago, April 4, 1973, at Chicago. Final score: Chicago 7, St. Louis 1.
— Wayne Gretzky, Edmonton, April 8, 1981, at Montreal. Final score: Edmonton 6, Montreal 3.
— Paul Coffey, Edmonton, May 14, 1985, at Edmonton. Final score: Edmonton 10, Chicago 5.
— Doug Gilmour, St. Louis, April 15, 1986, at Minnesota. Final score: St. Louis 6, Minnesota 3.
— Risto Siltanen, Quebec, April 14, 1987, at Hartford. Final score: Quebec 7, Hartford 5.
— Patrik Sundstrom, New Jersey, April 22, 1988, at New Jersey. Final score: New Jersey 10, Washington 4.
— Geoff Courtnall, St. Louis, April 23, 1998, at St. Louis. Final score: St. Louis 8, Los Angeles 3.

### MOST ASSISTS, ONE PERIOD:
**3 —** Three assists by one player in one period of a playoff game has been recorded on 81 occasions. Brad Richards of the Dallas Stars is the most recent to equal this mark with 3 assists in the third period at San Jose, April 27, 2008. Final score: Dallas 5, San Jose 2.
— Wayne Gretzky has had 3 assists in one period 5 times; Raymond Bourque, 3 times; Toe Blake, Jean Beliveau, Doug Harvey and Bobby Orr, twice each. Joe Primeau of Toronto was the first player to be credited with 3 assists in one period of a playoff game; third period at Boston vs. NY Rangers, April 7, 1932. Final score: Toronto 6, NY Rangers 2.

## POINTS

### MOST POINTS IN PLAYOFFS, CAREER:
**382 — Wayne Gretzky, Edmonton, Los Angeles, St. Louis, NY Rangers,** 122G, 260A
295 — Mark Messier, Edmonton, NY Rangers, 109G, 186A
233 — Jari Kurri, Edmonton, Los Angeles, NY Rangers, Anaheim, 106G, 127A
214 — Glenn Anderson, Edmonton, Toronto, NY Rangers, St. Louis, 93G, 121A
196 — Paul Coffey, Edmonton, Pittsburgh, Los Angeles, Detroit, Philadelphia, Carolina, 59G, 137A

### MOST POINTS, ONE PLAYOFF YEAR:
**47 — Wayne Gretzky, Edmonton,** in 1985. 17 goals, 30 assists in 18 games.
44 — Mario Lemieux, Pittsburgh, in 1991. 16 goals, 28 assists in 23 games.
43 — Wayne Gretzky, Edmonton, in 1988. 12 goals, 31 assists in 19 games.
40 — Wayne Gretzky, Los Angeles, in 1993. 15 goals, 25 assists in 24 games.
38 — Wayne Gretzky, Edmonton, in 1983. 12 goals, 26 assists in 16 games.

### MOST POINTS IN ONE SERIES (OTHER THAN FINAL):
**19 — Rick Middleton, Boston,** in 1983 DF, 7 games vs. Buffalo. 5 goals, 14 assists.
18 — Wayne Gretzky, Edmonton, in 1985 CF, 6 games vs. Chicago. 4 goals, 14 assists.
17 — Mario Lemieux, Pittsburgh, in 1992 DSF, 6 games vs. Washington. 7 goals, 10 assists.
16 — Barry Pederson, Boston, in 1983 DF, 7 games vs. Buffalo. 7 goals, 9 assists.
— Doug Gilmour, Toronto, in 1994 CSF, 7 games vs. San Jose. 3 goals, 13 assists.
15 — Jari Kurri, Edmonton, in 1985 CF, 6 games vs. Chicago. 12 goals, 3 assists.
— Wayne Gretzky, Edmonton, in 1987 DSF, 5 games vs. Los Angeles. 2 goals, 13 assists.
— Tim Kerr, Philadelphia, in 1989 DF, 7 games vs. Pittsburgh. 10 goals, 5 assists.
— Mario Lemieux, Pittsburgh, in 1991 CF, 6 games vs. Boston. 6 goals, 9 assists.

**MOST POINTS IN FINAL SERIES:**

**13 — Wayne Gretzky, Edmonton,** in 1988, 4 games plus suspended game vs. Boston. 3 goals, 10 assists.
12 — Gordie Howe, Detroit, in 1955, 7 games vs. Montreal. 5 goals, 7 assists.
— Yvan Cournoyer, Montreal, in 1973, 6 games vs. Chicago. 6 goals, 6 assists.
— Jacques Lemaire, Montreal, in 1973, 6 games vs. Chicago. 3 goals, 9 assists.
— Mario Lemieux, Pittsburgh, in 1991, 5 games vs. Minnesota. 5 goals, 7 assists.

**MOST POINTS, ONE GAME:**

**8 — Patrik Sundstrom, New Jersey,** April 22, 1988, at New Jersey in 10-4 win over Washington. Sundstrom had 3 goals, 5 assists.
**— Mario Lemieux, Pittsburgh,** April 25, 1989, at Pittsburgh in 10-7 win over Philadelphia. Lemieux had 5 goals, 3 assists.
7 — Wayne Gretzky, Edmonton, April 17, 1983, at Calgary in 10-2 win. Gretzky had 4 goals, 3 assists.
— Wayne Gretzky, Edmonton, April 25,1985, at Winnipeg in 8-3 win. Gretzky had 3 goals, 4 assists.
— Wayne Gretzky, Edmonton, April 9, 1987, at Edmonton in 13-3 win over Los Angeles. Gretzky had 1 goal, 6 assists.
6 — Dickie Moore, Montreal, March 25, 1954, at Montreal in 8-1 win over Boston. Moore had 2 goals, 4 assists.
— Phil Esposito, Boston, April 2, 1969, at Boston in 10-0 win over Toronto. Esposito had 4 goals, 2 assists.
— Darryl Sittler, Toronto, April 22, 1976, at Toronto in 8-5 win over Philadelphia. Sittler had 5 goals, 1 assist.
— Guy Lafleur, Montreal, April 11, 1977, at Montreal in 7-2 win over St. Louis. Lafleur had 3 goals, 3 assists.
— Mikko Leinonen, NY Rangers, April 8, 1982, at NY Rangers in 7-3 win over Philadelphia. Leinonen had 6 assists.
— Paul Coffey, Edmonton, May 14, 1985, at Edmonton in 10-5 win over Chicago. Coffey had 1 goal, 5 assists.
— John Anderson, Hartford, April 12, 1986, at Hartford in 9-4 win over Quebec. Anderson had 2 goals, 4 assists.
— Mario Lemieux, Pittsburgh, April 23, 1992, at Pittsburgh in 6-4 win over Washington. Lemieux had 3 goals, 3 assists.
— Geoff Courtnall, St. Louis, April 23, 1998, at St. Louis in 8-3 win over Los Angeles. Courtnall had 1 goal, 5 assists.

**MOST POINTS, ONE PERIOD:**

**4 — Maurice Richard,** Montreal, March 29, 1945, at Montreal, third period, in 10-3 win vs. Toronto. 3 goals, 1 assist.
**— Dickie Moore,** Montreal, March 25, 1954, at Montreal, first period, in 8-1 win vs. Boston. 2 goals, 2 assists.
**— Barry Pederson,** Boston, April 8, 1982, at Boston, second period, in 7-3 win vs. Buffalo. 3 goals, 1 assist.
**— Peter McNab,** Boston, April 11, 1982, at Buffalo, second period, in 5-2 win vs. Buffalo. 1 goal, 3 assists.
**— Tim Kerr,** Philadelphia, April 13, 1985, at NY Rangers, second period, in 6-5 win vs. NY Rangers. 4 goals.
**— Ken Linseman,** Boston, April 14, 1985, at Boston, second period, in 7-6 win vs. Montreal. 2 goals, 2 assists.
**— Wayne Gretzky,** Edmonton, April 12, 1987, at Los Angeles, third period, in 6-3 win vs. Los Angeles. 1 goal, 3 assists.
**— Glenn Anderson,** Edmonton, April 6, 1988, at Edmonton, third period, in 7-4 win vs. Winnipeg. 3 goals, 1 assist.
**— Mario Lemieux,** Pittsburgh, April 25, 1989, at Pittsburgh, first period, in 10-7 win vs. Philadelphia. 4 goals.
**— Dave Gagner,** Minnesota North Stars, April 8, 1991, at Minnesota, first period, in 6-5 loss vs. Chicago. 2 goals, 2 assists.
**— Mario Lemieux,** Pittsburgh, April 23, 1992, at Pittsburgh, second period, in 6-4 win vs. Washington. 2 goals, 2 assists.
**— Alexander Mogilny,** New Jersey, April 28, 2001, at New Jersey, second period, in 6-5 win vs. Toronto. 1 goal, 3 assists.
**— Brad Richards,** Dallas, April 27, 2008, at San Jose, third period, in 5-2 win vs. San Jose. 1 goal, 3 assists.

## POWER-PLAY GOALS

**MOST POWER-PLAY GOALS IN PLAYOFFS, CAREER:**

**38 — Brett Hull, St. Louis, Dallas, Detroit**
35 — Mike Bossy, NY Islanders
34 — Dino Ciccarelli, Minnesota, Washington, Detroit
— Wayne Gretzky, Edmonton, Los Angeles, St. Louis, NY Rangers
29 — Mario Lemieux, Pittsburgh

**MOST POWER-PLAY GOALS, ONE PLAYOFF YEAR:**

**9 — Mike Bossy, NY Islanders,** 1981. 18 games vs. Toronto, Edmonton, NY Rangers and Minnesota.
**— Cam Neely, Boston,** 1991. 19 games vs. Hartford, Montreal and Pittsburgh.
8 — Tim Kerr, Philadelphia, 1989. 19 games.
— John Druce, Washington, 1990. 15 games.
— Brian Propp, Minnesota, 1991. 23 games.
— Mario Lemieux, Pittsburgh, 1992. 15 games.

**MOST POWER-PLAY GOALS, ONE PLAYOFF SERIES:**

**6 — Chris Kontos, Los Angeles,** 1989 DSF vs. Edmonton, won by Los Angeles 4-3.
5 — Andy Bathgate, Detroit, 1966 SF vs. Chicago, won by Detroit 4-2.
— Denis Potvin, NY Islanders, 1981 QF vs. Edmonton, won by NY Islanders 4-2.
— Ken Houston, Calgary, 1981 QF vs. Philadelphia, won by Calgary 4-3.
— Rick Vaive, Chicago, 1988 DSF vs. St. Louis, won by St. Louis 4-1.
— Tim Kerr, Philadelphia, 1989 DF vs. Pittsburgh, won by Philadelphia 4-3.
— Mario Lemieux, Pittsburgh, 1989 DF vs. Philadelphia, won by Philadelphia 4-3.
— John Druce, Washington, 1990 DF vs. NY Rangers, won by Washington 4-1.
— Pat LaFontaine, Buffalo, 1992 DSF vs. Boston, won by Boston 4-3.
— Adam Graves, NY Rangers, 1996 CQF vs Montreal, won by NY Rangers 4-2.

**MOST POWER-PLAY GOALS, ONE GAME:**

**3 — Syd Howe, Detroit,** March 23, 1939, at Detroit vs. Montreal. Detroit won 7-3.
**— Sid Smith, Toronto,** April 10, 1949, at Detroit. Toronto won 3-1.
**— Phil Esposito, Boston,** April 2, 1969, at Boston vs. Toronto. Boston won 10-0.
**— John Bucyk, Boston,** April 21, 1974, at Boston vs. Chicago. Boston won 8-6.
**— Denis Potvin, NY Islanders,** April 17, 1981, at NY Islanders vs. Edmonton. NY Islanders won 6-3.
**— Tim Kerr, Philadelphia,** April 13, 1985, at NY Rangers. Philadelphia won 6-5.
**— Jari Kurri, Edmonton,** April 9, 1987, at Edmonton vs. Los Angeles. Edmonton won 13-3.
**— Mark Johnson, New Jersey,** April 22, 1988, at New Jersey vs. Washington. New Jersey won 10-4.
**— Dino Ciccarelli, Detroit,** April 29, 1993, at Toronto. Detroit won 7-3.
**— Dino Ciccarelli, Detroit,** May 11, 1995, at Dallas. Detroit won 5-1.
**— Valeri Kamensky, Colorado,** April 24, 1997, at Colorado vs. Chicago. Colorado won 7-0.

**MOST POWER-PLAY GOALS, ONE PERIOD:**

**3 — Tim Kerr, Philadelphia,** April 13, 1985, at NY Rangers, second period in 6-5 win.
2 — Two power-play goals have been scored by one player in one period on 55 occasions. Charlie Conacher of Toronto was the first to score two power-play goals in one period, setting the mark with two power-play goals in the second period at Toronto vs. Boston, March 26, 1936. Final score: Toronto 8, Boston 3. Brad Richards of the Tampa Bay Lightning is the most recent to equal this mark with two power-play goals in the second period at Calgary, June 5, 2004. Final score: Tampa Bay 3, Calgary 2.

## SHORTHAND GOALS

**MOST SHORTHAND GOALS IN PLAYOFFS, CAREER:**

**14 — Mark Messier, Edmonton, NY Rangers**
11 — Wayne Gretzky, Edmonton, Los Angeles, St. Louis
10 — Jari Kurri, Edmonton, Los Angeles, NY Rangers
8 — Ed Westfall, Boston, NY Islanders
— Hakan Loob, Calgary

**MOST SHORTHAND GOALS, ONE PLAYOFF YEAR:**

**3 — Derek Sanderson, Boston,** 1969. 1 vs. Toronto in QF, won by Boston 4-0; 2 vs. Montreal in SF, won by Montreal, 4-2.
**— Bill Barber, Philadelphia,** 1980. All vs. Minnesota in SF, won by Philadelphia 4-1.
**— Lorne Henning, NY Islanders,** 1980. 1 vs. Boston in QF, won by NY Islanders 4-1; 1 vs. Buffalo in SF, won by NY Islanders 4-2, 1 vs. Philadelphia in F, won by NY Islanders 4-2.
**— Wayne Gretzky, Edmonton,** 1983. 2 vs. Winnipeg in DSF, won by Edmonton 3-0; 1 vs. Calgary in DF, won by Edmonton 4-1.
**— Wayne Presley, Chicago,** 1989. All vs. Detroit in DSF, won by Chicago 4-2.
**— Todd Marchant, Edmonton,** 1997. 1 vs. Dallas in CQF, won by Edmonton 4-3; 2 vs. Colorado in CSF, won by Colorado 4-1.

*In 1969, Boston's Derek Sanderson became the first player in NHL history to score three shorthand goals in one playoff year. Later, Sanderson and Ken Hodge each scored a shorthand goal during the same Bruins penalty in a 6-5 win over the Rangers in game one of the 1972 Stanley Cup Final.*

**MOST SHORTHAND GOALS, ONE PLAYOFF SERIES:**
**3 — Bill Barber, Philadelphia,** 1980 SF vs. Minnesota, won by Philadelphia 4-1.
**— Wayne Presley, Chicago,** 1989 DSF vs. Detroit, won by Chicago 4-2.
2 — Mac Colville, NY Rangers, 1940 SF vs. Boston, won by NY Rangers 4-2.
— Jerry Toppazzini, Boston, 1958 SF vs. NY Rangers, won by Boston 4-2.
— Dave Keon, Toronto, 1963 F vs. Detroit, won by Toronto 4-1.
— Bob Pulford, Toronto, 1964 F vs. Detroit, won by Toronto 4-3.
— Serge Savard, Montreal, 1968 F vs. St. Louis, won by Montreal 4-0.
— Derek Sanderson, Boston, 1969 SF vs. Montreal, won by Montreal 4-2.
— Bryan Trottier, NY Islanders, 1980 PR vs. Los Angeles, won by NY Islanders 3-1.
— Bobby Lalonde, Boston, 1981 PR vs. Minnesota, won by Minnesota 3-0.
— Butch Goring, NY Islanders, 1981 SF vs. NY Rangers, won by NY Islanders 4-0.
— Wayne Gretzky, Edmonton, 1983 DSF vs. Winnipeg, won by Edmonton 3-0.
— Mark Messier, Edmonton, 1983 DF vs. Calgary, won by Edmonton 4-1.
— Jari Kurri, Edmonton, 1983 CF vs. Chicago, won by Edmonton 4-0.
— Wayne Gretzky, Edmonton, 1985 DF vs. Winnipeg, won by Edmonton 4-0.
— Kevin Lowe, Edmonton, 1987 F vs. Philadelphia, won by Edmonton 4-3.
— Bob Gould, Washington, 1988 DSF vs. Philadelphia, won by Washington 4-3.
— Dave Poulin, Philadelphia, 1989 DF vs. Pittsburgh, won by Philadelphia 4-3.
— Russ Courtnall, Montreal, 1991 DF vs. Boston, won by Boston 4-3.
— Sergei Fedorov, Detroit, 1992 DSF vs. Minnesota, won by Detroit 4-3.
— Mark Messier, NY Rangers, 1992 DSF vs. New Jersey, won by NY Rangers 4-3.
— Tom Fitzgerald, NY Islanders, 1993 DF vs. Pittsburgh, won by NY Islanders 4-3.
— Mark Osborne, Toronto, 1994 CSF vs. San Jose, won by Toronto 4-3.
— Tony Amonte, Chicago, 1997 CQF vs. Colorado, won by Colorado 4-2.
— Brian Rolston, New Jersey, 1997 CQF vs. Montreal, won by New Jersey 4-1.
— Rod Brind'Amour, Philadelphia, 1997 CQF vs. Pittsburgh, won by Philadelphia 4-1.
— Todd Marchant, Edmonton, 1997 CSF vs. Colorado, won by Colorado 4-1.
— Jeremy Roenick, Phoenix, 1998 CQF vs. Detroit, won by Detroit 4-2.
— Vincent Damphousse, San Jose, 1999 CQF vs. Colorado, won by Colorado 4-2.
— Dixon Ward, Buffalo, 1999 CF vs. Toronto, won by Buffalo 4-1.
— Curtis Brown, Buffalo, 2001 CSF vs. Pittsburgh, won by Pittsburgh 4-3.
— John Madden, New Jersey, 2006 CQF vs. NY Rangers, won by New Jersey 4-0.

**MOST SHORTHAND GOALS, ONE GAME:**
**2 — Dave Keon, Toronto,** April 18, 1963, at Toronto, in 3-1 win vs. Detroit.
**— Bryan Trottier, NY Islanders,** April 8, 1980, at NY Islanders, in 8-1 win vs. Los Angeles.
**— Bobby Lalonde, Boston,** April 11, 1981, at Minnesota, in 6-3 loss vs. Minnesota.
**— Wayne Gretzky, Edmonton,** April 6, 1983, at Edmonton, in 6-3 win vs. Winnipeg.
**— Jari Kurri, Edmonton,** April 24, 1983, at Edmonton, in 8-3 win vs. Chicago.
**— Wayne Gretzky, Edmonton,** April 25, 1985, at Winnipeg, in 8-3 win by Edmonton.
**— Mark Messier, NY Rangers,** April 21, 1992, at NY Rangers, in 7-3 loss vs. New Jersey.
**— Tom Fitzgerald, NY Islanders,** May 8, 1993, at NY Islanders, in 6-5 win vs. Pittsburgh.
**— Rod Brind'Amour, Philadelphia,** April 26, 1997, at Philadelphia, in 6-3 win vs. Pittsburgh.
**— Jeremy Roenick, Phoenix,** April 24, 1998, at Detroit, in 7-4 win by Phoenix.
**— Vincent Damphousse, San Jose,** April 30, 1999, at Colorado, in 7-3 win by San Jose.
**— John Madden, New Jersey,** April 24, 2006, at New Jersey, in 4-1 win vs. NY Rangers.

**MOST SHORTHAND GOALS, ONE PERIOD:**
**2 — Bryan Trottier, NY Islanders,** April 8, 1980, second period, at NY Islanders, in 8-1 win vs. Los Angeles.
**— Bobby Lalonde, Boston,** April 11, 1981, third period, at Minnesota, in 6-3 loss vs. Minnesota.
**— Jari Kurri, Edmonton,** April 24, 1983, third period, at Edmonton, in 8-4 win vs. Chicago.
**— Rod Brind'Amour, Philadelphia,** April 26, 1997, first period, at Philadelphia, in 6-3 win vs. Pittsburgh.
**— Jeremy Roenick, Phoenix,** April 24, 1998, second period, at Detroit, in 7-4 win by Phoenix.
**— Vincent Damphousse, San Jose,** April 30, 1999, third period, at Colorado, in 7-3 win vs. Colorado.

## GAME-WINNING GOALS

**MOST GAME-WINNING GOALS IN PLAYOFFS, CAREER:**
**24 — Wayne Gretzky, Edmonton, Los Angeles, St. Louis, NY Rangers**
**— Brett Hull, St. Louis, Dallas, Detroit**
19 — Claude Lemieux, Montreal, New Jersey, Colorado
— Joe Sakic, Colorado
18 — Maurice Richard, Montreal
— Joe Sakic, Colorado

**MOST GAME-WINNING GOALS, ONE PLAYOFF YEAR:**
**7 — Brad Richards, Tampa Bay,** 2004. 23 games.
6 — Joe Sakic, Colorado, 1996. 22 games.
— Joe Nieuwendyk, Dallas, 1999. 23 games.
5 — Mike Bossy, NY Islanders, 1983. 19 games.
— Jari Kurri, Edmonton, 1987. 21 games.
— Bobby Smith, Minnesota, 1991. 23 games.
— Mario Lemieux, Pittsburgh, 1992. 15 games.
— Fernando Pisani, Edmonton, 2006. 24 games.
— Johan Franzen, Detroit, 2008. 16 games.

**MOST GAME-WINNING GOALS, ONE PLAYOFF SERIES:**
**4 — Mike Bossy, NY Islanders,** 1983 CF vs. Boston, won by NY Islanders 4-2.

## OVERTIME GOALS

**MOST OVERTIME GOALS IN PLAYOFFS, CAREER:**
**8 — Joe Sakic, Colorado** (2 in 1996; 1 in 1998; 1 in 2001; 2 in 2004; 1 in 2006; 1 in 2008)
6 — Maurice Richard, Montreal
5 — Glenn Anderson, Edmonton, Toronto, St. Louis
4 — Bob Nystrom, NY Islanders
— Dale Hunter, Quebec, Washington
— Wayne Gretzky, Edmonton, Los Angeles
— Stephane Richer, Montreal, New Jersey
— Joe Murphy, Edmonton, Chicago
— Esa Tikkanen, Edmonton, NY Rangers
— Jaromir Jagr, Pittsburgh
— Kirk Muller, Montreal, Dallas
— Jeremy Roenick, Chicago, Philadelphia
— Chris Drury, Colorado, Buffalo
— Jamie Langenbrunner, Dallas, New Jersey

**MOST OVERTIME GOALS, ONE PLAYOFF YEAR:**
**3 — Mel Hill, Boston,** 1939. All vs. NY Rangers in best-of-seven SF, won by Boston 4-3.
**— Maurice Richard, Montreal,** 1951. 2 vs. Detroit in best-of-seven SF, won by Montreal 4-2; 1 vs. Toronto best-of-seven F, won by Toronto 4-1.

**MOST OVERTIME GOALS, ONE PLAYOFF SERIES:**
**3 — Mel Hill, Boston,** 1939, SF vs. NY Rangers, won by Boston 4-3. Hill scored at 59:25 of overtime March 21 for a 2-1 win; at 8:24 of overtime, March 23 for a 3-2 win; and at 48:00 of overtime, April 2 for a 2-1 win.

## SCORING BY A DEFENSEMAN

**MOST GOALS BY A DEFENSEMAN, ONE PLAYOFF YEAR:**
**12 — Paul Coffey, Edmonton,** 1985. 18 games.
11 — Brian Leetch, NY Rangers, 1994. 23 games.
9 — Bobby Orr, Boston, 1970. 14 games.
— Brad Park, Boston, 1978. 15 games.
8 — Denis Potvin, NY Islanders, 1981. 18 games.
— Raymond Bourque, Boston, 1983. 17 games.
— Denis Potvin, NY Islanders, 1983. 20 games.
— Paul Coffey, Edmonton, 1984. 19 games.

**MOST GOALS BY A DEFENSEMAN, ONE GAME:**
**3 — Bobby Orr, Boston,** April 11, 1971, at Montreal.
Final score: Boston 5, Montreal 2.
**— Dick Redmond, Chicago,** April 4, 1973, at Chicago.
Final score: Chicago 7, St. Louis 1.
**— Denis Potvin, NY Islanders,** April 17, 1981, at NY Islanders.
Final score: NY Islanders 6, Edmonton 3.
**— Paul Reinhart, Calgary,** April 14, 1983, at Edmonton.
Final score: Edmonton 6, Calgary 3.
**— Doug Halward, Vancouver,** April 7, 1984, at Vancouver.
Final score: Vancouver 7, Calgary 0.
**— Paul Reinhart, Calgary,** April 8, 1984, at Vancouver.
Final score: Calgary 5, Vancouver 1.
**— Al Iafrate, Washington,** April 26, 1993, at Washington.
Final score: Washington 6, NY Islanders 4.
**— Eric Desjardins, Montreal,** June 3, 1993, at Montreal.
Final score: Montreal 3, Los Angeles 2.
**— Gary Suter, Chicago,** April 24, 1994, at Chicago.
Final score: Chicago 4, Toronto 3.
**— Brian Leetch, NY Rangers,** May 22, 1995, at Philadelphia.
Final score: Philadelphia 4, NY Rangers 3.
**— Andy Delmore, Philadelphia,** May 7, 2000, at Philadelphia.
Final score: Philadelphia 6, Pittsburgh 3.

**MOST ASSISTS BY A DEFENSEMAN, ONE PLAYOFF YEAR:**
**25 — Paul Coffey, Edmonton,** 1985. 18 games.
24 — Al MacInnis, Calgary, 1989. 22 games.
23 — Brian Leetch, NY Rangers, 1994. 23 games.
19 — Bobby Orr, Boston, 1972. 15 games.
18 — Raymond Bourque, Boston, 1988. 23 games.
— Raymond Bourque, Boston, 1991. 19 games.
— Larry Murphy, Pittsburgh, 1991. 23 games.

**MOST ASSISTS BY A DEFENSEMAN, ONE GAME:**
**5 — Paul Coffey, Edmonton,** May 14, 1985, at Edmonton vs. Chicago. Edmonton won 10-5.
**— Risto Siltanen, Quebec,** April 14, 1987, at Hartford. Quebec won 7-5.

**MOST POINTS BY A DEFENSEMAN, ONE PLAYOFF YEAR:**
**37 — Paul Coffey, Edmonton,** 1985. 12 goals, 25 assists in 18 games.
34 — Brian Leetch, NY Rangers, 1994. 11 goals, 23 assists in 23 games.
31 — Al MacInnis, Calgary, 1989. 7 goals, 24 assists in 22 games.
25 — Denis Potvin, NY Islanders, 1981. 8 goals, 17 assists in 18 games.
— Raymond Bourque, Boston, 1991. 7 goals, 18 assists in 19 games.

**MOST POINTS BY A DEFENSEMAN, ONE GAME:**
**6 — Paul Coffey, Edmonton,** May 14, 1985, at Edmonton vs. Chicago. 1 goal, 5 assists. Edmonton won 10-5.
5 — Eddie Bush, Detroit, April 9, 1942, at Detroit vs. Toronto. 1 goal, 4 assists. Detroit won 5-2.
— Bob Dailey, Philadelphia, May 1, 1980, at Philadelphia vs. Minnesota. 1 goal, 4 assists. Philadelphia won 7-0.
— Denis Potvin, NY Islanders, April 17, 1981, at NY Islanders vs. Edmonton. 3 goals, 2 assists. NY Islanders won 6-3.
— Risto Siltanen, Quebec, April 14, 1987, at Hartford. 5 assists. Quebec won 7-5.

## SCORING BY A ROOKIE

**MOST GOALS BY A ROOKIE, ONE PLAYOFF YEAR:**
**14 — Dino Ciccarelli, Minnesota,** 1981. 19 games.
11 — Jeremy Roenick, Chicago, 1990. 20 games.
10 — Claude Lemieux, Montreal, 1986. 20 games.
9 — Pat Flatley, NY Islanders, 1984. 21 games
8 — Steve Christoff, Minnesota, 1980. 14 games.
— Brad Palmer, Minnesota, 1981. 19 games.
— Mike Krushelnyski, Boston, 1983. 17 games.
— Bob Joyce, Boston, 1988. 23 games.

**MOST POINTS BY A ROOKIE, ONE PLAYOFF YEAR:**
**21 — Dino Ciccarelli, Minnesota,** 1981. 14 goals, 7 assists in 19 games.
20 — Don Maloney, NY Rangers, 1979. 7 goals, 13 assists in 18 games.

## THREE-OR-MORE-GOAL GAMES

**MOST THREE-OR-MORE-GOAL GAMES IN PLAYOFFS, CAREER:**
**10 — Wayne Gretzky, Edmonton, Los Angeles, NY Rangers.** Eight three-goal games; two four-goal games.
7 — Maurice Richard, Montreal. Four three-goal games; two four-goal games; one five-goal game.
— Jari Kurri, Edmonton. Six three-goal games; one four-goal game.
6 — Dino Ciccarelli, Minnesota, Washington, Detroit. Five three-goal games; one four-goal game.
5 — Mike Bossy, NY Islanders. Four three-goal games; one four-goal game.

**MOST THREE-OR-MORE-GOAL GAMES, ONE PLAYOFF YEAR:**
**4 — Jari Kurri, Edmonton,** 1985. 1 four-goal game, 3 three-goal games.
3 — Mark Messier, Edmonton, 1983. 3 three-goal games.
— Mike Bossy, NY Islanders, 1983. 1 four-goal game, 2 three-goal games
2 — Newsy Lalonde, Montreal, 1919. 1 five-goal game, 1 four-goal game.
— Maurice Richard, Montreal, 1944. 1 five-goal game; 1 three-goal game.
— Doug Bentley, Chicago, 1944. 2 three-goal games.
— Norm Ullman, Detroit, 1964. 2 three-goal games.
— Phil Esposito, Boston, 1970. 2 three-goal games.
— Pit Martin, Chicago, 1973. 2 three-goal games.
— Rick MacLeish, Philadelphia, 1975. 2 three-goal games.
— Lanny McDonald, Toronto, 1977. 1 four-goal game; 1 three-goal game.
— Wayne Gretzky, Edmonton, 1981. 2 three-goal games.
— Wayne Gretzky, Edmonton, 1983. 2 four-goal games.
— Wayne Gretzky, Edmonton, 1985. 2 three-goal games.
— Petr Klima, Detroit, 1988. 2 three-goal games.
— Cam Neely, Boston, 1991. 2 three-goal games.
— Wayne Gretzky, NY Rangers, 1997. 2 three-goal games.
— Daniel Alfredsson, Ottawa, 1998. 2 three-goal games.
— Patrick Marleau, San Jose, 2004. 2 three-goal games.
— Johan Franzen, Detroit, 2008. 2 three-goal games.

**MOST THREE-OR-MORE-GOAL GAMES, ONE PLAYOFF SERIES:**
**3 — Jari Kurri, Edmonton,** 1985 CF vs. Chicago, won by Edmonton 4-2. Kurri scored 3 goals May 7 at Edmonton in 7-3 win, 3 goals May 14 at Edmonton in 10-5 win and 4 goals May 16 at Chicago in 8-2 win.
2 — Doug Bentley, Chicago, 1944 SF vs. Detroit, won by Chicago 4-1. Bentley scored 3 goals March 28 at Chicago in 7-1 win and 3 goals March 30 at Detroit in 5-2 win.
— Norm Ullman, Detroit, 1964 SF vs. Chicago, won by Detroit 4-3. Ullman scored 3 goals March 29 at Chicago in 5-4 win and 3 goals April 7 at Detroit in 7-2 win.
— Mark Messier, Edmonton, 1983 DF vs. Calgary, won by Edmonton 4-1. Messier scored 4 goals April 14 at Edmonton in 6-3 win and 3 goals April 17 at Calgary in 10-2 win.
— Mike Bossy, NY Islanders, 1983 CF vs. Boston, won by NY Islanders 4-2. Bossy scored 3 goals May 3 at NY Islanders in 8-3 win and 4 goals May 7 at New York in 8-4 win.
— Johan Franzen, Detroit, 2008 CSF vs. Colorado, won by Detroit 4-0. Franzen scored 3 goals Apr. 26 at Detroit in 5-1 win and 3 goals May 1 at Colorado in 8-2 win.

## SCORING STREAKS

**LONGEST CONSECUTIVE GOAL-SCORING STREAK, ONE PLAYOFF YEAR:**
**10 Games — Reggie Leach, Philadelphia,** 1976. Streak started April 17 at Toronto and ended May 9 at Montreal. He scored one goal in each of eight games; two in one game; and five in another; a total of 15 goals.

**LONGEST CONSECUTIVE POINT-SCORING STREAK, ONE PLAYOFF YEAR:**
**18 games — Bryan Trottier, NY Islanders,** 1981. 11 goals, 18 assists, 29 points.
17 games — Wayne Gretzky, Edmonton, 1988. 12 goals, 29 assists, 41 points.
— Al MacInnis, Calgary, 1989. 7 goals, 19 assists, 26 points.

**LONGEST CONSECUTIVE POINT-SCORING STREAK, MORE THAN ONE PLAYOFF YEAR:**
**27 games — Bryan Trottier, NY Islanders,** 1980, 1981 and 1982. 7 games in 1980 (3 goals, 5 assists, 8 points), 18 games in 1981 (11 goals, 18 assists, 29 points), and two games in 1982 (2 goals, 3 assists, 5 points). Total points, 42.
19 games — Wayne Gretzky, Edmonton, Los Angeles, 1988 and 1989. 17 games in 1988 (12 goals, 29 assists, 41 points with Edmonton), 2 games in 1989 (1 goal, 2 assists, 3 points with Los Angeles). Total points, 44.
— Al MacInnis, Calgary, 1989 and 1990. 17 games in 1989 (7 goals, 19 assists, 26 points), and two games in 1990 (2 goals, 1 assist, 3 points). Total points, 29.

## FASTEST GOALS

**FASTEST GOAL FROM START OF GAME:**
**0:06 — Don Kozak, Los Angeles,** April 17, 1977, at Los Angeles vs. Boston and goaltender Gerry Cheevers. Los Angeles won 7-4.
0:07 — Bob Gainey, Montreal, May 5, 1977, at NY Islanders vs. goaltender Chico Resch. Montreal won 2-1.
— Terry Murray, Philadelphia, April 12, 1981, at Quebec vs. goaltender Dan Bouchard. Quebec won 4-3 in overtime.

**FASTEST GOAL FROM START OF PERIOD (OTHER THAN FIRST):**
**0:06 — Pelle Eklund, Philadelphia,** April 25, 1989, at Pittsburgh vs. goaltender Tom Barrasso, second period. Pittsburgh won 10-7.
0:09 — Bill Collins, Minnesota, April 9, 1968, at Minnesota vs. Los Angeles and goaltender Wayne Rutledge, third period. Minnesota won 7-5.
— Dave Balon, Minnesota, April 25, 1968, at St. Louis vs. goaltender Glenn Hall, third period. Minnesota won 5-1.
— Murray Oliver, Minnesota, April 8, 1971, at St. Louis vs. goaltender Ernie Wakely, third period. St. Louis won 4-2.
— Clark Gillies, NY Islanders, April 15, 1977, at Buffalo vs. goaltender Don Edwards, third period. NY Islanders won 4-3.
— Eric Vail, Atlanta, April 11, 1978, at Atlanta vs. Detroit and goaltender Ron Low, third period. Detroit won 5-3.
— Stan Smyl, Vancouver, April 10, 1979, at Philadelphia vs. goaltender Wayne Stephenson, third period. Vancouver won 3-2.
— Wayne Gretzky, Edmonton, April 6, 1983, at Edmonton vs. Winnipeg and goaltender Brian Hayward, second period. Edmonton won 6-3.
— Mark Messier, Edmonton, April 16, 1984, at Calgary vs. goaltender Don Edwards, third period. Edmonton won 5-3.
— Brian Skrudland, Montreal, May 18, 1986, at Calgary vs. goaltender Mike Vernon, first overtime period. Montreal won 3-2.

**FASTEST TWO GOALS:**
**0:05 — Norm Ullman, Detroit,** April 11, 1965, at Detroit vs. Chicago and goaltender Glenn Hall. Ullman scored at 17:35 and 17:40 of second period. Detroit won 4-2.

**FASTEST TWO GOALS FROM START OF A GAME:**
**1:08 — Dick Duff, Toronto,** April 9, 1963, at Toronto vs. Detroit and goaltender Terry Sawchuk. Duff scored at 0:49 and 1:08. Toronto won 4-2.

**FASTEST TWO GOALS FROM START OF A PERIOD:**
**0:35 — Pat LaFontaine, NY Islanders,** May 19, 1984, at Edmonton vs. goaltender Andy Moog. LaFontaine scored at 0:13 and 0:35 of third period. Edmonton won 5-2.

## PENALTIES

**MOST PENALTY MINUTES IN PLAYOFFS, CAREER:**
**729 — Dale Hunter, Quebec, Washington, Colorado**
541 — Chris Nilan, Montreal, NY Rangers, Boston
529 — Claude Lemieux, Montreal, New Jersey, Colorado, Phoenix, Dallas
471 — Rick Tocchet, Philadelphia, Pittsburgh, Boston, Phoenix
466 — Willi Plett, Atlanta, Calgary, Minnesota, Boston

**MOST PENALTIES, ONE GAME:**
**8 — Forbes Kennedy, Toronto,** April 2, 1969, at Boston. Kennedy was assessed 4 minors, 2 majors, 1 10-minute misconduct, 1 game misconduct. Boston won 10-0.
**— Kim Clackson, Pittsburgh,** April 14, 1980, at Boston. Clackson was assessed 5 minors, 2 majors, 1 10-minute misconduct. Boston won 6-2.

**MOST PENALTY MINUTES, ONE GAME:**
**42 — Dave Schultz, Philadelphia,** April 22, 1976, at Toronto. Schultz was assessed 1 minor, 2 majors, 1 10-minute misconduct and 2 game-misconducts. Toronto won 8-5.

**MOST PENALTIES, ONE PERIOD AND MOST PENALTY MINUTES, ONE PERIOD:**
**6 Penalties; 39 Minutes — Ed Hospodar, NY Rangers,** April 9, 1981, at Los Angeles, first period. Hospodar was assessed 2 minors, 1 major, 1 10-minute misconduct, 2 game misconducts. Los Angeles won 5-4.

## GOALTENDING

**MOST PLAYOFF GAMES APPEARED IN BY A GOALTENDER, CAREER:**
**247 — Patrick Roy, Montreal, Colorado**
176 — Martin Brodeur, New Jersey
161 — Ed Belfour, Chicago, Dallas, Toronto
150 — Grant Fuhr, Edmonton, Buffalo, St. Louis
138 — Mike Vernon, Calgary, Detroit, San Jose, Florida

**MOST MINUTES PLAYED BY A GOALTENDER, CAREER:**
**15,209 — Patrick Roy, Montreal, Colorado**
10,949 — Martin Brodeur, New Jersey
9,945 — Ed Belfour, Chicago, Dallas, Toronto
8,834 — Grant Fuhr, Edmonton, Buffalo, St. Louis
8,214 — Mike Vernon, Calgary, Detroit, San Jose, Florida

**MOST MINUTES PLAYED BY A GOALTENDER, ONE PLAYOFF YEAR:**
**1,655 — Miikka Kiprusoff, Calgary,** 2004. 26 games.
1,544 — Kirk McLean, Vancouver, 1994. 24 games.
— Ed Belfour, Dallas, 1999. 23 games.
1,540 — Ron Hextall, Philadelphia, 1987. 26 games.
1,505 — Martin Brodeur, New Jersey, 2001. 25 games.

**MOST SHUTOUTS IN PLAYOFFS, CAREER:**
**23 — Patrick Roy, Montreal, Colorado**
**— Martin Brodeur, New Jersey**
16 — Curtis Joseph, St. Louis, Edmonton, Toronto

**MOST SHUTOUTS, ONE PLAYOFF YEAR:**
**7 — Martin Brodeur, New Jersey,** 2003. 24 games.
6 — Dominik Hasek, Detroit, 2002. 23 games.
5 — Jean-Sebastien Giguere, Anaheim, 2003. 21 games.
— Nikolai Khabibulin, Tampa Bay, 2004. 23 games.
— Miikka Kiprusoff, Calgary, 2004. 26 games.

**MOST SHUTOUTS, ONE PLAYOFF SERIES:**
**3 — Clint Benedict, Mtl. Maroons,** 1926 F vs. Victoria. 4 games.
**— Dave Kerr, NY Rangers,** 1940 SF vs. Boston. 6 games.
**— Frank McCool, Toronto,** 1945 F vs. Detroit. 7 games.
**— Turk Broda, Toronto,** 1950 SF vs. Detroit. 7 games.
**— Felix Potvin, Toronto,** 1994 CQF vs. Chicago. 6 games.
**— Martin Brodeur, New Jersey,** 1995 CQF vs. Boston. 5 games.
**— Brent Johnson, St. Louis,** 2002 CQF vs. Chicago. 5 games.
**— Patrick Lalime, Ottawa,** 2002 CQF vs. Philadelphia. 5 games.
**— Jean-Sebastien Giguere, Anaheim,** 2003 CF vs. Minnesota. 4 games.
**— Martin Brodeur, New Jersey,** 2003 F vs. Anaheim. 7 games.
**— Ed Belfour, Toronto,** 2004 CQF vs. Ottawa. 7 games.
**— Nikolai Khabibulin, Tampa Bay,** 2004 CQF vs. NY Islanders. 5 games.

**MOST WINS BY A GOALTENDER, CAREER:**
**151 — Patrick Roy, Montreal, Colorado**
98 — Martin Brodeur, New Jersey
92 — Grant Fuhr, Edmonton, Buffalo, St. Louis
88 — Billy Smith, NY Islanders
— Ed Belfour, Chicago, Dallas, Toronto

**MOST WINS BY A GOALTENDER, ONE PLAYOFF YEAR:**
**16 — Sixteen wins** by a goaltender in one playoff year has been recorded on 17 occasions. Marc-Andre Fleury of the Pittsburgh Penguins is the most recent to equal this mark, posting a record of 16 wins and 8 losses in 24 games in 2009. It was first accomplished by Grant Fuhr in 1988.

**MOST CONSECUTIVE WINS BY A GOALTENDER, MORE THAN ONE PLAYOFF YEAR:**
**14 — Tom Barrasso, Pittsburgh,** 1992, 1993; 3 wins vs. NY Rangers in 1992 DF, won by Pittsburgh 4-2; 4 wins vs. Boston in 1992 CF, won by Pittsburgh 4-0; 4 wins vs. Chicago in 1992 F, won by Pittsburgh 4-0; 3 wins vs. New Jersey in 1993 DSF, won by Pittsburgh 4-1.

**MOST CONSECUTIVE WINS BY A GOALTENDER, ONE PLAYOFF YEAR:**
**11 — Ed Belfour, Chicago,** 1992. 3 wins vs. St. Louis in DSF, won by Chicago 4-2; 4 wins vs. Detroit in DF, won by Chicago 4-0; and 4 wins vs. Edmonton in CF, won by Chicago 4-0.
**— Tom Barrasso, Pittsburgh,** 1992. 3 wins vs. NY Rangers in DF, won by Pittsburgh 4-2; 4 wins vs. Boston in CF, won by Pittsburgh 4-0; and 4 wins vs. Chicago in F, won by Pittsburgh 4-0.
**— Patrick Roy, Montreal,** 1993. 4 wins vs. Quebec in DSF, won by Montreal 4-2; 4 wins vs. Buffalo in DF, won by Montreal 4-0; and 3 wins vs. NY Islanders in CF, won by Montreal 4-1.

**LONGEST SHUTOUT SEQUENCE:**
**270:08 — George Hainsworth,** Montreal, 1930. Hainsworth's shutout streak began after Murray Murdoch scored a goal for the NY Rangers at 15:34 of the first period in the first game of a SF series on March 28, 1930. Hainsworth did not allow another goal in the final 113:18 of that game, won by Montreal 2-1 at 8:52 of the 4th overtime period. Hainsworth then shutout the NY Rangers in the next and final game of the series on March 30, 1930, won by Montreal 2-0. The streak continued with a 3-0 win over Boston in the opening game of the F series on April 1, 1930. His streak ended on April 3, 1930 when Boston's Eddie Shore scored at 16:50 of the second period in the second game of the F series.

**MOST CONSECUTIVE SHUTOUTS:**
**3 — Clint Benedict, Mtl. Maroons,** 1926. Benedict shut out Ottawa 1-0, Mar. 27; he then shut out Victoria twice, 3-0, Mar. 30; 3-0, Apr. 1. Mtl. Maroons won NHL F vs. Ottawa 2 goals to 1 and won the best-of-five F vs. Victoria 3-1.
**— John Ross Roach, NY Rangers,** 1929. Roach shut out NY Americans twice, 0-0, Mar. 19; 1-0, Mar. 21; he then shut out Toronto 1-0, Mar. 24. NY Rangers won QF vs. NY Americans 1 goal to 0 and won the best-of-three SF vs. Toronto 2-0.
**— Frank McCool, Toronto,** 1945. McCool shut out Detroit 1-0, April 6; 2-0, April 8; 1-0, April 12. Toronto won the best-of-seven F 4-3.
**— Brent Johnson, St. Louis,** 2002. Johnson shut out Chicago three times; 2-0, April 20; 4-0, April 21; 1-0, April 23. St. Louis won the best-of-seven CQF 4-1.
**— Patrick Lalime, Ottawa,** 2002. Lalime shut out Philadelphia three times; 3-0, April 20; 3-0, April 22; 3-0, April 24. Ottawa won the best-of-seven CQF 4-1.
**— Jean-Sebastien Giguere, Anaheim,** 2003. Giguere shut out Minnesota 1-0, May 10; 2-0, May 12; 4-0, May 14. Anaheim won the best-of-seven CF 4-0.

# Early Playoff Records

## 1893-1918
## Team Records

**MOST GOALS, BOTH TEAMS, ONE GAME:**
**25 — Ottawa Silver Seven, Dawson City** at Ottawa, Jan. 16, 1905. Ottawa 23, Dawson City 2. Ottawa won best-of-three series 2-0.

**MOST GOALS, ONE TEAM, ONE GAME:**
**23 — Ottawa Silver Seven** at Ottawa, Jan. 16, 1905. Ottawa defeated Dawson City 23-2.

**MOST GOALS, BOTH TEAMS, BEST-OF-THREE SERIES:**
**42 — Ottawa Silver Seven, Queen's University** at Ottawa, 1906. Ottawa defeated Queen's 16-7, Feb. 27, and 12-7, Feb. 28.

**MOST GOALS, ONE TEAM, BEST-OF-THREE SERIES:**
**32 — Ottawa Silver Seven** in 1905 at Ottawa. Defeated Dawson City 9-2, Jan. 13, and 23-2, Jan. 16.

**MOST GOALS, BOTH TEAMS, BEST-OF-FIVE SERIES:**
**39 — Toronto Arenas, Vancouver Millionaires** at Toronto, 1918. Toronto won 5-3, Mar. 20; 6-3, Mar. 26; 2-1, Mar. 30. Vancouver won 6-4, Mar. 23, and 8-1, Mar. 28. Toronto scored 18 goals; Vancouver 21.

**MOST GOALS, ONE TEAM, BEST-OF-FIVE SERIES:**
**26 — Vancouver Millionaires** in 1915 at Vancouver. Defeated Ottawa Senators 6-2, Mar. 22; 8-3, Mar. 24; and 12-3, Mar. 26.

## Individual Records

**MOST GOALS IN PLAYOFFS:**
**63 — Frank McGee, Ottawa Silver Seven,** in 22 playoff games. Seven goals in four games, 1903; 21 goals in eight games, 1904; 18 goals in four games, 1905; 17 goals in six games, 1906.

**MOST GOALS, ONE PLAYOFF SERIES:**
**15 — Frank McGee, Ottawa Silver Seven,** in two games in 1905 at Ottawa. Scored one goal, Jan. 13, in 9-2 victory over Dawson City and 14 goals, Jan. 16, in 23-2 victory.

**MOST GOALS, ONE PLAYOFF GAME:**
**14 — Frank McGee, Ottawa Silver Seven,** at Ottawa, Jan. 16, 1905, in 23-2 victory over Dawson City.

**FASTEST THREE GOALS:**
**40 Seconds — Marty Walsh, Ottawa Senators,** at Ottawa, March 16, 1911, at 3:00, 3:10, and 3:40 of third period. Ottawa defeated Port Arthur 13-4.

*Pittsburgh's Marc-Andre Fleury became the 17th goalie in NHL history to post 16 wins in one playoff year. Fleury was the only netminder to see action during the Penguins Stanley Cup run in 2009.*

## All-Time Playoff Goal Leaders since 1918

**(40 or more goals)**

| Player | Teams | Yrs. | GP | G |
|---|---|---|---|---|
| Wayne Gretzky | Edm., L.A., St.L., NYR | 16 | 208 | 122 |
| Mark Messier | Edm., NYR, Van. | 17 | 236 | 109 |
| Jari Kurri | Edm., L.A., NYR, Ana., Col. | 15 | 200 | 106 |
| Brett Hull | Cgy., St.L., Dal., Det., Phx. | 19 | 202 | 103 |
| Glenn Anderson | Edm., Tor., NYR, St.L. | 15 | 225 | 93 |
| Mike Bossy | NYI | 10 | 129 | 85 |
| Joe Sakic | Que., Col. | 13 | 172 | 84 |
| Maurice Richard | Mtl. | 15 | 133 | 82 |
| Claude Lemieux | Mtl., N.J., Col., Phx., Dal., S.J. | 18 | 234 | 80 |
| Jean Beliveau | Mtl. | 17 | 162 | 79 |
| Jaromir Jagr | Pit., Wsh., NYR | 15 | 169 | 77 |
| Mario Lemieux | Pit. | 8 | 107 | 76 |
| Dino Ciccarelli | Min., Wsh., Det., T.B., Fla. | 14 | 141 | 73 |
| Esa Tikkanen | Edm., NYR, St.L., N.J., Van., Fla., Wsh. | 13 | 186 | 72 |
| Bryan Trottier | NYI, Pit. | 17 | 221 | 71 |
| Steve Yzerman | Det. | 20 | 196 | 70 |
| Gordie Howe | Det., Hfd. | 20 | 157 | 68 |
| Joe Nieuwendyk | Cgy., Dal., N.J., Tor., Fla. | 16 | 158 | 66 |
| Denis Savard | Chi., Mtl., T.B. | 16 | 169 | 66 |
| Yvan Cournoyer | Mtl. | 12 | 147 | 64 |
| Peter Forsberg | Que., Col., Phi., Nsh. | 13 | 151 | 64 |
| Brian Propp | Phi., Bos., Min., Hfd. | 13 | 160 | 64 |
| Bobby Smith | Min., Mtl. | 13 | 184 | 64 |
| Bobby Hull | Chi., Wpg., Hfd. | 14 | 119 | 62 |
| Phil Esposito | Chi., Bos., NYR | 15 | 130 | 61 |
| Jacques Lemaire | Mtl. | 11 | 145 | 61 |
| Joe Mullen | St.L., Cgy., Pit., Bos. | 15 | 143 | 60 |
| Doug Gilmour | St.L., Cgy., Tor., N.J., Chi., Buf., Mtl. | 17 | 182 | 60 |
| *Brendan Shanahan | N.J., St.L., Hfd., Det., NYR | 19 | 184 | 60 |
| Stan Mikita | Chi. | 18 | 155 | 59 |
| Paul Coffey | Edm., Pit., L.A., Det., Hfd., Phi., Chi., Car., Bos. | 16 | 194 | 59 |
| Guy Lafleur | Mtl., NYR, Que. | 14 | 128 | 58 |
| Bernie Geoffrion | Mtl., NYR | 16 | 132 | 58 |
| Luc Robitaille | L.A., Pit., NYR, Det. | 15 | 159 | 58 |
| *Mike Modano | Min., Dal. | 15 | 174 | 58 |
| Cam Neely | Van., Bos. | 9 | 93 | 57 |
| Steve Larmer | Chi., NYR | 13 | 140 | 56 |
| Denis Potvin | NYI | 14 | 185 | 56 |
| Rick MacLeish | Phi., Hfd., Pit., Det. | 11 | 114 | 54 |
| Steve Thomas | Tor., Chi., NYI, N.J., Ana., Det. | 16 | 174 | 54 |
| Bill Barber | Phi. | 11 | 129 | 53 |
| Stephane Richer | Mtl., N.J., T.B., St.L., Pit. | 13 | 134 | 53 |
| Jeremy Roenick | Chi., Phx., Phi., L.A., S.J. | 17 | 154 | 53 |
| Rick Tocchet | Phi., Pit., L.A., Bos., Wsh., Phx. | 13 | 145 | 52 |
| Sergei Fedorov | Det., Ana., CBJ, Wsh. | 15 | 183 | 52 |
| Frank Mahovlich | Tor., Det., Mtl. | 14 | 137 | 51 |
| Brian Bellows | Min., Mtl., T.B., Ana., Wsh. | 13 | 143 | 51 |
| *Rod Brind'Amour | St.L., Phi., Car. | 12 | 159 | 51 |
| Steve Shutt | Mtl., L.A. | 12 | 99 | 50 |
| *Mark Recchi | Pit., Phi., Mtl., Car., Atl., T.B., Bos. | 13 | 151 | 50 |
| Henri Richard | Mtl. | 18 | 180 | 49 |
| Reggie Leach | Bos., Cal., Phi., Det. | 8 | 94 | 47 |
| *Chris Drury | Col., Cgy., Buf., NYR | 8 | 130 | 47 |
| Ted Lindsay | Det., Chi. | 16 | 133 | 47 |
| Clark Gillies | NYI, Buf. | 13 | 164 | 47 |
| Kevin Stevens | Pit., Bos., L.A., NYR, Phi. | 7 | 103 | 46 |
| Dickie Moore | Mtl., Tor., St.L. | 14 | 135 | 46 |
| Ron Francis | Hfd., Pit., Car., Tor. | 17 | 171 | 46 |
| *Nicklas Lidstrom | Det. | 17 | 235 | 46 |
| Rick Middleton | NYR, Bos. | 12 | 114 | 45 |
| *Alex Kovalev | NYR, Pit., Mtl. | 10 | 116 | 44 |
| Lanny McDonald | Tor., Col., Cgy. | 13 | 117 | 44 |
| Scott Young | Hfd., Pit., Que., Col., Ana., St.L., Dal. | 14 | 141 | 44 |
| *Daniel Alfredsson | Ott. | 11 | 101 | 43 |
| Ken Linseman | Phi., Edm., Bos., Tor. | 11 | 113 | 43 |
| Mike Gartner | Wsh., Min., NYR, Tor., Phx. | 15 | 122 | 43 |
| Dave Andreychuk | Buf., Tor., N.J., Bos., Col., T.B. | 18 | 162 | 43 |
| *Vyacheslav Kozlov | Det., Buf., Atl. | 10 | 118 | 42 |
| Bernie Nicholls | L.A., NYR, Edm., N.J., Chi., S.J. | 13 | 118 | 42 |
| Bobby Clarke | Phi. | 13 | 136 | 42 |
| John LeClair | Mtl., Phi., Pit. | 14 | 154 | 42 |
| Adam Oates | Det., St.L., Bos., Wsh., Phi., Ana., Edm. | 15 | 163 | 42 |
| Dale Hunter | Que., Wsh., Col. | 18 | 186 | 42 |
| John Bucyk | Det., Bos. | 14 | 124 | 41 |
| Vincent Damphousse | Tor., Edm., Mtl., S.J. | 14 | 140 | 41 |
| Raymond Bourque | Bos., Col. | 21 | 214 | 41 |
| Tim Kerr | Phi., NYR, Hfd. | 10 | 81 | 40 |
| Peter McNab | Buf., Bos., Van., N.J. | 10 | 107 | 40 |
| *Patrik Elias | N.J. | 12 | 133 | 40 |
| Bob Bourne | NYI, L.A. | 13 | 139 | 40 |
| John Tonelli | NYI, Cgy., L.A., Chi., Que. | 13 | 172 | 40 |

*Active

## All-Time Playoff Assist Leaders since 1918

**(65 or more assists)**

| Player | Teams | Yrs. | GP | A |
|---|---|---|---|---|
| Wayne Gretzky | Edm., L.A., St.L., NYR | 16 | 208 | 260 |
| Mark Messier | Edm., NYR, Van. | 17 | 236 | 186 |
| Raymond Bourque | Bos., Col. | 21 | 214 | 139 |
| Paul Coffey | Edm., Pit., L.A., Det., Hfd., Phi., Chi., Car., Bos. | 16 | 194 | 137 |
| Doug Gilmour | St.L., Cgy., Tor., N.J., Chi., Buf., Mtl. | 17 | 182 | 128 |
| Jari Kurri | Edm., L.A., NYR, Ana., Col. | 15 | 200 | 127 |
| Sergei Fedorov | Det., Ana., CBJ, Wsh. | 15 | 183 | 124 |
| Al MacInnis | Cgy., St.L. | 19 | 177 | 121 |
| Glenn Anderson | Edm., Tor., NYR, St.L. | 15 | 225 | 121 |
| *Nicklas Lidstrom | Det. | 17 | 235 | 119 |
| Larry Robinson | Mtl., L.A. | 20 | 227 | 116 |
| Steve Yzerman | Det. | 20 | 196 | 115 |
| Larry Murphy | L.A., Wsh., Min., Pit., Tor., Det. | 20 | 215 | 115 |
| Adam Oates | Det., St.L., Bos., Wsh., Phi., Ana., Edm. | 15 | 163 | 114 |
| Bryan Trottier | NYI, Pit. | 17 | 221 | 113 |
| *Chris Chelios | Mtl., Chi., Det. | 24 | 266 | 113 |
| Denis Savard | Chi., Mtl., T.B. | 16 | 169 | 109 |
| Denis Potvin | NYI | 14 | 185 | 108 |
| Peter Forsberg | Que., Col., Phi., Nsh. | 13 | 151 | 107 |
| Jaromir Jagr | Pit., Wsh., NYR | 15 | 169 | 104 |
| Joe Sakic | Que., Col. | 13 | 172 | 104 |
| Jean Beliveau | Mtl. | 17 | 162 | 97 |
| Ron Francis | Hfd., Pit., Car., Tor. | 17 | 171 | 97 |
| Mario Lemieux | Pit. | 8 | 107 | 96 |
| Bobby Smith | Min., Mtl. | 13 | 184 | 96 |
| *Sergei Zubov | NYR, Pit., Dal. | 13 | 164 | 93 |
| Gordie Howe | Det., Hfd. | 20 | 157 | 92 |
| Scott Stevens | Wsh., St.L., N.J. | 20 | 233 | 92 |
| Stan Mikita | Chi. | 18 | 155 | 91 |
| Brad Park | NYR, Bos., Det. | 17 | 161 | 90 |
| *Mike Modano | Min., Dal. | 15 | 174 | 87 |
| Brett Hull | Cgy., St.L., Dal., Det., Phx. | 19 | 202 | 87 |
| Craig Janney | Bos., St.L., S.J., Wpg., Phx., T.B., NYI | 11 | 120 | 86 |
| Brian Propp | Phi., Bos., Min., Hfd. | 13 | 160 | 84 |
| *Chris Pronger | Hfd., St.L., Edm., Ana. | 13 | 147 | 80 |
| Henri Richard | Mtl. | 18 | 180 | 80 |
| Jacques Lemaire | Mtl. | 11 | 145 | 78 |
| Claude Lemieux | Mtl., N.J., Col., Phx., Dal., S.J. | 18 | 234 | 78 |
| Ken Linseman | Phi., Edm., Bos., Tor. | 11 | 113 | 77 |
| Bobby Clarke | Phi. | 13 | 136 | 77 |
| Guy Lafleur | Mtl., NYR, Que. | 14 | 128 | 76 |
| Phil Esposito | Chi., Bos., NYR | 15 | 130 | 76 |
| Dale Hunter | Que., Wsh., Col. | 18 | 186 | 76 |
| Mike Bossy | NYI | 10 | 129 | 75 |
| Steve Larmer | Chi., NYR | 13 | 140 | 75 |
| John Tonelli | NYI, Cgy., L.A., Chi., Que. | 13 | 172 | 75 |
| *Brendan Shanahan | N.J., St.L., Hfd., Det., NYR | 19 | 184 | 74 |
| *Patrik Elias | N.J. | 12 | 133 | 73 |
| *Mark Recchi | Pit., Phi., Mtl., Car., Atl., T.B., Bos. | 13 | 151 | 73 |
| *Scott Niedermayer | N.J., Ana. | 15 | 202 | 73 |
| Peter Stastny | Que., N.J., St.L. | 12 | 93 | 72 |
| Bernie Nicholls | L.A., NYR, Edm., N.J., Chi., S.J. | 13 | 118 | 72 |
| Brian Bellows | Min., Mtl., T.B., Ana., Wsh. | 13 | 143 | 71 |
| Gilbert Perreault | Buf. | 11 | 90 | 70 |
| Geoff Courtnall | Bos., Edm., Wsh., St.L., Van. | 15 | 156 | 70 |
| Brian Leetch | NYR, Tor., Bos. | 8 | 95 | 69 |
| Dale Hawerchuk | Wpg., Buf., St.L., Phi. | 15 | 97 | 69 |
| Alex Delvecchio | Det. | 14 | 121 | 69 |
| Jeremy Roenick | Chi., Phx., Phi., L.A., S.J. | 17 | 154 | 69 |
| Luc Robitaille | L.A., Pit., NYR, Det. | 15 | 159 | 69 |
| Bobby Hull | Chi., Wpg., Hfd. | 14 | 119 | 67 |
| Sandis Ozolinsh | S.J., Col., Car., Fla., Ana., NYR | 10 | 137 | 67 |
| Frank Mahovlich | Tor., Det., Mtl. | 14 | 137 | 67 |
| Igor Larionov | Van., S.J., Det., Fla., N.J. | 13 | 150 | 67 |
| Bobby Orr | Bos., Chi. | 8 | 74 | 66 |
| Bernie Federko | St.L., Det. | 11 | 91 | 66 |
| Jean Ratelle | NYR, Bos. | 15 | 123 | 66 |
| Charlie Huddy | Edm., L.A., Buf., St.L. | 14 | 183 | 66 |
| Trevor Linden | Van., NYI, Mtl., Wsh. | 12 | 124 | 65 |

## All-Time Playoff Point Leaders since 1918

**(110 or more points)**

| Player | Teams | Yrs. | GP | G | A | Pts. |
|---|---|---|---|---|---|---|
| Wayne Gretzky | Edm., L.A., St.L., NYR | 16 | 208 | 122 | 260 | 382 |
| Mark Messier | Edm., NYR, Van. | 17 | 236 | 109 | 186 | 295 |
| Jari Kurri | Edm., L.A., NYR, Ana., Col. | 15 | 200 | 106 | 127 | 233 |
| Glenn Anderson | Edm., Tor., NYR, St.L. | 15 | 225 | 93 | 121 | 214 |
| Paul Coffey | Edm., Pit., L.A., Det., Hfd., Phi., Chi., Car., Bos. | 16 | 194 | 59 | 137 | 196 |
| Brett Hull | Cgy., St.L., Dal., Det., Phx. | 19 | 202 | 103 | 87 | 190 |
| Joe Sakic | Que., Col. | 13 | 172 | 84 | 104 | 188 |
| Doug Gilmour | St.L., Cgy., Tor., N.J., Chi., Buf., Mtl. | 17 | 182 | 60 | 128 | 188 |
| Steve Yzerman | Det. | 20 | 196 | 70 | 115 | 185 |
| Bryan Trottier | NYI, Pit. | 17 | 221 | 71 | 113 | 184 |
| Jaromir Jagr | Pit., Wsh., NYR | 15 | 169 | 77 | 104 | 181 |
| Raymond Bourque | Bos., Col. | 21 | 214 | 41 | 139 | 180 |
| Jean Beliveau | Mtl. | 17 | 162 | 79 | 97 | 176 |
| Sergei Fedorov | Det., Ana., CBJ, Wsh. | 15 | 183 | 52 | 124 | 176 |
| Denis Savard | Chi., Mtl., T.B. | 16 | 169 | 66 | 109 | 175 |
| Mario Lemieux | Pit. | 8 | 107 | 76 | 96 | 172 |
| Peter Forsberg | Que., Col., Phi., Nsh. | 13 | 151 | 64 | 107 | 171 |
| *Nicklas Lidstrom | Det. | 17 | 235 | 46 | 119 | 165 |
| Denis Potvin | NYI | 14 | 185 | 56 | 108 | 164 |
| Mike Bossy | NYI | 10 | 129 | 85 | 75 | 160 |
| Gordie Howe | Det., Hfd. | 20 | 157 | 68 | 92 | 160 |
| Al MacInnis | Cgy., St.L. | 19 | 177 | 39 | 121 | 160 |
| Bobby Smith | Min., Mtl. | 13 | 184 | 64 | 96 | 160 |
| Claude Lemieux | Mtl., N.J., Col., Phx., Dal., S.J. | 18 | 234 | 80 | 78 | 158 |
| Adam Oates | Det., St.L., Bos., Wsh., Phi., Ana., Edm. | 15 | 163 | 42 | 114 | 156 |
| Larry Murphy | L.A., Wsh., Min., Pit., Tor., Det. | 20 | 215 | 37 | 115 | 152 |
| Stan Mikita | Chi. | 18 | 155 | 59 | 91 | 150 |
| Brian Propp | Phi., Bos., Min., Hfd. | 13 | 160 | 64 | 84 | 148 |
| *Mike Modano | Min., Dal. | 15 | 174 | 58 | 87 | 145 |
| Larry Robinson | Mtl., L.A. | 20 | 227 | 28 | 116 | 144 |
| *Chris Chelios | Mtl., Chi., Det. | 24 | 266 | 31 | 113 | 144 |
| Ron Francis | Hfd., Pit., Car., Tor. | 17 | 171 | 46 | 97 | 143 |
| Jacques Lemaire | Mtl. | 11 | 145 | 61 | 78 | 139 |
| Phil Esposito | Chi., Bos., NYR | 15 | 130 | 61 | 76 | 137 |
| Guy Lafleur | Mtl., NYR, Que. | 14 | 128 | 58 | 76 | 134 |
| *Brendan Shanahan | N.J., St.L., Hfd., Det., NYR | 19 | 184 | 60 | 74 | 134 |
| Esa Tikkanen | Edm., NYR, St.L., N.J., Van., Fla., Wsh. | 13 | 186 | 72 | 60 | 132 |
| Steve Larmer | Chi., NYR | 13 | 140 | 56 | 75 | 131 |
| Bobby Hull | Chi., Wpg., Hfd. | 14 | 119 | 62 | 67 | 129 |
| Henri Richard | Mtl. | 18 | 180 | 49 | 80 | 129 |
| Yvan Cournoyer | Mtl. | 12 | 147 | 64 | 63 | 127 |
| Luc Robitaille | L.A., Pit., NYR, Det. | 15 | 159 | 58 | 69 | 127 |
| Maurice Richard | Mtl. | 15 | 133 | 82 | 44 | 126 |
| Brad Park | NYR, Bos., Det. | 17 | 161 | 35 | 90 | 125 |
| *Mark Recchi | Pit., Phi., Mtl., Car., Atl., T.B., Bos. | 13 | 151 | 50 | 73 | 123 |
| Brian Bellows | Min., Mtl., T.B., Ana., Wsh. | 13 | 143 | 51 | 71 | 122 |
| Jeremy Roenick | Chi., Phx., Phi., L.A., S.J. | 17 | 154 | 53 | 69 | 122 |
| Ken Linseman | Phi., Edm., Bos., Tor. | 11 | 113 | 43 | 77 | 120 |
| Bobby Clarke | Phi. | 13 | 136 | 42 | 77 | 119 |
| Bernie Geoffrion | Mtl., NYR | 16 | 132 | 58 | 60 | 118 |
| Frank Mahovlich | Tor., Det., Mtl. | 14 | 137 | 51 | 67 | 118 |
| Dino Ciccarelli | Min., Wsh., Det., T.B., Fla. | 14 | 141 | 73 | 45 | 118 |
| Dale Hunter | Que., Wsh., Col. | 18 | 186 | 42 | 76 | 118 |
| Scott Stevens | Wsh., St.L., N.J. | 20 | 233 | 26 | 92 | 118 |
| *Sergei Zubov | NYR, Pit., Dal. | 13 | 164 | 24 | 93 | 117 |
| Joe Nieuwendyk | Cgy., Dal., N.J., Tor., Fla. | 16 | 158 | 66 | 50 | 116 |
| John Tonelli | NYI, Cgy., L.A., Chi., Que. | 13 | 172 | 40 | 75 | 115 |
| Bernie Nicholls | L.A., NYR, Edm., N.J., Chi., S.J. | 13 | 118 | 42 | 72 | 114 |
| *Patrik Elias | N.J. | 12 | 133 | 40 | 73 | 113 |
| Rick Tocchet | Phi., Pit., L.A., Bos., Wsh., Phx. | 13 | 145 | 52 | 60 | 112 |
| *Rod Brind'Amour | St.L., Phi., Car. | 12 | 159 | 51 | 60 | 111 |
| Craig Janney | Bos., St.L., S.J., Wpg., Phx., T.B., NYI | 11 | 120 | 24 | 86 | 110 |
| Dickie Moore | Mtl., Tor., St.L. | 14 | 135 | 46 | 64 | 110 |

*In 2009, Pittsburgh's Evgeni Malkin was the first player to lead the NHL in scoring during the regular season and the playoffs since the Penguins' magnificent Mario Lemieux in 1992.*

# Leading Playoff Scorers, 1918–2009

| Season | Player, Team | Games Played | Goals | Assists | Points |
|---|---|---|---|---|---|
| 2008-09 | Evgeni Malkin, Pittsburgh | 24 | 14 | 22 | 36 |
| 2007-08 | Henrik Zetterberg, Detroit | 22 | 13 | 14 | 27 |
| | Sidney Crosby, Pittsburgh | 20 | 6 | 21 | 27 |
| 2006-07 | Daniel Alfredsson, Ottawa | 20 | 14 | 8 | 22 |
| | Dany Heatley, Ottawa | 20 | 7 | 15 | 22 |
| | Jason Spezza, Ottawa | 20 | 7 | 15 | 22 |
| 2005-06 | Eric Staal, Carolina | 25 | 9 | 19 | 28 |
| 2004-05 | *Season Cancelled* | | | | |
| 2003-04 | Brad Richards, Tampa Bay | 23 | 12 | 14 | 26 |
| 2002-03 | Jamie Langenbrunner, New Jersey | 24 | 11 | 7 | 18 |
| | Scott Niedermayer, New Jersey | 24 | 2 | 16 | 18 |
| 2001-02 | Peter Forsberg, Colorado | 20 | 9 | 18 | 27 |
| 2000-01 | Joe Sakic, Colorado | 21 | 13 | 13 | 26 |
| 99-2000 | Brett Hull, Dallas | 23 | 11 | 13 | 24 |
| 1998-99 | Peter Forsberg, Colorado | 19 | 8 | 16 | 24 |
| 1997-98 | Steve Yzerman, Detroit | 22 | 6 | 18 | 24 |
| 1996-97 | Eric Lindros, Philadelphia | 19 | 12 | 14 | 26 |
| 1995-96 | Joe Sakic, Colorado | 22 | 18 | 16 | 34 |
| 1994-95 | Sergei Fedorov, Detroit | 17 | 7 | 17 | 24 |
| 1993-94 | Brian Leetch, NY Rangers | 23 | 11 | 23 | 34 |
| 1992-93 | Wayne Gretzky, Los Angeles | 24 | 15 | 25 | 40 |
| 1991-92 | Mario Lemieux, Pittsburgh | 15 | 16 | 18 | 34 |
| 1990-91 | Mario Lemieux, Pittsburgh | 23 | 16 | 28 | 44 |
| 1989-90 | Craig Simpson, Edmonton | 22 | 16 | 15 | 31 |
| | Mark Messier, Edmonton | 22 | 9 | 22 | 31 |
| 1988-89 | Al MacInnis, Calgary | 22 | 7 | 24 | 31 |
| 1987-88 | Wayne Gretzky, Edmonton | 19 | 12 | 31 | 43 |
| 1986-87 | Wayne Gretzky, Edmonton | 21 | 5 | 29 | 34 |
| 1985-86 | Doug Gilmour, St. Louis | 19 | 9 | 12 | 21 |
| | Bernie Federko, St. Louis | 19 | 7 | 14 | 21 |
| 1984-85 | Wayne Gretzky, Edmonton | 18 | 17 | 30 | 47 |
| 1983-84 | Wayne Gretzky, Edmonton | 19 | 13 | 22 | 35 |
| 1982-83 | Wayne Gretzky, Edmonton | 16 | 12 | 26 | 38 |
| 1981-82 | Bryan Trottier, NY Islanders | 19 | 6 | 23 | 29 |
| 1980-81 | Mike Bossy, NY Islanders | 18 | 17 | 18 | 35 |
| 1979-80 | Bryan Trottier, NY Islanders | 21 | 12 | 17 | 29 |
| 1978-79 | Jacques Lemaire, Montreal | 16 | 11 | 12 | 23 |
| | Guy Lafleur, Montreal | 16 | 10 | 13 | 23 |
| 1977-78 | Guy Lafleur, Montreal | 15 | 10 | 11 | 21 |
| | Larry Robinson, Montreal | 15 | 4 | 17 | 21 |
| 1976-77 | Guy Lafleur, Montreal | 14 | 9 | 17 | 26 |
| 1975-76 | Reggie Leach, Philadelphia | 16 | 19 | 5 | 24 |
| 1974-75 | Rick MacLeish, Philadelphia | 17 | 11 | 9 | 20 |
| 1973-74 | Rick MacLeish, Philadelphia | 17 | 13 | 9 | 22 |
| 1972-73 | Yvan Cournoyer, Montreal | 17 | 15 | 10 | 25 |
| 1971-72 | Phil Esposito, Boston | 15 | 9 | 15 | 24 |
| | Bobby Orr, Boston | 15 | 5 | 19 | 24 |
| 1970-71 | Frank Mahovlich, Montreal | 20 | 14 | 13 | 27 |
| 1969-70 | Phil Esposito, Boston | 14 | 13 | 14 | 27 |
| 1968-69 | Phil Esposito, Boston | 10 | 8 | 10 | 18 |
| 1967-68 | Bill Goldsworthy, Minnesota | 14 | 8 | 7 | 15 |
| 1966-67 | Jim Pappin, Toronto | 12 | 7 | 8 | 15 |
| 1965-66 | Norm Ullman, Detroit | 12 | 6 | 9 | 15 |
| 1964-65 | Bobby Hull, Chicago | 14 | 10 | 7 | 17 |
| 1963-64 | Gordie Howe, Detroit | 14 | 9 | 10 | 19 |
| 1962-63 | Gordie Howe, Detroit | 11 | 7 | 9 | 16 |
| | Norm Ullman, Detroit | 11 | 4 | 12 | 16 |
| 1961-62 | Stan Mikita, Chicago | 12 | 6 | 15 | 21 |
| 1960-61 | Gordie Howe, Detroit | 11 | 4 | 11 | 15 |
| | Pierre Pilote, Chicago | 12 | 3 | 12 | 15 |
| 1959-60 | Henri Richard, Montreal | 8 | 3 | 9 | 12 |
| | Bernie Geoffrion, Montreal | 8 | 2 | 10 | 12 |
| 1958-59 | Dickie Moore, Montreal | 11 | 5 | 12 | 17 |
| 1957-58 | Fleming MacKell, Boston | 12 | 5 | 14 | 19 |
| 1956-57 | Bernie Geoffrion, Montreal | 11 | 11 | 7 | 18 |
| 1955-56 | Jean Béliveau, Montreal | 10 | 12 | 7 | 19 |
| 1954-55 | Gordie Howe, Detroit | 11 | 9 | 11 | 20 |
| 1953-54 | Dickie Moore, Montreal | 11 | 5 | 8 | 13 |
| 1952-53 | Ed Sandford, Boston | 11 | 8 | 3 | 11 |
| 1951-52 | Ted Lindsay, Detroit | 8 | 5 | 2 | 7 |
| | Floyd Curry, Montreal | 11 | 4 | 3 | 7 |
| | Metro Prystai, Detroit | 8 | 2 | 5 | 7 |
| | Gordie Howe, Detroit | 8 | 2 | 5 | 7 |
| 1950-51 | Maurice Richard, Montreal | 11 | 9 | 4 | 13 |
| | Max Bentley, Toronto | 11 | 2 | 11 | 13 |
| 1949-50 | Pentti Lund, NY Rangers | 12 | 6 | 5 | 11 |
| 1948-49 | Gordie Howe, Detroit | 11 | 8 | 3 | 11 |
| 1947-48 | Ted Kennedy, Toronto | 9 | 8 | 6 | 14 |
| 1946-47 | Maurice Richard, Montreal | 10 | 6 | 5 | 11 |
| 1945-46 | Elmer Lach, Montreal | 9 | 5 | 12 | 17 |
| 1944-45 | Joe Carveth, Detroit | 14 | 5 | 6 | 11 |
| 1943-44 | Toe Blake, Montreal | 9 | 7 | 11 | 18 |
| 1942-43 | Carl Liscombe, Detroit | 10 | 6 | 8 | 14 |
| 1941-42 | Don Grosso, Detroit | 12 | 8 | 6 | 14 |
| | Syl Apps, Toronto | 13 | 5 | 9 | 14 |
| 1940-41 | Milt Schmidt, Boston | 11 | 5 | 6 | 11 |
| 1939-40 | Phil Watson, NY Rangers | 12 | 3 | 6 | 9 |
| | Neil Colville, NY Rangers | 12 | 2 | 7 | 9 |
| 1938-39 | Bill Cowley, Boston | 12 | 3 | 11 | 14 |
| 1937-38 | Johnny Gottselig, Chicago | 10 | 5 | 3 | 8 |
| | Gordie Drillon, Toronto | 7 | 7 | 1 | 8 |
| 1936-37 | Marty Barry, Detroit | 10 | 4 | 7 | 11 |
| 1935-36 | Frank Boll, Toronto | 9 | 7 | 3 | 10 |
| 1934-35 | Baldy Northcott, Mtl. Maroons | 7 | 4 | 1 | 5 |
| | Busher Jackson, Toronto | 7 | 3 | 2 | 5 |
| | Cy Wentworth, Mtl. Maroons | 7 | 3 | 2 | 5 |
| | Charlie Conacher, Toronto | 7 | 1 | 4 | 5 |
| 1933-34 | Larry Aurie, Detroit | 9 | 3 | 7 | 10 |
| 1932-33 | Cecil Dillon, NY Rangers | 8 | 8 | 2 | 10 |
| 1931-32 | Frank Boucher, NY Rangers | 7 | 3 | 6 | 9 |
| 1930-31 | Cooney Weiland, Boston | 5 | 6 | 3 | 9 |
| 1929-30 | Marty Barry, Boston | 6 | 3 | 3 | 6 |
| | Cooney Weiland, Boston | 6 | 1 | 5 | 6 |
| 1928-29 | Andy Blair, Toronto | 4 | 3 | 0 | 3 |
| | Butch Keeling, NY Rangers | 6 | 3 | 0 | 3 |
| | Ace Bailey, Toronto | 4 | 1 | 2 | 3 |
| 1927-28 | Frank Boucher, NY Rangers | 9 | 7 | 3 | 10 |
| 1926-27 | Harry Oliver, Boston | 8 | 4 | 2 | 6 |
| | Percy Galbraith, Boston | 8 | 3 | 3 | 6 |
| 1925-26 | Nels Stewart, Mtl. Maroons | 8 | 6 | 3 | 9 |
| 1924-25 | Howie Morenz, Montreal | 6 | 7 | 1 | 8 |
| 1923-24 | Howie Morenz, Montreal | 6 | 7 | 3 | 10 |
| 1922-23 | Punch Broadbent, Ottawa | 8 | 6 | 1 | 7 |
| 1921-22 | Babe Dye, Toronto | 7 | 11 | 1 | 12 |
| 1920-21 | Cy Denneny, Ottawa | 7 | 4 | 2 | 6 |
| 1919-20 | Frank Nighbor, Ottawa | 5 | 6 | 1 | 7 |
| | Jack Darragh, Ottawa | 5 | 5 | 2 | 7 |
| 1918-19 | Newsy Lalonde, Montreal | 10 | 17 | 2 | 19 |
| 1917-18 | Alf Skinner, Toronto | 7 | 8 | 3 | 11 |

# Three-or-more-Goal Games, Playoffs 1918 –2009

| Player | Team | Date | City | Total Goals | Opposing Goaltender | Score | |
|---|---|---|---|---|---|---|---|
| Wayne Gretzky (10) | Edm. | Apr. 11/81 | Edm. | 3 | Richard Sevigny | Edm. 6 | Mtl. 2 |
| | | Apr. 19/81 | Edm. | 3 | Billy Smith | Edm. 5 | NYI 2 |
| | | Apr. 6/83 | Edm. | 4 | Brian Hayward | Edm. 6 | Wpg. 3 |
| | | Apr. 17/83 | Cgy. | 4 | Reggie Lemelin | Edm. 10 | Cgy. 2 |
| | | Apr. 25/85 | Wpg. | 3 | Brian Hayward (2) | | |
| | | | | | Marc Behrend (1) | Edm. 8 | Wpg. 3 |
| | | May 25/85 | Edm. | 3 | Pelle Lindbergh | Edm. 4 | Phi. 3 |
| | | Apr. 24/86 | Cgy. | 3 | Mike Vernon | Edm. 7 | Cgy. 4 |
| | L.A. | May 29/93 | Tor. | 3 | Felix Potvin | L.A. 5 | Tor. 4 |
| | NYR | Apr. 23/97 | NYR | 3 | John Vanbiesbrouck | NYR 3 | Fla. 2 |
| | | May 18/97 | Phi. | 3 | Garth Snow | NYR 5 | Phi. 4 |
| Maurice Richard (7) | Mtl. | Mar. 23/44 | Mtl. | 5 | Paul Bibeault | Mtl. 5 | Tor. 1 |
| | | Apr. 6/44 | Chi. | 3 | Mike Karakas | Mtl. 3 | Chi. 1 |
| | | Mar. 29/45 | Mtl. | 4 | Frank McCool | Mtl. 10 | Tor. 3 |
| | | Apr. 14/53 | Bos. | 3 | Gord Henry | Mtl. 7 | Bos. 3 |
| | | Mar. 20/56 | Mtl. | 3 | Gump Worsley | Mtl. 7 | NYR 1 |
| | | Apr. 6/57 | Mtl. | 4 | Don Simmons | Mtl. 5 | Bos. 1 |
| | | Apr. 1/58 | Det. | 3 | Terry Sawchuk | Mtl. 4 | Det. 3 |
| Jari Kurri (7) | Edm. | Apr. 4/84 | Edm. | 3 | Doug Soetaert (1) | | |
| | | | | | Mike Veisor (2) | Edm. 9 | Wpg. 2 |
| | | Apr. 25/85 | Wpg. | 3 | Brian Hayward (2) | | |
| | | | | | Marc Behrend (1) | Edm. 8 | Wpg. 3 |
| | | May 7/85 | Edm. | 3 | Murray Bannerman | Edm. 7 | Chi. 3 |
| | | May 14/85 | Edm. | 3 | Murray Bannerman | Edm. 10 | Chi. 5 |
| | | May 16/85 | Chi. | 4 | Murray Bannerman | Edm. 8 | Chi. 2 |
| | | Apr. 9/87 | Edm. | 4 | Rollie Melanson (2) | | |
| | | | | | Darren Eliot (2) | Edm. 13 | L.A. 3 |
| | | May 18/90 | Bos. | 3 | Andy Moog (2) | | |
| | | | | | Reggie Lemelin (1) | Edm. 7 | Bos. 2 |
| Dino Ciccarelli (6) | Min. | May 5/81 | Min. | 3 | Pat Riggin | Min. 7 | Cgy. 4 |
| | | Apr. 10/82 | Min. | 3 | Murray Bannerman | Min. 7 | Chi. 1 |
| | Wsh. | Apr. 5/90 | N.J. | 3 | Sean Burke | Wsh. 5 | N.J. 4 |
| | | Apr. 25/92 | Pit. | 4 | Tom Barrasso (1) | | |
| | | | | | Ken Wregget (3) | Wsh. 7 | Pit. 2 |
| | Det. | Apr. 29/93 | Tor. | 3 | Felix Potvin (2) | | |
| | | | | | Daren Puppa (1) | Det. 7 | Tor. 3 |
| | | May 11/95 | Dal. | 3 | Andy Moog (2) | | |
| | | | | | Darcy Wakaluk (1) | Det. 5 | Dal. 1 |
| Mike Bossy (5) | NYI | Apr. 16/79 | NYI | 3 | Tony Esposito | NYI 6 | Chi. 2 |
| | | May 8/82 | NYI | 3 | Richard Brodeur | NYI 6 | Van. 5 |
| | | Apr. 10/83 | Wsh. | 3 | Al Jensen | NYI 6 | Wsh. 3 |
| | | May 3/83 | NYI | 3 | Pete Peeters | NYI 8 | Bos. 3 |
| | | May 7/83 | NYI | 4 | Pete Peeters | NYI 8 | Bos. 4 |
| Phil Esposito (4) | Bos. | Apr. 2/69 | Bos. | 4 | Bruce Gamble | Bos. 10 | Tor. 0 |
| | | Apr. 8/70 | Bos. | 3 | Ed Giacomin | Bos. 8 | NYR 2 |
| | | Apr. 19/70 | Chi. | 3 | Tony Esposito | Bos. 6 | Chi. 3 |
| | | Apr. 8/75 | Bos. | 3 | Tony Esposito (2) | | |
| | | | | | Michel Dumas (1) | Bos. 8 | Chi. 2 |
| Mark Messier (4) | Edm. | Apr. 14/83 | Edm. | 4 | Reggie Lemelin | Edm. 6 | Cgy. 3 |
| | | Apr. 17/83 | Cgy. | 3 | Reggie Lemelin (1) | Edm. 10 | Cgy. 2 |
| | | | | | Don Edwards (2) | | |
| | | Apr. 26/83 | Edm. | 3 | Murray Bannerman | Edm. 8 | Chi. 2 |
| | NYR | May 25/94 | N.J. | 3 | Martin Brodeur (2) | NYR 4 | N.J. 2 |
| | | | | | ENG (1) | | |
| Steve Yzerman (4) | Det. | Apr. 6/89 | Det. | 3 | Alain Chevrier | Chi. 5 | Det. 4 |
| | | Apr. 4/91 | St.L. | 3 | Vincent Riendeau (2) | Det. 6 | St.L. 3 |
| | | | | | Pat Jablonski (1) | | |
| | | May 8/96 | St.L. | 3 | Jon Casey | St.L. 5 | Det. 4 |
| | | Apr. 21/99 | Det. | 3 | Guy Hebert (2) | Det. 5 | Ana. 3 |
| | | | | | Pat Jablonski (1) | | |
| Bernie Geoffrion (3) | Mtl. | Mar. 27/52 | Mtl. | 3 | Jim Henry | Mtl. 4 | Bos. 0 |
| | | Apr. 7/55 | Mtl. | 3 | Terry Sawchuk | Mtl. 4 | Det. 2 |
| | | Mar. 30/57 | Mtl. | 3 | Gump Worsley | Mtl. 8 | NYR 3 |
| Norm Ullman (3) | Det. | Mar. 29/64 | Chi. | 3 | Glenn Hall | Det. 5 | Chi. 4 |
| | | Apr. 7/64 | Det. | 3 | Glenn Hall (2) | | |
| | | | | | Denis DeJordy (1) | Det. 7 | Chi. 2 |
| | | Apr. 11/65 | Det. | 3 | Glenn Hall | Det. 4 | Chi. 2 |
| John Bucyk (3) | Bos. | May 3/70 | St.L. | 3 | Jacques Plante (1) | | |
| | | | | | Ernie Wakely (2) | Bos. 6 | St.L. 1 |
| | | Apr. 20/72 | Bos. | 3 | Jacques Caron (1) | | |
| | | | | | Ernie Wakely (2) | Bos. 10 | St.L. 2 |
| | | Apr. 21/74 | Bos. | 3 | Tony Esposito | Bos. 8 | Chi. 6 |
| Rick MacLeish (3) | Phi. | Apr. 11/74 | Phi. | 3 | Phil Myre | Phi. 5 | Atl. 1 |
| | | Apr. 13/75 | Phi. | 3 | Gord McRae | Phi. 6 | Tor. 3 |
| | | May 13/75 | Phi. | 3 | Glenn Resch | Phi. 4 | NYI 1 |
| Denis Savard (3) | Chi. | Apr. 19/82 | Chi. | 3 | Mike Liut | Chi. 7 | StL. 4 |
| | | Apr. 10/86 | Chi. | 4 | Ken Wregget | Tor. 6 | Chi. 4 |
| | | Apr. 9/88 | St.L. | 3 | Greg Millen | Chi. 6 | St.L. 3 |
| Tim Kerr (3) | Phi. | Apr. 13/85 | NYR | 4 | Glen Hanlon | Phi. 6 | NYR 5 |
| | | Apr. 20/87 | Phi. | 3 | Kelly Hrudey | Phi. 4 | NYI 2 |
| | | Apr. 19/89 | Pit. | 3 | Tom Barrasso | Phi. 4 | Pit. 2 |
| Cam Neely (3) | Bos. | Apr. 9/87 | Mtl. | 3 | Patrick Roy | Mtl. 4 | Bos. 3 |
| | | Apr. 5/91 | Bos. | 3 | Peter Sidorkiewicz | Bos. 4 | Hfd. 3 |
| | | Apr. 25/91 | Bos. | 3 | Patrick Roy | Bos. 4 | Mtl. 1 |
| Petr Klima (3) | Det. | Apr. 7/88 | Tor. | 3 | Allan Bester (2) | | |
| | | | | | Ken Wregett (1) | Det. 6 | Tor. 2 |
| | | Apr. 21/88 | St.L. | 3 | Greg Millen | Det. 6 | St.L. 0 |
| | Edm. | May 4/91 | Edm. | 3 | Jon Casey | Edm. 7 | Min. 2 |

| Player | Team | Date | City | Total Goals | Opposing Goaltender | Score | |
|---|---|---|---|---|---|---|---|
| Esa Tikkanen (3) | Edm. | May 22/88 | Edm. | 3 | Reggie Lemelin | Edm. 6 | Bos. 3 |
| | | Apr. 16/91 | Cgy. | 3 | Mike Vernon | Edm. 5 | Cgy. 4 |
| | | Apr. 26/92 | L.A. | 3 | Kelly Hrudey (2) | Edm. 5 | L.A. 2 |
| | | | | | Tom Askey (1) | | |
| Mike Gartner (3) | NYR | Apr. 13/90 | NYR | 3 | Mark Fitzpatrick (2) | | |
| | | | | | Glenn Healy (1) | NYR 6 | NYI 5 |
| | | Apr. 27/92 | NYR | 3 | Chris Terreri | NYR 8 | N.J. 5 |
| | Tor. | Apr. 25/96 | Tor. | 3 | Jon Casey | Tor. 5 | St.L. 4 |
| Mario Lemieux (3) | Pit. | Apr. 25/89 | Pit. | 5 | Ron Hextall | Pit. 10 | Phi. 7 |
| | | Apr. 23/92 | Pit. | 3 | Don Beaupre | Pit. 6 | Wsh. 4 |
| | | May 11/96 | Pit. | 3 | Mike Richter | Pit. 7 | NYR 3 |
| Patrick Marleau (3) | S.J. | Apr. 10/04 | S.J. | 3 | Chris Osgood | S.J. 3 | St.L. 1 |
| | | Apr. 22/04 | S.J. | 3 | David Aebischer | S.J. 5 | Col. 2 |
| | | Apr. 27/06 | S.J. | 3 | Chris Mason | Nsh. 4 | S.J. 5 |
| Newsy Lalonde (2) | Mtl. | Mar. 1/19 | Mtl. | 5 | Clint Benedict | Mtl. 6 | Ott. 3 |
| | | Mar. 22/19 | Sea. | 4 | Hap Holmes | Mtl. 4 | Sea. 2 |
| Howie Morenz (2) | Mtl. | Mar. 22/24 | Mtl. | 3 | Charles Reid | Mtl. 6 | Cgy.T. 1 |
| | | Mar. 27/25 | Mtl. | 3 | Hap Holmes | Mtl. 4 | Vic. 2 |
| Doug Bentley (2) | Chi. | Mar. 28/44 | Chi. | 3 | Connie Dion | Chi. 7 | Det. 1 |
| | | Mar. 30/44 | Det. | 3 | Connie Dion | Chi. 5 | Det. 2 |
| Toe Blake (2) | Mtl. | Mar. 22/38 | Mtl. | 3 | Mike Karakas | Mtl. 6 | Chi. 4 |
| | | Mar. 26/46 | Chi. | 3 | Mike Karakas | Mtl. 7 | Chi. 2 |
| Ted Kennedy (2) | Tor. | Apr. 14/45 | Tor. | 3 | Harry Lumley | Det. 5 | Tor. 3 |
| | | Mar. 27/48 | Tor. | 4 | Frank Brimsek | Tor. 5 | Bos. 3 |
| F. St. Marseille (2) | St.L. | Apr. 28/70 | St.L. | 3 | Al Smith | St.L. 5 | Pit. 0 |
| | | Apr. 6/72 | Min. | 3 | Cesare Maniago | Min. 6 | St.L. 5 |
| Bobby Hull (2) | Chi. | Apr. 7/63 | Det. | 3 | Terry Sawchuk | Det. 7 | Chi. 4 |
| | | Apr. 9/72 | Pit. | 3 | Jim Rutherford | Chi. 6 | Pit. 5 |
| Pit Martin (2) | Chi. | Apr. 4/73 | Chi. | 3 | Wayne Stephenson | Chi. 7 | St.L. 1 |
| | | May 10/73 | Chi. | 3 | Ken Dryden | Mtl. 6 | Chi. 4 |
| Yvan Cournoyer (2) | Mtl. | Apr. 5/73 | Mtl. | 3 | Dave Dryden | Mtl. 7 | Buf. 3 |
| | | Apr. 11/74 | Mtl. | 3 | Ed Giacomin | Mtl. 4 | NYR 1 |
| Guy Lafleur (2) | Mtl. | May 1/75 | Mtl. | 3 | Roger Crozier (1) | | |
| | | | | | Gerry Desjardins (2) | Mtl. 7 | Buf. 0 |
| | | Apr. 11/77 | Mtl. | 3 | Ed Staniowski | Mtl. 7 | St.L. 2 |
| Lanny McDonald (2) | Tor. | Apr. 9/77 | Pit. | 3 | Denis Herron | Tor. 5 | Pit. 2 |
| | | Apr. 17/77 | Tor. | 4 | Wayne Stephenson | Phi. 6 | Tor. 5 |
| Bill Barber (2) | Phi. | May 4/80 | Min. | 4 | Gilles Meloche | Phi. 5 | Min. 3 |
| | | Apr. 9/81 | Phi. | 3 | Dan Bouchard | Phi. 8 | Que. 5 |
| Bryan Trottier (2) | NYI | Apr. 8/80 | NYI | 3 | Doug Keans | NYI 8 | L.A. 1 |
| | | Apr. 9/81 | NYI | 3 | Michel Larocque | NYI 5 | Tor. 1 |
| Butch Goring (2) | L.A. | Apr. 9/77 | L.A. | 3 | Phil Myre | L.A. 4 | Atl. 2 |
| | NYI | May 17/81 | Min. | 3 | Gilles Meloche | NYI 7 | Min. 5 |
| Paul Reinhart (2) | Cgy. | Apr. 14/83 | Edm. | 3 | Andy Moog | Edm. 6 | Cgy. 3 |
| | | Apr. 8/84 | Van | 3 | Richard Brodeur | Cgy. 5 | Van. 1 |
| Brian Propp (2) | Phi. | Apr. 22/81 | Phi. | 3 | Pat Riggin | Phi. 9 | Cgy. 4 |
| | | Apr. 21/85 | Phi. | 3 | Billy Smith | Phi. 5 | NYI 2 |
| Peter Stastny (2) | Que. | Apr. 5/83 | Bos. | 3 | Pete Peeters | Bos. 4 | Que. 3 |
| | | Apr. 11/87 | Que. | 3 | Mike Liut (2) | | |
| | | | | | Steve Weeks (1) | Que. 5 | Hfd. 1 |
| Michel Goulet (2) | Que. | Apr. 23/85 | Que. | 3 | Steve Penney | Que. 7 | Mtl. 6 |
| | | Apr. 12/87 | Que. | 3 | Mike Liut | Que. 4 | Hfd. 1 |
| Glenn Anderson (2) | Edm. | Apr. 26/83 | Edm. | 4 | Murray Bannerman | Edm. 8 | Chi. 2 |
| | | Apr. 6/88 | Wpg. | 3 | Daniel Berthiaume | Edm. 7 | Wpg. 4 |
| Peter Zezel (2) | Phi. | Apr. 13/86 | NYR | 3 | John Vanbiesbrouck | Phi. 7 | NYR 1 |
| | St.L. | Apr. 11/89 | St.L. | 3 | Jon Casey (2) | | |
| | | | | | Kari Takko (1) | St.L. 6 | Min. 1 |
| Geoff Courtnall (2) | Van. | Apr. 4/91 | L.A. | 3 | Kelly Hrudey | Van. 6 | L.A. 5 |
| | | Apr. 30/92 | Van. | 3 | Rick Tabaracci | Van. 5 | Win. 0 |
| Joe Sakic (2) | Que. | May 6/95 | Que. | 3 | Mike Richter | Que. 5 | NYR 4 |
| | Col. | Apr. 25/96 | Col. | 3 | Corey Hirsch | Col. 5 | Van. 4 |
| Daniel Alfredsson (2) | Ott. | Apr. 28/98 | Ott. | 3 | Martin Brodeur | Ott. 4 | N.J. 3 |
| | | May 11/98 | Ott. | 3 | Olaf Kolzig | Ott. 4 | Wsh. 3 |
| Johan Franzen (2) | Det. | Apr. 26/08 | Det. | 3 | Jose Theodore (2) | | |
| | | | | | Peter Budaj (1) | Det. 5 | Col. 1 |
| | | May 1/08 | Col. | 3 | Jose Theodore (1) | Det. 8 | Col. 2 |
| | | | | | Peter Budaj (2) | | |
| Harry Meeking | Tor. | Mar. 11/18 | Tor. | 3 | Georges Vezina | Tor. 7 | Mtl. 3 |
| Alf Skinner | Tor. | Mar. 23/18 | Tor. | 3 | Hugh Lehman | Van.M. 6 | Tor. 4 |
| Joe Malone | Mtl. | Feb. 23/19 | Mtl. | 3 | Clint Benedict | Mtl. 8 | Ott. 4 |
| Odie Cleghorn | Mtl. | Feb. 27/19 | Ott. | 3 | Clint Benedict | Mtl. 5 | Ott. 3 |
| Jack Darragh | Ott. | Apr. 1/20 | Tor. | 3 | Hap Holmes | Ott. 6 | Sea. 1 |
| George Boucher | Ott. | Mar. 10/21 | Ott. | 3 | Jake Forbes | Ott. 5 | Tor. 0 |
| Babe Dye | Tor. | Mar. 28/22 | Tor. | 4 | Hugh Lehman | Tor. 5 | Van.M. 1 |
| Percy Galbraith | Bos. | Mar. 31/27 | Bos. | 3 | Hugh Lehman | Bos. 4 | Chi. 4 |
| Busher Jackson | Tor. | Apr. 5/32 | NYR | 3 | John Ross Roach | Tor. 6 | NYR 4 |
| Frank Boucher | NYR | Apr. 9/32 | Tor. | 3 | Lorne Chabot | Tor. 6 | NYR 4 |
| Charlie Conacher | Tor. | Mar. 26/36 | Tor. | 3 | Tiny Thompson | Tor. 8 | Bos. 3 |
| Syd Howe | Det. | Mar. 23/39 | Det. | 3 | Claude Bourque | Det. 7 | Mtl. 3 |
| Bryan Hextall | NYR | Apr. 3/40 | NYR | 3 | Turk Broda | NYR 6 | Tor. 2 |
| Joe Benoit | Mtl. | Mar. 22/41 | Mtl. | 3 | Sam LoPresti | Mtl. 4 | Chi. 3 |
| Syl Apps | Tor. | Mar. 25/41 | Tor. | 3 | Frank Brimsek | Tor. 7 | Bos. 2 |
| Jack McGill | Bos. | Mar. 29/42 | Bos. | 3 | Johnny Mowers | Det. 6 | Bos. 4 |
| Don Metz | Tor. | Apr. 14/42 | Tor. | 3 | Johnny Mowers | Tor. 9 | Det. 3 |
| Mud Bruneteau | Det. | Apr. 1/43 | Det. | 3 | Frank Brimsek | Det. 6 | Bos. 2 |
| Don Grosso | Det. | Apr. 7/43 | Bos. | 3 | Frank Brimsek | Det. 4 | Bos. 0 |
| Carl Liscombe | Det. | Apr. 3/45 | Bos. | 4 | Paul Bibeault | Det. 5 | Bos. 3 |
| Billy Reay | Mtl. | Apr. 1/47 | Bos. | 4 | Frank Brimsek | Mtl. 5 | Bos. 1 |
| Gerry Plamondon | Mtl. | Mar. 24/49 | Det. | 3 | Harry Lumley | Mtl. 4 | Det. 3 |
| Sid Smith | Tor. | Apr. 10/49 | Det. | 3 | Harry Lumley | Tor. 3 | Det. 1 |

# Three-or-more-Goal Games, Playoffs — *continued*

| Player | Team | Date | City | Total Goals | Opposing Goaltender | Score | |
|---|---|---|---|---|---|---|---|
| Pentti Lund | NYR | Apr. 2/50 | NYR | 3 | Bill Durnan | NYR 4 | Mtl. 1 |
| Ted Lindsay | Det. | Apr. 5/55 | Det. | 4 | Charlie Hodge (1) | | |
| | | | | | Jacques Plante (3) | Det. 7 | Mtl. 1 |
| Gordie Howe | Det. | Apr. 10/55 | Det. | 3 | Jacques Plante | Det. 5 | Mtl. 1 |
| Phil Goyette | Mtl. | Mar. 25/58 | Mtl. | 3 | Terry Sawchuk | Mtl. 8 | Det. 1 |
| Jerry Toppazzini | Bos. | Apr. 5/58 | Bos. | 3 | Gump Worsley | Bos. 8 | NYR 2 |
| Bob Pulford | Tor. | Apr. 19/62 | Tor. | 3 | Glenn Hall | Tor. 8 | Chi. 4 |
| Dave Keon | Tor. | Apr. 9/64 | Mtl. | 3 | Charlie Hodge (2) | Tor. 3 | Mtl. 1 |
| | | | | | ENG (1) | | |
| Henri Richard | Mtl. | Apr. 20/67 | Mtl. | 3 | Terry Sawchuk (2) | | |
| | | | | | Johnny Bower (1) | Mtl. 6 | Tor. 2 |
| Rosaire Paiement | Phi. | Apr. 13/68 | Phi. | 3 | Glenn Hall (1) | | |
| | | | | | Seth Martin (2) | Phi. 6 | St.L. 1 |
| Jean Beliveau | Mtl. | Apr. 20/68 | Mtl. | 3 | Denis DeJordy | Mtl. 4 | Chi. 1 |
| Red Berenson | St.L. | Apr. 15/69 | St.L. | 3 | Gerry Desjardins | St.L. 4 | L.A. 0 |
| Ken Schinkel | Pit. | Apr. 11/70 | Oak. | 3 | Gary Smith | Pit. 5 | Oak. 2 |
| Jim Pappin | Chi. | Apr. 11/71 | Phi. | 3 | Bruce Gamble | Chi. 6 | Phi. 2 |
| Bobby Orr | Bos. | Apr. 11/71 | Mtl. | 3 | Ken Dryden | Bos. 5 | Mtl. 2 |
| Jacques Lemaire | Mtl. | Apr. 20/71 | Mtl. | 3 | Gump Worsley | Mtl. 7 | Min. 2 |
| Vic Hadfield | NYR | Apr. 22/71 | NYR | 3 | Tony Esposito | NYR 4 | Chi. 1 |
| Fred Stanfield | Bos. | Apr. 18/72 | Bos. | 3 | Jacques Caron | Bos. 6 | St.L. 1 |
| Ken Hodge | Bos. | Apr. 30/72 | Bos. | 3 | Ed Giacomin | Bos. 6 | NYR 5 |
| Dick Redmond | Chi. | Apr. 4/73 | Chi. | 3 | Wayne Stephenson | Chi. 7 | St.L. 1 |
| Steve Vickers | NYR | Apr. 10/73 | Bos. | 3 | Ross Brooks (2) | | |
| | | | | | Eddie Johnston (1) | NYR 6 | Bos. 3 |
| Tom Williams | L.A. | Apr. 14/74 | L.A. | 3 | Mike Veisor | L.A. 5 | Chi. 1 |
| Marcel Dionne | L.A. | Apr. 15/76 | L.A. | 3 | Gilles Gilbert | L.A. 6 | Bos. 4 |
| Don Saleski | Phi. | Apr. 20/76 | Phi. | 3 | Wayne Thomas | Phi. 7 | Tor. 1 |
| Darryl Sittler | Tor. | Apr. 22/76 | Tor. | 5 | Bernie Parent | Tor. 8 | Phi. 5 |
| Reggie Leach | Phi. | May 6/76 | Phi. | 5 | Gilles Gilbert | Phi. 6 | Bos. 3 |
| Jim Lorentz | Buf. | Apr. 7/77 | Min. | 3 | Pete LoPresti (2) | | |
| | | | | | Gary Smith (1) | Buf. 7 | Min. 1 |
| Bobby Schmautz | Bos. | Apr. 11/77 | Bos. | 3 | Rogie Vachon | Bos. 8 | L.A. 3 |
| Billy Harris | NYI | Apr. 23/77 | Mtl. | 3 | Ken Dryden | Mtl. 4 | NYI 3 |
| George Ferguson | Tor. | Apr. 11/78 | Tor. | 3 | Rogie Vachon | Tor. 7 | L.A. 3 |
| Jean Ratelle | Bos. | May 3/79 | Bos. | 3 | Ken Dryden | Bos. 4 | Mtl. 3 |
| Stan Jonathan | Bos. | May 8/79 | Bos. | 3 | Ken Dryden | Bos. 5 | Mtl. 2 |
| Ron Duguay | NYR | Apr. 20/80 | NYR | 3 | Pete Peeters | NYR 4 | Phi. 2 |
| Steve Shutt | Mtl. | Apr. 22/80 | Mtl. | 3 | Gilles Meloche | Mtl. 6 | Min. 2 |
| Gilbert Perreault | Buf. | May 6/80 | NYI | 3 | Billy Smith (2) | | |
| | | | | | ENG (1) | Buf. 7 | NYI 4 |
| Paul Holmgren | Phi. | May 15/80 | Phi. | 3 | Billy Smith | Phi. 8 | NYI 3 |
| Steve Payne | Min. | Apr. 8/81 | Bos. | 3 | Rogie Vachon | Min. 5 | Bos. 4 |
| Denis Potvin | NYI | Apr. 17/81 | NYI | 3 | Andy Moog | NYI 6 | Edm. 3 |
| Barry Pederson | Bos. | Apr. 8/82 | Bos. | 3 | Don Edwards | Bos. 7 | Buf. 3 |
| Duane Sutter | NYI | Apr. 15/83 | NYI | 3 | Glen Hanlon | NYI 5 | NYR 0 |
| Doug Halward | Van. | Apr. 7/84 | Van. | 3 | Reggie Lemelin (2) | | |
| | | | | | Don Edwards (1) | Van. 7 | Cgy. 0 |
| Jorgen Pettersson | St.L. | Apr. 8/84 | Det. | 3 | Eddie Mio | St.L. 3 | Det. 2 |
| Clark Gillies | NYI | May 12/84 | NYI | 3 | Grant Fuhr | NYI 6 | Edm. 1 |
| Ken Linseman | Bos. | Apr. 14/85 | Bos. | 3 | Steve Penney | Bos. 7 | Mtl. 6 |
| Dave Andreychuk | Buf. | Apr. 14/85 | Buf. | 3 | Dan Bouchard | Buf. 7 | Que. 4 |
| Greg Paslawski | St.L. | Apr. 15/86 | Min. | 3 | Don Beaupre | St.L. 6 | Min. 3 |
| Doug Risebrough | Cgy. | May 4/86 | Cgy. | 3 | Rick Wamsley | Cgy. 8 | St.L. 2 |
| Mike McPhee | Mtl. | Apr. 11/87 | Bos. | 3 | Doug Keans | Mtl. 5 | Bos. 4 |
| John Ogrodnick | Que. | Apr. 14/87 | Hfd. | 3 | Mike Liut | Que. 7 | Hfd. 5 |
| Pelle Eklund | Phi. | May 10/87 | Mtl. | 3 | Patrick Roy (1) | | |
| | | | | | Brian Hayward (2) | Phi. 6 | Mtl. 3 |
| John Tucker | Buf. | Apr. 9/88 | Bos. | 4 | Andy Moog | Buf. 6 | Bos. 2 |
| Tony Hrkac | St.L. | Apr. 10/88 | St.L. | 4 | Darren Pang | St.L. 6 | Chi. 5 |
| Hakan Loob | Cgy. | Apr. 10/88 | Cgy. | 3 | Glenn Healy | Cgy. 7 | L.A. 3 |
| Ed Olczyk | Tor. | Apr. 12/88 | Tor. | 3 | Greg Stefan (2) | | |
| | | | | | Glen Hanlon (1) | Tor. 6 | Det. 5 |
| Aaron Broten | N.J. | Apr. 20/88 | N.J. | 3 | Pete Peeters | N.J. 5 | Wsh. 2 |
| Mark Johnson | N.J. | Apr. 22/88 | Wsh. | 4 | Pete Peeters | N.J. 10 | Wsh. 4 |
| Patrik Sundstrom | N.J. | Apr. 22/88 | Wsh. | 3 | Pete Peeters (2) | | |
| | | | | | Clint Malarchuk (1) | N.J. 10 | Wsh. 4 |
| Bob Brooke | Min. | Apr. 5/89 | St.L. | 3 | Greg Millen | St.L. 4 | Min. 3 |
| Chris Kontos | L.A. | Apr. 6/89 | L.A. | 3 | Grant Fuhr | L.A. 5 | Edm. 2 |
| Wayne Presley | Chi. | Apr. 13/89 | Chi. | 3 | Greg Stefan (1) | | |
| | | | | | Glen Hanlon (2) | Chi. 7 | Det. 1 |
| Tony Granato | L.A. | Apr. 10/90 | L.A. | 3 | Mike Vernon (1) | | |
| | | | | | Rick Wamsley (2) | L.A. 12 | Cgy. 4 |
| Tomas Sandstrom | L.A. | Apr. 10/90 | L.A. | 3 | Mike Vernon (1) | | |
| | | | | | Rick Wamsley (2) | L.A. 12 | Cgy. 4 |
| Dave Taylor | L.A. | Apr. 10/90 | L.A. | 3 | Mike Vernon (1) | | |
| | | | | | Rick Wamsley (2) | L.A. 12 | Cgy. 4 |
| Bernie Nicholls | NYR | Apr. 19/90 | NYR | 3 | Mike Liut | NYR 7 | Wsh. 3 |
| John Druce | Wsh. | Apr. 21/90 | NYR | 3 | John Vanbiesbrouck | Wsh. 6 | NYR 3 |
| Adam Oates | St.L. | Apr. 12/91 | St.L. | 3 | Tim Chevaldae | St.L. 6 | Det. 1 |
| Luc Robitaille | L.A. | Apr. 26/91 | L.A. | 3 | Grant Fuhr | L.A. 5 | Edm. 2 |
| Ray Sheppard | Det. | Apr. 24/92 | Min. | 3 | Jon Casey | Min. 5 | Det. 2 |
| Pavel Bure | Van. | Apr. 28/92 | Wpg. | 3 | Rick Tabaracci | Van. 8 | Wpg. 3 |
| Joe Murphy | Edm. | May 6/92 | Edm. | 3 | Kirk McLean | Edm. 5 | Van. 2 |
| Ron Francis | Pit. | May 9/92 | Pit. | 3 | Mike Richter (2) | | |
| | | | | | John V'brouck (1) | Pit. 5 | NYR. 4 |
| Kevin Stevens | Pit. | May 21/92 | Bos. | 4 | Andy Moog | Pit. 5 | Bos. 2 |
| Dirk Graham | Chi. | Jun. 1/92 | Chi. | 3 | Tom Barrasso | Pit. 6 | Chi. 5 |
| Brian Noonan | Chi. | Apr. 18/93 | Chi. | 3 | Curtis Joseph | St.L. 4 | Chi. 3 |
| Dale Hunter | Wsh. | Apr. 20/93 | Wsh. | 3 | Glenn Healy | NYI 5 | Wsh. 4 |
| Teemu Selanne | Wpg. | Apr. 23/93 | Wpg. | 3 | Kirk McLean | Wpg. 5 | Van. 4 |
| Ray Ferraro | NYI | Apr. 26/93 | Wsh. | 4 | Don Beaupre | Wsh. 6 | NYI 4 |
| Al Iafrate | Wsh. | Apr. 26/93 | Wsh. | 3 | Glenn Healy (2) | | |
| | | | | | Mark Fitzpatrick (1) | Wsh. 6 | NYI 4 |
| Paul DiPietro | Mtl. | Apr. 28/93 | Mtl. | 3 | Ron Hextall | Mtl. 6 | Que. 2 |
| Wendel Clark | Tor. | May 27/93 | L.A. | 3 | Kelly Hrudey | L.A. 5 | Tor. 4 |
| Eric Desjardins | Mtl. | Jun. 3/93 | Mtl. | 3 | Kelly Hrudey | Mtl. 3 | L.A. 2 |
| Tony Amonte | Chi. | Apr. 23/94 | Chi. | 4 | Felix Potvin | Chi. 5 | Tor. 4 |
| Gary Suter | Chi. | Apr. 24/94 | Chi. | 3 | Felix Potvin | Chi. 4 | Tor. 3 |
| Ulf Dahlen | S.J. | May 6/94 | S.J. | 3 | Felix Potvin | S.J. 5 | Tor. 2 |
| Mike Sullivan | Cgy. | May 11/95 | S.J. | 3 | Arturs Irbe (2) | | |
| | | | | | Wade Flaherty (1) | Cgy. 9 | S.J. 2 |
| Theoren Fleury | Cgy. | May 13/95 | S.J. | 4 | Arturs Irbe (3) | | |
| | | | | | ENG (1) | Cgy. 6 | S.J. 4 |
| Brendan Shanahan | St.L. | May 13/95 | Van. | 3 | Kirk McLean | St.L. 5 | Van. 2 |
| John LeClair | Phi. | May 21/95 | Phi. | 3 | Mike Richter | Phi. 5 | NYR 4 |
| Brian Leetch | NYR | May 22/95 | Phi. | 3 | Ron Hextall | Phi. 4 | NYR 3 |
| Trevor Linden | Van. | Apr. 25/96 | Col. | 3 | Patrick Roy | Col. 5 | Van. 4 |
| Jaromir Jagr | Pit. | May 11/96 | Pit. | 3 | Mike Richter | Pit. 7 | NYR 3 |
| Peter Forsberg | Col. | Jun. 6/96 | Col. | 3 | John Vanbiesbrouck | Col. 8 | Fla. 1 |
| Valeri Zelepukin | N.J. | Apr. 22/97 | Mtl. | 3 | Jocelyn Thibault | N.J. 6 | Mtl. 4 |
| Valeri Kamensky | Col. | Apr. 24/97 | Col. | 3 | Jeff Hackett (2) | | |
| | | | | | Chris Terreri (1) | Col. 7 | Chi. 0 |
| Eric Lindros | Phi. | May 20/97 | NYR | 3 | Mike Richter | Phi. 6 | NYR 3 |
| Matthew Barnaby | Buf. | May 10/98 | Buf. | 3 | Andy Moog (2) | Buf. 6 | Mtl. 3 |
| | | | | | ENG (1) | | |
| Martin Straka | Pit. | Apr. 25/99 | Pit. | 3 | Martin Brodeur | Pit. 4 | N.J. 2 |
| Martin Lapointe | Det. | Apr. 15/00 | Det. | 3 | Stephane Fiset (2) | Det. 8 | L.A. 5 |
| | | | | | Jamie Storr (1) | | |
| Doug Weight | Edm. | Apr. 16/00 | Edm. | 3 | Ed Belfour | Edm. 5 | Dal. 2 |
| Bill Guerin | Edm. | Apr. 18/00 | Edm. | 3 | Ed Belfour | Dal. 4 | Edm. 3 |
| Scott Young | St.L. | Apr. 23/00 | S.J. | 3 | Steve Shields | St.L. 6 | S.J. 2 |
| Andy Delmore | Phi. | May 7/00 | Phi. | 3 | Ron Tugnutt (2) | Phi. 6 | Pit. 3 |
| | | | | | Peter Skudra (1) | | |
| Brett Hull | Det. | Apr. 27/02 | Van. | 3 | Peter Skudra | Det. 6 | Van. 4 |
| Keith Tkachuk | St.L. | May 7/02 | St.L. | 3 | Dominik Hasek | St.L. 6 | Det. 1 |
| Darren McCarty | Det. | May 18/02 | Det. | 3 | Patrick Roy | Det. 5 | Col. 3 |
| Alexander Mogilny | Tor. | Apr. 9/03 | Phi. | 3 | Roman Cechmanek (2) | Tor. 5 | Phi. 3 |
| | | | | | ENG (1) | | |
| Mike Sillinger | St.L. | Apr. 12/04 | St.L. | 3 | Evgeni Nabokov (2) | St.L. 4 | S.J. 1 |
| | | | | | ENG (1) | | |
| Keith Primeau | Phi. | May 2/04 | Phi. | 3 | Ed Belfour (2) | Phi. 7 | Tor. 2 |
| | | | | | Trevor Kidd (1) | | |
| J.P. Dumont | Buf. | Apr. 24/06 | Buf. | 3 | Antero Niittymaki (1) | Phi. 2 | Buf. 8 |
| | | | | | Robert Esche (2) | | |
| John Madden | N.J. | Apr. 24/06 | N.J. | 3 | Kevin Weekes | NYR 1 | N.J. 4 |
| Jason Pominville | Buf. | Apr. 24/06 | Buf. | 3 | Antero Niittymaki (2) | Phi. 2 | Buf. 8 |
| | | | | | Robert Esche (1) | | |
| Joffrey Lupul | Ana. | May 9/06 | Col. | 4 | Jose Theodore | Ana. 4 | Col. 3 |
| Michael Nylander | NYR | Apr. 17/07 | NYR | 3 | Kari Lehtonen | NYR 7 | Atl. 0 |
| Andy McDonald | Ana. | Apr. 25/07 | Ana. | 3 | Dany Sabourin (1) | Ana. 5 | Van. 1 |
| | | | | | Roberto Luongo (2) | | |
| Pavel Datsyuk | Det. | May 12/08 | Dal. | 3 | Marty Turco | Det. 5 | Dal. 2 |
| Alex Ovechkin | Wsh. | May 4/09 | Wsh. | 3 | Marc-Andre Fleury | Wsh. 4 | Pit. 3 |
| Sidney Crosby | Pit. | May 4/09 | Wsh. | 3 | Semyon Varlamov | Wsh. 4 | Pit. 3 |
| Patrick Kane | Chi. | May 11/09 | Chi. | 3 | Roberto Luongo | Chi. 7 | Van. 5 |
| Evgeni Malkin | Pit. | May 21/09 | Pit. | 3 | Cam Ward | Pit. 7 | Car. 4 |

*Patrick Kane poses with the pucks from his first career playoff hat trick scored in Chicago's 7-5 win over Vancouver on May 11, 2009.*

# Overtime Games since 1918

**Abbreviations:** Teams/Cities: — **Ana.** - Anaheim; **Atl.** - Atlanta; **Bos.** - Boston; **Buf.** - Buffalo; **Cgy.** - Calgary; **Cgy. T.** - Calgary Tigers (Western Canada Hockey League); **Car.** - Carolina; **Chi.** - Chicago; **Col.** - Colorado; **Dal.** - Dallas; **Det.** - Detroit; **Edm.** - Edmonton; **Edm. E.** - Edmonton Eskimos (WCHL); **Fla.** - Florida; **Hfd.** - Hartford; **L.A.** - Los Angeles; **Min.** - Minnesota; **Mtl.** - Montreal; **Mtl. M.** - Montreal Maroons; **Nsh.** - Nashville, **N.J.** - New Jersey; **NYA** - NY Americans; **NYI** - New York Islanders; **NYR** - New York Rangers; **Oak.** - Oakland; **Ott.** - Ottawa; **Phi.** - Philadelphia; **Phx.** - Phoenix; **Pit.** - Pittsburgh; **Que.** - Quebec; **St.L.** - St. Louis; **Sea.** - Seattle Metropolitans (Pacific Coast Hockey Association); **S.J.** - San Jose; **T.B.** - Tampa Bay; **Tor.** - Toronto; **Van.** - Vancouver; **Van. M.** - Vancouver Millionaires (PCHA); **Vic.** - Victoria Cougars (WCHL); **Wpg.** - Winnipeg; **Wsh.** - Washington.

**SERIES** — **CF** - conference final; **CQF** - conference quarter-final; **CSF** - conference semi-final; **DF** - division final; **DSF** - division semi-final; **F** - final; **PRE** - preliminary round; **QF** - quarter-final; **SF** - semi-final.

| Date | City | Series | Score | | Scorer | Overtime | Series Winner |
|---|---|---|---|---|---|---|---|
| Mar. 26/19 | Sea. | F | Mtl. 0 | Sea. 0 | no scorer | 20:00 | .... |
| Mar. 29/19 | Sea. | F | Mtl. 4 | Sea. 3 | Jack McDonald | 15:57 | .... |
| Mar. 20/22 | Tor. | F | Tor. 2 | Van. M. 1 | Babe Dye | 4:50 | Tor. |
| Mar. 29/23 | Van. | F | Ott. 2 | Edm. E. 1 | Cy Denneny | 2:08 | Ott. |
| Mar. 31/27 | Mtl. | QF | Mtl. 1 | Mtl. M. 0 | Howie Morenz | 12:05 | Mtl. |
| Apr. 7/27 | Bos. | F | Ott. 0 | Bos. 0 | no scorer | 20:00 | Ott. |
| Apr. 11/27 | Ott. | F | Bos. 1 | Ott. 1 | no scorer | 20:00 | Ott. |
| Apr. 3/28 | Mtl. | QF | Mtl. M. 1 | Mtl. 0 | Russell Oatman | 8:20 | Mtl. M. |
| Apr. 7/28 | Mtl. | F | NYR 2 | Mtl. M. 1 | Frank Boucher | 7:05 | NYR |
| Mar. 21/29 | NYR | QF | NYR 1 | NYA 0 | Butch Keeling | 29:50 | NYR |
| Mar. 26/29 | Tor. | SF | NYR 2 | Tor. 1 | Frank Boucher | 2:03 | NYR |
| Mar. 20/30 | Mtl. | SF | Bos. 2 | Mtl. M. 1 | Harry Oliver | 45:35 | Bos. |
| Mar. 25/30 | Bos. | SF | Mtl. M. 1 | Bos. 0 | Archie Wilcox | 26:27 | Bos. |
| Mar. 26/30 | Mtl. | QF | Chi. 2 | Mtl. 2 | Howie Morenz (Mtl.) | 51:43 | Mtl. |
| Mar. 28/30 | Mtl. | SF | Mtl. 2 | NYR 1 | Gus Rivers | 68:52 | Mtl. |
| Mar. 24/31 | Bos. | SF | Bos. 5 | Mtl. 4 | Cooney Weiland | 18:56 | Mtl. |
| Mar. 26/31 | Chi. | QF | Chi. 2 | Tor. 1 | Stew Adams | 19:20 | Chi. |
| Mar. 28/31 | Mtl. | SF | Mtl. 4 | Bos. 3 | Georges Mantha | 5:10 | Mtl. |
| Apr. 1/31 | Mtl. | SF | Mtl. 3 | Bos. 2 | Wildor Larochelle | 19:00 | Mtl. |
| Apr. 5/31 | Chi. | F | Chi. 2 | Mtl. 1 | Johnny Gottselig | 24:50 | Mtl. |
| Apr. 9/31 | Mtl. | F | Chi. 3 | Mtl. 2 | Cy Wentworth | 53:50 | Mtl. |
| Mar. 26/32 | Mtl. | SF | NYR 4 | Mtl. 3 | Fred Cook | 59:32 | NYR |
| Apr. 2/32 | Tor. | SF | Tor. 3 | Mtl. M. 2 | Bob Gracie | 17:59 | Tor. |
| Mar. 25/33 | Bos. | SF | Bos. 2 | Tor. 1 | Marty Barry | 14:14 | Tor. |
| Mar. 28/33 | Bos. | SF | Tor. 1 | Bos. 0 | Busher Jackson | 15:03 | Tor. |
| Mar. 30/33 | Tor. | SF | Bos. 2 | Tor. 1 | Eddie Shore | 4:23 | Tor. |
| Apr. 3/33 | Tor. | SF | Tor. 1 | Bos. 0 | Ken Doraty | 104:46 | Tor. |
| Apr. 13/33 | Tor. | F | NYR 1 | Tor. 0 | Bill Cook | 7:33 | NYR |
| Mar. 22/34 | Tor. | SF | Det. 2 | Tor. 1 | Herbie Lewis | 1:33 | Det. |
| Mar. 25/34 | Chi. | QF | Chi. 1 | Mtl. 1 | Mush March (Chi) | 11:05 | Chi. |
| Apr. 3/34 | Det. | F | Chi. 2 | Det. 1 | Paul Thompson | 21:10 | Chi. |
| Apr. 10/34 | Chi. | F | Chi. 1 | Det. 0 | Mush March | 30:05 | Chi. |
| Mar. 23/35 | Bos. | SF | Bos. 1 | Tor. 0 | Dit Clapper | 33:26 | Tor. |
| Mar. 26/35 | Chi. | QF | Mtl. M. 1 | Chi. 0 | Baldy Northcott | 4:02 | Mtl. M. |
| Mar. 30/35 | Tor. | SF | Tor. 2 | Bos. 1 | Pep Kelly | 1:36 | Tor. |
| Apr. 4/35 | Tor. | F | Mtl. M. 3 | Tor. 2 | Dave Trottier | 5:28 | Mtl. M. |
| Mar. 24/36 | Mtl. | SF | Det. 1 | Mtl. M. 0 | Mud Bruneteau | 116:30 | Det. |
| Apr. 9/36 | Tor. | F | Tor. 4 | Det. 3 | Buzz Boll | 0:31 | Det. |
| Mar. 25/37 | NYR | QF | NYR 2 | Tor. 1 | Babe Pratt | 13:05 | NYR |
| Apr. 1/37 | Mtl. | SF | Det. 2 | Mtl. 1 | Hec Kilrea | 51:49 | Det. |
| Mar. 22/38 | NYR | QF | NYA 2 | NYR 1 | John Sorrell | 21:25 | NYA |
| Mar. 24/38 | Tor. | SF | Tor. 1 | Bos. 0 | George Parsons | 21:31 | Tor. |
| Mar. 26/38 | Mtl. | QF | Chi. 3 | Mtl. 2 | Paul Thompson | 11:49 | Chi. |
| Mar. 27/38 | NYR | QF | NYA 3 | NYR 2 | Lorne Carr | 60:40 | NYA |
| Mar. 29/38 | Bos. | SF | Tor. 3 | Bos. 2 | Gordie Drillon | 10:04 | Tor. |
| Mar. 31/38 | Chi. | SF | Chi. 1 | NYA 0 | Cully Dahlstrom | 33:01 | Chi. |
| Mar. 21/39 | NYR | SF | Bos. 2 | NYR 1 | Mel Hill | 59:25 | Bos. |
| Mar. 23/39 | Bos. | SF | Bos. 3 | NYR 2 | Mel Hill | 8:24 | Bos. |
| Mar. 26/39 | Det. | QF | Det. 1 | Mtl. 0 | Marty Barry | 7:47 | Det. |
| Mar. 30/39 | Bos. | SF | NYR 2 | Bos. 1 | Clint Smith | 17:19 | Bos. |
| Apr. 1/39 | Tor. | SF | Tor. 5 | Det. 4 | Gordie Drillon | 5:42 | Tor. |
| Apr. 2/39 | Bos. | SF | Bos. 2 | NYR 1 | Mel Hill | 48:00 | Bos. |
| Apr. 9/39 | Bos. | F | Tor. 3 | Bos. 2 | Doc Romnes | 10:38 | Bos. |
| Mar. 19/40 | Det. | QF | Det. 2 | NYA 1 | Syd Howe | 0:25 | Det. |
| Mar. 19/40 | Tor. | QF | Tor. 3 | Chi. 2 | Syl Apps | 6:35 | Tor. |
| Apr. 2/40 | NYR | F | NYR 2 | Tor. 1 | Alf Pike | 15:30 | NYR |
| Apr. 11/40 | Tor. | F | NYR 2 | Tor. 1 | Muzz Patrick | 31:43 | NYR |
| Apr. 13/40 | Tor. | F | NYR 3 | Tor. 2 | Bryan Hextall | 2:07 | NYR |
| Mar. 20/41 | Det. | QF | Det. 2 | NYR 1 | Syd Howe | 12:01 | Det. |
| Mar. 22/41 | Mtl. | QF | Mtl. 4 | Chi. 3 | Charlie Sands | 34:04 | Chi. |
| Mar. 29/41 | Bos. | SF | Tor. 2 | Bos. 1 | Pete Langelle | 17:31 | Bos. |
| Mar. 30/41 | Chi. | SF | Det. 2 | Chi. 1 | Gus Giesebrecht | 9:15 | Det. |
| Mar. 22/42 | Chi. | QF | Bos. 2 | Chi. 1 | Des Smith | 6:51 | Bos. |
| Mar. 21/43 | Bos. | SF | Bos. 5 | Mtl. 4 | Don Gallinger | 12:30 | Bos. |
| Mar. 23/43 | Det. | SF | Tor. 3 | Det. 2 | Jack McLean | 70:18 | Det. |
| Mar. 25/43 | Mtl. | SF | Bos. 3 | Mtl. 2 | Busher Jackson | 3:20 | Bos. |
| Mar. 30/43 | Tor. | SF | Det. 3 | Tor. 2 | Adam Brown | 9:21 | Det. |
| Mar. 30/43 | Bos. | SF | Bos. 5 | Mtl. 4 | Ab DeMarco | 3:41 | Bos. |
| Apr. 13/44 | Mtl. | F | Mtl. 5 | Chi. 4 | Toe Blake | 9:12 | Mtl. |
| Mar. 27/45 | Tor. | SF | Tor. 4 | Mtl. 3 | Gus Bodnar | 12:36 | Tor. |
| Mar. 29/45 | Det. | SF | Det. 3 | Bos. 2 | Mud Bruneteau | 17:12 | Det. |
| Apr. 21/45 | Tor. | F | Det. 1 | Tor. 0 | Eddie Bruneteau | 14:16 | Tor. |
| Mar. 28/46 | Bos. | SF | Bos. 4 | Det. 3 | Don Gallinger | 9:51 | Bos. |
| Mar. 30/46 | Mtl. | F | Mtl. 4 | Bos. 3 | Maurice Richard | 9:08 | Mtl. |
| Apr. 2/46 | Mtl. | F | Mtl. 3 | Bos. 2 | Jimmy Peters | 16:55 | Mtl. |
| Apr. 7/46 | Bos. | F | Bos. 3 | Mtl. 2 | Terry Reardon | 15:13 | Mtl. |
| Mar. 26/47 | Tor. | SF | Tor. 3 | Det. 2 | Howie Meeker | 3:05 | Tor. |
| Mar. 27/47 | Mtl. | SF | Mtl. 2 | Bos. 1 | Ken Mosdell | 5:38 | Mtl. |
| Apr. 3/47 | Mtl. | SF | Mtl. 4 | Bos. 3 | John Quilty | 36:40 | Mtl. |
| Apr. 15/47 | Tor. | F | Tor. 2 | Mtl. 1 | Syl Apps | 16:36 | Tor. |
| Mar. 24/48 | Tor. | SF | Tor. 5 | Bos. 4 | Nick Metz | 17:03 | Tor. |
| Mar. 22/49 | Det. | SF | Det. 2 | Mtl. 1 | Max McNab | 44:52 | Det. |
| Mar. 24/49 | Det. | SF | Mtl. 4 | Det. 3 | Gerry Plamondon | 2:59 | Det. |
| Mar. 26/49 | Tor. | SF | Bos. 5 | Tor. 4 | Woody Dumart | 16:14 | Tor. |
| Apr. 8/49 | Det. | F | Tor. 3 | Det. 2 | Joe Klukay | 17:31 | Tor. |
| Apr. 4/50 | Tor. | SF | Det. 2 | Tor. 1 | Leo Reise Jr. | 20:38 | Det. |
| Apr. 4/50 | Mtl. | SF | Mtl. 3 | NYR 2 | Elmer Lach | 15:19 | NYR |
| Apr. 9/50 | Det. | SF | Det. 1 | Tor. 0 | Leo Reise Jr. | 8:39 | Det. |
| Apr. 18/50 | Det. | F | NYR 4 | Det. 3 | Don Raleigh | 8:34 | Det. |
| Apr. 20/50 | Det. | F | NYR 2 | Det. 1 | Don Raleigh | 1:38 | Det. |
| Apr. 23/50 | Det. | F | Det. 4 | NYR 3 | Pete Babando | 28:31 | Det. |
| Mar. 27/51 | Det. | SF | Mtl. 3 | Det. 2 | Maurice Richard | 61:09 | Mtl. |
| Mar. 29/51 | Det. | SF | Mtl. 1 | Det. 0 | Maurice Richard | 42:20 | Mtl. |
| Mar. 31/51 | Tor. | SF | Bos. 1 | Tor. 1 | no scorer | 20:00 | Tor. |
| Apr. 11/51 | Tor. | F | Tor. 3 | Mtl. 2 | Sid Smith | 5:51 | Tor. |
| Apr. 14/51 | Tor. | F | Mtl. 3 | Tor. 2 | Maurice Richard | 2:55 | Tor. |
| Apr. 17/51 | Mtl. | F | Tor. 2 | Mtl. 1 | Ted Kennedy | 4:47 | Tor. |
| Apr. 19/51 | Mtl. | F | Tor. 3 | Mtl. 2 | Harry Watson | 5:15 | Tor. |
| Apr. 21/51 | Tor. | F | Tor. 3 | Mtl. 2 | Bill Barilko | 2:53 | Tor. |
| Apr. 6/52 | Bos. | SF | Mtl. 3 | Bos. 2 | Paul Masnick | 27:49 | Mtl. |
| Mar. 29/53 | Bos. | SF | Bos. 2 | Det. 1 | Jack McIntyre | 12:29 | Bos. |
| Mar. 29/53 | Chi. | SF | Chi. 2 | Mtl. 1 | Al Dewsbury | 5:18 | Mtl. |
| Apr. 16/53 | Mtl. | F | Mtl. 1 | Bos. 0 | Elmer Lach | 1:22 | Mtl. |
| Apr. 1/54 | Det. | SF | Det. 4 | Tor. 3 | Ted Lindsay | 21:01 | Det. |
| Apr. 11/54 | Det. | F | Mtl. 1 | Det. 0 | Ken Mosdell | 5:45 | Det. |
| Apr. 16/54 | Det. | F | Det. 2 | Mtl. 1 | Tony Leswick | 4:29 | Det. |
| Mar. 29/55 | Bos. | SF | Mtl. 4 | Bos. 3 | Don Marshall | 3:05 | Mtl. |
| Mar. 24/56 | Tor. | SF | Det. 5 | Tor. 4 | Ted Lindsay | 4:22 | Det. |
| Mar. 28/57 | NYR | SF | NYR 4 | Mtl. 3 | Andy Hebenton | 13:38 | Mtl. |
| Apr. 4/57 | Mtl. | SF | Mtl. 4 | NYR 3 | Maurice Richard | 1:11 | Mtl. |
| Mar. 27/58 | NYR | SF | Bos. 4 | NYR 3 | Jerry Toppazzini | 4:46 | Bos. |
| Mar. 30/58 | Det. | SF | Mtl. 2 | Det. 1 | André Pronovost | 11:52 | Mtl. |
| Apr. 17/58 | Mtl. | F | Mtl. 3 | Bos. 2 | Maurice Richard | 5:45 | Mtl. |
| Mar. 28/59 | Tor. | SF | Tor. 3 | Bos. 2 | Gerry Ehman | 5:02 | Tor. |
| Mar. 31/59 | Tor. | SF | Tor. 3 | Bos. 2 | Frank Mahovlich | 11:21 | Tor. |
| Apr. 14/59 | Tor. | F | Tor. 3 | Mtl. 2 | Dick Duff | 10:06 | Mtl. |
| Mar. 26/60 | Mtl. | SF | Mtl. 4 | Chi. 3 | Doug Harvey | 8:38 | Mtl. |
| Mar. 27/60 | Det. | SF | Tor. 5 | Det. 4 | Frank Mahovlich | 43:00 | Tor. |
| Mar. 29/60 | Det. | SF | Det. 2 | Tor. 1 | Gerry Melnyk | 1:54 | Tor. |
| Mar. 22/61 | Tor. | SF | Tor. 3 | Det. 2 | George Armstrong | 24:51 | Det. |
| Mar. 26/61 | Chi. | SF | Chi. 2 | Mtl. 1 | Murray Balfour | 52:12 | Chi. |
| Apr. 5/62 | Tor. | SF | Tor. 3 | NYR 2 | Red Kelly | 24:23 | Tor. |
| Apr. 2/64 | Det. | SF | Chi. 3 | Det. 2 | Murray Balfour | 8:21 | Det. |
| Apr. 14/64 | Tor. | F | Det. 4 | Tor. 3 | Larry Jeffrey | 7:52 | Tor. |
| Apr. 23/64 | Det. | F | Tor. 4 | Det. 3 | Bob Baun | 1:43 | Tor. |
| Apr. 6/65 | Tor. | SF | Tor. 3 | Mtl. 2 | Dave Keon | 4:17 | Mtl. |
| Apr. 13/65 | Tor. | SF | Mtl. 4 | Tor. 3 | Claude Provost | 16:33 | Mtl. |
| May 5/66 | Det. | F | Mtl. 3 | Det. 2 | Henri Richard | 2:20 | Mtl. |
| Apr. 13/67 | NYR | SF | Mtl. 2 | NYR 1 | John Ferguson | 6:28 | Mtl. |
| Apr. 25/67 | Tor. | F | Tor. 3 | Mtl. 2 | Bob Pulford | 28:26 | Tor. |
| Apr. 10/68 | St.L. | QF | St.L. 3 | Phi. 2 | Larry Keenan | 24:10 | St.L. |
| Apr. 16/68 | St.L. | QF | Phi. 2 | St.L. 1 | Don Blackburn | 31:18 | St.L. |
| Apr. 16/68 | Min. | QF | Min. 4 | L.A. 3 | Milan Marcetta | 9:11 | Min. |
| Apr. 22/68 | Min. | SF | Min. 3 | St.L. 2 | Parker MacDonald | 3:41 | St.L. |
| Apr. 27/68 | St.L. | SF | St.L. 4 | Min. 3 | Gary Sabourin | 1:32 | St.L. |
| Apr. 28/68 | Mtl. | SF | Mtl. 4 | Chi. 3 | Jacques Lemaire | 2:14 | Mtl. |
| Apr. 29/68 | St.L. | SF | St.L. 3 | Min. 2 | Bill McCreary | 17:27 | St.L. |
| May 3/68 | St.L. | SF | St.L. 2 | Min. 1 | Ron Schock | 22:50 | St.L. |
| May 5/68 | St.L. | F | Mtl. 3 | St.L. 2 | Jacques Lemaire | 1:41 | Mtl. |
| May 9/68 | Mtl. | F | Mtl. 4 | St.L. 3 | Bobby Rousseau | 1:13 | Mtl. |
| Apr. 2/69 | Oak. | QF | L.A. 5 | Oak. 4 | Ted Irvine | 0:19 | L.A. |
| Apr. 10/69 | Mtl. | SF | Mtl. 3 | Bos. 2 | Ralph Backstrom | 0:42 | Mtl. |
| Apr. 13/69 | Mtl. | SF | Mtl. 4 | Bos. 3 | Mickey Redmond | 4:55 | Mtl. |
| Apr. 24/69 | Bos. | SF | Mtl. 2 | Bos. 1 | Jean Béliveau | 31:28 | Mtl. |
| Apr. 12/70 | Oak. | QF | Pit. 3 | Oak. 2 | Michel Briere | 8:28 | Pit. |
| May 10/70 | Bos. | F | Bos. 4 | St.L. 3 | Bobby Orr | 0:40 | Bos. |
| Apr. 15/71 | Tor. | QF | NYR 2 | Tor. 1 | Bob Nevin | 9:07 | NYR |
| Apr. 18/71 | Chi. | SF | NYR 2 | Chi. 1 | Pete Stemkowski | 1:37 | Chi. |
| Apr. 27/71 | Chi. | SF | Chi. 3 | NYR 2 | Bobby Hull | 6:35 | Chi. |
| Apr. 29/71 | NYR | SF | NYR 3 | Chi. 2 | Pete Stemkowski | 41:29 | Chi. |
| May 4/71 | Chi. | F | Chi. 2 | Mtl. 1 | Jim Pappin | 21:11 | Mtl. |
| Apr. 6/72 | Bos. | QF | Tor. 4 | Bos. 3 | Jim Harrison | 2:58 | Bos. |
| Apr. 6/72 | Min. | QF | Min. 6 | St.L. 5 | Bill Goldsworthy | 1:36 | St.L. |
| Apr. 9/72 | Pit. | QF | Chi. 6 | Pit. 5 | Pit Martin | 0:12 | Chi. |
| Apr. 16/72 | Min. | QF | St.L. 2 | Min. 1 | Kevin O'Shea | 10:07 | St.L. |
| Apr. 1/73 | Mtl. | QF | Buf. 3 | Mtl. 2 | René Robert | 9:18 | Mtl. |
| Apr. 10/73 | Phi. | QF | Phi. 3 | Min. 2 | Gary Dornhoefer | 8:35 | Phi. |
| Apr. 14/73 | Mtl. | SF | Phi. 5 | Mtl. 4 | Rick MacLeish | 2:56 | Mtl. |
| Apr. 17/73 | Mtl. | SF | Mtl. 4 | Phi. 3 | Larry Robinson | 6:45 | Mtl. |
| Apr. 14/74 | Tor. | QF | Bos. 4 | Tor. 3 | Ken Hodge | 1:27 | Bos. |
| Apr. 14/74 | Atl. | QF | Phi. 4 | Atl. 3 | Dave Schultz | 5:40 | Phi. |
| Apr. 16/74 | Mtl. | QF | NYR 3 | Mtl. 2 | Ron Harris | 4:07 | NYR |
| Apr. 23/74 | Chi. | SF | Chi. 4 | Bos. 3 | Jim Pappin | 3:48 | Bos. |
| Apr. 28/74 | NYR | SF | NYR 2 | Phi. 1 | Rod Gilbert | 4:20 | Phi. |
| May 9/74 | Bos. | F | Phi. 3 | Bos. 2 | Bobby Clarke | 12:01 | Phi. |
| Apr. 8/75 | L.A. | PRE | L.A. 3 | Tor. 2 | Mike Murphy | 8:53 | Tor. |
| Apr. 10/75 | Tor. | PRE | Tor. 3 | L.A. 2 | Blaine Stoughton | 10:19 | Tor. |
| Apr. 10/75 | Chi. | PRE | Chi. 4 | Bos. 3 | Ivan Boldirev | 7:33 | Chi. |
| Apr. 11/75 | NYR | PRE | NYI 4 | NYR 3 | J.P. Parise | 0:11 | NYI |
| Apr. 17/75 | Chi. | QF | Chi. 5 | Buf. 4 | Stan Mikita | 2:31 | Buf. |
| Apr. 19/75 | Tor. | QF | Phi. 4 | Tor. 3 | André Dupont | 1:45 | Phi. |
| Apr. 22/75 | Mtl. | QF | Mtl. 5 | Van. 4 | Guy Lafleur | 17:06 | Mtl. |
| Apr. 27/75 | Buf. | SF | Buf. 6 | Mtl. 5 | Danny Gare | 4:42 | Buf. |
| May 1/75 | Phi. | SF | Phi. 5 | NYI 4 | Bobby Clarke | 2:56 | Phi. |
| May 6/75 | Buf. | SF | Buf. 5 | Mtl. 4 | René Robert | 5:56 | Buf. |
| May 7/75 | NYI | SF | NYI 4 | Phi. 3 | Jude Drouin | 1:53 | Phi. |
| May 20/75 | Buf. | F | Buf. 5 | Phi. 4 | René Robert | 18:29 | Phi. |
| Apr. 8/76 | Buf. | PRE | Buf. 3 | St.L. 2 | Danny Gare | 11:43 | Buf. |

# Overtime Games since 1918 — *continued*

| Date | City | Series | Score | | Scorer | Overtime | Series Winner |
|---|---|---|---|---|---|---|---|
| Apr. 9/76 | Buf. | PRE | Buf. 2 | St.L. 1 | Don Luce | 14:27 | Buf. |
| Apr. 13/76 | Bos. | QF | L.A. 3 | Bos. 2 | Butch Goring | 0:27 | Bos. |
| Apr. 13/76 | Buf. | QF | Buf. 3 | NYI 2 | Danny Gare | 14:04 | NYI |
| Apr. 22/76 | L.A. | QF | L.A. 4 | Bos. 3 | Butch Goring | 18:28 | Bos. |
| Apr. 29/76 | Phi. | SF | Phi. 2 | Bos. 1 | Reggie Leach | 13:38 | Phi. |
| Apr. 15/77 | Tor. | QF | Phi. 4 | Tor. 3 | Rick MacLeish | 2:55 | Phi. |
| Apr. 17/77 | Tor. | QF | Phi. 6 | Tor. 5 | Reggie Leach | 19:10 | Phi. |
| Apr. 24/77 | Phi. | SF | Bos. 4 | Phi. 3 | Rick Middleton | 2:57 | Bos. |
| Apr. 26/77 | Phi. | SF | Bos. 5 | Phi. 4 | Terry O'Reilly | 30:07 | Bos. |
| May 3/77 | Mtl. | SF | NYI 4 | Mtl. 3 | Billy Harris | 3:58 | Mtl. |
| May 14/77 | Bos. | F | Mtl. 2 | Bos. 1 | Jacques Lemaire | 4:32 | Mtl. |
| Apr. 11/78 | Phi. | PRE | Phi. 3 | Col. 2 | Mel Bridgman | 0:23 | Phi. |
| Apr. 13/78 | NYR | PRE | NYR 4 | Buf. 3 | Don Murdoch | 1:37 | Buf. |
| Apr. 19/78 | Bos. | QF | Bos. 4 | Chi. 3 | Terry O'Reilly | 1:50 | Bos. |
| Apr. 19/78 | NYI | QF | NYI 3 | Tor. 2 | Mike Bossy | 2:50 | Tor. |
| Apr. 21/78 | Chi. | QF | Bos. 4 | Chi. 3 | Peter McNab | 10:17 | Bos. |
| Apr. 25/78 | NYI | QF | NYI 2 | Tor. 1 | Bob Nystrom | 8:02 | Tor. |
| Apr. 29/78 | NYI | QF | Tor. 2 | NYI 1 | Lanny McDonald | 4:13 | Tor. |
| May 2/78 | Bos. | SF | Bos. 3 | Phi. 2 | Rick Middleton | 1:43 | Bos. |
| May 16/78 | Mtl. | F | Mtl. 3 | Bos. 2 | Guy Lafleur | 13:09 | Mtl. |
| May 21/78 | Bos. | F | Bos. 4 | Mtl. 3 | Bobby Schmautz | 6:22 | Mtl. |
| Apr. 12/79 | L.A. | PRE | NYR 2 | L.A. 1 | Phil Esposito | 6:11 | NYR |
| Apr. 14/79 | Buf. | PRE | Pit. 4 | Buf. 3 | George Ferguson | 0:47 | Pit. |
| Apr. 16/79 | Phi. | QF | Phi. 3 | NYR 2 | Ken Linseman | 0:44 | NYR |
| Apr. 18/79 | NYI | QF | NYI 1 | Chi. 0 | Mike Bossy | 2:31 | NYI |
| Apr. 21/79 | Tor. | QF | Mtl. 4 | Tor. 3 | Cam Connor | 25:25 | Mtl. |
| Apr. 22/79 | Tor. | QF | Mtl. 5 | Tor. 4 | Larry Robinson | 4:14 | Mtl. |
| Apr. 28/79 | NYI | SF | NYI 4 | NYR 3 | Denis Potvin | 8:02 | NYR |
| May 3/79 | NYR | SF | NYI 3 | NYR 2 | Bob Nystrom | 3:40 | NYR |
| May 3/79 | Bos. | SF | Bos. 4 | Mtl. 3 | Jean Ratelle | 3:46 | Mtl. |
| May 10/79 | Mtl. | SF | Mtl. 5 | Bos. 4 | Yvon Lambert | 9:33 | Mtl. |
| May 19/79 | NYR | F | Mtl. 4 | NYR 3 | Serge Savard | 7:25 | Mtl. |
| Apr. 8/80 | NYR | PRE | NYR 2 | Atl. 1 | Steve Vickers | 0:33 | NYR |
| Apr. 8/80 | Phi. | PRE | Phi. 4 | Edm. 3 | Bobby Clarke | 8:06 | Phi. |
| Apr. 8/80 | Chi. | PRE | Chi. 3 | St.L. 2 | Doug Lecuyer | 12:34 | Chi. |
| Apr. 11/80 | Hfd. | PRE | Mtl. 4 | Hfd. 3 | Yvon Lambert | 0:29 | Mtl. |
| Apr. 11/80 | Tor. | PRE | Min. 4 | Tor. 3 | Al MacAdam | 0:32 | Min. |
| Apr. 11/80 | L.A. | PRE | NYI 4 | L.A. 3 | Ken Morrow | 6:55 | NYI |
| Apr. 11/80 | Edm. | PRE | Phi. 3 | Edm. 2 | Ken Linseman | 23:56 | Phi. |
| Apr. 16/80 | Bos. | QF | NYI 2 | Bos. 1 | Clark Gillies | 1:02 | NYI |
| Apr. 17/80 | Bos. | QF | NYI 5 | Bos. 4 | Bob Bourne | 1:24 | NYI |
| Apr. 21/80 | NYI | QF | Bos. 4 | NYI 3 | Terry O'Reilly | 17:13 | NYI |
| May 1/80 | Buf. | SF | NYI 2 | Buf. 1 | Bob Nystrom | 21:20 | NYI |
| May 13/80 | Phi. | F | NYI 4 | Phi. 3 | Denis Potvin | 4:07 | NYI |
| May 24/80 | NYI | F | NYI 5 | Phi. 4 | Bob Nystrom | 7:11 | NYI |
| Apr. 8/81 | Buf. | PRE | Buf. 3 | Van. 2 | Alan Haworth | 5:00 | Buf. |
| Apr. 8/81 | Bos. | PRE | Min. 5 | Bos. 4 | Steve Payne | 3:34 | Min. |
| Apr. 11/81 | Chi. | PRE | Cgy. 5 | Chi. 4 | Willi Plett | 35:17 | Cgy. |
| Apr. 12/81 | Que. | PRE | Que. 4 | Phi. 3 | Dale Hunter | 0:37 | Phi. |
| Apr. 14/81 | St.L. | PRE | St.L. 4 | Pit. 3 | Mike Crombeen | 25:16 | St.L. |
| Apr. 16/81 | Buf. | QF | Min. 4 | Buf. 3 | Steve Payne | 0:22 | Min. |
| Apr. 20/81 | Min. | QF | Buf. 5 | Min. 4 | Craig Ramsay | 16:32 | Min. |
| Apr. 20/81 | Edm. | QF | NYI 5 | Edm. 4 | Ken Morrow | 5:41 | NYI |
| Apr. 7/82 | Min. | DSF | Chi. 3 | Min. 2 | Greg Fox | 3:34 | Chi. |
| Apr. 8/82 | Edm. | DSF | Edm. 3 | L.A. 2 | Wayne Gretzky | 6:20 | L.A. |
| Apr. 8/82 | Van. | DSF | Van. 2 | Cgy. 1 | Tiger Williams | 14:20 | Van. |
| Apr. 10/82 | Pit. | DSF | Pit. 2 | NYI 1 | Rick Kehoe | 4:14 | NYI |
| Apr. 10/82 | L.A. | DSF | L.A. 6 | Edm. 5 | Daryl Evans | 2:35 | L.A. |
| Apr. 13/82 | Mtl. | DSF | Que. 3 | Mtl. 2 | Dale Hunter | 0:22 | Que. |
| Apr. 13/82 | NYI | DSF | NYI 4 | Pit. 3 | John Tonelli | 6:19 | NYI |
| Apr. 16/82 | Van. | DF | L.A. 3 | Van. 2 | Steve Bozek | 4:33 | Van. |
| Apr. 18/82 | Que. | DF | Que. 3 | Bos. 2 | Wilf Paiement | 11:44 | Que. |
| Apr. 18/82 | NYR | DF | NYI 4 | NYR 3 | Bryan Trottier | 3:00 | NYI |
| Apr. 18/82 | L.A. | DF | Van. 4 | L.A. 3 | Colin Campbell | 1:23 | Van. |
| Apr. 21/82 | St.L. | DF | St.L. 3 | Chi. 2 | Bernie Federko | 3:28 | Chi. |
| Apr. 23/82 | Que. | DF | Bos. 6 | Que. 5 | Peter McNab | 10:54 | Que. |
| Apr. 27/82 | Chi. | CF | Van. 2 | Chi. 1 | Jim Nill | 28:58 | Van. |
| May 1/82 | Que. | CF | NYI 5 | Que. 4 | Wayne Merrick | 16:52 | NYI |
| May 8/82 | NYI | F | NYI 6 | Van. 5 | Mike Bossy | 19:58 | NYI |
| Apr. 5/83 | Bos. | DSF | Bos. 4 | Que. 3 | Barry Pederson | 1:46 | Bos. |
| Apr. 6/83 | Cgy. | DSF | Cgy. 4 | Van. 3 | Eddy Beers | 12:27 | Cgy. |
| Apr. 7/83 | Min. | DSF | Min. 5 | Tor. 4 | Bobby Smith | 5:03 | Min. |
| Apr. 10/83 | Tor. | DSF | Min. 5 | Tor. 4 | Dino Ciccarelli | 8:05 | Min. |
| Apr. 10/83 | Van. | DSF | Cgy. 4 | Van. 3 | Greg Meredith | 1:06 | Cgy. |
| Apr. 18/83 | Min. | DF | Chi. 4 | Min. 3 | Rich Preston | 10:34 | Chi. |
| Apr. 24/83 | Bos. | DF | Bos. 3 | Buf. 2 | Brad Park | 1:52 | Bos. |
| Apr. 5/84 | Edm. | DSF | Edm. 5 | Wpg. 4 | Randy Gregg | 0:21 | Edm. |
| Apr. 7/84 | Det. | DSF | St.L. 4 | Det. 3 | Mark Reeds | 37:07 | St.L. |
| Apr. 8/84 | Det. | DSF | St.L. 3 | Det. 2 | Jorgen Pettersson | 2:42 | St.L. |
| Apr. 10/84 | NYI | DSF | NYI 3 | NYR 2 | Ken Morrow | 8:56 | NYI |
| Apr. 13/84 | Min. | DF | St.L. 4 | Min. 3 | Doug Gilmour | 16:16 | Min. |
| Apr. 13/84 | Edm. | DF | Cgy. 6 | Edm. 5 | Carey Wilson | 3:42 | Edm. |
| Apr. 13/84 | NYI | DF | NYI 5 | Wsh. 4 | Anders Kallur | 7:35 | NYI |
| Apr. 16/84 | Mtl. | DF | Que. 4 | Mtl. 3 | Bo Berglund | 3:00 | Mtl. |
| Apr. 20/84 | Cgy. | DF | Cgy. 5 | Edm. 4 | Lanny McDonald | 1:04 | Edm. |
| Apr. 22/84 | Min. | DF | Min. 4 | St.L. 3 | Steve Payne | 6:00 | Min. |
| Apr. 10/85 | Phi. | DSF | Phi. 5 | NYR 4 | Mark Howe | 8:01 | Phi. |
| Apr. 10/85 | Wsh. | DSF | Wsh. 4 | NYI 3 | Alan Haworth | 2:28 | NYI |
| Apr. 10/85 | Edm. | DSF | Edm. 3 | L.A. 2 | Lee Fogolin | 3:01 | Edm. |
| Apr. 10/85 | Wpg. | DSF | Wpg. 5 | Cgy. 4 | Brian Mullen | 7:56 | Wpg. |
| Apr. 11/85 | Wsh. | DSF | Wsh. 2 | NYI 1 | Mike Gartner | 21:23 | NYI |
| Apr. 13/85 | L.A. | DSF | Edm. 4 | L.A. 3 | Glenn Anderson | 0:46 | Edm. |
| Apr. 18/85 | Mtl. | DF | Que. 2 | Mtl. 1 | Mark Kumpel | 12:23 | Que. |
| Apr. 23/85 | Que. | DF | Que. 7 | Mtl. 6 | Dale Hunter | 18:36 | Que. |

| Date | City | Series | Score | | Scorer | Overtime | Series Winner |
|---|---|---|---|---|---|---|---|
| Apr. 25/85 | Min. | DF | Chi. 7 | Min. 6 | Darryl Sutter | 21:57 | Chi. |
| Apr. 28/85 | Chi. | DF | Min. 5 | Chi. 4 | Dennis Maruk | 1:14 | Chi. |
| Apr. 30/85 | Min. | DF | Chi. 6 | Min. 5 | Darryl Sutter | 15:41 | Chi. |
| May 2/85 | Mtl. | DF | Que. 3 | Mtl. 2 | Peter Stastny | 2:22 | Que. |
| May 5/85 | Que. | CF | Que. 2 | Phi. 1 | Peter Stastny | 6:20 | Phi. |
| Apr. 9/86 | Que. | DSF | Hfd. 3 | Que. 2 | Sylvain Turgeon | 2:36 | Hfd. |
| Apr. 12/86 | Wpg. | DSF | Cgy. 4 | Wpg. 3 | Lanny McDonald | 8:25 | Cgy. |
| Apr. 17/86 | Wsh. | DF | NYR 4 | Wsh. 3 | Brian MacLellan | 1:16 | NYR |
| Apr. 20/86 | Edm. | DF | Edm. 6 | Cgy. 5 | Glenn Anderson | 1:04 | Cgy. |
| Apr. 23/86 | Hfd. | DF | Hfd. 2 | Mtl. 1 | Kevin Dineen | 1:07 | Mtl. |
| Apr. 23/86 | NYR | DF | NYR 6 | Wsh. 5 | Bob Brooke | 2:40 | NYR |
| Apr. 26/86 | St L. | DF | St L. 4 | Tor. 3 | Mark Reeds | 7:11 | St L. |
| Apr. 29/86 | Mtl. | DF | Mtl. 2 | Hfd. 1 | Claude Lemieux | 5:55 | Mtl. |
| May 5/86 | NYR | CF | Mtl. 4 | NYR 3 | Claude Lemieux | 9:41 | Mtl. |
| May 12/86 | St L. | CF | St L. 6 | Cgy. 5 | Doug Wickenheiser | 7:30 | Cgy. |
| May 18/86 | Cgy. | F | Mtl. 3 | Cgy. 2 | Brian Skrudland | 0:09 | Mtl. |
| Apr. 8/87 | Hfd. | DSF | Hfd. 3 | Que. 2 | Paul MacDermid | 2:20 | Que. |
| Apr. 9/87 | Mtl. | DSF | Mtl. 4 | Bos. 3 | Mats Naslund | 2:38 | Mtl. |
| Apr. 9/87 | St.L. | DSF | Tor. 3 | St.L. 2 | Rick Lanz | 10:17 | Tor. |
| Apr. 11/87 | Wpg. | DSF | Cgy. 3 | Wpg. 2 | Mike Bullard | 3:53 | Wpg. |
| Apr. 11/87 | Chi. | DSF | Det. 4 | Chi. 3 | Shawn Burr | 4:51 | Det. |
| Apr. 16/87 | Que. | DSF | Que. 5 | Hfd. 4 | Peter Stastny | 6:05 | Que. |
| Apr. 18/87 | Wsh. | DSF | NYI 3 | Wsh. 2 | Pat LaFontaine | 68:47 | NYI |
| Apr. 21/87 | Edm. | DF | Edm. 3 | Wpg. 2 | Glenn Anderson | 0:36 | Edm. |
| Apr. 26/87 | Que. | DF | Mtl. 3 | Que. 2 | Mats Naslund | 5:30 | Mtl. |
| Apr. 27/87 | Tor. | DF | Tor. 3 | Det. 2 | Mike Allison | 9:31 | Det. |
| May 4/87 | Phi. | CF | Phi. 4 | Mtl. 3 | Ilkka Sinislao | 9:11 | Phi. |
| May 20/87 | Edm. | F | Edm. 3 | Phi. 2 | Jari Kurri | 6:50 | Edm. |
| Apr. 6/88 | NYI | DSF | NYI 4 | N.J. 3 | Pat LaFontaine | 6:11 | N.J. |
| Apr. 10/88 | Phi. | DSF | Phi. 5 | Wsh. 4 | Murray Craven | 1:18 | Wsh. |
| Apr. 10/88 | N.J. | DSF | NYI 5 | N.J. 4 | Brent Sutter | 15:07 | N.J. |
| Apr. 10/88 | Buf. | DSF | Buf. 6 | Bos. 5 | John Tucker | 5:32 | Bos. |
| Apr. 12/88 | Det. | DSF | Tor. 6 | Det. 5 | Ed Olczyk | 0:34 | Det. |
| Apr. 16/88 | Wsh. | DSF | Wsh. 5 | Phi. 4 | Dale Hunter | 5:57 | Wsh. |
| Apr. 21/88 | Cgy. | DF | Edm. 5 | Cgy. 4 | Wayne Gretzky | 7:54 | Edm. |
| May 4/88 | Bos. | CF | N.J. 3 | Bos. 2 | Doug Brown | 17:46 | Bos. |
| May 9/88 | Det. | CF | Edm. 4 | Det. 3 | Jari Kurri | 11:02 | Edm. |
| Apr. 5/89 | St.L. | DSF | St.L. 4 | Min. 3 | Brett Hull | 11:55 | St.L. |
| Apr. 5/89 | Cgy. | DSF | Van. 4 | Cgy. 3 | Paul Reinhart | 2:47 | Cgy. |
| Apr. 6/89 | St.L. | DSF | St.L. 4 | Min. 3 | Rick Meagher | 5:30 | St.L. |
| Apr. 6/89 | Det. | DSF | Chi. 5 | Det. 4 | Duane Sutter | 14:36 | Chi. |
| Apr. 8/89 | Hfd. | DSF | Mtl. 5 | Hfd. 4 | Stephane Richer | 5:01 | Mtl. |
| Apr. 8/89 | Phi. | DSF | Wsh. 4 | Phi. 3 | Kelly Miller | 0:51 | Phi. |
| Apr. 9/89 | Hfd. | DSF | Mtl. 4 | Hfd. 3 | Russ Courtnall | 15:12 | Mtl. |
| Apr. 15/89 | Cgy. | DSF | Cgy. 4 | Van. 3 | Joel Otto | 19:21 | Cgy. |
| Apr. 18/89 | Cgy. | DF | Cgy. 4 | L.A. 3 | Doug Gilmour | 7:47 | Cgy. |
| Apr. 19/89 | Mtl. | DF | Mtl. 3 | Bos. 2 | Bobby Smith | 12:24 | Mtl. |
| Apr. 20/89 | St.L. | DF | St.L. 5 | Chi. 4 | Tony Hrkac | 33:49 | Chi. |
| Apr. 21/89 | Phi. | DF | Pit. 4 | Phi. 3 | Phil Bourque | 12:08 | Phi. |
| May 8/89 | Chi. | CF | Cgy. 2 | Chi. 1 | Al MacInnis | 15:05 | Cgy. |
| May 9/89 | Mtl. | CF | Phi. 2 | Mtl. 1 | Dave Poulin | 5:02 | Mtl. |
| May 19/89 | Mtl. | F | Mtl. 4 | Cgy. 3 | Ryan Walter | 38:08 | Cgy. |
| Apr. 5/90 | N.J. | DSF | Wsh. 5 | N.J. 4 | Dino Ciccarelli | 5:34 | Wsh. |
| Apr. 6/90 | Edm. | DSF | Edm. 3 | Wpg. 2 | Mark Lamb | 4:21 | Edm. |
| Apr. 8/90 | Tor. | DSF | St.L. 6 | Tor. 5 | Sergio Momesso | 6:04 | St.L. |
| Apr. 8/90 | L.A. | DSF | L.A. 2 | Cgy. 1 | Tony Granato | 8:37 | L.A. |
| Apr. 9/90 | Mtl. | DSF | Mtl. 2 | Buf. 1 | Brian Skrudland | 12:35 | Mtl. |
| Apr. 9/90 | NYI | DSF | NYI 4 | NYR 3 | Brent Sutter | 20:59 | NYR |
| Apr. 10/90 | Wpg. | DSF | Wpg. 4 | Edm. 3 | Dave Ellett | 21:08 | Edm. |
| Apr. 14/90 | L.A. | DSF | L.A. 4 | Cgy. 3 | Mike Krushelnyski | 23:14 | L.A. |
| Apr. 15/90 | Hfd. | DSF | Hfd. 3 | Bos. 2 | Kevin Dineen | 12:30 | Bos. |
| Apr. 21/90 | Bos. | DF | Bos. 5 | Mtl. 4 | Garry Galley | 3:42 | Bos. |
| Apr. 24/90 | L.A. | DF | Edm. 6 | L.A. 5 | Joe Murphy | 4:42 | Edm. |
| Apr. 25/90 | Wsh. | DF | Wsh. 4 | NYR 3 | Rod Langway | 0:34 | Wsh. |
| Apr. 27/90 | NYR | DF | Wsh. 2 | NYR 1 | John Druce | 6:48 | Wsh. |
| May 15/90 | Bos. | F | Edm. 3 | Bos. 2 | Petr Klima | 55:13 | Edm. |
| Apr. 4/91 | Chi. | DSF | Min. 4 | Chi. 3 | Brian Propp | 4:14 | Min. |
| Apr. 5/91 | Pit. | DSF | Pit. 5 | N.J. 4 | Jaromir Jagr | 8:52 | Pit. |
| Apr. 6/91 | L.A. | DSF | L.A. 3 | Van. 2 | Wayne Gretzky | 11:08 | L.A. |
| Apr. 8/91 | Van. | DSF | Van. 2 | L.A. 1 | Cliff Ronning | 3:12 | L.A. |
| Apr. 11/91 | NYR | DSF | Wsh. 5 | NYR 4 | Dino Ciccarelli | 6:44 | Wsh. |
| Apr. 11/91 | Mtl. | DSF | Mtl. 4 | Buf. 3 | Russ Courtnall | 5:56 | Mtl. |
| Apr. 14/91 | Edm. | DSF | Cgy. 2 | Edm. 1 | Theoren Fleury | 4:40 | Edm. |
| Apr. 16/91 | Cgy. | DSF | Edm. 5 | Cgy. 4 | Esa Tikkanen | 6:58 | Edm. |
| Apr. 18/91 | L.A. | DF | L.A. 4 | Edm. 3 | Luc Robitaille | 2:13 | Edm. |
| Apr. 19/91 | Bos. | DF | Mtl. 4 | Bos. 3 | Stephane Richer | 0:27 | Bos. |
| Apr. 19/91 | Pit. | DF | Pit. 7 | Wsh. 6 | Kevin Stevens | 8:10 | Pit. |
| Apr. 20/91 | L.A. | DF | Edm. 4 | L.A. 3 | Petr Klima | 24:48 | Edm. |
| Apr. 22/91 | Edm. | DF | Edm. 4 | L.A. 3 | Esa Tikkanen | 20:48 | Edm. |
| Apr. 27/91 | Mtl. | DF | Mtl. 3 | Bos. 2 | Shayne Corson | 17:47 | Bos. |
| Apr. 28/91 | Edm. | DF | Edm. 4 | L.A. 3 | Craig MacTavish | 16:57 | Edm. |
| May 3/91 | Bos. | CF | Bos. 5 | Pit. 4 | Vladimir Ruzicka | 8:14 | Pit. |
| Apr. 21/92 | Bos. | DSF | Bos. 3 | Buf. 2 | Adam Oates | 11:14 | Bos. |
| Apr. 22/92 | Min. | DSF | Det. 5 | Min. 4 | Yves Racine | 1:15 | Det. |
| Apr. 22/92 | St.L. | DSF | St.L. 5 | Chi. 4 | Brett Hull | 23:33 | Chi. |
| Apr. 25/92 | Buf. | DSF | Bos. 5 | Buf. 4 | Ted Donato | 2:08 | Bos. |
| Apr. 28/92 | Min. | DSF | Det. 1 | Min. 0 | Sergei Fedorov | 16:13 | Det. |
| Apr. 29/92 | Hfd. | DSF | Hfd. 2 | Mtl. 1 | Yvon Corriveau | 0:24 | Mtl. |
| May 1/92 | Mtl. | DSF | Mtl. 3 | Hfd. 2 | Russ Courtnall | 25:26 | Mtl. |
| May 3/92 | Van. | DF | Edm. 4 | Van. 3 | Joe Murphy | 8:36 | Edm. |
| May 5/92 | Mtl. | DF | Bos. 3 | Mtl. 2 | Peter Douris | 3:12 | Bos. |
| May 7/92 | Pit. | DF | NYR 6 | Pit. 5 | Kris King | 1:29 | Pit. |
| May 9/92 | Pit. | DF | Pit. 5 | NYR 4 | Ron Francis | 2:47 | Pit. |
| May 17/92 | Pit. | CF | Pit. 4 | Bos. 3 | Jaromir Jagr | 9:44 | Pit. |

*Chris Kunitz (#14) hugs Bill Guerin while the Penguins rush over to celebrate Guerin's overtime goal that gave Pittsburgh a 3-2 win over Philadelphia in game two of their first-round series.*

| Date | City | Series | Score | | Scorer | Overtime | Series Winner |
|---|---|---|---|---|---|---|---|
| May 20/92 | Edm. | CF | Chi. 4 | Edm. 3 | Jeremy Roenick | 2:45 | Chi. |
| Apr. 18/93 | Bos. | DSF | Buf. 5 | Bos. 4 | Bob Sweeney | 11:03 | Buf. |
| Apr. 18/93 | Que. | DSF | Que. 3 | Mtl. 2 | Scott Young | 16:49 | Mtl. |
| Apr. 20/93 | Wsh. | DSF | NYI 5 | Wsh. 4 | Brian Mullen | 34:50 | NYI |
| Apr. 22/93 | Mtl. | DSF | Mtl. 2 | Que. 1 | Vincent Damphousse | 10:30 | Mtl. |
| Apr. 22/93 | Buf. | DSF | Buf. 4 | Bos. 3 | Yuri Khmylev | 1:05 | Buf. |
| Apr. 22/93 | NYI | DSF | NYI 4 | Wsh. 3 | Ray Ferraro | 4:46 | NYI |
| Apr. 24/93 | Buf. | DSF | Buf. 6 | Bos. 5 | Brad May | 4:48 | Buf. |
| Apr. 24/93 | NYI | DSF | NYI 4 | Wsh. 3 | Ray Ferraro | 25:40 | NYI |
| Apr. 25/93 | St.L. | DSF | St.L. 4 | Chi. 3 | Craig Janney | 10:43 | St.L. |
| Apr. 26/93 | Que. | DSF | Mtl. 5 | Que. 4 | Kirk Muller | 8:17 | Mtl. |
| Apr. 27/93 | Det. | DSF | Tor. 5 | Det. 4 | Mike Foligno | 2:05 | Tor. |
| Apr. 27/93 | Van. | DSF | Wpg. 4 | Van. 3 | Teemu Selanne | 6:18 | Van. |
| Apr. 29/93 | Wpg. | DSF | Van. 4 | Wpg. 3 | Greg Adams | 4:30 | Van. |
| May 1/93 | Det. | DSF | Tor. 4 | Det. 3 | Nikolai Borschevsky | 2:35 | Tor. |
| May 3/93 | Tor. | DF | Tor. 2 | St.L. 1 | Doug Gilmour | 23:16 | Tor. |
| May 4/93 | Mtl. | DF | Mtl. 4 | Buf. 3 | Guy Carbonneau | 2:50 | Mtl. |
| May 5/93 | Tor. | DF | St.L. 2 | Tor. 1 | Jeff Brown | 23:03 | Tor. |
| May 6/93 | Buf. | DF | Mtl. 4 | Buf. 3 | Gilbert Dionne | 8:28 | Mtl. |
| May 8/93 | Buf. | DF | Mtl. 4 | Buf. 3 | Kirk Muller | 11:37 | Mtl. |
| May 11/93 | Van. | DF | L.A. 4 | Van. 3 | Gary Shuchuk | 26:31 | L.A. |
| May 14/93 | Pit. | DF | NYI 4 | Pit. 3 | Dave Volek | 5:16 | NYI |
| May 18/93 | Mtl. | CF | Mtl. 4 | NYI 3 | Stephan Lebeau | 26:21 | Mtl. |
| May 20/93 | NYI | CF | Mtl. 2 | NYI 1 | Guy Carbonneau | 12:34 | Mtl. |
| May 25/93 | Tor. | CF | Tor. 3 | L.A. 2 | Glenn Anderson | 19:20 | L.A. |
| May 27/93 | L.A. | CF | L.A. 5 | Tor. 4 | Wayne Gretzky | 1:41 | L.A. |
| Jun. 3/93 | Mtl. | F | Mtl. 3 | L.A. 2 | Eric Desjardins | 0:51 | Mtl. |
| Jun. 5/93 | L.A. | F | Mtl. 4 | L.A. 3 | John LeClair | 0:34 | Mtl. |
| Jun. 7/93 | L.A. | F | Mtl. 3 | L.A. 2 | John LeClair | 14:37 | Mtl. |
| Apr. 20/94 | Tor. | CQF | Tor. 1 | Chi. 0 | Todd Gill | 2:15 | Tor. |
| Apr. 22/94 | St.L. | CQF | Dal. 5 | St.L. 4 | Paul Cavallini | 8:34 | Dal. |
| Apr. 24/94 | Chi. | CQF | Chi. 4 | Tor. 3 | Jeremy Roenick | 1:23 | Tor. |
| Apr. 25/94 | Bos. | CQF | Mtl. 2 | Bos. 1 | Kirk Muller | 17:18 | Bos. |
| Apr. 26/94 | Cgy. | CQF | Van. 2 | Cgy. 1 | Geoff Courtnall | 7:15 | Van. |
| Apr. 27/94 | Buf. | CQF | Buf. 1 | N.J. 0 | Dave Hannan | 65:43 | N.J. |
| Apr. 28/94 | Van. | CQF | Van. 3 | Cgy. 2 | Trevor Linden | 16:43 | Van. |
| Apr. 30/94 | Cgy. | CQF | Van. 4 | Cgy. 3 | Pavel Bure | 22:20 | Van. |
| May 3/94 | N.J. | CSF | Bos. 6 | N.J. 5 | Don Sweeney | 9:08 | N.J. |
| May 7/94 | Bos. | CSF | N.J. 5 | Bos. 4 | Stephane Richer | 14:19 | N.J. |
| May 8/94 | Van. | CSF | Van. 2 | Dal. 1 | Sergio Momesso | 11:01 | Van. |
| May 12/94 | Tor. | CSF | Tor. 3 | S.J. 2 | Mike Gartner | 8:53 | Tor. |
| May 15/94 | NYR | CF | N.J. 4 | NYR 3 | Stephane Richer | 35:23 | NYR |
| May 16/94 | Tor. | CF | Tor. 3 | Van. 2 | Peter Zezel | 16:55 | Van. |
| May 19/94 | N.J. | CF | NYR 3 | N.J. 2 | Stephane Matteau | 26:13 | NYR |
| May 24/94 | Van. | CF | Van. 4 | Tor. 3 | Greg Adams | 20:14 | Van. |
| May 27/94 | NYR | CF | NYR 2 | N.J. 1 | Stephane Matteau | 24:24 | NYR |
| May 31/94 | NYR | F | Van. 3 | NYR 2 | Greg Adams | 19:26 | NYR |
| May 7/95 | Phi. | CQF | Phi. 4 | Buf. 3 | Karl Dykhuis | 10:06 | Phi. |
| May 9/95 | Cgy. | CQF | S.J. 5 | Cgy. 4 | Ulf Dahlen | 12:21 | S.J. |
| May 12/95 | NYR | CQF | NYR 3 | Que. 2 | Steve Larmer | 8:09 | NYR |
| May 12/95 | N.J. | CQF | N.J. 1 | Bos. 0 | Randy McKay | 8:51 | N.J. |
| May 14/95 | Pit. | CQF | Pit. 6 | Wsh. 5 | Luc Robitaille | 4:30 | Pit. |
| May 15/95 | St.L. | CQF | Van. 6 | St.L. 5 | Cliff Ronning | 1:48 | Van. |
| May 17/95 | Tor. | CQF | Tor. 5 | Chi. 4 | Randy Wood | 10:00 | Chi. |
| May 19/95 | Cgy. | CQF | S.J. 5 | Cgy. 4 | Ray Whitney | 21:54 | S.J. |
| May 21/95 | Phi. | CSF | Phi. 5 | NYR 4 | Eric Desjardins | 7:03 | Phi. |
| May 21/95 | Chi. | CSF | Chi. 2 | Van. 1 | Joe Murphy | 9:04 | Chi. |
| May 22/95 | Phi. | CSF | Phi. 4 | NYR 3 | Kevin Haller | 0:25 | Phi. |
| May 25/95 | Van. | CSF | Chi. 3 | Van. 2 | Chris Chelios | 6:22 | Chi. |
| May 26/95 | N.J. | CSF | N.J. 2 | Pit. 1 | Neal Broten | 18:36 | N.J. |
| May 27/95 | Van. | CSF | Chi. 4 | Van. 3 | Chris Chelios | 5:35 | Chi. |
| Jun. 1/95 | Det. | CF | Det. 2 | Chi. 1 | Nicklas Lidstrom | 1:01 | Det. |
| Jun. 6/95 | Chi. | CF | Det. 4 | Chi. 3 | Vladimir Konstantinov | 29:25 | Det. |
| Jun. 7/95 | N.J. | CF | Phi. 3 | N.J. 2 | Eric Lindros | 4:19 | N.J. |
| Jun. 11/95 | Det. | CF | Det. 2 | Chi. 1 | Vyacheslav Kozlov | 22:25 | Det. |
| Apr. 16/96 | NYR | CQF | Mtl. 3 | NYR 2 | Vincent Damphousse | 5:04 | NYR |
| Apr. 18/96 | Tor. | CQF | Tor. 5 | St.L. 4 | Mats Sundin | 4:02 | St.L. |
| Apr. 18/96 | Phi. | CQF | T.B. 2 | Phi. 1 | Brian Bellows | 9:05 | Phi. |

| Date | City | Series | Score | | Scorer | Overtime | Series Winner |
|---|---|---|---|---|---|---|---|
| Apr. 21/96 | St.L. | CQF | St.L. 3 | Tor. 2 | Glenn Anderson | 1:24 | St.L. |
| Apr. 21/96 | T.B. | CQF | T.B. 5 | Phi. 4 | Alexander Selivanov | 2:04 | Phi. |
| Apr. 23/96 | Cgy. | CQF | Chi. 2 | Cgy. 1 | Joe Murphy | 50:02 | Chi. |
| Apr. 24/96 | Wsh. | CQF | Pit. 3 | Wsh. 2 | Petr Nedved | 79:15 | Pit. |
| Apr. 25/96 | Col. | CQF | Col. 5 | Van. 4 | Joe Sakic | 0:51 | Col. |
| Apr. 25/96 | Tor. | CQF | Tor. 5 | St.L. 4 | Mike Gartner | 7:31 | St.L. |
| May 2/96 | Col. | CSF | Chi. 3 | Col. 2 | Jeremy Roenick | 6:29 | Col. |
| May 6/96 | Chi. | CSF | Chi. 4 | Col. 3 | Sergei Krivokrasov | 0:46 | Col. |
| May 8/96 | St.L. | CSF | St.L. 5 | Det. 4 | Igor Kravchuk | 3:23 | Det. |
| May 8/96 | Chi. | CSF | Col. 3 | Chi. 2 | Joe Sakic | 44:33 | Col. |
| May 9/96 | Fla. | CSF | Fla. 4 | Phi. 3 | Dave Lowry | 4:06 | Fla. |
| May 12/96 | Phi. | CSF | Fla. 2 | Phi. 1 | Mike Hough | 28:05 | Fla. |
| May 13/96 | Chi. | CSF | Col. 4 | Chi. 3 | Sandis Ozolinsh | 25:18 | Col. |
| May 16/96 | Det. | CSF | Det. 1 | St.L. 0 | Steve Yzerman | 21:15 | Det. |
| May 19/96 | Det. | CF | Col. 3 | Det. 2 | Mike Keane | 17:31 | Col. |
| Jun. 10/96 | Fla. | F | Col. 1 | Fla. 0 | Uwe Krupp | 44:31 | Col. |
| Apr. 20/97 | Chi. | CQF | Chi. 4 | Col. 3 | Sergei Krivokrasov | 31:03 | Col. |
| Apr. 20/97 | Edm. | CQF | Edm. 4 | Dal. 3 | Kelly Buchberger | 9:15 | Edm. |
| Apr. 22/97 | NYR | CQF | NYR 4 | Fla. 3 | Esa Tikkanen | 16:29 | NYR |
| Apr. 23/97 | Ott. | CQF | Ott. 1 | Buf. 0 | Daniel Alfredsson | 2:34 | Buf. |
| Apr. 24/97 | Mtl. | CQF | Mtl. 4 | N.J. 3 | Patrice Brisebois | 47:37 | N.J. |
| Apr. 25/97 | Fla. | CQF | NYR 3 | Fla. 2 | Esa Tikkanen | 12:02 | NYR |
| Apr. 25/97 | Dal. | CQF | Edm. 1 | Dal. 0 | Ryan Smyth | 20:22 | Edm. |
| Apr. 27/97 | Phx. | CQF | Ana. 3 | Phx. 2 | Paul Kariya | 7:29 | Ana. |
| Apr. 29/97 | Buf. | CQF | Buf. 3 | Ott. 2 | Derek Plante | 5:24 | Buf. |
| Apr. 29/97 | Dal. | CQF | Edm. 4 | Dal. 3 | Todd Marchant | 12:26 | Edm. |
| May 2/97 | Det. | CSF | Det. 2 | Ana. 1 | Martin Lapointe | 0:59 | Det. |
| May 4/97 | Det. | CSF | Det. 3 | Ana. 2 | Vyacheslav Kozlov | 41:31 | Det. |
| May 8/97 | Ana. | CSF | Det. 3 | Ana. 2 | Brendan Shanahan | 37:03 | Det. |
| May 9/97 | Phi. | CSF | Buf. 5 | Phi. 4 | Ed Ronan | 6:24 | Phi. |
| May 9/97 | Edm. | CSF | Col. 3 | Edm. 2 | Claude Lemieux | 8:35 | Col. |
| May 11/97 | N.J. | CSF | NYR 2 | N.J. 1 | Adam Graves | 14:08 | NYR |
| Apr. 22/98 | N.J. | CQF | Ott. 2 | N.J. 1 | Bruce Gardiner | 5:58 | Ott. |
| Apr. 23/98 | Pit. | CQF | Mtl. 3 | Pit. 2 | Benoit Brunet | 18:43 | Mtl. |
| Apr. 24/98 | Wsh. | CQF | Bos. 4 | Wsh. 3 | Darren Van Impe | 20:54 | Wsh. |
| Apr. 26/98 | Ott. | CQF | Ott. 2 | N.J. 1 | Alexei Yashin | 2:47 | Ott. |
| Apr. 26/98 | Bos. | CQF | Wsh. 3 | Bos. 2 | Joe Juneau | 26:31 | Wsh. |
| Apr. 26/98 | Edm. | CQF | Col. 5 | Edm. 4 | Joe Sakic | 15:25 | Edm. |
| Apr. 28/98 | S.J. | CQF | S.J. 1 | Dal. 0 | Andrei Zyuzin | 6:31 | Dal. |
| May 1/98 | Phi. | CQF | Buf. 3 | Phi. 2 | Michal Grosek | 5:40 | Buf. |
| May 2/98 | S.J. | CQF | Dal. 3 | S.J. 2 | Mike Keane | 3:43 | Dal. |
| May 3/98 | Bos. | CQF | Wsh. 3 | Bos. 2 | Brian Bellows | 15:24 | Wsh. |
| May 3/98 | Buf. | CSF | Buf. 3 | Mtl. 2 | Geoff Sanderson | 2:37 | Buf. |
| May 11/98 | Edm. | CSF | Dal. 1 | Edm. 0 | Benoit Hogue | 13:07 | Dal. |
| May 12/98 | Mtl. | CSF | Buf. 5 | Mtl. 4 | Michael Peca | 21:24 | Buf. |
| May 12/98 | St.L. | CSF | Det. 3 | St.L. 2 | Brendan Shanahan | 31:12 | Det. |
| May 25/98 | Wsh. | CF | Wsh. 3 | Buf. 2 | Todd Krygier | 3:01 | Wsh. |
| May 28/98 | Buf. | CF | Wsh. 4 | Buf. 3 | Peter Bondra | 9:37 | Wsh. |
| Jun. 3/98 | Dal. | CF | Dal. 3 | Det. 2 | Jamie Langenbrunner | 0:46 | Det. |
| Jun. 4/98 | Buf. | CF | Wsh. 3 | Buf. 2 | Joe Juneau | 6:24 | Wsh. |
| Jun. 11/98 | Det. | F | Det. 5 | Wsh. 4 | Kris Draper | 15:24 | Det. |
| Apr. 23/99 | Ott. | CQF | Buf. 3 | Ott. 2 | Miroslav Satan | 30:35 | Buf. |
| Apr. 24/99 | Car. | CQF | Car. 3 | Bos. 2 | Ray Sheppard | 17:05 | Bos. |
| Apr. 24/99 | Phx. | CQF | Phx. 4 | St.L. 3 | Shane Doan | 8:58 | St.L. |
| Apr. 26/99 | S.J. | CQF | Col. 2 | S.J. 1 | Milan Hejduk | 7:53 | Col. |
| Apr. 27/99 | Edm. | CQF | Dal. 3 | Edm. 2 | Joe Nieuwendyk | 57:34 | Dal. |
| Apr. 30/99 | Tor. | CQF | Tor. 2 | Phi. 1 | Yanic Perreault | 11:51 | Tor. |
| Apr. 30/99 | Car. | CQF | Bos. 4 | Car. 3 | Anson Carter | 34:45 | Bos. |
| Apr. 30/99 | Phx. | CQF | St.L. 2 | Phx. 1 | Scott Young | 5:43 | St.L. |
| May 2/99 | Pit. | CQF | Pit. 3 | N.J. 2 | Jaromir Jagr | 8:59 | Pit. |
| May 3/99 | S.J. | CQF | Col. 3 | S.J. 2 | Milan Hejduk | 13:12 | Col. |
| May 4/99 | Phx. | CQF | St.L. 1 | Phx. 0 | Pierre Turgeon | 17:59 | St.L. |
| May 7/99 | Col. | CSF | Det. 3 | Col. 2 | Kirk Maltby | 4:18 | Col. |
| May 8/99 | Dal. | CSF | Dal. 5 | St.L. 4 | Joe Nieuwendyk | 8:22 | Dal. |
| May 10/99 | St.L. | CSF | St.L. 3 | Dal. 2 | Pavol Demitra | 2:43 | Dal. |
| May 12/99 | St.L. | CSF | St.L. 3 | Dal. 2 | Pierre Turgeon | 5:52 | Dal. |
| May 13/99 | Pit. | CSF | Tor. 3 | Pit. 2 | Sergei Berezin | 2:18 | Tor. |
| May 17/99 | Pit. | CSF | Tor. 4 | Pit. 3 | Garry Valk | 1:57 | Tor. |

# Overtime Games since 1918 *— continued*

| Date | City | Series | Score | | Scorer | Overtime | Series Winner |
|---|---|---|---|---|---|---|---|
| May 17/99 | St.L. | CSF | Dal. 2 | St.L. 1 | Mike Modano | 2:21 | Dal. |
| May 28/99 | Col. | CF | Col. 3 | Dal. 2 | Chris Drury | 19:29 | Dal. |
| Jun. 8/99 | Dal. | F | Buf. 3 | Dal. 2 | Jason Woolley | 15:30 | Dal. |
| Jun. 19/99 | Buf. | F | Dal. 2 | Buf. 1 | Brett Hull | 54:51 | Dal. |
| Apr. 15/00 | Pit. | CQF | Pit. 2 | Wsh. 1 | Jaromir Jagr | 5:49 | Pit. |
| Apr. 18/00 | Buf. | CQF | Buf. 3 | Phi. 2 | Stu Barnes | 4:42 | Phi. |
| Apr. 22/00 | Tor. | CQF | Tor. 2 | Ott. 1 | Steve Thomas | 14:47 | Tor. |
| May 2/00 | Pit. | CSF | Phi. 4 | Pit. 3 | Andy Delmore | 11:01 | Phi. |
| May 3/00 | Det. | CSF | Col. 3 | Det. 2 | Chris Drury | 10:21 | Col. |
| May 4/00 | Pit. | CSF | Phi. 2 | Pit. 1 | Keith Primeau | 92:01 | Phi. |
| May 23/00 | Dal. | CF | Dal. 3 | Col. 2 | Joe Nieuwendyk | 12:10 | Dal. |
| Jun. 8/00 | N.J. | F | Dal. 1 | N.J. 0 | Mike Modano | 46:21 | N.J. |
| Jun. 10/00 | Dal. | F | N.J. 2 | Dal. 1 | Jason Arnott | 28:20 | N.J. |
| Apr. 11/01 | Dal. | CQF | Dal. 2 | Edm. 1 | Jamie Langenbrunner | 2:08 | Dal. |
| Apr. 13/01 | Ott. | CQF | Tor. 1 | Ott. 0 | Mats Sundin | 10:49 | Tor. |
| Apr. 14/01 | Phi. | CQF | Buf. 4 | Phi. 3 | Jay McKee | 18:02 | Buf. |
| Apr. 15/01 | Edm. | CQF | Dal. 3 | Edm. 2 | Benoit Hogue | 19:48 | Dal. |
| Apr. 16/01 | Tor. | CQF | Tor. 3 | Ott. 2 | Cory Cross | 2:16 | Tor. |
| Apr. 16/01 | Van. | CQF | Col. 4 | Van. 3 | Peter Forsberg | 2:50 | Col. |
| Apr. 17/01 | Buf. | CQF | Buf. 4 | Phi. 3 | Curtis Brown | 6:13 | Buf. |
| Apr. 17/01 | Edm. | CQF | Edm. 2 | Dal. 1 | Mike Comrie | 17:19 | Dal. |
| Apr. 18/01 | Car. | CQF | Car. 3 | N.J. 2 | Rod Brind'Amour | :46 | N.J. |
| Apr. 18/01 | Pit. | CQF | Wsh. 4 | Pit. 3 | Jeff Halpern | 4:01 | Pit. |
| Apr. 18/01 | L.A. | CQF | L.A. 4 | Det. 3 | Eric Belanger | 2:36 | L.A. |
| Apr. 19/01 | Dal. | CQF | Dal. 4 | Edm. 3 | Kirk Muller | 8:01 | Dal. |
| Apr. 19/01 | St.L. | CQF | St.L. 3 | S.J. 2 | Bryce Salvador | 9:54 | St.L. |
| Apr. 23/01 | Pit. | CQF | Pit. 4 | Wsh. 3 | Martin Straka | 13:04 | Pit. |
| Apr. 23/01 | L.A. | CQF | L.A. 3 | Det. 2 | Adam Deadmarsh | 4:48 | L.A. |
| Apr. 26/01 | Col. | CSF | L.A. 4 | Col. 3 | Jaroslav Modry | 14:23 | Col. |
| Apr. 28/01 | N.J. | CSF | N.J. 6 | Tor. 5 | Randy McKay | 5:31 | N.J. |
| May 1/01 | Tor. | CSF | N.J. 3 | Tor. 2 | Brian Rafalski | 7:00 | N.J. |
| May 1/01 | St.L. | CSF | St.L. 3 | Dal. 2 | Cory Stillman | 29:26 | St.L. |
| May 5/01 | Buf. | CSF | Buf. 3 | Pit. 2 | Stu Barnes | 8:34 | Pit. |
| May 6/01 | L.A. | CSF | L.A. 1 | Col. 0 | Glen Murray | 22:41 | Col. |
| May 8/01 | Pit. | CSF | Pit. 3 | Buf. 2 | Martin Straka | 11:29 | Pit. |
| May 10/01 | Buf. | CSF | Pit. 3 | Buf. 2 | Darius Kasparaitis | 13:01 | Pit. |
| May 16/01 | St.L. | CF | St.L. 4 | Col. 3 | Scott Young | 30:27 | Col. |
| May 18/01 | St.L. | CF | Col. 4 | St.L. 3 | Stephane Yelle | 4:23 | Col. |
| May 21/01 | Col. | CF | Col. 2 | St.L. 1 | Joe Sakic | :24 | Col. |
| Apr. 17/02 | Phi. | CQF | Phi. 1 | Ott. 0 | Ruslan Fedotenko | 7:47 | Ott. |
| Apr. 17/02 | Det. | CQF | Van. 4 | Det. 3 | Henrik Sedin | 13:59 | Det. |
| Apr. 19/02 | Car. | CQF | Car. 2 | N.J. 1 | Bates Battaglia | 15:26 | Car. |
| Apr. 24/02 | Car. | CQF | Car. 3 | N.J. 2 | Josef Vasicek | 8:16 | Car. |
| Apr. 25/02 | Col. | CQF | L.A. 1 | Col. 0 | Craig Johnson | 2:19 | Col. |
| Apr. 26/02 | Phi. | CQF | Ott. 2 | Phi. 1 | Martin Havlat | 7:33 | Ott. |
| May 4/02 | Tor. | CSF | Tor. 3 | Ott. 2 | Gary Roberts | 44:30 | Tor. |
| May 7/02 | Mtl. | CSF | Mtl. 2 | Car. 1 | Donald Audette | 2:26 | Car. |
| May 9/02 | Mtl. | CSF | Car. 4 | Mtl. 3 | Niclas Wallin | 3:14 | Car. |
| May 13/02 | S.J. | CSF | Col. 2 | S.J. 1 | Peter Forsberg | 2:47 | Col. |
| May 19/02 | Car. | CF | Car. 2 | Tor. 1 | Niclas Wallin | 13:42 | Car. |
| May 20/02 | Det. | CF | Col. 4 | Det. 3 | Chris Drury | 2:17 | Det. |
| May 21/02 | Tor. | CF | Car. 2 | Tor. 1 | Jeff O'Neill | 6:01 | Car. |
| May 22/02 | Col. | CF | Det. 2 | Col. 1 | Fredrik Olausson | 12:44 | Det. |
| May 27/02 | Det. | CF | Col. 2 | Det. 1 | Peter Forsberg | 6:24 | Det. |
| May 28/02 | Tor. | CF | Car. 2 | Tor. 1 | Martin Gelinas | 8:05 | Car. |
| Jun. 4/02 | Det. | F | Car. 3 | Det. 2 | Ron Francis | :58 | Det. |
| Jun. 8/02 | Car. | F | Det. 3 | Car. 2 | Igor Larionov | 54:47 | Det. |
| Apr. 10/03 | Det. | CQF | Ana. 2 | Det. 1 | Paul Kariya | 43:18 | Ana. |
| Apr. 14/03 | NYI | CQF | Ott. 3 | NYI 2 | Todd White | 22:25 | Ott. |
| Apr. 14/03 | Tor. | CQF | Tor. 4 | Phi. 3 | Tomas Kaberle | 27:20 | Phi. |
| Apr. 15/03 | Wsh. | CQF | T.B. 4 | Wsh. 3 | Vincent Lecavalier | 2:29 | T.B. |
| Apr. 16/03 | Tor. | CQF | Phi. 3 | Tor. 2 | Mark Recchi | 53:54 | Phi. |
| Apr. 16/03 | Ana. | CQF | Ana. 3 | Det. 2 | Steve Rucchin | 6:53 | Ana. |
| Apr. 20/03 | Wsh. | CQF | T.B. 2 | Wsh. 1 | Martin St. Louis | 44:03 | T.B. |
| Apr. 21/03 | Tor. | CQF | Tor. 2 | Phi. 1 | Travis Green | 30:51 | Phi. |
| Apr. 21/03 | Min. | CQF | Min. 3 | Col. 2 | Richard Park | 4:22 | Min. |
| Apr. 22/03 | Col. | CQF | Min. 3 | Col. 2 | Andrew Brunette | 3:25 | Min. |
| Apr. 24/03 | Dal. | CSF | Ana. 4 | Dal. 3 | Petr Sykora | 80:48 | Ana. |
| Apr. 25/03 | Van. | CSF | Van. 4 | Min. 3 | Trent Klatt | 3:42 | Min. |
| Apr. 26/03 | N.J. | CSF | N.J. 3 | T.B. 2 | Jamie Langenbrunner | 2:09 | N.J. |
| Apr. 26/03 | Dal. | CSF | Ana. 3 | Dal. 2 | Mike Leclerc | 1:44 | Ana. |
| Apr. 29/03 | Phi. | CSF | Ott. 3 | Phi. 2 | Wade Redden | 6:43 | Ott. |
| May 2/03 | Min. | CSF | Van. 3 | Min. 2 | Brent Sopel | 15:52 | Min. |
| May 2/03 | N.J. | CSF | N.J. 2 | T.B. 1 | Grant Marshall | 51:12 | N.J. |
| May 10/03 | Min. | CF | Ana. 1 | Min. 0 | Petr Sykora | 28:06 | Ana. |
| May 10/03 | Ott. | CF | Ott. 3 | N.J. 2 | Shaun Van Allen | 3:08 | N.J. |
| May 21/03 | N.J. | CF | Ott. 2 | N.J. 1 | Chris Phillips | 15:51 | N.J. |
| May 31/03 | Ana. | F | Ana. 3 | N.J. 2 | Ruslan Salei | 6:59 | N.J. |
| Jun. 2/03 | Ana. | F | Ana. 1 | N.J. 0 | Steve Thomas | 0:39 | N.J. |
| Apr. 8/04 | S.J. | CQF | S.J. 1 | St.L. 0 | Niko Dimitrakos | 9:16 | S.J. |
| Apr. 9/04 | Bos. | CQF | Bos. 2 | Mtl. 1 | Patrice Bergeron | 1:26 | Mtl. |
| Apr. 12/04 | Dal. | CQF | Dal. 4 | Col. 3 | Steve Ott | 2:11 | Col. |
| Apr. 13/04 | Mtl. | CQF | Bos. 4 | Mtl. 3 | Glen Murray | 29:27 | Mtl. |
| Apr. 14/04 | Dal. | CQF | Col. 3 | Dal. 2 | Marek Svatos | 25:21 | Col. |
| Apr. 16/04 | T.B. | CQF | T.B. 3 | NYI 2 | Martin St. Louis | 4:07 | T.B. |
| Apr. 17/04 | Cgy. | CQF | Van. 5 | Cgy. 4 | Brendan Morrison | 42:28 | Cgy. |
| Apr. 18/04 | Ott. | CQF | Ott. 2 | Tor. 1 | Mike Fisher | 21:47 | Tor. |
| Apr. 19/04 | Van. | CQF | Cgy. 3 | Van. 2 | Martin Gelinas | 1:25 | Cgy. |
| Apr. 22/04 | Det. | CQF | Cgy. 2 | Det. 1 | Marcus Nilson | 2:39 | Cgy. |
| Apr. 27/04 | Mtl. | CSF | T.B. 4 | Mtl 3 | Brad Richards | 1:05 | T.B. |
| Apr. 28/04 | Col | CSF | Col. 1 | S.J. 0 | Joe Sakic | 5:15 | S.J. |
| May 1/04 | S.J. | CSF | Col. 2 | S.J. 1 | Joe Sakic | 1:54 | S.J. |
| May 3/04 | Cgy | CSF | Cgy. 1 | Det. 0 | Martin Gelinas | 19:13 | Cgy. |
| May 4/04 | Phi. | CSF | Phi. 3 | Tor. 2 | Jeremy Roenick | 7:39 | Phi. |

| Date | City | Series | Score | | Scorer | Overtime | Series Winner |
|---|---|---|---|---|---|---|---|
| May 9/04 | S.J. | CF | Cgy. 4 | S.J. 3 | Steve Montador | 18:43 | Cgy. |
| May 20/04 | Phi. | CF | Phi. 5 | T.B. 4 | Simon Gagne | 18:18 | T.B. |
| Jun. 3/04 | T.B. | F | Cgy. 3 | T.B. 2 | Oleg Saprykin | 14:40 | T.B. |
| Jun. 5/04 | Cgy. | F | T.B. 3 | Cgy. 2 | Martin St. Louis | 20:33 | T.B. |
| Apr. 21/06 | Det. | CQF | Det. 3 | Edm. 2 | Kirk Maltby | 22:39 | Edm. |
| Apr. 21/06 | Cgy. | CQF | Cgy. 2 | Ana. 1 | Darren McCarty | 9:45 | Ana. |
| Apr. 22/06 | Buf. | CQF | Buf. 3 | Phi. 2 | Daniel Briere | 27:31 | Buf. |
| Apr. 24/06 | Car. | CQF | Mtl. 6 | Car. 5 | Michael Ryder | 22:32 | Car. |
| Apr. 24/06 | Dal. | CQF | Col. 5 | Dal. 4 | Joe Sakic | 4:36 | Col. |
| Apr. 25/06 | Edm. | CQF | Edm. 4 | Det. 3 | Jarret Stoll | 28:44 | Edm. |
| Apr. 26/06 | Mtl. | CQF | Car. 2 | Mtl. 1 | Eric Staal | 3:38 | Car. |
| Apr. 26/06 | Col. | CQF | Col. 4 | Dal. 3 | Alex Tanguay | 1:09 | Col. |
| Apr. 27/06 | Ana. | CQF | Ana. 3 | Cgy. 2 | Sean O'Donnell | 1:36 | Ana. |
| Apr. 30/06 | Dal. | CQF | Col. 3 | Dal. 2 | Andrew Brunette | 13:55 | Col. |
| May 2/06 | Mtl. | CQF | Car. 2 | Mtl. 1 | Cory Stillman | 1:19 | Car. |
| May 5/06 | Ott. | CSF | Buf. 7 | Ott. 6 | Chris Drury | 0:18 | Buf. |
| May 8/06 | Car. | CSF | Car. 3 | N.J. 2 | Niclas Wallin | 3:09 | Car. |
| May 9/06 | Col. | CSF | Ana. 4 | Col. 3 | Joffrey Lupul | 16:30 | Ana. |
| May 10/06 | Buf. | CSF | Buf. 3 | Ott. 2 | J.P. Dumont | 5:05 | Buf. |
| May 10/06 | Edm. | CSF | Edm. 3 | S.J. 2 | Shawn Horcoff | 42:24 | Edm. |
| May 13/06 | Ott. | CSF | Buf. 3 | Ott. 2 | Jason Pominville | 2:26 | Buf. |
| May 28/06 | Car. | CF | Car. 4 | Buf. 3 | Cory Stillman | 8:46 | Car. |
| May 30/06 | Buf. | CF | Buf. 2 | Car. 1 | Daniel Briere | 4:22 | Car. |
| June 14/06 | Car. | F | Edm. 4 | Car. 3 | Fernando Pisani | 3:31 | Car. |
| Apr. 11/07 | Nsh. | CQF | S.J. 5 | Nsh. 4 | Patrick Rissmiller | 28:14 | S.J. |
| Apr. 11/07 | Van. | CQF | Van. 5 | Dal. 4 | Henrik Sedin | 78:06 | Van. |
| Apr. 15/07 | Dal. | CQF | Van. 2 | Dal. 1 | Taylor Pyatt | 7:47 | Van. |
| Apr. 18/07 | T.B. | CQF | N.J. 4 | T.B. 3 | Scott Gomez | 12:54 | N.J. |
| Apr. 19/07 | Van. | CQF | Dal. 1 | Van. 0 | Brenden Morrow | 6:22 | Van. |
| Apr. 22/07 | Cgy. | CQF | Det. 2 | Cgy. 1 | Johan Franzen | 24:23 | Det. |
| Apr. 27/07 | Ana. | CSF | Van. 2 | Ana. 1 | Jeff Cowan | 27:49 | Ana. |
| Apr. 28/07 | N.J. | CSF | N.J. 3 | Ott. 2 | Jamie Langenbrunner | 21:55 | Ott. |
| Apr. 29/07 | NYR | CSF | NYR 2 | Buf. 1 | Michal Rozsival | 36:43 | Buf. |
| May 1/07 | Van. | CSF | Ana. 3 | Van. 2 | Travis Moen | 2:07 | Ana. |
| May 2/07 | S.J. | CSF | Det. 3 | S.J. 2 | Mathieu Schnieder | 16:04 | Det. |
| May 3/07 | Ana. | CSF | Ana. 2 | Van. 1 | Scott Niedermayer | 24:30 | Ana. |
| May 4/07 | Buf. | CSF | Buf. 2 | NYR 1 | Maxim Afinogenov | 4:39 | Buf. |
| May 12/07 | Buf. | CF | Ott. 4 | Buf. 3 | Joe Corvo | 24:58 | Ott. |
| May 13/07 | Det. | CF | Ana. 4 | Det. 3 | Scott Niedermayer | 14:17 | Ana. |
| May 19/07 | Buf. | CF | Ott. 3 | Buf. 2 | Daniel Alfredsson | 9:32 | Ott. |
| May 20/07 | Det. | CF | Ana. 2 | Det. 1 | Teemu Selanne | 11:57 | Ana. |
| Apr. 9/08 | Min. | CQF | Col. 3 | Min. 2 | Joe Sakic | 11:11 | Col. |
| Apr. 11/08 | Min. | CQF | Min. 3 | Col. 2 | Keith Carney | 1:14 | Col. |
| Apr. 12/08 | Mtl. | CQF | Mtl. 3 | Bos. 2 | Alex Kovalev | 2:30 | Mtl. |
| Apr. 13/08 | Mtl. | CQF | Bos. 2 | Mtl.1 | Marc Savard | 9:25 | Mtl. |
| Apr. 13/08 | NYR | CQF | N.J. 4 | NYR 3 | John Madden | 6:01 | NYR |
| Apr. 14/08 | Col. | CQF | Min. 3 | Col. 2 | Pierre-Marc Bouchard | 11:58 | Col. |
| Apr. 17/08 | Phi. | CQF | Phi. 4 | Wsh. 3 | Mike Knuble | 26:40 | Phi. |
| Apr. 18/08 | Det. | CQF | Det. 2 | Nsh. 1 | Johan Franzen | 1:48 | Det. |
| Apr. 22/08 | Wsh. | CQF | Phi. 3 | Wsh. 2 | Joffrey Lupul | 6:06 | Phi. |
| Apr. 24/08 | Mtl. | CSF | Mtl. 4 | Phi. 3 | Tom Kostopoulos | 0:48 | Phi. |
| Apr. 25/08 | S.J. | CSF | Dal. 3 | S.J. 2 | Brenden Morrow | 4:39 | Dal. |
| Apr. 29/08 | Dal. | CSF | Dal. 2 | S.J. 1 | Mattias Norstrom | 4:37 | Dal. |
| May 2/08 | S.J. | CSF | S.J. 3 | Dal. 2 | Joe Pavelski | 1:05 | Dal. |
| May 4/08 | Pit. | CSF | Pit. 3 | NYR 2 | Marian Hossa | 7:10 | Pit. |
| May 4/08 | Dal. | CSF | Dal. 2 | S.J. 1 | Brenden Morrow | 69:03 | Dal. |
| June 2/08 | Det. | F | Pit. 3 | Det. 2 | Petr Sykora | 49:57 | Det. |
| Apr. 16/09 | Chi. | CQF | Chi. 3 | Cgy. 2 | Martin Havlat | 0:12 | Chi. |
| Apr. 17/09 | Pit. | CQF | Pit. 3 | Phi. 2 | Bill Guerin | 18:29 | Pit. |
| Apr. 17/09 | N.J. | CQF | Car. 2 | N.J. 1 | Tim Gleason | 2:40 | Car. |
| Apr. 19/09 | Car. | CQF | N.J. 3 | Car. 2 | Travis Zajac | 4:58 | Car. |
| Apr. 21/09 | St.L. | CQF | Van. 3 | St.L. 2 | Alex Burrows | 19:41 | Van. |
| Apr. 25/09 | S.J. | CQF | S.J. 3 | Ana. 2 | Patrick Marleau | 6:02 | Ana. |
| May 3/09 | Det. | CSF | Ana. 4 | Det. 3 | Todd Marchant | 41:15 | Det. |
| May 6/09 | Pit. | CSF | Pit. 3 | Wsh. 2 | Kris Letang | 11:23 | Pit. |
| May 6/09 | Car. | CSF | Car. 3 | Bos. 2 | Jussi Jokinen | 2:48 | Car. |
| May 7/09 | Chi. | CSF | Chi. 2 | Van. 1 | Andrew Ladd | 2:52 | Chi. |
| May 9/09 | Wsh. | CSF | Pit. 4 | Wsh. 3 | Evgeni Malkin | 3:28 | Pit. |
| May 11/09 | Pit. | CSF | Wsh. 5 | Pit. 4 | David Steckel | 6:22 | Pit. |
| May 14/09 | Bos. | CSF | Car. 3 | Bos. 2 | Scott Walker | 18:46 | Car. |
| May 19/09 | Det. | CF | Det. 3 | Chi. 2 | Mikael Samuelsson | 5:14 | Det. |
| May 22/09 | Chi. | CF | Chi. 4 | Det. 3 | Patrick Sharp | 1:52 | Det. |
| May 27/09 | Det. | CF | Det. 2 | Chi. 1 | Darren Helm | 3:58 | Det. |

## Ten Longest Overtime Games

| Date | City | Series | Score | | Scorer | Overtime | Series Winner |
|---|---|---|---|---|---|---|---|
| Mar. 24/36 | Mtl. | SF | Det. 1 | Mtl. M. 0 | Mud Bruneteau | 116:30 | Det. |
| Apr. 3/33 | Tor. | SF | Tor. 1 | Bos. 0 | Ken Doraty | 104:46 | Tor. |
| May 4/00 | Pit. | CSF | Phi. 2 | Pit. 1 | Keith Primeau | 92:01 | Phi. |
| Apr. 24/03 | Dal. | CSF | Ana. 4 | Dal. 3 | Petr Sykora | 80:48 | Ana. |
| Apr. 24/96 | Wsh. | CQF | Pit. 3 | Wsh. 2 | Petr Nedved | 79:15 | Pit. |
| Apr. 11/07 | Van. | CQF | Van. 5 | Dal. 4 | Henrik Sedin | 78:06 | Van. |
| Mar. 23/43 | Det. | SF | Tor. 3 | Det. 2 | Jack McLean | 70:18 | Det. |
| May 4/08 | Dal. | CSF | Dal. 2 | S.J. 1 | Brenden Morrow | 69:03 | Dal. |
| Mar. 28/30 | Mtl. | SF | Mtl. 2 | NYR 1 | Gus Rivers | 68:52 | Mtl. |
| Apr. 18/87 | Wsh. | DSF | NYI 3 | Wsh. 2 | Pat LaFontaine | 68:47 | NYI |

# Overtime Record of Current Teams

(Listed by number of OT games played)

| | Overall | | | | Home | | | | | Road | | | | |
|---|---|---|---|---|---|---|---|---|---|---|---|---|---|---|
| Team | GP | W | L | T | GP | W | L | T | Last OT Game | GP | W | L | T | Last OT Game |
| Montreal | 131 | 73 | 56 | 2 | 63 | 39 | 23 | 1 | Apr. 24/08 | 68 | 34 | 33 | 1 | Apr. 13/08 |
| Toronto | 106 | 54 | 51 | 1 | 68 | 36 | 31 | 1 | May 4/04 | 38 | 18 | 20 | 0 | Apr. 18/04 |
| Boston | 105 | 41 | 61 | 3 | 48 | 22 | 25 | 1 | May 14/09 | 57 | 19 | 36 | 2 | May 6/09 |
| Detroit | 88 | 39 | 49 | 0 | 53 | 20 | 33 | 0 | May 27/09 | 35 | 19 | 16 | 0 | May 22/09 |
| Chicago | 67 | 33 | 32 | 2 | 33 | 19 | 13 | 1 | May 22/09 | 34 | 14 | 19 | 1 | May 27/09 |
| NY Rangers | 67 | 31 | 36 | 0 | 29 | 13 | 16 | 0 | Apr. 13/08 | 38 | 18 | 20 | 0 | May 4/08 |
| Dallas[1] | 64 | 28 | 36 | 0 | 32 | 13 | 19 | 0 | May 4/08 | 32 | 15 | 17 | 0 | May 2/08 |
| Philadelphia | 63 | 30 | 33 | 0 | 27 | 14 | 13 | 0 | Apr. 17/08 | 36 | 16 | 20 | 0 | Apr. 17/09 |
| Colorado[2] | 56 | 32 | 24 | 0 | 22 | 10 | 12 | 0 | Apr. 14/08 | 34 | 22 | 12 | 0 | Apr. 11/08 |
| Buffalo | 56 | 31 | 25 | 0 | 32 | 20 | 12 | 0 | May 19/07 | 24 | 11 | 13 | 0 | Apr. 29/07 |
| St. Louis | 51 | 27 | 24 | 0 | 27 | 20 | 7 | 0 | Apr. 21/09 | 24 | 7 | 17 | 0 | Apr. 8/04 |
| Vancouver | 43 | 21 | 22 | 0 | 18 | 7 | 11 | 0 | May 1/07 | 25 | 14 | 11 | 0 | May 7/09 |
| Edmonton | 42 | 24 | 18 | 0 | 23 | 13 | 10 | 0 | May 10/06 | 19 | 11 | 8 | 0 | Jun. 14/06 |
| Calgary[3] | 41 | 17 | 24 | 0 | 19 | 6 | 13 | 0 | Apr. 22/07 | 22 | 11 | 11 | 0 | Apr. 16/09 |
| NY Islanders | 40 | 29 | 11 | 0 | 18 | 14 | 4 | 0 | Apr. 14/03 | 22 | 15 | 7 | 0 | Apr. 16/04 |
| New Jersey[4] | 39 | 14 | 25 | 0 | 16 | 6 | 10 | 0 | Apr. 17/09 | 23 | 8 | 15 | 0 | Apr. 19/09 |
| Washington | 36 | 15 | 21 | 0 | 14 | 5 | 9 | 0 | May 9/09 | 22 | 10 | 12 | 0 | May 11/09 |
| Los Angeles | 35 | 17 | 18 | 0 | 19 | 11 | 8 | 0 | May 6/01 | 16 | 6 | 10 | 0 | Apr. 25/02 |
| Carolina[5] | 34 | 21 | 13 | 0 | 20 | 12 | 8 | 0 | May 6/09 | 14 | 9 | 5 | 0 | May 14/09 |
| Pittsburgh | 34 | 20 | 14 | 0 | 22 | 13 | 9 | 0 | May 11/09 | 12 | 7 | 5 | 0 | May 9/09 |
| Ottawa | 22 | 11 | 11 | 0 | 8 | 4 | 4 | 0 | May 13/06 | 14 | 7 | 7 | 0 | May 19/07 |
| Anaheim | 21 | 15 | 6 | 0 | 7 | 5 | 2 | 0 | May 3/07 | 14 | 10 | 4 | 0 | May 3/09 |
| San Jose | 21 | 7 | 14 | 0 | 12 | 4 | 8 | 0 | Apr. 25/09 | 9 | 3 | 6 | 0 | May 4/08 |
| Tampa Bay | 12 | 7 | 5 | 0 | 4 | 2 | 2 | 0 | Apr. 18/07 | 8 | 5 | 3 | 0 | Jun. 5/04 |
| Phoenix[6] | 12 | 5 | 7 | 0 | 8 | 3 | 5 | 0 | May 4/99 | 4 | 2 | 2 | 0 | Apr. 27/93 |
| Minnesota | 8 | 4 | 4 | 0 | 5 | 2 | 3 | 0 | Apr. 11/08 | 3 | 2 | 1 | 0 | Apr. 14/08 |
| Florida | 5 | 2 | 3 | 0 | 3 | 1 | 2 | 0 | Apr. 25/97 | 2 | 1 | 1 | 0 | Apr. 22/97 |
| Nashville | 2 | 0 | 2 | 0 | 1 | 0 | 1 | 0 | Apr. 11/07 | 1 | 0 | 1 | 0 | Apr. 18/08 |

[1] Totals include those of Minnesota North Stars 1967-93.
[2] Totals include those of Quebec 1979-95.
[3] Totals include those of Atlanta Flames 1972-80.
[4] Totals include those of Kansas City and Colorado Rockies 1974-82.
[5] Totals include those of Hartford 1979-97.
[6] Totals include those of Winnipeg 1979-96.

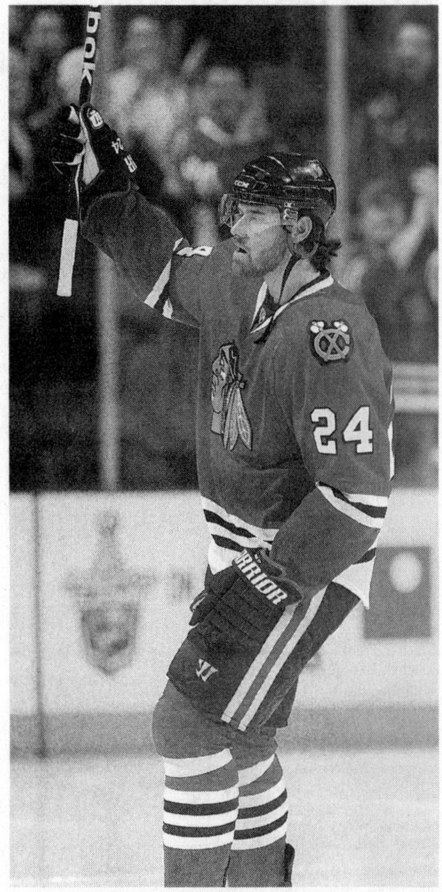


*Martin Havlat ended the shortest overtime game of the 2009 playoffs (and the third shortest of all time) when he scored after just 12 seconds in a 3-2 win over Calgary in Chicago's first playoff game since 2002.*

# Penalty Shots in Stanley Cup Playoff Games

| Date | Player, Team | Goaltender, Team | Scored | Final Score | Series |
|---|---|---|---|---|---|
| Mar. 25/37 | Lionel Conacher, Mtl. Maroons | Tiny Thompson, Boston | No | Mtl. M. 0 at Bos. 4 | QF |
| Apr. 15/37 | Alex Shibicky, NY Rangers | Earl Robertson, Detroit | No | NYR 0 at Det. 3 | F |
| Mar. 24/38 | Mush March, Chicago | Wilf Cude, Montreal | No | Mtl. 0 at Chi. 4 | QF |
| Mar. 29/38 | Lorne Carr, NY Americans | Mike Karakas, Chicago | No | Chi. 1 at NYA 3 | SF |
| Apr. 10/38 | Art Wiebe, Chicago | Turk Broda, Toronto | No | Tor. 1 at Chi. 2 | F |
| Mar. 24/42 | Charlie Sands, Montreal | Johnny Mowers, Detroit | No | Det. 0 at Mtl. 5 | QF |
| Apr. 13/44 | Virgil Johnson, Chicago | Bill Durnan, Montreal | No | Chi. 4 at Mtl. 5* | F |
| Apr. 9/68 | Wayne Connelly, Minnesota | Terry Sawchuk, Los Angeles | Yes | L.A. 5 at Min. 7 | QF |
| Apr. 27/68 | Jim Roberts, St. Louis | Cesare Maniago, Minnesota | No | St.L. 4 at Min. 3 | SF |
| May 16/71 | Frank Mahovlich, Montreal | Tony Esposito, Chicago | No | Chi. 3 at Mtl. 4 | F |
| May 7/75 | Bill Barber, Philadelphia | Glenn Resch, NY Islanders | No | Phi. 3 at NYI 4* | SF |
| Apr. 20/79 | Mike Walton, Chicago | Glenn Resch, NY Islanders | No | NYI 4 at Chi. 0 | QF |
| Apr. 9/81 | Peter McNab, Boston | Don Beaupre, Minnesota | No | Min. 5 at Bos. 4* | PR |
| Apr. 17/81 | Anders Hedberg, NY Rangers | Mike Liut, St. Louis | Yes | NYR 6 at St.L. 4 | QF |
| Apr. 9/83 | Denis Potvin, NY Islanders | Pat Riggin, Washington | No | NYI 6 at Wsh. 2 | DSF |
| Apr. 28/84 | Wayne Gretzky, Edmonton | Don Beaupre, Minnesota | Yes | Edm. 8 at Min. 5 | CF |
| May 1/84 | Mats Naslund, Montreal | Billy Smith, NY Islanders | No | Mtl. 1 at NYI 3 | CF |
| Apr. 14/85 | Bob Carpenter, Washington | Billy Smith, NY Islanders | No | Wsh. 4 at NYI. 6 | DF |
| May 28/85 | Ron Sutter, Philadelphia | Grant Fuhr, Edmonton | No | Phi. 3 at Edm. 5 | F |
| May 30/85 | Dave Poulin, Philadelphia | Grant Fuhr, Edmonton | No | Phi. 3 at Edm. 8 | F |
| Apr. 9/88 | John Tucker, Buffalo | Andy Moog, Boston | Yes | Bos. 2 at Buf. 6 | DSF |
| Apr. 9/88 | Petr Klima, Detroit | Allan Bester, Toronto | Yes | Det. 6 at Tor. 3 | DSF |
| Apr. 8/89 | Neal Broten, Minnesota | Greg Millen, St. Louis | Yes | St.L. 5 at Min. 3 | DSF |
| Apr. 4/90 | Al MacInnis, Calgary | Kelly Hrudey, Los Angeles | Yes | L.A. 5 at Cgy. 3 | DSF |
| Apr. 5/90 | Randy Wood, NY Islanders | Mike Richter, NY Rangers | No | NYI 1 at NYR 2 | DSF |
| May 3/90 | Kelly Miller, Washington | Andy Moog, Boston | No | Wsh. 3 at Bos. 5 | CF |
| May 18/90 | Petr Klima, Edmonton | Reggie Lemelin, Boston | No | Edm. 7 at Bos. 2 | F |
| Apr. 6/91 | Basil McRae, Minnesota | Ed Belfour, Chicago | Yes | Min. 2 at Chi. 5 | DSF |
| Apr. 10/91 | Steve Duchesne, Los Angeles | Kirk McLean, Vancouver | Yes | L.A. 6 at Van. 1 | DSF |
| May 11/92 | Jaromir Jagr, Pittsburgh | John Vanbiesbrouck, NYR | Yes | Pit. 3 at NYR 2 | DF |
| May 13/92 | Shawn McEachern, Pittsburgh | John Vanbiesbrouck, NYR | No | NYR 1 at Pit. 5 | DF |
| June 7/94 | Pavel Bure, Vancouver | Mike Richter, NYR | No | NYR 4 at Van. 2 | F |
| May 9/95 | Patrick Poulin, Chicago | Felix Potvin, Toronto | No | Tor. 3 at Chi. 0 | CQF |
| May 10/95 | Michal Pivonka, Washington | Tom Barrasso, Pittsburgh | No | Pit. 2 at Wsh. 6 | CQF |
| Apr. 24/96 | Joe Juneau, Washington | Ken Wregget, Pittsburgh | No | Pit. 3 at Wsh. 2** | CQF |
| May 11/97 | Eric Lindros, Philadelphia | Steve Shields, Buffalo | Yes | Phi. 6 at Buf. 3 | CSF |
| Apr. 23/98 | Aleksey Morozov, Pittsburgh | Andy Moog, Montreal | No | Mtl. 3 at Pit. 2** | CQF |
| Apr. 22/99 | Mats Sundin, Toronto | John Vanbiesbrouck, Phi. | No | Phi. 3 at Tor. 0 | CQF |
| May 29/99 | Mats Sundin, Toronto | Dominik Hasek, Buffalo | Yes | Tor. 2 at Buf. 5 | CF |
| Apr. 16/00 | Eric Desjardins, Philadelphia | Dominik Hasek, Buffalo | No | Phi. 2 at Buf. 0 | CQF |
| Apr. 11/01 | Mark Recchi, Philadelphia | Dominik Hasek, Buffalo | No | Buf. 2 at Phi. 1 | CQF |
| May 2/01 | Martin Straka, Pittsburgh | Dominik Hasek, Buffalo | No | Buf. 5 at Pit. 2 | CSF |
| May 12/01 | Joe Sakic, Colorado | Roman Turek, St. Louis | Yes | St.L. 1 at Col. 4 | CF |
| Apr. 21/02 | Todd Bertuzzi, Vancouver | Dominik Hasek, Detroit | No | Det. 3 at Van. 1 | CQF |
| Apr. 24/02 | Shawn Bates, NY Islanders | Curtis Joseph, Toronto | Yes | Tor. 3 at NYI 4 | CQF |
| Apr. 26/02 | Mike Johnson, Phoenix | Evgeni Nabokov, San Jose | Yes | Phx. 1 at S.J. 4 | CQF |
| Apr. 15/03 | Dainius Zubrus, Washington | Nikolai Khabibulin, Tampa Bay | No | T.B. 4 at Wsh. 3 | CQF |
| Apr. 21/03 | Robert Reichel, Toronto | Roman Cechmanek, Philadelphia | No | Phi. 1 at Tor. 2 | CQF |
| Apr. 7/04 | Steve Sullivan, Nashville | Manny Legace, Detroit | No | Nsh. 1 at Det. 3 | CQF |
| Apr. 28/06 | Derek Roy, Buffalo | Robert Esche, Philadelphia | No | Buf. 4 at Phi. 5 | CQF |
| June 5/06 | Chris Pronger, Edmonton*** | Cam Ward, Carolina | Yes | Edm. 4 at Car. 5 | F |
| Apr. 21/07 | Daniel Cleary, Detroit | Miikka Kiprusoff, Calgary | Yes | Cgy. 1 at Det. 5 | CQF |
| June 5/07 | Antoine Vermette, Ottawa | J.S. Giguere, Anaheim | No | Ott. 2 at Ana. 6 | F |
| Apr. 9/08 | Ryan Smyth, Colorado | Niklas Backstrom, Minnesota | No | Col. 3 at Min. 2 | CQF |
| Apr. 15/08 | Mike Richards, Philadelphia | Cristobal Huet, Washington | Yes | Wsh. 3 at Phi. 6 | CQF |
| Apr. 18/08 | John Madden, New Jersey | Henrik Lundqvist, NY Rangers | No | NYR 5 at N.J. 3 | CQF |
| Apr. 24/08 | Andrei Kostitsyn, Montreal | Martin Biron, Philadelphia | No | Phi. 3 at Mtl. 4 | CSF |
| Apr. 29/08 | Niklas Hagman, Dallas | Evgeni Nabokov, San Jose | No | S.J. 1 at Dal. 2 | CSF |
| May 1/08 | Evgeni Malkin, Pittsburgh | Henrik Lundqvist, NY Rangers | No | Pit. 0 at NYR 3 | CSF |

* Game was decided in overtime, but shot taken during regulation time.
** Shot taken in overtime.
*** First penalty shot scored in Stanley Cup Final history

*Anaheim's Todd Marchant ended the longest game of the 2009 playoffs. He scored at 1:15 of the third overtime period to give the Ducks a 4-3 win over Detroit in game two of their second-round series.*

# All-Time Playoff NHL Coaching Register

## Playoffs, 1917-2009

| Coach | Team | Games Coached | Wins | Losses | T | Years | Cup Wins | Career |
|---|---|---|---|---|---|---|---|---|
| Abel, Sid | Chicago | 7 | 3 | 4 | | 1 | | |
| | Detroit | 69 | 29 | 40 | | 8 | | |
| | Totals | 76 | 32 | 44 | | 9 | | 1952-76 |
| Adams, Jack | Detroit | 105 | 52 | 52 | 1 | 15 | 3 | 1927-47 |
| Allen, Keith | Philadelphia | 11 | 3 | 8 | | 2 | | 1967-69 |
| Arbour, Al | St. Louis | 11 | 4 | 7 | | 1 | | |
| | NY Islanders | 198 | 119 | 79 | | 15 | 4 | |
| | Totals | 209 | 123 | 86 | | 16 | 4 | 1970-08 |
| Babcock, Mike | Anaheim | 21 | 15 | 6 | | 1 | | |
| | Detroit | 69 | 43 | 26 | | 4 | 1 | |
| | Totals | 90 | 58 | 32 | | 5 | 1 | 2002-09 |
| Barber, Bill | Philadelphia | 11 | 3 | 8 | | 2 | | 2000-02 |
| Berenson, Red | St. Louis | 14 | 5 | 9 | | 2 | | 1979-82 |
| Bergeron, Michel | Quebec | 68 | 31 | 37 | | 7 | | 1980-90 |
| Berry, Bob | Los Angeles | 10 | 2 | 8 | | 3 | | |
| | Montreal | 8 | 2 | 6 | | 2 | | |
| | St. Louis | 15 | 7 | 8 | | 2 | | |
| | Totals | 33 | 11 | 22 | | 7 | | 1978-94 |
| Beverley, Nick | Toronto | 6 | 2 | 4 | | 1 | | 1995-96 |
| Blackburn, Don | Hartford | 3 | 0 | 3 | | 1 | | 1979-81 |
| Blair, Wren | Minnesota | 14 | 7 | 7 | | 1 | | 1967-70 |
| Blake, Toe | Montreal | 119 | 82 | 37 | | 13 | 8 | 1955-68 |
| Boileau, Marc | Pittsburgh | 9 | 5 | 4 | | 1 | | 1973-76 |
| Boivin, Leo | St. Louis | 3 | 1 | 2 | | 1 | | 1975-78 |
| Boucher, Frank | NY Rangers | 27 | 13 | 14 | | 4 | 1 | 1939-54 |
| Boucher, Georges | Mtl. Maroons | 2 | 0 | 2 | 0 | 1 | | 1930-50 |
| Boudreau, Bruce | Washington | 21 | 10 | 11 | | 2 | | 2007-09 |
| Bowman, Scotty | St. Louis | 52 | 26 | 26 | | 4 | | |
| | Montreal | 98 | 70 | 28 | | 8 | 5 | |
| | Buffalo | 36 | 18 | 18 | | 5 | | |
| | Pittsburgh | 33 | 23 | 10 | | 2 | 1 | |
| | Detroit | 134 | 86 | 48 | | 9 | 3 | |
| | Totals | 353 | 223 | 130 | | 28 | 9 | 1967-02 |
| Bowness, Rick | Boston | 15 | 8 | 7 | | 1 | | 1988-05 |
| Brooks, Herb | NY Rangers | 24 | 12 | 12 | | 3 | | |
| | New Jersey | 5 | 1 | 4 | | 1 | | |
| | Pittsburgh | 11 | 6 | 5 | | 1 | | |
| | Totals | 40 | 19 | 21 | | 5 | | 1981-00 |
| Brophy, John | Toronto | 19 | 9 | 10 | | 2 | | 1986-89 |
| Burns, Charlie | Minnesota | 6 | 2 | 4 | | 1 | | 1969-75 |
| Burns, Pat | Montreal | 56 | 30 | 26 | | 4 | | |
| | Toronto | 46 | 23 | 23 | | 3 | | |
| | Boston | 18 | 8 | 10 | | 2 | | |
| | New Jersey | 29 | 17 | 12 | | 2 | 1 | |
| | Totals | 149 | 78 | 71 | | 11 | 1 | 1988-05 |
| Bylsma, Dan | Pittsburgh | 24 | 16 | 8 | | 1 | 1 | 2008-09 |
| Campbell, Colin | NY Rangers | 36 | 18 | 18 | | 3 | | 1994-98 |
| Carbonneau, Guy | Montreal | 12 | 5 | 7 | | 1 | | 2006-09 |
| Carlyle, Randy | Anaheim | 56 | 34 | 22 | | 4 | 1 | 2005-09 |
| Carpenter, Doug | Toronto | 5 | 1 | 4 | | 1 | | 1984-91 |
| Carroll, Dick | Toronto | 2 | 1 | 1 | 0 | 1 | 1 | 1917-19 |
| Carroll, Frank | Toronto | 2 | 0 | 2 | 0 | 1 | | 1920-21 |
| Cassidy, Bruce | Washington | 6 | 2 | 4 | | 1 | | 2002-04 |
| Cheevers, Gerry | Boston | 34 | 15 | 19 | | 4 | | 1980-85 |
| Cherry, Don | Boston | 55 | 31 | 24 | | 5 | | 1974-80 |
| Clancy, King | Toronto | 14 | 2 | 12 | | 3 | | 1937-56 |
| Clapper, Dit | Boston | 25 | 8 | 17 | | 4 | | 1945-49 |
| Cleghorn, Odie | Pittsburgh | 4 | 1 | 2 | 1 | 2 | | 1925-29 |
| Cleghorn, Sprague | Mtl. Maroons | 4 | 1 | 1 | 2 | 1 | | 1931-32 |
| Constantine, Kevin | San Jose | 25 | 11 | 14 | | 2 | | |
| | Pittsburgh | 19 | 8 | 11 | | 2 | | |
| | New Jersey | 6 | 2 | 4 | | 1 | | |
| | Totals | 50 | 21 | 29 | | 5 | | 1993-02 |
| Crawford, Marc | Quebec | 6 | 2 | 4 | | 1 | | |
| | Colorado | 46 | 29 | 17 | | 3 | 1 | |
| | Vancouver | 27 | 12 | 15 | | 3 | | |
| | Totals | 79 | 43 | 36 | | 7 | 1 | 1994-08 |
| Creighton, Fred | Atlanta | 9 | 2 | 7 | | 4 | | 1974-80 |
| Crisp, Terry | Calgary | 37 | 22 | 15 | | 3 | 1 | |
| | Tampa Bay | 6 | 2 | 4 | | 1 | | |
| | Totals | 43 | 24 | 19 | | 4 | 1 | 1987-98 |
| Crozier, Joe | Buffalo | 6 | 2 | 4 | | 1 | | 1971-81 |
| Cunniff, John | New Jersey | 6 | 2 | 4 | | 1 | | 1982-91 |
| Curry, Alex | Ottawa | 2 | 0 | 1 | 1 | 1 | | 1925-26 |
| Dandurand, Leo | Montreal | 8 | 5 | 3 | 0 | 4 | 1 | 1921-35 |
| Day, Hap | Toronto | 80 | 49 | 31 | | 9 | 5 | 1940-50 |
| Demers, Jacques | St. Louis | 33 | 16 | 17 | | 3 | | |
| | Detroit | 38 | 20 | 18 | | 3 | | |
| | Montreal | 27 | 19 | 8 | | 2 | 1 | |
| | Totals | 98 | 55 | 43 | | 8 | 1 | 1979-99 |
| Denneny, Cy | Boston | 5 | 5 | 0 | 0 | 1 | 1 | 1928-33 |
| Dudley, Rick | Buffalo | 12 | 4 | 8 | | 2 | | 1989-04 |
| Dugal, Jules | Montreal | 3 | 1 | 2 | | 1 | | 1938-39 |
| Duncan, Art | Toronto | 2 | 0 | 1 | 1 | 1 | | 1926-32 |
| Dutton, Red | NY Americans | 11 | 4 | 7 | | 3 | | 1936-40 |
| Esposito, Phil | NY Rangers | 10 | 2 | 8 | | 2 | | 1986-89 |
| Evans, Jack | Hartford | 16 | 8 | 8 | | 2 | | 1975-88 |
| Ferguson, John | Winnipeg | 3 | 0 | 3 | | 1 | | 1975-86 |
| Francis, Bob | Phoenix | 10 | 2 | 8 | | 2 | | 1999-04 |
| Francis, Emile | NY Rangers | 75 | 34 | 41 | | 9 | | |
| | St. Louis | 14 | 5 | 9 | | 2 | | |
| | Totals | 89 | 39 | 50 | | 11 | | 1965-83 |
| Ftorek, Robbie | Los Angeles | 16 | 5 | 11 | | 2 | | |
| | New Jersey | 7 | 3 | 4 | | 1 | | |
| | Boston | 6 | 2 | 4 | | 1 | | |
| | Totals | 29 | 10 | 19 | | 4 | | 1987-03 |
| Gainey, Bob | Minnesota | 30 | 17 | 13 | | 2 | | |
| | Dallas | 14 | 6 | 8 | | 2 | | |
| | Montreal | 10 | 2 | 8 | | 2 | | |
| | Totals | 54 | 25 | 29 | | 6 | | 1990-09 |
| Geoffrion, Bernie | Atlanta | 4 | 0 | 4 | | 1 | | 1968-80 |
| Gerard, Eddie | Mtl. Maroons | 21 | 8 | 8 | 5 | 5 | 1 | 1917-35 |
| Gill, David | Ottawa | 8 | 3 | 2 | 3 | 2 | 1 | 1926-29 |
| Glover, Fred | Oakland | 11 | 3 | 8 | | 2 | | 1968-74 |
| Gordon, Jackie | Minnesota | 25 | 11 | 14 | | 3 | | 1970-75 |
| Goring, Butch | Boston | 3 | 0 | 3 | | 1 | | 1985-01 |
| Gorman, Tommy | NY Americans | 2 | 0 | 1 | 1 | 1 | | |
| | Chicago | 8 | 6 | 1 | 1 | 1 | 1 | |
| | Mtl. Maroons | 15 | 7 | 6 | 2 | 3 | 1 | |
| | Totals | 25 | 13 | 8 | 4 | 5 | 2 | 1925-38 |
| Gottselig, Johnny | Chicago | 4 | 0 | 4 | | 1 | | 1944-48 |
| Granato, Tony | Colorado | 18 | 9 | 9 | | 2 | | 2002-09 |
| Green, Ted | Edmonton | 16 | 8 | 8 | | 1 | | 1991-94 |
| Green, Pete | Ottawa | 8 | 3 | 4 | 1 | 4 | 3 | 1919-25 |
| Guidolin, Bep | Boston | 21 | 11 | 10 | | 2 | | 1972-76 |
| Harris, Ted | Minnesota | 2 | 0 | 2 | | 1 | | 1975-78 |
| Hart, Cecil | Montreal | 37 | 16 | 17 | 4 | 8 | 2 | 1926-39 |
| Hartley, Bob | Colorado | 80 | 49 | 31 | | 4 | 1 | |
| | Atlanta | 4 | 0 | 4 | | 1 | | |
| | Totals | 84 | 49 | 35 | | 5 | 1 | 1998-08 |
| Hartsburg, Craig | Chicago | 16 | 8 | 8 | | 2 | | |
| | Anaheim | 4 | 0 | 4 | | 1 | | |
| | Totals | 20 | 8 | 12 | | 3 | | 1995-09 |
| Harvey, Doug | NY Rangers | 6 | 2 | 4 | | 1 | | 1961-62 |
| Hay, Don | Phoenix | 7 | 3 | 4 | | 1 | | 1996-01 |
| Helmer, Rosie | NY Americans | 5 | 2 | 3 | 0 | 1 | | 1935-36 |
| Henning, Lorne | Minnesota | 5 | 2 | 3 | | 1 | | 1985-01 |
| Hitchcock, Ken | Dallas | 80 | 47 | 33 | | 5 | 1 | |
| | Philadelphia | 37 | 19 | 18 | | 3 | | |
| | Columbus | 4 | 0 | 4 | | 1 | | |
| | Totals | 121 | 66 | 55 | | 9 | 1 | 1995-09 |
| Hlinka, Ivan | Pittsburgh | 18 | 9 | 9 | | 1 | | 2000-02 |
| Holmgren, Paul | Philadelphia | 19 | 10 | 9 | | 1 | | 1988-96 |
| Imlach, Punch | Toronto | 92 | 44 | 48 | | 11 | 4 | 1958-80 |
| Inglis, Bill | Buffalo | 3 | 1 | 2 | | 1 | | 1978-79 |
| Irvin, Dick | Chicago | 9 | 5 | 3 | 1 | 1 | | |
| | Toronto | 66 | 33 | 32 | 1 | 9 | 1 | |
| | Montreal | 115 | 62 | 53 | | 14 | 3 | |
| | Totals | 190 | 100 | 88 | 2 | 24 | 4 | 1928-56 |
| Ivan, Tommy | Detroit | 67 | 36 | 31 | | 7 | 3 | 1947-58 |
| Johnson, Tom | Boston | 22 | 15 | 7 | | 2 | 1 | 1970-73 |
| Johnson, Bob | Calgary | 52 | 25 | 27 | | 5 | | |
| | Pittsburgh | 24 | 16 | 8 | | 1 | 1 | |
| | Totals | 76 | 41 | 35 | | 6 | 1 | 1982-91 |
| Johnston, Eddie | Chicago | 7 | 3 | 4 | | 1 | | |
| | Pittsburgh | 46 | 22 | 24 | | 5 | | |
| | Totals | 53 | 25 | 28 | | 6 | | 1979-97 |
| Julien, Claude | Montreal | 11 | 4 | 7 | | 1 | | |
| | Boston | 18 | 10 | 8 | | 2 | | |
| | Totals | 29 | 14 | 15 | | 3 | | 2002-09 |
| Kasper, Steve | Boston | 5 | 1 | 4 | | 1 | | 1995-97 |
| Keenan, Mike | Philadelphia | 57 | 32 | 25 | | 4 | | |
| | Chicago | 60 | 33 | 27 | | 4 | | |
| | NY Rangers | 23 | 16 | 7 | | 1 | 1 | |
| | St. Louis | 20 | 10 | 10 | | 2 | | |
| | Calgary | 13 | 5 | 8 | | 2 | | |
| | Totals | 173 | 96 | 77 | | 13 | 1 | 1984-09 |
| Kelly, Pat | Colorado | 2 | 0 | 2 | | 1 | | 1977-79 |
| Kelly, Red | Los Angeles | 18 | 7 | 11 | | 2 | | |
| | Pittsburgh | 14 | 6 | 8 | | 2 | | |
| | Toronto | 30 | 11 | 19 | | 4 | | |
| | Totals | 62 | 24 | 38 | | 8 | | 1967-77 |
| King, Dave | Calgary | 20 | 8 | 12 | | 3 | | 1992-03 |
| Kromm, Bobby | Detroit | 7 | 3 | 4 | | 1 | | 1977-80 |
| Lalonde, Newsy | Montreal | 11 | 5 | 4 | 2 | 4 | | |
| | Ottawa | 2 | 0 | 1 | 1 | 1 | | |
| | Totals | 13 | 5 | 5 | 3 | 5 | | 1917-35 |
| Lamoriello, Lou | New Jersey | 20 | 10 | 10 | | 2 | | 2005-07 |
| Laviolette, Peter | NY Islanders | 12 | 4 | 8 | | 2 | | |
| | Carolina | 25 | 16 | 9 | | 1 | 1 | |
| | Totals | 37 | 20 | 17 | | 3 | 1 | 2001-08 |
| Lemaire, Jacques | Montreal | 27 | 15 | 12 | | 2 | | |
| | New Jersey | 56 | 34 | 22 | | 4 | 1 | |
| | Minnesota | 29 | 11 | 18 | | 3 | | |
| | Totals | 112 | 60 | 52 | | 9 | 1 | 1983-09 |
| Lewis, Dave | Minnesota | 16 | 6 | 10 | | 2 | | 1998-07 |
| Ley, Rick | Hartford | 13 | 5 | 8 | | 2 | | |
| | Vancouver | 11 | 4 | 7 | | 1 | | |
| | Totals | 24 | 9 | 15 | | 3 | | 1989-96 |
| Long, Barry | Winnipeg | 11 | 3 | 8 | | 2 | | 1983-86 |
| Loughlin, Clem | Chicago | 4 | 1 | 2 | 1 | 2 | | 1934-37 |
| Low, Ron | Edmonton | 28 | 10 | 18 | | 3 | | 1994-02 |
| Lowe, Kevin | Edmonton | 5 | 1 | 4 | | 1 | | 1999-00 |

| Coach | Team | Games Coached | Wins | Losses | Ties | Years | Cup Wins | Career |
|---|---|---|---|---|---|---|---|---|
| **MacLean, Doug** | **Florida** | **27** | **13** | **14** | | **2** | | **1995-04** |
| **MacNeil, Al** | Montreal | 20 | 12 | 8 | | 1 | 1 | |
| | Atlanta | 4 | 1 | 3 | | 1 | | |
| | Calgary | 19 | 9 | 10 | | 2 | | |
| | **Totals** | **43** | **22** | **21** | | **4** | **1** | **1970-03** |
| **MacTavish, Craig** | **Edmonton** | **36** | **19** | **17** | | **3** | | **2000-09** |
| **Magnuson, Keith** | **Chicago** | **3** | **0** | **3** | | **1** | | **1980-82** |
| **Mahoney, Bill** | **Minnesota** | **16** | **7** | **9** | | **1** | | **1983-85** |
| **Maloney, Dan** | Toronto | 10 | 6 | 4 | | 1 | | |
| | Winnipeg | 15 | 5 | 10 | | 2 | | |
| | **Totals** | **25** | **11** | **14** | | **3** | | **1984-89** |
| **Maloney, Phil** | **Vancouver** | **7** | **1** | **6** | | **2** | | **1973-77** |
| **Martin, Jacques** | St. Louis | 16 | 7 | 9 | | 2 | | |
| | Ottawa | 69 | 31 | 38 | | 8 | | |
| | **Totals** | **85** | **38** | **47** | | **10** | | **1986-08** |
| **Maurice, Paul** | **Carolina** | **53** | **25** | **37** | | **4** | | **1995-09** |
| **McCammon, Bob** | Philadelphia | 10 | 1 | 9 | | 3 | | |
| | Vancouver | 7 | 3 | 4 | | 1 | | |
| | **Totals** | **17** | **4** | **13** | | **4** | | **1978-91** |
| **McLellan, John** | **Toronto** | **11** | **3** | **8** | | **2** | | **1969-73** |
| **McLellan, Todd** | **San Jose** | **6** | **2** | **4** | | **1** | | **2008-09** |
| **McVie, Tom** | **New Jersey** | **14** | **6** | **8** | | **2** | | **1975-92** |
| **Melrose, Barry** | **Los Angeles** | **24** | **13** | **11** | | **1** | | **1992-09** |
| **Milbury, Mike** | **Boston** | **40** | **23** | **17** | | **2** | | **1989-99** |
| **Muckler, John** | Edmonton | 40 | 25 | 15 | | 2 | 1 | |
| | Buffalo | 27 | 11 | 16 | | 4 | | |
| | **Totals** | **67** | **36** | **31** | | **6** | **1** | **1968-00** |
| **Muldoon, Pete** | **Chicago** | **2** | **0** | **1** | **1** | **1** | | **1926-27** |
| **Munro, Dunc** | **Mtl. Maroons** | **4** | **1** | **3** | **0** | **1** | | **1929-31** |
| **Murdoch, Bob** | Chicago | 5 | 1 | 4 | | 1 | | |
| | Winnipeg | 7 | 3 | 4 | | 1 | | |
| | **Totals** | **12** | **4** | **8** | | **2** | | **1987-91** |
| **Murphy, Mike** | **Los Angeles** | **5** | **1** | **4** | | **1** | | **1986-98** |
| **Murray, Terry** | Washington | 39 | 18 | 21 | | 4 | | |
| | Philadelphia | 46 | 28 | 18 | | 3 | | |
| | Florida | 4 | 0 | 4 | | 1 | | |
| | **Totals** | **89** | **46** | **43** | | **8** | | **1989-09** |
| **Murray, Andy** | Los Angeles | 24 | 10 | 14 | | 3 | | |
| | St. Louis | 4 | 0 | 4 | | 1 | | |
| | **Totals** | **28** | **10** | **18** | | **4** | | **1999-09** |
| **Murray, Bryan** | Washington | 53 | 24 | 29 | | 7 | | |
| | Detroit | 25 | 10 | 15 | | 3 | | |
| | Ottawa | 34 | 18 | 16 | | 3 | | |
| | **Totals** | **112** | **52** | **60** | | **13** | | **1981-08** |
| **Neale, Harry** | **Vancouver** | **14** | **3** | **11** | | **4** | | **1978-86** |
| **Neilson, Roger** | Toronto | 19 | 8 | 11 | | 2 | | |
| | Buffalo | 8 | 4 | 4 | | 1 | | |
| | Vancouver | 21 | 12 | 9 | | 2 | | |
| | NY Rangers | 29 | 13 | 16 | | 3 | | |
| | Philadelphia | 29 | 14 | 15 | | 3 | | |
| | **Totals** | **106** | **51** | **55** | | **11** | | **1977-02** |
| **Nolan, Ted** | Buffalo | 12 | 5 | 7 | | 1 | | |
| | NY Islanders | 5 | 1 | 4 | | 1 | | |
| | **Totals** | **17** | **6** | **11** | | **2** | | **1995-08** |
| **Nykoluk, Mike** | **Toronto** | **7** | **1** | **6** | | **2** | | **1980-84** |
| **O'Connell, Mike** | **Boston** | **5** | **1** | **4** | | **1** | | **2002-03** |
| **O'Donoghue, George** | **Toronto** | **2** | **1** | **0** | **1** | **1** | **1** | **1921-23** |
| **Oliver, Murray** | **Minnesota** | **9** | **4** | **5** | | **1** | | **1982-83** |
| **O'Reilly, Terry** | **Boston *** | **37** | **17** | **19** | **1** | **3** | | **1986-89** |

* Playoff game May 24, 1988 suspended due to power failure. Score tied.

| Coach | Team | Games Coached | Wins | Losses | Ties | Years | Cup Wins | Career |
|---|---|---|---|---|---|---|---|---|
| **Paddock, John** | **Winnipeg** | **13** | **5** | **8** | | **2** | | **1991-08** |
| **Page, Pierre** | Minnesota | 12 | 4 | 8 | | 2 | | |
| | Quebec | 6 | 2 | 4 | | 1 | | |
| | Calgary | 4 | 0 | 4 | | 1 | | |
| | **Totals** | **22** | **6** | **16** | | **4** | | **1988-98** |
| **Patrick, Lester** | **NY Rangers** | **65** | **32** | **26** | **7** | **12** | **2** | **1926-39** |
| **Patrick, Frank** | **Boston** | **6** | **2** | **4** | **0** | **2** | | **1934-36** |
| **Patrick, Craig** | NY Rangers | 17 | 7 | 10 | | 2 | | |
| | Pittsburgh | 5 | 1 | 4 | | 1 | | |
| | **Totals** | **22** | **8** | **14** | | **3** | | **1980-97** |
| **Patrick, Lynn** | NY Rangers | 12 | 7 | 5 | | 1 | | |
| | Boston * | 28 | 9 | 18 | 1 | 4 | | |
| | **Totals** | **40** | **16** | **23** | **1** | **5** | | **1948-76** |

* Playoff game March 31, 1951 suspended due to Toronto city curfew. Score tied.

| Coach | Team | Games Coached | Wins | Losses | Ties | Years | Cup Wins | Career |
|---|---|---|---|---|---|---|---|---|
| **Perron, Jean** | **Montreal** | **48** | **30** | **18** | | **3** | **1** | **1985-89** |
| **Perry, Don** | **Los Angeles** | **10** | **4** | **6** | | **1** | | **1981-84** |
| **Pilous, Rudy** | **Chicago** | **41** | **19** | **22** | | **5** | **1** | **1957-63** |
| **Plager, Barclay** | **St. Louis** | **4** | **1** | **3** | | **1** | | **1977-83** |
| **Playfair, Jim** | **Calgary** | **6** | **2** | **4** | | **1** | | **2006-07** |
| **Pleau, Larry** | **Hartford** | **10** | **2** | **8** | | **2** | | **1980-89** |
| **Polano, Nick** | **Detroit** | **7** | **1** | **6** | | **2** | | **1982-85** |
| **Powers, Eddie** | **Toronto** | **2** | **0** | **2** | **0** | **1** | | **1924-26** |
| **Primeau, Joe** | **Toronto *** | **15** | **8** | **6** | **1** | **2** | **1** | **1950-53** |

* Playoff game March 31, 1951 suspended due to Toronto city curfew. Score tied.

| Coach | Team | Games Coached | Wins | Losses | Ties | Years | Cup Wins | Career |
|---|---|---|---|---|---|---|---|---|
| **Pronovost, Marcel** | **Buffalo** | **8** | **3** | **5** | | **1** | | **1977-79** |
| **Pulford, Bob** | Los Angeles | 26 | 10 | 16 | | 4 | | |
| | Chicago | 45 | 17 | 28 | | 6 | | |
| | **Totals** | **71** | **27** | **44** | | **10** | | **1972-00** |

| Coach | Team | Games Coached | Wins | Losses | Ties | Years | Cup Wins | Career |
|---|---|---|---|---|---|---|---|---|
| **Quenneville, Joel** | St. Louis | 68 | 34 | 34 | | 7 | | |
| | Colorado | 19 | 8 | 11 | | 2 | | |
| | Chicago | 17 | 9 | 8 | | 1 | | |
| | **Totals** | **104** | **51** | **53** | | **10** | | **1996-09** |
| **Quinn, Pat** | Philadelphia | 39 | 22 | 17 | | 3 | | |
| | Los Angeles | 3 | 0 | 3 | | 1 | | |
| | Vancouver | 61 | 31 | 30 | | 5 | | |
| | Toronto | 80 | 41 | 39 | | 6 | | |
| | **Totals** | **183** | **94** | **89** | | **15** | | **1978-06** |
| **Reay, Billy** | **Chicago** | **116** | **56** | **60** | | **12** | | **1957-77** |
| **Renney, Tom** | **NY Rangers** | **24** | **11** | **13** | | **3** | | **1996-09** |
| **Risebrough, Doug** | **Calgary** | **7** | **3** | **4** | | **1** | | **1990-92** |
| **Roberts, Jim** | **Hartford** | **7** | **3** | **4** | | **1** | | **1981-97** |
| **Robinson, Larry** | Los Angeles | 4 | 0 | 4 | | 1 | | |
| | New Jersey | 48 | 31 | 17 | | 2 | 1 | |
| | **Totals** | **52** | **31** | **21** | | **3** | **1** | **1995-06** |
| **Ross, Art** | **Boston** | **65** | **27** | **33** | **5** | **11** | **1** | **1917-45** |
| **Ruel, Claude** | **Montreal** | **27** | **18** | **9** | | **3** | **1** | **1968-81** |
| **Ruff, Lindy** | **Buffalo** | **88** | **52** | **36** | | **6** | | **1997-09** |
| **Sather, Glen** | **Edmonton *** | **127** | **89** | **37** | **1** | **10** | **4** | **1979-04** |

* Playoff game May 24, 1988 suspended due to power failure. Score tied.

| Coach | Team | Games Coached | Wins | Losses | Ties | Years | Cup Wins | Career |
|---|---|---|---|---|---|---|---|---|
| **Sator, Ted** | NY Rangers | 16 | 8 | 8 | | 1 | | |
| | Buffalo | 11 | 3 | 8 | | 2 | | |
| | **Totals** | **27** | **11** | **16** | | **3** | | **1985-89** |
| **Schinkel, Ken** | **Pittsburgh** | **6** | **2** | **4** | | **2** | | **1972-77** |
| **Schmidt, Milt** | **Boston** | **34** | **15** | **19** | | **4** | | **1954-76** |
| **Schoenfeld, Jim** | New Jersey | 20 | 11 | 9 | | 1 | | |
| | Washington | 24 | 10 | 14 | | 3 | | |
| | Phoenix | 13 | 5 | 8 | | 2 | | |
| | **Totals** | **57** | **26** | **31** | | **6** | | **1985-99** |
| **Shero, Fred** | Philadelphia | 83 | 48 | 35 | | 6 | 2 | |
| | NY Rangers | 27 | 15 | 12 | | 2 | | |
| | **Totals** | **110** | **63** | **47** | | **8** | **2** | **1971-81** |
| **Simpson, Terry** | NY Islanders | 20 | 9 | 11 | | 2 | | |
| | Winnipeg | 6 | 2 | 4 | | 1 | | |
| | **Totals** | **26** | **11** | **15** | | **3** | | **1986-96** |
| **Sinden, Harry** | **Boston** | **43** | **24** | **19** | | **5** | **1** | **1966-85** |
| **Skinner, Jimmy** | **Detroit** | **26** | **14** | **12** | | **3** | **1** | **1954-58** |
| **Smith, Alf** | **Ottawa** | **5** | **1** | **4** | **0** | **1** | | **1918-19** |
| **Smith, Floyd** | **Buffalo** | **32** | **16** | **16** | | **3** | | **1971-80** |
| **Smythe, Conn** | **Toronto** | **4** | **2** | **2** | **0** | **1** | | **1927-31** |
| **Sonmor, Glen** | **Minnesota** | **47** | **26** | **21** | | **4** | | **1978-87** |
| **Stasiuk, Vic** | **Philadelphia** | **4** | **0** | **4** | | **1** | | **1969-73** |
| **Stevens, John** | **Philadelphia** | **23** | **11** | **12** | | **2** | | **2006-09** |
| **Stewart, Ron** | **Los Angeles** | **2** | **0** | **2** | | **1** | | **1975-78** |
| **Stewart, Bill** | **Chicago** | **10** | **7** | **3** | | **1** | **1** | **1937-39** |
| **Sutter, Darryl** | Chicago | 26 | 11 | 15 | | 3 | | |
| | San Jose | 42 | 18 | 24 | | 5 | | |
| | Calgary | 33 | 18 | 15 | | 2 | | |
| | **Totals** | **101** | **47** | **54** | | **10** | | **1992-06** |
| **Sutter, Brent** | **New Jersey** | **12** | **4** | **8** | | **2** | | **2007-09** |
| **Sutter, Brian** | St. Louis | 41 | 20 | 21 | | 4 | | |
| | Boston | 22 | 7 | 15 | | 3 | | |
| | Chicago | 5 | 1 | 4 | | 1 | | |
| | **Totals** | **68** | **28** | **40** | | **8** | | **1988-05** |
| **Talbot, Jean-Guy** | St. Louis | 5 | 1 | 4 | | 1 | | |
| | NY Rangers | 3 | 1 | 2 | | 1 | | |
| | **Totals** | **8** | **2** | **6** | | **2** | | **1972-78** |
| **Tessier, Orval** | **Chicago** | **18** | **9** | **9** | | **2** | | **1982-85** |
| **Therrien, Michel** | Montreal | 12 | 6 | 6 | | 1 | | |
| | Pittsburgh | 25 | 15 | 10 | | 2 | | |
| | **Totals** | **37** | **21** | **16** | | **3** | | **2000-09** |
| **Thompson, Paul** | **Chicago** | **19** | **7** | **12** | | **4** | | **1938-45** |
| **Tippett, Dave** | **Dallas** | **47** | **21** | **26** | | **5** | | **2002-09** |
| **Tobin, Bill** | **Chicago** | **4** | **1** | **2** | **1** | **2** | | **1929-32** |
| **Tortorella, John** | NY Rangers | 7 | 3 | 4 | | 1 | | |
| | Tampa Bay | 45 | 24 | 21 | | 4 | 1 | |
| | **Totals** | **52** | **27** | **25** | | **5** | **1** | **1999-09** |
| **Tremblay, Mario** | **Montreal** | **11** | **3** | **8** | | **2** | | **1995-97** |
| **Trotz, Barry** | **Nashville** | **22** | **6** | **16** | | **4** | | **1998-09** |
| **Ubriaco, Gene** | **Pittsburgh** | **11** | **7** | **4** | | **1** | | **1988-90** |
| **Vigneault, Alain** | Montreal | 10 | 4 | 6 | | 1 | | |
| | Vancouver | 22 | 11 | 11 | | 2 | | |
| | **Totals** | **32** | **15** | **17** | | **3** | | **1997-09** |
| **Watson, Phil** | **NY Rangers** | **16** | **4** | **12** | | **3** | | **1955-63** |
| **Watt, Tom** | Winnipeg | 7 | 1 | 6 | | 2 | | |
| | Vancouver | 3 | 0 | 3 | | 1 | | |
| | **Totals** | **10** | **1** | **9** | | **3** | | **1981-92** |
| **Webster, Tom** | **Los Angeles** | **28** | **12** | **16** | | **3** | | **1986-92** |
| **Weiland, Cooney** | **Boston** | **17** | **10** | **7** | | **2** | **1** | **1939-41** |
| **White, Bill** | **Chicago** | **2** | **0** | **2** | | **1** | | **1976-77** |
| **Wilson, Ron** | Anaheim | 11 | 4 | 7 | | 1 | | |
| | Washington | 32 | 15 | 17 | | 3 | | |
| | San Jose | 52 | 28 | 24 | | 4 | | |
| | **Totals** | **95** | **47** | **48** | | **8** | | **1993-09** |
| **Wilson, Johnny** | **Pittsburgh** | **12** | **4** | **8** | | **2** | | **1969-80** |
| **Young, Garry** | **St. Louis** | **2** | **0** | **2** | | **1** | | **1972-76** |

# Key to Prospect, NHL Player and Goaltender Registers

Demographics: Position, shooting side (catching hand for goaltenders), height, weight, place and date of birth as well as draft information, if any, is located on this line.

Major and tier-II junior, NCAA, minor pro, European and NHL clubs form a permanent part of each player's data panel. If a player sees action with more than one club in any of the above categories, a separate line is included for each one.

Olympic Team statistics are also listed.

Player's NHL organization as of August 101, 2009. This includes players under contract, unsigned draft choices and other players on reserve lists. Free agents as of this date show a blank here.

The complete career data panels of players with NHL experience who announced their retirement before the start of the 2008-09 season are included in the Player Register and Golatender Register.

These newly-retired players also show a blank here.

Each NHL club's minor-pro affiliates are listed on page 14.

**DATSYUK, Pavel** (daht-SOOK, PAH-vehl) **DET.**

Center. Shoots left. 5'11" 194 lbs. Born, Sverdlovsk, USSR, July 20, 1978. Detroit's 8th choice, 171st overall, in 1998 Entry Draft.

| | | | Regular Season | | | | | | | | | | | | | | Playoffs | | | | | | | | |
|---|---|---|---|---|---|---|---|---|---|---|---|---|---|---|---|---|---|---|---|---|---|---|---|---|---|
| Season | Club | League | GP | G | A | Pts | PIM | PP | SH | GW | S | % | +/- | TF | F% | Min | GP | G | A | Pts | PIM | PP | SH | GW | Min |
| 1996-97 | Yekaterinburg 2 | Russia-3 | 18 | 2 | 2 | 4 | 4 | .... | .... | .... | .... | .... | .... | .... | .... | .... | .... | .... | .... | .... | .... | .... | .... | .... | .... |
| | Yekaterinburg | Russia | 36 | 12 | 10 | 22 | 12 | .... | .... | .... | .... | .... | .... | .... | .... | .... | .... | .... | .... | .... | .... | .... | .... | .... | .... |
| 1997-98 | Yekaterinburg | Russia | 24 | 3 | 5 | 8 | 4 | .... | .... | .... | .... | .... | .... | .... | .... | .... | .... | .... | .... | .... | .... | .... | .... | .... | .... |
| | Yekaterinburg 2 | Russia-3 | 22 | 7 | 8 | 15 | 4 | .... | .... | .... | .... | .... | .... | .... | .... | .... | .... | .... | .... | .... | .... | .... | .... | .... | .... |
| 1998-99 | Yekaterinburg 2 | Russia-4 | 10 | 14 | 14 | 28 | 4 | .... | .... | .... | .... | .... | .... | .... | .... | .... | .... | .... | .... | .... | .... | .... | .... | .... | .... |
| | Yekaterinburg | Russia-2 | 35 | 21 | 23 | 44 | 14 | .... | .... | .... | .... | .... | .... | .... | .... | .... | 9 | 3 | 7 | 10 | 0 | .... | .... | .... | .... |
| 99-2000 | Yekaterinburg | Russia | 15 | 1 | 3 | 4 | 4 | .... | .... | .... | .... | .... | .... | .... | .... | .... | .... | .... | .... | .... | .... | .... | .... | .... | .... |
| 2000-01 | Ak Bars Kazan | Russia | 42 | 9 | 18 | 27 | 10 | .... | .... | .... | .... | .... | .... | .... | .... | .... | 4 | 0 | 1 | 1 | 2 | .... | .... | .... | .... |
| **2001-02 ♦** | **Detroit** | **NHL** | **70** | **11** | **24** | **35** | **4** | **2** | **0** | **1** | **79** | **13.9** | **4** | **794** | **47.7** | **13:39** | **21** | **3** | **3** | **6** | [illegible] | **1** | **0** | **1** | **10:40** |
| | Russia | Olympics | 6 | 1 | 2 | 3 | 0 | .... | .... | .... | .... | .... | .... | .... | .... | .... | .... | .... | .... | .... | .... | .... | .... | .... | .... |
| **2002-03** | **Detroit** | **NHL** | **64** | **12** | **39** | **51** | **16** | **1** | **0** | **1** | **82** | **14.6** | **20** | **778** | **48.2** | **15:28** | **4** | **0** | **0** | **0** | **0** | **0** | **0** | **0** | **18:48** |
| **2003-04** | **Detroit** | **NHL** | **75** | **30** | **38** | **68** | **35** | **8** | **1** | **4** | **136** | **22.1** | **–2** | **1314** | **54.0** | **18:16** | **12** | **0** | **6** | **6** | **2** | **0** | **0** | **0** | **17:23** |
| 2004-05 | Dynamo Moscow | Russia | 47 | 15 | 17 | 32 | 16 | .... | .... | .... | .... | .... | .... | .... | .... | .... | 10 | *6 | 3 | 9 | 4 | .... | .... | .... | .... |
| **2005-06** | **Detroit** | **NHL** | **75** | **28** | **59** | **87** | **22** | **11** | **0** | **4** | **145** | **19.3** | **26** | **1059** | **53.1** | **17:53** | **5** | **0** | **3** | **3** | **0** | **0** | **0** | **0** | **20:05** |
| | Russia | Olympics | 8 | 1 | 7 | 8 | 10 | .... | .... | .... | .... | .... | .... | .... | .... | .... | .... | .... | .... | .... | .... | .... | .... | .... | .... |
| **2006-07** | **Detroit** | **NHL** | **79** | **27** | **60** | **87** | **20** | **5** | **2** | **5** | **207** | **13.0** | **36** | **845** | **56.2** | **19:57** | **18** | **8** | **8** | **16** | **8** | **4** | **0** | **2** | **22:03** |
| **2007-08 ♦** | **Detroit** | **NHL** | **82** | **31** | **66** | **97** | **20** | **10** | **1** | **6** | **264** | **11.7** | **41** | **833** | **54.4** | **21:23** | **22** | **10** | **13** | **23** | **6** | **4** | **0** | **1** | **21:40** |
| **2008-09** | **Detroit** | **NHL** | **81** | **32** | **65** | **97** | **22** | **11** | **1** | **3** | **248** | **12.9** | **34** | **1135** | **56.0** | **19:13** | **16** | **1** | **8** | **9** | **9** | **1** | **0** | **0** | **20:05** |
| | **NHL Totals** | | **526** | **171** | **351** | **522** | **139** | **48** | **5** | **24** | **1161** | **14.7** | | **6758** | **53.1** | **18:09** | [illegible] | **22** | **41** | **63** | **27** | [illegible] | **0** | **4** | **18:24** |

Lady Byng Memorial Trophy (2006, 2007, 2008, 2009) • Frank J. Selke Trophy (2008, 2009) • NHL Second All-Star Team (2009)

Played in NHL All-Star Game (2004, 2008)

• Spent majority of 1999-2000 season on **Kazan** (Russia) reserve squad. Signed as a free agent by **Dynamo Moscow** (Russia), June 19, 2004.

Diamond (♦) indicates member of Stanley Cup-winning team.

"Did not play" Indicates that a player did not participate in a professional, junior or college league for an entire season.

Asterisks (*) indicates league leader in individual statistical categories.

All trades, free agent signings and other transactions involving NHL clubs are listed in chronological order. First draft selection for players who re-enter the NHL Entry Draft is noted here. Other special notes are also listed here. These are highlighted with a bullet (•).

Dates for trades or free agent signings often differ depending upon source. Signings can be reported based on when contracts are filed with NHL Central Registry or on the date a club announces that it has made a trade or come to terms with a free agent.

All-Star Team selections and awards are listed below player's year-by-year data.

NHL All-Star Game appearances are listed above trade notes.

THIS 78TH EDITION OF THE *NHL Official Guide & Record Book* is the 11th to include additional statistical categories for forwards and defensemen in the National Hockey League. These categories are, from left to right in the sample panel above, power-play goals (PP), shorthand goals (SH), game-winning goals (GW), shots on goal (S), percentage of shots that score (%), plus-minus rating (+/–), total faceoffs taken (TF), faceoff winning percentage (F%), and average time-on-ice per game played (Min).

To integrate this data, the Player Register has been is split into two sections. The Prospect Register presents data on players who have yet to play in the NHL. The NHL Player Register, containing more information and a photo of each player, lists all active players who have appeared in an NHL regular-season or playoff game at any time.

Goaltenders, whether prospects or active NHLers, are included in one register. With the addition of the shootout to NHL regular-season play, the column formerly used to record tie games for goaltenders has been renamed "O/T." For NHL goaltenders beginning in 2005-06, it lists overtime losses and shootout losses; previous to 2005-06, it lists tie games.

**Registers (with their starting page) are presented in the following order: Prospects (279), NHL Players (352), Goaltenders (585), Retired Players (610) and Retired Goaltenders (650).**

**League abbreviations, page 662. Late additions to the Registers, page 609.**

Some information is unavailable at press time. Readers are encouraged to contribute. See page 5 for contact names and addresses.

## Pronunciation of Player Names

United Press International phonetic style.

| | |
|---|---|
| AY | long A as in mate |
| A | short A as in cat |
| AI | nasal A as on air |
| AH | short A as in father |
| AW | broad A as in talk |
| EE | long E as in meat |
| EH | short E as in get |
| UH | hollow E as in the |
| AY | French long E with acute accent as in Pathe |
| IH | middle E as in pretty |
| EW | EW dipthong as in few |
| IGH | long I as in time |
| EE | French long I as in machine |
| IH | short I as in pity |
| OH | long O as in note |
| AH | short O as in hot |
| AW | broad O as in fought |
| OI | OI dipthong as in noise |
| OO | long double OO as in fool |
| U | short double O as in foot |
| OW | OW dipthong as in how |
| EW | long U as in mule |
| OO | long U as in rule |
| U | middle U as in put |
| UH | short U as in shut or hurt |
| K | hard C as in cat |
| S | soft C as in cease |
| SH | soft CH as in machine |
| CH | hard CH or TCH as in catch |
| Z | hard S as in bells |
| S | soft S as in sun |
| G | hard G as in gang |
| J | soft G as in general |
| ZH | soft J as in French version of Joliet |
| KH | gutteral CH as in Scottish version of Loch |

# 2009-10 Prospect Register

**Note:** The 2009-10 Prospect Register lists forwards and defensemen only. Goaltenders are listed separately. The Prospect Register lists every player drafted in the 2009 Entry Draft, players on NHL Reserve Lists and other players who have not yet played in the NHL. Trades and roster changes are current as of August 10, 2009.

**Abbreviations: GP** – games played; **G** – goals; **A** – assists; **Pts** – points; **PIM** – penalties in minutes; ***** – league-leading total.

**NHL Player Register begins on page 352.**
**Goaltender Register begins on page 585.**
**League Abbreviations are listed on page 662.**

## ABNEY, Cameron (AB-nee, KAM-ih-RUHN) EDM.

Right wing. Shoots right. 6'4", 192 lbs. Born, Aldergrove, B.C., May 23, 1991.
(Edmonton's 4th choice, 82nd overall, in 2009 Entry Draft).

| | | | Regular Season | | | | | Playoffs | | | | |
|---|---|---|---|---|---|---|---|---|---|---|---|---|
| Season | Club | League | GP | G | A | Pts | PIM | GP | G | A | Pts | PIM |
| 2007-08 | North Delta Devils | PIJHL | 42 | 12 | 14 | 26 | 110 | 5 | 1 | 0 | 1 | 27 |
| | Everett Silvertips | WHL | 4 | 0 | 0 | 0 | 0 | .... | .... | .... | .... | .... |
| 2008-09 | Everett Silvertips | WHL | 48 | 1 | 3 | 4 | 103 | 5 | 0 | 0 | 0 | 2 |

## ADAM, Luke (A-duhm, LEWK) BUF.

Center. Shoots left. 6'2", 203 lbs. Born, St. John's, Nfld., June 18, 1990.
(Buffalo's 3rd choice, 44th overall, in 2008 Entry Draft).

| | | | Regular Season | | | | | Playoffs | | | | |
|---|---|---|---|---|---|---|---|---|---|---|---|---|
| Season | Club | League | GP | G | A | Pts | PIM | GP | G | A | Pts | PIM |
| 2006-07 | St. John's | QMJHL | 63 | 6 | 9 | 15 | 51 | 4 | 0 | 2 | 2 | 4 |
| 2007-08 | St. John's | QMJHL | 70 | 36 | 30 | 66 | 72 | 6 | 3 | 5 | 8 | 8 |
| 2008-09 | Montreal | QMJHL | 47 | 22 | 27 | 49 | 59 | .... | .... | .... | .... | .... |

## ADAMS, Mark (A-duhmz, MAHRK) BUF.

Defense. Shoots right. 6'1", 187 lbs. Born, Boston, MA, May 23, 1991.
(Buffalo's 4th choice, 134th overall, in 2009 Entry Draft).

| | | | Regular Season | | | | | Playoffs | | | | |
|---|---|---|---|---|---|---|---|---|---|---|---|---|
| Season | Club | League | GP | G | A | Pts | PIM | GP | G | A | Pts | PIM |
| 2007-08 | Malden Cath. | High-MA | 23 | 4 | 13 | 17 | .... | .... | .... | .... | .... | .... |
| 2008-09 | Malden Cath. | High-MA | 23 | 6 | 23 | 29 | .... | .... | .... | .... | .... | .... |
| | Bos. Jr. Bruins | EJHL | 32 | 5 | 10 | 15 | 18 | .... | .... | .... | .... | .... |

• Signed Letter of Intent to attend **Providence College** (Hockey East) in fall of 2010.

## AHNELOV, Jonas (AH-neh-lawv, YOH-nuhs) PHX.

Defense. Shoots left. 6'3", 205 lbs. Born, Huddinge, Sweden, December 11, 1987.
(Phoenix's 3rd choice, 88th overall, in 2006 Entry Draft).

| | | | Regular Season | | | | | Playoffs | | | | |
|---|---|---|---|---|---|---|---|---|---|---|---|---|
| Season | Club | League | GP | G | A | Pts | PIM | GP | G | A | Pts | PIM |
| 2003-04 | Huddinge IK U18 | Swe-U18 | 6 | 0 | 3 | 3 | 8 | .... | .... | .... | .... | .... |
| | Huddinge IK Jr. | Swe-Jr. | 9 | 0 | 1 | 1 | 6 | .... | .... | .... | .... | .... |
| 2004-05 | Huddinge IK U18 | Swe-U18 | 2 | 0 | 0 | 0 | 2 | .... | .... | .... | .... | .... |
| | Huddinge IK Jr. | Swe-Jr. | 29 | 3 | 3 | 6 | 94 | 3 | 0 | 0 | 0 | 2 |
| 2005-06 | Frolunda Jr. | Swe-Jr. | 29 | 4 | 11 | 15 | 84 | 7 | 2 | 4 | 6 | 22 |
| | Frolunda | Sweden | 15 | 0 | 0 | 0 | 2 | .... | .... | .... | .... | .... |
| 2006-07 | Frolunda Jr. | Swe-Jr. | 9 | 4 | 5 | 9 | 22 | 8 | 2 | 3 | 5 | 8 |
| | Frolunda | Sweden | 46 | 1 | 3 | 4 | 20 | .... | .... | .... | .... | .... |
| 2007-08 | Boras HC | Sweden-2 | 1 | 0 | 0 | 0 | 0 | .... | .... | .... | .... | .... |
| | Frolunda | Sweden | 51 | 3 | 4 | 7 | 30 | 6 | 0 | 0 | 0 | 0 |
| 2008-09 | San Antonio | AHL | 43 | 1 | 6 | 7 | 35 | .... | .... | .... | .... | .... |

## AIELLO, Anthony (igh-EHL-oh, AN-thu-nee) MIN.

Defense. Shoots left. 6'1", 187 lbs. Born, Braintree, MA, May 19, 1986.
(Minnesota's 6th choice, 129th overall, in 2005 Entry Draft).

| | | | Regular Season | | | | | Playoffs | | | | |
|---|---|---|---|---|---|---|---|---|---|---|---|---|
| Season | Club | League | GP | G | A | Pts | PIM | GP | G | A | Pts | PIM |
| 2003-04 | Thayer Academy | High-MA | 33 | 11 | 26 | 37 | .... | .... | .... | .... | .... | .... |
| 2004-05 | Thayer Academy | High-MA | 30 | 7 | 27 | 34 | 42 | .... | .... | .... | .... | .... |
| 2005-06 | Boston College | H-East | 40 | 1 | 8 | 9 | 50 | .... | .... | .... | .... | .... |
| 2006-07 | Boston College | H-East | 22 | 1 | 8 | 9 | 24 | .... | .... | .... | .... | .... |
| 2007-08 | Boston College | H-East | 43 | 3 | 10 | 13 | 40 | .... | .... | .... | .... | .... |
| 2008-09 | Boston College | H-East | 27 | 0 | 4 | 4 | 28 | .... | .... | .... | .... | .... |

## ALBERS, Paul (AL-buhrs, PAWL)

Defense. Shoots left. 6'1", 189 lbs. Born, Melville, Sask., October 15, 1985.

| | | | Regular Season | | | | | Playoffs | | | | |
|---|---|---|---|---|---|---|---|---|---|---|---|---|
| Season | Club | League | GP | G | A | Pts | PIM | GP | G | A | Pts | PIM |
| 2001-02 | Calgary Hitmen | WHL | 54 | 1 | 5 | 6 | 32 | 7 | 0 | 0 | 0 | 6 |
| 2002-03 | Calgary Hitmen | WHL | 72 | 4 | 20 | 24 | 51 | 5 | 0 | 0 | 0 | 0 |
| 2003-04 | Calgary Hitmen | WHL | 8 | 0 | 1 | 1 | 6 | .... | .... | .... | .... | .... |
| | Regina Pats | WHL | 54 | 5 | 18 | 23 | 30 | 4 | 0 | 0 | 0 | 2 |
| 2004-05 | Regina Pats | WHL | 23 | 0 | 4 | 4 | 6 | .... | .... | .... | .... | .... |
| | Vancouver Giants | WHL | 48 | 4 | 19 | 23 | 42 | 6 | 2 | 3 | 5 | 0 |
| 2005-06 | Vancouver Giants | WHL | 70 | 17 | 45 | 62 | 33 | 18 | 3 | *16 | 19 | 8 |
| 2006-07 | Houston Aeros | AHL | 5 | 0 | 0 | 0 | 2 | .... | .... | .... | .... | .... |
| | Texas Wildcatters | ECHL | 68 | 12 | 31 | 43 | 32 | 9 | 1 | 5 | 6 | 8 |
| 2007-08 | Houston Aeros | AHL | 69 | 5 | 16 | 21 | 26 | 4 | 0 | 0 | 0 | 0 |
| 2008-09 | Houston Aeros | AHL | 73 | 4 | 7 | 11 | 52 | 12 | 0 | 1 | 1 | 2 |

WHL West First All-Star Team (2006) • Memorial Cup Tournament All-Star Team (2006) • ECHL All-Rookie Team (2007)

Signed as a free agent by **Minnesota**, July 5, 2006.

## ALBERT, John (AL-buhrt, JAWN) ATL.

Center. Shoots left. 5'9", 180 lbs. Born, Cleveland, OH, January 19, 1989.
(Atlanta's 3rd choice, 175th overall, in 2007 Entry Draft).

| | | | Regular Season | | | | | Playoffs | | | | |
|---|---|---|---|---|---|---|---|---|---|---|---|---|
| Season | Club | League | GP | G | A | Pts | PIM | GP | G | A | Pts | PIM |
| 2004-05 | Cleveland Barons | MWEHL | 67 | 34 | 60 | 94 | .... | .... | .... | .... | .... | .... |
| | Cleveland Barons | NAHL | 3 | 0 | 0 | 0 | 0 | .... | .... | .... | .... | .... |
| 2005-06 | USNTDP | U-17 | 19 | 8 | 15 | 23 | 25 | .... | .... | .... | .... | .... |
| | USNTDP | NAHL | 36 | 8 | 15 | 23 | 23 | .... | .... | .... | .... | .... |
| 2006-07 | USNTDP | U-18 | 41 | 8 | 16 | 24 | 10 | .... | .... | .... | .... | .... |
| | USNTDP | NAHL | 15 | 4 | 9 | 13 | 4 | .... | .... | .... | .... | .... |
| 2007-08 | Ohio State | CCHA | 41 | 4 | 17 | 21 | 10 | .... | .... | .... | .... | .... |
| 2008-09 | Ohio State | CCHA | 42 | 11 | 28 | 39 | 20 | .... | .... | .... | .... | .... |

## ALCEN, Johan (AL-sehn, YOH-hahn) COL.

Right wing. Shoots left. 6'1", 189 lbs. Born, Sandviken, Sweden, March 11, 1988.
(Colorado's 9th choice, 195th overall, in 2007 Entry Draft).

| | | | Regular Season | | | | | Playoffs | | | | |
|---|---|---|---|---|---|---|---|---|---|---|---|---|
| Season | Club | League | GP | G | A | Pts | PIM | GP | G | A | Pts | PIM |
| 2003-04 | Sandvikens IK | Sweden-4 | STATISTICS NOT AVAILABLE | | | | | | | | | |
| 2004-05 | Brynas IF Gavle Jr. | Swe-Jr. | 30 | 9 | 12 | 21 | 16 | .... | .... | .... | .... | .... |
| 2005-06 | Brynas U18 | Swe-U18 | 2 | 1 | 3 | 4 | 4 | .... | .... | .... | .... | .... |
| | Brynas IF Gavle Jr. | Swe-Jr. | 39 | 16 | 19 | 35 | 48 | 2 | 0 | 2 | 2 | 0 |
| | Brynas IF Gavle | Sweden | 3 | 0 | 0 | 0 | 0 | .... | .... | .... | .... | .... |
| 2006-07 | Brynas IF Gavle Jr. | Swe-Jr. | 26 | 17 | 29 | 46 | 46 | 4 | 1 | 1 | 2 | 0 |
| | IFK Arboga IK | Sweden-2 | 2 | 0 | 0 | 0 | 2 | .... | .... | .... | .... | .... |
| | Brynas IF Gavle | Sweden | 32 | 0 | 0 | 0 | 0 | 1 | 0 | 0 | 0 | 0 |
| 2007-08 | Brynas IF Gavle Jr. | Swe-Jr. | 7 | 12 | 9 | 21 | 6 | .... | .... | .... | .... | .... |
| | Brynas IF Gavle | Sweden | 39 | 4 | 6 | 10 | 14 | .... | .... | .... | .... | .... |
| | Brynas IF Gavle | Sweden-Q | 10 | 1 | 2 | 3 | 2 | .... | .... | .... | .... | .... |
| 2008-09 | Brynas IF Gavle Jr. | Swe-Jr. | 1 | 3 | 4 | 7 | 0 | .... | .... | .... | .... | .... |
| | Brynas IF Gavle | Sweden | 50 | 1 | 1 | 2 | 20 | 4 | 0 | 0 | 0 | 2 |

## ALEXANDROV, Yuri (al-ehx-AN-drawv, YOO-ree) BOS.

Defense. Shoots left. 6'1", 185 lbs. Born, Cherepovets, USSR, June 24, 1988.
(Boston's 2nd choice, 37th overall, in 2006 Entry Draft).

| | | | Regular Season | | | | | Playoffs | | | | |
|---|---|---|---|---|---|---|---|---|---|---|---|---|
| Season | Club | League | GP | G | A | Pts | PIM | GP | G | A | Pts | PIM |
| 2003-04 | Cherepovets 2 | Russia-3 | 32 | 0 | 2 | 2 | 10 | 4 | 0 | 0 | 0 | 0 |
| 2004-05 | Cherepovets 2 | Russia-3 | STATISTICS NOT AVAILABLE | | | | | | | | | |
| 2005-06 | Cherepovets | Russia | 37 | 1 | 0 | 1 | 18 | 2 | 0 | 0 | 0 | 2 |
| 2006-07 | Cherepovets | Russia | 45 | 1 | 1 | 2 | 38 | 5 | 0 | 0 | 0 | 8 |
| 2007-08 | Cherepovets | Russia | 45 | 5 | 4 | 9 | 32 | 8 | 0 | 0 | 0 | 8 |
| 2008-09 | Cherepovets | Rus-KHL | 26 | 3 | 5 | 8 | 40 | .... | .... | .... | .... | .... |

## ALIU, Akim (ah-lee-OO, a-KEEM) CHI.

Center. Shoots right. 6'2", 200 lbs. Born, Okene, Nigeria, April 24, 1989.
(Chicago's 3rd choice, 56th overall, in 2007 Entry Draft).

| | | | Regular Season | | | | | Playoffs | | | | |
|---|---|---|---|---|---|---|---|---|---|---|---|---|
| Season | Club | League | GP | G | A | Pts | PIM | GP | G | A | Pts | PIM |
| 2004-05 | Toronto Marlboros | GTHL | 68 | 35 | 50 | 85 | 197 | .... | .... | .... | .... | .... |
| 2005-06 | Windsor Spitfires | OHL | 18 | 3 | 4 | 7 | 25 | .... | .... | .... | .... | .... |
| | Sudbury Wolves | OHL | 29 | 7 | 6 | 13 | 54 | 6 | 0 | 1 | 1 | 7 |
| 2006-07 | Sudbury Wolves | OHL | 53 | 20 | 22 | 42 | 104 | 21 | 1 | 5 | 6 | 50 |
| 2007-08 | London Knights | OHL | 60 | 28 | 33 | 61 | 133 | 5 | 2 | 1 | 3 | 15 |
| | Rockford IceHogs | AHL | 2 | 0 | 0 | 0 | 2 | .... | .... | .... | .... | .... |
| 2008-09 | London Knights | OHL | 16 | 8 | 10 | 18 | 30 | .... | .... | .... | .... | .... |
| | Sudbury Wolves | OHL | 29 | 10 | 16 | 26 | 61 | 6 | 2 | 1 | 3 | 14 |
| | Rockford IceHogs | AHL | 5 | 2 | 0 | 2 | 14 | 1 | 1 | 0 | 1 | 0 |

## ALMOND, Cody (al-MUHND, KOH-dee) MIN.

Center. Shoots left. 6'2", 199 lbs. Born, Calgary, Alta., July 24, 1989.
(Minnesota's 3rd choice, 140th overall, in 2007 Entry Draft).

| | | | Regular Season | | | | | Playoffs | | | | |
|---|---|---|---|---|---|---|---|---|---|---|---|---|
| Season | Club | League | GP | G | A | Pts | PIM | GP | G | A | Pts | PIM |
| 2004-05 | Cgy. Stampeders | SAMHL | 30 | 28 | 15 | 43 | 108 | .... | .... | .... | .... | .... |
| 2005-06 | Kelowna Rockets | WHL | 23 | 2 | 1 | 3 | 7 | 8 | 0 | 0 | 0 | 0 |
| 2006-07 | Kelowna Rockets | WHL | 68 | 15 | 28 | 43 | 72 | .... | .... | .... | .... | .... |
| 2007-08 | Kelowna Rockets | WHL | 69 | 22 | 34 | 56 | 114 | 7 | 1 | 2 | 3 | 2 |
| 2008-09 | Kelowna Rockets | WHL | 70 | 33 | 33 | 66 | 105 | 22 | 10 | 17 | 27 | *51 |

## ALMQVIST, Adam (AHLM-kwihst, A-duhm) DET.

Defense. Shoots left. 5'10", 169 lbs. Born, Jonkoping, Sweden, February 27, 1991.
(Detroit's 7th choice, 210th overall, in 2009 Entry Draft).

| | | | Regular Season | | | | | Playoffs | | | | |
|---|---|---|---|---|---|---|---|---|---|---|---|---|
| Season | Club | League | GP | G | A | Pts | PIM | GP | G | A | Pts | PIM |
| 2006-07 | HV 71 U18 | Swe-U18 | 1 | 0 | 0 | 0 | 0 | 1 | 0 | 0 | 0 | 0 |
| 2007-08 | HV 71 U18 | Swe-U18 | 18 | 8 | 12 | 20 | 28 | .... | .... | .... | .... | .... |
| | HV 71 Jr. | Swe-Jr. | 23 | 1 | 6 | 7 | 12 | 3 | 0 | 0 | 0 | 4 |
| 2008-09 | HV 71 Jr. | Swe-Jr. | 41 | 8 | 28 | 36 | 44 | .... | .... | .... | .... | .... |

## AMBUHL, Andres (AM-b'yool, AWN-drehs) NYR

Right wing. Shoots right. 5'10", 190 lbs. Born, Davos, Switz., September 14, 1983.

| | | | Regular Season | | | | | Playoffs | | | | |
|---|---|---|---|---|---|---|---|---|---|---|---|---|
| Season | Club | League | GP | G | A | Pts | PIM | GP | G | A | Pts | PIM |
| 2000-01 | HC Davos Jr. | Swiss-Jr. | 31 | 24 | 17 | 41 | 36 | 6 | 4 | 3 | 7 | 6 |
| | HC Davos | Swiss | 3 | 0 | 1 | 1 | 0 | .... | .... | .... | .... | .... |
| 2001-02 | HC Davos | Swiss | 38 | 5 | 3 | 8 | 26 | 6 | 1 | 0 | 1 | 4 |
| | HC Davos Jr. | Swiss-Jr. | 3 | 2 | 2 | 4 | 12 | 1 | 0 | 1 | 1 | 2 |
| 2002-03 | HC Davos | Swiss | 40 | 6 | 11 | 17 | 18 | 17 | 0 | 2 | 2 | 10 |
| 2003-04 | HC Davos | Swiss | 487 | 6 | 16 | 22 | 40 | 6 | 0 | 1 | 1 | 2 |
| 2004-05 | HC Davos | Swiss | 43 | 7 | 11 | 18 | 67 | 15 | 3 | 2 | 5 | 12 |
| 2005-06 | HC Davos | Swiss | 44 | 7 | 14 | 21 | 50 | 15 | 4 | 1 | 5 | 12 |
| | Switzerland | Olympics | 1 | 0 | 0 | 0 | 0 | .... | .... | .... | .... | .... |
| 2006-07 | HC Davos | Swiss | 44 | 5 | 13 | 18 | 88 | 19 | 2 | 2 | 4 | 20 |
| 2007-08 | HC Davos | Swiss | 49 | 11 | 15 | 26 | 46 | 13 | 5 | 3 | 8 | 8 |
| 2008-09 | HC Davos | Swiss | 50 | 17 | 24 | 41 | 90 | 21 | 4 | 3 | 7 | 44 |

Signed as a free agent by **NY Rangers**, May 27, 2009.

## ANDERSEN, Niclas (AN-duhr-suhn, NIHK-luhs) L.A.

Defense. Shoots left. 6'1", 207 lbs. Born, Grums, Sweden, April 28, 1988.
(Los Angeles' 6th choice, 114th overall, in 2006 Entry Draft).

| | | | Regular Season | | | | | Playoffs | | | | |
|---|---|---|---|---|---|---|---|---|---|---|---|---|
| Season | Club | League | GP | G | A | Pts | PIM | GP | G | A | Pts | PIM |
| 2003-04 | Grums IK | Sweden-3 | 30 | 4 | 5 | 9 | 45 | .... | .... | .... | .... | .... |
| 2004-05 | Leksands IF Jr. | Swe-Jr. | 26 | 3 | 2 | 5 | 91 | 5 | 0 | 2 | 2 | 2 |
| 2005-06 | Leksands IF U18 | Swe-U18 | 3 | 0 | 3 | 3 | 8 | 2 | 0 | 0 | 0 | 10 |
| | Leksands IF Jr. | Swe-Jr. | 36 | 5 | 6 | 11 | 214 | .... | .... | .... | .... | .... |
| | Leksands IF | Sweden | 8 | 0 | 0 | 0 | 8 | .... | .... | .... | .... | .... |
| | Leksands IF | Sweden-Q | 3 | 0 | 0 | 0 | 2 | .... | .... | .... | .... | .... |
| 2006-07 | Leksands IF Jr. | Swe-Jr. | 4 | 1 | 1 | 2 | 47 | .... | .... | .... | .... | .... |
| | Leksands IF | Sweden-2 | 35 | 0 | 5 | 5 | 38 | .... | .... | .... | .... | .... |
| 2007-08 | AIK IF Solna | Sweden-2 | 3 | 1 | 1 | 2 | 2 | .... | .... | .... | .... | .... |
| | Brynas IF Gavle Jr. | Swe-Jr. | 5 | 0 | 1 | 1 | 35 | .... | .... | .... | .... | .... |
| | Brynas IF Gavle | Sweden | 38 | 0 | 3 | 3 | 26 | .... | .... | .... | .... | .... |
| | Brynas IF Gavle | Sweden-Q | 10 | 1 | 2 | 3 | 10 | .... | .... | .... | .... | .... |
| 2008-09 | Brynas IF Gavle | Sweden | 55 | 0 | 8 | 8 | 60 | 4 | 0 | 0 | 0 | 4 |

## ANDERSON, Chad (AN-duhr-suhn, CHAD)

Defense. Shoots right. 6'4", 217 lbs. Born, Chisago City, MN, June 16, 1982.

| | | | Regular Season | | | | | Playoffs | | | | |
|---|---|---|---|---|---|---|---|---|---|---|---|---|
| Season | Club | League | GP | G | A | Pts | PIM | GP | G | A | Pts | PIM |
| 2000-01 | Tri-City Storm | USHL | 50 | 0 | 1 | 1 | 34 | 7 | 0 | 1 | 1 | 2 |
| 2001-02 | Tri-City Storm | USHL | 60 | 3 | 10 | 13 | 53 | .... | .... | .... | .... | .... |
| 2002-03 | Tri-City Storm | USHL | 60 | 8 | 20 | 28 | 119 | 3 | 0 | 0 | 0 | 10 |
| 2003-04 | Alaska Anchorage | WCHA | 38 | 2 | 6 | 8 | 24 | .... | .... | .... | .... | .... |
| 2004-05 | Alaska Anchorage | WCHA | 36 | 4 | 11 | 15 | 46 | .... | .... | .... | .... | .... |
| 2005-06 | Alaska Anchorage | WCHA | 30 | 3 | 3 | 6 | 49 | .... | .... | .... | .... | .... |
| 2006-07 | Alaska Anchorage | WCHA | 34 | 7 | 13 | 20 | 96 | .... | .... | .... | .... | .... |
| | Las Vegas | ECHL | 2 | 0 | 0 | 0 | 0 | .... | .... | .... | .... | .... |
| 2007-08 | Philadelphia | AHL | 55 | 2 | 11 | 13 | 35 | 12 | 0 | 2 | 2 | 8 |
| 2008-09 | Hamilton Bulldogs | AHL | 56 | 5 | 2 | 7 | 55 | 5 | 0 | 2 | 2 | 6 |

Signed as a free agent by **Montreal**, August 6, 2008.

## ANDERSSON, Joakim (AN-duhr-suhn, YOH-ah-kihm) DET.

Center. Shoots left. 6'2", 198 lbs. Born, Munkedal, Sweden, February 5, 1989.
(Detroit's 2nd choice, 88th overall, in 2007 Entry Draft).

| | | | Regular Season | | | | | Playoffs | | | | |
|---|---|---|---|---|---|---|---|---|---|---|---|---|
| Season | Club | League | GP | G | A | Pts | PIM | GP | G | A | Pts | PIM |
| 2004-05 | Munkedals BK | Sweden-5 | STATISTICS NOT AVAILABLE | | | | | | | | | |
| 2005-06 | Frolunda U18 | Swe-U18 | 1 | 0 | 0 | 0 | 0 | 2 | 0 | 1 | 1 | 0 |
| | Frolunda Jr. | Swe-Jr. | 35 | 9 | 11 | 20 | 10 | 7 | 2 | 5 | 7 | 4 |
| 2006-07 | Frolunda U18 | Swe-U18 | 2 | 1 | 2 | 3 | 2 | 6 | 3 | 2 | 5 | 28 |
| | Frolunda Jr. | Swe-Jr. | 41 | 20 | 26 | 46 | 60 | 8 | 0 | 7 | 7 | 4 |
| | Frolunda | Sweden | 1 | 0 | 0 | 0 | 0 | .... | .... | .... | .... | .... |
| 2007-08 | Boras HC | Sweden-2 | 33 | 6 | 17 | 23 | 26 | .... | .... | .... | .... | .... |
| | Frolunda Jr. | Swe-Jr. | 6 | 8 | 2 | 10 | 30 | 5 | 6 | 3 | 9 | 4 |
| | Frolunda | Sweden | 9 | 1 | 0 | 1 | 2 | 4 | 1 | 1 | 2 | 0 |
| 2008-09 | Boras HC | Sweden-2 | 4 | 2 | 2 | 4 | 2 | .... | .... | .... | .... | .... |
| | Frolunda | Sweden | 49 | 6 | 6 | 12 | 22 | 11 | 0 | 0 | 0 | 4 |
| | Grand Rapids | AHL | 1 | 0 | 1 | 1 | 2 | 10 | 1 | 2 | 3 | 4 |

## ANDERSSON, Peter (AN-duhr-suhn, PEE-tuhr) VAN.

Defense. Shoots left. 6'3", 194 lbs. Born, Kvidinge, Sweden, April 13, 1991.
(Vancouver's 5th choice, 143rd overall, in 2009 Entry Draft).

| | | | Regular Season | | | | | Playoffs | | | | |
|---|---|---|---|---|---|---|---|---|---|---|---|---|
| Season | Club | League | GP | G | A | Pts | PIM | GP | G | A | Pts | PIM |
| 2007-08 | Frolunda U18 | Swe-U18 | 12 | 2 | 3 | 5 | 18 | 5 | 0 | 1 | 1 | 14 |
| | Frolunda Jr. | Swe-Jr. | 8 | 0 | 2 | 2 | 4 | 1 | 0 | 0 | 0 | 0 |
| | Frolunda | Sweden | 1 | 0 | 0 | 0 | 0 | .... | .... | .... | .... | .... |
| 2008-09 | Frolunda U18 | Swe-U18 | 5 | 0 | 1 | 1 | 4 | 5 | 1 | 1 | 2 | 2 |
| | Frolunda Jr. | Swe-Jr. | 36 | 3 | 5 | 8 | 42 | 4 | 0 | 1 | 1 | 0 |

## ANDRONOV, Sergei (an-DROH-nahv, SAIR-gay) ST.L.

Right wing. Shoots left. 6'2", 183 lbs. Born, Penza, USSR, July 19, 1989.
(St. Louis' 3rd choice, 78th overall, in 2009 Entry Draft).

| | | | Regular Season | | | | | Playoffs | | | | |
|---|---|---|---|---|---|---|---|---|---|---|---|---|
| Season | Club | League | GP | G | A | Pts | PIM | GP | G | A | Pts | PIM |
| 2006-07 | Lada Togliatti | Russia | 3 | 0 | 0 | 0 | 2 | .... | .... | .... | .... | .... |
| 2007-08 | Lada Togliatti 2 | Russia-3 | 16 | 10 | 2 | 12 | 16 | 8 | 7 | 2 | 9 | 0 |
| | Lada Togliatti | Russia | 38 | 2 | 5 | 7 | 2 | 4 | 1 | 0 | 1 | 6 |
| 2008-09 | Lada Togliatti 2 | Russia-3 | 7 | 5 | 2 | 7 | 6 | 3 | 0 | 2 | 2 | 32 |
| | Lada Togliatti | Rus-KHL | 47 | 9 | 5 | 14 | 22 | 5 | 0 | 1 | 1 | 8 |

## ANGELIDIS, Mike (AN-gehl-EE-dihs, MIGHK) CAR.

Left wing. Shoots left. 6'1", 210 lbs. Born, Woodbridge, Ont., June 27, 1985.

| | | | Regular Season | | | | | Playoffs | | | | |
|---|---|---|---|---|---|---|---|---|---|---|---|---|
| Season | Club | League | GP | G | A | Pts | PIM | GP | G | A | Pts | PIM |
| 2002-03 | Owen Sound | OHL | 65 | 7 | 10 | 17 | 81 | 4 | 1 | 1 | 2 | 0 |
| 2003-04 | Owen Sound | OHL | 66 | 9 | 9 | 18 | 118 | 7 | 4 | 1 | 5 | 4 |
| 2004-05 | Owen Sound | OHL | 41 | 9 | 10 | 19 | 126 | 8 | 3 | 2 | 5 | 10 |
| 2005-06 | Owen Sound | OHL | 68 | 53 | 25 | 78 | 167 | 11 | 5 | 9 | 14 | 38 |
| 2006-07 | Albany River Rats | AHL | 27 | 4 | 5 | 9 | 44 | 4 | 0 | 0 | 0 | 10 |
| | Florida Everblades | ECHL | 24 | 10 | 8 | 18 | 54 | .... | .... | .... | .... | .... |
| 2007-08 | Albany River Rats | AHL | 74 | 11 | 16 | 27 | 151 | 7 | 0 | 2 | 2 | 6 |
| 2008-09 | Albany River Rats | AHL | 67 | 15 | 10 | 25 | 142 | .... | .... | .... | .... | .... |

OHL First All-Star Team (2006) • Canadian Major Junior Humanitarian Player of the Year (2006)

Signed as a free agent by **Carolina**, July 27, 2006.

## ANIKEYENKO, Vitali (ah-nih-KEH-ehn-koh, vih-TAL-ee) OTT.

Defense. Shoots right. 6'3", 198 lbs. Born, Kiev, USSR, January 2, 1987.
(Ottawa's 2nd choice, 70th overall, in 2005 Entry Draft).

| | | | Regular Season | | | | | Playoffs | | | | |
|---|---|---|---|---|---|---|---|---|---|---|---|---|
| Season | Club | League | GP | G | A | Pts | PIM | GP | G | A | Pts | PIM |
| 2003-04 | Yaroslavl 2 | Russia-3 | 40 | 2 | 9 | 11 | 68 | .... | .... | .... | .... | .... |
| 2004-05 | Yaroslavl 2 | Russia-3 | 58 | 3 | 11 | 14 | 62 | .... | .... | .... | .... | .... |
| 2005-06 | Yaroslavl 2 | Russia-3 | 19 | 3 | 5 | 8 | 20 | .... | .... | .... | .... | .... |
| | Yaroslavl | Russia | 26 | 0 | 1 | 1 | 28 | 1 | 0 | 0 | 0 | 0 |
| 2006-07 | Yaroslavl 2 | Russia-3 | 15 | 1 | 6 | 7 | 59 | .... | .... | .... | .... | .... |
| | Yaroslavl | Russia | 25 | 1 | 3 | 4 | 16 | 3 | 0 | 0 | 0 | 12 |
| 2007-08 | Novokuznetsk | Russia | 10 | 1 | 1 | 2 | 10 | .... | .... | .... | .... | .... |
| | Yaroslavl | Russia | 40 | 4 | 9 | 13 | 48 | 16 | 0 | 0 | 0 | 20 |
| 2008-09 | Yaroslavl | Rus-KHL | 40 | 2 | 10 | 12 | 44 | 19 | 0 | 2 | 2 | 10 |

## ANSHAKOV, Sergei (an-sha-KAHV, SAIR-gay) PIT.

Left wing. Shoots left. 6'3", 179 lbs. Born, Moscow, USSR, January 13, 1984.
(Los Angeles' 2nd choice, 50th overall, in 2002 Entry Draft).

| | | | Regular Season | | | | | Playoffs | | | | |
|---|---|---|---|---|---|---|---|---|---|---|---|---|
| Season | Club | League | GP | G | A | Pts | PIM | GP | G | A | Pts | PIM |
| 2000-01 | Dyn'o Moscow 18 | Exhib. | 6 | 7 | 1 | 8 | 2 | .... | .... | .... | .... | .... |
| 2001-02 | HK CSKA 2 | Russia-3 | 3 | 3 | 1 | 4 | 0 | .... | .... | .... | .... | .... |
| | HK CSKA Moscow | Russia-2 | 46 | 20 | 12 | 22 | 10 | .... | .... | .... | .... | .... |
| 2002-03 | CSKA Moscow | Russia | 25 | 1 | 2 | 3 | 4 | .... | .... | .... | .... | .... |
| 2003-04 | CSKA Moscow | Russia | 33 | 3 | 2 | 5 | 12 | .... | .... | .... | .... | .... |
| 2004-05 | CSKA Moscow | Russia | 11 | 0 | 0 | 0 | 2 | .... | .... | .... | .... | .... |
| | Ufa | Russia | 23 | 9 | 3 | 12 | 4 | .... | .... | .... | .... | .... |
| 2005-06 | Ufa | Russia | 6 | 1 | 1 | 2 | 12 | .... | .... | .... | .... | .... |
| | Dynamo Moscow | Russia | 1 | 0 | 0 | 0 | 0 | .... | .... | .... | .... | .... |
| | HK MVD-THK Tver | Russia-3 | 1 | 2 | 0 | 2 | 0 | .... | .... | .... | .... | .... |
| | MVD | Russia | 12 | 1 | 3 | 4 | 2 | 2 | 0 | 1 | 1 | 0 |
| 2006-07 | CSKA Moscow | Russia | 29 | 2 | 3 | 5 | 12 | .... | .... | .... | .... | .... |
| | Sibir Novosibirsk 2 | Russia-3 | 2 | 2 | 1 | 3 | 0 | .... | .... | .... | .... | .... |
| | Sibir Novosibirsk | Russia | 17 | 2 | 4 | 6 | 4 | 3 | 1 | 0 | 1 | 2 |
| 2007-08 | Khabarovsk 2 | Russia-3 | 2 | 0 | 0 | 0 | 2 | .... | .... | .... | .... | .... |
| | Amur Khabarovsk | Russia | 22 | 4 | 2 | 6 | 4 | .... | .... | .... | .... | .... |
| 2008-09 | Nizhnekamsk | Rus-KHL | 41 | 7 | 3 | 10 | 10 | 2 | 0 | 0 | 0 | 0 |

Traded to **Pittsburgh** by **Los Angeles** with Martin Strbak for Martin Straka, November 30, 2003.

## ANTHONY, Steven (AN-thuh-nee, STEE-vehn) VAN.

Left wing. Shoots left. 6'1", 205 lbs. Born, Halifax, N.S., March 21, 1991.
(Vancouver's 7th choice, 187th overall, in 2009 Entry Draft).

| | | | Regular Season | | | | | Playoffs | | | | |
|---|---|---|---|---|---|---|---|---|---|---|---|---|
| Season | Club | League | GP | G | A | Pts | PIM | GP | G | A | Pts | PIM |
| 2006-07 | Dartmouth | NSMHL | 35 | 33 | 31 | 64 | 78 | 9 | 8 | 16 | 24 | 10 |
| 2007-08 | Saint John | QMJHL | 55 | 6 | 8 | 14 | 38 | 10 | 1 | 1 | 2 | 2 |
| 2008-09 | Saint John | QMJHL | 67 | 19 | 29 | 48 | 47 | 4 | 1 | 2 | 3 | 4 |

## ANTTILA, Marko (AN-tih-la, MAHR-koh) CHI.

Right wing. Shoots right. 6'7", 226 lbs. Born, Lempaala, Finland, May 27, 1985.
(Chicago's 17th choice, 260th overall, in 2004 Entry Draft).

| | | | Regular Season | | | | | Playoffs | | | | |
|---|---|---|---|---|---|---|---|---|---|---|---|---|
| Season | Club | League | GP | G | A | Pts | PIM | GP | G | A | Pts | PIM |
| 2002-03 | LeKi Lempaala U18 | Fin-U18 | 11 | 17 | 8 | 25 | 41 | .... | .... | .... | .... | .... |
| 2003-04 | LeKi Lempaala Jr. | Fin-Jr. | 12 | 11 | 11 | 22 | 26 | .... | .... | .... | .... | .... |
| | LeKi Lempaala | Finland-4 | 21 | 18 | 18 | 36 | 20 | .... | .... | .... | .... | .... |
| 2004-05 | Ilves Tampere Jr. | Fin-Jr. | 27 | 14 | 6 | 20 | 44 | 9 | 5 | 7 | 12 | 14 |
| | Ilves Tampere | Finland | 28 | 2 | 1 | 3 | 10 | 3 | 0 | 0 | 0 | 0 |
| 2005-06 | Ilves Tampere Jr. | Fin-Jr. | 10 | 4 | 2 | 6 | 6 | 2 | 1 | 1 | 2 | 4 |
| | Ilves Tampere | Finland | 50 | 4 | 3 | 7 | 46 | 4 | 0 | 0 | 0 | 0 |
| 2006-07 | Ilves Tampere | Finland | 53 | 2 | 2 | 4 | 34 | 7 | 1 | 0 | 1 | 8 |
| 2007-08 | Ilves Tampere | Finland | 56 | 14 | 9 | 23 | 90 | 9 | 2 | 2 | 4 | 4 |
| 2008-09 | Ilves Tampere | Finland | 53 | 8 | 14 | 22 | 69 | 3 | 0 | 0 | 0 | 2 |

**ARCHER, Andrew** (AHR-chuhr, AN-droo)

Defense. Shoots right. 6'4", 213 lbs. Born, Calgary, Alta., May 15, 1983.
(Montreal's 7th choice, 203rd overall, in 2001 Entry Draft).

| | | | Regular Season | | | | | Playoffs | | | | |
|---|---|---|---|---|---|---|---|---|---|---|---|---|
| Season | Club | League | GP | G | A | Pts | PIM | GP | G | A | Pts | PIM |
| 99-2000 | Oshawa Generals | OHL | 47 | 0 | 1 | 1 | 24 | 3 | 0 | 1 | 1 | 2 |
| 2000-01 | Oshawa Generals | OHL | 2 | 0 | 0 | 0 | 4 | .... | .... | .... | .... | .... |
| | Guelph Storm | OHL | 50 | 0 | 2 | 2 | 59 | 4 | 0 | 0 | 0 | 4 |
| 2001-02 | Guelph Storm | OHL | 58 | 3 | 10 | 13 | 76 | 9 | 0 | 2 | 2 | 16 |
| 2002-03 | Guelph Storm | OHL | 65 | 2 | 16 | 18 | 138 | 11 | 2 | 2 | 4 | 18 |
| 2003-04 | Hamilton Bulldogs | AHL | 30 | 0 | 1 | 1 | 23 | 3 | 0 | 0 | 0 | 0 |
| | Columbus | ECHL | 6 | 0 | 1 | 1 | 19 | .... | .... | .... | .... | .... |
| 2004-05 | Hamilton Bulldogs | AHL | 68 | 1 | 10 | 11 | 112 | 3 | 0 | 0 | 0 | 2 |
| 2005-06 | Hamilton Bulldogs | AHL | 42 | 0 | 3 | 3 | 62 | .... | .... | .... | .... | .... |
| 2006-07 | Hamilton Bulldogs | AHL | 16 | 0 | 1 | 1 | 24 | 19 | 0 | 3 | 3 | 21 |
| 2007-08 | Hamilton Bulldogs | AHL | 64 | 1 | 10 | 11 | 49 | .... | .... | .... | .... | .... |
| 2008-09 | Rockford IceHogs | AHL | 36 | 2 | 6 | 8 | 92 | .... | .... | .... | .... | .... |

• Missed majority of 2003-04 season recovering from hernia injury suffered in training camp, September 15, 2003. • Missed majority of 2006-07 season recovering from off-season knee surgery.

**ARDELAN, Mark** (AHR-deh-lan, MAHRK) **PIT.**

Defense. Shoots left. 5'11", 202 lbs. Born, Regina, Sask., March 16, 1983.

| | | | Regular Season | | | | | Playoffs | | | | |
|---|---|---|---|---|---|---|---|---|---|---|---|---|
| Season | Club | League | GP | G | A | Pts | PIM | GP | G | A | Pts | PIM |
| 99-2000 | Brandon | WHL | 63 | 4 | 16 | 20 | 60 | .... | .... | .... | .... | .... |
| 2000-01 | Brandon | WHL | 66 | 2 | 14 | 16 | 65 | 6 | 0 | 1 | 1 | 9 |
| 2001-02 | Vancouver Giants | WHL | 66 | 8 | 29 | 37 | 50 | .... | .... | .... | .... | .... |
| 2002-03 | Vancouver Giants | WHL | 71 | 13 | 35 | 48 | 64 | 4 | 0 | 1 | 1 | 0 |
| 2003-04 | Prince Albert | WHL | 72 | 19 | 54 | 73 | 29 | 6 | 1 | 4 | 5 | 0 |
| 2004-05 | Portland Pirates | AHL | 1 | 0 | 1 | 1 | 2 | .... | .... | .... | .... | .... |
| | South Carolina | ECHL | 72 | 15 | 32 | 47 | 24 | 4 | 0 | 0 | 0 | 2 |
| 2005-06 | Manchester | AHL | 62 | 9 | 21 | 30 | 36 | 7 | 2 | 0 | 2 | 0 |
| 2006-07 | Iowa Stars | AHL | 79 | 8 | 30 | 38 | 32 | 11 | 0 | 5 | 5 | 4 |
| 2007-08 | Wilkes-Barre | AHL | 60 | 7 | 20 | 27 | 33 | 23 | 6 | 7 | 13 | 2 |
| 2008-09 | Iserlohn Roosters | Germany | 34 | 7 | 15 | 22 | 6 | .... | .... | .... | .... | .... |
| | Lukko Rauma | Finland | 22 | 1 | 7 | 8 | 16 | .... | .... | .... | .... | .... |

Signed as a free agent by **Pittsburgh**, July 16, 2007.

**ARMSTRONG, John** (AHRM-stawng, JAWN) **CGY.**

Center. Shoots right. 6'2", 188 lbs. Born, Unionville, Ont., February 26, 1988.
(Calgary's 2nd choice, 87th overall, in 2006 Entry Draft).

| | | | Regular Season | | | | | Playoffs | | | | |
|---|---|---|---|---|---|---|---|---|---|---|---|---|
| Season | Club | League | GP | G | A | Pts | PIM | GP | G | A | Pts | PIM |
| 2004-05 | Plymouth Whalers | OHL | 52 | 6 | 13 | 19 | 39 | 4 | 0 | 0 | 0 | 4 |
| 2005-06 | Plymouth Whalers | OHL | 65 | 14 | 23 | 37 | 75 | 13 | 4 | 7 | 11 | 18 |
| 2006-07 | Plymouth Whalers | OHL | 34 | 8 | 13 | 21 | 26 | .... | .... | .... | .... | .... |
| | Peterborough | OHL | 27 | 11 | 13 | 24 | 34 | .... | .... | .... | .... | .... |
| 2007-08 | Peterborough | OHL | 65 | 21 | 36 | 57 | 77 | 5 | 0 | 1 | 1 | 6 |
| 2008-09 | Quad City Flames | AHL | 68 | 5 | 15 | 20 | 72 | .... | .... | .... | .... | .... |

**ARNIEL, Jamie** (ahr-NEEL, JAY-mee) **BOS.**

Center. Shoots right. 5'11", 191 lbs. Born, Kingston, Ont., November 16, 1989.
(Boston's 4th choice, 97th overall, in 2008 Entry Draft).

| | | | Regular Season | | | | | Playoffs | | | | |
|---|---|---|---|---|---|---|---|---|---|---|---|---|
| Season | Club | League | GP | G | A | Pts | PIM | GP | G | A | Pts | PIM |
| 2005-06 | Guelph Storm | OHL | 61 | 11 | 8 | 19 | 30 | 15 | 2 | 0 | 2 | 4 |
| 2006-07 | Guelph Storm | OHL | 68 | 31 | 31 | 62 | 51 | 4 | 2 | 2 | 4 | 0 |
| 2007-08 | Guelph Storm | OHL | 20 | 9 | 4 | 13 | 16 | .... | .... | .... | .... | .... |
| | Sarnia Sting | OHL | 40 | 18 | 16 | 34 | 22 | 9 | 2 | 2 | 4 | 6 |
| 2008-09 | Sarnia Sting | OHL | 63 | 32 | 36 | 68 | 28 | 5 | 1 | 2 | 3 | 4 |
| | Providence Bruins | AHL | .... | .... | .... | .... | .... | 8 | 1 | 0 | 1 | 0 |

**ASHTON, Carter** (ASH-tuhn, KAHR-tuhr) **T.B.**

Right wing. Shoots left. 6'3", 205 lbs. Born, Winnipeg, Man., April 1, 1991.
(Tampa Bay's 2nd choice, 29th overall, in 2009 Entry Draft).

| | | | Regular Season | | | | | Playoffs | | | | |
|---|---|---|---|---|---|---|---|---|---|---|---|---|
| Season | Club | League | GP | G | A | Pts | PIM | GP | G | A | Pts | PIM |
| 2006-07 | Sask. Contacts | SMHL | 41 | 28 | 38 | 66 | 99 | .... | .... | .... | .... | .... |
| | Lethbridge | WHL | 2 | 0 | 0 | 0 | 0 | .... | .... | .... | .... | .... |
| 2007-08 | Lethbridge | WHL | 40 | 5 | 4 | 9 | 21 | 19 | 0 | 1 | 1 | 12 |
| 2008-09 | Lethbridge | WHL | 70 | 30 | 20 | 50 | 93 | 11 | 1 | 2 | 3 | 15 |

**ASTON, Peter** (AS-tuhn, PEE-tuhr) **FLA.**

Defense. Shoots right. 6'1", 205 lbs. Born, Toronto, Ont., February 24, 1986.
(Florida's 5th choice, 155th overall, in 2006 Entry Draft).

| | | | Regular Season | | | | | Playoffs | | | | |
|---|---|---|---|---|---|---|---|---|---|---|---|---|
| Season | Club | League | GP | G | A | Pts | PIM | GP | G | A | Pts | PIM |
| 2002-03 | Pickering Panthers | OPJHL | 45 | 4 | 20 | 24 | 52 | .... | .... | .... | .... | .... |
| 2003-04 | Peterborough | OHL | 36 | 2 | 3 | 5 | 17 | .... | .... | .... | .... | .... |
| 2004-05 | Peterborough | OHL | 52 | 0 | 15 | 15 | 16 | 14 | 0 | 4 | 4 | 6 |
| 2005-06 | Peterborough | OHL | 16 | 4 | 15 | 19 | 10 | .... | .... | .... | .... | .... |
| | Windsor Spitfires | OHL | 49 | 12 | 21 | 33 | 21 | 7 | 2 | 1 | 3 | 2 |
| 2006-07 | Assat Pori | Finland | 21 | 2 | 1 | 3 | 14 | .... | .... | .... | .... | .... |
| | Oshawa Generals | OHL | 41 | 8 | 24 | 32 | 38 | 9 | 1 | 7 | 8 | 8 |
| 2007-08 | Rochester | AHL | 56 | 3 | 10 | 13 | 35 | .... | .... | .... | .... | .... |
| | Florida Everblades | ECHL | 6 | 1 | 2 | 3 | 4 | 2 | 0 | 1 | 1 | 2 |
| 2008-09 | Rochester | AHL | 53 | 2 | 8 | 10 | 24 | .... | .... | .... | .... | .... |

**ATKINSON, Cam** (AT-kihn-suhn, KAM-ih-RUHN) **CBJ**

Right wing. Shoots right. 5'9", 165 lbs. Born, Riverside, CT, June 5, 1989.
(Columbus' 8th choice, 157th overall, in 2008 Entry Draft).

| | | | Regular Season | | | | | Playoffs | | | | |
|---|---|---|---|---|---|---|---|---|---|---|---|---|
| Season | Club | League | GP | G | A | Pts | PIM | GP | G | A | Pts | PIM |
| 2005-06 | Avon Old Farms | High-CT | 25 | 15 | 20 | 35 | 16 | .... | .... | .... | .... | .... |
| 2006-07 | Avon Old Farms | High-CT | 27 | 28 | 24 | 52 | 12 | .... | .... | .... | .... | .... |
| 2007-08 | Avon Old Farms | High-CT | 28 | 26 | 37 | 63 | 10 | .... | .... | .... | .... | .... |
| 2008-09 | Boston College | H-East | 36 | 7 | 12 | 19 | 28 | .... | .... | .... | .... | .... |

**ATYUSHOV, Vitali** (a-tew-SHAWF, vih-TAL-ee) **OTT.**

Defense. Shoots left. 6'1", 205 lbs. Born, Penza, USSR, July 4, 1979.
(Ottawa's 8th choice, 276th overall, in 2002 Entry Draft).

| | | | Regular Season | | | | | Playoffs | | | | |
|---|---|---|---|---|---|---|---|---|---|---|---|---|
| Season | Club | League | GP | G | A | Pts | PIM | GP | G | A | Pts | PIM |
| 1997-98 | Krylja Sovetov | Russia | 4 | 0 | 0 | 0 | 2 | .... | .... | .... | .... | .... |
| 1998-99 | Dizelist Penza 2 | Russia-4 | 2 | 1 | 1 | 2 | 2 | .... | .... | .... | .... | .... |
| | Dizelist Penza | Russia-2 | 22 | 0 | 0 | 0 | 22 | .... | .... | .... | .... | .... |
| | Krylja Sovetov | Russia | 17 | 1 | 0 | 1 | 20 | .... | .... | .... | .... | .... |
| | Krylja Sovetov | Russia-Q | 21 | 0 | 5 | 5 | 50 | .... | .... | .... | .... | .... |
| 99-2000 | Perm | Russia | 38 | 4 | 0 | 4 | 50 | 3 | 0 | 0 | 0 | 12 |
| 2000-01 | Perm | Russia | 44 | 3 | 9 | 12 | 32 | .... | .... | .... | .... | .... |
| 2001-02 | Perm | Russia | 51 | 4 | 8 | 12 | 66 | .... | .... | .... | .... | .... |
| 2002-03 | Ak Bars Kazan | Russia | 33 | 0 | 9 | 9 | 12 | 2 | 0 | 0 | 0 | 0 |
| 2003-04 | Magnitogorsk | Russia | 56 | 5 | 9 | 14 | 26 | 14 | 2 | 3 | 5 | 6 |
| 2004-05 | Magnitogorsk | Russia | 58 | 6 | 18 | 24 | 42 | 5 | 2 | 0 | 2 | 0 |
| 2005-06 | Magnitogorsk | Russia | 51 | 7 | 12 | 19 | 64 | 11 | 2 | 0 | 2 | 4 |
| 2006-07 | Magnitogorsk | Russia | 54 | 7 | 20 | 27 | 46 | 15 | 3 | 9 | 12 | 10 |
| 2007-08 | Magnitogorsk | Russia | 56 | 10 | 33 | 43 | 32 | 10 | 1 | 4 | 5 | 2 |
| 2008-09 | Magnitogorsk | Rus-KHL | 55 | 8 | 27 | 35 | 34 | 12 | 1 | 6 | 7 | 8 |

**AUBIN, Brent** (OH-behn, BREHNT)

Right wing. Shoots left. 5'9", 181 lbs. Born, St-Sophie, Que., June 18, 1986.

| | | | Regular Season | | | | | Playoffs | | | | |
|---|---|---|---|---|---|---|---|---|---|---|---|---|
| Season | Club | League | GP | G | A | Pts | PIM | GP | G | A | Pts | PIM |
| 2002-03 | Rouyn-Noranda | QMJHL | 65 | 14 | 20 | 34 | 98 | 4 | 1 | 0 | 1 | 6 |
| 2003-04 | Rouyn-Noranda | QMJHL | 70 | 29 | 36 | 65 | 116 | 11 | 4 | 3 | 7 | 22 |
| 2004-05 | Rouyn-Noranda | QMJHL | 70 | 41 | 43 | 84 | 78 | 10 | 5 | 4 | 9 | 14 |
| 2005-06 | Rouyn-Noranda | QMJHL | 40 | 31 | 33 | 64 | 58 | .... | .... | .... | .... | .... |
| | Quebec Remparts | QMJHL | 32 | 26 | 27 | 53 | 34 | 23 | 12 | 15 | 27 | 24 |
| 2006-07 | Quebec Remparts | QMJHL | 68 | 51 | 54 | 105 | 124 | 5 | 3 | 5 | 8 | 8 |
| | Toronto Marlies | AHL | 8 | 0 | 2 | 2 | 4 | .... | .... | .... | .... | .... |
| 2007-08 | Toronto Marlies | AHL | 75 | 10 | 12 | 22 | 76 | 17 | 5 | 0 | 5 | 6 |
| 2008-09 | Toronto Marlies | AHL | 50 | 6 | 11 | 17 | 49 | .... | .... | .... | .... | .... |

Signed as a free agent by **Toronto**, September 15, 2006.

**AUBIN, Mathieu** (oh-BEHN, MAT-yew)

Center. Shoots right. 6'2", 202 lbs. Born, Sorel, Que., September 18, 1986.
(Montreal's 4th choice, 130th overall, in 2005 Entry Draft).

| | | | Regular Season | | | | | Playoffs | | | | |
|---|---|---|---|---|---|---|---|---|---|---|---|---|
| Season | Club | League | GP | G | A | Pts | PIM | GP | G | A | Pts | PIM |
| 2001-02 | Antoine-Girouard | QAAA | 19 | 5 | 10 | 15 | 10 | .... | .... | .... | .... | .... |
| 2002-03 | Antoine-Girouard | QAAA | 42 | 19 | 35 | 54 | 28 | .... | .... | .... | .... | .... |
| | Sherbrooke | QMJHL | 1 | 0 | 0 | 0 | 0 | .... | .... | .... | .... | .... |
| 2003-04 | Lewiston | QMJHL | 68 | 19 | 23 | 42 | 34 | 7 | 1 | 1 | 2 | 2 |
| 2004-05 | Lewiston | QMJHL | 49 | 19 | 26 | 45 | 24 | 8 | 3 | 6 | 9 | 6 |
| 2005-06 | Lewiston | QMJHL | 70 | 47 | 56 | 103 | 63 | 6 | 3 | 4 | 7 | 4 |
| 2006-07 | Hamilton Bulldogs | AHL | 17 | 2 | 3 | 5 | 4 | .... | .... | .... | .... | .... |
| | Cincinnati | ECHL | 38 | 12 | 25 | 37 | 32 | 10 | 4 | 5 | 9 | 10 |
| 2007-08 | Hamilton Bulldogs | AHL | 20 | 2 | 4 | 6 | 8 | .... | .... | .... | .... | .... |
| | Cincinnati | ECHL | 47 | 30 | 27 | 57 | 56 | 22 | 8 | 6 | 14 | 34 |
| 2008-09 | Hamilton Bulldogs | AHL | 32 | 7 | 5 | 12 | 29 | 5 | 0 | 0 | 0 | 0 |

**AUGER, Chris** (AW-zhay, KRIHS) **CHI.**

Center. Shoots left. 5'10", 161 lbs. Born, Belleville, Ont., December 16, 1987.
(Chicago's 8th choice, 169th overall, in 2006 Entry Draft).

| | | | Regular Season | | | | | Playoffs | | | | |
|---|---|---|---|---|---|---|---|---|---|---|---|---|
| Season | Club | League | GP | G | A | Pts | PIM | GP | G | A | Pts | PIM |
| 2004-05 | Wellington Dukes | OPJHL | 44 | 25 | 30 | 55 | 16 | 14 | 9 | 11 | 20 | 37 |
| 2005-06 | Wellington Dukes | OPJHL | 47 | 41 | 51 | 92 | 46 | 12 | 8 | 14 | 22 | 2 |
| 2006-07 | U. Mass-Lowell | H-East | 34 | 2 | 10 | 12 | 6 | .... | .... | .... | .... | .... |
| 2007-08 | U. Mass-Lowell | H-East | 33 | 4 | 10 | 14 | 16 | .... | .... | .... | .... | .... |
| 2008-09 | U. Mass-Lowell | H-East | 14 | 2 | 1 | 3 | 0 | .... | .... | .... | .... | .... |

OPJHL East MVP (2006)

**AULIE, Keith** (AW-lee, KEETH) **CGY.**

Defense. Shoots left. 6'6", 208 lbs. Born, Regina, Sask., June 11, 1989.
(Calgary's 3rd choice, 116th overall, in 2007 Entry Draft).

| | | | Regular Season | | | | | Playoffs | | | | |
|---|---|---|---|---|---|---|---|---|---|---|---|---|
| Season | Club | League | GP | G | A | Pts | PIM | GP | G | A | Pts | PIM |
| 2004-05 | Notre Dame | SJHL | 38 | 2 | 7 | 9 | 53 | .... | .... | .... | .... | .... |
| 2005-06 | Brandon | WHL | 38 | 0 | 2 | 2 | 32 | 4 | 0 | 0 | 0 | 4 |
| 2006-07 | Brandon | WHL | 66 | 1 | 8 | 9 | 82 | 11 | 0 | 2 | 2 | 14 |
| 2007-08 | Brandon | WHL | 72 | 5 | 12 | 17 | 81 | 6 | 0 | 3 | 3 | 11 |
| 2008-09 | Brandon | WHL | 58 | 6 | 27 | 33 | 83 | 12 | 2 | 7 | 9 | 12 |

WHL East First All-Star Team (2009)

**AVTSIN, Alexander** (AV-tsihn, al-ehx-AN-duhr) **MTL.**

Right wing. Shoots right. 6'2", 188 lbs. Born, Moscow, USSR, March 19, 1991.
(Montreal's 4th choice, 109th overall, in 2009 Entry Draft).

| | | | Regular Season | | | | | Playoffs | | | | |
|---|---|---|---|---|---|---|---|---|---|---|---|---|
| Season | Club | League | GP | G | A | Pts | PIM | GP | G | A | Pts | PIM |
| 2008-09 | Dyn'o Moscow 2 | Russia-3 | STATISTICS NOT AVAILABLE | | | | | | | | | |

**AXELSSON, Anton** (AHX-ehl-suhn, AN-tawn) **DET.**

Left wing. Shoots left. 6', 183 lbs. Born, Ytterby, Sweden, January 16, 1986.
(Detroit's 5th choice, 192nd overall, in 2004 Entry Draft).

| | | | Regular Season | | | | | Playoffs | | | | |
|---|---|---|---|---|---|---|---|---|---|---|---|---|
| Season | Club | League | GP | G | A | Pts | PIM | GP | G | A | Pts | PIM |
| 2003-04 | V.Frolunda Jr. | Swe-Jr. | 28 | 7 | 10 | 17 | 14 | 10 | 2 | 3 | 5 | 2 |
| 2004-05 | Frolunda Jr. | Swe-Jr. | 33 | 12 | 30 | 42 | 14 | 6 | 2 | 5 | 7 | 0 |
| 2005-06 | Frolunda Jr. | Swe-Jr. | 12 | 6 | 11 | 17 | 2 | 1 | 0 | 1 | 1 | 0 |
| | Frolunda | Sweden | 39 | 3 | 3 | 6 | 8 | 11 | 0 | 0 | 0 | 6 |
| 2006-07 | Frolunda Jr. | Swe-Jr. | 2 | 4 | 2 | 6 | 4 | .... | .... | .... | .... | .... |
| | Kungalvs IK | Sweden-3 | 1 | 1 | 3 | 4 | 0 | .... | .... | .... | .... | .... |
| | Frolunda | Sweden | 52 | 5 | 7 | 12 | 14 | .... | .... | .... | .... | .... |
| 2007-08 | Timra IK | Sweden | 54 | 10 | 10 | 20 | 10 | 11 | 2 | 2 | 4 | 4 |
| 2008-09 | Timra IK | Sweden | 52 | 6 | 9 | 15 | 0 | 7 | 1 | 0 | 1 | 0 |

**AXELSSON, Dick** (AHX-ehl-suhn, DIHK) **DET.**

Wing. Shoots left. 6'2", 198 lbs. Born, Stockholm, Sweden, April 25, 1987.
(Detroit's 3rd choice, 62nd overall, in 2006 Entry Draft).

| | | | Regular Season | | | | | Playoffs | | | | |
|---|---|---|---|---|---|---|---|---|---|---|---|---|
| Season | Club | League | GP | G | A | Pts | PIM | GP | G | A | Pts | PIM |
| 2003-04 | Huddinge IK U18 | Swe-U18 | 13 | 3 | 1 | 4 | 38 | .... | .... | .... | .... | .... |
| 2004-05 | Huddinge IK U18 | Swe-U18 | 1 | 0 | 0 | 0 | 0 | .... | .... | .... | .... | .... |
| | Huddinge IK Jr. | Swe-Jr. | 31 | 12 | 4 | 16 | 34 | 3 | 1 | 0 | 1 | 0 |
| 2005-06 | Huddinge IK Jr. | Swe-Jr. | 28 | 19 | 15 | 34 | 157 | .... | .... | .... | .... | .... |
| 2006-07 | Huddinge IK | Sweden-2 | 33 | 16 | 15 | 31 | 145 | .... | .... | .... | .... | .... |
| 2007-08 | Djurgarden | Sweden | 47 | 12 | 13 | 25 | 44 | 5 | 1 | 0 | 1 | 2 |
| 2008-09 | Djurgarden | Sweden | 18 | 5 | 7 | 12 | 10 | .... | .... | .... | .... | .... |
| | Farjestad | Sweden | 21 | 6 | 12 | 18 | 32 | 9 | 1 | 3 | 4 | 2 |

**AXELSSON, Emil** (AHX-ehl-suhn, eh-MIHL) **NYI**

Defense. Shoots left. 6'3", 198 lbs. Born, Orebro, Sweden, March 19, 1986.
(NY Islanders' 7th choice, 210th overall, in 2004 Entry Draft).

| | | | Regular Season | | | | | Playoffs | | | | |
|---|---|---|---|---|---|---|---|---|---|---|---|---|
| Season | Club | League | GP | G | A | Pts | PIM | GP | G | A | Pts | PIM |
| 2002-03 | HC Orebro 90 Jr. | Swe-Jr. | 27 | 7 | 9 | 16 | 2 | .... | .... | .... | .... | .... |
| 2003-04 | HC Orebro 90 | Sweden-2 | 49 | 4 | 0 | 4 | 116 | .... | .... | .... | .... | .... |
| 2004-05 | Linkopings HC Jr. | Swe-Jr. | 21 | 0 | 1 | 1 | 32 | .... | .... | .... | .... | .... |
| 2005-06 | IFK Arboga IK | Sweden-2 | 39 | 1 | 2 | 3 | 30 | .... | .... | .... | .... | .... |
| 2006-07 | IFK Arboga IK | Sweden-2 | 38 | 1 | 5 | 6 | 85 | .... | .... | .... | .... | .... |
| | Linkopings HC | Sweden | 2 | 0 | 0 | 0 | 0 | .... | .... | .... | .... | .... |
| | VIK Vasteras HK | Sweden-2 | 5 | 0 | 0 | 0 | 2 | 2 | 0 | 0 | 0 | 0 |
| 2007-08 | VIK Vasteras HK | Sweden-2 | 54 | 0 | 5 | 5 | 151 | 5 | 0 | 0 | 0 | 4 |
| 2008-09 | Vasteras Jr. | Swe-Jr. | 1 | 0 | 1 | 1 | 2 | .... | .... | .... | .... | .... |
| | IFK Arboga IK | Sweden-3 | 3 | 1 | 0 | 1 | 4 | .... | .... | .... | .... | .... |
| | VIK Vasteras HK | Sweden-2 | 8 | 0 | 0 | 0 | 2 | .... | .... | .... | .... | .... |

**AZEVEDO, Justin** (a-zeh-VAY-doh, JUHS-tihn) **L.A.**

Center. Shoots right. 5'7", 180 lbs. Born, West Lorne, Ont., April 1, 1988.
(Los Angeles' 8th choice, 153rd overall, in 2008 Entry Draft).

| | | | Regular Season | | | | | Playoffs | | | | |
|---|---|---|---|---|---|---|---|---|---|---|---|---|
| Season | Club | League | GP | G | A | Pts | PIM | GP | G | A | Pts | PIM |
| 2004-05 | Kitchener Rangers | OHL | 58 | 18 | 21 | 39 | 34 | 15 | 3 | 1 | 4 | 14 |
| 2005-06 | Kitchener Rangers | OHL | 60 | 29 | 40 | 69 | 80 | 5 | 0 | 3 | 3 | 12 |
| 2006-07 | Kitchener Rangers | OHL | 50 | 17 | 39 | 56 | 42 | 9 | 4 | 11 | 15 | 22 |
| 2007-08 | Kitchener Rangers | OHL | 67 | 43 | *81 | *124 | 69 | 20 | 10 | *26 | *36 | 33 |
| 2008-09 | Manchester | AHL | 49 | 12 | 24 | 36 | 31 | .... | .... | .... | .... | .... |

OHL First All-Star Team (2008) • Memorial Cup All-Star Team (2008) • Ed Chynoweth Trophy (Memorial Cup Tournament - Leading Scorer) (2008) • Canadian Major Junior First All-Star Team (2008) • Canadian Major Junior Player of the Year (2008)

**BABIN, Noah** (BA-bihn, NOH-ah)

Defense. Shoots right. 6', 200 lbs. Born, Palm Beach Gardens, FL, March 11, 1984.

| | | | Regular Season | | | | | Playoffs | | | | |
|---|---|---|---|---|---|---|---|---|---|---|---|---|
| Season | Club | League | GP | G | A | Pts | PIM | GP | G | A | Pts | PIM |
| 2002-03 | Green Bay | USHL | 57 | 3 | 11 | 14 | 54 | .... | .... | .... | .... | .... |
| 2003-04 | U. of Notre Dame | CCHA | 31 | 0 | 1 | 1 | 20 | .... | .... | .... | .... | .... |
| 2004-05 | U. of Notre Dame | CCHA | 38 | 5 | 6 | 11 | 34 | .... | .... | .... | .... | .... |
| 2005-06 | U. of Notre Dame | CCHA | 35 | 3 | 12 | 15 | 20 | .... | .... | .... | .... | .... |
| 2006-07 | U. of Notre Dame | CCHA | 42 | 2 | 20 | 22 | 32 | .... | .... | .... | .... | .... |
| | Albany River Rats | AHL | 11 | 1 | 6 | 7 | 2 | 5 | 0 | 0 | 0 | 2 |
| 2007-08 | Albany River Rats | AHL | 46 | 0 | 4 | 4 | 20 | .... | .... | .... | .... | .... |
| 2008-09 | Albany River Rats | AHL | 45 | 0 | 5 | 5 | 23 | .... | .... | .... | .... | .... |
| | Florida Everblades | ECHL | 18 | 3 | 8 | 11 | 2 | .... | .... | .... | .... | .... |

Signed as a free agent by **Carolina**, March 26, 2007.

**BAGNALL, Drew** (BAG-nuhl, DROO) **L.A.**

Defense. Shoots left. 6'3", 222 lbs. Born, Oakbank, Man., October 26, 1983.
(Dallas' 9th choice, 195th overall, in 2003 Entry Draft).

| | | | Regular Season | | | | | Playoffs | | | | |
|---|---|---|---|---|---|---|---|---|---|---|---|---|
| Season | Club | League | GP | G | A | Pts | PIM | GP | G | A | Pts | PIM |
| 2000-01 | Battlefords | SJHL | 58 | 7 | 20 | 27 | 205 | .... | .... | .... | .... | .... |
| 2001-02 | Battlefords | SJHL | 60 | 16 | 23 | 39 | 247 | .... | .... | .... | .... | .... |
| 2002-03 | Battlefords | SJHL | 55 | 17 | 46 | 63 | 248 | 4 | 0 | 1 | 1 | 4 |
| 2003-04 | St. Lawrence | ECAC | 40 | 5 | 13 | 18 | 61 | .... | .... | .... | .... | .... |
| 2004-05 | St. Lawrence | ECAC | 37 | 7 | 12 | 19 | 68 | .... | .... | .... | .... | .... |
| 2005-06 | St. Lawrence | ECAC | 24 | 1 | 9 | 10 | 32 | .... | .... | .... | .... | .... |
| 2006-07 | St. Lawrence | ECAC | 39 | 6 | 19 | 25 | 74 | .... | .... | .... | .... | .... |
| 2007-08 | Manchester | AHL | 54 | 1 | 11 | 12 | 115 | 4 | 0 | 0 | 0 | 4 |
| | Reading Royals | ECHL | 10 | 1 | 2 | 3 | 32 | .... | .... | .... | .... | .... |
| 2008-09 | Manchester | AHL | 79 | 0 | 6 | 6 | 150 | .... | .... | .... | .... | .... |

Traded to **Florida** by **Dallas** with Dallas' 2nd round compensatory choice (later traded to Phoenix - Phoenix selected Enver Lisin) in 2004 Entry Draft for Valeri Bure, March 8, 2004. Signed as a free agent by **Los Angeles**, August 23, 2007.

**BAIER, Paul** (BAI-uhr, PAWL)

Defense. Shoots right. 6'3", 212 lbs. Born, Summit, NJ, February 2, 1985.
(Los Angeles' 2nd choice, 95th overall, in 2004 Entry Draft).

| | | | Regular Season | | | | | Playoffs | | | | |
|---|---|---|---|---|---|---|---|---|---|---|---|---|
| Season | Club | League | GP | G | A | Pts | PIM | GP | G | A | Pts | PIM |
| 2002-03 | Deerfield Academy | High-MA | 25 | 2 | 15 | 17 | 24 | .... | .... | .... | .... | .... |
| 2003-04 | Deerfield Academy | High-MA | 23 | 6 | 4 | 10 | 22 | .... | .... | .... | .... | .... |
| 2004-05 | Brown U. | ECAC | 32 | 2 | 8 | 10 | 24 | .... | .... | .... | .... | .... |
| 2005-06 | Brown U. | ECAC | 30 | 0 | 6 | 6 | 18 | .... | .... | .... | .... | .... |
| 2006-07 | Brown U. | ECAC | 32 | 1 | 4 | 5 | 55 | .... | .... | .... | .... | .... |
| 2007-08 | Brown U. | ECAC | 31 | 2 | 5 | 7 | 38 | .... | .... | .... | .... | .... |
| | Rochester | AHL | 9 | 1 | 3 | 4 | 5 | .... | .... | .... | .... | .... |
| 2008-09 | Portland Pirates | AHL | 62 | 3 | 8 | 11 | 67 | 3 | 0 | 0 | 0 | 6 |

**BAILEY, Jason** (BAY-lee, JAY-sohn) **ANA.**

Right wing. Shoots right. 6', 205 lbs. Born, Ottawa, Ont., June 4, 1987.
(Anaheim's 3rd choice, 63rd overall, in 2005 Entry Draft).

| | | | Regular Season | | | | | Playoffs | | | | |
|---|---|---|---|---|---|---|---|---|---|---|---|---|
| Season | Club | League | GP | G | A | Pts | PIM | GP | G | A | Pts | PIM |
| 2003-04 | Nepean Raiders | CJHL | 45 | 14 | 14 | 28 | 119 | 18 | 2 | 7 | 9 | 35 |
| 2004-05 | USNTDP | U-18 | 26 | 3 | 2 | 5 | 91 | .... | .... | .... | .... | .... |
| | USNTDP | NAHL | 13 | 2 | 4 | 6 | 50 | .... | .... | .... | .... | .... |
| 2005-06 | U. of Michigan | CCHA | 27 | 5 | 2 | 7 | 57 | .... | .... | .... | .... | .... |
| 2006-07 | U. of Michigan | CCHA | 19 | 0 | 0 | 0 | 28 | .... | .... | .... | .... | .... |
| | Ottawa 67's | OHL | 35 | 7 | 9 | 16 | 88 | 4 | 0 | 0 | 0 | 6 |
| 2007-08 | Ottawa 67's | OHL | 34 | 8 | 9 | 17 | 78 | 4 | 0 | 2 | 2 | 11 |
| 2008-09 | Bakersfield | ECHL | 35 | 0 | 2 | 2 | 44 | 2 | 0 | 0 | 0 | 0 |
| | Iowa Chops | AHL | 2 | 0 | 0 | 0 | 0 | .... | .... | .... | .... | .... |

**BAINES, Ajay** (BAYNZ, AY-JAY)

Center. Shoots left. 5'9", 183 lbs. Born, Kamloops, B.C., March 25, 1978.

| | | | Regular Season | | | | | Playoffs | | | | |
|---|---|---|---|---|---|---|---|---|---|---|---|---|
| Season | Club | League | GP | G | A | Pts | PIM | GP | G | A | Pts | PIM |
| 1994-95 | Kamloops | Minor-BC | 52 | 45 | 79 | 124 | 139 | .... | .... | .... | .... | .... |
| 1995-96 | Kamloops Blazers | WHL | 68 | 14 | 29 | 43 | 43 | .... | .... | .... | .... | .... |
| 1996-97 | Kamloops Blazers | WHL | 70 | 32 | 43 | 75 | 106 | 5 | 4 | 1 | 5 | 6 |
| 1997-98 | Kamloops Blazers | WHL | 72 | 34 | 25 | 59 | 88 | .... | .... | .... | .... | .... |
| 1998-99 | Kamloops Blazers | WHL | 72 | 33 | 32 | 65 | 145 | 15 | 7 | 6 | 13 | 20 |
| 99-2000 | Greenville Grrrowl | ECHL | 67 | 24 | 31 | 55 | 102 | 15 | 2 | 5 | 7 | 13 |
| 2000-01 | Norfolk Admirals | AHL | 73 | 18 | 18 | 36 | 92 | 9 | 0 | 1 | 1 | 2 |
| 2001-02 | Norfolk Admirals | AHL | 80 | 16 | 28 | 44 | 70 | 4 | 0 | 1 | 1 | 0 |
| 2002-03 | Norfolk Admirals | AHL | 74 | 8 | 14 | 22 | 108 | 9 | 2 | 1 | 3 | 18 |
| 2003-04 | Norfolk Admirals | AHL | 80 | 15 | 27 | 42 | 81 | 8 | 1 | 3 | 4 | 13 |
| 2004-05 | Norfolk Admirals | AHL | 70 | 7 | 16 | 23 | 60 | 6 | 3 | 2 | 5 | 16 |
| 2005-06 | Norfolk Admirals | AHL | 32 | 4 | 4 | 8 | 45 | .... | .... | .... | .... | .... |
| | Omaha | AHL | 24 | 8 | 4 | 12 | 26 | .... | .... | .... | .... | .... |
| 2006-07 | Hamilton Bulldogs | AHL | 77 | 13 | 13 | 26 | 72 | 22 | 6 | 4 | 10 | 8 |
| 2007-08 | Hamilton Bulldogs | AHL | 58 | 6 | 3 | 9 | 61 | .... | .... | .... | .... | .... |
| 2008-09 | Iowa Chops | AHL | 79 | 7 | 24 | 31 | 53 | .... | .... | .... | .... | .... |

Fred T. Hunt Memorial Award (AHL – Sportsmanship) (2009)

Signed as a free agent by **Chicago**, August 1, 2001. Signed as a free agent by **Hamilton** (AHL), August 4, 2006.

**BALAN, Stanislav** (BAY-luhn, STAN-ihs-lahv) **NSH.**

Center. Shoots left. 6'2", 161 lbs. Born, Hodonin, Czech., January 30, 1986.
(Nashville's 8th choice, 209th overall, in 2004 Entry Draft).

| | | | Regular Season | | | | | Playoffs | | | | |
|---|---|---|---|---|---|---|---|---|---|---|---|---|
| Season | Club | League | GP | G | A | Pts | PIM | GP | G | A | Pts | PIM |
| 2001-02 | HC Zlin Jr. | CzRep-Jr. | 48 | 21 | 23 | 44 | 60 | 4 | 1 | 1 | 2 | 0 |
| 2002-03 | HC Zlin Jr. | CzRep-Jr. | 35 | 24 | 21 | 45 | 59 | 3 | 2 | 0 | 2 | 16 |
| 2003-04 | HC Zlin Jr. | CzRep-Jr. | 53 | 23 | 33 | 56 | 122 | 5 | 2 | 0 | 2 | 31 |
| | HC Hame Zlin | CzRep | 4 | 1 | 0 | 1 | 2 | .... | .... | .... | .... | .... |
| 2004-05 | SHK Hodonin | CzRep-3 | 5 | 3 | 2 | 5 | 20 | .... | .... | .... | .... | .... |
| | HC Zlin Jr. | CzRep-Jr. | 37 | 10 | 13 | 23 | 131 | 2 | 0 | 0 | 0 | 2 |
| 2005-06 | Portland | WHL | 67 | 14 | 23 | 37 | 102 | 12 | 1 | 4 | 5 | 18 |
| 2006-07 | HC Hame Zlin | CzRep | 44 | 4 | 3 | 7 | 48 | 5 | 0 | 0 | 0 | 2 |
| | Trebic | CzRep-2 | 7 | 3 | 2 | 5 | 12 | .... | .... | .... | .... | .... |
| 2007-08 | RI Okna Zlin | CzRep | 57 | 4 | 6 | 10 | 54 | .... | .... | .... | .... | .... |
| 2008-09 | HC Dukla Jihlava | CzRep-2 | 5 | 4 | 3 | 7 | 4 | .... | .... | .... | .... | .... |
| | RI Okna Zlin | CzRep | 46 | 5 | 3 | 8 | 61 | 4 | 0 | 0 | 0 | 0 |

**BALDWIN, Gord** (BAHLD-wihn, GOHRD) **CGY.**

Defense. Shoots left. 6'5", 199 lbs. Born, Winnipeg, Man., March 1, 1987.
(Calgary's 2nd choice, 69th overall, in 2005 Entry Draft).

| | | | Regular Season | | | | | Playoffs | | | | |
|---|---|---|---|---|---|---|---|---|---|---|---|---|
| Season | Club | League | GP | G | A | Pts | PIM | GP | G | A | Pts | PIM |
| 2003-04 | Wpg. Thrashers | MMHL | 39 | 5 | 16 | 21 | 66 | .... | .... | .... | .... | .... |
| 2004-05 | Medicine Hat | WHL | 66 | 3 | 8 | 11 | 73 | .... | .... | .... | .... | .... |
| 2005-06 | Medicine Hat | WHL | 71 | 4 | 20 | 24 | 119 | 13 | 0 | 9 | 9 | 22 |
| 2006-07 | Medicine Hat | WHL | 53 | 7 | 19 | 26 | 70 | 23 | 2 | 6 | 8 | 32 |
| 2007-08 | Quad City Flames | AHL | 37 | 0 | 5 | 5 | 26 | .... | .... | .... | .... | .... |
| | Las Vegas | ECHL | 12 | 0 | 1 | 1 | 9 | .... | .... | .... | .... | .... |
| 2008-09 | Quad City Flames | AHL | 55 | 2 | 4 | 6 | 39 | .... | .... | .... | .... | .... |
| | Las Vegas | ECHL | 3 | 0 | 1 | 1 | 23 | .... | .... | .... | .... | .... |

**BARANOV, Konstantin** (buh-RA-nawf, KAWN-stan-tihn) **PHI.**

Right wing. Shoots left. 6'2", 185 lbs. Born, Omsk, USSR, January 11, 1982.
(Philadelphia's 3rd choice, 126th overall, in 2002 Entry Draft).

| | | | Regular Season | | | | | Playoffs | | | | |
|---|---|---|---|---|---|---|---|---|---|---|---|---|
| Season | Club | League | GP | G | A | Pts | PIM | GP | G | A | Pts | PIM |
| 1998-99 | Omsk 2 | Russia-4 | 23 | 18 | 8 | 26 | 40 | .... | .... | .... | .... | .... |
| | Avangard Omsk | Russia | 1 | 0 | 0 | 0 | 0 | 2 | 0 | 0 | 0 | 0 |
| 99-2000 | Omsk 2 | Russia-3 | 33 | 15 | 8 | 23 | 46 | .... | .... | .... | .... | .... |
| | Avangard Omsk | Russia | 1 | 0 | 0 | 0 | 2 | .... | .... | .... | .... | .... |
| 2000-01 | Kristall Saratov | Russia-2 | 26 | 6 | 9 | 15 | 26 | .... | .... | .... | .... | .... |
| | Ufa | Russia | 8 | 1 | 0 | 1 | 4 | .... | .... | .... | .... | .... |
| 2001-02 | Avangard Omsk | Russia | 5 | 0 | 0 | 0 | 6 | .... | .... | .... | .... | .... |
| | Mechel | Russia | 6 | 1 | 2 | 3 | 2 | .... | .... | .... | .... | .... |
| | Lada Togliatti | Russia | 20 | 2 | 4 | 6 | 18 | 3 | 0 | 2 | 2 | 0 |
| 2002-03 | Avangard Omsk | Russia | 6 | 0 | 1 | 1 | 2 | .... | .... | .... | .... | .... |
| | Ufa | Russia | 11 | 2 | 2 | 4 | 0 | .... | .... | .... | .... | .... |
| | CSKA Moscow | Russia | 14 | 4 | 1 | 5 | 10 | .... | .... | .... | .... | .... |
| | Omsk 2 | Russia-3 | 3 | 4 | 6 | 10 | 2 | .... | .... | .... | .... | .... |
| 2003-04 | Avangard Omsk | Russia | 51 | 6 | 10 | 16 | 50 | 11 | 2 | 2 | 4 | 6 |
| 2004-05 | Omsk 2 | Russia-3 | 7 | 5 | 7 | 12 | 20 | .... | .... | .... | .... | .... |
| | Avangard Omsk | Russia | 21 | 3 | 2 | 5 | 16 | .... | .... | .... | .... | .... |
| 2005-06 | Dynamo Moscow | Russia | 19 | 0 | 5 | 5 | 10 | .... | .... | .... | .... | .... |
| | SKA St. Petersburg | Russia | 12 | 1 | 2 | 3 | 18 | 3 | 0 | 0 | 0 | 2 |
| 2006-07 | Amur Khabarovsk | Russia | 7 | 0 | 1 | 1 | 16 | .... | .... | .... | .... | .... |
| | Novokuznetsk | Russia | 21 | 2 | 2 | 4 | 28 | 3 | 3 | 1 | 4 | 0 |
| 2007-08 | Avtomobilist | Russia-2 | 4 | 0 | 0 | 0 | 26 | .... | .... | .... | .... | .... |
| | Avtomobilist 2 | Russia-3 | 6 | 3 | 2 | 5 | 10 | .... | .... | .... | .... | .... |
| | HK Dmitrov | Russia-2 | 33 | 5 | 14 | 19 | 56 | 2 | 1 | 0 | 1 | 0 |
| 2008-09 | Gazovik Tyumen | Russia-2 | 31 | 5 | 11 | 16 | 50 | .... | .... | .... | .... | .... |
| | Kapitan Stupino | Russia-2 | 21 | 8 | 13 | 21 | 36 | 9 | 1 | 3 | 4 | 16 |

**BARBERIO, Mark** (bahr-BAIR-ee-oh, MAHRK) **T.B.**

Defense. Shoots left. 6', 201 lbs. Born, Montreal, Que., March 23, 1990.
(Tampa Bay's 5th choice, 152nd overall, in 2008 Entry Draft).

| | | | Regular Season | | | | | Playoffs | | | | |
|---|---|---|---|---|---|---|---|---|---|---|---|---|
| Season | Club | League | GP | G | A | Pts | PIM | GP | G | A | Pts | PIM |
| 2005-06 | Lac St-Louis Lions | QAAA | 43 | 2 | 12 | 14 | 80 | 10 | 1 | 7 | 8 | 26 |
| 2006-07 | Cape Breton | QMJHL | 41 | 2 | 8 | 10 | 42 | .... | .... | .... | .... | .... |
| | Moncton Wildcats | QMJHL | 19 | 1 | 6 | 7 | 21 | 7 | 0 | 2 | 2 | 8 |
| 2007-08 | Moncton Wildcats | QMJHL | 70 | 11 | 35 | 46 | 75 | .... | .... | .... | .... | .... |
| 2008-09 | Moncton Wildcats | QMJHL | 66 | 15 | 30 | 45 | 42 | 10 | 0 | 4 | 4 | 8 |

QMJHL All-Rookie Team (2007)

**BARRIBALL, Jay** (BEHR-ih-bahl, JAY) **ST.L.**

Left wing. Shoots left. 5'9", 171 lbs. Born, Prior Lake, MN, May 27, 1987.
(San Jose's 6th choice, 203rd overall, in 2006 Entry Draft).

| | | | Regular Season | | | | | Playoffs | | | | |
|---|---|---|---|---|---|---|---|---|---|---|---|---|
| Season | Club | League | GP | G | A | Pts | PIM | GP | G | A | Pts | PIM |
| 2004-05 | Holy Angels | High-MN | 30 | 32 | 49 | 81 | .... | .... | .... | .... | .... | .... |
| 2005-06 | Holy Angels | High-MN | 20 | 28 | 38 | 66 | .... | .... | .... | .... | .... | .... |
| | Sioux Falls | USHL | 13 | 5 | 7 | 12 | 2 | 5 | 2 | 1 | 3 | 0 |
| 2006-07 | U. of Minnesota | WCHA | 44 | 20 | 23 | 43 | 16 | .... | .... | .... | .... | .... |
| 2007-08 | U. of Minnesota | WCHA | 41 | 6 | 15 | 21 | 34 | .... | .... | .... | .... | .... |
| 2008-09 | U. of Minnesota | WCHA | 34 | 11 | 23 | 34 | 52 | .... | .... | .... | .... | .... |

Traded to **St. Louis** by **San Jose** with Ville Nieminen and New Jersey's 1st round choice (previously acquired, St. Louis selected David Perron) in 2007 Entry Draft for Bill Guerin, February 27, 2007.

**BARRIE, Tyson** (BAIR-ree, TIGH-suhn) **COL.**

Defense. Shoots right. 5'10", 190 lbs. Born, Victoria, B.C., July 26, 1991.
(Colorado's 4th choice, 64th overall, in 2009 Entry Draft).

| | | | Regular Season | | | | | Playoffs | | | | |
|---|---|---|---|---|---|---|---|---|---|---|---|---|
| Season | Club | League | GP | G | A | Pts | PIM | GP | G | A | Pts | PIM |
| 2006-07 | Juan de Fuca | Minor-BC | 72 | 43 | 87 | 130 | .... | .... | .... | .... | .... | .... |
| | Kelowna Rockets | WHL | 7 | 0 | 3 | 3 | 2 | .... | .... | .... | .... | .... |
| 2007-08 | Kelowna Rockets | WHL | 64 | 9 | 34 | 43 | 32 | 7 | 1 | 3 | 4 | 0 |
| 2008-09 | Kelowna Rockets | WHL | 68 | 12 | 40 | 52 | 31 | 22 | 4 | 14 | 18 | 12 |

Canadian Major Junior All-Rookie Team (2008)

**BARTKOWSKI, Matthew** (bahrt-KOW-skee, MA-thew) **FLA.**

Defense. Shoots left. 6'1", 196 lbs. Born, Pittsburgh, PA, June 4, 1988.
(Florida's 5th choice, 190th overall, in 2008 Entry Draft).

| | | | Regular Season | | | | | Playoffs | | | | |
|---|---|---|---|---|---|---|---|---|---|---|---|---|
| Season | Club | League | GP | G | A | Pts | PIM | GP | G | A | Pts | PIM |
| 2006-07 | Lincoln Stars | USHL | 57 | 3 | 6 | 9 | 95 | 3 | 0 | 0 | 0 | 2 |
| 2007-08 | Lincoln Stars | USHL | 60 | 4 | 37 | 41 | 135 | 8 | 1 | 4 | 5 | 10 |
| 2008-09 | Ohio State | CCHA | 41 | 5 | 15 | 20 | 46 | .... | .... | .... | .... | .... |

CCHA All-Rookie Team (2009) • USHL First All-Star Team (2008)

**BARTULIS, Oskars** (bahr-TEW-lihs, AWZ-kahrz) **PHI.**

Defense. Shoots left. 6'2", 195 lbs. Born, Ogre, Latvia, January 21, 1987.
(Philadelphia's 2nd choice, 91st overall, in 2005 Entry Draft).

| | | | Regular Season | | | | | Playoffs | | | | |
|---|---|---|---|---|---|---|---|---|---|---|---|---|
| Season | Club | League | GP | G | A | Pts | PIM | GP | G | A | Pts | PIM |
| 2001-02 | Prizma '83 Riga | EEHL-B | 3 | 1 | 0 | 1 | 2 | .... | .... | .... | .... | .... |
| | Prizma '83 Riga | Latvia | 6 | 0 | 1 | 1 | 2 | .... | .... | .... | .... | .... |
| 2002-03 | Prizma '83 Riga | EEHL-B | 12 | 5 | 5 | 10 | 12 | .... | .... | .... | .... | .... |
| | Vilki Riga | Latvia | .... | 0 | 1 | 1 | 12 | .... | .... | .... | .... | .... |
| 2003-04 | CSKA Moscow 2 | Russia-3 | 65 | 3 | 9 | 12 | .... | .... | .... | .... | .... | .... |
| 2004-05 | Moncton Wildcats | QMJHL | 62 | 5 | 19 | 24 | 55 | 12 | 1 | 1 | 2 | 16 |
| 2005-06 | Moncton Wildcats | QMJHL | 54 | 6 | 25 | 31 | 84 | 21 | 1 | 9 | 10 | 22 |
| 2006-07 | Cape Breton | QMJHL | 55 | 13 | 35 | 48 | 52 | 16 | 3 | 9 | 12 | 24 |
| 2007-08 | Philadelphia | AHL | 57 | 1 | 20 | 21 | 42 | .... | .... | .... | .... | .... |
| 2008-09 | Philadelphia | AHL | 80 | 2 | 11 | 13 | 59 | 4 | 0 | 0 | 0 | 4 |

QMJHL All-Rookie Team (2005) • Canadian Major Junior All-Rookie Team (2005) • QMJHL Second All-Star Team (2007)

**BASHKIROV, Ruslan** (bash-KIHR-ahv, roos-LAHN) **OTT.**

Left wing. Shoots left. 5'11", 199 lbs. Born, Moscow, USSR, March 7, 1989.
(Ottawa's 2nd choice, 60th overall, in 2007 Entry Draft).

| | | | Regular Season | | | | | Playoffs | | | | |
|---|---|---|---|---|---|---|---|---|---|---|---|---|
| Season | Club | League | GP | G | A | Pts | PIM | GP | G | A | Pts | PIM |
| 2005-06 | Spartak Moscow 2 | Russia-3 | 35 | 16 | 9 | 25 | 44 | .... | .... | .... | .... | .... |
| 2006-07 | Quebec Remparts | QMJHL | 64 | 30 | 37 | 67 | 117 | 5 | 1 | 3 | 4 | 6 |
| 2007-08 | Mytischi | Russia | 4 | 0 | 0 | 0 | 0 | .... | .... | .... | .... | .... |
| | Kristall Elektrostal | Russia-2 | 12 | 4 | 0 | 4 | 22 | .... | .... | .... | .... | .... |
| 2008-09 | Lada Togliatti | Rus-KHL | 2 | 0 | 0 | 0 | 2 | .... | .... | .... | .... | .... |
| | Rys Podolsk | Russia-2 | 48 | 9 | 8 | 17 | 20 | 3 | 1 | 3 | 4 | 2 |

Signed as a free agent by **Mytischi** (Russia), August 23, 2007.

**BATHGATE, Andy** (BATH-gayt, AHN-dee) **PIT.**

Center. Shoots left. 6', 164 lbs. Born, Brampton, Ont., February 26, 1991.
(Pittsburgh's 6th choice, 151st overall, in 2009 Entry Draft).

| | | | Regular Season | | | | | Playoffs | | | | |
|---|---|---|---|---|---|---|---|---|---|---|---|---|
| Season | Club | League | GP | G | A | Pts | PIM | GP | G | A | Pts | PIM |
| 2007-08 | Georgetown | OPJHL | 40 | 14 | 30 | 44 | 24 | 10 | 1 | 6 | 7 | 10 |
| | Belleville Bulls | OHL | 5 | 0 | 1 | 1 | 2 | 5 | 0 | 0 | 0 | 0 |
| 2008-09 | Belleville Bulls | OHL | 44 | 4 | 12 | 16 | 10 | .... | .... | .... | .... | .... |

**BEACH, Kyle** (BEECH, KIGH-uhl) **CHI.**

Center. Shoots right. 6'3", 203 lbs. Born, Vancouver, B.C., January 13, 1990.
(Chicago's 1st choice, 11th overall, in 2008 Entry Draft).

| | | | Regular Season | | | | | Playoffs | | | | |
|---|---|---|---|---|---|---|---|---|---|---|---|---|
| Season | Club | League | GP | G | A | Pts | PIM | GP | G | A | Pts | PIM |
| 2005-06 | Okanagan Rockets | Minor-BC | 25 | 23 | 18 | 41 | 220 | .... | .... | .... | .... | .... |
| | Everett Silvertips | WHL | 4 | 2 | 1 | 3 | 4 | 9 | 1 | 3 | 4 | 31 |
| 2006-07 | Everett Silvertips | WHL | 65 | 29 | 32 | 61 | 196 | 11 | 5 | 6 | 11 | 19 |
| 2007-08 | Everett Silvertips | WHL | 60 | 27 | 33 | 60 | 222 | 4 | 0 | 0 | 0 | 4 |
| 2008-09 | Everett Silvertips | WHL | 30 | 9 | 21 | 30 | 106 | .... | .... | .... | .... | .... |
| | Lethbridge | WHL | 24 | 15 | 18 | 33 | 59 | 10 | 1 | 1 | 2 | 31 |
| | Rockford IceHogs | AHL | 2 | 0 | 0 | 0 | 15 | 1 | 0 | 0 | 0 | 0 |

WHL Rookie of the Year (2007)

**BEAULIEU, Josh** (BOI-l'yew, JAWSH) **PHI.**

Right wing. Shoots left. 6'1", 180 lbs. Born, Windsor, Ont., January 10, 1987.
(Philadelphia's 4th choice, 152nd overall, in 2005 Entry Draft).

| | | | Regular Season | | | | | Playoffs | | | | |
|---|---|---|---|---|---|---|---|---|---|---|---|---|
| Season | Club | League | GP | G | A | Pts | PIM | GP | G | A | Pts | PIM |
| 2003-04 | London Knights | OHL | 41 | 3 | 6 | 9 | 32 | 9 | 0 | 0 | 0 | 5 |
| 2004-05 | London Knights | OHL | 65 | 9 | 13 | 22 | 159 | 13 | 2 | 3 | 5 | 13 |
| 2005-06 | London Knights | OHL | 60 | 15 | 13 | 28 | 140 | 18 | 4 | 5 | 9 | 12 |
| 2006-07 | London Knights | OHL | 44 | 10 | 6 | 16 | 93 | 10 | 3 | 6 | 9 | 31 |
| 2007-08 | Philadelphia | AHL | 50 | 3 | 3 | 6 | 50 | .... | .... | .... | .... | .... |
| 2008-09 | Philadelphia | AHL | 40 | 1 | 1 | 2 | 36 | .... | .... | .... | .... | .... |

**BEAVERSON, Luke** (BEE-vuhr-suhn, LEWK) **FLA.**

Defense. Shoots left. 6'4", 208 lbs. Born, St. Paul, MN, December 11, 1984.
(Florida's 7th choice, 283rd overall, in 2004 Entry Draft).

| | | | Regular Season | | | | | Playoffs | | | | |
|---|---|---|---|---|---|---|---|---|---|---|---|---|
| Season | Club | League | GP | G | A | Pts | PIM | GP | G | A | Pts | PIM |
| 2003-04 | Green Bay | USHL | 57 | 1 | 6 | 7 | 141 | .... | .... | .... | .... | .... |
| 2004-05 | Alaska Anchorage | WCHA | 37 | 0 | 2 | 2 | 48 | .... | .... | .... | .... | .... |
| 2005-06 | Alaska Anchorage | WCHA | 34 | 1 | 3 | 4 | 53 | .... | .... | .... | .... | .... |
| 2006-07 | Alaska Anchorage | WCHA | 37 | 5 | 4 | 9 | 44 | .... | .... | .... | .... | .... |
| 2007-08 | Alaska-Anchorage | WCHA | 30 | 1 | 2 | 3 | 24 | .... | .... | .... | .... | .... |
| | Rochester | AHL | 6 | 0 | 0 | 0 | 13 | .... | .... | .... | .... | .... |
| 2008-09 | Rochester | AHL | 15 | 0 | 1 | 1 | 21 | .... | .... | .... | .... | .... |
| | Florida Everblades | ECHL | 28 | 0 | 3 | 3 | 36 | .... | .... | .... | .... | .... |

**BECK, Taylor** (BEHK, TAY-luhr) **NSH.**

Left wing. Shoots right. 6'2", 211 lbs. Born, St. Catharines, Ont., May 13, 1991.
(Nashville's 4th choice, 70th overall, in 2009 Entry Draft).

| | | | Regular Season | | | | | Playoffs | | | | |
|---|---|---|---|---|---|---|---|---|---|---|---|---|
| Season | Club | League | GP | G | A | Pts | PIM | GP | G | A | Pts | PIM |
| 2006-07 | Niagara Falls | Minor-ON | 69 | 64 | 75 | 139 | 76 | .... | .... | .... | .... | .... |
| 2007-08 | Guelph Storm | OHL | 56 | 7 | 14 | 21 | 43 | 7 | 0 | 0 | 0 | 4 |
| 2008-09 | Guelph Storm | OHL | 67 | 22 | 36 | 58 | 36 | 4 | 0 | 0 | 0 | 2 |

**BELLAMY, Rob** (BEHL-ah-mee, RAWB) **PHI.**

Right wing. Shoots right. 6', 205 lbs. Born, Providence, RI, May 30, 1985.
(Philadelphia's 1st choice, 92nd overall, in 2004 Entry Draft).

| | | | Regular Season | | | | | Playoffs | | | | |
|---|---|---|---|---|---|---|---|---|---|---|---|---|
| Season | Club | League | GP | G | A | Pts | PIM | GP | G | A | Pts | PIM |
| 2002-03 | Berkshire Bears | High-MA | 32 | 21 | 21 | 42 | 128 | .... | .... | .... | .... | .... |
| 2003-04 | N.E. Jr. Coyotes | EJHL | 36 | 19 | 21 | 40 | 95 | .... | .... | .... | .... | .... |
| 2004-05 | U. of Maine | H-East | 28 | 3 | 4 | 7 | 34 | .... | .... | .... | .... | .... |
| 2005-06 | U. of Maine | H-East | 40 | 6 | 9 | 15 | 77 | .... | .... | .... | .... | .... |
| 2006-07 | U. of Maine | H-East | 37 | 1 | 7 | 8 | 82 | .... | .... | .... | .... | .... |
| 2007-08 | U. of Maine | H-East | 33 | 5 | 13 | 18 | 61 | .... | .... | .... | .... | .... |
| | Philadelphia | AHL | 1 | 0 | 0 | 0 | 0 | .... | .... | .... | .... | .... |
| 2008-09 | Philadelphia | AHL | 51 | 2 | 3 | 5 | 18 | .... | .... | .... | .... | .... |

**BELLEMORE, Brett** (BEHL-mohr, BREHT) **CAR.**

Defense. Shoots right. 6'4", 205 lbs. Born, Windsor, Ont., June 25, 1988.
(Carolina's 5th choice, 162nd overall, in 2007 Entry Draft).

| | | | Regular Season | | | | | Playoffs | | | | |
|---|---|---|---|---|---|---|---|---|---|---|---|---|
| Season | Club | League | GP | G | A | Pts | PIM | GP | G | A | Pts | PIM |
| 2005-06 | Plymouth Whalers | OHL | 46 | 0 | 0 | 0 | 16 | 10 | 0 | 0 | 0 | 0 |
| 2006-07 | Plymouth Whalers | OHL | 50 | 0 | 12 | 12 | 50 | 20 | 0 | 5 | 5 | 28 |
| 2007-08 | Plymouth Whalers | OHL | 56 | 6 | 18 | 24 | 70 | 4 | 0 | 2 | 2 | 8 |
| | Albany River Rats | AHL | 4 | 0 | 0 | 0 | 6 | 5 | 0 | 0 | 0 | 6 |
| 2008-09 | Plymouth Whalers | OHL | 29 | 2 | 10 | 12 | 39 | 11 | 1 | 2 | 3 | 16 |
| | Albany River Rats | AHL | 6 | 0 | 0 | 0 | 4 | .... | .... | .... | .... | .... |

**BENDFELD, Jordan** (BENHD-felhd, JOHR-dahn) **EDM.**

Defense. Shoots right. 6'2", 222 lbs. Born, Leduc, Alta., February 9, 1988.
(Edmonton's 5th choice, 193rd overall, in 2008 Entry Draft).

| | | | Regular Season | | | | | Playoffs | | | | |
|---|---|---|---|---|---|---|---|---|---|---|---|---|
| Season | Club | League | GP | G | A | Pts | PIM | GP | G | A | Pts | PIM |
| 2003-04 | Leduc Oil Kings | AMHL | 36 | 0 | 9 | 9 | 22 | .... | .... | .... | .... | .... |
| 2004-05 | Leduc Oil Kings | AMHL | 21 | 1 | 5 | 6 | 96 | .... | .... | .... | .... | .... |
| | Medicine Hat | WHL | 16 | 0 | 0 | 0 | 4 | 2 | 0 | 0 | 0 | 2 |
| 2005-06 | Medicine Hat | WHL | 65 | 2 | 10 | 12 | 92 | 13 | 0 | 4 | 4 | 27 |
| 2006-07 | Medicine Hat | WHL | 72 | 9 | 21 | 30 | 136 | 23 | 0 | 5 | 5 | *62 |
| 2007-08 | Medicine Hat | WHL | 72 | 6 | 19 | 25 | 160 | 5 | 0 | 2 | 2 | 2 |
| 2008-09 | Stockton Thunder | ECHL | 17 | 1 | 2 | 3 | 25 | .... | .... | .... | .... | .... |

• Re-entered NHL Entry Draft. Originally Phoenix's 6th choice, 152nd overall, in 2006 Entry Draft.

• Missed majority of 2008-09 season recovering from knee injury suffered in game vs. Ontario (ECHL), November, 2008.

**BENN, Jamie** (BEHN, JAY-mee) **DAL.**

Left wing. Shoots left. 6'2", 185 lbs. Born, Victoria, B.C., July 18, 1989.
(Dallas' 5th choice, 129th overall, in 2007 Entry Draft).

| | | | Regular Season | | | | | Playoffs | | | | |
|---|---|---|---|---|---|---|---|---|---|---|---|---|
| Season | Club | League | GP | G | A | Pts | PIM | GP | G | A | Pts | PIM |
| 2004-05 | Peninsula Eagles | Minor-BC | STATISTICS NOT AVAILABLE | | | | | | | | | |
| | Peninsula Panthers | VIJHL | 4 | 1 | 2 | 3 | 2 | 2 | 0 | 0 | 0 | 0 |
| 2005-06 | Peninsula Panthers | VIJHL | 38 | 31 | 24 | 55 | 92 | 7 | 5 | 7 | 10 | 20 |
| 2006-07 | Victoria Grizzlies | BCHL | 53 | 42 | 23 | 65 | 78 | 11 | 5 | 4 | 9 | 12 |
| 2007-08 | Kelowna Rockets | WHL | 51 | 33 | 32 | 65 | 68 | 7 | 3 | 8 | 11 | 4 |
| 2008-09 | Kelowna Rockets | WHL | 56 | 46 | 36 | 82 | 71 | 19 | *13 | *20 | *33 | 18 |

WHL West First All-Star Team (2009)

**BENNETT, Mac** (BEHN-neht, MAK) **MTL.**

Defense. Shoots left. 5'11", 171 lbs. Born, Warwick, RI, March 25, 1991.
(Montreal's 3rd choice, 79th overall, in 2009 Entry Draft).

| | | | Regular Season | | | | | Playoffs | | | | |
|---|---|---|---|---|---|---|---|---|---|---|---|---|
| Season | Club | League | GP | G | A | Pts | PIM | GP | G | A | Pts | PIM |
| 2006-07 | Hotchkiss | High-CT | 25 | 7 | 6 | 13 | .... | .... | .... | .... | .... | .... |
| 2007-08 | Hotchkiss | High-CT | 25 | 6 | 9 | 15 | .... | .... | .... | .... | .... | .... |
| 2008-09 | Hotchkiss | High-CT | 15 | 4 | 11 | 15 | .... | .... | .... | .... | .... | .... |
| | Neponset Valley | Minor-MA | 16 | 5 | 19 | 24 | .... | .... | .... | .... | .... | .... |

**BENNETT, Spencer** (BEHN-neht, SPEHN-suhr) **CGY.**

Left wing. Shoots left. 6'3", 185 lbs. Born, White Rock, B.C., October 31, 1990.
(Calgary's 4th choice, 141st overall, in 2009 Entry Draft).

| | | | Regular Season | | | | | Playoffs | | | | |
|---|---|---|---|---|---|---|---|---|---|---|---|---|
| Season | Club | League | GP | G | A | Pts | PIM | GP | G | A | Pts | PIM |
| 2006-07 | Delta Ice Hawks | PIJHL | 40 | 6 | 12 | 18 | 14 | 3 | 0 | 0 | 0 | 2 |
| | Burnaby Express | BCHL | 7 | 1 | 0 | 1 | 2 | 13 | 1 | 1 | 2 | 2 |
| 2007-08 | Burnaby Express | BCHL | 58 | 6 | 11 | 17 | 41 | 5 | 1 | 2 | 3 | 4 |
| 2008-09 | Surrey Eagles | BCHL | 60 | 20 | 21 | 41 | 32 | 9 | 2 | 4 | 6 | 7 |

• Signed Letter of Intent to attend **University of Alaska-Anchorage** (WCHA) in fall of 2010.

### BENOIT, Andre (behn-WAH, AWN-dray) MTL.

Defense. Shoots left. 5'11", 197 lbs. Born, St. Albert, Ont., January 6, 1984.

| | | | Regular Season | | | | | Playoffs | | | | |
|---|---|---|---|---|---|---|---|---|---|---|---|---|
| Season | Club | League | GP | G | A | Pts | PIM | GP | G | A | Pts | PIM |
| 2000-01 | Kitchener Rangers | OHL | 65 | 16 | 19 | 35 | 37 | .... | .... | .... | .... | .... |
| 2001-02 | Kitchener Rangers | OHL | 62 | 13 | 32 | 45 | 77 | 4 | 1 | 0 | 1 | 8 |
| 2002-03 | Kitchener Rangers | OHL | 65 | 22 | 45 | 67 | 77 | 21 | 1 | 16 | 17 | 16 |
| 2003-04 | Kitchener Rangers | OHL | 65 | 24 | 51 | 75 | 67 | 5 | 1 | 1 | 2 | 6 |
| 2004-05 | Kitchener Rangers | OHL | 67 | 24 | 53 | 77 | 72 | 15 | 5 | 13 | 18 | 6 |
| 2005-06 | Hamilton Bulldogs | AHL | 70 | 7 | 19 | 26 | 60 | .... | .... | .... | .... | .... |
| 2006-07 | Hamilton Bulldogs | AHL | 64 | 10 | 21 | 31 | 41 | 22 | 2 | 11 | 13 | 22 |
| 2007-08 | Tappara Tampere | Finland | 54 | 12 | 26 | 38 | 96 | 11 | 2 | 3 | 5 | 10 |
| 2008-09 | Sodertalje SK | Sweden | 54 | 4 | 16 | 20 | 34 | .... | .... | .... | .... | .... |
| | Sodertalje SK | Sweden-Q | 10 | 0 | 2 | 2 | 10 | .... | .... | .... | .... | .... |

Signed as a free agent by **Montreal**, January 9, 2006. Signed as a free agent by **Tappara Tampere** (Finland), June 21, 2007. Signed as a free agent by **Montreal**, May 13, 2009.

### BERGIN, Mike (BUHR-gihn, MIGHK) DAL.

Defense. Shoots left. 6'3", 197 lbs. Born, Kanata, Ont., June 30, 1988.
(Dallas' 5th choice, 209th overall, in 2008 Entry Draft).

| | | | Regular Season | | | | | Playoffs | | | | |
|---|---|---|---|---|---|---|---|---|---|---|---|---|
| Season | Club | League | GP | G | A | Pts | PIM | GP | G | A | Pts | PIM |
| 2006-07 | Smiths Falls Bears | CJHL | 53 | 10 | 35 | 45 | 116 | 11 | 2 | 7 | 9 | 18 |
| 2007-08 | Smiths Falls Bears | CJHL | 45 | 14 | 27 | 41 | 60 | 15 | 2 | 5 | 7 | 19 |
| 2008-09 | RPI Engineers | ECAC | 6 | 0 | 1 | 1 | 6 | .... | .... | .... | .... | .... |

• Missed majority of 2008-09 season recovering from shoulder injury suffered in game vs. Massachusetts (Hockey East), October 21, 2008.

### BERGLUND, Kristofer (BUHR-gluhnd, KRIHS-toh-fuhr) ST.L.

Defense. Shoots left. 5'10", 180 lbs. Born, Umea, Sweden, August 12, 1988.
(St. Louis' 8th choice, 125th overall, in 2008 Entry Draft).

| | | | Regular Season | | | | | Playoffs | | | | |
|---|---|---|---|---|---|---|---|---|---|---|---|---|
| Season | Club | League | GP | G | A | Pts | PIM | GP | G | A | Pts | PIM |
| 2003-04 | Bjorkloven U18 | Swe-U18 | 10 | 4 | 4 | 8 | 2 | .... | .... | .... | .... | .... |
| 2004-05 | Bjorkloven U18 | Swe-U18 | STATISTICS NOT AVAILABLE | | | | | | | | | |
| 2005-06 | Bjorkloven Jr. | Swe-Jr. | 38 | 3 | 11 | 14 | 36 | 6 | 0 | 3 | 3 | 8 |
| | IF Bjorkloven Umea | Sweden-2 | 1 | 0 | 0 | 0 | 0 | .... | .... | .... | .... | .... |
| 2006-07 | Bjorkloven Jr. | Swe-Jr. | 30 | 4 | 22 | 26 | 38 | .... | .... | .... | .... | .... |
| | Tegs SK Umea | Sweden-3 | 2 | 0 | 1 | 1 | 2 | .... | .... | .... | .... | .... |
| | IF Bjorkloven Umea | Sweden-2 | 42 | 0 | 4 | 4 | 18 | .... | .... | .... | .... | .... |
| 2007-08 | Bjorkloven Jr. | Swe-Jr. | 1 | 0 | 0 | 0 | 0 | .... | .... | .... | .... | .... |
| | IF Bjorkloven Umea | Sweden-2 | 42 | 4 | 21 | 25 | 14 | 2 | 0 | 1 | 1 | 0 |
| 2008-09 | Lulea HF | Sweden | 52 | 3 | 22 | 25 | 36 | 5 | 0 | 3 | 3 | 4 |

### BERNARD, Ashton (buhr-NARD, ASH-tuhn) N.J.

Left wing. Shoots left. 6'4", 195 lbs. Born, Eskasoni, N.S., February 5, 1990.
(New Jersey's 6th choice, 174th overall, in 2009 Entry Draft).

| | | | Regular Season | | | | | Playoffs | | | | |
|---|---|---|---|---|---|---|---|---|---|---|---|---|
| Season | Club | League | GP | G | A | Pts | PIM | GP | G | A | Pts | PIM |
| 2005-06 | Cape Breton West | NSMHL | 29 | 6 | 4 | 10 | 115 | 11 | 0 | 1 | 1 | 45 |
| 2006-07 | Rouyn-Noranda | QMJHL | 26 | 0 | 0 | 0 | 50 | 1 | 0 | 0 | 0 | 0 |
| 2007-08 | Rouyn-Noranda | QMJHL | 26 | 1 | 0 | 1 | 115 | .... | .... | .... | .... | .... |
| | Shawinigan | QMJHL | 26 | 1 | 1 | 2 | 94 | 1 | 0 | 0 | 0 | 0 |
| 2008-09 | Shawinigan | QMJHL | 53 | 3 | 1 | 4 | 111 | 1 | 0 | 0 | 0 | 5 |

### BERNIKOV, Ruslan (BAIR-nih-kahf, roos-LAHN) DAL.

Right wing. Shoots left. 6'3", 216 lbs. Born, Vidnoye, USSR, December 4, 1977.
(Dallas' 6th choice, 139th overall, in 2000 Entry Draft).

| | | | Regular Season | | | | | Playoffs | | | | |
|---|---|---|---|---|---|---|---|---|---|---|---|---|
| Season | Club | League | GP | G | A | Pts | PIM | GP | G | A | Pts | PIM |
| 1996-97 | Dyn'o Moscow 2 | Russia-3 | 32 | 11 | 4 | 15 | 20 | .... | .... | .... | .... | .... |
| | Dynamo Moscow | Russia | 2 | 0 | 0 | 0 | 0 | .... | .... | .... | .... | .... |
| 1997-98 | Yekaterinburg 2 | Russia-3 | 2 | 1 | 1 | 2 | 0 | .... | .... | .... | .... | .... |
| | Yekaterinburg | Russia | 43 | 7 | 7 | 14 | 55 | .... | .... | .... | .... | .... |
| 1998-99 | Dynamo Moscow | Russia | 6 | 0 | 1 | 1 | 2 | .... | .... | .... | .... | .... |
| | Krylja Sovetov | Russia | 20 | 3 | 1 | 4 | 24 | .... | .... | .... | .... | .... |
| | CSKA Moscow | Russia | 1 | 0 | 0 | 0 | 0 | .... | .... | .... | .... | .... |
| | Cherepovets | Russia | 5 | 0 | 0 | 0 | 0 | 1 | 0 | 0 | 0 | 0 |
| 99-2000 | Dynamo Moscow | Russia | 6 | 2 | 1 | 3 | 2 | .... | .... | .... | .... | .... |
| | Amur Khabarovsk | Russia | 14 | 3 | 6 | 9 | 10 | 5 | 3 | 1 | 4 | 2 |
| 2000-01 | Amur Khabarovsk | Russia | 33 | 1 | 4 | 5 | 40 | .... | .... | .... | .... | .... |
| 2001-02 | Amur Khabarovsk | Russia | 38 | 7 | 10 | 17 | 20 | .... | .... | .... | .... | .... |
| 2002-03 | Krylja Sovetov | Russia | 50 | 15 | 10 | 25 | 40 | .... | .... | .... | .... | .... |
| 2003-04 | Lada Togliatti | Russia | 49 | 8 | 10 | 18 | 51 | 6 | 0 | 0 | 0 | 4 |
| 2004-05 | Lada Togliatti | Russia | 16 | 3 | 1 | 4 | 14 | .... | .... | .... | .... | .... |
| | Cherepovets | Russia | 33 | 9 | 6 | 15 | 8 | .... | .... | .... | .... | .... |
| 2005-06 | Mytischi | Russia | 21 | 2 | 3 | 5 | 40 | .... | .... | .... | .... | .... |
| | Ak Bars Kazan | Russia | 5 | 0 | 0 | 0 | 0 | .... | .... | .... | .... | .... |
| | Ufa | Russia | 16 | 3 | 2 | 5 | 26 | 6 | 1 | 0 | 1 | 4 |
| 2006-07 | Ufa | Russia | 32 | 6 | 3 | 9 | 14 | 5 | 1 | 1 | 2 | 6 |
| | Ufa 2 | Russia-3 | 4 | 4 | 3 | 7 | 28 | .... | .... | .... | .... | .... |
| 2007-08 | Sibir Novosibirsk | Russia | 20 | 3 | 4 | 7 | 16 | .... | .... | .... | .... | .... |
| | Nizhnekamsk | Russia | 27 | 8 | 3 | 11 | 34 | 5 | 1 | 2 | 3 | 2 |
| 2008-09 | Nizhnekamsk | Rus-KHL | 16 | 1 | 2 | 3 | 39 | .... | .... | .... | .... | .... |
| | Vityaz Chekhov | Rus-KHL | 10 | 0 | 2 | 2 | 4 | .... | .... | .... | .... | .... |

### BERRY, Alex (BAIR-ee, AL-ehx) TOR.

Right wing. Shoots right. 6'2", 212 lbs. Born, Danvers, MA, March 6, 1986.
(Toronto's 3rd choice, 153rd overall, in 2005 Entry Draft).

| | | | Regular Season | | | | | Playoffs | | | | |
|---|---|---|---|---|---|---|---|---|---|---|---|---|
| Season | Club | League | GP | G | A | Pts | PIM | GP | G | A | Pts | PIM |
| 2003-04 | Cushing | High-MA | 31 | 19 | 16 | 35 | 50 | .... | .... | .... | .... | .... |
| 2004-05 | Bos. Jr. Bruins | EJHL | 53 | 17 | 25 | 42 | 170 | .... | .... | .... | .... | .... |
| 2005-06 | Massachusetts | H-East | 24 | 1 | 1 | 2 | 33 | .... | .... | .... | .... | .... |
| 2006-07 | Massachusetts | H-East | 29 | 7 | 6 | 13 | 34 | .... | .... | .... | .... | .... |
| 2007-08 | Massachusetts | H-East | 34 | 10 | 7 | 17 | 63 | .... | .... | .... | .... | .... |
| 2008-09 | Massachusetts | H-East | 37 | 11 | 19 | 30 | 83 | .... | .... | .... | .... | .... |
| | Toronto Marlies | AHL | 8 | 0 | 0 | 0 | 15 | .... | .... | .... | .... | .... |

### BERTILSSON, Simon (BUHR-tihl-suhn, SEE-muhn) PHI.

Defense. Shoots left. 6', 185 lbs. Born, Karlskoga, Sweden, April 19, 1991.
(Philadelphia's 2nd choice, 87th overall, in 2009 Entry Draft).

| | | | Regular Season | | | | | Playoffs | | | | |
|---|---|---|---|---|---|---|---|---|---|---|---|---|
| Season | Club | League | GP | G | A | Pts | PIM | GP | G | A | Pts | PIM |
| 2006-07 | Bofors U18 | Swe-U18 | 19 | 8 | 10 | 18 | 6 | .... | .... | .... | .... | .... |
| 2007-08 | Brynas U18 | Swe-U18 | 4 | 1 | 1 | 2 | 27 | 5 | 0 | 0 | 0 | 4 |
| | Brynas IF Gavle Jr. | Swe-Jr. | 27 | 2 | 3 | 5 | 52 | 7 | 0 | 0 | 0 | 8 |
| 2008-09 | Brynas U18 | Swe-U18 | 5 | 2 | 3 | 5 | 50 | 1 | 2 | 0 | 2 | 4 |
| | Brynas IF Gavle Jr. | Swe-Jr. | 30 | 9 | 22 | 31 | 54 | 6 | 0 | 1 | 1 | 0 |
| | Brynas IF Gavle | Sweden | 21 | 0 | 1 | 1 | 2 | 4 | 0 | 0 | 0 | 0 |

### BERTRAM, Dan (BUHR-truhm, DAN) CHI.

Right wing. Shoots right. 5'11", 182 lbs. Born, Calgary, Alta., January 14, 1987.
(Chicago's 3rd choice, 54th overall, in 2005 Entry Draft).

| | | | Regular Season | | | | | Playoffs | | | | |
|---|---|---|---|---|---|---|---|---|---|---|---|---|
| Season | Club | League | GP | G | A | Pts | PIM | GP | G | A | Pts | PIM |
| 2003-04 | Camrose Kodiaks | AJHL | 44 | 22 | 33 | 55 | .... | .... | .... | .... | .... | .... |
| 2004-05 | Boston College | H-East | 39 | 9 | 8 | 17 | 58 | .... | .... | .... | .... | .... |
| 2005-06 | Boston College | H-East | 39 | 10 | 16 | 26 | 38 | .... | .... | .... | .... | .... |
| 2006-07 | Boston College | H-East | 40 | 8 | 17 | 25 | 48 | .... | .... | .... | .... | .... |
| 2007-08 | Boston College | H-East | 43 | 10 | 27 | 37 | 26 | .... | .... | .... | .... | .... |
| 2008-09 | Rockford IceHogs | AHL | 56 | 4 | 6 | 10 | 63 | 3 | 0 | 0 | 0 | 0 |

AJHL Rookie of the Year (2004)

### BERUBE, Jean-Sebastien (beh-ROO-bay, ZHAWN-seh-BAS-tee-yeh N.J.

Left wing. Shoots left. 6'3", 195 lbs. Born, Matane, Que., July 20, 1990.
(New Jersey's 9th choice, 205th overall, in 2008 Entry Draft).

| | | | Regular Season | | | | | Playoffs | | | | |
|---|---|---|---|---|---|---|---|---|---|---|---|---|
| Season | Club | League | GP | G | A | Pts | PIM | GP | G | A | Pts | PIM |
| 2006-07 | Rouyn-Noranda | QMJHL | 40 | 3 | 7 | 10 | 22 | 16 | 0 | 0 | 0 | 4 |
| 2007-08 | Rouyn-Noranda | QMJHL | 64 | 12 | 12 | 24 | 118 | 17 | 1 | 3 | 4 | 16 |
| 2008-09 | Rouyn-Noranda | QMJHL | 64 | 15 | 11 | 26 | 143 | 6 | 0 | 1 | 1 | 10 |

### BICKEL, Stu (BIH-kuhl, STEW) ANA.

Defense. Shoots right. 6'4", 215 lbs. Born, Chanhassen, MN, October 2, 1986.

| | | | Regular Season | | | | | Playoffs | | | | |
|---|---|---|---|---|---|---|---|---|---|---|---|---|
| Season | Club | League | GP | G | A | Pts | PIM | GP | G | A | Pts | PIM |
| 2004-05 | Green Bay | USHL | 13 | 0 | 0 | 0 | 20 | .... | .... | .... | .... | .... |
| 2005-06 | Green Bay | USHL | 14 | 0 | 0 | 0 | 25 | .... | .... | .... | .... | .... |
| 2006-07 | Sioux Falls | USHL | 57 | 2 | 11 | 13 | *215 | 8 | 0 | 3 | 3 | 29 |
| 2007-08 | U. of Minnesota | WCHA | 45 | 1 | 6 | 7 | *92 | .... | .... | .... | .... | .... |
| 2008-09 | Iowa Chops | AHL | 21 | 0 | 1 | 1 | 51 | .... | .... | .... | .... | .... |

Signed as a free agent by **Anaheim**, July 2, 2008.

### BIEGA, Alex (bee-AY-guh, AL-ehx) BUF.

Defense. Shoots right. 5'10", 191 lbs. Born, Montreal, Que., April 4, 1988.
(Buffalo's 5th choice, 147th overall, in 2006 Entry Draft).

| | | | Regular Season | | | | | Playoffs | | | | |
|---|---|---|---|---|---|---|---|---|---|---|---|---|
| Season | Club | League | GP | G | A | Pts | PIM | GP | G | A | Pts | PIM |
| 2004-05 | Salisbury School | High-CT | 27 | 9 | 22 | 31 | 45 | .... | .... | .... | .... | .... |
| 2005-06 | Salisbury School | High-CT | 28 | 10 | 17 | 27 | 51 | .... | .... | .... | .... | .... |
| 2006-07 | Harvard Crimson | ECAC | 33 | 6 | 12 | 18 | 36 | .... | .... | .... | .... | .... |
| 2007-08 | Harvard Crimson | ECAC | 34 | 3 | 19 | 22 | 28 | .... | .... | .... | .... | .... |
| 2008-09 | Harvard Crimson | ECAC | 31 | 4 | 16 | 20 | 46 | .... | .... | .... | .... | .... |

ECAC All-Rookie Team (2007)

### BIELKE, Dominik (BIGHL-keh, DOHM-ihn-ihk) S.J.

Defense. Shoots left. 6'3", 190 lbs. Born, Berlin, Germany, October 23, 1990.
(San Jose's 5th choice, 207th overall, in 2009 Entry Draft).

| | | | Regular Season | | | | | Playoffs | | | | |
|---|---|---|---|---|---|---|---|---|---|---|---|---|
| Season | Club | League | GP | G | A | Pts | PIM | GP | G | A | Pts | PIM |
| 2005-06 | Eisb. Jrs. Berl. Jr. | Ger-Jr. | 28 | 1 | 0 | 1 | 16 | 2 | 0 | 0 | 0 | 2 |
| 2006-07 | Eisb. Jrs. Berl. Jr. | Ger-Jr. | 33 | 12 | 22 | 34 | 36 | 3 | 1 | 1 | 2 | 6 |
| | Eisb. Jrs. Berlin | German-3 | 3 | 0 | 0 | 0 | 2 | .... | .... | .... | .... | .... |
| 2007-08 | Eisb. Jrs. Berl. Jr. | Ger-Jr. | 10 | 7 | 6 | 13 | 22 | 3 | 0 | 0 | 0 | 16 |
| | Eisb. Jrs. Berlin | German-3 | 46 | 5 | 7 | 12 | 74 | 7 | 2 | 4 | 6 | 12 |
| 2008-09 | Eisb. Jrs. Berlin | German-3 | 47 | 14 | 25 | 39 | 104 | .... | .... | .... | .... | .... |
| | Eisbaren Berlin | Germany | 7 | 0 | 1 | 1 | 2 | .... | .... | .... | .... | .... |

### BIGOS, Kyle (BEE-gohs, KIGHL) EDM.

Defense. Shoots right. 6'5", 230 lbs. Born, Upland, CA, May 12, 1989.
(Edmonton's 5th choice, 99th overall, in 2009 Entry Draft).

| | | | Regular Season | | | | | Playoffs | | | | |
|---|---|---|---|---|---|---|---|---|---|---|---|---|
| Season | Club | League | GP | G | A | Pts | PIM | GP | G | A | Pts | PIM |
| 2006-07 | Notre Dame | SMHL | 39 | 12 | 24 | 36 | 165 | .... | .... | .... | .... | .... |
| | Notre Dame | SJHL | 3 | 0 | 0 | 0 | 0 | .... | .... | .... | .... | .... |
| 2007-08 | Vernon Vipers | BCHL | 58 | 2 | 15 | 17 | 152 | 10 | 0 | 2 | 2 | 28 |
| 2008-09 | Vernon Vipers | BCHL | 58 | 8 | 25 | 33 | 126 | 17 | 2 | 4 | 6 | 37 |

• Signed Letter of Intent to attend **Merrimack College** (Hockey East) in fall of 2009.

### BILLINGSLEY, Tim (BIHL-ihngz-lee, TIHM) PHX.

Defense. Shoots right. 6'1", 177 lbs. Born, Ottawa, Ont., January 17, 1990.
(Phoenix's 8th choice, 189th overall, in 2008 Entry Draft).

| | | | Regular Season | | | | | Playoffs | | | | |
|---|---|---|---|---|---|---|---|---|---|---|---|---|
| Season | Club | League | GP | G | A | Pts | PIM | GP | G | A | Pts | PIM |
| 2005-06 | Cumberland | Minor-ON | 31 | 6 | 12 | 18 | 16 | .... | .... | .... | .... | .... |
| 2006-07 | St. Michael's | OHL | 49 | 2 | 6 | 8 | 24 | .... | .... | .... | .... | .... |
| 2007-08 | St. Michael's | OHL | 68 | 5 | 22 | 27 | 95 | 2 | 0 | 0 | 0 | 2 |
| 2008-09 | St. Michael's | OHL | 45 | 0 | 8 | 8 | 64 | 11 | 0 | 3 | 3 | 18 |

### BIRCH, Braden (BUHRCH, BRAY-duhn) CHI.

Defense. Shoots left. 6'3", 185 lbs. Born, Hamilton, Ont., September 25, 1989.
(Chicago's 6th choice, 179th overall, in 2008 Entry Draft).

| | | | Regular Season | | | | | Playoffs | | | | |
|---|---|---|---|---|---|---|---|---|---|---|---|---|
| Season | Club | League | GP | G | A | Pts | PIM | GP | G | A | Pts | PIM |
| 2006-07 | Stoney Creek | OJHL-B | 43 | 10 | 11 | 21 | 86 | .... | .... | .... | .... | .... |
| 2007-08 | Nanaimo Clippers | BCHL | 19 | 0 | 2 | 2 | 15 | .... | .... | .... | .... | .... |
| | Oakville Blades | OPJHL | 13 | 1 | 4 | 5 | 6 | 19 | 0 | 2 | 2 | 4 |
| 2008-09 | Oakville Blades | OJHL | 35 | 7 | 18 | 25 | 46 | 27 | 4 | 6 | 10 | 20 |

• Signed Letter of Intent to attend **Cornell University** (ECAC) in fall of 2009.

### BIRKHOLZ, Josh (BUHRK-hohlz, JAWSH) FLA.

Right wing. Shoots right. 6'1", 182 lbs. Born, St. Louis Park, MN, March 28, 1991.
(Florida's 3rd choice, 67th overall, in 2009 Entry Draft).

| | | | Regular Season | | | | | Playoffs | | | | |
|---|---|---|---|---|---|---|---|---|---|---|---|---|
| Season | Club | League | GP | G | A | Pts | PIM | GP | G | A | Pts | PIM |
| 2005-06 | Blake Bears | High-MN | 29 | 3 | 2 | 5 | 12 | .... | .... | .... | .... | .... |
| 2006-07 | Blake Bears | High-MN | 21 | 11 | 8 | 19 | 20 | .... | .... | .... | .... | .... |
| 2007-08 | Blake Bears | High-MN | 30 | 34 | 24 | 58 | 42 | .... | .... | .... | .... | .... |
| 2008-09 | Fargo Force | USHL | 55 | 21 | 15 | 36 | 52 | 9 | 3 | 2 | 5 | 4 |

• Signed Letter of Intent to attend **University of Minnesota** (WCHA) in fall of 2009.

**BJORKLUND, Henrik** (B'YOURK-luhnd, HEHN-rihk) **CGY.**

Right wing. Shoots right. 6'2", 202 lbs. Born, Karlstad, Sweden, September 22, 1990.
(Calgary's 3rd choice, 111th overall, in 2009 Entry Draft).

| | | | Regular Season | | | | | Playoffs | | | | |
|---|---|---|---|---|---|---|---|---|---|---|---|---|
| Season | Club | League | GP | G | A | Pts | PIM | GP | G | A | Pts | PIM |
| 2005-06 | Farjestad U18 | Swe-U18 | 10 | 3 | 2 | 5 | 6 | 5 | 1 | 0 | 1 | 2 |
| 2006-07 | Farjestad U18 | Swe-U18 | 14 | 13 | 12 | 25 | 53 | 8 | 4 | 3 | 7 | 20 |
| | Farjestad | Sweden | 1 | 0 | 0 | 0 | 0 | .... | .... | .... | .... | .... |
| 2007-08 | Farjestad U18 | Swe-U18 | 29 | 31 | 28 | 59 | 104 | 8 | 8 | 3 | 11 | 12 |
| | Farjestad | Sweden | 1 | 0 | 0 | 0 | 0 | 2 | 0 | 0 | 0 | 0 |
| | Skare BK | Sweden-3 | 17 | 7 | 4 | 11 | 6 | .... | .... | .... | .... | .... |
| 2008-09 | Farjestad | Sweden | 10 | 0 | 0 | 0 | 0 | .... | .... | .... | .... | .... |
| | Skare Jr. | Swe-Jr. | 1 | 2 | 0 | 2 | 4 | .... | .... | .... | .... | .... |
| | Skare BK Karlstad | Sweden-3 | 38 | 21 | 14 | 35 | 83 | 3 | 3 | 2 | 5 | 2 |

**BLACKER, Jesse** (BLA-kuhr, JEH-see) **TOR.**

Defense. Shoots right. 6'1", 190 lbs. Born, Toronto, Ont., April 19, 1991.
(Toronto's 3rd choice, 58th overall, in 2009 Entry Draft).

| | | | Regular Season | | | | | Playoffs | | | | |
|---|---|---|---|---|---|---|---|---|---|---|---|---|
| Season | Club | League | GP | G | A | Pts | PIM | GP | G | A | Pts | PIM |
| 2007-08 | Chatham Maroons | OJHL-B | 8 | 1 | 2 | 3 | 25 | .... | .... | .... | .... | .... |
| | Windsor Spitfires | OHL | 17 | 0 | 4 | 4 | 6 | 5 | 0 | 1 | 1 | 2 |
| 2008-09 | Windsor Spitfires | OHL | 67 | 4 | 17 | 21 | 54 | 20 | 0 | 4 | 4 | 18 |

**BLANCHARD, Nicolas** (BLAN-shard, NIHK-oh-las) **CAR.**

Center/Right wing. Shoots left. 6'1", 200 lbs. Born, Granby, Que., May 31, 1987.
(Carolina's 8th choice, 192nd overall, in 2005 Entry Draft).

| | | | Regular Season | | | | | Playoffs | | | | |
|---|---|---|---|---|---|---|---|---|---|---|---|---|
| Season | Club | League | GP | G | A | Pts | PIM | GP | G | A | Pts | PIM |
| 2003-04 | Antoine-Girouard | QAAA | 42 | 24 | 28 | 52 | 28 | 13 | 9 | 6 | 15 | 4 |
| 2004-05 | Chicoutimi | QMJHL | 69 | 13 | 26 | 39 | 31 | 17 | 2 | 2 | 4 | 10 |
| 2005-06 | Chicoutimi | QMJHL | 60 | 15 | 29 | 44 | 51 | 9 | 1 | 2 | 3 | 4 |
| 2006-07 | Chicoutimi | QMJHL | 62 | 22 | 35 | 57 | 41 | 4 | 0 | 2 | 2 | 8 |
| | Albany River Rats | AHL | 7 | 1 | 2 | 3 | 2 | 5 | 0 | 0 | 0 | 2 |
| 2007-08 | Albany River Rats | AHL | 64 | 11 | 12 | 23 | 70 | 7 | 0 | 2 | 2 | 2 |
| 2008-09 | Albany River Rats | AHL | 55 | 7 | 12 | 19 | 132 | .... | .... | .... | .... | .... |

**BLIZNAK, Mario** (BLIZH-nak, MAHR-ee-oh) **VAN.**

Center. Shoots left. 6', 200 lbs. Born, Trencin, Czech., March 6, 1987.
(Vancouver's 6th choice, 205th overall, in 2005 Entry Draft).

| | | | Regular Season | | | | | Playoffs | | | | |
|---|---|---|---|---|---|---|---|---|---|---|---|---|
| Season | Club | League | GP | G | A | Pts | PIM | GP | G | A | Pts | PIM |
| 2003-04 | Dubnica U18 | Svk-U18 | 46 | 25 | 26 | 51 | 62 | .... | .... | .... | .... | .... |
| | Dubnica Jr. | Slovak-Jr. | 2 | 1 | 0 | 1 | 2 | .... | .... | .... | .... | .... |
| 2004-05 | Dubnica U18 | Svk-U18 | 14 | 5 | 8 | 13 | 45 | .... | .... | .... | .... | .... |
| | Dubnica Jr. | Slovak-Jr. | 36 | 22 | 17 | 39 | 38 | .... | .... | .... | .... | .... |
| | Dubnica | Slovakia | 19 | 0 | 0 | 0 | 14 | .... | .... | .... | .... | .... |
| 2005-06 | Vancouver Giants | WHL | 69 | 9 | 12 | 21 | 29 | 18 | 4 | 1 | 5 | 14 |
| 2006-07 | Vancouver Giants | WHL | 47 | 8 | 14 | 22 | 20 | 22 | 6 | 6 | 12 | 14 |
| 2007-08 | Vancouver Giants | WHL | 67 | 19 | 32 | 51 | 36 | 10 | 3 | 5 | 8 | 2 |
| 2008-09 | Manitoba Moose | AHL | 64 | 7 | 9 | 16 | 24 | 21 | 3 | 2 | 5 | 8 |

**BLOMQVIST, Anton** (BLAWM-kvihst, AN-tawn) **CBJ**

Defense. Shoots left. 6'4", 189 lbs. Born, Kristianstad, Sweden, March 7, 1990.
(Columbus' 5th choice, 167th overall, in 2009 Entry Draft).

| | | | Regular Season | | | | | Playoffs | | | | |
|---|---|---|---|---|---|---|---|---|---|---|---|---|
| Season | Club | League | GP | G | A | Pts | PIM | GP | G | A | Pts | PIM |
| 2005-06 | Osby IK | Sweden-3 | 22 | 1 | 1 | 2 | 6 | .... | .... | .... | .... | .... |
| 2006-07 | Linkopings HC U18 | Swe-U18 | 10 | 2 | 1 | 3 | 16 | .... | .... | .... | .... | .... |
| | Linkopings HC Jr. | Swe-Jr. | 1 | 0 | 1 | 1 | 0 | .... | .... | .... | .... | .... |
| 2007-08 | Malmo U18 | Swe-U18 | 20 | 2 | 2 | 4 | 57 | 2 | 0 | 0 | 0 | 2 |
| | Malmo Jr. | Swe-Jr. | 18 | 0 | 1 | 1 | 20 | 5 | 0 | 1 | 1 | 2 |
| 2008-09 | Malmo Jr. | Swe-Jr. | 31 | 2 | 14 | 16 | 73 | .... | .... | .... | .... | .... |
| | Malmo | Sweden-2 | 13 | 0 | 3 | 3 | 8 | .... | .... | .... | .... | .... |

**BLOOD, Ben** (BLUHD, BEHN) **OTT.**

Defense. Shoots left. 6'3", 218 lbs. Born, Plymouth, MN, March 15, 1989.
(Ottawa's 4th choice, 120th overall, in 2007 Entry Draft).

| | | | Regular Season | | | | | Playoffs | | | | |
|---|---|---|---|---|---|---|---|---|---|---|---|---|
| Season | Club | League | GP | G | A | Pts | PIM | GP | G | A | Pts | PIM |
| 2005-06 | Shat.-St. Mary's | High-MN | 73 | 3 | 22 | 25 | 32 | .... | .... | .... | .... | .... |
| 2006-07 | Shat.-St. Mary's | High-MN | 63 | 11 | 25 | 36 | 144 | .... | .... | .... | .... | .... |
| 2007-08 | Des Moines | USHL | 11 | 0 | 7 | 7 | 17 | .... | .... | .... | .... | .... |
| | Indiana Ice | USHL | 46 | 10 | 6 | 16 | 83 | 4 | 1 | 2 | 3 | 14 |
| 2008-09 | North Dakota | WCHA | 31 | 0 | 1 | 1 | 12 | .... | .... | .... | .... | .... |

**BLOODOFF, Evan** (BLUHD-awf, EH-vuhn) **PHX.**

Left wing. Shoots left. 5'11", 190 lbs. Born, Nelson, B.C., November 21, 1990.
(Phoenix's 6th choice, 157th overall, in 2009 Entry Draft).

| | | | Regular Season | | | | | Playoffs | | | | |
|---|---|---|---|---|---|---|---|---|---|---|---|---|
| Season | Club | League | GP | G | A | Pts | PIM | GP | G | A | Pts | PIM |
| 2005-06 | Castlegar Rebels | Minor-BC | 50 | 32 | 21 | 53 | .... | .... | .... | .... | .... | .... |
| 2006-07 | Kelowna Rockets | WHL | 59 | 4 | 4 | 8 | 20 | .... | .... | .... | .... | .... |
| 2007-08 | Kelowna Rockets | WHL | 69 | 15 | 12 | 27 | 69 | 7 | 1 | 0 | 1 | 4 |
| 2008-09 | Kelowna Rockets | WHL | 71 | 12 | 9 | 21 | 77 | 22 | 3 | 3 | 6 | 10 |

**BLUM, Jonathon** (BLUHM, JAWN-ah-thuhn) **NSH.**

Defense. Shoots right. 6'1", 183 lbs. Born, Long Beach, CA, January 30, 1989.
(Nashville's 1st choice, 23rd overall, in 2007 Entry Draft).

| | | | Regular Season | | | | | Playoffs | | | | |
|---|---|---|---|---|---|---|---|---|---|---|---|---|
| Season | Club | League | GP | G | A | Pts | PIM | GP | G | A | Pts | PIM |
| 2004-05 | California Wave | Minor-CA | 55 | 15 | 50 | 65 | 65 | .... | .... | .... | .... | .... |
| 2005-06 | Vancouver Giants | WHL | 61 | 7 | 17 | 24 | 25 | 18 | 1 | 7 | 8 | 16 |
| 2006-07 | Vancouver Giants | WHL | 72 | 8 | 43 | 51 | 48 | 22 | 3 | 6 | 9 | 8 |
| 2007-08 | Vancouver Giants | WHL | 64 | 18 | 45 | 63 | 44 | 10 | 3 | 4 | 7 | 10 |
| 2008-09 | Vancouver Giants | WHL | 51 | 16 | 50 | 66 | 30 | 17 | 7 | 11 | 18 | 6 |
| | Milwaukee | AHL | .... | .... | .... | .... | .... | 5 | 0 | 0 | 0 | 0 |

WHL West Second All-Star Team (2008) • WHL West First All-Star Team (2009) • WHL Defenseman of the Year (2009) • Canadian Major Junior First All-Star Team (2009) • Canadian Major Junior Defenseman of the Year (2009)

**BODNARCHUK, Andrew** (BAWD-nahr-chuhk, AN-droo) **BOS.**

Defense. Shoots left. 5'11", 172 lbs. Born, Drumheller, Alta., July 11, 1988.
(Boston's 5th choice, 128th overall, in 2006 Entry Draft).

| | | | Regular Season | | | | | Playoffs | | | | |
|---|---|---|---|---|---|---|---|---|---|---|---|---|
| Season | Club | League | GP | G | A | Pts | PIM | GP | G | A | Pts | PIM |
| 2003-04 | Dartmouth | NSMHL | 58 | 16 | 23 | 39 | 81 | .... | .... | .... | .... | .... |
| 2004-05 | St. Paul's School | High-NH | 36 | 3 | 15 | 18 | .... | .... | .... | .... | .... | .... |
| 2005-06 | Halifax | QMJHL | 68 | 6 | 17 | 23 | 136 | 11 | 0 | 2 | 2 | 22 |
| 2006-07 | Halifax | QMJHL | 63 | 16 | 41 | 57 | 96 | 12 | 1 | 10 | 11 | 25 |
| | Providence Bruins | AHL | .... | .... | .... | .... | .... | 1 | 0 | 0 | 0 | 0 |
| 2007-08 | Halifax | QMJHL | 65 | 10 | 33 | 43 | 89 | 14 | 0 | 9 | 9 | 16 |
| 2008-09 | Providence Bruins | AHL | 62 | 1 | 8 | 9 | 33 | 15 | 0 | 2 | 2 | 22 |

QMJHL All-Rookie Team (2006)

**BODROV, Denis** (bawd-RAWV, DEH-nihs) **PHI.**

Defense. Shoots left. 6', 185 lbs. Born, Togliatti, USSR, August 22, 1986.
(Philadelphia's 4th choice, 55th overall, in 2006 Entry Draft).

| | | | Regular Season | | | | | Playoffs | | | | |
|---|---|---|---|---|---|---|---|---|---|---|---|---|
| Season | Club | League | GP | G | A | Pts | PIM | GP | G | A | Pts | PIM |
| 2002-03 | Lada Togliatti 2 | Russia-3 | 9 | 0 | 0 | 0 | 2 | .... | .... | .... | .... | .... |
| 2003-04 | Lada Togliatti 2 | Russia-3 | 45 | 3 | 4 | 7 | 58 | .... | .... | .... | .... | .... |
| 2004-05 | CSK VVS Samara | Russia-2 | 33 | 1 | 6 | 7 | 57 | .... | .... | .... | .... | .... |
| 2005-06 | Lada Togliatti | Russia | 35 | 2 | 2 | 4 | 42 | 8 | 0 | 0 | 0 | 8 |
| 2006-07 | Lada Togliatti | Russia | 49 | 1 | 5 | 6 | 70 | 3 | 0 | 1 | 1 | 6 |
| 2007-08 | Lada Togliatti 2 | Russia-3 | 8 | 3 | 4 | 7 | 38 | .... | .... | .... | .... | .... |
| | Lada Togliatti | Russia | 46 | 2 | 9 | 11 | 74 | 4 | 1 | 0 | 1 | 2 |
| 2008-09 | Lada Togliatti | Rus-KHL | 24 | 1 | 5 | 6 | 20 | .... | .... | .... | .... | .... |
| | Mytischi | Rus-KHL | 21 | 1 | 4 | 5 | 24 | 4 | 0 | 1 | 1 | 0 |

**BOLT, Bobby** (BOHLT, BAW-bee) **ANA.**

Left wing. Shoots left. 6'4", 228 lbs. Born, Thunder Bay, Ont., April 29, 1987.
(Anaheim's 4th choice, 127th overall, in 2005 Entry Draft).

| | | | Regular Season | | | | | Playoffs | | | | |
|---|---|---|---|---|---|---|---|---|---|---|---|---|
| Season | Club | League | GP | G | A | Pts | PIM | GP | G | A | Pts | PIM |
| 2003-04 | Strathroy Rockets | OHA-B | 39 | 5 | 14 | 19 | 41 | .... | .... | .... | .... | .... |
| | London Knights | OHL | 8 | 1 | 0 | 1 | 2 | .... | .... | .... | .... | .... |
| 2004-05 | Kingston | OHL | 67 | 11 | 14 | 25 | 92 | .... | .... | .... | .... | .... |
| 2005-06 | Kingston | OHL | 68 | 5 | 10 | 15 | 89 | 6 | 0 | 0 | 0 | 4 |
| 2006-07 | Kingston | OHL | 62 | 22 | 28 | 50 | 70 | 5 | 0 | 6 | 6 | 4 |
| | Portland Pirates | AHL | 5 | 1 | 1 | 2 | 2 | .... | .... | .... | .... | .... |
| 2007-08 | Portland Pirates | AHL | 4 | 0 | 0 | 0 | 0 | .... | .... | .... | .... | .... |
| | Augusta Lynx | ECHL | 62 | 15 | 11 | 26 | 45 | 5 | 1 | 0 | 1 | 7 |
| 2008-09 | Bakersfield | ECHL | 11 | 0 | 1 | 1 | 23 | 5 | 0 | 2 | 2 | 13 |

**BONINO, Nick** (boh-NEE-noh, NIHK) **ANA.**

Center. Shoots left. 6'1", 180 lbs. Born, Hartford, CT, April 20, 1988.
(San Jose's 6th choice, 173rd overall, in 2007 Entry Draft).

| | | | Regular Season | | | | | Playoffs | | | | |
|---|---|---|---|---|---|---|---|---|---|---|---|---|
| Season | Club | League | GP | G | A | Pts | PIM | GP | G | A | Pts | PIM |
| 2003-04 | Farmington | High-CT | 24 | 44 | 23 | 67 | 10 | .... | .... | .... | .... | .... |
| 2004-05 | Farmington | High-CT | 24 | 68 | 23 | 91 | 12 | .... | .... | .... | .... | .... |
| 2005-06 | Avon Old Farms | High-CT | 25 | 26 | 30 | 56 | 10 | .... | .... | .... | .... | .... |
| 2006-07 | Avon Old Farms | High-CT | 26 | 24 | 42 | 66 | 14 | .... | .... | .... | .... | .... |
| 2007-08 | Boston University | H-East | 39 | 16 | 13 | 29 | 10 | .... | .... | .... | .... | .... |
| 2008-09 | Boston University | H-East | 44 | 18 | 32 | 50 | 30 | .... | .... | .... | .... | .... |

NCAA Championship All-Tournament Team (2009)

Traded to **Anaheim** by **San Jose** with Timo Pielmeier and future considerations for Travis Moen and Kent Huskins, March 4, 2009.

**BONNEAU, Jimmy** (BAW-noh, JIHM-mee)

Left wing. Shoots left. 6'3", 214 lbs. Born, Baie-Comeau, Que., March 22, 1985.
(Montreal's 10th choice, 241st overall, in 2003 Entry Draft).

| | | | Regular Season | | | | | Playoffs | | | | |
|---|---|---|---|---|---|---|---|---|---|---|---|---|
| Season | Club | League | GP | G | A | Pts | PIM | GP | G | A | Pts | PIM |
| 2000-01 | Jonquiere Elites | QAAA | 1 | 0 | 0 | 0 | 0 | .... | .... | .... | .... | .... |
| 2001-02 | Jonquiere Elites | QAAA | 40 | 5 | 10 | 15 | 55 | 3 | 1 | 1 | 2 | 2 |
| 2002-03 | Montreal Rocket | QMJHL | 65 | 1 | 5 | 6 | 261 | 7 | 0 | 0 | 0 | 12 |
| 2003-04 | PEI Rocket | QMJHL | 70 | 7 | 12 | 19 | 263 | 11 | 1 | 0 | 1 | 12 |
| 2004-05 | PEI Rocket | QMJHL | 70 | 11 | 11 | 22 | 234 | .... | .... | .... | .... | .... |
| 2005-06 | Long Beach | ECHL | 65 | 1 | 5 | 6 | 137 | .... | .... | .... | .... | .... |
| 2006-07 | Hamilton Bulldogs | AHL | 9 | 0 | 0 | 0 | 59 | .... | .... | .... | .... | .... |
| | Cincinnati | ECHL | 46 | 2 | 5 | 7 | 89 | 10 | 0 | 0 | 0 | 23 |
| 2007-08 | Hamilton Bulldogs | AHL | 6 | 1 | 0 | 1 | 5 | .... | .... | .... | .... | .... |
| | Cincinnati | ECHL | 18 | 0 | 4 | 4 | 61 | 3 | 0 | 0 | 0 | 0 |
| 2008-09 | Portland Pirates | AHL | 46 | 0 | 6 | 6 | 122 | .... | .... | .... | .... | .... |

Signed as a free agent by **Buffalo**, August 13, 2008.

**BOOGAARD, Aaron** (BOO-gard, AIR-ruhn) **PIT.**

Right wing. Shoots right. 6'3", 220 lbs. Born, Newmarket, Ont., August 11, 1986.
(Minnesota's 9th choice, 175th overall, in 2004 Entry Draft).

| | | | Regular Season | | | | | Playoffs | | | | |
|---|---|---|---|---|---|---|---|---|---|---|---|---|
| Season | Club | League | GP | G | A | Pts | PIM | GP | G | A | Pts | PIM |
| 2002-03 | Calgary Hitmen | WHL | 39 | 3 | 0 | 3 | 52 | 5 | 0 | 0 | 0 | 0 |
| 2003-04 | Calgary Hitmen | WHL | 12 | 0 | 1 | 1 | 24 | .... | .... | .... | .... | .... |
| | Tri-City Americans | WHL | 23 | 3 | 1 | 4 | 33 | 6 | 0 | 0 | 0 | 8 |
| 2004-05 | Tri-City Americans | WHL | 65 | 4 | 11 | 15 | 96 | 5 | 0 | 0 | 0 | 4 |
| 2005-06 | Tri-City Americans | WHL | 65 | 6 | 4 | 10 | 211 | 5 | 0 | 2 | 2 | 4 |
| 2006-07 | Tri-City Americans | WHL | 69 | 10 | 11 | 21 | 173 | 5 | 1 | 0 | 1 | 14 |
| 2007-08 | Wilkes-Barre | AHL | 2 | 0 | 0 | 0 | 5 | .... | .... | .... | .... | .... |
| | Wheeling Nailers | ECHL | 58 | 6 | 9 | 15 | 105 | .... | .... | .... | .... | .... |
| 2008-09 | Wilkes-Barre | AHL | 41 | 2 | 1 | 3 | 112 | 1 | 0 | 0 | 0 | 0 |

Signed as a free agent by **Pittsburgh**, April 23, 2007.

**BOROWIECKI, Mark** (boh-roh-WIH-kee, MAHRK) **OTT.**

Defense. Shoots left. 6'1", 195 lbs. Born, Ottawa, Ont., July 12, 1989.
(Ottawa's 6th choice, 139th overall, in 2008 Entry Draft).

| | | | Regular Season | | | | | Playoffs | | | | |
|---|---|---|---|---|---|---|---|---|---|---|---|---|
| Season | Club | League | GP | G | A | Pts | PIM | GP | G | A | Pts | PIM |
| 2006-07 | Smiths Falls Bears | CJHL | 53 | 3 | 25 | 28 | 85 | 6 | 0 | 0 | 0 | 10 |
| 2007-08 | Smiths Falls Bears | CJHL | 46 | 2 | 24 | 26 | 80 | 15 | 1 | 10 | 11 | 22 |
| 2008-09 | Clarkson Knights | ECAC | 33 | 1 | 1 | 2 | 24 | .... | .... | .... | .... | .... |

### BORTUZZO, Robert (bohr-TOOZ-oh, RAW-buhrt) PIT.

Defense. Shoots right. 6'3", 196 lbs. Born, Thunder Bay, Ont., March 18, 1989.
(Pittsburgh's 3rd choice, 78th overall, in 2007 Entry Draft).

| | | | Regular Season | | | | | Playoffs | | | | |
|---|---|---|---|---|---|---|---|---|---|---|---|---|
| Season | Club | League | GP | G | A | Pts | PIM | GP | G | A | Pts | PIM |
| 2005-06 | F-Wm. North Stars | SIJHL | 40 | 4 | 18 | 22 | .... | .... | .... | .... | .... | .... |
| 2006-07 | Kitchener Rangers | OHL | 63 | 2 | 12 | 14 | 67 | 9 | 1 | 2 | 3 | 8 |
| 2007-08 | Kitchener Rangers | OHL | 52 | 3 | 15 | 18 | 61 | 18 | 0 | 8 | 8 | 14 |
| 2008-09 | Kitchener Rangers | OHL | 23 | 1 | 16 | 17 | 24 | .... | .... | .... | .... | .... |

### BOUCHARD, Francois (BOO-shahrd, frahn-SWUH) WSH.

Right wing. Shoots left. 6'1", 195 lbs. Born, Sherbrooke, Que., April 26, 1988.
(Washington's 4th choice, 35th overall, in 2006 Entry Draft).

| | | | Regular Season | | | | | Playoffs | | | | |
|---|---|---|---|---|---|---|---|---|---|---|---|---|
| Season | Club | League | GP | G | A | Pts | PIM | GP | G | A | Pts | PIM |
| 2004-05 | Baie-Comeau | QMJHL | 54 | 11 | 13 | 24 | 13 | 6 | 1 | 1 | 2 | 2 |
| 2005-06 | Baie-Comeau | QMJHL | 69 | 33 | 69 | 102 | 66 | 4 | 1 | 0 | 1 | 6 |
| 2006-07 | Baie-Comeau | QMJHL | 68 | 45 | *80 | *125 | 72 | 11 | 7 | 11 | 18 | 4 |
| 2007-08 | Baie-Comeau | QMJHL | 68 | 36 | 56 | 92 | 70 | 5 | 1 | 1 | 2 | 6 |
| | Hershey Bears | AHL | 4 | 1 | 0 | 1 | 2 | 1 | 0 | 0 | 0 | 2 |
| 2008-09 | Hershey Bears | AHL | 64 | 15 | 20 | 35 | 34 | 11 | 1 | 2 | 3 | 8 |

QMJHL Second All-Star Team (2007)

### BOUMA, Lance (BOW-ma, LANTZ) CGY.

Center. Shoots left. 6'1", 210 lbs. Born, Provost, Alta., March 25, 1990.
(Calgary's 3rd choice, 78th overall, in 2008 Entry Draft).

| | | | Regular Season | | | | | Playoffs | | | | |
|---|---|---|---|---|---|---|---|---|---|---|---|---|
| Season | Club | League | GP | G | A | Pts | PIM | GP | G | A | Pts | PIM |
| 2005-06 | Wainwright | RAMHL | 37 | 21 | 29 | 50 | .... | .... | .... | .... | .... | .... |
| | Vancouver Giants | WHL | 5 | 1 | 3 | 4 | 0 | .... | .... | .... | .... | .... |
| 2006-07 | Vancouver Giants | WHL | 49 | 3 | 5 | 8 | 31 | 22 | 3 | 3 | 6 | 12 |
| 2007-08 | Vancouver Giants | WHL | 71 | 12 | 23 | 35 | 93 | 10 | 0 | 1 | 1 | 8 |
| 2008-09 | Vancouver Giants | WHL | 48 | 9 | 16 | 25 | 116 | 17 | 7 | 5 | 12 | 30 |

### BOURDON, Marc-Andre (boor-DOHN, MAHRK-AHN-dray) PHI.

Defense. Shoots left. 6', 206 lbs. Born, St-Hyacinthe, Que., September 17, 1989.
(Philadelphia's 2nd choice, 67th overall, in 2008 Entry Draft).

| | | | Regular Season | | | | | Playoffs | | | | |
|---|---|---|---|---|---|---|---|---|---|---|---|---|
| Season | Club | League | GP | G | A | Pts | PIM | GP | G | A | Pts | PIM |
| 2006-07 | Rouyn-Noranda | QMJHL | 63 | 2 | 26 | 28 | 80 | 16 | 0 | 4 | 4 | 21 |
| 2007-08 | Rouyn-Noranda | QMJHL | 69 | 12 | 47 | 59 | 114 | 17 | 2 | 16 | 18 | 25 |
| 2008-09 | Rouyn-Noranda | QMJHL | 37 | 11 | 27 | 38 | 89 | .... | .... | .... | .... | .... |
| | Rimouski Oceanic | QMJHL | 17 | 7 | 15 | 22 | 23 | 13 | 1 | 12 | 13 | 25 |

QMJHL First All-Star Team (2008, 2009) • Canadian Major Junior Second All-Star Team (2008)

### BOURQUE, Gabriel (BOHRK, gah-BREE-ehl) NSH.

Left wing. Shoots left. 5'9", 185 lbs. Born, Rimouski, Que., September 23, 1990.
(Nashville's 9th choice, 132nd overall, in 2009 Entry Draft).

| | | | Regular Season | | | | | Playoffs | | | | |
|---|---|---|---|---|---|---|---|---|---|---|---|---|
| Season | Club | League | GP | G | A | Pts | PIM | GP | G | A | Pts | PIM |
| 2006-07 | Ecole Notre Dame | QAAA | 43 | 15 | 35 | 50 | 115 | 13 | 8 | 16 | 24 | 14 |
| 2007-08 | Baie-Comeau | QMJHL | 65 | 10 | 18 | 28 | 38 | 5 | 0 | 0 | 0 | 0 |
| 2008-09 | Baie-Comeau | QMJHL | 60 | 22 | 39 | 61 | 82 | 5 | 0 | 2 | 2 | 16 |

### BOURQUE, Ryan (BOHRK, RIGH-uhn) NYR

Center. Shoots left. 5'9", 163 lbs. Born, Boxford, MA, January 3, 1991.
(NY Rangers' 3rd choice, 80th overall, in 2009 Entry Draft).

| | | | Regular Season | | | | | Playoffs | | | | |
|---|---|---|---|---|---|---|---|---|---|---|---|---|
| Season | Club | League | GP | G | A | Pts | PIM | GP | G | A | Pts | PIM |
| 2006-07 | Cushing | High-MA | 29 | 19 | 31 | 50 | .... | .... | .... | .... | .... | .... |
| 2007-08 | USNTDP | NAHL | 34 | 11 | 9 | 20 | 14 | .... | .... | .... | .... | .... |
| | USNTDP | U-17 | 7 | 4 | 3 | 7 | 10 | .... | .... | .... | .... | .... |
| | USNTDP | U-18 | 27 | 4 | 12 | 16 | 18 | .... | .... | .... | .... | .... |
| 2008-09 | USNTDP | NAHL | 14 | 7 | 9 | 16 | 10 | .... | .... | .... | .... | .... |
| | USNTDP | U-18 | 43 | 14 | 24 | 38 | 48 | .... | .... | .... | .... | .... |

### BOURRET, Alex (BUHR-ray, AL-ehx)

Right wing. Shoots left. 5'11", 205 lbs. Born, Drummondville, Que., October 5, 1986.
(Atlanta's 1st choice, 16th overall, in 2005 Entry Draft).

| | | | Regular Season | | | | | Playoffs | | | | |
|---|---|---|---|---|---|---|---|---|---|---|---|---|
| Season | Club | League | GP | G | A | Pts | PIM | GP | G | A | Pts | PIM |
| 2001-02 | Magog | QAAA | 40 | 26 | 34 | 60 | 105 | .... | .... | .... | .... | .... |
| 2002-03 | Sherbrooke | QMJHL | 61 | 13 | 15 | 28 | 73 | 12 | 1 | 1 | 2 | 10 |
| 2003-04 | Lewiston | QMJHL | 65 | 22 | 41 | 63 | 94 | 7 | 4 | 5 | 9 | 20 |
| 2004-05 | Lewiston | QMJHL | 65 | 31 | 55 | 86 | 172 | 8 | 6 | 8 | 14 | 25 |
| 2005-06 | Shawinigan | QMJHL | 67 | 44 | 70 | 114 | 133 | 7 | 3 | 4 | 7 | 14 |
| 2006-07 | Chicago Wolves | AHL | 45 | 11 | 21 | 32 | 46 | .... | .... | .... | .... | .... |
| | Hartford Wolf Pack | AHL | 23 | 5 | 13 | 18 | 12 | 7 | 3 | 8 | 11 | 2 |
| 2007-08 | Hartford Wolf Pack | AHL | 54 | 9 | 24 | 33 | 78 | 5 | 1 | 3 | 4 | 17 |
| 2008-09 | San Antonio | AHL | 48 | 3 | 11 | 14 | 44 | .... | .... | .... | .... | .... |

QMJHL Second All-Star Team (2005, 2006)

Traded to **NY Rangers** by **Atlanta** for Pascal Dupuis and NY Rangers' 3rd round choice (later traded to Pittsburgh - Pittsburgh selected Robert Bortuzzo) in 2007 Entry Draft, February 27, 2007. Traded to **Phoenix** by **NY Rangers** for Pittsburgh's 3rd round choice (previously acquired, NY Rangers selected Tomas Kundratek) in 2008 Entry Draft, June 21, 2008.

### BOWMAN, Drayson (BOH-muhn, DRAY-suhn) CAR.

Center/Left wing. Shoots left. 6'1", 190 lbs. Born, Grand Rapids, MI, March 8, 1989.
(Carolina's 2nd choice, 72nd overall, in 2007 Entry Draft).

| | | | Regular Season | | | | | Playoffs | | | | |
|---|---|---|---|---|---|---|---|---|---|---|---|---|
| Season | Club | League | GP | G | A | Pts | PIM | GP | G | A | Pts | PIM |
| 2004-05 | Kimberly | KIJHL | 47 | 29 | 30 | 59 | 108 | .... | .... | .... | .... | .... |
| | Spokane Chiefs | WHL | 4 | 0 | 0 | 0 | 0 | .... | .... | .... | .... | .... |
| 2005-06 | Spokane Chiefs | WHL | 72 | 17 | 17 | 34 | 51 | .... | .... | .... | .... | .... |
| 2006-07 | Spokane Chiefs | WHL | 61 | 24 | 19 | 43 | 55 | 6 | 2 | 5 | 7 | 4 |
| 2007-08 | Spokane Chiefs | WHL | 66 | 42 | 40 | 82 | 62 | 21 | 11 | 9 | 20 | 8 |
| 2008-09 | Spokane Chiefs | WHL | 62 | 47 | 36 | 83 | 107 | 12 | 8 | 5 | 13 | 8 |

WHL West Second All-Star Team (2008, 2009) • Memorial Cup All-Star Team (2008)

### BOZAK, Tyler (BOH-zak, TIGH-luhr) TOR.

Center. Shoots right. 6', 165 lbs. Born, Regina, Sask., March 19, 1986.

| | | | Regular Season | | | | | Playoffs | | | | |
|---|---|---|---|---|---|---|---|---|---|---|---|---|
| Season | Club | League | GP | G | A | Pts | PIM | GP | G | A | Pts | PIM |
| 2003-04 | Regina Pat Cdns. | SMHL | 42 | 17 | 19 | 36 | 40 | .... | .... | .... | .... | .... |
| 2004-05 | Victoria Salsa | BCHL | 55 | 15 | 16 | 31 | 24 | 5 | 0 | 2 | 2 | 2 |
| 2005-06 | Victoria Salsa | BCHL | 56 | 31 | 38 | 69 | 26 | 16 | 8 | 8 | 16 | 14 |
| 2006-07 | Victoria Grizzlies | BCHL | 59 | 45 | 83 | 128 | 45 | .... | .... | .... | .... | .... |
| 2007-08 | U. of Denver | WCHA | 41 | 18 | 16 | 34 | 22 | .... | .... | .... | .... | .... |
| 2008-09 | U. of Denver | WCHA | 19 | 8 | 15 | 23 | 10 | .... | .... | .... | .... | .... |

WCHA All-Rookie Team (2008)

Signed as a free agent by **Toronto**, April 3, 2009.

### BRADFORD, Brock (BRAD-fohrd, BRAWK) BOS.

Center. Shoots right. 5'9", 168 lbs. Born, Burnaby, B.C., January 7, 1987.
(Boston's 8th choice, 217th overall, in 2005 Entry Draft).

| | | | Regular Season | | | | | Playoffs | | | | |
|---|---|---|---|---|---|---|---|---|---|---|---|---|
| Season | Club | League | GP | G | A | Pts | PIM | GP | G | A | Pts | PIM |
| 2002-03 | Richmond | PIJHL | 18 | 12 | 12 | 24 | .... | .... | .... | .... | .... | .... |
| | Coquitlam Express | BCHL | 36 | 11 | 23 | 34 | 14 | .... | .... | .... | .... | .... |
| 2003-04 | Coquitlam Express | BCHL | 57 | 36 | 49 | 85 | .... | .... | .... | .... | .... | .... |
| 2004-05 | Omaha Lancers | USHL | 60 | 24 | 33 | 57 | 16 | 5 | 0 | 1 | 1 | 0 |
| 2005-06 | Boston College | H-East | 42 | 6 | 12 | 18 | 8 | .... | .... | .... | .... | .... |
| 2006-07 | Boston College | H-East | 42 | 19 | 26 | 45 | 28 | .... | .... | .... | .... | .... |
| 2007-08 | Boston College | H-East | 5 | 3 | 2 | 5 | 2 | .... | .... | .... | .... | .... |
| 2008-09 | Boston College | H-East | 37 | *25 | 17 | 42 | 19 | .... | .... | .... | .... | .... |

Hockey East Second All-Star Team (2009)

### BRAUN, Constantin (BRAWN, kawn-stuhn-TIHN) L.A.

Left wing. Shoots left. 6'3", 198 lbs. Born, Lampertheim, West Germany, March 11, 1988.
(Los Angeles' 9th choice, 164th overall, in 2006 Entry Draft).

| | | | Regular Season | | | | | Playoffs | | | | |
|---|---|---|---|---|---|---|---|---|---|---|---|---|
| Season | Club | League | GP | G | A | Pts | PIM | GP | G | A | Pts | PIM |
| 2003-04 | Mannheim Jr. | Ger-Jr. | 30 | 12 | 5 | 17 | 42 | .... | .... | .... | .... | .... |
| 2004-05 | Eisb. Jrs. Berlin | German-3 | 1 | 0 | 0 | 0 | 0 | .... | .... | .... | .... | .... |
| | Eisb. Jrs. Berl. Jr. | Ger-Jr. | 29 | 14 | 20 | 34 | 125 | 6 | 5 | 4 | 9 | 16 |
| 2005-06 | Eisb. Jrs. Berl. Jr. | Ger-Jr. | 7 | 8 | 4 | 12 | 14 | 1 | 1 | 0 | 1 | 6 |
| | Eisbaren Berlin | Germany | 6 | 0 | 0 | 0 | 0 | .... | .... | .... | .... | .... |
| | Eisb. Jrs. Berlin | German-3 | 24 | 13 | 10 | 23 | 34 | .... | .... | .... | .... | .... |
| 2006-07 | Eisb. Jrs. Berlin | German-3 | 10 | 4 | 3 | 7 | 37 | 2 | 2 | 1 | 3 | 0 |
| | Eisbaren Berlin | Germany | 34 | 1 | 3 | 4 | 14 | .... | .... | .... | .... | .... |
| 2007-08 | Eisb. Jrs. Berlin | German-3 | 2 | 0 | 0 | 0 | 0 | .... | .... | .... | .... | .... |
| | Eisbaren Berlin | Germany | 50 | 4 | 7 | 11 | 32 | 14 | 3 | 7 | 10 | 2 |
| 2008-09 | Eisbaren Berlin | Germany | 43 | 6 | 9 | 15 | 20 | 12 | 0 | 2 | 2 | 2 |

### BRAUN, Justin (BRAWN, JUHS-tihn) S.J.

Defense. Shoots right. 6'1", 180 lbs. Born, St. Paul, MN, February 10, 1987.
(San Jose's 7th choice, 201st overall, in 2007 Entry Draft).

| | | | Regular Season | | | | | Playoffs | | | | |
|---|---|---|---|---|---|---|---|---|---|---|---|---|
| Season | Club | League | GP | G | A | Pts | PIM | GP | G | A | Pts | PIM |
| 2004-05 | White Bear Lake | High-MN | STATISTICS NOT AVAILABLE | | | | | | | | | |
| | Green Bay | USHL | 10 | 0 | 0 | 0 | 2 | .... | .... | .... | .... | .... |
| 2005-06 | Green Bay | USHL | 59 | 2 | 11 | 13 | 69 | 3 | 0 | 0 | 0 | 2 |
| 2006-07 | Massachusetts | H-East | 39 | 4 | 10 | 14 | 20 | .... | .... | .... | .... | .... |
| 2007-08 | Massachusetts | H-East | 36 | 4 | 16 | 20 | 20 | .... | .... | .... | .... | .... |
| 2008-09 | Massachusetts | H-East | 39 | 7 | 16 | 23 | 50 | .... | .... | .... | .... | .... |

Hockey East All-Rookie Team (2007) • Hockey East Second All-Star Team (2009)

### BRENNAN, Mike (BREH-nan, MIGHK) CHI.

Defense. Shoots right. 6', 190 lbs. Born, Smithtown, NY, January 24, 1986.

| | | | Regular Season | | | | | Playoffs | | | | |
|---|---|---|---|---|---|---|---|---|---|---|---|---|
| Season | Club | League | GP | G | A | Pts | PIM | GP | G | A | Pts | PIM |
| 2002-03 | USNTDP | U-17 | 18 | 2 | 4 | 6 | 8 | .... | .... | .... | .... | .... |
| | USNTDP | NAHL | 44 | 1 | 2 | 3 | 89 | .... | .... | .... | .... | .... |
| 2003-04 | USNTDP | U-17 | 43 | 2 | 5 | 7 | 58 | .... | .... | .... | .... | .... |
| | USNTDP | NAHL | 11 | 2 | 3 | 5 | 19 | .... | .... | .... | .... | .... |
| 2004-05 | Boston College | H-East | 40 | 2 | 6 | 8 | 46 | .... | .... | .... | .... | .... |
| 2005-06 | Boston College | H-East | 40 | 2 | 9 | 11 | 89 | .... | .... | .... | .... | .... |
| 2006-07 | Boston College | H-East | 42 | 0 | 11 | 11 | 89 | .... | .... | .... | .... | .... |
| 2007-08 | Boston College | H-East | 44 | 3 | 5 | 8 | 52 | .... | .... | .... | .... | .... |
| 2008-09 | Rockford IceHogs | AHL | 64 | 0 | 6 | 6 | 77 | 2 | 0 | 0 | 0 | 2 |

NCAA Championship All-Tournament Team (2008)

Signed as a free agent by **Chicago**, April 16, 2008.

### BRENNAN, T.J. (BREH-nan, TEE-JAY) BUF.

Defense. Shoots left. 6', 204 lbs. Born, Willingboro, NJ, April 3, 1989.
(Buffalo's 1st choice, 31st overall, in 2007 Entry Draft).

| | | | Regular Season | | | | | Playoffs | | | | |
|---|---|---|---|---|---|---|---|---|---|---|---|---|
| Season | Club | League | GP | G | A | Pts | PIM | GP | G | A | Pts | PIM |
| 2005-06 | Phi. Little Flyers | AtJHL | 42 | 9 | 23 | 32 | .... | .... | .... | .... | .... | .... |
| 2006-07 | Saint John | QMJHL | 68 | 16 | 25 | 41 | 79 | 4 | 1 | 1 | 2 | 4 |
| 2007-08 | St. John's | QMJHL | 65 | 16 | 25 | 41 | 92 | 6 | 2 | 4 | 6 | 12 |
| 2008-09 | Montreal | QMJHL | 59 | 5 | 29 | 34 | 63 | 10 | 4 | 8 | 12 | 34 |

### BRITTAIN, Josh (BRIH-tehn, JAWSH) ANA.

Left wing. Shoots left. 6'4", 216 lbs. Born, Milton, Ont., January 3, 1990.
(Anaheim's 5th choice, 71st overall, in 2008 Entry Draft).

| | | | Regular Season | | | | | Playoffs | | | | |
|---|---|---|---|---|---|---|---|---|---|---|---|---|
| Season | Club | League | GP | G | A | Pts | PIM | GP | G | A | Pts | PIM |
| 2005-06 | Tor. Jr. Canadiens | GTHL | 33 | 19 | 21 | 40 | 47 | .... | .... | .... | .... | .... |
| 2006-07 | Kingston | OHL | 54 | 5 | 12 | 17 | 38 | 2 | 0 | 0 | 0 | 0 |
| 2007-08 | Kingston | OHL | 68 | 28 | 23 | 51 | 106 | .... | .... | .... | .... | .... |
| 2008-09 | Kingston | OHL | 27 | 17 | 7 | 24 | 31 | .... | .... | .... | .... | .... |
| | Barrie Colts | OHL | 41 | 15 | 13 | 28 | 65 | 5 | 1 | 2 | 3 | 4 |

## BRODA, Joel — (BROH-da, JOHL) — WSH.

Center. Shoots left. 6'1", 200 lbs. Born, Yorkton, Sask., November 24, 1989.
(Washington's 6th choice, 144th overall, in 2008 Entry Draft).

| | | | Regular Season | | | | | Playoffs | | | | |
|---|---|---|---|---|---|---|---|---|---|---|---|---|
| Season | Club | League | GP | G | A | Pts | PIM | GP | G | A | Pts | PIM |
| 2004-05 | Beardy's | SMHL | 44 | 13 | 13 | 26 | 28 | .... | .... | .... | .... | .... |
| | Tri-City Americans | WHL | 2 | 0 | 0 | 0 | 0 | .... | .... | .... | .... | .... |
| 2005-06 | Tri-City Americans | WHL | 51 | 3 | 1 | 4 | 10 | 5 | 0 | 0 | 0 | 0 |
| 2006-07 | Tri-City Americans | WHL | 71 | 16 | 28 | 44 | 62 | 6 | 2 | 0 | 2 | 0 |
| 2007-08 | Tri-City Americans | WHL | 3 | 2 | 1 | 3 | 2 | .... | .... | .... | .... | .... |
| | Moose Jaw | WHL | 70 | 28 | 22 | 50 | 72 | 6 | 1 | 1 | 2 | 0 |
| 2008-09 | Moose Jaw | WHL | 39 | *36 | 12 | 48 | 45 | .... | .... | .... | .... | .... |
| | Calgary Hitmen | WHL | 28 | *17 | 22 | 39 | 19 | 18 | 11 | 13 | 24 | 8 |

WHL East Second All-Star Team (2009)

## BRODEUR, Mathieu — (broh-DUHR, MA-tyew) — PHX.

Defense. Shoots left. 6'5", 190 lbs. Born, Laval, Que., June 21, 1990.
(Phoenix's 5th choice, 76th overall, in 2008 Entry Draft).

| | | | Regular Season | | | | | Playoffs | | | | |
|---|---|---|---|---|---|---|---|---|---|---|---|---|
| Season | Club | League | GP | G | A | Pts | PIM | GP | G | A | Pts | PIM |
| 2006-07 | Laurentides | QAAA | 44 | 5 | 7 | 12 | 58 | 15 | 2 | 4 | 6 | 18 |
| 2007-08 | Cape Breton | QMJHL | 69 | 1 | 6 | 7 | 27 | 11 | 0 | 0 | 0 | 6 |
| 2008-09 | Cape Breton | QMJHL | 61 | 3 | 12 | 15 | 15 | 11 | 1 | 3 | 4 | 4 |

## BRODIE, T.J. — (BROH-dee, TEE-JAY) — CGY.

Defense. Shoots left. 6'1", 176 lbs. Born, Chatham, Ont., June 7, 1990.
(Calgary's 5th choice, 114th overall, in 2008 Entry Draft).

| | | | Regular Season | | | | | Playoffs | | | | |
|---|---|---|---|---|---|---|---|---|---|---|---|---|
| Season | Club | League | GP | G | A | Pts | PIM | GP | G | A | Pts | PIM |
| 2006-07 | Leamington Flyers | OJHL-B | 43 | 8 | 38 | 46 | 104 | 5 | 1 | 2 | 3 | 12 |
| | Saginaw Spirit | OHL | 20 | 0 | 4 | 4 | 23 | 3 | 0 | 1 | 1 | 2 |
| 2007-08 | Saginaw Spirit | OHL | 68 | 4 | 26 | 30 | 73 | 4 | 0 | 3 | 3 | 2 |
| 2008-09 | Saginaw Spirit | OHL | 63 | 12 | 38 | 50 | 67 | 8 | 3 | 6 | 9 | 8 |

## BROPHEY, Evan — (BROH-fee, EH-vuhn) — CHI.

Center/Left wing. Shoots left. 6'1", 203 lbs. Born, Kitchener, Ont., December 3, 1986.
(Chicago's 4th choice, 68th overall, in 2005 Entry Draft).

| | | | Regular Season | | | | | Playoffs | | | | |
|---|---|---|---|---|---|---|---|---|---|---|---|---|
| Season | Club | League | GP | G | A | Pts | PIM | GP | G | A | Pts | PIM |
| 2002-03 | Barrie Colts | OHL | 61 | 12 | 14 | 26 | 36 | 6 | 0 | 0 | 0 | 2 |
| 2003-04 | Barrie Colts | OHL | 67 | 14 | 11 | 25 | 63 | 12 | 4 | 3 | 7 | 4 |
| 2004-05 | Barrie Colts | OHL | 10 | 3 | 7 | 10 | 13 | .... | .... | .... | .... | .... |
| | Belleville Bulls | OHL | 53 | 25 | 36 | 61 | 42 | 5 | 2 | 1 | 3 | 2 |
| 2005-06 | Belleville Bulls | OHL | 22 | 9 | 17 | 26 | 39 | .... | .... | .... | .... | .... |
| | Plymouth Whalers | OHL | 40 | 10 | 25 | 35 | 42 | 13 | 4 | 7 | 11 | 18 |
| 2006-07 | Plymouth Whalers | OHL | 68 | 36 | 71 | 107 | 91 | 20 | 9 | 14 | 23 | 26 |
| 2007-08 | Rockford IceHogs | AHL | 74 | 4 | 15 | 19 | 64 | 1 | 0 | 0 | 0 | 0 |
| 2008-09 | Rockford IceHogs | AHL | 79 | 16 | 23 | 39 | 65 | 4 | 1 | 0 | 1 | 0 |

## BROSNIHAN, Pat — (BRAWS-nih-han, PAT) — PHX.

Right wing. Shoots right. 6'4", 214 lbs. Born, Worcester, MA, August 20, 1986.
(Phoenix's 5th choice, 212th overall, in 2005 Entry Draft).

| | | | Regular Season | | | | | Playoffs | | | | |
|---|---|---|---|---|---|---|---|---|---|---|---|---|
| Season | Club | League | GP | G | A | Pts | PIM | GP | G | A | Pts | PIM |
| 2003-04 | Worcester | High-MA | 25 | 28 | 26 | 54 | 30 | .... | .... | .... | .... | .... |
| 2004-05 | Worcester | High-MA | 26 | 20 | 44 | 64 | 48 | .... | .... | .... | .... | .... |
| 2005-06 | Yale | ECAC | 19 | 0 | 1 | 1 | 31 | .... | .... | .... | .... | .... |
| 2006-07 | Yale | ECAC | 27 | 3 | 2 | 5 | 37 | .... | .... | .... | .... | .... |
| 2007-08 | Yale | ECAC | 19 | 3 | 1 | 4 | 14 | .... | .... | .... | .... | .... |
| 2008-09 | Yale | ECAC | 33 | 6 | 2 | 8 | 24 | .... | .... | .... | .... | .... |

## BROWN, Chris — (BROWN, KRIHS) — PHX.

Center. Shoots right. 6'2", 191 lbs. Born, Houston, TX, February 3, 1991.
(Phoenix's 2nd choice, 36th overall, in 2009 Entry Draft).

| | | | Regular Season | | | | | Playoffs | | | | |
|---|---|---|---|---|---|---|---|---|---|---|---|---|
| Season | Club | League | GP | G | A | Pts | PIM | GP | G | A | Pts | PIM |
| 2007-08 | USNTDP | NAHL | 43 | 8 | 6 | 14 | 66 | 3 | 0 | 0 | 0 | 0 |
| | USNTDP | U-17 | 17 | 5 | 1 | 6 | 8 | .... | .... | .... | .... | .... |
| 2008-09 | USNTDP | NAHL | 15 | 6 | 2 | 8 | 37 | .... | .... | .... | .... | .... |
| | USNTDP | U-18 | 47 | 14 | 16 | 30 | 83 | .... | .... | .... | .... | .... |

• Signed Letter of Intent to attend **University of Michigan** (CCHA) in fall of 2009.

## BRUESS, Trevor — (BREW-ehs, TREH-vuhr) — WSH.

Right wing. Shoots right. 6', 209 lbs. Born, Minneapolis, MN, January 6, 1986.

| | | | Regular Season | | | | | Playoffs | | | | |
|---|---|---|---|---|---|---|---|---|---|---|---|---|
| Season | Club | League | GP | G | A | Pts | PIM | GP | G | A | Pts | PIM |
| 2004-05 | Fargo-Moorhead | NAHL | 51 | 11 | 17 | 28 | 72 | .... | .... | .... | .... | .... |
| 2005-06 | Lincoln Stars | USHL | 56 | 10 | 17 | 27 | 108 | 9 | 1 | 0 | 1 | 8 |
| 2006-07 | Minnesota State | WCHA | 37 | 3 | 11 | 14 | 102 | .... | .... | .... | .... | .... |
| 2007-08 | Minnesota State | WCHA | 38 | 9 | 21 | 30 | 54 | .... | .... | .... | .... | .... |
| 2008-09 | Minnesota State | WCHA | 35 | 12 | 5 | 17 | 117 | .... | .... | .... | .... | .... |

Signed as a free agent by **Washington**, March 20, 2009.

## BUBNICK, Jimmy — (BUHB-nihk, JIH-mee) — ATL.

Center. Shoots right. 6'2", 194 lbs. Born, Esterhazy, Sask., January 19, 1991.
(Atlanta's 7th choice, 155th overall, in 2009 Entry Draft).

| | | | Regular Season | | | | | Playoffs | | | | |
|---|---|---|---|---|---|---|---|---|---|---|---|---|
| Season | Club | League | GP | G | A | Pts | PIM | GP | G | A | Pts | PIM |
| 2006-07 | Sask. Contacts | SMHL | 41 | 33 | 37 | 70 | 32 | .... | .... | .... | .... | .... |
| | Kamloops Blazers | WHL | 2 | 0 | 1 | 1 | 0 | .... | .... | .... | .... | .... |
| 2007-08 | Kamloops Blazers | WHL | 64 | 9 | 18 | 27 | 24 | 4 | 0 | 0 | 0 | 4 |
| 2008-09 | Kamloops Blazers | WHL | 72 | 25 | 32 | 57 | 41 | 4 | 0 | 1 | 1 | 6 |

## BUCKLEY, Brendan — (BUHK-lee, BREHN-duhn)

Defense. Shoots right. 6'1", 205 lbs. Born, Boston, MA, February 26, 1977.
(Anaheim's 3rd choice, 117th overall, in 1996 Entry Draft).

| | | | Regular Season | | | | | Playoffs | | | | |
|---|---|---|---|---|---|---|---|---|---|---|---|---|
| Season | Club | League | GP | G | A | Pts | PIM | GP | G | A | Pts | PIM |
| 1994-95 | Boston Jr. Bruins | Exhib. | 48 | 22 | 43 | 65 | 164 | .... | .... | .... | .... | .... |
| 1995-96 | Boston College | H-East | 34 | 0 | 4 | 4 | 72 | .... | .... | .... | .... | .... |
| 1996-97 | Boston College | H-East | 38 | 2 | 6 | 8 | 90 | .... | .... | .... | .... | .... |
| 1997-98 | Boston College | H-East | 41 | 1 | 12 | 13 | 69 | .... | .... | .... | .... | .... |
| 1998-99 | Boston College | H-East | 43 | 1 | 13 | 14 | 75 | .... | .... | .... | .... | .... |
| 99-2000 | Cincinnati | AHL | 4 | 0 | 0 | 0 | 6 | .... | .... | .... | .... | .... |
| | Quad City | UHL | 61 | 1 | 10 | 11 | 73 | 9 | 1 | 0 | 1 | 10 |
| 2000-01 | Wilkes-Barre | AHL | 63 | 2 | 8 | 10 | 62 | 21 | 0 | 2 | 2 | 33 |
| 2001-02 | Wilkes-Barre | AHL | 80 | 1 | 19 | 20 | 116 | .... | .... | .... | .... | .... |
| 2002-03 | Wilkes-Barre | AHL | 80 | 2 | 6 | 8 | 99 | 6 | 0 | 0 | 0 | 2 |
| 2003-04 | Wilkes-Barre | AHL | 45 | 2 | 4 | 6 | 61 | .... | .... | .... | .... | .... |
| | Syracuse Crunch | AHL | 30 | 0 | 4 | 4 | 40 | 7 | 0 | 0 | 0 | 14 |
| 2004-05 | Worcester IceCats | AHL | 63 | 3 | 13 | 16 | 128 | .... | .... | .... | .... | .... |
| 2005-06 | Peoria Rivermen | AHL | 73 | 2 | 9 | 11 | 104 | 4 | 0 | 0 | 0 | 4 |
| 2006-07 | Manchester | AHL | 63 | 2 | 7 | 9 | 107 | 16 | 0 | 3 | 3 | 13 |
| 2007-08 | Iserlohn Roosters | Germany | 43 | 0 | 4 | 4 | 119 | 6 | 1 | 0 | 1 | 31 |
| 2008-09 | Worcester Sharks | AHL | 67 | 1 | 8 | 9 | 92 | 10 | 1 | 2 | 3 | 18 |

Signed as a free agent by **Pittsburgh**, September 28, 2000. Traded to **Columbus** by **Pittsburgh** for Pauli Levokari, February 10, 2004. Signed as a free agent by **Worcester** (AHL), October 25, 2004. Signed as a free agent by **Los Angeles**, July 10, 2006. Signed as a free agent by **San Jose**, July 15, 2008.

## BUDISH, Zach — (BOO-dihsh, ZAK) — NSH.

Right wing. Shoots right. 6'3", 223 lbs. Born, Edina, MN, May 9, 1991.
(Nashville's 2nd choice, 41st overall, in 2009 Entry Draft).

| | | | Regular Season | | | | | Playoffs | | | | |
|---|---|---|---|---|---|---|---|---|---|---|---|---|
| Season | Club | League | GP | G | A | Pts | PIM | GP | G | A | Pts | PIM |
| 2006-07 | Edina Hornets | High-MN | 31 | 22 | 25 | 47 | .... | .... | .... | .... | .... | .... |
| 2007-08 | Edina Hornets | High-MN | 30 | 26 | 37 | 63 | .... | .... | .... | .... | .... | .... |
| 2008-09 | Edina Hornets | High-MN | DID NOT PLAY – INJURED | | | | | | | | | |
| | Team Southwest | UMHSEL | 15 | 14 | 13 | 27 | 12 | .... | .... | .... | .... | .... |

• Missed entire 2008-09 High School season recovering from a knee injury suffered during football season. • Signed Letter of Intent to attend **University of Minnesota** (WCHA) in fall of 2009.

## BUMAGIN, Alexander — (buh-MAH-gihn, al-EHX-AN-duhr) — EDM.

Wing. Shoots left. 6', 180 lbs. Born, Togliatti, USSR, March 1, 1987.
(Edmonton's 5th choice, 170th overall, in 2006 Entry Draft).

| | | | Regular Season | | | | | Playoffs | | | | |
|---|---|---|---|---|---|---|---|---|---|---|---|---|
| Season | Club | League | GP | G | A | Pts | PIM | GP | G | A | Pts | PIM |
| 2002-03 | Lada Togliatti 2 | Russia-3 | 9 | 4 | 1 | 5 | 2 | .... | .... | .... | .... | .... |
| 2003-04 | Lada Togliatti 2 | Russia-3 | 22 | 4 | 9 | 13 | 12 | 4 | 0 | 1 | 1 | 4 |
| 2004-05 | Lada Togliatti | Russia | 7 | 2 | 0 | 2 | 2 | .... | .... | .... | .... | .... |
| | Lada Togliatti 2 | Russia-3 | STATISTICS NOT AVAILABLE | | | | | | | | | |
| | Lada Togliatti | Russia | 7 | 2 | 0 | 2 | 2 | .... | .... | .... | .... | .... |
| 2005-06 | Lada Togliatti | Russia | 40 | 9 | 12 | 21 | 28 | 8 | 0 | 3 | 3 | 4 |
| 2006-07 | Lada Togliatti | Russia | 41 | 2 | 3 | 5 | 18 | 3 | 0 | 0 | 0 | 0 |
| 2007-08 | Mytischi | Russia | 31 | 8 | 7 | 15 | 37 | 5 | 0 | 0 | 0 | 0 |
| 2008-09 | Mytischi | Rus-KHL | 40 | 4 | 7 | 11 | 20 | 6 | 2 | 1 | 3 | 0 |

## BURAVCHIKOV, Vyacheslav — (burh-AV-chih-kawf, V'YATCH-ih-slav) — BUF.

Defense. Shoots left. 6'1", 189 lbs. Born, Moscow, USSR, May 22, 1987.
(Buffalo's 7th choice, 191st overall, in 2005 Entry Draft).

| | | | Regular Season | | | | | Playoffs | | | | |
|---|---|---|---|---|---|---|---|---|---|---|---|---|
| Season | Club | League | GP | G | A | Pts | PIM | GP | G | A | Pts | PIM |
| 2003-04 | Krylja Sovetov 2 | Russia-3 | STATISTICS NOT AVAILABLE | | | | | | | | | |
| 2004-05 | Krylja Sovetov 2 | Russia-3 | 15 | 5 | 6 | 11 | 22 | .... | .... | .... | .... | .... |
| | Krylja Sovetov | Russia-2 | 26 | 4 | 1 | 5 | 14 | 3 | 0 | 0 | 0 | 2 |
| 2005-06 | Mytischi | Russia | 43 | 1 | 2 | 3 | 24 | 9 | 1 | 0 | 1 | 4 |
| 2006-07 | Ak Bars Kazan | Russia | 35 | 0 | 3 | 3 | 20 | .... | .... | .... | .... | .... |
| 2007-08 | Ak Bars Kazan | Russia | 46 | 1 | 0 | 1 | 12 | 10 | 1 | 0 | 1 | 4 |
| 2008-09 | Ak Bars Kazan | Rus-KHL | 44 | 4 | 6 | 10 | 14 | 18 | 0 | 1 | 1 | 16 |

## BURKE, Greg — (BUHRK, GREHG) — WSH.

Left wing. Shoots left. 6'3", 205 lbs. Born, Portsmouth, NH, May 16, 1990.
(Washington's 7th choice, 174th overall, in 2008 Entry Draft).

| | | | Regular Season | | | | | Playoffs | | | | |
|---|---|---|---|---|---|---|---|---|---|---|---|---|
| Season | Club | League | GP | G | A | Pts | PIM | GP | G | A | Pts | PIM |
| 2006-07 | N.H. Jr. Monarchs | EJHL | 34 | 6 | 12 | 18 | 22 | .... | .... | .... | .... | .... |
| 2007-08 | N.H. Jr. Monarchs | EJHL | 40 | 21 | 25 | 46 | 46 | 6 | 5 | 4 | 9 | 6 |
| 2008-09 | Cedar Rapids | USHL | 8 | 2 | 0 | 2 | 8 | .... | .... | .... | .... | .... |

• Missed majority of 2008-09 season recovering from shoulder injury. • Signed Letter of Intent to attend **University of New Hampshire** (Hockey East) in fall of 2009.

## BURKI, Codey — (BUHR-kee, KOH-dee) — COL.

Center. Shoots left. 6', 190 lbs. Born, Winnipeg, Man., November 17, 1987.
(Colorado's 3rd choice, 59th overall, in 2006 Entry Draft).

| | | | Regular Season | | | | | Playoffs | | | | |
|---|---|---|---|---|---|---|---|---|---|---|---|---|
| Season | Club | League | GP | G | A | Pts | PIM | GP | G | A | Pts | PIM |
| 2004-05 | Brandon | WHL | 68 | 10 | 13 | 23 | 48 | 24 | 6 | 5 | 11 | 13 |
| 2005-06 | Brandon | WHL | 70 | 27 | 34 | 61 | 69 | 6 | 0 | 3 | 3 | 2 |
| 2006-07 | Brandon | WHL | 70 | 36 | 49 | 85 | 83 | 11 | 6 | 5 | 11 | 4 |
| 2007-08 | Lake Erie Monsters | AHL | 40 | 2 | 7 | 9 | 22 | .... | .... | .... | .... | .... |
| | Johnstown Chiefs | ECHL | 12 | 3 | 4 | 7 | 14 | 4 | 0 | 0 | 0 | 4 |
| 2008-09 | Lake Erie Monsters | AHL | 54 | 9 | 10 | 19 | 32 | .... | .... | .... | .... | .... |
| | Johnstown Chiefs | ECHL | 14 | 1 | 4 | 5 | 14 | .... | .... | .... | .... | .... |

## BURLON, Brandon — (BUHR-lohn, BRAN-duhn) — N.J.

Defense. Shoots left. 6', 190 lbs. Born, Nobleton, Ont., March 5, 1990.
(New Jersey's 2nd choice, 52nd overall, in 2008 Entry Draft).

| | | | Regular Season | | | | | Playoffs | | | | |
|---|---|---|---|---|---|---|---|---|---|---|---|---|
| Season | Club | League | GP | G | A | Pts | PIM | GP | G | A | Pts | PIM |
| 2005-06 | Vaughan Kings | GTHL | 55 | 19 | 29 | 48 | 38 | .... | .... | .... | .... | .... |
| 2006-07 | St. Michael's | OPJHL | 45 | 4 | 19 | 23 | 46 | 4 | 0 | 1 | 1 | 4 |
| 2007-08 | St. Michael's | OPJHL | 32 | 7 | 17 | 24 | 41 | 10 | 2 | 4 | 6 | 8 |
| 2008-09 | U. of Michigan | CCHA | 33 | 5 | 10 | 15 | 14 | .... | .... | .... | .... | .... |

CCHA All-Rookie Team (2009)

**BUSTO, Michael** (BUHS-toh, MIGH-kuhl) **MTL.**

Defense. Shoots right. 6'2", 231 lbs. Born, Burnaby, B.C., June 20, 1986.

| | | | Regular Season | | | | | Playoffs | | | | |
|---|---|---|---|---|---|---|---|---|---|---|---|---|
| Season | Club | League | GP | G | A | Pts | PIM | GP | G | A | Pts | PIM |
| 2001-02 | Moose Jaw | WHL | 3 | 0 | 0 | 0 | 2 | .... | .... | .... | .... | .... |
| 2002-03 | Moose Jaw | WHL | 50 | 1 | 7 | 8 | 54 | 7 | 1 | 0 | 1 | 0 |
| 2003-04 | Moose Jaw | WHL | 42 | 4 | 13 | 17 | 51 | .... | .... | .... | .... | .... |
| | Swift Current | WHL | 26 | 0 | 0 | 0 | 29 | 5 | 0 | 0 | 0 | 2 |
| 2004-05 | Kootenay Ice | WHL | 71 | 8 | 21 | 29 | 79 | 16 | 1 | 5 | 6 | 27 |
| 2005-06 | Kootenay Ice | WHL | 69 | 8 | 35 | 43 | 77 | 4 | 0 | 4 | 4 | 4 |
| 2006-07 | Kootenay Ice | WHL | 70 | 20 | 43 | 63 | 79 | 6 | 1 | 2 | 3 | 9 |
| 2007-08 | Charlotte | ECHL | 48 | 4 | 12 | 16 | 10 | .... | .... | .... | .... | .... |
| 2008-09 | Charlotte | ECHL | 54 | 3 | 8 | 11 | 41 | .... | .... | .... | .... | .... |

WHL East First All-Star Team (2007)

Signed as a free agent by **NY Rangers**, April 27, 2007. Traded to **Montreal** by **NY Rangers** with Scott Gomez and Tom Pyatt for Chris Higgins, Ryan McDonagh and Pavel Valentenko, June 30, 2009.

**BUT, Anton** (BOOT, AN-tawn) **T.B.**

Left wing. Shoots left. 6'1", 189 lbs. Born, Kharkov, USSR, July 3, 1980.
(New Jersey's 7th choice, 119th overall, in 1998 Entry Draft).

| | | | Regular Season | | | | | Playoffs | | | | |
|---|---|---|---|---|---|---|---|---|---|---|---|---|
| Season | Club | League | GP | G | A | Pts | PIM | GP | G | A | Pts | PIM |
| 1995-96 | Yaroslavl 2 | CIS-2 | 60 | 30 | 12 | 42 | 10 | .... | .... | .... | .... | .... |
| 1996-97 | Yaroslavl 2 | Russia-3 | 70 | 30 | 20 | 50 | 20 | .... | .... | .... | .... | .... |
| 1997-98 | Yaroslavl 2 | Russia-2 | 48 | 12 | 5 | 17 | 28 | .... | .... | .... | .... | .... |
| 1998-99 | Yaroslavl 2 | Russia-3 | 22 | 12 | 8 | 20 | 59 | .... | .... | .... | .... | .... |
| | Torpedo Yaroslavl | Russia | 5 | 0 | 0 | 0 | 0 | .... | .... | .... | .... | .... |
| 99-2000 | Yaroslavl 2 | Russia-3 | 1 | 0 | 0 | 0 | 2 | .... | .... | .... | .... | .... |
| | Torpedo Yaroslavl | Russia | 26 | 2 | 5 | 7 | 16 | 8 | 2 | 1 | 3 | 0 |
| 2000-01 | Yaroslavl | Russia | 42 | 14 | 6 | 20 | 14 | 11 | 1 | 3 | 4 | 8 |
| 2001-02 | Yaroslavl | Russia | 48 | 14 | 11 | 25 | 14 | 6 | 0 | 1 | 1 | 2 |
| 2002-03 | Yaroslavl | Russia | 44 | 16 | 13 | 29 | 16 | 9 | 1 | 2 | 3 | 6 |
| 2003-04 | Yaroslavl | Russia | 51 | 11 | 10 | 21 | 24 | 3 | 0 | 0 | 0 | 0 |
| 2004-05 | Yaroslavl | Russia | 60 | 12 | 22 | 34 | 58 | 8 | 3 | 3 | 6 | 0 |
| 2005-06 | Yaroslavl | Russia | 49 | 16 | 21 | 37 | 26 | 11 | 2 | 1 | 3 | 2 |
| 2006-07 | SKA St. Petersburg | Russia | 52 | 13 | 13 | 26 | 61 | 2 | 0 | 1 | 1 | 2 |
| 2007-08 | SKA St. Petersburg | Russia | 57 | 15 | 13 | 28 | 40 | 9 | 4 | 1 | 5 | 6 |
| 2008-09 | CSKA Moscow | Rus-KHL | 55 | 12 | 21 | 33 | 36 | 8 | 2 | 1 | 3 | 2 |

Rights traded to **Tampa Bay** by **New Jersey** with Josef Boumedienne and Sascha Goc for Andrei Zyuzin, November 9, 2001.

**BUTCHER, Matt** (BUH-chuhr, MAT) **VAN.**

Center. Shoots left. 6'1", 188 lbs. Born, Bellingham, WA, January 1, 1987.
(Vancouver's 4th choice, 138th overall, in 2005 Entry Draft).

| | | | Regular Season | | | | | Playoffs | | | | |
|---|---|---|---|---|---|---|---|---|---|---|---|---|
| Season | Club | League | GP | G | A | Pts | PIM | GP | G | A | Pts | PIM |
| 2003-04 | Chilliwack Chiefs | BCHL | 48 | 7 | 18 | 25 | 73 | 11 | 3 | 1 | 4 | 14 |
| 2004-05 | Chilliwack Chiefs | BCHL | 59 | 27 | 28 | 55 | 94 | .... | .... | .... | .... | .... |
| 2005-06 | Chilliwack Chiefs | BCHL | 57 | 38 | 63 | 101 | 109 | 10 | 12 | 11 | 23 | 12 |
| 2006-07 | Northern Mich. | CCHA | 40 | 0 | 4 | 4 | 28 | .... | .... | .... | .... | .... |
| 2007-08 | Northern Mich. | CCHA | 44 | 8 | 15 | 23 | 45 | .... | .... | .... | .... | .... |
| 2008-09 | Northern Mich. | CCHA | 14 | 2 | 3 | 5 | 16 | .... | .... | .... | .... | .... |

**BUTTON, Ryan** (BUH-tuhn, RIGH-uhn) **BOS.**

Defense. Shoots left. 6'2", 185 lbs. Born, Edmonton, Alta., March 26, 1991.
(Boston's 2nd choice, 86th overall, in 2009 Entry Draft).

| | | | Regular Season | | | | | Playoffs | | | | |
|---|---|---|---|---|---|---|---|---|---|---|---|---|
| Season | Club | League | GP | G | A | Pts | PIM | GP | G | A | Pts | PIM |
| 2006-07 | Edmonton CAC | AMHL | 28 | 2 | 6 | 8 | 74 | .... | .... | .... | .... | .... |
| 2007-08 | Prince Albert | WHL | 58 | 0 | 8 | 8 | 30 | .... | .... | .... | .... | .... |
| 2008-09 | Prince Albert | WHL | 70 | 5 | 32 | 37 | 43 | .... | .... | .... | .... | .... |

**BYRON, Paul** (BIGH-ruhn, PAWL) **BUF.**

Center. Shoots left. 5'8", 135 lbs. Born, Ottawa, Ont., April 27, 1989.
(Buffalo's 6th choice, 179th overall, in 2007 Entry Draft).

| | | | Regular Season | | | | | Playoffs | | | | |
|---|---|---|---|---|---|---|---|---|---|---|---|---|
| Season | Club | League | GP | G | A | Pts | PIM | GP | G | A | Pts | PIM |
| 2005-06 | Ottawa West | OJHL-B | 33 | 20 | 23 | 43 | 33 | 7 | 3 | 8 | 11 | 4 |
| 2006-07 | Gatineau | QMJHL | 68 | 21 | 23 | 44 | 46 | 5 | 5 | 1 | 6 | 2 |
| 2007-08 | Gatineau | QMJHL | 52 | 37 | 31 | 68 | 25 | 19 | *21 | 11 | 32 | 12 |
| 2008-09 | Gatineau | QMJHL | 64 | 33 | 66 | 99 | 32 | 10 | 2 | 14 | 16 | 4 |

QMJHL Second All-Star Team (2009)

**CALLA, Brady** (KAL-luh, BRAY-dee) **FLA.**

Right wing. Shoots right. 6', 190 lbs. Born, North Vancouver, B.C., March 14, 1988.
(Florida's 2nd choice, 73rd overall, in 2006 Entry Draft).

| | | | Regular Season | | | | | Playoffs | | | | |
|---|---|---|---|---|---|---|---|---|---|---|---|---|
| Season | Club | League | GP | G | A | Pts | PIM | GP | G | A | Pts | PIM |
| 2004-05 | Everett Silvertips | WHL | 68 | 11 | 10 | 21 | 38 | 11 | 1 | 1 | 2 | 0 |
| 2005-06 | Everett Silvertips | WHL | 66 | 8 | 25 | 33 | 52 | 11 | 1 | 2 | 3 | 4 |
| 2006-07 | Everett Silvertips | WHL | 29 | 3 | 6 | 9 | 23 | .... | .... | .... | .... | .... |
| | Moose Jaw | WHL | 39 | 12 | 20 | 32 | 19 | .... | .... | .... | .... | .... |
| 2007-08 | Moose Jaw | WHL | 14 | 2 | 8 | 10 | 10 | .... | .... | .... | .... | .... |
| | Kamloops Blazers | WHL | 52 | 10 | 20 | 30 | 52 | 4 | 0 | 2 | 2 | 4 |
| | Rochester | AHL | 6 | 2 | 2 | 4 | 2 | .... | .... | .... | .... | .... |
| 2008-09 | Kamloops Blazers | WHL | 19 | 5 | 8 | 13 | 31 | .... | .... | .... | .... | .... |
| | Spokane Chiefs | WHL | 31 | 11 | 14 | 25 | 27 | 12 | 1 | 3 | 4 | 6 |
| | Rochester | AHL | 8 | 0 | 1 | 1 | 9 | .... | .... | .... | .... | .... |

**CALLAHAN, Mitchell** (kal-AH-han, MIH-chuhl) **DET.**

Right wing. Shoots right. 5'11", 175 lbs. Born, Whittier, CA, August 17, 1991.
(Detroit's 6th choice, 180th overall, in 2009 Entry Draft).

| | | | Regular Season | | | | | Playoffs | | | | |
|---|---|---|---|---|---|---|---|---|---|---|---|---|
| Season | Club | League | GP | G | A | Pts | PIM | GP | G | A | Pts | PIM |
| 2007-08 | L.A. Jr. Kings | Minor-CA | 52 | 32 | 37 | 69 | 62 | .... | .... | .... | .... | .... |
| 2008-09 | Kelowna Rockets | WHL | 70 | 14 | 13 | 27 | 188 | 22 | 1 | 3 | 4 | 43 |

**CALVERT, Matthew** (KAL-vuhrt, MA-thew) **CBJ**

Left wing. Shoots left. 5'9", 175 lbs. Born, Brandon, Man., December 24, 1989.
(Columbus' 5th choice, 127th overall, in 2008 Entry Draft).

| | | | Regular Season | | | | | Playoffs | | | | |
|---|---|---|---|---|---|---|---|---|---|---|---|---|
| Season | Club | League | GP | G | A | Pts | PIM | GP | G | A | Pts | PIM |
| 2005-06 | Brandon | MMHL | 38 | 24 | 30 | 54 | 48 | 6 | 3 | 6 | 9 | 18 |
| 2006-07 | Brandon | MMHL | 30 | 28 | 55 | 83 | 46 | 16 | 5 | 13 | 18 | 16 |
| | Winkler Flyers | MJHL | 1 | 0 | 0 | 0 | 15 | .... | .... | .... | .... | .... |
| 2007-08 | Brandon | WHL | 72 | 24 | 40 | 64 | 53 | 6 | 1 | 2 | 3 | 2 |
| 2008-09 | Brandon | WHL | 58 | 28 | 39 | 67 | 58 | 12 | 9 | 8 | 17 | 22 |

**CAMERON, Bryan** (KAM-ih-RUHN, BRIGH-uhn)

Center. Shoots right. 5'10", 180 lbs. Born, Brampton, Ont., February 25, 1989.
(Los Angeles' 4th choice, 82nd overall, in 2007 Entry Draft).

| | | | Regular Season | | | | | Playoffs | | | | |
|---|---|---|---|---|---|---|---|---|---|---|---|---|
| Season | Club | League | GP | G | A | Pts | PIM | GP | G | A | Pts | PIM |
| 2004-05 | Toronto Marlboros | GTHL | 75 | 73 | 47 | 120 | 76 | .... | .... | .... | .... | .... |
| 2005-06 | Belleville Bulls | OHL | 64 | 20 | 9 | 29 | 46 | 6 | 1 | 2 | 3 | 6 |
| 2006-07 | Belleville Bulls | OHL | 60 | 33 | 25 | 58 | 50 | 15 | 4 | 8 | 12 | 15 |
| 2007-08 | Belleville Bulls | OHL | 68 | 41 | 37 | 78 | 56 | 21 | 4 | 9 | 13 | 10 |
| 2008-09 | Belleville Bulls | OHL | 64 | 37 | 44 | 81 | 51 | 17 | 7 | 7 | 14 | 18 |

OHL First All-Star Team (2009)

**CAMERON, Randy** (KAM-ih-RUHN, RAN-dee)

Center. Shoots right. 5'11", 175 lbs. Born, Cornwall, P.E.I., January 28, 1989.
(Detroit's 3rd choice, 148th overall, in 2007 Entry Draft).

| | | | Regular Season | | | | | Playoffs | | | | |
|---|---|---|---|---|---|---|---|---|---|---|---|---|
| Season | Club | League | GP | G | A | Pts | PIM | GP | G | A | Pts | PIM |
| 2005-06 | Summerside | MJrHL | 52 | 21 | 50 | 71 | 16 | 11 | 2 | 6 | 8 | 6 |
| 2006-07 | Moncton Wildcats | QMJHL | 70 | 17 | 22 | 39 | 44 | 7 | 1 | 1 | 2 | 0 |
| 2007-08 | Moncton Wildcats | QMJHL | 62 | 12 | 27 | 39 | 30 | .... | .... | .... | .... | .... |
| 2008-09 | Moncton Wildcats | QMJHL | 56 | 19 | 32 | 51 | 24 | 10 | 3 | 5 | 8 | 14 |

**CAMPBELL, Andrew** (KAM-buhl, AN-droo) **L.A.**

Defense. Shoots left. 6'4", 196 lbs. Born, Caledonia, Ont., February 4, 1988.
(Los Angeles' 5th choice, 74th overall, in 2008 Entry Draft).

| | | | Regular Season | | | | | Playoffs | | | | |
|---|---|---|---|---|---|---|---|---|---|---|---|---|
| Season | Club | League | GP | G | A | Pts | PIM | GP | G | A | Pts | PIM |
| 2005-06 | Sault Ste. Marie | OHL | 31 | 1 | 3 | 4 | 23 | 3 | 0 | 0 | 0 | 4 |
| 2006-07 | Sault Ste. Marie | OHL | 63 | 4 | 14 | 18 | 75 | 13 | 0 | 1 | 1 | 6 |
| 2007-08 | Sault Ste. Marie | OHL | 68 | 13 | 22 | 35 | 64 | 14 | 2 | 3 | 5 | 13 |
| 2008-09 | Manchester | AHL | 72 | 3 | 5 | 8 | 72 | .... | .... | .... | .... | .... |

**CAMPBELL, Max** (KAM-behl, MAX) **NYR**

Center. Shoots left. 6', 178 lbs. Born, Strathroy, Ont., December 21, 1988.
(NY Rangers' 3rd choice, 138th overall, in 2007 Entry Draft).

| | | | Regular Season | | | | | Playoffs | | | | |
|---|---|---|---|---|---|---|---|---|---|---|---|---|
| Season | Club | League | GP | G | A | Pts | PIM | GP | G | A | Pts | PIM |
| 2005-06 | Strathroy Rockets | OJHL-B | 48 | 17 | 18 | 35 | 10 | .... | .... | .... | .... | .... |
| 2006-07 | Strathroy Rockets | OJHL-B | 46 | 46 | 49 | 95 | 84 | .... | .... | .... | .... | .... |
| 2007-08 | Western Mich. | CCHA | 38 | 6 | 16 | 22 | 10 | .... | .... | .... | .... | .... |
| 2008-09 | Western Mich. | CCHA | 40 | 16 | 15 | 31 | 44 | .... | .... | .... | .... | .... |

**CAPORUSSO, Louie** (kap-oh-ROO-soh, LOO-ee) **OTT.**

Center/Left wing. Shoots left. 5'10", 186 lbs. Born, Toronto, Ont., June 21, 1989.
(Ottawa's 3rd choice, 90th overall, in 2007 Entry Draft).

| | | | Regular Season | | | | | Playoffs | | | | |
|---|---|---|---|---|---|---|---|---|---|---|---|---|
| Season | Club | League | GP | G | A | Pts | PIM | GP | G | A | Pts | PIM |
| 2004-05 | Tor. Red Wings | GTHL | 53 | 38 | 28 | 66 | 28 | .... | .... | .... | .... | .... |
| 2005-06 | St. Michael's | OPJHL | 48 | 29 | 44 | 73 | 44 | 25 | 8 | 10 | 18 | 16 |
| 2006-07 | St. Michael's | OPJHL | 37 | 23 | 27 | 50 | 45 | 20 | 14 | 19 | 33 | 14 |
| 2007-08 | U. of Michigan | CCHA | 33 | 12 | 9 | 21 | 18 | .... | .... | .... | .... | .... |
| 2008-09 | U. of Michigan | CCHA | 41 | *24 | 25 | 49 | 30 | .... | .... | .... | .... | .... |

CCHA First All-Star Team (2009) • NCAA West First All-American Team (2009)

**CAREY, Paul** (KAIR-ee, PAWL) **COL.**

Center. Shoots left. 6', 175 lbs. Born, Boston, MA, September 24, 1988.
(Colorado's 7th choice, 135th overall, in 2007 Entry Draft).

| | | | Regular Season | | | | | Playoffs | | | | |
|---|---|---|---|---|---|---|---|---|---|---|---|---|
| Season | Club | League | GP | G | A | Pts | PIM | GP | G | A | Pts | PIM |
| 2005-06 | Salisbury School | High-CT | 27 | 14 | 11 | 25 | 18 | .... | .... | .... | .... | .... |
| 2006-07 | Salisbury School | High-CT | 24 | 16 | 11 | 27 | 16 | .... | .... | .... | .... | .... |
| 2007-08 | Indiana Ice | USHL | 60 | 34 | 32 | 66 | 32 | 4 | 1 | 2 | 3 | 2 |
| 2008-09 | Boston College | H-East | 24 | 5 | 4 | 9 | 8 | .... | .... | .... | .... | .... |

USHL All-Rookie Team (2008) • USHL Second All-Star Team (2008)

**CARLE, Mathieu** (KAHRL, MA-tyew) **MTL.**

Defense. Shoots right. 6', 204 lbs. Born, Gatineau, Que., September 30, 1987.
(Montreal's 3rd choice, 53rd overall, in 2006 Entry Draft).

| | | | Regular Season | | | | | Playoffs | | | | |
|---|---|---|---|---|---|---|---|---|---|---|---|---|
| Season | Club | League | GP | G | A | Pts | PIM | GP | G | A | Pts | PIM |
| 2004-05 | Acadie-Bathurst | QMJHL | 69 | 4 | 29 | 33 | 53 | .... | .... | .... | .... | .... |
| 2005-06 | Acadie-Bathurst | QMJHL | 67 | 18 | 51 | 69 | 122 | 17 | 1 | 14 | 15 | 29 |
| 2006-07 | Acadie-Bathurst | QMJHL | 38 | 12 | 39 | 51 | 52 | .... | .... | .... | .... | .... |
| | Rouyn-Noranda | QMJHL | 25 | 4 | 15 | 19 | 27 | 16 | 6 | 10 | 16 | 16 |
| 2007-08 | Hamilton Bulldogs | AHL | 64 | 7 | 17 | 24 | 43 | .... | .... | .... | .... | .... |
| 2008-09 | Hamilton Bulldogs | AHL | 59 | 7 | 22 | 29 | 43 | 6 | 0 | 2 | 2 | 4 |

QMJHL All-Rookie Team (2004)

**CARLSON, John** (KAHRL-suhn, JAWN) **WSH.**

Defense. Shoots right. 6'3", 211 lbs. Born, Natick, MA, January 10, 1990.
(Washington's 2nd choice, 27th overall, in 2008 Entry Draft).

| | | | Regular Season | | | | | Playoffs | | | | |
|---|---|---|---|---|---|---|---|---|---|---|---|---|
| Season | Club | League | GP | G | A | Pts | PIM | GP | G | A | Pts | PIM |
| 2005-06 | N.J. Rockets | AtJHL | 38 | 2 | 10 | 12 | 42 | .... | .... | .... | .... | .... |
| 2006-07 | N.J. Rockets | AtJHL | 44 | 12 | 38 | 50 | 96 | .... | .... | .... | .... | .... |
| | Indiana Ice | USHL | 2 | 0 | 0 | 0 | 6 | .... | .... | .... | .... | .... |
| 2007-08 | Indiana Ice | USHL | 59 | 12 | 31 | 43 | 72 | 4 | 1 | 0 | 1 | 0 |
| 2008-09 | London Knights | OHL | 59 | 16 | 60 | 76 | 65 | 14 | 7 | 15 | 22 | 16 |
| | Hershey Bears | AHL | .... | .... | .... | .... | .... | 16 | 2 | 1 | 3 | 0 |

OHL Second All-Star Team (2009) • USHL All-Rookie Team (2008) • USHL Second All-Star Team (2008)

## CARLSSON, Jonathan (KAHRL-suhn, JAWN-ah-thuhn) CHI.

Defense. Shoots right. 6'1", 198 lbs. Born, Uppsala, Sweden, August 5, 1988.
(Chicago's 4th choice, 162nd overall, in 2008 Entry Draft).

| | | | Regular Season | | | | | Playoffs | | | | |
|---|---|---|---|---|---|---|---|---|---|---|---|---|
| Season | Club | League | GP | G | A | Pts | PIM | GP | G | A | Pts | PIM |
| 2004-05 | Brynas IF Gavle Jr. | Swe-Jr. | 19 | 1 | 0 | 1 | 6 | .... | .... | .... | .... | .... |
| 2005-06 | Brynas U18 | Swe-U18 | 1 | 0 | 0 | 0 | 0 | .... | .... | .... | .... | .... |
| | Brynas IF Gavle Jr. | Swe-Jr. | 37 | 2 | 9 | 11 | 24 | 2 | 0 | 1 | 1 | 0 |
| 2006-07 | Brynas IF Gavle Jr. | Swe-Jr. | 39 | 12 | 5 | 17 | 16 | 4 | 2 | 1 | 3 | 6 |
| | Brynas IF Gavle | Sweden | 6 | 1 | 0 | 1 | 2 | .... | .... | .... | .... | .... |
| 2007-08 | Brynas IF Gavle Jr. | Swe-Jr. | 8 | 3 | 2 | 5 | 6 | 4 | 2 | 0 | 2 | 0 |
| | IF Bjorkloven Umea | Sweden-2 | 16 | 2 | 3 | 5 | 6 | .... | .... | .... | .... | .... |
| | Brynas IF Gavle | Sweden | 26 | 0 | 0 | 0 | 27 | .... | .... | .... | .... | .... |
| | Brynas IF Gavle | Sweden-Q | 9 | 0 | 0 | 0 | 2 | .... | .... | .... | .... | .... |
| 2008-09 | Brynas IF Gavle | Sweden | 55 | 0 | 1 | 1 | 78 | 4 | 0 | 0 | 0 | 4 |

## CARMAN, Michael (KAR-mahn, MIGH-kuhl) COL.

Center. Shoots left. 6', 180 lbs. Born, Augusta, GA, April 14, 1988.
(Colorado's 4th choice, 81st overall, in 2006 Entry Draft).

| | | | Regular Season | | | | | Playoffs | | | | |
|---|---|---|---|---|---|---|---|---|---|---|---|---|
| Season | Club | League | GP | G | A | Pts | PIM | GP | G | A | Pts | PIM |
| 2003-04 | Holy Angels | High-MN | 29 | 19 | 40 | 59 | .... | .... | .... | .... | .... | .... |
| 2004-05 | USNTDP | U-17 | 14 | 2 | 9 | 11 | 40 | .... | .... | .... | .... | .... |
| | USNTDP | NAHL | 39 | 12 | 15 | 27 | 38 | 10 | 2 | 4 | 6 | 10 |
| 2005-06 | USNTDP | U-18 | 43 | 15 | 23 | 38 | 78 | .... | .... | .... | .... | .... |
| | USNTDP | NAHL | 17 | 6 | 10 | 16 | 24 | .... | .... | .... | .... | .... |
| 2006-07 | U. of Minnesota | WCHA | 41 | 9 | 11 | 20 | 55 | .... | .... | .... | .... | .... |
| 2007-08 | U. of Minnesota | WCHA | 23 | 4 | 7 | 11 | 28 | .... | .... | .... | .... | .... |
| 2008-09 | U. of Minnesota | WCHA | 32 | 8 | 9 | 17 | 32 | .... | .... | .... | .... | .... |

## CARON, Jordan (kuh-RAWN, JOHR-dihn) BOS.

Right wing. Shoots left. 6'3", 202 lbs. Born, Sayabec, Que., November 2, 1990.
(Boston's 1st choice, 25th overall, in 2009 Entry Draft).

| | | | Regular Season | | | | | Playoffs | | | | |
|---|---|---|---|---|---|---|---|---|---|---|---|---|
| Season | Club | League | GP | G | A | Pts | PIM | GP | G | A | Pts | PIM |
| 2005-06 | Notre Dame | SMHL | 35 | 8 | 16 | 24 | 32 | .... | .... | .... | .... | .... |
| 2006-07 | Rimouski Oceanic | QMJHL | 59 | 18 | 22 | 40 | 41 | .... | .... | .... | .... | .... |
| 2007-08 | Rimouski Oceanic | QMJHL | 46 | 20 | 23 | 43 | 42 | 9 | 3 | 1 | 4 | 18 |
| 2008-09 | Rimouski Oceanic | QMJHL | 56 | 36 | 31 | 67 | 66 | 13 | 6 | 5 | 11 | 16 |

## CARPENTIER, Hugo (kar-PUHNT-yay, HEW-goh) CGY.

Center. Shoots left. 6'2", 200 lbs. Born, Hull, Que., March 17, 1988.
(Calgary's 4th choice, 118th overall, in 2006 Entry Draft).

| | | | Regular Season | | | | | Playoffs | | | | |
|---|---|---|---|---|---|---|---|---|---|---|---|---|
| Season | Club | League | GP | G | A | Pts | PIM | GP | G | A | Pts | PIM |
| 2004-05 | Rouyn-Noranda | QMJHL | 49 | 6 | 9 | 15 | 32 | 5 | 0 | 1 | 1 | 6 |
| 2005-06 | Rouyn-Noranda | QMJHL | 70 | 31 | 39 | 70 | 64 | 5 | 1 | 2 | 3 | 4 |
| 2006-07 | Rouyn-Noranda | QMJHL | 69 | 17 | 37 | 54 | 86 | 16 | 0 | 6 | 6 | 24 |
| 2007-08 | Rouyn-Noranda | QMJHL | 69 | 27 | 38 | 65 | 114 | 17 | 14 | 8 | 22 | 20 |
| 2008-09 | Quad City Flames | AHL | 17 | 2 | 2 | 4 | 8 | .... | .... | .... | .... | .... |
| | Las Vegas | ECHL | 45 | 9 | 15 | 24 | 33 | 8 | 0 | 3 | 3 | 0 |

## CARUANA, Matt (CAHR-wah-na, MAT)

Forward. Shoots left. 6', 185 lbs. Born, Oshawa, Ont., June 7, 1985.

| | | | Regular Season | | | | | Playoffs | | | | |
|---|---|---|---|---|---|---|---|---|---|---|---|---|
| Season | Club | League | GP | G | A | Pts | PIM | GP | G | A | Pts | PIM |
| 2004-05 | Niagara University | CHA | 36 | 8 | 8 | 16 | 32 | .... | .... | .... | .... | .... |
| 2005-06 | Niagara University | CHA | 36 | 12 | 24 | 36 | 20 | .... | .... | .... | .... | .... |
| 2006-07 | Niagara University | CHA | 37 | 14 | 24 | 38 | 26 | .... | .... | .... | .... | .... |
| 2007-08 | Niagara University | CHA | 37 | 17 | 22 | 39 | 30 | .... | .... | .... | .... | .... |
| | Portland Pirates | AHL | 5 | 0 | 1 | 1 | 2 | 13 | 0 | 0 | 0 | 2 |
| 2008-09 | Iowa Chops | AHL | 41 | 5 | 6 | 11 | 8 | .... | .... | .... | .... | .... |
| | Bakersfield | ECHL | 18 | 10 | 4 | 14 | 12 | .... | .... | .... | .... | .... |

CHA Second All-Star Team (2008)

Signed as a free agent by **Anaheim**, April 4, 2008.

## CARUSO, Michael (kah-ROO-soh, MIGH-kuhl) FLA.

Defense. Shoots left. 6'2", 191 lbs. Born, Mississauga, Ont., July 5, 1988.
(Florida's 3rd choice, 103rd overall, in 2006 Entry Draft).

| | | | Regular Season | | | | | Playoffs | | | | |
|---|---|---|---|---|---|---|---|---|---|---|---|---|
| Season | Club | League | GP | G | A | Pts | PIM | GP | G | A | Pts | PIM |
| 2004-05 | Guelph Storm | OHL | 56 | 0 | 3 | 3 | 31 | 4 | 0 | 0 | 0 | 2 |
| 2005-06 | Guelph Storm | OHL | 66 | 1 | 15 | 16 | 85 | 15 | 1 | 2 | 3 | 24 |
| 2006-07 | Guelph Storm | OHL | 64 | 4 | 16 | 20 | 119 | 4 | 0 | 0 | 0 | 8 |
| 2007-08 | Guelph Storm | OHL | 62 | 10 | 24 | 34 | 103 | 10 | 2 | 6 | 8 | 22 |
| 2008-09 | Rochester | AHL | 73 | 1 | 9 | 10 | 66 | .... | .... | .... | .... | .... |

## CASAVANT, Benjamin (ka-SA-vant, BEHN-jah-mihn) WSH.

Left wing. Shoots left. 6'1", 200 lbs. Born, St-Hyacinthe, Que., January 21, 1991.
(Washington's 7th choice, 205th overall, in 2009 Entry Draft).

| | | | Regular Season | | | | | Playoffs | | | | |
|---|---|---|---|---|---|---|---|---|---|---|---|---|
| Season | Club | League | GP | G | A | Pts | PIM | GP | G | A | Pts | PIM |
| 2006-07 | C.A.-Girouord | QAAA | 44 | 21 | 26 | 47 | 38 | 4 | 1 | 3 | 4 | 2 |
| 2007-08 | Rouyn-Noranda | QMJHL | 2 | 0 | 0 | 0 | 0 | .... | .... | .... | .... | .... |
| | PEI Rocket | QMJHL | 30 | 7 | 7 | 14 | 11 | 4 | 1 | 1 | 2 | 0 |
| 2008-09 | PEI Rocket | QMJHL | 68 | 39 | 41 | 80 | 49 | 5 | 2 | 0 | 2 | 0 |

## CAYER, Julien (KAY-uhr, JOO-lee-ehn) DET.

Center. Shoots left. 6'4", 186 lbs. Born, Longueuil, Que., July 6, 1989.
(Detroit's 4th choice, 151st overall, in 2008 Entry Draft).

| | | | Regular Season | | | | | Playoffs | | | | |
|---|---|---|---|---|---|---|---|---|---|---|---|---|
| Season | Club | League | GP | G | A | Pts | PIM | GP | G | A | Pts | PIM |
| 2005-06 | C.C. Lemoyne | QAAA | 42 | 11 | 21 | 32 | 46 | 8 | 1 | 2 | 3 | 14 |
| 2006-07 | St-Jerome | QJHL | 45 | 6 | 23 | 29 | 84 | 10 | 1 | 3 | 4 | 2 |
| 2007-08 | Northwood | High-NY | 42 | 24 | 32 | 56 | 56 | .... | .... | .... | .... | .... |
| 2008-09 | Clarkson Knights | ECAC | 29 | 4 | 6 | 10 | 30 | .... | .... | .... | .... | .... |

## CHAMPAGNE, Joel (sham-PAYN, JOHL) TOR.

Center. Shoots left. 6'4", 210 lbs. Born, Chateauguay, Que., January 24, 1990.
(Toronto's 5th choice, 129th overall, in 2008 Entry Draft).

| | | | Regular Season | | | | | Playoffs | | | | |
|---|---|---|---|---|---|---|---|---|---|---|---|---|
| Season | Club | League | GP | G | A | Pts | PIM | GP | G | A | Pts | PIM |
| 2005-06 | Chateauguay | QAAA | 42 | 9 | 29 | 38 | 22 | 19 | 7 | 10 | 17 | 20 |
| 2006-07 | Chicoutimi | QMJHL | 62 | 6 | 16 | 22 | 51 | 4 | 0 | 0 | 0 | 6 |
| 2007-08 | Chicoutimi | QMJHL | 70 | 18 | 22 | 40 | 45 | 6 | 1 | 1 | 2 | 6 |
| 2008-09 | Chicoutimi | QMJHL | 28 | 10 | 11 | 21 | 34 | .... | .... | .... | .... | .... |
| | PEI Rocket | QMJHL | 24 | 14 | 26 | 40 | 18 | 3 | 0 | 1 | 1 | 4 |

## CHAPPELL, Chris (CHA-puhl, KRIHS) NYR

Left wing. Shoots left. 6'4", 212 lbs. Born, Pickering, Ont., March 21, 1988.

| | | | Regular Season | | | | | Playoffs | | | | |
|---|---|---|---|---|---|---|---|---|---|---|---|---|
| Season | Club | League | GP | G | A | Pts | PIM | GP | G | A | Pts | PIM |
| 2003-04 | Pickering Panthers | OPJHL | 10 | 2 | 2 | 4 | 2 | .... | .... | .... | .... | .... |
| 2004-05 | Pickering Panthers | OPJHL | 49 | 8 | 27 | 35 | 11 | .... | .... | .... | .... | .... |
| 2005-06 | Saginaw Spirit | OHL | 60 | 8 | 12 | 20 | 53 | 4 | 0 | 0 | 0 | 2 |
| 2006-07 | Saginaw Spirit | OHL | 66 | 10 | 14 | 24 | 47 | 6 | 0 | 1 | 1 | 6 |
| 2007-08 | Saginaw Spirit | OHL | 54 | 14 | 20 | 34 | 55 | 4 | 2 | 1 | 3 | 4 |
| 2008-09 | Saginaw Spirit | OHL | 68 | 38 | 38 | 76 | 88 | 8 | 2 | 6 | 8 | 8 |

Signed as a free agent by **NY Rangers**, July 2, 2009.

## CHAPUT, Stefan (sha-PEW, STEH-fan) CAR.

Center. Shoots left. 6', 190 lbs. Born, Montreal, Que., March 11, 1988.
(Carolina's 4th choice, 153rd overall, in 2006 Entry Draft).

| | | | Regular Season | | | | | Playoffs | | | | |
|---|---|---|---|---|---|---|---|---|---|---|---|---|
| Season | Club | League | GP | G | A | Pts | PIM | GP | G | A | Pts | PIM |
| 2003-04 | West Island Lions | QAAA | 29 | 7 | 12 | 19 | 32 | 7 | 1 | 3 | 4 | 4 |
| 2004-05 | West Island Lions | QAAA | 39 | 29 | 25 | 54 | 86 | 5 | 2 | 2 | 4 | 16 |
| | Lewiston | QMJHL | 8 | 2 | 3 | 5 | 2 | 8 | 1 | 0 | 1 | 2 |
| 2005-06 | Lewiston | QMJHL | 69 | 19 | 29 | 48 | 44 | 6 | 0 | 1 | 1 | 4 |
| 2006-07 | Lewiston | QMJHL | 57 | 17 | 29 | 46 | 43 | 17 | 6 | 5 | 11 | 20 |
| 2007-08 | Lewiston | QMJHL | 62 | 33 | 36 | 69 | 56 | 6 | 2 | 1 | 3 | 12 |
| | Albany River Rats | AHL | 1 | 0 | 0 | 0 | 0 | .... | .... | .... | .... | .... |
| 2008-09 | Albany River Rats | AHL | 15 | 4 | 7 | 11 | 10 | .... | .... | .... | .... | .... |

## CHARLEBOIS, Joe (SHAHR-luh-boi, JOH) CHI.

Defense. Shoots right. 6'1", 210 lbs. Born, Potsdam, NY, February 18, 1986.
(Chicago's 10th choice, 188th overall, in 2005 Entry Draft).

| | | | Regular Season | | | | | Playoffs | | | | |
|---|---|---|---|---|---|---|---|---|---|---|---|---|
| Season | Club | League | GP | G | A | Pts | PIM | GP | G | A | Pts | PIM |
| 2002-03 | Cornwall Colts | CJHL | 59 | 2 | 18 | 20 | .... | .... | .... | .... | .... | .... |
| 2003-04 | USNTDP | U-18 | 35 | 0 | 2 | 2 | 10 | .... | .... | .... | .... | .... |
| | USNTDP | NAHL | 12 | 1 | 0 | 1 | 6 | 7 | 0 | 1 | 1 | 4 |
| 2004-05 | Sioux City | USHL | 59 | 1 | 24 | 25 | 146 | 7 | 1 | 1 | 2 | 6 |
| 2005-06 | New Hampshire | H-East | 32 | 2 | 3 | 5 | 35 | .... | .... | .... | .... | .... |
| 2006-07 | New Hampshire | H-East | 39 | 0 | 4 | 4 | 50 | .... | .... | .... | .... | .... |
| 2007-08 | New Hampshire | H-East | 38 | 1 | 8 | 9 | 40 | .... | .... | .... | .... | .... |
| 2008-09 | New Hampshire | H-East | 18 | 0 | 9 | 9 | 36 | .... | .... | .... | .... | .... |
| | Rockford IceHogs | AHL | 13 | 0 | 2 | 2 | 15 | .... | .... | .... | .... | .... |

## CHIAROT, Ben (CHAIR-awt, BEHN) ATL.

Defense. Shoots left. 6'2", 211 lbs. Born, Hamilton, Ont., May 9, 1991.
(Atlanta's 5th choice, 120th overall, in 2009 Entry Draft).

| | | | Regular Season | | | | | Playoffs | | | | |
|---|---|---|---|---|---|---|---|---|---|---|---|---|
| Season | Club | League | GP | G | A | Pts | PIM | GP | G | A | Pts | PIM |
| 2006-07 | Mississauga Reps | GTHL | 60 | 21 | 42 | 63 | 166 | .... | .... | .... | .... | .... |
| 2007-08 | Guelph Storm | OHL | 31 | 0 | 0 | 0 | 14 | .... | .... | .... | .... | .... |
| 2008-09 | Guelph Storm | OHL | 67 | 2 | 10 | 12 | 111 | 4 | 0 | 3 | 3 | 8 |

## CHIASSON, Alex (CHAY-sahn,, Al-ehx) DAL.

Right wing. Shoots right. 6'4", 187 lbs. Born, Montreal, Que., October 1, 1990.
(Dallas' 2nd choice, 38th overall, in 2009 Entry Draft).

| | | | Regular Season | | | | | Playoffs | | | | |
|---|---|---|---|---|---|---|---|---|---|---|---|---|
| Season | Club | League | GP | G | A | Pts | PIM | GP | G | A | Pts | PIM |
| 2007-08 | Northwood | High-NY | 45 | 35 | 46 | 81 | .... | .... | .... | .... | .... | .... |
| 2008-09 | Des Moines | USHL | 56 | 17 | 33 | 50 | 101 | .... | .... | .... | .... | .... |

• Signed Letter of Intent to attend **Boston University** (Hockey East) in fall of 2009.

## CHOUINARD, Joel (SHWEE-nahrd, JOHL) COL.

Defense. Shoots left. 6'1", 186 lbs. Born, Longueuil, Que., April 8, 1990.
(Colorado's 5th choice, 167th overall, in 2008 Entry Draft).

| | | | Regular Season | | | | | Playoffs | | | | |
|---|---|---|---|---|---|---|---|---|---|---|---|---|
| Season | Club | League | GP | G | A | Pts | PIM | GP | G | A | Pts | PIM |
| 2005-06 | Magog | QAAA | 44 | 4 | 14 | 18 | 70 | 13 | 1 | 5 | 6 | 6 |
| 2006-07 | Magog | QAAA | 33 | 8 | 30 | 38 | 88 | .... | .... | .... | .... | .... |
| | Victoriaville Tigres | QMJHL | 23 | 3 | 3 | 6 | 20 | 6 | 0 | 1 | 1 | 0 |
| 2007-08 | Victoriaville Tigres | QMJHL | 69 | 7 | 28 | 35 | 95 | 6 | 2 | 0 | 2 | 4 |
| 2008-09 | Victoriaville Tigres | QMJHL | 64 | 12 | 23 | 35 | 65 | 4 | 0 | 1 | 1 | 6 |

## CICHY, Michael (KEE-chee, MIGH-kuhl) MTL.

Center. Shoots left. 5'10", 185 lbs. Born, New Britain, CT, July 8, 1990.
(Montreal's 7th choice, 199th overall, in 2009 Entry Draft).

| | | | Regular Season | | | | | Playoffs | | | | |
|---|---|---|---|---|---|---|---|---|---|---|---|---|
| Season | Club | League | GP | G | A | Pts | PIM | GP | G | A | Pts | PIM |
| 2006-07 | USNTDP | NAHL | 32 | 2 | 8 | 10 | 35 | .... | .... | .... | .... | .... |
| | USNTDP | U-17 | 7 | 4 | 1 | 5 | 4 | .... | .... | .... | .... | .... |
| 2007-08 | Tri-City Storm | USHL | 59 | 16 | 29 | 45 | 45 | .... | .... | .... | .... | .... |
| 2008-09 | Tri-City Storm | USHL | 26 | *10 | 19 | 29 | 11 | .... | .... | .... | .... | .... |
| | Indiana Ice | USHL | 30 | *24 | 23 | 47 | 12 | 13 | 6 | *19 | *25 | 6 |

• Signed Letter of Intent to attend **University of North Dakota** (WCHA) in fall of 2009. • USHL First All-Star Team (2009)

## CIZIKAS, Casey (sih-ZEE-kuhs, KAY-see) NYI

Center. Shoots left. 5'10", 190 lbs. Born, Toronto, Ont., February 27, 1991.
(NY Islanders' 5th choice, 92nd overall, in 2009 Entry Draft).

| | | | Regular Season | | | | | Playoffs | | | | |
|---|---|---|---|---|---|---|---|---|---|---|---|---|
| Season | Club | League | GP | G | A | Pts | PIM | GP | G | A | Pts | PIM |
| 2006-07 | Mississauga Reps | GTHL | 77 | 46 | 60 | 106 | 88 | .... | .... | .... | .... | .... |
| 2007-08 | St. Michael's | OHL | 62 | 18 | 23 | 41 | 41 | 4 | 1 | 2 | 3 | 6 |
| 2008-09 | St. Michael's | OHL | 55 | 16 | 20 | 36 | 39 | 11 | 5 | 4 | 9 | 11 |

## CLACKSON, Matt (KLAK-suhn, MA-thyew) PHI.

Left wing. Shoots right. 6', 196 lbs. Born, Saskatoon, Sask., April 26, 1985.
(Philadelphia's 6th choice, 215th overall, in 2005 Entry Draft).

| | | | Regular Season | | | | | Playoffs | | | | |
|---|---|---|---|---|---|---|---|---|---|---|---|---|
| Season | Club | League | GP | G | A | Pts | PIM | GP | G | A | Pts | PIM |
| 2002-03 | Pittsburgh Hornets | MWEHL | 64 | 22 | 22 | 44 | 169 | .... | .... | .... | .... | .... |
| 2003-04 | Chicago Steel | USHL | 42 | 5 | 4 | 9 | 108 | 5 | 0 | 1 | 1 | 8 |
| 2004-05 | Chicago Steel | USHL | 56 | 10 | 15 | 25 | 270 | .... | .... | .... | .... | .... |
| 2005-06 | Western Mich. | CCHA | 34 | 1 | 1 | 2 | 52 | .... | .... | .... | .... | .... |
| 2006-07 | Western Mich. | CCHA | 36 | 0 | 8 | 8 | 80 | .... | .... | .... | .... | .... |
| 2007-08 | Western Mich. | CCHA | 35 | 3 | 3 | 6 | 87 | .... | .... | .... | .... | .... |
| | Philadelphia | AHL | 2 | 0 | 0 | 0 | 19 | .... | .... | .... | .... | .... |
| 2008-09 | Philadelphia | AHL | 80 | 3 | 6 | 9 | 263 | 4 | 0 | 0 | 0 | 4 |

## CLARK, Matt (KLAHRK, MAT) ANA.

Defense. Shoots right. 6'3", 205 lbs. Born, Lakewood, CO, October 17, 1990.
(Anaheim's 3rd choice, 37th overall, in 2009 Entry Draft).

| | | | Regular Season | | | | | Playoffs | | | | |
|---|---|---|---|---|---|---|---|---|---|---|---|---|
| Season | Club | League | GP | G | A | Pts | PIM | GP | G | A | Pts | PIM |
| 2006-07 | Brampton Capitals | OPJHL | 47 | 2 | 7 | 9 | 50 | 8 | 1 | 1 | 2 | 19 |
| 2007-08 | Brampton Capitals | OPJHL | 46 | 6 | 11 | 17 | 64 | 8 | 1 | 4 | 5 | 45 |
| 2008-09 | Brampton | OHL | 63 | 3 | 20 | 23 | 91 | 21 | 0 | 5 | 5 | 37 |

## CLICHE, Marc-Andre (KLEESH, MAHRK-AWN-dray) L.A.

Center. Shoots right. 6'1", 195 lbs. Born, Rouyn-Noranda, Que., March 23, 1987.
(NY Rangers' 3rd choice, 56th overall, in 2005 Entry Draft).

| | | | Regular Season | | | | | Playoffs | | | | |
|---|---|---|---|---|---|---|---|---|---|---|---|---|
| Season | Club | League | GP | G | A | Pts | PIM | GP | G | A | Pts | PIM |
| 2003-04 | Lewiston | QMJHL | 52 | 8 | 10 | 18 | 17 | 7 | 1 | 2 | 3 | 0 |
| 2004-05 | Lewiston | QMJHL | 19 | 4 | 4 | 8 | 8 | .... | .... | .... | .... | .... |
| 2005-06 | Lewiston | QMJHL | 66 | 37 | 45 | 82 | 60 | 6 | 2 | 2 | 4 | 0 |
| 2006-07 | Lewiston | QMJHL | 52 | 24 | 30 | 54 | 42 | 16 | 6 | 16 | 22 | 10 |
| 2007-08 | Manchester | AHL | 52 | 11 | 10 | 21 | 25 | 4 | 0 | 1 | 1 | 2 |
| 2008-09 | Manchester | AHL | 31 | 5 | 4 | 9 | 19 | .... | .... | .... | .... | .... |

Traded to **Los Angeles** by **NY Rangers** with Jason Ward, Jan Marek and NY Rangers' 3rd round choice (later traded to Buffalo - Buffalo selected Corey Fienhage) in 2008 Entry Draft for Sean Avery and John Seymour, February 5, 2007. • Missed majority of 2008-09 season recovering from shoulder injury suffered in training camp.

## CLIFFORD, Kyle (KLIHF-fuhrd, KIGHL) L.A.

Left wing. Shoots left. 6'1", 200 lbs. Born, Ayr, Ont., January 13, 1991.
(Los Angeles' 2nd choice, 35th overall, in 2009 Entry Draft).

| | | | Regular Season | | | | | Playoffs | | | | |
|---|---|---|---|---|---|---|---|---|---|---|---|---|
| Season | Club | League | GP | G | A | Pts | PIM | GP | G | A | Pts | PIM |
| 2006-07 | Cambridge Hawks | Minor-ON | 70 | 31 | 49 | 80 | 119 | .... | .... | .... | .... | .... |
| 2007-08 | Barrie Colts | OHL | 66 | 1 | 14 | 15 | 83 | 9 | 0 | 1 | 1 | 4 |
| 2008-09 | Barrie Colts | OHL | 60 | 16 | 12 | 28 | 133 | 5 | 0 | 0 | 0 | 13 |

## CLITSOME, Grant (KLIHT-suhm, GRANT) CBJ

Defense. Shoots left. 6', 208 lbs. Born, Gloucester, Ont., April 14, 1985.
(Columbus' 12th choice, 271st overall, in 2004 Entry Draft).

| | | | Regular Season | | | | | Playoffs | | | | |
|---|---|---|---|---|---|---|---|---|---|---|---|---|
| Season | Club | League | GP | G | A | Pts | PIM | GP | G | A | Pts | PIM |
| 2003-04 | Nepean Raiders | CJHL | 55 | 13 | 26 | 39 | 67 | 17 | 1 | 10 | 11 | 6 |
| 2004-05 | Clarkson Knights | ECAC | 39 | 2 | 11 | 13 | 36 | .... | .... | .... | .... | .... |
| 2005-06 | Clarkson Knights | ECAC | 34 | 2 | 17 | 19 | 20 | .... | .... | .... | .... | .... |
| 2006-07 | Clarkson Knights | ECAC | 38 | 7 | 12 | 19 | 38 | .... | .... | .... | .... | .... |
| 2007-08 | Clarkson Knights | ECAC | 39 | 5 | 17 | 22 | 28 | .... | .... | .... | .... | .... |
| | Syracuse Crunch | AHL | .... | .... | .... | .... | .... | 1 | 0 | 0 | 0 | 0 |
| 2008-09 | Syracuse Crunch | AHL | 73 | 4 | 15 | 19 | 74 | .... | .... | .... | .... | .... |

ECAC First All-Star Team (2008) • NCAA East Second All-American Team (2008)

## CLUNE, Richard (KLOON, RIH-chuhrd) L.A.

Left wing. Shoots left. 6', 196 lbs. Born, Toronto, Ont., April 25, 1987.
(Dallas' 3rd choice, 71st overall, in 2005 Entry Draft).

| | | | Regular Season | | | | | Playoffs | | | | |
|---|---|---|---|---|---|---|---|---|---|---|---|---|
| Season | Club | League | GP | G | A | Pts | PIM | GP | G | A | Pts | PIM |
| 2003-04 | Sarnia Sting | OHL | 58 | 3 | 13 | 16 | 72 | 5 | 0 | 1 | 1 | 0 |
| 2004-05 | Sarnia Sting | OHL | 68 | 21 | 13 | 34 | 103 | .... | .... | .... | .... | .... |
| 2005-06 | Sarnia Sting | OHL | 61 | 20 | 32 | 52 | 126 | .... | .... | .... | .... | .... |
| 2006-07 | Barrie Colts | OHL | 67 | 32 | 46 | 78 | 151 | 8 | 3 | 4 | 7 | 8 |
| | Iowa Stars | AHL | 1 | 0 | 0 | 0 | 2 | .... | .... | .... | .... | .... |
| 2007-08 | Iowa Stars | AHL | 38 | 3 | 5 | 8 | 137 | .... | .... | .... | .... | .... |
| | Idaho Steelheads | ECHL | 19 | 1 | 9 | 10 | 41 | .... | .... | .... | .... | .... |
| 2008-09 | Manchester | AHL | 35 | 3 | 6 | 9 | 87 | .... | .... | .... | .... | .... |

Traded to **Los Angeles** by **Dallas** for Lauri Tukonen, July 21, 2008.

## COHEN, Colby (KOH-uhn, KOHL-bee) COL.

Defense. Shoots right. 6'2", 200 lbs. Born, Villanova, PA, April 25, 1989.
(Colorado's 2nd choice, 45th overall, in 2007 Entry Draft).

| | | | Regular Season | | | | | Playoffs | | | | |
|---|---|---|---|---|---|---|---|---|---|---|---|---|
| Season | Club | League | GP | G | A | Pts | PIM | GP | G | A | Pts | PIM |
| 2004-05 | Syracuse Stars | EmJHL | 50 | 13 | 30 | 41 | .... | .... | .... | .... | .... | .... |
| 2005-06 | USNTDP | U-17 | 18 | 2 | 3 | 5 | 22 | .... | .... | .... | .... | .... |
| | USNTDP | NAHL | 37 | 5 | 9 | 14 | 33 | 10 | 1 | 1 | 2 | 0 |
| 2006-07 | USNTDP | U-17 | 4 | 1 | 3 | 4 | 0 | .... | .... | .... | .... | .... |
| | Lincoln Stars | USHL | 53 | 13 | 47 | 60 | 110 | 4 | 0 | 0 | 0 | 2 |
| 2007-08 | Boston University | H-East | 39 | 3 | 13 | 16 | 34 | .... | .... | .... | .... | .... |
| 2008-09 | Boston University | H-East | 43 | 8 | 24 | 32 | 65 | .... | .... | .... | .... | .... |

USHL Second All-Star Team (2007) • NCAA Championship All-Tournament Team (2009) • NCAA Championship Tournament MVP (2009)

## COLBERT, Will (KOHL-buhrt, WIHL) S.J.

Defense. Shoots left. 6'3", 225 lbs. Born, Arnprior, Ont., February 6, 1985.
(San Jose's 7th choice, 183rd overall, in 2005 Entry Draft).

| | | | Regular Season | | | | | Playoffs | | | | |
|---|---|---|---|---|---|---|---|---|---|---|---|---|
| Season | Club | League | GP | G | A | Pts | PIM | GP | G | A | Pts | PIM |
| 2001-02 | Pembroke | CJHL | 52 | 2 | 6 | 8 | 20 | .... | .... | .... | .... | .... |
| 2002-03 | Ottawa 67's | OHL | 56 | 1 | 6 | 7 | 23 | 23 | 1 | 5 | 6 | 7 |
| 2003-04 | Ottawa 67's | OHL | 55 | 3 | 18 | 21 | 28 | 7 | 0 | 4 | 4 | 0 |
| 2004-05 | Ottawa 67's | OHL | 68 | 6 | 26 | 32 | 65 | 21 | 3 | 8 | 11 | 8 |
| 2005-06 | St. FX University | AUAA | 28 | 3 | 8 | 11 | 10 | 3 | 0 | 0 | 0 | 2 |
| 2006-07 | St. FX University | AUAA | 27 | 2 | 9 | 11 | 28 | 8 | 0 | 5 | 5 | 16 |
| 2007-08 | St. FX University | AUAA | 28 | 2 | 13 | 15 | 22 | 3 | 0 | 1 | 1 | 6 |
| 2008-09 | St. FX University | AUAA | 26 | 5 | 12 | 17 | 24 | 2 | 0 | 0 | 0 | 0 |

• Re-entered NHL Entry Draft. Originally Ottawa's 7th choice, 228th overall, in 2003 Entry Draft.

CIS All-Rookie Team (2006)

## COLBORNE, Joe (KOHL-bohrn, JOH) BOS.

Center. Shoots left. 6'5", 206 lbs. Born, Calgary, Alta., January 30, 1990.
(Boston's 1st choice, 16th overall, in 2008 Entry Draft).

| | | | Regular Season | | | | | Playoffs | | | | |
|---|---|---|---|---|---|---|---|---|---|---|---|---|
| Season | Club | League | GP | G | A | Pts | PIM | GP | G | A | Pts | PIM |
| 2005-06 | Notre Dame | SMHL | 48 | 13 | 14 | 27 | 26 | .... | .... | .... | .... | .... |
| 2006-07 | Camrose Kodiaks | AJHL | 53 | 20 | 28 | 48 | 44 | 16 | 5 | 1 | 6 | 10 |
| 2007-08 | Camrose Kodiaks | AJHL | 55 | 33 | *57 | 90 | 48 | 18 | 8 | 8 | *16 | 26 |
| 2008-09 | U. of Denver | WCHA | 40 | 10 | 21 | 31 | 24 | .... | .... | .... | .... | .... |

WCHA All-Rookie Team (2009)

## COLE, Brad (KOHL, BRAD) CGY.

Defense. Shoots left. 6'4", 200 lbs. Born, Miniota, Man., October 21, 1986.

| | | | Regular Season | | | | | Playoffs | | | | |
|---|---|---|---|---|---|---|---|---|---|---|---|---|
| Season | Club | League | GP | G | A | Pts | PIM | GP | G | A | Pts | PIM |
| 2003-04 | Seattle | WHL | 6 | 0 | 0 | 0 | 12 | .... | .... | .... | .... | .... |
| | Kootenay Ice | WHL | 52 | 0 | 1 | 1 | 39 | 4 | 1 | 0 | 1 | 2 |
| 2004-05 | Kootenay Ice | WHL | 39 | 1 | 2 | 3 | 35 | 8 | 0 | 1 | 1 | 2 |
| 2005-06 | Kootenay Ice | WHL | 16 | 1 | 2 | 3 | 20 | .... | .... | .... | .... | .... |
| | Saskatoon Blades | WHL | 56 | 3 | 12 | 15 | 64 | 9 | 1 | 0 | 1 | 23 |
| 2006-07 | Saskatoon Blades | WHL | 63 | 16 | 25 | 41 | 83 | .... | .... | .... | .... | .... |
| 2007-08 | Quad City Flames | AHL | 25 | 1 | 4 | 5 | 13 | .... | .... | .... | .... | .... |
| | Las Vegas | ECHL | 19 | 0 | 4 | 4 | 11 | .... | .... | .... | .... | .... |
| 2008-09 | Quad City Flames | AHL | 73 | 3 | 8 | 11 | 53 | .... | .... | .... | .... | .... |

Signed as a free agent by **Calgary**, May 22, 2007.

## COLE, Ian (KOHL, EE-an) ST.L.

Defense. Shoots left. 6'1", 217 lbs. Born, Ann Arbour, MI, February 21, 1989.
(St. Louis' 2nd choice, 18th overall, in 2007 Entry Draft).

| | | | Regular Season | | | | | Playoffs | | | | |
|---|---|---|---|---|---|---|---|---|---|---|---|---|
| Season | Club | League | GP | G | A | Pts | PIM | GP | G | A | Pts | PIM |
| 2004-05 | Det. Victory Honda | MWEHL | 60 | 15 | 25 | 40 | .... | .... | .... | .... | .... | .... |
| 2005-06 | USNTDP | U-17 | 18 | 2 | 1 | 3 | 14 | .... | .... | .... | .... | .... |
| | USNTDP | NAHL | 40 | 2 | 8 | 10 | 75 | 12 | 0 | 3 | 3 | 14 |
| 2006-07 | USNTDP | U-18 | 42 | 6 | 11 | 17 | 36 | .... | .... | .... | .... | .... |
| | USNTDP | NAHL | 16 | 2 | 7 | 9 | 28 | .... | .... | .... | .... | .... |
| 2007-08 | U. of Notre Dame | CCHA | 43 | 8 | 12 | 20 | 40 | .... | .... | .... | .... | .... |
| 2008-09 | U. of Notre Dame | CCHA | 38 | 6 | 20 | 26 | 58 | .... | .... | .... | .... | .... |

CCHA First All-Star Team (2009) • NCAA West First All-American Team (2009)

## COLLINS, Dan (KAW-lihnz, DAN) FLA.

Right wing. Shoots right. 6'1", 185 lbs. Born, Syracuse, NY, February 26, 1987.
(Florida's 3rd choice, 90th overall, in 2005 Entry Draft).

| | | | Regular Season | | | | | Playoffs | | | | |
|---|---|---|---|---|---|---|---|---|---|---|---|---|
| Season | Club | League | GP | G | A | Pts | PIM | GP | G | A | Pts | PIM |
| 2002-03 | Syracuse | OPJHL | 35 | 14 | 12 | 26 | 58 | .... | .... | .... | .... | .... |
| 2003-04 | Plymouth Whalers | OHL | 59 | 9 | 13 | 22 | 30 | 9 | 0 | 1 | 1 | 0 |
| 2004-05 | Plymouth Whalers | OHL | 68 | 25 | 21 | 46 | 60 | 4 | 0 | 0 | 0 | 6 |
| 2005-06 | Plymouth Whalers | OHL | 44 | 26 | 23 | 49 | 56 | 4 | 3 | 2 | 5 | 2 |
| 2006-07 | Plymouth Whalers | OHL | 66 | 26 | 42 | 68 | 87 | 20 | 9 | 11 | 20 | 30 |
| 2007-08 | Rochester | AHL | 35 | 5 | 6 | 11 | 21 | .... | .... | .... | .... | .... |
| | Florida Everblades | ECHL | 28 | 4 | 14 | 18 | 34 | .... | .... | .... | .... | .... |
| 2008-09 | Rochester | AHL | 56 | 5 | 2 | 7 | 25 | .... | .... | .... | .... | .... |

## COLLINS, Sean (KAW-lihnz, SHAWN) CBJ

Center. Shoots left. 6'2", 186 lbs. Born, Saskatoon, Sask., December 29, 1988.
(Columbus' 9th choice, 187th overall, in 2008 Entry Draft).

| | | | Regular Season | | | | | Playoffs | | | | |
|---|---|---|---|---|---|---|---|---|---|---|---|---|
| Season | Club | League | GP | G | A | Pts | PIM | GP | G | A | Pts | PIM |
| 2006-07 | Waywayseecappo | MJHL | 70 | 20 | 69 | 89 | 34 | .... | .... | .... | .... | .... |
| 2007-08 | Waywayseecappo | MJHL | 60 | 51 | 64 | 115 | 34 | 7 | 9 | 4 | 13 | 10 |
| 2008-09 | Cornell Big Red | ECAC | 33 | 3 | 3 | 6 | 16 | .... | .... | .... | .... | .... |

## COMRIE, Adam (KAWM-ree, A-duhm) FLA.

Defense. Shoots left. 6'4", 205 lbs. Born, Kanata, Ont., July 31, 1990.
(Florida's 3rd choice, 80th overall, in 2008 Entry Draft).

| | | | Regular Season | | | | | Playoffs | | | | |
|---|---|---|---|---|---|---|---|---|---|---|---|---|
| Season | Club | League | GP | G | A | Pts | PIM | GP | G | A | Pts | PIM |
| 2006-07 | Ohio | USHL | 19 | 6 | 4 | 10 | 28 | .... | .... | .... | .... | .... |
| | Omaha Lancers | USHL | 38 | 1 | 6 | 7 | 27 | 5 | 0 | 0 | 0 | 4 |
| 2007-08 | Saginaw Spirit | OHL | 58 | 10 | 18 | 28 | 90 | 4 | 0 | 0 | 0 | 4 |
| 2008-09 | Saginaw Spirit | OHL | 52 | 9 | 21 | 30 | 70 | 8 | 0 | 2 | 2 | 8 |

## CONBOY, Andrew (KAWN-boi, AN-droo) MTL.

Left wing. Shoots left. 6'4", 192 lbs. Born, Burnsville, MN, May 16, 1988.
(Montreal's 7th choice, 142nd overall, in 2007 Entry Draft).

| | | | Regular Season | | | | | Playoffs | | | | |
|---|---|---|---|---|---|---|---|---|---|---|---|---|
| Season | Club | League | GP | G | A | Pts | PIM | GP | G | A | Pts | PIM |
| 2005-06 | Wichita Falls | NAHL | 51 | 7 | 8 | 15 | 158 | 5 | 0 | 2 | 2 | 2 |
| 2006-07 | Omaha Lancers | USHL | 56 | 25 | 25 | 50 | 105 | .... | .... | .... | .... | .... |
| 2007-08 | Omaha Lancers | USHL | 58 | 17 | 21 | 38 | 188 | 14 | *9 | 1 | 10 | 24 |
| 2008-09 | Michigan State | CCHA | 21 | 3 | 2 | 5 | 76 | .... | .... | .... | .... | .... |
| | Hamilton Bulldogs | AHL | 15 | 0 | 1 | 1 | 6 | 1 | 0 | 0 | 0 | 2 |

## CONDON, Nate (KOHN-duhn, NAY-thun) COL.

Center. Shoots left. 6', 180 lbs. Born, Wausau, WI, May 29, 1990.
(Colorado's 7th choice, 200th overall, in 2008 Entry Draft).

| | | | Regular Season | | | | | Playoffs | | | | |
|---|---|---|---|---|---|---|---|---|---|---|---|---|
| Season | Club | League | GP | G | A | Pts | PIM | GP | G | A | Pts | PIM |
| 2004-05 | Wausau West | High-WI | 22 | 1 | 4 | 5 | 4 | .... | .... | .... | .... | .... |
| 2005-06 | Wausau West | High-WI | 22 | 21 | 22 | 43 | 6 | .... | .... | .... | .... | .... |
| | Team Wisconsin | UMHSEL | 24 | 16 | 13 | 29 | 10 | .... | .... | .... | .... | .... |
| 2006-07 | Wausau West | High-WI | 21 | 21 | 27 | 48 | 10 | .... | .... | .... | .... | .... |
| | Team Wisconsin | UMHSEL | 23 | 14 | 9 | 23 | 6 | .... | .... | .... | .... | .... |
| 2007-08 | Wausau West | High-WI | 23 | 33 | 26 | 59 | 10 | .... | .... | .... | .... | .... |
| | Team Wisconsin | UMHSEL | 24 | 20 | 25 | 45 | 6 | .... | .... | .... | .... | .... |
| 2008-09 | Fargo Force | USHL | 58 | 11 | 18 | 29 | 20 | 10 | 1 | 5 | 6 | 2 |

• Signed Letter of Intent to attend **University of Minnesota** (WCHA) in fall of 2009.

## CONDRA, Erik (KAWN-druh, AIR-ihk) OTT.

Right wing. Shoots right. 6', 194 lbs. Born, Trenton, MI, August 6, 1986.
(Ottawa's 7th choice, 211th overall, in 2006 Entry Draft).

| | | | Regular Season | | | | | Playoffs | | | | |
|---|---|---|---|---|---|---|---|---|---|---|---|---|
| Season | Club | League | GP | G | A | Pts | PIM | GP | G | A | Pts | PIM |
| 2004-05 | Lincoln Stars | USHL | 60 | 30 | 30 | 60 | 56 | 4 | 0 | 2 | 2 | 4 |
| 2005-06 | U. of Notre Dame | CCHA | 36 | 6 | 28 | 34 | 32 | .... | .... | .... | .... | .... |
| 2006-07 | U. of Notre Dame | CCHA | 42 | 14 | 34 | 48 | 18 | .... | .... | .... | .... | .... |
| 2007-08 | U. of Notre Dame | CCHA | 41 | 15 | 23 | 38 | 26 | .... | .... | .... | .... | .... |
| 2008-09 | U. of Notre Dame | CCHA | 40 | 13 | 25 | 38 | 34 | .... | .... | .... | .... | .... |

CCHA All-Rookie Team (2006) • CCHA Second All-Star Team (2009) • NCAA West Second All-American Team (2009)

**CONNAUTON, Kevin** (kuh-NAW-tuhn, KEH-vihn) **VAN.**

Defense. Shoots left. 6'1", 185 lbs. Born, Edmonton, Alta., February 23, 1990.
(Vancouver's 3rd choice, 83rd overall, in 2009 Entry Draft).

| | | | Regular Season | | | | | Playoffs | | | | |
|---|---|---|---|---|---|---|---|---|---|---|---|---|
| Season | Club | League | GP | G | A | Pts | PIM | GP | G | A | Pts | PIM |
| 2007-08 | Spruce Grove | AJHL | 56 | 13 | 32 | 45 | 59 | 15 | 5 | 0 | 5 | 18 |
| 2008-09 | Western Mich. | CCHA | 40 | 7 | 11 | 18 | 44 | .... | .... | .... | .... | .... |

**CONNELLY, Brian** (KAW-nuh-lee, BRIGH-uhn) **CHI.**

Defense. Shoots left. 5'9", 170 lbs. Born, Bloomington, MN, June 10, 1986.

| | | | Regular Season | | | | | Playoffs | | | | |
|---|---|---|---|---|---|---|---|---|---|---|---|---|
| Season | Club | League | GP | G | A | Pts | PIM | GP | G | A | Pts | PIM |
| 2004-05 | Bloomington-Jeff. | High-MN | .... | 18 | 45 | 63 | .... | .... | .... | .... | .... | .... |
| | Tri-City Storm | USHL | 20 | 0 | 3 | 3 | 12 | 9 | 0 | 1 | 1 | 2 |
| 2005-06 | Tri-City Storm | USHL | 54 | 3 | 9 | 12 | 16 | 5 | 1 | 0 | 1 | 0 |
| 2006-07 | Colorado College | WCHA | 35 | 2 | 15 | 17 | 22 | .... | .... | .... | .... | .... |
| 2007-08 | Colorado College | WCHA | 41 | 3 | 16 | 19 | 32 | .... | .... | .... | .... | .... |
| 2008-09 | Colorado College | WCHA | 38 | 3 | 24 | 27 | 46 | .... | .... | .... | .... | .... |
| | Rockford IceHogs | AHL | 9 | 1 | 2 | 3 | 6 | 3 | 0 | 0 | 0 | 2 |

Signed to an ATO (tryout) contract by **Chicago**, March 23, 2009.

**CORMIER, Kevin** (KOHR-mee-ay, KEH-vihn) **N.J.**

Right wing. Shoots left. 6'3", 235 lbs. Born, Moncton, N.B., January 27, 1986.
(Phoenix's 6th choice, 168th overall, in 2004 Entry Draft).

| | | | Regular Season | | | | | Playoffs | | | | |
|---|---|---|---|---|---|---|---|---|---|---|---|---|
| Season | Club | League | GP | G | A | Pts | PIM | GP | G | A | Pts | PIM |
| 2003-04 | Moncton | MJrHL | 42 | 3 | 2 | 5 | 235 | 4 | 0 | 0 | 0 | 52 |
| | Halifax | QMJHL | 1 | 0 | 0 | 0 | 5 | .... | .... | .... | .... | .... |
| 2004-05 | Halifax | QMJHL | 60 | 2 | 5 | 7 | 235 | 9 | 0 | 0 | 0 | 8 |
| 2005-06 | Halifax | QMJHL | 69 | 16 | 11 | 27 | 202 | 11 | 0 | 1 | 1 | 18 |
| 2006-07 | Rimouski Oceanic | QMJHL | 28 | 5 | 4 | 9 | 97 | .... | .... | .... | .... | .... |
| | Shawinigan | QMJHL | 25 | 7 | 5 | 12 | 70 | 3 | 0 | 0 | 0 | 4 |
| 2007-08 | Arizona Sundogs | CHL | 23 | 3 | 2 | 5 | 104 | .... | .... | .... | .... | .... |
| 2008-09 | Lowell Devils | AHL | 1 | 0 | 0 | 0 | 5 | .... | .... | .... | .... | .... |
| | Trenton Devils | ECHL | 29 | 2 | 2 | 4 | 94 | 3 | 0 | 0 | 0 | 0 |

Traded to **New Jersey** by **Phoenix** for Sean Zimmerman, September 12, 2008.

**CORMIER, Patrice** (KOHR-mee-ay, pa-TREEZ) **N.J.**

Center. Shoots left. 6'2", 200 lbs. Born, Moncton, N.B., June 14, 1990.
(New Jersey's 3rd choice, 54th overall, in 2008 Entry Draft).

| | | | Regular Season | | | | | Playoffs | | | | |
|---|---|---|---|---|---|---|---|---|---|---|---|---|
| Season | Club | League | GP | G | A | Pts | PIM | GP | G | A | Pts | PIM |
| 2006-07 | Rimouski Oceanic | QMJHL | 53 | 11 | 10 | 21 | 73 | .... | .... | .... | .... | .... |
| 2007-08 | Rimouski Oceanic | QMJHL | 51 | 18 | 23 | 41 | 84 | 9 | 4 | 5 | 9 | 10 |
| 2008-09 | Rimouski Oceanic | QMJHL | 54 | 23 | 28 | 51 | 118 | 13 | 4 | 6 | 10 | 30 |

**CORNET, Philippe** (kohr-NAY, fihl-LEEP) **EDM.**

Left wing. Shoots left. 6', 173 lbs. Born, Val-Senneville, Que., March 28, 1990.
(Edmonton's 3rd choice, 133rd overall, in 2008 Entry Draft).

| | | | Regular Season | | | | | Playoffs | | | | |
|---|---|---|---|---|---|---|---|---|---|---|---|---|
| Season | Club | League | GP | G | A | Pts | PIM | GP | G | A | Pts | PIM |
| 2006-07 | Rimouski Oceanic | QMJHL | 46 | 7 | 14 | 21 | 8 | .... | .... | .... | .... | .... |
| 2007-08 | Rimouski Oceanic | QMJHL | 61 | 23 | 26 | 49 | 24 | 9 | 3 | 3 | 6 | 6 |
| 2008-09 | Rimouski Oceanic | QMJHL | 63 | 29 | 48 | 77 | 34 | 13 | 4 | 11 | 15 | 14 |

**CORRENTE, Matthew** (kohr-REHN-tay, MA-thew) **N.J.**

Defense. Shoots right. 6', 200 lbs. Born, Mississauga, Ont., March 17, 1988.
(New Jersey's 1st choice, 30th overall, in 2006 Entry Draft).

| | | | Regular Season | | | | | Playoffs | | | | |
|---|---|---|---|---|---|---|---|---|---|---|---|---|
| Season | Club | League | GP | G | A | Pts | PIM | GP | G | A | Pts | PIM |
| 2004-05 | Saginaw Spirit | OHL | 62 | 6 | 9 | 15 | 89 | .... | .... | .... | .... | .... |
| 2005-06 | Saginaw Spirit | OHL | 61 | 6 | 24 | 30 | 172 | 4 | 1 | 1 | 2 | 8 |
| 2006-07 | Saginaw Spirit | OHL | 29 | 2 | 13 | 15 | 67 | .... | .... | .... | .... | .... |
| | Mississauga | OHL | 14 | 1 | 10 | 11 | 27 | 5 | 0 | 1 | 1 | 8 |
| 2007-08 | Niagara Ice Dogs | OHL | 21 | 2 | 13 | 15 | 64 | 10 | 0 | 5 | 5 | 33 |
| 2008-09 | Lowell Devils | AHL | 67 | 6 | 12 | 18 | 161 | .... | .... | .... | .... | .... |

**COSTELLO, Jeff** (kaw-STEHL-oh, JEHF) **OTT.**

Left wing. Shoots left. 5'11", 198 lbs. Born, Milwaukee, WI, November 20, 1990.
(Ottawa's 6th choice, 146th overall, in 2009 Entry Draft).

| | | | Regular Season | | | | | Playoffs | | | | |
|---|---|---|---|---|---|---|---|---|---|---|---|---|
| Season | Club | League | GP | G | A | Pts | PIM | GP | G | A | Pts | PIM |
| 2005-06 | Catholic Memorial | High-WI | .... | 13 | 16 | 29 | .... | .... | .... | .... | .... | .... |
| 2006-07 | Catholic Memorial | High-WI | .... | 34 | 20 | 54 | .... | .... | .... | .... | .... | .... |
| 2007-08 | Catholic Memorial | High-WI | 22 | 31 | 17 | 48 | 60 | .... | .... | .... | .... | .... |
| | Team Wisconsin | UMHSEL | .... | 18 | 18 | 36 | .... | .... | .... | .... | .... | .... |
| 2008-09 | Cedar Rapids | USHL | 54 | 24 | 9 | 33 | 73 | 5 | 0 | 2 | 2 | 0 |

• Signed Letter of Intent to attend **University of Notre Dame** (CCHA) in fall of 2010.

**COUTURE, Derek** (koh-TYOOR, DAIR-ihk)

Right wing. Shoots right. 6'2", 206 lbs. Born, Calgary, Alta., April 24, 1984.

| | | | Regular Season | | | | | Playoffs | | | | |
|---|---|---|---|---|---|---|---|---|---|---|---|---|
| Season | Club | League | GP | G | A | Pts | PIM | GP | G | A | Pts | PIM |
| 2001-02 | Saskatoon Blades | WHL | 61 | 6 | 10 | 16 | 159 | 7 | 0 | 0 | 0 | 10 |
| 2002-03 | Saskatoon Blades | WHL | 70 | 17 | 20 | 37 | 160 | 6 | 1 | 2 | 3 | 13 |
| 2003-04 | Saskatoon Blades | WHL | 45 | 3 | 9 | 12 | 99 | .... | .... | .... | .... | .... |
| 2004-05 | Seattle | WHL | 71 | 20 | 18 | 38 | 154 | 12 | 3 | 6 | 9 | 18 |
| 2005-06 | Omaha | AHL | 66 | 7 | 12 | 19 | 88 | .... | .... | .... | .... | .... |
| 2006-07 | Omaha | AHL | 46 | 3 | 6 | 9 | 76 | 6 | 0 | 1 | 1 | 4 |
| 2007-08 | Quad City Flames | AHL | 76 | 10 | 8 | 18 | 129 | .... | .... | .... | .... | .... |
| 2008-09 | Binghamton | AHL | 18 | 2 | 3 | 5 | 21 | .... | .... | .... | .... | .... |
| | Elmira Jackals | ECHL | 21 | 6 | 14 | 20 | 53 | 7 | 1 | 3 | 4 | 37 |

Signed as a free agent by **Calgary**, August 5, 2005.

**COUTURE, Logan** (koh-TYOOR, LOH-guhn) **S.J.**

Center. Shoots left. 6'1", 195 lbs. Born, Guelph, Ont., March 28, 1989.
(San Jose's 1st choice, 9th overall, in 2007 Entry Draft).

| | | | Regular Season | | | | | Playoffs | | | | |
|---|---|---|---|---|---|---|---|---|---|---|---|---|
| Season | Club | League | GP | G | A | Pts | PIM | GP | G | A | Pts | PIM |
| 2004-05 | St. Thomas Stars | OJHL-B | 48 | 24 | 22 | 46 | .... | .... | .... | .... | .... | .... |
| 2005-06 | Ottawa 67's | OHL | 65 | 25 | 39 | 64 | 52 | 6 | 3 | 4 | 7 | 0 |
| 2006-07 | Ottawa 67's | OHL | 54 | 26 | 52 | 78 | 24 | 5 | 1 | 7 | 8 | 4 |
| 2007-08 | Ottawa 67's | OHL | 51 | 21 | 37 | 58 | 37 | 4 | 2 | 1 | 3 | 0 |
| 2008-09 | Ottawa 67's | OHL | 62 | 39 | 48 | 87 | 46 | 7 | 3 | 7 | 10 | 6 |
| | Worcester Sharks | AHL | 4 | 0 | 0 | 0 | 7 | 12 | 2 | 1 | 3 | 11 |

**COWEN, Jared** (KOW-ehn, JAIR-ehd) **OTT.**

Defense. Shoots left. 6'5", 222 lbs. Born, Saskatoon, Sask., January 25, 1991.
(Ottawa's 1st choice, 9th overall, in 2009 Entry Draft).

| | | | Regular Season | | | | | Playoffs | | | | |
|---|---|---|---|---|---|---|---|---|---|---|---|---|
| Season | Club | League | GP | G | A | Pts | PIM | GP | G | A | Pts | PIM |
| 2006-07 | Sask. Contacts | SMHL | 41 | 6 | 22 | 28 | 103 | .... | .... | .... | .... | .... |
| | Spokane Chiefs | WHL | 6 | 0 | 2 | 2 | 2 | 6 | 0 | 1 | 1 | 6 |
| 2007-08 | Spokane Chiefs | WHL | 68 | 4 | 14 | 18 | 62 | 21 | 1 | 3 | 4 | 17 |
| 2008-09 | Spokane Chiefs | WHL | 48 | 7 | 14 | 21 | 45 | .... | .... | .... | .... | .... |

**COWICK, Corey** (KOW-ihk, KOH-ree) **OTT.**

Left wing. Shoots left. 6'3", 203 lbs. Born, Gloucester, Ont., August 1, 1989.
(Ottawa's 7th choice, 160th overall, in 2009 Entry Draft).

| | | | Regular Season | | | | | Playoffs | | | | |
|---|---|---|---|---|---|---|---|---|---|---|---|---|
| Season | Club | League | GP | G | A | Pts | PIM | GP | G | A | Pts | PIM |
| 2006-07 | Oshawa Generals | OHL | 67 | 4 | 4 | 8 | 54 | 9 | 0 | 0 | 0 | 2 |
| 2007-08 | Oshawa Generals | OHL | 63 | 11 | 14 | 25 | 79 | 15 | 1 | 1 | 2 | 22 |
| 2008-09 | Ottawa 67's | OHL | 68 | 34 | 26 | 60 | 48 | 7 | 7 | 2 | 9 | 14 |

**CRACKNELL, Adam** (krak-NEHL, A-duhm) **ST.L.**

Right wing. Shoots right. 6'1", 191 lbs. Born, Prince Albert, Sask., July 15, 1985.
(Calgary's 10th choice, 279th overall, in 2004 Entry Draft).

| | | | Regular Season | | | | | Playoffs | | | | |
|---|---|---|---|---|---|---|---|---|---|---|---|---|
| Season | Club | League | GP | G | A | Pts | PIM | GP | G | A | Pts | PIM |
| 2002-03 | Kootenay Ice | WHL | 67 | 7 | 4 | 11 | 37 | 11 | 0 | 0 | 0 | 2 |
| 2003-04 | Kootenay Ice | WHL | 72 | 26 | 35 | 61 | 63 | 4 | 1 | 1 | 2 | 2 |
| 2004-05 | Kootenay Ice | WHL | 72 | 19 | 29 | 48 | 65 | 16 | 8 | 8 | 16 | 6 |
| 2005-06 | Kootenay Ice | WHL | 72 | 42 | 51 | 93 | 85 | 6 | 1 | 4 | 5 | 6 |
| | Omaha | AHL | 6 | 1 | 2 | 3 | 2 | .... | .... | .... | .... | .... |
| 2006-07 | Las Vegas | ECHL | 31 | 8 | 14 | 22 | 35 | 8 | 3 | 3 | 6 | 6 |
| 2007-08 | Quad City Flames | AHL | 4 | 1 | 0 | 1 | 0 | .... | .... | .... | .... | .... |
| | Las Vegas | ECHL | 61 | 29 | 30 | 59 | 47 | 21 | 9 | 13 | 22 | 4 |
| 2008-09 | Quad City Flames | AHL | 79 | 10 | 16 | 26 | 36 | .... | .... | .... | .... | .... |

WHL West Second All-Star Team (2006)

Signed as a free agent by **St. Louis**, July 23, 2009.

**CRAWFORD, Nick** (KRAW-fuhrd, NIHK) **BUF.**

Defense. Shoots left. 6'1", 188 lbs. Born, Brampton, Ont., February 23, 1990.
(Buffalo's 8th choice, 164th overall, in 2008 Entry Draft).

| | | | Regular Season | | | | | Playoffs | | | | |
|---|---|---|---|---|---|---|---|---|---|---|---|---|
| Season | Club | League | GP | G | A | Pts | PIM | GP | G | A | Pts | PIM |
| 2006-07 | Saginaw Spirit | OHL | 63 | 1 | 7 | 8 | 32 | 5 | 0 | 1 | 1 | 0 |
| 2007-08 | Saginaw Spirit | OHL | 68 | 4 | 16 | 20 | 58 | 4 | 1 | 1 | 2 | 2 |
| 2008-09 | Saginaw Spirit | OHL | 65 | 7 | 35 | 42 | 41 | 8 | 1 | 4 | 5 | 4 |

**CROSS, Tommy** (KRAWS, TAW-mee) **BOS.**

Defense. Shoots left. 6'3", 210 lbs. Born, Hartford, CT, September 12, 1989.
(Boston's 2nd choice, 35th overall, in 2007 Entry Draft).

| | | | Regular Season | | | | | Playoffs | | | | |
|---|---|---|---|---|---|---|---|---|---|---|---|---|
| Season | Club | League | GP | G | A | Pts | PIM | GP | G | A | Pts | PIM |
| 2004-05 | Simsbury | High-CT | 23 | 5 | 40 | 45 | 18 | .... | .... | .... | .... | .... |
| 2005-06 | Simsbury | High-CT | 22 | 15 | 35 | 50 | .... | .... | .... | .... | .... | .... |
| 2006-07 | Westminster | High-CT | 25 | 8 | 12 | 20 | 20 | .... | .... | .... | .... | .... |
| | USNTDP | NAHL | 2 | 0 | 2 | 2 | 0 | .... | .... | .... | .... | .... |
| | USNTDP | U-18 | 11 | 0 | 1 | 1 | 8 | .... | .... | .... | .... | .... |
| 2007-08 | Westminster | High-CT | 25 | 9 | 12 | 21 | .... | .... | .... | .... | .... | .... |
| | Ohio | USHL | 9 | 0 | 4 | 4 | 8 | .... | .... | .... | .... | .... |
| 2008-09 | Boston College | H-East | 24 | 0 | 8 | 8 | 24 | .... | .... | .... | .... | .... |

**CROWDER, Paul** (KROW-duhr, PAWL) **NYR**

Center. Shoots right. 6'3", 202 lbs. Born, Victoria, B.C., February 12, 1985.

| | | | Regular Season | | | | | Playoffs | | | | |
|---|---|---|---|---|---|---|---|---|---|---|---|---|
| Season | Club | League | GP | G | A | Pts | PIM | GP | G | A | Pts | PIM |
| 2002-03 | Powell River Kings | BCHL | STATISTICS NOT AVAILABLE | | | | | | | | | |
| 2003-04 | Powell River Kings | BCHL | 58 | 19 | 39 | 58 | 57 | 7 | 1 | 3 | 4 | 2 |
| 2004-05 | South Surrey | BCHL | 20 | 2 | 9 | 11 | 20 | .... | .... | .... | .... | .... |
| | Coquitlam Express | BCHL | 27 | 12 | 25 | 37 | 32 | 1 | 0 | 0 | 0 | 0 |
| 2005-06 | Burnaby Express | BCHL | 14 | 3 | 10 | 13 | 13 | .... | .... | .... | .... | .... |
| 2006-07 | Alaska Anchorage | WCHA | 37 | 11 | 13 | 24 | 26 | .... | .... | .... | .... | .... |
| 2007-08 | Alaska-Anchorage | WCHA | 35 | 7 | 16 | 23 | 10 | .... | .... | .... | .... | .... |
| 2008-09 | Alaska-Anchorage | WCHA | 35 | 14 | 19 | 33 | 44 | .... | .... | .... | .... | .... |
| | Hartford Wolf Pack | AHL | 11 | 0 | 3 | 3 | 6 | 5 | 0 | 0 | 0 | 4 |

Signed as a free agent by **NY Rangers**, March 19, 2009.

**CROWDER, Tim** (KROW-duhr, TIHM) **PIT.**

Right wing. Shoots right. 6'2", 180 lbs. Born, Victoria, B.C., October 16, 1986.
(Pittsburgh's 5th choice, 126th overall, in 2005 Entry Draft).

| | | | Regular Season | | | | | Playoffs | | | | |
|---|---|---|---|---|---|---|---|---|---|---|---|---|
| Season | Club | League | GP | G | A | Pts | PIM | GP | G | A | Pts | PIM |
| 2002-03 | Powell River Kings | BCHL | 52 | 6 | 6 | 12 | .... | .... | .... | .... | .... | .... |
| 2003-04 | Powell River Kings | BCHL | 57 | 21 | 34 | 55 | 44 | 7 | 3 | 3 | 6 | 8 |
| 2004-05 | South Surrey | BCHL | 56 | 23 | 27 | 50 | 30 | .... | .... | .... | .... | .... |
| 2005-06 | Michigan State | CCHA | 44 | 17 | 13 | 30 | 29 | .... | .... | .... | .... | .... |
| 2006-07 | Michigan State | CCHA | 41 | 14 | 11 | 25 | 18 | .... | .... | .... | .... | .... |
| 2007-08 | Michigan State | CCHA | 42 | 15 | 23 | 38 | 36 | .... | .... | .... | .... | .... |
| 2008-09 | Michigan State | CCHA | 24 | 4 | 9 | 13 | 14 | .... | .... | .... | .... | .... |

**CUMA, Tyler** (KOO-ma, TIGH-luhr) **MIN.**

Defense. Shoots left. 6'2", 180 lbs. Born, Toronto, Ont., January 19, 1990.
(Minnesota's 1st choice, 23rd overall, in 2008 Entry Draft).

| | | | Regular Season | | | | | Playoffs | | | | |
|---|---|---|---|---|---|---|---|---|---|---|---|---|
| Season | Club | League | GP | G | A | Pts | PIM | GP | G | A | Pts | PIM |
| 2005-06 | Mississauga Reps | GTHL | 40 | 15 | 20 | 35 | 52 | .... | .... | .... | .... | .... |
| 2006-07 | Ottawa 67's | OHL | 63 | 3 | 16 | 19 | 55 | 5 | 0 | 2 | 2 | 6 |
| 2007-08 | Ottawa 67's | OHL | 59 | 4 | 28 | 32 | 69 | 4 | 1 | 1 | 2 | 2 |
| 2008-09 | Ottawa 67's | OHL | 21 | 1 | 8 | 9 | 27 | .... | .... | .... | .... | .... |

• Missed majority of 2008-09 season recovering from knee injury suffered at Team Canada (juniors) training camp, December 12, 2008.

**CUNDARI, Mark** (kuhn-DAHR-ee, MAHRK) **ST.L.**

Defense. Shoots left. 5'9", 199 lbs. Born, Woodbridge, Ont., April 23, 1990.

| | | | Regular Season | | | | | Playoffs | | | | |
|---|---|---|---|---|---|---|---|---|---|---|---|---|
| Season | Club | League | GP | G | A | Pts | PIM | GP | G | A | Pts | PIM |
| 2005-06 | Vaughan Vipers | OPJHL | 2 | 0 | 0 | 0 | 0 | .... | .... | .... | .... | .... |
| 2006-07 | Windsor Spitfires | OHL | 62 | 6 | 16 | 22 | 130 | .... | .... | .... | .... | .... |
| 2007-08 | Windsor Spitfires | OHL | 63 | 6 | 17 | 23 | 141 | 3 | 0 | 0 | 0 | 10 |
| 2008-09 | Windsor Spitfires | OHL | 60 | 10 | 22 | 32 | 143 | 20 | 1 | 8 | 9 | 38 |

Signed as a free agent by **St. Louis**, September 24, 2008.

**CUNNING, Cam** (KUH-nihng, KAM) **CGY.**

Left wing. Shoots left. 6', 197 lbs. Born, Powell River, B.C., June 4, 1985.
(Calgary's 8th choice, 240th overall, in 2003 Entry Draft).

| | | | Regular Season | | | | | Playoffs | | | | |
|---|---|---|---|---|---|---|---|---|---|---|---|---|
| Season | Club | League | GP | G | A | Pts | PIM | GP | G | A | Pts | PIM |
| 2002-03 | Kamloops Blazers | WHL | 71 | 7 | 12 | 19 | 54 | 6 | 1 | 0 | 1 | 2 |
| 2003-04 | Kamloops Blazers | WHL | 65 | 14 | 13 | 27 | 62 | 5 | 1 | 1 | 2 | 10 |
| 2004-05 | Kamloops Blazers | WHL | 39 | 14 | 8 | 22 | 63 | .... | .... | .... | .... | .... |
| | Vancouver Giants | WHL | 30 | 3 | 7 | 10 | 19 | 6 | 1 | 3 | 4 | 14 |
| 2005-06 | Red Deer Rebels | WHL | 40 | 19 | 13 | 32 | 52 | .... | .... | .... | .... | .... |
| | Omaha | AHL | 30 | 2 | 4 | 6 | 24 | .... | .... | .... | .... | .... |
| 2006-07 | Omaha | AHL | 60 | 12 | 5 | 17 | 45 | 6 | 0 | 2 | 2 | 2 |
| 2007-08 | Quad City Flames | AHL | 68 | 11 | 4 | 15 | 80 | .... | .... | .... | .... | .... |
| 2008-09 | Quad City Flames | AHL | 63 | 7 | 14 | 21 | 38 | .... | .... | .... | .... | .... |

**CUNTI, Luca** (KOON-tee, LOO-ka) **T.B.**

Center. Shoots left. 6', 190 lbs. Born, Zurich, Switz., July 4, 1989.
(Tampa Bay's 2nd choice, 75th overall, in 2007 Entry Draft).

| | | | Regular Season | | | | | Playoffs | | | | |
|---|---|---|---|---|---|---|---|---|---|---|---|---|
| Season | Club | League | GP | G | A | Pts | PIM | GP | G | A | Pts | PIM |
| 2004-05 | GCK Zurich Jr. | Swiss-Jr. | 32 | 12 | 10 | 22 | 18 | .... | .... | .... | .... | .... |
| 2005-06 | GCK Lions Zurich | Swiss-2 | 7 | 0 | 0 | 0 | 2 | .... | .... | .... | .... | .... |
| | GCK Zurich Jr. | Swiss-Jr. | 48 | 20 | 24 | 44 | 34 | .... | .... | .... | .... | .... |
| | EHC Dubendorf | Swiss-3 | 6 | 1 | 5 | 6 | 0 | 6 | 2 | 2 | 4 | 0 |
| 2006-07 | GCK Zurich Jr. | Swiss-Jr. | 13 | 9 | 7 | 16 | 22 | .... | .... | .... | .... | .... |
| | Switzerland U20 | Swiss-2 | 3 | 0 | 0 | 0 | 2 | .... | .... | .... | .... | .... |
| | HC Thurgau | Swiss-2 | 5 | 1 | 0 | 1 | 6 | .... | .... | .... | .... | .... |
| | GCK Lions Zurich | Swiss-2 | 5 | 1 | 1 | 2 | 0 | .... | .... | .... | .... | .... |
| | SC Weinfelden | Swiss-3 | 1 | 2 | 0 | 2 | 0 | .... | .... | .... | .... | .... |
| | EHC Dubendorf | Swiss-3 | 11 | 8 | 8 | 16 | 18 | 15 | 6 | 9 | 15 | 18 |
| 2007-08 | Chicago Steel | USHL | 34 | 11 | 21 | 32 | 37 | 6 | 2 | 3 | 5 | 2 |
| 2008-09 | Rimouski Oceanic | QMJHL | 57 | 20 | 25 | 45 | 32 | 13 | 4 | 5 | 9 | 12 |

**CURRY, Sean** (KUH-ree, SHAWN) **PHI.**

Defense. Shoots right. 6'4", 230 lbs. Born, Burnsville, MN, April 29, 1982.
(Carolina's 6th choice, 211th overall, in 2001 Entry Draft).

| | | | Regular Season | | | | | Playoffs | | | | |
|---|---|---|---|---|---|---|---|---|---|---|---|---|
| Season | Club | League | GP | G | A | Pts | PIM | GP | G | A | Pts | PIM |
| 99-2000 | Burnsville | High-MN | 23 | 8 | 18 | 26 | .... | .... | .... | .... | .... | .... |
| 2000-01 | Tri-City Americans | WHL | 72 | 5 | 12 | 17 | 113 | .... | .... | .... | .... | .... |
| 2001-02 | Tri-City Americans | WHL | 36 | 6 | 6 | 12 | 84 | .... | .... | .... | .... | .... |
| | Medicine Hat | WHL | 24 | 4 | 13 | 17 | 43 | .... | .... | .... | .... | .... |
| 2002-03 | Lowell | AHL | 35 | 0 | 2 | 2 | 62 | .... | .... | .... | .... | .... |
| | Florida Everblades | ECHL | 32 | 1 | 6 | 7 | 77 | 1 | 0 | 0 | 0 | 0 |
| 2003-04 | Lowell | AHL | 74 | 1 | 8 | 9 | 66 | .... | .... | .... | .... | .... |
| 2004-05 | Lowell | AHL | 61 | 2 | 7 | 9 | 103 | 7 | 0 | 1 | 1 | 4 |
| 2005-06 | Providence Bruins | AHL | 72 | 4 | 4 | 8 | 144 | 6 | 0 | 1 | 1 | 20 |
| 2006-07 | Providence Bruins | AHL | 64 | 5 | 8 | 13 | 122 | 13 | 2 | 9 | 11 | 28 |
| 2007-08 | Providence Bruins | AHL | 72 | 13 | 25 | 38 | 139 | 10 | 0 | 4 | 4 | 27 |
| 2008-09 | Philadelphia | AHL | 80 | 5 | 13 | 18 | 72 | 4 | 0 | 0 | 0 | 2 |

Signed as a free agent by **Boston**, August 8, 2007. Signed as a free agent by **Philadelphia**, July 1, 2008.

**CZARNIK, Robert** (CHAHR-nihk, RAW-buhrt) **L.A.**

Right wing. Shoots right. 6', 178 lbs. Born, Detroit, MI, January 25, 1990.
(Los Angeles' 4th choice, 63rd overall, in 2008 Entry Draft).

| | | | Regular Season | | | | | Playoffs | | | | |
|---|---|---|---|---|---|---|---|---|---|---|---|---|
| Season | Club | League | GP | G | A | Pts | PIM | GP | G | A | Pts | PIM |
| 2005-06 | Det. Honeybaked | MWEHL | .... | 53 | 78 | 131 | .... | .... | .... | .... | .... | .... |
| 2006-07 | USNTDP | U-17 | 19 | 10 | 2 | 12 | 22 | .... | .... | .... | .... | .... |
| | USNTDP | NAHL | 46 | 7 | 10 | 17 | 46 | .... | .... | .... | .... | .... |
| 2007-08 | USNTDP | U-18 | 43 | 15 | 18 | 33 | 30 | .... | .... | .... | .... | .... |
| | USNTDP | NAHL | 14 | 4 | 2 | 6 | 12 | .... | .... | .... | .... | .... |
| 2008-09 | U. of Michigan | CCHA | 39 | 5 | 11 | 16 | 32 | .... | .... | .... | .... | .... |

**DADONOV, Evgeni** (do-DON-nauv, ehv-GEH-nee) **FLA.**

Right wing. Shoots left. 5'10", 178 lbs. Born, Chelyabinsk, USSR, March 12, 1989.
(Florida's 3rd choice, 71st overall, in 2007 Entry Draft).

| | | | Regular Season | | | | | Playoffs | | | | |
|---|---|---|---|---|---|---|---|---|---|---|---|---|
| Season | Club | League | GP | G | A | Pts | PIM | GP | G | A | Pts | PIM |
| 2005-06 | Chelyabinsk 2 | Russia-3 | 12 | 1 | 4 | 5 | 2 | .... | .... | .... | .... | .... |
| | Chelyabinsk | Russia-2 | .... | .... | .... | .... | .... | 1 | 0 | 0 | 0 | 0 |
| 2006-07 | Chelyabinsk 2 | Russia-3 | 4 | 2 | 0 | 2 | 14 | .... | .... | .... | .... | .... |
| | Chelyabinsk | Russia | 24 | 1 | 1 | 2 | 8 | .... | .... | .... | .... | .... |
| 2007-08 | Chelyabinsk 2 | Russia-3 | 12 | 4 | 7 | 11 | 32 | .... | .... | .... | .... | .... |
| | Chelyabinsk | Russia | 43 | 7 | 13 | 20 | 20 | 2 | 0 | 0 | 0 | 0 |
| 2008-09 | Chelyabinsk | Rus-KHL | 40 | 11 | 4 | 15 | 8 | 3 | 0 | 0 | 0 | 2 |

**D'AGOSTINO, Nicholas** (DA-goh-STEE-noh, NIHK-oh-las) **PIT.**

Defense. Shoots left. 6'1", 177 lbs. Born, Mississauga, Ont., June 24, 1990.
(Pittsburgh's 4th choice, 210th overall, in 2008 Entry Draft).

| | | | Regular Season | | | | | Playoffs | | | | |
|---|---|---|---|---|---|---|---|---|---|---|---|---|
| Season | Club | League | GP | G | A | Pts | PIM | GP | G | A | Pts | PIM |
| 2006-07 | Tor. Young Nats | GTHL | 30 | 5 | 21 | 26 | .... | 5 | 0 | 4 | 4 | .... |
| | Young Nats | Exhib. | 8 | 1 | 5 | 6 | .... | .... | .... | .... | .... | .... |
| 2007-08 | St. Michael's | OPJHL | 46 | 5 | 18 | 23 | 22 | 12 | 0 | 3 | 3 | 8 |
| 2008-09 | St. Michael's | OJHL | 43 | 9 | 24 | 33 | 34 | 6 | 2 | 3 | 5 | 8 |

• Signed Letter of Intent to attend **Cornell University** (ECAC) in fall of 2009.

**DALPE, Zac** (DAL-pee, ZAK) **CAR.**

Right wing. Shoots right. 6'1", 195 lbs. Born, Paris, Ont., November 1, 1989.
(Carolina's 2nd choice, 45th overall, in 2008 Entry Draft).

| | | | Regular Season | | | | | Playoffs | | | | |
|---|---|---|---|---|---|---|---|---|---|---|---|---|
| Season | Club | League | GP | G | A | Pts | PIM | GP | G | A | Pts | PIM |
| 2006-07 | Stratford Cullitons | OJHL-B | 52 | 30 | 43 | 73 | 68 | .... | .... | .... | .... | .... |
| 2007-08 | Penticton Vees | BCHL | 46 | 27 | 36 | 63 | 14 | 15 | 8 | 9 | 17 | 4 |
| 2008-09 | Ohio State | CCHA | 37 | 13 | 12 | 25 | 25 | .... | .... | .... | .... | .... |

CCHA All-Rookie Team (2009)

**D'AMIGO, Jerry** (dah-MEE-goh, JAIR-ree) **TOR.**

Right wing. Shoots left. 5'11", 196 lbs. Born, Binghamton, NY, February 19, 1991.
(Toronto's 6th choice, 158th overall, in 2009 Entry Draft).

| | | | Regular Season | | | | | Playoffs | | | | |
|---|---|---|---|---|---|---|---|---|---|---|---|---|
| Season | Club | League | GP | G | A | Pts | PIM | GP | G | A | Pts | PIM |
| 2007-08 | USNTDP | NAHL | 44 | 5 | 12 | 17 | 59 | 3 | 1 | 1 | 2 | 6 |
| | USNTDP | U-17 | 17 | 5 | 4 | 9 | 10 | .... | .... | .... | .... | .... |
| 2008-09 | USNTDP | NAHL | 11 | 8 | 6 | 14 | 4 | .... | .... | .... | .... | .... |
| | USNTDP | U-18 | 42 | 15 | 27 | 42 | 57 | .... | .... | .... | .... | .... |

• Signed Letter of Intent to attend **R.P.I.** (ECAC) in fall of 2009.

**DANIELS, Drew** (DA-nyehlz, DROO) **S.J.**

Right wing. Shoots right. 6'1", 158 lbs. Born, Suffern, NY, June 7, 1989.
(San Jose's 7th choice, 194th overall, in 2008 Entry Draft).

| | | | Regular Season | | | | | Playoffs | | | | |
|---|---|---|---|---|---|---|---|---|---|---|---|---|
| Season | Club | League | GP | G | A | Pts | PIM | GP | G | A | Pts | PIM |
| 2006-07 | Kent Prep School | High-CT | .... | 12 | 22 | 34 | .... | .... | .... | .... | .... | .... |
| 2007-08 | Kent Prep School | High-CT | 25 | 12 | 35 | 47 | 14 | .... | .... | .... | .... | .... |
| 2008-09 | Sioux City | USHL | 53 | 9 | 19 | 28 | 24 | .... | .... | .... | .... | .... |

• Signed Letter of Intent to attend **Northeastern University** (Hockey East) in fall of 2009.

**DANIELS, Justin** (DA-nyehlz, JUHS-tihn) **S.J.**

Center. Shoots right. 6'1", 156 lbs. Born, Suffern, NY, June 7, 1989.
(San Jose's 1st choice, 62nd overall, in 2008 Entry Draft).

| | | | Regular Season | | | | | Playoffs | | | | |
|---|---|---|---|---|---|---|---|---|---|---|---|---|
| Season | Club | League | GP | G | A | Pts | PIM | GP | G | A | Pts | PIM |
| 2006-07 | Kent Prep School | High-CT | .... | 14 | 32 | 46 | .... | .... | .... | .... | .... | .... |
| 2007-08 | Kent Prep School | High-CT | 25 | 17 | 37 | 54 | 10 | .... | .... | .... | .... | .... |
| 2008-09 | Sioux City | USHL | 56 | 9 | 28 | 37 | 17 | .... | .... | .... | .... | .... |

• Signed Letter of Intent to attend **Northeastern University** (Hockey East) in fall of 2009.

**DANIS-PEPIN, Simon** (da-NEE-peh-PEHN, see-MOHN) **CHI.**

Defense. Shoots right. 6'7", 217 lbs. Born, Gatineau, Que., April 11, 1988.
(Chicago's 3rd choice, 61st overall, in 2006 Entry Draft).

| | | | Regular Season | | | | | Playoffs | | | | |
|---|---|---|---|---|---|---|---|---|---|---|---|---|
| Season | Club | League | GP | G | A | Pts | PIM | GP | G | A | Pts | PIM |
| 2003-04 | Gatineau Intrepide | QAAA | 33 | 2 | 14 | 16 | 20 | 2 | 0 | 0 | 0 | 0 |
| 2004-05 | Gatineau Intrepide | QAAA | 39 | 6 | 31 | 37 | 64 | 14 | 6 | 7 | 13 | 25 |
| 2005-06 | N.H. Jr. Monarchs | EJHL | 2 | 0 | 0 | 0 | 0 | .... | .... | .... | .... | .... |
| | U. of Maine | H-East | 23 | 0 | 5 | 5 | 14 | .... | .... | .... | .... | .... |
| 2006-07 | U. of Maine | H-East | 40 | 2 | 4 | 6 | 18 | .... | .... | .... | .... | .... |
| 2007-08 | U. of Maine | H-East | 34 | 4 | 8 | 12 | 20 | .... | .... | .... | .... | .... |
| 2008-09 | U. of Maine | H-East | 36 | 0 | 13 | 13 | 29 | .... | .... | .... | .... | .... |

**DASILVA, Dan** (duh-SIHL-vah, DAN) **PHX.**

Right wing. Shoots right. 6'1", 195 lbs. Born, Saskatoon, Sask., April 30, 1985.

| | | | Regular Season | | | | | Playoffs | | | | |
|---|---|---|---|---|---|---|---|---|---|---|---|---|
| Season | Club | League | GP | G | A | Pts | PIM | GP | G | A | Pts | PIM |
| 2002-03 | Portland | WHL | 64 | 9 | 13 | 22 | 81 | 7 | 0 | 4 | 4 | 16 |
| 2003-04 | Portland | WHL | 65 | 36 | 20 | 56 | 120 | 5 | 0 | 1 | 1 | 6 |
| 2004-05 | Portland | WHL | 71 | 31 | 42 | 73 | 127 | 5 | 1 | 1 | 2 | 6 |
| 2005-06 | Lowell | AHL | 25 | 3 | 2 | 5 | 27 | .... | .... | .... | .... | .... |
| | San Diego Gulls | ECHL | 4 | 5 | 3 | 8 | 2 | .... | .... | .... | .... | .... |
| 2006-07 | Albany River Rats | AHL | 43 | 11 | 8 | 19 | 33 | .... | .... | .... | .... | .... |
| | Arizona Sundogs | CHL | 14 | 9 | 13 | 22 | 10 | .... | .... | .... | .... | .... |
| 2007-08 | Lake Erie Monsters | AHL | 54 | 9 | 14 | 23 | 50 | .... | .... | .... | .... | .... |
| 2008-09 | Worcester Sharks | AHL | 26 | 6 | 7 | 13 | 27 | 12 | 3 | 7 | 10 | 6 |
| | Phoenix | ECHL | 36 | 9 | 12 | 21 | 40 | .... | .... | .... | .... | .... |

Signed as a free agent by **Colorado**, October 11, 2005.

**DAUGAVINS, Kaspars** (DAH-gah-vihnsh, KAS-purz) **OTT.**

Left wing. Shoots left. 5'11", 204 lbs. Born, Riga, Latvia, May 18, 1988.
(Ottawa's 3rd choice, 91st overall, in 2006 Entry Draft).

| | | | Regular Season | | | | | Playoffs | | | | |
|---|---|---|---|---|---|---|---|---|---|---|---|---|
| Season | Club | League | GP | G | A | Pts | PIM | GP | G | A | Pts | PIM |
| 2003-04 | HK Riga 2000 | EEHL | 2 | 0 | 1 | 1 | 0 | .... | .... | .... | .... | .... |
| | Prizma/Riga 86 | Latvia | 14 | 6 | 6 | 12 | 10 | 2 | 1 | 1 | 2 | 4 |
| 2004-05 | CSKA Moscow 2 | Russia-3 | STATISTICS NOT AVAILABLE | | | | | | | | | |
| 2005-06 | HK Riga 2000 | Latvia | .... | 4 | 6 | 10 | 16 | .... | .... | .... | .... | .... |
| | HK Riga 2000 | BelOpen | 45 | 4 | 11 | 15 | 16 | .... | .... | .... | .... | .... |
| 2006-07 | St. Michael's | OHL | 61 | 18 | 42 | 60 | 64 | .... | .... | .... | .... | .... |
| | Binghamton | AHL | 11 | 2 | 0 | 2 | 9 | .... | .... | .... | .... | .... |
| 2007-08 | St. Michael's | OHL | 62 | 40 | 34 | 74 | 42 | 4 | 2 | 1 | 3 | 4 |
| | Binghamton | AHL | 3 | 0 | 1 | 1 | 0 | .... | .... | .... | .... | .... |
| 2008-09 | Binghamton | AHL | 23 | 2 | 1 | 3 | 9 | .... | .... | .... | .... | .... |
| | St. Michael's | OHL | 30 | 11 | 17 | 28 | 35 | 11 | 2 | 7 | 9 | 14 |

OHL All-Rookie Team (2007)

**D'AVERSA, Jonathan** (dah-VEHR-sah, JAWN-ah-thuhn) **PIT.**

Defense. Shoots right. 6'2", 200 lbs. Born, Richmond Hill, Ont., March 2, 1986.

| | | | Regular Season | | | | | Playoffs | | | | |
|---|---|---|---|---|---|---|---|---|---|---|---|---|
| Season | Club | League | GP | G | A | Pts | PIM | GP | G | A | Pts | PIM |
| 2002-03 | Stouffville Spirit | OPJHL | 49 | 4 | 21 | 25 | 18 | .... | .... | .... | .... | .... |
| 2003-04 | Sudbury Wolves | OHL | 63 | 1 | 14 | 15 | 22 | 7 | 0 | 1 | 1 | 2 |
| 2004-05 | Sudbury Wolves | OHL | 67 | 5 | 24 | 29 | 42 | 12 | 4 | 6 | 10 | 8 |
| 2005-06 | Sudbury Wolves | OHL | 62 | 7 | 39 | 46 | 83 | 10 | 2 | 0 | 2 | 17 |
| 2006-07 | Sudbury Wolves | OHL | 67 | 13 | 47 | 60 | 53 | 21 | 3 | 15 | 18 | 16 |
| 2007-08 | Wilkes-Barre | AHL | 27 | 4 | 2 | 6 | 6 | .... | .... | .... | .... | .... |
| | Wheeling Nailers | ECHL | 25 | 1 | 13 | 14 | 10 | .... | .... | .... | .... | .... |
| 2008-09 | Wilkes-Barre | AHL | 68 | 1 | 22 | 23 | 36 | 11 | 0 | 2 | 2 | 4 |
| | Wheeling Nailers | ECHL | 3 | 1 | 3 | 4 | 2 | .... | .... | .... | .... | .... |

Signed as a free agent by **Pittsburgh**, May 24, 2007.

**DAVIS, Nathan** (DAY-vihs, NAY-thuhn) **CHI.**

Center/Left wing. Shoots left. 6'1", 193 lbs. Born, Cleveland, OH, May 23, 1986.
(Chicago's 6th choice, 113th overall, in 2005 Entry Draft).

| | | | Regular Season | | | | | Playoffs | | | | |
|---|---|---|---|---|---|---|---|---|---|---|---|---|
| Season | Club | League | GP | G | A | Pts | PIM | GP | G | A | Pts | PIM |
| 2002-03 | USNTDP | NAHL | 20 | 2 | 3 | 5 | 23 | .... | .... | .... | .... | .... |
| 2003-04 | USNTDP | U-18 | 46 | 7 | 8 | 15 | 16 | .... | .... | .... | .... | .... |
| | USNTDP | NAHL | 11 | 3 | 6 | 9 | 17 | .... | .... | .... | .... | .... |
| 2004-05 | Miami U. | CCHA | 38 | 14 | 11 | 25 | 30 | .... | .... | .... | .... | .... |
| 2005-06 | Miami U. | CCHA | 37 | 20 | 20 | 40 | 34 | .... | .... | .... | .... | .... |
| 2006-07 | Miami U. | CCHA | 42 | 21 | 29 | 50 | 24 | .... | .... | .... | .... | .... |
| 2007-08 | Miami U. | CCHA | 21 | 8 | 9 | 17 | 14 | .... | .... | .... | .... | .... |
| 2008-09 | Rockford IceHogs | AHL | 49 | 5 | 7 | 12 | 16 | .... | .... | .... | .... | .... |

CCHA First All-Star Team (2006) • CCHA Second All-Star Team (2007) • NCAA West Second All-American Team (2007)

**DAY, Brian** (DAY, BRIGH-uhn) **NYI**

Right wing. Shoots right. 6', 186 lbs. Born, Boston, MA, August 4, 1988.
(NY Islanders' 11th choice, 171st overall, in 2006 Entry Draft).

| | | | Regular Season | | | | | Playoffs | | | | |
|---|---|---|---|---|---|---|---|---|---|---|---|---|
| Season | Club | League | GP | G | A | Pts | PIM | GP | G | A | Pts | PIM |
| 2003-04 | Gov. Dummer | High-MA | 25 | 8 | 15 | 23 | .... | .... | .... | .... | .... | .... |
| 2004-05 | Gov. Dummer | High-MA | 25 | 11 | 13 | 24 | 30 | .... | .... | .... | .... | .... |
| 2005-06 | Gov. Dummer | High-MA | 28 | 9 | 13 | 22 | 34 | .... | .... | .... | .... | .... |
| 2006-07 | Gov. Academy | High-MA | 27 | 20 | 18 | 38 | .... | .... | .... | .... | .... | .... |
| 2007-08 | Colgate | ECAC | 41 | 9 | 13 | 22 | 53 | .... | .... | .... | .... | .... |
| 2008-09 | Colgate | ECAC | 34 | 14 | 13 | 27 | 26 | .... | .... | .... | .... | .... |

**De COSTE, Kyle** (duh KAWS-tuh, KIGH-uhl) **T.B.**

Right wing. Shoots right. 6'1", 178 lbs. Born, London, Ont., June 30, 1990.
(Tampa Bay's 4th choice, 147th overall, in 2008 Entry Draft).

| | | | Regular Season | | | | | Playoffs | | | | |
|---|---|---|---|---|---|---|---|---|---|---|---|---|
| Season | Club | League | GP | G | A | Pts | PIM | GP | G | A | Pts | PIM |
| 2005-06 | Elgin | Minor-ON | 58 | 20 | 18 | 38 | 40 | .... | .... | .... | .... | .... |
| 2006-07 | Brampton | OHL | 45 | 1 | 3 | 4 | 29 | 3 | 1 | 0 | 1 | 0 |
| 2007-08 | Brampton | OHL | 66 | 10 | 12 | 22 | 48 | 5 | 0 | 0 | 0 | 2 |
| 2008-09 | Brampton | OHL | 37 | 8 | 6 | 14 | 51 | .... | .... | .... | .... | .... |
| | Sault Ste. Marie | OHL | 26 | 7 | 7 | 14 | 25 | .... | .... | .... | .... | .... |

**DE HAAN, Calvin** (DUH HAWN, CAL-vihn) **NYI**

Defense. Shoots left. 6', 170 lbs. Born, Ottawa, Ont., May 9, 1991.
(NY Islanders' 2nd choice, 12th overall, in 2009 Entry Draft).

| | | | Regular Season | | | | | Playoffs | | | | |
|---|---|---|---|---|---|---|---|---|---|---|---|---|
| Season | Club | League | GP | G | A | Pts | PIM | GP | G | A | Pts | PIM |
| 2006-07 | Ottawa Valley | Minor-ON | 32 | 4 | 22 | 26 | 20 | .... | .... | .... | .... | .... |
| 2007-08 | Kemptville 73's | CJHL | 58 | 3 | 39 | 42 | 14 | .... | .... | .... | .... | .... |
| 2008-09 | Oshawa Generals | OHL | 68 | 8 | 55 | 63 | 40 | .... | .... | .... | .... | .... |

**DEE, Robby** (DEE, RAW-bee) **EDM.**

Center/Wing. Shoots left. 6'2", 185 lbs. Born, Minneapolis, MN, April 9, 1987.
(Edmonton's 4th choice, 86th overall, in 2005 Entry Draft).

| | | | Regular Season | | | | | Playoffs | | | | |
|---|---|---|---|---|---|---|---|---|---|---|---|---|
| Season | Club | League | GP | G | A | Pts | PIM | GP | G | A | Pts | PIM |
| 2004-05 | Breck Mustangs | High-MN | 28 | 49 | 38 | 87 | 14 | .... | .... | .... | .... | .... |
| 2005-06 | Omaha Lancers | USHL | 32 | 6 | 6 | 12 | 20 | 3 | 1 | 0 | 1 | 2 |
| 2006-07 | Omaha Lancers | USHL | 34 | 11 | 14 | 25 | 60 | .... | .... | .... | .... | .... |
| 2007-08 | U. of Maine | H-East | 24 | 1 | 2 | 3 | 18 | .... | .... | .... | .... | .... |
| 2008-09 | U. of Maine | H-East | 33 | 6 | 5 | 11 | 24 | .... | .... | .... | .... | .... |

**DEGON, Marvin** (DEE-gawn, MAR-vihn) **MTL.**

Defense. Shoots right. 5'11", 190 lbs. Born, Worcester, MA, July 20, 1983.

| | | | Regular Season | | | | | Playoffs | | | | |
|---|---|---|---|---|---|---|---|---|---|---|---|---|
| Season | Club | League | GP | G | A | Pts | PIM | GP | G | A | Pts | PIM |
| 2002-03 | Massachusetts | H-East | 36 | 2 | 14 | 16 | 14 | .... | .... | .... | .... | .... |
| 2003-04 | Massachusetts | H-East | 36 | 5 | 15 | 20 | 18 | .... | .... | .... | .... | .... |
| 2004-05 | Massachusetts | H-East | 38 | 10 | 8 | 18 | 44 | .... | .... | .... | .... | .... |
| 2005-06 | Massachusetts | H-East | 36 | 10 | 19 | 29 | 33 | .... | .... | .... | .... | .... |
| | Hartford Wolf Pack | AHL | 14 | 2 | 4 | 6 | 4 | 13 | 0 | 5 | 5 | 6 |
| 2006-07 | Hartford Wolf Pack | AHL | 71 | 8 | 26 | 34 | 40 | 7 | 0 | 1 | 1 | 0 |
| 2007-08 | Hamilton Bulldogs | AHL | 79 | 9 | 22 | 31 | 56 | .... | .... | .... | .... | .... |
| 2008-09 | Wolfsburg | Germany | 52 | 11 | 29 | 40 | 42 | 10 | 3 | 2 | 5 | 8 |

Signed as a free agent by **Montreal**, July 5, 2007.

**DEGRAY, John** (DIH-gray, JAWN) **ANA.**

Defense. Shoots left. 6'4", 216 lbs. Born, Richmond Hill, Ont., March 14, 1988.
(Anaheim's 3rd choice, 83rd overall, in 2006 Entry Draft).

| | | | Regular Season | | | | | Playoffs | | | | |
|---|---|---|---|---|---|---|---|---|---|---|---|---|
| Season | Club | League | GP | G | A | Pts | PIM | GP | G | A | Pts | PIM |
| 2003-04 | Richmond Hill | Minor-ON | 76 | 5 | 35 | 40 | 107 | .... | .... | .... | .... | .... |
| 2004-05 | Brampton | OHL | 52 | 2 | 8 | 10 | 51 | 6 | 0 | 0 | 0 | 2 |
| 2005-06 | Brampton | OHL | 68 | 0 | 10 | 10 | 103 | 11 | 0 | 0 | 0 | 8 |
| 2006-07 | Brampton | OHL | 65 | 4 | 13 | 17 | 75 | 4 | 1 | 0 | 1 | 10 |
| 2007-08 | Brampton | OHL | 67 | 4 | 13 | 17 | 140 | 5 | 0 | 0 | 0 | 12 |
| | Portland Pirates | AHL | 6 | 0 | 0 | 0 | 0 | 3 | 0 | 0 | 0 | 0 |
| 2008-09 | Iowa Chops | AHL | 62 | 2 | 5 | 7 | 67 | .... | .... | .... | .... | .... |

**DEILERT, Alexander** (DAY-luhrt, al-ehx-AN-duhr) **CGY.**

Defense. Shoots right. 5'11", 180 lbs. Born, Stockholm, Sweden, February 10, 1989.
(Calgary's 7th choice, 198th overall, in 2008 Entry Draft).

| | | | Regular Season | | | | | Playoffs | | | | |
|---|---|---|---|---|---|---|---|---|---|---|---|---|
| Season | Club | League | GP | G | A | Pts | PIM | GP | G | A | Pts | PIM |
| 2004-05 | Hammarby U18 | Swe-U18 | 2 | 2 | 1 | 3 | .... | .... | .... | .... | .... | .... |
| 2005-06 | Djurgarden U18 | Swe-U18 | 24 | 6 | 8 | 14 | 41 | 4 | 0 | 0 | 0 | 4 |
| 2006-07 | Djurgarden U18 | Swe-U18 | 11 | 2 | 2 | 4 | 41 | 2 | 0 | 1 | 1 | 6 |
| | Djurgarden Jr. | Swe-Jr. | 28 | 1 | 4 | 5 | 10 | 7 | 0 | 0 | 0 | 0 |
| 2007-08 | Djurgarden Jr. | Swe-Jr. | 38 | 6 | 12 | 18 | 70 | 7 | 1 | 2 | 3 | 14 |
| 2008-09 | Djurgarden Jr. | Swe-Jr. | 19 | 4 | 7 | 11 | 45 | .... | .... | .... | .... | .... |
| | Almtuna | Sweden-2 | 6 | 0 | 1 | 1 | 2 | .... | .... | .... | .... | .... |
| | Djurgarden | Sweden | 6 | 0 | 0 | 0 | 0 | .... | .... | .... | .... | .... |
| | Frisk | Norway | 4 | 0 | 1 | 1 | 0 | .... | .... | .... | .... | .... |

**DEL ZOTTO, Michael** (DEHL ZAW-toh, MIGH-kuhl) **NYR**

Defense. Shoots left. 6'1", 200 lbs. Born, Stouffville, Ont., June 24, 1990.
(NY Rangers' 1st choice, 20th overall, in 2008 Entry Draft).

| | | | Regular Season | | | | | Playoffs | | | | |
|---|---|---|---|---|---|---|---|---|---|---|---|---|
| Season | Club | League | GP | G | A | Pts | PIM | GP | G | A | Pts | PIM |
| 2005-06 | Markham Waxers | Minor-ON | 73 | 30 | 90 | 120 | 90 | .... | .... | .... | .... | .... |
| 2006-07 | Oshawa Generals | OHL | 64 | 10 | 47 | 57 | 78 | 9 | 3 | 9 | 12 | 14 |
| 2007-08 | Oshawa Generals | OHL | 64 | 16 | 47 | 63 | 82 | 15 | 2 | 6 | 8 | 38 |
| 2008-09 | Oshawa Generals | OHL | 34 | 7 | 26 | 33 | 48 | .... | .... | .... | .... | .... |
| | London Knights | OHL | 28 | 6 | 24 | 30 | 30 | 14 | 3 | 16 | 19 | 18 |

**DELAHEY, Matt** (dehl-A-hay, MAT) **N.J.**

Defense. Shoots left. 6'2", 205 lbs. Born, Moose Jaw, Sask., September 25, 1989.
(New Jersey's 5th choice, 112th overall, in 2008 Entry Draft).

| | | | Regular Season | | | | | Playoffs | | | | |
|---|---|---|---|---|---|---|---|---|---|---|---|---|
| Season | Club | League | GP | G | A | Pts | PIM | GP | G | A | Pts | PIM |
| 2004-05 | Moose Jaw | SMHL | STATISTICS NOT AVAILABLE | | | | | | | | | |
| | Regina Pats | WHL | 1 | 0 | 0 | 0 | 0 | .... | .... | .... | .... | .... |
| 2005-06 | Moose Jaw | SMHL | STATISTICS NOT AVAILABLE | | | | | | | | | |
| | Regina Pats | WHL | 3 | 0 | 0 | 0 | 2 | 1 | 0 | 0 | 0 | 0 |
| 2006-07 | Regina Pats | WHL | 60 | 1 | 5 | 6 | 42 | 10 | 0 | 0 | 0 | 4 |
| 2007-08 | Regina Pats | WHL | 68 | 3 | 16 | 19 | 68 | 6 | 0 | 3 | 3 | 6 |
| 2008-09 | Regina Pats | WHL | 57 | 6 | 22 | 28 | 93 | .... | .... | .... | .... | .... |

**DELISLE, Daniel** (deh-LIGH-uhl, DAN-yehl) **CHI.**

Center/Left wing. Shoots left. 6'4", 222 lbs. Born, Minneapolis, MN, September 24, 1990.
(Chicago's 3rd choice, 89th overall, in 2009 Entry Draft).

| | | | Regular Season | | | | | Playoffs | | | | |
|---|---|---|---|---|---|---|---|---|---|---|---|---|
| Season | Club | League | GP | G | A | Pts | PIM | GP | G | A | Pts | PIM |
| 2006-07 | Totino-Grace | High-MN | .... | 21 | 26 | 47 | .... | .... | .... | .... | .... | .... |
| 2007-08 | Totino-Grace | High-MN | 27 | 25 | 31 | 56 | 26 | .... | .... | .... | .... | .... |
| 2008-09 | Totino-Grace | High-MN | 27 | 32 | 24 | 56 | 16 | .... | .... | .... | .... | .... |
| | Team Northeast | UMHSEL | 24 | 12 | 11 | 23 | .... | .... | .... | .... | .... | .... |

• Signed Letter of Intent to attend **University of Minnesota-Duluth** (WCHA) in fall of 2009.

**DELISLE, Steven** (deh-LIH-uhl, STEE-vehn) **CBJ**

Defense. Shoots right. 6'6", 209 lbs. Born, Levise, Que., July 30, 1990.
(Columbus' 3rd choice, 107th overall, in 2008 Entry Draft).

| | | | Regular Season | | | | | Playoffs | | | | |
|---|---|---|---|---|---|---|---|---|---|---|---|---|
| Season | Club | League | GP | G | A | Pts | PIM | GP | G | A | Pts | PIM |
| 2006-07 | Gatineau | QMJHL | 56 | 1 | 11 | 12 | 47 | 5 | 0 | 0 | 0 | 0 |
| 2007-08 | Gatineau | QMJHL | 70 | 6 | 23 | 29 | 82 | 19 | 0 | 10 | 10 | 16 |
| 2008-09 | Gatineau | QMJHL | 63 | 5 | 25 | 30 | 94 | 10 | 2 | 3 | 5 | 15 |

**DELLA ROVERE, Stefan** (DEHL-ah ROH-vair, STEH-fan) **WSH.**

Left wing. Shoots left. 5'11", 196 lbs. Born, Richmond Hill, Ont., February 25, 1990.
(Washington's 8th choice, 204th overall, in 2008 Entry Draft).

| | | | Regular Season | | | | | Playoffs | | | | |
|---|---|---|---|---|---|---|---|---|---|---|---|---|
| Season | Club | League | GP | G | A | Pts | PIM | GP | G | A | Pts | PIM |
| 2005-06 | Tor. Jr. Canadiens | GTHL | 47 | 25 | 31 | 56 | 69 | .... | .... | .... | .... | .... |
| 2006-07 | Barrie Colts | OHL | 48 | 7 | 7 | 14 | 37 | 6 | 0 | 0 | 0 | 0 |
| 2007-08 | Barrie Colts | OHL | 68 | 13 | 19 | 32 | 171 | 9 | 1 | 2 | 3 | 16 |
| 2008-09 | Barrie Colts | OHL | 57 | 27 | 24 | 51 | 146 | 5 | 2 | 2 | 4 | 19 |
| | South Carolina | ECHL | 2 | 0 | 1 | 1 | 6 | .... | .... | .... | .... | .... |

**DELORY, James** (deh-LOR-ee, JAYMZ) **FLA.**

Defense. Shoots right. 6'4", 220 lbs. Born, Scarborough, Ont., March 3, 1988.
(San Jose's 3rd choice, 98th overall, in 2006 Entry Draft).

| | | | Regular Season | | | | | Playoffs | | | | |
|---|---|---|---|---|---|---|---|---|---|---|---|---|
| Season | Club | League | GP | G | A | Pts | PIM | GP | G | A | Pts | PIM |
| 2004-05 | Oshawa Generals | OHL | 61 | 1 | 4 | 5 | 82 | .... | .... | .... | .... | .... |
| 2005-06 | Oshawa Generals | OHL | 67 | 6 | 26 | 32 | 136 | .... | .... | .... | .... | .... |
| 2006-07 | Oshawa Generals | OHL | 61 | 4 | 21 | 25 | 167 | 9 | 0 | 4 | 4 | 16 |
| 2007-08 | Oshawa Generals | OHL | 54 | 2 | 20 | 22 | 154 | 15 | 1 | 8 | 9 | 26 |
| 2008-09 | Oshawa Generals | OHL | 33 | 4 | 6 | 10 | 53 | .... | .... | .... | .... | .... |
| | Florida Everblades | ECHL | 1 | 0 | 0 | 0 | 0 | .... | .... | .... | .... | .... |

Signed as a free agent by **Florida**, July 3, 2008.

**DEMEN-WILLAUME, Richard** (deh-MEHN-WIHL-awm, RIH-kahrd) **COL.**

Defense. Shoots left. 6'3", 210 lbs. Born, Asa, Sweden, January 28, 1986.
(Colorado's 4th choice, 154th overall, in 2004 Entry Draft).

| | | | Regular Season | | | | | Playoffs | | | | |
|---|---|---|---|---|---|---|---|---|---|---|---|---|
| Season | Club | League | GP | G | A | Pts | PIM | GP | G | A | Pts | PIM |
| 2001-02 | V.Frolunda U18 | Swe-U18 | 13 | 2 | 2 | 4 | 14 | 3 | 1 | 0 | 1 | 2 |
| | V.Frolunda Jr. | Swe-Jr. | 1 | 0 | 0 | 0 | 0 | .... | .... | .... | .... | .... |
| 2002-03 | V.Frolunda Jr. | Swe-Jr. | 22 | 0 | 6 | 6 | 14 | 5 | 0 | 1 | 1 | 6 |
| | V.Frolunda U18 | Swe-U18 | 1 | 0 | 0 | 0 | 2 | 7 | 1 | 2 | 3 | 4 |
| 2003-04 | V.Frolunda Jr. | Swe-Jr. | 35 | 6 | 7 | 13 | 22 | .... | .... | .... | .... | .... |
| 2004-05 | Frolunda | Sweden | 9 | 0 | 0 | 0 | 0 | 1 | 0 | 0 | 0 | 0 |
| | Frolunda Jr. | Swe-Jr. | 32 | 3 | 12 | 15 | 63 | 6 | 1 | 1 | 2 | 22 |
| 2005-06 | Frolunda Jr. | Swe-Jr. | 10 | 4 | 8 | 12 | 8 | 6 | 3 | 5 | 8 | 31 |
| | Frolunda | Sweden | 42 | 2 | 1 | 3 | 26 | .... | .... | .... | .... | .... |
| 2006-07 | Arizona Sundogs | CHL | 9 | 0 | 2 | 2 | 16 | .... | .... | .... | .... | .... |
| 2007-08 | Rogle | Sweden-2 | 52 | 10 | 10 | 20 | 50 | .... | .... | .... | .... | .... |
| 2008-09 | Rogle | Sweden | 24 | 5 | 7 | 12 | 32 | .... | .... | .... | .... | .... |
| | Rogle | Sweden-Q | 4 | 0 | 0 | 0 | 2 | .... | .... | .... | .... | .... |

**DEMERS, Jason** (duh-MAIRZ, JAY-suhn) **S.J.**

Defense. Shoots right. 6'1", 195 lbs. Born, Dorval, Que., June 9, 1988.
(San Jose's 6th choice, 186th overall, in 2008 Entry Draft).

| | | | Regular Season | | | | | Playoffs | | | | |
|---|---|---|---|---|---|---|---|---|---|---|---|---|
| Season | Club | League | GP | G | A | Pts | PIM | GP | G | A | Pts | PIM |
| 2004-05 | Moncton Wildcats | QMJHL | 25 | 0 | 1 | 1 | 10 | .... | .... | .... | .... | .... |
| 2005-06 | Moncton Wildcats | QMJHL | 21 | 1 | 3 | 4 | 15 | .... | .... | .... | .... | .... |
| | Victoriaville Tigres | QMJHL | 33 | 2 | 13 | 15 | 58 | 5 | 0 | 2 | 2 | 10 |
| 2006-07 | Victoriaville Tigres | QMJHL | 69 | 5 | 19 | 24 | 98 | 6 | 0 | 0 | 0 | 2 |
| 2007-08 | Victoriaville Tigres | QMJHL | 67 | 9 | 55 | 64 | 91 | 6 | 1 | 5 | 6 | 6 |
| 2008-09 | Worcester Sharks | AHL | 78 | 2 | 31 | 33 | 54 | 12 | 0 | 4 | 4 | 6 |

### DEMERS, Julien (duh-MAIRZ, JOO-lee-ehn) S.J.

Defense. Shoots left. 6', 218 lbs. Born, Ottawa, Ont., September 25, 1989.
(San Jose's 4th choice, 146th overall, in 2008 Entry Draft).

| | | | Regular Season | | | | | Playoffs | | | | |
|---|---|---|---|---|---|---|---|---|---|---|---|---|
| Season | Club | League | GP | G | A | Pts | PIM | GP | G | A | Pts | PIM |
| 2006-07 | Nepean Raiders | CJHL | 35 | 7 | 24 | 31 | 38 | .... | .... | .... | .... | .... |
| | Ottawa 67's | OHL | 31 | 2 | 4 | 6 | 29 | 5 | 0 | 0 | 0 | 6 |
| 2007-08 | Ottawa 67's | OHL | 65 | 5 | 28 | 33 | 94 | 4 | 0 | 2 | 2 | 0 |
| 2008-09 | Ottawa 67's | OHL | 61 | 7 | 35 | 42 | 60 | 7 | 0 | 11 | 11 | 2 |

### DENISOV, Denis (den-NEES-ahf, deh-NEES) BUF.

Left wing. Shoots left. 6', 183 lbs. Born, Kalinin, USSR, December 31, 1981.
(Buffalo's 4th choice, 149th overall, in 2000 Entry Draft).

| | | | Regular Season | | | | | Playoffs | | | | |
|---|---|---|---|---|---|---|---|---|---|---|---|---|
| Season | Club | League | GP | G | A | Pts | PIM | GP | G | A | Pts | PIM |
| 1997-98 | HK CSKA Moscow | Russia | 7 | 0 | 0 | 0 | 4 | .... | .... | .... | .... | .... |
| 1998-99 | HK CSKA Moscow | Russia-2 | 42 | 1 | 6 | 7 | 16 | .... | .... | .... | .... | .... |
| 99-2000 | HK Moscow | Russia-2 | 39 | 1 | 8 | 9 | 16 | .... | .... | .... | .... | .... |
| 2000-01 | HK Moscow | Russia-2 | 41 | 0 | 3 | 3 | 6 | .... | .... | .... | .... | .... |
| 2001-02 | Krylja Sovetov | Russia | 47 | 3 | 4 | 7 | 37 | .... | .... | .... | .... | .... |
| | Krylja Sovetov 2 | Russia-3 | 3 | 0 | 1 | 1 | 18 | .... | .... | .... | .... | .... |
| 2002-03 | Ufa | Russia | 50 | 2 | 8 | 10 | 12 | 3 | 0 | 1 | 1 | 0 |
| 2003-04 | Ak Bars Kazan | Russia | 51 | 4 | 11 | 15 | 34 | 7 | 0 | 0 | 0 | 4 |
| 2004-05 | Ak Bars Kazan | Russia | 57 | 4 | 7 | 11 | 30 | 4 | 0 | 0 | 0 | 2 |
| 2005-06 | Ak Bars Kazan | Russia | 22 | 0 | 2 | 2 | 51 | 2 | 0 | 0 | 0 | 4 |
| 2006-07 | Avangard Omsk | Russia | 52 | 2 | 10 | 12 | 32 | 9 | 1 | 2 | 3 | 4 |
| 2007-08 | Avangard Omsk | Russia | 51 | 7 | 12 | 19 | 34 | 4 | 0 | 2 | 2 | 4 |
| 2008-09 | Dynamo Moscow | Rus-KHL | 56 | 7 | 15 | 22 | 95 | 10 | 2 | 2 | 4 | 10 |

### DENISOV, Vladimir (den-NEES-ahf)

Defense. Shoots left. 5'11", 207 lbs. Born, Novopolotzk, USSR, June 29, 1984.

| | | | Regular Season | | | | | Playoffs | | | | |
|---|---|---|---|---|---|---|---|---|---|---|---|---|
| Season | Club | League | GP | G | A | Pts | PIM | GP | G | A | Pts | PIM |
| 2003-04 | Yunior Minsk | Belarus | 1 | 0 | 0 | 0 | 2 | .... | .... | .... | .... | .... |
| | Novopolotsk | Belarus | 41 | 3 | 8 | 11 | 107 | 2 | 0 | 0 | 0 | 8 |
| 2004-05 | Dynamo Minsk | Belarus | 1 | 0 | 0 | 0 | 0 | .... | .... | .... | .... | .... |
| | Keramin Minsk 2 | Bel-2 | 9 | 3 | 2 | 5 | 20 | .... | .... | .... | .... | .... |
| | Keramin Minsk | Belarus | 12 | 0 | 1 | 1 | 12 | 4 | 0 | 0 | 0 | 0 |
| 2005-06 | Keramin Minsk 2 | Belarus-2 | 1 | 0 | 1 | 1 | 0 | .... | .... | .... | .... | .... |
| | Keramin Minsk | Belarus | 39 | 1 | 3 | 4 | 71 | .... | .... | .... | .... | .... |
| 2006-07 | Lada Togliatti | Russia | 39 | 0 | 3 | 3 | 76 | 3 | 0 | 0 | 0 | 6 |
| 2007-08 | Lake Erie Monsters | AHL | 66 | 2 | 6 | 8 | 111 | .... | .... | .... | .... | .... |
| | Johnstown Chiefs | ECHL | 5 | 0 | 2 | 2 | 26 | .... | .... | .... | .... | .... |
| 2008-09 | Hartford Wolf Pack | AHL | 62 | 5 | 15 | 20 | 117 | 2 | 0 | 0 | 0 | 2 |

Signed as a free agent by **NY Rangers**, July 10, 2008.

### DENNY, Chad (DEHN-ee, CHAD) ATL.

Defense. Shoots left. 6'3", 225 lbs. Born, Sydney, N.S., March 27, 1987.
(Atlanta's 3rd choice, 49th overall, in 2005 Entry Draft).

| | | | Regular Season | | | | | Playoffs | | | | |
|---|---|---|---|---|---|---|---|---|---|---|---|---|
| Season | Club | League | GP | G | A | Pts | PIM | GP | G | A | Pts | PIM |
| 2003-04 | Lewiston | QMJHL | 41 | 3 | 6 | 9 | 19 | 7 | 0 | 0 | 0 | 11 |
| 2004-05 | Lewiston | QMJHL | 53 | 8 | 18 | 26 | 98 | 8 | 2 | 2 | 4 | 14 |
| 2005-06 | Lewiston | QMJHL | 62 | 19 | 28 | 47 | 150 | 6 | 0 | 3 | 3 | 10 |
| 2006-07 | Lewiston | QMJHL | 59 | 17 | 48 | 65 | 89 | 17 | 10 | 9 | 19 | 32 |
| 2007-08 | Chicago Wolves | AHL | 11 | 2 | 4 | 6 | 19 | .... | .... | .... | .... | .... |
| | Gwinnett | ECHL | 48 | 7 | 6 | 13 | 48 | 8 | 0 | 0 | 0 | 12 |
| 2008-09 | Chicago Wolves | AHL | 40 | 4 | 6 | 10 | 24 | .... | .... | .... | .... | .... |
| | Gwinnett | ECHL | 2 | 1 | 0 | 1 | 2 | .... | .... | .... | .... | .... |

### DERLYUK, Roman (duhr-LYUHK, ROH-muhn) FLA.

Defense. Shoots left. 6'3", 198 lbs. Born, Leningrad, USSR, October 27, 1986.
(Florida's 7th choice, 164th overall, in 2005 Entry Draft).

| | | | Regular Season | | | | | Playoffs | | | | |
|---|---|---|---|---|---|---|---|---|---|---|---|---|
| Season | Club | League | GP | G | A | Pts | PIM | GP | G | A | Pts | PIM |
| 2003-04 | Lokom. St. Pete. | Russia-3 | STATISTICS NOT AVAILABLE | | | | | | | | | |
| 2004-05 | Spartak St. Pet. | Russia-2 | 51 | 0 | 3 | 3 | 74 | .... | .... | .... | .... | .... |
| 2005-06 | SKA St. Petersburg | Russia | 32 | 0 | 3 | 3 | 63 | 2 | 1 | 0 | 1 | 0 |
| | St. Petersburg 2 | Russia-3 | 2 | 0 | 1 | 1 | 0 | .... | .... | .... | .... | .... |
| 2006-07 | SKA St. Petersburg | Russia | 6 | 0 | 1 | 1 | 4 | .... | .... | .... | .... | .... |
| | St. Petersburg 2 | Russia-3 | 6 | 1 | 4 | 5 | 6 | .... | .... | .... | .... | .... |
| | THK Tver | Russia-3 | 2 | 0 | 2 | 2 | 0 | .... | .... | .... | .... | .... |
| | MVD | Russia | 19 | 0 | 3 | 3 | 14 | 1 | 0 | 0 | 0 | 0 |
| 2007-08 | MVD 2 | Russia-3 | 24 | 1 | 5 | 6 | 36 | .... | .... | .... | .... | .... |
| | MVD | Russia | 26 | 3 | 3 | 6 | 26 | 3 | 0 | 0 | 0 | 2 |
| 2008-09 | MVD | Rus-KHL | 54 | 3 | 8 | 11 | 50 | .... | .... | .... | .... | .... |

### DESBIENS, Guillaume (deh-BYEHN, GEE-OHM) VAN.

Right wing. Shoots right. 6'2", 205 lbs. Born, Alma, Que., April 20, 1985.
(Atlanta's 3rd choice, 116th overall, in 2003 Entry Draft).

| | | | Regular Season | | | | | Playoffs | | | | |
|---|---|---|---|---|---|---|---|---|---|---|---|---|
| Season | Club | League | GP | G | A | Pts | PIM | GP | G | A | Pts | PIM |
| 2001-02 | Rouyn-Noranda | QMJHL | 65 | 14 | 10 | 24 | 115 | 4 | 1 | 1 | 2 | 9 |
| 2002-03 | Rouyn-Noranda | QMJHL | 64 | 15 | 18 | 33 | 233 | 4 | 0 | 0 | 0 | 4 |
| 2003-04 | Rouyn-Noranda | QMJHL | 58 | 20 | 21 | 41 | 199 | 11 | 2 | 2 | 4 | 24 |
| 2004-05 | Rouyn-Noranda | QMJHL | 56 | 27 | 16 | 43 | 206 | 10 | 1 | 4 | 5 | 25 |
| 2005-06 | Chicago Wolves | AHL | 3 | 0 | 0 | 0 | 7 | .... | .... | .... | .... | .... |
| | Gwinnett | ECHL | 65 | 33 | 27 | 60 | 187 | 17 | 10 | 6 | 16 | 38 |
| 2006-07 | Chicago Wolves | AHL | 54 | 3 | 6 | 9 | 118 | 6 | 0 | 1 | 1 | 2 |
| 2007-08 | Chicago Wolves | AHL | 23 | 2 | 1 | 3 | 30 | 1 | 0 | 1 | 1 | 0 |
| | Gwinnett | ECHL | 10 | 2 | 5 | 7 | 46 | 8 | 3 | 6 | 9 | 10 |
| 2008-09 | Manitoba Moose | AHL | 78 | 21 | 26 | 47 | 158 | 22 | 4 | 8 | 12 | 18 |

Signed as a free agent by **Manitoba** (AHL), December 15, 2008. Signed as a free agent by **Vancouver**, July 22, 2009.

### DESCHAMPS, Nicolas (day-SHAWMP, NIHK-oh-las) ANA.

Center. Shoots left. 6'1", 185 lbs. Born, Lasalle, Que., January 6, 1990.
(Anaheim's 2nd choice, 35th overall, in 2008 Entry Draft).

| | | | Regular Season | | | | | Playoffs | | | | |
|---|---|---|---|---|---|---|---|---|---|---|---|---|
| Season | Club | League | GP | G | A | Pts | PIM | GP | G | A | Pts | PIM |
| 2005-06 | C.C. Lemoyne | QAAA | 23 | 5 | 4 | 9 | 14 | 8 | 0 | 0 | 0 | 12 |
| 2006-07 | C.C. Lemoyne | QAAA | 35 | 20 | 28 | 48 | 60 | 10 | 4 | 7 | 11 | 22 |
| 2007-08 | Chicoutimi | QMJHL | 70 | 24 | 43 | 67 | 63 | 6 | 2 | 3 | 5 | 6 |
| 2008-09 | Chicoutimi | QMJHL | 65 | 24 | 41 | 65 | 40 | 4 | 3 | 1 | 4 | 12 |
| | Iowa Chops | AHL | 2 | 0 | 1 | 1 | 0 | .... | .... | .... | .... | .... |

QMJHL All-Rookie Team (2008) • Canadian Major Junior All-Rookie Team (2008)

### DESIMONE, Phil (dih-SEE-mohn, FIHL) WSH.

Center. Shoots left. 6', 185 lbs. Born, East Amherst, NY, March 19, 1987.
(Washington's 4th choice, 84th overall, in 2007 Entry Draft).

| | | | Regular Season | | | | | Playoffs | | | | |
|---|---|---|---|---|---|---|---|---|---|---|---|---|
| Season | Club | League | GP | G | A | Pts | PIM | GP | G | A | Pts | PIM |
| 2004-05 | Sioux City | USHL | 44 | 2 | 7 | 9 | 28 | 6 | 0 | 1 | 1 | 4 |
| 2005-06 | Sioux City | USHL | 60 | 15 | 38 | 53 | 71 | .... | .... | .... | .... | .... |
| 2006-07 | Sioux City | USHL | 60 | 26 | 47 | 73 | 60 | 7 | 6 | 6 | 12 | 2 |
| 2007-08 | New Hampshire | H-East | 38 | 3 | 10 | 13 | 28 | .... | .... | .... | .... | .... |
| 2008-09 | New Hampshire | H-East | 38 | 7 | 11 | 18 | 46 | .... | .... | .... | .... | .... |

USHL First All-Star Team (2007) • USHL Player of the Year (2007)

### DESLAURIERS, Nicolas (duh-LOHR-ree-AY, NIH-koh-las) L.A.

Defense. Shoots left. 6', 198 lbs. Born, LaSalle, Que., February 22, 1991.
(Los Angeles' 3rd choice, 84th overall, in 2009 Entry Draft).

| | | | Regular Season | | | | | Playoffs | | | | |
|---|---|---|---|---|---|---|---|---|---|---|---|---|
| Season | Club | League | GP | G | A | Pts | PIM | GP | G | A | Pts | PIM |
| 2006-07 | Chateauguay | QAAA | 43 | 2 | 10 | 12 | 28 | 3 | 1 | 0 | 1 | 4 |
| 2007-08 | Rouyn-Noranda | QMJHL | 42 | 2 | 7 | 9 | 38 | 4 | 0 | 0 | 0 | 0 |
| 2008-09 | Rouyn-Noranda | QMJHL | 68 | 11 | 19 | 30 | 80 | 6 | 2 | 2 | 4 | 8 |

### DESHARNAIS, David (day-hahr-NAY, DAY-vihd) MTL.

Center. Shoots left. 5'7", 182 lbs. Born, Quebec, Que., September 14, 1986.

| | | | Regular Season | | | | | Playoffs | | | | |
|---|---|---|---|---|---|---|---|---|---|---|---|---|
| Season | Club | League | GP | G | A | Pts | PIM | GP | G | A | Pts | PIM |
| 2003-04 | Chicoutimi | QMJHL | 70 | 23 | 28 | 51 | 12 | 18 | 4 | 7 | 11 | 8 |
| 2004-05 | Chicoutimi | QMJHL | 68 | 32 | 65 | 97 | 39 | 17 | 5 | 10 | 15 | 8 |
| 2005-06 | Chicoutimi | QMJHL | 63 | 33 | 85 | 118 | 44 | 9 | 2 | 9 | 11 | 4 |
| 2006-07 | Chicoutimi | QMJHL | 61 | 38 | 70 | 108 | 32 | 4 | 1 | 5 | 6 | 2 |
| | Bridgeport | AHL | 7 | 1 | 1 | 2 | 4 | .... | .... | .... | .... | .... |
| 2007-08 | Hamilton Bulldogs | AHL | 4 | 0 | 1 | 1 | 6 | .... | .... | .... | .... | .... |
| | Cincinnati | ECHL | 68 | 29 | 77 | 106 | 18 | 22 | 9 | 24 | 33 | 18 |
| 2008-09 | Hamilton Bulldogs | AHL | 77 | 24 | 34 | 58 | 20 | 6 | 1 | 3 | 4 | 4 |

Signed as a free agent by **Montreal**, November 5, 2008.

### DESPRES, Simon (duh-PRAY, see-MOHN) PIT.

Defense. Shoots left. 6'4", 205 lbs. Born, Laval, Que., July 27, 1991.
(Pittsburgh's 1st choice, 30th overall, in 2009 Entry Draft).

| | | | Regular Season | | | | | Playoffs | | | | |
|---|---|---|---|---|---|---|---|---|---|---|---|---|
| Season | Club | League | GP | G | A | Pts | PIM | GP | G | A | Pts | PIM |
| 2006-07 | Laval-Bourassa | QAAA | 42 | 8 | 31 | 39 | 36 | 5 | 0 | 2 | 2 | 8 |
| 2007-08 | Saint John | QMJHL | 64 | 1 | 13 | 14 | 30 | 14 | 0 | 4 | 4 | 18 |
| 2008-09 | Saint John | QMJHL | 66 | 2 | 30 | 32 | 74 | 4 | 0 | 4 | 4 | 2 |

QMJHL All-Rookie Team (2008)

### DEVANE, Jamie (deh-VAYN, JAY-mee) TOR.

Left wing. Shoots left. 6'4", 212 lbs. Born, Mississauga, Ont., February 20, 1991.
(Toronto's 4th choice, 68th overall, in 2009 Entry Draft).

| | | | Regular Season | | | | | Playoffs | | | | |
|---|---|---|---|---|---|---|---|---|---|---|---|---|
| Season | Club | League | GP | G | A | Pts | PIM | GP | G | A | Pts | PIM |
| 2007-08 | Vaughan Kings | GTHL | 15 | 4 | 11 | 15 | 24 | .... | .... | .... | .... | .... |
| | Vaughan Vipers | OPJHL | 19 | 2 | 0 | 2 | 17 | 1 | 0 | 0 | 0 | 0 |
| 2008-09 | Plymouth Whalers | OHL | 64 | 5 | 12 | 17 | 92 | 11 | 0 | 0 | 0 | 17 |

### DIBENEDETTO, Justin (dih-behn-ih-DEH-toh, JUHS-tihn) NYI

Center. Shoots left. 5'11", 194 lbs. Born, Etobicoke, Ont., August 25, 1988.
(NY Islanders' 13th choice, 175th overall, in 2008 Entry Draft).

| | | | Regular Season | | | | | Playoffs | | | | |
|---|---|---|---|---|---|---|---|---|---|---|---|---|
| Season | Club | League | GP | G | A | Pts | PIM | GP | G | A | Pts | PIM |
| 2004-05 | St. Michael's | OHL | 64 | 3 | 6 | 9 | 37 | 9 | 0 | 0 | 0 | 0 |
| 2005-06 | St. Michael's | OHL | 61 | 17 | 13 | 30 | 58 | 4 | 1 | 0 | 1 | 11 |
| 2006-07 | Sarnia Sting | OHL | 58 | 28 | 35 | 63 | 46 | 4 | 2 | 1 | 3 | 4 |
| 2007-08 | Sarnia Sting | OHL | 58 | 39 | 54 | 93 | 61 | 9 | 3 | 7 | 10 | 12 |
| 2008-09 | Sarnia Sting | OHL | 62 | 45 | 48 | 93 | 85 | 5 | 0 | 3 | 3 | 12 |
| | Bridgeport | AHL | .... | .... | .... | .... | .... | 3 | 1 | 0 | 1 | 4 |

OHL Second All-Star Team (2009)

### DIDOMENICO, Christopher dee-DOH-mehn-ih-koh,KRIHS-toh-fuhr TOR.

Center. Shoots right. 5'11", 165 lbs. Born, Toronto, Ont., February 20, 1989.
(Toronto's 5th choice, 164th overall, in 2007 Entry Draft).

| | | | Regular Season | | | | | Playoffs | | | | |
|---|---|---|---|---|---|---|---|---|---|---|---|---|
| Season | Club | League | GP | G | A | Pts | PIM | GP | G | A | Pts | PIM |
| 2005-06 | North York | GTHL | 36 | 28 | 35 | 63 | .... | .... | .... | .... | .... | .... |
| | North York | OPJHL | 2 | 2 | 0 | 2 | 0 | .... | .... | .... | .... | .... |
| 2006-07 | Saint John | QMJHL | 70 | 25 | 50 | 75 | 60 | .... | .... | .... | .... | .... |
| 2007-08 | Saint John | QMJHL | 70 | 39 | 56 | 95 | 103 | 14 | 8 | 11 | 19 | 20 |
| 2008-09 | Saint John | QMJHL | 26 | 11 | 23 | 34 | 34 | .... | .... | .... | .... | .... |
| | Drummondville | QMJHL | 25 | 8 | 17 | 25 | 28 | 15 | 4 | *31 | 35 | 24 |

QMJHL All-Rookie Team (2007)

### DIETRICH, Robert (DEET-rihkh, RAW-buhrt) NSH.

Defense. Shoots right. 5'10", 174 lbs. Born, Ordzhonikidze, USSR, July 25, 1986.
(Nashville's 8th choice, 174th overall, in 2007 Entry Draft).

| | | | Regular Season | | | | | Playoffs | | | | |
|---|---|---|---|---|---|---|---|---|---|---|---|---|
| Season | Club | League | GP | G | A | Pts | PIM | GP | G | A | Pts | PIM |
| 2001-02 | Kaufbeuren Jr. | Ger-Jr. | 9 | 1 | 2 | 3 | 2 | .... | .... | .... | .... | .... |
| 2002-03 | Mannheim Jr. | Ger-Jr. | 33 | 4 | 13 | 17 | 39 | 3 | 0 | 1 | 1 | 4 |
| 2003-04 | EC Peiting | German-3 | 42 | 15 | 9 | 24 | 83 | .... | .... | .... | .... | .... |
| 2004-05 | ETC Crimmitschau | German-2 | 45 | 3 | 14 | 17 | 34 | 10 | 0 | 0 | 0 | 6 |
| 2005-06 | Straubing Tigers | German-2 | 46 | 5 | 3 | 8 | 55 | 15 | 0 | 1 | 1 | 8 |
| | Dusseldorf | Germany | 4 | 0 | 0 | 0 | 2 | .... | .... | .... | .... | .... |
| 2006-07 | Dusseldorf | Germany | 52 | 3 | 19 | 22 | 28 | 9 | 2 | 4 | 6 | 22 |
| 2007-08 | Dusseldorf | Germany | 9 | 1 | 1 | 2 | 12 | 13 | 1 | 2 | 3 | 4 |
| 2008-09 | Milwaukee | AHL | 63 | 4 | 15 | 19 | 32 | 11 | 1 | 7 | 8 | 2 |

## DINGLE, Ryan (DIHN-guhl, RIGH-uhn) PHI.

Left wing. Shoots left. 5'10", 190 lbs. Born, Steamboat Springs, CO, April 4, 1984.

| | | | Regular Season | | | | | Playoffs | | | | |
|---|---|---|---|---|---|---|---|---|---|---|---|---|
| **Season** | **Club** | **League** | **GP** | **G** | **A** | **Pts** | **PIM** | **GP** | **G** | **A** | **Pts** | **PIM** |
| 2001-02 | Des Moines | USHL | 61 | 7 | 10 | 17 | 63 | 3 | 1 | 0 | 1 | 2 |
| 2002-03 | Des Moines | USHL | 26 | 8 | 6 | 14 | 16 | .... | .... | .... | .... | .... |
| | Tri-City Storm | USHL | 32 | 17 | 17 | 34 | 31 | 3 | 0 | 0 | 0 | 6 |
| 2003-04 | Tri-City Storm | USHL | 38 | 13 | 23 | 36 | 14 | 9 | 3 | 7 | 10 | 4 |
| 2004-05 | U. of Denver | WCHA | 41 | 6 | 12 | 18 | 32 | .... | .... | .... | .... | .... |
| 2005-06 | U. of Denver | WCHA | 38 | 27 | 16 | 43 | 37 | .... | .... | .... | .... | .... |
| 2006-07 | U. of Denver | WCHA | 40 | 22 | 15 | 37 | 38 | .... | .... | .... | .... | .... |
| | Portland Pirates | AHL | 4 | 0 | 1 | 1 | 4 | .... | .... | .... | .... | .... |
| 2007-08 | Portland Pirates | AHL | 19 | 1 | 5 | 6 | 10 | 2 | 0 | 1 | 1 | 0 |
| | Augusta Lynx | ECHL | 50 | 10 | 17 | 27 | 51 | 5 | 0 | 1 | 1 | 4 |
| 2008-09 | Iowa Chops | AHL | 70 | 11 | 7 | 18 | 21 | .... | .... | .... | .... | .... |

Signed as a free agent by **Anaheim**, March 26, 2007. Traded to **Philadelphia** by **Anaheim** with Chris Pronger for Joffrey Lupul, Luca Sbisa, Philadelphia's 1st round choices in 2009 (later traded to Columbus - Columbus selected John Moore) and 2010 Entry Drafts and future considerations, June 26, 2009.

## DIXON, Stephen (DIHX-uhn, STEE-vehn) ANA.

Center. Shoots left. 5'11", 188 lbs. Born, Halifax, N.S., September 7, 1985.
(Pittsburgh's 9th choice, 229th overall, in 2003 Entry Draft).

| | | | Regular Season | | | | | Playoffs | | | | |
|---|---|---|---|---|---|---|---|---|---|---|---|---|
| **Season** | **Club** | **League** | **GP** | **G** | **A** | **Pts** | **PIM** | **GP** | **G** | **A** | **Pts** | **PIM** |
| 2001-02 | Cape Breton | QMJHL | 64 | 16 | 15 | 31 | 12 | 16 | 3 | 5 | 8 | 12 |
| 2002-03 | Cape Breton | QMJHL | 72 | 28 | 42 | 70 | 54 | 4 | 0 | 0 | 0 | 6 |
| 2003-04 | Cape Breton | QMJHL | 55 | 22 | 50 | 72 | 33 | 5 | 1 | 0 | 1 | 0 |
| 2004-05 | Cape Breton | QMJHL | 45 | 17 | 34 | 51 | 40 | .... | .... | .... | .... | .... |
| 2005-06 | Wilkes-Barre | AHL | 80 | 12 | 17 | 29 | 45 | 11 | 0 | 1 | 1 | 4 |
| 2006-07 | Wilkes-Barre | AHL | 80 | 17 | 24 | 41 | 43 | 11 | 2 | 3 | 5 | 6 |
| 2007-08 | Portland Pirates | AHL | 80 | 17 | 28 | 45 | 43 | 18 | 6 | 4 | 10 | 10 |
| 2008-09 | Brynas IF Gavle | Sweden | 53 | 8 | 19 | 27 | 32 | 4 | 0 | 0 | 0 | 2 |

Traded to **Anaheim** by **Pittsburgh** for Tim Brent, June 23, 2007.

## DOBRYSHKIN, Yuri (doh-BRIHSH-kihn, YOO-ree) ATL.

Right wing. Shoots right. 6', 189 lbs. Born, Penza, USSR, July 19, 1979.
(Atlanta's 7th choice, 159th overall, in 1999 Entry Draft).

| | | | Regular Season | | | | | Playoffs | | | | |
|---|---|---|---|---|---|---|---|---|---|---|---|---|
| **Season** | **Club** | **League** | **GP** | **G** | **A** | **Pts** | **PIM** | **GP** | **G** | **A** | **Pts** | **PIM** |
| 1996-97 | Krylja Sovetov 2 | Russia-3 | 35 | 13 | 5 | 18 | 42 | .... | .... | .... | .... | .... |
| | Krylja Sovetov | Russia | 2 | 0 | 0 | 0 | 0 | 2 | 0 | 0 | 0 | 0 |
| 1997-98 | Krylja Sovetov 2 | Russia-3 | 26 | 12 | 5 | 17 | 68 | .... | .... | .... | .... | .... |
| | Krylja Sovetov | Russia | 22 | 4 | 0 | 4 | 12 | .... | .... | .... | .... | .... |
| 1998-99 | Krylja Sovetov | Russia | 50 | 11 | 5 | 16 | 86 | .... | .... | .... | .... | .... |
| 99-2000 | Ak Bars Kazan | Russia | 27 | 6 | 9 | 15 | 24 | 17 | 2 | 0 | 2 | 10 |
| 2000-01 | Ak Bars Kazan | Russia | 40 | 10 | 5 | 15 | 32 | 4 | 2 | 0 | 2 | 2 |
| 2001-02 | Ak Bars Kazan | Russia | 38 | 9 | 8 | 17 | 22 | 11 | 0 | 2 | 2 | 6 |
| 2002-03 | Cherepovets | Russia | 49 | 19 | 7 | 26 | 82 | 12 | 5 | 2 | 7 | 12 |
| 2003-04 | Cherepovets | Russia | 53 | 11 | 7 | 18 | 75 | .... | .... | .... | .... | .... |
| 2004-05 | Magnitogorsk | Russia | 54 | 14 | 6 | 20 | 42 | 2 | 0 | 0 | 0 | 0 |
| 2005-06 | Magnitogorsk | Russia | 15 | 3 | 1 | 4 | 22 | 8 | 0 | 0 | 0 | 0 |
| | Magnitogorsk 2 | Russia-3 | 2 | 3 | 1 | 4 | 2 | .... | .... | .... | .... | .... |
| 2006-07 | CSKA Moscow | Russia | 50 | 5 | 10 | 15 | 65 | 12 | 3 | 0 | 3 | 12 |
| 2007-08 | Nizhny Novgorod | Russia | 48 | 15 | 6 | 21 | 60 | .... | .... | .... | .... | .... |
| 2008-09 | Nizhny Novgorod | Rus-KHL | 19 | 2 | 1 | 3 | 12 | .... | .... | .... | .... | .... |
| | Mytischi | Rus-KHL | 8 | 1 | 0 | 1 | 2 | 2 | 0 | 0 | 0 | 0 |

## DODGE, Nick (DAWGE, NIHK) CAR.

Right wing. Shoots right. 5'10", 185 lbs. Born, Oakville, Ont., May 1, 1986.
(Carolina's 5th choice, 183rd overall, in 2006 Entry Draft).

| | | | Regular Season | | | | | Playoffs | | | | |
|---|---|---|---|---|---|---|---|---|---|---|---|---|
| **Season** | **Club** | **League** | **GP** | **G** | **A** | **Pts** | **PIM** | **GP** | **G** | **A** | **Pts** | **PIM** |
| 2004-05 | Clarkson Knights | ECAC | 37 | 6 | 12 | 18 | 42 | .... | .... | .... | .... | .... |
| 2005-06 | Clarkson Knights | ECAC | 38 | 16 | 25 | 41 | 72 | .... | .... | .... | .... | .... |
| 2006-07 | Clarkson Knights | ECAC | 36 | 18 | 21 | 39 | 32 | .... | .... | .... | .... | .... |
| 2007-08 | Clarkson Knights | ECAC | 39 | 12 | 14 | 26 | 26 | .... | .... | .... | .... | .... |
| 2008-09 | Albany River Rats | AHL | 80 | 13 | 26 | 39 | 34 | .... | .... | .... | .... | .... |

ECAC First All-Star Team (2007) • NCAA East Second All-American Team (2007)

## DOHERTY, Taylor (DOHR-eh-tee, TAY-luhr) S.J.

Defense. Shoots right. 6'7", 218 lbs. Born, Cambridge, Ont., March 2, 1991.
(San Jose's 2nd choice, 57th overall, in 2009 Entry Draft).

| | | | Regular Season | | | | | Playoffs | | | | |
|---|---|---|---|---|---|---|---|---|---|---|---|---|
| **Season** | **Club** | **League** | **GP** | **G** | **A** | **Pts** | **PIM** | **GP** | **G** | **A** | **Pts** | **PIM** |
| 2006-07 | Cambridge Hawks | Minor-ON | 70 | 10 | 37 | 47 | 169 | .... | .... | .... | .... | .... |
| 2007-08 | Kingston | OHL | 64 | 6 | 14 | 20 | 118 | .... | .... | .... | .... | .... |
| 2008-09 | Kingston | OHL | 68 | 2 | 18 | 20 | 140 | .... | .... | .... | .... | .... |

## DONALLY, Ryan (DAWN-ah-lee, RIGH-uhn) ANA.

Left wing. Shoots left. 6'5", 223 lbs. Born, Tecumseh, Ont., February 4, 1985.
(Calgary's 3rd choice, 97th overall, in 2003 Entry Draft).

| | | | Regular Season | | | | | Playoffs | | | | |
|---|---|---|---|---|---|---|---|---|---|---|---|---|
| **Season** | **Club** | **League** | **GP** | **G** | **A** | **Pts** | **PIM** | **GP** | **G** | **A** | **Pts** | **PIM** |
| 2001-02 | Windsor Spitfires | OHL | 53 | 6 | 7 | 13 | 77 | 16 | 0 | 2 | 2 | 6 |
| 2002-03 | Windsor Spitfires | OHL | 65 | 11 | 15 | 26 | 108 | 7 | 0 | 1 | 1 | 8 |
| 2003-04 | Windsor Spitfires | OHL | 44 | 8 | 14 | 22 | 93 | .... | .... | .... | .... | .... |
| 2004-05 | Windsor Spitfires | OHL | 29 | 2 | 3 | 5 | 87 | .... | .... | .... | .... | .... |
| | Kitchener Rangers | OHL | 21 | 1 | 2 | 3 | 45 | 13 | 0 | 0 | 0 | 12 |
| 2005-06 | Kitchener Rangers | OHL | 8 | 0 | 0 | 0 | 29 | .... | .... | .... | .... | .... |
| | Sudbury Wolves | OHL | 39 | 5 | 5 | 10 | 76 | 10 | 0 | 1 | 1 | 27 |
| 2006-07 | Omaha | AHL | 18 | 3 | 2 | 5 | 38 | .... | .... | .... | .... | .... |
| | Las Vegas | ECHL | 33 | 3 | 5 | 8 | 79 | 3 | 0 | 0 | 0 | 4 |
| 2007-08 | Quad City Flames | AHL | 10 | 0 | 0 | 0 | 21 | .... | .... | .... | .... | .... |
| | Las Vegas | ECHL | 53 | 15 | 22 | 37 | 176 | 4 | 2 | 2 | 4 | 6 |
| 2008-09 | Iowa Chops | AHL | 72 | 5 | 4 | 9 | 159 | .... | .... | .... | .... | .... |

Signed as a free agent by **Anaheim**, July 22, 2008.

## DONIKA, Mikhail (DAW-nih-ka, mih-kigh-EHL) DAL.

Defense. Shoots left. 6', 185 lbs. Born, Yaroslavl, USSR, May 15, 1979.
(Dallas' 11th choice, 272nd overall, in 1999 Entry Draft).

| | | | Regular Season | | | | | Playoffs | | | | |
|---|---|---|---|---|---|---|---|---|---|---|---|---|
| **Season** | **Club** | **League** | **GP** | **G** | **A** | **Pts** | **PIM** | **GP** | **G** | **A** | **Pts** | **PIM** |
| 1996-97 | Yaroslavl 2 | Russia-3 | 15 | 3 | 5 | 8 | 6 | .... | .... | .... | .... | .... |
| | Torpedo Yaroslavl | Russia | 22 | 1 | 0 | 1 | 6 | 2 | 0 | 0 | 0 | 0 |
| 1997-98 | Yaroslavl 2 | Russia-2 | 19 | 1 | 2 | 3 | 32 | .... | .... | .... | .... | .... |
| | Torpedo Yaroslavl | Russia | 30 | 0 | 2 | 2 | 14 | .... | .... | .... | .... | .... |
| 1998-99 | Yaroslavl 2 | Russia-3 | 6 | 2 | 1 | 3 | 4 | .... | .... | .... | .... | .... |
| | Torpedo Yaroslavl | Russia | 37 | 0 | 1 | 1 | 10 | .... | .... | .... | .... | .... |
| 99-2000 | Torpedo Yaroslavl | Russia | 35 | 0 | 1 | 1 | 22 | 10 | 0 | 0 | 0 | 4 |
| 2000-01 | Dynamo Moscow | Russia | 43 | 1 | 3 | 4 | 12 | .... | .... | .... | .... | .... |
| 2001-02 | Amur Khabarovsk | Russia | 51 | 1 | 3 | 4 | 66 | .... | .... | .... | .... | .... |
| 2002-03 | Spartak Moscow | Russia | 51 | 4 | 7 | 11 | 16 | .... | .... | .... | .... | .... |
| 2003-04 | Spartak Moscow | Russia-2 | 55 | 4 | 14 | 18 | 14 | 12 | 2 | 1 | 3 | 2 |
| 2004-05 | Spartak Moscow | Russia | 49 | 0 | 2 | 2 | 34 | .... | .... | .... | .... | .... |
| 2005-06 | Perm | Russia | 26 | 0 | 0 | 0 | 18 | .... | .... | .... | .... | .... |
| | Sibir Novosibirsk | Russia | 14 | 1 | 3 | 4 | 8 | 3 | 0 | 1 | 1 | 0 |
| 2006-07 | Nizhny Novgorod | Russia-2 | 47 | 8 | 16 | 24 | 38 | 14 | 3 | 0 | 3 | 14 |
| 2007-08 | Nizhny Novgorod | Russia | 31 | 0 | 5 | 5 | 28 | .... | .... | .... | .... | .... |
| | Lada Togliatti | Russia | 2 | 0 | 0 | 0 | 0 | .... | .... | .... | .... | .... |
| | Yunost Minsk | Belarus | 10 | 1 | 1 | 2 | 2 | .... | .... | .... | .... | .... |
| | Yunior Minsk | Belarus-2 | .... | .... | .... | .... | .... | 1 | 0 | 0 | 0 | 0 |
| 2008-09 | Khanty-Mansiisk | Russia-2 | 46 | 3 | 11 | 14 | 46 | 15 | 1 | 1 | 2 | 16 |

## DONOVAN, Matt (DAWN-uh-vuhn, MAT) NYI

Defense. Shoots left. 5'11", 185 lbs. Born, Edmond, OK, May 9, 1990.
(NY Islanders' 8th choice, 96th overall, in 2008 Entry Draft).

| | | | Regular Season | | | | | Playoffs | | | | |
|---|---|---|---|---|---|---|---|---|---|---|---|---|
| **Season** | **Club** | **League** | **GP** | **G** | **A** | **Pts** | **PIM** | **GP** | **G** | **A** | **Pts** | **PIM** |
| 2006-07 | Dallas Stars AAA | NTHL | .... | 22 | 46 | 68 | 54 | .... | .... | .... | .... | .... |
| 2007-08 | Cedar Rapids | USHL | 59 | 12 | 18 | 30 | 41 | 3 | 0 | 1 | 1 | 4 |
| 2008-09 | Cedar Rapids | USHL | 57 | 19 | 32 | 51 | 43 | 5 | 0 | 4 | 4 | 2 |

• Signed Letter of Intent to attend **University of Denver** (WCHA) in fall of 2009. • USHL All-Rookie Team (2008) • USHL First All-Star Team (2009)

## DOVGAN, Viktor (DAWV-guhn, VIHK-tohr) WSH.

Defense. Shoots left. 6'2", 205 lbs. Born, Moscow, USSR, February 27, 1987.
(Washington's 7th choice, 209th overall, in 2005 Entry Draft).

| | | | Regular Season | | | | | Playoffs | | | | |
|---|---|---|---|---|---|---|---|---|---|---|---|---|
| **Season** | **Club** | **League** | **GP** | **G** | **A** | **Pts** | **PIM** | **GP** | **G** | **A** | **Pts** | **PIM** |
| 2003-04 | CSKA Moscow 2 | Russia-3 | STATISTICS NOT AVAILABLE | | | | | | | | | |
| 2004-05 | CSKA Moscow 2 | Russia-3 | STATISTICS NOT AVAILABLE | | | | | | | | | |
| 2005-06 | CSKA Moscow 2 | Russia-3 | STATISTICS NOT AVAILABLE | | | | | | | | | |
| | CSK VVS Samara | Russia-2 | 8 | 1 | 2 | 3 | 20 | 3 | 0 | 1 | 1 | 4 |
| 2006-07 | Hershey Bears | AHL | 1 | 0 | 0 | 0 | 2 | .... | .... | .... | .... | .... |
| | South Carolina | ECHL | 56 | 5 | 6 | 11 | 95 | .... | .... | .... | .... | .... |
| 2007-08 | CSKA Moscow | Russia | 16 | 0 | 0 | 0 | 10 | .... | .... | .... | .... | .... |
| 2008-09 | Hershey Bears | AHL | 2 | 0 | 0 | 0 | 2 | .... | .... | .... | .... | .... |
| | South Carolina | ECHL | 53 | 2 | 10 | 12 | 52 | .... | .... | .... | .... | .... |

## DOWD, Nic (DOWD, NIHK) L.A.

Center. Shoots right. 6'1", 175 lbs. Born, Huntsville, AL, May 27, 1990.
(Los Angeles' 10th choice, 198th overall, in 2009 Entry Draft).

| | | | Regular Season | | | | | Playoffs | | | | |
|---|---|---|---|---|---|---|---|---|---|---|---|---|
| **Season** | **Club** | **League** | **GP** | **G** | **A** | **Pts** | **PIM** | **GP** | **G** | **A** | **Pts** | **PIM** |
| 2007-08 | Culver Academy | High-IN | 45 | 15 | 31 | 46 | 38 | .... | .... | .... | .... | .... |
| 2008-09 | Wenatchee Wild | NAHL | 43 | 16 | 33 | 49 | 71 | 13 | 8 | *14 | *22 | 34 |

• Signed Letter of Intent to attend **St. Cloud State University** (WCHA) in fall of 2010.

## DOWZAK, Tysen (DOW-zak, TIGH-suhn) NYR

Defense. Shoots left. 6'5", 226 lbs. Born, Fergus Falls, MN, March 8, 1988.

| | | | Regular Season | | | | | Playoffs | | | | |
|---|---|---|---|---|---|---|---|---|---|---|---|---|
| **Season** | **Club** | **League** | **GP** | **G** | **A** | **Pts** | **PIM** | **GP** | **G** | **A** | **Pts** | **PIM** |
| 2005-06 | Kelowna Rockets | WHL | 43 | 1 | 3 | 4 | 68 | 8 | 0 | 0 | 0 | 16 |
| 2006-07 | Kelowna Rockets | WHL | 55 | 3 | 4 | 7 | 68 | .... | .... | .... | .... | .... |
| 2007-08 | Kelowna Rockets | WHL | 68 | 0 | 13 | 13 | 91 | 7 | 0 | 1 | 1 | 13 |
| | Texas Wildcatters | ECHL | .... | .... | .... | .... | .... | 5 | 0 | 0 | 0 | 4 |
| 2008-09 | Kelowna Rockets | WHL | 54 | 0 | 14 | 14 | 77 | 22 | 0 | 4 | 4 | 14 |
| | Hartford Wolf Pack | AHL | 1 | 0 | 0 | 0 | 2 | .... | .... | .... | .... | .... |
| | Charlotte | ECHL | 4 | 0 | 0 | 0 | 9 | .... | .... | .... | .... | .... |

Signed as a free agent by **NY Rangers**, October 14, 2008.

## DOYLE, Chris (DOYL, KRIHS) NYR

Center. Shoots left. 6', 194 lbs. Born, Charlottetown, P.E.I., March 22, 1990.
(NY Rangers' 6th choice, 141st overall, in 2008 Entry Draft).

| | | | Regular Season | | | | | Playoffs | | | | |
|---|---|---|---|---|---|---|---|---|---|---|---|---|
| **Season** | **Club** | **League** | **GP** | **G** | **A** | **Pts** | **PIM** | **GP** | **G** | **A** | **Pts** | **PIM** |
| 2006-07 | PEI Rocket | QMJHL | 50 | 18 | 18 | 36 | 50 | 7 | 1 | 3 | 4 | 4 |
| 2007-08 | PEI Rocket | QMJHL | 63 | 27 | 36 | 63 | 81 | 4 | 1 | 5 | 6 | 6 |
| 2008-09 | PEI Rocket | QMJHL | 59 | 30 | 42 | 72 | 79 | 5 | 2 | 2 | 4 | 8 |

## DRAVECKY, Vladimir (dra-VEH-kee, vla-DIH-meer)

Right wing. Shoots left. 5'11", 195 lbs. Born, Kosice, Czech., June 3, 1985.

| | | | Regular Season | | | | | Playoffs | | | | |
|---|---|---|---|---|---|---|---|---|---|---|---|---|
| **Season** | **Club** | **League** | **GP** | **G** | **A** | **Pts** | **PIM** | **GP** | **G** | **A** | **Pts** | **PIM** |
| 2002-03 | Trebisov | Slovak-2 | 2 | 0 | 1 | 1 | 0 | .... | .... | .... | .... | .... |
| 2003-04 | Presov Jr. | Slovak-Jr. | 1 | 0 | 1 | 1 | 0 | .... | .... | .... | .... | .... |
| | Presov | Slovak-2 | 4 | 1 | 1 | 2 | 4 | 7 | 7 | 2 | 9 | 4 |
| | HC Kosice | Slovakia | 43 | 1 | 3 | 4 | 4 | .... | .... | .... | .... | .... |
| 2004-05 | HC Kosice Jr. | Slovak-Jr. | 10 | 4 | 10 | 14 | 8 | 5 | 1 | 3 | 4 | 2 |
| | HC Kosice | Slovakia | 51 | 5 | 6 | 11 | 8 | 10 | 0 | 1 | 1 | 0 |
| 2005-06 | HC Kosice | Slovakia | 54 | 8 | 18 | 26 | 18 | 8 | 1 | 0 | 1 | 8 |
| | HKm Humenne | Slovak-2 | 1 | 3 | 4 | 0 | .... | .... | .... | .... | .... | .... |
| 2006-07 | HC Kosice | Slovakia | 52 | 9 | 14 | 23 | 16 | 11 | 5 | 3 | 8 | 2 |
| | HKm Humenne | Slovak-2 | 1 | 2 | 1 | 3 | 2 | .... | .... | .... | .... | .... |
| 2007-08 | Manchester | AHL | 31 | 3 | 9 | 12 | 19 | .... | .... | .... | .... | .... |
| | Reading Royals | ECHL | 26 | 4 | 20 | 24 | 20 | 6 | 0 | 1 | 1 | 4 |
| 2008-09 | Manchester | AHL | 80 | 6 | 18 | 24 | 42 | .... | .... | .... | .... | .... |

Signed as a free agent by **Los Angeles**, May 31, 2007.

### DRAZENOVIC, Nicholas — (DRAY-zehn-oh-vihk, NIH-koh-las) ST.L.

Center. Shoots left. 6', 185 lbs. Born, Prince George, B.C., January 14, 1987.
(St. Louis' 6th choice, 171st overall, in 2005 Entry Draft).

| | | | Regular Season | | | | | Playoffs | | | | |
|---|---|---|---|---|---|---|---|---|---|---|---|---|
| Season | Club | League | GP | G | A | Pts | PIM | GP | G | A | Pts | PIM |
| 2003-04 | Prince George | WHL | 65 | 7 | 30 | 37 | 38 | .... | .... | .... | .... | .... |
| 2004-05 | Prince George | WHL | 72 | 18 | 38 | 56 | 24 | .... | .... | .... | .... | .... |
| 2005-06 | Prince George | WHL | 71 | 30 | 33 | 63 | 51 | 5 | 0 | 0 | 0 | 4 |
| 2006-07 | Prince George | WHL | 58 | 18 | 32 | 50 | 63 | 15 | 9 | 10 | 19 | 6 |
| 2007-08 | Peoria Rivermen | AHL | 69 | 16 | 26 | 42 | 38 | .... | .... | .... | .... | .... |
| 2008-09 | Peoria Rivermen | AHL | 76 | 12 | 21 | 33 | 43 | 5 | 1 | 0 | 1 | 2 |

### DROZDETSKY, Alexander — (drawz-DEHT-skee, al-EHX-AN-duhr) PHI.

Right wing. Shoots left. 6', 180 lbs. Born, Moscow, USSR, November 10, 1981.
(Philadelphia's 2nd choice, 94th overall, in 2000 Entry Draft).

| | | | Regular Season | | | | | Playoffs | | | | |
|---|---|---|---|---|---|---|---|---|---|---|---|---|
| Season | Club | League | GP | G | A | Pts | PIM | GP | G | A | Pts | PIM |
| 1997-98 | St. Petersburg 2 | Russia-3 | 19 | 0 | 1 | 1 | 0 | .... | .... | .... | .... | .... |
| 1998-99 | St. Petersburg 2 | Russia-4 | 24 | 5 | 3 | 8 | 12 | .... | .... | .... | .... | .... |
| 99-2000 | St. Petersburg 2 | Russia-3 | 4 | 4 | 1 | 5 | 2 | .... | .... | .... | .... | .... |
| | SKA St. Petersburg | Russia | 32 | 2 | 0 | 2 | 10 | 4 | 0 | 0 | 0 | 0 |
| 2000-01 | SKA St. Petersburg | Russia | 42 | 6 | 7 | 13 | 74 | .... | .... | .... | .... | .... |
| 2001-02 | CSKA Moscow | Russia | 49 | 11 | 6 | 17 | 26 | .... | .... | .... | .... | .... |
| 2002-03 | CSKA Moscow | Russia | 46 | 14 | 13 | 27 | 30 | .... | .... | .... | .... | .... |
| 2003-04 | Ak Bars Kazan | Russia | 57 | 16 | 15 | 31 | 62 | 1 | 0 | 0 | 0 | 2 |
| 2004-05 | Ak Bars Kazan | Russia | 32 | 3 | 4 | 7 | 28 | .... | .... | .... | .... | .... |
| | Ak Bars Kazan 2 | Russia-3 | .... | 10 | 8 | 18 | .... | .... | .... | .... | .... | .... |
| | Nizhnekamsk | Russia | 7 | 5 | 1 | 6 | 4 | .... | .... | .... | .... | .... |
| 2005-06 | Avangard Omsk | Russia | 30 | 6 | 6 | 12 | 26 | .... | .... | .... | .... | .... |
| | SKA St. Petersburg | Russia | 16 | 4 | 10 | 14 | 6 | 3 | 0 | 0 | 0 | 0 |
| 2006-07 | SKA St. Petersburg | Russia | 45 | 11 | 15 | 26 | 66 | 3 | 0 | 2 | 2 | 0 |
| 2007-08 | St. Petersburg 2 | Russia-3 | 12 | 9 | 9 | 18 | 6 | .... | .... | .... | .... | .... |
| | Spartak Moscow | Russia | 32 | 11 | 6 | 17 | 40 | 5 | 4 | 3 | 7 | 2 |
| 2008-09 | Spartak Moscow | Rus-KHL | 47 | 14 | 13 | 27 | 38 | 6 | 1 | 3 | 4 | 2 |

### DUCHENE, Matt — (DOO-shayn, MAT) COL.

Center. Shoots left. 5'11", 200 lbs. Born, Haliburton, Ont., January 16, 1991.
(Colorado's 1st choice, 3rd overall, in 2009 Entry Draft).

| | | | Regular Season | | | | | Playoffs | | | | |
|---|---|---|---|---|---|---|---|---|---|---|---|---|
| Season | Club | League | GP | G | A | Pts | PIM | GP | G | A | Pts | PIM |
| 2006-07 | Cent. Ont. Wolves | Minor-ON | 52 | 69 | 37 | 106 | 36 | .... | .... | .... | .... | .... |
| 2007-08 | Brampton | OHL | 64 | 30 | 20 | 50 | 22 | 5 | 1 | 1 | 2 | 10 |
| 2008-09 | Brampton | OHL | 57 | 31 | 48 | 79 | 42 | 21 | 14 | 12 | 26 | 21 |

### DUCO, Mike — (DOO-koh, MIGHK) FLA.

Left wing. Shoots left. 5'10", 200 lbs. Born, Toronto, Ont., July 8, 1987.

| | | | Regular Season | | | | | Playoffs | | | | |
|---|---|---|---|---|---|---|---|---|---|---|---|---|
| Season | Club | League | GP | G | A | Pts | PIM | GP | G | A | Pts | PIM |
| 2003-04 | Kitchener Rangers | OHL | 5 | 1 | 2 | 3 | 4 | 4 | 0 | 1 | 1 | 4 |
| 2004-05 | Kitchener Rangers | OHL | 62 | 24 | 26 | 50 | 78 | 15 | 0 | 0 | 0 | 11 |
| 2005-06 | Kitchener Rangers | OHL | 59 | 22 | 22 | 44 | 113 | 5 | 2 | 1 | 3 | 10 |
| 2006-07 | Kitchener Rangers | OHL | 54 | 20 | 20 | 40 | 121 | 9 | 1 | 1 | 2 | 12 |
| 2007-08 | Kitchener Rangers | OHL | 62 | 32 | 22 | 54 | 173 | 20 | *16 | 6 | 22 | 37 |
| 2008-09 | Rochester | AHL | 68 | 14 | 14 | 28 | 147 | .... | .... | .... | .... | .... |

Signed as a free agent by **Florida**, October 8, 2007.

### DUFFY, Matt — (DUHF-ee, MAT) FLA.

Defense. Shoots right. 6'2", 180 lbs. Born, Portland, ME, March 21, 1986.
(Florida's 5th choice, 104th overall, in 2005 Entry Draft).

| | | | Regular Season | | | | | Playoffs | | | | |
|---|---|---|---|---|---|---|---|---|---|---|---|---|
| Season | Club | League | GP | G | A | Pts | PIM | GP | G | A | Pts | PIM |
| 2003-04 | N.H. Jr. Monarchs | EJHL | 33 | 9 | 13 | 22 | .... | .... | .... | .... | .... | .... |
| 2004-05 | N.H. Jr. Monarchs | EJHL | 54 | 19 | 26 | 45 | 147 | .... | .... | .... | .... | .... |
| 2005-06 | U. of Maine | H-East | 28 | 3 | 5 | 8 | 43 | .... | .... | .... | .... | .... |
| 2006-07 | U. of Maine | H-East | 39 | 5 | 5 | 10 | 41 | .... | .... | .... | .... | .... |
| 2007-08 | U. of Maine | H-East | 30 | 6 | 2 | 8 | 16 | .... | .... | .... | .... | .... |
| 2008-09 | U. of Maine | H-East | 39 | 7 | 10 | 17 | 64 | .... | .... | .... | .... | .... |
| | Rochester | AHL | 9 | 2 | 4 | 6 | 4 | .... | .... | .... | .... | .... |
| | Florida Everblades | ECHL | 2 | 0 | 0 | 0 | 0 | 3 | 0 | 1 | 1 | 2 |

### DUMONT, Gabriel — (doo-MAWNT, gah-BREE-ehl) MTL.

Center. Shoots right. 5'9", 182 lbs. Born, Ville Degelis, Que., October 6, 1990.
(Montreal's 5th choice, 139th overall, in 2009 Entry Draft).

| | | | Regular Season | | | | | Playoffs | | | | |
|---|---|---|---|---|---|---|---|---|---|---|---|---|
| Season | Club | League | GP | G | A | Pts | PIM | GP | G | A | Pts | PIM |
| 2006-07 | Ecole Notre Dame | QAAA | 39 | 30 | 42 | 72 | 127 | 13 | 11 | 12 | 23 | 20 |
| | Drummondville | QMJHL | 8 | 1 | 1 | 2 | 6 | 6 | 0 | 2 | 2 | 0 |
| 2007-08 | Drummondville | QMJHL | 59 | 11 | 14 | 25 | 103 | .... | .... | .... | .... | .... |
| 2008-09 | Drummondville | QMJHL | 51 | 28 | 21 | 49 | 63 | 19 | 6 | 13 | 19 | 32 |

### DUMOULIN, Brian — (DOO-moh-lihn, BRIGH-uhn) CAR.

Defense. Shoots left. 6'3", 205 lbs. Born, Biddeford, ME, September 6, 1991.
(Carolina's 2nd choice, 51st overall, in 2009 Entry Draft).

| | | | Regular Season | | | | | Playoffs | | | | |
|---|---|---|---|---|---|---|---|---|---|---|---|---|
| Season | Club | League | GP | G | A | Pts | PIM | GP | G | A | Pts | PIM |
| 2007-08 | Biddeford Tigers | High-ME | 24 | 13 | 48 | 61 | 10 | .... | .... | .... | .... | .... |
| 2008-09 | N.H. Jr. Monarchs | EJHL | 41 | 7 | 23 | 30 | 30 | 7 | 0 | 3 | 3 | 2 |

• Signed Letter of Intent to attend **Boston College** (Hockey East) in fall of 2009.

### DUPONT, Brodie — (DOO-pawnt, BROH-dee) NYR

Center. Shoots left. 6'2", 210 lbs. Born, Russell, Man., February 17, 1987.
(NY Rangers' 4th choice, 66th overall, in 2005 Entry Draft).

| | | | Regular Season | | | | | Playoffs | | | | |
|---|---|---|---|---|---|---|---|---|---|---|---|---|
| Season | Club | League | GP | G | A | Pts | PIM | GP | G | A | Pts | PIM |
| 2003-04 | Swan Valley | MJHL | 51 | 25 | 16 | 41 | 88 | 12 | 5 | 1 | 6 | 36 |
| | Calgary Hitmen | WHL | 2 | 0 | 1 | 1 | 0 | .... | .... | .... | .... | .... |
| 2004-05 | Calgary Hitmen | WHL | 70 | 14 | 11 | 25 | 111 | 12 | 2 | 8 | 10 | 21 |
| 2005-06 | Calgary Hitmen | WHL | 72 | 30 | 23 | 53 | 123 | 13 | 4 | 5 | 9 | 24 |
| 2006-07 | Calgary Hitmen | WHL | 70 | 37 | 33 | 70 | 90 | 18 | 9 | 7 | 16 | 33 |
| 2007-08 | Hartford Wolf Pack | AHL | 66 | 9 | 13 | 22 | 75 | 1 | 0 | 0 | 0 | 0 |
| 2008-09 | Hartford Wolf Pack | AHL | 79 | 18 | 24 | 42 | 112 | 6 | 0 | 2 | 2 | 15 |

### EAKIN, Cody — (EE-kihn, KOH-dee) WSH.

Center. Shoots left. 5'11", 187 lbs. Born, Winnipeg, Man., May 24, 1991.
(Washington's 3rd choice, 85th overall, in 2009 Entry Draft).

| | | | Regular Season | | | | | Playoffs | | | | |
|---|---|---|---|---|---|---|---|---|---|---|---|---|
| Season | Club | League | GP | G | A | Pts | PIM | GP | G | A | Pts | PIM |
| 2006-07 | Winnipeg Wild | MMHL | 38 | 29 | 35 | 64 | 62 | 7 | 5 | 4 | 9 | 10 |
| | Swift Current | WHL | 3 | 0 | 0 | 0 | 0 | .... | .... | .... | .... | .... |
| 2007-08 | Swift Current | WHL | 55 | 11 | 6 | 17 | 52 | 12 | 3 | 4 | 7 | 6 |
| 2008-09 | Swift Current | WHL | 54 | 24 | 24 | 48 | 42 | 7 | 3 | 0 | 3 | 10 |

### EAVES, Ben — (EEVZ, BEHN) NSH.

Center. Shoots right. 5'9", 182 lbs. Born, Minneapolis, MN, March 27, 1982.
(Pittsburgh's 6th choice, 131st overall, in 2001 Entry Draft).

| | | | Regular Season | | | | | Playoffs | | | | |
|---|---|---|---|---|---|---|---|---|---|---|---|---|
| Season | Club | League | GP | G | A | Pts | PIM | GP | G | A | Pts | PIM |
| 1998-99 | Minnesota Selects | USAHA | 71 | 68 | 88 | 156 | 12 | .... | .... | .... | .... | .... |
| 99-2000 | Shat.-St. Mary's | High-MN | 57 | 47 | 71 | 118 | 16 | .... | .... | .... | .... | .... |
| 2000-01 | Boston College | H-East | 40 | 13 | 26 | 39 | 12 | .... | .... | .... | .... | .... |
| 2001-02 | Boston College | H-East | 23 | 13 | 26 | 39 | 12 | .... | .... | .... | .... | .... |
| 2002-03 | Boston College | H-East | 36 | 18 | *39 | *57 | 18 | .... | .... | .... | .... | .... |
| 2003-04 | Boston College | H-East | 26 | 9 | 25 | 34 | 4 | .... | .... | .... | .... | .... |
| 2004-05 | Wilkes-Barre | AHL | 43 | 4 | 6 | 10 | 12 | 7 | 0 | 0 | 0 | 0 |
| | Wheeling Nailers | ECHL | 2 | 1 | 0 | 1 | 0 | .... | .... | .... | .... | .... |
| 2005-06 | Wilkes-Barre | AHL | 5 | 1 | 2 | 3 | 0 | .... | .... | .... | .... | .... |
| 2006-07 | DID NOT PLAY | | | | | | | | | | | |
| 2007-08 | Blues Espoo | Finland | 10 | 3 | 4 | 7 | 4 | 13 | 7 | 5 | 12 | 8 |
| 2008-09 | Blues Espoo | Finland | 22 | 3 | 15 | 18 | 18 | 14 | 4 | *20 | *24 | 6 |

Hockey East Second All-Star Team (2002) • Hockey East First All-Star Team (2003) • Hockey East Player of the Year (2003) (co-winner - Michael Ayers) • NCAA East First All-American Team (2003)

Signed as a free agent by **Nashville**, July 20, 2009.

### EBERLE, Jordan — (EH-buhr-lee, JOHR-dahn) EDM.

Center. Shoots right. 5'10", 174 lbs. Born, Regina, Sask., May 15, 1990.
(Edmonton's 1st choice, 22nd overall, in 2008 Entry Draft).

| | | | Regular Season | | | | | Playoffs | | | | |
|---|---|---|---|---|---|---|---|---|---|---|---|---|
| Season | Club | League | GP | G | A | Pts | PIM | GP | G | A | Pts | PIM |
| 2005-06 | Calgary Buffaloes | AMHL | 31 | 14 | 20 | 34 | 6 | 11 | 7 | 1 | 8 | 8 |
| 2006-07 | Regina Pats | WHL | 66 | 28 | 27 | 55 | 32 | 6 | 2 | 5 | 7 | 2 |
| 2007-08 | Regina Pats | WHL | 70 | 42 | 33 | 75 | 20 | 5 | 2 | 4 | 6 | 7 |
| 2008-09 | Regina Pats | WHL | 61 | 35 | 39 | 74 | 20 | .... | .... | .... | .... | .... |
| | Springfield Falcons | AHL | 9 | 3 | 6 | 9 | 4 | .... | .... | .... | .... | .... |

WHL East First All-Star Team (2008)

### ECKFORD, Tyler — (EHK-fuhrd, TIGH-luhr) N.J.

Defense. Shoots left. 6'1", 200 lbs. Born, Vancouver, B.C., September 8, 1985.
(New Jersey's 5th choice, 217th overall, in 2004 Entry Draft).

| | | | Regular Season | | | | | Playoffs | | | | |
|---|---|---|---|---|---|---|---|---|---|---|---|---|
| Season | Club | League | GP | G | A | Pts | PIM | GP | G | A | Pts | PIM |
| 2003-04 | South Surrey | BCHL | 58 | 7 | 30 | 37 | 101 | 13 | 2 | 8 | 10 | 34 |
| 2004-05 | South Surrey | BCHL | 60 | 22 | 43 | 65 | 93 | 25 | 4 | 15 | 19 | 46 |
| 2005-06 | Alaska | CCHA | 38 | 3 | 15 | 18 | 43 | .... | .... | .... | .... | .... |
| 2006-07 | Alaska | CCHA | 39 | 5 | 17 | 22 | 54 | .... | .... | .... | .... | .... |
| 2007-08 | Alaska | CCHA | 35 | 8 | 23 | 31 | 55 | .... | .... | .... | .... | .... |
| 2008-09 | Lowell Devils | AHL | 72 | 2 | 25 | 27 | 59 | .... | .... | .... | .... | .... |

CCHA All-Rookie Team (2006) • CCHA First All-Star Team (2008) • NCAA West First All-American Team (2008)

### EHRHARDT, Travis — (AIR-hahrt, TRA-vihs) DET.

Defense. Shoots left. 6', 197 lbs. Born, Calgary, Alta., April 12, 1989.

| | | | Regular Season | | | | | Playoffs | | | | |
|---|---|---|---|---|---|---|---|---|---|---|---|---|
| Season | Club | League | GP | G | A | Pts | PIM | GP | G | A | Pts | PIM |
| 2004-05 | Cgy. North Stars | AMHL | 11 | 0 | 0 | 0 | 0 | .... | .... | .... | .... | .... |
| | Moose Jaw | WHL | 2 | 0 | 1 | 1 | 2 | .... | .... | .... | .... | .... |
| 2005-06 | Moose Jaw | WHL | 45 | 1 | 10 | 11 | 37 | 18 | 0 | 2 | 2 | 18 |
| 2006-07 | Moose Jaw | WHL | 69 | 0 | 29 | 29 | 83 | .... | .... | .... | .... | .... |
| 2007-08 | Moose Jaw | WHL | 18 | 3 | 9 | 12 | 27 | .... | .... | .... | .... | .... |
| | Portland | WHL | 54 | 7 | 22 | 29 | 53 | .... | .... | .... | .... | .... |
| 2008-09 | Portland | WHL | 68 | 9 | 28 | 37 | 109 | .... | .... | .... | .... | .... |
| | Manitoba Moose | AHL | 3 | 0 | 0 | 0 | 0 | .... | .... | .... | .... | .... |

Signed as a free agent by **Detroit**, July 7, 2009.

### EKBOM, Viktor — (EHK-bawm, VIHK-tohr) PIT.

Defense. Shoots left. 6'2", 194 lbs. Born, Falkoping, Sweden, June 1, 1989.
(Pittsburgh's 7th choice, 181st overall, in 2009 Entry Draft).

| | | | Regular Season | | | | | Playoffs | | | | |
|---|---|---|---|---|---|---|---|---|---|---|---|---|
| Season | Club | League | GP | G | A | Pts | PIM | GP | G | A | Pts | PIM |
| 2004-05 | Skovde IK Jr. | Swe-Jr. | 37 | 3 | 3 | 6 | 24 | .... | .... | .... | .... | .... |
| 2005-06 | Skovde IK Jr. | Swe-Jr. | .... | 3 | 2 | 5 | .... | .... | .... | .... | .... | .... |
| | Skovde IK | Sweden-3 | 17 | 1 | 1 | 2 | 0 | .... | .... | .... | .... | .... |
| 2006-07 | Skovde IK | Sweden-3 | 36 | 3 | 14 | 17 | 30 | .... | .... | .... | .... | .... |
| 2007-08 | Linkopings HC Jr. | Swe-Jr. | 25 | 3 | 7 | 10 | 10 | 5 | 0 | 2 | 2 | 6 |
| | IK Oskarshamn | Sweden-2 | 9 | 0 | 0 | 0 | 2 | .... | .... | .... | .... | .... |
| 2008-09 | IK Oskarshamn | Sweden-2 | 29 | 2 | 4 | 6 | 22 | .... | .... | .... | .... | .... |
| | Linkopings HC | Sweden | 14 | 0 | 1 | 1 | 6 | 5 | 0 | 0 | 0 | 2 |
| | Linkopings HC Jr. | Swe-Jr. | .... | .... | .... | .... | .... | 5 | 1 | 1 | 2 | 2 |

### EKHOLM, Mattias — (EHK-hohlm, ma-TEE-uhs) NSH.

Defense. Shoots left. 6'4", 196 lbs. Born, Borlange, Sweden, May 24, 1990.
(Nashville's 7th choice, 102nd overall, in 2009 Entry Draft).

| | | | Regular Season | | | | | Playoffs | | | | |
|---|---|---|---|---|---|---|---|---|---|---|---|---|
| Season | Club | League | GP | G | A | Pts | PIM | GP | G | A | Pts | PIM |
| 2006-07 | Mora IK U18 | Swe-U18 | 5 | 2 | 2 | 4 | 6 | .... | .... | .... | .... | .... |
| | Mora IK Jr. | Swe-Jr. | 36 | 0 | 4 | 4 | 28 | 2 | 0 | 0 | 0 | 0 |
| 2007-08 | Mora IK U18 | Swe-U18 | 9 | 4 | 5 | 9 | 12 | .... | .... | .... | .... | .... |
| | Mora IK Jr. | Swe-Jr. | 37 | 5 | 7 | 12 | 54 | .... | .... | .... | .... | .... |
| | Mora IK | Sweden | 1 | 0 | 0 | 0 | 0 | .... | .... | .... | .... | .... |
| | Mora IK | Sweden-Q | 6 | 0 | 0 | 0 | 2 | .... | .... | .... | .... | .... |
| 2008-09 | Mora IK Jr. | Swe-Jr. | 21 | 3 | 5 | 8 | 32 | .... | .... | .... | .... | .... |
| | Mora IK | Sweden-2 | 38 | 2 | 11 | 13 | 12 | 3 | 0 | 0 | 0 | 4 |

## EKMAN-LARSSON, Oliver (EHK-man-LAHR-suhn, AW-lih-vuhr) PHX.

Defense. Shoots left. 6'2", 176 lbs. Born, Karlskrona, Sweden, July 17, 1991.
(Phoenix's 1st choice, 6th overall, in 2009 Entry Draft).

| | | | Regular Season | | | | | Playoffs | | | | |
|---|---|---|---|---|---|---|---|---|---|---|---|---|
| Season | Club | League | GP | G | A | Pts | PIM | GP | G | A | Pts | PIM |
| 2005-06 | Tingsryds AIF Jr. | Swe-Jr. | 1 | 0 | 0 | 0 | 2 | .... | .... | .... | .... | .... |
| 2006-07 | Tingsryds AIF U18 | Swe-U18 | 23 | 0 | 3 | 3 | 28 | .... | .... | .... | .... | .... |
| 2007-08 | Tingsryds AIF U18 | Swe-U18 | 12 | 2 | 3 | 5 | 57 | .... | .... | .... | .... | .... |
| | Tingsryds AIF Jr. | Swe-Jr. | 7 | 2 | 4 | 6 | 16 | .... | .... | .... | .... | .... |
| | Tingsryds AIF | Sweden-3 | 27 | 3 | 5 | 8 | 10 | .... | .... | .... | .... | .... |
| 2008-09 | Leksands IF | Sweden-2 | 47 | 5 | 16 | 21 | 38 | .... | .... | .... | .... | .... |

## ELKINS, Corey (EHL-kihns, KOH-ree) L.A.

Left wing. Shoots left. 6'2", 215 lbs. Born, West Bloomfield, MI, February 23, 1985.

| | | | Regular Season | | | | | Playoffs | | | | |
|---|---|---|---|---|---|---|---|---|---|---|---|---|
| Season | Club | League | GP | G | A | Pts | PIM | GP | G | A | Pts | PIM |
| 2002-03 | Det. Compuware | NAHL | 49 | 8 | 11 | 19 | 37 | .... | .... | .... | .... | .... |
| 2003-04 | St. Louis | USHL | 57 | 12 | 17 | 29 | 36 | .... | .... | .... | .... | .... |
| 2004-05 | Sioux City | USHL | 58 | 19 | 23 | 42 | 27 | 13 | 4 | 1 | 5 | 8 |
| 2005-06 | Ohio State | CCHA | 9 | 0 | 0 | 0 | 0 | .... | .... | .... | .... | .... |
| 2006-07 | Ohio State | CCHA | 26 | 7 | 7 | 14 | 10 | .... | .... | .... | .... | .... |
| 2007-08 | Ohio State | CCHA | 25 | 2 | 3 | 5 | 12 | .... | .... | .... | .... | .... |
| 2008-09 | Ohio State | CCHA | 42 | 18 | 23 | 41 | 18 | .... | .... | .... | .... | .... |

Signed as a free agent by **Los Angeles**, March 31, 2009.

## ELLER, Lars (EHL-uhr, LARZ) ST.L.

Center. Shoots left. 6'1", 192 lbs. Born, Herlev, Denmark, May 8, 1989.
(St. Louis' 1st choice, 13th overall, in 2007 Entry Draft).

| | | | Regular Season | | | | | Playoffs | | | | |
|---|---|---|---|---|---|---|---|---|---|---|---|---|
| Season | Club | League | GP | G | A | Pts | PIM | GP | G | A | Pts | PIM |
| 2004-05 | Rodovre IK Jr. | Den-Jr. | 28 | 21 | 26 | 47 | 20 | .... | .... | .... | .... | .... |
| | Rodovre | Denmark | 1 | 3 | 1 | 4 | 0 | .... | .... | .... | .... | .... |
| 2005-06 | Frolunda U18 | Swe-U18 | 8 | 2 | 4 | 6 | 10 | 2 | 0 | 0 | 0 | 0 |
| | Frolunda Jr. | Swe-Jr. | 36 | 7 | 7 | 14 | 6 | 2 | 0 | 0 | 0 | 0 |
| 2006-07 | Frolunda U18 | Swe-U18 | 3 | 1 | 4 | 5 | 6 | 6 | 3 | 2 | 5 | 8 |
| | Frolunda Jr. | Swe-Jr. | 39 | 18 | 37 | 55 | 58 | 8 | 4 | 1 | 5 | 24 |
| 2007-08 | Boras HC | Sweden-2 | 19 | 2 | 6 | 8 | 8 | .... | .... | .... | .... | .... |
| | Frolunda Jr. | Swe-Jr. | 9 | 4 | 4 | 8 | 10 | 7 | 5 | 6 | 11 | 14 |
| | Frolunda | Sweden | 14 | 0 | 2 | 2 | 4 | 7 | 0 | 1 | 1 | 2 |
| 2008-09 | Frolunda | Sweden | 48 | 12 | 17 | 29 | 28 | 10 | 3 | 1 | 4 | 12 |

## ELLERBY, Keaton (EHL-uhr-bee, KEE-tuhn) FLA.

Defense. Shoots left. 6'4", 186 lbs. Born, Strathmore, Alta., November 5, 1988.
(Florida's 1st choice, 10th overall, in 2007 Entry Draft).

| | | | Regular Season | | | | | Playoffs | | | | |
|---|---|---|---|---|---|---|---|---|---|---|---|---|
| Season | Club | League | GP | G | A | Pts | PIM | GP | G | A | Pts | PIM |
| 2003-04 | Okotoks Oilers | AMHA | 30 | 7 | 32 | 39 | 69 | .... | .... | .... | .... | .... |
| 2004-05 | Kamloops Blazers | WHL | 60 | 0 | 1 | 1 | 77 | 6 | 0 | 0 | 0 | 16 |
| 2005-06 | Kamloops Blazers | WHL | 68 | 2 | 6 | 8 | 121 | .... | .... | .... | .... | .... |
| 2006-07 | Kamloops Blazers | WHL | 69 | 2 | 23 | 25 | 120 | 4 | 1 | 2 | 3 | 12 |
| 2007-08 | Kamloops Blazers | WHL | 16 | 0 | 3 | 3 | 29 | .... | .... | .... | .... | .... |
| | Moose Jaw | WHL | 53 | 2 | 21 | 23 | 81 | 5 | 0 | 2 | 2 | 15 |
| 2008-09 | Rochester | AHL | 75 | 3 | 20 | 23 | 44 | .... | .... | .... | .... | .... |

## ELLINGTON, Taylor (EHL-ihng-tuhn, TAY-luhr) VAN.

Defense. Shoots left. 6', 205 lbs. Born, Victoria, B.C., October 31, 1988.
(Vancouver's 2nd choice, 33rd overall, in 2007 Entry Draft).

| | | | Regular Season | | | | | Playoffs | | | | |
|---|---|---|---|---|---|---|---|---|---|---|---|---|
| Season | Club | League | GP | G | A | Pts | PIM | GP | G | A | Pts | PIM |
| 2004-05 | Everett Silvertips | WHL | 47 | 0 | 0 | 0 | 48 | 8 | 0 | 1 | 1 | 4 |
| 2005-06 | Everett Silvertips | WHL | 63 | 0 | 7 | 7 | 62 | 15 | 1 | 2 | 3 | 16 |
| 2006-07 | Everett Silvertips | WHL | 60 | 5 | 8 | 13 | 65 | 6 | 1 | 0 | 1 | 2 |
| 2007-08 | Everett Silvertips | WHL | 48 | 3 | 11 | 14 | 66 | 4 | 0 | 0 | 0 | 0 |
| 2008-09 | Everett Silvertips | WHL | 69 | 6 | 26 | 32 | 130 | 5 | 0 | 5 | 5 | 6 |
| | Manitoba Moose | AHL | 1 | 1 | 0 | 1 | 0 | .... | .... | .... | .... | .... |

## ELLIOTT, Stefan (ehl-LEE-awt, STEH-fan) COL.

Defense. Shoots right. 6'1", 180 lbs. Born, Vancouver, B.C., January 30, 1991.
(Colorado's 3rd choice, 49th overall, in 2009 Entry Draft).

| | | | Regular Season | | | | | Playoffs | | | | |
|---|---|---|---|---|---|---|---|---|---|---|---|---|
| Season | Club | League | GP | G | A | Pts | PIM | GP | G | A | Pts | PIM |
| 2006-07 | Van. NW Giants | Minor-BC | 36 | 12 | 19 | 31 | 18 | .... | .... | .... | .... | .... |
| | Saskatoon Blades | WHL | 1 | 0 | 0 | 0 | 0 | .... | .... | .... | .... | .... |
| 2007-08 | Saskatoon Blades | WHL | 67 | 9 | 31 | 40 | 17 | .... | .... | .... | .... | .... |
| 2008-09 | Saskatoon Blades | WHL | 71 | 16 | 39 | 55 | 26 | 7 | 1 | 3 | 4 | 4 |

Canadian Major Junior Scholastic Player of the Year (2009)

## ELLIS, Ryan (EHL-ihs, RIGH-uhn) NSH.

Defense. Shoots right. 5'9", 180 lbs. Born, Hamilton, Ont., January 3, 1991.
(Nashville's 1st choice, 11th overall, in 2009 Entry Draft).

| | | | Regular Season | | | | | Playoffs | | | | |
|---|---|---|---|---|---|---|---|---|---|---|---|---|
| Season | Club | League | GP | G | A | Pts | PIM | GP | G | A | Pts | PIM |
| 2006-07 | Cambridge Hawks | Minor-ON | 75 | 37 | 56 | 93 | 151 | .... | .... | .... | .... | .... |
| 2007-08 | Windsor Spitfires | OHL | 63 | 15 | 48 | 63 | 51 | 5 | 2 | 3 | 5 | 2 |
| 2008-09 | Windsor Spitfires | OHL | 57 | 22 | *67 | 89 | 57 | 20 | 8 | *23 | 31 | 20 |

Canadian Major Junior All-Rookie Team (2008) • OHL First All-Star Team (2009) • Canadian Major Junior First All-Star Team (2009)

## ELO, Eero (EH-loh, EE-roh) MIN.

Left wing. Shoots right. 6'3", 189 lbs. Born, Rauma, Finland, April 26, 1990.
(Minnesota's 4th choice, 145th overall, in 2008 Entry Draft).

| | | | Regular Season | | | | | Playoffs | | | | |
|---|---|---|---|---|---|---|---|---|---|---|---|---|
| Season | Club | League | GP | G | A | Pts | PIM | GP | G | A | Pts | PIM |
| 2005-06 | Lukko Rauma U18 | Fin-U18 | 30 | 10 | 10 | 20 | 18 | .... | .... | .... | .... | .... |
| 2006-07 | Lukko Rauma U18 | Fin-U18 | 18 | 8 | 12 | 20 | 36 | .... | .... | .... | .... | .... |
| | Lukko Rauma Jr. | Fin-Jr. | 22 | 1 | 2 | 3 | 8 | .... | .... | .... | .... | .... |
| 2007-08 | Lukko Rauma U18 | Fin-U18 | 5 | 2 | 3 | 5 | 2 | 2 | 2 | 1 | 3 | 0 |
| | Lukko Rauma Jr. | Fin-Jr. | 42 | 12 | 15 | 27 | 34 | .... | .... | .... | .... | .... |
| 2008-09 | Suomi U20 | Finland-2 | 1 | 0 | 0 | 0 | 0 | .... | .... | .... | .... | .... |
| | Lukko Rauma Jr. | Fin-Jr. | 42 | 20 | 26 | 46 | 38 | 8 | 7 | 3 | 10 | 14 |

## EMMERSON, Riley (EHM-uhr-sohn, RIGH-lee)

Right wing. Shoots left. 6'8", 230 lbs. Born, Burnaby, B.C., February 7, 1986.
(Minnesota's 7th choice, 199th overall, in 2005 Entry Draft).

| | | | Regular Season | | | | | Playoffs | | | | |
|---|---|---|---|---|---|---|---|---|---|---|---|---|
| Season | Club | League | GP | G | A | Pts | PIM | GP | G | A | Pts | PIM |
| 2003-04 | Chilliwack Chiefs | BCHL | 52 | 0 | 6 | 6 | 137 | 6 | 0 | 0 | 0 | 0 |
| 2004-05 | Tri-City Americans | WHL | 35 | 0 | 0 | 0 | 61 | .... | .... | .... | .... | .... |
| 2005-06 | Tri-City Americans | WHL | 66 | 1 | 1 | 2 | 109 | 2 | 0 | 0 | 0 | 0 |
| 2006-07 | Texas Wildcatters | ECHL | 42 | 2 | 1 | 3 | 99 | .... | .... | .... | .... | .... |
| 2007-08 | Texas Wildcatters | ECHL | 51 | 2 | 2 | 4 | 142 | 4 | 0 | 0 | 0 | 16 |
| 2008-09 | Rochester | AHL | 42 | 0 | 0 | 0 | 107 | .... | .... | .... | .... | .... |
| | Florida Everblades | ECHL | 1 | 0 | 0 | 0 | 4 | .... | .... | .... | .... | .... |

## EMMERTON, Cory (EHM-uhr-tuhn, KOH-ree) DET.

Center. Shoots left. 6', 177 lbs. Born, St. Thomas, Ont., June 1, 1988.
(Detroit's 1st choice, 41st overall, in 2006 Entry Draft).

| | | | Regular Season | | | | | Playoffs | | | | |
|---|---|---|---|---|---|---|---|---|---|---|---|---|
| Season | Club | League | GP | G | A | Pts | PIM | GP | G | A | Pts | PIM |
| 2003-04 | Elgin | Minor-ON | 32 | 33 | 24 | 57 | 26 | .... | .... | .... | .... | .... |
| 2004-05 | Kingston | OHL | 58 | 17 | 21 | 38 | 8 | .... | .... | .... | .... | .... |
| 2005-06 | Kingston | OHL | 66 | 26 | 64 | 90 | 32 | 6 | 2 | 0 | 2 | 6 |
| 2006-07 | Kingston | OHL | 40 | 29 | 37 | 66 | 22 | 5 | 5 | 2 | 7 | 2 |
| | Grand Rapids | AHL | .... | .... | .... | .... | .... | 2 | 0 | 0 | 0 | 0 |
| 2007-08 | Kingston | OHL | 24 | 13 | 18 | 31 | 6 | .... | .... | .... | .... | .... |
| | Brampton | OHL | 30 | 12 | 18 | 30 | 10 | 5 | 0 | 2 | 2 | 2 |
| | Grand Rapids | AHL | 7 | 0 | 1 | 1 | 0 | .... | .... | .... | .... | .... |
| 2008-09 | Grand Rapids | AHL | 69 | 10 | 25 | 35 | 18 | 9 | 1 | 0 | 1 | 2 |

## ENGELLAND, Deryk (ehn-GUHL-uhnd, DEH-rihk)

Defense. Shoots right. 6'2", 202 lbs. Born, Edmonton, Alta., April 5, 1982.
(New Jersey's 11th choice, 194th overall, in 2000 Entry Draft).

| | | | Regular Season | | | | | Playoffs | | | | |
|---|---|---|---|---|---|---|---|---|---|---|---|---|
| Season | Club | League | GP | G | A | Pts | PIM | GP | G | A | Pts | PIM |
| 1998-99 | Moose Jaw | WHL | 2 | 0 | 0 | 0 | 0 | .... | .... | .... | .... | .... |
| 99-2000 | Moose Jaw | WHL | 55 | 0 | 5 | 5 | 62 | 4 | 0 | 0 | 0 | 0 |
| 2000-01 | Moose Jaw | WHL | 65 | 4 | 11 | 15 | 157 | 4 | 0 | 0 | 0 | 10 |
| 2001-02 | Moose Jaw | WHL | 56 | 7 | 10 | 17 | 102 | 12 | 0 | 2 | 2 | 27 |
| 2002-03 | Moose Jaw | WHL | 65 | 3 | 8 | 11 | 199 | 13 | 1 | 1 | 2 | 20 |
| 2003-04 | Lowell | AHL | 26 | 0 | 0 | 0 | 34 | .... | .... | .... | .... | .... |
| | Las Vegas | ECHL | 35 | 2 | 11 | 13 | 63 | 2 | 0 | 0 | 0 | 0 |
| 2004-05 | Las Vegas | ECHL | 72 | 5 | 16 | 21 | 138 | .... | .... | .... | .... | .... |
| 2005-06 | Hershey Bears | AHL | 37 | 0 | 4 | 4 | 77 | 1 | 0 | 0 | 0 | 0 |
| | South Carolina | ECHL | 35 | 3 | 13 | 16 | 20 | .... | .... | .... | .... | .... |
| 2006-07 | Hershey Bears | AHL | 44 | 4 | 6 | 10 | 95 | 14 | 0 | 0 | 0 | 14 |
| | Reading Royals | ECHL | 6 | 0 | 3 | 3 | 8 | .... | .... | .... | .... | .... |
| 2007-08 | Wilkes-Barre | AHL | 80 | 2 | 15 | 17 | 141 | 23 | 1 | 3 | 4 | 14 |
| 2008-09 | Wilkes-Barre | AHL | 80 | 3 | 11 | 14 | 143 | 12 | 0 | 2 | 2 | 6 |

Signed as a free agent by **Calgary**, July, 2003. Signed as a free agent by **Pittsburgh**, July 16, 2007.

## ENGQVIST, Andreas (ENG-kvihst, awn-DRAY-uhs) MTL.

Center. Shoots right. 6'4", 200 lbs. Born, Stockholm, Sweden, December 23, 1987.

| | | | Regular Season | | | | | Playoffs | | | | |
|---|---|---|---|---|---|---|---|---|---|---|---|---|
| Season | Club | League | GP | G | A | Pts | PIM | GP | G | A | Pts | PIM |
| 2004-05 | Spanga U18 | Swe-U18 | 6 | 3 | 6 | 9 | 6 | .... | .... | .... | .... | .... |
| | Spanga Jr. | Swe-Jr. | 13 | 15 | 9 | 24 | 12 | .... | .... | .... | .... | .... |
| 2005-06 | Djurgarden Jr. | Swe-Jr. | 26 | 6 | 13 | 19 | 6 | 4 | 1 | 1 | 2 | 2 |
| | Djurgarden | Sweden | 1 | 0 | 0 | 0 | 0 | .... | .... | .... | .... | .... |
| 2006-07 | Djurgarden Jr. | Swe-Jr. | 5 | 1 | 3 | 4 | 4 | 7 | 3 | 4 | 7 | 10 |
| | Djurgarden | Sweden | 43 | 1 | 3 | 4 | 16 | .... | .... | .... | .... | .... |
| 2007-08 | Djurgarden Jr. | Swe-Jr. | 1 | 1 | 0 | 1 | 0 | .... | .... | .... | .... | .... |
| | Djurgarden | Sweden | 51 | 5 | 7 | 12 | 16 | 5 | 0 | 0 | 0 | 0 |
| 2008-09 | Djurgarden | Sweden | 31 | 9 | 7 | 16 | 12 | .... | .... | .... | .... | .... |

Signed as a free agent by **Montreal**, July 13, 2009.

## ENLUND, Jonas (EHN-luhnd, YOH-nuhs) ATL.

Center. Shoots left. 6', 185 lbs. Born, Helsinki, Finland, November 3, 1987.
(Atlanta's 5th choice, 165th overall, in 2006 Entry Draft).

| | | | Regular Season | | | | | Playoffs | | | | |
|---|---|---|---|---|---|---|---|---|---|---|---|---|
| Season | Club | League | GP | G | A | Pts | PIM | GP | G | A | Pts | PIM |
| 2002-03 | HIFK Helsinki U18 | Fin-U18 | 24 | 11 | 3 | 14 | 0 | 2 | 1 | 0 | 1 | 0 |
| 2003-04 | HIFK Helsinki U18 | Fin-U18 | 30 | 15 | 16 | 31 | 30 | 7 | 3 | 5 | 8 | 2 |
| | HIFK Helsinki Jr. | Fin-Jr. | 3 | 0 | 0 | 0 | 0 | .... | .... | .... | .... | .... |
| 2004-05 | HIFK Helsinki U18 | Fin-U18 | .... | .... | .... | .... | .... | 7 | 4 | 3 | 7 | 8 |
| | HIFK Helsinki Jr. | Fin-Jr. | 38 | 15 | 15 | 30 | 18 | 2 | 1 | 1 | 2 | 0 |
| 2005-06 | Suomi U20 | Finland-2 | 4 | 1 | 1 | 2 | 0 | .... | .... | .... | .... | .... |
| | HIFK Helsinki Jr. | Fin-Jr. | 37 | 24 | 18 | 42 | 14 | .... | .... | .... | .... | .... |
| 2006-07 | Tappara Jr. | Fin-Jr. | 10 | 2 | 7 | 9 | 12 | 4 | 3 | 0 | 3 | 2 |
| | Suomi U20 | Finland-2 | 5 | 0 | 1 | 1 | 0 | .... | .... | .... | .... | .... |
| | Tappara Tampere | Finland | 46 | 2 | 1 | 3 | 8 | 5 | 0 | 0 | 0 | 0 |
| 2007-08 | Tappara Tampere | Finland | 56 | 19 | 22 | 41 | 10 | 11 | 3 | 3 | 6 | 4 |
| 2008-09 | Tappara Tampere | Finland | 58 | 11 | 16 | 27 | 26 | 3 | 2 | 2 | 4 | 2 |

## ENNIS, Tyler (EH-nihs, TIGH-luhr) BUF.

Center. Shoots left. 5'9", 146 lbs. Born, Edmonton, Alta., October 6, 1989.
(Buffalo's 2nd choice, 26th overall, in 2008 Entry Draft).

| | | | Regular Season | | | | | Playoffs | | | | |
|---|---|---|---|---|---|---|---|---|---|---|---|---|
| Season | Club | League | GP | G | A | Pts | PIM | GP | G | A | Pts | PIM |
| 2004-05 | K of C Pats | AMHL | 36 | 15 | 17 | 32 | 10 | .... | .... | .... | .... | .... |
| 2005-06 | Medicine Hat | WHL | 43 | 3 | 7 | 10 | 10 | 7 | 0 | 0 | 0 | 0 |
| 2006-07 | Medicine Hat | WHL | 71 | 26 | 24 | 50 | 30 | 22 | 8 | 4 | 12 | 6 |
| 2007-08 | Medicine Hat | WHL | 70 | 43 | 48 | 91 | 42 | 5 | 0 | 4 | 4 | 6 |
| 2008-09 | Medicine Hat | WHL | 61 | 43 | 42 | 85 | 21 | 11 | 8 | 11 | 19 | 10 |

WHL East First All-Star Team (2008, 2009)

**ERIXON, Tim** (AIR-ihx-uhn, TIHM) **CGY.**

Defense. Shoots left. 6'2", 189 lbs. Born, Port Chester, NY, February 24, 1991.
(Calgary's 1st choice, 23rd overall, in 2009 Entry Draft).

| | | | Regular Season | | | | | Playoffs | | | | |
|---|---|---|---|---|---|---|---|---|---|---|---|---|
| **Season** | **Club** | **League** | **GP** | **G** | **A** | **Pts** | **PIM** | **GP** | **G** | **A** | **Pts** | **PIM** |
| 2005-06 | Skelleftea U18 | Swe-U18 | 9 | 0 | 2 | 2 | 4 | .... | .... | .... | .... | .... |
| 2006-07 | Skelleftea U18 | Swe-U18 | 8 | 2 | 2 | 4 | 20 | .... | .... | .... | .... | .... |
| | Skelleftea Jr. | Swe-Jr. | 8 | 0 | 2 | 2 | 2 | 2 | 0 | 0 | 0 | 4 |
| 2007-08 | Skelleftea U18 | Swe-U18 | 4 | 0 | 1 | 1 | 10 | .... | .... | .... | .... | .... |
| | Skelleftea Jr. | Swe-Jr. | 28 | 3 | 11 | 14 | 78 | 1 | 0 | 1 | 1 | 4 |
| | Skelleftea AIK HK | Sweden | 2 | 0 | 0 | 0 | 0 | .... | .... | .... | .... | .... |
| 2008-09 | Skelleftea AIK U18 | Swe-U18 | 1 | 0 | 2 | 2 | 10 | 5 | 1 | 5 | 6 | 14 |
| | Skelleftea AIK Jr. | Swe-Jr. | 9 | 2 | 12 | 14 | 10 | 5 | 1 | 2 | 3 | 4 |
| | Malmo | Sweden-2 | 3 | 0 | 2 | 2 | 0 | .... | .... | .... | .... | .... |
| | Skelleftea AIK | Sweden | 45 | 2 | 5 | 7 | 12 | 9 | 0 | 0 | 0 | 4 |

**ERSTAD, Travis** (UHR-stad, TRA-vihs) **ST.L.**

Center/Right wing. Shoots right. 6'4", 199 lbs. Born, Madison, WI, November 9, 1988.
(St. Louis' 8th choice, 100th overall, in 2007 Entry Draft).

| | | | Regular Season | | | | | Playoffs | | | | |
|---|---|---|---|---|---|---|---|---|---|---|---|---|
| **Season** | **Club** | **League** | **GP** | **G** | **A** | **Pts** | **PIM** | **GP** | **G** | **A** | **Pts** | **PIM** |
| 2005-06 | Stevens Point High | High-WI | STATISTICS NOT AVAILABLE | | | | | | | | | |
| 2006-07 | Stevens Point High | High-WI | 24 | 31 | 33 | 64 | .... | .... | .... | .... | .... | .... |
| | Lincoln Stars | USHL | 8 | 0 | 0 | 0 | 4 | 3 | 1 | 0 | 1 | 0 |
| 2007-08 | Lincoln Stars | USHL | 52 | 9 | 10 | 19 | 104 | 8 | 1 | 2 | 3 | 8 |
| 2008-09 | Wisc-Stevens Pt. | NCHA | 26 | 10 | 7 | 17 | 56 | .... | .... | .... | .... | .... |

**ESPOSITO, Angelo** (EHS-poh-ZEE-toh, AN-jul-loh) **ATL.**

Center. Shoots left. 6'1", 180 lbs. Born, Montreal, Que., February 20, 1989.
(Pittsburgh's 1st choice, 20th overall, in 2007 Entry Draft).

| | | | Regular Season | | | | | Playoffs | | | | |
|---|---|---|---|---|---|---|---|---|---|---|---|---|
| **Season** | **Club** | **League** | **GP** | **G** | **A** | **Pts** | **PIM** | **GP** | **G** | **A** | **Pts** | **PIM** |
| 2004-05 | Shat.-St. Mary's | High-MN | 68 | 31 | 35 | 66 | 47 | .... | .... | .... | .... | .... |
| 2005-06 | Quebec Remparts | QMJHL | 57 | 39 | 59 | 98 | 45 | 23 | 6 | 5 | 11 | 4 |
| 2006-07 | Quebec Remparts | QMJHL | 60 | 27 | 52 | 79 | 63 | 5 | 4 | 3 | 7 | 2 |
| 2007-08 | Quebec Remparts | QMJHL | 56 | 30 | 39 | 69 | 69 | 11 | 4 | 6 | 10 | 6 |
| | Chicago Wolves | AHL | 1 | 0 | 0 | 0 | 0 | .... | .... | .... | .... | .... |
| 2008-09 | Montreal | QMJHL | 35 | 24 | 18 | 42 | 25 | .... | .... | .... | .... | .... |

QMJHL All-Rookie Team (2006) • QMJHL Offensive Rookie of the Year (2006)

Traded to **Atlanta** by **Pittsburgh** with Colby Armstrong, Erik Christensen and Pittsburgh's 1st round choice (Daultan Leveille) in 2008 Entry Draft for Marian Hossa and Pascal Dupuis, February 26, 2008.

**EVSEEV, Vladislav** (yehv-SAY-ehv, VLA-dih-slav) **BOS.**

Left wing. Shoots left. 6'2", 196 lbs. Born, Moscow, USSR, September 10, 1984.
(Boston's 2nd choice, 56th overall, in 2002 Entry Draft).

| | | | Regular Season | | | | | Playoffs | | | | |
|---|---|---|---|---|---|---|---|---|---|---|---|---|
| **Season** | **Club** | **League** | **GP** | **G** | **A** | **Pts** | **PIM** | **GP** | **G** | **A** | **Pts** | **PIM** |
| 99-2000 | Dyn'o Moscow 2 | Russia-3 | 5 | 2 | 3 | 5 | 6 | .... | .... | .... | .... | .... |
| 2000-01 | Dyn'o Moscow 2 | Russia-3 | 6 | 5 | 2 | 7 | 2 | .... | .... | .... | .... | .... |
| 2001-02 | CSKA Moscow 2 | Russia-3 | 8 | 2 | 1 | 3 | 2 | .... | .... | .... | .... | .... |
| | HK CSKA Moscow | Russia-2 | 15 | 2 | 5 | 7 | 10 | .... | .... | .... | .... | .... |
| 2002-03 | Dynamo Moscow | Russia | 22 | 1 | 1 | 2 | 2 | 1 | 0 | 0 | 0 | 0 |
| 2003-04 | Vityaz Podolsk | Russia-2 | 8 | 1 | 2 | 3 | 2 | 7 | 0 | 0 | 0 | 2 |
| 2004-05 | Dynamo Moscow | Russia | 12 | 1 | 1 | 2 | 2 | .... | .... | .... | .... | .... |
| | Ufa | Russia | 5 | 0 | 0 | 0 | 2 | .... | .... | .... | .... | .... |
| 2005-06 | Cherepovets | Russia | 30 | 3 | 0 | 3 | 18 | .... | .... | .... | .... | .... |
| 2006-07 | Dynamo Moscow | Russia | 30 | 1 | 3 | 4 | 32 | 2 | 0 | 0 | 0 | 0 |
| 2007-08 | Dynamo Moscow | Russia | 3 | 0 | 0 | 0 | 12 | .... | .... | .... | .... | .... |
| | Vityaz Chekhov | Russia | 30 | 5 | 5 | 10 | 10 | .... | .... | .... | .... | .... |
| 2008-09 | Vityaz Chekhov | Rus-KHL | 52 | 4 | 3 | 7 | 16 | .... | .... | .... | .... | .... |

**EZHOV, Denis** (YEHZH-awf, DEH-nihs) **BUF.**

Defense. Shoots left. 5'11", 200 lbs. Born, Togliatti, USSR, February 28, 1985.
(Buffalo's 5th choice, 114th overall, in 2003 Entry Draft).

| | | | Regular Season | | | | | Playoffs | | | | |
|---|---|---|---|---|---|---|---|---|---|---|---|---|
| **Season** | **Club** | **League** | **GP** | **G** | **A** | **Pts** | **PIM** | **GP** | **G** | **A** | **Pts** | **PIM** |
| 99-2000 | Lada Togliatti 2 | Russia-3 | 4 | 0 | 0 | 0 | 4 | .... | .... | .... | .... | .... |
| 2000-01 | Lada Togliatti 2 | Russia-3 | STATISTICS NOT AVAILABLE | | | | | | | | | |
| 2001-02 | Lada Togliatti 2 | Russia-3 | 4 | 2 | 4 | 6 | 6 | .... | .... | .... | .... | .... |
| | Lada Togliatti | Russia | 15 | 0 | 0 | 0 | 6 | .... | .... | .... | .... | .... |
| 2002-03 | Lada Togliatti 2 | Russia-3 | 15 | 2 | 7 | 9 | 4 | .... | .... | .... | .... | .... |
| | CSK VVS Samara | Russia-2 | 9 | 0 | 1 | 1 | 8 | .... | .... | .... | .... | .... |
| 2003-04 | Novokuznetsk | Russia | 19 | 0 | 1 | 1 | 2 | 3 | 0 | 0 | 0 | 0 |
| | CSKA Moscow 2 | Russia-3 | 4 | 1 | 2 | 3 | 2 | .... | .... | .... | .... | .... |
| 2004-05 | Novokuznetsk | Russia | 28 | 0 | 0 | 0 | 16 | 4 | 0 | 0 | 0 | 2 |
| 2005-06 | Mytischi | Russia | 24 | 1 | 0 | 1 | 10 | .... | .... | .... | .... | .... |
| | Kristall Elektrostal | Russia-3 | STATISTICS NOT AVAILABLE | | | | | | | | | |
| 2006-07 | Chelyabinsk | Russia | 54 | 2 | 6 | 8 | 73 | .... | .... | .... | .... | .... |
| 2007-08 | Chelyabinsk | Russia | 57 | 4 | 9 | 13 | 64 | 3 | 0 | 0 | 0 | 10 |
| 2008-09 | Omsk | Rus-KHL | 55 | 2 | 8 | 10 | 58 | 8 | 1 | 0 | 1 | 2 |

**FADDEN, Mitch** (FA-dehn, MIHTCH) **T.B.**

Center. Shoots left. 6', 174 lbs. Born, Victoria, B.C., April 3, 1988.
(Tampa Bay's 4th choice, 107th overall, in 2007 Entry Draft).

| | | | Regular Season | | | | | Playoffs | | | | |
|---|---|---|---|---|---|---|---|---|---|---|---|---|
| **Season** | **Club** | **League** | **GP** | **G** | **A** | **Pts** | **PIM** | **GP** | **G** | **A** | **Pts** | **PIM** |
| 2003-04 | Victoria Cougars | VIJHL | 47 | 36 | 31 | 67 | 63 | 11 | 11 | 4 | 15 | 24 |
| | Seattle | WHL | 2 | 0 | 0 | 0 | 0 | .... | .... | .... | .... | .... |
| 2004-05 | Seattle | WHL | 64 | 9 | 12 | 21 | 30 | 12 | 2 | 0 | 2 | 4 |
| 2005-06 | Seattle | WHL | 38 | 9 | 11 | 20 | 19 | .... | .... | .... | .... | .... |
| | Lethbridge | WHL | 30 | 11 | 17 | 28 | 22 | 6 | 2 | 5 | 7 | 14 |
| 2006-07 | Lethbridge | WHL | 71 | 36 | 48 | 84 | 54 | .... | .... | .... | .... | .... |
| 2007-08 | Lethbridge | WHL | 72 | 34 | 55 | 89 | 72 | 19 | 5 | 15 | 20 | 19 |
| 2008-09 | Lethbridge | WHL | 9 | 2 | 3 | 5 | 8 | .... | .... | .... | .... | .... |
| | Tri-City Americans | WHL | 54 | 35 | 36 | 71 | 41 | 10 | 3 | 13 | 16 | 8 |

WHL East Second All-Star Team (2008)

**FAHEY, Brian** (FAY-hee, BRIGH-uhn) **COL.**

Defense. Shoots right. 6'1", 215 lbs. Born, Des Plaines, IL, March 2, 1981.
(Colorado's 7th choice, 119th overall, in 2000 Entry Draft).

| | | | Regular Season | | | | | Playoffs | | | | |
|---|---|---|---|---|---|---|---|---|---|---|---|---|
| **Season** | **Club** | **League** | **GP** | **G** | **A** | **Pts** | **PIM** | **GP** | **G** | **A** | **Pts** | **PIM** |
| 1997-98 | USNTDP | U-18 | 17 | 1 | 10 | 11 | 12 | .... | .... | .... | .... | .... |
| | USNTDP | USHL | 5 | 1 | 1 | 2 | 8 | .... | .... | .... | .... | .... |
| | USNTDP | NAHL | 39 | 5 | 10 | 15 | 35 | 7 | 0 | 0 | 0 | 2 |
| 1998-99 | USNTDP | U-18 | 6 | 1 | 0 | 1 | 4 | .... | .... | .... | .... | .... |
| | USNTDP | USHL | 52 | 9 | 9 | 18 | 34 | .... | .... | .... | .... | .... |
| 99-2000 | U. of Wisconsin | WCHA | 41 | 6 | 11 | 17 | 42 | .... | .... | .... | .... | .... |
| 2000-01 | U. of Wisconsin | WCHA | 38 | 1 | 5 | 6 | 16 | .... | .... | .... | .... | .... |
| 2001-02 | U. of Wisconsin | WCHA | 38 | 2 | 8 | 10 | 55 | .... | .... | .... | .... | .... |
| 2002-03 | U. of Wisconsin | WCHA | 39 | 5 | 4 | 9 | 34 | .... | .... | .... | .... | .... |
| 2003-04 | Worcester IceCats | AHL | 2 | 0 | 0 | 0 | 2 | .... | .... | .... | .... | .... |
| | Atlantic City | ECHL | 55 | 11 | 26 | 37 | 49 | 2 | 0 | 0 | 0 | 2 |
| | Hershey Bears | AHL | 12 | 0 | 1 | 1 | 6 | .... | .... | .... | .... | .... |
| 2004-05 | Worcester IceCats | AHL | 20 | 0 | 4 | 4 | 12 | .... | .... | .... | .... | .... |
| | Atlantic City | ECHL | 46 | 10 | 16 | 26 | 47 | 3 | 0 | 2 | 2 | 0 |
| 2005-06 | Iowa Stars | AHL | 64 | 6 | 11 | 17 | 74 | 7 | 0 | 1 | 1 | 8 |
| | Idaho Steelheads | ECHL | 3 | 1 | 1 | 2 | 4 | .... | .... | .... | .... | .... |
| 2006-07 | Chicago Wolves | AHL | 75 | 11 | 18 | 29 | 81 | 15 | 3 | 2 | 5 | 20 |
| 2007-08 | Chicago Wolves | AHL | 76 | 14 | 23 | 37 | 123 | 24 | 2 | 8 | 10 | 24 |
| 2008-09 | Hartford Wolf Pack | AHL | 66 | 4 | 20 | 24 | 67 | 5 | 0 | 1 | 1 | 6 |

WCHA All-Rookie Team (2000) • ECHL All-Rookie Team (2004)

Signed as a free agent by **Chicago** (AHL), August 31, 2006. Signed as a free agent by **NY Rangers**, July 17, 2008. Traded to **Colorado** by **NY Rangers** for Nigel Wiliams, July 16, 2009.

**FAIRCHILD, Cade** (FAIR-chighld, KAYD) **ST.L.**

Defense. Shoots left. 5'10", 190 lbs. Born, Duluth, MN, January 15, 1989.
(St. Louis' 7th choice, 96th overall, in 2007 Entry Draft).

| | | | Regular Season | | | | | Playoffs | | | | |
|---|---|---|---|---|---|---|---|---|---|---|---|---|
| **Season** | **Club** | **League** | **GP** | **G** | **A** | **Pts** | **PIM** | **GP** | **G** | **A** | **Pts** | **PIM** |
| 2004-05 | Duluth East | High-MN | 29 | 10 | 32 | 42 | .... | .... | .... | .... | .... | .... |
| 2005-06 | USNTDP | U-17 | 18 | 2 | 7 | 9 | 4 | .... | .... | .... | .... | .... |
| | USNTDP | NAHL | 36 | 8 | 9 | 17 | 10 | 2 | 0 | 0 | 0 | 0 |
| 2006-07 | USNTDP | U-18 | 36 | 3 | 16 | 19 | 34 | .... | .... | .... | .... | .... |
| | USNTDP | NAHL | 13 | 1 | 6 | 7 | 16 | .... | .... | .... | .... | .... |
| 2007-08 | U. of Minnesota | WCHA | 40 | 2 | 13 | 15 | 22 | .... | .... | .... | .... | .... |
| 2008-09 | U. of Minnesota | WCHA | 35 | 9 | 24 | 33 | 52 | .... | .... | .... | .... | .... |

WCHA All-Rookie Team (2008)

**FALK, Justin** (FAWLK, JUHS-tihn) **MIN.**

Defense. Shoots left. 6'5", 215 lbs. Born, Snowflake, Man., October 11, 1988.
(Minnesota's 2nd choice, 110th overall, in 2007 Entry Draft).

| | | | Regular Season | | | | | Playoffs | | | | |
|---|---|---|---|---|---|---|---|---|---|---|---|---|
| **Season** | **Club** | **League** | **GP** | **G** | **A** | **Pts** | **PIM** | **GP** | **G** | **A** | **Pts** | **PIM** |
| 2004-05 | Swan Valley | MJHL | 56 | 0 | 8 | 8 | 46 | .... | .... | .... | .... | .... |
| | Calgary Hitmen | WHL | 4 | 0 | 0 | 0 | 2 | 5 | 0 | 0 | 0 | 0 |
| 2005-06 | Calgary Hitmen | WHL | 5 | 0 | 2 | 2 | 0 | .... | .... | .... | .... | .... |
| | Spokane Chiefs | WHL | 48 | 0 | 8 | 8 | 35 | .... | .... | .... | .... | .... |
| 2006-07 | Spokane Chiefs | WHL | 62 | 3 | 12 | 15 | 88 | 6 | 0 | 0 | 0 | 8 |
| 2007-08 | Spokane Chiefs | WHL | 72 | 4 | 22 | 26 | 98 | 21 | 1 | 4 | 5 | 12 |
| 2008-09 | Houston Aeros | AHL | 65 | 0 | 3 | 3 | 44 | 20 | 0 | 2 | 2 | 4 |

Memorial Cup All-Star Team (2008)

**FALLSTROM, Alexander** (FAHL-struhm, al-ehx-AN-duhr) **MIN.**

Right wing. Shoots right. 6'2", 192 lbs. Born, Goteborg, Sweden, September 15, 1990.
(Minnesota's 4th choice, 116th overall, in 2009 Entry Draft).

| | | | Regular Season | | | | | Playoffs | | | | |
|---|---|---|---|---|---|---|---|---|---|---|---|---|
| **Season** | **Club** | **League** | **GP** | **G** | **A** | **Pts** | **PIM** | **GP** | **G** | **A** | **Pts** | **PIM** |
| 2005-06 | Djurgarden U18 | Swe-U18 | 11 | 1 | 2 | 3 | 2 | .... | .... | .... | .... | .... |
| 2006-07 | Djurgarden U18 | Swe-U18 | 33 | 22 | 15 | 37 | 52 | 3 | 2 | 1 | 3 | 2 |
| | Djurgarden Jr. | Swe-Jr. | 2 | 0 | 0 | 0 | 0 | 1 | 0 | 0 | 0 | 0 |
| 2007-08 | Shat.-St. Mary's | High-MN | 62 | 20 | 27 | 47 | 56 | .... | .... | .... | .... | .... |
| 2008-09 | Shat.-St. Mary's | High-MN | 52 | 40 | 47 | 87 | 52 | .... | .... | .... | .... | .... |

• Signed Letter of Intent to attend **Harvard University** (ECAC) in fall of 2009.

**FAST, T.J.** (FAST, TEE-JAY) **ST.L.**

Defense. Shoots left. 6'1", 190 lbs. Born, Calgary, Alta., September 2, 1987.
(Los Angeles' 3rd choice, 60th overall, in 2005 Entry Draft).

| | | | Regular Season | | | | | Playoffs | | | | |
|---|---|---|---|---|---|---|---|---|---|---|---|---|
| **Season** | **Club** | **League** | **GP** | **G** | **A** | **Pts** | **PIM** | **GP** | **G** | **A** | **Pts** | **PIM** |
| 2003-04 | Cgy. North Stars | AMHL | 31 | 7 | 7 | 14 | 42 | .... | .... | .... | .... | .... |
| 2004-05 | Camrose Kodiaks | AJHL | 58 | 8 | 28 | 36 | 40 | .... | .... | .... | .... | .... |
| 2005-06 | U. of Denver | WCHA | 39 | 1 | 6 | 7 | 26 | .... | .... | .... | .... | .... |
| 2006-07 | U. of Denver | WCHA | 19 | 0 | 4 | 4 | 14 | .... | .... | .... | .... | .... |
| | Tri-City Americans | WHL | 26 | 3 | 19 | 22 | 30 | 6 | 0 | 1 | 1 | 14 |
| 2007-08 | Tri-City Americans | WHL | 71 | 17 | 37 | 54 | 92 | 16 | 1 | 8 | 9 | 16 |
| 2008-09 | Peoria Rivermen | AHL | 46 | 1 | 4 | 5 | 12 | .... | .... | .... | .... | .... |
| | Alaska Aces | ECHL | 9 | 0 | 1 | 1 | 6 | 18 | 0 | 5 | 5 | 11 |

AJHL All-Rookie Team (2005) • WHL West First All-Star Team (2008)

Traded to **St. Louis** by **Los Angeles** for St. Louis' 5th round choice (later traded to Florida – Florida selected Wade Megan) in 2009 Entry Draft, June 4, 2008.

**FAYNE, Mark** (FAYN, MAHRK) **N.J.**

Defense. Shoots right. 6'4", 220 lbs. Born, Nashua, NH, May 15, 1987.
(New Jersey's 5th choice, 155th overall, in 2005 Entry Draft).

| | | | Regular Season | | | | | Playoffs | | | | |
|---|---|---|---|---|---|---|---|---|---|---|---|---|
| **Season** | **Club** | **League** | **GP** | **G** | **A** | **Pts** | **PIM** | **GP** | **G** | **A** | **Pts** | **PIM** |
| 2003-04 | Nobles | High-MA | 20 | 3 | 5 | 8 | 14 | .... | .... | .... | .... | .... |
| 2004-05 | Nobles | High-MA | 24 | 1 | 17 | 18 | 16 | .... | .... | .... | .... | .... |
| 2005-06 | Nobles | High-MA | 29 | 10 | 24 | 34 | .... | .... | .... | .... | .... | .... |
| 2006-07 | Providence College | H-East | 36 | 5 | 7 | 12 | 43 | .... | .... | .... | .... | .... |
| 2007-08 | Providence College | H-East | 36 | 2 | 4 | 6 | 18 | .... | .... | .... | .... | .... |
| 2008-09 | Providence College | H-East | 33 | 4 | 5 | 9 | 30 | .... | .... | .... | .... | .... |

**FEDOROV, Yevgeny** (FEH-duh-rahf, yehv-GEH-nee) **DAL.**

Center. Shoots left. 5'10", 187 lbs. Born, Sverdlovsk, USSR, November 11, 1980.
(Los Angeles' 6th choice, 201st overall, in 2000 Entry Draft).

| | | | Regular Season | | | | | Playoffs | | | | |
|---|---|---|---|---|---|---|---|---|---|---|---|---|
| Season | Club | League | GP | G | A | Pts | PIM | GP | G | A | Pts | PIM |
| 1997-98 | Krylja Sovetov 2 | Russia-3 | 20 | 1 | 6 | 7 | 48 | .... | .... | .... | .... | .... |
| | Krylja Sovetov | Russia | 32 | 1 | 0 | 1 | 12 | .... | .... | .... | .... | .... |
| 1998-99 | Krylja Sovetov | Russia | 52 | 5 | 3 | 8 | 61 | .... | .... | .... | .... | .... |
| 99-2000 | Perm | Russia | 37 | 5 | 5 | 10 | 20 | 3 | 0 | 1 | 1 | 4 |
| 2000-01 | Perm | Russia | 43 | 9 | 9 | 18 | 18 | .... | .... | .... | .... | .... |
| 2001-02 | Ak Bars Kazan | Russia | 45 | 10 | 12 | 22 | 12 | 11 | 0 | 0 | 0 | 2 |
| 2002-03 | Ak Bars Kazan | Russia | 46 | 4 | 11 | 15 | 26 | 5 | 1 | 0 | 1 | 2 |
| 2003-04 | Ak Bars Kazan | Russia | 47 | 7 | 4 | 11 | 14 | 4 | 0 | 0 | 0 | 0 |
| 2004-05 | Ak Bars Kazan | Russia | 47 | 4 | 10 | 14 | 10 | .... | .... | .... | .... | .... |
| 2005-06 | Dynamo Moscow | Russia | 35 | 7 | 9 | 16 | 16 | .... | .... | .... | .... | .... |
| 2006-07 | Dynamo Moscow | Russia | 48 | 15 | 9 | 24 | 42 | 3 | 0 | 0 | 0 | 0 |
| 2007-08 | Magnitogorsk | Russia | 49 | 9 | 10 | 19 | 64 | 13 | 1 | 1 | 2 | 2 |
| 2008-09 | Magnitogorsk | Rus-KHL | 54 | 0 | 4 | 4 | 14 | 11 | 1 | 1 | 2 | 8 |

Traded to **Dallas** by **Los Angeles** for Dallas' 6th round choice (later traded to Chicago - Chicago selected Braden Birch) in 2008 Entry Draft, December 10, 2007.

**FENTON, P.J.** (FEHN-tuhn, PEE-JAY)

Left wing. Shoots left. 5'11", 180 lbs. Born, Springfield, MA, August 26, 1985.
(San Jose's 6th choice, 162nd overall, in 2005 Entry Draft).

| | | | Regular Season | | | | | Playoffs | | | | |
|---|---|---|---|---|---|---|---|---|---|---|---|---|
| Season | Club | League | GP | G | A | Pts | PIM | GP | G | A | Pts | PIM |
| 2002-03 | N.E. Jr. Coyotes | EJHL | 35 | 8 | 17 | 25 | .... | .... | .... | .... | .... | .... |
| 2003-04 | N.E. Jr. Coyotes | EJHL | 37 | 16 | 17 | 33 | 61 | .... | .... | .... | .... | .... |
| 2004-05 | Massachusetts | H-East | 36 | 12 | 12 | 24 | 24 | .... | .... | .... | .... | .... |
| 2005-06 | Massachusetts | H-East | 35 | 5 | 12 | 17 | 61 | .... | .... | .... | .... | .... |
| 2006-07 | Massachusetts | H-East | 39 | 10 | 15 | 25 | 16 | .... | .... | .... | .... | .... |
| 2007-08 | Massachusetts | H-East | 36 | 9 | 19 | 28 | 24 | .... | .... | .... | .... | .... |
| | Worcester Sharks | AHL | 4 | 0 | 0 | 0 | 4 | .... | .... | .... | .... | .... |
| 2008-09 | Worcester Sharks | AHL | 52 | 6 | 8 | 14 | 22 | .... | .... | .... | .... | .... |
| | Phoenix | ECHL | 14 | 9 | 2 | 11 | 0 | .... | .... | .... | .... | .... |

Hockey East All-Rookie Team (2005)

**FERGUSON, Simon** (fuhr-GUH-suhn, SIGH-muhn)

Right wing. Shoots right. 6', 200 lbs. Born, Edmonton, Alta., April 6, 1983.

| | | | Regular Season | | | | | Playoffs | | | | |
|---|---|---|---|---|---|---|---|---|---|---|---|---|
| Season | Club | League | GP | G | A | Pts | PIM | GP | G | A | Pts | PIM |
| 99-2000 | Lethbridge | WHL | 51 | 1 | 6 | 7 | 100 | .... | .... | .... | .... | .... |
| 2000-01 | Lethbridge | WHL | 63 | 5 | 18 | 23 | 169 | 5 | 0 | 0 | 0 | 36 |
| 2001-02 | Lethbridge | WHL | 70 | 13 | 25 | 38 | 207 | 4 | 0 | 1 | 1 | 10 |
| 2002-03 | Lethbridge | WHL | 37 | 15 | 17 | 32 | 141 | .... | .... | .... | .... | .... |
| | Kelowna Rockets | WHL | 30 | 12 | 11 | 23 | 112 | 19 | 5 | 7 | 12 | 55 |
| 2003-04 | Kelowna Rockets | WHL | 68 | 15 | 23 | 38 | 186 | 17 | 5 | 5 | 10 | 30 |
| 2004-05 | Edmonton | AHL | 10 | 0 | 1 | 1 | 12 | .... | .... | .... | .... | .... |
| | Greenville Grrrowl | ECHL | 50 | 10 | 30 | 40 | 244 | 7 | 1 | 3 | 4 | 31 |
| 2005-06 | Portland Pirates | AHL | 77 | 13 | 25 | 38 | 129 | 19 | 2 | 3 | 5 | 31 |
| 2006-07 | Portland Pirates | AHL | 66 | 7 | 4 | 11 | 128 | .... | .... | .... | .... | .... |
| | Augusta Lynx | ECHL | 2 | 0 | 2 | 2 | 4 | .... | .... | .... | .... | .... |
| 2007-08 | Portland Pirates | AHL | 60 | 6 | 12 | 18 | 103 | 18 | 2 | 0 | 2 | 29 |
| 2008-09 | San Antonio | AHL | 73 | 5 | 5 | 10 | 203 | .... | .... | .... | .... | .... |

Signed as a free agent by **San Antonio** (AHL), August 25, 2008.

**FERNHOLM, Daniel** (FUHRN-hohlm, DAN-yehl) **PIT.**

Defense. Shoots left. 6'4", 218 lbs. Born, Stockholm, Sweden, December 20, 1983.
(Pittsburgh's 4th choice, 101st overall, in 2002 Entry Draft).

| | | | Regular Season | | | | | Playoffs | | | | |
|---|---|---|---|---|---|---|---|---|---|---|---|---|
| Season | Club | League | GP | G | A | Pts | PIM | GP | G | A | Pts | PIM |
| 99-2000 | Mora IK Jr. | Swe-Jr. | 33 | 3 | 3 | 6 | 8 | 1 | 0 | 0 | 0 | 0 |
| 2000-01 | Mora IK Jr. | Swe-Jr. | 3 | 0 | 1 | 1 | 2 | .... | .... | .... | .... | .... |
| | Mora IK | Sweden-2 | 2 | 0 | 0 | 0 | 0 | .... | .... | .... | .... | .... |
| 2001-02 | Djurgarden Jr. | Swe-Jr. | 8 | 6 | 13 | 19 | 12 | 3 | 0 | 0 | 0 | 0 |
| 2002-03 | Huddinge IK | Sweden-2 | 39 | 6 | 10 | 16 | 20 | 2 | 1 | 0 | 1 | 0 |
| | Huddinge IK Jr. | Swe-Jr. | 1 | 0 | 0 | 0 | 2 | .... | .... | .... | .... | .... |
| 2003-04 | Hammarby | Sweden-2 | 15 | 1 | 3 | 4 | 6 | .... | .... | .... | .... | .... |
| | Djurgarden | Sweden | 37 | 4 | 7 | 11 | 28 | 4 | 0 | 0 | 0 | 4 |
| 2004-05 | Djurgarden Jr. | Swe-Jr. | 2 | 0 | 0 | 0 | 4 | .... | .... | .... | .... | .... |
| | HC Forst Bolzano | Italy | 7 | 0 | 2 | 2 | 2 | .... | .... | .... | .... | .... |
| | Djurgarden | Sweden | 31 | 3 | 2 | 5 | 22 | 11 | 0 | 0 | 0 | 14 |
| 2005-06 | Wilkes-Barre | AHL | 27 | 1 | 6 | 7 | 10 | .... | .... | .... | .... | .... |
| | Wheeling Nailers | ECHL | 29 | 2 | 4 | 6 | 20 | 9 | 1 | 3 | 4 | 6 |
| 2006-07 | Wheeling Nailers | ECHL | 13 | 0 | 3 | 3 | 14 | .... | .... | .... | .... | .... |
| | Djurgarden | Sweden | 32 | 4 | 12 | 16 | 16 | .... | .... | .... | .... | .... |
| 2007-08 | Linkopings HC | Sweden | 54 | 8 | 21 | 29 | 28 | 16 | 3 | 7 | 10 | 20 |
| 2008-09 | Linkopings HC | Sweden | 40 | 5 | 8 | 13 | 22 | 7 | 2 | 2 | 4 | 6 |

**FERRARO, Landon** (fuh-RAHR-oh, LAN-duhn) **DET.**

Center. Shoots right. 5'11", 165 lbs. Born, Trail, B.C., August 8, 1991.
(Detroit's 1st choice, 32nd overall, in 2009 Entry Draft).

| | | | Regular Season | | | | | Playoffs | | | | |
|---|---|---|---|---|---|---|---|---|---|---|---|---|
| Season | Club | League | GP | G | A | Pts | PIM | GP | G | A | Pts | PIM |
| 2006-07 | Van. NW Giants | Minor-BC | 25 | 21 | 13 | 34 | 77 | .... | .... | .... | .... | .... |
| | Red Deer Rebels | WHL | 4 | 0 | 0 | 0 | 0 | 1 | 0 | 0 | 0 | 0 |
| 2007-08 | Red Deer Rebels | WHL | 54 | 13 | 11 | 24 | 65 | .... | .... | .... | .... | .... |
| 2008-09 | Red Deer Rebels | WHL | 68 | 37 | 18 | 55 | 99 | .... | .... | .... | .... | .... |

**FERRIERO, Benn** (fuh-RAIR-oh, BEHN) **PHX.**

Center. Shoots right. 5'10", 191 lbs. Born, Boston, MA, April 29, 1987.
(Phoenix's 8th choice, 196th overall, in 2006 Entry Draft).

| | | | Regular Season | | | | | Playoffs | | | | |
|---|---|---|---|---|---|---|---|---|---|---|---|---|
| Season | Club | League | GP | G | A | Pts | PIM | GP | G | A | Pts | PIM |
| 2001-02 | Gov. Dummer | High-MA | STATISTICS NOT AVAILABLE | | | | | | | | | |
| 2002-03 | Gov. Dummer | High-MA | .... | 8 | 10 | 18 | .... | .... | .... | .... | .... | .... |
| 2003-04 | Gov. Dummer | High-MA | 28 | 19 | 24 | 43 | .... | .... | .... | .... | .... | .... |
| 2004-05 | Gov. Dummer | High-MA | 28 | 15 | 27 | 42 | .... | .... | .... | .... | .... | .... |
| 2005-06 | Boston College | H-East | 42 | 16 | 9 | 25 | 36 | .... | .... | .... | .... | .... |
| 2006-07 | Boston College | H-East | 42 | 23 | 23 | 46 | 43 | .... | .... | .... | .... | .... |
| 2007-08 | Boston College | H-East | 44 | 17 | 25 | 42 | 71 | .... | .... | .... | .... | .... |
| 2008-09 | Boston College | H-East | 37 | 8 | 18 | 26 | 44 | .... | .... | .... | .... | .... |

Hockey East All-Rookie Team (2006)

**FIENHAGE, Corey** (fihn-AW-gee, KOH-ree) **BUF.**

Defense. Shoots right. 6'2", 190 lbs. Born, Topeka, KS, May 4, 1990.
(Buffalo's 4th choice, 81st overall, in 2008 Entry Draft).

| | | | Regular Season | | | | | Playoffs | | | | |
|---|---|---|---|---|---|---|---|---|---|---|---|---|
| Season | Club | League | GP | G | A | Pts | PIM | GP | G | A | Pts | PIM |
| 2005-06 | Eastview High | High-MN | 25 | 1 | 6 | 7 | 32 | .... | .... | .... | .... | .... |
| 2006-07 | Eastview High | High-MN | 20 | 4 | 11 | 15 | .... | .... | .... | .... | .... | .... |
| | Team Southeast | UMWEHL | 11 | 4 | 4 | 8 | .... | .... | .... | .... | .... | .... |
| 2007-08 | Eastview High | High-MN | 26 | 6 | 10 | 16 | 87 | .... | .... | .... | .... | .... |
| | Team Southeast | UMWEHL | 12 | 2 | 4 | 6 | .... | .... | .... | .... | .... | .... |
| | Indiana Ice | USHL | 12 | 1 | 2 | 3 | 12 | 2 | 0 | 0 | 0 | 0 |
| 2008-09 | North Dakota | WCHA | 9 | 0 | 1 | 1 | 28 | .... | .... | .... | .... | .... |

**FIGREN, Robin** (FIH-grehn, RAW-bihn) **NYI**

Wing. Shoots right. 5'11", 176 lbs. Born, Stockholm, Sweden, March 7, 1988.
(NY Islanders' 3rd choice, 70th overall, in 2006 Entry Draft).

| | | | Regular Season | | | | | Playoffs | | | | |
|---|---|---|---|---|---|---|---|---|---|---|---|---|
| Season | Club | League | GP | G | A | Pts | PIM | GP | G | A | Pts | PIM |
| 2003-04 | Hammarby U18 | Swe-U18 | 11 | 5 | 5 | 10 | 22 | .... | .... | .... | .... | .... |
| 2004-05 | Frolunda U18 | Swe-U18 | 12 | 13 | 8 | 21 | 94 | 7 | 4 | 4 | 8 | 10 |
| | Frolunda Jr. | Swe-Jr. | 4 | 1 | 2 | 3 | 0 | .... | .... | .... | .... | .... |
| 2005-06 | Frolunda Jr. | Swe-Jr. | 38 | 10 | 18 | 28 | 72 | 7 | 4 | 2 | 6 | 6 |
| | Frolunda | Sweden | 2 | 0 | 0 | 0 | 0 | .... | .... | .... | .... | .... |
| | Frolunda U18 | Swe-U18 | 1 | 1 | 0 | 1 | 2 | 2 | 2 | 0 | 2 | 0 |
| 2006-07 | Calgary Hitmen | WHL | 62 | 10 | 17 | 27 | 54 | 18 | 4 | 4 | 8 | 18 |
| 2007-08 | Edmonton | WHL | 35 | 18 | 13 | 31 | 46 | .... | .... | .... | .... | .... |
| 2008-09 | Djurgarden | Sweden | 49 | 3 | 6 | 9 | 28 | .... | .... | .... | .... | .... |
| | Bridgeport | AHL | 3 | 0 | 1 | 1 | 2 | .... | .... | .... | .... | .... |

**FINLEY, Joe** (FIHN-lee, JOH) **WSH.**

Defense. Shoots left. 6'7", 245 lbs. Born, Edina, MN, June 29, 1987.
(Washington's 2nd choice, 27th overall, in 2005 Entry Draft).

| | | | Regular Season | | | | | Playoffs | | | | |
|---|---|---|---|---|---|---|---|---|---|---|---|---|
| Season | Club | League | GP | G | A | Pts | PIM | GP | G | A | Pts | PIM |
| 2004-05 | Sioux Falls | USHL | 55 | 3 | 10 | 13 | 181 | .... | .... | .... | .... | .... |
| 2005-06 | North Dakota | WCHA | 43 | 0 | 3 | 3 | 96 | .... | .... | .... | .... | .... |
| 2006-07 | North Dakota | WCHA | 41 | 1 | 6 | 7 | 72 | .... | .... | .... | .... | .... |
| 2007-08 | North Dakota | WCHA | 43 | 4 | 11 | 15 | 79 | .... | .... | .... | .... | .... |
| 2008-09 | North Dakota | WCHA | 27 | 2 | 8 | 10 | 56 | .... | .... | .... | .... | .... |
| | Hershey Bears | AHL | 1 | 0 | 0 | 0 | 7 | .... | .... | .... | .... | .... |

**FISCHER, David** (FIH-shuhr, DAY-vihd) **MTL.**

Defense. Shoots right. 6'4", 206 lbs. Born, Minneapolis, MN, February 19, 1988.
(Montreal's 1st choice, 20th overall, in 2006 Entry Draft).

| | | | Regular Season | | | | | Playoffs | | | | |
|---|---|---|---|---|---|---|---|---|---|---|---|---|
| Season | Club | League | GP | G | A | Pts | PIM | GP | G | A | Pts | PIM |
| 2003-04 | Apple Valley | High-MN | 27 | 2 | 9 | 11 | 10 | .... | .... | .... | .... | .... |
| 2004-05 | Apple Valley | High-MN | 28 | 8 | 20 | 28 | 36 | .... | .... | .... | .... | .... |
| 2005-06 | Apple Valley | High-MN | 28 | 8 | 31 | 39 | 22 | .... | .... | .... | .... | .... |
| 2006-07 | U. of Minnesota | WCHA | 42 | 0 | 5 | 5 | 14 | .... | .... | .... | .... | .... |
| 2007-08 | U. of Minnesota | WCHA | 45 | 2 | 12 | 14 | 18 | .... | .... | .... | .... | .... |
| 2008-09 | U. of Minnesota | WCHA | 31 | 2 | 11 | 13 | 16 | .... | .... | .... | .... | .... |

**FLAAKE, Jerome** (FLAH-keh, juh-ROHM) **TOR.**

Left wing. Shoots left. 6'2", 187 lbs. Born, Guben, East Germany, March 2, 1990.
(Toronto's 6th choice, 130th overall, in 2008 Entry Draft).

| | | | Regular Season | | | | | Playoffs | | | | |
|---|---|---|---|---|---|---|---|---|---|---|---|---|
| Season | Club | League | GP | G | A | Pts | PIM | GP | G | A | Pts | PIM |
| 2005-06 | Riessersee Jr. | Ger-Jr. | 36 | 20 | 18 | 38 | 36 | 3 | 0 | 2 | 2 | 0 |
| 2006-07 | Heil./Mann. Jr. | Ger-Jr. | 36 | 32 | 31 | 63 | 36 | 6 | 4 | 3 | 7 | 8 |
| 2007-08 | Kolner Haie | Germany | 30 | 0 | 1 | 1 | 4 | .... | .... | .... | .... | .... |
| | Koln Jr. | Ger-Jr. | 32 | 33 | 41 | 74 | 68 | 4 | 2 | 4 | 6 | 41 |
| 2008-09 | Kolner Haie | Germany | 43 | 5 | 11 | 16 | 22 | .... | .... | .... | .... | .... |

**FLEMMING, Brett** (FLEH-mihng, BREHT) **WSH.**

Defense. Shoots right. 5'11", 178 lbs. Born, Regina, Sask., February 26, 1991.
(Washington's 5th choice, 145th overall, in 2009 Entry Draft).

| | | | Regular Season | | | | | Playoffs | | | | |
|---|---|---|---|---|---|---|---|---|---|---|---|---|
| Season | Club | League | GP | G | A | Pts | PIM | GP | G | A | Pts | PIM |
| 2006-07 | Burlington Eagles | Minor-ON | 67 | 15 | 36 | 51 | 130 | .... | .... | .... | .... | .... |
| 2007-08 | St. Michael's | OHL | 47 | 1 | 9 | 10 | 30 | 4 | 0 | 0 | 0 | 6 |
| 2008-09 | St. Michael's | OHL | 64 | 3 | 25 | 28 | 89 | 10 | 1 | 3 | 4 | 2 |

**FLETCHER, Justin** (FLEH-chuhr, JUHS-tihn) **ST.L.**

Defense. Shoots left. 5'11", 190 lbs. Born, Maryville, IL, March 30, 1983.

| | | | Regular Season | | | | | Playoffs | | | | |
|---|---|---|---|---|---|---|---|---|---|---|---|---|
| Season | Club | League | GP | G | A | Pts | PIM | GP | G | A | Pts | PIM |
| 2000-01 | Sioux City | USHL | 38 | 0 | 5 | 5 | 28 | 3 | 0 | 0 | 0 | 0 |
| 2001-02 | Sioux City | USHL | 56 | 3 | 10 | 13 | 48 | 12 | 2 | 1 | 3 | 6 |
| 2002-03 | Sioux City | USHL | 60 | 12 | 31 | 43 | 28 | 4 | 0 | 3 | 3 | 6 |
| 2003-04 | St. Cloud State | WCHA | 29 | 6 | 7 | 13 | 22 | .... | .... | .... | .... | .... |
| 2004-05 | St. Cloud State | WCHA | 36 | 8 | 14 | 22 | 86 | .... | .... | .... | .... | .... |
| 2005-06 | St. Cloud State | WCHA | 40 | 6 | 21 | 27 | 55 | .... | .... | .... | .... | .... |
| 2006-07 | St. Cloud State | WCHA | 38 | 6 | 18 | 24 | 37 | .... | .... | .... | .... | .... |
| | Springfield Falcons | AHL | 10 | 3 | 1 | 4 | 4 | .... | .... | .... | .... | .... |
| 2007-08 | Norfolk Admirals | AHL | 39 | 1 | 4 | 5 | 37 | .... | .... | .... | .... | .... |
| | Rockford IceHogs | AHL | 20 | 4 | 7 | 11 | 43 | 11 | 0 | 1 | 1 | 6 |
| 2008-09 | Peoria Rivermen | AHL | 68 | 8 | 24 | 32 | 50 | 7 | 0 | 2 | 2 | 6 |

Signed as a free agent by **Tampa Bay**, April 30, 2007. Signed as a free agent by **St. Louis**, July 20, 2009.

## FLOOD, Mark (FLUD, MAHRK) NYI

Defense. Shoots right. 6'1", 190 lbs. Born, Charlottetown, P.E.I., September 29, 1984.
(Montreal's 8th choice, 188th overall, in 2003 Entry Draft).

| | | | Regular Season | | | | | Playoffs | | | | |
|---|---|---|---|---|---|---|---|---|---|---|---|---|
| Season | Club | League | GP | G | A | Pts | PIM | GP | G | A | Pts | PIM |
| 2000-01 | Charlotwn AAA | PEIHA | STATISTICS NOT AVAILABLE | | | | | | | | | |
| | Charlotwn Abbies | MJrHL | 11 | 0 | 2 | 2 | 2 | .... | .... | .... | .... | .... |
| 2001-02 | Peterborough | OHL | 57 | 1 | 4 | 5 | 21 | 6 | 0 | 0 | 0 | 2 |
| 2002-03 | Peterborough | OHL | 68 | 5 | 24 | 29 | 18 | 7 | 1 | 2 | 3 | 0 |
| 2003-04 | Peterborough | OHL | 68 | 15 | 29 | 44 | 30 | .... | .... | .... | .... | .... |
| 2004-05 | Peterborough | OHL | 60 | 4 | 38 | 42 | 14 | 14 | 2 | 7 | 9 | 0 |
| 2005-06 | Syracuse Crunch | AHL | 9 | 1 | 1 | 2 | 2 | .... | .... | .... | .... | .... |
| | Dayton Bombers | ECHL | 50 | 11 | 14 | 25 | 20 | .... | .... | .... | .... | .... |
| 2006-07 | Syracuse Crunch | AHL | 8 | 1 | 1 | 2 | 2 | .... | .... | .... | .... | .... |
| | Albany River Rats | AHL | 36 | 3 | 7 | 10 | 20 | .... | .... | .... | .... | .... |
| 2007-08 | Albany River Rats | AHL | 53 | 10 | 12 | 22 | 18 | .... | .... | .... | .... | .... |
| 2008-09 | Albany River Rats | AHL | 76 | 6 | 25 | 31 | 27 | .... | .... | .... | .... | .... |

Signed as a free agent by **Columbus**, August 22, 2005. Traded to **Carolina** by **Columbus** for Derrick Walser, November 29, 2006. Signed as a free agent by **NY Islanders**, July 6, 2009.

## FLYNN, Ryan (FLIHN, RIGH-uhn) NSH.

Right wing. Shoots right. 6'2", 216 lbs. Born, St. Paul, MN, March 22, 1988.
(Nashville's 4th choice, 176th overall, in 2006 Entry Draft).

| | | | Regular Season | | | | | Playoffs | | | | |
|---|---|---|---|---|---|---|---|---|---|---|---|---|
| Season | Club | League | GP | G | A | Pts | PIM | GP | G | A | Pts | PIM |
| 2003-04 | Centennial | High-MN | 30 | 29 | 39 | 68 | .... | .... | .... | .... | .... | .... |
| 2004-05 | USNTDP | U-17 | 14 | 4 | 5 | 9 | 12 | .... | .... | .... | .... | .... |
| | USNTDP | NAHL | 41 | 11 | 8 | 19 | 31 | 9 | 2 | 4 | 6 | 7 |
| 2005-06 | USNTDP | U-18 | 42 | 10 | 12 | 22 | 57 | .... | .... | .... | .... | .... |
| | USNTDP | NAHL | 17 | 6 | 5 | 11 | 20 | .... | .... | .... | .... | .... |
| 2006-07 | U. of Minnesota | WCHA | 43 | 5 | 8 | 13 | 58 | .... | .... | .... | .... | .... |
| 2007-08 | U. of Minnesota | WCHA | 38 | 4 | 11 | 15 | 51 | .... | .... | .... | .... | .... |
| 2008-09 | U. of Minnesota | WCHA | 37 | 6 | 13 | 19 | 62 | .... | .... | .... | .... | .... |

## FOLIGNO, Marcus (foh-LEE-noh, MAHR-kuhs) BUF.

Left wing. Shoots left. 6'2", 200 lbs. Born, Buffalo, NY, August 10, 1991.
(Buffalo's 3rd choice, 104th overall, in 2009 Entry Draft).

| | | | Regular Season | | | | | Playoffs | | | | |
|---|---|---|---|---|---|---|---|---|---|---|---|---|
| Season | Club | League | GP | G | A | Pts | PIM | GP | G | A | Pts | PIM |
| 2006-07 | Sudbury | Minor-ON | 30 | 21 | 15 | 36 | 70 | .... | .... | .... | .... | .... |
| 2007-08 | Sudbury Wolves | OHL | 66 | 5 | 6 | 11 | 38 | .... | .... | .... | .... | .... |
| 2008-09 | Sudbury Wolves | OHL | 65 | 12 | 18 | 30 | 96 | 6 | 1 | 2 | 3 | 9 |

## FORD, Matthew (FOHRD, MA-thew)

Right wing. Shoots right. 6'1", 206 lbs. Born, West Hills, CA, October 9, 1984.
(Chicago's 16th choice, 256th overall, in 2004 Entry Draft).

| | | | Regular Season | | | | | Playoffs | | | | |
|---|---|---|---|---|---|---|---|---|---|---|---|---|
| Season | Club | League | GP | G | A | Pts | PIM | GP | G | A | Pts | PIM |
| 2003-04 | Sioux Falls | USHL | 60 | *37 | 31 | 68 | 60 | .... | .... | .... | .... | .... |
| 2004-05 | U. of Wisconsin | WCHA | 21 | 5 | 5 | 10 | 18 | .... | .... | .... | .... | .... |
| 2005-06 | U. of Wisconsin | WCHA | 31 | 5 | 2 | 7 | 14 | .... | .... | .... | .... | .... |
| 2006-07 | U. of Wisconsin | WCHA | 39 | 7 | 6 | 13 | 38 | .... | .... | .... | .... | .... |
| 2007-08 | U. of Wisconsin | WCHA | 33 | 4 | 5 | 9 | 30 | .... | .... | .... | .... | .... |
| 2008-09 | Hartford Wolf Pack | AHL | 25 | 1 | 2 | 3 | 10 | .... | .... | .... | .... | .... |
| | Lake Erie Monsters | AHL | 5 | 0 | 0 | 0 | 2 | .... | .... | .... | .... | .... |
| | Charlotte | ECHL | 28 | 21 | 17 | 38 | 25 | 6 | 2 | 3 | 5 | 21 |

USHL Rookie of the Year (2004)

## FORNEY, Michael (FOHR-NEE, MIGH-kuhl) ATL.

Right wing. Shoots right. 6'2", 185 lbs. Born, Thief River Falls, MN, May 14, 1988.
(Atlanta's 3rd choice, 80th overall, in 2006 Entry Draft).

| | | | Regular Season | | | | | Playoffs | | | | |
|---|---|---|---|---|---|---|---|---|---|---|---|---|
| Season | Club | League | GP | G | A | Pts | PIM | GP | G | A | Pts | PIM |
| 2002-03 | Thief River Falls | High-MN | 28 | 4 | 10 | 14 | .... | .... | .... | .... | .... | .... |
| 2003-04 | Thief River Falls | High-MN | 24 | 14 | 22 | 36 | .... | .... | .... | .... | .... | .... |
| 2004-05 | Thief River Falls | High-MN | 28 | 34 | 33 | 67 | .... | .... | .... | .... | .... | .... |
| 2005-06 | Thief River Falls | High-MN | 21 | 23 | 37 | 60 | 28 | .... | .... | .... | .... | .... |
| | Des Moines | USHL | 3 | 0 | 0 | 0 | 0 | .... | .... | .... | .... | .... |
| 2006-07 | North Dakota | WCHA | 16 | 0 | 2 | 2 | 10 | .... | .... | .... | .... | .... |
| 2007-08 | North Dakota | WCHA | 3 | 0 | 0 | 0 | 2 | .... | .... | .... | .... | .... |
| 2008-09 | Green Bay | USHL | 59 | 26 | 34 | 60 | 53 | 7 | 3 | 7 | 10 | 2 |

## FORTIER, Olivier (FOHR-t'yay, OH-lihv-ee-ay) MTL.

Center. Shoots left. 5'11", 181 lbs. Born, Quebec City, Que., May 2, 1989.
(Montreal's 4th choice, 65th overall, in 2007 Entry Draft).

| | | | Regular Season | | | | | Playoffs | | | | |
|---|---|---|---|---|---|---|---|---|---|---|---|---|
| Season | Club | League | GP | G | A | Pts | PIM | GP | G | A | Pts | PIM |
| 2004-05 | St-Francois | QAAA | 31 | 7 | 17 | 24 | 8 | 4 | 2 | 1 | 3 | 4 |
| 2005-06 | Drummondville | QMJHL | 13 | 2 | 2 | 4 | 14 | .... | .... | .... | .... | .... |
| | Rimouski Oceanic | QMJHL | 27 | 4 | 8 | 12 | 16 | .... | .... | .... | .... | .... |
| 2006-07 | Rimouski Oceanic | QMJHL | 69 | 28 | 36 | 64 | 28 | .... | .... | .... | .... | .... |
| 2007-08 | Rimouski Oceanic | QMJHL | 67 | 23 | 23 | 46 | 37 | 3 | 1 | 0 | 1 | 4 |
| 2008-09 | Rimouski Oceanic | QMJHL | 29 | 8 | 27 | 35 | 12 | 13 | 4 | 5 | 9 | 12 |

## FORTUNUS, Maxime (fohr-TOON-uhs, MAX-eem) DAL.

Defense. Shoots right. 6'1", 190 lbs. Born, La Prairie, Que., July 28, 1983.

| | | | Regular Season | | | | | Playoffs | | | | |
|---|---|---|---|---|---|---|---|---|---|---|---|---|
| Season | Club | League | GP | G | A | Pts | PIM | GP | G | A | Pts | PIM |
| 99-2000 | Baie-Comeau | QMJHL | 68 | 6 | 15 | 21 | 36 | 6 | 0 | 0 | 0 | 2 |
| 2000-01 | Baie-Comeau | QMJHL | 71 | 10 | 31 | 41 | 106 | 11 | 2 | 4 | 6 | 6 |
| 2001-02 | Baie-Comeau | QMJHL | 72 | 11 | 30 | 41 | 76 | 5 | 0 | 1 | 1 | 2 |
| 2002-03 | Baie-Comeau | QMJHL | 69 | 12 | 32 | 44 | 44 | 12 | 2 | 4 | 6 | 6 |
| 2003-04 | Baie-Comeau | QMJHL | 5 | 1 | 0 | 1 | 15 | .... | .... | .... | .... | .... |
| | Houston Aeros | AHL | 12 | 0 | 2 | 2 | 2 | 1 | 0 | 0 | 0 | 0 |
| | Louisiana | ECHL | 64 | 3 | 15 | 18 | 27 | 4 | 1 | 1 | 2 | 0 |
| 2004-05 | Houston Aeros | AHL | 13 | 0 | 0 | 0 | 4 | .... | .... | .... | .... | .... |
| | Louisiana | ECHL | 59 | 8 | 16 | 24 | 26 | .... | .... | .... | .... | .... |
| 2005-06 | Manitoba Moose | AHL | 76 | 3 | 10 | 13 | 36 | 13 | 0 | 0 | 0 | 10 |
| 2006-07 | Manitoba Moose | AHL | 72 | 2 | 18 | 20 | 64 | 13 | 1 | 4 | 5 | 10 |
| 2007-08 | Manitoba Moose | AHL | 65 | 8 | 13 | 21 | 28 | 6 | 0 | 1 | 1 | 4 |
| 2008-09 | Manitoba Moose | AHL | 58 | 7 | 12 | 19 | 18 | 22 | 3 | 7 | 10 | 2 |

Signed as a free agent by **Dallas**, July 3, 2008.

## FOSS, Jeffrey (FAWS, JEHF-ree) NSH.

Defense. Shoots right. 6'2", 205 lbs. Born, Fargo, ND, December 12, 1988.
(Nashville's 5th choice, 166th overall, in 2008 Entry Draft).

| | | | Regular Season | | | | | Playoffs | | | | |
|---|---|---|---|---|---|---|---|---|---|---|---|---|
| Season | Club | League | GP | G | A | Pts | PIM | GP | G | A | Pts | PIM |
| 2004-05 | Moorhead Spuds | High-MN | 22 | 1 | 4 | 5 | 6 | .... | .... | .... | .... | .... |
| 2005-06 | Moorhead Spuds | High-MN | 26 | 4 | 17 | 21 | 16 | .... | .... | .... | .... | .... |
| | Team Great Plains | UMWEHL | 11 | 4 | 9 | 13 | .... | .... | .... | .... | .... | .... |
| 2006-07 | Moorhead Spuds | High-MN | 26 | 15 | 31 | 46 | 28 | .... | .... | .... | .... | .... |
| | Team Great Plains | UMWEHL | 12 | 3 | 13 | 16 | .... | .... | .... | .... | .... | .... |
| | Sioux Falls | USHL | 11 | 0 | 1 | 1 | 10 | 4 | 0 | 1 | 1 | 2 |
| 2007-08 | RPI Engineers | ECAC | 38 | 1 | 3 | 4 | 28 | .... | .... | .... | .... | .... |
| 2008-09 | RPI Engineers | ECAC | 39 | 2 | 9 | 11 | 58 | .... | .... | .... | .... | .... |

## FOUCAULT, Kris (foo-KOH, KRIHS) MIN.

Left wing. Shoots left. 6'1", 202 lbs. Born, Calgary, Alta., December 12, 1990.
(Minnesota's 3rd choice, 103rd overall, in 2009 Entry Draft).

| | | | Regular Season | | | | | Playoffs | | | | |
|---|---|---|---|---|---|---|---|---|---|---|---|---|
| Season | Club | League | GP | G | A | Pts | PIM | GP | G | A | Pts | PIM |
| 2006-07 | Calgary Buffaloes | AMHL | 35 | 7 | 6 | 13 | 46 | .... | .... | .... | .... | .... |
| | Swift Current | WHL | 3 | 0 | 0 | 0 | 0 | .... | .... | .... | .... | .... |
| 2007-08 | Kootenay Ice | WHL | 33 | 0 | 3 | 3 | 12 | 8 | 2 | 1 | 3 | 2 |
| 2008-09 | Kootenay Ice | WHL | 4 | 0 | 1 | 1 | 4 | .... | .... | .... | .... | .... |
| | Canmore Eagles | AJHL | 32 | 18 | 23 | 41 | 84 | .... | .... | .... | .... | .... |
| | Calgary Hitmen | WHL | 22 | 9 | 7 | 16 | 12 | 18 | 11 | 5 | 16 | 10 |

## FOURNIER, Gleason (FOHR-nyay, GLEE-suhn) DET.

Defense. Shoots left. 6', 176 lbs. Born, Rimouski, Que., September 8, 1991.
(Detroit's 4th choice, 90th overall, in 2009 Entry Draft).

| | | | Regular Season | | | | | Playoffs | | | | |
|---|---|---|---|---|---|---|---|---|---|---|---|---|
| Season | Club | League | GP | G | A | Pts | PIM | GP | G | A | Pts | PIM |
| 2006-07 | Ecole Notre Dame | QAAA | 44 | 3 | 17 | 20 | 32 | 13 | 0 | 2 | 2 | 30 |
| 2007-08 | Rimouski Oceanic | QMJHL | 56 | 3 | 8 | 11 | 26 | 3 | 0 | 0 | 0 | 0 |
| 2008-09 | Rimouski Oceanic | QMJHL | 66 | 3 | 25 | 28 | 64 | 4 | 0 | 0 | 0 | 0 |

## FOX, T.J. (FAWX, TEE-JAY)

Left wing. Shoots left. 6'1", 200 lbs. Born, Oswego, NY, June 11, 1984.

| | | | Regular Season | | | | | Playoffs | | | | |
|---|---|---|---|---|---|---|---|---|---|---|---|---|
| Season | Club | League | GP | G | A | Pts | PIM | GP | G | A | Pts | PIM |
| 2002-03 | Green Bay | USHL | 32 | 3 | 3 | 6 | 24 | .... | .... | .... | .... | .... |
| 2003-04 | Chicago Steel | USHL | 56 | 11 | 16 | 27 | 62 | 5 | 1 | 0 | 1 | 4 |
| 2004-05 | Chicago Steel | USHL | 60 | 21 | 29 | 50 | 90 | 7 | 2 | 3 | 5 | 8 |
| 2005-06 | Union College | ECAC | 30 | 8 | 12 | 20 | 34 | .... | .... | .... | .... | .... |
| 2006-07 | Union College | ECAC | 36 | 13 | 24 | 37 | 54 | .... | .... | .... | .... | .... |
| 2007-08 | Worcester Sharks | AHL | 71 | 12 | 12 | 24 | 33 | .... | .... | .... | .... | .... |
| 2008-09 | Worcester Sharks | AHL | 79 | 7 | 11 | 18 | 15 | 9 | 3 | 0 | 3 | 4 |

Signed as a free agent by **San Jose**, March 8, 2007.

## FRANK, Chris (FRANK, KRIHS) PHX.

Defense. Shoots left. 6'1", 231 lbs. Born, Lynnwood, WA, January 8, 1986.
(Phoenix's 7th choice, 188th overall, in 2006 Entry Draft).

| | | | Regular Season | | | | | Playoffs | | | | |
|---|---|---|---|---|---|---|---|---|---|---|---|---|
| Season | Club | League | GP | G | A | Pts | PIM | GP | G | A | Pts | PIM |
| 2003-04 | Cowichan Valley | BCHL | 55 | 3 | 16 | 19 | 277 | 6 | 1 | 0 | 1 | 26 |
| 2004-05 | Cowichan Valley | BCHL | 55 | 6 | 30 | 36 | 207 | .... | .... | .... | .... | .... |
| 2005-06 | Western Mich. | CCHA | 38 | 2 | 2 | 4 | 127 | .... | .... | .... | .... | .... |
| 2006-07 | Western Mich. | CCHA | 36 | 2 | 10 | 12 | *109 | .... | .... | .... | .... | .... |
| 2007-08 | Western Mich. | CCHA | 37 | 2 | 4 | 6 | 91 | .... | .... | .... | .... | .... |
| 2008-09 | Western Mich. | CCHA | 38 | 2 | 10 | 12 | 83 | .... | .... | .... | .... | .... |
| | San Antonio | AHL | 12 | 0 | 1 | 1 | 35 | .... | .... | .... | .... | .... |

## FRANSSON, Cody (FRAN-suhn, KOH-dee) NSH.

Defense. Shoots right. 6'5", 214 lbs. Born, Salmon Arm, B.C., August 8, 1987.
(Nashville's 3rd choice, 79th overall, in 2005 Entry Draft).

| | | | Regular Season | | | | | Playoffs | | | | |
|---|---|---|---|---|---|---|---|---|---|---|---|---|
| Season | Club | League | GP | G | A | Pts | PIM | GP | G | A | Pts | PIM |
| 2002-03 | Sicamous | Minor-BC | 65 | 44 | 82 | 126 | 42 | .... | .... | .... | .... | .... |
| | Vancouver Giants | WHL | 3 | 0 | 0 | 0 | 0 | .... | .... | .... | .... | .... |
| 2003-04 | Beaver Valley | KIJHL | 48 | 10 | 22 | 32 | 70 | .... | .... | .... | .... | .... |
| | Trail Smoke Eaters | BCHL | 2 | 0 | 1 | 1 | 0 | .... | .... | .... | .... | .... |
| | Vancouver Giants | WHL | 2 | 0 | 0 | 0 | 0 | .... | .... | .... | .... | .... |
| 2004-05 | Vancouver Giants | WHL | 64 | 2 | 11 | 13 | 44 | 4 | 0 | 1 | 1 | 0 |
| 2005-06 | Vancouver Giants | WHL | 71 | 15 | 40 | 55 | 61 | 18 | 5 | 15 | 20 | 12 |
| 2006-07 | Vancouver Giants | WHL | 59 | 17 | 34 | 51 | 88 | 19 | 3 | 4 | 7 | 10 |
| 2007-08 | Milwaukee | AHL | 76 | 11 | 25 | 36 | 40 | 6 | 0 | 2 | 2 | 2 |
| 2008-09 | Milwaukee | AHL | 76 | 11 | 41 | 52 | 47 | 11 | 3 | 5 | 8 | 8 |

WHL West Second All-Star Team (2006) • WHL West First All-Star Team (2007) • Memorial Cup Tournament All-Star Team (2007) • AHL Second All-Star Team (2009)

## FRANSSON, Johan (FRAN-suhn, YOH-han) L.A.

Defense. Shoots left. 6'1", 183 lbs. Born, Kalix, Sweden, February 18, 1985.
(Dallas' 2nd choice, 34th overall, in 2004 Entry Draft).

| | | | Regular Season | | | | | Playoffs | | | | |
|---|---|---|---|---|---|---|---|---|---|---|---|---|
| Season | Club | League | GP | G | A | Pts | PIM | GP | G | A | Pts | PIM |
| 2000-01 | Kalix HF | Sweden-3 | 19 | 0 | 6 | 6 | 8 | .... | .... | .... | .... | .... |
| 2001-02 | Lulea HF U18 | Swe-U18 | 5 | 2 | 0 | 2 | 0 | .... | .... | .... | .... | .... |
| | Lulea HF Jr. | Swe-Jr. | 29 | 4 | 4 | 8 | 28 | 5 | 0 | 1 | 1 | 8 |
| 2002-03 | Lulea HF Jr. | Swe-Jr. | 24 | 2 | 4 | 6 | 67 | .... | .... | .... | .... | .... |
| | Lulea HF U18 | Swe-U18 | 2 | 0 | 0 | 0 | 2 | .... | .... | .... | .... | .... |
| | Lulea HF | Sweden | 3 | 0 | 0 | 0 | 0 | .... | .... | .... | .... | .... |
| 2003-04 | Lulea HF Jr. | Swe-Jr. | 5 | 0 | 2 | 2 | 10 | .... | .... | .... | .... | .... |
| | Lulea HF | Sweden | 44 | 3 | 3 | 6 | 28 | 2 | 0 | 0 | 0 | 4 |
| 2004-05 | Lulea HF Jr. | Swe-Jr. | 1 | 1 | 1 | 2 | 0 | 7 | 1 | 2 | 3 | 4 |
| | Lulea HF | Sweden | 43 | 1 | 6 | 7 | 30 | 3 | 0 | 0 | 0 | 0 |
| 2005-06 | Lulea HF | Sweden | 50 | 3 | 5 | 8 | 74 | 6 | 1 | 1 | 2 | 6 |
| 2006-07 | Frolunda | Sweden | 35 | 0 | 6 | 6 | 18 | .... | .... | .... | .... | .... |
| | Assat Pori | Finland | 6 | 0 | 1 | 1 | 2 | .... | .... | .... | .... | .... |
| | Linkopings HC | Sweden | 8 | 0 | 0 | 0 | 4 | 15 | 0 | 0 | 0 | 2 |
| 2007-08 | Linkopings HC | Sweden | 48 | 5 | 9 | 14 | 24 | 16 | 0 | 5 | 5 | 16 |
| 2008-09 | Linkopings HC | Sweden | 40 | 3 | 7 | 10 | 24 | .... | .... | .... | .... | .... |
| | HC Lugano | Swiss | 7 | 2 | 3 | 5 | 2 | 4 | 2 | 0 | 2 | 0 |

Rights traded to **Los Angeles** by **Dallas** with Jaroslav Modry, Dallas' 2nd (Oscar Moller) and 3rd (Bryan Cameron) round choices in 2007 Entry Draft and Dallas' 1st round choice (later traded to Phoenix - Phoenix selected Viktor Tikhonov) in 2008 Entry Draft for Mattias Norstrom, Konstantin Pushkarev and Los Angeles' 3rd (Sergei Korostin) and 4th (later traded to Columbus - Columbus selected Maxim Mayorov) round choices in 2007 Entry Draft, February 27, 2007.

**FRATTIN, Matt** (FRA-tihn, MAT) **TOR.**

Right wing. Shoots right. 5'11", 187 lbs. Born, Edmonton, Alta., January 3, 1988.
(Toronto's 2nd choice, 99th overall, in 2007 Entry Draft).

| | | | Regular Season | | | | | Playoffs | | | | |
|---|---|---|---|---|---|---|---|---|---|---|---|---|
| **Season** | **Club** | **League** | **GP** | **G** | **A** | **Pts** | **PIM** | **GP** | **G** | **A** | **Pts** | **PIM** |
| 2004-05 | Gregg Distributors | AMHL | 34 | 12 | 13 | 25 | 14 | | | | | |
| 2005-06 | Gregg Distributors | AMHL | 34 | 20 | 17 | 37 | 48 | 6 | 5 | 1 | 6 | 4 |
| | Ft. Saskatchewan | AJHL | 3 | 2 | 0 | 2 | 0 | | | | | |
| 2006-07 | Ft. Saskatchewan | AJHL | 58 | 49 | 34 | 83 | 75 | 15 | 5 | 6 | 11 | 10 |
| 2007-08 | North Dakota | WCHA | 43 | 4 | 11 | 15 | 18 | | | | | |
| 2008-09 | North Dakota | WCHA | 42 | 13 | 12 | 25 | 48 | | | | | |

**FREDHEIM, Kris** (FREHD-highm, KRIHS) **VAN.**

Defense. Shoots right. 6'2", 174 lbs. Born, Campbell River, B.C., February 23, 1987.
(Vancouver's 5th choice, 185th overall, in 2005 Entry Draft).

| | | | Regular Season | | | | | Playoffs | | | | |
|---|---|---|---|---|---|---|---|---|---|---|---|---|
| **Season** | **Club** | **League** | **GP** | **G** | **A** | **Pts** | **PIM** | **GP** | **G** | **A** | **Pts** | **PIM** |
| 2003-04 | Notre Dame | SMHL | 41 | 9 | 21 | 30 | 38 | | | | | |
| 2004-05 | Notre Dame | SJHL | 50 | 2 | 15 | 17 | 28 | | | | | |
| 2005-06 | Notre Dame | SJHL | 52 | 12 | 23 | 35 | 75 | 11 | 2 | 9 | 11 | 15 |
| 2006-07 | Colorado College | WCHA | 23 | 1 | 3 | 4 | 16 | | | | | |
| 2007-08 | Colorado College | WCHA | 34 | 1 | 4 | 5 | 24 | | | | | |
| 2008-09 | Colorado College | WCHA | 32 | 2 | 5 | 7 | 40 | | | | | |

**FRETTER, Colton** (FREH-tuhr, KOHL-tuhn)

Right wing. Shoots right. 5'10", 187 lbs. Born, Harrow, Ont., March 12, 1982.
(Atlanta's 8th choice, 230th overall, in 2002 Entry Draft).

| | | | Regular Season | | | | | Playoffs | | | | |
|---|---|---|---|---|---|---|---|---|---|---|---|---|
| **Season** | **Club** | **League** | **GP** | **G** | **A** | **Pts** | **PIM** | **GP** | **G** | **A** | **Pts** | **PIM** |
| 99-2000 | Chatham Maroons | OHA-B | 40 | 12 | 22 | 34 | 34 | | | | | |
| 2000-01 | Chatham Maroons | OHA-B | 54 | 33 | 39 | 72 | .... | 15 | 7 | 6 | 13 | .... |
| 2001-02 | Chatham Maroons | OHA-B | 52 | 51 | 53 | 104 | 62 | 15 | 5 | 3 | 8 | 2 |
| 2002-03 | Michigan State | CCHA | 35 | 7 | 15 | 22 | 36 | | | | | |
| 2003-04 | Michigan State | CCHA | 39 | 6 | 11 | 17 | 22 | | | | | |
| 2004-05 | Michigan State | CCHA | 40 | 20 | 24 | 44 | 28 | | | | | |
| 2005-06 | Michigan State | CCHA | 45 | 10 | 19 | 29 | 28 | | | | | |
| 2006-07 | Gwinnett | ECHL | 51 | 36 | 32 | 68 | 46 | 4 | 3 | 0 | 3 | 4 |
| 2007-08 | Chicago Wolves | AHL | 8 | 1 | 3 | 4 | 2 | | | | | |
| | Gwinnett | ECHL | 2 | 2 | 0 | 2 | 4 | | | | | |
| | Bridgeport | AHL | 18 | 9 | 2 | 11 | 14 | | | | | |
| 2008-09 | Portland Pirates | AHL | 80 | 24 | 16 | 40 | 43 | 5 | 0 | 1 | 1 | 0 |

ECHL All-Rookie Team (2007) • ECHL Rookie of the Year (2007)

Signed as a free agent by **Buffalo**, August 4, 2008. Signed as a free agent by **Springfield** (AHL), August 3, 2009.

**FRISCHMON, Trevor** (FRIHCH-muhn, TREH-vuhr) **CBJ**

Center. Shoots left. 5'11", 197 lbs. Born, Ham Lake, MN, August 5, 1981.

| | | | Regular Season | | | | | Playoffs | | | | |
|---|---|---|---|---|---|---|---|---|---|---|---|---|
| **Season** | **Club** | **League** | **GP** | **G** | **A** | **Pts** | **PIM** | **GP** | **G** | **A** | **Pts** | **PIM** |
| 99-2000 | Lincoln Stars | USHL | 4 | 1 | 1 | 2 | 48 | 8 | 0 | 2 | 2 | 0 |
| 2000-01 | Lincoln Stars | USHL | 55 | 13 | 18 | 31 | 49 | 11 | 4 | 1 | 5 | 0 |
| 2001-02 | Lincoln Stars | USHL | 58 | 17 | 28 | 45 | 38 | 4 | 0 | 2 | 2 | 2 |
| 2002-03 | Colorado College | WCHA | 38 | 3 | 4 | 7 | 22 | | | | | |
| 2003-04 | Colorado College | WCHA | 39 | 10 | 7 | 17 | 34 | | | | | |
| 2004-05 | Colorado College | WCHA | 42 | 10 | 16 | 26 | 24 | | | | | |
| 2005-06 | Colorado College | WCHA | 41 | 7 | 9 | 16 | 41 | | | | | |
| 2006-07 | Syracuse Crunch | AHL | 33 | 0 | 7 | 7 | 10 | | | | | |
| | Dayton Bombers | ECHL | 24 | 5 | 8 | 13 | 14 | 20 | 3 | 5 | 8 | 24 |
| 2007-08 | Syracuse Crunch | AHL | 59 | 5 | 11 | 16 | 38 | 13 | 1 | 2 | 3 | 10 |
| | Charlotte | ECHL | 7 | 1 | 4 | 5 | 2 | | | | | |
| 2008-09 | Syracuse Crunch | AHL | 80 | 5 | 20 | 25 | 57 | | | | | |

Signed as a free agent by **Columbus**, July 3, 2009.

**FRITSCHE, Tom** (FRIHCH, TAWM) **COL.**

Left wing. Shoots left. 5'11", 183 lbs. Born, Parma, OH, September 30, 1986.
(Colorado's 3rd choice, 47th overall, in 2005 Entry Draft).

| | | | Regular Season | | | | | Playoffs | | | | |
|---|---|---|---|---|---|---|---|---|---|---|---|---|
| **Season** | **Club** | **League** | **GP** | **G** | **A** | **Pts** | **PIM** | **GP** | **G** | **A** | **Pts** | **PIM** |
| 2002-03 | USNTDP | U-17 | 19 | 7 | 11 | 18 | 16 | | | | | |
| | USNTDP | NAHL | 44 | 14 | 9 | 23 | 43 | | | | | |
| 2003-04 | USNTDP | U-18 | 46 | 19 | 23 | 42 | 46 | | | | | |
| | USNTDP | NAHL | 11 | 5 | 4 | 9 | 0 | | | | | |
| 2004-05 | Ohio State | CCHA | 42 | 11 | *34 | 45 | 38 | | | | | |
| 2005-06 | Ohio State | CCHA | 37 | 11 | 19 | 30 | 16 | | | | | |
| 2006-07 | Ohio State | CCHA | 19 | 5 | 8 | 13 | 8 | | | | | |
| 2007-08 | Ohio State | CCHA | 39 | 5 | 14 | 19 | 28 | | | | | |
| | Lake Erie Monsters | AHL | 15 | 2 | 3 | 5 | 2 | | | | | |
| 2008-09 | Lake Erie Monsters | AHL | 48 | 10 | 10 | 20 | 40 | | | | | |

CCHA All-Rookie Team (2005) • CCHA Second All-Star Team (2005)

**FROESE, Byron** (FROHZ, BIGH-ruhn) **CHI.**

Center. Shoots right. 5'11", 191 lbs. Born, Winkler, Man., March 12, 1991.
(Chicago's 4th choice, 119th overall, in 2009 Entry Draft).

| | | | Regular Season | | | | | Playoffs | | | | |
|---|---|---|---|---|---|---|---|---|---|---|---|---|
| **Season** | **Club** | **League** | **GP** | **G** | **A** | **Pts** | **PIM** | **GP** | **G** | **A** | **Pts** | **PIM** |
| 2007-08 | Pembina Valley | MMHL | 23 | 14 | 20 | 34 | 8 | 11 | 7 | 7 | 14 | 8 |
| 2008-09 | Everett Silvertips | WHL | 72 | 19 | 38 | 57 | 30 | 5 | 0 | 3 | 3 | 4 |

**FROSHAUG , Mats** (FRAWZ-howg, MATS) **VAN.**

Center. Shoots left. 6'1", 198 lbs. Born, Oslo, Norway, July 31, 1988.
(Vancouver's 4th choice, 161st overall, in 2008 Entry Draft).

| | | | Regular Season | | | | | Playoffs | | | | |
|---|---|---|---|---|---|---|---|---|---|---|---|---|
| **Season** | **Club** | **League** | **GP** | **G** | **A** | **Pts** | **PIM** | **GP** | **G** | **A** | **Pts** | **PIM** |
| 2004-05 | Sunne IK U18 | Swe-U18 | 18 | 8 | 8 | 16 | 35 | | | | | |
| | Sunne IK Jr. | Swe-Jr. | 16 | 0 | 3 | 3 | 4 | | | | | |
| 2005-06 | Sunne IK U18 | Swe-U18 | 16 | 8 | 11 | 19 | 10 | | | | | |
| | Sunne IK Jr. | Swe-Jr. | 17 | 14 | 10 | 24 | 6 | | | | | |
| | Sunne IK | Sweden-3 | 14 | 1 | 1 | 2 | 0 | | | | | |
| 2006-07 | Linkopings HC Jr. | Swe-Jr. | 37 | 10 | 11 | 21 | 20 | 5 | 0 | 1 | 1 | 6 |
| 2007-08 | Linkopings HC Jr. | Swe-Jr. | 35 | 18 | 18 | 36 | 41 | 5 | 3 | 4 | 7 | 2 |
| | Nykoping | Sweden-2 | 2 | 0 | 1 | 1 | 2 | | | | | |
| | Linkopings HC | Sweden | 2 | 0 | 0 | 0 | 0 | | | | | |
| 2008-09 | Linkopings HC Jr. | Swe-Jr. | 7 | 2 | 6 | 8 | 2 | | | | | |
| | Linkopings HC | Sweden | 20 | 0 | 1 | 1 | 0 | | | | | |
| | Lulea HF | Sweden | 14 | 0 | 1 | 1 | 0 | | | | | |
| | Sparta Sarpsborg | Norway | 7 | 2 | 6 | 8 | 6 | 14 | 1 | 3 | 4 | 2 |

**FULTON, Jordan** (FUL-tuhn, JOHR-dahn) **CGY.**

Center. Shoots left. 6'1", 191 lbs. Born, St. Louis Park, MN, September 12, 1987.
(Calgary's 6th choice, 179th overall, in 2006 Entry Draft).

| | | | Regular Season | | | | | Playoffs | | | | |
|---|---|---|---|---|---|---|---|---|---|---|---|---|
| **Season** | **Club** | **League** | **GP** | **G** | **A** | **Pts** | **PIM** | **GP** | **G** | **A** | **Pts** | **PIM** |
| 2002-03 | Breck Mustangs | High-MN | 26 | 24 | 7 | 31 | 12 | | | | | |
| 2003-04 | Breck Mustangs | High-MN | 31 | 30 | 36 | 66 | 24 | | | | | |
| 2004-05 | Breck Mustangs | High-MN | 28 | 29 | 41 | 70 | 68 | | | | | |
| 2005-06 | Breck Mustangs | High-MN | 28 | 45 | 36 | 81 | 76 | | | | | |
| 2006-07 | U. Minn-Duluth | WCHA | 38 | 3 | 7 | 10 | 22 | | | | | |
| 2007-08 | U. Minn-Duluth | WCHA | 36 | 5 | 9 | 14 | 40 | | | | | |
| 2008-09 | U. Minn-Duluth | WCHA | 42 | 12 | 5 | 17 | 60 | | | | | |

**GAGNON, Aaron** (GAN-YAWN, AIR-ruhn) **DAL.**

Center. Shoots right. 5'10", 185 lbs. Born, Quesnel, B.C., April 24, 1986.
(Phoenix's 8th choice, 240th overall, in 2004 Entry Draft).

| | | | Regular Season | | | | | Playoffs | | | | |
|---|---|---|---|---|---|---|---|---|---|---|---|---|
| **Season** | **Club** | **League** | **GP** | **G** | **A** | **Pts** | **PIM** | **GP** | **G** | **A** | **Pts** | **PIM** |
| 2001-02 | North Okanoghan | Minor-BC | 41 | 59 | 59 | 118 | 60 | | | | | |
| | Seattle | WHL | 2 | 0 | 0 | 0 | 0 | | | | | |
| 2002-03 | Seattle | WHL | 60 | 5 | 13 | 18 | 14 | 15 | 3 | 2 | 5 | 4 |
| 2003-04 | Seattle | WHL | 63 | 21 | 15 | 36 | 29 | | | | | |
| 2004-05 | Seattle | WHL | 72 | 31 | 34 | 65 | 29 | 12 | 4 | 5 | 9 | 16 |
| 2005-06 | Seattle | WHL | 62 | 24 | 21 | 45 | 40 | 7 | 5 | 3 | 8 | 6 |
| 2006-07 | Seattle | WHL | 59 | 42 | 38 | 80 | 58 | 11 | 6 | 2 | 8 | 10 |
| 2007-08 | Iowa Stars | AHL | 25 | 0 | 1 | 1 | 8 | | | | | |
| | Idaho Steelheads | ECHL | 22 | 7 | 14 | 21 | 4 | 4 | 1 | 1 | 2 | 2 |
| 2008-09 | Grand Rapids | AHL | 61 | 8 | 11 | 19 | 28 | 10 | 1 | 2 | 3 | 2 |

WHL West First All-Star Team (2005, 2007)

Signed as a free agent by **Dallas**, February 2, 2007.

**GARDINER, Jake** (GAHR-dih-nuhr, JAYK) **ANA.**

Defense. Shoots left. 6'1", 182 lbs. Born, Deephaven, MN, July 4, 1990.
(Anaheim's 1st choice, 17th overall, in 2008 Entry Draft).

| | | | Regular Season | | | | | Playoffs | | | | |
|---|---|---|---|---|---|---|---|---|---|---|---|---|
| **Season** | **Club** | **League** | **GP** | **G** | **A** | **Pts** | **PIM** | **GP** | **G** | **A** | **Pts** | **PIM** |
| 2005-06 | Minnetonka High | High-MN | 21 | 2 | 14 | 16 | 6 | | | | | |
| 2006-07 | Minnetonka High | High-MN | 19 | 10 | 22 | 32 | 20 | | | | | |
| | Team Southwest | UMWEHL | 11 | 4 | 3 | 7 | | | | | | |
| 2007-08 | Minnetonka High | High-MN | 24 | 20 | 28 | 48 | 14 | | | | | |
| | Team Southwest | UMWEHL | 11 | 8 | 7 | 15 | | | | | | |
| 2008-09 | U. of Wisconsin | WCHA | 39 | 3 | 18 | 21 | 16 | | | | | |

WCHA All-Rookie Team (2009)

**GAULTON, Mitch** (GAWL-tuhn, MIHTCH) **NYR**

Defense. Shoots left. 6', 207 lbs. Born, St. Catherines, Ont., April 25, 1990.
(NY Rangers' 7th choice, 171st overall, in 2008 Entry Draft).

| | | | Regular Season | | | | | Playoffs | | | | |
|---|---|---|---|---|---|---|---|---|---|---|---|---|
| **Season** | **Club** | **League** | **GP** | **G** | **A** | **Pts** | **PIM** | **GP** | **G** | **A** | **Pts** | **PIM** |
| 2005-06 | Tor. Red Wings | GTHL | 55 | 22 | 26 | 48 | 71 | | | | | |
| 2006-07 | Erie Otters | OHL | 54 | 5 | 11 | 16 | 53 | | | | | |
| 2007-08 | Erie Otters | OHL | 20 | 2 | 5 | 7 | 19 | | | | | |
| 2008-09 | Erie Otters | OHL | 22 | 1 | 5 | 6 | 4 | 5 | 0 | 0 | 0 | 4 |

**GAUNCE, Cameron** (GAWNS, KAM-ih-RUHN) **COL.**

Defense. Shoots left. 6'1", 203 lbs. Born, Sudbury, Ont., March 19, 1990.
(Colorado's 1st choice, 50th overall, in 2008 Entry Draft).

| | | | Regular Season | | | | | Playoffs | | | | |
|---|---|---|---|---|---|---|---|---|---|---|---|---|
| **Season** | **Club** | **League** | **GP** | **G** | **A** | **Pts** | **PIM** | **GP** | **G** | **A** | **Pts** | **PIM** |
| 2005-06 | Markham Waxers | Minor-ON | 72 | 11 | 60 | 71 | 122 | | | | | |
| 2006-07 | Markham Waxers | OPJHL | 45 | 2 | 12 | 14 | 68 | 11 | 0 | 3 | 3 | 26 |
| 2007-08 | St. Michael's | OHL | 63 | 10 | 30 | 40 | 99 | 4 | 0 | 1 | 1 | 6 |
| 2008-09 | St. Michael's | OHL | 67 | 17 | 47 | 64 | 110 | 11 | 4 | 6 | 10 | 20 |

OHL Second All-Star Team (2009)

**GAZDIC, Luke** (GAZ-dihk, LEWK) **DAL.**

Left wing. Shoots left. 6'3", 210 lbs. Born, Toronto, Ont., July 25, 1989.
(Dallas' 8th choice, 172nd overall, in 2007 Entry Draft).

| | | | Regular Season | | | | | Playoffs | | | | |
|---|---|---|---|---|---|---|---|---|---|---|---|---|
| **Season** | **Club** | **League** | **GP** | **G** | **A** | **Pts** | **PIM** | **GP** | **G** | **A** | **Pts** | **PIM** |
| 2005-06 | Wexford Raiders | OPJHL | 47 | 17 | 16 | 33 | 105 | | | | | |
| | North York | GTHL | 38 | 13 | 16 | 29 | 24 | | | | | |
| 2006-07 | Erie Otters | OHL | 58 | 5 | 8 | 13 | 136 | | | | | |
| 2007-08 | Erie Otters | OHL | 67 | 17 | 12 | 29 | 144 | | | | | |
| 2008-09 | Erie Otters | OHL | 63 | 20 | 10 | 30 | 127 | 5 | 0 | 0 | 0 | 9 |
| | Idaho Steelheads | ECHL | 2 | 1 | 0 | 1 | 14 | 2 | 0 | 0 | 0 | 0 |

**GEDIG, Curtis** (GEH-dihg, KUHR-tihs) **N.J.**

Defense. Shoots left. 6'3", 190 lbs. Born, Penticton, B.C., September 14, 1991.
(New Jersey's 7th choice, 204th overall, in 2009 Entry Draft).

| | | | Regular Season | | | | | Playoffs | | | | |
|---|---|---|---|---|---|---|---|---|---|---|---|---|
| **Season** | **Club** | **League** | **GP** | **G** | **A** | **Pts** | **PIM** | **GP** | **G** | **A** | **Pts** | **PIM** |
| 2007-08 | Okanagan Rockets | Minor-BC | 40 | 4 | 14 | 18 | 36 | | | | | |
| | Princeton Posse | KIJHL | 9 | 0 | 2 | 2 | 4 | 1 | 0 | 0 | 0 | 0 |
| 2008-09 | Merritt | BCHL | 16 | 2 | 4 | 6 | 2 | | | | | |
| | Cowichan Valley | BCHL | 30 | 2 | 10 | 12 | 16 | 10 | 0 | 3 | 3 | 2 |

**GELECH, Randall** (GEH-lehkh, RAN-duhl)

Center. Shoots right. 6'3", 220 lbs. Born, Wynard, Sask., February 2, 1984.
(Phoenix's 5th choice, 208th overall, in 2003 Entry Draft).

| | | | Regular Season | | | | | Playoffs | | | | |
|---|---|---|---|---|---|---|---|---|---|---|---|---|
| **Season** | **Club** | **League** | **GP** | **G** | **A** | **Pts** | **PIM** | **GP** | **G** | **A** | **Pts** | **PIM** |
| 2000-01 | Kelowna Rockets | WHL | 51 | 1 | 9 | 10 | 19 | 6 | 0 | 0 | 0 | 4 |
| 2001-02 | Kelowna Rockets | WHL | 48 | 6 | 2 | 8 | 33 | 15 | 2 | 1 | 3 | 15 |
| 2002-03 | Kelowna Rockets | WHL | 67 | 25 | 20 | 45 | 93 | 19 | 8 | 4 | 12 | 17 |
| 2003-04 | Kelowna Rockets | WHL | 71 | 30 | 19 | 49 | 117 | 17 | 10 | 4 | 14 | 22 |
| 2004-05 | Utah Grizzlies | AHL | 76 | 15 | 12 | 27 | 72 | | | | | |
| 2005-06 | San Antonio | AHL | 75 | 9 | 12 | 21 | 39 | | | | | |
| 2006-07 | San Antonio | AHL | 79 | 17 | 17 | 34 | 64 | | | | | |
| 2007-08 | Grand Rapids | AHL | 70 | 7 | 8 | 15 | 37 | | | | | |
| 2008-09 | Grand Rapids | AHL | 5 | 0 | 0 | 0 | 2 | | | | | |
| | Rochester | AHL | 56 | 9 | 9 | 18 | 33 | | | | | |

Memorial Cup Tournament All-Star Team (2004)

Signed as a free agent by **Detroit**, July 16, 2007.

## GELINAS, Eric (ZHEHL-ih-nuh, AIR-ihk) N.J.

Defense. Shoots left. 6'4", 190 lbs. Born, Vanier, Ont., May 8, 1991.
(New Jersey's 2nd choice, 54th overall, in 2009 Entry Draft).

| | | | Regular Season | | | | | Playoffs | | | | |
|---|---|---|---|---|---|---|---|---|---|---|---|---|
| Season | Club | League | GP | G | A | Pts | PIM | GP | G | A | Pts | PIM |
| 2006-07 | C.C. Lemoyne | QAAA | 44 | 5 | 14 | 19 | 50 | 10 | 1 | 4 | 5 | 14 |
| 2007-08 | Lewiston | QMJHL | 54 | 3 | 16 | 19 | 34 | 5 | 0 | 0 | 0 | 2 |
| 2008-09 | Lewiston | QMJHL | 67 | 10 | 29 | 39 | 80 | 4 | 0 | 1 | 1 | 12 |

## GENDUR, Dan (JEHN-duhr, DAN) VAN.

Right wing. Shoots right. 5'11", 195 lbs. Born, Vancouver, B.C., May 21, 1987.
(Vancouver's 6th choice, 206th overall, in 2007 Entry Draft).

| | | | Regular Season | | | | | Playoffs | | | | |
|---|---|---|---|---|---|---|---|---|---|---|---|---|
| Season | Club | League | GP | G | A | Pts | PIM | GP | G | A | Pts | PIM |
| 2003-04 | Victoria Cougars | VIJHL | 31 | 26 | 30 | 56 | 70 | .... | .... | .... | .... | .... |
| | Cowichan Valley | BCHL | 17 | 3 | 8 | 11 | 22 | 1 | 0 | 0 | 0 | 0 |
| 2004-05 | Prince George | WHL | 60 | 2 | 6 | 8 | 75 | .... | .... | .... | .... | .... |
| 2005-06 | Prince George | WHL | 19 | 2 | 1 | 3 | 24 | .... | .... | .... | .... | .... |
| 2006-07 | Prince George | WHL | 13 | 2 | 5 | 7 | 18 | .... | .... | .... | .... | .... |
| | Everett Silvertips | WHL | 48 | 20 | 22 | 42 | 44 | 12 | 4 | 4 | 8 | 8 |
| 2007-08 | Everett Silvertips | WHL | 60 | 29 | 55 | 84 | 68 | 4 | 1 | 2 | 3 | 8 |
| 2008-09 | Manitoba Moose | AHL | 10 | 1 | 0 | 1 | 2 | .... | .... | .... | .... | .... |
| | Victoria | ECHL | 52 | 9 | 29 | 38 | 97 | 2 | 1 | 2 | 3 | 0 |

WHL West Second All-Star Team (2008)

## GENEROUS, Matt (GEHN-uhr-uhs, MAT) BUF.

Defense. Shoots right. 6'3", 185 lbs. Born, Methuen, MA, May 4, 1985.
(Buffalo's 8th choice, 208th overall, in 2005 Entry Draft).

| | | | Regular Season | | | | | Playoffs | | | | |
|---|---|---|---|---|---|---|---|---|---|---|---|---|
| Season | Club | League | GP | G | A | Pts | PIM | GP | G | A | Pts | PIM |
| 2003-04 | N.E. Jr. Falcons | EJHL | 43 | 6 | 9 | 15 | 134 | .... | .... | .... | .... | .... |
| 2004-05 | N.E. Jr. Falcons | EJHL | 49 | 8 | 16 | 24 | 105 | .... | .... | .... | .... | .... |
| 2005-06 | St. Lawrence | ECAC | 34 | 4 | 11 | 15 | 34 | .... | .... | .... | .... | .... |
| 2006-07 | St. Lawrence | ECAC | 37 | 3 | 6 | 9 | 34 | .... | .... | .... | .... | .... |
| 2007-08 | St. Lawrence | ECAC | 33 | 3 | 12 | 15 | 31 | .... | .... | .... | .... | .... |
| 2008-09 | St. Lawrence | ECAC | 35 | 8 | 9 | 17 | 34 | .... | .... | .... | .... | .... |
| | Portland Pirates | AHL | 4 | 1 | 0 | 1 | 13 | 4 | 0 | 0 | 0 | 0 |

ECAC All-Rookie Team (2006)

## GENOWAY, Colby (JEHN-oh-way, KOHL-bee) VAN.

Right wing. Shoots right. 6'1", 201 lbs. Born, Morden, Man., December 12, 1983.

| | | | Regular Season | | | | | Playoffs | | | | |
|---|---|---|---|---|---|---|---|---|---|---|---|---|
| Season | Club | League | GP | G | A | Pts | PIM | GP | G | A | Pts | PIM |
| 2002-03 | North Dakota | WCHA | 31 | 1 | 2 | 3 | 24 | .... | .... | .... | .... | .... |
| 2003-04 | North Dakota | WCHA | 40 | 11 | 23 | 34 | 22 | .... | .... | .... | .... | .... |
| 2004-05 | North Dakota | WCHA | 42 | 13 | 31 | 44 | 38 | .... | .... | .... | .... | .... |
| | Hartford Wolf Pack | AHL | 4 | 0 | 0 | 0 | 0 | .... | .... | .... | .... | .... |
| 2005-06 | Hartford Wolf Pack | AHL | 77 | 26 | 35 | 61 | 78 | 13 | 4 | 8 | 12 | 10 |
| 2006-07 | Portland Pirates | AHL | 41 | 8 | 21 | 29 | 36 | .... | .... | .... | .... | .... |
| | Manitoba Moose | AHL | 32 | 1 | 11 | 12 | 12 | 13 | 1 | 1 | 2 | 6 |
| 2007-08 | Manitoba Moose | AHL | 67 | 15 | 34 | 49 | 37 | 6 | 0 | 4 | 4 | 6 |
| 2008-09 | Ilves Tampere | Finland | 11 | 7 | 7 | 14 | 8 | | | | | |

Signed as a free agent by **Anaheim**, July 11, 2006. Traded to **Vancouver** by **Anaheim** for Joe Rullier, January 24, 2007.

## GEOFFRION, Blake (JEHF-REE-ohn, BLAYK) NSH.

Left wing. Shoots left. 6'1", 192 lbs. Born, Plantation, FL, February 3, 1988.
(Nashville's 1st choice, 56th overall, in 2006 Entry Draft).

| | | | Regular Season | | | | | Playoffs | | | | |
|---|---|---|---|---|---|---|---|---|---|---|---|---|
| Season | Club | League | GP | G | A | Pts | PIM | GP | G | A | Pts | PIM |
| 2003-04 | Culver Academy | High-IN | 45 | .... | .... | 65 | .... | .... | .... | .... | .... | .... |
| 2004-05 | USNTDP | U-17 | 11 | 2 | 3 | 5 | 24 | .... | .... | .... | .... | .... |
| | USNTDP | NAHL | 37 | 7 | 15 | 22 | 62 | 10 | 2 | 5 | 7 | 23 |
| 2005-06 | USNTDP | U-18 | 41 | 12 | 14 | 26 | 38 | .... | .... | .... | .... | .... |
| | USNTDP | NAHL | 13 | 6 | 9 | 15 | 30 | .... | .... | .... | .... | .... |
| 2006-07 | U. of Wisconsin | WCHA | 36 | 2 | 4 | 6 | 62 | .... | .... | .... | .... | .... |
| 2007-08 | U. of Wisconsin | WCHA | 36 | 10 | 20 | 30 | 52 | .... | .... | .... | .... | .... |
| 2008-09 | U. of Wisconsin | WCHA | 35 | 15 | 13 | 28 | 73 | .... | .... | .... | .... | .... |

## GERGEN, Michael (GUHR-gehn, MIGH-kuhl) PIT.

Left wing. Shoots left. 5'11", 185 lbs. Born, Hastings, MN, February 17, 1987.
(Pittsburgh's 2nd choice, 61st overall, in 2005 Entry Draft).

| | | | Regular Season | | | | | Playoffs | | | | |
|---|---|---|---|---|---|---|---|---|---|---|---|---|
| Season | Club | League | GP | G | A | Pts | PIM | GP | G | A | Pts | PIM |
| 2003-04 | Shat.-St. Mary's | High-MN | 71 | 29 | 26 | 55 | 52 | .... | .... | .... | .... | .... |
| 2004-05 | Shat.-St. Mary's | High-MN | 69 | 64 | 53 | 117 | 110 | .... | .... | .... | .... | .... |
| 2005-06 | U. Minn-Duluth | WCHA | 39 | 14 | 8 | 22 | 63 | .... | .... | .... | .... | .... |
| 2006-07 | U. Minn-Duluth | WCHA | 39 | 5 | 11 | 16 | 34 | .... | .... | .... | .... | .... |
| 2007-08 | U. Minn-Duluth | WCHA | 33 | 6 | 7 | 13 | 49 | .... | .... | .... | .... | .... |
| 2008-09 | U. Minn-Duluth | WCHA | 42 | 9 | 9 | 18 | 40 | .... | .... | .... | .... | .... |

Signed as a free agent by **Salzburg** (Austria), May 13, 2009.

## GIFFORD, Brian (GIH-fuhrd, BRIGH-uhn) PIT.

Center. Shoots left. 6'1", 173 lbs. Born, Fargo, ND, November 12, 1985.
(Pittsburgh's 5th choice, 85th overall, in 2004 Entry Draft).

| | | | Regular Season | | | | | Playoffs | | | | |
|---|---|---|---|---|---|---|---|---|---|---|---|---|
| Season | Club | League | GP | G | A | Pts | PIM | GP | G | A | Pts | PIM |
| 2002-03 | Moorhead Spuds | High-MN | 30 | 18 | 20 | 38 | 32 | .... | .... | .... | .... | .... |
| 2003-04 | Moorhead Spuds | High-MN | 26 | 19 | 37 | 56 | 26 | .... | .... | .... | .... | .... |
| 2004-05 | Indiana Ice | USHL | 55 | 13 | 10 | 23 | 80 | 3 | 1 | 0 | 1 | 0 |
| 2005-06 | Indiana Ice | USHL | 56 | 12 | 14 | 26 | 55 | 5 | 0 | 2 | 2 | 0 |
| 2006-07 | U. of Denver | WCHA | 40 | 3 | 10 | 13 | 49 | .... | .... | .... | .... | .... |
| 2007-08 | U. of Denver | WCHA | 36 | 2 | 5 | 7 | 16 | .... | .... | .... | .... | .... |
| 2008-09 | U. of Denver | WCHA | 40 | 4 | 8 | 12 | 40 | .... | .... | .... | .... | .... |

## GILBERT, David (zhihl-BAIR, DAY-vihd) CHI.

Center. Shoots left. 6'2", 176 lbs. Born, Chateauguay, Que., February 9, 1991.
(Chicago's 8th choice, 209th overall, in 2009 Entry Draft).

| | | | Regular Season | | | | | Playoffs | | | | |
|---|---|---|---|---|---|---|---|---|---|---|---|---|
| Season | Club | League | GP | G | A | Pts | PIM | GP | G | A | Pts | PIM |
| 2006-07 | Antoine-Girouard | QAAA | 44 | 19 | 26 | 45 | 10 | 4 | 2 | 1 | 3 | 2 |
| 2007-08 | Antoine-Girouard | QAAA | 29 | 29 | 24 | 53 | 54 | .... | .... | .... | .... | .... |
| | Quebec Remparts | QMJHL | 28 | 7 | 7 | 14 | 12 | 11 | 1 | 0 | 1 | 2 |
| 2008-09 | Quebec Remparts | QMJHL | 67 | 11 | 32 | 43 | 24 | 17 | 6 | 2 | 8 | 11 |

## GILIATI, Stefano (jihl-ee-A-tee, steh-FA-noh) TOR.

Left wing. Shoots left. 5'11", 200 lbs. Born, Montreal, Que., October 7, 1987.

| | | | Regular Season | | | | | Playoffs | | | | |
|---|---|---|---|---|---|---|---|---|---|---|---|---|
| Season | Club | League | GP | G | A | Pts | PIM | GP | G | A | Pts | PIM |
| 2004-05 | Shawinigan | QMJHL | 54 | 9 | 5 | 14 | 23 | 3 | 0 | 0 | 0 | 2 |
| 2005-06 | Lewiston | QMJHL | 70 | 21 | 28 | 49 | 72 | 6 | 2 | 0 | 2 | 6 |
| 2006-07 | Lewiston | QMJHL | 68 | 24 | 33 | 57 | 73 | 17 | 4 | 11 | 15 | 22 |
| 2007-08 | Lewiston | QMJHL | 65 | 40 | 47 | 87 | 103 | .... | .... | .... | .... | .... |
| | Toronto Marlies | AHL | 1 | 0 | 0 | 0 | 0 | .... | .... | .... | .... | .... |
| 2008-09 | Toronto Marlies | AHL | 53 | 6 | 9 | 15 | 16 | .... | .... | .... | .... | .... |

QMJHL First All-Star Team (2008)

Signed as a free agent by **Toronto**, April 3, 2008.

## GILROY, Matt (GIHL-roy, MAT) NYR

Defense. Shoots right. 6'2", 195 lbs. Born, North Bellmore, NY, July 30, 1984.

| | | | Regular Season | | | | | Playoffs | | | | |
|---|---|---|---|---|---|---|---|---|---|---|---|---|
| Season | Club | League | GP | G | A | Pts | PIM | GP | G | A | Pts | PIM |
| 2000-01 | St. Mary's Gaels | High-NY | STATISTICS NOT AVAILABLE | | | | | | | | | |
| 2001-02 | St. Mary's Gaels | High-NY | STATISTICS NOT AVAILABLE | | | | | | | | | |
| 2002-03 | St. Mary's Gaels | High-NY | STATISTICS NOT AVAILABLE | | | | | | | | | |
| 2003-04 | NY Apple Core | EJHL | STATISTICS NOT AVAILABLE | | | | | | | | | |
| 2004-05 | Walpole Stars | EJHL | 55 | 24 | 29 | 53 | 20 | .... | .... | .... | .... | .... |
| 2005-06 | Boston University | H-East | 36 | 2 | 6 | 8 | 10 | .... | .... | .... | .... | .... |
| 2006-07 | Boston University | H-East | 39 | 9 | 17 | 26 | 14 | .... | .... | .... | .... | .... |
| 2007-08 | Boston University | H-East | 40 | 6 | 15 | 21 | 12 | .... | .... | .... | .... | .... |
| 2008-09 | Boston University | H-East | 45 | 8 | 29 | 37 | 12 | .... | .... | .... | .... | .... |

Hockey East First All-Star Team (2008, 2009) • NCAA East First All-American Team (2008, 2009) • Hobey Baker Memorial Award (Top U.S. Collegiate Player) (2009)

Signed as a free agent by **NY Rangers**, April 17, 2009.

## GIMAYEV, Sergei (gih-MIGH-ehv, SAIR-gay) OTT.

Defense. Shoots left. 6'1", 183 lbs. Born, Moscow, USSR, February 16, 1984.
(Ottawa's 6th choice, 166th overall, in 2003 Entry Draft).

| | | | Regular Season | | | | | Playoffs | | | | |
|---|---|---|---|---|---|---|---|---|---|---|---|---|
| Season | Club | League | GP | G | A | Pts | PIM | GP | G | A | Pts | PIM |
| 2001-02 | CSKA Moscow 2 | Russia-3 | 36 | 0 | 10 | 10 | 50 | .... | .... | .... | .... | .... |
| 2002-03 | Cherepovets | Russia | 11 | 0 | 0 | 0 | 4 | .... | .... | .... | .... | .... |
| 2003-04 | Cherepovets | Russia | 50 | 1 | 3 | 4 | 32 | .... | .... | .... | .... | .... |
| 2004-05 | Cherepovets | Russia | 5 | 0 | 1 | 1 | 2 | .... | .... | .... | .... | .... |
| | Sibir Novosibirsk | Russia | 31 | 1 | 6 | 7 | 34 | .... | .... | .... | .... | .... |
| 2005-06 | Dynamo Moscow | Russia | 46 | 1 | 3 | 4 | 36 | 2 | 0 | 0 | 0 | 0 |
| 2006-07 | Dynamo Moscow | Russia | 23 | 0 | 2 | 2 | 28 | 2 | 0 | 0 | 0 | 6 |
| 2007-08 | Cherepovets | Russia | 39 | 1 | 0 | 1 | 30 | 8 | 1 | 1 | 2 | 4 |
| 2008-09 | Barys Astana | Rus-KHL | 45 | 0 | 2 | 2 | 79 | .... | .... | .... | .... | .... |

## GIONTA, Stephen (jee-OHN-tuh, STEE-vehn) N.J.

Right wing. Shoots right. 5'7", 180 lbs. Born, Rochester, NY, October 9, 1983.

| | | | Regular Season | | | | | Playoffs | | | | |
|---|---|---|---|---|---|---|---|---|---|---|---|---|
| Season | Club | League | GP | G | A | Pts | PIM | GP | G | A | Pts | PIM |
| 2002-03 | Boston College | H-East | 33 | 5 | 10 | 15 | 36 | .... | .... | .... | .... | .... |
| 2003-04 | Boston College | H-East | 41 | 9 | 15 | 24 | 36 | .... | .... | .... | .... | .... |
| 2004-05 | Boston College | H-East | 38 | 8 | 11 | 19 | 44 | .... | .... | .... | .... | .... |
| 2005-06 | Boston College | H-East | 37 | 11 | 21 | 32 | 66 | .... | .... | .... | .... | .... |
| | Albany River Rats | AHL | 3 | 5 | 1 | 6 | 2 | .... | .... | .... | .... | .... |
| 2006-07 | Lowell Devils | AHL | 67 | 7 | 8 | 15 | 15 | .... | .... | .... | .... | .... |
| 2007-08 | Lowell Devils | AHL | 63 | 16 | 13 | 29 | 33 | .... | .... | .... | .... | .... |
| 2008-09 | Lowell Devils | AHL | 52 | 2 | 9 | 11 | 30 | .... | .... | .... | .... | .... |

Signed to an ATO (tryout) contract by **Albany** (AHL), April 12, 2006. Signed as a free agent by **New Jersey**, September 26, 2006. Signed as a free agent by **New Jersey**, July 31, 2009.

## GLADSKIKH, Evgeny (glad-SKEEKH, ehv-GEH-nee) VAN.

Right wing. Shoots left. 6', 198 lbs. Born, Magnitogorsk, USSR, April 24, 1982.
(Vancouver's 3rd choice, 114th overall, in 2001 Entry Draft).

| | | | Regular Season | | | | | Playoffs | | | | |
|---|---|---|---|---|---|---|---|---|---|---|---|---|
| Season | Club | League | GP | G | A | Pts | PIM | GP | G | A | Pts | PIM |
| 1998-99 | Magnitogorsk 2 | Russia-4 | 16 | 3 | 3 | 6 | 6 | .... | .... | .... | .... | .... |
| 99-2000 | Magnitogorsk 2 | Russia-3 | 39 | 17 | 2 | 19 | 24 | .... | .... | .... | .... | .... |
| | Magnitogorsk | Russia | 1 | 0 | 0 | 0 | 0 | .... | .... | .... | .... | .... |
| 2000-01 | Magnitogorsk 2 | Russia-3 | 11 | 10 | 7 | 17 | 6 | .... | .... | .... | .... | .... |
| | Magnitogorsk | Russia | 31 | 3 | 5 | 8 | 10 | 12 | 0 | 2 | 2 | 2 |
| 2001-02 | Magnitogorsk | Russia | 32 | 5 | 6 | 11 | 6 | 4 | 0 | 0 | 0 | 4 |
| 2002-03 | Magnitogorsk | Russia | 42 | 4 | 7 | 11 | 18 | 3 | 0 | 0 | 0 | 2 |
| 2003-04 | Magnitogorsk | Russia | 47 | 13 | 13 | 26 | 22 | 14 | 3 | 1 | 4 | 10 |
| 2004-05 | Magnitogorsk 2 | Russia-3 | 2 | 0 | 2 | 2 | 0 | .... | .... | .... | .... | .... |
| | Magnitogorsk | Russia | 42 | 11 | 12 | 23 | 24 | 4 | 1 | 0 | 1 | 4 |
| 2005-06 | Magnitogorsk | Russia | 43 | 12 | 8 | 20 | 20 | 7 | 1 | 1 | 2 | 2 |
| 2006-07 | Magnitogorsk | Russia | 47 | 5 | 9 | 14 | 16 | 15 | 2 | 4 | 6 | 6 |
| 2007-08 | Magnitogorsk | Russia | 52 | 12 | 12 | 24 | 12 | 12 | 2 | 2 | 4 | 2 |
| 2008-09 | Omsk | Rus-KHL | 17 | 1 | 4 | 5 | 4 | .... | .... | .... | .... | .... |
| | Mytischi | Rus-KHL | 26 | 2 | 8 | 10 | 22 | 7 | 1 | 0 | 1 | 2 |

## GLASS, Andrew (GLAS, AN-droo) WSH.

Left wing. Shoots left. 6', 175 lbs. Born, Wrentham, MA, July 14, 1989.
(Washington's 10th choice, 199th overall, in 2007 Entry Draft).

| | | | Regular Season | | | | | Playoffs | | | | |
|---|---|---|---|---|---|---|---|---|---|---|---|---|
| Season | Club | League | GP | G | A | Pts | PIM | GP | G | A | Pts | PIM |
| 2003-04 | Junior Bruins | Minor-MA | 61 | 15 | 23 | 38 | 2 | .... | .... | .... | .... | .... |
| 2004-05 | Little Bruins | Minor-MA | 33 | 5 | 13 | 18 | 15 | .... | .... | .... | .... | .... |
| | Nobles | High-MA | 29 | 7 | 15 | 22 | 6 | .... | .... | .... | .... | .... |
| 2005-06 | Little Bruins | Minor-MA | 19 | 9 | 11 | 20 | 17 | .... | .... | .... | .... | .... |
| | Nobles | High-MA | 29 | 15 | 24 | 39 | 8 | .... | .... | .... | .... | .... |
| 2006-07 | Little Bruins | Minor-MA | 12 | 7 | 8 | 15 | 4 | .... | .... | .... | .... | .... |
| | Nobles | High-MA | 18 | 7 | 10 | 17 | 6 | .... | .... | .... | .... | .... |
| 2007-08 | Nobles | High-MA | 29 | 27 | 23 | 50 | | .... | .... | .... | .... | .... |
| 2008-09 | Boston University | H-East | 15 | 2 | 1 | 3 | 2 | .... | .... | .... | .... | .... |

## GLASSER, Matthew (GLAS-uhr, MA-thew) EDM.

Left wing. Shoots left. 5'10", 175 lbs. Born, Saskatoon, Sask., January 11, 1987.
(Edmonton's 8th choice, 220th overall, in 2005 Entry Draft).

| | | | Regular Season | | | | | Playoffs | | | | |
|---|---|---|---|---|---|---|---|---|---|---|---|---|
| Season | Club | League | GP | G | A | Pts | PIM | GP | G | A | Pts | PIM |
| 2003-04 | Fort McMurray | AJHL | 55 | 13 | 12 | 25 | 24 | .... | .... | .... | .... | .... |
| 2004-05 | Fort McMurray | AJHL | 62 | 25 | 24 | 49 | 14 | .... | .... | .... | .... | .... |
| 2005-06 | Fort McMurray | AJHL | 58 | 15 | 20 | 35 | 36 | 17 | 5 | 2 | 7 | 38 |
| 2006-07 | U. of Denver | WCHA | 12 | 0 | 0 | 0 | 2 | .... | .... | .... | .... | .... |
| 2007-08 | U. of Denver | WCHA | 40 | 6 | 2 | 8 | 20 | .... | .... | .... | .... | .... |
| 2008-09 | U. of Denver | WCHA | 40 | 4 | 3 | 7 | 18 | .... | .... | .... | .... | .... |

## GLAZACHEV, Konstantin (GLAH-zuh-chehv, KAWN-stan-tihn) NSH.

Left wing. Shoots right. 6', 186 lbs. Born, Arkhangelsk, USSR, February 18, 1985.
(Nashville's 2nd choice, 35th overall, in 2003 Entry Draft).

| | | | Regular Season | | | | | Playoffs | | | | |
|---|---|---|---|---|---|---|---|---|---|---|---|---|
| Season | Club | League | GP | G | A | Pts | PIM | GP | G | A | Pts | PIM |
| 2001-02 | Yaroslavl 2 | Russia-3 | 7 | 5 | 6 | 11 | 6 | .... | .... | .... | .... | .... |
| 2002-03 | Yaroslavl 2 | Russia-3 | STATISTICS NOT AVAILABLE | | | | | | | | | |
| | Yaroslavl | Russia | 13 | 3 | 4 | 7 | 4 | 4 | 0 | 0 | 0 | 0 |
| 2003-04 | Yaroslavl 2 | Russia-3 | 9 | 6 | 5 | 11 | 8 | .... | .... | .... | .... | .... |
| | Yaroslavl | Russia | 35 | 4 | 3 | 7 | 4 | 2 | 0 | 0 | 0 | 0 |
| 2004-05 | Sibir Novosibirsk | Russia | 24 | 4 | 9 | 13 | 6 | .... | .... | .... | .... | .... |
| | Yaroslavl | Russia | 9 | 0 | 3 | 3 | 2 | .... | .... | .... | .... | .... |
| | Yaroslavl 2 | Russia-3 | 20 | 17 | 9 | 26 | 14 | .... | .... | .... | .... | .... |
| 2005-06 | Yaroslavl | Russia | 29 | 7 | 4 | 11 | 8 | 9 | 0 | 2 | 2 | 0 |
| 2006-07 | Yaroslavl | Russia | 14 | 4 | 1 | 5 | 10 | .... | .... | .... | .... | .... |
| | Yaroslavl 2 | Russia-3 | 4 | 2 | 5 | 7 | 0 | .... | .... | .... | .... | .... |
| | Amur Khabarovsk | Russia | 22 | 4 | 7 | 11 | 14 | .... | .... | .... | .... | .... |
| 2007-08 | Novokuznetsk | Russia | 50 | 7 | 9 | 16 | 10 | .... | .... | .... | .... | .... |
| 2008-09 | Barys Astana | Rus-KHL | 56 | 28 | 24 | 52 | 30 | 3 | 3 | 0 | 3 | 2 |

## GLEASON, Joe (GLEE-suhn, JOH) CHI.

Defense. Shoots right. 5'9", 178 lbs. Born, Edina, MN, March 30, 1990.
(Chicago's 7th choice, 192nd overall, in 2008 Entry Draft).

| | | | Regular Season | | | | | Playoffs | | | | |
|---|---|---|---|---|---|---|---|---|---|---|---|---|
| Season | Club | League | GP | G | A | Pts | PIM | GP | G | A | Pts | PIM |
| 2006-07 | Edina Hornets | High-MN | 21 | 10 | 23 | 33 | .... | .... | .... | .... | .... | .... |
| | Team Southwest | UMWEHL | 11 | 4 | 6 | 10 | .... | .... | .... | .... | .... | .... |
| 2007-08 | Edina Hornets | High-MN | 23 | 9 | 33 | 42 | .... | .... | .... | .... | .... | .... |
| | Team Southwest | UMWEHL | 12 | 6 | 14 | 20 | .... | .... | .... | .... | .... | .... |
| 2008-09 | Des Moines | USHL | 59 | 5 | 16 | 21 | 40 | .... | .... | .... | .... | .... |

• Signed Letter of Intent to attend **University of North Dakota** (WCHA) in fall of 2009.

## GLENNIE, Scott (GLEH-nee, SKAWT) DAL.

Right wing. Shoots right. 6'1", 177 lbs. Born, Oakville, Ont., February 22, 1991.
(Dallas' 1st choice, 8th overall, in 2009 Entry Draft).

| | | | Regular Season | | | | | Playoffs | | | | |
|---|---|---|---|---|---|---|---|---|---|---|---|---|
| Season | Club | League | GP | G | A | Pts | PIM | GP | G | A | Pts | PIM |
| 2006-07 | Winnipeg Wild | MMHL | 38 | 31 | 37 | 68 | 64 | 7 | 3 | 3 | 6 | 16 |
| 2007-08 | Brandon | WHL | 61 | 26 | 32 | 58 | 50 | 6 | 1 | 0 | 1 | 7 |
| 2008-09 | Brandon | WHL | 55 | 28 | 42 | 70 | 25 | 12 | 3 | 15 | 18 | 11 |

## GLUKHOV, Alexei (GLUH-khawv, al-EHX-ay) T.B.

Right wing. Shoots left. 6'3", 176 lbs. Born, Voskresensk, USSR, April 5, 1984.
(Tampa Bay's 12th choice, 286th overall, in 2002 Entry Draft).

| | | | Regular Season | | | | | Playoffs | | | | |
|---|---|---|---|---|---|---|---|---|---|---|---|---|
| Season | Club | League | GP | G | A | Pts | PIM | GP | G | A | Pts | PIM |
| 99-2000 | Voskresensk 2 | Russia-3 | 10 | 2 | 2 | 4 | 2 | .... | .... | .... | .... | .... |
| 2000-01 | Voskresensk | Russia-2 | 9 | 0 | 1 | 1 | 6 | .... | .... | .... | .... | .... |
| 2001-02 | Voskresensk 2 | Russia-3 | 34 | 8 | 22 | 30 | 54 | .... | .... | .... | .... | .... |
| | Voskresensk | Russia-2 | 4 | 0 | 0 | 0 | 0 | .... | .... | .... | .... | .... |
| 2002-03 | Voskresensk | Russia-2 | 38 | 4 | 4 | 8 | 30 | .... | .... | .... | .... | .... |
| 2003-04 | Voskresensk | Russia | 28 | 0 | 0 | 0 | 12 | .... | .... | .... | .... | .... |
| 2004-05 | Kristall Elektrostal | Russia-2 | 16 | 2 | 2 | 4 | 20 | .... | .... | .... | .... | .... |
| | Voskresensk | Russia | 9 | 0 | 0 | 0 | 6 | .... | .... | .... | .... | .... |
| | Victoria | ECHL | 32 | 5 | 12 | 17 | 12 | .... | .... | .... | .... | .... |
| | Springfield Falcons | AHL | 3 | 0 | 1 | 1 | 6 | .... | .... | .... | .... | .... |
| 2005-06 | Mytischi | Russia | 45 | 2 | 14 | 16 | 70 | 9 | 2 | 1 | 3 | 10 |
| 2006-07 | Cherepovets | Russia | 52 | 2 | 14 | 16 | 97 | 5 | 0 | 0 | 0 | 4 |
| 2007-08 | Cherepovets | Russia | 57 | 7 | 13 | 20 | 86 | 8 | 2 | 0 | 2 | 12 |
| 2008-09 | Mytischi | Rus-KHL | 43 | 10 | 10 | 20 | 28 | 7 | 1 | 1 | 2 | 4 |

Signed to PTO (tryout) contract by **Springfield** (AHL), April 14, 2005.

## GODFREY, Josh (GAWD-free, JAWSH) WSH.

Defense. Shoots right. 6'1", 202 lbs. Born, Collingwood, Ont., January 15, 1988.
(Washington's 2nd choice, 34th overall, in 2007 Entry Draft).

| | | | Regular Season | | | | | Playoffs | | | | |
|---|---|---|---|---|---|---|---|---|---|---|---|---|
| Season | Club | League | GP | G | A | Pts | PIM | GP | G | A | Pts | PIM |
| 2004-05 | Guelph Storm | OHL | 18 | 0 | 4 | 4 | 9 | 1 | 0 | 0 | 0 | 0 |
| 2005-06 | Guelph Storm | OHL | 33 | 2 | 8 | 10 | 38 | .... | .... | .... | .... | .... |
| | Sault Ste. Marie | OHL | 30 | 6 | 5 | 11 | 26 | 1 | 0 | 1 | 1 | 0 |
| 2006-07 | Sault Ste. Marie | OHL | 68 | 24 | 33 | 57 | 80 | 13 | 9 | 5 | 14 | 18 |
| 2007-08 | Sault Ste. Marie | OHL | 60 | 17 | 34 | 51 | 61 | 14 | 5 | 1 | 6 | 20 |
| | Hershey Bears | AHL | .... | .... | .... | .... | .... | 1 | 0 | 0 | 0 | 0 |
| 2008-09 | Hershey Bears | AHL | 13 | 0 | 6 | 6 | 21 | .... | .... | .... | .... | .... |
| | South Carolina | ECHL | 37 | 5 | 20 | 25 | 30 | 6 | 1 | 3 | 4 | 10 |

## GOGGIN, Mark (GAW-gihn, MAHRK) BOS.

Center. Shoots left. 5'11", 184 lbs. Born, Chicago, IL, July 29, 1990.
(Boston's 6th choice, 197th overall, in 2008 Entry Draft).

| | | | Regular Season | | | | | Playoffs | | | | |
|---|---|---|---|---|---|---|---|---|---|---|---|---|
| Season | Club | League | GP | G | A | Pts | PIM | GP | G | A | Pts | PIM |
| 2006-07 | Choate-Rosemary | High-CT | .... | 15 | 20 | 35 | .... | .... | .... | .... | .... | .... |
| 2007-08 | Choate-Rosemary | High-CT | 21 | 15 | 21 | 36 | 10 | .... | .... | .... | .... | .... |
| | USNTDP | U-17 | 3 | 1 | 1 | 2 | 0 | .... | .... | .... | .... | .... |
| | USNTDP | NAHL | 5 | 1 | 1 | 2 | 2 | .... | .... | .... | .... | .... |
| 2008-09 | Choate-Rosemary | High-CT | 25 | 14 | 20 | 34 | .... | .... | .... | .... | .... | .... |
| | Chicago Steel | USHL | 17 | 5 | 4 | 9 | 10 | .... | .... | .... | .... | .... |

• Signed Letter of Intent to attend **Dartmouth College** (ECAC) in fall of 2009.

## GOGULLA, Philip (GOH-goo-lah, FIHL-ihp) BUF.

Right wing. Shoots left. 6'2", 176 lbs. Born, Dusseldorf, West Germany, July 31, 1987.
(Buffalo's 2nd choice, 48th overall, in 2005 Entry Draft).

| | | | Regular Season | | | | | Playoffs | | | | |
|---|---|---|---|---|---|---|---|---|---|---|---|---|
| Season | Club | League | GP | G | A | Pts | PIM | GP | G | A | Pts | PIM |
| 2002-03 | Krefelder EV Jr. | Ger-Jr. | 32 | 11 | 23 | 34 | 42 | 2 | 0 | 0 | 0 | 2 |
| 2003-04 | Krefelder EV Jr. | Ger-Jr. | 35 | 35 | 44 | 79 | 22 | 2 | 0 | 2 | 2 | 27 |
| 2004-05 | Essen | German-2 | 3 | 0 | 0 | 0 | 0 | .... | .... | .... | .... | .... |
| | Koln Jr. | Ger-Jr. | 7 | 4 | 5 | 9 | 18 | .... | .... | .... | .... | .... |
| | Kolner Haie | Germany | 47 | 1 | 1 | 2 | 14 | 7 | 0 | 0 | 0 | 2 |
| 2005-06 | Kolner Haie | Germany | 48 | 7 | 15 | 22 | 49 | 9 | 3 | 2 | 5 | 40 |
| 2006-07 | Kolner Haie | Germany | 44 | 8 | 13 | 21 | 26 | 7 | 0 | 0 | 0 | 8 |
| 2007-08 | Kolner Haie | Germany | 51 | 11 | 33 | 44 | 30 | 14 | 3 | 9 | 12 | 6 |
| 2008-09 | Kolner Haie | Germany | 48 | 17 | 21 | 38 | 58 | .... | .... | .... | .... | .... |

## GOLOUBEF, Cody (GOH-luh-behf, KOH-dee) CBJ

Defense. Shoots right. 6', 195 lbs. Born, Mississauga, Ont., November 30, 1989.
(Columbus' 2nd choice, 37th overall, in 2008 Entry Draft).

| | | | Regular Season | | | | | Playoffs | | | | |
|---|---|---|---|---|---|---|---|---|---|---|---|---|
| Season | Club | League | GP | G | A | Pts | PIM | GP | G | A | Pts | PIM |
| 2003-04 | Toronto Marlboros | GTHL | 89 | 10 | 27 | 37 | 44 | .... | .... | .... | .... | .... |
| 2004-05 | Toronto Marlboros | GTHL | 69 | 14 | 47 | 61 | 56 | .... | .... | .... | .... | .... |
| 2005-06 | Milton Icehawks | OPJHL | 42 | 9 | 29 | 38 | 38 | 7 | 1 | 3 | 4 | 10 |
| 2006-07 | Oakville Blades | OPJHL | 9 | 5 | 5 | 10 | 46 | 10 | 2 | 10 | 12 | 18 |
| 2007-08 | U. of Wisconsin | WCHA | 40 | 4 | 6 | 10 | 36 | .... | .... | .... | .... | .... |
| 2008-09 | U. of Wisconsin | WCHA | 36 | 5 | 8 | 13 | 38 | .... | .... | .... | .... | .... |

• Missed majority of 2006-07 season due to injury.

## GONCHAROV, Maxim (gohn-CHAR-ahv, mahx-EEM) PHX.

Defense. Shoots right. 6', 176 lbs. Born, Moscow, USSR, June 15, 1989.
(Phoenix's 6th choice, 123rd overall, in 2007 Entry Draft).

| | | | Regular Season | | | | | Playoffs | | | | |
|---|---|---|---|---|---|---|---|---|---|---|---|---|
| Season | Club | League | GP | G | A | Pts | PIM | GP | G | A | Pts | PIM |
| 2005-06 | CSKA Moscow 2 | Russia-3 | STATISTICS NOT AVAILABLE | | | | | | | | | |
| 2006-07 | CSKA Moscow 2 | Russia-3 | STATISTICS NOT AVAILABLE | | | | | | | | | |
| | CSKA Moscow | Russia | 18 | 0 | 0 | 0 | 10 | 5 | 0 | 0 | 0 | 2 |
| 2007-08 | CSKA Moscow | Russia | 47 | 3 | 2 | 5 | 38 | 6 | 0 | 2 | 2 | 0 |
| | CSKA Moscow 2 | Russia-3 | 4 | 0 | 2 | 2 | 35 | 3 | 0 | 0 | 0 | 8 |
| 2008-09 | CSKA Moscow | Rus-KHL | 47 | 7 | 8 | 15 | 50 | 7 | 0 | 0 | 0 | 4 |

## GOTOVETS, Kirill (goh-TOH-vets, kih-RIHL) T.B.

Defense. Shoots left. 5'11", 175 lbs. Born, Minsk, USSR, June 25, 1991.
(Tampa Bay's 7th choice, 183rd overall, in 2009 Entry Draft).

| | | | Regular Season | | | | | Playoffs | | | | |
|---|---|---|---|---|---|---|---|---|---|---|---|---|
| Season | Club | League | GP | G | A | Pts | PIM | GP | G | A | Pts | PIM |
| 2007-08 | Yunior Minsk | Belarus-2 | 45 | 2 | 8 | 10 | 54 | .... | .... | .... | .... | .... |
| 2008-09 | Shat.-St. Mary's | High-MN | 50 | 6 | 23 | 29 | 66 | .... | .... | .... | .... | .... |

• Signed Letter of Intent to attend **Cornell University** (ECAC) in fall of 2010.

## GOULET, Alain (goo-LAY, AL-eh) BOS.

Defense. Shoots right. 6'3", 195 lbs. Born, Kapuskasing, Ont., September 22, 1988.
(Boston's 4th choice, 159th overall, in 2007 Entry Draft).

| | | | Regular Season | | | | | Playoffs | | | | |
|---|---|---|---|---|---|---|---|---|---|---|---|---|
| Season | Club | League | GP | G | A | Pts | PIM | GP | G | A | Pts | PIM |
| 2005-06 | Ottawa Jr. Sens | CJHL | 41 | 6 | 14 | 20 | 22 | .... | .... | .... | .... | .... |
| 2006-07 | Aurora Tigers | OPJHL | 43 | 10 | 32 | 42 | 34 | 25 | 5 | 16 | 21 | 32 |
| 2007-08 | Nebraska-Omaha | CCHA | 37 | 6 | 8 | 14 | 14 | .... | .... | .... | .... | .... |
| 2008-09 | Nebraska-Omaha | CCHA | 17 | 2 | 3 | 5 | 21 | .... | .... | .... | .... | .... |
| | Gatineau | QMJHL | 32 | 16 | 19 | 35 | 10 | 10 | 0 | 10 | 10 | 18 |

## GOULET, Stephane (goo-LAY, STEH-fan)

Right wing. Shoots left. 6'3", 185 lbs. Born, Levis, Que., January 7, 1986.
(Edmonton's 8th choice, 208th overall, in 2004 Entry Draft).

| | | | Regular Season | | | | | Playoffs | | | | |
|---|---|---|---|---|---|---|---|---|---|---|---|---|
| Season | Club | League | GP | G | A | Pts | PIM | GP | G | A | Pts | PIM |
| 2002-03 | Levis | QAAA | 42 | 39 | 29 | 68 | 70 | .... | .... | .... | .... | .... |
| 2003-04 | Quebec Remparts | QMJHL | 54 | 6 | 8 | 14 | 14 | 5 | 0 | 0 | 0 | 2 |
| 2004-05 | Moncton Wildcats | QMJHL | 69 | 22 | 25 | 47 | 37 | 12 | 3 | 7 | 10 | 12 |
| 2005-06 | Moncton Wildcats | QMJHL | 67 | 51 | 42 | 93 | 80 | 13 | 7 | 8 | 15 | 16 |
| 2006-07 | Grand Rapids | AHL | 2 | 0 | 0 | 0 | 2 | .... | .... | .... | .... | .... |
| | Stockton Thunder | ECHL | 69 | 17 | 23 | 40 | 58 | 5 | 0 | 1 | 1 | 2 |
| 2007-08 | Springfield Falcons | AHL | 36 | 9 | 5 | 14 | 22 | .... | .... | .... | .... | .... |
| | Stockton Thunder | ECHL | 12 | 4 | 10 | 14 | 10 | 6 | 5 | 4 | 9 | 0 |
| 2008-09 | Springfield Falcons | AHL | 18 | 1 | 3 | 4 | 6 | .... | .... | .... | .... | .... |
| | Stockton Thunder | ECHL | 12 | 3 | 6 | 9 | 18 | .... | .... | .... | .... | .... |

## GRABNER, Michael (GRAB-nuhr, MIGH-kuhl) VAN.

Right wing. Shoots left. 6', 187 lbs. Born, Villach, Austria, October 5, 1987.
(Vancouver's 1st choice, 14th overall, in 2006 Entry Draft).

| | | | Regular Season | | | | | Playoffs | | | | |
|---|---|---|---|---|---|---|---|---|---|---|---|---|
| Season | Club | League | GP | G | A | Pts | PIM | GP | G | A | Pts | PIM |
| 2002-03 | EC Villacher SV Jr. | Austria-Jr. | 13 | 6 | 4 | 10 | 4 | .... | .... | .... | .... | .... |
| 2003-04 | EC Villacher SV Jr. | Austria-Jr. | 23 | 32 | 5 | 37 | 58 | .... | .... | .... | .... | .... |
| | EC Villacher SV | Austria | 18 | 2 | 1 | 3 | 0 | .... | .... | .... | .... | .... |
| | Austria | WJ18-B | 5 | 3 | 1 | 4 | 4 | .... | .... | .... | .... | .... |
| 2004-05 | Spokane Chiefs | WHL | 58 | 13 | 11 | 24 | 18 | .... | .... | .... | .... | .... |
| 2005-06 | Spokane Chiefs | WHL | 67 | 36 | 14 | 50 | 28 | .... | .... | .... | .... | .... |
| 2006-07 | Spokane Chiefs | WHL | 55 | 39 | 16 | 55 | 34 | 6 | 0 | 1 | 1 | 2 |
| | Manitoba Moose | AHL | 2 | 1 | 1 | 2 | 0 | 6 | 0 | 0 | 0 | 0 |
| 2007-08 | Manitoba Moose | AHL | 74 | 22 | 22 | 44 | 8 | 6 | 3 | 0 | 3 | 2 |
| 2008-09 | Manitoba Moose | AHL | 66 | 30 | 18 | 48 | 20 | 20 | 10 | 7 | 17 | 2 |

## GRACHEV, Yevgeny (gra-CHAWF, yehv-GEH-nee) NYR

Center. Shoots left. 6'4", 217 lbs. Born, Khabarovsk, USSR, February 21, 1990.
(NY Rangers' 3rd choice, 75th overall, in 2008 Entry Draft).

| | | | Regular Season | | | | | Playoffs | | | | |
|---|---|---|---|---|---|---|---|---|---|---|---|---|
| Season | Club | League | GP | G | A | Pts | PIM | GP | G | A | Pts | PIM |
| 2005-06 | Yaroslavl 2 | Russia-3 | 1 | 0 | 0 | 0 | 2 | .... | .... | .... | .... | .... |
| 2006-07 | Yaroslavl 2 | Russia-3 | 28 | 7 | 6 | 13 | 6 | .... | .... | .... | .... | .... |
| 2007-08 | Yaroslavl 2 | Russia-3 | STATISTICS NOT AVAILABLE | | | | | | | | | |
| | Yaroslavl | Russia | 1 | 0 | 0 | 0 | 0 | .... | .... | .... | .... | .... |
| 2008-09 | Brampton | OHL | 60 | 40 | 40 | 80 | 22 | 19 | 11 | 14 | 25 | 4 |

OHL Rookie of the Year (2009)

## GRACIK, Juraj (GRAH-chihk, YUHR-ay) ATL.

Right wing. Shoots right. 6'3", 187 lbs. Born, Topolcany, Czech., August 14, 1986.
(Atlanta's 5th choice, 142nd overall, in 2004 Entry Draft).

| | | | Regular Season | | | | | Playoffs | | | | |
|---|---|---|---|---|---|---|---|---|---|---|---|---|
| Season | Club | League | GP | G | A | Pts | PIM | GP | G | A | Pts | PIM |
| 2002-03 | Topolcany Jr. | Slovak-Jr. | 24 | 10 | 7 | 17 | 28 | .... | .... | .... | .... | .... |
| 2003-04 | Topolcany Jr. | Slovak-Jr. | 28 | 22 | 12 | 34 | 78 | .... | .... | .... | .... | .... |
| | Topolcany | Slovak-2 | 28 | 16 | 8 | 24 | 8 | 4 | 1 | 0 | 1 | 0 |
| 2004-05 | Tri-City Americans | WHL | 33 | 4 | 2 | 6 | 18 | .... | .... | .... | .... | .... |
| 2005-06 | Tri-City Americans | WHL | 53 | 22 | 23 | 45 | 36 | .... | .... | .... | .... | .... |
| 2006-07 | Bratislava | Slovakia | 37 | 5 | 1 | 6 | 6 | 3 | 0 | 0 | 0 | 0 |
| | HC Topolcany | Slovak-2 | 7 | 8 | 1 | 9 | 18 | .... | .... | .... | .... | .... |
| | Ruzinov | Slovak-2 | 13 | 7 | 5 | 12 | 16 | 3 | 1 | 1 | 2 | 0 |
| 2007-08 | Bratislava | Slovakia | 40 | 3 | 4 | 7 | 10 | 11 | 0 | 0 | 0 | 0 |
| | Ruzinov | Slovak-2 | 10 | 5 | 3 | 8 | 10 | 4 | 1 | 2 | 3 | 4 |
| 2008-09 | Ruzinov | Slovak-2 | 6 | 5 | 2 | 7 | 26 | 2 | 1 | 1 | 2 | 2 |
| | Bratislava | Slovakia | 50 | 1 | 3 | 4 | 8 | 12 | 2 | 2 | 4 | 4 |

Signed as a free agent by **Bratislava** (Slovakia), October 14, 2006.

## GRANT, Alex (GRANT, AL-ehx) PIT.

Defense. Shoots right. 6'2", 185 lbs. Born, Antigonish, N.S., January 20, 1989.
(Pittsburgh's 6th choice, 118th overall, in 2007 Entry Draft).

| | | | Regular Season | | | | | Playoffs | | | | |
|---|---|---|---|---|---|---|---|---|---|---|---|---|
| Season | Club | League | GP | G | A | Pts | PIM | GP | G | A | Pts | PIM |
| 2004-05 | Antigonish | MJrHL | 50 | 7 | 9 | 16 | 36 | 3 | 1 | 1 | 2 | 2 |
| 2005-06 | Saint John | QMJHL | 47 | 4 | 9 | 13 | 58 | .... | .... | .... | .... | .... |
| 2006-07 | Saint John | QMJHL | 68 | 12 | 20 | 32 | 108 | .... | .... | .... | .... | .... |
| 2007-08 | Saint John | QMJHL | 70 | 15 | 33 | 48 | 96 | 14 | 3 | 11 | 14 | 12 |
| 2008-09 | Saint John | QMJHL | 37 | 9 | 22 | 31 | 51 | .... | .... | .... | .... | .... |
| | Shawinigan | QMJHL | 23 | 4 | 15 | 19 | 11 | 21 | 4 | 5 | 9 | 18 |

## GRANT, Derek (GRANT, DAIR-ihk) OTT.

Center. Shoots left. 6'3", 188 lbs. Born, Abbotsford, B.C., April 20, 1990.
(Ottawa's 5th choice, 119th overall, in 2008 Entry Draft).

| | | | Regular Season | | | | | Playoffs | | | | |
|---|---|---|---|---|---|---|---|---|---|---|---|---|
| Season | Club | League | GP | G | A | Pts | PIM | GP | G | A | Pts | PIM |
| 2006-07 | Abbotsford Pilots | PIJHL | 47 | 31 | 20 | 51 | 42 | 11 | 6 | 5 | 11 | 20 |
| 2007-08 | Langley Chiefs | BCHL | 57 | 24 | 39 | 63 | 44 | 12 | 5 | 5 | 10 | 15 |
| 2008-09 | Langley Chiefs | BCHL | 35 | 25 | 35 | 60 | 22 | 4 | 2 | 1 | 3 | 2 |

• Signed Letter of Intent to attend **Michigan State University** (CCHA) in fall of 2009.

## GRANTHAM, Ryley (GRAN-thum, RIGH-lee) CGY.

Center. Shoots left. 6'3", 207 lbs. Born, Hanna, Alta., January 7, 1988.
(Calgary's 6th choice, 168th overall, in 2008 Entry Draft).

| | | | Regular Season | | | | | Playoffs | | | | |
|---|---|---|---|---|---|---|---|---|---|---|---|---|
| Season | Club | League | GP | G | A | Pts | PIM | GP | G | A | Pts | PIM |
| 2005-06 | Brooks Bandits | AJHL | 43 | 6 | 3 | 9 | 98 | 13 | 2 | 0 | 2 | 16 |
| 2006-07 | Brooks Bandits | AJHL | .... | 3 | 11 | 14 | .... | .... | .... | .... | .... | .... |
| | Moose Jaw | WHL | 33 | 1 | 1 | 2 | 50 | .... | .... | .... | .... | .... |
| 2007-08 | Moose Jaw | WHL | 66 | 10 | 9 | 19 | 163 | 6 | 0 | 0 | 0 | 8 |
| 2008-09 | Moose Jaw | WHL | 38 | 8 | 5 | 13 | 132 | .... | .... | .... | .... | .... |
| | Kelowna Rockets | WHL | 29 | 4 | 12 | 16 | 61 | 22 | 4 | 1 | 5 | 16 |

## GRATCHEV, Maxim (GRAT-chehv, max-EEM)

Left wing. Shoots left. 5'11", 196 lbs. Born, Novosibirsk, USSR, September 26, 1988.
(NY Islanders' 3rd choice, 106th overall, in 2007 Entry Draft).

| | | | Regular Season | | | | | Playoffs | | | | |
|---|---|---|---|---|---|---|---|---|---|---|---|---|
| Season | Club | League | GP | G | A | Pts | PIM | GP | G | A | Pts | PIM |
| 2003-04 | Thayer Academy | High-MA | .... | 7 | 9 | 16 | .... | .... | .... | .... | .... | .... |
| 2004-05 | Quebec Remparts | QMJHL | 54 | 7 | 11 | 18 | 36 | .... | .... | .... | .... | .... |
| 2005-06 | Quebec Remparts | QMJHL | 22 | 5 | 5 | 10 | 40 | .... | .... | .... | .... | .... |
| | Rimouski Oceanic | QMJHL | 33 | 6 | 11 | 17 | 57 | .... | .... | .... | .... | .... |
| 2006-07 | Rimouski Oceanic | QMJHL | 70 | 35 | 42 | 77 | 88 | .... | .... | .... | .... | .... |
| 2007-08 | Rimouski Oceanic | QMJHL | 39 | 9 | 20 | 29 | 48 | 9 | 2 | 0 | 2 | 12 |
| 2008-09 | Lewiston | QMJHL | 64 | 30 | 31 | 61 | 108 | .... | .... | .... | .... | .... |
| | Bridgeport | AHL | 1 | 0 | 0 | 0 | 2 | 1 | 0 | 0 | 0 | 0 |

## GREENING, Colin (GREEN-ihng, KAW-lihn) OTT.

Center/Left wing. Shoots left. 6'2", 213 lbs. Born, St. John's, Nfld., March 9, 1986.
(Ottawa's 8th choice, 204th overall, in 2005 Entry Draft).

| | | | Regular Season | | | | | Playoffs | | | | |
|---|---|---|---|---|---|---|---|---|---|---|---|---|
| Season | Club | League | GP | G | A | Pts | PIM | GP | G | A | Pts | PIM |
| 2002-03 | St. John's | NFAHA | 60 | 24 | 34 | 58 | 48 | .... | .... | .... | .... | .... |
| 2003-04 | Upper Canada | High-ON | 53 | 30 | 43 | 73 | 40 | .... | .... | .... | .... | .... |
| 2004-05 | Upper Canada | High-ON | 35 | 24 | 22 | 46 | 24 | .... | .... | .... | .... | .... |
| 2005-06 | Nanaimo Clippers | BCHL | 56 | 27 | 35 | 62 | 46 | 5 | 3 | 0 | 3 | 2 |
| 2006-07 | Cornell Big Red | ECAC | 31 | 11 | 8 | 19 | 26 | .... | .... | .... | .... | .... |
| 2007-08 | Cornell Big Red | ECAC | 36 | 14 | 19 | 33 | 41 | .... | .... | .... | .... | .... |
| 2008-09 | Cornell Big Red | ECAC | 36 | 15 | 16 | 31 | 28 | .... | .... | .... | .... | .... |

ECAC Second All-Star Team (2008, 2009)

## GREENOP, Richard (GREEN-awp, RIH-chuhrd) TOR.

Center. Shoots right. 6'3", 210 lbs. Born, Oshawa, Ont., February 24, 1989.
(Chicago's 7th choice, 156th overall, in 2007 Entry Draft).

| | | | Regular Season | | | | | Playoffs | | | | |
|---|---|---|---|---|---|---|---|---|---|---|---|---|
| Season | Club | League | GP | G | A | Pts | PIM | GP | G | A | Pts | PIM |
| 2005-06 | Oshawa | OPJHL | 47 | 10 | 4 | 14 | 97 | .... | .... | .... | .... | .... |
| 2006-07 | Windsor Spitfires | OHL | 48 | 3 | 9 | 12 | 149 | .... | .... | .... | .... | .... |
| 2007-08 | Windsor Spitfires | OHL | 60 | 2 | 3 | 5 | 194 | 5 | 0 | 0 | 0 | 2 |
| 2008-09 | Windsor Spitfires | OHL | 60 | 4 | 4 | 8 | 156 | 15 | 0 | 0 | 0 | 28 |

Signed as a free agent by **Toronto**, July 6, 2009.

## GREGOIRE, Jason (GREHG-wahr, JAY-suhn) NYI

Left wing. Shoots left. 5'11", 175 lbs. Born, Winnipeg, Man., February 24, 1989.
(NY Islanders' 2nd choice, 76th overall, in 2007 Entry Draft).

| | | | Regular Season | | | | | Playoffs | | | | |
|---|---|---|---|---|---|---|---|---|---|---|---|---|
| Season | Club | League | GP | G | A | Pts | PIM | GP | G | A | Pts | PIM |
| 2005-06 | Winnipeg South | MJHL | 57 | 22 | 28 | 50 | 46 | 14 | 12 | 11 | 23 | .... |
| 2006-07 | Lincoln Stars | USHL | 32 | 16 | 20 | 36 | 10 | 4 | 4 | 0 | 4 | 2 |
| 2007-08 | Lincoln Stars | USHL | 54 | *37 | 32 | 69 | 41 | 8 | 3 | 9 | *12 | 6 |
| 2008-09 | North Dakota | WCHA | 42 | 12 | 17 | 29 | 28 | .... | .... | .... | .... | .... |

USHL First All-Star Team (2008) • USHL Player of the Year (2008)

## GROT, Denis (GROHT, DEH-nihs) VAN.

Defense. Shoots left. 6'1", 185 lbs. Born, Minsk, USSR, January 6, 1984.
(Vancouver's 2nd choice, 55th overall, in 2002 Entry Draft).

| | | | Regular Season | | | | | Playoffs | | | | |
|---|---|---|---|---|---|---|---|---|---|---|---|---|
| Season | Club | League | GP | G | A | Pts | PIM | GP | G | A | Pts | PIM |
| 2000-01 | Yaroslavl 2 | Russia-3 | 34 | 5 | 1 | 6 | 10 | .... | .... | .... | .... | .... |
| | Russia | Nat-Tm | 5 | 0 | 2 | 2 | 8 | .... | .... | .... | .... | .... |
| 2001-02 | Yaroslavl 2 | Russia-3 | 14 | 1 | 0 | 1 | 10 | .... | .... | .... | .... | .... |
| | Elektrostal 2 | Russia-3 | 3 | 0 | 1 | 1 | 2 | .... | .... | .... | .... | .... |
| | Elektrostal | Russia-2 | 33 | 1 | 1 | 2 | 42 | .... | .... | .... | .... | .... |
| 2002-03 | HK Lipetsk | Russia-2 | 27 | 4 | 4 | 8 | 28 | .... | .... | .... | .... | .... |
| 2003-04 | Yaroslavl | Russia | 31 | 0 | 2 | 2 | 4 | 3 | 0 | 0 | 0 | 2 |
| 2004-05 | Yaroslavl 2 | Russia-3 | 20 | 2 | 3 | 5 | 22 | .... | .... | .... | .... | .... |
| | Yaroslavl | Russia | 1 | 0 | 0 | 0 | 2 | .... | .... | .... | .... | .... |
| | Sibir Novosibirsk | Russia | 23 | 0 | 4 | 4 | 32 | .... | .... | .... | .... | .... |
| | Amur Khabarovsk | Russia-2 | 9 | 1 | 5 | 6 | 2 | 12 | 0 | 0 | 0 | 31 |
| 2005-06 | Spartak Moscow | Russia | 48 | 1 | 4 | 5 | 28 | 3 | 0 | 0 | 0 | 0 |
| 2006-07 | Nizhnekamsk | Russia | 38 | 2 | 7 | 9 | 59 | 1 | 0 | 0 | 0 | 2 |
| 2007-08 | Nizhnekamsk | Russia | 48 | 0 | 3 | 3 | 32 | 5 | 0 | 0 | 0 | 4 |
| 2008-09 | Sibir Novosibirsk | Rus-KHL | 54 | 0 | 5 | 5 | 36 | .... | .... | .... | .... | .... |

## GROULX, Danny (GROO, DA-nee) S.J.

Defense. Shoots left. 6', 205 lbs. Born, LaSalle, Que., June 23, 1981.

| | | | Regular Season | | | | | Playoffs | | | | |
|---|---|---|---|---|---|---|---|---|---|---|---|---|
| Season | Club | League | GP | G | A | Pts | PIM | GP | G | A | Pts | PIM |
| 1996-97 | Charles-Lemoyne | QAAA | 40 | 2 | 26 | 28 | .... | 15 | 3 | 15 | 18 | .... |
| 1997-98 | Val-d'Or Foreurs | QMJHL | 63 | 4 | 16 | 20 | 61 | 19 | 1 | 4 | 5 | 18 |
| 1998-99 | Val-d'Or Foreurs | QMJHL | 36 | 3 | 26 | 29 | 55 | .... | .... | .... | .... | .... |
| | Acadie-Bathurst | QMJHL | 36 | 2 | 15 | 17 | 51 | 18 | 0 | 2 | 2 | 6 |
| 99-2000 | Victoriaville Tigres | QMJHL | 66 | 12 | 55 | 67 | 131 | 6 | 0 | 4 | 4 | 14 |
| 2000-01 | Victoriaville Tigres | QMJHL | 72 | 16 | 71 | 87 | 164 | 13 | 2 | 19 | 21 | 46 |
| 2001-02 | Victoriaville Tigres | QMJHL | 68 | 29 | 83 | 112 | 165 | 22 | 9 | *30 | 39 | 68 |
| 2002-03 | Grand Rapids | AHL | 71 | 3 | 7 | 10 | 52 | 7 | 0 | 1 | 1 | 7 |
| 2003-04 | Grand Rapids | AHL | 79 | 8 | 13 | 21 | 93 | 3 | 0 | 0 | 0 | 0 |
| 2004-05 | Grand Rapids | AHL | 53 | 1 | 11 | 12 | 90 | .... | .... | .... | .... | .... |
| | Manitoba Moose | AHL | 16 | 2 | 6 | 8 | 16 | 13 | 1 | 3 | 4 | 14 |
| 2005-06 | Kassel Huskies | Germany | 51 | 2 | 11 | 13 | 93 | 5 | 0 | 1 | 1 | 6 |
| 2006-07 | Hamilton Bulldogs | AHL | 58 | 0 | 16 | 16 | 62 | 22 | 6 | 6 | 12 | 14 |
| 2007-08 | Manitoba Moose | AHL | 58 | 4 | 20 | 24 | 32 | 6 | 2 | 1 | 3 | 12 |
| 2008-09 | Rockford IceHogs | AHL | 80 | 6 | 34 | 40 | 58 | 4 | 0 | 2 | 2 | 2 |

QMJHL First All-Star Team (2001, 2002) • Canadian Major Junior First All-Star Team (2002) • Memorial Cup Tournament All-Star Team (2002) • Stafford Smythe Memorial Trophy (Memorial Cup Tournament MVP) (2002)

Signed as a free agent by **Detroit**, August 12, 2002. Loaned to **Manitoba** (AHL) by **Detroit** (Grand Rapids-AHL) for cash, March 15, 2005. Signed as a free agent by **Kassel** (Germany), August 25, 2005. Signed as a free agent by **San Jose**, July 16, 2009.

## GROULX, Samuel (GROOL, SAM-ew-uhl) S.J.

Defense. Shoots left. 6'2", 165 lbs. Born, Gatineau, Que., June 28, 1990.
(San Jose's 2nd choice, 92nd overall, in 2008 Entry Draft).

| | | | Regular Season | | | | | Playoffs | | | | |
|---|---|---|---|---|---|---|---|---|---|---|---|---|
| Season | Club | League | GP | G | A | Pts | PIM | GP | G | A | Pts | PIM |
| 2005-06 | Gatineau Intrepide | QAAA | 44 | 1 | 13 | 14 | 24 | 3 | 0 | 0 | 0 | 4 |
| 2006-07 | Gatineau Intrepide | QAAA | 36 | 2 | 9 | 11 | 62 | 3 | 0 | 1 | 1 | 8 |
| | Quebec Remparts | QMJHL | 9 | 1 | 1 | 2 | 2 | 1 | 0 | 0 | 0 | 0 |
| 2007-08 | Quebec Remparts | QMJHL | 70 | 5 | 20 | 25 | 100 | 11 | 0 | 3 | 3 | 14 |
| 2008-09 | Quebec Remparts | QMJHL | 61 | 3 | 22 | 25 | 86 | 17 | 2 | 6 | 8 | 18 |

QMJHL All-Rookie Team (2008)

## GRYBA, Eric (GREE-buh, AIR-ihk) OTT.

Defense. Shoots right. 6'3", 215 lbs. Born, Saskatoon, Sask., April 14, 1988.
(Ottawa's 2nd choice, 68th overall, in 2006 Entry Draft).

| | | | Regular Season | | | | | Playoffs | | | | |
|---|---|---|---|---|---|---|---|---|---|---|---|---|
| Season | Club | League | GP | G | A | Pts | PIM | GP | G | A | Pts | PIM |
| 2003-04 | Sask. Contacts | SMHL | 39 | 1 | 10 | 11 | 89 | 10 | 4 | 8 | 12 | 20 |
| 2004-05 | Sask. Contacts | SMHL | 32 | 11 | 29 | 40 | 83 | 11 | 5 | 7 | 12 | 22 |
| 2005-06 | Green Bay | USHL | 56 | 3 | 12 | 15 | *205 | 3 | 1 | 1 | 2 | 27 |
| 2006-07 | Boston University | H-East | 38 | 1 | 3 | 4 | 76 | .... | .... | .... | .... | .... |
| 2007-08 | Boston University | H-East | 32 | 1 | 1 | 2 | 54 | .... | .... | .... | .... | .... |
| 2008-09 | Boston University | H-East | 45 | 0 | 6 | 6 | 106 | .... | .... | .... | .... | .... |

## GUNNARSSON, Carl (GUHN-nuhr-suhn, KARL) TOR.

Defense. Shoots left. 6'2", 189 lbs. Born, Orebro, Sweden, November 9, 1986.
(Toronto's 6th choice, 194th overall, in 2007 Entry Draft).

| | | | Regular Season | | | | | Playoffs | | | | |
|---|---|---|---|---|---|---|---|---|---|---|---|---|
| Season | Club | League | GP | G | A | Pts | PIM | GP | G | A | Pts | PIM |
| 2003-04 | HC Orebro 90 | Sweden-2 | 43 | 0 | 4 | 4 | 16 | .... | .... | .... | .... | .... |
| 2004-05 | Linkopings HC U18 | Swe-U18 | 1 | 0 | 1 | 1 | 2 | .... | .... | .... | .... | .... |
| | Linkopings HC Jr. | Swe-Jr. | 22 | 2 | 5 | 7 | 24 | .... | .... | .... | .... | .... |
| 2005-06 | Linkopings HC Jr. | Swe-Jr. | 30 | 7 | 6 | 13 | 26 | 4 | 1 | 0 | 1 | 4 |
| | IFK Arboga IK | Sweden-2 | 12 | 1 | 5 | 6 | 8 | .... | .... | .... | .... | .... |
| | Linkopings HC | Sweden | 14 | 0 | 0 | 0 | 0 | .... | .... | .... | .... | .... |
| 2006-07 | Linkopings HC Jr. | Swe-Jr. | 6 | 0 | 5 | 5 | 6 | .... | .... | .... | .... | .... |
| | VIK Vasteras HK | Sweden-2 | 15 | 2 | 3 | 5 | 14 | .... | .... | .... | .... | .... |
| | Linkopings HC | Sweden | 30 | 2 | 2 | 4 | 8 | 15 | 0 | 4 | 4 | 4 |
| 2007-08 | Linkopings HC | Sweden | 53 | 2 | 7 | 9 | 26 | 16 | 0 | 4 | 4 | 10 |
| 2008-09 | Linkopings HC | Sweden | 53 | 6 | 10 | 16 | 26 | 7 | 0 | 1 | 1 | 2 |

## GUSTAFSSON, Anton (goos-TAHF-suhn, AN-tawn) WSH.

Center. Shoots left. 6'2", 194 lbs. Born, Karlskoga, Sweden, February 25, 1990.
(Washington's 1st choice, 21st overall, in 2008 Entry Draft).

| | | | Regular Season | | | | | Playoffs | | | | |
|---|---|---|---|---|---|---|---|---|---|---|---|---|
| Season | Club | League | GP | G | A | Pts | PIM | GP | G | A | Pts | PIM |
| 2005-06 | Karlskoga HC | Sweden-4 | .... | 3 | 0 | 3 | 0 | .... | .... | .... | .... | .... |
| 2006-07 | Frolunda U18 | Swe-U18 | 8 | 3 | 4 | 7 | 8 | 6 | 3 | 1 | 4 | 2 |
| | Frolunda Jr. | Swe-Jr. | 26 | 5 | 3 | 8 | 24 | 8 | 0 | 0 | 0 | 8 |
| 2007-08 | Frolunda U18 | Swe-U18 | 1 | 0 | 1 | 1 | 2 | .... | .... | .... | .... | .... |
| | Frolunda Jr. | Swe-Jr. | 33 | 15 | 17 | 32 | 55 | 2 | 1 | 0 | 1 | 2 |
| | Frolunda | Sweden | 1 | 0 | 0 | 0 | 0 | .... | .... | .... | .... | .... |
| 2008-09 | Bofors | Sweden-2 | 25 | 6 | 4 | 10 | 22 | .... | .... | .... | .... | .... |
| | Frolunda Jr. | Swe-Jr. | 2 | 0 | 0 | 0 | 4 | 5 | 3 | 4 | 7 | 4 |

## HAGELIN, Carl (HAG-eh-lihn, KARL) NYR

Left wing. Shoots left. 5'11", 176 lbs. Born, Sodertalje, Sweden, August 23, 1988.
(NY Rangers' 4th choice, 168th overall, in 2007 Entry Draft).

| | | | Regular Season | | | | | Playoffs | | | | |
|---|---|---|---|---|---|---|---|---|---|---|---|---|
| Season | Club | League | GP | G | A | Pts | PIM | GP | G | A | Pts | PIM |
| 2004-05 | Sodertalje SK U18 | Swe-U18 | 14 | 10 | 7 | 17 | 16 | 2 | 0 | 2 | 2 | 0 |
| 2005-06 | Sodertalje SK U18 | Swe-U18 | 7 | 4 | 8 | 12 | 2 | .... | .... | .... | .... | .... |
| | Sodertalje SK Jr. | Swe-Jr. | 41 | 20 | 20 | 40 | 42 | 4 | 1 | 2 | 3 | 22 |
| 2006-07 | Sodertalje SK Jr. | Swe-Jr. | 40 | 24 | 31 | 55 | 42 | 3 | 1 | 5 | 6 | 20 |
| 2007-08 | U. of Michigan | CCHA | 41 | 11 | 11 | 22 | 28 | .... | .... | .... | .... | .... |
| 2008-09 | U. of Michigan | CCHA | 41 | 13 | 18 | 31 | 32 | .... | .... | .... | .... | .... |

## HAMBLY, Tim (HAM-blee, TIHM)

Defense. Shoots left. 6', 185 lbs. Born, White Bear Lake, MN, June 23, 1983.

| | | | Regular Season | | | | | Playoffs | | | | |
|---|---|---|---|---|---|---|---|---|---|---|---|---|
| Season | Club | League | GP | G | A | Pts | PIM | GP | G | A | Pts | PIM |
| 2000-01 | Waterloo | USHL | 17 | 1 | 8 | 9 | 4 | .... | .... | .... | .... | .... |
| 2001-02 | U. Minn-Duluth | WCHA | 39 | 1 | 10 | 11 | 26 | .... | .... | .... | .... | .... |
| 2002-03 | U. Minn-Duluth | WCHA | 29 | 2 | 3 | 5 | 18 | .... | .... | .... | .... | .... |
| 2003-04 | U. Minn-Duluth | WCHA | 39 | 5 | 19 | 24 | 52 | .... | .... | .... | .... | .... |
| 2004-05 | U. Minn-Duluth | WCHA | 34 | 5 | 15 | 20 | 36 | .... | .... | .... | .... | .... |
| | Las Vegas | ECHL | 8 | 0 | 2 | 2 | 4 | .... | .... | .... | .... | .... |
| 2005-06 | Iowa Stars | AHL | 2 | 0 | 0 | 0 | 4 | .... | .... | .... | .... | .... |
| | Omaha | AHL | 45 | 1 | 16 | 17 | 33 | .... | .... | .... | .... | .... |
| | Las Vegas | ECHL | 31 | 9 | 12 | 21 | 23 | 9 | 3 | 2 | 5 | 4 |
| 2006-07 | Omaha | AHL | 67 | 3 | 15 | 18 | 28 | 5 | 1 | 0 | 1 | 0 |
| 2007-08 | Quad City Flames | AHL | 72 | 4 | 26 | 30 | 40 | .... | .... | .... | .... | .... |
| 2008-09 | Rockford IceHogs | AHL | 79 | 4 | 25 | 29 | 51 | 4 | 0 | 0 | 0 | 0 |

Signed as a free agent by **Chicago**, June 24, 2008.

## HAMBURG, Anthony (HAM-buhrg, AN-thuh-nee) MIN.

Center. Shoots right. 6'1", 185 lbs. Born, Houston, TX, August 30, 1991.
(Minnesota's 8th choice, 193rd overall, in 2009 Entry Draft).

| | | | Regular Season | | | | | Playoffs | | | | |
|---|---|---|---|---|---|---|---|---|---|---|---|---|
| Season | Club | League | GP | G | A | Pts | PIM | GP | G | A | Pts | PIM |
| 2007-08 | Dallas Stars AAA | Exhib. | 65 | 20 | 57 | 77 | 68 | .... | .... | .... | .... | .... |
| 2008-09 | Dallas Stars AAA | T1EHL | 46 | 16 | 38 | 54 | 38 | .... | .... | .... | .... | .... |
| | Dallas Stars AAA | Exhib. | 24 | 13 | 32 | 45 | 38 | .... | .... | .... | .... | .... |

## HAMILL, Zach (HA-mihl, ZAK) BOS.

Center. Shoots right. 5'11", 180 lbs. Born, Vancouver, B.C., September 23, 1988.
(Boston's 1st choice, 8th overall, in 2007 Entry Draft).

| | | | Regular Season | | | | | Playoffs | | | | |
|---|---|---|---|---|---|---|---|---|---|---|---|---|
| Season | Club | League | GP | G | A | Pts | PIM | GP | G | A | Pts | PIM |
| 2002-03 | Port Coquitlam | Minor-BC | 61 | 120 | 83 | 203 | .... | .... | .... | .... | .... | .... |
| 2003-04 | Port Coquitlam | PIJHL | 39 | 30 | 31 | 51 | 50 | .... | .... | .... | .... | .... |
| | Everett Silvertips | WHL | 4 | 0 | 2 | 2 | 0 | 20 | 3 | 2 | 5 | 2 |
| 2004-05 | Everett Silvertips | WHL | 57 | 8 | 25 | 33 | 29 | 11 | 2 | 3 | 5 | 8 |
| 2005-06 | Everett Silvertips | WHL | 53 | 21 | 38 | 59 | 28 | 15 | 3 | 11 | 14 | 4 |
| 2006-07 | Everett Silvertips | WHL | 69 | 32 | *61 | *93 | 90 | 12 | 2 | 8 | 10 | 16 |
| 2007-08 | Everett Silvertips | WHL | 67 | 26 | 49 | 75 | 88 | 4 | 0 | 3 | 3 | 2 |
| | Providence Bruins | AHL | 7 | 0 | 5 | 5 | 6 | 9 | 1 | 3 | 4 | 0 |
| 2008-09 | Providence Bruins | AHL | 65 | 13 | 13 | 26 | 40 | 16 | 1 | 5 | 6 | 4 |

WHL West First All-Star Team (2007) • Canadian Major Junior First All-Star Team (2007)

## HAMILTON, Mike (HAM-ihl-tuhn, MIGHK)

Left wing. Shoots left. 6'1", 190 lbs. Born, Vancouver, B.C., May 2, 1983.
(Atlanta's 6th choice, 175th overall, in 2003 Entry Draft).

| | | | Regular Season | | | | | Playoffs | | | | |
|---|---|---|---|---|---|---|---|---|---|---|---|---|
| Season | Club | League | GP | G | A | Pts | PIM | GP | G | A | Pts | PIM |
| 99-2000 | Peninsula Panthers | VIJHL | 44 | 33 | 42 | 75 | 94 | .... | .... | .... | .... | .... |
| 2000-01 | Peninsula Panthers | VIJHL | 19 | 15 | 20 | 35 | 106 | .... | .... | .... | .... | .... |
| | Victoria Salsa | BCHL | 31 | 2 | 5 | 7 | 18 | .... | .... | .... | .... | .... |
| 2001-02 | Victoria Salsa | BCHL | 13 | 5 | 2 | 7 | 14 | .... | .... | .... | .... | .... |
| | Merritt | BCHL | 45 | 23 | 36 | 59 | 64 | .... | .... | .... | .... | .... |
| 2002-03 | Merritt | BCHL | 56 | 42 | 51 | 95 | 133 | .... | .... | .... | .... | .... |
| 2003-04 | U. of Maine | H-East | 29 | 7 | 6 | 13 | 40 | .... | .... | .... | .... | .... |
| 2004-05 | U. of Maine | H-East | 38 | 3 | 15 | 18 | 49 | .... | .... | .... | .... | .... |
| 2005-06 | U. of Maine | H-East | 30 | 1 | 10 | 11 | 56 | .... | .... | .... | .... | .... |
| 2006-07 | U. of Maine | H-East | 40 | 9 | 13 | 22 | 63 | .... | .... | .... | .... | .... |
| 2007-08 | Gwinnett | ECHL | 72 | 23 | 27 | 50 | 121 | 8 | 2 | 6 | 8 | 16 |
| | Chicago Wolves | AHL | .... | .... | .... | .... | .... | 6 | 1 | 0 | 1 | 2 |
| 2008-09 | Chicago Wolves | AHL | 30 | 3 | 2 | 5 | 29 | .... | .... | .... | .... | .... |
| | Houston Aeros | AHL | 17 | 1 | 4 | 5 | 6 | .... | .... | .... | .... | .... |
| | Las Vegas | ECHL | 22 | 6 | 6 | 12 | 43 | 16 | 3 | 4 | 7 | 27 |

Signed as a free agent by **Chicago** (AHL), September 24, 2007. Signed as a free agent by **Houston** (AHL), December 3, 2008.

## HAMILTON, Ryan (HAM-ihl-tuhn, RIGH-uhn) TOR.

Left wing. Shoots left. 6'2", 215 lbs. Born, Oshawa, Ont., April 15, 1985.

| | | | Regular Season | | | | | Playoffs | | | | |
|---|---|---|---|---|---|---|---|---|---|---|---|---|
| Season | Club | League | GP | G | A | Pts | PIM | GP | G | A | Pts | PIM |
| 2002-03 | Couchiching | OPJHL | 11 | 5 | 8 | 13 | 2 | .... | .... | .... | .... | .... |
| | Peterborough Bees | OPJHL | 27 | 3 | 10 | 13 | 43 | .... | .... | .... | .... | .... |
| | Trenton Sting | OPJHL | 17 | 3 | 8 | 11 | 24 | .... | .... | .... | .... | .... |
| | Barrie Colts | OHL | 24 | 3 | 2 | 5 | 10 | 6 | 1 | 0 | 1 | 0 |
| 2003-04 | Kingston | OPJHL | 14 | 1 | 5 | 6 | 23 | .... | .... | .... | .... | .... |
| | Barrie Colts | OHL | 46 | 17 | 10 | 27 | 21 | 7 | 0 | 1 | 1 | 8 |
| 2004-05 | Barrie Colts | OHL | 37 | 13 | 11 | 24 | 6 | 6 | 2 | 0 | 2 | 2 |
| 2005-06 | Barrie Colts | OHL | 63 | 46 | 26 | 72 | 58 | 14 | 8 | 9 | 17 | 11 |
| | Houston Aeros | AHL | .... | .... | .... | .... | .... | 1 | 0 | 0 | 0 | 0 |
| 2006-07 | Houston Aeros | AHL | 62 | 7 | 9 | 16 | 36 | .... | .... | .... | .... | .... |
| 2007-08 | Houston Aeros | AHL | 72 | 20 | 19 | 39 | 38 | 2 | 1 | 0 | 1 | 0 |
| 2008-09 | Houston Aeros | AHL | 29 | 8 | 4 | 12 | 24 | .... | .... | .... | .... | .... |
| | Toronto Marlies | AHL | 36 | 7 | 6 | 13 | 33 | 6 | 1 | 2 | 3 | 4 |

Signed as a free agent by **Minnesota**, July 5, 2006. Traded to **Toronto** by **Minnesota** for Robbie Earl, January 21, 2009.

## HAMONIC, Travis (HA-mohn-ihk, TRA-vihs) NYI

Defense. Shoots right. 6', 192 lbs. Born, Winnipeg, Man., August 16, 1990.
(NY Islanders' 4th choice, 53rd overall, in 2008 Entry Draft).

| | | | Regular Season | | | | | Playoffs | | | | |
|---|---|---|---|---|---|---|---|---|---|---|---|---|
| Season | Club | League | GP | G | A | Pts | PIM | GP | G | A | Pts | PIM |
| 2006-07 | Winnipeg Saints | MJHL | .... | 2 | 13 | 15 | .... | .... | .... | .... | .... | .... |
| | Moose Jaw | WHL | 22 | 0 | 3 | 3 | 30 | .... | .... | .... | .... | .... |
| 2007-08 | Moose Jaw | WHL | 61 | 5 | 17 | 22 | 101 | 6 | 0 | 1 | 1 | 6 |
| 2008-09 | Moose Jaw | WHL | 57 | 13 | 27 | 40 | 126 | .... | .... | .... | .... | .... |

## HANOWSKI, Ben (ha-NOW-skee, BEHN) PIT.

Wing. Shoots left. 6'2", 198 lbs. Born, Little Falls, MN, October 18, 1990.
(Pittsburgh's 3rd choice, 63rd overall, in 2009 Entry Draft).

| | | | Regular Season | | | | | Playoffs | | | | |
|---|---|---|---|---|---|---|---|---|---|---|---|---|
| Season | Club | League | GP | G | A | Pts | PIM | GP | G | A | Pts | PIM |
| 2005-06 | Little Falls Flyers | High-MN | 31 | 35 | 29 | 64 | .... | .... | .... | .... | .... | .... |
| 2006-07 | Little Falls Flyers | High-MN | 29 | 40 | 71 | 111 | .... | .... | .... | .... | .... | .... |
| 2007-08 | Little Falls Flyers | High-MN | 26 | 48 | 47 | 95 | .... | .... | .... | .... | .... | .... |
| | Team North | UMHSEL | .... | 17 | 16 | 33 | .... | .... | .... | .... | .... | .... |
| 2008-09 | Little Falls Flyers | High-MN | 31 | 73 | 62 | 135 | 16 | .... | .... | .... | .... | .... |
| | Team North | UMHSEL | 19 | 14 | 8 | 22 | .... | .... | .... | .... | .... | .... |

• Signed Letter of Intent to attend **St. Cloud State University** (WCHA) in fall of 2009.

## HANSEN, Jake (HAHN-suhn, JAYK) CBJ

Wing. Shoots right. 6'2", 182 lbs. Born, St.Paul, MN, August 21, 1989.
(Columbus' 4th choice, 68th overall, in 2007 Entry Draft).

| | | | Regular Season | | | | | Playoffs | | | | |
|---|---|---|---|---|---|---|---|---|---|---|---|---|
| Season | Club | League | GP | G | A | Pts | PIM | GP | G | A | Pts | PIM |
| 2005-06 | White Bear Lake | High-MN | | STATISTICS NOT AVAILABLE | | | | | | | | |
| 2006-07 | White Bear Lake | High-MN | 25 | 28 | 43 | 71 | .... | .... | .... | .... | .... | .... |
| | Sioux Falls | USHL | 15 | 4 | 4 | 8 | 14 | 7 | 0 | 2 | 2 | 6 |
| 2007-08 | Sioux Falls | USHL | 60 | 31 | 27 | 58 | 57 | 3 | 1 | 0 | 1 | 0 |
| 2008-09 | U. of Minnesota | WCHA | 33 | 2 | 5 | 7 | 38 | .... | .... | .... | .... | .... |

USHL Second All-Star Team (2008)

## HARJU, Johan (HAHR-yoo, YOH-hahn) T.B.

Left wing. Shoots left. 6'3", 205 lbs. Born, Overtornea, Sweden, May 15, 1986.
(Tampa Bay's 6th choice, 167th overall, in 2007 Entry Draft).

| | | | Regular Season | | | | | Playoffs | | | | |
|---|---|---|---|---|---|---|---|---|---|---|---|---|
| Season | Club | League | GP | G | A | Pts | PIM | GP | G | A | Pts | PIM |
| 2002-03 | Lulea HF U18 | Swe-U18 | 11 | 7 | 2 | 9 | 14 | .... | .... | .... | .... | .... |
| | Lulea HF Jr. | Swe-Jr. | 7 | 2 | 0 | 2 | 0 | .... | .... | .... | .... | .... |
| 2003-04 | Lulea HF U18 | Swe-U18 | 3 | 1 | 3 | 4 | 0 | 7 | 4 | 3 | 7 | 8 |
| | Lulea HF Jr. | Swe-Jr. | 35 | 14 | 12 | 26 | 8 | .... | .... | .... | .... | .... |
| 2004-05 | Lulea HF Jr. | Swe-Jr. | 33 | 18 | 13 | 31 | 14 | 7 | 2 | 2 | 4 | 2 |
| | Pitea HC | Sweden-2 | 1 | 0 | 0 | 0 | 0 | .... | .... | .... | .... | .... |
| | Lulea HF | Sweden | 4 | 0 | 0 | 0 | 0 | .... | .... | .... | .... | .... |
| 2005-06 | Lulea HF Jr. | Swe-Jr. | 17 | 14 | 9 | 23 | 4 | 4 | 3 | 1 | 4 | 8 |
| | Lulea HF | Sweden | 39 | 3 | 1 | 4 | 8 | 4 | 0 | 0 | 0 | 20 |
| 2006-07 | Lulea HF | Sweden | 55 | 12 | 10 | 22 | 30 | 4 | 2 | 0 | 2 | 4 |
| 2007-08 | Lulea HF | Sweden | 51 | 20 | 8 | 28 | 55 | .... | .... | .... | .... | .... |
| 2008-09 | Lulea HF | Sweden | 55 | 27 | 22 | 49 | 30 | 5 | 4 | 1 | 5 | 0 |

## HARTIKAINEN, Teemu (har-tih-KIGH-nehn, TEE-moo) EDM.

Center. Shoots left. 6'1", 198 lbs. Born, Kuopio, Finland, May 3, 1990.
(Edmonton's 4th choice, 163rd overall, in 2008 Entry Draft).

| | | | Regular Season | | | | | Playoffs | | | | |
|---|---|---|---|---|---|---|---|---|---|---|---|---|
| Season | Club | League | GP | G | A | Pts | PIM | GP | G | A | Pts | PIM |
| 2006-07 | KalPa Kuopio U18 | Fin-U18 | 19 | 24 | 13 | 37 | 51 | .... | .... | .... | .... | .... |
| | KalPa Kuopio Jr. | Fin-Jr. | 11 | 2 | 1 | 3 | 0 | 3 | 0 | 0 | 0 | 4 |
| 2007-08 | KalPa Kuopio U18 | Fin-U18 | 7 | 9 | 6 | 15 | 6 | .... | .... | .... | .... | .... |
| | KalPa Kuopio Jr. | Fin-Jr. | 37 | 10 | 7 | 17 | 24 | 11 | 1 | 4 | 5 | 6 |
| | KalPa Kuopio | Finland | 1 | 0 | 0 | 0 | 0 | .... | .... | .... | .... | .... |
| 2008-09 | Suomi U20 | Finland-2 | 3 | 0 | 2 | 2 | 8 | .... | .... | .... | .... | .... |
| | KalPa Kuopio | Finland | 51 | 17 | 6 | 23 | 12 | 12 | 3 | 0 | 3 | 0 |

## HAULA, Erik (HOW-la, AIR-ihk) MIN.

Left wing. Shoots left. 5'11", 170 lbs. Born, Pori, Finland, March 23, 1991.
(Minnesota's 7th choice, 182nd overall, in 2009 Entry Draft).

| | | | Regular Season | | | | | Playoffs | | | | |
|---|---|---|---|---|---|---|---|---|---|---|---|---|
| Season | Club | League | GP | G | A | Pts | PIM | GP | G | A | Pts | PIM |
| 2006-07 | Assat Pori U18 | Fin-U18 | 29 | 19 | 24 | 43 | 24 | 6 | 1 | 3 | 4 | 4 |
| 2007-08 | Assat Pori U18 | Fin-U18 | 3 | 1 | 1 | 2 | 0 | 2 | 4 | 2 | 6 | 14 |
| | Assat Pori Jr. | Fin-Jr. | 40 | 7 | 15 | 22 | 26 | 12 | 2 | 0 | 2 | 4 |
| 2008-09 | Shat.-St. Mary's | High-MN | 53 | 26 | 58 | 84 | 46 | .... | .... | .... | .... | .... |

• Signed Letter of Intent to attend **University of Minnesota** (WCHA) in fall of 2010.

## HAUSWIRTH, Jake (HAWZ-wuhrth, JAYK) WSH.

Left wing. Shoots left. 6'5", 200 lbs. Born, Merrill, WI, February 16, 1988.

| | | | Regular Season | | | | | Playoffs | | | | |
|---|---|---|---|---|---|---|---|---|---|---|---|---|
| Season | Club | League | GP | G | A | Pts | PIM | GP | G | A | Pts | PIM |
| 2006-07 | Marquette | NAHL | 55 | 21 | 19 | 40 | 74 | .... | .... | .... | .... | .... |
| 2007-08 | Omaha Lancers | USHL | 57 | 13 | 10 | 23 | 36 | 13 | 2 | 4 | 6 | 10 |
| 2008-09 | Omaha Lancers | USHL | 58 | 28 | 24 | 52 | 22 | 3 | 1 | 0 | 1 | 0 |

Signed as a free agent by **Washington**, May 26, 2009.

## HAYES, Jimmy (HAYZ, JIH-mee) TOR.

Right wing. Shoots right. 6'5", 210 lbs. Born, Boston, MA, November 21, 1989.
(Toronto's 2nd choice, 60th overall, in 2008 Entry Draft).

| | | | Regular Season | | | | | Playoffs | | | | |
|---|---|---|---|---|---|---|---|---|---|---|---|---|
| Season | Club | League | GP | G | A | Pts | PIM | GP | G | A | Pts | PIM |
| 2006-07 | USNTDP | U-17 | 42 | 17 | 14 | 31 | 37 | .... | .... | .... | .... | .... |
| | USNTDP | NAHL | 14 | 6 | 8 | 14 | 4 | .... | .... | .... | .... | .... |
| 2007-08 | USNTDP | U-18 | 18 | 2 | 5 | 7 | 6 | .... | .... | .... | .... | .... |
| | USNTDP | NAHL | 19 | 2 | 8 | 10 | 6 | .... | .... | .... | .... | .... |
| | Lincoln Stars | USHL | 21 | 4 | 11 | 15 | 18 | 8 | 4 | 5 | 9 | 8 |
| 2008-09 | Boston College | H-East | 36 | 8 | 5 | 13 | 22 | .... | .... | .... | .... | .... |

## HEDMAN, Anton (HEHD-man, AN-tawn) BOS.

Center. Shoots left. 6'2", 207 lbs. Born, Stockholm, Sweden, May 15, 1986.
(Boston's 7th choice, 255th overall, in 2004 Entry Draft).

| | | | Regular Season | | | | | Playoffs | | | | |
|---|---|---|---|---|---|---|---|---|---|---|---|---|
| Season | Club | League | GP | G | A | Pts | PIM | GP | G | A | Pts | PIM |
| 2003-04 | Stocksund Jr. | Swe-Jr. | 14 | 5 | 5 | 10 | 14 | .... | .... | .... | .... | .... |
| 2004-05 | Djurgarden Jr. | Swe-Jr. | 32 | 14 | 9 | 23 | 119 | .... | .... | .... | .... | .... |
| 2005-06 | Sudbury Wolves | OHL | 60 | 18 | 16 | 34 | 126 | 8 | 1 | 3 | 4 | 19 |
| 2006-07 | Owen Sound | OHL | 39 | 12 | 12 | 24 | 73 | .... | .... | .... | .... | .... |
| | Guelph Storm | OHL | 28 | 5 | 7 | 12 | 38 | 4 | 0 | 1 | 1 | 8 |
| 2007-08 | Almtuna | Sweden-2 | 9 | 0 | 2 | 2 | 47 | .... | .... | .... | .... | .... |
| | Hammarby | Sweden-2 | 11 | 1 | 2 | 3 | 12 | .... | .... | .... | .... | .... |
| | VIK Vasteras HK | Sweden-2 | 9 | 0 | 1 | 1 | 39 | .... | .... | .... | .... | .... |
| 2008-09 | Vaxjo Lakers HC | Sweden-2 | 49 | 2 | 7 | 9 | 73 | 4 | 0 | 0 | 0 | 12 |

## HEDMAN, Oscar (HEHD-man, AWZ-kuhr) WSH.

Defense. Shoots left. 6', 209 lbs. Born, Ornskoldsvik, Sweden, April 21, 1986.
(Washington's 8th choice, 132nd overall, in 2004 Entry Draft).

| | | | Regular Season | | | | | Playoffs | | | | |
|---|---|---|---|---|---|---|---|---|---|---|---|---|
| Season | Club | League | GP | G | A | Pts | PIM | GP | G | A | Pts | PIM |
| 2002-03 | MODO U18 | Swe-U18 | 14 | 4 | 5 | 9 | 8 | 6 | 2 | 1 | 3 | 32 |
| | Malmo Jr. | Swe-Jr. | 5 | 0 | 1 | 1 | 2 | .... | .... | .... | .... | .... |
| 2003-04 | Malmo Jr. | Swe-Jr. | 25 | 7 | 11 | 18 | 28 | 8 | 3 | 3 | 6 | 6 |
| | MODO U18 | Swe-U18 | 3 | 3 | 1 | 4 | 2 | 2 | 0 | 3 | 3 | 0 |
| | MODO | Sweden | 24 | 1 | 2 | 3 | 6 | 6 | 0 | 0 | 0 | 0 |
| 2004-05 | MODO Jr. | Swe-Jr. | 7 | 2 | 2 | 4 | 12 | 5 | 0 | 1 | 1 | 4 |
| | MODO | Sweden | 43 | 1 | 3 | 4 | 18 | 4 | 0 | 0 | 0 | 0 |
| 2005-06 | MODO Jr. | Swe-Jr. | 7 | 3 | 2 | 5 | 10 | .... | .... | .... | .... | .... |
| | MODO | Sweden | 44 | 3 | 2 | 5 | 30 | 5 | 0 | 1 | 1 | 0 |
| 2006-07 | MODO | Sweden | 55 | 2 | 7 | 9 | 42 | 20 | 1 | 4 | 5 | 14 |
| 2007-08 | MODO | Sweden | 53 | 4 | 9 | 13 | 30 | 5 | 1 | 1 | 2 | 0 |
| 2008-09 | Frolunda | Sweden | 55 | 5 | 6 | 11 | 26 | 11 | 0 | 0 | 0 | 14 |

### HEDMAN, Victor (HEHD-muhn, VIHK-tohr) T.B.

Defense. Shoots left. 6'6", 220 lbs. Born, Ornskoldsvik, Sweden, December 18, 1990.
(Tampa Bay's 1st choice, 2nd overall, in 2009 Entry Draft).

| | | | Regular Season | | | | | Playoffs | | | | |
|---|---|---|---|---|---|---|---|---|---|---|---|---|
| Season | Club | League | GP | G | A | Pts | PIM | GP | G | A | Pts | PIM |
| 2005-06 | MODO U18 | Swe-U18 | 8 | 3 | 3 | 6 | 14 | 2 | 0 | 0 | 0 | 0 |
| | MODO Jr. | Swe-Jr. | 10 | 0 | 1 | 1 | 8 | .... | .... | .... | .... | .... |
| 2006-07 | MODO U18 | Swe-U18 | 3 | 3 | 0 | 3 | 29 | .... | .... | .... | .... | .... |
| | MODO Jr. | Swe-Jr. | 34 | 13 | 12 | 25 | 30 | 5 | 1 | 1 | 2 | 44 |
| 2007-08 | MODO Jr. | Swe-Jr. | 6 | 2 | 1 | 3 | 26 | 3 | 2 | 0 | 2 | 4 |
| | MODO | Sweden | 39 | 2 | 2 | 4 | 44 | 5 | 1 | 0 | 1 | 4 |
| 2008-09 | MODO Jr. | Swe-Jr. | 2 | 0 | 2 | 2 | 10 | 5 | 0 | 1 | 1 | 2 |
| | MODO | Sweden | 43 | 7 | 14 | 21 | 52 | .... | .... | .... | .... | .... |

### HEGARTY, Ryan (HEH-gahr-tee, RIGH-uhn) ANA.

Defense. Shoots left. 6', 196 lbs. Born, Stoneham, MA, May 16, 1990.
(Anaheim's 8th choice, 113th overall, in 2008 Entry Draft).

| | | | Regular Season | | | | | Playoffs | | | | |
|---|---|---|---|---|---|---|---|---|---|---|---|---|
| Season | Club | League | GP | G | A | Pts | PIM | GP | G | A | Pts | PIM |
| 2006-07 | USNTDP | U-17 | 15 | 1 | 2 | 3 | 10 | .... | .... | .... | .... | .... |
| | USNTDP | NAHL | 43 | 2 | 2 | 4 | 54 | 6 | 0 | 0 | 0 | 4 |
| 2007-08 | USNTDP | U-18 | 41 | 5 | 8 | 13 | 38 | .... | .... | .... | .... | .... |
| | USNTDP | NAHL | 14 | 2 | 8 | 10 | 18 | .... | .... | .... | .... | .... |
| 2008-09 | U. of Maine | H-East | 24 | 0 | 3 | 3 | 22 | .... | .... | .... | .... | .... |

### HEIKKINEN, Ilkka (HAY-kih-nehn, IHL-ka) NYR

Defense. Shoots left. 6'2", 191 lbs. Born, Rauma, Finland, November 13, 1984.

| | | | Regular Season | | | | | Playoffs | | | | |
|---|---|---|---|---|---|---|---|---|---|---|---|---|
| Season | Club | League | GP | G | A | Pts | PIM | GP | G | A | Pts | PIM |
| 2004-05 | Lukko Rauma | Finland | 48 | 0 | 2 | 2 | 8 | 9 | 0 | 0 | 0 | 0 |
| 2005-06 | Lukko Rauma | Finland | 55 | 5 | 10 | 15 | 46 | .... | .... | .... | .... | .... |
| 2006-07 | Lukko Rauma | Finland | 55 | 7 | 17 | 24 | 71 | 3 | 0 | 0 | 0 | 0 |
| 2007-08 | HIFK Helsinki | Finland | 51 | 11 | 26 | 37 | 96 | 7 | 0 | 2 | 2 | 6 |
| 2008-09 | HIFK Helsinki | Finland | 54 | 8 | 26 | 34 | 22 | 2 | 0 | 1 | 1 | 0 |

Signed as a free agent by **NY Rangers**, May 20, 2009.

### HELGESON, Seth (HEHL-guh-suhn, SEHTH) N.J.

Defense. Shoots left. 6'5", 220 lbs. Born, Faribault, MN, October 8, 1990.
(New Jersey's 4th choice, 114th overall, in 2009 Entry Draft).

| | | | Regular Season | | | | | Playoffs | | | | |
|---|---|---|---|---|---|---|---|---|---|---|---|---|
| Season | Club | League | GP | G | A | Pts | PIM | GP | G | A | Pts | PIM |
| 2006-07 | Faribault Falcons | High-MN | 27 | 19 | 17 | 36 | | .... | .... | .... | .... | .... |
| 2007-08 | Sioux City | USHL | 58 | 3 | 8 | 11 | 41 | 4 | 0 | 1 | 1 | 2 |
| 2008-09 | Sioux City | USHL | 58 | 4 | 12 | 16 | 64 | .... | .... | .... | .... | .... |

• Signed Letter of Intent to attend **University of Minnesota** (WCHA) in fall of 2009.

### HELLGREN, Jens (HEHL-grehn, YEHNZ) COL.

Defense. Shoots left. 6'3", 192 lbs. Born, Bjorbo, Sweden, March 6, 1989.
(Colorado's 8th choice, 155th overall, in 2007 Entry Draft).

| | | | Regular Season | | | | | Playoffs | | | | |
|---|---|---|---|---|---|---|---|---|---|---|---|---|
| Season | Club | League | GP | G | A | Pts | PIM | GP | G | A | Pts | PIM |
| 2004-05 | Leksands IF U18 | Swe-U18 | STATISTICS NOT AVAILABLE | | | | | | | | | |
| 2005-06 | Frolunda U18 | Swe-U18 | 12 | 1 | 0 | 1 | 2 | 2 | 0 | 0 | 0 | 2 |
| | Frolunda Jr. | Swe-Jr. | 22 | 0 | 0 | 0 | 4 | 6 | 0 | 0 | 0 | 0 |
| 2006-07 | Frolunda U18 | Swe-U18 | 3 | 0 | 2 | 2 | 0 | 4 | 2 | 2 | 4 | 6 |
| | Frolunda Jr. | Swe-Jr. | 40 | 4 | 6 | 10 | 26 | 7 | 0 | 0 | 0 | 2 |
| 2007-08 | Frolunda Jr. | Swe-Jr. | 40 | 4 | 10 | 14 | 20 | 8 | 0 | 1 | 1 | 2 |
| 2008-09 | Boras HC | Sweden-2 | 45 | 2 | 6 | 8 | 16 | .... | .... | .... | .... | .... |

### HELLSTROM, Alexander (HEHL-struhm, al-EHX-AN-duhr) ST.L.

Defense. Shoots left. 6'3", 210 lbs. Born, Falun, Sweden, April 17, 1987.
(St. Louis' 9th choice, 184th overall, in 2006 Entry Draft).

| | | | Regular Season | | | | | Playoffs | | | | |
|---|---|---|---|---|---|---|---|---|---|---|---|---|
| Season | Club | League | GP | G | A | Pts | PIM | GP | G | A | Pts | PIM |
| 2003-04 | Bjorkloven U18 | Swe-U18 | 7 | 0 | 2 | 2 | 8 | .... | .... | .... | .... | .... |
| 2004-05 | Bjorkloven U18 | Swe-U18 | STATISTICS NOT AVAILABLE | | | | | | | | | |
| | Bjorkloven Jr. | Swe-Jr. | 3 | 0 | 2 | 2 | 2 | .... | .... | .... | .... | .... |
| | IF Bjorkloven Umea | Sweden-2 | 15 | 0 | 1 | 1 | 8 | .... | .... | .... | .... | .... |
| 2005-06 | Bjorkloven Jr. | Swe-Jr. | 11 | 1 | 3 | 4 | 20 | 6 | 0 | 3 | 3 | 4 |
| | IF Bjorkloven Umea | Sweden-2 | 31 | 1 | 0 | 1 | 45 | .... | .... | .... | .... | .... |
| 2006-07 | Bjorkloven Jr. | Swe-Jr. | 8 | 2 | 2 | 4 | 26 | .... | .... | .... | .... | .... |
| | IF Bjorkloven Umea | Sweden-2 | 55 | 0 | 7 | 7 | 153 | 6 | 0 | 0 | 0 | 6 |
| 2007-08 | Peoria Rivermen | AHL | 35 | 3 | 2 | 5 | 38 | .... | .... | .... | .... | .... |
| 2008-09 | Peoria Rivermen | AHL | 40 | 0 | 1 | 1 | 37 | .... | .... | .... | .... | .... |
| | Alaska Aces | ECHL | 9 | 0 | 3 | 3 | 7 | .... | .... | .... | .... | .... |

### HENNIGAR, Rob (HEHN-ih-guhr, RAWB) NYI

Center. Shoots left. 5'11", 194 lbs. Born, Jordan, Ont., April 4, 1983.

| | | | Regular Season | | | | | Playoffs | | | | |
|---|---|---|---|---|---|---|---|---|---|---|---|---|
| Season | Club | League | GP | G | A | Pts | PIM | GP | G | A | Pts | PIM |
| 2000-01 | Windsor Spitfires | OHL | 43 | 7 | 13 | 20 | 27 | 5 | 0 | 1 | 1 | 4 |
| 2001-02 | Windsor Spitfires | OHL | 67 | 15 | 32 | 47 | 51 | 16 | 5 | 7 | 12 | 10 |
| 2002-03 | Windsor Spitfires | OHL | 68 | 29 | 46 | 75 | 56 | 7 | 3 | 4 | 7 | 6 |
| 2003-04 | Windsor Spitfires | OHL | 68 | 32 | 47 | 79 | 64 | 4 | 1 | 2 | 3 | 0 |
| 2004-05 | New Brunswick | AUAA | 28 | 9 | 26 | 35 | 26 | .... | .... | .... | .... | .... |
| 2005-06 | New Brunswick | AUAA | 28 | 9 | 33 | 42 | 32 | .... | .... | .... | .... | .... |
| 2006-07 | New Brunswick | AUAA | 25 | 13 | 29 | 42 | 14 | .... | .... | .... | .... | .... |
| 2007-08 | New Brunswick | AUAA | 27 | 15 | 43 | 58 | 12 | .... | .... | .... | .... | .... |
| 2008-09 | Bridgeport | AHL | 34 | 3 | 10 | 13 | 18 | 4 | 1 | 0 | 1 | 2 |
| | Utah Grizzlies | ECHL | 38 | 15 | 44 | 59 | 40 | .... | .... | .... | .... | .... |

Signed as a free agent by **NY Islanders**, April 9, 2008.

### HENRICH, Adam (HEHN-rihch, A-duhm)

Left wing. Shoots left. 6'4", 231 lbs. Born, Thornhill, Ont., January 19, 1984.
(Tampa Bay's 1st choice, 60th overall, in 2002 Entry Draft).

| | | | Regular Season | | | | | Playoffs | | | | |
|---|---|---|---|---|---|---|---|---|---|---|---|---|
| Season | Club | League | GP | G | A | Pts | PIM | GP | G | A | Pts | PIM |
| 99-2000 | Don Mills Flyers | GTHL | 54 | 30 | 52 | 82 | 86 | .... | .... | .... | .... | .... |
| 2000-01 | Brampton | OHL | 48 | 5 | 4 | 9 | 27 | 9 | 0 | 0 | 0 | 6 |
| 2001-02 | Brampton | OHL | 66 | 33 | 30 | 63 | 92 | .... | .... | .... | .... | .... |
| 2002-03 | Brampton | OHL | 63 | 31 | 33 | 64 | 84 | 11 | 4 | 1 | 5 | 25 |
| 2003-04 | Brampton | OHL | 65 | 29 | 29 | 58 | 146 | 12 | 5 | 1 | 6 | 24 |
| 2004-05 | Springfield Falcons | AHL | 63 | 10 | 16 | 26 | 97 | .... | .... | .... | .... | .... |
| | Johnstown Chiefs | ECHL | 6 | 2 | 1 | 3 | 15 | .... | .... | .... | .... | .... |
| 2005-06 | Springfield Falcons | AHL | 12 | 0 | 3 | 3 | 14 | .... | .... | .... | .... | .... |
| | Johnstown Chiefs | ECHL | 51 | 18 | 23 | 41 | 78 | 5 | 2 | 4 | 6 | 8 |
| 2006-07 | Springfield Falcons | AHL | 27 | 3 | 6 | 9 | 31 | .... | .... | .... | .... | .... |
| | Johnstown Chiefs | ECHL | 32 | 15 | 19 | 34 | 119 | 2 | 0 | 0 | 0 | 2 |
| 2007-08 | Norfolk Admirals | AHL | 43 | 14 | 17 | 31 | 88 | .... | .... | .... | .... | .... |
| | Wheeling Nailers | ECHL | 12 | 10 | 10 | 20 | 34 | .... | .... | .... | .... | .... |
| 2008-09 | Wilkes-Barre | AHL | 37 | 3 | 8 | 11 | 34 | 2 | 0 | 0 | 0 | 0 |

Signed as a free agent by **Pittsburgh**, July 8, 2008.

### HENRIQUE, Adam (HEHN-reek, A-duhm) N.J.

Center. Shoots left. 5'11", 190 lbs. Born, Brantford, Ont., February 6, 1990.
(New Jersey's 4th choice, 82nd overall, in 2008 Entry Draft).

| | | | Regular Season | | | | | Playoffs | | | | |
|---|---|---|---|---|---|---|---|---|---|---|---|---|
| Season | Club | League | GP | G | A | Pts | PIM | GP | G | A | Pts | PIM |
| 2006-07 | Windsor Spitfires | OHL | 62 | 23 | 21 | 44 | 20 | .... | .... | .... | .... | .... |
| 2007-08 | Windsor Spitfires | OHL | 66 | 20 | 24 | 44 | 28 | 5 | 2 | 3 | 5 | 4 |
| 2008-09 | Windsor Spitfires | OHL | 56 | 30 | 33 | 63 | 47 | 20 | 8 | 9 | 17 | 19 |

### HENRY, Jordan (HEHN-ree, JOHR-duhn) FLA.

Defense. Shoots right. 6'2", 198 lbs. Born, Milo, Alta., February 11, 1986.

| | | | Regular Season | | | | | Playoffs | | | | |
|---|---|---|---|---|---|---|---|---|---|---|---|---|
| Season | Club | League | GP | G | A | Pts | PIM | GP | G | A | Pts | PIM |
| 2003-04 | Moose Jaw | WHL | 61 | 0 | 4 | 4 | 82 | 10 | 0 | 0 | 0 | 6 |
| 2004-05 | Moose Jaw | WHL | 68 | 2 | 12 | 14 | 137 | 5 | 2 | 0 | 2 | 26 |
| 2005-06 | Moose Jaw | WHL | 40 | 1 | 12 | 13 | 104 | .... | .... | .... | .... | .... |
| | Red Deer Rebels | WHL | 29 | 2 | 8 | 10 | 51 | .... | .... | .... | .... | .... |
| 2006-07 | Red Deer Rebels | WHL | 72 | 7 | 25 | 32 | 162 | 7 | 0 | 4 | 4 | 26 |
| 2007-08 | Rochester | AHL | 49 | 3 | 5 | 8 | 73 | .... | .... | .... | .... | .... |
| | Florida Everblades | ECHL | 20 | 2 | 2 | 4 | 14 | .... | .... | .... | .... | .... |
| 2008-09 | Rochester | AHL | 69 | 4 | 12 | 16 | 111 | .... | .... | .... | .... | .... |

Signed as a free agent by **Florida**, October 8, 2007.

### HERSLEY, Patrik (HUHRS-lee, PAT-rihk) PHI.

Defense. Shoots right. 6'3", 205 lbs. Born, Malmo, Sweden, June 23, 1986.
(Los Angeles' 5th choice, 139th overall, in 2005 Entry Draft).

| | | | Regular Season | | | | | Playoffs | | | | |
|---|---|---|---|---|---|---|---|---|---|---|---|---|
| Season | Club | League | GP | G | A | Pts | PIM | GP | G | A | Pts | PIM |
| 2002-03 | Malmo U18 | Swe-U18 | 9 | 3 | 4 | 7 | 53 | 4 | 1 | 2 | 3 | 4 |
| | Malmo Jr. | Swe-Jr. | 16 | 0 | 2 | 2 | 4 | 1 | 0 | 0 | 0 | 0 |
| 2003-04 | Malmo U18 | Swe-U18 | 2 | 2 | 0 | 2 | 4 | .... | .... | .... | .... | .... |
| | Malmo Jr. | Swe-Jr. | 17 | 1 | 4 | 5 | 16 | 8 | 0 | 2 | 2 | 2 |
| 2004-05 | Malmo Jr. | Swe-Jr. | 31 | 8 | 14 | 22 | 104 | 3 | 2 | 1 | 3 | 6 |
| | Malmo | Sweden | 8 | 0 | 1 | 1 | 0 | .... | .... | .... | .... | .... |
| | Malmo | Sweden-Q | 6 | 0 | 0 | 0 | 2 | .... | .... | .... | .... | .... |
| 2005-06 | Malmo Jr. | Swe-Jr. | 13 | 10 | 9 | 19 | 38 | .... | .... | .... | .... | .... |
| | Malmo | Sweden-2 | 41 | 6 | 8 | 14 | 38 | .... | .... | .... | .... | .... |
| 2006-07 | Malmo Jr. | Swe-Jr. | 2 | 1 | 3 | 4 | 14 | .... | .... | .... | .... | .... |
| | Malmo | Sweden | 28 | 1 | 1 | 2 | 10 | .... | .... | .... | .... | .... |
| | IK Pantern Malmo | Sweden-3 | 2 | 1 | 1 | 2 | 8 | .... | .... | .... | .... | .... |
| 2007-08 | Manchester | AHL | 42 | 1 | 8 | 9 | 27 | .... | .... | .... | .... | .... |
| | Reading Royals | ECHL | 20 | 3 | 15 | 18 | 18 | 13 | 3 | 6 | 9 | 10 |
| 2008-09 | Philadelphia | AHL | 5 | 0 | 0 | 0 | 2 | .... | .... | .... | .... | .... |
| | Reading Royals | ECHL | 15 | 0 | 4 | 4 | 8 | .... | .... | .... | .... | .... |

Traded to **Philadelphia** by **Los Angeles** with Ned Lukacevic for Denis Gauthier and Philadelphia's 2nd round choice in 2010 Entry Draft, July 1, 2008. • Missed majority of 2008-09 season recovering from a shoulder injury.

### HESHKA, Shaun (HEHSH-kah, SHAWN) PHX.

Defense. Shoots right. 6'1", 198 lbs. Born, Melville, Sask., July 30, 1985.

| | | | Regular Season | | | | | Playoffs | | | | |
|---|---|---|---|---|---|---|---|---|---|---|---|---|
| Season | Club | League | GP | G | A | Pts | PIM | GP | G | A | Pts | PIM |
| 2002-03 | Melville | SJHL | 53 | 6 | 14 | 20 | 53 | .... | .... | .... | .... | .... |
| 2003-04 | Everett Silvertips | WHL | 66 | 3 | 7 | 10 | 25 | 21 | 0 | 2 | 2 | 8 |
| 2004-05 | Everett Silvertips | WHL | 72 | 12 | 26 | 38 | 21 | 11 | 2 | 0 | 2 | 6 |
| 2005-06 | Everett Silvertips | WHL | 66 | 10 | 49 | 59 | 91 | 14 | 3 | 10 | 13 | 10 |
| 2006-07 | Manitoba Moose | AHL | 57 | 2 | 4 | 6 | 14 | 7 | 0 | 0 | 0 | 8 |
| | Victoria | ECHL | 3 | 0 | 1 | 1 | 4 | .... | .... | .... | .... | .... |
| 2007-08 | Manitoba Moose | AHL | 77 | 9 | 21 | 30 | 59 | 6 | 0 | 1 | 1 | 4 |
| 2008-09 | Manitoba Moose | AHL | 77 | 3 | 23 | 26 | 25 | 22 | 0 | 5 | 5 | 12 |

WHL West First All-Star Team (2006)

Signed as a free agent by **Vancouver**, July 24, 2006. Traded to **Phoenix** by **Vancouver** for Phoenix's 7th round choice (Steven Anthony) in 2009 Entry Draft, June 27, 2009.

### HESKETH, Troy (HEHS-kehth, TROY) EDM.

Defense. Shoots left. 6'2", 178 lbs. Born, Minnetonka, MN, July 5, 1991.
(Edmonton's 3rd choice, 71st overall, in 2009 Entry Draft).

| | | | Regular Season | | | | | Playoffs | | | | |
|---|---|---|---|---|---|---|---|---|---|---|---|---|
| Season | Club | League | GP | G | A | Pts | PIM | GP | G | A | Pts | PIM |
| 2007-08 | Minnetonka High | High-MN | 9 | 0 | 0 | 0 | 2 | .... | .... | .... | .... | .... |
| 2008-09 | Minnetonka High | High-MN | 28 | 7 | 15 | 22 | 46 | .... | .... | .... | .... | .... |
| | Team Southwest | UMHSEL | 22 | 2 | 7 | 9 | .... | .... | .... | .... | .... | .... |

• Signed Letter of Intent to attend **University of Wisconsin** (WCHA) in fall of 2011.

### HEXTALL, Brett (HEHX-tahl, BREHT) PHX.

Center. Shoots right. 5'10", 176 lbs. Born, Philadelphia, PA, April 2, 1988.
(Phoenix's 7th choice, 159th overall, in 2008 Entry Draft).

| | | | Regular Season | | | | | Playoffs | | | | |
|---|---|---|---|---|---|---|---|---|---|---|---|---|
| Season | Club | League | GP | G | A | Pts | PIM | GP | G | A | Pts | PIM |
| 2006-07 | Penticton Vees | BCHL | 59 | 18 | 27 | 45 | 156 | 11 | 2 | 2 | 4 | 8 |
| 2007-08 | Penticton Vees | BCHL | 54 | 24 | 48 | 72 | 52 | 15 | *12 | 3 | 15 | 12 |
| 2008-09 | North Dakota | WCHA | 42 | 12 | 24 | 36 | 91 | .... | .... | .... | .... | .... |

**HICKEY, Chris** (HIH-kee, KRIHS) **MIN.**

Center. Shoots right. 6'1", 196 lbs. Born, St. Paul, MN, September 2, 1988.
(Minnesota's 7th choice, 192nd overall, in 2006 Entry Draft).

| | | | Regular Season | | | | | Playoffs | | | | |
|---|---|---|---|---|---|---|---|---|---|---|---|---|
| Season | Club | League | GP | G | A | Pts | PIM | GP | G | A | Pts | PIM |
| 2003-04 | Cretin-Derham | High-MN | 27 | 19 | 13 | 32 | 32 | .... | .... | .... | .... | .... |
| 2004-05 | Cretin-Derham | High-MN | 28 | 25 | 21 | 46 | 48 | .... | .... | .... | .... | .... |
| 2005-06 | Cretin-Derham | High-MN | 31 | 37 | 28 | 65 | 36 | .... | .... | .... | .... | .... |
| 2006-07 | Cretin-Derham | High-MN | 17 | 21 | 15 | 36 | .... | .... | .... | .... | .... | .... |
| | Tri-City Storm | USHL | 1 | 0 | 0 | 0 | 0 | .... | .... | .... | .... | .... |
| 2007-08 | Tri-City Storm | USHL | 55 | 15 | 16 | 31 | 34 | .... | .... | .... | .... | .... |
| 2008-09 | U. of Wisconsin | WCHA | 8 | 1 | 0 | 1 | 4 | .... | .... | .... | .... | .... |

**HICKEY, Thomas** (HIH-kee, TAW-muhs) **L.A.**

Defense. Shoots left. 6', 191 lbs. Born, Calgary, Alta., February 8, 1989.
(Los Angeles' 1st choice, 4th overall, in 2007 Entry Draft).

| | | | Regular Season | | | | | Playoffs | | | | |
|---|---|---|---|---|---|---|---|---|---|---|---|---|
| Season | Club | League | GP | G | A | Pts | PIM | GP | G | A | Pts | PIM |
| 2003-04 | Cgy. Royals | CBHL | 32 | 13 | 25 | 38 | 51 | .... | .... | .... | .... | .... |
| 2004-05 | Calgary Royals | AMHL | 33 | 9 | 13 | 22 | 36 | .... | .... | .... | .... | .... |
| | Seattle | WHL | 5 | 2 | 1 | 3 | 6 | .... | .... | .... | .... | .... |
| 2005-06 | Seattle | WHL | 69 | 1 | 27 | 28 | 53 | 7 | 1 | 3 | 4 | 10 |
| 2006-07 | Seattle | WHL | 68 | 9 | 41 | 50 | 70 | 11 | 3 | 4 | 7 | 4 |
| 2007-08 | Seattle | WHL | 63 | 11 | 34 | 45 | 49 | 9 | 1 | 9 | 10 | 4 |
| 2008-09 | Seattle | WHL | 57 | 16 | 35 | 51 | 30 | 5 | 2 | 1 | 3 | 4 |
| | Manchester | AHL | 7 | 1 | 6 | 7 | 2 | .... | .... | .... | .... | .... |

WHL West Second All-Star Team (2007) • WHL West First All-Star Team (2008, 2009)

**HILLIER, Ryan** (HIHL-lee-uhr, RIGH-uhn) **NYR**

Left wing. Shoots left. 6'1", 195 lbs. Born, Halifax, N.S., January 25, 1988.
(NY Rangers' 3rd choice, 84th overall, in 2006 Entry Draft).

| | | | Regular Season | | | | | Playoffs | | | | |
|---|---|---|---|---|---|---|---|---|---|---|---|---|
| Season | Club | League | GP | G | A | Pts | PIM | GP | G | A | Pts | PIM |
| 2003-04 | Dartmouth | NSMHL | 55 | 31 | 36 | 67 | 97 | .... | .... | .... | .... | .... |
| 2004-05 | Halifax | QMJHL | 21 | 1 | 1 | 2 | 13 | 7 | 0 | 2 | 2 | 2 |
| 2005-06 | Halifax | QMJHL | 68 | 19 | 38 | 57 | 76 | 11 | 2 | 2 | 4 | 12 |
| 2006-07 | Halifax | QMJHL | 70 | 32 | 27 | 59 | 79 | 12 | 3 | 6 | 9 | 20 |
| 2007-08 | Halifax | QMJHL | 70 | 34 | 38 | 72 | 55 | 14 | 8 | 7 | 15 | 22 |
| 2008-09 | Charlotte | ECHL | 66 | 10 | 16 | 26 | 33 | .... | .... | .... | .... | .... |

**HJALMARSSON, Simon** (H'YAHL-muhr-suhn, SEE-muhn) **ST.L.**

Right wing. Shoots left. 5'11", 161 lbs. Born, Varnamo, Sweden, February 1, 1989.
(St. Louis' 4th choice, 39th overall, in 2007 Entry Draft).

| | | | Regular Season | | | | | Playoffs | | | | |
|---|---|---|---|---|---|---|---|---|---|---|---|---|
| Season | Club | League | GP | G | A | Pts | PIM | GP | G | A | Pts | PIM |
| 2004-05 | Gislaveds SK Jr. | Swe-Jr. | | STATISTICS NOT AVAILABLE | | | | | | | | |
| 2005-06 | Frolunda U18 | Swe-U18 | 6 | 2 | 3 | 5 | 4 | 2 | 0 | 0 | 0 | 2 |
| | Frolunda Jr. | Swe-Jr. | 31 | 8 | 10 | 18 | 8 | 7 | 2 | 3 | 5 | 2 |
| 2006-07 | Frolunda U18 | Swe-U18 | 3 | 4 | 3 | 7 | 33 | 6 | 3 | 8 | 11 | 2 |
| | Gislaveds SK | Sweden-3 | 2 | 0 | 1 | 1 | 0 | .... | .... | .... | .... | .... |
| | Frolunda Jr. | Swe-Jr. | 41 | 31 | 23 | 54 | 91 | 8 | 1 | 1 | 2 | 6 |
| 2007-08 | Boras HC | Sweden-2 | 10 | 2 | 4 | 6 | 4 | .... | .... | .... | .... | .... |
| | Frolunda | Sweden | 1 | 0 | 0 | 0 | 2 | .... | .... | .... | .... | .... |
| | Frolunda Jr. | Swe-Jr. | 37 | 16 | 30 | 46 | 104 | 8 | 3 | 9 | 12 | 8 |
| 2008-09 | Boras HC | Sweden-2 | 40 | 14 | 19 | 33 | 28 | .... | .... | .... | .... | .... |
| | Frolunda Jr. | Swe-Jr. | 2 | 2 | 0 | 2 | 2 | 5 | 8 | 2 | 10 | 2 |

**HOBBS, Danny** (HAWBZ, DA-nee) **NYR**

Center/Right wing. Shoots left. 5'11", 178 lbs. Born, Shawville, Ont., June 21, 1989.
(NY Rangers' 6th choice, 198th overall, in 2007 Entry Draft).

| | | | Regular Season | | | | | Playoffs | | | | |
|---|---|---|---|---|---|---|---|---|---|---|---|---|
| Season | Club | League | GP | G | A | Pts | PIM | GP | G | A | Pts | PIM |
| 2005-06 | Stanstead | QJHL | 46 | 58 | 32 | 90 | 15 | .... | .... | .... | .... | .... |
| 2006-07 | Ohio | USHL | 60 | 10 | 11 | 21 | 36 | 4 | 0 | 2 | 2 | 2 |
| 2007-08 | Ohio | USHL | 54 | 15 | 16 | 31 | 22 | .... | .... | .... | .... | .... |
| 2008-09 | Massachusetts | H-East | 24 | 1 | 1 | 2 | 20 | .... | .... | .... | .... | .... |

**HOBSON, Adam** (HAWB-sohn, A-duhm) **CHI.**

Center. Shoots left. 6', 210 lbs. Born, Lund, Sweden, January 9, 1987.
(Chicago's 12th choice, 203rd overall, in 2005 Entry Draft).

| | | | Regular Season | | | | | Playoffs | | | | |
|---|---|---|---|---|---|---|---|---|---|---|---|---|
| Season | Club | League | GP | G | A | Pts | PIM | GP | G | A | Pts | PIM |
| 2002-03 | Abbotsford Pilots | PIJHL | 38 | 20 | 28 | 48 | .... | .... | .... | .... | .... | .... |
| | Spokane Chiefs | WHL | 1 | 0 | 0 | 0 | 2 | .... | .... | .... | .... | .... |
| 2003-04 | Spokane Chiefs | WHL | 63 | 4 | 5 | 9 | 35 | 4 | 0 | 0 | 0 | 0 |
| 2004-05 | Spokane Chiefs | WHL | 72 | 10 | 27 | 37 | 47 | .... | .... | .... | .... | .... |
| 2005-06 | Spokane Chiefs | WHL | 72 | 23 | 27 | 50 | 124 | .... | .... | .... | .... | .... |
| 2006-07 | Spokane Chiefs | WHL | 43 | 14 | 18 | 32 | 59 | 6 | 3 | 0 | 3 | 6 |
| 2007-08 | Rockford IceHogs | AHL | 25 | 1 | 4 | 5 | 36 | .... | .... | .... | .... | .... |
| | Pensacola | ECHL | 24 | 10 | 5 | 15 | 30 | .... | .... | .... | .... | .... |
| 2008-09 | Rockford IceHogs | AHL | 41 | 5 | 9 | 14 | 50 | 4 | 0 | 0 | 0 | 2 |
| | Fresno Falcons | ECHL | 26 | 4 | 10 | 14 | 30 | .... | .... | .... | .... | .... |
| | Gwinnett | ECHL | 6 | 2 | 3 | 5 | 7 | .... | .... | .... | .... | .... |

**HODGSON, Cody** (HAWJ-suhn, KOH-dee) **VAN.**

Center. Shoots right. 6', 185 lbs. Born, Toronto, Ont., February 18, 1990.
(Vancouver's 1st choice, 10th overall, in 2008 Entry Draft).

| | | | Regular Season | | | | | Playoffs | | | | |
|---|---|---|---|---|---|---|---|---|---|---|---|---|
| Season | Club | League | GP | G | A | Pts | PIM | GP | G | A | Pts | PIM |
| 2005-06 | Markham Waxers | Minor-ON | 30 | 27 | 24 | 51 | 22 | 15 | 13 | 14 | 27 | 8 |
| 2006-07 | Brampton | OHL | 63 | 23 | 23 | 46 | 24 | 4 | 1 | 3 | 4 | 0 |
| 2007-08 | Brampton | OHL | 68 | 40 | 45 | 85 | 36 | 5 | 5 | 0 | 5 | 2 |
| 2008-09 | Brampton | OHL | 53 | 43 | 49 | 92 | 33 | 21 | 11 | 20 | 31 | 18 |
| | Manitoba Moose | AHL | .... | .... | .... | .... | .... | 11 | 2 | 4 | 6 | 4 |

OHL First All-Star Team (2009) • OHL Player of the Year (2009) • Canadian Major Junior First All-Star Team (2009)

**HOEFFEL, Mike** (HOH-fuhl, MIGHK) **N.J.**

Left wing. Shoots left. 6'2", 185 lbs. Born, North Oaks, MN, April 9, 1989.
(New Jersey's 1st choice, 57th overall, in 2007 Entry Draft).

| | | | Regular Season | | | | | Playoffs | | | | |
|---|---|---|---|---|---|---|---|---|---|---|---|---|
| Season | Club | League | GP | G | A | Pts | PIM | GP | G | A | Pts | PIM |
| 2004-05 | Hill-Murray | High-MN | 26 | 24 | 19 | 43 | 10 | .... | .... | .... | .... | .... |
| 2005-06 | Hill-Murray | High-MN | 30 | 27 | 46 | 73 | 20 | .... | .... | .... | .... | .... |
| 2006-07 | USNTDP | U-18 | 33 | 10 | 2 | 12 | 18 | .... | .... | .... | .... | .... |
| | USNTDP | NAHL | 11 | 6 | 5 | 11 | 10 | .... | .... | .... | .... | .... |
| 2007-08 | U. of Minnesota | WCHA | 45 | 9 | 10 | 19 | 22 | .... | .... | .... | .... | .... |
| 2008-09 | U. of Minnesota | WCHA | 35 | 12 | 8 | 20 | 38 | .... | .... | .... | .... | .... |

**HOFFMAN, Mike** (HAWF-muhn, MIGHK) **OTT.**

Center/Left wing. Shoots left. 6', 170 lbs. Born, Kitchener, Ont., November 24, 1989.
(Ottawa's 5th choice, 130th overall, in 2009 Entry Draft).

| | | | Regular Season | | | | | Playoffs | | | | |
|---|---|---|---|---|---|---|---|---|---|---|---|---|
| Season | Club | League | GP | G | A | Pts | PIM | GP | G | A | Pts | PIM |
| 2006-07 | Kitchener | OJHL-B | 47 | 28 | 29 | 57 | 70 | 6 | 3 | 5 | 8 | 6 |
| | Kitchener Rangers | OHL | 2 | 0 | 0 | 0 | 2 | 4 | 0 | 0 | 0 | 0 |
| 2007-08 | Gatineau | QMJHL | 19 | 5 | 7 | 12 | 16 | .... | .... | .... | .... | .... |
| | Drummondville | QMJHL | 43 | 19 | 17 | 36 | 77 | .... | .... | .... | .... | .... |
| 2008-09 | Drummondville | QMJHL | 62 | 52 | 42 | 94 | 86 | 19 | 21 | 13 | 34 | 26 |

QMJHL First All-Star Team (2009)

**HOFFMAN, Mike** (HAWF-muhn, MIGHK)

Right wing. Shoots right. 6'5", 250 lbs. Born, Weymouth, MA, September 20, 1980.

| | | | Regular Season | | | | | Playoffs | | | | |
|---|---|---|---|---|---|---|---|---|---|---|---|---|
| Season | Club | League | GP | G | A | Pts | PIM | GP | G | A | Pts | PIM |
| 2002-03 | Connecticut | MAAC | 28 | 2 | 8 | 10 | 24 | .... | .... | .... | .... | .... |
| 2003-04 | Connecticut | MAAC | 3 | 0 | 0 | 0 | 2 | .... | .... | .... | .... | .... |
| | Worcester IceCats | AHL | 15 | 0 | 0 | 0 | 20 | .... | .... | .... | .... | .... |
| | Peoria Rivermen | ECHL | 25 | 2 | 7 | 9 | 16 | 8 | 0 | 1 | 1 | 6 |
| 2004-05 | Cleveland Barons | AHL | 58 | 1 | 7 | 8 | 170 | .... | .... | .... | .... | .... |
| 2005-06 | Toronto Marlies | AHL | 54 | 2 | 5 | 7 | 103 | 1 | 0 | 0 | 0 | 0 |
| 2006-07 | Manchester | AHL | 35 | 6 | 7 | 13 | 96 | .... | .... | .... | .... | .... |
| | Portland Pirates | AHL | 21 | 4 | 5 | 9 | 43 | .... | .... | .... | .... | .... |
| 2007-08 | Portland Pirates | AHL | 38 | 5 | 3 | 8 | 81 | 11 | 1 | 1 | 2 | 11 |
| 2008-09 | Chicago Wolves | AHL | 61 | 2 | 2 | 4 | 89 | .... | .... | .... | .... | .... |

Signed as a free agent by **Cleveland** (AHL), September 22, 2004. Signed as a free agent by **Toronto**, August 12, 2005. Signed to a PTO (tryout) contract by **Manchester** (AHL), October 25, 2006. Signed as a free agent by **Anaheim**, February 23, 2007. Signed as a free agent by **Atlanta**, July 9, 2008.

**HOLDEN, Nick** (HOHL-dehn, NIHK) **CBJ**

Defense. Shoots left. 6'4", 200 lbs. Born, St. Albert, Alta., May 15, 1987.

| | | | Regular Season | | | | | Playoffs | | | | |
|---|---|---|---|---|---|---|---|---|---|---|---|---|
| Season | Club | League | GP | G | A | Pts | PIM | GP | G | A | Pts | PIM |
| 2004-05 | Camrose Kodiaks | AJHL | 4 | 0 | 0 | 0 | 0 | .... | .... | .... | .... | .... |
| 2005-06 | Sherwood Park | AJHL | 57 | 7 | 23 | 30 | 46 | .... | .... | .... | .... | .... |
| 2006-07 | Chilliwack Bruins | WHL | 67 | 8 | 23 | 31 | 62 | 5 | 1 | 1 | 2 | 6 |
| 2007-08 | Chilliwack Bruins | WHL | 70 | 22 | 38 | 60 | 54 | 4 | 1 | 3 | 4 | 0 |
| | Syracuse Crunch | AHL | 1 | 0 | 0 | 0 | 2 | .... | .... | .... | .... | .... |
| 2008-09 | Syracuse Crunch | AHL | 61 | 4 | 18 | 22 | 46 | .... | .... | .... | .... | .... |

Signed as a free agent by **Columbus**, March 28, 2008.

**HOLLAND, Peter** (HAW-luhnd, PEE-tuhr) **ANA.**

Center. Shoots left. 6'2", 185 lbs. Born, Toronto, Ont., January 14, 1991.
(Anaheim's 1st choice, 15th overall, in 2009 Entry Draft).

| | | | Regular Season | | | | | Playoffs | | | | |
|---|---|---|---|---|---|---|---|---|---|---|---|---|
| Season | Club | League | GP | G | A | Pts | PIM | GP | G | A | Pts | PIM |
| 2006-07 | Brampton | Minor-ON | 60 | 59 | 60 | 119 | 107 | .... | .... | .... | .... | .... |
| 2007-08 | Guelph Storm | OHL | 62 | 8 | 15 | 23 | 31 | 10 | 0 | 1 | 1 | 4 |
| 2008-09 | Guelph Storm | OHL | 68 | 28 | 39 | 67 | 42 | 4 | 4 | 0 | 4 | 2 |

**HOLLOWAY, Bud** (HAHL-OH-way, BUHD) **L.A.**

Center. Shoots right. 6'1", 196 lbs. Born, Wapella, Sask., March 1, 1988.
(Los Angeles' 5th choice, 86th overall, in 2006 Entry Draft).

| | | | Regular Season | | | | | Playoffs | | | | |
|---|---|---|---|---|---|---|---|---|---|---|---|---|
| Season | Club | League | GP | G | A | Pts | PIM | GP | G | A | Pts | PIM |
| 2003-04 | Yorkton Harvest | SMHL | 43 | 15 | 21 | 36 | 22 | .... | .... | .... | .... | .... |
| | Seattle | WHL | 2 | 0 | 0 | 0 | 0 | .... | .... | .... | .... | .... |
| 2004-05 | Seattle | WHL | 67 | 4 | 11 | 15 | 27 | 12 | 0 | 1 | 1 | 0 |
| 2005-06 | Seattle | WHL | 72 | 21 | 13 | 34 | 18 | 7 | 3 | 2 | 5 | 4 |
| 2006-07 | Seattle | WHL | 71 | 27 | 38 | 65 | 50 | 11 | 3 | 3 | 6 | 8 |
| 2007-08 | Seattle | WHL | 70 | 43 | 40 | 83 | 55 | 12 | 5 | 5 | 10 | 4 |
| 2008-09 | Manchester | AHL | 38 | 7 | 5 | 12 | 6 | .... | .... | .... | .... | .... |
| | Ontario Reign | ECHL | 23 | 14 | 8 | 22 | 8 | 7 | 5 | 9 | 14 | 8 |

**HOLOS, Jonas** (hoh-LAWS, YOH-nuhs) **COL.**

Defense. Shoots right. 5'11", 196 lbs. Born, Sarpsborg, Norway, August 27, 1987.
(Colorado's 6th choice, 170th overall, in 2008 Entry Draft).

| | | | Regular Season | | | | | Playoffs | | | | |
|---|---|---|---|---|---|---|---|---|---|---|---|---|
| Season | Club | League | GP | G | A | Pts | PIM | GP | G | A | Pts | PIM |
| 2002-03 | Sarpsborg Jr. | Norway-Jr. | 20 | 1 | 1 | 2 | 0 | .... | .... | .... | .... | .... |
| 2003-04 | Sarpsborg Jr. | Norway-Jr. | 35 | 10 | 7 | 17 | 24 | 1 | 0 | 1 | 1 | 2 |
| | Sarpsborg | Norway | 1 | 0 | 0 | 0 | 0 | .... | .... | .... | .... | .... |
| 2004-05 | Sarpsborg Jr. | Norway-Jr. | 1 | 1 | 1 | 2 | 0 | 1 | 0 | 0 | 0 | 0 |
| | Sarpsborg | Norway | 41 | 3 | 2 | 5 | 18 | 4 | 0 | 0 | 0 | 2 |
| 2005-06 | Sarpsborg | Norway | 26 | 3 | 4 | 7 | 14 | 6 | 0 | 0 | 0 | 0 |
| 2006-07 | Sarpsborg 2 | Norway-2 | 1 | 2 | 0 | 2 | 0 | .... | .... | .... | .... | .... |
| | Sarpsborg | Norway | 40 | 11 | 19 | 30 | 32 | 13 | 2 | 2 | 4 | 18 |
| 2007-08 | Sarpsborg | Norway | 40 | 2 | 20 | 22 | 67 | 6 | 1 | 0 | 1 | 2 |
| 2008-09 | Farjestad | Sweden | 55 | 8 | 8 | 16 | 12 | 13 | 3 | 3 | 6 | 8 |

**HOLZAPFEL, Riley** (HOHL-za-fehl, RIGH-lee) **ATL.**

Center. Shoots left. 6', 190 lbs. Born, Regina, Sask., August 18, 1988.
(Atlanta's 2nd choice, 43rd overall, in 2006 Entry Draft).

| | | | Regular Season | | | | | Playoffs | | | | |
|---|---|---|---|---|---|---|---|---|---|---|---|---|
| Season | Club | League | GP | G | A | Pts | PIM | GP | G | A | Pts | PIM |
| 2004-05 | Moose Jaw | WHL | 63 | 15 | 13 | 28 | 32 | 5 | 1 | 2 | 3 | 8 |
| 2005-06 | Moose Jaw | WHL | 64 | 19 | 38 | 57 | 46 | 22 | 7 | 9 | 16 | 20 |
| 2006-07 | Moose Jaw | WHL | 72 | 39 | 43 | 82 | 94 | .... | .... | .... | .... | .... |
| 2007-08 | Moose Jaw | WHL | 49 | 18 | 23 | 41 | 43 | 6 | 3 | 5 | 8 | 12 |
| | Chicago Wolves | AHL | 1 | 0 | 0 | 0 | 0 | .... | .... | .... | .... | .... |
| 2008-09 | Chicago Wolves | AHL | 73 | 13 | 19 | 32 | 38 | .... | .... | .... | .... | .... |

WHL East First All-Star Team (2007)

**HOLZER, Korbinian** (HOHL-zuhr, kohr-BEEHN-yuhn) **TOR.**

Defense. Shoots right. 6'3", 190 lbs. Born, Munich, West Germany, February 16, 1988.
(Toronto's 4th choice, 111th overall, in 2006 Entry Draft).

| | | | Regular Season | | | | | Playoffs | | | | |
|---|---|---|---|---|---|---|---|---|---|---|---|---|
| Season | Club | League | GP | G | A | Pts | PIM | GP | G | A | Pts | PIM |
| 2004-05 | EC Bad Tolz Jr. | Ger-Jr. | 34 | 7 | 11 | 18 | 66 | 5 | 0 | 2 | 2 | 2 |
| 2005-06 | EC Bad Tolz Jr. | Ger-Jr. | 2 | 1 | 1 | 2 | 6 | .... | .... | .... | .... | .... |
| | Tolzer Lowen | German-2 | 46 | 3 | 3 | 6 | 94 | .... | .... | .... | .... | .... |
| 2006-07 | Regensburg | German-2 | 42 | 2 | 6 | 8 | 68 | 4 | 0 | 0 | 0 | 2 |
| 2007-08 | Dusseldorf | Germany | 35 | 2 | 5 | 7 | 66 | 13 | 0 | 2 | 2 | 20 |
| 2008-09 | Dusseldorf | Germany | 38 | 4 | 5 | 9 | 89 | 16 | 0 | 1 | 1 | 18 |

**HORAK, Roman** (HOH-rak, ROH-muhn) **NYR**

Center. Shoots left. 6', 189 lbs. Born, Ceske Budejovice, Czechoslovakia, May 21, 1991.
(NY Rangers' 4th choice, 127th overall, in 2009 Entry Draft).

| | | | Regular Season | | | | | Playoffs | | | | |
|---|---|---|---|---|---|---|---|---|---|---|---|---|
| **Season** | **Club** | **League** | **GP** | **G** | **A** | **Pts** | **PIM** | **GP** | **G** | **A** | **Pts** | **PIM** |
| 2004-05 | C. Budejovice U17 | CzR-U17 | 2 | 0 | 0 | 0 | 0 | .... | .... | .... | .... | .... |
| 2005-06 | C. Budejovice U17 | CzR-U17 | 34 | 5 | 3 | 8 | 10 | 3 | 0 | 0 | 0 | 4 |
| 2006-07 | C. Budejovice U17 | CzR-U17 | 24 | 22 | 16 | 38 | 38 | 2 | 1 | 0 | 1 | 4 |
| | C. Budejovice Jr. | CzRep-Jr. | 16 | 1 | 4 | 5 | 6 | 1 | 0 | 0 | 0 | 0 |
| 2007-08 | C. Budejovice U17 | CzR-U17 | 2 | 3 | 2 | 5 | 0 | .... | .... | .... | .... | .... |
| | C. Budejovice Jr. | CzRep-Jr. | 34 | 17 | 11 | 28 | 14 | 3 | 0 | 1 | 1 | 0 |
| | C. Budejovice | CzRep | 1 | 0 | 0 | 0 | 0 | .... | .... | .... | .... | .... |
| 2008-09 | C. Budejovice Jr. | CzRep-Jr. | 31 | 16 | 17 | 33 | 14 | 2 | 0 | 0 | 0 | 0 |
| | C. Budejovice | CzRep | 17 | 1 | 0 | 1 | 0 | .... | .... | .... | .... | .... |

**HOWSE, Ryan** (HOWS, RIGH-uhn) **CGY.**

Left wing. Shoots left. 5'11", 195 lbs. Born, Prince George, B.C., July 6, 1991.
(Calgary's 2nd choice, 74th overall, in 2009 Entry Draft).

| | | | Regular Season | | | | | Playoffs | | | | |
|---|---|---|---|---|---|---|---|---|---|---|---|---|
| **Season** | **Club** | **League** | **GP** | **G** | **A** | **Pts** | **PIM** | **GP** | **G** | **A** | **Pts** | **PIM** |
| 2006-07 | Cariboo Cougars | Minor-BC | 30 | 21 | 16 | 37 | 40 | .... | .... | .... | .... | .... |
| | Chilliwack Bruins | WHL | 5 | 1 | 0 | 1 | 2 | 1 | 0 | 0 | 0 | 0 |
| 2007-08 | Chilliwack Bruins | WHL | 54 | 10 | 7 | 17 | 12 | 4 | 1 | 1 | 2 | 2 |
| 2008-09 | Chilliwack Bruins | WHL | 61 | 31 | 13 | 44 | 12 | .... | .... | .... | .... | .... |

**HRABAL, Josef** (huh-RA-buhl, YOH-sehf) **EDM.**

Defense. Shoots left. 6'1", 176 lbs. Born, Prerov, Czech., August 17, 1985.
(Edmonton's 11th choice, 248th overall, in 2003 Entry Draft).

| | | | Regular Season | | | | | Playoffs | | | | |
|---|---|---|---|---|---|---|---|---|---|---|---|---|
| **Season** | **Club** | **League** | **GP** | **G** | **A** | **Pts** | **PIM** | **GP** | **G** | **A** | **Pts** | **PIM** |
| 2001-02 | HC Vsetin U17 | CzR-U17 | 38 | 4 | 2 | 6 | 18 | .... | .... | .... | .... | .... |
| 2002-03 | HC Vsetin Jr. | CzRep-Jr. | 30 | 6 | 7 | 13 | 12 | 9 | 2 | 4 | 6 | 10 |
| | HC Vsetin | CzRep | 6 | 0 | 0 | 0 | 4 | .... | .... | .... | .... | .... |
| 2003-04 | HC Vsetin Jr. | CzRep-Jr. | 46 | 12 | 8 | 20 | 54 | 7 | 1 | 0 | 1 | 2 |
| | HC Vsetin | CzRep | 13 | 0 | 0 | 0 | 2 | .... | .... | .... | .... | .... |
| 2004-05 | HC Vsetin | CzRep | 23 | 0 | 2 | 2 | 8 | .... | .... | .... | .... | .... |
| | HC Kometa Brno | CzRep-2 | 1 | 0 | 0 | 0 | 0 | .... | .... | .... | .... | .... |
| | HC Olomouc | CzRep-2 | 7 | 0 | 0 | 0 | 6 | .... | .... | .... | .... | .... |
| | HC Vsetin Jr. | CzRep-Jr. | 19 | 6 | 8 | 14 | 42 | 8 | 3 | 4 | 7 | 16 |
| 2005-06 | HC Vsetin | CzRep | 34 | 3 | 9 | 12 | 34 | .... | .... | .... | .... | .... |
| | HC Vsetin Jr. | CzRep-Jr. | 1 | 1 | 0 | 1 | 2 | .... | .... | .... | .... | .... |
| | HC Vsetin | CzRep-Q | .... | .... | .... | .... | .... | 6 | 0 | 2 | 2 | 2 |
| 2006-07 | Cherepovets | Russia | 20 | 3 | 4 | 7 | 24 | 5 | 0 | 1 | 1 | 2 |
| | HC Vsetin | CzRep | 21 | 3 | 7 | 10 | 30 | .... | .... | .... | .... | .... |
| 2007-08 | Cherepovets | Russia | 56 | 3 | 11 | 14 | 73 | 8 | 0 | 1 | 1 | 12 |
| 2008-09 | MODO | Sweden | 6 | 0 | 1 | 1 | 2 | .... | .... | .... | .... | .... |
| | Stockton Thunder | ECHL | 8 | 0 | 4 | 4 | 8 | .... | .... | .... | .... | .... |
| | Springfield Falcons | AHL | 17 | 0 | 1 | 1 | 14 | .... | .... | .... | .... | .... |

**HROMAS, Karel** (huh-ROM-mahs, KAH-rehl) **CHI.**

Left wing. Shoots left. 6'2", 208 lbs. Born, Beroun, Czech., January 27, 1986.
(Chicago's 8th choice, 123rd overall, in 2004 Entry Draft).

| | | | Regular Season | | | | | Playoffs | | | | |
|---|---|---|---|---|---|---|---|---|---|---|---|---|
| **Season** | **Club** | **League** | **GP** | **G** | **A** | **Pts** | **PIM** | **GP** | **G** | **A** | **Pts** | **PIM** |
| 2000-01 | Sparta U17 | CzR-U17 | 34 | 4 | 18 | 22 | 6 | .... | .... | .... | .... | .... |
| 2001-02 | Sparta U17 | CzR-U17 | 39 | 19 | 15 | 34 | 55 | 6 | 3 | 2 | 5 | 6 |
| 2002-03 | Sparta U17 | CzR-U17 | 1 | 3 | 1 | 4 | 0 | .... | .... | .... | .... | .... |
| | Sparta Jr. | CzRep-Jr. | 32 | 6 | 7 | 13 | 14 | 3 | 0 | 1 | 1 | 4 |
| 2003-04 | Sparta Jr. | CzRep-Jr. | 21 | 10 | 10 | 20 | 16 | .... | .... | .... | .... | .... |
| | HC Sparta Praha | CzRep | 13 | 0 | 0 | 0 | 0 | 2 | 0 | 0 | 0 | 0 |
| 2004-05 | Everett Silvertips | WHL | 65 | 18 | 11 | 29 | 22 | 11 | 2 | 2 | 4 | 4 |
| 2005-06 | Everett Silvertips | WHL | 52 | 11 | 11 | 22 | 14 | 14 | 2 | 0 | 2 | 10 |
| 2006-07 | HC Sparta Praha | CzRep | 48 | 1 | 0 | 1 | 20 | 11 | 1 | 0 | 1 | 0 |
| 2007-08 | HC Sparta Praha | CzRep | 52 | 0 | 1 | 1 | 42 | 4 | 0 | 0 | 0 | 0 |
| 2008-09 | HC Sparta Praha | CzRep | 52 | 2 | 4 | 6 | 64 | 11 | 0 | 3 | 3 | 20 |

**HUGHES, Bobby** (HEWZ, BAW-bee) **CAR.**

Center. Shoots left. 5'10", 180 lbs. Born, Richmond Hill, Ont., November 11, 1987.
(Carolina's 3rd choice, 123rd overall, in 2006 Entry Draft).

| | | | Regular Season | | | | | Playoffs | | | | |
|---|---|---|---|---|---|---|---|---|---|---|---|---|
| **Season** | **Club** | **League** | **GP** | **G** | **A** | **Pts** | **PIM** | **GP** | **G** | **A** | **Pts** | **PIM** |
| 2003-04 | Kingston | OHL | 62 | 11 | 16 | 27 | 20 | 5 | 0 | 1 | 1 | 2 |
| 2004-05 | Kingston | OHL | 66 | 17 | 38 | 55 | 36 | .... | .... | .... | .... | .... |
| 2005-06 | Kingston | OHL | 56 | 35 | 40 | 75 | 47 | 6 | 1 | 1 | 2 | 4 |
| 2006-07 | Kingston | OHL | 59 | 40 | 56 | 96 | 76 | 5 | 0 | 3 | 3 | 0 |
| | Albany River Rats | AHL | .... | .... | .... | .... | .... | 1 | 0 | 0 | 0 | 0 |
| 2007-08 | Albany River Rats | AHL | 26 | 6 | 10 | 16 | 4 | .... | .... | .... | .... | .... |
| 2008-09 | Albany River Rats | AHL | 27 | 4 | 3 | 7 | 8 | .... | .... | .... | .... | .... |
| | Florida Everblades | ECHL | 2 | 0 | 1 | 1 | 0 | .... | .... | .... | .... | .... |

**HUNTER, Dylan** (HUHN-tuhr, DIH-luhn)

Left wing. Shoots left. 5'11", 198 lbs. Born, Quebec City, Que., May 21, 1985.
(Buffalo's 8th choice, 273rd overall, in 2004 Entry Draft).

| | | | Regular Season | | | | | Playoffs | | | | |
|---|---|---|---|---|---|---|---|---|---|---|---|---|
| **Season** | **Club** | **League** | **GP** | **G** | **A** | **Pts** | **PIM** | **GP** | **G** | **A** | **Pts** | **PIM** |
| 2001-02 | London Knights | OHL | 54 | 6 | 21 | 27 | 38 | 6 | 1 | 1 | 2 | 10 |
| 2002-03 | London Knights | OHL | 68 | 11 | 31 | 42 | 41 | 14 | 3 | 3 | 6 | 8 |
| 2003-04 | London Knights | OHL | 64 | 26 | 53 | 79 | 47 | 15 | 4 | 10 | 14 | 10 |
| 2004-05 | London Knights | OHL | 67 | 31 | 73 | 104 | 64 | 18 | 10 | 11 | 21 | 16 |
| 2005-06 | London Knights | OHL | 62 | 32 | 85 | 117 | 50 | 19 | 13 | 23 | 36 | 16 |
| 2006-07 | Rochester | AHL | 67 | 8 | 20 | 28 | 42 | 6 | 1 | 2 | 3 | 2 |
| 2007-08 | Rochester | AHL | 70 | 20 | 27 | 47 | 69 | .... | .... | .... | .... | .... |
| 2008-09 | Portland Pirates | AHL | 45 | 3 | 13 | 16 | 24 | .... | .... | .... | .... | .... |

OHL First All-Star Team (2005) • OHL Second All-Star Team (2006)

**HUTCHINGS, Alex** (HUH-chihngz, Al-ehx) **T.B.**

Left wing. Shoots right. 5'10", 173 lbs. Born, Burlington, Ont., November 7, 1990.
(Tampa Bay's 4th choice, 93rd overall, in 2009 Entry Draft).

| | | | Regular Season | | | | | Playoffs | | | | |
|---|---|---|---|---|---|---|---|---|---|---|---|---|
| **Season** | **Club** | **League** | **GP** | **G** | **A** | **Pts** | **PIM** | **GP** | **G** | **A** | **Pts** | **PIM** |
| 2006-07 | Barrie Colts | OHL | 30 | 1 | 4 | 5 | 24 | .... | .... | .... | .... | .... |
| 2007-08 | Barrie Colts | OHL | 68 | 29 | 25 | 54 | 48 | 9 | 0 | 5 | 5 | 18 |
| 2008-09 | Barrie Colts | OHL | 63 | 34 | 34 | 68 | 60 | 5 | 3 | 4 | 7 | 6 |

**IGNATUSHKIN, Igor** (ihg-nah-TOOSH-kihn, EE-gohr) **WSH.**

Center. Shoots left. 5'11", 161 lbs. Born, Elektrostal, USSR, April 7, 1984.
(Washington's 12th choice, 242nd overall, in 2002 Entry Draft).

| | | | Regular Season | | | | | Playoffs | | | | |
|---|---|---|---|---|---|---|---|---|---|---|---|---|
| **Season** | **Club** | **League** | **GP** | **G** | **A** | **Pts** | **PIM** | **GP** | **G** | **A** | **Pts** | **PIM** |
| 99-2000 | Elektrostal 2 | Russia-3 | 5 | 0 | 0 | 0 | 0 | .... | .... | .... | .... | .... |
| 2000-01 | Team Center 84 | Exhib. | 5 | 1 | 1 | 2 | 0 | .... | .... | .... | .... | .... |
| | Elektrostal 2 | Russia-3 | | STATISTICS NOT AVAILABLE | | | | | | | | |
| 2001-02 | Elektrostal 2 | Russia-3 | 6 | 2 | 3 | 5 | 6 | .... | .... | .... | .... | .... |
| | Elektrostal | Russia-2 | 46 | 1 | 4 | 5 | 20 | .... | .... | .... | .... | .... |
| 2002-03 | Elektrostal | Russia-2 | 36 | 9 | 10 | 19 | 8 | .... | .... | .... | .... | .... |
| 2003-04 | Kristall Elektrostal | Russia-2 | 49 | 6 | 2 | 8 | 22 | .... | .... | .... | .... | .... |
| 2004-05 | Kristall Elektrostal | Russia-2 | 45 | 9 | 3 | 12 | 28 | .... | .... | .... | .... | .... |
| | Leninogorsk | Russia-2 | 6 | 1 | 1 | 2 | 6 | 4 | 1 | 0 | 1 | 4 |
| 2005-06 | Mytischi | Russia | 7 | 0 | 0 | 0 | 2 | .... | .... | .... | .... | .... |
| | Kristall Elektrostal | Russia-3 | | STATISTICS NOT AVAILABLE | | | | | | | | |
| 2006-07 | Kristall Elektrostal | Russia-2 | 49 | 14 | 23 | 37 | 48 | .... | .... | .... | .... | .... |
| 2007-08 | Khabarovsk 2 | Russia-3 | 2 | 0 | 0 | 0 | 0 | .... | .... | .... | .... | .... |
| | Amur Khabarovsk | Russia | 49 | 4 | 4 | 8 | 12 | 4 | 0 | 0 | 0 | 2 |
| 2008-09 | Amur Khabarovsk | Rus-KHL | 49 | 6 | 8 | 14 | 16 | .... | .... | .... | .... | .... |

**ILLO, Radoslav** (IHL-oh, RAD-oh-slav) **ANA.**

Center. Shoots left. 6', 178 lbs. Born, Povazska Bystrica, Czechoslovakia, January 21, 1990.
(Anaheim's 6th choice, 136th overall, in 2009 Entry Draft).

| | | | Regular Season | | | | | Playoffs | | | | |
|---|---|---|---|---|---|---|---|---|---|---|---|---|
| **Season** | **Club** | **League** | **GP** | **G** | **A** | **Pts** | **PIM** | **GP** | **G** | **A** | **Pts** | **PIM** |
| 2005-06 | P. Bystrica U18 | Svk-U18 | 4 | 1 | 1 | 2 | 2 | .... | .... | .... | .... | .... |
| 2006-07 | Bratislava U18 | Svk-U18 | 26 | 9 | 14 | 23 | 12 | .... | .... | .... | .... | .... |
| 2007-08 | Hampton Roads | MJHL | .... | 48 | 38 | 86 | .... | .... | .... | .... | .... | .... |
| 2008-09 | Tri-City Storm | USHL | 47 | 21 | 12 | 33 | 37 | .... | .... | .... | .... | .... |

**ILVONEN, Harri** (ihl-VOH-nehn, HAIR-ree) **MIN.**

Defense. Shoots left. 6'2", 187 lbs. Born, Helsinki, Finland, November 3, 1988.
(Minnesota's 4th choice, 170th overall, in 2007 Entry Draft).

| | | | Regular Season | | | | | Playoffs | | | | |
|---|---|---|---|---|---|---|---|---|---|---|---|---|
| **Season** | **Club** | **League** | **GP** | **G** | **A** | **Pts** | **PIM** | **GP** | **G** | **A** | **Pts** | **PIM** |
| 2004-05 | Tappara U18 | Fin-U18 | 27 | 2 | 10 | 12 | 14 | 2 | 0 | 0 | 0 | 2 |
| 2005-06 | Tappara U18 | Fin-U18 | 10 | 3 | 5 | 8 | 10 | 3 | 0 | 2 | 2 | 4 |
| | Tappara Jr. | Fin-Jr. | 24 | 2 | 1 | 3 | 24 | .... | .... | .... | .... | .... |
| 2006-07 | Tappara Jr. | Fin-Jr. | 39 | 9 | 21 | 30 | 38 | 10 | 0 | 2 | 2 | 22 |
| | Suomi U20 | Finland-2 | 10 | 0 | 2 | 2 | 12 | .... | .... | .... | .... | .... |
| | Tappara Tampere | Finland | 7 | 0 | 0 | 0 | 2 | .... | .... | .... | .... | .... |
| 2007-08 | Suomi U20 | Finland-2 | 4 | 0 | 2 | 2 | 2 | .... | .... | .... | .... | .... |
| | Tappara Jr. | Fin-Jr. | 14 | 2 | 10 | 12 | 22 | .... | .... | .... | .... | .... |
| | Tappara Tampere | Finland | 2 | 0 | 0 | 0 | 0 | .... | .... | .... | .... | .... |
| | LeKi Lempaala | Finland-2 | 7 | 0 | 1 | 1 | 4 | .... | .... | .... | .... | .... |
| | HPK Hameenlinna | Finland | 9 | 2 | 2 | 4 | 2 | .... | .... | .... | .... | .... |
| 2008-09 | LeKi Lempaala | Finland-2 | 21 | 4 | 3 | 7 | 8 | .... | .... | .... | .... | .... |

**IRMEN, Danny** (UHR-mehn, DA-nee) **MIN.**

Center. Shoots right. 6', 190 lbs. Born, Fargo, ND, September 6, 1984.
(Minnesota's 3rd choice, 78th overall, in 2003 Entry Draft).

| | | | Regular Season | | | | | Playoffs | | | | |
|---|---|---|---|---|---|---|---|---|---|---|---|---|
| **Season** | **Club** | **League** | **GP** | **G** | **A** | **Pts** | **PIM** | **GP** | **G** | **A** | **Pts** | **PIM** |
| 2001-02 | Lincoln Stars | USHL | 61 | 17 | 36 | 53 | .... | .... | .... | .... | .... | .... |
| 2002-03 | Lincoln Stars | USHL | 45 | 21 | 34 | 55 | 78 | 10 | 8 | 6 | 14 | 17 |
| 2003-04 | U. of Minnesota | WCHA | 44 | 14 | 8 | 22 | 40 | .... | .... | .... | .... | .... |
| 2004-05 | U. of Minnesota | WCHA | 44 | 24 | 19 | 43 | 66 | .... | .... | .... | .... | .... |
| 2005-06 | U. of Minnesota | WCHA | 30 | 16 | 22 | 38 | 40 | .... | .... | .... | .... | .... |
| | Houston Aeros | AHL | 4 | 0 | 2 | 2 | 0 | 7 | 0 | 0 | 0 | 4 |
| 2006-07 | Houston Aeros | AHL | 80 | 17 | 20 | 37 | 45 | .... | .... | .... | .... | .... |
| 2007-08 | Houston Aeros | AHL | 77 | 10 | 13 | 23 | 51 | 5 | 0 | 1 | 1 | 0 |
| 2008-09 | Houston Aeros | AHL | 69 | 7 | 11 | 18 | 39 | 20 | 2 | 0 | 2 | 8 |

USHL Second All-Star Team (2003) • USHL Playoff MVP (2003)

**ISAKOV, Evgeni** (ih-SA-kawf, ehv-GEH-nee) **PIT.**

Right wing. Shoots left. 6'1", 196 lbs. Born, Krasnoyarsk, USSR, October 13, 1984.
(Pittsburgh's 6th choice, 161st overall, in 2003 Entry Draft).

| | | | Regular Season | | | | | Playoffs | | | | |
|---|---|---|---|---|---|---|---|---|---|---|---|---|
| **Season** | **Club** | **League** | **GP** | **G** | **A** | **Pts** | **PIM** | **GP** | **G** | **A** | **Pts** | **PIM** |
| 99-2000 | Rubin Tyumen 2 | Russia-3 | 7 | 0 | 2 | 2 | 16 | .... | .... | .... | .... | .... |
| 2000-01 | Rubin Tyumen 2 | Russia-3 | .... | .... | .... | .... | .... | .... | .... | .... | .... | .... |
| | Gazovik Tyumen | Russia-3 | 11 | 1 | 1 | 2 | 12 | .... | .... | .... | .... | .... |
| 2001-02 | Gazovik Tyumen | Russia-2 | 19 | 2 | 2 | 4 | 2 | .... | .... | .... | .... | .... |
| | Elektrostal | Russia-2 | 29 | 3 | 2 | 5 | 24 | .... | .... | .... | .... | .... |
| | Elektrostal 2 | Russia-3 | 11 | 3 | 3 | 6 | 43 | .... | .... | .... | .... | .... |
| 2002-03 | Cherepovets | Russia | 36 | 0 | 3 | 3 | 12 | 1 | 0 | 0 | 0 | 0 |
| 2003-04 | Cherepovets | Russia | 38 | 3 | 2 | 5 | 18 | .... | .... | .... | .... | .... |
| | Cherepovets 2 | Russia-3 | 14 | 4 | 8 | 12 | 48 | .... | .... | .... | .... | .... |
| 2004-05 | Kristall Saratov | Russia-2 | 1 | 0 | 0 | 0 | 0 | .... | .... | .... | .... | .... |
| | Tyumen 2 | Russia-3 | 2 | 1 | 3 | 4 | 14 | .... | .... | .... | .... | .... |
| | Gazovik Tyumen | Russia-2 | 4 | 0 | 2 | 2 | 2 | 3 | 0 | 0 | 0 | 2 |
| 2005-06 | Gazovik Tyumen | Russia-2 | 46 | 9 | 12 | 21 | 90 | 3 | 0 | 0 | 0 | 6 |
| 2006-07 | Gazovik Tyumen | Russia-2 | 51 | 6 | 11 | 17 | 48 | .... | .... | .... | .... | .... |
| | Tyumen 2 | Russia-3 | 2 | 1 | 2 | 3 | 0 | .... | .... | .... | .... | .... |
| 2007-08 | Gazovik Tyumen | Russia-2 | 43 | 10 | 11 | 21 | 119 | .... | .... | .... | .... | .... |
| 2008-09 | Khanty-Mansiisk | Russia-2 | 18 | 1 | 4 | 5 | 12 | .... | .... | .... | .... | .... |
| | Metallurg Serov | Russia-2 | 33 | 11 | 18 | 29 | 40 | 3 | 1 | 0 | 1 | 22 |

**JACKSON, Scott** (JAK-suhn, SKAWT) **T.B.**

Defense. Shoots left. 6'4", 213 lbs. Born, Salmon Arm, B.C., February 5, 1987.
(St. Louis' 2nd choice, 37th overall, in 2005 Entry Draft).

| | | | Regular Season | | | | | Playoffs | | | | |
|---|---|---|---|---|---|---|---|---|---|---|---|---|
| **Season** | **Club** | **League** | **GP** | **G** | **A** | **Pts** | **PIM** | **GP** | **G** | **A** | **Pts** | **PIM** |
| 2002-03 | Sicamous Eagles | KIJHL | 45 | 2 | 20 | 22 | 20 | .... | .... | .... | .... | .... |
| | Seattle | WHL | 2 | 0 | 0 | 0 | 2 | .... | .... | .... | .... | .... |
| 2003-04 | Seattle | WHL | 66 | 4 | 9 | 13 | 17 | .... | .... | .... | .... | .... |
| 2004-05 | Seattle | WHL | 72 | 6 | 16 | 22 | 46 | 12 | 1 | 2 | 3 | 4 |
| 2005-06 | Seattle | WHL | 57 | 3 | 23 | 26 | 48 | 7 | 1 | 4 | 5 | 12 |
| 2006-07 | Seattle | WHL | 71 | 4 | 31 | 35 | 52 | 11 | 0 | 5 | 5 | 9 |
| 2007-08 | Seattle | WHL | 58 | 6 | 17 | 23 | 44 | 12 | 2 | 2 | 4 | 8 |
| 2008-09 | Norfolk Admirals | AHL | 34 | 0 | 4 | 4 | 14 | .... | .... | .... | .... | .... |
| | Mississippi | ECHL | 3 | 1 | 0 | 1 | 2 | .... | .... | .... | .... | .... |

Signed as a free agent by **Tampa Bay**, July 3, 2008.

**JENKS, A.J.** (JEHKS, AY-JAY) **FLA.**

Left wing. Shoots left. 6'2", 206 lbs. Born, Detroit, MI, June 27, 1990.
(Florida's 4th choice, 100th overall, in 2008 Entry Draft).

| | | | Regular Season | | | | | Playoffs | | | | |
|---|---|---|---|---|---|---|---|---|---|---|---|---|
| Season | Club | League | GP | G | A | Pts | PIM | GP | G | A | Pts | PIM |
| 2004-05 | Det. Compuware | MWEHL | 28 | 7 | 12 | 19 | 54 | .... | .... | .... | .... | .... |
| 2005-06 | Det. Honeybaked | MWEHL | 21 | 7 | 10 | 17 | 23 | .... | .... | .... | .... | .... |
| 2006-07 | Plymouth Whalers | OHL | 68 | 9 | 14 | 23 | 50 | 20 | 0 | 1 | 1 | 8 |
| 2007-08 | Plymouth Whalers | OHL | 68 | 26 | 29 | 55 | 94 | 4 | 1 | 0 | 1 | 4 |
| 2008-09 | Plymouth Whalers | OHL | 61 | 21 | 31 | 52 | 78 | 11 | 1 | 2 | 3 | 18 |

**JENSEN, Christian** (JEHN-suhn, KRIHS-tyehn) **S.J.**

Defense. Shoots right. 6'3", 190 lbs. Born, Brooklyn, NY, January 6, 1986.
(San Jose's 10th choice, 289th overall, in 2004 Entry Draft).

| | | | Regular Season | | | | | Playoffs | | | | |
|---|---|---|---|---|---|---|---|---|---|---|---|---|
| Season | Club | League | GP | G | A | Pts | PIM | GP | G | A | Pts | PIM |
| 2003-04 | New Jersey Jrs. | AtJHL | 48 | 6 | 23 | 29 | 62 | .... | .... | .... | .... | .... |
| 2004-05 | Jersey Hitmen | EJHL | 48 | 1 | 9 | 10 | 22 | .... | .... | .... | .... | .... |
| 2005-06 | Chicago Steel | USHL | 24 | 0 | 4 | 4 | 8 | .... | .... | .... | .... | .... |
| | Waterloo | USHL | 18 | 1 | 4 | 5 | 14 | .... | .... | .... | .... | .... |
| 2006-07 | RPI Engineers | ECAC | 24 | 1 | 3 | 4 | 28 | .... | .... | .... | .... | .... |
| 2007-08 | RPI Engineers | ECAC | 31 | 2 | 5 | 7 | 41 | .... | .... | .... | .... | .... |
| 2008-09 | RPI Engineers | ECAC | 6 | 1 | 0 | 1 | 8 | .... | .... | .... | .... | .... |

**JENSEN, Nick** (JEHN-suhn, NIHK) **DET.**

Defense. Shoots right. 6'1", 187 lbs. Born, St. Paul, MN, September 21, 1990.
(Detroit's 5th choice, 150th overall, in 2009 Entry Draft).

| | | | Regular Season | | | | | Playoffs | | | | |
|---|---|---|---|---|---|---|---|---|---|---|---|---|
| Season | Club | League | GP | G | A | Pts | PIM | GP | G | A | Pts | PIM |
| 2006-07 | Rogers Royals | High-MN | 21 | 20 | 17 | 37 | .... | .... | .... | .... | .... | .... |
| 2007-08 | Rogers Royals | High-MN | 14 | 14 | 13 | 27 | .... | .... | .... | .... | .... | .... |
| 2008-09 | Green Bay | USHL | 52 | 5 | 17 | 22 | 27 | 7 | 0 | 1 | 1 | 2 |

• Signed Letter of Intent to attend **St. Cloud State University** (WCHA) in fall of 2009.

**JESSIMAN, Hugh** (JEHS-ih-muhn, HEW) **NSH.**

Right wing. Shoots right. 6'6", 235 lbs. Born, New York, NY, March 28, 1984.
(NY Rangers' 1st choice, 12th overall, in 2003 Entry Draft).

| | | | Regular Season | | | | | Playoffs | | | | |
|---|---|---|---|---|---|---|---|---|---|---|---|---|
| Season | Club | League | GP | G | A | Pts | PIM | GP | G | A | Pts | PIM |
| 2001-02 | Brunswick Bruins | High-CT | 18 | 25 | 27 | 52 | 40 | .... | .... | .... | .... | .... |
| 2002-03 | Dartmouth | ECAC | 34 | 23 | 24 | 47 | 48 | .... | .... | .... | .... | .... |
| 2003-04 | Dartmouth | ECAC | 34 | 16 | 17 | 33 | 71 | .... | .... | .... | .... | .... |
| 2004-05 | Dartmouth | ECAC | 12 | 1 | 1 | 2 | 18 | .... | .... | .... | .... | .... |
| 2005-06 | Hartford Wolf Pack | AHL | 46 | 7 | 12 | 19 | 66 | 2 | 0 | 0 | 0 | 0 |
| | Charlotte | ECHL | 25 | 13 | 10 | 23 | 56 | .... | .... | .... | .... | .... |
| 2006-07 | Hartford Wolf Pack | AHL | 49 | 7 | 6 | 13 | 79 | 7 | 1 | 0 | 1 | 9 |
| | Charlotte | ECHL | 20 | 12 | 10 | 22 | 52 | .... | .... | .... | .... | .... |
| 2007-08 | Hartford Wolf Pack | AHL | 71 | 18 | 24 | 42 | 154 | 5 | 0 | 1 | 1 | 21 |
| 2008-09 | Hartford Wolf Pack | AHL | 6 | 0 | 0 | 0 | 2 | .... | .... | .... | .... | .... |
| | Milwaukee | AHL | 63 | 20 | 7 | 27 | 100 | 10 | 2 | 0 | 2 | 10 |

ECAC All-Rookie Team (2003) • ECAC Rookie of the Year (2003) • ECAC Second All-Star Team (2004)

Traded to **Nashville** by **NY Rangers** for future considerations, October 30, 2008.

**JOHANSSON, Marcus** (yoh-HAHN-suhn, MAHR-kuhs) **WSH.**

Center. Shoots left. 5'11", 189 lbs. Born, Landskrona, Sweden, October 6, 1990.
(Washington's 1st choice, 24th overall, in 2009 Entry Draft).

| | | | Regular Season | | | | | Playoffs | | | | |
|---|---|---|---|---|---|---|---|---|---|---|---|---|
| Season | Club | League | GP | G | A | Pts | PIM | GP | G | A | Pts | PIM |
| 2005-06 | Malmo U18 | Swe-U18 | 12 | 0 | 7 | 7 | 0 | 6 | 0 | 4 | 4 | 0 |
| 2006-07 | Farjestad U18 | Swe-U18 | 12 | 5 | 9 | 14 | 8 | 8 | 7 | 3 | 10 | 2 |
| 2007-08 | Farjestad U18 | Swe-U18 | 24 | 12 | 26 | 38 | 16 | 8 | 4 | 8 | 12 | 0 |
| | Skare BK | Sweden-3 | 19 | 2 | 10 | 12 | 10 | .... | .... | .... | .... | .... |
| | Farjestad | Sweden | .... | .... | .... | .... | .... | 3 | 0 | 0 | 0 | 0 |
| 2008-09 | Farjestad U18 | Swe-U18 | 2 | 2 | 0 | 2 | 0 | .... | .... | .... | .... | .... |
| | Skare BK Karlstad | Sweden-3 | 5 | 5 | 5 | 10 | 0 | .... | .... | .... | .... | .... |
| | Farjestad | Sweden | 45 | 5 | 5 | 10 | 10 | 6 | 0 | 0 | 0 | 0 |

**JOHANSSON, Mikael** (yoh-HAHN-suhn, MIGH-kuhl) **MTL.**

Center. Shoots left. 5'10", 189 lbs. Born, Arvika, Sweden, June 27, 1985.
(Detroit's 8th choice, 289th overall, in 2003 Entry Draft).

| | | | Regular Season | | | | | Playoffs | | | | |
|---|---|---|---|---|---|---|---|---|---|---|---|---|
| Season | Club | League | GP | G | A | Pts | PIM | GP | G | A | Pts | PIM |
| 2001-02 | Truro Bearcats | MJrHL | 31 | 1 | 13 | 14 | 34 | 6 | 0 | 0 | 0 | 6 |
| 2002-03 | Arvika HC | Sweden-3 | 30 | 13 | 28 | 41 | 89 | .... | .... | .... | .... | .... |
| 2003-04 | Skare BK Karlstad | Sweden-3 | 10 | 1 | 5 | 6 | 6 | .... | .... | .... | .... | .... |
| 2004-05 | Bofors | Sweden-2 | 45 | 5 | 7 | 12 | 22 | 5 | 0 | 0 | 0 | 0 |
| 2005-06 | Farjestad | Sweden | 46 | 1 | 5 | 6 | 16 | 18 | 0 | 2 | 2 | 4 |
| 2006-07 | Farjestad | Sweden | 55 | 7 | 9 | 16 | 42 | 8 | 2 | 3 | 5 | 4 |
| 2007-08 | Farjestad | Sweden | 53 | 15 | 24 | 39 | 80 | 11 | 4 | 5 | 9 | 37 |
| 2008-09 | Farjestad | Sweden | 49 | 6 | 28 | 34 | 20 | 11 | 1 | 3 | 4 | 2 |

Signed as a free agent by **Montreal**, May 27, 2009.

**JOHNSON, Jamie** (JAHN-suhn, JAY-mee) **FLA.**

Center. Shoots right. 5'11", 185 lbs. Born, Port Franks, Ont., January 23, 1982.

| | | | Regular Season | | | | | Playoffs | | | | |
|---|---|---|---|---|---|---|---|---|---|---|---|---|
| Season | Club | League | GP | G | A | Pts | PIM | GP | G | A | Pts | PIM |
| 99-2000 | Sarnia Sting | OHL | 61 | 6 | 14 | 20 | 24 | 7 | 0 | 2 | 2 | 2 |
| 2000-01 | Sarnia Sting | OHL | 9 | 0 | 5 | 5 | 7 | .... | .... | .... | .... | .... |
| | Oshawa Generals | OHL | 56 | 8 | 38 | 46 | 14 | .... | .... | .... | .... | .... |
| 2001-02 | Oshawa Generals | OHL | 68 | 17 | 61 | 78 | 46 | 5 | 2 | 4 | 6 | 2 |
| 2002-03 | Oshawa Generals | OHL | 68 | 24 | 76 | 100 | 34 | 13 | 1 | 13 | 14 | 16 |
| 2003-04 | Louisiana | ECHL | 71 | 12 | 45 | 57 | 46 | 9 | 3 | 6 | 9 | 4 |
| 2004-05 | Augusta Lynx | ECHL | 72 | 22 | 58 | 80 | 26 | .... | .... | .... | .... | .... |
| 2005-06 | Augusta Lynx | ECHL | 7 | 2 | 4 | 6 | 6 | .... | .... | .... | .... | .... |
| | Iowa Stars | AHL | 68 | 9 | 28 | 37 | 24 | 7 | 0 | 4 | 4 | 21 |
| 2006-07 | Augusta Lynx | ECHL | 31 | 14 | 30 | 44 | 26 | .... | .... | .... | .... | .... |
| | Iowa Stars | AHL | 8 | 1 | 3 | 4 | 2 | .... | .... | .... | .... | .... |
| | Bridgeport | AHL | 34 | 5 | 11 | 16 | 18 | .... | .... | .... | .... | .... |
| 2007-08 | Albany River Rats | AHL | 79 | 21 | 37 | 58 | 28 | 7 | 0 | 2 | 2 | 0 |
| 2008-09 | TPS Turku | Finland | 42 | 8 | 20 | 28 | 24 | 6 | 0 | 3 | 3 | 2 |

Signed as a free agent by **Florida**, July 15, 2009.

**JOHNSON, Nick** (JAWN-suhn, NIHK) **PIT.**

Right wing. Shoots right. 6'1", 183 lbs. Born, Calgary, Alta., December 24, 1985.
(Pittsburgh's 4th choice, 67th overall, in 2004 Entry Draft).

| | | | Regular Season | | | | | Playoffs | | | | |
|---|---|---|---|---|---|---|---|---|---|---|---|---|
| Season | Club | League | GP | G | A | Pts | PIM | GP | G | A | Pts | PIM |
| 2002-03 | St. Albert Saints | AJHL | 60 | 21 | 30 | 51 | 10 | .... | .... | .... | .... | .... |
| 2003-04 | St. Albert Saints | AJHL | 51 | 35 | 36 | 71 | 33 | 4 | 0 | 2 | 2 | 0 |
| 2004-05 | Dartmouth | ECAC | 35 | 18 | 17 | 35 | 16 | .... | .... | .... | .... | .... |
| 2005-06 | Dartmouth | ECAC | 33 | 15 | 10 | 25 | 24 | .... | .... | .... | .... | .... |
| 2006-07 | Dartmouth | ECAC | 33 | 14 | 16 | 30 | 46 | .... | .... | .... | .... | .... |
| 2007-08 | Dartmouth | ECAC | 32 | 10 | 25 | 35 | 20 | .... | .... | .... | .... | .... |
| | Wilkes-Barre | AHL | 4 | 0 | 1 | 1 | 0 | 10 | 0 | 1 | 1 | 2 |
| 2008-09 | Wheeling Nailers | ECHL | 18 | 14 | 10 | 24 | 19 | .... | .... | .... | .... | .... |
| | Wilkes-Barre | AHL | 56 | 14 | 17 | 31 | 30 | 12 | 4 | 6 | 10 | 8 |

ECAC All-Rookie Team 2005) • ECAC First All-Star Team (2008)

**JOHNSON, Patrick** (JAWN-suhn, PAT-rihk) **MTL.**

Left wing. Shoots left. 5'9", 158 lbs. Born, Madison, WI, April 21, 1989.
(Montreal's 5th choice, 206th overall, in 2008 Entry Draft).

| | | | Regular Season | | | | | Playoffs | | | | |
|---|---|---|---|---|---|---|---|---|---|---|---|---|
| Season | Club | League | GP | G | A | Pts | PIM | GP | G | A | Pts | PIM |
| 2006-07 | Lincoln Stars | USHL | 49 | 11 | 16 | 27 | 50 | 4 | 1 | 0 | 1 | 14 |
| 2007-08 | U. of Wisconsin | WCHA | 40 | 8 | 13 | 21 | 36 | .... | .... | .... | .... | .... |
| 2008-09 | U. of Wisconsin | WCHA | 35 | 3 | 4 | 7 | 44 | .... | .... | .... | .... | .... |

**JOHNSTON, Stephen** (JAWN-stuhn, STEE-vehn) **DET.**

Left wing. Shoots left. 6'1", 175 lbs. Born, Guelph, Ont., February 24, 1990.
(Detroit's 5th choice, 181st overall, in 2008 Entry Draft).

| | | | Regular Season | | | | | Playoffs | | | | |
|---|---|---|---|---|---|---|---|---|---|---|---|---|
| Season | Club | League | GP | G | A | Pts | PIM | GP | G | A | Pts | PIM |
| 2005-06 | Guelph AAA | Minor-ON | 57 | 26 | 30 | 56 | 32 | .... | .... | .... | .... | .... |
| 2006-07 | Guelph AAA | Minor-ON | STATISTICS NOT AVAILABLE | | | | | | | | | |
| | John F. Ross | High-ON | 48 | 37 | 39 | 76 | .... | .... | .... | .... | .... | .... |
| 2007-08 | Belleville Bulls | OHL | 56 | 2 | 7 | 9 | 12 | 21 | 5 | 2 | 7 | 6 |
| 2008-09 | Belleville Bulls | OHL | 58 | 14 | 22 | 36 | 38 | 8 | 0 | 2 | 2 | 13 |

**JOKINEN, Justin** (YOH-kihn-ihn, JUHS-tihn) **BUF.**

Right wing. Shoots right. 6'2", 165 lbs. Born, Cloquet, MN, November 25, 1989.
(Buffalo's 5th choice, 101st overall, in 2008 Entry Draft).

| | | | Regular Season | | | | | Playoffs | | | | |
|---|---|---|---|---|---|---|---|---|---|---|---|---|
| Season | Club | League | GP | G | A | Pts | PIM | GP | G | A | Pts | PIM |
| 2005-06 | Cloquet | High-MN | .... | 7 | 11 | 18 | .... | .... | .... | .... | .... | .... |
| 2006-07 | Cloquet | High-MN | .... | 26 | 25 | 51 | 18 | .... | .... | .... | .... | .... |
| | Team North | UMWEHL | 11 | 6 | 5 | 11 | .... | .... | .... | .... | .... | .... |
| 2007-08 | Cloquet | High-MN | 30 | 22 | 21 | 43 | .... | .... | .... | .... | .... | .... |
| | Team North | UMWEHL | 12 | 5 | 13 | 18 | .... | .... | .... | .... | .... | .... |
| 2008-09 | Minnesota State | WCHA | 24 | 3 | 2 | 5 | 6 | .... | .... | .... | .... | .... |

**JONES, Matt** (JOHNZ, MAT) **S.J.**

Right wing. Shoots right. 6'4", 210 lbs. Born, Kentwood, MI, January 13, 1986.

| | | | Regular Season | | | | | Playoffs | | | | |
|---|---|---|---|---|---|---|---|---|---|---|---|---|
| Season | Club | League | GP | G | A | Pts | PIM | GP | G | A | Pts | PIM |
| 2005-06 | Sioux City | USHL | 51 | 11 | 8 | 19 | 71 | .... | .... | .... | .... | .... |
| 2006-07 | Merrimack College | H-East | 32 | 4 | 2 | 6 | 70 | .... | .... | .... | .... | .... |
| 2007-08 | Merrimack College | H-East | 34 | 15 | 7 | 22 | 60 | .... | .... | .... | .... | .... |
| | Worcester Sharks | AHL | 7 | 2 | 1 | 3 | 8 | .... | .... | .... | .... | .... |
| 2008-09 | Worcester Sharks | AHL | 46 | 2 | 6 | 8 | 19 | .... | .... | .... | .... | .... |
| | Phoenix | ECHL | 2 | 0 | 0 | 0 | 2 | .... | .... | .... | .... | .... |

Signed as a free agent by **San Jose**, March 28, 2008.

**JONSSON, Per** (YAWN-suhn, PAIR) **CGY.**

Defense. Shoots left. 6', 172 lbs. Born, Karlstad, Sweden, April 20, 1988.
(Calgary's 8th choice, 209th overall, in 2006 Entry Draft).

| | | | Regular Season | | | | | Playoffs | | | | |
|---|---|---|---|---|---|---|---|---|---|---|---|---|
| Season | Club | League | GP | G | A | Pts | PIM | GP | G | A | Pts | PIM |
| 2004-05 | Farjestad U18 | Swe-U18 | 12 | 2 | 2 | 4 | 10 | 2 | 0 | 0 | 0 | 2 |
| 2005-06 | Farjestad U18 | Swe-U18 | 14 | 3 | 1 | 4 | 38 | 8 | 1 | 1 | 2 | 22 |
| 2006-07 | Farjestad | Sweden | 11 | 0 | 1 | 1 | 0 | .... | .... | .... | .... | .... |
| | Skare BK Karlstad | Sweden-3 | 25 | 3 | 4 | 7 | 42 | .... | .... | .... | .... | .... |
| 2007-08 | Skare BK | Sweden-3 | 38 | 3 | 15 | 18 | 102 | .... | .... | .... | .... | .... |
| | Farjestad | Sweden | 16 | 0 | 1 | 1 | 0 | .... | .... | .... | .... | .... |
| 2008-09 | Bofors | Sweden-2 | 14 | 1 | 1 | 2 | 22 | .... | .... | .... | .... | .... |
| | Malmo | Sweden-2 | 28 | 1 | 1 | 2 | 12 | .... | .... | .... | .... | .... |
| | Farjestad | Sweden | .... | .... | .... | .... | .... | 1 | 0 | 0 | 0 | 0 |

**JORDAN, Michal** (JOHR-duhn, MEE-khuhl) **CAR.**

Defense. Shoots left. 6'1", 184 lbs. Born, Zlin, Czech., July 17, 1990.
(Carolina's 3rd choice, 105th overall, in 2008 Entry Draft).

| | | | Regular Season | | | | | Playoffs | | | | |
|---|---|---|---|---|---|---|---|---|---|---|---|---|
| Season | Club | League | GP | G | A | Pts | PIM | GP | G | A | Pts | PIM |
| 2005-06 | HC Zlin U17 | CzR-U17 | 43 | 7 | 15 | 22 | 12 | 5 | 0 | 1 | 1 | 2 |
| 2006-07 | HC Zlin U17 | CzR-U17 | 1 | 0 | 0 | 0 | 4 | .... | .... | .... | .... | .... |
| | HC Zlin Jr. | CzRep-Jr. | 40 | 7 | 11 | 18 | 20 | 12 | 1 | 5 | 6 | 12 |
| 2007-08 | Windsor Spitfires | OHL | 22 | 1 | 5 | 6 | 12 | .... | .... | .... | .... | .... |
| | Plymouth Whalers | OHL | 39 | 5 | 17 | 22 | 32 | 4 | 0 | 3 | 3 | 6 |
| 2008-09 | Plymouth Whalers | OHL | 58 | 12 | 30 | 42 | 39 | 11 | 0 | 3 | 3 | 12 |

**JOSEFSON, Jacob** (JOH-sehf-suhn, YA-kuhb) **N.J.**

Center. Shoots left. 6', 185 lbs. Born, Stockholm, Sweden, March 2, 1991.
(New Jersey's 1st choice, 20th overall, in 2009 Entry Draft).

| | | | Regular Season | | | | | Playoffs | | | | |
|---|---|---|---|---|---|---|---|---|---|---|---|---|
| Season | Club | League | GP | G | A | Pts | PIM | GP | G | A | Pts | PIM |
| 2005-06 | Djurgarden U18 | Swe-U18 | 5 | 1 | 1 | 2 | 0 | .... | .... | .... | .... | .... |
| 2006-07 | Djurgarden U18 | Swe-U18 | 25 | 14 | 17 | 31 | 22 | 3 | 0 | 0 | 0 | 0 |
| 2007-08 | Djurgarden U18 | Swe-U18 | 4 | 1 | 2 | 3 | 12 | 6 | 0 | 6 | 6 | 4 |
| | Djurgarden Jr. | Swe-Jr. | 34 | 14 | 17 | 31 | 22 | 7 | 2 | 3 | 5 | 8 |
| | Djurgarden | Sweden | 1 | 0 | 0 | 0 | 0 | .... | .... | .... | .... | .... |
| 2008-09 | Djurgarden Jr. | Swe-Jr. | 5 | 1 | 2 | 3 | 8 | 6 | 1 | 3 | 4 | 4 |
| | Djurgarden | Sweden | 50 | 5 | 11 | 16 | 14 | .... | .... | .... | .... | .... |
| | Djurgarden U18 | Swe-U18 | .... | .... | .... | .... | .... | 1 | 0 | 0 | 0 | 0 |

**JOSI, Roman** (YAW-see, ROH-man) **NSH.**

Defense. Shoots left. 6'1", 198 lbs. Born, Bern, Switzerland, June 1, 1990.
(Nashville's 3rd choice, 38th overall, in 2008 Entry Draft).

| | | | Regular Season | | | | | Playoffs | | | | |
|---|---|---|---|---|---|---|---|---|---|---|---|---|
| Season | Club | League | GP | G | A | Pts | PIM | GP | G | A | Pts | PIM |
| 2005-06 | SC Bern Future Jr. | Swiss-Jr. | 5 | 0 | 0 | 0 | 0 | .... | .... | .... | .... | .... |
| 2006-07 | SC Bern Future Jr. | Swiss-Jr. | 33 | 14 | 16 | 30 | 28 | 14 | 1 | 3 | 4 | 2 |
| | Switzerland U20 | Swiss-2 | 5 | 1 | 1 | 2 | 2 | .... | .... | .... | .... | .... |
| | SC Bern | Swiss | 3 | 0 | 1 | 1 | 0 | .... | .... | .... | .... | .... |
| 2007-08 | Switzerland U20 | Swiss-2 | 2 | 0 | 1 | 1 | 0 | .... | .... | .... | .... | .... |
| | HC Neuchatel | Swiss-2 | 3 | 2 | 0 | 2 | 4 | .... | .... | .... | .... | .... |
| | SC Bern | Swiss | 35 | 2 | 6 | 8 | 10 | 6 | 0 | 0 | 0 | 0 |
| 2008-09 | SC Bern | Swiss | 42 | 7 | 17 | 24 | 16 | 6 | 0 | 0 | 0 | 2 |

**JOUDREY, Andrew** (JOO-dree, AN-droo)

Center. Shoots left. 5'11", 191 lbs. Born, Halifax, N.S., July 15, 1984.
(Washington's 5th choice, 249th overall, in 2003 Entry Draft).

| | | | Regular Season | | | | | Playoffs | | | | |
|---|---|---|---|---|---|---|---|---|---|---|---|---|
| Season | Club | League | GP | G | A | Pts | PIM | GP | G | A | Pts | PIM |
| 2000-01 | Dartmouth | NSMHL | 82 | 51 | 70 | 121 | .... | .... | .... | .... | .... | .... |
| 2001-02 | Notre Dame | SJHL | 57 | 24 | 38 | 62 | 14 | .... | .... | .... | .... | .... |
| 2002-03 | Notre Dame | SJHL | 53 | 27 | 51 | 78 | 16 | .... | .... | .... | .... | .... |
| 2003-04 | U. of Wisconsin | WCHA | 42 | 7 | 15 | 22 | 2 | .... | .... | .... | .... | .... |
| 2004-05 | U. of Wisconsin | WCHA | 41 | 7 | 17 | 24 | 18 | .... | .... | .... | .... | .... |
| 2005-06 | U. of Wisconsin | WCHA | 37 | 8 | 10 | 18 | 14 | .... | .... | .... | .... | .... |
| 2006-07 | U. of Wisconsin | WCHA | 40 | 9 | 20 | 29 | 18 | .... | .... | .... | .... | .... |
| | Hershey Bears | AHL | 5 | 2 | 1 | 3 | 0 | 10 | 0 | 2 | 2 | 0 |
| 2007-08 | Hershey Bears | AHL | 61 | 11 | 14 | 25 | 22 | 5 | 0 | 1 | 1 | 0 |
| 2008-09 | Hershey Bears | AHL | 69 | 7 | 20 | 27 | 22 | 22 | 1 | 3 | 4 | 6 |

**KABLUKOV, Ilja** (ka-BLOO-hahv, IHL-yah) **VAN.**

Center. Shoots left. 6'2", 183 lbs. Born, Moscow, USSR, January 18, 1988.
(Vancouver's 4th choice, 146th overall, in 2007 Entry Draft).

| | | | Regular Season | | | | | Playoffs | | | | |
|---|---|---|---|---|---|---|---|---|---|---|---|---|
| Season | Club | League | GP | G | A | Pts | PIM | GP | G | A | Pts | PIM |
| 2005-06 | CSKA Moscow 2 | Russia-3 | STATISTICS NOT AVAILABLE | | | | | | | | | |
| 2006-07 | CSKA Moscow 2 | Russia-3 | STATISTICS NOT AVAILABLE | | | | | | | | | |
| | CSKA Moscow | Russia | 24 | 0 | 0 | 0 | 2 | 2 | 0 | 0 | 0 | 2 |
| 2007-08 | CSKA Moscow | Russia | 50 | 4 | 9 | 13 | 18 | 6 | 1 | 3 | 4 | 2 |
| | CSKA Moscow 2 | Russia-3 | .... | .... | .... | .... | .... | 2 | 1 | 3 | 4 | 2 |
| 2008-09 | Nizhny Novgorod | Rus-KHL | 42 | 1 | 3 | 4 | 8 | 3 | 0 | 0 | 0 | 4 |

**KADRI, Nazem** (KAH-dree, NA-zihm) **TOR.**

Center. Shoots left. 6', 167 lbs. Born, London, Ont., October 6, 1990.
(Toronto's 1st choice, 7th overall, in 2009 Entry Draft).

| | | | Regular Season | | | | | Playoffs | | | | |
|---|---|---|---|---|---|---|---|---|---|---|---|---|
| Season | Club | League | GP | G | A | Pts | PIM | GP | G | A | Pts | PIM |
| 2005-06 | Lon. Jr. Knights | Minor-ON | 62 | 49 | 43 | 92 | 82 | .... | .... | .... | .... | .... |
| 2006-07 | Kitchener Rangers | OHL | 62 | 7 | 15 | 22 | 30 | 9 | 0 | 2 | 2 | 4 |
| 2007-08 | Kitchener Rangers | OHL | 68 | 25 | 40 | 65 | 57 | 20 | 9 | 17 | 26 | 26 |
| 2008-09 | London Knights | OHL | 56 | 25 | 53 | 78 | 31 | 14 | 9 | 12 | 21 | 22 |

**KAIP, Rylan** (KAYP, RIH-luhn) **ATL.**

Center. Shoots left. 6'1", 195 lbs. Born, Wilcox, Sask., March 19, 1984.
(Atlanta's 9th choice, 269th overall, in 2003 Entry Draft).

| | | | Regular Season | | | | | Playoffs | | | | |
|---|---|---|---|---|---|---|---|---|---|---|---|---|
| Season | Club | League | GP | G | A | Pts | PIM | GP | G | A | Pts | PIM |
| 2000-01 | Notre Dame | SJHL | 5 | 0 | 0 | 0 | 0 | 1 | 0 | 0 | 0 | 0 |
| 2001-02 | Notre Dame | SJHL | 61 | 14 | 18 | 32 | 77 | .... | .... | .... | .... | .... |
| 2002-03 | Notre Dame | SJHL | 57 | 20 | 36 | 56 | 164 | 6 | 1 | 6 | 7 | 21 |
| 2003-04 | Notre Dame | SJHL | 54 | 30 | 36 | 66 | 133 | 4 | 1 | 1 | 2 | 6 |
| 2004-05 | North Dakota | WCHA | 22 | 0 | 4 | 4 | 20 | .... | .... | .... | .... | .... |
| 2005-06 | North Dakota | WCHA | 42 | 3 | 5 | 8 | 76 | .... | .... | .... | .... | .... |
| 2006-07 | North Dakota | WCHA | 38 | 5 | 7 | 12 | 55 | .... | .... | .... | .... | .... |
| 2007-08 | North Dakota | WCHA | 42 | 8 | 7 | 15 | 81 | .... | .... | .... | .... | .... |
| 2008-09 | Chicago Wolves | AHL | 42 | 1 | 2 | 3 | 17 | .... | .... | .... | .... | .... |

**KAMPFER, Steven** (KAMP-fuhr, STEE-vehn) **ANA.**

Defense. Shoots right. 5'11", 204 lbs. Born, Ann Arbour, MI, September 24, 1988.
(Anaheim's 5th choice, 93rd overall, in 2007 Entry Draft).

| | | | Regular Season | | | | | Playoffs | | | | |
|---|---|---|---|---|---|---|---|---|---|---|---|---|
| Season | Club | League | GP | G | A | Pts | PIM | GP | G | A | Pts | PIM |
| 2004-05 | Sioux City | USHL | 47 | 6 | 13 | 19 | 91 | 13 | 2 | 5 | 7 | 12 |
| 2005-06 | Sioux City | USHL | 56 | 6 | 10 | 16 | 99 | .... | .... | .... | .... | .... |
| 2006-07 | U. of Michigan | CCHA | 35 | 1 | 3 | 4 | 24 | .... | .... | .... | .... | .... |
| 2007-08 | U. of Michigan | CCHA | 42 | 2 | 15 | 17 | 36 | .... | .... | .... | .... | .... |
| 2008-09 | U. of Michigan | CCHA | 25 | 1 | 12 | 13 | 24 | .... | .... | .... | .... | .... |

**KANA, Tomas** (KA-nah, TAW-mahsh) **ST.L.**

Center. Shoots right. 6', 208 lbs. Born, Opava, Czech., November 29, 1987.
(St. Louis' 3rd choice, 31st overall, in 2006 Entry Draft).

| | | | Regular Season | | | | | Playoffs | | | | |
|---|---|---|---|---|---|---|---|---|---|---|---|---|
| Season | Club | League | GP | G | A | Pts | PIM | GP | G | A | Pts | PIM |
| 2002-03 | HC Vitkovice U17 | CzR-U17 | 44 | 20 | 14 | 34 | 72 | 2 | 2 | 0 | 2 | 4 |
| | HC Vitkovice Jr. | CzRep-Jr. | 3 | 2 | 0 | 2 | 4 | .... | .... | .... | .... | .... |
| 2003-04 | HC Vitkovice U17 | CzR-U17 | 8 | 2 | 9 | 11 | 33 | 7 | 4 | 5 | 9 | 18 |
| | HC Vitkovice Jr. | CzRep-Jr. | 50 | 12 | 7 | 19 | 78 | .... | .... | .... | .... | .... |
| 2004-05 | HC Vitkovice Jr. | CzRep-Jr. | 46 | 12 | 22 | 34 | 155 | 2 | 0 | 0 | 0 | 2 |
| | HC Vitkovice Steel | CzRep | 1 | 0 | 0 | 0 | 0 | .... | .... | .... | .... | .... |
| 2005-06 | HC Vitkovice Steel | CzRep | 42 | 5 | 9 | 14 | 50 | 6 | 0 | 1 | 1 | 2 |
| | HC Vitkovice Jr. | CzRep-Jr. | 5 | 4 | 3 | 7 | 16 | .... | .... | .... | .... | .... |
| 2006-07 | HC Vitkovice Steel | CzRep | 44 | 9 | 7 | 16 | 54 | .... | .... | .... | .... | .... |
| | BK Mlada Boleslav | CzRep-2 | 6 | 2 | 1 | 3 | 16 | 6 | 1 | 0 | 1 | 16 |
| 2007-08 | Alaska Aces | ECHL | 12 | 2 | 0 | 2 | 4 | .... | .... | .... | .... | .... |
| | HC Sareza Ostrava | CzRep-2 | 8 | 3 | 0 | 3 | 6 | .... | .... | .... | .... | .... |
| | HC Vitkovice Steel | CzRep | 8 | 1 | 1 | 2 | 6 | .... | .... | .... | .... | .... |
| | Usti n. L. | CzRep | 17 | 4 | 4 | 8 | 18 | .... | .... | .... | .... | .... |
| | Usti n. L. | CzRep-Q | .... | .... | .... | .... | .... | 3 | 0 | 0 | 0 | 2 |
| 2008-09 | Peoria Rivermen | AHL | 18 | 1 | 0 | 1 | 15 | .... | .... | .... | .... | .... |
| | Alaska Aces | ECHL | 30 | 6 | 14 | 20 | 65 | 21 | 1 | 2 | 3 | 10 |

**KANE, Evander** (KAYN, ee-VAN-duhr) **ATL.**

Center. Shoots left. 6'1", 180 lbs. Born, Vancouver, B.C., August 2, 1991.
(Atlanta's 1st choice, 4th overall, in 2009 Entry Draft).

| | | | Regular Season | | | | | Playoffs | | | | |
|---|---|---|---|---|---|---|---|---|---|---|---|---|
| Season | Club | League | GP | G | A | Pts | PIM | GP | G | A | Pts | PIM |
| 2006-07 | Greater Van. | Minor-BC | 30 | 22 | 32 | 54 | 150 | .... | .... | .... | .... | .... |
| | Vancouver Giants | WHL | 8 | 1 | 0 | 1 | 11 | 5 | 0 | 0 | 0 | 0 |
| 2007-08 | Vancouver Giants | WHL | 65 | 24 | 17 | 41 | 66 | 10 | 1 | 2 | 3 | 8 |
| 2008-09 | Vancouver Giants | WHL | 61 | 48 | 48 | 96 | 89 | 17 | 7 | 8 | 15 | 45 |

WHL West First All-Star Team (2009)

**KARIYA, Martin** (kah-REE-ah, MAR-tihn)

Right wing. Shoots right. 5'9", 175 lbs. Born, Vancouver, B.C., October 5, 1981.

| | | | Regular Season | | | | | Playoffs | | | | |
|---|---|---|---|---|---|---|---|---|---|---|---|---|
| Season | Club | League | GP | G | A | Pts | PIM | GP | G | A | Pts | PIM |
| 1998-99 | Victoria Salsa | BCJHL | 59 | 25 | 80 | 105 | 14 | .... | .... | .... | .... | .... |
| 99-2000 | U. of Maine | H-East | 35 | 8 | 17 | 25 | 6 | .... | .... | .... | .... | .... |
| 2000-01 | U. of Maine | H-East | 39 | 12 | 14 | 36 | 10 | .... | .... | .... | .... | .... |
| 2001-02 | U. of Maine | H-East | 43 | 16 | 28 | 44 | 14 | .... | .... | .... | .... | .... |
| 2002-03 | U. of Maine | H-East | 39 | 14 | 36 | 50 | 6 | .... | .... | .... | .... | .... |
| | Portland Pirates | AHL | .... | .... | .... | .... | .... | 3 | 0 | 0 | 0 | 0 |
| 2003-04 | Bridgeport | AHL | 70 | 8 | 17 | 25 | 16 | 7 | 0 | 1 | 1 | 2 |
| 2004-05 | HC Nikko Icebucks | AsianHL | 15 | 6 | 12 | 18 | 20 | .... | .... | .... | .... | .... |
| 2005-06 | Stjernen Hockey | Norway | 39 | 15 | 37 | 52 | 49 | 11 | 3 | 10 | 13 | 8 |
| 2006-07 | Blues Espoo | Finland | 51 | 18 | *43 | *61 | 58 | .... | .... | .... | .... | .... |
| 2007-08 | Peoria Rivermen | AHL | 71 | 16 | 37 | 53 | 29 | .... | .... | .... | .... | .... |
| 2008-09 | Langnau | Swiss | 50 | 14 | 40 | 54 | 22 | 5 | 0 | 2 | 2 | 2 |

Hockey East First All-Star Team (2003)

Signed to a PTO (tryout) contract by **Portland** (AHL), April 9, 2003. Signed as a free agent by **Bridgeport** (AHL), July 7, 2003. Signed as a free agent by **St. Louis**, June 1, 2007.

**KARLSSON, Erik** (KAHRL-suhn, AIR-ihk) **OTT.**

Defense. Shoots right. 5'11", 169 lbs. Born, Landsbro, Sweden, May 31, 1990.
(Ottawa's 1st choice, 15th overall, in 2008 Entry Draft).

| | | | Regular Season | | | | | Playoffs | | | | |
|---|---|---|---|---|---|---|---|---|---|---|---|---|
| Season | Club | League | GP | G | A | Pts | PIM | GP | G | A | Pts | PIM |
| 2006-07 | Sodertalje SK U18 | Swe-U18 | 2 | 0 | 1 | 1 | 33 | .... | .... | .... | .... | .... |
| | Sodertalje SK Jr. | Swe-Jr. | 10 | 2 | 8 | 10 | 8 | .... | .... | .... | .... | .... |
| 2007-08 | Frolunda U18 | Swe-U18 | 3 | 1 | 2 | 3 | 2 | 2 | 0 | 1 | 1 | 10 |
| | Frolunda Jr. | Swe-Jr. | 38 | 13 | 24 | 37 | 68 | 5 | 1 | 0 | 1 | 4 |
| | Frolunda | Sweden | 7 | 1 | 0 | 1 | 0 | 6 | 0 | 0 | 0 | 0 |
| 2008-09 | Frolunda Jr. | Swe-Jr. | 1 | 0 | 2 | 2 | 2 | .... | .... | .... | .... | .... |
| | Boras HC | Sweden-2 | 7 | 0 | 1 | 1 | 14 | .... | .... | .... | .... | .... |
| | Frolunda | Sweden | 45 | 5 | 5 | 10 | 10 | 11 | 1 | 2 | 3 | 24 |

**KARLSSON, Mattias** (KARL-suhn, mat-TEE-uhs) **OTT.**

Defense. Shoots left. 6'2", 228 lbs. Born, Stora, Sweden, April 15, 1985.
(Ottawa's 4th choice, 135th overall, in 2003 Entry Draft).

| | | | Regular Season | | | | | Playoffs | | | | |
|---|---|---|---|---|---|---|---|---|---|---|---|---|
| Season | Club | League | GP | G | A | Pts | PIM | GP | G | A | Pts | PIM |
| 2001-02 | Brynas U18 | Swe-U18 | 5 | 2 | 1 | 3 | 6 | .... | .... | .... | .... | .... |
| | Brynas IF Gavle Jr. | Swe-Jr. | 13 | 0 | 1 | 1 | 12 | .... | .... | .... | .... | .... |
| 2002-03 | Brynas IF Gavle Jr. | Swe-Jr. | 27 | 11 | 6 | 17 | 93 | 2 | 0 | 0 | 0 | 4 |
| | Brynas IF Gavle | Sweden | 3 | 0 | 0 | 0 | 0 | .... | .... | .... | .... | .... |
| | Brynas IF Gavle | Sweden-Q | 3 | 0 | 0 | 0 | 0 | .... | .... | .... | .... | .... |
| 2003-04 | Brynas IF Gavle Jr. | Swe-Jr. | 20 | 5 | 8 | 13 | 67 | 5 | 0 | 4 | 4 | 10 |
| | Brynas IF Gavle | Sweden | 39 | 0 | 0 | 0 | 6 | .... | .... | .... | .... | .... |
| 2004-05 | Brynas IF Gavle Jr. | Swe-Jr. | 13 | 3 | 5 | 8 | 40 | .... | .... | .... | .... | .... |
| | Almtuna | Sweden-2 | 22 | 0 | 2 | 2 | 18 | .... | .... | .... | .... | .... |
| | Brynas IF Gavle | Sweden | 9 | 0 | 0 | 0 | 2 | .... | .... | .... | .... | .... |
| | Brynas IF Gavle | Sweden-Q | 1 | 0 | 0 | 0 | 0 | .... | .... | .... | .... | .... |
| 2005-06 | Almtuna Jr. | Swe-Jr. | 2 | 0 | 1 | 1 | 4 | .... | .... | .... | .... | .... |
| | Almtuna | Sweden-2 | 32 | 3 | 4 | 7 | 40 | .... | .... | .... | .... | .... |
| 2006-07 | Bofors | Sweden-2 | 44 | 11 | 21 | 32 | 34 | .... | .... | .... | .... | .... |
| 2007-08 | Binghamton | AHL | 2 | 0 | 0 | 0 | 0 | .... | .... | .... | .... | .... |
| | Farjestad | Sweden | 13 | 2 | 2 | 4 | 4 | 12 | 1 | 3 | 4 | 20 |
| 2008-09 | Binghamton | AHL | 73 | 9 | 42 | 51 | 40 | .... | .... | .... | .... | .... |

AHL All-Rookie Team (2009)

**KASSIAN, Matt** (KAS-ee-uhn, MAT) **MIN.**

Left wing. Shoots left. 6'5", 245 lbs. Born, Edmonton, Alta., October 28, 1986.
(Minnesota's 2nd choice, 57th overall, in 2005 Entry Draft).

| | | | Regular Season | | | | | Playoffs | | | | |
|---|---|---|---|---|---|---|---|---|---|---|---|---|
| Season | Club | League | GP | G | A | Pts | PIM | GP | G | A | Pts | PIM |
| 2002-03 | Sherwood Park | AJHL | 33 | 5 | 7 | 12 | 38 | .... | .... | .... | .... | .... |
| 2003-04 | Vancouver Giants | WHL | 37 | 1 | 0 | 1 | 42 | 3 | 0 | 0 | 0 | 4 |
| 2004-05 | Vancouver Giants | WHL | 41 | 0 | 3 | 3 | 89 | .... | .... | .... | .... | .... |
| | Kamloops Blazers | WHL | 28 | 3 | 0 | 3 | 83 | 6 | 1 | 2 | 3 | 14 |
| 2005-06 | Kamloops Blazers | WHL | 67 | 5 | 6 | 11 | 147 | .... | .... | .... | .... | .... |
| 2006-07 | Kamloops Blazers | WHL | 72 | 8 | 10 | 18 | 162 | 4 | 0 | 1 | 1 | 0 |
| 2007-08 | Houston Aeros | AHL | 19 | 0 | 0 | 0 | 48 | .... | .... | .... | .... | .... |
| | Texas Wildcatters | ECHL | 47 | 6 | 4 | 10 | 90 | .... | .... | .... | .... | .... |
| 2008-09 | Houston Aeros | AHL | 56 | 1 | 2 | 3 | 130 | 4 | 0 | 0 | 0 | 10 |

**KASSIAN, Zack** (KA-see-uhn, ZAK) **BUF.**

Right wing. Shoots right. 6'3", 210 lbs. Born, Windsor, Ont., January 24, 1991.
(Buffalo's 1st choice, 13th overall, in 2009 Entry Draft).

| | | | Regular Season | | | | | Playoffs | | | | |
|---|---|---|---|---|---|---|---|---|---|---|---|---|
| Season | Club | League | GP | G | A | Pts | PIM | GP | G | A | Pts | PIM |
| 2006-07 | Wind. Jr. Spitfires | Minor-ON | 57 | 32 | 48 | 80 | 136 | .... | .... | .... | .... | .... |
| 2007-08 | Peterborough | OHL | 58 | 9 | 12 | 21 | 74 | 5 | 1 | 0 | 1 | 2 |
| 2008-09 | Peterborough | OHL | 61 | 24 | 39 | 63 | 136 | 4 | 0 | 2 | 2 | 8 |

**KATIC, Mark** (KA-tihk, MAHRK) **NYI**

Defense. Shoots left. 5'10", 180 lbs. Born, Timmins, Ont., May 9, 1989.
(NY Islanders' 1st choice, 62nd overall, in 2007 Entry Draft).

| | | | Regular Season | | | | | Playoffs | | | | |
|---|---|---|---|---|---|---|---|---|---|---|---|---|
| Season | Club | League | GP | G | A | Pts | PIM | GP | G | A | Pts | PIM |
| 2003-04 | Timmins Majors | GNMHL | 40 | 12 | 20 | 32 | 35 | .... | .... | .... | .... | .... |
| 2004-05 | Timmins Majors | GNMHL | 35 | 11 | 21 | 32 | 74 | .... | .... | .... | .... | .... |
| 2005-06 | Sarnia Sting | OHL | 51 | 5 | 29 | 34 | 33 | .... | .... | .... | .... | .... |
| 2006-07 | Sarnia Sting | OHL | 68 | 5 | 35 | 40 | 31 | 4 | 1 | 3 | 4 | 8 |
| 2007-08 | Sarnia Sting | OHL | 45 | 5 | 26 | 31 | 28 | 6 | 0 | 3 | 3 | 8 |
| 2008-09 | Sarnia Sting | OHL | 63 | 13 | 41 | 54 | 45 | 4 | 1 | 0 | 1 | 6 |

### KAZIONOV, Denis (ka-zee-OH-nahv, DEH-nihs) T.B.

Left wing. Shoots left. 6'3", 187 lbs. Born, Perm, USSR, December 8, 1987.
(Tampa Bay's 4th choice, 198th overall, in 2006 Entry Draft).

| | | | Regular Season | | | | | Playoffs | | | | |
|---|---|---|---|---|---|---|---|---|---|---|---|---|
| Season | Club | League | GP | G | A | Pts | PIM | GP | G | A | Pts | PIM |
| 2003-04 | CSKA Moscow 2 | Russia-3 | 2 | 0 | 1 | 1 | 2 | .... | .... | .... | .... | .... |
| 2004-05 | Dyn'o Moscow 2 | Russia-3 | STATISTICS NOT AVAILABLE | | | | | .... | .... | .... | .... | .... |
| 2005-06 | MVD | Russia | 26 | 0 | 0 | 0 | 12 | 3 | 0 | 0 | 0 | 0 |
| | HK MVD-THK Tver | Russia-3 | 31 | 6 | 13 | 19 | 34 | .... | .... | .... | .... | .... |
| 2006-07 | THK Tver | Russia-3 | 13 | 23 | 15 | 38 | 42 | .... | .... | .... | .... | .... |
| | MVD | Russia | 24 | 2 | 0 | 2 | 8 | 2 | 0 | 0 | 0 | 2 |
| 2007-08 | Novokuznetsk | Russia | 8 | 0 | 0 | 0 | 8 | .... | .... | .... | .... | .... |
| | Avangard Omsk 2 | Russia-3 | 13 | 10 | 6 | 16 | 16 | .... | .... | .... | .... | .... |
| | Avangard Omsk | Russia | 18 | 0 | 0 | 0 | 4 | 3 | 0 | 0 | 0 | 6 |
| 2008-09 | Amur Khabarovsk | Rus-KHL | 6 | 0 | 0 | 0 | 6 | .... | .... | .... | .... | .... |
| | Trebic | CzRep-2 | 2 | 0 | 1 | 1 | 2 | .... | .... | .... | .... | .... |
| | BK Mlada Boleslav | CzRep | 33 | 4 | 6 | 10 | 99 | .... | .... | .... | .... | .... |
| | BK Mlada Boleslav | CzRep-Q | .... | .... | .... | .... | .... | 2 | 0 | 0 | 0 | 0 |

### KAZIONOV, Dmitri (ka-zee-OH-nahv, dih-MEE-tree) T.B.

Center. Shoots left. 6'3", 185 lbs. Born, Moscow, USSR, May 13, 1984.
(Tampa Bay's 2nd choice, 100th overall, in 2002 Entry Draft).

| | | | Regular Season | | | | | Playoffs | | | | |
|---|---|---|---|---|---|---|---|---|---|---|---|---|
| Season | Club | League | GP | G | A | Pts | PIM | GP | G | A | Pts | PIM |
| 99-2000 | Dyn'o Moscow 2 | Russia-3 | 2 | 1 | 0 | 1 | 0 | .... | .... | .... | .... | .... |
| 2000-01 | THK Tver | Russia-2 | 33 | 1 | 1 | 2 | 6 | .... | .... | .... | .... | .... |
| 2001-02 | HK CSKA Moscow | Russia-2 | 2 | 0 | 1 | 1 | 0 | .... | .... | .... | .... | .... |
| | HK CSKA 2 | Russia-3 | 10 | 1 | 0 | 1 | 4 | .... | .... | .... | .... | .... |
| | Lada Togliatti | Russia | 3 | 0 | 0 | 0 | 0 | .... | .... | .... | .... | .... |
| | Lada Togliatti 2 | Russia-3 | 16 | 10 | 9 | 19 | 0 | .... | .... | .... | .... | .... |
| 2002-03 | Lada Togliatti | Russia | 5 | 0 | 1 | 1 | 4 | .... | .... | .... | .... | .... |
| | Lada Togliatti 2 | Russia-3 | 34 | 14 | 13 | 27 | 26 | .... | .... | .... | .... | .... |
| 2003-04 | Lada Togliatti 2 | Russia-3 | 5 | 3 | 2 | 5 | 0 | 4 | 0 | 0 | 0 | 0 |
| | Lada Togliatti | Russia | 47 | 5 | 5 | 10 | 34 | 5 | 0 | 0 | 0 | 4 |
| 2004-05 | Lada Togliatti | Russia | 46 | 3 | 7 | 10 | 32 | 2 | 0 | 0 | 0 | 0 |
| | Lada Togliatti 2 | Russia-3 | 2 | 1 | 0 | 1 | 4 | .... | .... | .... | .... | .... |
| 2005-06 | Lada Togliatti | Russia | 13 | 0 | 3 | 3 | 18 | .... | .... | .... | .... | .... |
| | Dynamo Moscow | Russia | 27 | 2 | 2 | 4 | 24 | 4 | 1 | 0 | 1 | 6 |
| 2006-07 | Ak Bars Kazan | Russia | 48 | 10 | 11 | 21 | 34 | 13 | 2 | 3 | 5 | 4 |
| 2007-08 | Ak Bars Kazan | Russia | 56 | 7 | 13 | 20 | 46 | 10 | 0 | 3 | 3 | 16 |
| 2008-09 | Ak Bars Kazan | Rus-KHL | 55 | 10 | 11 | 21 | 30 | 21 | 2 | 6 | 8 | 12 |

### KEEFE, Adam (KEEF, A-duhm)

Right wing. Shoots right. 5'10", 200 lbs. Born, Brampton, Ont., April 26, 1984.

| | | | Regular Season | | | | | Playoffs | | | | |
|---|---|---|---|---|---|---|---|---|---|---|---|---|
| Season | Club | League | GP | G | A | Pts | PIM | GP | G | A | Pts | PIM |
| 2000-01 | Sudbury Wolves | OHL | 50 | 4 | 10 | 14 | 62 | 8 | 0 | 0 | 0 | 2 |
| 2001-02 | Sudbury Wolves | OHL | 16 | 1 | 2 | 3 | 46 | .... | .... | .... | .... | .... |
| | Kitchener Rangers | OHL | 49 | 0 | 2 | 2 | 208 | 3 | 0 | 0 | 0 | 14 |
| 2002-03 | Kitchener Rangers | OHL | 45 | 8 | 8 | 16 | 168 | 21 | 0 | 1 | 1 | 19 |
| 2003-04 | Kitchener Rangers | OHL | 67 | 18 | 20 | 38 | 205 | 5 | 1 | 3 | 4 | 12 |
| 2004-05 | Kitchener Rangers | OHL | 67 | 16 | 30 | 46 | 286 | 14 | 3 | 4 | 7 | 44 |
| 2005-06 | Manitoba Moose | AHL | 31 | 3 | 2 | 5 | 158 | .... | .... | .... | .... | .... |
| | Toledo Storm | ECHL | 28 | 11 | 10 | 21 | 174 | 11 | 2 | 0 | 2 | 50 |
| 2006-07 | Manitoba Moose | AHL | 22 | 2 | 2 | 4 | 91 | .... | .... | .... | .... | .... |
| | Grand Rapids | AHL | 16 | 0 | 3 | 3 | 97 | .... | .... | .... | .... | .... |
| | Victoria | ECHL | 8 | 0 | 0 | 0 | 27 | .... | .... | .... | .... | .... |
| 2007-08 | Grand Rapids | AHL | 32 | 1 | 0 | 1 | 124 | .... | .... | .... | .... | .... |
| | San Antonio | AHL | 34 | 1 | 0 | 1 | 121 | 1 | 0 | 0 | 0 | 0 |
| 2008-09 | San Antonio | AHL | 41 | 2 | 1 | 3 | 185 | .... | .... | .... | .... | .... |

Signed as a free agent by **San Antonio** (AHL), August 25, 2008.

### KELLER, Justin (KEHL-uhr, JUHS-tihn)

Left wing. Shoots left. 5'11", 185 lbs. Born, Nelson, B.C., March 4, 1986.
(Tampa Bay's 8th choice, 245th overall, in 2004 Entry Draft).

| | | | Regular Season | | | | | Playoffs | | | | |
|---|---|---|---|---|---|---|---|---|---|---|---|---|
| Season | Club | League | GP | G | A | Pts | PIM | GP | G | A | Pts | PIM |
| 2001-02 | Spokane Chiefs | WHL | 25 | 7 | 6 | 13 | 10 | .... | .... | .... | .... | .... |
| | Saskatoon Blades | WHL | 36 | 7 | 6 | 13 | 6 | 2 | 0 | 0 | 0 | 2 |
| 2002-03 | Saskatoon Blades | WHL | 2 | 0 | 0 | 0 | 0 | .... | .... | .... | .... | .... |
| | Regina Pats | WHL | 16 | 3 | 3 | 6 | 6 | .... | .... | .... | .... | .... |
| 2003-04 | Kelowna Rockets | WHL | 72 | 25 | 21 | 46 | 44 | 17 | 4 | 5 | 9 | 18 |
| 2004-05 | Kelowna Rockets | WHL | 72 | 31 | 22 | 53 | 103 | 23 | 12 | 10 | 22 | 44 |
| 2005-06 | Kelowna Rockets | WHL | 72 | *51 | 37 | 88 | 82 | 12 | 3 | 6 | 9 | 14 |
| 2006-07 | Springfield Falcons | AHL | 60 | 13 | 11 | 24 | 26 | .... | .... | .... | .... | .... |
| 2007-08 | Norfolk Admirals | AHL | 70 | 15 | 22 | 37 | 45 | .... | .... | .... | .... | .... |
| 2008-09 | Norfolk Admirals | AHL | 58 | 18 | 19 | 37 | 52 | .... | .... | .... | .... | .... |

WHL West First All-Star Team (2006)

### KELLER, Ryan (KEHL-uhr, RIGH-uhn) OTT.

Center. Shoots right. 5'10", 186 lbs. Born, Saskatoon, Sask., January 6, 1984.

| | | | Regular Season | | | | | Playoffs | | | | |
|---|---|---|---|---|---|---|---|---|---|---|---|---|
| Season | Club | League | GP | G | A | Pts | PIM | GP | G | A | Pts | PIM |
| 2001-02 | Saskatoon Blades | WHL | 52 | 18 | 23 | 41 | 58 | 7 | 1 | 2 | 3 | 14 |
| 2002-03 | Saskatoon Blades | WHL | 66 | 38 | 41 | 79 | 101 | 6 | 7 | 1 | 8 | 8 |
| 2003-04 | Saskatoon Blades | WHL | 72 | 24 | 20 | 44 | 59 | .... | .... | .... | .... | .... |
| 2004-05 | Saskatoon Blades | WHL | 67 | 40 | 33 | 73 | 63 | 4 | 1 | 1 | 2 | 9 |
| 2005-06 | Grand Rapids | AHL | 10 | 1 | 0 | 1 | 14 | 13 | 0 | 0 | 0 | 0 |
| | Muskegon Fury | UHL | 65 | 41 | 40 | 81 | 79 | 3 | 2 | 2 | 4 | 0 |
| 2006-07 | Grand Rapids | AHL | 38 | 9 | 8 | 17 | 26 | .... | .... | .... | .... | .... |
| | Syracuse Crunch | AHL | 22 | 5 | 9 | 14 | 14 | .... | .... | .... | .... | .... |
| 2007-08 | Blues Espoo | Finland | 47 | 22 | 22 | 44 | 24 | 17 | 3 | 6 | 9 | 22 |
| 2008-09 | Blues Espoo | Finland | 54 | 21 | 34 | 55 | 38 | 14 | *9 | 7 | 16 | 4 |

Signed as a free agent by **Ottawa**, June 1, 2009.

### KEMP, T.J. (KEHMP, TEE-JAY)

Defense. Shoots left. 5'11", 197 lbs. Born, Pickering, Ont., July 3, 1981.

| | | | Regular Season | | | | | Playoffs | | | | |
|---|---|---|---|---|---|---|---|---|---|---|---|---|
| Season | Club | League | GP | G | A | Pts | PIM | GP | G | A | Pts | PIM |
| 2001-02 | Mercyhurst | MAAC | 31 | 6 | 13 | 19 | 18 | .... | .... | .... | .... | .... |
| 2002-03 | Mercyhurst | MAAC | 37 | 11 | 16 | 27 | 39 | .... | .... | .... | .... | .... |
| 2003-04 | Mercyhurst | AH | 34 | 5 | 21 | 26 | 42 | .... | .... | .... | .... | .... |
| 2004-05 | Mercyhurst | AH | 31 | 10 | 18 | 28 | 78 | .... | .... | .... | .... | .... |
| | Missouri | UHL | 6 | 1 | 2 | 3 | 4 | .... | .... | .... | .... | .... |
| 2005-06 | Peoria Rivermen | AHL | 3 | 0 | 0 | 0 | 2 | .... | .... | .... | .... | .... |
| | Iowa Stars | AHL | 3 | 0 | 0 | 0 | 0 | .... | .... | .... | .... | .... |
| | Milwaukee | AHL | 2 | 0 | 0 | 0 | 2 | .... | .... | .... | .... | .... |
| | Bridgeport | AHL | 6 | 0 | 0 | 0 | 0 | .... | .... | .... | .... | .... |
| | Reading Royals | ECHL | 60 | 13 | 27 | 40 | 54 | 4 | 1 | 1 | 2 | 2 |
| 2006-07 | Manchester | AHL | 65 | 5 | 33 | 38 | 56 | 14 | 2 | 5 | 7 | 12 |
| 2007-08 | Springfield Falcons | AHL | 73 | 8 | 38 | 46 | 44 | .... | .... | .... | .... | .... |
| 2008-09 | Wilkes-Barre | AHL | 22 | 1 | 8 | 9 | 22 | .... | .... | .... | .... | .... |
| | Hamilton Bulldogs | AHL | 45 | 1 | 17 | 18 | 18 | 5 | 0 | 0 | 0 | 4 |

Signed as a free agent by **Edmonton**, July 17, 2007. Signed as a free agent by **Pittsburgh**, July 8, 2008. Traded to **Montreal** by **Pittsburgh** for future considerations, January 5, 2009.

### KEMPE, Mario (KEHM-peh, MAHR-ee-oh) PHI.

Center. Shoots left. 6', 185 lbs. Born, Kramfors, Sweden, September 19, 1988.
(Philadelphia's 4th choice, 122nd overall, in 2007 Entry Draft).

| | | | Regular Season | | | | | Playoffs | | | | |
|---|---|---|---|---|---|---|---|---|---|---|---|---|
| Season | Club | League | GP | G | A | Pts | PIM | GP | G | A | Pts | PIM |
| 2003-04 | Hoga Kusten | Sweden-4 | STATISTICS NOT AVAILABLE | | | | | | | | | |
| 2004-05 | MODO U18 | Swe-U18 | 14 | 5 | 7 | 12 | 40 | 4 | 1 | 1 | 2 | 4 |
| 2005-06 | MODO U18 | Swe-U18 | 6 | 4 | 2 | 6 | 29 | 2 | 0 | 2 | 2 | 0 |
| | MODO Jr. | Swe-Jr. | 36 | 20 | 12 | 32 | 16 | 2 | 0 | 0 | 0 | 10 |
| 2006-07 | St. John's | QMJHL | 62 | 23 | 19 | 42 | 51 | 4 | 0 | 0 | 0 | 2 |
| 2007-08 | St. John's | QMJHL | 48 | 25 | 24 | 49 | 36 | 6 | 4 | 3 | 7 | 8 |
| 2008-09 | Rogle | Sweden | 30 | 2 | 8 | 10 | 8 | .... | .... | .... | .... | .... |
| | Philadelphia | AHL | 5 | 0 | 0 | 0 | 2 | 3 | 0 | 0 | 0 | 2 |

### KENNEDY, Matt (KEH-nuh-dee, MAT) CAR.

Right wing. Shoots right. 6'2", 202 lbs. Born, Richmond Hill, Ont., March 4, 1989.
(Carolina's 4th choice, 131st overall, in 2009 Entry Draft).

| | | | Regular Season | | | | | Playoffs | | | | |
|---|---|---|---|---|---|---|---|---|---|---|---|---|
| Season | Club | League | GP | G | A | Pts | PIM | GP | G | A | Pts | PIM |
| 2005-06 | Seguin Bruins | OPJHL | 47 | 11 | 16 | 27 | 71 | 6 | 0 | 0 | 0 | 8 |
| | Guelph Storm | OHL | 13 | 1 | 0 | 1 | 31 | 13 | 0 | 2 | 2 | 8 |
| 2006-07 | Guelph Storm | OHL | 63 | 10 | 12 | 22 | 78 | 4 | 1 | 1 | 2 | 10 |
| 2007-08 | Guelph Storm | OHL | 45 | 17 | 4 | 21 | 99 | 10 | 3 | 1 | 4 | 25 |
| 2008-09 | Guelph Storm | OHL | 67 | 33 | 40 | 73 | 95 | 4 | 3 | 2 | 5 | 0 |
| | Syracuse Crunch | AHL | 4 | 1 | 0 | 1 | 2 | .... | .... | .... | .... | .... |

### KESSEL, Blake (KEH-suhl, BLAYK) NYI

Defense. Shoots right. 6'1", 210 lbs. Born, Madison, WI, April 13, 1989.
(NY Islanders' 4th choice, 166th overall, in 2007 Entry Draft).

| | | | Regular Season | | | | | Playoffs | | | | |
|---|---|---|---|---|---|---|---|---|---|---|---|---|
| Season | Club | League | GP | G | A | Pts | PIM | GP | G | A | Pts | PIM |
| 2005-06 | Madison Capitols | MAHL | 62 | 33 | 47 | 80 | .... | .... | .... | .... | .... | .... |
| 2006-07 | Waterloo | USHL | 59 | 11 | 27 | 38 | 38 | 9 | 1 | 5 | 6 | 8 |
| 2007-08 | Waterloo | USHL | 59 | 19 | 38 | 57 | 26 | 11 | 1 | *10 | 11 | 12 |
| 2008-09 | New Hampshire | H-East | 37 | 6 | 7 | 13 | 24 | .... | .... | .... | .... | .... |

USHL All-Rookie Team (2007) • USHL Defenseman of the Year (2008) • USHL First All-Star Team (2008)

### KHOMITSKI, Vadim (khoh-MIHT-skee, va-DEEM) DAL.

Defense. Shoots left. 6'1", 185 lbs. Born, Voskresensk, USSR, July 21, 1982.
(Dallas' 5th choice, 123rd overall, in 2000 Entry Draft).

| | | | Regular Season | | | | | Playoffs | | | | |
|---|---|---|---|---|---|---|---|---|---|---|---|---|
| Season | Club | League | GP | G | A | Pts | PIM | GP | G | A | Pts | PIM |
| 1998-99 | Voskresensk | Russia | 9 | 0 | 0 | 0 | 10 | .... | .... | .... | .... | .... |
| 99-2000 | Voskresensk | Russia-2 | 17 | 0 | 0 | 0 | 31 | .... | .... | .... | .... | .... |
| | HK Moscow | Russia-2 | 11 | 0 | 1 | 1 | 10 | .... | .... | .... | .... | .... |
| 2000-01 | HK Moscow | Russia-2 | 44 | 2 | 7 | 9 | 89 | .... | .... | .... | .... | .... |
| 2001-02 | HK CSKA Moscow | Russia-2 | 68 | 2 | 18 | 20 | 63 | .... | .... | .... | .... | .... |
| 2002-03 | CSKA Moscow | Russia | 51 | 3 | 2 | 5 | 58 | .... | .... | .... | .... | .... |
| 2003-04 | CSKA Moscow | Russia | 54 | 3 | 3 | 6 | 46 | .... | .... | .... | .... | .... |
| 2004-05 | CSKA Moscow | Russia | 60 | 1 | 5 | 6 | 105 | .... | .... | .... | .... | .... |
| 2005-06 | CSKA Moscow | Russia | 51 | 5 | 6 | 11 | 110 | 7 | 0 | 0 | 0 | 6 |
| 2006-07 | Iowa Stars | AHL | 9 | 1 | 6 | 7 | 24 | .... | .... | .... | .... | .... |
| | Mytischi | Russia | 29 | 6 | 5 | 11 | 50 | 9 | 1 | 1 | 2 | 22 |
| 2007-08 | Iowa Stars | AHL | 7 | 1 | 0 | 1 | 10 | .... | .... | .... | .... | .... |
| | Mytischi | Russia | 27 | 1 | 3 | 4 | 34 | 5 | 1 | 2 | 3 | 8 |
| 2008-09 | Mytischi | Rus-KHL | 45 | 2 | 4 | 6 | 68 | 7 | 2 | 0 | 2 | 25 |

### KHOMUTOV, Ivan (khoh-moo-TAWF, ee-VAHN) N.J.

Center. Shoots left. 6'3", 220 lbs. Born, Saratov, USSR, March 11, 1985.
(New Jersey's 3rd choice, 93rd overall, in 2003 Entry Draft).

| | | | Regular Season | | | | | Playoffs | | | | |
|---|---|---|---|---|---|---|---|---|---|---|---|---|
| Season | Club | League | GP | G | A | Pts | PIM | GP | G | A | Pts | PIM |
| 2001-02 | HK CSKA 2 | Russia-3 | 30 | 11 | 8 | 19 | 14 | .... | .... | .... | .... | .... |
| 2002-03 | Elektrostal | Russia-2 | 20 | 1 | 1 | 2 | 8 | .... | .... | .... | .... | .... |
| 2003-04 | London Knights | OHL | 40 | 9 | 12 | 21 | 25 | 15 | 3 | 1 | 4 | 7 |
| 2004-05 | Albany River Rats | AHL | 66 | 6 | 11 | 17 | 30 | .... | .... | .... | .... | .... |
| 2005-06 | Albany River Rats | AHL | 60 | 9 | 20 | 29 | 44 | .... | .... | .... | .... | .... |
| 2006-07 | Lowell Devils | AHL | 3 | 1 | 1 | 2 | 2 | .... | .... | .... | .... | .... |
| | Trenton Titans | ECHL | 5 | 0 | 1 | 1 | 2 | .... | .... | .... | .... | .... |
| 2007-08 | Lowell Devils | AHL | 72 | 13 | 19 | 32 | 53 | .... | .... | .... | .... | .... |
| 2008-09 | CSKA Moscow | Rus-KHL | 47 | 9 | 7 | 16 | 32 | 7 | 1 | 0 | 1 | 4 |

### KILLORN, Alexander (KIHL-ohrn, al-ehx-AN-duhr) T.B.

Center. Shoots left. 6', 161 lbs. Born, Halifax, N.S., September 14, 1989.
(Tampa Bay's 3rd choice, 77th overall, in 2007 Entry Draft).

| | | | Regular Season | | | | | Playoffs | | | | |
|---|---|---|---|---|---|---|---|---|---|---|---|---|
| Season | Club | League | GP | G | A | Pts | PIM | GP | G | A | Pts | PIM |
| 2005-06 | Lac St-Louis Lions | QAAA | 43 | 18 | 34 | 52 | 94 | 10 | 9 | 6 | 15 | 8 |
| 2006-07 | Deerfield Academy | High-MA | 25 | 18 | 14 | 32 | .... | .... | .... | .... | .... | .... |
| 2007-08 | Deerfield Academy | High-MA | 24 | 28 | 27 | 55 | .... | .... | .... | .... | .... | .... |
| 2008-09 | Harvard Crimson | ECAC | 30 | 6 | 8 | 14 | 46 | .... | .... | .... | .... | .... |

### KINCH, Matt (KIHNCH, MATT)

Defense. Shoots left. 5'11", 185 lbs. Born, Red Deer, Alta., February 17, 1980.
(Buffalo's 8th choice, 146th overall, in 1999 Entry Draft).

| | | | Regular Season | | | | | Playoffs | | | | |
|---|---|---|---|---|---|---|---|---|---|---|---|---|
| Season | Club | League | GP | G | A | Pts | PIM | GP | G | A | Pts | PIM |
| 1995-96 | Red Deer | AMHL | 35 | 6 | 17 | 23 | 31 | .... | .... | .... | .... | .... |
| | Calgary Hitmen | WHL | 1 | 0 | 1 | 1 | 2 | .... | .... | .... | .... | .... |
| 1996-97 | Calgary Hitmen | WHL | 64 | 10 | 22 | 32 | 31 | .... | .... | .... | .... | .... |
| 1997-98 | Calgary Hitmen | WHL | 55 | 7 | 24 | 31 | 13 | 18 | 3 | 2 | 5 | 4 |
| 1998-99 | Calgary Hitmen | WHL | 68 | 14 | 69 | 83 | 16 | 21 | 8 | 15 | 23 | 59 |
| 99-2000 | Calgary Hitmen | WHL | 62 | 14 | 61 | 75 | 24 | 13 | 2 | 12 | 14 | 8 |
| 2000-01 | Calgary Hitmen | WHL | 70 | 18 | 66 | 84 | 52 | 12 | 3 | 6 | 9 | 6 |
| 2001-02 | Hartford Wolf Pack | AHL | 40 | 1 | 7 | 8 | 4 | .... | .... | .... | .... | .... |
| | Charlotte | ECHL | 26 | 3 | 12 | 15 | 13 | 5 | 3 | 2 | 5 | 0 |
| 2002-03 | Hartford Wolf Pack | AHL | 66 | 7 | 22 | 29 | 28 | 2 | 0 | 0 | 0 | 0 |
| 2003-04 | Hartford Wolf Pack | AHL | 67 | 1 | 19 | 20 | 38 | 1 | 0 | 0 | 0 | 0 |
| 2004-05 | Salzburg | Austria | 37 | 1 | 12 | 13 | 18 | .... | .... | .... | .... | .... |
| 2005-06 | Langnau | Swiss | 25 | 1 | 4 | 5 | 14 | .... | .... | .... | .... | .... |
| | ERC Ingolstadt | Germany | 16 | 1 | 2 | 3 | 16 | 7 | 0 | 0 | 0 | 4 |
| 2006-07 | Straubing Tigers | Germany | 51 | 4 | 20 | 24 | 36 | .... | .... | .... | .... | .... |
| 2007-08 | Binghamton | AHL | 73 | 9 | 16 | 25 | 73 | .... | .... | .... | .... | .... |
| 2008-09 | Worcester Sharks | AHL | 3 | 0 | 2 | 2 | 0 | .... | .... | .... | .... | .... |
| | Wolfsburg | Germany | 23 | 3 | 4 | 7 | 12 | 10 | 1 | 2 | 3 | 10 |

WHL East First All-Star Team (1999, 2001) • Memorial Cup Tournament All-Star Team (1999) • Canadian Major Junior Sportsman of the Year (1999) • WHL East Second All-Star Team (2000) • Canadian Major Junior First All-Star Team (2001)

Signed as a free agent by **NY Rangers**, June 26, 2001. Signed as a free agent by **Salzburg** (Austria), August 11, 2004. Signed as a free agent by **Ottawa**, July 17, 2007. Signed as a free agent by **San Jose**, July 17, 2008.

### KINDL, Jakub (KEEHN-duhl, YA-kuhb) DET.

Defense. Shoots left. 6'3", 199 lbs. Born, Sumperk, Czech., February 10, 1987.
(Detroit's 1st choice, 19th overall, in 2005 Entry Draft).

| | | | Regular Season | | | | | Playoffs | | | | |
|---|---|---|---|---|---|---|---|---|---|---|---|---|
| Season | Club | League | GP | G | A | Pts | PIM | GP | G | A | Pts | PIM |
| 2002-03 | HC Pardubice U17 | CzR-U17 | 3 | 0 | 3 | 3 | 10 | .... | .... | .... | .... | .... |
| | HC Pardubice Jr. | CzRep-Jr. | 27 | 0 | 3 | 3 | 46 | .... | .... | .... | .... | .... |
| | Pardubice | CzRep | 1 | 0 | 0 | 0 | 0 | .... | .... | .... | .... | .... |
| 2003-04 | HC Pardubice U17 | CzR-U17 | 2 | 0 | 1 | 1 | 6 | .... | .... | .... | .... | .... |
| | HC Pardubice Jr. | CzRep-Jr. | 48 | 4 | 14 | 18 | 108 | .... | .... | .... | .... | .... |
| | Hr. Kralove | CzRep-2 | 1 | 0 | 0 | 0 | 0 | 1 | 0 | 0 | 0 | 0 |
| 2004-05 | Kitchener Rangers | OHL | 62 | 3 | 11 | 14 | 92 | 12 | 0 | 0 | 0 | 22 |
| 2005-06 | Kitchener Rangers | OHL | 60 | 12 | 46 | 58 | 112 | 5 | 1 | 0 | 1 | 10 |
| | Grand Rapids | AHL | 3 | 0 | 1 | 1 | 2 | .... | .... | .... | .... | .... |
| 2006-07 | Kitchener Rangers | OHL | 54 | 11 | 44 | 55 | 142 | 9 | 2 | 9 | 11 | 8 |
| | Grand Rapids | AHL | .... | .... | .... | .... | .... | 7 | 0 | 2 | 2 | 0 |
| 2007-08 | Grand Rapids | AHL | 75 | 3 | 14 | 17 | 82 | .... | .... | .... | .... | .... |
| 2008-09 | Grand Rapids | AHL | 78 | 6 | 27 | 33 | 76 | 10 | 2 | 1 | 3 | 2 |

OHL Second All-Star Team (2007)

### KING, Dwight (KIHNG, DWIGHT) L.A.

Center/Left wing. Shoots left. 6'3", 218 lbs. Born, Meadowlake, Sask., July 5, 1989.
(Los Angeles' 6th choice, 109th overall, in 2007 Entry Draft).

| | | | Regular Season | | | | | Playoffs | | | | |
|---|---|---|---|---|---|---|---|---|---|---|---|---|
| Season | Club | League | GP | G | A | Pts | PIM | GP | G | A | Pts | PIM |
| 2004-05 | Beardy's | SMHL | 44 | 26 | 30 | 56 | 16 | 3 | 0 | 1 | 1 | 4 |
| | Lethbridge | WHL | 7 | 0 | 0 | 0 | 2 | 4 | 0 | 0 | 0 | 2 |
| 2005-06 | Lethbridge | WHL | 68 | 8 | 8 | 16 | 22 | 6 | 0 | 0 | 0 | 6 |
| 2006-07 | Lethbridge | WHL | 62 | 12 | 32 | 44 | 39 | .... | .... | .... | .... | .... |
| 2007-08 | Lethbridge | WHL | 72 | 34 | 35 | 69 | 56 | 19 | 8 | 6 | 14 | 12 |
| 2008-09 | Lethbridge | WHL | 64 | 25 | 35 | 60 | 51 | 11 | 1 | 7 | 8 | 2 |

### KISHEL, Scott (KIH-shuhl, SKAWT) MTL.

Defense. Shoots left. 6', 172 lbs. Born, Virginia, MN, April 21, 1989.
(Montreal's 9th choice, 192nd overall, in 2007 Entry Draft).

| | | | Regular Season | | | | | Playoffs | | | | |
|---|---|---|---|---|---|---|---|---|---|---|---|---|
| Season | Club | League | GP | G | A | Pts | PIM | GP | G | A | Pts | PIM |
| 2004-05 | Virginia Blue Devils | High-MN | .... | 4 | 9 | 13 | .... | .... | .... | .... | .... | .... |
| 2005-06 | Virginia Blue Devils | High-MN | .... | 5 | 25 | 30 | .... | .... | .... | .... | .... | .... |
| 2006-07 | Virginia Blue Devils | High-MN | 24 | 14 | 34 | 48 | .... | .... | .... | .... | .... | .... |
| 2007-08 | Sioux Falls | USHL | 57 | 3 | 11 | 14 | 34 | 3 | 0 | 0 | 0 | 0 |
| 2008-09 | U. Minn-Duluth | WCHA | 12 | 0 | 2 | 2 | 2 | .... | .... | .... | .... | .... |

### KIVISTO, Tommi (K'VIHS-toh, TAW-mee) CAR.

Defense. Shoots left. 6'1", 195 lbs. Born, Vantaa, Finland, June 7, 1991.
(Carolina's 6th choice, 208th overall, in 2009 Entry Draft).

| | | | Regular Season | | | | | Playoffs | | | | |
|---|---|---|---|---|---|---|---|---|---|---|---|---|
| Season | Club | League | GP | G | A | Pts | PIM | GP | G | A | Pts | PIM |
| 2006-07 | Jokerit U18 | Fin-U18 | 24 | 0 | 2 | 2 | 10 | .... | .... | .... | .... | .... |
| 2007-08 | Jokerit U18 | Fin-U18 | 26 | 6 | 10 | 16 | 50 | 4 | 0 | 3 | 3 | 4 |
| | Jokerit Helsinki Jr. | Fin-Jr. | 9 | 2 | 0 | 2 | 4 | 4 | 0 | 3 | 3 | 2 |
| 2008-09 | Red Deer Rebels | WHL | 65 | 1 | 21 | 22 | 49 | .... | .... | .... | .... | .... |

### KLASSEN, Sam (klah-SIHN, SAM) NYR

Defense. Shoots left. 6'1", 196 lbs. Born, Watrous, Sask., January 1, 1989.

| | | | Regular Season | | | | | Playoffs | | | | |
|---|---|---|---|---|---|---|---|---|---|---|---|---|
| Season | Club | League | GP | G | A | Pts | PIM | GP | G | A | Pts | PIM |
| 2006-07 | Humboldt Broncos | SJHL | 32 | 2 | 9 | 11 | 74 | .... | .... | .... | .... | .... |
| | Saskatoon Blades | WHL | 39 | 1 | 5 | 6 | 52 | .... | .... | .... | .... | .... |
| 2007-08 | Saskatoon Blades | WHL | 71 | 1 | 24 | 25 | 103 | .... | .... | .... | .... | .... |
| 2008-09 | Saskatoon Blades | WHL | 72 | 2 | 18 | 20 | 92 | 7 | 0 | 1 | 1 | 10 |

Signed as a free agent by **NY Rangers**, July 27, 2009.

### KLEMENTYEV, Anton (kluh-MEHN-tee-ehv, AN-tawn) NYI

Defense. Shoots right. 6'1", 198 lbs. Born, Togliatti, USSR, March 25, 1990.
(NY Islanders' 6th choice, 122nd overall, in 2009 Entry Draft).

| | | | Regular Season | | | | | Playoffs | | | | |
|---|---|---|---|---|---|---|---|---|---|---|---|---|
| Season | Club | League | GP | G | A | Pts | PIM | GP | G | A | Pts | PIM |
| 2006-07 | Yaroslavl 2 | Russia-3 | 36 | 2 | 6 | 8 | 69 | .... | .... | .... | .... | .... |
| 2007-08 | Yaroslavl 2 | Russia-3 | | STATISTICS NOT AVAILABLE | | | | | | | | |
| 2008-09 | Yaroslavl 2 | Russia-3 | | STATISTICS NOT AVAILABLE | | | | | | | | |
| | Yaroslavl | Rus-KHL | 1 | 0 | 0 | 0 | 0 | .... | .... | .... | .... | .... |

### KLINGBERG, Carl (KLIHNG-buhrg, KAHRL) ATL.

Left wing. Shoots right. 6'3", 205 lbs. Born, Goteborg, Sweden, January 28, 1991.
(Atlanta's 2nd choice, 34th overall, in 2009 Entry Draft).

| | | | Regular Season | | | | | Playoffs | | | | |
|---|---|---|---|---|---|---|---|---|---|---|---|---|
| Season | Club | League | GP | G | A | Pts | PIM | GP | G | A | Pts | PIM |
| 2006-07 | Frolunda U18 | Swe-U18 | 7 | 3 | 1 | 4 | 0 | .... | .... | .... | .... | .... |
| | Frolunda Jr. | Swe-Jr. | 2 | 0 | 0 | 0 | 0 | .... | .... | .... | .... | .... |
| 2007-08 | Frolunda U18 | Swe-U18 | 31 | 19 | 24 | 43 | 22 | 5 | 2 | 1 | 3 | 8 |
| 2008-09 | Frolunda U18 | Swe-U18 | 3 | 4 | 1 | 5 | 0 | 5 | 2 | 2 | 4 | 2 |
| | Frolunda Jr. | Swe-Jr. | 35 | 13 | 13 | 26 | 34 | 2 | 0 | 0 | 0 | 4 |
| | Boras HC | Sweden-2 | 8 | 4 | 2 | 6 | 2 | .... | .... | .... | .... | .... |
| | Frolunda | Sweden | 10 | 2 | 1 | 3 | 0 | .... | .... | .... | .... | .... |

### KLINKHAMMER, Robert (KLIHNK-ham-uhr, RAW-buhrt) CHI.

Left wing. Shoots left. 6'3", 209 lbs. Born, Lethbridge, Alta., August 12, 1986.

| | | | Regular Season | | | | | Playoffs | | | | |
|---|---|---|---|---|---|---|---|---|---|---|---|---|
| Season | Club | League | GP | G | A | Pts | PIM | GP | G | A | Pts | PIM |
| 2003-04 | Lethbridge Y | AMHL | 29 | 20 | 22 | 42 | 8 | .... | .... | .... | .... | .... |
| | Lethbridge | WHL | 25 | 2 | 3 | 5 | 12 | .... | .... | .... | .... | .... |
| 2004-05 | Lethbridge | WHL | 72 | 14 | 12 | 26 | 81 | 5 | 0 | 1 | 1 | 4 |
| 2005-06 | Lethbridge | WHL | 35 | 5 | 7 | 12 | 15 | .... | .... | .... | .... | .... |
| | Seattle | WHL | 32 | 3 | 5 | 8 | 37 | 7 | 0 | 1 | 1 | 6 |
| 2006-07 | Seattle | WHL | 1 | 0 | 0 | 0 | 9 | .... | .... | .... | .... | .... |
| | Portland | WHL | 37 | 23 | 19 | 42 | 70 | .... | .... | .... | .... | .... |
| | Brandon | WHL | 28 | 10 | 21 | 31 | 29 | 11 | 4 | 4 | 8 | 22 |
| 2007-08 | Norfolk Admirals | AHL | 66 | 12 | 12 | 24 | 41 | .... | .... | .... | .... | .... |
| 2008-09 | Rockford IceHogs | AHL | 76 | 15 | 18 | 33 | 32 | 4 | 0 | 1 | 1 | 0 |

Signed as a free agent by **Tampa Bay**, July, 2007. Signed as a free agent by **Chicago**, June 8, 2009.

### KLOTZ, Garrett (KLAWTZ, GAIR-reht) PHI.

Left wing. Shoots left. 6'6", 225 lbs. Born, Regina, Sask., November 27, 1988.
(Philadelphia's 3rd choice, 66th overall, in 2007 Entry Draft).

| | | | Regular Season | | | | | Playoffs | | | | |
|---|---|---|---|---|---|---|---|---|---|---|---|---|
| Season | Club | League | GP | G | A | Pts | PIM | GP | G | A | Pts | PIM |
| 2004-05 | Reg. Midget Hawks | SMMHL | | STATISTICS NOT AVAILABLE | | | | | | | | |
| | Reg. Pat Canadians | SMHL | 5 | 0 | 1 | 1 | 0 | .... | .... | .... | .... | .... |
| 2005-06 | Red Deer Rebels | WHL | 35 | 2 | 0 | 2 | 26 | .... | .... | .... | .... | .... |
| 2006-07 | Saskatoon Blades | WHL | 63 | 2 | 2 | 4 | 107 | .... | .... | .... | .... | .... |
| 2007-08 | Saskatoon Blades | WHL | 52 | 1 | 3 | 4 | 96 | .... | .... | .... | .... | .... |
| 2008-09 | Philadelphia | AHL | 36 | 0 | 1 | 1 | 59 | .... | .... | .... | .... | .... |

### KNACKSTEDT, Jordan (NAK-stehd, JOHR-dahn) BOS.

Right wing. Shoots right. 6'2", 195 lbs. Born, Saskatoon, Sask., September 28, 1988.
(Boston's 6th choice, 189th overall, in 2007 Entry Draft).

| | | | Regular Season | | | | | Playoffs | | | | |
|---|---|---|---|---|---|---|---|---|---|---|---|---|
| Season | Club | League | GP | G | A | Pts | PIM | GP | G | A | Pts | PIM |
| 2003-04 | Beardy's | SMHL | 44 | 22 | 19 | 41 | 20 | 4 | 2 | 1 | 3 | 0 |
| 2004-05 | Red Deer Rebels | WHL | 52 | 1 | 2 | 3 | 34 | 7 | 0 | 0 | 0 | 2 |
| 2005-06 | Red Deer Rebels | WHL | 72 | 12 | 28 | 40 | 36 | .... | .... | .... | .... | .... |
| 2006-07 | Red Deer Rebels | WHL | 33 | 10 | 7 | 17 | 54 | .... | .... | .... | .... | .... |
| | Moose Jaw | WHL | 39 | 13 | 26 | 39 | 44 | .... | .... | .... | .... | .... |
| 2007-08 | Moose Jaw | WHL | 72 | 31 | 54 | 85 | 116 | 6 | 1 | 1 | 2 | 8 |
| | Providence Bruins | AHL | 5 | 2 | 0 | 2 | 2 | 4 | 1 | 0 | 1 | 0 |
| 2008-09 | Providence Bruins | AHL | 71 | 10 | 16 | 26 | 55 | 16 | 3 | 1 | 4 | 11 |

### KNIGHT, Corban (NIGHT, KOHR-buhn) FLA.

Center. Shoots right. 6'1", 180 lbs. Born, Oliver, B.C., September 10, 1990.
(Florida's 5th choice, 135th overall, in 2009 Entry Draft).

| | | | Regular Season | | | | | Playoffs | | | | |
|---|---|---|---|---|---|---|---|---|---|---|---|---|
| Season | Club | League | GP | G | A | Pts | PIM | GP | G | A | Pts | PIM |
| 2006-07 | UFA Bisons | AMHL | 36 | 6 | 18 | 24 | 44 | 8 | 2 | 4 | 6 | 16 |
| 2007-08 | UFA Bisons | AMHL | 36 | 29 | 36 | 65 | 64 | 6 | 5 | 4 | 9 | 10 |
| | Okotoks Oilers | AJHL | 4 | 1 | 0 | 1 | 0 | 7 | 0 | 0 | 0 | 0 |
| 2008-09 | Okotoks Oilers | AJHL | 61 | 34 | 38 | 72 | 55 | 9 | 10 | 2 | 12 | 12 |

• Signed Letter of Intent to attend **University of North Dakota** (WCHA) in fall of 2010.

### KNODEL, Eric (NOH-dehl, AIR-ihk) TOR.

Defense. Shoots left. 6'6", 216 lbs. Born, West Chesteer, PA, June 8, 1990.
(Toronto's 5th choice, 128th overall, in 2009 Entry Draft).

| | | | Regular Season | | | | | Playoffs | | | | |
|---|---|---|---|---|---|---|---|---|---|---|---|---|
| Season | Club | League | GP | G | A | Pts | PIM | GP | G | A | Pts | PIM |
| 2007-08 | Phi. Jr. Flyers | AYHL | 16 | 5 | 6 | 11 | 6 | .... | .... | .... | .... | .... |
| | Phi. Jr. Flyers | Exhib. | 35 | 11 | 17 | 28 | 30 | .... | .... | .... | .... | .... |
| 2008-09 | Phi. Jr. Flyers | AYHL | 16 | 2 | 13 | 15 | 12 | .... | .... | .... | .... | .... |
| | Phi. Jr. Flyers | Exhib. | 35 | 11 | 19 | 30 | 18 | .... | .... | .... | .... | .... |

### KNYAZEV, Igor (kuh-NYA-zhev, EE-gohr) PHX.

Defense. Shoots left. 6', 208 lbs. Born, Elektrostal, USSR, January 27, 1983.
(Carolina's 1st choice, 15th overall, in 2001 Entry Draft).

| | | | Regular Season | | | | | Playoffs | | | | |
|---|---|---|---|---|---|---|---|---|---|---|---|---|
| Season | Club | League | GP | G | A | Pts | PIM | GP | G | A | Pts | PIM |
| 99-2000 | Spartak Moscow 2 | Russia-3 | 13 | 2 | 4 | 6 | 74 | .... | .... | .... | .... | .... |
| | Spartak Moscow | Russia-2 | 26 | 1 | 1 | 2 | 6 | .... | .... | .... | .... | .... |
| 2000-01 | Spartak Moscow | Russia-2 | 53 | 6 | 5 | 11 | 101 | .... | .... | .... | .... | .... |
| 2001-02 | Spartak Moscow | Russia | 3 | 0 | 0 | 0 | 8 | .... | .... | .... | .... | .... |
| | Spartak Moscow 2 | Russia-3 | 2 | 0 | 1 | 1 | 0 | .... | .... | .... | .... | .... |
| | Ak Bars Kazan | Russia | 14 | 0 | 1 | 1 | 4 | 3 | 0 | 0 | 0 | 0 |
| 2002-03 | Lowell | AHL | 68 | 2 | 5 | 7 | 68 | .... | .... | .... | .... | .... |
| 2003-04 | Springfield Falcons | AHL | 72 | 1 | 6 | 7 | 61 | .... | .... | .... | .... | .... |
| 2004-05 | Voskresensk | Russia | 29 | 0 | 2 | 2 | 57 | .... | .... | .... | .... | .... |
| 2005-06 | Mytischi | Russia | 21 | 3 | 1 | 4 | 36 | .... | .... | .... | .... | .... |
| 2006-07 | Dynamo Moscow | Russia | 14 | 0 | 2 | 2 | 22 | .... | .... | .... | .... | .... |
| | Vityaz Chekhov | Russia | 12 | 0 | 0 | 0 | 82 | 3 | 0 | 0 | 0 | 2 |
| 2007-08 | MVD | Russia | 8 | 0 | 2 | 2 | 6 | 3 | 0 | 2 | 2 | 2 |
| 2008-09 | MVD | Rus-KHL | 8 | 0 | 1 | 1 | 8 | .... | .... | .... | .... | .... |

Traded to **Phoenix** by **Carolina** with David Tanabe for Danny Markov and Edmonton's 3rd round choice (previously acquired, later traded to NY Rangers - NY Rangers selected Billy Ryan) in 2004 Entry Draft, June 21, 2003. Signed as a free agent by **Voskresensk** (Russia), September, 2004.

## KOHN, Dustin
(KOHN, DUHS-tihn) **NYI**

Defense. Shoots left. 6'2", 182 lbs. Born, Edmonton, Alta., February 2, 1987.
(NY Islanders' 2nd choice, 46th overall, in 2005 Entry Draft).

| | | | Regular Season | | | | | Playoffs | | | | |
|---|---|---|---|---|---|---|---|---|---|---|---|---|
| Season | Club | League | GP | G | A | Pts | PIM | GP | G | A | Pts | PIM |
| 2003-04 | Calgary Hitmen | WHL | 52 | 3 | 6 | 9 | 13 | 7 | 0 | 1 | 1 | 2 |
| 2004-05 | Calgary Hitmen | WHL | 71 | 8 | 35 | 43 | 61 | 12 | 0 | 4 | 4 | 6 |
| 2005-06 | Calgary Hitmen | WHL | 38 | 2 | 12 | 14 | 20 | .... | .... | .... | .... | .... |
| | Brandon | WHL | 31 | 2 | 13 | 15 | 30 | 6 | 0 | 4 | 4 | 10 |
| | Bridgeport | AHL | 2 | 0 | 0 | 0 | 0 | .... | .... | .... | .... | .... |
| 2006-07 | Brandon | WHL | 61 | 5 | 45 | 50 | 77 | 11 | 1 | 8 | 9 | 18 |
| 2007-08 | Bridgeport | AHL | 62 | 3 | 9 | 12 | 28 | .... | .... | .... | .... | .... |
| 2008-09 | Bridgeport | AHL | 58 | 4 | 13 | 17 | 45 | 5 | 0 | 0 | 0 | 4 |

## KOLARIK, Chad
(kah-LOHR-ihk, CHAD) **PHX.**

Center. Shoots right. 5'10", 175 lbs. Born, Abington, PA, January 26, 1986.
(Phoenix's 7th choice, 199th overall, in 2004 Entry Draft).

| | | | Regular Season | | | | | Playoffs | | | | |
|---|---|---|---|---|---|---|---|---|---|---|---|---|
| Season | Club | League | GP | G | A | Pts | PIM | GP | G | A | Pts | PIM |
| 2002-03 | USNTDP | U-17 | 21 | 14 | 10 | 24 | 4 | .... | .... | .... | .... | .... |
| | USNTDP | NAHL | 44 | 16 | 22 | 38 | 43 | .... | .... | .... | .... | .... |
| 2003-04 | USNTDP | U-18 | 45 | 18 | 20 | 38 | 16 | .... | .... | .... | .... | .... |
| | USNTDP | NAHL | 10 | 3 | 4 | 7 | 4 | .... | .... | .... | .... | .... |
| 2004-05 | U. of Michigan | CCHA | 42 | 18 | 17 | 35 | 53 | .... | .... | .... | .... | .... |
| 2005-06 | U. of Michigan | CCHA | 41 | 12 | 26 | 38 | 30 | .... | .... | .... | .... | .... |
| 2006-07 | U. of Michigan | CCHA | 41 | 18 | 27 | 45 | 24 | .... | .... | .... | .... | .... |
| 2007-08 | U. of Michigan | CCHA | 39 | 30 | 26 | 56 | 24 | .... | .... | .... | .... | .... |
| | San Antonio | AHL | .... | .... | .... | .... | .... | 7 | 4 | 2 | 6 | 0 |
| 2008-09 | San Antonio | AHL | 76 | 20 | 30 | 50 | 47 | .... | .... | .... | .... | .... |

CCHA First All-Star Team (2008) • NCAA West Second All-American Team (2008)

## KOLOMATIS, David
(koh-loh-MA-tihs, DAY-vihd) **L.A.**

Defense. Shoots right. 5'11", 189 lbs. Born, Livingston, NJ, February 25, 1989.
(Los Angeles' 6th choice, 126th overall, in 2009 Entry Draft).

| | | | Regular Season | | | | | Playoffs | | | | |
|---|---|---|---|---|---|---|---|---|---|---|---|---|
| Season | Club | League | GP | G | A | Pts | PIM | GP | G | A | Pts | PIM |
| 2005-06 | USNTDP | NAHL | 16 | 1 | 0 | 1 | 4 | .... | .... | .... | .... | .... |
| | USNTDP | U-17 | 3 | 0 | 0 | 0 | 2 | .... | .... | .... | .... | .... |
| 2006-07 | Owen Sound | OHL | 67 | 4 | 16 | 20 | 54 | 4 | 0 | 0 | 0 | 0 |
| 2007-08 | Owen Sound | OHL | 68 | 9 | 36 | 45 | 68 | .... | .... | .... | .... | .... |
| 2008-09 | Owen Sound | OHL | 63 | 18 | 28 | 46 | 52 | 4 | 2 | 2 | 4 | 0 |
| | Providence Bruins | AHL | 4 | 0 | 0 | 0 | 0 | 16 | 0 | 1 | 1 | 2 |

## KOLOSOV, Sergei
(KOH-leh-sawf, SAIR-gay) **DET.**

Defense. Shoots left. 6'4", 210 lbs. Born, Novopolotsk, USSR, May 22, 1986.
(Detroit's 3rd choice, 151st overall, in 2004 Entry Draft).

| | | | Regular Season | | | | | Playoffs | | | | |
|---|---|---|---|---|---|---|---|---|---|---|---|---|
| Season | Club | League | GP | G | A | Pts | PIM | GP | G | A | Pts | PIM |
| 2003-04 | Dynamo Minsk | Belarus | STATISTICS NOT AVAILABLE | | | | | | | | | |
| 2004-05 | Dynamo Minsk | BelOpen | 37 | 2 | 6 | 8 | 24 | .... | .... | .... | .... | .... |
| | Yunost-Minsk | BelOpen | 1 | 0 | 0 | 0 | 2 | 9 | 0 | 0 | 0 | 4 |
| 2005-06 | Cedar Rapids | USHL | 50 | 2 | 8 | 10 | 66 | 8 | 0 | 0 | 0 | 10 |
| 2006-07 | Cedar Rapids | USHL | 51 | 1 | 10 | 11 | 79 | 5 | 0 | 0 | 0 | 4 |
| 2007-08 | Dynamo Minsk | Belarus | 55 | 5 | 9 | 14 | 83 | .... | .... | .... | .... | .... |
| 2008-09 | Grand Rapids | AHL | 70 | 4 | 7 | 11 | 36 | 10 | 0 | 0 | 0 | 9 |

## KOLTSOV, Kirill
(kohlt-SAHV, kih-RIHL) **VAN.**

Defense. Shoots left. 5'11", 183 lbs. Born, Chelyabinsk, USSR, February 1, 1983.
(Vancouver's 1st choice, 49th overall, in 2002 Entry Draft).

| | | | Regular Season | | | | | Playoffs | | | | |
|---|---|---|---|---|---|---|---|---|---|---|---|---|
| Season | Club | League | GP | G | A | Pts | PIM | GP | G | A | Pts | PIM |
| 1998-99 | Streetsville Derbys | OPJHL | 20 | 5 | 7 | 12 | 4 | .... | .... | .... | .... | .... |
| 99-2000 | Omsk 2 | Russia-3 | 27 | 0 | 7 | 7 | 30 | .... | .... | .... | .... | .... |
| | Avangard Omsk | Russia | 2 | 0 | 0 | 0 | 0 | .... | .... | .... | .... | .... |
| 2000-01 | Avangard Omsk | Russia | 39 | 0 | 1 | 1 | 20 | 16 | 1 | 3 | 4 | 12 |
| 2001-02 | Avangard Omsk | Russia | 41 | 1 | 5 | 6 | 34 | 11 | 1 | 0 | 1 | 8 |
| 2002-03 | Avangard Omsk | Russia | 45 | 4 | 8 | 12 | 54 | 12 | 1 | 3 | 4 | 8 |
| 2003-04 | Manitoba Moose | AHL | 74 | 7 | 25 | 32 | 62 | .... | .... | .... | .... | .... |
| 2004-05 | Manitoba Moose | AHL | 28 | 3 | 14 | 17 | 42 | .... | .... | .... | .... | .... |
| | Avangard Omsk | Russia | 22 | 2 | 2 | 4 | 46 | 10 | 0 | 1 | 1 | 18 |
| 2005-06 | Avangard Omsk | Russia | 43 | 9 | 8 | 17 | 98 | 13 | 4 | 5 | 9 | 10 |
| 2006-07 | Avangard Omsk | Russia | 51 | 9 | 31 | 40 | 46 | 9 | 3 | 3 | 6 | 12 |
| 2007-08 | Ufa | Russia | 50 | 5 | 18 | 23 | 42 | 11 | 0 | 6 | 6 | 6 |
| 2008-09 | Ufa | Rus-KHL | 49 | 5 | 20 | 25 | 81 | 3 | 0 | 0 | 0 | 2 |

## KOPER, Levko
(KOE-puhr, LEHV-koh) **ATL.**

Left wing. Shoots left. 6', 180 lbs. Born, Edmonton, Alta., October 5, 1990.
(Atlanta's 8th choice, 185th overall, in 2009 Entry Draft).

| | | | Regular Season | | | | | Playoffs | | | | |
|---|---|---|---|---|---|---|---|---|---|---|---|---|
| Season | Club | League | GP | G | A | Pts | PIM | GP | G | A | Pts | PIM |
| 2005-06 | SSAC Bulldogs | Minor-AB | 36 | 39 | 50 | 89 | 34 | .... | .... | .... | .... | .... |
| | Boston Athletics | AMHL | 1 | 0 | 1 | 1 | 0 | .... | .... | .... | .... | .... |
| 2006-07 | Spokane Chiefs | WHL | 50 | 3 | 2 | 5 | 14 | 5 | 0 | 0 | 0 | 0 |
| 2007-08 | Spokane Chiefs | WHL | 69 | 12 | 14 | 26 | 45 | 21 | 4 | 5 | 9 | 14 |
| 2008-09 | Spokane Chiefs | WHL | 71 | 23 | 36 | 59 | 57 | 12 | 3 | 7 | 10 | 6 |

## KORNEEV, Konstantin
(kor-NEE-ehv, KAWN-stan-tihn) **MTL.**

Defense. Shoots right. 5'11", 181 lbs. Born, Moscow, USSR, June 5, 1984.
(Montreal's 6th choice, 275th overall, in 2002 Entry Draft).

| | | | Regular Season | | | | | Playoffs | | | | |
|---|---|---|---|---|---|---|---|---|---|---|---|---|
| Season | Club | League | GP | G | A | Pts | PIM | GP | G | A | Pts | PIM |
| 99-2000 | Krylja Sovetov 2 | Russia-3 | 1 | 0 | 0 | 0 | 0 | .... | .... | .... | .... | .... |
| 2000-01 | Russia Jr. | Exhib. | 12 | 0 | 4 | 4 | 10 | .... | .... | .... | .... | .... |
| 2001-02 | Krylja Sovetov 2 | Russia-3 | 26 | 9 | 19 | 28 | 44 | .... | .... | .... | .... | .... |
| | Krylja Sovetov | Russia | 4 | 0 | 2 | 2 | 0 | 2 | 0 | 0 | 0 | 2 |
| 2002-03 | Krylja Sovetov | Russia | 49 | 2 | 8 | 10 | 28 | .... | .... | .... | .... | .... |
| 2003-04 | Ak Bars Kazan | Russia | 55 | 1 | 4 | 5 | 8 | 8 | 0 | 1 | 1 | 2 |
| 2004-05 | Ak Bars Kazan 2 | Russia-3 | .... | 6 | 16 | 22 | .... | .... | .... | .... | .... | .... |
| | Ak Bars Kazan | Russia | 35 | 0 | 4 | 4 | 10 | 1 | 0 | 0 | 0 | 0 |
| 2005-06 | Ak Bars Kazan | Russia | 30 | 1 | 3 | 4 | 14 | 4 | 0 | 0 | 0 | 0 |
| 2006-07 | CSKA Moscow | Russia | 54 | 8 | 14 | 22 | 40 | 12 | 2 | 4 | 6 | 6 |
| 2007-08 | CSKA Moscow | Russia | 57 | 6 | 18 | 24 | 52 | 6 | 0 | 1 | 1 | 0 |
| 2008-09 | CSKA Moscow | Rus-KHL | 54 | 6 | 18 | 24 | 46 | 8 | 1 | 0 | 1 | 6 |

## KOROSTIN, Sergei
(koh-ROH-stihn, SAIR-gay) **DAL.**

Right wing. Shoots left. 5'11", 180 lbs. Born, Prokopjevsk, USSR, July 5, 1989.
(Dallas' 2nd choice, 64th overall, in 2007 Entry Draft).

| | | | Regular Season | | | | | Playoffs | | | | |
|---|---|---|---|---|---|---|---|---|---|---|---|---|
| Season | Club | League | GP | G | A | Pts | PIM | GP | G | A | Pts | PIM |
| 2005-06 | Dyn'o Moscow 2 | Russia-3 | STATISTICS NOT AVAILABLE | | | | | | | | | |
| | Dynamo Moscow | Russia | 1 | 0 | 0 | 0 | 0 | .... | .... | .... | .... | .... |
| 2006-07 | Dyn'o Moscow 2 | Russia-3 | STATISTICS NOT AVAILABLE | | | | | | | | | |
| | Dynamo Moscow | Russia | 7 | 0 | 0 | 0 | 8 | .... | .... | .... | .... | .... |
| 2007-08 | Dynamo Moscow | Russia | 2 | 0 | 0 | 0 | 2 | .... | .... | .... | .... | .... |
| | Prokopjevsk | Russia-3 | 2 | 2 | 2 | 4 | 0 | .... | .... | .... | .... | .... |
| | Texas Tornado | NAHL | 19 | 8 | 10 | 18 | 12 | 3 | 2 | 0 | 2 | 2 |
| 2008-09 | London Knights | OHL | 13 | 2 | 5 | 7 | 17 | .... | .... | .... | .... | .... |
| | Peterborough | OHL | 36 | 11 | 18 | 29 | 16 | 4 | 1 | 2 | 3 | 0 |

## KOSMACHEV, Dmitry
(kaws-ma-CHEHV, dih-MEE-tree) **CBJ**

Defense. Shoots right. 6'3", 227 lbs. Born, Nizhny Novgorod, USSR, June 7, 1985.
(Columbus' 3rd choice, 71st overall, in 2003 Entry Draft).

| | | | Regular Season | | | | | Playoffs | | | | |
|---|---|---|---|---|---|---|---|---|---|---|---|---|
| Season | Club | League | GP | G | A | Pts | PIM | GP | G | A | Pts | PIM |
| 2001-02 | HK CSKA 2 | Russia-3 | 6 | 1 | 0 | 1 | 2 | .... | .... | .... | .... | .... |
| | HK CSKA Moscow | Russia-2 | 49 | 0 | 1 | 1 | 12 | .... | .... | .... | .... | .... |
| 2002-03 | CSKA Moscow | Russia | 27 | 0 | 0 | 0 | 2 | .... | .... | .... | .... | .... |
| 2003-04 | CSKA Moscow | Russia | 34 | 0 | 2 | 2 | 12 | .... | .... | .... | .... | .... |
| 2004-05 | Nizhny Novgorod | Russia-2 | 34 | 3 | 4 | 7 | 22 | 15 | 0 | 1 | 1 | 0 |
| 2005-06 | Mytischi | Russia | 38 | 2 | 2 | 4 | 14 | 9 | 0 | 0 | 0 | 4 |
| | Kristall Elektrostal | Russia-3 | STATISTICS NOT AVAILABLE | | | | | | | | | |
| 2006-07 | Mytischi | Russia | 32 | 0 | 0 | 0 | 18 | 9 | 0 | 0 | 0 | 2 |
| 2007-08 | Mytischi | Russia | 56 | 0 | 6 | 6 | 34 | 4 | 0 | 0 | 0 | 2 |
| 2008-09 | Ak Bars Kazan | Rus-KHL | 28 | 0 | 3 | 3 | 24 | .... | .... | .... | .... | .... |

## KOSTKA, Mike
(KOHST-kuh, MIGHK)

Defense. Shoots right. 6'2", 210 lbs. Born, Ajax, Ont., November 28, 1985.

| | | | Regular Season | | | | | Playoffs | | | | |
|---|---|---|---|---|---|---|---|---|---|---|---|---|
| Season | Club | League | GP | G | A | Pts | PIM | GP | G | A | Pts | PIM |
| 2001-02 | Ajax Axemen | OPJHL | 19 | 1 | 4 | 5 | 8 | .... | .... | .... | .... | .... |
| 2002-03 | Ajax Axemen | OPJHL | 39 | 4 | 11 | 15 | 32 | .... | .... | .... | .... | .... |
| 2003-04 | Aurora Tigers | OPJHL | 42 | 9 | 27 | 36 | 4 | .... | .... | .... | .... | .... |
| 2004-05 | Massachusetts | H-East | 32 | 1 | 5 | 6 | 14 | .... | .... | .... | .... | .... |
| 2005-06 | Massachusetts | H-East | 36 | 2 | 6 | 8 | 20 | .... | .... | .... | .... | .... |
| 2006-07 | Massachusetts | H-East | 39 | 3 | 15 | 18 | 20 | .... | .... | .... | .... | .... |
| 2007-08 | Massachusetts | H-East | 36 | 9 | 12 | 21 | 20 | .... | .... | .... | .... | .... |
| | Rochester | AHL | 1 | 0 | 0 | 0 | 2 | .... | .... | .... | .... | .... |
| 2008-09 | Portland Pirates | AHL | 80 | 4 | 26 | 30 | 33 | 4 | 1 | 0 | 1 | 6 |

Hockey East Second All-Star Team (2008)

Signed as a free agent by **Buffalo**, March 25, 2008.

## KOZEK, Andrew
(KOH-zehk, AN-droo) **ATL.**

Left wing. Shoots left. 5'10", 190 lbs. Born, Revelstoke, B.C., May 26, 1986.
(Atlanta's 4th choice, 53rd overall, in 2005 Entry Draft).

| | | | Regular Season | | | | | Playoffs | | | | |
|---|---|---|---|---|---|---|---|---|---|---|---|---|
| Season | Club | League | GP | G | A | Pts | PIM | GP | G | A | Pts | PIM |
| 2003-04 | South Surrey | BCHL | 58 | 19 | 22 | 41 | 67 | .... | .... | .... | .... | .... |
| 2004-05 | South Surrey | BCHL | 60 | 48 | 49 | 97 | 81 | .... | .... | .... | .... | .... |
| 2005-06 | North Dakota | WCHA | 46 | 7 | 6 | 13 | 22 | .... | .... | .... | .... | .... |
| 2006-07 | North Dakota | WCHA | 41 | 5 | 6 | 11 | 12 | .... | .... | .... | .... | .... |
| 2007-08 | North Dakota | WCHA | 42 | 18 | 3 | 21 | 18 | .... | .... | .... | .... | .... |
| 2008-09 | North Dakota | WCHA | 38 | 8 | 12 | 20 | 40 | .... | .... | .... | .... | .... |
| | Chicago Wolves | AHL | 5 | 2 | 0 | 2 | 2 | .... | .... | .... | .... | .... |

## KOZUN, Brandon
(KOH-zuhn, BRAN-duhn) **L.A.**

Right wing. Shoots right. 5'8", 162 lbs. Born, Los Angeles, CA, March 8, 1990.
(Los Angeles' 8th choice, 179th overall, in 2009 Entry Draft).

| | | | Regular Season | | | | | Playoffs | | | | |
|---|---|---|---|---|---|---|---|---|---|---|---|---|
| Season | Club | League | GP | G | A | Pts | PIM | GP | G | A | Pts | PIM |
| 2006-07 | Calgary Royals | AJHL | 39 | 20 | 22 | 42 | 38 | 4 | 2 | 1 | 3 | 2 |
| | Calgary Hitmen | WHL | 11 | 1 | 1 | 2 | 4 | .... | .... | .... | .... | .... |
| 2007-08 | Calgary Hitmen | WHL | 69 | 19 | 34 | 53 | 46 | 16 | 4 | 14 | 18 | 6 |
| 2008-09 | Calgary Hitmen | WHL | 72 | 40 | 68 | 108 | 58 | 18 | 7 | 12 | 19 | 8 |

WHL East First All-Star Team (2009)

## KREIDER, Chris
(KRIGH-duhr, KRIHS) **NYR**

Center. Shoots left. 6'2", 201 lbs. Born, Boxford, MA, April 30, 1991.
(NY Rangers' 1st choice, 19th overall, in 2009 Entry Draft).

| | | | Regular Season | | | | | Playoffs | | | | |
|---|---|---|---|---|---|---|---|---|---|---|---|---|
| Season | Club | League | GP | G | A | Pts | PIM | GP | G | A | Pts | PIM |
| 2005-06 | Masconomet | High-MA | 19 | 5 | 10 | 15 | .... | .... | .... | .... | .... | .... |
| 2006-07 | Masconomet | High-MA | 20 | 28 | 13 | 41 | .... | .... | .... | .... | .... | .... |
| 2007-08 | Andover | High-MA | 24 | 26 | 15 | 41 | .... | .... | .... | .... | .... | .... |
| 2008-09 | Andover | High-MA | 26 | 33 | 23 | 56 | 10 | .... | .... | .... | .... | .... |
| | Valley Jr. Warriors | Minor-MA | 5 | 4 | 2 | 6 | .... | .... | .... | .... | .... | .... |

• Signed Letter of Intent to attend **Boston College** (Hockey East) in fall of 2010.

## KRIKUNOV, Ilia
(krih-koo-NAWF, IHL-yah) **VAN.**

Left wing. Shoots left. 5'11", 169 lbs. Born, Elektrostal, USSR, February 27, 1984.
(Vancouver's 8th choice, 223rd overall, in 2002 Entry Draft).

| | | | Regular Season | | | | | Playoffs | | | | |
|---|---|---|---|---|---|---|---|---|---|---|---|---|
| Season | Club | League | GP | G | A | Pts | PIM | GP | G | A | Pts | PIM |
| 2000-01 | Elektrostal 2 | Russia-3 | 4 | 0 | 0 | 0 | 2 | .... | .... | .... | .... | .... |
| 2001-02 | Elektrostal 2 | Russia-3 | 5 | 3 | 6 | 9 | 4 | .... | .... | .... | .... | .... |
| | Elektrostal | Russia-2 | 48 | 12 | 10 | 22 | 28 | .... | .... | .... | .... | .... |
| 2002-03 | Elektrostal | Russia-2 | 48 | 19 | 9 | 28 | 34 | .... | .... | .... | .... | .... |
| 2003-04 | Voskresensk | Russia | 50 | 10 | 9 | 19 | 14 | .... | .... | .... | .... | .... |
| 2004-05 | Voskresensk | Russia | 58 | 9 | 14 | 23 | 20 | .... | .... | .... | .... | .... |
| 2005-06 | Mytischi | Russia | 46 | 10 | 5 | 15 | 57 | 8 | 1 | 1 | 2 | 2 |
| | Kristall Elektrostal | Russia-3 | STATISTICS NOT AVAILABLE | | | | | | | | | |
| 2006-07 | Mytischi | Russia | 48 | 9 | 6 | 15 | 56 | 9 | 2 | 1 | 3 | 12 |
| 2007-08 | Mytischi | Russia | 34 | 7 | 12 | 19 | 18 | 5 | 1 | 1 | 2 | 4 |
| 2008-09 | Mytischi | Rus-KHL | 5 | 0 | 1 | 1 | 0 | .... | .... | .... | .... | .... |
| | Nizhny Novgorod | Rus-KHL | 27 | 6 | 6 | 12 | 10 | 3 | 0 | 2 | 2 | 0 |

**KRISTO, Danny** (KRIHS-toh, DAN-ee) **MTL.**

Right wing. Shoots right. 5'11", 180 lbs. Born, Edina, MN, June 18, 1990.
(Montreal's 1st choice, 56th overall, in 2008 Entry Draft).

| | | | Regular Season | | | | | Playoffs | | | | |
|---|---|---|---|---|---|---|---|---|---|---|---|---|
| **Season** | **Club** | **League** | **GP** | **G** | **A** | **Pts** | **PIM** | **GP** | **G** | **A** | **Pts** | **PIM** |
| 2006-07 | USNTDP | U-17 | 14 | 4 | 5 | 9 | 0 | .... | .... | .... | .... | .... |
| | USNTDP | NAHL | 39 | 8 | 10 | 18 | 34 | 6 | 0 | 1 | 1 | 2 |
| 2007-08 | USNTDP | U-18 | 43 | 18 | 14 | 32 | 18 | .... | .... | .... | .... | .... |
| | USNTDP | NAHL | 14 | 4 | 4 | 8 | 6 | .... | .... | .... | .... | .... |
| 2008-09 | Omaha Lancers | USHL | 50 | 22 | 35 | 57 | 18 | 3 | 3 | 0 | 3 | 2 |

• Signed Letter of Intent to attend **University of North Dakota** (WCHA) in fall of 2009.

**KRUEGER, Justin** (KROO-guhr, JUHS-tihn) **CAR.**

Defense. Shoots right. 6'2", 205 lbs. Born, Dusseldorf, West Germany, October 6, 1986.
(Carolina's 6th choice, 213th overall, in 2006 Entry Draft).

| | | | Regular Season | | | | | Playoffs | | | | |
|---|---|---|---|---|---|---|---|---|---|---|---|---|
| **Season** | **Club** | **League** | **GP** | **G** | **A** | **Pts** | **PIM** | **GP** | **G** | **A** | **Pts** | **PIM** |
| 2002-03 | HC Davos Jr. | Swiss-Jr. | 12 | 0 | 0 | 0 | 4 | 2 | 0 | 0 | 0 | 0 |
| 2003-04 | HC Davos Jr. | Swiss-Jr. | 33 | 2 | 0 | 2 | 14 | .... | .... | .... | .... | .... |
| 2004-05 | HC Davos Jr. | Swiss-Jr. | 38 | 5 | 12 | 17 | 76 | 4 | 1 | 2 | 3 | 2 |
| 2005-06 | Penticton Vees | BCHL | 55 | 7 | 15 | 22 | 25 | .... | .... | .... | .... | .... |
| 2006-07 | Cornell Big Red | ECAC | 31 | 1 | 5 | 6 | 24 | .... | .... | .... | .... | .... |
| 2007-08 | Cornell Big Red | ECAC | 35 | 4 | 5 | 9 | 33 | .... | .... | .... | .... | .... |
| 2008-09 | Cornell Big Red | ECAC | 35 | 1 | 4 | 5 | 24 | .... | .... | .... | .... | .... |

**KRUGER, Marcus** (KROO-guhr, MAHR-kuhs) **CHI.**

Center. Shoots left. 5'11", 172 lbs. Born, Stockholm, Sweden, May 27, 1990.
(Chicago's 5th choice, 149th overall, in 2009 Entry Draft).

| | | | Regular Season | | | | | Playoffs | | | | |
|---|---|---|---|---|---|---|---|---|---|---|---|---|
| **Season** | **Club** | **League** | **GP** | **G** | **A** | **Pts** | **PIM** | **GP** | **G** | **A** | **Pts** | **PIM** |
| 2006-07 | Djurgarden U18 | Swe-U18 | 23 | 5 | 14 | 19 | 10 | 3 | 2 | 1 | 3 | 2 |
| 2007-08 | Djurgarden U18 | Swe-U18 | 22 | 11 | 20 | 31 | 22 | 7 | 3 | 8 | 11 | 6 |
| | Djurgarden Jr. | Swe-Jr. | 22 | 3 | 13 | 16 | 16 | 7 | 5 | 3 | 8 | 0 |
| 2008-09 | Djurgarden Jr. | Swe-Jr. | 34 | 9 | 30 | 39 | 24 | 6 | 1 | 5 | 6 | 2 |
| | Djurgarden | Sweden | 15 | 2 | 2 | 4 | 2 | .... | .... | .... | .... | .... |

**KRYSANOV, Anton** (KREE-sa-nahf, AN-tawn) **PHX.**

Center. Shoots left. 6'3", 198 lbs. Born, Togliatti, USSR, March 25, 1987.
(Phoenix's 4th choice, 148th overall, in 2005 Entry Draft).

| | | | Regular Season | | | | | Playoffs | | | | |
|---|---|---|---|---|---|---|---|---|---|---|---|---|
| **Season** | **Club** | **League** | **GP** | **G** | **A** | **Pts** | **PIM** | **GP** | **G** | **A** | **Pts** | **PIM** |
| 2002-03 | Lada Togliatti 2 | Russia-3 | 9 | 1 | 3 | 4 | 2 | .... | .... | .... | .... | .... |
| 2003-04 | Lada Togliatti 2 | Russia-3 | 18 | 2 | 3 | 5 | 2 | .... | .... | .... | .... | .... |
| 2004-05 | Lada Togliatti 2 | Russia-3 | 34 | 13 | 13 | 26 | 32 | .... | .... | .... | .... | .... |
| | Lada Togliatti | Russia | 15 | 1 | 0 | 1 | 2 | .... | .... | .... | .... | .... |
| 2005-06 | Lada Togliatti | Russia | 46 | 3 | 3 | 6 | 24 | 8 | 0 | 0 | 0 | 2 |
| 2006-07 | Lada Togliatti | Russia | 48 | 1 | 15 | 16 | 14 | 3 | 0 | 0 | 0 | 4 |
| 2007-08 | Lada Togliatti 2 | Russia-3 | 2 | 2 | 1 | 3 | 2 | .... | .... | .... | .... | .... |
| | Lada Togliatti | Russia | 54 | 9 | 11 | 20 | 22 | 4 | 0 | 1 | 1 | 0 |
| 2008-09 | Lada Togliatti | Rus-KHL | 46 | 8 | 10 | 18 | 14 | 5 | 0 | 3 | 3 | 4 |

**KRYUKOV, Artem** (KREE-oo-kahf, AHR-tehm) **BUF.**

Center. Shoots left. 6'3", 180 lbs. Born, Novosibirsk, USSR, March 5, 1982.
(Buffalo's 1st choice, 15th overall, in 2000 Entry Draft).

| | | | Regular Season | | | | | Playoffs | | | | |
|---|---|---|---|---|---|---|---|---|---|---|---|---|
| **Season** | **Club** | **League** | **GP** | **G** | **A** | **Pts** | **PIM** | **GP** | **G** | **A** | **Pts** | **PIM** |
| 1997-98 | Torpedo Yaroslavl | Russia | 7 | 0 | 0 | 0 | 2 | .... | .... | .... | .... | .... |
| 1998-99 | Yaroslavl 2 | Russia-3 | 20 | 2 | 2 | 4 | 6 | .... | .... | .... | .... | .... |
| 99-2000 | Yaroslavl 2 | Russia-3 | 14 | 1 | 1 | 2 | 12 | .... | .... | .... | .... | .... |
| | Torpedo Yaroslavl | Russia | 3 | 0 | 0 | 0 | 4 | .... | .... | .... | .... | .... |
| 2000-01 | Yaroslavl 2 | Russia-3 | 6 | 0 | 0 | 0 | 2 | 11 | 0 | 0 | 0 | 8 |
| | SKA St. Petersburg | Russia | 14 | 0 | 2 | 2 | 14 | .... | .... | .... | .... | .... |
| 2001-02 | Yaroslavl | Russia | 15 | 1 | 3 | 4 | 10 | 6 | 1 | 0 | 1 | 8 |
| 2002-03 | Sibir Novosibirsk | Russia | 9 | 0 | 0 | 0 | 27 | .... | .... | .... | .... | .... |
| 2003-04 | Yaroslavl 2 | Russia-3 | 30 | 5 | 4 | 9 | 26 | .... | .... | .... | .... | .... |
| | Yaroslavl | Russia | 4 | 0 | 2 | 2 | 0 | .... | .... | .... | .... | .... |
| 2004-05 | Yaroslavl | Russia | 60 | 8 | 9 | 17 | 44 | 7 | 1 | 0 | 1 | 4 |
| 2005-06 | Yaroslavl | Russia | 33 | 1 | 2 | 3 | 42 | 1 | 0 | 0 | 0 | 0 |
| | Yaroslavl 2 | Russia-3 | 6 | 3 | 3 | 6 | 18 | .... | .... | .... | .... | .... |
| 2006-07 | Vityaz Chekhov | Russia | 12 | 0 | 0 | 0 | 20 | .... | .... | .... | .... | .... |
| | Yaroslavl 2 | Russia-3 | 13 | 4 | 10 | 14 | 10 | .... | .... | .... | .... | .... |
| | Yaroslavl | Russia | 19 | 1 | 3 | 4 | 20 | .... | .... | .... | .... | .... |
| 2007-08 | SKA St. Petersburg | Russia | 51 | 7 | 8 | 15 | 54 | 9 | 0 | 2 | 2 | 8 |
| 2008-09 | SKA St. Petersburg | Rus-KHL | 50 | 8 | 3 | 11 | 48 | .... | .... | .... | .... | .... |

**KUBALIK, Tomas** (koo-BAHL-ihk, TAW-mahsh) **CBJ**

Right wing. Shoots right. 6'2", 194 lbs. Born, Plzen, Czech., May 1, 1990.
(Columbus' 6th choice, 135th overall, in 2008 Entry Draft).

| | | | Regular Season | | | | | Playoffs | | | | |
|---|---|---|---|---|---|---|---|---|---|---|---|---|
| **Season** | **Club** | **League** | **GP** | **G** | **A** | **Pts** | **PIM** | **GP** | **G** | **A** | **Pts** | **PIM** |
| 2003-04 | HC Plzen U17 | CzR-U17 | 4 | 0 | 0 | 0 | 0 | .... | .... | .... | .... | .... |
| 2004-05 | HC Plzen U17 | CzR-U17 | 37 | 4 | 1 | 5 | 18 | .... | .... | .... | .... | .... |
| 2005-06 | HC Plzen U17 | CzR-U17 | 35 | 26 | 21 | 47 | 91 | 6 | 1 | 5 | 6 | 16 |
| | HC Plzen Jr. | CzRep-Jr. | 5 | 1 | 2 | 3 | 6 | .... | .... | .... | .... | .... |
| 2006-07 | HC Plzen U17 | CzR-U17 | 2 | 4 | 1 | 5 | 6 | 8 | 5 | 5 | 10 | 30 |
| | HC Plzen Jr. | CzRep-Jr. | 34 | 23 | 15 | 38 | 76 | 3 | 1 | 2 | 3 | 24 |
| | Plzen | CzRep | 23 | 1 | 0 | 1 | 18 | .... | .... | .... | .... | .... |
| 2007-08 | HC Plzen Jr. | CzRep-Jr. | 22 | 8 | 13 | 21 | 50 | 5 | 1 | 3 | 4 | 22 |
| | Beroun | CzRep-2 | 7 | 0 | 0 | 0 | 2 | .... | .... | .... | .... | .... |
| | Plzen | CzRep | 20 | 2 | 1 | 3 | 8 | 1 | 0 | 0 | 0 | 0 |
| 2008-09 | HC Plzen Jr. | CzRep-Jr. | 4 | 1 | 2 | 3 | 10 | .... | .... | .... | .... | .... |
| | Plzen | CzRep | 32 | 1 | 1 | 2 | 64 | 17 | 1 | 0 | 1 | 8 |

**KUDELKA, Tomas** (koo-DEHL-kah, TAW-mahsh) **OTT.**

Defense. Shoots left. 6'3", 206 lbs. Born, Gottwaldov, Czech., March 10, 1987.
(Ottawa's 6th choice, 136th overall, in 2005 Entry Draft).

| | | | Regular Season | | | | | Playoffs | | | | |
|---|---|---|---|---|---|---|---|---|---|---|---|---|
| **Season** | **Club** | **League** | **GP** | **G** | **A** | **Pts** | **PIM** | **GP** | **G** | **A** | **Pts** | **PIM** |
| 2002-03 | HC Zlin U17 | CzR-U17 | 45 | 1 | 16 | 17 | 28 | 3 | 1 | 0 | 1 | 12 |
| 2003-04 | HC Zlin U17 | CzR-U17 | 1 | 0 | 0 | 0 | 2 | 3 | 0 | 0 | 0 | 0 |
| | HC Zlin Jr. | CzRep-Jr. | 51 | 1 | 12 | 13 | 95 | 7 | 0 | 0 | 0 | 0 |
| | HC Hame Zlin | CzRep | 3 | 0 | 0 | 0 | 0 | .... | .... | .... | .... | .... |
| 2004-05 | HC Zlin Jr. | CzRep-Jr. | 38 | 9 | 8 | 17 | 38 | .... | .... | .... | .... | .... |
| | HC Hame Zlin | CzRep | 4 | 0 | 0 | 0 | 6 | .... | .... | .... | .... | .... |
| 2005-06 | Lethbridge | WHL | 64 | 6 | 25 | 31 | 77 | 6 | 1 | 1 | 2 | 12 |
| | Binghamton | AHL | 5 | 0 | 0 | 0 | 4 | .... | .... | .... | .... | .... |
| 2006-07 | Lethbridge | WHL | 59 | 14 | 27 | 41 | 74 | .... | .... | .... | .... | .... |
| | Binghamton | AHL | 11 | 1 | 2 | 3 | 8 | .... | .... | .... | .... | .... |
| 2007-08 | Binghamton | AHL | 35 | 1 | 1 | 2 | 17 | .... | .... | .... | .... | .... |
| | Elmira Jackals | ECHL | 23 | 5 | 14 | 19 | 26 | 1 | 0 | 0 | 0 | 0 |
| 2008-09 | Binghamton | AHL | 76 | 7 | 16 | 23 | 67 | .... | .... | .... | .... | .... |

**KUGRYSHEV, Dmitry** (koo-GRIH-shev, dih-MEE-tree) **WSH.**

Right wing. Shoots right. 5'11", 192 lbs. Born, Balakovo, USSR, January 18, 1990.
(Washington's 4th choice, 58th overall, in 2008 Entry Draft).

| | | | Regular Season | | | | | Playoffs | | | | |
|---|---|---|---|---|---|---|---|---|---|---|---|---|
| **Season** | **Club** | **League** | **GP** | **G** | **A** | **Pts** | **PIM** | **GP** | **G** | **A** | **Pts** | **PIM** |
| 2005-06 | CSKA Moscow 2 | Russia-3 | STATISTICS NOT AVAILABLE | | | | | | | | | |
| 2006-07 | CSKA Moscow 2 | Russia-3 | STATISTICS NOT AVAILABLE | | | | | | | | | |
| 2007-08 | CSKA Moscow 2 | Russia-3 | 29 | 25 | 25 | 50 | 60 | 7 | 5 | 6 | 11 | 6 |
| 2008-09 | Quebec Remparts | QMJHL | 57 | 34 | 40 | 74 | 38 | 17 | 6 | 14 | 20 | 24 |

QMJHL All-Rookie Team (2009)

**KULDA , Arturs** (KOOL-da, AHR-tuhrs) **ATL.**

Defense. Shoots left. 6'2", 210 lbs. Born, Riga, Latvia, July 25, 1988.
(Atlanta's 7th choice, 200th overall, in 2006 Entry Draft).

| | | | Regular Season | | | | | Playoffs | | | | |
|---|---|---|---|---|---|---|---|---|---|---|---|---|
| **Season** | **Club** | **League** | **GP** | **G** | **A** | **Pts** | **PIM** | **GP** | **G** | **A** | **Pts** | **PIM** |
| 2003-04 | Prizma/Riga 86 | Latvia | 11 | 0 | 0 | 0 | 8 | 2 | 0 | 0 | 0 | 0 |
| 2004-05 | CSKA Moscow 2 | Russia-3 | STATISTICS NOT AVAILABLE | | | | | | | | | |
| 2005-06 | CSKA Moscow 2 | Russia-3 | 44 | 5 | 12 | 17 | .... | .... | .... | .... | .... | .... |
| 2006-07 | Peterborough | OHL | 58 | 2 | 9 | 11 | 83 | .... | .... | .... | .... | .... |
| 2007-08 | Peterborough | OHL | 55 | 7 | 27 | 34 | 87 | 5 | 1 | 3 | 4 | 6 |
| | Chicago Wolves | AHL | 5 | 0 | 1 | 1 | 10 | 22 | 1 | 5 | 6 | 32 |
| 2008-09 | Chicago Wolves | AHL | 57 | 1 | 14 | 15 | 59 | .... | .... | .... | .... | .... |

**KULIKOV, Dmitry** (kool-YIH-kawf, dih-MEE-tree) **FLA.**

Defense. Shoots left. 6', 183 lbs. Born, Lipetsk, USSR, October 29, 1990.
(Florida's 1st choice, 14th overall, in 2009 Entry Draft).

| | | | Regular Season | | | | | Playoffs | | | | |
|---|---|---|---|---|---|---|---|---|---|---|---|---|
| **Season** | **Club** | **League** | **GP** | **G** | **A** | **Pts** | **PIM** | **GP** | **G** | **A** | **Pts** | **PIM** |
| 2007-08 | Yaroslavl 2 | Russia-3 | STATISTICS NOT AVAILABLE | | | | | | | | | |
| 2008-09 | Drummondville | QMJHL | 57 | 12 | 50 | 62 | 46 | 19 | 2 | 18 | 20 | 16 |

QMJHL All-Rookie Team (2009) • QMJHL First All-Star Team (2009) • QMJHL Rookie of the Year (2009) • Canadian Major Junior Second All-Star Team (2009)

**KULYASH, Denis** (kuh-L'YASH, DEH-nihs) **NSH.**

Defense. Shoots left. 6'3", 199 lbs. Born, Omsk, USSR, May 31, 1983.
(Nashville's 9th choice, 243rd overall, in 2004 Entry Draft).

| | | | Regular Season | | | | | Playoffs | | | | |
|---|---|---|---|---|---|---|---|---|---|---|---|---|
| **Season** | **Club** | **League** | **GP** | **G** | **A** | **Pts** | **PIM** | **GP** | **G** | **A** | **Pts** | **PIM** |
| 2003-04 | CSK VVS Samara 2 | Russia-3 | STATISTICS NOT AVAILABLE | | | | | | | | | |
| | CSKA Moscow | Russia | 10 | 1 | 0 | 1 | 8 | .... | .... | .... | .... | .... |
| 2004-05 | CSKA Moscow | Russia | 59 | 8 | 10 | 18 | 58 | .... | .... | .... | .... | .... |
| 2005-06 | Dynamo Moscow | Russia | 44 | 12 | 5 | 17 | 117 | 4 | 0 | 2 | 2 | 6 |
| 2006-07 | Dynamo Moscow | Russia | 48 | 3 | 9 | 12 | 58 | 2 | 0 | 0 | 0 | 2 |
| 2007-08 | CSKA Moscow | Russia | 53 | 9 | 13 | 22 | 79 | 6 | 1 | 1 | 2 | 34 |
| 2008-09 | CSKA Moscow | Rus-KHL | 56 | 16 | 10 | 26 | 62 | 8 | 2 | 1 | 3 | 20 |

**KUNDRATEK, Tomas** (kuhn-DRAT-ehk, TAW-mahsh) **NYR**

Defense. Shoots right. 6'1", 190 lbs. Born, Prerov, Czech., December 26, 1989.
(NY Rangers' 4th choice, 90th overall, in 2008 Entry Draft).

| | | | Regular Season | | | | | Playoffs | | | | |
|---|---|---|---|---|---|---|---|---|---|---|---|---|
| **Season** | **Club** | **League** | **GP** | **G** | **A** | **Pts** | **PIM** | **GP** | **G** | **A** | **Pts** | **PIM** |
| 2003-04 | HC Prerov U17 | CzR-U17 | 6 | 0 | 0 | 0 | 0 | .... | .... | .... | .... | .... |
| 2004-05 | HC Prerov U17 | CzR-U17 | 38 | 2 | 7 | 9 | 26 | 4 | 0 | 1 | 1 | 4 |
| 2005-06 | HC Trinec U17 | CzR-U17 | 39 | 5 | 13 | 18 | 96 | 2 | 0 | 1 | 1 | 10 |
| | HC Trinec Jr. | CzRep-Jr. | 12 | 1 | 1 | 2 | 16 | 7 | 1 | 1 | 2 | 4 |
| 2006-07 | HC Trinec Jr. | CzRep-Jr. | 33 | 4 | 13 | 17 | 93 | 3 | 1 | 1 | 2 | 10 |
| | HC Ocelari Trinec | CzRep | 22 | 0 | 1 | 1 | 4 | 4 | 0 | 0 | 0 | 6 |
| 2007-08 | HC Trinec Jr. | CzRep-Jr. | 14 | 3 | 6 | 9 | 28 | .... | .... | .... | .... | .... |
| | Prostejov | CzRep-2 | 15 | 1 | 0 | 1 | 10 | .... | .... | .... | .... | .... |
| | HC Havirov | CzRep-2 | 2 | 0 | 0 | 0 | 2 | .... | .... | .... | .... | .... |
| | HC Ocelari Trinec | CzRep | 14 | 0 | 1 | 1 | 10 | 7 | 0 | 2 | 2 | 8 |
| 2008-09 | Medicine Hat | WHL | 51 | 4 | 19 | 23 | 63 | 11 | 0 | 6 | 6 | 12 |
| | Hartford Wolf Pack | AHL | .... | .... | .... | .... | .... | 1 | 0 | 0 | 0 | 0 |

**KVETON, David** (KVEH-tuhn, DAY-vihd) **NYR**

Right wing. Shoots left. 6', 190 lbs. Born, Novy Jicin, Czech., January 3, 1988.
(NY Rangers' 4th choice, 104th overall, in 2006 Entry Draft).

| | | | Regular Season | | | | | Playoffs | | | | |
|---|---|---|---|---|---|---|---|---|---|---|---|---|
| **Season** | **Club** | **League** | **GP** | **G** | **A** | **Pts** | **PIM** | **GP** | **G** | **A** | **Pts** | **PIM** |
| 2003-04 | HC Vsetin U17 | CzR-U17 | 14 | 9 | 11 | 20 | 35 | .... | .... | .... | .... | .... |
| | HC Vsetin Jr. | CzRep-Jr. | 41 | 12 | 11 | 23 | 14 | 5 | 2 | 3 | 5 | 2 |
| | TJ Novy Jicin | CzRep-3 | 1 | 0 | 1 | 1 | 0 | .... | .... | .... | .... | .... |
| | HC Vsetin | CzRep | 1 | 0 | 0 | 0 | 0 | .... | .... | .... | .... | .... |
| 2004-05 | HC Vsetin U17 | CzR-U17 | 1 | 1 | 0 | 1 | 0 | .... | .... | .... | .... | .... |
| | HC Vsetin Jr. | CzRep-Jr. | 36 | 21 | 27 | 48 | 66 | 8 | 6 | 5 | 11 | 4 |
| | TJ Novy Jicin | CzRep-3 | 7 | 0 | 1 | 1 | 6 | .... | .... | .... | .... | .... |
| | HC Vsetin | CzRep | 6 | 1 | 0 | 1 | 0 | .... | .... | .... | .... | .... |
| 2005-06 | HC Vsetin Jr. | CzRep-Jr. | 1 | 1 | 1 | 2 | 0 | 1 | 0 | 1 | 1 | 0 |
| | HC Sareza Ostrava | CzRep-2 | 7 | 2 | 1 | 3 | 2 | .... | .... | .... | .... | .... |
| | HC Vsetin | CzRep | 45 | 6 | 4 | 10 | 18 | .... | .... | .... | .... | .... |
| | TJ Novy Jicin | CzRep-3 | .... | .... | .... | .... | .... | 5 | 5 | 0 | 5 | 18 |
| | HC Vsetin | CzRep-Q | .... | .... | .... | .... | .... | 3 | 1 | 1 | 2 | 2 |
| 2006-07 | Gatineau | QMJHL | 31 | 5 | 27 | 32 | 17 | 5 | 0 | 0 | 0 | 4 |
| | HC Vsetin | CzRep | 19 | 2 | 0 | 2 | 8 | .... | .... | .... | .... | .... |
| 2007-08 | HC Ocelari Trinec | CzRep | 28 | 10 | 5 | 15 | 10 | .... | .... | .... | .... | .... |
| 2008-09 | HC Ocelari Trinec | CzRep | 46 | 22 | 22 | 44 | 20 | 5 | 3 | 2 | 5 | 16 |

**KYTNAR, Milan** (KIHT-nahr, MEE-lan) **EDM.**

Center. Shoots left. 6', 180 lbs. Born, Topolcany, Czech., May 19, 1989.
(Edmonton's 5th choice, 127th overall, in 2007 Entry Draft).

| | | | Regular Season | | | | | Playoffs | | | | |
|---|---|---|---|---|---|---|---|---|---|---|---|---|
| Season | Club | League | GP | G | A | Pts | PIM | GP | G | A | Pts | PIM |
| 2003-04 | Topolcany U18 | Svk-U18 | 42 | 17 | 22 | 39 | 90 | .... | .... | .... | .... | .... |
| 2004-05 | Topolcany U18 | Svk-U18 | 53 | 36 | 65 | 101 | 105 | .... | .... | .... | .... | .... |
| | Topolcany Jr. | Slovak-Jr. | 10 | 2 | 2 | 4 | 8 | .... | .... | .... | .... | .... |
| 2005-06 | HK Trnava U18 | Svk-U18 | 30 | 18 | 23 | 41 | 106 | .... | .... | .... | .... | .... |
| | HK Trnava Jr. | Slovak-Jr. | 12 | 1 | 2 | 3 | 20 | .... | .... | .... | .... | .... |
| | Topolcany U18 | Svk-U18 | 8 | 4 | 4 | 8 | 4 | .... | .... | .... | .... | .... |
| | Topolcany Jr. | Slovak-Jr. | 6 | 6 | 4 | 10 | 8 | .... | .... | .... | .... | .... |
| 2006-07 | HC Topolcany U18 | Svk-U18 | 53 | 37 | 54 | 91 | 84 | .... | .... | .... | .... | .... |
| | HC Topolcany | Slovak-2 | 22 | 4 | 7 | 11 | 53 | 5 | 1 | 1 | 2 | 4 |
| 2007-08 | Kelowna Rockets | WHL | 62 | 9 | 13 | 22 | 66 | 7 | 0 | 0 | 0 | 4 |
| 2008-09 | Saskatoon Blades | WHL | 65 | 27 | 37 | 64 | 89 | 7 | 3 | 1 | 4 | 14 |

**LAAKSO, Teemu** (LAK-soh, TEE-moo) **NSH.**

Defense. Shoots right. 6'1", 208 lbs. Born, Tuusula, Finland, August 27, 1987.
(Nashville's 2nd choice, 78th overall, in 2005 Entry Draft).

| | | | Regular Season | | | | | Playoffs | | | | |
|---|---|---|---|---|---|---|---|---|---|---|---|---|
| Season | Club | League | GP | G | A | Pts | PIM | GP | G | A | Pts | PIM |
| 2002-03 | KJT Jarvenpaa U18 | Fin-U18 | 18 | 2 | 5 | 7 | 24 | .... | .... | .... | .... | .... |
| 2003-04 | HIFK Helsinki Jr. | Fin-Jr. | 41 | 3 | 6 | 9 | 20 | 3 | 0 | 1 | 1 | 0 |
| 2004-05 | HIFK Helsinki U18 | Fin-U18 | .... | .... | .... | .... | .... | 1 | 0 | 0 | 0 | 0 |
| | HIFK Helsinki Jr. | Fin-Jr. | 20 | 5 | 4 | 9 | 18 | .... | .... | .... | .... | .... |
| | HIFK Helsinki | Finland | 15 | 0 | 2 | 2 | 2 | .... | .... | .... | .... | .... |
| 2005-06 | HIFK Helsinki Jr. | Fin-Jr. | 6 | 1 | 2 | 3 | 32 | .... | .... | .... | .... | .... |
| | Suomi U20 | Finland-2 | 6 | 2 | 0 | 2 | 10 | .... | .... | .... | .... | .... |
| | HIFK Helsinki | Finland | 47 | 2 | 1 | 3 | 20 | 8 | 1 | 0 | 1 | 0 |
| 2006-07 | Suomi U20 | Finland-2 | 2 | 0 | 1 | 1 | 4 | .... | .... | .... | .... | .... |
| | HIFK Helsinki | Finland | 50 | 3 | 6 | 9 | 70 | 5 | 0 | 1 | 1 | 0 |
| 2007-08 | HIFK Helsinki | Finland | 53 | 3 | 7 | 10 | 40 | 7 | 0 | 0 | 0 | 2 |
| 2008-09 | Milwaukee | AHL | 42 | 2 | 7 | 9 | 50 | .... | .... | .... | .... | .... |

**LABRECQUE, Dave** (lah-BREHK, DAYV) **PHI.**

Center. Shoots left. 6', 170 lbs. Born, Vanier, Que., January 27, 1990.
(Philadelphia's 4th choice, 153rd overall, in 2009 Entry Draft).

| | | | Regular Season | | | | | Playoffs | | | | |
|---|---|---|---|---|---|---|---|---|---|---|---|---|
| Season | Club | League | GP | G | A | Pts | PIM | GP | G | A | Pts | PIM |
| 2005-06 | Sem. St-Francois | QAAA | 43 | 18 | 30 | 48 | 82 | 3 | 2 | 1 | 3 | 2 |
| 2006-07 | Sem. St-Francois | QAAA | 38 | 21 | 39 | 60 | 92 | 18 | 13 | 17 | 30 | 28 |
| | Shawinigan | QMJHL | 4 | 1 | 0 | 1 | 0 | .... | .... | .... | .... | .... |
| 2007-08 | Que. AssurExperts | QJHL | 36 | 17 | 30 | 47 | 22 | .... | .... | .... | .... | .... |
| | Shawinigan | QMJHL | 22 | 4 | 7 | 11 | 26 | 5 | 1 | 2 | 3 | 6 |
| 2008-09 | Shawinigan | QMJHL | 59 | 13 | 48 | 61 | 76 | 20 | 3 | 16 | 19 | 34 |

**LABRIE, Pierre-Cedric** (la-BREE, pee-AIR-SEH-DRIHK) **VAN.**

Left wing. Shoots right. 6'2", 218 lbs. Born, Baie Comeau, Que., December 6, 1986.

| | | | Regular Season | | | | | Playoffs | | | | |
|---|---|---|---|---|---|---|---|---|---|---|---|---|
| Season | Club | League | GP | G | A | Pts | PIM | GP | G | A | Pts | PIM |
| 2003-04 | Coaticook | QJHL | 46 | 13 | 12 | 25 | 96 | .... | .... | .... | .... | .... |
| | Quebec Remparts | QMJHL | 1 | 0 | 0 | 0 | 0 | .... | .... | .... | .... | .... |
| 2004-05 | Coaticook | QJHL | 15 | 3 | 4 | 7 | 59 | .... | .... | .... | .... | .... |
| 2005-06 | Restigouche Tigers | MJrHL | 54 | 43 | 43 | 86 | 153 | .... | .... | .... | .... | .... |
| | Baie-Comeau | QMJHL | .... | .... | .... | .... | .... | 4 | 2 | 2 | 4 | 6 |
| 2006-07 | Baie-Comeau | QMJHL | 68 | 35 | 28 | 63 | 113 | 11 | 8 | 6 | 14 | 35 |
| 2007-08 | Manitoba Moose | AHL | 67 | 7 | 11 | 18 | 108 | 3 | 0 | 0 | 0 | 2 |
| 2008-09 | Manitoba Moose | AHL | 63 | 6 | 9 | 15 | 79 | 14 | 0 | 1 | 1 | 37 |

Signed as a free agent by **Vancouver**, July 3, 2007.

**LAGACE, Jacob** (LEH-gah-see, JAY-kawb) **BUF.**

Left wing. Shoots left. 5'11", 190 lbs. Born, Beloeil, Que., January 9, 1990.
(Buffalo's 7th choice, 134th overall, in 2008 Entry Draft).

| | | | Regular Season | | | | | Playoffs | | | | |
|---|---|---|---|---|---|---|---|---|---|---|---|---|
| Season | Club | League | GP | G | A | Pts | PIM | GP | G | A | Pts | PIM |
| 2005-06 | C.A.-Girouord | QAAA | 38 | 10 | 11 | 21 | .... | 8 | 0 | 2 | 2 | 4 |
| 2006-07 | C.A.-Girouord | QAAA | 44 | 24 | 29 | 53 | 46 | 4 | 1 | 4 | 5 | 2 |
| 2007-08 | Chicoutimi | QMJHL | 67 | 23 | 39 | 62 | 40 | 6 | 3 | 2 | 5 | 7 |
| 2008-09 | Chicoutimi | QMJHL | 64 | 32 | 37 | 69 | 52 | 4 | 1 | 2 | 3 | 4 |

QMJHL All-Rookie Team (2008)

**LAGERSTROM, Tony** (LA-guhr-struhm, TOH-nee) **CHI.**

Center. Shoots left. 6'1", 189 lbs. Born, Stockholm, Sweden, July 19, 1988.
(Chicago's 4th choice, 76th overall, in 2006 Entry Draft).

| | | | Regular Season | | | | | Playoffs | | | | |
|---|---|---|---|---|---|---|---|---|---|---|---|---|
| Season | Club | League | GP | G | A | Pts | PIM | GP | G | A | Pts | PIM |
| 2003-04 | Huddinge IK U18 | Swe-U18 | 12 | 5 | 1 | 6 | 6 | .... | .... | .... | .... | .... |
| 2004-05 | Sodertalje SK U18 | Swe-U18 | 2 | 3 | 2 | 5 | 4 | 1 | 0 | 0 | 0 | 0 |
| | Sodertalje SK Jr. | Swe-Jr. | 28 | 13 | 11 | 24 | 16 | 3 | 2 | 1 | 3 | 2 |
| 2005-06 | Sodertalje SK U18 | Swe-U18 | 7 | 9 | 5 | 14 | 2 | 1 | 0 | 0 | 0 | 0 |
| | Sodertalje SK Jr. | Swe-Jr. | 37 | 14 | 19 | 33 | 69 | 4 | 1 | 2 | 3 | 14 |
| | Sodertalje SK | Sweden | 1 | 0 | 0 | 0 | 0 | .... | .... | .... | .... | .... |
| 2006-07 | Sodertalje SK Jr. | Swe-Jr. | 23 | 7 | 11 | 18 | 16 | 3 | 0 | 3 | 3 | 6 |
| | Sodertalje SK | Sweden-2 | 36 | 0 | 1 | 1 | 2 | .... | .... | .... | .... | .... |
| 2007-08 | Sodertalje SK Jr. | Swe-Jr. | 3 | 1 | 2 | 3 | 0 | .... | .... | .... | .... | .... |
| | Huddinge IK | Sweden-2 | 37 | 9 | 5 | 14 | 30 | .... | .... | .... | .... | .... |
| 2008-09 | Mora IK | Sweden-2 | 45 | 12 | 18 | 30 | 14 | 3 | 0 | 0 | 0 | 0 |

**LAHTI, Janne** (LAH-tee, yah-NAY) **MTL.**

Left wing. Shoots left. 6', 200 lbs. Born, Riihimaki, Finland, July 20, 1982.

| | | | Regular Season | | | | | Playoffs | | | | |
|---|---|---|---|---|---|---|---|---|---|---|---|---|
| Season | Club | League | GP | G | A | Pts | PIM | GP | G | A | Pts | PIM |
| 1998-99 | HPK U18 | Fin-U18 | 36 | 10 | 6 | 16 | 18 | .... | .... | .... | .... | .... |
| 99-2000 | HPK U18 | Fin-U18 | 12 | 5 | 7 | 12 | 2 | .... | .... | .... | .... | .... |
| | HPK Jr. | Fin-Jr. | 18 | 6 | 5 | 11 | 8 | .... | .... | .... | .... | .... |
| 2000-01 | HPK Jr. | Fin-Jr. | 35 | 9 | 11 | 20 | 16 | .... | .... | .... | .... | .... |
| 2001-02 | HPK Hameenlinna | Finland | 36 | 1 | 0 | 1 | 2 | 4 | 0 | 0 | 0 | 0 |
| | HPK Jr. | Fin-Jr. | 22 | 22 | 11 | 33 | 18 | 4 | 1 | 3 | 4 | 2 |
| 2002-03 | HPK Hameenlinna | Finland | 17 | 1 | 0 | 1 | 2 | 1 | 0 | 0 | 0 | 0 |
| | HPK Jr. | Fin-Jr. | 22 | 23 | 19 | 42 | 35 | .... | .... | .... | .... | .... |
| 2003-04 | HPK Hameenlinna | Finland | 43 | 14 | 6 | 20 | 26 | 8 | 1 | 0 | 1 | 0 |
| 2004-05 | HPK Hameenlinna | Finland | 52 | 6 | 9 | 15 | 22 | 8 | 2 | 2 | 4 | 4 |
| | Haukat Jarvenpaa | Finland-2 | 4 | 2 | 2 | 4 | 2 | .... | .... | .... | .... | .... |
| 2005-06 | HPK Hameenlinna | Finland | 51 | 9 | 13 | 22 | 30 | 13 | 5 | 4 | 9 | 6 |
| 2006-07 | HPK Hameenlinna | Finland | 56 | 20 | 14 | 34 | 87 | 9 | 8 | 1 | 9 | 4 |
| 2007-08 | Hamilton Bulldogs | AHL | 65 | 9 | 9 | 18 | 47 | .... | .... | .... | .... | .... |
| 2008-09 | Jokerit Helsinki | Finland | 41 | 9 | 8 | 17 | 10 | 5 | 1 | 3 | 4 | 2 |

Signed as a free agent by **Montreal**, May 31, 2007.

**LAJUNEN, Jani** (LA-joo-nehn, YAH-nee) **NSH.**

Center. Shoots left. 6'1", 184 lbs. Born, Helsinki, Finland, June 16, 1990.
(Nashville's 6th choice, 201st overall, in 2008 Entry Draft).

| | | | Regular Season | | | | | Playoffs | | | | |
|---|---|---|---|---|---|---|---|---|---|---|---|---|
| Season | Club | League | GP | G | A | Pts | PIM | GP | G | A | Pts | PIM |
| 2005-06 | K-Vantaa U18 | Fin-U18 | 2 | 0 | 0 | 0 | 0 | .... | .... | .... | .... | .... |
| 2006-07 | Blues Espoo U18 | Fin-U18 | 28 | 5 | 12 | 17 | 20 | 6 | 1 | 1 | 2 | 4 |
| 2007-08 | Blues Espoo U18 | Fin-U18 | 1 | 1 | 0 | 1 | 2 | 4 | 2 | 2 | 4 | 0 |
| | Blues Espoo Jr. | Fin-Jr. | 25 | 4 | 10 | 14 | 14 | 3 | 0 | 0 | 0 | 0 |
| | Blues Espoo | Finland | 1 | 0 | 0 | 0 | 0 | .... | .... | .... | .... | .... |
| 2008-09 | Suomi U20 | Finland-2 | 2 | 2 | 2 | 4 | 0 | .... | .... | .... | .... | .... |
| | Blues Espoo Jr. | Fin-Jr. | 25 | 16 | 10 | 26 | 24 | 8 | 2 | 1 | 3 | 12 |

**LALIBERTE, David** (la-lih-BUHR-tee, DAY-vihd) **PHI.**

Right wing. Shoots right. 6'1", 194 lbs. Born, St-Jean-Sur-Richelieu, Que., March 17, 1986.
(Philadelphia's 3rd choice, 124th overall, in 2004 Entry Draft).

| | | | Regular Season | | | | | Playoffs | | | | |
|---|---|---|---|---|---|---|---|---|---|---|---|---|
| Season | Club | League | GP | G | A | Pts | PIM | GP | G | A | Pts | PIM |
| 2001-02 | Antoine-Girouard | QAAA | 41 | 21 | 21 | 42 | 14 | 15 | 8 | 9 | 17 | 6 |
| 2002-03 | Montreal Rocket | QMJHL | 66 | 15 | 14 | 29 | 10 | 6 | 3 | 0 | 3 | 2 |
| 2003-04 | PEI Rocket | QMJHL | 70 | 21 | 22 | 43 | 51 | 11 | 1 | 3 | 4 | 6 |
| 2004-05 | PEI Rocket | QMJHL | 41 | 23 | 13 | 36 | 36 | .... | .... | .... | .... | .... |
| 2005-06 | PEI Rocket | QMJHL | 34 | 12 | 11 | 23 | 41 | 6 | 3 | 1 | 4 | 6 |
| 2006-07 | PEI Rocket | QMJHL | 68 | 50 | 48 | 98 | 86 | 7 | 5 | 4 | 9 | 4 |
| 2007-08 | Philadelphia | AHL | 27 | 3 | 6 | 9 | 13 | .... | .... | .... | .... | .... |
| | Wheeling Nailers | ECHL | 27 | 10 | 14 | 24 | 16 | .... | .... | .... | .... | .... |
| 2008-09 | Philadelphia | AHL | 70 | 28 | 20 | 48 | 43 | 4 | 0 | 1 | 1 | 4 |

**LALONDE, Shawn** (la-LAWND, SHAWN) **CHI.**

Defense. Shoots right. 6'1", 175 lbs. Born, Ottawa, Ont., March 10, 1990.
(Chicago's 2nd choice, 68th overall, in 2008 Entry Draft).

| | | | Regular Season | | | | | Playoffs | | | | |
|---|---|---|---|---|---|---|---|---|---|---|---|---|
| Season | Club | League | GP | G | A | Pts | PIM | GP | G | A | Pts | PIM |
| 2005-06 | Cumberland | Minor-ON | 60 | 18 | 36 | 54 | 98 | .... | .... | .... | .... | .... |
| 2006-07 | Belleville Bulls | OHL | 58 | 6 | 20 | 26 | 71 | 13 | 1 | 1 | 2 | 6 |
| 2007-08 | Belleville Bulls | OHL | 66 | 9 | 22 | 31 | 67 | 21 | 2 | 7 | 9 | 25 |
| 2008-09 | Belleville Bulls | OHL | 66 | 19 | 34 | 53 | 73 | 17 | 3 | 9 | 12 | 36 |

**LALONDE-McNICOLL, Cedric** (la-LAWND mihk-NIH-kohl, SEH-DRIHK) **COL.**

Center. Shoots left. 5'10", 176 lbs. Born, Longueuil, Que., August 28, 1988.

| | | | Regular Season | | | | | Playoffs | | | | |
|---|---|---|---|---|---|---|---|---|---|---|---|---|
| Season | Club | League | GP | G | A | Pts | PIM | GP | G | A | Pts | PIM |
| 2004-05 | C.C. Lemoyne | QAAA | 41 | 20 | 24 | 44 | 30 | 4 | 2 | 2 | 4 | 21 |
| | Shawinigan | QMJHL | 1 | 0 | 1 | 1 | 0 | 1 | 0 | 0 | 0 | 0 |
| 2005-06 | Shawinigan | QMJHL | 67 | 13 | 17 | 30 | 34 | 10 | 1 | 7 | 8 | 2 |
| 2006-07 | Shawinigan | QMJHL | 47 | 16 | 30 | 46 | 14 | 4 | 4 | 1 | 5 | 0 |
| 2007-08 | Shawinigan | QMJHL | 69 | 43 | 40 | 83 | 20 | 5 | 0 | 8 | 8 | 6 |
| 2008-09 | Shawinigan | QMJHL | 65 | 38 | 66 | 104 | 22 | .... | .... | .... | .... | .... |

Canadian Major Junior Second All-Star Team (2009) • Canadian Major Junior Sportsman of the Year (2008, 2009)

Signed as a free agent by **Colorado**, March 6, 2009.

**LAMMERS, John** (LA-muhrs, JAWN)

Left wing. Shoots left. 5'11", 184 lbs. Born, Bowmanville, Ont., January 29, 1986.
(Dallas' 5th choice, 86th overall, in 2004 Entry Draft).

| | | | Regular Season | | | | | Playoffs | | | | |
|---|---|---|---|---|---|---|---|---|---|---|---|---|
| Season | Club | League | GP | G | A | Pts | PIM | GP | G | A | Pts | PIM |
| 2001-02 | Langley Bantams | Minor-BC | 64 | 51 | 69 | 120 | 30 | .... | .... | .... | .... | .... |
| | Lethbridge | WHL | 5 | 0 | 0 | 0 | 0 | .... | .... | .... | .... | .... |
| 2002-03 | Lethbridge | WHL | 53 | 17 | 15 | 32 | 11 | .... | .... | .... | .... | .... |
| 2003-04 | Lethbridge | WHL | 62 | 21 | 24 | 45 | 31 | .... | .... | .... | .... | .... |
| 2004-05 | Lethbridge | WHL | 66 | 17 | 30 | 47 | 43 | 5 | 0 | 0 | 0 | 2 |
| 2005-06 | Everett Silvertips | WHL | 70 | 38 | 37 | 75 | 25 | 15 | 5 | 6 | 11 | 12 |
| 2006-07 | Iowa Stars | AHL | 52 | 6 | 8 | 14 | 14 | .... | .... | .... | .... | .... |
| | Idaho Steelheads | ECHL | 9 | 2 | 2 | 4 | 4 | 22 | 7 | 12 | 19 | 2 |
| 2007-08 | Iowa Stars | AHL | 1 | 0 | 0 | 0 | 0 | .... | .... | .... | .... | .... |
| | Idaho Steelheads | ECHL | 36 | 27 | 16 | 43 | 22 | 4 | 0 | 3 | 3 | 2 |
| | Assat Pori | Finland | 23 | 0 | 4 | 4 | 24 | .... | .... | .... | .... | .... |
| 2008-09 | Houston Aeros | AHL | 57 | 12 | 14 | 26 | 40 | 18 | 0 | 8 | 8 | 4 |

**LANDER, Anton** (LAN-duhr, AN-tawn) **EDM.**

Center. Shoots left. 6', 194 lbs. Born, Sundsvall, Sweden, April 24, 1991.
(Edmonton's 2nd choice, 40th overall, in 2009 Entry Draft).

| | | | Regular Season | | | | | Playoffs | | | | |
|---|---|---|---|---|---|---|---|---|---|---|---|---|
| Season | Club | League | GP | G | A | Pts | PIM | GP | G | A | Pts | PIM |
| 2005-06 | Timra IK U18 | Swe-U18 | 14 | 1 | 6 | 7 | 14 | .... | .... | .... | .... | .... |
| 2006-07 | Timra IK U18 | Swe-U18 | 12 | 6 | 10 | 16 | 14 | 2 | 1 | 2 | 3 | 0 |
| | Timra IK Jr. | Swe-Jr. | 10 | 2 | 1 | 3 | 10 | .... | .... | .... | .... | .... |
| 2007-08 | Timra IK U18 | Swe-U18 | 4 | 6 | 4 | 10 | 8 | .... | .... | .... | .... | .... |
| | Timra IK Jr. | Swe-Jr. | 18 | 5 | 14 | 19 | 39 | .... | .... | .... | .... | .... |
| | Timra IK | Sweden | 32 | 1 | 2 | 3 | 4 | 10 | 0 | 0 | 0 | 0 |
| 2008-09 | Timra IK Jr. | Swe-Jr. | 8 | 5 | 1 | 6 | 8 | .... | .... | .... | .... | .... |
| | Timra IK | Sweden | 47 | 4 | 6 | 10 | 12 | 7 | 0 | 0 | 0 | 4 |

**LANNON, Ryan** (LA-nuhn, RIGH-uhn) **MIN.**

Defense. Shoots left. 6'1", 198 lbs. Born, Worcester, MA, December 14, 1982.
(Pittsburgh's 10th choice, 239th overall, in 2002 Entry Draft).

| | | | Regular Season | | | | | Playoffs | | | | |
|---|---|---|---|---|---|---|---|---|---|---|---|---|
| Season | Club | League | GP | G | A | Pts | PIM | GP | G | A | Pts | PIM |
| 1998-99 | USNTDP | NAHL | 56 | 3 | 4 | 7 | 36 | .... | .... | .... | .... | .... |
| 99-2000 | Cushing | High-MA | STATISTICS NOT AVAILABLE | | | | | | | | | |
| 2000-01 | Cushing | High-MA | STATISTICS NOT AVAILABLE | | | | | | | | | |
| 2001-02 | Harvard Crimson | ECAC | 34 | 0 | 2 | 2 | 38 | .... | .... | .... | .... | .... |
| 2002-03 | Harvard Crimson | ECAC | 34 | 3 | 11 | 14 | 39 | .... | .... | .... | .... | .... |
| 2003-04 | Harvard Crimson | ECAC | 35 | 0 | 9 | 9 | 36 | .... | .... | .... | .... | .... |
| 2004-05 | Harvard Crimson | ECAC | 33 | 1 | 12 | 13 | 34 | .... | .... | .... | .... | .... |
| 2005-06 | Wilkes-Barre | AHL | 74 | 2 | 8 | 10 | 65 | 11 | 0 | 0 | 0 | 8 |
| 2006-07 | Wilkes-Barre | AHL | 68 | 0 | 19 | 19 | 71 | 11 | 0 | 2 | 2 | 14 |
| 2007-08 | Wilkes-Barre | AHL | 75 | 3 | 10 | 13 | 29 | 23 | 1 | 6 | 7 | 2 |
| 2008-09 | San Antonio | AHL | 63 | 0 | 5 | 5 | 33 | .... | .... | .... | .... | .... |

Signed as a free agent by **Phoenix**, July 15, 2008. Signed as a free agent by **Minnesota** July 23, 2009.

**LAPOINT, Derrick** (luh-POYNT, DAIR-ihk) **FLA.**

Defense. Shoots left. 6'3", 175 lbs. Born, Eau Claire, MA, May 13, 1988.
(Florida's 4th choice, 116th overall, in 2006 Entry Draft).

| | | | Regular Season | | | | | Playoffs | | | | |
|---|---|---|---|---|---|---|---|---|---|---|---|---|
| Season | Club | League | GP | G | A | Pts | PIM | GP | G | A | Pts | PIM |
| 2004-05 | Eau Claire North | High-WI | 23 | 9 | 28 | 37 | 14 | | | | | |
| 2005-06 | Eau Claire North | High-WI | 23 | 6 | 26 | 32 | 34 | | | | | |
| 2006-07 | Green Bay | USHL | 59 | 13 | 36 | 49 | 48 | 4 | 0 | 2 | 2 | 2 |
| 2007-08 | North Dakota | WCHA | 31 | 2 | 5 | 7 | 34 | | | | | |
| 2008-09 | North Dakota | WCHA | 32 | 1 | 4 | 5 | 12 | | | | | |

USHL All-Rookie Team (2007) • USHL First All-Star Team (2007)

**LARKIN, Thomas** (LAHR-kihn, TAW-muhs) **CBJ**

Defense. Shoots right. 6'5", 206 lbs. Born, London, England, December 31, 1990.
(Columbus' 4th choice, 137th overall, in 2009 Entry Draft).

| | | | Regular Season | | | | | Playoffs | | | | |
|---|---|---|---|---|---|---|---|---|---|---|---|---|
| Season | Club | League | GP | G | A | Pts | PIM | GP | G | A | Pts | PIM |
| 2006-07 | Exeter | High-NH | 28 | 1 | 7 | 8 | 5 | | | | | |
| 2007-08 | Exeter | High-NH | 29 | 6 | 15 | 21 | 18 | | | | | |
| 2008-09 | Exeter | High-NH | 35 | 14 | 38 | 52 | 30 | | | | | |
| | Little Bruins | Minor-MA | 18 | 1 | 1 | 2 | 10 | | | | | |

• Signed Letter of Intent to attend **Colgate University** (ECAC) in fall of 2009.

**LARSEN, Philip** (LAHR-suhn, FIHL-ihp) **DAL.**

Defense. Shoots right. 5'11", 185 lbs. Born, Esbjerg, Denmark, December 7, 1989.
(Dallas' 3rd choice, 149th overall, in 2008 Entry Draft).

| | | | Regular Season | | | | | Playoffs | | | | |
|---|---|---|---|---|---|---|---|---|---|---|---|---|
| Season | Club | League | GP | G | A | Pts | PIM | GP | G | A | Pts | PIM |
| 2004-05 | Esbjerg IK Jr. | Den-Jr. | 10 | 1 | 0 | 1 | 2 | | | | | |
| 2005-06 | Rogle Jr. | Swe-Jr. | 32 | 1 | 4 | 5 | 24 | | | | | |
| | Rogle | Sweden-2 | 13 | 0 | 0 | 0 | 0 | | | | | |
| 2006-07 | Frolunda U18 | Swe-U18 | 3 | 1 | 2 | 3 | 2 | 4 | 2 | 1 | 3 | 8 |
| | Frolunda Jr. | Swe-Jr. | 37 | 3 | 15 | 18 | 50 | 8 | 0 | 1 | 1 | 6 |
| | Frolunda | Sweden | 5 | 0 | 0 | 0 | 0 | | | | | |
| 2007-08 | Frolunda Jr. | Swe-Jr. | 8 | 1 | 4 | 5 | 12 | 7 | 0 | 4 | 4 | 6 |
| | Boras HC | Sweden-2 | 24 | 5 | 5 | 10 | 32 | | | | | |
| | Frolunda | Sweden | 16 | 0 | 0 | 0 | 2 | | | | | |
| 2008-09 | Frolunda Jr. | Swe-Jr. | 1 | 1 | 0 | 1 | 0 | | | | | |
| | Frolunda | Sweden | 53 | 2 | 15 | 17 | 18 | 11 | 2 | 1 | 3 | 4 |

**LARSON, Nick** (LAHR-suhn, NIHK-oh-las) **CGY.**

Left wing. Shoots left. 6'1", 182 lbs. Born, St.Paul, MN, November 14, 1989.
(Calgary's 4th choice, 108th overall, in 2008 Entry Draft).

| | | | Regular Season | | | | | Playoffs | | | | |
|---|---|---|---|---|---|---|---|---|---|---|---|---|
| Season | Club | League | GP | G | A | Pts | PIM | GP | G | A | Pts | PIM |
| 2006-07 | St. Thomas | High-MN | 25 | 20 | 30 | 50 | | | | | | |
| | Team Southeast | UMWEHL | 11 | 5 | 6 | 11 | | | | | | |
| 2007-08 | Waterloo | USHL | 57 | 19 | 19 | 38 | 66 | 9 | 3 | 2 | 5 | 31 |
| 2008-09 | Waterloo | USHL | 51 | 19 | 17 | 36 | 144 | 3 | 0 | 0 | 0 | 4 |

• Signed Letter of Intent to attend **University of Notre Dame** (CCHA) in fall of 2009.

**LASU, Nicklas** (LA-soo, NIHK-luhs) **ATL.**

Left wing. Shoots left. 5'11", 176 lbs. Born, Molndal, Sweden, September 16, 1989.
(Atlanta's 5th choice, 124th overall, in 2008 Entry Draft).

| | | | Regular Season | | | | | Playoffs | | | | |
|---|---|---|---|---|---|---|---|---|---|---|---|---|
| Season | Club | League | GP | G | A | Pts | PIM | GP | G | A | Pts | PIM |
| 2005-06 | Frolunda U18 | Swe-U18 | 14 | 3 | 3 | 6 | 2 | 2 | 1 | 0 | 1 | 2 |
| 2006-07 | Frolunda U18 | Swe-U18 | 5 | 5 | 5 | 10 | 12 | 7 | 2 | 6 | 8 | 6 |
| | Frolunda Jr. | Swe-Jr. | 39 | 11 | 14 | 25 | 30 | 7 | 0 | 0 | 0 | 4 |
| 2007-08 | Frolunda Jr. | Swe-Jr. | 41 | 19 | 34 | 53 | 42 | 8 | 5 | 5 | 10 | 4 |
| | Frolunda | Sweden | 2 | 0 | 0 | 0 | 0 | | | | | |
| 2008-09 | Frolunda Jr. | Swe-Jr. | 4 | 3 | 1 | 4 | 33 | | | | | |
| | Boras HC | Sweden-2 | 21 | 4 | 6 | 10 | 35 | | | | | |
| | Frolunda | Sweden | 14 | 3 | 1 | 4 | 4 | 11 | 0 | 1 | 1 | 8 |

**LATTA, Michael** (LA-tuh, MIGH-kuhl) **NSH.**

Center. Shoots right. 5'11", 207 lbs. Born, Kitchener, Ont., May 25, 1991.
(Nashville's 5th choice, 72nd overall, in 2009 Entry Draft).

| | | | Regular Season | | | | | Playoffs | | | | |
|---|---|---|---|---|---|---|---|---|---|---|---|---|
| Season | Club | League | GP | G | A | Pts | PIM | GP | G | A | Pts | PIM |
| 2006-07 | Waterloo Wolves | Minor-ON | 73 | 52 | 66 | 118 | 213 | | | | | |
| 2007-08 | Ottawa 67's | OHL | 50 | 14 | 14 | 28 | 78 | 4 | 0 | 1 | 1 | 2 |
| 2008-09 | Ottawa 67's | OHL | 23 | 8 | 13 | 21 | 32 | | | | | |
| | Guelph Storm | OHL | 42 | 14 | 22 | 36 | 60 | 4 | 0 | 2 | 2 | 12 |

**LAURIDSEN, Oliver** (LAWR-ihd-suhn, AW-lih-vuhr) **PHI.**

Defense. Shoots left. 6'6", 220 lbs. Born, Gentofte, Denmark, March 24, 1989.
(Philadelphia's 6th choice, 196th overall, in 2009 Entry Draft).

| | | | Regular Season | | | | | Playoffs | | | | |
|---|---|---|---|---|---|---|---|---|---|---|---|---|
| Season | Club | League | GP | G | A | Pts | PIM | GP | G | A | Pts | PIM |
| 2004-05 | IC Gentofte Jr. | Den-Jr. | 24 | 4 | 12 | 16 | 22 | | | | | |
| | IC Gentofte | Den-2 | 8 | 0 | 1 | 1 | 0 | | | | | |
| 2005-06 | Rogle Jr. | Swe-Jr. | 28 | 1 | 1 | 2 | 32 | | | | | |
| 2006-07 | Linkopings HC Jr. | Swe-Jr. | 34 | 0 | 2 | 2 | 95 | 5 | 0 | 0 | 0 | 8 |
| 2007-08 | Linkopings HC U18 | Swe-U18 | 2 | 1 | 3 | 4 | 0 | | | | | |
| | Tranas AIF | Sweden-3 | 1 | 0 | 0 | 0 | 0 | | | | | |
| | Linkopings HC Jr. | Swe-Jr. | 35 | 5 | 6 | 11 | 159 | 1 | 0 | 1 | 1 | 0 |
| 2008-09 | St. Cloud State | WCHA | 28 | 0 | 1 | 1 | 38 | | | | | |

**LAVIN, Joseph** (LA-vihn, JOH-sehf) **CHI.**

Defense. Shoots left. 6'1", 195 lbs. Born, Worcester, MA, July 17, 1989.
(Chicago's 6th choice, 126th overall, in 2007 Entry Draft).

| | | | Regular Season | | | | | Playoffs | | | | |
|---|---|---|---|---|---|---|---|---|---|---|---|---|
| Season | Club | League | GP | G | A | Pts | PIM | GP | G | A | Pts | PIM |
| 2004-05 | Boston Jr. Bruins | EmJHL | 64 | 11 | 44 | 55 | | | | | | |
| 2005-06 | USNTDP | U-17 | 19 | 2 | 1 | 3 | 30 | | | | | |
| | USNTDP | NAHL | 37 | 8 | 10 | 18 | 16 | 12 | 3 | 2 | 5 | 4 |
| 2006-07 | USNTDP | U-18 | 23 | 1 | 0 | 1 | 18 | | | | | |
| | USNTDP | NAHL | 18 | 1 | 8 | 9 | 22 | 6 | 0 | 2 | 2 | 4 |
| 2007-08 | Providence College | H-East | 36 | 0 | 8 | 8 | 26 | | | | | |
| 2008-09 | Providence College | H-East | 12 | 0 | 1 | 1 | 10 | | | | | |

**LAVRENTIEV, Anton** (lahv-REHN-tee-yehv, AN-tawn) **NSH.**

Defense. Shoots right. 6'4", 196 lbs. Born, Kazan, USSR, August 25, 1983.
(Nashville's 7th choice, 178th overall, in 2001 Entry Draft).

| | | | Regular Season | | | | | Playoffs | | | | |
|---|---|---|---|---|---|---|---|---|---|---|---|---|
| Season | Club | League | GP | G | A | Pts | PIM | GP | G | A | Pts | PIM |
| 2000-01 | Ak Bars Kazan 2 | Russia-3 | STATISTICS NOT AVAILABLE | | | | | | | | | |
| 2001-02 | Sudbury Wolves | OHL | 10 | 0 | 0 | 0 | 17 | | | | | |
| | Ak Bars Kazan 2 | Russia-3 | STATISTICS NOT AVAILABLE | | | | | | | | | |
| 2002-03 | Yuzhny Ural Orsk | Russia-2 | 13 | 0 | 1 | 1 | 14 | | | | | |
| 2003-04 | HK Rybinsk | Russia-2 | 31 | 2 | 1 | 3 | 49 | | | | | |
| 2004-05 | Novopolotsk | BelOpen | 23 | 2 | 3 | 5 | 26 | 1 | 0 | 0 | 0 | 2 |
| 2005-06 | Naber. Chelny | Russia-3 | 70 | 8 | 6 | 14 | 214 | | | | | |
| 2006-07 | Naber. Chelny | Russia-3 | 67 | 10 | 21 | 31 | 270 | | | | | |
| 2007-08 | Naber. Chelny | Russia-3 | 63 | 9 | 10 | 19 | 127 | | | | | |
| 2008-09 | Naber. Chelny | Russia-3 | 60 | 8 | 7 | 15 | 160 | | | | | |

**LAWRENCE, Chris** (LOH-rehnts, KRIHS) **T.B.**

Center. Shoots right. 6'4", 199 lbs. Born, Toronto, Ont., February 5, 1987.
(Tampa Bay's 3rd choice, 89th overall, in 2005 Entry Draft).

| | | | Regular Season | | | | | Playoffs | | | | |
|---|---|---|---|---|---|---|---|---|---|---|---|---|
| Season | Club | League | GP | G | A | Pts | PIM | GP | G | A | Pts | PIM |
| 2003-04 | Sault Ste. Marie | OHL | 62 | 7 | 6 | 13 | 34 | | | | | |
| 2004-05 | Sault Ste. Marie | OHL | 68 | 11 | 40 | 51 | 57 | 7 | 3 | 3 | 6 | 4 |
| 2005-06 | Sault Ste. Marie | OHL | 29 | 3 | 14 | 17 | 31 | | | | | |
| | Mississauga | OHL | 38 | 20 | 16 | 36 | 60 | | | | | |
| 2006-07 | Mississauga | OHL | 64 | 47 | 41 | 88 | 113 | 5 | 3 | 1 | 4 | 14 |
| 2007-08 | Norfolk Admirals | AHL | 53 | 5 | 11 | 16 | 32 | | | | | |
| 2008-09 | Norfolk Admirals | AHL | 48 | 5 | 3 | 8 | 37 | | | | | |
| | Augusta Lynx | ECHL | 7 | 1 | 2 | 3 | 25 | | | | | |
| | Mississippi | ECHL | 3 | 0 | 1 | 1 | 5 | | | | | |

**LAWSON, Kyle** (LAW-suhn, KIGHL) **CAR.**

Defense. Shoots right. 5'11", 192 lbs. Born, Southfield, MI, January 11, 1987.
(Carolina's 9th choice, 198th overall, in 2005 Entry Draft).

| | | | Regular Season | | | | | Playoffs | | | | |
|---|---|---|---|---|---|---|---|---|---|---|---|---|
| Season | Club | League | GP | G | A | Pts | PIM | GP | G | A | Pts | PIM |
| 2003-04 | Det. Honeybaked | MWEHL | 61 | 17 | 41 | 58 | 68 | | | | | |
| | Texarkana Bandits | NAHL | | | | | | 3 | 0 | 1 | 1 | 0 |
| 2004-05 | USNTDP | U-18 | 23 | 2 | 12 | 14 | 6 | | | | | |
| | USNTDP | NAHL | 8 | 1 | 3 | 4 | 0 | | | | | |
| 2005-06 | Tri-City Storm | USHL | 49 | 9 | 13 | 22 | 40 | 1 | 0 | 0 | 0 | 0 |
| 2006-07 | U. of Notre Dame | CCHA | 38 | 4 | 15 | 19 | 14 | | | | | |
| 2007-08 | U. of Notre Dame | CCHA | 45 | 5 | 21 | 26 | 36 | | | | | |
| 2008-09 | U. of Notre Dame | CCHA | 40 | 4 | 19 | 23 | 44 | | | | | |

CCHA All-Rookie Team (2007) • NCAA Championship All-Tournament Team (2008) • CCHA Second All-Star Team (2009)

**LEBLANC, Louis** (luh-BLAWNK, LOU-ee) **MTL.**

Center. Shoots right. 6', 174 lbs. Born, Pointe-Claire, Que., January 26, 1991.
(Montreal's 1st choice, 18th overall, in 2009 Entry Draft).

| | | | Regular Season | | | | | Playoffs | | | | |
|---|---|---|---|---|---|---|---|---|---|---|---|---|
| Season | Club | League | GP | G | A | Pts | PIM | GP | G | A | Pts | PIM |
| 2006-07 | Lac St-Louis Lions | QAAA | 40 | 31 | 18 | 49 | 72 | 22 | 14 | 7 | 21 | 10 |
| 2007-08 | Lac St-Louis Lions | QAAA | 43 | 54 | 37 | 91 | 152 | 14 | 8 | 14 | 22 | 76 |
| 2008-09 | Omaha Lancers | USHL | 60 | 28 | 31 | 59 | 78 | 3 | 2 | 1 | 3 | 2 |

USHL All-Rookie Team (2009) • USHL Rookie of the Year (2009)

• Signed Letter of Intent to attend **Harvard University** (ECAC) in fall of 2009.

**LEBLANC, Peter** (luh-BLAHNK, PEE-tuhr) **CHI.**

Center. Shoots left. 5'10", 196 lbs. Born, Hamilton, Ont., February 3, 1988.
(Chicago's 9th choice, 186th overall, in 2006 Entry Draft).

| | | | Regular Season | | | | | Playoffs | | | | |
|---|---|---|---|---|---|---|---|---|---|---|---|---|
| Season | Club | League | GP | G | A | Pts | PIM | GP | G | A | Pts | PIM |
| 2004-05 | Hamilton | OPJHL | 49 | 14 | 22 | 36 | | | | | | |
| 2005-06 | Hamilton | OPJHL | 22 | 10 | 12 | 22 | 25 | | | | | |
| 2006-07 | New Hampshire | H-East | 39 | 1 | 4 | 5 | 4 | | | | | |
| 2007-08 | New Hampshire | H-East | 37 | 5 | 10 | 15 | 37 | | | | | |
| 2008-09 | New Hampshire | H-East | 38 | 14 | 16 | 30 | 8 | | | | | |

OPJHL Rookie of the Year (2005)

• Missed majority of 2005-06 season due to mononucleosis.

**LEDDY, Nick** (LEH-dee, NIHK) **MIN.**

Defense. Shoots left. 5'11", 179 lbs. Born, Eden Prairie, MN, March 20, 1991.
(Minnesota's 1st choice, 16th overall, in 2009 Entry Draft).

| | | | Regular Season | | | | | Playoffs | | | | |
|---|---|---|---|---|---|---|---|---|---|---|---|---|
| Season | Club | League | GP | G | A | Pts | PIM | GP | G | A | Pts | PIM |
| 2006-07 | Eden Prairie Eagles | High-MN | 28 | 2 | 16 | 18 | 10 | | | | | |
| 2007-08 | Eden Prairie Eagles | High-MN | 27 | 6 | 22 | 28 | 14 | | | | | |
| | USNTDP | U-18 | 4 | 0 | 2 | 2 | | | | | | |
| 2008-09 | Eden Prairie Eagles | High-MN | 31 | 12 | 33 | 45 | 26 | | | | | |
| | Team Southwest | UMHSEL | 24 | 9 | 11 | 20 | | | | | | |

• Signed Letter of Intent to attend **University of Minnesota** (WCHA) in fall of 2009.

**LEE, Anders** (LEE, AN-duhrz) **NYI**

Center. Shoots left. 6'2", 209 lbs. Born, St.Paul, MN, July 3, 1990.
(NY Islanders' 7th choice, 152nd overall, in 2009 Entry Draft).

| | | | Regular Season | | | | | Playoffs | | | | |
|---|---|---|---|---|---|---|---|---|---|---|---|---|
| Season | Club | League | GP | G | A | Pts | PIM | GP | G | A | Pts | PIM |
| 2006-07 | St. Thomas | High-MN | 31 | 24 | 17 | 41 | | | | | | |
| 2007-08 | Edina Hornets | High-MN | 31 | 32 | 22 | 54 | | | | | | |
| 2008-09 | Edina Hornets | High-MN | 31 | 25 | 59 | 84 | 30 | | | | | |
| | Team Southwest | UMHSEL | 18 | 12 | 17 | 29 | | | | | | |

• Signed Letter of Intent to attend **University of Notre Dame** (CCHA) in fall of 2010.

**LEE, Carter** (LEE, KAHR-tuhr) **S.J.**

Right wing. Shoots right. 6'1", 190 lbs. Born, Toms River, NJ, July 2, 1984.
(San Jose's 11th choice, 276th overall, in 2003 Entry Draft).

| | | | Regular Season | | | | | Playoffs | | | | |
|---|---|---|---|---|---|---|---|---|---|---|---|---|
| Season | Club | League | GP | G | A | Pts | PIM | GP | G | A | Pts | PIM |
| 2001-02 | Christian Bros. | High-NJ | 34 | 10 | 9 | 19 | 45 | | | | | |
| 2002-03 | Canterbury | High-CT | 35 | 38 | 22 | 60 | 40 | | | | | |
| 2003-04 | Canterbury | High-CT | 30 | 19 | 26 | 45 | 40 | | | | | |
| 2004-05 | Northeastern | H-East | 11 | 2 | 1 | 3 | 4 | | | | | |
| 2005-06 | Northeastern | H-East | 9 | 0 | 1 | 1 | 21 | | | | | |
| 2006-07 | Lake Superior | CCHA | DID NOT PLAY – TRANSFERRED COLLEGES | | | | | | | | | |
| 2007-08 | Lake Superior | CCHA | 17 | 1 | 1 | 2 | 8 | | | | | |
| 2008-09 | Lake Superior | CCHA | 12 | 2 | 2 | 4 | 2 | | | | | |

## LEE, Chris (LEE, KRIHS) PIT.

Defense. Shoots left. 6', 185 lbs. Born, MacTier, Ont., October 3, 1980.

| | | | Regular Season | | | | | Playoffs | | | | |
|---|---|---|---|---|---|---|---|---|---|---|---|---|
| Season | Club | League | GP | G | A | Pts | PIM | GP | G | A | Pts | PIM |
| 2004-05 | Florida Everblades | ECHL | 68 | 5 | 22 | 27 | 16 | 15 | 2 | 9 | 11 | 6 |
| 2005-06 | Florida Everblades | ECHL | 52 | 10 | 27 | 37 | 56 | 8 | 2 | 1 | 3 | 4 |
| 2006-07 | Albany River Rats | AHL | 3 | 0 | 1 | 1 | 4 | .... | .... | .... | .... | .... |
| | Bridgeport | AHL | 1 | 0 | 0 | 0 | 0 | .... | .... | .... | .... | .... |
| | Omaha | AHL | 32 | 4 | 13 | 17 | 16 | 6 | 3 | 0 | 3 | 6 |
| | Florida Everblades | ECHL | 37 | 6 | 19 | 25 | 22 | 9 | 3 | 1 | 4 | 0 |
| 2007-08 | Iowa Stars | AHL | 68 | 7 | 21 | 28 | 42 | .... | .... | .... | .... | .... |
| 2008-09 | Bridgeport | AHL | 66 | 6 | 24 | 30 | 36 | 5 | 0 | 3 | 3 | 2 |

Signed as a free agent by **NY Islanders**, July 3, 2008. Signed as a free agent by **Pittsburgh**, July 5, 2009.

## LEE, John (LEE, JAWN) FLA.

Defense. Shoots right. 6'2", 173 lbs. Born, Fargo, ND, January 16, 1989.
(Florida's 5th choice, 131st overall, in 2007 Entry Draft).

| | | | Regular Season | | | | | Playoffs | | | | |
|---|---|---|---|---|---|---|---|---|---|---|---|---|
| Season | Club | League | GP | G | A | Pts | PIM | GP | G | A | Pts | PIM |
| 2004-05 | Moorhead Spuds | High-MN | 3 | 0 | 1 | 1 | 0 | .... | .... | .... | .... | .... |
| 2005-06 | Moorhead Spuds | High-MN | 26 | 6 | 21 | 27 | 50 | .... | .... | .... | .... | .... |
| 2006-07 | Moorhead Spuds | High-MN | 26 | 6 | 33 | 39 | 62 | .... | .... | .... | .... | .... |
| | Waterloo | USHL | 27 | 2 | 7 | 9 | 56 | 9 | 0 | 3 | 3 | 4 |
| 2007-08 | Waterloo | USHL | 59 | 1 | 11 | 12 | 106 | 11 | 0 | 4 | 4 | 24 |
| 2008-09 | U. of Denver | WCHA | 39 | 0 | 5 | 5 | 38 | .... | .... | .... | .... | .... |

## LEGAULT, Maxime (luh-GOH, max-EEM) BUF.

Right wing. Shoots right. 6'2", 195 lbs. Born, Ste. Agathe, Que., March 28, 1989.
(Buffalo's 6th choice, 194th overall, in 2009 Entry Draft).

| | | | Regular Season | | | | | Playoffs | | | | |
|---|---|---|---|---|---|---|---|---|---|---|---|---|
| Season | Club | League | GP | G | A | Pts | PIM | GP | G | A | Pts | PIM |
| 2005-06 | Laval-Laurentides | QAAA | 36 | 13 | 15 | 28 | 138 | 4 | 2 | 1 | 3 | 21 |
| 2006-07 | Shawinigan | QMJHL | 55 | 7 | 12 | 19 | 98 | 4 | 0 | 0 | 0 | 4 |
| 2007-08 | Shawinigan | QMJHL | 31 | 6 | 4 | 10 | 61 | .... | .... | .... | .... | .... |
| 2008-09 | Shawinigan | QMJHL | 63 | 28 | 16 | 44 | 66 | 21 | 10 | 3 | 13 | 23 |

## LEGEIN, Stefan (LEE-gihn, STEH-fan) CBJ

Right wing. Shoots right. 5'10", 185 lbs. Born, Oakville, Ont., November 24, 1988.
(Columbus' 2nd choice, 37th overall, in 2007 Entry Draft).

| | | | Regular Season | | | | | Playoffs | | | | |
|---|---|---|---|---|---|---|---|---|---|---|---|---|
| Season | Club | League | GP | G | A | Pts | PIM | GP | G | A | Pts | PIM |
| 2003-04 | Tor. Red Wings | GTHL | 33 | 19 | 14 | 33 | 63 | .... | .... | .... | .... | .... |
| 2004-05 | Milton Icehawks | OPJHL | 26 | 7 | 12 | 19 | 18 | .... | .... | .... | .... | .... |
| | Mississauga | OHL | 49 | 3 | 5 | 8 | 37 | 5 | 0 | 1 | 1 | 0 |
| 2005-06 | Mississauga | OHL | 59 | 7 | 9 | 16 | 101 | .... | .... | .... | .... | .... |
| 2006-07 | Mississauga | OHL | 64 | 43 | 32 | 75 | 115 | 5 | 3 | 2 | 5 | 0 |
| 2007-08 | Niagara Ice Dogs | OHL | 30 | 24 | 13 | 37 | 80 | 10 | 7 | 11 | 18 | 28 |
| | Syracuse Crunch | AHL | .... | .... | .... | .... | .... | 2 | 0 | 0 | 0 | 0 |
| 2008-09 | Syracuse Crunch | AHL | 26 | 1 | 0 | 1 | 4 | .... | .... | .... | .... | .... |

OHL Second All-Star Team (2008)

## LEHTERA, Jori (LEH-tuhr-a, YOHR-ee) ST.L.

Center. Shoots left. 6'2", 191 lbs. Born, Helsinki, Finland, December 23, 1987.
(St. Louis' 4th choice, 65th overall, in 2008 Entry Draft).

| | | | Regular Season | | | | | Playoffs | | | | |
|---|---|---|---|---|---|---|---|---|---|---|---|---|
| Season | Club | League | GP | G | A | Pts | PIM | GP | G | A | Pts | PIM |
| 2003-04 | Jokerit U18 | Fin-U18 | 19 | 0 | 6 | 6 | 2 | 5 | 3 | 1 | 4 | 0 |
| 2004-05 | Jokerit U18 | Fin-U18 | 30 | 13 | 37 | 50 | 24 | 7 | 6 | 5 | 11 | 2 |
| 2005-06 | Suomi U20 | Finland-2 | 2 | 0 | 0 | 0 | 0 | .... | .... | .... | .... | .... |
| | Jokerit Helsinki Jr. | Fin-Jr. | 39 | 14 | 33 | 47 | 16 | 4 | 1 | 4 | 5 | 0 |
| 2006-07 | Suomi U20 | Finland-2 | 10 | 4 | 7 | 11 | 10 | .... | .... | .... | .... | .... |
| | Jokerit Helsinki Jr. | Fin-Jr. | 24 | 18 | 48 | 66 | 20 | 5 | 1 | 7 | 8 | 2 |
| | Jokerit Helsinki | Finland | 28 | 6 | 6 | 12 | 14 | .... | .... | .... | .... | .... |
| 2007-08 | Tappara Tampere | Finland | 54 | 13 | 29 | 42 | 32 | 11 | 4 | 2 | 6 | 8 |
| 2008-09 | Tappara Tampere | Finland | 58 | 9 | 38 | 47 | 34 | 3 | 4 | 5 | 9 | 4 |
| | Peoria Rivermen | AHL | 7 | 0 | 1 | 1 | 2 | 7 | 1 | 1 | 2 | 10 |

## LEHTIVUORI, Joonas (leh-tee-VWOO-aw-ree, YOH-nuhs) PHI.

Defense. Shoots left. 5'11", 170 lbs. Born, Tampere, Finland, July 19, 1988.
(Philadelphia's 6th choice, 101st overall, in 2006 Entry Draft).

| | | | Regular Season | | | | | Playoffs | | | | |
|---|---|---|---|---|---|---|---|---|---|---|---|---|
| Season | Club | League | GP | G | A | Pts | PIM | GP | G | A | Pts | PIM |
| 2004-05 | Ilves Tampere U18 | Fin-U18 | 25 | 5 | 11 | 16 | 12 | 5 | 1 | 1 | 2 | 8 |
| 2005-06 | Ilves Tampere U18 | Fin-U18 | 2 | 0 | 1 | 1 | 0 | 6 | 1 | 4 | 5 | 4 |
| | Ilves Tampere Jr. | Fin-Jr. | 39 | 9 | 16 | 25 | 22 | 3 | 0 | 0 | 0 | 4 |
| | Ilves Tampere | Finland | 1 | 0 | 0 | 0 | 0 | .... | .... | .... | .... | .... |
| 2006-07 | Ilves Tampere Jr. | Fin-Jr. | 15 | 3 | 8 | 11 | 51 | 5 | 0 | 1 | 1 | 2 |
| | Suomi U20 | Finland-2 | 2 | 0 | 0 | 0 | 0 | .... | .... | .... | .... | .... |
| | Ilves Tampere | Finland | 40 | 0 | 0 | 0 | 18 | 4 | 0 | 0 | 0 | 0 |
| 2007-08 | Suomi U20 | Finland-2 | 2 | 0 | 1 | 1 | 2 | .... | .... | .... | .... | .... |
| | Ilves Tampere | Finland | 48 | 8 | 13 | 21 | 10 | 9 | 1 | 1 | 2 | 2 |
| 2008-09 | Ilves Tampere | Finland | 44 | 4 | 8 | 12 | 16 | 3 | 0 | 0 | 0 | 0 |

## LEMIEUX, Francis (leh-M'YOO, FRAN-sihs)

Center. Shoots right. 5'11", 187 lbs. Born, Sherbrooke, Que., February 22, 1984.

| | | | Regular Season | | | | | Playoffs | | | | |
|---|---|---|---|---|---|---|---|---|---|---|---|---|
| Season | Club | League | GP | G | A | Pts | PIM | GP | G | A | Pts | PIM |
| 2001-02 | Chicoutimi | QMJHL | 66 | 17 | 22 | 39 | 44 | 3 | 0 | 0 | 0 | 0 |
| 2002-03 | Chicoutimi | QMJHL | 66 | 28 | 35 | 63 | 36 | 4 | 0 | 0 | 0 | 2 |
| 2003-04 | Chicoutimi | QMJHL | 70 | 22 | 44 | 66 | 49 | 18 | 6 | 4 | 10 | 10 |
| 2004-05 | Chicoutimi | QMJHL | 70 | 32 | 50 | 82 | 52 | 13 | 4 | 5 | 9 | 6 |
| 2005-06 | Hamilton Bulldogs | AHL | 67 | 18 | 23 | 41 | 76 | .... | .... | .... | .... | .... |
| 2006-07 | Hamilton Bulldogs | AHL | 44 | 6 | 11 | 17 | 34 | 11 | 0 | 2 | 2 | 6 |
| 2007-08 | Hamilton Bulldogs | AHL | 33 | 0 | 6 | 6 | 27 | .... | .... | .... | .... | .... |
| | Grand Rapids | AHL | 26 | 6 | 5 | 11 | 28 | .... | .... | .... | .... | .... |
| 2008-09 | Grand Rapids | AHL | 58 | 13 | 16 | 29 | 48 | 7 | 0 | 1 | 1 | 8 |

Signed as a free agent by **Montreal**, December 8, 2005. Traded to **Detroit** by **Montreal** for Brett Engelhardt, February 8, 2008.

## LEMTYUGOV, Nikolai (LEHM-tyuh-gawf, NIH-koh-ligh) ST.L.

Right wing. Shoots left. 6', 200 lbs. Born, Miass, USSR, January 15, 1986.
(St. Louis' 7th choice, 219th overall, in 2005 Entry Draft).

| | | | Regular Season | | | | | Playoffs | | | | |
|---|---|---|---|---|---|---|---|---|---|---|---|---|
| Season | Club | League | GP | G | A | Pts | PIM | GP | G | A | Pts | PIM |
| 2003-04 | CSKA Moscow 2 | Russia-3 | STATISTICS NOT AVAILABLE | | | | | | | | | |
| 2004-05 | CSKA Moscow 2 | Russia-3 | STATISTICS NOT AVAILABLE | | | | | | | | | |
| | CSKA Moscow | Russia | 11 | 1 | 1 | 2 | 16 | .... | .... | .... | .... | .... |
| 2005-06 | CSKA Moscow | Russia | 37 | 9 | 11 | 20 | 45 | 7 | 1 | 1 | 2 | 8 |
| 2006-07 | Cherepovets | Russia | 52 | 11 | 8 | 19 | 50 | 5 | 0 | 1 | 1 | 8 |
| 2007-08 | Peoria Rivermen | AHL | 69 | 22 | 15 | 37 | 71 | .... | .... | .... | .... | .... |
| 2008-09 | Cherepovets | Rus-KHL | 21 | 7 | 4 | 11 | 8 | .... | .... | .... | .... | .... |

## LERG, Bryan (LEHRG, BRIGH-uhn) EDM.

Center. Shoots left. 5'10", 175 lbs. Born, Livonia, MI, January 20, 1986.

| | | | Regular Season | | | | | Playoffs | | | | |
|---|---|---|---|---|---|---|---|---|---|---|---|---|
| Season | Club | League | GP | G | A | Pts | PIM | GP | G | A | Pts | PIM |
| 2002-03 | USNTDP | U-17 | 19 | 11 | 6 | 17 | 5 | .... | .... | .... | .... | .... |
| | USNTDP | NAHL | 46 | 10 | 12 | 22 | 32 | .... | .... | .... | .... | .... |
| 2003-04 | USNTDP | U-18 | 46 | 22 | 25 | 47 | .... | .... | .... | .... | .... | .... |
| | USNTDP | NAHL | 11 | 5 | 7 | 12 | 10 | .... | .... | .... | .... | .... |
| 2004-05 | Michigan State | CCHA | 41 | 10 | 5 | 15 | 14 | .... | .... | .... | .... | .... |
| 2005-06 | Michigan State | CCHA | 45 | 15 | 23 | 38 | 26 | .... | .... | .... | .... | .... |
| 2006-07 | Michigan State | CCHA | 41 | 23 | 13 | 36 | 21 | .... | .... | .... | .... | .... |
| 2007-08 | Michigan State | CCHA | 42 | 20 | 19 | 39 | 18 | .... | .... | .... | .... | .... |
| | Springfield Falcons | AHL | 4 | 0 | 2 | 2 | 2 | .... | .... | .... | .... | .... |
| 2008-09 | Springfield Falcons | AHL | 42 | 9 | 8 | 17 | 24 | .... | .... | .... | .... | .... |
| | Stockton Thunder | ECHL | 7 | 2 | 8 | 10 | 4 | .... | .... | .... | .... | .... |

Signed as a free agent by **Edmonton**, April 2, 2008.

## LETESTU, Mark (luh-TEHS- too, MAHRK) PIT.

Center. Shoots right. 5'11", 195 lbs. Born, Elk Point, Alta., February 4, 1985.

| | | | Regular Season | | | | | Playoffs | | | | |
|---|---|---|---|---|---|---|---|---|---|---|---|---|
| Season | Club | League | GP | G | A | Pts | PIM | GP | G | A | Pts | PIM |
| 2003-04 | Bonnyville Pontiacs | AJHL | 58 | 22 | 27 | 49 | 24 | .... | .... | .... | .... | .... |
| 2004-05 | Bonnyville Pontiacs | AJHL | 63 | 39 | 47 | 86 | 32 | .... | .... | .... | .... | .... |
| 2005-06 | Bonnyville Pontiacs | AJHL | 58 | 50 | 55 | 105 | 59 | .... | .... | .... | .... | .... |
| 2006-07 | Western Mich. | CCHA | 37 | 24 | 22 | 46 | 14 | .... | .... | .... | .... | .... |
| | Wilkes-Barre | AHL | 3 | 0 | 0 | 0 | 0 | 2 | 0 | 0 | 0 | 2 |
| 2007-08 | Wilkes-Barre | AHL | 52 | 6 | 12 | 18 | 28 | 13 | 0 | 3 | 3 | 0 |
| | Wheeling Nailers | ECHL | 6 | 1 | 2 | 3 | 4 | .... | .... | .... | .... | .... |
| 2008-09 | Wilkes-Barre | AHL | 73 | 24 | 37 | 61 | 6 | 12 | 2 | 8 | 10 | 4 |

Signed as a free agent by **Pittsburgh**, March 22, 2007.

## LEVEILLE, Daultan (leh-VAY-yay, DAWL-tuhn) ATL.

Center. Shoots left. 5'11", 163 lbs. Born, St. Catharines, Ont., August 10, 1990.
(Atlanta's 2nd choice, 29th overall, in 2008 Entry Draft).

| | | | Regular Season | | | | | Playoffs | | | | |
|---|---|---|---|---|---|---|---|---|---|---|---|---|
| Season | Club | League | GP | G | A | Pts | PIM | GP | G | A | Pts | PIM |
| 2005-06 | St. Catharines | Minor-ON | 46 | 25 | 31 | 56 | 32 | .... | .... | .... | .... | .... |
| 2006-07 | St. Catharines | OJHL-B | 48 | 19 | 26 | 45 | 30 | .... | .... | .... | .... | .... |
| 2007-08 | St. Catharines | OJHL-B | 45 | 29 | 27 | 56 | 38 | 16 | *14 | 16 | 30 | 14 |
| 2008-09 | Michigan State | CCHA | 38 | 9 | 8 | 17 | 12 | .... | .... | .... | .... | .... |

## LINDGREN, Perttu (LIHND-gruhn, PUHR-too) DAL.

Center. Shoots left. 6', 185 lbs. Born, Tampere, Finland, August 26, 1987.
(Dallas' 4th choice, 75th overall, in 2005 Entry Draft).

| | | | Regular Season | | | | | Playoffs | | | | |
|---|---|---|---|---|---|---|---|---|---|---|---|---|
| Season | Club | League | GP | G | A | Pts | PIM | GP | G | A | Pts | PIM |
| 2003-04 | Ilves Tampere U18 | Fin-U18 | 24 | 11 | 17 | 28 | 26 | .... | .... | .... | .... | .... |
| | Ilves Tampere Jr. | Fin-Jr. | 2 | 0 | 0 | 0 | 0 | .... | .... | .... | .... | .... |
| 2004-05 | Ilves Tampere Jr. | Fin-Jr. | 38 | 12 | 29 | 41 | 2 | 10 | 7 | 10 | 17 | 4 |
| | Ilves Tampere | Finland | 2 | 0 | 0 | 0 | 0 | .... | .... | .... | .... | .... |
| 2005-06 | Ilves Tampere Jr. | Fin-Jr. | 2 | 1 | 0 | 1 | 0 | .... | .... | .... | .... | .... |
| | Suomi U20 | Finland-2 | 3 | 0 | 3 | 3 | 0 | .... | .... | .... | .... | .... |
| | Ilves Tampere | Finland | 51 | 13 | 24 | 37 | 16 | 4 | 0 | 0 | 0 | 0 |
| 2006-07 | Suomi U20 | Finland-2 | 2 | 1 | 1 | 2 | 2 | .... | .... | .... | .... | .... |
| | Ilves Tampere | Finland | 43 | 4 | 22 | 26 | 38 | 7 | 4 | 2 | 6 | 2 |
| 2007-08 | Iowa Stars | AHL | 69 | 10 | 24 | 34 | 6 | .... | .... | .... | .... | .... |
| 2008-09 | Lukko Rauma | Finland | 49 | 5 | 19 | 24 | 16 | 7 | 1 | 0 | 1 | 6 |

Assigned to **Rauma** (Finland) by **Dallas**, October 2, 2008.

## LINDSTROM, Mattias (LIHND-struhm, ma-TEE-uhs) CAR.

Left wing. Shoots left. 6'4", 203 lbs. Born, Lulea, Sweden, March 21, 1991.
(Carolina's 3rd choice, 88th overall, in 2009 Entry Draft).

| | | | Regular Season | | | | | Playoffs | | | | |
|---|---|---|---|---|---|---|---|---|---|---|---|---|
| Season | Club | League | GP | G | A | Pts | PIM | GP | G | A | Pts | PIM |
| 2007-08 | Skelleftea U18 | Swe-U18 | 3 | 1 | 0 | 1 | 0 | .... | .... | .... | .... | .... |
| | Skelleftea Jr. | Swe-Jr. | 21 | 5 | 1 | 6 | 40 | .... | .... | .... | .... | .... |
| 2008-09 | Skelleftea AIK U18 | Swe-U18 | 2 | 0 | 0 | 0 | 6 | 5 | 0 | 1 | 1 | 10 |
| | Skelleftea AIK Jr. | Swe-Jr. | 31 | 8 | 5 | 13 | 46 | 5 | 2 | 0 | 2 | 0 |
| | Skelleftea AIK | Sweden | 7 | 1 | 0 | 1 | 0 | 7 | 1 | 0 | 1 | 0 |

## LINGLET, Charles (LIHNG-leht, CHAHR-uhlz)

Left wing. Shoots left. 6'2", 205 lbs. Born, Montreal, Que., June 22, 1982.

| | | | Regular Season | | | | | Playoffs | | | | |
|---|---|---|---|---|---|---|---|---|---|---|---|---|
| Season | Club | League | GP | G | A | Pts | PIM | GP | G | A | Pts | PIM |
| 99-2000 | Baie-Comeau | QMJHL | 64 | 14 | 20 | 34 | 13 | 6 | 3 | 3 | 6 | 4 |
| 2000-01 | Baie-Comeau | QMJHL | 70 | 21 | 34 | 55 | 61 | 11 | 2 | 2 | 4 | 10 |
| 2001-02 | Baie-Comeau | QMJHL | 72 | 52 | 71 | 123 | 34 | 5 | 1 | 3 | 4 | 2 |
| 2002-03 | Baie-Comeau | QMJHL | 47 | 21 | 27 | 48 | 35 | 12 | 3 | 8 | 11 | 18 |
| 2003-04 | Utah Grizzlies | AHL | 7 | 0 | 0 | 0 | 2 | .... | .... | .... | .... | .... |
| | Alaska Aces | ECHL | 62 | 20 | 35 | 55 | 61 | 7 | 2 | 5 | 7 | 4 |
| 2004-05 | Alaska Aces | ECHL | 72 | 28 | 34 | 62 | 44 | 15 | 6 | 10 | 16 | 14 |
| 2005-06 | Peoria Rivermen | AHL | 38 | 14 | 7 | 21 | 10 | .... | .... | .... | .... | .... |
| | Las Vegas | ECHL | 16 | 5 | 9 | 14 | 15 | 12 | 5 | 4 | 9 | 20 |
| 2006-07 | Peoria Rivermen | AHL | 73 | 31 | 29 | 60 | 30 | .... | .... | .... | .... | .... |
| 2007-08 | Peoria Rivermen | AHL | 80 | 24 | 42 | 66 | 65 | .... | .... | .... | .... | .... |
| 2008-09 | Peoria Rivermen | AHL | 37 | 1 | 8 | 9 | 23 | .... | .... | .... | .... | .... |
| | Springfield Falcons | AHL | 21 | 7 | 9 | 16 | 6 | .... | .... | .... | .... | .... |

QMJHL First All-Star Team (2002)

Signed as a free agent by **St. Louis**, January 1, 2007.

## LIVINGSTON, James (LIH-vihng-stuhn, JAYMZ) ST.L.

Right wing. Shoots right. 6'1", 203 lbs. Born, Halifax, N.S., March 8, 1990.
(St. Louis' 5th choice, 70th overall, in 2008 Entry Draft).

| | | | Regular Season | | | | | Playoffs | | | | |
|---|---|---|---|---|---|---|---|---|---|---|---|---|
| Season | Club | League | GP | G | A | Pts | PIM | GP | G | A | Pts | PIM |
| 2005-06 | York Simcoe | Minor-ON | 51 | 25 | 32 | 57 | .... | .... | .... | .... | .... | .... |
| 2006-07 | Sault Ste. Marie | OHL | 60 | 2 | 5 | 7 | 95 | 13 | 1 | 0 | 1 | 15 |
| 2007-08 | Sault Ste. Marie | OHL | 68 | 21 | 23 | 44 | 135 | 14 | 2 | 3 | 5 | 14 |
| 2008-09 | Sault Ste. Marie | OHL | 66 | 20 | 17 | 37 | 98 | .... | .... | .... | .... | .... |

## LOGINOV, Denis (LOG-gih-nawv, DEH-nihs) ATL.

Center. Shoots left. 6'1", 211 lbs. Born, Kazan, USSR, May 5, 1985.
(Atlanta's 7th choice, 203rd overall, in 2003 Entry Draft).

| | | | Regular Season | | | | | Playoffs | | | | |
|---|---|---|---|---|---|---|---|---|---|---|---|---|
| Season | Club | League | GP | G | A | Pts | PIM | GP | G | A | Pts | PIM |
| 99-2000 | Ak Bars Kazan 2 | Russia-3 | 4 | 0 | 0 | 0 | 0 | .... | .... | .... | .... | .... |
| 2000-01 | Ak Bars Kazan 2 | Russia-3 | STATISTICS NOT AVAILABLE | | | | | | | | | |
| 2001-02 | Ak Bars Kazan 2 | Russia-3 | 38 | 6 | 10 | 16 | 40 | .... | .... | .... | .... | .... |
| | Team Volga | Exhib. | 3 | 0 | 3 | 3 | 27 | .... | .... | .... | .... | .... |
| 2002-03 | Ak Bars Kazan 2 | Russia-3 | 52 | 17 | 24 | 41 | 98 | .... | .... | .... | .... | .... |
| • | Perm | Russia | 1 | 0 | 0 | 0 | 0 | .... | .... | .... | .... | .... |
| 2003-04 | Ak Bars Kazan | Russia | 16 | 2 | 1 | 3 | 0 | 7 | 1 | 0 | 1 | 6 |
| 2004-05 | Ak Bars Kazan | Russia | 2 | 0 | 0 | 0 | 0 | .... | .... | .... | .... | .... |
| 2005-06 | Almetjevsk | Russia-2 | 7 | 1 | 0 | 1 | 8 | .... | .... | .... | .... | .... |
| | Ak Bars Kazan | Russia | 16 | 1 | 1 | 2 | 10 | .... | .... | .... | .... | .... |
| 2006-07 | Ak Bars Kazan 2 | Russia-3 | STATISTICS NOT AVAILABLE | | | | | | | | | |
| 2007-08 | Nizhnekamsk | Russia | 6 | 0 | 0 | 0 | 6 | .... | .... | .... | .... | .... |
| | Volzhsk | Russia-2 | 10 | 2 | 3 | 5 | 14 | .... | .... | .... | .... | .... |
| | Orenburg | Russia-2 | 12 | 3 | 3 | 6 | 30 | .... | .... | .... | .... | .... |
| 2008-09 | Rys Podolsk | Russia-2 | 51 | 10 | 5 | 15 | 97 | 3 | 0 | 1 | 1 | 2 |

## LOKTIONOV, Andrei (lawk-too-OH-nawf, ahn-DRAY) L.A.

Center. Shoots left. 5'11", 177 lbs. Born, Voskresensk, USSR, May 30, 1990.
(Los Angeles' 7th choice, 123rd overall, in 2008 Entry Draft).

| | | | Regular Season | | | | | Playoffs | | | | |
|---|---|---|---|---|---|---|---|---|---|---|---|---|
| Season | Club | League | GP | G | A | Pts | PIM | GP | G | A | Pts | PIM |
| 2005-06 | Spartak Moscow 2 | Russia-3 | 4 | 1 | 1 | 2 | 2 | .... | .... | .... | .... | .... |
| 2006-07 | Yaroslavl 2 | Russia-3 | 31 | 7 | 21 | 28 | 26 | .... | .... | .... | .... | .... |
| 2007-08 | Yaroslavl 2 | Russia-3 | STATISTICS NOT AVAILABLE | | | | | | | | | |
| | Yaroslavl | Russia | 5 | 0 | 1 | 1 | 0 | 1 | 0 | 0 | 0 | 0 |
| 2008-09 | Windsor Spitfires | OHL | 51 | 24 | 42 | 66 | 16 | 20 | 11 | 22 | 33 | 2 |

## LONG, Colin (LAWNG, KAW-lihn) PHX.

Center. Shoots right. 5'11", 186 lbs. Born, Santa Ana, CA, June 19, 1989.
(Phoenix's 6th choice, 99th overall, in 2008 Entry Draft).

| | | | Regular Season | | | | | Playoffs | | | | |
|---|---|---|---|---|---|---|---|---|---|---|---|---|
| Season | Club | League | GP | G | A | Pts | PIM | GP | G | A | Pts | PIM |
| 2005-06 | Kelowna Rockets | WHL | 20 | 1 | 3 | 4 | 6 | 3 | 0 | 0 | 0 | 0 |
| 2006-07 | Kelowna Rockets | WHL | 69 | 11 | 17 | 28 | 38 | .... | .... | .... | .... | .... |
| 2007-08 | Kelowna Rockets | WHL | 72 | 31 | 69 | 100 | 41 | 7 | 2 | 10 | 12 | 6 |
| 2008-09 | Kelowna Rockets | WHL | 68 | 33 | 58 | 91 | 28 | 22 | 4 | 12 | 16 | 16 |

WHL West First All-Star Team (2008) • WHL West Second All-Star Team (2009)

## LOPRIENO, Joe (loh-PRE-eh-noh, JOH) S.J.

Defense. Shoots right. 6'3", 225 lbs. Born, Bloomingdale, IL, October 8, 1986.

| | | | Regular Season | | | | | Playoffs | | | | |
|---|---|---|---|---|---|---|---|---|---|---|---|---|
| Season | Club | League | GP | G | A | Pts | PIM | GP | G | A | Pts | PIM |
| 2004-05 | Chicago Steel | USHL | 50 | 0 | 3 | 3 | 78 | 1 | 0 | 0 | 0 | 6 |
| 2005-06 | Chicago Steel | USHL | 45 | 3 | 10 | 13 | 73 | .... | .... | .... | .... | .... |
| 2006-07 | Merrimack College | H-East | 32 | 1 | 3 | 4 | 66 | .... | .... | .... | .... | .... |
| 2007-08 | Merrimack College | H-East | 34 | 2 | 3 | 5 | 74 | .... | .... | .... | .... | .... |
| 2008-09 | Merrimack College | H-East | 22 | 2 | 2 | 4 | 50 | .... | .... | .... | .... | .... |

Signed as a free agent by **San Jose**, March 30, 2009.

## LORENZ, Sean (lohr-EHNZ, SHAWN) MIN.

Defense. Shoots right. 6'1", 191 lbs. Born, Littleton, CO, March 10, 1990.
(Minnesota's 3rd choice, 115th overall, in 2008 Entry Draft).

| | | | Regular Season | | | | | Playoffs | | | | |
|---|---|---|---|---|---|---|---|---|---|---|---|---|
| Season | Club | League | GP | G | A | Pts | PIM | GP | G | A | Pts | PIM |
| 2006-07 | USNTDP | U-17 | 6 | 6 | 9 | 15 | 28 | .... | .... | .... | .... | .... |
| | USNTDP | NAHL | 45 | 1 | 7 | 8 | 26 | 6 | 0 | 0 | 0 | 2 |
| 2007-08 | USNTDP | U-18 | 50 | 0 | 8 | 8 | 28 | .... | .... | .... | .... | .... |
| | USNTDP | NAHL | 14 | 2 | 1 | 3 | 4 | .... | .... | .... | .... | .... |
| 2008-09 | U. of Notre Dame | CCHA | 40 | 0 | 3 | 3 | 18 | .... | .... | .... | .... | .... |

## LOVE, Mitch (LUHV, MIHTCH)

Defense. Shoots left. 6', 200 lbs. Born, Quesnel, B.C., June 15, 1984.

| | | | Regular Season | | | | | Playoffs | | | | |
|---|---|---|---|---|---|---|---|---|---|---|---|---|
| Season | Club | League | GP | G | A | Pts | PIM | GP | G | A | Pts | PIM |
| 2000-01 | Moose Jaw | WHL | 51 | 5 | 4 | 9 | 97 | 4 | 0 | 0 | 0 | 2 |
| 2001-02 | Moose Jaw | WHL | 16 | 0 | 1 | 1 | 40 | .... | .... | .... | .... | .... |
| | Swift Current | WHL | 52 | 5 | 11 | 16 | 132 | 12 | 0 | 0 | 0 | 37 |
| 2002-03 | Swift Current | WHL | 70 | 2 | 15 | 17 | *327 | 4 | 1 | 0 | 1 | 16 |
| 2003-04 | Everett Silvertips | WHL | 70 | 12 | 15 | 27 | 163 | 21 | 2 | 6 | 8 | 47 |
| 2004-05 | Everett Silvertips | WHL | 59 | 9 | 20 | 29 | 142 | 4 | 0 | 2 | 2 | 6 |
| 2005-06 | Lowell | AHL | 27 | 0 | 4 | 4 | 68 | .... | .... | .... | .... | .... |
| 2006-07 | Albany River Rats | AHL | 69 | 1 | 5 | 6 | 184 | .... | .... | .... | .... | .... |
| 2007-08 | Lake Erie Monsters | AHL | 59 | 2 | 5 | 7 | 213 | .... | .... | .... | .... | .... |
| | Johnstown Chiefs | ECHL | 4 | 0 | 0 | 0 | 16 | .... | .... | .... | .... | .... |
| 2008-09 | Houston Aeros | AHL | 63 | 2 | 4 | 6 | 214 | 16 | 1 | 0 | 1 | 32 |

Signed as a free agent by **Colorado**, October 25, 2005.

## LoVECCHIO, Jeff (LOH-veh-kee-oh, JEHF) BOS.

Left wing. Shoots left. 6'2", 198 lbs. Born, Arlington Heights, IL, August 26, 1985.

| | | | Regular Season | | | | | Playoffs | | | | |
|---|---|---|---|---|---|---|---|---|---|---|---|---|
| Season | Club | League | GP | G | A | Pts | PIM | GP | G | A | Pts | PIM |
| 2003-04 | River City Lancers | USHL | 58 | 16 | 13 | 29 | 29 | 3 | 0 | 1 | 1 | 2 |
| 2004-05 | Omaha Lancers | USHL | 57 | 17 | 27 | 44 | 82 | 5 | 1 | 0 | 1 | 0 |
| 2005-06 | Western Mich. | CCHA | 40 | 7 | 11 | 18 | 46 | .... | .... | .... | .... | .... |
| 2006-07 | Western Mich. | CCHA | 37 | 19 | 16 | 35 | 24 | .... | .... | .... | .... | .... |
| 2007-08 | Western Mich. | CCHA | 36 | 9 | 12 | 21 | 28 | .... | .... | .... | .... | .... |
| | Providence Bruins | AHL | 14 | 3 | 2 | 5 | 6 | 6 | 0 | 1 | 1 | 2 |
| 2008-09 | | | DID NOT PLAY – INJURED | | | | | | | | | |

Signed as a free agent by **Boston**, March 18, 2008. • Missed entire 2008-09 season recovering from a head injury.

## LUCENIUS, Niclas (loo-SEHN-ee-uhs, NIHK-luhs) ATL.

Center. Shoots left. 6', 190 lbs. Born, Turku, Finland, May 3, 1989.
(Atlanta's 2nd choice, 115th overall, in 2007 Entry Draft).

| | | | Regular Season | | | | | Playoffs | | | | |
|---|---|---|---|---|---|---|---|---|---|---|---|---|
| Season | Club | League | GP | G | A | Pts | PIM | GP | G | A | Pts | PIM |
| 2005-06 | Tappara U18 | Fin-U18 | 11 | 6 | 5 | 11 | 10 | 3 | 2 | 0 | 2 | 25 |
| | Tappara Jr. | Fin-Jr. | 23 | 5 | 4 | 9 | 18 | .... | .... | .... | .... | .... |
| 2006-07 | Tappara U18 | Fin-U18 | 7 | 5 | 3 | 8 | 32 | .... | .... | .... | .... | .... |
| | Tappara Jr. | Fin-Jr. | 33 | 14 | 14 | 28 | 44 | 10 | 2 | 3 | 5 | 14 |
| | Tappara Tampere | Finland | 5 | 0 | 0 | 0 | 0 | .... | .... | .... | .... | .... |
| 2007-08 | Suomi U20 | Finland-2 | 5 | 1 | 2 | 3 | 12 | .... | .... | .... | .... | .... |
| | Tappara Jr. | Fin-Jr. | 15 | 6 | 13 | 19 | 28 | .... | .... | .... | .... | .... |
| | Tappara Tampere | Finland | 28 | 0 | 2 | 2 | 10 | .... | .... | .... | .... | .... |
| | LeKi Lempaala | Finland-2 | 6 | 2 | 1 | 3 | 4 | 3 | 0 | 2 | 2 | 4 |
| 2008-09 | Suomi U20 | Finland-2 | 6 | 2 | 4 | 6 | 0 | .... | .... | .... | .... | .... |
| | Tappara Jr. | Fin-Jr. | 1 | 0 | 0 | 0 | 0 | .... | .... | .... | .... | .... |
| | Kiekko-Vantaa | Finland-2 | 2 | 0 | 0 | 0 | 2 | .... | .... | .... | .... | .... |
| | Tappara Tampere | Finland | 46 | 6 | 5 | 11 | 32 | 3 | 0 | 0 | 0 | 2 |

## LUCIA, Tony (loo-CHEE-ah, TOH-nee) S.J.

Left wing. Shoots left. 6', 180 lbs. Born, Wayzata, MN, August 23, 1987.
(San Jose's 8th choice, 193rd overall, in 2005 Entry Draft).

| | | | Regular Season | | | | | Playoffs | | | | |
|---|---|---|---|---|---|---|---|---|---|---|---|---|
| Season | Club | League | GP | G | A | Pts | PIM | GP | G | A | Pts | PIM |
| 2003-04 | Wayzata | High-MN | 31 | 13 | 22 | 35 | .... | .... | .... | .... | .... | .... |
| 2004-05 | Wayzata | High-MN | 24 | 27 | 36 | 63 | 32 | .... | .... | .... | .... | .... |
| | Omaha Lancers | USHL | 11 | 1 | 0 | 1 | 0 | .... | .... | .... | .... | .... |
| 2005-06 | Omaha Lancers | USHL | 56 | 12 | 23 | 35 | 25 | 5 | 0 | 0 | 0 | 2 |
| 2006-07 | U. of Minnesota | WCHA | 43 | 7 | 12 | 19 | 28 | .... | .... | .... | .... | .... |
| 2007-08 | U. of Minnesota | WCHA | 44 | 7 | 11 | 18 | 41 | .... | .... | .... | .... | .... |
| 2008-09 | U. of Minnesota | WCHA | 34 | 9 | 8 | 17 | 43 | .... | .... | .... | .... | .... |

## LUDWIG, Trevor (LUHD-wihg, TREH-vuhr) DAL.

Defense. Shoots left. 6'1", 200 lbs. Born, Rhinelander, WI, May 24, 1985.
(Dallas' 7th choice, 183rd overall, in 2004 Entry Draft).

| | | | Regular Season | | | | | Playoffs | | | | |
|---|---|---|---|---|---|---|---|---|---|---|---|---|
| Season | Club | League | GP | G | A | Pts | PIM | GP | G | A | Pts | PIM |
| 2002-03 | Texas Tornado | NAHL | 55 | 4 | 5 | 9 | 39 | .... | .... | .... | .... | .... |
| 2003-04 | Texas Tornado | NAHL | 54 | 5 | 25 | 30 | 50 | .... | .... | .... | .... | .... |
| 2004-05 | Providence College | H-East | 33 | 1 | 6 | 7 | 36 | .... | .... | .... | .... | .... |
| 2005-06 | Providence College | H-East | 27 | 0 | 2 | 2 | 6 | .... | .... | .... | .... | .... |
| 2006-07 | Providence College | H-East | 26 | 0 | 2 | 2 | 37 | .... | .... | .... | .... | .... |
| 2007-08 | Providence College | H-East | 29 | 1 | 3 | 4 | 28 | .... | .... | .... | .... | .... |
| | Iowa Stars | AHL | 7 | 0 | 3 | 3 | 12 | .... | .... | .... | .... | .... |
| 2008-09 | Manitoba Moose | AHL | 16 | 0 | 0 | 0 | 18 | .... | .... | .... | .... | .... |
| | Idaho Steelheads | ECHL | 35 | 2 | 8 | 10 | 41 | 4 | 0 | 0 | 0 | 13 |

NAHL All-Rookie Team (2003) • NAHL First All-Star Team (2004)

## LUKACEVIC, Ned (loo-kuh-SAY-vihk, NEHD)

Left wing. Shoots left. 6', 185 lbs. Born, Podgorica, Serbia, February 11, 1986.
(Los Angeles' 3rd choice, 110th overall, in 2004 Entry Draft).

| | | | Regular Season | | | | | Playoffs | | | | |
|---|---|---|---|---|---|---|---|---|---|---|---|---|
| Season | Club | League | GP | G | A | Pts | PIM | GP | G | A | Pts | PIM |
| 2000-01 | Port Coquitlam | Minor-BC | 60 | 42 | 48 | 90 | .... | .... | .... | .... | .... | .... |
| 2001-02 | Port Coquitlam | Minor-BC | 70 | 40 | 55 | 95 | 60 | .... | .... | .... | .... | .... |
| | Spokane Chiefs | WHL | 1 | 1 | 0 | 1 | 0 | .... | .... | .... | .... | .... |
| 2002-03 | Spokane Chiefs | WHL | 31 | 0 | 4 | 4 | 29 | 4 | 0 | 1 | 1 | 0 |
| 2003-04 | Spokane Chiefs | WHL | 72 | 19 | 14 | 33 | 65 | 4 | 1 | 1 | 2 | 2 |
| 2004-05 | Spokane Chiefs | WHL | 71 | 18 | 28 | 46 | 52 | .... | .... | .... | .... | .... |
| 2005-06 | Swift Current | WHL | 63 | 25 | 28 | 53 | 71 | 4 | 1 | 0 | 1 | 5 |
| | Manchester | AHL | .... | .... | .... | .... | .... | 7 | 1 | 0 | 1 | 4 |
| 2006-07 | Manchester | AHL | 12 | 1 | 0 | 1 | 9 | .... | .... | .... | .... | .... |
| | Reading Royals | ECHL | 53 | 7 | 17 | 24 | 38 | .... | .... | .... | .... | .... |
| 2007-08 | Reading Royals | ECHL | 61 | 17 | 19 | 36 | 52 | 8 | 0 | 2 | 2 | 2 |
| 2008-09 | Providence Bruins | AHL | 52 | 3 | 5 | 8 | 6 | 8 | 0 | 1 | 1 | 5 |
| | Reading Royals | ECHL | 13 | 4 | 3 | 7 | 10 | .... | .... | .... | .... | .... |

Traded to **Philadelphia** by **Los Angeles** with Patrik Hersley for Denis Gauthier and Philadelphia's 2nd round choice in 2010 Entry Draft, July 1, 2008. Traded to **Boston** by **Philadelphia** with a conditional 4th round choice in 2009 Entry Draft for Andrew Alberts, October 14, 2008.

## LUNDBOHM, Bryan (LUHND-bawm, BRIGH-uhn)

Center. Shoots right. 5'10", 185 lbs. Born, Roseau, MN, August 24, 1977.

| | | | Regular Season | | | | | Playoffs | | | | |
|---|---|---|---|---|---|---|---|---|---|---|---|---|
| Season | Club | League | GP | G | A | Pts | PIM | GP | G | A | Pts | PIM |
| 1996-97 | Lincoln Stars | USHL | 52 | 12 | 33 | 45 | 33 | 14 | 8 | 4 | 12 | 20 |
| 1997-98 | Lincoln Stars | USHL | 55 | 26 | 38 | 64 | 10 | 9 | 2 | 7 | 9 | 0 |
| 1998-99 | North Dakota | WCHA | 32 | 2 | 9 | 11 | 4 | .... | .... | .... | .... | .... |
| 99-2000 | North Dakota | WCHA | 44 | 22 | 22 | 44 | 14 | .... | .... | .... | .... | .... |
| 2000-01 | North Dakota | WCHA | 46 | *32 | 37 | 69 | 38 | .... | .... | .... | .... | .... |
| 2001-02 | Milwaukee | AHL | 79 | 11 | 23 | 34 | 63 | .... | .... | .... | .... | .... |
| 2002-03 | Milwaukee | AHL | 80 | 9 | 17 | 26 | 63 | 6 | 1 | 5 | 6 | 0 |
| 2003-04 | HC Sierre | Swiss-2 | 10 | 6 | 8 | 14 | 8 | .... | .... | .... | .... | .... |
| | Milwaukee | AHL | 28 | 6 | 8 | 14 | 8 | .... | .... | .... | .... | .... |
| 2004-05 | Fort Worth | CHL | 26 | 10 | 20 | 30 | 28 | .... | .... | .... | .... | .... |
| | Grand Rapids | AHL | 3 | 0 | 0 | 0 | 0 | .... | .... | .... | .... | .... |
| | Milwaukee | AHL | 47 | 7 | 12 | 19 | 36 | 4 | 0 | 0 | 0 | 0 |
| 2005-06 | Houston Aeros | AHL | 78 | 9 | 21 | 30 | 46 | 8 | 3 | 5 | 8 | 4 |
| 2006-07 | Houston Aeros | AHL | 77 | 9 | 21 | 30 | 34 | .... | .... | .... | .... | .... |
| 2007-08 | KalPa Kuopio | Finland | 5 | 0 | 1 | 1 | 0 | .... | .... | .... | .... | .... |
| | Vojens | Denmark | 33 | 12 | 15 | 27 | 12 | 13 | 4 | 4 | 8 | 6 |
| 2008-09 | Houston Aeros | AHL | 50 | 5 | 7 | 12 | 19 | 17 | 1 | 3 | 4 | 6 |

USHL First All-Star Team (1998) • WCHA First All-Star Team (2001) • NCAA West Second All-American Team (2001) • NCAA Championship All-Tournament Team (2001)

Signed as a free agent by **Nashville**, May 1, 2001. Signed as a free agent by **Sierre** (Swiss-2), September 5, 2003. Signed as a free agent by **Milwaukee** (AHL), November 25, 2003. • Missed majority of 2003-04 season recovering from groin injury suffered in game vs. Philadelphia (AHL), January 31, 2004. Signed as a free agent by **Fort Worth** (CHL), October 19, 2004. Signed as a free agent by **Grand Rapids** (AHL), November 17, 2004. Signed as a free agent by **Milwaukee** (AHL), December 28, 2004. Signed as a free agent by **Minnesota**, July 15, 2008.

## LYAMIN, Kirill (L'YAH-mihn, kih-RIHL) OTT.

Defense. Shoots left. 6'3", 198 lbs. Born, Moscow, USSR, January 13, 1986.
(Ottawa's 2nd choice, 58th overall, in 2004 Entry Draft).

| | | | Regular Season | | | | | Playoffs | | | | |
|---|---|---|---|---|---|---|---|---|---|---|---|---|
| Season | Club | League | GP | G | A | Pts | PIM | GP | G | A | Pts | PIM |
| 2001-02 | Moscow 18 | Exhib. | 5 | 0 | 3 | 3 | 4 | .... | .... | .... | .... | .... |
| 2002-03 | CSKA Moscow 2 | Russia-3 | 5 | 0 | 0 | 0 | 10 | .... | .... | .... | .... | .... |
| | Moscow 18 | Exhib. | 5 | 0 | 0 | 0 | 6 | .... | .... | .... | .... | .... |
| 2003-04 | CSKA Moscow 2 | Russia-3 | STATISTICS NOT AVAILABLE | | | | | | | | | |
| | CSKA Moscow | Russia | 28 | 0 | 3 | 3 | 12 | .... | .... | .... | .... | .... |
| 2004-05 | CSKA Moscow 2 | Russia-3 | STATISTICS NOT AVAILABLE | | | | | | | | | |
| 2005-06 | CSKA Moscow | Russia | 25 | 0 | 1 | 1 | 28 | 2 | 0 | 0 | 0 | 0 |
| 2006-07 | CSKA Moscow | Russia | 47 | 1 | 7 | 8 | 48 | 12 | 1 | 0 | 1 | 8 |
| 2007-08 | Mytischi | Russia | 40 | 1 | 6 | 7 | 77 | 3 | 0 | 0 | 0 | 0 |
| 2008-09 | Spartak Moscow | Rus-KHL | 54 | 1 | 7 | 8 | 82 | 6 | 0 | 0 | 0 | 4 |

## LYNCH, Kevin (LIHNCH, KEH-vihn) CBJ

Center. Shoots right. 6'1", 190 lbs. Born, Grosse Pointe, MI, April 23, 1991.
(Columbus' 2nd choice, 56th overall, in 2009 Entry Draft).

| | | | Regular Season | | | | | Playoffs | | | | |
|---|---|---|---|---|---|---|---|---|---|---|---|---|
| Season | Club | League | GP | G | A | Pts | PIM | GP | G | A | Pts | PIM |
| 2006-07 | Det. Honeybaked | MWEHL | 28 | 14 | 14 | 28 | 16 | .... | .... | .... | .... | .... |
| | Det. Honeybaked | Exhib. | 24 | 22 | 10 | 32 | .... | .... | .... | .... | .... | .... |
| 2007-08 | USNTDP | NAHL | 43 | 11 | 4 | 15 | 24 | 3 | 2 | 0 | 2 | 2 |
| | USNTDP | U-17 | 17 | 6 | 2 | 8 | 18 | .... | .... | .... | .... | .... |
| 2008-09 | USNTDP | NAHL | 16 | 8 | 7 | 15 | 14 | .... | .... | .... | .... | .... |
| | USNTDP | U-18 | 47 | 16 | 17 | 33 | 40 | .... | .... | .... | .... | .... |

• Signed Letter of Intent to attend **University of Michigan** (CCHA) in fall of 2009.

## LYUBUSHIN, Mikhail (l'yoo-BOOSH-ihn, mih-kigh-EHL) L.A.

Defense. Shoots left. 6'1", 183 lbs. Born, Moscow, USSR, July 24, 1983.
(Los Angeles' 9th choice, 215th overall, in 2002 Entry Draft).

| | | | Regular Season | | | | | Playoffs | | | | |
|---|---|---|---|---|---|---|---|---|---|---|---|---|
| Season | Club | League | GP | G | A | Pts | PIM | GP | G | A | Pts | PIM |
| 99-2000 | Vityaz Podolsk 2 | Russia-3 | 24 | 2 | 2 | 4 | 69 | .... | .... | .... | .... | .... |
| 2000-01 | Krylja Sovetov | Russia-2 | 2 | 0 | 1 | 1 | 0 | 1 | 0 | 0 | 0 | 0 |
| 2001-02 | Krylja Sovetov 2 | Russia-3 | 20 | 3 | 6 | 9 | 24 | .... | .... | .... | .... | .... |
| | THK Tver | Russia-2 | 22 | 1 | 0 | 1 | 18 | .... | .... | .... | .... | .... |
| | Krylja Sovetov | Russia | 13 | 0 | 1 | 1 | 14 | 3 | 0 | 0 | 0 | 0 |
| 2002-03 | Krylja Sovetov | Russia | 49 | 0 | 6 | 6 | 26 | .... | .... | .... | .... | .... |
| 2003-04 | Dynamo Moscow | Russia | 38 | 1 | 2 | 3 | 18 | 2 | 0 | 0 | 0 | 2 |
| 2004-05 | Voskresensk | Russia | 21 | 1 | 2 | 3 | 16 | .... | .... | .... | .... | .... |
| | Vityaz Chekhov | Russia-2 | 8 | 0 | 2 | 2 | 6 | 14 | 1 | 0 | 1 | 8 |
| 2005-06 | Cherepovets | Russia | 23 | 1 | 4 | 5 | 10 | .... | .... | .... | .... | .... |
| | Avangard Omsk | Russia | 26 | 0 | 1 | 1 | 20 | 8 | 0 | 0 | 0 | 4 |
| 2006-07 | Avangard Omsk | Russia | 21 | 0 | 1 | 1 | 16 | 3 | 0 | 0 | 0 | 2 |
| | Avangard Omsk 2 | Russia-3 | 2 | 0 | 1 | 1 | 4 | .... | .... | .... | .... | .... |
| 2007-08 | Avangard Omsk | Russia | 42 | 1 | 3 | 4 | 28 | 4 | 0 | 0 | 0 | 2 |
| 2008-09 | Omsk | Rus-KHL | 4 | 0 | 1 | 1 | 4 | .... | .... | .... | .... | .... |
| | Nizhny Novgorod | Rus-KHL | 25 | 0 | 2 | 2 | 32 | 2 | 0 | 0 | 0 | 2 |

## MacARTHUR, Pete (muh-KAR-thuhr, PEET) CHI.

Left wing. Shoots left. 5'10", 180 lbs. Born, Clifton Park, NY, June 20, 1985.

| | | | Regular Season | | | | | Playoffs | | | | |
|---|---|---|---|---|---|---|---|---|---|---|---|---|
| Season | Club | League | GP | G | A | Pts | PIM | GP | G | A | Pts | PIM |
| 2003-04 | Waterloo | USHL | 52 | 18 | 24 | 42 | 33 | 10 | 2 | 8 | 10 | 11 |
| 2004-05 | Boston University | H-East | 40 | 13 | 14 | 27 | 32 | .... | .... | .... | .... | .... |
| 2005-06 | Boston University | H-East | 40 | 14 | 25 | 39 | 38 | .... | .... | .... | .... | .... |
| 2006-07 | Boston University | H-East | 39 | 16 | 20 | 36 | 26 | .... | .... | .... | .... | .... |
| 2007-08 | Boston University | H-East | 40 | 21 | 24 | 45 | 24 | .... | .... | .... | .... | .... |
| | Bridgeport | AHL | 9 | 0 | 1 | 1 | 6 | .... | .... | .... | .... | .... |
| 2008-09 | Rockford IceHogs | AHL | 64 | 14 | 11 | 25 | 27 | 4 | 0 | 0 | 0 | 0 |
| | Fresno Falcons | ECHL | 3 | 2 | 2 | 4 | 2 | .... | .... | .... | .... | .... |

Signed as a free agent by **Chicago**, July 9, 2009.

## MacDERMID, Lane (MAK-duhr-mihd, LAYN) BOS.

Left wing. Shoots left. 6'3", 199 lbs. Born, Hartford, CT, August 25, 1989.
(Boston's 3rd choice, 112th overall, in 2009 Entry Draft).

| | | | Regular Season | | | | | Playoffs | | | | |
|---|---|---|---|---|---|---|---|---|---|---|---|---|
| Season | Club | League | GP | G | A | Pts | PIM | GP | G | A | Pts | PIM |
| 2005-06 | Owen Sound | OJHL-B | 48 | 1 | 7 | 8 | .... | .... | .... | .... | .... | .... |
| 2006-07 | Owen Sound | OHL | 57 | 2 | 5 | 7 | 115 | 4 | 1 | 0 | 1 | 2 |
| 2007-08 | Owen Sound | OHL | 66 | 13 | 11 | 24 | 190 | .... | .... | .... | .... | .... |
| 2008-09 | Owen Sound | OHL | 26 | 8 | 6 | 14 | 85 | .... | .... | .... | .... | .... |
| | Windsor Spitfires | OHL | 38 | 7 | 14 | 21 | 112 | 20 | 4 | 5 | 9 | 38 |

## MacDONALD, Franklin (MAK-DAWN-uhld, FRAN-klihn)

Defense. Shoots left. 6', 198 lbs. Born, Sydney, N.S., April 8, 1985.

| | | | Regular Season | | | | | Playoffs | | | | |
|---|---|---|---|---|---|---|---|---|---|---|---|---|
| Season | Club | League | GP | G | A | Pts | PIM | GP | G | A | Pts | PIM |
| 2002-03 | Truro Bearcats | MJrHL | 48 | 2 | 10 | 12 | 65 | .... | .... | .... | .... | .... |
| 2003-04 | Halifax | QMJHL | 63 | 4 | 8 | 12 | 52 | .... | .... | .... | .... | .... |
| 2004-05 | Halifax | QMJHL | 65 | 5 | 11 | 16 | 93 | 13 | 0 | 5 | 5 | 24 |
| 2005-06 | Halifax | QMJHL | 58 | 12 | 33 | 45 | 129 | 11 | 4 | 2 | 6 | 22 |
| 2006-07 | Rochester | AHL | 11 | 0 | 2 | 2 | 12 | .... | .... | .... | .... | .... |
| | Florida Everblades | ECHL | 56 | 4 | 20 | 24 | 58 | 16 | 1 | 5 | 6 | 20 |
| 2007-08 | Rochester | AHL | 51 | 1 | 13 | 14 | 49 | .... | .... | .... | .... | .... |
| | Florida Everblades | ECHL | 11 | 2 | 6 | 8 | 20 | 3 | 0 | 1 | 1 | 0 |
| 2008-09 | Rochester | AHL | 61 | 1 | 8 | 9 | 28 | .... | .... | .... | .... | .... |

Signed as a free agent by **Florida**, September 14, 2006.

## MACENAUER, Maxime (MAY-sehn-owr, mahx-EEM) ANA.

Center. Shoots left. 6', 198 lbs. Born, Laval, Que., January 4, 1989.
(Anaheim's 3rd choice, 63rd overall, in 2007 Entry Draft).

| | | | Regular Season | | | | | Playoffs | | | | |
|---|---|---|---|---|---|---|---|---|---|---|---|---|
| Season | Club | League | GP | G | A | Pts | PIM | GP | G | A | Pts | PIM |
| 2004-05 | Ecole Montpetit | QAAA | 37 | 17 | 22 | 39 | 56 | 3 | 0 | 0 | 0 | 0 |
| 2005-06 | Rimouski Oceanic | QMJHL | 41 | 8 | 14 | 22 | 30 | .... | .... | .... | .... | .... |
| 2006-07 | Rouyn-Noranda | QMJHL | 14 | 1 | 3 | 4 | 10 | .... | .... | .... | .... | .... |
| 2007-08 | Rouyn-Noranda | QMJHL | 67 | 23 | 37 | 60 | 53 | 17 | 6 | 10 | 16 | 8 |
| 2008-09 | Rouyn-Noranda | QMJHL | 35 | 15 | 9 | 24 | 34 | .... | .... | .... | .... | .... |
| | Shawinigan | QMJHL | 19 | 7 | 9 | 16 | 18 | 21 | 5 | 9 | 14 | 20 |

## MACKENZIE, Drew (muh-KEHN-zee , DROO) BUF.

Defense. Shoots left. 6'2", 200 lbs. Born, Stamford, CT, December 17, 1988.
(Buffalo's 8th choice, 209th overall, in 2007 Entry Draft).

| | | | Regular Season | | | | | Playoffs | | | | |
|---|---|---|---|---|---|---|---|---|---|---|---|---|
| Season | Club | League | GP | G | A | Pts | PIM | GP | G | A | Pts | PIM |
| 2004-05 | Taft Rhinos | High-CT | .... | 0 | 1 | 1 | .... | .... | .... | .... | .... | .... |
| 2005-06 | Taft Rhinos | High-CT | .... | 0 | 11 | 11 | .... | .... | .... | .... | .... | .... |
| 2006-07 | Taft Rhinos | High-CT | 24 | 3 | 10 | 13 | 10 | .... | .... | .... | .... | .... |
| 2007-08 | Waterloo | USHL | 57 | 4 | 14 | 18 | 103 | 11 | 0 | 6 | 6 | 4 |
| 2008-09 | U. of Vermont | H-East | 31 | 1 | 9 | 10 | 14 | .... | .... | .... | .... | .... |

## MACLEAN, Brett (muh-KLAIN, BREHT) PHX.

Left wing. Shoots right. 6'2", 197 lbs. Born, Port Elgin, Ont., December 24, 1988.
(Phoenix's 3rd choice, 32nd overall, in 2007 Entry Draft).

| | | | Regular Season | | | | | Playoffs | | | | |
|---|---|---|---|---|---|---|---|---|---|---|---|---|
| Season | Club | League | GP | G | A | Pts | PIM | GP | G | A | Pts | PIM |
| 2003-04 | Listowel Cyclones | OJHL-B | 9 | 4 | 6 | 10 | 10 | 2 | 3 | 2 | 5 | 12 |
| | Grey-Bruce | Minor-ON | 66 | 71 | 47 | 118 | 117 | .... | .... | .... | .... | .... |
| 2004-05 | Erie Otters | OHL | 68 | 7 | 16 | 23 | 31 | 6 | 1 | 1 | 2 | 6 |
| 2005-06 | Erie Otters | OHL | 13 | 3 | 5 | 8 | 6 | .... | .... | .... | .... | .... |
| | Oshawa Generals | OHL | 35 | 13 | 25 | 38 | 29 | .... | .... | .... | .... | .... |
| 2006-07 | Oshawa Generals | OHL | 68 | 47 | 53 | 100 | 43 | 7 | 6 | 9 | 15 | 9 |
| 2007-08 | Oshawa Generals | OHL | 61 | *61 | 58 | 119 | 42 | 15 | 5 | 11 | 16 | 12 |
| 2008-09 | San Antonio | AHL | 74 | 21 | 19 | 40 | 33 | .... | .... | .... | .... | .... |

OHL Second All-Star Team (2007) • OHL First All-Star Team (2008) • Canadian Major Junior Second All-Star Team (2008)

## MacMILLAN, Logan (muhk-MIHL-uhn , LOH-guhn) ANA.

Center. Shoots left. 6'2", 200 lbs. Born, Charlottetown, P.E.I., July 5, 1989.
(Anaheim's 1st choice, 19th overall, in 2007 Entry Draft).

| | | | Regular Season | | | | | Playoffs | | | | |
|---|---|---|---|---|---|---|---|---|---|---|---|---|
| Season | Club | League | GP | G | A | Pts | PIM | GP | G | A | Pts | PIM |
| 2004-05 | Notre Dame | SJHL | 41 | 9 | 19 | 28 | 27 | .... | .... | .... | .... | .... |
| 2005-06 | Halifax | QMJHL | 62 | 9 | 9 | 18 | 31 | 11 | 1 | 0 | 1 | 0 |
| 2006-07 | Halifax | QMJHL | 68 | 20 | 35 | 55 | 82 | 12 | 9 | 11 | 20 | 6 |
| 2007-08 | Halifax | QMJHL | 46 | 15 | 26 | 41 | 77 | 15 | 3 | 10 | 13 | 20 |
| 2008-09 | Halifax | QMJHL | 15 | 4 | 6 | 10 | 27 | .... | .... | .... | .... | .... |
| | Rimouski Oceanic | QMJHL | 28 | 5 | 16 | 21 | 37 | 13 | 3 | 3 | 6 | 20 |

## MacWILLIAM, Andrew (MAK-WIHL-yuhm, AN-droo) TOR.

Defense. Shoots left. 6'2", 214 lbs. Born, Calgary, Alta., March 25, 1990.
(Toronto's 8th choice, 188th overall, in 2008 Entry Draft).

| | | | Regular Season | | | | | Playoffs | | | | |
|---|---|---|---|---|---|---|---|---|---|---|---|---|
| Season | Club | League | GP | G | A | Pts | PIM | GP | G | A | Pts | PIM |
| 2006-07 | Calgary Royals | AMHL | 35 | 5 | 13 | 18 | 125 | .... | .... | .... | .... | .... |
| | Camrose Kodiaks | AJHL | 2 | 0 | 0 | 0 | 0 | 1 | 0 | 0 | 0 | 0 |
| 2007-08 | Camrose Kodiaks | AJHL | 54 | 0 | 13 | 13 | 130 | 18 | 0 | 5 | 5 | 49 |
| 2008-09 | Camrose Kodiaks | AJHL | 57 | 8 | 21 | 29 | 220 | 11 | 0 | 4 | 4 | 39 |

• Signed Letter of Intent to attend **University of North Dakota** (WCHA) in fall of 2009.

## MADSEN, Morten (MAD-sehn, MOHR-tuhn) MIN.

Right wing. Shoots left. 6'2", 205 lbs. Born, Rodovre, Denmark, January 16, 1987.
(Minnesota's 5th choice, 122nd overall, in 2005 Entry Draft).

| | | | Regular Season | | | | | Playoffs | | | | |
|---|---|---|---|---|---|---|---|---|---|---|---|---|
| Season | Club | League | GP | G | A | Pts | PIM | GP | G | A | Pts | PIM |
| 2003-04 | V.Frolunda U18 | Swe-U18 | 11 | 13 | 8 | 21 | 0 | 7 | 3 | 1 | 4 | 4 |
| | V.Frolunda Jr. | Swe-Jr. | 16 | 3 | 2 | 5 | 0 | 1 | 0 | 0 | 0 | 0 |
| 2004-05 | Frolunda U18 | Swe-U18 | 2 | 1 | 2 | 3 | 0 | 6 | 7 | 7 | 14 | 6 |
| | Frolunda Jr. | Swe-Jr. | 32 | 7 | 14 | 21 | 14 | 6 | 3 | 2 | 5 | 0 |
| 2005-06 | Frolunda Jr. | Swe-Jr. | 36 | 10 | 32 | 42 | 60 | 7 | 5 | 3 | 8 | 4 |
| | Frolunda | Sweden | 5 | 0 | 0 | 0 | 2 | .... | .... | .... | .... | .... |
| 2006-07 | Victoriaville Tigres | QMJHL | 62 | 32 | 68 | 100 | 86 | 6 | 3 | 6 | 9 | 4 |
| 2007-08 | Houston Aeros | AHL | 50 | 3 | 17 | 20 | 18 | 3 | 1 | 0 | 1 | 0 |
| 2008-09 | Houston Aeros | AHL | 56 | 6 | 16 | 22 | 33 | 1 | 0 | 1 | 1 | 0 |

## MAGGIO, Daniel (MA-jee-oh, DAN-yehl) NYR

Defense. Shoots right. 6'3", 198 lbs. Born, Windsor, Ont., March 4, 1991.
(NY Rangers' 6th choice, 170th overall, in 2009 Entry Draft).

| | | | Regular Season | | | | | Playoffs | | | | |
|---|---|---|---|---|---|---|---|---|---|---|---|---|
| Season | Club | League | GP | G | A | Pts | PIM | GP | G | A | Pts | PIM |
| 2006-07 | Wind. Jr. Spitfires | Minor-ON | 59 | 16 | 38 | 54 | 94 | .... | .... | .... | .... | .... |
| 2007-08 | Sudbury Wolves | OHL | 64 | 5 | 15 | 20 | 96 | .... | .... | .... | .... | .... |
| 2008-09 | Sudbury Wolves | OHL | 44 | 2 | 14 | 16 | 60 | 6 | 1 | 0 | 1 | 12 |

## MAGNAN-GRENIER, Olivier (MAHG-nah-GREH-n'yay) N.J.

Defense. Shoots left. 6'2", 205 lbs. Born, Sherbrooke, Que., May 1, 1986.
(New Jersey's 6th choice, 148th overall, in 2006 Entry Draft).

| | | | Regular Season | | | | | Playoffs | | | | |
|---|---|---|---|---|---|---|---|---|---|---|---|---|
| Season | Club | League | GP | G | A | Pts | PIM | GP | G | A | Pts | PIM |
| 2004-05 | Rouyn-Noranda | QMJHL | 70 | 5 | 15 | 20 | 82 | 10 | 0 | 2 | 2 | 14 |
| 2005-06 | Rouyn-Noranda | QMJHL | 69 | 14 | 27 | 41 | 97 | 5 | 0 | 1 | 1 | 6 |
| 2006-07 | Lowell Devils | AHL | 24 | 1 | 1 | 2 | 13 | .... | .... | .... | .... | .... |
| | Trenton Titans | ECHL | 45 | 1 | 9 | 10 | 63 | 1 | 0 | 0 | 0 | 0 |
| 2007-08 | Lowell Devils | AHL | 75 | 1 | 15 | 16 | 69 | .... | .... | .... | .... | .... |
| 2008-09 | Lowell Devils | AHL | 76 | 2 | 8 | 10 | 66 | .... | .... | .... | .... | .... |

## MAKAROV, Igor (MAK-ah-rahv, EE-gohr) CHI.

Right wing. Shoots right. 6'1", 183 lbs. Born, Moscow, USSR, September 19, 1987.
(Chicago's 2nd choice, 33rd overall, in 2006 Entry Draft).

| | | | Regular Season | | | | | Playoffs | | | | |
|---|---|---|---|---|---|---|---|---|---|---|---|---|
| Season | Club | League | GP | G | A | Pts | PIM | GP | G | A | Pts | PIM |
| 2003-04 | Krylja Sovetov 2 | Russia-3 | 1 | 0 | 0 | 0 | 0 | .... | .... | .... | .... | .... |
| 2004-05 | Krylja Sovetov 2 | Russia-3 | 38 | 13 | 15 | 28 | 44 | .... | .... | .... | .... | .... |
| | Krylja Sovetov | Russia-2 | 6 | 2 | 2 | 4 | 4 | 1 | 0 | 0 | 0 | 0 |
| 2005-06 | Krylja Sovetov | Russia-2 | 35 | 9 | 7 | 16 | 20 | 17 | 3 | 4 | 7 | 20 |
| 2006-07 | SKA St. Petersburg | Russia | 49 | 7 | 2 | 9 | 47 | 3 | 1 | 0 | 1 | 2 |
| 2007-08 | St. Petersburg 2 | Russia-3 | 3 | 1 | 3 | 4 | 2 | 2 | 1 | 2 | 3 | 2 |
| | SKA St. Petersburg | Russia | 50 | 4 | 11 | 15 | 26 | 9 | 2 | 1 | 3 | 35 |
| 2008-09 | SKA St. Petersburg | Rus-KHL | 42 | 9 | 8 | 17 | 61 | 3 | 1 | 0 | 1 | 2 |

## MAKI, Ryan (MA-kee, RIGH-uhn) NSH.

Right wing. Shoots right. 6'2", 210 lbs. Born, Medford, NJ, April 23, 1985.
(Nashville's 5th choice, 176th overall, in 2005 Entry Draft).

| | | | Regular Season | | | | | Playoffs | | | | |
|---|---|---|---|---|---|---|---|---|---|---|---|---|
| Season | Club | League | GP | G | A | Pts | PIM | GP | G | A | Pts | PIM |
| 2001-02 | USNTDP | U-17 | 17 | 3 | 11 | 14 | 6 | .... | .... | .... | .... | .... |
| | USNTDP | NAHL | 31 | 4 | 11 | 15 | 24 | .... | .... | .... | .... | .... |
| 2002-03 | USNTDP | U-18 | 42 | 5 | 6 | 11 | 18 | .... | .... | .... | .... | .... |
| | USNTDP | NAHL | 10 | 1 | 0 | 1 | 8 | .... | .... | .... | .... | .... |
| 2003-04 | Harvard Crimson | ECAC | 34 | 4 | 4 | 8 | 18 | .... | .... | .... | .... | .... |
| 2004-05 | Harvard Crimson | ECAC | 30 | 10 | 9 | 19 | 20 | .... | .... | .... | .... | .... |
| 2005-06 | Harvard Crimson | ECAC | 33 | 10 | 12 | 22 | 32 | .... | .... | .... | .... | .... |
| 2006-07 | Harvard Crimson | ECAC | 32 | 12 | 11 | 23 | 36 | .... | .... | .... | .... | .... |
| | Milwaukee | AHL | 2 | 0 | 1 | 1 | 0 | 2 | 0 | 0 | 0 | 0 |
| 2007-08 | Milwaukee | AHL | 54 | 2 | 3 | 5 | 23 | 3 | 0 | 0 | 0 | 2 |
| | Cincinnati | ECHL | 5 | 1 | 0 | 1 | 4 | 6 | 1 | 0 | 1 | 4 |
| 2008-09 | Milwaukee | AHL | 65 | 12 | 13 | 25 | 37 | 11 | 1 | 1 | 2 | 4 |

## MALENKYKH, Vladimir (MAH-lihn-keh, vla-DIH-meer) PIT.

Defense. Shoots left. 6'1", 187 lbs. Born, Togliatti, USSR, October 1, 1980.
(Pittsburgh's 7th choice, 157th overall, in 1999 Entry Draft).

| | | | Regular Season | | | | | Playoffs | | | | |
|---|---|---|---|---|---|---|---|---|---|---|---|---|
| Season | Club | League | GP | G | A | Pts | PIM | GP | G | A | Pts | PIM |
| 1997-98 | Lada Togliatti 2 | Russia-3 | 39 | 6 | 4 | 10 | 112 | .... | .... | .... | .... | .... |
| 1998-99 | Lada Togliatti 2 | Russia-4 | 38 | 6 | 3 | 9 | 68 | .... | .... | .... | .... | .... |
| | Lada Togliatti | Russia | 9 | 0 | 0 | 0 | 2 | .... | .... | .... | .... | .... |
| 99-2000 | Lada Togliatti 2 | Russia-3 | 34 | 7 | 9 | 16 | 98 | .... | .... | .... | .... | .... |
| | CSK VVS Samara | Russia | 7 | 0 | 1 | 1 | 14 | .... | .... | .... | .... | .... |
| | Lada Togliatti | Russia | 1 | 0 | 0 | 0 | 0 | .... | .... | .... | .... | .... |
| | CSK VVS Samara 2 | Russia-3 | 1 | 0 | 1 | 1 | 2 | .... | .... | .... | .... | .... |
| 2000-01 | Lada Togliatti | Russia | 25 | 1 | 1 | 2 | 14 | 5 | 0 | 0 | 0 | 26 |
| 2001-02 | Lada Togliatti | Russia | 47 | 5 | 4 | 9 | 88 | 4 | 0 | 0 | 0 | 2 |
| 2002-03 | Lada Togliatti | Russia | 30 | 3 | 1 | 4 | 36 | 10 | 0 | 0 | 0 | 6 |
| 2003-04 | Lada Togliatti | Russia | 44 | 2 | 4 | 6 | 42 | 3 | 0 | 0 | 0 | 0 |
| 2004-05 | Lada Togliatti | Russia | 37 | 1 | 4 | 5 | 20 | .... | .... | .... | .... | .... |
| 2005-06 | Magnitogorsk | Russia | 36 | 0 | 2 | 2 | 8 | 11 | 0 | 1 | 1 | 16 |
| | Magnitogorsk 2 | Russia-3 | 5 | 1 | 1 | 2 | 2 | .... | .... | .... | .... | .... |
| 2006-07 | Magnitogorsk | Russia | 54 | 2 | 9 | 11 | 92 | 15 | 1 | 2 | 3 | 28 |
| 2007-08 | Magnitogorsk 2 | Russia-3 | 1 | 1 | 0 | 1 | 0 | .... | .... | .... | .... | .... |
| | Magnitogorsk | Russia | 19 | 0 | 2 | 2 | 18 | 12 | 0 | 0 | 0 | 8 |
| 2008-09 | Magnitogorsk | Rus-KHL | 53 | 3 | 4 | 7 | 22 | 12 | 3 | 0 | 3 | 35 |

## MALONE, Brad (MA-lohn, BRAD) COL.

Center/Left wing. Shoots left. 6'2", 207 lbs. Born, Miramichi, N.B., May 20, 1989.
(Colorado's 5th choice, 105th overall, in 2007 Entry Draft).

| | | | Regular Season | | | | | Playoffs | | | | |
|---|---|---|---|---|---|---|---|---|---|---|---|---|
| Season | Club | League | GP | G | A | Pts | PIM | GP | G | A | Pts | PIM |
| 2005-06 | Cushing | High-MA | STATISTICS NOT AVAILABLE | | | | | | | | | |
| 2006-07 | Sioux Falls | USHL | 57 | 14 | 19 | 33 | 134 | 8 | 3 | 1 | 4 | 24 |
| 2007-08 | North Dakota | WCHA | 34 | 1 | 2 | 3 | 44 | .... | .... | .... | .... | .... |
| 2008-09 | North Dakota | WCHA | 41 | 5 | 12 | 17 | 75 | .... | .... | .... | .... | .... |

## MARCHAND, Brad (mahr-SHAND, BRAD) BOS.

Center. Shoots left. 5'9", 183 lbs. Born, Halifax, N.S., May 11, 1988.
(Boston's 4th choice, 71st overall, in 2006 Entry Draft).

| | | | Regular Season | | | | | Playoffs | | | | |
|---|---|---|---|---|---|---|---|---|---|---|---|---|
| Season | Club | League | GP | G | A | Pts | PIM | GP | G | A | Pts | PIM |
| 2003-04 | Dartmouth | NSMHL | 60 | 47 | 47 | 94 | 104 | .... | .... | .... | .... | .... |
| 2004-05 | Moncton Wildcats | QMJHL | 61 | 9 | 20 | 29 | 52 | 11 | 1 | 0 | 1 | 7 |
| 2005-06 | Moncton Wildcats | QMJHL | 68 | 29 | 37 | 66 | 83 | 20 | 5 | 14 | 19 | 34 |
| 2006-07 | Val-d'Or Foreurs | QMJHL | 57 | 33 | 47 | 80 | 108 | 20 | *16 | *24 | *40 | 36 |
| 2007-08 | Val-d'Or Foreurs | QMJHL | 33 | 21 | 23 | 44 | 36 | .... | .... | .... | .... | .... |
| | Halifax | QMJHL | 26 | 10 | 19 | 29 | 40 | 14 | 3 | 16 | 19 | 18 |
| 2008-09 | Providence Bruins | AHL | 79 | 18 | 41 | 59 | 67 | 16 | 7 | 8 | 15 | 26 |

## MARCINKO, Tomas (mahr-TSIHN-koh, TAW-mahsh) NYI

Center. Shoots right. 6'4", 187 lbs. Born, Poprad, Czech., April 11, 1988.
(NY Islanders' 6th choice, 115th overall, in 2006 Entry Draft).

| | | | Regular Season | | | | | Playoffs | | | | |
|---|---|---|---|---|---|---|---|---|---|---|---|---|
| Season | Club | League | GP | G | A | Pts | PIM | GP | G | A | Pts | PIM |
| 2003-04 | HC Kosice U18 | Svk-U18 | 42 | 19 | 23 | 42 | 60 | 2 | 0 | 0 | 0 | 4 |
| | HC Kosice Jr. | Slovak-Jr. | 7 | 0 | 2 | 2 | 4 | 3 | 0 | 1 | 1 | 0 |
| 2004-05 | HC Kosice Jr. | Slovak-Jr. | 38 | 11 | 18 | 29 | 28 | 8 | 1 | 2 | 3 | 6 |
| | HC Kosice | Slovakia | 6 | 0 | 0 | 0 | 0 | .... | .... | .... | .... | .... |
| | HC Kosice | Slovakia | 6 | 0 | 0 | 0 | 0 | .... | .... | .... | .... | .... |
| 2005-06 | HC Kosice Jr. | Slovak-Jr. | 35 | 26 | 21 | 47 | 50 | 3 | 1 | 0 | 1 | 4 |
| | HKm Humenne | Slovak-2 | 9 | 3 | 5 | 8 | 10 | .... | .... | .... | .... | .... |
| | HC Kosice | Slovakia | 18 | 2 | 0 | 2 | 2 | 5 | 0 | 0 | 0 | 0 |
| 2006-07 | Barrie Colts | OHL | 56 | 19 | 21 | 40 | 56 | 8 | 0 | 1 | 1 | 8 |
| 2007-08 | Barrie Colts | OHL | 48 | 19 | 26 | 45 | 54 | 9 | 4 | 3 | 7 | 14 |
| 2008-09 | Bridgeport | AHL | 58 | 4 | 7 | 11 | 30 | 4 | 0 | 0 | 0 | 0 |

## MAREK, Jan (MAIR-ehk, YAHN) L.A.

Center. Shoots right. 5'10", 185 lbs. Born, Jindrichuv Hradec, Czech., December 31, 1979.
(NY Rangers' 10th choice, 243rd overall, in 2003 Entry Draft).

| | | | Regular Season | | | | | Playoffs | | | | |
|---|---|---|---|---|---|---|---|---|---|---|---|---|
| Season | Club | League | GP | G | A | Pts | PIM | GP | G | A | Pts | PIM |
| 1998-99 | Trinec | CzRep | 32 | 2 | 2 | 4 | 2 | 6 | 0 | 0 | 0 | 0 |
| 99-2000 | HC Trinec Jr. | CzRep-Jr. | 6 | 5 | 5 | 10 | 10 | 1 | 0 | 0 | 0 | 0 |
| | HC Slezan Opava | CzRep-2 | 3 | 0 | 1 | 1 | 4 | .... | .... | .... | .... | .... |
| | Jind. Hradec | CzRep-2 | 4 | 0 | 3 | 3 | 10 | .... | .... | .... | .... | .... |
| | HC Ocelari Trinec | CzRep | 32 | 1 | 5 | 6 | 4 | 2 | 0 | 0 | 0 | 0 |
| 2000-01 | HC Ocelari Trinec | CzRep | 38 | 7 | 4 | 11 | 2 | .... | .... | .... | .... | .... |
| 2001-02 | HC Ocelari Trinec | CzRep | 52 | 13 | 27 | 40 | 44 | 6 | 1 | 3 | 4 | 6 |
| 2002-03 | HC Ocelari Trinec | CzRep | 51 | *32 | 30 | 62 | 42 | 12 | 6 | 4 | 10 | 22 |
| 2003-04 | HC Sparta Praha | CzRep | 50 | 21 | 30 | 51 | 62 | 11 | 4 | 9 | 13 | 26 |
| 2004-05 | HC Sparta Praha | CzRep | 38 | 7 | 21 | 28 | 26 | 5 | 2 | 2 | 4 | 2 |
| 2005-06 | HC Sparta Praha | CzRep | 48 | 22 | 32 | *54 | 66 | 17 | 4 | 4 | 8 | 24 |
| 2006-07 | Magnitogorsk | Russia | 47 | 17 | 30 | 47 | 70 | 15 | 7 | 10 | 17 | 10 |
| 2007-08 | Magnitogorsk | Russia | 49 | 16 | 32 | 48 | 40 | 11 | 4 | 3 | 7 | 2 |
| 2008-09 | Magnitogorsk | Rus-KHL | 53 | *38 | 37 | 75 | 62 | 12 | 6 | 4 | 10 | 26 |

Traded to **Los Angeles** by **NY Rangers** with Jason Ward, Marc-Andre Cliche and NY Rangers' 3rd round choice (later traded to Buffalo - Buffalo selected Corey Fienhage) in 2008 Entry Draft for Sean Avery and John Seymour, February 5, 2007.

## MAROON, Patrick (ma-ROON, PAT-rihk) PHI.

Left wing. Shoots left. 6'4", 225 lbs. Born, St Louis, MO, April 23, 1988.
(Philadelphia's 6th choice, 161st overall, in 2007 Entry Draft).

| | | | Regular Season | | | | | Playoffs | | | | |
|---|---|---|---|---|---|---|---|---|---|---|---|---|
| Season | Club | League | GP | G | A | Pts | PIM | GP | G | A | Pts | PIM |
| 2005-06 | Texarkana Bandits | NAHL | 57 | 23 | 37 | 60 | 61 | 8 | 3 | 1 | 4 | 22 |
| 2006-07 | St. Louis Bandits | NAHL | 57 | 40 | 55 | *95 | 152 | 12 | *10 | *13 | *23 | 12 |
| 2007-08 | London Knights | OHL | 64 | 35 | 55 | 90 | 57 | 5 | 0 | 1 | 1 | 10 |
| | Philadelphia | AHL | 1 | 0 | 0 | 0 | 0 | .... | .... | .... | .... | .... |
| 2008-09 | Philadelphia | AHL | 80 | 23 | 31 | 54 | 62 | 4 | 1 | 2 | 3 | 13 |

## MARQUARDT, Matt (MAR-kwart, MAT) BOS.

Left wing. Shoots left. 6'3", 222 lbs. Born, North Bay, Ont., July 19, 1987.
(Columbus' 10th choice, 194th overall, in 2006 Entry Draft).

| | | | Regular Season | | | | | Playoffs | | | | |
|---|---|---|---|---|---|---|---|---|---|---|---|---|
| Season | Club | League | GP | G | A | Pts | PIM | GP | G | A | Pts | PIM |
| 2003-04 | Huntsville Wildcats | OPJHL | STATISTICS NOT AVAILABLE | | | | | | | | | |
| | Brockville Braves | CJHL | 11 | 1 | 2 | 3 | 17 | .... | .... | .... | .... | .... |
| 2004-05 | Brockville Braves | CJHL | 55 | 19 | 22 | 41 | 78 | 7 | 2 | 1 | 3 | 8 |
| 2005-06 | Moncton Wildcats | QMJHL | 68 | 16 | 9 | 25 | 69 | 20 | 5 | 3 | 8 | 12 |
| 2006-07 | Moncton Wildcats | QMJHL | 67 | 41 | 29 | 70 | 68 | 7 | 1 | 3 | 4 | 14 |
| 2007-08 | Moncton Wildcats | QMJHL | 35 | 20 | 13 | 33 | 38 | .... | .... | .... | .... | .... |
| | Baie-Comeau | QMJHL | 33 | 23 | 13 | 36 | 33 | 5 | 1 | 1 | 2 | 6 |
| 2008-09 | Providence Bruins | AHL | 71 | 9 | 13 | 22 | 45 | 9 | 1 | 1 | 2 | 2 |

CJHL Rookie of the Year (2005)

Traded to **Boston** by **Columbus** for Jonathon Sigalet, May 27, 2008.

## MARSHALL, Kevin (MAR-shuhl, KEH-vihn) PHI.

Defense. Shoots left. 6'1", 200 lbs. Born, Boucherville, Que., March 10, 1989.
(Philadelphia's 2nd choice, 41st overall, in 2007 Entry Draft).

| | | | Regular Season | | | | | Playoffs | | | | |
|---|---|---|---|---|---|---|---|---|---|---|---|---|
| Season | Club | League | GP | G | A | Pts | PIM | GP | G | A | Pts | PIM |
| 2004-05 | C.C. Lemoyne | QAAA | 39 | 2 | 9 | 11 | 88 | 5 | 0 | 1 | 1 | 16 |
| 2005-06 | Lewiston | QMJHL | 60 | 1 | 10 | 11 | 112 | 6 | 0 | 1 | 1 | 14 |
| 2006-07 | Lewiston | QMJHL | 70 | 5 | 27 | 32 | 141 | 17 | 0 | 7 | 7 | 38 |
| 2007-08 | Lewiston | QMJHL | 66 | 11 | 24 | 35 | 143 | 6 | 1 | 1 | 2 | 12 |
| 2008-09 | Quebec Remparts | QMJHL | 61 | 9 | 29 | 38 | 125 | 17 | 1 | 10 | 11 | 32 |

QMJHL Second All-Star Team (2008)

## MARSHALL, Matt (MAR-shuhl, MAT) T.B.

Center/Right wing. Shoots right. 6'1", 175 lbs. Born, Boston, MA, August 30, 1988.
(Tampa Bay's 5th choice, 150th overall, in 2007 Entry Draft).

| | | | Regular Season | | | | | Playoffs | | | | |
|---|---|---|---|---|---|---|---|---|---|---|---|---|
| Season | Club | League | GP | G | A | Pts | PIM | GP | G | A | Pts | PIM |
| 2005-06 | Hingham | High-MA | STATISTICS NOT AVAILABLE | | | | | | | | | |
| 2006-07 | Nobles | High-MA | 27 | 14 | 10 | 24 | 6 | .... | .... | .... | .... | .... |
| 2007-08 | Nobles | High-MA | 29 | 25 | 26 | 51 | | .... | .... | .... | .... | .... |
| 2008-09 | U. of Vermont | H-East | 24 | 1 | 3 | 4 | 12 | .... | .... | .... | .... | .... |

## MARTIN, Jesse (MAHR-tihn, JEH-see) ATL.

Center. Shoots right. 5'11", 170 lbs. Born, Edmonton, Alta., September 7, 1988.
(Atlanta's 6th choice, 195th overall, in 2006 Entry Draft).

| | | | Regular Season | | | | | Playoffs | | | | |
|---|---|---|---|---|---|---|---|---|---|---|---|---|
| Season | Club | League | GP | G | A | Pts | PIM | GP | G | A | Pts | PIM |
| 2003-04 | K of C Pats | AMHL | 34 | 10 | 11 | 21 | 6 | .... | .... | .... | .... | .... |
| 2004-05 | K of C Pats | AMHL | 30 | 17 | 28 | 45 | 70 | 8 | 4 | 8 | 12 | .... |
| 2005-06 | Spruce Grove | AJHL | 40 | 15 | 29 | 44 | 122 | .... | .... | .... | .... | .... |
| 2006-07 | Tri-City Storm | USHL | 59 | 19 | 37 | 56 | 31 | 9 | 2 | 4 | 6 | 4 |
| 2007-08 | U. of Denver | WCHA | 41 | 7 | 8 | 15 | 26 | .... | .... | .... | .... | .... |
| 2008-09 | U. of Denver | WCHA | 37 | 10 | 13 | 23 | 34 | .... | .... | .... | .... | .... |

## MARTIN, Matt (MAHR-tihn, MA-thew) NYI

Left wing. Shoots left. 6'2", 192 lbs. Born, Windsor, Ont., May 8, 1989.
(NY Islanders' 11th choice, 148th overall, in 2008 Entry Draft).

| | | | Regular Season | | | | | Playoffs | | | | |
|---|---|---|---|---|---|---|---|---|---|---|---|---|
| Season | Club | League | GP | G | A | Pts | PIM | GP | G | A | Pts | PIM |
| 2005-06 | Blenheim Blast | OHA-C | 40 | 11 | 12 | 23 | 102 | .... | .... | .... | .... | .... |
| 2006-07 | Sarnia Blast | OJHL-B | 9 | 2 | 5 | 7 | 16 | .... | .... | .... | .... | .... |
| | Sarnia Sting | OHL | 39 | 3 | 3 | 6 | 52 | 4 | 0 | 0 | 0 | 0 |
| 2007-08 | Sarnia Sting | OHL | 66 | 25 | 13 | 38 | 155 | 9 | 3 | 3 | 6 | 16 |
| 2008-09 | Sarnia Sting | OHL | 61 | 35 | 30 | 65 | 142 | 5 | 3 | 0 | 3 | 10 |

## MARTINEZ, Alec (mar-TEE-nehz, AL-ehk) L.A.

Defense. Shoots left. 6'1", 214 lbs. Born, Rochester Hills, MI, July 26, 1987.
(Los Angeles' 5th choice, 95th overall, in 2007 Entry Draft).

| | | | Regular Season | | | | | Playoffs | | | | |
|---|---|---|---|---|---|---|---|---|---|---|---|---|
| Season | Club | League | GP | G | A | Pts | PIM | GP | G | A | Pts | PIM |
| 2004-05 | Cedar Rapids | USHL | 58 | 10 | 11 | 21 | 30 | 11 | 1 | 2 | 3 | 8 |
| 2005-06 | Miami U. | CCHA | 39 | 3 | 8 | 11 | 31 | .... | .... | .... | .... | .... |
| 2006-07 | Miami U. | CCHA | 42 | 9 | 15 | 24 | 40 | .... | .... | .... | .... | .... |
| 2007-08 | Miami U. | CCHA | 42 | 9 | 23 | 32 | 42 | .... | .... | .... | .... | .... |
| 2008-09 | Manchester | AHL | 72 | 8 | 15 | 23 | 42 | .... | .... | .... | .... | .... |

CCHA First All-Star Team (2008) • NCAA West Second All-American Team (2008)

## MARVIN, Aaron (MAHR-vihn, AIR-ruhn) CGY.

Forward. Shoots left. 6'2", 191 lbs. Born, Warrod, MN, May 27, 1988.
(Calgary's 3rd choice, 89th overall, in 2006 Entry Draft).

| | | | Regular Season | | | | | Playoffs | | | | |
|---|---|---|---|---|---|---|---|---|---|---|---|---|
| Season | Club | League | GP | G | A | Pts | PIM | GP | G | A | Pts | PIM |
| 2004-05 | Warroad Warriors | High-MN | 31 | 23 | 25 | 48 | 18 | .... | .... | .... | .... | .... |
| 2005-06 | Warroad Warriors | High-MN | 23 | 9 | 21 | 30 | 40 | .... | .... | .... | .... | .... |
| 2006-07 | Tri-City Storm | USHL | 13 | 1 | 3 | 4 | 8 | 9 | 1 | 0 | 1 | 8 |
| 2007-08 | St. Cloud State | WCHA | 40 | 3 | 10 | 13 | 33 | .... | .... | .... | .... | .... |
| 2008-09 | St. Cloud State | WCHA | 38 | 10 | 17 | 27 | 46 | .... | .... | .... | .... | .... |

## MASHINTER, Brandon (ma-SHIHN-tuhr, BRAN-duhn) S.J.

Center. Shoots left. 6'4", 235 lbs. Born, Bradford, Ont., September 20, 1988.

| Season | Club | League | Regular Season GP | G | A | Pts | PIM | Playoffs GP | G | A | Pts | PIM |
|---|---|---|---|---|---|---|---|---|---|---|---|---|
| 2004-05 | Tor. T-Birds | OPJHL | 49 | 3 | 6 | 9 | 19 | .... | .... | .... | .... | .... |
| | Sarnia Sting | OHL | 8 | 0 | 0 | 0 | 9 | .... | .... | .... | .... | .... |
| 2005-06 | Sarnia Sting | OHL | 65 | 6 | 1 | 7 | 65 | .... | .... | .... | .... | .... |
| 2006-07 | Sarnia Sting | OHL | 55 | 7 | 8 | 15 | 49 | 4 | 0 | 2 | 2 | 0 |
| 2007-08 | Kitchener Rangers | OHL | 62 | 10 | 10 | 20 | 84 | 20 | 2 | 2 | 4 | 16 |
| 2008-09 | Kitchener Rangers | OHL | 21 | 14 | 12 | 26 | 24 | .... | .... | .... | .... | .... |
| | Belleville Bulls | OHL | 31 | 20 | 12 | 32 | 32 | 17 | 8 | 3 | 11 | 13 |

Signed as a free agent by **San Jose**, July, 2009.

## MASSE, Dany (ma-SAY, DA-nee) MTL.

Left wing. Shoots left. 5'10", 188 lbs. Born, La Pocatière, Que., May 12, 1988.

| Season | Club | League | Regular Season GP | G | A | Pts | PIM | Playoffs GP | G | A | Pts | PIM |
|---|---|---|---|---|---|---|---|---|---|---|---|---|
| 2004-05 | Val-d'Or Foreurs | QMJHL | 58 | 2 | 8 | 10 | 43 | .... | .... | .... | .... | .... |
| 2005-06 | Val-d'Or Foreurs | QMJHL | 67 | 9 | 20 | 29 | 64 | 5 | 0 | 0 | 0 | 0 |
| 2006-07 | Acadie-Bathurst | QMJHL | 69 | 26 | 30 | 56 | 84 | 12 | 1 | 6 | 7 | 12 |
| 2007-08 | Acadie-Bathurst | QMJHL | 70 | 29 | 50 | 79 | 38 | 12 | 1 | 6 | 7 | 14 |
| 2008-09 | Drummondville | QMJHL | 68 | 44 | 66 | 110 | 52 | 19 | 15 | 21 | 36 | 18 |

QMJHL First All-Star Team (2009)

Signed as a free agent by **Montreal**, April 15, 2009.

## MATSON, Taylor (MAT-suhn, TAY-luhr) VAN.

Center. Shoots right. 5'10", 165 lbs. Born, Mound, MN, September 16, 1988.
(Vancouver's 5th choice, 176th overall, in 2007 Entry Draft).

| Season | Club | League | Regular Season GP | G | A | Pts | PIM | Playoffs GP | G | A | Pts | PIM |
|---|---|---|---|---|---|---|---|---|---|---|---|---|
| 2005-06 | Holy Angels | High-MN | 27 | 30 | 40 | 70 | 28 | .... | .... | .... | .... | .... |
| 2006-07 | Holy Angels | High-MN | 11 | 16 | 15 | 31 | 16 | .... | .... | .... | .... | .... |
| | Des Moines | USHL | 10 | 1 | 2 | 3 | 6 | 6 | 0 | 1 | 1 | 10 |
| 2007-08 | Des Moines | USHL | 55 | 13 | 24 | 37 | 38 | .... | .... | .... | .... | .... |
| 2008-09 | U. of Minnesota | WCHA | 13 | 1 | 0 | 1 | 2 | .... | .... | .... | .... | .... |

## MATSUMOTO, Jonathan (mat-suh-MOH-toh, JAWN-ah-thuhn) PHI.

Center. Shoots left. 6', 184 lbs. Born, Ottawa, Ont., October 13, 1986.
(Philadelphia's 5th choice, 79th overall, in 2006 Entry Draft).

| Season | Club | League | Regular Season GP | G | A | Pts | PIM | Playoffs GP | G | A | Pts | PIM |
|---|---|---|---|---|---|---|---|---|---|---|---|---|
| 2002-03 | Cumberland | CJHL | 8 | 2 | 3 | 5 | 2 | 10 | 4 | 7 | 11 | 2 |
| 2003-04 | Cumberland | CJHL | 51 | 31 | 32 | 63 | 26 | 7 | 5 | 5 | 10 | 6 |
| 2004-05 | Bowling Green | CCHA | 36 | 18 | 14 | 32 | 22 | .... | .... | .... | .... | .... |
| 2005-06 | Bowling Green | CCHA | 36 | 20 | 28 | 48 | 43 | .... | .... | .... | .... | .... |
| 2006-07 | Bowling Green | CCHA | 38 | 11 | 22 | 33 | 70 | .... | .... | .... | .... | .... |
| | Philadelphia | AHL | 16 | 2 | 2 | 4 | 10 | .... | .... | .... | .... | .... |
| 2007-08 | Philadelphia | AHL | 77 | 20 | 24 | 44 | 52 | 12 | 2 | 2 | 4 | 10 |
| 2008-09 | Philadelphia | AHL | 78 | 29 | 34 | 63 | 77 | 4 | 1 | 2 | 3 | 4 |

## McBAIN, Jamie (muhk-BAYN, JAY-mee) CAR.

Defense. Shoots right. 6'2", 200 lbs. Born, Edina, MN, February 25, 1988.
(Carolina's 1st choice, 63rd overall, in 2006 Entry Draft).

| Season | Club | League | Regular Season GP | G | A | Pts | PIM | Playoffs GP | G | A | Pts | PIM |
|---|---|---|---|---|---|---|---|---|---|---|---|---|
| 2003-04 | Shat.-St. Mary's | High-MN | 73 | 6 | 27 | 33 | .... | .... | .... | .... | .... | .... |
| 2004-05 | USNTDP | U-17 | 14 | 1 | 6 | 7 | 16 | .... | .... | .... | .... | .... |
| | USNTDP | NAHL | 38 | 2 | 7 | 9 | 22 | 10 | 0 | 3 | 3 | 4 |
| 2005-06 | USNTDP | U-18 | 41 | 9 | 16 | 25 | 35 | .... | .... | .... | .... | .... |
| | USNTDP | NAHL | 14 | 0 | 5 | 5 | 6 | .... | .... | .... | .... | .... |
| 2006-07 | U. of Wisconsin | WCHA | 36 | 3 | 15 | 18 | 36 | .... | .... | .... | .... | .... |
| 2007-08 | U. of Wisconsin | WCHA | 35 | 5 | 19 | 24 | 18 | .... | .... | .... | .... | .... |
| 2008-09 | U. of Wisconsin | WCHA | 40 | 7 | 30 | 37 | 30 | .... | .... | .... | .... | .... |
| | Albany River Rats | AHL | 10 | 1 | 1 | 2 | 2 | .... | .... | .... | .... | .... |

WCHA All-Rookie Team (2007) • WCHA First All-Star Team (2009) • WCHA Player of the Year (2009) • NCAA West First All-American Team (2009)

## McCARTHY, John (muh-KAHR-thee, JAWN) S.J.

Left wing. Shoots left. 6'1", 200 lbs. Born, Boston, MA, August 9, 1986.
(San Jose's 5th choice, 202nd overall, in 2006 Entry Draft).

| Season | Club | League | Regular Season GP | G | A | Pts | PIM | Playoffs GP | G | A | Pts | PIM |
|---|---|---|---|---|---|---|---|---|---|---|---|---|
| 2004-05 | Des Moines | USHL | 60 | 8 | 10 | 18 | 32 | .... | .... | .... | .... | .... |
| 2005-06 | Boston University | H-East | 33 | 2 | 2 | 4 | 12 | .... | .... | .... | .... | .... |
| 2006-07 | Boston University | H-East | 39 | 2 | 3 | 5 | 18 | .... | .... | .... | .... | .... |
| 2007-08 | Boston University | H-East | 38 | 4 | 3 | 7 | 24 | .... | .... | .... | .... | .... |
| 2008-09 | Boston University | H-East | 45 | 6 | 23 | 29 | 24 | .... | .... | .... | .... | .... |

## McCOLLEM, Matthew (muh-KAHL-uhm, MA-thew) ST.L.

Left wing. Shoots left. 6', 185 lbs. Born, Somerville, MA, May 6, 1988.
(St. Louis' 8th choice, 154th overall, in 2006 Entry Draft).

| Season | Club | League | Regular Season GP | G | A | Pts | PIM | Playoffs GP | G | A | Pts | PIM |
|---|---|---|---|---|---|---|---|---|---|---|---|---|
| 2004-05 | Belmont Hill | High-MA | .... | 2 | 7 | 9 | .... | .... | .... | .... | .... | .... |
| 2005-06 | Belmont Hill | High-MA | .... | 15 | 11 | 26 | .... | .... | .... | .... | .... | .... |
| 2006-07 | Belmont Hill | High-MA | 28 | 16 | 19 | 35 | 64 | .... | .... | .... | .... | .... |
| 2007-08 | Harvard Crimson | ECAC | 31 | 5 | 9 | 14 | 28 | .... | .... | .... | .... | .... |
| 2008-09 | Harvard Crimson | ECAC | 29 | 6 | 8 | 14 | 28 | .... | .... | .... | .... | .... |

## McCUE, Matt (muh-KEW, MAHT) ANA.

Defense. Shoots left. 6'1", 218 lbs. Born, Cochrane, Alta., July 5, 1988.

| Season | Club | League | Regular Season GP | G | A | Pts | PIM | Playoffs GP | G | A | Pts | PIM |
|---|---|---|---|---|---|---|---|---|---|---|---|---|
| 2003-04 | Medicine Hat | AMHL | 28 | 2 | 7 | 9 | 101 | .... | .... | .... | .... | .... |
| | Spokane Chiefs | WHL | 3 | 0 | 0 | 0 | 0 | .... | .... | .... | .... | .... |
| 2004-05 | Spokane Chiefs | WHL | 21 | 1 | 2 | 3 | 35 | .... | .... | .... | .... | .... |
| 2005-06 | Spokane Chiefs | WHL | 56 | 5 | 10 | 15 | 125 | .... | .... | .... | .... | .... |
| 2006-07 | Spokane Chiefs | WHL | 4 | 1 | 1 | 2 | 4 | .... | .... | .... | .... | .... |
| | Chilliwack Bruins | WHL | 32 | 2 | 5 | 7 | 71 | 5 | 0 | 0 | 0 | 14 |
| 2007-08 | Chilliwack Bruins | WHL | 42 | 0 | 4 | 4 | 111 | .... | .... | .... | .... | .... |
| | Brandon | WHL | 28 | 0 | 7 | 7 | 84 | 6 | 1 | 0 | 1 | 12 |
| 2008-09 | Brandon | WHL | 9 | 1 | 1 | 2 | 35 | .... | .... | .... | .... | .... |
| | Medicine Hat | WHL | 52 | 5 | 18 | 23 | 160 | 9 | 1 | 2 | 3 | 12 |

• Missed majority of 2004-05 season recovering from a leg injury. Signed as a free agent by **Anaheim**, December 30, 2008.

## McCUTCHEON, Mark (muh-KUH-chuhn, MAHRK)

Center. Shoots right. 6', 190 lbs. Born, Ithaca, NY, May 21, 1984.
(Colorado's 3rd choice, 146th overall, in 2003 Entry Draft).

| Season | Club | League | Regular Season GP | G | A | Pts | PIM | Playoffs GP | G | A | Pts | PIM |
|---|---|---|---|---|---|---|---|---|---|---|---|---|
| 2001-02 | N.E. Jr. Coyotes | EJHL | 36 | 24 | 26 | 50 | 84 | .... | .... | .... | .... | .... |
| 2002-03 | N.E. Jr. Coyotes | EJHL | 35 | 27 | 22 | 49 | 76 | 10 | 8 | 5 | 13 | 24 |
| 2003-04 | Cornell Big Red | ECAC | 32 | 0 | 4 | 4 | 12 | .... | .... | .... | .... | .... |
| 2004-05 | Cornell Big Red | ECAC | 22 | 0 | 5 | 5 | 12 | .... | .... | .... | .... | .... |
| 2005-06 | Cornell Big Red | ECAC | 34 | 9 | 6 | 15 | 34 | .... | .... | .... | .... | .... |
| 2006-07 | Cornell Big Red | ECAC | 29 | 10 | 10 | 20 | 32 | .... | .... | .... | .... | .... |
| 2007-08 | Lake Erie Monsters | AHL | 63 | 2 | 7 | 9 | 73 | .... | .... | .... | .... | .... |
| 2008-09 | Lake Erie Monsters | AHL | 65 | 6 | 11 | 17 | 70 | .... | .... | .... | .... | .... |
| | Johnstown Chiefs | ECHL | 9 | 3 | 1 | 4 | 14 | .... | .... | .... | .... | .... |

## McDONAGH, Ryan (muhk-DUHN-uh, RIGH-uhn) NYR

Defense. Shoots left. 6'1", 211 lbs. Born, St.Paul, MN, June 13, 1989.
(Montreal's 1st choice, 12th overall, in 2007 Entry Draft).

| Season | Club | League | Regular Season GP | G | A | Pts | PIM | Playoffs GP | G | A | Pts | PIM |
|---|---|---|---|---|---|---|---|---|---|---|---|---|
| 2004-05 | Cretin-Derham | High-MN | 28 | 12 | 18 | 30 | .... | .... | .... | .... | .... | .... |
| 2005-06 | Cretin-Derham | High-MN | 25 | 12 | 33 | 45 | .... | .... | .... | .... | .... | .... |
| 2006-07 | Cretin-Derham | High-MN | 26 | 14 | 26 | 40 | .... | .... | .... | .... | .... | .... |
| 2007-08 | U. of Wisconsin | WCHA | 40 | 5 | 7 | 12 | 42 | .... | .... | .... | .... | .... |
| 2008-09 | U. of Wisconsin | WCHA | 36 | 5 | 11 | 16 | 59 | .... | .... | .... | .... | .... |

WCHA All-Rookie Team (2008)

Traded to **NY Rangers** by **Montreal** with Chris Higgins and Pavel Valentenko for Scott Gomez, Tom Pyatt and Mike Busto, June 30, 2009.

## McDONALD, Colin (muhk-DAWN-uhld, KAW-lihn) EDM.

Right wing. Shoots right. 6'3", 205 lbs. Born, New Haven, CT, September 30, 1984.
(Edmonton's 2nd choice, 51st overall, in 2003 Entry Draft).

| Season | Club | League | Regular Season GP | G | A | Pts | PIM | Playoffs GP | G | A | Pts | PIM |
|---|---|---|---|---|---|---|---|---|---|---|---|---|
| 2001-02 | N.E. Jr. Coyotes | EJHL | 39 | 16 | 20 | 36 | 50 | .... | .... | .... | .... | .... |
| 2002-03 | N.E. Jr. Coyotes | EJHL | 44 | 28 | 40 | *68 | 59 | .... | .... | .... | .... | .... |
| 2003-04 | Providence College | H-East | 37 | 10 | 6 | 16 | 47 | .... | .... | .... | .... | .... |
| 2004-05 | Providence College | H-East | 26 | 11 | 5 | 16 | 14 | .... | .... | .... | .... | .... |
| 2005-06 | Providence College | H-East | 36 | 9 | 19 | 28 | 29 | .... | .... | .... | .... | .... |
| 2006-07 | Providence College | H-East | 36 | 13 | 4 | 17 | 30 | .... | .... | .... | .... | .... |
| 2007-08 | Springfield Falcons | AHL | 73 | 12 | 11 | 23 | 46 | .... | .... | .... | .... | .... |
| 2008-09 | Springfield Falcons | AHL | 77 | 10 | 12 | 22 | 65 | .... | .... | .... | .... | .... |
| | Stockton Thunder | ECHL | 3 | 0 | 2 | 2 | 0 | .... | .... | .... | .... | .... |

Hockey East All-Rookie Team (2004)

## McGRATH, Evan (muh-GRATH, EH-vuhn) DET.

Center. Shoots left. 6', 190 lbs. Born, Oakville, Ont., January 14, 1986.
(Detroit's 2nd choice, 128th overall, in 2004 Entry Draft).

| Season | Club | League | Regular Season GP | G | A | Pts | PIM | Playoffs GP | G | A | Pts | PIM |
|---|---|---|---|---|---|---|---|---|---|---|---|---|
| 2001-02 | Oakville Blades | OPJHL | 49 | 43 | 44 | 87 | 24 | .... | .... | .... | .... | .... |
| 2002-03 | Kitchener Rangers | OHL | 64 | 16 | 31 | 47 | 40 | 21 | 6 | 2 | 8 | 6 |
| 2003-04 | Kitchener Rangers | OHL | 68 | 15 | 36 | 51 | 28 | 5 | 2 | 1 | 3 | 2 |
| 2004-05 | Kitchener Rangers | OHL | 67 | 28 | 59 | 87 | 51 | 15 | 7 | 6 | 13 | 6 |
| 2005-06 | Kitchener Rangers | OHL | 67 | 37 | 77 | 114 | 63 | 5 | 1 | 3 | 4 | 4 |
| 2006-07 | Grand Rapids | AHL | 59 | 6 | 8 | 14 | 41 | 7 | 0 | 0 | 0 | 0 |
| | Toledo Storm | ECHL | 9 | 6 | 9 | 15 | 12 | .... | .... | .... | .... | .... |
| 2007-08 | Grand Rapids | AHL | 78 | 18 | 17 | 35 | 26 | .... | .... | .... | .... | .... |
| 2008-09 | Grand Rapids | AHL | 68 | 17 | 30 | 47 | 24 | .... | .... | .... | .... | .... |

OHL All-Rookie Team (2003)

## McGUIRK, Brian (muh-GUHRK, BRIGH-uhn)

Left wing. Shoots left. 6', 191 lbs. Born, Danvers, MA, July 11, 1985.
(Columbus' 10th choice, 231st overall, in 2004 Entry Draft).

| Season | Club | League | Regular Season GP | G | A | Pts | PIM | Playoffs GP | G | A | Pts | PIM |
|---|---|---|---|---|---|---|---|---|---|---|---|---|
| 2003-04 | Gov. Dummer | High-MA | 25 | 16 | 16 | 32 | .... | .... | .... | .... | .... | .... |
| 2004-05 | Boston University | H-East | 33 | 0 | 1 | 1 | 18 | .... | .... | .... | .... | .... |
| 2005-06 | Boston University | H-East | 39 | 5 | 4 | 9 | 18 | .... | .... | .... | .... | .... |
| 2006-07 | Boston University | H-East | 36 | 1 | 4 | 5 | 24 | .... | .... | .... | .... | .... |
| 2007-08 | Boston University | H-East | 37 | 4 | 9 | 13 | 53 | .... | .... | .... | .... | .... |
| | Syracuse Crunch | AHL | 6 | 2 | 1 | 3 | 11 | .... | .... | .... | .... | .... |
| 2008-09 | Syracuse Crunch | AHL | 60 | 2 | 4 | 6 | 39 | .... | .... | .... | .... | .... |

## McINTYRE, David (MAK-ihn-tigh-uhr, DAY-vihd) N.J.

Center. Shoots left. 6', 190 lbs. Born, Oakville, Ont., February 4, 1987.
(Dallas' 4th choice, 138th overall, in 2006 Entry Draft).

| Season | Club | League | Regular Season GP | G | A | Pts | PIM | Playoffs GP | G | A | Pts | PIM |
|---|---|---|---|---|---|---|---|---|---|---|---|---|
| 2004-05 | Newmarket | OPJHL | 46 | 17 | 14 | 31 | 33 | 16 | 8 | 7 | 15 | 20 |
| 2005-06 | Newmarket | OPJHL | 46 | 42 | 50 | 92 | 143 | 11 | 4 | 8 | 12 | 42 |
| 2006-07 | Colgate | ECAC | 40 | 9 | 8 | 17 | 75 | .... | .... | .... | .... | .... |
| 2007-08 | Colgate | ECAC | 39 | 15 | 17 | 32 | 38 | .... | .... | .... | .... | .... |
| 2008-09 | Colgate | ECAC | 37 | 21 | 22 | 43 | 54 | .... | .... | .... | .... | .... |

ECAC First All-Star Team (2009) • NCAA East First All-American Team (2009)

Traded to **Anaheim** by **Dallas** with future considerations for Brian Sutherby, December 14, 2008. Traded to **New Jersey** by **Anaheim** for Sheldon Brookbank, February 3, 2009.

## McKELVIE, Zach (muh-KEHL-vee, ZAK) BOS.

Defense. Shoots . 6'2", 197 lbs. Born, St. Paul, MN, February 22, 1985.

| Season | Club | League | Regular Season GP | G | A | Pts | PIM | Playoffs GP | G | A | Pts | PIM |
|---|---|---|---|---|---|---|---|---|---|---|---|---|
| 2004-05 | Bozeman IceDogs | NAHL | 53 | 0 | 6 | 6 | 108 | .... | .... | .... | .... | .... |
| 2005-06 | Army | AH | 32 | 2 | 8 | 10 | 64 | .... | .... | .... | .... | .... |
| 2006-07 | Army | AH | 34 | 3 | 9 | 12 | 48 | .... | .... | .... | .... | .... |
| 2007-08 | Army | AH | 35 | 4 | 13 | 17 | 48 | .... | .... | .... | .... | .... |
| 2008-09 | Army | AH | 33 | 5 | 12 | 17 | 48 | .... | .... | .... | .... | .... |

Signed as a free agent by **Boston**, July 13, 2009.

## McKENZIE, Curtis (muh-KEHN-zee, KUHR-tihs) DAL.

Left wing. Shoots left. 6'2", 192 lbs. Born, Golden, B.C., February 22, 1991.
(Dallas' 5th choice, 159th overall, in 2009 Entry Draft).

| Season | Club | League | Regular Season GP | G | A | Pts | PIM | Playoffs GP | G | A | Pts | PIM |
|---|---|---|---|---|---|---|---|---|---|---|---|---|
| 2007-08 | Penticton Vees | BCHL | 49 | 3 | 7 | 10 | 81 | 7 | 0 | 1 | 1 | 9 |
| 2008-09 | Penticton Vees | BCHL | 53 | 30 | 34 | 64 | 90 | 10 | 3 | 7 | 10 | 81 |

• Signed Letter of Intent to attend **Miami University** (CCHA) in fall of 2009.

## McKENZIE, Ian (muh-KEHN-zee, EE-an) NSH.

Right wing. Shoots right. 6'5", 232 lbs. Born, Weyburn, Sask., May 23, 1987.

| | | | Regular Season | | | | | Playoffs | | | | |
|---|---|---|---|---|---|---|---|---|---|---|---|---|
| Season | Club | League | GP | G | A | Pts | PIM | GP | G | A | Pts | PIM |
| 2003-04 | Saskatoon Blazers | SMHL | STATISTICS NOT AVAILABLE | | | | | | | | | |
| | Moose Jaw | WHL | 8 | 0 | 0 | 0 | 0 | .... | .... | .... | .... | .... |
| 2004-05 | Moose Jaw | WHL | 44 | 3 | 4 | 7 | 18 | 5 | 0 | 0 | 0 | 11 |
| 2005-06 | Moose Jaw | WHL | 42 | 4 | 3 | 7 | 68 | 22 | 5 | 3 | 8 | 8 |
| 2006-07 | Moose Jaw | WHL | 6 | 1 | 0 | 1 | 10 | .... | .... | .... | .... | .... |
| | Seattle | WHL | 60 | 12 | 9 | 21 | 77 | 11 | 2 | 1 | 3 | 17 |
| 2007-08 | Seattle | WHL | 68 | 19 | 21 | 40 | 103 | 12 | 8 | 6 | 14 | 12 |
| 2008-09 | Milwaukee | AHL | 26 | 3 | 1 | 4 | 31 | .... | .... | .... | .... | .... |
| | Cincinnati | ECHL | 40 | 12 | 3 | 15 | 56 | 8 | 4 | 4 | 8 | 8 |

Signed as a free agent by **Nashville**, May 6, 2008.

## McKENZIE, Jim (muh-KEHN-zee, JIHM)

Right wing. Shoots right. 6'2", 204 lbs. Born, St. Paul, MN, June 10, 1984.
(Ottawa's 7th choice, 141st overall, in 2004 Entry Draft).

| | | | Regular Season | | | | | Playoffs | | | | |
|---|---|---|---|---|---|---|---|---|---|---|---|---|
| Season | Club | League | GP | G | A | Pts | PIM | GP | G | A | Pts | PIM |
| 2000-01 | Hill-Murray | High-MN | 27 | 9 | 13 | 22 | .... | .... | .... | .... | .... | .... |
| 2001-02 | USNTDP | U-18 | 13 | 7 | 8 | 15 | 10 | .... | .... | .... | .... | .... |
| | USNTDP | USHL | 2 | 0 | 1 | 1 | 9 | .... | .... | .... | .... | .... |
| | USNTDP | NAHL | 4 | 0 | 2 | 2 | 4 | .... | .... | .... | .... | .... |
| | Green Bay | USHL | 17 | 1 | 2 | 3 | 34 | .... | .... | .... | .... | .... |
| 2002-03 | Sioux Falls | USHL | 45 | 6 | 18 | 24 | 108 | .... | .... | .... | .... | .... |
| 2003-04 | Sioux Falls | USHL | 59 | 26 | 38 | 64 | 168 | .... | .... | .... | .... | .... |
| 2004-05 | Michigan State | CCHA | 34 | 11 | 7 | 18 | 44 | .... | .... | .... | .... | .... |
| 2005-06 | Michigan State | CCHA | 43 | 11 | 17 | 28 | 85 | .... | .... | .... | .... | .... |
| 2006-07 | Michigan State | CCHA | 35 | 12 | 18 | 30 | 56 | .... | .... | .... | .... | .... |
| 2007-08 | Binghamton | AHL | 18 | 2 | 1 | 3 | 15 | .... | .... | .... | .... | .... |
| | Elmira Jackals | ECHL | 43 | 9 | 10 | 19 | 43 | 6 | 1 | 0 | 1 | 6 |
| 2008-09 | Binghamton | AHL | 44 | 1 | 4 | 5 | 18 | .... | .... | .... | .... | .... |

## McLAREN, Frazer (muh-KLAIR-uhn, FRAY-zuhr) S.J.

Left wing. Shoots left. 6'5", 235 lbs. Born, Winnipeg, Man., October 29, 1987.
(San Jose's 8th choice, 203rd overall, in 2007 Entry Draft).

| | | | Regular Season | | | | | Playoffs | | | | |
|---|---|---|---|---|---|---|---|---|---|---|---|---|
| Season | Club | League | GP | G | A | Pts | PIM | GP | G | A | Pts | PIM |
| 2002-03 | Kelvin | High-MB | 56 | 27 | 24 | 51 | 136 | .... | .... | .... | .... | .... |
| 2003-04 | Portland | WHL | 50 | 0 | 3 | 3 | 44 | 1 | 0 | 0 | 0 | 0 |
| 2004-05 | Portland | WHL | 71 | 6 | 5 | 11 | 124 | 7 | 0 | 0 | 0 | 10 |
| 2005-06 | Portland | WHL | 70 | 12 | 6 | 18 | 194 | 12 | 0 | 2 | 2 | 27 |
| 2006-07 | Portland | WHL | 61 | 19 | 12 | 31 | 186 | .... | .... | .... | .... | .... |
| 2007-08 | Portland | WHL | 18 | 4 | 3 | 7 | 45 | .... | .... | .... | .... | .... |
| | Moose Jaw | WHL | 48 | 15 | 18 | 33 | 119 | 6 | 1 | 1 | 2 | 8 |
| | Worcester Sharks | AHL | 4 | 0 | 1 | 1 | 17 | .... | .... | .... | .... | .... |
| 2008-09 | Worcester Sharks | AHL | 75 | 7 | 1 | 8 | 181 | 12 | 1 | 4 | 5 | *50 |

## McMILLAN, Brandon (muhk-MIHL-uhn, BRAN-duhn) ANA.

Center. Shoots left. 5'11", 188 lbs. Born, Richmond, B.C., March 22, 1990.
(Anaheim's 7th choice, 85th overall, in 2008 Entry Draft).

| | | | Regular Season | | | | | Playoffs | | | | |
|---|---|---|---|---|---|---|---|---|---|---|---|---|
| Season | Club | League | GP | G | A | Pts | PIM | GP | G | A | Pts | PIM |
| 2006-07 | Kelowna Rockets | WHL | 55 | 2 | 10 | 12 | 27 | .... | .... | .... | .... | .... |
| 2007-08 | Kelowna Rockets | WHL | 71 | 15 | 26 | 41 | 56 | 7 | 0 | 0 | 0 | 6 |
| 2008-09 | Kelowna Rockets | WHL | 70 | 14 | 35 | 49 | 75 | 22 | 0 | 5 | 5 | 20 |

## McMILLAN, Carson (muhk-MIHL-lihn, KAHR-suhn) MIN.

Right wing. Shoots right. 6'1", 194 lbs. Born, Brandon, Man., September 10, 1988.
(Minnesota's 5th choice, 200th overall, in 2007 Entry Draft).

| | | | Regular Season | | | | | Playoffs | | | | |
|---|---|---|---|---|---|---|---|---|---|---|---|---|
| Season | Club | League | GP | G | A | Pts | PIM | GP | G | A | Pts | PIM |
| 2003-04 | Crocus Plains | High-MB | STATISTICS NOT AVAILABLE | | | | | | | | | |
| | Brandon | MMHL | 4 | 0 | 0 | 0 | 0 | .... | .... | .... | .... | .... |
| 2004-05 | Brandon | MMHL | 40 | 17 | 19 | 36 | 34 | 5 | 3 | 4 | 7 | 8 |
| | Winkler Flyers | MJHL | 4 | 1 | 1 | 2 | 2 | .... | .... | .... | .... | .... |
| 2005-06 | Calgary Hitmen | WHL | 59 | 3 | 2 | 5 | 42 | 13 | 0 | 0 | 0 | 2 |
| 2006-07 | Calgary Hitmen | WHL | 72 | 7 | 15 | 22 | 76 | 18 | 2 | 0 | 2 | 17 |
| 2007-08 | Calgary Hitmen | WHL | 72 | 16 | 26 | 42 | 87 | 16 | 1 | 0 | 1 | 22 |
| 2008-09 | Calgary Hitmen | WHL | 68 | 31 | 41 | 72 | 93 | 18 | 3 | 8 | 11 | 18 |

## McNABB, Brayden (muhk-NAB, BRAY-duhn) BUF.

Defense. Shoots left. 6'4", 200 lbs. Born, Saskatoon, Sask., January 21, 1991.
(Buffalo's 2nd choice, 66th overall, in 2009 Entry Draft).

| | | | Regular Season | | | | | Playoffs | | | | |
|---|---|---|---|---|---|---|---|---|---|---|---|---|
| Season | Club | League | GP | G | A | Pts | PIM | GP | G | A | Pts | PIM |
| 2006-07 | Notre Dame | SMHL | 41 | 5 | 13 | 18 | 72 | .... | .... | .... | .... | .... |
| | Kootenay Ice | WHL | 3 | 0 | 0 | 0 | 0 | .... | .... | .... | .... | .... |
| 2007-08 | Kootenay Ice | WHL | 65 | 2 | 9 | 11 | 63 | 10 | 0 | 1 | 1 | 10 |
| 2008-09 | Kootenay Ice | WHL | 67 | 10 | 26 | 36 | 140 | 4 | 0 | 5 | 5 | 2 |

## McNEILL, Patrick (muhk-NEEL, PAT-rihk) WSH.

Defense. Shoots left. 6', 198 lbs. Born, Strathroy, Ont., March 17, 1987.
(Washington's 4th choice, 118th overall, in 2005 Entry Draft).

| | | | Regular Season | | | | | Playoffs | | | | |
|---|---|---|---|---|---|---|---|---|---|---|---|---|
| Season | Club | League | GP | G | A | Pts | PIM | GP | G | A | Pts | PIM |
| 2002-03 | Strathroy Rockets | OHA-B | 45 | 6 | 13 | 19 | 53 | .... | .... | .... | .... | .... |
| 2003-04 | Saginaw Spirit | OHL | 57 | 3 | 11 | 14 | 28 | .... | .... | .... | .... | .... |
| 2004-05 | Saginaw Spirit | OHL | 66 | 7 | 26 | 33 | 31 | .... | .... | .... | .... | .... |
| 2005-06 | Saginaw Spirit | OHL | 68 | 21 | 56 | 77 | 64 | 4 | 1 | 3 | 4 | 6 |
| 2006-07 | Saginaw Spirit | OHL | 58 | 22 | 36 | 58 | 49 | 6 | 3 | 2 | 5 | 6 |
| 2007-08 | Hershey Bears | AHL | 48 | 1 | 13 | 14 | 16 | 2 | 0 | 0 | 0 | 0 |
| | South Carolina | ECHL | 19 | 5 | 11 | 16 | 16 | 5 | 0 | 2 | 2 | 4 |
| 2008-09 | Hershey Bears | AHL | 46 | 3 | 15 | 18 | 20 | 10 | 0 | 3 | 3 | 4 |

OHL Second All-Star Team (2006)

## McPHERSON, Corbin (muhk-FUHR-suhn, KOHR-bihn) N.J.

Defense. Shoots left. 6'4", 210 lbs. Born, Folsom, CA, September 7, 1988.
(New Jersey's 3rd choice, 87th overall, in 2007 Entry Draft).

| | | | Regular Season | | | | | Playoffs | | | | |
|---|---|---|---|---|---|---|---|---|---|---|---|---|
| Season | Club | League | GP | G | A | Pts | PIM | GP | G | A | Pts | PIM |
| 2005-06 | San Jose Jr. Sharks | Minor-CA | 59 | 5 | 16 | 21 | 45 | .... | .... | .... | .... | .... |
| 2006-07 | Cowichan Valley | BCHL | 44 | 4 | 10 | 14 | 63 | 18 | 1 | 3 | 4 | 14 |
| 2007-08 | Cowichan Valley | BCHL | 55 | 3 | 14 | 17 | 84 | .... | .... | .... | .... | .... |
| 2008-09 | Colgate | ECAC | 37 | 0 | 5 | 5 | 50 | .... | .... | .... | .... | .... |

## McQUAID, Adam (muhk-WAYD, A-duhm) BOS.

Defense. Shoots right. 6'4", 197 lbs. Born, Charlottetown, P.E.I., October 12, 1986.
(Columbus' 2nd choice, 55th overall, in 2005 Entry Draft).

| | | | Regular Season | | | | | Playoffs | | | | |
|---|---|---|---|---|---|---|---|---|---|---|---|---|
| Season | Club | League | GP | G | A | Pts | PIM | GP | G | A | Pts | PIM |
| 2003-04 | Sudbury Wolves | OHL | 47 | 3 | 6 | 9 | 25 | 7 | 0 | 1 | 1 | 2 |
| 2004-05 | Sudbury Wolves | OHL | 66 | 3 | 16 | 19 | 98 | 8 | 0 | 2 | 2 | 10 |
| 2005-06 | Sudbury Wolves | OHL | 68 | 3 | 14 | 17 | 107 | 10 | 0 | 1 | 1 | 16 |
| 2006-07 | Sudbury Wolves | OHL | 65 | 9 | 22 | 31 | 110 | 21 | 1 | 5 | 6 | 24 |
| 2007-08 | Providence Bruins | AHL | 68 | 1 | 8 | 9 | 73 | 10 | 0 | 0 | 0 | 9 |
| 2008-09 | Providence Bruins | AHL | 78 | 4 | 11 | 15 | 141 | 16 | 0 | 3 | 3 | 26 |

Traded to **Boston** by **Columbus** for Boston's 5th round choice (later traded to Dallas - Dallas selected Jamie Benn) in 2007 Entry Draft, May 16, 2007.

## McRAE, Philip (muh-KRAY, FIHL-ihp) ST.L.

Center. Shoots left. 6'2", 191 lbs. Born, Minneapolis, MN, March 15, 1990.
(St. Louis' 2nd choice, 33rd overall, in 2008 Entry Draft).

| | | | Regular Season | | | | | Playoffs | | | | |
|---|---|---|---|---|---|---|---|---|---|---|---|---|
| Season | Club | League | GP | G | A | Pts | PIM | GP | G | A | Pts | PIM |
| 2005-06 | USNTDP | U-17 | 15 | 1 | 1 | 2 | 0 | .... | .... | .... | .... | .... |
| | USNTDP | NAHL | 33 | 8 | 8 | 16 | 9 | 10 | 1 | 2 | 3 | 2 |
| 2006-07 | London Knights | OHL | 63 | 2 | 8 | 10 | 27 | 16 | 0 | 0 | 0 | 6 |
| 2007-08 | London Knights | OHL | 66 | 18 | 28 | 46 | 61 | 4 | 0 | 0 | 0 | 7 |
| 2008-09 | London Knights | OHL | 59 | 29 | 31 | 60 | 54 | 14 | 5 | 5 | 10 | 12 |

## MECKLER, David (MEHK-luhr, DAY-vihd) L.A.

Center. Shoots right. 6', 209 lbs. Born, Highland Park, IL, July 9, 1987.
(Los Angeles' 7th choice, 134th overall, in 2006 Entry Draft).

| | | | Regular Season | | | | | Playoffs | | | | |
|---|---|---|---|---|---|---|---|---|---|---|---|---|
| Season | Club | League | GP | G | A | Pts | PIM | GP | G | A | Pts | PIM |
| 2004-05 | Waterloo | USHL | 60 | 30 | 15 | 45 | 32 | 5 | 3 | 2 | 5 | 2 |
| 2005-06 | Yale | ECAC | 31 | 7 | 3 | 10 | 28 | .... | .... | .... | .... | .... |
| 2006-07 | London Knights | OHL | 67 | 38 | 35 | 73 | 53 | 16 | *15 | 7 | 22 | 20 |
| 2007-08 | Manchester | AHL | 76 | 23 | 13 | 36 | 24 | 4 | 1 | 1 | 2 | 2 |
| 2008-09 | Manchester | AHL | 74 | 14 | 15 | 29 | 28 | .... | .... | .... | .... | .... |

## MEDVEC, Kyle (MEHD-vek, KIGHL) MIN.

Defense. Shoots left. 6'6", 205 lbs. Born, Westminster, CO, June 16, 1988.
(Minnesota's 4th choice, 102nd overall, in 2006 Entry Draft).

| | | | Regular Season | | | | | Playoffs | | | | |
|---|---|---|---|---|---|---|---|---|---|---|---|---|
| Season | Club | League | GP | G | A | Pts | PIM | GP | G | A | Pts | PIM |
| 2003-04 | Apple Valley | High-MN | 27 | 1 | 12 | 13 | 30 | .... | .... | .... | .... | .... |
| 2004-05 | Apple Valley | High-MN | 23 | 4 | 16 | 20 | 18 | .... | .... | .... | .... | .... |
| 2005-06 | Apple Valley | High-MN | 28 | 13 | 22 | 35 | 44 | .... | .... | .... | .... | .... |
| | Sioux City | USHL | 3 | 0 | 0 | 0 | 0 | .... | .... | .... | .... | .... |
| 2006-07 | Sioux City | USHL | 57 | 4 | 14 | 18 | 83 | 7 | 0 | 0 | 0 | 4 |
| 2007-08 | U. of Vermont | H-East | 30 | 1 | 4 | 5 | 18 | .... | .... | .... | .... | .... |
| 2008-09 | U. of Vermont | H-East | 39 | 2 | 10 | 12 | 40 | .... | .... | .... | .... | .... |

## MEGALINSKY, Dmitri (meh-gahl-IHN-skee, dih-MEE-tree) OTT.

Defense. Shoots left. 6'2", 212 lbs. Born, Perm, USSR, April 15, 1985.
(Ottawa's 7th choice, 186th overall, in 2005 Entry Draft).

| | | | Regular Season | | | | | Playoffs | | | | |
|---|---|---|---|---|---|---|---|---|---|---|---|---|
| Season | Club | League | GP | G | A | Pts | PIM | GP | G | A | Pts | PIM |
| 2003-04 | HK Voronezh | Russia-2 | 42 | 4 | 8 | 12 | 159 | .... | .... | .... | .... | .... |
| | Yaroslavl | Russia | 1 | 0 | 0 | 0 | 0 | .... | .... | .... | .... | .... |
| | Yaroslavl 2 | Russia-3 | 11 | 0 | 4 | 4 | 16 | .... | .... | .... | .... | .... |
| 2004-05 | Yaroslavl | Russia | 1 | 0 | 0 | 0 | 2 | .... | .... | .... | .... | .... |
| | Yaroslavl 2 | Russia-3 | 30 | 6 | 12 | 18 | 82 | .... | .... | .... | .... | .... |
| 2005-06 | Yaroslavl 2 | Russia-3 | 12 | 4 | 10 | 14 | 6 | .... | .... | .... | .... | .... |
| | Yaroslavl | Russia | 20 | 0 | 1 | 1 | 8 | 8 | 0 | 0 | 0 | 6 |
| 2006-07 | Khimik | Russia-2 | 33 | 4 | 7 | 11 | 34 | 7 | 0 | 1 | 1 | 16 |
| 2007-08 | Vityaz Chekhov | Russia | 25 | 2 | 7 | 9 | 20 | .... | .... | .... | .... | .... |
| 2008-09 | Vityaz Chekhov | Rus-KHL | 52 | 2 | 5 | 7 | 72 | .... | .... | .... | .... | .... |

## MEGAN, Wade (MEE-guhn, WAYD) FLA.

Center. Shoots left. 6'1", 185 lbs. Born, Canton, NY, July 22, 1990.
(Florida's 6th choice, 138th overall, in 2009 Entry Draft).

| | | | Regular Season | | | | | Playoffs | | | | |
|---|---|---|---|---|---|---|---|---|---|---|---|---|
| Season | Club | League | GP | G | A | Pts | PIM | GP | G | A | Pts | PIM |
| 2007-08 | Kent Prep School | High-CT | 34 | 24 | 29 | 53 | .... | .... | .... | .... | .... | .... |
| 2008-09 | Kent Prep School | High-CT | 32 | 27 | 36 | 63 | 18 | .... | .... | .... | .... | .... |
| | Neponset Valley | Minor-MA | 16 | 8 | 8 | 16 | .... | .... | .... | .... | .... | .... |

• Signed Letter of Intent to attend **Boston University** (Hockey East) in fall of 2009.

## MELYAKOV, Igor (mehl-yuh-KAHF, EE-gohr) L.A.

Left wing. Shoots left. 5'10", 190 lbs. Born, Lipetsk, USSR, December 23, 1976.
(Los Angeles' 6th choice, 137th overall, in 1995 Entry Draft).

| | | | Regular Season | | | | | Playoffs | | | | |
|---|---|---|---|---|---|---|---|---|---|---|---|---|
| Season | Club | League | GP | G | A | Pts | PIM | GP | G | A | Pts | PIM |
| 1993-94 | Torpedo Yaroslavl | CIS | 39 | 4 | 3 | 7 | 10 | 4 | 0 | 0 | 0 | 0 |
| 1994-95 | Torpedo Yaroslavl | CIS | 50 | 6 | 8 | 14 | 34 | 4 | 0 | 1 | 1 | 0 |
| 1995-96 | Torpedo Yaroslavl | CIS | 39 | 5 | 1 | 6 | 6 | 3 | 0 | 0 | 0 | 2 |
| 1996-97 | Torpedo Yaroslavl | Russia | 8 | 0 | 0 | 0 | 0 | .... | .... | .... | .... | .... |
| | Nizhny Novgorod | Russia | 12 | 2 | 3 | 5 | 10 | .... | .... | .... | .... | .... |
| 1997-98 | Nizhny Novgorod | Russia | 13 | 3 | 3 | 6 | 6 | .... | .... | .... | .... | .... |
| 1998-99 | Nizhny Novgorod | Russia-2 | 36 | 13 | 17 | 30 | 14 | .... | .... | .... | .... | .... |
| 99-2000 | Nizhny Novgorod | Russia | 34 | 1 | 8 | 9 | 10 | 5 | 1 | 0 | 1 | 4 |
| 2000-01 | Nizhny Novgorod | Russia | 24 | 2 | 3 | 5 | 10 | .... | .... | .... | .... | .... |
| 2001-02 | HK Lipetsk | Russia-2 | 68 | 16 | 37 | 53 | 94 | .... | .... | .... | .... | .... |
| 2002-03 | Voskresensk | Russia-2 | 48 | 9 | 22 | 31 | 16 | .... | .... | .... | .... | .... |
| 2003-04 | Nizhny Novgorod | Russia | 45 | 5 | 10 | 15 | 18 | .... | .... | .... | .... | .... |
| | Nizh. Novgorod 2 | Russia-3 | 4 | 1 | 6 | 7 | 4 | .... | .... | .... | .... | .... |
| 2004-05 | Nizhny Novgorod | Russia-2 | 52 | 14 | 30 | 44 | 32 | 11 | 2 | 4 | 6 | 18 |
| 2005-06 | Magnitogorsk | Russia | 25 | 7 | 8 | 15 | 10 | 3 | 0 | 0 | 0 | 2 |
| 2006-07 | Novokuznetsk | Russia | 22 | 0 | 1 | 1 | 6 | .... | .... | .... | .... | .... |
| | Nizhny Novgorod | Russia-2 | 16 | 2 | 6 | 8 | 10 | 12 | 2 | 5 | 7 | 6 |
| 2007-08 | Nizhny Novgorod | Russia | 8 | 1 | 0 | 1 | 6 | .... | .... | .... | .... | .... |
| | Zauralje Kurgan | Russia-2 | 24 | 2 | 11 | 13 | 38 | .... | .... | .... | .... | .... |
| 2008-09 | Zauralje Kurgan | Russia-2 | 46 | 3 | 22 | 25 | 32 | .... | .... | .... | .... | .... |

**MERCIER, Justin** (MUHR-see-uhr, JUHS-tihn) **COL.**

Forward. Shoots left. 5'11", 190 lbs. Born, Erie, PA, June 25, 1987.
(Colorado's 8th choice, 168th overall, in 2005 Entry Draft).

| | | | Regular Season | | | | | Playoffs | | | | |
|---|---|---|---|---|---|---|---|---|---|---|---|---|
| **Season** | **Club** | **League** | **GP** | **G** | **A** | **Pts** | **PIM** | **GP** | **G** | **A** | **Pts** | **PIM** |
| 2003-04 | St. Louis | USHL | 60 | 12 | 9 | 21 | .... | .... | .... | .... | .... | .... |
| 2004-05 | USNTDP | U-18 | 26 | 1 | 7 | 8 | 31 | .... | .... | .... | .... | .... |
| | USNTDP | NAHL | 16 | 4 | 3 | 7 | 33 | .... | .... | .... | .... | .... |
| 2005-06 | Miami U. | CCHA | 35 | 3 | 7 | 10 | 32 | .... | .... | .... | .... | .... |
| 2006-07 | Miami U. | CCHA | 40 | 10 | 15 | 25 | 59 | .... | .... | .... | .... | .... |
| 2007-08 | Miami U. | CCHA | 42 | 25 | 15 | 40 | 42 | .... | .... | .... | .... | .... |
| 2008-09 | Miami U. | CCHA | 40 | 14 | 15 | 29 | 58 | .... | .... | .... | .... | .... |

**MESTERY, Eric** (MEHS-tuhr-ee, AIR-ihk) **WSH.**

Defense. Shoots left. 6'5", 203 lbs. Born, Winnipeg, Man., May 28, 1990.
(Washington's 3rd choice, 57th overall, in 2008 Entry Draft).

| | | | Regular Season | | | | | Playoffs | | | | |
|---|---|---|---|---|---|---|---|---|---|---|---|---|
| **Season** | **Club** | **League** | **GP** | **G** | **A** | **Pts** | **PIM** | **GP** | **G** | **A** | **Pts** | **PIM** |
| 2005-06 | Wpg. Thrashers | MMHL | 39 | 5 | 18 | 23 | 28 | .... | .... | .... | .... | .... |
| 2006-07 | Tri-City Americans | WHL | 43 | 1 | 6 | 7 | 20 | .... | .... | .... | .... | .... |
| 2007-08 | Tri-City Americans | WHL | 71 | 2 | 14 | 16 | 65 | 16 | 2 | 1 | 3 | 10 |
| 2008-09 | Tri-City Americans | WHL | 16 | 0 | 6 | 6 | 10 | .... | .... | .... | .... | .... |
| | Lethbridge | WHL | 42 | 1 | 11 | 12 | 30 | 11 | 0 | 1 | 1 | 2 |

**MIKUS, Juraj** (MEE-kuhsh, YUHR-ay) **L.A.**

Right wing. Shoots right. 6'1", 200 lbs. Born, Skalica, Czech., February 22, 1987.
(Montreal's 3rd choice, 121st overall, in 2005 Entry Draft).

| | | | Regular Season | | | | | Playoffs | | | | |
|---|---|---|---|---|---|---|---|---|---|---|---|---|
| **Season** | **Club** | **League** | **GP** | **G** | **A** | **Pts** | **PIM** | **GP** | **G** | **A** | **Pts** | **PIM** |
| 2003-04 | HK 36 Skalica U18 | Svk-U18 | 34 | 18 | 17 | 35 | 26 | 9 | 10 | 5 | 15 | 12 |
| | HK 36 Skalica Jr. | Slovak-Jr. | 8 | 3 | 7 | 10 | 16 | .... | .... | .... | .... | .... |
| | HK 36 Skalica | Slovakia | 2 | 1 | 0 | 1 | 0 | 4 | 0 | 0 | 0 | 0 |
| 2004-05 | HK 36 Skalica U18 | Svk-U18 | 3 | 1 | 7 | 8 | 2 | .... | .... | .... | .... | .... |
| | HK 36 Skalica Jr. | Slovak-Jr. | 30 | 17 | 18 | 35 | 40 | 9 | 6 | 8 | 14 | 18 |
| | HK 36 Skalica | Slovakia | 46 | 6 | 6 | 12 | 16 | .... | .... | .... | .... | .... |
| 2005-06 | HK 36 Skalica Jr. | Slovak-Jr. | 4 | 1 | 0 | 1 | 2 | 2 | 1 | 2 | 3 | 2 |
| | HK 36 Skalica | Slovakia | 47 | 4 | 7 | 11 | 56 | 7 | 2 | 1 | 3 | 14 |
| 2006-07 | Chicoutimi | QMJHL | 60 | 29 | 42 | 71 | 36 | 4 | 1 | 1 | 2 | 4 |
| 2007-08 | HK 36 Skalica | Slovakia | 54 | 21 | 22 | 43 | 52 | 13 | 8 | 5 | 13 | 36 |
| 2008-09 | HK 36 Skalica | Slovakia | 56 | 31 | 59 | 90 | 52 | 17 | 7 | 16 | 23 | 18 |

Signed as a free agent by **Los Angeles**, July 21, 2009.

**MIKUS, Juraj** (MEE-kuhsh, YUHR-ay) **TOR.**

Defense. Shoots left. 6'4", 185 lbs. Born, Trencin, Czech., November 30, 1988.
(Toronto's 4th choice, 134th overall, in 2007 Entry Draft).

| | | | Regular Season | | | | | Playoffs | | | | |
|---|---|---|---|---|---|---|---|---|---|---|---|---|
| **Season** | **Club** | **League** | **GP** | **G** | **A** | **Pts** | **PIM** | **GP** | **G** | **A** | **Pts** | **PIM** |
| 2004-05 | Piestany U18 | Svk-U18 | 2 | 1 | 2 | 3 | 2 | .... | .... | .... | .... | .... |
| | Dukla Trencin U18 | Svk-U18 | 39 | 2 | 7 | 9 | 20 | 5 | 0 | 0 | 0 | 0 |
| 2005-06 | Piestany Jr. | Slovak-Jr. | 6 | 0 | 4 | 4 | 2 | .... | .... | .... | .... | .... |
| | Dukla Trencin Jr. | Slovak-Jr. | 17 | 1 | 4 | 5 | 2 | .... | .... | .... | .... | .... |
| | Dukla Trencin U18 | Svk-U18 | 40 | 3 | 18 | 21 | 36 | 7 | 1 | 5 | 6 | 12 |
| 2006-07 | Dukla Trencin Jr. | Slovak-Jr. | 42 | 9 | 15 | 24 | 72 | 7 | 2 | 1 | 3 | 10 |
| | P. Bystrica | Slovak-2 | 7 | 0 | 3 | 3 | 2 | 1 | 0 | 0 | 0 | 0 |
| | Dukla Trencin | Slovakia | 22 | 0 | 0 | 0 | 2 | 7 | 0 | 0 | 0 | 0 |
| 2007-08 | HK VSR SR 20 | Slovakia | 21 | 1 | 4 | 5 | 30 | .... | .... | .... | .... | .... |
| | Dukla Trencin | Slovakia | 14 | 0 | 3 | 3 | 4 | 14 | 0 | 1 | 1 | 2 |
| 2008-09 | HC Dukla Senica | Slovak-2 | 9 | 1 | 1 | 2 | 4 | 1 | 0 | 0 | 0 | 0 |
| | Dukla Trencin | Slovakia | 51 | 2 | 1 | 3 | 18 | 4 | 2 | 0 | 2 | 0 |
| | Dukla Trencin Jr. | Slovak-Jr. | .... | .... | .... | .... | .... | 2 | 0 | 0 | 0 | 2 |

**MILLER, Tyler** (MIHL-luhr, TIGH-luhr) **N.J.**

Defense. Shoots left. 6'4", 230 lbs. Born, Placentia, CA, September 15, 1986.
(New Jersey's 5th choice, 107th overall, in 2006 Entry Draft).

| | | | Regular Season | | | | | Playoffs | | | | |
|---|---|---|---|---|---|---|---|---|---|---|---|---|
| **Season** | **Club** | **League** | **GP** | **G** | **A** | **Pts** | **PIM** | **GP** | **G** | **A** | **Pts** | **PIM** |
| 2004-05 | South Surrey | BCHL | 53 | 3 | 9 | 12 | 85 | .... | .... | .... | .... | .... |
| 2005-06 | Penticton Vees | BCHL | 60 | 16 | 32 | 48 | 73 | .... | .... | .... | .... | .... |
| 2006-07 | Northern Mich. | CCHA | 37 | 2 | 12 | 14 | 12 | .... | .... | .... | .... | .... |
| 2007-08 | Northern Mich. | CCHA | 42 | 2 | 7 | 9 | 53 | .... | .... | .... | .... | .... |
| 2008-09 | Northern Mich. | CCHA | 16 | 0 | 2 | 2 | 14 | .... | .... | .... | .... | .... |

**MILLS, Brad** (MIHLS, BRAD) **N.J.**

Right wing. Shoots right. 6', 195 lbs. Born, Terrace, B.C., May 3, 1983.

| | | | Regular Season | | | | | Playoffs | | | | |
|---|---|---|---|---|---|---|---|---|---|---|---|---|
| **Season** | **Club** | **League** | **GP** | **G** | **A** | **Pts** | **PIM** | **GP** | **G** | **A** | **Pts** | **PIM** |
| 2002-03 | Fort McMurray | AJHL | 62 | 20 | 47 | 67 | 73 | .... | .... | .... | .... | .... |
| 2003-04 | Yale | ECAC | 27 | 4 | 7 | 11 | 18 | .... | .... | .... | .... | .... |
| 2004-05 | Yale | ECAC | 27 | 12 | 14 | 26 | 30 | .... | .... | .... | .... | .... |
| 2005-06 | Yale | ECAC | 22 | 8 | 8 | 16 | 65 | .... | .... | .... | .... | .... |
| 2006-07 | Yale | ECAC | 20 | 2 | 6 | 8 | 39 | .... | .... | .... | .... | .... |
| | Lowell Devils | AHL | 8 | 0 | 1 | 1 | 4 | .... | .... | .... | .... | .... |
| 2007-08 | Lowell Devils | AHL | 16 | 1 | 2 | 3 | 44 | .... | .... | .... | .... | .... |
| | Trenton Devils | ECHL | 26 | 9 | 7 | 16 | 67 | .... | .... | .... | .... | .... |
| 2008-09 | Lowell Devils | AHL | 75 | 5 | 16 | 21 | 108 | .... | .... | .... | .... | .... |

Signed as a free agent by **Lowell** (AHL), June 17, 2008. Signed as a free agent by **New Jersey**, June 1, 2009.

**MIRNOV, Igor** (mihr-NAWF, EE-gohr) **OTT.**

Left wing. Shoots left. 6', 187 lbs. Born, Chita, USSR, September 19, 1984.
(Ottawa's 2nd choice, 67th overall, in 2003 Entry Draft).

| | | | Regular Season | | | | | Playoffs | | | | |
|---|---|---|---|---|---|---|---|---|---|---|---|---|
| **Season** | **Club** | **League** | **GP** | **G** | **A** | **Pts** | **PIM** | **GP** | **G** | **A** | **Pts** | **PIM** |
| 2001-02 | Dyn'o Moscow 2 | Russia-3 | 30 | 33 | 17 | 50 | 34 | .... | .... | .... | .... | .... |
| | Dynamo Moscow | Russia | 6 | 0 | 0 | 0 | 0 | .... | .... | .... | .... | .... |
| 2002-03 | Dynamo Moscow | Russia | 50 | 3 | 7 | 10 | 49 | 5 | 0 | 0 | 0 | 2 |
| 2003-04 | Dynamo Moscow | Russia | 53 | 11 | 10 | 21 | 26 | 3 | 0 | 0 | 0 | 2 |
| 2004-05 | Dynamo Moscow | Russia | 55 | 13 | 13 | 26 | 50 | 9 | 2 | 4 | 6 | 0 |
| 2005-06 | Dynamo Moscow | Russia | 32 | 8 | 10 | 18 | 36 | 4 | 0 | 2 | 2 | 4 |
| 2006-07 | Dynamo Moscow | Russia | 49 | 21 | 25 | 46 | 54 | 3 | 2 | 1 | 3 | 4 |
| 2007-08 | Dynamo Moscow | Russia | 24 | 3 | 3 | 6 | 16 | .... | .... | .... | .... | .... |
| | Magnitogorsk | Russia | 23 | 9 | 6 | 15 | 20 | 13 | 3 | 1 | 4 | 4 |
| 2008-09 | Magnitogorsk | Rus-KHL | 39 | 11 | 8 | 19 | 24 | 11 | 2 | 7 | 9 | 8 |

**MISHARIN, Georgy** (mih-SHAHR-ihn, g'YOHR-gee) **MIN.**

Defense. Shoots left. 6', 198 lbs. Born, Yekaterinburg, USSR, May 11, 1985.
(Minnesota's 6th choice, 207th overall, in 2003 Entry Draft).

| | | | Regular Season | | | | | Playoffs | | | | |
|---|---|---|---|---|---|---|---|---|---|---|---|---|
| **Season** | **Club** | **League** | **GP** | **G** | **A** | **Pts** | **PIM** | **GP** | **G** | **A** | **Pts** | **PIM** |
| 2001-02 | Yekaterinburg 2 | Russia-3 | STATISTICS NOT AVAILABLE | | | | | | | | | |
| | Magnitogorsk 2 | Russia-3 | STATISTICS NOT AVAILABLE | | | | | | | | | |
| 2002-03 | Yekaterinburg | Russia-2 | 28 | 1 | 3 | 4 | 16 | .... | .... | .... | .... | .... |
| 2003-04 | Saginaw Spirit | OHL | 65 | 5 | 22 | 27 | 42 | .... | .... | .... | .... | .... |
| 2004-05 | Nizhnekamsk | Russia | 47 | 1 | 3 | 4 | 38 | 3 | 0 | 0 | 0 | 4 |
| 2005-06 | CSKA Moscow | Russia | 50 | 4 | 9 | 13 | 46 | 7 | 0 | 0 | 0 | 31 |
| 2006-07 | Dynamo Moscow | Russia | 48 | 3 | 7 | 10 | 70 | 3 | 0 | 1 | 1 | 12 |
| 2007-08 | CSKA Moscow | Russia | 50 | 6 | 5 | 11 | 42 | 6 | 0 | 3 | 3 | 6 |
| 2008-09 | CSKA Moscow | Rus-KHL | 54 | 3 | 12 | 15 | 52 | 8 | 0 | 1 | 1 | 6 |

Signed as a free agent by **Dynamo Moscow** (Russia), August 31, 2006.

**MISKOVIC, Zach** (MIHS-koh-vihch, ZAK) **WSH.**

Defense. Shoots right. 6'1", 195 lbs. Born, River Forest, IL, May 8, 1985.

| | | | Regular Season | | | | | Playoffs | | | | |
|---|---|---|---|---|---|---|---|---|---|---|---|---|
| **Season** | **Club** | **League** | **GP** | **G** | **A** | **Pts** | **PIM** | **GP** | **G** | **A** | **Pts** | **PIM** |
| 2002-03 | Cedar Rapids | USHL | 60 | 2 | 6 | 8 | 91 | 7 | 0 | 0 | 0 | 12 |
| 2003-04 | Cedar Rapids | USHL | 60 | 6 | 15 | 21 | 139 | 4 | 1 | 1 | 2 | 2 |
| 2004-05 | Cedar Rapids | USHL | 60 | 4 | 16 | 20 | 149 | 8 | 1 | 0 | 1 | 14 |
| 2005-06 | St. Lawrence | ECAC | 40 | 1 | 15 | 16 | 30 | .... | .... | .... | .... | .... |
| 2006-07 | St. Lawrence | ECAC | 39 | 2 | 10 | 12 | 48 | .... | .... | .... | .... | .... |
| 2007-08 | St. Lawrence | ECAC | 37 | 8 | 12 | 20 | 36 | .... | .... | .... | .... | .... |
| 2008-09 | St. Lawrence | ECAC | 38 | 16 | 9 | 25 | 32 | .... | .... | .... | .... | .... |

ECAC First All-Star Team (2009) • NCAA East First All-American Team (2009)

Signed as a free agent by **Washington**, March 25, 2009.

**MITCHELL, Dale** (MIH-chuhl, DAYL) **TOR.**

Right wing. Shoots right. 5'9", 205 lbs. Born, Etobicoke, Ont., April 9, 1989.
(Toronto's 1st choice, 74th overall, in 2007 Entry Draft).

| | | | Regular Season | | | | | Playoffs | | | | |
|---|---|---|---|---|---|---|---|---|---|---|---|---|
| **Season** | **Club** | **League** | **GP** | **G** | **A** | **Pts** | **PIM** | **GP** | **G** | **A** | **Pts** | **PIM** |
| 2005-06 | Oshawa Generals | OHL | 65 | 20 | 23 | 43 | 63 | .... | .... | .... | .... | .... |
| 2006-07 | Oshawa Generals | OHL | 67 | 43 | 37 | 80 | 81 | 9 | 1 | 4 | 5 | 12 |
| 2007-08 | Oshawa Generals | OHL | 63 | 24 | 36 | 60 | 79 | 15 | 10 | 6 | 16 | 23 |
| | Toronto Marlies | AHL | .... | .... | .... | .... | .... | 2 | 0 | 1 | 1 | 2 |
| 2008-09 | Windsor Spitfires | OHL | 66 | 33 | 35 | 68 | 87 | 20 | 14 | 15 | 29 | 24 |

**MITCHELL, Garrett** (MIH-chuhl, GAIR-reht) **WSH.**

Right wing. Shoots right. 5'11", 185 lbs. Born, Regina, Sask., September 2, 1991.
(Washington's 6th choice, 175th overall, in 2009 Entry Draft).

| | | | Regular Season | | | | | Playoffs | | | | |
|---|---|---|---|---|---|---|---|---|---|---|---|---|
| **Season** | **Club** | **League** | **GP** | **G** | **A** | **Pts** | **PIM** | **GP** | **G** | **A** | **Pts** | **PIM** |
| 2006-07 | Regina | SMHL | 42 | 14 | 11 | 25 | 140 | .... | .... | .... | .... | .... |
| | Regina Pats | WHL | 4 | 0 | 1 | 1 | 2 | .... | .... | .... | .... | .... |
| 2007-08 | Regina Pats | WHL | 62 | 8 | 5 | 13 | 73 | 6 | 1 | 0 | 1 | 6 |
| 2008-09 | Regina Pats | WHL | 71 | 10 | 5 | 15 | 140 | .... | .... | .... | .... | .... |

**MITERA, Mark** (MIH-tair-a, MAHRK) **ANA.**

Defense. Shoots left. 6'3", 211 lbs. Born, Royal Oak, MI, October 22, 1987.
(Anaheim's 1st choice, 19th overall, in 2006 Entry Draft).

| | | | Regular Season | | | | | Playoffs | | | | |
|---|---|---|---|---|---|---|---|---|---|---|---|---|
| **Season** | **Club** | **League** | **GP** | **G** | **A** | **Pts** | **PIM** | **GP** | **G** | **A** | **Pts** | **PIM** |
| 2003-04 | USNTDP | U-17 | 16 | 2 | 6 | 8 | 22 | .... | .... | .... | .... | .... |
| | USNTDP | NAHL | 43 | 2 | 13 | 15 | 69 | 7 | 0 | 2 | 2 | 10 |
| 2004-05 | USNTDP | U-18 | 45 | 5 | 10 | 15 | 91 | .... | .... | .... | .... | .... |
| | USNTDP | NAHL | 16 | 2 | 6 | 8 | 32 | .... | .... | .... | .... | .... |
| 2005-06 | U. of Michigan | CCHA | 39 | 0 | 10 | 10 | 59 | .... | .... | .... | .... | .... |
| 2006-07 | U. of Michigan | CCHA | 41 | 1 | 17 | 18 | 52 | .... | .... | .... | .... | .... |
| 2007-08 | U. of Michigan | CCHA | 43 | 2 | 21 | 23 | 60 | .... | .... | .... | .... | .... |
| 2008-09 | U. of Michigan | CCHA | 8 | 1 | 2 | 3 | 4 | .... | .... | .... | .... | .... |
| | Iowa Chops | AHL | 5 | 0 | 2 | 2 | 2 | .... | .... | .... | .... | .... |

CCHA Second All-Star Team (2008)

**MONAST, Guillaume** (moh-NAST, GEE-OHM) **DAL.**

Defense. Shoots right. 6'2", 201 lbs. Born, Longueuil, Que., May 12, 1988.

| | | | Regular Season | | | | | Playoffs | | | | |
|---|---|---|---|---|---|---|---|---|---|---|---|---|
| **Season** | **Club** | **League** | **GP** | **G** | **A** | **Pts** | **PIM** | **GP** | **G** | **A** | **Pts** | **PIM** |
| 2005-06 | Val-d'Or Foreurs | QMJHL | 65 | 2 | 7 | 9 | 54 | 5 | 0 | 0 | 0 | 0 |
| 2006-07 | Val-d'Or Foreurs | QMJHL | 35 | 0 | 4 | 4 | 31 | .... | .... | .... | .... | .... |
| | Halifax | QMJHL | 32 | 3 | 11 | 14 | 28 | 12 | 2 | 7 | 9 | 6 |
| 2007-08 | Halifax | QMJHL | 65 | 8 | 22 | 30 | 68 | 15 | 2 | 4 | 6 | 22 |
| 2008-09 | Quebec Remparts | QMJHL | 63 | 5 | 38 | 43 | 59 | 17 | 3 | 7 | 10 | 22 |

Signed as a free agent by **Dallas**, September 25, 2008.

**MONTGOMERY, Kevin** (mawnt-GUHM-uhr-ee, KEH-vihn) **COL.**

Defense. Shoots left. 6'1", 185 lbs. Born, Rochester, NY, April 4, 1988.
(Colorado's 5th choice, 110th overall, in 2006 Entry Draft).

| | | | Regular Season | | | | | Playoffs | | | | |
|---|---|---|---|---|---|---|---|---|---|---|---|---|
| **Season** | **Club** | **League** | **GP** | **G** | **A** | **Pts** | **PIM** | **GP** | **G** | **A** | **Pts** | **PIM** |
| 2003-04 | Syracuse Jr. Stars | EmJHL | 62 | 7 | 28 | 35 | .... | .... | .... | .... | .... | .... |
| 2004-05 | USNTDP | U-17 | 8 | 1 | 4 | 5 | 4 | .... | .... | .... | .... | .... |
| | USNTDP | NAHL | 38 | 4 | 12 | 16 | 46 | 9 | 1 | 3 | 4 | 6 |
| 2005-06 | USNTDP | U-18 | 42 | 2 | 10 | 12 | 61 | .... | .... | .... | .... | .... |
| | USNTDP | NAHL | 17 | 4 | 6 | 10 | 15 | .... | .... | .... | .... | .... |
| 2006-07 | Ohio State | CCHA | 17 | 1 | 4 | 5 | 18 | .... | .... | .... | .... | .... |
| | London Knights | OHL | 31 | 1 | 16 | 17 | 50 | 9 | 0 | 0 | 0 | 6 |
| 2007-08 | London Knights | OHL | 63 | 9 | 34 | 43 | 95 | 5 | 0 | 1 | 1 | 4 |
| | Lake Erie Monsters | AHL | 5 | 0 | 0 | 0 | 2 | .... | .... | .... | .... | .... |
| 2008-09 | London Knights | OHL | 46 | 2 | 34 | 36 | 41 | 14 | 0 | 4 | 4 | 6 |
| | Lake Erie Monsters | AHL | 5 | 0 | 1 | 1 | 2 | .... | .... | .... | .... | .... |

**MOON, Nathan** (MOON, NAY-thun) **PIT.**

Center. Shoots right. 5'11", 179 lbs. Born, Belleville, Ont., January 4, 1990.
(Pittsburgh's 1st choice, 120th overall, in 2008 Entry Draft).

| | | | Regular Season | | | | | Playoffs | | | | |
|---|---|---|---|---|---|---|---|---|---|---|---|---|
| **Season** | **Club** | **League** | **GP** | **G** | **A** | **Pts** | **PIM** | **GP** | **G** | **A** | **Pts** | **PIM** |
| 2006-07 | Kingston | OHL | 56 | 13 | 27 | 40 | 39 | 5 | 2 | 0 | 2 | 0 |
| 2007-08 | Kingston | OHL | 68 | 35 | 42 | 77 | 79 | .... | .... | .... | .... | .... |
| 2008-09 | Kingston | OHL | 62 | 32 | 40 | 72 | 81 | .... | .... | .... | .... | .... |

### MOORE, John (MOOR, JAWN) CBJ

Defense. Shoots left. 6'2", 189 lbs. Born, Winnetka, IL, November 19, 1990.
(Columbus' 1st choice, 21st overall, in 2009 Entry Draft).

| | | | Regular Season | | | | | Playoffs | | | | |
|---|---|---|---|---|---|---|---|---|---|---|---|---|
| Season | Club | League | GP | G | A | Pts | PIM | GP | G | A | Pts | PIM |
| 2006-07 | Chicago Mission | MWEHL | 31 | 1 | 12 | 13 | 26 | .... | .... | .... | .... | .... |
| | Chicago Mission | Exhib. | 30 | 13 | 37 | 50 | 14 | .... | .... | .... | .... | .... |
| 2007-08 | Chicago Steel | USHL | 56 | 4 | 11 | 15 | 26 | 7 | 0 | 2 | 2 | 2 |
| 2008-09 | Chicago Steel | USHL | 57 | 14 | 25 | 39 | 50 | .... | .... | .... | .... | .... |

USHL First All-Star Team (2009) • USHL Defenseman of the Year (2009)

### MOORE, Mike (MOOR, MIGHK) S.J.

Defense. Shoots left. 6'1", 200 lbs. Born, Calgary, Alta., December 12, 1984.

| | | | Regular Season | | | | | Playoffs | | | | |
|---|---|---|---|---|---|---|---|---|---|---|---|---|
| Season | Club | League | GP | G | A | Pts | PIM | GP | G | A | Pts | PIM |
| 2003-04 | South Surrey | BCHL | 52 | 6 | 21 | 27 | 148 | 10 | 0 | 2 | 2 | 6 |
| 2004-05 | Princeton | ECAC | 25 | 3 | 7 | 10 | 22 | .... | .... | .... | .... | .... |
| 2005-06 | Princeton | ECAC | 30 | 0 | 4 | 4 | 42 | .... | .... | .... | .... | .... |
| 2006-07 | Princeton | ECAC | 32 | 4 | 10 | 14 | 50 | .... | .... | .... | .... | .... |
| 2007-08 | Princeton | ECAC | 34 | 7 | 17 | 24 | 40 | .... | .... | .... | .... | .... |
| | Worcester Sharks | AHL | 3 | 0 | 0 | 0 | 16 | .... | .... | .... | .... | .... |
| 2008-09 | Worcester Sharks | AHL | 76 | 5 | 13 | 18 | 132 | 12 | 0 | 1 | 1 | 17 |

ECAC First All-Star Team (2008) • NCAA East First All-American Team (2008)

Signed as a free agent by **San Jose**, April 8, 2008.

### MORIN, Jeremy (moh-REHN, JAIR-eh-mee) ATL.

Left wing. Shoots right. 6'1", 189 lbs. Born, Auburn, NY, April 16, 1991.
(Atlanta's 3rd choice, 45th overall, in 2009 Entry Draft).

| | | | Regular Season | | | | | Playoffs | | | | |
|---|---|---|---|---|---|---|---|---|---|---|---|---|
| Season | Club | League | GP | G | A | Pts | PIM | GP | G | A | Pts | PIM |
| 2006-07 | Syracuse Stars | EJHL | 45 | 26 | 28 | 54 | 80 | .... | .... | .... | .... | .... |
| 2007-08 | USNTDP | NAHL | 30 | 17 | 17 | 34 | 26 | .... | .... | .... | .... | .... |
| | USNTDP | U-17 | 7 | 11 | 1 | 12 | 4 | .... | .... | .... | .... | .... |
| | USNTDP | U-18 | 28 | 20 | 14 | 34 | 36 | .... | .... | .... | .... | .... |
| 2008-09 | USNTDP | NAHL | 14 | 12 | 15 | 27 | 28 | .... | .... | .... | .... | .... |
| | USNTDP | U-18 | 41 | 21 | 11 | 32 | 79 | .... | .... | .... | .... | .... |

### MORNEAU, Samuel (mohr-NOH, SAM-ew-l) CAR.

Left wing. Shoots left. 5'11", 190 lbs. Born, Cowansville, Que., February 10, 1990.
(Carolina's 5th choice, 195th overall, in 2008 Entry Draft).

| | | | Regular Season | | | | | Playoffs | | | | |
|---|---|---|---|---|---|---|---|---|---|---|---|---|
| Season | Club | League | GP | G | A | Pts | PIM | GP | G | A | Pts | PIM |
| 2006-07 | Acadie-Bathurst | QMJHL | 51 | 6 | 10 | 16 | 34 | 10 | 1 | 0 | 1 | 0 |
| 2007-08 | Baie-Comeau | QMJHL | 68 | 23 | 19 | 42 | 54 | 5 | 0 | 1 | 1 | 8 |
| 2008-09 | Val-d'Or Foreurs | QMJHL | 64 | 25 | 29 | 54 | 81 | .... | .... | .... | .... | .... |

### MORRIS, Mike (MOHR-his, MIGHK)

Right wing. Shoots right. 6'1", 185 lbs. Born, Dorchester, MA, July 14, 1983.
(San Jose's 1st choice, 27th overall, in 2002 Entry Draft).

| | | | Regular Season | | | | | Playoffs | | | | |
|---|---|---|---|---|---|---|---|---|---|---|---|---|
| Season | Club | League | GP | G | A | Pts | PIM | GP | G | A | Pts | PIM |
| 2000-01 | St. Sebastian's | High-MA | 28 | 20 | 28 | 48 | 18 | .... | .... | .... | .... | .... |
| 2001-02 | St. Sebastian's | High-MA | 31 | 29 | 29 | 58 | 26 | .... | .... | .... | .... | .... |
| 2002-03 | Northeastern | H-East | 26 | 9 | 12 | 21 | 16 | .... | .... | .... | .... | .... |
| 2003-04 | Northeastern | H-East | 34 | 10 | 20 | 30 | 14 | .... | .... | .... | .... | .... |
| 2004-05 | Northeastern | H-East | 34 | 19 | 20 | 39 | 22 | .... | .... | .... | .... | .... |
| 2005-06 | Northeastern | H-East | DID NOT PLAY – INJURED | | | | | | | | | |
| 2006-07 | Northeastern | H-East | 20 | 7 | 11 | 18 | 22 | .... | .... | .... | .... | .... |
| 2007-08 | Worcester Sharks | AHL | 9 | 1 | 1 | 2 | 2 | .... | .... | .... | .... | .... |
| 2008-09 | Worcester Sharks | AHL | 17 | 5 | 6 | 11 | 6 | .... | .... | .... | .... | .... |

Hockey East Second All-Star Team (2005)

• Missed entire 2005-06 season with post-concussion syndrome. • Missed majority of 2007-08 season recovering from a sports hernia injury. • Missed remainder of 2008-09 season recovering from head injury suffered in game vs. San Antonio (AHL), November 23, 2008

### MOTIN, Johan (MOH-tihn, YOH-han) EDM.

Defense. Shoots right. 6'1", 202 lbs. Born, Karlskoga, Sweden, October 10, 1989.
(Edmonton's 2nd choice, 103rd overall, in 2008 Entry Draft).

| | | | Regular Season | | | | | Playoffs | | | | |
|---|---|---|---|---|---|---|---|---|---|---|---|---|
| Season | Club | League | GP | G | A | Pts | PIM | GP | G | A | Pts | PIM |
| 2005-06 | Farjestad U18 | Swe-U18 | 14 | 0 | 7 | 7 | 6 | 8 | 0 | 2 | 2 | 8 |
| 2006-07 | Farjestad U18 | Swe-U18 | 1 | 0 | 0 | 0 | 0 | 1 | 1 | 1 | 2 | 0 |
| | Skare BK Karlstad | Sweden-3 | 18 | 0 | 4 | 4 | 30 | .... | .... | .... | .... | .... |
| | Farjestad | Sweden | 22 | 0 | 4 | 4 | 8 | 9 | 0 | 0 | 0 | 2 |
| 2007-08 | Farjestad | Sweden | 28 | 0 | 2 | 2 | 10 | .... | .... | .... | .... | .... |
| | Bofors | Sweden-2 | 15 | 2 | 3 | 5 | 18 | .... | .... | .... | .... | .... |
| | Skare BK | Sweden-3 | 3 | 0 | 2 | 2 | 2 | .... | .... | .... | .... | .... |
| 2008-09 | Skare BK Karlstad | Sweden-3 | 8 | 0 | 3 | 3 | 8 | .... | .... | .... | .... | .... |
| | Farjestad | Sweden | 52 | 0 | 3 | 3 | 28 | 13 | 0 | 1 | 1 | 6 |

### MOZYAKIN, Sergei (mohz-YA-kihn, SAIR-gay) CBJ

Left wing. Shoots right. 5'10", 171 lbs. Born, Yaroslavl, USSR, March 30, 1981.
(Columbus' 13th choice, 263rd overall, in 2002 Entry Draft).

| | | | Regular Season | | | | | Playoffs | | | | |
|---|---|---|---|---|---|---|---|---|---|---|---|---|
| Season | Club | League | GP | G | A | Pts | PIM | GP | G | A | Pts | PIM |
| 1998-99 | Val-d'Or Foreurs | QMJHL | 4 | 0 | 1 | 1 | 2 | .... | .... | .... | .... | .... |
| 99-2000 | HK Moscow 2 | Russia-3 | 6 | 9 | 3 | 12 | 6 | .... | .... | .... | .... | .... |
| | HK Moscow | Russia-2 | 44 | 23 | 25 | 48 | 10 | .... | .... | .... | .... | .... |
| 2000-01 | HK Moscow | Russia-2 | 37 | 22 | 28 | 50 | 18 | .... | .... | .... | .... | .... |
| | CSKA Moscow | Russia | 9 | 0 | 2 | 2 | 0 | .... | .... | .... | .... | .... |
| 2001-02 | HK CSKA Moscow | Russia-2 | 54 | 34 | 30 | 64 | 10 | 12 | 9 | 12 | 21 | 4 |
| 2002-03 | CSKA Moscow | Russia | 33 | 12 | 15 | 27 | 18 | .... | .... | .... | .... | .... |
| 2003-04 | CSKA Moscow | Russia | 45 | 21 | 19 | 40 | 6 | .... | .... | .... | .... | .... |
| 2004-05 | CSKA Moscow | Russia | 49 | 11 | 12 | 23 | 22 | .... | .... | .... | .... | .... |
| 2005-06 | CSKA Moscow | Russia | 51 | 20 | *31 | *51 | 28 | 7 | 1 | 2 | 3 | 4 |
| 2006-07 | Mytischi | Russia | 54 | 27 | 33 | 60 | 10 | 9 | 5 | 3 | 8 | 4 |
| 2007-08 | Mytischi | Russia | 57 | *37 | 29 | *66 | 22 | 5 | 3 | 1 | 4 | 0 |
| 2008-09 | Mytischi | Rus-KHL | 56 | 36 | *42 | *78 | 14 | 7 | 2 | 5 | 7 | 0 |

### MULLEN, Patrick (MUHL-uhn, PA-trihk) L.A.

Defense. Shoots right. 5'10", 180 lbs. Born, Pittsburgh, PA, May 6, 1986.

| | | | Regular Season | | | | | Playoffs | | | | |
|---|---|---|---|---|---|---|---|---|---|---|---|---|
| Season | Club | League | GP | G | A | Pts | PIM | GP | G | A | Pts | PIM |
| 2004-05 | Sioux City | USHL | 60 | 14 | 23 | 37 | 8 | .... | .... | .... | .... | .... |
| 2005-06 | U. of Denver | WCHA | 37 | 7 | 10 | 17 | 24 | .... | .... | .... | .... | .... |
| | U. of Denver | WCHA | 37 | 7 | 10 | 17 | 24 | .... | .... | .... | .... | .... |
| 2006-07 | U. of Denver | WCHA | 37 | 5 | 12 | 17 | 20 | .... | .... | .... | .... | .... |
| 2007-08 | U. of Denver | WCHA | 40 | 4 | 18 | 22 | 65 | .... | .... | .... | .... | .... |
| 2008-09 | U. of Denver | WCHA | 38 | 4 | 21 | 25 | 39 | .... | .... | .... | .... | .... |

Signed as a free agent by **Los Angeles**, April 3, 2009.

### MURATOV, Yevgeny (muhr-A-tahf, yehv-GEH-nee) EDM.

Left wing. Shoots right. 5'10", 178 lbs. Born, Nizhny Tagil, USSR, January 28, 1981.
(Edmonton's 10th choice, 274th overall, in 2000 Entry Draft).

| | | | Regular Season | | | | | Playoffs | | | | |
|---|---|---|---|---|---|---|---|---|---|---|---|---|
| Season | Club | League | GP | G | A | Pts | PIM | GP | G | A | Pts | PIM |
| 1997-98 | Nizhnekamsk 2 | Russia-3 | 39 | 7 | 7 | 14 | 2 | .... | .... | .... | .... | .... |
| 1998-99 | Nizhnekamsk 2 | Russia-4 | 37 | 26 | 9 | 35 | 32 | .... | .... | .... | .... | .... |
| | Nizhnekamsk | Russia | 4 | 0 | 0 | 0 | 0 | 3 | 1 | 0 | 1 | 2 |
| 99-2000 | Nizhnekamsk | Russia | 29 | 9 | 7 | 16 | 2 | .... | .... | .... | .... | .... |
| | Ak Bars Kazan | Russia | 8 | 2 | 2 | 4 | 2 | 9 | 0 | 0 | 0 | 2 |
| 2000-01 | Nizhnekamsk | Russia | 42 | 9 | 8 | 17 | 14 | 4 | 0 | 0 | 0 | 0 |
| 2001-02 | Nizhnekamsk | Russia | 45 | 5 | 13 | 18 | 4 | .... | .... | .... | .... | .... |
| 2002-03 | Nizhnekamsk | Russia | 51 | 10 | 11 | 21 | 41 | .... | .... | .... | .... | .... |
| 2003-04 | Nizhnekamsk | Russia | 20 | 1 | 6 | 7 | 8 | .... | .... | .... | .... | .... |
| 2004-05 | Novokuznetsk | Russia | 58 | 15 | 13 | 28 | 12 | 4 | 1 | 2 | 3 | 0 |
| 2005-06 | SKA St. Petersburg | Russia | 49 | 13 | 10 | 23 | 16 | 3 | 0 | 1 | 1 | 0 |
| 2006-07 | SKA St. Petersburg | Russia | 42 | 5 | 9 | 14 | 14 | 1 | 0 | 0 | 0 | 0 |
| | St. Petersburg 2 | Russia-3 | 5 | 5 | 5 | 10 | 2 | .... | .... | .... | .... | .... |
| 2007-08 | Nizhnekamsk | Russia | 22 | 2 | 5 | 7 | 8 | .... | .... | .... | .... | .... |
| | Sibir Novosibirsk | Russia | 30 | 3 | 2 | 5 | 6 | .... | .... | .... | .... | .... |
| 2008-09 | Sibir Novosibirsk | Rus-KHL | 47 | 10 | 13 | 23 | 10 | .... | .... | .... | .... | .... |

Signed as a free agent by **Nizhnekamsk** (Russia), August 5, 2007.

### MURPHY, Colin (MUHR-fee, KOHL-ihn)

Left wing. Shoots left. 6', 195 lbs. Born, Fort McMurray, Alta., April 11, 1980.

| | | | Regular Season | | | | | Playoffs | | | | |
|---|---|---|---|---|---|---|---|---|---|---|---|---|
| Season | Club | League | GP | G | A | Pts | PIM | GP | G | A | Pts | PIM |
| 2001-02 | Michigan Tech | WCHA | 38 | 8 | 19 | 27 | 40 | .... | .... | .... | .... | .... |
| 2002-03 | Michigan Tech | WCHA | 37 | 20 | 20 | 40 | 42 | .... | .... | .... | .... | .... |
| 2003-04 | Michigan Tech | WCHA | 33 | 15 | 17 | 32 | 28 | .... | .... | .... | .... | .... |
| 2004-05 | Michigan Tech | WCHA | 37 | 11 | *42 | 53 | 40 | .... | .... | .... | .... | .... |
| | St. John's | AHL | 12 | 1 | 7 | 8 | 34 | 5 | 1 | 3 | 4 | 17 |
| 2005-06 | Toronto Marlies | AHL | 53 | 16 | 17 | 33 | 44 | 4 | 0 | 0 | 0 | 0 |
| 2006-07 | Toronto Marlies | AHL | 73 | 20 | 36 | 56 | 126 | .... | .... | .... | .... | .... |
| 2007-08 | Toronto Marlies | AHL | 68 | 11 | 27 | 38 | 152 | 11 | 2 | 3 | 5 | 34 |
| 2008-09 | Portland Pirates | AHL | 50 | 13 | 17 | 30 | 50 | 5 | 0 | 0 | 0 | 4 |

WCHA First All-Star Team (2005) • NCAA West Second All-American Team (2005)

Signed as a free agent by **Toronto**, March 18, 2005. Signed as a free agent by **Buffalo**, August 4, 2008.

### MURSAK , Jan (MUHR-sak, YAHN) DET.

Left wing. Shoots right. 5'11", 167 lbs. Born, Maribor, Yugoslavia, January 20, 1988.
(Detroit's 5th choice, 182nd overall, in 2006 Entry Draft).

| | | | Regular Season | | | | | Playoffs | | | | |
|---|---|---|---|---|---|---|---|---|---|---|---|---|
| Season | Club | League | GP | G | A | Pts | PIM | GP | G | A | Pts | PIM |
| 2002-03 | HK Maribor U18 | Sloven-U18 | 13 | 27 | 18 | 45 | 14 | .... | .... | .... | .... | .... |
| 2003-04 | HK Maribor U18 | Sloven-U18 | 22 | 27 | 17 | 44 | 14 | .... | .... | .... | .... | .... |
| | HK Maribor Jr. | Sloven-Jr. | 19 | 8 | 8 | 16 | 37 | .... | .... | .... | .... | .... |
| | HK Maribor | Slovenia | 14 | 3 | 3 | 6 | 16 | .... | .... | .... | .... | .... |
| 2004-05 | HK Maribor Jr. | Sloven-Jr. | 19 | 17 | 16 | 33 | 39 | .... | .... | .... | .... | .... |
| | HK Maribor | Slovenia | 24 | 16 | 29 | 45 | 10 | .... | .... | .... | .... | .... |
| 2005-06 | C. Budejovice Jr. | CzRep-Jr. | 43 | 15 | 15 | 30 | 32 | 5 | 0 | 2 | 2 | 2 |
| 2006-07 | Saginaw Spirit | OHL | 62 | 27 | 53 | 80 | 50 | 6 | 1 | 2 | 3 | 10 |
| | Grand Rapids | AHL | .... | .... | .... | .... | .... | 7 | 0 | 2 | 2 | 2 |
| 2007-08 | Saginaw Spirit | OHL | 26 | 6 | 20 | 26 | 15 | .... | .... | .... | .... | .... |
| | Belleville Bulls | OHL | 31 | 11 | 27 | 38 | 8 | 21 | 9 | 15 | 24 | 10 |
| 2008-09 | Grand Rapids | AHL | 51 | 2 | 7 | 9 | 25 | 6 | 0 | 1 | 1 | 0 |

### MYERS, Tyler (MIGH-uhrz, TIGH-luhr) BUF.

Defense. Shoots right. 6'7", 204 lbs. Born, Houston, TX, February 1, 1990.
(Buffalo's 1st choice, 12th overall, in 2008 Entry Draft).

| | | | Regular Season | | | | | Playoffs | | | | |
|---|---|---|---|---|---|---|---|---|---|---|---|---|
| Season | Club | League | GP | G | A | Pts | PIM | GP | G | A | Pts | PIM |
| 2005-06 | Notre Dame | SMHL | 34 | 4 | 6 | 10 | 78 | .... | .... | .... | .... | .... |
| | Kelowna Rockets | WHL | 9 | 0 | 1 | 1 | 2 | 8 | 1 | 0 | 1 | 2 |
| 2006-07 | Kelowna Rockets | WHL | 59 | 2 | 13 | 15 | 78 | .... | .... | .... | .... | .... |
| 2007-08 | Kelowna Rockets | WHL | 65 | 6 | 13 | 19 | 97 | 7 | 1 | 2 | 3 | 12 |
| 2008-09 | Kelowna Rockets | WHL | 58 | 9 | 33 | 42 | 105 | 22 | 5 | 15 | 20 | 29 |

WHL West Second All-Star Team (2009)

### NAGY, Kory (NAH-gee, KOHR-ee) N.J.

Left wing. Shoots left. 5'11", 195 lbs. Born, London, Ont., October 12, 1989.
(New Jersey's 6th choice, 142nd overall, in 2008 Entry Draft).

| | | | Regular Season | | | | | Playoffs | | | | |
|---|---|---|---|---|---|---|---|---|---|---|---|---|
| Season | Club | League | GP | G | A | Pts | PIM | GP | G | A | Pts | PIM |
| 2005-06 | Lindsay Muskies | OPJHL | 47 | 11 | 12 | 23 | 14 | 4 | 0 | 0 | 0 | 0 |
| | Oshawa Generals | OHL | 16 | 0 | 1 | 1 | 8 | .... | .... | .... | .... | .... |
| 2006-07 | Oshawa Generals | OHL | 64 | 0 | 5 | 5 | 18 | 9 | 0 | 0 | 0 | 4 |
| 2007-08 | Oshawa Generals | OHL | 57 | 5 | 12 | 17 | 47 | 15 | 6 | 3 | 9 | 4 |
| 2008-09 | Oshawa Generals | OHL | 63 | 17 | 38 | 55 | 83 | .... | .... | .... | .... | .... |

### NASH, Riley (NASH, RIGH-lee) EDM.

Center. Shoots right. 6'1", 175 lbs. Born, Consort, Alta., May 9, 1989.
(Edmonton's 3rd choice, 21st overall, in 2007 Entry Draft).

| | | | Regular Season | | | | | Playoffs | | | | |
|---|---|---|---|---|---|---|---|---|---|---|---|---|
| Season | Club | League | GP | G | A | Pts | PIM | GP | G | A | Pts | PIM |
| 2005-06 | Thompson Blazers | Minor-BC | 31 | 29 | 31 | 60 | 100 | .... | .... | .... | .... | .... |
| | Salmon Arm | BCHL | 1 | 0 | 0 | 0 | 0 | 5 | 1 | 2 | 3 | 0 |
| 2006-07 | Salmon Arm | BCHL | 55 | 38 | 46 | 84 | 87 | 11 | 4 | 7 | 11 | 31 |
| 2007-08 | Cornell Big Red | ECAC | 36 | 12 | 20 | 32 | 28 | .... | .... | .... | .... | .... |
| 2008-09 | Cornell Big Red | ECAC | 36 | 13 | 22 | 35 | 34 | .... | .... | .... | .... | .... |

ECAC All-Rookie Team (2008) • ECAC Rookie of the Year (2008) • ECAC First All-Star Team (2009)

**NASLUND, Fredrik** (NAZ-luhnd, FREHD-rihk) **DAL.**

Left wing. Shoots right. 6'4", 211 lbs. Born, Stockholm, Sweden, February 11, 1986.
(Dallas' 6th choice, 104th overall, in 2004 Entry Draft).

| | | | Regular Season | | | | | Playoffs | | | | |
|---|---|---|---|---|---|---|---|---|---|---|---|---|
| Season | Club | League | GP | G | A | Pts | PIM | GP | G | A | Pts | PIM |
| 2002-03 | Vasteras Jr. | Swe-Jr. | 34 | 12 | 9 | 21 | 8 | .... | .... | .... | .... | .... |
| 2003-04 | Vasteras Jr. | Swe-Jr. | 17 | 13 | 15 | 28 | 6 | 3 | 0 | 1 | 1 | 4 |
| | Vasteras | Sweden-2 | 32 | 2 | 4 | 6 | 0 | .... | .... | .... | .... | .... |
| 2004-05 | Vasteras | Sweden-2 | 3 | 0 | 0 | 0 | 0 | .... | .... | .... | .... | .... |
| | Vasteras Jr. | Swe-Jr. | 21 | 7 | 7 | 14 | 2 | .... | .... | .... | .... | .... |
| 2005-06 | Peterborough | OHL | 66 | 9 | 21 | 30 | 30 | 19 | 6 | 5 | 11 | 6 |
| 2006-07 | Nykoping | Sweden-2 | 45 | 13 | 13 | 26 | 38 | 5 | 2 | 2 | 4 | 4 |
| 2007-08 | Nybro Vikings IF | Sweden-2 | 33 | 7 | 12 | 19 | 14 | .... | .... | .... | .... | .... |
| 2008-09 | Nybro Vikings IF | Sweden-2 | STATISTICS NOT AVAILABLE | | | | | | | | | |

**NATTINEN, Joonas** (NA-tih-nuhn, YOH-nuhs) **MTL.**

Center. Shoots right. 6'2", 187 lbs. Born, Jamsa, Finland, January 3, 1991.
(Montreal's 2nd choice, 65th overall, in 2009 Entry Draft).

| | | | Regular Season | | | | | Playoffs | | | | |
|---|---|---|---|---|---|---|---|---|---|---|---|---|
| Season | Club | League | GP | G | A | Pts | PIM | GP | G | A | Pts | PIM |
| 2006-07 | JyP Jyvaskyla U18 | Fin-U18 | 30 | 10 | 25 | 35 | 22 | 8 | 5 | 7 | 12 | 0 |
| 2007-08 | JyP Jyvaskyla U18 | Fin-U18 | 34 | 14 | 34 | 48 | 22 | 2 | 0 | 0 | 0 | 0 |
| | JyP Jyvaskyla Jr. | Fin-Jr. | 8 | 0 | 2 | 2 | 2 | 3 | 0 | 2 | 2 | 2 |
| 2008-09 | Suomi U20 | Finland-2 | 5 | 2 | 2 | 4 | 0 | .... | .... | .... | .... | .... |
| | Blues Espoo Jr. | Fin-Jr. | 30 | 9 | 29 | 38 | 6 | 10 | 3 | 10 | 13 | 4 |
| | Blues Espoo | Finland | 14 | 0 | 0 | 0 | 4 | .... | .... | .... | .... | .... |

**NEAL, Michael** (NEEL, MIGH-kuhl) **DAL.**

Left wing. Shoots left. 6'2", 188 lbs. Born, Whitby, Ont., April 3, 1989.
(Dallas' 7th choice, 149th overall, in 2007 Entry Draft).

| | | | Regular Season | | | | | Playoffs | | | | |
|---|---|---|---|---|---|---|---|---|---|---|---|---|
| Season | Club | League | GP | G | A | Pts | PIM | GP | G | A | Pts | PIM |
| 2004-05 | Whitby Wildcats | Minor-ON | 52 | 20 | 29 | 49 | 67 | .... | .... | .... | .... | .... |
| 2005-06 | Belleville Bulls | OHL | 46 | 1 | 3 | 4 | 6 | .... | .... | .... | .... | .... |
| 2006-07 | Belleville Bulls | OHL | 52 | 4 | 4 | 8 | 25 | 15 | 0 | 1 | 1 | 6 |
| 2007-08 | Belleville Bulls | OHL | .... | .... | .... | .... | .... | 7 | 0 | 0 | 0 | 2 |
| 2008-09 | Belleville Bulls | OHL | 3 | 0 | 0 | 0 | 0 | .... | .... | .... | .... | .... |
| | Sarnia Sting | OHL | 63 | 9 | 12 | 21 | 48 | 5 | 0 | 1 | 1 | 4 |

• Missed entire 2007-08 regular season recovering from knee injury.

**NELSON, Levi** (NELH-suhn, LEE-vigh) **BOS.**

Center. Shoots left. 5'11", 167 lbs. Born, Calgary, Alta., April 28, 1988.
(Boston's 6th choice, 158th overall, in 2006 Entry Draft).

| | | | Regular Season | | | | | Playoffs | | | | |
|---|---|---|---|---|---|---|---|---|---|---|---|---|
| Season | Club | League | GP | G | A | Pts | PIM | GP | G | A | Pts | PIM |
| 2004-05 | Cgy. North Stars | AMHL | 35 | 15 | 13 | 28 | 70 | .... | .... | .... | .... | .... |
| | Swift Current | WHL | 2 | 1 | 0 | 1 | 0 | .... | .... | .... | .... | .... |
| 2005-06 | Swift Current | WHL | 63 | 21 | 17 | 38 | 63 | 4 | 0 | 0 | 0 | 4 |
| 2006-07 | Swift Current | WHL | 66 | 18 | 34 | 52 | 125 | 6 | 4 | 3 | 7 | 4 |
| | Providence Bruins | AHL | 1 | 0 | 0 | 0 | 2 | 4 | 1 | 0 | 1 | 2 |
| 2007-08 | Swift Current | WHL | 67 | 25 | 36 | 61 | 152 | 12 | 7 | 8 | 15 | 16 |
| 2008-09 | Providence Bruins | AHL | 59 | 2 | 5 | 7 | 37 | 5 | 1 | 1 | 2 | 2 |
| | Reading Royals | ECHL | 8 | 2 | 1 | 3 | 28 | .... | .... | .... | .... | .... |

**NEMISZ, Greg** (NEH-mihtz, GREHG) **CGY.**

Center. Shoots right. 6'3", 195 lbs. Born, Courtice, Ont., June 5, 1990.
(Calgary's 1st choice, 25th overall, in 2008 Entry Draft).

| | | | Regular Season | | | | | Playoffs | | | | |
|---|---|---|---|---|---|---|---|---|---|---|---|---|
| Season | Club | League | GP | G | A | Pts | PIM | GP | G | A | Pts | PIM |
| 2005-06 | Clarington | Minor-ON | 32 | 29 | 24 | 53 | 24 | .... | .... | .... | .... | .... |
| 2006-07 | Windsor Spitfires | OHL | 62 | 11 | 23 | 34 | 23 | .... | .... | .... | .... | .... |
| 2007-08 | Windsor Spitfires | OHL | 68 | 34 | 33 | 67 | 52 | 5 | 2 | 1 | 3 | 8 |
| 2008-09 | Windsor Spitfires | OHL | 65 | 36 | 41 | 77 | 48 | 20 | 8 | 12 | 20 | 22 |

OHL Second All-Star Team (2009)

**NEPRYAYEV, Ivan** (neh-pree-YIGH-ehv, IGH-vuhn) **WSH.**

Center. Shoots left. 6'1", 180 lbs. Born, Yaroslavl, USSR, February 4, 1982.
(Washington's 5th choice, 163rd overall, in 2000 Entry Draft).

| | | | Regular Season | | | | | Playoffs | | | | |
|---|---|---|---|---|---|---|---|---|---|---|---|---|
| Season | Club | League | GP | G | A | Pts | PIM | GP | G | A | Pts | PIM |
| 1997-98 | Torpedo Yaroslavl | Russia | 6 | 0 | 0 | 0 | 0 | .... | .... | .... | .... | .... |
| 1998-99 | Yaroslavl 2 | Russia-3 | 15 | 1 | 0 | 1 | 0 | .... | .... | .... | .... | .... |
| 99-2000 | Yaroslavl 2 | Russia-3 | 40 | 8 | 14 | 22 | .... | .... | .... | .... | .... | .... |
| 2000-01 | Yaroslavl | Russia | 10 | 0 | 0 | 0 | 2 | .... | .... | .... | .... | .... |
| 2001-02 | Yaroslavl 2 | Russia-3 | 2 | 1 | 0 | 1 | 18 | .... | .... | .... | .... | .... |
| | Yaroslavl | Russia | 36 | 3 | 8 | 11 | 28 | .... | .... | .... | .... | .... |
| 2002-03 | Yaroslavl | Russia | 26 | 3 | 6 | 9 | 12 | 6 | 1 | 0 | 1 | 0 |
| 2003-04 | Yaroslavl 2 | Russia-3 | 13 | 5 | 10 | 15 | 12 | .... | .... | .... | .... | .... |
| 2004-05 | Yaroslavl | Russia | 56 | 10 | 10 | 20 | 73 | 9 | 1 | 0 | 1 | 16 |
| 2005-06 | Yaroslavl | Russia | 43 | 7 | 16 | 23 | 70 | 11 | 0 | 0 | 0 | 8 |
| | Russia | Olympics | 2 | 0 | 0 | 0 | 2 | .... | .... | .... | .... | .... |
| 2006-07 | Yaroslavl | Russia | 52 | 17 | 9 | 26 | 66 | 7 | 0 | 4 | 4 | 2 |
| 2007-08 | Yaroslavl | Russia | 56 | 9 | 17 | 26 | 84 | 15 | 3 | 6 | 9 | 41 |
| 2008-09 | Dynamo Moscow | Rus-KHL | 52 | 14 | 13 | 27 | 48 | 12 | 0 | 4 | 4 | 10 |

**NESBITT, Derek** (NEHZ-biht, DAIR-ihk)

Right wing. Shoots left. 6', 185 lbs. Born, Egmondville, Ont., April 16, 1982.

| | | | Regular Season | | | | | Playoffs | | | | |
|---|---|---|---|---|---|---|---|---|---|---|---|---|
| Season | Club | League | GP | G | A | Pts | PIM | GP | G | A | Pts | PIM |
| 2001-02 | Ferris State | CCHA | 36 | 9 | 11 | 20 | 16 | .... | .... | .... | .... | .... |
| 2002-03 | Ferris State | CCHA | 42 | 20 | 33 | 53 | 26 | .... | .... | .... | .... | .... |
| 2003-04 | Ferris State | CCHA | 38 | 11 | 17 | 28 | 36 | .... | .... | .... | .... | .... |
| 2004-05 | Ferris State | CCHA | 38 | 19 | 21 | 40 | 44 | .... | .... | .... | .... | .... |
| | Bossier-Shreve. | CHL | 7 | 0 | 5 | 5 | 0 | .... | .... | .... | .... | .... |
| 2005-06 | Gwinnett | ECHL | 71 | 26 | 43 | 69 | 6 | 17 | 6 | 7 | 13 | 8 |
| 2006-07 | Idaho Steelheads | ECHL | 66 | 30 | 51 | 81 | 32 | 22 | 6 | 12 | 18 | 8 |
| 2007-08 | Rockford IceHogs | AHL | 46 | 17 | 18 | 35 | 6 | 12 | 3 | 3 | 6 | 12 |
| | Gwinnett | ECHL | 26 | 11 | 28 | 39 | 4 | .... | .... | .... | .... | .... |
| 2008-09 | San Antonio | AHL | 49 | 6 | 9 | 15 | 6 | .... | .... | .... | .... | .... |
| | Manitoba Moose | AHL | 5 | 0 | 4 | 4 | 0 | 1 | 0 | 0 | 0 | 0 |

Signed as a free agent by **Phoenix**, July 2, 2008.

**NESS, Aaron** (NEHS, AIR-uhn) **NYI**

Defense. Shoots left. 5'10", 157 lbs. Born, Bemidji, MN, May 18, 1990.
(NY Islanders' 3rd choice, 40th overall, in 2008 Entry Draft).

| | | | Regular Season | | | | | Playoffs | | | | |
|---|---|---|---|---|---|---|---|---|---|---|---|---|
| Season | Club | League | GP | G | A | Pts | PIM | GP | G | A | Pts | PIM |
| 2005-06 | Roseau Rams | High-MN | 30 | 3 | 18 | 21 | 8 | .... | .... | .... | .... | .... |
| 2006-07 | Roseau Rams | High-MN | 31 | 13 | 38 | 51 | 12 | .... | .... | .... | .... | .... |
| | Team Great Plains | UMWEHL | 11 | 0 | 8 | 8 | .... | .... | .... | .... | .... | .... |
| 2007-08 | Roseau Rams | High-MN | 31 | 28 | 44 | 72 | 16 | .... | .... | .... | .... | .... |
| | Great Plains | UMWEHL | 11 | 2 | 11 | 13 | .... | .... | .... | .... | .... | .... |
| 2008-09 | U. of Minnesota | WCHA | 37 | 2 | 15 | 17 | 16 | .... | .... | .... | .... | .... |

**NESTRASIL, Andrej** (NEHS-tra-shihl, ahn-DRAY) **DET.**

Right wing. Shoots left. 6'2", 200 lbs. Born, Prague, Czechoslovakia, February 22, 1991.
(Detroit's 3rd choice, 75th overall, in 2009 Entry Draft).

| | | | Regular Season | | | | | Playoffs | | | | |
|---|---|---|---|---|---|---|---|---|---|---|---|---|
| Season | Club | League | GP | G | A | Pts | PIM | GP | G | A | Pts | PIM |
| 2004-05 | Slavia U17 | CzR-U17 | 3 | 0 | 1 | 1 | 2 | .... | .... | .... | .... | .... |
| 2005-06 | Slavia U17 | CzR-U17 | 41 | 6 | 12 | 18 | 18 | .... | .... | .... | .... | .... |
| 2006-07 | Slavia U17 | CzR-U17 | 43 | 24 | 37 | 61 | 75 | 5 | 2 | 2 | 4 | 6 |
| 2007-08 | Slavia U17 | CzR-U17 | .... | .... | .... | .... | .... | 2 | 1 | 0 | 1 | 2 |
| | HC Slavia Praha Jr. | CzRep-Jr. | 40 | 12 | 16 | 28 | 58 | 5 | 1 | 2 | 3 | 4 |
| 2008-09 | Victoriaville Tigres | QMJHL | 66 | 22 | 35 | 57 | 67 | 4 | 2 | 1 | 3 | 10 |

**NEUBER, Kyle** (NEW-buhr, KIGHL) **CBJ**

Right wing. Shoots right. 6'2", 225 lbs. Born, London, Ont., March 22, 1989.
(Columbus' 6th choice, 197th overall, in 2009 Entry Draft).

| | | | Regular Season | | | | | Playoffs | | | | |
|---|---|---|---|---|---|---|---|---|---|---|---|---|
| Season | Club | League | GP | G | A | Pts | PIM | GP | G | A | Pts | PIM |
| 2006-07 | St. Michael's | OHL | 26 | 0 | 1 | 1 | 70 | .... | .... | .... | .... | .... |
| | St. Michael's | OPJHL | 4 | 2 | 0 | 2 | 12 | 15 | 0 | 3 | 3 | 39 |
| 2007-08 | St. Michael's | OHL | 54 | 4 | 4 | 8 | 133 | 4 | 0 | 0 | 0 | 8 |
| 2008-09 | St. Michael's | OHL | 59 | 9 | 3 | 12 | 135 | 10 | 0 | 0 | 0 | 25 |

**NICASTRO, Max** (nih-KAS-troh, MAX) **DET.**

Defense. Shoots right. 6'2", 189 lbs. Born, Thousand Oaks, CA, March 2, 1990.
(Detroit's 2nd choice, 91st overall, in 2008 Entry Draft).

| | | | Regular Season | | | | | Playoffs | | | | |
|---|---|---|---|---|---|---|---|---|---|---|---|---|
| Season | Club | League | GP | G | A | Pts | PIM | GP | G | A | Pts | PIM |
| 2006-07 | L.A. Jr. Kings | Minor-CA | 48 | 17 | 19 | 36 | 44 | .... | .... | .... | .... | .... |
| 2007-08 | Chicago Steel | USHL | 58 | 6 | 14 | 20 | 78 | 7 | 1 | 2 | 3 | 12 |
| 2008-09 | Chicago Steel | USHL | 57 | 9 | 22 | 31 | 84 | .... | .... | .... | .... | .... |

• Signed Letter of Intent to attend **Boston University** (Hockey East) in fall of 2009.

**NICKERSON, Matt** (NIH-kuhr-suhn, MAT) **EDM.**

Defense. Shoots right. 6'4", 230 lbs. Born, New London, CT, January 11, 1985.
(Dallas' 4th choice, 99th overall, in 2003 Entry Draft).

| | | | Regular Season | | | | | Playoffs | | | | |
|---|---|---|---|---|---|---|---|---|---|---|---|---|
| Season | Club | League | GP | G | A | Pts | PIM | GP | G | A | Pts | PIM |
| 2000-01 | Victoria Salsa | BCHL | .... | .... | .... | .... | 196 | .... | .... | .... | .... | .... |
| 2001-02 | Texas Tornado | NAHL | 47 | 1 | 12 | 13 | 97 | 6 | 0 | 0 | 0 | 6 |
| 2002-03 | Texas Tornado | NAHL | 47 | 6 | 23 | 29 | 277 | 6 | 0 | 1 | 1 | *18 |
| 2003-04 | Clarkson Knights | ECAC | 38 | 5 | 9 | 14 | *179 | .... | .... | .... | .... | .... |
| 2004-05 | Victoriaville Tigres | QMJHL | 48 | 1 | 11 | 12 | 182 | 6 | 0 | 1 | 1 | 27 |
| 2005-06 | Assat Pori | Finland | 36 | 5 | 8 | 13 | *236 | 14 | 1 | 0 | 1 | 50 |
| 2006-07 | Iowa Stars | AHL | 40 | 0 | 3 | 3 | 97 | .... | .... | .... | .... | .... |
| | Idaho Steelheads | ECHL | 13 | 1 | 1 | 2 | 73 | .... | .... | .... | .... | .... |
| 2007-08 | Assat Pori | Finland | 25 | 1 | 6 | 7 | 106 | .... | .... | .... | .... | .... |
| | Ilves Tampere | Finland | 13 | 3 | 3 | 6 | 39 | 9 | 0 | 2 | 2 | 24 |
| 2008-09 | Ilves Tampere | Finland | 40 | 1 | 1 | 2 | *156 | 3 | 1 | 0 | 1 | 0 |

Signed as a free agent by **HIFK Helsinki** (Finland), October 4, 2007. Signed as a free agent by **Edmonton**, July 13, 2009.

**NIEMI, Jyri** (nee-YEH-mee, YEW-ree) **NYI**

Defense. Shoots left. 6'2", 192 lbs. Born, Hameenkyro, Finland, June 15, 1990.
(NY Islanders' 6th choice, 72nd overall, in 2008 Entry Draft).

| | | | Regular Season | | | | | Playoffs | | | | |
|---|---|---|---|---|---|---|---|---|---|---|---|---|
| Season | Club | League | GP | G | A | Pts | PIM | GP | G | A | Pts | PIM |
| 2006-07 | HPK U18 | Fin-U18 | 1 | 0 | 1 | 1 | 4 | .... | .... | .... | .... | .... |
| | HPK Jr. | Fin-Jr. | 40 | 7 | 5 | 12 | 82 | .... | .... | .... | .... | .... |
| 2007-08 | Saskatoon Blades | WHL | 49 | 14 | 20 | 34 | 57 | .... | .... | .... | .... | .... |
| 2008-09 | Saskatoon Blades | WHL | 60 | 7 | 25 | 32 | 74 | 6 | 1 | 6 | 7 | 10 |

**NIGRO, Anthony** (NIGH-groh, AN-thuh-nee) **ST.L.**

Center. Shoots left. 6', 182 lbs. Born, Vaughan, Ont., January 11, 1990.
(St. Louis' 9th choice, 155th overall, in 2008 Entry Draft).

| | | | Regular Season | | | | | Playoffs | | | | |
|---|---|---|---|---|---|---|---|---|---|---|---|---|
| Season | Club | League | GP | G | A | Pts | PIM | GP | G | A | Pts | PIM |
| 2006-07 | Guelph Storm | OHL | 56 | 4 | 13 | 17 | 26 | 4 | 0 | 0 | 0 | 2 |
| 2007-08 | Guelph Storm | OHL | 67 | 24 | 24 | 48 | 65 | 10 | 2 | 3 | 5 | 7 |
| 2008-09 | Guelph Storm | OHL | 25 | 7 | 11 | 18 | 31 | .... | .... | .... | .... | .... |
| | Ottawa 67's | OHL | 42 | 23 | 28 | 51 | 28 | 7 | 4 | 4 | 8 | 4 |

**NIKITIN, Nikita** (nih-KEE-tihn, nih-KEE-tuh) **ST.L.**

Defense. Shoots left. 6'3", 178 lbs. Born, Omsk, USSR, June 16, 1986.
(St. Louis' 5th choice, 136th overall, in 2004 Entry Draft).

| | | | Regular Season | | | | | Playoffs | | | | |
|---|---|---|---|---|---|---|---|---|---|---|---|---|
| Season | Club | League | GP | G | A | Pts | PIM | GP | G | A | Pts | PIM |
| 2002-03 | Omsk 2 | Russia-3 | 34 | 3 | 7 | 10 | 4 | .... | .... | .... | .... | .... |
| 2003-04 | Omsk 2 | Russia-3 | 34 | 3 | 8 | 11 | 22 | .... | .... | .... | .... | .... |
| 2004-05 | Avangard Omsk | Russia | 12 | 0 | 0 | 0 | 2 | 3 | 0 | 0 | 0 | 0 |
| | Omsk 2 | Russia-3 | 31 | 3 | 8 | 11 | 20 | .... | .... | .... | .... | .... |
| 2005-06 | Avangard Omsk | Russia | 43 | 1 | 2 | 3 | 22 | 13 | 1 | 2 | 3 | 6 |
| | Omsk 2 | Russia-3 | 1 | 0 | 0 | 0 | 0 | .... | .... | .... | .... | .... |
| 2006-07 | Avangard Omsk | Russia | 54 | 1 | 15 | 16 | 99 | 9 | 0 | 4 | 4 | 35 |
| 2007-08 | Avangard Omsk | Russia | 57 | 3 | 11 | 14 | 48 | 4 | 0 | 1 | 1 | 2 |
| 2008-09 | Omsk | Rus-KHL | 53 | 4 | 11 | 15 | 28 | 9 | 1 | 2 | 3 | 8 |

## NIKULIN, Ilja (nih-KOO-lihn, IHL-yah) ATL.

Defense. Shoots left. 6'3", 211 lbs. Born, Moscow, USSR, March 12, 1982.
(Atlanta's 2nd choice, 31st overall, in 2000 Entry Draft).

| | | | Regular Season | | | | | Playoffs | | | | |
|---|---|---|---|---|---|---|---|---|---|---|---|---|
| Season | Club | League | GP | G | A | Pts | PIM | GP | G | A | Pts | PIM |
| 1998-99 | Dyn'o Moscow 2 | Russia-3 | 23 | 0 | 2 | 2 | 18 | .... | .... | .... | .... | .... |
| 99-2000 | Dyn'o Moscow 2 | Russia-3 | 4 | 2 | 1 | 3 | 10 | .... | .... | .... | .... | .... |
| | THK Tver | Russia-2 | 39 | 3 | 6 | 9 | 84 | .... | .... | .... | .... | .... |
| 2000-01 | Dynamo Moscow | Russia | 44 | 0 | 4 | 4 | 61 | .... | .... | .... | .... | .... |
| 2001-02 | Dyn'o Moscow 2 | Russia-3 | 2 | 0 | 1 | 1 | 2 | .... | .... | .... | .... | .... |
| | Dynamo Moscow | Russia | 47 | 2 | 1 | 3 | 44 | 3 | 0 | 0 | 0 | 0 |
| 2002-03 | Dynamo Moscow | Russia | 40 | 1 | 4 | 5 | 46 | 5 | 0 | 1 | 1 | 4 |
| 2003-04 | Dynamo Moscow | Russia | 54 | 1 | 5 | 6 | 56 | 3 | 0 | 0 | 0 | 2 |
| 2004-05 | Dynamo Moscow | Russia | 50 | 1 | 9 | 10 | 65 | 10 | 0 | 3 | 3 | 8 |
| 2005-06 | Ak Bars Kazan | Russia | 49 | 9 | 9 | 18 | 48 | 13 | 4 | 0 | 4 | 36 |
| 2006-07 | Ak Bars Kazan | Russia | 51 | 11 | 14 | 25 | 99 | 16 | 4 | 5 | 9 | 18 |
| 2007-08 | Ak Bars Kazan | Russia | 57 | 3 | 15 | 18 | 95 | 10 | 1 | 3 | 4 | 14 |
| 2008-09 | Ak Bars Kazan | Rus-KHL | 53 | 7 | 26 | 33 | 72 | 17 | 2 | 8 | 10 | 22 |

## NILL, Trevor (NIHL, TREH-vuhr) ST.L.

Center. Shoots right. 6'1", 194 lbs. Born, Detroit, MI, April 11, 1989.
(St. Louis' 10th choice, 190th overall, in 2007 Entry Draft).

| | | | Regular Season | | | | | Playoffs | | | | |
|---|---|---|---|---|---|---|---|---|---|---|---|---|
| Season | Club | League | GP | G | A | Pts | PIM | GP | G | A | Pts | PIM |
| 2004-05 | Det. Compuware | MWEHL | 25 | 10 | 8 | 18 | 8 | 4 | 2 | 1 | 3 | 0 |
| 2005-06 | Det. Compuware | MWEHL | 21 | 4 | 9 | 13 | 20 | 4 | 1 | 0 | 1 | 2 |
| 2006-07 | Det. Compuware | MWEHL | 24 | 6 | 10 | 16 | 23 | 6 | 2 | 4 | 6 | 2 |
| 2007-08 | Penticton Vees | BCHL | 53 | 5 | 6 | 11 | 16 | 11 | 0 | 2 | 2 | 0 |
| 2008-09 | Michigan State | CCHA | 34 | 1 | 2 | 3 | 6 | .... | .... | .... | .... | .... |

## NOLAN, Jordan (NOH-luhn, JOHR-dahn) L.A.

Center. Shoots left. 6'3", 216 lbs. Born, St. Catharines, Ont., June 23, 1989.
(Los Angeles' 9th choice, 186th overall, in 2009 Entry Draft).

| | | | Regular Season | | | | | Playoffs | | | | |
|---|---|---|---|---|---|---|---|---|---|---|---|---|
| Season | Club | League | GP | G | A | Pts | PIM | GP | G | A | Pts | PIM |
| 2005-06 | Erie Otters | OHL | 33 | 3 | 4 | 7 | 20 | .... | .... | .... | .... | .... |
| 2006-07 | Windsor Spitfires | OHL | 60 | 11 | 16 | 27 | 100 | .... | .... | .... | .... | .... |
| 2007-08 | Windsor Spitfires | OHL | 62 | 13 | 14 | 27 | 69 | 5 | 3 | 0 | 3 | 2 |
| 2008-09 | Sault Ste. Marie | OHL | 64 | 16 | 27 | 43 | 158 | .... | .... | .... | .... | .... |

## NOREAU, Maxim (NOHR-oh, max-EEM)

Defense. Shoots right. 5'11", 190 lbs. Born, Montreal, Que., May 14, 1987.

| | | | Regular Season | | | | | Playoffs | | | | |
|---|---|---|---|---|---|---|---|---|---|---|---|---|
| Season | Club | League | GP | G | A | Pts | PIM | GP | G | A | Pts | PIM |
| 2004-05 | Victoriaville Tigres | QMJHL | 65 | 5 | 8 | 13 | 47 | 7 | 0 | 0 | 0 | 8 |
| 2005-06 | Victoriaville Tigres | QMJHL | 69 | 22 | 43 | 65 | 116 | 5 | 2 | 4 | 6 | 7 |
| 2006-07 | Victoriaville Tigres | QMJHL | 69 | 17 | 53 | 70 | 106 | 6 | 2 | 1 | 3 | 8 |
| 2007-08 | Houston Aeros | AHL | 50 | 8 | 8 | 16 | 48 | 5 | 0 | 0 | 0 | 4 |
| | Texas Wildcatters | ECHL | 2 | 0 | 3 | 3 | 0 | .... | .... | .... | .... | .... |
| 2008-09 | Houston Aeros | AHL | 77 | 14 | 25 | 39 | 49 | 20 | 4 | 7 | 11 | 2 |

Signed as a free agent by **Minnesota**, May 22, 2008.

## NYQUIST, Gustav (NEW-kwihst, GUHS-tav) DET.

Right wing. Shoots left. 5'10", 169 lbs. Born, Halmstad, Sweden, September 1, 1989.
(Detroit's 3rd choice, 121st overall, in 2008 Entry Draft).

| | | | Regular Season | | | | | Playoffs | | | | |
|---|---|---|---|---|---|---|---|---|---|---|---|---|
| Season | Club | League | GP | G | A | Pts | PIM | GP | G | A | Pts | PIM |
| 2005-06 | Malmo U18 | Swe-U18 | 14 | 9 | 3 | 12 | 10 | 6 | 1 | 3 | 4 | 0 |
| 2006-07 | Malmo Jr. | Swe-Jr. | 42 | 21 | 23 | 44 | 57 | 4 | 2 | 2 | 4 | 6 |
| 2007-08 | Malmo Jr. | Swe-Jr. | 24 | 11 | 20 | 31 | 20 | 7 | 5 | 5 | 10 | 6 |
| 2008-09 | U. of Maine | H-East | 38 | 13 | 19 | 32 | 28 | .... | .... | .... | .... | .... |

Hockey East All-Rookie Team (2009)

## OBERG, Evan (OH-buhrg, EH-vuhn) VAN.

Defense. Shoots left. 6', 165 lbs. Born, Forestburg, Alta., February 16, 1988.

| | | | Regular Season | | | | | Playoffs | | | | |
|---|---|---|---|---|---|---|---|---|---|---|---|---|
| Season | Club | League | GP | G | A | Pts | PIM | GP | G | A | Pts | PIM |
| 2005-06 | Camrose Kodiaks | AJHL | 44 | 4 | 9 | 13 | 56 | 14 | 1 | 1 | 2 | 14 |
| 2006-07 | Camrose Kodiaks | AJHL | 52 | 9 | 14 | 23 | 86 | 16 | 3 | 11 | 14 | 24 |
| | Camrose Kodiaks | RB-Cup | .... | .... | .... | .... | .... | 4 | 1 | 5 | 6 | 2 |
| 2007-08 | U. Minn-Duluth | WCHA | 24 | 1 | 2 | 3 | 10 | .... | .... | .... | .... | .... |
| 2008-09 | U. Minn-Duluth | WCHA | 43 | 7 | 20 | 27 | 50 | .... | .... | .... | .... | .... |

Signed as a free agent by **Vancouver**, April 10, 2009.

## O'BRIEN, James (oh-BRIGH-uhn, JAYMZ) OTT.

Center. Shoots right. 6'3", 198 lbs. Born, Maplewood, MN, January 29, 1989.
(Ottawa's 1st choice, 29th overall, in 2007 Entry Draft).

| | | | Regular Season | | | | | Playoffs | | | | |
|---|---|---|---|---|---|---|---|---|---|---|---|---|
| Season | Club | League | GP | G | A | Pts | PIM | GP | G | A | Pts | PIM |
| 2003-04 | Det. Caesars | MWEHL | 68 | 19 | 24 | 43 | 72 | .... | .... | .... | .... | .... |
| 2004-05 | USNTDP | U-17 | 13 | 6 | 6 | 12 | 10 | .... | .... | .... | .... | .... |
| | USNTDP | NAHL | 40 | 10 | 12 | 22 | 41 | 1 | 0 | 0 | 0 | 0 |
| 2005-06 | USNTDP | U-18 | 38 | 11 | 14 | 25 | 62 | .... | .... | .... | .... | .... |
| | USNTDP | NAHL | 13 | 6 | 10 | 16 | 14 | .... | .... | .... | .... | .... |
| 2006-07 | U. of Minnesota | WCHA | 43 | 7 | 8 | 15 | 51 | .... | .... | .... | .... | .... |
| 2007-08 | Seattle | WHL | 70 | 21 | 34 | 55 | 66 | 12 | 2 | 6 | 8 | 14 |
| 2008-09 | Seattle | WHL | 63 | 27 | 35 | 62 | 55 | 5 | 1 | 0 | 1 | 10 |
| | Binghamton | AHL | 6 | 0 | 1 | 1 | 0 | .... | .... | .... | .... | .... |

## O'DELL, Eric (OH-DEHL, AIR-ihk) ATL.

Center. Shoots right. 6', 174 lbs. Born, Ottawa, Ont., June 21, 1990.
(Anaheim's 3rd choice, 39th overall, in 2008 Entry Draft).

| | | | Regular Season | | | | | Playoffs | | | | |
|---|---|---|---|---|---|---|---|---|---|---|---|---|
| Season | Club | League | GP | G | A | Pts | PIM | GP | G | A | Pts | PIM |
| 2006-07 | Ottawa West | OJHL-B | 40 | 28 | 20 | 48 | 45 | .... | .... | .... | .... | .... |
| | Ottawa Jr. Sens | CJHL | 2 | 1 | 0 | 1 | 0 | .... | .... | .... | .... | .... |
| 2007-08 | Cumberland | CJHL | 34 | 23 | 33 | 56 | 12 | .... | .... | .... | .... | .... |
| | Sudbury Wolves | OHL | 26 | 14 | 18 | 32 | 19 | .... | .... | .... | .... | .... |
| 2008-09 | Sudbury Wolves | OHL | 65 | 33 | 30 | 63 | 55 | 6 | 0 | 4 | 4 | 4 |

Traded to **Atlanta** by **Anaheim** for Erik Christensen, March 4 , 2009.

## OLIVER, Nick (aw-LIH-vuhr, NIHK) NSH.

Center/Left wing. Shoots left. 6'3", 205 lbs. Born, Grand Forks, ND, May 4, 1991.
(Nashville's 8th choice, 110th overall, in 2009 Entry Draft).

| | | | Regular Season | | | | | Playoffs | | | | |
|---|---|---|---|---|---|---|---|---|---|---|---|---|
| Season | Club | League | GP | G | A | Pts | PIM | GP | G | A | Pts | PIM |
| 2006-07 | Roseau Rams | High-MN | 31 | 12 | 14 | 26 | 51 | .... | .... | .... | .... | .... |
| 2007-08 | Roseau Rams | High-MN | 30 | 17 | 25 | 42 | 45 | .... | .... | .... | .... | .... |
| 2008-09 | Roseau Rams | High-MN | 11 | 5 | 11 | 16 | .... | .... | .... | .... | .... | .... |
| | Fargo Force | USHL | 12 | 1 | 1 | 2 | 11 | 1 | 0 | 0 | 0 | 0 |

• Signed Letter of Intent to attend **St. Cloud State University** (WCHA) in fall of 2010.

## OLSEN, Dylan (OHL-suhn, DIH-luhn) CHI.

Defense. Shoots left. 6'2", 206 lbs. Born, Salt Lake City, UT, January 3, 1991.
(Chicago's 1st choice, 28th overall, in 2009 Entry Draft).

| | | | Regular Season | | | | | Playoffs | | | | |
|---|---|---|---|---|---|---|---|---|---|---|---|---|
| Season | Club | League | GP | G | A | Pts | PIM | GP | G | A | Pts | PIM |
| 2006-07 | Calgary Blazers | SAMHL | 53 | 19 | 41 | 60 | 119 | .... | .... | .... | .... | .... |
| | Camrose Kodiaks | AJHL | 2 | 1 | 0 | 1 | 0 | .... | .... | .... | .... | .... |
| 2007-08 | Camrose Kodiaks | AJHL | 49 | 8 | 16 | 24 | 45 | 16 | 1 | 5 | 6 | 6 |
| 2008-09 | Camrose Kodiaks | AJHL | 53 | 10 | 19 | 29 | 123 | 10 | 1 | 6 | 7 | 12 |

• Signed Letter of Intent to attend **University of Minnesota-Duluth** (WCHA) in fall of 2009.

## OLSON, Drew (OHL-suhn, DROO) CBJ

Defense. Shoots left. 6', 206 lbs. Born, Brainerd, MN, April 4, 1990.
(Columbus' 4th choice, 118th overall, in 2008 Entry Draft).

| | | | Regular Season | | | | | Playoffs | | | | |
|---|---|---|---|---|---|---|---|---|---|---|---|---|
| Season | Club | League | GP | G | A | Pts | PIM | GP | G | A | Pts | PIM |
| 2006-07 | Brainerd | High-MN | STATISTICS NOT AVAILABLE | | | | | | | | | |
| | Team North | UMWEHL | 11 | 2 | 4 | 6 | .... | .... | .... | .... | .... | .... |
| 2007-08 | Brainerd | High-MN | 27 | 20 | 16 | 36 | .... | .... | .... | .... | .... | .... |
| | Team North | UMWEHL | 11 | 3 | 4 | 7 | .... | .... | .... | .... | .... | .... |
| 2008-09 | Omaha Lancers | USHL | 39 | 2 | 6 | 8 | 43 | .... | .... | .... | .... | .... |

• Signed Letter of Intent to attend **University of Minnesota-Duluth** (WCHA) in fall of 2009.

## OLVER, Mark (AWL-vuhr, MAHRK) COL.

Center. Shoots left. 5'10", 155 lbs. Born, Burnaby, B.C., January 1, 1988.
(Colorado's 4th choice, 140th overall, in 2008 Entry Draft).

| | | | Regular Season | | | | | Playoffs | | | | |
|---|---|---|---|---|---|---|---|---|---|---|---|---|
| Season | Club | League | GP | G | A | Pts | PIM | GP | G | A | Pts | PIM |
| 2005-06 | Omaha Lancers | USHL | 59 | 5 | 20 | 25 | 72 | 2 | 0 | 0 | 0 | 0 |
| 2006-07 | Omaha Lancers | USHL | 57 | 29 | 35 | 64 | 84 | 5 | 3 | 3 | 6 | 18 |
| 2007-08 | Northern Mich. | CCHA | 39 | 21 | 17 | 38 | 59 | .... | .... | .... | .... | .... |
| 2008-09 | Northern Mich. | CCHA | 40 | 16 | 19 | 35 | 84 | .... | .... | .... | .... | .... |

CCHA All-Rookie Team (2008)

## OMARK, Linus (OH-mahrk, LIH-nuhs) EDM.

Left wing. Shoots left. 5'9", 170 lbs. Born, Overtornea, Sweden, February 5, 1987.
(Edmonton's 4th choice, 97th overall, in 2007 Entry Draft).

| | | | Regular Season | | | | | Playoffs | | | | |
|---|---|---|---|---|---|---|---|---|---|---|---|---|
| Season | Club | League | GP | G | A | Pts | PIM | GP | G | A | Pts | PIM |
| 2003-04 | Lulea HF U18 | Swe-U18 | 14 | 14 | 8 | 22 | 18 | 7 | 3 | 4 | 7 | 0 |
| | Lulea HF Jr. | Swe-Jr. | 1 | 0 | 0 | 0 | 0 | .... | .... | .... | .... | .... |
| 2004-05 | Lulea HF U18 | Swe-U18 | 1 | 2 | 0 | 2 | 0 | .... | .... | .... | .... | .... |
| | Lulea HF Jr. | Swe-Jr. | 32 | 8 | 9 | 17 | 44 | 7 | 4 | 2 | 6 | 2 |
| 2005-06 | Lulea HF Jr. | Swe-Jr. | 32 | 22 | 21 | 43 | 56 | 5 | 1 | 2 | 3 | 28 |
| | Lulea HF | Sweden | 19 | 0 | 1 | 1 | 10 | 3 | 0 | 0 | 0 | 0 |
| 2006-07 | Lulea HF | Sweden | 50 | 8 | 9 | 17 | 32 | 4 | 1 | 0 | 1 | 2 |
| 2007-08 | Lulea HF | Sweden | 55 | 11 | 21 | 32 | 46 | .... | .... | .... | .... | .... |
| 2008-09 | Lulea HF | Sweden | 53 | 23 | 32 | 55 | 66 | 5 | 0 | 5 | 5 | 4 |

## O'MARRA, Ryan (oh-MAHR-ah, RIGH-uhn) EDM.

Center. Shoots right. 6'2", 207 lbs. Born, Tokyo, Japan, June 9, 1987.
(NY Islanders' 1st choice, 15th overall, in 2005 Entry Draft).

| | | | Regular Season | | | | | Playoffs | | | | |
|---|---|---|---|---|---|---|---|---|---|---|---|---|
| Season | Club | League | GP | G | A | Pts | PIM | GP | G | A | Pts | PIM |
| 2002-03 | Miss. Senators | GTHL | 76 | 51 | 60 | 111 | 83 | .... | .... | .... | .... | .... |
| | Georgetown | OPJHL | 3 | 0 | 2 | 2 | 0 | .... | .... | .... | .... | .... |
| | Streetsville Derbys | OPJHL | 6 | 0 | 1 | 1 | 2 | .... | .... | .... | .... | .... |
| 2003-04 | Erie Otters | OHL | 63 | 16 | 16 | 32 | 33 | 9 | 5 | 5 | 10 | 6 |
| 2004-05 | Erie Otters | OHL | 64 | 25 | 38 | 63 | 60 | 6 | 4 | 1 | 5 | 0 |
| 2005-06 | Erie Otters | OHL | 61 | 27 | 50 | 77 | 134 | .... | .... | .... | .... | .... |
| | Bridgeport | AHL | 8 | 4 | 1 | 5 | 4 | 3 | 0 | 1 | 1 | 2 |
| 2006-07 | Erie Otters | OHL | 13 | 8 | 6 | 14 | 26 | .... | .... | .... | .... | .... |
| | Saginaw Spirit | OHL | 33 | 18 | 19 | 37 | 48 | 3 | 2 | 1 | 3 | 4 |
| 2007-08 | Springfield Falcons | AHL | 31 | 2 | 7 | 9 | 31 | .... | .... | .... | .... | .... |
| | Stockton Thunder | ECHL | 24 | 11 | 9 | 20 | 45 | 6 | 2 | 7 | 9 | 10 |
| 2008-09 | Springfield Falcons | AHL | 62 | 1 | 9 | 10 | 49 | .... | .... | .... | .... | .... |

Traded to **Edmonton** by **NY Islanders** with Robert Nilsson and NY Islanders' 1st round choice (Alex Plante) in 2007 Entry Draft for Ryan Smyth, February 27, 2007.

## O'NEILL, Will (oh-NEEL, WIHL) ATL.

Defense. Shoots left. 6', 193 lbs. Born, Boston, MA, April 28, 1988.
(Atlanta's 8th choice, 210th overall, in 2006 Entry Draft).

| | | | Regular Season | | | | | Playoffs | | | | |
|---|---|---|---|---|---|---|---|---|---|---|---|---|
| Season | Club | League | GP | G | A | Pts | PIM | GP | G | A | Pts | PIM |
| 2004-05 | Tabor | High-MA | .... | 1 | 16 | 17 | .... | .... | .... | .... | .... | .... |
| 2005-06 | Tabor | High-MA | 28 | 5 | 25 | 30 | 38 | .... | .... | .... | .... | .... |
| 2006-07 | Omaha Lancers | USHL | 57 | 4 | 9 | 13 | 73 | 5 | 0 | 0 | 0 | 8 |
| 2007-08 | Omaha Lancers | USHL | 58 | 5 | 19 | 24 | 95 | 14 | 1 | 6 | 7 | 38 |
| 2008-09 | U. of Maine | H-East | 34 | 4 | 12 | 16 | 82 | .... | .... | .... | .... | .... |

## O'REILLY, Ryan (oh-RIGH-lee, RIGH-uhn) COL.

Center. Shoots left. 6', 200 lbs. Born, Clinton, Ont., February 7, 1991.
(Colorado's 2nd choice, 33rd overall, in 2009 Entry Draft).

| | | | Regular Season | | | | | Playoffs | | | | |
|---|---|---|---|---|---|---|---|---|---|---|---|---|
| Season | Club | League | GP | G | A | Pts | PIM | GP | G | A | Pts | PIM |
| 2006-07 | Tor. Jr. Canadiens | GTHL | 50 | 31 | 43 | 74 | .... | .... | .... | .... | .... | .... |
| | Tor. Canadiens | OPJHL | 1 | 1 | 0 | 1 | 0 | .... | .... | .... | .... | .... |
| 2007-08 | Erie Otters | OHL | 61 | 19 | 33 | 52 | 14 | .... | .... | .... | .... | .... |
| 2008-09 | Erie Otters | OHL | 68 | 16 | 50 | 66 | 26 | 5 | 0 | 5 | 5 | 2 |

**ORLOV, Dmitri** (ohr-LAWF, dih-MEE-tree) **WSH.**

Defense. Shoots left. 5'11", 202 lbs. Born, Novokuznetsk, USSR, July 23, 1991.
(Washington's 2nd choice, 55th overall, in 2009 Entry Draft).

| | | | Regular Season | | | | | Playoffs | | | | |
|---|---|---|---|---|---|---|---|---|---|---|---|---|
| Season | Club | League | GP | G | A | Pts | PIM | GP | G | A | Pts | PIM |
| 2007-08 | Novokuznetsk | Russia | 6 | 0 | 0 | 0 | 0 | .... | .... | .... | .... | .... |
| 2008-09 | Novokuznetsk 2 | Russia-3 | STATISTICS NOT AVAILABLE | | | | | | | | | |
| | Novokuznetsk | Rus-KHL | 16 | 1 | 0 | 1 | 4 | .... | .... | .... | .... | .... |

**ORLOV, Maxim** (ohr-LAHF, max-EEM) **WSH.**

Center. Shoots left. 6', 176 lbs. Born, Moscow, USSR, March 31, 1981.
(Washington's 9th choice, 219th overall, in 1999 Entry Draft).

| | | | Regular Season | | | | | Playoffs | | | | |
|---|---|---|---|---|---|---|---|---|---|---|---|---|
| Season | Club | League | GP | G | A | Pts | PIM | GP | G | A | Pts | PIM |
| 1998-99 | CSKA Moscow | Russia | 2 | 0 | 0 | 0 | 2 | 1 | 0 | 0 | 0 | 0 |
| 99-2000 | CSKA Moscow | Russia | 25 | 0 | 0 | 0 | 2 | 2 | 0 | 0 | 0 | 2 |
| 2000-01 | CSKA Moscow | Russia | 41 | 5 | 4 | 9 | 14 | .... | .... | .... | .... | .... |
| 2001-02 | CSKA Moscow 2 | Russia-3 | 7 | 7 | 4 | 11 | 4 | .... | .... | .... | .... | .... |
| | CSKA Moscow | Russia | 35 | 3 | 5 | 8 | 14 | .... | .... | .... | .... | .... |
| 2002-03 | MGU Moscow | Russia-3 | 2 | 0 | 0 | 0 | 0 | .... | .... | .... | .... | .... |
| | Leninogorsk | Russia-2 | 25 | 3 | 8 | 11 | 24 | .... | .... | .... | .... | .... |
| 2003-04 | Leninogorsk | Russia-2 | 35 | 5 | 9 | 14 | 39 | 2 | 0 | 0 | 0 | 0 |
| 2004-05 | Kristall Saratov | Russia-2 | 47 | 13 | 23 | 36 | 46 | 4 | 0 | 0 | 0 | 2 |
| 2005-06 | Ufa 2 | Russia-3 | 20 | 8 | 8 | 16 | 10 | .... | .... | .... | .... | .... |
| | Ufa | Russia | 5 | 0 | 0 | 0 | 0 | .... | .... | .... | .... | .... |
| 2006-07 | Toros Neftekamsk | Russia-2 | 55 | 5 | 22 | 27 | 46 | .... | .... | .... | .... | .... |
| 2007-08 | Toros Neftekamsk | Russia-2 | 50 | 7 | 12 | 19 | 20 | 3 | 1 | 2 | 3 | 0 |
| 2008-09 | Toros Neftekamsk | Russia-2 | 41 | 10 | 9 | 19 | 14 | 7 | 3 | 0 | 3 | 6 |

**ORPIK, Andrew** (OHR-pihk, AN-droo) **BUF.**

Defense. Shoots right. 6'3", 200 lbs. Born, East Amherst, NY, March 12, 1986.
(Buffalo's 9th choice, 227th overall, in 2005 Entry Draft).

| | | | Regular Season | | | | | Playoffs | | | | |
|---|---|---|---|---|---|---|---|---|---|---|---|---|
| Season | Club | League | GP | G | A | Pts | PIM | GP | G | A | Pts | PIM |
| 2003-04 | Thayer Academy | High-MA | 32 | 9 | 8 | 17 | 18 | .... | .... | .... | .... | .... |
| 2004-05 | Thayer Academy | High-MA | 31 | 8 | 12 | 20 | 24 | .... | .... | .... | .... | .... |
| 2005-06 | Boston College | H-East | 40 | 3 | 5 | 8 | 32 | .... | .... | .... | .... | .... |
| 2006-07 | Boston College | H-East | 38 | 3 | 6 | 9 | 22 | .... | .... | .... | .... | .... |
| 2007-08 | Boston College | H-East | 41 | 7 | 6 | 13 | 57 | .... | .... | .... | .... | .... |
| 2008-09 | Boston College | H-East | 36 | 5 | 12 | 17 | 36 | .... | .... | .... | .... | .... |

**OSLUND, Nick** (OZ-luhnd, NIHK) **DET.**

Right wing. Shoots right. 6'3", 195 lbs. Born, Burnsville, MN, November 15, 1987.
(Detroit's 6th choice, 191st overall, in 2006 Entry Draft).

| | | | Regular Season | | | | | Playoffs | | | | |
|---|---|---|---|---|---|---|---|---|---|---|---|---|
| Season | Club | League | GP | G | A | Pts | PIM | GP | G | A | Pts | PIM |
| 2004-05 | Burnsville | High-MN | 27 | 29 | 18 | 47 | 28 | .... | .... | .... | .... | .... |
| 2005-06 | Burnsville | High-MN | 26 | 22 | 30 | 52 | 30 | .... | .... | .... | .... | .... |
| 2006-07 | Tri-City Storm | USHL | 56 | 7 | 14 | 21 | 24 | 9 | 0 | 1 | 1 | 0 |
| 2007-08 | St. Cloud State | WCHA | 38 | 4 | 1 | 5 | 27 | .... | .... | .... | .... | .... |
| 2008-09 | St. Cloud State | WCHA | 35 | 4 | 3 | 7 | 26 | .... | .... | .... | .... | .... |

**OSTRCIL, Radim** (AWS-tuhr-chihl, RA-dihm) **BOS.**

Defense. Shoots left. 5'11", 194 lbs. Born, Vsetin, Czech., January 15, 1989.
(Boston's 5th choice, 169th overall, in 2007 Entry Draft).

| | | | Regular Season | | | | | Playoffs | | | | |
|---|---|---|---|---|---|---|---|---|---|---|---|---|
| Season | Club | League | GP | G | A | Pts | PIM | GP | G | A | Pts | PIM |
| 2002-03 | HC Vsetin U17 | CzR-U17 | 33 | 1 | 2 | 3 | 8 | 11 | 1 | 1 | 2 | 2 |
| 2003-04 | HC Vsetin U17 | CzR-U17 | 43 | 0 | 12 | 12 | 44 | 2 | 0 | 0 | 0 | 0 |
| 2004-05 | HC Vsetin U17 | CzR-U17 | 31 | 8 | 15 | 23 | 85 | 3 | 1 | 3 | 4 | 4 |
| | HC Vsetin Jr. | CzRep-Jr. | 19 | 0 | 3 | 3 | 14 | 3 | 0 | 0 | 0 | 2 |
| 2005-06 | HC Vsetin U17 | CzR-U17 | 1 | 1 | 1 | 2 | 0 | 3 | 2 | 2 | 4 | 0 |
| | HC Vsetin Jr. | CzRep-Jr. | 41 | 6 | 8 | 14 | 50 | 5 | 1 | 1 | 2 | 6 |
| | Hr. Kralove | CzRep-2 | 1 | 0 | 0 | 0 | 0 | 1 | 0 | 0 | 0 | 0 |
| | HC Vsetin | CzRep | 3 | 0 | 0 | 0 | 6 | .... | .... | .... | .... | .... |
| 2006-07 | HC Vsetin Jr. | CzRep-Jr. | 25 | 8 | 13 | 21 | 69 | 8 | 4 | 4 | 8 | 6 |
| | HC Vsetin | CzRep | 37 | 1 | 1 | 2 | 20 | .... | .... | .... | .... | .... |
| 2007-08 | Ottawa 67's | OHL | 59 | 0 | 13 | 13 | 69 | 4 | 0 | 0 | 0 | 2 |
| 2008-09 | HC Olomouc Jr. | CzRep-Jr. | 5 | 3 | 2 | 5 | 10 | .... | .... | .... | .... | .... |
| | HC Olomouc | CzRep-2 | 38 | 1 | 3 | 4 | 18 | 5 | 0 | 0 | 0 | 4 |

**OULAHEN, Ryan** (OO-la-hehn, RIGH-uhn) **DET.**

Center. Shoots left. 6', 180 lbs. Born, Newmarket, Ont., March 26, 1985.
(Detroit's 3rd choice, 164th overall, in 2003 Entry Draft).

| | | | Regular Season | | | | | Playoffs | | | | |
|---|---|---|---|---|---|---|---|---|---|---|---|---|
| Season | Club | League | GP | G | A | Pts | PIM | GP | G | A | Pts | PIM |
| 2000-01 | Wexford Raiders | Minor-ON | 66 | 38 | 58 | 96 | 18 | .... | .... | .... | .... | .... |
| 2001-02 | Newmarket | OPJHL | 48 | 18 | 17 | 35 | 4 | .... | .... | .... | .... | .... |
| 2002-03 | Brampton | OHL | 61 | 21 | 22 | 43 | 6 | 11 | 2 | 1 | 3 | 2 |
| 2003-04 | Brampton | OHL | 57 | 17 | 18 | 35 | 26 | 12 | 3 | 7 | 10 | 6 |
| 2004-05 | Brampton | OHL | 64 | 27 | 31 | 58 | 22 | 5 | 1 | 4 | 5 | 4 |
| 2005-06 | Grand Rapids | AHL | 75 | 9 | 10 | 19 | 20 | 16 | 0 | 0 | 0 | 2 |
| 2006-07 | Grand Rapids | AHL | 79 | 11 | 16 | 27 | 42 | 7 | 0 | 2 | 2 | 4 |
| 2007-08 | Grand Rapids | AHL | 75 | 14 | 16 | 30 | 47 | .... | .... | .... | .... | .... |
| 2008-09 | Grand Rapids | AHL | 73 | 19 | 12 | 31 | 31 | .... | .... | .... | .... | .... |

**PAAJARVI-SVENSSON, Magnus** pe-ya-YAR-vee-SVEHN-suhn, MAG-nuhs **EDM.**

Left wing. Shoots left. 6'1", 201 lbs. Born, Norrkoping, Sweden, April 12, 1991.
(Edmonton's 1st choice, 10th overall, in 2009 Entry Draft).

| | | | Regular Season | | | | | Playoffs | | | | |
|---|---|---|---|---|---|---|---|---|---|---|---|---|
| Season | Club | League | GP | G | A | Pts | PIM | GP | G | A | Pts | PIM |
| 2005-06 | Malmo U18 | Swe-U18 | 13 | 2 | 3 | 5 | 4 | 1 | 0 | 0 | 0 | 0 |
| | Malmo Jr. | Swe-Jr. | 2 | 0 | 0 | 0 | 0 | .... | .... | .... | .... | .... |
| 2006-07 | Malmo U18 | Swe-U18 | 3 | 3 | 3 | 6 | 0 | .... | .... | .... | .... | .... |
| | Malmo Jr. | Swe-Jr. | 20 | 4 | 2 | 6 | 6 | 4 | 0 | 1 | 1 | 0 |
| 2007-08 | Timra IK U18 | Swe-U18 | 5 | 1 | 6 | 7 | 4 | .... | .... | .... | .... | .... |
| | Timra IK Jr. | Swe-Jr. | 18 | 7 | 15 | 22 | 6 | .... | .... | .... | .... | .... |
| | Timra IK | Sweden | 35 | 1 | 2 | 3 | 2 | 11 | 0 | 0 | 0 | 2 |
| 2008-09 | Timra IK Jr. | Swe-Jr. | 1 | 0 | 0 | 0 | 0 | .... | .... | .... | .... | .... |
| | Timra IK | Sweden | 50 | 7 | 10 | 17 | 4 | 7 | 1 | 0 | 1 | 0 |

**PACAN, David** (PAY-cuhn, DAY-vihd) **CHI.**

Center. Shoots right. 6'3", 187 lbs. Born, Ottawa, Ont., March 31, 1991.
(Chicago's 6th choice, 177th overall, in 2009 Entry Draft).

| | | | Regular Season | | | | | Playoffs | | | | |
|---|---|---|---|---|---|---|---|---|---|---|---|---|
| Season | Club | League | GP | G | A | Pts | PIM | GP | G | A | Pts | PIM |
| 2007-08 | Cumberland | CJHL | 60 | 12 | 22 | 34 | 30 | 6 | 3 | 7 | 10 | 6 |
| 2008-09 | Cumberland | CJHL | 58 | 22 | 38 | 60 | 78 | 6 | 2 | 6 | 8 | 6 |

• Signed Letter of Intent to attend **University of Vermont** (Hockey East) in fall of 2009.

**PACKARD, Dennis** (PA-kuhrd, DEH-nihs)

Left wing. Shoots left. 6'4", 235 lbs. Born, St. Catherines, Ont., February 9, 1982.
(Tampa Bay's 8th choice, 219th overall, in 2001 Entry Draft).

| | | | Regular Season | | | | | Playoffs | | | | |
|---|---|---|---|---|---|---|---|---|---|---|---|---|
| Season | Club | League | GP | G | A | Pts | PIM | GP | G | A | Pts | PIM |
| 99-2000 | USNTDP | U-18 | 6 | 0 | 1 | 1 | 2 | .... | .... | .... | .... | .... |
| | USNTDP | USHL | 55 | 11 | 14 | 25 | 85 | .... | .... | .... | .... | .... |
| 2000-01 | Harvard Crimson | ECAC | 33 | 4 | 4 | 8 | 28 | .... | .... | .... | .... | .... |
| 2001-02 | Harvard Crimson | ECAC | 32 | 9 | 10 | 19 | 34 | .... | .... | .... | .... | .... |
| 2002-03 | Harvard Crimson | ECAC | 30 | 8 | 8 | 16 | 32 | .... | .... | .... | .... | .... |
| 2003-04 | Harvard Crimson | ECAC | 36 | 11 | 11 | 22 | 16 | .... | .... | .... | .... | .... |
| 2004-05 | Springfield Falcons | AHL | 47 | 2 | 8 | 10 | 25 | .... | .... | .... | .... | .... |
| | Johnstown Chiefs | ECHL | 15 | 3 | 4 | 7 | 6 | .... | .... | .... | .... | .... |
| 2005-06 | Springfield Falcons | AHL | 46 | 3 | 6 | 9 | 34 | .... | .... | .... | .... | .... |
| | Johnstown Chiefs | ECHL | 16 | 2 | 9 | 11 | 12 | 5 | 0 | 1 | 1 | 4 |
| 2006-07 | Providence Bruins | AHL | 68 | 6 | 12 | 18 | 55 | 13 | 1 | 1 | 2 | 2 |
| 2007-08 | Worcester Sharks | AHL | 76 | 11 | 19 | 30 | 31 | .... | .... | .... | .... | .... |
| 2008-09 | Bridgeport | AHL | 36 | 0 | 3 | 3 | 21 | 2 | 0 | 0 | 0 | 4 |
| | Utah Grizzlies | ECHL | 11 | 5 | 6 | 11 | 8 | .... | .... | .... | .... | .... |

Signed as a free agent by **Boston**, July 17, 2006. Signed as a free agent by **Bridgeport** (AHL), November 25, 2008.

**PAINCHAUD, Chad** (PAYN-show, CHAD)

Left wing. Shoots left. 6'1", 185 lbs. Born, Mississauga, Ont., May 27, 1986.
(Atlanta's 4th choice, 106th overall, in 2004 Entry Draft).

| | | | Regular Season | | | | | Playoffs | | | | |
|---|---|---|---|---|---|---|---|---|---|---|---|---|
| Season | Club | League | GP | G | A | Pts | PIM | GP | G | A | Pts | PIM |
| 2002-03 | Mississauga Reps | GTHL | 52 | 47 | 47 | 94 | .... | .... | .... | .... | .... | .... |
| 2003-04 | Mississauga | OHL | 68 | 17 | 25 | 42 | 25 | 24 | 4 | 6 | 10 | 23 |
| 2004-05 | Mississauga | OHL | 8 | 3 | 3 | 6 | 11 | .... | .... | .... | .... | .... |
| | Sarnia Sting | OHL | 49 | 18 | 16 | 34 | 22 | .... | .... | .... | .... | .... |
| 2005-06 | Sarnia Sting | OHL | 49 | 31 | 34 | 65 | 65 | .... | .... | .... | .... | .... |
| 2006-07 | Gwinnett | ECHL | 72 | 22 | 32 | 54 | 71 | 4 | 0 | 5 | 5 | 4 |
| 2007-08 | Chicago Wolves | AHL | 22 | 1 | 2 | 3 | 13 | .... | .... | .... | .... | .... |
| | Gwinnett | ECHL | 10 | 8 | 6 | 14 | 17 | 4 | 0 | 1 | 1 | 0 |
| 2008-09 | Iowa Chops | AHL | 16 | 3 | 3 | 6 | 0 | .... | .... | .... | .... | .... |
| | Bakersfield | ECHL | 57 | 20 | 44 | 64 | 46 | 7 | 2 | 8 | 10 | 23 |

Traded to **Anaheim** by **Atlanta** with Ken Klee and Brad Larsen for Mathieu Schneider, September 26, 2008.

**PALIN, Brett** (PAY-lihn, BREHT) **CGY.**

Defense. Shoots right. 6'1", 200 lbs. Born, Nanaimo, B.C., June 23, 1984.

| | | | Regular Season | | | | | Playoffs | | | | |
|---|---|---|---|---|---|---|---|---|---|---|---|---|
| Season | Club | League | GP | G | A | Pts | PIM | GP | G | A | Pts | PIM |
| 2000-01 | Kelowna Rockets | WHL | 39 | 0 | 0 | 0 | 25 | .... | .... | .... | .... | .... |
| 2001-02 | Kelowna Rockets | WHL | 70 | 0 | 1 | 1 | 88 | 15 | 0 | 0 | 0 | 4 |
| 2002-03 | Kelowna Rockets | WHL | 71 | 1 | 17 | 18 | 118 | 19 | 0 | 4 | 4 | 12 |
| 2003-04 | Kelowna Rockets | WHL | 72 | 1 | 16 | 17 | 106 | 17 | 0 | 5 | 5 | 24 |
| 2004-05 | Kelowna Rockets | WHL | 72 | 4 | 21 | 25 | 71 | 24 | 4 | 6 | 10 | 52 |
| 2005-06 | Omaha | AHL | 64 | 0 | 5 | 5 | 46 | .... | .... | .... | .... | .... |
| 2006-07 | Omaha | AHL | 78 | 1 | 9 | 10 | 71 | 6 | 1 | 0 | 1 | 0 |
| 2007-08 | Quad City Flames | AHL | 67 | 0 | 10 | 10 | 68 | .... | .... | .... | .... | .... |
| 2008-09 | Quad City Flames | AHL | 57 | 5 | 10 | 15 | 40 | .... | .... | .... | .... | .... |

Signed as a free agent by **Calgary**, August 5, 2005.

**PALMIERI, Kyle** (pawl-mee-AIR-ee, KIGHL) **ANA.**

Center/Right wing. Shoots right. 5'10", 191 lbs. Born, Smithtown, NY, February 1, 1991.
(Anaheim's 2nd choice, 26th overall, in 2009 Entry Draft).

| | | | Regular Season | | | | | Playoffs | | | | |
|---|---|---|---|---|---|---|---|---|---|---|---|---|
| Season | Club | League | GP | G | A | Pts | PIM | GP | G | A | Pts | PIM |
| 2007-08 | USNTDP | NAHL | 32 | 15 | 10 | 25 | 43 | .... | .... | .... | .... | .... |
| | USNTDP | U-17 | 7 | 5 | 0 | 5 | 8 | .... | .... | .... | .... | .... |
| | USNTDP | U-18 | 27 | 9 | 9 | 18 | 20 | .... | .... | .... | .... | .... |
| 2008-09 | USNTDP | NAHL | 5 | 1 | 1 | 2 | 2 | .... | .... | .... | .... | .... |
| | USNTDP | U-18 | 28 | 14 | 14 | 28 | 49 | .... | .... | .... | .... | .... |

**PALMIERI, Nick** (pawl-mee-AIR-ee, NIHK) **N.J.**

Right wing. Shoots right. 6'3", 215 lbs. Born, Utica, NY, July 12, 1989.
(New Jersey's 2nd choice, 79th overall, in 2007 Entry Draft).

| | | | Regular Season | | | | | Playoffs | | | | |
|---|---|---|---|---|---|---|---|---|---|---|---|---|
| Season | Club | League | GP | G | A | Pts | PIM | GP | G | A | Pts | PIM |
| 2004-05 | Northwood | High-NY | STATISTICS NOT AVAILABLE | | | | | | | | | |
| 2005-06 | Erie Otters | OHL | 68 | 13 | 10 | 23 | 79 | .... | .... | .... | .... | .... |
| 2006-07 | Erie Otters | OHL | 56 | 24 | 21 | 45 | 99 | .... | .... | .... | .... | .... |
| 2007-08 | Erie Otters | OHL | 50 | 28 | 18 | 46 | 122 | .... | .... | .... | .... | .... |
| | Lowell Devils | AHL | 9 | 1 | 0 | 1 | 4 | .... | .... | .... | .... | .... |
| 2008-09 | Erie Otters | OHL | 18 | 7 | 5 | 12 | 41 | .... | .... | .... | .... | .... |
| | Belleville Bulls | OHL | 43 | 20 | 9 | 29 | 75 | 17 | 14 | 3 | 17 | 27 |

• Signed Letter of Intent to attend **University of Notre Dame** (CCHA) in fall of 2009.

**PALUSHAJ, Aaron** (puh-LOO-shigh, AIR-ruhn) **ST.L.**

Right wing. Shoots right. 5'11", 187 lbs. Born, Livonia, MI, September 7, 1989.
(St. Louis' 5th choice, 44th overall, in 2007 Entry Draft).

| | | | Regular Season | | | | | Playoffs | | | | |
|---|---|---|---|---|---|---|---|---|---|---|---|---|
| Season | Club | League | GP | G | A | Pts | PIM | GP | G | A | Pts | PIM |
| 2005-06 | Des Moines | USHL | 58 | 10 | 23 | 33 | 53 | 11 | 2 | 4 | 6 | 15 |
| 2006-07 | Des Moines | USHL | 56 | 22 | 45 | 67 | 62 | 8 | 6 | 5 | 11 | 6 |
| 2007-08 | U. of Michigan | CCHA | 43 | 10 | *34 | 44 | 22 | .... | .... | .... | .... | .... |
| 2008-09 | U. of Michigan | CCHA | 39 | 13 | *37 | *50 | 26 | .... | .... | .... | .... | .... |
| | Peoria Rivermen | AHL | 4 | 2 | 0 | 2 | 4 | 4 | 0 | 1 | 1 | 2 |

CCHA First All-Star Team (2009) • NCAA West First All-American Team (2009)

**PANIK, Richard** (PAH-nihk, RIH-chuhrd) **T.B.**

Right wing. Shoots left. 6'2", 203 lbs. Born, Martin, Czechoslovakia, February 7, 1991.
(Tampa Bay's 3rd choice, 52nd overall, in 2009 Entry Draft).

| | | | Regular Season | | | | | Playoffs | | | | |
|---|---|---|---|---|---|---|---|---|---|---|---|---|
| Season | Club | League | GP | G | A | Pts | PIM | GP | G | A | Pts | PIM |
| 2005-06 | MHC Martin U18 | Svk-U18 | 40 | 11 | 13 | 24 | 20 | 4 | 4 | 2 | 6 | 4 |
| 2006-07 | HC Trinec U17 | CzR-U17 | 12 | 10 | 6 | 16 | 48 | 3 | 1 | 4 | 5 | 8 |
| | HC Trinec Jr. | CzRep-Jr. | 27 | 16 | 9 | 25 | 30 | 4 | 1 | 4 | 5 | 6 |
| 2007-08 | HC Trinec Jr. | CzRep-Jr. | 39 | 35 | 27 | 62 | 70 | 8 | 8 | 4 | 12 | 52 |
| | HC Ocelari Trinec | CzRep | 6 | 0 | 0 | 0 | 0 | .... | .... | .... | .... | .... |
| 2008-09 | HC Trinec Jr. | CzRep-Jr. | 16 | 10 | 9 | 19 | 36 | 8 | 6 | 1 | 7 | 41 |
| | HC Havirov | CzRep-2 | 3 | 2 | 1 | 3 | 0 | .... | .... | .... | .... | .... |
| | HC Ocelari Trinec | CzRep | 15 | 1 | 1 | 2 | 4 | 4 | 0 | 0 | 0 | 0 |

## PAQUETTE, Danick (pa-KETT, DA-nihk) ATL.

Right wing. Shoots right. 6', 210 lbs. Born, Montreal, Que., July 17, 1990.
(Atlanta's 3rd choice, 64th overall, in 2008 Entry Draft).

| | | | Regular Season | | | | | Playoffs | | | | |
|---|---|---|---|---|---|---|---|---|---|---|---|---|
| Season | Club | League | GP | G | A | Pts | PIM | GP | G | A | Pts | PIM |
| 2005-06 | Ecole Montpetit | QAAA | 36 | 17 | 16 | 33 | 191 | 3 | 0 | 1 | 1 | 6 |
| 2006-07 | Lewiston | QMJHL | 63 | 4 | 14 | 18 | 112 | 14 | 0 | 0 | 0 | 18 |
| 2007-08 | Lewiston | QMJHL | 63 | 29 | 13 | 42 | 213 | 5 | 1 | 2 | 3 | 30 |
| 2008-09 | Lewiston | QMJHL | 61 | 25 | 25 | 50 | 230 | 2 | 1 | 2 | 3 | 25 |
| | Chicago Wolves | AHL | 4 | 0 | 0 | 0 | 12 | .... | .... | .... | .... | .... |

## PARADIS, Philippe (PAIR-a-dee, fihl-EEP) CAR.

Center. Shoots left. 6'2", 205 lbs. Born, Dolbeau, Que., January 2, 1991.
(Carolina's 1st choice, 27th overall, in 2009 Entry Draft).

| | | | Regular Season | | | | | Playoffs | | | | |
|---|---|---|---|---|---|---|---|---|---|---|---|---|
| Season | Club | League | GP | G | A | Pts | PIM | GP | G | A | Pts | PIM |
| 2006-07 | Jonquiere Elites | QAAA | 38 | 5 | 12 | 17 | 76 | 3 | 1 | 1 | 2 | 6 |
| 2007-08 | Shawinigan | QMJHL | 45 | 11 | 12 | 23 | 44 | 3 | 0 | 0 | 0 | 0 |
| 2008-09 | Shawinigan | QMJHL | 66 | 19 | 31 | 50 | 74 | 21 | 6 | 6 | 12 | 20 |

## PARSE, Scott (PARS, SKAWT) L.A.

Center. Shoots right. 6', 193 lbs. Born, Portage, MI, September 5, 1984.
(Los Angeles' 5th choice, 174th overall, in 2004 Entry Draft).

| | | | Regular Season | | | | | Playoffs | | | | |
|---|---|---|---|---|---|---|---|---|---|---|---|---|
| Season | Club | League | GP | G | A | Pts | PIM | GP | G | A | Pts | PIM |
| 2002-03 | Tri-City Storm | USHL | 48 | 21 | 23 | 44 | 32 | 3 | 2 | 1 | 3 | 8 |
| 2003-04 | Nebraska-Omaha | CCHA | 39 | 16 | 19 | 35 | 52 | .... | .... | .... | .... | .... |
| 2004-05 | Nebraska-Omaha | CCHA | 39 | 19 | 30 | 49 | 32 | .... | .... | .... | .... | .... |
| 2005-06 | Nebraska-Omaha | CCHA | 41 | 20 | *41 | *61 | 40 | .... | .... | .... | .... | .... |
| 2006-07 | Nebraska-Omaha | CCHA | 40 | 24 | 28 | 52 | 36 | .... | .... | .... | .... | .... |
| | Grand Rapids | AHL | 10 | 2 | 5 | 7 | 6 | 7 | 1 | 0 | 1 | 8 |
| 2007-08 | Manchester | AHL | 14 | 0 | 3 | 3 | 4 | .... | .... | .... | .... | .... |
| | Reading Royals | ECHL | 18 | 5 | 11 | 16 | 14 | .... | .... | .... | .... | .... |
| 2008-09 | Manchester | AHL | 74 | 15 | 24 | 39 | 38 | .... | .... | .... | .... | .... |

USHL All-Rookie Team (2003) • CCHA First All-Star Team (2005, 2007) • CCHA - Player of the Year (2006) • NCAA West First All-American Team (2006) • NCAA West Second All-American Team (2007)

## PARSHIN, Denis (PAHR-shihn, DEH-nihs) COL.

Right wing. Shoots left. 5'10", 165 lbs. Born, Rybinsk, USSR, February 1, 1986.
(Colorado's 3rd choice, 72nd overall, in 2004 Entry Draft).

| | | | Regular Season | | | | | Playoffs | | | | |
|---|---|---|---|---|---|---|---|---|---|---|---|---|
| Season | Club | League | GP | G | A | Pts | PIM | GP | G | A | Pts | PIM |
| 2002-03 | CSKA Moscow 2 | Russia-3 | 4 | 1 | 0 | 1 | 2 | .... | .... | .... | .... | .... |
| 2003-04 | CSKA Moscow | Russia | 27 | 2 | 4 | 6 | 4 | .... | .... | .... | .... | .... |
| | CSKA Moscow 2 | Russia-3 | STATISTICS NOT AVAILABLE | | | | | | | | | |
| 2004-05 | CSKA Moscow | Russia | 42 | 3 | 4 | 7 | 18 | .... | .... | .... | .... | .... |
| 2005-06 | CSKA Moscow 2 | Russia-3 | STATISTICS NOT AVAILABLE | | | | | | | | | |
| | CSKA Moscow | Russia | 37 | 2 | 8 | 10 | 22 | 6 | 0 | 2 | 2 | 2 |
| 2006-07 | CSKA Moscow | Russia | 54 | 18 | 14 | 32 | 24 | 12 | 2 | 2 | 4 | 8 |
| 2007-08 | CSKA Moscow | Russia | 56 | 12 | 23 | 35 | 46 | 6 | 1 | 0 | 1 | 0 |
| 2008-09 | CSKA Moscow | Rus-KHL | 48 | 13 | 14 | 27 | 34 | 8 | 1 | 0 | 1 | 6 |

## PASHNIN, Mikhail (pahsh-NIHN, mih-KHIGH-eel) NYR

Defense. Shoots left. 5'11", 187 lbs. Born, Chelyabinsk, USSR, May 11, 1989.
(NY Rangers' 7th choice, 200th overall, in 2009 Entry Draft).

| | | | Regular Season | | | | | Playoffs | | | | |
|---|---|---|---|---|---|---|---|---|---|---|---|---|
| Season | Club | League | GP | G | A | Pts | PIM | GP | G | A | Pts | PIM |
| 2005-06 | Mechel 2 | Russia-3 | 25 | 0 | 5 | 5 | 30 | .... | .... | .... | .... | .... |
| 2006-07 | Mechel 2 | Russia-3 | 12 | 1 | 3 | 4 | 26 | .... | .... | .... | .... | .... |
| | Mechel | Russia-2 | 41 | 0 | 2 | 2 | 40 | 4 | 0 | 0 | 0 | 8 |
| 2007-08 | Mechel 2 | Russia-3 | 8 | 4 | 1 | 5 | 12 | .... | .... | .... | .... | .... |
| | Mechel | Russia-2 | 49 | 2 | 5 | 7 | 58 | .... | .... | .... | .... | .... |
| 2008-09 | Mechel 2 | Russia-3 | 3 | 0 | 1 | 1 | 4 | .... | .... | .... | .... | .... |
| | Mechel | Russia-2 | 35 | 2 | 4 | 6 | 40 | 7 | 0 | 2 | 2 | 8 |

## PATERYN, Greg (PA-tuhr-ihn, GREHG) MTL.

Defense. Shoots right. 6'2", 219 lbs. Born, Sterling Heights, MI, June 20, 1990.
(Toronto's 4th choice, 128th overall, in 2008 Entry Draft).

| | | | Regular Season | | | | | Playoffs | | | | |
|---|---|---|---|---|---|---|---|---|---|---|---|---|
| Season | Club | League | GP | G | A | Pts | PIM | GP | G | A | Pts | PIM |
| 2004-05 | Brother Rice | High-MI | 29 | 2 | 8 | 10 | 42 | .... | .... | .... | .... | .... |
| 2005-06 | Brother Rice | High-MI | 24 | 0 | 8 | 8 | 34 | .... | .... | .... | .... | .... |
| 2006-07 | Brother Rice | High-MI | 27 | 9 | 19 | 28 | 44 | .... | .... | .... | .... | .... |
| 2007-08 | Ohio | USHL | 60 | 3 | 24 | 27 | 145 | .... | .... | .... | .... | .... |
| 2008-09 | U. of Michigan | CCHA | 28 | 0 | 5 | 5 | 32 | .... | .... | .... | .... | .... |

Traded to **Montreal** by **Toronto** with Toronto's 2nd round choice (later traded to Chicago) in 2010 Entry Draft for Mikhail Grabovski, July 3, 2008.

## PATTERSON, Gaelan (PA-tuhr-suhn, GAY-luhn) CGY.

Center. Shoots left. 6', 204 lbs. Born, La Ronge, Sask., August 22, 1990.
(Calgary's 6th choice, 201st overall, in 2009 Entry Draft).

| | | | Regular Season | | | | | Playoffs | | | | |
|---|---|---|---|---|---|---|---|---|---|---|---|---|
| Season | Club | League | GP | G | A | Pts | PIM | GP | G | A | Pts | PIM |
| 2005-06 | Beardy's | SMHL | 38 | 7 | 10 | 17 | 16 | .... | .... | .... | .... | .... |
| 2006-07 | Saskatoon Blades | WHL | 53 | 3 | 1 | 4 | 24 | .... | .... | .... | .... | .... |
| 2007-08 | Saskatoon Blades | WHL | 51 | 4 | 6 | 10 | 38 | .... | .... | .... | .... | .... |
| 2008-09 | Saskatoon Blades | WHL | 71 | 22 | 35 | 57 | 41 | 7 | 1 | 1 | 2 | 2 |

## PAUKOVICH, Geoff (paw-KOH-vihch, JEHF) EDM.

Left wing. Shoots left. 6'4", 208 lbs. Born, Englewood, CO, April 24, 1986.
(Edmonton's 4th choice, 57th overall, in 2004 Entry Draft).

| | | | Regular Season | | | | | Playoffs | | | | |
|---|---|---|---|---|---|---|---|---|---|---|---|---|
| Season | Club | League | GP | G | A | Pts | PIM | GP | G | A | Pts | PIM |
| 2002-03 | Tri-City Storm | USHL | 31 | 1 | 3 | 4 | 29 | .... | .... | .... | .... | .... |
| 2003-04 | USNTDP | U-18 | 44 | 6 | 9 | 15 | 46 | .... | .... | .... | .... | .... |
| | USNTDP | NAHL | 11 | 4 | 2 | 6 | 31 | .... | .... | .... | .... | .... |
| 2004-05 | U. of Denver | WCHA | 41 | 12 | 10 | 22 | 120 | .... | .... | .... | .... | .... |
| 2005-06 | U. of Denver | WCHA | 37 | 4 | 6 | 10 | 72 | .... | .... | .... | .... | .... |
| 2006-07 | U. of Denver | WCHA | 39 | 8 | 9 | 17 | 65 | .... | .... | .... | .... | .... |
| 2007-08 | Stockton Thunder | ECHL | 70 | 13 | 13 | 26 | 94 | 6 | 1 | 0 | 1 | 4 |
| 2008-09 | Springfield Falcons | AHL | 46 | 5 | 4 | 9 | 51 | .... | .... | .... | .... | .... |
| | Stockton Thunder | ECHL | 6 | 1 | 0 | 1 | 4 | .... | .... | .... | .... | .... |

## PELECH, Michael (PEH-lehch, MIGH-kuhl) L.A.

Center/Left wing. Shoots left. 6'3", 206 lbs. Born, Toronto, Ont., October 6, 1989.
(Los Angeles' 7th choice, 156th overall, in 2009 Entry Draft).

| | | | Regular Season | | | | | Playoffs | | | | |
|---|---|---|---|---|---|---|---|---|---|---|---|---|
| Season | Club | League | GP | G | A | Pts | PIM | GP | G | A | Pts | PIM |
| 2004-05 | St. Mike's B's | OPJHL | 47 | 12 | 25 | 37 | 22 | 23 | 1 | 7 | 8 | 20 |
| 2005-06 | Kitchener Rangers | OHL | 48 | 3 | 6 | 9 | 32 | 2 | 0 | 0 | 0 | 0 |
| 2006-07 | St. Michael's | OHL | 65 | 12 | 35 | 47 | 54 | .... | .... | .... | .... | .... |
| 2007-08 | St. Michael's | OHL | 68 | 17 | 32 | 49 | 72 | 4 | 1 | 1 | 2 | 6 |
| 2008-09 | St. Michael's | OHL | 68 | 19 | 46 | 65 | 121 | 11 | 4 | 9 | 13 | 23 |

## PELTZ, Brad (PEHLTZ, BRAD) OTT.

Left wing. Shoots right. 6'1", 185 lbs. Born, New York, NY, October 2, 1989.
(Ottawa's 8th choice, 190th overall, in 2009 Entry Draft).

| | | | Regular Season | | | | | Playoffs | | | | |
|---|---|---|---|---|---|---|---|---|---|---|---|---|
| Season | Club | League | GP | G | A | Pts | PIM | GP | G | A | Pts | PIM |
| 2005-06 | Avon Old Farms | High-CT | 19 | 2 | 0 | 2 | 6 | .... | .... | .... | .... | .... |
| 2006-07 | Avon Old Farms | High-CT | 26 | 8 | 7 | 15 | 8 | .... | .... | .... | .... | .... |
| 2007-08 | Avon Old Farms | High-CT | 27 | 12 | 19 | 31 | 12 | .... | .... | .... | .... | .... |
| 2008-09 | Avon Old Farms | High-CT | DID NOT PLAY – INJURED | | | | | | | | | |

• Signed Letter of Intent to attend **Yale University** (ECAC) in fall of 2010.

## PELUSO, Anthony (puh-LOO-soh, AN-toh-nee) ST.L.

Defense. Shoots right. 6'3", 230 lbs. Born, North York, Ont., April 18, 1989.
(St. Louis' 9th choice, 160th overall, in 2007 Entry Draft).

| | | | Regular Season | | | | | Playoffs | | | | |
|---|---|---|---|---|---|---|---|---|---|---|---|---|
| Season | Club | League | GP | G | A | Pts | PIM | GP | G | A | Pts | PIM |
| 2004-05 | Richmond Hill | Minor-ON | 30 | 22 | 20 | 42 | 80 | .... | .... | .... | .... | .... |
| 2005-06 | Erie Otters | OHL | 68 | 5 | 3 | 8 | 66 | .... | .... | .... | .... | .... |
| 2006-07 | Erie Otters | OHL | 52 | 7 | 3 | 10 | 176 | .... | .... | .... | .... | .... |
| 2007-08 | Erie Otters | OHL | 21 | 3 | 3 | 6 | 41 | .... | .... | .... | .... | .... |
| | Sault Ste. Marie | OHL | 42 | 4 | 11 | 15 | 83 | 14 | 2 | 1 | 3 | 12 |
| 2008-09 | Sault Ste. Marie | OHL | 36 | 9 | 6 | 15 | 68 | .... | .... | .... | .... | .... |
| | Brampton | OHL | 27 | 11 | 11 | 22 | 57 | 21 | 8 | 7 | 15 | 29 |

## PELUSO, Chris (puh-LOO-soh, KRIHS) PIT.

Defense. Shoots left. 5'11", 180 lbs. Born, Wadena, MN, August 21, 1986.
(Pittsburgh's 9th choice, 194th overall, in 2004 Entry Draft).

| | | | Regular Season | | | | | Playoffs | | | | |
|---|---|---|---|---|---|---|---|---|---|---|---|---|
| Season | Club | League | GP | G | A | Pts | PIM | GP | G | A | Pts | PIM |
| 2003-04 | Brainerd | High-MN | 25 | 10 | 33 | 43 | .... | .... | .... | .... | .... | .... |
| 2004-05 | Sioux Falls | USHL | 53 | 1 | 7 | 8 | 54 | .... | .... | .... | .... | .... |
| 2005-06 | Sioux Falls | USHL | 57 | 5 | 19 | 24 | 49 | 14 | 0 | 4 | 4 | 8 |
| 2006-07 | Bemidji State | CHA | 26 | 0 | 6 | 6 | 24 | .... | .... | .... | .... | .... |
| 2007-08 | Bemidji State | CHA | 36 | 1 | 9 | 10 | 26 | .... | .... | .... | .... | .... |
| 2008-09 | Bemidji State | CHA | 35 | 0 | 13 | 13 | 34 | .... | .... | .... | .... | .... |

## PENNER, Jeff (PEH-nuhr, JEHF) BOS.

Defense. Shoots left. 5'10", 191 lbs. Born, Steinbach, Man., April 13, 1987.

| | | | Regular Season | | | | | Playoffs | | | | |
|---|---|---|---|---|---|---|---|---|---|---|---|---|
| Season | Club | League | GP | G | A | Pts | PIM | GP | G | A | Pts | PIM |
| 2005-06 | Dauphin Kings | MJHL | 44 | 8 | 27 | 35 | 46 | .... | .... | .... | .... | .... |
| 2006-07 | Dauphin Kings | MJHL | 45 | 9 | 44 | 53 | .... | .... | .... | .... | .... | .... |
| 2007-08 | Alaska | CCHA | 35 | 5 | 7 | 12 | 49 | .... | .... | .... | .... | .... |
| | Providence Bruins | AHL | 2 | 0 | 0 | 0 | 0 | .... | .... | .... | .... | .... |
| 2008-09 | Providence Bruins | AHL | 80 | 10 | 18 | 28 | 50 | 16 | 6 | 5 | 11 | 8 |

MJHL Rookie All-Star Team (2006) • MJHL First All-Star Team (2007)

Signed as a free agent by **Boston**, March 29, 2008.

## PERKOVICH, Nathan (puhr-KOH-vihch, NAY-thuhn) N.J.

Right wing. Shoots right. 6'5", 195 lbs. Born, Canton, MI, October 15, 1985.
(New Jersey's 6th choice, 250th overall, in 2004 Entry Draft).

| | | | Regular Season | | | | | Playoffs | | | | |
|---|---|---|---|---|---|---|---|---|---|---|---|---|
| Season | Club | League | GP | G | A | Pts | PIM | GP | G | A | Pts | PIM |
| 2003-04 | Cedar Rapids | USHL | 35 | 1 | 7 | 8 | 23 | 4 | 1 | 0 | 1 | 0 |
| 2004-05 | Chicago Steel | USHL | 37 | 6 | 2 | 8 | 55 | 7 | 2 | 2 | 4 | 4 |
| 2005-06 | Chicago Steel | USHL | 56 | 28 | 24 | 52 | 121 | .... | .... | .... | .... | .... |
| 2006-07 | Lake Superior | CCHA | 42 | 15 | 7 | 22 | 59 | .... | .... | .... | .... | .... |
| 2007-08 | Lake Superior | CCHA | 36 | 17 | 8 | 25 | 52 | .... | .... | .... | .... | .... |
| 2008-09 | Lake Superior | CCHA | 35 | 12 | 12 | 24 | 68 | .... | .... | .... | .... | .... |
| | Trenton Devils | ECHL | .... | .... | .... | .... | .... | 6 | 1 | 3 | 4 | 4 |

## PERREAULT, Mathieu (pair-OH, MA-tyew) WSH.

Center. Shoots left. 5'10", 175 lbs. Born, Drummondville, Que., January 5, 1988.
(Washington's 10th choice, 177th overall, in 2006 Entry Draft).

| | | | Regular Season | | | | | Playoffs | | | | |
|---|---|---|---|---|---|---|---|---|---|---|---|---|
| Season | Club | League | GP | G | A | Pts | PIM | GP | G | A | Pts | PIM |
| 2004-05 | Magog | QAAA | 41 | 25 | 47 | 72 | 68 | 9 | 5 | 10 | 15 | 12 |
| 2005-06 | Acadie-Bathurst | QMJHL | 62 | 18 | 34 | 52 | 42 | 17 | 10 | 11 | 21 | 8 |
| 2006-07 | Acadie-Bathurst | QMJHL | 67 | 41 | 78 | 119 | 66 | 12 | 6 | 8 | 14 | 8 |
| 2007-08 | Acadie-Bathurst | QMJHL | 65 | 34 | *80 | *114 | 61 | 12 | 3 | 19 | 22 | 6 |
| | Hershey Bears | AHL | .... | .... | .... | .... | .... | 3 | 0 | 0 | 0 | 0 |
| 2008-09 | Hershey Bears | AHL | 77 | 11 | 39 | 50 | 36 | 21 | 2 | 6 | 8 | 8 |

QMJHL First All-Star Team (2007) • QMJHL Player of the Year (2007) • QMJHL Second All-Star Team (2008) • Canadian Major Junior Second All-Star Team (2007, 2008)

## PERRY, Todd (PAIHR-ee, TAWD)

Defense. Shoots left. 6'3", 215 lbs. Born, Ingleside, Ont., December 13, 1986.

| | | | Regular Season | | | | | Playoffs | | | | |
|---|---|---|---|---|---|---|---|---|---|---|---|---|
| Season | Club | League | GP | G | A | Pts | PIM | GP | G | A | Pts | PIM |
| 2002-03 | Brockville Braves | CJHL | 55 | 3 | 28 | 31 | .... | .... | .... | .... | .... | .... |
| 2003-04 | Brockville Braves | CJHL | 38 | 7 | 16 | 23 | .... | .... | .... | .... | .... | .... |
| 2004-05 | Boston College | H-East | 4 | 0 | 0 | 0 | 0 | .... | .... | .... | .... | .... |
| | Barrie Colts | OHL | 29 | 0 | 8 | 8 | 46 | 6 | 0 | 0 | 0 | 13 |
| 2005-06 | Barrie Colts | OHL | 67 | 4 | 20 | 24 | 165 | 14 | 2 | 3 | 5 | 29 |
| 2006-07 | London Knights | OHL | 67 | 1 | 18 | 19 | 129 | 16 | 2 | 4 | 6 | 36 |
| 2007-08 | Toronto Marlies | AHL | 8 | 0 | 1 | 1 | 8 | .... | .... | .... | .... | .... |
| | Columbia Inferno | ECHL | 55 | 6 | 22 | 28 | 73 | 13 | 0 | 0 | 0 | 14 |
| 2008-09 | Toronto Marlies | AHL | 70 | 2 | 5 | 7 | 81 | 6 | 0 | 2 | 2 | 6 |

Signed by **Barrie** (OHL) after leaving **Boston College** (H-East), January 2, 2005. Signed as a free agent by **Toronto** (AHL), October 3, 2007.

### PERSSON, Dennis (PAIR-suhn, DEH-nihs) BUF.

Defense. Shoots left. 6'1", 181 lbs. Born, Nykoping, Sweden, June 2, 1988.
(Buffalo's 1st choice, 24th overall, in 2006 Entry Draft).

| | | | Regular Season | | | | | Playoffs | | | | |
|---|---|---|---|---|---|---|---|---|---|---|---|---|
| Season | Club | League | GP | G | A | Pts | PIM | GP | G | A | Pts | PIM |
| 2004-05 | Vasteras U18 | Swe-U18 | 3 | 0 | 1 | 1 | 2 | 4 | 0 | 1 | 1 | 0 |
| | Vasteras Jr. | Swe-Jr. | 27 | 3 | 3 | 6 | 24 | .... | .... | .... | .... | .... |
| 2005-06 | Vasteras Jr. | Swe-Jr. | 28 | 11 | 15 | 26 | 22 | .... | .... | .... | .... | .... |
| | VIK Vasteras HK | Sweden-2 | 19 | 0 | 2 | 2 | 6 | .... | .... | .... | .... | .... |
| 2006-07 | Djurgarden | Sweden | 9 | 0 | 0 | 0 | 2 | .... | .... | .... | .... | .... |
| | Almtuna | Sweden-2 | 3 | 0 | 0 | 0 | 2 | .... | .... | .... | .... | .... |
| | Nykoping | Sweden-2 | 29 | 4 | 4 | 8 | 38 | .... | .... | .... | .... | .... |
| | Djurgarden Jr. | Swe-Jr. | 11 | 1 | 3 | 4 | 8 | 5 | 2 | 3 | 5 | 2 |
| 2007-08 | Djurgarden Jr. | Swe-Jr. | 4 | 0 | 0 | 0 | 10 | .... | .... | .... | .... | .... |
| | Djurgarden | Sweden | 21 | 0 | 1 | 1 | 6 | .... | .... | .... | .... | .... |
| | Nykoping | Sweden-2 | 21 | 1 | 3 | 4 | 14 | .... | .... | .... | .... | .... |
| 2008-09 | Timra IK | Sweden | 46 | 1 | 5 | 6 | 24 | 7 | 0 | 0 | 0 | 0 |
| | Timra IK Jr. | Swe-Jr. | 1 | 0 | 0 | 0 | 0 | .... | .... | .... | .... | .... |
| | Portland Pirates | AHL | 8 | 0 | 2 | 2 | 6 | 3 | 0 | 0 | 0 | 0 |

### PERVYSHIN, Andrei (pair-VIHSH-ihn, AWN-dray) ST.L.

Defense. Shoots left. 5'8", 156 lbs. Born, Arkhangelsk, USSR, February 2, 1985.
(St. Louis' 11th choice, 253rd overall, in 2003 Entry Draft).

| | | | Regular Season | | | | | Playoffs | | | | |
|---|---|---|---|---|---|---|---|---|---|---|---|---|
| Season | Club | League | GP | G | A | Pts | PIM | GP | G | A | Pts | PIM |
| 2003-04 | Spartak Moscow | Russia-2 | 59 | 3 | 6 | 9 | 14 | 13 | 0 | 1 | 1 | 4 |
| 2004-05 | Ak Bars Kazan 2 | Russia-3 | .... | 0 | 1 | 1 | .... | .... | .... | .... | .... | .... |
| | Ak Bars Kazan | Russia | 52 | 0 | 3 | 3 | 10 | 2 | 0 | 0 | 0 | 0 |
| 2005-06 | Ak Bars Kazan | Russia | 48 | 3 | 7 | 10 | 22 | 13 | 0 | 3 | 3 | 14 |
| 2006-07 | Ak Bars Kazan | Russia | 45 | 5 | 8 | 13 | 71 | 12 | 2 | 3 | 5 | 8 |
| 2007-08 | Ak Bars Kazan | Russia | 55 | 7 | 8 | 15 | 40 | 10 | 1 | 1 | 2 | 2 |
| 2008-09 | Ak Bars Kazan | Rus-KHL | 54 | 6 | 21 | 27 | 28 | 21 | 1 | 9 | 10 | 10 |

### PESTUNOV, Dmitri (pehs-too-NAWF, dih-MEE-tree) PHX.

Center. Shoots left. 5'9", 196 lbs. Born, Ust-Kamenogorsk, USSR, January 22, 1985.
(Phoenix's 2nd choice, 80th overall, in 2003 Entry Draft).

| | | | Regular Season | | | | | Playoffs | | | | |
|---|---|---|---|---|---|---|---|---|---|---|---|---|
| Season | Club | League | GP | G | A | Pts | PIM | GP | G | A | Pts | PIM |
| 2002-03 | Magnitogorsk | Russia | 32 | 4 | 0 | 4 | 0 | .... | .... | .... | .... | .... |
| 2003-04 | Magnitogorsk | Russia | 51 | 6 | 7 | 13 | 40 | 14 | 0 | 3 | 3 | 25 |
| | Magnitogorsk 2 | Russia-3 | 6 | 3 | 15 | 18 | 2 | 3 | 0 | 2 | 2 | 4 |
| 2004-05 | Magnitogorsk | Russia | 37 | 4 | 4 | 8 | 46 | .... | .... | .... | .... | .... |
| | Spartak Moscow | Russia | 12 | 1 | 1 | 2 | 14 | .... | .... | .... | .... | .... |
| 2005-06 | Magnitogorsk | Russia | 48 | 6 | 13 | 19 | 58 | 4 | 0 | 1 | 1 | 0 |
| 2006-07 | Magnitogorsk | Russia | 53 | 5 | 18 | 23 | 26 | 11 | 0 | 0 | 0 | 8 |
| 2007-08 | Spartak Moscow | Russia | 51 | 8 | 17 | 25 | 56 | 5 | 0 | 0 | 0 | 16 |
| 2008-09 | Omsk | Rus-KHL | 56 | 7 | 34 | 41 | 58 | 9 | 0 | 3 | 3 | 16 |

Signed as a free agent by **Spartak Moscow** (Russia), February 16, 2005.

### PETERSEN, Nick (PEE-tuhr-suhn, NIHK) PIT.

Right wing. Shoots right. 6'2", 186 lbs. Born, Wakefield, Que., May 27, 1989.
(Pittsburgh's 4th choice, 121st overall, in 2009 Entry Draft).

| | | | Regular Season | | | | | Playoffs | | | | |
|---|---|---|---|---|---|---|---|---|---|---|---|---|
| Season | Club | League | GP | G | A | Pts | PIM | GP | G | A | Pts | PIM |
| 2006-07 | Georgetown Prep. | High-MD | .... | 28 | 14 | 42 | .... | .... | .... | .... | .... | .... |
| | Wsh. Jr. Nationals | AtJHL | 40 | 24 | 34 | 58 | 40 | .... | .... | .... | .... | .... |
| 2007-08 | Shawinigan | QMJHL | 51 | 11 | 18 | 29 | 38 | 5 | 5 | 1 | 6 | 8 |
| 2008-09 | Shawinigan | QMJHL | 68 | 37 | 53 | 90 | 42 | 21 | 10 | 12 | 22 | 22 |

### PETERSSON, Andre (PEH-tuhr-suhn, AHN-dray) OTT.

Right wing. Shoots right. 5'9", 174 lbs. Born, Olofstrom, Sweden, September 11, 1990.
(Ottawa's 4th choice, 109th overall, in 2008 Entry Draft).

| | | | Regular Season | | | | | Playoffs | | | | |
|---|---|---|---|---|---|---|---|---|---|---|---|---|
| Season | Club | League | GP | G | A | Pts | PIM | GP | G | A | Pts | PIM |
| 2005-06 | Tingsryds AIF U18 | Swe-U18 | 9 | 5 | 3 | 8 | 0 | .... | .... | .... | .... | .... |
| 2006-07 | HV 71 U18 | Swe-U18 | 10 | 14 | 10 | 24 | 6 | 2 | 1 | 2 | 3 | 0 |
| | HV 71 Jr. | Swe-Jr. | 6 | 1 | 1 | 2 | 8 | .... | .... | .... | .... | .... |
| 2007-08 | HV 71 U18 | Swe-U18 | 4 | 4 | 5 | 9 | 4 | .... | .... | .... | .... | .... |
| | HV 71 Jr. | Swe-Jr. | 36 | 16 | 22 | 38 | 34 | 3 | 0 | 0 | 0 | 2 |
| 2008-09 | HV 71 Jonkoping | Sweden | 10 | 0 | 1 | 1 | 0 | .... | .... | .... | .... | .... |
| | HV 71 Jr. | Swe-Jr. | 36 | 24 | 31 | 55 | 28 | 7 | 7 | 4 | 11 | 8 |

### PETRECKI, Nicholas (peh-TREH-kee, NIH-koh-las) S.J.

Defense. Shoots left. 6'3", 215 lbs. Born, Schenectady, NY, July 11, 1989.
(San Jose's 2nd choice, 28th overall, in 2007 Entry Draft).

| | | | Regular Season | | | | | Playoffs | | | | |
|---|---|---|---|---|---|---|---|---|---|---|---|---|
| Season | Club | League | GP | G | A | Pts | PIM | GP | G | A | Pts | PIM |
| 2004-05 | Capital District | EmJHL | 53 | 5 | 18 | 23 | 159 | .... | .... | .... | .... | .... |
| 2005-06 | Omaha Lancers | USHL | 53 | 0 | 3 | 3 | 110 | 5 | 0 | 0 | 0 | 0 |
| 2006-07 | Omaha Lancers | USHL | 54 | 11 | 14 | 25 | 177 | 5 | 0 | 0 | 0 | 10 |
| 2007-08 | Boston College | H-East | 42 | 5 | 7 | 12 | *102 | .... | .... | .... | .... | .... |
| 2008-09 | Boston College | H-East | 35 | 0 | 7 | 7 | *161 | .... | .... | .... | .... | .... |

USHL Second All-Star Team (2007)

### PETROV, Kirill (peh-TRAWF, kih-RIHL) NYI

Right wing. Shoots left. 6'3", 198 lbs. Born, Kazan, USSR, April 13, 1990.
(NY Islanders' 7th choice, 73rd overall, in 2008 Entry Draft).

| | | | Regular Season | | | | | Playoffs | | | | |
|---|---|---|---|---|---|---|---|---|---|---|---|---|
| Season | Club | League | GP | G | A | Pts | PIM | GP | G | A | Pts | PIM |
| 2005-06 | Ak Bars Kazan 2 | Russia-3 | STATISTICS NOT AVAILABLE | | | | | | | | | |
| 2006-07 | Ak Bars Kazan 2 | Russia-3 | STATISTICS NOT AVAILABLE | | | | | | | | | |
| | Ak Bars Kazan | Russia | 9 | 1 | 1 | 2 | 8 | 3 | 0 | 0 | 0 | 2 |
| 2007-08 | Ak Bars Kazan | Russia | 47 | 4 | 6 | 10 | 54 | 8 | 1 | 1 | 2 | 0 |
| 2008-09 | Ak Bars Kazan 2 | Russia-3 | 9 | 4 | 10 | 14 | 26 | .... | .... | .... | .... | .... |
| | Ak Bars Kazan | Rus-KHL | 6 | 1 | 0 | 1 | 2 | .... | .... | .... | .... | .... |

### PETRY, Jeff (PEH-tree, JEHF) EDM.

Defense. Shoots right. 6'3", 180 lbs. Born, Ann Arbor, MI, December 9, 1987.
(Edmonton's 1st choice, 45th overall, in 2006 Entry Draft).

| | | | Regular Season | | | | | Playoffs | | | | |
|---|---|---|---|---|---|---|---|---|---|---|---|---|
| Season | Club | League | GP | G | A | Pts | PIM | GP | G | A | Pts | PIM |
| 2004-05 | St. Mary's Prep | High-MI | 23 | 2 | 8 | 10 | .... | 6 | 2 | 5 | 7 | .... |
| 2005-06 | Det. Caesers | MWEHL | 33 | 7 | 21 | 28 | 24 | .... | .... | .... | .... | .... |
| | Des Moines | USHL | 48 | 1 | 14 | 15 | 68 | 11 | 2 | 5 | 7 | 8 |
| 2006-07 | Des Moines | USHL | 55 | 18 | 27 | 45 | 71 | 8 | 0 | 6 | 6 | 10 |
| 2007-08 | Michigan State | CCHA | 42 | 3 | 21 | 24 | 28 | .... | .... | .... | .... | .... |
| 2008-09 | Michigan State | CCHA | 38 | 2 | 12 | 14 | 32 | .... | .... | .... | .... | .... |

USHL First All-Star Team (2007) • USHL Defenseman of the Year (2007) • CCHA All-Rookie Team (2008)

### PHILLIPS, Paul (FIHL-ihps, PAWL) CHI.

Defense. Shoots left. 6'1", 195 lbs. Born, Darien, IL, July 16, 1991.
(Chicago's 7th choice, 195th overall, in 2009 Entry Draft).

| | | | Regular Season | | | | | Playoffs | | | | |
|---|---|---|---|---|---|---|---|---|---|---|---|---|
| Season | Club | League | GP | G | A | Pts | PIM | GP | G | A | Pts | PIM |
| 2006-07 | Chicago Fury | MWEHL | 26 | 7 | 5 | 12 | 40 | .... | .... | .... | .... | .... |
| 2007-08 | Cedar Rapids | USHL | 43 | 1 | 2 | 3 | 25 | 3 | 0 | 0 | 0 | 4 |
| 2008-09 | Cedar Rapids | USHL | 60 | 8 | 25 | 33 | 56 | 5 | 0 | 0 | 0 | 6 |

• Signed Letter of Intent to attend **University of Denver** (WCHA) in fall of 2009.

### PIERRO-ZABOTEL, Casey (PEE-air-oh-ZA-boh-tuhl, KAY-see) PIT.

Center. Shoots left. 6'1", 205 lbs. Born, Ashcroft, B.C., November 8, 1988.
(Pittsburgh's 4th choice, 80th overall, in 2007 Entry Draft).

| | | | Regular Season | | | | | Playoffs | | | | |
|---|---|---|---|---|---|---|---|---|---|---|---|---|
| Season | Club | League | GP | G | A | Pts | PIM | GP | G | A | Pts | PIM |
| 2004-05 | Merritt | BCHL | 58 | 6 | 6 | 12 | 19 | 5 | 0 | 0 | 0 | 0 |
| 2005-06 | Merritt | BCHL | 60 | 20 | 35 | 55 | 29 | 9 | 9 | 4 | 13 | 10 |
| 2006-07 | Merritt | BCHL | 55 | 51 | 65 | 116 | 42 | 7 | 8 | 3 | 11 | 13 |
| 2007-08 | Vancouver Giants | WHL | 49 | 19 | 29 | 48 | 8 | 10 | 2 | 4 | 6 | 4 |
| 2008-09 | Vancouver Giants | WHL | 72 | 36 | *79 | *115 | 52 | 17 | 4 | 13 | 17 | 16 |

WHL West First All-Star Team (2009) • Canadian Major Junior Second All-Star Team (2009)

### PIKKARAINEN, Ilkka (pih-kar-AY-nihn, IHL-kah) N.J.

Right wing. Shoots right. 6'2", 220 lbs. Born, Sonkajarvi, Finland, April 19, 1981.
(New Jersey's 9th choice, 218th overall, in 2002 Entry Draft).

| | | | Regular Season | | | | | Playoffs | | | | |
|---|---|---|---|---|---|---|---|---|---|---|---|---|
| Season | Club | League | GP | G | A | Pts | PIM | GP | G | A | Pts | PIM |
| 1998-99 | HIFK Helsinki U18 | Fin-U18 | 24 | 6 | 12 | 18 | 26 | 2 | 1 | 0 | 1 | 27 |
| | HIFK Helsinki Jr. | Fin-Jr. | 13 | 6 | 1 | 7 | 12 | .... | .... | .... | .... | .... |
| 99-2000 | HIFK Helsinki Jr. | Fin-Jr. | 28 | 3 | 2 | 5 | 14 | 3 | 1 | 1 | 2 | 2 |
| 2000-01 | HIFK Helsinki Jr. | Fin-Jr. | 38 | 27 | 31 | 58 | 186 | 9 | 2 | 5 | 7 | 26 |
| | HIFK Helsinki | Finland | 4 | 0 | 0 | 0 | 8 | 2 | 0 | 0 | 0 | 0 |
| 2001-02 | HIFK Helsinki | Finland | 54 | 9 | 9 | 18 | 111 | .... | .... | .... | .... | .... |
| 2002-03 | HIFK Helsinki | Finland | 47 | 11 | 12 | 23 | 40 | .... | .... | .... | .... | .... |
| 2003-04 | Albany River Rats | AHL | 63 | 8 | 10 | 18 | 118 | .... | .... | .... | .... | .... |
| 2004-05 | Albany River Rats | AHL | 71 | 12 | 12 | 24 | 102 | .... | .... | .... | .... | .... |
| 2005-06 | Albany River Rats | AHL | 62 | 9 | 11 | 20 | 85 | .... | .... | .... | .... | .... |
| 2006-07 | HIFK Helsinki | Finland | 53 | 17 | 20 | 37 | 140 | 5 | 0 | 1 | 1 | 2 |
| 2007-08 | HIFK Helsinki | Finland | 37 | 8 | 10 | 18 | 100 | 7 | 1 | 2 | 3 | 6 |
| 2008-09 | HIFK Helsinki | Finland | 54 | 24 | 13 | 37 | 149 | 2 | 0 | 0 | 0 | 0 |

### PINIZZOTTO, Steve (pih-nih-ZAW-toh, STEEV) WSH.

Center. Shoots right. 6'1", 200 lbs. Born, Mississauga, Ont., April 26, 1984.

| | | | Regular Season | | | | | Playoffs | | | | |
|---|---|---|---|---|---|---|---|---|---|---|---|---|
| Season | Club | League | GP | G | A | Pts | PIM | GP | G | A | Pts | PIM |
| 2001-02 | Oakville Blades | OPJHL | 34 | 10 | 16 | 26 | 40 | .... | .... | .... | .... | .... |
| 2002-03 | Oakville Blades | OPJHL | 44 | 16 | 24 | 40 | 152 | 2 | 0 | 0 | 0 | 2 |
| 2003-04 | Oakville Blades | OPJHL | 39 | 17 | 34 | 51 | 177 | .... | .... | .... | .... | .... |
| 2004-05 | Oakville Blades | OPJHL | 48 | 33 | 62 | 95 | 86 | .... | .... | .... | .... | .... |
| 2005-06 | RIT Tigers | NCAA | 20 | 7 | 6 | 13 | 32 | .... | .... | .... | .... | .... |
| 2006-07 | RIT Tigers | AH | 34 | 13 | 31 | 44 | 76 | .... | .... | .... | .... | .... |
| | Hershey Bears | AHL | 5 | 0 | 0 | 0 | 4 | .... | .... | .... | .... | .... |
| 2007-08 | Hershey Bears | AHL | 23 | 0 | 4 | 4 | 12 | 5 | 0 | 0 | 0 | 13 |
| | South Carolina | ECHL | 40 | 15 | 17 | 32 | 58 | 10 | 1 | 2 | 3 | 34 |
| 2008-09 | Hershey Bears | AHL | 45 | 4 | 7 | 11 | 61 | 21 | 3 | 2 | 5 | 28 |
| | South Carolina | ECHL | 11 | 4 | 6 | 10 | 19 | .... | .... | .... | .... | .... |

Signed as a free agent by **Washington**, March 16, 2007.

### PIRRI, Brandon (PIHR-ee, BRAN-duhn) CHI.

Center. Shoots left. 6', 160 lbs. Born, Toronto, Ont., April 10, 1991.
(Chicago's 2nd choice, 59th overall, in 2009 Entry Draft).

| | | | Regular Season | | | | | Playoffs | | | | |
|---|---|---|---|---|---|---|---|---|---|---|---|---|
| Season | Club | League | GP | G | A | Pts | PIM | GP | G | A | Pts | PIM |
| 2006-07 | Tor. Young Nats | GTHL | 44 | 54 | 72 | 128 | 18 | .... | .... | .... | .... | .... |
| 2007-08 | Streetsville Derbys | OPJHL | 40 | 18 | 32 | 50 | 42 | .... | .... | .... | .... | .... |
| 2008-09 | Streetsville Derbys | OJHL | 18 | 21 | 28 | 49 | 24 | .... | .... | .... | .... | .... |
| | Georgetown | OJHL | 26 | 25 | 20 | 45 | 22 | .... | .... | .... | .... | .... |

• Signed Letter of Intent to attend **R.P.I.** (ECAC) in fall of 2009.

### PISTILLI, Matthew (pihs-TIHL-lee, MATH-yew) CAR.

Right wing. Shoots right. 6'2", 219 lbs. Born, Montreal, Que., October 17, 1988.

| | | | Regular Season | | | | | Playoffs | | | | |
|---|---|---|---|---|---|---|---|---|---|---|---|---|
| Season | Club | League | GP | G | A | Pts | PIM | GP | G | A | Pts | PIM |
| 2004-05 | Trois-Rivieres | QAAA | 41 | 20 | 28 | 48 | 34 | .... | .... | .... | .... | .... |
| | Shawinigan | QMJHL | 2 | 1 | 1 | 2 | 6 | .... | .... | .... | .... | .... |
| 2005-06 | Shawinigan | QMJHL | 34 | 5 | 5 | 10 | 20 | .... | .... | .... | .... | .... |
| | Gatineau | QMJHL | 32 | 10 | 13 | 23 | 16 | 17 | 2 | 2 | 4 | 8 |
| 2006-07 | Gatineau | QMJHL | 65 | 22 | 29 | 51 | 44 | 5 | 1 | 1 | 2 | 2 |
| 2007-08 | Gatineau | QMJHL | 63 | 37 | 56 | 93 | 51 | 19 | 11 | 17 | 28 | 14 |
| 2008-09 | Shawinigan | QMJHL | 63 | 45 | 41 | 86 | 37 | 21 | 13 | 7 | 20 | 4 |

Signed as a free agent by **Carolina**, May 20, 2009.

**PITTON, Jason** (PIH-tuhn, JAY-suhn)

Left wing. Shoots left. 6'3", 216 lbs. Born, Mississauga, Ont., May 23, 1986.
(NY Islanders' 9th choice, 244th overall, in 2004 Entry Draft).

| | | | Regular Season | | | | | Playoffs | | | | |
|---|---|---|---|---|---|---|---|---|---|---|---|---|
| Season | Club | League | GP | G | A | Pts | PIM | GP | G | A | Pts | PIM |
| 2002-03 | Brampton Capitals | OPJHL | 47 | 23 | 18 | 41 | 46 | .... | .... | .... | .... | .... |
| | Sault Ste. Marie | OHL | 1 | 0 | 0 | 0 | 0 | .... | .... | .... | .... | .... |
| 2003-04 | Sault Ste. Marie | OHL | 67 | 9 | 11 | 20 | 37 | .... | .... | .... | .... | .... |
| 2004-05 | Sault Ste. Marie | OHL | 68 | 23 | 19 | 42 | 35 | 7 | 2 | 2 | 4 | 4 |
| 2005-06 | Sault Ste. Marie | OHL | 37 | 18 | 9 | 27 | 29 | .... | .... | .... | .... | .... |
| | Guelph Storm | OHL | 31 | 10 | 5 | 15 | 21 | 15 | 5 | 3 | 8 | 18 |
| 2006-07 | Bridgeport | AHL | 76 | 9 | 10 | 19 | 65 | .... | .... | .... | .... | .... |
| 2007-08 | Bridgeport | AHL | 21 | 1 | 4 | 5 | 16 | .... | .... | .... | .... | .... |
| | Utah Grizzlies | ECHL | 23 | 5 | 8 | 13 | 29 | .... | .... | .... | .... | .... |
| 2008-09 | Bridgeport | AHL | 39 | 2 | 2 | 4 | 47 | .... | .... | .... | .... | .... |

**PLANTE, Alex** (PLAWNT, AL-ehx) **EDM.**

Defense. Shoots right. 6'4", 225 lbs. Born, Brandon, Man., May 9, 1989.
(Edmonton's 2nd choice, 15th overall, in 2007 Entry Draft).

| | | | Regular Season | | | | | Playoffs | | | | |
|---|---|---|---|---|---|---|---|---|---|---|---|---|
| Season | Club | League | GP | G | A | Pts | PIM | GP | G | A | Pts | PIM |
| 2004-05 | Brandon | MMHL | 37 | 5 | 21 | 26 | 120 | .... | .... | .... | .... | .... |
| | Calgary Hitmen | WHL | 8 | 0 | 0 | 0 | 6 | 11 | 0 | 0 | 0 | 17 |
| 2005-06 | Calgary Hitmen | WHL | 54 | 1 | 3 | 4 | 72 | 13 | 0 | 0 | 0 | 6 |
| 2006-07 | Calgary Hitmen | WHL | 58 | 8 | 30 | 38 | 81 | 13 | 5 | 6 | 11 | 14 |
| 2007-08 | Calgary Hitmen | WHL | 36 | 1 | 1 | 2 | 28 | 15 | 0 | 4 | 4 | 10 |
| 2008-09 | Calgary Hitmen | WHL | 68 | 8 | 37 | 45 | 157 | 18 | 6 | 9 | 15 | 41 |

**PLEKHANOV, Andrey** (pleh-HAN-awf, AWN-dray) **CBJ**

Defense. Shoots right. 6'2", 206 lbs. Born, Nizhnekamsk, USSR, July 12, 1986.
(Columbus' 5th choice, 96th overall, in 2004 Entry Draft).

| | | | Regular Season | | | | | Playoffs | | | | |
|---|---|---|---|---|---|---|---|---|---|---|---|---|
| Season | Club | League | GP | G | A | Pts | PIM | GP | G | A | Pts | PIM |
| 2003-04 | Nizhnekamsk 2 | Russia-3 | STATISTICS NOT AVAILABLE | | | | | | | | | |
| 2004-05 | Sarnia Sting | OHL | 2 | 0 | 0 | 0 | 0 | .... | .... | .... | .... | .... |
| | Nizhnekamsk | Russia | 2 | 0 | 0 | 0 | 2 | .... | .... | .... | .... | .... |
| | Leninogorsk | Russia-2 | 1 | 0 | 0 | 0 | 4 | .... | .... | .... | .... | .... |
| | Perm 2 | Russia-3 | 2 | 0 | 0 | 0 | 4 | .... | .... | .... | .... | .... |
| 2005-06 | Nizhnekamsk | Russia | 45 | 1 | 1 | 2 | 22 | 5 | 0 | 0 | 0 | 0 |
| 2006-07 | Nizhnekamsk | Russia | 16 | 1 | 2 | 3 | 28 | .... | .... | .... | .... | .... |
| 2007-08 | Elmira Jackals | ECHL | 7 | 0 | 1 | 1 | 2 | .... | .... | .... | .... | .... |
| | Syracuse Crunch | AHL | 40 | 9 | 16 | 25 | 10 | 8 | 1 | 2 | 3 | 2 |
| 2008-09 | Syracuse Crunch | AHL | 54 | 2 | 17 | 19 | 50 | .... | .... | .... | .... | .... |

**PONICH, Brett** (PAW-nihch, BREHT) **ST.L.**

Defense. Shoots left. 6'6", 215 lbs. Born, Edmonton, Alta., February 22, 1991.
(St. Louis' 2nd choice, 48th overall, in 2009 Entry Draft).

| | | | Regular Season | | | | | Playoffs | | | | |
|---|---|---|---|---|---|---|---|---|---|---|---|---|
| Season | Club | League | GP | G | A | Pts | PIM | GP | G | A | Pts | PIM |
| 2006-07 | Leduc Oil Kings | AMHL | 35 | 1 | 10 | 11 | 64 | 13 | 1 | 6 | 7 | 24 |
| | Portland | WHL | 2 | 0 | 0 | 0 | 0 | .... | .... | .... | .... | .... |
| 2007-08 | Portland | WHL | 64 | 0 | 3 | 3 | 63 | .... | .... | .... | .... | .... |
| 2008-09 | Portland | WHL | 72 | 1 | 17 | 18 | 117 | .... | .... | .... | .... | .... |

**POPE, Matt** (POHP, MAT) **VAN.**

Right wing. Shoots right. 6'1", 200 lbs. Born, Langley, B.C., August 5, 1984.

| | | | Regular Season | | | | | Playoffs | | | | |
|---|---|---|---|---|---|---|---|---|---|---|---|---|
| Season | Club | League | GP | G | A | Pts | PIM | GP | G | A | Pts | PIM |
| 2003-04 | Langley Hornets | BCHL | 60 | 27 | 44 | 71 | 92 | .... | .... | .... | .... | .... |
| 2004-05 | Bemidji State | CHA | 37 | 7 | 7 | 14 | 28 | .... | .... | .... | .... | .... |
| 2005-06 | Bemidji State | CHA | 37 | 7 | 14 | 21 | 44 | .... | .... | .... | .... | .... |
| 2006-07 | Bemidji State | CHA | 33 | 5 | 8 | 13 | 14 | .... | .... | .... | .... | .... |
| 2007-08 | Bemidji State | CHA | 36 | 14 | 9 | 23 | 40 | .... | .... | .... | .... | .... |
| 2008-09 | Binghamton | AHL | 4 | 2 | 1 | 3 | 4 | .... | .... | .... | .... | .... |
| | Manitoba Moose | AHL | 8 | 2 | 3 | 5 | 6 | 12 | 3 | 3 | 6 | 2 |
| | Bakersfield | ECHL | 54 | 30 | 33 | 63 | 72 | .... | .... | .... | .... | .... |

Signed as a free agent by **Vancouver**, July 2, 2009.

**POPOV, Andrei** (PAH-pawv, AWN-dray) **PHI.**

Right wing. Shoots left. 6', 187 lbs. Born, Chelyabinsk, USSR, July 15, 1988.
(Philadelphia's 10th choice, 205th overall, in 2006 Entry Draft).

| | | | Regular Season | | | | | Playoffs | | | | |
|---|---|---|---|---|---|---|---|---|---|---|---|---|
| Season | Club | League | GP | G | A | Pts | PIM | GP | G | A | Pts | PIM |
| 2003-04 | Chelyabinsk 2 | Russia-3 | 6 | 3 | 0 | 3 | 4 | .... | .... | .... | .... | .... |
| 2004-05 | Chelyabinsk 2 | Russia-3 | 17 | 7 | 1 | 8 | 4 | .... | .... | .... | .... | .... |
| 2005-06 | Chelyabinsk 2 | Russia-3 | 2 | 1 | 4 | 5 | 0 | .... | .... | .... | .... | .... |
| | Chelyabinsk | Russia-2 | 37 | 8 | 8 | 16 | 26 | 5 | 2 | 0 | 2 | 2 |
| 2006-07 | Chelyabinsk 2 | Russia-3 | 2 | 1 | 1 | 2 | 0 | .... | .... | .... | .... | .... |
| | Chelyabinsk | Russia | 44 | 2 | 10 | 12 | 36 | .... | .... | .... | .... | .... |
| 2007-08 | Chelyabinsk 2 | Russia-3 | 6 | 4 | 3 | 7 | 4 | .... | .... | .... | .... | .... |
| | Chelyabinsk | Russia | 33 | 5 | 2 | 7 | 12 | 2 | 0 | 0 | 0 | 4 |
| 2008-09 | Chelyabinsk | Rus-KHL | 54 | 4 | 5 | 9 | 38 | 3 | 0 | 0 | 0 | 0 |

**POSPISIL, Tomas** (PAWS-pih-shihl, TAW-mahsh) **ATL.**

Right wing. Shoots right. 6', 180 lbs. Born, Sumperk, Czech., August 25, 1987.
(Atlanta's 6th choice, 135th overall, in 2005 Entry Draft).

| | | | Regular Season | | | | | Playoffs | | | | |
|---|---|---|---|---|---|---|---|---|---|---|---|---|
| Season | Club | League | GP | G | A | Pts | PIM | GP | G | A | Pts | PIM |
| 2002-03 | HC Trinec U17 | CzR-U17 | 41 | 24 | 28 | 52 | 44 | 2 | 0 | 1 | 1 | 2 |
| | HC Trinec Jr. | CzRep-Jr. | 2 | 0 | 0 | 0 | 0 | 2 | 0 | 0 | 0 | 0 |
| 2003-04 | HC Trinec U17 | CzR-U17 | 3 | 3 | 3 | 6 | 14 | 5 | 5 | 2 | 7 | 26 |
| | HC Trinec Jr. | CzRep-Jr. | 45 | 14 | 11 | 25 | 40 | 2 | 1 | 1 | 2 | 0 |
| 2004-05 | HC Ocelari Trinec | CzRep | 14 | 0 | 0 | 0 | 0 | .... | .... | .... | .... | .... |
| | HC Trinec Jr. | CzRep-Jr. | 38 | 19 | 18 | 37 | 44 | 5 | 4 | 1 | 5 | 27 |
| 2005-06 | Sarnia Sting | OHL | 60 | 25 | 30 | 55 | 61 | .... | .... | .... | .... | .... |
| 2006-07 | Sarnia Sting | OHL | 55 | 29 | 38 | 67 | 38 | 4 | 1 | 5 | 6 | 4 |
| 2007-08 | Chicago Wolves | AHL | 11 | 0 | 2 | 2 | 2 | .... | .... | .... | .... | .... |
| | Gwinnett | ECHL | 54 | 18 | 23 | 41 | 18 | 8 | 2 | 3 | 5 | 6 |
| 2008-09 | Chicago Wolves | AHL | 31 | 1 | 1 | 2 | 14 | .... | .... | .... | .... | .... |
| | Albany River Rats | AHL | 17 | 1 | 3 | 4 | 4 | .... | .... | .... | .... | .... |
| | Gwinnett | ECHL | 2 | 2 | 1 | 3 | 2 | .... | .... | .... | .... | .... |

**POSTMA, Paul** (POHST-muh, PAWL) **ATL.**

Defense. Shoots right. 6'2", 180 lbs. Born, Red Deer, Alta., February 22, 1989.
(Atlanta's 4th choice, 205th overall, in 2007 Entry Draft).

| | | | Regular Season | | | | | Playoffs | | | | |
|---|---|---|---|---|---|---|---|---|---|---|---|---|
| Season | Club | League | GP | G | A | Pts | PIM | GP | G | A | Pts | PIM |
| 2004-05 | Red Deer | AMHL | 36 | 6 | 5 | 11 | 24 | .... | .... | .... | .... | .... |
| | Swift Current | WHL | 4 | 0 | 0 | 0 | 0 | .... | .... | .... | .... | .... |
| 2005-06 | Swift Current | WHL | 58 | 2 | 9 | 11 | 6 | 4 | 0 | 0 | 0 | 0 |
| 2006-07 | Swift Current | WHL | 70 | 5 | 19 | 24 | 42 | 6 | 0 | 1 | 1 | 0 |
| 2007-08 | Swift Current | WHL | 2 | 0 | 0 | 0 | 2 | .... | .... | .... | .... | .... |
| | Calgary Hitmen | WHL | 66 | 14 | 28 | 42 | 30 | 16 | 6 | 4 | 10 | 4 |
| 2008-09 | Calgary Hitmen | WHL | 70 | 23 | 61 | 84 | 28 | 18 | 5 | 8 | 13 | 10 |

WHL East First All-Star Team (2009) • Canadian Major Junior Second All-Star Team (2009)

**PRICE, Jeremy** (PRIGHS, JAIR-eh-mee) **VAN.**

Defense. Shoots right. 6'1", 175 lbs. Born, Milton, Ont., September 26, 1990.
(Vancouver's 4th choice, 113th overall, in 2009 Entry Draft).

| | | | Regular Season | | | | | Playoffs | | | | |
|---|---|---|---|---|---|---|---|---|---|---|---|---|
| Season | Club | League | GP | G | A | Pts | PIM | GP | G | A | Pts | PIM |
| 2006-07 | Milton Icehawks | OPJHL | 37 | 1 | 6 | 7 | 51 | 5 | 2 | 1 | 3 | 9 |
| 2007-08 | Milton Icehawks | OPJHL | 44 | 10 | 22 | 32 | 28 | 10 | 0 | 6 | 6 | 4 |
| 2008-09 | Nepean Raiders | CJHL | 55 | 12 | 29 | 41 | 50 | 14 | 2 | 4 | 6 | 14 |

• Signed Letter of Intent to attend **Colgate University** (ECAC) in fall of 2009.

**PRYOR, Nick** (PRIGH-uhr, NIHK) **ANA.**

Defense. Shoots left. 5'11", 184 lbs. Born, St. Paul, MN, September 9, 1990.
(Anaheim's 10th choice, 208th overall, in 2008 Entry Draft).

| | | | Regular Season | | | | | Playoffs | | | | |
|---|---|---|---|---|---|---|---|---|---|---|---|---|
| Season | Club | League | GP | G | A | Pts | PIM | GP | G | A | Pts | PIM |
| 2006-07 | USNTDP | U-17 | 7 | 2 | 3 | 5 | 2 | .... | .... | .... | .... | .... |
| | USNTDP | NAHL | 37 | 1 | 3 | 4 | 10 | 4 | 1 | 0 | 1 | 0 |
| 2007-08 | USNTDP | U-18 | 41 | 3 | 9 | 12 | 6 | .... | .... | .... | .... | .... |
| | USNTDP | NAHL | 12 | 0 | 2 | 2 | 6 | .... | .... | .... | .... | .... |
| 2008-09 | Des Moines | USHL | 31 | 6 | 12 | 18 | 26 | .... | .... | .... | .... | .... |
| | Waterloo | USHL | 12 | 1 | 5 | 6 | 10 | .... | .... | .... | .... | .... |

• Signed Letter of Intent to attend **University of Wisconsin** (WCHA) in fall of 2009.

**PUUSTINEN, Juuso** (POOS-tih-nehn, YUH-soh) **CGY.**

Right wing. Shoots right. 6'1", 185 lbs. Born, Kuopio, Finland, April 5, 1988.
(Calgary's 5th choice, 149th overall, in 2006 Entry Draft).

| | | | Regular Season | | | | | Playoffs | | | | |
|---|---|---|---|---|---|---|---|---|---|---|---|---|
| Season | Club | League | GP | G | A | Pts | PIM | GP | G | A | Pts | PIM |
| 2004-05 | KalPa Kuopio U18 | Fin-U18 | 26 | 14 | 15 | 29 | 81 | 6 | 1 | 2 | 3 | 4 |
| | KalPa Kuopio Jr. | Fin-Jr. | 1 | 0 | 0 | 0 | 0 | .... | .... | .... | .... | .... |
| 2005-06 | KalPa Kuopio U18 | Fin-U18 | 7 | 8 | 7 | 15 | 18 | 1 | 0 | 0 | 0 | 2 |
| | KalPa Kuopio Jr. | Fin-Jr. | 29 | 9 | 5 | 14 | 46 | 5 | 0 | 0 | 0 | 0 |
| 2006-07 | Suomi U20 | Finland-2 | 2 | 0 | 1 | 1 | 2 | .... | .... | .... | .... | .... |
| | Kamloops Blazers | WHL | 64 | 32 | 39 | 71 | 52 | 4 | 0 | 3 | 3 | 4 |
| 2007-08 | Kamloops Blazers | WHL | 60 | 27 | 26 | 53 | 26 | 4 | 1 | 1 | 2 | 2 |
| 2008-09 | Blues Espoo | Finland | 53 | 13 | 20 | 33 | 14 | 14 | 1 | 1 | 2 | 4 |

**PYATT, Tom** (PIGH-at, TAWM) **MTL.**

Center. Shoots left. 5'11", 183 lbs. Born, Thunder Bay, Ont., February 14, 1987.
(NY Rangers' 6th choice, 107th overall, in 2005 Entry Draft).

| | | | Regular Season | | | | | Playoffs | | | | |
|---|---|---|---|---|---|---|---|---|---|---|---|---|
| Season | Club | League | GP | G | A | Pts | PIM | GP | G | A | Pts | PIM |
| 2003-04 | Saginaw Spirit | OHL | 67 | 9 | 9 | 18 | 21 | .... | .... | .... | .... | .... |
| 2004-05 | Saginaw Spirit | OHL | 57 | 18 | 30 | 48 | 14 | .... | .... | .... | .... | .... |
| 2005-06 | Saginaw Spirit | OHL | 58 | 24 | 29 | 53 | 29 | 4 | 1 | 2 | 3 | 4 |
| 2006-07 | Saginaw Spirit | OHL | 58 | 43 | 38 | 81 | 18 | 6 | 3 | 5 | 8 | 0 |
| | Hartford Wolf Pack | AHL | 1 | 0 | 0 | 0 | 0 | .... | .... | .... | .... | .... |
| 2007-08 | Hartford Wolf Pack | AHL | 41 | 4 | 7 | 11 | 6 | 3 | 0 | 0 | 0 | 0 |
| | Charlotte | ECHL | 16 | 6 | 9 | 15 | 8 | 3 | 0 | 0 | 0 | 0 |
| 2008-09 | Hartford Wolf Pack | AHL | 73 | 15 | 22 | 37 | 22 | 4 | 0 | 0 | 0 | 2 |

Traded to **Montreal** by **NY Rangers** with Scott Gomez and Mike Busto for Chris Higgins, Ryan McDonagh and Pavel Valentenko, June 30, 2009.

**PYETT, Logan** (PIGH-eht, LOH-guhn) **DET.**

Defense. Shoots right. 5'10", 199 lbs. Born, Regina, Sask., May 26, 1988.
(Detroit's 7th choice, 212th overall, in 2006 Entry Draft).

| | | | Regular Season | | | | | Playoffs | | | | |
|---|---|---|---|---|---|---|---|---|---|---|---|---|
| Season | Club | League | GP | G | A | Pts | PIM | GP | G | A | Pts | PIM |
| 2002-03 | Balgonie | SSMHL | 35 | 27 | 46 | 73 | 40 | .... | .... | .... | .... | .... |
| 2003-04 | Regina Pat Cdns. | SMHL | 44 | 18 | 27 | 45 | 34 | .... | .... | .... | .... | .... |
| | Regina Pats | WHL | 2 | 0 | 1 | 1 | 0 | 3 | 0 | 0 | 0 | 0 |
| 2004-05 | Regina Pats | WHL | 67 | 5 | 19 | 24 | 67 | .... | .... | .... | .... | .... |
| 2005-06 | Regina Pats | WHL | 71 | 10 | 35 | 45 | 89 | 6 | 1 | 6 | 7 | 12 |
| 2006-07 | Regina Pats | WHL | 71 | 14 | 48 | 62 | 84 | 10 | 3 | 6 | 9 | 4 |
| 2007-08 | Regina Pats | WHL | 62 | 20 | 34 | 54 | 54 | 6 | 1 | 3 | 4 | 0 |
| 2008-09 | Grand Rapids | AHL | 61 | 3 | 11 | 14 | 12 | 1 | 0 | 0 | 0 | 0 |

WHL East First All-Star Team (2008) • Canadian Major Junior Second All-Star Team (2008)

**QUAILER, Steve** (KWAY-luhr, STEEV) **MTL.**

Left wing. Shoots left. 6'4", 187 lbs. Born, Arvada, CO, August 5, 1989.
(Montreal's 2nd choice, 86th overall, in 2008 Entry Draft).

| | | | Regular Season | | | | | Playoffs | | | | |
|---|---|---|---|---|---|---|---|---|---|---|---|---|
| Season | Club | League | GP | G | A | Pts | PIM | GP | G | A | Pts | PIM |
| 2006-07 | Rocky Mountain | Minor-CO | 53 | 14 | 23 | 37 | 25 | .... | .... | .... | .... | .... |
| 2007-08 | Sioux City | USHL | 60 | 19 | 30 | 49 | 55 | 4 | 1 | 2 | 3 | 4 |
| 2008-09 | Northeastern | H-East | 41 | 10 | 15 | 25 | 12 | .... | .... | .... | .... | .... |

USHL All-Rookie Team (2008) • Hockey East All-Rookie Team (2009)

### QUIST, William (KVIHST, WILL-yuhm) EDM.

Left wing. Shoots left. 6'3", 185 lbs. Born, Nybro, Sweden, July 31, 1989.
(Edmonton's 6th choice, 157th overall, in 2007 Entry Draft).

| | | | Regular Season | | | | | Playoffs | | | | |
|---|---|---|---|---|---|---|---|---|---|---|---|---|
| Season | Club | League | GP | G | A | Pts | PIM | GP | G | A | Pts | PIM |
| 2005-06 | Tingsryds AIF U18 | Swe-U18 | 12 | 6 | 3 | 9 | 12 | .... | .... | .... | .... | .... |
| | Tingsryds AIF Jr. | Swe-Jr. | 10 | 0 | 4 | 4 | 14 | .... | .... | .... | .... | .... |
| 2006-07 | Tingsryds AIF U18 | Swe-U18 | 16 | 8 | 10 | 18 | 18 | .... | .... | .... | .... | .... |
| | Tingsryds AIF Jr. | Swe-Jr. | 22 | 10 | 15 | 25 | 86 | .... | .... | .... | .... | .... |
| | Tingsryds AIF | Sweden-3 | 7 | 0 | 0 | 0 | 0 | 1 | 0 | 0 | 0 | 0 |
| 2007-08 | Linkopings HC U18 | Swe-U18 | 2 | 1 | 0 | 1 | 2 | .... | .... | .... | .... | .... |
| | Linkopings HC Jr. | Swe-Jr. | 9 | 3 | 2 | 5 | 31 | .... | .... | .... | .... | .... |
| | Tingsryds AIF U18 | Swe-U18 | 4 | 1 | 2 | 3 | 6 | .... | .... | .... | .... | .... |
| | Tingsryds AIF Jr. | Swe-Jr. | 6 | 4 | 7 | 11 | 4 | .... | .... | .... | .... | .... |
| | Tingsryds AIF | Sweden-3 | 17 | 6 | 7 | 13 | 6 | .... | .... | .... | .... | .... |
| 2008-09 | Olofstroms IK | Sweden-3 | 1 | 0 | 0 | 0 | 2 | .... | .... | .... | .... | .... |
| | Nybro Vikings IF | Sweden-2 | 53 | 11 | 2 | 13 | 47 | .... | .... | .... | .... | .... |

### RABBIT, Wacey (RA-biht, WAY-see)

Center. Shoots left. 5'10", 169 lbs. Born, Lethbridge, Alta., November 16, 1986.
(Boston's 6th choice, 154th overall, in 2005 Entry Draft).

| | | | Regular Season | | | | | Playoffs | | | | |
|---|---|---|---|---|---|---|---|---|---|---|---|---|
| Season | Club | League | GP | G | A | Pts | PIM | GP | G | A | Pts | PIM |
| 2001-02 | Cgy. North Stars | AMHL | 35 | 24 | 28 | 52 | .... | .... | .... | .... | .... | .... |
| | Saskatoon Blades | WHL | 3 | 0 | 1 | 1 | 0 | .... | .... | .... | .... | .... |
| 2002-03 | Saskatoon Blades | WHL | 62 | 21 | 24 | 45 | 33 | 5 | 1 | 3 | 4 | 6 |
| 2003-04 | Saskatoon Blades | WHL | 60 | 9 | 8 | 17 | 51 | .... | .... | .... | .... | .... |
| 2004-05 | Saskatoon Blades | WHL | 70 | 22 | 45 | 67 | 70 | 4 | 1 | 2 | 3 | 0 |
| 2005-06 | Saskatoon Blades | WHL | 64 | 28 | 28 | 56 | 45 | 10 | 5 | 3 | 8 | 4 |
| 2006-07 | Vancouver Giants | WHL | 30 | 11 | 25 | 36 | 34 | 22 | *11 | 9 | 20 | 16 |
| | Providence Bruins | AHL | 22 | 1 | 2 | 3 | 25 | .... | .... | .... | .... | .... |
| 2007-08 | Providence Bruins | AHL | 66 | 9 | 17 | 26 | 51 | 4 | 2 | 0 | 2 | 2 |
| 2008-09 | Providence Bruins | AHL | 74 | 16 | 18 | 34 | 74 | 14 | 1 | 5 | 6 | 8 |

### RAHIMI, Daniel (RA-hih-mee, DAN-yehl) VAN.

Defense. Shoots left. 6'3", 221 lbs. Born, Umea, Sweden, April 28, 1987.
(Vancouver's 2nd choice, 82nd overall, in 2006 Entry Draft).

| | | | Regular Season | | | | | Playoffs | | | | |
|---|---|---|---|---|---|---|---|---|---|---|---|---|
| Season | Club | League | GP | G | A | Pts | PIM | GP | G | A | Pts | PIM |
| 2003-04 | Bjorkloven U18 | Swe-U18 | 10 | 0 | 3 | 3 | 14 | .... | .... | .... | .... | .... |
| 2004-05 | Bjorkloven U18 | Swe-U18 | STATISTICS NOT AVAILABLE | | | | | | | | | |
| | Bjorkloven Jr. | Swe-Jr. | 3 | 1 | 0 | 1 | 8 | .... | .... | .... | .... | .... |
| 2005-06 | Bjorkloven Jr. | Swe-Jr. | 40 | 3 | 10 | 13 | 78 | 6 | 3 | 2 | 5 | 37 |
| | IF Bjorkloven Umea | Sweden-2 | 6 | 0 | 0 | 0 | 4 | .... | .... | .... | .... | .... |
| 2006-07 | Manitoba Moose | AHL | 1 | 0 | 0 | 0 | 0 | 4 | 0 | 0 | 0 | 2 |
| | Bjorkloven Jr. | Swe-Jr. | 8 | 0 | 2 | 2 | 18 | .... | .... | .... | .... | .... |
| | IF Bjorkloven Umea | Sweden-2 | 43 | 0 | 3 | 3 | 112 | 6 | 0 | 0 | 0 | 6 |
| 2007-08 | Manitoba Moose | AHL | 41 | 3 | 2 | 5 | 37 | .... | .... | .... | .... | .... |
| | Victoria | ECHL | 19 | 0 | 5 | 5 | 14 | .... | .... | .... | .... | .... |
| 2008-09 | Manitoba Moose | AHL | 58 | 1 | 5 | 6 | 49 | .... | .... | .... | .... | .... |

### RAI, Prab (RIGH, PRAB) VAN.

Center. Shoots left. 5'11", 191 lbs. Born, Surrey, B.C., November 22, 1989.
(Vancouver's 3rd choice, 131st overall, in 2008 Entry Draft).

| | | | Regular Season | | | | | Playoffs | | | | |
|---|---|---|---|---|---|---|---|---|---|---|---|---|
| Season | Club | League | GP | G | A | Pts | PIM | GP | G | A | Pts | PIM |
| 2006-07 | Prince George | WHL | 24 | 2 | 3 | 5 | 12 | .... | .... | .... | .... | .... |
| | Seattle | WHL | 38 | 5 | 14 | 19 | 18 | 8 | 1 | 4 | 5 | 0 |
| 2007-08 | Seattle | WHL | 72 | 20 | 45 | 65 | 21 | 11 | 2 | 4 | 6 | 4 |
| 2008-09 | Seattle | WHL | 61 | 25 | 40 | 65 | 29 | 5 | 1 | 1 | 2 | 0 |

### RAJALA, Toni (ray-YAH-lah, TOH-nee) EDM.

Left wing. Shoots left. 5'10", 163 lbs. Born, Parkano, Finland, March 29, 1991.
(Edmonton's 6th choice, 101st overall, in 2009 Entry Draft).

| | | | Regular Season | | | | | Playoffs | | | | |
|---|---|---|---|---|---|---|---|---|---|---|---|---|
| Season | Club | League | GP | G | A | Pts | PIM | GP | G | A | Pts | PIM |
| 2006-07 | Ilves Tampere U18 | Fin-U18 | 30 | 18 | 26 | 44 | 32 | 3 | 2 | 1 | 3 | 4 |
| | Ilves Tampere Jr. | Fin-Jr. | 1 | 0 | 0 | 0 | 0 | .... | .... | .... | .... | .... |
| 2007-08 | Ilves Tampere U18 | Fin-U18 | 13 | 10 | 15 | 25 | 18 | .... | .... | .... | .... | .... |
| | Ilves Tampere Jr. | Fin-Jr. | 33 | 13 | 22 | 35 | 10 | 5 | 1 | 3 | 4 | 8 |
| 2008-09 | Suomi U20 | Finland-2 | 4 | 1 | 2 | 3 | 2 | .... | .... | .... | .... | .... |
| | Ilves Tampere Jr. | Fin-Jr. | 31 | 14 | 17 | 31 | 18 | .... | .... | .... | .... | .... |
| | Ilves Tampere | Finland | 21 | 2 | 3 | 5 | 0 | 3 | 0 | 0 | 0 | 2 |

### RAKHSHANI, Rhett (rahk-SHAH-nee, REHT) NYI

Right wing. Shoots right. 5'10", 170 lbs. Born, Orange, CA, March 6, 1988.
(NY Islanders' 4th choice, 100th overall, in 2006 Entry Draft).

| | | | Regular Season | | | | | Playoffs | | | | |
|---|---|---|---|---|---|---|---|---|---|---|---|---|
| Season | Club | League | GP | G | A | Pts | PIM | GP | G | A | Pts | PIM |
| 2003-04 | California Wave | Minor-CA | 56 | 54 | 67 | 121 | .... | .... | .... | .... | .... | .... |
| 2004-05 | USNTDP | U-17 | 14 | 6 | 5 | 11 | 32 | .... | .... | .... | .... | .... |
| | USNTDP | NAHL | 40 | 12 | 15 | 27 | 21 | 9 | 1 | 4 | 5 | 2 |
| 2005-06 | USNTDP | U-18 | 43 | 11 | 12 | 23 | 30 | .... | .... | .... | .... | .... |
| | USNTDP | NAHL | 16 | 13 | 13 | 26 | 35 | .... | .... | .... | .... | .... |
| 2006-07 | U. of Denver | WCHA | 40 | 10 | 26 | 36 | 38 | .... | .... | .... | .... | .... |
| 2007-08 | U. of Denver | WCHA | 37 | 14 | 14 | 28 | 52 | .... | .... | .... | .... | .... |
| 2008-09 | U. of Denver | WCHA | 38 | 15 | 22 | 37 | 50 | .... | .... | .... | .... | .... |

### RANDELL, Tyler (RAN-duhl, TIGH-luhr) BOS.

Right wing. Shoots right. 6'1", 199 lbs. Born, Scarborough, Ont., June 15, 1991.
(Boston's 4th choice, 176th overall, in 2009 Entry Draft).

| | | | Regular Season | | | | | Playoffs | | | | |
|---|---|---|---|---|---|---|---|---|---|---|---|---|
| Season | Club | League | GP | G | A | Pts | PIM | GP | G | A | Pts | PIM |
| 2006-07 | Brampton | Minor-ON | 63 | 53 | 38 | 91 | 81 | .... | .... | .... | .... | .... |
| 2007-08 | Belleville Bulls | OHL | 62 | 5 | 6 | 11 | 24 | 19 | 0 | 0 | 0 | 0 |
| 2008-09 | Belleville Bulls | OHL | 36 | 10 | 5 | 15 | 60 | .... | .... | .... | .... | .... |
| | Kitchener Rangers | OHL | 37 | 14 | 8 | 22 | 39 | .... | .... | .... | .... | .... |

### RATCHUK, Michael (RAT-chuhk, MIGH-kuhl) PHI.

Defense. Shoots left. 5'10", 180 lbs. Born, Buffalo, NY, February 20, 1988.
(Philadelphia's 3rd choice, 42nd overall, in 2006 Entry Draft).

| | | | Regular Season | | | | | Playoffs | | | | |
|---|---|---|---|---|---|---|---|---|---|---|---|---|
| Season | Club | League | GP | G | A | Pts | PIM | GP | G | A | Pts | PIM |
| 2004-05 | USNTDP | U-17 | 15 | 1 | 4 | 5 | 16 | .... | .... | .... | .... | .... |
| | USNTDP | NAHL | 33 | 3 | 6 | 9 | 14 | 10 | 1 | 1 | 2 | 2 |
| 2005-06 | USNTDP | U-18 | 39 | 8 | 14 | 22 | 52 | .... | .... | .... | .... | .... |
| | USNTDP | NAHL | 16 | 4 | 4 | 8 | 4 | .... | .... | .... | .... | .... |
| 2006-07 | Michigan State | CCHA | 40 | 4 | 8 | 12 | 28 | .... | .... | .... | .... | .... |
| 2007-08 | Michigan State | CCHA | 42 | 6 | 19 | 25 | 48 | .... | .... | .... | .... | .... |
| | Philadelphia | AHL | 3 | 1 | 2 | 3 | 2 | 5 | 0 | 1 | 1 | 0 |
| 2008-09 | Philadelphia | AHL | 77 | 5 | 12 | 17 | 44 | 4 | 0 | 1 | 1 | 2 |

### RAU, Chad (ROW, CHAD) TOR.

Center. Shoots right. 5'11", 185 lbs. Born, Eden Prairie, MN, January 18, 1987.
(Toronto's 6th choice, 228th overall, in 2005 Entry Draft).

| | | | Regular Season | | | | | Playoffs | | | | |
|---|---|---|---|---|---|---|---|---|---|---|---|---|
| Season | Club | League | GP | G | A | Pts | PIM | GP | G | A | Pts | PIM |
| 2004-05 | Des Moines | USHL | 57 | 31 | 40 | 71 | 32 | .... | .... | .... | .... | .... |
| 2005-06 | Colorado College | WCHA | 42 | 13 | 17 | 30 | 8 | .... | .... | .... | .... | .... |
| 2006-07 | Colorado College | WCHA | 39 | 14 | 17 | 31 | 4 | .... | .... | .... | .... | .... |
| 2007-08 | Colorado College | WCHA | 40 | *28 | 14 | 42 | 8 | .... | .... | .... | .... | .... |
| 2008-09 | Colorado College | WCHA | 38 | 18 | 19 | 37 | 6 | .... | .... | .... | .... | .... |

USHL All-Rookie Team (2005) • USHL First All-Star Team (2005) • USHL Rookie of the Year (2005) • WCHA First All-Star Team (2008, 2009) • NCAA West Second All-American Team (2008, 2009)

### REAVES, Ryan (REEVZ, RIGH-uhn) ST.L.

Right wing. Shoots right. 6'1", 220 lbs. Born, Winnipeg, Man., January 20, 1987.
(St. Louis' 4th choice, 156th overall, in 2005 Entry Draft).

| | | | Regular Season | | | | | Playoffs | | | | |
|---|---|---|---|---|---|---|---|---|---|---|---|---|
| Season | Club | League | GP | G | A | Pts | PIM | GP | G | A | Pts | PIM |
| 2004-05 | Brandon | WHL | 64 | 7 | 9 | 16 | 79 | 23 | 2 | 4 | 6 | 43 |
| 2005-06 | Brandon | WHL | 68 | 14 | 14 | 28 | 91 | 6 | 0 | 1 | 1 | 8 |
| 2006-07 | Brandon | WHL | 69 | 15 | 20 | 35 | 76 | 11 | 1 | 4 | 5 | 19 |
| 2007-08 | Peoria Rivermen | AHL | 31 | 4 | 3 | 7 | 46 | .... | .... | .... | .... | .... |
| | Alaska Aces | ECHL | 9 | 2 | 0 | 2 | 42 | 2 | 0 | 0 | 0 | 22 |
| 2008-09 | Peoria Rivermen | AHL | 57 | 8 | 9 | 17 | 130 | 4 | 0 | 0 | 0 | 2 |

### REDMOND, Zach (REHD-muhnd, ZAK) ATL.

Defense. Shoots right. 6'2", 197 lbs. Born, Houston, TX, July 26, 1988.
(Atlanta's 7th choice, 184th overall, in 2008 Entry Draft).

| | | | Regular Season | | | | | Playoffs | | | | |
|---|---|---|---|---|---|---|---|---|---|---|---|---|
| Season | Club | League | GP | G | A | Pts | PIM | GP | G | A | Pts | PIM |
| 2005-06 | Sioux Falls | USHL | 48 | 4 | 7 | 11 | 57 | 11 | 1 | 2 | 3 | 4 |
| 2006-07 | Sioux Falls | USHL | 60 | 8 | 31 | 39 | 37 | 8 | 3 | 7 | 10 | 8 |
| 2007-08 | Ferris State | CCHA | 37 | 6 | 13 | 19 | 33 | .... | .... | .... | .... | .... |
| 2008-09 | Ferris State | CCHA | 38 | 3 | 21 | 24 | 48 | .... | .... | .... | .... | .... |

### REED, Harrison (REED, HAIR-rih-suhn) CAR.

Center/Right wing. Shoots right. 6'1", 185 lbs. Born, Newmarket, Ont., January 18, 1988.
(Carolina's 2nd choice, 93rd overall, in 2006 Entry Draft).

| | | | Regular Season | | | | | Playoffs | | | | |
|---|---|---|---|---|---|---|---|---|---|---|---|---|
| Season | Club | League | GP | G | A | Pts | PIM | GP | G | A | Pts | PIM |
| 2004-05 | Petrolia Jets | OJHL-B | 43 | 11 | 18 | 29 | 43 | .... | .... | .... | .... | .... |
| | London Knights | OHL | 6 | 0 | 0 | 0 | 0 | 4 | 0 | 1 | 1 | 0 |
| 2005-06 | Sarnia Sting | OHL | 68 | 26 | 24 | 50 | 50 | .... | .... | .... | .... | .... |
| 2006-07 | Sarnia Sting | OHL | 67 | 29 | 52 | 81 | 30 | 4 | 0 | 4 | 4 | 8 |
| 2007-08 | Sarnia Sting | OHL | 28 | 6 | 12 | 18 | 20 | .... | .... | .... | .... | .... |
| | Guelph Storm | OHL | 41 | 8 | 21 | 29 | 20 | 10 | 3 | 2 | 5 | 12 |
| 2008-09 | Albany River Rats | AHL | 70 | 5 | 4 | 9 | 22 | .... | .... | .... | .... | .... |
| | Florida Everblades | ECHL | 1 | 1 | 1 | 2 | 0 | .... | .... | .... | .... | .... |

### REESE, Dylan (REES, DIH-luhn)

Defense. Shoots right. 6', 205 lbs. Born, Pittsburgh, PA, August 29, 1984.
(NY Rangers' 9th choice, 209th overall, in 2003 Entry Draft).

| | | | Regular Season | | | | | Playoffs | | | | |
|---|---|---|---|---|---|---|---|---|---|---|---|---|
| Season | Club | League | GP | G | A | Pts | PIM | GP | G | A | Pts | PIM |
| 2000-01 | Pittsburgh Hornets | MWEHL | 66 | 14 | 42 | 66 | .... | .... | .... | .... | .... | .... |
| 2001-02 | Pittsburgh Forge | NAHL | 48 | 7 | 16 | 23 | 70 | 7 | 0 | 2 | 2 | 4 |
| 2002-03 | Pittsburgh Forge | NAHL | 56 | 11 | 30 | 41 | 98 | 5 | 2 | 3 | 5 | 6 |
| 2003-04 | Harvard Crimson | ECAC | 21 | 1 | 4 | 5 | 18 | .... | .... | .... | .... | .... |
| 2004-05 | Harvard Crimson | ECAC | 34 | 7 | 12 | 19 | 44 | .... | .... | .... | .... | .... |
| 2005-06 | Harvard Crimson | ECAC | 33 | 4 | 15 | 19 | 36 | .... | .... | .... | .... | .... |
| 2006-07 | Harvard Crimson | ECAC | 33 | 9 | 9 | 18 | 26 | .... | .... | .... | .... | .... |
| | Hartford Wolf Pack | AHL | 10 | 0 | 4 | 4 | 12 | 2 | 0 | 0 | 0 | 2 |
| 2007-08 | San Antonio | AHL | 59 | 1 | 6 | 7 | 49 | 3 | 1 | 1 | 2 | 4 |
| 2008-09 | San Antonio | AHL | 75 | 1 | 27 | 28 | 64 | .... | .... | .... | .... | .... |

ECAC Second All-Star Team (2006, 2007)

Signed as a free agent by **San Antonio** (AHL), September 5, 2007.

### REGAN, Eric (REE-guhn, AIR-ihk) ANA.

Defenseman. Shoots right. 6'2", 205 lbs. Born, Whitby, Ont., May 20, 1988.

| | | | Regular Season | | | | | Playoffs | | | | |
|---|---|---|---|---|---|---|---|---|---|---|---|---|
| Season | Club | League | GP | G | A | Pts | PIM | GP | G | A | Pts | PIM |
| 2004-05 | Erie Otters | OHL | 61 | 2 | 2 | 4 | 6 | 6 | 0 | 0 | 0 | 0 |
| 2005-06 | Erie Otters | OHL | 25 | 0 | 3 | 3 | 14 | .... | .... | .... | .... | .... |
| | Oshawa Generals | OHL | 35 | 3 | 10 | 13 | 16 | .... | .... | .... | .... | .... |
| 2006-07 | Oshawa Generals | OHL | 64 | 3 | 42 | 45 | 64 | 9 | 1 | 1 | 2 | 7 |
| 2007-08 | Oshawa Generals | OHL | 67 | 8 | 40 | 48 | 56 | 15 | 1 | 7 | 8 | 26 |
| 2008-09 | Iowa Chops | AHL | 59 | 1 | 7 | 8 | 36 | .... | .... | .... | .... | .... |

Signed as a free agent by **Anaheim**, September 22, 2008.

### REGNER, Brent (REHG-nuhr, BREHNT) CBJ

Defense. Shoots right. 5'11", 175 lbs. Born, Westlock, Alta., May 17, 1989.
(Columbus' 7th choice, 137th overall, in 2008 Entry Draft).

| | | | Regular Season | | | | | Playoffs | | | | |
|---|---|---|---|---|---|---|---|---|---|---|---|---|
| Season | Club | League | GP | G | A | Pts | PIM | GP | G | A | Pts | PIM |
| 2004-05 | Ft. Saskatchewan | AMHL | 36 | 2 | 13 | 15 | 24 | .... | .... | .... | .... | .... |
| 2005-06 | Ft. Saskatchewan | AMHL | 36 | 9 | 25 | 34 | 30 | 14 | 1 | 7 | 8 | 2 |
| | Vancouver Giants | WHL | 1 | 0 | 0 | 0 | 0 | .... | .... | .... | .... | .... |
| 2006-07 | Vancouver Giants | WHL | 64 | 1 | 5 | 6 | 19 | 22 | 0 | 6 | 6 | 10 |
| 2007-08 | Vancouver Giants | WHL | 72 | 8 | 39 | 47 | 45 | 10 | 0 | 10 | 10 | 10 |
| 2008-09 | Vancouver Giants | WHL | 70 | 15 | 52 | 67 | 42 | 17 | 2 | 11 | 13 | 6 |

WHL West Second All-Star Team (2009)

## REID, Cameron (REED, KAM-uhr-UHN) NSH.

Center. Shoots left. 6'2", 187 lbs. Born, Delta, B.C., August 25, 1991.
(Nashville's 10th choice, 192nd overall, in 2009 Entry Draft).

| | | | Regular Season | | | | | Playoffs | | | | |
|---|---|---|---|---|---|---|---|---|---|---|---|---|
| Season | Club | League | GP | G | A | Pts | PIM | GP | G | A | Pts | PIM |
| 2007-08 | Victoria Grizzlies | BCHL | 55 | 10 | 16 | 26 | 25 | 11 | 2 | 3 | 5 | 4 |
| 2008-09 | Victoria Grizzlies | BCHL | 41 | 6 | 17 | 23 | 32 | .... | .... | .... | .... | .... |
| | Westside Warriors | BCHL | 17 | 6 | 11 | 17 | 10 | 8 | 4 | 3 | 7 | 0 |

• Signed Letter of Intent to attend **University of New Hampshire** (Hockey East) in fall of 2009.

## REUL, Denis (ROIL, DEH-nihs)

Defense. Shoots right. 6'4", 214 lbs. Born, Marktredwitz, West Germany, June 29, 1989.
(Boston's 3rd choice, 130th overall, in 2007 Entry Draft).

| | | | Regular Season | | | | | Playoffs | | | | |
|---|---|---|---|---|---|---|---|---|---|---|---|---|
| Season | Club | League | GP | G | A | Pts | PIM | GP | G | A | Pts | PIM |
| 2004-05 | Mannheimer ERC | German-5 | 1 | 0 | 0 | 0 | 0 | .... | .... | .... | .... | .... |
| | Mannheim Jr. | Ger-Jr. | 34 | 0 | 3 | 3 | 18 | 7 | 1 | 0 | 1 | 12 |
| 2005-06 | Mannheim Jr. | Ger-Jr. | 36 | 6 | 13 | 19 | 40 | 5 | 0 | 1 | 1 | 4 |
| 2006-07 | Heilbronner Falken | German-3 | 16 | 0 | 1 | 1 | 16 | .... | .... | .... | .... | .... |
| | Heil./Mann. Jr. | Ger-Jr. | 34 | 9 | 17 | 26 | 82 | 6 | 0 | 1 | 1 | 16 |
| 2007-08 | Lewiston | QMJHL | 67 | 3 | 11 | 14 | 99 | 6 | 0 | 0 | 0 | 4 |
| 2008-09 | Lewiston | QMJHL | 60 | 4 | 14 | 18 | 91 | 4 | 0 | 0 | 0 | 10 |
| | Providence Bruins | AHL | 5 | 0 | 1 | 1 | 6 | .... | .... | .... | .... | .... |

Signed as a free agent by **Lewiston** (QMJHL), Asugust 14, 2007.

## RIENDEAU, Yannick (ree-EHN-doh, YAH-nihk) BOS.

Right wing. Shoots left. 5'11", 187 lbs. Born, Boucherville, Que., June 18, 1988.

| | | | Regular Season | | | | | Playoffs | | | | |
|---|---|---|---|---|---|---|---|---|---|---|---|---|
| Season | Club | League | GP | G | A | Pts | PIM | GP | G | A | Pts | PIM |
| 2004-05 | Rouyn-Noranda | QMJHL | 58 | 10 | 15 | 25 | 22 | 6 | 0 | 1 | 1 | 0 |
| 2005-06 | Rouyn-Noranda | QMJHL | 67 | 27 | 38 | 65 | 40 | 5 | 0 | 2 | 2 | 6 |
| 2006-07 | Rouyn-Noranda | QMJHL | 67 | 32 | 40 | 72 | 38 | 10 | 9 | 5 | 14 | 6 |
| 2007-08 | HC Chamonix | France | 24 | 11 | 11 | 22 | 87 | 5 | 7 | 7 | 14 | 20 |
| | Rouyn-Noranda | QMJHL | 42 | 23 | 26 | 49 | 18 | 17 | 8 | 13 | 21 | 14 |
| 2008-09 | Drummondville | QMJHL | 64 | 58 | 68 | 126 | 31 | 19 | 29 | 23 | 52 | 16 |

QMJHL First All-Star Team (2009) • Canadian Major Junior First All-Star Team (2009)

Signed as a free agent by **Boston**, April 2, 2009.

## RINALDO, Zac (rih-NAL-doh, ZAK) PHI.

Center. Shoots left. 5'11", 169 lbs. Born, Mississauga, Ont., June 15, 1990.
(Philadelphia's 4th choice, 178th overall, in 2008 Entry Draft).

| | | | Regular Season | | | | | Playoffs | | | | |
|---|---|---|---|---|---|---|---|---|---|---|---|---|
| Season | Club | League | GP | G | A | Pts | PIM | GP | G | A | Pts | PIM |
| 2006-07 | Hamilton | OPJHL | 44 | 16 | 16 | 32 | 193 | 16 | 4 | 4 | 8 | 48 |
| | St. Michael's | OHL | 6 | 0 | 0 | 0 | 2 | .... | .... | .... | .... | .... |
| 2007-08 | St. Michael's | OHL | 63 | 7 | 7 | 14 | 191 | 4 | 0 | 0 | 0 | 9 |
| 2008-09 | St. Michael's | OHL | 34 | 6 | 7 | 13 | *112 | .... | .... | .... | .... | .... |
| | London Knights | OHL | 22 | 4 | 13 | 17 | *89 | 8 | 1 | 1 | 2 | 26 |

## RISSANEN, Rasmus (RIH-sa-nehn, RAS-mus) CAR.

Defense. Shoots left. 6'2", 185 lbs. Born, Kuopio, Finland, July 13, 1991.
(Carolina's 5th choice, 178th overall, in 2009 Entry Draft).

| | | | Regular Season | | | | | Playoffs | | | | |
|---|---|---|---|---|---|---|---|---|---|---|---|---|
| Season | Club | League | GP | G | A | Pts | PIM | GP | G | A | Pts | PIM |
| 2006-07 | KalPa Kuopio U18 | Fin-U18 | 9 | 1 | 1 | 2 | 28 | 3 | 0 | 1 | 1 | 8 |
| 2007-08 | KalPa Kuopio U18 | Fin-U18 | 29 | 7 | 9 | 16 | 99 | 2 | 0 | 0 | 0 | 8 |
| | KalPa Kuopio Jr. | Fin-Jr. | 5 | 0 | 0 | 0 | 10 | .... | .... | .... | .... | .... |
| 2008-09 | KalPa Kuopio Jr. | Fin-Jr. | 29 | 1 | 8 | 9 | 56 | 4 | 0 | 1 | 1 | 6 |

## ROBAK, Colby (ROH-bak, KOHL-bee) FLA.

Defense. Shoots left. 6'3", 194 lbs. Born, Dauphin, Man., April 24, 1990.
(Florida's 2nd choice, 46th overall, in 2008 Entry Draft).

| | | | Regular Season | | | | | Playoffs | | | | |
|---|---|---|---|---|---|---|---|---|---|---|---|---|
| Season | Club | League | GP | G | A | Pts | PIM | GP | G | A | Pts | PIM |
| 2005-06 | Parkland Rangers | MMHL | 40 | 14 | 20 | 34 | 14 | .... | .... | .... | .... | .... |
| 2006-07 | Brandon | WHL | 39 | 2 | 3 | 5 | 12 | 1 | 0 | 0 | 0 | 0 |
| 2007-08 | Brandon | WHL | 71 | 6 | 24 | 30 | 25 | 6 | 0 | 2 | 2 | 8 |
| 2008-09 | Brandon | WHL | 65 | 13 | 29 | 42 | 41 | 12 | 6 | 8 | 14 | 4 |

## RODIN, Anton (ROH-dihn, AN-tawn) VAN.

Right wing. Shoots left. 5'11", 174 lbs. Born, Stockholm, Sweden, November 21, 1990.
(Vancouver's 2nd choice, 53rd overall, in 2009 Entry Draft).

| | | | Regular Season | | | | | Playoffs | | | | |
|---|---|---|---|---|---|---|---|---|---|---|---|---|
| Season | Club | League | GP | G | A | Pts | PIM | GP | G | A | Pts | PIM |
| 2006-07 | Brynas U18 | Swe-U18 | 14 | 7 | 4 | 11 | 4 | 3 | 0 | 0 | 0 | 2 |
| | Brynas IF Gavle Jr. | Swe-Jr. | 1 | 0 | 0 | 0 | 0 | .... | .... | .... | .... | .... |
| 2007-08 | Brynas U18 | Swe-U18 | 6 | 2 | 7 | 9 | 8 | 5 | 2 | 5 | 7 | 0 |
| | Brynas IF Gavle Jr. | Swe-Jr. | 35 | 8 | 11 | 19 | 36 | 7 | 1 | 0 | 1 | 0 |
| 2008-09 | Brynas IF Gavle Jr. | Swe-Jr. | 37 | 29 | 26 | 55 | 34 | 7 | 2 | 10 | 12 | 4 |
| | IK Oskarshamn | Sweden-2 | 6 | 0 | 0 | 0 | 2 | .... | .... | .... | .... | .... |

## RODWELL, Derek (RAWD-wehl, DAIR-ihk) N.J.

Left wing. Shoots right. 6'1", 190 lbs. Born, Taber, Alta., July 8, 1990.
(New Jersey's 5th choice, 144th overall, in 2009 Entry Draft).

| | | | Regular Season | | | | | Playoffs | | | | |
|---|---|---|---|---|---|---|---|---|---|---|---|---|
| Season | Club | League | GP | G | A | Pts | PIM | GP | G | A | Pts | PIM |
| 2007-08 | Okotoks Oilers | AJHL | 62 | 9 | 10 | 19 | 69 | 9 | 0 | 3 | 3 | 6 |
| 2008-09 | Okotoks Oilers | AJHL | 41 | 17 | 12 | 29 | 69 | 9 | 1 | 2 | 3 | 6 |

• Signed Letter of Intent to attend **University of North Dakota** (WCHA) in fall of 2010.

## ROE, Garrett (ROH, GAIR-eht) L.A.

Left wing. Shoots left. 5'8", 162 lbs. Born, Vienna, VA, February 22, 1988.
(Los Angeles' 9th choice, 183rd overall, in 2008 Entry Draft).

| | | | Regular Season | | | | | Playoffs | | | | |
|---|---|---|---|---|---|---|---|---|---|---|---|---|
| Season | Club | League | GP | G | A | Pts | PIM | GP | G | A | Pts | PIM |
| 2004-05 | Indiana Ice | USHL | 49 | 6 | 15 | 21 | 62 | 3 | 0 | 3 | 3 | 4 |
| 2005-06 | Indiana Ice | USHL | 49 | 21 | 32 | 53 | 93 | 2 | 3 | 0 | 3 | 0 |
| 2006-07 | Indiana Ice | USHL | 57 | 24 | 39 | 63 | 143 | 6 | 3 | 10 | 13 | 8 |
| 2007-08 | St. Cloud State | WCHA | 39 | 18 | 27 | 45 | 55 | .... | .... | .... | .... | .... |
| 2008-09 | St. Cloud State | WCHA | 38 | 17 | 31 | 48 | 72 | .... | .... | .... | .... | .... |

WCHA All-Rookie Team (2008)

## ROGERS, Andy (RAW-juhrs, AN-dee)

Defense. Shoots left. 6'5", 206 lbs. Born, Calgary, Alta., August 25, 1986.
(Tampa Bay's 1st choice, 30th overall, in 2004 Entry Draft).

| | | | Regular Season | | | | | Playoffs | | | | |
|---|---|---|---|---|---|---|---|---|---|---|---|---|
| Season | Club | League | GP | G | A | Pts | PIM | GP | G | A | Pts | PIM |
| 2000-01 | Calgary AA Gold | CMHA | 32 | 2 | 7 | 9 | 32 | .... | .... | .... | .... | .... |
| 2001-02 | Calgary AAA Gold | CBHL | 30 | 1 | 13 | 14 | 80 | .... | .... | .... | .... | .... |
| 2002-03 | Calgary Hitmen | WHL | 25 | 0 | 3 | 3 | 17 | .... | .... | .... | .... | .... |
| 2003-04 | Calgary Hitmen | WHL | 64 | 1 | 3 | 4 | 89 | 7 | 0 | 0 | 0 | 11 |
| 2004-05 | Calgary Hitmen | WHL | 18 | 1 | 4 | 5 | 36 | .... | .... | .... | .... | .... |
| | Prince George | WHL | 30 | 1 | 5 | 6 | 49 | .... | .... | .... | .... | .... |
| 2005-06 | Prince George | WHL | 21 | 0 | 3 | 3 | 51 | .... | .... | .... | .... | .... |
| 2006-07 | Springfield Falcons | AHL | 48 | 0 | 7 | 7 | 39 | .... | .... | .... | .... | .... |
| 2007-08 | Norfolk Admirals | AHL | 30 | 0 | 1 | 1 | 35 | .... | .... | .... | .... | .... |
| | Mississippi | ECHL | 4 | 1 | 0 | 1 | 10 | .... | .... | .... | .... | .... |
| 2008-09 | Norfolk Admirals | AHL | 34 | 0 | 2 | 2 | 38 | .... | .... | .... | .... | .... |
| | Toronto Marlies | AHL | 1 | 0 | 0 | 0 | 0 | 2 | 0 | 0 | 0 | 2 |

Traded to **Toronto** by **Tampa Bay** with Olaf Kolzig, Jamie Heward and Carolina's 4th round choice (previously acquired – later forfeited) in 2009 Entry Draft for Richard Petiot, March 4, 2009.

## ROGERS, Brandon (RAW-juhrs, BRAN-duhn) MIN.

Defense. Shoots right. 6'1", 195 lbs. Born, Rochester, NH, February 27, 1982.
(Anaheim's 6th choice, 118th overall, in 2001 Entry Draft).

| | | | Regular Season | | | | | Playoffs | | | | |
|---|---|---|---|---|---|---|---|---|---|---|---|---|
| Season | Club | League | GP | G | A | Pts | PIM | GP | G | A | Pts | PIM |
| 1998-99 | Hotchkiss | High-CT | 22 | 8 | 13 | 21 | .... | .... | .... | .... | .... | .... |
| 99-2000 | Hotchkiss | High-CT | 25 | 9 | 12 | 21 | 35 | .... | .... | .... | .... | .... |
| 2000-01 | Hotchkiss | High-CT | 22 | 10 | 13 | 23 | 45 | .... | .... | .... | .... | .... |
| 2001-02 | U. of Michigan | CCHA | 32 | 2 | 1 | 3 | 30 | .... | .... | .... | .... | .... |
| 2002-03 | U. of Michigan | CCHA | 43 | 4 | 21 | 25 | 65 | .... | .... | .... | .... | .... |
| 2003-04 | U. of Michigan | CCHA | 43 | 7 | 16 | 23 | 46 | .... | .... | .... | .... | .... |
| 2004-05 | U. of Michigan | CCHA | 42 | 5 | 22 | 27 | 70 | .... | .... | .... | .... | .... |
| 2005-06 | Omaha | AHL | 42 | 0 | 8 | 8 | 24 | .... | .... | .... | .... | .... |
| | Norfolk Admirals | AHL | 27 | 3 | 7 | 10 | 28 | 2 | 0 | 0 | 0 | 4 |
| 2006-07 | Norfolk Admirals | AHL | 64 | 0 | 9 | 9 | 92 | 6 | 0 | 0 | 0 | 14 |
| 2007-08 | Houston Aeros | AHL | 63 | 4 | 24 | 28 | 77 | 5 | 0 | 1 | 1 | 2 |
| 2008-09 | Houston Aeros | AHL | 74 | 3 | 29 | 32 | 80 | 20 | 0 | 3 | 3 | 12 |

CCHA Second All-Star Team (2004) • Yanick Dupre Memorial Award (AHL - Outstanding Humanitarian Contribution) (2009)

Signed as a free agent by **Minnesota**, July 15, 2008.

## ROGERS, Doug (RAW-juhrs, DUHG) NYI

Center. Shoots right. 6', 175 lbs. Born, Watertown, MA, January 20, 1988.
(NY Islanders' 7th choice, 119th overall, in 2006 Entry Draft).

| | | | Regular Season | | | | | Playoffs | | | | |
|---|---|---|---|---|---|---|---|---|---|---|---|---|
| Season | Club | League | GP | G | A | Pts | PIM | GP | G | A | Pts | PIM |
| 2003-04 | St. Sebastian's | High-MA | 28 | 24 | 24 | 48 | .... | .... | .... | .... | .... | .... |
| 2004-05 | St. Sebastian's | High-MA | 28 | 17 | 26 | 43 | .... | .... | .... | .... | .... | .... |
| 2005-06 | St. Sebastian's | High-MA | 28 | 24 | 38 | 62 | 20 | .... | .... | .... | .... | .... |
| 2006-07 | Harvard Crimson | ECAC | 33 | 7 | 17 | 24 | 18 | .... | .... | .... | .... | .... |
| 2007-08 | Harvard Crimson | ECAC | 34 | 13 | 19 | 32 | 30 | .... | .... | .... | .... | .... |
| 2008-09 | Harvard Crimson | ECAC | 31 | 8 | 13 | 21 | 40 | .... | .... | .... | .... | .... |

## ROGERS, Kyle (RAW-juhrs, KIGHL) TOR.

Right wing. Shoots right. 6'3", 215 lbs. Born, Philadelphia, PA, December 20, 1984.

| | | | Regular Season | | | | | Playoffs | | | | |
|---|---|---|---|---|---|---|---|---|---|---|---|---|
| Season | Club | League | GP | G | A | Pts | PIM | GP | G | A | Pts | PIM |
| 2005-06 | Niagara University | CHA | 28 | 2 | 2 | 4 | 12 | .... | .... | .... | .... | .... |
| 2006-07 | Niagara University | CHA | 35 | 6 | 7 | 13 | 37 | .... | .... | .... | .... | .... |
| 2007-08 | Niagara University | CHA | 34 | 10 | 13 | 23 | 40 | .... | .... | .... | .... | .... |
| | Toronto Marlies | AHL | 2 | 0 | 0 | 0 | 0 | 10 | 0 | 0 | 0 | 7 |
| 2008-09 | Toronto Marlies | AHL | 71 | 4 | 7 | 11 | 63 | 4 | 1 | 0 | 1 | 0 |

Signed as a free agent by **Toronto**, March 29, 2008.

## ROHLFS, David (ROHLFS, DAY-vihd)

Right wing. Shoots right. 6'3", 225 lbs. Born, Ann Arbor, MI, June 4, 1984.
(Edmonton's 7th choice, 154th overall, in 2003 Entry Draft).

| | | | Regular Season | | | | | Playoffs | | | | |
|---|---|---|---|---|---|---|---|---|---|---|---|---|
| Season | Club | League | GP | G | A | Pts | PIM | GP | G | A | Pts | PIM |
| 2000-01 | Det. Compuware | MWEHL | 70 | 35 | 21 | 56 | .... | .... | .... | .... | .... | .... |
| | Det. Compuware | NAHL | 4 | 0 | 1 | 1 | 0 | .... | .... | .... | .... | .... |
| 2001-02 | Det. Compuware | NAHL | 60 | 13 | 10 | 23 | 36 | .... | .... | .... | .... | .... |
| 2002-03 | Det. Compuware | NAHL | 53 | 30 | 14 | 44 | 36 | 5 | 2 | 1 | 3 | 8 |
| 2003-04 | U. of Michigan | CCHA | 43 | 7 | 6 | 13 | 26 | .... | .... | .... | .... | .... |
| 2004-05 | U. of Michigan | CCHA | 34 | 5 | 5 | 10 | 14 | .... | .... | .... | .... | .... |
| 2005-06 | U. of Michigan | CCHA | 40 | 2 | 10 | 12 | 43 | .... | .... | .... | .... | .... |
| 2006-07 | U. of Michigan | CCHA | 41 | 17 | 17 | 34 | 30 | .... | .... | .... | .... | .... |
| 2007-08 | Springfield Falcons | AHL | 2 | 0 | 0 | 0 | 2 | .... | .... | .... | .... | .... |
| | Stockton Thunder | ECHL | 65 | 16 | 16 | 32 | 41 | 2 | 0 | 0 | 0 | 0 |
| 2008-09 | Stockton Thunder | ECHL | 55 | 7 | 5 | 12 | 31 | 12 | 2 | 3 | 5 | 6 |

## ROMAN, Ondrej (ROH-mahn, AWN-dray) DAL.

Center. Shoots left. 6', 168 lbs. Born, Ostrava, Czech., April 8, 1989.
(Dallas' 6th choice, 136th overall, in 2007 Entry Draft).

| | | | Regular Season | | | | | Playoffs | | | | |
|---|---|---|---|---|---|---|---|---|---|---|---|---|
| Season | Club | League | GP | G | A | Pts | PIM | GP | G | A | Pts | PIM |
| 2002-03 | HC Ostrava U17 | CzR-U17 | 6 | 1 | 1 | 2 | 0 | .... | .... | .... | .... | .... |
| 2003-04 | HC Ostrava U17 | CzR-U17 | 55 | 38 | 27 | 65 | 61 | .... | .... | .... | .... | .... |
| 2004-05 | HC Ostrava U17 | CzR-U17 | 8 | 8 | 16 | 24 | 22 | .... | .... | .... | .... | .... |
| | HC Ostrava Jr. | CzRep-Jr. | 7 | 2 | 2 | 4 | 6 | .... | .... | .... | .... | .... |
| | HC Vitkovice U17 | CzR-U17 | 2 | 0 | 3 | 3 | 2 | .... | .... | .... | .... | .... |
| | HC Vitkovice Jr. | CzRep-Jr. | 30 | 8 | 3 | 11 | 12 | .... | .... | .... | .... | .... |
| 2005-06 | HC Vitkovice U17 | CzR-U17 | .... | .... | .... | .... | .... | 4 | 1 | 8 | 9 | 0 |
| | HC Vitkovice Jr. | CzRep-Jr. | 46 | 17 | 27 | 44 | 42 | 5 | 0 | 3 | 3 | 4 |
| | HC Vitkovice Steel | CzRep | 1 | 0 | 0 | 0 | 0 | .... | .... | .... | .... | .... |
| 2006-07 | Spokane Chiefs | WHL | 70 | 4 | 44 | 48 | 42 | 6 | 1 | 4 | 5 | 0 |
| 2007-08 | Spokane Chiefs | WHL | 72 | 15 | 46 | 61 | 28 | 21 | 9 | 11 | 20 | 6 |
| 2008-09 | HC Vitkovice Jr. | CzRep-Jr. | 4 | 1 | 3 | 4 | 0 | .... | .... | .... | .... | .... |
| | HC Vitkovice Steel | CzRep | 26 | 3 | 6 | 9 | 2 | .... | .... | .... | .... | .... |
| | Spokane Chiefs | WHL | 32 | 10 | 22 | 32 | 19 | 12 | 1 | 4 | 5 | 10 |

## ROMANO, Tony (roh-MAHN-oh, TOH-nee) NYI

Center. Shoots right. 5'11", 175 lbs. Born, Smithtown, NY, January 5, 1988.
(New Jersey's 7th choice, 178th overall, in 2006 Entry Draft).

| | | | Regular Season | | | | | Playoffs | | | | |
|---|---|---|---|---|---|---|---|---|---|---|---|---|
| Season | Club | League | GP | G | A | Pts | PIM | GP | G | A | Pts | PIM |
| 2004-05 | New York Bobcats | AtJHL | .... | 47 | 54 | 101 | .... | .... | .... | .... | .... | .... |
| 2005-06 | New York Bobcats | AtJHL | 40 | *50 | 52 | *102 | 38 | .... | .... | .... | .... | .... |
| 2006-07 | Cornell Big Red | ECAC | 29 | 9 | 10 | 19 | 18 | .... | .... | .... | .... | .... |
| 2007-08 | London Knights | OHL | 66 | 12 | 10 | 22 | 40 | 4 | 1 | 0 | 1 | 0 |
| 2008-09 | Peterborough | OHL | 65 | 36 | 33 | 69 | 86 | 2 | 2 | 1 | 3 | 4 |

Rights traded to **NY Islanders** by **New Jersey** for Ben Walter and future considerations, June 30, 2009.

## ROSEHILL, Jay (ROHZ-hihl, JAY) TOR.

Defense. Shoots left. 6'3", 195 lbs. Born, Olds, Alta., July 16, 1985.
(Tampa Bay's 6th choice, 227th overall, in 2003 Entry Draft).

| | | | Regular Season | | | | | Playoffs | | | | |
|---|---|---|---|---|---|---|---|---|---|---|---|---|
| Season | Club | League | GP | G | A | Pts | PIM | GP | G | A | Pts | PIM |
| 2002-03 | Olds Grizzlys | AJHL | 59 | 1 | 4 | 5 | 219 | .... | .... | .... | .... | .... |
| 2003-04 | Olds Grizzlys | AJHL | 42 | 4 | 12 | 16 | 172 | 14 | 2 | 2 | 4 | .... |
| 2004-05 | U. Minn-Duluth | WCHA | 34 | 0 | 5 | 5 | 103 | .... | .... | .... | .... | .... |
| 2005-06 | Springfield Falcons | AHL | 45 | 1 | 2 | 3 | 68 | .... | .... | .... | .... | .... |
| | Johnstown Chiefs | ECHL | 5 | 0 | 0 | 0 | 13 | 5 | 0 | 0 | 0 | 4 |
| 2006-07 | Springfield Falcons | AHL | 64 | 0 | 6 | 6 | 85 | .... | .... | .... | .... | .... |
| | Johnstown Chiefs | ECHL | 1 | 0 | 0 | 0 | 2 | .... | .... | .... | .... | .... |
| 2007-08 | Norfolk Admirals | AHL | 66 | 3 | 4 | 7 | 194 | .... | .... | .... | .... | .... |
| | Mississippi | ECHL | 2 | 0 | 0 | 0 | 6 | .... | .... | .... | .... | .... |
| 2008-09 | Norfolk Admirals | AHL | 57 | 5 | 7 | 12 | 221 | .... | .... | .... | .... | .... |
| | Toronto Marlies | AHL | 13 | 2 | 1 | 3 | 54 | 6 | 0 | 0 | 0 | 4 |

Signed as a free agent by **Toronto**, July 6 2009.

## ROSS, Nick (RAWS, NIHK) PHX.

Defense. Shoots left. 6'1", 188 lbs. Born, Edmonton, Alta., February 10, 1989.
(Phoenix's 2nd choice, 30th overall, in 2007 Entry Draft).

| | | | Regular Season | | | | | Playoffs | | | | |
|---|---|---|---|---|---|---|---|---|---|---|---|---|
| Season | Club | League | GP | G | A | Pts | PIM | GP | G | A | Pts | PIM |
| 2004-05 | Lethbridge | AMHL | 33 | 8 | 20 | 28 | 123 | .... | .... | .... | .... | .... |
| | Regina Pats | WHL | 10 | 0 | 1 | 1 | 2 | .... | .... | .... | .... | .... |
| 2005-06 | Regina Pats | WHL | 62 | 7 | 16 | 23 | 38 | 6 | 0 | 1 | 1 | 2 |
| 2006-07 | Regina Pats | WHL | 70 | 7 | 24 | 31 | 87 | 10 | 1 | 5 | 6 | 14 |
| 2007-08 | Regina Pats | WHL | 41 | 3 | 25 | 28 | 60 | .... | .... | .... | .... | .... |
| | Kamloops Blazers | WHL | 31 | 5 | 14 | 19 | 55 | 4 | 0 | 2 | 2 | 10 |
| | San Antonio | AHL | 4 | 1 | 0 | 1 | 0 | .... | .... | .... | .... | .... |
| 2008-09 | Kamloops Blazers | WHL | 40 | 4 | 18 | 22 | 51 | .... | .... | .... | .... | .... |
| | Vancouver Giants | WHL | 34 | 7 | 14 | 21 | 32 | 17 | 1 | 8 | 9 | 14 |

## ROUSSEL, Charles-Olivier (roo-SEHL, CHAR-uhlz-OH-lihv-ee-ay) NSH.

Defense. Shoots right. 6'1", 201 lbs. Born, St. Eustache, Que., September 13, 1991.
(Nashville's 3rd choice, 42nd overall, in 2009 Entry Draft).

| | | | Regular Season | | | | | Playoffs | | | | |
|---|---|---|---|---|---|---|---|---|---|---|---|---|
| Season | Club | League | GP | G | A | Pts | PIM | GP | G | A | Pts | PIM |
| 2006-07 | Laurentides | QAAA | 44 | 8 | 24 | 32 | 90 | 15 | 2 | 9 | 11 | 24 |
| 2007-08 | Shawinigan | QMJHL | 50 | 3 | 13 | 16 | 28 | 5 | 1 | 2 | 3 | 2 |
| 2008-09 | Shawinigan | QMJHL | 68 | 11 | 33 | 44 | 77 | 21 | 5 | 13 | 18 | 14 |

QMJHL Second All-Star Team (2009)

## RUDENKO, Konstantin (roo-DEHN-koh, KAWN-stan-tihn) PHI.

Left wing. Shoots right. 5'11", 180 lbs. Born, Ust-Kamenogorsk, USSR, July 23, 1981.
(Philadelphia's 3rd choice, 160th overall, in 1999 Entry Draft).

| | | | Regular Season | | | | | Playoffs | | | | |
|---|---|---|---|---|---|---|---|---|---|---|---|---|
| Season | Club | League | GP | G | A | Pts | PIM | GP | G | A | Pts | PIM |
| 1997-98 | Omsk 2 | Russia-3 | 22 | 7 | 8 | 15 | 4 | .... | .... | .... | .... | .... |
| 1998-99 | Cherepovets | Russia | 28 | 15 | 9 | 24 | 67 | .... | .... | .... | .... | .... |
| | Cherepovets 2 | Russia-3 | 3 | 0 | 1 | 1 | 4 | .... | .... | .... | .... | .... |
| 99-2000 | St. Petersburg 2 | Russia-3 | 7 | 2 | 4 | 6 | 2 | .... | .... | .... | .... | .... |
| | SKA St. Petersburg | Russia | 19 | 1 | 1 | 2 | 10 | 1 | 0 | 0 | 0 | 0 |
| 2000-01 | Yaroslavl | Russia | 18 | 2 | 3 | 5 | 28 | 9 | 2 | 1 | 3 | 8 |
| 2001-02 | Yaroslavl 2 | Russia-3 | 2 | 1 | 1 | 2 | 2 | .... | .... | .... | .... | .... |
| | Yaroslavl | Russia | 8 | 0 | 2 | 2 | 12 | 1 | 0 | 0 | 0 | 0 |
| 2002-03 | Yaroslavl | Russia | 20 | 3 | 4 | 7 | 20 | 2 | 0 | 0 | 0 | 0 |
| 2003-04 | Yaroslavl 2 | Russia-3 | 4 | 4 | 2 | 6 | 4 | .... | .... | .... | .... | .... |
| | Yaroslavl | Russia | 43 | 10 | 12 | 22 | 18 | 3 | 0 | 0 | 0 | 0 |
| 2004-05 | Yaroslavl 2 | Russia-3 | 20 | 13 | 14 | 27 | 42 | .... | .... | .... | .... | .... |
| | Yaroslavl | Russia | 21 | 1 | 0 | 1 | 8 | 2 | 0 | 0 | 0 | 0 |
| 2005-06 | Yaroslavl | Russia | 49 | 11 | 17 | 28 | 55 | 11 | 1 | 2 | 3 | 0 |
| 2006-07 | Yaroslavl | Russia | 35 | 11 | 8 | 19 | 30 | 7 | 2 | 2 | 4 | 6 |
| 2007-08 | Yaroslavl | Russia | 46 | 6 | 16 | 22 | 28 | 7 | 0 | 1 | 1 | 8 |
| 2008-09 | Yaroslavl | Rus-KHL | 48 | 10 | 18 | 28 | 26 | 19 | 4 | 8 | 12 | 24 |

## RUEGSEGGER, Tyler (ROOG-suh-guhr, TIGH-luhr) TOR.

Center. Shoots right. 5'11", 170 lbs. Born, Denver, CO, January 19, 1988.
(Toronto's 6th choice, 166th overall, in 2006 Entry Draft).

| | | | Regular Season | | | | | Playoffs | | | | |
|---|---|---|---|---|---|---|---|---|---|---|---|---|
| Season | Club | League | GP | G | A | Pts | PIM | GP | G | A | Pts | PIM |
| 2004-05 | Shat.-St. Mary's | High-MN | 69 | 26 | 54 | 80 | 30 | .... | .... | .... | .... | .... |
| 2005-06 | Shat.-St. Mary's | High-MN | 60 | 38 | 51 | 89 | 70 | .... | .... | .... | .... | .... |
| 2006-07 | U. of Denver | WCHA | 40 | 15 | 19 | 34 | 25 | .... | .... | .... | .... | .... |
| 2007-08 | U. of Denver | WCHA | 31 | 10 | 12 | 22 | 39 | .... | .... | .... | .... | .... |
| 2008-09 | U. of Denver | WCHA | 35 | 15 | 11 | 26 | 40 | .... | .... | .... | .... | .... |

## RUFENACH, Bryan (RUHF-ehn-ak, BRIGH-uhn) DET.

Defense. Shoots left. 5'11", 184 lbs. Born, Cameron, Ont., April 15, 1989.
(Detroit's 5th choice, 208th overall, in 2007 Entry Draft).

| | | | Regular Season | | | | | Playoffs | | | | |
|---|---|---|---|---|---|---|---|---|---|---|---|---|
| Season | Club | League | GP | G | A | Pts | PIM | GP | G | A | Pts | PIM |
| 2005-06 | Lindsay Muskies | OPJHL | 48 | 11 | 15 | 26 | 50 | 4 | 1 | 1 | 2 | 6 |
| 2006-07 | Lindsay Muskies | OPJHL | 31 | 11 | 21 | 32 | 28 | 5 | 1 | 2 | 3 | 8 |
| 2007-08 | Clarkson Knights | ECAC | 35 | 3 | 3 | 6 | 12 | .... | .... | .... | .... | .... |
| 2008-09 | Clarkson Knights | ECAC | 34 | 9 | 9 | 18 | 32 | .... | .... | .... | .... | .... |

## RUGGERI, Rosario (ROO-zhee-AIR-ee, roh-ZAHR-ee-oh)

Defense. Shoots right. 6'1", 215 lbs. Born, Montreal, Que., June 8, 1984.
(Philadelphia's 2nd choice, 105th overall, in 2002 Entry Draft).

| | | | Regular Season | | | | | Playoffs | | | | |
|---|---|---|---|---|---|---|---|---|---|---|---|---|
| Season | Club | League | GP | G | A | Pts | PIM | GP | G | A | Pts | PIM |
| 99-2000 | Lac St-Louis Lions | QAAA | 40 | 0 | 7 | 7 | 70 | .... | .... | .... | .... | .... |
| 2000-01 | Lac St-Louis Lions | QAAA | 24 | 6 | 11 | 17 | 117 | 5 | 1 | 3 | 4 | 4 |
| | Montreal Rocket | QMJHL | 9 | 0 | 0 | 0 | 8 | .... | .... | .... | .... | .... |
| 2001-02 | Chicoutimi | QMJHL | 60 | 2 | 15 | 17 | 131 | 4 | 1 | 1 | 2 | 10 |
| 2002-03 | Chicoutimi | QMJHL | 70 | 10 | 37 | 47 | 64 | 3 | 0 | 0 | 0 | 21 |
| 2003-04 | Chicoutimi | QMJHL | 65 | 12 | 36 | 48 | 98 | 18 | 2 | 2 | 4 | 28 |
| 2004-05 | Philadelphia | AHL | 5 | 0 | 0 | 0 | 0 | .... | .... | .... | .... | .... |
| | Trenton Titans | ECHL | 49 | 2 | 12 | 14 | 77 | 20 | 0 | 2 | 2 | 26 |
| 2005-06 | Philadelphia | AHL | 2 | 0 | 0 | 0 | 2 | .... | .... | .... | .... | .... |
| | Trenton Titans | ECHL | 32 | 2 | 8 | 10 | 28 | .... | .... | .... | .... | .... |
| 2006-07 | Philadelphia | AHL | 15 | 0 | 2 | 2 | 0 | .... | .... | .... | .... | .... |
| | Trenton Titans | ECHL | 49 | 4 | 25 | 29 | 46 | 5 | 0 | 0 | 0 | 6 |
| 2007-08 | Lowell Devils | AHL | 60 | 4 | 14 | 18 | 26 | .... | .... | .... | .... | .... |
| 2008-09 | Lowell Devils | AHL | 49 | 2 | 2 | 4 | 51 | .... | .... | .... | .... | .... |
| | Trenton Devils | ECHL | 2 | 0 | 0 | 0 | 2 | .... | .... | .... | .... | .... |

Signed as a free agent by **New Jersey**, August, 2008.

## RUNDBLAD, David (RUHND-blahd, DAY-vihd) ST.L.

Defense. Shoots right. 6'2", 189 lbs. Born, Lycksele, Sweden, October 8, 1990.
(St. Louis' 1st choice, 17th overall, in 2009 Entry Draft).

| | | | Regular Season | | | | | Playoffs | | | | |
|---|---|---|---|---|---|---|---|---|---|---|---|---|
| Season | Club | League | GP | G | A | Pts | PIM | GP | G | A | Pts | PIM |
| 2004-05 | Lycksele SK | Sweden-4 | 1 | 0 | 0 | 0 | 0 | .... | .... | .... | .... | .... |
| 2005-06 | Lycksele SK | Sweden-4 | 11 | 5 | 2 | 7 | 2 | .... | .... | .... | .... | .... |
| 2006-07 | Skelleftea U18 | Swe-U18 | 4 | 1 | 1 | 2 | 0 | .... | .... | .... | .... | .... |
| | Skelleftea Jr. | Swe-Jr. | 14 | 3 | 4 | 7 | 12 | 2 | 0 | 0 | 0 | 2 |
| 2007-08 | Skelleftea U18 | Swe-U18 | 4 | 3 | 2 | 5 | 29 | .... | .... | .... | .... | .... |
| | Skelleftea Jr. | Swe-Jr. | 35 | 11 | 15 | 26 | 44 | 2 | 1 | 3 | 4 | 6 |
| | Skelleftea AIK HK | Sweden | 6 | 0 | 0 | 0 | 2 | .... | .... | .... | .... | .... |
| 2008-09 | Skelleftea AIK Jr. | Swe-Jr. | 10 | 8 | 7 | 15 | 2 | .... | .... | .... | .... | .... |
| | Skelleftea AIK | Sweden | 45 | 0 | 10 | 10 | 8 | 10 | 1 | 1 | 2 | 2 |

## RUSSELL, Ryan (RUH-sehl, RIGH-uhn) MTL.

Center. Shoots left. 5'10", 175 lbs. Born, Caroline, Alta., May 2, 1987.
(NY Rangers' 9th choice, 211th overall, in 2005 Entry Draft).

| | | | Regular Season | | | | | Playoffs | | | | |
|---|---|---|---|---|---|---|---|---|---|---|---|---|
| Season | Club | League | GP | G | A | Pts | PIM | GP | G | A | Pts | PIM |
| 2003-04 | Kootenay Ice | WHL | 67 | 3 | 9 | 12 | 27 | 4 | 0 | 0 | 0 | 0 |
| 2004-05 | Kootenay Ice | WHL | 66 | 32 | 21 | 53 | 18 | 16 | 6 | 7 | 13 | 12 |
| 2005-06 | Kootenay Ice | WHL | 72 | 33 | 42 | 75 | 30 | 6 | 3 | 5 | 8 | 2 |
| 2006-07 | Kootenay Ice | WHL | 58 | 30 | 46 | 76 | 40 | 7 | 3 | 6 | 9 | 2 |
| 2007-08 | Hamilton Bulldogs | AHL | 25 | 2 | 1 | 3 | 4 | .... | .... | .... | .... | .... |
| | Cincinnati | ECHL | 12 | 6 | 4 | 10 | 4 | 15 | 3 | 4 | 7 | 0 |
| 2008-09 | Hamilton Bulldogs | AHL | 79 | 20 | 19 | 39 | 24 | 6 | 1 | 3 | 4 | 2 |

Traded to **Montreal** by **NY Rangers** for Montreal's 7th round choice (David Skokan) in 2007 Entry Draft, May 31, 2007.

## RUST, Matt (RUHST, MAT) FLA.

Center. Shoots left. 5'10", 192 lbs. Born, Bloomfield Hills, MI, March 23, 1989.
(Florida's 4th choice, 101st overall, in 2007 Entry Draft).

| | | | Regular Season | | | | | Playoffs | | | | |
|---|---|---|---|---|---|---|---|---|---|---|---|---|
| Season | Club | League | GP | G | A | Pts | PIM | GP | G | A | Pts | PIM |
| 2004-05 | Det. Honeybaked | MWEHL | 50 | 16 | 24 | 40 | .... | .... | .... | .... | .... | .... |
| 2005-06 | USNTDP | U-17 | 20 | 5 | 5 | 10 | 22 | .... | .... | .... | .... | .... |
| | USNTDP | NAHL | 36 | 9 | 8 | 17 | 36 | 12 | 2 | 0 | 2 | 0 |
| 2006-07 | USNTDP | U-18 | 36 | 3 | 16 | 19 | 34 | .... | .... | .... | .... | .... |
| | USNTDP | NAHL | 15 | 9 | 6 | 15 | 31 | .... | .... | .... | .... | .... |
| 2007-08 | U. of Michigan | CCHA | 38 | 12 | 11 | 23 | 69 | .... | .... | .... | .... | .... |
| 2008-09 | U. of Michigan | CCHA | 37 | 11 | 11 | 22 | 39 | .... | .... | .... | .... | .... |

## RUTH, Theo (ROOTH, THEE-oh) CBJ

Defense. Shoots right. 6', 201 lbs. Born, Naperville, IL, February 14, 1989.
(Washington's 3rd choice, 46th overall, in 2007 Entry Draft).

| | | | Regular Season | | | | | Playoffs | | | | |
|---|---|---|---|---|---|---|---|---|---|---|---|---|
| Season | Club | League | GP | G | A | Pts | PIM | GP | G | A | Pts | PIM |
| 2004-05 | Chicago Mission | MAHL | 46 | 8 | 8 | 16 | .... | .... | .... | .... | .... | .... |
| 2005-06 | USNTDP | U-17 | 18 | 2 | 3 | 5 | 22 | .... | .... | .... | .... | .... |
| | USNTDP | NAHL | 36 | 1 | 2 | 3 | 33 | 12 | 0 | 2 | 2 | 8 |
| 2006-07 | USNTDP | U-18 | 39 | 2 | 6 | 8 | 52 | .... | .... | .... | .... | .... |
| | USNTDP | NAHL | 9 | 3 | 6 | 9 | 14 | .... | .... | .... | .... | .... |
| 2007-08 | U. of Notre Dame | CCHA | 42 | 2 | 3 | 5 | 36 | .... | .... | .... | .... | .... |
| 2008-09 | U. of Notre Dame | CCHA | 36 | 2 | 5 | 7 | 42 | .... | .... | .... | .... | .... |

Traded to **Columbus** by **Washington** for Sergei Fedorov, February 26, 2008.

## RUZICKA, Vladimir (roo-ZHEECH-kuh, vla-DIH-meer) PHX.

Center. Shoots left. 6'1", 196 lbs. Born, Most, Czech., February 17, 1989.
(Phoenix's 5th choice, 103rd overall, in 2007 Entry Draft).

| | | | Regular Season | | | | | Playoffs | | | | |
|---|---|---|---|---|---|---|---|---|---|---|---|---|
| Season | Club | League | GP | G | A | Pts | PIM | GP | G | A | Pts | PIM |
| 2002-03 | Slavia U17 | CzR-U17 | 20 | 1 | 5 | 6 | 2 | 1 | 0 | 0 | 0 | 0 |
| 2003-04 | Slavia U17 | CzR-U17 | 51 | 18 | 35 | 53 | 24 | 7 | 5 | 8 | 13 | 4 |
| 2004-05 | Slavia U17 | CzR-U17 | 38 | 22 | 39 | 61 | 38 | 6 | 4 | 4 | 8 | 10 |
| 2005-06 | Slavia U17 | CzR-U17 | 3 | 3 | 6 | 9 | 22 | 6 | 5 | 7 | 12 | 14 |
| | HC Slavia Praha Jr. | CzRep-Jr. | 37 | 15 | 26 | 41 | 42 | 1 | 0 | 1 | 1 | 0 |
| | HC Slavia Praha | CzRep | 13 | 1 | 1 | 2 | 4 | .... | .... | .... | .... | .... |
| 2006-07 | HC Slavia Praha Jr. | CzRep-Jr. | 37 | 24 | 34 | 58 | 54 | 4 | 1 | 2 | 3 | 4 |
| | HC Slavia Praha | CzRep | 3 | 0 | 0 | 0 | 0 | .... | .... | .... | .... | .... |
| 2007-08 | HC Slavia Praha Jr. | CzRep-Jr. | 1 | 0 | 0 | 0 | 4 | 1 | 0 | 0 | 0 | 2 |
| | HC Slavia Praha | CzRep | 42 | 7 | 8 | 15 | 18 | 19 | 1 | 0 | 1 | 4 |
| 2008-09 | HC Slavia Praha | CzRep | 36 | 5 | 6 | 11 | 14 | 14 | 2 | 1 | 3 | 6 |

## RYAN, Ben (RIGH-uhn, BEHN) NSH.

Center. Shoots right. 5'11", 190 lbs. Born, Detroit, MI, October 16, 1988.
(Nashville's 5th choice, 114th overall, in 2007 Entry Draft).

| | | | Regular Season | | | | | Playoffs | | | | |
|---|---|---|---|---|---|---|---|---|---|---|---|---|
| Season | Club | League | GP | G | A | Pts | PIM | GP | G | A | Pts | PIM |
| 2005-06 | Des Moines | USHL | 60 | 14 | 23 | 37 | 38 | 11 | 4 | 1 | 5 | 4 |
| 2006-07 | Des Moines | USHL | 59 | 22 | 42 | 64 | 66 | 8 | 3 | 5 | 8 | 8 |
| 2007-08 | U. of Notre Dame | CCHA | 47 | 10 | 16 | 26 | 22 | .... | .... | .... | .... | .... |
| 2008-09 | U. of Notre Dame | CCHA | 39 | 12 | 15 | 27 | 30 | .... | .... | .... | .... | .... |

**RYAN, Kenny** (RIGH-uhn, KEH-nee) **TOR.**

Right wing. Shoots right. 6', 204 lbs. Born, Franklin Village, MI, July 10, 1991.
(Toronto's 2nd choice, 50th overall, in 2009 Entry Draft).

| | | | Regular Season | | | | | Playoffs | | | | |
|---|---|---|---|---|---|---|---|---|---|---|---|---|
| Season | Club | League | GP | G | A | Pts | PIM | GP | G | A | Pts | PIM |
| 2006-07 | Det. Honeybaked | MWEHL | 31 | 16 | 17 | 33 | 34 | .... | .... | .... | .... | .... |
| | Det. Honeybaked | Exhib. | 34 | 17 | 24 | 41 | .... | .... | .... | .... | .... | .... |
| 2007-08 | USNTDP | NAHL | 36 | 10 | 8 | 18 | 53 | .... | .... | .... | .... | .... |
| | USNTDP | U-17 | 13 | 0 | 5 | 5 | 12 | .... | .... | .... | .... | .... |
| 2008-09 | USNTDP | NAHL | 16 | 4 | 9 | 13 | 12 | .... | .... | .... | .... | .... |
| | USNTDP | U-18 | 46 | 23 | 13 | 36 | 38 | .... | .... | .... | .... | .... |

• Signed Letter of Intent to attend **Boston College** (Hockey East) in fall of 2009.

**RYDER, Dan** (RIGH-duhr, DAN)

Center. Shoots right. 5'11", 193 lbs. Born, Bonavista, Nfld., January 12, 1987.
(Calgary's 3rd choice, 74th overall, in 2005 Entry Draft).

| | | | Regular Season | | | | | Playoffs | | | | |
|---|---|---|---|---|---|---|---|---|---|---|---|---|
| Season | Club | League | GP | G | A | Pts | PIM | GP | G | A | Pts | PIM |
| 2003-04 | Peterborough | OHL | 63 | 20 | 32 | 52 | 16 | .... | .... | .... | .... | .... |
| 2004-05 | Peterborough | OHL | 68 | 29 | 53 | 82 | 55 | .... | .... | .... | .... | .... |
| 2005-06 | Peterborough | OHL | 65 | 38 | 44 | 82 | 57 | 19 | *15 | 16 | 31 | 22 |
| 2006-07 | Peterborough | OHL | 29 | 24 | 35 | 59 | 21 | .... | .... | .... | .... | .... |
| | Plymouth Whalers | OHL | 28 | 16 | 17 | 33 | 4 | 20 | 8 | 9 | 17 | 10 |
| 2007-08 | Quad City Flames | AHL | 6 | 1 | 4 | 5 | 2 | .... | .... | .... | .... | .... |
| 2008-09 | Quad City Flames | AHL | 19 | 3 | 6 | 9 | 14 | .... | .... | .... | .... | .... |
| | Las Vegas | ECHL | 4 | 0 | 0 | 0 | 15 | .... | .... | .... | .... | .... |
| | Providence Bruins | AHL | 20 | 1 | 5 | 6 | 4 | 8 | 0 | 1 | 1 | 0 |

**RYNO, Johan** (RYUH-noh, YOH-han) **DET.**

Right wing. Shoots left. 6'4", 198 lbs. Born, Orebro, Sweden, June 5, 1986.
(Detroit's 6th choice, 137th overall, in 2005 Entry Draft).

| | | | Regular Season | | | | | Playoffs | | | | |
|---|---|---|---|---|---|---|---|---|---|---|---|---|
| Season | Club | League | GP | G | A | Pts | PIM | GP | G | A | Pts | PIM |
| 2003-04 | IFK Hallsberg | Sweden-3 | 28 | 9 | 18 | 27 | 30 | .... | .... | .... | .... | .... |
| 2004-05 | IFK Kumla Jr. | Swe-Jr. | 29 | 20 | 18 | 38 | 14 | .... | .... | .... | .... | .... |
| | IFK Arboga IK | Sweden-2 | 2 | 0 | 0 | 0 | 0 | .... | .... | .... | .... | .... |
| 2005-06 | IK Oskarshamn | Sweden-2 | 34 | 13 | 10 | 23 | 64 | .... | .... | .... | .... | .... |
| 2006-07 | Frolunda Jr. | Swe-Jr. | 2 | 1 | 0 | 1 | 2 | .... | .... | .... | .... | .... |
| | Frolunda | Sweden | 14 | 0 | 0 | 0 | 14 | .... | .... | .... | .... | .... |
| | AIK IF Solna | Sweden-2 | 14 | 2 | 7 | 9 | 14 | .... | .... | .... | .... | .... |
| | Timra IK | Sweden | 25 | 5 | 6 | 11 | 8 | 5 | 0 | 1 | 1 | 0 |
| 2007-08 | Grand Rapids | AHL | 12 | 3 | 4 | 7 | 8 | .... | .... | .... | .... | .... |
| | Djurgarden | Sweden | 30 | 2 | 7 | 9 | 18 | 5 | 0 | 0 | 0 | 0 |
| 2008-09 | AIK IF Solna | Sweden-2 | STATISTICS NOT AVAILABLE | | | | | | | | | |

**SACCHETTI, Nico** (SA-sheh-tee, NEE-koh) **DAL.**

Center. Shoots right. 5'11", 189 lbs. Born, Virginia, MN, August 21, 1989.
(Dallas' 1st choice, 50th overall, in 2007 Entry Draft).

| | | | Regular Season | | | | | Playoffs | | | | |
|---|---|---|---|---|---|---|---|---|---|---|---|---|
| Season | Club | League | GP | G | A | Pts | PIM | GP | G | A | Pts | PIM |
| 2004-05 | Virginia Blue Devils | High-MN | 29 | 25 | 29 | 54 | .... | .... | .... | .... | .... | .... |
| 2005-06 | Virginia Blue Devils | High-MN | 27 | 29 | 45 | 74 | .... | .... | .... | .... | .... | .... |
| 2006-07 | Virginia Blue Devils | High-MN | 25 | 38 | 52 | 90 | 22 | .... | .... | .... | .... | .... |
| 2007-08 | Omaha Lancers | USHL | 56 | 10 | 14 | 24 | 51 | 14 | 1 | 2 | 3 | 10 |
| 2008-09 | U. of Minnesota | WCHA | 36 | 4 | 3 | 7 | 43 | .... | .... | .... | .... | .... |

**SACKRISON, Andy** (sak-RIH-suhn, AN-dee) **ST.L.**

Center. Shoots left. 6'1", 197 lbs. Born, St. Louis Park, MN, November 12, 1987.
(St. Louis' 7th choice, 124th overall, in 2006 Entry Draft).

| | | | Regular Season | | | | | Playoffs | | | | |
|---|---|---|---|---|---|---|---|---|---|---|---|---|
| Season | Club | League | GP | G | A | Pts | PIM | GP | G | A | Pts | PIM |
| 2004-05 | St. Louis Park | High-MN | 26 | 18 | 15 | 33 | .... | .... | .... | .... | .... | .... |
| 2005-06 | St. Louis Park | High-MN | 25 | 42 | 27 | 69 | .... | .... | .... | .... | .... | .... |
| 2006-07 | Tri-City Storm | USHL | 59 | 12 | 15 | 27 | 19 | 9 | 2 | 0 | 2 | 6 |
| 2007-08 | Minnesota State | WCHA | 36 | 6 | 14 | 20 | 4 | .... | .... | .... | .... | .... |
| 2008-09 | Minnesota State | WCHA | 31 | 3 | 5 | 8 | 18 | .... | .... | .... | .... | .... |

**SALLINEN, Jere** (sa-LIGH-nehn, YAIR-ray) **MIN.**

Right wing. Shoots left. 6', 183 lbs. Born, Espoo, Finland, October 26, 1990.
(Minnesota's 6th choice, 163rd overall, in 2009 Entry Draft).

| | | | Regular Season | | | | | Playoffs | | | | |
|---|---|---|---|---|---|---|---|---|---|---|---|---|
| Season | Club | League | GP | G | A | Pts | PIM | GP | G | A | Pts | PIM |
| 2006-07 | Blues Espoo U18 | Fin-U18 | 26 | 9 | 3 | 12 | 44 | 7 | 2 | 2 | 4 | 16 |
| 2007-08 | Blues Espoo U18 | Fin-U18 | 13 | 8 | 10 | 18 | 16 | 4 | 1 | 5 | 6 | 12 |
| | Blues Espoo Jr. | Fin-Jr. | 36 | 11 | 19 | 30 | 94 | 3 | 0 | 2 | 2 | 8 |
| | Blues Espoo | Finland | 6 | 0 | 0 | 0 | 2 | .... | .... | .... | .... | .... |
| 2008-09 | Blues Espoo Jr. | Fin-Jr. | 9 | 1 | 2 | 3 | 31 | .... | .... | .... | .... | .... |

**SALMONSSON, Johannes** (sal-MUHN-suhn, yoh-HA-nuhs) **PIT.**

Left wing. Shoots left. 6'2", 183 lbs. Born, Uppsala, Sweden, February 7, 1986.
(Pittsburgh's 2nd choice, 31st overall, in 2004 Entry Draft).

| | | | Regular Season | | | | | Playoffs | | | | |
|---|---|---|---|---|---|---|---|---|---|---|---|---|
| Season | Club | League | GP | G | A | Pts | PIM | GP | G | A | Pts | PIM |
| 2002-03 | Almtuna | Sweden-2 | 26 | 10 | 14 | 24 | 4 | .... | .... | .... | .... | .... |
| 2003-04 | Djurgarden Jr. | Swe-Jr. | 6 | 4 | 9 | 13 | 6 | .... | .... | .... | .... | .... |
| | Djurgarden | Sweden | 25 | 0 | 3 | 3 | 4 | .... | .... | .... | .... | .... |
| | Almtuna | Sweden-2 | 2 | 0 | 0 | 0 | 0 | .... | .... | .... | .... | .... |
| 2004-05 | Almtuna | Sweden-2 | 8 | 0 | 2 | 2 | 6 | .... | .... | .... | .... | .... |
| | Djurgarden Jr. | Swe-Jr. | 4 | 2 | 0 | 2 | 4 | .... | .... | .... | .... | .... |
| | Djurgarden | Sweden | 30 | 2 | 2 | 4 | 6 | 9 | 0 | 0 | 0 | 0 |
| 2005-06 | Spokane Chiefs | WHL | 54 | 12 | 15 | 27 | 30 | .... | .... | .... | .... | .... |
| 2006-07 | Brynas IF Gavle Jr. | Swe-Jr. | 2 | 0 | 7 | 7 | 0 | .... | .... | .... | .... | .... |
| | Brynas IF Gavle | Sweden | 45 | 8 | 3 | 11 | 28 | .... | .... | .... | .... | .... |
| 2007-08 | Brynas IF Gavle Jr. | Swe-Jr. | 2 | 0 | 2 | 2 | 2 | .... | .... | .... | .... | .... |
| | Brynas IF Gavle | Sweden | 9 | 0 | 1 | 1 | 2 | .... | .... | .... | .... | .... |
| | Rogle | Sweden-2 | 34 | 15 | 9 | 24 | 36 | .... | .... | .... | .... | .... |
| 2008-09 | Rogle | Sweden | 33 | 5 | 4 | 9 | 12 | .... | .... | .... | .... | .... |

Signed as a free agent by **Brynas** (Sweden), September 18, 2006.

**SAMSON, Jerome** (SAM-sohn, jeh-ROHM) **CAR.**

Right wing. Shoots right. 6', 195 lbs. Born, Greenfield Park, Que., September 4, 1987.

| | | | Regular Season | | | | | Playoffs | | | | |
|---|---|---|---|---|---|---|---|---|---|---|---|---|
| Season | Club | League | GP | G | A | Pts | PIM | GP | G | A | Pts | PIM |
| 2004-05 | Moncton Wildcats | QMJHL | 63 | 6 | 11 | 17 | 22 | 12 | 1 | 4 | 5 | 8 |
| 2005-06 | Moncton Wildcats | QMJHL | 62 | 20 | 32 | 52 | 46 | 21 | 6 | 12 | 18 | 15 |
| 2006-07 | Moncton Wildcats | QMJHL | 38 | 19 | 33 | 52 | 20 | .... | .... | .... | .... | .... |
| | Val-d'Or Foreurs | QMJHL | 33 | 25 | 22 | 47 | 16 | 20 | 14 | 12 | 26 | 10 |
| 2007-08 | Albany River Rats | AHL | 65 | 21 | 18 | 39 | 38 | 7 | 1 | 1 | 2 | 2 |
| 2008-09 | Albany River Rats | AHL | 70 | 22 | 32 | 54 | 56 | .... | .... | .... | .... | .... |

Signed as a free agent by **Carolina**, July 2, 2007.

**SAMUELSSON, Jesper** (SA-mewl-suhn, YEHS-puhr) **DET.**

Center. Shoots left. 5'11", 178 lbs. Born, Stockholm, Sweden, June 13, 1988.
(Detroit's 6th choice, 211th overall, in 2008 Entry Draft).

| | | | Regular Season | | | | | Playoffs | | | | |
|---|---|---|---|---|---|---|---|---|---|---|---|---|
| Season | Club | League | GP | G | A | Pts | PIM | GP | G | A | Pts | PIM |
| 2004-05 | Hasten | Sweden-3 | 1 | 0 | 0 | 0 | 0 | .... | .... | .... | .... | .... |
| 2005-06 | Hasten | Sweden-3 | 36 | 8 | 11 | 19 | 67 | .... | .... | .... | .... | .... |
| 2006-07 | Hasten | Sweden-3 | 36 | 15 | 29 | 44 | 38 | .... | .... | .... | .... | .... |
| 2007-08 | HC Vita Hasten | Sweden-3 | 40 | 20 | 42 | 62 | 73 | .... | .... | .... | .... | .... |
| 2008-09 | Timra IK Jr. | Swe-Jr. | 4 | 2 | 0 | 2 | 2 | .... | .... | .... | .... | .... |
| | Sundsvall | Sweden-2 | 13 | 1 | 5 | 6 | 38 | .... | .... | .... | .... | .... |
| | Timra IK | Sweden | 40 | 2 | 1 | 3 | 10 | 3 | 0 | 0 | 0 | 0 |

**SAMUELSSON, Philip** (SAM-yuhl-suhn, FIHL-ihp) **PIT.**

Defense. Shoots left. 6'3", 198 lbs. Born, Leksand, Sweden, July 26, 1991.
(Pittsburgh's 2nd choice, 61st overall, in 2009 Entry Draft).

| | | | Regular Season | | | | | Playoffs | | | | |
|---|---|---|---|---|---|---|---|---|---|---|---|---|
| Season | Club | League | GP | G | A | Pts | PIM | GP | G | A | Pts | PIM |
| 2006-07 | P.F. Chang's | Minor-AZ | 54 | 9 | 31 | 40 | 70 | .... | .... | .... | .... | .... |
| 2007-08 | P.F. Chang's | Minor-AZ | 41 | 8 | 25 | 33 | 48 | .... | .... | .... | .... | .... |
| 2008-09 | Chicago Steel | USHL | 54 | 0 | 22 | 22 | 60 | .... | .... | .... | .... | .... |
| | USNTDP | U-18 | 4 | 0 | 0 | 0 | 6 | .... | .... | .... | .... | .... |

• Signed Letter of Intent to attend **Boston College** (Hockey East) in fall of 2009.

**SAMUELS-THOMAS, Jordan** (SAM-yewlz-TAW-muhs, JOHR-dahn) **ATL.**

Left wing. Shoots left. 6'3", 198 lbs. Born, Hartford, CT, May 28, 1990.
(Atlanta's 9th choice, 203rd overall, in 2009 Entry Draft).

| | | | Regular Season | | | | | Playoffs | | | | |
|---|---|---|---|---|---|---|---|---|---|---|---|---|
| Season | Club | League | GP | G | A | Pts | PIM | GP | G | A | Pts | PIM |
| 2006-07 | Hartford | AtJHL | 43 | 21 | 37 | 58 | 44 | .... | .... | .... | .... | .... |
| 2007-08 | Waterloo | USHL | 56 | 8 | 3 | 11 | 65 | 11 | 0 | 2 | 2 | 10 |
| 2008-09 | Waterloo | USHL | 59 | 32 | 22 | 54 | 59 | 3 | 2 | 1 | 3 | 2 |

• Signed Letter of Intent to attend **Bowling Green University** (CCHA) in fall of 2009.

**SANDIN, Emil** (san-DEEN, eh-MIHL) **OTT.**

Left wing. Shoots left. 5'11", 181 lbs. Born, Uppsala, Sweden, February 28, 1988.
(Ottawa's 7th choice, 199th overall, in 2008 Entry Draft).

| | | | Regular Season | | | | | Playoffs | | | | |
|---|---|---|---|---|---|---|---|---|---|---|---|---|
| Season | Club | League | GP | G | A | Pts | PIM | GP | G | A | Pts | PIM |
| 2004-05 | Brynas IF Gavle Jr. | Swe-Jr. | 2 | 0 | 0 | 0 | 0 | .... | .... | .... | .... | .... |
| 2005-06 | Brynas U18 | Swe-U18 | 4 | 2 | 3 | 5 | 14 | .... | .... | .... | .... | .... |
| | Brynas IF Gavle Jr. | Swe-Jr. | 31 | 9 | 9 | 18 | 8 | 2 | 2 | 0 | 2 | 0 |
| 2006-07 | Brynas IF Gavle Jr. | Swe-Jr. | 39 | 10 | 20 | 30 | 40 | 4 | 1 | 0 | 1 | 4 |
| 2007-08 | Brynas IF Gavle Jr. | Swe-Jr. | 28 | 10 | 25 | 35 | 50 | 7 | 1 | 4 | 5 | 8 |
| | Brynas IF Gavle | Sweden | 19 | 0 | 4 | 4 | 0 | .... | .... | .... | .... | .... |
| | Brynas IF Gavle | Sweden-Q | 2 | 0 | 0 | 0 | 0 | .... | .... | .... | .... | .... |
| 2008-09 | Brynas IF Gavle | Sweden | 53 | 6 | 11 | 17 | 6 | 4 | 0 | 0 | 0 | 4 |

**SANGUINETTI, Bobby** (san-GIH-neh-tee, BAW-bee) **NYR**

Defense. Shoots right. 6'3", 190 lbs. Born, Trenton, NJ, February 29, 1988.
(NY Rangers' 1st choice, 21st overall, in 2006 Entry Draft).

| | | | Regular Season | | | | | Playoffs | | | | |
|---|---|---|---|---|---|---|---|---|---|---|---|---|
| Season | Club | League | GP | G | A | Pts | PIM | GP | G | A | Pts | PIM |
| 2003-04 | Lawrenceville | High-NJ | 26 | 4 | 17 | 21 | .... | .... | .... | .... | .... | .... |
| 2004-05 | Owen Sound | OHL | 67 | 4 | 20 | 24 | 12 | 5 | 0 | 2 | 2 | 0 |
| 2005-06 | Owen Sound | OHL | 68 | 14 | 51 | 65 | 44 | 11 | 5 | 10 | 15 | 4 |
| 2006-07 | Owen Sound | OHL | 67 | 23 | 30 | 53 | 48 | 4 | 3 | 3 | 6 | 2 |
| | Hartford Wolf Pack | AHL | 5 | 0 | 3 | 3 | 2 | 7 | 0 | 1 | 1 | 2 |
| 2007-08 | Brampton | OHL | 61 | 29 | 41 | 70 | 38 | 5 | 1 | 3 | 4 | 10 |
| | Hartford Wolf Pack | AHL | 6 | 0 | 1 | 1 | 2 | 5 | 0 | 0 | 0 | 2 |
| 2008-09 | Hartford Wolf Pack | AHL | 78 | 6 | 36 | 42 | 42 | 6 | 1 | 4 | 5 | 6 |

OHL Second All-Star Team (2008)

**SANNITZ, Raffaele** (ZAH-nihts, ra-FIGH-ehl-lay) **CBJ**

Center. Shoots left. 6'1", 205 lbs. Born, Mendrisio, Switz., May 18, 1983.
(Columbus' 9th choice, 204th overall, in 2001 Entry Draft).

| | | | Regular Season | | | | | Playoffs | | | | |
|---|---|---|---|---|---|---|---|---|---|---|---|---|
| Season | Club | League | GP | G | A | Pts | PIM | GP | G | A | Pts | PIM |
| 1997-98 | HC Lugano Jr. | Swiss-Jr. | 33 | 7 | 12 | 19 | 54 | .... | .... | .... | .... | .... |
| 1998-99 | HC Lugano Jr. | Swiss-Jr. | 38 | 5 | 12 | 17 | 62 | .... | .... | .... | .... | .... |
| | HC Lugano | Swiss | 8 | 0 | 1 | 1 | 0 | .... | .... | .... | .... | .... |
| 99-2000 | HC Lugano Jr. | Swiss-Jr. | 33 | 13 | 16 | 29 | 47 | .... | .... | .... | .... | .... |
| | HC Lugano | Swiss | 1 | 0 | 0 | 0 | 2 | .... | .... | .... | .... | .... |
| 2000-01 | HC Sierre | Swiss-2 | 2 | 0 | 0 | 0 | 0 | .... | .... | .... | .... | .... |
| | HC Lugano Jr. | Swiss-Jr. | 35 | 22 | 30 | 52 | 152 | 2 | 0 | 0 | 0 | 0 |
| | HC Lugano | Swiss | 13 | 1 | 0 | 1 | 0 | 2 | 0 | 0 | 0 | 0 |
| 2001-02 | HC Lugano Jr. | Swiss-Jr. | 14 | 14 | 13 | 27 | 18 | 3 | 3 | 2 | 5 | 4 |
| | HC Lugano | Swiss | 38 | 3 | 4 | 7 | 37 | 12 | 1 | 1 | 2 | 2 |
| 2002-03 | HC Lugano | Swiss | 14 | 1 | 1 | 2 | 37 | .... | .... | .... | .... | .... |
| 2003-04 | HC Lugano | Swiss | 48 | 7 | 9 | 16 | 20 | 16 | 2 | 1 | 3 | 8 |
| | EHC Chur | Swiss-2 | 2 | 2 | 1 | 3 | 2 | .... | .... | .... | .... | .... |
| 2004-05 | Syracuse Crunch | AHL | 53 | 6 | 3 | 9 | 38 | .... | .... | .... | .... | .... |
| | Dayton Bombers | ECHL | 2 | 0 | 3 | 3 | 0 | .... | .... | .... | .... | .... |
| 2005-06 | HC Lugano | Swiss | 33 | 5 | 9 | 14 | 85 | 17 | 4 | 8 | 12 | 16 |
| 2006-07 | HC Lugano | Swiss | 38 | 6 | 20 | 26 | 50 | 6 | 3 | 3 | 6 | 41 |
| 2007-08 | HC Lugano | Swiss | 50 | 7 | 10 | 17 | 36 | 5 | 3 | 1 | 4 | 31 |
| 2008-09 | HC Lugano | Swiss | 43 | 5 | 17 | 22 | 64 | 7 | 4 | 0 | 4 | 10 |

• Missed majority of 2002-03 season recovering from shoulder injury suffered in game vs. Kloten (Swiss), October 12, 2002.

**SANTORELLI, Mark** (san-toh-REHL-ee, MAHRK) **NSH.**

Center. Shoots right. 6'1", 189 lbs. Born, Burnaby, B.C., August 6, 1988.
(Nashville's 6th choice, 119th overall, in 2007 Entry Draft).

| | | | Regular Season | | | | | Playoffs | | | | |
|---|---|---|---|---|---|---|---|---|---|---|---|---|
| Season | Club | League | GP | G | A | Pts | PIM | GP | G | A | Pts | PIM |
| 2003-04 | Abbotsford Pilots | PIJHL | 40 | 12 | 19 | 31 | 33 | .... | .... | .... | .... | .... |
| | Chilliwack Chiefs | BCHL | 1 | 0 | 1 | 1 | 0 | .... | .... | .... | .... | .... |
| 2004-05 | Salmon Arm | BCHL | 59 | 9 | 16 | 25 | 10 | 11 | 2 | 3 | 5 | 6 |
| 2005-06 | Salmon Arm | BCHL | 20 | 2 | 10 | 12 | 11 | .... | .... | .... | .... | .... |
| | Burnaby Express | BCHL | 39 | 15 | 28 | 43 | 16 | 20 | 2 | 14 | 16 | 14 |
| 2006-07 | Chilliwack Bruins | WHL | 72 | 29 | 53 | 82 | 46 | 5 | 2 | 3 | 5 | 2 |
| 2007-08 | Chilliwack Bruins | WHL | 72 | 27 | *74 | *101 | 40 | 4 | 1 | 4 | 5 | 4 |
| | Milwaukee | AHL | 1 | 0 | 0 | 0 | 0 | 2 | 0 | 0 | 0 | 0 |
| 2008-09 | Milwaukee | AHL | 53 | 1 | 6 | 7 | 8 | .... | .... | .... | .... | .... |
| | Cincinnati | ECHL | 6 | 1 | 2 | 3 | 0 | 15 | 1 | 6 | 7 | 0 |

WHL West Second All-Star Team (2008)

**SAPONARI, Vinny** (sa-pawn-AIR-ee, VIH-nee) **ATL.**

Right wing. Shoots right. 6', 179 lbs. Born, Powder Springs, GA, February 15, 1990.
(Atlanta's 4th choice, 94th overall, in 2008 Entry Draft).

| | | | Regular Season | | | | | Playoffs | | | | |
|---|---|---|---|---|---|---|---|---|---|---|---|---|
| Season | Club | League | GP | G | A | Pts | PIM | GP | G | A | Pts | PIM |
| 2006-07 | USNTDP | U-17 | 4 | 11 | 6 | 17 | .... | .... | .... | .... | .... | .... |
| | USNTDP | U-18 | 21 | 4 | 3 | 7 | 6 | .... | .... | .... | .... | .... |
| | USNTDP | NAHL | 35 | 9 | 10 | 19 | 43 | .... | .... | .... | .... | .... |
| 2007-08 | USNTDP | U-18 | 42 | 12 | 16 | 28 | 42 | .... | .... | .... | .... | .... |
| | USNTDP | NAHL | 15 | 1 | 7 | 8 | 0 | .... | .... | .... | .... | .... |
| 2008-09 | Boston University | H-East | 44 | 8 | 9 | 17 | 39 | .... | .... | .... | .... | .... |

**SAUVE, Maxime** (soh-VAY, max-EEM) **BOS.**

Center. Shoots left. 6', 183 lbs. Born, Tours, France, January 30, 1990.
(Boston's 2nd choice, 47th overall, in 2008 Entry Draft).

| | | | Regular Season | | | | | Playoffs | | | | |
|---|---|---|---|---|---|---|---|---|---|---|---|---|
| Season | Club | League | GP | G | A | Pts | PIM | GP | G | A | Pts | PIM |
| 2005-06 | Laval-Laurentides | QAAA | 41 | 16 | 30 | 46 | 54 | 5 | 1 | 3 | 4 | 2 |
| 2006-07 | Quebec Remparts | QMJHL | 60 | 10 | 6 | 16 | 24 | 2 | 0 | 0 | 0 | 2 |
| 2007-08 | Quebec Remparts | QMJHL | 38 | 12 | 20 | 32 | 22 | .... | .... | .... | .... | .... |
| | Val-d'Or Foreurs | QMJHL | 32 | 14 | 19 | 33 | 8 | 4 | 2 | 3 | 5 | 2 |
| 2008-09 | Val-d'Or Foreurs | QMJHL | 64 | 27 | 49 | 76 | 43 | .... | .... | .... | .... | .... |

**SAUVE, Yann** (soh-VAY, YAHN) **VAN.**

Defense. Shoots left. 6'3", 209 lbs. Born, Montreal, Que., February 18, 1990.
(Vancouver's 2nd choice, 41st overall, in 2008 Entry Draft).

| | | | Regular Season | | | | | Playoffs | | | | |
|---|---|---|---|---|---|---|---|---|---|---|---|---|
| Season | Club | League | GP | G | A | Pts | PIM | GP | G | A | Pts | PIM |
| 2005-06 | Chateauguay | QAAA | 42 | 14 | 15 | 29 | 63 | 19 | 2 | 12 | 14 | 44 |
| 2006-07 | Saint John | QMJHL | 60 | 2 | 13 | 15 | 75 | .... | .... | .... | .... | .... |
| 2007-08 | Saint John | QMJHL | 69 | 6 | 15 | 21 | 92 | 14 | 1 | 2 | 3 | 23 |
| 2008-09 | Saint John | QMJHL | 61 | 5 | 25 | 30 | 64 | 4 | 0 | 2 | 2 | 8 |

**SAVARD, David** (suh-VAHRD, DAY-vihd) **CBJ**

Defense. Shoots right. 6'1", 200 lbs. Born, St. Hyacinthe, Que., October 22, 1990.
(Columbus' 3rd choice, 94th overall, in 2009 Entry Draft).

| | | | Regular Season | | | | | Playoffs | | | | |
|---|---|---|---|---|---|---|---|---|---|---|---|---|
| Season | Club | League | GP | G | A | Pts | PIM | GP | G | A | Pts | PIM |
| 2006-07 | Sem. St-Francois | QAAA | 44 | 10 | 16 | 26 | 52 | 18 | 1 | 12 | 13 | 10 |
| 2007-08 | Baie-Comeau | QMJHL | 35 | 1 | 6 | 7 | 22 | .... | .... | .... | .... | .... |
| | Moncton Wildcats | QMJHL | 32 | 0 | 5 | 5 | 18 | .... | .... | .... | .... | .... |
| 2008-09 | Moncton Wildcats | QMJHL | 68 | 9 | 35 | 44 | 33 | 10 | 5 | 5 | 10 | 10 |

**SAWYER, Jean-Claude** (SOI-uhr, ZHAWN-KLOHD) **CHI.**

Defense. Shoots left. 6'3", 194 lbs. Born, Saint John, N.B., August 12, 1986.
(Minnesota's 8th choice, 161st overall, in 2004 Entry Draft).

| | | | Regular Season | | | | | Playoffs | | | | |
|---|---|---|---|---|---|---|---|---|---|---|---|---|
| Season | Club | League | GP | G | A | Pts | PIM | GP | G | A | Pts | PIM |
| 2002-03 | Cape Breton | QMJHL | 31 | 3 | 2 | 5 | 44 | 3 | 0 | 0 | 0 | 2 |
| 2003-04 | Cape Breton | QMJHL | 56 | 5 | 13 | 18 | 48 | 2 | 0 | 0 | 0 | 2 |
| 2004-05 | Cape Breton | QMJHL | 58 | 10 | 22 | 32 | 53 | 5 | 2 | 2 | 4 | 4 |
| 2005-06 | Cape Breton | QMJHL | 69 | 12 | 41 | 53 | 108 | 9 | 4 | 0 | 4 | 15 |
| 2006-07 | Cape Breton | QMJHL | 68 | 15 | 62 | 77 | 87 | 16 | 3 | 16 | 19 | 6 |
| 2007-08 | Rockford IceHogs | AHL | 4 | 0 | 0 | 0 | 4 | .... | .... | .... | .... | .... |
| | Pensacola | ECHL | 65 | 7 | 25 | 32 | 50 | .... | .... | .... | .... | .... |
| 2008-09 | Rockford IceHogs | AHL | 19 | 3 | 1 | 4 | 19 | .... | .... | .... | .... | .... |
| | Fresno Falcons | ECHL | 6 | 1 | 2 | 3 | 6 | .... | .... | .... | .... | .... |
| | Gwinnett | ECHL | 31 | 5 | 17 | 22 | 35 | 5 | 1 | 0 | 1 | 2 |

QMJHL Second All-Star Team (2007)

Signed as a free agent by **Chicago**, July 2, 2007.

**SCALZO, Mario** (SKAL-zoh, MAHR-ee-oh)

Defense. Shoots left. 5'9", 187 lbs. Born, St-Hubert, Que., November 11, 1984.

| | | | Regular Season | | | | | Playoffs | | | | |
|---|---|---|---|---|---|---|---|---|---|---|---|---|
| Season | Club | League | GP | G | A | Pts | PIM | GP | G | A | Pts | PIM |
| 2001-02 | Antoine-Girouard | QAAA | 40 | 8 | 27 | 35 | 50 | .... | .... | .... | .... | .... |
| | Victoriaville Tigres | QMJHL | 1 | 0 | 1 | 1 | 0 | 1 | 0 | 0 | 0 | 0 |
| 2002-03 | Victoriaville Tigres | QMJHL | 72 | 10 | 34 | 44 | 134 | 4 | 0 | 3 | 3 | 6 |
| 2003-04 | Victoriaville Tigres | QMJHL | 68 | 16 | 52 | 68 | 113 | .... | .... | .... | .... | .... |
| 2004-05 | Victoriaville Tigres | QMJHL | 39 | 11 | 19 | 30 | 73 | .... | .... | .... | .... | .... |
| | Rimouski Oceanic | QMJHL | 23 | 13 | 31 | 44 | 31 | 13 | 7 | 14 | 21 | 10 |
| 2005-06 | Iowa Stars | AHL | 74 | 4 | 29 | 33 | 42 | 7 | 0 | 2 | 2 | 8 |
| 2006-07 | Iowa Stars | AHL | 73 | 4 | 21 | 25 | 89 | 9 | 0 | 3 | 3 | 10 |
| 2007-08 | Iowa Stars | AHL | 15 | 1 | 8 | 9 | 10 | .... | .... | .... | .... | .... |
| | Norfolk Admirals | AHL | 48 | 4 | 16 | 20 | 27 | .... | .... | .... | .... | .... |
| 2008-09 | Salzburg | Austria | 47 | 10 | 30 | 40 | 116 | .... | .... | .... | .... | .... |

QMJHL All-Rookie Team (2003) • QMJHL Second All-Star Team (2004) • QMJHL First All-Star Team (2005) • Memorial Cup All-Star Team (2005)

Signed as a free agent by **Dallas**, August 5, 2005. Traded to **Tampa Bay** by **Dallas** for Bryce Lampman, November 19, 2007.

**SCANDELLA, Marco** (skan-DEHL-a, MAHR-koh) **MIN.**

Defense. Shoots left. 6'2", 190 lbs. Born, Montreal, Que., February 23, 1990.
(Minnesota's 2nd choice, 55th overall, in 2008 Entry Draft).

| | | | Regular Season | | | | | Playoffs | | | | |
|---|---|---|---|---|---|---|---|---|---|---|---|---|
| Season | Club | League | GP | G | A | Pts | PIM | GP | G | A | Pts | PIM |
| 2005-06 | Ecole Montpetit | QAAA | 42 | 3 | 4 | 7 | 40 | 3 | 0 | 0 | 0 | 2 |
| 2006-07 | Mtl. Predators | QAAA | 42 | 7 | 13 | 20 | 66 | 3 | 0 | 1 | 1 | 10 |
| 2007-08 | Val-d'Or Foreurs | QMJHL | 65 | 4 | 10 | 14 | 35 | 4 | 0 | 1 | 1 | 4 |
| 2008-09 | Val-d'Or Foreurs | QMJHL | 58 | 10 | 27 | 37 | 64 | .... | .... | .... | .... | .... |
| | Houston Aeros | AHL | 2 | 0 | 0 | 0 | 0 | 6 | 0 | 0 | 0 | 2 |

**SCEVIOUR, Colton** (SEE-vee-yuhr, KOHL-tuhn) **DAL.**

Center/Right wing. Shoots right. 6', 201 lbs. Born, Red Deer, Alta., April 20, 1989.
(Dallas' 3rd choice, 112th overall, in 2007 Entry Draft).

| | | | Regular Season | | | | | Playoffs | | | | |
|---|---|---|---|---|---|---|---|---|---|---|---|---|
| Season | Club | League | GP | G | A | Pts | PIM | GP | G | A | Pts | PIM |
| 2004-05 | Red Deer | AMHL | 36 | 15 | 22 | 37 | 32 | .... | .... | .... | .... | .... |
| | Portland | WHL | 6 | 1 | 0 | 1 | 6 | 4 | 0 | 0 | 0 | 0 |
| 2005-06 | Portland | WHL | 58 | 3 | 6 | 9 | 25 | 12 | 0 | 1 | 1 | 4 |
| 2006-07 | Portland | WHL | 49 | 12 | 26 | 38 | 38 | .... | .... | .... | .... | .... |
| 2007-08 | Portland | WHL | 17 | 2 | 8 | 10 | 9 | .... | .... | .... | .... | .... |
| | Lethbridge | WHL | 52 | 31 | 23 | 54 | 36 | 19 | 3 | 10 | 13 | 15 |
| 2008-09 | Lethbridge | WHL | 69 | 29 | 51 | 80 | 48 | 11 | 4 | 3 | 7 | 12 |

**SCHAEFFER, Kevin** (SHAY-fuhr, KEH-vihn)

Defense. Shoots right. 6', 203 lbs. Born, Huntington, NY, October 16, 1984.
(Nashville's 7th choice, 193rd overall, in 2004 Entry Draft).

| | | | Regular Season | | | | | Playoffs | | | | |
|---|---|---|---|---|---|---|---|---|---|---|---|---|
| Season | Club | League | GP | G | A | Pts | PIM | GP | G | A | Pts | PIM |
| 2002-03 | NY Apple Core | EJHL | 65 | 20 | 38 | 58 | 60 | .... | .... | .... | .... | .... |
| 2003-04 | Boston University | H-East | 38 | 5 | 12 | 17 | 20 | .... | .... | .... | .... | .... |
| 2004-05 | Boston University | H-East | 41 | 2 | 12 | 14 | 26 | .... | .... | .... | .... | .... |
| 2005-06 | Boston University | H-East | 40 | 4 | 9 | 13 | 18 | .... | .... | .... | .... | .... |
| 2006-07 | Boston University | H-East | 33 | 6 | 4 | 10 | 22 | .... | .... | .... | .... | .... |
| 2007-08 | Providence Bruins | AHL | 31 | 1 | 1 | 2 | 6 | .... | .... | .... | .... | .... |
| | Reading Royals | ECHL | 19 | 2 | 5 | 7 | 21 | 11 | 1 | 3 | 4 | 8 |
| 2008-09 | Binghamton | AHL | 3 | 0 | 0 | 0 | 0 | .... | .... | .... | .... | .... |
| | Providence Bruins | AHL | 48 | 0 | 3 | 3 | 14 | 5 | 0 | 0 | 0 | 2 |
| | Reading Royals | ECHL | 6 | 0 | 0 | 0 | 6 | .... | .... | .... | .... | .... |

Hockey East All-Rookie Team (2004)

**SCHENN, Brayden** (SHEHN, BRAY-duhn) **L.A.**

Center. Shoots left. 6', 198 lbs. Born, Saskatoon, Sask., August 22, 1991.
(Los Angeles' 1st choice, 5th overall, in 2009 Entry Draft).

| | | | Regular Season | | | | | Playoffs | | | | |
|---|---|---|---|---|---|---|---|---|---|---|---|---|
| Season | Club | League | GP | G | A | Pts | PIM | GP | G | A | Pts | PIM |
| 2006-07 | Sask. Contacts | SMHL | 41 | 27 | 43 | 70 | 63 | .... | .... | .... | .... | .... |
| 2007-08 | Brandon | WHL | 66 | 28 | 43 | 71 | 48 | 6 | 2 | 1 | 3 | 14 |
| 2008-09 | Brandon | WHL | 70 | 32 | 56 | 88 | 82 | 12 | 8 | 10 | 18 | 12 |

WHL Rookie of the Year (2008) • Canadian Major Junior All-Rookie Team (2008) • WHL East Second All-Star Team (2009)

**SCHEVJEV, Maxim** (shehv-YAWF-yehv, max-EEM) **BUF.**

Center. Shoots left. 6', 178 lbs. Born, Noginsk, USSR, July 5, 1984.
(Buffalo's 7th choice, 178th overall, in 2002 Entry Draft).

| | | | Regular Season | | | | | Playoffs | | | | |
|---|---|---|---|---|---|---|---|---|---|---|---|---|
| Season | Club | League | GP | G | A | Pts | PIM | GP | G | A | Pts | PIM |
| 99-2000 | Elektrostal 2 | Russia-3 | 11 | 0 | 1 | 1 | 2 | .... | .... | .... | .... | .... |
| 2000-01 | Elektrostal | Russia-2 | 7 | 0 | 0 | 0 | 6 | .... | .... | .... | .... | .... |
| 2001-02 | Elektrostal 2 | Russia-3 | 6 | 1 | 2 | 3 | 2 | .... | .... | .... | .... | .... |
| | Elektrostal | Russia-2 | 49 | 6 | 9 | 15 | 34 | .... | .... | .... | .... | .... |
| 2002-03 | Amur Khabarovsk | Russia | 21 | 0 | 0 | 0 | 10 | .... | .... | .... | .... | .... |
| | Khabarovsk 2 | Russia-3 | 5 | 2 | 1 | 3 | 4 | .... | .... | .... | .... | .... |
| 2003-04 | Kristall Elektrostal | Russia-2 | 26 | 4 | 5 | 9 | 20 | .... | .... | .... | .... | .... |
| | Voskresensk | Russia | 18 | 1 | 0 | 1 | 2 | .... | .... | .... | .... | .... |
| 2004-05 | Kristall Elektrostal | Russia-2 | 48 | 4 | 7 | 11 | 109 | .... | .... | .... | .... | .... |
| 2005-06 | Yuzhny Ural Orsk | Russia-2 | 38 | 3 | 10 | 13 | 38 | .... | .... | .... | .... | .... |
| | Yuzhny Ural Orsk 2 | Russia-3 | 3 | 1 | 3 | 4 | 0 | .... | .... | .... | .... | .... |
| | Kristall Elektrostal | Russia-3 | STATISTICS NOT AVAILABLE | | | | | | | | | |
| 2006-07 | Kristall Elektrostal | Russia-2 | 47 | 4 | 7 | 11 | 52 | .... | .... | .... | .... | .... |
| 2007-08 | Kristall Elektrostal | Russia-2 | 58 | 6 | 11 | 17 | 68 | .... | .... | .... | .... | .... |
| 2008-09 | Titan Klin | Russia-2 | 13 | 2 | 0 | 2 | 4 | .... | .... | .... | .... | .... |
| | HK Bryansk | Russia-3 | STATISTICS NOT AVAILABLE | | | | | | | | | |

**SCHIESTEL, Drew** (SHIGHS-tuhl, DROO) **BUF.**

Defense. Shoots right. 6'1", 180 lbs. Born, Hamilton, Ont., March 9, 1989.
(Buffalo's 2nd choice, 59th overall, in 2007 Entry Draft).

| | | | Regular Season | | | | | Playoffs | | | | |
|---|---|---|---|---|---|---|---|---|---|---|---|---|
| Season | Club | League | GP | G | A | Pts | PIM | GP | G | A | Pts | PIM |
| 2004-05 | Hamilton Reps | Minor-ON | 68 | 21 | 27 | 46 | .... | .... | .... | .... | .... | .... |
| 2005-06 | Mississauga | OHL | 40 | 1 | 4 | 5 | 42 | .... | .... | .... | .... | .... |
| 2006-07 | Mississauga | OHL | 66 | 6 | 15 | 21 | 40 | 5 | 0 | 6 | 6 | 2 |
| 2007-08 | Niagara Ice Dogs | OHL | 68 | 8 | 29 | 37 | 40 | 10 | 1 | 6 | 7 | 10 |
| 2008-09 | Niagara Ice Dogs | OHL | 63 | 10 | 38 | 48 | 75 | 12 | 2 | 6 | 8 | 14 |

**SCHIRA, Craig** (SHIH-rah, KRAYG) **OTT.**

Defense. Shoots right. 6', 196 lbs. Born, Spiritwood, Sask., April 21, 1988.

| | | | Regular Season | | | | | Playoffs | | | | |
|---|---|---|---|---|---|---|---|---|---|---|---|---|
| Season | Club | League | GP | G | A | Pts | PIM | GP | G | A | Pts | PIM |
| 2003-04 | Saskatoon Blazers | SMHL | 39 | 2 | 10 | 12 | 20 | .... | .... | .... | .... | .... |
| | Regina Pats | WHL | 2 | 0 | 0 | 0 | 2 | .... | .... | .... | .... | .... |
| 2004-05 | Regina Pats | WHL | 60 | 1 | 7 | 8 | 25 | .... | .... | .... | .... | .... |
| 2005-06 | Regina Pats | WHL | 71 | 5 | 28 | 33 | 72 | 6 | 1 | 1 | 2 | 2 |
| 2006-07 | Regina Pats | WHL | 71 | 3 | 23 | 26 | 74 | 10 | 0 | 0 | 0 | 4 |
| 2007-08 | Regina Pats | WHL | 2 | 0 | 1 | 1 | 0 | .... | .... | .... | .... | .... |
| | Vancouver Giants | WHL | 63 | 8 | 22 | 30 | 58 | 10 | 0 | 1 | 1 | 0 |
| 2008-09 | Vancouver Giants | WHL | 71 | 16 | 43 | 59 | 46 | 17 | 2 | 4 | 6 | 4 |

Signed as a free agent by **Ottawa**, March 9, 2009.

**SCHNEIDER, Andy** (SHNIGH-duhr, AN-dee)

Defense. Shoots left. 6'1", 215 lbs. Born, Grand Forks, ND, July 31, 1981.
(Pittsburgh's 7th choice, 156th overall, in 2001 Entry Draft).

| | | | Regular Season | | | | | Playoffs | | | | |
|---|---|---|---|---|---|---|---|---|---|---|---|---|
| Season | Club | League | GP | G | A | Pts | PIM | GP | G | A | Pts | PIM |
| 1998-99 | Lincoln Stars | USHL | 9 | 0 | 4 | 4 | 8 | 4 | 0 | 0 | 0 | 2 |
| 99-2000 | Lincoln Stars | USHL | 46 | 7 | 10 | 17 | 102 | 10 | 6 | 4 | 10 | 27 |
| 2000-01 | Lincoln Stars | USHL | 54 | 12 | 24 | 36 | 134 | .... | .... | .... | .... | .... |
| 2001-02 | North Dakota | WCHA | 35 | 3 | 11 | 14 | 65 | .... | .... | .... | .... | .... |
| 2002-03 | North Dakota | WCHA | 43 | 11 | 30 | 41 | 52 | .... | .... | .... | .... | .... |
| 2003-04 | North Dakota | WCHA | 39 | 2 | 10 | 12 | 54 | .... | .... | .... | .... | .... |
| 2004-05 | North Dakota | WCHA | 42 | 2 | 8 | 10 | 58 | .... | .... | .... | .... | .... |
| 2005-06 | Wilkes-Barre | AHL | 50 | 3 | 13 | 16 | 54 | .... | .... | .... | .... | .... |
| | Wheeling Nailers | ECHL | 4 | 0 | 1 | 1 | 2 | .... | .... | .... | .... | .... |
| 2006-07 | Dusseldorf | Germany | 48 | 6 | 20 | 26 | 73 | 9 | 3 | 7 | 10 | 18 |
| 2007-08 | Portland Pirates | AHL | 57 | 3 | 8 | 11 | 81 | 11 | 2 | 3 | 5 | 6 |
| 2008-09 | Toronto Marlies | AHL | 32 | 0 | 5 | 5 | 42 | .... | .... | .... | .... | .... |
| | Adler Mannheim | Germany | 7 | 0 | 1 | 1 | 10 | .... | .... | .... | .... | .... |

Signed as a free agent by **Toronto**, July 27, 2008.

## SCHROEDER, Jordan (SHRAY-duhr, JOHR-dahn) VAN.

Center. Shoots right. 5'8", 175 lbs. Born, Burnsville, MN, September 29, 1990.
(Vancouver's 1st choice, 22nd overall, in 2009 Entry Draft).

| | | | Regular Season | | | | | Playoffs | | | | |
|---|---|---|---|---|---|---|---|---|---|---|---|---|
| **Season** | **Club** | **League** | **GP** | **G** | **A** | **Pts** | **PIM** | **GP** | **G** | **A** | **Pts** | **PIM** |
| 2005-06 | St. Thomas | High-MN | 31 | 27 | 35 | 62 | .... | .... | .... | .... | .... | .... |
| | Team Southeast | UMHSEL | .... | 7 | 14 | 21 | .... | .... | .... | .... | .... | .... |
| 2006-07 | USNTDP | NAHL | 31 | 12 | 11 | 23 | 10 | .... | .... | .... | .... | .... |
| | USNTDP | U-17 | 8 | 2 | 8 | 10 | 2 | .... | .... | .... | .... | .... |
| | USNTDP | U-18 | 17 | 6 | 13 | 19 | 4 | .... | .... | .... | .... | .... |
| 2007-08 | USNTDP | NAHL | 14 | 1 | 8 | 9 | 4 | .... | .... | .... | .... | .... |
| | USNTDP | U-18 | 41 | 21 | 23 | 44 | 12 | .... | .... | .... | .... | .... |
| 2008-09 | U. of Minnesota | WCHA | 35 | 13 | 32 | 45 | 29 | .... | .... | .... | .... | .... |

## SCHULTZ, Ian (SHUHLTZ, EE-an) ST.L.

Right wing. Shoots right. 6'2", 205 lbs. Born, Calgary, Alta., February 4, 1990.
(St. Louis' 6th choice, 87th overall, in 2008 Entry Draft).

| | | | Regular Season | | | | | Playoffs | | | | |
|---|---|---|---|---|---|---|---|---|---|---|---|---|
| **Season** | **Club** | **League** | **GP** | **G** | **A** | **Pts** | **PIM** | **GP** | **G** | **A** | **Pts** | **PIM** |
| 2006-07 | Calgary Buffaloes | AMHL | 32 | 13 | 25 | 38 | 92 | 7 | 2 | 7 | 9 | 26 |
| | Calgary Hitmen | WHL | 1 | 1 | 0 | 1 | 0 | .... | .... | .... | .... | .... |
| 2007-08 | Calgary Hitmen | WHL | 67 | 15 | 15 | 30 | 128 | 16 | 2 | 7 | 9 | 19 |
| 2008-09 | Calgary Hitmen | WHL | 58 | 15 | 26 | 41 | 127 | 18 | 5 | 7 | 12 | 24 |

## SCHULTZ, Justin (SHUHLTZ, JUHS-tihn) ANA.

Defense. Shoots right. 6'2", 180 lbs. Born, Kelowna, B.C., July 6, 1990.
(Anaheim's 4th choice, 43rd overall, in 2008 Entry Draft).

| | | | Regular Season | | | | | Playoffs | | | | |
|---|---|---|---|---|---|---|---|---|---|---|---|---|
| **Season** | **Club** | **League** | **GP** | **G** | **A** | **Pts** | **PIM** | **GP** | **G** | **A** | **Pts** | **PIM** |
| 2006-07 | Westside Warriors | Minor-BC | .... | 29 | 29 | 58 | 29 | .... | .... | .... | .... | .... |
| 2007-08 | Westside Warriors | BCHL | 57 | 9 | 31 | 40 | 28 | 11 | 3 | 5 | 8 | 4 |
| 2008-09 | Westside Warriors | BCHL | 49 | 15 | 35 | 50 | 29 | 6 | 1 | 2 | 3 | 2 |

• Signed Letter of Intent to attend **University of Wisconsin** (WCHA) in fall of 2009.

## SCHUTZ, Felix (SCHUTZ, FEEL-ihx) BUF.

Center. Shoots left. 5'11", 187 lbs. Born, Erding, West Germany, November 3, 1987.
(Buffalo's 4th choice, 117th overall, in 2006 Entry Draft).

| | | | Regular Season | | | | | Playoffs | | | | |
|---|---|---|---|---|---|---|---|---|---|---|---|---|
| **Season** | **Club** | **League** | **GP** | **G** | **A** | **Pts** | **PIM** | **GP** | **G** | **A** | **Pts** | **PIM** |
| 2003-04 | Mannheim Jr. | Ger-Jr. | 30 | 22 | 22 | 44 | 12 | .... | .... | .... | .... | .... |
| 2004-05 | EV Landshut Jr. | Ger-Jr. | 9 | 6 | 8 | 14 | 33 | 2 | 2 | 3 | 5 | 0 |
| | Landshut Cann. | German-2 | 24 | 1 | 2 | 3 | 8 | 5 | 0 | 0 | 0 | 2 |
| 2005-06 | Saint John | QMJHL | 65 | 21 | 31 | 52 | 61 | .... | .... | .... | .... | .... |
| 2006-07 | Saint John | QMJHL | 18 | 4 | 7 | 11 | 16 | .... | .... | .... | .... | .... |
| | Val-d'Or Foreurs | QMJHL | 27 | 15 | 18 | 33 | 28 | 20 | 5 | 10 | 15 | 22 |
| 2007-08 | ERC Ingolstadt | Germany | 46 | 12 | 13 | 25 | 76 | 3 | 0 | 1 | 1 | 2 |
| 2008-09 | Portland Pirates | AHL | 78 | 15 | 27 | 42 | 61 | 5 | 1 | 1 | 2 | 2 |

QMJHL All-Rookie Team (2006)

## SCOTT, Greg (SKAWT, GREHG) TOR.

Right wing. Shoots right. 6', 178 lbs. Born, Victoria, B.C., June 3, 1988.

| | | | Regular Season | | | | | Playoffs | | | | |
|---|---|---|---|---|---|---|---|---|---|---|---|---|
| **Season** | **Club** | **League** | **GP** | **G** | **A** | **Pts** | **PIM** | **GP** | **G** | **A** | **Pts** | **PIM** |
| 2004-05 | Peninsula Panthers | VIJHL | 48 | 34 | 40 | 74 | 65 | .... | .... | .... | .... | .... |
| | Victoria Salsa | BCHL | 7 | 1 | 1 | 2 | 0 | .... | .... | .... | .... | .... |
| 2005-06 | Seattle | WHL | 69 | 8 | 14 | 22 | 37 | 7 | 1 | 3 | 4 | 4 |
| 2006-07 | Seattle | WHL | 72 | 18 | 14 | 32 | 62 | 11 | 0 | 2 | 2 | 2 |
| 2007-08 | Seattle | WHL | 72 | 38 | 37 | 75 | 56 | 12 | 5 | 4 | 9 | 9 |
| 2008-09 | Seattle | WHL | 65 | 32 | 44 | 76 | 39 | 5 | 0 | 6 | 6 | 2 |

Signed as a free agent by **Toronto**, July 3, 2008.

## SDAO, Michael (S'DAY-oh, MIGH-kuhl) OTT.

Defense. Shoots left. 6'4", 221 lbs. Born, Bloomington, MN, July 3, 1989.
(Ottawa's 9th choice, 191st overall, in 2009 Entry Draft).

| | | | Regular Season | | | | | Playoffs | | | | |
|---|---|---|---|---|---|---|---|---|---|---|---|---|
| **Season** | **Club** | **League** | **GP** | **G** | **A** | **Pts** | **PIM** | **GP** | **G** | **A** | **Pts** | **PIM** |
| 2005-06 | Culver Academy | High-IN | 40 | 1 | 6 | 7 | 38 | .... | .... | .... | .... | .... |
| 2006-07 | Culver Academy | High-IN | 43 | 1 | 6 | 7 | 85 | .... | .... | .... | .... | .... |
| 2007-08 | Lincoln Stars | USHL | 53 | 3 | 6 | 9 | 178 | 8 | 0 | 1 | 1 | 20 |
| 2008-09 | Lincoln Stars | USHL | 51 | 3 | 7 | 10 | 162 | 7 | 0 | 0 | 0 | *33 |

• Signed Letter of Intent to attend **Princeton University** (ECAC) in fall of 2009.

## SEABROOK, Keith (SEE-bruk, KEETH) CGY.

Defense. Shoots right. 6', 198 lbs. Born, Delta, B.C., August 2, 1988.
(Washington's 5th choice, 52nd overall, in 2006 Entry Draft).

| | | | Regular Season | | | | | Playoffs | | | | |
|---|---|---|---|---|---|---|---|---|---|---|---|---|
| **Season** | **Club** | **League** | **GP** | **G** | **A** | **Pts** | **PIM** | **GP** | **G** | **A** | **Pts** | **PIM** |
| 2004-05 | Coquitlam Express | BCHL | 58 | 8 | 20 | 28 | 70 | .... | .... | .... | .... | .... |
| 2005-06 | Burnaby Express | BCHL | 57 | 10 | 24 | 34 | 81 | .... | .... | .... | .... | .... |
| 2006-07 | U. of Denver | WCHA | 37 | 2 | 11 | 13 | 24 | .... | .... | .... | .... | .... |
| 2007-08 | Calgary Hitmen | WHL | 59 | 4 | 13 | 17 | 47 | 14 | 0 | 5 | 5 | 13 |
| 2008-09 | Calgary Hitmen | WHL | 64 | 15 | 40 | 55 | 58 | 18 | 4 | 11 | 15 | 26 |

• Left **University of Denver** (WCHA) and signed with **Calgary** (WHL), July 30, 2007. Traded to **Calgary** by **Washington** for future considerations, July 17, 2009.

## SEDOV, Pavel (se-DAHF, PAH-vehl) T.B.

Right wing. Shoots left. 6'3", 200 lbs. Born, Voskresensk, USSR, January 12, 1982.
(Tampa Bay's 5th choice, 161st overall, in 2000 Entry Draft).

| | | | Regular Season | | | | | Playoffs | | | | |
|---|---|---|---|---|---|---|---|---|---|---|---|---|
| **Season** | **Club** | **League** | **GP** | **G** | **A** | **Pts** | **PIM** | **GP** | **G** | **A** | **Pts** | **PIM** |
| 99-2000 | Voskresensk | Russia-2 | 10 | 0 | 0 | 0 | 2 | .... | .... | .... | .... | .... |
| | Voskresensk 2 | Russia-3 | 21 | 5 | 5 | 10 | 26 | .... | .... | .... | .... | .... |
| 2000-01 | Voskresensk | Russia-2 | 38 | 2 | 1 | 3 | 10 | .... | .... | .... | .... | .... |
| 2001-02 | Voskresensk 2 | Russia-3 | 12 | 4 | 1 | 5 | 0 | .... | .... | .... | .... | .... |
| | Voskresensk | Russia-2 | 18 | 3 | 1 | 4 | 0 | .... | .... | .... | .... | .... |
| 2002-03 | Voskresensk | Russia-2 | 25 | 1 | 5 | 6 | 6 | .... | .... | .... | .... | .... |
| | Voskresensk 2 | Russia-3 | 7 | 2 | 4 | 6 | 4 | .... | .... | .... | .... | .... |
| 2003-04 | THK Tver | Russia-2 | 26 | 2 | 6 | 8 | 6 | .... | .... | .... | .... | .... |
| | Voskresensk | Russia | 10 | 1 | 0 | 1 | 2 | .... | .... | .... | .... | .... |
| | Voskresensk 2 | Russia-3 | STATISTICS NOT AVAILABLE | | | | | | | | | |
| 2004-05 | HK Tver | Russia-3 | STATISTICS NOT AVAILABLE | | | | | | | | | |
| | HK Dmitrov | Russia-3 | STATISTICS NOT AVAILABLE | | | | | | | | | |
| | HK Ryazan | Russia-4 | STATISTICS NOT AVAILABLE | | | | | | | | | |
| 2005-06 | | | DID NOT PLAY | | | | | | | | | |
| 2006-07 | HK Ryazan | Russia-3 | 70 | 24 | 29 | 53 | 16 | .... | .... | .... | .... | .... |
| 2007-08 | HK Ryazan | Russia-2 | 50 | 6 | 10 | 16 | 14 | .... | .... | .... | .... | .... |
| 2008-09 | HK Ryazan | Russia-2 | 63 | 13 | 13 | 26 | 18 | 8 | 3 | 4 | 7 | 2 |

## SEITSONEN, Aki (SIGHT-soh-nehn, AH-kee)

Center. Shoots right. 6'3", 206 lbs. Born, Riihimaki, Finland, February 5, 1986.
(Calgary's 4th choice, 118th overall, in 2004 Entry Draft).

| | | | Regular Season | | | | | Playoffs | | | | |
|---|---|---|---|---|---|---|---|---|---|---|---|---|
| **Season** | **Club** | **League** | **GP** | **G** | **A** | **Pts** | **PIM** | **GP** | **G** | **A** | **Pts** | **PIM** |
| 2002-03 | HPK U18 | Fin-U18 | 28 | 15 | 18 | 33 | 6 | 2 | 1 | 1 | 2 | 0 |
| | HPK Jr. | Fin-Jr. | 1 | 1 | 0 | 1 | 0 | .... | .... | .... | .... | .... |
| 2003-04 | Prince Albert | WHL | 71 | 16 | 24 | 40 | 18 | 5 | 0 | 0 | 0 | 0 |
| 2004-05 | Prince Albert | WHL | 67 | 24 | 28 | 52 | 14 | 17 | 5 | 9 | 14 | 10 |
| 2005-06 | Prince Albert | WHL | 66 | 20 | 15 | 35 | 22 | .... | .... | .... | .... | .... |
| | Omaha | AHL | 7 | 0 | 0 | 0 | 2 | .... | .... | .... | .... | .... |
| 2006-07 | Omaha | AHL | 13 | 1 | 3 | 4 | 0 | .... | .... | .... | .... | .... |
| | Las Vegas | ECHL | 59 | 14 | 18 | 32 | 16 | 5 | 0 | 2 | 2 | 2 |
| 2007-08 | Las Vegas | ECHL | 70 | 18 | 18 | 36 | 14 | 21 | 7 | 3 | 10 | 4 |
| 2008-09 | Quad City Flames | AHL | 45 | 4 | 2 | 6 | 10 | .... | .... | .... | .... | .... |

## SEMIN, Dmitri (SEH-min, dih-MEE-tree) ST.L.

Center. Shoots left. 5'10", 185 lbs. Born, Moscow, USSR, August 14, 1983.
(St. Louis' 4th choice, 159th overall, in 2001 Entry Draft).

| | | | Regular Season | | | | | Playoffs | | | | |
|---|---|---|---|---|---|---|---|---|---|---|---|---|
| **Season** | **Club** | **League** | **GP** | **G** | **A** | **Pts** | **PIM** | **GP** | **G** | **A** | **Pts** | **PIM** |
| 99-2000 | Spartak Moscow 2 | Russia-3 | 27 | 9 | 10 | 19 | 10 | .... | .... | .... | .... | .... |
| | Spartak Moscow | Russia-2 | 1 | 0 | 0 | 0 | 0 | .... | .... | .... | .... | .... |
| 2000-01 | Spartak Moscow | Russia-2 | 21 | 6 | 3 | 9 | 4 | 11 | 2 | 3 | 5 | 4 |
| 2001-02 | Spartak Moscow 2 | Russia-3 | 4 | 5 | 0 | 5 | 4 | .... | .... | .... | .... | .... |
| | Spartak Moscow | Russia | 44 | 2 | 6 | 8 | 14 | .... | .... | .... | .... | .... |
| 2002-03 | Spartak Moscow | Russia | 51 | 9 | 13 | 22 | 30 | .... | .... | .... | .... | .... |
| 2003-04 | Spartak Moscow | Russia-2 | 60 | 15 | 23 | 38 | 34 | 13 | 2 | 2 | 4 | 2 |
| 2004-05 | Spartak Moscow | Russia | 53 | 7 | 7 | 14 | 34 | .... | .... | .... | .... | .... |
| 2005-06 | Spartak Moscow | Russia | 51 | 12 | 14 | 26 | 38 | 3 | 0 | 1 | 1 | 0 |
| 2006-07 | Yaroslavl | Russia | 41 | 13 | 13 | 26 | 30 | 7 | 3 | 2 | 5 | 2 |
| 2007-08 | Yaroslavl | Russia | 54 | 9 | 14 | 23 | 46 | 16 | 1 | 2 | 3 | 10 |
| 2008-09 | Yaroslavl | Rus-KHL | 53 | 7 | 13 | 20 | 28 | 16 | 4 | 5 | 9 | 33 |

## SEPPANEN, Timo (SEH-pah-nehn, TEE-moh) PIT.

Defense. Shoots left. 6'1", 209 lbs. Born, Helsinki, Finland, July 22, 1987.
(Pittsburgh's 5th choice, 185th overall, in 2006 Entry Draft).

| | | | Regular Season | | | | | Playoffs | | | | |
|---|---|---|---|---|---|---|---|---|---|---|---|---|
| **Season** | **Club** | **League** | **GP** | **G** | **A** | **Pts** | **PIM** | **GP** | **G** | **A** | **Pts** | **PIM** |
| 2002-03 | HIFK Helsinki U18 | Fin-U18 | 24 | 2 | 5 | 7 | 12 | 2 | 2 | 0 | 2 | 0 |
| 2003-04 | HIFK Helsinki U18 | Fin-U18 | 7 | 2 | 5 | 7 | 32 | 4 | 0 | 2 | 2 | 6 |
| | HIFK Helsinki Jr. | Fin-Jr. | 29 | 0 | 4 | 4 | 6 | 7 | 0 | 0 | 0 | 2 |
| 2004-05 | HIFK Helsinki U18 | Fin-U18 | .... | .... | .... | .... | .... | 7 | 2 | 3 | 5 | 26 |
| | HIFK Helsinki Jr. | Fin-Jr. | 39 | 3 | 4 | 7 | 32 | 3 | 0 | 0 | 0 | 4 |
| 2005-06 | Suomi U20 | Finland-2 | 6 | 2 | 2 | 4 | 10 | .... | .... | .... | .... | .... |
| | HIFK Helsinki Jr. | Fin-Jr. | 30 | 7 | 11 | 18 | 65 | .... | .... | .... | .... | .... |
| | HIFK Helsinki | Finland | 21 | 0 | 0 | 0 | 2 | 5 | 0 | 1 | 1 | 0 |
| 2006-07 | HIFK Helsinki Jr. | Fin-Jr. | 12 | 2 | 2 | 4 | 10 | .... | .... | .... | .... | .... |
| | Suomi U20 | Finland-2 | 6 | 1 | 0 | 1 | 6 | .... | .... | .... | .... | .... |
| | HIFK Helsinki | Finland | 12 | 0 | 0 | 0 | 10 | .... | .... | .... | .... | .... |
| | HPK Jr. | Fin-Jr. | 9 | 1 | 4 | 5 | 8 | 3 | 1 | 2 | 3 | 0 |
| | HPK Hameenlinna | Finland | 16 | 2 | 1 | 3 | 10 | .... | .... | .... | .... | .... |
| 2007-08 | HIFK Helsinki Jr. | Fin-Jr. | 1 | 1 | 0 | 1 | 2 | .... | .... | .... | .... | .... |
| | HIFK Helsinki | Finland | 3 | 0 | 0 | 0 | 0 | .... | .... | .... | .... | .... |
| | KalPa Kuopio | Finland | 49 | 6 | 6 | 12 | 30 | .... | .... | .... | .... | .... |
| 2008-09 | KalPa Kuopio | Finland | 57 | 3 | 7 | 10 | 42 | 12 | 2 | 2 | 4 | 12 |

## SERSEN, Michal (suhr-SEHN, MEE-khahl) T.B.

Defense. Shoots left. 6'2", 200 lbs. Born, Celnica, Czech., December 28, 1985.
(Pittsburgh's 7th choice, 130th overall, in 2004 Entry Draft).

| | | | Regular Season | | | | | Playoffs | | | | |
|---|---|---|---|---|---|---|---|---|---|---|---|---|
| **Season** | **Club** | **League** | **GP** | **G** | **A** | **Pts** | **PIM** | **GP** | **G** | **A** | **Pts** | **PIM** |
| 2002-03 | Bratislava Jr. | Slovak-Jr. | 33 | 5 | 4 | 9 | 51 | .... | .... | .... | .... | .... |
| | Bratislava | Slovakia | 17 | 0 | 0 | 0 | 0 | .... | .... | .... | .... | .... |
| 2003-04 | Rimouski Oceanic | QMJHL | 45 | 7 | 18 | 25 | 30 | 9 | 1 | 5 | 6 | 6 |
| 2004-05 | Rimouski Oceanic | QMJHL | 67 | 9 | 33 | 42 | 74 | 13 | 0 | 8 | 8 | 18 |
| 2005-06 | Quebec Remparts | QMJHL | 63 | 22 | 57 | 79 | 76 | 23 | 3 | 18 | 21 | 36 |
| 2006-07 | Bratislava | Slovakia | 42 | 1 | 4 | 5 | 28 | 14 | 0 | 1 | 1 | 2 |
| 2007-08 | Bratislava | Slovakia | 54 | 9 | 9 | 18 | 58 | 18 | 1 | 2 | 3 | 6 |
| 2008-09 | Bratislava | Slovakia | 40 | 4 | 12 | 16 | 49 | .... | .... | .... | .... | .... |

QMJHL Second All-Star Team (2006) • Memorial Cup Tournament All-Star Team (2006)

Signed as a free agent by **Bratislava** (Slovakia), October 14, 2006. Traded to **Tampa Bay** by **Pittsburgh** for Tampa Bay's 5th round choice (Alex Velischek) in 2009 Entry Draft, October 1, 2008.

## SERTICH, Marty (SUHR-tihch, MAHR-tee) COL.

Center. Shoots left. 5'9", 165 lbs. Born, Roseville, MN, October 13, 1982.

| | | | Regular Season | | | | | Playoffs | | | | |
|---|---|---|---|---|---|---|---|---|---|---|---|---|
| **Season** | **Club** | **League** | **GP** | **G** | **A** | **Pts** | **PIM** | **GP** | **G** | **A** | **Pts** | **PIM** |
| 2001-02 | Sioux Falls | USHL | 61 | 19 | 33 | 52 | 30 | 3 | 1 | 0 | 1 | 0 |
| 2002-03 | Colorado College | WCHA | 42 | 9 | 20 | 29 | 26 | .... | .... | .... | .... | .... |
| 2003-04 | Colorado College | WCHA | 39 | 11 | 28 | 39 | 12 | .... | .... | .... | .... | .... |
| 2004-05 | Colorado College | WCHA | 42 | 27 | 37 | *64 | 26 | .... | .... | .... | .... | .... |
| 2005-06 | Colorado College | WCHA | 42 | 14 | 36 | 50 | 55 | .... | .... | .... | .... | .... |
| 2006-07 | Iowa Stars | AHL | 44 | 13 | 20 | 33 | 24 | 2 | 0 | 1 | 1 | 0 |
| 2007-08 | Iowa Stars | AHL | 79 | 27 | 25 | 52 | 42 | .... | .... | .... | .... | .... |
| 2008-09 | Lake Erie Monsters | AHL | 24 | 7 | 8 | 15 | 22 | .... | .... | .... | .... | .... |

WCHA Second All-Star Team (2006)

Signed as a free agent by **Dallas**, July 10, 2006. Traded to **Colorado** by **Dallas** for future considerations, June 10, 2008.

## SEVERYN, C.J. (SEH-vuhr-ihn, SEE-JAY) CGY.

Left wing. Shoots left. 6', 185 lbs. Born, Beaver, PA, June 2, 1989.
(Calgary's 5th choice, 186th overall, in 2007 Entry Draft).

| | | | Regular Season | | | | | Playoffs | | | | |
|---|---|---|---|---|---|---|---|---|---|---|---|---|
| **Season** | **Club** | **League** | **GP** | **G** | **A** | **Pts** | **PIM** | **GP** | **G** | **A** | **Pts** | **PIM** |
| 2004-05 | Pittsburgh Hornets | MWEHL | 65 | 27 | 44 | 71 | .... | .... | .... | .... | .... | .... |
| 2005-06 | USNTDP | U-17 | 19 | 2 | 3 | 5 | 40 | .... | .... | .... | .... | .... |
| | USNTDP | NAHL | 32 | 2 | 13 | 15 | 77 | 12 | 1 | 0 | 1 | 12 |
| 2006-07 | USNTDP | U-18 | 42 | 8 | 8 | 16 | 32 | .... | .... | .... | .... | .... |
| | USNTDP | NAHL | 15 | 0 | 3 | 3 | 22 | .... | .... | .... | .... | .... |
| 2007-08 | Ohio State | CCHA | 32 | 0 | 2 | 2 | 20 | .... | .... | .... | .... | .... |
| 2008-09 | Ohio State | CCHA | 33 | 9 | 3 | 12 | 24 | .... | .... | .... | .... | .... |

**SEXTON, Ben** (SEHKS-tuhn, BEHN) **BOS.**

Center. Shoots right. 5'11", 192 lbs. Born, Ottawa, Ont., June 6, 1991.
(Boston's 5th choice, 206th overall, in 2009 Entry Draft).

| | | | Regular Season | | | | | Playoffs | | | | |
|---|---|---|---|---|---|---|---|---|---|---|---|---|
| Season | Club | League | GP | G | A | Pts | PIM | GP | G | A | Pts | PIM |
| 2007-08 | Nepean Raiders | CJHL | 48 | 15 | 15 | 30 | 71 | 6 | 1 | 5 | 6 | 4 |
| 2008-09 | Nepean Raiders | CJHL | 38 | 14 | 21 | 35 | 54 | 11 | 3 | 9 | 12 | 22 |

• Signed Letter of Intent to attend **Clarkson University** (ECAC) in fall of 2009.

**SEXTON, Dan** (SEHKS-tuhn, DAN) **ANA.**

Right wing. Shoots right. 5'10", 166 lbs. Born, Apple Valley, MN, April 29, 1987.

| | | | Regular Season | | | | | Playoffs | | | | |
|---|---|---|---|---|---|---|---|---|---|---|---|---|
| Season | Club | League | GP | G | A | Pts | PIM | GP | G | A | Pts | PIM |
| 2005-06 | Wichita Falls | NAHL | 58 | 22 | 37 | 59 | 16 | 5 | 2 | 1 | 3 | 0 |
| 2006-07 | Sioux Falls | USHL | 58 | 14 | 10 | 24 | 20 | 8 | 8 | 1 | 9 | 0 |
| 2007-08 | Bowling Green | CCHA | 38 | 7 | 14 | 21 | 42 | .... | .... | .... | .... | .... |
| 2008-09 | Bowling Green | CCHA | 38 | 17 | 22 | 39 | 20 | .... | .... | .... | .... | .... |

Signed as a free agent by **Anaheim**, April 7, 2009.

**SHADILOV, Igor** (sha-DEE-lahf, EE-gohr) **WSH.**

Defense. Shoots left. 6'2", 189 lbs. Born, Moscow, USSR, June 7, 1980.
(Washington's 10th choice, 249th overall, in 1999 Entry Draft).

| | | | Regular Season | | | | | Playoffs | | | | |
|---|---|---|---|---|---|---|---|---|---|---|---|---|
| Season | Club | League | GP | G | A | Pts | PIM | GP | G | A | Pts | PIM |
| 1996-97 | Dyn'o Moscow 2 | Russia-3 | 30 | 3 | 7 | 10 | 30 | .... | .... | .... | .... | .... |
| 1997-98 | Dynamo Moscow | Russia | 38 | 1 | 0 | 1 | 6 | .... | .... | .... | .... | .... |
| 1998-99 | Dyn'o Moscow 2 | Russia-3 | 28 | 2 | 9 | 11 | 15 | .... | .... | .... | .... | .... |
| | Dynamo Moscow | Russia | 2 | 0 | 0 | 0 | 0 | .... | .... | .... | .... | .... |
| | Krylja Sovetov | Russia | 9 | 0 | 0 | 0 | 0 | .... | .... | .... | .... | .... |
| 99-2000 | THK Tver | Russia-2 | 14 | 0 | 3 | 3 | 6 | .... | .... | .... | .... | .... |
| | Dynamo Moscow | Russia | 26 | 0 | 2 | 2 | 8 | 16 | 0 | 0 | 0 | 2 |
| 2000-01 | Dynamo Moscow | Russia | 34 | 1 | 5 | 6 | 12 | .... | .... | .... | .... | .... |
| 2001-02 | Cherepovets | Russia | 33 | 7 | 3 | 10 | 10 | 4 | 0 | 0 | 0 | 2 |
| 2002-03 | Cherepovets | Russia | 32 | 3 | 3 | 6 | 28 | 12 | 1 | 3 | 4 | 4 |
| 2003-04 | Dynamo Moscow | Russia | 56 | 4 | 8 | 12 | 16 | 3 | 0 | 1 | 1 | 2 |
| 2004-05 | Dynamo Moscow | Russia | 34 | 0 | 5 | 5 | 12 | .... | .... | .... | .... | .... |
| 2005-06 | Ak Bars Kazan | Russia | 49 | 3 | 9 | 12 | 20 | 13 | 1 | 1 | 2 | 6 |
| 2006-07 | Ak Bars Kazan | Russia | 49 | 5 | 10 | 15 | 32 | 16 | 1 | 1 | 2 | 41 |
| 2007-08 | Ufa | Russia | 45 | 5 | 11 | 16 | 18 | 16 | 0 | 2 | 2 | 8 |
| 2008-09 | Ufa | Rus-KHL | 29 | 5 | 9 | 14 | 10 | .... | .... | .... | .... | .... |

**SHAFIGULIN, Grigory** (sha-fih-GOO-lihn, grih-GOH-ree) **NSH.**

Center. Shoots left. 6'2", 185 lbs. Born, Chelyabinsk, USSR, January 13, 1985.
(Nashville's 8th choice, 98th overall, in 2003 Entry Draft).

| | | | Regular Season | | | | | Playoffs | | | | |
|---|---|---|---|---|---|---|---|---|---|---|---|---|
| Season | Club | League | GP | G | A | Pts | PIM | GP | G | A | Pts | PIM |
| 2000-01 | Chelyabinsk 2 | Russia-3 | 6 | 3 | 2 | 5 | 8 | .... | .... | .... | .... | .... |
| 2001-02 | Yaroslavl 2 | Russia-3 | 19 | 2 | 2 | 4 | 12 | .... | .... | .... | .... | .... |
| 2002-03 | Yaroslavl 2 | Russia-3 | 33 | 18 | 12 | 30 | 46 | 7 | 0 | 4 | 4 | 31 |
| | Yaroslavl | Russia | 11 | 0 | 1 | 1 | 4 | 8 | 0 | 0 | 0 | 4 |
| 2003-04 | Yaroslavl | Russia | 29 | 3 | 0 | 3 | 4 | 2 | 0 | 0 | 0 | 0 |
| | Yaroslavl 2 | Russia-3 | 11 | 3 | 8 | 11 | 22 | .... | .... | .... | .... | .... |
| 2004-05 | Yaroslavl 2 | Russia-3 | 1 | 0 | 2 | 2 | 0 | .... | .... | .... | .... | .... |
| | Yaroslavl | Russia | 46 | 5 | 6 | 11 | 49 | 9 | 0 | 0 | 0 | 10 |
| 2005-06 | Yaroslavl | Russia | 32 | 3 | 6 | 9 | 20 | 3 | 0 | 0 | 0 | 6 |
| | Yaroslavl 2 | Russia-3 | 7 | 1 | 3 | 4 | 18 | .... | .... | .... | .... | .... |
| 2006-07 | Yaroslavl | Russia | 54 | 5 | 16 | 21 | 46 | 7 | 3 | 0 | 3 | 14 |
| 2007-08 | Ak Bars Kazan | Russia | 39 | 5 | 5 | 10 | 112 | 8 | 1 | 0 | 1 | 4 |
| 2008-09 | Ak Bars Kazan | Rus-KHL | 28 | 4 | 5 | 9 | 18 | .... | .... | .... | .... | .... |
| | Vityaz Chekhov | Rus-KHL | 14 | 3 | 5 | 8 | 6 | .... | .... | .... | .... | .... |

**SHARP, MacGregor** (SHAHRP, muh-GREHG-uhr) **ANA.**

Center. Shoots right. 6'1", 195 lbs. Born, Vancouver, B.C., October 1, 1985.

| | | | Regular Season | | | | | Playoffs | | | | |
|---|---|---|---|---|---|---|---|---|---|---|---|---|
| Season | Club | League | GP | G | A | Pts | PIM | GP | G | A | Pts | PIM |
| 2002-03 | Camrose Kodiaks | AJHL | 60 | 23 | 25 | 48 | 96 | .... | .... | .... | .... | .... |
| 2003-04 | Camrose Kodiaks | AJHL | 44 | 20 | 26 | 46 | 45 | .... | .... | .... | .... | .... |
| 2004-05 | Camrose Kodiaks | AJHL | 57 | 19 | 30 | 49 | 32 | .... | .... | .... | .... | .... |
| 2005-06 | U. Minn-Duluth | WCHA | 40 | 6 | 8 | 14 | 31 | .... | .... | .... | .... | .... |
| 2006-07 | U. Minn-Duluth | WCHA | 38 | 11 | 16 | 27 | 35 | .... | .... | .... | .... | .... |
| 2007-08 | U. Minn-Duluth | WCHA | 36 | 7 | 10 | 17 | 14 | .... | .... | .... | .... | .... |
| 2008-09 | U. Minn-Duluth | WCHA | 43 | 26 | 24 | 50 | 20 | .... | .... | .... | .... | .... |
| | Iowa Chops | AHL | 6 | 1 | 1 | 2 | 4 | .... | .... | .... | .... | .... |

Signed as a free agent by **Anaheim**, April 1, 2009.

**SHARROW, Jim** (SHA-row, JIHM)

Defense. Shoots right. 6'2", 198 lbs. Born, Framingham, MA, January 31, 1985.
(Atlanta's 2nd choice, 110th overall, in 2003 Entry Draft).

| | | | Regular Season | | | | | Playoffs | | | | |
|---|---|---|---|---|---|---|---|---|---|---|---|---|
| Season | Club | League | GP | G | A | Pts | PIM | GP | G | A | Pts | PIM |
| 2001-02 | USNTDP | U-17 | 17 | 2 | 11 | 13 | 2 | .... | .... | .... | .... | .... |
| | USNTDP | NAHL | 44 | 3 | 5 | 8 | 28 | .... | .... | .... | .... | .... |
| 2002-03 | Halifax | QMJHL | 70 | 2 | 14 | 16 | 54 | 25 | 2 | 4 | 6 | 24 |
| 2003-04 | Halifax | QMJHL | 52 | 12 | 26 | 38 | 67 | .... | .... | .... | .... | .... |
| 2004-05 | Halifax | QMJHL | 69 | 16 | 31 | 47 | 76 | 13 | 5 | 6 | 11 | 6 |
| 2005-06 | Chicago Wolves | AHL | 47 | 2 | 17 | 19 | 17 | .... | .... | .... | .... | .... |
| | Gwinnett | ECHL | 23 | 3 | 7 | 10 | 12 | .... | .... | .... | .... | .... |
| 2006-07 | Chicago Wolves | AHL | 42 | 4 | 14 | 18 | 38 | .... | .... | .... | .... | .... |
| 2007-08 | Manitoba Moose | AHL | 44 | 5 | 17 | 22 | 26 | 2 | 0 | 1 | 1 | 0 |
| 2008-09 | Manitoba Moose | AHL | 17 | 1 | 5 | 6 | 4 | .... | .... | .... | .... | .... |
| | Rockford IceHogs | AHL | 50 | 3 | 5 | 8 | 40 | 4 | 0 | 1 | 1 | 0 |

QMJHL All-Rookie Team (2003)

Traded to **Vancouver** by **Atlanta** for Jesse Schultz, June 23, 2007. Traded to **Chicago** by **Vancouver** for future considerations, December 9, 2008.

**SHATTENKIRK, Kevin** (SHAH-tehn-kuhrk, KEH-vihn) **COL.**

Defense. Shoots right. 5'11", 193 lbs. Born, Greenwich, CT, January 29, 1989.
(Colorado's 1st choice, 14th overall, in 2007 Entry Draft).

| | | | Regular Season | | | | | Playoffs | | | | |
|---|---|---|---|---|---|---|---|---|---|---|---|---|
| Season | Club | League | GP | G | A | Pts | PIM | GP | G | A | Pts | PIM |
| 2004-05 | Brunswick Bruins | High-CT | 22 | 10 | 18 | 28 | .... | .... | .... | .... | .... | .... |
| 2005-06 | USNTDP | U-17 | 13 | 4 | 4 | 8 | 4 | .... | .... | .... | .... | .... |
| | USNTDP | NAHL | 28 | 6 | 9 | 15 | 17 | 12 | 3 | 7 | 10 | 10 |
| 2006-07 | USNTDP | U-18 | 43 | 8 | 19 | 27 | 36 | .... | .... | .... | .... | .... |
| | USNTDP | NAHL | 14 | 5 | 8 | 13 | 26 | .... | .... | .... | .... | .... |
| 2007-08 | Boston University | H-East | 40 | 4 | 17 | 21 | 38 | .... | .... | .... | .... | .... |
| 2008-09 | Boston University | H-East | 43 | 7 | 21 | 28 | 40 | .... | .... | .... | .... | .... |

Hockey East All-Rookie Team (2008) • Hockey East Second All-Star Team (2009) • NCAA East Second All-American Team (2009)

**SHATTOCK, Tyler** (SHA-tuhk, TIGH-luhr) **ST.L.**

Right wing. Shoots right. 6'3", 198 lbs. Born, Vernon, B.C., February 10, 1990.
(St. Louis' 4th choice, 108th overall, in 2009 Entry Draft).

| | | | Regular Season | | | | | Playoffs | | | | |
|---|---|---|---|---|---|---|---|---|---|---|---|---|
| Season | Club | League | GP | G | A | Pts | PIM | GP | G | A | Pts | PIM |
| 2005-06 | Thompson Blazers | Minor-BC | STATISTICS NOT AVAILABLE | | | | | | | | | |
| | Kamloops Blazers | WHL | 2 | 0 | 1 | 1 | 2 | .... | .... | .... | .... | .... |
| 2006-07 | Kamloops Blazers | WHL | 58 | 7 | 9 | 16 | 51 | 4 | 0 | 0 | 0 | 0 |
| 2007-08 | Kamloops Blazers | WHL | 48 | 9 | 14 | 23 | 45 | 4 | 1 | 1 | 2 | 4 |
| 2008-09 | Kamloops Blazers | WHL | 68 | 30 | 39 | 69 | 82 | 4 | 0 | 1 | 1 | 6 |

**SHEFER, Andrei** (SHEH-fuhr, AWN-dray) **L.A.**

Left wing. Shoots left. 6'1", 194 lbs. Born, Yekaterinburg, USSR, July 26, 1981.
(Los Angeles' 1st choice, 43rd overall, in 1999 Entry Draft).

| | | | Regular Season | | | | | Playoffs | | | | |
|---|---|---|---|---|---|---|---|---|---|---|---|---|
| Season | Club | League | GP | G | A | Pts | PIM | GP | G | A | Pts | PIM |
| 1997-98 | Yekaterinburg 2 | Russia-3 | 16 | 3 | 3 | 6 | 18 | .... | .... | .... | .... | .... |
| 1998-99 | Cherepovets 3 | Russia-4 | 6 | 2 | 2 | 4 | 18 | .... | .... | .... | .... | .... |
| | Cherepovets 2 | Russia-3 | 21 | 6 | 5 | 11 | 20 | .... | .... | .... | .... | .... |
| | Cherepovets | Russia | 8 | 1 | 0 | 1 | 4 | .... | .... | .... | .... | .... |
| 99-2000 | Halifax | QMJHL | 72 | 34 | 42 | 76 | 30 | 10 | 0 | 5 | 5 | 4 |
| 2000-01 | SKA St. Petersburg | Russia | 11 | 6 | 1 | 7 | 4 | .... | .... | .... | .... | .... |
| | Cherepovets | Russia | 20 | 1 | 1 | 2 | 10 | 6 | 1 | 0 | 1 | 0 |
| 2001-02 | Cherepovets 2 | Russia-3 | 3 | 1 | 2 | 3 | 2 | .... | .... | .... | .... | .... |
| | Cherepovets | Russia | 8 | 0 | 0 | 0 | 6 | .... | .... | .... | .... | .... |
| | SKA St. Petersburg | Russia | 28 | 4 | 4 | 8 | 10 | .... | .... | .... | .... | .... |
| 2002-03 | Cherepovets | Russia | 37 | 2 | 4 | 6 | 10 | 10 | 0 | 0 | 0 | 0 |
| | Cherepovets 2 | Russia-3 | 3 | 1 | 2 | 3 | 2 | .... | .... | .... | .... | .... |
| 2003-04 | Cherepovets | Russia | 55 | 4 | 6 | 10 | 46 | .... | .... | .... | .... | .... |
| 2004-05 | Cherepovets | Russia | 46 | 1 | 11 | 12 | 18 | .... | .... | .... | .... | .... |
| 2005-06 | Cherepovets | Russia | 45 | 2 | 1 | 3 | 32 | 4 | 0 | 1 | 1 | 0 |
| 2006-07 | CSKA Moscow | Russia | 45 | 7 | 7 | 14 | 48 | 2 | 0 | 0 | 0 | 2 |
| 2007-08 | CSKA Moscow | Russia | 53 | 3 | 14 | 17 | 34 | 6 | 1 | 1 | 2 | 0 |
| 2008-09 | Cherepovets | Rus-KHL | 37 | 3 | 5 | 8 | 16 | .... | .... | .... | .... | .... |

**SHELAST, Tyler** (SHEE-last, TIGH-luhr) **DAL.**

Wing. Shoots right. 6'1", 202 lbs. Born, Edmonton, Alta., December 26, 1984.

| | | | Regular Season | | | | | Playoffs | | | | |
|---|---|---|---|---|---|---|---|---|---|---|---|---|
| Season | Club | League | GP | G | A | Pts | PIM | GP | G | A | Pts | PIM |
| 2003-04 | Powell River Kings | BCHL | 58 | 25 | 42 | 67 | 131 | 7 | 1 | 3 | 4 | 6 |
| 2004-05 | Michigan Tech | WCHA | 37 | 11 | 8 | 19 | 42 | .... | .... | .... | .... | .... |
| 2005-06 | Michigan Tech | WCHA | 37 | 9 | 9 | 18 | 44 | .... | .... | .... | .... | .... |
| 2006-07 | Michigan Tech | WCHA | 38 | 15 | 9 | 24 | 18 | .... | .... | .... | .... | .... |
| 2007-08 | Michigan Tech | WCHA | 39 | 16 | 10 | 26 | 26 | .... | .... | .... | .... | .... |
| | Iowa Stars | AHL | 11 | 1 | 1 | 2 | 0 | .... | .... | .... | .... | .... |
| 2008-09 | Hamilton Bulldogs | AHL | 17 | 2 | 1 | 3 | 4 | .... | .... | .... | .... | .... |
| | Idaho Steelheads | ECHL | 31 | 9 | 12 | 21 | 23 | 4 | 0 | 0 | 0 | 4 |

Signed as a free agent by **Dallas**, March 19, 2008.

**SHIELDS, David** (SHEELDZ, DAY-vihd) **ST.L.**

Defense. Shoots right. 6'3", 218 lbs. Born, Buffalo, NY, January 27, 1991.
(St. Louis' 5th choice, 168th overall, in 2009 Entry Draft).

| | | | Regular Season | | | | | Playoffs | | | | |
|---|---|---|---|---|---|---|---|---|---|---|---|---|
| Season | Club | League | GP | G | A | Pts | PIM | GP | G | A | Pts | PIM |
| 2006-07 | Maksymum | Minor-NY | 37 | 4 | 16 | 20 | 60 | .... | .... | .... | .... | .... |
| 2007-08 | Erie Otters | OHL | 60 | 1 | 3 | 4 | 31 | .... | .... | .... | .... | .... |
| 2008-09 | Erie Otters | OHL | 61 | 1 | 16 | 17 | 28 | 5 | 0 | 0 | 0 | 5 |

**SHIROKOV, Sergei** (sheer-OH-kawv, SAIR-gay) **VAN.**

Wing. Shoots right. 5'10", 176 lbs. Born, Ozery, USSR, March 10, 1986.
(Vancouver's 3rd choice, 163rd overall, in 2006 Entry Draft).

| | | | Regular Season | | | | | Playoffs | | | | |
|---|---|---|---|---|---|---|---|---|---|---|---|---|
| Season | Club | League | GP | G | A | Pts | PIM | GP | G | A | Pts | PIM |
| 2001-02 | HK CSKA 2 | Russia-3 | 18 | 2 | 3 | 5 | 0 | .... | .... | .... | .... | .... |
| 2002-03 | CSKA Moscow 2 | Russia-3 | 2 | 0 | 0 | 0 | 0 | .... | .... | .... | .... | .... |
| 2003-04 | CSKA Moscow 2 | Russia-3 | 66 | 39 | 41 | 80 | 66 | .... | .... | .... | .... | .... |
| 2004-05 | CSKA Moscow 2 | Russia-3 | 25 | 16 | 13 | 29 | 47 | .... | .... | .... | .... | .... |
| | CSKA Moscow | Russia | 8 | 0 | 0 | 0 | 0 | .... | .... | .... | .... | .... |
| | CSKA Moscow | Russia | 8 | 0 | 0 | 0 | 0 | .... | .... | .... | .... | .... |
| 2005-06 | CSKA Moscow | Russia | 39 | 7 | 7 | 14 | 26 | 4 | 0 | 0 | 0 | 0 |
| 2006-07 | CSKA Moscow | Russia | 52 | 16 | 19 | 35 | 36 | 12 | 4 | 6 | 10 | 4 |
| 2007-08 | CSKA Moscow | Russia | 57 | 12 | 21 | 33 | 28 | 6 | 0 | 3 | 3 | 4 |
| 2008-09 | CSKA Moscow | Rus-KHL | 56 | 17 | 23 | 40 | 36 | 8 | 1 | 3 | 4 | 4 |

**SHORE, Drew** (SHOHR, DROO) **FLA.**

Center. Shoots right. 6'3", 190 lbs. Born, Denver, CO, January 29, 1991.
(Florida's 2nd choice, 44th overall, in 2009 Entry Draft).

| | | | Regular Season | | | | | Playoffs | | | | |
|---|---|---|---|---|---|---|---|---|---|---|---|---|
| Season | Club | League | GP | G | A | Pts | PIM | GP | G | A | Pts | PIM |
| 2006-07 | Det. Honeybaked | MWEHL | 31 | 9 | 25 | 34 | 20 | .... | .... | .... | .... | .... |
| | Det. Honeybaked | Exhib. | 34 | 17 | 23 | 40 | .... | .... | .... | .... | .... | .... |
| 2007-08 | USNTDP | NAHL | 35 | 9 | 16 | 25 | 12 | 3 | 0 | 1 | 1 | 0 |
| | USNTDP | U-17 | 16 | 4 | 8 | 12 | 6 | .... | .... | .... | .... | .... |
| 2008-09 | USNTDP | NAHL | 15 | 7 | 7 | 14 | 16 | .... | .... | .... | .... | .... |
| | USNTDP | U-18 | 47 | 10 | 25 | 35 | 30 | .... | .... | .... | .... | .... |

• Signed Letter of Intent to attend **University of Denver** (WCHA) in fall of 2009.

## SIDDALL, Matt (sih-DUHL, MAT) ATL.

Right wing. Shoots right. 6'1", 210 lbs. Born, North Vancouver, B.C., September 26, 1984.
(Atlanta's 9th choice, 270th overall, in 2004 Entry Draft).

| | | | Regular Season | | | | | Playoffs | | | | |
|---|---|---|---|---|---|---|---|---|---|---|---|---|
| Season | Club | League | GP | G | A | Pts | PIM | GP | G | A | Pts | PIM |
| 2003-04 | Powell River Kings | BCHL | 45 | 25 | 36 | 61 | 216 | 7 | 4 | 2 | 6 | 10 |
| 2004-05 | Northern Mich. | CCHA | 33 | 4 | 4 | 8 | 62 | .... | .... | .... | .... | .... |
| 2005-06 | Northern Mich. | CCHA | 36 | 6 | 6 | 12 | 72 | .... | .... | .... | .... | .... |
| 2006-07 | Northern Mich. | CCHA | 37 | 4 | 16 | 20 | 107 | .... | .... | .... | .... | .... |
| 2007-08 | Northern Mich. | CCHA | 41 | 18 | 18 | 36 | *116 | .... | .... | .... | .... | .... |
| 2008-09 | Chicago Wolves | AHL | 20 | 0 | 1 | 1 | 19 | .... | .... | .... | .... | .... |
| | Gwinnett | ECHL | 40 | 17 | 20 | 37 | 153 | 2 | 0 | 1 | 1 | 6 |

## SIDORENKO, Kirill (sih-dohr-EHN-koh, kih-RIHL) DAL.

Center. Shoots left. 6'3", 187 lbs. Born, Omsk, USSR, March 30, 1983.
(Dallas' 9th choice, 180th overall, in 2002 Entry Draft).

| | | | Regular Season | | | | | Playoffs | | | | |
|---|---|---|---|---|---|---|---|---|---|---|---|---|
| Season | Club | League | GP | G | A | Pts | PIM | GP | G | A | Pts | PIM |
| 1998-99 | Omsk 2 | Russia-4 | 2 | 0 | 0 | 0 | 2 | .... | .... | .... | .... | .... |
| 99-2000 | Omsk 2 | Russia-3 | 26 | 2 | 11 | 13 | 14 | .... | .... | .... | .... | .... |
| 2000-01 | Omsk 2 | Russia-3 | 30 | 8 | 7 | 15 | 44 | .... | .... | .... | .... | .... |
| 2001-02 | Mostovik Kurgan | Russia-2 | 50 | 11 | 6 | 17 | 64 | .... | .... | .... | .... | .... |
| 2002-03 | Sibir Novosibirsk | Russia | 30 | 1 | 1 | 2 | 2 | .... | .... | .... | .... | .... |
| 2003-04 | Energiya Kemerovo | Russia-2 | 14 | 1 | 1 | 2 | 6 | .... | .... | .... | .... | .... |
| | Zauralje Kurgan | Russia-2 | 32 | 3 | 3 | 6 | 6 | 4 | 0 | 0 | 0 | 27 |
| 2004-05 | Omsk 2 | Russia-3 | 18 | 7 | 4 | 11 | 12 | .... | .... | .... | .... | .... |
| | CSK VVS Samara | Russia-2 | 16 | 2 | 2 | 4 | 0 | .... | .... | .... | .... | .... |
| 2005-06 | CSK VVS Samara | Russia-2 | 47 | 8 | 11 | 19 | 62 | .... | .... | .... | .... | .... |
| | Krylja Sovetov | Russia-2 | 6 | 3 | 3 | 6 | 8 | 17 | 1 | 3 | 4 | 4 |
| 2006-07 | Krylja Sovetov 2 | Russia-3 | 4 | 2 | 1 | 3 | 6 | .... | .... | .... | .... | .... |
| | Krylja Sovetov | Russia | 35 | 5 | 4 | 9 | 22 | .... | .... | .... | .... | .... |
| 2007-08 | Titan Klin | Russia-2 | 53 | 6 | 12 | 18 | 43 | .... | .... | .... | .... | .... |
| 2008-09 | Kristall Saratov | Russia-2 | 56 | 17 | 9 | 26 | 54 | .... | .... | .... | .... | .... |

## SILFVERBERG, Jakob (SIHL-vuhr-buhrg, YA-kuhb) OTT.

Left wing. Shoots right. 6'2", 185 lbs. Born, Gavle, Sweden, October 13, 1990.
(Ottawa's 2nd choice, 39th overall, in 2009 Entry Draft).

| | | | Regular Season | | | | | Playoffs | | | | |
|---|---|---|---|---|---|---|---|---|---|---|---|---|
| Season | Club | League | GP | G | A | Pts | PIM | GP | G | A | Pts | PIM |
| 2005-06 | Brynas U18 | Swe-U18 | 8 | 0 | 0 | 0 | 0 | .... | .... | .... | .... | .... |
| 2006-07 | Brynas U18 | Swe-U18 | 14 | 3 | 8 | 11 | 6 | 3 | 0 | 0 | 0 | 0 |
| | Brynas IF Gavle Jr. | Swe-Jr. | 6 | 1 | 3 | 4 | 0 | .... | .... | .... | .... | .... |
| 2007-08 | Brynas U18 | Swe-U18 | 5 | 5 | 3 | 8 | 2 | 5 | 3 | 4 | 7 | 2 |
| | Brynas IF Gavle Jr. | Swe-Jr. | 30 | 8 | 12 | 20 | 8 | 7 | 3 | 0 | 3 | 2 |
| 2008-09 | Brynas IF Gavle Jr. | Swe-Jr. | 30 | 14 | 24 | 38 | 6 | .... | .... | .... | .... | .... |
| | Brynas IF Gavle | Sweden | 16 | 3 | 1 | 4 | 2 | 4 | 0 | 0 | 0 | 2 |

## SIMEK, Juraj (SEE-mehk, YUHR-ay) T.B.

Wing. Shoots left. 6'1", 192 lbs. Born, Presov, Czech., September 29, 1987.
(Vancouver's 4th choice, 167th overall, in 2006 Entry Draft).

| | | | Regular Season | | | | | Playoffs | | | | |
|---|---|---|---|---|---|---|---|---|---|---|---|---|
| Season | Club | League | GP | G | A | Pts | PIM | GP | G | A | Pts | PIM |
| 2002-03 | SC Bern Jr. | Swiss-Jr. | 2 | 1 | 0 | 1 | 0 | 2 | 0 | 0 | 0 | 0 |
| 2003-04 | Kloten Flyers Jr. | Swiss-Jr. | 36 | 8 | 6 | 14 | 28 | .... | .... | .... | .... | .... |
| 2004-05 | Kloten Flyers | Swiss | 18 | 0 | 0 | 0 | 0 | .... | .... | .... | .... | .... |
| | Kloten Flyers Jr. | Swiss-Jr. | 39 | 17 | 13 | 30 | 62 | 9 | 2 | 3 | 5 | 10 |
| | Kloten Flyers | Swiss | 18 | 0 | 0 | 0 | 2 | .... | .... | .... | .... | .... |
| 2005-06 | Kloten Flyers Jr. | Swiss-Jr. | 45 | 24 | 44 | 68 | 202 | .... | .... | .... | .... | .... |
| | Kloten Flyers | Swiss | 8 | 0 | 1 | 1 | 4 | .... | .... | .... | .... | .... |
| | EHC Biel-Bienne | Swiss-2 | 3 | 0 | 0 | 0 | 2 | .... | .... | .... | .... | .... |
| 2006-07 | Brandon | WHL | 58 | 28 | 29 | 57 | 41 | 9 | 1 | 5 | 6 | 6 |
| 2007-08 | Manitoba Moose | AHL | 66 | 7 | 10 | 17 | 30 | 1 | 1 | 0 | 1 | 0 |
| 2008-09 | Norfolk Admirals | AHL | 63 | 9 | 13 | 22 | 49 | .... | .... | .... | .... | .... |

Traded to **Tampa Bay** by **Vancouver** with Lukas Krajicek for Shane O'Brien and Michel Ouellet, October 6, 2008.

## SIMS, Shane (SIHMZ, SHAYN) NYI

Defense. Shoots right. 6', 192 lbs. Born, East Amherst, NY, April 30, 1988.
(NY Islanders' 8th choice, 126th overall, in 2006 Entry Draft).

| | | | Regular Season | | | | | Playoffs | | | | |
|---|---|---|---|---|---|---|---|---|---|---|---|---|
| Season | Club | League | GP | G | A | Pts | PIM | GP | G | A | Pts | PIM |
| 2004-05 | Buffalo Lightning | OPJHL | 48 | 14 | 26 | 40 | 47 | .... | .... | .... | .... | .... |
| 2005-06 | Des Moines | USHL | 59 | 10 | 12 | 22 | 80 | 11 | 2 | 0 | 2 | 12 |
| 2006-07 | Des Moines | USHL | 59 | 10 | 19 | 29 | 137 | 8 | 1 | 3 | 4 | 8 |
| 2007-08 | Ohio State | CCHA | 39 | 1 | 10 | 11 | 45 | .... | .... | .... | .... | .... |
| 2008-09 | Ohio State | CCHA | 42 | 7 | 17 | 24 | 42 | .... | .... | .... | .... | .... |

USHL All-Rookie Team (2006)

## SINDEL, Jakub (SHIHN-dehl, YA-kuhb) CHI.

Center. Shoots right. 6', 172 lbs. Born, Jihlava, Czech., January 24, 1986.
(Chicago's 5th choice, 54th overall, in 2004 Entry Draft).

| | | | Regular Season | | | | | Playoffs | | | | |
|---|---|---|---|---|---|---|---|---|---|---|---|---|
| Season | Club | League | GP | G | A | Pts | PIM | GP | G | A | Pts | PIM |
| 99-2000 | Slavia U17 | CzR-U17 | 32 | 10 | 6 | 16 | 6 | .... | .... | .... | .... | .... |
| 2000-01 | Slavia U17 | CzR-U17 | 26 | 12 | 15 | 27 | 2 | 6 | 1 | 0 | 1 | 0 |
| 2001-02 | Slavia U17 | CzR-U17 | 34 | 32 | 14 | 46 | 34 | 2 | 0 | 1 | 1 | 2 |
| | HC Slavia Praha Jr. | CzRep-Jr. | 14 | 7 | 4 | 11 | 10 | .... | .... | .... | .... | .... |
| 2002-03 | HC Slavia Praha Jr. | CzRep-Jr. | 35 | 12 | 11 | 23 | 39 | 2 | 0 | 1 | 1 | 0 |
| 2003-04 | HC Sparta Praha | CzRep | 34 | 5 | 1 | 6 | 14 | 13 | 1 | 1 | 2 | 2 |
| | Sparta Jr. | CzRep-Jr. | 13 | 8 | 14 | 22 | 4 | .... | .... | .... | .... | .... |
| | HC Dukla Jihlava | CzRep-2 | 1 | 0 | 0 | 0 | 0 | .... | .... | .... | .... | .... |
| 2004-05 | Sparta Jr. | CzRep-Jr. | 9 | 5 | 16 | 21 | 16 | .... | .... | .... | .... | .... |
| | HC Sparta Praha | CzRep | 10 | 0 | 2 | 2 | 0 | .... | .... | .... | .... | .... |
| | Trebic | CzRep-2 | 5 | 0 | 0 | 0 | 0 | .... | .... | .... | .... | .... |
| | Brandon | WHL | 35 | 16 | 13 | 29 | 12 | 24 | 7 | 4 | 11 | 22 |
| 2005-06 | HC Sparta Praha | CzRep | 12 | 1 | 1 | 2 | 6 | .... | .... | .... | .... | .... |
| | Plzen | CzRep | 31 | 11 | 8 | 19 | 18 | .... | .... | .... | .... | .... |
| 2006-07 | Plzen | CzRep | 50 | 16 | 10 | 26 | 30 | .... | .... | .... | .... | .... |
| | BK Mlada Boleslav | CzRep-2 | 4 | 1 | 0 | 1 | 4 | 8 | 5 | 5 | 10 | 20 |
| 2007-08 | Plzen | CzRep | 45 | 19 | 4 | 23 | 16 | 4 | 0 | 2 | 2 | 4 |
| | BK Mlada Boleslav | CzRep-2 | .... | .... | .... | .... | .... | 11 | 5 | 2 | 7 | 8 |
| 2008-09 | Plzen | CzRep | 22 | 4 | 4 | 8 | 12 | .... | .... | .... | .... | .... |
| | Pelicans Lahti | Finland | 23 | 7 | 8 | 15 | 12 | 8 | 2 | 2 | 4 | 8 |

## SIPOTZ, Brian (SIHP-awtz, BRIGH-uhn)

Defense. Shoots right. 6'7", 235 lbs. Born, South Bend, IN, September 16, 1981.
(Atlanta's 3rd choice, 100th overall, in 2001 Entry Draft).

| | | | Regular Season | | | | | Playoffs | | | | |
|---|---|---|---|---|---|---|---|---|---|---|---|---|
| Season | Club | League | GP | G | A | Pts | PIM | GP | G | A | Pts | PIM |
| 99-2000 | Culver Academy | High-IN | 45 | 14 | 22 | 36 | 56 | .... | .... | .... | .... | .... |
| 2000-01 | Miami U. | CCHA | 32 | 0 | 1 | 1 | 48 | .... | .... | .... | .... | .... |
| 2001-02 | Miami U. | CCHA | 25 | 0 | 1 | 1 | 28 | .... | .... | .... | .... | .... |
| 2002-03 | Miami U. | CCHA | 26 | 0 | 0 | 0 | 24 | .... | .... | .... | .... | .... |
| 2003-04 | Miami U. | CCHA | 36 | 0 | 3 | 3 | 39 | .... | .... | .... | .... | .... |
| 2004-05 | Chicago Wolves | AHL | 75 | 2 | 6 | 8 | 31 | 18 | 1 | 2 | 3 | 6 |
| | Gwinnett | ECHL | 2 | 0 | 0 | 0 | 0 | .... | .... | .... | .... | .... |
| 2005-06 | Chicago Wolves | AHL | 57 | 2 | 12 | 14 | 41 | .... | .... | .... | .... | .... |
| 2006-07 | Chicago Wolves | AHL | 73 | 2 | 10 | 12 | 36 | 8 | 0 | 0 | 0 | 2 |
| 2007-08 | Chicago Wolves | AHL | 54 | 1 | 4 | 5 | 22 | 21 | 0 | 4 | 4 | 14 |
| 2008-09 | Chicago Wolves | AHL | 66 | 2 | 5 | 7 | 36 | .... | .... | .... | .... | .... |

## SKACHKOV, Evgeny (skatch-KAWF, yehv-GEH-nee) ST.L.

Left wing. Shoots right. 6', 187 lbs. Born, Penza, USSR, July 14, 1984.
(St. Louis' 10th choice, 221st overall, in 2003 Entry Draft).

| | | | Regular Season | | | | | Playoffs | | | | |
|---|---|---|---|---|---|---|---|---|---|---|---|---|
| Season | Club | League | GP | G | A | Pts | PIM | GP | G | A | Pts | PIM |
| 2000-01 | Dizelist Penza | Russia-2 | 9 | 0 | 0 | 0 | 0 | .... | .... | .... | .... | .... |
| 2001-02 | Kapitan Stupino | Russia-3 | STATISTICS NOT AVAILABLE | | | | | | | | | |
| 2002-03 | Stupino | Russia-3 | STATISTICS NOT AVAILABLE | | | | | | | | | |
| | Kapitan Stupino | EEHL | 34 | 4 | 4 | 8 | 2 | .... | .... | .... | .... | .... |
| 2003-04 | CSKA Moscow | Russia | 1 | 0 | 0 | 0 | 2 | .... | .... | .... | .... | .... |
| | CSKA Moscow 2 | Russia-3 | DID NOT PLAY – INJURED | | | | | | | | | |
| 2004-05 | Spartak Moscow | Russia | 9 | 0 | 2 | 2 | 0 | .... | .... | .... | .... | .... |
| 2005-06 | Spartak Moscow 2 | Russia-3 | 55 | 25 | 31 | 56 | 98 | .... | .... | .... | .... | .... |
| | Spartak Moscow | Russia | 2 | 0 | 0 | 0 | 6 | .... | .... | .... | .... | .... |
| 2006-07 | Chelyabinsk | Russia | 52 | 13 | 9 | 22 | 52 | .... | .... | .... | .... | .... |
| 2007-08 | Chelyabinsk | Russia | 53 | 14 | 13 | 27 | 58 | 3 | 1 | 0 | 1 | 6 |
| 2008-09 | Chelyabinsk | Rus-KHL | 54 | 14 | 18 | 32 | 56 | .... | .... | .... | .... | .... |

## SKOKAN, David (SKOH-kahn, DAY-vihd) NYR

Center. Shoots left. 6', 191 lbs. Born, Poprad, Czech., December 6, 1988.
(NY Rangers' 5th choice, 193rd overall, in 2007 Entry Draft).

| | | | Regular Season | | | | | Playoffs | | | | |
|---|---|---|---|---|---|---|---|---|---|---|---|---|
| Season | Club | League | GP | G | A | Pts | PIM | GP | G | A | Pts | PIM |
| 2003-04 | Poprad U18 | Svk-U18 | 38 | 17 | 28 | 45 | 110 | 6 | 1 | 5 | 6 | 37 |
| | HK SKP Poprad Jr. | Slovak-Jr. | 7 | 2 | 0 | 2 | 7 | .... | .... | .... | .... | .... |
| 2004-05 | Poprad U18 | Svk-U18 | 4 | 4 | 6 | 10 | 37 | .... | .... | .... | .... | .... |
| | HK SKP Poprad Jr. | Slovak-Jr. | 24 | 5 | 19 | 24 | 52 | .... | .... | .... | .... | .... |
| | HK SKP Poprad | Slovakia | 8 | 0 | 0 | 0 | 6 | 2 | 0 | 0 | 0 | 25 |
| 2005-06 | Rimouski Oceanic | QMJHL | 53 | 6 | 15 | 21 | 143 | .... | .... | .... | .... | .... |
| 2006-07 | Rimouski Oceanic | QMJHL | 52 | 14 | 21 | 35 | 62 | .... | .... | .... | .... | .... |
| 2007-08 | Rimouski Oceanic | QMJHL | 53 | 19 | 21 | 40 | 92 | 8 | 0 | 5 | 5 | 10 |
| 2008-09 | HK Poprad | Slovakia | 33 | 9 | 9 | 18 | 115 | .... | .... | .... | .... | .... |
| | HK Poprad | Slovak-Q | 1 | 0 | 0 | 0 | 25 | .... | .... | .... | .... | .... |

## SLANEY, Robert (SLAY-nee, RAW-buhrt) TOR.

Left wing. Shoots left. 6'2", 203 lbs. Born, Upper Island Cove, Nfld., October 13, 1988.

| | | | Regular Season | | | | | Playoffs | | | | |
|---|---|---|---|---|---|---|---|---|---|---|---|---|
| Season | Club | League | GP | G | A | Pts | PIM | GP | G | A | Pts | PIM |
| 2005-06 | Cape Breton | QMJHL | 54 | 3 | 4 | 7 | 21 | 7 | 0 | 3 | 3 | 4 |
| 2006-07 | Cape Breton | QMJHL | 58 | 13 | 12 | 25 | 67 | 15 | 5 | 5 | 10 | 8 |
| 2007-08 | Cape Breton | QMJHL | 64 | 26 | 29 | 55 | 63 | 11 | 6 | 3 | 9 | 10 |
| 2008-09 | Cape Breton | QMJHL | 63 | 36 | 45 | 81 | 78 | 7 | 5 | 4 | 9 | 18 |

Canadian Major Junior Scholastic Player of the Year (2008)

Signed as a free agent by **Toronto**, April 14, 2009.

## SMITH, Austin (SMIHTH, AUZ-tihn) DAL.

Right wing. Shoots right. 5'11", 160 lbs. Born, Dallas, TX, November 7, 1988.
(Dallas' 4th choice, 128th overall, in 2007 Entry Draft).

| | | | Regular Season | | | | | Playoffs | | | | |
|---|---|---|---|---|---|---|---|---|---|---|---|---|
| Season | Club | League | GP | G | A | Pts | PIM | GP | G | A | Pts | PIM |
| 2003-04 | Dallas Jesuit Prep | High-TX | STATISTICS NOT AVAILABLE | | | | | | | | | |
| 2004-05 | Dallas Jesuit Prep | High-TX | STATISTICS NOT AVAILABLE | | | | | | | | | |
| | Alliance Bulldogs | NTHL | 53 | 29 | 46 | 75 | 24 | .... | .... | .... | .... | .... |
| 2005-06 | The Gunnery | High-CT | 31 | 23 | 20 | 43 | 22 | .... | .... | .... | .... | .... |
| 2006-07 | The Gunnery | High-CT | 30 | 25 | 38 | 63 | 36 | .... | .... | .... | .... | .... |
| 2007-08 | Penticton Vees | BCHL | 60 | 32 | 35 | 67 | 42 | 15 | 11 | 11 | 22 | 12 |
| 2008-09 | Colgate | ECAC | 37 | 17 | 14 | 31 | 24 | .... | .... | .... | .... | .... |

## SMITH, Barron (SMIHTH, BAIR-uhn) TOR.

Defense. Shoots right. 6'4", 191 lbs. Born, Hinsdale, IL, April 2, 1991.
(Toronto's 7th choice, 188th overall, in 2009 Entry Draft).

| | | | Regular Season | | | | | Playoffs | | | | |
|---|---|---|---|---|---|---|---|---|---|---|---|---|
| Season | Club | League | GP | G | A | Pts | PIM | GP | G | A | Pts | PIM |
| 2006-07 | Chicago Mission | MWEHL | 30 | 1 | 5 | 6 | 58 | .... | .... | .... | .... | .... |
| 2007-08 | Chicago Steel | USHL | 41 | 1 | 4 | 5 | 65 | 7 | 0 | 0 | 0 | 20 |
| 2008-09 | London Knights | OHL | 14 | 0 | 0 | 0 | 21 | .... | .... | .... | .... | .... |
| | Peterborough | OHL | 20 | 0 | 2 | 2 | 36 | .... | .... | .... | .... | .... |

## SMITH, Ben (SMIHTH, BEHN) CHI.

Right wing. Shoots right. 5'11", 195 lbs. Born, Winston-Salem, NC, July 11, 1988.
(Chicago's 5th choice, 169th overall, in 2008 Entry Draft).

| | | | Regular Season | | | | | Playoffs | | | | |
|---|---|---|---|---|---|---|---|---|---|---|---|---|
| Season | Club | League | GP | G | A | Pts | PIM | GP | G | A | Pts | PIM |
| 2006-07 | Boston College | H-East | 42 | 10 | 8 | 18 | 10 | .... | .... | .... | .... | .... |
| 2007-08 | Boston College | H-East | 44 | 25 | 25 | 50 | 12 | .... | .... | .... | .... | .... |
| 2008-09 | Boston College | H-East | 37 | 6 | 11 | 17 | 6 | .... | .... | .... | .... | .... |

NCAA Championship All-Tournament Team (2008)

## SMITH, Brendan (SMIHTH, BREHN-duhn) DET.

Defense. Shoots left. 6'1", 170 lbs. Born, Toronto, Ont., February 8, 1989.
(Detroit's 1st choice, 27th overall, in 2007 Entry Draft).

| | | | Regular Season | | | | | Playoffs | | | | |
|---|---|---|---|---|---|---|---|---|---|---|---|---|
| Season | Club | League | GP | G | A | Pts | PIM | GP | G | A | Pts | PIM |
| 2004-05 | Toronto Marlboros | GTHL | 66 | 22 | 63 | 85 | 120 | .... | .... | .... | .... | .... |
| 2005-06 | St. Michael's | OPJHL | 39 | 5 | 21 | 26 | 55 | 17 | 1 | 5 | 6 | 44 |
| 2006-07 | St. Michael's | OPJHL | 39 | 12 | 24 | 36 | 90 | 16 | 6 | 14 | 20 | 30 |
| 2007-08 | U. of Wisconsin | WCHA | 22 | 2 | 10 | 12 | 26 | .... | .... | .... | .... | .... |
| 2008-09 | U. of Wisconsin | WCHA | 31 | 9 | 14 | 23 | 75 | .... | .... | .... | .... | .... |

## SMITH, Craig (SMIHTH, KRAYG) NSH.

Center. Shoots right. 6'1", 189 lbs. Born, Madison, WI, September 5, 1989.
(Nashville's 6th choice, 98th overall, in 2009 Entry Draft).

| | | | Regular Season | | | | | Playoffs | | | | |
|---|---|---|---|---|---|---|---|---|---|---|---|---|
| Season | Club | League | GP | G | A | Pts | PIM | GP | G | A | Pts | PIM |
| 2004-05 | Madison Lancers | High-WI | 20 | 16 | 24 | 40 | .... | .... | .... | .... | .... | .... |
| 2005-06 | Madison Lancers | High-WI | 20 | 35 | 26 | 61 | .... | .... | .... | .... | .... | .... |
| 2006-07 | Waterloo | USHL | 45 | 8 | 10 | 18 | 28 | 4 | 0 | 1 | 1 | 8 |
| 2007-08 | Waterloo | USHL | 58 | 13 | 10 | 23 | 90 | 11 | 2 | 3 | 5 | 8 |
| 2008-09 | Waterloo | USHL | 54 | 28 | 48 | 76 | 108 | 3 | 1 | 3 | 4 | 26 |

• Signed Letter of Intent to attend **University of Wisconsin** (WCHA) in fall of 2009. • USHL First All-Star Team (2009)

## SMITH, Derek (SMIHTH, dair-IHK) OTT.

Defense. Shoots left. 6'1", 200 lbs. Born, Belleville, Ont., October 13, 1984.

| | | | Regular Season | | | | | Playoffs | | | | |
|---|---|---|---|---|---|---|---|---|---|---|---|---|
| Season | Club | League | GP | G | A | Pts | PIM | GP | G | A | Pts | PIM |
| 2002-03 | Wellington Dukes | OPJHL | 21 | 6 | 10 | 16 | 26 | .... | .... | .... | .... | .... |
| 2003-04 | Wellington Dukes | OPJHL | 44 | 8 | 26 | 34 | 34 | .... | .... | .... | .... | .... |
| 2004-05 | Lake Superior | CCHA | 38 | 1 | 4 | 5 | 28 | .... | .... | .... | .... | .... |
| 2005-06 | Lake Superior | CCHA | 36 | 2 | 8 | 10 | 18 | .... | .... | .... | .... | .... |
| 2006-07 | Lake Superior | CCHA | 43 | 10 | 20 | 30 | 10 | .... | .... | .... | .... | .... |
| 2007-08 | Binghamton | AHL | 52 | 2 | 11 | 13 | 18 | .... | .... | .... | .... | .... |
| | Elmira Jackals | ECHL | 1 | 0 | 1 | 1 | 0 | .... | .... | .... | .... | .... |
| 2008-09 | Binghamton | AHL | 75 | 7 | 17 | 24 | 49 | .... | .... | .... | .... | .... |

Signed as a free agent by **Ottawa**, April 12, 2007.

## SMITH, Reilly (SMIHTH, RIGH-lee) DAL.

Right wing. Shoots left. 6', 157 lbs. Born, Toronto, Ont., April 1, 1991.
(Dallas' 3rd choice, 69th overall, in 2009 Entry Draft).

| | | | Regular Season | | | | | Playoffs | | | | |
|---|---|---|---|---|---|---|---|---|---|---|---|---|
| Season | Club | League | GP | G | A | Pts | PIM | GP | G | A | Pts | PIM |
| 2007-08 | Tor. Young Nats | GTHL | 70 | 80 | 77 | 157 | 56 | .... | .... | .... | .... | .... |
| | St. Michael's | OPJHL | 13 | 2 | 7 | 9 | 22 | 1 | 0 | 0 | 0 | 2 |
| 2008-09 | St. Michael's | OJHL | 49 | 27 | 48 | 75 | 44 | 6 | 9 | 6 | 15 | 10 |

• Signed Letter of Intent to attend **Miami University** (CCHA) in fall of 2010.

## SMOLYANINOV, Vitali (smoh-LEE-ya-NEE-nohv, vih-TAL-ee) T.B.

Left wing. Shoots left. 6'3", 205 lbs. Born, Nizhnekamsk, USSR, August 5, 1983.
(Tampa Bay's 12th choice, 261st overall, in 2001 Entry Draft).

| | | | Regular Season | | | | | Playoffs | | | | |
|---|---|---|---|---|---|---|---|---|---|---|---|---|
| Season | Club | League | GP | G | A | Pts | PIM | GP | G | A | Pts | PIM |
| 1998-99 | Nizhnekamsk 2 | Russia-4 | 12 | 1 | 0 | 1 | 0 | .... | .... | .... | .... | .... |
| 99-2000 | Nizhnekamsk 2 | Russia-3 | 54 | 7 | 7 | 14 | 28 | .... | .... | .... | .... | .... |
| 2000-01 | Nizhnekamsk 2 | Russia-3 | STATISTICS NOT AVAILABLE | | | | | | | | | |
| 2001-02 | Nizhnekamsk | Russia | 1 | 0 | 0 | 0 | 0 | .... | .... | .... | .... | .... |
| 2002-03 | HK Voronezh | Russia-2 | 14 | 1 | 1 | 2 | 12 | .... | .... | .... | .... | .... |
| 2003-04 | Karaganda | Kazakh. | 9 | 2 | 3 | 5 | 0 | .... | .... | .... | .... | .... |
| | Karaganda | Russia-2 | 19 | 0 | 1 | 1 | 32 | .... | .... | .... | .... | .... |
| 2004-05 | Karaganda | Kazakh. | 7 | 5 | 3 | 8 | 2 | .... | .... | .... | .... | .... |
| | Karaganda | Russia-2 | 20 | 1 | 5 | 6 | 10 | .... | .... | .... | .... | .... |
| 2005-06 | Irtysh Pavlodar | Kazakh. | 14 | 8 | 6 | 14 | 12 | .... | .... | .... | .... | .... |
| | Irtysh Pavlodar | Russia-3 | STATISTICS NOT AVAILABLE | | | | | | | | | |
| 2006-07 | Barys Astana | Russia-3 | 42 | 8 | 19 | 27 | 36 | .... | .... | .... | .... | .... |
| | Barys Astana | Kazakh. | 22 | 10 | 6 | 16 | 52 | .... | .... | .... | .... | .... |
| 2007-08 | Barys Astana | Russia-2 | 51 | 18 | 21 | 39 | 54 | 7 | 1 | 1 | 2 | 2 |
| 2008-09 | Barys Astana | Rus-KHL | 14 | 1 | 2 | 3 | 10 | .... | .... | .... | .... | .... |
| | Khanty-Mansiisk | Russia-2 | 2 | 0 | 1 | 1 | 2 | .... | .... | .... | .... | .... |
| | Gazovik Tyumen | Russia-2 | 20 | 7 | 7 | 14 | 12 | 8 | 3 | 0 | 3 | 6 |

## SNEEP, Carl (SNEEP, KAHRL) PIT.

Defense. Shoots right. 6'4", 210 lbs. Born, St. Louis Park, MN, November 5, 1987.
(Pittsburgh's 2nd choice, 32nd overall, in 2006 Entry Draft).

| | | | Regular Season | | | | | Playoffs | | | | |
|---|---|---|---|---|---|---|---|---|---|---|---|---|
| Season | Club | League | GP | G | A | Pts | PIM | GP | G | A | Pts | PIM |
| 2004-05 | Brainerd | High-MN | 26 | 20 | 21 | 41 | 25 | .... | .... | .... | .... | .... |
| 2005-06 | Brainerd | High-MN | 26 | 14 | 23 | 37 | 34 | .... | .... | .... | .... | .... |
| | Lincoln Stars | USHL | 13 | 1 | 3 | 4 | 9 | 9 | 0 | 1 | 1 | 6 |
| 2006-07 | Boston College | H-East | 38 | 1 | 9 | 10 | 8 | .... | .... | .... | .... | .... |
| 2007-08 | Boston College | H-East | 44 | 3 | 12 | 15 | 15 | .... | .... | .... | .... | .... |
| 2008-09 | Boston College | H-East | 33 | 2 | 9 | 11 | 26 | .... | .... | .... | .... | .... |

## SNELLMAN , Niko (SNEHL-mahn, NEE-KOH) NSH.

Left wing. Shoots left. 6'3", 208 lbs. Born, Tampere, Finland, March 12, 1988.
(Nashville's 2nd choice, 105th overall, in 2006 Entry Draft).

| | | | Regular Season | | | | | Playoffs | | | | |
|---|---|---|---|---|---|---|---|---|---|---|---|---|
| Season | Club | League | GP | G | A | Pts | PIM | GP | G | A | Pts | PIM |
| 2004-05 | Ilves Tampere U18 | Fin-U18 | 22 | 5 | 1 | 6 | 44 | 5 | 0 | 0 | 0 | 2 |
| 2005-06 | Ilves Tampere U18 | Fin-U18 | 6 | 3 | 8 | 11 | 28 | 6 | 2 | 5 | 7 | 64 |
| | Ilves Tampere Jr. | Fin-Jr. | 23 | 4 | 4 | 8 | 74 | 3 | 0 | 0 | 0 | 4 |
| 2006-07 | Regina Pats | WHL | 32 | 5 | 5 | 10 | 65 | .... | .... | .... | .... | .... |
| 2007-08 | Ilves Tampere Jr. | Fin-Jr. | 31 | 5 | 11 | 16 | 137 | 1 | 0 | 0 | 0 | 0 |
| | Ilves Tampere | Finland | .... | .... | .... | .... | .... | 1 | 0 | 1 | 1 | 0 |
| 2008-09 | Ilves Jr. | Finland-Jr. | 5 | 0 | 0 | 0 | 8 | .... | .... | .... | .... | .... |
| | LeKi Lempaala | Finland-2 | 11 | 1 | 0 | 1 | 27 | 2 | 0 | 0 | 0 | 4 |

## SNETSINGER, Brad (SNEHT-sihng-uhr, BRAD) N.J.

Left wing. Shoots left. 6'2", 190 lbs. Born, Ajax, Ont., April 8, 1987.

| | | | Regular Season | | | | | Playoffs | | | | |
|---|---|---|---|---|---|---|---|---|---|---|---|---|
| Season | Club | League | GP | G | A | Pts | PIM | GP | G | A | Pts | PIM |
| 2003-04 | Milton IceHawks | OPJHL | 40 | 10 | 9 | 19 | 30 | .... | .... | .... | .... | .... |
| | Mississauga | OHL | 8 | 2 | 1 | 3 | 2 | 1 | 0 | 0 | 0 | 0 |
| 2004-05 | Mississauga | OHL | 54 | 8 | 5 | 13 | 30 | 5 | 0 | 0 | 0 | 0 |
| 2005-06 | Windsor Spitfires | OHL | 60 | 29 | 15 | 44 | 29 | 7 | 2 | 3 | 5 | 8 |
| 2006-07 | Windsor Spitfires | OHL | 63 | 29 | 33 | 62 | 86 | .... | .... | .... | .... | .... |
| 2007-08 | Windsor Spitfires | OHL | 68 | 37 | 52 | 89 | 45 | 2 | 0 | 0 | 0 | 5 |
| 2008-09 | Lowell Devils | AHL | 8 | 1 | 0 | 1 | 6 | .... | .... | .... | .... | .... |
| | Trenton Devils | ECHL | 49 | 21 | 28 | 49 | 22 | 7 | 0 | 2 | 2 | 10 |

Signed as a free agent by **New Jersey**, December 20, 2007.

## SODERBERG, Carl (SOH-dehr-buhrg, KAHRL) BOS.

Center. Shoots left. 6'3", 198 lbs. Born, Malmo, Sweden, October 12, 1985.
(St. Louis' 2nd choice, 49th overall, in 2004 Entry Draft).

| | | | Regular Season | | | | | Playoffs | | | | |
|---|---|---|---|---|---|---|---|---|---|---|---|---|
| Season | Club | League | GP | G | A | Pts | PIM | GP | G | A | Pts | PIM |
| 2000-01 | Skane | Exhib. | 8 | 1 | 2 | 3 | 2 | .... | .... | .... | .... | .... |
| | Malmo U18 | Swe-U18 | 3 | 1 | 1 | 2 | 0 | .... | .... | .... | .... | .... |
| 2001-02 | Malmo U18 | Swe-U18 | 13 | 9 | 20 | 29 | 18 | .... | .... | .... | .... | .... |
| | Malmo Jr. | Swe-Jr. | 4 | 0 | 2 | 2 | 2 | 7 | 0 | 2 | 2 | 4 |
| 2002-03 | Malmo U18 | Swe-U18 | 4 | 6 | 3 | 9 | 25 | .... | .... | .... | .... | .... |
| | Malmo Jr. | Swe-Jr. | 28 | 17 | 18 | 35 | 22 | 6 | 2 | 4 | 6 | 8 |
| 2003-04 | Malmo | Sweden | 24 | 1 | 1 | 2 | 8 | .... | .... | .... | .... | .... |
| | Malmo U18 | Swe-U18 | 27 | 23 | 25 | 48 | 30 | 6 | 1 | 2 | 3 | 10 |
| | Malmo | Sweden-Q | 8 | 1 | 1 | 2 | 4 | .... | .... | .... | .... | .... |
| 2004-05 | Morrums GoIS IK | Sweden-2 | 14 | 5 | 6 | 11 | 8 | .... | .... | .... | .... | .... |
| | Malmo Jr. | Swe-Jr. | 12 | 13 | 6 | 19 | 43 | 3 | 2 | 1 | 3 | 12 |
| | Malmo | Sweden | 38 | 0 | 5 | 5 | 8 | .... | .... | .... | .... | .... |
| | Malmo | Sweden-Q | 7 | 0 | 0 | 0 | 0 | .... | .... | .... | .... | .... |
| 2005-06 | Malmo | Sweden-2 | 49 | 20 | 27 | 47 | 47 | .... | .... | .... | .... | .... |
| 2006-07 | Malmo | Sweden | 31 | 12 | 18 | 30 | 14 | .... | .... | .... | .... | .... |
| 2007-08 | Malmo | Sweden-2 | 42 | 22 | 36 | 58 | 18 | .... | .... | .... | .... | .... |
| 2008-09 | Malmo | Sweden-2 | 45 | 18 | 41 | 59 | 26 | .... | .... | .... | .... | .... |

Traded to **Boston** by **St. Louis** for Hannu Toivonen, July 23, 2007.

## SOIN, Sergei (SOY-ihn, SAIR-gay) NSH.

Center/Left wing. Shoots left. 6', 185 lbs. Born, Moscow, USSR, March 31, 1982.
(Colorado's 3rd choice, 50th overall, in 2000 Entry Draft).

| | | | Regular Season | | | | | Playoffs | | | | |
|---|---|---|---|---|---|---|---|---|---|---|---|---|
| Season | Club | League | GP | G | A | Pts | PIM | GP | G | A | Pts | PIM |
| 1997-98 | Krylja Sovetov 2 | Russia-3 | 2 | 0 | 0 | 0 | 0 | .... | .... | .... | .... | .... |
| 1998-99 | Krylja Sovetov | Russia | 34 | 1 | 4 | 5 | 12 | .... | .... | .... | .... | .... |
| 99-2000 | Krylja Sovetov 2 | Russia-3 | 8 | 2 | 3 | 5 | 12 | .... | .... | .... | .... | .... |
| | Krylja Sovetov | Russia-2 | 32 | 8 | 8 | 16 | 28 | 14 | 0 | 2 | 2 | 6 |
| 2000-01 | Krylja Sovetov 2 | Russia-3 | 8 | 2 | 3 | 5 | 12 | .... | .... | .... | .... | .... |
| | Krylja Sovetov | Russia-2 | 19 | 6 | 3 | 9 | 8 | 11 | 2 | 2 | 4 | 2 |
| 2001-02 | Krylja Sovetov 2 | Russia-3 | 5 | 2 | 6 | 8 | 20 | .... | .... | .... | .... | .... |
| | Krylja Sovetov | Russia | 41 | 5 | 7 | 12 | 8 | .... | .... | .... | .... | .... |
| 2002-03 | Krylja Sovetov | Russia | 49 | 8 | 6 | 14 | 40 | .... | .... | .... | .... | .... |
| 2003-04 | CSKA Moscow | Russia | 49 | 1 | 6 | 7 | 32 | .... | .... | .... | .... | .... |
| 2004-05 | CSKA Moscow | Russia | 19 | 3 | 3 | 6 | 10 | .... | .... | .... | .... | .... |
| 2005-06 | Cherepovets | Russia | 48 | 5 | 12 | 17 | 36 | 4 | 1 | 1 | 2 | 0 |
| 2006-07 | Cherepovets | Russia | 52 | 12 | 12 | 24 | 78 | 5 | 2 | 1 | 3 | 0 |
| 2007-08 | Cherepovets | Russia | 52 | 9 | 11 | 20 | 22 | 7 | 1 | 1 | 2 | 4 |
| 2008-09 | Cherepovets | Rus-KHL | 51 | 7 | 19 | 26 | 38 | .... | .... | .... | .... | .... |

Traded to **Nashville** by **Colorado** for Tomas Slovak, June 21, 2003.

## SOINTU, Matias (SOYN-too, mat-TEE-uhs) T.B.

Right wing. Shoots left. 5'10", 154 lbs. Born, Tampere, Finland, February 10, 1990.
(Tampa Bay's 7th choice, 182nd overall, in 2008 Entry Draft).

| | | | Regular Season | | | | | Playoffs | | | | |
|---|---|---|---|---|---|---|---|---|---|---|---|---|
| Season | Club | League | GP | G | A | Pts | PIM | GP | G | A | Pts | PIM |
| 2006-07 | Ilves Tampere U18 | Fin-U18 | 34 | 22 | 23 | 45 | 32 | 3 | 0 | 0 | 0 | 0 |
| 2007-08 | Ilves Tampere U18 | Fin-U18 | 10 | 8 | 6 | 14 | 6 | .... | .... | .... | .... | .... |
| | Ilves Tampere Jr. | Fin-Jr. | 41 | 21 | 19 | 40 | 38 | 5 | 3 | 1 | 4 | 4 |
| 2008-09 | Suomi U20 | Finland-2 | 3 | 1 | 1 | 2 | 2 | .... | .... | .... | .... | .... |
| | Ilves Tampere Jr. | Fin-Jr. | 7 | 1 | 1 | 2 | 6 | .... | .... | .... | .... | .... |

## SOL, Cody (SAWL, KOH-dee) ATL.

Defense. Shoots left. 6'4", 215 lbs. Born, Woodstock, Ont., February 11, 1991.
(Atlanta's 6th choice, 125th overall, in 2009 Entry Draft).

| | | | Regular Season | | | | | Playoffs | | | | |
|---|---|---|---|---|---|---|---|---|---|---|---|---|
| Season | Club | League | GP | G | A | Pts | PIM | GP | G | A | Pts | PIM |
| 2007-08 | St. Mary's Lincolns | OJHL-B | 20 | 2 | 2 | 4 | 30 | .... | .... | .... | .... | .... |
| | Saginaw Spirit | OHL | 12 | 0 | 0 | 0 | 4 | 1 | 0 | 0 | 0 | 0 |
| 2008-09 | Saginaw Spirit | OHL | 66 | 1 | 6 | 7 | 128 | 8 | 0 | 2 | 2 | 14 |

## SOLAREV, Ilja (SOH-luh-rehv, IHL-yuh) T.B.

Left wing. Shoots left. 6'3", 176 lbs. Born, Perm, USSR, August 2, 1982.
(Tampa Bay's 13th choice, 281st overall, in 2001 Entry Draft).

| | | | Regular Season | | | | | Playoffs | | | | |
|---|---|---|---|---|---|---|---|---|---|---|---|---|
| Season | Club | League | GP | G | A | Pts | PIM | GP | G | A | Pts | PIM |
| 1997-98 | Perm 2 | Russia-3 | 4 | 1 | 0 | 1 | 0 | .... | .... | .... | .... | .... |
| 1998-99 | Perm 2 | Russia-4 | 20 | 2 | 6 | 8 | 10 | .... | .... | .... | .... | .... |
| 99-2000 | Perm 2 | Russia-3 | 35 | 3 | 2 | 5 | 24 | .... | .... | .... | .... | .... |
| 2000-01 | Perm 2 | Russia-3 | STATISTICS NOT AVAILABLE | | | | | | | | | |
| | Perm | Russia | 5 | 0 | 1 | 1 | 0 | .... | .... | .... | .... | .... |
| 2001-02 | Leninogorsk | Russia-2 | 31 | 3 | 5 | 8 | 20 | .... | .... | .... | .... | .... |
| | HK Tambov | Russia-3 | 2 | 0 | 0 | 0 | 0 | .... | .... | .... | .... | .... |
| 2002-03 | Perm 2 | Russia-3 | STATISTICS NOT AVAILABLE | | | | | | | | | |
| | HK Brest | Belarus | STATISTICS NOT AVAILABLE | | | | | | | | | |
| 2003-04 | Motor Barnaul | Russia-2 | 34 | 6 | 6 | 12 | 20 | 1 | 0 | 0 | 0 | 0 |
| 2004-05 | Energiya Kemerovo | Russia-2 | 36 | 3 | 2 | 5 | 28 | .... | .... | .... | .... | .... |
| 2005-06 | HK Lipetsk | Russia-2 | 49 | 4 | 6 | 10 | 30 | 3 | 0 | 0 | 0 | 0 |
| 2006-07 | Satpayev | Russia-2 | 44 | 17 | 16 | 33 | 24 | .... | .... | .... | .... | .... |
| | Satpayev | Kazakh. | 21 | 7 | 2 | 9 | 12 | .... | .... | .... | .... | .... |
| 2007-08 | Satpayev | Russia-2 | 29 | 10 | 10 | 20 | 24 | .... | .... | .... | .... | .... |
| | Barys Astana | Russia-2 | 22 | 4 | 9 | 13 | 26 | 7 | 2 | 1 | 3 | 6 |
| 2008-09 | Barys Astana | Rus-KHL | 46 | 8 | 7 | 15 | 24 | .... | .... | .... | .... | .... |

## SONNE, Brett (SOHNE, BREHT) ST.L.

Center/Left wing. Shoots left. 5'11", 184 lbs. Born, Chilliwack, B.C., March 16, 1989.
(St. Louis' 6th choice, 85th overall, in 2007 Entry Draft).

| | | | Regular Season | | | | | Playoffs | | | | |
|---|---|---|---|---|---|---|---|---|---|---|---|---|
| Season | Club | League | GP | G | A | Pts | PIM | GP | G | A | Pts | PIM |
| 2004-05 | Port Coquitlam | PIJHL | 47 | 21 | 34 | 55 | 125 | .... | .... | .... | .... | .... |
| | Calgary Hitmen | WHL | 6 | 0 | 0 | 0 | 2 | .... | .... | .... | .... | .... |
| 2005-06 | Calgary Hitmen | WHL | 64 | 12 | 9 | 21 | 38 | 13 | 1 | 2 | 3 | 8 |
| 2006-07 | Calgary Hitmen | WHL | 71 | 21 | 9 | 30 | 65 | 18 | 5 | 1 | 6 | 22 |
| 2007-08 | Calgary Hitmen | WHL | 29 | 8 | 12 | 20 | 12 | 16 | 3 | 1 | 4 | 14 |
| 2008-09 | Calgary Hitmen | WHL | 62 | 48 | 52 | 100 | 58 | 14 | 7 | 9 | 16 | 18 |

WHL East First All-Star Team (2009) • WHL Player of the Year (2009) • Canadian Major Junior Second All-Star Team (2009)

## SOPANEN, Vili (SOH-puh-nehn, VIHL-ee) N.J.

Right wing. Shoots right. 6'4", 205 lbs. Born, Valkeala, Finland, October 21, 1987.
(New Jersey's 5th choice, 177th overall, in 2007 Entry Draft).

| | | | Regular Season | | | | | Playoffs | | | | |
|---|---|---|---|---|---|---|---|---|---|---|---|---|
| Season | Club | League | GP | G | A | Pts | PIM | GP | G | A | Pts | PIM |
| 2003-04 | K-Reipas U18 | Fin-U18 | 20 | 1 | 2 | 3 | 14 | .... | .... | .... | .... | .... |
| 2004-05 | K-Reipas U18 | Fin-U18 | 25 | 11 | 15 | 26 | 4 | 3 | 0 | 2 | 2 | 22 |
| 2005-06 | Pelicans Lahti Jr. | Fin-Jr. | 38 | 15 | 17 | 32 | 22 | .... | .... | .... | .... | .... |
| | Pelicans Lahti | Finland | 3 | 0 | 0 | 0 | 0 | .... | .... | .... | .... | .... |
| 2006-07 | Pelicans Lahti Jr. | Fin-Jr. | 33 | 18 | 21 | 39 | 40 | 15 | 5 | 13 | 18 | 18 |
| | Suomi U20 | Finland-2 | 6 | 1 | 1 | 2 | 4 | .... | .... | .... | .... | .... |
| | Pelicans Lahti | Finland | 7 | 1 | 0 | 1 | 0 | .... | .... | .... | .... | .... |
| 2007-08 | Pelicans Lahti Jr. | Fin-Jr. | 2 | 1 | 1 | 2 | 0 | .... | .... | .... | .... | .... |
| | Pelicans Lahti | Finland | 54 | 15 | 15 | 30 | 8 | 6 | 0 | 4 | 4 | 2 |
| 2008-09 | Pelicans Lahti | Finland | 58 | 11 | 17 | 28 | 30 | 10 | 1 | 1 | 2 | 6 |

## SORYAL, Justin (SOHR-yahl, JUHS-tihn)

Left wing. Shoots left. 6'2", 210 lbs. Born, Newmarket, Ont., June 29, 2007.

| | | | Regular Season | | | | | Playoffs | | | | |
|---|---|---|---|---|---|---|---|---|---|---|---|---|
| Season | Club | League | GP | G | A | Pts | PIM | GP | G | A | Pts | PIM |
| 2003-04 | Aurora Tigers | OPJHL | 3 | 0 | 0 | 0 | 2 | .... | .... | .... | .... | .... |
| 2004-05 | Peterborough | OHL | 29 | 0 | 1 | 1 | 54 | 14 | 0 | 1 | 1 | 21 |
| 2005-06 | Peterborough | OHL | 53 | 3 | 3 | 6 | 136 | 17 | 0 | 1 | 1 | 16 |
| 2006-07 | Peterborough | OHL | 60 | 26 | 27 | 53 | 125 | .... | .... | .... | .... | .... |
| 2007-08 | Peterborough | OHL | 59 | 17 | 22 | 39 | 140 | 5 | 2 | 0 | 2 | 8 |
| 2008-09 | Hartford Wolf Pack | AHL | 43 | 3 | 7 | 10 | 114 | .... | .... | .... | .... | .... |

Signed as a free agent by **NY Rangers**, March 12, 2008.

## SOUTHORN, Jordon (SUH-thohrn, JOHR-dahn) BUF.

Defense. Shoots left. 6'2", 185 lbs. Born, Montreal, Que., May 15, 1990.
(Buffalo's 6th choice, 104th overall, in 2008 Entry Draft).

| | | | Regular Season | | | | | Playoffs | | | | |
|---|---|---|---|---|---|---|---|---|---|---|---|---|
| Season | Club | League | GP | G | A | Pts | PIM | GP | G | A | Pts | PIM |
| 2005-06 | Lac St-Louis Tigres | Minor-QC | 26 | 7 | 15 | 22 | 90 | .... | .... | .... | .... | .... |
| 2006-07 | PEI Rocket | QMJHL | 58 | 5 | 5 | 10 | 76 | 7 | 0 | 0 | 0 | 2 |
| 2007-08 | PEI Rocket | QMJHL | 69 | 12 | 19 | 31 | 70 | 4 | 0 | 1 | 1 | 4 |
| 2008-09 | PEI Rocket | QMJHL | 64 | 6 | 35 | 41 | 71 | 5 | 0 | 2 | 2 | 10 |

## SPALING, Nick (SPAHL-ihng, NIHK) NSH.

Center. Shoots left. 6'1", 190 lbs. Born, Palmerston, Ont., September 19, 1988.
(Nashville's 3rd choice, 58th overall, in 2007 Entry Draft).

| | | | Regular Season | | | | | Playoffs | | | | |
|---|---|---|---|---|---|---|---|---|---|---|---|---|
| Season | Club | League | GP | G | A | Pts | PIM | GP | G | A | Pts | PIM |
| 2004-05 | Listowel Cyclones | OJHL-B | 61 | 25 | 27 | 52 | 58 | .... | .... | .... | .... | .... |
| 2005-06 | Kitchener Rangers | OHL | 62 | 10 | 15 | 25 | 22 | 5 | 0 | 3 | 3 | 0 |
| 2006-07 | Kitchener Rangers | OHL | 61 | 23 | 36 | 59 | 41 | 9 | 2 | 3 | 5 | 4 |
| 2007-08 | Kitchener Rangers | OHL | 56 | 38 | 34 | 72 | 18 | 20 | 14 | 16 | 30 | 9 |
| 2008-09 | Milwaukee | AHL | 79 | 12 | 23 | 35 | 28 | 11 | 0 | 3 | 3 | 8 |

## SPANG, Dan (SPANG, DAN)

Defense. Shoots left. 6', 199 lbs. Born, Winchester, MA, August 18, 1983.
(San Jose's 2nd choice, 52nd overall, in 2002 Entry Draft).

| | | | Regular Season | | | | | Playoffs | | | | |
|---|---|---|---|---|---|---|---|---|---|---|---|---|
| Season | Club | League | GP | G | A | Pts | PIM | GP | G | A | Pts | PIM |
| 2000-01 | Winchester High | High-MA | 24 | 8 | 37 | 45 | 14 | .... | .... | .... | .... | .... |
| 2001-02 | Winchester High | High-MA | 6 | 9 | 8 | 17 | 14 | .... | .... | .... | .... | .... |
| 2002-03 | Boston University | H-East | 27 | 3 | 6 | 9 | 14 | .... | .... | .... | .... | .... |
| 2003-04 | Boston University | H-East | 38 | 5 | 9 | 14 | 12 | .... | .... | .... | .... | .... |
| 2004-05 | Boston University | H-East | 41 | 3 | 13 | 16 | 22 | .... | .... | .... | .... | .... |
| 2005-06 | Boston University | H-East | 40 | 9 | 22 | 31 | 14 | .... | .... | .... | .... | .... |
| | Cleveland Barons | AHL | 8 | 0 | 0 | 0 | 8 | .... | .... | .... | .... | .... |
| 2006-07 | Worcester Sharks | AHL | 48 | 4 | 21 | 25 | 18 | .... | .... | .... | .... | .... |
| 2007-08 | Worcester Sharks | AHL | 77 | 8 | 23 | 31 | 41 | .... | .... | .... | .... | .... |
| 2008-09 | Quad City Flames | AHL | 30 | 1 | 7 | 8 | 10 | .... | .... | .... | .... | .... |
| | Syracuse Crunch | AHL | 24 | 3 | 10 | 13 | 6 | .... | .... | .... | .... | .... |
| | Las Vegas | ECHL | 17 | 2 | 10 | 12 | 10 | 16 | 5 | 10 | 15 | 2 |

Hockey East First All-Star Team (2006) • NCAA East First All-American Team (2006)

• Missed majority of 2001-02 season recovering from head injuries suffered in automobile accident, October, 2001. Signed as a free agent by **Quad City** (AHL), July 22, 2008.

## SPINA, David (SPEE-nuh, DAY-vihd) PHX.

Left wing. Shoots left. 5'10", 185 lbs. Born, Mesa, AZ, June 5, 1983.

| | | | Regular Season | | | | | Playoffs | | | | |
|---|---|---|---|---|---|---|---|---|---|---|---|---|
| Season | Club | League | GP | G | A | Pts | PIM | GP | G | A | Pts | PIM |
| 99-2000 | Texas Tornado | NAHL | 54 | 15 | 26 | 41 | 31 | .... | .... | .... | .... | .... |
| 2000-01 | USNTDP | USHL | 23 | 3 | 7 | 10 | 28 | .... | .... | .... | .... | .... |
| 2001-02 | Boston College | H-East | 36 | 13 | 13 | 26 | 39 | .... | .... | .... | .... | .... |
| 2002-03 | Boston College | H-East | 37 | 17 | 20 | 37 | 34 | .... | .... | .... | .... | .... |
| 2003-04 | Boston College | H-East | 25 | 6 | 6 | 12 | 20 | .... | .... | .... | .... | .... |
| 2004-05 | Boston College | H-East | 40 | 13 | 15 | 28 | 42 | .... | .... | .... | .... | .... |
| | Utah Grizzlies | AHL | 9 | 0 | 0 | 0 | 2 | .... | .... | .... | .... | .... |
| 2005-06 | Springfield Falcons | AHL | 54 | 11 | 13 | 24 | 36 | .... | .... | .... | .... | .... |
| | South Carolina | ECHL | 11 | 7 | 0 | 7 | 6 | .... | .... | .... | .... | .... |
| 2006-07 | Springfield Falcons | AHL | 73 | 15 | 20 | 35 | 80 | .... | .... | .... | .... | .... |
| | Johnstown Chiefs | ECHL | 6 | 4 | 2 | 6 | 4 | .... | .... | .... | .... | .... |
| 2007-08 | San Antonio | AHL | 76 | 21 | 29 | 50 | 35 | 7 | 3 | 0 | 3 | 2 |
| 2008-09 | San Antonio | AHL | 63 | 16 | 38 | 54 | 55 | .... | .... | .... | .... | .... |

Signed as a free agent by **Phoenix**, July 2, 2008.

## SPRUNGER, Julien (SRUHN-guhr, JEW-lee-ehn)

Right wing. Shoots right. 6'4", 197 lbs. Born, Fribourg, Switz., January 4, 1986.
(Minnesota's 7th choice, 117th overall, in 2004 Entry Draft).

| | | | Regular Season | | | | | Playoffs | | | | |
|---|---|---|---|---|---|---|---|---|---|---|---|---|
| Season | Club | League | GP | G | A | Pts | PIM | GP | G | A | Pts | PIM |
| 2002-03 | Fribourg Jr. | Swiss-Jr. | 24 | 21 | 19 | 40 | 32 | .... | .... | .... | .... | .... |
| | Fribourg | Swiss | 2 | 0 | 0 | 0 | 0 | .... | .... | .... | .... | .... |
| | HC Dudingen | Swiss-3 | 9 | 7 | 1 | 8 | .... | 2 | 1 | 1 | 2 | .... |
| 2003-04 | Fribourg | Swiss | 42 | 2 | 3 | 5 | 14 | 4 | 0 | 0 | 0 | 4 |
| 2004-05 | Fribourg Jr. | Swiss-Jr. | 4 | 3 | 4 | 7 | 4 | .... | .... | .... | .... | .... |
| | Chaux-de-Fonds | Swiss-2 | 1 | 0 | 0 | 0 | 0 | .... | .... | .... | .... | .... |
| | Fribourg | Swiss | 41 | 9 | 7 | 16 | 35 | 11 | 2 | 1 | 3 | 14 |
| 2005-06 | Fribourg Jr. | Swiss-Jr. | 2 | 2 | 1 | 3 | 6 | .... | .... | .... | .... | .... |
| | Fribourg | Swiss | 38 | 19 | 14 | 33 | 36 | 10 | 5 | 2 | 7 | 25 |
| | Fribourg | Swiss-Q | .... | .... | .... | .... | .... | 5 | 2 | 1 | 3 | 4 |
| 2006-07 | Fribourg | Swiss | 34 | 10 | 10 | 20 | 46 | .... | .... | .... | .... | .... |
| 2007-08 | Fribourg | Swiss | 49 | 27 | 20 | 47 | 34 | 5 | 2 | 1 | 3 | 20 |
| 2008-09 | Fribourg | Swiss | 47 | 25 | 21 | 46 | 56 | 10 | 6 | 4 | 10 | 6 |

## SPURGEON, Jared (SPUHR-juhn, JAIR-uhd) NYI

Defense. Shoots right. 5'8", 175 lbs. Born, Edmonton, Alta., November 29, 1989.
(NY Islanders' 12th choice, 156th overall, in 2008 Entry Draft).

| | | | Regular Season | | | | | Playoffs | | | | |
|---|---|---|---|---|---|---|---|---|---|---|---|---|
| Season | Club | League | GP | G | A | Pts | PIM | GP | G | A | Pts | PIM |
| 2004-05 | K of C Pats | AMHL | 26 | 9 | 21 | 30 | 16 | .... | .... | .... | .... | .... |
| 2005-06 | Spokane Chiefs | WHL | 46 | 3 | 9 | 12 | 28 | .... | .... | .... | .... | .... |
| 2006-07 | Spokane Chiefs | WHL | 38 | 4 | 15 | 19 | 16 | .... | .... | .... | .... | .... |
| 2007-08 | Spokane Chiefs | WHL | 69 | 12 | 31 | 43 | 19 | 21 | 0 | 5 | 5 | 16 |
| 2008-09 | Spokane Chiefs | WHL | 59 | 10 | 35 | 45 | 37 | 12 | 2 | 3 | 5 | 10 |

## SPURGEON, Tyler (SPUHR-juhn, TIGH-luhr)

Center. Shoots left. 5'11", 188 lbs. Born, Edmonton, Alta., April 10, 1986.
(Edmonton's 9th choice, 242nd overall, in 2004 Entry Draft).

| | | | Regular Season | | | | | Playoffs | | | | |
|---|---|---|---|---|---|---|---|---|---|---|---|---|
| Season | Club | League | GP | G | A | Pts | PIM | GP | G | A | Pts | PIM |
| 2001-02 | Edmonton MLAC | AMHL | 35 | 39 | 36 | 75 | 12 | .... | .... | .... | .... | .... |
| | Kelowna Rockets | WHL | 2 | 0 | 1 | 1 | 0 | .... | .... | .... | .... | .... |
| 2002-03 | Kelowna Rockets | WHL | 50 | 7 | 6 | 13 | 21 | 19 | 2 | 5 | 7 | 6 |
| 2003-04 | Kelowna Rockets | WHL | 49 | 8 | 16 | 24 | 24 | 17 | 4 | 5 | 9 | 9 |
| 2004-05 | Kelowna Rockets | WHL | 72 | 21 | 41 | 62 | 32 | 24 | 11 | 6 | 17 | 12 |
| 2005-06 | Kelowna Rockets | WHL | 39 | 7 | 17 | 24 | 22 | 12 | 0 | 3 | 3 | 14 |
| 2006-07 | Wilkes-Barre | AHL | 34 | 5 | 10 | 15 | 10 | 6 | 1 | 0 | 1 | 4 |
| | Stockton Thunder | ECHL | 39 | 12 | 17 | 29 | 26 | .... | .... | .... | .... | .... |
| 2007-08 | Springfield Falcons | AHL | 12 | 1 | 7 | 8 | 2 | .... | .... | .... | .... | .... |
| 2008-09 | Springfield Falcons | AHL | 73 | 6 | 14 | 20 | 35 | .... | .... | .... | .... | .... |

## STAAL, Jared (STAWL, JAIR-uhd) PHX.

Right wing. Shoots right. 6'3", 198 lbs. Born, Thunder Bay, Ont., August 21, 1990.
(Phoenix's 3rd choice, 49th overall, in 2008 Entry Draft).

| | | | Regular Season | | | | | Playoffs | | | | |
|---|---|---|---|---|---|---|---|---|---|---|---|---|
| Season | Club | League | GP | G | A | Pts | PIM | GP | G | A | Pts | PIM |
| 2005-06 | Thunder Bay Kings | Minor-ON | 64 | 24 | 25 | 49 | 72 | .... | .... | .... | .... | .... |
| 2006-07 | Sudbury Wolves | OHL | 63 | 2 | 1 | 3 | 18 | 21 | 1 | 0 | 1 | 2 |
| 2007-08 | Sudbury Wolves | OHL | 60 | 21 | 28 | 49 | 44 | .... | .... | .... | .... | .... |
| 2008-09 | Sudbury Wolves | OHL | 67 | 19 | 33 | 52 | 38 | 6 | 0 | 1 | 1 | 2 |
| | San Antonio | AHL | 5 | 0 | 0 | 0 | 0 | .... | .... | .... | .... | .... |

## STAHLBERG, Viktor (STAHL-buhrg, VIHK-tohr) TOR.

Left wing. Shoots left. 6'3", 196 lbs. Born, Stockholm, Sweden, January 17, 1986.
(Toronto's 5th choice, 161st overall, in 2006 Entry Draft).

| | | | Regular Season | | | | | Playoffs | | | | |
|---|---|---|---|---|---|---|---|---|---|---|---|---|
| Season | Club | League | GP | G | A | Pts | PIM | GP | G | A | Pts | PIM |
| 2003-04 | Molndal U18 | Swe-U18 | 13 | 14 | 13 | 27 | .... | .... | .... | .... | .... | .... |
| | Molndal Jr. | Swe-Jr. | 18 | 25 | 10 | 35 | .... | .... | .... | .... | .... | .... |
| | IF Molndal Hockey | Sweden-4 | .... | 11 | 9 | 20 | .... | .... | .... | .... | .... | .... |
| 2004-05 | Molndal Jr. | Swe-Jr. | 11 | 16 | 7 | 23 | .... | .... | .... | .... | .... | .... |
| | IF Molndal Hockey | Sweden-3 | 29 | 6 | 9 | 15 | 54 | .... | .... | .... | .... | .... |
| 2005-06 | Frolunda Jr. | Swe-Jr. | 41 | 27 | 26 | 53 | 89 | 7 | 6 | 5 | 11 | 6 |
| 2006-07 | U. of Vermont | H-East | 39 | 7 | 8 | 15 | 53 | .... | .... | .... | .... | .... |
| 2007-08 | U. of Vermont | H-East | 39 | 10 | 13 | 23 | 34 | .... | .... | .... | .... | .... |
| 2008-09 | U. of Vermont | H-East | 39 | 24 | 22 | 46 | 32 | .... | .... | .... | .... | .... |
| | Toronto Marlies | AHL | .... | .... | .... | .... | .... | 2 | 0 | 1 | 1 | 0 |

Hockey East First All-Star Team (2009) • NCAA East First All-American Team (2009)

## STASYUK, Denis (stah-S'YUHK, DEH-nihs) FLA.

Center. Shoots left. 6'1", 165 lbs. Born, Novokuznetsk, USSR, September 2, 1985.
(Florida's 9th choice, 171st overall, in 2003 Entry Draft).

| | | | Regular Season | | | | | Playoffs | | | | |
|---|---|---|---|---|---|---|---|---|---|---|---|---|
| Season | Club | League | GP | G | A | Pts | PIM | GP | G | A | Pts | PIM |
| 2002-03 | Novokuznetsk 2 | Russia-3 | STATISTICS NOT AVAILABLE | | | | | | | | | |
| | Novokuznetsk | Russia | 11 | 1 | 0 | 1 | 0 | .... | .... | .... | .... | .... |
| 2003-04 | Novokuznetsk 2 | Russia-3 | STATISTICS NOT AVAILABLE | | | | | | | | | |
| | Novokuznetsk | Russia | 5 | 0 | 0 | 0 | 0 | .... | .... | .... | .... | .... |
| 2004-05 | Amur Khabarovsk | Russia-2 | 44 | 11 | 10 | 21 | 12 | 10 | 1 | 2 | 3 | 6 |
| 2005-06 | Novokuznetsk | Russia | 41 | 7 | 2 | 9 | 18 | 3 | 0 | 0 | 0 | 0 |
| 2006-07 | Novokuznetsk | Russia | 26 | 0 | 1 | 1 | 16 | 3 | 0 | 0 | 0 | 0 |
| 2007-08 | Novokuznetsk | Russia | 33 | 4 | 2 | 6 | 14 | .... | .... | .... | .... | .... |
| 2008-09 | Novokuznetsk | Rus-KHL | 44 | 2 | 8 | 10 | 12 | .... | .... | .... | .... | .... |

## STEFANOVICH, Mikhail (steh-fan-AWV-ihch, mih-kigh-EHL) TOR.

Right wing. Shoots right. 6'2", 202 lbs. Born, Minsk, USSR, November 27, 1989.
(Toronto's 3rd choice, 98th overall, in 2008 Entry Draft).

| | | | Regular Season | | | | | Playoffs | | | | |
|---|---|---|---|---|---|---|---|---|---|---|---|---|
| Season | Club | League | GP | G | A | Pts | PIM | GP | G | A | Pts | PIM |
| 2004-05 | Dynamo Minsk 2 | Belarus-2 | 19 | 3 | 7 | 10 | 8 | .... | .... | .... | .... | .... |
| | HK Gomel 2 | Belarus-2 | 14 | 3 | 0 | 3 | 6 | .... | .... | .... | .... | .... |
| 2005-06 | HK Gomel 2 | Belarus-2 | 37 | 18 | 12 | 30 | 64 | .... | .... | .... | .... | .... |
| 2006-07 | HK Gomel 2 | Belarus-2 | 3 | 3 | 1 | 4 | 4 | .... | .... | .... | .... | .... |
| | HK Gomel | Belarus | 41 | 16 | 9 | 25 | 43 | 5 | 1 | 0 | 1 | 2 |
| 2007-08 | HK Gomel | Belarus | 1 | 0 | 0 | 0 | 0 | .... | .... | .... | .... | .... |
| | Quebec Remparts | QMJHL | 62 | 32 | 34 | 66 | 32 | 11 | 4 | 4 | 8 | 10 |
| 2008-09 | Quebec Remparts | QMJHL | 56 | 49 | 27 | 76 | 17 | 17 | 11 | 5 | 16 | 6 |

## STEFISHEN, Taylor (STEH-fih-shehn, TAY-luhr) NSH.

Left wing. Shoots right. 5'11", 191 lbs. Born, North Vancouver, B.C., August 15, 1990.
(Nashville's 4th choice, 136th overall, in 2008 Entry Draft).

| | | | Regular Season | | | | | Playoffs | | | | |
|---|---|---|---|---|---|---|---|---|---|---|---|---|
| Season | Club | League | GP | G | A | Pts | PIM | GP | G | A | Pts | PIM |
| 2006-07 | Langley Chiefs | BCHL | 59 | 25 | 31 | 56 | 73 | 7 | 5 | 1 | 6 | 8 |
| 2007-08 | Langley Chiefs | BCHL | 57 | 33 | 48 | 81 | 71 | 12 | 6 | 10 | 16 | 19 |
| 2008-09 | Ohio State | CCHA | 15 | 3 | 5 | 8 | 2 | .... | .... | .... | .... | .... |

## STEJSKAL, Joe (STAY-kuhl, JOH) MTL.

Defense. Shoots right. 6'3", 211 lbs. Born, Grand Rapids, MN, April 30, 1988.
(Montreal's 6th choice, 133rd overall, in 2007 Entry Draft).

| | | | Regular Season | | | | | Playoffs | | | | |
|---|---|---|---|---|---|---|---|---|---|---|---|---|
| Season | Club | League | GP | G | A | Pts | PIM | GP | G | A | Pts | PIM |
| 2003-04 | Grand Rapids | High-MN | .... | 1 | 7 | 8 | .... | .... | .... | .... | .... | .... |
| 2004-05 | Grand Rapids | High-MN | .... | 2 | 8 | 10 | .... | .... | .... | .... | .... | .... |
| 2005-06 | Grand Rapids | High-MN | .... | 7 | 18 | 25 | .... | .... | .... | .... | .... | .... |
| 2006-07 | Grand Rapids | High-MN | 24 | 11 | 17 | 28 | 42 | .... | .... | .... | .... | .... |
| 2007-08 | Dartmouth | ECAC | 32 | 1 | 4 | 5 | 46 | .... | .... | .... | .... | .... |
| 2008-09 | Dartmouth | ECAC | 29 | 7 | 5 | 12 | 53 | .... | .... | .... | .... | .... |

**STEPAN, Derek** (STEH-pan, DAIR-ihk) **NYR**

Center. Shoots right. 6', 175 lbs. Born, Hastings, MN, June 18, 1990.
(NY Rangers' 2nd choice, 51st overall, in 2008 Entry Draft).

| | | | Regular Season | | | | | Playoffs | | | | |
|---|---|---|---|---|---|---|---|---|---|---|---|---|
| Season | Club | League | GP | G | A | Pts | PIM | GP | G | A | Pts | PIM |
| 2006-07 | Shat.-St. Mary's | High-MN | 63 | 38 | 32 | 70 | 22 | .... | .... | .... | .... | .... |
| 2007-08 | Shat.-St. Mary's | High-MN | 60 | 44 | 67 | 111 | 22 | .... | .... | .... | .... | .... |
| 2008-09 | U. of Wisconsin | WCHA | 40 | 9 | 24 | 33 | 6 | .... | .... | .... | .... | .... |

**STEPHENSON, Logan** (STEE-vehn-suhn, LOH-guhn)

Defense. Shoots left. 6'3", 197 lbs. Born, Saskatoon, Sask., February 19, 1986.
(Phoenix's 2nd choice, 35th overall, in 2004 Entry Draft).

| | | | Regular Season | | | | | Playoffs | | | | |
|---|---|---|---|---|---|---|---|---|---|---|---|---|
| Season | Club | League | GP | G | A | Pts | PIM | GP | G | A | Pts | PIM |
| 2001-02 | Notre Dame | SMHL | 37 | 4 | 2 | 6 | 74 | .... | .... | .... | .... | .... |
| | Tri-City Americans | WHL | .... | .... | .... | .... | .... | 3 | 0 | 0 | 0 | 0 |
| 2002-03 | Tri-City Americans | WHL | 50 | 0 | 6 | 6 | 121 | .... | .... | .... | .... | .... |
| 2003-04 | Tri-City Americans | WHL | 69 | 3 | 8 | 11 | 112 | 11 | 1 | 1 | 2 | 10 |
| 2004-05 | Tri-City Americans | WHL | 59 | 6 | 9 | 15 | 86 | 5 | 0 | 0 | 0 | 2 |
| 2005-06 | Tri-City Americans | WHL | 71 | 10 | 43 | 53 | 162 | 5 | 1 | 0 | 1 | 18 |
| 2006-07 | San Antonio | AHL | 73 | 3 | 5 | 8 | 90 | .... | .... | .... | .... | .... |
| 2007-08 | San Antonio | AHL | 74 | 1 | 7 | 8 | 94 | 7 | 0 | 1 | 1 | 6 |
| 2008-09 | San Antonio | AHL | 19 | 1 | 1 | 2 | 40 | .... | .... | .... | .... | .... |
| | Iowa Chops | AHL | 25 | 0 | 2 | 2 | 21 | .... | .... | .... | .... | .... |
| | Rockford IceHogs | AHL | 16 | 1 | 2 | 3 | 31 | 4 | 0 | 0 | 0 | 14 |

WHL West Second All-Star Team (2006)

Traded to **Anaheim** by **Phoenix** for Joakim Lindstrom, December 3, 2008. Traded to **Chicago** by **Anaheim** with Samuel Pahlsson and future considerations for James Wisniewski and Petri Kontiola, March 4, 2009.

**STOA, Ryan** (STOH-ah, RIGH-uhn) **COL.**

Center. Shoots left. 6'3", 200 lbs. Born, Bloomington, MN, April 13, 1987.
(Colorado's 1st choice, 34th overall, in 2005 Entry Draft).

| | | | Regular Season | | | | | Playoffs | | | | |
|---|---|---|---|---|---|---|---|---|---|---|---|---|
| Season | Club | League | GP | G | A | Pts | PIM | GP | G | A | Pts | PIM |
| 2003-04 | USNTDP | U-17 | 18 | 9 | 8 | 17 | .... | .... | .... | .... | .... | .... |
| | USNTDP | NAHL | 42 | 10 | 12 | 22 | 26 | 7 | 7 | 1 | 8 | 2 |
| 2004-05 | USNTDP | U-18 | 23 | 4 | 11 | 15 | 16 | .... | .... | .... | .... | .... |
| | USNTDP | NAHL | 15 | 10 | 13 | 23 | 20 | .... | .... | .... | .... | .... |
| 2005-06 | U. of Minnesota | WCHA | 41 | 10 | 15 | 25 | 43 | .... | .... | .... | .... | .... |
| 2006-07 | U. of Minnesota | WCHA | 41 | 12 | 12 | 24 | 44 | .... | .... | .... | .... | .... |
| 2007-08 | U. of Minnesota | WCHA | 2 | 1 | 1 | 2 | 2 | .... | .... | .... | .... | .... |
| 2008-09 | U. of Minnesota | WCHA | 36 | 24 | 22 | 46 | 76 | .... | .... | .... | .... | .... |

WCHA First All-Star Team (2009) • NCAA West First All-American Team (2009)

• Missed remainder of 2007-08 season recovering from knee injury suffered in game vs. University of Michigan, October 13, 2007.

**STOESZ, Myles** (STOHZ, MIGH-uhlz) **N.J.**

Left wing. Shoots right. 6'2", 210 lbs. Born, Steinbach, Man., February 15, 1987.
(Atlanta's 8th choice, 207th overall, in 2005 Entry Draft).

| | | | Regular Season | | | | | Playoffs | | | | |
|---|---|---|---|---|---|---|---|---|---|---|---|---|
| Season | Club | League | GP | G | A | Pts | PIM | GP | G | A | Pts | PIM |
| 2003-04 | Spokane Chiefs | WHL | 43 | 1 | 1 | 2 | 133 | 0 | 0 | 0 | 0 | 0 |
| 2004-05 | Spokane Chiefs | WHL | 67 | 1 | 8 | 9 | 238 | .... | .... | .... | .... | .... |
| 2005-06 | Spokane Chiefs | WHL | 56 | 0 | 2 | 2 | 260 | .... | .... | .... | .... | .... |
| 2006-07 | Chilliwack Bruins | WHL | 40 | 3 | 2 | 5 | 135 | .... | .... | .... | .... | .... |
| | Regina Pats | WHL | 29 | 4 | 2 | 6 | 89 | 9 | 0 | 0 | 0 | 21 |
| 2007-08 | Gwinnett | ECHL | 64 | 4 | 2 | 6 | *291 | 1 | 0 | 0 | 0 | 0 |
| 2008-09 | Gwinnett | ECHL | 43 | 4 | 3 | 7 | 158 | .... | .... | .... | .... | .... |
| | Trenton Devils | ECHL | 10 | 0 | 0 | 0 | 30 | 3 | 0 | 0 | 0 | 9 |

Traded to **New Jersey** by **Atlanta** with Niclas Havelid for Anssi Salmela, March 1, 2009.

**STOKES, Ryan** (STOHKS, RIGH-uhn)

Defense. Shoots left. 6'3", 180 lbs. Born, Sarnia, Ont., June 23, 1983.

| | | | Regular Season | | | | | Playoffs | | | | |
|---|---|---|---|---|---|---|---|---|---|---|---|---|
| Season | Club | League | GP | G | A | Pts | PIM | GP | G | A | Pts | PIM |
| 2001-02 | Barrie Colts | OHL | 53 | 0 | 5 | 5 | 31 | 20 | 0 | 0 | 0 | 16 |
| 2002-03 | Mississauga | OHL | 59 | 2 | 7 | 9 | 139 | 5 | 0 | 1 | 1 | 22 |
| 2003-04 | Mississauga | OHL | 66 | 4 | 20 | 24 | 179 | 24 | 2 | 9 | 11 | 74 |
| 2004-05 | Houston Aeros | AHL | 7 | 0 | 0 | 0 | 7 | .... | .... | .... | .... | .... |
| | Pensacola | ECHL | 59 | 1 | 15 | 16 | 119 | .... | .... | .... | .... | .... |
| 2005-06 | Houston Aeros | AHL | 75 | 2 | 3 | 5 | 164 | 6 | 0 | 1 | 1 | 10 |
| 2006-07 | Houston Aeros | AHL | 72 | 2 | 8 | 10 | 158 | .... | .... | .... | .... | .... |
| 2007-08 | Rockford IceHogs | AHL | 55 | 4 | 6 | 10 | 93 | 12 | 0 | 0 | 0 | 14 |
| 2008-09 | Providence Bruins | AHL | 20 | 1 | 1 | 2 | 51 | 9 | 0 | 0 | 0 | 24 |

Signed as a free agent by **Minnesota**, May 25, 2004. Signed as a free agent by **Boston**, August 28, 2008.

**STOLYAROV, Gennady** (stohl-yah-RAWF, gehn-AH-dee) **DET.**

Right wing. Shoots left. 6'4", 187 lbs. Born, Moscow, USSR, August 20, 1986.
(Detroit's 7th choice, 257th overall, in 2004 Entry Draft).

| | | | Regular Season | | | | | Playoffs | | | | |
|---|---|---|---|---|---|---|---|---|---|---|---|---|
| Season | Club | League | GP | G | A | Pts | PIM | GP | G | A | Pts | PIM |
| 2003-04 | Dyn'o Moscow 2 | Russia-3 | | STATISTICS NOT AVAILABLE | | | | | | | | |
| | THK Tver | Russia-2 | 24 | 3 | 1 | 4 | 4 | .... | .... | .... | .... | .... |
| 2004-05 | Vityaz Chekhov | Russia-2 | 25 | 0 | 1 | 1 | 2 | .... | .... | .... | .... | .... |
| 2005-06 | Kapitan Stupino | Russia-2 | 17 | 3 | 5 | 8 | 20 | 5 | 1 | 2 | 3 | 36 |
| | Dynamo Moscow | Russia | 12 | 0 | 0 | 0 | 4 | 3 | 0 | 1 | 1 | 0 |
| 2006-07 | Dynamo Moscow | Russia | 37 | 6 | 3 | 9 | 39 | 2 | 0 | 0 | 0 | 0 |
| 2007-08 | Dynamo Moscow | Russia | 37 | 3 | 3 | 6 | 22 | 8 | 1 | 0 | 1 | 2 |
| 2008-09 | Dynamo Moscow | Rus-KHL | 3 | 0 | 0 | 0 | 4 | .... | .... | .... | .... | .... |
| | Barys Astana | Rus-KHL | 41 | 12 | 9 | 21 | 24 | 3 | 0 | 0 | 0 | 4 |

**STONE, Michael** (STOHN, MIGH-kuhl) **PHX.**

Defense. Shoots right. 6'3", 200 lbs. Born, Winnipeg, Man., June 7, 1990.
(Phoenix's 4th choice, 69th overall, in 2008 Entry Draft).

| | | | Regular Season | | | | | Playoffs | | | | |
|---|---|---|---|---|---|---|---|---|---|---|---|---|
| Season | Club | League | GP | G | A | Pts | PIM | GP | G | A | Pts | PIM |
| 2005-06 | Wpg. Thrashers | MMHL | 40 | 14 | 18 | 32 | 14 | .... | .... | .... | .... | .... |
| 2006-07 | Calgary Hitmen | WHL | 55 | 2 | 18 | 20 | 32 | 17 | 0 | 3 | 3 | 14 |
| 2007-08 | Calgary Hitmen | WHL | 71 | 10 | 25 | 35 | 28 | 14 | 3 | 4 | 7 | 10 |
| 2008-09 | Calgary Hitmen | WHL | 69 | 19 | 42 | 61 | 87 | 18 | 2 | 11 | 13 | 16 |

WHL East Second All-Star Team (2009)

**STONER, Clayton** (STOH-nuhr, KLAY-tuhn) **MIN.**

Defense. Shoots left. 6'4", 212 lbs. Born, Port McNeill, B.C., February 19, 1985.
(Minnesota's 4th choice, 79th overall, in 2004 Entry Draft).

| | | | Regular Season | | | | | Playoffs | | | | |
|---|---|---|---|---|---|---|---|---|---|---|---|---|
| Season | Club | League | GP | G | A | Pts | PIM | GP | G | A | Pts | PIM |
| 2000-01 | Campbell River | VIJHL | 47 | 4 | 16 | 20 | 57 | .... | .... | .... | .... | .... |
| 2001-02 | Campbell River | VIJHL | 42 | 12 | 35 | 47 | 199 | .... | .... | .... | .... | .... |
| 2002-03 | Tri-City Americans | WHL | 58 | 4 | 12 | 16 | 85 | .... | .... | .... | .... | .... |
| 2003-04 | Tri-City Americans | WHL | 71 | 7 | 24 | 31 | 109 | 11 | 1 | 1 | 2 | 8 |
| 2004-05 | Tri-City Americans | WHL | 60 | 12 | 34 | 46 | 81 | 4 | 0 | 3 | 3 | 2 |
| 2005-06 | Houston Aeros | AHL | 73 | 6 | 18 | 24 | 92 | 3 | 1 | 1 | 2 | 7 |
| 2006-07 | Houston Aeros | AHL | 65 | 1 | 6 | 7 | 104 | .... | .... | .... | .... | .... |
| 2007-08 | Houston Aeros | AHL | 56 | 3 | 12 | 15 | 78 | .... | .... | .... | .... | .... |
| 2008-09 | Houston Aeros | AHL | 63 | 2 | 22 | 24 | 81 | 20 | 1 | 4 | 5 | 27 |

WHL West Second All-Star Team (2005)

**STRAIT, Brian** (STRAYT, BRIGH-uhn) **PIT.**

Defense. Shoots left. 6'1", 200 lbs. Born, Boston, MA, January 4, 1988.
(Pittsburgh's 3rd choice, 65th overall, in 2006 Entry Draft).

| | | | Regular Season | | | | | Playoffs | | | | |
|---|---|---|---|---|---|---|---|---|---|---|---|---|
| Season | Club | League | GP | G | A | Pts | PIM | GP | G | A | Pts | PIM |
| 2003-04 | NMH School | High-MA | 30 | 5 | 15 | 20 | .... | .... | .... | .... | .... | .... |
| 2004-05 | USNTDP | U-17 | 18 | 1 | 5 | 6 | 8 | .... | .... | .... | .... | .... |
| | USNTDP | NAHL | 42 | 4 | 8 | 12 | 42 | 10 | 0 | 2 | 2 | 2 |
| 2005-06 | USNTDP | U-18 | 40 | 2 | 7 | 9 | 31 | .... | .... | .... | .... | .... |
| | USNTDP | NAHL | 15 | 0 | 5 | 5 | 41 | .... | .... | .... | .... | .... |
| 2006-07 | Boston University | H-East | 36 | 3 | 3 | 6 | 47 | .... | .... | .... | .... | .... |
| 2007-08 | Boston University | H-East | 37 | 0 | 10 | 10 | 20 | .... | .... | .... | .... | .... |
| 2008-09 | Boston University | H-East | 38 | 2 | 5 | 7 | 67 | .... | .... | .... | .... | .... |

**SUBBAN, P.K.** (soo-BAHN, PEE-KAY) **MTL.**

Defense. Shoots right. 6', 207 lbs. Born, Toronto, Ont., May 13, 1989.
(Montreal's 3rd choice, 43rd overall, in 2007 Entry Draft).

| | | | Regular Season | | | | | Playoffs | | | | |
|---|---|---|---|---|---|---|---|---|---|---|---|---|
| Season | Club | League | GP | G | A | Pts | PIM | GP | G | A | Pts | PIM |
| 2004-05 | Markham | GTHL | 67 | 15 | 28 | 43 | 179 | .... | .... | .... | .... | .... |
| 2005-06 | Belleville Bulls | OHL | 52 | 5 | 7 | 12 | 70 | 3 | 0 | 0 | 0 | 2 |
| 2006-07 | Belleville Bulls | OHL | 68 | 15 | 41 | 56 | 89 | 15 | 5 | 8 | 13 | 26 |
| 2007-08 | Belleville Bulls | OHL | 58 | 8 | 38 | 46 | 100 | 21 | 8 | 15 | 23 | 28 |
| 2008-09 | Belleville Bulls | OHL | 56 | 14 | 62 | 76 | 94 | 17 | 3 | 12 | 15 | 22 |

OHL First All-Star Team (2009)

**SUBBOTIN, Dmitri** (soo-BOH-tihn, dih-MEE-tree) **CBJ**

Left wing. Shoots left. 6'1", 200 lbs. Born, Tomsk, USSR, October 20, 1977.
(NY Rangers' 3rd choice, 76th overall, in 1996 Entry Draft).

| | | | Regular Season | | | | | Playoffs | | | | |
|---|---|---|---|---|---|---|---|---|---|---|---|---|
| Season | Club | League | GP | G | A | Pts | PIM | GP | G | A | Pts | PIM |
| 1993-94 | Yekaterinburg | CIS | 12 | 0 | 3 | 3 | 4 | .... | .... | .... | .... | .... |
| 1994-95 | Yekaterinburg | CIS | 52 | 9 | 6 | 15 | 75 | 2 | 0 | 0 | 0 | 2 |
| 1995-96 | CSKA Moscow | CIS | 41 | 6 | 5 | 11 | 62 | 3 | 0 | 0 | 0 | 0 |
| 1996-97 | CSKA Moscow | Russia-2 | 8 | 1 | 0 | 1 | 8 | .... | .... | .... | .... | .... |
| | HK CSKA Moscow | Russia | 17 | 5 | 3 | 8 | 22 | 2 | 0 | 0 | 0 | 2 |
| 1997-98 | HK CSKA Moscow | Russia | 16 | 1 | 1 | 2 | 47 | .... | .... | .... | .... | .... |
| 1998-99 | Dynamo Moscow | Russia | 1 | 0 | 1 | 1 | 0 | .... | .... | .... | .... | .... |
| | Lada Togliatti | Russia | 31 | 8 | 3 | 11 | 47 | 7 | 0 | 0 | 0 | 4 |
| 99-2000 | Lada Togliatti | Russia | 27 | 10 | 4 | 14 | 26 | 7 | 1 | 1 | 2 | 4 |
| | Lada Togliatti 2 | Russia-3 | 2 | 0 | 1 | 1 | 0 | .... | .... | .... | .... | .... |
| 2000-01 | Dynamo Moscow | Russia | 39 | 11 | 15 | 26 | 48 | .... | .... | .... | .... | .... |
| 2001-02 | Magnitogorsk | Russia | 38 | 8 | 3 | 11 | 18 | 9 | 0 | 2 | 2 | 10 |
| 2002-03 | Cherepovets | Russia | 10 | 0 | 1 | 1 | 31 | .... | .... | .... | .... | .... |
| | CSKA Moscow | Russia | 20 | 3 | 9 | 12 | 6 | .... | .... | .... | .... | .... |
| 2003-04 | CSKA Moscow | Russia | 20 | 0 | 3 | 3 | 14 | .... | .... | .... | .... | .... |
| | Avangard Omsk | Russia | 26 | 6 | 6 | 12 | 36 | 11 | 2 | 3 | 5 | 6 |
| 2004-05 | Avangard Omsk | Russia | 55 | 5 | 6 | 11 | 66 | 7 | 0 | 0 | 0 | 10 |
| 2005-06 | Ufa | Russia | 5 | 0 | 1 | 1 | 8 | .... | .... | .... | .... | .... |
| | MVD | Russia | 27 | 6 | 8 | 14 | 52 | 4 | 1 | 3 | 4 | 4 |
| 2006-07 | MVD | Russia | 51 | 16 | 20 | 36 | 96 | 2 | 0 | 1 | 1 | 6 |
| 2007-08 | Vityaz Chekhov | Russia | 44 | 12 | 13 | 25 | 22 | .... | .... | .... | .... | .... |
| 2008-09 | MVD | Rus-KHL | 19 | 0 | 6 | 6 | 6 | .... | .... | .... | .... | .... |

Claimed by **Columbus** from **NY Rangers** in Expansion Draft, June 23, 2000.

**SUCHARSKI, Nick** (soo-CHAR-skee, NIHK) **CBJ**

Left wing. Shoots left. 6'2", 185 lbs. Born, Toronto, Ont., November 15, 1987.
(Columbus' 6th choice, 136th overall, in 2006 Entry Draft).

| | | | Regular Season | | | | | Playoffs | | | | |
|---|---|---|---|---|---|---|---|---|---|---|---|---|
| Season | Club | League | GP | G | A | Pts | PIM | GP | G | A | Pts | PIM |
| 2003-04 | Wexford Raiders | OPJHL | 43 | 15 | 29 | 44 | 48 | .... | .... | .... | .... | .... |
| 2004-05 | Wexford Raiders | OPJHL | 46 | 26 | 27 | 53 | 78 | 13 | 6 | 10 | 16 | 20 |
| 2005-06 | Michigan State | CCHA | 36 | 2 | 5 | 7 | 18 | .... | .... | .... | .... | .... |
| 2006-07 | Michigan State | CCHA | 41 | 9 | 15 | 24 | 32 | .... | .... | .... | .... | .... |
| 2007-08 | Michigan State | CCHA | 41 | 9 | 17 | 26 | 32 | .... | .... | .... | .... | .... |
| 2008-09 | Michigan State | CCHA | 6 | 0 | 1 | 1 | 6 | .... | .... | .... | .... | .... |

**SULLIVAN, Sean** (SUHL-ih-vuhn, SHAWN) **PHX.**

Defense. Shoots left. 6', 188 lbs. Born, Boston, MA, March 29, 1984.
(Phoenix's 7th choice, 272nd overall, in 2003 Entry Draft).

| | | | Regular Season | | | | | Playoffs | | | | |
|---|---|---|---|---|---|---|---|---|---|---|---|---|
| Season | Club | League | GP | G | A | Pts | PIM | GP | G | A | Pts | PIM |
| 2001-02 | St. Sebastian's | High-MA | 31 | 3 | 11 | 14 | 4 | .... | .... | .... | .... | .... |
| 2002-03 | St. Sebastian's | High-MA | 41 | 9 | 30 | 39 | 59 | .... | .... | .... | .... | .... |
| 2003-04 | Boston University | H-East | 36 | 2 | 5 | 7 | 14 | .... | .... | .... | .... | .... |
| 2004-05 | Boston University | H-East | 41 | 1 | 3 | 4 | 10 | .... | .... | .... | .... | .... |
| 2005-06 | Boston University | H-East | 40 | 3 | 14 | 17 | 32 | .... | .... | .... | .... | .... |
| 2006-07 | Boston University | H-East | 38 | 3 | 12 | 15 | 12 | .... | .... | .... | .... | .... |
| | San Antonio | AHL | 7 | 0 | 0 | 0 | 0 | .... | .... | .... | .... | .... |
| 2007-08 | San Antonio | AHL | 34 | 0 | 8 | 8 | 13 | 1 | 0 | 0 | 0 | 4 |
| | Arizona Sundogs | CHL | 22 | 9 | 16 | 25 | 19 | .... | .... | .... | .... | .... |
| 2008-09 | San Antonio | AHL | 65 | 9 | 23 | 32 | 24 | .... | .... | .... | .... | .... |

NCAA East Second All-American Team (2007)

## SUMMERS, Chris (SUHM-mehrs, KRIHS) PHX.

Defense. Shoots left. 6'2", 180 lbs. Born, Ann Arbor, MI, February 5, 1988.
(Phoenix's 2nd choice, 29th overall, in 2006 Entry Draft).

| | | | Regular Season | | | | | Playoffs | | | | |
|---|---|---|---|---|---|---|---|---|---|---|---|---|
| Season | Club | League | GP | G | A | Pts | PIM | GP | G | A | Pts | PIM |
| 2004-05 | USNTDP | U-17 | 13 | 2 | 2 | 4 | 10 | .... | .... | .... | .... | .... |
| | USNTDP | NAHL | 31 | 2 | 5 | 7 | 20 | 7 | 1 | 0 | 1 | 0 |
| 2005-06 | USNTDP | U-18 | 42 | 4 | 9 | 13 | 67 | .... | .... | .... | .... | .... |
| | USNTDP | NAHL | 17 | 2 | 2 | 4 | 20 | .... | .... | .... | .... | .... |
| 2006-07 | U. of Michigan | CCHA | 41 | 6 | 8 | 14 | 58 | .... | .... | .... | .... | .... |
| 2007-08 | U. of Michigan | CCHA | 41 | 2 | 11 | 13 | 65 | .... | .... | .... | .... | .... |
| 2008-09 | U. of Michigan | CCHA | 41 | 4 | 13 | 17 | 40 | .... | .... | .... | .... | .... |

## SWEATT, Bill (SWEHT, BIHL) CHI.

Left wing. Shoots left. 6', 180 lbs. Born, Elburn, IL, September 21, 1988.
(Chicago's 2nd choice, 38th overall, in 2007 Entry Draft).

| | | | Regular Season | | | | | Playoffs | | | | |
|---|---|---|---|---|---|---|---|---|---|---|---|---|
| Season | Club | League | GP | G | A | Pts | PIM | GP | G | A | Pts | PIM |
| 2003-04 | Team Illinois | MWEHL | 74 | 33 | 37 | 70 | .... | .... | .... | .... | .... | .... |
| 2004-05 | USNTDP | U-17 | 11 | 5 | 10 | 15 | 54 | .... | .... | .... | .... | .... |
| | USNTDP | NAHL | 41 | 7 | 9 | 16 | 12 | 10 | 4 | 3 | 7 | 6 |
| 2005-06 | USNTDP | U-18 | 42 | 19 | 11 | 30 | 24 | .... | .... | .... | .... | .... |
| | USNTDP | NAHL | 17 | 10 | 15 | 25 | 4 | .... | .... | .... | .... | .... |
| 2006-07 | Colorado College | WCHA | 30 | 9 | 17 | 26 | 18 | .... | .... | .... | .... | .... |
| 2007-08 | Colorado College | WCHA | 37 | 10 | 17 | 27 | 38 | .... | .... | .... | .... | .... |
| 2008-09 | Colorado College | WCHA | 37 | 12 | 11 | 23 | 28 | .... | .... | .... | .... | .... |

## SWEETLAND, Andrew (SWEET-land, AN-droo) FLA.

Left wing. Shoots left. 6'2", 204 lbs. Born, Bonavista, Nfld., October 21, 1986.

| | | | Regular Season | | | | | Playoffs | | | | |
|---|---|---|---|---|---|---|---|---|---|---|---|---|
| Season | Club | League | GP | G | A | Pts | PIM | GP | G | A | Pts | PIM |
| 2004-05 | Couchiching | OPJHL | 42 | 34 | 24 | 58 | 8 | .... | .... | .... | .... | .... |
| 2005-06 | Couchiching | OPJHL | 30 | 18 | 15 | 33 | 6 | .... | .... | .... | .... | .... |
| 2006-07 | Amherst Ramblers | MJAHL | 54 | 56 | 61 | 117 | 20 | 6 | 3 | 8 | 11 | 0 |
| 2007-08 | U. of Maine | H-East | 28 | 8 | 9 | 17 | 2 | .... | .... | .... | .... | .... |
| 2008-09 | Rochester | AHL | 48 | 1 | 2 | 3 | 12 | .... | .... | .... | .... | .... |
| | Florida Everblades | ECHL | 23 | 10 | 13 | 23 | 8 | 11 | 2 | 4 | 6 | 2 |

Signed as a free agent by **Florida**, March 31, 2008.

## SWIFT, Michael (SWIHFT, MIGH-kuhl) N.J.

Center. Shoots left. 5'9", 170 lbs. Born, Peterborough, Ont., March 26, 1987.

| | | | Regular Season | | | | | Playoffs | | | | |
|---|---|---|---|---|---|---|---|---|---|---|---|---|
| Season | Club | League | GP | G | A | Pts | PIM | GP | G | A | Pts | PIM |
| 2003-04 | Mississauga | OHL | 9 | 2 | 2 | 4 | 6 | .... | .... | .... | .... | .... |
| 2004-05 | Mississauga | OHL | 67 | 15 | 17 | 32 | 46 | 5 | 0 | 0 | 0 | 4 |
| 2005-06 | Mississauga | OHL | 65 | 22 | 32 | 54 | 46 | .... | .... | .... | .... | .... |
| 2006-07 | Mississauga | OHL | 67 | 34 | 59 | 93 | 76 | 5 | 0 | 1 | 1 | 6 |
| | Laredo Bucks | CHL | .... | .... | .... | .... | .... | 12 | 1 | 3 | 4 | 8 |
| 2007-08 | Niagara Ice Dogs | OHL | 68 | 38 | 62 | 100 | 130 | 10 | 9 | 9 | 18 | 22 |
| 2008-09 | Lowell Devils | AHL | 52 | 12 | 15 | 27 | 50 | .... | .... | .... | .... | .... |

Signed as a free agent by **New Jersey**, April 19, 2008.

## SZWARZ, Jordan (SWAWRZ, JOHR-dahn) PHX.

Right wing. Shoots right. 5'11", 189 lbs. Born, Burlington, Ont., May 14, 1991.
(Phoenix's 4th choice, 97th overall, in 2009 Entry Draft).

| | | | Regular Season | | | | | Playoffs | | | | |
|---|---|---|---|---|---|---|---|---|---|---|---|---|
| Season | Club | League | GP | G | A | Pts | PIM | GP | G | A | Pts | PIM |
| 2006-07 | Burlington Eagles | Minor-ON | 66 | 56 | 54 | 110 | 88 | .... | .... | .... | .... | .... |
| 2007-08 | Saginaw Spirit | OHL | 65 | 12 | 21 | 33 | 56 | 4 | 0 | 0 | 0 | 2 |
| 2008-09 | Saginaw Spirit | OHL | 67 | 17 | 34 | 51 | 76 | 8 | 1 | 5 | 6 | 10 |

## TALBOT, Julian (TAL-buht, JOO-lee-uhn) ST.L.

Center. Shoots left. 5'11", 181 lbs. Born, Wahnapitae, Ont., March 24, 1985.

| | | | Regular Season | | | | | Playoffs | | | | |
|---|---|---|---|---|---|---|---|---|---|---|---|---|
| Season | Club | League | GP | G | A | Pts | PIM | GP | G | A | Pts | PIM |
| 2002-03 | Ottawa 67's | OHL | 62 | 10 | 18 | 28 | 13 | 23 | 1 | 7 | 8 | 2 |
| 2003-04 | Ottawa 67's | OHL | 68 | 18 | 31 | 49 | 56 | 7 | 1 | 4 | 5 | 6 |
| 2004-05 | Ottawa 67's | OHL | 68 | 25 | 41 | 66 | 50 | 21 | 8 | 12 | 20 | 31 |
| 2005-06 | Ottawa 67's | OHL | 65 | 30 | 47 | 77 | 70 | 3 | 1 | 2 | 3 | 8 |
| 2006-07 | Providence Bruins | AHL | 7 | 1 | 2 | 3 | 0 | .... | .... | .... | .... | .... |
| | Alaska Aces | ECHL | 66 | 20 | 33 | 53 | 54 | 15 | 9 | 11 | 20 | 8 |
| 2007-08 | Peoria Rivermen | AHL | 78 | 24 | 26 | 50 | 53 | .... | .... | .... | .... | .... |
| 2008-09 | Peoria Rivermen | AHL | 65 | 20 | 23 | 43 | 43 | 7 | 0 | 1 | 1 | 4 |

Signed as a free agent by **St. Louis**, March 19, 2008.

## TANGRADI, Eric (tan-GRAY-dee, AIR-ihk) PIT.

Center. Shoots left. 6'3", 214 lbs. Born, Philadelphia, PA, February 10, 1989.
(Anaheim's 2nd choice, 42nd overall, in 2007 Entry Draft).

| | | | Regular Season | | | | | Playoffs | | | | |
|---|---|---|---|---|---|---|---|---|---|---|---|---|
| Season | Club | League | GP | G | A | Pts | PIM | GP | G | A | Pts | PIM |
| 2005-06 | Wyoming Prep | High-PA | 38 | 21 | 23 | 44 | 120 | .... | .... | .... | .... | .... |
| 2006-07 | Belleville Bulls | OHL | 65 | 5 | 15 | 20 | 32 | 15 | 8 | 9 | 17 | 14 |
| 2007-08 | Belleville Bulls | OHL | 56 | 24 | 36 | 60 | 41 | 21 | 7 | 11 | 18 | 20 |
| 2008-09 | Belleville Bulls | OHL | 55 | 38 | 50 | 88 | 61 | 16 | 8 | 13 | 21 | 12 |

Traded to **Pittsburgh** by **Anaheim** with Chris Kunitz for Ryan Whitney, February 26, 2009.

## TARDY, Maxwell (TAHR-dee, MAX-wehl) ST.L.

Center. Shoots right. 5'11", 173 lbs. Born, Duluth, MN, October 27, 1990.
(St. Louis' 6th choice, 202nd overall, in 2009 Entry Draft).

| | | | Regular Season | | | | | Playoffs | | | | |
|---|---|---|---|---|---|---|---|---|---|---|---|---|
| Season | Club | League | GP | G | A | Pts | PIM | GP | G | A | Pts | PIM |
| 2007-08 | Duluth East | High-MN | 9 | 1 | 3 | 4 | 8 | .... | .... | .... | .... | .... |
| 2008-09 | Duluth East | High-MN | 30 | 35 | 25 | 60 | 24 | .... | .... | .... | .... | .... |
| | Team North | UMHSEL | 24 | 19 | 20 | 39 | .... | .... | .... | .... | .... | .... |

• Signed Letter of Intent to attend **University of Minnesota-Duluth** (WCHA) in fall of 2010.

## TARKIR, Zach (TAHR-kihr, ZAK)

Defense. Shoots right. 6'1", 195 lbs. Born, Fresno, CA, June 28, 1984.
(New Jersey's 4th choice, 167th overall, in 2003 Entry Draft).

| | | | Regular Season | | | | | Playoffs | | | | |
|---|---|---|---|---|---|---|---|---|---|---|---|---|
| Season | Club | League | GP | G | A | Pts | PIM | GP | G | A | Pts | PIM |
| 2001-02 | Great Falls | AWHL | 24 | 3 | 5 | 8 | .... | 8 | 0 | 3 | 3 | .... |
| 2002-03 | Chilliwack Chiefs | BCHL | 53 | 5 | 28 | 33 | 86 | .... | .... | .... | .... | .... |
| 2003-04 | Northern Mich. | CCHA | 36 | 2 | 3 | 5 | 40 | .... | .... | .... | .... | .... |
| 2004-05 | Northern Mich. | CCHA | 35 | 2 | 8 | 10 | 51 | .... | .... | .... | .... | .... |
| 2005-06 | Northern Mich. | CCHA | 39 | 3 | 11 | 14 | 57 | .... | .... | .... | .... | .... |
| 2006-07 | Northern Mich. | CCHA | 41 | 7 | 13 | 20 | 46 | .... | .... | .... | .... | .... |
| | Lowell Devils | AHL | 2 | 0 | 0 | 0 | 0 | .... | .... | .... | .... | .... |
| 2007-08 | Lowell Devils | AHL | 11 | 0 | 5 | 5 | 2 | .... | .... | .... | .... | .... |
| | Trenton Devils | ECHL | 49 | 1 | 14 | 15 | 32 | .... | .... | .... | .... | .... |
| 2008-09 | Portland Pirates | AHL | 32 | 3 | 4 | 7 | 20 | .... | .... | .... | .... | .... |
| | South Carolina | ECHL | 24 | 1 | 7 | 8 | 29 | 23 | 5 | 10 | 15 | 24 |

## TASSONE, Matthew (tah-SOH-nee, MA-thew) DAL.

Center. Shoots left. 6', 200 lbs. Born, Edmonton, Alta., September 28, 1989.
(Dallas' 4th choice, 176th overall, in 2008 Entry Draft).

| | | | Regular Season | | | | | Playoffs | | | | |
|---|---|---|---|---|---|---|---|---|---|---|---|---|
| Season | Club | League | GP | G | A | Pts | PIM | GP | G | A | Pts | PIM |
| 2005-06 | Ft. Saskatchewan | AMHL | 25 | 14 | 19 | 33 | 91 | 12 | 4 | 8 | 12 | 24 |
| | Swift Current | WHL | 4 | 0 | 1 | 1 | 0 | .... | .... | .... | .... | .... |
| 2006-07 | Swift Current | WHL | 38 | 6 | 2 | 8 | 60 | .... | .... | .... | .... | .... |
| 2007-08 | Swift Current | WHL | 60 | 19 | 17 | 36 | 111 | 12 | 3 | 5 | 8 | 12 |
| 2008-09 | Swift Current | WHL | 52 | 36 | 19 | 55 | 100 | .... | .... | .... | .... | .... |

## TATAR, Tomas (TAH-tahr, TAW-mahsh) DET.

Center. Shoots left. 5'11", 176 lbs. Born, Ilava, Czechoslovakia, December 1, 1990.
(Detroit's 2nd choice, 60th overall, in 2009 Entry Draft).

| | | | Regular Season | | | | | Playoffs | | | | |
|---|---|---|---|---|---|---|---|---|---|---|---|---|
| Season | Club | League | GP | G | A | Pts | PIM | GP | G | A | Pts | PIM |
| 2004-05 | Dubnica U18 | Svk-U18 | 1 | 0 | 0 | 0 | 0 | .... | .... | .... | .... | .... |
| 2005-06 | Dubnica U18 | Svk-U18 | 43 | 11 | 15 | 26 | 18 | .... | .... | .... | .... | .... |
| 2006-07 | Dubnica Jr. | Slovak-Jr. | 6 | 3 | 0 | 3 | 2 | .... | .... | .... | .... | .... |
| | Dukla Trencin U18 | Svk-U18 | 48 | 33 | 44 | 77 | 42 | .... | .... | .... | .... | .... |
| 2007-08 | Dukla Trencin U18 | Svk-U18 | 4 | 9 | 4 | 13 | 0 | .... | .... | .... | .... | .... |
| | Dukla Trencin Jr. | Slovak-Jr. | 42 | 41 | 35 | 76 | 32 | .... | .... | .... | .... | .... |
| 2008-09 | HC 07 Detva | Slovak-2 | 1 | 1 | 1 | 2 | 2 | .... | .... | .... | .... | .... |
| | HKm Zvolen | Slovakia | 48 | 7 | 8 | 15 | 20 | 13 | 5 | 3 | 8 | 4 |

## TAVARES, John (tah-VAHR-ehs, JAWN) NYI

Center. Shoots left. 6', 195 lbs. Born, Mississauga, Ont., September 20, 1990.
(NY Islanders' 1st choice, 1st overall, in 2009 Entry Draft).

| | | | Regular Season | | | | | Playoffs | | | | |
|---|---|---|---|---|---|---|---|---|---|---|---|---|
| Season | Club | League | GP | G | A | Pts | PIM | GP | G | A | Pts | PIM |
| 2004-05 | Toronto Marlboros | GTHL | 72 | 91 | 67 | 158 | .... | .... | .... | .... | .... | .... |
| | Milton Icehawks | OPJHL | 20 | 13 | 15 | 28 | 10 | .... | .... | .... | .... | .... |
| 2005-06 | Oshawa Generals | OHL | 65 | 45 | 32 | 77 | 72 | .... | .... | .... | .... | .... |
| 2006-07 | Oshawa Generals | OHL | 67 | 72 | 62 | 134 | 60 | 9 | 7 | 12 | 19 | 6 |
| 2007-08 | Oshawa Generals | OHL | 59 | 40 | 78 | 118 | 69 | 15 | 3 | 13 | 16 | 20 |
| 2008-09 | Oshawa Generals | OHL | 32 | *26 | 28 | *54 | 32 | .... | .... | .... | .... | .... |
| | London Knights | OHL | 24 | *32 | 18 | *50 | 22 | 14 | 10 | 11 | 21 | 8 |

Canadian Major Junior Rookie of the Year (2006) • OHL First All-Star Team (2007) • Canadian Major Junior First All-Star Team (2007, 2009) • Canadian Major Junior Player of the Year (2007) • OHL Second All-Star Team (2009)

## TAYLOR, Justin (TAY-luhr, JUHS-tihn)

Center. Shoots left. 5'11", 184 lbs. Born, London, Ont., February 8, 1989.
(Washington's 8th choice, 180th overall, in 2007 Entry Draft).

| | | | Regular Season | | | | | Playoffs | | | | |
|---|---|---|---|---|---|---|---|---|---|---|---|---|
| Season | Club | League | GP | G | A | Pts | PIM | GP | G | A | Pts | PIM |
| 2005-06 | Wellington Dukes | OPJHL | 48 | 18 | 13 | 31 | 12 | 12 | 0 | 3 | 3 | 8 |
| 2006-07 | Wellington Dukes | OPJHL | 37 | 20 | 32 | 52 | 36 | .... | .... | .... | .... | .... |
| | London Knights | OHL | 31 | 6 | 12 | 18 | 18 | 16 | 4 | 6 | 10 | 17 |
| 2007-08 | London Knights | OHL | 68 | 26 | 29 | 55 | 79 | 5 | 0 | 0 | 0 | 5 |
| 2008-09 | London Knights | OHL | 64 | 37 | 30 | 67 | 104 | 14 | 6 | 6 | 12 | 12 |

## TAYLOR, Max (TAY-luhr, MAX)

Center. Shoots left. 5'10", 185 lbs. Born, Ottawa, Ont., December 20, 1983.

| | | | Regular Season | | | | | Playoffs | | | | |
|---|---|---|---|---|---|---|---|---|---|---|---|---|
| Season | Club | League | GP | G | A | Pts | PIM | GP | G | A | Pts | PIM |
| 2003-04 | St. Lawrence | ECAC | 35 | 1 | 6 | 7 | 10 | .... | .... | .... | .... | .... |
| 2004-05 | St. Lawrence | ECAC | 37 | 11 | 15 | 26 | 18 | .... | .... | .... | .... | .... |
| 2005-06 | St. Lawrence | ECAC | 34 | 4 | 11 | 15 | 24 | .... | .... | .... | .... | .... |
| 2006-07 | St. Lawrence | ECAC | 39 | 13 | 18 | 31 | 32 | .... | .... | .... | .... | .... |
| 2007-08 | Texas Wildcatters | ECHL | 59 | 25 | 20 | 45 | 51 | 6 | 5 | 6 | 11 | 10 |
| | Toronto Marlies | AHL | 13 | 2 | 3 | 5 | 28 | .... | .... | .... | .... | .... |
| 2008-09 | Toronto Marlies | AHL | 15 | 6 | 2 | 8 | 4 | .... | .... | .... | .... | .... |
| | Reading Royals | ECHL | 4 | 5 | 0 | 5 | 0 | .... | .... | .... | .... | .... |

Signed as a free agent by **Toronto** (AHL), March 11, 2008. • Missed majority of 2008-09 season recovering from a head injury.

## TEDENBY, Mattias (TEH-dehn-bew, muh-TIGH-uhs) N.J.

Left wing. Shoots left. 5'10", 175 lbs. Born, Vetlanda, Sweden, February 21, 1990.
(New Jersey's 1st choice, 24th overall, in 2008 Entry Draft).

| | | | Regular Season | | | | | Playoffs | | | | |
|---|---|---|---|---|---|---|---|---|---|---|---|---|
| Season | Club | League | GP | G | A | Pts | PIM | GP | G | A | Pts | PIM |
| 2005-06 | HV 71 U18 | Swe-U18 | 13 | 8 | 7 | 15 | 24 | 5 | 1 | 0 | 1 | 10 |
| 2006-07 | HV 71 U18 | Swe-U18 | 2 | 4 | 0 | 4 | 2 | 5 | 7 | 2 | 9 | 14 |
| | HV 71 Jr. | Swe-Jr. | 27 | 10 | 10 | 20 | 43 | 4 | 3 | 1 | 4 | 2 |
| 2007-08 | HV 71 U18 | Swe-U18 | 1 | 1 | 0 | 1 | 0 | .... | .... | .... | .... | .... |
| | HV 71 Jr. | Swe-Jr. | 25 | 14 | 16 | 30 | 14 | 2 | 0 | 0 | 0 | 0 |
| | HV 71 Jonkoping | Sweden | 23 | 3 | 3 | 6 | 6 | 5 | 0 | 0 | 0 | 0 |
| 2008-09 | IK Oskarshamn | Sweden-2 | 13 | 2 | 9 | 11 | 6 | .... | .... | .... | .... | .... |
| | HV 71 Jonkoping | Sweden | 32 | 3 | 1 | 4 | 6 | 18 | 6 | 3 | 9 | 6 |

**TENKANEN, Valtteri** (TEHN-kah-nehn, vahl-TEH-ree) **L.A.**

Center. Shoots left. 5'11", 182 lbs. Born, Jamsa, Finland, March 27, 1985.
(Los Angeles' 10th choice, 264th overall, in 2004 Entry Draft).

| | | | Regular Season | | | | | Playoffs | | | | |
|---|---|---|---|---|---|---|---|---|---|---|---|---|
| Season | Club | League | GP | G | A | Pts | PIM | GP | G | A | Pts | PIM |
| 2001-02 | JYP Jyvaskyla U18 | Fin-U18 | 25 | 14 | 12 | 26 | 2 | 7 | 1 | 0 | 1 | 0 |
| | JYP Jyvaskyla Jr. | Fin-Jr. | 3 | 0 | 1 | 1 | 0 | .... | .... | .... | .... | .... |
| 2002-03 | JYP Jyvaskyla U18 | Fin-U18 | 1 | 2 | 1 | 3 | 0 | .... | .... | .... | .... | .... |
| | JYP Jyvaskyla Jr. | Fin-Jr. | 30 | 8 | 7 | 15 | 14 | 4 | 1 | 1 | 2 | 0 |
| 2003-04 | Suomi U20 | Finland-2 | 2 | 0 | 1 | 1 | 0 | .... | .... | .... | .... | .... |
| | JYP Jyvaskyla Jr. | Fin-Jr. | 10 | 3 | 2 | 5 | 2 | 9 | 2 | 3 | 5 | 0 |
| | JYP Jyvaskyla | Finland | 25 | 1 | 3 | 4 | 2 | 2 | 0 | 0 | 0 | 0 |
| 2004-05 | JYP Jyvaskyla Jr. | Fin-Jr. | 12 | 1 | 5 | 6 | 14 | 6 | 2 | 1 | 3 | 25 |
| | JYP Jyvaskyla | Finland | 10 | 0 | 1 | 1 | 0 | .... | .... | .... | .... | .... |
| 2005-06 | JYP Jyvaskyla | Finland | 35 | 0 | 6 | 6 | 4 | 3 | 0 | 1 | 1 | 0 |
| 2006-07 | JYP Jyvaskyla | Finland | 34 | 4 | 9 | 13 | 4 | .... | .... | .... | .... | .... |
| 2007-08 | JYP Jyvaskyla | Finland | 13 | 0 | 0 | 0 | 2 | .... | .... | .... | .... | .... |
| | SaiPa | Finland | 25 | 3 | 6 | 9 | 29 | .... | .... | .... | .... | .... |
| | SaPKo Savonlinna | Finland-2 | 2 | 1 | 3 | 4 | 0 | .... | .... | .... | .... | .... |
| 2008-09 | SaiPa | Finland | 36 | 6 | 3 | 9 | 4 | 3 | 0 | 0 | 0 | 0 |

**TERESCHENKO, Alexei** (teh-reh-SHEHN-koh, al-EHX-ay) **DAL.**

Center. Shoots left. 5'11", 176 lbs. Born, Mozhaisk, USSR, December 16, 1980.
(Dallas' 4th choice, 91st overall, in 2000 Entry Draft).

| | | | Regular Season | | | | | Playoffs | | | | |
|---|---|---|---|---|---|---|---|---|---|---|---|---|
| Season | Club | League | GP | G | A | Pts | PIM | GP | G | A | Pts | PIM |
| 1996-97 | Dyn'o Moscow 2 | Russia-3 | 9 | 0 | 0 | 0 | 2 | .... | .... | .... | .... | .... |
| 1997-98 | Dynamo Moscow | Russia | 26 | 6 | 7 | 13 | 30 | .... | .... | .... | .... | .... |
| 1998-99 | Dyn'o Moscow 2 | Russia-3 | 28 | 4 | 17 | 21 | 20 | .... | .... | .... | .... | .... |
| | THK Tver | Russia-2 | 12 | 3 | 4 | 7 | 4 | .... | .... | .... | .... | .... |
| | Dynamo Moscow | Russia | 1 | 0 | 1 | 1 | 0 | 2 | 0 | 0 | 0 | 0 |
| 99-2000 | Dynamo Moscow | Russia | 27 | 1 | 1 | 2 | 10 | 17 | 1 | 1 | 2 | 8 |
| 2000-01 | Dynamo Moscow | Russia | 39 | 3 | 2 | 5 | 18 | .... | .... | .... | .... | .... |
| 2001-02 | Yaroslavl 2 | Russia-3 | 1 | 0 | 0 | 0 | 0 | .... | .... | .... | .... | .... |
| | Dynamo Moscow | Russia | 40 | 3 | 6 | 9 | 20 | 3 | 0 | 0 | 0 | 0 |
| 2002-03 | Dynamo Moscow | Russia | 40 | 7 | 9 | 16 | 14 | 5 | 1 | 0 | 1 | 2 |
| 2003-04 | Dynamo Moscow | Russia | 47 | 8 | 12 | 20 | 26 | 3 | 0 | 0 | 0 | 4 |
| 2004-05 | Dynamo Moscow | Russia | 31 | 3 | 6 | 9 | 8 | 10 | 0 | 1 | 1 | 2 |
| 2005-06 | Ak Bars Kazan | Russia | 36 | 3 | 12 | 15 | 12 | 10 | 0 | 4 | 4 | 12 |
| 2006-07 | Ak Bars Kazan | Russia | 53 | 8 | 22 | 30 | 38 | 16 | 3 | 6 | 9 | 6 |
| 2007-08 | Ufa | Russia | 51 | 16 | 24 | 40 | 22 | 16 | 5 | 4 | 9 | 6 |
| 2008-09 | Ufa | Rus-KHL | 55 | 29 | 29 | 58 | 22 | 4 | 0 | 1 | 1 | 8 |

**TERNAVSKY, Artem** (tuhr-NAV-skee, AHR-tehm) **WSH.**

Defense. Shoots left. 6'2", 208 lbs. Born, Magnitogorsk, USSR, June 2, 1983.
(Washington's 4th choice, 160th overall, in 2001 Entry Draft).

| | | | Regular Season | | | | | Playoffs | | | | |
|---|---|---|---|---|---|---|---|---|---|---|---|---|
| Season | Club | League | GP | G | A | Pts | PIM | GP | G | A | Pts | PIM |
| 99-2000 | CSKA Moscow 2 | Russia-3 | 2 | 0 | 1 | 1 | 0 | .... | .... | .... | .... | .... |
| | HK Moscow 2 | Russia-3 | 25 | 0 | 4 | 4 | 42 | .... | .... | .... | .... | .... |
| 2000-01 | Sherbrooke | QMJHL | 65 | 3 | 15 | 18 | 143 | .... | .... | .... | .... | .... |
| 2001-02 | Mostovik Kurgan | Russia-2 | 25 | 0 | 0 | 0 | 46 | .... | .... | .... | .... | .... |
| 2002-03 | Sibir Novosibirsk | Russia | 42 | 1 | 1 | 2 | 20 | .... | .... | .... | .... | .... |
| 2003-04 | Ufa | Russia | 12 | 0 | 0 | 0 | 4 | .... | .... | .... | .... | .... |
| | Magnitogorsk 2 | Russia-3 | 7 | 1 | 0 | 1 | 0 | .... | .... | .... | .... | .... |
| 2004-05 | Nizhny Novgorod | Russia-2 | 16 | 0 | 1 | 1 | 18 | .... | .... | .... | .... | .... |
| | Motor Barnaul | Russia-2 | 8 | 0 | 1 | 1 | 14 | .... | .... | .... | .... | .... |
| 2005-06 | Karaganda | Kazakh. | 17 | 1 | 1 | 2 | 12 | .... | .... | .... | .... | .... |
| | Karaganda | Russia-2 | 39 | 3 | 2 | 5 | 26 | 6 | 0 | 1 | 1 | 2 |
| 2006-07 | Gazovik Tyumen | Russia-2 | 56 | 3 | 12 | 15 | 78 | 3 | 1 | 0 | 1 | 4 |
| | Ust-Kamenogorsk | Kazakh. | 14 | 3 | 2 | 5 | 12 | .... | .... | .... | .... | .... |
| 2007-08 | Novokuznetsk | Russia | 56 | 6 | 7 | 13 | 46 | .... | .... | .... | .... | .... |
| 2008-09 | CSKA Moscow | Rus-KHL | 53 | 4 | 3 | 7 | 40 | 8 | 0 | 0 | 0 | 8 |

**TERRY, Chris** (TAIR-ee, KRIHS) **CAR.**

Left wing. Shoots left. 5'10", 190 lbs. Born, Brampton, Ont., April 7, 1989.
(Carolina's 4th choice, 132nd overall, in 2007 Entry Draft).

| | | | Regular Season | | | | | Playoffs | | | | |
|---|---|---|---|---|---|---|---|---|---|---|---|---|
| Season | Club | League | GP | G | A | Pts | PIM | GP | G | A | Pts | PIM |
| 2003-04 | Markham | GTHL | 66 | 39 | 50 | 89 | .... | .... | .... | .... | .... | .... |
| 2004-05 | Markham | GTHL | 60 | 42 | 53 | 95 | 113 | 9 | 0 | 9 | 9 | 14 |
| 2005-06 | Plymouth Whalers | OHL | 64 | 9 | 19 | 28 | 72 | 11 | 3 | 2 | 5 | 4 |
| 2006-07 | Plymouth Whalers | OHL | 68 | 22 | 44 | 66 | 98 | 20 | 8 | 10 | 18 | 21 |
| 2007-08 | Plymouth Whalers | OHL | 68 | 44 | 57 | 101 | 107 | 4 | 4 | 3 | 7 | 6 |
| | Albany River Rats | AHL | 1 | 0 | 0 | 0 | 0 | .... | .... | .... | .... | .... |
| 2008-09 | Plymouth Whalers | OHL | 53 | 39 | 55 | 94 | 75 | 11 | 7 | 9 | 16 | 18 |

**TESSIER, Kelsey** (TEHS-ee-ay, KEHL-see) **COL.**

Center. Shoots right. 5'9", 168 lbs. Born, Moncton, N.B., January 16, 1990.
(Colorado's 3rd choice, 110th overall, in 2008 Entry Draft).

| | | | Regular Season | | | | | Playoffs | | | | |
|---|---|---|---|---|---|---|---|---|---|---|---|---|
| Season | Club | League | GP | G | A | Pts | PIM | GP | G | A | Pts | PIM |
| 2005-06 | Colorado Outlaws | Minor-CO | STATISTICS NOT AVAILABLE | | | | | | | | | |
| 2006-07 | Quebec Remparts | QMJHL | 63 | 23 | 27 | 50 | 40 | 5 | 1 | 5 | 6 | 0 |
| 2007-08 | Quebec Remparts | QMJHL | 68 | 36 | 45 | 81 | 73 | 11 | 8 | 7 | 15 | 10 |
| 2008-09 | Quebec Remparts | QMJHL | 64 | 25 | 35 | 60 | 43 | 17 | 9 | 2 | 11 | 21 |

**TEUBERT, Colten** (TEW-buhrt, KOHL-tuhn) **L.A.**

Defense. Shoots right. 6'4", 187 lbs. Born, White Rock, B.C., March 8, 1990.
(Los Angeles' 2nd choice, 13th overall, in 2008 Entry Draft).

| | | | Regular Season | | | | | Playoffs | | | | |
|---|---|---|---|---|---|---|---|---|---|---|---|---|
| Season | Club | League | GP | G | A | Pts | PIM | GP | G | A | Pts | PIM |
| 2005-06 | South West Hawks | Minor-BC | 29 | 8 | 12 | 20 | 122 | .... | .... | .... | .... | .... |
| | Regina Pats | WHL | 14 | 0 | 2 | 2 | 16 | 6 | 0 | 1 | 1 | 4 |
| 2006-07 | Regina Pats | WHL | 63 | 3 | 8 | 11 | 91 | 10 | 0 | 1 | 1 | 13 |
| 2007-08 | Regina Pats | WHL | 66 | 7 | 16 | 23 | 135 | 6 | 1 | 4 | 5 | 6 |
| 2008-09 | Regina Pats | WHL | 60 | 12 | 25 | 37 | 136 | .... | .... | .... | .... | .... |
| | Ontario Reign | ECHL | 8 | 0 | 1 | 1 | 10 | 6 | 0 | 1 | 1 | 19 |

**THANG, Ryan** (THAYNG, RIGH-uhn) **NSH.**

Left wing. Shoots right. 5'11", 189 lbs. Born, Chicago, IL, May 11, 1987.
(Nashville's 4th choice, 81st overall, in 2007 Entry Draft).

| | | | Regular Season | | | | | Playoffs | | | | |
|---|---|---|---|---|---|---|---|---|---|---|---|---|
| Season | Club | League | GP | G | A | Pts | PIM | GP | G | A | Pts | PIM |
| 2004-05 | Sioux Falls | USHL | 58 | 9 | 22 | 31 | 45 | .... | .... | .... | .... | .... |
| 2005-06 | Sioux Falls | USHL | 32 | 8 | 14 | 22 | 52 | .... | .... | .... | .... | .... |
| | Omaha Lancers | USHL | 25 | 15 | 15 | 30 | 26 | 5 | 2 | 1 | 3 | 2 |
| 2006-07 | U. of Notre Dame | CCHA | 42 | 20 | 21 | 41 | 22 | .... | .... | .... | .... | .... |
| 2007-08 | U. of Notre Dame | CCHA | 47 | 18 | 14 | 32 | 48 | .... | .... | .... | .... | .... |
| 2008-09 | U. of Notre Dame | CCHA | 33 | 10 | 9 | 19 | 36 | .... | .... | .... | .... | .... |

CCHA All-Rookie Team (2007)

**THURESSON, Andreas** (THUR-reh-suhn, an-DRAY-uhs) **NSH.**

Center. Shoots right. 6'1", 204 lbs. Born, Kristianstad, Sweden, November 18, 1987.
(Nashville's 7th choice, 144th overall, in 2007 Entry Draft).

| | | | Regular Season | | | | | Playoffs | | | | |
|---|---|---|---|---|---|---|---|---|---|---|---|---|
| Season | Club | League | GP | G | A | Pts | PIM | GP | G | A | Pts | PIM |
| 2003-04 | Malmo U18 | Swe-U18 | 3 | 0 | 0 | 0 | 4 | .... | .... | .... | .... | .... |
| | Tyringe SoSS | Sweden-3 | 12 | 0 | 1 | 1 | 0 | .... | .... | .... | .... | .... |
| | Malmo Jr. | Swe-Jr. | 19 | 2 | 2 | 4 | 16 | 8 | 0 | 0 | 0 | 6 |
| 2004-05 | Malmo U18 | Swe-U18 | 3 | 1 | 1 | 2 | 4 | .... | .... | .... | .... | .... |
| | Malmo Jr. | Swe-Jr. | 30 | 4 | 4 | 8 | 28 | 3 | 2 | 1 | 3 | 2 |
| 2005-06 | Malmo U18 | Swe-U18 | 2 | 1 | 0 | 1 | 4 | .... | .... | .... | .... | .... |
| | Malmo Jr. | Swe-Jr. | 38 | 15 | 18 | 33 | 71 | .... | .... | .... | .... | .... |
| | Malmo | Sweden-2 | 20 | 0 | 2 | 2 | 10 | .... | .... | .... | .... | .... |
| 2006-07 | Malmo | Sweden | 48 | 10 | 5 | 15 | 26 | .... | .... | .... | .... | .... |
| | Malmo | Sweden-Q | 10 | 2 | 2 | 4 | 2 | .... | .... | .... | .... | .... |
| 2007-08 | Milwaukee | AHL | 77 | 11 | 7 | 18 | 37 | 6 | 0 | 0 | 0 | 4 |
| 2008-09 | Milwaukee | AHL | 74 | 14 | 15 | 29 | 32 | 11 | 3 | 1 | 4 | 4 |

**TIMMINS, Scott** (TIHM-mihnz, SKAWT) **FLA.**

Center. Shoots left. 5'11", 191 lbs. Born, Hamilton, Ont., September 11, 1989.
(Florida's 7th choice, 165th overall, in 2009 Entry Draft).

| | | | Regular Season | | | | | Playoffs | | | | |
|---|---|---|---|---|---|---|---|---|---|---|---|---|
| Season | Club | League | GP | G | A | Pts | PIM | GP | G | A | Pts | PIM |
| 2005-06 | Burlington | OPJHL | 31 | 8 | 4 | 12 | 8 | 4 | 1 | 1 | 2 | 0 |
| 2006-07 | Kitchener Rangers | OHL | 42 | 2 | 5 | 7 | 8 | .... | .... | .... | .... | .... |
| 2007-08 | Kitchener Rangers | OHL | 62 | 17 | 12 | 29 | 46 | 20 | 3 | 5 | 8 | 10 |
| 2008-09 | Kitchener Rangers | OHL | 38 | 25 | 24 | 49 | 28 | .... | .... | .... | .... | .... |
| | Windsor Spitfires | OHL | 28 | 10 | 14 | 24 | 33 | 20 | 6 | 10 | 16 | 26 |

**TKACHENKO, Ivan** (t'kuh-CHEHN-koh, ee-VAHN) **CBJ**

Left wing. Shoots left. 5'10", 187 lbs. Born, Yaroslavl, USSR, November 9, 1979.
(Columbus' 5th choice, 98th overall, in 2002 Entry Draft).

| | | | Regular Season | | | | | Playoffs | | | | |
|---|---|---|---|---|---|---|---|---|---|---|---|---|
| Season | Club | League | GP | G | A | Pts | PIM | GP | G | A | Pts | PIM |
| 1997-98 | Yaroslavl 2 | Russia-2 | STATISTICS NOT AVAILABLE | | | | | | | | | |
| | Torpedo Yaroslavl | Russia | .... | .... | .... | .... | .... | 1 | 0 | 0 | 0 | 0 |
| 1998-99 | Yaroslavl 2 | Russia-3 | 28 | 15 | 13 | 28 | 26 | .... | .... | .... | .... | .... |
| 99-2000 | Yaroslavl 2 | Russia-3 | 1 | 1 | 0 | 1 | 0 | .... | .... | .... | .... | .... |
| | Motor Zavolzhje | Russia-2 | 43 | 15 | 14 | 29 | 22 | .... | .... | .... | .... | .... |
| | Nizhnekamsk 2 | Russia-3 | 8 | 6 | 3 | 9 | 24 | .... | .... | .... | .... | .... |
| | Nizhnekamsk | Russia | 5 | 1 | 0 | 1 | 0 | 4 | 0 | 1 | 1 | 0 |
| 2000-01 | Nizhnekamsk | Russia | 28 | 2 | 2 | 4 | 14 | 4 | 0 | 1 | 1 | 0 |
| 2001-02 | Yaroslavl 2 | Russia-3 | 1 | 0 | 1 | 1 | 2 | .... | .... | .... | .... | .... |
| | Yaroslavl | Russia | 44 | 13 | 20 | 33 | 57 | 9 | 5 | 2 | 7 | 4 |
| 2002-03 | Yaroslavl | Russia | 44 | 11 | 6 | 17 | 57 | 10 | 2 | 3 | 5 | 6 |
| 2003-04 | Yaroslavl | Russia | 56 | 7 | 11 | 18 | 22 | 3 | 0 | 0 | 0 | 0 |
| 2004-05 | Yaroslavl | Russia | 59 | 15 | 15 | 30 | 30 | 9 | 2 | 3 | 5 | 8 |
| 2005-06 | Yaroslavl | Russia | 45 | 10 | 21 | 31 | 30 | 11 | 1 | 2 | 3 | 16 |
| | Yaroslavl 2 | Russia-3 | 1 | 0 | 1 | 1 | 2 | .... | .... | .... | .... | .... |
| 2006-07 | Yaroslavl | Russia | 52 | 9 | 24 | 33 | 30 | 7 | 1 | 2 | 3 | 6 |
| 2007-08 | Yaroslavl | Russia | 56 | 14 | 15 | 29 | 34 | 16 | 1 | 3 | 4 | 6 |
| 2008-09 | Yaroslavl | Rus-KHL | 56 | 14 | 13 | 27 | 40 | 19 | 3 | 5 | 8 | 10 |

**TOCHKIN, Kellan** (TAWCH-kihn, KEHL-uhn) **VAN.**

Right wing. Shoots right. 5'9", 170 lbs. Born, Abbotsford, B.C., February 15, 1991.

| | | | Regular Season | | | | | Playoffs | | | | |
|---|---|---|---|---|---|---|---|---|---|---|---|---|
| Season | Club | League | GP | G | A | Pts | PIM | GP | G | A | Pts | PIM |
| 2006-07 | Fraser Valley | Minor-BC | 37 | 34 | 34 | 68 | 48 | .... | .... | .... | .... | .... |
| | Everett Silvertips | WHL | 3 | 0 | 0 | 0 | 2 | .... | .... | .... | .... | .... |
| 2007-08 | Ridge Meadow | PIJHL | 32 | 24 | 35 | 59 | 56 | 10 | 3 | 8 | 11 | 2 |
| | Langley Chiefs | BCHL | 1 | 0 | 1 | 1 | 0 | .... | .... | .... | .... | .... |
| 2008-09 | Everett Silvertips | WHL | 72 | 20 | 54 | 74 | 37 | 2 | 1 | 0 | 1 | 2 |

Signed as a free agent by **Vancouver**, July 27, 2009.

**TOEWS, David** (TAYVZ, DAY-vihd) **NYI**

Center. Shoots right. 5'10", 175 lbs. Born, Winnipeg, Man., June 7, 1990.
(NY Islanders' 5th choice, 66th overall, in 2008 Entry Draft).

| | | | Regular Season | | | | | Playoffs | | | | |
|---|---|---|---|---|---|---|---|---|---|---|---|---|
| Season | Club | League | GP | G | A | Pts | PIM | GP | G | A | Pts | PIM |
| 2005-06 | Colorado Outlaws | Minor-CO | STATISTICS NOT AVAILABLE | | | | | | | | | |
| 2006-07 | Shat.-St. Mary's | High-MN | 61 | 34 | 47 | 81 | 52 | .... | .... | .... | .... | .... |
| 2007-08 | Shat.-St. Mary's | High-MN | 51 | 44 | 56 | 100 | 20 | .... | .... | .... | .... | .... |
| 2008-09 | North Dakota | WCHA | 23 | 5 | 6 | 11 | 4 | .... | .... | .... | .... | .... |

**TOPOL, Sergei** (TOH-puhl, SAIR-gay) **VAN.**

Center. Shoots left. 6'2", 183 lbs. Born, Omsk, USSR, February 15, 1985.
(Vancouver's 8th choice, 252nd overall, in 2003 Entry Draft).

| | | | Regular Season | | | | | Playoffs | | | | |
|---|---|---|---|---|---|---|---|---|---|---|---|---|
| Season | Club | League | GP | G | A | Pts | PIM | GP | G | A | Pts | PIM |
| 2002-03 | Omsk 2 | Russia-3 | 45 | 16 | 5 | 21 | 18 | .... | .... | .... | .... | .... |
| 2003-04 | Omsk 2 | Russia-3 | 39 | 25 | 14 | 39 | 10 | .... | .... | .... | .... | .... |
| | Avangard Omsk | Russia | 9 | 0 | 0 | 0 | 2 | .... | .... | .... | .... | .... |
| 2004-05 | Mechel | Russia-2 | 19 | 1 | 0 | 1 | 6 | .... | .... | .... | .... | .... |
| | Mechel 2 | Russia-3 | 5 | 2 | 1 | 3 | 8 | .... | .... | .... | .... | .... |
| | Omsk 2 | Russia-3 | 18 | 6 | 4 | 10 | 4 | .... | .... | .... | .... | .... |
| | Avangard Omsk | Russia | 2 | 1 | 0 | 1 | 0 | .... | .... | .... | .... | .... |
| 2005-06 | Omsk 2 | Russia-3 | 33 | 24 | 15 | 39 | 26 | .... | .... | .... | .... | .... |
| | Avangard Omsk | Russia | 17 | 1 | 0 | 1 | 12 | .... | .... | .... | .... | .... |
| 2006-07 | Avangard Omsk 2 | Russia-3 | 26 | 18 | 14 | 32 | 30 | .... | .... | .... | .... | .... |
| | Avangard Omsk | Russia | 27 | 0 | 1 | 1 | 12 | 1 | 0 | 0 | 0 | 2 |
| 2007-08 | Avtomobilist | Russia-2 | 16 | 0 | 7 | 7 | 10 | .... | .... | .... | .... | .... |
| | Avtomobilist 2 | Russia-3 | 6 | 6 | 4 | 10 | 14 | .... | .... | .... | .... | .... |
| | Nizhny Tagil | Russia-2 | 6 | 1 | 0 | 1 | 0 | .... | .... | .... | .... | .... |
| 2008-09 | Yermak Angarsk | Russia-2 | 50 | 17 | 8 | 25 | 38 | 4 | 0 | 1 | 1 | 2 |

## TORP, Nichlas (TOHRP, NIHK-luhs) MTL.

Defense. Shoots left. 5'10", 197 lbs. Born, Jonkoping, Sweden, April 10, 1989.
(Montreal's 8th choice, 163rd overall, in 2007 Entry Draft).

| | | | Regular Season | | | | | Playoffs | | | | |
|---|---|---|---|---|---|---|---|---|---|---|---|---|
| Season | Club | League | GP | G | A | Pts | PIM | GP | G | A | Pts | PIM |
| 2004-05 | HV 71 U18 | Swe-U18 | 11 | 5 | 2 | 7 | 20 | .... | .... | .... | .... | .... |
| 2005-06 | HV 71 U18 | Swe-U18 | 8 | 3 | 1 | 4 | 45 | 5 | 1 | 1 | 2 | 12 |
| | HV 71 Jr. | Swe-Jr. | 7 | 0 | 0 | 0 | 34 | .... | .... | .... | .... | .... |
| 2006-07 | HV 71 U18 | Swe-U18 | 1 | 0 | 0 | 0 | 2 | 3 | 1 | 0 | 1 | 43 |
| | HV 71 Jr. | Swe-Jr. | 17 | 3 | 1 | 4 | 42 | 4 | 0 | 2 | 2 | 10 |
| 2007-08 | HV 71 Jonkoping | Sweden | DID NOT PLAY – INJURED | | | | | | | | | |
| 2008-09 | HV 71 Jr. | Swe-Jr. | 4 | 0 | 1 | 1 | 22 | .... | .... | .... | .... | .... |
| | HV 71 Jonkoping | Sweden | 44 | 0 | 2 | 2 | 43 | 12 | 0 | 0 | 0 | 0 |

## TORQUATO, Zack (tohr-KAH-toh, ZAK)

Center. Shoots right. 6', 195 lbs. Born, Sault Ste Marie, Ont., June 8, 1989.
(Detroit's 4th choice, 178th overall, in 2007 Entry Draft).

| | | | Regular Season | | | | | Playoffs | | | | |
|---|---|---|---|---|---|---|---|---|---|---|---|---|
| Season | Club | League | GP | G | A | Pts | PIM | GP | G | A | Pts | PIM |
| 2004-05 | Stratford Cullitons | OJHL-B | 47 | 34 | 41 | 75 | 52 | .... | .... | .... | .... | .... |
| 2005-06 | Saginaw Spirit | OHL | 65 | 19 | 18 | 37 | 56 | 4 | 1 | 0 | 1 | 6 |
| 2006-07 | Saginaw Spirit | OHL | 22 | 10 | 13 | 23 | 24 | .... | .... | .... | .... | .... |
| | Erie Otters | OHL | 43 | 20 | 26 | 46 | 69 | .... | .... | .... | .... | .... |
| 2007-08 | Erie Otters | OHL | 66 | 25 | 42 | 67 | 112 | .... | .... | .... | .... | .... |
| | Grand Rapids | AHL | 11 | 1 | 0 | 1 | 8 | .... | .... | .... | .... | .... |
| 2008-09 | Erie Otters | OHL | 66 | 29 | 34 | 63 | 78 | 5 | 2 | 4 | 6 | 11 |
| | Grand Rapids | AHL | 1 | 0 | 0 | 0 | 0 | .... | .... | .... | .... | .... |

## TREMBLAY, Jonathan (TRAHM-blay, JAWN-ah-thuhn)

Right wing. Shoots right. 6'3", 240 lbs. Born, Fauquier, Ont., March 3, 1984.
(San Jose's 6th choice, 201st overall, in 2003 Entry Draft).

| | | | Regular Season | | | | | Playoffs | | | | |
|---|---|---|---|---|---|---|---|---|---|---|---|---|
| Season | Club | League | GP | G | A | Pts | PIM | GP | G | A | Pts | PIM |
| 2001-02 | Timmins Majors | GNML | STATISTICS NOT AVAILABLE | | | | | | | | | |
| | Acadie-Bathurst | QMJHL | 2 | 0 | 0 | 0 | 5 | 1 | 0 | 0 | 0 | 0 |
| 2002-03 | Acadie-Bathurst | QMJHL | 62 | 0 | 1 | 1 | 232 | 9 | 0 | 0 | 0 | 45 |
| 2003-04 | Acadie-Bathurst | QMJHL | 60 | 3 | 0 | 3 | *316 | .... | .... | .... | .... | .... |
| 2004-05 | Cleveland Barons | AHL | 1 | 0 | 0 | 0 | 0 | .... | .... | .... | .... | .... |
| | Johnstown Chiefs | ECHL | 46 | 2 | 3 | 5 | 136 | .... | .... | .... | .... | .... |
| 2005-06 | Toledo Storm | ECHL | 1 | 0 | 0 | 0 | 0 | .... | .... | .... | .... | .... |
| | Kalamazoo Wings | UHL | 8 | 0 | 0 | 0 | 20 | .... | .... | .... | .... | .... |
| | Quad City | UHL | 37 | 0 | 2 | 2 | 62 | .... | .... | .... | .... | .... |
| 2006-07 | Worcester Sharks | AHL | 3 | 0 | 0 | 0 | 5 | .... | .... | .... | .... | .... |
| | Fresno Falcons | ECHL | 63 | 0 | 2 | 2 | 133 | .... | .... | .... | .... | .... |
| 2007-08 | Worcester Sharks | AHL | 17 | 0 | 1 | 1 | 37 | .... | .... | .... | .... | .... |
| 2008-09 | Quad City Flames | AHL | 5 | 0 | 0 | 0 | 0 | .... | .... | .... | .... | .... |
| | Providence Bruins | AHL | 41 | 1 | 0 | 1 | 63 | .... | .... | .... | .... | .... |
| | Wichita Thunder | CHL | 4 | 0 | 0 | 0 | 14 | .... | .... | .... | .... | .... |

Signed as a free agent by **Quad City** (AHL), July 22, 2008.

## TREMBLAY, Nick (TRAWM-blay, NIHK-oh-las) BOS.

Center. Shoots left. 5'11", 190 lbs. Born, Ottawa, Ont., April 5, 1988.
(Boston's 5th choice, 173rd overall, in 2008 Entry Draft).

| | | | Regular Season | | | | | Playoffs | | | | |
|---|---|---|---|---|---|---|---|---|---|---|---|---|
| Season | Club | League | GP | G | A | Pts | PIM | GP | G | A | Pts | PIM |
| 2005-06 | Champlain College | QJHL | 48 | 13 | 22 | 35 | 36 | 9 | 1 | 1 | 2 | 8 |
| 2006-07 | Champlain College | QJHL | 53 | 26 | 26 | 52 | 58 | 7 | 1 | 2 | 3 | 2 |
| 2007-08 | Smiths Falls Bears | CJHL | 57 | *51 | 59 | *110 | 12 | 9 | 5 | 8 | 13 | 10 |
| 2008-09 | Clarkson Knights | ECAC | 36 | 4 | 7 | 11 | 22 | .... | .... | .... | .... | .... |

## TREVELYAN, T.J. (truh-VEHL-yuhn, TEE-JAY)

Left wing. Shoots left. 5'10", 187 lbs. Born, Mississauga, Ont., March 6, 1984.

| | | | Regular Season | | | | | Playoffs | | | | |
|---|---|---|---|---|---|---|---|---|---|---|---|---|
| Season | Club | League | GP | G | A | Pts | PIM | GP | G | A | Pts | PIM |
| 2002-03 | St. Lawrence | ECAC | 34 | 10 | 12 | 22 | 38 | .... | .... | .... | .... | .... |
| 2003-04 | St. Lawrence | ECAC | 38 | *23 | 16 | 39 | 62 | .... | .... | .... | .... | .... |
| 2004-05 | St. Lawrence | ECAC | 38 | *25 | 20 | 45 | 61 | .... | .... | .... | .... | .... |
| 2005-06 | St. Lawrence | ECAC | 40 | 20 | 28 | *48 | 43 | .... | .... | .... | .... | .... |
| 2006-07 | Providence Bruins | AHL | 60 | 28 | 24 | 52 | 41 | 13 | 3 | 6 | 9 | 12 |
| | Long Beach | ECHL | 15 | 9 | 8 | 17 | 16 | .... | .... | .... | .... | .... |
| 2007-08 | Providence Bruins | AHL | 72 | 18 | 20 | 38 | 23 | 10 | 5 | 3 | 8 | 6 |
| 2008-09 | Iowa Chops | AHL | 76 | 23 | 24 | 47 | 18 | .... | .... | .... | .... | .... |

ECAC First All-Star Team (2005, 2006) • ECAC Player of the Year (2006) • NCAA East First All-American Team (2006)

Signed as a free agent by **Boston**, August 17, 2006.

## TRIVINO, Corey (trih-VEE-noh, KOH-ree) NYI

Center. Shoots left. 6'1", 170 lbs. Born, Etobicoke, Ont., January 12, 1990.
(NY Islanders' 2nd choice, 36th overall, in 2008 Entry Draft).

| | | | Regular Season | | | | | Playoffs | | | | |
|---|---|---|---|---|---|---|---|---|---|---|---|---|
| Season | Club | League | GP | G | A | Pts | PIM | GP | G | A | Pts | PIM |
| 2005-06 | Toronto Marlboros | GTHL | 30 | 17 | 22 | 39 | 4 | .... | .... | .... | .... | .... |
| 2006-07 | Stouffville Spirit | OPJHL | 49 | 24 | 34 | 58 | 24 | 9 | 1 | 6 | 7 | 16 |
| 2007-08 | Stouffville Spirit | OPJHL | 39 | 19 | 50 | 69 | 22 | 15 | 5 | 17 | 22 | 10 |
| 2008-09 | Boston University | H-East | 32 | 6 | 7 | 13 | 14 | .... | .... | .... | .... | .... |

## TROPP, Corey (TROHP, KOHR-ee) BUF.

Right wing. Shoots right. 6', 183 lbs. Born, Grosse Pointe, MI, July 25, 1989.
(Buffalo's 3rd choice, 89th overall, in 2007 Entry Draft).

| | | | Regular Season | | | | | Playoffs | | | | |
|---|---|---|---|---|---|---|---|---|---|---|---|---|
| Season | Club | League | GP | G | A | Pts | PIM | GP | G | A | Pts | PIM |
| 2005-06 | Sioux Falls | USHL | 46 | 7 | 8 | 15 | 21 | 14 | 2 | 3 | 5 | 8 |
| 2006-07 | Sioux Falls | USHL | 54 | 26 | 36 | 62 | 76 | 8 | 4 | 9 | *13 | 0 |
| 2007-08 | Michigan State | CCHA | 42 | 6 | 11 | 17 | 16 | .... | .... | .... | .... | .... |
| 2008-09 | Michigan State | CCHA | 21 | 3 | 8 | 11 | 45 | .... | .... | .... | .... | .... |

## TROTTER, Brock (TRAW-tuhr, BRAWK) MTL.

Center. Shoots right. 5'10", 170 lbs. Born, Brandon, Man., September 18, 1987.

| | | | Regular Season | | | | | Playoffs | | | | |
|---|---|---|---|---|---|---|---|---|---|---|---|---|
| Season | Club | League | GP | G | A | Pts | PIM | GP | G | A | Pts | PIM |
| 2003-04 | Dauphin Kings | MJHL | 63 | 32 | 33 | 65 | 108 | .... | .... | .... | .... | .... |
| 2004-05 | Lincoln Stars | USHL | 60 | 20 | 38 | 58 | 84 | 4 | 2 | 3 | 5 | 0 |
| 2005-06 | U. of Denver | WCHA | 5 | 3 | 2 | 5 | 2 | .... | .... | .... | .... | .... |
| 2006-07 | U. of Denver | WCHA | 40 | 16 | 24 | 40 | 22 | .... | .... | .... | .... | .... |
| 2007-08 | U. of Denver | WCHA | 24 | 13 | 18 | 31 | 18 | .... | .... | .... | .... | .... |
| | Hamilton Bulldogs | AHL | 21 | 3 | 6 | 9 | 4 | .... | .... | .... | .... | .... |
| 2008-09 | Hamilton Bulldogs | AHL | 76 | 18 | 31 | 49 | 32 | 6 | 0 | 1 | 1 | 13 |

• Missed majority of 2005-06 season recovering from achilles tendon injury suffered in game vs. North Dakota (WCHA), October 29, 2005. Signed as a free agent by **Montreal**, February 7, 2008.

## TRUKHNO, Vyacheslav (trookh-NOH, V'YTACH-ih-slav) EDM.

Left wing. Shoots left. 6'1", 197 lbs. Born, Khimki, USSR, February 22, 1987.
(Edmonton's 6th choice, 120th overall, in 2005 Entry Draft).

| | | | Regular Season | | | | | Playoffs | | | | |
|---|---|---|---|---|---|---|---|---|---|---|---|---|
| Season | Club | League | GP | G | A | Pts | PIM | GP | G | A | Pts | PIM |
| 2002-03 | Rungstead IK | Den-2 | 1 | 2 | 3 | 5 | 0 | .... | .... | .... | .... | .... |
| | Rungstead | Denmark | 27 | 7 | 4 | 11 | 8 | 12 | 0 | 1 | 1 | 8 |
| 2003-04 | Rungstead | Denmark | 35 | 12 | 11 | 23 | 18 | 7 | 0 | 0 | 0 | 8 |
| 2004-05 | PEI Rocket | QMJHL | 64 | 25 | 34 | 59 | 57 | .... | .... | .... | .... | .... |
| 2005-06 | PEI Rocket | QMJHL | 60 | 28 | 68 | 96 | 81 | 3 | 2 | 2 | 4 | 0 |
| 2006-07 | Gatineau | QMJHL | 60 | 25 | 77 | 102 | 67 | 5 | 0 | 6 | 6 | 19 |
| 2007-08 | Springfield Falcons | AHL | 64 | 14 | 21 | 35 | 44 | .... | .... | .... | .... | .... |
| 2008-09 | Springfield Falcons | AHL | 56 | 7 | 19 | 26 | 35 | .... | .... | .... | .... | .... |

QMJHL All-Rookie Team (2005) • Canadian Major Junior All-Rookie Team (2005) • QMJHL First All-Star Team (2007)

## TRUNEV, Maxim (troo-NAWF, max-EEM) MTL.

Right wing. Shoots right. 5'11", 174 lbs. Born, Kirovo-Chepetsk, USSR, September 7, 1990.
(Montreal's 4th choice, 138th overall, in 2008 Entry Draft).

| | | | Regular Season | | | | | Playoffs | | | | |
|---|---|---|---|---|---|---|---|---|---|---|---|---|
| Season | Club | League | GP | G | A | Pts | PIM | GP | G | A | Pts | PIM |
| 2005-06 | Cherepovets 2 | Russia-3 | STATISTICS NOT AVAILABLE | | | | | | | | | |
| 2006-07 | Cherepovets 2 | Russia-3 | STATISTICS NOT AVAILABLE | | | | | | | | | |
| 2007-08 | Cherepovets 2 | Russia-3 | STATISTICS NOT AVAILABLE | | | | | | | | | |
| | Cherepovets | Russia | 1 | 0 | 0 | 0 | 0 | .... | .... | .... | .... | .... |
| 2008-09 | Cherepovets | Rus-KHL | 32 | 4 | 1 | 5 | 8 | .... | .... | .... | .... | .... |

## TUOMAINEN, Miikka (too-oh-MAY-nehn, MEE-kah) ATL.

Left wing. Shoots left. 6'3", 207 lbs. Born, Turku, Finland, May 22, 1986.
(Atlanta's 7th choice, 204th overall, in 2004 Entry Draft).

| | | | Regular Season | | | | | Playoffs | | | | |
|---|---|---|---|---|---|---|---|---|---|---|---|---|
| Season | Club | League | GP | G | A | Pts | PIM | GP | G | A | Pts | PIM |
| 2001-02 | TuTo Turku U18 | Fin-U18 | 14 | 8 | 5 | 13 | 14 | .... | .... | .... | .... | .... |
| | TuTo Turku Jr. | Fin-Jr. | 1 | 1 | 0 | 1 | 0 | .... | .... | .... | .... | .... |
| 2002-03 | TuTo Turku U18 | Fin-U18 | 24 | 3 | 4 | 7 | 52 | 4 | 0 | 0 | 0 | 0 |
| | TuTo Turku Jr. | Fin-Jr. | 2 | 0 | 0 | 0 | 4 | .... | .... | .... | .... | .... |
| | TuTo Turku | Finland-2 | 6 | 0 | 0 | 0 | 0 | .... | .... | .... | .... | .... |
| 2003-04 | TuTo Turku Jr. | Fin-Jr. | 20 | 10 | 7 | 17 | 6 | .... | .... | .... | .... | .... |
| | TuTo Turku U18 | Fin-U18 | 20 | 10 | 7 | 17 | 6 | .... | .... | .... | .... | .... |
| | TuTo Turku | Finland-2 | 30 | 4 | 3 | 7 | 2 | .... | .... | .... | .... | .... |
| 2004-05 | TuTo Turku Jr. | Fin-Jr. | 5 | 1 | 4 | 5 | 0 | .... | .... | .... | .... | .... |
| | TuTo Turku | Finland-2 | 42 | 4 | 4 | 8 | 22 | 7 | 1 | 0 | 1 | 2 |
| 2005-06 | Lukko Rauma Jr. | Fin-Jr. | 16 | 5 | 3 | 8 | 4 | 9 | 5 | 3 | 8 | 8 |
| | Suomi U20 | Finland-2 | 2 | 0 | 0 | 0 | 2 | .... | .... | .... | .... | .... |
| | Lukko Rauma | Finland | 33 | 2 | 2 | 4 | 12 | .... | .... | .... | .... | .... |
| 2006-07 | Lukko Rauma Jr. | Fin-Jr. | 5 | 0 | 1 | 1 | 0 | .... | .... | .... | .... | .... |
| | Lukko Rauma | Finland | 54 | 6 | 8 | 14 | 77 | 3 | 1 | 0 | 1 | 0 |
| 2007-08 | Lukko Rauma | Finland | 50 | 1 | 2 | 3 | 55 | 3 | 0 | 0 | 0 | 0 |
| 2008-09 | Lukko Rauma | Finland | 58 | 5 | 10 | 15 | 16 | 6 | 1 | 1 | 2 | 25 |

## TUREK, Ryan (TOOR-ehk, RIGH-uhn) ST.L.

Center. Shoots right. 6', 188 lbs. Born, Southfield, MI, September 22, 1987.
(St. Louis' 5th choice, 94th overall, in 2006 Entry Draft).

| | | | Regular Season | | | | | Playoffs | | | | |
|---|---|---|---|---|---|---|---|---|---|---|---|---|
| Season | Club | League | GP | G | A | Pts | PIM | GP | G | A | Pts | PIM |
| 2004-05 | Omaha Lancers | USHL | 45 | 3 | 8 | 11 | 52 | 4 | 1 | 0 | 1 | 2 |
| 2005-06 | Omaha Lancers | USHL | 52 | 17 | 11 | 28 | 71 | 5 | 1 | 1 | 2 | 2 |
| 2006-07 | Michigan State | CCHA | 31 | 0 | 2 | 2 | 18 | .... | .... | .... | .... | .... |
| 2007-08 | Michigan State | CCHA | 35 | 0 | 5 | 5 | 16 | .... | .... | .... | .... | .... |
| 2008-09 | Michigan State | CCHA | 14 | 0 | 2 | 2 | 20 | .... | .... | .... | .... | .... |
| | Alaska Aces | ECHL | 35 | 3 | 3 | 6 | 26 | 19 | 1 | 6 | 7 | 8 |

## TURNBULL, Joshua (TUHRN-buhl, JAWSH-oo-uh) L.A.

Center. Shoots right. 5'10", 172 lbs. Born, Hayward, WI, July 12, 1988.
(Los Angeles' 8th choice, 137th overall, in 2007 Entry Draft).

| | | | Regular Season | | | | | Playoffs | | | | |
|---|---|---|---|---|---|---|---|---|---|---|---|---|
| Season | Club | League | GP | G | A | Pts | PIM | GP | G | A | Pts | PIM |
| 2005-06 | Duluth East | High-MN | STATISTICS NOT AVAILABLE | | | | | | | | | |
| 2006-07 | Waterloo | USHL | 60 | 25 | 29 | 54 | 66 | 9 | 3 | 1 | 4 | 12 |
| 2007-08 | U. of Wisconsin | WCHA | 37 | 4 | 7 | 11 | 44 | .... | .... | .... | .... | .... |
| 2008-09 | U. of Wisconsin | WCHA | 24 | 4 | 2 | 6 | 26 | .... | .... | .... | .... | .... |

USHL All-Rookie Team (2007)

## TURNBULL, Travis (TUHRN-buhl, TRA-vihs) BUF.

Forward. Shoots right. 6', 193 lbs. Born, Chesterfield, MO, July 7, 1986.

| | | | Regular Season | | | | | Playoffs | | | | |
|---|---|---|---|---|---|---|---|---|---|---|---|---|
| Season | Club | League | GP | G | A | Pts | PIM | GP | G | A | Pts | PIM |
| 2003-04 | Sioux City | USHL | 56 | 7 | 12 | 19 | 73 | 7 | 0 | 0 | 0 | 9 |
| 2004-05 | Sioux City | USHL | 44 | 17 | 21 | 38 | 103 | 13 | 4 | 2 | 6 | 61 |
| 2005-06 | U. of Michigan | CCHA | 41 | 9 | 9 | 18 | 67 | .... | .... | .... | .... | .... |
| 2006-07 | U. of Michigan | CCHA | 41 | 8 | 9 | 17 | 54 | .... | .... | .... | .... | .... |
| 2007-08 | U. of Michigan | CCHA | 43 | 15 | 12 | 27 | 48 | .... | .... | .... | .... | .... |
| 2008-09 | U. of Michigan | CCHA | 41 | 8 | 20 | 28 | 74 | .... | .... | .... | .... | .... |
| | Portland Pirates | AHL | 3 | 0 | 0 | 0 | 5 | 5 | 0 | 0 | 0 | 4 |

Signed as a free agent by **Buffalo**, April 6, 2009.

**TURNER, Brennan** (TUHR-nuhr, BREH-nuhn) **CHI.**

Defense. Shoots left. 6'3", 221 lbs. Born, Winnipeg, Man., December 5, 1986.
(Chicago's 8th choice, 134th overall, in 2005 Entry Draft).

| | | | Regular Season | | | | | Playoffs | | | | |
|---|---|---|---|---|---|---|---|---|---|---|---|---|
| Season | Club | League | GP | G | A | Pts | PIM | GP | G | A | Pts | PIM |
| 2003-04 | Notre Dame | SJHL | 35 | 2 | 8 | 10 | 110 | .... | .... | .... | .... | .... |
| 2004-05 | Notre Dame | SJHL | 41 | 5 | 12 | 17 | 207 | 8 | 0 | 1 | 1 | 25 |
| 2005-06 | Yale | ECAC | 16 | 0 | 2 | 2 | 53 | .... | .... | .... | .... | .... |
| 2006-07 | Yale | ECAC | 27 | 0 | 0 | 0 | 71 | .... | .... | .... | .... | .... |
| 2007-08 | Yale | ECAC | 15 | 0 | 1 | 1 | 22 | .... | .... | .... | .... | .... |
| | Rockford IceHogs | AHL | 4 | 0 | 0 | 0 | 14 | .... | .... | .... | .... | .... |
| 2008-09 | Rockford IceHogs | AHL | 3 | 0 | 1 | 1 | 5 | .... | .... | .... | .... | .... |
| | Fresno Falcons | ECHL | 29 | 2 | 2 | 4 | 87 | .... | .... | .... | .... | .... |
| | Gwinnett | ECHL | 40 | 1 | 13 | 14 | 70 | 5 | 0 | 1 | 1 | 8 |

**TYRELL, Dana** (TIH-rehl, DAY-nuh) **T.B.**

Center/Right wing. Shoots left. 5'10", 185 lbs. Born, Airdrie, Alta., April 23, 1989.
(Tampa Bay's 1st choice, 47th overall, in 2007 Entry Draft).

| | | | Regular Season | | | | | Playoffs | | | | |
|---|---|---|---|---|---|---|---|---|---|---|---|---|
| Season | Club | League | GP | G | A | Pts | PIM | GP | G | A | Pts | PIM |
| 2003-04 | Airdrie Xtreme | AMBHL | 35 | 21 | 47 | 68 | 28 | 7 | 6 | 4 | 10 | .... |
| 2004-05 | UFA Bisons | AMHL | 34 | 16 | 23 | 39 | 32 | 16 | 8 | 9 | *17 | .... |
| | Prince George | WHL | 1 | 0 | 0 | 0 | 2 | .... | .... | .... | .... | .... |
| 2005-06 | Prince George | WHL | 69 | 7 | 11 | 18 | 44 | 5 | 0 | 0 | 0 | 2 |
| 2006-07 | Prince George | WHL | 72 | 30 | 26 | 56 | 51 | 15 | 1 | 6 | 7 | 4 |
| 2007-08 | Prince George | WHL | 68 | 25 | 40 | 65 | 47 | .... | .... | .... | .... | .... |
| | Norfolk Admirals | AHL | 11 | 1 | 5 | 6 | 6 | .... | .... | .... | .... | .... |
| 2008-09 | Prince George | WHL | 30 | 19 | 21 | 40 | 27 | .... | .... | .... | .... | .... |

**ULLSTROM, David** (UHL-struhm, DAY-vihd) **NYI**

Center. Shoots left. 6'3", 198 lbs. Born, Jonkoping, Sweden, April 22, 1989.
(NY Islanders' 9th choice, 102nd overall, in 2008 Entry Draft).

| | | | Regular Season | | | | | Playoffs | | | | |
|---|---|---|---|---|---|---|---|---|---|---|---|---|
| Season | Club | League | GP | G | A | Pts | PIM | GP | G | A | Pts | PIM |
| 2005-06 | HV 71 U18 | Swe-U18 | 13 | 5 | 8 | 13 | 14 | 5 | 4 | 1 | 5 | 14 |
| | HV 71 Jr. | Swe-Jr. | 1 | 0 | 0 | 0 | 0 | .... | .... | .... | .... | .... |
| 2006-07 | HV 71 U18 | Swe-U18 | 1 | 0 | 0 | 0 | 2 | 5 | 2 | 6 | 8 | 10 |
| | HV 71 Jr. | Swe-Jr. | 39 | 16 | 14 | 30 | 30 | 4 | 0 | 2 | 2 | 0 |
| 2007-08 | HV 71 Jr. | Swe-Jr. | 40 | 27 | 27 | 54 | 86 | 3 | 2 | 2 | 4 | 0 |
| | HV 71 Jonkoping | Sweden | 7 | 0 | 0 | 0 | 0 | .... | .... | .... | .... | .... |
| 2008-09 | HV 71 Jr. | Swe-Jr. | 2 | 0 | 0 | 0 | 0 | .... | .... | .... | .... | .... |
| | Boras HC | Sweden-2 | 15 | 9 | 7 | 16 | 22 | .... | .... | .... | .... | .... |
| | HV 71 Jonkoping | Sweden | 19 | 1 | 3 | 4 | 6 | 14 | 1 | 0 | 1 | 4 |

**URBOM, Alexander** (OOR-bohm, al-ehx-AN-duhr) **N.J.**

Defense. Shoots left. 6'3", 195 lbs. Born, Stockholm, Sweden, December 20, 1990.
(New Jersey's 3rd choice, 73rd overall, in 2009 Entry Draft).

| | | | Regular Season | | | | | Playoffs | | | | |
|---|---|---|---|---|---|---|---|---|---|---|---|---|
| Season | Club | League | GP | G | A | Pts | PIM | GP | G | A | Pts | PIM |
| 2005-06 | Djurgarden U18 | Swe-U18 | 2 | 0 | 0 | 0 | 0 | .... | .... | .... | .... | .... |
| 2006-07 | Djurgarden U18 | Swe-U18 | 31 | 6 | 11 | 17 | 36 | 3 | 0 | 1 | 1 | 2 |
| 2007-08 | Djurgarden U18 | Swe-U18 | 7 | 2 | 6 | 8 | 6 | 5 | 1 | 0 | 1 | 2 |
| | Djurgarden Jr. | Swe-Jr. | 39 | 3 | 8 | 11 | 54 | 7 | 0 | 1 | 1 | 2 |
| 2008-09 | Djurgarden Jr. | Swe-Jr. | 16 | 5 | 6 | 11 | 45 | .... | .... | .... | .... | .... |
| | Djurgarden | Sweden | 28 | 0 | 0 | 0 | 2 | .... | .... | .... | .... | .... |
| | Djurgarden U18 | Swe-U18 | .... | .... | .... | .... | .... | 5 | 1 | 0 | 1 | 2 |

**UTKIN, Dmitri** (OOT-kihn, dih-MEE-tree) **BOS.**

Left wing. Shoots left. 6', 170 lbs. Born, Yaroslavl, USSR, June 10, 1984.
(Boston's 5th choice, 228th overall, in 2002 Entry Draft).

| | | | Regular Season | | | | | Playoffs | | | | |
|---|---|---|---|---|---|---|---|---|---|---|---|---|
| Season | Club | League | GP | G | A | Pts | PIM | GP | G | A | Pts | PIM |
| 2000-01 | Yaroslavl 2 | Russia-3 | 49 | 12 | 1 | 13 | 10 | .... | .... | .... | .... | .... |
| 2001-02 | Yaroslavl 2 | Russia-3 | 32 | 15 | 7 | 22 | 33 | .... | .... | .... | .... | .... |
| 2002-03 | Yaroslavl | Russia | 4 | 0 | 1 | 1 | 0 | .... | .... | .... | .... | .... |
| 2003-04 | Spartak Moscow | Russia-2 | 57 | 10 | 10 | 20 | 8 | 13 | 3 | 3 | 6 | 2 |
| 2004-05 | Keramin Minsk | BelOpen | 8 | 2 | 0 | 2 | 31 | .... | .... | .... | .... | .... |
| | HK Brest | BelOpen | 20 | 4 | 12 | 16 | 4 | .... | .... | .... | .... | .... |
| | HK Riga 2000 | BelOpen | .... | .... | .... | .... | .... | 3 | 0 | 0 | 0 | 0 |
| | HK Riga 2000 | Latvia | .... | .... | .... | .... | .... | 6 | 3 | 2 | 5 | 0 |
| 2005-06 | Spartak Moscow | Russia | 33 | 3 | 1 | 4 | 4 | 2 | 0 | 0 | 0 | 0 |
| | Spartak Moscow 2 | Russia-3 | 10 | 5 | 2 | 7 | 8 | .... | .... | .... | .... | .... |
| 2006-07 | Chelyabinsk | Russia | 50 | 6 | 8 | 14 | 20 | .... | .... | .... | .... | .... |
| 2007-08 | Chelyabinsk 2 | Russia-3 | 16 | 4 | 3 | 7 | 2 | .... | .... | .... | .... | .... |
| | Chelyabinsk | Russia | 5 | 1 | 0 | 1 | 2 | .... | .... | .... | .... | .... |
| | Avtomobilist | Russia-2 | 11 | 2 | 0 | 2 | 0 | 6 | 1 | 0 | 1 | 0 |
| 2008-09 | Mechel | Russia-2 | 40 | 13 | 8 | 21 | 40 | .... | .... | .... | .... | .... |
| | Khanty-Mansiisk | Russia-2 | 8 | 4 | 3 | 7 | 0 | 16 | 2 | 7 | 9 | 4 |

**VAIVE, Justin** (VIGHV, JUHS-tihn) **ANA.**

Left wing. Shoots left. 6'5", 210 lbs. Born, Buffalo, NY, July 8, 1989.
(Anaheim's 4th choice, 92nd overall, in 2007 Entry Draft).

| | | | Regular Season | | | | | Playoffs | | | | |
|---|---|---|---|---|---|---|---|---|---|---|---|---|
| Season | Club | League | GP | G | A | Pts | PIM | GP | G | A | Pts | PIM |
| 2004-05 | Toronto Marlboros | GTHL | 72 | 38 | 64 | 102 | .... | .... | .... | .... | .... | .... |
| 2005-06 | USNTDP | U-17 | 13 | 3 | 5 | 8 | 18 | .... | .... | .... | .... | .... |
| | USNTDP | NAHL | 24 | 4 | 8 | 12 | 34 | 5 | 1 | 1 | 2 | 6 |
| 2006-07 | USNTDP | U-18 | 43 | 7 | 8 | 15 | 49 | .... | .... | .... | .... | .... |
| | USNTDP | NAHL | 15 | 4 | 1 | 5 | 22 | .... | .... | .... | .... | .... |
| 2007-08 | Miami U. | CCHA | 41 | 3 | 7 | 10 | 65 | .... | .... | .... | .... | .... |
| 2008-09 | Miami U. | CCHA | 37 | 6 | 6 | 12 | 44 | .... | .... | .... | .... | .... |

**VALENTENKO, Pavel** (val-ehn-TEHN-koh, PAH-vehl) **NYR**

Defense. Shoots left. 6'2", 218 lbs. Born, Nizhnekamsk, USSR, October 20, 1987.
(Montreal's 5th choice, 139th overall, in 2006 Entry Draft).

| | | | Regular Season | | | | | Playoffs | | | | |
|---|---|---|---|---|---|---|---|---|---|---|---|---|
| Season | Club | League | GP | G | A | Pts | PIM | GP | G | A | Pts | PIM |
| 2002-03 | Lada Togliatti 2 | Russia-3 | 6 | 0 | 0 | 0 | 4 | .... | .... | .... | .... | .... |
| 2003-04 | Nizhnekamsk 2 | Russia-3 | 26 | 0 | 1 | 1 | 28 | .... | .... | .... | .... | .... |
| 2004-05 | Nizhnekamsk 2 | Russia-3 | STATISTICS NOT AVAILABLE | | | | | | | | | |
| 2005-06 | Nizhnekamsk 2 | Russia-3 | STATISTICS NOT AVAILABLE | | | | | | | | | |
| | Nizhnekamsk | Russia | 2 | 0 | 0 | 0 | 2 | .... | .... | .... | .... | .... |
| 2006-07 | Nizhnekamsk | Russia | 50 | 0 | 2 | 2 | 62 | 4 | 0 | 0 | 0 | 2 |
| 2007-08 | Hamilton Bulldogs | AHL | 57 | 1 | 15 | 16 | 58 | .... | .... | .... | .... | .... |
| 2008-09 | Hamilton Bulldogs | AHL | 4 | 0 | 2 | 2 | 2 | .... | .... | .... | .... | .... |
| | Dynamo Moscow | Rus-KHL | 8 | 0 | 1 | 1 | 8 | 1 | 0 | 0 | 0 | 2 |

• Missed majority of 2008-09 season recovering from an injury. Traded to **NY Rangers** by **Montreal** with Chris Higgins and Ryan McDonagh for Scott Gomez, Tom Pyatt and Mike Busto, June 30, 2009.

**VALENTINE, Scott** (VAL-ehn-tighn, SKAWT) **ANA.**

Defense. Shoots left. 6', 196 lbs. Born, Ottawa, Ont., May 2, 1991.
(Anaheim's 7th choice, 166th overall, in 2009 Entry Draft).

| | | | Regular Season | | | | | Playoffs | | | | |
|---|---|---|---|---|---|---|---|---|---|---|---|---|
| Season | Club | League | GP | G | A | Pts | PIM | GP | G | A | Pts | PIM |
| 2007-08 | Hawkesbury | CJHL | 51 | 2 | 15 | 17 | 81 | 11 | 3 | 4 | 7 | 18 |
| | London Knights | OHL | 3 | 0 | 0 | 0 | 2 | .... | .... | .... | .... | .... |
| 2008-09 | London Knights | OHL | 17 | 0 | 0 | 0 | 20 | .... | .... | .... | .... | .... |
| | Oshawa Generals | OHL | 26 | 1 | 8 | 9 | 51 | .... | .... | .... | .... | .... |

**VALETTE, Craig** (va-LEHT, KRAIG)

Center. Shoots left. 6', 200 lbs. Born, Shellbrook, Sask., October 7, 1982.

| | | | Regular Season | | | | | Playoffs | | | | |
|---|---|---|---|---|---|---|---|---|---|---|---|---|
| Season | Club | League | GP | G | A | Pts | PIM | GP | G | A | Pts | PIM |
| 1998-99 | Sask. Contacts | SMHL | 36 | 19 | 22 | 41 | .... | .... | .... | .... | .... | .... |
| 99-2000 | Saskatoon Blades | WHL | 47 | 2 | 1 | 3 | 25 | 3 | 0 | 0 | 0 | 0 |
| 2000-01 | Saskatoon Blades | WHL | 24 | 2 | 0 | 2 | 19 | .... | .... | .... | .... | .... |
| | Portland | WHL | 39 | 8 | 6 | 14 | 39 | 16 | 0 | 2 | 2 | 27 |
| 2001-02 | Portland | WHL | 67 | 8 | 14 | 22 | 160 | 7 | 2 | 1 | 3 | 6 |
| 2002-03 | Portland | WHL | 71 | 30 | 26 | 56 | 192 | 7 | 5 | 4 | 9 | 18 |
| 2003-04 | Cleveland Barons | AHL | 56 | 6 | 10 | 16 | 77 | 5 | 0 | 0 | 0 | 2 |
| 2004-05 | Cleveland Barons | AHL | 79 | 6 | 6 | 12 | 94 | .... | .... | .... | .... | .... |
| 2005-06 | Cleveland Barons | AHL | 69 | 5 | 6 | 11 | 95 | .... | .... | .... | .... | .... |
| 2006-07 | Worcester Sharks | AHL | 55 | 15 | 11 | 26 | 77 | 1 | 0 | 0 | 0 | 0 |
| 2007-08 | Worcester Sharks | AHL | 69 | 4 | 10 | 14 | 97 | .... | .... | .... | .... | .... |
| 2008-09 | Syracuse Crunch | AHL | 6 | 0 | 0 | 0 | 2 | .... | .... | .... | .... | .... |
| | Houston Aeros | AHL | 15 | 0 | 2 | 2 | 15 | .... | .... | .... | .... | .... |
| | Stockton Thunder | ECHL | 43 | 9 | 16 | 25 | 65 | 14 | 6 | 7 | 13 | 19 |

Signed as a free agent by **San Jose**, April 4, 2003. Signed as a free agent by **Houston** (AHL), November 4, 2008.

**VANDE VELDE, Chris** (VAN-deh VEHLD, KRIHS) **EDM.**

Center. Shoots left. 6'2", 204 lbs. Born, Moorhead, MN, March 15, 1987.
(Edmonton's 5th choice, 97th overall, in 2005 Entry Draft).

| | | | Regular Season | | | | | Playoffs | | | | |
|---|---|---|---|---|---|---|---|---|---|---|---|---|
| Season | Club | League | GP | G | A | Pts | PIM | GP | G | A | Pts | PIM |
| 2003-04 | Moorhead Spuds | High-MN | 29 | 19 | 24 | 43 | .... | .... | .... | .... | .... | .... |
| 2004-05 | Moorhead Spuds | High-MN | 30 | 35 | 32 | 67 | 28 | .... | .... | .... | .... | .... |
| | Lincoln Stars | USHL | 7 | 1 | 4 | 5 | 0 | 4 | 0 | 2 | 2 | 0 |
| 2005-06 | Lincoln Stars | USHL | 56 | 16 | 20 | 36 | 70 | 9 | 1 | 3 | 4 | 10 |
| 2006-07 | North Dakota | WCHA | 38 | 3 | 6 | 9 | 37 | .... | .... | .... | .... | .... |
| 2007-08 | North Dakota | WCHA | 43 | 15 | 17 | 32 | 38 | .... | .... | .... | .... | .... |
| 2008-09 | North Dakota | WCHA | 43 | 18 | 17 | 35 | 69 | .... | .... | .... | .... | .... |

**vanRIEMSDYK, James** (VAN REEMZ-dighk, JAYMZ) **PHI.**

Left wing. Shoots left. 6'3", 205 lbs. Born, Middletown, NJ, May 4, 1989.
(Philadelphia's 1st choice, 2nd overall, in 2007 Entry Draft).

| | | | Regular Season | | | | | Playoffs | | | | |
|---|---|---|---|---|---|---|---|---|---|---|---|---|
| Season | Club | League | GP | G | A | Pts | PIM | GP | G | A | Pts | PIM |
| 2004-05 | Christian Bros. | High-NJ | 30 | 36 | 24 | 60 | .... | .... | .... | .... | .... | .... |
| 2005-06 | USNTDP | U-17 | 11 | 7 | 5 | 12 | 18 | .... | .... | .... | .... | .... |
| | USNTDP | U-18 | 14 | 1 | 3 | 4 | 6 | .... | .... | .... | .... | .... |
| | USNTDP | NAHL | 37 | 18 | 11 | 29 | 36 | 7 | 1 | 0 | 1 | 8 |
| 2006-07 | USNTDP | U-18 | 39 | 25 | 28 | 53 | 48 | .... | .... | .... | .... | .... |
| | USNTDP | NAHL | 12 | 13 | 12 | 25 | 37 | .... | .... | .... | .... | .... |
| 2007-08 | New Hampshire | H-East | 31 | 11 | 23 | 34 | 36 | .... | .... | .... | .... | .... |
| 2008-09 | New Hampshire | H-East | 36 | 17 | 23 | 40 | 47 | .... | .... | .... | .... | .... |
| | Philadelphia | AHL | 7 | 1 | 1 | 2 | 2 | 4 | 0 | 0 | 0 | 2 |

Hockey East All-Rookie Team (2008) • Hockey East Second All-Star Team (2009)

**VARONE, Philip** (vah-ROHN, FIHL-ihp) **S.J.**

Center. Shoots left. 5'10", 186 lbs. Born, Vaughan, Ont., December 4, 1990.
(San Jose's 3rd choice, 147th overall, in 2009 Entry Draft).

| | | | Regular Season | | | | | Playoffs | | | | |
|---|---|---|---|---|---|---|---|---|---|---|---|---|
| Season | Club | League | GP | G | A | Pts | PIM | GP | G | A | Pts | PIM |
| 2006-07 | Kitchener | OJHL-B | 20 | 10 | 11 | 21 | 21 | .... | .... | .... | .... | .... |
| | Kitchener Rangers | OHL | 13 | 1 | 3 | 4 | 2 | .... | .... | .... | .... | .... |
| 2007-08 | Kitchener Rangers | OHL | 35 | 5 | 20 | 25 | 12 | .... | .... | .... | .... | .... |
| | London Knights | OHL | 31 | 10 | 26 | 36 | 14 | 5 | 1 | 1 | 2 | 7 |
| 2008-09 | London Knights | OHL | 58 | 19 | 33 | 52 | 32 | 14 | 10 | 9 | 19 | 19 |

**VASYUNOV, Alexander** (vahs-YUH-nawv, al-EHX-AN-duhr) **N.J.**

Left wing. Shoots right. 6', 190 lbs. Born, Yaroslavl, USSR, April 22, 1988.
(New Jersey's 2nd choice, 58th overall, in 2006 Entry Draft).

| | | | Regular Season | | | | | Playoffs | | | | |
|---|---|---|---|---|---|---|---|---|---|---|---|---|
| Season | Club | League | GP | G | A | Pts | PIM | GP | G | A | Pts | PIM |
| 2004-05 | Yaroslavl 2 | Russia-3 | 28 | 10 | 2 | 12 | 6 | .... | .... | .... | .... | .... |
| 2005-06 | Yaroslavl 2 | Russia-3 | 29 | 29 | 6 | 35 | 14 | .... | .... | .... | .... | .... |
| | Yaroslavl | Russia | 2 | 0 | 0 | 0 | 2 | .... | .... | .... | .... | .... |
| 2006-07 | Yaroslavl | Russia | 17 | 0 | 0 | 0 | 4 | .... | .... | .... | .... | .... |
| | Yaroslavl 2 | Russia-3 | 30 | 16 | 9 | 25 | 52 | .... | .... | .... | .... | .... |
| 2007-08 | Yaroslavl | Russia | 22 | 4 | 0 | 4 | 4 | 16 | 2 | 0 | 2 | 2 |
| 2008-09 | Yaroslavl | Rus-KHL | 2 | 0 | 0 | 0 | 0 | .... | .... | .... | .... | .... |
| | Lowell Devils | AHL | 69 | 15 | 13 | 28 | 12 | .... | .... | .... | .... | .... |

**VATANEN, Sami** (VAH-ta-nehn, SA-mee) **ANA.**

Defense. Shoots right. 5'9", 163 lbs. Born, Jyvaskyla, Finland, June 3, 1991.
(Anaheim's 5th choice, 106th overall, in 2009 Entry Draft).

| | | | Regular Season | | | | | Playoffs | | | | |
|---|---|---|---|---|---|---|---|---|---|---|---|---|
| Season | Club | League | GP | G | A | Pts | PIM | GP | G | A | Pts | PIM |
| 2006-07 | JyP Jyvaskyla U18 | Fin-U18 | .... | .... | .... | .... | .... | 7 | 1 | 0 | 1 | 2 |
| 2007-08 | JyP Jyvaskyla U18 | Fin-U18 | 35 | 9 | 29 | 38 | 30 | 1 | 0 | 0 | 0 | 0 |
| | JyP Jyvaskyla Jr. | Fin-Jr. | .... | .... | .... | .... | .... | 2 | 0 | 0 | 0 | 0 |
| 2008-09 | JyP Jyvaskyla U18 | Fin-U18 | 2 | 0 | 0 | 0 | 0 | 1 | 1 | 1 | 2 | 14 |
| | Suomi U20 | Finland-2 | 2 | 0 | 0 | 0 | 2 | .... | .... | .... | .... | .... |
| | D Team Jyvaskyla | Finland-2 | 5 | 1 | 1 | 2 | 8 | .... | .... | .... | .... | .... |
| | JyP Jyvaskyla Jr. | Fin-Jr. | 20 | 3 | 7 | 10 | 22 | .... | .... | .... | .... | .... |

## VEILLEUX, Keven (VAY-oo, KEH-vihn) PIT.

Center. Shoots right. 6'5", 202 lbs. Born, Saint-Renee, Que., June 27, 1989.
(Pittsburgh's 2nd choice, 51st overall, in 2007 Entry Draft).

| | | | Regular Season | | | | | Playoffs | | | | |
|---|---|---|---|---|---|---|---|---|---|---|---|---|
| Season | Club | League | GP | G | A | Pts | PIM | GP | G | A | Pts | PIM |
| 2004-05 | Levis | QAAA | 11 | 1 | 0 | 1 | 0 | 2 | 0 | 1 | 1 | 0 |
| 2005-06 | Levis | QAAA | 26 | 12 | 23 | 35 | 53 | .... | .... | .... | .... | .... |
| | Victoriaville Tigres | QMJHL | 33 | 2 | 13 | 15 | 4 | 5 | 0 | 1 | 1 | 2 |
| 2006-07 | Victoriaville Tigres | QMJHL | 70 | 20 | 35 | 55 | 53 | 6 | 1 | 5 | 6 | 4 |
| 2007-08 | Victoriaville Tigres | QMJHL | 42 | 10 | 32 | 42 | 54 | .... | .... | .... | .... | .... |
| | Rimouski Oceanic | QMJHL | 19 | 7 | 15 | 22 | 22 | 9 | 3 | 4 | 7 | 2 |
| 2008-09 | Rimouski Oceanic | QMJHL | 29 | 15 | 33 | 48 | 47 | 13 | 7 | 12 | 19 | 31 |

## VELISCHEK, Alex (VEHL-ih-shehk, Al-ehx) PIT.

Defense. Shoots left. 6', 200 lbs. Born, Quebec City, Que., December 17, 1990.
(Pittsburgh's 5th choice, 123rd overall, in 2009 Entry Draft).

| | | | Regular Season | | | | | Playoffs | | | | |
|---|---|---|---|---|---|---|---|---|---|---|---|---|
| Season | Club | League | GP | G | A | Pts | PIM | GP | G | A | Pts | PIM |
| 2005-06 | Delbarton | High-NJ | 26 | 8 | 14 | 22 | 18 | .... | .... | .... | .... | .... |
| 2006-07 | Delbarton | High-NJ | 24 | 12 | 14 | 26 | 26 | .... | .... | .... | .... | .... |
| 2007-08 | Delbarton | High-NJ | 27 | 9 | 14 | 23 | 36 | .... | .... | .... | .... | .... |
| 2008-09 | Delbarton | High-NJ | 30 | 16 | 35 | 51 | 42 | .... | .... | .... | .... | .... |

• Signed Letter of Intent to attend **Providence College** (Hockey East) in fall of 2009.

## VEY, Linden (VAY, LIHN-duhn) L.A.

Right wing. Shoots right. 5'11", 176 lbs. Born, Wakaw, Sask., July 17, 1991.
(Los Angeles' 5th choice, 96th overall, in 2009 Entry Draft).

| | | | Regular Season | | | | | Playoffs | | | | |
|---|---|---|---|---|---|---|---|---|---|---|---|---|
| Season | Club | League | GP | G | A | Pts | PIM | GP | G | A | Pts | PIM |
| 2006-07 | Beardy's | SMHL | 44 | 28 | 44 | 72 | 26 | .... | .... | .... | .... | .... |
| | Medicine Hat | WHL | 2 | 0 | 0 | 0 | 2 | .... | .... | .... | .... | .... |
| 2007-08 | Medicine Hat | WHL | 48 | 8 | 9 | 17 | 21 | 5 | 0 | 1 | 1 | 2 |
| 2008-09 | Medicine Hat | WHL | 71 | 24 | 48 | 72 | 20 | 11 | 2 | 5 | 7 | 2 |

## VIEDENSKY, Marek (vee-ehd-EHN-skee, MAR-ehk) S.J.

Center. Shoots right. 6'4", 185 lbs. Born, Handlova, Czechoslovakia, August 18, 1990.
(San Jose's 4th choice, 189th overall, in 2009 Entry Draft).

| | | | Regular Season | | | | | Playoffs | | | | |
|---|---|---|---|---|---|---|---|---|---|---|---|---|
| Season | Club | League | GP | G | A | Pts | PIM | GP | G | A | Pts | PIM |
| 2004-05 | Prievidza U18 | Svk-U18 | 10 | 2 | 1 | 3 | 2 | .... | .... | .... | .... | .... |
| 2005-06 | Prievidza U18 | Svk-U18 | 31 | 18 | 18 | 36 | 18 | .... | .... | .... | .... | .... |
| 2006-07 | Dukla Trencin U18 | Svk-U18 | 12 | 6 | 12 | 18 | 6 | .... | .... | .... | .... | .... |
| | Dukla Trencin Jr. | Slovak-Jr. | 30 | 5 | 3 | 8 | 8 | 7 | 1 | 1 | 2 | 16 |
| 2007-08 | Dukla Trencin U18 | Svk-U18 | 2 | 0 | 1 | 1 | 0 | .... | .... | .... | .... | .... |
| | Dukla Trencin Jr. | Slovak-Jr. | 33 | 11 | 15 | 26 | 24 | 7 | 1 | 1 | 2 | 6 |
| 2008-09 | Prince George | WHL | 59 | 16 | 24 | 40 | 34 | 4 | 2 | 0 | 2 | 2 |

## VIGILANTE, John (vih-jih-LAN-tee, JAWN)

Left wing. Shoots left. 6', 190 lbs. Born, Dearborn, MI, May 24, 1985.

| | | | Regular Season | | | | | Playoffs | | | | |
|---|---|---|---|---|---|---|---|---|---|---|---|---|
| Season | Club | League | GP | G | A | Pts | PIM | GP | G | A | Pts | PIM |
| 2002-03 | Plymouth Whalers | OHL | 65 | 15 | 24 | 39 | 31 | 18 | 6 | 3 | 9 | 8 |
| 2003-04 | Plymouth Whalers | OHL | 66 | 30 | 38 | 68 | 25 | 9 | 1 | 7 | 8 | 8 |
| 2004-05 | Plymouth Whalers | OHL | 68 | 24 | 38 | 62 | 17 | 4 | 0 | 0 | 0 | 0 |
| 2005-06 | Plymouth Whalers | OHL | 55 | 24 | 53 | 77 | 34 | 13 | 4 | 12 | 16 | 0 |
| 2006-07 | Milwaukee | AHL | 62 | 8 | 19 | 27 | 10 | 2 | 0 | 0 | 0 | 2 |
| 2007-08 | Milwaukee | AHL | 73 | 15 | 31 | 46 | 12 | 6 | 0 | 1 | 1 | 0 |
| 2008-09 | Syracuse Crunch | AHL | 52 | 7 | 8 | 15 | 14 | .... | .... | .... | .... | .... |
| | Quad City Flames | AHL | 24 | 7 | 8 | 15 | 2 | .... | .... | .... | .... | .... |

Signed as a free agent by **Nashville**. December 7, 2005. Signed as a free agent by **Columbus**. July 8, 2008.

## VINCOUR, Tomas (VIHN-tsoh-oor, TAW-mahsh) DAL.

Center. Shoots right. 6'2", 203 lbs. Born, Brno, Czechoslovakia, November 19, 1990.
(Dallas' 4th choice, 129th overall, in 2009 Entry Draft).

| | | | Regular Season | | | | | Playoffs | | | | |
|---|---|---|---|---|---|---|---|---|---|---|---|---|
| Season | Club | League | GP | G | A | Pts | PIM | GP | G | A | Pts | PIM |
| 2004-05 | Brno U17 | CzR-U17 | 42 | 23 | 13 | 36 | 36 | .... | .... | .... | .... | .... |
| 2005-06 | Brno U17 | CzR-U17 | 21 | 13 | 14 | 27 | 77 | .... | .... | .... | .... | .... |
| | Brno Jr. | CzRep-Jr. | 28 | 8 | 10 | 18 | 61 | .... | .... | .... | .... | .... |
| | Brno | CzRep-2 | 1 | 0 | 0 | 0 | 0 | .... | .... | .... | .... | .... |
| 2006-07 | Brno U17 | CzR-U17 | 1 | 0 | 0 | 0 | 0 | 2 | 0 | 2 | 2 | 0 |
| | Brno Jr. | CzRep-Jr. | 41 | 15 | 24 | 39 | 58 | .... | .... | .... | .... | .... |
| | Brno | CzRep-2 | 4 | 0 | 1 | 1 | 0 | .... | .... | .... | .... | .... |
| 2007-08 | Edmonton | WHL | 65 | 16 | 23 | 39 | 36 | .... | .... | .... | .... | .... |
| 2008-09 | Edmonton | WHL | 49 | 17 | 19 | 36 | 23 | .... | .... | .... | .... | .... |

## VISHNYAKOV, Albert (vihsh-nyeh-KAWF, al-BAIRT) T.B.

Left wing. Shoots right. 6', 185 lbs. Born, Almyetevsk, USSR, December 30, 1983.
(Tampa Bay's 9th choice, 273rd overall, in 2003 Entry Draft).

| | | | Regular Season | | | | | Playoffs | | | | |
|---|---|---|---|---|---|---|---|---|---|---|---|---|
| Season | Club | League | GP | G | A | Pts | PIM | GP | G | A | Pts | PIM |
| 99-2000 | Almetjevsk 2 | Russia-3 | 41 | 11 | 5 | 16 | 68 | .... | .... | .... | .... | .... |
| 2000-01 | Almetjevsk | Russia-2 | 29 | 0 | 0 | 0 | 2 | .... | .... | .... | .... | .... |
| 2001-02 | Ak Bars Kazan | Russia | 9 | 0 | 1 | 1 | 2 | .... | .... | .... | .... | .... |
| | Nizhny Novgorod | Russia | 6 | 1 | 0 | 1 | 0 | .... | .... | .... | .... | .... |
| | Nizh. Novgorod 2 | Russia-3 | 4 | 2 | 2 | 4 | 10 | .... | .... | .... | .... | .... |
| 2002-03 | Ak Bars Kazan | Russia | 47 | 7 | 6 | 13 | 47 | 5 | 1 | 0 | 1 | 0 |
| 2003-04 | Nizhnekamsk | Russia | 10 | 2 | 3 | 5 | 10 | .... | .... | .... | .... | .... |
| | Ak Bars Kazan 2 | Russia-3 | STATISTICS NOT AVAILABLE | | | | | | | | | |
| | Ak Bars Kazan | Russia | 10 | 1 | 1 | 2 | 8 | .... | .... | .... | .... | .... |
| 2004-05 | Dynamo Moscow | Russia | 28 | 1 | 2 | 3 | 10 | .... | .... | .... | .... | .... |
| 2005-06 | Dynamo Moscow | Russia | 48 | 9 | 3 | 12 | 78 | 3 | 0 | 0 | 0 | 0 |
| 2006-07 | Dynamo Moscow | Russia | 33 | 9 | 6 | 15 | 36 | 1 | 0 | 0 | 0 | 0 |
| 2007-08 | Spartak Moscow | Russia | 8 | 2 | 0 | 2 | 14 | .... | .... | .... | .... | .... |
| | Novokuznetsk | Russia | 19 | 1 | 7 | 8 | 12 | .... | .... | .... | .... | .... |
| 2008-09 | Novokuznetsk | Rus-KHL | 50 | 6 | 9 | 15 | 28 | .... | .... | .... | .... | .... |

## VITALE, Joe (vih-TA-lee, JOH) PIT.

Center. Shoots right. 6', 205 lbs. Born, St. Louis, MO, August 20, 1985.
(Pittsburgh's 7th choice, 195th overall, in 2005 Entry Draft).

| | | | Regular Season | | | | | Playoffs | | | | |
|---|---|---|---|---|---|---|---|---|---|---|---|---|
| Season | Club | League | GP | G | A | Pts | PIM | GP | G | A | Pts | PIM |
| 2003-04 | St. Louis Jr. Blues | CSJHL | 43 | 21 | 29 | 50 | 42 | .... | .... | .... | .... | .... |
| 2004-05 | Sioux Falls | USHL | 53 | 11 | 20 | 31 | 62 | .... | .... | .... | .... | .... |
| 2005-06 | Northeastern | H-East | 31 | 8 | 8 | 16 | 71 | .... | .... | .... | .... | .... |
| 2006-07 | Northeastern | H-East | 35 | 7 | 9 | 16 | 54 | .... | .... | .... | .... | .... |
| 2007-08 | Northeastern | H-East | 37 | 12 | 23 | 35 | 75 | .... | .... | .... | .... | .... |
| 2008-09 | Northeastern | H-East | 40 | 7 | 20 | 27 | 68 | .... | .... | .... | .... | .... |
| | Wilkes-Barre | AHL | 5 | 2 | 2 | 4 | 2 | 12 | 0 | 0 | 0 | 12 |

Hockey East Second All-Star Team (2008)

## VOGELHUBER, Trent (VOH-guhl-hew-buhr, TREHNT) CBJ

Right wing. Shoots right. 6'2", 185 lbs. Born, Cleveland, OH, July 13, 1988.
(Columbus' 7th choice, 211th overall, in 2007 Entry Draft).

| | | | Regular Season | | | | | Playoffs | | | | |
|---|---|---|---|---|---|---|---|---|---|---|---|---|
| Season | Club | League | GP | G | A | Pts | PIM | GP | G | A | Pts | PIM |
| 2004-05 | Ohio AAA | Ind. | 67 | 32 | 30 | 62 | 77 | .... | .... | .... | .... | .... |
| 2005-06 | Ohio AAA | GLHL | 44 | 27 | 52 | 79 | 28 | .... | .... | .... | .... | .... |
| 2006-07 | St. Louis Bandits | NAHL | 31 | 10 | 16 | 26 | 24 | .... | .... | .... | .... | .... |
| 2007-08 | Des Moines | USHL | 2 | 0 | 1 | 1 | 0 | .... | .... | .... | .... | .... |
| 2008-09 | Miami U. | CCHA | 29 | 2 | 2 | 4 | 22 | .... | .... | .... | .... | .... |

## VOLOSHENKO, Roman (voh-loh-SHEHN-koh, ROH-muhn) MIN.

Left wing. Shoots right. 6'1", 207 lbs. Born, Brest, USSR, May 12, 1986.
(Minnesota's 2nd choice, 42nd overall, in 2004 Entry Draft).

| | | | Regular Season | | | | | Playoffs | | | | |
|---|---|---|---|---|---|---|---|---|---|---|---|---|
| Season | Club | League | GP | G | A | Pts | PIM | GP | G | A | Pts | PIM |
| 2001-02 | Krylja Sovetov 2 | Russia-3 | 8 | 2 | 3 | 5 | 0 | .... | .... | .... | .... | .... |
| 2002-03 | Krylja Sovetov 2 | Russia-3 | 6 | 3 | 1 | 4 | 2 | .... | .... | .... | .... | .... |
| | Krylja Sovetov | Russia | 5 | 0 | 1 | 1 | 2 | .... | .... | .... | .... | .... |
| 2003-04 | Krylja Sovetov | Russia-2 | 46 | 7 | 8 | 15 | 40 | 4 | 1 | 1 | 2 | 4 |
| 2004-05 | Krylja Sovetov 2 | Russia-3 | 1 | 0 | 0 | 0 | 2 | .... | .... | .... | .... | .... |
| | Krylja Sovetov | Russia-2 | 38 | 16 | 13 | 29 | 22 | 3 | 0 | 1 | 1 | 2 |
| 2005-06 | Houston Aeros | AHL | 69 | 33 | 27 | 60 | 36 | 7 | 0 | 1 | 1 | 0 |
| 2006-07 | Houston Aeros | AHL | 76 | 11 | 19 | 30 | 22 | .... | .... | .... | .... | .... |
| 2007-08 | Dynamo Moscow | Russia | 18 | 1 | 1 | 2 | 6 | 3 | 0 | 0 | 0 | 2 |
| 2008-09 | Dynamo Moscow | Rus-KHL | 5 | 0 | 0 | 0 | 2 | .... | .... | .... | .... | .... |
| | MVD | Rus-KHL | 10 | 1 | 1 | 2 | 2 | .... | .... | .... | .... | .... |

## VOROBIEV, Dmitri (voh-roh-BEE-ehf, dih-MEE-tree) TOR.

Defense. Shoots left. 6'2", 211 lbs. Born, Togliatti, USSR, October 18, 1985.
(Toronto's 3rd choice, 157th overall, in 2004 Entry Draft).

| | | | Regular Season | | | | | Playoffs | | | | |
|---|---|---|---|---|---|---|---|---|---|---|---|---|
| Season | Club | League | GP | G | A | Pts | PIM | GP | G | A | Pts | PIM |
| 2002-03 | Lada Togliatti 2 | Russia-3 | 31 | 3 | 5 | 8 | 12 | .... | .... | .... | .... | .... |
| 2003-04 | Lada Togliatti 2 | Russia-3 | 10 | 1 | 1 | 2 | 4 | .... | .... | .... | .... | .... |
| | Lada Togliatti | Russia | 23 | 1 | 0 | 1 | 12 | 4 | 0 | 0 | 0 | 4 |
| 2004-05 | Lada Togliatti | Russia | 53 | 2 | 6 | 8 | 30 | 10 | 0 | 0 | 0 | 8 |
| 2005-06 | Lada Togliatti | Russia | 42 | 1 | 7 | 8 | 73 | 8 | 0 | 0 | 0 | 8 |
| 2006-07 | Lada Togliatti | Russia | 54 | 10 | 7 | 17 | 48 | 3 | 0 | 0 | 0 | 6 |
| 2007-08 | Lada Togliatti | Russia | 55 | 16 | 12 | 28 | 74 | 4 | 3 | 0 | 3 | 2 |
| 2008-09 | Lada Togliatti | Rus-KHL | 39 | 4 | 14 | 18 | 18 | .... | .... | .... | .... | .... |
| | Ufa | Rus-KHL | 5 | 0 | 0 | 0 | 0 | .... | .... | .... | .... | .... |

## VOROSHNIN, Pavel (vo-rohsh-NIHN, PAH-vehl) BUF.

Defense. Shoots left. 6'2", 183 lbs. Born, Chelyabinsk, USSR, March 23, 1984.
(Buffalo's 7th choice, 172nd overall, in 2003 Entry Draft).

| | | | Regular Season | | | | | Playoffs | | | | |
|---|---|---|---|---|---|---|---|---|---|---|---|---|
| Season | Club | League | GP | G | A | Pts | PIM | GP | G | A | Pts | PIM |
| 2001-02 | Chelyabinsk | Russia-2 | 32 | 0 | 2 | 2 | 10 | .... | .... | .... | .... | .... |
| 2002-03 | Mississauga | OHL | 68 | 9 | 27 | 36 | 81 | 1 | 0 | 0 | 0 | 2 |
| 2003-04 | Mississauga | OHL | 18 | 0 | 4 | 4 | 6 | .... | .... | .... | .... | .... |
| | Owen Sound | OHL | 40 | 3 | 18 | 21 | 36 | 7 | 0 | 2 | 2 | 4 |
| 2004-05 | Metallurg Serov | Russia-2 | 34 | 0 | 1 | 1 | 12 | .... | .... | .... | .... | .... |
| 2005-06 | Lada Togliatti | Russia | 33 | 0 | 1 | 1 | 18 | 8 | 0 | 1 | 1 | 0 |
| 2006-07 | Lada Togliatti | Russia | 3 | 0 | 0 | 0 | 2 | .... | .... | .... | .... | .... |
| | Mytischi | Russia | 9 | 0 | 1 | 1 | 0 | .... | .... | .... | .... | .... |
| 2007-08 | Mytischi | Russia | 18 | 0 | 0 | 0 | 12 | .... | .... | .... | .... | .... |
| 2008-09 | Khimik | Rus-KHL | 41 | 1 | 5 | 6 | 28 | .... | .... | .... | .... | .... |

## VOYNOV, Viatcheslav (VOY-nawf, v'ya-cheh-SLAV) L.A.

Defense. Shoots right. 5'11", 186 lbs. Born, Chelyabinsk, USSR, January 15, 1990.
(Los Angeles' 3rd choice, 32nd overall, in 2008 Entry Draft).

| | | | Regular Season | | | | | Playoffs | | | | |
|---|---|---|---|---|---|---|---|---|---|---|---|---|
| Season | Club | League | GP | G | A | Pts | PIM | GP | G | A | Pts | PIM |
| 2005-06 | Chelyabinsk 2 | Russia-3 | 2 | 0 | 0 | 0 | 0 | .... | .... | .... | .... | .... |
| 2006-07 | Chelyabinsk | Russia | 31 | 0 | 0 | 0 | 12 | .... | .... | .... | .... | .... |
| 2007-08 | Chelyabinsk 2 | Russia-3 | 2 | 1 | 0 | 1 | 0 | .... | .... | .... | .... | .... |
| | Chelyabinsk | Russia | 36 | 1 | 3 | 4 | 20 | 2 | 0 | 0 | 0 | 0 |
| 2008-09 | Manchester | AHL | 61 | 8 | 15 | 23 | 46 | .... | .... | .... | .... | .... |

## WAHL, Mitch (WAWL, MIHTCH) CGY.

Center. Shoots right. 6', 175 lbs. Born, Long Beach, CA, January 22, 1990.
(Calgary's 2nd choice, 48th overall, in 2008 Entry Draft).

| | | | Regular Season | | | | | Playoffs | | | | |
|---|---|---|---|---|---|---|---|---|---|---|---|---|
| Season | Club | League | GP | G | A | Pts | PIM | GP | G | A | Pts | PIM |
| 2005-06 | L.A. Jr. Kings | Minor-CA | 64 | 40 | 50 | 90 | 95 | .... | .... | .... | .... | .... |
| | Spokane Chiefs | WHL | 2 | 0 | 0 | 0 | 0 | .... | .... | .... | .... | .... |
| 2006-07 | Spokane Chiefs | WHL | 69 | 16 | 32 | 48 | 50 | 4 | 0 | 1 | 1 | 5 |
| 2007-08 | Spokane Chiefs | WHL | 67 | 20 | 53 | 73 | 63 | 21 | 6 | 8 | 14 | 20 |
| 2008-09 | Spokane Chiefs | WHL | 63 | 32 | 35 | 67 | 78 | 12 | 2 | 11 | 13 | 6 |

Memorial Cup All-Star Team (2008)

**WALKER, Julian** (WAH-kuhr, JEW-lee-ehn) **MIN.**

Wing. Shoots right. 6'2", 209 lbs. Born, Bern, Switz., September 10, 1986.
(Minnesota's 6th choice, 162nd overall, in 2006 Entry Draft).

| | | | Regular Season | | | | | Playoffs | | | | |
|---|---|---|---|---|---|---|---|---|---|---|---|---|
| **Season** | **Club** | **League** | **GP** | **G** | **A** | **Pts** | **PIM** | **GP** | **G** | **A** | **Pts** | **PIM** |
| 2001-02 | SC Bern Jr. | Swiss-Jr. | .... | .... | .... | .... | .... | 1 | 0 | 0 | 0 | 0 |
| 2002-03 | SC Bern Jr. | Swiss-Jr. | 34 | 2 | 5 | 7 | 14 | 3 | 0 | 0 | 0 | 4 |
| 2003-04 | SC Bern Jr. | Swiss-Jr. | 35 | 15 | 15 | 30 | 91 | 7 | 2 | 3 | 5 | 8 |
| 2004-05 | SC Bern Jr. | Swiss-Jr. | 42 | 25 | 32 | 57 | 84 | 9 | 1 | 11 | 12 | 10 |
| | SC Langenthal | Swiss-2 | 3 | 0 | 0 | 0 | 0 | .... | .... | .... | .... | .... |
| 2005-06 | EHC Basel Jr. | Swiss-Jr. | 6 | 3 | 2 | 5 | 6 | .... | .... | .... | .... | .... |
| | EHC Olten | Swiss-2 | 2 | 0 | 0 | 0 | 2 | .... | .... | .... | .... | .... |
| | EHC Basel | Swiss | 36 | 2 | 0 | 2 | 41 | 5 | 1 | 0 | 1 | 6 |
| 2006-07 | EHC Basel | Swiss | 40 | 4 | 4 | 8 | 16 | 13 | 0 | 1 | 1 | 6 |
| | EHC Olten | Swiss-2 | 8 | 8 | 4 | 12 | 0 | .... | .... | .... | .... | .... |
| 2007-08 | EHC Basel | Swiss | 50 | 0 | 6 | 6 | 22 | 8 | 2 | 0 | 2 | 10 |
| | EHC Basel | Swiss-Q | .... | .... | .... | .... | .... | 4 | 2 | 1 | 3 | 2 |
| 2008-09 | HC Ambri-Piotta | Swiss | 50 | 11 | 14 | 25 | 36 | 9 | 0 | 0 | 0 | 8 |

**WALSH, Dustin** (WAWLSH, DUHS-tihn) **MTL.**

Center. Shoots left. 6'3", 181 lbs. Born, Shannonville, Ont., March 20, 1991.
(Montreal's 6th choice, 169th overall, in 2009 Entry Draft).

| | | | Regular Season | | | | | Playoffs | | | | |
|---|---|---|---|---|---|---|---|---|---|---|---|---|
| **Season** | **Club** | **League** | **GP** | **G** | **A** | **Pts** | **PIM** | **GP** | **G** | **A** | **Pts** | **PIM** |
| 2007-08 | Quinte West Pack | OPJHL | 22 | 11 | 7 | 18 | 10 | .... | .... | .... | .... | .... |
| 2008-09 | Trenton Hercs | OJHL | 32 | 22 | 20 | 42 | 20 | .... | .... | .... | .... | .... |
| | Kingston | OJHL | 12 | 10 | 11 | 21 | 8 | 25 | 13 | 11 | 24 | 10 |

• Signed Letter of Intent to attend **Dartmouth University** (ECAC) in fall of 2009.

**WALSKY, Eric** (WAHL-sky, AIR-ihk) **VAN.**

Right wing. Shoots right. 5'11", 196 lbs. Born, Anchorage, AK, September 30, 1984.

| | | | Regular Season | | | | | Playoffs | | | | |
|---|---|---|---|---|---|---|---|---|---|---|---|---|
| **Season** | **Club** | **League** | **GP** | **G** | **A** | **Pts** | **PIM** | **GP** | **G** | **A** | **Pts** | **PIM** |
| 2002-03 | Anchorage East | High-AK | .... | 32 | 32 | 64 | .... | .... | .... | .... | .... | .... |
| 2003-04 | River City Lancers | USHL | 45 | 9 | 16 | 25 | 16 | 3 | 0 | 0 | 0 | 0 |
| 2004-05 | Alaska Anchorage | WCHA | 16 | 3 | 4 | 7 | 2 | .... | .... | .... | .... | .... |
| 2005-06 | Alaska Anchorage | WCHA | 35 | 3 | 12 | 15 | 14 | .... | .... | .... | .... | .... |
| 2006-07 | Colorado College | WCHA | DID NOT PLAY – TRANSFERRED COLLEGES | | | | | | | | | |
| 2007-08 | Colorado College | WCHA | 41 | 12 | 8 | 20 | 14 | .... | .... | .... | .... | .... |
| 2008-09 | Colorado College | WCHA | 38 | 12 | 24 | 36 | 24 | .... | .... | .... | .... | .... |
| | Manitoba Moose | AHL | 5 | 0 | 2 | 2 | 0 | .... | .... | .... | .... | .... |

Signed as a free agent by **Vancouver**, March 20, 2009.

**WARG, Stefan** (WAHRG, STEH-fan) **ANA.**

Defense. Shoots right. 6'3", 204 lbs. Born, Stockholm, Sweden, February 6, 1990.
(Anaheim's 9th choice, 143rd overall, in 2008 Entry Draft).

| | | | Regular Season | | | | | Playoffs | | | | |
|---|---|---|---|---|---|---|---|---|---|---|---|---|
| **Season** | **Club** | **League** | **GP** | **G** | **A** | **Pts** | **PIM** | **GP** | **G** | **A** | **Pts** | **PIM** |
| 2006-07 | Vasteras U18 | Swe-U18 | 14 | 0 | 6 | 6 | 14 | 5 | 0 | 0 | 0 | 6 |
| 2007-08 | Vasteras U18 | Swe-U18 | 1 | 0 | 0 | 0 | 12 | .... | .... | .... | .... | .... |
| | Vasteras Jr. | Swe-Jr. | 33 | 2 | 6 | 8 | 61 | 3 | 0 | 0 | 0 | 14 |
| | VIK Vasteras HK | Sweden-2 | 3 | 0 | 0 | 0 | 0 | .... | .... | .... | .... | .... |
| 2008-09 | Seattle | WHL | 70 | 1 | 16 | 17 | 80 | 5 | 0 | 0 | 0 | 2 |

**WARN, Max** (VAHRN, MAX) **DAL.**

Left wing. Shoots left. 6'2", 194 lbs. Born, Helsinki, Finland, June 10, 1988.
(Dallas' 5th choice, 150th overall, in 2006 Entry Draft).

| | | | Regular Season | | | | | Playoffs | | | | |
|---|---|---|---|---|---|---|---|---|---|---|---|---|
| **Season** | **Club** | **League** | **GP** | **G** | **A** | **Pts** | **PIM** | **GP** | **G** | **A** | **Pts** | **PIM** |
| 2004-05 | HIFK Helsinki U18 | Fin-U18 | 22 | 6 | 9 | 15 | 30 | 7 | 1 | 3 | 4 | 4 |
| | HIFK Helsinki Jr. | Fin-Jr. | 4 | 0 | 0 | 0 | 0 | 2 | 0 | 0 | 0 | 0 |
| 2005-06 | HIFK Helsinki U18 | Fin-U18 | 7 | 5 | 4 | 9 | 6 | 7 | 4 | 2 | 6 | 6 |
| | HIFK Helsinki Jr. | Fin-Jr. | 24 | 3 | 10 | 13 | 39 | .... | .... | .... | .... | .... |
| 2006-07 | HIFK Helsinki Jr. | Fin-Jr. | 13 | 5 | 6 | 11 | 10 | 10 | 4 | 6 | 10 | 6 |
| | HIFK Helsinki | Finland | 1 | 0 | 0 | 0 | 0 | .... | .... | .... | .... | .... |
| 2007-08 | Suomi U20 | Finland-2 | 4 | 0 | 0 | 0 | 4 | .... | .... | .... | .... | .... |
| | HPK Hameenlinna | Finland | 4 | 0 | 0 | 0 | 0 | .... | .... | .... | .... | .... |
| | Kiekko-Vantaa | Finland-2 | 1 | 2 | 0 | 2 | 0 | .... | .... | .... | .... | .... |
| | HIFK Helsinki Jr. | Fin-Jr. | 14 | 3 | 3 | 6 | 12 | .... | .... | .... | .... | .... |
| | HIFK Helsinki | Finland | 23 | 0 | 0 | 0 | 4 | 5 | 0 | 0 | 0 | 0 |
| 2008-09 | HIFK Helsinki | Finland | 51 | 5 | 11 | 16 | 26 | 2 | 0 | 0 | 0 | 0 |

**WARSOFSKY, David** (wawr-SAWF-skee, DAY-vihd) **ST.L.**

Defense. Shoots left. 5'8", 164 lbs. Born, Marshfield, MA, May 30, 1990.
(St. Louis' 7th choice, 95th overall, in 2008 Entry Draft).

| | | | Regular Season | | | | | Playoffs | | | | |
|---|---|---|---|---|---|---|---|---|---|---|---|---|
| **Season** | **Club** | **League** | **GP** | **G** | **A** | **Pts** | **PIM** | **GP** | **G** | **A** | **Pts** | **PIM** |
| 2005-06 | Cushing | High-MA | .... | 8 | 26 | 34 | .... | .... | .... | .... | .... | .... |
| 2006-07 | Cushing | High-MA | 29 | 15 | 34 | 49 | 55 | .... | .... | .... | .... | .... |
| 2007-08 | USNTDP | U-18 | 41 | 5 | 29 | 34 | 26 | .... | .... | .... | .... | .... |
| | USNTDP | NAHL | 15 | 4 | 2 | 6 | 8 | .... | .... | .... | .... | .... |
| 2008-09 | Boston University | H-East | 45 | 3 | 20 | 23 | 28 | .... | .... | .... | .... | .... |

**WATHIER, Francis** (waw-TEE-ay, FRAN-sihs) **DAL.**

Left wing. Shoots left. 6'3", 198 lbs. Born, St Isidore, Ont., December 7, 1984.
(Dallas' 8th choice, 185th overall, in 2003 Entry Draft).

| | | | Regular Season | | | | | Playoffs | | | | |
|---|---|---|---|---|---|---|---|---|---|---|---|---|
| **Season** | **Club** | **League** | **GP** | **G** | **A** | **Pts** | **PIM** | **GP** | **G** | **A** | **Pts** | **PIM** |
| 2001-02 | Hull Olympiques | QMJHL | 63 | 1 | 3 | 4 | 68 | 12 | 1 | 2 | 3 | 30 |
| 2002-03 | Hull Olympiques | QMJHL | 72 | 9 | 18 | 27 | 143 | 20 | 1 | 6 | 7 | 20 |
| 2003-04 | Gatineau | QMJHL | 51 | 9 | 16 | 25 | 127 | 15 | 0 | 2 | 2 | 23 |
| 2004-05 | Gatineau | QMJHL | 67 | 15 | 20 | 35 | 96 | 10 | 0 | 2 | 2 | 8 |
| 2005-06 | Iowa Stars | AHL | 11 | 0 | 1 | 1 | 26 | .... | .... | .... | .... | .... |
| 2006-07 | Iowa Stars | AHL | 57 | 14 | 3 | 17 | 78 | 12 | 0 | 4 | 4 | 25 |
| | Idaho Steelheads | ECHL | 17 | 4 | 9 | 13 | 31 | 7 | 1 | 1 | 2 | 4 |
| 2007-08 | Iowa Stars | AHL | 19 | 2 | 3 | 5 | 17 | .... | .... | .... | .... | .... |
| 2008-09 | Iowa Chops | AHL | 77 | 6 | 10 | 16 | 127 | .... | .... | .... | .... | .... |

• Missed majority of 2005-06 season recovering from two shoulder injuries.

**WATKINS, Matt** (WAHT-kihns, MAT) **DAL.**

Right wing. Shoots left. 5'10", 180 lbs. Born, Aylesbury, Sask., November 22, 1986.
(Dallas' 6th choice, 160th overall, in 2005 Entry Draft).

| | | | Regular Season | | | | | Playoffs | | | | |
|---|---|---|---|---|---|---|---|---|---|---|---|---|
| **Season** | **Club** | **League** | **GP** | **G** | **A** | **Pts** | **PIM** | **GP** | **G** | **A** | **Pts** | **PIM** |
| 2003-04 | Tisdale Trojans | SMHL | 44 | 34 | 37 | 71 | 52 | .... | .... | .... | .... | .... |
| 2004-05 | Vernon Vipers | BCHL | 60 | 36 | 38 | 74 | 53 | .... | .... | .... | .... | .... |
| 2005-06 | North Dakota | WCHA | 46 | 5 | 4 | 9 | 45 | .... | .... | .... | .... | .... |
| 2006-07 | North Dakota | WCHA | 38 | 6 | 11 | 17 | 31 | .... | .... | .... | .... | .... |
| 2007-08 | North Dakota | WCHA | 43 | 8 | 10 | 18 | 34 | .... | .... | .... | .... | .... |
| 2008-09 | North Dakota | WCHA | 41 | 7 | 7 | 14 | 40 | .... | .... | .... | .... | .... |

**WATSON, Ryan** (WAWT-suhn , RIGH-uhn) **FLA.**

Left wing. Shoots left. 6'1", 175 lbs. Born, Cambridge, Ont., March 1, 1988.
(Florida's 7th choice, 191st overall, in 2007 Entry Draft).

| | | | Regular Season | | | | | Playoffs | | | | |
|---|---|---|---|---|---|---|---|---|---|---|---|---|
| **Season** | **Club** | **League** | **GP** | **G** | **A** | **Pts** | **PIM** | **GP** | **G** | **A** | **Pts** | **PIM** |
| 2005-06 | Cambridge | OJHL-B | 46 | 7 | 19 | 26 | 58 | 16 | 5 | 5 | 10 | 14 |
| 2006-07 | Cambridge | OJHL-B | 37 | 27 | 29 | 56 | 55 | 9 | 2 | 7 | 9 | 18 |
| 2007-08 | Western Mich. | CCHA | 34 | 4 | 4 | 8 | 16 | .... | .... | .... | .... | .... |
| 2008-09 | Western Mich. | CCHA | 35 | 4 | 2 | 6 | 22 | .... | .... | .... | .... | .... |

**WATT, J.D.** (WAHT , JAY-DEE) **CGY.**

Right wing. Shoots right. 6'1", 198 lbs. Born, Calgary, Alta., May 25, 1987.
(Calgary's 4th choice, 111th overall, in 2005 Entry Draft).

| | | | Regular Season | | | | | Playoffs | | | | |
|---|---|---|---|---|---|---|---|---|---|---|---|---|
| **Season** | **Club** | **League** | **GP** | **G** | **A** | **Pts** | **PIM** | **GP** | **G** | **A** | **Pts** | **PIM** |
| 2003-04 | Drumheller | AJHL | 59 | 20 | 17 | 37 | 245 | .... | .... | .... | .... | .... |
| | Vancouver Giants | WHL | 3 | 1 | 0 | 1 | 0 | 10 | 0 | 3 | 3 | 14 |
| 2004-05 | Vancouver Giants | WHL | 66 | 6 | 7 | 13 | 213 | .... | .... | .... | .... | .... |
| 2005-06 | Vancouver Giants | WHL | 58 | 8 | 29 | 37 | 199 | 18 | 4 | 3 | 7 | 42 |
| 2006-07 | Vancouver Giants | WHL | 70 | 34 | 19 | 53 | 182 | 21 | 2 | 3 | 5 | 72 |
| 2007-08 | Red Deer Rebels | WHL | 29 | 7 | 8 | 15 | 87 | .... | .... | .... | .... | .... |
| | Regina Pats | WHL | 29 | 6 | 16 | 22 | 82 | 6 | 2 | 6 | 8 | 19 |
| 2008-09 | Quad City Flames | AHL | 42 | 0 | 2 | 2 | 146 | .... | .... | .... | .... | .... |
| | Las Vegas | ECHL | 18 | 5 | 9 | 14 | 51 | 16 | 3 | 4 | 7 | 70 |

**WAUGH, Geoff** (WAW, JEHF)

Defense. Shoots right. 6'4", 215 lbs. Born, Winnipeg, Man., August 25, 1983.
(Dallas' 6th choice, 78th overall, in 2002 Entry Draft).

| | | | Regular Season | | | | | Playoffs | | | | |
|---|---|---|---|---|---|---|---|---|---|---|---|---|
| **Season** | **Club** | **League** | **GP** | **G** | **A** | **Pts** | **PIM** | **GP** | **G** | **A** | **Pts** | **PIM** |
| 2000-01 | Kindersley Klippers | SJHL | 57 | 2 | 5 | 7 | 74 | .... | .... | .... | .... | .... |
| 2001-02 | Kindersley Klippers | SJHL | 59 | 4 | 21 | 25 | 125 | 18 | 0 | 8 | 8 | 59 |
| 2002-03 | Northern Mich. | CCHA | 39 | 0 | 7 | 7 | 41 | .... | .... | .... | .... | .... |
| 2003-04 | Northern Mich. | CCHA | 41 | 2 | 13 | 15 | 72 | .... | .... | .... | .... | .... |
| 2004-05 | Northern Mich. | CCHA | 39 | 2 | 8 | 10 | 89 | .... | .... | .... | .... | .... |
| 2005-06 | Northern Mich. | CCHA | 39 | 0 | 7 | 7 | 74 | .... | .... | .... | .... | .... |
| 2006-07 | Springfield Falcons | AHL | 10 | 0 | 0 | 0 | 25 | .... | .... | .... | .... | .... |
| | Johnstown Chiefs | ECHL | 56 | 1 | 12 | 13 | 91 | 2 | 1 | 0 | 1 | 4 |
| 2007-08 | Binghamton | AHL | 71 | 3 | 3 | 6 | 139 | .... | .... | .... | .... | .... |
| 2008-09 | Binghamton | AHL | 27 | 0 | 2 | 2 | 23 | .... | .... | .... | .... | .... |
| | Portland Pirates | AHL | 13 | 0 | 1 | 1 | 33 | 2 | 0 | 0 | 0 | 2 |
| | Elmira Jackals | ECHL | 2 | 0 | 0 | 0 | 11 | .... | .... | .... | .... | .... |

Signed as a free agent by **Ottawa**, August 11, 2008.

**WEBER, Will** (WEH-buhr, WIHL) **CBJ**

Defense. Shoots left. 6'4", 205 lbs. Born, Gaylord, MI, October 28, 1988.
(Columbus' 3rd choice, 53rd overall, in 2007 Entry Draft).

| | | | Regular Season | | | | | Playoffs | | | | |
|---|---|---|---|---|---|---|---|---|---|---|---|---|
| **Season** | **Club** | **League** | **GP** | **G** | **A** | **Pts** | **PIM** | **GP** | **G** | **A** | **Pts** | **PIM** |
| 2003-04 | Gaylord | High-MI | STATISTICS NOT AVAILABLE | | | | | | | | | |
| 2004-05 | Gaylord | High-MI | STATISTICS NOT AVAILABLE | | | | | | | | | |
| 2005-06 | Gaylord | High-MI | STATISTICS NOT AVAILABLE | | | | | | | | | |
| 2006-07 | Gaylord | High-MI | 25 | 18 | 20 | 38 | 104 | .... | .... | .... | .... | .... |
| 2007-08 | Chicago Steel | USHL | 46 | 8 | 10 | 18 | 137 | .... | .... | .... | .... | .... |
| 2008-09 | Miami U. | CCHA | 38 | 3 | 2 | 5 | 75 | .... | .... | .... | .... | .... |

**WEISE, Dale** (WIHGS, DAYL) **NYR**

Right wing. Shoots right. 6'2", 209 lbs. Born, Winnipeg, Man., August 5, 1988.
(NY Rangers' 5th choice, 111th overall, in 2008 Entry Draft).

| | | | Regular Season | | | | | Playoffs | | | | |
|---|---|---|---|---|---|---|---|---|---|---|---|---|
| **Season** | **Club** | **League** | **GP** | **G** | **A** | **Pts** | **PIM** | **GP** | **G** | **A** | **Pts** | **PIM** |
| 2005-06 | Swift Current | WHL | 53 | 4 | 14 | 18 | 57 | 4 | 0 | 0 | 0 | 2 |
| 2006-07 | Swift Current | WHL | 67 | 18 | 25 | 43 | 94 | 6 | 0 | 1 | 1 | 8 |
| 2007-08 | Swift Current | WHL | 53 | 29 | 22 | 51 | 84 | 12 | 7 | 6 | 13 | 20 |
| 2008-09 | Hartford Wolf Pack | AHL | 74 | 11 | 12 | 23 | 64 | 6 | 3 | 1 | 4 | 2 |

**WELLER, Justin** (WEHL-uhr, JUHS-tihn) **PHX.**

Defense. Shoots right. 6'2", 205 lbs. Born, Daysland, Alta., July 26, 1991.
(Phoenix's 5th choice, 105th overall, in 2009 Entry Draft).

| | | | Regular Season | | | | | Playoffs | | | | |
|---|---|---|---|---|---|---|---|---|---|---|---|---|
| **Season** | **Club** | **League** | **GP** | **G** | **A** | **Pts** | **PIM** | **GP** | **G** | **A** | **Pts** | **PIM** |
| 2006-07 | Sherwood Park | AMHL | 35 | 0 | 8 | 8 | 46 | 9 | 3 | 2 | 5 | 10 |
| 2007-08 | Red Deer Rebels | WHL | 49 | 0 | 3 | 3 | 40 | .... | .... | .... | .... | .... |
| 2008-09 | Red Deer Rebels | WHL | 32 | 0 | 4 | 4 | 30 | .... | .... | .... | .... | .... |

**WELLER, Shawn** (WEHL-uhr, SHAWN) **OTT.**

Left wing. Shoots left. 6'1", 199 lbs. Born, Glens Falls, NY, July 8, 1986.
(Ottawa's 3rd choice, 77th overall, in 2004 Entry Draft).

| | | | Regular Season | | | | | Playoffs | | | | |
|---|---|---|---|---|---|---|---|---|---|---|---|---|
| Season | Club | League | GP | G | A | Pts | PIM | GP | G | A | Pts | PIM |
| 2001-02 | South Glen Falls | High-NY | 25 | 32 | 21 | 53 | .... | .... | .... | .... | .... | .... |
| 2002-03 | Capital District | EJHL | STATISTICS NOT AVAILABLE | | | | | | | | | |
| 2003-04 | Capital District | EJHL | 37 | 18 | 25 | 43 | 110 | 3 | 3 | 3 | 6 | 6 |
| | Capital District | Exhib. | 30 | 16 | 19 | 35 | 78 | .... | .... | .... | .... | .... |
| 2004-05 | Clarkson Knights | ECAC | 33 | 3 | 11 | 14 | 72 | .... | .... | .... | .... | .... |
| 2005-06 | Clarkson Knights | ECAC | 37 | 14 | 10 | 24 | *103 | .... | .... | .... | .... | .... |
| 2006-07 | Clarkson Knights | ECAC | 39 | 19 | 21 | 40 | 62 | .... | .... | .... | .... | .... |
| | Binghamton | AHL | 5 | 0 | 0 | 0 | 4 | .... | .... | .... | .... | .... |
| 2007-08 | Binghamton | AHL | 59 | 8 | 8 | 16 | 40 | .... | .... | .... | .... | .... |
| | Elmira Jackals | ECHL | 10 | 4 | 5 | 9 | 11 | .... | .... | .... | .... | .... |
| 2008-09 | Binghamton | AHL | 70 | 4 | 5 | 9 | 57 | .... | .... | .... | .... | .... |
| | Elmira Jackals | ECHL | 4 | 1 | 1 | 2 | 2 | .... | .... | .... | .... | .... |

**WELLWOOD, Eric** (WEHL-wud, AIR-ihk) **PHI.**

Left wing. Shoots left. 5'11", 168 lbs. Born, Windsor, Ont., March 6, 1990.
(Philadelphia's 5th choice, 172nd overall, in 2009 Entry Draft).

| | | | Regular Season | | | | | Playoffs | | | | |
|---|---|---|---|---|---|---|---|---|---|---|---|---|
| Season | Club | League | GP | G | A | Pts | PIM | GP | G | A | Pts | PIM |
| 2006-07 | Tecumseh Chiefs | OJHL-B | 34 | 10 | 10 | 20 | 33 | .... | .... | .... | .... | .... |
| | Windsor Spitfires | OHL | 23 | 2 | 5 | 7 | 0 | .... | .... | .... | .... | .... |
| 2007-08 | Windsor Spitfires | OHL | 68 | 9 | 7 | 16 | 12 | 5 | 0 | 0 | 0 | 2 |
| 2008-09 | Windsor Spitfires | OHL | 61 | 16 | 18 | 34 | 12 | 20 | 10 | 11 | 21 | 12 |

**WEREK, Ethan** (WAIR-ehk, EE-thuhn) **NYR**

Center. Shoots left. 6'1", 190 lbs. Born, Markham, Ont., June 7, 1991.
(NY Rangers' 2nd choice, 47th overall, in 2009 Entry Draft).

| | | | Regular Season | | | | | Playoffs | | | | |
|---|---|---|---|---|---|---|---|---|---|---|---|---|
| Season | Club | League | GP | G | A | Pts | PIM | GP | G | A | Pts | PIM |
| 2006-07 | Toronto Marlboros | GTHL | 55 | 59 | 69 | 128 | 72 | .... | .... | .... | .... | .... |
| 2007-08 | Stouffville Spirit | OPJHL | 37 | 29 | 41 | 70 | 76 | 15 | 6 | 13 | 19 | 44 |
| 2008-09 | Kingston | OHL | 66 | 32 | 32 | 64 | 83 | .... | .... | .... | .... | .... |

**WERNER, Steve** (WUHR-nuhr, STEEV)

Right wing. Shoots right. 6'1", 200 lbs. Born, Washington, DC, August 8, 1984.
(Washington's 2nd choice, 83rd overall, in 2003 Entry Draft).

| | | | Regular Season | | | | | Playoffs | | | | |
|---|---|---|---|---|---|---|---|---|---|---|---|---|
| Season | Club | League | GP | G | A | Pts | PIM | GP | G | A | Pts | PIM |
| 99-2000 | Wsh. Jr. Capitals | MetroHL | 42 | 32 | 45 | 77 | .... | .... | .... | .... | .... | .... |
| 2000-01 | USNTDP | U-17 | 13 | 5 | 2 | 7 | 2 | .... | .... | .... | .... | .... |
| | USNTDP | NAHL | 56 | 7 | 21 | 28 | 24 | .... | .... | .... | .... | .... |
| 2001-02 | USNTDP | U-18 | 34 | 10 | 16 | 26 | 10 | .... | .... | .... | .... | .... |
| | USNTDP | USHL | 10 | 2 | 3 | 5 | 9 | .... | .... | .... | .... | .... |
| | USNTDP | NAHL | 10 | 4 | 1 | 5 | 23 | .... | .... | .... | .... | .... |
| 2002-03 | Massachusetts | H-East | 37 | 16 | 22 | 38 | 4 | .... | .... | .... | .... | .... |
| 2003-04 | Massachusetts | H-East | 33 | 7 | 17 | 24 | 18 | .... | .... | .... | .... | .... |
| 2004-05 | Massachusetts | H-East | 38 | 14 | 13 | 27 | 12 | .... | .... | .... | .... | .... |
| 2005-06 | Massachusetts | H-East | 35 | 13 | 14 | 27 | 26 | .... | .... | .... | .... | .... |
| | Hershey Bears | AHL | 4 | 0 | 3 | 3 | 2 | .... | .... | .... | .... | .... |
| 2006-07 | Hershey Bears | AHL | 26 | 3 | 3 | 6 | 26 | .... | .... | .... | .... | .... |
| | South Carolina | ECHL | 26 | 10 | 7 | 17 | 14 | .... | .... | .... | .... | .... |
| 2007-08 | Hershey Bears | AHL | 8 | 1 | 4 | 5 | 2 | .... | .... | .... | .... | .... |
| | Springfield Falcons | AHL | 30 | 9 | 4 | 13 | 23 | .... | .... | .... | .... | .... |
| 2008-09 | Milwaukee | AHL | 37 | 7 | 8 | 15 | 18 | .... | .... | .... | .... | .... |
| | Cincinnati | ECHL | 2 | 1 | 3 | 4 | 0 | .... | .... | .... | .... | .... |

Hockey East All-Rookie Team (2003)

**WESSBECKER, John** (WEHS-beh-kuhr, JAWN) **T.B.**

Defense. Shoots right. 6'1", 180 lbs. Born, Edina, MN, September 15, 1986.
(Tampa Bay's 9th choice, 225th overall, in 2005 Entry Draft).

| | | | Regular Season | | | | | Playoffs | | | | |
|---|---|---|---|---|---|---|---|---|---|---|---|---|
| Season | Club | League | GP | G | A | Pts | PIM | GP | G | A | Pts | PIM |
| 2004-05 | Blake Bears | High-MN | 16 | 6 | 16 | 22 | 38 | .... | .... | .... | .... | .... |
| 2005-06 | Massachusetts | H-East | 36 | 0 | 3 | 3 | 30 | .... | .... | .... | .... | .... |
| 2006-07 | Massachusetts | H-East | 38 | 1 | 0 | 1 | 14 | .... | .... | .... | .... | .... |
| 2007-08 | Massachusetts | H-East | 14 | 0 | 3 | 3 | 2 | .... | .... | .... | .... | .... |
| 2008-09 | Massachusetts | H-East | 35 | 1 | 4 | 5 | 34 | .... | .... | .... | .... | .... |

**WESTGARTH, Brett** (WEHST-garth, BREHT) **NYI**

Defense. Shoots right. 6'2", 215 lbs. Born, Amherstburg, Ont., February 4, 1982.

| | | | Regular Season | | | | | Playoffs | | | | |
|---|---|---|---|---|---|---|---|---|---|---|---|---|
| Season | Club | League | GP | G | A | Pts | PIM | GP | G | A | Pts | PIM |
| 2002-03 | Princeton | ECAC | 27 | 1 | 0 | 1 | 30 | .... | .... | .... | .... | .... |
| 2003-04 | Princeton | ECAC | 23 | 0 | 1 | 1 | 18 | .... | .... | .... | .... | .... |
| 2004-05 | | | DID NOT PLAY | | | | | | | | | |
| 2005-06 | Princeton | ECAC | 31 | 3 | 8 | 11 | 30 | .... | .... | .... | .... | .... |
| 2006-07 | Princeton | ECAC | 33 | 0 | 11 | 11 | 32 | .... | .... | .... | .... | .... |
| | Syracuse Crunch | AHL | 5 | 0 | 1 | 1 | 6 | .... | .... | .... | .... | .... |
| 2007-08 | Iowa Stars | AHL | 37 | 2 | 3 | 5 | 89 | .... | .... | .... | .... | .... |
| | Flint Generals | IHL | 27 | 2 | 10 | 12 | 39 | .... | .... | .... | .... | .... |
| 2008-09 | Worcester Sharks | AHL | 77 | 2 | 7 | 9 | 137 | 9 | 0 | 0 | 0 | 42 |

Signed as a free agent by **San Jose**, July 17, 2008. Signed as a free agent by **NY Islanders**, July 2, 2009.

**WEY, Patrick** (WAY, PAT-rihk) **WSH.**

Defense. Shoots right. 6'2", 209 lbs. Born, Pittsburgh, PA, March 21, 1991.
(Washington's 4th choice, 115th overall, in 2009 Entry Draft).

| | | | Regular Season | | | | | Playoffs | | | | |
|---|---|---|---|---|---|---|---|---|---|---|---|---|
| Season | Club | League | GP | G | A | Pts | PIM | GP | G | A | Pts | PIM |
| 2006-07 | Pittsburgh Hornets | MWEHL | 18 | 0 | 5 | 5 | 14 | .... | .... | .... | .... | .... |
| 2007-08 | Waterloo | USHL | 35 | 1 | 5 | 6 | 30 | 8 | 1 | 0 | 1 | 2 |
| 2008-09 | Waterloo | USHL | 58 | 7 | 27 | 34 | 75 | 3 | 0 | 0 | 0 | 0 |

• Signed Letter of Intent to attend **Boston College** (Hockey East) in fall of 2009.

**WHARTON, Kyle** (WAWR-tuhn, KIGHL)

Defense. Shoots left. 6'3", 196 lbs. Born, Ottawa, Ont., March 3, 1986.
(Columbus' 3rd choice, 59th overall, in 2004 Entry Draft).

| | | | Regular Season | | | | | Playoffs | | | | |
|---|---|---|---|---|---|---|---|---|---|---|---|---|
| Season | Club | League | GP | G | A | Pts | PIM | GP | G | A | Pts | PIM |
| 2001-02 | Ottawa Valley | Minor-ON | 34 | 18 | 24 | 42 | .... | .... | .... | .... | .... | .... |
| 2002-03 | Ottawa 67's | OHL | 39 | 3 | 5 | 8 | 16 | .... | .... | .... | .... | .... |
| 2003-04 | Ottawa 67's | OHL | 43 | 4 | 10 | 14 | 50 | 7 | 2 | 3 | 5 | 4 |
| 2004-05 | Ottawa 67's | OHL | 29 | 1 | 12 | 13 | 23 | .... | .... | .... | .... | .... |
| | Sault Ste. Marie | OHL | 28 | 4 | 12 | 16 | 22 | 7 | 1 | 5 | 6 | 4 |
| 2005-06 | Sault Ste. Marie | OHL | 34 | 6 | 16 | 22 | 62 | .... | .... | .... | .... | .... |
| | Guelph Storm | OHL | 24 | 2 | 14 | 16 | 34 | 15 | 4 | 8 | 12 | 20 |
| 2006-07 | Syracuse Crunch | AHL | 2 | 0 | 0 | 0 | 4 | .... | .... | .... | .... | .... |
| | Eisbaren Berlin | Germany | 30 | 2 | 6 | 8 | 36 | 3 | 0 | 0 | 0 | 14 |
| 2007-08 | Syracuse Crunch | AHL | 13 | 2 | 1 | 3 | 29 | .... | .... | .... | .... | .... |
| | Elmira Jackals | ECHL | 32 | 4 | 7 | 11 | 46 | .... | .... | .... | .... | .... |
| 2008-09 | Syracuse Crunch | AHL | 18 | 1 | 2 | 3 | 14 | .... | .... | .... | .... | .... |
| | Johnstown Chiefs | ECHL | 17 | 2 | 6 | 8 | 22 | .... | .... | .... | .... | .... |

Assigned to **Berlin** (Germany) by **Columbus**, October 25, 2006.

**WHITE, Patrick** (WIGHT, PAT-rihk) **VAN.**

Center. Shoots right. 6'1", 186 lbs. Born, Grand Rapids, MN, January 20, 1989.
(Vancouver's 1st choice, 25th overall, in 2007 Entry Draft).

| | | | Regular Season | | | | | Playoffs | | | | |
|---|---|---|---|---|---|---|---|---|---|---|---|---|
| Season | Club | League | GP | G | A | Pts | PIM | GP | G | A | Pts | PIM |
| 2003-04 | Grand Rapids | High-MN | .... | 3 | 6 | 9 | .... | .... | .... | .... | .... | .... |
| 2004-05 | Grand Rapids | High-MN | .... | 17 | 15 | 32 | .... | .... | .... | .... | .... | .... |
| 2005-06 | Grand Rapids | High-MN | .... | 24 | 28 | 52 | .... | .... | .... | .... | .... | .... |
| 2006-07 | Grand Rapids | High-MN | .... | 19 | 35 | 54 | .... | .... | .... | .... | .... | .... |
| | Tri-City Storm | USHL | 12 | 8 | 1 | 9 | 4 | .... | .... | .... | .... | .... |
| 2007-08 | U. of Minnesota | WCHA | 45 | 6 | 4 | 10 | 20 | .... | .... | .... | .... | .... |
| 2008-09 | U. of Minnesota | WCHA | 36 | 7 | 9 | 16 | 18 | .... | .... | .... | .... | .... |

**WHITE, Ryan** (WIGHT, RIGH-uhn) **MTL.**

Center. Shoots right. 6', 190 lbs. Born, Brandon, Man., March 17, 1988.
(Montreal's 4th choice, 66th overall, in 2006 Entry Draft).

| | | | Regular Season | | | | | Playoffs | | | | |
|---|---|---|---|---|---|---|---|---|---|---|---|---|
| Season | Club | League | GP | G | A | Pts | PIM | GP | G | A | Pts | PIM |
| 2003-04 | Brandon | MMHL | 39 | 21 | 41 | 62 | 90 | 11 | 7 | 7 | 14 | 22 |
| 2004-05 | Calgary Hitmen | WHL | 63 | 9 | 14 | 23 | 95 | 12 | 2 | 1 | 3 | 26 |
| 2005-06 | Calgary Hitmen | WHL | 72 | 20 | 33 | 53 | 121 | 13 | 3 | 4 | 7 | 18 |
| 2006-07 | Calgary Hitmen | WHL | 72 | 34 | 55 | 89 | 97 | 18 | 6 | 8 | 14 | 36 |
| 2007-08 | Calgary Hitmen | WHL | 68 | 28 | 44 | 72 | 98 | 16 | 6 | 11 | 17 | 8 |
| 2008-09 | Hamilton Bulldogs | AHL | 80 | 11 | 18 | 29 | 68 | 6 | 3 | 1 | 4 | 9 |

WHL East First All-Star Team (2007) • WHL East Second All-Star Team (2008)

**WHITMORE, Derek** (WHIHT-mohr, DAIR-ihk) **BUF.**

Forward. Shoots left. 5'11", 185 lbs. Born, Rochester, NY, December 17, 1984.

| | | | Regular Season | | | | | Playoffs | | | | |
|---|---|---|---|---|---|---|---|---|---|---|---|---|
| Season | Club | League | GP | G | A | Pts | PIM | GP | G | A | Pts | PIM |
| 2002-03 | Waterloo | USHL | 58 | 15 | 13 | 28 | 51 | 6 | 1 | 0 | 1 | 0 |
| 2003-04 | Waterloo | USHL | 10 | 2 | 0 | 2 | 6 | .... | .... | .... | .... | .... |
| | Lincoln Stars | USHL | 45 | 19 | 23 | 42 | 22 | .... | .... | .... | .... | .... |
| 2004-05 | Bowling Green | CCHA | 33 | 11 | 6 | 17 | 14 | .... | .... | .... | .... | .... |
| 2005-06 | Bowling Green | CCHA | 34 | 13 | 6 | 19 | 17 | .... | .... | .... | .... | .... |
| 2006-07 | Bowling Green | CCHA | 38 | 19 | 10 | 29 | 20 | .... | .... | .... | .... | .... |
| 2007-08 | Bowling Green | CCHA | 38 | 27 | 10 | 37 | 33 | .... | .... | .... | .... | .... |
| | Rochester | AHL | 8 | 1 | 0 | 1 | 2 | .... | .... | .... | .... | .... |
| 2008-09 | Portland Pirates | AHL | 77 | 11 | 11 | 22 | 17 | 5 | 1 | 1 | 2 | 2 |

CCHA Second All-Star Team (2008)

Signed as a free agent by **Buffalo**, March 26, 2008.

**WICK, Roman** (WIHK, ROH-muhn) **OTT.**

Right wing. Shoots left. 6'2", 192 lbs. Born, Kloten, Switz., December 30, 1985.
(Ottawa's 8th choice, 156th overall, in 2004 Entry Draft).

| | | | Regular Season | | | | | Playoffs | | | | |
|---|---|---|---|---|---|---|---|---|---|---|---|---|
| Season | Club | League | GP | G | A | Pts | PIM | GP | G | A | Pts | PIM |
| 2000-01 | Kloten Flyers Jr. | Swiss-Jr. | 26 | 4 | 1 | 5 | 6 | 5 | 1 | 0 | 1 | 2 |
| 2001-02 | Kloten Flyers Jr. | Swiss-Jr. | 34 | 19 | 27 | 46 | 32 | 8 | 1 | 2 | 3 | 4 |
| 2002-03 | Kloten Flyers Jr. | Swiss-Jr. | 28 | 29 | 22 | 51 | 68 | 2 | 0 | 1 | 1 | 0 |
| | Kloten Flyers | Swiss | 9 | 1 | 0 | 1 | 4 | 1 | 0 | 0 | 0 | 0 |
| 2003-04 | Kloten Flyers | Swiss | 20 | 1 | 1 | 2 | 6 | .... | .... | .... | .... | .... |
| | Kloten Flyers | Swiss-Q | 7 | 3 | 1 | 4 | 0 | .... | .... | .... | .... | .... |
| | GCK Lions Zurich | Swiss-2 | 6 | 4 | 0 | 4 | 6 | .... | .... | .... | .... | .... |
| 2004-05 | Red Deer Rebels | WHL | 66 | 32 | 38 | 70 | 25 | 7 | 1 | 2 | 3 | 6 |
| 2005-06 | Red Deer Rebels | WHL | 23 | 7 | 10 | 17 | 8 | .... | .... | .... | .... | .... |
| | Lethbridge | WHL | 38 | 14 | 17 | 31 | 20 | 6 | 4 | 3 | 7 | 6 |
| 2006-07 | Kloten Flyers | Swiss | 44 | 12 | 11 | 23 | 20 | 11 | 1 | 1 | 2 | 2 |
| 2007-08 | Kloten Flyers | Swiss | 50 | 12 | 15 | 27 | 46 | 4 | 1 | 2 | 3 | 2 |
| 2008-09 | Kloten Flyers | Swiss | 45 | 24 | 13 | 37 | 38 | 15 | 5 | *10 | *15 | 12 |

**WIDEMAN, Chris** (WIGHD-muhn, KRIHS) **OTT.**

Defense. Shoots right. 5'10", 170 lbs. Born, St. Louis, MO, January 7, 1990.
(Ottawa's 4th choice, 100th overall, in 2009 Entry Draft).

| | | | Regular Season | | | | | Playoffs | | | | |
|---|---|---|---|---|---|---|---|---|---|---|---|---|
| Season | Club | League | GP | G | A | Pts | PIM | GP | G | A | Pts | PIM |
| 2006-07 | St.L. AAA Blues | Minor-MO | 62 | 9 | 21 | 30 | 122 | .... | .... | .... | .... | .... |
| | St. Louis Bandits | NAHL | 1 | 0 | 0 | 0 | 0 | 7 | 0 | 1 | 1 | 4 |
| 2007-08 | Cedar Rapids | USHL | 53 | 2 | 12 | 14 | 51 | 1 | 0 | 0 | 0 | 0 |
| 2008-09 | Miami U. | CCHA | 39 | 0 | 26 | 26 | 56 | .... | .... | .... | .... | .... |

**WIERCIOCH, Patrick** (WEER-kawsh, PAT-rihk) **OTT.**

Defense. Shoots left. 6'5", 197 lbs. Born, Burnaby, B.C., September 12, 1990.
(Ottawa's 2nd choice, 42nd overall, in 2008 Entry Draft).

| | | | Regular Season | | | | | Playoffs | | | | |
|---|---|---|---|---|---|---|---|---|---|---|---|---|
| Season | Club | League | GP | G | A | Pts | PIM | GP | G | A | Pts | PIM |
| 2006-07 | Burnaby Express | BCHL | 42 | 9 | 16 | 25 | 46 | 14 | 3 | 4 | 7 | 10 |
| 2007-08 | Omaha Lancers | USHL | 40 | 3 | 18 | 21 | 24 | 14 | 2 | 9 | 11 | 22 |
| 2008-09 | U. of Denver | WCHA | 36 | 12 | 23 | 35 | 26 | .... | .... | .... | .... | .... |

WCHA All-Rookie Team (2009) • WCHA Second All-Star Team (2009)

## WILD, Cody (WIGHLD, KOH-dee) EDM.

Defense. Shoots left. 6'1", 185 lbs. Born, Limestone, ME, June 5, 1987.
(Edmonton's 4th choice, 140th overall, in 2006 Entry Draft).

| | | | Regular Season | | | | | Playoffs | | | | |
|---|---|---|---|---|---|---|---|---|---|---|---|---|
| Season | Club | League | GP | G | A | Pts | PIM | GP | G | A | Pts | PIM |
| 2003-04 | Bos. Jr. Bruins | EJHL | 53 | 5 | 24 | 29 | 12 | .... | .... | .... | .... | .... |
| 2004-05 | Bos. Jr. Bruins | EJHL | 64 | 16 | 36 | 52 | 44 | .... | .... | .... | .... | .... |
| 2005-06 | Providence College | H-East | 36 | 6 | 15 | 21 | 24 | .... | .... | .... | .... | .... |
| 2006-07 | Providence College | H-East | 32 | 6 | 8 | 14 | 28 | .... | .... | .... | .... | .... |
| 2007-08 | Providence College | H-East | 32 | 4 | 18 | 22 | 28 | .... | .... | .... | .... | .... |
| | Springfield Falcons | AHL | 13 | 1 | 2 | 3 | 8 | .... | .... | .... | .... | .... |
| 2008-09 | Springfield Falcons | AHL | 59 | 4 | 14 | 18 | 42 | .... | .... | .... | .... | .... |
| | Stockton Thunder | ECHL | 6 | 1 | 2 | 3 | 8 | .... | .... | .... | .... | .... |

Hockey East All-Rookie Team (2006)

## WILLIAMS, Nigel (WIHL-yuhms, NIGH-juhl) NYR

Defense. Shoots left. 6'4", 226 lbs. Born, Aurora, IL, April 18, 1988.
(Colorado's 2nd choice, 51st overall, in 2006 Entry Draft).

| | | | Regular Season | | | | | Playoffs | | | | |
|---|---|---|---|---|---|---|---|---|---|---|---|---|
| Season | Club | League | GP | G | A | Pts | PIM | GP | G | A | Pts | PIM |
| 2004-05 | Team Illinois | MWEHL | 60 | 14 | 18 | 32 | .... | .... | .... | .... | .... | .... |
| | USNTDP | U-17 | 3 | 2 | 1 | 3 | 4 | .... | .... | .... | .... | .... |
| 2005-06 | USNTDP | U-18 | 40 | 3 | 6 | 9 | 40 | .... | .... | .... | .... | .... |
| | USNTDP | NAHL | 19 | 3 | 4 | 7 | 23 | .... | .... | .... | .... | .... |
| 2006-07 | U. of Wisconsin | WCHA | 1 | 0 | 0 | 0 | 2 | .... | .... | .... | .... | .... |
| | Saginaw Spirit | OHL | 46 | 17 | 19 | 36 | 92 | 6 | 2 | 1 | 3 | 10 |
| 2007-08 | Saginaw Spirit | OHL | 29 | 5 | 19 | 24 | 60 | .... | .... | .... | .... | .... |
| | Belleville Bulls | OHL | 38 | 10 | 12 | 22 | 40 | 21 | 7 | 11 | 18 | 20 |
| 2008-09 | Lake Erie Monsters | AHL | 70 | 7 | 14 | 21 | 55 | .... | .... | .... | .... | .... |

Traded to **NY Rangers** by **Colorado** for Brian Fahey, July 16, 2009.

## WILSON, Colin (WIHL-suhn, KAW-lihn) NSH.

Center. Shoots left. 6'1", 215 lbs. Born, Greenwich, CT, October 20, 1989.
(Nashville's 1st choice, 7th overall, in 2008 Entry Draft).

| | | | Regular Season | | | | | Playoffs | | | | |
|---|---|---|---|---|---|---|---|---|---|---|---|---|
| Season | Club | League | GP | G | A | Pts | PIM | GP | G | A | Pts | PIM |
| 2005-06 | USNTDP | U-17 | 15 | 9 | 7 | 16 | 2 | .... | .... | .... | .... | .... |
| | USNTDP | U-18 | 16 | 2 | 4 | 6 | 8 | .... | .... | .... | .... | .... |
| | USNTDP | NAHL | 34 | 10 | 11 | 21 | 10 | 2 | 0 | 0 | 0 | 2 |
| 2006-07 | USNTDP | U-18 | 41 | 19 | 31 | 50 | 32 | .... | .... | .... | .... | .... |
| | USNTDP | NAHL | 15 | 11 | 13 | 24 | 21 | .... | .... | .... | .... | .... |
| 2007-08 | Boston University | H-East | 37 | 12 | 23 | 35 | 22 | .... | .... | .... | .... | .... |
| 2008-09 | Boston University | H-East | 43 | 17 | *38 | *55 | 52 | .... | .... | .... | .... | .... |

Hockey East All-Rookie Team (2008) • Hockey East Rookie of the Year (2008) • Hockey East First All-Star Team (2009) • NCAA East First All-American Team (2009) • NCAA Championship All-Tournament Team (2009)

## WILSON, Garrett (WIHL-suhn, GAIR-reht) FLA.

Left wing. Shoots left. 6'2", 199 lbs. Born, Barrie, Ont., March 16, 1991.
(Florida's 4th choice, 107th overall, in 2009 Entry Draft).

| | | | Regular Season | | | | | Playoffs | | | | |
|---|---|---|---|---|---|---|---|---|---|---|---|---|
| Season | Club | League | GP | G | A | Pts | PIM | GP | G | A | Pts | PIM |
| 2007-08 | Tecumseh Chiefs | OJHL-B | 46 | 11 | 26 | 37 | 40 | 14 | 13 | 8 | 21 | 22 |
| | Windsor Spitfires | OHL | 7 | 1 | 0 | 1 | 2 | 3 | 0 | 0 | 0 | 0 |
| 2008-09 | Owen Sound | OHL | 53 | 17 | 18 | 35 | 44 | 4 | 1 | 3 | 4 | 7 |

## WILSON, Kelsey (WIHL-suhn, KEHL-see) NSH.

Left wing. Shoots left. 6'1", 214 lbs. Born, Sault Ste. Marie, Ont., January 22, 1986.

| | | | Regular Season | | | | | Playoffs | | | | |
|---|---|---|---|---|---|---|---|---|---|---|---|---|
| Season | Club | League | GP | G | A | Pts | PIM | GP | G | A | Pts | PIM |
| 2003-04 | Sarnia Sting | OHL | 62 | 5 | 11 | 16 | 106 | 5 | 0 | 0 | 0 | 4 |
| 2004-05 | Sarnia Sting | OHL | 37 | 0 | 3 | 3 | 118 | .... | .... | .... | .... | .... |
| | Guelph Storm | OHL | 23 | 7 | 4 | 11 | 78 | 4 | 0 | 0 | 0 | 9 |
| 2005-06 | Guelph Storm | OHL | 67 | 38 | 31 | 69 | 196 | 15 | 12 | 6 | 18 | 33 |
| 2006-07 | Milwaukee | AHL | 74 | 9 | 10 | 19 | 215 | 4 | 0 | 0 | 0 | 6 |
| 2007-08 | Milwaukee | AHL | 66 | 8 | 11 | 19 | 179 | 6 | 1 | 0 | 1 | 22 |
| 2008-09 | Milwaukee | AHL | 80 | 15 | 17 | 32 | 160 | 10 | 1 | 2 | 3 | 20 |

Signed as a free agent by **Nashville**, October 6, 2006.

## WILSON, Kyle (WIHL-suhn, KIGHL) WSH.

Center. Shoots right. 6'1", 200 lbs. Born, Oakville, Ont., December 15, 1984.
(Minnesota's 12th choice, 272nd overall, in 2004 Entry Draft).

| | | | Regular Season | | | | | Playoffs | | | | |
|---|---|---|---|---|---|---|---|---|---|---|---|---|
| Season | Club | League | GP | G | A | Pts | PIM | GP | G | A | Pts | PIM |
| 2000-01 | Strathroy Rockets | OHA-B | 33 | 12 | 17 | 29 | 15 | 5 | 2 | 2 | 4 | 2 |
| 2001-02 | Strathroy Rockets | OHA-B | 53 | 42 | 25 | 67 | 16 | .... | .... | .... | .... | .... |
| 2002-03 | Colgate | ECAC | 33 | 4 | 2 | 6 | 15 | .... | .... | .... | .... | .... |
| 2003-04 | Colgate | ECAC | 37 | 14 | 17 | 31 | 23 | .... | .... | .... | .... | .... |
| 2004-05 | Colgate | ECAC | 30 | 5 | 18 | 23 | 12 | .... | .... | .... | .... | .... |
| 2005-06 | Colgate | ECAC | 39 | *23 | 18 | 41 | 22 | .... | .... | .... | .... | .... |
| 2006-07 | San Antonio | AHL | 7 | 1 | 0 | 1 | 2 | .... | .... | .... | .... | .... |
| | South Carolina | ECHL | 5 | 3 | 2 | 5 | 4 | .... | .... | .... | .... | .... |
| | Hershey Bears | AHL | 54 | 24 | 30 | 54 | 26 | 19 | 7 | 9 | 16 | 8 |
| 2007-08 | Hershey Bears | AHL | 80 | 30 | 31 | 61 | 26 | 5 | 0 | 3 | 3 | 2 |
| 2008-09 | Hershey Bears | AHL | 80 | 28 | 30 | 58 | 31 | 22 | 3 | 7 | 10 | 2 |

ECAC Second All-Star Team (2006)

Signed as a free agent by **San Antonio** (AHL), October 6, 2006. Signed as a free agent by **Washington**, July 5, 2007.

## WILSON, Ryan (WIHL-suhn, RIGH-uhn) COL.

Defense. Shoots left. 6'1", 207 lbs. Born, Windsor, Ont., February 3, 1987.

| | | | Regular Season | | | | | Playoffs | | | | |
|---|---|---|---|---|---|---|---|---|---|---|---|---|
| Season | Club | League | GP | G | A | Pts | PIM | GP | G | A | Pts | PIM |
| 2003-04 | St. Michael's | OHL | 58 | 3 | 22 | 25 | 88 | 18 | 3 | 7 | 10 | 16 |
| 2004-05 | St. Michael's | OHL | 68 | 13 | 24 | 37 | 149 | 10 | 4 | 5 | 9 | 12 |
| 2005-06 | St. Michael's | OHL | 64 | 12 | 49 | 61 | 145 | 4 | 1 | 3 | 4 | 12 |
| 2006-07 | Sarnia Sting | OHL | 68 | 17 | 58 | 75 | 136 | 4 | 1 | 3 | 4 | 14 |
| 2007-08 | Sarnia Sting | OHL | 58 | 7 | 64 | 71 | 84 | 9 | 0 | 7 | 7 | 19 |
| 2008-09 | Quad City Flames | AHL | 60 | 4 | 16 | 20 | 56 | .... | .... | .... | .... | .... |
| | Lake Erie Monsters | AHL | 8 | 0 | 2 | 2 | 25 | .... | .... | .... | .... | .... |

Signed as a free agent by **Calgary**, July 1, 2008. Traded to **Colorado** by **Calgary** with Lawrence Nycholat and Montreal's 2nd round choice (previously acquired, Colorado selected Stefan Elliott) in 2009 Entry Draft for Jordan Leopold, March 4, 2009.

## WINGELS, Tommy (WIHN-guhls, TAW-mee) S.J.

Center. Shoots right. 6', 184 lbs. Born, Evanston, IL, April 12, 1988.
(San Jose's 5th choice, 177th overall, in 2008 Entry Draft).

| | | | Regular Season | | | | | Playoffs | | | | |
|---|---|---|---|---|---|---|---|---|---|---|---|---|
| Season | Club | League | GP | G | A | Pts | PIM | GP | G | A | Pts | PIM |
| 2006-07 | Cedar Rapids | USHL | 47 | 10 | 18 | 28 | 52 | 6 | 3 | 0 | 3 | 6 |
| 2007-08 | Miami U. | CCHA | 42 | 15 | 14 | 29 | 22 | .... | .... | .... | .... | .... |
| 2008-09 | Miami U. | CCHA | 41 | 11 | 17 | 28 | 66 | .... | .... | .... | .... | .... |

NCAA Championship All-Tournament Team (2009)

## WINKLER, Scott (WIHNK-luhr, SKAWT) DAL.

Center. Shoots right. 6'2", 194 lbs. Born, Asker, Norway, February 22, 1990.
(Dallas' 2nd choice, 89th overall, in 2008 Entry Draft).

| | | | Regular Season | | | | | Playoffs | | | | |
|---|---|---|---|---|---|---|---|---|---|---|---|---|
| Season | Club | League | GP | G | A | Pts | PIM | GP | G | A | Pts | PIM |
| 2005-06 | Frisk Asker IF/NTG | Norway-Jr. | 3 | 1 | 0 | 1 | 0 | .... | .... | .... | .... | .... |
| 2006-07 | Frisk Asker IF/NTG | Norway-Jr. | 26 | 34 | 30 | 64 | 20 | 8 | 5 | 3 | 8 | 2 |
| | Asker 2 | Norway-2 | 25 | 6 | 6 | 12 | 2 | .... | .... | .... | .... | .... |
| 2007-08 | Russell Stover | Minor-MO | 70 | 40 | 52 | 92 | 36 | .... | .... | .... | .... | .... |
| 2008-09 | Cedar Rapids | USHL | 55 | 10 | 26 | 36 | 35 | 5 | 0 | 2 | 2 | 0 |

• Signed Letter of Intent to attend **Colorado College** (WCHA) in fall of 2009.

## WINNETT, Ben (wih-NEHT, BEHN) TOR.

Left wing. Shoots right. 5'11", 173 lbs. Born, New Westminster, B.C., April 3, 1989.
(Toronto's 3rd choice, 104th overall, in 2007 Entry Draft).

| | | | Regular Season | | | | | Playoffs | | | | |
|---|---|---|---|---|---|---|---|---|---|---|---|---|
| Season | Club | League | GP | G | A | Pts | PIM | GP | G | A | Pts | PIM |
| 2005-06 | Salmon Arm | BCHL | 60 | 18 | 31 | 49 | 31 | 1 | 1 | 1 | 2 | 6 |
| 2006-07 | Salmon Arm | BCHL | 39 | 27 | 30 | 57 | 58 | 11 | 3 | 7 | 10 | 12 |
| 2007-08 | U. of Michigan | CCHA | 41 | 6 | 5 | 11 | 12 | .... | .... | .... | .... | .... |
| 2008-09 | U. of Michigan | CCHA | 32 | 4 | 7 | 11 | 16 | .... | .... | .... | .... | .... |

## WITKOWSKI, Luke (wiht-KOW-skee, LEWK) T.B.

Defense. Shoots right. 6'2", 200 lbs. Born, Holland, MI, April 14, 1990.
(Tampa Bay's 6th choice, 160th overall, in 2008 Entry Draft).

| | | | Regular Season | | | | | Playoffs | | | | |
|---|---|---|---|---|---|---|---|---|---|---|---|---|
| Season | Club | League | GP | G | A | Pts | PIM | GP | G | A | Pts | PIM |
| 2006-07 | Team nXi Majors | Minor-MI | 59 | 18 | 22 | 40 | 172 | .... | .... | .... | .... | .... |
| 2007-08 | Ohio | USHL | 58 | 3 | 10 | 13 | 139 | .... | .... | .... | .... | .... |
| 2008-09 | Fargo Force | USHL | 55 | 6 | 16 | 22 | 118 | 10 | 2 | 1 | 3 | 29 |

• Signed Letter of Intent to attend **Western Michigan University** (CCHA) in fall of 2009.

## WOHLBERG, David (WOHL-buhrg, DAY-vihd) N.J.

Center. Shoots left. 6'1", 190 lbs. Born, South Lyon, MI, July 18, 1990.
(New Jersey's 7th choice, 172nd overall, in 2008 Entry Draft).

| | | | Regular Season | | | | | Playoffs | | | | |
|---|---|---|---|---|---|---|---|---|---|---|---|---|
| Season | Club | League | GP | G | A | Pts | PIM | GP | G | A | Pts | PIM |
| 2006-07 | USNTDP | U-17 | 12 | 2 | 6 | 8 | 42 | .... | .... | .... | .... | .... |
| | USNTDP | NAHL | 45 | 10 | 10 | 20 | 99 | 6 | 3 | 0 | 3 | 6 |
| 2007-08 | USNTDP | U-18 | 37 | 9 | 7 | 16 | 48 | .... | .... | .... | .... | .... |
| | USNTDP | NAHL | 22 | 10 | 5 | 15 | 27 | .... | .... | .... | .... | .... |
| 2008-09 | U. of Michigan | CCHA | 40 | 15 | 15 | 30 | 51 | .... | .... | .... | .... | .... |

CCHA All-Rookie Team (2009) • CCHA Rookie of the Year (2009)

## WRENN, William (REHN, WILL-yuhm) S.J.

Defense. Shoots right. 6'1", 190 lbs. Born, Anchorage, AK, March 16, 1991.
(San Jose's 1st choice, 43rd overall, in 2009 Entry Draft).

| | | | Regular Season | | | | | Playoffs | | | | |
|---|---|---|---|---|---|---|---|---|---|---|---|---|
| Season | Club | League | GP | G | A | Pts | PIM | GP | G | A | Pts | PIM |
| 2007-08 | USNTDP | NAHL | 43 | 0 | 5 | 5 | 36 | 3 | 0 | 0 | 0 | 15 |
| | USNTDP | U-17 | 17 | 0 | 2 | 2 | 14 | .... | .... | .... | .... | .... |
| 2008-09 | USNTDP | NAHL | 13 | 1 | 4 | 5 | 37 | .... | .... | .... | .... | .... |
| | USNTDP | U-18 | 47 | 5 | 7 | 12 | 46 | .... | .... | .... | .... | .... |

• Signed Letter of Intent to attend **University of Denver** (WCHA) in fall of 2009.

## WRIGHT, James (RIGHT, JAYMZ) T.B.

Center. Shoots left. 6'3", 175 lbs. Born, Saskatoon, Sask., March 24, 1990.
(Tampa Bay's 2nd choice, 117th overall, in 2008 Entry Draft).

| | | | Regular Season | | | | | Playoffs | | | | |
|---|---|---|---|---|---|---|---|---|---|---|---|---|
| Season | Club | League | GP | G | A | Pts | PIM | GP | G | A | Pts | PIM |
| 2005-06 | Sask. Contacts | SMHL | 41 | 13 | 19 | 32 | 43 | .... | .... | .... | .... | .... |
| | Vancouver Giants | WHL | 2 | 0 | 0 | 0 | 2 | .... | .... | .... | .... | .... |
| 2006-07 | Vancouver Giants | WHL | 48 | 5 | 7 | 12 | 31 | 14 | 3 | 1 | 4 | 0 |
| 2007-08 | Vancouver Giants | WHL | 60 | 13 | 23 | 36 | 21 | 6 | 1 | 0 | 1 | 2 |
| 2008-09 | Vancouver Giants | WHL | 71 | 21 | 26 | 47 | 54 | 17 | 3 | 7 | 10 | 13 |

## WUDRICK, Geordie (WUD-rihk, JOHR-dee) L.A.

Left wing. Shoots left. 6'3", 213 lbs. Born, New Westminster, B.C., April 9, 1990.
(Los Angeles' 6th choice, 88th overall, in 2008 Entry Draft).

| | | | Regular Season | | | | | Playoffs | | | | |
|---|---|---|---|---|---|---|---|---|---|---|---|---|
| Season | Club | League | GP | G | A | Pts | PIM | GP | G | A | Pts | PIM |
| 2005-06 | Notre Dame | SMHL | 42 | 14 | 16 | 30 | 30 | .... | .... | .... | .... | .... |
| | Swift Current | WHL | 14 | 0 | 1 | 1 | 4 | 4 | 0 | 0 | 0 | 2 |
| 2006-07 | Swift Current | WHL | 67 | 13 | 11 | 24 | 60 | 6 | 1 | 1 | 2 | 4 |
| 2007-08 | Swift Current | WHL | 66 | 20 | 24 | 44 | 72 | 12 | 5 | 2 | 7 | 12 |
| 2008-09 | Swift Current | WHL | 69 | 35 | 22 | 57 | 77 | 7 | 0 | 2 | 2 | 6 |

**WYMAN, James** (WIGH-muhn, JAYMZ) **MTL.**

Right wing. Shoots right. 6'2", 201 lbs. Born, Edina, MN, February 27, 1986.
(Montreal's 3rd choice, 100th overall, in 2004 Entry Draft).

| | | | Regular Season | | | | | Playoffs | | | | |
|---|---|---|---|---|---|---|---|---|---|---|---|---|
| **Season** | **Club** | **League** | **GP** | **G** | **A** | **Pts** | **PIM** | **GP** | **G** | **A** | **Pts** | **PIM** |
| 2001-02 | Blake Bears | High-MN | 26 | 7 | 5 | 12 | .... | .... | .... | .... | .... | .... |
| 2002-03 | Blake Bears | High-MN | 28 | 17 | 23 | 40 | 12 | .... | .... | .... | .... | .... |
| 2003-04 | Blake Bears | High-MN | 27 | 31 | 24 | 55 | 4 | .... | .... | .... | .... | .... |
| | Team Southwest | UMEHL | 24 | 8 | 8 | 16 | .... | .... | .... | .... | .... | .... |
| 2004-05 | Dartmouth | ECAC | 33 | 5 | 6 | 11 | 4 | .... | .... | .... | .... | .... |
| 2005-06 | Dartmouth | ECAC | 28 | 8 | 12 | 20 | 6 | .... | .... | .... | .... | .... |
| 2006-07 | Dartmouth | ECAC | 33 | 13 | 11 | 24 | 20 | .... | .... | .... | .... | .... |
| 2007-08 | Dartmouth | ECAC | 29 | 15 | 15 | 30 | 18 | .... | .... | .... | .... | .... |
| | Hamilton Bulldogs | AHL | 8 | 0 | 1 | 1 | 5 | .... | .... | .... | .... | .... |
| 2008-09 | Hamilton Bulldogs | AHL | 52 | 6 | 5 | 11 | 8 | 6 | 0 | 1 | 1 | 2 |
| | Cincinnati | ECHL | 15 | 0 | 8 | 8 | 4 | .... | .... | .... | .... | .... |

**YACHMENEV, Denis** (YATCH-muh-nehv, DEH-nihs) **FLA.**

Left wing. Shoots left. 6'1", 185 lbs. Born, Chelyabinsk, USSR, June 4, 1984.
(Florida's 9th choice, 200th overall, in 2002 Entry Draft).

| | | | Regular Season | | | | | Playoffs | | | | |
|---|---|---|---|---|---|---|---|---|---|---|---|---|
| **Season** | **Club** | **League** | **GP** | **G** | **A** | **Pts** | **PIM** | **GP** | **G** | **A** | **Pts** | **PIM** |
| 2000-01 | Chelyabinsk 2 | Russia-3 | 36 | 40 | 27 | 67 | .... | .... | .... | .... | .... | .... |
| 2001-02 | North Bay | OHL | 65 | 17 | 12 | 29 | 32 | 5 | 2 | 0 | 2 | 0 |
| 2002-03 | Saginaw Spirit | OHL | 68 | 17 | 28 | 45 | 69 | .... | .... | .... | .... | .... |
| 2003-04 | Amur Khabarovsk | Russia | 25 | 0 | 1 | 1 | 4 | .... | .... | .... | .... | .... |
| | Omsk 2 | Russia-3 | 13 | 12 | 4 | 16 | 10 | .... | .... | .... | .... | .... |
| 2004-05 | Amur Khabarovsk | Russia-2 | 42 | 7 | 14 | 21 | 28 | 13 | 3 | 1 | 4 | 8 |
| 2005-06 | Amur Khabarovsk | Russia-2 | 46 | 9 | 14 | 23 | 43 | 11 | 2 | 3 | 5 | 6 |
| 2006-07 | Sibir Novosibirsk 2 | Russia-3 | 6 | 0 | 3 | 3 | 8 | .... | .... | .... | .... | .... |
| | Sibir Novosibirsk | Russia | 16 | 0 | 0 | 0 | 8 | 1 | 0 | 0 | 0 | 0 |
| 2007-08 | Chelyabinsk | Russia | 40 | 2 | 7 | 9 | 22 | 2 | 0 | 0 | 0 | 0 |
| 2008-09 | Chelyabinsk | Rus-KHL | 8 | 0 | 0 | 0 | 2 | .... | .... | .... | .... | .... |
| | Chelyabinsk 2 | Russia-3 | 49 | 29 | 20 | 49 | 48 | .... | .... | .... | .... | .... |

**YEMELIN, Alexei** (yeh-MUH-lehn, al-EHX-ay) **MTL.**

Defense. Shoots left. 6', 187 lbs. Born, Togliatti, USSR, April 25, 1986.
(Montreal's 2nd choice, 84th overall, in 2004 Entry Draft).

| | | | Regular Season | | | | | Playoffs | | | | |
|---|---|---|---|---|---|---|---|---|---|---|---|---|
| **Season** | **Club** | **League** | **GP** | **G** | **A** | **Pts** | **PIM** | **GP** | **G** | **A** | **Pts** | **PIM** |
| 2002-03 | Lada Togliatti 2 | Russia-3 | 31 | 1 | 1 | 2 | 20 | .... | .... | .... | .... | .... |
| 2003-04 | Lada Togliatti 2 | Russia-3 | 2 | 0 | 0 | 0 | 10 | .... | .... | .... | .... | .... |
| | CSK VVS Samara | Russia-2 | 52 | 2 | 4 | 6 | 180 | 1 | 0 | 0 | 0 | 18 |
| 2004-05 | Lada Togliatti | Russia | 12 | 0 | 1 | 1 | 24 | 2 | 0 | 0 | 0 | 2 |
| 2005-06 | Lada Togliatti | Russia | 44 | 6 | 6 | 12 | 131 | 6 | 0 | 1 | 1 | *47 |
| 2006-07 | Lada Togliatti | Russia | 43 | 2 | 5 | 7 | 74 | 3 | 0 | 0 | 0 | 4 |
| 2007-08 | Ak Bars Kazan | Russia | 56 | 0 | 5 | 5 | 123 | 10 | 0 | 1 | 1 | 10 |
| 2008-09 | Ak Bars Kazan | Rus-KHL | 51 | 0 | 3 | 3 | 58 | 7 | 1 | 0 | 1 | 20 |

**YIP, Brandon** (YIHP, BRAN-duhn) **COL.**

Right wing. Shoots right. 6'1", 180 lbs. Born, Vancouver, B.C., April 25, 1985.
(Colorado's 7th choice, 239th overall, in 2004 Entry Draft).

| | | | Regular Season | | | | | Playoffs | | | | |
|---|---|---|---|---|---|---|---|---|---|---|---|---|
| **Season** | **Club** | **League** | **GP** | **G** | **A** | **Pts** | **PIM** | **GP** | **G** | **A** | **Pts** | **PIM** |
| 2003-04 | Coquitlam Express | BCHL | 56 | 31 | 38 | 69 | 87 | 4 | 1 | 2 | 3 | 14 |
| 2004-05 | Coquitlam Express | BCHL | 43 | 20 | 42 | 62 | 92 | 7 | 6 | 1 | 7 | 12 |
| 2005-06 | Boston University | H-East | 39 | 9 | 22 | 31 | 59 | .... | .... | .... | .... | .... |
| 2006-07 | Boston University | H-East | 18 | 5 | 6 | 11 | 29 | .... | .... | .... | .... | .... |
| 2007-08 | Boston University | H-East | 37 | 11 | 12 | 23 | 28 | .... | .... | .... | .... | .... |
| 2008-09 | Boston University | H-East | 45 | 20 | 23 | 43 | 118 | .... | .... | .... | .... | .... |

Hockey East All-Rookie Team (2006) • Hockey East Rookie of the Year (2006)

**YOUNG, Gus** (YUHNG, GUHS) **COL.**

Defense. Shoots left. 6'2", 190 lbs. Born, Dedham, MA, July 10, 1991.
(Colorado's 7th choice, 184th overall, in 2009 Entry Draft).

| | | | Regular Season | | | | | Playoffs | | | | |
|---|---|---|---|---|---|---|---|---|---|---|---|---|
| **Season** | **Club** | **League** | **GP** | **G** | **A** | **Pts** | **PIM** | **GP** | **G** | **A** | **Pts** | **PIM** |
| 2006-07 | Nobles | High-MA | 31 | 3 | 10 | 13 | 14 | .... | .... | .... | .... | .... |
| 2007-08 | Nobles | High-MA | 29 | 6 | 9 | 15 | .... | .... | .... | .... | .... | .... |
| | Little Bruins | Minor-MA | 11 | 0 | 6 | 6 | .... | .... | .... | .... | .... | .... |
| 2008-09 | Nobles | High-MA | 29 | 5 | 29 | 34 | 16 | .... | .... | .... | .... | .... |
| | Cape Cod Whalers | Minor-MA | STATISTICS NOT AVAILABLE | | | | | | | | | |

• Signed Letter of Intent to attend **Yale University** (ECAC) in fall of 2010.

**YOUNG, Harry** (YUHNG, HAIR-ee) **N.J.**

Defense. Shoots left. 6'5", 200 lbs. Born, Windsor, Ont., November 12, 1989.
(New Jersey's 8th choice, 202nd overall, in 2008 Entry Draft).

| | | | Regular Season | | | | | Playoffs | | | | |
|---|---|---|---|---|---|---|---|---|---|---|---|---|
| **Season** | **Club** | **League** | **GP** | **G** | **A** | **Pts** | **PIM** | **GP** | **G** | **A** | **Pts** | **PIM** |
| 2005-06 | Guelph Storm | OHL | 44 | 0 | 4 | 4 | 20 | .... | .... | .... | .... | .... |
| 2006-07 | Guelph Storm | OHL | 7 | 0 | 2 | 2 | 11 | .... | .... | .... | .... | .... |
| | Windsor Spitfires | OHL | 47 | 0 | 3 | 3 | 72 | .... | .... | .... | .... | .... |
| 2007-08 | Windsor Spitfires | OHL | 68 | 2 | 12 | 14 | 155 | 5 | 0 | 1 | 1 | 8 |
| 2008-09 | Windsor Spitfires | OHL | 46 | 8 | 4 | 12 | 138 | 20 | 1 | 4 | 5 | *41 |

**YUNKOV, Mikhail** (yuhn-KAWF, mih-kigh-EHL) **WSH.**

Center. Shoots left. 6', 180 lbs. Born, Voskresensk, USSR, February 16, 1986.
(Washington's 5th choice, 62nd overall, in 2004 Entry Draft).

| | | | Regular Season | | | | | Playoffs | | | | |
|---|---|---|---|---|---|---|---|---|---|---|---|---|
| **Season** | **Club** | **League** | **GP** | **G** | **A** | **Pts** | **PIM** | **GP** | **G** | **A** | **Pts** | **PIM** |
| 2001-02 | Krylja Sovetov 2 | Russia-3 | 4 | 0 | 1 | 1 | 0 | .... | .... | .... | .... | .... |
| 2002-03 | Krylja Sovetov | Russia | 7 | 1 | 0 | 1 | 2 | .... | .... | .... | .... | .... |
| | Krylja Sovetov 2 | Russia-3 | 3 | 0 | 1 | 1 | 0 | .... | .... | .... | .... | .... |
| 2003-04 | Krylja Sovetov | Russia-2 | 38 | 5 | 10 | 15 | 12 | 4 | 0 | 1 | 1 | 0 |
| | Krylja Sovetov 2 | Russia-3 | STATISTICS NOT AVAILABLE | | | | | | | | | |
| 2004-05 | Krylja Sovetov 2 | Russia-3 | 1 | 0 | 0 | 0 | 0 | .... | .... | .... | .... | .... |
| | Krylja Sovetov | Russia-2 | 38 | 9 | 14 | 23 | 22 | 3 | 0 | 1 | 1 | 4 |
| 2005-06 | Ak Bars Kazan | Russia | 33 | 3 | 4 | 7 | 35 | 11 | 0 | 1 | 1 | 6 |
| 2006-07 | Ak Bars Kazan | Russia | 47 | 3 | 6 | 9 | 12 | 16 | 1 | 2 | 3 | 8 |
| 2007-08 | Spartak Moscow | Russia | 57 | 4 | 6 | 10 | 20 | 5 | 1 | 0 | 1 | 6 |
| 2008-09 | Spartak Moscow | Rus-KHL | 54 | 7 | 14 | 21 | 30 | 6 | 0 | 2 | 2 | 6 |

**ZABORSKY, Tomas** (za-BOHR-skee, TAW-mahsh) **NYR**

Wing. Shoots left. 6'1", 188 lbs. Born, Banska Bystrica, Czech., November 14, 1987.
(NY Rangers' 5th choice, 137th overall, in 2006 Entry Draft).

| | | | Regular Season | | | | | Playoffs | | | | |
|---|---|---|---|---|---|---|---|---|---|---|---|---|
| **Season** | **Club** | **League** | **GP** | **G** | **A** | **Pts** | **PIM** | **GP** | **G** | **A** | **Pts** | **PIM** |
| 2003-04 | Dukla Trencin U18 | Svk-U18 | 46 | 20 | 12 | 32 | 8 | 7 | 4 | 2 | 6 | 4 |
| 2004-05 | Dukla Trencin U18 | Svk-U18 | 46 | 44 | 25 | 69 | 53 | 7 | 4 | 4 | 8 | 39 |
| | Dukla Trencin Jr. | Slovak-Jr. | 7 | 1 | 2 | 3 | 0 | 1 | 0 | 1 | 1 | 0 |
| 2005-06 | Dukla Trencin | Slovakia | 4 | 0 | 0 | 0 | 2 | .... | .... | .... | .... | .... |
| | Dukla Trencin Jr. | Slovak-Jr. | 42 | 39 | 22 | 61 | 18 | 7 | 10 | 5 | 15 | 2 |
| | P. Bystrica | Slovak-2 | 5 | 0 | 1 | 1 | 2 | .... | .... | .... | .... | .... |
| 2006-07 | Saginaw Spirit | OHL | 59 | 19 | 24 | 43 | 18 | 6 | 1 | 2 | 3 | 4 |
| 2007-08 | Saginaw Spirit | OHL | 68 | 31 | 39 | 70 | 42 | 4 | 2 | 1 | 3 | 2 |
| | Hartford Wolf Pack | AHL | 2 | 0 | 1 | 1 | 0 | .... | .... | .... | .... | .... |
| 2008-09 | Hartford Wolf Pack | AHL | 8 | 1 | 2 | 3 | 2 | .... | .... | .... | .... | .... |
| | Charlotte | ECHL | 28 | 4 | 8 | 12 | 14 | .... | .... | .... | .... | .... |
| | Dayton Bombers | ECHL | 19 | 10 | 6 | 16 | 14 | .... | .... | .... | .... | .... |

**ZACKRISSON, Patrik** (ZAK-rihs-suhn, PAT-rihk) **S.J.**

Right wing. Shoots right. 5'11", 190 lbs. Born, Ekero, Sweden, March 27, 1987.
(San Jose's 5th choice, 165th overall, in 2007 Entry Draft).

| | | | Regular Season | | | | | Playoffs | | | | |
|---|---|---|---|---|---|---|---|---|---|---|---|---|
| **Season** | **Club** | **League** | **GP** | **G** | **A** | **Pts** | **PIM** | **GP** | **G** | **A** | **Pts** | **PIM** |
| 2002-03 | Ska IK | Sweden-3 | 17 | 3 | 6 | 9 | 4 | .... | .... | .... | .... | .... |
| 2003-04 | V.Frolunda U18 | Swe-U18 | 14 | 5 | 9 | 14 | 4 | 7 | 2 | 3 | 5 | 0 |
| | V.Frolunda Jr. | Swe-Jr. | 2 | 0 | 1 | 1 | 0 | .... | .... | .... | .... | .... |
| 2004-05 | Frolunda U18 | Swe-U18 | 2 | 2 | 1 | 3 | 29 | 6 | 3 | 3 | 6 | 4 |
| | Frolunda Jr. | Swe-Jr. | 32 | 16 | 9 | 25 | 22 | 6 | 1 | 2 | 3 | 0 |
| 2005-06 | Frolunda Jr. | Swe-Jr. | 39 | 26 | 19 | 45 | 34 | 7 | 4 | 5 | 9 | 4 |
| | Frolunda | Sweden | 10 | 0 | 1 | 1 | 0 | .... | .... | .... | .... | .... |
| 2006-07 | Rogle | Sweden-2 | 38 | 17 | 23 | 40 | 32 | .... | .... | .... | .... | .... |
| 2007-08 | Linkopings HC | Sweden | 55 | 4 | 9 | 13 | 35 | 16 | 3 | 1 | 4 | 12 |
| 2008-09 | Linkopings HC | Sweden | 54 | 15 | 19 | 34 | 12 | 7 | 1 | 3 | 4 | 2 |

**ZAGRAPAN, Marek** (ZAG-rah-pahn, MAIR-ehk) **BUF.**

Center. Shoots left. 6'1", 195 lbs. Born, Presov, Czech., December 6, 1986.
(Buffalo's 1st choice, 13th overall, in 2005 Entry Draft).

| | | | Regular Season | | | | | Playoffs | | | | |
|---|---|---|---|---|---|---|---|---|---|---|---|---|
| **Season** | **Club** | **League** | **GP** | **G** | **A** | **Pts** | **PIM** | **GP** | **G** | **A** | **Pts** | **PIM** |
| 2001-02 | HC Zlin U17 | CzR-U17 | 48 | 23 | 14 | 37 | 24 | 6 | 1 | 0 | 1 | 2 |
| 2002-03 | HC Zlin U17 | CzR-U17 | 15 | 18 | 16 | 34 | 14 | 3 | 1 | 0 | 1 | 6 |
| | HC Zlin Jr. | CzRep-Jr. | 25 | 9 | 13 | 22 | 10 | .... | .... | .... | .... | .... |
| | HC Hame Zlin | CzRep | 13 | 1 | 1 | 2 | 10 | .... | .... | .... | .... | .... |
| 2003-04 | HC Zlin Jr. | CzRep-Jr. | 42 | 23 | 12 | 35 | 40 | 7 | 1 | 3 | 4 | 4 |
| | HC Hame Zlin | CzRep | 5 | 0 | 0 | 0 | 0 | .... | .... | .... | .... | .... |
| | HC Kometa Brno | CzRep-2 | 5 | 0 | 1 | 1 | 0 | .... | .... | .... | .... | .... |
| 2004-05 | Chicoutimi | QMJHL | 59 | 32 | 50 | 82 | 50 | 17 | 11 | 6 | 17 | 28 |
| 2005-06 | Chicoutimi | QMJHL | 59 | 35 | 52 | 87 | 63 | 8 | 4 | 6 | 10 | 4 |
| 2006-07 | Rochester | AHL | 71 | 17 | 21 | 38 | 39 | 6 | 1 | 0 | 1 | 2 |
| 2007-08 | Rochester | AHL | 76 | 18 | 22 | 40 | 66 | .... | .... | .... | .... | .... |
| 2008-09 | Portland Pirates | AHL | 80 | 21 | 28 | 49 | 44 | 5 | 2 | 1 | 3 | 2 |

Signed as a free agent by **Cherepovets** (KHL), June 2, 2009.

**ZAHN, Teigan** (ZAWN, TEE-guhn) **CHI.**

Defense. Shoots left. 6'1", 217 lbs. Born, Regina, Sask., January 4, 1990.
(Chicago's 3rd choice, 132nd overall, in 2008 Entry Draft).

| | | | Regular Season | | | | | Playoffs | | | | |
|---|---|---|---|---|---|---|---|---|---|---|---|---|
| **Season** | **Club** | **League** | **GP** | **G** | **A** | **Pts** | **PIM** | **GP** | **G** | **A** | **Pts** | **PIM** |
| 2005-06 | Moose Jaw | SMHL | STATISTICS NOT AVAILABLE | | | | | | | | | |
| | Saskatoon Blades | WHL | 1 | 0 | 0 | 0 | 2 | .... | .... | .... | .... | .... |
| 2006-07 | Saskatoon Blades | WHL | 39 | 0 | 3 | 3 | 68 | .... | .... | .... | .... | .... |
| 2007-08 | Saskatoon Blades | WHL | 69 | 4 | 15 | 19 | 104 | .... | .... | .... | .... | .... |
| 2008-09 | Saskatoon Blades | WHL | 62 | 5 | 11 | 16 | 160 | 7 | 1 | 2 | 3 | 12 |

**ZALEWSKI, Steven** (zuh-LEH-skee, STEE-vehn) **S.J.**

Center. Shoots left. 6', 195 lbs. Born, Utica, NY, August 20, 1986.
(San Jose's 5th choice, 153rd overall, in 2004 Entry Draft).

| | | | Regular Season | | | | | Playoffs | | | | |
|---|---|---|---|---|---|---|---|---|---|---|---|---|
| **Season** | **Club** | **League** | **GP** | **G** | **A** | **Pts** | **PIM** | **GP** | **G** | **A** | **Pts** | **PIM** |
| 2003-04 | Northwood | High-NY | 40 | 32 | 34 | 66 | 22 | .... | .... | .... | .... | .... |
| 2004-05 | Clarkson Knights | ECAC | 39 | 12 | 7 | 19 | 60 | .... | .... | .... | .... | .... |
| 2005-06 | Clarkson Knights | ECAC | 35 | 9 | 13 | 22 | 50 | .... | .... | .... | .... | .... |
| 2006-07 | Clarkson Knights | ECAC | 39 | 16 | 18 | 34 | 44 | .... | .... | .... | .... | .... |
| 2007-08 | Clarkson Knights | ECAC | 38 | 21 | 12 | 33 | 34 | .... | .... | .... | .... | .... |
| | Worcester Sharks | AHL | 7 | 2 | 4 | 6 | 0 | .... | .... | .... | .... | .... |
| 2008-09 | Worcester Sharks | AHL | 75 | 13 | 26 | 39 | 26 | 12 | 0 | 1 | 1 | 6 |

ECAC First All-Star Team (2008)

**ZAPLETAL, Jan** (ZAH-pleht-tuhl, YAHN) **T.B.**

Defense. Shoots right. 6'3", 190 lbs. Born, Brno, Czech., August 21, 1986.
(Tampa Bay's 6th choice, 188th overall, in 2004 Entry Draft).

| | | | Regular Season | | | | | Playoffs | | | | |
|---|---|---|---|---|---|---|---|---|---|---|---|---|
| **Season** | **Club** | **League** | **GP** | **G** | **A** | **Pts** | **PIM** | **GP** | **G** | **A** | **Pts** | **PIM** |
| 2001-02 | HC Ytong Brno Jr. | CzRep-Jr. | 27 | 3 | 0 | 3 | 8 | .... | .... | .... | .... | .... |
| 2002-03 | HC Vsetin Jr. | CzRep-Jr. | 39 | 5 | 7 | 12 | 10 | 10 | 0 | 0 | 0 | 2 |
| 2003-04 | HC Vsetin Jr. | CzRep-Jr. | 51 | 2 | 4 | 6 | 26 | 4 | 0 | 0 | 0 | 0 |
| 2004-05 | Regina Pats | WHL | 55 | 3 | 2 | 5 | 20 | .... | .... | .... | .... | .... |
| 2005-06 | HC Vsetin Jr. | CzRep-Jr. | 9 | 0 | 3 | 3 | 2 | .... | .... | .... | .... | .... |
| | HC Vsetin | CzRep | 16 | 0 | 0 | 0 | 10 | .... | .... | .... | .... | .... |
| | Jind. Hradec | CzRep-2 | 20 | 0 | 0 | 0 | 16 | .... | .... | .... | .... | .... |
| 2006-07 | VSK Technika Brno | CzRep-3 | 22 | 1 | 5 | 6 | 32 | .... | .... | .... | .... | .... |
| 2007-08 | HC Olomouc | CzRep-2 | 10 | 0 | 0 | 0 | 10 | .... | .... | .... | .... | .... |
| | HC TJ Sternberk | CzRep-3 | 11 | 2 | 3 | 5 | 12 | .... | .... | .... | .... | .... |
| | SHK Hodonin | CzRep-3 | 16 | 2 | 2 | 4 | 22 | 3 | 0 | 1 | 1 | 2 |
| 2008-09 | HC TJ Sternberk | CzRep-3 | 39 | 5 | 7 | 12 | 48 | 5 | 2 | 0 | 2 | 6 |

**ZELISKA, Lukas** (zeh-LIHS-kah, LOO-kahsh) **NYR**

Center. Shoots right. 5'11", 175 lbs. Born, Martin, Czech., January 8, 1988.
(NY Rangers' 7th choice, 204th overall, in 2006 Entry Draft).

| | | | Regular Season | | | | | Playoffs | | | | |
|---|---|---|---|---|---|---|---|---|---|---|---|---|
| **Season** | **Club** | **League** | **GP** | **G** | **A** | **Pts** | **PIM** | **GP** | **G** | **A** | **Pts** | **PIM** |
| 2003-04 | HC Trinec U17 | CzR-U17 | 48 | 39 | 41 | 80 | 166 | 5 | 2 | 2 | 4 | 4 |
| | HC Trinec Jr. | CzRep-Jr. | 7 | 1 | 1 | 2 | 2 | .... | .... | .... | .... | .... |
| 2004-05 | HC Trinec U17 | CzR-U17 | 11 | 7 | 11 | 18 | 40 | .... | .... | .... | .... | .... |
| | HC Trinec Jr. | CzRep-Jr. | 13 | 1 | 2 | 3 | 6 | .... | .... | .... | .... | .... |
| 2005-06 | HC Trinec Jr. | CzRep-Jr. | 29 | 8 | 3 | 11 | 81 | 7 | 4 | 1 | 5 | 22 |
| | HC Ocelari Trinec | CzRep | 1 | 0 | 0 | 0 | 0 | .... | .... | .... | .... | .... |
| 2006-07 | Prince Albert | WHL | 61 | 4 | 25 | 29 | 77 | 5 | 1 | 4 | 5 | 4 |
| 2007-08 | Prostejov | CzRep-2 | 2 | 0 | 0 | 0 | 0 | .... | .... | .... | .... | .... |
| | HC Trinec Jr. | CzRep-Jr. | 38 | 23 | 29 | 52 | 236 | 7 | 2 | 4 | 6 | 10 |
| 2008-09 | HC Ocelari Trinec | CzRep | 14 | 0 | 0 | 0 | 0 | .... | .... | .... | .... | .... |
| | HC Havirov | CzRep-2 | 32 | 10 | 5 | 15 | 52 | 4 | 0 | 1 | 1 | 6 |

**ZHARKOV, Vladimir** (zhar-KAWV, vla-DIH-meer) **N.J.**

Right wing. Shoots left. 6'1", 195 lbs. Born, Elektrostal, USSR, January 10, 1988.
(New Jersey's 4th choice, 77th overall, in 2006 Entry Draft).

| | | | Regular Season | | | | | Playoffs | | | | |
|---|---|---|---|---|---|---|---|---|---|---|---|---|
| **Season** | **Club** | **League** | **GP** | **G** | **A** | **Pts** | **PIM** | **GP** | **G** | **A** | **Pts** | **PIM** |
| 2004-05 | CSKA Moscow 2 | Russia-3 | STATISTICS NOT AVAILABLE | | | | | | | | | |
| 2005-06 | CSKA Moscow | Russia | 4 | 0 | 1 | 1 | 4 | 1 | 0 | 0 | 0 | 0 |
| | CSKA Moscow 2 | Russia-3 | 48 | 17 | 22 | 39 | 86 | .... | .... | .... | .... | .... |
| 2006-07 | CSKA Moscow | Russia | 47 | 4 | 1 | 5 | 18 | 12 | 0 | 1 | 1 | 2 |
| 2007-08 | CSKA Moscow | Russia | 30 | 5 | 2 | 7 | 6 | .... | .... | .... | .... | .... |
| | CSKA Moscow 2 | Russia-3 | 4 | 3 | 4 | 7 | 4 | 12 | 8 | 7 | 15 | 8 |
| 2008-09 | Lowell Devils | AHL | 69 | 11 | 23 | 34 | 26 | .... | .... | .... | .... | .... |

**ZIMAKOV, Sergei** (zih-MAH-kahv, SAIR-gay) **WSH.**

Defense. Shoots left. 6'1", 194 lbs. Born, Moscow, USSR, January 15, 1978.
(Washington's 4th choice, 58th overall, in 1996 Entry Draft).

| | | | Regular Season | | | | | Playoffs | | | | |
|---|---|---|---|---|---|---|---|---|---|---|---|---|
| **Season** | **Club** | **League** | **GP** | **G** | **A** | **Pts** | **PIM** | **GP** | **G** | **A** | **Pts** | **PIM** |
| 1994-95 | Omaha Lancers | USHL | 48 | 14 | 46 | 60 | 22 | .... | .... | .... | .... | .... |
| 1995-96 | Krylja Sovetov | CIS | 49 | 2 | 7 | 9 | 36 | .... | .... | .... | .... | .... |
| 1996-97 | Krylja Sovetov | Russia | 39 | 4 | 3 | 7 | 57 | 2 | 0 | 0 | 0 | 0 |
| 1997-98 | Krylja Sovetov | Russia | 42 | 4 | 1 | 5 | 48 | .... | .... | .... | .... | .... |
| 1998-99 | Ak Bars Kazan | Russia | 28 | 1 | 0 | 1 | 6 | 8 | 0 | 1 | 1 | 6 |
| 99-2000 | Perm | Russia | 31 | 1 | 2 | 3 | 34 | 3 | 0 | 1 | 1 | 0 |
| 2000-01 | CSKA Moscow 2 | Russia-3 | 3 | 2 | 2 | 4 | 2 | .... | .... | .... | .... | .... |
| | CSKA Moscow | Russia | 26 | 1 | 5 | 6 | 28 | .... | .... | .... | .... | .... |
| 2001-02 | CSKA Moscow | Russia | 42 | 3 | 10 | 13 | 74 | .... | .... | .... | .... | .... |
| 2002-03 | Ufa | Russia | 11 | 0 | 0 | 0 | 8 | .... | .... | .... | .... | .... |
| | Ufa 2 | Russia-3 | STATISTICS NOT AVAILABLE | | | | | | | | | |
| 2003-04 | Spartak Moscow | Russia-2 | 60 | 11 | 17 | 28 | 38 | 12 | 0 | 1 | 1 | 10 |
| 2004-05 | Spartak Moscow | Russia | 23 | 2 | 2 | 4 | 20 | .... | .... | .... | .... | .... |
| 2005-06 | Spartak Moscow | Russia | 46 | 3 | 11 | 14 | 55 | 3 | 0 | 0 | 0 | 4 |
| 2006-07 | Vityaz Chekhov | Russia | 36 | 3 | 2 | 5 | 38 | 3 | 0 | 0 | 0 | 0 |
| 2007-08 | Spartak Moscow | Russia | 11 | 1 | 1 | 2 | 10 | .... | .... | .... | .... | .... |
| | Krylja Sovetov | Russia-2 | 17 | 7 | 5 | 12 | 34 | .... | .... | .... | .... | .... |
| 2008-09 | MHK Krylja Sov. | Russia-2 | 55 | 6 | 10 | 16 | 75 | 15 | 2 | 6 | 8 | 16 |

**ZIMMERMAN, Sean** (ZIH-mehr-man, SHAWN) **PHX.**

Defense. Shoots right. 6'2", 210 lbs. Born, Denver, CO, May 24, 1987.
(New Jersey's 6th choice, 170th overall, in 2005 Entry Draft).

| | | | Regular Season | | | | | Playoffs | | | | |
|---|---|---|---|---|---|---|---|---|---|---|---|---|
| **Season** | **Club** | **League** | **GP** | **G** | **A** | **Pts** | **PIM** | **GP** | **G** | **A** | **Pts** | **PIM** |
| 2002-03 | Spokane Braves | KIJHL | 45 | 3 | 5 | 8 | 70 | .... | .... | .... | .... | .... |
| 2003-04 | Spokane Chiefs | WHL | 67 | 4 | 4 | 8 | 16 | 4 | 0 | 0 | 0 | 0 |
| 2004-05 | Spokane Chiefs | WHL | 71 | 2 | 14 | 16 | 36 | .... | .... | .... | .... | .... |
| 2005-06 | Spokane Chiefs | WHL | 72 | 2 | 19 | 21 | 44 | .... | .... | .... | .... | .... |
| | Albany River Rats | AHL | 6 | 0 | 0 | 0 | 4 | .... | .... | .... | .... | .... |
| 2006-07 | Spokane Chiefs | WHL | 60 | 2 | 12 | 14 | 69 | 6 | 0 | 2 | 2 | 2 |
| | Lowell Devils | AHL | 1 | 0 | 0 | 0 | 2 | .... | .... | .... | .... | .... |
| 2007-08 | Lowell Devils | AHL | 66 | 0 | 6 | 6 | 47 | .... | .... | .... | .... | .... |
| | Trenton Devils | ECHL | 8 | 0 | 1 | 1 | 10 | .... | .... | .... | .... | .... |
| 2008-09 | San Antonio | AHL | 36 | 2 | 0 | 2 | 30 | .... | .... | .... | .... | .... |
| | Arizona Sundogs | CHL | 20 | 0 | 3 | 3 | 20 | .... | .... | .... | .... | .... |

Traded to **Phoenix** by **New Jersey** for Kevin Cormier, September 12, 2008.

**ZUBAREV, Andrei** (ZOO-bah-rehv, AWN-dray) **ATL.**

Defense. Shoots left. 6'1", 202 lbs. Born, Ufa, USSR, March 3, 1987.
(Atlanta's 7th choice, 187th overall, in 2005 Entry Draft).

| | | | Regular Season | | | | | Playoffs | | | | |
|---|---|---|---|---|---|---|---|---|---|---|---|---|
| **Season** | **Club** | **League** | **GP** | **G** | **A** | **Pts** | **PIM** | **GP** | **G** | **A** | **Pts** | **PIM** |
| 2003-04 | Ufa 2 | Russia-3 | STATISTICS NOT AVAILABLE | | | | | | | | | |
| | Ufa | Russia | 6 | 0 | 1 | 1 | 4 | .... | .... | .... | .... | .... |
| 2004-05 | Ufa 2 | Russia-3 | 28 | 2 | 4 | 6 | 32 | .... | .... | .... | .... | .... |
| | Ufa | Russia | 5 | 0 | 0 | 0 | 4 | .... | .... | .... | .... | .... |
| 2005-06 | Ak Bars Kazan | Russia | 40 | 2 | 11 | 13 | 40 | .... | .... | .... | .... | .... |
| 2006-07 | Ak Bars Kazan | Russia | 20 | 0 | 0 | 0 | 32 | .... | .... | .... | .... | .... |
| 2007-08 | Ak Bars Kazan | Russia | 39 | 4 | 3 | 7 | 86 | 2 | 0 | 0 | 0 | 0 |
| 2008-09 | Mytischi | Rus-KHL | 35 | 0 | 4 | 4 | 65 | 7 | 2 | 3 | 5 | 29 |

# 2009-10 NHL Player Register

**Note:** The 2009-10 NHL Player Register lists forwards and defensemen only. Goaltenders are listed separately. The NHL Player Register lists every active skater who played in the NHL in 2008-09 plus additional players with NHL experience. Trades and roster changes are current as of August 10, 2009.

**Abbreviations: GP** – games played; **G** – goals; **A** – assists; **Pts** – points; **PIM** – penalties in minutes; **PP** – power-play goals; **SH** – shorthanded goals; **GW** – game-winning goals; **S** – shots; **%** – shooting percentage; **+/–** – plus/minus; **TF** – total faceoffs taken; **F%** – faceoff winning percentage; **Min** – average time on ice per game; ***** – league-leading total ♦ – member of Stanley Cup-winning team.

**Prospect Register begins on page 279.**
**Goaltender Register begins on page 585.**
**League abbreviations are listed on page 662.**

## ABDELKADER, Justin

(abdehl-KAY-duhr, JUHS-tihn) **DET.**

Left wing. Shoots left. 6'1", 215 lbs. Born, Muskegon, MI, February 25, 1987. Detroit's 2nd choice, 42nd overall, in 2005 Entry Draft.

| Season | Club | League | GP | G | A | Pts | PIM | PP | SH | GW | S | % | +/- | TF | F% | Min | GP | G | A | Pts | PIM | PP | SH | GW | Min |
|---|---|---|---|---|---|---|---|---|---|---|---|---|---|---|---|---|---|---|---|---|---|---|---|---|---|
| | | | **Regular Season** | | | | | | | | | | | | | | **Playoffs** | | | | | | | | |
| 2003-04 | Muskegon M.S. | High-MI | 28 | 37 | 43 | 80 | .... | .... | .... | .... | .... | .... | .... | .... | .... | .... | .... | .... | .... | .... | .... | .... | .... | .... | .... |
| 2004-05 | Cedar Rapids | USHL | 60 | 27 | 25 | 52 | 86 | .... | .... | .... | .... | .... | .... | .... | .... | .... | 11 | 0 | 4 | 4 | 8 | .... | .... | .... | .... |
| 2005-06 | Michigan State | CCHA | 44 | 10 | 12 | 22 | 83 | .... | .... | .... | .... | .... | .... | .... | .... | .... | .... | .... | .... | .... | .... | .... | .... | .... | .... |
| 2006-07 | Michigan State | CCHA | 38 | 15 | 18 | 33 | 91 | .... | .... | .... | .... | .... | .... | .... | .... | .... | .... | .... | .... | .... | .... | .... | .... | .... | .... |
| **2007-08** | Michigan State | CCHA | 42 | 19 | 21 | 40 | 107 | .... | .... | .... | .... | .... | .... | .... | .... | .... | .... | .... | .... | .... | .... | .... | .... | .... | .... |
| | **Detroit** | **NHL** | **2** | **0** | **0** | **0** | **2** | **0** | **0** | **0** | **6** | **0.0** | **0** | **12** | **41.7** | **12:13** | .... | .... | .... | .... | .... | .... | .... | .... | .... |
| **2008-09** | **Detroit** | **NHL** | **2** | **0** | **0** | **0** | **0** | **0** | **0** | **0** | **2** | **0.0** | **0** | **7** | **57.1** | **9:18** | **10** | **2** | **1** | **3** | **0** | **0** | **0** | **0** | **6:58** |
| | Grand Rapids | AHL | 76 | 24 | 28 | 52 | 102 | .... | .... | .... | .... | .... | .... | .... | .... | .... | 10 | 6 | 2 | 8 | 23 | .... | .... | .... | .... |
| | **NHL Totals** | | **4** | **0** | **0** | **0** | **2** | **0** | **0** | **0** | **8** | **0.0** | | **19** | **47.4** | **10:45** | **10** | **2** | **1** | **3** | **0** | **0** | **0** | **0** | **6:58** |

NCAA Championship All-Tournament Team (2007) • NCAA Championship Tournament MVP (2007) • AHL All-Rookie Team (2009)

## ADAMS, Craig

(A-duhmz, KRAYG) **PIT.**

Right wing. Shoots right. 6', 197 lbs. Born, Seria, Brunei, April 26, 1977. Hartford's 9th choice, 223rd overall, in 1996 Entry Draft.

| Season | Club | League | GP | G | A | Pts | PIM | PP | SH | GW | S | % | +/- | TF | F% | Min | GP | G | A | Pts | PIM | PP | SH | GW | Min |
|---|---|---|---|---|---|---|---|---|---|---|---|---|---|---|---|---|---|---|---|---|---|---|---|---|---|
| 1995-96 | Harvard Crimson | ECAC | 34 | 8 | 9 | 17 | 56 | .... | .... | .... | .... | .... | .... | .... | .... | .... | .... | .... | .... | .... | .... | .... | .... | .... | .... |
| 1996-97 | Harvard Crimson | ECAC | 32 | 6 | 4 | 10 | 36 | .... | .... | .... | .... | .... | .... | .... | .... | .... | .... | .... | .... | .... | .... | .... | .... | .... | .... |
| 1997-98 | Harvard Crimson | ECAC | 12 | 6 | 6 | 12 | 12 | .... | .... | .... | .... | .... | .... | .... | .... | .... | .... | .... | .... | .... | .... | .... | .... | .... | .... |
| 1998-99 | Harvard Crimson | ECAC | 31 | 9 | 14 | 23 | 53 | .... | .... | .... | .... | .... | .... | .... | .... | .... | .... | .... | .... | .... | .... | .... | .... | .... | .... |
| 99-2000 | Cincinnati | IHL | 73 | 12 | 12 | 24 | 124 | .... | .... | .... | .... | .... | .... | .... | .... | .... | 8 | 0 | 1 | 1 | 14 | .... | .... | .... | .... |
| **2000-01** | **Carolina** | **NHL** | **44** | **1** | **0** | **1** | **20** | **0** | **0** | **0** | **15** | **6.7** | **–7** | **4** | **25.0** | **4:30** | **3** | **0** | **0** | **0** | **0** | **0** | **0** | **0** | **3:45** |
| | Cincinnati | IHL | 4 | 0 | 1 | 1 | 9 | .... | .... | .... | .... | .... | .... | .... | .... | .... | 1 | 0 | 0 | 0 | 2 | .... | .... | .... | .... |
| **2001-02** | **Carolina** | **NHL** | **33** | **0** | **1** | **1** | **38** | **0** | **0** | **0** | **17** | **0.0** | **2** | **9** | **33.3** | **5:54** | **1** | **0** | **0** | **0** | **0** | **0** | **0** | **0** | **7:41** |
| | Lowell | AHL | 22 | 5 | 4 | 9 | 51 | .... | .... | .... | .... | .... | .... | .... | .... | .... | .... | .... | .... | .... | .... | .... | .... | .... | .... |
| **2002-03** | **Carolina** | **NHL** | **81** | **6** | **12** | **18** | **71** | **1** | **0** | **1** | **107** | **5.6** | **–11** | **20** | **35.0** | **12:12** | .... | .... | .... | .... | .... | .... | .... | .... | .... |
| **2003-04** | **Carolina** | **NHL** | **80** | **7** | **10** | **17** | **69** | **0** | **1** | **0** | **110** | **6.4** | **–5** | **20** | **45.0** | **13:41** | .... | .... | .... | .... | .... | .... | .... | .... | .... |
| 2004-05 | HC Milano | Italy | 30 | 15 | 14 | 29 | 57 | .... | .... | .... | .... | .... | .... | .... | .... | .... | 15 | 4 | 7 | 11 | 26 | .... | .... | .... | .... |
| **2005-06♦** | **Carolina** | **NHL** | **67** | **10** | **11** | **21** | **51** | **1** | **1** | **2** | **68** | **14.7** | **1** | **13** | **53.9** | **12:18** | **25** | **0** | **0** | **0** | **10** | **0** | **0** | **0** | **8:16** |
| | Lowell | AHL | 13 | 4 | 3 | 7 | 20 | .... | .... | .... | .... | .... | .... | .... | .... | .... | .... | .... | .... | .... | .... | .... | .... | .... | .... |
| **2006-07** | **Carolina** | **NHL** | **82** | **7** | **7** | **14** | **54** | **0** | **1** | **1** | **71** | **9.9** | **–9** | **36** | **30.6** | **10:04** | .... | .... | .... | .... | .... | .... | .... | .... | .... |
| **2007-08** | **Carolina** | **NHL** | **40** | **2** | **3** | **5** | **34** | **0** | **0** | **0** | **31** | **6.5** | **–8** | **11** | **27.3** | **9:48** | .... | .... | .... | .... | .... | .... | .... | .... | .... |
| | **Chicago** | **NHL** | **35** | **2** | **4** | **6** | **24** | **0** | **1** | **1** | **32** | **6.3** | **–8** | **30** | **53.3** | **11:56** | .... | .... | .... | .... | .... | .... | .... | .... | .... |
| **2008-09** | **Chicago** | **NHL** | **36** | **2** | **4** | **6** | **22** | **1** | **0** | **0** | **38** | **5.3** | **–3** | **16** | **37.5** | **8:43** | .... | .... | .... | .... | .... | .... | .... | .... | .... |
| | **♦ Pittsburgh** | **NHL** | **9** | **0** | **1** | **1** | **0** | **0** | **0** | **0** | **9** | **0.0** | **0** | **5** | **40.0** | **8:34** | **24** | **3** | **2** | **5** | **16** | **0** | **0** | **0** | **9:45** |
| | **NHL Totals** | | **507** | **37** | **53** | **90** | **383** | **3** | **4** | **5** | **498** | **7.4** | | **164** | **39.6** | **10:30** | **53** | **3** | **2** | **5** | **26** | **0** | **0** | **0** | **8:40** |

• Rights transferred to **Carolina** after **Hartford** franchise relocated, June 25, 1997. • Missed majority of 1997-98 season recovering from shoulder injury suffered in game vs. University of Wisconsin (WCHA), December 27, 1997. Signed as a free agent by **Milano**, (Italy), July 28, 2004. Signed as a free agent by **Anaheim**, August 25, 2005. Traded to **Carolina** by **Anaheim** for Bruno St. Jacques, October 3, 2005. Traded to **Chicago** by **Carolina** for future considerations, January 17, 2008. Claimed on waivers by **Pittsburgh** from **Chicago**, March 4, 2009.

## AFINOGENOV, Maxim

(ah-fihn-ah-GEHN-ahf, max-IHM)

Right wing. Shoots left. 6', 191 lbs. Born, Moscow, USSR, September 4, 1979. Buffalo's 3rd choice, 69th overall, in 1997 Entry Draft.

| Season | Club | League | GP | G | A | Pts | PIM | PP | SH | GW | S | % | +/- | TF | F% | Min | GP | G | A | Pts | PIM | PP | SH | GW | Min |
|---|---|---|---|---|---|---|---|---|---|---|---|---|---|---|---|---|---|---|---|---|---|---|---|---|---|
| 1996-97 | Dynamo Moscow | Russia | 29 | 6 | 5 | 11 | 10 | .... | .... | .... | .... | .... | .... | .... | .... | .... | 4 | 0 | 2 | 2 | 0 | .... | .... | .... | .... |
| | Dynamo Moscow | EuroHL | 3 | 0 | 0 | 0 | 0 | .... | .... | .... | .... | .... | .... | .... | .... | .... | 3 | 1 | 0 | 1 | 4 | .... | .... | .... | .... |
| 1997-98 | Dynamo Moscow | Russia | 35 | 10 | 5 | 15 | 53 | .... | .... | .... | .... | .... | .... | .... | .... | .... | .... | .... | .... | .... | .... | .... | .... | .... | .... |
| | Dynamo Moscow | EuroHL | 6 | 3 | 1 | 4 | 27 | .... | .... | .... | .... | .... | .... | .... | .... | .... | .... | .... | .... | .... | .... | .... | .... | .... | .... |
| 1998-99 | Dynamo Moscow | Russia | 38 | 8 | 13 | 21 | 24 | .... | .... | .... | .... | .... | .... | .... | .... | .... | 16 | *10 | 6 | *16 | 14 | .... | .... | .... | .... |
| | Dynamo Moscow | EuroHL | 5 | 3 | 5 | 8 | 29 | .... | .... | .... | .... | .... | .... | .... | .... | .... | 4 | 2 | 1 | 3 | 27 | .... | .... | .... | .... |
| **99-2000** | **Buffalo** | **NHL** | **65** | **16** | **18** | **34** | **41** | **2** | **0** | **2** | **128** | **12.5** | **–4** | **0** | **0.0** | **13:09** | **5** | **0** | **1** | **1** | **2** | **0** | **0** | **0** | **12:53** |
| | Rochester | AHL | 15 | 6 | 12 | 18 | 8 | .... | .... | .... | .... | .... | .... | .... | .... | .... | 8 | 3 | 1 | 4 | 4 | .... | .... | .... | .... |
| **2000-01** | **Buffalo** | **NHL** | **78** | **14** | **22** | **36** | **40** | **3** | **0** | **5** | **190** | **7.4** | **1** | **2** | **0.0** | **14:32** | **11** | **2** | **3** | **5** | **4** | **0** | **0** | **0** | **10:56** |
| **2001-02** | **Buffalo** | **NHL** | **81** | **21** | **19** | **40** | **69** | **3** | **1** | **0** | **234** | **9.0** | **–9** | **1** | **100.0** | **15:22** | .... | .... | .... | .... | .... | .... | .... | .... | .... |
| | Russia | Olympics | 6 | 2 | 2 | 4 | 4 | .... | .... | .... | .... | .... | .... | .... | .... | .... | .... | .... | .... | .... | .... | .... | .... | .... | .... |
| **2002-03** | **Buffalo** | **NHL** | **35** | **5** | **6** | **11** | **21** | **2** | **0** | **2** | **77** | **6.5** | **–12** | **4** | **50.0** | **13:24** | .... | .... | .... | .... | .... | .... | .... | .... | .... |
| **2003-04** | **Buffalo** | **NHL** | **73** | **17** | **14** | **31** | **57** | **3** | **0** | **4** | **148** | **11.5** | **–4** | **9** | **22.2** | **13:46** | .... | .... | .... | .... | .... | .... | .... | .... | .... |
| 2004-05 | Dynamo Moscow | Russia | 36 | 13 | 14 | 27 | 91 | .... | .... | .... | .... | .... | .... | .... | .... | .... | 10 | 4 | 4 | 8 | 8 | .... | .... | .... | .... |
| **2005-06** | **Buffalo** | **NHL** | **77** | **22** | **51** | **73** | **84** | **11** | **0** | **3** | **241** | **9.1** | **6** | **17** | **17.7** | **16:20** | **18** | **3** | **5** | **8** | **10** | **0** | **0** | **0** | **16:53** |
| | Russia | Olympics | 8 | 0 | 1 | 1 | 10 | .... | .... | .... | .... | .... | .... | .... | .... | .... | .... | .... | .... | .... | .... | .... | .... | .... | .... |
| **2006-07** | **Buffalo** | **NHL** | **56** | **23** | **38** | **61** | **66** | **7** | **0** | **3** | **151** | **15.2** | **19** | **3** | **66.7** | **17:03** | **15** | **5** | **4** | **9** | **6** | **3** | **0** | **2** | **15:24** |
| **2007-08** | **Buffalo** | **NHL** | **56** | **10** | **18** | **28** | **42** | **1** | **0** | **1** | **114** | **8.8** | **–16** | **5** | **20.0** | **16:03** | .... | .... | .... | .... | .... | .... | .... | .... | .... |
| **2008-09** | **Buffalo** | **NHL** | **48** | **6** | **14** | **20** | **20** | **0** | **0** | **0** | **93** | **6.5** | **–7** | **3** | **0.0** | **12:36** | .... | .... | .... | .... | .... | .... | .... | .... | .... |
| | **NHL Totals** | | **569** | **134** | **200** | **334** | **440** | **32** | **1** | **20** | **1376** | **9.7** | | **44** | **25.0** | **14:48** | **49** | **10** | **13** | **23** | **22** | **3** | **0** | **2** | **14:41** |

• Missed majority of 2002-03 season recovering from head injury suffered prior to training camp, August, 2002. Signed as a free agent by **Dynamo Moscow** (Russia), June 19, 2004.

## ALBERTS, Andrew

(AL-buhrts, AN-droo) **CAR.**

Defense. Shoots left. 6'5", 218 lbs. Born, Minneapolis, MN, June 30, 1981. Boston's 5th choice, 179th overall, in 2001 Entry Draft.

| Season | Club | League | Regular Season GP | G | A | Pts | PIM | PP | SH | GW | S | % | +/- | TF | F% | Min | Playoffs GP | G | A | Pts | PIM | PP | SH | GW | Min |
|---|---|---|---|---|---|---|---|---|---|---|---|---|---|---|---|---|---|---|---|---|---|---|---|---|---|
| 1998-99 | Benide | High-MN | 26 | 10 | 25 | 35 | .... | .... | .... | .... | .... | .... | .... | .... | .... | .... | .... | .... | .... | .... | .... | .... | .... | .... | .... |
| 99-2000 | Waterloo | USHL | 49 | 2 | 2 | 4 | 55 | .... | .... | .... | .... | .... | .... | .... | .... | .... | 4 | 0 | 0 | 0 | 12 | .... | .... | .... | .... |
| 2000-01 | Waterloo | USHL | 54 | 4 | 10 | 14 | 128 | .... | .... | .... | .... | .... | .... | .... | .... | .... | .... | .... | .... | .... | .... | .... | .... | .... | .... |
| 2001-02 | Boston College | H-East | 38 | 2 | 10 | 12 | 52 | .... | .... | .... | .... | .... | .... | .... | .... | .... | .... | .... | .... | .... | .... | .... | .... | .... | .... |
| 2002-03 | Boston College | H-East | 39 | 6 | 16 | 22 | 60 | .... | .... | .... | .... | .... | .... | .... | .... | .... | .... | .... | .... | .... | .... | .... | .... | .... | .... |
| 2003-04 | Boston College | H-East | 42 | 4 | 12 | 16 | 64 | .... | .... | .... | .... | .... | .... | .... | .... | .... | .... | .... | .... | .... | .... | .... | .... | .... | .... |
| 2004-05 | Boston College | H-East | 30 | 4 | 12 | 16 | 67 | .... | .... | .... | .... | .... | .... | .... | .... | .... | .... | .... | .... | .... | .... | .... | .... | .... | .... |
| | Providence Bruins | AHL | 8 | 0 | 0 | 0 | 16 | .... | .... | .... | .... | .... | .... | .... | .... | .... | 16 | 1 | 4 | 5 | 40 | .... | .... | .... | .... |
| **2005-06** | **Boston** | **NHL** | **73** | **1** | **6** | **7** | **68** | **0** | **1** | **0** | **30** | **3.3** | **3** | **2** | **50.0** | **12:50** | .... | .... | .... | .... | .... | .... | .... | .... | .... |
| | Providence Bruins | AHL | 6 | 0 | 1 | 1 | 7 | .... | .... | .... | .... | .... | .... | .... | .... | .... | .... | .... | .... | .... | .... | .... | .... | .... | .... |
| **2006-07** | **Boston** | **NHL** | **76** | **0** | **10** | **10** | **124** | **0** | **0** | **0** | **41** | **0.0** | **−15** | **1** | **0.0** | **19:40** | .... | .... | .... | .... | .... | .... | .... | .... | .... |
| **2007-08** | **Boston** | **NHL** | **35** | **0** | **2** | **2** | **39** | **0** | **0** | **0** | **25** | **0.0** | **4** | **2** | **50.0** | **20:37** | **2** | **0** | **0** | **0** | **0** | **0** | **0** | **0** | **11:07** |
| **2008-09** | **Philadelphia** | **NHL** | **79** | **1** | **12** | **13** | **61** | **0** | **0** | **0** | **46** | **2.2** | **6** | **0** | **0.0** | **15:48** | **6** | **0** | **1** | **1** | **10** | **0** | **0** | **0** | **13:40** |
| | **NHL Totals** | | **263** | **2** | **30** | **32** | **292** | **0** | **1** | **0** | **142** | **1.4** | | **5** | **40.0** | **16:44** | **8** | **0** | **1** | **1** | **10** | **0** | **0** | **0** | **13:02** |

Hockey East Second All-Star Team (2004) • NCAA East First All-American Team (2004, 2005) • Hockey East First All-Star Team (2005)

• Missed majority of 2007-08 season recovering from post-concussion symptoms. Traded to **Philadelphia** by **Boston** for Ned Lukacevic and Philadelphia's 4th round choice (Lane MacDermid) in 2009 Entry Draft, October 14, 2008. Signed as a free agent by **Carolina**, July 15, 2009.

## ALFREDSSON, Daniel

(AHL-frehd-suhn, DAN-yehl) **OTT.**

Right wing. Shoots right. 5'11", 208 lbs. Born, Gothenburg, Sweden, December 11, 1972. Ottawa's 5th choice, 133rd overall, in 1994 Entry Draft.

| Season | Club | League | Regular Season GP | G | A | Pts | PIM | PP | SH | GW | S | % | +/- | TF | F% | Min | Playoffs GP | G | A | Pts | PIM | PP | SH | GW | Min |
|---|---|---|---|---|---|---|---|---|---|---|---|---|---|---|---|---|---|---|---|---|---|---|---|---|---|
| 1990-91 | Molndal Hockey | Sweden-2 | 3 | 0 | 0 | 0 | 2 | .... | .... | .... | .... | .... | .... | .... | .... | .... | 8 | 4 | 4 | 8 | 4 | .... | .... | .... | .... |
| 1991-92 | Molndal | Sweden-2 | 32 | 12 | 8 | 20 | 43 | .... | .... | .... | .... | .... | .... | .... | .... | .... | .... | .... | .... | .... | .... | .... | .... | .... | .... |
| 1992-93 | V.Frolunda | Sweden | 20 | 1 | 5 | 6 | 8 | .... | .... | .... | .... | .... | .... | .... | .... | .... | .... | .... | .... | .... | .... | .... | .... | .... | .... |
| 1993-94 | V.Frolunda | Sweden | 39 | 20 | 10 | 30 | 18 | .... | .... | .... | .... | .... | .... | .... | .... | .... | 4 | 1 | 1 | 2 | .... | .... | .... | .... | .... |
| 1994-95 | V.Frolunda | Sweden | 22 | 7 | 11 | 18 | 22 | .... | .... | .... | .... | .... | .... | .... | .... | .... | .... | .... | .... | .... | .... | .... | .... | .... | .... |
| **1995-96** | **Ottawa** | **NHL** | **82** | **26** | **35** | **61** | **28** | **8** | **2** | **3** | **212** | **12.3** | **−18** | .... | .... | .... | .... | .... | .... | .... | .... | .... | .... | .... | .... |
| **1996-97** | **Ottawa** | **NHL** | **76** | **24** | **47** | **71** | **30** | **11** | **1** | **1** | **247** | **9.7** | **5** | .... | .... | .... | **7** | **5** | **2** | **7** | **6** | **3** | **0** | **2** | .... |
| **1997-98** | **Ottawa** | **NHL** | **55** | **17** | **28** | **45** | **18** | **7** | **0** | **7** | **149** | **11.4** | **7** | .... | .... | .... | **11** | **7** | **2** | **9** | **20** | **2** | **1** | **1** | .... |
| | Sweden | Olympics | 4 | 2 | 3 | 5 | 2 | .... | .... | .... | .... | .... | .... | .... | .... | .... | .... | .... | .... | .... | .... | .... | .... | .... | .... |
| **1998-99** | **Ottawa** | **NHL** | **58** | **11** | **22** | **33** | **14** | **3** | **0** | **5** | **163** | **6.7** | **8** | **7** | **57.1** | **17:22** | **4** | **1** | **2** | **3** | **4** | **1** | **0** | **0** | **22:23** |
| **99-2000** | **Ottawa** | **NHL** | **57** | **21** | **38** | **59** | **28** | **4** | **2** | **0** | **164** | **12.8** | **11** | **3** | **66.7** | **18:45** | **6** | **1** | **3** | **4** | **2** | **1** | **0** | **0** | **20:22** |
| **2000-01** | **Ottawa** | **NHL** | **68** | **24** | **46** | **70** | **30** | **10** | **0** | **3** | **206** | **11.7** | **11** | **8** | **50.0** | **18:47** | **4** | **1** | **0** | **1** | **2** | **0** | **0** | **0** | **21:20** |
| **2001-02** | **Ottawa** | **NHL** | **78** | **37** | **34** | **71** | **45** | **9** | **1** | **4** | **243** | **15.2** | **3** | **30** | **30.0** | **20:19** | **12** | **7** | **6** | **13** | **4** | **3** | **0** | **3** | **21:43** |
| | Sweden | Olympics | 4 | 1 | 4 | 5 | 2 | .... | .... | .... | .... | .... | .... | .... | .... | .... | .... | .... | .... | .... | .... | .... | .... | .... | .... |
| **2002-03** | **Ottawa** | **NHL** | **78** | **27** | **51** | **78** | **42** | **9** | **0** | **6** | **240** | **11.3** | **15** | **40** | **40.0** | **19:32** | **18** | **4** | **4** | **8** | **12** | **4** | **0** | **1** | **18:00** |
| **2003-04** | **Ottawa** | **NHL** | **77** | **32** | **48** | **80** | **24** | **9** | **0** | **5** | **230** | **13.9** | **12** | **33** | **24.2** | **19:24** | **7** | **1** | **2** | **3** | **2** | **0** | **0** | **0** | **20:03** |
| 2004-05 | Frolunda | Sweden | 15 | 8 | 9 | 17 | 10 | .... | .... | .... | .... | .... | .... | .... | .... | .... | 14 | *12 | 6 | *18 | 8 | .... | .... | .... | .... |
| **2005-06** | **Ottawa** | **NHL** | **77** | **43** | **60** | **103** | **50** | **16** | **5** | **8** | **249** | **17.3** | **29** | **44** | **20.5** | **21:41** | **10** | **2** | **8** | **10** | **4** | **1** | **0** | **0** | **21:10** |
| | Sweden | Olympics | 8 | 5 | 5 | 10 | 4 | .... | .... | .... | .... | .... | .... | .... | .... | .... | .... | .... | .... | .... | .... | .... | .... | .... | .... |
| **2006-07** | **Ottawa** | **NHL** | **77** | **29** | **58** | **87** | **42** | **7** | **2** | **7** | **240** | **12.1** | **42** | **43** | **34.9** | **21:35** | **20** | ***14** | **8** | ***22** | **10** | **6** | **1** | **4** | **23:20** |
| **2007-08** | **Ottawa** | **NHL** | **70** | **40** | **49** | **89** | **34** | **9** | **7** | **5** | **217** | **18.4** | **15** | **39** | **53.9** | **22:17** | **2** | **0** | **0** | **0** | **0** | **0** | **0** | **0** | **19:20** |
| **2008-09** | **Ottawa** | **NHL** | **79** | **24** | **50** | **74** | **24** | **8** | **1** | **3** | **204** | **11.8** | **7** | **17** | **23.5** | **20:53** | .... | .... | .... | .... | .... | .... | .... | .... | .... |
| | **NHL Totals** | | **932** | **355** | **566** | **921** | **409** | **110** | **21** | **57** | **2764** | **12.8** | | **264** | **34.8** | **20:10** | **101** | **43** | **37** | **80** | **66** | **21** | **2** | **11** | **20:57** |

NHL All-Rookie Team (1996) • Calder Memorial Trophy (1996) • NHL Second All-Star Team (2006)

Played in NHL All-Star Game (1996, 1997, 1998, 2004, 2008)

Signed as a free agent by **Frolunda** (Sweden), November 10, 2004.

## ALLEN, Bryan

(AHL-lehn, BRIGH-uhn) **FLA.**

Defense. Shoots left. 6'4", 220 lbs. Born, Kingston, Ont., August 21, 1980. Vancouver's 1st choice, 4th overall, in 1998 Entry Draft.

| Season | Club | League | Regular Season GP | G | A | Pts | PIM | PP | SH | GW | S | % | +/- | TF | F% | Min | Playoffs GP | G | A | Pts | PIM | PP | SH | GW | Min |
|---|---|---|---|---|---|---|---|---|---|---|---|---|---|---|---|---|---|---|---|---|---|---|---|---|---|
| 1995-96 | Ernestown Jets | OHA-C | 36 | 1 | 16 | 17 | 71 | .... | .... | .... | .... | .... | .... | .... | .... | .... | .... | .... | .... | .... | .... | .... | .... | .... | .... |
| 1996-97 | Oshawa Generals | OHL | 60 | 2 | 4 | 6 | 76 | .... | .... | .... | .... | .... | .... | .... | .... | .... | 18 | 1 | 3 | 4 | 26 | .... | .... | .... | .... |
| 1997-98 | Oshawa Generals | OHL | 48 | 6 | 13 | 19 | 126 | .... | .... | .... | .... | .... | .... | .... | .... | .... | 5 | 0 | 5 | 5 | 18 | .... | .... | .... | .... |
| 1998-99 | Oshawa Generals | OHL | 37 | 7 | 15 | 22 | 77 | .... | .... | .... | .... | .... | .... | .... | .... | .... | 15 | 0 | 3 | 3 | 26 | .... | .... | .... | .... |
| 99-2000 | Oshawa Generals | OHL | 3 | 0 | 2 | 2 | 12 | .... | .... | .... | .... | .... | .... | .... | .... | .... | 3 | 0 | 0 | 0 | 13 | .... | .... | .... | .... |
| | Syracuse Crunch | AHL | 9 | 1 | 1 | 2 | 11 | .... | .... | .... | .... | .... | .... | .... | .... | .... | 2 | 0 | 0 | 0 | 2 | .... | .... | .... | .... |
| **2000-01** | **Vancouver** | **NHL** | **6** | **0** | **0** | **0** | **0** | **0** | **0** | **0** | **2** | **0.0** | **0** | **0** | **0.0** | **9:20** | **2** | **0** | **0** | **0** | **2** | **0** | **0** | **0** | **13:47** |
| | Kansas City | IHL | 75 | 5 | 20 | 25 | 99 | .... | .... | .... | .... | .... | .... | .... | .... | .... | .... | .... | .... | .... | .... | .... | .... | .... | .... |
| **2001-02** | **Vancouver** | **NHL** | **11** | **0** | **0** | **0** | **6** | **0** | **0** | **0** | **4** | **0.0** | **1** | **0** | **0.0** | **10:47** | .... | .... | .... | .... | .... | .... | .... | .... | .... |
| | Manitoba Moose | AHL | 68 | 7 | 18 | 25 | 121 | .... | .... | .... | .... | .... | .... | .... | .... | .... | 5 | 0 | 1 | 1 | 8 | .... | .... | .... | .... |
| **2002-03** | **Vancouver** | **NHL** | **48** | **5** | **3** | **8** | **73** | **0** | **0** | **1** | **43** | **11.6** | **8** | **0** | **0.0** | **12:56** | **1** | **0** | **0** | **0** | **2** | **0** | **0** | **0** | **10:35** |
| | Manitoba Moose | AHL | 7 | 0 | 1 | 1 | 4 | .... | .... | .... | .... | .... | .... | .... | .... | .... | .... | .... | .... | .... | .... | .... | .... | .... | .... |
| **2003-04** | **Vancouver** | **NHL** | **74** | **2** | **5** | **7** | **94** | **0** | **0** | **0** | **70** | **2.9** | **−10** | **0** | **0.0** | **16:51** | **4** | **0** | **0** | **0** | **2** | **0** | **0** | **0** | **14:37** |
| 2004-05 | Voskresensk | Russia | 19 | 0 | 3 | 3 | 34 | .... | .... | .... | .... | .... | .... | .... | .... | .... | .... | .... | .... | .... | .... | .... | .... | .... | .... |
| **2005-06** | **Vancouver** | **NHL** | **77** | **7** | **10** | **17** | **115** | **1** | **0** | **0** | **88** | **8.0** | **4** | **0** | **0.0** | **20:27** | .... | .... | .... | .... | .... | .... | .... | .... | .... |
| **2006-07** | **Florida** | **NHL** | **82** | **4** | **21** | **25** | **112** | **0** | **0** | **0** | **99** | **4.0** | **7** | **1** | **0.0** | **21:36** | .... | .... | .... | .... | .... | .... | .... | .... | .... |
| **2007-08** | **Florida** | **NHL** | **73** | **2** | **14** | **16** | **67** | **0** | **0** | **0** | **67** | **3.0** | **5** | **0** | **0.0** | **21:17** | .... | .... | .... | .... | .... | .... | .... | .... | .... |
| **2008-09** | **Florida** | **NHL** | **2** | **0** | **1** | **1** | **0** | **0** | **0** | **0** | **5** | **0.0** | **2** | **0** | **0.0** | **27:11** | .... | .... | .... | .... | .... | .... | .... | .... | .... |
| | **NHL Totals** | | **373** | **20** | **54** | **74** | **467** | **1** | **0** | **1** | **378** | **5.3** | | **1** | **0.0** | **18:45** | **7** | **0** | **0** | **0** | **6** | **0** | **0** | **0** | **13:48** |

OHL First All-Star Team (1999)

• Missed majority of 1999-2000 season recovering from knee injury suffered in training camp, September 21, 1999. Signed as a free agent by **Voskresensk** (Russia), December 20, 2004. Traded to **Florida** by **Vancouver** with Todd Bertuzzi and Alex Auld for Roberto Luongo, Lukas Krajicek and Florida's 6th round choice (Sergei Shirokov) in 2006 Entry Draft, June 23, 2006. • Missed majority of 2008-09 season recovering from off-season arthroscopic knee surgery and follow-up cartilage surgery (October 27, 2008).

## ALZNER, Karl

(ALZ-nuhr, KARL) **WSH.**

Defense. Shoots left. 6'2", 205 lbs. Born, Burnaby, B.C., September 24, 1988. Washington's 1st choice, 5th overall, in 2007 Entry Draft.

| Season | Club | League | Regular Season GP | G | A | Pts | PIM | PP | SH | GW | S | % | +/- | TF | F% | Min | Playoffs GP | G | A | Pts | PIM | PP | SH | GW | Min |
|---|---|---|---|---|---|---|---|---|---|---|---|---|---|---|---|---|---|---|---|---|---|---|---|---|---|
| 2002-03 | Burnaby W.C. | Minor-BC | 64 | 17 | 31 | 48 | 24 | .... | .... | .... | .... | .... | .... | .... | .... | .... | .... | .... | .... | .... | .... | .... | .... | .... | .... |
| 2003-04 | Richmond | PIJHL | 41 | 3 | 9 | 12 | 8 | .... | .... | .... | .... | .... | .... | .... | .... | .... | 13 | 0 | 2 | 2 | 0 | .... | .... | .... | .... |
| | Calgary Hitmen | WHL | 1 | 0 | 0 | 0 | 0 | .... | .... | .... | .... | .... | .... | .... | .... | .... | .... | .... | .... | .... | .... | .... | .... | .... | .... |
| 2004-05 | Calgary Hitmen | WHL | 66 | 0 | 10 | 10 | 19 | .... | .... | .... | .... | .... | .... | .... | .... | .... | 12 | 0 | 3 | 3 | 9 | .... | .... | .... | .... |
| 2005-06 | Calgary Hitmen | WHL | 70 | 4 | 20 | 24 | 28 | .... | .... | .... | .... | .... | .... | .... | .... | .... | 13 | 1 | 3 | 4 | 4 | .... | .... | .... | .... |
| 2006-07 | Calgary Hitmen | WHL | 63 | 8 | 39 | 47 | 32 | .... | .... | .... | .... | .... | .... | .... | .... | .... | 18 | 1 | 12 | 13 | 4 | .... | .... | .... | .... |
| 2007-08 | Calgary Hitmen | WHL | 60 | 7 | 29 | 36 | 15 | .... | .... | .... | .... | .... | .... | .... | .... | .... | 16 | 6 | 2 | 8 | 4 | .... | .... | .... | .... |
| **2008-09** | **Washington** | **NHL** | **30** | **1** | **4** | **5** | **2** | **0** | **0** | **0** | **31** | **3.2** | **−1** | **0** | **0.0** | **19:25** | .... | .... | .... | .... | .... | .... | .... | .... | .... |
| | Hershey Bears | AHL | 48 | 4 | 16 | 20 | 10 | .... | .... | .... | .... | .... | .... | .... | .... | .... | 10 | 0 | 2 | 2 | 2 | .... | .... | .... | .... |
| | **NHL Totals** | | **30** | **1** | **4** | **5** | **2** | **0** | **0** | **0** | **31** | **3.2** | | **0** | **0.0** | **19:25** | .... | .... | .... | .... | .... | .... | .... | .... | .... |

WHL East Second All-Star Team (2007) • Canadian Major Junior Second All-Star Team (2007) • WHL East First All-Star Team (2008) • WHL Defenseman of the Year (2008) • WHL Player of the Year (2008) • Canadian Major Junior First All-Star Team (2008) • Canadian Major Junior Defenseman of the Year (2008)



## ANDERSSON, Jonas

(AN-duhr-suhn, YOH-nuhs) **NSH.**

Right wing. Shoots left. 6'3", 204 lbs. Born, Stockholm, Sweden, February 24, 1981. Nashville's 2nd choice, 33rd overall, in 1999 Entry Draft.

| Season | Club | League | Regular Season GP | G | A | Pts | PIM | PP | SH | GW | S | % | +/- | TF | F% | Min | Playoffs GP | G | A | Pts | PIM | PP | SH | GW | Min |
|---|---|---|---|---|---|---|---|---|---|---|---|---|---|---|---|---|---|---|---|---|---|---|---|---|---|
| 1997-98 | AIK Solna Jr. | Swe-Jr. | 33 | 14 | 16 | 30 | 32 | .... | .... | .... | .... | .... | .... | .... | .... | .... | .... | .... | .... | .... | .... | .... | .... | .... | .... |
| 1998-99 | AIK Solna Jr. | Swe-Jr. | 16 | 3 | 7 | 10 | 18 | .... | .... | .... | .... | .... | .... | .... | .... | .... | .... | .... | .... | .... | .... | .... | .... | .... | .... |
| | London Knights | Britain | 12 | 2 | 3 | 5 | 0 | .... | .... | .... | .... | .... | .... | .... | .... | .... | .... | .... | .... | .... | .... | .... | .... | .... | .... |
| 99-2000 | North Bay | OHL | 67 | 31 | 36 | 67 | 27 | .... | .... | .... | .... | .... | .... | .... | .... | .... | 6 | 2 | 2 | 4 | 2 | .... | .... | .... | .... |
| | Milwaukee | IHL | 2 | 1 | 0 | 1 | 0 | .... | .... | .... | .... | .... | .... | .... | .... | .... | 2 | 0 | 0 | 0 | 2 | .... | .... | .... | .... |
| 2000-01 | Milwaukee | IHL | 52 | 6 | 7 | 13 | 44 | .... | .... | .... | .... | .... | .... | .... | .... | .... | 5 | 0 | 0 | 0 | 2 | .... | .... | .... | .... |
| **2001-02** | **Nashville** | **NHL** | **5** | **0** | **0** | **0** | **2** | **0** | **0** | **0** | **4** | **0.0** | **−2** | **0** | **0.0** | **9:06** | .... | .... | .... | .... | .... | .... | .... | .... | .... |
| | Milwaukee | AHL | 71 | 13 | 17 | 30 | 19 | .... | .... | .... | .... | .... | .... | .... | .... | .... | .... | .... | .... | .... | .... | .... | .... | .... | .... |
| 2002-03 | Milwaukee | AHL | 49 | 7 | 4 | 11 | 12 | .... | .... | .... | .... | .... | .... | .... | .... | .... | 5 | 0 | 1 | 1 | 4 | .... | .... | .... | .... |
| 2003-04 | | DID NOT PLAY – INJURED | | | | | | | | | | | | | | | | | | | | | | | |
| 2004-05 | Sodertalje SK | Sweden | 34 | 0 | 4 | 4 | 8 | .... | .... | .... | .... | .... | .... | .... | .... | .... | .... | .... | .... | .... | .... | .... | .... | .... | .... |
| | Brynas IF Gavle | Sweden | 7 | 2 | 0 | 2 | 2 | .... | .... | .... | .... | .... | .... | .... | .... | .... | .... | .... | .... | .... | .... | .... | .... | .... | .... |

| | | | Regular Season | | | | | | | | | | | | | | Playoffs | | | | | | | | |
|---|---|---|---|---|---|---|---|---|---|---|---|---|---|---|---|---|---|---|---|---|---|---|---|---|---|
| Season | Club | League | GP | G | A | Pts | PIM | PP | SH | GW | S | % | +/- | TF | F% | Min | GP | G | A | Pts | PIM | PP | SH | GW | Min |
| 2005-06 | Ilves Tampere | Finland | 48 | 8 | 10 | 18 | 26 | .... | .... | .... | .... | .... | .... | .... | .... | .... | 4 | 2 | 0 | 2 | 0 | .... | .... | .... | .... |
| 2006-07 | HPK Hameenlinna | Finland | 23 | 6 | 7 | 13 | 20 | .... | .... | .... | .... | .... | .... | .... | .... | .... | 9 | 0 | 1 | 1 | 8 | .... | .... | .... | .... |
| 2007-08 | HPK Hameenlinna | Finland | 42 | 11 | 13 | 24 | 42 | .... | .... | .... | .... | .... | .... | .... | .... | .... | .... | .... | .... | .... | .... | .... | .... | .... | .... |
| | Karpat Oulu | Finland | 13 | 1 | 7 | 8 | 4 | .... | .... | .... | .... | .... | .... | .... | .... | .... | 10 | 3 | 7 | 10 | 4 | .... | .... | .... | .... |
| 2008-09 | Karpat Oulu | Finland | 55 | 24 | 33 | 57 | 54 | .... | .... | .... | .... | .... | .... | .... | .... | .... | 15 | 6 | 4 | 10 | 10 | .... | .... | .... | .... |
| | **NHL Totals** | | **5** | **0** | **0** | **0** | **2** | **0** | **0** | **0** | **4** | **0.0** | | **0** | **0.0** | **9:06** | .... | .... | .... | .... | .... | .... | .... | .... | .... |

• Missed entire 2003-04 season recovering from wrist injury suffered in training camp, September 30, 2003. Signed as a free agent by **Sodertalje** (Sweden), April 28, 2004. Signed as a free agent by **Gavle** (Sweden), January 22, 2005.

## ANISIMOV, Artem

(a-NEE-see-mawv, AHR-tehm) **NYR**

Center. Shoots left. 6'4", 194 lbs. Born, Yaroslavl, USSR, May 24, 1988. NY Rangers' 2nd choice, 54th overall, in 2006 Entry Draft.

| | | | | | | | | | | | | | | | | | | | | | | | | | |
|---|---|---|---|---|---|---|---|---|---|---|---|---|---|---|---|---|---|---|---|---|---|---|---|---|---|
| 2004-05 | Yaroslavl 2 | Russia-3 | 24 | 3 | 5 | 8 | 10 | .... | .... | .... | .... | .... | .... | .... | .... | .... | .... | .... | .... | .... | .... | .... | .... | .... | .... |
| 2005-06 | Yaroslavl 2 | Russia-3 | 32 | 15 | 12 | 27 | 28 | .... | .... | .... | .... | .... | .... | .... | .... | .... | .... | .... | .... | .... | .... | .... | .... | .... | .... |
| | Yaroslavl | Russia | 10 | 0 | 1 | 1 | 4 | .... | .... | .... | .... | .... | .... | .... | .... | .... | .... | .... | .... | .... | .... | .... | .... | .... | .... |
| 2006-07 | Yaroslavl 2 | Russia-3 | 2 | 2 | 0 | 2 | 0 | .... | .... | .... | .... | .... | .... | .... | .... | .... | .... | .... | .... | .... | .... | .... | .... | .... | .... |
| | Yaroslavl | Russia | 39 | 2 | 8 | 10 | 26 | .... | .... | .... | .... | .... | .... | .... | .... | .... | 7 | 3 | 2 | 5 | 4 | .... | .... | .... | .... |
| 2007-08 | Hartford | AHL | 74 | 16 | 27 | 43 | 30 | .... | .... | .... | .... | .... | .... | .... | .... | .... | 5 | 1 | 0 | 1 | 2 | .... | .... | .... | .... |
| **2008-09** | **NY Rangers** | **NHL** | **1** | **0** | **0** | **0** | **0** | **0** | **0** | **0** | **1** | **0.0** | **0** | **5** | **40.0** | **9:27** | **1** | **0** | **0** | **0** | **0** | **0** | **0** | **0** | **5:35** |
| | Hartford | AHL | 80 | 37 | 44 | 81 | 50 | .... | .... | .... | .... | .... | .... | .... | .... | .... | 6 | 2 | 0 | 2 | 0 | .... | .... | .... | .... |
| | **NHL Totals** | | **1** | **0** | **0** | **0** | **0** | **0** | **0** | **0** | **1** | **0.0** | | **5** | **40.0** | **9:27** | **1** | **0** | **0** | **0** | **0** | **0** | **0** | **0** | **5:35** |

## ANTROPOV, Nik

(an-TROH-pahv, NIHK) **ATL.**

Center. Shoots left. 6'6", 230 lbs. Born, Ust-Kamenogorsk, USSR, February 18, 1980. Toronto's 1st choice, 10th overall, in 1998 Entry Draft.

| | | | | | | | | | | | | | | | | | | | | | | | | | |
|---|---|---|---|---|---|---|---|---|---|---|---|---|---|---|---|---|---|---|---|---|---|---|---|---|---|
| 1996-97 | Ust-Kamenogorsk | Russia-2 | 8 | 2 | 1 | 3 | 6 | .... | .... | .... | .... | .... | .... | .... | .... | .... | .... | .... | .... | .... | .... | .... | .... | .... | .... |
| 1997-98 | Ust-Kamenogorsk | Russia-2 | 42 | 15 | 24 | 39 | 62 | .... | .... | .... | .... | .... | .... | .... | .... | .... | .... | .... | .... | .... | .... | .... | .... | .... | .... |
| 1998-99 | Dynamo Moscow | Russia | 30 | 5 | 9 | 14 | 30 | .... | .... | .... | .... | .... | .... | .... | .... | .... | 11 | 0 | 1 | 1 | 4 | .... | .... | .... | .... |
| **99-2000** | **Toronto** | **NHL** | **66** | **12** | **18** | **30** | **41** | **0** | **0** | **2** | **89** | **13.5** | **14** | **501** | **46.3** | **12:48** | **3** | **0** | **0** | **0** | **4** | **0** | **0** | **0** | **10:14** |
| | St. John's | AHL | 2 | 0 | 0 | 0 | 4 | .... | .... | .... | .... | .... | .... | .... | .... | .... | .... | .... | .... | .... | .... | .... | .... | .... | .... |
| **2000-01** | **Toronto** | **NHL** | **52** | **6** | **11** | **17** | **30** | **0** | **0** | **1** | **71** | **8.5** | **5** | **431** | **44.3** | **10:02** | **9** | **2** | **1** | **3** | **12** | **1** | **0** | **1** | **11:04** |
| **2001-02** | **Toronto** | **NHL** | **11** | **1** | **1** | **2** | **4** | **0** | **0** | **0** | **12** | **8.3** | **–1** | **31** | **38.7** | **8:57** | .... | .... | .... | .... | .... | .... | .... | .... | .... |
| | St. John's | AHL | 34 | 11 | 24 | 35 | 47 | .... | .... | .... | .... | .... | .... | .... | .... | .... | .... | .... | .... | .... | .... | .... | .... | .... | .... |
| **2002-03** | **Toronto** | **NHL** | **72** | **16** | **29** | **45** | **124** | **2** | **1** | **6** | **102** | **15.7** | **11** | **621** | **40.1** | **15:00** | **3** | **0** | **0** | **0** | **0** | **0** | **0** | **0** | **19:17** |
| **2003-04** | **Toronto** | **NHL** | **62** | **13** | **18** | **31** | **62** | **1** | **1** | **2** | **89** | **14.6** | **7** | **309** | **40.8** | **15:18** | **13** | **0** | **2** | **2** | **18** | **0** | **0** | **0** | **15:56** |
| 2004-05 | Ak Bars Kazan | Russia | 10 | 2 | 3 | 5 | 6 | .... | .... | .... | .... | .... | .... | .... | .... | .... | .... | .... | .... | .... | .... | .... | .... | .... | .... |
| | Yaroslavl | Russia | 26 | 4 | 15 | 19 | 44 | .... | .... | .... | .... | .... | .... | .... | .... | .... | 9 | 3 | 4 | 7 | 18 | .... | .... | .... | .... |
| **2005-06** | **Toronto** | **NHL** | **57** | **12** | **19** | **31** | **56** | **2** | **1** | **0** | **113** | **10.6** | **13** | **172** | **34.3** | **15:34** | .... | .... | .... | .... | .... | .... | .... | .... | .... |
| | Kazakhstan | Olympics | 5 | 1 | 0 | 1 | 4 | .... | .... | .... | .... | .... | .... | .... | .... | .... | .... | .... | .... | .... | .... | .... | .... | .... | .... |
| **2006-07** | **Toronto** | **NHL** | **54** | **18** | **15** | **33** | **44** | **4** | **0** | **4** | **125** | **14.4** | **8** | **34** | **35.3** | **16:36** | .... | .... | .... | .... | .... | .... | .... | .... | .... |
| **2007-08** | **Toronto** | **NHL** | **72** | **26** | **30** | **56** | **92** | **12** | **0** | **5** | **165** | **15.8** | **10** | **271** | **42.1** | **20:07** | .... | .... | .... | .... | .... | .... | .... | .... | .... |
| **2008-09** | **Toronto** | **NHL** | **63** | **21** | **25** | **46** | **24** | **6** | **0** | **2** | **171** | **12.3** | **–13** | **195** | **41.0** | **17:13** | .... | .... | .... | .... | .... | .... | .... | .... | .... |
| | **NY Rangers** | **NHL** | **18** | **7** | **6** | **13** | **6** | **2** | **0** | **2** | **53** | **13.2** | **–1** | **4** | **0.0** | **17:05** | **7** | **2** | **1** | **3** | **6** | **1** | **0** | **0** | **16:42** |
| | **NHL Totals** | | **527** | **132** | **172** | **304** | **483** | **29** | **3** | **24** | **990** | **13.3** | | **2569** | **41.8** | **15:24** | **35** | **4** | **4** | **8** | **40** | **2** | **0** | **1** | **14:38** |

Signed as a free agent by **Kazan** (Russia), October 27, 2004. Signed as a free agent by **Yaroslavl** (Russia), December 20, 2004. Traded to **NY Rangers** by **Toronto** for NY Ranger's 2nd round choice (Kenny Ryan) in 2009 Entry Draft, March 4, 2009. Signed as a free agent by **Atlanta**, July 2, 2009.

## ARMSTRONG, Colby

(AHRM-stawng, KOHL-bee) **ATL.**

Right wing. Shoots right. 6'2", 195 lbs. Born, Lloydminster, Sask., November 23, 1982. Pittsburgh's 1st choice, 21st overall, in 2001 Entry Draft.

| | | | | | | | | | | | | | | | | | | | | | | | | | |
|---|---|---|---|---|---|---|---|---|---|---|---|---|---|---|---|---|---|---|---|---|---|---|---|---|---|
| 1998-99 | Sask. Contacts | SMHL | 33 | 21 | 19 | 40 | 103 | .... | .... | .... | .... | .... | .... | .... | .... | .... | .... | .... | .... | .... | .... | .... | .... | .... | .... |
| | Red Deer Rebels | WHL | 1 | 0 | 1 | 1 | 0 | .... | .... | .... | .... | .... | .... | .... | .... | .... | .... | .... | .... | .... | .... | .... | .... | .... | .... |
| 99-2000 | Red Deer Rebels | WHL | 68 | 13 | 25 | 38 | 122 | .... | .... | .... | .... | .... | .... | .... | .... | .... | 2 | 0 | 1 | 1 | 11 | .... | .... | .... | .... |
| 2000-01 | Red Deer Rebels | WHL | 72 | 36 | 42 | 78 | 156 | .... | .... | .... | .... | .... | .... | .... | .... | .... | 21 | 6 | 6 | 12 | 29 | .... | .... | .... | .... |
| 2001-02 | Red Deer Rebels | WHL | 64 | 27 | 41 | 68 | 115 | .... | .... | .... | .... | .... | .... | .... | .... | .... | 23 | 6 | 10 | 16 | 32 | .... | .... | .... | .... |
| 2002-03 | Wilkes-Barre | AHL | 73 | 7 | 11 | 18 | 76 | .... | .... | .... | .... | .... | .... | .... | .... | .... | 3 | 0 | 0 | 0 | 4 | .... | .... | .... | .... |
| 2003-04 | Wilkes-Barre | AHL | 67 | 10 | 17 | 27 | 71 | .... | .... | .... | .... | .... | .... | .... | .... | .... | 24 | 3 | 1 | 4 | 45 | .... | .... | .... | .... |
| 2004-05 | Wilkes-Barre | AHL | 80 | 18 | 37 | 55 | 89 | .... | .... | .... | .... | .... | .... | .... | .... | .... | 10 | 4 | 2 | 6 | 14 | .... | .... | .... | .... |
| **2005-06** | **Pittsburgh** | **NHL** | **47** | **16** | **24** | **40** | **58** | **7** | **2** | **3** | **86** | **18.6** | **15** | **44** | **27.3** | **19:04** | .... | .... | .... | .... | .... | .... | .... | .... | .... |
| | Wilkes-Barre | AHL | 31 | 11 | 18 | 29 | 44 | .... | .... | .... | .... | .... | .... | .... | .... | .... | .... | .... | .... | .... | .... | .... | .... | .... | .... |
| **2006-07** | **Pittsburgh** | **NHL** | **80** | **12** | **22** | **34** | **67** | **1** | **1** | **3** | **145** | **8.3** | **2** | **13** | **15.4** | **16:50** | **5** | **0** | **1** | **1** | **11** | **0** | **0** | **0** | **15:18** |
| **2007-08** | **Pittsburgh** | **NHL** | **54** | **9** | **15** | **24** | **50** | **0** | **0** | **2** | **84** | **10.7** | **6** | **12** | **25.0** | **15:24** | .... | .... | .... | .... | .... | .... | .... | .... | .... |
| | **Atlanta** | **NHL** | **18** | **4** | **7** | **11** | **6** | **1** | **0** | **1** | **29** | **13.8** | **–2** | **3** | **0.0** | **18:02** | .... | .... | .... | .... | .... | .... | .... | .... | .... |
| **2008-09** | **Atlanta** | **NHL** | **82** | **22** | **18** | **40** | **75** | **3** | **0** | **2** | **141** | **15.6** | **5** | **28** | **28.6** | **15:09** | .... | .... | .... | .... | .... | .... | .... | .... | .... |
| | **NHL Totals** | | **281** | **63** | **86** | **149** | **256** | **12** | **3** | **11** | **485** | **13.0** | | **100** | **25.0** | **16:31** | **5** | **0** | **1** | **1** | **11** | **0** | **0** | **0** | **15:18** |

Traded to **Atlanta** by **Pittsburgh** with Erik Christensen, Angelo Esposito and Pittsburgh's 1st round choice (Daultan Leveille) in 2008 Entry Draft for Marian Hossa and Pascal Dupuis, February 26, 2008.

## ARMSTRONG, Derek

(AHRM-strawng, DAIR-ihk)

Center. Shoots right. 6', 197 lbs. Born, Ottawa, Ont., April 23, 1973. NY Islanders' 5th choice, 128th overall, in 1992 Entry Draft.

| | | | | | | | | | | | | | | | | | | | | | | | | | |
|---|---|---|---|---|---|---|---|---|---|---|---|---|---|---|---|---|---|---|---|---|---|---|---|---|---|
| 1989-90 | Hawkesbury | CJHL | 48 | 8 | 10 | 18 | 30 | .... | .... | .... | .... | .... | .... | .... | .... | .... | .... | .... | .... | .... | .... | .... | .... | .... | .... |
| 1990-91 | Hawkesbury | CJHL | 54 | 27 | 45 | 72 | 49 | .... | .... | .... | .... | .... | .... | .... | .... | .... | .... | .... | .... | .... | .... | .... | .... | .... | .... |
| | Sudbury Wolves | OHL | 2 | 0 | 2 | 2 | 0 | .... | .... | .... | .... | .... | .... | .... | .... | .... | .... | .... | .... | .... | .... | .... | .... | .... | .... |
| 1991-92 | Sudbury Wolves | OHL | 66 | 31 | 54 | 85 | 22 | .... | .... | .... | .... | .... | .... | .... | .... | .... | 9 | 2 | 2 | 4 | 2 | .... | .... | .... | .... |
| 1992-93 | Sudbury Wolves | OHL | 66 | 44 | 62 | 106 | 56 | .... | .... | .... | .... | .... | .... | .... | .... | .... | 14 | 9 | 10 | 19 | 26 | .... | .... | .... | .... |
| **1993-94** | **NY Islanders** | **NHL** | **1** | **0** | **0** | **0** | **0** | **0** | **0** | **0** | **2** | **0.0** | **0** | .... | .... | .... | .... | .... | .... | .... | .... | .... | .... | .... | .... |
| | Salt Lake | IHL | 76 | 23 | 35 | 58 | 61 | .... | .... | .... | .... | .... | .... | .... | .... | .... | .... | .... | .... | .... | .... | .... | .... | .... | .... |
| 1994-95 | Denver Grizzlies | IHL | 59 | 13 | 18 | 31 | 65 | .... | .... | .... | .... | .... | .... | .... | .... | .... | 6 | 0 | 2 | 2 | 0 | .... | .... | .... | .... |
| **1995-96** | **NY Islanders** | **NHL** | **19** | **1** | **3** | **4** | **14** | **0** | **0** | **0** | **23** | **4.3** | **–6** | .... | .... | .... | .... | .... | .... | .... | .... | .... | .... | .... | .... |
| | Worcester IceCats | AHL | 51 | 11 | 15 | 26 | 33 | .... | .... | .... | .... | .... | .... | .... | .... | .... | 4 | 2 | 1 | 3 | 0 | .... | .... | .... | .... |
| **1996-97** | **NY Islanders** | **NHL** | **50** | **6** | **7** | **13** | **33** | **0** | **0** | **2** | **36** | **16.7** | **–8** | .... | .... | .... | .... | .... | .... | .... | .... | .... | .... | .... | .... |
| | Utah Grizzlies | IHL | 17 | 4 | 8 | 12 | 10 | .... | .... | .... | .... | .... | .... | .... | .... | .... | 6 | 0 | 4 | 4 | 4 | .... | .... | .... | .... |
| **1997-98** | **Ottawa** | **NHL** | **9** | **2** | **0** | **2** | **9** | **0** | **0** | **1** | **8** | **25.0** | **1** | .... | .... | .... | .... | .... | .... | .... | .... | .... | .... | .... | .... |
| | Detroit Vipers | IHL | 10 | 0 | 1 | 1 | 2 | .... | .... | .... | .... | .... | .... | .... | .... | .... | .... | .... | .... | .... | .... | .... | .... | .... | .... |
| | Hartford | AHL | 54 | 16 | 30 | 46 | 40 | .... | .... | .... | .... | .... | .... | .... | .... | .... | 15 | 2 | 6 | 8 | 22 | .... | .... | .... | .... |
| **1998-99** | **NY Rangers** | **NHL** | **3** | **0** | **0** | **0** | **0** | **0** | **0** | **0** | **1** | **0.0** | **0** | **0** | **0.0** | **2:50** | .... | .... | .... | .... | .... | .... | .... | .... | .... |
| | Hartford | AHL | 59 | 29 | 51 | 80 | 73 | .... | .... | .... | .... | .... | .... | .... | .... | .... | 7 | 5 | 4 | 9 | 10 | .... | .... | .... | .... |
| **99-2000** | **NY Rangers** | **NHL** | **1** | **0** | **0** | **0** | **0** | **0** | **0** | **0** | **1** | **0.0** | **0** | **3** | **33.3** | **3:10** | .... | .... | .... | .... | .... | .... | .... | .... | .... |
| | Hartford | AHL | 77 | 28 | 54 | 82 | 101 | .... | .... | .... | .... | .... | .... | .... | .... | .... | 23 | 7 | 16 | 23 | 24 | .... | .... | .... | .... |
| **2000-01** | **NY Rangers** | **NHL** | **3** | **0** | **0** | **0** | **0** | **0** | **0** | **0** | **6** | **0.0** | **0** | **30** | **50.0** | **11:22** | .... | .... | .... | .... | .... | .... | .... | .... | .... |
| | Hartford | AHL | 75 | 32 | *69 | *101 | 73 | .... | .... | .... | .... | .... | .... | .... | .... | .... | 5 | 0 | 6 | 6 | 6 | .... | .... | .... | .... |
| 2001-02 | SC Bern | Swiss | 44 | 17 | 36 | 53 | 62 | .... | .... | .... | .... | .... | .... | .... | .... | .... | 6 | 3 | 5 | 8 | 8 | .... | .... | .... | .... |
| **2002-03** | **Los Angeles** | **NHL** | **66** | **12** | **26** | **38** | **30** | **2** | **0** | **1** | **106** | **11.3** | **5** | **708** | **50.0** | **15:40** | .... | .... | .... | .... | .... | .... | .... | .... | .... |
| | Manchester | AHL | 2 | 3 | 0 | 3 | 4 | .... | .... | .... | .... | .... | .... | .... | .... | .... | .... | .... | .... | .... | .... | .... | .... | .... | .... |
| **2003-04** | **Los Angeles** | **NHL** | **57** | **14** | **21** | **35** | **33** | **5** | **0** | **1** | **101** | **13.9** | **4** | **912** | **52.0** | **17:00** | .... | .... | .... | .... | .... | .... | .... | .... | .... |
| 2004-05 | Geneve | Swiss | 9 | 6 | 7 | 13 | 18 | .... | .... | .... | .... | .... | .... | .... | .... | .... | .... | .... | .... | .... | .... | .... | .... | .... | .... |
| | Rapperswil | Swiss | 3 | 1 | 3 | 4 | 4 | .... | .... | .... | .... | .... | .... | .... | .... | .... | .... | .... | .... | .... | .... | .... | .... | .... | .... |
| **2005-06** | **Los Angeles** | **NHL** | **62** | **13** | **28** | **41** | **46** | **7** | **0** | **1** | **100** | **13.0** | **–2** | **546** | **50.7** | **15:31** | .... | .... | .... | .... | .... | .... | .... | .... | .... |
| **2006-07** | **Los Angeles** | **NHL** | **67** | **11** | **33** | **44** | **62** | **3** | **0** | **0** | **109** | **10.1** | **13** | **842** | **47.9** | **15:04** | .... | .... | .... | .... | .... | .... | .... | .... | .... |
| **2007-08** | **Los Angeles** | **NHL** | **77** | **8** | **27** | **35** | **63** | **1** | **0** | **2** | **118** | **6.8** | **4** | **750** | **50.7** | **13:17** | .... | .... | .... | .... | .... | .... | .... | .... | .... |
| **2008-09** | **Los Angeles** | **NHL** | **56** | **5** | **4** | **9** | **63** | **1** | **0** | **1** | **42** | **11.9** | **–11** | **240** | **47.9** | **8:29** | .... | .... | .... | .... | .... | .... | .... | .... | .... |
| | **NHL Totals** | | **471** | **72** | **149** | **221** | **353** | **19** | **0** | **9** | **653** | **11.0** | | **4031** | **50.1** | **14:05** | .... | .... | .... | .... | .... | .... | .... | .... | .... |

AHL Second All-Star Team (2000) • Jack A. Butterfield Trophy (AHL – Playoff MVP) (2000) • AHL First All-Star Team (2001) • John P. Sollenberger Trophy (AHL – Leading Scorer) (2001) • Les Cunningham Award (AHL – MVP) (2001)

Signed as a free agent by **Ottawa**, July 28, 1997. • Loaned to **Hartford** (AHL) by **Ottawa**, October 28, 1997. Signed as a free agent by **NY Rangers**, August 10, 1998. Signed as a free agent by **Bern** (Swiss) with NY Rangers retaining NHL rights, July 18, 2001. Traded to **Los Angeles** by **NY Rangers** for Los Angeles' 6th round choice (Chris Holt) in 2003 Entry Draft, July 16, 2002. Signed as a free agent by **Geneve** (Swiss), October 12, 2004. Signed as a free agent by **Rapperswil** (Swiss), February 13, 2005.

## ARMSTRONG, Riley
(AHRM-stawng, RIGH-lee) **CGY.**

Right wing. Shoots right. 5'11", 180 lbs. Born, Saskatoon, Sask., November 8, 1984.

| Season | Club | League | GP | G | A | Pts | PIM | PP | SH | GW | S | % | +/- | TF | F% | Min | Playoffs GP | G | A | Pts | PIM | PP | SH | GW | Min |
|---|---|---|---|---|---|---|---|---|---|---|---|---|---|---|---|---|---|---|---|---|---|---|---|---|---|
| 2001-02 | Yorkton Terriers | SMHL | 42 | 43 | 34 | 77 | .... | .... | .... | .... | .... | .... | .... | .... | .... | .... | .... | .... | .... | .... | .... | .... | .... | .... | .... |
| 2002-03 | Kootenay Ice | WHL | 65 | 6 | 10 | 16 | 69 | .... | .... | .... | .... | .... | .... | .... | .... | .... | 10 | 0 | 1 | 1 | 14 | .... | .... | .... | .... |
| 2003-04 | Everett Silvertips | WHL | 69 | 18 | 26 | 44 | 119 | .... | .... | .... | .... | .... | .... | .... | .... | .... | 21 | 5 | 4 | 9 | 46 | .... | .... | .... | .... |
| 2004-05 | Cleveland Barons | AHL | 70 | 8 | 11 | 19 | 117 | .... | .... | .... | .... | .... | .... | .... | .... | .... | .... | .... | .... | .... | .... | .... | .... | .... | .... |
| 2005-06 | Cleveland Barons | AHL | 64 | 4 | 5 | 9 | 67 | .... | .... | .... | .... | .... | .... | .... | .... | .... | .... | .... | .... | .... | .... | .... | .... | .... | .... |
| 2006-07 | Worcester Sharks | AHL | 73 | 19 | 17 | 36 | 108 | .... | .... | .... | .... | .... | .... | .... | .... | .... | 6 | 0 | 1 | 1 | 12 | .... | .... | .... | .... |
| 2007-08 | Worcester Sharks | AHL | 64 | 15 | 19 | 34 | 91 | .... | .... | .... | .... | .... | .... | .... | .... | .... | .... | .... | .... | .... | .... | .... | .... | .... | .... |
| **2008-09** | **San Jose** | **NHL** | **2** | **0** | **0** | **0** | **2** | **0** | **0** | **0** | **1** | **0.0** | **–1** | **0** | **0.0** | **7:26** | .... | .... | .... | .... | .... | .... | .... | .... | .... |
| | Worcester Sharks | AHL | 71 | 25 | 17 | 42 | 101 | .... | .... | .... | .... | .... | .... | .... | .... | .... | 12 | 3 | 10 | 13 | 46 | .... | .... | .... | .... |
| | **NHL Totals** | | **2** | **0** | **0** | **0** | **2** | **0** | **0** | **0** | **1** | **0.0** | | **0** | **0.0** | **7:26** | .... | .... | .... | .... | .... | .... | .... | .... | .... |

Signed as a free agent by **San Jose**, September 15, 2004. Signed as a free agent by **Calgary**, July 2, 2009.

## ARNASON, Tyler
(AHR-na-suhn, TIGH-luhr) **NYR**

Center. Shoots left. 5'11", 204 lbs. Born, Oklahoma City, OK, March 16, 1979. Chicago's 6th choice, 183rd overall, in 1998 Entry Draft.

| Season | Club | League | GP | G | A | Pts | PIM | PP | SH | GW | S | % | +/- | TF | F% | Min | Playoffs GP | G | A | Pts | PIM | PP | SH | GW | Min |
|---|---|---|---|---|---|---|---|---|---|---|---|---|---|---|---|---|---|---|---|---|---|---|---|---|---|
| 1996-97 | Winnipeg South | MJHL | 50 | 35 | 50 | 85 | 15 | .... | .... | .... | .... | .... | .... | .... | .... | .... | 6 | 3 | 3 | 6 | 18 | .... | .... | .... | .... |
| 1997-98 | Fargo-Moorhead | USHL | 52 | 37 | 45 | 82 | 16 | .... | .... | .... | .... | .... | .... | .... | .... | .... | 4 | 1 | 1 | 2 | 2 | .... | .... | .... | .... |
| 1998-99 | St. Cloud State | WCHA | 38 | 14 | 17 | 31 | 16 | .... | .... | .... | .... | .... | .... | .... | .... | .... | .... | .... | .... | .... | .... | .... | .... | .... | .... |
| 99-2000 | St. Cloud State | WCHA | 39 | 19 | 30 | 49 | 18 | .... | .... | .... | .... | .... | .... | .... | .... | .... | .... | .... | .... | .... | .... | .... | .... | .... | .... |
| 2000-01 | St. Cloud State | WCHA | 41 | 28 | 28 | 56 | 14 | .... | .... | .... | .... | .... | .... | .... | .... | .... | .... | .... | .... | .... | .... | .... | .... | .... | .... |
| **2001-02** | **Chicago** | **NHL** | **21** | **3** | **1** | **4** | **4** | **0** | **0** | **0** | **19** | **15.8** | **–3** | **112** | **41.1** | **9:28** | **3** | **0** | **0** | **0** | **0** | **0** | **0** | **0** | **7:43** |
| | Norfolk Admirals | AHL | 60 | 26 | 30 | 56 | 42 | .... | .... | .... | .... | .... | .... | .... | .... | .... | .... | .... | .... | .... | .... | .... | .... | .... | .... |
| **2002-03** | **Chicago** | **NHL** | **82** | **19** | **20** | **39** | **20** | **3** | **0** | **6** | **178** | **10.7** | **7** | **626** | **40.3** | **14:30** | .... | .... | .... | .... | .... | .... | .... | .... | .... |
| **2003-04** | **Chicago** | **NHL** | **82** | **22** | **33** | **55** | **16** | **6** | **0** | **2** | **222** | **9.9** | **–13** | **904** | **43.1** | **16:34** | .... | .... | .... | .... | .... | .... | .... | .... | .... |
| 2004-05 | Brynas IF Gavle | Sweden | 4 | 0 | 0 | 0 | 0 | .... | .... | .... | .... | .... | .... | .... | .... | .... | .... | .... | .... | .... | .... | .... | .... | .... | .... |
| **2005-06** | **Chicago** | **NHL** | **60** | **13** | **28** | **41** | **40** | **5** | **0** | **1** | **161** | **8.1** | **5** | **492** | **44.7** | **14:58** | .... | .... | .... | .... | .... | .... | .... | .... | .... |
| | **Ottawa** | **NHL** | **19** | **0** | **4** | **4** | **4** | **0** | **0** | **0** | **42** | **0.0** | **–4** | **172** | **51.7** | **12:19** | .... | .... | .... | .... | .... | .... | .... | .... | .... |
| **2006-07** | **Colorado** | **NHL** | **82** | **16** | **33** | **49** | **26** | **1** | **0** | **3** | **211** | **7.6** | **–8** | **422** | **43.8** | **14:20** | .... | .... | .... | .... | .... | .... | .... | .... | .... |
| **2007-08** | **Colorado** | **NHL** | **70** | **10** | **21** | **31** | **16** | **3** | **0** | **1** | **179** | **5.6** | **–1** | **792** | **47.4** | **15:16** | **10** | **2** | **3** | **5** | **2** | **1** | **0** | **0** | **14:12** |
| **2008-09** | **Colorado** | **NHL** | **71** | **5** | **17** | **22** | **14** | **2** | **0** | **1** | **108** | **4.6** | **–16** | **721** | **46.1** | **13:19** | .... | .... | .... | .... | .... | .... | .... | .... | .... |
| | **NHL Totals** | | **487** | **88** | **157** | **245** | **140** | **20** | **0** | **14** | **1120** | **7.9** | | **4241** | **44.5** | **14:31** | **13** | **2** | **3** | **5** | **2** | **1** | **0** | **0** | **12:42** |

USHL First All-Star Team (1998) • WCHA All-Rookie Team (1999) • WCHA Second All-Star Team (2000) • AHL All-Rookie Team (2002) • Dudley "Red" Garrett Memorial Award (AHL – Rookie of the Year) (2002) • NHL All-Rookie Team (2003)

Signed as a free agent by **Gavle** (Sweden), October 29, 2004. Traded to **Ottawa** by **Chicago** for Brandon Bochenski and Ottawa's 2nd round choice (Simon Danis-Pepin) in 2006 Entry Draft, March 9, 2006. Signed as a free agent by **Colorado**, July 1, 2006. Signed as a free agent by **NY Rangers**, July 3, 2009.

## ARNOTT, Jason
(AHR-nawt, JAY-suhn) **NSH.**

Center. Shoots right. 6'5", 220 lbs. Born, Collingwood, Ont., October 11, 1974. Edmonton's 1st choice, 7th overall, in 1993 Entry Draft.

| Season | Club | League | GP | G | A | Pts | PIM | PP | SH | GW | S | % | +/- | TF | F% | Min | Playoffs GP | G | A | Pts | PIM | PP | SH | GW | Min |
|---|---|---|---|---|---|---|---|---|---|---|---|---|---|---|---|---|---|---|---|---|---|---|---|---|---|
| 1989-90 | Stayner Siskins | OHA-C | 34 | 21 | 31 | 52 | 12 | .... | .... | .... | .... | .... | .... | .... | .... | .... | .... | .... | .... | .... | .... | .... | .... | .... | .... |
| 1990-91 | Lindsay Bears | OHA-B | 42 | 17 | 44 | 61 | 10 | .... | .... | .... | .... | .... | .... | .... | .... | .... | 8 | 9 | 8 | 17 | 6 | .... | .... | .... | .... |
| 1991-92 | Oshawa Generals | OHL | 57 | 9 | 15 | 24 | 12 | .... | .... | .... | .... | .... | .... | .... | .... | .... | .... | .... | .... | .... | .... | .... | .... | .... | .... |
| 1992-93 | Oshawa Generals | OHL | 56 | 41 | 57 | 98 | 74 | .... | .... | .... | .... | .... | .... | .... | .... | .... | 13 | 9 | 9 | 18 | 20 | .... | .... | .... | .... |
| **1993-94** | **Edmonton** | **NHL** | **78** | **33** | **35** | **68** | **104** | **10** | **0** | **4** | **194** | **17.0** | **1** | .... | .... | .... | .... | .... | .... | .... | .... | .... | .... | .... | .... |
| **1994-95** | **Edmonton** | **NHL** | **42** | **15** | **22** | **37** | **128** | **7** | **0** | **1** | **156** | **9.6** | **–14** | .... | .... | .... | .... | .... | .... | .... | .... | .... | .... | .... | .... |
| **1995-96** | **Edmonton** | **NHL** | **64** | **28** | **31** | **59** | **87** | **8** | **0** | **5** | **244** | **11.5** | **–6** | .... | .... | .... | .... | .... | .... | .... | .... | .... | .... | .... | .... |
| **1996-97** | **Edmonton** | **NHL** | **67** | **19** | **38** | **57** | **92** | **10** | **1** | **2** | **248** | **7.7** | **–21** | .... | .... | .... | **12** | **3** | **6** | **9** | **18** | **1** | **0** | **0** | .... |
| **1997-98** | **Edmonton** | **NHL** | **35** | **5** | **13** | **18** | **78** | **1** | **0** | **0** | **100** | **5.0** | **–16** | .... | .... | .... | .... | .... | .... | .... | .... | .... | .... | .... | .... |
| | **New Jersey** | **NHL** | **35** | **5** | **10** | **15** | **21** | **3** | **0** | **2** | **99** | **5.1** | **–8** | .... | .... | .... | **5** | **0** | **2** | **2** | **0** | **0** | **0** | **0** | .... |
| **1998-99** | **New Jersey** | **NHL** | **74** | **27** | **27** | **54** | **79** | **8** | **0** | **3** | **200** | **13.5** | **10** | **872** | **49.3** | **15:24** | **7** | **2** | **2** | **4** | **4** | **1** | **0** | **0** | **16:48** |
| **99-2000** ♦ | **New Jersey** | **NHL** | **76** | **22** | **34** | **56** | **51** | **7** | **0** | **4** | **244** | **9.0** | **22** | **1172** | **46.9** | **17:05** | **23** | **8** | **12** | **20** | **18** | **3** | **0** | **1** | **16:29** |
| **2000-01** | **New Jersey** | **NHL** | **54** | **21** | **34** | **55** | **75** | **8** | **0** | **3** | **138** | **15.2** | **23** | **760** | **49.6** | **16:12** | **23** | **8** | **7** | **15** | **16** | **5** | **0** | **0** | **15:49** |
| **2001-02** | **New Jersey** | **NHL** | **63** | **22** | **19** | **41** | **59** | **8** | **0** | **1** | **169** | **13.0** | **3** | **934** | **47.8** | **17:13** | .... | .... | .... | .... | .... | .... | .... | .... | .... |
| | **Dallas** | **NHL** | **10** | **3** | **1** | **4** | **6** | **2** | **0** | **2** | **28** | **10.7** | **–1** | **77** | **52.0** | **18:13** | .... | .... | .... | .... | .... | .... | .... | .... | .... |
| **2002-03** | **Dallas** | **NHL** | **72** | **23** | **24** | **47** | **51** | **7** | **0** | **6** | **169** | **13.6** | **9** | **1130** | **53.3** | **16:12** | **11** | **3** | **2** | **5** | **6** | **1** | **0** | **0** | **15:35** |
| **2003-04** | **Dallas** | **NHL** | **73** | **21** | **36** | **57** | **66** | **5** | **0** | **5** | **143** | **14.7** | **23** | **1203** | **53.0** | **17:00** | **5** | **1** | **1** | **2** | **2** | **1** | **0** | **0** | **17:23** |
| 2004-05 | | | DID NOT PLAY | | | | | | | | | | | | | | | | | | | | | | |
| **2005-06** | **Dallas** | **NHL** | **81** | **32** | **44** | **76** | **102** | **11** | **1** | **5** | **167** | **19.2** | **13** | **1306** | **51.2** | **17:12** | **5** | **0** | **3** | **3** | **4** | **0** | **0** | **0** | **20:04** |
| **2006-07** | **Nashville** | **NHL** | **68** | **27** | **27** | **54** | **48** | **12** | **0** | **6** | **190** | **14.2** | **15** | **1145** | **50.6** | **17:59** | **5** | **2** | **1** | **3** | **2** | **1** | **0** | **0** | **19:17** |
| **2007-08** | **Nashville** | **NHL** | **79** | **28** | **44** | **72** | **54** | **13** | **0** | **3** | **248** | **11.3** | **19** | **1260** | **48.7** | **18:59** | **4** | **1** | **0** | **1** | **4** | **0** | **0** | **1** | **18:29** |
| **2008-09** | **Nashville** | **NHL** | **65** | **33** | **24** | **57** | **49** | **9** | **0** | **5** | **196** | **16.8** | **2** | **1037** | **50.6** | **18:55** | .... | .... | .... | .... | .... | .... | .... | .... | .... |
| | **NHL Totals** | | **1036** | **364** | **463** | **827** | **1150** | **129** | **2** | **57** | **2933** | **12.4** | | **10896** | **50.2** | **17:15** | **100** | **28** | **36** | **64** | **74** | **13** | **0** | **2** | **16:44** |

NHL All-Rookie Team (1994)

Played in NHL All-Star Game (1997, 2008)

Traded to **New Jersey** by **Edmonton** with Bryan Muir for Valeri Zelepukin and Bill Guerin, January 4, 1998. Traded to **Dallas** by **New Jersey** with Randy McKay and New Jersey's 1st round choice (later traded to Columbus – later traded to Buffalo – Buffalo selected Daniel Paille) in 2002 Entry Draft for Joe Nieuwendyk and Jamie Langenbrunner, March 19, 2002. Signed as a free agent by **Nashville**, July 2, 2006.

## ARTYUKHIN, Evgeny
(ahr-TYEW-khin, ehv-GEH-nee) **T.B.**

Right wing. Shoots left. 6'5", 254 lbs. Born, Moscow, USSR, April 4, 1983. Tampa Bay's 4th choice, 94th overall, in 2001 Entry Draft.

| Season | Club | League | GP | G | A | Pts | PIM | PP | SH | GW | S | % | +/- | TF | F% | Min | Playoffs GP | G | A | Pts | PIM | PP | SH | GW | Min |
|---|---|---|---|---|---|---|---|---|---|---|---|---|---|---|---|---|---|---|---|---|---|---|---|---|---|
| 99-2000 | Vityaz Podolsk 2 | Russia-3 | 26 | 9 | 8 | 17 | 46 | .... | .... | .... | .... | .... | .... | .... | .... | .... | .... | .... | .... | .... | .... | .... | .... | .... | .... |
| | Vityaz Podolsk | Russia-2 | 3 | 0 | 0 | 0 | 2 | .... | .... | .... | .... | .... | .... | .... | .... | .... | .... | .... | .... | .... | .... | .... | .... | .... | .... |
| 2000-01 | Vityaz Podolsk | Russia | 24 | 0 | 1 | 1 | 14 | .... | .... | .... | .... | .... | .... | .... | .... | .... | .... | .... | .... | .... | .... | .... | .... | .... | .... |
| 2001-02 | Vityaz Podolsk 2 | Russia-3 | 4 | 3 | 1 | 4 | 6 | .... | .... | .... | .... | .... | .... | .... | .... | .... | .... | .... | .... | .... | .... | .... | .... | .... | .... |
| | Vityaz Podolsk | Russia-2 | 49 | 15 | 7 | 22 | 94 | .... | .... | .... | .... | .... | .... | .... | .... | .... | 12 | 0 | 1 | 1 | 18 | .... | .... | .... | .... |
| 2002-03 | Moncton Wildcats | QMJHL | 53 | 13 | 27 | 40 | 204 | .... | .... | .... | .... | .... | .... | .... | .... | .... | 6 | 1 | 2 | 3 | 29 | .... | .... | .... | .... |
| 2003-04 | Hershey Bears | AHL | 36 | 3 | 3 | 6 | 111 | .... | .... | .... | .... | .... | .... | .... | .... | .... | .... | .... | .... | .... | .... | .... | .... | .... | .... |
| | Pensacola | ECHL | 6 | 1 | 0 | 1 | 14 | .... | .... | .... | .... | .... | .... | .... | .... | .... | .... | .... | .... | .... | .... | .... | .... | .... | .... |
| 2004-05 | Springfield | AHL | 62 | 9 | 19 | 28 | 142 | .... | .... | .... | .... | .... | .... | .... | .... | .... | .... | .... | .... | .... | .... | .... | .... | .... | .... |
| **2005-06** | **Tampa Bay** | **NHL** | **72** | **4** | **13** | **17** | **90** | **1** | **0** | **0** | **79** | **5.1** | **–4** | **0** | **0.0** | **8:43** | **5** | **1** | **0** | **1** | **6** | **0** | **0** | **0** | **8:14** |
| | Springfield | AHL | 4 | 2 | 1 | 3 | 4 | .... | .... | .... | .... | .... | .... | .... | .... | .... | .... | .... | .... | .... | .... | .... | .... | .... | .... |
| 2006-07 | Yaroslavl | Russia | 44 | 5 | 8 | 13 | 183 | .... | .... | .... | .... | .... | .... | .... | .... | .... | 1 | 0 | 0 | 0 | 0 | .... | .... | .... | .... |
| 2007-08 | Avangard Omsk | Russia | 19 | 3 | 2 | 5 | 40 | .... | .... | .... | .... | .... | .... | .... | .... | .... | .... | .... | .... | .... | .... | .... | .... | .... | .... |
| | CSKA Moscow | Russia | 23 | 3 | 5 | 8 | 99 | .... | .... | .... | .... | .... | .... | .... | .... | .... | 6 | 4 | 0 | 4 | 6 | .... | .... | .... | .... |
| **2008-09** | **Tampa Bay** | **NHL** | **73** | **6** | **10** | **16** | **151** | **1** | **0** | **0** | **100** | **6.0** | **1** | **2** | **0.0** | **10:40** | .... | .... | .... | .... | .... | .... | .... | .... | .... |
| | **NHL Totals** | | **145** | **10** | **23** | **33** | **241** | **2** | **0** | **0** | **179** | **5.6** | | **2** | **0.0** | **9:42** | **5** | **1** | **0** | **1** | **6** | **0** | **0** | **0** | **8:14** |

Signed as a free agent by **Yaroslavl** (Russia), August 5, 2006.

## ASHAM, Arron
(ASH-uhm, AIR-ruhn) **PHI.**

Right wing. Shoots right. 5'11", 205 lbs. Born, Portage La Prairie, Man., April 13, 1978. Montreal's 3rd choice, 71st overall, in 1996 Entry Draft.

| Season | Club | League | GP | G | A | Pts | PIM | PP | SH | GW | S | % | +/- | TF | F% | Min | Playoffs GP | G | A | Pts | PIM | PP | SH | GW | Min |
|---|---|---|---|---|---|---|---|---|---|---|---|---|---|---|---|---|---|---|---|---|---|---|---|---|---|
| 1993-94 | Portage | MAHA | 21 | 18 | 19 | 37 | 82 | .... | .... | .... | .... | .... | .... | .... | .... | .... | .... | .... | .... | .... | .... | .... | .... | .... | .... |
| 1994-95 | Red Deer Rebels | WHL | 62 | 11 | 16 | 27 | 126 | .... | .... | .... | .... | .... | .... | .... | .... | .... | .... | .... | .... | .... | .... | .... | .... | .... | .... |
| 1995-96 | Red Deer Rebels | WHL | 70 | 32 | 45 | 77 | 174 | .... | .... | .... | .... | .... | .... | .... | .... | .... | 10 | 6 | 3 | 9 | 20 | .... | .... | .... | .... |
| 1996-97 | Red Deer Rebels | WHL | 67 | 45 | 51 | 96 | 149 | .... | .... | .... | .... | .... | .... | .... | .... | .... | 16 | 12 | 14 | 26 | 36 | .... | .... | .... | .... |
| 1997-98 | Red Deer Rebels | WHL | 67 | 43 | 49 | 92 | 153 | .... | .... | .... | .... | .... | .... | .... | .... | .... | 5 | 0 | 2 | 2 | 8 | .... | .... | .... | .... |
| | Fredericton | AHL | 2 | 1 | 1 | 2 | 0 | .... | .... | .... | .... | .... | .... | .... | .... | .... | 2 | 0 | 1 | 1 | 0 | .... | .... | .... | .... |
| **1998-99** | **Montreal** | **NHL** | **7** | **0** | **0** | **0** | **0** | **0** | **0** | **0** | **5** | **0.0** | **–4** | **0** | **0.0** | **7:27** | .... | .... | .... | .... | .... | .... | .... | .... | .... |
| | Fredericton | AHL | 60 | 16 | 18 | 34 | 118 | .... | .... | .... | .... | .... | .... | .... | .... | .... | 13 | 8 | 6 | 14 | 11 | .... | .... | .... | .... |
| **99-2000** | **Montreal** | **NHL** | **33** | **4** | **2** | **6** | **24** | **0** | **1** | **1** | **29** | **13.8** | **–7** | **1** | **0.0** | **10:14** | .... | .... | .... | .... | .... | .... | .... | .... | .... |
| | Quebec Citadelles | AHL | 13 | 4 | 5 | 9 | 32 | .... | .... | .... | .... | .... | .... | .... | .... | .... | 2 | 0 | 0 | 0 | 2 | .... | .... | .... | .... |
| **2000-01** | **Montreal** | **NHL** | **46** | **2** | **3** | **5** | **59** | **0** | **0** | **0** | **32** | **6.3** | **–9** | **3** | **100.0** | **8:28** | .... | .... | .... | .... | .... | .... | .... | .... | .... |
| | Quebec Citadelles | AHL | 15 | 7 | 9 | 16 | 51 | .... | .... | .... | .... | .... | .... | .... | .... | .... | 7 | 1 | 2 | 3 | 2 | .... | .... | .... | .... |
| **2001-02** | **Montreal** | **NHL** | **35** | **5** | **4** | **9** | **55** | **0** | **0** | **0** | **30** | **16.7** | **7** | **4** | **25.0** | **8:13** | **3** | **0** | **1** | **1** | **0** | **0** | **0** | **0** | **5:39** |
| | Quebec Citadelles | AHL | 24 | 9 | 14 | 23 | 35 | .... | .... | .... | .... | .... | .... | .... | .... | .... | .... | .... | .... | .... | .... | .... | .... | .... | .... |

| | | | Regular Season | | | | | | | | | | | | | | Playoffs | | | | | | | | |
|---|---|---|---|---|---|---|---|---|---|---|---|---|---|---|---|---|---|---|---|---|---|---|---|---|---|
| Season | Club | League | GP | G | A | Pts | PIM | PP | SH | GW | S | % | +/- | TF | F% | Min | GP | G | A | Pts | PIM | PP | SH | GW | Min |
| **2002-03** | **NY Islanders** | **NHL** | **78** | **15** | **19** | **34** | **57** | **4** | **0** | **1** | **114** | **13.2** | **1** | **17** | **41.2** | **12:13** | **5** | **0** | **0** | **0** | **16** | **0** | **0** | **0** | **15:09** |
| **2003-04** | **NY Islanders** | **NHL** | **79** | **12** | **12** | **24** | **92** | **1** | **0** | **0** | **108** | **11.1** | **–12** | **23** | **34.8** | **13:13** | **5** | **0** | **1** | **1** | **4** | **0** | **0** | **0** | **8:44** |
| 2004-05 | EHC Visp | Swiss-2 | 5 | 2 | 4 | 6 | 6 | .... | .... | .... | .... | .... | .... | .... | .... | .... | 4 | 1 | 1 | 2 | 8 | .... | .... | .... | .... |
| **2005-06** | **NY Islanders** | **NHL** | **63** | **9** | **15** | **24** | **103** | **2** | **1** | **0** | **99** | **9.1** | **–5** | **63** | **41.3** | **13:33** | .... | .... | .... | .... | .... | .... | .... | .... | .... |
| **2006-07** | **NY Islanders** | **NHL** | **80** | **11** | **12** | **23** | **63** | **0** | **0** | **2** | **85** | **12.9** | **3** | **10** | **60.0** | **9:20** | **5** | **1** | **0** | **1** | **0** | **0** | **0** | **0** | **10:08** |
| **2007-08** | **New Jersey** | **NHL** | **77** | **6** | **4** | **10** | **84** | **0** | **0** | **2** | **68** | **8.8** | **–6** | **3** | **0.0** | **8:33** | **5** | **0** | **1** | **1** | **2** | **0** | **0** | **0** | **5:04** |
| **2008-09** | **Philadelphia** | **NHL** | **78** | **8** | **12** | **20** | **155** | **0** | **0** | **1** | **74** | **10.8** | **0** | **15** | **46.7** | **8:45** | **6** | **1** | **1** | **2** | **6** | **0** | **0** | **1** | **7:55** |
| | **NHL Totals** | | **576** | **72** | **83** | **155** | **692** | **7** | **2** | **7** | **644** | **11.2** | | **139** | **41.7** | **10:25** | **29** | **2** | **4** | **6** | **28** | **0** | **0** | **1** | **8:58** |

Traded to **NY Islanders** by **Montreal** with Montreal's 5th round choice (Marcus Paulsson) in 2002 Entry Draft for Mariusz Czerkawski, June 22, 2002. Signed as a free agent by **Visp** (Swiss-2), January 19, 2005. Signed as a free agent by **New Jersey**, August 7, 2007. Signed as a free agent by **Philadelphia**, July 7, 2008.

## AUCOIN, Adrian

(oh-KOIN, AY-dree-uhn) **PHX.**

Defense. Shoots right. 6'2", 212 lbs. Born, Ottawa, Ont., July 3, 1973. Vancouver's 7th choice, 117th overall, in 1992 Entry Draft.

| Season | Club | League | GP | G | A | Pts | PIM | PP | SH | GW | S | % | +/- | TF | F% | Min | GP | G | A | Pts | PIM | PP | SH | GW | Min |
|---|---|---|---|---|---|---|---|---|---|---|---|---|---|---|---|---|---|---|---|---|---|---|---|---|---|
| 1989-90 | Nepean Raiders | CJHL | 54 | 2 | 14 | 16 | 95 | .... | .... | .... | .... | .... | .... | .... | .... | .... | 4 | 0 | 1 | 1 | .... | .... | .... | .... | .... |
| 1990-91 | Nepean Raiders | CJHL | 56 | 17 | 33 | 50 | 125 | .... | .... | .... | .... | .... | .... | .... | .... | .... | .... | .... | .... | .... | .... | .... | .... | .... | .... |
| 1991-92 | Boston University | H-East | 32 | 2 | 10 | 12 | 60 | .... | .... | .... | .... | .... | .... | .... | .... | .... | .... | .... | .... | .... | .... | .... | .... | .... | .... |
| 1992-93 | Canada | Nat-Tm | 42 | 8 | 10 | 18 | 71 | .... | .... | .... | .... | .... | .... | .... | .... | .... | .... | .... | .... | .... | .... | .... | .... | .... | .... |
| 1993-94 | Canada | Nat-Tm | 59 | 5 | 12 | 17 | 80 | .... | .... | .... | .... | .... | .... | .... | .... | .... | .... | .... | .... | .... | .... | .... | .... | .... | .... |
| | Canada | Olympics | 4 | 0 | 0 | 0 | 2 | .... | .... | .... | .... | .... | .... | .... | .... | .... | .... | .... | .... | .... | .... | .... | .... | .... | .... |
| | Hamilton | AHL | 13 | 1 | 2 | 3 | 19 | .... | .... | .... | .... | .... | .... | .... | .... | .... | 4 | 0 | 2 | 2 | 6 | .... | .... | .... | .... |
| **1994-95** | Syracuse Crunch | AHL | 71 | 13 | 18 | 31 | 52 | .... | .... | .... | .... | .... | .... | .... | .... | .... | .... | .... | .... | .... | .... | .... | .... | .... | .... |
| | **Vancouver** | **NHL** | **1** | **1** | **0** | **1** | **0** | **0** | **0** | **0** | **2** | **50.0** | **1** | .... | .... | .... | **4** | **1** | **0** | **1** | **0** | **1** | **0** | **0** | .... |
| **1995-96** | **Vancouver** | **NHL** | **49** | **4** | **14** | **18** | **34** | **2** | **0** | **0** | **85** | **4.7** | **8** | .... | .... | .... | **6** | **0** | **0** | **0** | **2** | **0** | **0** | **0** | .... |
| | Syracuse Crunch | AHL | 29 | 5 | 13 | 18 | 47 | .... | .... | .... | .... | .... | .... | .... | .... | .... | .... | .... | .... | .... | .... | .... | .... | .... | .... |
| **1996-97** | **Vancouver** | **NHL** | **70** | **5** | **16** | **21** | **63** | **1** | **0** | **0** | **116** | **4.3** | **0** | .... | .... | .... | .... | .... | .... | .... | .... | .... | .... | .... | .... |
| **1997-98** | **Vancouver** | **NHL** | **35** | **3** | **3** | **6** | **21** | **1** | **0** | **1** | **44** | **6.8** | **–4** | .... | .... | .... | .... | .... | .... | .... | .... | .... | .... | .... | .... |
| **1998-99** | **Vancouver** | **NHL** | **82** | **23** | **11** | **34** | **77** | **18** | **2** | **3** | **174** | **13.2** | **–14** | **1** | **100.0** | **23:52** | .... | .... | .... | .... | .... | .... | .... | .... | .... |
| **99-2000** | **Vancouver** | **NHL** | **57** | **10** | **14** | **24** | **30** | **4** | **0** | **1** | **126** | **7.9** | **7** | **0** | **0.0** | **23:06** | .... | .... | .... | .... | .... | .... | .... | .... | .... |
| **2000-01** | **Vancouver** | **NHL** | **47** | **3** | **13** | **16** | **20** | **1** | **0** | **0** | **99** | **3.0** | **13** | **0** | **0.0** | **18:21** | .... | .... | .... | .... | .... | .... | .... | .... | .... |
| | **Tampa Bay** | **NHL** | **26** | **1** | **11** | **12** | **25** | **1** | **0** | **0** | **60** | **1.7** | **–8** | **0** | **0.0** | **23:34** | .... | .... | .... | .... | .... | .... | .... | .... | .... |
| **2001-02** | **NY Islanders** | **NHL** | **81** | **12** | **22** | **34** | **62** | **7** | **0** | **1** | **232** | **5.2** | **23** | **0** | **0.0** | **28:54** | **7** | **2** | **5** | **7** | **4** | **2** | **0** | **0** | **32:19** |
| **2002-03** | **NY Islanders** | **NHL** | **73** | **8** | **27** | **35** | **70** | **5** | **0** | **1** | **175** | **4.6** | **–5** | **0** | **0.0** | **29:01** | **5** | **1** | **2** | **3** | **4** | **0** | **0** | **0** | **31:43** |
| **2003-04** | **NY Islanders** | **NHL** | **81** | **13** | **31** | **44** | **54** | **4** | **0** | **2** | **213** | **6.1** | **29** | **0** | **0.0** | **26:38** | **5** | **0** | **0** | **0** | **6** | **0** | **0** | **0** | **28:21** |
| 2004-05 | MODO | Sweden | 14 | 2 | 4 | 6 | 32 | .... | .... | .... | .... | .... | .... | .... | .... | .... | 6 | 1 | 0 | 1 | 16 | .... | .... | .... | .... |
| **2005-06** | **Chicago** | **NHL** | **33** | **1** | **5** | **6** | **38** | **1** | **0** | **0** | **59** | **1.7** | **–13** | **0** | **0.0** | **22:58** | .... | .... | .... | .... | .... | .... | .... | .... | .... |
| **2006-07** | **Chicago** | **NHL** | **59** | **4** | **12** | **16** | **50** | **2** | **0** | **3** | **96** | **4.2** | **–22** | **0** | **0.0** | **20:50** | .... | .... | .... | .... | .... | .... | .... | .... | .... |
| **2007-08** | **Calgary** | **NHL** | **76** | **10** | **25** | **35** | **37** | **5** | **0** | **1** | **121** | **8.3** | **13** | **0** | **0.0** | **20:58** | **7** | **0** | **3** | **3** | **4** | **0** | **0** | **0** | **18:13** |
| **2008-09** | **Calgary** | **NHL** | **81** | **10** | **24** | **34** | **46** | **3** | **0** | **3** | **126** | **7.9** | **–8** | **0** | **0.0** | **22:18** | **6** | **2** | **1** | **3** | **2** | **0** | **0** | **0** | **21:10** |
| | **NHL Totals** | | **851** | **108** | **228** | **336** | **627** | **55** | **2** | **16** | **1728** | **6.3** | | **1** | **100.0** | **24:04** | **40** | **6** | **11** | **17** | **22** | **3** | **0** | **0** | **26:02** |

Played in NHL All-Star Game (2004)

• Missed majority of 1997-98 season recovering from ankle (October 4, 1997 vs. Anaheim) and groin (November 1, 1997 vs. Pittsburgh) injuries. Traded to **Tampa Bay** by **Vancouver** with Vancouver's 2nd round choice (Alexander Polushin) in 2001 Entry Draft for Dan Cloutier, February 7, 2001. Traded to **NY Islanders** by **Tampa Bay** with Alexander Kharitonov for Mathieu Biron and NY Islanders' 2nd round choice (later traded to Washington – later traded to Vancouver – Vancouver selected Denis Grot) in 2002 Entry Draft, June 22, 2001. Signed as a free agent by **MODO** (Sweden), December 21, 2004. Signed as a free agent by **Chicago**, August 2, 2005. Traded to **Calgary** by **Chicago** with Chicago's 7th round choice (C.J. Severyn) in 2007 Entry Draft for Andrei Zyuzin and Steve Marr, June 22, 2007. Signed as a free agent by **Phoenix**, July 2, 2009.

## AUCOIN, Keith

(oh-KOIN, KEETH) **WSH.**

Center. Shoots right. 5'8", 165 lbs. Born, Waltham, MA, November 6, 1978.

| Season | Club | League | GP | G | A | Pts | PIM | PP | SH | GW | S | % | +/- | TF | F% | Min | GP | G | A | Pts | PIM | PP | SH | GW | Min |
|---|---|---|---|---|---|---|---|---|---|---|---|---|---|---|---|---|---|---|---|---|---|---|---|---|---|
| 1997-98 | Norwich U. | ECAC-3 | 26 | 19 | 14 | 33 | .... | .... | .... | .... | .... | .... | .... | .... | .... | .... | .... | .... | .... | .... | .... | .... | .... | .... | .... |
| 1998-99 | Norwich U. | ECAC-3 | 31 | 33 | 39 | 72 | .... | .... | .... | .... | .... | .... | .... | .... | .... | .... | .... | .... | .... | .... | .... | .... | .... | .... | .... |
| 99-2000 | Norwich U. | ECAC-3 | 31 | 36 | 41 | 77 | 14 | .... | .... | .... | .... | .... | .... | .... | .... | .... | .... | .... | .... | .... | .... | .... | .... | .... | .... |
| 2000-01 | Norwich U. | ECAC-3 | 28 | 26 | 30 | 56 | 26 | .... | .... | .... | .... | .... | .... | .... | .... | .... | .... | .... | .... | .... | .... | .... | .... | .... | .... |
| 2001-02 | Lowell | AHL | 30 | 6 | 10 | 16 | 8 | .... | .... | .... | .... | .... | .... | .... | .... | .... | .... | .... | .... | .... | .... | .... | .... | .... | .... |
| | Florida Everblades | ECHL | 1 | 0 | 2 | 2 | 0 | .... | .... | .... | .... | .... | .... | .... | .... | .... | .... | .... | .... | .... | .... | .... | .... | .... | .... |
| | BC Icemen | UHL | 44 | 23 | 35 | 58 | 42 | .... | .... | .... | .... | .... | .... | .... | .... | .... | 10 | 3 | 5 | 8 | 4 | .... | .... | .... | .... |
| 2002-03 | Providence Bruins | AHL | 78 | 25 | 49 | 74 | 71 | .... | .... | .... | .... | .... | .... | .... | .... | .... | 4 | 0 | 1 | 1 | 6 | .... | .... | .... | .... |
| 2003-04 | Cincinnati | AHL | 80 | 18 | 30 | 48 | 64 | .... | .... | .... | .... | .... | .... | .... | .... | .... | 9 | 0 | 3 | 3 | 4 | .... | .... | .... | .... |
| 2004-05 | Memphis | CHL | 5 | 4 | 5 | 9 | 10 | .... | .... | .... | .... | .... | .... | .... | .... | .... | .... | .... | .... | .... | .... | .... | .... | .... | .... |
| | Providence Bruins | AHL | 72 | 21 | 45 | 66 | 49 | .... | .... | .... | .... | .... | .... | .... | .... | .... | 17 | 4 | *14 | 18 | 18 | .... | .... | .... | .... |
| **2005-06** | **Carolina** | **NHL** | **7** | **0** | **1** | **1** | **4** | **0** | **0** | **0** | **3** | **0.0** | **–4** | **4** | **100.0** | **5:19** | .... | .... | .... | .... | .... | .... | .... | .... | .... |
| | Lowell | AHL | 72 | 29 | 56 | 85 | 68 | .... | .... | .... | .... | .... | .... | .... | .... | .... | .... | .... | .... | .... | .... | .... | .... | .... | .... |
| **2006-07** | **Carolina** | **NHL** | **8** | **0** | **1** | **1** | **0** | **0** | **0** | **0** | **6** | **0.0** | **1** | **29** | **65.5** | **6:17** | .... | .... | .... | .... | .... | .... | .... | .... | .... |
| | Albany River Rats | AHL | 65 | 27 | 72 | 99 | 108 | .... | .... | .... | .... | .... | .... | .... | .... | .... | 5 | 1 | 3 | 4 | 7 | .... | .... | .... | .... |
| **2007-08** | **Carolina** | **NHL** | **38** | **5** | **8** | **13** | **10** | **0** | **0** | **0** | **65** | **7.7** | **3** | **327** | **37.9** | **13:28** | .... | .... | .... | .... | .... | .... | .... | .... | .... |
| | Albany River Rats | AHL | 38 | 8 | 37 | 45 | 38 | .... | .... | .... | .... | .... | .... | .... | .... | .... | .... | .... | .... | .... | .... | .... | .... | .... | .... |
| **2008-09** | **Washington** | **NHL** | **12** | **2** | **4** | **6** | **4** | **1** | **0** | **0** | **15** | **13.3** | **5** | **83** | **39.8** | **10:19** | .... | .... | .... | .... | .... | .... | .... | .... | .... |
| | Hershey Bears | AHL | 70 | 25 | *71 | 96 | 73 | .... | .... | .... | .... | .... | .... | .... | .... | .... | 21 | 5 | *18 | 23 | 16 | .... | .... | .... | .... |
| | **NHL Totals** | | **65** | **7** | **14** | **21** | **18** | **1** | **0** | **0** | **89** | **7.9** | | **443** | **40.6** | **11:07** | .... | .... | .... | .... | .... | .... | .... | .... | .... |

ECAC-3 First All-Star Team (2000, 2001) • ECAC-3 Player of the Year (2000, 2001) • AHL Second All-Star Team (2006, 2007) • AHL First All-Star Team (2009)

Signed as a free agent by **Lowell** (AHL), June 19, 2001. Signed as a free agent by **Providence** (AHL), August 2, 2002. Signed as a free agent by **Anaheim**, August 29, 2003. Signed to a PTO (tryout) contract by **Providence** (AHL), November 4, 2004, Signed as a free agent by **Providence** (AHL), December 9, 2004. Signed as a free agent by **Carolina**, August 4, 2005. Signed as a free agent by **Washington**, July 3, 2008.

## AVERY, Sean

(AY-vuhr-ee, SHAWN) **NYR**

Center. Shoots left. 5'10", 195 lbs. Born, Pickering, Ont., April 10, 1980.

| Season | Club | League | GP | G | A | Pts | PIM | PP | SH | GW | S | % | +/- | TF | F% | Min | GP | G | A | Pts | PIM | PP | SH | GW | Min |
|---|---|---|---|---|---|---|---|---|---|---|---|---|---|---|---|---|---|---|---|---|---|---|---|---|---|
| 1995-96 | Markham | Minor-ON | 70 | 34 | 81 | 115 | 180 | .... | .... | .... | .... | .... | .... | .... | .... | .... | .... | .... | .... | .... | .... | .... | .... | .... | .... |
| | Markham Waxers | MTJHL | 1 | 0 | 0 | 0 | 4 | .... | .... | .... | .... | .... | .... | .... | .... | .... | .... | .... | .... | .... | .... | .... | .... | .... | .... |
| 1996-97 | Owen Sound | OHL | 58 | 10 | 21 | 31 | 86 | .... | .... | .... | .... | .... | .... | .... | .... | .... | 4 | 1 | 0 | 1 | 4 | .... | .... | .... | .... |
| 1997-98 | Owen Sound | OHL | 47 | 13 | 41 | 54 | 105 | .... | .... | .... | .... | .... | .... | .... | .... | .... | .... | .... | .... | .... | .... | .... | .... | .... | .... |
| 1998-99 | Owen Sound | OHL | 28 | 22 | 23 | 45 | 70 | .... | .... | .... | .... | .... | .... | .... | .... | .... | .... | .... | .... | .... | .... | .... | .... | .... | .... |
| | Kingston | OHL | 33 | 14 | 25 | 39 | 88 | .... | .... | .... | .... | .... | .... | .... | .... | .... | 5 | 1 | 3 | 4 | 13 | .... | .... | .... | .... |
| 99-2000 | Kingston | OHL | 55 | 28 | 56 | 84 | 215 | .... | .... | .... | .... | .... | .... | .... | .... | .... | 5 | 2 | 2 | 4 | 26 | .... | .... | .... | .... |
| 2000-01 | Cincinnati | AHL | 58 | 8 | 15 | 23 | 304 | .... | .... | .... | .... | .... | .... | .... | .... | .... | 4 | 1 | 0 | 1 | 19 | .... | .... | .... | .... |
| **2001-02** | **Detroit** | **NHL** | **36** | **2** | **2** | **4** | **68** | **0** | **0** | **1** | **30** | **6.7** | **1** | **299** | **51.8** | **7:51** | .... | .... | .... | .... | .... | .... | .... | .... | .... |
| | Cincinnati | AHL | 36 | 14 | 7 | 21 | 106 | .... | .... | .... | .... | .... | .... | .... | .... | .... | .... | .... | .... | .... | .... | .... | .... | .... | .... |
| **2002-03** | **Detroit** | **NHL** | **39** | **5** | **6** | **11** | **120** | **0** | **0** | **2** | **40** | **12.5** | **7** | **224** | **58.0** | **7:03** | .... | .... | .... | .... | .... | .... | .... | .... | .... |
| | Grand Rapids | AHL | 15 | 6 | 6 | 12 | 82 | .... | .... | .... | .... | .... | .... | .... | .... | .... | .... | .... | .... | .... | .... | .... | .... | .... | .... |
| | **Los Angeles** | **NHL** | **12** | **1** | **3** | **4** | **33** | **0** | **0** | **0** | **19** | **5.3** | **0** | **49** | **46.9** | **13:50** | .... | .... | .... | .... | .... | .... | .... | .... | .... |
| | Manchester | AHL | .... | .... | .... | .... | .... | .... | .... | .... | .... | .... | .... | .... | .... | .... | 3 | 2 | 1 | 3 | 8 | .... | .... | .... | .... |
| **2003-04** | **Los Angeles** | **NHL** | **76** | **9** | **19** | **28** | ***261** | **0** | **0** | **2** | **125** | **7.2** | **2** | **124** | **54.8** | **11:41** | .... | .... | .... | .... | .... | .... | .... | .... | .... |
| 2004-05 | Pelicans Lahti | Finland | 2 | 3 | 0 | 3 | 26 | .... | .... | .... | .... | .... | .... | .... | .... | .... | .... | .... | .... | .... | .... | .... | .... | .... | .... |
| | Motor City | UHL | 16 | 15 | 11 | 26 | 149 | .... | .... | .... | .... | .... | .... | .... | .... | .... | .... | .... | .... | .... | .... | .... | .... | .... | .... |
| **2005-06** | **Los Angeles** | **NHL** | **75** | **15** | **24** | **39** | ***257** | **1** | **3** | **1** | **189** | **7.9** | **–5** | **226** | **44.3** | **13:37** | .... | .... | .... | .... | .... | .... | .... | .... | .... |
| **2006-07** | **Los Angeles** | **NHL** | **55** | **10** | **18** | **28** | **116** | **1** | **1** | **2** | **160** | **6.3** | **–10** | **180** | **47.2** | **16:52** | .... | .... | .... | .... | .... | .... | .... | .... | .... |
| | **NY Rangers** | **NHL** | **29** | **8** | **12** | **20** | **58** | **1** | **0** | **0** | **89** | **9.0** | **11** | **110** | **52.7** | **17:49** | **10** | **1** | **4** | **5** | **27** | **0** | **0** | **0** | **19:27** |
| **2007-08** | **NY Rangers** | **NHL** | **57** | **15** | **18** | **33** | **154** | **2** | **0** | **4** | **125** | **12.0** | **6** | **28** | **39.3** | **15:50** | **8** | **4** | **3** | **7** | **6** | **1** | **0** | **1** | **14:14** |
| **2008-09** | **Dallas** | **NHL** | **23** | **3** | **7** | **10** | **77** | **0** | **0** | **0** | **49** | **6.1** | **2** | **12** | **41.7** | **14:59** | .... | .... | .... | .... | .... | .... | .... | .... | .... |
| | Hartford | AHL | 8 | 2 | 1 | 3 | 8 | .... | .... | .... | .... | .... | .... | .... | .... | .... | .... | .... | .... | .... | .... | .... | .... | .... | .... |
| | **NY Rangers** | **NHL** | **18** | **5** | **7** | **12** | **34** | **2** | **0** | **0** | **50** | **10.0** | **4** | **6** | **66.7** | **16:44** | **6** | **0** | **2** | **2** | **24** | **0** | **0** | **0** | **17:38** |
| | **NHL Totals** | | **420** | **73** | **116** | **189** | **1178** | **7** | **4** | **12** | **876** | **8.3** | | **1258** | **50.8** | **13:24** | **24** | **5** | **9** | **14** | **57** | **1** | **0** | **1** | **17:15** |

Signed as a free agent by **Detroit**, September 21, 1999. Traded to **Los Angeles** by **Detroit** with Maxim Kuznetsov, Detroit's 1st round choice (Jeff Tambellini) in 2003 Entry Draft and Detroit's 2nd round choice (later traded to Boston – Boston selected Martins Karsums) in 2004 Entry Draft for Mathieu Schneider, March 11, 2003. Signed as a free agent by **Lahti** (Finland), November 24, 2004. Signed as a free agent by **Motor City** (UHL), February 11, 2005. Traded to **NY Rangers** by **Los Angeles** with John Seymour for Jason Ward, Jan Marek, Marc-Andre Cliche and NY Rangers' 3rd round choice (later traded to Buffalo - Buffalo selected Corey Fienhage) in 2008 Entry Draft, February 5, 2007. Signed as a free agent by **Dallas**, July 2, 2008. Claimed on waivers by **NY Rangers** from **Dallas**, March 3, 2009.

## AXELSSON, P.J.

(AHX-ehl-suhn, PEE-JAY)

Left wing. Shoots left. 6'1", 188 lbs. Born, Kungalv, Sweden, February 26, 1975. Boston's 7th choice, 177th overall, in 1995 Entry Draft.

| | | | Regular Season | | | | | | | | | | | | | | Playoffs | | | | | | | | |
|---|---|---|---|---|---|---|---|---|---|---|---|---|---|---|---|---|---|---|---|---|---|---|---|---|---|
| Season | Club | League | GP | G | A | Pts | PIM | PP | SH | GW | S | % | +/- | TF | F% | Min | GP | G | A | Pts | PIM | PP | SH | GW | Min |
| 1992-93 | V.Frolunda Jr. | Swe-Jr. | 16 | 9 | 5 | 14 | 12 | .... | .... | .... | .... | .... | .... | .... | .... | .... | .... | .... | .... | .... | .... | .... | .... | .... | .... |
| | V.Frolunda | Sweden | 1 | 0 | 0 | 0 | 0 | .... | .... | .... | .... | .... | .... | .... | .... | .... | .... | .... | .... | .... | .... | .... | .... | .... | .... |
| 1993-94 | V.Frolunda | Sweden | 11 | 0 | 0 | 0 | 4 | .... | .... | .... | .... | .... | .... | .... | .... | .... | 4 | 0 | 0 | 0 | 0 | .... | .... | .... | .... |
| 1994-95 | V.Frolunda Jr. | Swe-Jr. | 19 | 16 | 9 | 25 | 22 | .... | .... | .... | .... | .... | .... | .... | .... | .... | .... | .... | .... | .... | .... | .... | .... | .... | .... |
| | V.Frolunda | Sweden | 11 | 2 | 1 | 3 | 6 | .... | .... | .... | .... | .... | .... | .... | .... | .... | 5 | 0 | 0 | 0 | 0 | .... | .... | .... | .... |
| 1995-96 | V.Frolunda | Sweden | 36 | 15 | 5 | 20 | 10 | .... | .... | .... | .... | .... | .... | .... | .... | .... | 13 | 3 | 0 | 3 | 10 | .... | .... | .... | .... |
| 1996-97 | V.Frolunda | Sweden | 50 | 19 | 15 | 34 | 34 | .... | .... | .... | .... | .... | .... | .... | .... | .... | 3 | 0 | 2 | 2 | 0 | .... | .... | .... | .... |
| | V.Frolunda | EuroHL | 3 | 1 | 1 | 2 | 0 | .... | .... | .... | .... | .... | .... | .... | .... | .... | 3 | 0 | 0 | 0 | 2 | .... | .... | .... | .... |
| **1997-98** | **Boston** | **NHL** | **82** | **8** | **19** | **27** | **38** | **2** | **0** | **1** | **144** | **5.6** | **–14** | .... | .... | .... | **6** | **1** | **0** | **1** | **0** | **0** | **0** | **0** | .... |
| **1998-99** | **Boston** | **NHL** | **77** | **7** | **10** | **17** | **18** | **0** | **0** | **2** | **146** | **4.8** | **–14** | **8** | **75.0** | **16:38** | **12** | **1** | **1** | **2** | **4** | **0** | **0** | **0** | **15:11** |
| **99-2000** | **Boston** | **NHL** | **81** | **10** | **16** | **26** | **24** | **0** | **0** | **4** | **186** | **5.4** | **1** | **22** | **27.3** | **16:43** | .... | .... | .... | .... | .... | .... | .... | .... | .... |
| **2000-01** | **Boston** | **NHL** | **81** | **8** | **15** | **23** | **27** | **0** | **0** | **2** | **146** | **5.5** | **–12** | **41** | **36.6** | **12:30** | .... | .... | .... | .... | .... | .... | .... | .... | .... |
| **2001-02** | **Boston** | **NHL** | **78** | **7** | **17** | **24** | **16** | **0** | **2** | **0** | **127** | **5.5** | **6** | **17** | **35.3** | **14:42** | **6** | **2** | **1** | **3** | **6** | **0** | **1** | **1** | **16:48** |
| | Sweden | Olympics | 4 | 0 | 0 | 0 | 2 | .... | .... | .... | .... | .... | .... | .... | .... | .... | .... | .... | .... | .... | .... | .... | .... | .... | .... |
| **2002-03** | **Boston** | **NHL** | **66** | **17** | **19** | **36** | **24** | **2** | **2** | **1** | **122** | **13.9** | **8** | **17** | **23.5** | **16:37** | **5** | **0** | **0** | **0** | **6** | **0** | **0** | **0** | **13:23** |
| **2003-04** | **Boston** | **NHL** | **68** | **6** | **14** | **20** | **42** | **0** | **0** | **1** | **107** | **5.6** | **2** | **13** | **15.4** | **16:19** | **7** | **0** | **0** | **0** | **4** | **0** | **0** | **0** | **14:43** |
| 2004-05 | Frolunda | Sweden | 45 | 8 | 9 | 17 | 95 | .... | .... | .... | .... | .... | .... | .... | .... | .... | 14 | 1 | *10 | 11 | 18 | .... | .... | .... | .... |
| **2005-06** | **Boston** | **NHL** | **59** | **10** | **18** | **28** | **4** | **1** | **2** | **1** | **113** | **8.8** | **–3** | **27** | **40.7** | **17:36** | .... | .... | .... | .... | .... | .... | .... | .... | .... |
| | Sweden | Olympics | 8 | 3 | 3 | 6 | 0 | .... | .... | .... | .... | .... | .... | .... | .... | .... | .... | .... | .... | .... | .... | .... | .... | .... | .... |
| **2006-07** | **Boston** | **NHL** | **55** | **11** | **16** | **27** | **52** | **3** | **2** | **0** | **81** | **13.6** | **–10** | **38** | **34.2** | **19:34** | .... | .... | .... | .... | .... | .... | .... | .... | .... |
| **2007-08** | **Boston** | **NHL** | **75** | **13** | **16** | **29** | **15** | **0** | **2** | **2** | **100** | **13.0** | **11** | **45** | **37.8** | **17:36** | **7** | **0** | **0** | **0** | **2** | **0** | **0** | **0** | **16:57** |
| **2008-09** | **Boston** | **NHL** | **75** | **6** | **24** | **30** | **16** | **2** | **0** | **0** | **87** | **6.9** | **–1** | **47** | **34.0** | **16:14** | **11** | **0** | **1** | **1** | **2** | **0** | **0** | **0** | **14:03** |
| | **NHL Totals** | | **797** | **103** | **184** | **287** | **276** | **10** | **10** | **14** | **1359** | **7.6** | | **275** | **34.9** | **16:18** | **54** | **4** | **3** | **7** | **24** | **0** | **1** | **1** | **15:08** |

Signed as a free agent by **Frolunda** (Sweden), September 15, 2004. Signed as a free agent by **Frolunda** (Sweden), July 28, 2009.

## BABCHUK, Anton

(bab-CHUHK, AN-tawn) **CAR.**

Defense. Shoots right. 6'5", 212 lbs. Born, Kiev, USSR, May 6, 1984. Chicago's 1st choice, 21st overall, in 2002 Entry Draft.

| Season | Club | League | GP | G | A | Pts | PIM | PP | SH | GW | S | % | +/- | TF | F% | Min | GP | G | A | Pts | PIM | PP | SH | GW | Min |
|---|---|---|---|---|---|---|---|---|---|---|---|---|---|---|---|---|---|---|---|---|---|---|---|---|---|
| 99-2000 | Elektrostal 2 | Russia-3 | 6 | 0 | 0 | 0 | 8 | .... | .... | .... | .... | .... | .... | .... | .... | .... | .... | .... | .... | .... | .... | .... | .... | .... | .... |
| | Elektrostal 2 | Russia-3 | 18 | 0 | 1 | 1 | 18 | .... | .... | .... | .... | .... | .... | .... | .... | .... | .... | .... | .... | .... | .... | .... | .... | .... | .... |
| 2000-01 | Elektrostal | Russia-2 | 7 | 0 | 0 | 0 | 12 | .... | .... | .... | .... | .... | .... | .... | .... | .... | .... | .... | .... | .... | .... | .... | .... | .... | .... |
| | Russia 17 | Nat-Tm | 15 | 1 | 3 | 4 | 12 | .... | .... | .... | .... | .... | .... | .... | .... | .... | .... | .... | .... | .... | .... | .... | .... | .... | .... |
| 2001-02 | Elektrostal | Russia-2 | 40 | 7 | 8 | 15 | 90 | .... | .... | .... | .... | .... | .... | .... | .... | .... | .... | .... | .... | .... | .... | .... | .... | .... | .... |
| | Elektrostal 2 | Russia-3 | 3 | 0 | 0 | 0 | 8 | .... | .... | .... | .... | .... | .... | .... | .... | .... | .... | .... | .... | .... | .... | .... | .... | .... | .... |
| 2002-03 | Ak Bars Kazan | Russia | 10 | 0 | 0 | 0 | 4 | .... | .... | .... | .... | .... | .... | .... | .... | .... | .... | .... | .... | .... | .... | .... | .... | .... | .... |
| | St. Petersburg | Russia | 20 | 3 | 0 | 3 | 10 | .... | .... | .... | .... | .... | .... | .... | .... | .... | .... | .... | .... | .... | .... | .... | .... | .... | .... |
| | Spartak St. Pet. | Russia-2 | 1 | 1 | 0 | 1 | 0 | .... | .... | .... | .... | .... | .... | .... | .... | .... | .... | .... | .... | .... | .... | .... | .... | .... | .... |
| **2003-04** | **Chicago** | **NHL** | **5** | **0** | **2** | **2** | **2** | **0** | **0** | **0** | **11** | **0.0** | **–1** | **0** | **0.0** | **12:43** | .... | .... | .... | .... | .... | .... | .... | .... | .... |
| | Norfolk Admirals | AHL | 73 | 8 | 14 | 22 | 89 | .... | .... | .... | .... | .... | .... | .... | .... | .... | 8 | 0 | 2 | 2 | 6 | .... | .... | .... | .... |
| 2004-05 | Norfolk Admirals | AHL | 66 | 8 | 16 | 24 | 88 | .... | .... | .... | .... | .... | .... | .... | .... | .... | 2 | 0 | 0 | 0 | 2 | .... | .... | .... | .... |
| **2005-06** | **Chicago** | **NHL** | **17** | **2** | **3** | **5** | **16** | **1** | **0** | **0** | **24** | **8.3** | **–5** | **0** | **0.0** | **16:38** | .... | .... | .... | .... | .... | .... | .... | .... | .... |
| | Norfolk Admirals | AHL | 24 | 5 | 7 | 12 | 22 | .... | .... | .... | .... | .... | .... | .... | .... | .... | .... | .... | .... | .... | .... | .... | .... | .... | .... |
| | ♦ **Carolina** | **NHL** | **22** | **3** | **2** | **5** | **6** | **2** | **0** | **0** | **32** | **9.4** | **–2** | **0** | **0.0** | **13:22** | .... | .... | .... | .... | .... | .... | .... | .... | .... |
| | Lowell | AHL | 5 | 1 | 3 | 4 | 0 | .... | .... | .... | .... | .... | .... | .... | .... | .... | .... | .... | .... | .... | .... | .... | .... | .... | .... |
| **2006-07** | **Carolina** | **NHL** | **52** | **2** | **12** | **14** | **30** | **0** | **0** | **2** | **63** | **3.2** | **–6** | **0** | **0.0** | **17:26** | .... | .... | .... | .... | .... | .... | .... | .... | .... |
| | Albany River Rats | AHL | 9 | 1 | 6 | 7 | 2 | .... | .... | .... | .... | .... | .... | .... | .... | .... | .... | .... | .... | .... | .... | .... | .... | .... | .... |
| 2007-08 | Avangard Omsk | Russia | 57 | 9 | 17 | 26 | 30 | .... | .... | .... | .... | .... | .... | .... | .... | .... | 4 | 1 | 1 | 2 | 6 | .... | .... | .... | .... |
| **2008-09** | **Carolina** | **NHL** | **72** | **16** | **19** | **35** | **16** | **9** | **0** | **4** | **127** | **12.6** | **13** | **0** | **0.0** | **18:04** | **13** | **0** | **1** | **1** | **10** | **0** | **0** | **0** | **16:03** |
| | **NHL Totals** | | **168** | **23** | **38** | **61** | **70** | **12** | **0** | **6** | **257** | **8.9** | | **0** | **0.0** | **16:57** | **13** | **0** | **1** | **1** | **10** | **0** | **0** | **0** | **16:03** |

Traded to **Carolina** by **Chicago** for Danny Richmond and Columbus' 4th round choice (previously acquired, later traded to Toronto - Toronto selected James Reimer) in 2006 Entry Draft, January 20, 2006.

## BACKES, David

(BA-kuhs, DAY-vihd) **ST.L.**

Center. Shoots right. 6'3", 220 lbs. Born, Blaine, MN, May 1, 1984. St. Louis' 2nd choice, 62nd overall, in 2003 Entry Draft.

| Season | Club | League | GP | G | A | Pts | PIM | PP | SH | GW | S | % | +/- | TF | F% | Min | GP | G | A | Pts | PIM | PP | SH | GW | Min |
|---|---|---|---|---|---|---|---|---|---|---|---|---|---|---|---|---|---|---|---|---|---|---|---|---|---|
| 99-2000 | Spring Lake Park | High-MN | 24 | 17 | 20 | 37 | .... | .... | .... | .... | .... | .... | .... | .... | .... | .... | .... | .... | .... | .... | .... | .... | .... | .... | .... |
| 2000-01 | Spring Lake Park | High-MN | 24 | 29 | 46 | 75 | .... | .... | .... | .... | .... | .... | .... | .... | .... | .... | .... | .... | .... | .... | .... | .... | .... | .... | .... |
| 2001-02 | Chicago Steel | USHL | 25 | 31 | 36 | 67 | .... | .... | .... | .... | .... | .... | .... | .... | .... | .... | 2 | 1 | 1 | 2 | | .... | .... | .... | .... |
| | Lincoln Stars | USHL | 30 | 11 | 10 | 21 | 54 | .... | .... | .... | .... | .... | .... | .... | .... | .... | 3 | 0 | 0 | 0 | 2 | .... | .... | .... | .... |
| 2002-03 | Lincoln Stars | USHL | 57 | 28 | 41 | 69 | 126 | .... | .... | .... | .... | .... | .... | .... | .... | .... | 7 | 4 | 1 | 5 | 17 | .... | .... | .... | .... |
| 2003-04 | Minnesota State | WCHA | 39 | 16 | 21 | 37 | 66 | .... | .... | .... | .... | .... | .... | .... | .... | .... | .... | .... | .... | .... | .... | .... | .... | .... | .... |
| 2004-05 | Minnesota State | WCHA | 38 | 17 | 23 | 40 | 55 | .... | .... | .... | .... | .... | .... | .... | .... | .... | .... | .... | .... | .... | .... | .... | .... | .... | .... |
| 2005-06 | Minnesota State | WCHA | 38 | 13 | 29 | 42 | 91 | .... | .... | .... | .... | .... | .... | .... | .... | .... | .... | .... | .... | .... | .... | .... | .... | .... | .... |
| | Peoria Rivermen | AHL | 12 | 5 | 5 | 10 | 10 | .... | .... | .... | .... | .... | .... | .... | .... | .... | 3 | 1 | 1 | 2 | 8 | .... | .... | .... | .... |
| **2006-07** | **St. Louis** | **NHL** | **49** | **10** | **13** | **23** | **37** | **2** | **0** | **2** | **89** | **11.2** | **6** | **26** | **46.2** | **13:25** | .... | .... | .... | .... | .... | .... | .... | .... | .... |
| | Peoria Rivermen | AHL | 31 | 10 | 3 | 13 | 47 | .... | .... | .... | .... | .... | .... | .... | .... | .... | .... | .... | .... | .... | .... | .... | .... | .... | .... |
| **2007-08** | **St. Louis** | **NHL** | **72** | **13** | **18** | **31** | **99** | **3** | **0** | **2** | **129** | **10.1** | **–11** | **67** | **44.8** | **14:41** | .... | .... | .... | .... | .... | .... | .... | .... | .... |
| **2008-09** | **St. Louis** | **NHL** | **82** | **31** | **23** | **54** | **165** | **6** | **2** | **1** | **208** | **14.9** | **–3** | **477** | **44.4** | **17:41** | **4** | **1** | **2** | **3** | **10** | **0** | **0** | **0** | **22:56** |
| | **NHL Totals** | | **203** | **54** | **54** | **108** | **301** | **11** | **2** | **5** | **426** | **12.7** | | **570** | **44.6** | **15:35** | **4** | **1** | **2** | **3** | **10** | **0** | **0** | **0** | **22:56** |

USHL First All-Star Team (2003) • WCHA All-Rookie Team (2004) • WCHA Second All-Star Team (2006) • NCAA West Second All-American Team (2006)

## BACKLUND, Mikael

(BAHK-luhnd, mih-KIGH-ehl) **CGY.**

Center. Shoots left. 6', 194 lbs. Born, Vasteras, Sweden, March 17, 1989. Calgary's 1st choice, 24th overall, in 2007 Entry Draft.

| Season | Club | League | GP | G | A | Pts | PIM | PP | SH | GW | S | % | +/- | TF | F% | Min | GP | G | A | Pts | PIM | PP | SH | GW | Min |
|---|---|---|---|---|---|---|---|---|---|---|---|---|---|---|---|---|---|---|---|---|---|---|---|---|---|
| 2004-05 | Vasteras U18 | Swe-U18 | 14 | 5 | 6 | 11 | 14 | .... | .... | .... | .... | .... | .... | .... | .... | .... | 4 | 2 | 1 | 3 | 2 | .... | .... | .... | .... |
| 2005-06 | Vasteras Jr. | Swe-Jr. | 25 | 15 | 16 | 31 | 30 | .... | .... | .... | .... | .... | .... | .... | .... | .... | .... | .... | .... | .... | .... | .... | .... | .... | .... |
| | VIK Vasteras HK | Sweden-2 | 12 | 2 | 2 | 4 | 14 | .... | .... | .... | .... | .... | .... | .... | .... | .... | .... | .... | .... | .... | .... | .... | .... | .... | .... |
| 2006-07 | Vasteras U18 | Swe-U18 | 2 | 2 | 1 | 3 | 2 | .... | .... | .... | .... | .... | .... | .... | .... | .... | 1 | 0 | 0 | 0 | 10 | .... | .... | .... | .... |
| | Vasteras Jr. | Swe-Jr. | 7 | 5 | 4 | 9 | 8 | .... | .... | .... | .... | .... | .... | .... | .... | .... | 5 | 1 | 0 | 1 | 4 | .... | .... | .... | .... |
| | VIK Vasteras HK | Sweden-2 | 18 | 1 | 2 | 3 | 14 | .... | .... | .... | .... | .... | .... | .... | .... | .... | .... | .... | .... | .... | .... | .... | .... | .... | .... |
| 2007-08 | Vasteras Jr. | Swe-Jr. | 9 | 7 | 6 | 13 | 20 | .... | .... | .... | .... | .... | .... | .... | .... | .... | .... | .... | .... | .... | .... | .... | .... | .... | .... |
| | VIK Vasteras HK | Sweden-2 | 46 | 11 | 4 | 15 | 28 | .... | .... | .... | .... | .... | .... | .... | .... | .... | 5 | 4 | 3 | 7 | 0 | .... | .... | .... | .... |
| **2008-09** | Vasteras Jr. | Swe-Jr. | 2 | 3 | 2 | 5 | 0 | .... | .... | .... | .... | .... | .... | .... | .... | .... | .... | .... | .... | .... | .... | .... | .... | .... | .... |
| | VIK Vasteras HK | Sweden-2 | 17 | 4 | 4 | 8 | 39 | .... | .... | .... | .... | .... | .... | .... | .... | .... | .... | .... | .... | .... | .... | .... | .... | .... | .... |
| | **Calgary** | **NHL** | **1** | **0** | **0** | **0** | **0** | **0** | **0** | **0** | **1** | **0.0** | **0** | **7** | **28.6** | **10:44** | .... | .... | .... | .... | .... | .... | .... | .... | .... |
| | Kelowna Rockets | WHL | 28 | 12 | 18 | 30 | 26 | .... | .... | .... | .... | .... | .... | .... | .... | .... | 19 | *13 | 10 | 23 | 26 | .... | .... | .... | .... |
| | **NHL Totals** | | **1** | **0** | **0** | **0** | **0** | **0** | **0** | **0** | **1** | **0.0** | | **7** | **28.6** | **10:44** | .... | .... | .... | .... | .... | .... | .... | .... | .... |

• Assigned to **Vasteras** (Sweden-2) by **Calgary**, October 4, 2008.

## BACKMAN, Christian

(BAK-man, KRIH-stan)

Defense. Shoots left. 6'4", 210 lbs. Born, Alingsas, Sweden, April 28, 1980. St. Louis' 1st choice, 24th overall, in 1998 Entry Draft.

| Season | Club | League | GP | G | A | Pts | PIM | PP | SH | GW | S | % | +/- | TF | F% | Min | GP | G | A | Pts | PIM | PP | SH | GW | Min |
|---|---|---|---|---|---|---|---|---|---|---|---|---|---|---|---|---|---|---|---|---|---|---|---|---|---|
| 1996-97 | V.Frolunda Jr. | Swe-Jr. | 26 | 2 | 5 | 7 | 16 | .... | .... | .... | .... | .... | .... | .... | .... | .... | .... | .... | .... | .... | .... | .... | .... | .... | .... |
| 1997-98 | V.Frolunda U18 | Swe-U18 | 4 | 4 | 1 | 5 | 2 | .... | .... | .... | .... | .... | .... | .... | .... | .... | 5 | 2 | 2 | 4 | 2 | .... | .... | .... | .... |
| | V.Frolunda Jr. | Swe-Jr. | 28 | 5 | 14 | 19 | 12 | .... | .... | .... | .... | .... | .... | .... | .... | .... | 2 | 0 | 1 | 1 | 4 | .... | .... | .... | .... |
| 1998-99 | V.Frolunda Jr. | Swe-Jr. | 4 | 0 | 2 | 2 | 4 | .... | .... | .... | .... | .... | .... | .... | .... | .... | .... | .... | .... | .... | .... | .... | .... | .... | .... |
| | V.Frolunda | Sweden | 49 | 0 | 4 | 4 | 4 | .... | .... | .... | .... | .... | .... | .... | .... | .... | 4 | 0 | 0 | 0 | 0 | .... | .... | .... | .... |
| 99-2000 | V.Frolunda Jr. | Swe-Jr. | 5 | 1 | 1 | 2 | 0 | .... | .... | .... | .... | .... | .... | .... | .... | .... | 3 | 1 | 1 | 2 | 0 | .... | .... | .... | .... |
| | Gislaveds SK | Sweden-2 | 21 | 5 | 2 | 7 | 8 | .... | .... | .... | .... | .... | .... | .... | .... | .... | .... | .... | .... | .... | .... | .... | .... | .... | .... |
| | V.Frolunda | Sweden | 27 | 1 | 0 | 1 | 14 | .... | .... | .... | .... | .... | .... | .... | .... | .... | 5 | 0 | 0 | 0 | 0 | .... | .... | .... | .... |
| 2000-01 | V.Frolunda | Sweden | 50 | 1 | 10 | 11 | 32 | .... | .... | .... | .... | .... | .... | .... | .... | .... | 3 | 0 | 2 | 2 | 2 | .... | .... | .... | .... |
| 2001-02 | V.Frolunda | Sweden | 44 | 7 | 4 | 11 | 38 | .... | .... | .... | .... | .... | .... | .... | .... | .... | 10 | 0 | 0 | 0 | 8 | .... | .... | .... | .... |
| **2002-03** | **St. Louis** | **NHL** | **4** | **0** | **0** | **0** | **0** | **0** | **0** | **0** | **4** | **0.0** | **–3** | **0** | **0.0** | **12:22** | .... | .... | .... | .... | .... | .... | .... | .... | .... |
| | Worcester IceCats | AHL | 72 | 8 | 19 | 27 | 66 | .... | .... | .... | .... | .... | .... | .... | .... | .... | 3 | 0 | 1 | 1 | 5 | .... | .... | .... | .... |
| **2003-04** | **St. Louis** | **NHL** | **66** | **5** | **13** | **18** | **16** | **1** | **0** | **0** | **92** | **5.4** | **3** | **0** | **0.0** | **19:20** | **5** | **0** | **2** | **2** | **4** | **0** | **0** | **0** | **23:06** |
| | Worcester IceCats | AHL | 4 | 1 | 2 | 3 | 2 | .... | .... | .... | .... | .... | .... | .... | .... | .... | .... | .... | .... | .... | .... | .... | .... | .... | .... |
| 2004-05 | Frolunda | Sweden | 50 | 4 | 15 | 19 | 40 | .... | .... | .... | .... | .... | .... | .... | .... | .... | 14 | 2 | 7 | 9 | 10 | .... | .... | .... | .... |

| | | | Regular Season | | | | | | | | | | | | | | Playoffs | | | | | | | | |
|---|---|---|---|---|---|---|---|---|---|---|---|---|---|---|---|---|---|---|---|---|---|---|---|---|---|
| Season | Club | League | GP | G | A | Pts | PIM | PP | SH | GW | S | % | +/- | TF | F% | Min | GP | G | A | Pts | PIM | PP | SH | GW | Min |
| 2005-06 | St. Louis | NHL | 52 | 6 | 12 | 18 | 48 | 3 | 0 | 1 | 70 | 8.6 | -15 | 0 | 0.0 | 24:49 | | | | | | | | | |
| | Sweden | Olympics | 8 | 1 | 2 | 3 | 6 | | | | | | | | | | | | | | | | | | |
| 2006-07 | St. Louis | NHL | 61 | 7 | 11 | 18 | 36 | 1 | 0 | 0 | 80 | 8.8 | 13 | 0 | 0.0 | 22:10 | | | | | | | | | |
| 2007-08 | St. Louis | NHL | 45 | 1 | 9 | 10 | 30 | 0 | 0 | 0 | 30 | 3.3 | -4 | 0 | 0.0 | 19:22 | | | | | | | | | |
| | NY Rangers | NHL | 18 | 2 | 6 | 8 | 20 | 1 | 0 | 0 | 21 | 9.5 | 2 | 0 | 0.0 | 18:49 | 8 | 0 | 0 | 0 | 12 | 0 | 0 | 0 | 18:16 |
| 2008-09 | Columbus | NHL | 56 | 2 | 5 | 7 | 32 | 1 | 0 | 1 | 54 | 3.7 | 5 | 1 | 0.0 | 15:39 | | | | | | | | | |
| | NHL Totals | | 302 | 23 | 56 | 79 | 182 | 7 | 0 | 2 | 351 | 6.6 | | 1 | 0.0 | 20:03 | 13 | 0 | 2 | 2 | 16 | 0 | 0 | 0 | 20:07 |

Signed as a free agent by **Frolunda** (Sweden), September 15, 2004. Traded to **NY Rangers** by **St. Louis** for NY Rangers' 4th round choice (later traded back to NY Rangers - NY Rangers selected Dale Weise) in 2008 Entry Draft, February 26, 2008. Traded to **Columbus** by **NY Rangers** with Fedor Tyutin for Nikolai Zherdev and Dan Fritsche, July 2, 2008.

## BACKSTROM, Nicklas

(BAK-struhm, NIHK-luhs) **WSH.**

Center. Shoots left. 6'1", 210 lbs. Born, Gavle, Sweden, November 23, 1987. Washington's 1st choice, 4th overall, in 2006 Entry Draft.

| Season | Club | League | GP | G | A | Pts | PIM | PP | SH | GW | S | % | +/- | TF | F% | Min | GP | G | A | Pts | PIM | PP | SH | GW | Min |
|---|---|---|---|---|---|---|---|---|---|---|---|---|---|---|---|---|---|---|---|---|---|---|---|---|---|
| 2001-02 | Brynas U18 | Swe-U18 | 2 | 0 | 0 | 0 | 0 | | | | | | | | | | | | | | | | | | |
| 2002-03 | Brynas U18 | Swe-U18 | STATISTICS NOT AVAILABLE | | | | | | | | | | | | | | | | | | | | | | |
| 2003-04 | Brynas U18 | Swe-U18 | 6 | 9 | 5 | 14 | 4 | | | | | | | | | | 3 | 0 | 3 | 3 | 0 | | | | |
| | Brynas IF Gavle Jr. | Swe-Jr. | 21 | 2 | 6 | 8 | 2 | | | | | | | | | | 5 | 0 | 0 | 0 | 4 | | | | |
| 2004-05 | Brynas IF Gavle Jr. | Swe-Jr. | 29 | 17 | 17 | 34 | 24 | | | | | | | | | | | | | | | | | | |
| | Brynas IF Gavle | Sweden | 19 | 0 | 0 | 0 | 2 | | | | | | | | | | | | | | | | | | |
| 2005-06 | Brynas IF Gavle | Sweden | 46 | 10 | 16 | 26 | 30 | | | | | | | | | | 4 | 1 | 0 | 1 | 2 | | | | |
| | Brynas IF Gavle Jr. | Swe-Jr. | | | | | | | | | | | | | | | 1 | 0 | 0 | 0 | 2 | | | | |
| 2006-07 | Brynas IF Gavle | Sweden | 45 | 12 | 28 | 40 | 46 | | | | | | | | | | 7 | 3 | 3 | 6 | 6 | | | | |
| 2007-08 | Washington | NHL | 82 | 14 | 55 | 69 | 24 | 3 | 0 | 4 | 153 | 9.2 | 13 | 874 | 46.3 | 19:00 | 7 | 4 | 2 | 6 | 2 | 3 | 0 | 0 | 20:26 |
| 2008-09 | Washington | NHL | 82 | 22 | 66 | 88 | 46 | 14 | 0 | 1 | 174 | 12.6 | 16 | 1171 | 48.7 | 19:57 | 14 | 3 | 12 | 15 | 8 | 2 | 0 | 0 | 21:40 |
| | NHL Totals | | 164 | 36 | 121 | 157 | 70 | 17 | 0 | 5 | 327 | 11.0 | | 2045 | 47.7 | 19:28 | 21 | 7 | 14 | 21 | 10 | 5 | 0 | 0 | 21:15 |

NHL All-Rookie Team (2008)

## BAILEY, Joshua

(BAY-lee, JAWSH) **NYI**

Center. Shoots left. 6'1", 188 lbs. Born, Oshawa, Ont., October 2, 1989. NY Islanders' 1st choice, 9th overall, in 2008 Entry Draft.

| Season | Club | League | GP | G | A | Pts | PIM | PP | SH | GW | S | % | +/- | TF | F% | Min | GP | G | A | Pts | PIM | PP | SH | GW | Min |
|---|---|---|---|---|---|---|---|---|---|---|---|---|---|---|---|---|---|---|---|---|---|---|---|---|---|
| 2004-05 | Clarington | Minor-ON | 69 | 53 | 59 | 112 | 38 | | | | | | | | | | | | | | | | | | |
| 2005-06 | Owen Sound | OHL | 55 | 7 | 19 | 26 | 8 | | | | | | | | | | 11 | 0 | 0 | 0 | 0 | | | | |
| 2006-07 | Owen Sound | OHL | 27 | 11 | 15 | 26 | 8 | | | | | | | | | | | | | | | | | | |
| | Windsor Spitfires | OHL | 42 | 11 | 24 | 35 | 16 | | | | | | | | | | | | | | | | | | |
| 2007-08 | Windsor Spitfires | OHL | 67 | 29 | 67 | 96 | 32 | | | | | | | | | | 5 | 1 | 5 | 6 | 2 | | | | |
| 2008-09 | NY Islanders | NHL | 68 | 7 | 18 | 25 | 16 | 3 | 0 | 0 | 74 | 9.5 | -14 | 807 | 41.1 | 15:29 | | | | | | | | | |
| | NHL Totals | | 68 | 7 | 18 | 25 | 16 | 3 | 0 | 0 | 74 | 9.5 | | 807 | 41.1 | 15:29 | | | | | | | | | |

## BALLARD, Keith

(BAL-uhrd, KEETH) **FLA.**

Defense. Shoots left. 5'11", 208 lbs. Born, Baudette, MN, November 26, 1982. Buffalo's 1st choice, 11th overall, in 2002 Entry Draft.

| Season | Club | League | GP | G | A | Pts | PIM | PP | SH | GW | S | % | +/- | TF | F% | Min | GP | G | A | Pts | PIM | PP | SH | GW | Min |
|---|---|---|---|---|---|---|---|---|---|---|---|---|---|---|---|---|---|---|---|---|---|---|---|---|---|
| 99-2000 | USNTDP | U-18 | 6 | 1 | 1 | 2 | 4 | | | | | | | | | | | | | | | | | | |
| | USNTDP | USHL | 58 | 12 | 21 | 33 | 119 | | | | | | | | | | | | | | | | | | |
| 2000-01 | Omaha Lancers | USHL | 56 | 22 | 29 | 51 | 168 | | | | | | | | | | 10 | 1 | 6 | 7 | 8 | | | | |
| 2001-02 | U. of Minnesota | WCHA | 41 | 10 | 13 | 23 | 42 | | | | | | | | | | | | | | | | | | |
| 2002-03 | U. of Minnesota | WCHA | 41 | 12 | 29 | 41 | 78 | | | | | | | | | | | | | | | | | | |
| 2003-04 | U. of Minnesota | WCHA | 37 | 11 | 25 | 36 | 83 | | | | | | | | | | | | | | | | | | |
| 2004-05 | Utah Grizzlies | AHL | 60 | 2 | 18 | 20 | 88 | | | | | | | | | | | | | | | | | | |
| 2005-06 | Phoenix | NHL | 82 | 8 | 31 | 39 | 99 | 1 | 3 | 1 | 102 | 7.8 | -18 | 0 | 0.0 | 19:59 | | | | | | | | | |
| 2006-07 | Phoenix | NHL | 69 | 5 | 22 | 27 | 59 | 2 | 0 | 0 | 79 | 6.3 | -7 | 0 | 0.0 | 22:00 | | | | | | | | | |
| 2007-08 | Phoenix | NHL | 82 | 6 | 15 | 21 | 85 | 2 | 1 | 1 | 105 | 5.7 | 7 | 0 | 0.0 | 21:16 | | | | | | | | | |
| 2008-09 | Florida | NHL | 82 | 6 | 28 | 34 | 72 | 1 | 0 | 1 | 106 | 5.7 | 14 | 1 | 0.0 | 22:23 | | | | | | | | | |
| | NHL Totals | | 315 | 25 | 96 | 121 | 315 | 6 | 4 | 3 | 392 | 6.4 | | 1 | 0.0 | 21:23 | | | | | | | | | |

USHL First All-Star Team (2001) • WCHA All-Rookie Team (2002) • WCHA First All-Star Team (2003, 2004) • NCAA West First All-American Team (2004)

Traded to **Colorado** by **Buffalo** for Steve Reinprecht, July 3, 2003. Traded to **Phoenix** by **Colorado** with Derek Morris for Ossi Vaananen, Chris Gratton and Phoenix's 2nd round choice (Paul Stastny) in 2005 Entry Draft, March 9, 2004. Traded to **Florida** by **Phoenix** with Nick Boynton and Ottawa's 2nd round choice (previously acquired, later traded back to Phoenix - Phoenix selected Jared Staal) in 2008 Entry Draft for Olli Jokinen, June 20, 2008.

## BARANKA, Ivan

(ba-RAN-kuh, IGH-vuhn) **NYR**

Defense. Shoots left. 6'3", 205 lbs. Born, Ilava, Czech., May 19, 1985. NY Rangers' 2nd choice, 50th overall, in 2003 Entry Draft.

| Season | Club | League | GP | G | A | Pts | PIM | PP | SH | GW | S | % | +/- | TF | F% | Min | GP | G | A | Pts | PIM | PP | SH | GW | Min |
|---|---|---|---|---|---|---|---|---|---|---|---|---|---|---|---|---|---|---|---|---|---|---|---|---|---|
| 2002-03 | Dubnica Jr. | Slovak-Jr. | 27 | 1 | 7 | 8 | 44 | | | | | | | | | | | | | | | | | | |
| | Dubnica | Slovak-2 | 2 | 0 | 0 | 0 | 0 | | | | | | | | | | | | | | | | | | |
| 2003-04 | Everett Silvertips | WHL | 58 | 3 | 12 | 15 | 69 | | | | | | | | | | 20 | 3 | 5 | 8 | 26 | | | | |
| 2004-05 | Everett Silvertips | WHL | 64 | 7 | 16 | 23 | 64 | | | | | | | | | | 11 | 3 | 1 | 4 | 6 | | | | |
| | Hartford | AHL | | | | | | | | | | | | | | | 1 | 0 | 0 | 0 | 0 | | | | |
| 2005-06 | Hartford | AHL | 59 | 5 | 16 | 21 | 87 | | | | | | | | | | | | | | | | | | |
| 2006-07 | Hartford | AHL | 54 | 3 | 20 | 23 | 50 | | | | | | | | | | | | | | | | | | |
| 2007-08 | NY Rangers | NHL | 1 | 0 | 1 | 1 | 0 | 0 | 0 | 0 | 1 | 0.0 | 1 | 0 | 0.0 | 12:44 | | | | | | | | | |
| | Hartford | AHL | 61 | 5 | 21 | 26 | 53 | | | | | | | | | | 5 | 0 | 2 | 2 | 2 | | | | |
| 2008-09 | Spartak Moscow | Rus-KHL | 47 | 2 | 8 | 10 | 50 | | | | | | | | | | 6 | 1 | 2 | 3 | 6 | | | | |
| | NHL Totals | | 1 | 0 | 1 | 1 | 0 | 0 | 0 | 0 | 1 | 0.0 | | 0 | 0.0 | 12:44 | | | | | | | | | |

## BARCH, Krys

(BAHRCH, KRIHS) **DAL.**

Right wing. Shoots left. 6'2", 220 lbs. Born, Hamilton, Ont., March 26, 1980. Washington's 3rd choice, 106th overall, in 1998 Entry Draft.

| Season | Club | League | GP | G | A | Pts | PIM | PP | SH | GW | S | % | +/- | TF | F% | Min | GP | G | A | Pts | PIM | PP | SH | GW | Min |
|---|---|---|---|---|---|---|---|---|---|---|---|---|---|---|---|---|---|---|---|---|---|---|---|---|---|
| 1995-96 | Georgetown | OPJHL | 41 | 6 | 8 | 14 | 10 | | | | | | | | | | | | | | | | | | |
| 1996-97 | Georgetown | OPJHL | 51 | 18 | 26 | 44 | 58 | | | | | | | | | | | | | | | | | | |
| 1997-98 | London Knights | OHL | 65 | 9 | 27 | 36 | 62 | | | | | | | | | | 16 | 4 | 3 | 7 | 16 | | | | |
| 1998-99 | London Knights | OHL | 66 | 18 | 20 | 38 | 66 | | | | | | | | | | 25 | 9 | 17 | 26 | 15 | | | | |
| 99-2000 | London Knights | OHL | 56 | 23 | 26 | 49 | 78 | | | | | | | | | | | | | | | | | | |
| | Portland Pirates | AHL | | | | | | | | | | | | | | | 4 | 0 | 2 | 2 | 2 | | | | |
| 2000-01 | Portland Pirates | AHL | 76 | 10 | 15 | 25 | 91 | | | | | | | | | | 2 | 0 | 0 | 0 | 0 | | | | |
| 2001-02 | Portland Pirates | AHL | 29 | 3 | 8 | 11 | 28 | | | | | | | | | | | | | | | | | | |
| | Richmond | ECHL | 25 | 6 | 4 | 10 | 43 | | | | | | | | | | | | | | | | | | |
| 2002-03 | Portland Pirates | AHL | 36 | 1 | 7 | 8 | 49 | | | | | | | | | | | | | | | | | | |
| 2003-04 | | | DID NOT PLAY | | | | | | | | | | | | | | | | | | | | | | |
| 2004-05 | Norfolk Admirals | AHL | 9 | 1 | 0 | 1 | 37 | | | | | | | | | | | | | | | | | | |
| | Greenville | ECHL | 55 | 11 | 19 | 30 | 154 | | | | | | | | | | 3 | 0 | 0 | 0 | 36 | | | | |
| 2005-06 | Iowa Stars | AHL | 43 | 7 | 6 | 13 | 129 | | | | | | | | | | 7 | 0 | 1 | 1 | 37 | | | | |
| | Greenville | ECHL | 14 | 10 | 4 | 14 | 75 | | | | | | | | | | | | | | | | | | |
| 2006-07 | Dallas | NHL | 26 | 3 | 2 | 5 | 107 | 0 | 0 | 2 | 12 | 25.0 | 2 | 1 | 0.0 | 5:38 | | | | | | | | | |
| | Iowa Stars | AHL | 31 | 3 | 5 | 8 | 110 | | | | | | | | | | | | | | | | | | |
| 2007-08 | Dallas | NHL | 48 | 1 | 2 | 3 | 105 | 0 | 0 | 0 | 23 | 4.3 | -3 | 2 | 0.0 | 6:30 | 3 | 0 | 0 | 0 | 2 | 0 | 0 | 0 | 2:21 |
| 2008-09 | Dallas | NHL | 72 | 4 | 5 | 9 | 133 | 0 | 0 | 1 | 27 | 14.8 | 1 | 7 | 28.6 | 6:27 | | | | | | | | | |
| | NHL Totals | | 146 | 8 | 9 | 17 | 345 | 0 | 0 | 3 | 62 | 12.9 | | 10 | 20.0 | 6:20 | 3 | 0 | 0 | 0 | 2 | 0 | 0 | 0 | 2:21 |

Signed as a free agent by **Dallas**, July 18, 2006.

## BARKER, Cam

(BAR-kuhr, KAM) **CHI.**

Defense. Shoots left. 6'3", 213 lbs. Born, Winnipeg, Man., April 4, 1986. Chicago's 1st choice, 3rd overall, in 2004 Entry Draft.

| Season | Club | League | GP | G | A | Pts | PIM | PP | SH | GW | S | % | +/- | TF | F% | Min | GP | G | A | Pts | PIM | PP | SH | GW | Min |
|---|---|---|---|---|---|---|---|---|---|---|---|---|---|---|---|---|---|---|---|---|---|---|---|---|---|
| 2001-02 | Cornwall Colts | CJHL | 72 | 6 | 23 | 29 | 132 | | | | | | | | | | | | | | | | | | |
| | Medicine Hat | WHL | 3 | 0 | 1 | 1 | 0 | | | | | | | | | | | | | | | | | | |
| 2002-03 | Medicine Hat | WHL | 64 | 10 | 37 | 47 | 79 | | | | | | | | | | 11 | 3 | 4 | 7 | 17 | | | | |
| 2003-04 | Medicine Hat | WHL | 69 | 21 | 44 | 65 | 105 | | | | | | | | | | 20 | 3 | 9 | 12 | 18 | | | | |
| 2004-05 | Medicine Hat | WHL | 52 | 15 | 33 | 48 | 99 | | | | | | | | | | 12 | 3 | 3 | 6 | 16 | | | | |
| 2005-06 | Chicago | NHL | 1 | 0 | 0 | 0 | 0 | 0 | 0 | 0 | 1 | 0.0 | 0 | 0 | 0.0 | 11:02 | | | | | | | | | |
| | Medicine Hat | WHL | 26 | 5 | 13 | 18 | 63 | | | | | | | | | | 13 | 4 | 8 | 12 | *59 | | | | |

| | | | Regular Season | | | | | | | | | | | | | | Playoffs | | | | | | | | |
|---|---|---|---|---|---|---|---|---|---|---|---|---|---|---|---|---|---|---|---|---|---|---|---|---|---|
| Season | Club | League | GP | G | A | Pts | PIM | PP | SH | GW | S | % | +/- | TF | F% | Min | GP | G | A | Pts | PIM | PP | SH | GW | Min |
| **2006-07** | **Chicago** | **NHL** | **35** | **1** | **7** | **8** | **44** | **1** | **0** | **0** | **38** | **2.6** | **–12** | **0** | **0.0** | **19:19** | .... | .... | .... | .... | .... | .... | .... | .... | .... |
| | Norfolk Admirals | AHL | 34 | 5 | 10 | 15 | 53 | .... | .... | .... | .... | .... | .... | .... | .... | .... | 6 | 1 | 3 | 4 | 13 | .... | .... | .... | .... |
| **2007-08** | **Chicago** | **NHL** | **45** | **6** | **12** | **18** | **52** | **2** | **0** | **0** | **42** | **14.3** | **–3** | **0** | **0.0** | **17:12** | .... | .... | .... | .... | .... | .... | .... | .... | .... |
| | Rockford IceHogs | AHL | 29 | 8 | 11 | 19 | 67 | .... | .... | .... | .... | .... | .... | .... | .... | .... | .... | .... | .... | .... | .... | .... | .... | .... | .... |
| **2008-09** | **Chicago** | **NHL** | **68** | **6** | **34** | **40** | **65** | **5** | **0** | **1** | **101** | **5.9** | **–6** | **1** | **0.0** | **18:20** | **17** | **3** | **6** | **9** | **2** | **0** | **0** | **0** | **16:39** |
| | Rockford IceHogs | AHL | 7 | 3 | 2 | 5 | 6 | .... | .... | .... | .... | .... | .... | .... | .... | .... | .... | .... | .... | .... | .... | .... | .... | .... | .... |
| | **NHL Totals** | | **149** | **13** | **53** | **66** | **161** | **8** | **0** | **1** | **182** | **7.1** | | **1** | **0.0** | **18:11** | **17** | **3** | **6** | **9** | **2** | **0** | **0** | **0** | **16:39** |

## BASS, Cody

(BAS, KOH-dee) **OTT.**

Center. Shoots right. 6', 213 lbs. Born, Owen Sound, Ont., January 7, 1987. Ottawa's 3rd choice, 95th overall, in 2005 Entry Draft.

| | | | | | | | | | | | | | | | | | | | | | | | | | |
|---|---|---|---|---|---|---|---|---|---|---|---|---|---|---|---|---|---|---|---|---|---|---|---|---|---|
| 2003-04 | Mississauga | OHL | 61 | 3 | 7 | 10 | 30 | .... | .... | .... | .... | .... | .... | .... | .... | .... | 24 | 2 | 3 | 5 | 21 | .... | .... | .... | .... |
| 2004-05 | Mississauga | OHL | 66 | 11 | 17 | 28 | 103 | .... | .... | .... | .... | .... | .... | .... | .... | .... | 5 | 1 | 1 | 2 | 8 | .... | .... | .... | .... |
| 2005-06 | Mississauga | OHL | 67 | 16 | 25 | 41 | 152 | .... | .... | .... | .... | .... | .... | .... | .... | .... | .... | .... | .... | .... | .... | .... | .... | .... | .... |
| | Binghamton | AHL | 9 | 1 | 0 | 1 | 2 | .... | .... | .... | .... | .... | .... | .... | .... | .... | .... | .... | .... | .... | .... | .... | .... | .... | .... |
| 2006-07 | Mississauga | OHL | 23 | 5 | 11 | 16 | 37 | .... | .... | .... | .... | .... | .... | .... | .... | .... | .... | .... | .... | .... | .... | .... | .... | .... | .... |
| | Saginaw Spirit | OHL | 30 | 5 | 24 | 29 | 49 | .... | .... | .... | .... | .... | .... | .... | .... | .... | 6 | 1 | 2 | 3 | 10 | .... | .... | .... | .... |
| | Binghamton | AHL | 5 | 0 | 2 | 2 | 9 | .... | .... | .... | .... | .... | .... | .... | .... | .... | .... | .... | .... | .... | .... | .... | .... | .... | .... |
| **2007-08** | **Ottawa** | **NHL** | **21** | **2** | **2** | **4** | **19** | **0** | **1** | **1** | **12** | **16.7** | **–1** | **73** | **43.8** | **5:19** | **4** | **1** | **0** | **1** | **6** | **0** | **0** | **0** | **8:21** |
| | Binghamton | AHL | 24 | 3 | 5 | 8 | 44 | .... | .... | .... | .... | .... | .... | .... | .... | .... | .... | .... | .... | .... | .... | .... | .... | .... | .... |
| **2008-09** | **Ottawa** | **NHL** | **12** | **0** | **0** | **0** | **15** | **0** | **0** | **0** | **5** | **0.0** | **–2** | **50** | **42.0** | **5:41** | .... | .... | .... | .... | .... | .... | .... | .... | .... |
| | Binghamton | AHL | 18 | 1 | 1 | 2 | 41 | .... | .... | .... | .... | .... | .... | .... | .... | .... | .... | .... | .... | .... | .... | .... | .... | .... | .... |
| | **NHL Totals** | | **33** | **2** | **2** | **4** | **34** | **0** | **1** | **1** | **17** | **11.8** | | **123** | **43.1** | **5:27** | **4** | **1** | **0** | **1** | **6** | **0** | **0** | **0** | **8:21** |

• Missed remainder of 2008-09 season recovering from shoulder injury suffered in game at Calgary, December 27, 2008.

## BATTAGLIA, Bates

(buh-TAG-lee-ah, BAYTS)

Left wing. Shoots left. 6'2", 205 lbs. Born, Chicago, IL, December 13, 1975. Anaheim's 6th choice, 132nd overall, in 1994 Entry Draft.

| | | | | | | | | | | | | | | | | | | | | | | | | | |
|---|---|---|---|---|---|---|---|---|---|---|---|---|---|---|---|---|---|---|---|---|---|---|---|---|---|
| 1992-93 | Team Illinois | MEHL | 60 | 42 | 42 | 84 | 68 | .... | .... | .... | .... | .... | .... | .... | .... | .... | .... | .... | .... | .... | .... | .... | .... | .... | .... |
| 1993-94 | Caledon | MTJHL | 44 | 15 | 33 | 48 | 104 | .... | .... | .... | .... | .... | .... | .... | .... | .... | .... | .... | .... | .... | .... | .... | .... | .... | .... |
| 1994-95 | Lake Superior | CCHA | 38 | 6 | 14 | 20 | 34 | .... | .... | .... | .... | .... | .... | .... | .... | .... | .... | .... | .... | .... | .... | .... | .... | .... | .... |
| 1995-96 | Lake Superior | CCHA | 40 | 13 | 22 | 35 | 48 | .... | .... | .... | .... | .... | .... | .... | .... | .... | .... | .... | .... | .... | .... | .... | .... | .... | .... |
| 1996-97 | Lake Superior | CCHA | 38 | 12 | 27 | 39 | 80 | .... | .... | .... | .... | .... | .... | .... | .... | .... | .... | .... | .... | .... | .... | .... | .... | .... | .... |
| **1997-98** | **Carolina** | **NHL** | **33** | **2** | **4** | **6** | **10** | **0** | **0** | **1** | **21** | **9.5** | **–1** | .... | .... | .... | .... | .... | .... | .... | .... | .... | .... | .... | .... |
| | New Haven | AHL | 48 | 15 | 21 | 36 | 48 | .... | .... | .... | .... | .... | .... | .... | .... | .... | 1 | 0 | 0 | 0 | 0 | .... | .... | .... | .... |
| **1998-99** | **Carolina** | **NHL** | **60** | **7** | **11** | **18** | **22** | **0** | **0** | **0** | **52** | **13.5** | **7** | **144** | **39.6** | **9:53** | **6** | **0** | **3** | **3** | **8** | **0** | **0** | **0** | **15:22** |
| **99-2000** | **Carolina** | **NHL** | **77** | **16** | **18** | **34** | **39** | **3** | **0** | **3** | **86** | **18.6** | **20** | **23** | **26.1** | **15:12** | .... | .... | .... | .... | .... | .... | .... | .... | .... |
| **2000-01** | **Carolina** | **NHL** | **80** | **12** | **15** | **27** | **76** | **2** | **0** | **3** | **133** | **9.0** | **–14** | **5** | **60.0** | **14:28** | **6** | **0** | **2** | **2** | **2** | **0** | **0** | **0** | **11:25** |
| **2001-02** | **Carolina** | **NHL** | **82** | **21** | **25** | **46** | **44** | **5** | **1** | **2** | **167** | **12.6** | **–6** | **12** | **33.3** | **19:05** | **23** | **5** | **9** | **14** | **14** | **1** | **0** | **1** | **20:42** |
| **2002-03** | **Carolina** | **NHL** | **70** | **5** | **14** | **19** | **90** | **0** | **1** | **1** | **96** | **5.2** | **–17** | **16** | **25.0** | **18:39** | .... | .... | .... | .... | .... | .... | .... | .... | .... |
| | **Colorado** | **NHL** | **13** | **1** | **5** | **6** | **10** | **1** | **0** | **1** | **27** | **3.7** | **–2** | **3** | **0.0** | **15:19** | **7** | **0** | **2** | **2** | **4** | **0** | **0** | **0** | **14:39** |
| **2003-04** | **Colorado** | **NHL** | **4** | **0** | **1** | **1** | **4** | **0** | **0** | **0** | **1** | **0.0** | **–1** | **1** | **100.0** | **11:04** | .... | .... | .... | .... | .... | .... | .... | .... | .... |
| | **Washington** | **NHL** | **66** | **4** | **6** | **10** | **38** | **0** | **0** | **1** | **69** | **5.8** | **–23** | **116** | **32.8** | **13:37** | .... | .... | .... | .... | .... | .... | .... | .... | .... |
| 2004-05 | Mississippi | ECHL | 25 | 6 | 11 | 17 | 24 | .... | .... | .... | .... | .... | .... | .... | .... | .... | 4 | 0 | 0 | 0 | 10 | .... | .... | .... | .... |
| 2005-06 | Toronto Marlies | AHL | 79 | 20 | 47 | 67 | 86 | .... | .... | .... | .... | .... | .... | .... | .... | .... | 5 | 1 | 1 | 2 | 6 | .... | .... | .... | .... |
| **2006-07** | **Toronto** | **NHL** | **82** | **12** | **19** | **31** | **45** | **0** | **0** | **0** | **94** | **12.8** | **9** | **4** | **0.0** | **12:27** | .... | .... | .... | .... | .... | .... | .... | .... | .... |
| **2007-08** | **Toronto** | **NHL** | **13** | **0** | **0** | **0** | **7** | **0** | **0** | **0** | **6** | **0.0** | **–6** | **1** | **0.0** | **4:46** | .... | .... | .... | .... | .... | .... | .... | .... | .... |
| | Toronto Marlies | AHL | 56 | 12 | 14 | 26 | 42 | .... | .... | .... | .... | .... | .... | .... | .... | .... | 19 | 6 | 2 | 8 | 28 | .... | .... | .... | .... |
| 2008-09 | Toronto Marlies | AHL | 59 | 17 | 34 | 51 | 55 | .... | .... | .... | .... | .... | .... | .... | .... | .... | 6 | 2 | 3 | 5 | 4 | .... | .... | .... | .... |
| | **NHL Totals** | | **580** | **80** | **118** | **198** | **385** | **11** | **2** | **12** | **752** | **10.6** | | **325** | **34.8** | **14:39** | **42** | **5** | **16** | **21** | **28** | **1** | **0** | **1** | **17:36** |

Traded to **Hartford** by **Anaheim** with Anaheim's 4th round choice (Josef Vasicek) in 1998 Entry Draft for Mark Janssens, March 18, 1997. Rights transferred to **Carolina** after **Hartford** franchise relocated, June 25, 1997. Traded to **Colorado** by **Carolina** for Radim Vrbata, March 11, 2003. Traded to **Washington** by **Colorado** with Jonas Johansson for Steve Konowalchuk and Washington's 3rd round choice (later traded to Carolina – Carolina selected Casey Borer) in 2004 Entry Draft, October 22, 2003. Signed as a free agent by **Mississippi** (ECHL), February 21, 2005. Signed to a PTO (tryout) contract by **Toronto** (AHL), October 2, 2005. Signed as a free agent by **Toronto**, July 8, 2006.

## BAUMGARTNER, Nolan

(BAWM-gahrt-nuhr, NOH-luhn) **VAN.**

Defense. Shoots right. 6'2", 205 lbs. Born, Calgary, Alta., March 23, 1976. Washington's 1st choice, 10th overall, in 1994 Entry Draft.

| | | | | | | | | | | | | | | | | | | | | | | | | | |
|---|---|---|---|---|---|---|---|---|---|---|---|---|---|---|---|---|---|---|---|---|---|---|---|---|---|
| 1991-92 | Cgy. AAA Flames | AMHL | 39 | 11 | 29 | 40 | 40 | .... | .... | .... | .... | .... | .... | .... | .... | .... | .... | .... | .... | .... | .... | .... | .... | .... | .... |
| 1992-93 | Kamloops Blazers | WHL | 43 | 0 | 5 | 5 | 30 | .... | .... | .... | .... | .... | .... | .... | .... | .... | 11 | 1 | 1 | 2 | 0 | .... | .... | .... | .... |
| 1993-94 | Kamloops Blazers | WHL | 69 | 13 | 42 | 55 | 109 | .... | .... | .... | .... | .... | .... | .... | .... | .... | 19 | 3 | 14 | 17 | 33 | .... | .... | .... | .... |
| 1994-95 | Kamloops Blazers | WHL | 62 | 8 | 36 | 44 | 71 | .... | .... | .... | .... | .... | .... | .... | .... | .... | 21 | 4 | 13 | 17 | 16 | .... | .... | .... | .... |
| **1995-96** | Kamloops Blazers | WHL | 28 | 13 | 15 | 28 | 45 | .... | .... | .... | .... | .... | .... | .... | .... | .... | 16 | 1 | 9 | 10 | 26 | .... | .... | .... | .... |
| | **Washington** | **NHL** | **1** | **0** | **0** | **0** | **0** | **0** | **0** | **0** | **0** | **0.0** | **–1** | .... | .... | .... | **1** | **0** | **0** | **0** | **10** | **0** | **0** | **0** | .... |
| 1996-97 | Portland Pirates | AHL | 8 | 2 | 2 | 4 | 4 | .... | .... | .... | .... | .... | .... | .... | .... | .... | .... | .... | .... | .... | .... | .... | .... | .... | .... |
| **1997-98** | **Washington** | **NHL** | **4** | **0** | **1** | **1** | **0** | **0** | **0** | **0** | **4** | **0.0** | **0** | .... | .... | .... | .... | .... | .... | .... | .... | .... | .... | .... | .... |
| | Portland Pirates | AHL | 70 | 2 | 24 | 26 | 70 | .... | .... | .... | .... | .... | .... | .... | .... | .... | 10 | 1 | 4 | 5 | 10 | .... | .... | .... | .... |
| **1998-99** | **Washington** | **NHL** | **5** | **0** | **0** | **0** | **0** | **0** | **0** | **0** | **1** | **0.0** | **–3** | **0** | **0.0** | **8:41** | .... | .... | .... | .... | .... | .... | .... | .... | .... |
| | Portland Pirates | AHL | 38 | 5 | 14 | 19 | 62 | .... | .... | .... | .... | .... | .... | .... | .... | .... | .... | .... | .... | .... | .... | .... | .... | .... | .... |
| **99-2000** | **Washington** | **NHL** | **8** | **0** | **1** | **1** | **2** | **0** | **0** | **0** | **6** | **0.0** | **1** | **0** | **0.0** | **10:31** | .... | .... | .... | .... | .... | .... | .... | .... | .... |
| | Portland Pirates | AHL | 71 | 5 | 18 | 23 | 56 | .... | .... | .... | .... | .... | .... | .... | .... | .... | 4 | 1 | 2 | 3 | 10 | .... | .... | .... | .... |
| **2000-01** | **Chicago** | **NHL** | **8** | **0** | **0** | **0** | **6** | **0** | **0** | **0** | **7** | **0.0** | **–4** | **2** | **50.0** | **12:40** | .... | .... | .... | .... | .... | .... | .... | .... | .... |
| | Norfolk Admirals | AHL | 63 | 5 | 28 | 33 | 75 | .... | .... | .... | .... | .... | .... | .... | .... | .... | 9 | 2 | 3 | 5 | 11 | .... | .... | .... | .... |
| 2001-02 | Norfolk Admirals | AHL | 76 | 10 | 24 | 34 | 72 | .... | .... | .... | .... | .... | .... | .... | .... | .... | 4 | 0 | 1 | 1 | 2 | .... | .... | .... | .... |
| **2002-03** | **Vancouver** | **NHL** | **8** | **1** | **2** | **3** | **4** | **1** | **0** | **0** | **7** | **14.3** | **4** | **0** | **0.0** | **11:36** | **2** | **0** | **0** | **0** | **0** | **0** | **0** | **0** | **11:07** |
| | Manitoba Moose | AHL | 59 | 8 | 31 | 39 | 82 | .... | .... | .... | .... | .... | .... | .... | .... | .... | 1 | 0 | 0 | 0 | 4 | .... | .... | .... | .... |
| **2003-04** | **Pittsburgh** | **NHL** | **5** | **0** | **0** | **0** | **2** | **0** | **0** | **0** | **6** | **0.0** | **–7** | **0** | **0.0** | **19:20** | .... | .... | .... | .... | .... | .... | .... | .... | .... |
| | **Vancouver** | **NHL** | **9** | **0** | **3** | **3** | **2** | **0** | **0** | **0** | **9** | **0.0** | **3** | **0** | **0.0** | **11:52** | .... | .... | .... | .... | .... | .... | .... | .... | .... |
| | Manitoba Moose | AHL | 55 | 6 | 21 | 27 | 101 | .... | .... | .... | .... | .... | .... | .... | .... | .... | .... | .... | .... | .... | .... | .... | .... | .... | .... |
| 2004-05 | Manitoba Moose | AHL | 78 | 9 | 30 | 39 | 51 | .... | .... | .... | .... | .... | .... | .... | .... | .... | 14 | 0 | 4 | 4 | 10 | .... | .... | .... | .... |
| **2005-06** | **Vancouver** | **NHL** | **70** | **5** | **29** | **34** | **30** | **4** | **1** | **1** | **73** | **6.8** | **11** | **1** | **0.0** | **16:29** | .... | .... | .... | .... | .... | .... | .... | .... | .... |
| **2006-07** | **Philadelphia** | **NHL** | **6** | **0** | **1** | **1** | **21** | **0** | **0** | **0** | **4** | **0.0** | **0** | **0** | **0.0** | **15:00** | .... | .... | .... | .... | .... | .... | .... | .... | .... |
| | Philadelphia | AHL | 51 | 6 | 20 | 26 | 46 | .... | .... | .... | .... | .... | .... | .... | .... | .... | .... | .... | .... | .... | .... | .... | .... | .... | .... |
| | **Dallas** | **NHL** | **7** | **0** | **2** | **2** | **0** | **0** | **0** | **0** | **4** | **0.0** | **0** | **0** | **0.0** | **12:14** | .... | .... | .... | .... | .... | .... | .... | .... | .... |
| 2007-08 | Iowa Stars | AHL | 56 | 5 | 13 | 18 | 47 | .... | .... | .... | .... | .... | .... | .... | .... | .... | .... | .... | .... | .... | .... | .... | .... | .... | .... |
| | Manitoba Moose | AHL | 18 | 0 | 6 | 6 | 10 | .... | .... | .... | .... | .... | .... | .... | .... | .... | 3 | 0 | 1 | 1 | 4 | .... | .... | .... | .... |
| 2008-09 | Manitoba Moose | AHL | 72 | 11 | 22 | 33 | 50 | .... | .... | .... | .... | .... | .... | .... | .... | .... | 22 | 0 | 5 | 5 | 22 | .... | .... | .... | .... |
| | **NHL Totals** | | **131** | **6** | **39** | **45** | **67** | **5** | **1** | **1** | **121** | **5.0** | | **3** | **33.3** | **14:43** | **3** | **0** | **0** | **0** | **10** | **0** | **0** | **0** | **11:06** |

Memorial Cup Tournement All-Star Team (1994, 1995) • WHL West First All-Star Team (1995, 1996) • Canadian Major Junior First All-Star Team (1995) • Canadian Major Junior Defenseman of the Year (1995)

Traded to **Chicago** by **Washington** for Remi Royer, July 20, 2000. Signed as a free agent by **Vancouver**, July 11, 2002. Claimed by **Pittsburgh** from **Vancouver** in Waiver Draft, October 3, 2003. Claimed on waivers by **Vancouver** from **Pittsburgh**, November 1, 2003. Signed as a free agent by **Philadelphia**, July 1, 2006. Claimed on waivers by **Dallas** from **Philadelphia**, February 24, 2007. Signed as a free agent by **Vancouver**, July 2, 2008.

## BAYDA, Ryan

(BAY-duh, RIGH-uhn)

Left wing. Shoots left. 5'11", 185 lbs. Born, Saskatoon, Sask., December 9, 1980. Carolina's 2nd choice, 80th overall, in 2000 Entry Draft.

| | | | | | | | | | | | | | | | | | | | | | | | | | |
|---|---|---|---|---|---|---|---|---|---|---|---|---|---|---|---|---|---|---|---|---|---|---|---|---|---|
| 1995-96 | Saskatoon Flyers | SMHL | 60 | 85 | 74 | 159 | 85 | .... | .... | .... | .... | .... | .... | .... | .... | .... | .... | .... | .... | .... | .... | .... | .... | .... | .... |
| 1996-97 | Sask. Contacts | SMHL | 44 | 22 | 23 | 45 | 18 | .... | .... | .... | .... | .... | .... | .... | .... | .... | .... | .... | .... | .... | .... | .... | .... | .... | .... |
| 1997-98 | Sask. Contacts | SMHL | 41 | 29 | 49 | 78 | 103 | .... | .... | .... | .... | .... | .... | .... | .... | .... | .... | .... | .... | .... | .... | .... | .... | .... | .... |
| 1998-99 | Vernon Vipers | BCHL | 45 | 24 | 58 | 82 | 15 | .... | .... | .... | .... | .... | .... | .... | .... | .... | .... | .... | .... | .... | .... | .... | .... | .... | .... |
| 99-2000 | North Dakota | WCHA | 44 | 17 | 23 | 40 | 30 | .... | .... | .... | .... | .... | .... | .... | .... | .... | .... | .... | .... | .... | .... | .... | .... | .... | .... |
| 2000-01 | North Dakota | WCHA | 46 | 25 | 34 | 59 | 48 | .... | .... | .... | .... | .... | .... | .... | .... | .... | .... | .... | .... | .... | .... | .... | .... | .... | .... |
| 2001-02 | North Dakota | WCHA | 37 | 19 | 28 | 47 | 52 | .... | .... | .... | .... | .... | .... | .... | .... | .... | .... | .... | .... | .... | .... | .... | .... | .... | .... |
| | Lowell | AHL | 3 | 1 | 1 | 2 | 0 | .... | .... | .... | .... | .... | .... | .... | .... | .... | 5 | 3 | 0 | 3 | 0 | .... | .... | .... | .... |
| **2002-03** | **Carolina** | **NHL** | **25** | **4** | **10** | **14** | **16** | **0** | **0** | **1** | **49** | **8.2** | **–5** | **2** | **100.0** | **17:15** | .... | .... | .... | .... | .... | .... | .... | .... | .... |
| | Lowell | AHL | 53 | 11 | 32 | 43 | 32 | .... | .... | .... | .... | .... | .... | .... | .... | .... | .... | .... | .... | .... | .... | .... | .... | .... | .... |
| **2003-04** | **Carolina** | **NHL** | **44** | **3** | **3** | **6** | **22** | **0** | **0** | **1** | **65** | **4.6** | **–14** | **4** | **0.0** | **10:57** | .... | .... | .... | .... | .... | .... | .... | .... | .... |
| | Lowell | AHL | 34 | 7 | 15 | 22 | 28 | .... | .... | .... | .... | .... | .... | .... | .... | .... | .... | .... | .... | .... | .... | .... | .... | .... | .... |
| 2004-05 | Lowell | AHL | 80 | 13 | 27 | 40 | 91 | .... | .... | .... | .... | .... | .... | .... | .... | .... | 9 | 3 | 3 | 6 | 4 | .... | .... | .... | .... |
| 2005-06 | Manitoba Moose | AHL | 59 | 13 | 25 | 38 | 52 | .... | .... | .... | .... | .... | .... | .... | .... | .... | 13 | 1 | 6 | 7 | 27 | .... | .... | .... | .... |

| | | | Regular Season | | | | | | | | | | | | | | Playoffs | | | | | | | | |
|---|---|---|---|---|---|---|---|---|---|---|---|---|---|---|---|---|---|---|---|---|---|---|---|---|---|
| Season | Club | League | GP | G | A | Pts | PIM | PP | SH | GW | S | % | +/- | TF | F% | Min | GP | G | A | Pts | PIM | PP | SH | GW | Min |
| **2006-07** | **Carolina** | **NHL** | **9** | **1** | **1** | **2** | **2** | **0** | **0** | **0** | **10** | **10.0** | **-1** | **0** | **0.0** | **8:41** | .... | .... | .... | .... | .... | .... | .... | .... | .... |
| | Albany River Rats | AHL | 55 | 29 | 25 | 54 | 66 | .... | .... | .... | .... | .... | .... | .... | .... | .... | 5 | 3 | 2 | 5 | 4 | .... | .... | .... | .... |
| **2007-08** | **Carolina** | **NHL** | **31** | **3** | **3** | **6** | **28** | **0** | **0** | **0** | **58** | **5.2** | **-2** | **2** | **0.0** | **12:36** | .... | .... | .... | .... | .... | .... | .... | .... | .... |
| | Albany River Rats | AHL | 21 | 7 | 10 | 17 | 6 | .... | .... | .... | .... | .... | .... | .... | .... | .... | .... | .... | .... | .... | .... | .... | .... | .... | .... |
| **2008-09** | **Carolina** | **NHL** | **70** | **5** | **7** | **12** | **26** | **0** | **0** | **0** | **62** | **8.1** | **2** | **18** | **44.4** | **10:27** | **15** | **2** | **2** | **4** | **18** | **0** | **0** | **0** | **6:21** |
| | **NHL Totals** | | **179** | **16** | **24** | **40** | **94** | **0** | **0** | **2** | **244** | **6.6** | | **26** | **38.5** | **11:48** | **15** | **2** | **2** | **4** | **18** | **0** | **0** | **0** | **6:21** |

BCHL Rookie of the Year (1999) • WCHA All-Rookie Team (2000) • WCHA Second All-Star Team (2001, 2002)

## BEAGLE, Jay

(BEE-guhl, JAY) **WSH.**

Right wing. Shoots right. 6'3", 208 lbs. Born, Calgary, Alta., October 16, 1985.

| | | | | | | | | | | | | | | | | | | | | | | | | | |
|---|---|---|---|---|---|---|---|---|---|---|---|---|---|---|---|---|---|---|---|---|---|---|---|---|---|
| 2003-04 | Calgary Royals | AJHL | 58 | 10 | 27 | 37 | 100 | .... | .... | .... | .... | .... | .... | .... | .... | .... | .... | .... | .... | .... | .... | .... | .... | .... | .... |
| 2004-05 | Calgary Royals | AJHL | 64 | 28 | 42 | 70 | 114 | .... | .... | .... | .... | .... | .... | .... | .... | .... | .... | .... | .... | .... | .... | .... | .... | .... | .... |
| 2005-06 | Alaska Anchorage | WCHA | 31 | 4 | 6 | 10 | 40 | .... | .... | .... | .... | .... | .... | .... | .... | .... | .... | .... | .... | .... | .... | .... | .... | .... | .... |
| 2006-07 | Alaska Anchorage | WCHA | 36 | 10 | 10 | 20 | 93 | .... | .... | .... | .... | .... | .... | .... | .... | .... | .... | .... | .... | .... | .... | .... | .... | .... | .... |
| | Idaho Steelheads | ECHL | 8 | 2 | 8 | 10 | 4 | .... | .... | .... | .... | .... | .... | .... | .... | .... | 18 | 1 | 2 | 3 | 22 | .... | .... | .... | .... |
| 2007-08 | Hershey Bears | AHL | 64 | 19 | 18 | 37 | 41 | .... | .... | .... | .... | .... | .... | .... | .... | .... | 5 | 0 | 1 | 1 | 2 | .... | .... | .... | .... |
| **2008-09** | **Washington** | **NHL** | **3** | **0** | **0** | **0** | **2** | **0** | **0** | **0** | **5** | **0.0** | **-3** | **13** | **38.5** | **7:36** | **4** | **0** | **0** | **0** | **0** | **0** | **0** | **0** | **3:33** |
| | Hershey Bears | AHL | 47 | 4 | 5 | 9 | 37 | .... | .... | .... | .... | .... | .... | .... | .... | .... | 18 | 1 | 3 | 4 | 16 | .... | .... | .... | .... |
| | **NHL Totals** | | **3** | **0** | **0** | **0** | **2** | **0** | **0** | **0** | **5** | **0.0** | | **13** | **38.5** | **7:36** | **4** | **0** | **0** | **0** | **0** | **0** | **0** | **0** | **3:33** |

Signed as a free agent by **Washington**, March 26, 2008.

## BEAUCHEMIN, Francois

(boh-sheh-MEH, frahn-SWUH) **TOR.**

Defense. Shoots left. 6', 207 lbs. Born, Sorel, Que., June 4, 1980. Montreal's 3rd choice, 75th overall, in 1998 Entry Draft.

| | | | | | | | | | | | | | | | | | | | | | | | | | |
|---|---|---|---|---|---|---|---|---|---|---|---|---|---|---|---|---|---|---|---|---|---|---|---|---|---|
| 1995-96 | Richelieu Riverains | QAAA | 40 | 9 | 23 | 32 | 59 | .... | .... | .... | .... | .... | .... | .... | .... | .... | .... | .... | .... | .... | .... | .... | .... | .... | .... |
| 1996-97 | Laval Titan | QMJHL | 66 | 7 | 21 | 28 | 132 | .... | .... | .... | .... | .... | .... | .... | .... | .... | 3 | 0 | 0 | 0 | 2 | .... | .... | .... | .... |
| 1997-98 | Laval Titan | QMJHL | 70 | 12 | 35 | 47 | 132 | .... | .... | .... | .... | .... | .... | .... | .... | .... | 16 | 1 | 3 | 4 | 23 | .... | .... | .... | .... |
| 1998-99 | Acadie-Bathurst | QMJHL | 31 | 4 | 17 | 21 | 53 | .... | .... | .... | .... | .... | .... | .... | .... | .... | 23 | 2 | 16 | 18 | 55 | .... | .... | .... | .... |
| 99-2000 | Acadie-Bathurst | QMJHL | 38 | 11 | 36 | 47 | 64 | .... | .... | .... | .... | .... | .... | .... | .... | .... | .... | .... | .... | .... | .... | .... | .... | .... | .... |
| | Moncton Wildcats | QMJHL | 33 | 8 | 31 | 39 | 35 | .... | .... | .... | .... | .... | .... | .... | .... | .... | 16 | 2 | 11 | 13 | 14 | .... | .... | .... | .... |
| 2000-01 | Quebec Citadelles | AHL | 56 | 3 | 6 | 9 | 44 | .... | .... | .... | .... | .... | .... | .... | .... | .... | .... | .... | .... | .... | .... | .... | .... | .... | .... |
| 2001-02 | Quebec Citadelles | AHL | 56 | 8 | 11 | 19 | 88 | .... | .... | .... | .... | .... | .... | .... | .... | .... | 3 | 0 | 1 | 1 | 0 | .... | .... | .... | .... |
| | Mississippi | ECHL | 7 | 1 | 3 | 4 | 2 | .... | .... | .... | .... | .... | .... | .... | .... | .... | .... | .... | .... | .... | .... | .... | .... | .... | .... |
| **2002-03** | **Montreal** | **NHL** | **1** | **0** | **0** | **0** | **0** | **0** | **0** | **0** | **1** | **0.0** | **-1** | **0** | **0.0** | **17:11** | .... | .... | .... | .... | .... | .... | .... | .... | .... |
| | Hamilton | AHL | 75 | 7 | 21 | 28 | 92 | .... | .... | .... | .... | .... | .... | .... | .... | .... | 23 | 1 | 9 | 10 | 16 | .... | .... | .... | .... |
| 2003-04 | Hamilton | AHL | 77 | 9 | 27 | 36 | 57 | .... | .... | .... | .... | .... | .... | .... | .... | .... | 10 | 2 | 4 | 6 | 18 | .... | .... | .... | .... |
| 2004-05 | Syracuse Crunch | AHL | 72 | 3 | 27 | 30 | 55 | .... | .... | .... | .... | .... | .... | .... | .... | .... | .... | .... | .... | .... | .... | .... | .... | .... | .... |
| **2005-06** | **Columbus** | **NHL** | **11** | **0** | **2** | **2** | **11** | **0** | **0** | **0** | **16** | **0.0** | **-6** | **0** | **0.0** | **17:16** | .... | .... | .... | .... | .... | .... | .... | .... | .... |
| | **Anaheim** | **NHL** | **61** | **8** | **26** | **34** | **41** | **4** | **0** | **3** | **121** | **6.6** | **8** | **1** | **0.0** | **24:14** | **16** | **3** | **6** | **9** | **11** | **3** | **0** | **0** | **27:26** |
| **2006-07♦** | **Anaheim** | **NHL** | **71** | **7** | **21** | **28** | **49** | **2** | **0** | **0** | **128** | **5.5** | **7** | **1** | **0.0** | **25:28** | **20** | **4** | **4** | **8** | **16** | **4** | **0** | **0** | **30:33** |
| **2007-08** | **Anaheim** | **NHL** | **82** | **2** | **19** | **21** | **59** | **0** | **0** | **2** | **144** | **1.4** | **-9** | **1** | **0.0** | **25:32** | **6** | **0** | **0** | **0** | **26** | **0** | **0** | **0** | **21:02** |
| **2008-09** | **Anaheim** | **NHL** | **20** | **4** | **1** | **5** | **12** | **0** | **0** | **2** | **45** | **8.9** | **-3** | **0** | **0.0** | **24:54** | **13** | **1** | **0** | **1** | **15** | **0** | **0** | **0** | **21:25** |
| | **NHL Totals** | | **246** | **21** | **69** | **90** | **172** | **6** | **0** | **7** | **455** | **4.6** | | **3** | **0.0** | **24:44** | **55** | **8** | **10** | **18** | **68** | **7** | **0** | **0** | **26:27** |

QMJHL All-Rookie Team (1997) • QMJHL Second All-Star Team (2000)

Claimed on waivers by **Columbus** from **Montreal**, September 15, 2004. Traded to **Anaheim** by **Columbus** with Tyler Wright for Sergei Fedorov and Anaheim's 5th round choice (Maxime Frechette) in 2006 Entry Draft, November 15, 2005. • Missed remainder of 2008-09 regular season recovering from knee injury suffered in game vs. Nashville, November 14, 2008.. Signed as a free agent by **Toronto**, July 6, 2009.

## BEECH, Kris

(BEECH, KRIHS)

Center. Shoots left. 6'3", 211 lbs. Born, Salmon Arm, B.C., February 5, 1981. Washington's 1st choice, 7th overall, in 1999 Entry Draft.

| | | | | | | | | | | | | | | | | | | | | | | | | | |
|---|---|---|---|---|---|---|---|---|---|---|---|---|---|---|---|---|---|---|---|---|---|---|---|---|---|
| 1996-97 | Sicamous Eagles | KIJHL | 49 | 34 | 36 | 70 | 80 | .... | .... | .... | .... | .... | .... | .... | .... | .... | .... | .... | .... | .... | .... | .... | .... | .... | .... |
| | Calgary Hitmen | WHL | 8 | 1 | 1 | 2 | 0 | .... | .... | .... | .... | .... | .... | .... | .... | .... | .... | .... | .... | .... | .... | .... | .... | .... | .... |
| 1997-98 | Calgary Hitmen | WHL | 58 | 10 | 25 | 35 | 24 | .... | .... | .... | .... | .... | .... | .... | .... | .... | 12 | 4 | 5 | 9 | 32 | .... | .... | .... | .... |
| 1998-99 | Calgary Hitmen | WHL | 68 | 26 | 41 | 67 | 103 | .... | .... | .... | .... | .... | .... | .... | .... | .... | 6 | 1 | 4 | 5 | 8 | .... | .... | .... | .... |
| 99-2000 | Calgary Hitmen | WHL | 66 | 32 | 54 | 86 | 99 | .... | .... | .... | .... | .... | .... | .... | .... | .... | 5 | 3 | 5 | 8 | 16 | .... | .... | .... | .... |
| **2000-01** | **Washington** | **NHL** | **4** | **0** | **0** | **0** | **2** | **0** | **0** | **0** | **0** | **0.0** | **-2** | **25** | **36.0** | **7:29** | .... | .... | .... | .... | .... | .... | .... | .... | .... |
| | Calgary Hitmen | WHL | 40 | 22 | 44 | 66 | 103 | .... | .... | .... | .... | .... | .... | .... | .... | .... | 10 | 2 | 8 | 10 | 26 | .... | .... | .... | .... |
| **2001-02** | **Pittsburgh** | **NHL** | **79** | **10** | **15** | **25** | **45** | **2** | **0** | **0** | **126** | **7.9** | **-25** | **604** | **45.2** | **13:33** | .... | .... | .... | .... | .... | .... | .... | .... | .... |
| **2002-03** | **Pittsburgh** | **NHL** | **12** | **0** | **1** | **1** | **6** | **0** | **0** | **0** | **6** | **0.0** | **-3** | **96** | **42.7** | **10:34** | .... | .... | .... | .... | .... | .... | .... | .... | .... |
| | Wilkes-Barre | AHL | 50 | 19 | 24 | 43 | 76 | .... | .... | .... | .... | .... | .... | .... | .... | .... | 5 | 1 | 1 | 2 | 0 | .... | .... | .... | .... |
| **2003-04** | **Pittsburgh** | **NHL** | **4** | **0** | **1** | **1** | **6** | **0** | **0** | **0** | **6** | **0.0** | **0** | **45** | **40.0** | **12:32** | .... | .... | .... | .... | .... | .... | .... | .... | .... |
| | Wilkes-Barre | AHL | 53 | 20 | 25 | 45 | 97 | .... | .... | .... | .... | .... | .... | .... | .... | .... | 22 | 9 | 6 | 15 | 22 | .... | .... | .... | .... |
| 2004-05 | Wilkes-Barre | AHL | 68 | 14 | 48 | 62 | 146 | .... | .... | .... | .... | .... | .... | .... | .... | .... | 11 | 4 | 6 | 10 | 14 | .... | .... | .... | .... |
| **2005-06** | **Nashville** | **NHL** | **5** | **1** | **2** | **3** | **0** | **0** | **0** | **0** | **6** | **16.7** | **1** | **81** | **54.3** | **14:40** | .... | .... | .... | .... | .... | .... | .... | .... | .... |
| | Milwaukee | AHL | 48 | 18 | 32 | 50 | 48 | .... | .... | .... | .... | .... | .... | .... | .... | .... | .... | .... | .... | .... | .... | .... | .... | .... | .... |
| | **Washington** | **NHL** | **5** | **0** | **0** | **0** | **4** | **0** | **0** | **0** | **6** | **0.0** | **0** | **36** | **50.0** | **9:24** | .... | .... | .... | .... | .... | .... | .... | .... | .... |
| | Hershey Bears | AHL | 10 | 8 | 6 | 14 | 6 | .... | .... | .... | .... | .... | .... | .... | .... | .... | 21 | 14 | 14 | 28 | 30 | .... | .... | .... | .... |
| **2006-07** | **Washington** | **NHL** | **64** | **8** | **18** | **26** | **46** | **3** | **0** | **0** | **77** | **10.4** | **-11** | **744** | **48.4** | **12:28** | .... | .... | .... | .... | .... | .... | .... | .... | .... |
| **2007-08** | **Columbus** | **NHL** | **16** | **5** | **4** | **9** | **2** | **2** | **0** | **0** | **24** | **20.8** | **3** | **205** | **53.2** | **13:00** | .... | .... | .... | .... | .... | .... | .... | .... | .... |
| | Syracuse Crunch | AHL | 16 | 5 | 10 | 15 | 22 | .... | .... | .... | .... | .... | .... | .... | .... | .... | .... | .... | .... | .... | .... | .... | .... | .... | .... |
| | **Vancouver** | **NHL** | **4** | **1** | **1** | **2** | **0** | **0** | **0** | **0** | **6** | **16.7** | **1** | **37** | **48.7** | **9:37** | .... | .... | .... | .... | .... | .... | .... | .... | .... |
| | **Pittsburgh** | **NHL** | **5** | **0** | **0** | **0** | **2** | **0** | **0** | **0** | **6** | **0.0** | **-1** | **34** | **50.0** | **8:14** | .... | .... | .... | .... | .... | .... | .... | .... | .... |
| 2008-09 | HV 71 Jonkoping | Sweden | 45 | 17 | 17 | 34 | 116 | .... | .... | .... | .... | .... | .... | .... | .... | .... | 18 | 3 | 3 | 6 | 22 | .... | .... | .... | .... |
| | **NHL Totals** | | **198** | **25** | **42** | **67** | **113** | **7** | **0** | **0** | **263** | **9.5** | | **1907** | **47.6** | **12:33** | .... | .... | .... | .... | .... | .... | .... | .... | .... |

Traded to **Pittsburgh** by **Washington** with Michal Sivek, Ross Lupaschuk and future considerations for Jaromir Jagr and Frantisek Kucera, July 11, 2001. Traded to **Nashville** by **Pittsburgh** for Nashville's 4th round choice (later traded to Florida - Florida selected Derrick Lapoint) in 2006 Entry Draft, September 9, 2005. Traded to **Washington** by **Nashville** with Nashville's 1st round choice (Semyon Varlamov) in 2006 Entry Draft for Brendan Witt, March 9, 2006. Signed as a free agent by **Columbus**, August 7, 2007. Claimed on waivers by **Vancouver** from **Columbus**, January 10, 2008. Claimed on waivers by **Washington** from **Vancouver**, January 23, 2008. Claimed on waivers by **Pittsburgh** from **Washington**, January 26, 2008. Signed as a free agent by **Jonkoping** (Sweden), October 13, 2008.

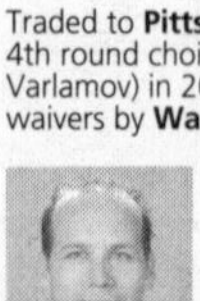

## BEGIN, Steve

(bay-ZHIN, STEEV) **BOS.**

Center. Shoots left. 6', 192 lbs. Born, Trois-Rivieres, Que., June 14, 1978. Calgary's 3rd choice, 40th overall, in 1996 Entry Draft.

| | | | | | | | | | | | | | | | | | | | | | | | | | |
|---|---|---|---|---|---|---|---|---|---|---|---|---|---|---|---|---|---|---|---|---|---|---|---|---|---|
| 1993-94 | Cap-d-Madelaine | QAAA | 8 | 0 | 1 | 1 | 6 | .... | .... | .... | .... | .... | .... | .... | .... | .... | 2 | 0 | 0 | 0 | 0 | .... | .... | .... | .... |
| 1994-95 | Cap-d-Madelaine | QAAA | 35 | 9 | 15 | 24 | 48 | .... | .... | .... | .... | .... | .... | .... | .... | .... | 3 | 0 | 0 | 0 | 2 | .... | .... | .... | .... |
| 1995-96 | Val-d'Or Foreurs | QMJHL | 64 | 13 | 23 | 36 | 218 | .... | .... | .... | .... | .... | .... | .... | .... | .... | 13 | 1 | 3 | 4 | 33 | .... | .... | .... | .... |
| 1996-97 | Val-d'Or Foreurs | QMJHL | 58 | 13 | 33 | 46 | 229 | .... | .... | .... | .... | .... | .... | .... | .... | .... | 10 | 0 | 3 | 3 | 8 | .... | .... | .... | .... |
| | Saint John Flames | AHL | .... | .... | .... | .... | .... | .... | .... | .... | .... | .... | .... | .... | .... | .... | 4 | 0 | 2 | 2 | 6 | .... | .... | .... | .... |
| **1997-98** | **Calgary** | **NHL** | **5** | **0** | **0** | **0** | **23** | **0** | **0** | **0** | **2** | **0.0** | **0** | .... | .... | .... | .... | .... | .... | .... | .... | .... | .... | .... | .... |
| | Val-d'Or Foreurs | QMJHL | 35 | 18 | 17 | 35 | 73 | .... | .... | .... | .... | .... | .... | .... | .... | .... | 15 | 2 | 12 | 14 | 34 | .... | .... | .... | .... |
| 1998-99 | Saint John Flames | AHL | 73 | 11 | 9 | 20 | 156 | .... | .... | .... | .... | .... | .... | .... | .... | .... | 7 | 2 | 0 | 2 | 18 | .... | .... | .... | .... |
| **99-2000** | **Calgary** | **NHL** | **13** | **1** | **1** | **2** | **18** | **0** | **0** | **0** | **3** | **33.3** | **-3** | **19** | **47.4** | **7:13** | .... | .... | .... | .... | .... | .... | .... | .... | .... |
| | Saint John Flames | AHL | 47 | 13 | 12 | 25 | 99 | .... | .... | .... | .... | .... | .... | .... | .... | .... | .... | .... | .... | .... | .... | .... | .... | .... | .... |
| **2000-01** | **Calgary** | **NHL** | **4** | **0** | **0** | **0** | **21** | **0** | **0** | **0** | **3** | **0.0** | **0** | **0** | **0.0** | **6:04** | .... | .... | .... | .... | .... | .... | .... | .... | .... |
| | Saint John Flames | AHL | 58 | 14 | 14 | 28 | 109 | .... | .... | .... | .... | .... | .... | .... | .... | .... | 19 | 10 | 7 | 17 | 18 | .... | .... | .... | .... |
| **2001-02** | **Calgary** | **NHL** | **51** | **7** | **5** | **12** | **79** | **1** | **0** | **0** | **65** | **10.8** | **-3** | **129** | **53.5** | **9:25** | .... | .... | .... | .... | .... | .... | .... | .... | .... |
| **2002-03** | **Calgary** | **NHL** | **50** | **3** | **1** | **4** | **51** | **0** | **0** | **1** | **59** | **5.1** | **-7** | **50** | **60.0** | **9:13** | .... | .... | .... | .... | .... | .... | .... | .... | .... |
| **2003-04** | **Montreal** | **NHL** | **52** | **10** | **5** | **15** | **41** | **0** | **1** | **1** | **91** | **11.0** | **6** | **436** | **48.6** | **12:32** | **9** | **0** | **1** | **1** | **10** | **0** | **0** | **0** | **12:26** |
| 2004-05 | Hamilton | AHL | 21 | 10 | 3 | 13 | 20 | .... | .... | .... | .... | .... | .... | .... | .... | .... | 4 | 0 | 2 | 2 | 8 | .... | .... | .... | .... |
| **2005-06** | **Montreal** | **NHL** | **76** | **11** | **12** | **23** | **113** | **1** | **2** | **2** | **134** | **8.2** | **9** | **573** | **50.1** | **14:19** | **2** | **0** | **0** | **0** | **2** | **0** | **0** | **0** | **13:42** |
| **2006-07** | **Montreal** | **NHL** | **52** | **5** | **5** | **10** | **46** | **0** | **0** | **0** | **64** | **7.8** | **-6** | **159** | **49.7** | **11:55** | .... | .... | .... | .... | .... | .... | .... | .... | .... |
| **2007-08** | **Montreal** | **NHL** | **44** | **3** | **5** | **8** | **48** | **0** | **0** | **0** | **67** | **4.5** | **0** | **69** | **34.8** | **11:38** | **12** | **0** | **3** | **3** | **8** | **0** | **0** | **0** | **12:45** |
| **2008-09** | **Montreal** | **NHL** | **42** | **6** | **4** | **10** | **27** | **0** | **0** | **1** | **65** | **9.2** | **-5** | **78** | **53.9** | **10:51** | .... | .... | .... | .... | .... | .... | .... | .... | .... |
| | **Dallas** | **NHL** | **20** | **1** | **1** | **2** | **15** | **0** | **0** | **0** | **25** | **4.0** | **-1** | **55** | **41.8** | **10:26** | .... | .... | .... | .... | .... | .... | .... | .... | .... |
| | **NHL Totals** | | **409** | **47** | **39** | **86** | **482** | **2** | **3** | **5** | **578** | **8.1** | | **1568** | **49.4** | **11:22** | **23** | **0** | **4** | **4** | **20** | **0** | **0** | **0** | **12:43** |

Jack A. Butterfield Trophy (AHL – Playoff MVP) (2001)

Traded to **Buffalo** by **Calgary** with Chris Drury for Steve Reinprecht and Rhett Warrener, July 3, 2003. Claimed by **Montreal** from **Buffalo** in Waiver Draft, October 3, 2003. Traded to **Dallas** by **Montreal** for Doug Janik, February 26, 2009. Signed as a free agent by **Boston**, July 1, 2009.

## BELAK, Wade

(BEE-lak, WAYD) **NSH.**

Right wing. Shoots right. 6'5", 225 lbs. Born, Saskatoon, Sask., July 3, 1976. Quebec's 1st choice, 12th overall, in 1994 Entry Draft.

| | | | Regular Season | | | | | | | | | | | | | | Playoffs | | | | | | | | |
|---|---|---|---|---|---|---|---|---|---|---|---|---|---|---|---|---|---|---|---|---|---|---|---|---|---|
| Season | Club | League | GP | G | A | Pts | PIM | PP | SH | GW | S | % | +/- | TF | F% | Min | GP | G | A | Pts | PIM | PP | SH | GW | Min |
| 1991-92 | North Battleford | SMBHL | 57 | 6 | 20 | 26 | 186 | .... | .... | .... | .... | .... | .... | .... | .... | .... | .... | .... | .... | .... | .... | .... | .... | .... | .... |
| 1992-93 | North Battleford | SJHL | 50 | 5 | 15 | 20 | 146 | .... | .... | .... | .... | .... | .... | .... | .... | .... | .... | .... | .... | .... | .... | .... | .... | .... | .... |
| | Saskatoon Blades | WHL | 7 | 0 | 0 | 0 | 23 | .... | .... | .... | .... | .... | .... | .... | .... | .... | 7 | 0 | 0 | 0 | 0 | .... | .... | .... | .... |
| 1993-94 | Saskatoon Blades | WHL | 69 | 4 | 13 | 17 | 226 | .... | .... | .... | .... | .... | .... | .... | .... | .... | 16 | 2 | 2 | 4 | 43 | .... | .... | .... | .... |
| 1994-95 | Saskatoon Blades | WHL | 72 | 4 | 14 | 18 | 290 | .... | .... | .... | .... | .... | .... | .... | .... | .... | 9 | 0 | 0 | 0 | 36 | .... | .... | .... | .... |
| | Cornwall Aces | AHL | .... | .... | .... | .... | .... | .... | .... | .... | .... | .... | .... | .... | .... | .... | 11 | 1 | 2 | 3 | 40 | .... | .... | .... | .... |
| 1995-96 | Saskatoon Blades | WHL | 63 | 3 | 15 | 18 | 207 | .... | .... | .... | .... | .... | .... | .... | .... | .... | 4 | 0 | 0 | 0 | 9 | .... | .... | .... | .... |
| | Cornwall Aces | AHL | 5 | 0 | 0 | 0 | 18 | .... | .... | .... | .... | .... | .... | .... | .... | .... | 2 | 0 | 0 | 0 | 2 | .... | .... | .... | .... |
| **1996-97** | **Colorado** | **NHL** | 5 | 0 | 0 | 0 | 11 | 0 | 0 | 0 | 1 | 0.0 | –1 | .... | .... | .... | .... | .... | .... | .... | .... | .... | .... | .... | .... |
| | Hershey Bears | AHL | 65 | 1 | 7 | 8 | 320 | .... | .... | .... | .... | .... | .... | .... | .... | .... | 16 | 0 | 1 | 1 | 61 | .... | .... | .... | .... |
| **1997-98** | **Colorado** | **NHL** | 8 | 1 | 1 | 2 | 27 | 0 | 0 | 1 | 2 | 50.0 | –3 | .... | .... | .... | .... | .... | .... | .... | .... | .... | .... | .... | .... |
| | Hershey Bears | AHL | 11 | 0 | 0 | 0 | 30 | .... | .... | .... | .... | .... | .... | .... | .... | .... | .... | .... | .... | .... | .... | .... | .... | .... | .... |
| **1998-99** | **Colorado** | **NHL** | 22 | 0 | 0 | 0 | 71 | 0 | 0 | 0 | 5 | 0.0 | –2 | 0 | 0.0 | 6:48 | .... | .... | .... | .... | .... | .... | .... | .... | .... |
| | Hershey Bears | AHL | 17 | 0 | 1 | 1 | 49 | .... | .... | .... | .... | .... | .... | .... | .... | .... | .... | .... | .... | .... | .... | .... | .... | .... | .... |
| | **Calgary** | **NHL** | 9 | 0 | 1 | 1 | 23 | 0 | 0 | 0 | 2 | 0.0 | 3 | 0 | 0.0 | 10:46 | .... | .... | .... | .... | .... | .... | .... | .... | .... |
| | Saint John Flames | AHL | 12 | 0 | 2 | 2 | 43 | .... | .... | .... | .... | .... | .... | .... | .... | .... | 6 | 0 | 1 | 1 | 23 | .... | .... | .... | .... |
| **99-2000** | **Calgary** | **NHL** | 40 | 0 | 2 | 2 | 122 | 0 | 0 | 0 | 11 | 0.0 | –4 | 1 | 0.0 | 7:33 | .... | .... | .... | .... | .... | .... | .... | .... | .... |
| **2000-01** | **Calgary** | **NHL** | 23 | 0 | 0 | 0 | 79 | 0 | 0 | 0 | 8 | 0.0 | –2 | 0 | 0.0 | 6:54 | .... | .... | .... | .... | .... | .... | .... | .... | .... |
| | **Toronto** | **NHL** | 16 | 1 | 1 | 2 | 31 | 0 | 0 | 0 | 8 | 12.5 | –4 | 0 | 0.0 | 13:38 | .... | .... | .... | .... | .... | .... | .... | .... | .... |
| **2001-02** | **Toronto** | **NHL** | 63 | 1 | 3 | 4 | 142 | 0 | 0 | 0 | 47 | 2.1 | 2 | 0 | 0.0 | 9:14 | 16 | 1 | 0 | 1 | 18 | 0 | 0 | 0 | 7:28 |
| **2002-03** | **Toronto** | **NHL** | 55 | 3 | 6 | 9 | 196 | 0 | 0 | 0 | 33 | 9.1 | –2 | 0 | 0.0 | 10:50 | 2 | 0 | 0 | 0 | 4 | 0 | 0 | 0 | 8:22 |
| **2003-04** | **Toronto** | **NHL** | 34 | 1 | 1 | 2 | 109 | 0 | 0 | 0 | 15 | 6.7 | 0 | 0 | 0.0 | 7:00 | 4 | 0 | 0 | 0 | 14 | 0 | 0 | 0 | 9:59 |
| 2004-05 | Coventry Blaze | Britain | 20 | 3 | 5 | 8 | 109 | .... | .... | .... | .... | .... | .... | .... | .... | .... | 8 | 1 | 1 | 2 | 16 | .... | .... | .... | .... |
| **2005-06** | **Toronto** | **NHL** | 55 | 0 | 3 | 3 | 109 | 0 | 0 | 0 | 16 | 0.0 | –13 | 0 | 0.0 | 9:59 | .... | .... | .... | .... | .... | .... | .... | .... | .... |
| **2006-07** | **Toronto** | **NHL** | 65 | 0 | 3 | 3 | 110 | 0 | 0 | 0 | 16 | 0.0 | –8 | 0 | 0.0 | 5:02 | .... | .... | .... | .... | .... | .... | .... | .... | .... |
| **2007-08** | **Toronto** | **NHL** | 30 | 1 | 0 | 1 | 66 | 0 | 0 | 0 | 13 | 7.7 | –2 | 1 | 0.0 | 4:02 | .... | .... | .... | .... | .... | .... | .... | .... | .... |
| | **Florida** | **NHL** | 17 | 0 | 0 | 0 | 12 | 0 | 0 | 0 | 4 | 0.0 | 0 | 0 | 0.0 | 4:09 | .... | .... | .... | .... | .... | .... | .... | .... | .... |
| **2008-09** | **Florida** | **NHL** | 15 | 0 | 0 | 0 | 25 | 0 | 0 | 0 | 4 | 0.0 | 0 | 0 | 0.0 | 4:25 | .... | .... | .... | .... | .... | .... | .... | .... | .... |
| | **Nashville** | **NHL** | 38 | 0 | 2 | 2 | 54 | 0 | 0 | 0 | 15 | 0.0 | –1 | 0 | 0.0 | 5:35 | .... | .... | .... | .... | .... | .... | .... | .... | .... |
| | **NHL Totals** | | **495** | **8** | **23** | **31** | **1187** | **0** | **0** | **1** | **200** | **4.0** | | **2** | **0.0** | **7:39** | **22** | **1** | **0** | **1** | **36** | **0** | **0** | **0** | **8:00** |

• Rights transferred to **Colorado** after **Quebec** franchise relocated, June 21, 1995. Traded to **Calgary** by **Colorado** with Rene Corbet, Robyn Regehr and Colorado's 2nd round compensatory choice (Jarret Stoll) in 2000 Entry Draft for Theoren Fleury and Chris Dingman, February 28, 1999. • Missed majority of 1999-2000 and 2000-01 seasons recovering from shoulder injury suffered in game vs. Colorado, February 10, 2000. Claimed on waivers by **Toronto** from **Calgary**, February 16, 2001. • Missed majority of 2003-04 season recovering from abdomen (November 20, 2003 vs. Edmonton) and knee (January 6, 2004 vs. Nashville) injuries. Signed as a free agent by **Coventry** (Britain), November 8, 2004. Traded to **Florida** by **Toronto** for Florida's 5th round choice (Jerome Flaake) in 2008 Entry Draft, February 26, 2008. Traded to **Nashville** by **Florida** for Nick Tarnasky, November 27, 2008.

## BELANGER, Eric

(buh-LAWN-zhay, AIR-ihk) **MIN.**

Center. Shoots left. 5'11", 187 lbs. Born, Sherbrooke, Que., December 16, 1977. Los Angeles' 5th choice, 96th overall, in 1996 Entry Draft.

| Season | Club | League | GP | G | A | Pts | PIM | PP | SH | GW | S | % | +/- | TF | F% | Min | GP | G | A | Pts | PIM | PP | SH | GW | Min |
|---|---|---|---|---|---|---|---|---|---|---|---|---|---|---|---|---|---|---|---|---|---|---|---|---|---|
| 1993-94 | Magog | QAAA | 32 | 19 | 24 | 43 | 24 | .... | .... | .... | .... | .... | .... | .... | .... | .... | 13 | 5 | 6 | 11 | 36 | .... | .... | .... | .... |
| 1994-95 | Beauport | QMJHL | 71 | 12 | 28 | 40 | 24 | .... | .... | .... | .... | .... | .... | .... | .... | .... | 18 | 5 | 9 | 14 | 25 | .... | .... | .... | .... |
| 1995-96 | Beauport | QMJHL | 59 | 35 | 48 | 83 | 18 | .... | .... | .... | .... | .... | .... | .... | .... | .... | 20 | 13 | 14 | 27 | 6 | .... | .... | .... | .... |
| 1996-97 | Beauport | QMJHL | 31 | 13 | 37 | 50 | 30 | .... | .... | .... | .... | .... | .... | .... | .... | .... | .... | .... | .... | .... | .... | .... | .... | .... | .... |
| | Rimouski Oceanic | QMJHL | 31 | 26 | 41 | 67 | 36 | .... | .... | .... | .... | .... | .... | .... | .... | .... | 4 | 2 | 3 | 5 | 10 | .... | .... | .... | .... |
| 1997-98 | Fredericton | AHL | 56 | 17 | 34 | 51 | 28 | .... | .... | .... | .... | .... | .... | .... | .... | .... | 4 | 2 | 1 | 3 | 2 | .... | .... | .... | .... |
| 1998-99 | Springfield | AHL | 33 | 8 | 18 | 26 | 10 | .... | .... | .... | .... | .... | .... | .... | .... | .... | 3 | 0 | 1 | 1 | 2 | .... | .... | .... | .... |
| | Long Beach | IHL | 1 | 0 | 0 | 0 | 0 | .... | .... | .... | .... | .... | .... | .... | .... | .... | .... | .... | .... | .... | .... | .... | .... | .... | .... |
| 99-2000 | Lowell | AHL | 65 | 15 | 25 | 40 | 20 | .... | .... | .... | .... | .... | .... | .... | .... | .... | 7 | 3 | 3 | 6 | 2 | .... | .... | .... | .... |
| **2000-01** | **Los Angeles** | **NHL** | 62 | 9 | 12 | 21 | 16 | 1 | 2 | 1 | 80 | 11.3 | 14 | 849 | 56.4 | 13:25 | 13 | 1 | 4 | 5 | 2 | 0 | 0 | 1 | 13:47 |
| | Lowell | AHL | 13 | 8 | 10 | 18 | 4 | .... | .... | .... | .... | .... | .... | .... | .... | .... | .... | .... | .... | .... | .... | .... | .... | .... | .... |
| **2001-02** | **Los Angeles** | **NHL** | 53 | 8 | 16 | 24 | 21 | 2 | 1 | 1 | 67 | 11.9 | 2 | 882 | 57.7 | 14:33 | 7 | 0 | 0 | 0 | 4 | 0 | 0 | 0 | 12:57 |
| **2002-03** | **Los Angeles** | **NHL** | 62 | 16 | 19 | 35 | 26 | 0 | 3 | 1 | 114 | 14.0 | –5 | 1143 | 51.8 | 17:42 | .... | .... | .... | .... | .... | .... | .... | .... | .... |
| **2003-04** | **Los Angeles** | **NHL** | 81 | 13 | 20 | 33 | 44 | 0 | 1 | 2 | 132 | 9.8 | –16 | 1418 | 53.7 | 17:01 | .... | .... | .... | .... | .... | .... | .... | .... | .... |
| 2004-05 | HC Forst Bolzano | Italy | 12 | 13 | 10 | 23 | 20 | .... | .... | .... | .... | .... | .... | .... | .... | .... | 9 | 3 | 7 | 10 | 33 | .... | .... | .... | .... |
| **2005-06** | **Los Angeles** | **NHL** | 65 | 17 | 20 | 37 | 62 | 5 | 0 | 1 | 119 | 14.3 | –5 | 1179 | 49.0 | 17:33 | .... | .... | .... | .... | .... | .... | .... | .... | .... |
| **2006-07** | **Carolina** | **NHL** | 56 | 8 | 12 | 20 | 14 | 3 | 0 | 1 | 100 | 8.0 | –2 | 689 | 53.4 | 14:51 | .... | .... | .... | .... | .... | .... | .... | .... | .... |
| | **Atlanta** | **NHL** | 24 | 9 | 6 | 15 | 12 | 1 | 0 | 0 | 49 | 18.4 | 0 | 517 | 52.6 | 19:29 | 4 | 1 | 0 | 1 | 12 | 1 | 0 | 0 | 16:47 |
| **2007-08** | **Minnesota** | **NHL** | 75 | 13 | 24 | 37 | 30 | 7 | 1 | 3 | 115 | 11.3 | –6 | 1195 | 49.1 | 17:13 | 6 | 0 | 0 | 0 | 4 | 0 | 0 | 0 | 18:34 |
| **2008-09** | **Minnesota** | **NHL** | 79 | 13 | 23 | 36 | 26 | 4 | 0 | 4 | 147 | 8.8 | –5 | 1205 | 52.0 | 17:50 | .... | .... | .... | .... | .... | .... | .... | .... | .... |
| | **NHL Totals** | | **557** | **106** | **152** | **258** | **251** | **23** | **8** | **14** | **923** | **11.5** | | **9077** | **52.6** | **16:33** | **30** | **2** | **4** | **6** | **22** | **1** | **0** | **1** | **14:57** |

Signed as a free agent by **Bolzano** (Italy), December 22, 2004. Traded to **Carolina** by **Los Angeles** with Tim Gleason for Oleg Tverdovsky and Jack Johnson, September 29, 2006. Traded to **Nashville** by **Carolina** for Josef Vasicek, February 9, 2007. Traded to **Atlanta** by **Nashville** for Vitaly Vishnevski, February 10, 2007. Signed as a free agent by **Minnesota**, July 3, 2007.

## BELESKEY, Matt

(beh-LEH-skee, MAT) **ANA.**

Left wing. Shoots left. 6', 208 lbs. Born, Windsor, Ont., June 7, 1988. Anaheim's 4th choice, 112th overall, in 2006 Entry Draft.

| Season | Club | League | GP | G | A | Pts | PIM | PP | SH | GW | S | % | +/- | TF | F% | Min | GP | G | A | Pts | PIM | PP | SH | GW | Min |
|---|---|---|---|---|---|---|---|---|---|---|---|---|---|---|---|---|---|---|---|---|---|---|---|---|---|
| 2004-05 | Belleville Bulls | OHL | 68 | 10 | 13 | 23 | 118 | .... | .... | .... | .... | .... | .... | .... | .... | .... | 5 | 0 | 0 | 0 | 18 | .... | .... | .... | .... |
| 2005-06 | Belleville Bulls | OHL | 61 | 20 | 20 | 40 | 119 | .... | .... | .... | .... | .... | .... | .... | .... | .... | 6 | 1 | 2 | 3 | 10 | .... | .... | .... | .... |
| 2006-07 | Belleville Bulls | OHL | 66 | 27 | 41 | 68 | 124 | .... | .... | .... | .... | .... | .... | .... | .... | .... | 15 | 4 | 10 | 14 | 18 | .... | .... | .... | .... |
| 2007-08 | Belleville Bulls | OHL | 62 | 41 | 49 | 90 | 106 | .... | .... | .... | .... | .... | .... | .... | .... | .... | 21 | 12 | 21 | 33 | 23 | .... | .... | .... | .... |
| **2008-09** | **Anaheim** | **NHL** | 2 | 0 | 0 | 0 | 0 | 0 | 0 | 0 | 0 | 0.0 | 0 | 2 | 0.0 | 11:10 | .... | .... | .... | .... | .... | .... | .... | .... | .... |
| | Iowa Chops | AHL | 58 | 11 | 24 | 35 | 58 | .... | .... | .... | .... | .... | .... | .... | .... | .... | .... | .... | .... | .... | .... | .... | .... | .... | .... |
| | **NHL Totals** | | **2** | **0** | **0** | **0** | **0** | **0** | **0** | **0** | **0** | **0.0** | | **2** | **0.0** | **11:09** | .... | .... | .... | .... | .... | .... | .... | .... | .... |

## BELL, Brendan

(BEHL, BREHN-duhn) **ST.L.**

Defense. Shoots left. 6'2", 211 lbs. Born, Ottawa, Ont., March 31, 1983. Toronto's 3rd choice, 65th overall, in 2001 Entry Draft.

| Season | Club | League | GP | G | A | Pts | PIM | PP | SH | GW | S | % | +/- | TF | F% | Min | GP | G | A | Pts | PIM | PP | SH | GW | Min |
|---|---|---|---|---|---|---|---|---|---|---|---|---|---|---|---|---|---|---|---|---|---|---|---|---|---|
| 1998-99 | Ott. Jr. Senators | CJHL | 54 | 7 | 20 | 27 | 46 | .... | .... | .... | .... | .... | .... | .... | .... | .... | .... | .... | .... | .... | .... | .... | .... | .... | .... |
| 99-2000 | Ottawa 67's | OHL | 48 | 1 | 32 | 33 | 34 | .... | .... | .... | .... | .... | .... | .... | .... | .... | 5 | 0 | 1 | 1 | 4 | .... | .... | .... | .... |
| 2000-01 | Ottawa 67's | OHL | 68 | 7 | 32 | 39 | 59 | .... | .... | .... | .... | .... | .... | .... | .... | .... | 20 | 1 | 11 | 12 | 22 | .... | .... | .... | .... |
| 2001-02 | Ottawa 67's | OHL | 67 | 10 | 36 | 46 | 56 | .... | .... | .... | .... | .... | .... | .... | .... | .... | 13 | 2 | 5 | 7 | 25 | .... | .... | .... | .... |
| 2002-03 | Ottawa 67's | OHL | 55 | 14 | 39 | 53 | 46 | .... | .... | .... | .... | .... | .... | .... | .... | .... | 23 | 8 | 19 | 27 | 25 | .... | .... | .... | .... |
| 2003-04 | St. John's | AHL | 74 | 7 | 18 | 25 | 72 | .... | .... | .... | .... | .... | .... | .... | .... | .... | .... | .... | .... | .... | .... | .... | .... | .... | .... |
| 2004-05 | St. John's | AHL | 75 | 6 | 25 | 31 | 57 | .... | .... | .... | .... | .... | .... | .... | .... | .... | 5 | 0 | 1 | 1 | 2 | .... | .... | .... | .... |
| **2005-06** | **Toronto** | **NHL** | 1 | 0 | 0 | 0 | 0 | 0 | 0 | 0 | 2 | 0.0 | 0 | 0 | 0.0 | 14:00 | .... | .... | .... | .... | .... | .... | .... | .... | .... |
| | Toronto Marlies | AHL | 70 | 6 | 37 | 43 | 99 | .... | .... | .... | .... | .... | .... | .... | .... | .... | 5 | 0 | 4 | 4 | 10 | .... | .... | .... | .... |
| **2006-07** | **Toronto** | **NHL** | 31 | 1 | 4 | 5 | 19 | 1 | 0 | 0 | 29 | 3.4 | –3 | 1 | 0.0 | 12:08 | .... | .... | .... | .... | .... | .... | .... | .... | .... |
| | **Phoenix** | **NHL** | 14 | 0 | 2 | 2 | 8 | 0 | 0 | 0 | 18 | 0.0 | –8 | 0 | 0.0 | 17:07 | .... | .... | .... | .... | .... | .... | .... | .... | .... |
| **2007-08** | **Phoenix** | **NHL** | 2 | 0 | 0 | 0 | 0 | 0 | 0 | 0 | 0 | 0.0 | –2 | 0 | 0.0 | 14:49 | .... | .... | .... | .... | .... | .... | .... | .... | .... |
| | San Antonio | AHL | 69 | 7 | 24 | 31 | 80 | .... | .... | .... | .... | .... | .... | .... | .... | .... | 7 | 2 | 5 | 7 | 10 | .... | .... | .... | .... |
| **2008-09** | **Ottawa** | **NHL** | 53 | 6 | 15 | 21 | 24 | 5 | 0 | 1 | 76 | 7.9 | –5 | 0 | 0.0 | 17:44 | .... | .... | .... | .... | .... | .... | .... | .... | .... |
| | Binghamton | AHL | 15 | 6 | 9 | 15 | 12 | .... | .... | .... | .... | .... | .... | .... | .... | .... | .... | .... | .... | .... | .... | .... | .... | .... | .... |
| | **NHL Totals** | | **101** | **7** | **21** | **28** | **51** | **6** | **0** | **1** | **125** | **5.6** | | **1** | **0.0** | **15:50** | .... | .... | .... | .... | .... | .... | .... | .... | .... |

OHL First All-Star Team (2003) • Canadian Major Junior First All-Star Team (2003) • Canadian Major Junior Defenseman of the Year (2003)

Traded to **Phoenix** by **Toronto** with Toronto's 2nd round choice (later traded to Nashville - Nashville selected Roman Josi) in 2008 Entry Draft for Yanic Perreault and Phoenix's 5th round choice (Joel Champagne) in 2008 Entry Draft, February 27, 2007. Signed as a free agent by **Ottawa**, July 11, 2008. Signed as a free agent by **St. Louis**, July 31, 2009.

## BELL, Mark

(BEHL, MAHRK)

Center. Shoots left. 6'4", 220 lbs. Born, St. Pauls, Ont., August 5, 1980. Chicago's 1st choice, 8th overall, in 1998 Entry Draft.

| Season | Club | League | GP | G | A | Pts | PIM | PP | SH | GW | S | % | +/- | TF | F% | Min | GP | G | A | Pts | PIM | PP | SH | GW | Min |
|---|---|---|---|---|---|---|---|---|---|---|---|---|---|---|---|---|---|---|---|---|---|---|---|---|---|
| 1995-96 | Stratford Cullitons | OHA-B | 47 | 8 | 15 | 23 | 32 | .... | .... | .... | .... | .... | .... | .... | .... | .... | .... | .... | .... | .... | .... | .... | .... | .... | .... |
| 1996-97 | Ottawa 67's | OHL | 65 | 8 | 12 | 20 | 40 | .... | .... | .... | .... | .... | .... | .... | .... | .... | 24 | 4 | 7 | 11 | 13 | .... | .... | .... | .... |
| 1997-98 | Ottawa 67's | OHL | 55 | 34 | 26 | 60 | 87 | .... | .... | .... | .... | .... | .... | .... | .... | .... | 13 | 6 | 5 | 11 | 14 | .... | .... | .... | .... |
| 1998-99 | Ottawa 67's | OHL | 44 | 29 | 26 | 55 | 69 | .... | .... | .... | .... | .... | .... | .... | .... | .... | 9 | 6 | 5 | 11 | 8 | .... | .... | .... | .... |
| 99-2000 | Ottawa 67's | OHL | 48 | 34 | 38 | 72 | 95 | .... | .... | .... | .... | .... | .... | .... | .... | .... | 2 | 0 | 1 | 1 | 0 | .... | .... | .... | .... |
| **2000-01** | **Chicago** | **NHL** | 13 | 0 | 1 | 1 | 4 | 0 | 0 | 0 | 14 | 0.0 | 0 | 141 | 48.9 | 12:00 | .... | .... | .... | .... | .... | .... | .... | .... | .... |
| | Norfolk Admirals | AHL | 61 | 15 | 27 | 42 | 126 | .... | .... | .... | .... | .... | .... | .... | .... | .... | 9 | 4 | 3 | 7 | 10 | .... | .... | .... | .... |

| | | | Regular Season | | | | | | | | | | | | | | Playoffs | | | | | | | | |
|---|---|---|---|---|---|---|---|---|---|---|---|---|---|---|---|---|---|---|---|---|---|---|---|---|---|
| Season | Club | League | GP | G | A | Pts | PIM | PP | SH | GW | S | % | +/- | TF | F% | Min | GP | G | A | Pts | PIM | PP | SH | GW | Min |
| **2001-02** | **Chicago** | **NHL** | **80** | **12** | **16** | **28** | **124** | **1** | **0** | **1** | **120** | **10.0** | **–6** | **47** | **42.6** | **12:39** | **5** | **0** | **0** | **0** | **8** | **0** | **0** | **0** | **9:18** |
| **2002-03** | **Chicago** | **NHL** | **82** | **14** | **15** | **29** | **113** | **0** | **2** | **0** | **127** | **11.0** | **0** | **377** | **52.5** | **14:04** | .... | .... | .... | .... | .... | .... | .... | .... | .... |
| **2003-04** | **Chicago** | **NHL** | **82** | **21** | **24** | **45** | **106** | **2** | **0** | **1** | **202** | **10.4** | **–14** | **387** | **48.3** | **17:37** | .... | .... | .... | .... | .... | .... | .... | .... | .... |
| 2004-05 | Trondheim IK | Norway | 25 | 10 | 17 | 27 | 87 | .... | .... | .... | .... | .... | .... | .... | .... | .... | 11 | 6 | 6 | 12 | 44 | .... | .... | .... | .... |
| **2005-06** | **Chicago** | **NHL** | **82** | **25** | **23** | **48** | **107** | **11** | **1** | **1** | **227** | **11.0** | **–14** | **1034** | **48.5** | **17:37** | .... | .... | .... | .... | .... | .... | .... | .... | .... |
| **2006-07** | **San Jose** | **NHL** | **71** | **11** | **10** | **21** | **83** | **3** | **0** | **2** | **116** | **9.5** | **–9** | **108** | **48.2** | **12:57** | **4** | **0** | **0** | **0** | **2** | **0** | **0** | **0** | **10:16** |
| **2007-08** | **Toronto** | **NHL** | **35** | **4** | **6** | **10** | **60** | **0** | **0** | **0** | **42** | **9.5** | **–2** | **179** | **41.3** | **9:45** | .... | .... | .... | .... | .... | .... | .... | .... | .... |
| 2008-09 | Toronto Marlies | AHL | 56 | 12 | 15 | 27 | 34 | .... | .... | .... | .... | .... | .... | .... | .... | .... | .... | .... | .... | .... | .... | .... | .... | .... | .... |
| | Hartford | AHL | 18 | 6 | 8 | 14 | 31 | .... | .... | .... | .... | .... | .... | .... | .... | .... | 5 | 1 | 0 | 1 | 4 | .... | .... | .... | .... |
| | **NHL Totals** | | **445** | **87** | **95** | **182** | **597** | **17** | **3** | **5** | **848** | **10.3** | | **2273** | **48.4** | **14:33** | **9** | **0** | **0** | **0** | **10** | **0** | **0** | **0** | **9:44** |

Signed as a free agent by **Trondheim** (Norway), November 6, 2004. Traded to **San Jose** by **Chicago** for Tom Preissing and Josh Hennessy, July 10, 2006. Traded to **Toronto** by **San Jose** with Vesa Toskala for Toronto's 1st (later traded to St. Louis – St. Louis selected Lars Eller) and 2nd (later traded to St. Louis – St. Louis selected Aaron Palushaj) round choices in 2007 Entry Draft and Toronto's 4th round choice (later traded to Nashville – Nashville selected Craig Smith) in 2009 Entry Draft, June 22, 2007. • Suspended by NHL for 15 games for substance abuse violations. • Missed majority of 2007-08 season recovering from facial injury suffered in game at Pittsburgh, January 3, 2008 and resulting surgery. Claimed on waivers by **NY Rangers** from **Toronto**, February 25, 2009.

## BELLE, Shawn
(BEHL, SHAWN) **MTL.**

Defense. Shoots left. 6'1", 233 lbs. Born, Edmonton, Alta., January 3, 1985. St. Louis' 1st choice, 30th overall, in 2003 Entry Draft.

| Season | Club | League | GP | G | A | Pts | PIM | PP | SH | GW | S | % | +/- | TF | F% | Min | GP | G | A | Pts | PIM | PP | SH | GW | Min |
|---|---|---|---|---|---|---|---|---|---|---|---|---|---|---|---|---|---|---|---|---|---|---|---|---|---|
| 99-2000 | K of C Squires | AMBHL | 34 | 7 | 20 | 27 | 36 | .... | .... | .... | .... | .... | .... | .... | .... | .... | .... | .... | .... | .... | .... | .... | .... | .... | .... |
| 2000-01 | K of C Squires | AMBHL | 39 | 18 | 30 | 48 | 69 | .... | .... | .... | .... | .... | .... | .... | .... | .... | .... | .... | .... | .... | .... | .... | .... | .... | .... |
| | Regina Pats | WHL | 4 | 0 | 3 | 3 | 0 | .... | .... | .... | .... | .... | .... | .... | .... | .... | .... | .... | .... | .... | .... | .... | .... | .... | .... |
| | Tri-City | WHL | 2 | 0 | 1 | 1 | 0 | .... | .... | .... | .... | .... | .... | .... | .... | .... | .... | .... | .... | .... | .... | .... | .... | .... | .... |
| 2001-02 | Tri-City | WHL | 64 | 1 | 17 | 18 | 51 | .... | .... | .... | .... | .... | .... | .... | .... | .... | 5 | 2 | 1 | 3 | 2 | .... | .... | .... | .... |
| 2002-03 | Tri-City | WHL | 66 | 7 | 14 | 21 | 79 | .... | .... | .... | .... | .... | .... | .... | .... | .... | .... | .... | .... | .... | .... | .... | .... | .... | .... |
| 2003-04 | Tri-City | WHL | 55 | 9 | 20 | 29 | 68 | .... | .... | .... | .... | .... | .... | .... | .... | .... | 11 | 3 | 5 | 8 | 15 | .... | .... | .... | .... |
| 2004-05 | Tri-City | WHL | 62 | 13 | 32 | 45 | 76 | .... | .... | .... | .... | .... | .... | .... | .... | .... | 5 | 1 | 1 | 2 | 6 | .... | .... | .... | .... |
| 2005-06 | Iowa Stars | AHL | 45 | 1 | 2 | 3 | 63 | .... | .... | .... | .... | .... | .... | .... | .... | .... | .... | .... | .... | .... | .... | .... | .... | .... | .... |
| | Houston Aeros | AHL | 16 | 1 | 1 | 2 | 18 | .... | .... | .... | .... | .... | .... | .... | .... | .... | 8 | 1 | 0 | 1 | 4 | .... | .... | .... | .... |
| **2006-07** | **Minnesota** | **NHL** | **9** | **0** | **1** | **1** | **0** | **0** | **0** | **0** | **3** | **0.0** | **4** | **0** | **0.0** | **9:56** | .... | .... | .... | .... | .... | .... | .... | .... | .... |
| | Houston Aeros | AHL | 57 | 4 | 14 | 18 | 73 | .... | .... | .... | .... | .... | .... | .... | .... | .... | .... | .... | .... | .... | .... | .... | .... | .... | .... |
| 2007-08 | Houston Aeros | AHL | 63 | 1 | 2 | 3 | 74 | .... | .... | .... | .... | .... | .... | .... | .... | .... | 3 | 0 | 0 | 0 | 2 | .... | .... | .... | .... |
| 2008-09 | Hamilton | AHL | 60 | 3 | 10 | 13 | 93 | .... | .... | .... | .... | .... | .... | .... | .... | .... | 6 | 1 | 0 | 1 | 16 | .... | .... | .... | .... |
| | **NHL Totals** | | **9** | **0** | **1** | **1** | **0** | **0** | **0** | **0** | **3** | **0.0** | | **0** | **0.0** | **9:56** | .... | .... | .... | .... | .... | .... | .... | .... | .... |

• Rights traded to **Dallas** by **St. Louis** for Jason Bacashihua, June 25, 2004. Traded to **Minnesota** by **Dallas** with Martin Skoula for Willie Mitchell and Minnesota's 2nd round choice (Nico Sacchetti) in 2007 Entry Draft, March 9, 2006. Traded to **Montreal** by **Minnesota** for Cory Locke, July 11, 2008.

## BENTIVOGLIO, Sean
(behn-tih-VOHG-lee-oh, SHAWN) **NYI**

Left wing. Shoots left. 5'10", 190 lbs. Born, Thorold, Ont., October 16, 1985.

| Season | Club | League | GP | G | A | Pts | PIM | PP | SH | GW | S | % | +/- | TF | F% | Min | GP | G | A | Pts | PIM | PP | SH | GW | Min |
|---|---|---|---|---|---|---|---|---|---|---|---|---|---|---|---|---|---|---|---|---|---|---|---|---|---|
| 2003-04 | Niagara University | CHA | 39 | 2 | 19 | 21 | 14 | .... | .... | .... | .... | .... | .... | .... | .... | .... | .... | .... | .... | .... | .... | .... | .... | .... | .... |
| 2004-05 | Niagara University | CHA | 36 | 9 | 18 | 27 | 20 | .... | .... | .... | .... | .... | .... | .... | .... | .... | .... | .... | .... | .... | .... | .... | .... | .... | .... |
| 2005-06 | Niagara University | CHA | 33 | 16 | 22 | 38 | 55 | .... | .... | .... | .... | .... | .... | .... | .... | .... | .... | .... | .... | .... | .... | .... | .... | .... | .... |
| 2006-07 | Niagara University | CHA | 37 | 16 | 30 | 46 | 53 | .... | .... | .... | .... | .... | .... | .... | .... | .... | .... | .... | .... | .... | .... | .... | .... | .... | .... |
| | Providence Bruins | AHL | 15 | 3 | 11 | 14 | 8 | .... | .... | .... | .... | .... | .... | .... | .... | .... | 13 | 3 | 6 | 9 | 14 | .... | .... | .... | .... |
| 2007-08 | Bridgeport | AHL | 68 | 9 | 23 | 32 | 28 | .... | .... | .... | .... | .... | .... | .... | .... | .... | .... | .... | .... | .... | .... | .... | .... | .... | .... |
| **2008-09** | **NY Islanders** | **NHL** | **1** | **0** | **0** | **0** | **2** | **0** | **0** | **0** | **2** | **0.0** | **0** | **1** | **0.0** | **11:31** | .... | .... | .... | .... | .... | .... | .... | .... | .... |
| | Bridgeport | AHL | 78 | 13 | 19 | 32 | 47 | .... | .... | .... | .... | .... | .... | .... | .... | .... | 4 | 1 | 1 | 2 | 4 | .... | .... | .... | .... |
| | **NHL Totals** | | **1** | **0** | **0** | **0** | **2** | **0** | **0** | **0** | **2** | **0.0** | | **1** | **0.0** | **11:31** | .... | .... | .... | .... | .... | .... | .... | .... | .... |

Signed as a free agent by **NY Islanders**, May 19, 2007.

## BERARD, Bryan
(buh-RAHRD, BRIGH-uhn)

Defense. Shoots left. 6'2", 220 lbs. Born, Woonsocket, RI, March 5, 1977. Ottawa's 1st choice, 1st overall, in 1995 Entry Draft.

| Season | Club | League | GP | G | A | Pts | PIM | PP | SH | GW | S | % | +/- | TF | F% | Min | GP | G | A | Pts | PIM | PP | SH | GW | Min |
|---|---|---|---|---|---|---|---|---|---|---|---|---|---|---|---|---|---|---|---|---|---|---|---|---|---|
| 1991-92 | Mount St. Charles | High-RI | 15 | 3 | 15 | 18 | 4 | .... | .... | .... | .... | .... | .... | .... | .... | .... | .... | .... | .... | .... | .... | .... | .... | .... | .... |
| 1992-93 | Mount St. Charles | High-RI | 15 | 8 | 12 | 20 | 18 | .... | .... | .... | .... | .... | .... | .... | .... | .... | .... | .... | .... | .... | .... | .... | .... | .... | .... |
| 1993-94 | Mount St. Charles | High-RI | 15 | 11 | 26 | 37 | 4.5 | .... | .... | .... | .... | .... | .... | .... | .... | .... | 4 | 3 | 3 | 6 | 6 | .... | .... | .... | .... |
| 1994-95 | Detroit | OHL | 58 | 20 | 55 | 75 | 97 | .... | .... | .... | .... | .... | .... | .... | .... | .... | 21 | 4 | 20 | 24 | 38 | .... | .... | .... | .... |
| 1995-96 | Detroit | OHL | 56 | 31 | 58 | 89 | 116 | .... | .... | .... | .... | .... | .... | .... | .... | .... | 17 | 7 | 18 | 25 | 41 | .... | .... | .... | .... |
| **1996-97** | **NY Islanders** | **NHL** | **82** | **8** | **40** | **48** | **86** | **3** | **0** | **1** | **172** | **4.7** | **1** | .... | .... | .... | .... | .... | .... | .... | .... | .... | .... | .... | .... |
| **1997-98** | **NY Islanders** | **NHL** | **75** | **14** | **32** | **46** | **59** | **8** | **1** | **2** | **192** | **7.3** | **–32** | .... | .... | .... | .... | .... | .... | .... | .... | .... | .... | .... | .... |
| | United States | Olympics | 2 | 0 | 0 | 0 | 0 | .... | .... | .... | .... | .... | .... | .... | .... | .... | .... | .... | .... | .... | .... | .... | .... | .... | .... |
| **1998-99** | **NY Islanders** | **NHL** | **31** | **4** | **11** | **15** | **26** | **2** | **0** | **3** | **72** | **5.6** | **–6** | **0** | **0.0** | **24:45** | .... | .... | .... | .... | .... | .... | .... | .... | .... |
| | **Toronto** | **NHL** | **38** | **5** | **14** | **19** | **22** | **2** | **0** | **2** | **63** | **7.9** | **7** | **0** | **0.0** | **22:38** | **17** | **1** | **8** | **9** | **8** | **1** | **0** | **0** | **21:11** |
| **99-2000** | **Toronto** | **NHL** | **64** | **3** | **27** | **30** | **42** | **1** | **0** | **0** | **98** | **3.1** | **11** | **0** | **0.0** | **19:34** | .... | .... | .... | .... | .... | .... | .... | .... | .... |
| **2000-01** | **Toronto** | **NHL** | DID NOT PLAY – INJURED | | | | | | | | | | | | | | | | | | | | | | |
| **2001-02** | **NY Rangers** | **NHL** | **82** | **2** | **21** | **23** | **60** | **0** | **0** | **0** | **132** | **1.5** | **–1** | **0** | **0.0** | **19:38** | .... | .... | .... | .... | .... | .... | .... | .... | .... |
| **2002-03** | **Boston** | **NHL** | **80** | **10** | **28** | **38** | **64** | **4** | **0** | **1** | **205** | **4.9** | **–4** | **0** | **0.0** | **21:21** | **3** | **1** | **0** | **1** | **2** | **0** | **0** | **0** | **21:50** |
| **2003-04** | **Chicago** | **NHL** | **58** | **13** | **34** | **47** | **53** | **6** | **0** | **0** | **203** | **6.4** | **–24** | **0** | **0.0** | **21:46** | .... | .... | .... | .... | .... | .... | .... | .... | .... |
| 2004-05 | | | DID NOT PLAY | | | | | | | | | | | | | | | | | | | | | | |
| **2005-06** | **Columbus** | **NHL** | **44** | **12** | **20** | **32** | **32** | **11** | **0** | **2** | **126** | **9.5** | **–29** | **0** | **0.0** | **22:40** | .... | .... | .... | .... | .... | .... | .... | .... | .... |
| **2006-07** | **Columbus** | **NHL** | **11** | **0** | **3** | **3** | **8** | **0** | **0** | **0** | **22** | **0.0** | **–4** | **0** | **0.0** | **18:58** | .... | .... | .... | .... | .... | .... | .... | .... | .... |
| **2007-08** | **NY Islanders** | **NHL** | **54** | **5** | **17** | **22** | **48** | **4** | **0** | **2** | **87** | **5.7** | **–17** | **0** | **0.0** | **17:38** | .... | .... | .... | .... | .... | .... | .... | .... | .... |
| 2008-09 | Vityaz Chekhov | Rus-KHL | 25 | 3 | 14 | 17 | 103 | .... | .... | .... | .... | .... | .... | .... | .... | .... | .... | .... | .... | .... | .... | .... | .... | .... | .... |
| | **NHL Totals** | | **619** | **76** | **247** | **323** | **500** | **41** | **1** | **13** | **1372** | **5.5** | | **0** | **0.0** | **20:49** | **20** | **2** | **8** | **10** | **10** | **1** | **0** | **0** | **21:17** |

OHL All-Rookie Team (1995) • OHL First All-Star Team (1995, 1996) • OHL Rookie of the Year (1995) • Canadian Major Junior First All-Star Team (1995, 1996) • Canadian Major Junior Rookie of the Year (1995) • Canadian Major Junior Defenseman of the Year (1996) • NHL All-Rookie Team (1997) • Calder Memorial Trophy (1997) • Bill Masterton Memorial Trophy (2004)

Traded to **NY Islanders** by **Ottawa** with Don Beaupre and Martin Straka for Damian Rhodes and Wade Redden, January 23, 1996. Traded to **Toronto** by **NY Islanders** with NY Islanders' 6th round choice (Jan Sochor) in 1999 Entry Draft for Felix Potvin and Toronto's 6th round choice (later traded to Tampa Bay – Tampa Bay selected Fedor Fedorov) in 1999 Entry Draft, January 9, 1999. • Missed remainder of 1999-2000 season and entire 2000-01 season recovering from eye injury suffered in game vs. Ottawa, March 11, 2000. Signed as a free agent by **NY Rangers**, October 5, 2001. Signed as a free agent by **Boston**, August 13, 2002. Signed as a free agent by **Chicago**, October 31, 2003. Signed as a free agent by **Columbus**, August 3, 2005. • Missed majority of 2006-07 season due to recurring back injury. Signed as a free agent by **NY Islanders**, October 9, 2007. Signed as a free agent by **Vityaz Chekhov** (Rus-KHL), November 16, 2008.

## BERGENHEIM, Sean
(BUHR-gehn-highm, SHAWN) **NYI**

Left wing. Shoots left. 5'10", 205 lbs. Born, Helsinki, Finland, February 8, 1984. NY Islanders' 1st choice, 22nd overall, in 2002 Entry Draft.

| Season | Club | League | GP | G | A | Pts | PIM | PP | SH | GW | S | % | +/- | TF | F% | Min | GP | G | A | Pts | PIM | PP | SH | GW | Min |
|---|---|---|---|---|---|---|---|---|---|---|---|---|---|---|---|---|---|---|---|---|---|---|---|---|---|
| 99-2000 | Jokerit U18 | Fin-U18 | 30 | 22 | 11 | 33 | 34 | .... | .... | .... | .... | .... | .... | .... | .... | .... | 3 | 1 | 0 | 1 | 0 | .... | .... | .... | .... |
| | Jokerit U18 | Fin-U18 | 17 | 10 | 8 | 18 | 14 | .... | .... | .... | .... | .... | .... | .... | .... | .... | 3 | 1 | 0 | 1 | 2 | .... | .... | .... | .... |
| 2000-01 | Jokerit U18 | Fin-U18 | 1 | 1 | 0 | 1 | 4 | .... | .... | .... | .... | .... | .... | .... | .... | .... | 6 | 9 | 5 | 14 | 8 | .... | .... | .... | .... |
| | Jokerit Helsinki Jr. | Fin-Jr. | 18 | 6 | 4 | 10 | 26 | .... | .... | .... | .... | .... | .... | .... | .... | .... | 2 | 0 | 0 | 0 | 4 | .... | .... | .... | .... |
| 2001-02 | Jokerit U18 | Fin-U18 | .... | .... | .... | .... | .... | .... | .... | .... | .... | .... | .... | .... | .... | .... | 5 | 6 | 2 | 8 | 18 | .... | .... | .... | .... |
| | Jokerit Helsinki Jr. | Fin-Jr. | 23 | 11 | 19 | 30 | 36 | .... | .... | .... | .... | .... | .... | .... | .... | .... | 1 | 0 | 0 | 0 | 2 | .... | .... | .... | .... |
| | Kiekko-Vantaa | Finland-2 | 4 | 0 | 0 | 0 | 52 | .... | .... | .... | .... | .... | .... | .... | .... | .... | .... | .... | .... | .... | .... | .... | .... | .... | .... |
| | Jokerit Helsinki | Finland | 28 | 2 | 2 | 4 | 4 | .... | .... | .... | .... | .... | .... | .... | .... | .... | .... | .... | .... | .... | .... | .... | .... | .... | .... |
| 2002-03 | Jokerit Helsinki Jr. | Fin-Jr. | 2 | 3 | 0 | 3 | 2 | .... | .... | .... | .... | .... | .... | .... | .... | .... | .... | .... | .... | .... | .... | .... | .... | .... | .... |
| | Jokerit Helsinki | Finland | 38 | 3 | 3 | 6 | 4 | .... | .... | .... | .... | .... | .... | .... | .... | .... | 2 | 0 | 0 | 0 | 0 | .... | .... | .... | .... |
| **2003-04** | **NY Islanders** | **NHL** | **18** | **1** | **1** | **2** | **4** | **0** | **1** | **0** | **12** | **8.3** | **–4** | **2** | **50.0** | **8:55** | .... | .... | .... | .... | .... | .... | .... | .... | .... |
| | Jokerit Helsinki | Finland | 20 | 2 | 2 | 4 | 18 | .... | .... | .... | .... | .... | .... | .... | .... | .... | 3 | 1 | 1 | 2 | 0 | .... | .... | .... | .... |
| | Bridgeport | AHL | .... | .... | .... | .... | .... | .... | .... | .... | .... | .... | .... | .... | .... | .... | 7 | 2 | 3 | 5 | 10 | .... | .... | .... | .... |
| 2004-05 | Bridgeport | AHL | 61 | 15 | 14 | 29 | 69 | .... | .... | .... | .... | .... | .... | .... | .... | .... | .... | .... | .... | .... | .... | .... | .... | .... | .... |
| **2005-06** | **NY Islanders** | **NHL** | **28** | **4** | **5** | **9** | **20** | **0** | **0** | **1** | **63** | **6.3** | **–11** | **14** | **28.6** | **13:17** | .... | .... | .... | .... | .... | .... | .... | .... | .... |
| | Bridgeport | AHL | 55 | 25 | 22 | 47 | 112 | .... | .... | .... | .... | .... | .... | .... | .... | .... | 7 | 0 | 2 | 2 | 24 | .... | .... | .... | .... |
| 2006-07 | Yaroslavl | Russia | 9 | 1 | 4 | 5 | 26 | .... | .... | .... | .... | .... | .... | .... | .... | .... | .... | .... | .... | .... | .... | .... | .... | .... | .... |
| | Frolunda | Sweden | 36 | 16 | 17 | 33 | 80 | .... | .... | .... | .... | .... | .... | .... | .... | .... | .... | .... | .... | .... | .... | .... | .... | .... | .... |
| **2007-08** | **NY Islanders** | **NHL** | **78** | **10** | **12** | **22** | **62** | **1** | **0** | **1** | **155** | **6.5** | **–3** | **15** | **60.0** | **11:15** | .... | .... | .... | .... | .... | .... | .... | .... | .... |
| **2008-09** | **NY Islanders** | **NHL** | **59** | **15** | **9** | **24** | **64** | **0** | **4** | **5** | **152** | **9.9** | **–2** | **22** | **40.9** | **14:15** | .... | .... | .... | .... | .... | .... | .... | .... | .... |
| | **NHL Totals** | | **183** | **30** | **27** | **57** | **150** | **1** | **5** | **7** | **382** | **7.9** | | **53** | **43.4** | **12:18** | .... | .... | .... | .... | .... | .... | .... | .... | .... |

Signed as a free agent by **Yaroslavl** (Russia), August 5, 2006. Signed as a free agent by **Frolunda** (Sweden), November 3, 2006.

## BERGERON, Marc-Andre

(BAIR-zhur-uhn, MAHRK-AWN-dray)

Defense. Shoots left. 5'9", 198 lbs. Born, St-Louis-de-France, Que., October 13, 1980.

| | | | Regular Season | | | | | | | | | | | | | | Playoffs | | | | | | | | |
|---|---|---|---|---|---|---|---|---|---|---|---|---|---|---|---|---|---|---|---|---|---|---|---|---|---|
| Season | Club | League | GP | G | A | Pts | PIM | PP | SH | GW | S | % | +/- | TF | F% | Min | GP | G | A | Pts | PIM | PP | SH | GW | Min |
| 1996-97 | Cap-d-Madeleine | QAAA | 4 | 0 | 1 | 1 | 0 | .... | .... | .... | .... | .... | .... | .... | .... | .... | 2 | 0 | 0 | 0 | 0 | .... | .... | .... | .... |
| 1997-98 | Baie-Comeau | QMJHL | 40 | 6 | 14 | 20 | 48 | .... | .... | .... | .... | .... | .... | .... | .... | .... | .... | .... | .... | .... | .... | .... | .... | .... | .... |
| 1998-99 | Baie-Comeau | QMJHL | 46 | 8 | 14 | 22 | 57 | .... | .... | .... | .... | .... | .... | .... | .... | .... | .... | .... | .... | .... | .... | .... | .... | .... | .... |
| | Shawinigan | QMJHL | 24 | 6 | 7 | 13 | 66 | .... | .... | .... | .... | .... | .... | .... | .... | .... | 5 | 2 | 2 | 4 | 24 | .... | .... | .... | .... |
| 99-2000 | Shawinigan | QMJHL | 70 | 24 | 50 | 74 | 173 | .... | .... | .... | .... | .... | .... | .... | .... | .... | 13 | 4 | 7 | 11 | 45 | .... | .... | .... | .... |
| 2000-01 | Shawinigan | QMJHL | 69 | 42 | 59 | 101 | 185 | .... | .... | .... | .... | .... | .... | .... | .... | .... | 10 | 4 | 11 | 15 | 24 | .... | .... | .... | .... |
| 2001-02 | Hamilton | AHL | 50 | 2 | 13 | 15 | 61 | .... | .... | .... | .... | .... | .... | .... | .... | .... | 9 | 1 | 4 | 5 | 8 | .... | .... | .... | .... |
| **2002-03** | **Edmonton** | **NHL** | **5** | **1** | **1** | **2** | **9** | **0** | **0** | **0** | **5** | **20.0** | **2** | **0** | **0.0** | **16:30** | **1** | **0** | **1** | **1** | **0** | **0** | **0** | **0** | **19:20** |
| | Hamilton | AHL | 66 | 8 | 31 | 39 | 73 | .... | .... | .... | .... | .... | .... | .... | .... | .... | 20 | 0 | 7 | 7 | 25 | .... | .... | .... | .... |
| **2003-04** | **Edmonton** | **NHL** | **54** | **9** | **17** | **26** | **26** | **3** | **0** | **0** | **105** | **8.6** | **13** | **0** | **0.0** | **17:39** | .... | .... | .... | .... | .... | .... | .... | .... | .... |
| | Toronto | AHL | 17 | 4 | 3 | 7 | 23 | .... | .... | .... | .... | .... | .... | .... | .... | .... | .... | .... | .... | .... | .... | .... | .... | .... | .... |
| 2004-05 | Brynas IF Gavle | Sweden | 10 | 3 | 2 | 5 | 72 | .... | .... | .... | .... | .... | .... | .... | .... | .... | .... | .... | .... | .... | .... | .... | .... | .... | .... |
| | Brynas IF Gavle | Sweden-Q | 9 | 1 | 2 | 3 | 8 | .... | .... | .... | .... | .... | .... | .... | .... | .... | .... | .... | .... | .... | .... | .... | .... | .... | .... |
| **2005-06** | **Edmonton** | **NHL** | **75** | **15** | **20** | **35** | **38** | **8** | **0** | **1** | **144** | **10.4** | **3** | **0** | **0.0** | **21:14** | **18** | **2** | **1** | **3** | **14** | **2** | **0** | **0** | **14:56** |
| **2006-07** | **Edmonton** | **NHL** | **55** | **8** | **17** | **25** | **28** | **6** | **0** | **3** | **111** | **7.2** | **-9** | **0** | **0.0** | **17:27** | .... | .... | .... | .... | .... | .... | .... | .... | .... |
| | **NY Islanders** | **NHL** | **23** | **6** | **15** | **21** | **10** | **4** | **0** | **1** | **55** | **10.9** | **5** | **0** | **0.0** | **23:07** | **5** | **1** | **1** | **2** | **6** | **1** | **0** | **1** | **27:21** |
| **2007-08** | **NY Islanders** | **NHL** | **46** | **9** | **9** | **18** | **16** | **8** | **0** | **1** | **96** | **9.4** | **-14** | **0** | **0.0** | **18:17** | .... | .... | .... | .... | .... | .... | .... | .... | .... |
| | **Anaheim** | **NHL** | **9** | **0** | **1** | **1** | **4** | **0** | **0** | **0** | **12** | **0.0** | **-2** | **0** | **0.0** | **12:50** | .... | .... | .... | .... | .... | .... | .... | .... | .... |
| **2008-09** | **Minnesota** | **NHL** | **72** | **14** | **18** | **32** | **30** | **7** | **0** | **3** | **140** | **10.0** | **5** | **0** | **0.0** | **16:54** | .... | .... | .... | .... | .... | .... | .... | .... | .... |
| | **NHL Totals** | | **339** | **62** | **98** | **160** | **161** | **36** | **0** | **9** | **668** | **9.3** | | **0** | **0.0** | **18:34** | **24** | **3** | **3** | **6** | **20** | **3** | **0** | **1** | **17:42** |

QMJHL First All-Star Team (2001) • Canadian Major Junior First All-Star Team (2001) • Canadian Major Junior Defenseman of the Year (2001) • AHL Second All-Star Team (2003)

Signed as a free agent by **Edmonton**, July 20, 2001. Signed as a free agent by **Gavle** (Sweden), January 23, 2005. Traded to **NY Islanders** by **Edmonton** with Edmonton's 3rd round choice (later traded back to Edmonton - later traded to Anaheim - later traded back to NY Islanders - NY Islanders selected Kirill Petrov) in 2008 Entry Draft for Denis Grebeshkov, February 18, 2007. Traded to **Anaheim** by **NY Islanders** for Edmonton's 3rd round choice (previously acquired, NY Islanders selected Kirill Petrov) in 2008 Entry Draft, February 26, 2008. Traded to **Minnesota** by **Anaheim** for Minnesota's 3rd round choice (Brandon McMillan) in 2008 Entry Draft, June 10, 2008.

## BERGERON, Patrice

(BUHR-zhuhr-uhn, pa-TREEC) **BOS.**

Center. Shoots right. 6'2", 194 lbs. Born, Ancienne-Lorette, Que., July 24, 1985. Boston's 2nd choice, 45th overall, in 2003 Entry Draft.

| | | | Regular Season | | | | | | | | | | | | | | Playoffs | | | | | | | | |
|---|---|---|---|---|---|---|---|---|---|---|---|---|---|---|---|---|---|---|---|---|---|---|---|---|---|
| Season | Club | League | GP | G | A | Pts | PIM | PP | SH | GW | S | % | +/- | TF | F% | Min | GP | G | A | Pts | PIM | PP | SH | GW | Min |
| 2000-01 | Ste-Foy | QAAA | 5 | 1 | 2 | 3 | 0 | .... | .... | .... | .... | .... | .... | .... | .... | .... | .... | .... | .... | .... | .... | .... | .... | .... | .... |
| 2001-02 | St-Francois | QAAA | 38 | 25 | 37 | 62 | 18 | .... | .... | .... | .... | .... | .... | .... | .... | .... | 8 | 6 | 4 | 10 | 10 | .... | .... | .... | .... |
| | Acadie-Bathurst | QMJHL | 4 | 0 | 1 | 1 | 0 | .... | .... | .... | .... | .... | .... | .... | .... | .... | .... | .... | .... | .... | .... | .... | .... | .... | .... |
| 2002-03 | Acadie-Bathurst | QMJHL | 70 | 23 | 50 | 73 | 62 | .... | .... | .... | .... | .... | .... | .... | .... | .... | 11 | 6 | 9 | 15 | 6 | .... | .... | .... | .... |
| **2003-04** | **Boston** | **NHL** | **71** | **16** | **23** | **39** | **22** | **7** | **0** | **2** | **133** | **12.0** | **5** | **699** | **49.4** | **16:21** | **7** | **1** | **3** | **4** | **0** | **0** | **0** | **1** | **17:13** |
| 2004-05 | Providence Bruins | AHL | 68 | 21 | 40 | 61 | 59 | .... | .... | .... | .... | .... | .... | .... | .... | .... | 16 | 5 | 7 | 12 | 4 | .... | .... | .... | .... |
| **2005-06** | **Boston** | **NHL** | **81** | **31** | **42** | **73** | **22** | **12** | **1** | **6** | **310** | **10.0** | **3** | **1447** | **54.7** | **20:36** | .... | .... | .... | .... | .... | .... | .... | .... | .... |
| **2006-07** | **Boston** | **NHL** | **77** | **22** | **48** | **70** | **26** | **14** | **0** | **6** | **224** | **9.8** | **-28** | **1560** | **51.2** | **20:49** | .... | .... | .... | .... | .... | .... | .... | .... | .... |
| **2007-08** | **Boston** | **NHL** | **10** | **3** | **4** | **7** | **2** | **2** | **0** | **0** | **24** | **12.5** | **2** | **175** | **50.3** | **18:10** | .... | .... | .... | .... | .... | .... | .... | .... | .... |
| **2008-09** | **Boston** | **NHL** | **64** | **8** | **31** | **39** | **16** | **1** | **1** | **1** | **155** | **5.2** | **2** | **1025** | **54.5** | **17:59** | **11** | **0** | **5** | **5** | **11** | **0** | **0** | **0** | **17:56** |
| | **NHL Totals** | | **303** | **80** | **148** | **228** | **88** | **36** | **2** | **15** | **846** | **9.5** | | **4906** | **52.6** | **19:01** | **18** | **1** | **8** | **9** | **11** | **0** | **0** | **1** | **17:39** |

QAAA Second All-Star Team (2002)

• Missed majority of 2007-08 season recovering from concussion suffered in game vs. Philadelphia, October 27, 2007.

## BERGFORS, Nicklas

(BUHRG-fohrs, NIHK-luhs) **N.J.**

Right wing. Shoots right. 5'11", 195 lbs. Born, Sodertalje, Sweden, March 7, 1987. New Jersey's 1st choice, 23rd overall, in 2005 Entry Draft.

| | | | Regular Season | | | | | | | | | | | | | | Playoffs | | | | | | | | |
|---|---|---|---|---|---|---|---|---|---|---|---|---|---|---|---|---|---|---|---|---|---|---|---|---|---|
| Season | Club | League | GP | G | A | Pts | PIM | PP | SH | GW | S | % | +/- | TF | F% | Min | GP | G | A | Pts | PIM | PP | SH | GW | Min |
| 2002-03 | Sodertalje SK U18 | Swe-U18 | 4 | 4 | 4 | 8 | 0 | .... | .... | .... | .... | .... | .... | .... | .... | .... | .... | .... | .... | .... | .... | .... | .... | .... | .... |
| | Sodertalje SK Jr. | Swe-Jr. | 13 | 1 | 5 | 6 | 4 | .... | .... | .... | .... | .... | .... | .... | .... | .... | .... | .... | .... | .... | .... | .... | .... | .... | .... |
| 2003-04 | Sodertalje SK U18 | Swe-U18 | 5 | 14 | 4 | 18 | 4 | .... | .... | .... | .... | .... | .... | .... | .... | .... | 2 | 0 | 1 | 1 | 6 | .... | .... | .... | .... |
| | Sodertalje SK Jr. | Swe-Jr. | 31 | 13 | 17 | 30 | 22 | .... | .... | .... | .... | .... | .... | .... | .... | .... | 2 | 1 | 1 | 2 | 0 | .... | .... | .... | .... |
| 2004-05 | Sodertalje SK Jr. | Swe-Jr. | 21 | 18 | 16 | 34 | 25 | .... | .... | .... | .... | .... | .... | .... | .... | .... | 3 | 0 | 3 | 3 | 4 | .... | .... | .... | .... |
| | Sodertalje SK | Sweden | 25 | 1 | 0 | 1 | 2 | .... | .... | .... | .... | .... | .... | .... | .... | .... | 2 | 0 | 0 | 0 | 0 | .... | .... | .... | .... |
| 2005-06 | Albany River Rats | AHL | 65 | 17 | 23 | 40 | 10 | .... | .... | .... | .... | .... | .... | .... | .... | .... | .... | .... | .... | .... | .... | .... | .... | .... | .... |
| 2006-07 | Lowell Devils | AHL | 60 | 13 | 19 | 32 | 8 | .... | .... | .... | .... | .... | .... | .... | .... | .... | .... | .... | .... | .... | .... | .... | .... | .... | .... |
| **2007-08** | **New Jersey** | **NHL** | **1** | **0** | **0** | **0** | **0** | **0** | **0** | **0** | **3** | **0.0** | **-1** | **1** | **0.0** | **11:17** | .... | .... | .... | .... | .... | .... | .... | .... | .... |
| | Lowell Devils | AHL | 66 | 12 | 15 | 27 | 22 | .... | .... | .... | .... | .... | .... | .... | .... | .... | .... | .... | .... | .... | .... | .... | .... | .... | .... |
| **2008-09** | **New Jersey** | **NHL** | **8** | **1** | **0** | **1** | **0** | **0** | **0** | **0** | **6** | **16.7** | **-1** | **0** | **0.0** | **5:48** | .... | .... | .... | .... | .... | .... | .... | .... | .... |
| | Lowell Devils | AHL | 66 | 22 | 29 | 51 | 14 | .... | .... | .... | .... | .... | .... | .... | .... | .... | .... | .... | .... | .... | .... | .... | .... | .... | .... |
| | **NHL Totals** | | **9** | **1** | **0** | **1** | **0** | **0** | **0** | **0** | **9** | **11.1** | | **1** | **0.0** | **6:24** | .... | .... | .... | .... | .... | .... | .... | .... | .... |

## BERGLUND, Patrik

(BUHRG-luhnd, PAT-rihk) **ST.L.**

Center. Shoots left. 6'3", 211 lbs. Born, Vasteras, Sweden, June 2, 1988. St. Louis' 2nd choice, 25th overall, in 2006 Entry Draft.

| | | | Regular Season | | | | | | | | | | | | | | Playoffs | | | | | | | | |
|---|---|---|---|---|---|---|---|---|---|---|---|---|---|---|---|---|---|---|---|---|---|---|---|---|---|
| Season | Club | League | GP | G | A | Pts | PIM | PP | SH | GW | S | % | +/- | TF | F% | Min | GP | G | A | Pts | PIM | PP | SH | GW | Min |
| 2002-03 | Vasteras U18 | Swe-U18 | 1 | 0 | 1 | 1 | 0 | .... | .... | .... | .... | .... | .... | .... | .... | .... | .... | .... | .... | .... | .... | .... | .... | .... | .... |
| 2003-04 | Vasteras U18 | Swe-U18 | 10 | 4 | 1 | 5 | 18 | .... | .... | .... | .... | .... | .... | .... | .... | .... | .... | .... | .... | .... | .... | .... | .... | .... | .... |
| 2004-05 | Vasteras U18 | Swe-U18 | 5 | 2 | 1 | 3 | 4 | .... | .... | .... | .... | .... | .... | .... | .... | .... | 3 | 0 | 1 | 1 | 6 | .... | .... | .... | .... |
| | Vasteras Jr. | Swe-Jr. | 25 | 5 | 5 | 10 | 14 | .... | .... | .... | .... | .... | .... | .... | .... | .... | .... | .... | .... | .... | .... | .... | .... | .... | .... |
| 2005-06 | Vasteras Jr. | Swe-Jr. | 27 | 17 | 12 | 29 | 38 | .... | .... | .... | .... | .... | .... | .... | .... | .... | .... | .... | .... | .... | .... | .... | .... | .... | .... |
| | VIK Vasteras HK | Sweden-2 | 21 | 3 | 1 | 4 | 4 | .... | .... | .... | .... | .... | .... | .... | .... | .... | .... | .... | .... | .... | .... | .... | .... | .... | .... |
| 2006-07 | VIK Vasteras HK | Sweden-2 | 35 | 21 | 27 | 48 | 30 | .... | .... | .... | .... | .... | .... | .... | .... | .... | 1 | 0 | 0 | 0 | 2 | .... | .... | .... | .... |
| | Vasteras Jr. | Swe-Jr. | .... | .... | .... | .... | .... | .... | .... | .... | .... | .... | .... | .... | .... | .... | 5 | 4 | 5 | 9 | 6 | .... | .... | .... | .... |
| 2007-08 | VIK Vasteras HK | Sweden-2 | 46 | 22 | 32 | 54 | 26 | .... | .... | .... | .... | .... | .... | .... | .... | .... | 5 | 1 | 2 | 3 | 6 | .... | .... | .... | .... |
| **2008-09** | **St. Louis** | **NHL** | **76** | **21** | **26** | **47** | **16** | **7** | **0** | **1** | **143** | **14.7** | **19** | **540** | **39.8** | **14:43** | **4** | **0** | **0** | **0** | **2** | **0** | **0** | **0** | **10:11** |
| | **NHL Totals** | | **76** | **21** | **26** | **47** | **16** | **7** | **0** | **1** | **143** | **14.7** | | **540** | **39.8** | **14:43** | **4** | **0** | **0** | **0** | **2** | **0** | **0** | **0** | **10:11** |

NHL All-Rookie Team (2009)

## BERNIER, Steve

(BAIRN-yay, STEEV) **VAN.**

Right wing. Shoots right. 6'2", 225 lbs. Born, Quebec City, Que., March 31, 1985. San Jose's 2nd choice, 16th overall, in 2003 Entry Draft.

| | | | Regular Season | | | | | | | | | | | | | | Playoffs | | | | | | | | |
|---|---|---|---|---|---|---|---|---|---|---|---|---|---|---|---|---|---|---|---|---|---|---|---|---|---|
| Season | Club | League | GP | G | A | Pts | PIM | PP | SH | GW | S | % | +/- | TF | F% | Min | GP | G | A | Pts | PIM | PP | SH | GW | Min |
| 1998-99 | Quebec AA Aces | QAHA | 28 | 33 | 23 | 56 | 24 | .... | .... | .... | .... | .... | .... | .... | .... | .... | .... | .... | .... | .... | .... | .... | .... | .... | .... |
| 99-2000 | Quebec AA Aces | QAHA | 26 | 12 | 23 | 35 | 42 | .... | .... | .... | .... | .... | .... | .... | .... | .... | .... | .... | .... | .... | .... | .... | .... | .... | .... |
| 2000-01 | Ste-Foy | QAAA | 39 | 17 | 35 | 52 | 48 | .... | .... | .... | .... | .... | .... | .... | .... | .... | 16 | 9 | 17 | 26 | 8 | .... | .... | .... | .... |
| 2001-02 | Moncton Wildcats | QMJHL | 66 | 31 | 28 | 59 | 51 | .... | .... | .... | .... | .... | .... | .... | .... | .... | .... | .... | .... | .... | .... | .... | .... | .... | .... |
| 2002-03 | Moncton Wildcats | QMJHL | 71 | 49 | 52 | 101 | 90 | .... | .... | .... | .... | .... | .... | .... | .... | .... | 2 | 1 | 0 | 1 | 2 | .... | .... | .... | .... |
| 2003-04 | Moncton Wildcats | QMJHL | 66 | 36 | 46 | 82 | 80 | .... | .... | .... | .... | .... | .... | .... | .... | .... | 20 | 7 | 10 | 17 | 17 | .... | .... | .... | .... |
| 2004-05 | Moncton Wildcats | QMJHL | 68 | 35 | 36 | 71 | 114 | .... | .... | .... | .... | .... | .... | .... | .... | .... | 12 | 6 | 13 | 19 | 22 | .... | .... | .... | .... |
| **2005-06** | **San Jose** | **NHL** | **39** | **14** | **13** | **27** | **35** | **2** | **1** | **1** | **75** | **18.7** | **4** | **8** | **62.5** | **14:08** | **11** | **1** | **5** | **6** | **8** | **1** | **0** | **1** | **15:17** |
| | Cleveland Barons | AHL | 49 | 20 | 23 | 43 | 33 | .... | .... | .... | .... | .... | .... | .... | .... | .... | .... | .... | .... | .... | .... | .... | .... | .... | .... |
| **2006-07** | **San Jose** | **NHL** | **62** | **15** | **16** | **31** | **29** | **6** | **0** | **4** | **104** | **14.4** | **5** | **18** | **27.8** | **13:35** | **11** | **0** | **1** | **1** | **2** | **0** | **0** | **0** | **10:39** |
| | Worcester Sharks | AHL | 10 | 3 | 4 | 7 | 2 | .... | .... | .... | .... | .... | .... | .... | .... | .... | .... | .... | .... | .... | .... | .... | .... | .... | .... |
| **2007-08** | **San Jose** | **NHL** | **59** | **13** | **10** | **23** | **62** | **4** | **0** | **0** | **96** | **13.5** | **-2** | **10** | **50.0** | **13:07** | .... | .... | .... | .... | .... | .... | .... | .... | .... |
| | **Buffalo** | **NHL** | **17** | **3** | **6** | **9** | **2** | **0** | **0** | **0** | **35** | **8.6** | **1** | **5** | **20.0** | **14:06** | .... | .... | .... | .... | .... | .... | .... | .... | .... |
| **2008-09** | **Vancouver** | **NHL** | **81** | **15** | **17** | **32** | **27** | **2** | **0** | **4** | **137** | **10.9** | **4** | **21** | **23.8** | **13:50** | **10** | **2** | **2** | **4** | **7** | **2** | **0** | **2** | **15:00** |
| | **NHL Totals** | | **258** | **60** | **62** | **122** | **155** | **14** | **1** | **9** | **447** | **13.4** | | **62** | **33.9** | **13:40** | **32** | **3** | **8** | **11** | **17** | **3** | **0** | **3** | **13:36** |

QMJHL All-Rookie Team (2002) • QMJHL Second All-Star Team (2003, 2004) • Canadian Major Junior Second All-Star Team (2003)

Traded to **Buffalo** by **San Jose** with San Jose's 1st round choice (Tyler Ennis) in 2008 Entry Draft for Brian Campbell and Buffalo's 7th round choice (Drew Daniels) in 2008 Entry Draft, February 26, 2008. Traded to **Vancouver** by **Buffalo** for Los Angeles' 3rd round choice (previously acquired, Buffalo selected Brayden McNabb) in 2009 Entry Draft and Vancouver's 2nd round choice in 2010 Entry Draft, July 4, 2008.

| | | | Regular Season | | | | | | | | | | | | | | Playoffs | | | | | | | | |
|---|---|---|---|---|---|---|---|---|---|---|---|---|---|---|---|---|---|---|---|---|---|---|---|---|---|
| Season | Club | League | GP | G | A | Pts | PIM | PP | SH | GW | S | % | +/- | TF | F% | Min | GP | G | A | Pts | PIM | PP | SH | GW | Min |

## BERTI, Adam

(BUHR-tee, A-duhm)

Left wing. Shoots left. 6'3", 198 lbs. Born, Scarborough, Ont., July 1, 1986. Chicago's 6th choice, 68th overall, in 2004 Entry Draft.

| Season | Club | League | GP | G | A | Pts | PIM | PP | SH | GW | S | % | +/- | TF | F% | Min | GP | G | A | Pts | PIM | PP | SH | GW | Min |
|---|---|---|---|---|---|---|---|---|---|---|---|---|---|---|---|---|---|---|---|---|---|---|---|---|---|
| 2002-03 | Oshawa Generals | OHL | 15 | 3 | 3 | 6 | 12 | .... | .... | .... | .... | .... | .... | .... | .... | .... | .... | .... | .... | .... | .... | .... | .... | .... | .... |
| 2003-04 | Oshawa Generals | OHL | 66 | 17 | 29 | 46 | 44 | .... | .... | .... | .... | .... | .... | .... | .... | .... | 7 | 0 | 2 | 2 | 4 | .... | .... | .... | .... |
| 2004-05 | Oshawa Generals | OHL | 66 | 23 | 28 | 51 | 53 | .... | .... | .... | .... | .... | .... | .... | .... | .... | .... | .... | .... | .... | .... | .... | .... | .... | .... |
| 2005-06 | Oshawa Generals | OHL | 23 | 16 | 18 | 34 | 28 | .... | .... | .... | .... | .... | .... | .... | .... | .... | .... | .... | .... | .... | .... | .... | .... | .... | .... |
| | Erie Otters | OHL | 39 | 17 | 12 | 29 | 24 | .... | .... | .... | .... | .... | .... | .... | .... | .... | .... | .... | .... | .... | .... | .... | .... | .... | .... |
| 2006-07 | Norfolk Admirals | AHL | 48 | 6 | 6 | 12 | 50 | .... | .... | .... | .... | .... | .... | .... | .... | .... | .... | .... | .... | .... | .... | .... | .... | .... | .... |
| **2007-08** | **Chicago** | **NHL** | **2** | **0** | **0** | **0** | **0** | **0** | **0** | **0** | **1** | **0.0** | **0** | **0** | **0.0** | **10:07** | .... | .... | .... | .... | .... | .... | .... | .... | .... |
| | Rockford IceHogs | AHL | 42 | 2 | 5 | 7 | 68 | .... | .... | .... | .... | .... | .... | .... | .... | .... | 5 | 1 | 0 | 1 | 2 | .... | .... | .... | .... |
| | Pensacola | ECHL | 4 | 2 | 3 | 5 | 0 | .... | .... | .... | .... | .... | .... | .... | .... | .... | .... | .... | .... | .... | .... | .... | .... | .... | .... |
| 2008-09 | Rockford IceHogs | AHL | 10 | 1 | 2 | 3 | 5 | .... | .... | .... | .... | .... | .... | .... | .... | .... | 1 | 0 | 0 | 0 | 0 | .... | .... | .... | .... |
| | Fresno Falcons | ECHL | 29 | 3 | 6 | 9 | 28 | .... | .... | .... | .... | .... | .... | .... | .... | .... | .... | .... | .... | .... | .... | .... | .... | .... | .... |
| | Gwinnett | ECHL | 39 | 10 | 24 | 34 | 16 | .... | .... | .... | .... | .... | .... | .... | .... | .... | 5 | 0 | 3 | 3 | 9 | .... | .... | .... | .... |
| | **NHL Totals** | | **2** | **0** | **0** | **0** | **0** | **0** | **0** | **0** | **1** | **0.0** | | **0** | **0.0** | **10:07** | .... | .... | .... | .... | .... | .... | .... | .... | .... |

## BERTUZZI, Todd

(buhr-TOO-zee, TAWD)

Right wing. Shoots left. 6'3", 231 lbs. Born, Sudbury, Ont., February 2, 1975. NY Islanders' 1st choice, 23rd overall, in 1993 Entry Draft.

| Season | Club | League | GP | G | A | Pts | PIM | PP | SH | GW | S | % | +/- | TF | F% | Min | GP | G | A | Pts | PIM | PP | SH | GW | Min |
|---|---|---|---|---|---|---|---|---|---|---|---|---|---|---|---|---|---|---|---|---|---|---|---|---|---|
| 1990-91 | Sudbury Legion | NOHA | 48 | 25 | 46 | 71 | 247 | .... | .... | .... | .... | .... | .... | .... | .... | .... | .... | .... | .... | .... | .... | .... | .... | .... | .... |
| | Sudbury Cubs | NOJHA | 3 | 3 | 2 | 5 | 10 | .... | .... | .... | .... | .... | .... | .... | .... | .... | .... | .... | .... | .... | .... | .... | .... | .... | .... |
| 1991-92 | Guelph Storm | OHL | 47 | 7 | 14 | 21 | 145 | .... | .... | .... | .... | .... | .... | .... | .... | .... | .... | .... | .... | .... | .... | .... | .... | .... | .... |
| 1992-93 | Guelph Storm | OHL | 59 | 27 | 32 | 59 | 164 | .... | .... | .... | .... | .... | .... | .... | .... | .... | 5 | 2 | 2 | 4 | 6 | .... | .... | .... | .... |
| 1993-94 | Guelph Storm | OHL | 61 | 28 | 54 | 82 | 165 | .... | .... | .... | .... | .... | .... | .... | .... | .... | 9 | 2 | 6 | 8 | 30 | .... | .... | .... | .... |
| 1994-95 | Guelph Storm | OHL | 62 | 54 | 65 | 119 | 58 | .... | .... | .... | .... | .... | .... | .... | .... | .... | 14 | *15 | 18 | 33 | 41 | .... | .... | .... | .... |
| **1995-96** | **NY Islanders** | **NHL** | **76** | **18** | **21** | **39** | **83** | **4** | **0** | **2** | **127** | **14.2** | **–14** | .... | .... | .... | .... | .... | .... | .... | .... | .... | .... | .... | .... |
| **1996-97** | **NY Islanders** | **NHL** | **64** | **10** | **13** | **23** | **68** | **3** | **0** | **1** | **79** | **12.7** | **–3** | .... | .... | .... | .... | .... | .... | .... | .... | .... | .... | .... | .... |
| | Utah Grizzlies | IHL | 13 | 5 | 5 | 10 | 16 | .... | .... | .... | .... | .... | .... | .... | .... | .... | .... | .... | .... | .... | .... | .... | .... | .... | .... |
| **1997-98** | **NY Islanders** | **NHL** | **52** | **7** | **11** | **18** | **58** | **1** | **0** | **1** | **63** | **11.1** | **–19** | .... | .... | .... | .... | .... | .... | .... | .... | .... | .... | .... | .... |
| | **Vancouver** | **NHL** | **22** | **6** | **9** | **15** | **63** | **1** | **1** | **1** | **39** | **15.4** | **2** | .... | .... | .... | .... | .... | .... | .... | .... | .... | .... | .... | .... |
| **1998-99** | **Vancouver** | **NHL** | **32** | **8** | **8** | **16** | **44** | **1** | **0** | **3** | **72** | **11.1** | **–6** | **191** | **43.5** | **18:28** | .... | .... | .... | .... | .... | .... | .... | .... | .... |
| **99-2000** | **Vancouver** | **NHL** | **80** | **25** | **25** | **50** | **126** | **4** | **0** | **2** | **173** | **14.5** | **–2** | **476** | **46.6** | **15:24** | .... | .... | .... | .... | .... | .... | .... | .... | .... |
| **2000-01** | **Vancouver** | **NHL** | **79** | **25** | **30** | **55** | **93** | **14** | **0** | **3** | **203** | **12.3** | **–18** | **84** | **45.2** | **17:13** | **4** | **2** | **2** | **4** | **8** | **0** | **0** | **0** | **19:01** |
| **2001-02** | **Vancouver** | **NHL** | **72** | **36** | **49** | **85** | **110** | **14** | **0** | **3** | **203** | **17.7** | **21** | **151** | **49.0** | **19:40** | **6** | **2** | **2** | **4** | **14** | **1** | **0** | **0** | **21:50** |
| **2002-03** | **Vancouver** | **NHL** | **82** | **46** | **51** | **97** | **144** | **25** | **0** | **7** | **243** | **18.9** | **2** | **208** | **47.1** | **20:34** | **14** | **2** | **4** | **6** | ***60** | **0** | **0** | **0** | **21:05** |
| **2003-04** | **Vancouver** | **NHL** | **69** | **17** | **43** | **60** | **122** | **8** | **0** | **2** | **156** | **10.9** | **21** | **111** | **45.1** | **21:00** | .... | .... | .... | .... | .... | .... | .... | .... | .... |
| 2004-05 | | | DID NOT PLAY – SUSPENDED | | | | | | | | | | | | | | | | | | | | | | |
| **2005-06** | **Vancouver** | **NHL** | **82** | **25** | **46** | **71** | **120** | **12** | **0** | **3** | **200** | **12.5** | **–17** | **363** | **43.8** | **19:08** | .... | .... | .... | .... | .... | .... | .... | .... | .... |
| | Canada | Olympics | 6 | 0 | 3 | 3 | 6 | .... | .... | .... | .... | .... | .... | .... | .... | .... | .... | .... | .... | .... | .... | .... | .... | .... | .... |
| **2006-07** | **Florida** | **NHL** | **7** | **1** | **6** | **7** | **13** | **1** | **0** | **0** | **8** | **12.5** | **–4** | **0** | **0.0** | **16:32** | .... | .... | .... | .... | .... | .... | .... | .... | .... |
| | **Detroit** | **NHL** | **8** | **2** | **2** | **4** | **6** | **0** | **0** | **0** | **15** | **13.3** | **3** | **2** | **50.0** | **15:32** | **16** | **3** | **4** | **7** | **15** | **1** | **0** | **0** | **14:25** |
| **2007-08** | **Anaheim** | **NHL** | **68** | **14** | **26** | **40** | **97** | **4** | **0** | **2** | **121** | **11.6** | **8** | **110** | **45.5** | **16:27** | **6** | **0** | **2** | **2** | **14** | **0** | **0** | **0** | **14:15** |
| **2008-09** | **Calgary** | **NHL** | **66** | **15** | **29** | **44** | **74** | **6** | **0** | **4** | **127** | **11.8** | **–13** | **45** | **46.7** | **18:36** | **6** | **1** | **1** | **2** | **8** | **0** | **0** | **0** | **17:25** |
| | **NHL Totals** | | **859** | **255** | **369** | **624** | **1221** | **98** | **1** | **34** | **1829** | **13.9** | | **1741** | **45.7** | **18:26** | **52** | **10** | **15** | **25** | **119** | **2** | **0** | **0** | **17:45** |

OHL Second All-Star Team (1995) • NHL First All-Star Team (2003)

Played in NHL All-Star Game (2003, 2004)

Traded to **Vancouver** by **NY Islanders** with Bryan McCabe and NY Islanders' 3rd round choice (Jarkko Ruutu) in 1998 Entry Draft for Trevor Linden, February 6, 1998. • Missed majority of 1998-99 season recovering from leg injury suffered in game vs. Washington, November 1, 1998. • Suspended indefinitely by NHL for deliberate injury to Steve Moore in game vs. Colorado, March 8, 2004. • Reinstated by NHL on August 8, 2005. Traded to **Florida** by **Vancouver** with Bryan Allen and Alex Auld for Roberto Luongo, Lukas Krajicek and Florida's 6th round choice (Sergei Shirokov) in 2006 Entry Draft, June 23, 2006. Traded to **Detroit** by **Florida** for Shawn Matthias and Detroit's 2nd round choice (later traded to Nashville - Nashville selected Nick Spaling) in 2007 Entry Draft, February 27, 2007. • Missed majority of 2006-07 season recovering from recurring back injury. Signed as a free agent by **Anaheim**, July 2, 2007. Signed as a free agent by **Calgary**, July 7, 2008.

## BETTS, Blair

(BEHTS, BLAIR)

Center. Shoots left. 6'3", 210 lbs. Born, Edmonton, Alta., February 16, 1980. Calgary's 2nd choice, 33rd overall, in 1998 Entry Draft.

| Season | Club | League | GP | G | A | Pts | PIM | PP | SH | GW | S | % | +/- | TF | F% | Min | GP | G | A | Pts | PIM | PP | SH | GW | Min |
|---|---|---|---|---|---|---|---|---|---|---|---|---|---|---|---|---|---|---|---|---|---|---|---|---|---|
| 1995-96 | Sherwood Park | AMHL | 34 | 22 | 19 | 41 | 69 | .... | .... | .... | .... | .... | .... | .... | .... | .... | .... | .... | .... | .... | .... | .... | .... | .... | .... |
| 1996-97 | Prince George | WHL | 58 | 12 | 18 | 30 | 19 | .... | .... | .... | .... | .... | .... | .... | .... | .... | 15 | 2 | 2 | 4 | 6 | .... | .... | .... | .... |
| 1997-98 | Prince George | WHL | 71 | 35 | 41 | 76 | 38 | .... | .... | .... | .... | .... | .... | .... | .... | .... | 11 | 4 | 6 | 10 | 8 | .... | .... | .... | .... |
| 1998-99 | Prince George | WHL | 42 | 20 | 22 | 42 | 39 | .... | .... | .... | .... | .... | .... | .... | .... | .... | 7 | 3 | 2 | 5 | 8 | .... | .... | .... | .... |
| 99-2000 | Prince George | WHL | 44 | 24 | 35 | 59 | 38 | .... | .... | .... | .... | .... | .... | .... | .... | .... | 13 | 11 | 11 | 22 | 6 | .... | .... | .... | .... |
| 2000-01 | Saint John Flames | AHL | 75 | 13 | 15 | 28 | 28 | .... | .... | .... | .... | .... | .... | .... | .... | .... | 19 | 2 | 3 | 5 | 4 | .... | .... | .... | .... |
| **2001-02** | **Calgary** | **NHL** | **6** | **1** | **0** | **1** | **2** | **0** | **0** | **1** | **4** | **25.0** | **–1** | **39** | **48.7** | **7:05** | .... | .... | .... | .... | .... | .... | .... | .... | .... |
| | Saint John Flames | AHL | 67 | 20 | 29 | 49 | 10 | .... | .... | .... | .... | .... | .... | .... | .... | .... | .... | .... | .... | .... | .... | .... | .... | .... | .... |
| **2002-03** | **Calgary** | **NHL** | **9** | **1** | **3** | **4** | **0** | **0** | **0** | **0** | **16** | **6.3** | **3** | **71** | **53.5** | **11:33** | .... | .... | .... | .... | .... | .... | .... | .... | .... |
| | Saint John Flames | AHL | 19 | 6 | 7 | 13 | 6 | .... | .... | .... | .... | .... | .... | .... | .... | .... | .... | .... | .... | .... | .... | .... | .... | .... | .... |
| **2003-04** | **Calgary** | **NHL** | **20** | **1** | **2** | **3** | **10** | **1** | **0** | **1** | **21** | **4.8** | **–1** | **248** | **54.0** | **12:46** | .... | .... | .... | .... | .... | .... | .... | .... | .... |
| 2004-05 | Hartford | AHL | 16 | 5 | 4 | 9 | 4 | .... | .... | .... | .... | .... | .... | .... | .... | .... | .... | .... | .... | .... | .... | .... | .... | .... | .... |
| **2005-06** | **NY Rangers** | **NHL** | **66** | **8** | **2** | **10** | **24** | **0** | **1** | **0** | **94** | **8.5** | **–10** | **817** | **53.4** | **12:55** | **4** | **1** | **1** | **2** | **2** | **0** | **0** | **0** | **16:12** |
| **2006-07** | **NY Rangers** | **NHL** | **82** | **9** | **4** | **13** | **24** | **1** | **1** | **0** | **120** | **7.5** | **–4** | **1186** | **52.3** | **14:02** | **10** | **0** | **0** | **0** | **4** | **0** | **0** | **0** | **11:15** |
| **2007-08** | **NY Rangers** | **NHL** | **75** | **2** | **5** | **7** | **20** | **0** | **0** | **0** | **85** | **2.4** | **–4** | **771** | **50.3** | **11:52** | **8** | **0** | **0** | **0** | **2** | **0** | **0** | **0** | **7:16** |
| **2008-09** | **NY Rangers** | **NHL** | **81** | **6** | **4** | **10** | **16** | **0** | **2** | **1** | **83** | **7.2** | **–5** | **884** | **49.3** | **10:37** | **6** | **0** | **0** | **0** | **0** | **0** | **0** | **0** | **9:08** |
| | **NHL Totals** | | **339** | **28** | **20** | **48** | **96** | **2** | **4** | **3** | **423** | **6.6** | | **4016** | **51.6** | **12:15** | **28** | **1** | **1** | **2** | **8** | **0** | **0** | **0** | **10:22** |

• Missed majority of 2002-03 season recovering from shoulder injury suffered in training camp, September 27, 2002. • Missed majority of 2003-04 season recovering from shoulder injuries suffered in games vs. Chicago (November 22, 2003) and Colorado (December 31, 2003). Traded to **NY Rangers** by **Calgary** with Jamie McLennan and Greg Moore for Chris Simon and NY Rangers' 7th round choice (Matt Schneider) in 2004 Entry Draft, March 6, 2004.

## BICKELL, Bryan

(BIH-kuhl, BRIGH-uhn) **CHI.**

Left wing. Shoots left. 6'4", 223 lbs. Born, Bowmanville, Ont., March 9, 1986. Chicago's 3rd choice, 41st overall, in 2004 Entry Draft.

| Season | Club | League | GP | G | A | Pts | PIM | PP | SH | GW | S | % | +/- | TF | F% | Min | GP | G | A | Pts | PIM | PP | SH | GW | Min |
|---|---|---|---|---|---|---|---|---|---|---|---|---|---|---|---|---|---|---|---|---|---|---|---|---|---|
| 2000-01 | Tor. Red Wings | GTHL | 68 | 24 | 26 | 50 | 20 | .... | .... | .... | .... | .... | .... | .... | .... | .... | 5 | 3 | 1 | 4 | 4 | .... | .... | .... | .... |
| 2001-02 | Tor. Red Wings | GTHL | 65 | 31 | 41 | 72 | 76 | .... | .... | .... | .... | .... | .... | .... | .... | .... | 2 | 2 | 2 | 4 | 0 | .... | .... | .... | .... |
| 2002-03 | Ottawa 67's | OHL | 50 | 7 | 10 | 17 | 4 | .... | .... | .... | .... | .... | .... | .... | .... | .... | 20 | 5 | 3 | 8 | 12 | .... | .... | .... | .... |
| 2003-04 | Ottawa 67's | OHL | 59 | 20 | 16 | 36 | 76 | .... | .... | .... | .... | .... | .... | .... | .... | .... | 7 | 3 | 0 | 3 | 11 | .... | .... | .... | .... |
| 2004-05 | Ottawa 67's | OHL | 66 | 22 | 32 | 54 | 95 | .... | .... | .... | .... | .... | .... | .... | .... | .... | 21 | 5 | 12 | 17 | 32 | .... | .... | .... | .... |
| 2005-06 | Ottawa 67's | OHL | 41 | 28 | 22 | 50 | 41 | .... | .... | .... | .... | .... | .... | .... | .... | .... | .... | .... | .... | .... | .... | .... | .... | .... | .... |
| | Windsor Spitfires | OHL | 26 | 17 | 16 | 33 | 19 | .... | .... | .... | .... | .... | .... | .... | .... | .... | 7 | 5 | 5 | 10 | 10 | .... | .... | .... | .... |
| **2006-07** | **Chicago** | **NHL** | **3** | **2** | **0** | **2** | **0** | **0** | **0** | **0** | **10** | **20.0** | **1** | **0** | **0.0** | **11:49** | .... | .... | .... | .... | .... | .... | .... | .... | .... |
| | Norfolk Admirals | AHL | 48 | 10 | 15 | 25 | 66 | .... | .... | .... | .... | .... | .... | .... | .... | .... | 2 | 0 | 0 | 0 | 0 | .... | .... | .... | .... |
| **2007-08** | **Chicago** | **NHL** | **4** | **0** | **0** | **0** | **2** | **0** | **0** | **0** | **3** | **0.0** | **–1** | **0** | **0.0** | **9:08** | .... | .... | .... | .... | .... | .... | .... | .... | .... |
| | Rockford IceHogs | AHL | 73 | 19 | 20 | 39 | 52 | .... | .... | .... | .... | .... | .... | .... | .... | .... | 12 | 2 | 3 | 5 | 11 | .... | .... | .... | .... |
| 2008-09 | Rockford IceHogs | AHL | 42 | 6 | 8 | 14 | 60 | .... | .... | .... | .... | .... | .... | .... | .... | .... | 4 | 0 | 2 | 2 | 4 | .... | .... | .... | .... |
| | **NHL Totals** | | **7** | **2** | **0** | **2** | **2** | **0** | **0** | **0** | **13** | **15.4** | | **0** | **0.0** | **10:17** | .... | .... | .... | .... | .... | .... | .... | .... | .... |

## BIEKSA, Kevin

(BEEKS-ah, KEH-vihn) **VAN.**

Defense. Shoots right. 6', 205 lbs. Born, Grimsby, Ont., June 16, 1981. Vancouver's 4th choice, 151st overall, in 2001 Entry Draft.

| Season | Club | League | GP | G | A | Pts | PIM | PP | SH | GW | S | % | +/- | TF | F% | Min | GP | G | A | Pts | PIM | PP | SH | GW | Min |
|---|---|---|---|---|---|---|---|---|---|---|---|---|---|---|---|---|---|---|---|---|---|---|---|---|---|
| 1997-98 | Burlington | OPJHL | 27 | 0 | 3 | 3 | 10 | .... | .... | .... | .... | .... | .... | .... | .... | .... | .... | .... | .... | .... | .... | .... | .... | .... | .... |
| 1998-99 | Burlington | OPJHL | 49 | 8 | 29 | 37 | 83 | .... | .... | .... | .... | .... | .... | .... | .... | .... | .... | .... | .... | .... | .... | .... | .... | .... | .... |
| 99-2000 | Burlington | OPJHL | 49 | 6 | 27 | 33 | 139 | .... | .... | .... | .... | .... | .... | .... | .... | .... | .... | .... | .... | .... | .... | .... | .... | .... | .... |
| 2000-01 | Bowling Green | CCHA | 35 | 4 | 9 | 13 | 90 | .... | .... | .... | .... | .... | .... | .... | .... | .... | .... | .... | .... | .... | .... | .... | .... | .... | .... |
| 2001-02 | Bowling Green | CCHA | 40 | 5 | 10 | 15 | 68 | .... | .... | .... | .... | .... | .... | .... | .... | .... | .... | .... | .... | .... | .... | .... | .... | .... | .... |
| 2002-03 | Bowling Green | CCHA | 34 | 8 | 17 | 25 | 92 | .... | .... | .... | .... | .... | .... | .... | .... | .... | .... | .... | .... | .... | .... | .... | .... | .... | .... |
| 2003-04 | Bowling Green | CCHA | 38 | 7 | 15 | 22 | 66 | .... | .... | .... | .... | .... | .... | .... | .... | .... | .... | .... | .... | .... | .... | .... | .... | .... | .... |
| | Manitoba Moose | AHL | 4 | 0 | 2 | 2 | 2 | .... | .... | .... | .... | .... | .... | .... | .... | .... | .... | .... | .... | .... | .... | .... | .... | .... | .... |
| 2004-05 | Manitoba Moose | AHL | 80 | 12 | 27 | 39 | 192 | .... | .... | .... | .... | .... | .... | .... | .... | .... | 14 | 1 | 1 | 2 | 52 | .... | .... | .... | .... |
| **2005-06** | **Vancouver** | **NHL** | **39** | **0** | **6** | **6** | **77** | **0** | **0** | **0** | **38** | **0.0** | **–1** | **0** | **0.0** | **16:06** | .... | .... | .... | .... | .... | .... | .... | .... | .... |
| | Manitoba Moose | AHL | 23 | 3 | 17 | 20 | 71 | .... | .... | .... | .... | .... | .... | .... | .... | .... | 13 | 0 | 10 | 10 | 38 | .... | .... | .... | .... |
| **2006-07** | **Vancouver** | **NHL** | **81** | **12** | **30** | **42** | **134** | **6** | **0** | **2** | **203** | **5.9** | **1** | **0** | **0.0** | **24:16** | **9** | **0** | **0** | **0** | **20** | **0** | **0** | **0** | **28:01** |

| | | | | | | | | Regular Season | | | | | | | | | Playoffs | | | | | | | | |
|---|---|---|---|---|---|---|---|---|---|---|---|---|---|---|---|---|---|---|---|---|---|---|---|---|---|
| Season | Club | League | GP | G | A | Pts | PIM | PP | SH | GW | S | % | +/- | TF | F% | Min | GP | G | A | Pts | PIM | PP | SH | GW | Min |
| 2007-08 | Vancouver | NHL | 34 | 2 | 10 | 12 | 90 | 1 | 0 | 1 | 64 | 3.1 | –11 | 0 | 0.0 | 23:24 | .... | .... | .... | .... | .... | .... | .... | .... | .... |
| | Manitoba Moose | AHL | 1 | 0 | 1 | 1 | 2 | .... | .... | .... | .... | .... | .... | .... | .... | .... | .... | .... | .... | .... | .... | .... | .... | .... | .... |
| 2008-09 | Vancouver | NHL | 72 | 11 | 32 | 43 | 97 | 5 | 0 | 2 | 153 | 7.2 | –4 | 0 | 0.0 | 23:29 | 10 | 0 | 5 | 5 | 14 | 0 | 0 | 0 | 24:08 |
| | NHL Totals | | 226 | 25 | 78 | 103 | 398 | 12 | 0 | 5 | 458 | 5.5 | | 0 | 0.0 | 22:29 | 19 | 0 | 5 | 5 | 34 | 0 | 0 | 0 | 25:58 |

AHL All-Rookie Team (2005)

## BISAILLON, Sebastien

(BIH-sigh-awn, suh-BAS-tee-yeh)

Defense. Shoots right. 6', 205 lbs. Born, Mont-Laurier, Que., December 8, 1986.

| | | | | | | | | | | | | | | | | | | | | | | | | | |
|---|---|---|---|---|---|---|---|---|---|---|---|---|---|---|---|---|---|---|---|---|---|---|---|---|---|
| 2002-03 | Val-d'Or Foreurs | QMJHL | 1 | 0 | 0 | 0 | 0 | .... | .... | .... | .... | .... | .... | .... | .... | .... | .... | .... | .... | .... | .... | .... | .... | .... | .... |
| 2003-04 | Val-d'Or Foreurs | QMJHL | 67 | 4 | 14 | 18 | 39 | .... | .... | .... | .... | .... | .... | .... | .... | .... | 7 | 2 | 0 | 2 | 2 | .... | .... | .... | .... |
| 2004-05 | Val-d'Or Foreurs | QMJHL | 69 | 15 | 33 | 48 | 39 | .... | .... | .... | .... | .... | .... | .... | .... | .... | .... | .... | .... | .... | .... | .... | .... | .... | .... |
| 2005-06 | Val-d'Or Foreurs | QMJHL | 63 | 35 | 36 | 71 | 56 | .... | .... | .... | .... | .... | .... | .... | .... | .... | 5 | 0 | 4 | 4 | 2 | .... | .... | .... | .... |
| 2006-07 | Edmonton | NHL | 2 | 0 | 0 | 0 | 0 | 0 | 0 | 0 | 3 | 0.0 | –1 | 0 | 0.0 | 14:12 | .... | .... | .... | .... | .... | .... | .... | .... | .... |
| | Val-d'Or Foreurs | QMJHL | 63 | 12 | 40 | 52 | 30 | .... | .... | .... | .... | .... | .... | .... | .... | .... | 20 | 2 | 10 | 12 | 12 | .... | .... | .... | .... |
| 2007-08 | Springfield | AHL | 21 | 3 | 7 | 10 | 10 | .... | .... | .... | .... | .... | .... | .... | .... | .... | .... | .... | .... | .... | .... | .... | .... | .... | .... |
| | Stockton Thunder | ECHL | 7 | 4 | 2 | 6 | 2 | .... | .... | .... | .... | .... | .... | .... | .... | .... | 6 | 0 | 1 | 1 | 2 | .... | .... | .... | .... |
| 2008-09 | Springfield | AHL | 31 | 5 | 7 | 12 | 21 | .... | .... | .... | .... | .... | .... | .... | .... | .... | .... | .... | .... | .... | .... | .... | .... | .... | .... |
| | Stockton Thunder | ECHL | 27 | 3 | 7 | 10 | 14 | .... | .... | .... | .... | .... | .... | .... | .... | .... | 3 | 0 | 1 | 1 | 2 | .... | .... | .... | .... |
| | NHL Totals | | 2 | 0 | 0 | 0 | 0 | 0 | 0 | 0 | 3 | 0.0 | | 0 | 0.0 | 14:12 | .... | .... | .... | .... | .... | .... | .... | .... | .... |

Signed as a free agent by **Edmonton**, September 27, 2006.

## BISSONNETTE, Paul

(bih-sawn-EHT, PAWL) **PIT.**

Defense. Shoots left. 6'2", 211 lbs. Born, Welland, Ont., March 11, 1985. Pittsburgh's 5th choice, 121st overall, in 2003 Entry Draft.

| | | | | | | | | | | | | | | | | | | | | | | | | | |
|---|---|---|---|---|---|---|---|---|---|---|---|---|---|---|---|---|---|---|---|---|---|---|---|---|---|
| 2001-02 | North Bay | OHL | 57 | 3 | 3 | 6 | 21 | .... | .... | .... | .... | .... | .... | .... | .... | .... | 5 | 0 | 0 | 0 | 2 | .... | .... | .... | .... |
| 2002-03 | Saginaw Spirit | OHL | 67 | 7 | 16 | 23 | 57 | .... | .... | .... | .... | .... | .... | .... | .... | .... | .... | .... | .... | .... | .... | .... | .... | .... | .... |
| 2003-04 | Saginaw Spirit | OHL | 67 | 5 | 14 | 19 | 96 | .... | .... | .... | .... | .... | .... | .... | .... | .... | .... | .... | .... | .... | .... | .... | .... | .... | .... |
| 2004-05 | Saginaw Spirit | OHL | 28 | 1 | 6 | 7 | 46 | .... | .... | .... | .... | .... | .... | .... | .... | .... | .... | .... | .... | .... | .... | .... | .... | .... | .... |
| | Owen Sound | OHL | 35 | 2 | 11 | 13 | 46 | .... | .... | .... | .... | .... | .... | .... | .... | .... | 8 | 1 | 3 | 4 | 2 | .... | .... | .... | .... |
| 2005-06 | Wilkes-Barre | AHL | 55 | 1 | 5 | 6 | 60 | .... | .... | .... | .... | .... | .... | .... | .... | .... | 11 | 0 | 1 | 1 | 4 | .... | .... | .... | .... |
| | Wheeling Nailers | ECHL | 14 | 3 | 7 | 10 | 4 | .... | .... | .... | .... | .... | .... | .... | .... | .... | .... | .... | .... | .... | .... | .... | .... | .... | .... |
| 2006-07 | Wilkes-Barre | AHL | 3 | 0 | 0 | 0 | 6 | .... | .... | .... | .... | .... | .... | .... | .... | .... | .... | .... | .... | .... | .... | .... | .... | .... | .... |
| | Wheeling Nailers | ECHL | 65 | 10 | 32 | 42 | 115 | .... | .... | .... | .... | .... | .... | .... | .... | .... | .... | .... | .... | .... | .... | .... | .... | .... | .... |
| 2007-08 | Wilkes-Barre | AHL | 46 | 3 | 5 | 8 | 145 | .... | .... | .... | .... | .... | .... | .... | .... | .... | 7 | 0 | 0 | 0 | 11 | .... | .... | .... | .... |
| | Wheeling Nailers | ECHL | 22 | 3 | 14 | 17 | 43 | .... | .... | .... | .... | .... | .... | .... | .... | .... | .... | .... | .... | .... | .... | .... | .... | .... | .... |
| 2008-09 | Pittsburgh | NHL | 15 | 0 | 1 | 1 | 22 | 0 | 0 | 0 | 4 | 0.0 | –1 | 0 | 0.0 | 3:31 | .... | .... | .... | .... | .... | .... | .... | .... | .... |
| | Wilkes-Barre | AHL | 57 | 9 | 7 | 16 | 176 | .... | .... | .... | .... | .... | .... | .... | .... | .... | 8 | 0 | 2 | 2 | 9 | .... | .... | .... | .... |
| | NHL Totals | | 15 | 0 | 1 | 1 | 22 | 0 | 0 | 0 | 4 | 0.0 | | 0 | 0.0 | 3:31 | .... | .... | .... | .... | .... | .... | .... | .... | .... |

## BITZ, Byron

(BIHTZ, BIGH-ruhn) **BOS.**

Right wing. Shoots right. 6'5", 215 lbs. Born, Saskatoon, Sask., July 21, 1984. Boston's 4th choice, 107th overall, in 2003 Entry Draft.

| | | | | | | | | | | | | | | | | | | | | | | | | | |
|---|---|---|---|---|---|---|---|---|---|---|---|---|---|---|---|---|---|---|---|---|---|---|---|---|---|
| 2000-01 | Saskatoon | SMBHL | 40 | 17 | 35 | 52 | .... | .... | .... | .... | .... | .... | .... | .... | .... | .... | .... | .... | .... | .... | .... | .... | .... | .... | .... |
| 2001-02 | Saskatoon | SMHL | 41 | 25 | 48 | 73 | 69 | .... | .... | .... | .... | .... | .... | .... | .... | .... | 11 | 12 | 10 | 22 | 9 | .... | .... | .... | .... |
| 2002-03 | Nanaimo Clippers | BCHL | 58 | 27 | 46 | 73 | 59 | .... | .... | .... | .... | .... | .... | .... | .... | .... | .... | .... | .... | .... | .... | .... | .... | .... | .... |
| 2003-04 | Cornell Big Red | ECAC | 31 | 5 | 16 | 21 | 36 | .... | .... | .... | .... | .... | .... | .... | .... | .... | .... | .... | .... | .... | .... | .... | .... | .... | .... |
| 2004-05 | Cornell Big Red | ECAC | 29 | 5 | 10 | 15 | 20 | .... | .... | .... | .... | .... | .... | .... | .... | .... | .... | .... | .... | .... | .... | .... | .... | .... | .... |
| 2005-06 | Cornell Big Red | ECAC | 35 | 10 | 18 | 28 | 52 | .... | .... | .... | .... | .... | .... | .... | .... | .... | .... | .... | .... | .... | .... | .... | .... | .... | .... |
| 2006-07 | Cornell Big Red | ECAC | 29 | 8 | 16 | 24 | 49 | .... | .... | .... | .... | .... | .... | .... | .... | .... | .... | .... | .... | .... | .... | .... | .... | .... | .... |
| 2007-08 | Providence Bruins | AHL | 61 | 13 | 14 | 27 | 70 | .... | .... | .... | .... | .... | .... | .... | .... | .... | 10 | 1 | 1 | 2 | 6 | .... | .... | .... | .... |
| 2008-09 | Boston | NHL | 35 | 4 | 3 | 7 | 18 | 0 | 0 | 0 | 31 | 12.9 | 0 | 50 | 42.0 | 10:22 | 5 | 1 | 1 | 2 | 2 | 0 | 0 | 0 | 11:27 |
| | Providence Bruins | AHL | 37 | 3 | 7 | 10 | 68 | .... | .... | .... | .... | .... | .... | .... | .... | .... | .... | .... | .... | .... | .... | .... | .... | .... | .... |
| | NHL Totals | | 35 | 4 | 3 | 7 | 18 | 0 | 0 | 0 | 31 | 12.9 | | 50 | 42.0 | 10:22 | 5 | 1 | 1 | 2 | 2 | 0 | 0 | 0 | 11:27 |

## BLAKE, Jason

(BLAYK, JAY-suhn) **TOR.**

Center. Shoots left. 5'10", 180 lbs. Born, Moorhead, MN, September 2, 1973.

| | | | | | | | | | | | | | | | | | | | | | | | | | |
|---|---|---|---|---|---|---|---|---|---|---|---|---|---|---|---|---|---|---|---|---|---|---|---|---|---|
| 1991-92 | Moorhead Spuds | High-MN | 25 | 30 | 30 | 60 | .... | .... | .... | .... | .... | .... | .... | .... | .... | .... | .... | .... | .... | .... | .... | .... | .... | .... | .... |
| 1992-93 | Waterloo | USHL | 45 | 24 | 27 | 51 | 107 | .... | .... | .... | .... | .... | .... | .... | .... | .... | .... | .... | .... | .... | .... | .... | .... | .... | .... |
| 1993-94 | Waterloo | USHL | 47 | 50 | 50 | 100 | 76 | .... | .... | .... | .... | .... | .... | .... | .... | .... | .... | .... | .... | .... | .... | .... | .... | .... | .... |
| 1994-95 | Ferris State | CCHA | 36 | 16 | 16 | 32 | 46 | .... | .... | .... | .... | .... | .... | .... | .... | .... | .... | .... | .... | .... | .... | .... | .... | .... | .... |
| 1995-96 | North Dakota | WCHA | DID NOT PLAY – TRANSFERRED COLLEGES | | | | | | | | | | | | | | | | | | | | | | |
| 1996-97 | North Dakota | WCHA | 43 | 19 | 32 | 51 | 44 | .... | .... | .... | .... | .... | .... | .... | .... | .... | .... | .... | .... | .... | .... | .... | .... | .... | .... |
| 1997-98 | North Dakota | WCHA | 38 | 24 | 27 | 51 | 62 | .... | .... | .... | .... | .... | .... | .... | .... | .... | .... | .... | .... | .... | .... | .... | .... | .... | .... |
| 1998-99 | North Dakota | WCHA | 38 | *28 | *41 | *69 | 49 | .... | .... | .... | .... | .... | .... | .... | .... | .... | .... | .... | .... | .... | .... | .... | .... | .... | .... |
| | Los Angeles | NHL | 1 | 1 | 0 | 1 | 0 | 0 | 0 | 0 | 5 | 20.0 | 1 | 14 | 35.7 | 17:13 | .... | .... | .... | .... | .... | .... | .... | .... | .... |
| | Orlando | IHL | 5 | 3 | 5 | 8 | 6 | .... | .... | .... | .... | .... | .... | .... | .... | .... | 13 | 3 | 4 | 7 | 20 | .... | .... | .... | .... |
| 99-2000 | Los Angeles | NHL | 64 | 5 | 18 | 23 | 26 | 0 | 0 | 1 | 131 | 3.8 | 4 | 269 | 43.9 | 11:17 | 3 | 0 | 0 | 0 | 0 | 0 | 0 | 0 | 9:35 |
| | Long Beach | IHL | 7 | 3 | 6 | 9 | 2 | .... | .... | .... | .... | .... | .... | .... | .... | .... | .... | .... | .... | .... | .... | .... | .... | .... | .... |
| 2000-01 | Los Angeles | NHL | 17 | 1 | 3 | 4 | 10 | 0 | 0 | 0 | 27 | 3.7 | –8 | 13 | 61.5 | 10:03 | .... | .... | .... | .... | .... | .... | .... | .... | .... |
| | Lowell | AHL | 2 | 0 | 1 | 1 | 2 | .... | .... | .... | .... | .... | .... | .... | .... | .... | .... | .... | .... | .... | .... | .... | .... | .... | .... |
| | NY Islanders | NHL | 30 | 4 | 8 | 12 | 24 | 1 | 1 | 0 | 73 | 5.5 | –12 | 118 | 44.1 | 15:43 | .... | .... | .... | .... | .... | .... | .... | .... | .... |
| 2001-02 | NY Islanders | NHL | 82 | 8 | 10 | 18 | 36 | 0 | 0 | 1 | 136 | 5.9 | –11 | 23 | 43.5 | 12:54 | 7 | 0 | 1 | 1 | 13 | 0 | 0 | 0 | 12:13 |
| 2002-03 | NY Islanders | NHL | 81 | 25 | 30 | 55 | 58 | 3 | 1 | 4 | 253 | 9.9 | 16 | 22 | 18.2 | 17:38 | 5 | 0 | 1 | 1 | 2 | 0 | 0 | 0 | 19:39 |
| 2003-04 | NY Islanders | NHL | 75 | 22 | 25 | 47 | 56 | 1 | 4 | 3 | 243 | 9.1 | 11 | 70 | 41.4 | 18:49 | 4 | 2 | 0 | 2 | 2 | 0 | 0 | 0 | 18:09 |
| 2004-05 | HC Lugano | Swiss | 7 | 2 | 2 | 4 | 4 | .... | .... | .... | .... | .... | .... | .... | .... | .... | .... | .... | .... | .... | .... | .... | .... | .... | .... |
| 2005-06 | NY Islanders | NHL | 76 | 28 | 29 | 57 | 60 | 12 | 2 | 2 | 304 | 9.2 | 0 | 152 | 42.8 | 18:47 | .... | .... | .... | .... | .... | .... | .... | .... | .... |
| | United States | Olympics | 6 | 0 | 0 | 0 | 2 | .... | .... | .... | .... | .... | .... | .... | .... | .... | .... | .... | .... | .... | .... | .... | .... | .... | .... |
| 2006-07 | NY Islanders | NHL | 82 | 40 | 29 | 69 | 34 | 14 | 0 | 7 | 305 | 13.1 | 1 | 117 | 57.3 | 18:09 | 5 | 1 | 2 | 3 | 2 | 0 | 0 | 0 | 17:04 |
| 2007-08 | Toronto | NHL | 82 | 15 | 37 | 52 | 28 | 2 | 0 | 0 | 332 | 4.5 | –4 | 28 | 50.0 | 17:49 | .... | .... | .... | .... | .... | .... | .... | .... | .... |
| 2008-09 | Toronto | NHL | 78 | 25 | 38 | 63 | 40 | 5 | 1 | 5 | 302 | 8.3 | –2 | 77 | 46.8 | 18:21 | .... | .... | .... | .... | .... | .... | .... | .... | .... |
| | NHL Totals | | 668 | 174 | 227 | 401 | 372 | 38 | 9 | 23 | 2111 | 8.2 | | 903 | 45.2 | 16:36 | 24 | 3 | 4 | 7 | 19 | 0 | 0 | 0 | 15:26 |

USHL Player of the Year (1994) • WCHA First All-Star Team (1997, 1998, 1999) • NCAA West Second All-American Team (1998) • WCHA Player of the Year (1999) • NCAA West First All-American Team (1999) • Bill Masterton Memorial Trophy (2008)

Played in NHL All-Star Game (2007)

Signed as a free agent by **Los Angeles**, April 20, 1999. Traded to **NY Islanders** by **Los Angeles** for NY Islanders' 5th round choice (Joel Andresen) in 2002 Entry Draft, January 3, 2001. Signed as a free agent by **Lugano** (Swiss), December 1, 2004. Signed as a free agent by **Toronto**, July 1, 2007.

## BLAKE, Rob

(BLAYK, RAWB) **S.J.**

Defense. Shoots right. 6'4", 225 lbs. Born, Simcoe, Ont., December 10, 1969. Los Angeles' 4th choice, 70th overall, in 1988 Entry Draft.

| | | | | | | | | | | | | | | | | | | | | | | | | | |
|---|---|---|---|---|---|---|---|---|---|---|---|---|---|---|---|---|---|---|---|---|---|---|---|---|---|
| 1985-86 | Brantford Classics | OHA-B | 39 | 3 | 13 | 16 | 43 | .... | .... | .... | .... | .... | .... | .... | .... | .... | .... | .... | .... | .... | .... | .... | .... | .... | .... |
| 1986-87 | Stratford Cullitons | OHA-B | 31 | 11 | 20 | 31 | 115 | .... | .... | .... | .... | .... | .... | .... | .... | .... | .... | .... | .... | .... | .... | .... | .... | .... | .... |
| 1987-88 | Bowling Green | CCHA | 43 | 5 | 8 | 13 | 88 | .... | .... | .... | .... | .... | .... | .... | .... | .... | .... | .... | .... | .... | .... | .... | .... | .... | .... |
| 1988-89 | Bowling Green | CCHA | 46 | 11 | 21 | 32 | 140 | .... | .... | .... | .... | .... | .... | .... | .... | .... | .... | .... | .... | .... | .... | .... | .... | .... | .... |
| 1989-90 | Bowling Green | CCHA | 42 | 23 | 36 | 59 | 140 | .... | .... | .... | .... | .... | .... | .... | .... | .... | .... | .... | .... | .... | .... | .... | .... | .... | .... |
| | Los Angeles | NHL | 4 | 0 | 0 | 0 | 4 | 0 | 0 | 0 | 3 | 0.0 | 0 | .... | .... | .... | 8 | 1 | 3 | 4 | 4 | 1 | 0 | 0 | .... |
| 1990-91 | Los Angeles | NHL | 75 | 12 | 34 | 46 | 125 | 9 | 0 | 2 | 150 | 8.0 | 3 | .... | .... | .... | 12 | 1 | 4 | 5 | 26 | 1 | 0 | 0 | .... |
| 1991-92 | Los Angeles | NHL | 57 | 7 | 13 | 20 | 102 | 5 | 0 | 0 | 131 | 5.3 | –5 | .... | .... | .... | 6 | 2 | 1 | 3 | 12 | 0 | 0 | 0 | .... |
| 1992-93 | Los Angeles | NHL | 76 | 16 | 43 | 59 | 152 | 10 | 0 | 4 | 243 | 6.6 | 18 | .... | .... | .... | 23 | 4 | 6 | 10 | 46 | 1 | 1 | 0 | .... |
| 1993-94 | Los Angeles | NHL | 84 | 20 | 48 | 68 | 137 | 7 | 0 | 6 | 304 | 6.6 | –7 | .... | .... | .... | .... | .... | .... | .... | .... | .... | .... | .... | .... |
| 1994-95 | Los Angeles | NHL | 24 | 4 | 7 | 11 | 38 | 4 | 0 | 1 | 76 | 5.3 | –16 | .... | .... | .... | .... | .... | .... | .... | .... | .... | .... | .... | .... |
| 1995-96 | Los Angeles | NHL | 6 | 1 | 2 | 3 | 8 | 0 | 0 | 0 | 13 | 7.7 | 0 | .... | .... | .... | .... | .... | .... | .... | .... | .... | .... | .... | .... |
| 1996-97 | Los Angeles | NHL | 62 | 8 | 23 | 31 | 82 | 4 | 0 | 1 | 169 | 4.7 | –28 | .... | .... | .... | .... | .... | .... | .... | .... | .... | .... | .... | .... |
| 1997-98 | Los Angeles | NHL | 81 | 23 | 27 | 50 | 94 | 11 | 0 | 4 | 261 | 8.8 | –3 | .... | .... | .... | 4 | 0 | 0 | 0 | 6 | 0 | 0 | 0 | .... |
| | Canada | Olympics | 6 | 1 | 1 | 2 | 2 | .... | .... | .... | .... | .... | .... | .... | .... | .... | .... | .... | .... | .... | .... | .... | .... | .... | .... |
| 1998-99 | Los Angeles | NHL | 62 | 12 | 23 | 35 | 128 | 5 | 1 | 2 | 216 | 5.6 | –7 | 0 | 0.0 | 24:52 | .... | .... | .... | .... | .... | .... | .... | .... | .... |
| 99-2000 | Los Angeles | NHL | 77 | 18 | 39 | 57 | 112 | 12 | 0 | 5 | 327 | 5.5 | 10 | 0 | 0.0 | 28:30 | 4 | 0 | 2 | 2 | 4 | 0 | 0 | 0 | 30:10 |

| | | | Regular Season | | | | | | | | | | | | | | Playoffs | | | | | | | | |
|---|---|---|---|---|---|---|---|---|---|---|---|---|---|---|---|---|---|---|---|---|---|---|---|---|---|
| Season | Club | League | GP | G | A | Pts | PIM | PP | SH | GW | S | % | +/- | TF | F% | Min | GP | G | A | Pts | PIM | PP | SH | GW | Min |
| 2000-01 | Los Angeles | NHL | 54 | 17 | 32 | 49 | 69 | 9 | 0 | 1 | 223 | 7.6 | –8 | 0 | 0.0 | 28:11 | .... | .... | .... | .... | .... | .... | .... | .... | .... |
| | ♦ Colorado | NHL | 13 | 2 | 8 | 10 | 8 | 1 | 0 | 1 | 44 | 4.5 | 11 | 0 | 0.0 | 26:03 | 23 | 6 | 13 | 19 | 16 | 3 | 0 | 0 | 29:26 |
| 2001-02 | Colorado | NHL | 75 | 16 | 40 | 56 | 58 | 10 | 0 | 2 | 229 | 7.0 | 16 | 0 | 0.0 | 27:35 | 20 | 6 | 6 | 12 | 16 | 1 | 0 | 0 | 26:38 |
| | Canada | Olympics | 6 | 1 | 2 | 3 | 2 | .... | .... | .... | .... | .... | .... | .... | .... | .... | .... | .... | .... | .... | .... | .... | .... | .... | .... |
| 2002-03 | Colorado | NHL | 79 | 17 | 28 | 45 | 57 | 8 | 2 | 3 | 269 | 6.3 | 20 | 0 | 0.0 | 26:21 | 7 | 1 | 2 | 3 | 8 | 0 | 0 | 0 | 27:28 |
| 2003-04 | Colorado | NHL | 74 | 13 | 33 | 46 | 61 | 8 | 0 | 3 | 242 | 5.4 | 6 | 1 | 0.0 | 24:23 | 9 | 0 | 5 | 5 | 6 | 0 | 0 | 0 | 20:17 |
| 2004-05 | | | | DID NOT PLAY | | | | | | | | | | | | | | | | | | | | | |
| 2005-06 | Colorado | NHL | 81 | 14 | 37 | 51 | 94 | 7 | 1 | 1 | 264 | 5.3 | 2 | 2 | 0.0 | 24:22 | 9 | 3 | 1 | 4 | 8 | 2 | 0 | 1 | 28:19 |
| | Canada | Olympics | 6 | 0 | 1 | 1 | 2 | .... | .... | .... | .... | .... | .... | .... | .... | .... | .... | .... | .... | .... | .... | .... | .... | .... | .... |
| 2006-07 | Los Angeles | NHL | 72 | 14 | 20 | 34 | 82 | 11 | 0 | 1 | 208 | 6.7 | –26 | 3 | 33.3 | 24:24 | .... | .... | .... | .... | .... | .... | .... | .... | .... |
| 2007-08 | Los Angeles | NHL | 71 | 9 | 22 | 31 | 98 | 5 | 0 | 2 | 144 | 6.3 | –19 | 8 | 50.0 | 22:44 | .... | .... | .... | .... | .... | .... | .... | .... | .... |
| 2008-09 | San Jose | NHL | 73 | 10 | 35 | 45 | 110 | 6 | 0 | 1 | 198 | 5.1 | 15 | 0 | 0.0 | 21:16 | 6 | 1 | 3 | 4 | 4 | 0 | 0 | 0 | 21:50 |
| | NHL Totals | | 1200 | 233 | 514 | 747 | 1619 | 132 | 4 | 40 | 3714 | 6.3 | | 14 | 35.7 | 25:14 | 131 | 25 | 46 | 71 | 156 | 9 | 1 | 1 | 26:49 |

CCHA Second All-Star Team (1989) • CCHA First All-Star Team (1990) • NCAA West First All-American Team (1990) • NHL All-Rookie Team (1991) • NHL First All-Star Team (1998) • James Norris Memorial Trophy (1998) • NHL Second All-Star Team (2000, 2001, 2002)

Played in NHL All-Star Game (1994, 1999, 2000, 2001, 2002, 2003, 2004)

• Missed majority of 1995-96 season recovering from knee injury suffered in game vs. Washington, October 20, 1995. Traded to **Colorado** by **Los Angeles** with Steve Reinprecht for Adam Deadmarsh, Aaron Miller, a player to be named later (Jared Aulin, March 22, 2001) and Colorado's 1st round choices in 2001 (Dave Steckel) and 2003 (Brian Boyle) Entry Drafts, February 21, 2001. Signed as a free agent by **Los Angeles**, July 1, 2006. Signed as a free agent by **San Jose**, July 3, 2008.

### BLUNDEN, Michael (BLUHN-dehn, MIGH-kuhl) CBJ

Right wing. Shoots right. 6'4", 207 lbs. Born, Toronto, Ont., December 15, 1986. Chicago's 2nd choice, 43rd overall, in 2005 Entry Draft.

| | | | | | | | | | | | | | | | | | | | | | | | | | |
|---|---|---|---|---|---|---|---|---|---|---|---|---|---|---|---|---|---|---|---|---|---|---|---|---|---|
| 2002-03 | Erie Otters | OHL | 63 | 10 | 7 | 17 | 55 | .... | .... | .... | .... | .... | .... | .... | .... | .... | .... | .... | .... | .... | .... | .... | .... | .... | .... |
| 2003-04 | Erie Otters | OHL | 52 | 22 | 17 | 39 | 53 | .... | .... | .... | .... | .... | .... | .... | .... | .... | 3 | 0 | 0 | 0 | 0 | .... | .... | .... | .... |
| 2004-05 | Erie Otters | OHL | 61 | 22 | 19 | 41 | 75 | .... | .... | .... | .... | .... | .... | .... | .... | .... | 2 | 0 | 0 | 0 | 2 | .... | .... | .... | .... |
| 2005-06 | Erie Otters | OHL | 60 | 46 | 38 | 84 | 63 | .... | .... | .... | .... | .... | .... | .... | .... | .... | .... | .... | .... | .... | .... | .... | .... | .... | .... |
| | Norfolk Admirals | AHL | 11 | 1 | 5 | 6 | 2 | .... | .... | .... | .... | .... | .... | .... | .... | .... | 1 | 0 | 0 | 0 | 0 | .... | .... | .... | .... |
| 2006-07 | Chicago | NHL | 9 | 0 | 0 | 0 | 10 | 0 | 0 | 0 | 10 | 0.0 | –5 | 1 | 0.0 | 11:23 | .... | .... | .... | .... | .... | .... | .... | .... | .... |
| | Norfolk Admirals | AHL | 17 | 4 | 5 | 9 | 15 | .... | .... | .... | .... | .... | .... | .... | .... | .... | .... | .... | .... | .... | .... | .... | .... | .... | .... |
| 2007-08 | Chicago | NHL | 1 | 0 | 0 | 0 | 0 | 0 | 0 | 0 | 1 | 0.0 | –1 | 0 | 0.0 | 7:51 | .... | .... | .... | .... | .... | .... | .... | .... | .... |
| | Rockford IceHogs | AHL | 74 | 16 | 21 | 37 | 83 | .... | .... | .... | .... | .... | .... | .... | .... | .... | 12 | 1 | 3 | 4 | 35 | .... | .... | .... | .... |
| 2008-09 | Rockford IceHogs | AHL | 37 | 3 | 7 | 10 | 42 | .... | .... | .... | .... | .... | .... | .... | .... | .... | .... | .... | .... | .... | .... | .... | .... | .... | .... |
| | Syracuse Crunch | AHL | 39 | 9 | 12 | 21 | 68 | .... | .... | .... | .... | .... | .... | .... | .... | .... | .... | .... | .... | .... | .... | .... | .... | .... | .... |
| | NHL Totals | | 10 | 0 | 0 | 0 | 10 | 0 | 0 | 0 | 11 | 0.0 | | 1 | 0.0 | 11:02 | .... | .... | .... | .... | .... | .... | .... | .... | .... |

• Missed majority of 2006-07 season recovering from shoulder injury sufffered in game vs. Hershey (AHL), December 10, 2006. Traded to **Columbus** by **Chicago** for Adam Pineault, January 10, 2008.

### BOCHENSKI, Brandon (boh-CHEHN-skee, BRAN-duhn) T.B.

Right wing. Shoots right. 6'1", 187 lbs. Born, Blaine, MN, April 4, 1982. Ottawa's 9th choice, 223rd overall, in 2001 Entry Draft.

| | | | | | | | | | | | | | | | | | | | | | | | | | |
|---|---|---|---|---|---|---|---|---|---|---|---|---|---|---|---|---|---|---|---|---|---|---|---|---|---|
| 99-2000 | Blaine Bengals | High-MN | 28 | 32 | 30 | 62 | .... | .... | .... | .... | .... | .... | .... | .... | .... | .... | .... | .... | .... | .... | .... | .... | .... | .... | .... |
| 2000-01 | Lincoln Stars | USHL | 55 | *47 | 33 | 80 | 22 | .... | .... | .... | .... | .... | .... | .... | .... | .... | 11 | 5 | 7 | 12 | 4 | .... | .... | .... | .... |
| 2001-02 | North Dakota | WCHA | 36 | 17 | 15 | 32 | 36 | .... | .... | .... | .... | .... | .... | .... | .... | .... | .... | .... | .... | .... | .... | .... | .... | .... | .... |
| 2002-03 | North Dakota | WCHA | 43 | 35 | 27 | 62 | 42 | .... | .... | .... | .... | .... | .... | .... | .... | .... | .... | .... | .... | .... | .... | .... | .... | .... | .... |
| 2003-04 | North Dakota | WCHA | 41 | 27 | 33 | 60 | 40 | .... | .... | .... | .... | .... | .... | .... | .... | .... | .... | .... | .... | .... | .... | .... | .... | .... | .... |
| 2004-05 | Binghamton | AHL | 75 | 34 | 36 | 70 | 16 | .... | .... | .... | .... | .... | .... | .... | .... | .... | 6 | 1 | 0 | 1 | 2 | .... | .... | .... | .... |
| 2005-06 | Ottawa | NHL | 20 | 6 | 7 | 13 | 14 | 2 | 0 | 0 | 39 | 15.4 | 7 | 4 | 50.0 | 12:17 | .... | .... | .... | .... | .... | .... | .... | .... | .... |
| | Binghamton | AHL | 33 | 22 | 24 | 46 | 36 | .... | .... | .... | .... | .... | .... | .... | .... | .... | .... | .... | .... | .... | .... | .... | .... | .... | .... |
| | Chicago | NHL | 20 | 2 | 2 | 4 | 8 | 0 | 0 | 0 | 23 | 8.7 | –9 | 8 | 37.5 | 8:53 | .... | .... | .... | .... | .... | .... | .... | .... | .... |
| | Norfolk Admirals | AHL | .... | .... | .... | .... | .... | .... | .... | .... | .... | .... | .... | .... | .... | .... | 3 | 1 | 1 | 2 | 0 | .... | .... | .... | .... |
| 2006-07 | Chicago | NHL | 10 | 2 | 0 | 2 | 2 | 0 | 0 | 0 | 20 | 10.0 | –2 | 1 | 0.0 | 9:59 | .... | .... | .... | .... | .... | .... | .... | .... | .... |
| | Norfolk Admirals | AHL | 35 | 33 | 33 | 66 | 31 | .... | .... | .... | .... | .... | .... | .... | .... | .... | .... | .... | .... | .... | .... | .... | .... | .... | .... |
| | Boston | NHL | 31 | 11 | 11 | 22 | 14 | 3 | 0 | 2 | 72 | 15.3 | 3 | 4 | 25.0 | 14:59 | .... | .... | .... | .... | .... | .... | .... | .... | .... |
| 2007-08 | Boston | NHL | 20 | 0 | 6 | 6 | 6 | 0 | 0 | 0 | 30 | 0.0 | 2 | 6 | 33.3 | 12:48 | .... | .... | .... | .... | .... | .... | .... | .... | .... |
| | Providence Bruins | AHL | 2 | 1 | 0 | 1 | 0 | .... | .... | .... | .... | .... | .... | .... | .... | .... | .... | .... | .... | .... | .... | .... | .... | .... | .... |
| | Anaheim | NHL | 12 | 2 | 2 | 4 | 6 | 1 | 0 | 0 | 17 | 11.8 | 2 | 1 | 0.0 | 12:28 | .... | .... | .... | .... | .... | .... | .... | .... | .... |
| | Nashville | NHL | 8 | 1 | 2 | 3 | 0 | 0 | 0 | 0 | 9 | 11.1 | 2 | 0 | 0.0 | 9:01 | 3 | 0 | 0 | 0 | 0 | 0 | 0 | 0 | 6:36 |
| 2008-09 | Tampa Bay | NHL | 7 | 0 | 1 | 1 | 2 | 0 | 0 | 0 | 11 | 0.0 | –3 | 0 | 0.0 | 10:47 | .... | .... | .... | .... | .... | .... | .... | .... | .... |
| | Norfolk Admirals | AHL | 69 | 27 | 26 | 53 | 48 | .... | .... | .... | .... | .... | .... | .... | .... | .... | .... | .... | .... | .... | .... | .... | .... | .... | .... |
| | NHL Totals | | 128 | 24 | 31 | 55 | 52 | 6 | 0 | 2 | 221 | 10.9 | | 24 | 33.3 | 12:02 | 3 | 0 | 0 | 0 | 0 | 0 | 0 | 0 | 6:36 |

USHL First All-Star Team (2001) • USHL Rookie of the Year (2001) • WCHA All-Rookie Team (2002) • WCHA Rookie of the Year (2002) • WCHA Second All-Star Team (2003) • WCHA First All-Star Team (2004) • NCAA West First All-American Team (2004) • AHL All-Rookie Team (2005)

Traded to **Chicago** by **Ottawa** with Ottawa's 2nd round choice (Simon Danis-Pepin) in 2006 Entry Draft for Tyler Arnason, March 9, 2006. Traded to **Boston** by **Chicago** for Kris Versteeg and future considerations, February 3, 2007. Traded to **Anaheim** by **Boston** for Shane Hnidy and Anaheim's 6th round choice (Nicholas Tremblay) in 2008 Entry Draft, January 2, 2008. Traded to **Nashville** by **Anaheim** for future considerations, February 26, 2008. Signed as a free agent by **Tampa Bay**, July 8, 2008.

### BODIE, Troy (BOH-dee, TROI) ANA.

Right wing. Shoots right. 6'4", 215 lbs. Born, Portage La Prairie, Man., January 25, 1985. Edmonton's 12th choice, 278th overall, in 2003 Entry Draft.

| | | | | | | | | | | | | | | | | | | | | | | | | | |
|---|---|---|---|---|---|---|---|---|---|---|---|---|---|---|---|---|---|---|---|---|---|---|---|---|---|
| 2001-02 | Central Plains | MMMHL | 40 | 22 | 21 | 43 | 10 | .... | .... | .... | .... | .... | .... | .... | .... | .... | .... | .... | .... | .... | .... | .... | .... | .... | .... |
| 2002-03 | Kelowna Rockets | WHL | 35 | 4 | 4 | 8 | 36 | .... | .... | .... | .... | .... | .... | .... | .... | .... | 11 | 1 | 1 | 2 | 2 | .... | .... | .... | .... |
| 2003-04 | Kelowna Rockets | WHL | 71 | 8 | 12 | 20 | 112 | .... | .... | .... | .... | .... | .... | .... | .... | .... | 17 | 7 | 3 | 10 | 6 | .... | .... | .... | .... |
| 2004-05 | Kelowna Rockets | WHL | 72 | 24 | 24 | 48 | 96 | .... | .... | .... | .... | .... | .... | .... | .... | .... | 24 | 4 | 13 | 17 | 26 | .... | .... | .... | .... |
| 2005-06 | Kelowna Rockets | WHL | 72 | 28 | 25 | 53 | 117 | .... | .... | .... | .... | .... | .... | .... | .... | .... | 12 | 5 | 4 | 9 | 8 | .... | .... | .... | .... |
| 2006-07 | Hamilton | AHL | 20 | 0 | 1 | 1 | 29 | .... | .... | .... | .... | .... | .... | .... | .... | .... | .... | .... | .... | .... | .... | .... | .... | .... | .... |
| | Stockton Thunder | ECHL | 46 | 21 | 17 | 38 | 80 | .... | .... | .... | .... | .... | .... | .... | .... | .... | 6 | 0 | 2 | 2 | 6 | .... | .... | .... | .... |
| 2007-08 | Springfield | AHL | 62 | 9 | 6 | 15 | 108 | .... | .... | .... | .... | .... | .... | .... | .... | .... | .... | .... | .... | .... | .... | .... | .... | .... | .... |
| 2008-09 | Anaheim | NHL | 4 | 0 | 0 | 0 | 0 | 0 | 0 | 0 | 5 | 0.0 | 0 | 2 | 50.0 | 8:09 | .... | .... | .... | .... | .... | .... | .... | .... | .... |
| | Iowa Chops | AHL | 71 | 15 | 12 | 27 | 105 | .... | .... | .... | .... | .... | .... | .... | .... | .... | .... | .... | .... | .... | .... | .... | .... | .... | .... |
| | NHL Totals | | 4 | 0 | 0 | 0 | 0 | 0 | 0 | 0 | 5 | 0.0 | | 2 | 50.0 | 8:09 | .... | .... | .... | .... | .... | .... | .... | .... | .... |

Signed as a free agent by **Anaheim**, July 22, 2008.

### BOEDKER, Mikkel (BAWD-kuhr, MIH-kehl) PHX.

Right wing. Shoots left. 5'11", 195 lbs. Born, Brondby, Denmark, December 16, 1989. Phoenix's 1st choice, 8th overall, in 2008 Entry Draft.

| | | | | | | | | | | | | | | | | | | | | | | | | | |
|---|---|---|---|---|---|---|---|---|---|---|---|---|---|---|---|---|---|---|---|---|---|---|---|---|---|
| 2004-05 | Rodovre IK | Den-2 | 1 | 0 | 1 | 1 | 0 | .... | .... | .... | .... | .... | .... | .... | .... | .... | .... | .... | .... | .... | .... | .... | .... | .... | .... |
| 2005-06 | Frolunda U18 | Swe-U18 | 5 | 2 | 0 | 2 | 0 | .... | .... | .... | .... | .... | .... | .... | .... | .... | 2 | 0 | 1 | 1 | 0 | .... | .... | .... | .... |
| | Frolunda Jr. | Swe-Jr. | 37 | 9 | 8 | 17 | 22 | .... | .... | .... | .... | .... | .... | .... | .... | .... | 2 | 1 | 2 | 3 | 0 | .... | .... | .... | .... |
| 2006-07 | Frolunda U18 | Swe-U18 | 3 | 3 | 2 | 5 | 2 | .... | .... | .... | .... | .... | .... | .... | .... | .... | 6 | 5 | 4 | 9 | 2 | .... | .... | .... | .... |
| | Frolunda Jr. | Swe-Jr. | 39 | 19 | 30 | 49 | 14 | .... | .... | .... | .... | .... | .... | .... | .... | .... | 8 | 6 | 5 | 11 | 6 | .... | .... | .... | .... |
| | Frolunda | Sweden | 2 | 0 | 0 | 0 | 0 | .... | .... | .... | .... | .... | .... | .... | .... | .... | .... | .... | .... | .... | .... | .... | .... | .... | .... |
| 2007-08 | Kitchener Rangers | OHL | 62 | 29 | 44 | 73 | 14 | .... | .... | .... | .... | .... | .... | .... | .... | .... | 20 | 9 | *26 | 35 | 2 | .... | .... | .... | .... |
| 2008-09 | Phoenix | NHL | 78 | 11 | 17 | 28 | 18 | 2 | 0 | 3 | 116 | 9.5 | –6 | 8 | 12.5 | 15:32 | .... | .... | .... | .... | .... | .... | .... | .... | .... |
| | NHL Totals | | 78 | 11 | 17 | 28 | 18 | 2 | 0 | 3 | 116 | 9.5 | | 8 | 12.5 | 15:32 | .... | .... | .... | .... | .... | .... | .... | .... | .... |

### BOGOSIAN, Zach (buh-GOH-zhuhn, ZAK) ATL.

Defense. Shoots right. 6'2", 200 lbs. Born, Massena, NY, July 15, 1990. Atlanta's 1st choice, 3rd overall, in 2008 Entry Draft.

| | | | | | | | | | | | | | | | | | | | | | | | | | |
|---|---|---|---|---|---|---|---|---|---|---|---|---|---|---|---|---|---|---|---|---|---|---|---|---|---|
| 2005-06 | Cushing | High-MA | 36 | 1 | 16 | 17 | .... | .... | .... | .... | .... | .... | .... | .... | .... | .... | .... | .... | .... | .... | .... | .... | .... | .... | .... |
| 2006-07 | Peterborough | OHL | 67 | 7 | 26 | 33 | 63 | .... | .... | .... | .... | .... | .... | .... | .... | .... | .... | .... | .... | .... | .... | .... | .... | .... | .... |
| 2007-08 | Peterborough | OHL | 60 | 11 | 50 | 61 | 72 | .... | .... | .... | .... | .... | .... | .... | .... | .... | 5 | 0 | 3 | 3 | 8 | .... | .... | .... | .... |
| 2008-09 | Atlanta | NHL | 47 | 9 | 10 | 19 | 47 | 2 | 1 | 1 | 90 | 10.0 | 11 | 0 | 0.0 | 18:06 | .... | .... | .... | .... | .... | .... | .... | .... | .... |
| | Chicago Wolves | AHL | 5 | 1 | 0 | 1 | 0 | .... | .... | .... | .... | .... | .... | .... | .... | .... | .... | .... | .... | .... | .... | .... | .... | .... | .... |
| | NHL Totals | | 47 | 9 | 10 | 19 | 47 | 2 | 1 | 1 | 90 | 10.0 | | 0 | 0.0 | 18:06 | .... | .... | .... | .... | .... | .... | .... | .... | .... |

OHL First All-Star Team (2008)

| | | | Regular Season | | | | | | | | | | | | | | | Playoffs | | | | | | | | |
|---|---|---|---|---|---|---|---|---|---|---|---|---|---|---|---|---|---|---|---|---|---|---|---|---|---|
| Season | Club | League | GP | G | A | Pts | PIM | PP | SH | GW | S | % | +/- | TF | F% | Min | GP | G | A | Pts | PIM | PP | SH | GW | Min |

## BOGUNIECKI, Eric

(BOH-guhn-ih-kee, AIR-ihk)

Center. Shoots right. 5'8", 198 lbs. Born, New Haven, CT, May 6, 1975. St. Louis' 6th choice, 193rd overall, in 1993 Entry Draft.

| | | | | | | | | | | | | | | | | | | | | | | | | | |
|---|---|---|---|---|---|---|---|---|---|---|---|---|---|---|---|---|---|---|---|---|---|---|---|---|---|
| 1992-93 | Westminster | High-CT | 24 | 30 | 24 | 54 | 55 | .... | .... | .... | .... | .... | .... | .... | .... | .... | .... | .... | .... | .... | .... | .... | .... | .... | .... |
| 1993-94 | New Hampshire | H-East | 40 | 17 | 16 | 33 | 66 | .... | .... | .... | .... | .... | .... | .... | .... | .... | .... | .... | .... | .... | .... | .... | .... | .... | .... |
| 1994-95 | New Hampshire | H-East | 34 | 12 | 16 | 28 | 62 | .... | .... | .... | .... | .... | .... | .... | .... | .... | .... | .... | .... | .... | .... | .... | .... | .... | .... |
| 1995-96 | New Hampshire | H-East | 32 | 23 | 28 | 51 | 46 | .... | .... | .... | .... | .... | .... | .... | .... | .... | .... | .... | .... | .... | .... | .... | .... | .... | .... |
| 1996-97 | New Hampshire | H-East | 36 | 26 | 31 | 57 | 58 | .... | .... | .... | .... | .... | .... | .... | .... | .... | .... | .... | .... | .... | .... | .... | .... | .... | .... |
| 1997-98 | Dayton Bombers | ECHL | 26 | 19 | 18 | 37 | 36 | .... | .... | .... | .... | .... | .... | .... | .... | .... | .... | .... | .... | .... | .... | .... | .... | .... | .... |
| | Fort Wayne | IHL | 35 | 4 | 8 | 12 | 29 | .... | .... | .... | .... | .... | .... | .... | .... | .... | 4 | 1 | 2 | 3 | 10 | .... | .... | .... | .... |
| 1998-99 | Fort Wayne | IHL | 72 | 32 | 34 | 66 | 100 | .... | .... | .... | .... | .... | .... | .... | .... | .... | 2 | 0 | 1 | 1 | 2 | .... | .... | .... | .... |
| 99-2000 | Florida | NHL | 4 | 0 | 0 | 0 | 2 | 0 | 0 | 0 | 5 | 0.0 | –1 | 25 | 36.0 | 8:35 | .... | .... | .... | .... | .... | .... | .... | .... | .... |
| | Louisville Panthers | AHL | 57 | 33 | 42 | 75 | 148 | .... | .... | .... | .... | .... | .... | .... | .... | .... | 4 | 3 | 2 | 5 | 20 | .... | .... | .... | .... |
| 2000-01 | Louisville Panthers | AHL | 28 | 13 | 12 | 25 | 56 | .... | .... | .... | .... | .... | .... | .... | .... | .... | .... | .... | .... | .... | .... | .... | .... | .... | .... |
| | St. Louis | NHL | 1 | 0 | 0 | 0 | 0 | 0 | 0 | 0 | 1 | 0.0 | –1 | 0 | 0.0 | 13:44 | .... | .... | .... | .... | .... | .... | .... | .... | .... |
| | Worcester IceCats | AHL | 45 | 17 | 28 | 45 | 100 | .... | .... | .... | .... | .... | .... | .... | .... | .... | 9 | 3 | 2 | 5 | 10 | .... | .... | .... | .... |
| 2001-02 | St. Louis | NHL | 8 | 0 | 1 | 1 | 4 | 0 | 0 | 0 | 10 | 0.0 | –2 | 21 | 38.1 | 11:42 | 1 | 0 | 1 | 1 | 0 | 0 | 0 | 0 | 8:01 |
| | Worcester IceCats | AHL | 63 | *38 | 46 | 84 | 181 | .... | .... | .... | .... | .... | .... | .... | .... | .... | 3 | 2 | 0 | 2 | 4 | .... | .... | .... | .... |
| 2002-03 | St. Louis | NHL | 80 | 22 | 27 | 49 | 38 | 3 | 1 | 5 | 117 | 18.8 | 22 | 5 | 40.0 | 14:00 | 7 | 1 | 2 | 3 | 2 | 1 | 0 | 0 | 13:09 |
| 2003-04 | St. Louis | NHL | 27 | 6 | 4 | 10 | 20 | 2 | 0 | 2 | 40 | 15.0 | –1 | 1 | 0.0 | 14:42 | 1 | 0 | 0 | 0 | 0 | 0 | 0 | 0 | 12:52 |
| | Worcester IceCats | AHL | 3 | 0 | 1 | 1 | 0 | .... | .... | .... | .... | .... | .... | .... | .... | .... | .... | .... | .... | .... | .... | .... | .... | .... | .... |
| 2004-05 | Worcester IceCats | AHL | 30 | 14 | 11 | 25 | 46 | .... | .... | .... | .... | .... | .... | .... | .... | .... | .... | .... | .... | .... | .... | .... | .... | .... | .... |
| | SC Langenthal | Swiss-2 | 10 | 5 | 3 | 8 | 47 | .... | .... | .... | .... | .... | .... | .... | .... | .... | .... | .... | .... | .... | .... | .... | .... | .... | .... |
| 2005-06 | St. Louis | NHL | 9 | 1 | 4 | 5 | 4 | 1 | 0 | 0 | 12 | 8.3 | –1 | 1 | 100.0 | 12:15 | .... | .... | .... | .... | .... | .... | .... | .... | .... |
| | Peoria Rivermen | AHL | 2 | 0 | 0 | 0 | 4 | .... | .... | .... | .... | .... | .... | .... | .... | .... | .... | .... | .... | .... | .... | .... | .... | .... | .... |
| | Pittsburgh | NHL | 38 | 5 | 6 | 11 | 29 | 1 | 0 | 0 | 36 | 13.9 | –2 | 74 | 48.7 | 10:50 | .... | .... | .... | .... | .... | .... | .... | .... | .... |
| 2006-07 | Syracuse Crunch | AHL | 6 | 0 | 0 | 0 | 8 | .... | .... | .... | .... | .... | .... | .... | .... | .... | .... | .... | .... | .... | .... | .... | .... | .... | .... |
| | NY Islanders | NHL | 11 | 0 | 0 | 0 | 8 | 0 | 0 | 0 | 2 | 0.0 | 0 | 0 | 0.0 | 4:54 | .... | .... | .... | .... | .... | .... | .... | .... | .... |
| | Bridgeport | AHL | 48 | 22 | 32 | 54 | 48 | .... | .... | .... | .... | .... | .... | .... | .... | .... | .... | .... | .... | .... | .... | .... | .... | .... | .... |
| 2007-08 | ERC Ingolstadt | Germany | 16 | 4 | 14 | 18 | 24 | .... | .... | .... | .... | .... | .... | .... | .... | .... | 3 | 1 | 3 | 4 | 2 | .... | .... | .... | .... |
| 2008-09 | Iowa Chops | AHL | 69 | 18 | 16 | 34 | 52 | .... | .... | .... | .... | .... | .... | .... | .... | .... | .... | .... | .... | .... | .... | .... | .... | .... | .... |
| | **NHL Totals** | | **178** | **34** | **42** | **76** | **105** | **7** | **1** | **7** | **223** | **15.2** | | **127** | **44.1** | **12:33** | **9** | **1** | **3** | **4** | **2** | **1** | **0** | **0** | **12:33** |

Hockey East Second All-Star Team (1997) • AHL First All-Star Team (2002) • Les Cunningham Award (AHL – MVP) (2002)

Signed as a free agent by **Florida**, July 7, 1999. Traded to **St. Louis** by **Florida** for Andrei Podkonicky, December 17, 2000. • Missed majority of 2003-04 season recovering from shoulder (September 23, 2003 in training camp) and head (February 28, 2004 vs. Vancouver) injuries. Signed as a free agent by **Langenthal** (Swiss-2), October 4, 2004. Traded to **Pittsburgh** by **St. Louis** for Steve Poapst, December 9, 2005. Signed as a free agent by **Columbus**, August 22, 2006. Traded to **NY Islanders** by **Columbus** for Ryan Caldwell, October 25, 2006. Signed as a free agent by **Ingolstadt** (Germany), June 29, 2007. Signed as a free agent by **Anaheim**, July 22, 2008.

## BOIS, Danny

(BOIZ, DA-nee) **CHI.**

Right wing. Shoots right. 6'1", 202 lbs. Born, Thunder Bay, Ont., June 1, 1983. Colorado's 2nd choice, 97th overall, in 2001 Entry Draft.

| | | | | | | | | | | | | | | | | | | | | | | | | | |
|---|---|---|---|---|---|---|---|---|---|---|---|---|---|---|---|---|---|---|---|---|---|---|---|---|---|
| 1998-99 | T. Bay Kings | TBMHL | 15 | 7 | 12 | 19 | 28 | .... | .... | .... | .... | .... | .... | .... | .... | .... | .... | .... | .... | .... | .... | .... | .... | .... | .... |
| 99-2000 | Wellington Dukes | OPJHL | 37 | 15 | 20 | 35 | 115 | .... | .... | .... | .... | .... | .... | .... | .... | .... | .... | .... | .... | .... | .... | .... | .... | .... | .... |
| 2000-01 | London Knights | OHL | 66 | 21 | 16 | 37 | 218 | .... | .... | .... | .... | .... | .... | .... | .... | .... | 5 | 2 | 1 | 3 | 19 | .... | .... | .... | .... |
| 2001-02 | London Knights | OHL | 62 | 16 | 14 | 30 | 256 | .... | .... | .... | .... | .... | .... | .... | .... | .... | 12 | 2 | 2 | 4 | 47 | .... | .... | .... | .... |
| 2002-03 | London Knights | OHL | 56 | 19 | 13 | 32 | 207 | .... | .... | .... | .... | .... | .... | .... | .... | .... | 13 | 4 | 6 | 10 | 38 | .... | .... | .... | .... |
| 2003-04 | London Knights | OHL | 52 | 14 | 25 | 39 | 242 | .... | .... | .... | .... | .... | .... | .... | .... | .... | 7 | 4 | 4 | 8 | 29 | .... | .... | .... | .... |
| 2004-05 | Binghamton | AHL | 72 | 2 | 4 | 6 | 287 | .... | .... | .... | .... | .... | .... | .... | .... | .... | 6 | 0 | 1 | 1 | 2 | .... | .... | .... | .... |
| 2005-06 | Binghamton | AHL | 79 | 18 | 17 | 35 | 224 | .... | .... | .... | .... | .... | .... | .... | .... | .... | .... | .... | .... | .... | .... | .... | .... | .... | .... |
| 2006-07 | Ottawa | NHL | 1 | 0 | 0 | 0 | 7 | 0 | 0 | 0 | 1 | 0.0 | 0 | 2 | 50.0 | 3:53 | .... | .... | .... | .... | .... | .... | .... | .... | .... |
| | Binghamton | AHL | 65 | 14 | 13 | 27 | 153 | .... | .... | .... | .... | .... | .... | .... | .... | .... | .... | .... | .... | .... | .... | .... | .... | .... | .... |
| 2007-08 | Binghamton | AHL | 54 | 8 | 13 | 21 | 153 | .... | .... | .... | .... | .... | .... | .... | .... | .... | .... | .... | .... | .... | .... | .... | .... | .... | .... |
| 2008-09 | Binghamton | AHL | 66 | 12 | 12 | 24 | 149 | .... | .... | .... | .... | .... | .... | .... | .... | .... | .... | .... | .... | .... | .... | .... | .... | .... | .... |
| | **NHL Totals** | | **1** | **0** | **0** | **0** | **7** | **0** | **0** | **0** | **1** | **0.0** | | **2** | **50.0** | **3:53** | .... | .... | .... | .... | .... | .... | .... | .... | .... |

Signed as a free agent by **Ottawa**, April 30, 2004. Signed as a free agent by **Chicago**, July 20, 2009.

## BOLDUC, Alexandre

(bohl-DUHK, ahl-ehx-AHN-druh) **VAN.**

Center. Shoots left. 6'1", 178 lbs. Born, Montreal, Que., June 26, 1985. St. Louis' 6th choice, 127th overall, in 2003 Entry Draft.

| | | | | | | | | | | | | | | | | | | | | | | | | | |
|---|---|---|---|---|---|---|---|---|---|---|---|---|---|---|---|---|---|---|---|---|---|---|---|---|---|
| 2000-01 | Notre Dame | SMHL | 61 | 17 | 35 | 52 | .... | .... | .... | .... | .... | .... | .... | .... | .... | .... | .... | .... | .... | .... | .... | .... | .... | .... | .... |
| 2001-02 | Rouyn-Noranda | QMJHL | 64 | 6 | 14 | 20 | 69 | .... | .... | .... | .... | .... | .... | .... | .... | .... | 4 | 1 | 1 | 2 | 4 | .... | .... | .... | .... |
| 2002-03 | Rouyn-Noranda | QMJHL | 66 | 14 | 29 | 43 | 131 | .... | .... | .... | .... | .... | .... | .... | .... | .... | 4 | 0 | 2 | 2 | 2 | .... | .... | .... | .... |
| 2003-04 | Rouyn-Noranda | QMJHL | 65 | 23 | 35 | 58 | 115 | .... | .... | .... | .... | .... | .... | .... | .... | .... | 11 | 3 | 4 | 7 | 18 | .... | .... | .... | .... |
| 2004-05 | Rouyn-Noranda | QMJHL | 33 | 7 | 10 | 17 | 46 | .... | .... | .... | .... | .... | .... | .... | .... | .... | .... | .... | .... | .... | .... | .... | .... | .... | .... |
| | Shawinigan | QMJHL | 29 | 7 | 11 | 18 | 14 | .... | .... | .... | .... | .... | .... | .... | .... | .... | 3 | 0 | 0 | 0 | 0 | .... | .... | .... | .... |
| 2005-06 | Manitoba Moose | AHL | 29 | 3 | 7 | 10 | 35 | .... | .... | .... | .... | .... | .... | .... | .... | .... | .... | .... | .... | .... | .... | .... | .... | .... | .... |
| | Bakersfield | ECHL | 24 | 10 | 6 | 16 | 56 | .... | .... | .... | .... | .... | .... | .... | .... | .... | 11 | 4 | 4 | 8 | 28 | .... | .... | .... | .... |
| 2006-07 | Manitoba Moose | AHL | 32 | 4 | 5 | 9 | 35 | .... | .... | .... | .... | .... | .... | .... | .... | .... | 5 | 0 | 0 | 0 | 8 | .... | .... | .... | .... |
| | Bakersfield | ECHL | 16 | 7 | 17 | 24 | 42 | .... | .... | .... | .... | .... | .... | .... | .... | .... | 6 | 2 | 4 | 6 | 9 | .... | .... | .... | .... |
| 2007-08 | Manitoba Moose | AHL | 70 | 18 | 19 | 37 | 93 | .... | .... | .... | .... | .... | .... | .... | .... | .... | 6 | 1 | 0 | 1 | 6 | .... | .... | .... | .... |
| 2008-09 | Vancouver | NHL | 7 | 0 | 1 | 1 | 4 | 0 | 0 | 0 | 7 | 0.0 | 1 | 13 | 38.5 | 7:20 | .... | .... | .... | .... | .... | .... | .... | .... | .... |
| | Manitoba Moose | AHL | 63 | 12 | 21 | 33 | 116 | .... | .... | .... | .... | .... | .... | .... | .... | .... | 13 | 5 | 4 | 9 | 14 | .... | .... | .... | .... |
| | **NHL Totals** | | **7** | **0** | **1** | **1** | **4** | **0** | **0** | **0** | **7** | **0.0** | | **13** | **38.5** | **7:20** | .... | .... | .... | .... | .... | .... | .... | .... | .... |

Signed as a free agent by **Vancouver**, July 2, 2008.

## BOLL, Jared

(BOWL, JAIR-ehd) **CBJ**

Right wing. Shoots right. 6'2", 210 lbs. Born, Charlotte, NC, May 13, 1986. Columbus' 4th choice, 101st overall, in 2005 Entry Draft.

| | | | | | | | | | | | | | | | | | | | | | | | | | |
|---|---|---|---|---|---|---|---|---|---|---|---|---|---|---|---|---|---|---|---|---|---|---|---|---|---|
| 2003-04 | Lincoln Stars | USHL | 57 | 6 | 8 | 14 | *176 | .... | .... | .... | .... | .... | .... | .... | .... | .... | .... | .... | .... | .... | .... | .... | .... | .... | .... |
| 2004-05 | Lincoln Stars | USHL | 59 | 23 | 24 | 47 | *294 | .... | .... | .... | .... | .... | .... | .... | .... | .... | 4 | 1 | 3 | 4 | 25 | .... | .... | .... | .... |
| 2005-06 | Plymouth Whalers | OHL | 65 | 19 | 22 | 41 | 205 | .... | .... | .... | .... | .... | .... | .... | .... | .... | 13 | 2 | 4 | 6 | 21 | .... | .... | .... | .... |
| 2006-07 | Plymouth Whalers | OHL | 66 | 28 | 27 | 55 | 198 | .... | .... | .... | .... | .... | .... | .... | .... | .... | 20 | 6 | 4 | 10 | *66 | .... | .... | .... | .... |
| 2007-08 | Columbus | NHL | 75 | 5 | 5 | 10 | 226 | 0 | 0 | 3 | 63 | 7.9 | –4 | 6 | 33.3 | 8:01 | .... | .... | .... | .... | .... | .... | .... | .... | .... |
| 2008-09 | Columbus | NHL | 75 | 4 | 10 | 14 | 180 | 1 | 0 | 0 | 73 | 5.5 | –6 | 4 | 0.0 | 8:54 | 1 | 0 | 0 | 0 | 0 | 0 | 0 | 0 | 5:17 |
| | **NHL Totals** | | **150** | **9** | **15** | **24** | **406** | **1** | **0** | **3** | **136** | **6.6** | | **10** | **20.0** | **8:27** | **1** | **0** | **0** | **0** | **0** | **0** | **0** | **0** | **5:17** |

## BOLLAND, Dave

(BOHL-uhnd, DAYV) **CHI.**

Center. Shoots right. 6', 181 lbs. Born, Toronto, Ont., June 5, 1986. Chicago's 2nd choice, 32nd overall, in 2004 Entry Draft.

| | | | | | | | | | | | | | | | | | | | | | | | | | |
|---|---|---|---|---|---|---|---|---|---|---|---|---|---|---|---|---|---|---|---|---|---|---|---|---|---|
| 2000-01 | Tor. Red Wings | GTHL | 95 | 79 | 67 | 146 | .... | .... | .... | .... | .... | .... | .... | .... | .... | .... | .... | .... | .... | .... | .... | .... | .... | .... | .... |
| 2001-02 | Tor. Red Wings | GTHL | 36 | 35 | 35 | 70 | 40 | .... | .... | .... | .... | .... | .... | .... | .... | .... | .... | .... | .... | .... | .... | .... | .... | .... | .... |
| 2002-03 | London Knights | OHL | 64 | 7 | 10 | 17 | 21 | .... | .... | .... | .... | .... | .... | .... | .... | .... | 14 | 2 | 1 | 3 | 2 | .... | .... | .... | .... |
| 2003-04 | London Knights | OHL | 65 | 37 | 30 | 67 | 58 | .... | .... | .... | .... | .... | .... | .... | .... | .... | 15 | 3 | 10 | 13 | 18 | .... | .... | .... | .... |
| 2004-05 | London Knights | OHL | 66 | 34 | 51 | 85 | 97 | .... | .... | .... | .... | .... | .... | .... | .... | .... | 18 | 11 | 14 | 25 | 30 | .... | .... | .... | .... |
| 2005-06 | London Knights | OHL | 59 | *57 | 73 | 130 | 104 | .... | .... | .... | .... | .... | .... | .... | .... | .... | 15 | *15 | 9 | 24 | 41 | .... | .... | .... | .... |
| 2006-07 | Chicago | NHL | 1 | 0 | 0 | 0 | 0 | 0 | 0 | 0 | 1 | 0.0 | –1 | 11 | 36.4 | 11:17 | .... | .... | .... | .... | .... | .... | .... | .... | .... |
| | Norfolk Admirals | AHL | 65 | 17 | 32 | 49 | 53 | .... | .... | .... | .... | .... | .... | .... | .... | .... | 6 | 0 | 4 | 4 | 17 | .... | .... | .... | .... |
| 2007-08 | Chicago | NHL | 39 | 4 | 13 | 17 | 28 | 0 | 0 | 0 | 49 | 8.2 | 6 | 385 | 46.5 | 13:43 | .... | .... | .... | .... | .... | .... | .... | .... | .... |
| | Rockford IceHogs | AHL | 16 | 6 | 4 | 10 | 22 | .... | .... | .... | .... | .... | .... | .... | .... | .... | 7 | 0 | 0 | 0 | 8 | .... | .... | .... | .... |
| 2008-09 | Chicago | NHL | 81 | 19 | 28 | 47 | 52 | 2 | 2 | 4 | 111 | 17.1 | 19 | 1177 | 44.4 | 16:27 | 17 | 4 | 8 | 12 | 24 | 1 | 1 | 1 | 18:43 |
| | **NHL Totals** | | **121** | **23** | **41** | **64** | **80** | **2** | **2** | **4** | **161** | **14.3** | | **1573** | **44.8** | **15:32** | **17** | **4** | **8** | **12** | **24** | **1** | **1** | **1** | **18:43** |

OHL First All-Star Team (2006) • Canadian Major Junior First All-Star Team (2006)

## BONK, Radek

(BOHNK, RA-dehk)

Center. Shoots left. 6'2", 210 lbs. Born, Krnov, Czech., January 9, 1976. Ottawa's 1st choice, 3rd overall, in 1994 Entry Draft.

| | | | Regular Season | | | | | | | | | | | | | | Playoffs | | | | | | | | |
|---|---|---|---|---|---|---|---|---|---|---|---|---|---|---|---|---|---|---|---|---|---|---|---|---|---|
| Season | Club | League | GP | G | A | Pts | PIM | PP | SH | GW | S | % | +/- | TF | F% | Min | GP | G | A | Pts | PIM | PP | SH | GW | Min |
| 1990-91 | Opava Jr. | Czech-Jr. | 35 | 47 | 42 | 89 | 25 | .... | .... | .... | .... | .... | .... | .... | .... | .... | .... | .... | .... | .... | .... | .... | .... | .... | .... |
| 1991-92 | AC ZPS Zlin Jr. | Czech-Jr. | 45 | 47 | 36 | 83 | 30 | .... | .... | .... | .... | .... | .... | .... | .... | .... | .... | .... | .... | .... | .... | .... | .... | .... | .... |
| 1992-93 | AC ZPS Zlin | Czech | 30 | 5 | 5 | 10 | 10 | .... | .... | .... | .... | .... | .... | .... | .... | .... | .... | .... | .... | .... | .... | .... | .... | .... | .... |
| 1993-94 | Las Vegas | IHL | 76 | 42 | 45 | 87 | 208 | .... | .... | .... | .... | .... | .... | .... | .... | .... | 5 | 1 | 2 | 3 | 10 | .... | .... | .... | .... |
| **1994-95** | Las Vegas | IHL | 33 | 7 | 13 | 20 | 62 | .... | .... | .... | .... | .... | .... | .... | .... | .... | .... | .... | .... | .... | .... | .... | .... | .... | .... |
| | **Ottawa** | **NHL** | **42** | **3** | **8** | **11** | **28** | **1** | **0** | **0** | **40** | **7.5** | **–5** | .... | .... | .... | .... | .... | .... | .... | .... | .... | .... | .... | .... |
| | P.E.I. Senators | AHL | .... | .... | .... | .... | .... | .... | .... | .... | .... | .... | .... | .... | .... | .... | 1 | 0 | 0 | 0 | 0 | .... | .... | .... | .... |
| **1995-96** | **Ottawa** | **NHL** | **76** | **16** | **19** | **35** | **36** | **5** | **0** | **1** | **161** | **9.9** | **–5** | .... | .... | .... | .... | .... | .... | .... | .... | .... | .... | .... | .... |
| **1996-97** | **Ottawa** | **NHL** | **53** | **5** | **13** | **18** | **14** | **0** | **1** | **0** | **82** | **6.1** | **–4** | .... | .... | .... | **7** | **0** | **1** | **1** | **4** | **0** | **0** | **0** | .... |
| **1997-98** | **Ottawa** | **NHL** | **65** | **7** | **9** | **16** | **16** | **1** | **0** | **0** | **93** | **7.5** | **–13** | .... | .... | .... | **5** | **0** | **0** | **0** | **2** | **0** | **0** | **0** | .... |
| **1998-99** | **Ottawa** | **NHL** | **81** | **16** | **16** | **32** | **48** | **0** | **1** | **6** | **110** | **14.5** | **15** | **1184** | **50.1** | **13:44** | **4** | **0** | **0** | **0** | **6** | **0** | **0** | **0** | **16:16** |
| **99-2000** | Pardubice | CzRep | 3 | 1 | 0 | 1 | 4 | .... | .... | .... | .... | .... | .... | .... | .... | .... | .... | .... | .... | .... | .... | .... | .... | .... | .... |
| | **Ottawa** | **NHL** | **80** | **23** | **37** | **60** | **53** | **10** | **0** | **5** | **167** | **13.8** | **–2** | **1654** | **52.0** | **18:14** | **6** | **0** | **0** | **0** | **8** | **0** | **0** | **0** | **15:37** |
| **2000-01** | **Ottawa** | **NHL** | **74** | **23** | **36** | **59** | **52** | **5** | **2** | **3** | **139** | **16.5** | **27** | **1506** | **51.2** | **18:16** | **2** | **0** | **0** | **0** | **2** | **0** | **0** | **0** | **14:32** |
| **2001-02** | **Ottawa** | **NHL** | **82** | **25** | **45** | **70** | **52** | **6** | **2** | **5** | **170** | **14.7** | **3** | **1530** | **51.0** | **17:57** | **12** | **3** | **7** | **10** | **6** | **2** | **0** | **1** | **18:53** |
| **2002-03** | **Ottawa** | **NHL** | **70** | **22** | **32** | **54** | **36** | **11** | **0** | **4** | **146** | **15.1** | **6** | **1218** | **46.2** | **17:32** | **18** | **6** | **5** | **11** | **10** | **2** | **0** | **0** | **17:43** |
| **2003-04** | **Ottawa** | **NHL** | **66** | **12** | **32** | **44** | **66** | **6** | **0** | **1** | **98** | **12.2** | **2** | **1184** | **44.9** | **17:38** | **7** | **0** | **2** | **2** | **0** | **0** | **0** | **0** | **18:29** |
| 2004-05 | HC Ocelari Trinec | CzRep | 27 | 6 | 10 | 16 | 44 | .... | .... | .... | .... | .... | .... | .... | .... | .... | .... | .... | .... | .... | .... | .... | .... | .... | .... |
| | HC Hame Zlin | CzRep | 6 | 3 | 2 | 5 | 4 | .... | .... | .... | .... | .... | .... | .... | .... | .... | 6 | 0 | 2 | 2 | 8 | .... | .... | .... | .... |
| **2005-06** | **Montreal** | **NHL** | **61** | **6** | **15** | **21** | **52** | **0** | **2** | **1** | **76** | **7.9** | **–3** | **963** | **47.4** | **15:10** | **6** | **2** | **0** | **2** | **2** | **0** | **0** | **1** | **15:36** |
| **2006-07** | **Montreal** | **NHL** | **74** | **13** | **10** | **23** | **54** | **1** | **2** | **1** | **111** | **11.7** | **0** | **1198** | **49.8** | **15:52** | .... | .... | .... | .... | .... | .... | .... | .... | .... |
| **2007-08** | **Nashville** | **NHL** | **79** | **14** | **15** | **29** | **40** | **6** | **0** | **1** | **138** | **10.1** | **–31** | **879** | **52.0** | **15:56** | **6** | **1** | **0** | **1** | **2** | **0** | **0** | **0** | **17:56** |
| **2008-09** | **Nashville** | **NHL** | **66** | **9** | **16** | **25** | **34** | **6** | **0** | **2** | **102** | **8.8** | **–12** | **751** | **59.9** | **15:27** | .... | .... | .... | .... | .... | .... | .... | .... | .... |
| | **NHL Totals** | | **969** | **194** | **303** | **497** | **581** | **58** | **10** | **30** | **1633** | **11.9** | | **12067** | **50.2** | **16:36** | **73** | **12** | **15** | **27** | **42** | **4** | **0** | **2** | **17:26** |

Garry F. Longman Memorial Trophy (IHL – Rookie of the Year) (1994)

Played in NHL All-Star Game (2000, 2001)

Traded to **Los Angeles** by **Ottawa** for Los Angeles' 3rd round choice (Shawn Weller) in 2004 Entry Draft, June 26, 2004. Traded to **Montreal** by **Los Angeles** with Cristobal Huet for Mathieu Garon and San Jose's 3rd round choice (previously acquired, Los Angeles selected Paul Baier) in 2004 Entry Draft, June 26, 2004. Signed as a free agent by **Trinec** (CzRep), September 17, 2004. Signed as a free agent by **Zlin** (CzRep), January 31, 2005. Signed as a free agent by **Nashville**, July 2, 2007.

## BOOGAARD, Derek

(BOO-gard, DAIR-ihk) **MIN.**

Left wing. Shoots right. 6'8", 257 lbs. Born, Saskatoon, Sask., June 23, 1982. Minnesota's 6th choice, 202nd overall, in 2001 Entry Draft.

| Season | Club | League | GP | G | A | Pts | PIM | PP | SH | GW | S | % | +/- | TF | F% | Min | GP | G | A | Pts | PIM | PP | SH | GW | Min |
|---|---|---|---|---|---|---|---|---|---|---|---|---|---|---|---|---|---|---|---|---|---|---|---|---|---|
| 1998-99 | Regina Caps | SJHL | 35 | 2 | 3 | 5 | 166 | .... | .... | .... | .... | .... | .... | .... | .... | .... | .... | .... | .... | .... | .... | .... | .... | .... | .... |
| 99-2000 | Regina Pats | WHL | 5 | 0 | 0 | 0 | 17 | .... | .... | .... | .... | .... | .... | .... | .... | .... | .... | .... | .... | .... | .... | .... | .... | .... | .... |
| | Prince George | WHL | 33 | 0 | 0 | 0 | 149 | .... | .... | .... | .... | .... | .... | .... | .... | .... | .... | .... | .... | .... | .... | .... | .... | .... | .... |
| 2000-01 | Prince George | WHL | 61 | 1 | 8 | 9 | 245 | .... | .... | .... | .... | .... | .... | .... | .... | .... | 6 | 1 | 0 | 1 | 31 | .... | .... | .... | .... |
| 2001-02 | Prince George | WHL | 2 | 0 | 0 | 0 | 16 | .... | .... | .... | .... | .... | .... | .... | .... | .... | .... | .... | .... | .... | .... | .... | .... | .... | .... |
| | Medicine Hat | WHL | 46 | 1 | 8 | 9 | 178 | .... | .... | .... | .... | .... | .... | .... | .... | .... | .... | .... | .... | .... | .... | .... | .... | .... | .... |
| 2002-03 | Medicine Hat | WHL | 27 | 1 | 2 | 3 | 65 | .... | .... | .... | .... | .... | .... | .... | .... | .... | .... | .... | .... | .... | .... | .... | .... | .... | .... |
| | Louisiana | ECHL | 33 | 1 | 2 | 3 | 240 | .... | .... | .... | .... | .... | .... | .... | .... | .... | 2 | 0 | 0 | 0 | 0 | .... | .... | .... | .... |
| 2003-04 | Houston Aeros | AHL | 53 | 0 | 4 | 4 | 207 | .... | .... | .... | .... | .... | .... | .... | .... | .... | 2 | 0 | 1 | 1 | 16 | .... | .... | .... | .... |
| 2004-05 | Houston Aeros | AHL | 56 | 1 | 4 | 5 | 259 | .... | .... | .... | .... | .... | .... | .... | .... | .... | 5 | 0 | 0 | 0 | 38 | .... | .... | .... | .... |
| **2005-06** | **Minnesota** | **NHL** | **65** | **2** | **4** | **6** | **158** | **0** | **0** | **1** | **15** | **13.3** | **2** | **0** | **0.0** | **5:23** | .... | .... | .... | .... | .... | .... | .... | .... | .... |
| **2006-07** | **Minnesota** | **NHL** | **48** | **0** | **1** | **1** | **120** | **0** | **0** | **0** | **11** | **0.0** | **0** | **0** | **0.0** | **4:38** | **4** | **0** | **1** | **1** | **20** | **0** | **0** | **0** | **5:59** |
| **2007-08** | **Minnesota** | **NHL** | **34** | **0** | **0** | **0** | **74** | **0** | **0** | **0** | **6** | **0.0** | **–5** | **0** | **0.0** | **3:56** | **6** | **0** | **0** | **0** | **24** | **0** | **0** | **0** | **4:48** |
| **2008-09** | **Minnesota** | **NHL** | **51** | **0** | **3** | **3** | **87** | **0** | **0** | **0** | **13** | **0.0** | **3** | **0** | **0.0** | **5:00** | .... | .... | .... | .... | .... | .... | .... | .... | .... |
| | **NHL Totals** | | **198** | **2** | **8** | **10** | **439** | **0** | **0** | **1** | **45** | **4.4** | | **0** | **0.0** | **4:51** | **10** | **0** | **1** | **1** | **44** | **0** | **0** | **0** | **5:16** |

## BOOTH, David

(BOOTH, DAY-vihd) **FLA.**

Left wing. Shoots left. 6', 212 lbs. Born, Detroit, MI, November 24, 1984. Florida's 3rd choice, 53rd overall, in 2004 Entry Draft.

| Season | Club | League | GP | G | A | Pts | PIM | PP | SH | GW | S | % | +/- | TF | F% | Min | GP | G | A | Pts | PIM | PP | SH | GW | Min |
|---|---|---|---|---|---|---|---|---|---|---|---|---|---|---|---|---|---|---|---|---|---|---|---|---|---|
| 2000-01 | Det. Compuware | NAHL | 42 | 17 | 13 | 30 | 44 | .... | .... | .... | .... | .... | .... | .... | .... | .... | 2 | 1 | 0 | 1 | 2 | .... | .... | .... | .... |
| 2001-02 | USNTDP | U-18 | 40 | 12 | 6 | 18 | 17 | .... | .... | .... | .... | .... | .... | .... | .... | .... | .... | .... | .... | .... | .... | .... | .... | .... | .... |
| | USNTDP | USHL | 12 | 4 | 3 | 7 | 6 | .... | .... | .... | .... | .... | .... | .... | .... | .... | .... | .... | .... | .... | .... | .... | .... | .... | .... |
| | USNTDP | NAHL | 6 | 1 | 3 | 4 | 18 | .... | .... | .... | .... | .... | .... | .... | .... | .... | .... | .... | .... | .... | .... | .... | .... | .... | .... |
| 2002-03 | Michigan State | CCHA | 39 | 17 | 19 | 36 | 53 | .... | .... | .... | .... | .... | .... | .... | .... | .... | .... | .... | .... | .... | .... | .... | .... | .... | .... |
| 2003-04 | Michigan State | CCHA | 30 | 8 | 10 | 18 | 30 | .... | .... | .... | .... | .... | .... | .... | .... | .... | .... | .... | .... | .... | .... | .... | .... | .... | .... |
| 2004-05 | Michigan State | CCHA | 29 | 7 | 9 | 16 | 30 | .... | .... | .... | .... | .... | .... | .... | .... | .... | .... | .... | .... | .... | .... | .... | .... | .... | .... |
| 2005-06 | Michigan State | CCHA | 37 | 13 | 22 | 35 | 50 | .... | .... | .... | .... | .... | .... | .... | .... | .... | .... | .... | .... | .... | .... | .... | .... | .... | .... |
| **2006-07** | **Florida** | **NHL** | **48** | **3** | **7** | **10** | **12** | **0** | **0** | **1** | **86** | **3.5** | **0** | **11** | **36.4** | **9:34** | .... | .... | .... | .... | .... | .... | .... | .... | .... |
| | Rochester | AHL | 25 | 7 | 7 | 14 | 26 | .... | .... | .... | .... | .... | .... | .... | .... | .... | 6 | 0 | 2 | 2 | 4 | .... | .... | .... | .... |
| **2007-08** | **Florida** | **NHL** | **73** | **22** | **18** | **40** | **26** | **1** | **0** | **6** | **228** | **9.6** | **13** | **38** | **34.2** | **16:10** | .... | .... | .... | .... | .... | .... | .... | .... | .... |
| **2008-09** | **Florida** | **NHL** | **72** | **31** | **29** | **60** | **38** | **11** | **0** | **5** | **246** | **12.6** | **10** | **17** | **41.2** | **17:05** | .... | .... | .... | .... | .... | .... | .... | .... | .... |
| | **NHL Totals** | | **193** | **56** | **54** | **110** | **76** | **12** | **0** | **12** | **560** | **10.0** | | **66** | **36.4** | **14:52** | .... | .... | .... | .... | .... | .... | .... | .... | .... |

CCHA All-Rookie Team (2003)

## BOOTLAND, Darryl

(BOOT-land, DAIR-uhl)

Right wing. Shoots right. 6'1", 197 lbs. Born, Toronto, Ont., November 2, 1981. Colorado's 12th choice, 252nd overall, in 2000 Entry Draft.

| Season | Club | League | GP | G | A | Pts | PIM | PP | SH | GW | S | % | +/- | TF | F% | Min | GP | G | A | Pts | PIM | PP | SH | GW | Min |
|---|---|---|---|---|---|---|---|---|---|---|---|---|---|---|---|---|---|---|---|---|---|---|---|---|---|
| 1997-98 | Orangeville | OHA-B | 44 | 22 | 26 | 48 | 177 | .... | .... | .... | .... | .... | .... | .... | .... | .... | .... | .... | .... | .... | .... | .... | .... | .... | .... |
| 1998-99 | Barrie Colts | OHL | 38 | 18 | 11 | 29 | 89 | .... | .... | .... | .... | .... | .... | .... | .... | .... | .... | .... | .... | .... | .... | .... | .... | .... | .... |
| | St. Michael's | OHL | 28 | 12 | 6 | 18 | 80 | .... | .... | .... | .... | .... | .... | .... | .... | .... | .... | .... | .... | .... | .... | .... | .... | .... | .... |
| 99-2000 | St. Michael's | OHL | 65 | 24 | 30 | 54 | 166 | .... | .... | .... | .... | .... | .... | .... | .... | .... | .... | .... | .... | .... | .... | .... | .... | .... | .... |
| 2000-01 | St. Michael's | OHL | 56 | 32 | 33 | 65 | 136 | .... | .... | .... | .... | .... | .... | .... | .... | .... | 11 | 3 | 1 | 4 | 20 | .... | .... | .... | .... |
| 2001-02 | St. Michael's | OHL | 61 | 41 | 56 | 97 | 137 | .... | .... | .... | .... | .... | .... | .... | .... | .... | 15 | 8 | 10 | 18 | 50 | .... | .... | .... | .... |
| 2002-03 | Toledo Storm | ECHL | 54 | 17 | 19 | 36 | 322 | .... | .... | .... | .... | .... | .... | .... | .... | .... | .... | .... | .... | .... | .... | .... | .... | .... | .... |
| | Grand Rapids | AHL | 16 | 1 | 4 | 5 | 41 | .... | .... | .... | .... | .... | .... | .... | .... | .... | 15 | 3 | 2 | 5 | 46 | .... | .... | .... | .... |
| **2003-04** | **Detroit** | **NHL** | **22** | **1** | **1** | **2** | **74** | **0** | **0** | **1** | **13** | **7.7** | **–3** | **1** | **100.0** | **6:07** | .... | .... | .... | .... | .... | .... | .... | .... | .... |
| | Grand Rapids | AHL | 54 | 12 | 2 | 14 | 175 | .... | .... | .... | .... | .... | .... | .... | .... | .... | 4 | 0 | 1 | 1 | 2 | .... | .... | .... | .... |
| 2004-05 | Grand Rapids | AHL | 78 | 14 | 20 | 34 | 336 | .... | .... | .... | .... | .... | .... | .... | .... | .... | .... | .... | .... | .... | .... | .... | .... | .... | .... |
| 2005-06 | Grand Rapids | AHL | 77 | 27 | 29 | 56 | 392 | .... | .... | .... | .... | .... | .... | .... | .... | .... | 16 | 5 | 7 | 12 | 50 | .... | .... | .... | .... |
| **2006-07** | **Detroit** | **NHL** | **6** | **0** | **0** | **0** | **9** | **0** | **0** | **0** | **4** | **0.0** | **0** | **2** | **100.0** | **4:08** | .... | .... | .... | .... | .... | .... | .... | .... | .... |
| | Grand Rapids | AHL | 68 | 18 | 13 | 31 | 222 | .... | .... | .... | .... | .... | .... | .... | .... | .... | 6 | 1 | 0 | 1 | 32 | .... | .... | .... | .... |
| **2007-08** | **NY Islanders** | **NHL** | **4** | **0** | **1** | **1** | **2** | **0** | **0** | **0** | **3** | **0.0** | **0** | **0** | **0.0** | **4:42** | .... | .... | .... | .... | .... | .... | .... | .... | .... |
| | Bridgeport | AHL | 28 | 2 | 8 | 10 | 93 | .... | .... | .... | .... | .... | .... | .... | .... | .... | .... | .... | .... | .... | .... | .... | .... | .... | .... |
| | Portland Pirates | AHL | 35 | 2 | 5 | 7 | 132 | .... | .... | .... | .... | .... | .... | .... | .... | .... | 16 | 1 | 1 | 2 | 21 | .... | .... | .... | .... |
| 2008-09 | Manitoba Moose | AHL | 14 | 5 | 4 | 9 | 42 | .... | .... | .... | .... | .... | .... | .... | .... | .... | .... | .... | .... | .... | .... | .... | .... | .... | .... |
| | Salzburg | Austria | 14 | 4 | 8 | 12 | 89 | .... | .... | .... | .... | .... | .... | .... | .... | .... | 14 | 4 | 6 | 10 | 62 | .... | .... | .... | .... |
| | **NHL Totals** | | **32** | **1** | **2** | **3** | **85** | **0** | **0** | **1** | **20** | **5.0** | | **3** | **100.0** | **5:34** | .... | .... | .... | .... | .... | .... | .... | .... | .... |

Signed as a free agent by **Detroit**, July 25, 2002. Signed as a free agent by **NY Islanders**, July 9, 2007. Traded to **Anaheim** by **NY Islanders** for Matt Keith, January 9, 2008.

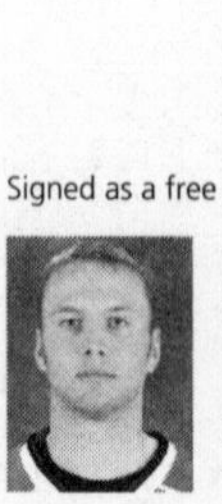

## BORER, Casey

(BOHR-uhr, KAY-see) **CAR.**

Defense. Shoots left. 6'2", 205 lbs. Born, Minneapolis, MN, July 28, 1985. Carolina's 3rd choice, 69th overall, in 2004 Entry Draft.

| Season | Club | League | GP | G | A | Pts | PIM | PP | SH | GW | S | % | +/- | TF | F% | Min | GP | G | A | Pts | PIM | PP | SH | GW | Min |
|---|---|---|---|---|---|---|---|---|---|---|---|---|---|---|---|---|---|---|---|---|---|---|---|---|---|
| 2002-03 | USNTDP | U-18 | 46 | 2 | 2 | 4 | 36 | .... | .... | .... | .... | .... | .... | .... | .... | .... | .... | .... | .... | .... | .... | .... | .... | .... | .... |
| | USNTDP | NAHL | 10 | 1 | 2 | 3 | 10 | .... | .... | .... | .... | .... | .... | .... | .... | .... | .... | .... | .... | .... | .... | .... | .... | .... | .... |
| 2003-04 | St. Cloud State | WCHA | 31 | 0 | 8 | 8 | 18 | .... | .... | .... | .... | .... | .... | .... | .... | .... | .... | .... | .... | .... | .... | .... | .... | .... | .... |
| 2004-05 | St. Cloud State | WCHA | 35 | 0 | 11 | 11 | 40 | .... | .... | .... | .... | .... | .... | .... | .... | .... | .... | .... | .... | .... | .... | .... | .... | .... | .... |
| 2005-06 | St. Cloud State | WCHA | 42 | 3 | 8 | 11 | 24 | .... | .... | .... | .... | .... | .... | .... | .... | .... | .... | .... | .... | .... | .... | .... | .... | .... | .... |
| 2006-07 | St. Cloud State | WCHA | 40 | 2 | 9 | 11 | 30 | .... | .... | .... | .... | .... | .... | .... | .... | .... | .... | .... | .... | .... | .... | .... | .... | .... | .... |
| | Albany River Rats | AHL | 1 | 0 | 0 | 0 | 0 | .... | .... | .... | .... | .... | .... | .... | .... | .... | .... | .... | .... | .... | .... | .... | .... | .... | .... |
| **2007-08** | **Carolina** | **NHL** | **11** | **1** | **2** | **3** | **4** | **0** | **0** | **0** | **5** | **20.0** | **–3** | **0** | **0.0** | **15:17** | .... | .... | .... | .... | .... | .... | .... | .... | .... |
| | Albany River Rats | AHL | 61 | 6 | 13 | 19 | 58 | .... | .... | .... | .... | .... | .... | .... | .... | .... | .... | .... | .... | .... | .... | .... | .... | .... | .... |
| **2008-09** | **Carolina** | **NHL** | **3** | **0** | **0** | **0** | **5** | **0** | **0** | **0** | **0** | **0.0** | **0** | **0** | **0.0** | **11:05** | .... | .... | .... | .... | .... | .... | .... | .... | .... |
| | Albany River Rats | AHL | 51 | 4 | 6 | 10 | 26 | .... | .... | .... | .... | .... | .... | .... | .... | .... | .... | .... | .... | .... | .... | .... | .... | .... | .... |
| | **NHL Totals** | | **14** | **1** | **2** | **3** | **9** | **0** | **0** | **0** | **5** | **20.0** | | **0** | **0.0** | **14:23** | .... | .... | .... | .... | .... | .... | .... | .... | .... |

## BOUCHARD, Pierre-Marc

(BOO-shahrd, PEE-air- MAHRK) **MIN.**

Center. Shoots left. 5'10", 173 lbs. Born, Sherbrooke, Que., April 27, 1984. Minnesota's 1st choice, 8th overall, in 2002 Entry Draft.

| | | | Regular Season | | | | | | | | | | | | | | Playoffs | | | | | | | | |
|---|---|---|---|---|---|---|---|---|---|---|---|---|---|---|---|---|---|---|---|---|---|---|---|---|---|
| Season | Club | League | GP | G | A | Pts | PIM | PP | SH | GW | S | % | +/- | TF | F% | Min | GP | G | A | Pts | PIM | PP | SH | GW | Min |
| 1998-99 | Mtl.-Bourassa | QAHA | 28 | 23 | 41 | 64 | .... | .... | .... | .... | .... | .... | .... | .... | .... | .... | .... | .... | .... | .... | .... | .... | .... | .... | .... |
| 99-2000 | Charles-Lemoyne | QAAA | 42 | 28 | *45 | *74 | 20 | .... | .... | .... | .... | .... | .... | .... | .... | .... | 9 | 4 | 8 | 12 | 6 | .... | .... | .... | .... |
| 2000-01 | Chicoutimi | QMJHL | 67 | 38 | 57 | 95 | 20 | .... | .... | .... | .... | .... | .... | .... | .... | .... | 6 | 5 | 8 | 13 | 0 | .... | .... | .... | .... |
| 2001-02 | Chicoutimi | QMJHL | 69 | 46 | *94 | *140 | 54 | .... | .... | .... | .... | .... | .... | .... | .... | .... | 4 | 2 | 3 | 5 | 4 | .... | .... | .... | .... |
| **2002-03** | **Minnesota** | **NHL** | **50** | **7** | **13** | **20** | **18** | **5** | **0** | **1** | **53** | **13.2** | **1** | **474** | **40.7** | **13:16** | **5** | **0** | **1** | **1** | **2** | **0** | **0** | **0** | **13:15** |
| **2003-04** | **Minnesota** | **NHL** | **61** | **4** | **18** | **22** | **22** | **2** | **0** | **0** | **60** | **6.7** | **−7** | **60** | **50.0** | **14:00** | .... | .... | .... | .... | .... | .... | .... | .... | .... |
| 2004-05 | Houston Aeros | AHL | 67 | 12 | 42 | 54 | 46 | .... | .... | .... | .... | .... | .... | .... | .... | .... | 5 | 0 | 1 | 1 | 0 | .... | .... | .... | .... |
| **2005-06** | **Minnesota** | **NHL** | **80** | **17** | **42** | **59** | **28** | **7** | **0** | **3** | **118** | **14.4** | **3** | **15** | **46.7** | **15:15** | .... | .... | .... | .... | .... | .... | .... | .... | .... |
| **2006-07** | **Minnesota** | **NHL** | **82** | **20** | **37** | **57** | **14** | **5** | **0** | **3** | **173** | **11.6** | **13** | **18** | **33.3** | **15:59** | **5** | **1** | **1** | **2** | **0** | **0** | **0** | **0** | **14:48** |
| **2007-08** | **Minnesota** | **NHL** | **81** | **13** | **50** | **63** | **34** | **6** | **0** | **4** | **129** | **10.1** | **11** | **10** | **40.0** | **16:51** | **6** | **2** | **2** | **4** | **2** | **1** | **0** | **1** | **17:47** |
| **2008-09** | **Minnesota** | **NHL** | **71** | **16** | **30** | **46** | **20** | **2** | **0** | **1** | **142** | **11.3** | **−5** | **19** | **57.9** | **16:59** | .... | .... | .... | .... | .... | .... | .... | .... | .... |
| | **NHL Totals** | | **425** | **77** | **190** | **267** | **136** | **27** | **0** | **12** | **675** | **11.4** | | **596** | **42.1** | **15:34** | **16** | **3** | **4** | **7** | **4** | **1** | **0** | **1** | **15:26** |

QMJHL Rookie of the Year (2001) • QMJHL First All-Star Team (2002) • Canadian Major Junior First All-Star Team (2002) • Canadian Major Junior Player of the Year (2002)

## BOUCHER, Philippe

(boo-SHAY, fihl-EEP)

Defense. Shoots right. 6'3", 218 lbs. Born, Ste-Apollinaire, Que., March 24, 1973. Buffalo's 1st choice, 13th overall, in 1991 Entry Draft.

| Season | Club | League | GP | G | A | Pts | PIM | PP | SH | GW | S | % | +/- | TF | F% | Min | GP | G | A | Pts | PIM | PP | SH | GW | Min |
|---|---|---|---|---|---|---|---|---|---|---|---|---|---|---|---|---|---|---|---|---|---|---|---|---|---|
| 1988-89 | Ste-Foy | QAAA | 5 | 0 | 0 | 0 | 2 | .... | .... | .... | .... | .... | .... | .... | .... | .... | .... | .... | .... | .... | .... | .... | .... | .... | .... |
| 1989-90 | Ste-Foy | QAAA | 42 | 26 | 60 | 86 | 76 | .... | .... | .... | .... | .... | .... | .... | .... | .... | 12 | 6 | *19 | 25 | 16 | .... | .... | .... | .... |
| 1990-91 | Granby Bisons | QMJHL | 69 | 21 | 46 | 67 | 92 | .... | .... | .... | .... | .... | .... | .... | .... | .... | .... | .... | .... | .... | .... | .... | .... | .... | .... |
| 1991-92 | Granby Bisons | QMJHL | 49 | 22 | 37 | 59 | 47 | .... | .... | .... | .... | .... | .... | .... | .... | .... | .... | .... | .... | .... | .... | .... | .... | .... | .... |
| | Laval Titan | QMJHL | 16 | 7 | 11 | 18 | 36 | .... | .... | .... | .... | .... | .... | .... | .... | .... | 10 | 5 | 6 | 11 | 8 | .... | .... | .... | .... |
| **1992-93** | Laval Titan | QMJHL | 16 | 12 | 15 | 27 | 37 | .... | .... | .... | .... | .... | .... | .... | .... | .... | 13 | 6 | 15 | 21 | 12 | .... | .... | .... | .... |
| | **Buffalo** | **NHL** | **18** | **0** | **4** | **4** | **14** | **0** | **0** | **0** | **28** | **0.0** | **1** | .... | .... | .... | .... | .... | .... | .... | .... | .... | .... | .... | .... |
| | Rochester | AHL | 5 | 4 | 3 | 7 | 8 | .... | .... | .... | .... | .... | .... | .... | .... | .... | 3 | 0 | 1 | 1 | 2 | .... | .... | .... | .... |
| **1993-94** | **Buffalo** | **NHL** | **38** | **6** | **8** | **14** | **29** | **4** | **0** | **1** | **67** | **9.0** | **−1** | .... | .... | .... | **7** | **1** | **1** | **2** | **2** | **1** | **0** | **0** | .... |
| | Rochester | AHL | 31 | 10 | 22 | 32 | 51 | .... | .... | .... | .... | .... | .... | .... | .... | .... | .... | .... | .... | .... | .... | .... | .... | .... | .... |
| **1994-95** | Rochester | AHL | 43 | 14 | 27 | 41 | 26 | .... | .... | .... | .... | .... | .... | .... | .... | .... | .... | .... | .... | .... | .... | .... | .... | .... | .... |
| | **Buffalo** | **NHL** | **9** | **1** | **4** | **5** | **0** | **0** | **0** | **0** | **15** | **6.7** | **6** | .... | .... | .... | .... | .... | .... | .... | .... | .... | .... | .... | .... |
| | **Los Angeles** | **NHL** | **6** | **1** | **0** | **1** | **4** | **0** | **0** | **0** | **15** | **6.7** | **−3** | .... | .... | .... | .... | .... | .... | .... | .... | .... | .... | .... | .... |
| **1995-96** | **Los Angeles** | **NHL** | **53** | **7** | **16** | **23** | **31** | **5** | **0** | **1** | **145** | **4.8** | **−26** | .... | .... | .... | .... | .... | .... | .... | .... | .... | .... | .... | .... |
| | Phoenix | IHL | 10 | 4 | 3 | 7 | 4 | .... | .... | .... | .... | .... | .... | .... | .... | .... | .... | .... | .... | .... | .... | .... | .... | .... | .... |
| **1996-97** | **Los Angeles** | **NHL** | **60** | **7** | **18** | **25** | **25** | **2** | **0** | **1** | **159** | **4.4** | **0** | .... | .... | .... | .... | .... | .... | .... | .... | .... | .... | .... | .... |
| **1997-98** | **Los Angeles** | **NHL** | **45** | **6** | **10** | **16** | **49** | **1** | **0** | **0** | **80** | **7.5** | **6** | .... | .... | .... | .... | .... | .... | .... | .... | .... | .... | .... | .... |
| | Long Beach | IHL | 2 | 0 | 1 | 1 | 4 | .... | .... | .... | .... | .... | .... | .... | .... | .... | .... | .... | .... | .... | .... | .... | .... | .... | .... |
| **1998-99** | **Los Angeles** | **NHL** | **45** | **2** | **6** | **8** | **32** | **1** | **0** | **0** | **87** | **2.3** | **−12** | **0** | **0.0** | **17:51** | .... | .... | .... | .... | .... | .... | .... | .... | .... |
| **99-2000** | **Los Angeles** | **NHL** | **1** | **0** | **0** | **0** | **0** | **0** | **0** | **0** | **3** | **0.0** | **0** | **0** | **0.0** | **17:04** | .... | .... | .... | .... | .... | .... | .... | .... | .... |
| | Long Beach | IHL | 14 | 4 | 11 | 15 | 8 | .... | .... | .... | .... | .... | .... | .... | .... | .... | 6 | 0 | 9 | 9 | 8 | .... | .... | .... | .... |
| **2000-01** | **Los Angeles** | **NHL** | **22** | **2** | **4** | **6** | **20** | **2** | **0** | **0** | **40** | **5.0** | **4** | **0** | **0.0** | **18:25** | **13** | **0** | **1** | **1** | **2** | **0** | **0** | **0** | **15:48** |
| | Manitoba Moose | IHL | 45 | 10 | 22 | 32 | 39 | .... | .... | .... | .... | .... | .... | .... | .... | .... | .... | .... | .... | .... | .... | .... | .... | .... | .... |
| **2001-02** | **Los Angeles** | **NHL** | **80** | **7** | **23** | **30** | **94** | **4** | **0** | **2** | **198** | **3.5** | **0** | **0** | **0.0** | **21:36** | **5** | **0** | **1** | **1** | **2** | **0** | **0** | **0** | **19:31** |
| **2002-03** | **Dallas** | **NHL** | **80** | **7** | **20** | **27** | **94** | **1** | **1** | **3** | **137** | **5.1** | **28** | **1** | **0.0** | **20:29** | **11** | **1** | **2** | **3** | **11** | **0** | **0** | **0** | **21:28** |
| **2003-04** | **Dallas** | **NHL** | **70** | **8** | **16** | **24** | **64** | **2** | **0** | **2** | **134** | **6.0** | **15** | **0** | **0.0** | **22:24** | **5** | **1** | **0** | **1** | **6** | **0** | **0** | **0** | **23:57** |
| 2004-05 | | | DID NOT PLAY | | | | | | | | | | | | | | | | | | | | | | |
| **2005-06** | **Dallas** | **NHL** | **66** | **16** | **27** | **43** | **77** | **8** | **0** | **3** | **174** | **9.2** | **28** | **1** | **100.0** | **23:25** | **5** | **0** | **1** | **1** | **2** | **0** | **0** | **0** | **21:35** |
| **2006-07** | **Dallas** | **NHL** | **76** | **19** | **32** | **51** | **104** | **12** | **0** | **4** | **222** | **8.6** | **2** | **1** | **0.0** | **22:54** | **7** | **0** | **1** | **1** | **6** | **0** | **0** | **0** | **27:22** |
| **2007-08** | **Dallas** | **NHL** | **38** | **2** | **12** | **14** | **26** | **0** | **1** | **0** | **72** | **2.8** | **3** | **0** | **0.0** | **21:31** | **3** | **0** | **0** | **0** | **4** | **0** | **0** | **0** | **20:04** |
| **2008-09** | **Dallas** | **NHL** | **16** | **0** | **3** | **3** | **15** | **0** | **0** | **0** | **29** | **0.0** | **−4** | **0** | **0.0** | **21:43** | .... | .... | .... | .... | .... | .... | .... | .... | .... |
| | **♦ Pittsburgh** | **NHL** | **25** | **3** | **3** | **6** | **24** | **0** | **0** | **0** | **37** | **8.1** | **10** | **0** | **0.0** | **19:05** | **9** | **1** | **3** | **4** | **4** | **1** | **0** | **1** | **11:23** |
| | **NHL Totals** | | **748** | **94** | **206** | **300** | **702** | **42** | **2** | **17** | **1642** | **5.7** | | **3** | **33.3** | **21:22** | **65** | **4** | **10** | **14** | **39** | **2** | **0** | **1** | **19:20** |

QMJHL Second All-Star Team (1991, 1992) • QMJHL Defensive Rookie of the Year (1991) • Canadian Major Junior Rookie of the Year (1991)

Played in NHL All-Star Game (2007)

Traded to **Los Angeles** by **Buffalo** with Denis Tsygurov and Grant Fuhr for Alexei Zhitnik, Robb Stauber, Charlie Huddy and Los Angeles' 5th round choice (Marian Menhart) in 1995 Entry Draft, February 14, 1995. • Missed majority of 1999-2000 season recovering from foot injury suffered in training camp, September, 1999. Signed as a free agent by **Dallas**, July 2, 2002. • Missed majority of 2007-08 season recovering from shoulder surgery, December 5, 2007. Traded to **Pittsburgh** by **Dallas** for Darryl Sydor, November 16, 2008.

## BOUCK, Tyler

(BOWK, TIGH-luhr)

Center. Shoots left. 6', 196 lbs. Born, Camrose, Alta., January 13, 1980. Dallas' 2nd choice, 57th overall, in 1998 Entry Draft.

| Season | Club | League | GP | G | A | Pts | PIM | PP | SH | GW | S | % | +/- | TF | F% | Min | GP | G | A | Pts | PIM | PP | SH | GW | Min |
|---|---|---|---|---|---|---|---|---|---|---|---|---|---|---|---|---|---|---|---|---|---|---|---|---|---|
| 1995-96 | Sherwood Park | AMHL | 22 | 10 | 21 | 31 | 58 | .... | .... | .... | .... | .... | .... | .... | .... | .... | .... | .... | .... | .... | .... | .... | .... | .... | .... |
| 1996-97 | Prince George | WHL | 12 | 0 | 2 | 2 | 11 | .... | .... | .... | .... | .... | .... | .... | .... | .... | .... | .... | .... | .... | .... | .... | .... | .... | .... |
| 1997-98 | Prince George | WHL | 65 | 11 | 26 | 37 | 90 | .... | .... | .... | .... | .... | .... | .... | .... | .... | 11 | 1 | 0 | 1 | 21 | .... | .... | .... | .... |
| 1998-99 | Prince George | WHL | 56 | 22 | 25 | 47 | 178 | .... | .... | .... | .... | .... | .... | .... | .... | .... | 2 | 0 | 2 | 2 | 10 | .... | .... | .... | .... |
| 99-2000 | Prince George | WHL | 57 | 30 | 33 | 63 | 183 | .... | .... | .... | .... | .... | .... | .... | .... | .... | 13 | 6 | 13 | 19 | 36 | .... | .... | .... | .... |
| **2000-01** | **Dallas** | **NHL** | **48** | **2** | **5** | **7** | **29** | **0** | **0** | **1** | **41** | **4.9** | **−3** | **1** | **0.0** | **8:59** | **1** | **0** | **0** | **0** | **0** | **0** | **0** | **0** | **9:02** |
| | Utah Grizzlies | IHL | 24 | 2 | 6 | 8 | 39 | .... | .... | .... | .... | .... | .... | .... | .... | .... | .... | .... | .... | .... | .... | .... | .... | .... | .... |
| **2001-02** | **Phoenix** | **NHL** | **7** | **0** | **0** | **0** | **4** | **0** | **0** | **0** | **3** | **0.0** | **−1** | **0** | **0.0** | **6:54** | .... | .... | .... | .... | .... | .... | .... | .... | .... |
| | Springfield | AHL | 21 | 1 | 2 | 3 | 33 | .... | .... | .... | .... | .... | .... | .... | .... | .... | .... | .... | .... | .... | .... | .... | .... | .... | .... |
| | Manitoba Moose | AHL | 20 | 4 | 4 | 8 | 25 | .... | .... | .... | .... | .... | .... | .... | .... | .... | .... | .... | .... | .... | .... | .... | .... | .... | .... |
| 2002-03 | Manitoba Moose | AHL | 76 | 10 | 28 | 38 | 103 | .... | .... | .... | .... | .... | .... | .... | .... | .... | 14 | 2 | 2 | 4 | 10 | .... | .... | .... | .... |
| **2003-04** | **Vancouver** | **NHL** | **18** | **1** | **2** | **3** | **23** | **0** | **1** | **0** | **12** | **8.3** | **−4** | **0** | **0.0** | **9:18** | **1** | **0** | **0** | **0** | **0** | **0** | **0** | **0** | **5:15** |
| | Manitoba Moose | AHL | 49 | 11 | 14 | 25 | 100 | .... | .... | .... | .... | .... | .... | .... | .... | .... | .... | .... | .... | .... | .... | .... | .... | .... | .... |
| 2004-05 | TPS Turku | Finland | 40 | 3 | 7 | 10 | 100 | .... | .... | .... | .... | .... | .... | .... | .... | .... | 6 | 1 | 0 | 1 | 12 | .... | .... | .... | .... |
| **2005-06** | **Vancouver** | **NHL** | **12** | **1** | **1** | **2** | **21** | **0** | **0** | **0** | **6** | **16.7** | **0** | **0** | **0.0** | **6:22** | .... | .... | .... | .... | .... | .... | .... | .... | .... |
| | Manitoba Moose | AHL | 8 | 0 | 1 | 1 | 8 | .... | .... | .... | .... | .... | .... | .... | .... | .... | .... | .... | .... | .... | .... | .... | .... | .... | .... |
| **2006-07** | **Vancouver** | **NHL** | **6** | **0** | **0** | **0** | **16** | **0** | **0** | **0** | **7** | **0.0** | **−1** | **0** | **0.0** | **7:55** | .... | .... | .... | .... | .... | .... | .... | .... | .... |
| | Manitoba Moose | AHL | 24 | 1 | 3 | 4 | 36 | .... | .... | .... | .... | .... | .... | .... | .... | .... | .... | .... | .... | .... | .... | .... | .... | .... | .... |
| 2007-08 | Portland Pirates | AHL | 79 | 11 | 18 | 29 | 86 | .... | .... | .... | .... | .... | .... | .... | .... | .... | 13 | 0 | 2 | 2 | 8 | .... | .... | .... | .... |
| 2008-09 | Portland Pirates | AHL | 63 | 7 | 16 | 23 | 80 | .... | .... | .... | .... | .... | .... | .... | .... | .... | 5 | 1 | 0 | 1 | 0 | .... | .... | .... | .... |
| | **NHL Totals** | | **91** | **4** | **8** | **12** | **93** | **0** | **1** | **1** | **69** | **5.8** | | **1** | **0.0** | **8:28** | **2** | **0** | **0** | **0** | **0** | **0** | **0** | **0** | **7:09** |

WHL West First All-Star Team (2000)

Traded to **Phoenix** by **Dallas** for Jyrki Lumme, June 23, 2001. Traded to **Vancouver** by **Phoenix** with Todd Warriner, Trevor Letowski and Phoenix's 3rd round choice (later traded back to Phoenix – Phoenix selected Dimitri Pestunov) in 2003 Entry Draft for Drake Berehowsky and Denis Pederson, December 28, 2001. Signed as a free agent by **Turku** (Finland), October 22, 2004. • Missed majority of 2005-06 season recovering from groin injury suffered in training camp (October 4, 2005) and as a healthy reserve. • Missed majority of 2006-07 season recovering from shoulder injury suffered in game vs. Hamilton (AHL), December 27, 2006. Signed as a free agent by **Buffalo**, August 8, 2008. Signed as a free agent by **Ingolstadt** (Germany), April 28, 2009.

## BOUILLON, Francis

(BOO-liawn, FRAN-sihs)

Defense. Shoots left. 5'8", 198 lbs. Born, New York, NY, October 17, 1975.

| Season | Club | League | GP | G | A | Pts | PIM | PP | SH | GW | S | % | +/- | TF | F% | Min | GP | G | A | Pts | PIM | PP | SH | GW | Min |
|---|---|---|---|---|---|---|---|---|---|---|---|---|---|---|---|---|---|---|---|---|---|---|---|---|---|
| 1991-92 | Mtl-Bourassa | QAAA | 42 | 2 | 5 | 7 | 28 | .... | .... | .... | .... | .... | .... | .... | .... | .... | 9 | 1 | 0 | 1 | 6 | .... | .... | .... | .... |
| 1992-93 | Laval Titan | QMJHL | 46 | 0 | 7 | 7 | 45 | .... | .... | .... | .... | .... | .... | .... | .... | .... | .... | .... | .... | .... | .... | .... | .... | .... | .... |
| 1993-94 | Laval Titan | QMJHL | 68 | 3 | 15 | 18 | 129 | .... | .... | .... | .... | .... | .... | .... | .... | .... | 19 | 2 | 9 | 11 | 48 | .... | .... | .... | .... |
| 1994-95 | Laval Titan | QMJHL | 72 | 8 | 25 | 33 | 115 | .... | .... | .... | .... | .... | .... | .... | .... | .... | 20 | 3 | 11 | 14 | 21 | .... | .... | .... | .... |
| 1995-96 | Granby | QMJHL | 68 | 11 | 35 | 46 | 156 | .... | .... | .... | .... | .... | .... | .... | .... | .... | 21 | 2 | 12 | 14 | 30 | .... | .... | .... | .... |
| 1996-97 | Wheeling Nailers | ECHL | 69 | 10 | 32 | 42 | 77 | .... | .... | .... | .... | .... | .... | .... | .... | .... | 3 | 0 | 2 | 2 | 10 | .... | .... | .... | .... |
| 1997-98 | Quebec Rafales | IHL | 71 | 8 | 27 | 35 | 76 | .... | .... | .... | .... | .... | .... | .... | .... | .... | .... | .... | .... | .... | .... | .... | .... | .... | .... |
| 1998-99 | Fredericton | AHL | 79 | 19 | 36 | 55 | 174 | .... | .... | .... | .... | .... | .... | .... | .... | .... | 5 | 2 | 1 | 3 | 0 | .... | .... | .... | .... |
| **99-2000** | **Montreal** | **NHL** | **74** | **3** | **13** | **16** | **38** | **2** | **0** | **1** | **76** | **3.9** | **−7** | **1** | **0.0** | **15:52** | .... | .... | .... | .... | .... | .... | .... | .... | .... |
| **2000-01** | **Montreal** | **NHL** | **29** | **0** | **6** | **6** | **26** | **0** | **0** | **0** | **24** | **0.0** | **3** | **0** | **0.0** | **13:24** | .... | .... | .... | .... | .... | .... | .... | .... | .... |
| | Quebec Citadelles | AHL | 4 | 0 | 0 | 0 | 0 | .... | .... | .... | .... | .... | .... | .... | .... | .... | .... | .... | .... | .... | .... | .... | .... | .... | .... |
| **2001-02** | **Montreal** | **NHL** | **28** | **0** | **5** | **5** | **33** | **0** | **0** | **0** | **24** | **0.0** | **−5** | **0** | **0.0** | **18:47** | .... | .... | .... | .... | .... | .... | .... | .... | .... |
| | Quebec Citadelles | AHL | 38 | 8 | 14 | 22 | 30 | .... | .... | .... | .... | .... | .... | .... | .... | .... | .... | .... | .... | .... | .... | .... | .... | .... | .... |
| **2002-03** | **Nashville** | **NHL** | **4** | **0** | **0** | **0** | **2** | **0** | **0** | **0** | **0** | **0.0** | **−1** | **0** | **0.0** | **12:52** | .... | .... | .... | .... | .... | .... | .... | .... | .... |
| | **Montreal** | **NHL** | **20** | **3** | **1** | **4** | **2** | **0** | **1** | **0** | **30** | **10.0** | **−1** | **0** | **0.0** | **20:24** | .... | .... | .... | .... | .... | .... | .... | .... | .... |
| | Hamilton | AHL | 29 | 1 | 12 | 13 | 31 | .... | .... | .... | .... | .... | .... | .... | .... | .... | .... | .... | .... | .... | .... | .... | .... | .... | .... |
| **2003-04** | **Montreal** | **NHL** | **73** | **2** | **16** | **18** | **70** | **0** | **0** | **0** | **86** | **2.3** | **1** | **0** | **0.0** | **19:39** | **11** | **0** | **0** | **0** | **7** | **0** | **0** | **0** | **18:00** |
| 2004-05 | Leksands IF | Sweden-2 | 31 | 10 | 21 | 31 | 46 | .... | .... | .... | .... | .... | .... | .... | .... | .... | .... | .... | .... | .... | .... | .... | .... | .... | .... |

| | | | Regular Season | | | | | | | | | | | | | | Playoffs | | | | | | | | |
|---|---|---|---|---|---|---|---|---|---|---|---|---|---|---|---|---|---|---|---|---|---|---|---|---|---|
| Season | Club | League | GP | G | A | Pts | PIM | PP | SH | GW | S | % | +/- | TF | F% | Min | GP | G | A | Pts | PIM | PP | SH | GW | Min |
| **2005-06** | **Montreal** | **NHL** | **67** | **3** | **19** | **22** | **34** | **3** | **0** | **1** | **75** | **4.0** | **-6** | **0** | **0.0** | **20:47** | **6** | **1** | **2** | **3** | **10** | **1** | **0** | **0** | **22:24** |
| **2006-07** | **Montreal** | **NHL** | **62** | **3** | **11** | **14** | **52** | **1** | **0** | **1** | **56** | **5.4** | **-10** | **0** | **0.0** | **18:19** | .... | .... | .... | .... | .... | .... | .... | .... | .... |
| **2007-08** | **Montreal** | **NHL** | **74** | **2** | **6** | **8** | **61** | **0** | **0** | **0** | **60** | **3.3** | **9** | **0** | **0.0** | **17:22** | **7** | **1** | **2** | **3** | **4** | **0** | **0** | **0** | **15:55** |
| **2008-09** | **Montreal** | **NHL** | **54** | **5** | **4** | **9** | **53** | **0** | **0** | **1** | **51** | **9.8** | **-7** | **0** | **0.0** | **16:30** | **1** | **0** | **0** | **0** | **0** | **0** | **0** | **0** | **1:46** |
| | **NHL Totals** | | **485** | **21** | **81** | **102** | **371** | **6** | **1** | **4** | **482** | **4.4** | | **1** | **0.0** | **17:54** | **25** | **2** | **4** | **6** | **21** | **1** | **0** | **0** | **17:49** |

Signed as a free agent by **Montreal**, August 18, 1998. • Missed majority of 2000-01 season recovering from ankle injury suffered in game vs. Calgary, December 31, 2000. Claimed by **Nashville** from **Montreal** in Waiver Draft, October 4, 2002. Claimed on waivers by **Montreal** from **Nashville**, October 25, 2002. Signed as a free agent by **Leksands** (Sweden-2), November 15, 2004.

## BOULERICE, Jesse

(BOO-luhr-ighs, JEH-see)

Right wing. Shoots right. 6'2", 215 lbs. Born, Plattsburgh, NY, August 10, 1978. Philadelphia's 4th choice, 133rd overall, in 1996 Entry Draft.

| Season | Club | League | GP | G | A | Pts | PIM | PP | SH | GW | S | % | +/- | TF | F% | Min | GP | G | A | Pts | PIM | PP | SH | GW | Min |
|---|---|---|---|---|---|---|---|---|---|---|---|---|---|---|---|---|---|---|---|---|---|---|---|---|---|
| 1994-95 | Hawkesbury | CJHL | 46 | 1 | 8 | 9 | 160 | .... | .... | .... | .... | .... | .... | .... | .... | .... | .... | .... | .... | .... | .... | .... | .... | .... | .... |
| 1995-96 | Detroit | OHL | 64 | 2 | 5 | 7 | 150 | .... | .... | .... | .... | .... | .... | .... | .... | .... | 16 | 0 | 0 | 0 | 12 | .... | .... | .... | .... |
| 1996-97 | Detroit | OHL | 33 | 10 | 14 | 24 | 209 | .... | .... | .... | .... | .... | .... | .... | .... | .... | .... | .... | .... | .... | .... | .... | .... | .... | .... |
| 1997-98 | Plymouth Whalers | OHL | 53 | 20 | 23 | 43 | 170 | .... | .... | .... | .... | .... | .... | .... | .... | .... | 13 | 2 | 4 | 6 | 35 | .... | .... | .... | .... |
| 1998-99 | Philadelphia | AHL | 24 | 1 | 2 | 3 | 82 | .... | .... | .... | .... | .... | .... | .... | .... | .... | .... | .... | .... | .... | .... | .... | .... | .... | .... |
| | New Orleans | ECHL | 12 | 0 | 1 | 1 | 38 | .... | .... | .... | .... | .... | .... | .... | .... | .... | .... | .... | .... | .... | .... | .... | .... | .... | .... |
| 99-2000 | Philadelphia | AHL | 40 | 3 | 4 | 7 | 85 | .... | .... | .... | .... | .... | .... | .... | .... | .... | 4 | 0 | 2 | 2 | 4 | .... | .... | .... | .... |
| | Trenton Titans | ECHL | 25 | 8 | 8 | 16 | 90 | .... | .... | .... | .... | .... | .... | .... | .... | .... | .... | .... | .... | .... | .... | .... | .... | .... | .... |
| 2000-01 | Philadelphia | AHL | 60 | 3 | 4 | 7 | 256 | .... | .... | .... | .... | .... | .... | .... | .... | .... | 10 | 1 | 1 | 2 | 28 | .... | .... | .... | .... |
| **2001-02** | **Philadelphia** | **NHL** | **3** | **0** | **0** | **0** | **5** | **0** | **0** | **0** | **1** | **0.0** | **-1** | **0** | **0.0** | **4:18** | .... | .... | .... | .... | .... | .... | .... | .... | .... |
| | Philadelphia | AHL | 41 | 2 | 5 | 7 | 204 | .... | .... | .... | .... | .... | .... | .... | .... | .... | .... | .... | .... | .... | .... | .... | .... | .... | .... |
| | Lowell | AHL | 15 | 2 | 4 | 6 | 80 | .... | .... | .... | .... | .... | .... | .... | .... | .... | 5 | 0 | 2 | 2 | 6 | .... | .... | .... | .... |
| **2002-03** | **Carolina** | **NHL** | **48** | **2** | **1** | **3** | **108** | **0** | **0** | **0** | **12** | **16.7** | **-2** | **0** | **0.0** | **3:54** | .... | .... | .... | .... | .... | .... | .... | .... | .... |
| **2003-04** | **Carolina** | **NHL** | **76** | **6** | **1** | **7** | **127** | **0** | **0** | **0** | **46** | **13.0** | **-5** | **0** | **0.0** | **6:32** | .... | .... | .... | .... | .... | .... | .... | .... | .... |
| 2004-05 | | | DID NOT PLAY | | | | | | | | | | | | | | | | | | | | | | |
| **2005-06** | **Carolina** | **NHL** | **26** | **0** | **0** | **0** | **51** | **0** | **0** | **0** | **3** | **0.0** | **-3** | **0** | **0.0** | **2:30** | .... | .... | .... | .... | .... | .... | .... | .... | .... |
| | **St. Louis** | **NHL** | **12** | **0** | **0** | **0** | **13** | **0** | **0** | **0** | **2** | **0.0** | **-4** | **0** | **0.0** | **2:39** | .... | .... | .... | .... | .... | .... | .... | .... | .... |
| 2006-07 | Albany River Rats | AHL | 16 | 4 | 3 | 7 | 36 | .... | .... | .... | .... | .... | .... | .... | .... | .... | .... | .... | .... | .... | .... | .... | .... | .... | .... |
| **2007-08** | **Philadelphia** | **NHL** | **5** | **0** | **0** | **0** | **29** | **0** | **0** | **0** | **1** | **0.0** | **-2** | **0** | **0.0** | **3:52** | .... | .... | .... | .... | .... | .... | .... | .... | .... |
| | Philadelphia | AHL | 36 | 2 | 4 | 6 | 101 | .... | .... | .... | .... | .... | .... | .... | .... | .... | 7 | 0 | 0 | 0 | 2 | .... | .... | .... | .... |
| **2008-09** | Lake Erie | AHL | 41 | 4 | 3 | 7 | 97 | .... | .... | .... | .... | .... | .... | .... | .... | .... | .... | .... | .... | .... | .... | .... | .... | .... | .... |
| | **Edmonton** | **NHL** | **2** | **0** | **0** | **0** | **0** | **0** | **0** | **0** | **0** | **0.0** | **0** | **0** | **0.0** | **3:43** | .... | .... | .... | .... | .... | .... | .... | .... | .... |
| | **NHL Totals** | | **172** | **8** | **2** | **10** | **333** | **0** | **0** | **0** | **65** | **12.3** | | **0** | **0.0** | **4:46** | .... | .... | .... | .... | .... | .... | .... | .... | .... |

Traded to **Carolina** by **Philadelphia** for Greg Koehler, February 13, 2002. Traded to **St. Louis** by **Carolina** with Mike Zigomanis, the rights to Magnus Kahnberg, Carolina's 1st round choice (later traded to New Jersey - New Jersey selected Matthew Corrente) in 2006 Entry Draft, Toronto's 4th round choice (previously acquired, St. Louis selected Reto Berra) in 2006 Entry Draft and Chicago's 4th round choice (previously acquired, St. Louis selected Cade Fairchild) in 2007 Entry Draft for Doug Weight and Erkki Rajamaki, January 30, 2006. Signed as a free agent by **Carolina**, August 2, 2006. Signed as a free agent by **Philadelphia**, October 3, 2007. Signed to a PTO (tryout) contract by **Lake Erie** (AHL), October 8, 2008. Signed as a free agent by **Colorado**, November 8, 2008. Claimed on waivers by **Edmonton** from **Colorado**, November 11, 2008.

## BOULTON, Eric

(BOHL-tuhn, AIR-ihk) **ATL.**

Left wing. Shoots left. 6'1", 225 lbs. Born, Halifax, N.S., August 17, 1976. NY Rangers' 12th choice, 234th overall, in 1994 Entry Draft.

| Season | Club | League | GP | G | A | Pts | PIM | PP | SH | GW | S | % | +/- | TF | F% | Min | GP | G | A | Pts | PIM | PP | SH | GW | Min |
|---|---|---|---|---|---|---|---|---|---|---|---|---|---|---|---|---|---|---|---|---|---|---|---|---|---|
| 1992-93 | Cole Harbour | MJrHL | 44 | 12 | 15 | 27 | 212 | .... | .... | .... | .... | .... | .... | .... | .... | .... | .... | .... | .... | .... | .... | .... | .... | .... | .... |
| 1993-94 | Oshawa Generals | OHL | 45 | 4 | 3 | 7 | 149 | .... | .... | .... | .... | .... | .... | .... | .... | .... | 5 | 0 | 0 | 0 | 16 | .... | .... | .... | .... |
| 1994-95 | Oshawa Generals | OHL | 27 | 7 | 5 | 12 | 125 | .... | .... | .... | .... | .... | .... | .... | .... | .... | .... | .... | .... | .... | .... | .... | .... | .... | .... |
| | Sarnia Sting | OHL | 24 | 3 | 7 | 10 | 134 | .... | .... | .... | .... | .... | .... | .... | .... | .... | 4 | 0 | 1 | 1 | 10 | .... | .... | .... | .... |
| 1995-96 | Sarnia Sting | OHL | 66 | 14 | 29 | 43 | 243 | .... | .... | .... | .... | .... | .... | .... | .... | .... | 9 | 0 | 3 | 3 | 29 | .... | .... | .... | .... |
| 1996-97 | Binghamton | AHL | 23 | 2 | 3 | 5 | 67 | .... | .... | .... | .... | .... | .... | .... | .... | .... | 3 | 0 | 0 | 0 | 4 | .... | .... | .... | .... |
| | Charlotte | ECHL | 44 | 14 | 11 | 25 | 325 | .... | .... | .... | .... | .... | .... | .... | .... | .... | 3 | 0 | 1 | 1 | 6 | .... | .... | .... | .... |
| 1997-98 | Charlotte | ECHL | 53 | 11 | 16 | 27 | 202 | .... | .... | .... | .... | .... | .... | .... | .... | .... | 4 | 1 | 0 | 1 | 0 | .... | .... | .... | .... |
| | Fort Wayne | IHL | 8 | 0 | 2 | 2 | 42 | .... | .... | .... | .... | .... | .... | .... | .... | .... | .... | .... | .... | .... | .... | .... | .... | .... | .... |
| 1998-99 | Kentucky | AHL | 34 | 3 | 3 | 6 | 154 | .... | .... | .... | .... | .... | .... | .... | .... | .... | 10 | 0 | 1 | 1 | 36 | .... | .... | .... | .... |
| | Florida Everblades | ECHL | 26 | 9 | 13 | 22 | 143 | .... | .... | .... | .... | .... | .... | .... | .... | .... | .... | .... | .... | .... | .... | .... | .... | .... | .... |
| | Houston Aeros | IHL | 7 | 1 | 0 | 1 | 41 | .... | .... | .... | .... | .... | .... | .... | .... | .... | .... | .... | .... | .... | .... | .... | .... | .... | .... |
| 99-2000 | Rochester | AHL | 76 | 2 | 2 | 4 | 276 | .... | .... | .... | .... | .... | .... | .... | .... | .... | 18 | 2 | 1 | 3 | 53 | .... | .... | .... | .... |
| **2000-01** | **Buffalo** | **NHL** | **35** | **1** | **2** | **3** | **94** | **0** | **0** | **0** | **20** | **5.0** | **-1** | **2** | **0.0** | **5:42** | .... | .... | .... | .... | .... | .... | .... | .... | .... |
| **2001-02** | **Buffalo** | **NHL** | **35** | **2** | **3** | **5** | **129** | **0** | **0** | **1** | **21** | **9.5** | **-1** | **0** | **0.0** | **6:08** | .... | .... | .... | .... | .... | .... | .... | .... | .... |
| **2002-03** | **Buffalo** | **NHL** | **58** | **1** | **5** | **6** | **178** | **0** | **0** | **0** | **33** | **3.0** | **1** | **6** | **33.3** | **6:35** | .... | .... | .... | .... | .... | .... | .... | .... | .... |
| **2003-04** | **Buffalo** | **NHL** | **44** | **1** | **2** | **3** | **110** | **0** | **0** | **0** | **20** | **5.0** | **-2** | **1** | **0.0** | **4:52** | .... | .... | .... | .... | .... | .... | .... | .... | .... |
| 2004-05 | Columbia Inferno | ECHL | 48 | 23 | 16 | 39 | 124 | .... | .... | .... | .... | .... | .... | .... | .... | .... | 4 | 2 | 3 | 5 | 8 | .... | .... | .... | .... |
| **2005-06** | **Atlanta** | **NHL** | **51** | **4** | **5** | **9** | **87** | **0** | **0** | **0** | **28** | **14.3** | **-4** | **2** | **50.0** | **4:54** | .... | .... | .... | .... | .... | .... | .... | .... | .... |
| **2006-07** | **Atlanta** | **NHL** | **45** | **3** | **4** | **7** | **49** | **0** | **0** | **0** | **42** | **7.1** | **2** | **2** | **50.0** | **6:16** | **4** | **0** | **0** | **0** | **24** | **0** | **0** | **0** | **5:04** |
| **2007-08** | **Atlanta** | **NHL** | **74** | **4** | **5** | **9** | **127** | **0** | **0** | **0** | **64** | **6.3** | **-10** | **4** | **25.0** | **7:27** | .... | .... | .... | .... | .... | .... | .... | .... | .... |
| **2008-09** | **Atlanta** | **NHL** | **76** | **3** | **10** | **13** | **176** | **0** | **0** | **0** | **71** | **4.2** | **-3** | **4** | **25.0** | **7:33** | .... | .... | .... | .... | .... | .... | .... | .... | .... |
| | **NHL Totals** | | **418** | **19** | **36** | **55** | **950** | **0** | **0** | **1** | **299** | **6.4** | | **21** | **28.6** | **6:23** | **4** | **0** | **0** | **0** | **24** | **0** | **0** | **0** | **5:04** |

Signed as a free agent by **Buffalo**, September 14, 1999. Signed as a free agent by **Columbia** (ECHL), November 24, 2004. Signed as a free agent by **Atlanta**, August 8, 2005.

## BOUMEDIENNE, Josef

(BOO-mih-dyehn, JOH-sehf)

Defense. Shoots left. 6'1", 200 lbs. Born, Stockholm, Sweden, January 12, 1978. New Jersey's 7th choice, 91st overall, in 1996 Entry Draft.

| Season | Club | League | GP | G | A | Pts | PIM | PP | SH | GW | S | % | +/- | TF | F% | Min | GP | G | A | Pts | PIM | PP | SH | GW | Min |
|---|---|---|---|---|---|---|---|---|---|---|---|---|---|---|---|---|---|---|---|---|---|---|---|---|---|
| 1994-95 | Huddinge IK Jr. | Swe-Jr. | 10 | 0 | 2 | 2 | 57 | .... | .... | .... | .... | .... | .... | .... | .... | .... | .... | .... | .... | .... | .... | .... | .... | .... | .... |
| 1995-96 | Huddinge IK Jr. | Swe-Jr. | 25 | 2 | 4 | 6 | 66 | .... | .... | .... | .... | .... | .... | .... | .... | .... | .... | .... | .... | .... | .... | .... | .... | .... | .... |
| | Huddinge IK | Sweden-2 | 7 | 0 | 0 | 0 | 14 | .... | .... | .... | .... | .... | .... | .... | .... | .... | .... | .... | .... | .... | .... | .... | .... | .... | .... |
| 1996-97 | Sodertalje SK | Sweden | 32 | 1 | 1 | 2 | 32 | .... | .... | .... | .... | .... | .... | .... | .... | .... | .... | .... | .... | .... | .... | .... | .... | .... | .... |
| 1997-98 | Sodertalje SK | Sweden | 26 | 3 | 3 | 6 | 28 | .... | .... | .... | .... | .... | .... | .... | .... | .... | .... | .... | .... | .... | .... | .... | .... | .... | .... |
| 1998-99 | Tappara Tampere | Finland | 51 | 6 | 8 | 14 | 119 | .... | .... | .... | .... | .... | .... | .... | .... | .... | .... | .... | .... | .... | .... | .... | .... | .... | .... |
| 99-2000 | Tappara Tampere | Finland | 50 | 8 | 24 | 32 | 160 | .... | .... | .... | .... | .... | .... | .... | .... | .... | 4 | 1 | 2 | 3 | 10 | .... | .... | .... | .... |
| 2000-01 | Albany River Rats | AHL | 79 | 8 | 28 | 36 | 117 | .... | .... | .... | .... | .... | .... | .... | .... | .... | .... | .... | .... | .... | .... | .... | .... | .... | .... |
| **2001-02** | **New Jersey** | **NHL** | **1** | **1** | **0** | **1** | **2** | **0** | **0** | **0** | **1** | **100.0** | **-1** | **0** | **0.0** | **20:23** | .... | .... | .... | .... | .... | .... | .... | .... | .... |
| | Albany River Rats | AHL | 9 | 0 | 3 | 3 | 10 | .... | .... | .... | .... | .... | .... | .... | .... | .... | .... | .... | .... | .... | .... | .... | .... | .... | .... |
| | **Tampa Bay** | **NHL** | **3** | **0** | **0** | **0** | **4** | **0** | **0** | **0** | **0** | **0.0** | **-1** | **0** | **0.0** | **10:58** | .... | .... | .... | .... | .... | .... | .... | .... | .... |
| | Springfield | AHL | 53 | 7 | 25 | 32 | 57 | .... | .... | .... | .... | .... | .... | .... | .... | .... | .... | .... | .... | .... | .... | .... | .... | .... | .... |
| **2002-03** | Binghamton | AHL | 26 | 2 | 15 | 17 | 62 | .... | .... | .... | .... | .... | .... | .... | .... | .... | .... | .... | .... | .... | .... | .... | .... | .... | .... |
| | **Washington** | **NHL** | **6** | **1** | **0** | **1** | **0** | **0** | **0** | **1** | **7** | **14.3** | **-1** | **0** | **0.0** | **19:33** | .... | .... | .... | .... | .... | .... | .... | .... | .... |
| | Portland Pirates | AHL | 44 | 8 | 22 | 30 | 77 | .... | .... | .... | .... | .... | .... | .... | .... | .... | .... | .... | .... | .... | .... | .... | .... | .... | .... |
| **2003-04** | **Washington** | **NHL** | **37** | **2** | **12** | **14** | **30** | **2** | **0** | **0** | **44** | **4.5** | **-10** | **0** | **0.0** | **23:02** | .... | .... | .... | .... | .... | .... | .... | .... | .... |
| | Portland Pirates | AHL | 13 | 1 | 8 | 9 | 10 | .... | .... | .... | .... | .... | .... | .... | .... | .... | .... | .... | .... | .... | .... | .... | .... | .... | .... |
| 2004-05 | Brynas IF Gavle | Sweden | 13 | 6 | 0 | 6 | 43 | .... | .... | .... | .... | .... | .... | .... | .... | .... | .... | .... | .... | .... | .... | .... | .... | .... | .... |
| | Karpat Oulu | Finland | 32 | 5 | 10 | 15 | 58 | .... | .... | .... | .... | .... | .... | .... | .... | .... | 12 | 1 | 5 | 6 | 12 | .... | .... | .... | .... |
| 2005-06 | ZSC Lions Zurich | Swiss | 17 | 1 | 10 | 11 | 22 | .... | .... | .... | .... | .... | .... | .... | .... | .... | .... | .... | .... | .... | .... | .... | .... | .... | .... |
| | Sodertalje SK | Sweden | 26 | 1 | 19 | 20 | 62 | .... | .... | .... | .... | .... | .... | .... | .... | .... | .... | .... | .... | .... | .... | .... | .... | .... | .... |
| | Sodertalje SK | Sweden-Q | 10 | 2 | 7 | 9 | 18 | .... | .... | .... | .... | .... | .... | .... | .... | .... | .... | .... | .... | .... | .... | .... | .... | .... | .... |
| 2006-07 | Karpat Oulu | Finland | 18 | 2 | 2 | 4 | 36 | .... | .... | .... | .... | .... | .... | .... | .... | .... | 10 | 1 | 3 | 4 | 16 | .... | .... | .... | .... |
| 2007-08 | Hershey Bears | AHL | 52 | 7 | 35 | 42 | 81 | .... | .... | .... | .... | .... | .... | .... | .... | .... | 1 | 0 | 0 | 0 | 2 | .... | .... | .... | .... |
| 2008-09 | Toronto Marlies | AHL | 19 | 0 | 7 | 7 | 29 | .... | .... | .... | .... | .... | .... | .... | .... | .... | .... | .... | .... | .... | .... | .... | .... | .... | .... |
| | Karpat Oulu | Finland | 17 | 3 | 7 | 10 | 32 | .... | .... | .... | .... | .... | .... | .... | .... | .... | 15 | 1 | 8 | 9 | 32 | .... | .... | .... | .... |
| | **NHL Totals** | | **47** | **4** | **12** | **16** | **36** | **2** | **0** | **1** | **52** | **7.7** | | **0** | **0.0** | **21:46** | .... | .... | .... | .... | .... | .... | .... | .... | .... |

Traded to **Tampa Bay** by **New Jersey** with Sascha Goc and the rights to Anton But for Andrei Zyuzin, November 9, 2001. Traded to **Ottawa** by **Tampa Bay** for Ottawa's 7th round choice (Fredrik Norrena) in 2002 Entry Draft, June 23, 2002. Traded to **Washington** by **Ottawa** for Dean Melanson, December 16, 2002. Signed as a free agent by **Gavle** (Sweden), September 25, 2004. Signed as a free agent by **Oulu** (Finland), November 10, 2004. Signed as a free agent by **Zurich** (Swiss), September 7, 2005. Signed as a free agent by **Toronto**, August 18, 2008.

## BOURQUE, Chris

(BOHRK, KRIHS) **WSH.**

Center. Shoots left. 5'10", 177 lbs. Born, Boston, MA, January 29, 1986. Washington's 4th choice, 33rd overall, in 2004 Entry Draft.

| Season | Club | League | GP | G | A | Pts | PIM | PP | SH | GW | S | % | +/- | TF | F% | Min | GP | G | A | Pts | PIM | PP | SH | GW | Min |
|---|---|---|---|---|---|---|---|---|---|---|---|---|---|---|---|---|---|---|---|---|---|---|---|---|---|
| 2002-03 | Cushing | High-MA | 28 | 31 | 26 | 57 | 49 | .... | .... | .... | .... | .... | .... | .... | .... | .... | .... | .... | .... | .... | .... | .... | .... | .... | .... |
| 2003-04 | Cushing | High-MA | 31 | 37 | 53 | 90 | 96 | .... | .... | .... | .... | .... | .... | .... | .... | .... | .... | .... | .... | .... | .... | .... | .... | .... | .... |
| 2004-05 | Boston University | H-East | 35 | 10 | 13 | 23 | 50 | .... | .... | .... | .... | .... | .... | .... | .... | .... | .... | .... | .... | .... | .... | .... | .... | .... | .... |
| | Portland Pirates | AHL | 6 | 1 | 1 | 2 | 2 | .... | .... | .... | .... | .... | .... | .... | .... | .... | .... | .... | .... | .... | .... | .... | .... | .... | .... |
| 2005-06 | Hershey Bears | AHL | 52 | 8 | 28 | 36 | 40 | .... | .... | .... | .... | .... | .... | .... | .... | .... | 1 | 0 | 0 | 0 | 0 | .... | .... | .... | .... |
| 2006-07 | Hershey Bears | AHL | 76 | 25 | 33 | 58 | 49 | .... | .... | .... | .... | .... | .... | .... | .... | .... | 19 | 2 | 6 | 8 | 18 | .... | .... | .... | .... |

| | | | Regular Season | | | | | | | | | | | | | | | Playoffs | | | | | | | | |
|---|---|---|---|---|---|---|---|---|---|---|---|---|---|---|---|---|---|---|---|---|---|---|---|---|
| Season | Club | League | GP | G | A | Pts | PIM | PP | SH | GW | S | % | +/- | TF | F% | Min | GP | G | A | Pts | PIM | PP | SH | GW | Min |
| **2007-08** | **Washington** | **NHL** | **4** | **0** | **0** | **0** | **2** | **0** | **0** | **0** | **4** | **0.0** | **0** | **1** | **0.0** | **8:42** | .... | .... | .... | .... | .... | .... | .... | .... | .... |
| | Hershey Bears | AHL | 73 | 28 | 35 | 63 | 56 | .... | .... | .... | .... | .... | .... | .... | .... | .... | 5 | 1 | 3 | 4 | 8 | .... | .... | .... | .... |
| **2008-09** | **Washington** | **NHL** | **8** | **1** | **0** | **1** | **0** | **0** | **0** | **0** | **11** | **9.1** | **0** | **0** | **0.0** | **9:46** | .... | .... | .... | .... | .... | .... | .... | .... | .... |
| | Hershey Bears | AHL | 69 | 21 | 52 | 73 | 57 | .... | .... | .... | .... | .... | .... | .... | .... | .... | 22 | 5 | 16 | 21 | 30 | .... | .... | .... | .... |
| | **NHL Totals** | | **12** | **1** | **0** | **1** | **2** | **0** | **0** | **0** | **15** | **6.7** | | **1** | **0.0** | **9:25** | .... | .... | .... | .... | .... | .... | .... | .... | .... |

Hockey East All-Rookie Team (2005)

## BOURQUE, Rene
(BOHRK, reh-NAY) **CGY.**

Left wing. Shoots left. 6'2", 213 lbs. Born, Lac La Biche, Alta., December 10, 1981.

| Season | Club | League | GP | G | A | Pts | PIM | PP | SH | GW | S | % | +/- | TF | F% | Min | GP | G | A | Pts | PIM | PP | SH | GW | Min |
|---|---|---|---|---|---|---|---|---|---|---|---|---|---|---|---|---|---|---|---|---|---|---|---|---|---|
| 2000-01 | U. of Wisconsin | WCHA | 32 | 10 | 5 | 15 | 18 | .... | .... | .... | .... | .... | .... | .... | .... | .... | .... | .... | .... | .... | .... | .... | .... | .... | .... |
| 2001-02 | U. of Wisconsin | WCHA | 38 | 12 | 7 | 19 | 26 | .... | .... | .... | .... | .... | .... | .... | .... | .... | .... | .... | .... | .... | .... | .... | .... | .... | .... |
| 2002-03 | U. of Wisconsin | WCHA | 40 | 19 | 8 | 27 | 54 | .... | .... | .... | .... | .... | .... | .... | .... | .... | .... | .... | .... | .... | .... | .... | .... | .... | .... |
| 2003-04 | U. of Wisconsin | WCHA | 42 | 16 | 20 | 36 | 74 | .... | .... | .... | .... | .... | .... | .... | .... | .... | .... | .... | .... | .... | .... | .... | .... | .... | .... |
| 2004-05 | Norfolk Admirals | AHL | 78 | 33 | 27 | 60 | 105 | .... | .... | .... | .... | .... | .... | .... | .... | .... | 6 | 1 | 0 | 1 | 8 | .... | .... | .... | .... |
| **2005-06** | **Chicago** | **NHL** | **77** | **16** | **18** | **34** | **56** | **4** | **0** | **2** | **180** | **8.9** | **3** | **11** | **36.4** | **15:20** | .... | .... | .... | .... | .... | .... | .... | .... | .... |
| **2006-07** | **Chicago** | **NHL** | **44** | **7** | **10** | **17** | **38** | **2** | **1** | **1** | **82** | **8.5** | **-4** | **9** | **22.2** | **16:01** | .... | .... | .... | .... | .... | .... | .... | .... | .... |
| | Norfolk Admirals | AHL | 1 | 0 | 0 | 0 | 0 | .... | .... | .... | .... | .... | .... | .... | .... | .... | .... | .... | .... | .... | .... | .... | .... | .... | .... |
| **2007-08** | **Chicago** | **NHL** | **62** | **10** | **14** | **24** | **42** | **0** | **5** | **2** | **103** | **9.7** | **6** | **8** | **25.0** | **15:16** | .... | .... | .... | .... | .... | .... | .... | .... | .... |
| **2008-09** | **Calgary** | **NHL** | **58** | **21** | **19** | **40** | **70** | **0** | **1** | **0** | **149** | **14.1** | **18** | **18** | **50.0** | **16:05** | **5** | **1** | **0** | **1** | **22** | **0** | **0** | **0** | **17:06** |
| | **NHL Totals** | | **241** | **54** | **61** | **115** | **206** | **6** | **7** | **5** | **514** | **10.5** | | **46** | **37.0** | **15:38** | **5** | **1** | **0** | **1** | **22** | **0** | **0** | **0** | **17:06** |

AHL All-Rookie Team (2005) • Dudley "Red" Garrett Memorial Trophy (AHL - Top Rookie) (2005)

Signed as a free agent by **Chicago**, July 29, 2004. Traded to **Calgary** by **Chicago** for future considerations, July 1, 2008.

## BOUWMEESTER, Jay
(BOW-mee-stuhr, JAY) **CGY.**

Defense. Shoots left. 6'4", 214 lbs. Born, Edmonton, Alta., September 27, 1983. Florida's 1st choice, 3rd overall, in 2002 Entry Draft.

| Season | Club | League | GP | G | A | Pts | PIM | PP | SH | GW | S | % | +/- | TF | F% | Min | GP | G | A | Pts | PIM | PP | SH | GW | Min |
|---|---|---|---|---|---|---|---|---|---|---|---|---|---|---|---|---|---|---|---|---|---|---|---|---|---|
| 1998-99 | Edmonton SSAC | AMHL | 32 | 14 | 29 | 43 | 36 | .... | .... | .... | .... | .... | .... | .... | .... | .... | .... | .... | .... | .... | .... | .... | .... | .... | .... |
| | Medicine Hat | WHL | 8 | 2 | 1 | 3 | 2 | .... | .... | .... | .... | .... | .... | .... | .... | .... | .... | .... | .... | .... | .... | .... | .... | .... | .... |
| 99-2000 | Medicine Hat | WHL | 64 | 13 | 21 | 34 | 26 | .... | .... | .... | .... | .... | .... | .... | .... | .... | .... | .... | .... | .... | .... | .... | .... | .... | .... |
| 2000-01 | Medicine Hat | WHL | 61 | 14 | 39 | 53 | 44 | .... | .... | .... | .... | .... | .... | .... | .... | .... | .... | .... | .... | .... | .... | .... | .... | .... | .... |
| 2001-02 | Medicine Hat | WHL | 61 | 11 | 50 | 61 | 42 | .... | .... | .... | .... | .... | .... | .... | .... | .... | .... | .... | .... | .... | .... | .... | .... | .... | .... |
| **2002-03** | **Florida** | **NHL** | **82** | **4** | **12** | **16** | **14** | **2** | **0** | **0** | **110** | **3.6** | **-29** | **0** | **0.0** | **20:09** | .... | .... | .... | .... | .... | .... | .... | .... | .... |
| **2003-04** | **Florida** | **NHL** | **61** | **2** | **18** | **20** | **30** | **0** | **0** | **0** | **85** | **2.4** | **-15** | **0** | **0.0** | **23:02** | .... | .... | .... | .... | .... | .... | .... | .... | .... |
| | San Antonio | AHL | 2 | 0 | 1 | 1 | 2 | .... | .... | .... | .... | .... | .... | .... | .... | .... | .... | .... | .... | .... | .... | .... | .... | .... | .... |
| 2004-05 | San Antonio | AHL | 64 | 4 | 13 | 17 | 50 | .... | .... | .... | .... | .... | .... | .... | .... | .... | .... | .... | .... | .... | .... | .... | .... | .... | .... |
| | Chicago Wolves | AHL | 18 | 6 | 3 | 9 | 12 | .... | .... | .... | .... | .... | .... | .... | .... | .... | 18 | 0 | 0 | 0 | 14 | .... | .... | .... | .... |
| **2005-06** | **Florida** | **NHL** | **82** | **5** | **41** | **46** | **79** | **0** | **0** | **0** | **189** | **2.6** | **1** | **1** | **0.0** | **25:29** | .... | .... | .... | .... | .... | .... | .... | .... | .... |
| | Canada | Olympics | 6 | 0 | 0 | 0 | 0 | .... | .... | .... | .... | .... | .... | .... | .... | .... | .... | .... | .... | .... | .... | .... | .... | .... | .... |
| **2006-07** | **Florida** | **NHL** | **82** | **12** | **30** | **42** | **66** | **3** | **0** | **3** | **174** | **6.9** | **23** | **0** | **0.0** | **26:09** | .... | .... | .... | .... | .... | .... | .... | .... | .... |
| **2007-08** | **Florida** | **NHL** | **82** | **15** | **22** | **37** | **72** | **4** | **0** | **0** | **182** | **8.2** | **-5** | **0** | **0.0** | **27:28** | .... | .... | .... | .... | .... | .... | .... | .... | .... |
| **2008-09** | **Florida** | **NHL** | **82** | **15** | **27** | **42** | **68** | **9** | **0** | **2** | **182** | **8.2** | **-2** | **0** | **0.0** | **26:59** | .... | .... | .... | .... | .... | .... | .... | .... | .... |
| | **NHL Totals** | | **471** | **53** | **150** | **203** | **329** | **18** | **0** | **5** | **922** | **5.7** | | **1** | **0.0** | **24:58** | .... | .... | .... | .... | .... | .... | .... | .... | .... |

WHL East First All-Star Team (2002) • NHL All-Rookie Team (2003)

Played in NHL All-Star Game (2007, 2009)

• Loaned to **Chicago** (AHL) by **Florida** (San Antonio-AHL) for cash, March 8, 2005. Traded to **Calgary** by **Florida** for Jordan Leopold and Phoenix's 3rd round choice (previously acquired, Florida selected Josh Birkholz) in 2009 Entry Draft, June 27, 2009.

## BOYCE, Darryl
(BOIS, DAIR-uhl) **TOR.**

Center. Shoots left. 6', 200 lbs. Born, Summerside, P.E.I., July 7, 1984.

| Season | Club | League | GP | G | A | Pts | PIM | PP | SH | GW | S | % | +/- | TF | F% | Min | GP | G | A | Pts | PIM | PP | SH | GW | Min |
|---|---|---|---|---|---|---|---|---|---|---|---|---|---|---|---|---|---|---|---|---|---|---|---|---|---|
| 2001-02 | St. Michael's | OHL | 67 | 10 | 11 | 21 | 71 | .... | .... | .... | .... | .... | .... | .... | .... | .... | 15 | 2 | 5 | 7 | 46 | .... | .... | .... | .... |
| 2002-03 | St. Michael's | OHL | 64 | 16 | 21 | 37 | 119 | .... | .... | .... | .... | .... | .... | .... | .... | .... | 19 | 1 | 3 | 4 | 28 | .... | .... | .... | .... |
| 2003-04 | St. Michael's | OHL | 64 | 13 | 24 | 37 | 110 | .... | .... | .... | .... | .... | .... | .... | .... | .... | 18 | 1 | 3 | 4 | 23 | .... | .... | .... | .... |
| 2004-05 | St. Michael's | OHL | 67 | 15 | 35 | 50 | 152 | .... | .... | .... | .... | .... | .... | .... | .... | .... | 10 | 2 | 5 | 7 | 28 | .... | .... | .... | .... |
| 2005-06 | New Brunswick | AUAA | 28 | 15 | 17 | 32 | 50 | .... | .... | .... | .... | .... | .... | .... | .... | .... | .... | .... | .... | .... | .... | .... | .... | .... | .... |
| 2006-07 | New Brunswick | AUAA | 25 | 14 | 19 | 33 | 63 | .... | .... | .... | .... | .... | .... | .... | .... | .... | .... | .... | .... | .... | .... | .... | .... | .... | .... |
| **2007-08** | Toronto Marlies | AHL | 41 | 8 | 16 | 24 | 71 | .... | .... | .... | .... | .... | .... | .... | .... | .... | .... | .... | .... | .... | .... | .... | .... | .... | .... |
| | **Toronto** | **NHL** | **1** | **0** | **0** | **0** | **0** | **0** | **0** | **0** | **0** | **0.0** | **0** | **2** | **100.0** | **3:20** | .... | .... | .... | .... | .... | .... | .... | .... | .... |
| 2008-09 | Toronto Marlies | AHL | 73 | 12 | 18 | 30 | 131 | .... | .... | .... | .... | .... | .... | .... | .... | .... | 6 | 2 | 0 | 2 | 27 | .... | .... | .... | .... |
| | **NHL Totals** | | **1** | **0** | **0** | **0** | **0** | **0** | **0** | **0** | **0** | **0.0** | | **2** | **100.0** | **3:20** | .... | .... | .... | .... | .... | .... | .... | .... | .... |

Signed as a free agent by **Toronto** (AHL), April, 2007. Signed as a free agent by **Toronto**, January 1, 2008.

## BOYCHUK, Johnny
(BOI-chuhk, JAW-nee) **BOS.**

Defense. Shoots right. 6'2", 225 lbs. Born, Edmonton, Alta., January 19, 1984. Colorado's 2nd choice, 61st overall, in 2002 Entry Draft.

| Season | Club | League | GP | G | A | Pts | PIM | PP | SH | GW | S | % | +/- | TF | F% | Min | GP | G | A | Pts | PIM | PP | SH | GW | Min |
|---|---|---|---|---|---|---|---|---|---|---|---|---|---|---|---|---|---|---|---|---|---|---|---|---|---|
| 1998-99 | Edm. Cycle | AMBHL | 36 | 8 | 20 | 28 | 59 | .... | .... | .... | .... | .... | .... | .... | .... | .... | .... | .... | .... | .... | .... | .... | .... | .... | .... |
| 99-2000 | Edm. Cycle | AMHL | 35 | 6 | 17 | 23 | 59 | .... | .... | .... | .... | .... | .... | .... | .... | .... | .... | .... | .... | .... | .... | .... | .... | .... | .... |
| 2000-01 | Calgary Hitmen | WHL | 66 | 4 | 8 | 12 | 61 | .... | .... | .... | .... | .... | .... | .... | .... | .... | 12 | 1 | 1 | 2 | 17 | .... | .... | .... | .... |
| 2001-02 | Calgary Hitmen | WHL | 70 | 8 | 32 | 40 | 85 | .... | .... | .... | .... | .... | .... | .... | .... | .... | 7 | 1 | 1 | 2 | 6 | .... | .... | .... | .... |
| 2002-03 | Calgary Hitmen | WHL | 40 | 8 | 18 | 26 | 58 | .... | .... | .... | .... | .... | .... | .... | .... | .... | .... | .... | .... | .... | .... | .... | .... | .... | .... |
| | Moose Jaw | WHL | 27 | 5 | 17 | 22 | 32 | .... | .... | .... | .... | .... | .... | .... | .... | .... | 13 | 2 | 6 | 8 | 29 | .... | .... | .... | .... |
| 2003-04 | Moose Jaw | WHL | 62 | 13 | 20 | 33 | 71 | .... | .... | .... | .... | .... | .... | .... | .... | .... | 10 | 1 | 9 | 10 | 9 | .... | .... | .... | .... |
| 2004-05 | Hershey Bears | AHL | 80 | 3 | 12 | 15 | 69 | .... | .... | .... | .... | .... | .... | .... | .... | .... | .... | .... | .... | .... | .... | .... | .... | .... | .... |
| 2005-06 | Lowell | AHL | 74 | 6 | 26 | 32 | 73 | .... | .... | .... | .... | .... | .... | .... | .... | .... | .... | .... | .... | .... | .... | .... | .... | .... | .... |
| 2006-07 | Albany River Rats | AHL | 80 | 10 | 18 | 28 | 125 | .... | .... | .... | .... | .... | .... | .... | .... | .... | 5 | 1 | 1 | 2 | 4 | .... | .... | .... | .... |
| **2007-08** | **Colorado** | **NHL** | **4** | **0** | **0** | **0** | **0** | **0** | **0** | **0** | **3** | **0.0** | **1** | **1** | **0.0** | **8:57** | .... | .... | .... | .... | .... | .... | .... | .... | .... |
| | Lake Erie | AHL | 60 | 8 | 18 | 26 | 63 | .... | .... | .... | .... | .... | .... | .... | .... | .... | .... | .... | .... | .... | .... | .... | .... | .... | .... |
| **2008-09** | **Boston** | **NHL** | **1** | **0** | **0** | **0** | **0** | **0** | **0** | **0** | **0** | **0.0** | **0** | **0** | **0.0** | **14:48** | .... | .... | .... | .... | .... | .... | .... | .... | .... |
| | Providence Bruins | AHL | 78 | 20 | 46 | 66 | 61 | .... | .... | .... | .... | .... | .... | .... | .... | .... | 16 | 3 | 5 | 8 | 19 | .... | .... | .... | .... |
| | **NHL Totals** | | **5** | **0** | **0** | **0** | **0** | **0** | **0** | **0** | **3** | **0.0** | | **1** | **0.0** | **10:07** | .... | .... | .... | .... | .... | .... | .... | .... | .... |

AHL First All-Star Team (2009) • Eddie Shore Award (AHL – Outstanding Defenseman) (2009)

Traded to **Boston** by **Colorado** for Matt Hendricks, June 24, 2008.

## BOYCHUK, Zach
(BOY-chuhk, ZAK) **CAR.**

Center. Shoots left. 5'10", 185 lbs. Born, Airdrie, Alta., October 4, 1989. Carolina's 1st choice, 14th overall, in 2008 Entry Draft.

| Season | Club | League | GP | G | A | Pts | PIM | PP | SH | GW | S | % | +/- | TF | F% | Min | GP | G | A | Pts | PIM | PP | SH | GW | Min |
|---|---|---|---|---|---|---|---|---|---|---|---|---|---|---|---|---|---|---|---|---|---|---|---|---|---|
| 2004-05 | UFA Bisons | AMHL | 36 | 13 | 14 | 27 | 18 | .... | .... | .... | .... | .... | .... | .... | .... | .... | 16 | 10 | 5 | 15 | .... | .... | .... | .... | .... |
| 2005-06 | Lethbridge | WHL | 64 | 18 | 33 | 51 | 30 | .... | .... | .... | .... | .... | .... | .... | .... | .... | 6 | 0 | 5 | 5 | 2 | .... | .... | .... | .... |
| 2006-07 | Lethbridge | WHL | 69 | 31 | 60 | 91 | 52 | .... | .... | .... | .... | .... | .... | .... | .... | .... | .... | .... | .... | .... | .... | .... | .... | .... | .... |
| 2007-08 | Lethbridge | WHL | 61 | 33 | 39 | 72 | 80 | .... | .... | .... | .... | .... | .... | .... | .... | .... | 18 | *13 | 8 | 21 | 6 | .... | .... | .... | .... |
| **2008-09** | **Carolina** | **NHL** | **2** | **0** | **0** | **0** | **0** | **0** | **0** | **0** | **0** | **0.0** | **0** | **1** | **0.0** | **12:03** | .... | .... | .... | .... | .... | .... | .... | .... | .... |
| | Lethbridge | WHL | 43 | 28 | 29 | 57 | 22 | .... | .... | .... | .... | .... | .... | .... | .... | .... | 11 | 7 | 6 | 13 | 12 | .... | .... | .... | .... |
| | Albany River Rats | AHL | 2 | 0 | 1 | 1 | 2 | .... | .... | .... | .... | .... | .... | .... | .... | .... | .... | .... | .... | .... | .... | .... | .... | .... | .... |
| | **NHL Totals** | | **2** | **0** | **0** | **0** | **0** | **0** | **0** | **0** | **0** | **0.0** | | **1** | **0.0** | **12:03** | .... | .... | .... | .... | .... | .... | .... | .... | .... |

WHL East Second All-Star Team (2007, 2008)

## BOYD, Dustin
(BOID, DUHS-tihn) **CGY.**

Center. Shoots left. 6', 198 lbs. Born, Winnipeg, Man., July 16, 1986. Calgary's 3rd choice, 98th overall, in 2004 Entry Draft.

| Season | Club | League | GP | G | A | Pts | PIM | PP | SH | GW | S | % | +/- | TF | F% | Min | GP | G | A | Pts | PIM | PP | SH | GW | Min |
|---|---|---|---|---|---|---|---|---|---|---|---|---|---|---|---|---|---|---|---|---|---|---|---|---|---|
| 2001-02 | Wpg. Warriors | MMMHL | 40 | 50 | 57 | 107 | 16 | .... | .... | .... | .... | .... | .... | .... | .... | .... | .... | .... | .... | .... | .... | .... | .... | .... | .... |
| 2002-03 | Moose Jaw | WHL | 63 | 11 | 17 | 28 | 15 | .... | .... | .... | .... | .... | .... | .... | .... | .... | 13 | 0 | 3 | 3 | 2 | .... | .... | .... | .... |
| 2003-04 | Moose Jaw | WHL | 72 | 18 | 20 | 38 | 40 | .... | .... | .... | .... | .... | .... | .... | .... | .... | 10 | 2 | 2 | 4 | 8 | .... | .... | .... | .... |
| 2004-05 | Moose Jaw | WHL | 66 | 26 | 35 | 61 | 57 | .... | .... | .... | .... | .... | .... | .... | .... | .... | 5 | 1 | 2 | 3 | 2 | .... | .... | .... | .... |
| 2005-06 | Moose Jaw | WHL | 64 | 48 | 42 | 90 | 34 | .... | .... | .... | .... | .... | .... | .... | .... | .... | 22 | 7 | 11 | 18 | 10 | .... | .... | .... | .... |
| **2006-07** | **Calgary** | **NHL** | **13** | **2** | **2** | **4** | **4** | **0** | **0** | **1** | **8** | **25.0** | **5** | **16** | **50.0** | **10:09** | .... | .... | .... | .... | .... | .... | .... | .... | .... |
| | Omaha | AHL | 66 | 27 | 33 | 60 | 34 | .... | .... | .... | .... | .... | .... | .... | .... | .... | 6 | 1 | 1 | 2 | 0 | .... | .... | .... | .... |

| | | | Regular Season | | | | | | | | | | | | | | Playoffs | | | | | | | | |
|---|---|---|---|---|---|---|---|---|---|---|---|---|---|---|---|---|---|---|---|---|---|---|---|---|---|
| Season | Club | League | GP | G | A | Pts | PIM | PP | SH | GW | S | % | +/- | TF | F% | Min | GP | G | A | Pts | PIM | PP | SH | GW | Min |
| **2007-08** | **Calgary** | **NHL** | **48** | **7** | **5** | **12** | **6** | **0** | **0** | **1** | **46** | **15.2** | **–11** | **129** | **50.4** | **9:49** | .... | .... | .... | .... | .... | .... | .... | .... | .... |
| | Quad City Flames | AHL | 18 | 2 | 7 | 9 | 4 | .... | .... | .... | .... | .... | .... | .... | .... | .... | .... | .... | .... | .... | .... | .... | .... | .... | .... |
| **2008-09** | **Calgary** | **NHL** | **71** | **11** | **11** | **22** | **10** | **1** | **1** | **3** | **74** | **14.9** | **–11** | **477** | **45.5** | **12:52** | **5** | **1** | **0** | **1** | **0** | **0** | **0** | **0** | **9:52** |
| | Quad City Flames | AHL | 5 | 2 | 0 | 2 | 2 | .... | .... | .... | .... | .... | .... | .... | .... | .... | .... | .... | .... | .... | .... | .... | .... | .... | .... |
| | **NHL Totals** | | **132** | **20** | **18** | **38** | **20** | **1** | **1** | **5** | **128** | **15.6** | | **622** | **46.6** | **11:30** | **5** | **1** | **0** | **1** | **0** | **0** | **0** | **0** | **9:52** |

WHL East First All-Star Team (2006)

## BOYES, Brad (BOIZ, BRAD) ST.L.

Center. Shoots right. 6', 200 lbs. Born, Mississauga, Ont., April 17, 1982. Toronto's 1st choice, 24th overall, in 2000 Entry Draft.

| Season | Club | League | GP | G | A | Pts | PIM | PP | SH | GW | S | % | +/- | TF | F% | Min | GP | G | A | Pts | PIM | PP | SH | GW | Min |
|---|---|---|---|---|---|---|---|---|---|---|---|---|---|---|---|---|---|---|---|---|---|---|---|---|---|
| 1997-98 | Mississauga Reps | MTHL | 44 | 27 | 50 | 77 | .... | .... | .... | .... | .... | .... | .... | .... | .... | .... | .... | .... | .... | .... | .... | .... | .... | .... | .... |
| 1998-99 | Erie Otters | OHL | 59 | 24 | 36 | 60 | 30 | .... | .... | .... | .... | .... | .... | .... | .... | .... | 5 | 1 | 2 | 3 | 10 | .... | .... | .... | .... |
| 99-2000 | Erie Otters | OHL | 68 | 36 | 46 | 82 | 38 | .... | .... | .... | .... | .... | .... | .... | .... | .... | 13 | 6 | 8 | 14 | 10 | .... | .... | .... | .... |
| 2000-01 | Erie Otters | OHL | 59 | 45 | 45 | 90 | 42 | .... | .... | .... | .... | .... | .... | .... | .... | .... | 15 | 10 | 13 | 23 | 8 | .... | .... | .... | .... |
| 2001-02 | Erie Otters | OHL | 47 | 36 | 41 | 77 | 42 | .... | .... | .... | .... | .... | .... | .... | .... | .... | 21 | 22 | *19 | 41 | 27 | .... | .... | .... | .... |
| 2002-03 | St. John's | AHL | 65 | 23 | 28 | 51 | 45 | .... | .... | .... | .... | .... | .... | .... | .... | .... | .... | .... | .... | .... | .... | .... | .... | .... | .... |
| | Cleveland Barons | AHL | 15 | 7 | 6 | 13 | 21 | .... | .... | .... | .... | .... | .... | .... | .... | .... | .... | .... | .... | .... | .... | .... | .... | .... | .... |
| **2003-04** | **San Jose** | **NHL** | **1** | **0** | **0** | **0** | **2** | **0** | **0** | **0** | **0** | **0.0** | **–2** | **0** | **0.0** | **13:03** | .... | .... | .... | .... | .... | .... | .... | .... | .... |
| | Cleveland Barons | AHL | 61 | 25 | 35 | 60 | 38 | .... | .... | .... | .... | .... | .... | .... | .... | .... | .... | .... | .... | .... | .... | .... | .... | .... | .... |
| | Providence Bruins | AHL | 17 | 6 | 6 | 12 | 13 | .... | .... | .... | .... | .... | .... | .... | .... | .... | 2 | 1 | 0 | 1 | 0 | .... | .... | .... | .... |
| 2004-05 | Providence Bruins | AHL | 80 | 33 | 42 | 75 | 58 | .... | .... | .... | .... | .... | .... | .... | .... | .... | 16 | 8 | 7 | 15 | 23 | .... | .... | .... | .... |
| **2005-06** | **Boston** | **NHL** | **82** | **26** | **43** | **69** | **30** | **8** | **0** | **3** | **203** | **12.8** | **11** | **265** | **53.6** | **15:46** | .... | .... | .... | .... | .... | .... | .... | .... | .... |
| **2006-07** | **Boston** | **NHL** | **62** | **13** | **21** | **34** | **25** | **1** | **1** | **1** | **139** | **9.4** | **–17** | **220** | **44.1** | **16:04** | .... | .... | .... | .... | .... | .... | .... | .... | .... |
| | **St. Louis** | **NHL** | **19** | **4** | **8** | **12** | **4** | **0** | **0** | **1** | **43** | **9.3** | **0** | **93** | **58.1** | **17:25** | .... | .... | .... | .... | .... | .... | .... | .... | .... |
| **2007-08** | **St. Louis** | **NHL** | **82** | **43** | **22** | **65** | **20** | **11** | **0** | **9** | **207** | **20.8** | **1** | **236** | **44.5** | **17:57** | .... | .... | .... | .... | .... | .... | .... | .... | .... |
| **2008-09** | **St. Louis** | **NHL** | **82** | **33** | **39** | **72** | **26** | **16** | **0** | **11** | **220** | **15.0** | **–20** | **315** | **49.2** | **19:08** | **4** | **2** | **1** | **3** | **0** | **1** | **0** | **0** | **21:34** |
| | **NHL Totals** | | **328** | **119** | **133** | **252** | **107** | **36** | **1** | **25** | **812** | **14.7** | | **1129** | **49.0** | **17:18** | **4** | **2** | **1** | **3** | **0** | **1** | **0** | **0** | **21:34** |

Canadian Major Junior Scholastic Player of the Year (2000) • OHL Second All-Star Team (2001) • OHL First All-Star Team (2002) • Canadian Major Junior Second All-Star Team (2002) • Canadian Major Junior Sportsman of the Year (2002) • AHL All-Rookie Team (2003) • AHL Second All-Star Team (2004) • NHL All-Rookie Team (2006)

Traded to **San Jose** by **Toronto** with Alyn McCauley and Toronto's 1st round choice (later traded to Boston – Boston selected Mark Stuart) in 2003 Entry Draft for Owen Nolan, March 5, 2003. Traded to **Boston** by **San Jose** for Jeff Jillson, March 9, 2004. Traded to **St. Louis** by **Boston** for Dennis Wideman, February 27, 2007.

## BOYLE, Brian (BOIL, BRIGH-uhn) NYR

Center. Shoots left. 6'7", 252 lbs. Born, Hingham, MA, December 18, 1984. Los Angeles' 2nd choice, 26th overall, in 2003 Entry Draft.

| Season | Club | League | GP | G | A | Pts | PIM | PP | SH | GW | S | % | +/- | TF | F% | Min | GP | G | A | Pts | PIM | PP | SH | GW | Min |
|---|---|---|---|---|---|---|---|---|---|---|---|---|---|---|---|---|---|---|---|---|---|---|---|---|---|
| 2000-01 | St. Sebastian's | High-MA | 25 | 20 | 19 | 39 | .... | .... | .... | .... | .... | .... | .... | .... | .... | .... | .... | .... | .... | .... | .... | .... | .... | .... | .... |
| 2001-02 | St. Sebastian's | High-MA | 28 | 21 | 26 | 47 | 22 | .... | .... | .... | .... | .... | .... | .... | .... | .... | .... | .... | .... | .... | .... | .... | .... | .... | .... |
| 2002-03 | St. Sebastian's | High-MA | 31 | 32 | 31 | 62 | 46 | .... | .... | .... | .... | .... | .... | .... | .... | .... | .... | .... | .... | .... | .... | .... | .... | .... | .... |
| 2003-04 | Boston College | H-East | 35 | 5 | 3 | 8 | 36 | .... | .... | .... | .... | .... | .... | .... | .... | .... | .... | .... | .... | .... | .... | .... | .... | .... | .... |
| 2004-05 | Boston College | H-East | 40 | 19 | 8 | 27 | 64 | .... | .... | .... | .... | .... | .... | .... | .... | .... | .... | .... | .... | .... | .... | .... | .... | .... | .... |
| 2005-06 | Boston College | H-East | 42 | 22 | *30 | 52 | 90 | .... | .... | .... | .... | .... | .... | .... | .... | .... | .... | .... | .... | .... | .... | .... | .... | .... | .... |
| 2006-07 | Boston College | H-East | 42 | 19 | *34 | *53 | *104 | .... | .... | .... | .... | .... | .... | .... | .... | .... | .... | .... | .... | .... | .... | .... | .... | .... | .... |
| | Manchester | AHL | 2 | 0 | 0 | 0 | 2 | .... | .... | .... | .... | .... | .... | .... | .... | .... | 16 | 3 | 5 | 8 | 13 | .... | .... | .... | .... |
| **2007-08** | **Los Angeles** | **NHL** | **8** | **4** | **1** | **5** | **4** | **0** | **0** | **0** | **19** | **21.1** | **4** | **80** | **46.3** | **13:38** | .... | .... | .... | .... | .... | .... | .... | .... | .... |
| | Manchester | AHL | 70 | 31 | 31 | 62 | 87 | .... | .... | .... | .... | .... | .... | .... | .... | .... | .... | .... | .... | .... | .... | .... | .... | .... | .... |
| **2008-09** | **Los Angeles** | **NHL** | **28** | **4** | **1** | **5** | **42** | **0** | **0** | **1** | **36** | **11.1** | **–9** | **225** | **45.3** | **10:08** | .... | .... | .... | .... | .... | .... | .... | .... | .... |
| | Manchester | AHL | 42 | 10 | 11 | 21 | 73 | .... | .... | .... | .... | .... | .... | .... | .... | .... | .... | .... | .... | .... | .... | .... | .... | .... | .... |
| | **NHL Totals** | | **36** | **8** | **2** | **10** | **46** | **0** | **0** | **1** | **55** | **14.5** | | **305** | **45.6** | **10:55** | .... | .... | .... | .... | .... | .... | .... | .... | .... |

Hockey East First All-Star Team (2006, 2007) • NCAA East Second All-American Team (2006) • NCAA East First All-American Team (2007) • NCAA Championship All-Tournament Team (2007)

Traded to **NY Rangers** by **Los Angeles** for NY Rangers' 3rd round choice in 2010 Entry Draft, June 27, 2009.

## BOYLE, Dan (BOIL, DAN) S.J.

Defense. Shoots right. 5'11", 190 lbs. Born, Ottawa, Ont., July 12, 1976.

| Season | Club | League | GP | G | A | Pts | PIM | PP | SH | GW | S | % | +/- | TF | F% | Min | GP | G | A | Pts | PIM | PP | SH | GW | Min |
|---|---|---|---|---|---|---|---|---|---|---|---|---|---|---|---|---|---|---|---|---|---|---|---|---|---|
| 1992-93 | Gloucester | CJHL | 55 | 22 | 51 | 73 | 60 | .... | .... | .... | .... | .... | .... | .... | .... | .... | .... | .... | .... | .... | .... | .... | .... | .... | .... |
| 1993-94 | Gloucester | CJHL | 53 | 27 | 54 | 81 | 155 | .... | .... | .... | .... | .... | .... | .... | .... | .... | .... | .... | .... | .... | .... | .... | .... | .... | .... |
| 1994-95 | Miami U. | CCHA | 35 | 8 | 18 | 26 | 24 | .... | .... | .... | .... | .... | .... | .... | .... | .... | .... | .... | .... | .... | .... | .... | .... | .... | .... |
| 1995-96 | Miami U. | CCHA | 36 | 7 | 20 | 27 | 70 | .... | .... | .... | .... | .... | .... | .... | .... | .... | .... | .... | .... | .... | .... | .... | .... | .... | .... |
| 1996-97 | Miami U. | CCHA | 40 | 11 | 43 | 54 | 52 | .... | .... | .... | .... | .... | .... | .... | .... | .... | .... | .... | .... | .... | .... | .... | .... | .... | .... |
| 1997-98 | Miami U. | CCHA | 37 | 14 | 26 | 40 | 58 | .... | .... | .... | .... | .... | .... | .... | .... | .... | .... | .... | .... | .... | .... | .... | .... | .... | .... |
| **1998-99** | **Florida** | **NHL** | **22** | **3** | **5** | **8** | **6** | **1** | **0** | **1** | **31** | **9.7** | **0** | **1** | **100.0** | **18:50** | .... | .... | .... | .... | .... | .... | .... | .... | .... |
| | Kentucky | AHL | 53 | 8 | 34 | 42 | 87 | .... | .... | .... | .... | .... | .... | .... | .... | .... | 12 | 3 | 5 | 8 | 16 | .... | .... | .... | .... |
| **99-2000** | **Florida** | **NHL** | **13** | **0** | **3** | **3** | **4** | **0** | **0** | **0** | **9** | **0.0** | **–2** | **0** | **0.0** | **16:57** | .... | .... | .... | .... | .... | .... | .... | .... | .... |
| | Louisville Panthers | AHL | 58 | 14 | 38 | 52 | 75 | .... | .... | .... | .... | .... | .... | .... | .... | .... | 4 | 0 | 2 | 2 | 8 | .... | .... | .... | .... |
| **2000-01** | **Florida** | **NHL** | **69** | **4** | **18** | **22** | **28** | **1** | **0** | **0** | **83** | **4.8** | **–14** | **0** | **0.0** | **16:56** | .... | .... | .... | .... | .... | .... | .... | .... | .... |
| | Louisville Panthers | AHL | 6 | 0 | 5 | 5 | 12 | .... | .... | .... | .... | .... | .... | .... | .... | .... | .... | .... | .... | .... | .... | .... | .... | .... | .... |
| **2001-02** | **Florida** | **NHL** | **25** | **3** | **3** | **6** | **12** | **1** | **0** | **0** | **31** | **9.7** | **–1** | **2** | **50.0** | **15:40** | .... | .... | .... | .... | .... | .... | .... | .... | .... |
| | **Tampa Bay** | **NHL** | **41** | **5** | **15** | **20** | **27** | **2** | **0** | **1** | **68** | **7.4** | **–15** | **0** | **0.0** | **22:28** | .... | .... | .... | .... | .... | .... | .... | .... | .... |
| **2002-03** | **Tampa Bay** | **NHL** | **77** | **13** | **40** | **53** | **44** | **8** | **0** | **1** | **136** | **9.6** | **9** | **2** | **0.0** | **24:31** | **11** | **0** | **7** | **7** | **6** | **0** | **0** | **0** | **27:45** |
| **2003-04**♦ | **Tampa Bay** | **NHL** | **78** | **9** | **30** | **39** | **60** | **3** | **0** | **2** | **137** | **6.6** | **23** | **0** | **0.0** | **22:46** | **23** | **2** | **8** | **10** | **16** | **1** | **0** | **0** | **21:27** |
| 2004-05 | Djurgarden | Sweden | 32 | 9 | 9 | 18 | 47 | .... | .... | .... | .... | .... | .... | .... | .... | .... | 12 | 2 | 3 | 5 | 26 | .... | .... | .... | .... |
| **2005-06** | **Tampa Bay** | **NHL** | **79** | **15** | **38** | **53** | **38** | **6** | **0** | **4** | **153** | **9.8** | **–8** | **1** | **0.0** | **23:26** | **5** | **1** | **3** | **4** | **6** | **0** | **0** | **0** | **25:54** |
| | Canada | Olympics | DID NOT PLAY | | | | | | | | | | | | | | | | | | | | | | |
| **2006-07** | **Tampa Bay** | **NHL** | **82** | **20** | **43** | **63** | **62** | **10** | **1** | **4** | **203** | **9.9** | **–5** | **1** | **0.0** | **27:03** | **6** | **0** | **1** | **1** | **2** | **0** | **0** | **0** | **28:03** |
| **2007-08** | **Tampa Bay** | **NHL** | **37** | **4** | **21** | **25** | **57** | **2** | **0** | **1** | **74** | **5.4** | **–29** | **0** | **0.0** | **27:24** | .... | .... | .... | .... | .... | .... | .... | .... | .... |
| **2008-09** | **San Jose** | **NHL** | **77** | **16** | **41** | **57** | **52** | **8** | **0** | **4** | **213** | **7.5** | **6** | **1** | **0.0** | **24:46** | **6** | **2** | **2** | **4** | **8** | **1** | **0** | **0** | **23:17** |
| | **NHL Totals** | | **600** | **92** | **257** | **349** | **390** | **42** | **1** | **18** | **1138** | **8.1** | | **8** | **25.0** | **22:57** | **51** | **5** | **21** | **26** | **38** | **2** | **0** | **0** | **24:14** |

CCHA First All-Star Team (1997, 1998) • NCAA West First All-American Team (1997, 1998) • AHL All-Rookie Team (1999 • AHL Second All-Star Team (1999, 2000) • NHL Second All-Star Team (2007, 2009)

Played in NHL All-Star Game (2009)

Signed as a free agent by **Florida**, March 30, 1998. Traded to **Tampa Bay** by **Florida** for Tampa Bay's 5th round choice (Martin Tuma) in 2003 Entry Draft, January 7, 2002. Signed as a free agent by **Djurgarden** (Sweden), November 14, 2004. • Missed majority of 2007-08 season recovering from off-ice wrist injury, September 22, 2007 and follow-up surgery, November 6, 2007. Traded to **San Jose** by **Tampa Bay** with Brad Lukowich for Matt Carle, Ty Wishart, San Jose's 1st round choice (later traded to Ottawa, later traded to NY Islanders, later traded to Columbus, later traded to Anaheim - Anaheim selected Kyle Palmieri) in 2009 Entry Draft and San Jose's 4th round choice in 2010 Entry Draft, July 4, 2008.

## BOYNTON, Nick (BOIN-tuhn, NIHK) ANA.

Defense. Shoots right. 6'2", 220 lbs. Born, Nobleton, Ont., January 14, 1979. Boston's 1st choice, 21st overall, in 1999 Entry Draft.

| Season | Club | League | GP | G | A | Pts | PIM | PP | SH | GW | S | % | +/- | TF | F% | Min | GP | G | A | Pts | PIM | PP | SH | GW | Min |
|---|---|---|---|---|---|---|---|---|---|---|---|---|---|---|---|---|---|---|---|---|---|---|---|---|---|
| 1993-94 | Caledon | MTJHL | 4 | 0 | 1 | 1 | 0 | .... | .... | .... | .... | .... | .... | .... | .... | .... | .... | .... | .... | .... | .... | .... | .... | .... | .... |
| 1994-95 | Caledon | MTJHL | 44 | 10 | 35 | 45 | 139 | .... | .... | .... | .... | .... | .... | .... | .... | .... | .... | .... | .... | .... | .... | .... | .... | .... | .... |
| 1995-96 | Ottawa 67's | OHL | 64 | 10 | 14 | 24 | 90 | .... | .... | .... | .... | .... | .... | .... | .... | .... | 4 | 0 | 3 | 3 | 10 | .... | .... | .... | .... |
| 1996-97 | Ottawa 67's | OHL | 63 | 13 | 51 | 64 | 143 | .... | .... | .... | .... | .... | .... | .... | .... | .... | 24 | 4 | *24 | 28 | 38 | .... | .... | .... | .... |
| 1997-98 | Ottawa 67's | OHL | 40 | 7 | 31 | 38 | 94 | .... | .... | .... | .... | .... | .... | .... | .... | .... | 13 | 0 | 4 | 4 | 24 | .... | .... | .... | .... |
| 1998-99 | Ottawa 67's | OHL | 51 | 11 | 48 | 59 | 83 | .... | .... | .... | .... | .... | .... | .... | .... | .... | 9 | 1 | 9 | 10 | 18 | .... | .... | .... | .... |
| **99-2000** | **Boston** | **NHL** | **5** | **0** | **0** | **0** | **0** | **0** | **0** | **0** | **6** | **0.0** | **–5** | **0** | **0.0** | **21:21** | .... | .... | .... | .... | .... | .... | .... | .... | .... |
| | Providence Bruins | AHL | 53 | 5 | 14 | 19 | 66 | .... | .... | .... | .... | .... | .... | .... | .... | .... | 12 | 1 | 0 | 1 | 6 | .... | .... | .... | .... |
| **2000-01** | **Boston** | **NHL** | **1** | **0** | **0** | **0** | **0** | **0** | **0** | **0** | **1** | **0.0** | **–1** | **0** | **0.0** | **14:27** | .... | .... | .... | .... | .... | .... | .... | .... | .... |
| | Providence Bruins | AHL | 78 | 6 | 27 | 33 | 105 | .... | .... | .... | .... | .... | .... | .... | .... | .... | 17 | 0 | 2 | 2 | 35 | .... | .... | .... | .... |
| **2001-02** | **Boston** | **NHL** | **80** | **4** | **14** | **18** | **107** | **0** | **0** | **1** | **136** | **2.9** | **18** | **0** | **0.0** | **18:30** | **6** | **1** | **2** | **3** | **8** | **0** | **0** | **0** | **21:30** |
| **2002-03** | **Boston** | **NHL** | **78** | **7** | **17** | **24** | **99** | **0** | **1** | **2** | **160** | **4.4** | **8** | **1** | **0.0** | **22:41** | **5** | **0** | **1** | **1** | **4** | **0** | **0** | **0** | **23:22** |
| **2003-04** | **Boston** | **NHL** | **81** | **6** | **24** | **30** | **98** | **1** | **1** | **1** | **178** | **3.4** | **17** | **0** | **0.0** | **22:32** | **7** | **0** | **2** | **2** | **2** | **0** | **0** | **0** | **24:44** |
| 2004-05 | Nottingham | Britain | 9 | 1 | 3 | 4 | 4 | .... | .... | .... | .... | .... | .... | .... | .... | .... | 6 | 1 | 2 | 3 | 22 | .... | .... | .... | .... |
| **2005-06** | **Boston** | **NHL** | **54** | **5** | **7** | **12** | **93** | **1** | **1** | **0** | **89** | **5.6** | **–7** | **1** | **100.0** | **20:39** | .... | .... | .... | .... | .... | .... | .... | .... | .... |
| **2006-07** | **Phoenix** | **NHL** | **59** | **2** | **9** | **11** | **138** | **1** | **0** | **0** | **53** | **3.8** | **–13** | **1** | **0.0** | **16:48** | .... | .... | .... | .... | .... | .... | .... | .... | .... |

| | | | Regular Season | | | | | | | | | | | | | | Playoffs | | | | | | | | |
|---|---|---|---|---|---|---|---|---|---|---|---|---|---|---|---|---|---|---|---|---|---|---|---|---|---|
| Season | Club | League | GP | G | A | Pts | PIM | PP | SH | GW | S | % | +/- | TF | F% | Min | GP | G | A | Pts | PIM | PP | SH | GW | Min |
| 2007-08 | Phoenix | NHL | 79 | 3 | 9 | 12 | 125 | 0 | 1 | 0 | 94 | 3.2 | –9 | 0 | 0.0 | 17:01 | .... | .... | .... | .... | .... | .... | .... | .... | .... |
| 2008-09 | Florida | NHL | 68 | 5 | 16 | 21 | 91 | 0 | 0 | 1 | 104 | 4.8 | 7 | 0 | 0.0 | 16:36 | .... | .... | .... | .... | .... | .... | .... | .... | .... |
| | NHL Totals | | 505 | 32 | 96 | 128 | 751 | 3 | 4 | 5 | 821 | 3.9 | | 3 | 33.3 | 19:21 | 18 | 1 | 5 | 6 | 14 | 0 | 0 | 0 | 23:16 |

• Re-entered NHL Entry Draft. Originally Washington's 1st choice, 9th overall, in 1997 Entry Draft.

OHL All-Rookie Team (1996) • Memorial Cup Tournament All-Star Team (1999) • Stafford Smythe Memorial Trophy (Memorial Cup Tournament - MVP) (1999) • NHL All-Rookie Team (2002)

Played in NHL All-Star Game (2004)

Signed as a free agent by **Nottingham** (Britain), January 26, 2005. Traded to **Phoenix** by **Boston** with Boston's 4th round choice (later traded to Toronto – Toronto selected Matt Frattin) in 2007 Entry Draft for Paul Mara and Phoenix's 3rd round choice (later traded to Anaheim - Anaheim selected Maxime Macenauer) in 2007 Entry Draft, June 26, 2006. Traded to **Florida** by **Phoenix** with Keith Ballard and Ottawa's 2nd round choice (previously acquired, later traded back to Phoenix – Phoenix selected Jared Staal) in 2008 Entry Draft for Olli Jokinen, June 20, 2008. Signed as a free agent by **Anaheim**, July 9, 2009.

## BRADLEY, Matt

(BRAD-lee, MAT) **WSH.**

Right wing. Shoots right. 6'3", 200 lbs. Born, Stittsville, Ont., June 13, 1978. San Jose's 4th choice, 102nd overall, in 1996 Entry Draft.

| | | | | | | | | | | | | | | | | | | | | | | | | | |
|---|---|---|---|---|---|---|---|---|---|---|---|---|---|---|---|---|---|---|---|---|---|---|---|---|---|
| 1994-95 | Cumberland | CJHL | 49 | 13 | 20 | 33 | 18 | .... | .... | .... | .... | .... | .... | .... | .... | .... | .... | .... | .... | .... | .... | .... | .... | .... | .... |
| 1995-96 | Kingston | OHL | 55 | 10 | 14 | 24 | 17 | .... | .... | .... | .... | .... | .... | .... | .... | .... | 6 | 0 | 1 | 1 | 6 | .... | .... | .... | .... |
| 1996-97 | Kingston | OHL | 65 | 24 | 24 | 48 | 41 | .... | .... | .... | .... | .... | .... | .... | .... | .... | 5 | 0 | 4 | 4 | 2 | .... | .... | .... | .... |
| | Kentucky | AHL | 1 | 0 | 1 | 1 | 0 | .... | .... | .... | .... | .... | .... | .... | .... | .... | .... | .... | .... | .... | .... | .... | .... | .... | .... |
| 1997-98 | Kingston | OHL | 55 | 33 | 50 | 83 | 24 | .... | .... | .... | .... | .... | .... | .... | .... | .... | 8 | 3 | 4 | 7 | 7 | .... | .... | .... | .... |
| 1998-99 | Kentucky | AHL | 79 | 23 | 20 | 43 | 57 | .... | .... | .... | .... | .... | .... | .... | .... | .... | 10 | 1 | 4 | 5 | 4 | .... | .... | .... | .... |
| 99-2000 | Kentucky | AHL | 80 | 22 | 19 | 41 | 81 | .... | .... | .... | .... | .... | .... | .... | .... | .... | 9 | 6 | 3 | 9 | 9 | .... | .... | .... | .... |
| **2000-01** | **San Jose** | **NHL** | **21** | **1** | **1** | **2** | **19** | **0** | **0** | **0** | **16** | **6.3** | **0** | **0** | **0.0** | **6:58** | .... | .... | .... | .... | .... | .... | .... | .... | .... |
| | Kentucky | AHL | 22 | 5 | 8 | 13 | 16 | .... | .... | .... | .... | .... | .... | .... | .... | .... | 1 | 1 | 0 | 1 | 5 | .... | .... | .... | .... |
| **2001-02** | **San Jose** | **NHL** | **54** | **9** | **13** | **22** | **43** | **0** | **0** | **2** | **63** | **14.3** | **22** | **2** | **0.0** | **8:27** | **10** | **0** | **0** | **0** | **0** | **0** | **0** | **0** | **5:16** |
| **2002-03** | **San Jose** | **NHL** | **46** | **2** | **3** | **5** | **37** | **0** | **0** | **0** | **21** | **9.5** | **–1** | **1** | **0.0** | **7:54** | .... | .... | .... | .... | .... | .... | .... | .... | .... |
| **2003-04** | **Pittsburgh** | **NHL** | **82** | **7** | **9** | **16** | **65** | **0** | **0** | **1** | **85** | **8.2** | **–27** | **29** | **41.4** | **12:48** | .... | .... | .... | .... | .... | .... | .... | .... | .... |
| 2004-05 | Bulldogs Dornbirn | Austria-2 | 6 | 5 | 2 | 7 | 18 | .... | .... | .... | .... | .... | .... | .... | .... | .... | .... | .... | .... | .... | .... | .... | .... | .... | .... |
| **2005-06** | **Washington** | **NHL** | **74** | **7** | **12** | **19** | **72** | **0** | **0** | **1** | **87** | **8.0** | **–8** | **25** | **52.0** | **12:36** | .... | .... | .... | .... | .... | .... | .... | .... | .... |
| **2006-07** | **Washington** | **NHL** | **57** | **4** | **9** | **13** | **47** | **0** | **0** | **0** | **77** | **5.2** | **–5** | **20** | **45.0** | **11:55** | .... | .... | .... | .... | .... | .... | .... | .... | .... |
| **2007-08** | **Washington** | **NHL** | **77** | **7** | **11** | **18** | **74** | **1** | **1** | **2** | **111** | **6.3** | **1** | **32** | **43.8** | **10:00** | **7** | **0** | **2** | **2** | **2** | **0** | **0** | **0** | **11:40** |
| **2008-09** | **Washington** | **NHL** | **81** | **5** | **6** | **11** | **59** | **0** | **0** | **1** | **98** | **5.1** | **–1** | **24** | **41.7** | **10:37** | **14** | **2** | **4** | **6** | **0** | **0** | **1** | **1** | **12:45** |
| | **NHL Totals** | | **492** | **42** | **64** | **106** | **416** | **1** | **1** | **7** | **558** | **7.5** | | **133** | **43.6** | **10:41** | **31** | **2** | **6** | **8** | **2** | **0** | **1** | **1** | **10:06** |

Traded to **Pittsburgh** by **San Jose** for Wayne Primeau, March 11, 2003. Signed as a free agent by **Dornbirn** (Austria-2), November 14, 2004. Signed as a free agent by **Washington**, August 18, 2005.

## BRASHEAR, Donald

(bra-SHEER, DAWN-uohld) **NYR**

Left wing. Shoots left. 6'3", 234 lbs. Born, Bedford, IN, January 7, 1972.

| | | | | | | | | | | | | | | | | | | | | | | | | | |
|---|---|---|---|---|---|---|---|---|---|---|---|---|---|---|---|---|---|---|---|---|---|---|---|---|---|
| 1988-89 | Ste-Foy | QAAA | 10 | 1 | 2 | 3 | 10 | .... | .... | .... | .... | .... | .... | .... | .... | .... | .... | .... | .... | .... | .... | .... | .... | .... | .... |
| 1989-90 | Longueuil | QMJHL | 64 | 12 | 14 | 26 | 169 | .... | .... | .... | .... | .... | .... | .... | .... | .... | 7 | 0 | 0 | 0 | 11 | .... | .... | .... | .... |
| 1990-91 | Longueuil | QMJHL | 68 | 12 | 26 | 38 | 195 | .... | .... | .... | .... | .... | .... | .... | .... | .... | 8 | 0 | 3 | 3 | 33 | .... | .... | .... | .... |
| 1991-92 | Verdun | QMJHL | 65 | 18 | 24 | 42 | 283 | .... | .... | .... | .... | .... | .... | .... | .... | .... | 18 | 4 | 2 | 6 | 98 | .... | .... | .... | .... |
| 1992-93 | Fredericton | AHL | 76 | 11 | 3 | 14 | 261 | .... | .... | .... | .... | .... | .... | .... | .... | .... | 5 | 0 | 0 | 0 | 8 | .... | .... | .... | .... |
| **1993-94** | **Montreal** | **NHL** | **14** | **2** | **2** | **4** | **34** | **0** | **0** | **0** | **15** | **13.3** | **0** | .... | .... | .... | **2** | **0** | **0** | **0** | **0** | **0** | **0** | **0** | .... |
| | Fredericton | AHL | 62 | 38 | 28 | 66 | 250 | .... | .... | .... | .... | .... | .... | .... | .... | .... | .... | .... | .... | .... | .... | .... | .... | .... | .... |
| **1994-95** | Fredericton | AHL | 29 | 10 | 9 | 19 | 182 | .... | .... | .... | .... | .... | .... | .... | .... | .... | 17 | 7 | 5 | 12 | 77 | .... | .... | .... | .... |
| | **Montreal** | **NHL** | **20** | **1** | **1** | **2** | **63** | **0** | **0** | **1** | **10** | **10.0** | **–5** | .... | .... | .... | .... | .... | .... | .... | .... | .... | .... | .... | .... |
| **1995-96** | **Montreal** | **NHL** | **67** | **0** | **4** | **4** | **223** | **0** | **0** | **0** | **25** | **0.0** | **–10** | .... | .... | .... | **6** | **0** | **0** | **0** | **2** | **0** | **0** | **0** | .... |
| **1996-97** | **Montreal** | **NHL** | **10** | **0** | **0** | **0** | **38** | **0** | **0** | **0** | **6** | **0.0** | **–2** | .... | .... | .... | .... | .... | .... | .... | .... | .... | .... | .... | .... |
| | **Vancouver** | **NHL** | **59** | **8** | **5** | **13** | **207** | **0** | **0** | **2** | **55** | **14.5** | **–6** | .... | .... | .... | .... | .... | .... | .... | .... | .... | .... | .... | .... |
| **1997-98** | **Vancouver** | **NHL** | **77** | **9** | **9** | **18** | ***372** | **0** | **0** | **1** | **64** | **14.1** | **–9** | .... | .... | .... | .... | .... | .... | .... | .... | .... | .... | .... | .... |
| **1998-99** | **Vancouver** | **NHL** | **82** | **8** | **10** | **18** | **209** | **2** | **0** | **1** | **112** | **7.1** | **–25** | **6** | **16.7** | **13:25** | .... | .... | .... | .... | .... | .... | .... | .... | .... |
| **99-2000** | **Vancouver** | **NHL** | **60** | **11** | **2** | **13** | **136** | **1** | **0** | **3** | **83** | **13.3** | **–9** | **11** | **36.4** | **13:07** | .... | .... | .... | .... | .... | .... | .... | .... | .... |
| **2000-01** | **Vancouver** | **NHL** | **79** | **9** | **19** | **28** | **145** | **0** | **0** | **1** | **127** | **7.1** | **0** | **6** | **16.7** | **13:27** | **4** | **0** | **0** | **0** | **0** | **0** | **0** | **0** | **14:47** |
| **2001-02** | **Vancouver** | **NHL** | **31** | **5** | **8** | **13** | **90** | **1** | **0** | **0** | **45** | **11.1** | **–8** | **4** | **25.0** | **13:58** | .... | .... | .... | .... | .... | .... | .... | .... | .... |
| | **Philadelphia** | **NHL** | **50** | **4** | **15** | **19** | **109** | **0** | **0** | **2** | **62** | **6.5** | **0** | **1** | **0.0** | **13:00** | **5** | **0** | **0** | **0** | **19** | **0** | **0** | **0** | **9:55** |
| **2002-03** | **Philadelphia** | **NHL** | **80** | **8** | **17** | **25** | **161** | **0** | **0** | **1** | **99** | **8.1** | **5** | **27** | **33.3** | **13:23** | **13** | **1** | **2** | **3** | **21** | **0** | **0** | **0** | **11:09** |
| **2003-04** | **Philadelphia** | **NHL** | **64** | **6** | **7** | **13** | **212** | **0** | **0** | **0** | **72** | **8.3** | **–1** | **18** | **38.9** | **11:02** | **18** | **1** | **3** | **4** | **61** | **1** | **0** | **0** | **8:56** |
| 2004-05 | Quebec RadioX | QNAHL | 47 | 18 | 32 | 50 | 260 | .... | .... | .... | .... | .... | .... | .... | .... | .... | 8 | 4 | 6 | 10 | 42 | .... | .... | .... | .... |
| **2005-06** | **Philadelphia** | **NHL** | **76** | **4** | **5** | **9** | **166** | **0** | **0** | **0** | **73** | **5.5** | **–2** | **7** | **28.6** | **8:36** | **1** | **0** | **0** | **0** | **0** | **0** | **0** | **0** | **4:20** |
| **2006-07** | **Washington** | **NHL** | **77** | **4** | **9** | **13** | **156** | **0** | **0** | **0** | **47** | **8.5** | **1** | **8** | **25.0** | **7:58** | .... | .... | .... | .... | .... | .... | .... | .... | .... |
| **2007-08** | **Washington** | **NHL** | **80** | **5** | **3** | **8** | **119** | **0** | **0** | **0** | **59** | **8.5** | **–7** | **1** | **0.0** | **7:52** | **7** | **1** | **1** | **2** | **0** | **0** | **0** | **0** | **7:30** |
| **2008-09** | **Washington** | **NHL** | **63** | **1** | **3** | **4** | **121** | **0** | **0** | **1** | **43** | **2.3** | **–6** | **0** | **0.0** | **8:15** | **4** | **0** | **0** | **0** | **18** | **0** | **0** | **0** | **3:25** |
| | **NHL Totals** | | **989** | **85** | **119** | **204** | **2561** | **4** | **0** | **13** | **997** | **8.5** | | **89** | **30.3** | **11:05** | **60** | **3** | **6** | **9** | **121** | **1** | **0** | **0** | **9:19** |

Signed as a free agent by **Montreal**, July 28, 1992. Traded to **Vancouver** by **Montreal** for Jassen Cullimore, November 13, 1996. Traded to **Philadelphia** by **Vancouver** with Vancouver's 6th round choice (later traded to Columbus – Columbus selected Jaroslav Balastik) in 2002 Entry Draft for Jan Hlavac and Tampa Bay's 3rd round choice (previously acquired, Vancouver selected Brett Skinner) in 2002 Entry Draft, December 17, 2001. Signed as a free agent by **Quebec** (QNAHL), September 21, 2004. Signed as a free agent by **Washington**, July 14, 2006. Signed as a free agent by **NY Rangers**, July 1, 2009.

## BRASSARD, Derick

(bruh-SAHRD, DAIR-ihk) **CBJ**

Center. Shoots left. 6'1", 190 lbs. Born, Hull, Que., September 22, 1987. Columbus' 1st choice, 6th overall, in 2006 Entry Draft.

| | | | | | | | | | | | | | | | | | | | | | | | | | |
|---|---|---|---|---|---|---|---|---|---|---|---|---|---|---|---|---|---|---|---|---|---|---|---|---|---|
| 2004-05 | Drummondville | QMJHL | 69 | 25 | 51 | 76 | 25 | .... | .... | .... | .... | .... | .... | .... | .... | .... | 6 | 1 | 5 | 6 | 6 | .... | .... | .... | .... |
| 2005-06 | Drummondville | QMJHL | 58 | 44 | 72 | 116 | 92 | .... | .... | .... | .... | .... | .... | .... | .... | .... | 7 | 5 | 4 | 9 | 10 | .... | .... | .... | .... |
| 2006-07 | Drummondville | QMJHL | 14 | 6 | 19 | 25 | 24 | .... | .... | .... | .... | .... | .... | .... | .... | .... | 12 | 9 | 15 | 24 | 12 | .... | .... | .... | .... |
| **2007-08** | **Columbus** | **NHL** | **17** | **1** | **1** | **2** | **6** | **0** | **0** | **0** | **13** | **7.7** | **–4** | **80** | **42.5** | **9:03** | .... | .... | .... | .... | .... | .... | .... | .... | .... |
| | Syracuse Crunch | AHL | 42 | 15 | 36 | 51 | 51 | .... | .... | .... | .... | .... | .... | .... | .... | .... | 13 | 4 | 9 | 13 | 10 | .... | .... | .... | .... |
| **2008-09** | **Columbus** | **NHL** | **31** | **10** | **15** | **25** | **17** | **3** | **0** | **1** | **59** | **16.9** | **12** | **332** | **48.5** | **14:25** | .... | .... | .... | .... | .... | .... | .... | .... | .... |
| | **NHL Totals** | | **48** | **11** | **16** | **27** | **23** | **3** | **0** | **1** | **72** | **15.3** | | **412** | **47.3** | **12:31** | .... | .... | .... | .... | .... | .... | .... | .... | .... |

QMJHL First All-Star Team (2006) • Canadian Major Junior Second All-Star Team (2006)

• Missed majority of 2006-07 season recovering from shoulder injury. • Missed majority of 2008-09 season recovering from shoulder injury suffered in game at Dallas, December 18, 2008.

## BRENNAN, Kip

(BREH-nan, KIHP)

Left wing. Shoots left. 6'4", 230 lbs. Born, Kingston, Ont., August 27, 1980. Los Angeles' 4th choice, 103rd overall, in 1998 Entry Draft.

| | | | | | | | | | | | | | | | | | | | | | | | | | |
|---|---|---|---|---|---|---|---|---|---|---|---|---|---|---|---|---|---|---|---|---|---|---|---|---|---|
| 1995-96 | St. Mike's B's | OPJHL | 40 | 0 | 11 | 11 | 155 | .... | .... | .... | .... | .... | .... | .... | .... | .... | 7 | 0 | 1 | 1 | 20 | .... | .... | .... | .... |
| 1996-97 | Windsor Spitfires | OHL | 42 | 0 | 10 | 10 | 156 | .... | .... | .... | .... | .... | .... | .... | .... | .... | 5 | 0 | 1 | 1 | 16 | .... | .... | .... | .... |
| 1997-98 | Windsor Spitfires | OHL | 24 | 0 | 7 | 7 | 103 | .... | .... | .... | .... | .... | .... | .... | .... | .... | .... | .... | .... | .... | .... | .... | .... | .... | .... |
| | Sudbury Wolves | OHL | 24 | 0 | 3 | 3 | 85 | .... | .... | .... | .... | .... | .... | .... | .... | .... | .... | .... | .... | .... | .... | .... | .... | .... | .... |
| 1998-99 | Sudbury Wolves | OHL | 38 | 9 | 12 | 21 | 160 | .... | .... | .... | .... | .... | .... | .... | .... | .... | .... | .... | .... | .... | .... | .... | .... | .... | .... |
| 99-2000 | Sudbury Wolves | OHL | 55 | 16 | 16 | 32 | 228 | .... | .... | .... | .... | .... | .... | .... | .... | .... | 12 | 3 | 3 | 6 | 67 | .... | .... | .... | .... |
| 2000-01 | Lowell | AHL | 23 | 2 | 3 | 5 | 117 | .... | .... | .... | .... | .... | .... | .... | .... | .... | .... | .... | .... | .... | .... | .... | .... | .... | .... |
| | Sudbury Wolves | OHL | 27 | 7 | 14 | 21 | 94 | .... | .... | .... | .... | .... | .... | .... | .... | .... | 12 | 5 | 6 | 11 | *92 | .... | .... | .... | .... |
| **2001-02** | **Los Angeles** | **NHL** | **4** | **0** | **0** | **0** | **22** | **0** | **0** | **0** | **0** | **0.0** | **1** | **0** | **0.0** | **4:40** | .... | .... | .... | .... | .... | .... | .... | .... | .... |
| | Manchester | AHL | 44 | 4 | 1 | 5 | 269 | .... | .... | .... | .... | .... | .... | .... | .... | .... | 4 | 0 | 1 | 1 | 26 | .... | .... | .... | .... |
| **2002-03** | **Los Angeles** | **NHL** | **19** | **0** | **0** | **0** | **57** | **0** | **0** | **0** | **6** | **0.0** | **0** | **2** | **0.0** | **4:52** | .... | .... | .... | .... | .... | .... | .... | .... | .... |
| | Manchester | AHL | 35 | 3 | 2 | 5 | 195 | .... | .... | .... | .... | .... | .... | .... | .... | .... | 3 | 0 | 0 | 0 | 0 | .... | .... | .... | .... |
| **2003-04** | **Los Angeles** | **NHL** | **18** | **1** | **0** | **1** | **79** | **0** | **0** | **0** | **6** | **16.7** | **–1** | **0** | **0.0** | **5:01** | .... | .... | .... | .... | .... | .... | .... | .... | .... |
| | Manchester | AHL | 2 | 0 | 0 | 0 | 6 | .... | .... | .... | .... | .... | .... | .... | .... | .... | .... | .... | .... | .... | .... | .... | .... | .... | .... |
| | **Atlanta** | **NHL** | **5** | **0** | **0** | **0** | **17** | **0** | **0** | **0** | **2** | **0.0** | **0** | **0** | **0.0** | **3:37** | .... | .... | .... | .... | .... | .... | .... | .... | .... |
| 2004-05 | Chicago Wolves | AHL | 48 | 7 | 6 | 13 | 267 | .... | .... | .... | .... | .... | .... | .... | .... | .... | 18 | 1 | 1 | 2 | *105 | .... | .... | .... | .... |
| **2005-06** | **Anaheim** | **NHL** | **12** | **0** | **1** | **1** | **35** | **0** | **0** | **0** | **5** | **0.0** | **–2** | **1** | **0.0** | **4:16** | .... | .... | .... | .... | .... | .... | .... | .... | .... |
| | Portland Pirates | AHL | 9 | 2 | 1 | 3 | 22 | .... | .... | .... | .... | .... | .... | .... | .... | .... | .... | .... | .... | .... | .... | .... | .... | .... | .... |
| 2006-07 | Hershey Bears | AHL | 26 | 4 | 2 | 6 | 67 | .... | .... | .... | .... | .... | .... | .... | .... | .... | 6 | 0 | 1 | 1 | 30 | .... | .... | .... | .... |
| | Toronto Marlies | AHL | 1 | 0 | 0 | 0 | 6 | .... | .... | .... | .... | .... | .... | .... | .... | .... | .... | .... | .... | .... | .... | .... | .... | .... | .... |
| | Long Beach | ECHL | 11 | 2 | 3 | 5 | 74 | .... | .... | .... | .... | .... | .... | .... | .... | .... | .... | .... | .... | .... | .... | .... | .... | .... | .... |
| **2007-08** | **NY Islanders** | **NHL** | **3** | **0** | **0** | **0** | **12** | **0** | **0** | **0** | **0** | **0.0** | **0** | **0** | **0.0** | **4:21** | .... | .... | .... | .... | .... | .... | .... | .... | .... |
| | Bridgeport | AHL | 49 | 2 | 1 | 3 | 247 | .... | .... | .... | .... | .... | .... | .... | .... | .... | .... | .... | .... | .... | .... | .... | .... | .... | .... |

| | | | Regular Season | | | | | | | | | | | | | | Playoffs | | | | | | | | |
|---|---|---|---|---|---|---|---|---|---|---|---|---|---|---|---|---|---|---|---|---|---|---|---|---|---|
| Season | Club | League | GP | G | A | Pts | PIM | PP | SH | GW | S | % | +/- | TF | F% | Min | GP | G | A | Pts | PIM | PP | SH | GW | Min |
| 2008-09 | HIFK Helsinki | Finland | 22 | 0 | 3 | 3 | 118 | | | | | | | | | | | | | | | | | | |
| | Hershey Bears | AHL | 22 | 1 | 3 | 4 | 88 | | | | | | | | | | 1 | 0 | 0 | 0 | 4 | | | | |
| | South Carolina | ECHL | 3 | 0 | 0 | 0 | 16 | | | | | | | | | | | | | | | | | | |
| | **NHL Totals** | | **61** | **1** | **1** | **2** | **222** | **0** | **0** | **0** | **19** | **5.3** | | **3** | **0.0** | **4:39** | | | | | | | | | |

Traded to **Atlanta** by **Los Angeles** for Jeff Cowan, March 9, 2004. • Spent the majority of the 2003-04 season serving as a healthy reserve. Signed as a free agent by **Chicago** (AHL), September 27, 2004. Traded to **Anaheim** by **Atlanta** for Mark Popovic, August 23, 2005. Signed as a free agent by **NY Islanders**, July 3, 2007. Signed as a free agent by **Hershey** (AHL), December 16, 2008.

## BRENT, Tim
(BREHNT, TIHM) **TOR.**

Center. Shoots right. 6', 197 lbs. Born, Cambridge, Ont., March 10, 1984. Anaheim's 3rd choice, 75th overall, in 2004 Entry Draft.

| Season | Club | League | GP | G | A | Pts | PIM | PP | SH | GW | S | % | +/- | TF | F% | Min | GP | G | A | Pts | PIM | PP | SH | GW | Min |
|---|---|---|---|---|---|---|---|---|---|---|---|---|---|---|---|---|---|---|---|---|---|---|---|---|---|
| 99-2000 | Cambridge | OHA-B | 40 | 19 | 16 | 35 | 42 | | | | | | | | | | | | | | | | | | |
| 2000-01 | St. Michael's | OHL | 64 | 9 | 19 | 28 | 31 | | | | | | | | | | 18 | 2 | 8 | 10 | 6 | | | | |
| 2001-02 | St. Michael's | OHL | 61 | 19 | 40 | 59 | 52 | | | | | | | | | | 14 | 7 | 12 | 19 | 20 | | | | |
| 2002-03 | St. Michael's | OHL | 60 | 24 | 42 | 66 | 74 | | | | | | | | | | 19 | 7 | 17 | 24 | 14 | | | | |
| 2003-04 | St. Michael's | OHL | 53 | 26 | 41 | 67 | 105 | | | | | | | | | | 18 | 4 | 13 | 17 | 24 | | | | |
| 2004-05 | Cincinnati | AHL | 46 | 5 | 13 | 18 | 42 | | | | | | | | | | 12 | 0 | 1 | 1 | 6 | | | | |
| 2005-06 | Portland Pirates | AHL | 37 | 15 | 9 | 24 | 32 | | | | | | | | | | 15 | 4 | 4 | 8 | 16 | | | | |
| **2006-07** | **Anaheim** | **NHL** | **15** | **1** | **0** | **1** | **6** | **0** | **0** | **0** | **14** | **7.1** | **–5** | **86** | **48.8** | **6:55** | | | | | | | | | |
| | Portland Pirates | AHL | 48 | 16 | 14 | 30 | 40 | | | | | | | | | | | | | | | | | | |
| **2007-08** | **Pittsburgh** | **NHL** | **1** | **0** | **0** | **0** | **0** | **0** | **0** | **0** | **0** | **0.0** | **–1** | **5** | **60.0** | **4:34** | | | | | | | | | |
| | Wilkes-Barre | AHL | 74 | 18 | 43 | 61 | 79 | | | | | | | | | | 23 | *12 | 15 | 27 | 10 | | | | |
| **2008-09** | **Chicago** | **NHL** | **2** | **0** | **0** | **0** | **2** | **0** | **0** | **0** | **0** | **0.0** | **0** | **10** | **50.0** | **8:21** | | | | | | | | | |
| | Rockford IceHogs | AHL | 64 | 20 | 42 | 62 | 59 | | | | | | | | | | 4 | 0 | 1 | 1 | 2 | | | | |
| | **NHL Totals** | | **18** | **1** | **0** | **1** | **8** | **0** | **0** | **0** | **14** | **7.1** | | **101** | **49.5** | **6:57** | | | | | | | | | |

• Re-entered NHL Entry Draft. Originally Anaheim's 2nd choice, 37th overall, in 2002 Entry Draft.

Traded to **Pittsburgh** by **Anaheim** for Stephen Dixon, June 23, 2007. Traded to **Chicago** by **Pittsburgh** for Danny Richmond, July 17, 2008. Signed as a free agent by **Toronto**, July 6 2009.

## BREWER, Eric
(BREW-uhr, AIR-ihk) **ST.L.**

Defense. Shoots left. 6'3", 220 lbs. Born, Vernon, B.C., April 17, 1979. NY Islanders' 2nd choice, 5th overall, in 1997 Entry Draft.

| Season | Club | League | GP | G | A | Pts | PIM | PP | SH | GW | S | % | +/- | TF | F% | Min | GP | G | A | Pts | PIM | PP | SH | GW | Min |
|---|---|---|---|---|---|---|---|---|---|---|---|---|---|---|---|---|---|---|---|---|---|---|---|---|---|
| 1994-95 | Kamloops | Minor-BC | 40 | 19 | 19 | 38 | 62 | | | | | | | | | | | | | | | | | | |
| 1995-96 | Prince George | WHL | 63 | 4 | 10 | 14 | 25 | | | | | | | | | | | | | | | | | | |
| 1996-97 | Prince George | WHL | 71 | 5 | 24 | 29 | 81 | | | | | | | | | | 15 | 2 | 4 | 6 | 16 | | | | |
| 1997-98 | Prince George | WHL | 34 | 5 | 28 | 33 | 45 | | | | | | | | | | 11 | 4 | 2 | 6 | 19 | | | | |
| **1998-99** | **NY Islanders** | **NHL** | **63** | **5** | **6** | **11** | **32** | **2** | **0** | **0** | **63** | **7.9** | **–14** | **0** | **0.0** | **15:28** | | | | | | | | | |
| **99-2000** | **NY Islanders** | **NHL** | **26** | **0** | **2** | **2** | **20** | **0** | **0** | **0** | **30** | **0.0** | **–11** | **0** | **0.0** | **18:33** | | | | | | | | | |
| | Lowell | AHL | 25 | 2 | 2 | 4 | 26 | | | | | | | | | | 7 | 0 | 0 | 0 | 0 | | | | |
| **2000-01** | **Edmonton** | **NHL** | **77** | **7** | **14** | **21** | **53** | **2** | **0** | **2** | **91** | **7.7** | **15** | **0** | **0.0** | **18:31** | **6** | **1** | **5** | **6** | **2** | **1** | **0** | **0** | **28:12** |
| **2001-02** | **Edmonton** | **NHL** | **81** | **7** | **18** | **25** | **45** | **6** | **0** | **2** | **165** | **4.2** | **–5** | **0** | **0.0** | **23:56** | | | | | | | | | |
| | Canada | Olympics | 6 | 2 | 0 | 2 | 0 | | | | | | | | | | | | | | | | | | |
| **2002-03** | **Edmonton** | **NHL** | **80** | **8** | **21** | **29** | **45** | **1** | **0** | **1** | **147** | **5.4** | **–11** | **1** | **100.0** | **24:56** | **6** | **1** | **3** | **4** | **6** | **0** | **0** | **0** | **25:31** |
| **2003-04** | **Edmonton** | **NHL** | **77** | **7** | **18** | **25** | **67** | **3** | **0** | **1** | **135** | **5.2** | **–6** | **0** | **0.0** | **24:40** | | | | | | | | | |
| 2004-05 | | | DID NOT PLAY | | | | | | | | | | | | | | | | | | | | | | |
| **2005-06** | **St. Louis** | **NHL** | **32** | **6** | **3** | **9** | **45** | **1** | **0** | **1** | **64** | **9.4** | **–17** | **0** | **0.0** | **23:28** | | | | | | | | | |
| **2006-07** | **St. Louis** | **NHL** | **82** | **6** | **23** | **29** | **69** | **2** | **0** | **1** | **111** | **5.4** | **–10** | **0** | **0.0** | **24:32** | | | | | | | | | |
| **2007-08** | **St. Louis** | **NHL** | **77** | **1** | **21** | **22** | **91** | **0** | **0** | **0** | **101** | **1.0** | **–18** | **0** | **0.0** | **24:38** | | | | | | | | | |
| **2008-09** | **St. Louis** | **NHL** | **28** | **1** | **5** | **6** | **24** | **1** | **0** | **0** | **49** | **2.0** | **–14** | **0** | **0.0** | **25:07** | | | | | | | | | |
| | **NHL Totals** | | **623** | **48** | **131** | **179** | **491** | **18** | **0** | **8** | **956** | **5.0** | | **1** | **100.0** | **22:36** | **12** | **2** | **8** | **10** | **8** | **1** | **0** | **0** | **26:51** |

WHL West Second All-Star Team (1998)

Played in NHL All-Star Game (2003)

Traded to **Edmonton** by **NY Islanders** with Josh Green and NY Islanders' 2nd round choice (Brad Winchester) in 2000 Entry Draft for Roman Hamrlik, June 24, 2000. Traded to **St. Louis** by **Edmonton** with Doug Lynch and Jeff Woywitka for Chris Pronger, August 2, 2005. • Missed majority of 2005-06 season recovering from shoulder injuries suffered in games at Columbus (November 16, 2005) and Atlanta (January 13, 2006). • Missed majority of 2008-09 season recovering from back injury suffered in game at Los Angeles, December 11, 2008.

## BRIERE, Daniel
(bree-AIR, DAN-yehl) **PHI.**

Center. Shoots right. 5'10", 179 lbs. Born, Gatineau, Que., October 6, 1977. Phoenix's 2nd choice, 24th overall, in 1996 Entry Draft.

| Season | Club | League | GP | G | A | Pts | PIM | PP | SH | GW | S | % | +/- | TF | F% | Min | GP | G | A | Pts | PIM | PP | SH | GW | Min |
|---|---|---|---|---|---|---|---|---|---|---|---|---|---|---|---|---|---|---|---|---|---|---|---|---|---|
| 1992-93 | Abitibi Regents | QAAA | 42 | 24 | 30 | 54 | 28 | | | | | | | | | | 3 | 0 | 3 | 3 | 8 | | | | |
| 1993-94 | Gatineau | QAAA | 44 | 56 | 47 | 103 | 56 | | | | | | | | | | | | | | | | | | |
| 1994-95 | Drummondville | QMJHL | 72 | 51 | 72 | 123 | 54 | | | | | | | | | | 4 | 2 | 3 | 5 | 2 | | | | |
| 1995-96 | Drummondville | QMJHL | 67 | *67 | *96 | *163 | 84 | | | | | | | | | | 6 | 6 | 12 | 18 | 8 | | | | |
| 1996-97 | Drummondville | QMJHL | 59 | 52 | 78 | 130 | 94 | | | | | | | | | | 8 | 7 | 7 | 14 | 14 | | | | |
| **1997-98** | **Phoenix** | **NHL** | **5** | **1** | **0** | **1** | **2** | **0** | **0** | **0** | **4** | **25.0** | **1** | | | | | | | | | | | | |
| | Springfield | AHL | 68 | 36 | 56 | 92 | 42 | | | | | | | | | | 4 | 1 | 2 | 3 | 4 | | | | |
| **1998-99** | **Phoenix** | **NHL** | **64** | **8** | **14** | **22** | **30** | **2** | **0** | **2** | **90** | **8.9** | **–3** | **484** | **47.5** | **11:13** | | | | | | | | | |
| | Las Vegas | IHL | 1 | 1 | 1 | 2 | 0 | | | | | | | | | | | | | | | | | | |
| | Springfield | AHL | 13 | 2 | 6 | 8 | 20 | | | | | | | | | | 3 | 0 | 1 | 1 | 2 | | | | |
| **99-2000** | **Phoenix** | **NHL** | **13** | **1** | **1** | **2** | **0** | **0** | **0** | **0** | **9** | **11.1** | **0** | **65** | **49.2** | **7:41** | **1** | **0** | **0** | **0** | **0** | **0** | **0** | **0** | **6:16** |
| | Springfield | AHL | 58 | 29 | 42 | 71 | 56 | | | | | | | | | | | | | | | | | | |
| **2000-01** | **Phoenix** | **NHL** | **30** | **11** | **4** | **15** | **12** | **9** | **0** | **1** | **43** | **25.6** | **–2** | **210** | **50.0** | **10:50** | | | | | | | | | |
| | Springfield | AHL | 30 | 21 | 25 | 46 | 30 | | | | | | | | | | | | | | | | | | |
| **2001-02** | **Phoenix** | **NHL** | **78** | **32** | **28** | **60** | **52** | **12** | **0** | **5** | **149** | **21.5** | **6** | **951** | **51.8** | **15:44** | **5** | **2** | **1** | **3** | **2** | **1** | **0** | **1** | **16:25** |
| **2002-03** | **Phoenix** | **NHL** | **68** | **17** | **29** | **46** | **50** | **4** | **0** | **3** | **142** | **12.0** | **–21** | **1108** | **52.5** | **17:02** | | | | | | | | | |
| | **Buffalo** | **NHL** | **14** | **7** | **5** | **12** | **12** | **5** | **0** | **1** | **39** | **17.9** | **1** | **206** | **50.0** | **17:49** | | | | | | | | | |
| **2003-04** | **Buffalo** | **NHL** | **82** | **28** | **37** | **65** | **70** | **11** | **0** | **3** | **194** | **14.4** | **–7** | **1066** | **47.1** | **18:20** | | | | | | | | | |
| 2004-05 | SC Bern | Swiss | 36 | 16 | 29 | 45 | 26 | | | | | | | | | | 11 | 1 | 6 | 7 | 2 | | | | |
| **2005-06** | **Buffalo** | **NHL** | **48** | **25** | **33** | **58** | **48** | **11** | **0** | **4** | **147** | **17.0** | **3** | **517** | **50.7** | **19:04** | **18** | **8** | **11** | **19** | **12** | **3** | **0** | **2** | **18:48** |
| **2006-07** | **Buffalo** | **NHL** | **81** | **32** | **63** | **95** | **89** | **9** | **0** | **6** | **234** | **13.7** | **17** | **1089** | **49.6** | **19:19** | **16** | **3** | **12** | **15** | **16** | **2** | **0** | **1** | **20:53** |
| **2007-08** | **Philadelphia** | **NHL** | **79** | **31** | **41** | **72** | **68** | **14** | **0** | **3** | **182** | **17.0** | **–22** | **1250** | **50.5** | **18:52** | **17** | **9** | **7** | **16** | **20** | **6** | **0** | **3** | **18:26** |
| **2008-09** | **Philadelphia** | **NHL** | **29** | **11** | **14** | **25** | **26** | **4** | **0** | **0** | **54** | **20.4** | **–1** | **147** | **46.3** | **15:39** | **6** | **1** | **3** | **4** | **8** | **1** | **0** | **0** | **16:41** |
| | **NHL Totals** | | **591** | **204** | **269** | **473** | **459** | **81** | **0** | **28** | **1287** | **15.9** | | **7093** | **50.0** | **16:34** | **63** | **23** | **34** | **57** | **58** | **13** | **0** | **7** | **18:38** |

QMJHL All-Rookie Team (1995) • QMJHL Offensive Rookie of the Year (1995) • QMJHL Second All-Star Team (1996, 1997) • AHL All-Rookie Team (1998) • AHL First All-Star Team (1998) • Dudley "Red" Garrett Memorial Award (AHL – Rookie of the Year) (1998)

Played in NHL All-Star Game (2007)

Traded to **Buffalo** by **Phoenix** with Phoenix's 3rd round choice (Andrej Sekera) in 2004 Entry Draft for Chris Gratton and Buffalo's 4th round choice (later traded to Edmonton – Edmonton selected Liam Reddox) in 2004 Entry Draft, March 10, 2003. Signed as a free agent by **Bern** (Swiss), September 28, 2004. Signed as a free agent by **Philadelphia**, July 1, 2007. • Missed majority of 2008-09 season recovering from abdominal surgery (October 25, 2008) and groin surgery (January 22, 2009).

## BRIND'AMOUR, Rod
(BRIHND-uh-MOHR, RAWD) **CAR.**

Center. Shoots left. 6'1", 205 lbs. Born, Ottawa, Ont., August 9, 1970. St. Louis' 1st choice, 9th overall, in 1988 Entry Draft.

| Season | Club | League | GP | G | A | Pts | PIM | PP | SH | GW | S | % | +/- | TF | F% | Min | GP | G | A | Pts | PIM | PP | SH | GW | Min |
|---|---|---|---|---|---|---|---|---|---|---|---|---|---|---|---|---|---|---|---|---|---|---|---|---|---|
| 1986-87 | Notre Dame | SMHL | 33 | 38 | 50 | 88 | 66 | | | | | | | | | | | | | | | | | | |
| 1987-88 | Notre Dame | SJHL | 56 | 46 | 61 | 107 | 136 | | | | | | | | | | | | | | | | | | |
| **1988-89** | Michigan State | CCHA | 42 | 27 | 32 | 59 | 63 | | | | | | | | | | | | | | | | | | |
| | **St. Louis** | **NHL** | | | | | | | | | | | | | | | **5** | **2** | **0** | **2** | **4** | **0** | **0** | **0** | |
| **1989-90** | **St. Louis** | **NHL** | **79** | **26** | **35** | **61** | **46** | **10** | **0** | **1** | **160** | **16.3** | **23** | | | | **12** | **5** | **8** | **13** | **6** | **1** | **0** | **0** | |
| **1990-91** | **St. Louis** | **NHL** | **78** | **17** | **32** | **49** | **93** | **4** | **0** | **3** | **169** | **10.1** | **2** | | | | **13** | **2** | **5** | **7** | **10** | **1** | **0** | **0** | |
| **1991-92** | **Philadelphia** | **NHL** | **80** | **33** | **44** | **77** | **100** | **8** | **4** | **5** | **202** | **16.3** | **–3** | | | | | | | | | | | | |
| **1992-93** | **Philadelphia** | **NHL** | **81** | **37** | **49** | **86** | **89** | **13** | **4** | **4** | **206** | **18.0** | **–8** | | | | | | | | | | | | |
| **1993-94** | **Philadelphia** | **NHL** | **84** | **35** | **62** | **97** | **85** | **14** | **1** | **4** | **230** | **15.2** | **–9** | | | | | | | | | | | | |
| **1994-95** | **Philadelphia** | **NHL** | **48** | **12** | **27** | **39** | **33** | **4** | **1** | **2** | **86** | **14.0** | **–4** | | | | **15** | **6** | **9** | **15** | **8** | **2** | **1** | **1** | |
| **1995-96** | **Philadelphia** | **NHL** | **82** | **26** | **61** | **87** | **110** | **4** | **4** | **5** | **213** | **12.2** | **20** | | | | **12** | **2** | **5** | **7** | **6** | **1** | **0** | **0** | |
| **1996-97** | **Philadelphia** | **NHL** | **82** | **27** | **32** | **59** | **41** | **8** | **2** | **3** | **205** | **13.2** | **2** | | | | **19** | ***13** | **8** | **21** | **10** | **4** | **2** | **1** | |
| **1997-98** | **Philadelphia** | **NHL** | **82** | **36** | **38** | **74** | **54** | **10** | **2** | **8** | **205** | **17.6** | **–2** | | | | **5** | **2** | **2** | **4** | **7** | **0** | **0** | **0** | |
| | Canada | Olympics | 6 | 1 | 2 | 3 | 0 | | | | | | | | | | | | | | | | | | |
| **1998-99** | **Philadelphia** | **NHL** | **82** | **24** | **50** | **74** | **47** | **10** | **0** | **3** | **191** | **12.6** | **3** | **1773** | **56.5** | **21:29** | **6** | **1** | **3** | **4** | **0** | **0** | **0** | **0** | **25:08** |
| **99-2000** | **Philadelphia** | **NHL** | **12** | **5** | **3** | **8** | **4** | **4** | **0** | **0** | **26** | **19.2** | **–1** | **291** | **60.5** | **20:50** | | | | | | | | | |
| | **Carolina** | **NHL** | **33** | **4** | **10** | **14** | **22** | **0** | **1** | **1** | **61** | **6.6** | **–12** | **704** | **55.5** | **20:35** | | | | | | | | | |
| **2000-01** | **Carolina** | **NHL** | **79** | **20** | **36** | **56** | **47** | **5** | **1** | **5** | **163** | **12.3** | **–7** | **1907** | **60.4** | **22:07** | **6** | **1** | **3** | **4** | **6** | **0** | **0** | **1** | **23:27** |

| | | | Regular Season | | | | | | | | | | | | | | Playoffs | | | | | | | | |
|---|---|---|---|---|---|---|---|---|---|---|---|---|---|---|---|---|---|---|---|---|---|---|---|---|---|
| Season | Club | League | GP | G | A | Pts | PIM | PP | SH | GW | S | % | +/- | TF | F% | Min | GP | G | A | Pts | PIM | PP | SH | GW | Min |
| 2001-02 | Carolina | NHL | 81 | 23 | 32 | 55 | 40 | 5 | 2 | 5 | 162 | 14.2 | 3 | 2058 | 59.2 | 22:07 | 23 | 4 | 8 | 12 | 16 | 2 | 1 | 1 | 24:52 |
| 2002-03 | Carolina | NHL | 48 | 14 | 23 | 37 | 37 | 7 | 1 | 0 | 110 | 12.7 | –9 | 1242 | 56.5 | 23:46 | .... | .... | .... | .... | .... | .... | .... | .... | .... |
| 2003-04 | Carolina | NHL | 78 | 12 | 26 | 38 | 28 | 1 | 0 | 1 | 141 | 8.5 | 0 | 1817 | 61.1 | 21:23 | .... | .... | .... | .... | .... | .... | .... | .... | .... |
| 2004-05 | Kloten Flyers | Swiss | 2 | 2 | 1 | 3 | 0 | .... | .... | .... | .... | .... | .... | .... | .... | .... | 5 | 2 | 4 | 6 | 6 | .... | .... | .... | .... |
| 2005-06♦ | Carolina | NHL | 78 | 31 | 39 | 70 | 68 | 19 | 2 | 5 | 198 | 15.7 | 8 | 2145 | 59.1 | 24:18 | 25 | 12 | 6 | 18 | 16 | 6 | 0 | 4 | 23:52 |
| 2006-07 | Carolina | NHL | 78 | 26 | 56 | 82 | 46 | 9 | 2 | 5 | 181 | 14.4 | 7 | 2047 | 59.3 | 23:19 | .... | .... | .... | .... | .... | .... | .... | .... | .... |
| 2007-08 | Carolina | NHL | 59 | 19 | 32 | 51 | 38 | 6 | 0 | 4 | 151 | 12.6 | 0 | 1460 | 58.3 | 22:27 | .... | .... | .... | .... | .... | .... | .... | .... | .... |
| 2008-09 | Carolina | NHL | 80 | 16 | 35 | 51 | 36 | 6 | 1 | 1 | 135 | 11.9 | –23 | 1488 | 61.0 | 18:58 | 18 | 1 | 3 | 4 | 8 | 0 | 0 | 0 | 15:23 |
| | **NHL Totals** | | **1404** | **443** | **722** | **1165** | **1064** | **147** | **28** | **65** | **3195** | **13.9** | | **16932** | **59.0** | **22:02** | **159** | **51** | **60** | **111** | **97** | **17** | **4** | **8** | **22:16** |

CCHA Rookie of the Year (1989) • NHL All-Rookie Team (1990) • Frank J. Selke Trophy (2006, 2007)

Played in NHL All-Star Game (1992)

Traded to **Philadelphia** by **St. Louis** with Dan Quinn for Ron Sutter and Murray Baron, September 22, 1991. Traded to **Carolina** by **Philadelphia** with Jean-Marc Pelletier and Philadelphia's 2nd round choice (later traded to Colorado – Colorado selected Agris Saviels) in 2000 Entry Draft for Keith Primeau and Carolina's 5th round choice (later traded to NY Islanders – NY Islanders selected Kristofer Ottosson) in 2000 Entry Draft, January 23, 2000. Signed as a free agent by **Kloten** (Swiss), February 16, 2005.

## BRINE, David

(BRIGHN, DAY-vihd) **FLA.**

Center. Shoots left. 6'1", 201 lbs. Born, Truro, N.S., January 6, 1985.

| | | | | | | | | | | | | | | | | | | | | | | | | | |
|---|---|---|---|---|---|---|---|---|---|---|---|---|---|---|---|---|---|---|---|---|---|---|---|---|---|
| 2002-03 | Truro Bearcats | MJrHL | 52 | 21 | 32 | 53 | 29 | .... | .... | .... | .... | .... | .... | .... | .... | .... | .... | .... | .... | .... | .... | .... | .... | .... | .... |
| 2003-04 | Halifax | QMJHL | 70 | 22 | 25 | 47 | 20 | .... | .... | .... | .... | .... | .... | .... | .... | .... | .... | .... | .... | .... | .... | .... | .... | .... | .... |
| 2004-05 | Halifax | QMJHL | 67 | 14 | 37 | 51 | 36 | .... | .... | .... | .... | .... | .... | .... | .... | .... | 13 | 6 | 7 | 13 | 8 | .... | .... | .... | .... |
| 2005-06 | Halifax | QMJHL | 70 | 34 | 66 | 100 | 80 | .... | .... | .... | .... | .... | .... | .... | .... | .... | 11 | 1 | 5 | 6 | 23 | .... | .... | .... | .... |
| | Manitoba Moose | AHL | .... | .... | .... | .... | .... | .... | .... | .... | .... | .... | .... | .... | .... | .... | 9 | 0 | 1 | 1 | 2 | .... | .... | .... | .... |
| 2006-07 | Rochester | AHL | 22 | 4 | 4 | 8 | 4 | .... | .... | .... | .... | .... | .... | .... | .... | .... | .... | .... | .... | .... | .... | .... | .... | .... | .... |
| | Florida Everblades | ECHL | 52 | 9 | 21 | 30 | 22 | .... | .... | .... | .... | .... | .... | .... | .... | .... | 15 | 6 | 4 | 10 | 22 | .... | .... | .... | .... |
| **2007-08** | **Florida** | **NHL** | **9** | **0** | **1** | **1** | **4** | **0** | **0** | **0** | **3** | **0.0** | **–1** | **44** | **38.6** | **6:02** | .... | .... | .... | .... | .... | .... | .... | .... | .... |
| | Rochester | AHL | 66 | 9 | 11 | 20 | 26 | .... | .... | .... | .... | .... | .... | .... | .... | .... | .... | .... | .... | .... | .... | .... | .... | .... | .... |
| 2008-09 | Rochester | AHL | 79 | 8 | 23 | 31 | 35 | .... | .... | .... | .... | .... | .... | .... | .... | .... | .... | .... | .... | .... | .... | .... | .... | .... | .... |
| | **NHL Totals** | | **9** | **0** | **1** | **1** | **4** | **0** | **0** | **0** | **3** | **0.0** | | **44** | **38.6** | **6:02** | .... | .... | .... | .... | .... | .... | .... | .... | .... |

Signed as a free agent by **Florida**, September 14, 2006.

## BRISEBOIS, Patrice

(BREES-bwah, pa-TREEZ)

Defense. Shoots right. 6'2", 197 lbs. Born, Montreal, Que., January 27, 1971. Montreal's 2nd choice, 30th overall, in 1989 Entry Draft.

| | | | | | | | | | | | | | | | | | | | | | | | | | |
|---|---|---|---|---|---|---|---|---|---|---|---|---|---|---|---|---|---|---|---|---|---|---|---|---|---|
| 1986-87 | Mtl-Bourassa | QAAA | 39 | 15 | 19 | 34 | 66 | .... | .... | .... | .... | .... | .... | .... | .... | .... | .... | .... | .... | .... | .... | .... | .... | .... | .... |
| 1987-88 | Laval Titan | QMJHL | 48 | 10 | 34 | 44 | 95 | .... | .... | .... | .... | .... | .... | .... | .... | .... | 6 | 0 | 2 | 2 | 2 | .... | .... | .... | .... |
| 1988-89 | Laval Titan | QMJHL | 50 | 20 | 45 | 65 | 95 | .... | .... | .... | .... | .... | .... | .... | .... | .... | 17 | 8 | 14 | 22 | 45 | .... | .... | .... | .... |
| 1989-90 | Laval Titan | QMJHL | 56 | 18 | 70 | 88 | 108 | .... | .... | .... | .... | .... | .... | .... | .... | .... | 13 | 7 | 9 | 16 | 26 | .... | .... | .... | .... |
| **1990-91** | Drummondville | QMJHL | 54 | 17 | 44 | 61 | 72 | .... | .... | .... | .... | .... | .... | .... | .... | .... | 14 | 6 | 18 | 24 | 49 | .... | .... | .... | .... |
| | **Montreal** | **NHL** | **10** | **0** | **2** | **2** | **4** | **0** | **0** | **0** | **11** | **0.0** | **1** | .... | .... | .... | .... | .... | .... | .... | .... | .... | .... | .... | .... |
| **1991-92** | **Montreal** | **NHL** | **26** | **2** | **8** | **10** | **20** | **0** | **0** | **1** | **37** | **5.4** | **9** | .... | .... | .... | **11** | **2** | **4** | **6** | **6** | **1** | **0** | **1** | .... |
| | Fredericton | AHL | 53 | 12 | 27 | 39 | 51 | .... | .... | .... | .... | .... | .... | .... | .... | .... | .... | .... | .... | .... | .... | .... | .... | .... | .... |
| **1992-93♦** | **Montreal** | **NHL** | **70** | **10** | **21** | **31** | **79** | **4** | **0** | **2** | **123** | **8.1** | **6** | .... | .... | .... | **20** | **0** | **4** | **4** | **18** | **0** | **0** | **0** | .... |
| **1993-94** | **Montreal** | **NHL** | **53** | **2** | **21** | **23** | **63** | **1** | **0** | **0** | **71** | **2.8** | **5** | .... | .... | .... | **7** | **0** | **4** | **4** | **6** | **0** | **0** | **0** | .... |
| **1994-95** | **Montreal** | **NHL** | **35** | **4** | **8** | **12** | **26** | **0** | **0** | **2** | **67** | **6.0** | **–2** | .... | .... | .... | .... | .... | .... | .... | .... | .... | .... | .... | .... |
| **1995-96** | **Montreal** | **NHL** | **69** | **9** | **27** | **36** | **65** | **3** | **0** | **1** | **127** | **7.1** | **10** | .... | .... | .... | **6** | **1** | **2** | **3** | **6** | **0** | **0** | **0** | .... |
| **1996-97** | **Montreal** | **NHL** | **49** | **2** | **13** | **15** | **24** | **0** | **0** | **1** | **72** | **2.8** | **–7** | .... | .... | .... | **3** | **1** | **1** | **2** | **24** | **0** | **0** | **1** | .... |
| **1997-98** | **Montreal** | **NHL** | **79** | **10** | **27** | **37** | **67** | **5** | **0** | **1** | **125** | **8.0** | **16** | .... | .... | .... | **10** | **1** | **0** | **1** | **0** | **0** | **0** | **0** | .... |
| **1998-99** | **Montreal** | **NHL** | **54** | **3** | **9** | **12** | **28** | **1** | **0** | **1** | **90** | **3.3** | **–8** | **0** | **0.0** | **22:26** | .... | .... | .... | .... | .... | .... | .... | .... | .... |
| **99-2000** | **Montreal** | **NHL** | **54** | **10** | **25** | **35** | **18** | **5** | **0** | **2** | **88** | **11.4** | **–1** | **0** | **0.0** | **23:14** | .... | .... | .... | .... | .... | .... | .... | .... | .... |
| **2000-01** | **Montreal** | **NHL** | **77** | **15** | **21** | **36** | **28** | **11** | **0** | **4** | **178** | **8.4** | **–31** | **1** | **100.0** | **24:43** | .... | .... | .... | .... | .... | .... | .... | .... | .... |
| **2001-02** | **Montreal** | **NHL** | **71** | **4** | **29** | **33** | **25** | **2** | **1** | **1** | **95** | **4.2** | **9** | **0** | **0.0** | **23:53** | **10** | **1** | **1** | **2** | **2** | **0** | **0** | **0** | **22:05** |
| **2002-03** | **Montreal** | **NHL** | **73** | **4** | **25** | **29** | **32** | **1** | **0** | **1** | **105** | **3.8** | **–14** | **0** | **0.0** | **23:23** | .... | .... | .... | .... | .... | .... | .... | .... | .... |
| **2003-04** | **Montreal** | **NHL** | **71** | **4** | **27** | **31** | **22** | **2** | **0** | **0** | **96** | **4.2** | **17** | **0** | **0.0** | **21:20** | **11** | **2** | **1** | **3** | **4** | **1** | **0** | **0** | **22:30** |
| 2004-05 | Kloten Flyers | Swiss | 10 | 3 | 1 | 4 | 2 | .... | .... | .... | .... | .... | .... | .... | .... | .... | .... | .... | .... | .... | .... | .... | .... | .... | .... |
| **2005-06** | **Colorado** | **NHL** | **80** | **10** | **28** | **38** | **55** | **4** | **0** | **2** | **107** | **9.3** | **1** | **2** | **0.0** | **22:19** | **9** | **0** | **1** | **1** | **4** | **0** | **0** | **0** | **22:19** |
| **2006-07** | **Colorado** | **NHL** | **33** | **1** | **10** | **11** | **22** | **1** | **0** | **0** | **36** | **2.8** | **–5** | **0** | **0.0** | **19:23** | .... | .... | .... | .... | .... | .... | .... | .... | .... |
| **2007-08** | **Montreal** | **NHL** | **43** | **3** | **8** | **11** | **26** | **2** | **0** | **0** | **42** | **7.1** | **–2** | **0** | **0.0** | **16:50** | **10** | **1** | **5** | **6** | **6** | **1** | **0** | **1** | **16:33** |
| **2008-09** | **Montreal** | **NHL** | **62** | **5** | **13** | **18** | **19** | **4** | **0** | **1** | **68** | **7.4** | **–3** | **0** | **0.0** | **15:54** | **1** | **0** | **0** | **0** | **0** | **0** | **0** | **0** | **16:07** |
| | **NHL Totals** | | **1009** | **98** | **322** | **420** | **623** | **46** | **1** | **20** | **1538** | **6.4** | | **3** | **33.3** | **21:43** | **98** | **9** | **23** | **32** | **76** | **3** | **0** | **3** | **20:45** |

QMJHL Second All-Star Team (1990) • QMJHL First All-Star Team (1991) • Canadian Major Junior Defenseman of the Year (1991) • Memorial Cup Tournament All-Star Team (1991)

Signed as a free agent by **Kloten** (Swiss), October 13, 2004. Signed as a free agent by **Colorado**, August 3, 2005. • Missed remainder of 2006-07 season recovering from back injury suffered in game vs. Dallas, December 27, 2006. Signed as a free agent by **Montreal**, August 3, 2007.

## BRODZIAK, Kyle

(brohd-ZEE-ak, KIGHL) **MIN.**

Center. Shoots right. 6'2", 209 lbs. Born, St. Paul, Alta., May 25, 1984. Edmonton's 9th choice, 214th overall, in 2003 Entry Draft.

| | | | | | | | | | | | | | | | | | | | | | | | | | |
|---|---|---|---|---|---|---|---|---|---|---|---|---|---|---|---|---|---|---|---|---|---|---|---|---|---|
| 99-2000 | Ft. Saskatchewan | AMBHL | 36 | 23 | 33 | 56 | 57 | .... | .... | .... | .... | .... | .... | .... | .... | .... | .... | .... | .... | .... | .... | .... | .... | .... | .... |
| | Moose Jaw | WHL | 2 | 0 | 0 | 0 | 0 | .... | .... | .... | .... | .... | .... | .... | .... | .... | .... | .... | .... | .... | .... | .... | .... | .... | .... |
| 2000-01 | Moose Jaw | WHL | 57 | 2 | 8 | 10 | 49 | .... | .... | .... | .... | .... | .... | .... | .... | .... | 3 | 0 | 0 | 0 | 0 | .... | .... | .... | .... |
| 2001-02 | Moose Jaw | WHL | 72 | 8 | 12 | 20 | 56 | .... | .... | .... | .... | .... | .... | .... | .... | .... | 12 | 0 | 3 | 3 | 11 | .... | .... | .... | .... |
| 2002-03 | Moose Jaw | WHL | 72 | 32 | 30 | 62 | 84 | .... | .... | .... | .... | .... | .... | .... | .... | .... | 13 | 5 | 3 | 8 | 16 | .... | .... | .... | .... |
| 2003-04 | Moose Jaw | WHL | 70 | 39 | 54 | 93 | 58 | .... | .... | .... | .... | .... | .... | .... | .... | .... | 10 | 5 | 4 | 9 | 10 | .... | .... | .... | .... |
| 2004-05 | Edmonton | AHL | 56 | 6 | 26 | 32 | 49 | .... | .... | .... | .... | .... | .... | .... | .... | .... | .... | .... | .... | .... | .... | .... | .... | .... | .... |
| **2005-06** | **Edmonton** | **NHL** | **10** | **0** | **0** | **0** | **4** | **0** | **0** | **0** | **7** | **0.0** | **–4** | **75** | **52.0** | **11:02** | .... | .... | .... | .... | .... | .... | .... | .... | .... |
| | Iowa Stars | AHL | 55 | 12 | 19 | 31 | 41 | .... | .... | .... | .... | .... | .... | .... | .... | .... | 7 | 1 | 3 | 4 | 2 | .... | .... | .... | .... |
| **2006-07** | **Edmonton** | **NHL** | **6** | **1** | **0** | **1** | **2** | **0** | **0** | **0** | **11** | **9.1** | **0** | **48** | **52.1** | **17:08** | .... | .... | .... | .... | .... | .... | .... | .... | .... |
| | Wilkes-Barre | AHL | 62 | 24 | 32 | 56 | 44 | .... | .... | .... | .... | .... | .... | .... | .... | .... | 11 | 1 | 5 | 6 | 14 | .... | .... | .... | .... |
| **2007-08** | **Edmonton** | **NHL** | **80** | **14** | **17** | **31** | **33** | **0** | **1** | **3** | **125** | **11.2** | **–6** | **297** | **51.5** | **12:55** | .... | .... | .... | .... | .... | .... | .... | .... | .... |
| **2008-09** | **Edmonton** | **NHL** | **79** | **11** | **16** | **27** | **21** | **1** | **1** | **3** | **99** | **11.1** | **4** | **947** | **51.6** | **12:43** | .... | .... | .... | .... | .... | .... | .... | .... | .... |
| | **NHL Totals** | | **175** | **26** | **33** | **59** | **60** | **1** | **2** | **6** | **242** | **10.7** | | **1367** | **51.6** | **12:52** | .... | .... | .... | .... | .... | .... | .... | .... | .... |

WHL East First All-Star Team (2004) • Canadian Major Junior Second All-Star Team (2004)

Traded to **Minnesota** by **Edmonton** with Edmonton's 6th round choice (Darcy Kuemper) in 2009 Entry Draft for Dallas's 4th round choice (previously acquired, Edmonton selected Kyle Bigos) in 2009 Entry Draft and Minnesota's 5th round choice (Olivier Roy) in 2009 Entry Draft, June 27, 2009.

## BROOKBANK, Sheldon

(BRUK-bank, SHEHL-duhn) **ANA.**

Defense. Shoots right. 6'2", 205 lbs. Born, Lanigan, Sask., October 3, 1980.

| | | | | | | | | | | | | | | | | | | | | | | | | | |
|---|---|---|---|---|---|---|---|---|---|---|---|---|---|---|---|---|---|---|---|---|---|---|---|---|---|
| 2000-01 | Humboldt | SJHL | 59 | 14 | 35 | 49 | 281 | .... | .... | .... | .... | .... | .... | .... | .... | .... | .... | .... | .... | .... | .... | .... | .... | .... | .... |
| 2001-02 | Grand Rapids | AHL | 6 | 0 | 1 | 1 | 24 | .... | .... | .... | .... | .... | .... | .... | .... | .... | .... | .... | .... | .... | .... | .... | .... | .... | .... |
| | Mississippi | ECHL | 62 | 8 | 21 | 29 | 137 | .... | .... | .... | .... | .... | .... | .... | .... | .... | 10 | 1 | 4 | 5 | 27 | .... | .... | .... | .... |
| 2002-03 | Grand Rapids | AHL | 69 | 2 | 11 | 13 | 136 | .... | .... | .... | .... | .... | .... | .... | .... | .... | 15 | 1 | 3 | 4 | 28 | .... | .... | .... | .... |
| 2003-04 | Cincinnati | AHL | 74 | 2 | 9 | 11 | 216 | .... | .... | .... | .... | .... | .... | .... | .... | .... | 9 | 0 | 2 | 2 | 20 | .... | .... | .... | .... |
| 2004-05 | Cincinnati | AHL | 60 | 1 | 11 | 12 | 181 | .... | .... | .... | .... | .... | .... | .... | .... | .... | 11 | 0 | 0 | 0 | 40 | .... | .... | .... | .... |
| 2005-06 | Milwaukee | AHL | 73 | 9 | 26 | 35 | 232 | .... | .... | .... | .... | .... | .... | .... | .... | .... | 21 | 1 | 8 | 9 | 49 | .... | .... | .... | .... |
| **2006-07** | **Nashville** | **NHL** | **3** | **0** | **1** | **1** | **12** | **0** | **0** | **0** | **3** | **0.0** | **0** | **0** | **0.0** | **8:16** | .... | .... | .... | .... | .... | .... | .... | .... | .... |
| | Milwaukee | AHL | 78 | 15 | 38 | 53 | 176 | .... | .... | .... | .... | .... | .... | .... | .... | .... | 4 | 0 | 0 | 0 | 6 | .... | .... | .... | .... |
| **2007-08** | **New Jersey** | **NHL** | **44** | **0** | **8** | **8** | **63** | **0** | **0** | **0** | **43** | **0.0** | **0** | **0** | **0.0** | **15:08** | .... | .... | .... | .... | .... | .... | .... | .... | .... |
| | Lowell Devils | AHL | 1 | 0 | 0 | 0 | 5 | .... | .... | .... | .... | .... | .... | .... | .... | .... | .... | .... | .... | .... | .... | .... | .... | .... | .... |
| **2008-09** | **New Jersey** | **NHL** | **15** | **0** | **0** | **0** | **25** | **0** | **0** | **0** | **6** | **0.0** | **1** | **0** | **0.0** | **8:51** | .... | .... | .... | .... | .... | .... | .... | .... | .... |
| | **Anaheim** | **NHL** | **29** | **1** | **3** | **4** | **51** | **0** | **0** | **0** | **24** | **4.2** | **3** | **0** | **0.0** | **13:50** | **13** | **0** | **0** | **0** | **18** | **0** | **0** | **0** | **11:13** |
| | **NHL Totals** | | **91** | **1** | **12** | **13** | **151** | **0** | **0** | **0** | **76** | **1.3** | | **0** | **0.0** | **13:27** | **13** | **0** | **0** | **0** | **18** | **0** | **0** | **0** | **11:13** |

AHL First All-Star Team (2007) • Eddie Shore Award (AHL - Outstanding Defenseman) (2007)

Signed as a free agent by **Anaheim**, July 21, 2003. Signed as a free agent by **Nashville**, August 4, 2005. Signed as a free agent by **Columbus**, July 1, 2007. Claimed on waivers by **New Jersey** from **Columbus**, October 2, 2007. Traded to **Anaheim** by **New Jersey** for David McIntyre, February 3, 2009.

## BROOKBANK, Wade (BRUK-bank, WAYD) PIT.

Left wing. Shoots left. 6'4", 225 lbs. Born, Lanigan, Sask., September 29, 1977.

| | | | Regular Season | | | | | | | | | | | | | | Playoffs | | | | | | | | |
|---|---|---|---|---|---|---|---|---|---|---|---|---|---|---|---|---|---|---|---|---|---|---|---|---|---|
| Season | Club | League | GP | G | A | Pts | PIM | PP | SH | GW | S | % | +/- | TF | F% | Min | GP | G | A | Pts | PIM | PP | SH | GW | Min |
| 1997-98 | Melville | SJHL | 58 | 8 | 21 | 29 | 330 | .... | .... | .... | .... | .... | .... | .... | .... | .... | .... | .... | .... | .... | .... | .... | .... | .... | .... |
| | Anchorage Aces | WCHL | 7 | 0 | 0 | 0 | 46 | .... | .... | .... | .... | .... | .... | .... | .... | .... | 4 | 0 | 0 | 0 | 20 | .... | .... | .... | .... |
| 1998-99 | Anchorage Aces | WCHL | 56 | 0 | 4 | 4 | 337 | .... | .... | .... | .... | .... | .... | .... | .... | .... | .... | .... | .... | .... | .... | .... | .... | .... | .... |
| 99-2000 | Oklahoma City | CHL | 68 | 3 | 9 | 12 | 354 | .... | .... | .... | .... | .... | .... | .... | .... | .... | 7 | 1 | 1 | 2 | 29 | .... | .... | .... | .... |
| 2000-01 | Orlando | IHL | 29 | 0 | 1 | 1 | 122 | .... | .... | .... | .... | .... | .... | .... | .... | .... | 4 | 0 | 0 | 0 | 6 | .... | .... | .... | .... |
| | Oklahoma City | CHL | 46 | 1 | 13 | 14 | 267 | .... | .... | .... | .... | .... | .... | .... | .... | .... | 5 | 0 | 0 | 0 | 24 | .... | .... | .... | .... |
| 2001-02 | Grand Rapids | AHL | 73 | 1 | 6 | 7 | 337 | .... | .... | .... | .... | .... | .... | .... | .... | .... | 3 | 0 | 1 | 1 | 14 | .... | .... | .... | .... |
| 2002-03 | Binghamton | AHL | 8 | 0 | 0 | 0 | 28 | .... | .... | .... | .... | .... | .... | .... | .... | .... | .... | .... | .... | .... | .... | .... | .... | .... | .... |
| **2003-04** | **Nashville** | **NHL** | **9** | **0** | **0** | **0** | **38** | **0** | **0** | **0** | **1** | **0.0** | **–4** | **0** | **0.0** | **3:28** | .... | .... | .... | .... | .... | .... | .... | .... | .... |
| | Milwaukee | AHL | 6 | 0 | 0 | 0 | 6 | .... | .... | .... | .... | .... | .... | .... | .... | .... | .... | .... | .... | .... | .... | .... | .... | .... | .... |
| | Binghamton | AHL | 4 | 0 | 0 | 0 | 31 | .... | .... | .... | .... | .... | .... | .... | .... | .... | .... | .... | .... | .... | .... | .... | .... | .... | .... |
| | **Vancouver** | **NHL** | **20** | **2** | **0** | **2** | **95** | **0** | **0** | **1** | **6** | **33.3** | **3** | **0** | **0.0** | **3:50** | .... | .... | .... | .... | .... | .... | .... | .... | .... |
| | Manitoba Moose | AHL | 4 | 0 | 0 | 0 | 12 | .... | .... | .... | .... | .... | .... | .... | .... | .... | .... | .... | .... | .... | .... | .... | .... | .... | .... |
| 2004-05 | Manitoba Moose | AHL | 68 | 0 | 10 | 10 | 285 | .... | .... | .... | .... | .... | .... | .... | .... | .... | 9 | 0 | 0 | 0 | 10 | .... | .... | .... | .... |
| **2005-06** | **Vancouver** | **NHL** | **32** | **1** | **2** | **3** | **81** | **0** | **0** | **0** | **10** | **10.0** | **3** | **0** | **0.0** | **4:56** | .... | .... | .... | .... | .... | .... | .... | .... | .... |
| **2006-07** | **Boston** | **NHL** | **7** | **1** | **0** | **1** | **15** | **0** | **0** | **0** | **1** | **100.0** | **–1** | **1** | **0.0** | **4:25** | .... | .... | .... | .... | .... | .... | .... | .... | .... |
| | Providence Bruins | AHL | 4 | 0 | 0 | 0 | 15 | .... | .... | .... | .... | .... | .... | .... | .... | .... | .... | .... | .... | .... | .... | .... | .... | .... | .... |
| | Wilkes-Barre | AHL | 39 | 1 | 0 | 1 | 116 | .... | .... | .... | .... | .... | .... | .... | .... | .... | 5 | 0 | 0 | 0 | 6 | .... | .... | .... | .... |
| **2007-08** | **Carolina** | **NHL** | **32** | **1** | **1** | **2** | **76** | **0** | **0** | **0** | **12** | **8.3** | **4** | **4** | **25.0** | **3:48** | .... | .... | .... | .... | .... | .... | .... | .... | .... |
| | Albany River Rats | AHL | 25 | 0 | 2 | 2 | 28 | .... | .... | .... | .... | .... | .... | .... | .... | .... | .... | .... | .... | .... | .... | .... | .... | .... | .... |
| **2008-09** | **Carolina** | **NHL** | **27** | **1** | **0** | **1** | **40** | **0** | **0** | **0** | **8** | **12.5** | **0** | **0** | **0.0** | **2:30** | .... | .... | .... | .... | .... | .... | .... | .... | .... |
| | Norfolk Admirals | AHL | 24 | 0 | 1 | 1 | 46 | .... | .... | .... | .... | .... | .... | .... | .... | .... | .... | .... | .... | .... | .... | .... | .... | .... | .... |
| | **NHL Totals** | | **127** | **6** | **3** | **9** | **345** | **0** | **0** | **1** | **38** | **15.8** | | **5** | **20.0** | **3:50** | .... | .... | .... | .... | .... | .... | .... | .... | .... |

Signed as a free agent by **Orlando** (IHL), September 1, 2000. Signed as a free agent by **Ottawa**, July 27, 2001. • Missed majority of 2002-03 season recovering from knee injury suffered in game vs. Wilkes-Barre (AHL), November 2, 2002. Claimed by **Nashville** from **Ottawa** in Waiver Draft, October 3, 2003. Traded to **Vancouver** by **Nashville** for future considerations, December 17, 2003. Claimed on waivers by **Ottawa** from **Vancouver**, December 19, 2003. Traded to **Florida** by **Ottawa** for future considerations, December 29, 2003. Claimed on waivers by **Vancouver** from **Florida**, January 3, 2004. • Missed majority of 2005-06 season recovering from two head injuries suffered during the season and serving as a healthy reserve. Signed as a free agent by **Boston**, July 21, 2006. Traded to **Pittsburgh** by **Boston** for future considerations, December 19, 2006. Signed as a free agent by **Carolina**, July 1, 2007. Traded to **Tampa Bay** by **Carolina** with Josef Melichar and future considerations for Jussi Jokinen, February 7, 2009. Signed as a free agent by **Pittsburgh**, July 31, 2009.

## BROOKS, Alex (BROOKS, AL-ehx)

Defense. Shoots right. 6'1", 195 lbs. Born, Madison, WI, August 21, 1976.

| Season | Club | League | GP | G | A | Pts | PIM | PP | SH | GW | S | % | +/- | TF | F% | Min | GP | G | A | Pts | PIM | PP | SH | GW | Min |
|---|---|---|---|---|---|---|---|---|---|---|---|---|---|---|---|---|---|---|---|---|---|---|---|---|---|
| 1993-94 | Madison Capitols | USHL | 13 | 3 | 11 | 14 | .... | .... | .... | .... | .... | .... | .... | .... | .... | .... | .... | .... | .... | .... | .... | .... | .... | .... | .... |
| 1994-95 | Madison West | High-WI | 24 | 13 | 28 | 41 | .... | .... | .... | .... | .... | .... | .... | .... | .... | .... | .... | .... | .... | .... | .... | .... | .... | .... | .... |
| 1995-96 | Green Bay | USHL | 46 | 3 | 22 | 25 | .... | .... | .... | .... | .... | .... | .... | .... | .... | .... | .... | .... | .... | .... | .... | .... | .... | .... | .... |
| 1996-97 | U. of Wisconsin | WCHA | DID NOT PLAY – INJURED | | | | | | | | | | | | | | | | | | | | | | |
| 1997-98 | U. of Wisconsin | WCHA | 40 | 1 | 4 | 5 | 72 | .... | .... | .... | .... | .... | .... | .... | .... | .... | .... | .... | .... | .... | .... | .... | .... | .... | .... |
| 1998-99 | U. of Wisconsin | WCHA | 37 | 0 | 3 | 3 | 73 | .... | .... | .... | .... | .... | .... | .... | .... | .... | .... | .... | .... | .... | .... | .... | .... | .... | .... |
| 99-2000 | U. of Wisconsin | WCHA | 41 | 4 | 10 | 14 | 78 | .... | .... | .... | .... | .... | .... | .... | .... | .... | .... | .... | .... | .... | .... | .... | .... | .... | .... |
| 2000-01 | U. of Wisconsin | WCHA | 41 | 3 | 16 | 19 | 76 | .... | .... | .... | .... | .... | .... | .... | .... | .... | .... | .... | .... | .... | .... | .... | .... | .... | .... |
| 2001-02 | Jokerit Helsinki | Finland | 53 | 1 | 3 | 4 | 109 | .... | .... | .... | .... | .... | .... | .... | .... | .... | 12 | 0 | 0 | 0 | 11 | .... | .... | .... | .... |
| 2002-03 | Albany River Rats | AHL | 66 | 0 | 7 | 7 | 56 | .... | .... | .... | .... | .... | .... | .... | .... | .... | .... | .... | .... | .... | .... | .... | .... | .... | .... |
| 2003-04 | Albany River Rats | AHL | 77 | 2 | 6 | 8 | 100 | .... | .... | .... | .... | .... | .... | .... | .... | .... | .... | .... | .... | .... | .... | .... | .... | .... | .... |
| 2004-05 | Albany River Rats | AHL | 63 | 0 | 6 | 6 | 83 | .... | .... | .... | .... | .... | .... | .... | .... | .... | .... | .... | .... | .... | .... | .... | .... | .... | .... |
| 2005-06 | Albany River Rats | AHL | 58 | 1 | 4 | 5 | 81 | .... | .... | .... | .... | .... | .... | .... | .... | .... | .... | .... | .... | .... | .... | .... | .... | .... | .... |
| **2006-07** | **New Jersey** | **NHL** | **19** | **0** | **1** | **1** | **4** | **0** | **0** | **0** | **4** | **0.0** | **–1** | **0** | **0.0** | **8:39** | .... | .... | .... | .... | .... | .... | .... | .... | .... |
| | Lowell Devils | AHL | 21 | 0 | 2 | 2 | 6 | .... | .... | .... | .... | .... | .... | .... | .... | .... | .... | .... | .... | .... | .... | .... | .... | .... | .... |
| 2007-08 | Peoria Rivermen | AHL | 70 | 0 | 8 | 8 | 90 | .... | .... | .... | .... | .... | .... | .... | .... | .... | .... | .... | .... | .... | .... | .... | .... | .... | .... |
| 2008-09 | Chicago Wolves | AHL | 50 | 0 | 10 | 10 | 58 | .... | .... | .... | .... | .... | .... | .... | .... | .... | .... | .... | .... | .... | .... | .... | .... | .... | .... |
| | **NHL Totals** | | **19** | **0** | **1** | **1** | **4** | **0** | **0** | **0** | **4** | **0.0** | | **0** | **0.0** | **8:39** | .... | .... | .... | .... | .... | .... | .... | .... | .... |

• Missed entire 1996-97 season recovering from back injury suffered during off-season training, August, 1996. Signed as a free agent by **New Jersey**, July 12, 2002. Signed as a free agent by **St. Louis**, August 9, 2007.

## BROUWER, Troy (BROW-uhr, TROI) CHI.

Right wing. Shoots right. 6'2", 213 lbs. Born, Vancouver, B.C., August 17, 1985. Chicago's 13th choice, 214th overall, in 2004 Entry Draft.

| Season | Club | League | GP | G | A | Pts | PIM | PP | SH | GW | S | % | +/- | TF | F% | Min | GP | G | A | Pts | PIM | PP | SH | GW | Min |
|---|---|---|---|---|---|---|---|---|---|---|---|---|---|---|---|---|---|---|---|---|---|---|---|---|---|
| 2001-02 | Moose Jaw | WHL | 13 | 0 | 0 | 0 | 7 | .... | .... | .... | .... | .... | .... | .... | .... | .... | .... | .... | .... | .... | .... | .... | .... | .... | .... |
| 2002-03 | Moose Jaw | WHL | 59 | 9 | 12 | 21 | 54 | .... | .... | .... | .... | .... | .... | .... | .... | .... | 13 | 1 | 2 | 3 | 14 | .... | .... | .... | .... |
| 2003-04 | Moose Jaw | WHL | 72 | 23 | 26 | 49 | 111 | .... | .... | .... | .... | .... | .... | .... | .... | .... | 10 | 3 | 0 | 3 | 12 | .... | .... | .... | .... |
| 2004-05 | Moose Jaw | WHL | 71 | 22 | 25 | 47 | 132 | .... | .... | .... | .... | .... | .... | .... | .... | .... | 5 | 1 | 2 | 3 | 8 | .... | .... | .... | .... |
| 2005-06 | Moose Jaw | WHL | 72 | 49 | 53 | *102 | 122 | .... | .... | .... | .... | .... | .... | .... | .... | .... | 17 | 10 | 4 | 14 | 34 | .... | .... | .... | .... |
| **2006-07** | **Chicago** | **NHL** | **10** | **0** | **0** | **0** | **7** | **0** | **0** | **0** | **7** | **0.0** | **–7** | **0** | **0.0** | **9:55** | .... | .... | .... | .... | .... | .... | .... | .... | .... |
| | Norfolk Admirals | AHL | 66 | 41 | 38 | 79 | 70 | .... | .... | .... | .... | .... | .... | .... | .... | .... | 6 | 1 | 0 | 1 | 4 | .... | .... | .... | .... |
| **2007-08** | **Chicago** | **NHL** | **2** | **0** | **1** | **1** | **0** | **0** | **0** | **0** | **0** | **0.0** | **1** | **0** | **0.0** | **11:56** | .... | .... | .... | .... | .... | .... | .... | .... | .... |
| | Rockford IceHogs | AHL | 75 | 35 | 19 | 54 | 154 | .... | .... | .... | .... | .... | .... | .... | .... | .... | 12 | 5 | 4 | 9 | 16 | .... | .... | .... | .... |
| **2008-09** | **Chicago** | **NHL** | **69** | **10** | **16** | **26** | **50** | **4** | **1** | **0** | **126** | **7.9** | **7** | **20** | **45.0** | **15:05** | **17** | **0** | **2** | **2** | **12** | **0** | **0** | **0** | **11:51** |
| | Rockford IceHogs | AHL | 5 | 2 | 6 | 8 | 20 | .... | .... | .... | .... | .... | .... | .... | .... | .... | .... | .... | .... | .... | .... | .... | .... | .... | .... |
| | **NHL Totals** | | **81** | **10** | **17** | **27** | **57** | **4** | **1** | **0** | **133** | **7.5** | | **20** | **45.0** | **14:22** | **17** | **0** | **2** | **2** | **12** | **0** | **0** | **0** | **11:51** |

WHL East First All-Star Team (2006) • Canadian Major Junior Second All-Star Team (2006) • AHL All-Rookie Team (2007) • AHL Second All-Star Team (2007)

## BROWN, Curtis (BROWN, KUHR-tihs)

Center/Left wing. Shoots left. 6', 200 lbs. Born, Unity, Sask., February 12, 1976. Buffalo's 2nd choice, 43rd overall, in 1994 Entry Draft.

| Season | Club | League | GP | G | A | Pts | PIM | PP | SH | GW | S | % | +/- | TF | F% | Min | GP | G | A | Pts | PIM | PP | SH | GW | Min |
|---|---|---|---|---|---|---|---|---|---|---|---|---|---|---|---|---|---|---|---|---|---|---|---|---|---|
| 1990-91 | Unity Bantams | SBHL | 60 | 93 | 104 | 197 | 55 | .... | .... | .... | .... | .... | .... | .... | .... | .... | .... | .... | .... | .... | .... | .... | .... | .... | .... |
| 1991-92 | Moose Jaw | SMHL | 36 | 35 | 30 | 65 | 44 | .... | .... | .... | .... | .... | .... | .... | .... | .... | .... | .... | .... | .... | .... | .... | .... | .... | .... |
| 1992-93 | Moose Jaw | WHL | 71 | 13 | 16 | 29 | 30 | .... | .... | .... | .... | .... | .... | .... | .... | .... | .... | .... | .... | .... | .... | .... | .... | .... | .... |
| 1993-94 | Moose Jaw | WHL | 72 | 27 | 38 | 65 | 82 | .... | .... | .... | .... | .... | .... | .... | .... | .... | .... | .... | .... | .... | .... | .... | .... | .... | .... |
| **1994-95** | Moose Jaw | WHL | 70 | 51 | 53 | 104 | 63 | .... | .... | .... | .... | .... | .... | .... | .... | .... | 10 | 8 | 7 | 15 | 20 | .... | .... | .... | .... |
| | **Buffalo** | **NHL** | **1** | **1** | **1** | **2** | **2** | **0** | **0** | **0** | **4** | **25.0** | **2** | .... | .... | .... | .... | .... | .... | .... | .... | .... | .... | .... | .... |
| **1995-96** | Moose Jaw | WHL | 25 | 20 | 18 | 38 | 30 | .... | .... | .... | .... | .... | .... | .... | .... | .... | .... | .... | .... | .... | .... | .... | .... | .... | .... |
| | Prince Albert | WHL | 19 | 12 | 21 | 33 | 8 | .... | .... | .... | .... | .... | .... | .... | .... | .... | 18 | 10 | 15 | 25 | 18 | .... | .... | .... | .... |
| | **Buffalo** | **NHL** | **4** | **0** | **0** | **0** | **0** | **0** | **0** | **0** | **1** | **0.0** | **0** | .... | .... | .... | .... | .... | .... | .... | .... | .... | .... | .... | .... |
| | Rochester | AHL | .... | .... | .... | .... | .... | .... | .... | .... | .... | .... | .... | .... | .... | .... | 12 | 0 | 1 | 1 | 2 | .... | .... | .... | .... |
| **1996-97** | **Buffalo** | **NHL** | **28** | **4** | **3** | **7** | **18** | **0** | **0** | **1** | **31** | **12.9** | **4** | .... | .... | .... | .... | .... | .... | .... | .... | .... | .... | .... | .... |
| | Rochester | AHL | 51 | 22 | 21 | 43 | 30 | .... | .... | .... | .... | .... | .... | .... | .... | .... | 10 | 4 | 6 | 10 | 4 | .... | .... | .... | .... |
| **1997-98** | **Buffalo** | **NHL** | **63** | **12** | **12** | **24** | **34** | **1** | **1** | **2** | **91** | **13.2** | **11** | .... | .... | .... | **13** | **1** | **2** | **3** | **10** | **1** | **0** | **0** | .... |
| **1998-99** | **Buffalo** | **NHL** | **78** | **16** | **31** | **47** | **56** | **5** | **1** | **3** | **128** | **12.5** | **23** | **1198** | **45.0** | **17:30** | **21** | **7** | **6** | **13** | **10** | **3** | **0** | **3** | **18:51** |
| **99-2000** | **Buffalo** | **NHL** | **74** | **22** | **29** | **51** | **42** | **5** | **0** | **4** | **149** | **14.8** | **19** | **1318** | **48.6** | **18:11** | **5** | **1** | **3** | **4** | **6** | **1** | **0** | **0** | **17:11** |
| **2000-01** | **Buffalo** | **NHL** | **70** | **10** | **22** | **32** | **34** | **2** | **1** | **0** | **105** | **9.5** | **15** | **1159** | **50.4** | **16:34** | **13** | **5** | **0** | **5** | **8** | **0** | **2** | **1** | **18:14** |
| **2001-02** | **Buffalo** | **NHL** | **82** | **20** | **17** | **37** | **32** | **4** | **1** | **5** | **171** | **11.7** | **–4** | **1608** | **49.0** | **17:48** | .... | .... | .... | .... | .... | .... | .... | .... | .... |
| **2002-03** | **Buffalo** | **NHL** | **74** | **15** | **16** | **31** | **40** | **3** | **4** | **4** | **144** | **10.4** | **4** | **1387** | **49.5** | **16:53** | .... | .... | .... | .... | .... | .... | .... | .... | .... |
| **2003-04** | **Buffalo** | **NHL** | **68** | **9** | **12** | **21** | **30** | **2** | **1** | **2** | **117** | **7.7** | **2** | **1182** | **51.5** | **16:36** | .... | .... | .... | .... | .... | .... | .... | .... | .... |
| | **San Jose** | **NHL** | **12** | **2** | **2** | **4** | **6** | **0** | **0** | **0** | **21** | **9.5** | **1** | **105** | **47.6** | **16:26** | **17** | **0** | **2** | **2** | **18** | **0** | **0** | **0** | **14:37** |
| 2004-05 | San Diego Gulls | ECHL | 47 | 9 | 29 | 38 | 24 | .... | .... | .... | .... | .... | .... | .... | .... | .... | .... | .... | .... | .... | .... | .... | .... | .... | .... |
| **2005-06** | **Chicago** | **NHL** | **71** | **5** | **10** | **15** | **38** | **0** | **1** | **0** | **84** | **6.0** | **–9** | **881** | **50.6** | **13:39** | .... | .... | .... | .... | .... | .... | .... | .... | .... |
| **2006-07** | **San Jose** | **NHL** | **78** | **8** | **12** | **20** | **56** | **0** | **2** | **3** | **84** | **9.5** | **–2** | **881** | **51.4** | **13:10** | **11** | **0** | **2** | **2** | **2** | **0** | **0** | **0** | **12:10** |
| **2007-08** | **San Jose** | **NHL** | **33** | **5** | **4** | **9** | **10** | **0** | **0** | **0** | **38** | **13.2** | **4** | **179** | **59.2** | **10:49** | **7** | **0** | **0** | **0** | **4** | **0** | **0** | **0** | **9:11** |
| 2008-09 | Kloten Flyers | Swiss | 44 | 10 | 13 | 23 | 28 | .... | .... | .... | .... | .... | .... | .... | .... | .... | 15 | 4 | 4 | 8 | 20 | .... | .... | .... | .... |
| | **NHL Totals** | | **736** | **129** | **171** | **300** | **398** | **22** | **12** | **24** | **1168** | **11.0** | | **9898** | **49.5** | **16:02** | **87** | **14** | **15** | **29** | **58** | **5** | **2** | **4** | **15:45** |

WHL East First All-Star Team (1995) • WHL East Second All-Star Team (1996)

Traded to **San Jose** by **Buffalo** with Andy Delmore for Jeff Jillson and San Jose's compensatory 7th round choice (Andrew Orpik) in 2005 Entry Draft, March 9, 2004. Signed as a free agent by **Chicago**, July 2, 2004. Signed as a free agent by **San Diego** (ECHL), November 16, 2004. Signed as a free agent by **San Jose**, July 3, 2006. Signed as a free agent by **Kloten** (Swiss), July 17, 2008.

## BROWN, Dustin
(BROWN, DUHS-tihn) **L.A.**

Left wing. Shoots right. 6', 207 lbs. Born, Ithaca, NY, November 4, 1984. Los Angeles' 1st choice, 13th overall, in 2003 Entry Draft.

| Season | Club | League | GP | G | A | Pts | PIM | PP | SH | GW | S | % | +/- | TF | F% | Min | Playoffs GP | G | A | Pts | PIM | PP | SH | GW | Min |
|---|---|---|---|---|---|---|---|---|---|---|---|---|---|---|---|---|---|---|---|---|---|---|---|---|---|
| 1998-99 | Ithaca | High-NY | 18 | 4 | 13 | 17 | .... | .... | .... | .... | .... | .... | .... | .... | .... | .... | .... | .... | .... | .... | .... | .... | .... | .... | .... |
| 99-2000 | Ithaca | High-NY | 24 | 33 | 21 | 53 | .... | .... | .... | .... | .... | .... | .... | .... | .... | .... | .... | .... | .... | .... | .... | .... | .... | .... | .... |
| 2000-01 | Guelph Storm | OHL | 53 | 23 | 22 | 45 | 45 | .... | .... | .... | .... | .... | .... | .... | .... | .... | 4 | 0 | 0 | 0 | 10 | .... | .... | .... | .... |
| 2001-02 | Guelph Storm | OHL | 63 | 41 | 32 | 73 | 56 | .... | .... | .... | .... | .... | .... | .... | .... | .... | 9 | 8 | 5 | 13 | 14 | .... | .... | .... | .... |
| 2002-03 | Guelph Storm | OHL | 58 | 34 | 42 | 76 | 89 | .... | .... | .... | .... | .... | .... | .... | .... | .... | 11 | 7 | 8 | 15 | 6 | .... | .... | .... | .... |
| **2003-04** | **Los Angeles** | **NHL** | **31** | **1** | **4** | **5** | **16** | **0** | **0** | **0** | **40** | **2.5** | **0** | **1** | **0.0** | **10:29** | .... | .... | .... | .... | .... | .... | .... | .... | .... |
| 2004-05 | Manchester | AHL | 79 | 29 | 45 | 74 | 96 | .... | .... | .... | .... | .... | .... | .... | .... | .... | 6 | 5 | 2 | 7 | 10 | .... | .... | .... | .... |
| **2005-06** | **Los Angeles** | **NHL** | **79** | **14** | **14** | **28** | **80** | **6** | **0** | **2** | **159** | **8.8** | **–10** | **15** | **66.7** | **13:59** | .... | .... | .... | .... | .... | .... | .... | .... | .... |
| **2006-07** | **Los Angeles** | **NHL** | **81** | **17** | **29** | **46** | **54** | **13** | **0** | **1** | **195** | **8.7** | **–21** | **77** | **49.4** | **18:43** | .... | .... | .... | .... | .... | .... | .... | .... | .... |
| **2007-08** | **Los Angeles** | **NHL** | **78** | **33** | **27** | **60** | **55** | **12** | **2** | **4** | **219** | **15.1** | **–13** | **40** | **50.0** | **20:18** | .... | .... | .... | .... | .... | .... | .... | .... | .... |
| **2008-09** | **Los Angeles** | **NHL** | **80** | **24** | **29** | **53** | **64** | **7** | **0** | **6** | **292** | **8.2** | **–15** | **54** | **46.3** | **19:24** | .... | .... | .... | .... | .... | .... | .... | .... | .... |
| | **NHL Totals** | | **349** | **89** | **103** | **192** | **269** | **38** | **2** | **13** | **905** | **9.8** | | **187** | **49.7** | **17:25** | .... | .... | .... | .... | .... | .... | .... | .... | .... |

OHL All-Rookie Team (2001) • Canadian Major Junior Scholastic Player of the Year (2003)
Played in NHL All-Star Game (2009)
• Missed majority of 2003-04 season recovering from ankle injury suffered in game vs. Chicago, November 29, 2003.

## BROWN, Mike
(BROWN, MIGHK) **ANA.**

Right wing. Shoots right. 6', 210 lbs. Born, Northbrook, IL, June 24, 1985. Vancouver's 4th choice, 159th overall, in 2004 Entry Draft.

| Season | Club | League | GP | G | A | Pts | PIM | PP | SH | GW | S | % | +/- | TF | F% | Min | Playoffs GP | G | A | Pts | PIM | PP | SH | GW | Min |
|---|---|---|---|---|---|---|---|---|---|---|---|---|---|---|---|---|---|---|---|---|---|---|---|---|---|
| 2000-01 | Chicago Chill | USAHA | 66 | 27 | 23 | 50 | .... | .... | .... | .... | .... | .... | .... | .... | .... | .... | .... | .... | .... | .... | .... | .... | .... | .... | .... |
| 2001-02 | USNTDP | U-17 | 17 | 6 | 4 | 10 | 13 | .... | .... | .... | .... | .... | .... | .... | .... | .... | .... | .... | .... | .... | .... | .... | .... | .... | .... |
| | USNTDP | NAHL | 46 | 5 | 11 | 16 | 56 | .... | .... | .... | .... | .... | .... | .... | .... | .... | .... | .... | .... | .... | .... | .... | .... | .... | .... |
| 2002-03 | USNTDP | U-18 | 34 | 5 | 3 | 8 | 16 | .... | .... | .... | .... | .... | .... | .... | .... | .... | .... | .... | .... | .... | .... | .... | .... | .... | .... |
| | USNTDP | NAHL | 9 | 0 | 3 | 3 | 29 | .... | .... | .... | .... | .... | .... | .... | .... | .... | .... | .... | .... | .... | .... | .... | .... | .... | .... |
| 2003-04 | U. of Michigan | CCHA | 42 | 8 | 5 | 13 | 51 | .... | .... | .... | .... | .... | .... | .... | .... | .... | .... | .... | .... | .... | .... | .... | .... | .... | .... |
| 2004-05 | U. of Michigan | CCHA | 35 | 3 | 5 | 8 | 95 | .... | .... | .... | .... | .... | .... | .... | .... | .... | .... | .... | .... | .... | .... | .... | .... | .... | .... |
| 2005-06 | Manitoba Moose | AHL | 73 | 7 | 8 | 15 | 139 | .... | .... | .... | .... | .... | .... | .... | .... | .... | 13 | 1 | 2 | 3 | 17 | .... | .... | .... | .... |
| 2006-07 | Manitoba Moose | AHL | 62 | 3 | 0 | 3 | 194 | .... | .... | .... | .... | .... | .... | .... | .... | .... | 13 | 0 | 2 | 2 | 16 | .... | .... | .... | .... |
| **2007-08** | **Vancouver** | **NHL** | **19** | **1** | **0** | **1** | **55** | **0** | **0** | **0** | **9** | **11.1** | **–2** | **0** | **0.0** | **6:19** | .... | .... | .... | .... | .... | .... | .... | .... | .... |
| | Manitoba Moose | AHL | 54 | 10 | 3 | 13 | 201 | .... | .... | .... | .... | .... | .... | .... | .... | .... | 6 | 2 | 0 | 2 | 11 | .... | .... | .... | .... |
| **2008-09** | **Vancouver** | **NHL** | **20** | **0** | **1** | **1** | **85** | **0** | **0** | **0** | **6** | **0.0** | **–5** | **2** | **0.0** | **5:29** | .... | .... | .... | .... | .... | .... | .... | .... | .... |
| | **Anaheim** | **NHL** | **28** | **2** | **1** | **3** | **60** | **0** | **0** | **2** | **38** | **5.3** | **–2** | **4** | **0.0** | **10:02** | **13** | **0** | **2** | **2** | **25** | **0** | **0** | **0** | **8:28** |
| | **NHL Totals** | | **67** | **3** | **2** | **5** | **200** | **0** | **0** | **2** | **53** | **5.7** | | **6** | **0.0** | **7:37** | **13** | **0** | **2** | **2** | **25** | **0** | **0** | **0** | **8:28** |

Traded to **Anaheim** by **Vancouver** for Nathan McIver, February 4, 2009.

## BRULE, Gilbert
(broo-LAY, zhihl-BAIR) **EDM.**

Center. Shoots right. 5'10", 180 lbs. Born, Edmonton, Alta., January 1, 1987. Columbus' 1st choice, 6th overall, in 2005 Entry Draft.

| Season | Club | League | GP | G | A | Pts | PIM | PP | SH | GW | S | % | +/- | TF | F% | Min | Playoffs GP | G | A | Pts | PIM | PP | SH | GW | Min |
|---|---|---|---|---|---|---|---|---|---|---|---|---|---|---|---|---|---|---|---|---|---|---|---|---|---|
| 2002-03 | Quesnel | BCHL | 48 | 32 | 25 | 57 | 71 | .... | .... | .... | .... | .... | .... | .... | .... | .... | .... | .... | .... | .... | .... | .... | .... | .... | .... |
| | Vancouver Giants | WHL | 1 | 0 | 0 | 0 | 0 | .... | .... | .... | .... | .... | .... | .... | .... | .... | 4 | 1 | 0 | 1 | 0 | .... | .... | .... | .... |
| 2003-04 | Vancouver Giants | WHL | 67 | 25 | 35 | 60 | 100 | .... | .... | .... | .... | .... | .... | .... | .... | .... | 11 | 4 | 5 | 9 | 10 | .... | .... | .... | .... |
| 2004-05 | Vancouver Giants | WHL | 70 | 39 | 48 | 87 | 169 | .... | .... | .... | .... | .... | .... | .... | .... | .... | 6 | 1 | 3 | 4 | 8 | .... | .... | .... | .... |
| **2005-06** | **Columbus** | **NHL** | **7** | **2** | **2** | **4** | **0** | **0** | **0** | **0** | **11** | **18.2** | **–2** | **60** | **43.3** | **13:11** | .... | .... | .... | .... | .... | .... | .... | .... | .... |
| | Vancouver Giants | WHL | 27 | 23 | 15 | 38 | 40 | .... | .... | .... | .... | .... | .... | .... | .... | .... | 18 | *16 | 14 | *30 | 44 | .... | .... | .... | .... |
| **2006-07** | **Columbus** | **NHL** | **78** | **9** | **10** | **19** | **28** | **3** | **0** | **0** | **98** | **9.2** | **–21** | **268** | **45.9** | **10:39** | .... | .... | .... | .... | .... | .... | .... | .... | .... |
| **2007-08** | **Columbus** | **NHL** | **61** | **1** | **8** | **9** | **24** | **0** | **0** | **1** | **74** | **1.4** | **–4** | **78** | **51.3** | **9:54** | .... | .... | .... | .... | .... | .... | .... | .... | .... |
| | Syracuse Crunch | AHL | 16 | 5 | 5 | 10 | 44 | .... | .... | .... | .... | .... | .... | .... | .... | .... | 13 | 2 | 3 | 5 | 16 | .... | .... | .... | .... |
| **2008-09** | **Edmonton** | **NHL** | **11** | **2** | **1** | **3** | **12** | **0** | **0** | **1** | **13** | **15.4** | **–3** | **5** | **80.0** | **9:52** | .... | .... | .... | .... | .... | .... | .... | .... | .... |
| | Springfield | AHL | 39 | 13 | 11 | 24 | 58 | .... | .... | .... | .... | .... | .... | .... | .... | .... | .... | .... | .... | .... | .... | .... | .... | .... | .... |
| | **NHL Totals** | | **157** | **14** | **21** | **35** | **64** | **3** | **0** | **2** | **196** | **7.1** | | **411** | **47.0** | **10:25** | .... | .... | .... | .... | .... | .... | .... | .... | .... |

WHL West First All-Star Team (2005) • Canadian Major Junior Second All-Star Team (2005) • Canadian Major Junior Scholastic Player of the Year (2005) • WHL West Second All-Star Team (2006) • Memorial Cup Tournament All-Star Team (2006) • Ed Chynoweth Trophy (Memorial Cup Tournament - Leading Scorer) (2006)
• Missed majority of 2005-06 season recovering from sternum (October 7, 2005 vs. Calgary) and leg (November 30, 2005 at Minnesota) injuries. Traded to **Edmonton** by **Columbus** for Raffi Torres, July 1, 2008.

## BRUNETTE, Andrew
(broo-NEHT, AN-droo) **MIN.**

Left wing. Shoots left. 6'1", 210 lbs. Born, Sudbury, Ont., August 24, 1973. Washington's 6th choice, 174th overall, in 1993 Entry Draft.

| Season | Club | League | GP | G | A | Pts | PIM | PP | SH | GW | S | % | +/- | TF | F% | Min | Playoffs GP | G | A | Pts | PIM | PP | SH | GW | Min |
|---|---|---|---|---|---|---|---|---|---|---|---|---|---|---|---|---|---|---|---|---|---|---|---|---|---|
| 1989-90 | Rayside-Balfour | NOHA | 32 | 38 | *65 | *103 | .... | .... | .... | .... | .... | .... | .... | .... | .... | .... | .... | .... | .... | .... | .... | .... | .... | .... | .... |
| | Rayside-Balfour | NOJHA | 4 | 1 | 1 | 2 | 0 | .... | .... | .... | .... | .... | .... | .... | .... | .... | .... | .... | .... | .... | .... | .... | .... | .... | .... |
| 1990-91 | Owen Sound | OHL | 63 | 15 | 20 | 35 | 15 | .... | .... | .... | .... | .... | .... | .... | .... | .... | .... | .... | .... | .... | .... | .... | .... | .... | .... |
| 1991-92 | Owen Sound | OHL | 66 | 51 | 47 | 98 | 42 | .... | .... | .... | .... | .... | .... | .... | .... | .... | 5 | 5 | 0 | 5 | 8 | .... | .... | .... | .... |
| 1992-93 | Owen Sound | OHL | 66 | *62 | *100 | *162 | 91 | .... | .... | .... | .... | .... | .... | .... | .... | .... | 8 | 8 | 6 | 14 | 16 | .... | .... | .... | .... |
| 1993-94 | Portland Pirates | AHL | 23 | 9 | 11 | 20 | 10 | .... | .... | .... | .... | .... | .... | .... | .... | .... | 2 | 0 | 1 | 1 | 0 | .... | .... | .... | .... |
| | Providence Bruins | AHL | 3 | 0 | 0 | 0 | 0 | .... | .... | .... | .... | .... | .... | .... | .... | .... | .... | .... | .... | .... | .... | .... | .... | .... | .... |
| | Hampton Roads | ECHL | 20 | 12 | 18 | 30 | 32 | .... | .... | .... | .... | .... | .... | .... | .... | .... | 7 | 7 | 6 | 13 | 18 | .... | .... | .... | .... |
| 1994-95 | Portland Pirates | AHL | 79 | 30 | 50 | 80 | 53 | .... | .... | .... | .... | .... | .... | .... | .... | .... | 7 | 3 | 3 | 6 | 10 | .... | .... | .... | .... |
| **1995-96** | **Washington** | **NHL** | **11** | **3** | **3** | **6** | **0** | **0** | **0** | **1** | **16** | **18.8** | **5** | .... | .... | .... | **6** | **1** | **3** | **4** | **0** | **0** | **0** | **0** | .... |
| | Portland Pirates | AHL | 69 | 28 | 66 | 94 | 125 | .... | .... | .... | .... | .... | .... | .... | .... | .... | 20 | 11 | 18 | 29 | 15 | .... | .... | .... | .... |
| **1996-97** | **Washington** | **NHL** | **23** | **4** | **7** | **11** | **12** | **2** | **0** | **0** | **23** | **17.4** | **–3** | .... | .... | .... | .... | .... | .... | .... | .... | .... | .... | .... | .... |
| | Portland Pirates | AHL | 50 | 22 | 51 | 73 | 48 | .... | .... | .... | .... | .... | .... | .... | .... | .... | 5 | 1 | 2 | 3 | 0 | .... | .... | .... | .... |
| **1997-98** | **Washington** | **NHL** | **28** | **11** | **12** | **23** | **12** | **4** | **0** | **2** | **42** | **26.2** | **2** | .... | .... | .... | .... | .... | .... | .... | .... | .... | .... | .... | .... |
| | Portland Pirates | AHL | 43 | 21 | 46 | 67 | 64 | .... | .... | .... | .... | .... | .... | .... | .... | .... | 10 | 1 | 11 | 12 | 12 | .... | .... | .... | .... |
| **1998-99** | **Nashville** | **NHL** | **77** | **11** | **20** | **31** | **26** | **7** | **0** | **1** | **65** | **16.9** | **–10** | **8** | **50.0** | **13:13** | .... | .... | .... | .... | .... | .... | .... | .... | .... |
| **99-2000** | **Atlanta** | **NHL** | **81** | **23** | **27** | **50** | **30** | **9** | **0** | **2** | **107** | **21.5** | **–32** | **8** | **25.0** | **15:42** | .... | .... | .... | .... | .... | .... | .... | .... | .... |
| **2000-01** | **Atlanta** | **NHL** | **77** | **15** | **44** | **59** | **26** | **6** | **0** | **4** | **104** | **14.4** | **–5** | **11** | **54.6** | **16:58** | .... | .... | .... | .... | .... | .... | .... | .... | .... |
| **2001-02** | **Minnesota** | **NHL** | **81** | **21** | **48** | **69** | **18** | **10** | **0** | **2** | **106** | **19.8** | **–4** | **111** | **58.6** | **16:02** | .... | .... | .... | .... | .... | .... | .... | .... | .... |
| **2002-03** | **Minnesota** | **NHL** | **82** | **18** | **28** | **46** | **30** | **9** | **0** | **2** | **97** | **18.6** | **–10** | **59** | **44.1** | **14:29** | **18** | **7** | **6** | **13** | **4** | **4** | **0** | **1** | **15:00** |
| **2003-04** | **Minnesota** | **NHL** | **82** | **15** | **34** | **49** | **12** | **7** | **0** | **3** | **90** | **16.7** | **3** | **49** | **46.9** | **15:32** | .... | .... | .... | .... | .... | .... | .... | .... | .... |
| 2004-05 | | | DID NOT PLAY | | | | | | | | | | | | | | | | | | | | | | |
| **2005-06** | **Colorado** | **NHL** | **82** | **24** | **39** | **63** | **48** | **11** | **0** | **2** | **129** | **18.6** | **9** | **18** | **33.3** | **15:01** | **9** | **3** | **6** | **9** | **8** | **1** | **0** | **1** | **17:47** |
| **2006-07** | **Colorado** | **NHL** | **82** | **27** | **56** | **83** | **36** | **9** | **0** | **2** | **173** | **15.6** | **–8** | **8** | **62.5** | **17:31** | .... | .... | .... | .... | .... | .... | .... | .... | .... |
| **2007-08** | **Colorado** | **NHL** | **82** | **19** | **40** | **59** | **14** | **7** | **0** | **2** | **125** | **15.2** | **5** | **8** | **37.5** | **15:33** | **10** | **5** | **3** | **8** | **2** | **3** | **0** | **0** | **17:02** |
| **2008-09** | **Minnesota** | **NHL** | **80** | **22** | **28** | **50** | **18** | **9** | **0** | **3** | **118** | **18.6** | **–5** | **9** | **22.2** | **16:57** | .... | .... | .... | .... | .... | .... | .... | .... | .... |
| | **NHL Totals** | | **868** | **213** | **386** | **599** | **282** | **90** | **0** | **26** | **1195** | **17.8** | | **289** | **49.1** | **15:42** | **43** | **16** | **18** | **34** | **14** | **8** | **0** | **2** | **16:13** |

OHL First All-Star Team (1993) • Canadian Major Junior Second All-Star Team (1993) • AHL Second All-Star Team (1995)
Claimed by **Nashville** from **Washington** in Expansion Draft, June 26, 1998. Traded to **Atlanta** by **Nashville** for Atlanta's 5th round choice (Matt Hendricks) in 2000 Entry Draft, June 21, 1999. Signed as a free agent by **Minnesota**, July 17, 2001. Signed as a free agent by **Colorado**, August 6, 2005. Signed as a free agent by **Minnesota**, July 1, 2008.

## BRUNNSTROM, Fabian
(BRUHN-struhm, FAY-bee-yehn) **DAL.**

Left wing. Shoots left. 6'2", 203 lbs. Born, Jonstorp, Sweden, February 6, 1985.

| Season | Club | League | GP | G | A | Pts | PIM | PP | SH | GW | S | % | +/- | TF | F% | Min | Playoffs GP | G | A | Pts | PIM | PP | SH | GW | Min |
|---|---|---|---|---|---|---|---|---|---|---|---|---|---|---|---|---|---|---|---|---|---|---|---|---|---|
| 2002-03 | Jonstorps IF | Sweden-3 | STATISTICS NOT AVAILABLE | | | | | | | | | | | | | | | | | | | | | | |
| 2003-04 | Helsingborgs HC | Sweden-4 | .... | 6 | 7 | 13 | .... | .... | .... | .... | .... | .... | .... | .... | .... | .... | .... | .... | .... | .... | .... | .... | .... | .... | .... |
| 2004-05 | Helsingborgs HC | Sweden-4 | .... | 18 | 11 | 29 | .... | .... | .... | .... | .... | .... | .... | .... | .... | .... | .... | .... | .... | .... | .... | .... | .... | .... | .... |
| 2005-06 | Jonstorps IF | Sweden-3 | 38 | 21 | 23 | 44 | 8 | .... | .... | .... | .... | .... | .... | .... | .... | .... | .... | .... | .... | .... | .... | .... | .... | .... | .... |
| | Rogle | Sweden-2 | 3 | 0 | 0 | 0 | 2 | .... | .... | .... | .... | .... | .... | .... | .... | .... | .... | .... | .... | .... | .... | .... | .... | .... | .... |
| 2006-07 | Boras HC | Sweden-3 | 49 | 38 | 41 | 79 | 32 | .... | .... | .... | .... | .... | .... | .... | .... | .... | 2 | 1 | 3 | 4 | 0 | .... | .... | .... | .... |
| 2007-08 | Farjestad | Sweden | 54 | 9 | 28 | 37 | 16 | .... | .... | .... | .... | .... | .... | .... | .... | .... | 12 | 1 | 0 | 1 | 6 | .... | .... | .... | .... |
| **2008-09** | **Dallas** | **NHL** | **55** | **17** | **12** | **29** | **8** | **4** | **0** | **5** | **81** | **21.0** | **–8** | **0** | **0.0** | **11:37** | .... | .... | .... | .... | .... | .... | .... | .... | .... |
| | Manitoba Moose | AHL | 1 | 0 | 0 | 0 | 0 | .... | .... | .... | .... | .... | .... | .... | .... | .... | .... | .... | .... | .... | .... | .... | .... | .... | .... |
| | **NHL Totals** | | **55** | **17** | **12** | **29** | **8** | **4** | **0** | **5** | **81** | **21.0** | | **0** | **0.0** | **11:37** | .... | .... | .... | .... | .... | .... | .... | .... | .... |

Signed as a free agent by **Dallas**, May 8, 2008.

## BRYLIN, Sergei

(BRIH-lin, SAIR-gay)

Left wing. Shoots left. 5'10", 190 lbs.  Born, Moscow, USSR, January 13, 1974. New Jersey's 2nd choice, 42nd overall, in 1992 Entry Draft.

| | | | Regular Season | | | | | | | | | | | | | | Playoffs | | | | | | | | |
|---|---|---|---|---|---|---|---|---|---|---|---|---|---|---|---|---|---|---|---|---|---|---|---|---|---|
| Season | Club | League | GP | G | A | Pts | PIM | PP | SH | GW | S | % | +/- | TF | F% | Min | GP | G | A | Pts | PIM | PP | SH | GW | Min |
| 1991-92 | CSKA Moscow | CIS | 44 | 1 | 6 | 7 | 4 | .... | .... | .... | .... | .... | .... | .... | .... | .... | .... | .... | .... | .... | .... | .... | .... | .... | .... |
| | CSKA Moscow 2 | CIS-3 | 1 | 0 | 0 | 0 | 0 | .... | .... | .... | .... | .... | .... | .... | .... | .... | .... | .... | .... | .... | .... | .... | .... | .... | .... |
| 1992-93 | CSKA Moscow | CIS | 42 | 5 | 4 | 9 | 36 | .... | .... | .... | .... | .... | .... | .... | .... | .... | .... | .... | .... | .... | .... | .... | .... | .... | .... |
| 1993-94 | CSKA Moscow | CIS | 39 | 4 | 6 | 10 | 36 | .... | .... | .... | .... | .... | .... | .... | .... | .... | .... | .... | .... | .... | .... | .... | .... | .... | .... |
| | Russian Penguins | IHL | 13 | 4 | 5 | 9 | 18 | .... | .... | .... | .... | .... | .... | .... | .... | .... | .... | .... | .... | .... | .... | .... | .... | .... | .... |
| 1994-95 | Albany River Rats | AHL | 63 | 19 | 35 | 54 | 78 | .... | .... | .... | .... | .... | .... | .... | .... | .... | .... | .... | .... | .... | .... | .... | .... | .... | .... |
| | ♦ New Jersey | NHL | 26 | 6 | 8 | 14 | 8 | 0 | 0 | 0 | 41 | 14.6 | 12 | .... | .... | .... | 12 | 1 | 2 | 3 | 4 | 0 | 0 | 0 | .... |
| 1995-96 | New Jersey | NHL | 50 | 4 | 5 | 9 | 26 | 0 | 0 | 1 | 51 | 7.8 | –2 | .... | .... | .... | .... | .... | .... | .... | .... | .... | .... | .... | .... |
| 1996-97 | New Jersey | NHL | 29 | 2 | 2 | 4 | 20 | 0 | 0 | 0 | 34 | 5.9 | –13 | .... | .... | .... | .... | .... | .... | .... | .... | .... | .... | .... | .... |
| | Albany River Rats | AHL | 43 | 17 | 24 | 41 | 38 | .... | .... | .... | .... | .... | .... | .... | .... | .... | 16 | 4 | 8 | 12 | 12 | .... | .... | .... | .... |
| 1997-98 | New Jersey | NHL | 18 | 2 | 3 | 5 | 0 | 0 | 0 | 0 | 20 | 10.0 | 4 | .... | .... | .... | .... | .... | .... | .... | .... | .... | .... | .... | .... |
| | Albany River Rats | AHL | 44 | 21 | 22 | 43 | 60 | .... | .... | .... | .... | .... | .... | .... | .... | .... | .... | .... | .... | .... | .... | .... | .... | .... | .... |
| 1998-99 | New Jersey | NHL | 47 | 5 | 10 | 15 | 28 | 3 | 0 | 1 | 51 | 9.8 | 8 | 184 | 50.5 | 12:55 | 5 | 3 | 1 | 4 | 4 | 1 | 0 | 1 | 18:21 |
| 99-2000♦ | New Jersey | NHL | 64 | 9 | 11 | 20 | 20 | 1 | 0 | 1 | 84 | 10.7 | 0 | 72 | 41.7 | 13:23 | 17 | 3 | 5 | 8 | 0 | 0 | 0 | 0 | 13:02 |
| 2000-01 | New Jersey | NHL | 75 | 23 | 29 | 52 | 24 | 3 | 1 | 0 | 130 | 17.7 | 25 | 43 | 44.2 | 15:31 | 20 | 3 | 4 | 7 | 6 | 1 | 0 | 1 | 13:07 |
| 2001-02 | New Jersey | NHL | 76 | 16 | 28 | 44 | 10 | 5 | 0 | 3 | 133 | 12.0 | 21 | 17 | 47.1 | 17:11 | 6 | 0 | 2 | 2 | 2 | 0 | 0 | 0 | 19:05 |
| 2002-03♦ | New Jersey | NHL | 52 | 11 | 8 | 19 | 16 | 3 | 1 | 1 | 86 | 12.8 | –2 | 90 | 32.2 | 16:11 | 19 | 1 | 3 | 4 | 8 | 0 | 0 | 1 | 17:03 |
| 2003-04 | New Jersey | NHL | 82 | 14 | 19 | 33 | 20 | 7 | 0 | 1 | 98 | 14.3 | 10 | 695 | 46.6 | 16:25 | 5 | 0 | 0 | 0 | 0 | 0 | 0 | 0 | 15:02 |
| 2004-05 | Voskresensk | Russia | 35 | 8 | 19 | 27 | 40 | .... | .... | .... | .... | .... | .... | .... | .... | .... | .... | .... | .... | .... | .... | .... | .... | .... | .... |
| 2005-06 | New Jersey | NHL | 82 | 15 | 22 | 37 | 46 | 4 | 0 | 3 | 126 | 11.9 | –4 | 807 | 48.7 | 15:44 | 9 | 2 | 0 | 2 | 2 | 0 | 0 | 0 | 16:34 |
| 2006-07 | New Jersey | NHL | 82 | 16 | 24 | 40 | 35 | 8 | 0 | 2 | 97 | 16.5 | –5 | 277 | 45.5 | 17:45 | 11 | 1 | 2 | 3 | 6 | 1 | 0 | 0 | 18:12 |
| 2007-08 | New Jersey | NHL | 82 | 6 | 10 | 16 | 20 | 0 | 0 | 1 | 65 | 9.2 | –5 | 192 | 45.8 | 13:33 | 5 | 1 | 0 | 1 | 0 | 0 | 0 | 0 | 11:39 |
| 2008-09 | St. Petersburg | Rus-KHL | 50 | 9 | 15 | 24 | 16 | .... | .... | .... | .... | .... | .... | .... | .... | .... | 3 | 0 | 2 | 2 | 2 | .... | .... | .... | .... |
| | NHL Totals | | 765 | 129 | 179 | 308 | 273 | 34 | 2 | 14 | 1016 | 12.7 | | 2377 | 46.7 | 15:32 | 109 | 15 | 19 | 34 | 32 | 3 | 0 | 3 | 15:26 |

Signed as a free agent by **Voskresensk** (Russia), November 4, 2004.

## BURISH, Adam

(BUHR-ish, A-duhm) **CHI.**

Right wing. Shoots right. 6'1", 200 lbs.  Born, Madison, WI, January 6, 1983. Chicago's 9th choice, 282nd overall, in 2002 Entry Draft.

| | | | Regular Season | | | | | | | | | | | | | | Playoffs | | | | | | | | |
|---|---|---|---|---|---|---|---|---|---|---|---|---|---|---|---|---|---|---|---|---|---|---|---|---|---|
| Season | Club | League | GP | G | A | Pts | PIM | PP | SH | GW | S | % | +/- | TF | F% | Min | GP | G | A | Pts | PIM | PP | SH | GW | Min |
| 2000-01 | Edgewood | High-WI | 22 | 25 | 30 | 55 | 22 | .... | .... | .... | .... | .... | .... | .... | .... | .... | .... | .... | .... | .... | .... | .... | .... | .... | .... |
| 2001-02 | Green Bay | USHL | 61 | 24 | 33 | 57 | 122 | .... | .... | .... | .... | .... | .... | .... | .... | .... | 1 | 0 | 0 | 0 | 0 | .... | .... | .... | .... |
| 2002-03 | U. of Wisconsin | WCHA | 19 | 0 | 6 | 6 | 32 | .... | .... | .... | .... | .... | .... | .... | .... | .... | .... | .... | .... | .... | .... | .... | .... | .... | .... |
| 2003-04 | U. of Wisconsin | WCHA | 43 | 6 | 13 | 19 | 63 | .... | .... | .... | .... | .... | .... | .... | .... | .... | .... | .... | .... | .... | .... | .... | .... | .... | .... |
| 2004-05 | U. of Wisconsin | WCHA | 41 | 13 | 7 | 20 | 41 | .... | .... | .... | .... | .... | .... | .... | .... | .... | .... | .... | .... | .... | .... | .... | .... | .... | .... |
| 2005-06 | U. of Wisconsin | WCHA | 42 | 9 | 24 | 33 | 67 | .... | .... | .... | .... | .... | .... | .... | .... | .... | .... | .... | .... | .... | .... | .... | .... | .... | .... |
| 2006-07 | Chicago | NHL | 9 | 0 | 0 | 0 | 2 | 0 | 0 | 0 | 12 | 0.0 | –4 | 6 | 50.0 | 11:08 | .... | .... | .... | .... | .... | .... | .... | .... | .... |
| | Norfolk Admirals | AHL | 64 | 11 | 10 | 21 | 146 | .... | .... | .... | .... | .... | .... | .... | .... | .... | 6 | 1 | 1 | 2 | 4 | .... | .... | .... | .... |
| 2007-08 | Chicago | NHL | 81 | 4 | 4 | 8 | 214 | 0 | 1 | 1 | 69 | 5.8 | –13 | 264 | 42.1 | 11:45 | .... | .... | .... | .... | .... | .... | .... | .... | .... |
| 2008-09 | Chicago | NHL | 66 | 6 | 3 | 9 | 93 | 0 | 0 | 2 | 83 | 7.2 | 3 | 124 | 39.5 | 9:12 | 17 | 3 | 2 | 5 | 30 | 0 | 0 | 1 | 11:02 |
| | NHL Totals | | 156 | 10 | 7 | 17 | 309 | 0 | 1 | 3 | 164 | 6.1 | | 394 | 41.4 | 10:38 | 17 | 3 | 2 | 5 | 30 | 0 | 0 | 1 | 11:02 |

NCAA Championship All-Tournament Team (2006)

## BURNS, Brent

(BUHRNZ, BREHNT) **MIN.**

Defense. Shoots right. 6'5", 219 lbs.  Born, Ajax, Ont., March 9, 1985. Minnesota's 1st choice, 20th overall, in 2003 Entry Draft.

| | | | Regular Season | | | | | | | | | | | | | | Playoffs | | | | | | | | |
|---|---|---|---|---|---|---|---|---|---|---|---|---|---|---|---|---|---|---|---|---|---|---|---|---|---|
| Season | Club | League | GP | G | A | Pts | PIM | PP | SH | GW | S | % | +/- | TF | F% | Min | GP | G | A | Pts | PIM | PP | SH | GW | Min |
| 2000-01 | North York | MTHL | 46 | 4 | 7 | 11 | 16 | .... | .... | .... | .... | .... | .... | .... | .... | .... | .... | .... | .... | .... | .... | .... | .... | .... | .... |
| 2001-02 | Couchiching | OPJHL | 68 | 15 | 25 | 40 | 14 | .... | .... | .... | .... | .... | .... | .... | .... | .... | .... | .... | .... | .... | .... | .... | .... | .... | .... |
| 2002-03 | Brampton | OHL | 68 | 15 | 25 | 40 | 14 | .... | .... | .... | .... | .... | .... | .... | .... | .... | 11 | 5 | 6 | 11 | 6 | .... | .... | .... | .... |
| 2003-04 | Minnesota | NHL | 36 | 1 | 5 | 6 | 12 | 0 | 0 | 0 | 34 | 2.9 | –10 | 7 | 28.6 | 13:29 | .... | .... | .... | .... | .... | .... | .... | .... | .... |
| | Houston Aeros | AHL | 1 | 0 | 1 | 1 | 2 | .... | .... | .... | .... | .... | .... | .... | .... | .... | .... | .... | .... | .... | .... | .... | .... | .... | .... |
| 2004-05 | Houston Aeros | AHL | 73 | 11 | 16 | 27 | 57 | .... | .... | .... | .... | .... | .... | .... | .... | .... | 5 | 0 | 0 | 0 | 4 | .... | .... | .... | .... |
| 2005-06 | Minnesota | NHL | 72 | 4 | 12 | 16 | 32 | 1 | 0 | 1 | 73 | 5.5 | –7 | 11 | 54.6 | 14:07 | .... | .... | .... | .... | .... | .... | .... | .... | .... |
| 2006-07 | Minnesota | NHL | 77 | 7 | 18 | 25 | 26 | 3 | 0 | 3 | 108 | 6.5 | 16 | 4 | 25.0 | 15:48 | 5 | 0 | 1 | 1 | 14 | 0 | 0 | 0 | 18:59 |
| 2007-08 | Minnesota | NHL | 82 | 15 | 28 | 43 | 80 | 8 | 0 | 4 | 158 | 9.5 | 12 | 1 | 100.0 | 23:06 | 6 | 0 | 2 | 2 | 6 | 0 | 0 | 0 | 27:35 |
| 2008-09 | Minnesota | NHL | 59 | 8 | 19 | 27 | 45 | 4 | 0 | 2 | 147 | 5.4 | –7 | 5 | 60.0 | 22:25 | .... | .... | .... | .... | .... | .... | .... | .... | .... |
| | NHL Totals | | 326 | 35 | 82 | 117 | 195 | 16 | 0 | 10 | 520 | 6.7 | | 28 | 46.4 | 18:12 | 11 | 0 | 3 | 3 | 20 | 0 | 0 | 0 | 23:40 |

• Spent majority of 2003-04 season on assignment to Team Canada and serving as a healthy reserve.

## BURROWS, Alexandre

(BUHR-ohz, al-ehx-AHN-druh) **VAN.**

Left wing. Shoots left. 6'1", 190 lbs.  Born, Pincourt, Que., April 11, 1981.

| | | | Regular Season | | | | | | | | | | | | | | Playoffs | | | | | | | | |
|---|---|---|---|---|---|---|---|---|---|---|---|---|---|---|---|---|---|---|---|---|---|---|---|---|---|
| Season | Club | League | GP | G | A | Pts | PIM | PP | SH | GW | S | % | +/- | TF | F% | Min | GP | G | A | Pts | PIM | PP | SH | GW | Min |
| 2000-01 | Shawinigan | QMJHL | 63 | 16 | 14 | 30 | 105 | .... | .... | .... | .... | .... | .... | .... | .... | .... | 10 | 2 | 1 | 3 | 8 | .... | .... | .... | .... |
| 2001-02 | Shawinigan | QMJHL | 64 | 35 | 35 | 70 | 184 | .... | .... | .... | .... | .... | .... | .... | .... | .... | 10 | 9 | 10 | 19 | 20 | .... | .... | .... | .... |
| 2002-03 | Greenville | ECHL | 53 | 9 | 17 | 26 | 201 | .... | .... | .... | .... | .... | .... | .... | .... | .... | .... | .... | .... | .... | .... | .... | .... | .... | .... |
| | Baton Rouge | ECHL | 13 | 4 | 2 | 6 | 64 | .... | .... | .... | .... | .... | .... | .... | .... | .... | .... | .... | .... | .... | .... | .... | .... | .... | .... |
| 2003-04 | Manitoba Moose | AHL | 2 | 0 | 0 | 0 | 0 | .... | .... | .... | .... | .... | .... | .... | .... | .... | .... | .... | .... | .... | .... | .... | .... | .... | .... |
| | Columbia Inferno | ECHL | 64 | 29 | 44 | 73 | 194 | .... | .... | .... | .... | .... | .... | .... | .... | .... | 4 | 2 | 0 | 2 | 28 | .... | .... | .... | .... |
| 2004-05 | Manitoba Moose | AHL | 72 | 9 | 17 | 26 | 107 | .... | .... | .... | .... | .... | .... | .... | .... | .... | 14 | 0 | 3 | 3 | 37 | .... | .... | .... | .... |
| | Columbia Inferno | ECHL | 4 | 5 | 1 | 6 | 4 | .... | .... | .... | .... | .... | .... | .... | .... | .... | .... | .... | .... | .... | .... | .... | .... | .... | .... |
| 2005-06 | Vancouver | NHL | 43 | 7 | 5 | 12 | 61 | 0 | 1 | 1 | 49 | 14.3 | 5 | 19 | 47.4 | 10:24 | .... | .... | .... | .... | .... | .... | .... | .... | .... |
| | Manitoba Moose | AHL | 33 | 12 | 18 | 30 | 57 | .... | .... | .... | .... | .... | .... | .... | .... | .... | 13 | 6 | 7 | 13 | 27 | .... | .... | .... | .... |
| 2006-07 | Vancouver | NHL | 81 | 3 | 6 | 9 | 93 | 0 | 0 | 1 | 70 | 4.3 | –7 | 16 | 43.8 | 11:26 | 11 | 1 | 0 | 1 | 14 | 0 | 0 | 0 | 10:34 |
| 2007-08 | Vancouver | NHL | 82 | 12 | 19 | 31 | 179 | 1 | 3 | 3 | 126 | 9.5 | 11 | 37 | 35.1 | 15:06 | .... | .... | .... | .... | .... | .... | .... | .... | .... |
| 2008-09 | Vancouver | NHL | 82 | 28 | 23 | 51 | 150 | 0 | 4 | 3 | 175 | 16.0 | 23 | 80 | 46.3 | 16:51 | 10 | 3 | 1 | 4 | 20 | 0 | 0 | 1 | 18:48 |
| | NHL Totals | | 288 | 50 | 53 | 103 | 483 | 1 | 8 | 8 | 420 | 11.9 | | 152 | 43.4 | 13:52 | 21 | 4 | 1 | 5 | 34 | 0 | 0 | 1 | 14:29 |

Signed as a free agent by **Manitoba** (AHL), October 21, 2003. Signed as a free agent by **Vancouver**, November 8, 2005.

## BUTLER, Chris

(BUHT-luhr, KRIHS) **BUF.**

Defense. Shoots left. 6'1", 178 lbs.  Born, St. Louis, MO, October 27, 1986. Buffalo's 4th choice, 96th overall, in 2005 Entry Draft.

| | | | Regular Season | | | | | | | | | | | | | | Playoffs | | | | | | | | |
|---|---|---|---|---|---|---|---|---|---|---|---|---|---|---|---|---|---|---|---|---|---|---|---|---|---|
| Season | Club | League | GP | G | A | Pts | PIM | PP | SH | GW | S | % | +/- | TF | F% | Min | GP | G | A | Pts | PIM | PP | SH | GW | Min |
| 2003-04 | Sioux City | USHL | 55 | 3 | 6 | 9 | 37 | .... | .... | .... | .... | .... | .... | .... | .... | .... | 7 | 0 | 1 | 1 | 6 | .... | .... | .... | .... |
| 2004-05 | Sioux City | USHL | 60 | 6 | 22 | 28 | 90 | .... | .... | .... | .... | .... | .... | .... | .... | .... | 13 | 1 | 6 | 7 | 10 | .... | .... | .... | .... |
| 2005-06 | U. of Denver | WCHA | 35 | 7 | 15 | 22 | 28 | .... | .... | .... | .... | .... | .... | .... | .... | .... | .... | .... | .... | .... | .... | .... | .... | .... | .... |
| 2006-07 | U. of Denver | WCHA | 39 | 10 | 17 | 27 | 42 | .... | .... | .... | .... | .... | .... | .... | .... | .... | .... | .... | .... | .... | .... | .... | .... | .... | .... |
| 2007-08 | U. of Denver | WCHA | 41 | 3 | 14 | 17 | 38 | .... | .... | .... | .... | .... | .... | .... | .... | .... | .... | .... | .... | .... | .... | .... | .... | .... | .... |
| 2008-09 | Buffalo | NHL | 47 | 2 | 4 | 6 | 18 | 0 | 0 | 1 | 36 | 5.6 | 11 | 0 | 0.0 | 16:43 | .... | .... | .... | .... | .... | .... | .... | .... | .... |
| | Portland Pirates | AHL | 27 | 2 | 10 | 12 | 14 | .... | .... | .... | .... | .... | .... | .... | .... | .... | 4 | 0 | 0 | 0 | 0 | .... | .... | .... | .... |
| | NHL Totals | | 47 | 2 | 4 | 6 | 18 | 0 | 0 | 1 | 36 | 5.6 | | 0 | 0.0 | 16:43 | .... | .... | .... | .... | .... | .... | .... | .... | .... |

USHL First All-Star Team (2005) • WCHA All-Rookie Team (2006) • WCHA Second All-Star Team (2008) • NCAA West Second All-American Team (2008)

## BYERS, Dane

(BIGH-uhrs, DAYN) **NYR**

Left wing. Shoots left. 6'3", 195 lbs.  Born, Nipawin, Sask., February 21, 1986. NY Rangers' 4th choice, 48th overall, in 2004 Entry Draft.

| | | | Regular Season | | | | | | | | | | | | | | Playoffs | | | | | | | | |
|---|---|---|---|---|---|---|---|---|---|---|---|---|---|---|---|---|---|---|---|---|---|---|---|---|---|
| Season | Club | League | GP | G | A | Pts | PIM | PP | SH | GW | S | % | +/- | TF | F% | Min | GP | G | A | Pts | PIM | PP | SH | GW | Min |
| 2002-03 | Prince Albert | WHL | 49 | 8 | 6 | 14 | 46 | .... | .... | .... | .... | .... | .... | .... | .... | .... | .... | .... | .... | .... | .... | .... | .... | .... | .... |
| 2003-04 | Prince Albert | WHL | 51 | 9 | 8 | 17 | 134 | .... | .... | .... | .... | .... | .... | .... | .... | .... | 6 | 1 | 2 | 3 | 17 | .... | .... | .... | .... |
| 2004-05 | Prince Albert | WHL | 65 | 11 | 9 | 20 | 181 | .... | .... | .... | .... | .... | .... | .... | .... | .... | 17 | 4 | 6 | 10 | 18 | .... | .... | .... | .... |
| 2005-06 | Prince Albert | WHL | 71 | 21 | 27 | 48 | 157 | .... | .... | .... | .... | .... | .... | .... | .... | .... | .... | .... | .... | .... | .... | .... | .... | .... | .... |
| | Hartford | AHL | 5 | 0 | 2 | 2 | 6 | .... | .... | .... | .... | .... | .... | .... | .... | .... | .... | .... | .... | .... | .... | .... | .... | .... | .... |
| 2006-07 | Hartford | AHL | 78 | 17 | 30 | 47 | 213 | .... | .... | .... | .... | .... | .... | .... | .... | .... | 7 | 2 | 0 | 2 | 16 | .... | .... | .... | .... |
| 2007-08 | NY Rangers | NHL | 1 | 0 | 0 | 0 | 0 | 0 | 0 | 0 | 0 | 0.0 | –1 | 0 | 0.0 | 5:05 | .... | .... | .... | .... | .... | .... | .... | .... | .... |
| | Hartford | AHL | 73 | 23 | 23 | 46 | 184 | .... | .... | .... | .... | .... | .... | .... | .... | .... | 5 | 2 | 1 | 3 | 2 | .... | .... | .... | .... |
| 2008-09 | Hartford | AHL | 9 | 4 | 3 | 7 | 18 | .... | .... | .... | .... | .... | .... | .... | .... | .... | 6 | 3 | 1 | 4 | 7 | .... | .... | .... | .... |
| | NHL Totals | | 1 | 0 | 0 | 0 | 0 | 0 | 0 | 0 | 0 | 0.0 | | 0 | 0.0 | 5:05 | .... | .... | .... | .... | .... | .... | .... | .... | .... |

• Missed majority of 2008-09 season recovering from knee injury.

## BYFUGLIEN, Dustin
(BUHF-lihn, DUHS-tihn) **CHI.**

Right wing. Shoots right. 6'3", 246 lbs. Born, Minneapolis, MN, March 27, 1985. Chicago's 8th choice, 245th overall, in 2003 Entry Draft.

| | | | Regular Season | | | | | | | | | | | | | | Playoffs | | | | | | | | |
|---|---|---|---|---|---|---|---|---|---|---|---|---|---|---|---|---|---|---|---|---|---|---|---|---|---|
| Season | Club | League | GP | G | A | Pts | PIM | PP | SH | GW | S | % | +/- | TF | F% | Min | GP | G | A | Pts | PIM | PP | SH | GW | Min |
| 2001-02 | Chicago Mission | MAHL | 52 | 32 | 30 | 62 | 40 | .... | .... | .... | .... | .... | .... | .... | .... | .... | .... | .... | .... | .... | .... | .... | .... | .... | .... |
| | Brandon | WHL | 3 | 0 | 0 | 0 | 0 | .... | .... | .... | .... | .... | .... | .... | .... | .... | .... | .... | .... | .... | .... | .... | .... | .... | .... |
| 2002-03 | Brandon | WHL | 8 | 1 | 1 | 2 | 4 | .... | .... | .... | .... | .... | .... | .... | .... | .... | .... | .... | .... | .... | .... | .... | .... | .... | .... |
| | Prince George | WHL | 48 | 9 | 28 | 37 | 74 | .... | .... | .... | .... | .... | .... | .... | .... | .... | 5 | 1 | 3 | 4 | 12 | .... | .... | .... | .... |
| 2003-04 | Prince George | WHL | 66 | 16 | 29 | 45 | 137 | .... | .... | .... | .... | .... | .... | .... | .... | .... | .... | .... | .... | .... | .... | .... | .... | .... | .... |
| 2004-05 | Prince George | WHL | 64 | 22 | 36 | 58 | 184 | .... | .... | .... | .... | .... | .... | .... | .... | .... | .... | .... | .... | .... | .... | .... | .... | .... | .... |
| **2005-06** | **Chicago** | **NHL** | **25** | **3** | **2** | **5** | **24** | **0** | **0** | **1** | **45** | **6.7** | **–6** | **0** | **0.0** | **17:19** | .... | .... | .... | .... | .... | .... | .... | .... | .... |
| | Norfolk Admirals | AHL | 53 | 8 | 15 | 23 | 75 | .... | .... | .... | .... | .... | .... | .... | .... | .... | 4 | 1 | 2 | 3 | 4 | .... | .... | .... | .... |
| **2006-07** | **Chicago** | **NHL** | **9** | **1** | **2** | **3** | **10** | **0** | **0** | **0** | **18** | **5.6** | **–2** | **0** | **0.0** | **17:18** | .... | .... | .... | .... | .... | .... | .... | .... | .... |
| | Norfolk Admirals | AHL | 63 | 16 | 28 | 44 | 146 | .... | .... | .... | .... | .... | .... | .... | .... | .... | 6 | 0 | 2 | 2 | 18 | .... | .... | .... | .... |
| **2007-08** | **Chicago** | **NHL** | **67** | **19** | **17** | **36** | **59** | **7** | **0** | **4** | **163** | **11.7** | **–7** | **1** | **0.0** | **17:02** | .... | .... | .... | .... | .... | .... | .... | .... | .... |
| | Rockford IceHogs | AHL | 8 | 2 | 5 | 7 | 25 | .... | .... | .... | .... | .... | .... | .... | .... | .... | .... | .... | .... | .... | .... | .... | .... | .... | .... |
| **2008-09** | **Chicago** | **NHL** | **77** | **15** | **16** | **31** | **81** | **3** | **0** | **4** | **202** | **7.4** | **7** | **11** | **18.2** | **14:52** | **17** | **3** | **6** | **9** | **26** | **1** | **0** | **0** | **17:11** |
| | **NHL Totals** | | **178** | **38** | **37** | **75** | **174** | **10** | **0** | **9** | **428** | **8.9** | | **12** | **16.7** | **16:09** | **17** | **3** | **6** | **9** | **26** | **1** | **0** | **0** | **17:11** |

AHL Second All-Star Team (2007)

## CALDER, Kyle
(KAWL-duhr, KIGHL)

Left wing. Shoots left. 5'11", 177 lbs. Born, Mannville, Alta., January 5, 1979. Chicago's 7th choice, 130th overall, in 1997 Entry Draft.

| Season | Club | League | GP | G | A | Pts | PIM | PP | SH | GW | S | % | +/- | TF | F% | Min | GP | G | A | Pts | PIM | PP | SH | GW | Min |
|---|---|---|---|---|---|---|---|---|---|---|---|---|---|---|---|---|---|---|---|---|---|---|---|---|---|
| 1994-95 | Leduc Oil Barons | AMHL | 27 | 25 | 32 | 57 | 22 | .... | .... | .... | .... | .... | .... | .... | .... | .... | .... | .... | .... | .... | .... | .... | .... | .... | .... |
| 1995-96 | Regina Pats | WHL | 27 | 1 | 7 | 8 | 10 | .... | .... | .... | .... | .... | .... | .... | .... | .... | 11 | 0 | 0 | 0 | 0 | .... | .... | .... | .... |
| 1996-97 | Regina Pats | WHL | 62 | 25 | 34 | 59 | 17 | .... | .... | .... | .... | .... | .... | .... | .... | .... | 5 | 3 | 0 | 3 | 6 | .... | .... | .... | .... |
| 1997-98 | Regina Pats | WHL | 62 | 27 | 50 | 77 | 58 | .... | .... | .... | .... | .... | .... | .... | .... | .... | 2 | 0 | 1 | 1 | 0 | .... | .... | .... | .... |
| 1998-99 | Regina Pats | WHL | 34 | 23 | 28 | 51 | 29 | .... | .... | .... | .... | .... | .... | .... | .... | .... | .... | .... | .... | .... | .... | .... | .... | .... | .... |
| | Kamloops Blazers | WHL | 27 | 19 | 18 | 37 | 30 | .... | .... | .... | .... | .... | .... | .... | .... | .... | 15 | 6 | 10 | 16 | 6 | .... | .... | .... | .... |
| **99-2000** | **Chicago** | **NHL** | **8** | **1** | **1** | **2** | **2** | **0** | **0** | **0** | **5** | **20.0** | **–3** | **2** | **0.0** | **9:59** | .... | .... | .... | .... | .... | .... | .... | .... | .... |
| | Cleveland | IHL | 74 | 14 | 22 | 36 | 43 | .... | .... | .... | .... | .... | .... | .... | .... | .... | 9 | 2 | 2 | 4 | 14 | .... | .... | .... | .... |
| **2000-01** | **Chicago** | **NHL** | **43** | **5** | **10** | **15** | **14** | **0** | **0** | **1** | **63** | **7.9** | **–4** | **2** | **0.0** | **12:43** | .... | .... | .... | .... | .... | .... | .... | .... | .... |
| | Norfolk Admirals | AHL | 37 | 12 | 15 | 27 | 21 | .... | .... | .... | .... | .... | .... | .... | .... | .... | 9 | 2 | 6 | 8 | 2 | .... | .... | .... | .... |
| **2001-02** | **Chicago** | **NHL** | **81** | **17** | **36** | **53** | **47** | **6** | **0** | **3** | **133** | **12.8** | **8** | **0** | **0.0** | **16:33** | **5** | **2** | **0** | **2** | **2** | **1** | **0** | **0** | **16:45** |
| **2002-03** | **Chicago** | **NHL** | **82** | **15** | **27** | **42** | **40** | **7** | **0** | **2** | **164** | **9.1** | **–6** | **4** | **25.0** | **16:43** | .... | .... | .... | .... | .... | .... | .... | .... | .... |
| **2003-04** | **Chicago** | **NHL** | **66** | **21** | **18** | **39** | **29** | **10** | **0** | **1** | **144** | **14.6** | **–18** | **13** | **30.8** | **17:08** | .... | .... | .... | .... | .... | .... | .... | .... | .... |
| 2004-05 | Sodertalje SK | Sweden | 12 | 5 | 1 | 6 | 6 | .... | .... | .... | .... | .... | .... | .... | .... | .... | 10 | 5 | 1 | 6 | 2 | .... | .... | .... | .... |
| **2005-06** | **Chicago** | **NHL** | **79** | **26** | **33** | **59** | **52** | **6** | **2** | **6** | **183** | **14.2** | **–4** | **13** | **46.2** | **18:23** | .... | .... | .... | .... | .... | .... | .... | .... | .... |
| **2006-07** | **Philadelphia** | **NHL** | **59** | **9** | **12** | **21** | **36** | **2** | **2** | **0** | **88** | **10.2** | **–31** | **10** | **30.0** | **15:02** | .... | .... | .... | .... | .... | .... | .... | .... | .... |
| | **Detroit** | **NHL** | **19** | **5** | **9** | **14** | **22** | **1** | **0** | **2** | **42** | **11.9** | **6** | **2** | **50.0** | **17:05** | **13** | **0** | **1** | **1** | **8** | **0** | **0** | **0** | **8:59** |
| **2007-08** | **Los Angeles** | **NHL** | **65** | **7** | **13** | **20** | **18** | **3** | **0** | **0** | **70** | **10.0** | **–11** | **18** | **38.9** | **13:00** | .... | .... | .... | .... | .... | .... | .... | .... | .... |
| **2008-09** | **Los Angeles** | **NHL** | **74** | **8** | **19** | **27** | **41** | **2** | **0** | **1** | **93** | **8.6** | **–1** | **3** | **33.3** | **13:10** | .... | .... | .... | .... | .... | .... | .... | .... | .... |
| | **NHL Totals** | | **576** | **114** | **178** | **292** | **301** | **37** | **4** | **16** | **985** | **11.6** | | **67** | **34.3** | **15:33** | **18** | **2** | **1** | **3** | **10** | **1** | **0** | **0** | **11:09** |

Signed as a free agent by **Sodertalje** (Sweden), January 20, 2005. Traded to **Philadelphia** by **Chicago** for Michael Handzus, August 4, 2006. Traded to **Chicago** by **Philadelphia** for Lasse Kukkonen and Chicago's 3rd round choice (Garrett Klotz) in 2007 Entry Draft, February 26, 2007. Traded to **Detroit** by **Chicago** for Jason Williams, February 26, 2007. Signed as a free agent by **Los Angeles**, July 2, 2007.

## CALDWELL, Ryan
(KAWLD-wehl, RIGH-uhn)

Defense. Shoots left. 6'2", 174 lbs. Born, Deloraine, Man., June 15, 1981. NY Islanders' 7th choice, 202nd overall, in 2000 Entry Draft.

| Season | Club | League | GP | G | A | Pts | PIM | PP | SH | GW | S | % | +/- | TF | F% | Min | GP | G | A | Pts | PIM | PP | SH | GW | Min |
|---|---|---|---|---|---|---|---|---|---|---|---|---|---|---|---|---|---|---|---|---|---|---|---|---|---|
| 1998-99 | Shat.-St. Mary's | High-MN | 29 | 24 | 55 | 79 | 22 | .... | .... | .... | .... | .... | .... | .... | .... | .... | .... | .... | .... | .... | .... | .... | .... | .... | .... |
| 99-2000 | Thunder Bay | USHL | 46 | 3 | 20 | 23 | 152 | .... | .... | .... | .... | .... | .... | .... | .... | .... | .... | .... | .... | .... | .... | .... | .... | .... | .... |
| 2000-01 | U. of Denver | WCHA | 36 | 3 | 20 | 23 | 76 | .... | .... | .... | .... | .... | .... | .... | .... | .... | .... | .... | .... | .... | .... | .... | .... | .... | .... |
| 2001-02 | U. of Denver | WCHA | 40 | 3 | 16 | 19 | 76 | .... | .... | .... | .... | .... | .... | .... | .... | .... | .... | .... | .... | .... | .... | .... | .... | .... | .... |
| 2002-03 | U. of Denver | WCHA | 38 | 5 | 14 | 19 | 58 | .... | .... | .... | .... | .... | .... | .... | .... | .... | .... | .... | .... | .... | .... | .... | .... | .... | .... |
| 2003-04 | U. of Denver | WCHA | 42 | 15 | 12 | 27 | 96 | .... | .... | .... | .... | .... | .... | .... | .... | .... | .... | .... | .... | .... | .... | .... | .... | .... | .... |
| 2004-05 | Bridgeport | AHL | 73 | 2 | 19 | 21 | 65 | .... | .... | .... | .... | .... | .... | .... | .... | .... | .... | .... | .... | .... | .... | .... | .... | .... | .... |
| **2005-06** | **NY Islanders** | **NHL** | **2** | **0** | **0** | **0** | **2** | **0** | **0** | **0** | **2** | **0.0** | **–2** | **0** | **0.0** | **16:33** | .... | .... | .... | .... | .... | .... | .... | .... | .... |
| | Bridgeport | AHL | 61 | 2 | 13 | 15 | 38 | .... | .... | .... | .... | .... | .... | .... | .... | .... | 7 | 1 | 1 | 2 | 2 | .... | .... | .... | .... |
| 2006-07 | Syracuse Crunch | AHL | 61 | 7 | 23 | 30 | 94 | .... | .... | .... | .... | .... | .... | .... | .... | .... | .... | .... | .... | .... | .... | .... | .... | .... | .... |
| **2007-08** | **Phoenix** | **NHL** | **2** | **0** | **0** | **0** | **2** | **0** | **0** | **0** | **1** | **0.0** | **0** | **0** | **0.0** | **6:08** | .... | .... | .... | .... | .... | .... | .... | .... | .... |
| | San Antonio | AHL | 71 | 3 | 18 | 21 | 94 | .... | .... | .... | .... | .... | .... | .... | .... | .... | 7 | 0 | 0 | 0 | 4 | .... | .... | .... | .... |
| 2008-09 | Dusseldorf | Germany | 47 | 4 | 14 | 18 | 132 | .... | .... | .... | .... | .... | .... | .... | .... | .... | 15 | 3 | 7 | 10 | 33 | .... | .... | .... | .... |
| | **NHL Totals** | | **4** | **0** | **0** | **0** | **4** | **0** | **0** | **0** | **3** | **0.0** | | **0** | **0.0** | **11:20** | .... | .... | .... | .... | .... | .... | .... | .... | .... |

WCHA All-Rookie Team (2001) • WCHA Second All-Star Team (2004) • NCAA West First All-American Team (2004) • NCAA Championship All-Tournament Team (2004)

Traded to **Columbus** by **NY Islanders** for Eric Boguniecki, October 25, 2006. Signed as a free agent by **Phoenix**, July 23, 2007.

## CALLAHAN, Joe
(kal-AH-han, JOH) **S.J.**

Defense. Shoots right. 6'3", 220 lbs. Born, Brockton, MA, December 20, 1982. Phoenix's 4th choice, 70th overall, in 2002 Entry Draft.

| Season | Club | League | GP | G | A | Pts | PIM | PP | SH | GW | S | % | +/- | TF | F% | Min | GP | G | A | Pts | PIM | PP | SH | GW | Min |
|---|---|---|---|---|---|---|---|---|---|---|---|---|---|---|---|---|---|---|---|---|---|---|---|---|---|
| 2001-02 | Yale | ECAC | 31 | 3 | 8 | 11 | 20 | .... | .... | .... | .... | .... | .... | .... | .... | .... | .... | .... | .... | .... | .... | .... | .... | .... | .... |
| 2002-03 | Yale | ECAC | 32 | 2 | 11 | 13 | 38 | .... | .... | .... | .... | .... | .... | .... | .... | .... | .... | .... | .... | .... | .... | .... | .... | .... | .... |
| 2003-04 | Yale | ECAC | 31 | 6 | 14 | 20 | 38 | .... | .... | .... | .... | .... | .... | .... | .... | .... | .... | .... | .... | .... | .... | .... | .... | .... | .... |
| | Springfield | AHL | 13 | 0 | 4 | 4 | 12 | .... | .... | .... | .... | .... | .... | .... | .... | .... | .... | .... | .... | .... | .... | .... | .... | .... | .... |
| 2004-05 | Utah Grizzlies | AHL | 75 | 4 | 7 | 11 | 66 | .... | .... | .... | .... | .... | .... | .... | .... | .... | .... | .... | .... | .... | .... | .... | .... | .... | .... |
| 2005-06 | San Antonio | AHL | 80 | 1 | 5 | 6 | 88 | .... | .... | .... | .... | .... | .... | .... | .... | .... | .... | .... | .... | .... | .... | .... | .... | .... | .... |
| 2006-07 | San Antonio | AHL | 78 | 1 | 13 | 14 | 65 | .... | .... | .... | .... | .... | .... | .... | .... | .... | .... | .... | .... | .... | .... | .... | .... | .... | .... |
| 2007-08 | Portland Pirates | AHL | 65 | 1 | 23 | 24 | 59 | .... | .... | .... | .... | .... | .... | .... | .... | .... | 18 | 1 | 11 | 12 | 25 | .... | .... | .... | .... |
| **2008-09** | **NY Islanders** | **NHL** | **18** | **0** | **2** | **2** | **4** | **0** | **0** | **0** | **6** | **0.0** | **5** | **1** | **0.0** | **15:00** | .... | .... | .... | .... | .... | .... | .... | .... | .... |
| | Bridgeport | AHL | 56 | 4 | 9 | 13 | 38 | .... | .... | .... | .... | .... | .... | .... | .... | .... | 5 | 1 | 2 | 3 | 4 | .... | .... | .... | .... |
| | **NHL Totals** | | **18** | **0** | **2** | **2** | **4** | **0** | **0** | **0** | **6** | **0.0** | | **1** | **0.0** | **15:00** | .... | .... | .... | .... | .... | .... | .... | .... | .... |

Signed as a free agent by **Anaheim**, July 12, 2007. Signed as a free agent by **NY Islanders**, July 8, 2008. Signed as a free agent by **San Jose**, July 16, 2009.

## CALLAHAN, Ryan
(kal-AH-han, RIGH-uhn) **NYR**

Right wing. Shoots right. 5'11", 188 lbs. Born, Rochester, NY, March 21, 1985. NY Rangers' 9th choice, 127th overall, in 2004 Entry Draft.

| Season | Club | League | GP | G | A | Pts | PIM | PP | SH | GW | S | % | +/- | TF | F% | Min | GP | G | A | Pts | PIM | PP | SH | GW | Min |
|---|---|---|---|---|---|---|---|---|---|---|---|---|---|---|---|---|---|---|---|---|---|---|---|---|---|
| 2002-03 | Guelph Storm | OHL | 59 | 14 | 17 | 31 | 47 | .... | .... | .... | .... | .... | .... | .... | .... | .... | 11 | 0 | 3 | 3 | 2 | .... | .... | .... | .... |
| 2003-04 | Guelph Storm | OHL | 68 | 36 | 32 | 68 | 86 | .... | .... | .... | .... | .... | .... | .... | .... | .... | 22 | *13 | 8 | 21 | 20 | .... | .... | .... | .... |
| 2004-05 | Guelph Storm | OHL | 60 | 28 | 26 | 54 | 108 | .... | .... | .... | .... | .... | .... | .... | .... | .... | 4 | 1 | 1 | 2 | 6 | .... | .... | .... | .... |
| 2005-06 | Guelph Storm | OHL | 62 | 52 | 32 | 84 | 126 | .... | .... | .... | .... | .... | .... | .... | .... | .... | 13 | 7 | 17 | 24 | 20 | .... | .... | .... | .... |
| **2006-07** | **NY Rangers** | **NHL** | **14** | **4** | **2** | **6** | **9** | **0** | **0** | **1** | **40** | **10.0** | **5** | **3** | **66.7** | **10:31** | **10** | **2** | **1** | **3** | **6** | **1** | **0** | **0** | **12:19** |
| | Hartford | AHL | 60 | 35 | 20 | 55 | 74 | .... | .... | .... | .... | .... | .... | .... | .... | .... | .... | .... | .... | .... | .... | .... | .... | .... | .... |
| **2007-08** | **NY Rangers** | **NHL** | **52** | **8** | **5** | **13** | **31** | **0** | **1** | **1** | **92** | **8.7** | **7** | **5** | **20.0** | **12:22** | **10** | **2** | **2** | **4** | **10** | **0** | **1** | **1** | **15:55** |
| | Hartford | AHL | 11 | 7 | 8 | 15 | 27 | .... | .... | .... | .... | .... | .... | .... | .... | .... | .... | .... | .... | .... | .... | .... | .... | .... | .... |
| **2008-09** | **NY Rangers** | **NHL** | **81** | **22** | **18** | **40** | **45** | **2** | **1** | **1** | **237** | **9.3** | **7** | **10** | **70.0** | **17:04** | **7** | **2** | **0** | **2** | **4** | **1** | **0** | **1** | **19:44** |
| | **NHL Totals** | | **147** | **34** | **25** | **59** | **85** | **2** | **2** | **3** | **369** | **9.2** | | **18** | **55.6** | **14:47** | **27** | **6** | **3** | **9** | **20** | **2** | **1** | **2** | **15:34** |

OHL Second All-Star Team (2006) • AHL All-Rookie Team (2007)

## CAMMALLERI, Michael
(kam-UH-LAIR-ee, MIGH-kuhl) **MTL.**

Center. Shoots left. 5'9", 185 lbs. Born, Richmond Hill, Ont., June 8, 1982. Los Angeles' 3rd choice, 49th overall, in 2001 Entry Draft.

| Season | Club | League | GP | G | A | Pts | PIM | PP | SH | GW | S | % | +/- | TF | F% | Min | GP | G | A | Pts | PIM | PP | SH | GW | Min |
|---|---|---|---|---|---|---|---|---|---|---|---|---|---|---|---|---|---|---|---|---|---|---|---|---|---|
| 1997-98 | Bramalea Blues | OPJHL | 46 | 36 | 52 | 88 | 30 | .... | .... | .... | .... | .... | .... | .... | .... | .... | .... | .... | .... | .... | .... | .... | .... | .... | .... |
| 1998-99 | Bramalea Blues | OPJHL | 41 | 31 | 72 | 103 | 51 | .... | .... | .... | .... | .... | .... | .... | .... | .... | .... | .... | .... | .... | .... | .... | .... | .... | .... |
| 99-2000 | U. of Michigan | CCHA | 39 | 13 | 13 | 26 | 32 | .... | .... | .... | .... | .... | .... | .... | .... | .... | .... | .... | .... | .... | .... | .... | .... | .... | .... |
| 2000-01 | U. of Michigan | CCHA | 42 | *29 | 32 | 61 | 24 | .... | .... | .... | .... | .... | .... | .... | .... | .... | .... | .... | .... | .... | .... | .... | .... | .... | .... |
| 2001-02 | U. of Michigan | CCHA | 29 | 23 | 21 | 44 | 28 | .... | .... | .... | .... | .... | .... | .... | .... | .... | .... | .... | .... | .... | .... | .... | .... | .... | .... |
| **2002-03** | **Los Angeles** | **NHL** | **28** | **5** | **3** | **8** | **22** | **2** | **0** | **2** | **40** | **12.5** | **–4** | **253** | **51.4** | **14:05** | .... | .... | .... | .... | .... | .... | .... | .... | .... |
| | Manchester | AHL | 13 | 5 | 15 | 20 | 12 | .... | .... | .... | .... | .... | .... | .... | .... | .... | .... | .... | .... | .... | .... | .... | .... | .... | .... |
| **2003-04** | **Los Angeles** | **NHL** | **31** | **9** | **6** | **15** | **20** | **2** | **0** | **2** | **53** | **17.0** | **1** | **280** | **53.6** | **13:18** | .... | .... | .... | .... | .... | .... | .... | .... | .... |
| | Manchester | AHL | 41 | 20 | 19 | 39 | 28 | .... | .... | .... | .... | .... | .... | .... | .... | .... | 1 | 0 | 1 | 1 | 0 | .... | .... | .... | .... |

| | | | Regular Season | | | | | | | | | | | | | | Playoffs | | | | | | | | |
|---|---|---|---|---|---|---|---|---|---|---|---|---|---|---|---|---|---|---|---|---|---|---|---|---|---|
| Season | Club | League | GP | G | A | Pts | PIM | PP | SH | GW | S | % | +/- | TF | F% | Min | GP | G | A | Pts | PIM | PP | SH | GW | Min |
| 2004-05 | Manchester | AHL | 79 | *46 | 63 | 109 | 60 | .... | .... | .... | .... | .... | .... | .... | .... | .... | 6 | 1 | 5 | 6 | 0 | .... | .... | .... | .... |
| **2005-06** | **Los Angeles** | **NHL** | **80** | **26** | **29** | **55** | **50** | **15** | **0** | **4** | **206** | **12.6** | **–14** | **578** | **53.5** | **16:45** | .... | .... | .... | .... | .... | .... | .... | .... | .... |
| **2006-07** | **Los Angeles** | **NHL** | **81** | **34** | **46** | **80** | **48** | **16** | **0** | **5** | **299** | **11.4** | **5** | **301** | **54.2** | **18:03** | .... | .... | .... | .... | .... | .... | .... | .... | .... |
| **2007-08** | **Los Angeles** | **NHL** | **63** | **19** | **28** | **47** | **30** | **10** | **0** | **1** | **210** | **9.0** | **–16** | **380** | **54.2** | **18:35** | .... | .... | .... | .... | .... | .... | .... | .... | .... |
| **2008-09** | **Calgary** | **NHL** | **81** | **39** | **43** | **82** | **44** | **19** | **0** | **6** | **255** | **15.3** | **–2** | **368** | **60.3** | **17:33** | **6** | **1** | **2** | **3** | **2** | **0** | **0** | **0** | **18:02** |
| | **NHL Totals** | | **364** | **132** | **155** | **287** | **214** | **64** | **0** | **20** | **1063** | **12.4** | | **2160** | **54.6** | **17:02** | **6** | **1** | **2** | **3** | **2** | **0** | **0** | **0** | **18:02** |

CCHA First All-Star Team (2001) • NCAA West Second All-American Team (2001) • CCHA Second All-Star Team (2002) • NCAA West First All-American Team (2002) • AHL Second All-Star Team (2005) • Willie Marshall Award (AHL - Top Goal-scorer) (2005)

• Missed majority of 2002-03 season recovering from head injury suffered in game vs. San Jose, January 28, 2003. Traded to **Calgary** by **Los Angeles** with Calgary's 2nd round choice (previously acquired, Calgary selected Mitch Wahl) in 2008 Entry Draft for Calgary's 1st round choice (later traded to Anaheim – Anaheim selected Jake Gardiner) in 2008 Entry Draft and Calgary's 2nd round choice (later traded to Carolina – Carolina selected Brian Dumoulin) in 2009 Entry Draft, June 20, 2008. Signed as a free agent by **Montreal**, July 1, 2009.

### CAMPBELL, Brian

(KAM-behl, BRIGH-uhn) **CHI.**

Defense. Shoots left. 6', 188 lbs. Born, Strathroy, Ont., May 23, 1979. Buffalo's 7th choice, 156th overall, in 1997 Entry Draft.

| Season | Club | League | GP | G | A | Pts | PIM | PP | SH | GW | S | % | +/- | TF | F% | Min | GP | G | A | Pts | PIM | PP | SH | GW | Min |
|---|---|---|---|---|---|---|---|---|---|---|---|---|---|---|---|---|---|---|---|---|---|---|---|---|---|
| 1994-95 | Petrolia Oil Barons | OHA-B | 49 | 11 | 27 | 38 | 43 | .... | .... | .... | .... | .... | .... | .... | .... | .... | .... | .... | .... | .... | .... | .... | .... | .... | .... |
| 1995-96 | Ottawa 67's | OHL | 66 | 5 | 22 | 27 | 23 | .... | .... | .... | .... | .... | .... | .... | .... | .... | 4 | 0 | 1 | 1 | 2 | .... | .... | .... | .... |
| 1996-97 | Ottawa 67's | OHL | 66 | 7 | 36 | 43 | 12 | .... | .... | .... | .... | .... | .... | .... | .... | .... | 24 | 2 | 11 | 13 | 8 | .... | .... | .... | .... |
| 1997-98 | Ottawa 67's | OHL | 66 | 14 | 39 | 53 | 31 | .... | .... | .... | .... | .... | .... | .... | .... | .... | 13 | 1 | 14 | 15 | 0 | .... | .... | .... | .... |
| 1998-99 | Ottawa 67's | OHL | 62 | 12 | 75 | 87 | 27 | .... | .... | .... | .... | .... | .... | .... | .... | .... | 9 | 2 | 10 | 12 | 6 | .... | .... | .... | .... |
| | Rochester | AHL | .... | .... | .... | .... | .... | .... | .... | .... | .... | .... | .... | .... | .... | .... | 2 | 0 | 0 | 0 | 0 | .... | .... | .... | .... |
| **99-2000** | **Buffalo** | **NHL** | **12** | **1** | **4** | **5** | **4** | **0** | **0** | **0** | **10** | **10.0** | **–2** | **0** | **0.0** | **15:48** | .... | .... | .... | .... | .... | .... | .... | .... | .... |
| | Rochester | AHL | 67 | 2 | 24 | 26 | 22 | .... | .... | .... | .... | .... | .... | .... | .... | .... | 21 | 0 | 3 | 3 | 0 | .... | .... | .... | .... |
| **2000-01** | **Buffalo** | **NHL** | **8** | **0** | **0** | **0** | **2** | **0** | **0** | **0** | **7** | **0.0** | **–2** | **0** | **0.0** | **15:40** | .... | .... | .... | .... | .... | .... | .... | .... | .... |
| | Rochester | AHL | 65 | 7 | 25 | 32 | 24 | .... | .... | .... | .... | .... | .... | .... | .... | .... | 4 | 0 | 1 | 1 | 0 | .... | .... | .... | .... |
| **2001-02** | **Buffalo** | **NHL** | **29** | **3** | **3** | **6** | **12** | **0** | **0** | **0** | **30** | **10.0** | **0** | **1** | **0.0** | **15:18** | .... | .... | .... | .... | .... | .... | .... | .... | .... |
| | Rochester | AHL | 45 | 2 | 35 | 37 | 13 | .... | .... | .... | .... | .... | .... | .... | .... | .... | .... | .... | .... | .... | .... | .... | .... | .... | .... |
| **2002-03** | **Buffalo** | **NHL** | **65** | **2** | **17** | **19** | **20** | **0** | **0** | **1** | **90** | **2.2** | **–8** | **1** | **0.0** | **18:40** | .... | .... | .... | .... | .... | .... | .... | .... | .... |
| **2003-04** | **Buffalo** | **NHL** | **53** | **3** | **8** | **11** | **12** | **0** | **0** | **0** | **45** | **6.7** | **–8** | **0** | **0.0** | **16:02** | .... | .... | .... | .... | .... | .... | .... | .... | .... |
| 2004-05 | Jokerit Helsinki | Finland | 44 | 12 | 13 | 25 | 12 | .... | .... | .... | .... | .... | .... | .... | .... | .... | 12 | 3 | 4 | 7 | 6 | .... | .... | .... | .... |
| **2005-06** | **Buffalo** | **NHL** | **79** | **12** | **32** | **44** | **16** | **5** | **0** | **5** | **105** | **11.4** | **–14** | **0** | **0.0** | **17:43** | **18** | **0** | **6** | **6** | **12** | **0** | **0** | **0** | **20:29** |
| **2006-07** | **Buffalo** | **NHL** | **82** | **6** | **42** | **48** | **35** | **1** | **0** | **1** | **92** | **6.5** | **28** | **0** | **0.0** | **21:53** | **16** | **3** | **4** | **7** | **14** | **2** | **0** | **0** | **21:39** |
| **2007-08** | **Buffalo** | **NHL** | **63** | **5** | **38** | **43** | **12** | **3** | **0** | **0** | **102** | **4.9** | **–1** | **0** | **0.0** | **25:06** | .... | .... | .... | .... | .... | .... | .... | .... | .... |
| | **San Jose** | **NHL** | **20** | **3** | **16** | **19** | **8** | **2** | **0** | **0** | **40** | **7.5** | **9** | **0** | **0.0** | **25:07** | **13** | **1** | **6** | **7** | **4** | **0** | **0** | **0** | **29:19** |
| **2008-09** | **Chicago** | **NHL** | **82** | **7** | **45** | **52** | **22** | **4** | **0** | **1** | **108** | **6.5** | **5** | **0** | **0.0** | **22:34** | **17** | **2** | **8** | **10** | **0** | **2** | **0** | **0** | **20:29** |
| | **NHL Totals** | | **493** | **42** | **205** | **247** | **143** | **15** | **0** | **8** | **629** | **6.7** | | **2** | **0.0** | **20:11** | **64** | **6** | **24** | **30** | **30** | **4** | **0** | **0** | **22:34** |

OHL First All-Star Team (1999) • OHL MVP (1999) • Canadian Major Junior First All-Star Team (1999) • Canadian Major Junior Player of the Year (1999) • George Parsons Trophy (Memorial Cup Tournament - Most Sportsmanlike Player) (1999) • NHL Second All-Star Team (2008)

Played in NHL All-Star Game (2007, 2008, 2009)

Signed as a free agent by **Jokerit Helsinki** (Finland), October 19, 2004. Traded to **San Jose** by **Buffalo** with Buffalo's 7th round choice (Drew Daniels) in 2008 Entry Draft for Steve Bernier and San Jose's 1st round choice (Tyler Ennis) in 2008 Entry Draft, February 26, 2008. Signed as a free agent by **Chicago**, July 1, 2008.

### CAMPBELL, Darcy

(KAM-behl, DAHR-see)

Defense. Shoots left. 6'1", 180 lbs. Born, Airdrie, Alta., May 12, 1984.

| Season | Club | League | GP | G | A | Pts | PIM | PP | SH | GW | S | % | +/- | TF | F% | Min | GP | G | A | Pts | PIM | PP | SH | GW | Min |
|---|---|---|---|---|---|---|---|---|---|---|---|---|---|---|---|---|---|---|---|---|---|---|---|---|---|
| 2002-03 | Canmore Eagles | AJHL | 62 | 10 | 37 | 47 | 112 | .... | .... | .... | .... | .... | .... | .... | .... | .... | 9 | 2 | 2 | 4 | 6 | .... | .... | .... | .... |
| 2003-04 | Canmore Eagles | AJHL | 24 | 6 | 15 | 21 | 25 | .... | .... | .... | .... | .... | .... | .... | .... | .... | 14 | 2 | 7 | 9 | 2 | .... | .... | .... | .... |
| | Olds Grizzlys | AJHL | 36 | 9 | 19 | 28 | 40 | .... | .... | .... | .... | .... | .... | .... | .... | .... | .... | .... | .... | .... | .... | .... | .... | .... | .... |
| 2004-05 | Alaska | CCHA | 37 | 2 | 10 | 12 | 56 | .... | .... | .... | .... | .... | .... | .... | .... | .... | .... | .... | .... | .... | .... | .... | .... | .... | .... |
| 2005-06 | Alaska | CCHA | 38 | 5 | 9 | 14 | 67 | .... | .... | .... | .... | .... | .... | .... | .... | .... | .... | .... | .... | .... | .... | .... | .... | .... | .... |
| **2006-07** | Alaska | CCHA | 39 | 4 | 20 | 24 | 54 | .... | .... | .... | .... | .... | .... | .... | .... | .... | .... | .... | .... | .... | .... | .... | .... | .... | .... |
| | **Columbus** | **NHL** | **1** | **0** | **0** | **0** | **0** | **0** | **0** | **0** | **0** | **0.0** | **0** | **0** | **0.0** | **5:41** | .... | .... | .... | .... | .... | .... | .... | .... | .... |
| 2007-08 | Syracuse Crunch | AHL | 28 | 1 | 5 | 6 | 26 | .... | .... | .... | .... | .... | .... | .... | .... | .... | .... | .... | .... | .... | .... | .... | .... | .... | .... |
| | Lake Erie | AHL | 8 | 1 | 0 | 1 | 2 | .... | .... | .... | .... | .... | .... | .... | .... | .... | .... | .... | .... | .... | .... | .... | .... | .... | .... |
| 2008-09 | Lake Erie | AHL | 74 | 7 | 8 | 15 | 61 | .... | .... | .... | .... | .... | .... | .... | .... | .... | .... | .... | .... | .... | .... | .... | .... | .... | .... |
| | **NHL Totals** | | **1** | **0** | **0** | **0** | **0** | **0** | **0** | **0** | **0** | **0.0** | | **0** | **0.0** | **5:41** | .... | .... | .... | .... | .... | .... | .... | .... | .... |

AJHL South All-Rookie Team (2003) • AJHL South First All-Star Team (2004)

Signed as a free agent by **Columbus**, March 24, 2007. Traded to **Colorado** by **Columbus** with Phillipe Dupuis for Mark Rycroft, January 22, 2008.

### CAMPBELL, Gregory

(KAM-behl, GREH-goh-ree) **FLA.**

Left wing. Shoots left. 6', 197 lbs. Born, London, Ont., December 17, 1983. Florida's 4th choice, 67th overall, in 2002 Entry Draft.

| Season | Club | League | GP | G | A | Pts | PIM | PP | SH | GW | S | % | +/- | TF | F% | Min | GP | G | A | Pts | PIM | PP | SH | GW | Min |
|---|---|---|---|---|---|---|---|---|---|---|---|---|---|---|---|---|---|---|---|---|---|---|---|---|---|
| 1998-99 | Aylmer Aces | OHA-B | 49 | 5 | 9 | 14 | 44 | .... | .... | .... | .... | .... | .... | .... | .... | .... | .... | .... | .... | .... | .... | .... | .... | .... | .... |
| 99-2000 | St. Thomas Stars | OHA-B | 51 | 12 | 8 | 20 | 51 | .... | .... | .... | .... | .... | .... | .... | .... | .... | .... | .... | .... | .... | .... | .... | .... | .... | .... |
| 2000-01 | Plymouth Whalers | OHL | 65 | 2 | 12 | 14 | 40 | .... | .... | .... | .... | .... | .... | .... | .... | .... | 10 | 0 | 0 | 0 | 7 | .... | .... | .... | .... |
| 2001-02 | Plymouth Whalers | OHL | 65 | 17 | 36 | 53 | 105 | .... | .... | .... | .... | .... | .... | .... | .... | .... | 6 | 0 | 2 | 2 | 13 | .... | .... | .... | .... |
| 2002-03 | Kitchener Rangers | OHL | 55 | 23 | 33 | 56 | 116 | .... | .... | .... | .... | .... | .... | .... | .... | .... | 21 | 15 | 4 | 19 | 34 | .... | .... | .... | .... |
| **2003-04** | **Florida** | **NHL** | **2** | **0** | **0** | **0** | **5** | **0** | **0** | **0** | **0** | **0.0** | **–1** | **1** | **0.0** | **9:09** | .... | .... | .... | .... | .... | .... | .... | .... | .... |
| | San Antonio | AHL | 76 | 13 | 16 | 29 | 73 | .... | .... | .... | .... | .... | .... | .... | .... | .... | .... | .... | .... | .... | .... | .... | .... | .... | .... |
| 2004-05 | San Antonio | AHL | 70 | 12 | 16 | 28 | 113 | .... | .... | .... | .... | .... | .... | .... | .... | .... | .... | .... | .... | .... | .... | .... | .... | .... | .... |
| **2005-06** | **Florida** | **NHL** | **64** | **3** | **6** | **9** | **40** | **0** | **0** | **0** | **59** | **5.1** | **–11** | **38** | **34.2** | **8:38** | .... | .... | .... | .... | .... | .... | .... | .... | .... |
| | Rochester | AHL | 11 | 3 | 3 | 6 | 30 | .... | .... | .... | .... | .... | .... | .... | .... | .... | .... | .... | .... | .... | .... | .... | .... | .... | .... |
| **2006-07** | **Florida** | **NHL** | **79** | **6** | **3** | **9** | **66** | **0** | **1** | **0** | **103** | **5.8** | **–10** | **588** | **45.2** | **10:34** | .... | .... | .... | .... | .... | .... | .... | .... | .... |
| **2007-08** | **Florida** | **NHL** | **81** | **5** | **13** | **18** | **72** | **0** | **2** | **1** | **113** | **4.4** | **–12** | **460** | **51.1** | **12:27** | .... | .... | .... | .... | .... | .... | .... | .... | .... |
| **2008-09** | **Florida** | **NHL** | **77** | **13** | **19** | **32** | **76** | **1** | **0** | **1** | **135** | **9.6** | **0** | **1018** | **50.0** | **16:47** | .... | .... | .... | .... | .... | .... | .... | .... | .... |
| | **NHL Totals** | | **303** | **27** | **41** | **68** | **259** | **1** | **3** | **2** | **410** | **6.6** | | **2105** | **48.6** | **12:14** | .... | .... | .... | .... | .... | .... | .... | .... | .... |

Memorial Cup Tournament All-Star Team (2003) • George Parsons Trophy (Memorial Cup Tournament - Most Sportsmanlike Player) (2003) • Ed Chynoweth Trophy (Memorial Cup Tournament - Leading Scorer) (2003)

### CAMPOLI, Chris

(kam-POH-lee, KRIHS) **OTT.**

Defense. Shoots left. 6', 190 lbs. Born, North York, Ont., July 9, 1984. NY Islanders' 8th choice, 227th overall, in 2004 Entry Draft.

| Season | Club | League | GP | G | A | Pts | PIM | PP | SH | GW | S | % | +/- | TF | F% | Min | GP | G | A | Pts | PIM | PP | SH | GW | Min |
|---|---|---|---|---|---|---|---|---|---|---|---|---|---|---|---|---|---|---|---|---|---|---|---|---|---|
| 2001-02 | Erie Otters | OHL | 68 | 2 | 24 | 26 | 117 | .... | .... | .... | .... | .... | .... | .... | .... | .... | 20 | 0 | 5 | 5 | 18 | .... | .... | .... | .... |
| 2002-03 | Erie Otters | OHL | 60 | 8 | 40 | 48 | 82 | .... | .... | .... | .... | .... | .... | .... | .... | .... | .... | .... | .... | .... | .... | .... | .... | .... | .... |
| 2003-04 | Erie Otters | OHL | 67 | 20 | 46 | 66 | 66 | .... | .... | .... | .... | .... | .... | .... | .... | .... | 8 | 0 | 6 | 6 | 16 | .... | .... | .... | .... |
| 2004-05 | Bridgeport | AHL | 79 | 15 | 34 | 49 | 78 | .... | .... | .... | .... | .... | .... | .... | .... | .... | .... | .... | .... | .... | .... | .... | .... | .... | .... |
| **2005-06** | **NY Islanders** | **NHL** | **80** | **9** | **25** | **34** | **46** | **2** | **0** | **2** | **123** | **7.3** | **–16** | **0** | **0.0** | **18:32** | .... | .... | .... | .... | .... | .... | .... | .... | .... |
| **2006-07** | **NY Islanders** | **NHL** | **51** | **1** | **13** | **14** | **23** | **0** | **0** | **0** | **41** | **2.4** | **–3** | **0** | **0.0** | **14:50** | **5** | **1** | **1** | **2** | **2** | **0** | **0** | **0** | **13:30** |
| | Bridgeport | AHL | 15 | 3 | 3 | 6 | 8 | .... | .... | .... | .... | .... | .... | .... | .... | .... | .... | .... | .... | .... | .... | .... | .... | .... | .... |
| **2007-08** | **NY Islanders** | **NHL** | **46** | **4** | **14** | **18** | **16** | **2** | **1** | **0** | **68** | **5.9** | **–1** | **0** | **0.0** | **19:09** | .... | .... | .... | .... | .... | .... | .... | .... | .... |
| **2008-09** | **NY Islanders** | **NHL** | **51** | **6** | **11** | **17** | **43** | **0** | **1** | **2** | **53** | **11.3** | **–20** | **0** | **0.0** | **19:50** | .... | .... | .... | .... | .... | .... | .... | .... | .... |
| | **Ottawa** | **NHL** | **25** | **5** | **8** | **13** | **12** | **2** | **0** | **2** | **38** | **13.2** | **4** | **0** | **0.0** | **18:58** | .... | .... | .... | .... | .... | .... | .... | .... | .... |
| | **NHL Totals** | | **253** | **25** | **71** | **96** | **140** | **6** | **2** | **6** | **323** | **7.7** | | **0** | **0.0** | **18:12** | **5** | **1** | **1** | **2** | **2** | **0** | **0** | **0** | **13:30** |

OHL Humanitarian Player of the Year (2004) • Canadian Major Junior Humanitarian Player of the Year (2004) • AHL All-Rookie Team (2005)

Traded to **Ottawa** by **NY Islanders** with Mike Comrie for Dean McAmmond and San Jose's 1st round choice (previously acquired, later traded to Columbus, later traded to Anahaim – Anaheim selected Kyle Palmieri) in 2009 Entry Draft, February 20, 2009.

### CAPUTI, Luca

(ka-POO-tee, LOO-ka) **PIT.**

Left wing. Shoots left. 6'2", 184 lbs. Born, Toronto, Ont., October 1, 1988. Pittsburgh's 5th choice, 111th overall, in 2007 Entry Draft.

| Season | Club | League | GP | G | A | Pts | PIM | PP | SH | GW | S | % | +/- | TF | F% | Min | GP | G | A | Pts | PIM | PP | SH | GW | Min |
|---|---|---|---|---|---|---|---|---|---|---|---|---|---|---|---|---|---|---|---|---|---|---|---|---|---|
| 2003-04 | Tor. Jr. Canadiens | GTHL | 53 | 52 | 55 | 107 | 127 | .... | .... | .... | .... | .... | .... | .... | .... | .... | .... | .... | .... | .... | .... | .... | .... | .... | .... |
| 2004-05 | Mississauga | OHL | 48 | 5 | 1 | 6 | 25 | .... | .... | .... | .... | .... | .... | .... | .... | .... | .... | .... | .... | .... | .... | .... | .... | .... | .... |
| 2005-06 | Mississauga | OHL | 32 | 3 | 0 | 3 | 43 | .... | .... | .... | .... | .... | .... | .... | .... | .... | .... | .... | .... | .... | .... | .... | .... | .... | .... |
| 2006-07 | Mississauga | OHL | 68 | 27 | 38 | 65 | 66 | .... | .... | .... | .... | .... | .... | .... | .... | .... | 5 | 2 | 1 | 3 | 0 | .... | .... | .... | .... |
| 2007-08 | Niagara Ice Dogs | OHL | 66 | 51 | 60 | 111 | 107 | .... | .... | .... | .... | .... | .... | .... | .... | .... | 10 | 8 | 9 | 17 | 14 | .... | .... | .... | .... |
| | Wilkes-Barre | AHL | .... | .... | .... | .... | .... | .... | .... | .... | .... | .... | .... | .... | .... | .... | 19 | 4 | 4 | 8 | 8 | .... | .... | .... | .... |

| Season | Club | League | GP | G | A | Pts | PIM | PP | SH | GW | S | % | +/- | TF | F% | Min | Playoffs GP | G | A | Pts | PIM | PP | SH | GW | Min |
|---|---|---|---|---|---|---|---|---|---|---|---|---|---|---|---|---|---|---|---|---|---|---|---|---|---|
| **2008-09** | **Pittsburgh** | **NHL** | **5** | **1** | **0** | **1** | **4** | **0** | **0** | **0** | **7** | **14.3** | **–1** | **0** | **0.0** | **10:16** | .... | .... | .... | .... | .... | .... | .... | .... | .... |
| | Wilkes-Barre | AHL | 66 | 18 | 27 | 45 | 45 | .... | .... | .... | .... | .... | .... | .... | .... | .... | 12 | 3 | 5 | 8 | 10 | .... | .... | .... | .... |
| | Wheeling Nailers | ECHL | 3 | 2 | 1 | 3 | 0 | .... | .... | .... | .... | .... | .... | .... | .... | .... | .... | .... | .... | .... | .... | .... | .... | .... | .... |
| | **NHL Totals** | | **5** | **1** | **0** | **1** | **4** | **0** | **0** | **0** | **7** | **14.3** | | **0** | **0.0** | **10:16** | .... | .... | .... | .... | .... | .... | .... | .... | .... |

OHL Second All-Star Team (2008)

## CARCILLO, Daniel
(KAR-sihl-oh, DAN-yuhl) **PHI.**

Left wing. Shoots left. 6', 205 lbs. Born, King City, Ont., January 28, 1985. Pittsburgh's 4th choice, 73rd overall, in 2003 Entry Draft.

| Season | Club | League | GP | G | A | Pts | PIM | PP | SH | GW | S | % | +/- | TF | F% | Min | Playoffs GP | G | A | Pts | PIM | PP | SH | GW | Min |
|---|---|---|---|---|---|---|---|---|---|---|---|---|---|---|---|---|---|---|---|---|---|---|---|---|---|
| 2001-02 | Milton Merchants | OHA-B | 47 | 15 | 16 | 31 | 162 | .... | .... | .... | .... | .... | .... | .... | .... | .... | .... | .... | .... | .... | .... | .... | .... | .... | .... |
| 2002-03 | Sarnia Sting | OHL | 68 | 29 | 37 | 66 | 157 | .... | .... | .... | .... | .... | .... | .... | .... | .... | 6 | 0 | 4 | 4 | 14 | .... | .... | .... | .... |
| 2003-04 | Sarnia Sting | OHL | 61 | 30 | 29 | 59 | 148 | .... | .... | .... | .... | .... | .... | .... | .... | .... | 4 | 1 | 2 | 3 | 12 | .... | .... | .... | .... |
| 2004-05 | Sarnia Sting | OHL | 12 | 2 | 7 | 9 | 40 | .... | .... | .... | .... | .... | .... | .... | .... | .... | .... | .... | .... | .... | .... | .... | .... | .... | .... |
| | Mississauga | OHL | 20 | 8 | 10 | 18 | 75 | .... | .... | .... | .... | .... | .... | .... | .... | .... | 5 | 3 | 1 | 4 | 18 | .... | .... | .... | .... |
| 2005-06 | Wilkes-Barre | AHL | 51 | 11 | 13 | 24 | 311 | .... | .... | .... | .... | .... | .... | .... | .... | .... | 11 | 1 | 0 | 1 | 47 | .... | .... | .... | .... |
| | Wheeling Nailers | ECHL | 6 | 3 | 2 | 5 | 32 | .... | .... | .... | .... | .... | .... | .... | .... | .... | .... | .... | .... | .... | .... | .... | .... | .... | .... |
| **2006-07** | Wilkes-Barre | AHL | 52 | 21 | 9 | 30 | 183 | .... | .... | .... | .... | .... | .... | .... | .... | .... | .... | .... | .... | .... | .... | .... | .... | .... | .... |
| | **Phoenix** | **NHL** | **18** | **4** | **3** | **7** | **74** | **3** | **0** | **0** | **32** | **12.5** | **–7** | **0** | **0.0** | **14:56** | .... | .... | .... | .... | .... | .... | .... | .... | .... |
| **2007-08** | **Phoenix** | **NHL** | **57** | **13** | **11** | **24** | ***324** | **3** | **0** | **1** | **106** | **12.3** | **1** | **5** | **80.0** | **12:43** | .... | .... | .... | .... | .... | .... | .... | .... | .... |
| | San Antonio | AHL | 5 | 2 | 1 | 3 | 16 | .... | .... | .... | .... | .... | .... | .... | .... | .... | .... | .... | .... | .... | .... | .... | .... | .... | .... |
| **2008-09** | **Phoenix** | **NHL** | **54** | **3** | **7** | **10** | ***174** | **2** | **0** | **0** | **95** | **3.2** | **–13** | **18** | **55.6** | **11:59** | .... | .... | .... | .... | .... | .... | .... | .... | .... |
| | **Philadelphia** | **NHL** | **20** | **0** | **4** | **4** | ***80** | **0** | **0** | **0** | **35** | **0.0** | **–2** | **2** | **100.0** | **10:16** | **5** | **1** | **1** | **2** | **5** | **0** | **0** | **0** | **8:11** |
| | **NHL Totals** | | **149** | **20** | **25** | **45** | **652** | **8** | **0** | **1** | **268** | **7.5** | | **25** | **64.0** | **12:23** | **5** | **1** | **1** | **2** | **5** | **0** | **0** | **0** | **8:11** |

Traded to **Phoenix** by **Pittsburgh** with Pittsburgh's 3rd round choice (later traded to NY Rangers - NY Rangers selected Tomas Kundratek) in 2008 Entry Draft for Georges Laraque, February 27, 2007. Traded to **Philadelphia** by **Phoenix** for Scottie Upshall and Philadelphia's 2nd round choice in 2011 Entry Draft, March 4, 2009.

## CARD, Mike
(KARD, MIGHK)

Defense. Shoots right. 6'1", 201 lbs. Born, Kitchener, Ont., February 18, 1986. Buffalo's 7th choice, 241st overall, in 2004 Entry Draft.

| Season | Club | League | GP | G | A | Pts | PIM | PP | SH | GW | S | % | +/- | TF | F% | Min | Playoffs GP | G | A | Pts | PIM | PP | SH | GW | Min |
|---|---|---|---|---|---|---|---|---|---|---|---|---|---|---|---|---|---|---|---|---|---|---|---|---|---|
| 2002-03 | Kelowna Rockets | WHL | 61 | 7 | 22 | 29 | 41 | .... | .... | .... | .... | .... | .... | .... | .... | .... | 19 | 2 | 6 | 8 | 12 | .... | .... | .... | .... |
| 2003-04 | Kelowna Rockets | WHL | 72 | 6 | 12 | 18 | 47 | .... | .... | .... | .... | .... | .... | .... | .... | .... | 17 | 2 | 4 | 6 | 20 | .... | .... | .... | .... |
| 2004-05 | Kelowna Rockets | WHL | 72 | 10 | 35 | 45 | 85 | .... | .... | .... | .... | .... | .... | .... | .... | .... | 24 | 2 | 5 | 7 | 38 | .... | .... | .... | .... |
| 2005-06 | Kelowna Rockets | WHL | 64 | 12 | 43 | 55 | 103 | .... | .... | .... | .... | .... | .... | .... | .... | .... | 12 | 0 | 3 | 3 | 8 | .... | .... | .... | .... |
| **2006-07** | **Buffalo** | **NHL** | **4** | **0** | **0** | **0** | **0** | **0** | **0** | **0** | **0** | **0.0** | **0** | **0** | **0.0** | **4:34** | .... | .... | .... | .... | .... | .... | .... | .... | .... |
| | Rochester | AHL | 50 | 1 | 8 | 9 | 38 | .... | .... | .... | .... | .... | .... | .... | .... | .... | 6 | 0 | 0 | 0 | 8 | .... | .... | .... | .... |
| | Florida Everblades | ECHL | 6 | 1 | 3 | 4 | 2 | .... | .... | .... | .... | .... | .... | .... | .... | .... | 9 | 1 | 4 | 5 | 14 | .... | .... | .... | .... |
| 2007-08 | Rochester | AHL | 23 | 1 | 4 | 5 | 32 | .... | .... | .... | .... | .... | .... | .... | .... | .... | .... | .... | .... | .... | .... | .... | .... | .... | .... |
| 2008-09 | Portland Pirates | AHL | 19 | 0 | 1 | 1 | 20 | .... | .... | .... | .... | .... | .... | .... | .... | .... | .... | .... | .... | .... | .... | .... | .... | .... | .... |
| | **NHL Totals** | | **4** | **0** | **0** | **0** | **0** | **0** | **0** | **0** | **0** | **0.0** | | **0** | **0.0** | **4:34** | .... | .... | .... | .... | .... | .... | .... | .... | .... |

• Missed majority of 2008-09 season recovering from head injury.

## CARKNER, Matt
(KARK-nehr, MAT) **OTT.**

Defense. Shoots right. 6'4", 226 lbs. Born, Winchester, Ont., November 3, 1980. Montreal's 2nd choice, 58th overall, in 1999 Entry Draft.

| Season | Club | League | GP | G | A | Pts | PIM | PP | SH | GW | S | % | +/- | TF | F% | Min | Playoffs GP | G | A | Pts | PIM | PP | SH | GW | Min |
|---|---|---|---|---|---|---|---|---|---|---|---|---|---|---|---|---|---|---|---|---|---|---|---|---|---|
| 1996-97 | Winchester | OHA-B | 29 | 1 | 18 | 19 | .... | .... | .... | .... | .... | .... | .... | .... | .... | .... | .... | .... | .... | .... | .... | .... | .... | .... | .... |
| 1997-98 | Peterborough | OHL | 57 | 0 | 6 | 6 | 121 | .... | .... | .... | .... | .... | .... | .... | .... | .... | 4 | 0 | 0 | 0 | 2 | .... | .... | .... | .... |
| 1998-99 | Peterborough | OHL | 60 | 2 | 16 | 18 | 173 | .... | .... | .... | .... | .... | .... | .... | .... | .... | 5 | 0 | 0 | 0 | 20 | .... | .... | .... | .... |
| 99-2000 | Peterborough | OHL | 62 | 3 | 13 | 16 | 177 | .... | .... | .... | .... | .... | .... | .... | .... | .... | 5 | 0 | 1 | 1 | 6 | .... | .... | .... | .... |
| 2000-01 | Peterborough | OHL | 53 | 8 | 8 | 16 | 128 | .... | .... | .... | .... | .... | .... | .... | .... | .... | 7 | 0 | 3 | 3 | 25 | .... | .... | .... | .... |
| 2001-02 | Cleveland Barons | AHL | 74 | 0 | 3 | 3 | 335 | .... | .... | .... | .... | .... | .... | .... | .... | .... | .... | .... | .... | .... | .... | .... | .... | .... | .... |
| 2002-03 | Cleveland Barons | AHL | 39 | 1 | 4 | 5 | 104 | .... | .... | .... | .... | .... | .... | .... | .... | .... | .... | .... | .... | .... | .... | .... | .... | .... | .... |
| 2003-04 | Cleveland Barons | AHL | 60 | 2 | 11 | 13 | 115 | .... | .... | .... | .... | .... | .... | .... | .... | .... | 9 | 0 | 3 | 3 | 39 | .... | .... | .... | .... |
| 2004-05 | Cleveland Barons | AHL | 73 | 0 | 10 | 10 | 192 | .... | .... | .... | .... | .... | .... | .... | .... | .... | .... | .... | .... | .... | .... | .... | .... | .... | .... |
| **2005-06** | **San Jose** | **NHL** | **1** | **0** | **1** | **1** | **2** | **0** | **0** | **0** | **0** | **0.0** | **0** | **0** | **0.0** | **6:01** | .... | .... | .... | .... | .... | .... | .... | .... | .... |
| | Cleveland Barons | AHL | 69 | 10 | 21 | 31 | 202 | .... | .... | .... | .... | .... | .... | .... | .... | .... | .... | .... | .... | .... | .... | .... | .... | .... | .... |
| 2006-07 | Wilkes-Barre | AHL | 75 | 6 | 24 | 30 | 167 | .... | .... | .... | .... | .... | .... | .... | .... | .... | 8 | 1 | 0 | 1 | 19 | .... | .... | .... | .... |
| 2007-08 | Binghamton | AHL | 67 | 10 | 15 | 25 | 218 | .... | .... | .... | .... | .... | .... | .... | .... | .... | .... | .... | .... | .... | .... | .... | .... | .... | .... |
| **2008-09** | **Ottawa** | **NHL** | **1** | **0** | **0** | **0** | **0** | **0** | **0** | **0** | **0** | **0.0** | **0** | **0** | **0.0** | **4:08** | .... | .... | .... | .... | .... | .... | .... | .... | .... |
| | Binghamton | AHL | 67 | 3 | 18 | 21 | 210 | .... | .... | .... | .... | .... | .... | .... | .... | .... | .... | .... | .... | .... | .... | .... | .... | .... | .... |
| | **NHL Totals** | | **2** | **0** | **1** | **1** | **2** | **0** | **0** | **0** | **0** | **0.0** | | **0** | **0.0** | **5:05** | .... | .... | .... | .... | .... | .... | .... | .... | .... |

Yanick Dupre Memorial Award (AHL - Outstanding Humanitarian Contribution) (2007)

Signed as a free agent by **San Jose**, June 6, 2001. • Missed majority of 2002-03 season recovering from knee injury suffered in game vs. Utah (AHL), January 4, 2003. Signed as a free agent by **Pittsburgh**, July 23, 2006. Signed as a free agent by **Ottawa**, July 3, 2007.

## CARLE, Matt
(KAHRL, MAT) **PHI.**

Defense. Shoots left. 6', 205 lbs. Born, Anchorage, AK, September 25, 1984. San Jose's 4th choice, 47th overall, in 2003 Entry Draft.

| Season | Club | League | GP | G | A | Pts | PIM | PP | SH | GW | S | % | +/- | TF | F% | Min | Playoffs GP | G | A | Pts | PIM | PP | SH | GW | Min |
|---|---|---|---|---|---|---|---|---|---|---|---|---|---|---|---|---|---|---|---|---|---|---|---|---|---|
| 99-2000 | Alaska All-Stars | AASHA | 42 | 14 | 28 | 42 | .... | .... | .... | .... | .... | .... | .... | .... | .... | .... | .... | .... | .... | .... | .... | .... | .... | .... | .... |
| 2000-01 | USNTDP | U-17 | 13 | 0 | 1 | 1 | .... | .... | .... | .... | .... | .... | .... | .... | .... | .... | .... | .... | .... | .... | .... | .... | .... | .... | .... |
| | USNTDP | NAHL | 55 | 1 | 4 | 5 | 33 | .... | .... | .... | .... | .... | .... | .... | .... | .... | .... | .... | .... | .... | .... | .... | .... | .... | .... |
| 2001-02 | USNTDP | U-18 | 45 | 3 | 13 | 16 | 30 | .... | .... | .... | .... | .... | .... | .... | .... | .... | .... | .... | .... | .... | .... | .... | .... | .... | .... |
| | USNTDP | NAHL | 7 | 1 | 2 | 3 | 0 | .... | .... | .... | .... | .... | .... | .... | .... | .... | .... | .... | .... | .... | .... | .... | .... | .... | .... |
| | USNTDP | USHL | 12 | 0 | 0 | 0 | 21 | .... | .... | .... | .... | .... | .... | .... | .... | .... | .... | .... | .... | .... | .... | .... | .... | .... | .... |
| 2002-03 | River City Lancers | USHL | 59 | 12 | 30 | 42 | 98 | .... | .... | .... | .... | .... | .... | .... | .... | .... | 11 | 2 | 2 | 4 | 20 | .... | .... | .... | .... |
| 2003-04 | U. of Denver | WCHA | 30 | 5 | 20 | 25 | 33 | .... | .... | .... | .... | .... | .... | .... | .... | .... | .... | .... | .... | .... | .... | .... | .... | .... | .... |
| 2004-05 | U. of Denver | WCHA | 43 | 13 | 31 | 44 | 68 | .... | .... | .... | .... | .... | .... | .... | .... | .... | .... | .... | .... | .... | .... | .... | .... | .... | .... |
| **2005-06** | U. of Denver | WCHA | 39 | 11 | *42 | 53 | 58 | .... | .... | .... | .... | .... | .... | .... | .... | .... | .... | .... | .... | .... | .... | .... | .... | .... | .... |
| | **San Jose** | **NHL** | **12** | **3** | **3** | **6** | **14** | **2** | **0** | **1** | **11** | **27.3** | **–2** | **0** | **0.0** | **16:07** | **11** | **0** | **3** | **3** | **4** | **0** | **0** | **0** | **15:17** |
| **2006-07** | **San Jose** | **NHL** | **77** | **11** | **31** | **42** | **30** | **8** | **0** | **1** | **111** | **9.9** | **9** | **1** | **0.0** | **18:08** | **11** | **2** | **3** | **5** | **0** | **1** | **0** | **1** | **14:51** |
| | Worcester Sharks | AHL | 3 | 0 | 2 | 2 | 0 | .... | .... | .... | .... | .... | .... | .... | .... | .... | .... | .... | .... | .... | .... | .... | .... | .... | .... |
| **2007-08** | **San Jose** | **NHL** | **62** | **2** | **13** | **15** | **26** | **2** | **0** | **1** | **63** | **3.2** | **–8** | **1** | **100.0** | **16:33** | **11** | **0** | **1** | **1** | **4** | **0** | **0** | **0** | **13:56** |
| **2008-09** | **Tampa Bay** | **NHL** | **12** | **1** | **1** | **2** | **6** | **0** | **0** | **0** | **13** | **7.7** | **1** | **0** | **0.0** | **21:58** | .... | .... | .... | .... | .... | .... | .... | .... | .... |
| | **Philadelphia** | **NHL** | **64** | **4** | **20** | **24** | **16** | **0** | **0** | **2** | **72** | **5.6** | **2** | **0** | **0.0** | **21:17** | **6** | **0** | **3** | **3** | **4** | **0** | **0** | **0** | **22:15** |
| | **NHL Totals** | | **227** | **21** | **68** | **89** | **92** | **12** | **0** | **5** | **270** | **7.8** | | **2** | **50.0** | **18:41** | **39** | **2** | **10** | **12** | **12** | **1** | **0** | **1** | **15:51** |

USHL First All-Star Team (2003) • USHL Defenseman of the Year (2003) • WCHA All-Rookie Team (2004) • WCHA First All-Star Team (2005, 2006) • NCAA West First All-American Team (2005, 2006) • NCAA Championship All-Tournament Team (2005) • WCHA Player of the Year (2006) • Hobey Baker Memorial Award (Top U.S. Collegiate Player) (2006) • NHL All-Rookie Team (2007)

Traded to **Tampa Bay** by **San Jose** with Ty Wishart, San Jose's 1st round choice (later traded to Ottawa, later traded to NY Islanders, later traded to Columbus, later traded to Anaheim – Anaheim selected Kyle Palmieri) in 2009 Entry Draft and San Jose's 4th round choice in 2010 Entry Draft for Dan Boyle and Brad Lukowich, July 4, 2008. Traded to **Philadelphia** by **Tampa Bay** with San Jose's 3rd round choice (previously acquired, Philadelphia selected Simon Bertilsson) in 2009 Entry Draft for Steve Eminger, Steve Downie and Tampa Bay's 4th round choice (previously acquired, Tampa Bay selected Alex Hutchings) in 2009 Entry Draft, November 7, 2008.

## CARSON, Brett
(KAR-suhn, BREHT) **CAR.**

Defense. Shoots right. 6'4", 210 lbs. Born, Regina, Sask., November 29, 1985. Carolina's 4th choice, 109th overall, in 2004 Entry Draft.

| Season | Club | League | GP | G | A | Pts | PIM | PP | SH | GW | S | % | +/- | TF | F% | Min | Playoffs GP | G | A | Pts | PIM | PP | SH | GW | Min |
|---|---|---|---|---|---|---|---|---|---|---|---|---|---|---|---|---|---|---|---|---|---|---|---|---|---|
| 99-2000 | Pipestone Valley | SSMHL | 8 | 0 | 0 | 0 | 0 | .... | .... | .... | .... | .... | .... | .... | .... | .... | .... | .... | .... | .... | .... | .... | .... | .... | .... |
| 2000-01 | Pipestone Valley | SSMHL | 31 | 5 | 17 | 22 | 20 | .... | .... | .... | .... | .... | .... | .... | .... | .... | .... | .... | .... | .... | .... | .... | .... | .... | .... |
| 2001-02 | Yorkton Terriers | SMHL | 41 | 16 | 37 | 53 | 32 | .... | .... | .... | .... | .... | .... | .... | .... | .... | .... | .... | .... | .... | .... | .... | .... | .... | .... |
| | Moose Jaw | WHL | 6 | 0 | 0 | 0 | 0 | .... | .... | .... | .... | .... | .... | .... | .... | .... | 12 | 2 | 0 | 2 | 0 | .... | .... | .... | .... |
| 2002-03 | Moose Jaw | WHL | 28 | 1 | 4 | 5 | 28 | .... | .... | .... | .... | .... | .... | .... | .... | .... | .... | .... | .... | .... | .... | .... | .... | .... | .... |
| | Calgary Hitmen | WHL | 30 | 3 | 6 | 9 | 4 | .... | .... | .... | .... | .... | .... | .... | .... | .... | 5 | 2 | 1 | 3 | 0 | .... | .... | .... | .... |
| 2003-04 | Calgary Hitmen | WHL | 71 | 5 | 27 | 32 | 49 | .... | .... | .... | .... | .... | .... | .... | .... | .... | 7 | 0 | 0 | 0 | 6 | .... | .... | .... | .... |
| 2004-05 | Calgary Hitmen | WHL | 61 | 8 | 16 | 24 | 61 | .... | .... | .... | .... | .... | .... | .... | .... | .... | 8 | 2 | 2 | 4 | 8 | .... | .... | .... | .... |
| 2005-06 | Calgary Hitmen | WHL | 72 | 11 | 29 | 40 | 62 | .... | .... | .... | .... | .... | .... | .... | .... | .... | 13 | 1 | 6 | 7 | 20 | .... | .... | .... | .... |
| 2006-07 | Albany River Rats | AHL | 63 | 2 | 16 | 18 | 26 | .... | .... | .... | .... | .... | .... | .... | .... | .... | 5 | 0 | 2 | 2 | 0 | .... | .... | .... | .... |
| | Florida Everblades | ECHL | 3 | 1 | 1 | 2 | 0 | .... | .... | .... | .... | .... | .... | .... | .... | .... | .... | .... | .... | .... | .... | .... | .... | .... | .... |
| 2007-08 | Albany River Rats | AHL | 77 | 2 | 22 | 24 | 32 | .... | .... | .... | .... | .... | .... | .... | .... | .... | 7 | 1 | 3 | 4 | 11 | .... | .... | .... | .... |

| | | | Regular Season | | | | | | | | | | | | | | Playoffs | | | | | | | | |
|---|---|---|---|---|---|---|---|---|---|---|---|---|---|---|---|---|---|---|---|---|---|---|---|---|---|
| Season | Club | League | GP | G | A | Pts | PIM | PP | SH | GW | S | % | +/- | TF | F% | Min | GP | G | A | Pts | PIM | PP | SH | GW | Min |
| 2008-09 | Carolina | NHL | 5 | 0 | 0 | 0 | 4 | 0 | 0 | 0 | 2 | 0.0 | –3 | 0 | 0.0 | 15:44 | .... | .... | .... | .... | .... | .... | .... | .... | .... |
| | Albany River Rats | AHL | 69 | 6 | 29 | 35 | 34 | .... | .... | .... | .... | .... | .... | .... | .... | .... | .... | .... | .... | .... | .... | .... | .... | .... | .... |
| | NHL Totals | | 5 | 0 | 0 | 0 | 4 | 0 | 0 | 0 | 2 | 0.0 | | 0 | 0.0 | 15:44 | .... | .... | .... | .... | .... | .... | .... | .... | .... |

WHL East First All-Star Team (2006)

## CARTER, Jeff

(KAHR-tuhr, JEHF) **PHI.**

Center. Shoots right. 6'3", 200 lbs. Born, London, Ont., January 1, 1985. Philadelphia's 1st choice, 11th overall, in 2003 Entry Draft.

| Season | Club | League | GP | G | A | Pts | PIM | PP | SH | GW | S | % | +/- | TF | F% | Min | GP | G | A | Pts | PIM | PP | SH | GW | Min |
|---|---|---|---|---|---|---|---|---|---|---|---|---|---|---|---|---|---|---|---|---|---|---|---|---|---|
| 2000-01 | Strathroy Rockets | OHA-B | 49 | 27 | 20 | 47 | 10 | .... | .... | .... | .... | .... | .... | .... | .... | .... | .... | .... | .... | .... | .... | .... | .... | .... | .... |
| 2001-02 | Sault Ste. Marie | OHL | 63 | 18 | 17 | 35 | 12 | .... | .... | .... | .... | .... | .... | .... | .... | .... | 4 | 0 | 0 | 0 | 2 | .... | .... | .... | .... |
| 2002-03 | Sault Ste. Marie | OHL | 61 | 35 | 36 | 71 | 55 | .... | .... | .... | .... | .... | .... | .... | .... | .... | 4 | 0 | 2 | 2 | 2 | .... | .... | .... | .... |
| 2003-04 | Sault Ste. Marie | OHL | 57 | 36 | 30 | 66 | 26 | .... | .... | .... | .... | .... | .... | .... | .... | .... | .... | .... | .... | .... | .... | .... | .... | .... | .... |
| | Philadelphia | AHL | .... | .... | .... | .... | .... | .... | .... | .... | .... | .... | .... | .... | .... | .... | 12 | 4 | 1 | 5 | 0 | .... | .... | .... | .... |
| 2004-05 | Sault Ste. Marie | OHL | 55 | 34 | 40 | 74 | 40 | .... | .... | .... | .... | .... | .... | .... | .... | .... | 7 | 5 | 5 | 10 | 6 | .... | .... | .... | .... |
| | Philadelphia | AHL | 3 | 0 | 1 | 1 | 4 | .... | .... | .... | .... | .... | .... | .... | .... | .... | 21 | 12 | 11 | 23 | 12 | .... | .... | .... | .... |
| 2005-06 | Philadelphia | NHL | 81 | 23 | 19 | 42 | 40 | 6 | 2 | 7 | 189 | 12.2 | 10 | 683 | 48.2 | 12:04 | 6 | 0 | 0 | 0 | 10 | 0 | 0 | 0 | 13:04 |
| 2006-07 | Philadelphia | NHL | 62 | 14 | 23 | 37 | 48 | 3 | 2 | 1 | 215 | 6.5 | –17 | 1062 | 45.4 | 19:00 | .... | .... | .... | .... | .... | .... | .... | .... | .... |
| 2007-08 | Philadelphia | NHL | 82 | 29 | 24 | 53 | 55 | 7 | 2 | 5 | 260 | 11.2 | 6 | 1378 | 47.7 | 18:51 | 17 | 6 | 5 | 11 | 12 | 3 | 0 | 1 | 20:08 |
| 2008-09 | Philadelphia | NHL | 82 | 46 | 38 | 84 | 68 | 13 | 4 | 12 | 342 | 13.5 | 23 | 1725 | 48.3 | 20:57 | 6 | 1 | 0 | 1 | 8 | 0 | 0 | 0 | 20:21 |
| | NHL Totals | | 307 | 112 | 104 | 216 | 211 | 29 | 10 | 25 | 1006 | 11.1 | | 4848 | 47.5 | 17:39 | 29 | 7 | 5 | 12 | 30 | 3 | 0 | 1 | 18:43 |

OHL Second All-Star Team (2004) • OHL First All-Star Team (2005) • Canadian Major Junior Sportsman of the Year (2005) • Canadian Major Junior First All-Star Team (2005)
Played in NHL All-Star Game (2009)

## CARTER, Ryan

(KAHR-tuhr, RIGH-uhn) **ANA.**

Center. Shoots left. 6'2", 202 lbs. Born, White Bear Lake, MN, August 3, 1983.

| Season | Club | League | GP | G | A | Pts | PIM | PP | SH | GW | S | % | +/- | TF | F% | Min | GP | G | A | Pts | PIM | PP | SH | GW | Min |
|---|---|---|---|---|---|---|---|---|---|---|---|---|---|---|---|---|---|---|---|---|---|---|---|---|---|
| 2002-03 | Green Bay | USHL | 55 | 19 | 17 | 36 | 94 | .... | .... | .... | .... | .... | .... | .... | .... | .... | .... | .... | .... | .... | .... | .... | .... | .... | .... |
| 2003-04 | Green Bay | USHL | 59 | 22 | 23 | 45 | 131 | .... | .... | .... | .... | .... | .... | .... | .... | .... | .... | .... | .... | .... | .... | .... | .... | .... | .... |
| 2004-05 | Minnesota State | WCHA | 37 | 15 | 8 | 23 | 44 | .... | .... | .... | .... | .... | .... | .... | .... | .... | .... | .... | .... | .... | .... | .... | .... | .... | .... |
| 2005-06 | Minnesota State | WCHA | 39 | 19 | 16 | 35 | 71 | .... | .... | .... | .... | .... | .... | .... | .... | .... | .... | .... | .... | .... | .... | .... | .... | .... | .... |
| 2006-07 | Portland Pirates | AHL | 76 | 16 | 20 | 36 | 85 | .... | .... | .... | .... | .... | .... | .... | .... | .... | .... | .... | .... | .... | .... | .... | .... | .... | .... |
| | ♦ Anaheim | NHL | .... | .... | .... | .... | .... | .... | .... | .... | .... | .... | .... | .... | .... | .... | 4 | 0 | 0 | 0 | 0 | 0 | 0 | 0 | 3:12 |
| 2007-08 | Anaheim | NHL | 34 | 4 | 4 | 8 | 36 | 0 | 0 | 1 | 56 | 7.1 | –2 | 299 | 61.5 | 10:29 | 6 | 0 | 0 | 0 | 6 | 0 | 0 | 0 | 11:03 |
| | Portland Pirates | AHL | 13 | 3 | 2 | 5 | 38 | .... | .... | .... | .... | .... | .... | .... | .... | .... | .... | .... | .... | .... | .... | .... | .... | .... | .... |
| 2008-09 | Anaheim | NHL | 48 | 3 | 6 | 9 | 52 | 0 | 0 | 1 | 40 | 7.5 | 3 | 304 | 48.0 | 9:06 | 10 | 2 | 3 | 5 | 0 | 1 | 0 | 0 | 12:14 |
| | NHL Totals | | 82 | 7 | 10 | 17 | 88 | 0 | 0 | 2 | 96 | 7.3 | | 603 | 54.7 | 9:40 | 20 | 2 | 3 | 5 | 6 | 1 | 0 | 0 | 10:04 |

Signed as a free agent by **Anaheim**, July 12, 2006.

## CAVANAGH, Tom

(KAV-a-naw, TAWM)

Left wing. Shoots left. 6', 200 lbs. Born, Warwick, RI, March 24, 1982. San Jose's 6th choice, 182nd overall, in 2001 Entry Draft.

| Season | Club | League | GP | G | A | Pts | PIM | PP | SH | GW | S | % | +/- | TF | F% | Min | GP | G | A | Pts | PIM | PP | SH | GW | Min |
|---|---|---|---|---|---|---|---|---|---|---|---|---|---|---|---|---|---|---|---|---|---|---|---|---|---|
| 1997-98 | Toll Gate Titans | High-RI | 15 | 5 | 17 | 22 | 6 | .... | .... | .... | .... | .... | .... | .... | .... | .... | 4 | 2 | 8 | 10 | 4 | .... | .... | .... | .... |
| 1998-99 | Toll Gate Titans | High-RI | 15 | 9 | 20 | 29 | 26 | .... | .... | .... | .... | .... | .... | .... | .... | .... | 5 | 5 | 4 | 9 | 6 | .... | .... | .... | .... |
| 99-2000 | Toll Gate Titans | High-RI | 18 | 25 | 29 | *54 | 28 | .... | .... | .... | .... | .... | .... | .... | .... | .... | 5 | 0 | 12 | 12 | 9 | .... | .... | .... | .... |
| 2000-01 | Exeter | High-NH | 31 | *42 | 40 | 82 | 34 | .... | .... | .... | .... | .... | .... | .... | .... | .... | .... | .... | .... | .... | .... | .... | .... | .... | .... |
| 2001-02 | Harvard Crimson | ECAC | 34 | 8 | 17 | 25 | 4 | .... | .... | .... | .... | .... | .... | .... | .... | .... | .... | .... | .... | .... | .... | .... | .... | .... | .... |
| 2002-03 | Harvard Crimson | ECAC | 34 | 14 | 13 | 27 | 31 | .... | .... | .... | .... | .... | .... | .... | .... | .... | .... | .... | .... | .... | .... | .... | .... | .... | .... |
| 2003-04 | Harvard Crimson | ECAC | 36 | 16 | 20 | 36 | 26 | .... | .... | .... | .... | .... | .... | .... | .... | .... | .... | .... | .... | .... | .... | .... | .... | .... | .... |
| 2004-05 | Harvard Crimson | ECAC | 34 | 10 | 19 | 29 | 22 | .... | .... | .... | .... | .... | .... | .... | .... | .... | .... | .... | .... | .... | .... | .... | .... | .... | .... |
| 2005-06 | Cleveland Barons | AHL | 62 | 10 | 11 | 21 | 36 | .... | .... | .... | .... | .... | .... | .... | .... | .... | .... | .... | .... | .... | .... | .... | .... | .... | .... |
| 2006-07 | Worcester Sharks | AHL | 74 | 12 | 32 | 44 | 56 | .... | .... | .... | .... | .... | .... | .... | .... | .... | 6 | 1 | 0 | 1 | 6 | .... | .... | .... | .... |
| 2007-08 | San Jose | NHL | 1 | 0 | 1 | 1 | 0 | 0 | 0 | 0 | 0 | 0.0 | 1 | 3 | 33.3 | 13:54 | .... | .... | .... | .... | .... | .... | .... | .... | .... |
| | Worcester Sharks | AHL | 77 | 19 | 36 | 55 | 55 | .... | .... | .... | .... | .... | .... | .... | .... | .... | .... | .... | .... | .... | .... | .... | .... | .... | .... |
| 2008-09 | San Jose | NHL | 17 | 1 | 1 | 2 | 4 | 0 | 0 | 0 | 9 | 11.1 | –2 | 57 | 45.6 | 7:44 | .... | .... | .... | .... | .... | .... | .... | .... | .... |
| | Worcester Sharks | AHL | 51 | 15 | 24 | 39 | 37 | .... | .... | .... | .... | .... | .... | .... | .... | .... | 12 | 3 | 2 | 5 | 8 | .... | .... | .... | .... |
| | NHL Totals | | 18 | 1 | 2 | 3 | 4 | 0 | 0 | 0 | 9 | 11.1 | | 60 | 45.0 | 8:04 | .... | .... | .... | .... | .... | .... | .... | .... | .... |

ECAC Second All-Star Team (2005)

## CHARA, Zdeno

(CHAH-rah, z'DEHN-oh) **BOS.**

Defense. Shoots left. 6'9", 255 lbs. Born, Trencin, Czech., March 18, 1977. NY Islanders' 3rd choice, 56th overall, in 1996 Entry Draft.

| Season | Club | League | GP | G | A | Pts | PIM | PP | SH | GW | S | % | +/- | TF | F% | Min | GP | G | A | Pts | PIM | PP | SH | GW | Min |
|---|---|---|---|---|---|---|---|---|---|---|---|---|---|---|---|---|---|---|---|---|---|---|---|---|---|
| 1994-95 | Dukla Trencin U18 | Svk-U18 | 30 | 22 | 22 | 44 | 113 | .... | .... | .... | .... | .... | .... | .... | .... | .... | .... | .... | .... | .... | .... | .... | .... | .... | .... |
| | Dukla Trencin Jr. | Slovak-Jr. | 2 | 0 | 0 | 0 | 0 | .... | .... | .... | .... | .... | .... | .... | .... | .... | .... | .... | .... | .... | .... | .... | .... | .... | .... |
| 1995-96 | Dukla Trencin Jr. | Slovak-Jr. | 22 | 1 | 13 | 14 | 80 | .... | .... | .... | .... | .... | .... | .... | .... | .... | .... | .... | .... | .... | .... | .... | .... | .... | .... |
| | HK VTJ Piestany | Slovak-2 | 10 | 1 | 3 | 4 | 10 | .... | .... | .... | .... | .... | .... | .... | .... | .... | .... | .... | .... | .... | .... | .... | .... | .... | .... |
| | Sparta Jr. | CzRep-Jr. | 15 | 1 | 2 | 3 | 42 | .... | .... | .... | .... | .... | .... | .... | .... | .... | .... | .... | .... | .... | .... | .... | .... | .... | .... |
| | HC Sparta Praha | CzRep | 1 | 0 | 0 | 0 | 0 | .... | .... | .... | .... | .... | .... | .... | .... | .... | .... | .... | .... | .... | .... | .... | .... | .... | .... |
| 1996-97 | Prince George | WHL | 49 | 3 | 19 | 22 | 120 | .... | .... | .... | .... | .... | .... | .... | .... | .... | 15 | 1 | 7 | 8 | 45 | .... | .... | .... | .... |
| 1997-98 | NY Islanders | NHL | 25 | 0 | 1 | 1 | 50 | 0 | 0 | 0 | 10 | 0.0 | 1 | .... | .... | .... | .... | .... | .... | .... | .... | .... | .... | .... | .... |
| | Kentucky | AHL | 48 | 4 | 9 | 13 | 125 | .... | .... | .... | .... | .... | .... | .... | .... | .... | 1 | 0 | 0 | 0 | 4 | .... | .... | .... | .... |
| 1998-99 | NY Islanders | NHL | 59 | 2 | 6 | 8 | 83 | 0 | 1 | 0 | 56 | 3.6 | –8 | 0 | 0.0 | 18:54 | .... | .... | .... | .... | .... | .... | .... | .... | .... |
| | Lowell | AHL | 23 | 2 | 2 | 4 | 47 | .... | .... | .... | .... | .... | .... | .... | .... | .... | .... | .... | .... | .... | .... | .... | .... | .... | .... |
| 99-2000 | NY Islanders | NHL | 65 | 2 | 9 | 11 | 57 | 0 | 0 | 1 | 47 | 4.3 | –27 | 0 | 0.0 | 22:52 | .... | .... | .... | .... | .... | .... | .... | .... | .... |
| 2000-01 | NY Islanders | NHL | 82 | 2 | 7 | 9 | 157 | 0 | 1 | 0 | 83 | 2.4 | –27 | 0 | 0.0 | 22:20 | .... | .... | .... | .... | .... | .... | .... | .... | .... |
| 2001-02 | Dukla Trencin | Slovakia | 8 | 2 | 2 | 4 | 32 | .... | .... | .... | .... | .... | .... | .... | .... | .... | .... | .... | .... | .... | .... | .... | .... | .... | .... |
| | Ottawa | NHL | 75 | 10 | 13 | 23 | 156 | 4 | 1 | 2 | 105 | 9.5 | 30 | 0 | 0.0 | 22:16 | 10 | 0 | 1 | 1 | 12 | 0 | 0 | 0 | 26:07 |
| 2002-03 | Ottawa | NHL | 74 | 9 | 30 | 39 | 116 | 3 | 0 | 2 | 168 | 5.4 | 29 | 0 | 0.0 | 24:57 | 18 | 1 | 6 | 7 | 14 | 0 | 0 | 0 | 25:07 |
| 2003-04 | Ottawa | NHL | 79 | 16 | 25 | 41 | 147 | 7 | 0 | 3 | 185 | 8.6 | 33 | 0 | 0.0 | 24:38 | 7 | 1 | 1 | 2 | 8 | 0 | 0 | 0 | 24:38 |
| 2004-05 | Farjestad | Sweden | 33 | 10 | 15 | 25 | 132 | .... | .... | .... | .... | .... | .... | .... | .... | .... | 13 | 3 | 5 | 8 | 82 | .... | .... | .... | .... |
| 2005-06 | Ottawa | NHL | 71 | 16 | 27 | 43 | 135 | 10 | 1 | 3 | 212 | 7.5 | 17 | 24 | 41.7 | 27:11 | 10 | 1 | 3 | 4 | 23 | 1 | 0 | 0 | 27:32 |
| | Slovakia | Olympics | 6 | 1 | 1 | 2 | 2 | .... | .... | .... | .... | .... | .... | .... | .... | .... | .... | .... | .... | .... | .... | .... | .... | .... | .... |
| 2006-07 | Boston | NHL | 80 | 11 | 32 | 43 | 100 | 9 | 0 | 3 | 204 | 5.4 | –21 | 1 | 0.0 | 27:58 | .... | .... | .... | .... | .... | .... | .... | .... | .... |
| 2007-08 | Boston | NHL | 77 | 17 | 34 | 51 | 114 | 9 | 1 | 0 | 207 | 8.2 | 14 | 0 | 0.0 | 26:50 | 7 | 1 | 1 | 2 | 12 | 1 | 0 | 0 | 25:52 |
| 2008-09 | Boston | NHL | 80 | 19 | 31 | 50 | 95 | 11 | 0 | 3 | 216 | 8.8 | 23 | 4 | 25.0 | 26:04 | 11 | 1 | 3 | 4 | 12 | 1 | 0 | 1 | 25:11 |
| | NHL Totals | | 767 | 104 | 215 | 319 | 1210 | 53 | 5 | 17 | 1493 | 7.0 | | 29 | 37.9 | 24:33 | 63 | 5 | 15 | 20 | 81 | 3 | 0 | 1 | 25:42 |

AHL All-Rookie Team (1998) • NHL First All-Star Team (2004, 2009) • NHL Second All-Star Team (2006, 2008) • James Norris Memorial Trophy (2009)
Played in NHL All-Star Game (2003, 2007, 2008, 2009)

Traded to **Ottawa** by **NY Islanders** with Bill Muckalt and NY Islanders' 1st round choice (Jason Spezza) in 2001 Entry Draft for Alexei Yashin, June 23, 2001. Signed as a free agent by **Farjestad** (Sweden), September 24, 2004. Signed as a free agent by **Boston**, July 1, 2006.

## CHEECHOO, Jonathan

(CHEE-choo, JAWN-ah-thuhn) **S.J.**

Right wing. Shoots right. 6'1", 200 lbs. Born, Moose Factory, Ont., July 15, 1980. San Jose's 2nd choice, 29th overall, in 1998 Entry Draft.

| Season | Club | League | GP | G | A | Pts | PIM | PP | SH | GW | S | % | +/- | TF | F% | Min | GP | G | A | Pts | PIM | PP | SH | GW | Min |
|---|---|---|---|---|---|---|---|---|---|---|---|---|---|---|---|---|---|---|---|---|---|---|---|---|---|
| 1996-97 | Kitchener | OHA-B | 43 | 35 | 41 | 76 | 33 | .... | .... | .... | .... | .... | .... | .... | .... | .... | .... | .... | .... | .... | .... | .... | .... | .... | .... |
| 1997-98 | Belleville Bulls | OHL | 64 | 31 | 45 | 76 | 62 | .... | .... | .... | .... | .... | .... | .... | .... | .... | 10 | 4 | 2 | 6 | 10 | .... | .... | .... | .... |
| 1998-99 | Belleville Bulls | OHL | 63 | 35 | 47 | 82 | 74 | .... | .... | .... | .... | .... | .... | .... | .... | .... | 21 | 15 | 15 | 30 | 27 | .... | .... | .... | .... |
| 99-2000 | Belleville Bulls | OHL | 66 | 45 | 46 | 91 | 102 | .... | .... | .... | .... | .... | .... | .... | .... | .... | 16 | 5 | 12 | 17 | 16 | .... | .... | .... | .... |
| 2000-01 | Kentucky | AHL | 75 | 32 | 34 | 66 | 63 | .... | .... | .... | .... | .... | .... | .... | .... | .... | 3 | 0 | 0 | 0 | 0 | .... | .... | .... | .... |
| 2001-02 | Cleveland Barons | AHL | 53 | 21 | 25 | 46 | 54 | .... | .... | .... | .... | .... | .... | .... | .... | .... | .... | .... | .... | .... | .... | .... | .... | .... | .... |
| 2002-03 | San Jose | NHL | 66 | 9 | 7 | 16 | 39 | 0 | 0 | 3 | 94 | 9.6 | –5 | 8 | 37.5 | 10:43 | .... | .... | .... | .... | .... | .... | .... | .... | .... |
| | Cleveland Barons | AHL | 9 | 3 | 4 | 7 | 16 | .... | .... | .... | .... | .... | .... | .... | .... | .... | .... | .... | .... | .... | .... | .... | .... | .... | .... |
| 2003-04 | San Jose | NHL | 81 | 28 | 19 | 47 | 33 | 8 | 0 | 9 | 175 | 16.0 | 5 | 7 | 14.3 | 16:12 | 17 | 4 | 6 | 10 | 10 | 1 | 0 | 0 | 17:37 |
| 2004-05 | HV 71 Jonkoping | Sweden | 20 | 5 | 0 | 5 | 10 | .... | .... | .... | .... | .... | .... | .... | .... | .... | .... | .... | .... | .... | .... | .... | .... | .... | .... |
| 2005-06 | San Jose | NHL | 82 | *56 | 37 | 93 | 58 | 24 | 2 | 11 | 317 | 17.7 | 23 | 20 | 20.0 | 19:57 | 11 | 4 | 5 | 9 | 8 | 1 | 0 | 1 | 24:00 |
| 2006-07 | San Jose | NHL | 76 | 37 | 32 | 69 | 69 | 15 | 0 | 5 | 250 | 14.8 | 11 | 32 | 31.3 | 17:34 | 11 | 3 | 3 | 6 | 6 | 1 | 0 | 1 | 16:25 |

| | | | Regular Season | | | | | | | | | | | | | | Playoffs | | | | | | | | |
|---|---|---|---|---|---|---|---|---|---|---|---|---|---|---|---|---|---|---|---|---|---|---|---|---|---|
| Season | Club | League | GP | G | A | Pts | PIM | PP | SH | GW | S | % | +/- | TF | F% | Min | GP | G | A | Pts | PIM | PP | SH | GW | Min |
| **2007-08** | **San Jose** | **NHL** | **69** | **23** | **14** | **37** | **46** | **10** | **0** | **4** | **220** | **10.5** | **11** | **20** | **20.0** | **16:36** | **13** | **4** | **4** | **8** | **4** | **0** | **0** | **1** | **18:21** |
| **2008-09** | **San Jose** | **NHL** | **66** | **12** | **17** | **29** | **59** | **5** | **1** | **4** | **152** | **7.9** | **–3** | **4** | **25.0** | **15:19** | **6** | **1** | **1** | **2** | **4** | **0** | **0** | **0** | **10:10** |
| | **NHL Totals** | | **440** | **165** | **126** | **291** | **304** | **62** | **3** | **36** | **1208** | **13.7** | | **91** | **25.3** | **16:15** | **58** | **16** | **19** | **35** | **32** | **3** | **0** | **3** | **18:00** |

OHL All-Rookie Team (1998) • AHL All-Rookie Team (2001) • Maurice "Rocket" Richard Trophy (2006)

Played in NHL All-Star Game (2007)

Signed as a free agent by **Jonkoping** (Sweden), December 21, 2004.

## CHELIOS, Chris

(CHELL-EE-ohs, KRIHS)

Defense. Shoots right. 6', 191 lbs. Born, Chicago, IL, January 25, 1962. Montreal's 5th choice, 40th overall, in 1981 Entry Draft.

| Season | Club | League | GP | G | A | Pts | PIM | PP | SH | GW | S | % | +/- | TF | F% | Min | GP | G | A | Pts | PIM | PP | SH | GW | Min |
|---|---|---|---|---|---|---|---|---|---|---|---|---|---|---|---|---|---|---|---|---|---|---|---|---|---|
| 1979-80 | Moose Jaw | SJHL | 53 | 12 | 31 | 43 | 118 | .... | .... | .... | .... | .... | .... | .... | .... | .... | .... | .... | .... | .... | .... | .... | .... | .... | .... |
| 1980-81 | Moose Jaw | SJHL | 54 | 23 | 64 | 87 | 175 | .... | .... | .... | .... | .... | .... | .... | .... | .... | .... | .... | .... | .... | .... | .... | .... | .... | .... |
| 1981-82 | U. of Wisconsin | WCHA | 43 | 6 | 43 | 49 | 50 | .... | .... | .... | .... | .... | .... | .... | .... | .... | .... | .... | .... | .... | .... | .... | .... | .... | .... |
| 1982-83 | U. of Wisconsin | WCHA | 26 | 9 | 17 | 26 | 50 | .... | .... | .... | .... | .... | .... | .... | .... | .... | .... | .... | .... | .... | .... | .... | .... | .... | .... |
| **1983-84** | United States | Nat-Tm | 60 | 14 | 35 | 49 | 58 | .... | .... | .... | .... | .... | .... | .... | .... | .... | .... | .... | .... | .... | .... | .... | .... | .... | .... |
| | United States | Olympics | 6 | 0 | 4 | 4 | 8 | .... | .... | .... | .... | .... | .... | .... | .... | .... | .... | .... | .... | .... | .... | .... | .... | .... | .... |
| | **Montreal** | **NHL** | **12** | **0** | **2** | **2** | **12** | **0** | **0** | **0** | **23** | **0.0** | **–5** | .... | .... | .... | **15** | **1** | **9** | **10** | **17** | **1** | **0** | **0** | .... |
| **1984-85** | **Montreal** | **NHL** | **74** | **9** | **55** | **64** | **87** | **2** | **1** | **0** | **199** | **4.5** | **11** | .... | .... | .... | **9** | **2** | **8** | **10** | **17** | **2** | **0** | **0** | .... |
| **1985-86 ♦** | **Montreal** | **NHL** | **41** | **8** | **26** | **34** | **67** | **2** | **0** | **0** | **101** | **7.9** | **4** | .... | .... | .... | **20** | **2** | **9** | **11** | **49** | **1** | **0** | **0** | .... |
| **1986-87** | **Montreal** | **NHL** | **71** | **11** | **33** | **44** | **124** | **6** | **0** | **2** | **141** | **7.8** | **–5** | .... | .... | .... | **17** | **4** | **9** | **13** | **38** | **2** | **1** | **0** | .... |
| **1987-88** | **Montreal** | **NHL** | **71** | **20** | **41** | **61** | **172** | **10** | **1** | **5** | **199** | **10.1** | **14** | .... | .... | .... | **11** | **3** | **1** | **4** | **29** | **1** | **0** | **0** | .... |
| **1988-89** | **Montreal** | **NHL** | **80** | **15** | **58** | **73** | **185** | **8** | **0** | **6** | **206** | **7.3** | **35** | .... | .... | .... | **21** | **4** | **15** | **19** | **28** | **1** | **0** | **2** | .... |
| **1989-90** | **Montreal** | **NHL** | **53** | **9** | **22** | **31** | **136** | **1** | **2** | **1** | **123** | **7.3** | **20** | .... | .... | .... | **5** | **0** | **1** | **1** | **8** | **0** | **0** | **0** | .... |
| **1990-91** | **Chicago** | **NHL** | **77** | **12** | **52** | **64** | **192** | **5** | **2** | **2** | **187** | **6.4** | **23** | .... | .... | .... | **6** | **1** | **7** | **8** | **46** | **1** | **0** | **0** | .... |
| **1991-92** | **Chicago** | **NHL** | **80** | **9** | **47** | **56** | **245** | **2** | **2** | **2** | **239** | **3.8** | **24** | .... | .... | .... | **18** | **6** | **15** | **21** | **37** | **3** | **0** | **1** | .... |
| **1992-93** | **Chicago** | **NHL** | **84** | **15** | **58** | **73** | **282** | **8** | **0** | **2** | **290** | **5.2** | **14** | .... | .... | .... | **4** | **0** | **2** | **2** | **14** | **0** | **0** | **0** | .... |
| **1993-94** | **Chicago** | **NHL** | **76** | **16** | **44** | **60** | **212** | **7** | **1** | **2** | **219** | **7.3** | **12** | .... | .... | .... | **6** | **1** | **1** | **2** | **8** | **1** | **0** | **0** | .... |
| **1994-95** | EHC Biel-Bienne | Swiss | 3 | 0 | 3 | 3 | 4 | .... | .... | .... | .... | .... | .... | .... | .... | .... | .... | .... | .... | .... | .... | .... | .... | .... | .... |
| | **Chicago** | **NHL** | **48** | **5** | **33** | **38** | **72** | **3** | **1** | **0** | **166** | **3.0** | **17** | .... | .... | .... | **16** | **4** | **7** | **11** | **12** | **0** | **1** | **3** | .... |
| **1995-96** | **Chicago** | **NHL** | **81** | **14** | **58** | **72** | **140** | **7** | **0** | **3** | **219** | **6.4** | **25** | .... | .... | .... | **9** | **0** | **3** | **3** | **8** | **0** | **0** | **0** | .... |
| **1996-97** | **Chicago** | **NHL** | **72** | **10** | **38** | **48** | **112** | **2** | **0** | **2** | **194** | **5.2** | **16** | .... | .... | .... | **6** | **0** | **1** | **1** | **8** | **0** | **0** | **0** | .... |
| **1997-98** | **Chicago** | **NHL** | **81** | **3** | **39** | **42** | **151** | **1** | **0** | **0** | **205** | **1.5** | **–7** | .... | .... | .... | .... | .... | .... | .... | .... | .... | .... | .... | .... |
| | United States | Olympics | 4 | 2 | 0 | 2 | 2 | .... | .... | .... | .... | .... | .... | .... | .... | .... | .... | .... | .... | .... | .... | .... | .... | .... | .... |
| **1998-99** | **Chicago** | **NHL** | **65** | **8** | **26** | **34** | **89** | **2** | **1** | **0** | **172** | **4.7** | **–4** | **4** | **25.0** | **27:19** | .... | .... | .... | .... | .... | .... | .... | .... | .... |
| | **Detroit** | **NHL** | **10** | **1** | **1** | **2** | **4** | **1** | **0** | **1** | **15** | **6.7** | **5** | **0** | **0.0** | **22:21** | **10** | **0** | **4** | **4** | **14** | **0** | **0** | **0** | **27:15** |
| **99-2000** | **Detroit** | **NHL** | **81** | **3** | **31** | **34** | **103** | **0** | **0** | **0** | **135** | **2.2** | **48** | **0** | **0.0** | **25:16** | **9** | **0** | **1** | **1** | **8** | **0** | **0** | **0** | **24:06** |
| **2000-01** | **Detroit** | **NHL** | **24** | **0** | **3** | **3** | **45** | **0** | **0** | **0** | **26** | **0.0** | **4** | **0** | **0.0** | **22:51** | **5** | **1** | **0** | **1** | **2** | **0** | **0** | **0** | **19:41** |
| **2001-02 ♦** | **Detroit** | **NHL** | **79** | **6** | **33** | **39** | **126** | **1** | **0** | **1** | **128** | **4.7** | **40** | **0** | **0.0** | **25:18** | **23** | **1** | **13** | **14** | **44** | **1** | **0** | **0** | **26:22** |
| | United States | Olympics | 6 | 1 | 0 | 1 | 4 | .... | .... | .... | .... | .... | .... | .... | .... | .... | .... | .... | .... | .... | .... | .... | .... | .... | .... |
| **2002-03** | **Detroit** | **NHL** | **66** | **2** | **17** | **19** | **78** | **0** | **1** | **1** | **92** | **2.2** | **4** | **0** | **0.0** | **24:15** | **4** | **0** | **0** | **0** | **2** | **0** | **0** | **0** | **25:43** |
| **2003-04** | **Detroit** | **NHL** | **69** | **2** | **19** | **21** | **61** | **0** | **0** | **0** | **113** | **1.8** | **12** | **0** | **0.0** | **21:21** | **8** | **0** | **1** | **1** | **4** | **0** | **0** | **0** | **21:13** |
| 2004-05 | Motor City | UHL | 23 | 5 | 19 | 24 | 25 | .... | .... | .... | .... | .... | .... | .... | .... | .... | .... | .... | .... | .... | .... | .... | .... | .... | .... |
| **2005-06** | **Detroit** | **NHL** | **81** | **4** | **7** | **11** | **108** | **1** | **1** | **0** | **83** | **4.8** | **22** | **4** | **25.0** | **18:29** | **6** | **0** | **0** | **0** | **6** | **0** | **0** | **0** | **19:25** |
| | United States | Olympics | 6 | 0 | 1 | 1 | 2 | .... | .... | .... | .... | .... | .... | .... | .... | .... | .... | .... | .... | .... | .... | .... | .... | .... | .... |
| **2006-07** | **Detroit** | **NHL** | **71** | **0** | **11** | **11** | **34** | **0** | **0** | **0** | **72** | **0.0** | **11** | **1** | **0.0** | **18:08** | **18** | **1** | **6** | **7** | **12** | **0** | **1** | **0** | **20:07** |
| **2007-08 ♦** | **Detroit** | **NHL** | **69** | **3** | **9** | **12** | **36** | **0** | **0** | **1** | **60** | **5.0** | **11** | **0** | **0.0** | **16:58** | **14** | **0** | **0** | **0** | **10** | **0** | **0** | **0** | **12:54** |
| **2008-09** | **Detroit** | **NHL** | **28** | **0** | **0** | **0** | **18** | **0** | **0** | **0** | **14** | **0.0** | **1** | **0** | **0.0** | **11:40** | **6** | **0** | **0** | **0** | **2** | **0** | **0** | **0** | **7:21** |
| | Grand Rapids | AHL | 2 | 0 | 1 | 1 | 2 | .... | .... | .... | .... | .... | .... | .... | .... | .... | .... | .... | .... | .... | .... | .... | .... | .... | .... |
| | **NHL Totals** | | **1644** | **185** | **763** | **948** | **2891** | **69** | **13** | **31** | **3621** | **5.1** | | **9** | **22.2** | **21:41** | **266** | **31** | **113** | **144** | **423** | **14** | **3** | **6** | **21:04** |

WCHA Second All-Star Team (1983) • NCAA Championship All-Tournament Team (1983) • NHL All-Rookie Team (1985) • NHL First All-Star Team (1989, 1993, 1995, 1996, 2002) • James Norris Memorial Trophy (1989, 1993, 1996) • NHL Second All-Star Team (1991, 1997) • Bud Light Plus/Minus Award (2002)

Played in NHL All-Star Game (1985, 1990, 1991, 1992, 1993, 1994, 1996, 1997, 1998, 2000, 2002)

Traded to **Chicago** by **Montreal** with Montreal's 2nd round choice (Michael Pomichter) in 1991 Entry Draft for Denis Savard, June 29, 1990. Traded to **Detroit** by **Chicago** for Anders Eriksson and Detroit's 1st round choices in 1999 (Steve McCarthy) and 2001 (Adam Munro) Entry Drafts, March 23, 1999. • Missed majority of 2000-01 season recovering from knee injury suffered in game vs. Dallas, November 17, 2000. Signed as a free agent by **Motor City** (UHL), February 1, 2005. • Missed majority of 2008-09 season recovering from broken leg suffered during exhbition game.

## CHIMERA, Jason

(chih-MAIR-uh, JAY-suhn) **CBJ**

Left wing. Shoots left. 6'2", 216 lbs. Born, Edmonton, Alta., May 2, 1979. Edmonton's 5th choice, 121st overall, in 1997 Entry Draft.

| Season | Club | League | GP | G | A | Pts | PIM | PP | SH | GW | S | % | +/- | TF | F% | Min | GP | G | A | Pts | PIM | PP | SH | GW | Min |
|---|---|---|---|---|---|---|---|---|---|---|---|---|---|---|---|---|---|---|---|---|---|---|---|---|---|
| 1994-95 | Edmonton Pats | AMHL | 33 | 27 | 31 | 58 | 42 | .... | .... | .... | .... | .... | .... | .... | .... | .... | .... | .... | .... | .... | .... | .... | .... | .... | .... |
| 1995-96 | Edmonton Pats | AMHL | 34 | 23 | 24 | 47 | 44 | .... | .... | .... | .... | .... | .... | .... | .... | .... | .... | .... | .... | .... | .... | .... | .... | .... | .... |
| 1996-97 | Medicine Hat | WHL | 71 | 16 | 23 | 39 | 64 | .... | .... | .... | .... | .... | .... | .... | .... | .... | 4 | 0 | 1 | 1 | 4 | .... | .... | .... | .... |
| 1997-98 | Medicine Hat | WHL | 72 | 34 | 32 | 66 | 93 | .... | .... | .... | .... | .... | .... | .... | .... | .... | .... | .... | .... | .... | .... | .... | .... | .... | .... |
| | Hamilton | AHL | 4 | 0 | 0 | 0 | 8 | .... | .... | .... | .... | .... | .... | .... | .... | .... | .... | .... | .... | .... | .... | .... | .... | .... | .... |
| 1998-99 | Medicine Hat | WHL | 37 | 18 | 22 | 40 | 84 | .... | .... | .... | .... | .... | .... | .... | .... | .... | .... | .... | .... | .... | .... | .... | .... | .... | .... |
| | Brandon | WHL | 21 | 14 | 12 | 26 | 32 | .... | .... | .... | .... | .... | .... | .... | .... | .... | 5 | 4 | 1 | 5 | 8 | .... | .... | .... | .... |
| 99-2000 | Hamilton | AHL | 78 | 15 | 13 | 28 | 77 | .... | .... | .... | .... | .... | .... | .... | .... | .... | 10 | 0 | 2 | 2 | 12 | .... | .... | .... | .... |
| **2000-01** | **Edmonton** | **NHL** | **1** | **0** | **0** | **0** | **0** | **0** | **0** | **0** | **0** | **0.0** | **0** | **0** | **0.0** | **6:58** | .... | .... | .... | .... | .... | .... | .... | .... | .... |
| | Hamilton | AHL | 78 | 29 | 25 | 54 | 93 | .... | .... | .... | .... | .... | .... | .... | .... | .... | .... | .... | .... | .... | .... | .... | .... | .... | .... |
| **2001-02** | **Edmonton** | **NHL** | **3** | **1** | **0** | **1** | **0** | **0** | **0** | **0** | **3** | **33.3** | **–3** | **0** | **0.0** | **12:44** | .... | .... | .... | .... | .... | .... | .... | .... | .... |
| | Hamilton | AHL | 77 | 26 | 51 | 77 | 158 | .... | .... | .... | .... | .... | .... | .... | .... | .... | 15 | 4 | 6 | 10 | 10 | .... | .... | .... | .... |
| **2002-03** | **Edmonton** | **NHL** | **66** | **14** | **9** | **23** | **36** | **0** | **1** | **4** | **90** | **15.6** | **–2** | **11** | **54.6** | **10:46** | **2** | **0** | **2** | **2** | **0** | **0** | **0** | **0** | **10:55** |
| **2003-04** | **Edmonton** | **NHL** | **60** | **4** | **8** | **12** | **57** | **0** | **0** | **1** | **79** | **5.1** | **–1** | **22** | **31.8** | **10:07** | .... | .... | .... | .... | .... | .... | .... | .... | .... |
| 2004-05 | AS Varese Hockey | Italy | 15 | 7 | 3 | 10 | 34 | .... | .... | .... | .... | .... | .... | .... | .... | .... | 5 | 2 | 1 | 3 | 31 | .... | .... | .... | .... |
| **2005-06** | **Columbus** | **NHL** | **80** | **17** | **13** | **30** | **95** | **1** | **1** | **5** | **127** | **13.4** | **–10** | **16** | **50.0** | **12:41** | .... | .... | .... | .... | .... | .... | .... | .... | .... |
| **2006-07** | **Columbus** | **NHL** | **82** | **15** | **21** | **36** | **91** | **2** | **2** | **2** | **151** | **9.9** | **2** | **38** | **36.8** | **15:22** | .... | .... | .... | .... | .... | .... | .... | .... | .... |
| **2007-08** | **Columbus** | **NHL** | **81** | **14** | **17** | **31** | **98** | **1** | **1** | **3** | **198** | **7.1** | **–5** | **35** | **45.7** | **17:30** | .... | .... | .... | .... | .... | .... | .... | .... | .... |
| **2008-09** | **Columbus** | **NHL** | **49** | **8** | **14** | **22** | **41** | **1** | **0** | **1** | **115** | **7.0** | **8** | **42** | **42.9** | **16:15** | **4** | **0** | **1** | **1** | **2** | **0** | **0** | **0** | **13:21** |
| | **NHL Totals** | | **422** | **73** | **82** | **155** | **418** | **5** | **5** | **16** | **763** | **9.6** | | **164** | **42.1** | **13:52** | **6** | **0** | **3** | **3** | **2** | **0** | **0** | **0** | **12:32** |

AHL First All-Star Team (2002)

Traded to **Phoenix** by **Edmonton** with Edmonton's 3rd round choice (later traded to Carolina – later traded to NY Rangers – NY Rangers selected Billy Ryan) in 2004 Entry Draft for New Jersey's 2nd round choice (previously acquired, Edmonton selected Geoff Paukovich) in 2004 Entry Draft and Buffalo's 4th round choice (previously acquired, Edmonton selected Liam Reddox) in 2004 Entry Draft, June 26, 2004. Signed as a free agent by **Varese** (Italy), December 15, 2004. Traded to **Columbus** by **Phoenix** with Cale Hulse and Mike Rupp for Geoff Sanderson and Tim Jackman, October 8, 2005.

## CHIPCHURA, Kyle

(chip-CHUHR-a, KIGHL) **MTL.**

Center. Shoots left. 6'2", 204 lbs. Born, Westlock, Alta., February 19, 1986. Montreal's 1st choice, 18th overall, in 2004 Entry Draft.

| Season | Club | League | GP | G | A | Pts | PIM | PP | SH | GW | S | % | +/- | TF | F% | Min | GP | G | A | Pts | PIM | PP | SH | GW | Min |
|---|---|---|---|---|---|---|---|---|---|---|---|---|---|---|---|---|---|---|---|---|---|---|---|---|---|
| 2000-01 | Spruce Grove | AMBHL | 36 | 26 | 34 | 60 | 48 | .... | .... | .... | .... | .... | .... | .... | .... | .... | .... | .... | .... | .... | .... | .... | .... | .... | .... |
| 2001-02 | Ft. Saskatchewan | AMHL | 33 | 15 | 36 | 51 | 78 | .... | .... | .... | .... | .... | .... | .... | .... | .... | 17 | 16 | 20 | 36 | .... | .... | .... | .... | .... |
| 2002-03 | Prince Albert | WHL | 63 | 9 | 21 | 30 | 89 | .... | .... | .... | .... | .... | .... | .... | .... | .... | .... | .... | .... | .... | .... | .... | .... | .... | .... |
| 2003-04 | Prince Albert | WHL | 64 | 15 | 33 | 48 | 118 | .... | .... | .... | .... | .... | .... | .... | .... | .... | 6 | 2 | 4 | 6 | 12 | .... | .... | .... | .... |
| 2004-05 | Prince Albert | WHL | 28 | 14 | 18 | 32 | 32 | .... | .... | .... | .... | .... | .... | .... | .... | .... | 14 | 4 | 7 | 11 | 25 | .... | .... | .... | .... |
| 2005-06 | Prince Albert | WHL | 59 | 21 | 34 | 55 | 81 | .... | .... | .... | .... | .... | .... | .... | .... | .... | .... | .... | .... | .... | .... | .... | .... | .... | .... |
| | Hamilton | AHL | 8 | 1 | 2 | 3 | 6 | .... | .... | .... | .... | .... | .... | .... | .... | .... | .... | .... | .... | .... | .... | .... | .... | .... | .... |
| 2006-07 | Hamilton | AHL | 80 | 12 | 27 | 39 | 56 | .... | .... | .... | .... | .... | .... | .... | .... | .... | 22 | 6 | 7 | 13 | 20 | .... | .... | .... | .... |
| **2007-08** | **Montreal** | **NHL** | **36** | **4** | **7** | **11** | **10** | **0** | **0** | **0** | **36** | **11.1** | **–1** | **317** | **43.9** | **11:22** | .... | .... | .... | .... | .... | .... | .... | .... | .... |
| | Hamilton | AHL | 39 | 10 | 11 | 21 | 27 | .... | .... | .... | .... | .... | .... | .... | .... | .... | .... | .... | .... | .... | .... | .... | .... | .... | .... |
| **2008-09** | **Montreal** | **NHL** | **13** | **0** | **3** | **3** | **5** | **0** | **0** | **0** | **5** | **0.0** | **–6** | **107** | **43.9** | **10:18** | .... | .... | .... | .... | .... | .... | .... | .... | .... |
| | Hamilton | AHL | 51 | 14 | 21 | 35 | 65 | .... | .... | .... | .... | .... | .... | .... | .... | .... | 6 | 3 | 0 | 3 | 2 | .... | .... | .... | .... |
| | **NHL Totals** | | **49** | **4** | **10** | **14** | **15** | **0** | **0** | **0** | **41** | **9.8** | | **424** | **43.9** | **11:05** | .... | | | | | | | | |

WHL East Second All-Star Team (2006)

## CHORNEY, Taylor

(CHOHR-nee, TAY-luhr) **EDM.**

Defense. Shoots left. 5'11", 182 lbs. Born, Thunder Bay, Ont., April 27, 1987. Edmonton's 2nd choice, 36th overall, in 2005 Entry Draft.

| | | | Regular Season | | | | | | | | | | | | | | Playoffs | | | | | | | | |
|---|---|---|---|---|---|---|---|---|---|---|---|---|---|---|---|---|---|---|---|---|---|---|---|---|---|
| Season | Club | League | GP | G | A | Pts | PIM | PP | SH | GW | S | % | +/- | TF | F% | Min | GP | G | A | Pts | PIM | PP | SH | GW | Min |
| 2003-04 | Shat.-St. Mary's | High-MN | 74 | 12 | 44 | 56 | 58 | .... | .... | .... | .... | .... | .... | .... | .... | .... | .... | .... | .... | .... | .... | .... | .... | .... | .... |
| 2004-05 | Shat.-St. Mary's | High-MN | 50 | 4 | 30 | 34 | 52 | .... | .... | .... | .... | .... | .... | .... | .... | .... | .... | .... | .... | .... | .... | .... | .... | .... | .... |
| 2005-06 | North Dakota | WCHA | 44 | 3 | 15 | 18 | 54 | .... | .... | .... | .... | .... | .... | .... | .... | .... | .... | .... | .... | .... | .... | .... | .... | .... | .... |
| 2006-07 | North Dakota | WCHA | 39 | 8 | 23 | 31 | 48 | .... | .... | .... | .... | .... | .... | .... | .... | .... | .... | .... | .... | .... | .... | .... | .... | .... | .... |
| 2007-08 | North Dakota | WCHA | 43 | 3 | 21 | 24 | 24 | .... | .... | .... | .... | .... | .... | .... | .... | .... | .... | .... | .... | .... | .... | .... | .... | .... | .... |
| **2008-09** | **Edmonton** | **NHL** | **2** | **0** | **0** | **0** | **0** | **0** | **0** | **0** | **0** | **0.0** | **-4** | **0** | **0.0** | **15:43** | .... | .... | .... | .... | .... | .... | .... | .... | .... |
| | Springfield | AHL | 68 | 5 | 16 | 21 | 22 | .... | .... | .... | .... | .... | .... | .... | .... | .... | .... | .... | .... | .... | .... | .... | .... | .... | .... |
| | **NHL Totals** | | **2** | **0** | **0** | **0** | **0** | **0** | **0** | **0** | **0** | **0.0** | | **0** | **0.0** | **15:43** | .... | .... | .... | .... | .... | .... | .... | .... | .... |

WCHA Second All-Star Team (2007) • NCAA West Second All-American Team (2007) • WCHA First All-Star Team (2008)

## CHRISTENSEN, Erik

(KRIHS-tehn-suhn, AIR-ihk) **ANA.**

Center. Shoots left. 6'1", 205 lbs. Born, Edmonton, Alta., December 17, 1983. Pittsburgh's 3rd choice, 69th overall, in 2002 Entry Draft.

| Season | Club | League | GP | G | A | Pts | PIM | PP | SH | GW | S | % | +/- | TF | F% | Min | GP | G | A | Pts | PIM | PP | SH | GW | Min |
|---|---|---|---|---|---|---|---|---|---|---|---|---|---|---|---|---|---|---|---|---|---|---|---|---|---|
| 1998-99 | Leduc Oil Kings | AMBHL | 36 | 34 | 42 | 76 | 70 | .... | .... | .... | .... | .... | .... | .... | .... | .... | .... | .... | .... | .... | .... | .... | .... | .... | .... |
| 99-2000 | Kamloops Blazers | WHL | 66 | 9 | 5 | 14 | 41 | .... | .... | .... | .... | .... | .... | .... | .... | .... | 4 | 0 | 0 | 0 | 2 | .... | .... | .... | .... |
| 2000-01 | Kamloops Blazers | WHL | 72 | 21 | 23 | 44 | 36 | .... | .... | .... | .... | .... | .... | .... | .... | .... | 4 | 1 | 1 | 2 | 0 | .... | .... | .... | .... |
| 2001-02 | Kamloops Blazers | WHL | 70 | 22 | 36 | 58 | 68 | .... | .... | .... | .... | .... | .... | .... | .... | .... | 4 | 0 | 0 | 0 | 4 | .... | .... | .... | .... |
| 2002-03 | Kamloops Blazers | WHL | 67 | *54 | 54 | *108 | 60 | .... | .... | .... | .... | .... | .... | .... | .... | .... | 6 | 1 | 7 | 8 | 14 | .... | .... | .... | .... |
| 2003-04 | Kamloops Blazers | WHL | 29 | 10 | 14 | 24 | 40 | .... | .... | .... | .... | .... | .... | .... | .... | .... | .... | .... | .... | .... | .... | .... | .... | .... | .... |
| | Brandon | WHL | 34 | 17 | 21 | 38 | 20 | .... | .... | .... | .... | .... | .... | .... | .... | .... | 11 | 8 | 4 | 12 | 8 | .... | .... | .... | .... |
| 2004-05 | Wilkes-Barre | AHL | 77 | 14 | 13 | 27 | 33 | .... | .... | .... | .... | .... | .... | .... | .... | .... | 11 | 1 | 6 | 7 | 4 | .... | .... | .... | .... |
| **2005-06** | **Pittsburgh** | **NHL** | **33** | **6** | **7** | **13** | **34** | **2** | **0** | **0** | **85** | **7.1** | **-3** | **381** | **53.0** | **14:17** | .... | .... | .... | .... | .... | .... | .... | .... | .... |
| | Wilkes-Barre | AHL | 48 | 24 | 22 | 46 | 50 | .... | .... | .... | .... | .... | .... | .... | .... | .... | 11 | 2 | 2 | 4 | 2 | .... | .... | .... | .... |
| **2006-07** | **Pittsburgh** | **NHL** | **61** | **18** | **15** | **33** | **26** | **6** | **0** | **1** | **133** | **13.5** | **-3** | **240** | **56.3** | **11:38** | **4** | **0** | **0** | **0** | **6** | **0** | **0** | **0** | **8:15** |
| | Wilkes-Barre | AHL | 16 | 12 | 12 | 24 | 8 | .... | .... | .... | .... | .... | .... | .... | .... | .... | .... | .... | .... | .... | .... | .... | .... | .... | .... |
| **2007-08** | **Pittsburgh** | **NHL** | **49** | **9** | **11** | **20** | **28** | **2** | **0** | **0** | **109** | **8.3** | **-3** | **314** | **58.6** | **12:37** | .... | .... | .... | .... | .... | .... | .... | .... | .... |
| | **Atlanta** | **NHL** | **10** | **2** | **2** | **4** | **2** | **0** | **0** | **0** | **23** | **8.7** | **-7** | **160** | **58.1** | **16:57** | .... | .... | .... | .... | .... | .... | .... | .... | .... |
| **2008-09** | **Atlanta** | **NHL** | **47** | **5** | **14** | **19** | **14** | **1** | **0** | **0** | **90** | **5.6** | **-7** | **427** | **54.6** | **14:16** | .... | .... | .... | .... | .... | .... | .... | .... | .... |
| | **Anaheim** | **NHL** | **17** | **2** | **7** | **9** | **6** | **1** | **0** | **0** | **32** | **6.3** | **-2** | **70** | **62.9** | **11:55** | **8** | **0** | **2** | **2** | **0** | **0** | **0** | **0** | **10:37** |
| | **NHL Totals** | | **217** | **42** | **56** | **98** | **110** | **12** | **0** | **1** | **472** | **8.9** | | **1592** | **56.0** | **13:06** | **12** | **0** | **2** | **2** | **6** | **0** | **0** | **0** | **9:50** |

WHL West First All-Star Team (2003) • Canadian Major Junior Second All-Star Team (2003)

Traded to **Atlanta** by **Pittsburgh** with Colby Armstrong, Angelo Esposito and Pittsburgh's 1st round choice (Daultan Leveille) in 2008 Entry Draft for Marian Hossa and Pascal Dupuis, February 26, 2008. Traded to **Anaheim** by **Atlanta** for Eric O'Dell, March 4, 2009.

## CHUCKO, Kris

(CHUH-koh, KRIHS) **CGY.**

Left wing. Shoots right. 6'2", 198 lbs. Born, Burnaby, B.C., March 13, 1986. Calgary's 1st choice, 24th overall, in 2004 Entry Draft.

| Season | Club | League | GP | G | A | Pts | PIM | PP | SH | GW | S | % | +/- | TF | F% | Min | GP | G | A | Pts | PIM | PP | SH | GW | Min |
|---|---|---|---|---|---|---|---|---|---|---|---|---|---|---|---|---|---|---|---|---|---|---|---|---|---|
| 2002-03 | Salmon Arm | BCHL | 59 | 14 | 19 | 33 | 80 | .... | .... | .... | .... | .... | .... | .... | .... | .... | 11 | 5 | 3 | 8 | 12 | .... | .... | .... | .... |
| 2003-04 | Salmon Arm | BCHL | 53 | 32 | 55 | 87 | 161 | .... | .... | .... | .... | .... | .... | .... | .... | .... | 14 | 10 | 9 | 19 | 36 | .... | .... | .... | .... |
| 2004-05 | U. of Minnesota | WCHA | 44 | 10 | 11 | 21 | 61 | .... | .... | .... | .... | .... | .... | .... | .... | .... | .... | .... | .... | .... | .... | .... | .... | .... | .... |
| 2005-06 | U. of Minnesota | WCHA | 33 | 4 | 9 | 13 | 40 | .... | .... | .... | .... | .... | .... | .... | .... | .... | .... | .... | .... | .... | .... | .... | .... | .... | .... |
| 2006-07 | Omaha | AHL | 80 | 14 | 14 | 28 | 72 | .... | .... | .... | .... | .... | .... | .... | .... | .... | 6 | 0 | 0 | 0 | 2 | .... | .... | .... | .... |
| 2007-08 | Quad City Flames | AHL | 80 | 15 | 15 | 30 | 38 | .... | .... | .... | .... | .... | .... | .... | .... | .... | .... | .... | .... | .... | .... | .... | .... | .... | .... |
| **2008-09** | **Calgary** | **NHL** | **2** | **0** | **0** | **0** | **2** | **0** | **0** | **0** | **0** | **0.0** | **0** | **1** | **0.0** | **7:02** | .... | .... | .... | .... | .... | .... | .... | .... | .... |
| | Quad City Flames | AHL | 74 | 28 | 23 | 51 | 59 | .... | .... | .... | .... | .... | .... | .... | .... | .... | .... | .... | .... | .... | .... | .... | .... | .... | .... |
| | **NHL Totals** | | **2** | **0** | **0** | **0** | **2** | **0** | **0** | **0** | **0** | **0.0** | | **1** | **0.0** | **7:02** | .... | .... | .... | .... | .... | .... | .... | .... | .... |

## CLARK, Brett

(KLAHRK, BREHT) **COL.**

Defense. Shoots left. 6', 195 lbs. Born, Wapella, Sask., December 23, 1976. Montreal's 7th choice, 154th overall, in 1996 Entry Draft.

| Season | Club | League | GP | G | A | Pts | PIM | PP | SH | GW | S | % | +/- | TF | F% | Min | GP | G | A | Pts | PIM | PP | SH | GW | Min |
|---|---|---|---|---|---|---|---|---|---|---|---|---|---|---|---|---|---|---|---|---|---|---|---|---|---|
| 1994-95 | Melville | SJHL | 62 | 19 | 32 | 51 | 77 | .... | .... | .... | .... | .... | .... | .... | .... | .... | .... | .... | .... | .... | .... | .... | .... | .... | .... |
| 1995-96 | U. of Maine | H-East | 39 | 7 | 31 | 38 | 22 | .... | .... | .... | .... | .... | .... | .... | .... | .... | .... | .... | .... | .... | .... | .... | .... | .... | .... |
| 1996-97 | Canada | Nat-Tm | 57 | 6 | 21 | 27 | 52 | .... | .... | .... | .... | .... | .... | .... | .... | .... | .... | .... | .... | .... | .... | .... | .... | .... | .... |
| **1997-98** | **Montreal** | **NHL** | **41** | **1** | **0** | **1** | **20** | **0** | **0** | **0** | **26** | **3.8** | **-3** | .... | .... | .... | .... | .... | .... | .... | .... | .... | .... | .... | .... |
| | Fredericton | AHL | 20 | 0 | 6 | 6 | 6 | .... | .... | .... | .... | .... | .... | .... | .... | .... | 4 | 0 | 1 | 1 | 17 | .... | .... | .... | .... |
| **1998-99** | **Montreal** | **NHL** | **61** | **2** | **2** | **4** | **16** | **0** | **0** | **0** | **36** | **5.6** | **-3** | **0** | **0.0** | **13:11** | .... | .... | .... | .... | .... | .... | .... | .... | .... |
| | Fredericton | AHL | 3 | 1 | 0 | 1 | 0 | .... | .... | .... | .... | .... | .... | .... | .... | .... | .... | .... | .... | .... | .... | .... | .... | .... | .... |
| **99-2000** | **Atlanta** | **NHL** | **14** | **0** | **1** | **1** | **4** | **0** | **0** | **0** | **13** | **0.0** | **-12** | **0** | **0.0** | **16:51** | .... | .... | .... | .... | .... | .... | .... | .... | .... |
| | Orlando | IHL | 63 | 9 | 17 | 26 | 31 | .... | .... | .... | .... | .... | .... | .... | .... | .... | 6 | 0 | 1 | 1 | 0 | .... | .... | .... | .... |
| **2000-01** | **Atlanta** | **NHL** | **28** | **1** | **2** | **3** | **14** | **0** | **0** | **0** | **35** | **2.9** | **-12** | **0** | **0.0** | **18:02** | .... | .... | .... | .... | .... | .... | .... | .... | .... |
| | Orlando | IHL | 43 | 2 | 9 | 11 | 32 | .... | .... | .... | .... | .... | .... | .... | .... | .... | 15 | 1 | 6 | 7 | 2 | .... | .... | .... | .... |
| **2001-02** | **Atlanta** | **NHL** | **2** | **0** | **0** | **0** | **0** | **0** | **0** | **0** | **0** | **0.0** | **-3** | **1** | **100.0** | **15:32** | .... | .... | .... | .... | .... | .... | .... | .... | .... |
| | Chicago Wolves | AHL | 42 | 3 | 17 | 20 | 18 | .... | .... | .... | .... | .... | .... | .... | .... | .... | .... | .... | .... | .... | .... | .... | .... | .... | .... |
| | Hershey Bears | AHL | 32 | 7 | 9 | 16 | 12 | .... | .... | .... | .... | .... | .... | .... | .... | .... | 8 | 0 | 2 | 2 | 6 | .... | .... | .... | .... |
| 2002-03 | Hershey Bears | AHL | 80 | 8 | 27 | 35 | 26 | .... | .... | .... | .... | .... | .... | .... | .... | .... | 5 | 0 | 4 | 4 | 4 | .... | .... | .... | .... |
| **2003-04** | **Colorado** | **NHL** | **12** | **1** | **1** | **2** | **6** | **0** | **0** | **0** | **14** | **7.1** | **3** | **0** | **0.0** | **10:26** | .... | .... | .... | .... | .... | .... | .... | .... | .... |
| | Hershey Bears | AHL | 64 | 11 | 21 | 32 | 37 | .... | .... | .... | .... | .... | .... | .... | .... | .... | .... | .... | .... | .... | .... | .... | .... | .... | .... |
| 2004-05 | Hershey Bears | AHL | 67 | 7 | 37 | 44 | 54 | .... | .... | .... | .... | .... | .... | .... | .... | .... | .... | .... | .... | .... | .... | .... | .... | .... | .... |
| **2005-06** | **Colorado** | **NHL** | **80** | **9** | **27** | **36** | **56** | **4** | **0** | **1** | **148** | **6.1** | **3** | **1** | **0.0** | **19:39** | **9** | **2** | **2** | **4** | **2** | **0** | **1** | **0** | **24:17** |
| **2006-07** | **Colorado** | **NHL** | **82** | **10** | **29** | **39** | **50** | **4** | **0** | **1** | **140** | **7.1** | **5** | **1** | **100.0** | **23:41** | .... | .... | .... | .... | .... | .... | .... | .... | .... |
| **2007-08** | **Colorado** | **NHL** | **57** | **5** | **16** | **21** | **33** | **1** | **0** | **0** | **87** | **5.7** | **5** | **0** | **0.0** | **23:09** | .... | .... | .... | .... | .... | .... | .... | .... | .... |
| **2008-09** | **Colorado** | **NHL** | **76** | **2** | **10** | **12** | **32** | **0** | **0** | **1** | **97** | **2.1** | **-16** | **0** | **0.0** | **22:20** | .... | .... | .... | .... | .... | .... | .... | .... | .... |
| | **NHL Totals** | | **453** | **31** | **88** | **119** | **231** | **9** | **0** | **3** | **596** | **5.2** | | **3** | **66.7** | **19:59** | **9** | **2** | **2** | **4** | **2** | **0** | **1** | **0** | **24:17** |

Claimed by **Atlanta** from **Montreal** in Expansion Draft, June 25, 1999. Traded to **Colorado** by **Atlanta** for Frederic Cassivi, January 24, 2002.

## CLARK, Chris

(KLAHRK, KRIHS) **WSH.**

Right wing. Shoots right. 6', 196 lbs. Born, South Windsor, CT, March 8, 1976. Calgary's 3rd choice, 77th overall, in 1994 Entry Draft.

| Season | Club | League | GP | G | A | Pts | PIM | PP | SH | GW | S | % | +/- | TF | F% | Min | GP | G | A | Pts | PIM | PP | SH | GW | Min |
|---|---|---|---|---|---|---|---|---|---|---|---|---|---|---|---|---|---|---|---|---|---|---|---|---|---|
| 1990-91 | South Windsor | High-CT | 23 | 16 | 15 | 31 | 24 | .... | .... | .... | .... | .... | .... | .... | .... | .... | .... | .... | .... | .... | .... | .... | .... | .... | .... |
| 1991-92 | Spring. Olympics | NEJHL | 49 | 21 | 29 | 50 | 56 | .... | .... | .... | .... | .... | .... | .... | .... | .... | .... | .... | .... | .... | .... | .... | .... | .... | .... |
| 1992-93 | Spring. Olympics | NEJHL | 43 | 17 | 60 | 77 | 120 | .... | .... | .... | .... | .... | .... | .... | .... | .... | .... | .... | .... | .... | .... | .... | .... | .... | .... |
| 1993-94 | Spring. Olympics | NEJHL | 35 | 31 | 26 | 57 | 185 | .... | .... | .... | .... | .... | .... | .... | .... | .... | .... | .... | .... | .... | .... | .... | .... | .... | .... |
| 1994-95 | Clarkson Knights | ECAC | 32 | 12 | 11 | 23 | 92 | .... | .... | .... | .... | .... | .... | .... | .... | .... | .... | .... | .... | .... | .... | .... | .... | .... | .... |
| 1995-96 | Clarkson Knights | ECAC | 38 | 10 | 8 | 18 | 108 | .... | .... | .... | .... | .... | .... | .... | .... | .... | .... | .... | .... | .... | .... | .... | .... | .... | .... |
| 1996-97 | Clarkson Knights | ECAC | 37 | 23 | 25 | 48 | *86 | .... | .... | .... | .... | .... | .... | .... | .... | .... | .... | .... | .... | .... | .... | .... | .... | .... | .... |
| 1997-98 | Clarkson Knights | ECAC | 35 | 18 | 21 | 39 | *106 | .... | .... | .... | .... | .... | .... | .... | .... | .... | .... | .... | .... | .... | .... | .... | .... | .... | .... |
| 1998-99 | Saint John Flames | AHL | 73 | 13 | 27 | 40 | 123 | .... | .... | .... | .... | .... | .... | .... | .... | .... | 7 | 2 | 4 | 6 | 15 | .... | .... | .... | .... |
| **99-2000** | **Calgary** | **NHL** | **22** | **0** | **1** | **1** | **14** | **0** | **0** | **0** | **17** | **0.0** | **-3** | **0** | **0.0** | **9:02** | .... | .... | .... | .... | .... | .... | .... | .... | .... |
| | Saint John Flames | AHL | 48 | 16 | 17 | 33 | 134 | .... | .... | .... | .... | .... | .... | .... | .... | .... | .... | .... | .... | .... | .... | .... | .... | .... | .... |
| **2000-01** | **Calgary** | **NHL** | **29** | **5** | **1** | **6** | **38** | **1** | **0** | **0** | **43** | **11.6** | **0** | **3** | **33.3** | **11:56** | .... | .... | .... | .... | .... | .... | .... | .... | .... |
| | Saint John Flames | AHL | 48 | 18 | 17 | 35 | 131 | .... | .... | .... | .... | .... | .... | .... | .... | .... | 18 | 4 | 10 | 14 | 49 | .... | .... | .... | .... |
| **2001-02** | **Calgary** | **NHL** | **64** | **10** | **7** | **17** | **79** | **2** | **1** | **4** | **109** | **9.2** | **-12** | **21** | **33.3** | **13:57** | .... | .... | .... | .... | .... | .... | .... | .... | .... |
| **2002-03** | **Calgary** | **NHL** | **81** | **10** | **12** | **22** | **126** | **2** | **0** | **2** | **156** | **6.4** | **-11** | **40** | **32.5** | **14:24** | .... | .... | .... | .... | .... | .... | .... | .... | .... |
| **2003-04** | **Calgary** | **NHL** | **82** | **10** | **15** | **25** | **106** | **4** | **0** | **2** | **137** | **7.3** | **-3** | **97** | **36.1** | **14:05** | **26** | **3** | **3** | **6** | **30** | **1** | **0** | **0** | **14:34** |
| 2004-05 | SC Bern | Swiss | 3 | 0 | 0 | 0 | 6 | .... | .... | .... | .... | .... | .... | .... | .... | .... | .... | .... | .... | .... | .... | .... | .... | .... | .... |
| | Storhamar | Norway | 15 | 10 | 4 | 14 | 86 | .... | .... | .... | .... | .... | .... | .... | .... | .... | 7 | 4 | 4 | 8 | 14 | .... | .... | .... | .... |
| **2005-06** | **Washington** | **NHL** | **78** | **20** | **19** | **39** | **110** | **1** | **3** | **0** | **144** | **13.9** | **9** | **209** | **49.3** | **15:24** | .... | .... | .... | .... | .... | .... | .... | .... | .... |
| **2006-07** | **Washington** | **NHL** | **74** | **30** | **24** | **54** | **66** | **9** | **4** | **2** | **164** | **18.3** | **-10** | **118** | **50.9** | **18:25** | .... | .... | .... | .... | .... | .... | .... | .... | .... |
| **2007-08** | **Washington** | **NHL** | **18** | **5** | **4** | **9** | **43** | **1** | **0** | **1** | **29** | **17.2** | **0** | **13** | **46.2** | **16:54** | .... | .... | .... | .... | .... | .... | .... | .... | .... |
| **2008-09** | **Washington** | **NHL** | **32** | **1** | **5** | **6** | **32** | **0** | **0** | **0** | **36** | **2.8** | **-3** | **6** | **50.0** | **11:34** | **8** | **1** | **0** | **1** | **8** | **0** | **0** | **0** | **6:32** |
| | **NHL Totals** | | **480** | **91** | **88** | **179** | **614** | **20** | **8** | **11** | **835** | **10.9** | | **507** | **45.0** | **14:35** | **34** | **4** | **3** | **7** | **38** | **1** | **0** | **0** | **12:41** |

ECAC Second All-Star Team (1998)

Signed as a free agent by **Bern** (Swiss), October 3, 2004. Signed as a free agent by **Storhamar** (Norway), December 29, 2004. Traded to **Washington** by **Calgary** with Calgary's 7th round choice (Andrew Glass) in 2007 Entry Draft for Washington's 7th round choice (Devin Didiomete) in 2006 Entry Draft and Washington's 6th round choice (later traded to Colorado - Colorado selected Jens Hellgren) in 2007 Entry Draft, August 4, 2005. • Missed majority of 2007-08 season recovering from groin injury. • Missed majority of 2008-09 season recovering from wrist surgery, February 4, 2009.

## CLARKE, Noah

(KLAHRK, NOH-uh)

Left wing. Shoots left. 5'9", 190 lbs. Born, La Verne, CA, June 11, 1979. Los Angeles' 10th choice, 250th overall, in 1999 Entry Draft.

| | | | Regular Season | | | | | | | | | | | | | | Playoffs | | | | | | | | |
|---|---|---|---|---|---|---|---|---|---|---|---|---|---|---|---|---|---|---|---|---|---|---|---|---|---|
| Season | Club | League | GP | G | A | Pts | PIM | PP | SH | GW | S | % | +/- | TF | F% | Min | GP | G | A | Pts | PIM | PP | SH | GW | Min |
| 1996-97 | Shat.-St. Mary's | High-MN | 30 | 33 | 44 | 77 | .... | .... | .... | .... | .... | .... | .... | .... | .... | .... | .... | .... | .... | .... | .... | .... | .... | .... | .... |
| 1997-98 | Des Moines | USHL | 54 | 19 | 30 | 49 | 29 | .... | .... | .... | .... | .... | .... | .... | .... | .... | 12 | 2 | 9 | 11 | 23 | .... | .... | .... | .... |
| 1998-99 | Des Moines | USHL | 52 | 31 | 32 | 63 | 47 | .... | .... | .... | .... | .... | .... | .... | .... | .... | 13 | 8 | 2 | 10 | 16 | .... | .... | .... | .... |
| 99-2000 | Colorado College | WCHA | 39 | 17 | 20 | 37 | 30 | .... | .... | .... | .... | .... | .... | .... | .... | .... | .... | .... | .... | .... | .... | .... | .... | .... | .... |
| 2000-01 | Colorado College | WCHA | 41 | 12 | 20 | 32 | 22 | .... | .... | .... | .... | .... | .... | .... | .... | .... | .... | .... | .... | .... | .... | .... | .... | .... | .... |
| 2001-02 | Colorado College | WCHA | 42 | 13 | 24 | 37 | 32 | .... | .... | .... | .... | .... | .... | .... | .... | .... | .... | .... | .... | .... | .... | .... | .... | .... | .... |
| 2002-03 | Colorado College | WCHA | 42 | 21 | *49 | 70 | 15 | .... | .... | .... | .... | .... | .... | .... | .... | .... | .... | .... | .... | .... | .... | .... | .... | .... | .... |
| | Manchester | AHL | 3 | 1 | 1 | 2 | 0 | .... | .... | .... | .... | .... | .... | .... | .... | .... | .... | .... | .... | .... | .... | .... | .... | .... | .... |
| **2003-04** | **Los Angeles** | **NHL** | **2** | **0** | **1** | **1** | **0** | **0** | **0** | **0** | **3** | **0.0** | **1** | **0** | **0.0** | **9:39** | .... | .... | .... | .... | .... | .... | .... | .... | .... |
| | Manchester | AHL | 71 | 25 | 26 | 51 | 24 | .... | .... | .... | .... | .... | .... | .... | .... | .... | 6 | 3 | 1 | 4 | 4 | .... | .... | .... | .... |
| 2004-05 | Manchester | AHL | 61 | 21 | 24 | 45 | 24 | .... | .... | .... | .... | .... | .... | .... | .... | .... | 6 | 1 | 0 | 1 | 4 | .... | .... | .... | .... |
| **2005-06** | **Los Angeles** | **NHL** | **5** | **0** | **0** | **0** | **0** | **0** | **0** | **0** | **3** | **0.0** | **0** | **3** | **33.3** | **7:23** | .... | .... | .... | .... | .... | .... | .... | .... | .... |
| | Manchester | AHL | 69 | 14 | 30 | 44 | 33 | .... | .... | .... | .... | .... | .... | .... | .... | .... | 7 | 4 | 4 | 8 | 2 | .... | .... | .... | .... |
| **2006-07** | **Los Angeles** | **NHL** | **13** | **2** | **0** | **2** | **4** | **0** | **1** | **0** | **11** | **18.2** | **-6** | **43** | **39.5** | **8:36** | .... | .... | .... | .... | .... | .... | .... | .... | .... |
| | Manchester | AHL | 63 | 24 | 33 | 57 | 27 | .... | .... | .... | .... | .... | .... | .... | .... | .... | 16 | 1 | 3 | 4 | 4 | .... | .... | .... | .... |
| **2007-08** | **New Jersey** | **NHL** | **1** | **1** | **0** | **1** | **0** | **0** | **0** | **0** | **3** | **33.3** | **0** | **0** | **0.0** | **10:39** | .... | .... | .... | .... | .... | .... | .... | .... | .... |
| | Lowell Devils | AHL | 47 | 14 | 17 | 31 | 25 | .... | .... | .... | .... | .... | .... | .... | .... | .... | .... | .... | .... | .... | .... | .... | .... | .... | .... |
| 2008-09 | Lukko Rauma | Finland | 25 | 2 | 7 | 9 | 10 | .... | .... | .... | .... | .... | .... | .... | .... | .... | 7 | 1 | 2 | 3 | 4 | .... | .... | .... | .... |
| | HC Ambri-Piotta | Swiss | 28 | 8 | 13 | 21 | 16 | .... | .... | .... | .... | .... | .... | .... | .... | .... | .... | .... | .... | .... | .... | .... | .... | .... | .... |
| | **NHL Totals** | | **21** | **3** | **1** | **4** | **4** | **0** | **1** | **0** | **20** | **15.0** | | **46** | **39.1** | **8:30** | .... | .... | .... | .... | .... | .... | .... | .... | .... |

USHL All-Rookie Team (1998) • USHL First All-Star Team (1999) • Curt Hammer Award (USHL - Most Gentlemanly Player) (1999) • WCHA All-Rookie Team (2000) • WCHA Second All-Star Team (2003) • NCAA West First All-American Team (2003) • AHL All-Rookie Team (2004)

Signed as a free agent by **New Jersey**, July 24, 2007.

## CLARKSON, David

(KLAHRK-suhn, DAYV-ihd) **N.J.**

Right wing. Shoots right. 6'1", 200 lbs. Born, Toronto, Ont., March 31, 1984.

| Season | Club | League | GP | G | A | Pts | PIM | PP | SH | GW | S | % | +/- | TF | F% | Min | GP | G | A | Pts | PIM | PP | SH | GW | Min |
|---|---|---|---|---|---|---|---|---|---|---|---|---|---|---|---|---|---|---|---|---|---|---|---|---|---|
| 2001-02 | Belleville Bulls | OHL | 22 | 2 | 7 | 9 | 34 | .... | .... | .... | .... | .... | .... | .... | .... | .... | 8 | 1 | 1 | 2 | 6 | .... | .... | .... | .... |
| 2002-03 | Belleville Bulls | OHL | 3 | 0 | 0 | 0 | 11 | .... | .... | .... | .... | .... | .... | .... | .... | .... | .... | .... | .... | .... | .... | .... | .... | .... | .... |
| | Kitchener Rangers | OHL | 54 | 17 | 11 | 28 | 122 | .... | .... | .... | .... | .... | .... | .... | .... | .... | 21 | 4 | 3 | 7 | 23 | .... | .... | .... | .... |
| 2003-04 | Kitchener Rangers | OHL | 55 | 22 | 17 | 39 | 173 | .... | .... | .... | .... | .... | .... | .... | .... | .... | .... | .... | .... | .... | .... | .... | .... | .... | .... |
| 2004-05 | Kitchener Rangers | OHL | 51 | 33 | 21 | 54 | 145 | .... | .... | .... | .... | .... | .... | .... | .... | .... | 15 | 6 | 2 | 8 | 40 | .... | .... | .... | .... |
| 2005-06 | Albany River Rats | AHL | 56 | 13 | 21 | 34 | 233 | .... | .... | .... | .... | .... | .... | .... | .... | .... | .... | .... | .... | .... | .... | .... | .... | .... | .... |
| **2006-07** | **New Jersey** | **NHL** | **7** | **3** | **1** | **4** | **6** | **2** | **0** | **1** | **18** | **16.7** | **-1** | **1** | **0.0** | **17:02** | **3** | **0** | **0** | **0** | **2** | **0** | **0** | **0** | **6:42** |
| | Lowell Devils | AHL | 67 | 20 | 18 | 38 | 150 | .... | .... | .... | .... | .... | .... | .... | .... | .... | .... | .... | .... | .... | .... | .... | .... | .... | .... |
| **2007-08** | **New Jersey** | **NHL** | **81** | **9** | **13** | **22** | **183** | **0** | **0** | **1** | **151** | **6.0** | **1** | **15** | **40.0** | **12:02** | **5** | **0** | **0** | **0** | **4** | **0** | **0** | **0** | **12:20** |
| **2008-09** | **New Jersey** | **NHL** | **82** | **17** | **15** | **32** | **164** | **4** | **0** | **3** | **158** | **10.8** | **-1** | **7** | **28.6** | **12:03** | **7** | **2** | **0** | **2** | **19** | **1** | **0** | **1** | **8:32** |
| | **NHL Totals** | | **170** | **29** | **29** | **58** | **353** | **6** | **0** | **5** | **327** | **8.9** | | **23** | **34.8** | **12:15** | **15** | **2** | **0** | **2** | **25** | **1** | **0** | **1** | **9:26** |

Signed as a free agent by **New Jersey**, August 12, 2005.

## CLEARY, Daniel

(KLIH-ree, DAN-yehl) **DET.**

Right wing. Shoots left. 6', 210 lbs. Born, Carbonear, Nfld., December 18, 1978. Chicago's 1st choice, 13th overall, in 1997 Entry Draft.

| Season | Club | League | GP | G | A | Pts | PIM | PP | SH | GW | S | % | +/- | TF | F% | Min | GP | G | A | Pts | PIM | PP | SH | GW | Min |
|---|---|---|---|---|---|---|---|---|---|---|---|---|---|---|---|---|---|---|---|---|---|---|---|---|---|
| 1993-94 | Kingston | MTJHL | 41 | 18 | 28 | 46 | 33 | .... | .... | .... | .... | .... | .... | .... | .... | .... | 2 | 0 | 1 | 1 | 0 | .... | .... | .... | .... |
| 1994-95 | Belleville Bulls | OHL | 62 | 26 | 55 | 81 | 62 | .... | .... | .... | .... | .... | .... | .... | .... | .... | 16 | 7 | 10 | 17 | 23 | .... | .... | .... | .... |
| 1995-96 | Belleville Bulls | OHL | 64 | 53 | 62 | 115 | 74 | .... | .... | .... | .... | .... | .... | .... | .... | .... | 14 | 10 | 17 | 27 | 40 | .... | .... | .... | .... |
| 1996-97 | Belleville Bulls | OHL | 64 | 32 | 48 | 80 | 88 | .... | .... | .... | .... | .... | .... | .... | .... | .... | 6 | 3 | 4 | 7 | 6 | .... | .... | .... | .... |
| **1997-98** | **Chicago** | **NHL** | **6** | **0** | **0** | **0** | **0** | **0** | **0** | **0** | **4** | **0.0** | **-2** | .... | .... | .... | .... | .... | .... | .... | .... | .... | .... | .... | .... |
| | Belleville Bulls | OHL | 30 | 16 | 31 | 47 | 14 | .... | .... | .... | .... | .... | .... | .... | .... | .... | 10 | 6 | *17 | *23 | 10 | .... | .... | .... | .... |
| | Indianapolis Ice | IHL | 4 | 2 | 1 | 3 | 6 | .... | .... | .... | .... | .... | .... | .... | .... | .... | .... | .... | .... | .... | .... | .... | .... | .... | .... |
| **1998-99** | **Chicago** | **NHL** | **35** | **4** | **5** | **9** | **24** | **0** | **0** | **0** | **49** | **8.2** | **-1** | **13** | **46.2** | **14:21** | .... | .... | .... | .... | .... | .... | .... | .... | .... |
| | Portland Pirates | AHL | 30 | 9 | 17 | 26 | 74 | .... | .... | .... | .... | .... | .... | .... | .... | .... | .... | .... | .... | .... | .... | .... | .... | .... | .... |
| | Hamilton | AHL | 9 | 0 | 1 | 1 | 7 | .... | .... | .... | .... | .... | .... | .... | .... | .... | 3 | 0 | 0 | 0 | 0 | .... | .... | .... | .... |
| **99-2000** | **Edmonton** | **NHL** | **17** | **3** | **2** | **5** | **8** | **0** | **0** | **1** | **18** | **16.7** | **-1** | **1** | **100.0** | **9:44** | **4** | **0** | **1** | **1** | **2** | **0** | **0** | **0** | **8:40** |
| | Hamilton | AHL | 58 | 22 | 52 | 74 | 108 | .... | .... | .... | .... | .... | .... | .... | .... | .... | 5 | 2 | 3 | 5 | 18 | .... | .... | .... | .... |
| **2000-01** | **Edmonton** | **NHL** | **81** | **14** | **21** | **35** | **37** | **2** | **0** | **2** | **107** | **13.1** | **5** | **13** | **23.1** | **12:58** | **6** | **1** | **1** | **2** | **8** | **1** | **0** | **0** | **14:09** |
| **2001-02** | **Edmonton** | **NHL** | **65** | **10** | **19** | **29** | **51** | **2** | **1** | **1** | **75** | **13.3** | **-1** | **5** | **60.0** | **12:43** | .... | .... | .... | .... | .... | .... | .... | .... | .... |
| **2002-03** | **Edmonton** | **NHL** | **57** | **4** | **13** | **17** | **31** | **0** | **0** | **1** | **89** | **4.5** | **5** | **5** | **40.0** | **11:58** | .... | .... | .... | .... | .... | .... | .... | .... | .... |
| **2003-04** | **Phoenix** | **NHL** | **68** | **6** | **11** | **17** | **42** | **0** | **3** | **0** | **83** | **7.2** | **-8** | **51** | **39.2** | **13:12** | .... | .... | .... | .... | .... | .... | .... | .... | .... |
| 2004-05 | Mora IK | Sweden | 47 | 11 | 26 | 37 | 138 | .... | .... | .... | .... | .... | .... | .... | .... | .... | .... | .... | .... | .... | .... | .... | .... | .... | .... |
| **2005-06** | **Detroit** | **NHL** | **77** | **3** | **12** | **15** | **40** | **0** | **0** | **1** | **106** | **2.8** | **5** | **286** | **45.8** | **10:30** | **6** | **0** | **1** | **1** | **6** | **0** | **0** | **0** | **10:44** |
| **2006-07** | **Detroit** | **NHL** | **71** | **20** | **20** | **40** | **24** | **6** | **2** | **5** | **135** | **14.8** | **6** | **411** | **51.1** | **15:28** | **18** | **4** | **8** | **12** | **30** | **1** | **2** | **0** | **16:28** |
| **2007-08♦** | **Detroit** | **NHL** | **63** | **20** | **22** | **42** | **33** | **5** | **0** | **3** | **177** | **11.3** | **21** | **110** | **50.9** | **17:23** | **22** | **2** | **1** | **3** | **4** | **0** | **1** | **0** | **17:50** |
| **2008-09** | **Detroit** | **NHL** | **74** | **14** | **26** | **40** | **46** | **3** | **0** | **3** | **163** | **8.6** | **0** | **121** | **55.4** | **16:56** | **23** | **9** | **6** | **15** | **12** | **0** | **0** | **3** | **16:55** |
| | **NHL Totals** | | **614** | **98** | **151** | **249** | **336** | **18** | **6** | **17** | **1006** | **9.7** | | **1016** | **49.1** | **13:47** | **79** | **16** | **18** | **34** | **62** | **2** | **3** | **3** | **15:58** |

OHL All-Rookie Team (1995) • OHL First All-Star Team (1996, 1997) • AHL Second All-Star Team (2000)

Traded to **Edmonton** by **Chicago** with Chad Kilger, Ethan Moreau and Christian Laflamme for Boris Mironov, Dean McAmmond and Jonas Elofsson, March 20, 1999. Signed as a free agent by **Phoenix**, July 15, 2003. Signed as a free agent by **Mora** (Sweden), September 6, 2004. Signed as a free agent by **Detroit**, October 4, 2005.

## CLOWE, Ryane

(KLOH, RIGH-uhn) **S.J.**

Right wing. Shoots left. 6'2", 225 lbs. Born, St. John's, Nfld., September 30, 1982. San Jose's 5th choice, 175th overall, in 2001 Entry Draft.

| Season | Club | League | GP | G | A | Pts | PIM | PP | SH | GW | S | % | +/- | TF | F% | Min | GP | G | A | Pts | PIM | PP | SH | GW | Min |
|---|---|---|---|---|---|---|---|---|---|---|---|---|---|---|---|---|---|---|---|---|---|---|---|---|---|
| 2000-01 | Rimouski Oceanic | QMJHL | 32 | 15 | 10 | 25 | 43 | .... | .... | .... | .... | .... | .... | .... | .... | .... | 11 | 8 | 1 | 9 | 12 | .... | .... | .... | .... |
| 2001-02 | Rimouski Oceanic | QMJHL | 53 | 28 | 45 | 73 | 120 | .... | .... | .... | .... | .... | .... | .... | .... | .... | 7 | 1 | 6 | 7 | 2 | .... | .... | .... | .... |
| 2002-03 | Rimouski Oceanic | QMJHL | 17 | 8 | 19 | 27 | 44 | .... | .... | .... | .... | .... | .... | .... | .... | .... | .... | .... | .... | .... | .... | .... | .... | .... | .... |
| | Montreal Rocket | QMJHL | 43 | 18 | 30 | 48 | 60 | .... | .... | .... | .... | .... | .... | .... | .... | .... | 7 | 3 | 7 | 10 | 6 | .... | .... | .... | .... |
| 2003-04 | Cleveland Barons | AHL | 72 | 11 | 29 | 40 | 97 | .... | .... | .... | .... | .... | .... | .... | .... | .... | 8 | 3 | 1 | 4 | 9 | .... | .... | .... | .... |
| 2004-05 | Cleveland Barons | AHL | 74 | 27 | 35 | 62 | 101 | .... | .... | .... | .... | .... | .... | .... | .... | .... | .... | .... | .... | .... | .... | .... | .... | .... | .... |
| **2005-06** | **San Jose** | **NHL** | **18** | **0** | **2** | **2** | **9** | **0** | **0** | **0** | **14** | **0.0** | **-2** | **2** | **0.0** | **9:40** | **1** | **0** | **0** | **0** | **0** | **0** | **0** | **0** | **5:06** |
| | Cleveland Barons | AHL | 35 | 13 | 21 | 34 | 35 | .... | .... | .... | .... | .... | .... | .... | .... | .... | .... | .... | .... | .... | .... | .... | .... | .... | .... |
| **2006-07** | **San Jose** | **NHL** | **58** | **16** | **18** | **34** | **78** | **4** | **0** | **3** | **93** | **17.2** | **4** | **5** | **60.0** | **13:11** | **11** | **4** | **2** | **6** | **17** | **0** | **0** | **1** | **15:19** |
| **2007-08** | **San Jose** | **NHL** | **15** | **3** | **5** | **8** | **22** | **2** | **0** | **0** | **22** | **13.6** | **-1** | **14** | **35.7** | **14:17** | **13** | **5** | **4** | **9** | **12** | **2** | **0** | **0** | **19:00** |
| **2008-09** | **San Jose** | **NHL** | **71** | **22** | **30** | **52** | **51** | **11** | **0** | **1** | **161** | **13.7** | **8** | **120** | **40.8** | **17:47** | **6** | **1** | **1** | **2** | **8** | **0** | **0** | **0** | **18:22** |
| | **NHL Totals** | | **162** | **41** | **55** | **96** | **160** | **17** | **0** | **4** | **290** | **14.1** | | **141** | **40.4** | **14:54** | **31** | **10** | **7** | **17** | **37** | **2** | **0** | **1** | **17:07** |

• Missed majority of 2007-08 season recovering from knee injury suffered in game at Columbus, October 27, 2007.

## CLUTTERBUCK, Cal

(KLUH-tuhr-buhck, KAL) **MIN.**

Right wing. Shoots right. 5'11", 213 lbs. Born, Welland, Ont., November 18, 1987. Minnesota's 3rd choice, 72nd overall, in 2006 Entry Draft.

| Season | Club | League | GP | G | A | Pts | PIM | PP | SH | GW | S | % | +/- | TF | F% | Min | GP | G | A | Pts | PIM | PP | SH | GW | Min |
|---|---|---|---|---|---|---|---|---|---|---|---|---|---|---|---|---|---|---|---|---|---|---|---|---|---|
| 2004-05 | St. Michael's | OHL | 38 | 10 | 6 | 16 | 55 | .... | .... | .... | .... | .... | .... | .... | .... | .... | .... | .... | .... | .... | .... | .... | .... | .... | .... |
| | Oshawa Generals | OHL | 27 | 9 | 9 | 18 | 42 | .... | .... | .... | .... | .... | .... | .... | .... | .... | .... | .... | .... | .... | .... | .... | .... | .... | .... |
| 2005-06 | Oshawa Generals | OHL | 66 | 35 | 33 | 68 | 139 | .... | .... | .... | .... | .... | .... | .... | .... | .... | .... | .... | .... | .... | .... | .... | .... | .... | .... |
| 2006-07 | Oshawa Generals | OHL | 65 | 35 | 54 | 89 | 153 | .... | .... | .... | .... | .... | .... | .... | .... | .... | 9 | 8 | 5 | 13 | 21 | .... | .... | .... | .... |
| **2007-08** | **Minnesota** | **NHL** | **2** | **0** | **0** | **0** | **0** | **0** | **0** | **0** | **0** | **0.0** | **0** | **1** | **100.0** | **7:05** | .... | .... | .... | .... | .... | .... | .... | .... | .... |
| | Houston Aeros | AHL | 73 | 11 | 13 | 24 | 97 | .... | .... | .... | .... | .... | .... | .... | .... | .... | 5 | 0 | 0 | 0 | 14 | .... | .... | .... | .... |
| **2008-09** | **Minnesota** | **NHL** | **78** | **11** | **7** | **18** | **76** | **1** | **0** | **1** | **136** | **8.1** | **-5** | **17** | **11.8** | **13:00** | .... | .... | .... | .... | .... | .... | .... | .... | .... |
| | Houston Aeros | AHL | 2 | 0 | 0 | 0 | 0 | .... | .... | .... | .... | .... | .... | .... | .... | .... | .... | .... | .... | .... | .... | .... | .... | .... | .... |
| | **NHL Totals** | | **80** | **11** | **7** | **18** | **76** | **1** | **0** | **1** | **136** | **8.1** | | **18** | **16.7** | **12:51** | .... | .... | .... | .... | .... | .... | .... | .... | .... |

## CLYMER, Ben

(KLIH-mehr, BEHN)

Right wing. Shoots right. 6'1", 200 lbs. Born, Bloomington, MN, April 11, 1978. Boston's 3rd choice, 27th overall, in 1997 Entry Draft.

| | | | Regular Season | | | | | | | | | | | | | | Playoffs | | | | | | | | |
|---|---|---|---|---|---|---|---|---|---|---|---|---|---|---|---|---|---|---|---|---|---|---|---|---|---|
| Season | Club | League | GP | G | A | Pts | PIM | PP | SH | GW | S | % | +/- | TF | F% | Min | GP | G | A | Pts | PIM | PP | SH | GW | Min |
| 1993-94 | Jefferson Jaguars | High-MN | 23 | 3 | 7 | 10 | 20 | .... | .... | .... | .... | .... | .... | .... | .... | .... | .... | .... | .... | .... | .... | .... | .... | .... | .... |
| 1994-95 | Jefferson Jaguars | High-MN | 28 | 11 | 22 | 33 | 36 | .... | .... | .... | .... | .... | .... | .... | .... | .... | .... | .... | .... | .... | .... | .... | .... | .... | .... |
| 1995-96 | Jefferson Jaguars | High-MN | 18 | 12 | 34 | 46 | 34 | .... | .... | .... | .... | .... | .... | .... | .... | .... | 5 | 0 | 6 | 6 | 6 | .... | .... | .... | .... |
| 1996-97 | U. of Minnesota | WCHA | 29 | 7 | 13 | 20 | 64 | .... | .... | .... | .... | .... | .... | .... | .... | .... | .... | .... | .... | .... | .... | .... | .... | .... | .... |
| 1997-98 | U. of Minnesota | WCHA | 1 | 0 | 0 | 0 | 2 | .... | .... | .... | .... | .... | .... | .... | .... | .... | .... | .... | .... | .... | .... | .... | .... | .... | .... |
| 1998-99 | Seattle | WHL | 70 | 12 | 44 | 56 | 93 | .... | .... | .... | .... | .... | .... | .... | .... | .... | 11 | 1 | 5 | 6 | 12 | .... | .... | .... | .... |
| **99-2000** | **Tampa Bay** | **NHL** | **60** | **2** | **6** | **8** | **87** | **2** | **0** | **0** | **98** | **2.0** | **-26** | **3** | **66.7** | **19:37** | .... | .... | .... | .... | .... | .... | .... | .... | .... |
| | Detroit Vipers | IHL | 19 | 1 | 9 | 10 | 30 | .... | .... | .... | .... | .... | .... | .... | .... | .... | .... | .... | .... | .... | .... | .... | .... | .... | .... |
| **2000-01** | **Tampa Bay** | **NHL** | **23** | **5** | **1** | **6** | **21** | **3** | **0** | **0** | **25** | **20.0** | **-7** | **8** | **25.0** | **13:03** | .... | .... | .... | .... | .... | .... | .... | .... | .... |
| | Detroit Vipers | IHL | 53 | 5 | 8 | 13 | 88 | .... | .... | .... | .... | .... | .... | .... | .... | .... | .... | .... | .... | .... | .... | .... | .... | .... | .... |
| **2001-02** | **Tampa Bay** | **NHL** | **81** | **14** | **20** | **34** | **36** | **4** | **0** | **2** | **151** | **9.3** | **-10** | **14** | **28.6** | **17:26** | .... | .... | .... | .... | .... | .... | .... | .... | .... |
| **2002-03** | **Tampa Bay** | **NHL** | **65** | **6** | **12** | **18** | **57** | **1** | **0** | **1** | **103** | **5.8** | **-2** | **15** | **0.0** | **13:39** | **11** | **0** | **2** | **2** | **6** | **0** | **0** | **0** | **13:30** |
| **2003-04♦** | **Tampa Bay** | **NHL** | **66** | **2** | **8** | **10** | **50** | **0** | **0** | **0** | **96** | **2.1** | **5** | **25** | **28.0** | **9:48** | **5** | **0** | **0** | **0** | **0** | **0** | **0** | **0** | **7:46** |
| 2004-05 | EHC Biel-Bienne | Swiss-2 | 19 | 11 | 12 | 23 | 30 | .... | .... | .... | .... | .... | .... | .... | .... | .... | 11 | 6 | 11 | 17 | 24 | .... | .... | .... | .... |
| **2005-06** | **Washington** | **NHL** | **77** | **16** | **17** | **33** | **72** | **3** | **0** | **3** | **149** | **10.7** | **-7** | **11** | **45.5** | **14:10** | .... | .... | .... | .... | .... | .... | .... | .... | .... |
| **2006-07** | **Washington** | **NHL** | **66** | **7** | **13** | **20** | **44** | **0** | **0** | **0** | **78** | **9.0** | **-17** | **7** | **14.3** | **13:57** | .... | .... | .... | .... | .... | .... | .... | .... | .... |
| 2007-08 | Hershey Bears | AHL | 50 | 11 | 16 | 27 | 83 | .... | .... | .... | .... | .... | .... | .... | .... | .... | .... | .... | .... | .... | .... | .... | .... | .... | .... |
| 2008-09 | Dynamo Minsk | Rus-KHL | 49 | 4 | 14 | 18 | 85 | .... | .... | .... | .... | .... | .... | .... | .... | .... | .... | .... | .... | .... | .... | .... | .... | .... | .... |
| | **NHL Totals** | | **438** | **52** | **77** | **129** | **367** | **13** | **0** | **6** | **700** | **7.4** | | **83** | **25.3** | **14:41** | **16** | **0** | **2** | **2** | **6** | **0** | **0** | **0** | **11:42** |

• Missed majority of 1997-98 season recovering from shoulder injury suffered in game vs. University of Michigan (CCHA), October 10, 1997. Signed as a free agent by **Tampa Bay**, October 2, 1999. Signed as a free agent by **Biel-Bienne** (Swiss-2), December 2, 2004. Signed as a free agent by **Washington**, August 8, 2005.

## COBURN, Braydon

(KOH-buhrn, BRAY-duhn) **PHI.**

Defense. Shoots left. 6'5", 220 lbs. Born, Calgary, Alta., February 27, 1985. Atlanta's 1st choice, 8th overall, in 2003 Entry Draft.

| Season | Club | League | GP | G | A | Pts | PIM | PP | SH | GW | S | % | +/- | TF | F% | Min | GP | G | A | Pts | PIM | PP | SH | GW | Min |
|---|---|---|---|---|---|---|---|---|---|---|---|---|---|---|---|---|---|---|---|---|---|---|---|---|---|
| 2000-01 | Notre Dame | SMHL | 32 | 3 | 19 | 22 | 70 | .... | .... | .... | .... | .... | .... | .... | .... | .... | .... | .... | .... | .... | .... | .... | .... | .... | .... |
| | Portland | WHL | 2 | 0 | 1 | 1 | 0 | .... | .... | .... | .... | .... | .... | .... | .... | .... | 14 | 0 | 4 | 4 | 2 | .... | .... | .... | .... |
| 2001-02 | Portland | WHL | 68 | 4 | 33 | 37 | 100 | .... | .... | .... | .... | .... | .... | .... | .... | .... | 7 | 1 | 1 | 2 | 9 | .... | .... | .... | .... |
| 2002-03 | Portland | WHL | 53 | 3 | 16 | 19 | 147 | .... | .... | .... | .... | .... | .... | .... | .... | .... | 7 | 0 | 1 | 1 | 8 | .... | .... | .... | .... |
| 2003-04 | Portland | WHL | 55 | 10 | 20 | 30 | 92 | .... | .... | .... | .... | .... | .... | .... | .... | .... | 5 | 0 | 1 | 1 | 10 | .... | .... | .... | .... |
| 2004-05 | Portland | WHL | 60 | 12 | 32 | 44 | 144 | .... | .... | .... | .... | .... | .... | .... | .... | .... | 7 | 1 | 5 | 6 | 6 | .... | .... | .... | .... |
| | Chicago Wolves | AHL | 3 | 0 | 1 | 1 | 5 | .... | .... | .... | .... | .... | .... | .... | .... | .... | 18 | 0 | 1 | 1 | 36 | .... | .... | .... | .... |
| **2005-06** | **Atlanta** | **NHL** | **9** | **0** | **1** | **1** | **4** | **0** | **0** | **0** | **4** | **0.0** | **-2** | **0** | **0.0** | **7:43** | .... | .... | .... | .... | .... | .... | .... | .... | .... |
| | Chicago Wolves | AHL | 73 | 6 | 20 | 26 | 134 | .... | .... | .... | .... | .... | .... | .... | .... | .... | .... | .... | .... | .... | .... | .... | .... | .... | .... |
| **2006-07** | **Atlanta** | **NHL** | **29** | **0** | **4** | **4** | **30** | **0** | **0** | **0** | **21** | **0.0** | **1** | **0** | **0.0** | **11:41** | .... | .... | .... | .... | .... | .... | .... | .... | .... |
| | Chicago Wolves | AHL | 15 | 1 | 10 | 11 | 36 | .... | .... | .... | .... | .... | .... | .... | .... | .... | .... | .... | .... | .... | .... | .... | .... | .... | .... |
| | **Philadelphia** | **NHL** | **20** | **3** | **4** | **7** | **16** | **1** | **0** | **0** | **33** | **9.1** | **-2** | **0** | **0.0** | **20:58** | .... | .... | .... | .... | .... | .... | .... | .... | .... |
| **2007-08** | **Philadelphia** | **NHL** | **78** | **9** | **27** | **36** | **74** | **5** | **0** | **2** | **113** | **8.0** | **17** | **0** | **0.0** | **21:14** | **14** | **0** | **6** | **6** | **14** | **0** | **0** | **0** | **22:25** |
| **2008-09** | **Philadelphia** | **NHL** | **80** | **7** | **21** | **28** | **97** | **3** | **0** | **0** | **130** | **5.4** | **7** | **0** | **0.0** | **24:37** | **6** | **0** | **3** | **3** | **7** | **0** | **0** | **0** | **26:29** |
| | **NHL Totals** | | **216** | **19** | **57** | **76** | **221** | **9** | **0** | **2** | **301** | **6.3** | | **0** | **0.0** | **20:37** | **20** | **0** | **9** | **9** | **21** | **0** | **0** | **0** | **23:38** |

WHL Rookie of the Year (2002) • WHL West First All-Star Team (2004, 2005) • Canadian Major Junior Second All-Star Team (2005)

Traded to **Philadelphia** by **Atlanta** for Alexei Zhitnik, February 24, 2007.

## COGLIANO, Andrew

(kawg-lee-A-noh, AN-droo) **EDM.**

Center. Shoots left. 5'10", 184 lbs. Born, Toronto, Ont., June 14, 1987. Edmonton's 1st choice, 25th overall, in 2005 Entry Draft.

| Season | Club | League | GP | G | A | Pts | PIM | PP | SH | GW | S | % | +/- | TF | F% | Min | GP | G | A | Pts | PIM | PP | SH | GW | Min |
|---|---|---|---|---|---|---|---|---|---|---|---|---|---|---|---|---|---|---|---|---|---|---|---|---|---|
| 2002-03 | Vaughan | GTHL | 58 | 39 | 54 | 93 | 122 | .... | .... | .... | .... | .... | .... | .... | .... | .... | .... | .... | .... | .... | .... | .... | .... | .... | .... |
| 2003-04 | St. Mike's B's | OPJHL | 36 | 26 | 47 | 73 | 14 | .... | .... | .... | .... | .... | .... | .... | .... | .... | 24 | 11 | 20 | 31 | 12 | .... | .... | .... | .... |
| 2004-05 | St. Mike's B's | OPJHL | 49 | 36 | *66 | *102 | 33 | .... | .... | .... | .... | .... | .... | .... | .... | .... | 25 | *22 | *24 | *46 | 20 | .... | .... | .... | .... |
| 2005-06 | U. of Michigan | CCHA | 39 | 12 | 16 | 28 | 38 | .... | .... | .... | .... | .... | .... | .... | .... | .... | .... | .... | .... | .... | .... | .... | .... | .... | .... |
| 2006-07 | U. of Michigan | CCHA | 38 | 24 | 26 | 50 | 12 | .... | .... | .... | .... | .... | .... | .... | .... | .... | .... | .... | .... | .... | .... | .... | .... | .... | .... |
| **2007-08** | **Edmonton** | **NHL** | **82** | **18** | **27** | **45** | **20** | **1** | **2** | **5** | **98** | **18.4** | **1** | **542** | **39.5** | **13:40** | .... | .... | .... | .... | .... | .... | .... | .... | .... |
| **2008-09** | **Edmonton** | **NHL** | **82** | **18** | **20** | **38** | **22** | **4** | **0** | **4** | **116** | **15.5** | **-6** | **702** | **37.2** | **14:24** | .... | .... | .... | .... | .... | .... | .... | .... | .... |
| | **NHL Totals** | | **164** | **36** | **47** | **83** | **42** | **5** | **2** | **9** | **214** | **16.8** | | **1244** | **38.2** | **14:02** | .... | .... | .... | .... | .... | .... | .... | .... | .... |

CCHA All-Rookie Team (2006)

## COLAIACOVO, Carlo

(koh-lee-A-KOH-voh, KAHR-loh) **ST.L.**

Defense. Shoots left. 6'1", 200 lbs. Born, Toronto, Ont., January 27, 1983. Toronto's 1st choice, 17th overall, in 2001 Entry Draft.

| Season | Club | League | GP | G | A | Pts | PIM | PP | SH | GW | S | % | +/- | TF | F% | Min | GP | G | A | Pts | PIM | PP | SH | GW | Min |
|---|---|---|---|---|---|---|---|---|---|---|---|---|---|---|---|---|---|---|---|---|---|---|---|---|---|
| 1998-99 | Mississauga Reps | GTHL | 44 | 10 | 12 | 23 | 28 | .... | .... | .... | .... | .... | .... | .... | .... | .... | .... | .... | .... | .... | .... | .... | .... | .... | .... |
| 99-2000 | Erie Otters | OHL | 52 | 4 | 18 | 22 | 12 | .... | .... | .... | .... | .... | .... | .... | .... | .... | 13 | 2 | 4 | 6 | 9 | .... | .... | .... | .... |
| 2000-01 | Erie Otters | OHL | 62 | 12 | 27 | 39 | 59 | .... | .... | .... | .... | .... | .... | .... | .... | .... | 14 | 4 | 7 | 11 | 16 | .... | .... | .... | .... |
| 2001-02 | Erie Otters | OHL | 60 | 13 | 27 | 40 | 49 | .... | .... | .... | .... | .... | .... | .... | .... | .... | 21 | 7 | 10 | 17 | 20 | .... | .... | .... | .... |
| **2002-03** | **Toronto** | **NHL** | **2** | **0** | **1** | **1** | **0** | **0** | **0** | **0** | **1** | **0.0** | **0** | **0** | **0.0** | **13:43** | .... | .... | .... | .... | .... | .... | .... | .... | .... |
| | Erie Otters | OHL | 35 | 14 | 21 | 35 | 12 | .... | .... | .... | .... | .... | .... | .... | .... | .... | .... | .... | .... | .... | .... | .... | .... | .... | .... |
| **2003-04** | **Toronto** | **NHL** | **2** | **0** | **1** | **1** | **2** | **0** | **0** | **0** | **0** | **0.0** | **1** | **0** | **0.0** | **13:56** | .... | .... | .... | .... | .... | .... | .... | .... | .... |
| | St. John's | AHL | 62 | 6 | 25 | 31 | 50 | .... | .... | .... | .... | .... | .... | .... | .... | .... | .... | .... | .... | .... | .... | .... | .... | .... | .... |
| 2004-05 | St. John's | AHL | 49 | 4 | 20 | 24 | 59 | .... | .... | .... | .... | .... | .... | .... | .... | .... | 5 | 0 | 1 | 1 | 2 | .... | .... | .... | .... |
| **2005-06** | **Toronto** | **NHL** | **21** | **2** | **5** | **7** | **17** | **1** | **0** | **0** | **21** | **9.5** | **0** | **1** | **0.0** | **15:26** | .... | .... | .... | .... | .... | .... | .... | .... | .... |
| | Toronto Marlies | AHL | 14 | 5 | 6 | 11 | 14 | .... | .... | .... | .... | .... | .... | .... | .... | .... | .... | .... | .... | .... | .... | .... | .... | .... | .... |
| **2006-07** | **Toronto** | **NHL** | **48** | **8** | **9** | **17** | **22** | **0** | **0** | **1** | **60** | **13.3** | **5** | **0** | **0.0** | **17:57** | .... | .... | .... | .... | .... | .... | .... | .... | .... |
| | Toronto Marlies | AHL | 5 | 1 | 5 | 6 | 4 | .... | .... | .... | .... | .... | .... | .... | .... | .... | .... | .... | .... | .... | .... | .... | .... | .... | .... |
| **2007-08** | **Toronto** | **NHL** | **28** | **2** | **4** | **6** | **10** | **0** | **0** | **1** | **30** | **6.7** | **-4** | **0** | **0.0** | **17:26** | .... | .... | .... | .... | .... | .... | .... | .... | .... |
| | Toronto Marlies | AHL | 2 | 0 | 0 | 0 | 0 | .... | .... | .... | .... | .... | .... | .... | .... | .... | .... | .... | .... | .... | .... | .... | .... | .... | .... |
| **2008-09** | **Toronto** | **NHL** | **10** | **0** | **1** | **1** | **6** | **0** | **0** | **0** | **9** | **0.0** | **-2** | **0** | **0.0** | **16:52** | .... | .... | .... | .... | .... | .... | .... | .... | .... |
| | **St. Louis** | **NHL** | **63** | **3** | **26** | **29** | **29** | **0** | **0** | **0** | **78** | **3.8** | **2** | **0** | **0.0** | **18:29** | **4** | **0** | **0** | **0** | **2** | **0** | **0** | **0** | **22:19** |
| | **NHL Totals** | | **174** | **15** | **47** | **62** | **86** | **1** | **0** | **2** | **199** | **7.5** | | **1** | **0.0** | **17:36** | **4** | **0** | **0** | **0** | **2** | **0** | **0** | **0** | **22:19** |

OHL Second All-Star Team (2002, 2003)

• Missed remainder of 2005-06 season recovering from head injury suffered in game at Ottawa, January 23, 2006. • Missed majority of 2007-08 season recovering from recurring knee injury. Traded to **St. Louis** by **Toronto** with Alex Steen for Lee Stempniak, November 24, 2008.

## COLE, Erik

(KOHL, AIR-ihk) **CAR.**

Left wing. Shoots left. 6'2", 205 lbs. Born, Oswego, NY, November 6, 1978. Carolina's 3rd choice, 71st overall, in 1998 Entry Draft.

| Season | Club | League | GP | G | A | Pts | PIM | PP | SH | GW | S | % | +/- | TF | F% | Min | GP | G | A | Pts | PIM | PP | SH | GW | Min |
|---|---|---|---|---|---|---|---|---|---|---|---|---|---|---|---|---|---|---|---|---|---|---|---|---|---|
| 1995-96 | Oswego | High-NY | 40 | 49 | 41 | 90 | .... | .... | .... | .... | .... | .... | .... | .... | .... | .... | .... | .... | .... | .... | .... | .... | .... | .... | .... |
| 1996-97 | Des Moines | USHL | 48 | 30 | 34 | 64 | 140 | .... | .... | .... | .... | .... | .... | .... | .... | .... | 5 | 2 | 0 | 2 | 6 | .... | .... | .... | .... |
| 1997-98 | Clarkson Knights | ECAC | 34 | 11 | 20 | 31 | 55 | .... | .... | .... | .... | .... | .... | .... | .... | .... | .... | .... | .... | .... | .... | .... | .... | .... | .... |
| 1998-99 | Clarkson Knights | ECAC | 36 | *22 | 20 | 42 | 50 | .... | .... | .... | .... | .... | .... | .... | .... | .... | .... | .... | .... | .... | .... | .... | .... | .... | .... |
| 99-2000 | Clarkson Knights | ECAC | 33 | 19 | 11 | 30 | 46 | .... | .... | .... | .... | .... | .... | .... | .... | .... | .... | .... | .... | .... | .... | .... | .... | .... | .... |
| | Cincinnati | IHL | 9 | 4 | 3 | 7 | 2 | .... | .... | .... | .... | .... | .... | .... | .... | .... | 7 | 1 | 1 | 2 | 2 | .... | .... | .... | .... |
| 2000-01 | Cincinnati | IHL | 69 | 23 | 20 | 43 | 28 | .... | .... | .... | .... | .... | .... | .... | .... | .... | 5 | 1 | 0 | 1 | 2 | .... | .... | .... | .... |
| **2001-02** | **Carolina** | **NHL** | **81** | **16** | **24** | **40** | **35** | **3** | **0** | **2** | **159** | **10.1** | **-10** | **17** | **47.1** | **16:04** | **23** | **6** | **3** | **9** | **30** | **1** | **0** | **1** | **18:27** |
| **2002-03** | **Carolina** | **NHL** | **53** | **14** | **13** | **27** | **72** | **6** | **2** | **3** | **125** | **11.2** | **1** | **56** | **39.3** | **17:08** | .... | .... | .... | .... | .... | .... | .... | .... | .... |
| **2003-04** | **Carolina** | **NHL** | **80** | **18** | **24** | **42** | **93** | **2** | **2** | **3** | **172** | **10.5** | **-4** | **15** | **46.7** | **18:06** | .... | .... | .... | .... | .... | .... | .... | .... | .... |
| 2004-05 | Eisbaren Berlin | Germany | 39 | 6 | 21 | 27 | 76 | .... | .... | .... | .... | .... | .... | .... | .... | .... | 8 | 5 | 1 | 6 | 37 | .... | .... | .... | .... |
| **2005-06♦** | **Carolina** | **NHL** | **60** | **30** | **29** | **59** | **54** | **3** | **3** | **8** | **164** | **18.3** | **19** | **19** | **36.8** | **19:18** | **2** | **0** | **0** | **0** | **0** | **0** | **0** | **0** | **15:29** |
| | United States | Olympics | 6 | 1 | 2 | 3 | 0 | .... | .... | .... | .... | .... | .... | .... | .... | .... | .... | .... | .... | .... | .... | .... | .... | .... | .... |
| **2006-07** | **Carolina** | **NHL** | **71** | **29** | **32** | **61** | **76** | **9** | **0** | **4** | **166** | **17.5** | **2** | **27** | **40.7** | **18:01** | .... | .... | .... | .... | .... | .... | .... | .... | .... |
| **2007-08** | **Carolina** | **NHL** | **73** | **22** | **29** | **51** | **76** | **10** | **0** | **4** | **216** | **10.2** | **5** | **38** | **23.7** | **19:22** | .... | .... | .... | .... | .... | .... | .... | .... | .... |

| | | | Regular Season | | | | | | | | | | | | | | Playoffs | | | | | | | | |
|---|---|---|---|---|---|---|---|---|---|---|---|---|---|---|---|---|---|---|---|---|---|---|---|---|---|
| Season | Club | League | GP | G | A | Pts | PIM | PP | SH | GW | S | % | +/- | TF | F% | Min | GP | G | A | Pts | PIM | PP | SH | GW | Min |
| **2008-09** | **Edmonton** | **NHL** | **63** | **16** | **11** | **27** | **63** | **5** | **0** | **1** | **145** | **11.0** | **−3** | **48** | **39.6** | **17:05** | | | | | | | | | |
| | **Carolina** | **NHL** | **17** | **2** | **13** | **15** | **10** | **0** | **0** | **0** | **33** | **6.1** | **3** | **1** | **100.0** | **19:36** | **18** | **0** | **5** | **5** | **22** | **0** | **0** | **0** | **17:17** |
| | **NHL Totals** | | **498** | **147** | **175** | **322** | **479** | **38** | **7** | **25** | **1180** | **12.5** | | **221** | **38.0** | **17:54** | **43** | **6** | **8** | **14** | **52** | **1** | **0** | **1** | **17:50** |

USHL Second All-Star Team (1997) • ECAC Rookie of the Year (1998) (co-winner - Willie Mitchell) • ECAC First All-Star Team (1999) • NCAA East Second All-American Team (1999) • ECAC Second All-Star Team (2000)

Signed as a free agent by **Berlin** (Germany), October 24, 2004. Traded to **Edmonton** by **Carolina** for Joni Pitkanen, July 1, 2008. Traded to **Carolina** by **Edmonton** with Edmonton's 5th round choice (Matt Kennedy) in 2009 Entry Draft for Patrick O'Sullivan and Carolina's 2nd round choice (later traded to Buffalo – later traded to Toronto – Toronto selected Jesse Blacker) in 2009 Entry Draft, March 4, 2009.

## COLLINS, Sean

(KAW-lihnz, SHAWN) **WSH.**

Defense. Shoots right. 6'1", 212 lbs. Born, Troy, MI, October 30, 1983.

| Season | Club | League | GP | G | A | Pts | PIM | PP | SH | GW | S | % | +/- | TF | F% | Min | GP | G | A | Pts | PIM | PP | SH | GW | Min |
|---|---|---|---|---|---|---|---|---|---|---|---|---|---|---|---|---|---|---|---|---|---|---|---|---|---|
| 2002-03 | Sioux City | USHL | 59 | 6 | 22 | 28 | 89 | | | | | | | | | | 4 | 0 | 1 | 1 | 2 | | | | |
| 2003-04 | Ohio State | CCHA | 41 | 3 | 12 | 15 | 57 | | | | | | | | | | | | | | | | | | |
| 2004-05 | Ohio State | CCHA | 40 | 9 | 17 | 26 | 40 | | | | | | | | | | | | | | | | | | |
| 2005-06 | Ohio State | CCHA | 39 | 7 | 11 | 18 | 63 | | | | | | | | | | | | | | | | | | |
| 2006-07 | Ohio State | CCHA | 37 | 9 | 19 | 28 | 50 | | | | | | | | | | | | | | | | | | |
| | Hershey Bears | AHL | 3 | 0 | 0 | 0 | 2 | | | | | | | | | | | | | | | | | | |
| 2007-08 | Hershey Bears | AHL | 12 | 0 | 0 | 0 | 11 | | | | | | | | | | | | | | | | | | |
| | South Carolina | ECHL | 31 | 1 | 13 | 14 | 16 | | | | | | | | | | 20 | 1 | 8 | 9 | 24 | | | | |
| **2008-09** | **Washington** | **NHL** | **15** | **1** | **1** | **2** | **12** | **0** | **0** | **0** | **14** | **7.1** | **1** | **0** | **0.0** | **14:32** | | | | | | | | | |
| | Hershey Bears | AHL | 39 | 1 | 7 | 8 | 38 | | | | | | | | | | 6 | 0 | 2 | 2 | 2 | | | | |
| | **NHL Totals** | | **15** | **1** | **1** | **2** | **12** | **0** | **0** | **0** | **14** | **7.1** | | **0** | **0.0** | **14:32** | | | | | | | | | |

Signed as a free agent by **Washington**, March 19, 2007.

## COLLITON, Jeremy

(KAW-lih-tuhn, JAIR-eh-mee)

Center. Shoots right. 6'2", 195 lbs. Born, Blackie, Alta., January 13, 1985. NY Islanders' 4th choice, 58th overall, in 2003 Entry Draft.

| Season | Club | League | GP | G | A | Pts | PIM | PP | SH | GW | S | % | +/- | TF | F% | Min | GP | G | A | Pts | PIM | PP | SH | GW | Min |
|---|---|---|---|---|---|---|---|---|---|---|---|---|---|---|---|---|---|---|---|---|---|---|---|---|---|
| 99-2000 | Airdrie Express | AMHL | 33 | 16 | 25 | 41 | 28 | | | | | | | | | | | | | | | | | | |
| 2000-01 | Crowsnest Pass | AJHL | 63 | 18 | 30 | 48 | 98 | | | | | | | | | | | | | | | | | | |
| 2001-02 | Prince Albert | WHL | 68 | 11 | 21 | 32 | 53 | | | | | | | | | | | | | | | | | | |
| 2002-03 | Prince Albert | WHL | 58 | 20 | 28 | 48 | 76 | | | | | | | | | | | | | | | | | | |
| 2003-04 | Prince Albert | WHL | 62 | 24 | 26 | 50 | 73 | | | | | | | | | | 6 | 5 | 5 | 10 | 8 | | | | |
| 2004-05 | Prince Albert | WHL | 41 | 16 | 30 | 46 | 25 | | | | | | | | | | 17 | 3 | 4 | 7 | 21 | | | | |
| **2005-06** | **NY Islanders** | **NHL** | **19** | **1** | **1** | **2** | **6** | **0** | **0** | **0** | **9** | **11.1** | **2** | **76** | **40.8** | **6:18** | | | | | | | | | |
| | Bridgeport | AHL | 66 | 20 | 32 | 52 | 44 | | | | | | | | | | 6 | 0 | 1 | 1 | 2 | | | | |
| **2006-07** | **NY Islanders** | **NHL** | **1** | **0** | **0** | **0** | **0** | **0** | **0** | **0** | **0** | **0.0** | **−1** | **0** | **0.0** | **4:40** | | | | | | | | | |
| | Bridgeport | AHL | 45 | 10 | 12 | 22 | 32 | | | | | | | | | | | | | | | | | | |
| **2007-08** | **NY Islanders** | **NHL** | **16** | **0** | **0** | **0** | **8** | **0** | **0** | **0** | **16** | **0.0** | **−4** | **104** | **51.9** | **8:46** | | | | | | | | | |
| | Bridgeport | AHL | 65 | 9 | 11 | 20 | 44 | | | | | | | | | | | | | | | | | | |
| **2008-09** | **NY Islanders** | **NHL** | **6** | **0** | **1** | **1** | **2** | **0** | **0** | **0** | **4** | **0.0** | **−2** | **70** | **64.3** | **11:03** | | | | | | | | | |
| | Bridgeport | AHL | 56 | 8 | 28 | 36 | 36 | | | | | | | | | | 2 | 0 | 1 | 1 | 0 | | | | |
| | **NHL Totals** | | **42** | **1** | **2** | **3** | **16** | **0** | **0** | **0** | **29** | **3.4** | | **250** | **52.0** | **7:53** | | | | | | | | | |

Signed as a free agent by **Rogle** (Sweden), June 19, 2009.

## COMEAU, Blake

(KOH-moh, BLAYK) **NYI**

Right wing. Shoots right. 6'1", 207 lbs. Born, Meadow Lake, Sask., February 18, 1986. NY Islanders' 2nd choice, 47th overall, in 2004 Entry Draft.

| Season | Club | League | GP | G | A | Pts | PIM | PP | SH | GW | S | % | +/- | TF | F% | Min | GP | G | A | Pts | PIM | PP | SH | GW | Min |
|---|---|---|---|---|---|---|---|---|---|---|---|---|---|---|---|---|---|---|---|---|---|---|---|---|---|
| 2001-02 | Sask. Contacts | SMHL | 42 | 27 | 33 | 60 | 72 | | | | | | | | | | | | | | | | | | |
| | Kelowna Rockets | WHL | 3 | 0 | 0 | 0 | 4 | | | | | | | | | | | | | | | | | | |
| 2002-03 | Kelowna Rockets | WHL | 54 | 5 | 18 | 23 | 77 | | | | | | | | | | 19 | 2 | 1 | 3 | 20 | | | | |
| 2003-04 | Kelowna Rockets | WHL | 71 | 10 | 23 | 33 | 123 | | | | | | | | | | 17 | 4 | 2 | 6 | 23 | | | | |
| 2004-05 | Kelowna Rockets | WHL | 65 | 24 | 23 | 47 | 108 | | | | | | | | | | 24 | 6 | 12 | 18 | 34 | | | | |
| 2005-06 | Kelowna Rockets | WHL | 60 | 21 | 53 | 74 | 85 | | | | | | | | | | 12 | 4 | 9 | 13 | 22 | | | | |
| | Bridgeport | AHL | | | | | | | | | | | | | | | 7 | 0 | 3 | 3 | 0 | | | | |
| **2006-07** | **NY Islanders** | **NHL** | **3** | **0** | **0** | **0** | **0** | **0** | **0** | **0** | **1** | **0.0** | **0** | **0** | **0.0** | **9:25** | | | | | | | | | |
| | Bridgeport | AHL | 61 | 12 | 31 | 43 | 46 | | | | | | | | | | | | | | | | | | |
| **2007-08** | **NY Islanders** | **NHL** | **51** | **8** | **7** | **15** | **22** | **1** | **0** | **1** | **67** | **11.9** | **1** | **27** | **29.6** | **11:40** | | | | | | | | | |
| | Bridgeport | AHL | 31 | 4 | 15 | 19 | 30 | | | | | | | | | | | | | | | | | | |
| **2008-09** | **NY Islanders** | **NHL** | **53** | **7** | **18** | **25** | **32** | **2** | **0** | **0** | **78** | **9.0** | **−17** | **45** | **31.1** | **16:17** | | | | | | | | | |
| | Bridgeport | AHL | 19 | 4 | 15 | 19 | 22 | | | | | | | | | | 2 | 0 | 0 | 0 | 0 | | | | |
| | **NHL Totals** | | **107** | **15** | **25** | **40** | **54** | **3** | **0** | **1** | **146** | **10.3** | | **72** | **30.6** | **13:53** | | | | | | | | | |

WHL West First All-Star Team (2006)

## COMMODORE, Mike

(KAWM-uh-dohr, MIGHK) **CBJ**

Defense. Shoots right. 6'5", 228 lbs. Born, Fort Saskatchewan, Alta., November 7, 1979. New Jersey's 2nd choice, 42nd overall, in 1999 Entry Draft.

| Season | Club | League | GP | G | A | Pts | PIM | PP | SH | GW | S | % | +/- | TF | F% | Min | GP | G | A | Pts | PIM | PP | SH | GW | Min |
|---|---|---|---|---|---|---|---|---|---|---|---|---|---|---|---|---|---|---|---|---|---|---|---|---|---|
| 1996-97 | Ft. Saskatchewan | AJHL | 51 | 3 | 8 | 11 | 244 | | | | | | | | | | | | | | | | | | |
| 1997-98 | North Dakota | WCHA | 29 | 0 | 5 | 5 | 74 | | | | | | | | | | | | | | | | | | |
| 1998-99 | North Dakota | WCHA | 39 | 5 | 8 | 13 | 154 | | | | | | | | | | | | | | | | | | |
| 99-2000 | North Dakota | WCHA | 38 | 5 | 7 | 12 | *154 | | | | | | | | | | | | | | | | | | |
| **2000-01** | **New Jersey** | **NHL** | **20** | **1** | **4** | **5** | **14** | **0** | **0** | **0** | **11** | **9.1** | **5** | **0** | **0.0** | **12:46** | | | | | | | | | |
| | Albany River Rats | AHL | 41 | 2 | 5 | 7 | 59 | | | | | | | | | | | | | | | | | | |
| **2001-02** | **New Jersey** | **NHL** | **37** | **0** | **1** | **1** | **30** | **0** | **0** | **0** | **22** | **0.0** | **−12** | **0** | **0.0** | **12:37** | | | | | | | | | |
| | Albany River Rats | AHL | 14 | 0 | 3 | 3 | 31 | | | | | | | | | | | | | | | | | | |
| **2002-03** | Cincinnati | AHL | 61 | 2 | 9 | 11 | 210 | | | | | | | | | | | | | | | | | | |
| | **Calgary** | **NHL** | **6** | **0** | **1** | **1** | **19** | **0** | **0** | **0** | **5** | **0.0** | **2** | **0** | **0.0** | **11:35** | | | | | | | | | |
| | Saint John Flames | AHL | 7 | 0 | 3 | 3 | 18 | | | | | | | | | | | | | | | | | | |
| **2003-04** | **Calgary** | **NHL** | **12** | **0** | **0** | **0** | **25** | **0** | **0** | **0** | **10** | **0.0** | **−4** | **0** | **0.0** | **15:17** | **20** | **0** | **2** | **2** | **19** | **0** | **0** | **0** | **11:34** |
| | Lowell | AHL | 37 | 5 | 11 | 16 | 75 | | | | | | | | | | | | | | | | | | |
| 2004-05 | Lowell | AHL | 73 | 6 | 29 | 35 | 175 | | | | | | | | | | 11 | 1 | 2 | 3 | 18 | | | | |
| **2005-06**♦ | **Carolina** | **NHL** | **72** | **3** | **10** | **13** | **138** | **0** | **0** | **2** | **72** | **4.2** | **12** | **1** | **0.0** | **15:30** | **25** | **2** | **2** | **4** | **33** | **0** | **1** | **0** | **19:27** |
| **2006-07** | **Carolina** | **NHL** | **82** | **7** | **22** | **29** | **113** | **0** | **2** | **1** | **136** | **5.1** | **0** | **0** | **0.0** | **19:54** | | | | | | | | | |
| **2007-08** | **Carolina** | **NHL** | **41** | **3** | **9** | **12** | **74** | **0** | **0** | **0** | **67** | **4.5** | **2** | **0** | **0.0** | **19:16** | | | | | | | | | |
| | **Ottawa** | **NHL** | **26** | **0** | **2** | **2** | **26** | **0** | **0** | **0** | **30** | **0.0** | **−9** | **0** | **0.0** | **16:33** | **4** | **0** | **2** | **2** | **0** | **0** | **0** | **0** | **20:14** |
| **2008-09** | **Columbus** | **NHL** | **81** | **5** | **19** | **24** | **100** | **0** | **0** | **0** | **103** | **4.9** | **11** | **3** | **66.7** | **22:54** | **4** | **0** | **0** | **0** | **18** | **0** | **0** | **0** | **21:32** |
| | **NHL Totals** | | **377** | **19** | **68** | **87** | **539** | **0** | **2** | **3** | **456** | **4.2** | | **4** | **50.0** | **18:02** | **53** | **2** | **6** | **8** | **70** | **0** | **1** | **0** | **16:42** |

NCAA Championship All-Tournament Team (2000)

Traded to **Anaheim** by **New Jersey** with Petr Sykora, Jean-Francois Damphousse and Igor Pohanka for Jeff Friesen, Oleg Tverdovsky and Maxim Balmochnykh, July 6, 2002. Traded to **Calgary** by **Anaheim** with Jean-Francois Damphousse for Rob Niedermayer, March 11, 2003. Traded to **Carolina** by **Calgary** for Atlanta's 3rd round choice (previously acquired, Calgary selected Gord Baldwin) in 2005 Entry Draft, July 29, 2005. Traded to **Ottawa** by **Carolina** with Cory Stillman for Joe Corvo and Patrick Eaves, February 11, 2008. Signed as a free agent by **Columbus**, July 1, 2008.

## COMRIE, Mike

(KAWM-ree, MIGHK)

Center. Shoots left. 5'10", 185 lbs. Born, Edmonton, Alta., September 11, 1980. Edmonton's 5th choice, 91st overall, in 1999 Entry Draft.

| Season | Club | League | GP | G | A | Pts | PIM | PP | SH | GW | S | % | +/- | TF | F% | Min | GP | G | A | Pts | PIM | PP | SH | GW | Min |
|---|---|---|---|---|---|---|---|---|---|---|---|---|---|---|---|---|---|---|---|---|---|---|---|---|---|
| 1995-96 | Edmonton SSAC | AMHL | 33 | 51 | 52 | 103 | | | | | | | | | | | | | | | | | | | |
| 1996-97 | St. Albert Saints | AJHL | 63 | 37 | 41 | 78 | 44 | | | | | | | | | | | | | | | | | | |
| 1997-98 | St. Albert Saints | AJHL | 58 | *60 | *78 | *138 | 134 | | | | | | | | | | 19 | *24 | *24 | *48 | 51 | | | | |
| 1998-99 | U. of Michigan | CCHA | 42 | 19 | 25 | 44 | 38 | | | | | | | | | | | | | | | | | | |
| 99-2000 | U. of Michigan | CCHA | 40 | 24 | 35 | 59 | 95 | | | | | | | | | | | | | | | | | | |
| **2000-01** | Kootenay Ice | WHL | 37 | 39 | 40 | 79 | 79 | | | | | | | | | | | | | | | | | | |
| | **Edmonton** | **NHL** | **41** | **8** | **14** | **22** | **14** | **3** | **0** | **1** | **62** | **12.9** | **6** | **372** | **43.3** | **11:23** | **6** | **1** | **2** | **3** | **0** | **1** | **0** | **1** | **15:00** |
| **2001-02** | **Edmonton** | **NHL** | **82** | **33** | **27** | **60** | **45** | **8** | **0** | **5** | **170** | **19.4** | **16** | **1198** | **47.3** | **17:32** | | | | | | | | | |
| **2002-03** | **Edmonton** | **NHL** | **69** | **20** | **31** | **51** | **90** | **8** | **0** | **6** | **170** | **11.8** | **−18** | **1069** | **47.1** | **17:51** | **6** | **1** | **0** | **1** | **10** | **0** | **0** | **0** | **13:07** |
| **2003-04** | **Philadelphia** | **NHL** | **21** | **4** | **5** | **9** | **12** | **0** | **0** | **1** | **36** | **11.1** | **2** | **165** | **50.9** | **12:51** | | | | | | | | | |
| | **Phoenix** | **NHL** | **28** | **8** | **7** | **15** | **16** | **1** | **1** | **1** | **65** | **12.3** | **−8** | **304** | **50.3** | **17:50** | | | | | | | | | |
| 2004-05 | Farjestad | Sweden | 10 | 1 | 6 | 7 | 10 | | | | | | | | | | | | | | | | | | |
| **2005-06** | **Phoenix** | **NHL** | **80** | **30** | **30** | **60** | **55** | **10** | **0** | **4** | **190** | **15.8** | **2** | **781** | **52.8** | **16:01** | | | | | | | | | |

| | | | Regular Season | | | | | | | | | | | | | | Playoffs | | | | | | | | |
|---|---|---|---|---|---|---|---|---|---|---|---|---|---|---|---|---|---|---|---|---|---|---|---|---|---|
| Season | Club | League | GP | G | A | Pts | PIM | PP | SH | GW | S | % | +/- | TF | F% | Min | GP | G | A | Pts | PIM | PP | SH | GW | Min |
| **2006-07** | **Phoenix** | **NHL** | **24** | **7** | **13** | **20** | **20** | **4** | **0** | **1** | **38** | **18.4** | **1** | **210** | **48.6** | **16:36** | .... | .... | .... | .... | .... | .... | .... | .... | .... |
| | **Ottawa** | **NHL** | **41** | **13** | **12** | **25** | **24** | **3** | **0** | **2** | **87** | **14.9** | **−1** | **244** | **50.0** | **14:27** | **20** | **2** | **4** | **6** | **17** | **0** | **0** | **0** | **12:41** |
| **2007-08** | **NY Islanders** | **NHL** | **76** | **21** | **28** | **49** | **87** | **4** | **0** | **3** | **194** | **10.8** | **−21** | **1227** | **46.0** | **19:11** | .... | .... | .... | .... | .... | .... | .... | .... | .... |
| **2008-09** | **NY Islanders** | **NHL** | **41** | **7** | **13** | **20** | **26** | **2** | **0** | **0** | **80** | **8.8** | **−8** | **390** | **41.3** | **16:28** | .... | .... | .... | .... | .... | .... | .... | .... | .... |
| | **Ottawa** | **NHL** | **22** | **3** | **4** | **7** | **6** | **0** | **0** | **1** | **41** | **7.3** | **−7** | **27** | **37.0** | **14:17** | .... | .... | .... | .... | .... | .... | .... | .... | .... |
| | **NHL Totals** | | **525** | **154** | **184** | **338** | **395** | **43** | **1** | **25** | **1133** | **13.6** | | **5987** | **47.4** | **16:26** | **32** | **4** | **6** | **10** | **27** | **1** | **0** | **1** | **13:12** |

CCHA All-Rookie Team (1999) • CCHA First All-Star Team (1999) • CCHA Rookie of the Year (1999) • CCHA First All-Star Team (2000) • NCAA West Second All-American Team (2000)

• Left **University of Michigan** (CCHA) and signed as a free agent by **Kootenay** (WHL), August 23, 2000. • Left **Kootenay** (WHL) and signed with **Edmonton**, December 30, 2000. Traded to **Philadelphia** by **Edmonton** for Jeff Woywitka, Philadelphia's 1st round choice (Rob Schremp) in 2004 Entry Draft and Philadelphia's 3rd round choice (Danny Syvret) in 2005 Entry Draft, December 16, 2003. Traded to **Phoenix** by **Philadelphia** for Sean Burke, Branko Radivojevic and Ben Eager, February 9, 2004. Signed as a free agent by **Farjestad** (Sweden), October 30, 2004. Traded to **Ottawa** by **Phoenix** for Alexei Kaigorodov, January 3, 2007. Signed as a free agent by **NY Islanders**, July 5, 2007. Traded to **Ottawa** by **NY Islanders** with Chris Campoli for Dean McAmmond and San Jose's 1st round choice (previously acquired, later traded to Columbus, later traded to Anaheim – Anaheim selected Kyle Palmieri) in 2009 Entry Draft, February 20, 2009.

## CONBOY, Tim

(KAWN-boi, TIHM) **CAR.**

Defense. Shoots right. 6'2", 210 lbs. Born, Farmington, MN, March 22, 1982. San Jose's 6th choice, 217th overall, in 2002 Entry Draft.

| Season | Club | League | GP | G | A | Pts | PIM | PP | SH | GW | S | % | +/- | TF | F% | Min | GP | G | A | Pts | PIM | PP | SH | GW | Min |
|---|---|---|---|---|---|---|---|---|---|---|---|---|---|---|---|---|---|---|---|---|---|---|---|---|---|
| 99-2000 | Brainerd | High-MN | 22 | 20 | 26 | 46 | .... | .... | .... | .... | .... | .... | .... | .... | .... | .... | .... | .... | .... | .... | .... | .... | .... | .... | .... |
| 2000-01 | Rochester | USHL | 51 | 5 | 9 | 14 | 256 | .... | .... | .... | .... | .... | .... | .... | .... | .... | .... | .... | .... | .... | .... | .... | .... | .... | .... |
| 2001-02 | Rochester | USHL | 14 | 1 | 6 | 7 | 65 | .... | .... | .... | .... | .... | .... | .... | .... | .... | .... | .... | .... | .... | .... | .... | .... | .... | .... |
| | Topeka | USHL | 29 | 4 | 15 | 19 | 128 | .... | .... | .... | .... | .... | .... | .... | .... | .... | .... | .... | .... | .... | .... | .... | .... | .... | .... |
| 2002-03 | St. Cloud State | WCHA | 31 | 3 | 12 | 15 | 48 | .... | .... | .... | .... | .... | .... | .... | .... | .... | .... | .... | .... | .... | .... | .... | .... | .... | .... |
| 2003-04 | St. Cloud State | WCHA | 32 | 5 | 5 | 10 | 68 | .... | .... | .... | .... | .... | .... | .... | .... | .... | .... | .... | .... | .... | .... | .... | .... | .... | .... |
| | Cleveland Barons | AHL | .... | .... | .... | .... | .... | .... | .... | .... | .... | .... | .... | .... | .... | .... | 3 | 0 | 3 | 3 | 4 | .... | .... | .... | .... |
| 2004-05 | Cleveland Barons | AHL | 61 | 4 | 11 | 15 | 134 | .... | .... | .... | .... | .... | .... | .... | .... | .... | .... | .... | .... | .... | .... | .... | .... | .... | .... |
| 2005-06 | Cleveland Barons | AHL | 78 | 6 | 14 | 20 | 124 | .... | .... | .... | .... | .... | .... | .... | .... | .... | .... | .... | .... | .... | .... | .... | .... | .... | .... |
| 2006-07 | Albany River Rats | AHL | 75 | 3 | 7 | 10 | 163 | .... | .... | .... | .... | .... | .... | .... | .... | .... | 5 | 0 | 1 | 1 | 6 | .... | .... | .... | .... |
| **2007-08** | **Carolina** | **NHL** | **19** | **0** | **5** | **5** | **60** | **0** | **0** | **0** | **16** | **0.0** | **1** | **0** | **0.0** | **6:58** | .... | .... | .... | .... | .... | .... | .... | .... | .... |
| | Albany River Rats | AHL | 52 | 2 | 2 | 4 | 191 | .... | .... | .... | .... | .... | .... | .... | .... | .... | 1 | 0 | 0 | 0 | 21 | .... | .... | .... | .... |
| **2008-09** | **Carolina** | **NHL** | **28** | **0** | **1** | **1** | **37** | **0** | **0** | **0** | **13** | **0.0** | **−1** | **0** | **0.0** | **5:21** | **3** | **0** | **0** | **0** | **9** | **0** | **0** | **0** | **4:22** |
| | Albany River Rats | AHL | 39 | 1 | 5 | 6 | 127 | .... | .... | .... | .... | .... | .... | .... | .... | .... | .... | .... | .... | .... | .... | .... | .... | .... | .... |
| | **NHL Totals** | | **47** | **0** | **6** | **6** | **97** | **0** | **0** | **0** | **29** | **0.0** | | **0** | **0.0** | **6:00** | **3** | **0** | **0** | **0** | **9** | **0** | **0** | **0** | **4:22** |

Signed as a free agent by **Carolina**, July 21, 2006.

## CONNER, Chris

(KAWN-uhr, KRIHS) **PIT.**

Wing. Shoots left. 5'8", 180 lbs. Born, Westland, MI, December 23, 1983.

| Season | Club | League | GP | G | A | Pts | PIM | PP | SH | GW | S | % | +/- | TF | F% | Min | GP | G | A | Pts | PIM | PP | SH | GW | Min |
|---|---|---|---|---|---|---|---|---|---|---|---|---|---|---|---|---|---|---|---|---|---|---|---|---|---|
| 2002-03 | Michigan Tech | WCHA | 38 | 13 | 24 | 37 | 8 | .... | .... | .... | .... | .... | .... | .... | .... | .... | .... | .... | .... | .... | .... | .... | .... | .... | .... |
| 2003-04 | Michigan Tech | WCHA | 38 | 25 | 14 | 39 | 12 | .... | .... | .... | .... | .... | .... | .... | .... | .... | .... | .... | .... | .... | .... | .... | .... | .... | .... |
| 2004-05 | Michigan Tech | WCHA | 37 | 14 | 10 | 24 | 6 | .... | .... | .... | .... | .... | .... | .... | .... | .... | .... | .... | .... | .... | .... | .... | .... | .... | .... |
| 2005-06 | Michigan Tech | WCHA | 38 | 17 | 12 | 29 | 18 | .... | .... | .... | .... | .... | .... | .... | .... | .... | .... | .... | .... | .... | .... | .... | .... | .... | .... |
| | Iowa Stars | AHL | 15 | 2 | 3 | 5 | 0 | .... | .... | .... | .... | .... | .... | .... | .... | .... | 7 | 1 | 1 | 2 | 2 | .... | .... | .... | .... |
| **2006-07** | **Dallas** | **NHL** | **11** | **1** | **2** | **3** | **4** | **0** | **0** | **0** | **18** | **5.6** | **−3** | **1** | **100.0** | **11:15** | .... | .... | .... | .... | .... | .... | .... | .... | .... |
| | Iowa Stars | AHL | 48 | 19 | 18 | 37 | 24 | .... | .... | .... | .... | .... | .... | .... | .... | .... | 12 | 2 | 5 | 7 | 2 | .... | .... | .... | .... |
| **2007-08** | **Dallas** | **NHL** | **22** | **3** | **2** | **5** | **6** | **0** | **0** | **0** | **27** | **11.1** | **0** | **1** | **100.0** | **12:00** | **1** | **0** | **0** | **0** | **0** | **0** | **0** | **0** | **4:17** |
| | Iowa Stars | AHL | 55 | 13 | 26 | 39 | 17 | .... | .... | .... | .... | .... | .... | .... | .... | .... | .... | .... | .... | .... | .... | .... | .... | .... | .... |
| **2008-09** | **Dallas** | **NHL** | **38** | **3** | **10** | **13** | **10** | **0** | **0** | **1** | **34** | **8.8** | **−5** | **1** | **0.0** | **10:56** | .... | .... | .... | .... | .... | .... | .... | .... | .... |
| | Peoria Rivermen | AHL | 30 | 16 | 12 | 28 | 10 | .... | .... | .... | .... | .... | .... | .... | .... | .... | .... | .... | .... | .... | .... | .... | .... | .... | .... |
| | **NHL Totals** | | **71** | **7** | **14** | **21** | **20** | **0** | **0** | **1** | **79** | **8.9** | | **3** | **66.7** | **11:19** | **1** | **0** | **0** | **0** | **0** | **0** | **0** | **0** | **4:17** |

WCHA Second All-Star Team (2004)

Signed as a free agent by **Dallas**, July 13, 2006. Signed as a free agent by **Pittsburgh**, July 5. 2009.

## CONNOLLY, Tim

(KAW-nuhl-lee, TIHM) **BUF.**

Center. Shoots right. 6'1", 190 lbs. Born, Syracuse, NY, May 7, 1981. NY Islanders' 1st choice, 5th overall, in 1999 Entry Draft.

| Season | Club | League | GP | G | A | Pts | PIM | PP | SH | GW | S | % | +/- | TF | F% | Min | GP | G | A | Pts | PIM | PP | SH | GW | Min |
|---|---|---|---|---|---|---|---|---|---|---|---|---|---|---|---|---|---|---|---|---|---|---|---|---|---|
| 1996-97 | Syracuse | MTJHL | 50 | 42 | 62 | 104 | 34 | .... | .... | .... | .... | .... | .... | .... | .... | .... | .... | .... | .... | .... | .... | .... | .... | .... | .... |
| 1997-98 | Erie Otters | OHL | 59 | 30 | 32 | 62 | 32 | .... | .... | .... | .... | .... | .... | .... | .... | .... | 7 | 1 | 6 | 7 | 6 | .... | .... | .... | .... |
| 1998-99 | Erie Otters | OHL | 46 | 34 | 34 | 68 | 50 | .... | .... | .... | .... | .... | .... | .... | .... | .... | .... | .... | .... | .... | .... | .... | .... | .... | .... |
| **99-2000** | **NY Islanders** | **NHL** | **81** | **14** | **20** | **34** | **44** | **2** | **1** | **1** | **114** | **12.3** | **−25** | **786** | **36.3** | **16:18** | .... | .... | .... | .... | .... | .... | .... | .... | .... |
| **2000-01** | **NY Islanders** | **NHL** | **82** | **10** | **31** | **41** | **42** | **5** | **0** | **0** | **171** | **5.8** | **−14** | **989** | **41.7** | **20:02** | .... | .... | .... | .... | .... | .... | .... | .... | .... |
| **2001-02** | **Buffalo** | **NHL** | **82** | **10** | **35** | **45** | **34** | **3** | **0** | **3** | **126** | **7.9** | **4** | **1074** | **39.6** | **16:58** | .... | .... | .... | .... | .... | .... | .... | .... | .... |
| **2002-03** | **Buffalo** | **NHL** | **80** | **12** | **13** | **25** | **32** | **6** | **0** | **2** | **159** | **7.5** | **−28** | **845** | **42.8** | **16:00** | .... | .... | .... | .... | .... | .... | .... | .... | .... |
| **2003-04** | **Buffalo** | **NHL** | DID NOT PLAY – INJURED | | | | | | | | | | | | | | | | | | | | | | |
| 2004-05 | Langnau | Swiss | 16 | 7 | 3 | 10 | 14 | .... | .... | .... | .... | .... | .... | .... | .... | .... | .... | .... | .... | .... | .... | .... | .... | .... | .... |
| **2005-06** | **Buffalo** | **NHL** | **63** | **16** | **39** | **55** | **28** | **7** | **0** | **3** | **99** | **16.2** | **5** | **844** | **42.5** | **18:00** | **8** | **5** | **6** | **11** | **0** | **1** | **1** | **1** | **17:29** |
| **2006-07** | **Buffalo** | **NHL** | **2** | **1** | **0** | **1** | **2** | **0** | **0** | **0** | **2** | **50.0** | **1** | **13** | **53.9** | **13:07** | **16** | **0** | **9** | **9** | **4** | **0** | **0** | **0** | **16:56** |
| **2007-08** | **Buffalo** | **NHL** | **48** | **7** | **33** | **40** | **8** | **3** | **1** | **3** | **111** | **6.3** | **4** | **463** | **48.0** | **18:41** | .... | .... | .... | .... | .... | .... | .... | .... | .... |
| **2008-09** | **Buffalo** | **NHL** | **48** | **18** | **29** | **47** | **22** | **5** | **1** | **5** | **126** | **14.3** | **12** | **544** | **42.1** | **19:07** | .... | .... | .... | .... | .... | .... | .... | .... | .... |
| | **NHL Totals** | | **486** | **88** | **200** | **288** | **212** | **31** | **3** | **17** | **908** | **9.7** | | **5558** | **41.4** | **17:43** | **24** | **5** | **15** | **20** | **4** | **1** | **1** | **1** | **17:07** |

Traded to **Buffalo** by **NY Islanders** with Taylor Pyatt for Michael Peca, June 24, 2001. • Missed entire 2003-04 season recovering from head injury suffered in pre-season game vs. Chicago, October 2, 2003. Signed as a free agent by **Langnau** (Swiss), October 10, 2004. • Missed majority of 2006-07 season recovering from concussion suffered in game vs. Ottawa, May 8, 2006.

## CONROY, Craig

(KAWN-roi, KRAYG) **CGY.**

Center. Shoots right. 6'2", 193 lbs. Born, Potsdam, NY, September 4, 1971. Montreal's 7th choice, 123rd overall, in 1990 Entry Draft.

| Season | Club | League | GP | G | A | Pts | PIM | PP | SH | GW | S | % | +/- | TF | F% | Min | GP | G | A | Pts | PIM | PP | SH | GW | Min |
|---|---|---|---|---|---|---|---|---|---|---|---|---|---|---|---|---|---|---|---|---|---|---|---|---|---|
| 1989-90 | Northwood | High-NY | 31 | 33 | 43 | 76 | .... | .... | .... | .... | .... | .... | .... | .... | .... | .... | .... | .... | .... | .... | .... | .... | .... | .... | .... |
| 1990-91 | Clarkson Knights | ECAC | 40 | 8 | 21 | 29 | 24 | .... | .... | .... | .... | .... | .... | .... | .... | .... | .... | .... | .... | .... | .... | .... | .... | .... | .... |
| 1991-92 | Clarkson Knights | ECAC | 31 | 19 | 17 | 36 | 36 | .... | .... | .... | .... | .... | .... | .... | .... | .... | .... | .... | .... | .... | .... | .... | .... | .... | .... |
| 1992-93 | Clarkson Knights | ECAC | 35 | 10 | 23 | 33 | 26 | .... | .... | .... | .... | .... | .... | .... | .... | .... | .... | .... | .... | .... | .... | .... | .... | .... | .... |
| 1993-94 | Clarkson Knights | ECAC | 34 | 26 | *40 | *66 | 46 | .... | .... | .... | .... | .... | .... | .... | .... | .... | .... | .... | .... | .... | .... | .... | .... | .... | .... |
| **1994-95** | Fredericton | AHL | 55 | 26 | 18 | 44 | 29 | .... | .... | .... | .... | .... | .... | .... | .... | .... | 11 | 7 | 3 | 10 | 6 | .... | .... | .... | .... |
| | **Montreal** | **NHL** | **6** | **1** | **0** | **1** | **0** | **0** | **0** | **0** | **4** | **25.0** | **−1** | .... | .... | .... | .... | .... | .... | .... | .... | .... | .... | .... | .... |
| **1995-96** | **Montreal** | **NHL** | **7** | **0** | **0** | **0** | **2** | **0** | **0** | **0** | **1** | **0.0** | **−4** | .... | .... | .... | .... | .... | .... | .... | .... | .... | .... | .... | .... |
| | Fredericton | AHL | 67 | 31 | 38 | 69 | 65 | .... | .... | .... | .... | .... | .... | .... | .... | .... | 10 | 5 | 7 | 12 | 6 | .... | .... | .... | .... |
| **1996-97** | Fredericton | AHL | 9 | 10 | 6 | 16 | 10 | .... | .... | .... | .... | .... | .... | .... | .... | .... | .... | .... | .... | .... | .... | .... | .... | .... | .... |
| | **St. Louis** | **NHL** | **61** | **6** | **11** | **17** | **43** | **0** | **0** | **1** | **74** | **8.1** | **0** | .... | .... | .... | **6** | **0** | **0** | **0** | **8** | **0** | **0** | **0** | .... |
| | Worcester IceCats | AHL | 5 | 5 | 6 | 11 | 2 | .... | .... | .... | .... | .... | .... | .... | .... | .... | .... | .... | .... | .... | .... | .... | .... | .... | .... |
| **1997-98** | **St. Louis** | **NHL** | **81** | **14** | **29** | **43** | **46** | **0** | **3** | **1** | **118** | **11.9** | **20** | .... | .... | .... | **10** | **1** | **2** | **3** | **8** | **0** | **0** | **1** | .... |
| **1998-99** | **St. Louis** | **NHL** | **69** | **14** | **25** | **39** | **38** | **0** | **1** | **1** | **134** | **10.4** | **14** | **1190** | **54.6** | **16:39** | **13** | **2** | **1** | **3** | **6** | **0** | **0** | **0** | **15:09** |
| **99-2000** | **St. Louis** | **NHL** | **79** | **12** | **15** | **27** | **36** | **1** | **2** | **3** | **98** | **12.2** | **5** | **1339** | **53.6** | **14:48** | **7** | **0** | **2** | **2** | **2** | **0** | **0** | **0** | **13:13** |
| **2000-01** | **St. Louis** | **NHL** | **69** | **11** | **14** | **25** | **46** | **0** | **3** | **2** | **101** | **10.9** | **2** | **729** | **55.1** | **14:01** | .... | .... | .... | .... | .... | .... | .... | .... | .... |
| | **Calgary** | **NHL** | **14** | **3** | **4** | **7** | **14** | **0** | **1** | **0** | **32** | **9.4** | **0** | **264** | **52.7** | **18:08** | .... | .... | .... | .... | .... | .... | .... | .... | .... |
| **2001-02** | **Calgary** | **NHL** | **81** | **27** | **48** | **75** | **32** | **7** | **2** | **4** | **146** | **18.5** | **24** | **1654** | **54.3** | **20:56** | .... | .... | .... | .... | .... | .... | .... | .... | .... |
| **2002-03** | **Calgary** | **NHL** | **79** | **22** | **37** | **59** | **36** | **5** | **0** | **2** | **143** | **15.4** | **−4** | **1579** | **57.0** | **19:47** | .... | .... | .... | .... | .... | .... | .... | .... | .... |
| **2003-04** | **Calgary** | **NHL** | **63** | **8** | **39** | **47** | **44** | **2** | **0** | **0** | **112** | **7.1** | **13** | **1402** | **53.9** | **19:13** | **26** | **6** | **11** | **17** | **12** | **2** | **0** | **1** | **20:23** |
| 2004-05 | | | DID NOT PLAY | | | | | | | | | | | | | | | | | | | | | | |
| **2005-06** | **Los Angeles** | **NHL** | **78** | **22** | **44** | **66** | **78** | **5** | **3** | **3** | **154** | **14.3** | **13** | **1429** | **51.2** | **19:13** | .... | .... | .... | .... | .... | .... | .... | .... | .... |
| | United States | Olympics | 6 | 1 | 4 | 5 | 2 | .... | .... | .... | .... | .... | .... | .... | .... | .... | .... | .... | .... | .... | .... | .... | .... | .... | .... |
| **2006-07** | **Los Angeles** | **NHL** | **52** | **5** | **11** | **16** | **38** | **4** | **0** | **2** | **73** | **6.8** | **−13** | **802** | **51.5** | **15:29** | .... | .... | .... | .... | .... | .... | .... | .... | .... |
| | **Calgary** | **NHL** | **28** | **8** | **13** | **21** | **18** | **0** | **1** | **0** | **39** | **20.5** | **10** | **443** | **50.3** | **16:00** | **6** | **1** | **1** | **2** | **8** | **0** | **0** | **0** | **15:33** |
| **2007-08** | **Calgary** | **NHL** | **79** | **12** | **22** | **34** | **71** | **1** | **0** | **4** | **116** | **10.3** | **6** | **1411** | **51.5** | **17:09** | **7** | **0** | **2** | **2** | **8** | **0** | **0** | **0** | **16:43** |
| **2008-09** | **Calgary** | **NHL** | **82** | **12** | **36** | **48** | **28** | **0** | **1** | **1** | **104** | **11.5** | **20** | **1382** | **52.8** | **15:22** | **6** | **0** | **1** | **1** | **0** | **0** | **0** | **0** | **12:35** |
| | **NHL Totals** | | **928** | **177** | **348** | **525** | **570** | **25** | **17** | **24** | **1449** | **12.2** | | **13624** | **53.5** | **17:18** | **81** | **10** | **20** | **30** | **52** | **2** | **0** | **2** | **17:00** |

ECAC First All-Star Team (1994) • NCAA East First All-American Team (1994) • NCAA Final Four All-Tournament Team (1994)

Traded to **St. Louis** by **Montreal** with Pierre Turgeon and Rory Fitzpatrick for Murray Baron, Shayne Corson and St. Louis' 5th round choice (Gennady Razin) in 1997 Entry Draft, October 29, 1996. Traded to **Calgary** by **St. Louis** with St. Louis' 7th round choice (David Moss) in 2001 Entry Draft for Cory Stillman, March 13, 2001. Signed as a free agent by **Los Angeles**, July 6, 2004. Traded to **Calgary** by **Los Angeles** for Jamie Lundmark, Calgary's 4th round choice (Dwight King) in 2007 Entry Draft and Calgary's 2nd round choice (later traded back to Calgary - Calgary selected Mitch Wahl) in 2008 Entry Draft, January 29, 2007.

## COOKE, Matt

(KUK, MAT) **PIT.**

Center. Shoots left. 5'11", 205 lbs. Born, Belleville, Ont., September 7, 1978. Vancouver's 8th choice, 144th overall, in 1997 Entry Draft.

| Season | Club | League | GP | G | A | Pts | PIM | PP | SH | GW | S | % | +/- | TF | F% | Min | GP | G | A | Pts | PIM | PP | SH | GW | Min |
|---|---|---|---|---|---|---|---|---|---|---|---|---|---|---|---|---|---|---|---|---|---|---|---|---|---|
| | | | Regular Season | | | | | | | | | | | | | | Playoffs | | | | | | | | |
| 1994-95 | Wellington Dukes | MTJHL | 46 | 9 | 23 | 32 | 62 | | | | | | | | | | | | | | | | | | |
| 1995-96 | Windsor Spitfires | OHL | 61 | 8 | 11 | 19 | 102 | | | | | | | | | | 7 | 1 | 3 | 4 | 6 | | | | |
| 1996-97 | Windsor Spitfires | OHL | 65 | 45 | 50 | 95 | 146 | | | | | | | | | | 5 | 5 | 5 | 10 | 10 | | | | |
| 1997-98 | Windsor Spitfires | OHL | 23 | 14 | 19 | 33 | 50 | | | | | | | | | | | | | | | | | | |
| | Kingston | OHL | 25 | 8 | 13 | 21 | 49 | | | | | | | | | | 12 | 8 | 8 | 16 | 20 | | | | |
| **1998-99** | **Vancouver** | **NHL** | **30** | **0** | **2** | **2** | **27** | **0** | **0** | **0** | **22** | **0.0** | **-12** | **189** | **40.2** | **8:07** | | | | | | | | | |
| | Syracuse Crunch | AHL | 37 | 15 | 18 | 33 | 119 | | | | | | | | | | | | | | | | | | |
| **99-2000** | **Vancouver** | **NHL** | **51** | **5** | **7** | **12** | **39** | **0** | **1** | **1** | **58** | **8.6** | **3** | **71** | **39.4** | **11:48** | | | | | | | | | |
| | Syracuse Crunch | AHL | 18 | 5 | 8 | 13 | 27 | | | | | | | | | | | | | | | | | | |
| **2000-01** | **Vancouver** | **NHL** | **81** | **14** | **13** | **27** | **94** | **0** | **2** | **0** | **121** | **11.6** | **5** | **321** | **43.0** | **14:35** | **4** | **0** | **0** | **0** | **4** | **0** | **0** | **0** | **12:04** |
| **2001-02** | **Vancouver** | **NHL** | **82** | **13** | **20** | **33** | **111** | **1** | **0** | **2** | **103** | **12.6** | **4** | **28** | **32.1** | **14:03** | **6** | **3** | **2** | **5** | **0** | **1** | **0** | **0** | **15:09** |
| **2002-03** | **Vancouver** | **NHL** | **82** | **15** | **27** | **42** | **82** | **1** | **4** | **0** | **118** | **12.7** | **21** | **31** | **35.5** | **13:24** | **14** | **2** | **1** | **3** | **12** | **0** | **0** | **0** | **14:07** |
| **2003-04** | **Vancouver** | **NHL** | **53** | **11** | **12** | **23** | **73** | **1** | **1** | **4** | **79** | **13.9** | **5** | **34** | **52.9** | **14:06** | **7** | **3** | **1** | **4** | **12** | **0** | **0** | **1** | **18:23** |
| 2004-05 | | | DID NOT PLAY | | | | | | | | | | | | | | | | | | | | | | |
| **2005-06** | **Vancouver** | **NHL** | **45** | **8** | **10** | **18** | **71** | **0** | **0** | **2** | **67** | **11.9** | **-8** | **25** | **24.0** | **13:57** | | | | | | | | | |
| **2006-07** | **Vancouver** | **NHL** | **81** | **10** | **20** | **30** | **64** | **1** | **0** | **3** | **133** | **7.5** | **0** | **19** | **47.4** | **15:37** | **1** | **0** | **0** | **0** | **2** | **0** | **0** | **0** | **9:51** |
| **2007-08** | **Vancouver** | **NHL** | **61** | **7** | **9** | **16** | **64** | **0** | **0** | **1** | **68** | **10.3** | **-4** | **26** | **42.3** | **13:24** | | | | | | | | | |
| | **Washington** | **NHL** | **17** | **3** | **4** | **7** | **27** | **0** | **1** | **0** | **18** | **16.7** | **5** | **2** | **50.0** | **12:19** | **7** | **0** | **0** | **0** | **4** | **0** | **0** | **0** | **13:55** |
| **2008-09 ♦** | **Pittsburgh** | **NHL** | **76** | **13** | **18** | **31** | **101** | **0** | **0** | **1** | **86** | **15.1** | **0** | **19** | **36.8** | **14:13** | **24** | **1** | **6** | **7** | **22** | **0** | **0** | **0** | **15:09** |
| | **NHL Totals** | | **659** | **99** | **142** | **241** | **753** | **4** | **9** | **14** | **873** | **11.3** | | **765** | **41.0** | **13:42** | **63** | **9** | **10** | **19** | **56** | **1** | **0** | **1** | **14:52** |

Traded to **Washington** by **Vancouver** for Matt Pettinger, February 26, 2008. Signed as a free agent by **Pittsburgh**, July 6, 2008.

## CORAZZINI, Carl

(koh-ra-ZEE-nee, KAHRL)

Center. Shoots right. 5'10", 182 lbs. Born, Framingham, MA, April 21, 1979.

| Season | Club | League | GP | G | A | Pts | PIM | PP | SH | GW | S | % | +/- | TF | F% | Min | GP | G | A | Pts | PIM | PP | SH | GW | Min |
|---|---|---|---|---|---|---|---|---|---|---|---|---|---|---|---|---|---|---|---|---|---|---|---|---|---|
| 1996-97 | St. Sebastian's | High-MA | 25 | 29 | 31 | 60 | | | | | | | | | | | | | | | | | | | |
| 1997-98 | Boston University | H-East | 36 | 9 | 6 | 15 | 4 | | | | | | | | | | | | | | | | | | |
| 1998-99 | Boston University | H-East | 37 | 15 | 9 | 24 | 12 | | | | | | | | | | | | | | | | | | |
| 99-2000 | Boston University | H-East | 42 | 22 | 20 | 42 | 44 | | | | | | | | | | | | | | | | | | |
| 2000-01 | Boston University | H-East | 35 | 16 | 20 | 36 | 48 | | | | | | | | | | | | | | | | | | |
| 2001-02 | Providence Bruins | AHL | 61 | 7 | 8 | 15 | 10 | | | | | | | | | | | | | | | | | | |
| 2002-03 | Providence Bruins | AHL | 33 | 7 | 6 | 13 | 4 | | | | | | | | | | 4 | 0 | 0 | 0 | 0 | | | | |
| | Atlantic City | ECHL | 27 | 13 | 8 | 21 | 14 | | | | | | | | | | | | | | | | | | |
| **2003-04** | **Boston** | **NHL** | **12** | **2** | **0** | **2** | **0** | **0** | **1** | **0** | **16** | **12.5** | **2** | **6** | **33.3** | **10:41** | | | | | | | | | |
| | Providence Bruins | AHL | 62 | 16 | 9 | 25 | 6 | | | | | | | | | | 2 | 1 | 0 | 1 | 2 | | | | |
| 2004-05 | Providence Bruins | AHL | 8 | 0 | 0 | 0 | 0 | | | | | | | | | | | | | | | | | | |
| | Hershey Bears | AHL | 52 | 10 | 13 | 23 | 6 | | | | | | | | | | | | | | | | | | |
| 2005-06 | Norfolk Admirals | AHL | 75 | 26 | 29 | 55 | 16 | | | | | | | | | | 4 | 2 | 2 | 4 | 0 | | | | |
| **2006-07** | **Chicago** | **NHL** | **7** | **0** | **1** | **1** | **2** | **0** | **0** | **0** | **5** | **0.0** | **0** | **1** | **0.0** | **10:47** | | | | | | | | | |
| | Norfolk Admirals | AHL | 68 | 28 | 29 | 57 | 18 | | | | | | | | | | 6 | 4 | 1 | 5 | 2 | | | | |
| 2007-08 | Grand Rapids | AHL | 80 | 24 | 36 | 60 | 14 | | | | | | | | | | | | | | | | | | |
| 2008-09 | Springfield | AHL | 55 | 7 | 12 | 19 | 18 | | | | | | | | | | | | | | | | | | |
| | Peoria Rivermen | AHL | 25 | 4 | 9 | 13 | 4 | | | | | | | | | | 7 | 2 | 0 | 2 | 6 | | | | |
| | **NHL Totals** | | **19** | **2** | **1** | **3** | **2** | **0** | **1** | **0** | **21** | **9.5** | | **7** | **28.6** | **10:44** | | | | | | | | | |

Hockey East All-Rookie Team (1998) • Hockey East First All-Star Team (2001) • NCAA East Second All-American Team (2001)

Signed as a free agent by **Boston**, August 8, 2001. Signed as a free agent by **Providence** (AHL), October 1, 2004. Traded to **Hershey** (AHL) by **Providence** (AHL) for Darrel Scoville, November 15, 2004. Signed as a free agent by **Norfolk** (AHL), October 18, 2005. Signed as a free agent by **Chicago**, July 17, 2006. Signed as a free agent by **Detroit**, July 16, 2007. Signed as a free agent by **Edmonton**, July 17, 2008.

## CORVO, Joe

(KOHR-voh, JOH) **CAR.**

Defense. Shoots right. 6', 204 lbs. Born, Oak Park, IL, June 20, 1977. Los Angeles' 4th choice, 83rd overall, in 1997 Entry Draft.

| Season | Club | League | GP | G | A | Pts | PIM | PP | SH | GW | S | % | +/- | TF | F% | Min | GP | G | A | Pts | PIM | PP | SH | GW | Min |
|---|---|---|---|---|---|---|---|---|---|---|---|---|---|---|---|---|---|---|---|---|---|---|---|---|---|
| 1995-96 | Western Mich. | CCHA | 41 | 5 | 25 | 30 | 38 | | | | | | | | | | | | | | | | | | |
| 1996-97 | Western Mich. | CCHA | 32 | 12 | 21 | 33 | 85 | | | | | | | | | | | | | | | | | | |
| 1997-98 | Western Mich. | CCHA | 32 | 5 | 12 | 17 | 93 | | | | | | | | | | | | | | | | | | |
| 1998-99 | Springfield | AHL | 50 | 5 | 15 | 20 | 32 | | | | | | | | | | | | | | | | | | |
| | Hampton Roads | ECHL | 5 | 0 | 0 | 0 | 15 | | | | | | | | | | 4 | 0 | 1 | 1 | 0 | | | | |
| 99-2000 | | | DID NOT PLAY | | | | | | | | | | | | | | | | | | | | | | |
| 2000-01 | Lowell | AHL | 77 | 10 | 23 | 33 | 31 | | | | | | | | | | 4 | 3 | 1 | 4 | 0 | | | | |
| 2001-02 | Manchester | AHL | 80 | 13 | 37 | 50 | 30 | | | | | | | | | | 5 | 0 | 5 | 5 | 0 | | | | |
| **2002-03** | **Los Angeles** | **NHL** | **50** | **5** | **7** | **12** | **14** | **2** | **0** | **0** | **84** | **6.0** | **2** | **0** | **0.0** | **18:37** | | | | | | | | | |
| | Manchester | AHL | 26 | 8 | 18 | 26 | 8 | | | | | | | | | | 3 | 0 | 0 | 0 | 0 | | | | |
| **2003-04** | **Los Angeles** | **NHL** | **72** | **8** | **17** | **25** | **36** | **0** | **0** | **3** | **150** | **5.3** | **7** | **1** | **0.0** | **21:09** | | | | | | | | | |
| 2004-05 | Chicago Wolves | AHL | 23 | 7 | 7 | 14 | 14 | | | | | | | | | | 18 | 4 | 5 | 9 | 12 | | | | |
| **2005-06** | **Los Angeles** | **NHL** | **81** | **14** | **26** | **40** | **38** | **7** | **0** | **3** | **190** | **7.4** | **16** | **0** | **0.0** | **19:59** | | | | | | | | | |
| **2006-07** | **Ottawa** | **NHL** | **76** | **8** | **29** | **37** | **42** | **3** | **0** | **2** | **160** | **5.0** | **8** | **0** | **0.0** | **18:04** | **20** | **2** | **7** | **9** | **6** | **1** | **0** | **1** | **17:18** |
| **2007-08** | **Ottawa** | **NHL** | **51** | **6** | **21** | **27** | **18** | **1** | **0** | **1** | **111** | **5.4** | **13** | **0** | **0.0** | **17:41** | | | | | | | | | |
| | **Carolina** | **NHL** | **23** | **7** | **14** | **21** | **8** | **5** | **0** | **2** | **56** | **12.5** | **4** | **0** | **0.0** | **20:46** | | | | | | | | | |
| **2008-09** | **Carolina** | **NHL** | **81** | **14** | **24** | **38** | **18** | **8** | **1** | **6** | **213** | **6.6** | **-1** | **0** | **0.0** | **24:19** | **18** | **2** | **5** | **7** | **4** | **1** | **0** | **1** | **25:27** |
| | **NHL Totals** | | **434** | **62** | **138** | **200** | **174** | **26** | **1** | **17** | **964** | **6.4** | | **1** | **0.0** | **20:16** | **38** | **4** | **12** | **16** | **10** | **2** | **0** | **2** | **21:10** |

CCHA All-Rookie Team (1996) • CCHA Second All-Star Team (1997)

• Missed entire 1999-2000 season after failing to come to contract terms with **Los Angeles.** Signed as a free agent by **Chicago** (AHL), February 24, 2005. Signed as a free agent by **Ottawa**, July 1, 2006. Traded to **Carolina** by **Ottawa** with Patrick Eaves for Cory Stillman and Mike Commodore, February 11, 2008

## COTE, Jean-Philippe

(KOH-tay, ZHAWN-fihl-EEP)

Defense. Shoots left. 6'3", 213 lbs. Born, Charlesbourg, Que., April 22, 1982. Toronto's 10th choice, 265th overall, in 2000 Entry Draft.

| Season | Club | League | GP | G | A | Pts | PIM | PP | SH | GW | S | % | +/- | TF | F% | Min | GP | G | A | Pts | PIM | PP | SH | GW | Min |
|---|---|---|---|---|---|---|---|---|---|---|---|---|---|---|---|---|---|---|---|---|---|---|---|---|---|
| 1998-99 | Ste-Foy | QAAA | 38 | 10 | 24 | 34 | 34 | | | | | | | | | | 17 | 1 | 8 | 9 | 17 | | | | |
| | Quebec Remparts | QMJHL | 8 | 0 | 0 | 0 | 2 | | | | | | | | | | | | | | | | | | |
| 99-2000 | Quebec Remparts | QMJHL | 34 | 0 | 10 | 10 | 15 | | | | | | | | | | | | | | | | | | |
| | Cape Breton | QMJHL | 28 | 0 | 4 | 4 | 21 | | | | | | | | | | 4 | 0 | 1 | 1 | 4 | | | | |
| 2000-01 | Cape Breton | QMJHL | 71 | 6 | 29 | 35 | 90 | | | | | | | | | | 12 | 0 | 0 | 0 | 18 | | | | |
| 2001-02 | Cape Breton | QMJHL | 61 | 4 | 20 | 24 | 72 | | | | | | | | | | 16 | 1 | 6 | 7 | 38 | | | | |
| 2002-03 | Cape Breton | QMJHL | 16 | 1 | 3 | 4 | 12 | | | | | | | | | | | | | | | | | | |
| | Acadie-Bathurst | QMJHL | 48 | 8 | 18 | 26 | 87 | | | | | | | | | | 11 | 2 | 3 | 5 | 20 | | | | |
| 2003-04 | Hamilton | AHL | 75 | 2 | 7 | 9 | 79 | | | | | | | | | | 10 | 0 | 4 | 4 | 24 | | | | |
| 2004-05 | Hamilton | AHL | 51 | 1 | 8 | 9 | 58 | | | | | | | | | | 4 | 0 | 1 | 1 | 0 | | | | |
| **2005-06** | **Montreal** | **NHL** | **8** | **0** | **0** | **0** | **4** | **0** | **0** | **0** | **2** | **0.0** | **2** | **0** | **0.0** | **11:02** | | | | | | | | | |
| | Hamilton | AHL | 61 | 3 | 8 | 11 | 113 | | | | | | | | | | | | | | | | | | |
| 2006-07 | Hamilton | AHL | 68 | 3 | 9 | 12 | 115 | | | | | | | | | | 6 | 0 | 0 | 0 | 2 | | | | |
| 2007-08 | Hamilton | AHL | 79 | 1 | 12 | 13 | 112 | | | | | | | | | | | | | | | | | | |
| 2008-09 | Wilkes-Barre | AHL | 50 | 2 | 10 | 12 | 74 | | | | | | | | | | 2 | 0 | 0 | 0 | 2 | | | | |
| | **NHL Totals** | | **8** | **0** | **0** | **0** | **4** | **0** | **0** | **0** | **2** | **0.0** | | **0** | **0.0** | **11:02** | | | | | | | | | |

Signed as a free agent by **Montreal**, August 19, 2004.

## COTE, Riley

(KOH-tay, RIGH-lee) **PHI.**

Right wing. Shoots left. 6'2", 220 lbs. Born, Winnipeg, Man., March 16, 1982.

| Season | Club | League | GP | G | A | Pts | PIM | PP | SH | GW | S | % | +/- | TF | F% | Min | GP | G | A | Pts | PIM | PP | SH | GW | Min |
|---|---|---|---|---|---|---|---|---|---|---|---|---|---|---|---|---|---|---|---|---|---|---|---|---|---|
| 1998-99 | Prince Albert | WHL | 37 | 3 | 2 | 5 | 63 | | | | | | | | | | 9 | 0 | 0 | 0 | 9 | | | | |
| 99-2000 | Prince Albert | WHL | 67 | 6 | 7 | 13 | 71 | | | | | | | | | | 3 | 1 | 0 | 1 | 2 | | | | |
| 2000-01 | Prince Albert | WHL | 64 | 17 | 35 | 52 | 114 | | | | | | | | | | | | | | | | | | |
| 2001-02 | Prince Albert | WHL | 67 | 28 | 23 | 51 | 134 | | | | | | | | | | | | | | | | | | |
| 2002-03 | St. John's | AHL | 6 | 0 | 0 | 0 | 5 | | | | | | | | | | | | | | | | | | |
| | Memphis | CHL | 51 | 8 | 6 | 14 | 241 | | | | | | | | | | 14 | 1 | 0 | 1 | 54 | | | | |
| 2003-04 | Syracuse Crunch | AHL | 9 | 0 | 0 | 0 | 19 | | | | | | | | | | | | | | | | | | |
| | Dayton Bombers | ECHL | 57 | 6 | 11 | 17 | 258 | | | | | | | | | | | | | | | | | | |
| 2004-05 | Philadelphia | AHL | 61 | 4 | 7 | 11 | 280 | | | | | | | | | | 13 | 0 | 0 | 0 | 6 | | | | |

| | | | Regular Season | | | | | | | | | | | | | | Playoffs | | | | | | | | |
|---|---|---|---|---|---|---|---|---|---|---|---|---|---|---|---|---|---|---|---|---|---|---|---|---|---|
| Season | Club | League | GP | G | A | Pts | PIM | PP | SH | GW | S | % | +/- | TF | F% | Min | GP | G | A | Pts | PIM | PP | SH | GW | Min |
| 2005-06 | Philadelphia | AHL | 70 | 3 | 1 | 4 | 259 | | | | | | | | | | | | | | | | | | |
| **2006-07** | **Philadelphia** | **NHL** | **8** | **0** | **0** | **0** | **11** | **0** | **0** | **0** | **3** | **0.0** | **0** | **0** | **0.0** | **4:30** | | | | | | | | | |
| | Philadelphia | AHL | 37 | 1 | 4 | 5 | 125 | | | | | | | | | | | | | | | | | | |
| **2007-08** | **Philadelphia** | **NHL** | **70** | **1** | **3** | **4** | **202** | **0** | **0** | **0** | **17** | **5.9** | **2** | **2** | **50.0** | **4:17** | **3** | **0** | **0** | **0** | **0** | **0** | **0** | **0** | **4:08** |
| **2008-09** | **Philadelphia** | **NHL** | **63** | **0** | **3** | **3** | **174** | **0** | **0** | **0** | **24** | **0.0** | **–7** | **0** | **0.0** | **4:10** | | | | | | | | | |
| | **NHL Totals** | | **141** | **1** | **6** | **7** | **387** | **0** | **0** | **0** | **44** | **2.3** | | **2** | **50.0** | **4:14** | **3** | **0** | **0** | **0** | **0** | **0** | **0** | **0** | **4:08** |

Signed as a free agent by **Philadelphia**, August 23, 2005.

## COWAN, Jeff

(KOW-an, JEHF)

Left wing. Shoots left. 6'2", 205 lbs. Born, Scarborough, Ont., September 27, 1976.

| Season | Club | League | GP | G | A | Pts | PIM | PP | SH | GW | S | % | +/- | TF | F% | Min | GP | G | A | Pts | PIM | PP | SH | GW | Min |
|---|---|---|---|---|---|---|---|---|---|---|---|---|---|---|---|---|---|---|---|---|---|---|---|---|---|
| 1992-93 | Guelph Platers | OHA-B | 45 | 8 | 8 | 16 | 22 | | | | | | | | | | | | | | | | | | |
| 1993-94 | Guelph Platers | OHA-B | 43 | 30 | 26 | 56 | 96 | | | | | | | | | | | | | | | | | | |
| | Guelph Storm | OHL | 17 | 1 | 0 | 1 | 5 | | | | | | | | | | | | | | | | | | |
| 1994-95 | Guelph Storm | OHL | 51 | 10 | 7 | 17 | 14 | | | | | | | | | | 14 | 1 | 1 | 2 | 0 | | | | |
| 1995-96 | Barrie Colts | OHL | 66 | 38 | 14 | 52 | 29 | | | | | | | | | | 5 | 1 | 2 | 3 | 6 | | | | |
| 1996-97 | Saint John Flames | AHL | 22 | 5 | 5 | 10 | 8 | | | | | | | | | | | | | | | | | | |
| | Roanoke Express | ECHL | 47 | 21 | 13 | 34 | 42 | | | | | | | | | | | | | | | | | | |
| 1997-98 | Saint John Flames | AHL | 69 | 15 | 13 | 28 | 23 | | | | | | | | | | 13 | 4 | 1 | 5 | 14 | | | | |
| 1998-99 | Saint John Flames | AHL | 71 | 7 | 12 | 19 | 117 | | | | | | | | | | 4 | 0 | 1 | 1 | 10 | | | | |
| **99-2000** | **Calgary** | **NHL** | **13** | **4** | **1** | **5** | **16** | **0** | **0** | **0** | **26** | **15.4** | **2** | **0** | **0.0** | **10:22** | | | | | | | | | |
| | Saint John Flames | AHL | 47 | 15 | 10 | 25 | 77 | | | | | | | | | | | | | | | | | | |
| **2000-01** | **Calgary** | **NHL** | **51** | **9** | **4** | **13** | **74** | **2** | **0** | **1** | **48** | **18.8** | **–8** | **5** | **20.0** | **9:06** | | | | | | | | | |
| **2001-02** | **Calgary** | **NHL** | **19** | **1** | **0** | **1** | **40** | **0** | **0** | **1** | **13** | **7.7** | **–3** | **2** | **50.0** | **7:44** | | | | | | | | | |
| | **Atlanta** | **NHL** | **38** | **4** | **1** | **5** | **50** | **0** | **0** | **1** | **51** | **7.8** | **–11** | **5** | **20.0** | **12:27** | | | | | | | | | |
| **2002-03** | **Atlanta** | **NHL** | **66** | **3** | **5** | **8** | **115** | **0** | **0** | **0** | **52** | **5.8** | **–15** | **10** | **30.0** | **8:24** | | | | | | | | | |
| **2003-04** | **Atlanta** | **NHL** | **58** | **9** | **15** | **24** | **68** | **1** | **0** | **1** | **74** | **12.2** | **2** | **9** | **22.2** | **10:04** | | | | | | | | | |
| | **Los Angeles** | **NHL** | **13** | **2** | **1** | **3** | **24** | **1** | **0** | **0** | **15** | **13.3** | **–1** | **2** | **50.0** | **11:43** | | | | | | | | | |
| 2004-05 | | | DID NOT PLAY | | | | | | | | | | | | | | | | | | | | | | |
| **2005-06** | **Los Angeles** | **NHL** | **46** | **8** | **1** | **9** | **73** | **0** | **0** | **0** | **53** | **15.1** | **–8** | **4** | **25.0** | **8:26** | | | | | | | | | |
| **2006-07** | **Los Angeles** | **NHL** | **21** | **0** | **2** | **2** | **32** | **0** | **0** | **0** | **28** | **0.0** | **–1** | **1** | **0.0** | **7:37** | | | | | | | | | |
| | **Vancouver** | **NHL** | **42** | **7** | **3** | **10** | **93** | **0** | **1** | **0** | **46** | **15.2** | **4** | **0** | **0.0** | **8:15** | **10** | **2** | **0** | **2** | **22** | **0** | **0** | **1** | **11:38** |
| **2007-08** | **Vancouver** | **NHL** | **46** | **0** | **1** | **1** | **110** | **0** | **0** | **0** | **35** | **0.0** | **–5** | **1** | **0.0** | **8:45** | | | | | | | | | |
| 2008-09 | Peoria Rivermen | AHL | 71 | 5 | 10 | 15 | 94 | | | | | | | | | | 7 | 1 | 1 | 2 | 0 | | | | |
| | **NHL Totals** | | **413** | **47** | **34** | **81** | **695** | **4** | **1** | **4** | **441** | **10.7** | | **39** | **25.6** | **9:13** | **10** | **2** | **0** | **2** | **22** | **0** | **0** | **1** | **11:38** |

Signed as a free agent by **Calgary**, October 2, 1995. Traded to **Atlanta** by **Calgary** with the rights to Kurtis Foster for Petr Buzek and Atlanta's 6th round choice (Adam Pardy) in 2004 Entry Draft, December 18, 2001. Traded to **Los Angeles** by **Atlanta** for Kip Brennan, March 9, 2004. Claimed on waivers by **Vancouver** from **Los Angeles**, December 30, 2006.

## CRABB, Joey

(KRAB, JOH-ee) **ATL.**

Right wing. Shoots right. 6'1", 195 lbs. Born, Anchorage, AK, April 3, 1983. NY Rangers' 7th choice, 226th overall, in 2002 Entry Draft.

| Season | Club | League | GP | G | A | Pts | PIM | PP | SH | GW | S | % | +/- | TF | F% | Min | GP | G | A | Pts | PIM | PP | SH | GW | Min |
|---|---|---|---|---|---|---|---|---|---|---|---|---|---|---|---|---|---|---|---|---|---|---|---|---|---|
| 99-2000 | USNTDP | NAHL | 55 | 13 | 10 | 23 | 69 | | | | | | | | | | 3 | 1 | 0 | 1 | 4 | | | | |
| 2000-01 | USNTDP | U-18 | 39 | 10 | 10 | 20 | 22 | | | | | | | | | | | | | | | | | | |
| | USNTDP | USHL | 21 | 2 | 3 | 5 | 18 | | | | | | | | | | | | | | | | | | |
| 2001-02 | Green Bay | USHL | 61 | 15 | 27 | 42 | 94 | | | | | | | | | | 7 | 4 | 8 | 12 | 21 | | | | |
| 2002-03 | Colorado College | WCHA | 35 | 4 | 4 | 8 | 40 | | | | | | | | | | | | | | | | | | |
| 2003-04 | Colorado College | WCHA | 39 | 15 | 12 | 27 | 20 | | | | | | | | | | | | | | | | | | |
| 2004-05 | Colorado College | WCHA | 43 | 16 | 16 | 32 | 44 | | | | | | | | | | | | | | | | | | |
| 2005-06 | Colorado College | WCHA | 42 | 18 | 25 | 43 | 45 | | | | | | | | | | | | | | | | | | |
| 2006-07 | Chicago Wolves | AHL | 63 | 7 | 15 | 22 | 25 | | | | | | | | | | 6 | 0 | 0 | 0 | 0 | | | | |
| 2007-08 | Chicago Wolves | AHL | 72 | 9 | 26 | 35 | 78 | | | | | | | | | | 24 | 1 | 4 | 5 | 20 | | | | |
| **2008-09** | **Atlanta** | **NHL** | **29** | **4** | **5** | **9** | **28** | **0** | **1** | **1** | **33** | **12.1** | **–2** | **33** | **39.4** | **12:13** | | | | | | | | | |
| | Chicago Wolves | AHL | 42 | 15 | 14 | 29 | 62 | | | | | | | | | | | | | | | | | | |
| | **NHL Totals** | | **29** | **4** | **5** | **9** | **28** | **0** | **1** | **1** | **33** | **12.1** | | **33** | **39.4** | **12:13** | | | | | | | | | |

Signed as a free agent by **Atlanta**, August 31, 2006.

## CRAIG, Ryan

(KRAIG, RIGH-uhn) **T.B.**

Center. Shoots left. 6'2", 212 lbs. Born, Abbotsford, B.C., January 6, 1982. Tampa Bay's 10th choice, 255th overall, in 2002 Entry Draft.

| Season | Club | League | GP | G | A | Pts | PIM | PP | SH | GW | S | % | +/- | TF | F% | Min | GP | G | A | Pts | PIM | PP | SH | GW | Min |
|---|---|---|---|---|---|---|---|---|---|---|---|---|---|---|---|---|---|---|---|---|---|---|---|---|---|
| 1997-98 | Abbotsford | Minor-BC | 80 | 118 | 120 | 238 | 110 | | | | | | | | | | | | | | | | | | |
| | Brandon | WHL | 1 | 0 | 0 | 0 | 0 | | | | | | | | | | | | | | | | | | |
| 1998-99 | Brandon | WHL | 54 | 11 | 12 | 23 | 46 | | | | | | | | | | 5 | 0 | 0 | 0 | 4 | | | | |
| 99-2000 | Brandon | WHL | 65 | 17 | 19 | 36 | 40 | | | | | | | | | | | | | | | | | | |
| 2000-01 | Brandon | WHL | 70 | 38 | 33 | 71 | 49 | | | | | | | | | | 6 | 3 | 0 | 3 | 7 | | | | |
| 2001-02 | Brandon | WHL | 52 | 29 | 35 | 64 | 52 | | | | | | | | | | 19 | 11 | 10 | 21 | 13 | | | | |
| 2002-03 | Brandon | WHL | 60 | 42 | 32 | 74 | 69 | | | | | | | | | | 17 | 5 | 8 | 13 | 29 | | | | |
| 2003-04 | Hershey Bears | AHL | 61 | 4 | 8 | 12 | 24 | | | | | | | | | | | | | | | | | | |
| | Pensacola | ECHL | 5 | 3 | 5 | 8 | 0 | | | | | | | | | | 2 | 0 | 1 | 1 | 0 | | | | |
| 2004-05 | Springfield | AHL | 80 | 27 | 14 | 41 | 50 | | | | | | | | | | | | | | | | | | |
| **2005-06** | **Tampa Bay** | **NHL** | **48** | **15** | **13** | **28** | **6** | **6** | **0** | **0** | **81** | **18.5** | **–4** | **95** | **46.3** | **15:21** | **5** | **0** | **0** | **0** | **10** | **0** | **0** | **0** | **12:59** |
| | Springfield | AHL | 28 | 12 | 10 | 22 | 14 | | | | | | | | | | | | | | | | | | |
| **2006-07** | **Tampa Bay** | **NHL** | **72** | **14** | **13** | **27** | **55** | **4** | **0** | **2** | **130** | **10.8** | **–11** | **110** | **40.0** | **15:20** | **6** | **0** | **0** | **0** | **12** | **0** | **0** | **0** | **7:02** |
| **2007-08** | **Tampa Bay** | **NHL** | **7** | **1** | **1** | **2** | **0** | **1** | **0** | **0** | **8** | **12.5** | **–1** | **1** | **100.0** | **13:04** | | | | | | | | | |
| | Norfolk Admirals | AHL | 2 | 1 | 2 | 3 | 2 | | | | | | | | | | | | | | | | | | |
| **2008-09** | **Tampa Bay** | **NHL** | **54** | **2** | **4** | **6** | **60** | **0** | **0** | **0** | **64** | **3.1** | **–7** | **222** | **49.6** | **10:16** | | | | | | | | | |
| | **NHL Totals** | | **181** | **32** | **31** | **63** | **121** | **11** | **0** | **2** | **283** | **11.3** | | **428** | **46.5** | **13:44** | **11** | **0** | **0** | **0** | **22** | **0** | **0** | **0** | **9:44** |

WHL East First All-Star Team (2003) • Canadian Major Junior Humanitarian Player of the Year (2003)
• Missed majority of 2007-08 season recovering from back and knee injuries.

## CROMBEEN, B.J.

(KRAWM-been, BEE-JAY) **ST.L.**

Right wing. Shoots right. 6'2", 212 lbs. Born, Denver, CO, July 10, 1985. Dallas' 3rd choice, 54th overall, in 2003 Entry Draft.

| Season | Club | League | GP | G | A | Pts | PIM | PP | SH | GW | S | % | +/- | TF | F% | Min | GP | G | A | Pts | PIM | PP | SH | GW | Min |
|---|---|---|---|---|---|---|---|---|---|---|---|---|---|---|---|---|---|---|---|---|---|---|---|---|---|
| 2000-01 | Newmarket | OPJHL | 35 | 14 | 14 | 28 | 63 | | | | | | | | | | | | | | | | | | |
| 2001-02 | Barrie Colts | OHL | 60 | 12 | 13 | 25 | 118 | | | | | | | | | | 20 | 1 | 1 | 2 | 31 | | | | |
| 2002-03 | Barrie Colts | OHL | 63 | 22 | 24 | 46 | 133 | | | | | | | | | | 6 | 1 | 0 | 1 | 8 | | | | |
| 2003-04 | Barrie Colts | OHL | 62 | 21 | 29 | 50 | 154 | | | | | | | | | | 12 | 5 | 7 | 12 | 35 | | | | |
| 2004-05 | Barrie Colts | OHL | 63 | 31 | 18 | 49 | 111 | | | | | | | | | | 6 | 2 | 4 | 6 | 35 | | | | |
| 2005-06 | Iowa Stars | AHL | 52 | 5 | 7 | 12 | 97 | | | | | | | | | | 5 | 1 | 0 | 1 | 9 | | | | |
| | Idaho Steelheads | ECHL | 8 | 5 | 3 | 8 | 5 | | | | | | | | | | | | | | | | | | |
| 2006-07 | Assat Pori | Finland | 55 | 13 | 9 | 22 | 152 | | | | | | | | | | | | | | | | | | |
| | Idaho Steelheads | ECHL | 13 | 7 | 4 | 11 | 43 | | | | | | | | | | 22 | 5 | 5 | 10 | 45 | | | | |
| **2007-08** | **Dallas** | **NHL** | **8** | **0** | **2** | **2** | **39** | **0** | **0** | **0** | **9** | **0.0** | **1** | **1** | **0.0** | **6:38** | **5** | **0** | **0** | **0** | **0** | **0** | **0** | **0** | **4:16** |
| | Iowa Stars | AHL | 65 | 14 | 14 | 28 | 158 | | | | | | | | | | | | | | | | | | |
| **2008-09** | **Dallas** | **NHL** | **15** | **1** | **4** | **5** | **26** | **0** | **0** | **0** | **12** | **8.3** | **–1** | **0** | **0.0** | **8:14** | | | | | | | | | |
| | **St. Louis** | **NHL** | **66** | **11** | **6** | **17** | **122** | **0** | **1** | **3** | **112** | **9.8** | **–8** | **7** | **42.9** | **13:45** | **4** | **0** | **0** | **0** | **12** | **0** | **0** | **0** | **9:46** |
| | **NHL Totals** | | **89** | **12** | **12** | **24** | **187** | **0** | **1** | **3** | **133** | **9.0** | | **8** | **37.5** | **12:11** | **9** | **0** | **0** | **0** | **12** | **0** | **0** | **0** | **6:43** |

Signed as a free agent by **Pori** (Finland), August 2, 2006. Claimed on waivers by **St. Louis** from **Dallas**, November 18, 2008.

## CROSBY, Sidney

(KRAWZ-bee, SIHD-nee) **PIT.**

Center. Shoots left. 5'11", 200 lbs. Born, Cole Harbour, N.S., August 7, 1987. Pittsburgh's 1st choice, 1st overall, in 2005 Entry Draft.

| Season | Club | League | GP | G | A | Pts | PIM | PP | SH | GW | S | % | +/- | TF | F% | Min | GP | G | A | Pts | PIM | PP | SH | GW | Min |
|---|---|---|---|---|---|---|---|---|---|---|---|---|---|---|---|---|---|---|---|---|---|---|---|---|---|
| 2001-02 | Dartmouth | NSMHL | 74 | 95 | 98 | 193 | 114 | | | | | | | | | | | | | | | | | | |
| 2002-03 | Shat.-St. Mary's | High-MN | 57 | 72 | 90 | 162 | | | | | | | | | | | | | | | | | | | |
| 2003-04 | Rimouski Oceanic | QMJHL | 59 | 54 | *81 | *135 | 74 | | | | | | | | | | 9 | 7 | 9 | 16 | 10 | | | | |
| 2004-05 | Rimouski Oceanic | QMJHL | 62 | *66 | *102 | *168 | 84 | | | | | | | | | | 13 | *14 | *17 | *31 | 16 | | | | |
| **2005-06** | **Pittsburgh** | **NHL** | **81** | **39** | **63** | **102** | **110** | **16** | **0** | **5** | **278** | **14.0** | **–1** | **1174** | **45.5** | **20:08** | | | | | | | | | |
| **2006-07** | **Pittsburgh** | **NHL** | **79** | **36** | **84** | ***120** | **60** | **13** | **0** | **4** | **250** | **14.4** | **10** | **1686** | **49.8** | **20:46** | **5** | **3** | **2** | **5** | **4** | **1** | **0** | **1** | **21:40** |

| Season | Club | League | GP | G | A | Pts | PIM | PP | SH | GW | S | % | +/- | TF | F% | Min | Playoffs GP | G | A | Pts | PIM | PP | SH | GW | Min |
|---|---|---|---|---|---|---|---|---|---|---|---|---|---|---|---|---|---|---|---|---|---|---|---|---|---|
| **2007-08** | **Pittsburgh** | **NHL** | **53** | **24** | **48** | **72** | **39** | **6** | **0** | **4** | **173** | **13.9** | **18** | **1103** | **51.4** | **20:51** | **20** | **6** | ***21** | ***27** | **12** | **2** | **0** | **1** | **20:42** |
| **2008-09 ♦** | **Pittsburgh** | **NHL** | **77** | **33** | **70** | **103** | **76** | **7** | **0** | **3** | **238** | **13.9** | **3** | **1615** | **51.3** | **21:57** | **24** | ***15** | **16** | **31** | **14** | **5** | **0** | **2** | **20:49** |
| | **NHL Totals** | | **290** | **132** | **265** | **397** | **285** | **42** | **0** | **16** | **939** | **14.1** | | **5578** | **49.6** | **20:55** | **49** | **24** | **39** | **63** | **30** | **8** | **0** | **4** | **20:51** |

(Regular Season: GP through Min; Playoffs: GP through Min)

QMJHL All-Rookie Team (2004) • QMJHL First All-Star Team (2004, 2005) • QMJHL Player of the Year (2004, 2005) • Canadian Major Junior First All-Star Team (2004, 2005) • Canadian Major Junior Rookie of the Year (2004) • Canadian Major Junior Player of the Year (2004, 2005) • Memorial Cup All-Star Team (2005) • Ed Chynoweth Trophy (Memorial Cup Tournament - Leading Scorer) (2005) • NHL All-Rookie Team (2006) • NHL First All-Star Team (2007) • Art Ross Trophy (2007) • Lester B. Pearson Award (2007) • Hart Memorial Trophy (2007)

Played in NHL All-Star Game (2007)

## CULLEN, Mark

(KUH-lehn, MAHRK) **CHI.**

Center. Shoots left. 5'11", 190 lbs. Born, Moorhead, MN, October 28, 1978.

| Season | Club | League | GP | G | A | Pts | PIM | PP | SH | GW | S | % | +/- | TF | F% | Min | Playoffs GP | G | A | Pts | PIM | PP | SH | GW | Min |
|---|---|---|---|---|---|---|---|---|---|---|---|---|---|---|---|---|---|---|---|---|---|---|---|---|---|
| 1996-97 | Fargo High | High-ND | 30 | 20 | 45 | 65 | .... | .... | .... | .... | .... | .... | .... | .... | .... | .... | .... | .... | .... | .... | .... | .... | .... | .... | .... |
| 1997-98 | Fargo-Moorhead | USHL | 30 | 17 | 37 | 54 | 16 | .... | .... | .... | .... | .... | .... | .... | .... | .... | 4 | 3 | 0 | 3 | 25 | .... | .... | .... | .... |
| 1998-99 | Colorado College | WCHA | 42 | 8 | 25 | 33 | 22 | .... | .... | .... | .... | .... | .... | .... | .... | .... | .... | .... | .... | .... | .... | .... | .... | .... | .... |
| 99-2000 | Colorado College | WCHA | 37 | 11 | 20 | 31 | 22 | .... | .... | .... | .... | .... | .... | .... | .... | .... | .... | .... | .... | .... | .... | .... | .... | .... | .... |
| 2000-01 | Colorado College | WCHA | 31 | 20 | 33 | 53 | 26 | .... | .... | .... | .... | .... | .... | .... | .... | .... | .... | .... | .... | .... | .... | .... | .... | .... | .... |
| 2001-02 | Colorado College | WCHA | 43 | 14 | 36 | 50 | 14 | .... | .... | .... | .... | .... | .... | .... | .... | .... | .... | .... | .... | .... | .... | .... | .... | .... | .... |
| 2002-03 | Houston Aeros | AHL | 72 | 22 | 25 | 47 | 20 | .... | .... | .... | .... | .... | .... | .... | .... | .... | 15 | 3 | 7 | 10 | 4 | .... | .... | .... | .... |
| 2003-04 | Houston Aeros | AHL | 53 | 10 | 28 | 38 | 28 | .... | .... | .... | .... | .... | .... | .... | .... | .... | 2 | 0 | 0 | 0 | 0 | .... | .... | .... | .... |
| 2004-05 | Houston Aeros | AHL | 64 | 10 | 24 | 34 | 26 | .... | .... | .... | .... | .... | .... | .... | .... | .... | 5 | 1 | 1 | 2 | 0 | .... | .... | .... | .... |
| **2005-06** | **Chicago** | **NHL** | **29** | **7** | **9** | **16** | **2** | **0** | **0** | **0** | **45** | **15.6** | **7** | **281** | **48.8** | **13:15** | .... | .... | .... | .... | .... | .... | .... | .... | .... |
| | Norfolk Admirals | AHL | 54 | 29 | 39 | 68 | 48 | .... | .... | .... | .... | .... | .... | .... | .... | .... | 4 | 2 | 2 | 4 | 0 | .... | .... | .... | .... |
| **2006-07** | **Philadelphia** | **NHL** | **3** | **0** | **0** | **0** | **0** | **0** | **0** | **0** | **4** | **0.0** | **–3** | **14** | **50.0** | **6:15** | .... | .... | .... | .... | .... | .... | .... | .... | .... |
| | Philadelphia | AHL | 56 | 16 | 36 | 52 | 34 | .... | .... | .... | .... | .... | .... | .... | .... | .... | .... | .... | .... | .... | .... | .... | .... | .... | .... |
| 2007-08 | Grand Rapids | AHL | 59 | 16 | 31 | 47 | 61 | .... | .... | .... | .... | .... | .... | .... | .... | .... | .... | .... | .... | .... | .... | .... | .... | .... | .... |
| 2008-09 | Manitoba Moose | AHL | 56 | 14 | 25 | 39 | 22 | .... | .... | .... | .... | .... | .... | .... | .... | .... | 20 | 4 | 9 | 13 | 0 | .... | .... | .... | .... |
| | **NHL Totals** | | **32** | **7** | **9** | **16** | **2** | **0** | **0** | **0** | **49** | **14.3** | | **295** | **48.8** | **12:36** | .... | .... | .... | .... | .... | .... | .... | .... | .... |

USHL All-Rookie Team (1998) • USHL Rookie of the Year (1998) • WCHA First All-Star Team (2001, 2002) • NCAA West Second All-American Team (2001) • Fred Hunt Memorial Trophy (AHL - Sportsmanship) (2006)

Signed as a free agent by **Minnesota**, April 8, 2002. Signed as a free agent by **Chicago**, August 4, 2005. Signed as a free agent by **Philadelphia**, July 5, 2006. Signed as a free agent by **Detroit**, July 16, 2007. Signed as a free agent by **Vancouver**, July 4, 2008. Signed as a free agent by **Chicago**, July 13, 2009.

## CULLEN, Matt

(KUH-lehn, MAT) **CAR.**

Center. Shoots left. 6'1", 200 lbs. Born, Virginia, MN, November 2, 1976. Anaheim's 2nd choice, 35th overall, in 1996 Entry Draft.

| Season | Club | League | GP | G | A | Pts | PIM | PP | SH | GW | S | % | +/- | TF | F% | Min | Playoffs GP | G | A | Pts | PIM | PP | SH | GW | Min |
|---|---|---|---|---|---|---|---|---|---|---|---|---|---|---|---|---|---|---|---|---|---|---|---|---|---|
| 1994-95 | Moorhead Spuds | High-MN | 28 | 47 | 42 | 89 | 78 | .... | .... | .... | .... | .... | .... | .... | .... | .... | .... | .... | .... | .... | .... | .... | .... | .... | .... |
| 1995-96 | St. Cloud State | WCHA | 39 | 12 | 29 | 41 | 28 | .... | .... | .... | .... | .... | .... | .... | .... | .... | .... | .... | .... | .... | .... | .... | .... | .... | .... |
| 1996-97 | St. Cloud State | WCHA | 36 | 15 | 30 | 45 | 70 | .... | .... | .... | .... | .... | .... | .... | .... | .... | .... | .... | .... | .... | .... | .... | .... | .... | .... |
| | Baltimore Bandits | AHL | 6 | 3 | 3 | 6 | 7 | .... | .... | .... | .... | .... | .... | .... | .... | .... | 3 | 0 | 2 | 2 | 0 | .... | .... | .... | .... |
| **1997-98** | **Anaheim** | **NHL** | **61** | **6** | **21** | **27** | **23** | **2** | **0** | **0** | **75** | **8.0** | **–4** | .... | .... | .... | .... | .... | .... | .... | .... | .... | .... | .... | .... |
| | Cincinnati | AHL | 18 | 15 | 12 | 27 | 2 | .... | .... | .... | .... | .... | .... | .... | .... | .... | .... | .... | .... | .... | .... | .... | .... | .... | .... |
| **1998-99** | **Anaheim** | **NHL** | **75** | **11** | **14** | **25** | **47** | **5** | **1** | **1** | **112** | **9.8** | **–12** | **1047** | **47.7** | **15:31** | **4** | **0** | **0** | **0** | **0** | **0** | **0** | **0** | **15:30** |
| | Cincinnati | AHL | 3 | 1 | 2 | 3 | 8 | .... | .... | .... | .... | .... | .... | .... | .... | .... | .... | .... | .... | .... | .... | .... | .... | .... | .... |
| **99-2000** | **Anaheim** | **NHL** | **80** | **13** | **26** | **39** | **24** | **1** | **0** | **1** | **137** | **9.5** | **5** | **1247** | **44.6** | **16:54** | .... | .... | .... | .... | .... | .... | .... | .... | .... |
| **2000-01** | **Anaheim** | **NHL** | **82** | **10** | **30** | **40** | **38** | **4** | **0** | **1** | **159** | **6.3** | **–23** | **1478** | **48.0** | **18:15** | .... | .... | .... | .... | .... | .... | .... | .... | .... |
| **2001-02** | **Anaheim** | **NHL** | **79** | **18** | **30** | **48** | **24** | **3** | **1** | **4** | **164** | **11.0** | **–1** | **1283** | **51.4** | **17:01** | .... | .... | .... | .... | .... | .... | .... | .... | .... |
| **2002-03** | **Anaheim** | **NHL** | **50** | **7** | **14** | **21** | **12** | **1** | **0** | **1** | **77** | **9.1** | **–4** | **271** | **50.6** | **14:18** | .... | .... | .... | .... | .... | .... | .... | .... | .... |
| | **Florida** | **NHL** | **30** | **6** | **6** | **12** | **22** | **2** | **1** | **1** | **54** | **11.1** | **–4** | **423** | **47.3** | **14:43** | .... | .... | .... | .... | .... | .... | .... | .... | .... |
| **2003-04** | **Florida** | **NHL** | **56** | **6** | **13** | **19** | **24** | **1** | **0** | **2** | **75** | **8.0** | **–2** | **735** | **50.6** | **14:12** | .... | .... | .... | .... | .... | .... | .... | .... | .... |
| 2004-05 | SG Cortina | Italy | 36 | *27 | 33 | 60 | 64 | .... | .... | .... | .... | .... | .... | .... | .... | .... | 18 | 8 | 14 | 22 | 32 | .... | .... | .... | .... |
| **2005-06 ♦** | **Carolina** | **NHL** | **78** | **25** | **24** | **49** | **40** | **8** | **0** | **5** | **214** | **11.7** | **4** | **583** | **52.1** | **16:26** | **25** | **4** | **14** | **18** | **12** | **2** | **0** | **1** | **15:37** |
| **2006-07** | **NY Rangers** | **NHL** | **80** | **16** | **25** | **41** | **52** | **2** | **3** | **2** | **217** | **7.4** | **0** | **1134** | **54.6** | **17:10** | **10** | **1** | **3** | **4** | **6** | **0** | **0** | **1** | **16:55** |
| **2007-08** | **Carolina** | **NHL** | **59** | **13** | **36** | **49** | **32** | **8** | **0** | **1** | **137** | **9.5** | **2** | **649** | **56.1** | **16:52** | .... | .... | .... | .... | .... | .... | .... | .... | .... |
| **2008-09** | **Carolina** | **NHL** | **69** | **22** | **21** | **43** | **20** | **4** | **2** | **2** | **139** | **15.8** | **11** | **884** | **51.7** | **16:48** | **18** | **3** | **3** | **6** | **14** | **0** | **1** | **0** | **16:41** |
| | **NHL Totals** | | **799** | **153** | **260** | **413** | **358** | **41** | **8** | **21** | **1560** | **9.8** | | **9734** | **50.1** | **16:25** | **57** | **8** | **20** | **28** | **32** | **2** | **1** | **2** | **16:11** |

WCHA Second All-Star Team (1997)

Traded to **Florida** by **Anaheim** with Pavel Trnka and Anaheim's 4th round choice (James Pemberton) in 2003 Entry Draft for Sandis Ozolinsh and Lance Ward, January 30, 2003. Signed as a free agent by **Carolina**, August 5, 2004. Signed as a free agent by **Cortina** (Italy), September 18, 2004. Signed as a free agent by **NY Rangers**, July 1, 2006. Traded to **Carolina** by **NY Rangers** for Andrew Hutchinson, Joe Barnes and Carolina's 3rd round choice (Evgeny Grachev) in 2008 Entry Draft, July 17, 2007.

## CULLIMORE, Jassen

(KUHL-ih-mohr, JAY-suhn)

Defense. Shoots left. 6'5", 235 lbs. Born, Simcoe, Ont., December 4, 1972. Vancouver's 2nd choice, 29th overall, in 1991 Entry Draft.

| Season | Club | League | GP | G | A | Pts | PIM | PP | SH | GW | S | % | +/- | TF | F% | Min | Playoffs GP | G | A | Pts | PIM | PP | SH | GW | Min |
|---|---|---|---|---|---|---|---|---|---|---|---|---|---|---|---|---|---|---|---|---|---|---|---|---|---|
| 1986-87 | Caledonia | OHA-C | 18 | 2 | 0 | 2 | 9 | .... | .... | .... | .... | .... | .... | .... | .... | .... | .... | .... | .... | .... | .... | .... | .... | .... | .... |
| 1987-88 | Simcoe Rams | OHA-C | 35 | 11 | 14 | 25 | 92 | .... | .... | .... | .... | .... | .... | .... | .... | .... | .... | .... | .... | .... | .... | .... | .... | .... | .... |
| 1988-89 | Peterborough | OHA-B | 29 | 11 | 17 | 28 | 88 | .... | .... | .... | .... | .... | .... | .... | .... | .... | .... | .... | .... | .... | .... | .... | .... | .... | .... |
| | Peterborough | OHL | 20 | 2 | 1 | 3 | 6 | .... | .... | .... | .... | .... | .... | .... | .... | .... | .... | .... | .... | .... | .... | .... | .... | .... | .... |
| 1989-90 | Peterborough | OHL | 59 | 2 | 6 | 8 | 61 | .... | .... | .... | .... | .... | .... | .... | .... | .... | 11 | 0 | 2 | 2 | 8 | .... | .... | .... | .... |
| 1990-91 | Peterborough | OHL | 62 | 8 | 16 | 24 | 74 | .... | .... | .... | .... | .... | .... | .... | .... | .... | 4 | 1 | 0 | 1 | 7 | .... | .... | .... | .... |
| 1991-92 | Peterborough | OHL | 54 | 9 | 37 | 46 | 65 | .... | .... | .... | .... | .... | .... | .... | .... | .... | 10 | 3 | 6 | 9 | 8 | .... | .... | .... | .... |
| 1992-93 | Hamilton | AHL | 56 | 5 | 7 | 12 | 60 | .... | .... | .... | .... | .... | .... | .... | .... | .... | .... | .... | .... | .... | .... | .... | .... | .... | .... |
| 1993-94 | Hamilton | AHL | 71 | 8 | 20 | 28 | 86 | .... | .... | .... | .... | .... | .... | .... | .... | .... | 3 | 0 | 1 | 1 | 2 | .... | .... | .... | .... |
| **1994-95** | Syracuse Crunch | AHL | 33 | 2 | 7 | 9 | 66 | .... | .... | .... | .... | .... | .... | .... | .... | .... | .... | .... | .... | .... | .... | .... | .... | .... | .... |
| | **Vancouver** | **NHL** | **34** | **1** | **2** | **3** | **39** | **0** | **0** | **0** | **30** | **3.3** | **–2** | .... | .... | .... | **11** | **0** | **0** | **0** | **12** | **0** | **0** | **0** | .... |
| **1995-96** | **Vancouver** | **NHL** | **27** | **1** | **1** | **2** | **21** | **0** | **0** | **1** | **12** | **8.3** | **4** | .... | .... | .... | .... | .... | .... | .... | .... | .... | .... | .... | .... |
| **1996-97** | **Vancouver** | **NHL** | **3** | **0** | **0** | **0** | **2** | **0** | **0** | **0** | **2** | **0.0** | **–2** | .... | .... | .... | .... | .... | .... | .... | .... | .... | .... | .... | .... |
| | **Montreal** | **NHL** | **49** | **2** | **6** | **8** | **42** | **0** | **1** | **1** | **52** | **3.8** | **4** | .... | .... | .... | **2** | **0** | **0** | **0** | **2** | **0** | **0** | **0** | .... |
| **1997-98** | **Montreal** | **NHL** | **3** | **0** | **0** | **0** | **4** | **0** | **0** | **0** | **1** | **0.0** | **0** | .... | .... | .... | .... | .... | .... | .... | .... | .... | .... | .... | .... |
| | Fredericton | AHL | 5 | 1 | 0 | 1 | 8 | .... | .... | .... | .... | .... | .... | .... | .... | .... | .... | .... | .... | .... | .... | .... | .... | .... | .... |
| | **Tampa Bay** | **NHL** | **25** | **1** | **2** | **3** | **22** | **1** | **0** | **0** | **17** | **5.9** | **–4** | .... | .... | .... | .... | .... | .... | .... | .... | .... | .... | .... | .... |
| **1998-99** | **Tampa Bay** | **NHL** | **78** | **5** | **12** | **17** | **81** | **1** | **1** | **1** | **73** | **6.8** | **–22** | **0** | **0.0** | **20:14** | .... | .... | .... | .... | .... | .... | .... | .... | .... |
| **99-2000** | Providence Bruins | AHL | 16 | 5 | 10 | 15 | 31 | .... | .... | .... | .... | .... | .... | .... | .... | .... | .... | .... | .... | .... | .... | .... | .... | .... | .... |
| | **Tampa Bay** | **NHL** | **46** | **1** | **1** | **2** | **66** | **0** | **0** | **0** | **23** | **4.3** | **–12** | **2** | **0.0** | **15:38** | .... | .... | .... | .... | .... | .... | .... | .... | .... |
| **2000-01** | **Tampa Bay** | **NHL** | **74** | **1** | **6** | **7** | **80** | **0** | **0** | **0** | **56** | **1.8** | **–6** | **0** | **0.0** | **19:43** | .... | .... | .... | .... | .... | .... | .... | .... | .... |
| **2001-02** | **Tampa Bay** | **NHL** | **78** | **4** | **9** | **13** | **58** | **0** | **0** | **1** | **84** | **4.8** | **–1** | **0** | **0.0** | **20:07** | .... | .... | .... | .... | .... | .... | .... | .... | .... |
| **2002-03** | **Tampa Bay** | **NHL** | **28** | **1** | **3** | **4** | **31** | **0** | **0** | **0** | **23** | **4.3** | **3** | **0** | **0.0** | **18:25** | **11** | **1** | **1** | **2** | **4** | **0** | **0** | **0** | **22:11** |
| **2003-04 ♦** | **Tampa Bay** | **NHL** | **79** | **2** | **5** | **7** | **58** | **0** | **0** | **1** | **78** | **2.6** | **8** | **0** | **0.0** | **19:02** | **11** | **0** | **2** | **2** | **6** | **0** | **0** | **0** | **15:15** |
| 2004-05 | | | DID NOT PLAY | | | | | | | | | | | | | | | | | | | | | | |
| **2005-06** | **Chicago** | **NHL** | **54** | **1** | **6** | **7** | **53** | **1** | **0** | **1** | **23** | **4.3** | **–24** | **0** | **0.0** | **16:58** | .... | .... | .... | .... | .... | .... | .... | .... | .... |
| **2006-07** | **Chicago** | **NHL** | **65** | **1** | **6** | **7** | **64** | **0** | **0** | **0** | **17** | **5.9** | **–6** | **0** | **0.0** | **16:17** | .... | .... | .... | .... | .... | .... | .... | .... | .... |
| **2007-08** | **Florida** | **NHL** | **65** | **3** | **10** | **13** | **38** | **0** | **0** | **1** | **55** | **5.5** | **21** | **1** | **100.0** | **18:04** | .... | .... | .... | .... | .... | .... | .... | .... | .... |
| | Rochester | AHL | 3 | 0 | 1 | 1 | 4 | .... | .... | .... | .... | .... | .... | .... | .... | .... | .... | .... | .... | .... | .... | .... | .... | .... | .... |
| **2008-09** | **Florida** | **NHL** | **68** | **2** | **8** | **10** | **37** | **0** | **0** | **0** | **52** | **3.8** | **–10** | **0** | **0.0** | **16:48** | .... | .... | .... | .... | .... | .... | .... | .... | .... |
| | **NHL Totals** | | **776** | **26** | **77** | **103** | **696** | **3** | **2** | **7** | **598** | **4.3** | | **3** | **33.3** | **18:19** | **35** | **1** | **3** | **4** | **24** | **0** | **0** | **0** | **18:43** |

OHL Second All-Star Team (1992)

Traded to **Montreal** by **Vancouver** for Donald Brashear, November 13, 1996. Claimed on waivers by **Tampa Bay** from **Montreal**, January 22, 1998. • Loaned to **Providence** (AHL) by **Tampa Bay**, October 1, 1999. • Missed majority of 2002-03 season recovering from elbow injury suffered in game vs. Vancouver, November 29, 2002. Signed as a free agent by **Chicago**, July 22, 2004. Traded to **Montreal** by **Chicago** with Tony Salmelainen for Sergei Samsonov, June 16, 2007. Signed as a free agent by **Florida**, October 26, 2007.

## CUMISKEY, Kyle

(kuh-MIHS-kee, KIGHL) **COL.**

Defense. Shoots left. 5'10", 185 lbs. Born, Abbotsford, B.C., December 2, 1986. Colorado's 9th choice, 222nd overall, in 2005 Entry Draft.

| Season | Club | League | GP | G | A | Pts | PIM | PP | SH | GW | S | % | +/- | TF | F% | Min | Playoffs GP | G | A | Pts | PIM | PP | SH | GW | Min |
|---|---|---|---|---|---|---|---|---|---|---|---|---|---|---|---|---|---|---|---|---|---|---|---|---|---|
| 2002-03 | Penticton | BCHL | 59 | 10 | 11 | 21 | 36 | .... | .... | .... | .... | .... | .... | .... | .... | .... | .... | .... | .... | .... | .... | .... | .... | .... | .... |
| 2003-04 | Kelowna Rockets | WHL | 54 | 2 | 7 | 9 | 20 | .... | .... | .... | .... | .... | .... | .... | .... | .... | 17 | 0 | 0 | 0 | 0 | .... | .... | .... | .... |
| 2004-05 | Kelowna Rockets | WHL | 72 | 4 | 36 | 40 | 47 | .... | .... | .... | .... | .... | .... | .... | .... | .... | 24 | 0 | 13 | 13 | 12 | .... | .... | .... | .... |
| 2005-06 | Kelowna Rockets | WHL | 51 | 6 | 24 | 30 | 52 | .... | .... | .... | .... | .... | .... | .... | .... | .... | 12 | 0 | 6 | 6 | 8 | .... | .... | .... | .... |
| **2006-07** | **Colorado** | **NHL** | **9** | **1** | **1** | **2** | **2** | **0** | **0** | **0** | **8** | **12.5** | **0** | **0** | **0.0** | **13:28** | .... | .... | .... | .... | .... | .... | .... | .... | .... |
| | Albany River Rats | AHL | 63 | 7 | 26 | 33 | 32 | .... | .... | .... | .... | .... | .... | .... | .... | .... | 5 | 0 | 2 | 2 | 6 | .... | .... | .... | .... |

| | | | Regular Season | | | | | | | | | | | | | | Playoffs | | | | | | | | |
|---|---|---|---|---|---|---|---|---|---|---|---|---|---|---|---|---|---|---|---|---|---|---|---|---|---|
| Season | Club | League | GP | G | A | Pts | PIM | PP | SH | GW | S | % | +/- | TF | F% | Min | GP | G | A | Pts | PIM | PP | SH | GW | Min |
| **2007-08** | **Colorado** | **NHL** | **38** | **0** | **5** | **5** | **16** | **0** | **0** | **0** | **19** | **0.0** | **–3** | **0** | **0.0** | **12:08** | .... | .... | .... | .... | .... | .... | .... | .... | .... |
| | Lake Erie | AHL | 5 | 1 | 1 | 2 | 4 | .... | .... | .... | .... | .... | .... | .... | .... | .... | .... | .... | .... | .... | .... | .... | .... | .... | .... |
| **2008-09** | **Colorado** | **NHL** | **6** | **0** | **0** | **0** | **0** | **0** | **0** | **0** | **2** | **0.0** | **–2** | **0** | **0.0** | **8:32** | .... | .... | .... | .... | .... | .... | .... | .... | .... |
| | Lake Erie | AHL | 28 | 5 | 12 | 17 | 16 | .... | .... | .... | .... | .... | .... | .... | .... | .... | .... | .... | .... | .... | .... | .... | .... | .... | .... |
| | **NHL Totals** | | **53** | **1** | **6** | **7** | **18** | **0** | **0** | **0** | **29** | **3.4** | | **0** | **0.0** | **11:57** | .... | .... | .... | .... | .... | .... | .... | .... | .... |

## D'AGOSTINI, Matt

(DAG-uh-stee-noh, MAT) **MTL.**

Right wing. Shoots right. 6', 200 lbs. Born, Sault Ste. Marie, Ont., October 23, 1986. Montreal's 5th choice, 190th overall, in 2005 Entry Draft.

| Season | Club | League | GP | G | A | Pts | PIM | PP | SH | GW | S | % | +/- | TF | F% | Min | GP | G | A | Pts | PIM | PP | SH | GW | Min |
|---|---|---|---|---|---|---|---|---|---|---|---|---|---|---|---|---|---|---|---|---|---|---|---|---|---|
| 2003-04 | Soo North Stars | GNML | 36 | 36 | 23 | 59 | 41 | .... | .... | .... | .... | .... | .... | .... | .... | .... | .... | .... | .... | .... | .... | .... | .... | .... | .... |
| 2004-05 | Guelph Storm | OHL | 59 | 24 | 22 | 46 | 29 | .... | .... | .... | .... | .... | .... | .... | .... | .... | 4 | 0 | 2 | 2 | 8 | .... | .... | .... | .... |
| 2005-06 | Guelph Storm | OHL | 66 | 25 | 54 | 79 | 81 | .... | .... | .... | .... | .... | .... | .... | .... | .... | 15 | 8 | 20 | 28 | 16 | .... | .... | .... | .... |
| 2006-07 | Hamilton | AHL | 63 | 21 | 28 | 49 | 33 | .... | .... | .... | .... | .... | .... | .... | .... | .... | 22 | 4 | 9 | 13 | 18 | .... | .... | .... | .... |
| **2007-08** | **Montreal** | **NHL** | **1** | **0** | **0** | **0** | **2** | **0** | **0** | **0** | **0** | **0.0** | **0** | **0** | **0.0** | **8:49** | .... | .... | .... | .... | .... | .... | .... | .... | .... |
| | Hamilton | AHL | 76 | 23 | 30 | 53 | 38 | .... | .... | .... | .... | .... | .... | .... | .... | .... | .... | .... | .... | .... | .... | .... | .... | .... | .... |
| **2008-09** | **Montreal** | **NHL** | **53** | **12** | **9** | **21** | **16** | **3** | **0** | **1** | **116** | **10.3** | **–17** | **9** | **33.3** | **13:25** | **3** | **0** | **0** | **0** | **0** | **0** | **0** | **0** | **11:49** |
| | Hamilton | AHL | 20 | 14 | 11 | 25 | 16 | .... | .... | .... | .... | .... | .... | .... | .... | .... | .... | .... | .... | .... | .... | .... | .... | .... | .... |
| | **NHL Totals** | | **54** | **12** | **9** | **21** | **18** | **3** | **0** | **1** | **116** | **10.3** | | **9** | **33.3** | **13:19** | **3** | **0** | **0** | **0** | **0** | **0** | **0** | **0** | **11:49** |

## DALEY, Trevor

(DAY-lee, TREH-vuhr) **DAL.**

Defense. Shoots left. 5'11", 207 lbs. Born, Toronto, Ont., October 9, 1983. Dallas' 5th choice, 43rd overall, in 2002 Entry Draft.

| Season | Club | League | GP | G | A | Pts | PIM | PP | SH | GW | S | % | +/- | TF | F% | Min | GP | G | A | Pts | PIM | PP | SH | GW | Min |
|---|---|---|---|---|---|---|---|---|---|---|---|---|---|---|---|---|---|---|---|---|---|---|---|---|---|
| 1998-99 | Vaughan Vipers | OPJHL | 44 | 10 | 36 | 46 | 79 | .... | .... | .... | .... | .... | .... | .... | .... | .... | .... | .... | .... | .... | .... | .... | .... | .... | .... |
| 99-2000 | Sault Ste. Marie | OHL | 54 | 16 | 30 | 46 | 77 | .... | .... | .... | .... | .... | .... | .... | .... | .... | 15 | 3 | 7 | 10 | 12 | .... | .... | .... | .... |
| 2000-01 | Sault Ste. Marie | OHL | 58 | 14 | 27 | 41 | 105 | .... | .... | .... | .... | .... | .... | .... | .... | .... | .... | .... | .... | .... | .... | .... | .... | .... | .... |
| 2001-02 | Sault Ste. Marie | OHL | 47 | 9 | 39 | 48 | 38 | .... | .... | .... | .... | .... | .... | .... | .... | .... | 6 | 2 | 2 | 4 | 4 | .... | .... | .... | .... |
| 2002-03 | Sault Ste. Marie | OHL | 57 | 20 | 33 | 53 | 128 | .... | .... | .... | .... | .... | .... | .... | .... | .... | 1 | 0 | 0 | 0 | 2 | .... | .... | .... | .... |
| **2003-04** | **Dallas** | **NHL** | **27** | **1** | **5** | **6** | **14** | **1** | **0** | **0** | **34** | **2.9** | **–6** | **0** | **0.0** | **16:02** | **1** | **0** | **0** | **0** | **0** | **0** | **0** | **0** | **10:21** |
| | Utah Grizzlies | AHL | 40 | 8 | 6 | 14 | 76 | .... | .... | .... | .... | .... | .... | .... | .... | .... | .... | .... | .... | .... | .... | .... | .... | .... | .... |
| 2004-05 | Hamilton | AHL | 78 | 7 | 27 | 34 | 109 | .... | .... | .... | .... | .... | .... | .... | .... | .... | 4 | 0 | 1 | 1 | 2 | .... | .... | .... | .... |
| **2005-06** | **Dallas** | **NHL** | **81** | **3** | **11** | **14** | **87** | **0** | **0** | **1** | **91** | **3.3** | **–2** | **0** | **0.0** | **18:40** | **3** | **0** | **0** | **0** | **0** | **0** | **0** | **0** | **11:30** |
| **2006-07** | **Dallas** | **NHL** | **74** | **4** | **8** | **12** | **63** | **0** | **0** | **1** | **68** | **5.9** | **2** | **0** | **0.0** | **19:23** | **7** | **1** | **0** | **1** | **4** | **0** | **0** | **0** | **22:26** |
| **2007-08** | **Dallas** | **NHL** | **82** | **5** | **19** | **24** | **85** | **0** | **0** | **1** | **87** | **5.7** | **–1** | **1** | **100.0** | **19:48** | **18** | **1** | **0** | **1** | **20** | **0** | **0** | **0** | **18:52** |
| **2008-09** | **Dallas** | **NHL** | **75** | **7** | **18** | **25** | **73** | **0** | **0** | **2** | **104** | **6.7** | **2** | **1** | **0.0** | **22:00** | .... | .... | .... | .... | .... | .... | .... | .... | .... |
| | **NHL Totals** | | **339** | **20** | **61** | **81** | **322** | **1** | **0** | **5** | **384** | **5.2** | | **2** | **50.0** | **19:37** | **29** | **2** | **0** | **2** | **24** | **0** | **0** | **0** | **18:40** |

## DALLMAN, Kevin

(DAL-mahn, KEH-vihn)

Defense. Shoots right. 5'11", 195 lbs. Born, Niagara Falls, Ont., February 26, 1981.

| Season | Club | League | GP | G | A | Pts | PIM | PP | SH | GW | S | % | +/- | TF | F% | Min | GP | G | A | Pts | PIM | PP | SH | GW | Min |
|---|---|---|---|---|---|---|---|---|---|---|---|---|---|---|---|---|---|---|---|---|---|---|---|---|---|
| 1996-97 | Niagara Falls | OHA-B | 3 | 0 | 1 | 1 | 2 | .... | .... | .... | .... | .... | .... | .... | .... | .... | .... | .... | .... | .... | .... | .... | .... | .... | .... |
| 1997-98 | Niagara Falls | OHA-B | 47 | 13 | 25 | 38 | 42 | .... | .... | .... | .... | .... | .... | .... | .... | .... | .... | .... | .... | .... | .... | .... | .... | .... | .... |
| 1998-99 | Guelph Storm | OHL | 68 | 8 | 30 | 38 | 52 | .... | .... | .... | .... | .... | .... | .... | .... | .... | 11 | 1 | 4 | 5 | 2 | .... | .... | .... | .... |
| 99-2000 | Guelph Storm | OHL | 67 | 13 | 46 | 59 | 38 | .... | .... | .... | .... | .... | .... | .... | .... | .... | 6 | 0 | 2 | 2 | 11 | .... | .... | .... | .... |
| 2000-01 | Guelph Storm | OHL | 66 | 25 | 52 | 77 | 88 | .... | .... | .... | .... | .... | .... | .... | .... | .... | 1 | 0 | 0 | 0 | 0 | .... | .... | .... | .... |
| 2001-02 | Guelph Storm | OHL | 67 | 23 | 63 | 86 | 68 | .... | .... | .... | .... | .... | .... | .... | .... | .... | 9 | 8 | 8 | 16 | 22 | .... | .... | .... | .... |
| 2002-03 | Providence Bruins | AHL | 72 | 2 | 19 | 21 | 53 | .... | .... | .... | .... | .... | .... | .... | .... | .... | .... | .... | .... | .... | .... | .... | .... | .... | .... |
| 2003-04 | Providence Bruins | AHL | 65 | 6 | 23 | 29 | 44 | .... | .... | .... | .... | .... | .... | .... | .... | .... | 2 | 0 | 0 | 0 | 0 | .... | .... | .... | .... |
| 2004-05 | Providence Bruins | AHL | 71 | 8 | 26 | 34 | 48 | .... | .... | .... | .... | .... | .... | .... | .... | .... | 17 | 4 | 6 | 10 | 20 | .... | .... | .... | .... |
| **2005-06** | **Boston** | **NHL** | **21** | **0** | **1** | **1** | **8** | **0** | **0** | **0** | **42** | **0.0** | **1** | **0** | **0.0** | **19:24** | .... | .... | .... | .... | .... | .... | .... | .... | .... |
| | **St. Louis** | **NHL** | **46** | **4** | **9** | **13** | **21** | **3** | **0** | **0** | **89** | **4.5** | **–15** | **11** | **18.2** | **18:49** | .... | .... | .... | .... | .... | .... | .... | .... | .... |
| **2006-07** | **Los Angeles** | **NHL** | **53** | **1** | **9** | **10** | **12** | **0** | **0** | **0** | **76** | **1.3** | **–13** | **20** | **20.0** | **12:48** | .... | .... | .... | .... | .... | .... | .... | .... | .... |
| | Manchester | AHL | 3 | 4 | 0 | 4 | 4 | .... | .... | .... | .... | .... | .... | .... | .... | .... | .... | .... | .... | .... | .... | .... | .... | .... | .... |
| **2007-08** | **Los Angeles** | **NHL** | **34** | **3** | **4** | **7** | **4** | **0** | **0** | **1** | **41** | **7.3** | **4** | **2** | **0.0** | **12:53** | .... | .... | .... | .... | .... | .... | .... | .... | .... |
| | Manchester | AHL | 5 | 1 | 4 | 5 | 2 | .... | .... | .... | .... | .... | .... | .... | .... | .... | .... | .... | .... | .... | .... | .... | .... | .... | .... |
| 2008-09 | Barys Astana | Rus-KHL | 53 | 29 | 30 | 59 | 137 | .... | .... | .... | .... | .... | .... | .... | .... | .... | 3 | 0 | 1 | 1 | 8 | .... | .... | .... | .... |
| | **NHL Totals** | | **154** | **8** | **23** | **31** | **45** | **3** | **0** | **1** | **248** | **3.2** | | **33** | **18.2** | **15:31** | .... | .... | .... | .... | .... | .... | .... | .... | .... |

Memorial Cup Tournament All-Star Team (2002)

Signed as a free agent by **Boston**, July 18, 2002. Claimed on waivers by **St. Louis** from **Boston**, December 3, 2005. Signed as a free agent by **Los Angeles**, July 10, 2006.

## DANDENAULT, Mathieu

(DAHN-deh-noh, MA-tyew)

Defense. Shoots right. 6', 208 lbs. Born, Sherbrooke, Que., February 3, 1976. Detroit's 2nd choice, 49th overall, in 1994 Entry Draft.

| Season | Club | League | GP | G | A | Pts | PIM | PP | SH | GW | S | % | +/- | TF | F% | Min | GP | G | A | Pts | PIM | PP | SH | GW | Min |
|---|---|---|---|---|---|---|---|---|---|---|---|---|---|---|---|---|---|---|---|---|---|---|---|---|---|
| 1990-91 | Gloucester | Minor-ON | 44 | 52 | 50 | 102 | 30 | .... | .... | .... | .... | .... | .... | .... | .... | .... | .... | .... | .... | .... | .... | .... | .... | .... | .... |
| 1991-92 | Vanier Voyageurs | OHA-B | 33 | 27 | 31 | 58 | 20 | .... | .... | .... | .... | .... | .... | .... | .... | .... | .... | .... | .... | .... | .... | .... | .... | .... | .... |
| | Gloucester | CJHL | 6 | 3 | 4 | 7 | 0 | .... | .... | .... | .... | .... | .... | .... | .... | .... | .... | .... | .... | .... | .... | .... | .... | .... | .... |
| 1992-93 | Gloucester | CJHL | 55 | 11 | 26 | 37 | 64 | .... | .... | .... | .... | .... | .... | .... | .... | .... | .... | .... | .... | .... | .... | .... | .... | .... | .... |
| 1993-94 | Sherbrooke | QMJHL | 67 | 17 | 36 | 53 | 67 | .... | .... | .... | .... | .... | .... | .... | .... | .... | 12 | 4 | 10 | 14 | 12 | .... | .... | .... | .... |
| 1994-95 | Sherbrooke | QMJHL | 67 | 37 | 70 | 107 | 76 | .... | .... | .... | .... | .... | .... | .... | .... | .... | 7 | 1 | 7 | 8 | 10 | .... | .... | .... | .... |
| **1995-96** | **Detroit** | **NHL** | **34** | **5** | **7** | **12** | **6** | **1** | **0** | **0** | **32** | **15.6** | **6** | .... | .... | .... | .... | .... | .... | .... | .... | .... | .... | .... | .... |
| | Adirondack | AHL | 4 | 0 | 0 | 0 | 0 | .... | .... | .... | .... | .... | .... | .... | .... | .... | .... | .... | .... | .... | .... | .... | .... | .... | .... |
| **1996-97** ♦ | **Detroit** | **NHL** | **65** | **3** | **9** | **12** | **28** | **0** | **0** | **0** | **81** | **3.7** | **–10** | .... | .... | .... | .... | .... | .... | .... | .... | .... | .... | .... | .... |
| **1997-98** ♦ | **Detroit** | **NHL** | **68** | **5** | **12** | **17** | **43** | **0** | **0** | **0** | **75** | **6.7** | **5** | .... | .... | .... | **3** | **1** | **0** | **1** | **0** | **1** | **0** | **0** | .... |
| **1998-99** | **Detroit** | **NHL** | **75** | **4** | **10** | **14** | **59** | **0** | **0** | **0** | **94** | **4.3** | **17** | **3** | **0.0** | **15:10** | **10** | **0** | **1** | **1** | **0** | **0** | **0** | **0** | **11:51** |
| **99-2000** | **Detroit** | **NHL** | **81** | **6** | **12** | **18** | **20** | **0** | **0** | **0** | **98** | **6.1** | **–12** | **1** | **100.0** | **12:10** | **6** | **0** | **0** | **0** | **2** | **0** | **0** | **0** | **8:31** |
| **2000-01** | **Detroit** | **NHL** | **73** | **10** | **15** | **25** | **38** | **2** | **0** | **2** | **95** | **10.5** | **11** | **0** | **0.0** | **16:06** | **6** | **0** | **1** | **1** | **0** | **0** | **0** | **0** | **14:11** |
| **2001-02** ♦ | **Detroit** | **NHL** | **81** | **8** | **12** | **20** | **44** | **2** | **0** | **3** | **97** | **8.2** | **–5** | **1** | **0.0** | **16:43** | **23** | **1** | **2** | **3** | **8** | **0** | **1** | **0** | **13:29** |
| **2002-03** | **Detroit** | **NHL** | **74** | **4** | **15** | **19** | **64** | **1** | **0** | **0** | **74** | **5.4** | **25** | **0** | **0.0** | **19:08** | **4** | **0** | **0** | **0** | **2** | **0** | **0** | **0** | **25:51** |
| **2003-04** | **Detroit** | **NHL** | **65** | **3** | **9** | **12** | **40** | **0** | **1** | **0** | **68** | **4.4** | **9** | **1** | **0.0** | **13:47** | **12** | **1** | **1** | **2** | **6** | **0** | **0** | **1** | **13:33** |
| 2004-05 | Asiago | Italy | 10 | 0 | 2 | 2 | 2 | .... | .... | .... | .... | .... | .... | .... | .... | .... | 9 | 1 | 6 | 7 | 4 | .... | .... | .... | .... |
| **2005-06** | **Montreal** | **NHL** | **82** | **5** | **15** | **20** | **83** | **0** | **0** | **1** | **101** | **5.0** | **8** | **0** | **0.0** | **18:38** | **6** | **0** | **3** | **3** | **4** | **0** | **0** | **0** | **19:48** |
| **2006-07** | **Montreal** | **NHL** | **68** | **2** | **6** | **8** | **40** | **0** | **0** | **0** | **54** | **3.7** | **–8** | **3** | **0.0** | **16:07** | .... | .... | .... | .... | .... | .... | .... | .... | .... |
| **2007-08** | **Montreal** | **NHL** | **61** | **9** | **5** | **14** | **34** | **0** | **1** | **0** | **69** | **13.0** | **–11** | **1** | **0.0** | **11:08** | **9** | **0** | **0** | **0** | **2** | **0** | **0** | **0** | **8:45** |
| **2008-09** | **Montreal** | **NHL** | **41** | **4** | **8** | **12** | **17** | **0** | **0** | **0** | **46** | **8.7** | **7** | **5** | **40.0** | **11:45** | **4** | **0** | **0** | **0** | **0** | **0** | **0** | **0** | **21:05** |
| | **NHL Totals** | | **868** | **68** | **135** | **203** | **516** | **6** | **2** | **6** | **984** | **6.9** | | **15** | **20.0** | **15:20** | **83** | **3** | **8** | **11** | **24** | **1** | **1** | **1** | **13:55** |

Signed as a free agent by **Asiago** (Italy), December 27, 2004. Signed as a free agent by **Montreal**, August 3, 2005.

## DARCHE, Mathieu

(DAHRSH, MA-thew) **MTL.**

Left wing. Shoots left. 6'1", 220 lbs. Born, St. Laurent, Que., November 26, 1976.

| Season | Club | League | GP | G | A | Pts | PIM | PP | SH | GW | S | % | +/- | TF | F% | Min | GP | G | A | Pts | PIM | PP | SH | GW | Min |
|---|---|---|---|---|---|---|---|---|---|---|---|---|---|---|---|---|---|---|---|---|---|---|---|---|---|
| 1995-96 | Choate-Rosemary | High-CT | STATISTICS NOT AVAILABLE | | | | | | | | | | | | | | | | | | | | | | |
| 1996-97 | McGill Redmen | OUAA | 23 | 1 | 2 | 3 | 27 | .... | .... | .... | .... | .... | .... | .... | .... | .... | .... | .... | .... | .... | .... | .... | .... | .... | .... |
| 1997-98 | McGill Redmen | OUAA | 40 | 28 | 17 | 45 | 69 | .... | .... | .... | .... | .... | .... | .... | .... | .... | .... | .... | .... | .... | .... | .... | .... | .... | .... |
| 1998-99 | McGill Redmen | OUAA | 32 | 16 | 24 | 40 | 60 | .... | .... | .... | .... | .... | .... | .... | .... | .... | .... | .... | .... | .... | .... | .... | .... | .... | .... |
| 99-2000 | McGill Redmen | OUAA | 33 | 31 | 41 | *72 | 38 | .... | .... | .... | .... | .... | .... | .... | .... | .... | 5 | 2 | 8 | 10 | 16 | .... | .... | .... | .... |
| **2000-01** | **Columbus** | **NHL** | **9** | **0** | **0** | **0** | **0** | **0** | **0** | **0** | **9** | **0.0** | **–4** | **1** | **0.0** | **10:07** | .... | .... | .... | .... | .... | .... | .... | .... | .... |
| | Syracuse Crunch | AHL | 66 | 16 | 24 | 40 | 21 | .... | .... | .... | .... | .... | .... | .... | .... | .... | 5 | 0 | 1 | 1 | 4 | .... | .... | .... | .... |
| **2001-02** | **Columbus** | **NHL** | **14** | **1** | **1** | **2** | **6** | **0** | **0** | **0** | **15** | **6.7** | **–5** | **3** | **33.3** | **9:49** | .... | .... | .... | .... | .... | .... | .... | .... | .... |
| | Syracuse Crunch | AHL | 63 | 22 | 23 | 45 | 26 | .... | .... | .... | .... | .... | .... | .... | .... | .... | 10 | 2 | 5 | 7 | 2 | .... | .... | .... | .... |
| **2002-03** | **Columbus** | **NHL** | **1** | **0** | **0** | **0** | **0** | **0** | **0** | **0** | **0** | **0.0** | **–1** | **0** | **0.0** | **6:57** | .... | .... | .... | .... | .... | .... | .... | .... | .... |
| | Syracuse Crunch | AHL | 76 | 32 | 32 | 64 | 38 | .... | .... | .... | .... | .... | .... | .... | .... | .... | .... | .... | .... | .... | .... | .... | .... | .... | .... |
| **2003-04** | **Nashville** | **NHL** | **2** | **0** | **0** | **0** | **0** | **0** | **0** | **0** | **1** | **0.0** | **–1** | **0** | **0.0** | **6:39** | .... | .... | .... | .... | .... | .... | .... | .... | .... |
| | Milwaukee | AHL | 76 | 28 | 31 | 59 | 41 | .... | .... | .... | .... | .... | .... | .... | .... | .... | 22 | 6 | 8 | 14 | 8 | .... | .... | .... | .... |
| 2004-05 | Hershey Bears | AHL | 79 | 29 | 25 | 54 | 49 | .... | .... | .... | .... | .... | .... | .... | .... | .... | .... | .... | .... | .... | .... | .... | .... | .... | .... |
| 2005-06 | Fuchse Duisburg | Germany | 52 | 12 | 13 | 25 | 88 | .... | .... | .... | .... | .... | .... | .... | .... | .... | 5 | 1 | 3 | 4 | 4 | .... | .... | .... | .... |
| **2006-07** | **San Jose** | **NHL** | **2** | **0** | **0** | **0** | **0** | **0** | **0** | **0** | **3** | **0.0** | **0** | **0** | **0.0** | **9:13** | .... | .... | .... | .... | .... | .... | .... | .... | .... |
| | Worcester Sharks | AHL | 76 | 35 | 45 | 80 | 72 | .... | .... | .... | .... | .... | .... | .... | .... | .... | 5 | 2 | 2 | 4 | 2 | .... | .... | .... | .... |

| | | | Regular Season | | | | | | | | | | | | | | Playoffs | | | | | | | | |
|---|---|---|---|---|---|---|---|---|---|---|---|---|---|---|---|---|---|---|---|---|---|---|---|---|---|
| Season | Club | League | GP | G | A | Pts | PIM | PP | SH | GW | S | % | +/- | TF | F% | Min | GP | G | A | Pts | PIM | PP | SH | GW | Min |
| **2007-08** | **Tampa Bay** | **NHL** | **73** | **7** | **15** | **22** | **20** | **1** | **1** | **0** | **120** | **5.8** | **-14** | **89** | **48.3** | **14:26** | .... | .... | .... | .... | .... | .... | .... | .... | .... |
| | Norfolk Admirals | AHL | 4 | 3 | 7 | 10 | 2 | .... | .... | .... | .... | .... | .... | .... | .... | .... | .... | .... | .... | .... | .... | .... | .... | .... | .... |
| 2008-09 | Portland Pirates | AHL | 80 | 31 | 35 | 66 | 37 | .... | .... | .... | .... | .... | .... | .... | .... | .... | 5 | 0 | 0 | 0 | 4 | .... | .... | .... | .... |
| | **NHL Totals** | | **101** | **8** | **16** | **24** | **26** | **1** | **1** | **0** | **148** | **5.4** | | **93** | **47.3** | **13:04** | .... | .... | .... | .... | .... | .... | .... | .... | .... |

OUAA East Second All-Star Team (1998) • OUAA East First All-Star Team (1999) • OUAA First All-Star Team (2000) • CIAU All-Canadian Team (2000)

Signed as a free agent by **Columbus**, May 16, 2000. Signed as a free agent by **Nashville**, September 10, 2003. Signed as a free agent by **Colorado**, July 26, 2004. Signed as a free agent by **San Jose**, July 10, 2006. Signed as a free agent by **Tampa Bay**, July 2, 2007. Signed as a free agent by **Buffalo**, July 24, 2008. Signed as a free agent by **Montreal**, July 2, 2009.

## DATSYUK, Pavel

(daht-SOOK, PAH-vehl) **DET.**

Center. Shoots left. 5'11", 194 lbs. Born, Sverdlovsk, USSR, July 20, 1978. Detroit's 8th choice, 171st overall, in 1998 Entry Draft.

| Season | Club | League | GP | G | A | Pts | PIM | PP | SH | GW | S | % | +/- | TF | F% | Min | GP | G | A | Pts | PIM | PP | SH | GW | Min |
|---|---|---|---|---|---|---|---|---|---|---|---|---|---|---|---|---|---|---|---|---|---|---|---|---|---|
| 1996-97 | Yekaterinburg 2 | Russia-3 | 18 | 2 | 2 | 4 | 4 | .... | .... | .... | .... | .... | .... | .... | .... | .... | .... | .... | .... | .... | .... | .... | .... | .... | .... |
| | Yekaterinburg | Russia | 36 | 12 | 10 | 22 | 12 | .... | .... | .... | .... | .... | .... | .... | .... | .... | .... | .... | .... | .... | .... | .... | .... | .... | .... |
| 1997-98 | Yekaterinburg | Russia | 24 | 3 | 5 | 8 | 4 | .... | .... | .... | .... | .... | .... | .... | .... | .... | .... | .... | .... | .... | .... | .... | .... | .... | .... |
| | Yekaterinburg 2 | Russia-3 | 22 | 7 | 8 | 15 | 4 | .... | .... | .... | .... | .... | .... | .... | .... | .... | .... | .... | .... | .... | .... | .... | .... | .... | .... |
| 1998-99 | Yekaterinburg 2 | Russia-4 | 10 | 14 | 14 | 28 | 4 | .... | .... | .... | .... | .... | .... | .... | .... | .... | .... | .... | .... | .... | .... | .... | .... | .... | .... |
| | Yekaterinburg | Russia-2 | 35 | 21 | 23 | 44 | 14 | .... | .... | .... | .... | .... | .... | .... | .... | .... | 9 | 3 | 7 | 10 | 10 | .... | .... | .... | .... |
| 99-2000 | Yekaterinburg | Russia | 15 | 1 | 3 | 4 | 4 | .... | .... | .... | .... | .... | .... | .... | .... | .... | .... | .... | .... | .... | .... | .... | .... | .... | .... |
| 2000-01 | Ak Bars Kazan | Russia | 42 | 9 | 18 | 27 | 10 | .... | .... | .... | .... | .... | .... | .... | .... | .... | 4 | 0 | 1 | 1 | 2 | .... | .... | .... | .... |
| **2001-02♦** | **Detroit** | **NHL** | **70** | **11** | **24** | **35** | **4** | **2** | **0** | **1** | **79** | **13.9** | **4** | **794** | **47.7** | **13:39** | **21** | **3** | **3** | **6** | **2** | **1** | **0** | **1** | **10:40** |
| | Russia | Olympics | 6 | 1 | 2 | 3 | 0 | .... | .... | .... | .... | .... | .... | .... | .... | .... | .... | .... | .... | .... | .... | .... | .... | .... | .... |
| **2002-03** | **Detroit** | **NHL** | **64** | **12** | **39** | **51** | **16** | **1** | **0** | **1** | **82** | **14.6** | **20** | **778** | **48.2** | **15:28** | **4** | **0** | **0** | **0** | **0** | **0** | **0** | **0** | **18:48** |
| **2003-04** | **Detroit** | **NHL** | **75** | **30** | **38** | **68** | **35** | **8** | **1** | **4** | **136** | **22.1** | **-2** | **1314** | **54.0** | **18:16** | **12** | **0** | **6** | **6** | **2** | **0** | **0** | **0** | **17:23** |
| 2004-05 | Dynamo Moscow | Russia | 47 | 15 | 17 | 32 | 16 | .... | .... | .... | .... | .... | .... | .... | .... | .... | 10 | *6 | 3 | 9 | 4 | .... | .... | .... | .... |
| **2005-06** | **Detroit** | **NHL** | **75** | **28** | **59** | **87** | **22** | **11** | **0** | **4** | **145** | **19.3** | **26** | **1059** | **53.1** | **17:53** | **5** | **0** | **3** | **3** | **0** | **0** | **0** | **0** | **20:05** |
| | Russia | Olympics | 8 | 1 | 7 | 8 | 10 | .... | .... | .... | .... | .... | .... | .... | .... | .... | .... | .... | .... | .... | .... | .... | .... | .... | .... |
| **2006-07** | **Detroit** | **NHL** | **79** | **27** | **60** | **87** | **20** | **5** | **2** | **5** | **207** | **13.0** | **36** | **845** | **56.2** | **19:57** | **18** | **8** | **8** | **16** | **8** | **4** | **0** | **2** | **22:03** |
| **2007-08♦** | **Detroit** | **NHL** | **82** | **31** | **66** | **97** | **20** | **10** | **1** | **6** | **264** | **11.7** | **41** | **833** | **54.4** | **21:23** | **22** | **10** | **13** | **23** | **6** | **4** | **0** | **1** | **21:40** |
| **2008-09** | **Detroit** | **NHL** | **81** | **32** | **65** | **97** | **22** | **11** | **1** | **3** | **248** | **12.9** | **34** | **1135** | **56.0** | **19:13** | **16** | **1** | **8** | **9** | **9** | **1** | **0** | **0** | **20:05** |
| | **NHL Totals** | | **526** | **171** | **351** | **522** | **139** | **48** | **5** | **24** | **1161** | **14.7** | | **6758** | **53.1** | **18:09** | **98** | **22** | **41** | **63** | **27** | **10** | **0** | **4** | **18:24** |

Lady Byng Memorial Trophy (2006, 2007, 2008, 2009) • Frank J. Selke Trophy (2008, 2009) • NHL Second All-Star Team (2009)

Played in NHL All-Star Game (2004, 2008)

• Spent majority of 1999-2000 season on **Kazan** (Russia) reserve squad. Signed as a free agent by **Dynamo Moscow** (Russia), June 19, 2004.

## DAVIS, Patrick

(DAY-vihs, PAT-rihk) **N.J.**

Right wing. Shoots right. 6'2", 195 lbs. Born, Sterling, MI, December 28, 1986. New Jersey's 4th choice, 99th overall, in 2005 Entry Draft.

| Season | Club | League | GP | G | A | Pts | PIM | PP | SH | GW | S | % | +/- | TF | F% | Min | GP | G | A | Pts | PIM | PP | SH | GW | Min |
|---|---|---|---|---|---|---|---|---|---|---|---|---|---|---|---|---|---|---|---|---|---|---|---|---|---|
| 2002-03 | Detroit Belle Tire | MWEHL | STATISTICS NOT AVAILABLE | | | | | .... | .... | .... | .... | .... | .... | .... | .... | .... | .... | .... | .... | .... | .... | .... | .... | .... | .... |
| | Sioux City | USHL | 16 | 3 | 2 | 5 | 8 | .... | .... | .... | .... | .... | .... | .... | .... | .... | 1 | 0 | 0 | 0 | 2 | .... | .... | .... | .... |
| 2003-04 | Kitchener Rangers | OHL | 27 | 8 | 10 | 18 | 21 | .... | .... | .... | .... | .... | .... | .... | .... | .... | .... | .... | .... | .... | .... | .... | .... | .... | .... |
| 2004-05 | Kitchener Rangers | OHL | 59 | 20 | 30 | 50 | 41 | .... | .... | .... | .... | .... | .... | .... | .... | .... | 14 | 3 | 4 | 7 | 20 | .... | .... | .... | .... |
| 2005-06 | Kitchener Rangers | OHL | 22 | 13 | 4 | 17 | 30 | .... | .... | .... | .... | .... | .... | .... | .... | .... | .... | .... | .... | .... | .... | .... | .... | .... | .... |
| | Windsor Spitfires | OHL | 38 | 22 | 29 | 51 | 64 | .... | .... | .... | .... | .... | .... | .... | .... | .... | 7 | 2 | 6 | 8 | 12 | .... | .... | .... | .... |
| | Albany River Rats | AHL | 3 | 0 | 0 | 0 | 2 | .... | .... | .... | .... | .... | .... | .... | .... | .... | .... | .... | .... | .... | .... | .... | .... | .... | .... |
| 2006-07 | Lowell Devils | AHL | 41 | 5 | 13 | 18 | 26 | .... | .... | .... | .... | .... | .... | .... | .... | .... | .... | .... | .... | .... | .... | .... | .... | .... | .... |
| 2007-08 | Lowell Devils | AHL | 60 | 7 | 12 | 19 | 58 | .... | .... | .... | .... | .... | .... | .... | .... | .... | .... | .... | .... | .... | .... | .... | .... | .... | .... |
| **2008-09** | **New Jersey** | **NHL** | **1** | **0** | **0** | **0** | **0** | **0** | **0** | **0** | **0** | **0.0** | **0** | **0** | **0.0** | **4:30** | .... | .... | .... | .... | .... | .... | .... | .... | .... |
| | Lowell Devils | AHL | 74 | 13 | 17 | 30 | 45 | .... | .... | .... | .... | .... | .... | .... | .... | .... | .... | .... | .... | .... | .... | .... | .... | .... | .... |
| | **NHL Totals** | | **1** | **0** | **0** | **0** | **0** | **0** | **0** | **0** | **0** | **0.0** | | **0** | **0.0** | **4:30** | .... | .... | .... | .... | .... | .... | .... | .... | .... |

## DAVISON, Rob

(DAY-vihs-ohn, RAWB) **N.J.**

Defense. Shoots left. 6'3", 220 lbs. Born, St. Catharines, Ont., May 1, 1980. San Jose's 4th choice, 98th overall, in 1998 Entry Draft.

| Season | Club | League | GP | G | A | Pts | PIM | PP | SH | GW | S | % | +/- | TF | F% | Min | GP | G | A | Pts | PIM | PP | SH | GW | Min |
|---|---|---|---|---|---|---|---|---|---|---|---|---|---|---|---|---|---|---|---|---|---|---|---|---|---|
| 1996-97 | St. Mike's B's | OPJHL | 45 | 2 | 6 | 8 | 93 | .... | .... | .... | .... | .... | .... | .... | .... | .... | 6 | 0 | 0 | 0 | 9 | .... | .... | .... | .... |
| 1997-98 | North Bay | OHL | 59 | 0 | 11 | 11 | 200 | .... | .... | .... | .... | .... | .... | .... | .... | .... | .... | .... | .... | .... | .... | .... | .... | .... | .... |
| 1998-99 | North Bay | OHL | 59 | 2 | 17 | 19 | 150 | .... | .... | .... | .... | .... | .... | .... | .... | .... | 4 | 0 | 1 | 1 | 12 | .... | .... | .... | .... |
| 99-2000 | North Bay | OHL | 67 | 4 | 6 | 10 | 194 | .... | .... | .... | .... | .... | .... | .... | .... | .... | 6 | 0 | 1 | 1 | 8 | .... | .... | .... | .... |
| 2000-01 | Kentucky | AHL | 72 | 0 | 4 | 4 | 230 | .... | .... | .... | .... | .... | .... | .... | .... | .... | 3 | 0 | 0 | 0 | 0 | .... | .... | .... | .... |
| 2001-02 | Cleveland Barons | AHL | 70 | 1 | 3 | 4 | 206 | .... | .... | .... | .... | .... | .... | .... | .... | .... | .... | .... | .... | .... | .... | .... | .... | .... | .... |
| **2002-03** | **San Jose** | **NHL** | **15** | **1** | **2** | **3** | **22** | **0** | **0** | **0** | **15** | **6.7** | **4** | **0** | **0.0** | **17:53** | .... | .... | .... | .... | .... | .... | .... | .... | .... |
| | Cleveland Barons | AHL | 42 | 1 | 3 | 4 | 82 | .... | .... | .... | .... | .... | .... | .... | .... | .... | .... | .... | .... | .... | .... | .... | .... | .... | .... |
| **2003-04** | **San Jose** | **NHL** | **55** | **0** | **3** | **3** | **92** | **0** | **0** | **0** | **33** | **0.0** | **-3** | **0** | **0.0** | **14:22** | **5** | **0** | **2** | **2** | **4** | **0** | **0** | **0** | **9:01** |
| 2004-05 | Cardiff Devils | Britain | 24 | 2 | 3 | 5 | 114 | .... | .... | .... | .... | .... | .... | .... | .... | .... | 8 | 0 | 1 | 1 | 12 | .... | .... | .... | .... |
| **2005-06** | **San Jose** | **NHL** | **69** | **1** | **5** | **6** | **76** | **0** | **0** | **0** | **36** | **2.8** | **6** | **0** | **0.0** | **13:50** | **1** | **0** | **0** | **0** | **0** | **0** | **0** | **0** | **8:00** |
| **2006-07** | **San Jose** | **NHL** | **22** | **0** | **2** | **2** | **27** | **0** | **0** | **0** | **14** | **0.0** | **-2** | **0** | **0.0** | **9:19** | .... | .... | .... | .... | .... | .... | .... | .... | .... |
| **2007-08** | **San Jose** | **NHL** | **15** | **0** | **0** | **0** | **21** | **0** | **0** | **0** | **10** | **0.0** | **-3** | **0** | **0.0** | **7:47** | .... | .... | .... | .... | .... | .... | .... | .... | .... |
| | **NY Islanders** | **NHL** | **19** | **1** | **1** | **2** | **32** | **0** | **1** | **0** | **22** | **4.5** | **-3** | **0** | **0.0** | **18:40** | .... | .... | .... | .... | .... | .... | .... | .... | .... |
| **2008-09** | **Vancouver** | **NHL** | **23** | **0** | **2** | **2** | **51** | **0** | **0** | **0** | **15** | **0.0** | **-4** | **0** | **0.0** | **10:05** | .... | .... | .... | .... | .... | .... | .... | .... | .... |
| | **NHL Totals** | | **218** | **3** | **15** | **18** | **321** | **0** | **1** | **0** | **145** | **2.1** | | **0** | **0.0** | **13:24** | **6** | **0** | **2** | **2** | **4** | **0** | **0** | **0** | **8:51** |

Signed as a free agent by **Cardiff** (Britain), October 5, 2004. Traded to **NY Islanders** by **San Jose** for NY Islanders' 7th round choice (Jason Demers) in 2008 Entry Draft, February 26, 2008. Signed as a free agent by **Vancouver**, July 10, 2008. • Missed majority of 2006-07, 2007-08 and 2008-09 seasons recovering from various injuries and serving as a healthy reserve. Signed as a free agent by **New Jersey**, July 31, 2009.

## DAWES, Nigel

(DAWZ, NIGH-juhl) **CGY.**

Left wing. Shoots left. 5'8", 190 lbs. Born, Winnipeg, Man., February 9, 1985. NY Rangers' 5th choice, 149th overall, in 2003 Entry Draft.

| Season | Club | League | GP | G | A | Pts | PIM | PP | SH | GW | S | % | +/- | TF | F% | Min | GP | G | A | Pts | PIM | PP | SH | GW | Min |
|---|---|---|---|---|---|---|---|---|---|---|---|---|---|---|---|---|---|---|---|---|---|---|---|---|---|
| 2000-01 | Wpg. Warriors | MMMHL | 36 | 55 | 41 | 96 | 74 | .... | .... | .... | .... | .... | .... | .... | .... | .... | .... | .... | .... | .... | .... | .... | .... | .... | .... |
| 2001-02 | Kootenay Ice | WHL | 54 | 15 | 19 | 34 | 14 | .... | .... | .... | .... | .... | .... | .... | .... | .... | 22 | 9 | 6 | 15 | 8 | .... | .... | .... | .... |
| 2002-03 | Kootenay Ice | WHL | 72 | 47 | 45 | 92 | 54 | .... | .... | .... | .... | .... | .... | .... | .... | .... | 11 | 4 | 8 | 12 | 6 | .... | .... | .... | .... |
| 2003-04 | Kootenay Ice | WHL | 56 | 47 | 23 | 70 | 31 | .... | .... | .... | .... | .... | .... | .... | .... | .... | 4 | 1 | 2 | 3 | 10 | .... | .... | .... | .... |
| | Hartford | AHL | 4 | 0 | 0 | 0 | 0 | .... | .... | .... | .... | .... | .... | .... | .... | .... | .... | .... | .... | .... | .... | .... | .... | .... | .... |
| 2004-05 | Kootenay Ice | WHL | 63 | 50 | 26 | 76 | 30 | .... | .... | .... | .... | .... | .... | .... | .... | .... | 12 | 5 | 10 | 15 | 5 | .... | .... | .... | .... |
| 2005-06 | Hartford | AHL | 77 | 35 | 31 | 66 | 21 | .... | .... | .... | .... | .... | .... | .... | .... | .... | 13 | 6 | 6 | 12 | 9 | .... | .... | .... | .... |
| **2006-07** | **NY Rangers** | **NHL** | **8** | **1** | **0** | **1** | **0** | **0** | **0** | **0** | **7** | **14.3** | **-4** | **1** | **0.0** | **6:44** | **1** | **0** | **0** | **0** | **0** | **0** | **0** | **0** | **9:02** |
| | Hartford | AHL | 65 | 27 | 33 | 60 | 29 | .... | .... | .... | .... | .... | .... | .... | .... | .... | 7 | 5 | 6 | 11 | 9 | .... | .... | .... | .... |
| **2007-08** | **NY Rangers** | **NHL** | **61** | **14** | **15** | **29** | **10** | **3** | **0** | **4** | **121** | **11.6** | **11** | **2** | **50.0** | **12:59** | **10** | **2** | **2** | **4** | **0** | **0** | **0** | **0** | **12:31** |
| | Hartford | AHL | 20 | 14 | 20 | 34 | 2 | .... | .... | .... | .... | .... | .... | .... | .... | .... | .... | .... | .... | .... | .... | .... | .... | .... | .... |
| **2008-09** | **NY Rangers** | **NHL** | **52** | **10** | **9** | **19** | **15** | **3** | **0** | **4** | **96** | **10.4** | **-2** | **0** | **0.0** | **13:03** | .... | .... | .... | .... | .... | .... | .... | .... | .... |
| | **Phoenix** | **NHL** | **12** | **0** | **2** | **2** | **0** | **0** | **0** | **0** | **19** | **0.0** | **-4** | **0** | **0.0** | **14:09** | .... | .... | .... | .... | .... | .... | .... | .... | .... |
| | **NHL Totals** | | **133** | **25** | **26** | **51** | **25** | **6** | **0** | **8** | **243** | **10.3** | | **3** | **33.3** | **12:44** | **11** | **2** | **2** | **4** | **0** | **0** | **0** | **0** | **12:12** |

WHL West Second All-Star Team (2003) • WHL West First All-Star Team (2004, 2005)

Traded to **Phoenix** by **NY Rangers** with Dmitri Kalinin and Petr Prucha for Derek Morris, March 4, 2009. Claimed on waivers by **Calgary**, July 15, 2009.

## DELMORE, Andy

(DEHL-mohr, AN-dee) **DET.**

Defense. Shoots right. 6', 200 lbs. Born, LaSalle, Ont., December 26, 1976.

| Season | Club | League | GP | G | A | Pts | PIM | PP | SH | GW | S | % | +/- | TF | F% | Min | GP | G | A | Pts | PIM | PP | SH | GW | Min |
|---|---|---|---|---|---|---|---|---|---|---|---|---|---|---|---|---|---|---|---|---|---|---|---|---|---|
| 1992-93 | Chatham | OHA-B | 47 | 4 | 21 | 25 | 38 | .... | .... | .... | .... | .... | .... | .... | .... | .... | .... | .... | .... | .... | .... | .... | .... | .... | .... |
| 1993-94 | North Bay | OHL | 45 | 2 | 7 | 9 | 33 | .... | .... | .... | .... | .... | .... | .... | .... | .... | 17 | 0 | 0 | 0 | 2 | .... | .... | .... | .... |
| 1994-95 | North Bay | OHL | 40 | 2 | 14 | 16 | 21 | .... | .... | .... | .... | .... | .... | .... | .... | .... | .... | .... | .... | .... | .... | .... | .... | .... | .... |
| | Sarnia Sting | OHL | 27 | 5 | 13 | 18 | 27 | .... | .... | .... | .... | .... | .... | .... | .... | .... | 3 | 0 | 0 | 0 | 2 | .... | .... | .... | .... |
| 1995-96 | Sarnia Sting | OHL | 64 | 21 | 38 | 59 | 45 | .... | .... | .... | .... | .... | .... | .... | .... | .... | 10 | 3 | 7 | 10 | 2 | .... | .... | .... | .... |
| 1996-97 | Sarnia Sting | OHL | 64 | 18 | 60 | 78 | 39 | .... | .... | .... | .... | .... | .... | .... | .... | .... | 12 | 2 | 10 | 12 | 10 | .... | .... | .... | .... |
| | Fredericton | AHL | 4 | 0 | 1 | 1 | 0 | .... | .... | .... | .... | .... | .... | .... | .... | .... | .... | .... | .... | .... | .... | .... | .... | .... | .... |
| 1997-98 | Philadelphia | AHL | 73 | 9 | 30 | 39 | 46 | .... | .... | .... | .... | .... | .... | .... | .... | .... | 18 | 4 | 4 | 8 | 21 | .... | .... | .... | .... |
| **1998-99** | **Philadelphia** | **NHL** | **2** | **0** | **1** | **1** | **0** | **0** | **0** | **0** | **2** | **0.0** | **-1** | **0** | **0.0** | **20:42** | .... | .... | .... | .... | .... | .... | .... | .... | .... |
| | Philadelphia | AHL | 70 | 5 | 18 | 23 | 51 | .... | .... | .... | .... | .... | .... | .... | .... | .... | 15 | 1 | 4 | 5 | 6 | .... | .... | .... | .... |
| **99-2000** | **Philadelphia** | **NHL** | **27** | **2** | **5** | **7** | **8** | **0** | **0** | **1** | **55** | **3.6** | **-1** | **0** | **0.0** | **17:17** | **18** | **5** | **2** | **7** | **14** | **1** | **0** | **1** | **17:33** |
| | Philadelphia | AHL | 39 | 12 | 14 | 26 | 31 | .... | .... | .... | .... | .... | .... | .... | .... | .... | .... | .... | .... | .... | .... | .... | .... | .... | .... |
| **2000-01** | **Philadelphia** | **NHL** | **66** | **5** | **9** | **14** | **16** | **2** | **0** | **0** | **119** | **4.2** | **2** | **0** | **0.0** | **17:39** | **2** | **1** | **0** | **1** | **2** | **0** | **0** | **1** | **15:20** |

| | | | Regular Season | | | | | | | | | | | | | | Playoffs | | | | | | | | |
|---|---|---|---|---|---|---|---|---|---|---|---|---|---|---|---|---|---|---|---|---|---|---|---|---|---|
| Season | Club | League | GP | G | A | Pts | PIM | PP | SH | GW | S | % | +/- | TF | F% | Min | GP | G | A | Pts | PIM | PP | SH | GW | Min |
| 2001-02 | Nashville | NHL | 73 | 16 | 22 | 38 | 22 | 11 | 0 | 3 | 175 | 9.1 | –13 | 0 | 0.0 | 19:40 | .... | .... | .... | .... | .... | .... | .... | .... | .... |
| 2002-03 | Nashville | NHL | 71 | 18 | 16 | 34 | 28 | 14 | 0 | 6 | 149 | 12.1 | –17 | 0 | 0.0 | 17:05 | .... | .... | .... | .... | .... | .... | .... | .... | .... |
| 2003-04 | Buffalo | NHL | 37 | 2 | 5 | 7 | 29 | 2 | 0 | 0 | 40 | 5.0 | –5 | 0 | 0.0 | 15:11 | .... | .... | .... | .... | .... | .... | .... | .... | .... |
| | Rochester | AHL | 8 | 0 | 2 | 2 | 2 | .... | .... | .... | .... | .... | .... | .... | .... | .... | .... | .... | .... | .... | .... | .... | .... | .... | .... |
| 2004-05 | Adler Mannheim | Germany | 50 | 7 | 16 | 23 | 59 | .... | .... | .... | .... | .... | .... | .... | .... | .... | 14 | 1 | 6 | 7 | 12 | .... | .... | .... | .... |
| 2005-06 | Columbus | NHL | 7 | 0 | 0 | 0 | 2 | 0 | 0 | 0 | 7 | 0.0 | –1 | 0 | 0.0 | 15:24 | .... | .... | .... | .... | .... | .... | .... | .... | .... |
| | Syracuse Crunch | AHL | 66 | 17 | 55 | 72 | 46 | .... | .... | .... | .... | .... | .... | .... | .... | .... | 6 | 0 | 1 | 1 | 19 | .... | .... | .... | .... |
| 2006-07 | Springfield | AHL | 47 | 12 | 12 | 24 | 22 | .... | .... | .... | .... | .... | .... | .... | .... | .... | .... | .... | .... | .... | .... | .... | .... | .... | .... |
| | Chicago Wolves | AHL | 28 | 5 | 11 | 16 | 10 | .... | .... | .... | .... | .... | .... | .... | .... | .... | 15 | 0 | 6 | 6 | 2 | .... | .... | .... | .... |
| 2007-08 | Hamburg Freezers | Germany | 51 | 10 | 25 | 35 | 90 | .... | .... | .... | .... | .... | .... | .... | .... | .... | 8 | 0 | 1 | 1 | 12 | .... | .... | .... | .... |
| 2008-09 | Hamburg Freezers | Germany | 52 | 9 | 22 | 31 | 70 | .... | .... | .... | .... | .... | .... | .... | .... | .... | 9 | 1 | 3 | 4 | 8 | .... | .... | .... | .... |
| | NHL Totals | | 283 | 43 | 58 | 101 | 105 | 29 | 0 | 10 | 547 | 7.9 | | 0 | 0.0 | 17:38 | 20 | 6 | 2 | 8 | 16 | 1 | 0 | 2 | 17:19 |

OHL First All-Star Team (1997) • AHL First All-Star Team (2006) • Eddie Shore Award (AHL - Outstanding Defenseman) (2006)

Signed as a free agent by **Philadelphia**, June 9, 1997. Traded to **Nashville** by **Philadelphia** for Nashville's 3rd round choice (later traded to Phoenix – Phoenix selected Joe Callahan) in 2002 Entry Draft, July 31, 2001. Traded to **Buffalo** by **Nashville** for Buffalo's 3rd round choice (later traded to Minnesota – Minnesota selected Clayton Stoner) in 2004 Entry Draft, June 27, 2003. Traded to **San Jose** by **Buffalo** with Curtis Brown for Jeff Jillson and San Jose's compensatory 7th round choice (Andrew Orpik) in 2005 Entry Draft, March 9, 2004. Traded to **Boston** by **San Jose** for future considerations, March 9, 2004. Signed as a free agent by **Mannheim** (Germany), July 21, 2004. Signed as a free agent by **Detroit**, August 16, 2005. Claimed on waivers by **Columbus** from **Detroit**, October 4, 2005. Signed as a free agent by **Tampa Bay**, July 1, 2006. Traded to **Atlanta** by **Tampa Bay** with Andre Deveaux for Stephen Baby and Kyle Wanvig, February 1, 2007. Signed as a free agent by **Hamburg** (Germany), June 13, 2007. Signed as a free agent by **Detroit**, July 28, 2009.

## DEMITRA, Pavol

(deh-MEET-rah, PAH-vohl) **VAN.**

Left wing. Shoots left. 6′, 200 lbs. Born, Dubnica, Czech., November 29, 1974. Ottawa's 9th choice, 227th overall, in 1993 Entry Draft.

| | | | | | | | | | | | | | | | | | | | | | | | | | |
|---|---|---|---|---|---|---|---|---|---|---|---|---|---|---|---|---|---|---|---|---|---|---|---|---|---|
| 1991-92 | Dubnica | Czech-2 | 28 | 13 | 10 | 23 | 12 | .... | .... | .... | .... | .... | .... | .... | .... | .... | .... | .... | .... | .... | .... | .... | .... | .... | .... |
| 1992-93 | Dubnica | Czech-2 | 4 | 3 | 0 | 3 | .... | .... | .... | .... | .... | .... | .... | .... | .... | .... | .... | .... | .... | .... | .... | .... | .... | .... | .... |
| | Dukla Trencin | Czech | 46 | 11 | 17 | 28 | 0 | .... | .... | .... | .... | .... | .... | .... | .... | .... | .... | .... | .... | .... | .... | .... | .... | .... | .... |
| 1993-94 | Ottawa | NHL | 12 | 1 | 1 | 2 | 4 | 1 | 0 | 0 | 10 | 10.0 | –7 | .... | .... | .... | .... | .... | .... | .... | .... | .... | .... | .... | .... |
| | P.E.I. Senators | AHL | 41 | 18 | 23 | 41 | 8 | .... | .... | .... | .... | .... | .... | .... | .... | .... | .... | .... | .... | .... | .... | .... | .... | .... | .... |
| 1994-95 | P.E.I. Senators | AHL | 61 | 26 | 48 | 74 | 23 | .... | .... | .... | .... | .... | .... | .... | .... | .... | 5 | 0 | 7 | 7 | 0 | .... | .... | .... | .... |
| | Ottawa | NHL | 16 | 4 | 3 | 7 | 0 | 1 | 0 | 0 | 21 | 19.0 | –4 | .... | .... | .... | .... | .... | .... | .... | .... | .... | .... | .... | .... |
| 1995-96 | Ottawa | NHL | 31 | 7 | 10 | 17 | 6 | 2 | 0 | 1 | 66 | 10.6 | –3 | .... | .... | .... | .... | .... | .... | .... | .... | .... | .... | .... | .... |
| | P.E.I. Senators | AHL | 48 | 28 | 53 | 81 | 44 | .... | .... | .... | .... | .... | .... | .... | .... | .... | .... | .... | .... | .... | .... | .... | .... | .... | .... |
| 1996-97 | Dukla Trencin | Slovakia | 1 | 1 | 1 | 2 | .... | .... | .... | .... | .... | .... | .... | .... | .... | .... | .... | .... | .... | .... | .... | .... | .... | .... | .... |
| | Las Vegas | IHL | 22 | 8 | 13 | 21 | 10 | .... | .... | .... | .... | .... | .... | .... | .... | .... | .... | .... | .... | .... | .... | .... | .... | .... | .... |
| | St. Louis | NHL | 8 | 3 | 0 | 3 | 2 | 2 | 0 | 1 | 15 | 20.0 | 0 | .... | .... | .... | 6 | 1 | 3 | 4 | 6 | 0 | 0 | 0 | .... |
| | Grand Rapids | IHL | 42 | 20 | 30 | 50 | 24 | .... | .... | .... | .... | .... | .... | .... | .... | .... | .... | .... | .... | .... | .... | .... | .... | .... | .... |
| 1997-98 | St. Louis | NHL | 61 | 22 | 30 | 52 | 22 | 4 | 4 | 6 | 147 | 15.0 | 11 | .... | .... | .... | 10 | 3 | 3 | 6 | 2 | 0 | 0 | 0 | .... |
| 1998-99 | St. Louis | NHL | 82 | 37 | 52 | 89 | 16 | 14 | 0 | 10 | 259 | 14.3 | 13 | 250 | 44.0 | 20:10 | 13 | 5 | 4 | 9 | 4 | 3 | 0 | 1 | 19:10 |
| 99-2000 | St. Louis | NHL | 71 | 28 | 47 | 75 | 8 | 8 | 0 | 4 | 241 | 11.6 | 34 | 41 | 39.0 | 19:13 | .... | .... | .... | .... | .... | .... | .... | .... | .... |
| 2000-01 | St. Louis | NHL | 44 | 20 | 25 | 45 | 16 | 5 | 0 | 5 | 124 | 16.1 | 27 | 8 | 37.5 | 18:03 | 15 | 2 | 4 | 6 | 2 | 0 | 0 | 1 | 18:13 |
| 2001-02 | St. Louis | NHL | 82 | 35 | 43 | 78 | 46 | 11 | 0 | 10 | 212 | 16.5 | 13 | 1224 | 48.1 | 19:11 | 10 | 4 | 7 | 11 | 6 | 2 | 1 | 1 | 19:45 |
| | Slovakia | Olympics | 2 | 1 | 2 | 3 | 2 | .... | .... | .... | .... | .... | .... | .... | .... | .... | .... | .... | .... | .... | .... | .... | .... | .... | .... |
| 2002-03 | St. Louis | NHL | 78 | 36 | 57 | 93 | 32 | 11 | 0 | 4 | 205 | 17.6 | 0 | 1253 | 46.1 | 19:47 | 7 | 2 | 4 | 6 | 2 | 1 | 0 | 0 | 18:20 |
| 2003-04 | St. Louis | NHL | 68 | 23 | 35 | 58 | 18 | 8 | 0 | 5 | 179 | 12.8 | 1 | 770 | 47.3 | 20:30 | 5 | 1 | 0 | 1 | 4 | 0 | 0 | 0 | 18:07 |
| 2004-05 | Dukla Trencin | Slovakia | 54 | *28 | *54 | *82 | 39 | .... | .... | .... | .... | .... | .... | .... | .... | .... | 12 | 4 | 13 | 17 | 14 | .... | .... | .... | .... |
| 2005-06 | Los Angeles | NHL | 58 | 25 | 37 | 62 | 42 | 7 | 5 | 7 | 184 | 13.6 | 21 | 114 | 49.1 | 21:04 | .... | .... | .... | .... | .... | .... | .... | .... | .... |
| | Slovakia | Olympics | 6 | 2 | 5 | 7 | 2 | .... | .... | .... | .... | .... | .... | .... | .... | .... | .... | .... | .... | .... | .... | .... | .... | .... | .... |
| 2006-07 | Minnesota | NHL | 71 | 25 | 39 | 64 | 28 | 9 | 1 | 4 | 175 | 14.3 | 0 | 513 | 47.8 | 20:39 | 5 | 1 | 3 | 4 | 0 | 0 | 0 | 0 | 19:47 |
| 2007-08 | Minnesota | NHL | 68 | 15 | 39 | 54 | 24 | 2 | 0 | 1 | 126 | 11.9 | 9 | 890 | 45.3 | 19:42 | 6 | 1 | 2 | 3 | 2 | 1 | 0 | 0 | 21:09 |
| 2008-09 | Vancouver | NHL | 69 | 20 | 33 | 53 | 20 | 4 | 0 | 1 | 143 | 14.0 | 6 | 242 | 54.6 | 17:29 | 6 | 1 | 2 | 3 | 2 | 1 | 0 | 0 | 17:38 |
| | NHL Totals | | 819 | 301 | 451 | 752 | 284 | 89 | 10 | 59 | 2107 | 14.3 | | 5305 | 47.0 | 19:37 | 83 | 21 | 32 | 53 | 30 | 8 | 1 | 3 | 18:58 |

Lady Byng Memorial Trophy (2000)

Played in NHL All-Star Game (1999, 2000, 2002)

Traded to **St. Louis** by **Ottawa** for Christer Olsson, November 27, 1996. Signed as a free agent by **Trencin** (Slovakia), September 17, 2004. Signed as a free agent by **Los Angeles**, August 2, 2005. Traded to **Minnesota** by **Los Angeles** for Patrick O'Sullivan and Edmonton's 1st round choice (previously acquired, Los Angeles selected Trevor Lewis) in 2006 Entry Draft, June 24, 2006. Signed as a free agent by **Vancouver**, July 10, 2008.

## DEVEAUX, Andre

(de-VOH, AWN-dray) **TOR.**

Center. Shoots right. 6′3″, 240 lbs. Born, Welland, Ont., February 23, 1984. Montreal's 4th choice, 182nd overall, in 2002 Entry Draft.

| | | | | | | | | | | | | | | | | | | | | | | | | | |
|---|---|---|---|---|---|---|---|---|---|---|---|---|---|---|---|---|---|---|---|---|---|---|---|---|---|
| 2000-01 | Belleville Bulls | OHL | 58 | 3 | 6 | 9 | 65 | .... | .... | .... | .... | .... | .... | .... | .... | .... | 10 | 3 | 6 | 9 | 6 | .... | .... | .... | .... |
| 2001-02 | Belleville Bulls | OHL | 64 | 8 | 13 | 21 | 89 | .... | .... | .... | .... | .... | .... | .... | .... | .... | 11 | 1 | 2 | 3 | 30 | .... | .... | .... | .... |
| 2002-03 | Belleville Bulls | OHL | 34 | 6 | 12 | 18 | 93 | .... | .... | .... | .... | .... | .... | .... | .... | .... | .... | .... | .... | .... | .... | .... | .... | .... | .... |
| | Owen Sound | OHL | 29 | 9 | 10 | 19 | 33 | .... | .... | .... | .... | .... | .... | .... | .... | .... | 4 | 2 | 2 | 4 | 6 | .... | .... | .... | .... |
| 2003-04 | Owen Sound | OHL | 64 | 16 | 30 | 46 | 151 | .... | .... | .... | .... | .... | .... | .... | .... | .... | 7 | 3 | 3 | 6 | 21 | .... | .... | .... | .... |
| 2004-05 | Springfield | AHL | 73 | 4 | 8 | 12 | 210 | .... | .... | .... | .... | .... | .... | .... | .... | .... | .... | .... | .... | .... | .... | .... | .... | .... | .... |
| 2005-06 | Springfield | AHL | 59 | 6 | 5 | 11 | 135 | .... | .... | .... | .... | .... | .... | .... | .... | .... | .... | .... | .... | .... | .... | .... | .... | .... | .... |
| | Johnstown Chiefs | ECHL | 11 | 4 | 7 | 11 | 36 | .... | .... | .... | .... | .... | .... | .... | .... | .... | 5 | 1 | 1 | 2 | 2 | .... | .... | .... | .... |
| 2006-07 | Springfield | AHL | 8 | 1 | 2 | 3 | 8 | .... | .... | .... | .... | .... | .... | .... | .... | .... | .... | .... | .... | .... | .... | .... | .... | .... | .... |
| | Johnstown Chiefs | ECHL | 21 | 6 | 8 | 14 | 51 | .... | .... | .... | .... | .... | .... | .... | .... | .... | .... | .... | .... | .... | .... | .... | .... | .... | .... |
| | Chicago Wolves | AHL | 28 | 4 | 4 | 8 | 105 | .... | .... | .... | .... | .... | .... | .... | .... | .... | 14 | 3 | 2 | 5 | 48 | .... | .... | .... | .... |
| 2007-08 | Chicago Wolves | AHL | 66 | 7 | 11 | 18 | 232 | .... | .... | .... | .... | .... | .... | .... | .... | .... | 24 | 0 | 2 | 2 | 67 | .... | .... | .... | .... |
| 2008-09 | Toronto | NHL | 21 | 0 | 1 | 1 | 75 | 0 | 0 | 0 | 15 | 0.0 | –3 | 7 | 28.6 | 7:14 | .... | .... | .... | .... | .... | .... | .... | .... | .... |
| | Toronto Marlies | AHL | 38 | 14 | 11 | 25 | 114 | .... | .... | .... | .... | .... | .... | .... | .... | .... | 6 | 0 | 3 | 3 | 14 | .... | .... | .... | .... |
| | NHL Totals | | 21 | 0 | 1 | 1 | 75 | 0 | 0 | 0 | 15 | 0.0 | | 7 | 28.6 | 7:14 | .... | .... | .... | .... | .... | .... | .... | .... | .... |

Signed as a free agent by **Tampa Bay**, September 15, 2004. Traded to **Atlanta** by **Tampa Bay** with Andy Delmore for and Stephen Baby and Kyle Wanvig, February 1, 2007. Signed as a free agent by **Toronto**, July 21, 2008.

## DEVEREAUX, Boyd

(DEH-vuhr-oh, BOID)

Center. Shoots left. 6′2″, 195 lbs. Born, Seaforth, Ont., April 16, 1978. Edmonton's 1st choice, 6th overall, in 1996 Entry Draft.

| | | | | | | | | | | | | | | | | | | | | | | | | | |
|---|---|---|---|---|---|---|---|---|---|---|---|---|---|---|---|---|---|---|---|---|---|---|---|---|---|
| 1992-93 | Seaforth Sailors | OHA-D | 34 | 7 | 20 | 27 | 13 | .... | .... | .... | .... | .... | .... | .... | .... | .... | .... | .... | .... | .... | .... | .... | .... | .... | .... |
| 1993-94 | Stratford Cullitons | OHA-B | 46 | 12 | 27 | 39 | 8 | .... | .... | .... | .... | .... | .... | .... | .... | .... | .... | .... | .... | .... | .... | .... | .... | .... | .... |
| 1994-95 | Stratford Cullitons | OHA-B | 45 | 31 | 74 | 105 | 21 | .... | .... | .... | .... | .... | .... | .... | .... | .... | .... | .... | .... | .... | .... | .... | .... | .... | .... |
| 1995-96 | Kitchener Rangers | OHL | 66 | 20 | 38 | 58 | 35 | .... | .... | .... | .... | .... | .... | .... | .... | .... | 12 | 3 | 7 | 10 | 4 | .... | .... | .... | .... |
| 1996-97 | Kitchener Rangers | OHL | 54 | 28 | 41 | 69 | 37 | .... | .... | .... | .... | .... | .... | .... | .... | .... | 13 | 4 | 11 | 15 | 8 | .... | .... | .... | .... |
| | Hamilton | AHL | .... | .... | .... | .... | .... | .... | .... | .... | .... | .... | .... | .... | .... | .... | 1 | 0 | 1 | 1 | 0 | .... | .... | .... | .... |
| 1997-98 | Edmonton | NHL | 38 | 1 | 4 | 5 | 6 | 0 | 0 | 0 | 27 | 3.7 | –5 | .... | .... | .... | .... | .... | .... | .... | .... | .... | .... | .... | .... |
| | Hamilton | AHL | 14 | 5 | 6 | 11 | 6 | .... | .... | .... | .... | .... | .... | .... | .... | .... | 9 | 1 | 1 | 2 | 8 | .... | .... | .... | .... |
| 1998-99 | Edmonton | NHL | 61 | 6 | 8 | 14 | 23 | 0 | 1 | 4 | 39 | 15.4 | 2 | 409 | 42.8 | 10:09 | 1 | 0 | 0 | 0 | 0 | 0 | 0 | 0 | 32:46 |
| | Hamilton | AHL | 7 | 4 | 6 | 10 | 2 | .... | .... | .... | .... | .... | .... | .... | .... | .... | 8 | 0 | 3 | 3 | 4 | .... | .... | .... | .... |
| 99-2000 | Edmonton | NHL | 76 | 8 | 19 | 27 | 20 | 0 | 1 | 2 | 108 | 7.4 | 7 | 241 | 34.9 | 12:36 | .... | .... | .... | .... | .... | .... | .... | .... | .... |
| 2000-01 | Detroit | NHL | 55 | 5 | 6 | 11 | 14 | 0 | 0 | 0 | 66 | 7.6 | 1 | 124 | 37.1 | 10:08 | 2 | 0 | 0 | 0 | 0 | 0 | 0 | 0 | 10:39 |
| 2001-02 ♦ | Detroit | NHL | 79 | 9 | 16 | 25 | 24 | 0 | 0 | 2 | 116 | 7.8 | 9 | 12 | 33.3 | 11:30 | 21 | 2 | 4 | 6 | 4 | 0 | 0 | 0 | 10:58 |
| 2002-03 | Detroit | NHL | 61 | 3 | 9 | 12 | 16 | 0 | 0 | 1 | 72 | 4.2 | 4 | 7 | 42.9 | 9:26 | .... | .... | .... | .... | .... | .... | .... | .... | .... |
| 2003-04 | Detroit | NHL | 61 | 6 | 9 | 15 | 20 | 0 | 0 | 2 | 62 | 9.7 | –1 | 14 | 50.0 | 9:58 | 3 | 1 | 0 | 1 | 0 | 0 | 0 | 0 | 6:36 |
| 2004-05 | | | Did not play | | | | | | | | | | | | | | | | | | | | | | |
| 2005-06 | Phoenix | NHL | 78 | 8 | 14 | 22 | 44 | 1 | 0 | 1 | 76 | 10.5 | –13 | 281 | 36.7 | 12:47 | .... | .... | .... | .... | .... | .... | .... | .... | .... |
| 2006-07 | Toronto | NHL | 33 | 8 | 11 | 19 | 12 | 0 | 0 | 0 | 57 | 14.0 | 4 | 42 | 26.2 | 15:17 | .... | .... | .... | .... | .... | .... | .... | .... | .... |
| | Toronto Marlies | AHL | 30 | 6 | 8 | 14 | 14 | .... | .... | .... | .... | .... | .... | .... | .... | .... | .... | .... | .... | .... | .... | .... | .... | .... | .... |
| 2007-08 | Toronto | NHL | 62 | 7 | 11 | 18 | 24 | 0 | 1 | 1 | 81 | 8.6 | –6 | 6 | 33.3 | 13:58 | .... | .... | .... | .... | .... | .... | .... | .... | .... |
| 2008-09 | Toronto | NHL | 23 | 6 | 5 | 11 | 2 | 0 | 3 | 0 | 41 | 14.6 | 3 | 9 | 44.4 | 13:42 | .... | .... | .... | .... | .... | .... | .... | .... | .... |
| | Toronto Marlies | AHL | 45 | 9 | 7 | 16 | 14 | .... | .... | .... | .... | .... | .... | .... | .... | .... | .... | .... | .... | .... | .... | .... | .... | .... | .... |
| | NHL Totals | | 627 | 67 | 112 | 179 | 205 | 1 | 6 | 13 | 745 | 9.0 | | 1145 | 38.3 | 11:44 | 27 | 3 | 4 | 7 | 4 | 0 | 0 | 0 | 11:16 |

Canadian Major Junior Scholastic Player of the Year (1996)

Signed as a free agent by **Detroit**, August 23, 2000. Signed as a free agent by **Phoenix**, July 5, 2004. Signed as a free agent by **Toronto**, October 7, 2006.

## de VRIES, Greg

(deh-VREES, GREHG)

Defense. Shoots left. 6'2", 205 lbs. Born, Sundridge, Ont., January 4, 1973.

| | | | Regular Season | | | | | | | | | | | | | | Playoffs | | | | | | | | |
|---|---|---|---|---|---|---|---|---|---|---|---|---|---|---|---|---|---|---|---|---|---|---|---|---|---|
| **Season** | **Club** | **League** | **GP** | **G** | **A** | **Pts** | **PIM** | **PP** | **SH** | **GW** | **S** | **%** | **+/-** | **TF** | **F%** | **Min** | **GP** | **G** | **A** | **Pts** | **PIM** | **PP** | **SH** | **GW** | **Min** |
| 1988-89 | Cortina Astros | Minor-ON | 35 | 28 | 40 | 68 | .... | .... | .... | .... | .... | .... | .... | .... | .... | .... | .... | .... | .... | .... | .... | .... | .... | .... | .... |
| 1989-90 | Aurora Eagles | OHA-B | 42 | 1 | 16 | 17 | 32 | .... | .... | .... | .... | .... | .... | .... | .... | .... | .... | .... | .... | .... | .... | .... | .... | .... | .... |
| 1990-91 | Stratford Cullitons | OHA-B | 40 | 8 | 32 | 40 | 120 | .... | .... | .... | .... | .... | .... | .... | .... | .... | 3 | 2 | 1 | 3 | 20 | .... | .... | .... | .... |
| 1991-92 | Thorold | OHA-B | 3 | 0 | 0 | 0 | 0 | .... | .... | .... | .... | .... | .... | .... | .... | .... | .... | .... | .... | .... | .... | .... | .... | .... | .... |
| | Bowling Green | CCHA | 24 | 0 | 3 | 3 | 20 | .... | .... | .... | .... | .... | .... | .... | .... | .... | .... | .... | .... | .... | .... | .... | .... | .... | .... |
| 1992-93 | Niagara Falls | OHL | 62 | 3 | 23 | 26 | 86 | .... | .... | .... | .... | .... | .... | .... | .... | .... | 4 | 0 | 1 | 1 | 6 | .... | .... | .... | .... |
| 1993-94 | Niagara Falls | OHL | 64 | 5 | 40 | 45 | 135 | .... | .... | .... | .... | .... | .... | .... | .... | .... | .... | .... | .... | .... | .... | .... | .... | .... | .... |
| | Cape Breton | AHL | 9 | 0 | 0 | 0 | 11 | .... | .... | .... | .... | .... | .... | .... | .... | .... | 1 | 0 | 0 | 0 | 0 | .... | .... | .... | .... |
| 1994-95 | Cape Breton | AHL | 77 | 5 | 19 | 24 | 68 | .... | .... | .... | .... | .... | .... | .... | .... | .... | .... | .... | .... | .... | .... | .... | .... | .... | .... |
| **1995-96** | **Edmonton** | **NHL** | **13** | **1** | **1** | **2** | **12** | **0** | **0** | **0** | **8** | **12.5** | **-2** | .... | .... | .... | .... | .... | .... | .... | .... | .... | .... | .... | .... |
| | Cape Breton | AHL | 58 | 9 | 30 | 39 | 174 | .... | .... | .... | .... | .... | .... | .... | .... | .... | .... | .... | .... | .... | .... | .... | .... | .... | .... |
| **1996-97** | **Edmonton** | **NHL** | **37** | **0** | **4** | **4** | **52** | **0** | **0** | **0** | **31** | **0.0** | **-2** | .... | .... | .... | **12** | **0** | **1** | **1** | **8** | **0** | **0** | **0** | .... |
| | Hamilton | AHL | 34 | 4 | 14 | 18 | 26 | .... | .... | .... | .... | .... | .... | .... | .... | .... | .... | .... | .... | .... | .... | .... | .... | .... | .... |
| **1997-98** | **Edmonton** | **NHL** | **65** | **7** | **4** | **11** | **80** | **1** | **0** | **0** | **53** | **13.2** | **-17** | .... | .... | .... | **7** | **0** | **0** | **0** | **21** | **0** | **0** | **0** | .... |
| **1998-99** | **Nashville** | **NHL** | **6** | **0** | **0** | **0** | **4** | **0** | **0** | **0** | **1** | **1.0** | **-4** | **0** | **0.0** | **18:11** | .... | .... | .... | .... | .... | .... | .... | .... | .... |
| | **Colorado** | **NHL** | **67** | **1** | **3** | **4** | **60** | **0** | **0** | **0** | **56** | **56.0** | **-3** | **1** | **100.0** | **16:23** | **19** | **0** | **2** | **2** | **22** | **0** | **0** | **0** | **12:09** |
| **99-2000** | **Colorado** | **NHL** | **69** | **2** | **7** | **9** | **73** | **0** | **0** | **0** | **40** | **5.0** | **-7** | **0** | **0.0** | **14:59** | **5** | **0** | **0** | **0** | **4** | **0** | **0** | **0** | **8:09** |
| **2000-01 ♦** | **Colorado** | **NHL** | **79** | **5** | **12** | **17** | **51** | **0** | **0** | **0** | **76** | **6.6** | **23** | **0** | **0.0** | **17:06** | **23** | **0** | **1** | **1** | **20** | **0** | **0** | **0** | **14:17** |
| **2001-02** | **Colorado** | **NHL** | **82** | **8** | **12** | **20** | **57** | **1** | **1** | **3** | **148** | **5.4** | **18** | **1** | **0.0** | **23:03** | **21** | **4** | **9** | **13** | **2** | **0** | **0** | **1** | **24:12** |
| **2002-03** | **Colorado** | **NHL** | **82** | **6** | **26** | **32** | **70** | **0** | **0** | **2** | **112** | **5.4** | **15** | **1** | **100.0** | **22:15** | **7** | **2** | **0** | **2** | **0** | **0** | **0** | **0** | **22:11** |
| **2003-04** | **NY Rangers** | **NHL** | **53** | **3** | **12** | **15** | **37** | **0** | **0** | **0** | **58** | **5.2** | **12** | **0** | **0.0** | **19:01** | .... | .... | .... | .... | .... | .... | .... | .... | .... |
| | **Ottawa** | **NHL** | **13** | **0** | **1** | **1** | **6** | **0** | **0** | **0** | **12** | **0.0** | **0** | **0** | **0.0** | **17:51** | **7** | **0** | **1** | **1** | **8** | **0** | **0** | **0** | **17:51** |
| 2004-05 | | | | DID NOT PLAY | | | | | | | | | | | | | | | | | | | | | |
| **2005-06** | **Atlanta** | **NHL** | **82** | **7** | **28** | **35** | **76** | **3** | **0** | **2** | **111** | **6.3** | **1** | **1** | **100.0** | **22:01** | .... | .... | .... | .... | .... | .... | .... | .... | .... |
| **2006-07** | **Atlanta** | **NHL** | **82** | **3** | **21** | **24** | **66** | **0** | **0** | **0** | **102** | **2.9** | **-3** | **0** | **0.0** | **22:14** | **4** | **1** | **0** | **1** | **4** | **0** | **0** | **0** | **19:17** |
| **2007-08** | **Nashville** | **NHL** | **77** | **4** | **11** | **15** | **71** | **0** | **0** | **1** | **66** | **6.1** | **7** | **0** | **0.0** | **18:52** | **6** | **1** | **0** | **1** | **2** | **0** | **0** | **1** | **19:41** |
| **2008-09** | **Nashville** | **NHL** | **71** | **1** | **4** | **5** | **65** | **0** | **0** | **0** | **38** | **2.6** | **-15** | **0** | **0.0** | **15:08** | .... | .... | .... | .... | .... | .... | .... | .... | .... |
| | **NHL Totals** | | **878** | **48** | **146** | **194** | **780** | **5** | **1** | **8** | **912** | **5.3** | | **4** | **75.0** | **19:16** | **111** | **8** | **14** | **22** | **91** | **0** | **0** | **2** | **17:13** |

Signed as a free agent by **Edmonton**, March 20, 1994. Traded to **Nashville** by **Edmonton** with Eric Fichaud and Drake Berehowsky for Mikhail Shtalenkov and Jim Dowd, October 1, 1998. Traded to **Colorado** by **Nashville** for Colorado's 3rd round choice (later traded back to Colorado - Colorado selected Branko Radivojevic) in 1999 Entry Draft, October 24, 1998. Signed as a free agent by **NY Rangers**, July 14, 2003. Traded to **Ottawa** by **NY Rangers** for Karel Rachunek and Alexandre Giroux, March 9, 2004. Traded to **Atlanta** by **Ottawa** with Marian Hossa for Dany Heatley, August 23, 2005. Signed as a free agent by **Nashville**, July 2, 2007.

## DIMITRAKOS, Niko

(DIH-mih-tra-kohs, NEE-KOH)

Right wing. Shoots right. 5'11", 205 lbs. Born, Somerville, MA, May 21, 1979. San Jose's 4th choice, 155th overall, in 1999 Entry Draft.

| | | | Regular Season | | | | | | | | | | | | | | Playoffs | | | | | | | | |
|---|---|---|---|---|---|---|---|---|---|---|---|---|---|---|---|---|---|---|---|---|---|---|---|---|---|
| **Season** | **Club** | **League** | **GP** | **G** | **A** | **Pts** | **PIM** | **PP** | **SH** | **GW** | **S** | **%** | **+/-** | **TF** | **F%** | **Min** | **GP** | **G** | **A** | **Pts** | **PIM** | **PP** | **SH** | **GW** | **Min** |
| 1994-95 | Matignon | High-MA | 23 | 10 | 12 | 22 | .... | .... | .... | .... | .... | .... | .... | .... | .... | .... | .... | .... | .... | .... | .... | .... | .... | .... | .... |
| 1995-96 | Matignon | High-MA | 25 | 12 | 28 | 40 | .... | .... | .... | .... | .... | .... | .... | .... | .... | .... | .... | .... | .... | .... | .... | .... | .... | .... | .... |
| 1996-97 | Matignon | High-MA | 25 | 23 | 32 | 55 | .... | .... | .... | .... | .... | .... | .... | .... | .... | .... | .... | .... | .... | .... | .... | .... | .... | .... | .... |
| 1997-98 | Avon Old Farms | High-CT | 26 | 27 | 28 | 55 | .... | .... | .... | .... | .... | .... | .... | .... | .... | .... | .... | .... | .... | .... | .... | .... | .... | .... | .... |
| 1998-99 | U. of Maine | H-East | 35 | 8 | 19 | 27 | 33 | .... | .... | .... | .... | .... | .... | .... | .... | .... | .... | .... | .... | .... | .... | .... | .... | .... | .... |
| 99-2000 | U. of Maine | H-East | 32 | 11 | 16 | 27 | 16 | .... | .... | .... | .... | .... | .... | .... | .... | .... | .... | .... | .... | .... | .... | .... | .... | .... | .... |
| 2000-01 | U. of Maine | H-East | 29 | 11 | 14 | 25 | 43 | .... | .... | .... | .... | .... | .... | .... | .... | .... | .... | .... | .... | .... | .... | .... | .... | .... | .... |
| 2001-02 | U. of Maine | H-East | 43 | 20 | 31 | 51 | 44 | .... | .... | .... | .... | .... | .... | .... | .... | .... | .... | .... | .... | .... | .... | .... | .... | .... | .... |
| **2002-03** | **San Jose** | **NHL** | **21** | **6** | **7** | **13** | **8** | **3** | **0** | **0** | **34** | **17.6** | **-7** | **2** | **50.0** | **14:15** | .... | .... | .... | .... | .... | .... | .... | .... | .... |
| | Cleveland Barons | AHL | 55 | 15 | 29 | 44 | 30 | .... | .... | .... | .... | .... | .... | .... | .... | .... | .... | .... | .... | .... | .... | .... | .... | .... | .... |
| **2003-04** | **San Jose** | **NHL** | **68** | **9** | **15** | **24** | **49** | **2** | **0** | **4** | **116** | **7.8** | **6** | **4** | **50.0** | **13:20** | **15** | **1** | **8** | **9** | **8** | **0** | **0** | **1** | **14:31** |
| | Cleveland Barons | AHL | 7 | 4 | 4 | 8 | 4 | .... | .... | .... | .... | .... | .... | .... | .... | .... | .... | .... | .... | .... | .... | .... | .... | .... | .... |
| 2004-05 | Langnau | Swiss | 3 | 0 | 1 | 1 | 2 | .... | .... | .... | .... | .... | .... | .... | .... | .... | 6 | 3 | 3 | 6 | 16 | .... | .... | .... | .... |
| **2005-06** | **San Jose** | **NHL** | **45** | **4** | **12** | **16** | **26** | **0** | **0** | **0** | **66** | **6.1** | **0** | **8** | **25.0** | **11:54** | .... | .... | .... | .... | .... | .... | .... | .... | .... |
| | **Philadelphia** | **NHL** | **19** | **5** | **4** | **9** | **6** | **1** | **0** | **1** | **27** | **18.5** | **4** | **2** | **50.0** | **10:52** | **5** | **0** | **0** | **0** | **2** | **0** | **0** | **0** | **10:07** |
| **2006-07** | **Philadelphia** | **NHL** | **5** | **0** | **0** | **0** | **6** | **0** | **0** | **0** | **4** | **0.0** | **-4** | **0** | **0.0** | **8:32** | .... | .... | .... | .... | .... | .... | .... | .... | .... |
| | Philadelphia | AHL | 45 | 15 | 13 | 28 | 34 | .... | .... | .... | .... | .... | .... | .... | .... | .... | .... | .... | .... | .... | .... | .... | .... | .... | .... |
| | Chicago Wolves | AHL | 17 | 4 | 10 | 14 | 20 | .... | .... | .... | .... | .... | .... | .... | .... | .... | 15 | 3 | 7 | 10 | 8 | .... | .... | .... | .... |
| 2007-08 | Binghamton | AHL | 64 | 20 | 20 | 40 | 67 | .... | .... | .... | .... | .... | .... | .... | .... | .... | .... | .... | .... | .... | .... | .... | .... | .... | .... |
| 2008-09 | Skelleftea AIK | Sweden | 54 | 22 | 22 | 44 | 59 | .... | .... | .... | .... | .... | .... | .... | .... | .... | 1 | 0 | 0 | 0 | 0 | .... | .... | .... | .... |
| | **NHL Totals** | | **158** | **24** | **38** | **62** | **95** | **6** | **0** | **5** | **247** | **9.7** | | **16** | **37.5** | **12:36** | **20** | **1** | **8** | **9** | **10** | **0** | **0** | **1** | **13:25** |

NCAA Championship All-Tournament Team (1999) • Hockey East Second All-Star Team (2002)

Signed as a free agent by **Langnau** (Swiss), February 2, 2005. Traded to **Philadelphia** by **San Jose** for Philadelphia's 3rd round choice (later traded to Columbus - Columbus selected Tommy Sestito) in 2006 Entry Draft, March 9, 2006. • Loaned to **Chicago** (AHL) by **Philadelphia** (AHL) for Jared Ross, March 1, 2007. Signed as a free agent by **Ottawa**, July 13, 2007.

## DiPENTA, Joe

(DIH-pehn-tah, JOH) **BUF.**

Defense. Shoots left. 6'2", 199 lbs. Born, Barrie, Ont., February 25, 1979. Florida's 2nd choice, 61st overall, in 1998 Entry Draft.

| | | | Regular Season | | | | | | | | | | | | | | Playoffs | | | | | | | | |
|---|---|---|---|---|---|---|---|---|---|---|---|---|---|---|---|---|---|---|---|---|---|---|---|---|---|
| **Season** | **Club** | **League** | **GP** | **G** | **A** | **Pts** | **PIM** | **PP** | **SH** | **GW** | **S** | **%** | **+/-** | **TF** | **F%** | **Min** | **GP** | **G** | **A** | **Pts** | **PIM** | **PP** | **SH** | **GW** | **Min** |
| 1996-97 | Smiths Falls Bears | CJHL | 54 | 13 | 22 | 35 | 92 | .... | .... | .... | .... | .... | .... | .... | .... | .... | .... | .... | .... | .... | .... | .... | .... | .... | .... |
| 1997-98 | Boston University | H-East | 38 | 2 | 16 | 18 | 50 | .... | .... | .... | .... | .... | .... | .... | .... | .... | .... | .... | .... | .... | .... | .... | .... | .... | .... |
| 1998-99 | Boston University | H-East | 36 | 2 | 15 | 17 | 72 | .... | .... | .... | .... | .... | .... | .... | .... | .... | .... | .... | .... | .... | .... | .... | .... | .... | .... |
| 99-2000 | Halifax | QMJHL | 63 | 13 | 43 | 56 | 83 | .... | .... | .... | .... | .... | .... | .... | .... | .... | 10 | 3 | 4 | 7 | 26 | .... | .... | .... | .... |
| 2000-01 | Philadelphia | AHL | 71 | 3 | 5 | 8 | 65 | .... | .... | .... | .... | .... | .... | .... | .... | .... | 10 | 1 | 2 | 3 | 15 | .... | .... | .... | .... |
| 2001-02 | Philadelphia | AHL | 61 | 2 | 4 | 6 | 71 | .... | .... | .... | .... | .... | .... | .... | .... | .... | .... | .... | .... | .... | .... | .... | .... | .... | .... |
| | Chicago Wolves | AHL | 15 | 0 | 2 | 2 | 15 | .... | .... | .... | .... | .... | .... | .... | .... | .... | 25 | 1 | 3 | 4 | 22 | .... | .... | .... | .... |
| **2002-03** | **Atlanta** | **NHL** | **3** | **1** | **1** | **2** | **0** | **0** | **0** | **0** | **2** | **50.0** | **3** | **0** | **0.0** | **15:47** | .... | .... | .... | .... | .... | .... | .... | .... | .... |
| | Chicago Wolves | AHL | 76 | 2 | 17 | 19 | 107 | .... | .... | .... | .... | .... | .... | .... | .... | .... | 9 | 0 | 1 | 1 | 7 | .... | .... | .... | .... |
| 2003-04 | Chicago Wolves | AHL | 73 | 0 | 6 | 6 | 105 | .... | .... | .... | .... | .... | .... | .... | .... | .... | 10 | 1 | 0 | 1 | 13 | .... | .... | .... | .... |
| 2004-05 | Manitoba Moose | AHL | 73 | 2 | 10 | 12 | 48 | .... | .... | .... | .... | .... | .... | .... | .... | .... | 14 | 0 | 5 | 5 | 2 | .... | .... | .... | .... |
| **2005-06** | **Anaheim** | **NHL** | **72** | **2** | **6** | **8** | **46** | **0** | **0** | **0** | **27** | **7.4** | **8** | **0** | **0.0** | **13:31** | **16** | **0** | **0** | **0** | **13** | **0** | **0** | **0** | **11:34** |
| **2006-07 ♦** | **Anaheim** | **NHL** | **76** | **2** | **6** | **8** | **48** | **0** | **0** | **1** | **33** | **6.1** | **1** | **1** | **0.0** | **12:09** | **16** | **0** | **0** | **0** | **4** | **0** | **0** | **0** | **8:12** |
| **2007-08** | **Anaheim** | **NHL** | **23** | **1** | **4** | **5** | **16** | **0** | **0** | **0** | **5** | **20.0** | **3** | **0** | **0.0** | **10:39** | .... | .... | .... | .... | .... | .... | .... | .... | .... |
| 2008-09 | Frolunda | Sweden | 47 | 1 | 5 | 6 | 71 | .... | .... | .... | .... | .... | .... | .... | .... | .... | 11 | 0 | 1 | 1 | 12 | .... | .... | .... | .... |
| | **NHL Totals** | | **174** | **6** | **17** | **23** | **110** | **0** | **0** | **1** | **67** | **9.0** | | **1** | **0.0** | **12:35** | **32** | **0** | **0** | **0** | **17** | **0** | **0** | **0** | **9:53** |

• Left **Boston University** (Hockey East) and signed with **Halifax** (QMJHL), May 2, 1999. Signed as a free agent by **Philadelphia**, July 12, 2000. Traded to **Atlanta** by **Philadelphia** for Jarrod Skalde, March 5, 2002. Signed as a free agent by **Vancouver**, August 19, 2004. Signed as a free agent by **Anaheim**, August 11, 2005. • Spent majority of 2007-08 season serving as a healthy reserve. Signed as a free agent by **Frolunda** (Sweden), July 15, 2008. Signed as a free agent by **Buffalo**, July 11, 2009.

## DiSALVATORE, Jon

(dih-SAL-vuh-tohr, JAWN) **MIN.**

Right wing. Shoots right. 6'1", 200 lbs. Born, Bangor, ME, March 30, 1981. San Jose's 2nd choice, 104th overall, in 2000 Entry Draft.

| | | | Regular Season | | | | | | | | | | | | | | Playoffs | | | | | | | | |
|---|---|---|---|---|---|---|---|---|---|---|---|---|---|---|---|---|---|---|---|---|---|---|---|---|---|
| **Season** | **Club** | **League** | **GP** | **G** | **A** | **Pts** | **PIM** | **PP** | **SH** | **GW** | **S** | **%** | **+/-** | **TF** | **F%** | **Min** | **GP** | **G** | **A** | **Pts** | **PIM** | **PP** | **SH** | **GW** | **Min** |
| 1997-98 | N.E. Jr. Coyotes | EJHL | 38 | 24 | 41 | 65 | .... | .... | .... | .... | .... | .... | .... | .... | .... | .... | .... | .... | .... | .... | .... | .... | .... | .... | .... |
| 1998-99 | N.E. Jr. Coyotes | EJHL | 48 | 44 | 76 | *120 | 38 | .... | .... | .... | .... | .... | .... | .... | .... | .... | .... | .... | .... | .... | .... | .... | .... | .... | .... |
| 99-2000 | Providence | H-East | 38 | 15 | 12 | 27 | 12 | .... | .... | .... | .... | .... | .... | .... | .... | .... | .... | .... | .... | .... | .... | .... | .... | .... | .... |
| 2000-01 | Providence | H-East | 36 | 9 | 16 | 25 | 29 | .... | .... | .... | .... | .... | .... | .... | .... | .... | .... | .... | .... | .... | .... | .... | .... | .... | .... |
| 2001-02 | Providence | H-East | 38 | 16 | 26 | 42 | 6 | .... | .... | .... | .... | .... | .... | .... | .... | .... | .... | .... | .... | .... | .... | .... | .... | .... | .... |
| 2002-03 | Providence | H-East | 36 | 19 | 29 | 48 | 12 | .... | .... | .... | .... | .... | .... | .... | .... | .... | .... | .... | .... | .... | .... | .... | .... | .... | .... |
| 2003-04 | Cleveland Barons | AHL | 74 | 22 | 24 | 46 | 30 | .... | .... | .... | .... | .... | .... | .... | .... | .... | 8 | 1 | 1 | 2 | 2 | .... | .... | .... | .... |
| 2004-05 | Worcester IceCats | AHL | 79 | 22 | 23 | 45 | 42 | .... | .... | .... | .... | .... | .... | .... | .... | .... | .... | .... | .... | .... | .... | .... | .... | .... | .... |
| **2005-06** | **St. Louis** | **NHL** | **5** | **0** | **0** | **0** | **2** | **0** | **0** | **0** | **3** | **0.0** | **-1** | **0** | **0.0** | **8:27** | .... | .... | .... | .... | .... | .... | .... | .... | .... |
| | Peoria Rivermen | AHL | 72 | 22 | 45 | 67 | 42 | .... | .... | .... | .... | .... | .... | .... | .... | .... | 4 | 0 | 0 | 0 | 0 | .... | .... | .... | .... |
| 2006-07 | Peoria Rivermen | AHL | 76 | 21 | 39 | 60 | 50 | .... | .... | .... | .... | .... | .... | .... | .... | .... | .... | .... | .... | .... | .... | .... | .... | .... | .... |
| 2007-08 | San Antonio | AHL | 66 | 22 | 24 | 46 | 46 | .... | .... | .... | .... | .... | .... | .... | .... | .... | 7 | 2 | 1 | 3 | 9 | .... | .... | .... | .... |
| 2008-09 | Lowell Devils | AHL | 76 | 20 | 33 | 53 | 32 | .... | .... | .... | .... | .... | .... | .... | .... | .... | .... | .... | .... | .... | .... | .... | .... | .... | .... |
| | **NHL Totals** | | **5** | **0** | **0** | **0** | **2** | **0** | **0** | **0** | **3** | **0.0** | | **0** | **0.0** | **8:27** | .... | .... | .... | .... | .... | .... | .... | .... | .... |

Signed as a free agent by **St. Louis**, June 30, 2004. Signed as a free agent by **Phoenix**, July 9, 2007. Signed as a free agent by **New Jersey**, July 17, 2008. Signed as a free agent by **Minnesota**, July 17, 2009.

## DOAN, Shane

(DOHN, SHAYN) **PHX.**

Right wing. Shoots right. 6'2", 224 lbs. Born, Halkirk, Alta., October 10, 1976. Winnipeg's 1st choice, 7th overall, in 1995 Entry Draft.

| | | | Regular Season | | | | | | | | | | | | | | Playoffs | | | | | | | | |
|---|---|---|---|---|---|---|---|---|---|---|---|---|---|---|---|---|---|---|---|---|---|---|---|---|---|
| Season | Club | League | GP | G | A | Pts | PIM | PP | SH | GW | S | % | +/- | TF | F% | Min | GP | G | A | Pts | PIM | PP | SH | GW | Min |
| 1991-92 | Killam Selects | AAHA | 56 | 80 | 84 | 164 | 74 | | | | | | | | | | | | | | | | | | |
| 1992-93 | Kamloops Blazers | WHL | 51 | 7 | 12 | 19 | 65 | | | | | | | | | | 13 | 0 | 1 | 1 | 8 | | | | |
| 1993-94 | Kamloops Blazers | WHL | 52 | 24 | 24 | 48 | 88 | | | | | | | | | | | | | | | | | | |
| 1994-95 | Kamloops Blazers | WHL | 71 | 37 | 57 | 94 | 106 | | | | | | | | | | 21 | 6 | 10 | 16 | 16 | | | | |
| **1995-96** | **Winnipeg** | **NHL** | **74** | **7** | **10** | **17** | **101** | **1** | **0** | **3** | **106** | **6.6** | **-9** | | | | **6** | **0** | **0** | **0** | **6** | **0** | **0** | **0** | |
| **1996-97** | **Phoenix** | **NHL** | **63** | **4** | **8** | **12** | **49** | **0** | **0** | **0** | **100** | **4.0** | **-3** | | | | **4** | **0** | **0** | **0** | **2** | **0** | **0** | **0** | |
| **1997-98** | **Phoenix** | **NHL** | **33** | **5** | **6** | **11** | **35** | **0** | **0** | **3** | **42** | **11.9** | **-3** | | | | **6** | **1** | **0** | **1** | **6** | **0** | **0** | **0** | |
| | Springfield | AHL | 39 | 21 | 21 | 42 | 64 | | | | | | | | | | | | | | | | | | |
| **1998-99** | **Phoenix** | **NHL** | **79** | **6** | **16** | **22** | **54** | **0** | **0** | **0** | **156** | **3.8** | **-5** | **6** | **16.7** | **12:42** | **7** | **2** | **2** | **4** | **6** | **0** | **0** | **2** | **17:58** |
| **99-2000** | **Phoenix** | **NHL** | **81** | **26** | **25** | **51** | **66** | **1** | **1** | **4** | **221** | **11.8** | **6** | **25** | **36.0** | **16:51** | **4** | **1** | **2** | **3** | **8** | **1** | **0** | **0** | **18:11** |
| **2000-01** | **Phoenix** | **NHL** | **76** | **26** | **37** | **63** | **89** | **6** | **1** | **6** | **220** | **11.8** | **0** | **15** | **40.0** | **19:32** | | | | | | | | | |
| **2001-02** | **Phoenix** | **NHL** | **81** | **20** | **29** | **49** | **61** | **6** | **0** | **2** | **205** | **9.8** | **11** | **52** | **44.2** | **18:10** | **5** | **2** | **2** | **4** | **6** | **0** | **0** | **0** | **17:21** |
| **2002-03** | **Phoenix** | **NHL** | **82** | **21** | **37** | **58** | **86** | **7** | **0** | **2** | **225** | **9.3** | **3** | **623** | **39.8** | **18:47** | | | | | | | | | |
| **2003-04** | **Phoenix** | **NHL** | **79** | **27** | **41** | **68** | **47** | **9** | **2** | **1** | **254** | **10.6** | **-11** | **55** | **40.0** | **21:46** | | | | | | | | | |
| 2004-05 | | | Did not play | | | | | | | | | | | | | | | | | | | | | | |
| **2005-06** | **Phoenix** | **NHL** | **82** | **30** | **36** | **66** | **123** | **17** | **0** | **7** | **254** | **11.8** | **-9** | **126** | **43.7** | **19:08** | | | | | | | | | |
| | Canada | Olympics | 6 | 2 | 1 | 3 | 2 | | | | | | | | | | | | | | | | | | |
| **2006-07** | **Phoenix** | **NHL** | **73** | **27** | **28** | **55** | **73** | **11** | **0** | **7** | **209** | **12.9** | **-14** | **174** | **39.1** | **20:27** | | | | | | | | | |
| **2007-08** | **Phoenix** | **NHL** | **80** | **28** | **50** | **78** | **59** | **9** | **2** | **5** | **243** | **11.5** | **4** | **187** | **41.2** | **20:46** | | | | | | | | | |
| **2008-09** | **Phoenix** | **NHL** | **82** | **31** | **42** | **73** | **72** | **10** | **0** | **4** | **230** | **13.5** | **5** | **362** | **44.2** | **20:15** | | | | | | | | | |
| | **NHL Totals** | | **965** | **258** | **365** | **623** | **915** | **77** | **6** | **44** | **2465** | **10.5** | | **1625** | **41.2** | **18:49** | **32** | **6** | **6** | **12** | **34** | **1** | **0** | **2** | **17:50** |

Memorial Cup Tournament All-Star Team (1995) • Stafford Smythe Memorial Trophy (Memorial Cup Tournament - MVP) (1995)
Played in NHL All-Star Game (2004, 2009)
• Transferred to **Phoenix** after **Winnipeg** franchise relocated, July 1, 1996.

## DOELL, Kevin

(DOH-ehl, KEH-vihn)

Center. Shoots left. 5'11", 190 lbs. Born, Saskatoon, Sask., July 15, 1979.

| Season | Club | League | GP | G | A | Pts | PIM | PP | SH | GW | S | % | +/- | TF | F% | Min | GP | G | A | Pts | PIM | PP | SH | GW | Min |
|---|---|---|---|---|---|---|---|---|---|---|---|---|---|---|---|---|---|---|---|---|---|---|---|---|---|
| 99-2000 | U. of Denver | WCHA | 40 | 8 | 15 | 23 | 18 | | | | | | | | | | | | | | | | | | |
| 2000-01 | U. of Denver | WCHA | 36 | 9 | 10 | 19 | 26 | | | | | | | | | | | | | | | | | | |
| 2001-02 | U. of Denver | WCHA | 41 | 20 | 23 | 43 | 28 | | | | | | | | | | | | | | | | | | |
| 2002-03 | U. of Denver | WCHA | 41 | 25 | 26 | 51 | 34 | | | | | | | | | | | | | | | | | | |
| 2003-04 | Chicago Wolves | AHL | 8 | 1 | 1 | 2 | 6 | | | | | | | | | | 1 | 0 | 0 | 0 | 0 | | | | |
| | Gwinnett | ECHL | 63 | 33 | 41 | 74 | 88 | | | | | | | | | | 13 | 1 | 6 | 7 | 12 | | | | |
| 2004-05 | Chicago Wolves | AHL | 45 | 4 | 8 | 12 | 69 | | | | | | | | | | | | | | | | | | |
| | Gwinnett | ECHL | 11 | 6 | 9 | 15 | 14 | | | | | | | | | | 8 | 2 | 1 | 3 | 14 | | | | |
| 2005-06 | Chicago Wolves | AHL | 78 | 17 | 34 | 51 | 72 | | | | | | | | | | | | | | | | | | |
| 2006-07 | Chicago Wolves | AHL | 80 | 14 | 19 | 33 | 107 | | | | | | | | | | 15 | 2 | 4 | 6 | 14 | | | | |
| **2007-08** | **Atlanta** | **NHL** | **8** | **0** | **1** | **1** | **4** | **0** | **0** | **0** | **6** | **0.0** | **-2** | **53** | **47.2** | **9:40** | | | | | | | | | |
| | Chicago Wolves | AHL | 68 | 16 | 17 | 33 | 75 | | | | | | | | | | 24 | 4 | 5 | 9 | 41 | | | | |
| 2008-09 | Leksands IF | Sweden-2 | 37 | 22 | 27 | 49 | 105 | | | | | | | | | | | | | | | | | | |
| | **NHL Totals** | | **8** | **0** | **1** | **1** | **4** | **0** | **0** | **0** | **6** | **0.0** | | **53** | **47.2** | **9:40** | | | | | | | | | |

ECHL All-Rookie Team (2004) • ECHL Rookie of the Year (2004)
Signed as a free agent by **Atlanta**, June 30, 2004. Signed as a free agent by **Leksands** (Sweden-2), July 31, 2008.

## DONOVAN, Shean

(DAW-nuh-vuhn, SHAWN) **OTT.**

Right wing. Shoots right. 6'3", 218 lbs. Born, Timmins, Ont., January 22, 1975. San Jose's 2nd choice, 28th overall, in 1993 Entry Draft.

| Season | Club | League | GP | G | A | Pts | PIM | PP | SH | GW | S | % | +/- | TF | F% | Min | GP | G | A | Pts | PIM | PP | SH | GW | Min |
|---|---|---|---|---|---|---|---|---|---|---|---|---|---|---|---|---|---|---|---|---|---|---|---|---|---|
| 1990-91 | Kanata Valley | CJHL | 44 | 8 | 5 | 13 | 8 | | | | | | | | | | | | | | | | | | |
| 1991-92 | Ottawa 67's | OHL | 58 | 11 | 8 | 19 | 14 | | | | | | | | | | 11 | 1 | 0 | 1 | 5 | | | | |
| 1992-93 | Ottawa 67's | OHL | 66 | 29 | 23 | 52 | 33 | | | | | | | | | | | | | | | | | | |
| 1993-94 | Ottawa 67's | OHL | 62 | 35 | 49 | 84 | 63 | | | | | | | | | | 17 | 10 | 11 | 21 | 14 | | | | |
| **1994-95** | Ottawa 67's | OHL | 29 | 22 | 19 | 41 | 41 | | | | | | | | | | | | | | | | | | |
| | **San Jose** | **NHL** | **14** | **0** | **0** | **0** | **6** | **0** | **0** | **0** | **13** | **0.0** | **-6** | | | | **7** | **0** | **1** | **1** | **6** | **0** | **0** | **0** | |
| | Kansas City | IHL | 5 | 0 | 2 | 2 | 7 | | | | | | | | | | 14 | 5 | 3 | 8 | 23 | | | | |
| **1995-96** | **San Jose** | **NHL** | **74** | **13** | **8** | **21** | **39** | **0** | **1** | **2** | **73** | **17.8** | **-17** | | | | | | | | | | | | |
| | Kansas City | IHL | 4 | 0 | 0 | 0 | 8 | | | | | | | | | | 5 | 0 | 0 | 0 | 8 | | | | |
| **1996-97** | **San Jose** | **NHL** | **73** | **9** | **6** | **15** | **42** | **0** | **1** | **0** | **115** | **7.8** | **-18** | | | | | | | | | | | | |
| | Kentucky | AHL | 3 | 1 | 3 | 4 | 18 | | | | | | | | | | | | | | | | | | |
| **1997-98** | **San Jose** | **NHL** | **20** | **3** | **3** | **6** | **22** | **0** | **0** | **0** | **24** | **12.5** | **3** | | | | | | | | | | | | |
| | **Colorado** | **NHL** | **47** | **5** | **7** | **12** | **48** | **0** | **0** | **0** | **57** | **8.8** | **3** | | | | | | | | | | | | |
| **1998-99** | **Colorado** | **NHL** | **68** | **7** | **12** | **19** | **37** | **1** | **0** | **1** | **81** | **8.6** | **4** | **9** | **22.2** | **8:46** | **5** | **0** | **0** | **0** | **2** | **0** | **0** | **0** | **4:55** |
| **99-2000** | **Colorado** | **NHL** | **18** | **1** | **0** | **1** | **8** | **0** | **0** | **0** | **13** | **7.7** | **-4** | **1** | **0.0** | **5:20** | | | | | | | | | |
| | **Atlanta** | **NHL** | **33** | **4** | **7** | **11** | **18** | **1** | **0** | **1** | **53** | **7.5** | **-13** | **22** | **31.8** | **14:19** | | | | | | | | | |
| **2000-01** | **Atlanta** | **NHL** | **63** | **12** | **11** | **23** | **47** | **1** | **3** | **1** | **93** | **12.9** | **-14** | **218** | **45.9** | **14:03** | | | | | | | | | |
| **2001-02** | **Atlanta** | **NHL** | **48** | **6** | **6** | **12** | **40** | **1** | **0** | **2** | **64** | **9.4** | **-16** | **12** | **50.0** | **13:30** | | | | | | | | | |
| | **Pittsburgh** | **NHL** | **13** | **2** | **1** | **3** | **4** | **0** | **0** | **0** | **18** | **11.1** | **-5** | **4** | **0.0** | **14:34** | | | | | | | | | |
| **2002-03** | **Pittsburgh** | **NHL** | **52** | **4** | **5** | **9** | **30** | **0** | **1** | **0** | **66** | **6.1** | **-6** | **37** | **24.3** | **13:01** | | | | | | | | | |
| | **Calgary** | **NHL** | **13** | **1** | **2** | **3** | **7** | **0** | **0** | **1** | **22** | **4.5** | **-2** | **3** | **66.7** | **15:39** | | | | | | | | | |
| **2003-04** | **Calgary** | **NHL** | **82** | **18** | **24** | **42** | **72** | **3** | **3** | **8** | **138** | **13.0** | **14** | **53** | **39.6** | **14:55** | **24** | **5** | **5** | **10** | **23** | **0** | **0** | **2** | **15:27** |
| 2004-05 | Geneve | Swiss | 12 | 5 | 3 | 8 | 30 | | | | | | | | | | | | | | | | | | |
| **2005-06** | **Calgary** | **NHL** | **80** | **9** | **11** | **20** | **82** | **0** | **1** | **0** | **132** | **6.8** | **9** | **26** | **30.8** | **11:47** | **7** | **0** | **0** | **0** | **6** | **0** | **0** | **0** | **11:24** |
| **2006-07** | **Boston** | **NHL** | **76** | **6** | **11** | **17** | **56** | **0** | **0** | **0** | **108** | **5.6** | **-13** | **41** | **43.9** | **14:09** | | | | | | | | | |
| **2007-08** | **Ottawa** | **NHL** | **82** | **5** | **7** | **12** | **73** | **0** | **0** | **3** | **91** | **5.5** | **-3** | **29** | **37.9** | **9:35** | **4** | **1** | **0** | **1** | **2** | **0** | **0** | **0** | **14:00** |
| **2008-09** | **Ottawa** | **NHL** | **65** | **5** | **5** | **10** | **34** | **0** | **0** | **1** | **58** | **8.6** | **-2** | **9** | **44.4** | **7:50** | | | | | | | | | |
| | **NHL Totals** | | **921** | **110** | **126** | **236** | **665** | **7** | **10** | **20** | **1219** | **9.0** | | **464** | **40.5** | **11:59** | **47** | **6** | **6** | **12** | **39** | **0** | **0** | **2** | **13:16** |

Traded to **Colorado** by **San Jose** with San Jose's 1st round choice (Alex Tanguay) in 1998 Entry Draft for Mike Ricci and Colorado's 2nd round choice (later traded to Buffalo – Buffalo selected Jaroslav Kristek) in 1998 Entry Draft, November 21, 1997. Traded to **Atlanta** by **Colorado** for Rick Tabaracci, December 8, 1999. Claimed on waivers by **Pittsburgh** from **Atlanta**, March 15, 2002. Traded to **Calgary** by **Pittsburgh** for Micki Dupont and Mathias Johansson, March 11, 2003. Signed as a free agent by **Geneve** (Swiss), November 13, 2004. Signed as a free agent by **Boston**, July 2, 2006. Traded to **Ottawa** by **Boston** for Peter Schaefer, July 17, 2007.

## DORSETT, Derek

(DOHRS-iht, DAIR-ihk) **CBJ**

Right wing. Shoots right. 5'11", 187 lbs. Born, Kindersley, Sask., December 20, 1986. Columbus' 9th choice, 189th overall, in 2006 Entry Draft.

| Season | Club | League | GP | G | A | Pts | PIM | PP | SH | GW | S | % | +/- | TF | F% | Min | GP | G | A | Pts | PIM | PP | SH | GW | Min |
|---|---|---|---|---|---|---|---|---|---|---|---|---|---|---|---|---|---|---|---|---|---|---|---|---|---|
| 2004-05 | Medicine Hat | WHL | 51 | 5 | 11 | 16 | 108 | | | | | | | | | | 13 | 5 | 1 | 6 | 35 | | | | |
| 2005-06 | Medicine Hat | WHL | 68 | 25 | 23 | 48 | *279 | | | | | | | | | | 13 | 8 | 4 | 12 | 53 | | | | |
| 2006-07 | Medicine Hat | WHL | 61 | 19 | 45 | 64 | 206 | | | | | | | | | | 17 | 8 | 8 | 16 | 56 | | | | |
| 2007-08 | Syracuse Crunch | AHL | 64 | 10 | 8 | 18 | 289 | | | | | | | | | | 12 | 0 | 1 | 1 | 56 | | | | |
| **2008-09** | **Columbus** | **NHL** | **52** | **4** | **1** | **5** | **150** | **0** | **0** | **1** | **59** | **6.8** | **-1** | **9** | **44.4** | **8:53** | **3** | **0** | **0** | **0** | **2** | **0** | **0** | **0** | **9:11** |
| | Syracuse Crunch | AHL | 7 | 1 | 5 | 6 | 35 | | | | | | | | | | | | | | | | | | |
| | **NHL Totals** | | **52** | **4** | **1** | **5** | **150** | **0** | **0** | **1** | **59** | **6.8** | | **9** | **44.4** | **8:53** | **3** | **0** | **0** | **0** | **2** | **0** | **0** | **0** | **9:11** |

## DOUGHTY, Drew

(DOW-tee, DROO) **L.A.**

Defense. Shoots right. 6'1", 203 lbs. Born, London, Ont., December 8, 1989. Los Angeles' 1st choice, 2nd overall, in 2008 Entry Draft.

| Season | Club | League | GP | G | A | Pts | PIM | PP | SH | GW | S | % | +/- | TF | F% | Min | GP | G | A | Pts | PIM | PP | SH | GW | Min |
|---|---|---|---|---|---|---|---|---|---|---|---|---|---|---|---|---|---|---|---|---|---|---|---|---|---|
| 2004-05 | Lon. Jr. Knights | Minor-ON | 55 | 19 | 30 | 49 | 31 | | | | | | | | | | | | | | | | | | |
| 2005-06 | Guelph Storm | OHL | 65 | 5 | 28 | 33 | 40 | | | | | | | | | | 14 | 0 | 13 | 13 | 18 | | | | |
| 2006-07 | Guelph Storm | OHL | 67 | 21 | 53 | 74 | 76 | | | | | | | | | | 4 | 2 | 3 | 5 | 8 | | | | |
| 2007-08 | Guelph Storm | OHL | 58 | 13 | 37 | 50 | 68 | | | | | | | | | | 10 | 3 | 6 | 9 | 14 | | | | |
| **2008-09** | **Los Angeles** | **NHL** | **81** | **6** | **21** | **27** | **56** | **3** | **0** | **1** | **126** | **4.8** | **-17** | **0** | **0.0** | **23:50** | | | | | | | | | |
| | **NHL Totals** | | **81** | **6** | **21** | **27** | **56** | **3** | **0** | **1** | **126** | **4.8** | | **0** | **0.0** | **23:50** | | | | | | | | | |

OHL First All-Star Team (2007, 2008) • Canadian Major Junior First All-Star Team (2008) • NHL All-Rookie Team (2009)

## DOWELL, Jake

(DOW-uhl, JAYK) **CHI.**

Center. Shoots left. 6', 202 lbs. Born, Eau Claire, WI, March 4, 1985. Chicago's 10th choice, 140th overall, in 2004 Entry Draft.

| | | | Regular Season | | | | | | | | | | | | | Playoffs | | | | | | | | |
|---|---|---|---|---|---|---|---|---|---|---|---|---|---|---|---|---|---|---|---|---|---|---|---|---|
| Season | Club | League | GP | G | A | Pts | PIM | PP | SH | GW | S | % | +/- | TF | F% | Min | GP | G | A | Pts | PIM | PP | SH | GW | Min |
| 2000-01 | Eau Claire Mem. | High-WI | 24 | 25 | 30 | 55 | .... | .... | .... | .... | .... | .... | .... | .... | .... | .... | .... | .... | .... | .... | .... | .... | .... | .... | .... |
| 2001-02 | USNTDP | U-17 | 11 | 5 | 1 | 6 | 14 | .... | .... | .... | .... | .... | .... | .... | .... | .... | .... | .... | .... | .... | .... | .... | .... | .... | .... |
| | USNTDP | NAHL | 44 | 5 | 12 | 17 | 51 | .... | .... | .... | .... | .... | .... | .... | .... | .... | .... | .... | .... | .... | .... | .... | .... | .... | .... |
| 2002-03 | USNTDP | U-18 | 54 | 8 | 17 | 25 | 54 | .... | .... | .... | .... | .... | .... | .... | .... | .... | .... | .... | .... | .... | .... | .... | .... | .... | .... |
| | USNTDP | NAHL | 9 | 2 | 2 | 4 | 13 | .... | .... | .... | .... | .... | .... | .... | .... | .... | .... | .... | .... | .... | .... | .... | .... | .... | .... |
| 2003-04 | U. of Wisconsin | WCHA | 37 | 6 | 13 | 19 | 48 | .... | .... | .... | .... | .... | .... | .... | .... | .... | .... | .... | .... | .... | .... | .... | .... | .... | .... |
| 2004-05 | U. of Wisconsin | WCHA | 38 | 12 | 14 | 26 | 74 | .... | .... | .... | .... | .... | .... | .... | .... | .... | .... | .... | .... | .... | .... | .... | .... | .... | .... |
| 2005-06 | U. of Wisconsin | WCHA | 43 | 5 | 15 | 20 | 42 | .... | .... | .... | .... | .... | .... | .... | .... | .... | .... | .... | .... | .... | .... | .... | .... | .... | .... |
| 2006-07 | U. of Wisconsin | WCHA | 41 | 19 | 6 | 25 | 54 | .... | .... | .... | .... | .... | .... | .... | .... | .... | .... | .... | .... | .... | .... | .... | .... | .... | .... |
| | Norfolk Admirals | AHL | 9 | 2 | 3 | 5 | 8 | .... | .... | .... | .... | .... | .... | .... | .... | .... | 6 | 0 | 3 | 3 | 4 | .... | .... | .... | .... |
| **2007-08** | **Chicago** | **NHL** | **19** | **2** | **1** | **3** | **10** | **0** | **1** | **0** | **19** | **10.5** | **1** | **170** | **46.5** | **11:56** | .... | .... | .... | .... | .... | .... | .... | .... | .... |
| | Rockford IceHogs | AHL | 49 | 7 | 10 | 17 | 64 | .... | .... | .... | .... | .... | .... | .... | .... | .... | 12 | 1 | 1 | 2 | 6 | .... | .... | .... | .... |
| **2008-09** | **Chicago** | **NHL** | **1** | **0** | **0** | **0** | **2** | **0** | **0** | **0** | **0** | **0.0** | **1** | **12** | **66.7** | **13:37** | .... | .... | .... | .... | .... | .... | .... | .... | .... |
| | Rockford IceHogs | AHL | 75 | 6 | 14 | 20 | 128 | .... | .... | .... | .... | .... | .... | .... | .... | .... | 4 | 0 | 0 | 0 | 0 | .... | .... | .... | .... |
| | **NHL Totals** | | **20** | **2** | **1** | **3** | **12** | **0** | **1** | **0** | **19** | **10.5** | | **182** | **47.8** | **12:01** | .... | .... | .... | .... | .... | .... | .... | .... | .... |

## DOWNEY, Aaron

(DOW-nee, AIR-ruhn)

Right wing. Shoots right. 6'1", 215 lbs. Born, Shelburne, Ont., August 27, 1974.

| | | | Regular Season | | | | | | | | | | | | | Playoffs | | | | | | | | |
|---|---|---|---|---|---|---|---|---|---|---|---|---|---|---|---|---|---|---|---|---|---|---|---|---|
| Season | Club | League | GP | G | A | Pts | PIM | PP | SH | GW | S | % | +/- | TF | F% | Min | GP | G | A | Pts | PIM | PP | SH | GW | Min |
| 1990-91 | Grand Valley | OHA-C | 27 | 6 | 8 | 14 | 57 | .... | .... | .... | .... | .... | .... | .... | .... | .... | .... | .... | .... | .... | .... | .... | .... | .... | .... |
| 1991-92 | Collingwood | OHA-B | 40 | 9 | 8 | 17 | 111 | .... | .... | .... | .... | .... | .... | .... | .... | .... | .... | .... | .... | .... | .... | .... | .... | .... | .... |
| 1992-93 | Guelph Storm | OHL | 53 | 3 | 3 | 6 | 88 | .... | .... | .... | .... | .... | .... | .... | .... | .... | 5 | 1 | 0 | 1 | 0 | .... | .... | .... | .... |
| 1993-94 | Cole Harbour | NSMHL | 35 | 8 | 20 | 28 | 210 | .... | .... | .... | .... | .... | .... | .... | .... | .... | .... | .... | .... | .... | .... | .... | .... | .... | .... |
| 1994-95 | Cole Harbour | NSMHL | 40 | 10 | 31 | 41 | 320 | .... | .... | .... | .... | .... | .... | .... | .... | .... | .... | .... | .... | .... | .... | .... | .... | .... | .... |
| 1995-96 | Hampton Roads | ECHL | 65 | 12 | 11 | 23 | 354 | .... | .... | .... | .... | .... | .... | .... | .... | .... | .... | .... | .... | .... | .... | .... | .... | .... | .... |
| 1996-97 | Manitoba Moose | IHL | 2 | 0 | 0 | 0 | 17 | .... | .... | .... | .... | .... | .... | .... | .... | .... | .... | .... | .... | .... | .... | .... | .... | .... | .... |
| | Portland Pirates | AHL | 3 | 0 | 0 | 0 | 19 | .... | .... | .... | .... | .... | .... | .... | .... | .... | .... | .... | .... | .... | .... | .... | .... | .... | .... |
| | Hampton Roads | ECHL | 64 | 8 | 8 | 16 | 338 | .... | .... | .... | .... | .... | .... | .... | .... | .... | 9 | 0 | 3 | 3 | 26 | .... | .... | .... | .... |
| 1997-98 | Providence Bruins | AHL | 78 | 5 | 10 | 15 | *407 | .... | .... | .... | .... | .... | .... | .... | .... | .... | .... | .... | .... | .... | .... | .... | .... | .... | .... |
| 1998-99 | Providence Bruins | AHL | 75 | 10 | 12 | 22 | *401 | .... | .... | .... | .... | .... | .... | .... | .... | .... | 19 | 1 | 1 | 2 | 46 | .... | .... | .... | .... |
| **99-2000** | **Boston** | **NHL** | **1** | **0** | **0** | **0** | **0** | **0** | **0** | **0** | **0** | **0.0** | **0** | **0** | **0.0** | **8:31** | .... | .... | .... | .... | .... | .... | .... | .... | .... |
| | Providence Bruins | AHL | 47 | 6 | 4 | 10 | 221 | .... | .... | .... | .... | .... | .... | .... | .... | .... | 14 | 1 | 0 | 1 | 24 | .... | .... | .... | .... |
| **2000-01** | **Chicago** | **NHL** | **3** | **0** | **0** | **0** | **6** | **0** | **0** | **0** | **2** | **0.0** | **–1** | **0** | **0.0** | **5:30** | .... | .... | .... | .... | .... | .... | .... | .... | .... |
| | Norfolk Admirals | AHL | 67 | 6 | 15 | 21 | 234 | .... | .... | .... | .... | .... | .... | .... | .... | .... | 9 | 0 | 0 | 0 | 4 | .... | .... | .... | .... |
| **2001-02** | **Chicago** | **NHL** | **36** | **1** | **0** | **1** | **76** | **0** | **0** | **1** | **10** | **10.0** | **–2** | **0** | **0.0** | **5:06** | **4** | **0** | **0** | **0** | **8** | **0** | **0** | **0** | **6:29** |
| | Norfolk Admirals | AHL | 12 | 0 | 2 | 2 | 21 | .... | .... | .... | .... | .... | .... | .... | .... | .... | .... | .... | .... | .... | .... | .... | .... | .... | .... |
| **2002-03** | **Dallas** | **NHL** | **43** | **1** | **1** | **2** | **69** | **0** | **0** | **0** | **14** | **7.1** | **1** | **0** | **0.0** | **4:47** | .... | .... | .... | .... | .... | .... | .... | .... | .... |
| **2003-04** | **Dallas** | **NHL** | **37** | **1** | **1** | **2** | **77** | **0** | **0** | **1** | **11** | **9.1** | **2** | **0** | **0.0** | **4:30** | .... | .... | .... | .... | .... | .... | .... | .... | .... |
| 2004-05 | | | DID NOT PLAY | | | | | | | | | | | | | | | | | | | | | | |
| **2005-06** | **St. Louis** | **NHL** | **17** | **2** | **0** | **2** | **45** | **0** | **0** | **0** | **11** | **18.2** | **0** | **0** | **0.0** | **3:56** | .... | .... | .... | .... | .... | .... | .... | .... | .... |
| | **Montreal** | **NHL** | **25** | **1** | **4** | **5** | **50** | **0** | **0** | **0** | **10** | **10.0** | **2** | **1** | **0.0** | **6:43** | **1** | **0** | **0** | **0** | **0** | **0** | **0** | **0** | **6:17** |
| **2006-07** | **Montreal** | **NHL** | **21** | **1** | **0** | **1** | **48** | **0** | **0** | **1** | **10** | **10.0** | **–6** | **0** | **0.0** | **4:59** | .... | .... | .... | .... | .... | .... | .... | .... | .... |
| | Providence Bruins | AHL | 15 | 0 | 0 | 0 | 30 | .... | .... | .... | .... | .... | .... | .... | .... | .... | 1 | 0 | 0 | 0 | 12 | .... | .... | .... | .... |
| **2007-08♦** | **Detroit** | **NHL** | **56** | **0** | **3** | **3** | **116** | **0** | **0** | **0** | **15** | **0.0** | **0** | **0** | **0.0** | **4:35** | .... | .... | .... | .... | .... | .... | .... | .... | .... |
| **2008-09** | **Detroit** | **NHL** | **4** | **1** | **1** | **2** | **7** | **0** | **0** | **0** | **2** | **50.0** | **0** | **0** | **0.0** | **5:13** | .... | .... | .... | .... | .... | .... | .... | .... | .... |
| | Grand Rapids | AHL | 65 | 2 | 7 | 9 | 126 | .... | .... | .... | .... | .... | .... | .... | .... | .... | 10 | 0 | 1 | 1 | 44 | .... | .... | .... | .... |
| | **NHL Totals** | | **243** | **8** | **10** | **18** | **494** | **0** | **0** | **3** | **85** | **9.4** | | **1** | **0.0** | **4:56** | **5** | **0** | **0** | **0** | **8** | **0** | **0** | **0** | **6:27** |

Signed as a free agent by **Boston**, January 20, 1998. Signed as a free agent by **Chicago**, August 13, 2000. Signed as a free agent by **Dallas**, July 3, 2002. • Spent majority of 2003-04 season serving as a healthy reserve. Signed as a free agent by **St. Louis**, August 1, 2005. Claimed on waivers by **Montreal** from **St. Louis**, January 23, 2006. • Spent majority of 2006-07 season serving as a healthy reserve. Signed as a free agent by **St. Louis**, August 1, 2005.Signed as a free agent by **Detroit**, October 3, 2007.

## DOWNIE, Steve

(DOW-nee, STEEV) **T.B.**

Right wing. Shoots right. 5'11", 200 lbs. Born, Newmarket, Ont., April 3, 1987. Philadelphia's 1st choice, 29th overall, in 2005 Entry Draft.

| | | | Regular Season | | | | | | | | | | | | | Playoffs | | | | | | | | |
|---|---|---|---|---|---|---|---|---|---|---|---|---|---|---|---|---|---|---|---|---|---|---|---|---|
| Season | Club | League | GP | G | A | Pts | PIM | PP | SH | GW | S | % | +/- | TF | F% | Min | GP | G | A | Pts | PIM | PP | SH | GW | Min |
| 2002-03 | Aurora Tigers | OPJHL | 34 | 12 | 13 | 25 | 55 | .... | .... | .... | .... | .... | .... | .... | .... | .... | .... | .... | .... | .... | .... | .... | .... | .... | .... |
| 2003-04 | Windsor Spitfires | OHL | 49 | 7 | 9 | 16 | 90 | .... | .... | .... | .... | .... | .... | .... | .... | .... | 4 | 0 | 1 | 1 | 27 | .... | .... | .... | .... |
| 2004-05 | Windsor Spitfires | OHL | 61 | 21 | 52 | 73 | 179 | .... | .... | .... | .... | .... | .... | .... | .... | .... | 11 | 4 | 5 | 9 | 49 | .... | .... | .... | .... |
| 2005-06 | Windsor Spitfires | OHL | 1 | 3 | 0 | 3 | 4 | .... | .... | .... | .... | .... | .... | .... | .... | .... | .... | .... | .... | .... | .... | .... | .... | .... | .... |
| | Peterborough | OHL | 34 | 16 | 34 | 50 | 109 | .... | .... | .... | .... | .... | .... | .... | .... | .... | 19 | 6 | 15 | 21 | 38 | .... | .... | .... | .... |
| 2006-07 | Peterborough | OHL | 28 | 23 | 36 | 59 | 92 | .... | .... | .... | .... | .... | .... | .... | .... | .... | .... | .... | .... | .... | .... | .... | .... | .... | .... |
| | Kitchener Rangers | OHL | 17 | 12 | 21 | 33 | 32 | .... | .... | .... | .... | .... | .... | .... | .... | .... | 9 | 8 | 14 | 22 | 15 | .... | .... | .... | .... |
| | Philadelphia | AHL | 1 | 0 | 0 | 0 | 0 | .... | .... | .... | .... | .... | .... | .... | .... | .... | .... | .... | .... | .... | .... | .... | .... | .... | .... |
| **2007-08** | **Philadelphia** | **NHL** | **32** | **6** | **6** | **12** | **73** | **0** | **1** | **1** | **25** | **24.0** | **2** | **15** | **33.3** | **9:51** | **6** | **0** | **1** | **1** | **10** | **0** | **0** | **0** | **6:04** |
| | Philadelphia | AHL | 21 | 5 | 12 | 17 | 114 | .... | .... | .... | .... | .... | .... | .... | .... | .... | .... | .... | .... | .... | .... | .... | .... | .... | .... |
| **2008-09** | **Philadelphia** | **NHL** | **6** | **0** | **0** | **0** | **11** | **0** | **0** | **0** | **1** | **0.0** | **–4** | **13** | **15.4** | **5:57** | .... | .... | .... | .... | .... | .... | .... | .... | .... |
| | Philadelphia | AHL | 4 | 1 | 7 | 8 | 23 | .... | .... | .... | .... | .... | .... | .... | .... | .... | .... | .... | .... | .... | .... | .... | .... | .... | .... |
| | **Tampa Bay** | **NHL** | **23** | **3** | **3** | **6** | **54** | **0** | **0** | **1** | **25** | **12.0** | **2** | **7** | **42.9** | **9:04** | .... | .... | .... | .... | .... | .... | .... | .... | .... |
| | Norfolk Admirals | AHL | 23 | 8 | 17 | 25 | 107 | .... | .... | .... | .... | .... | .... | .... | .... | .... | .... | .... | .... | .... | .... | .... | .... | .... | .... |
| | **NHL Totals** | | **61** | **9** | **9** | **18** | **138** | **0** | **1** | **2** | **51** | **17.6** | | **35** | **28.6** | **9:10** | **6** | **0** | **1** | **1** | **10** | **0** | **0** | **0** | **6:04** |

Traded to **Tampa Bay** by **Philadelphia** with Steve Eminger and Tampa Bay's 4th round choice (previously acquired, Tampa Bay selected Alex Hutchings) in 2009 Entry Draft for Matt Carle and San Jose's 3rd round choice (previously acquired, Philadelphia selected Simon Bertilsson) in 2009 Entry Draft, November 7, 2008.

## DRAPER, Kris

(DRAY-puhr, KRIHS) **DET.**

Center. Shoots left. 5'10", 188 lbs. Born, Toronto, Ont., May 24, 1971. Winnipeg's 4th choice, 62nd overall, in 1989 Entry Draft.

| | | | Regular Season | | | | | | | | | | | | | Playoffs | | | | | | | | |
|---|---|---|---|---|---|---|---|---|---|---|---|---|---|---|---|---|---|---|---|---|---|---|---|---|
| Season | Club | League | GP | G | A | Pts | PIM | PP | SH | GW | S | % | +/- | TF | F% | Min | GP | G | A | Pts | PIM | PP | SH | GW | Min |
| 1987-88 | Don Mills Flyers | MTHL | 40 | 35 | 32 | 67 | 46 | .... | .... | .... | .... | .... | .... | .... | .... | .... | .... | .... | .... | .... | .... | .... | .... | .... | .... |
| 1988-89 | Canada | Nat-Tm | 60 | 11 | 15 | 26 | 16 | .... | .... | .... | .... | .... | .... | .... | .... | .... | .... | .... | .... | .... | .... | .... | .... | .... | .... |
| 1989-90 | Canada | Nat-Tm | 61 | 12 | 22 | 34 | 44 | .... | .... | .... | .... | .... | .... | .... | .... | .... | .... | .... | .... | .... | .... | .... | .... | .... | .... |
| **1990-91** | Ottawa 67's | OHL | 39 | 19 | 42 | 61 | 35 | .... | .... | .... | .... | .... | .... | .... | .... | .... | 17 | 8 | 11 | 19 | 20 | .... | .... | .... | .... |
| | **Winnipeg** | **NHL** | **3** | **1** | **0** | **1** | **5** | **0** | **0** | **0** | **1** | **100.0** | **0** | .... | .... | .... | .... | .... | .... | .... | .... | .... | .... | .... | .... |
| | Moncton Hawks | AHL | 7 | 2 | 1 | 3 | 2 | .... | .... | .... | .... | .... | .... | .... | .... | .... | .... | .... | .... | .... | .... | .... | .... | .... | .... |
| **1991-92** | **Winnipeg** | **NHL** | **10** | **2** | **0** | **2** | **2** | **0** | **0** | **0** | **19** | **10.5** | **0** | .... | .... | .... | **2** | **0** | **0** | **0** | **0** | **0** | **0** | **0** | |
| | Moncton Hawks | AHL | 61 | 11 | 18 | 29 | 113 | .... | .... | .... | .... | .... | .... | .... | .... | .... | 4 | 0 | 1 | 1 | 6 | .... | .... | .... | .... |
| **1992-93** | **Winnipeg** | **NHL** | **7** | **0** | **0** | **0** | **2** | **0** | **0** | **0** | **5** | **0.0** | **–6** | .... | .... | .... | .... | .... | .... | .... | .... | .... | .... | .... | .... |
| | Moncton Hawks | AHL | 67 | 12 | 23 | 35 | 40 | .... | .... | .... | .... | .... | .... | .... | .... | .... | 5 | 2 | 2 | 4 | 18 | .... | .... | .... | .... |
| **1993-94** | **Detroit** | **NHL** | **39** | **5** | **8** | **13** | **31** | **0** | **1** | **0** | **55** | **9.1** | **11** | .... | .... | .... | **7** | **2** | **2** | **4** | **4** | **0** | **1** | **0** | |
| | Adirondack | AHL | 46 | 20 | 23 | 43 | 49 | .... | .... | .... | .... | .... | .... | .... | .... | .... | .... | .... | .... | .... | .... | .... | .... | .... | .... |
| **1994-95** | **Detroit** | **NHL** | **36** | **2** | **6** | **8** | **22** | **0** | **0** | **0** | **44** | **4.5** | **1** | .... | .... | .... | **18** | **4** | **1** | **5** | **12** | **0** | **1** | **1** | |
| **1995-96** | **Detroit** | **NHL** | **52** | **7** | **9** | **16** | **32** | **0** | **1** | **0** | **51** | **13.7** | **2** | .... | .... | .... | **18** | **4** | **2** | **6** | **18** | **0** | **1** | **0** | |
| **1996-97♦** | **Detroit** | **NHL** | **76** | **8** | **5** | **13** | **73** | **1** | **0** | **1** | **85** | **9.4** | **–11** | .... | .... | .... | **20** | **2** | **4** | **6** | **12** | **0** | **1** | **0** | |
| **1997-98♦** | **Detroit** | **NHL** | **64** | **13** | **10** | **23** | **45** | **1** | **0** | **4** | **96** | **13.5** | **5** | .... | .... | .... | **19** | **1** | **3** | **4** | **12** | **0** | **0** | **1** | |
| **1998-99** | **Detroit** | **NHL** | **80** | **4** | **14** | **18** | **79** | **0** | **1** | **1** | **78** | **5.1** | **2** | **887** | **54.6** | **12:43** | **10** | **0** | **1** | **1** | **6** | **0** | **0** | **0** | **11:35** |
| **99-2000** | **Detroit** | **NHL** | **51** | **5** | **7** | **12** | **28** | **0** | **0** | **3** | **76** | **6.6** | **3** | **380** | **57.6** | **13:33** | **9** | **2** | **0** | **2** | **6** | **0** | **0** | **0** | **12:26** |
| **2000-01** | **Detroit** | **NHL** | **75** | **8** | **17** | **25** | **38** | **0** | **1** | **1** | **123** | **6.5** | **17** | **997** | **56.5** | **13:26** | **6** | **0** | **1** | **1** | **2** | **0** | **0** | **0** | **16:08** |
| **2001-02♦** | **Detroit** | **NHL** | **82** | **15** | **15** | **30** | **56** | **0** | **2** | **3** | **137** | **10.9** | **26** | **756** | **53.2** | **15:35** | **23** | **2** | **3** | **5** | **20** | **0** | **0** | **0** | **17:00** |
| **2002-03** | **Detroit** | **NHL** | **82** | **14** | **21** | **35** | **82** | **0** | **1** | **2** | **142** | **9.9** | **6** | **1059** | **56.9** | **16:12** | **4** | **0** | **0** | **0** | **4** | **0** | **0** | **0** | **17:29** |
| **2003-04** | **Detroit** | **NHL** | **67** | **24** | **16** | **40** | **31** | **2** | **5** | **1** | **149** | **16.1** | **22** | **1058** | **56.9** | **17:44** | **12** | **1** | **3** | **4** | **6** | **0** | **0** | **0** | **18:29** |
| 2004-05 | | | DID NOT PLAY | | | | | | | | | | | | | | | | | | | | | | |
| **2005-06** | **Detroit** | **NHL** | **80** | **10** | **22** | **32** | **58** | **0** | **1** | **1** | **153** | **6.5** | **3** | **1287** | **57.7** | **17:46** | **6** | **0** | **0** | **0** | **6** | **0** | **0** | **0** | **19:58** |
| | Canada | Olympics | 6 | 0 | 0 | 0 | 0 | .... | .... | .... | .... | .... | .... | .... | .... | .... | .... | .... | .... | .... | .... | .... | .... | .... | .... |
| **2006-07** | **Detroit** | **NHL** | **81** | **14** | **15** | **29** | **58** | **0** | **5** | **1** | **157** | **8.9** | **7** | **1242** | **57.3** | **16:45** | **18** | **2** | **0** | **2** | **24** | **0** | **0** | **0** | **16:36** |
| **2007-08♦** | **Detroit** | **NHL** | **65** | **9** | **8** | **17** | **68** | **0** | **2** | **2** | **97** | **9.3** | **–2** | **944** | **58.6** | **15:38** | **22** | **3** | **1** | **4** | **10** | **0** | **0** | **1** | **15:27** |
| **2008-09** | **Detroit** | **NHL** | **79** | **7** | **10** | **17** | **40** | **0** | **1** | **2** | **93** | **7.5** | **–13** | **1000** | **60.3** | **11:59** | **8** | **1** | **0** | **1** | **0** | **0** | **0** | **0** | **8:37** |
| | **NHL Totals** | | **1029** | **148** | **183** | **331** | **750** | **4** | **21** | **22** | **1561** | **9.5** | | **9610** | **57.1** | **15:10** | **202** | **24** | **21** | **45** | **142** | **0** | **4** | **3** | **15:33** |

Frank J. Selke Trophy (2004)

Traded to **Detroit** by **Winnipeg** for future considerations, June 30, 1993.

## DREWISKE, Davis
(droo-WIHS-kee, DAY-vihs) **L.A.**

Defense. Shoots left. 6'2", 215 lbs. Born, Hudson, WI, November 22, 1984.

| | | | Regular Season | | | | | | | | | | | | | | Playoffs | | | | | | | | |
|---|---|---|---|---|---|---|---|---|---|---|---|---|---|---|---|---|---|---|---|---|---|---|---|---|---|
| Season | Club | League | GP | G | A | Pts | PIM | PP | SH | GW | S | % | +/- | TF | F% | Min | GP | G | A | Pts | PIM | PP | SH | GW | Min |
| 2003-04 | Des Moines | USHL | 60 | 4 | 19 | 23 | 63 | .... | .... | .... | .... | .... | .... | .... | .... | .... | 3 | 0 | 0 | 0 | 4 | .... | .... | .... | .... |
| 2004-05 | U. of Wisconsin | WCHA | 34 | 1 | 5 | 6 | 20 | .... | .... | .... | .... | .... | .... | .... | .... | .... | .... | .... | .... | .... | .... | .... | .... | .... | .... |
| 2005-06 | U. of Wisconsin | WCHA | 35 | 2 | 2 | 4 | 22 | .... | .... | .... | .... | .... | .... | .... | .... | .... | .... | .... | .... | .... | .... | .... | .... | .... | .... |
| 2006-07 | U. of Wisconsin | WCHA | 41 | 4 | 6 | 10 | 46 | .... | .... | .... | .... | .... | .... | .... | .... | .... | .... | .... | .... | .... | .... | .... | .... | .... | .... |
| 2007-08 | U. of Wisconsin | WCHA | 40 | 5 | 16 | 21 | 46 | .... | .... | .... | .... | .... | .... | .... | .... | .... | .... | .... | .... | .... | .... | .... | .... | .... | .... |
| | Manchester | AHL | 5 | 0 | 0 | 0 | 6 | .... | .... | .... | .... | .... | .... | .... | .... | .... | 4 | 0 | 1 | 1 | 6 | .... | .... | .... | .... |
| **2008-09** | **Los Angeles** | **NHL** | **17** | **0** | **3** | **3** | **18** | **0** | **0** | **0** | **21** | **0.0** | **1** | **0** | **0.0** | **17:19** | .... | .... | .... | .... | .... | .... | .... | .... | .... |
| | Manchester | AHL | 61 | 1 | 13 | 14 | 95 | .... | .... | .... | .... | .... | .... | .... | .... | .... | .... | .... | .... | .... | .... | .... | .... | .... | .... |
| | **NHL Totals** | | **17** | **0** | **3** | **3** | **18** | **0** | **0** | **0** | **21** | **0.0** | | **0** | **0.0** | **17:19** | .... | .... | .... | .... | .... | .... | .... | .... | .... |

Signed as a free agent by **Los Angeles**, April 1, 2008.

## DRURY, Chris
(DROO-ree, KRIHS) **NYR**

Center. Shoots right. 5'10", 190 lbs. Born, Trumbull, CT, August 20, 1976. Quebec's 5th choice, 72nd overall, in 1994 Entry Draft.

| | | | Regular Season | | | | | | | | | | | | | | Playoffs | | | | | | | | |
|---|---|---|---|---|---|---|---|---|---|---|---|---|---|---|---|---|---|---|---|---|---|---|---|---|---|
| Season | Club | League | GP | G | A | Pts | PIM | PP | SH | GW | S | % | +/- | TF | F% | Min | GP | G | A | Pts | PIM | PP | SH | GW | Min |
| 1991-92 | Fairfield Prep | High-CT | 25 | 22 | 27 | 49 | .... | .... | .... | .... | .... | .... | .... | .... | .... | .... | .... | .... | .... | .... | .... | .... | .... | .... | .... |
| 1992-93 | Fairfield Prep | High-CT | 24 | 25 | 32 | 57 | 15 | .... | .... | .... | .... | .... | .... | .... | .... | .... | .... | .... | .... | .... | .... | .... | .... | .... | .... |
| 1993-94 | Fairfield Prep | High-CT | 24 | 37 | 18 | 55 | .... | .... | .... | .... | .... | .... | .... | .... | .... | .... | .... | .... | .... | .... | .... | .... | .... | .... | .... |
| 1994-95 | Boston University | H-East | 39 | 12 | 15 | 27 | 38 | .... | .... | .... | .... | .... | .... | .... | .... | .... | .... | .... | .... | .... | .... | .... | .... | .... | .... |
| 1995-96 | Boston University | H-East | 37 | 35 | 33 | *68 | 46 | .... | .... | .... | .... | .... | .... | .... | .... | .... | .... | .... | .... | .... | .... | .... | .... | .... | .... |
| 1996-97 | Boston University | H-East | 41 | *38 | 24 | 62 | 64 | .... | .... | .... | .... | .... | .... | .... | .... | .... | .... | .... | .... | .... | .... | .... | .... | .... | .... |
| 1997-98 | Boston University | H-East | 38 | 28 | 29 | 57 | 88 | .... | .... | .... | .... | .... | .... | .... | .... | .... | .... | .... | .... | .... | .... | .... | .... | .... | .... |
| **1998-99** | **Colorado** | **NHL** | **79** | **20** | **24** | **44** | **62** | **6** | **0** | **3** | **138** | **14.5** | **9** | **418** | **46.9** | **13:15** | **19** | **6** | **2** | **8** | **4** | **0** | **0** | **4** | **11:28** |
| **99-2000** | **Colorado** | **NHL** | **82** | **20** | **47** | **67** | **42** | **7** | **0** | **2** | **213** | **9.4** | **8** | **1321** | **53.1** | **18:33** | **17** | **4** | **10** | **14** | **4** | **1** | **0** | **2** | **18:30** |
| **2000-01 •** | **Colorado** | **NHL** | **71** | **24** | **41** | **65** | **47** | **11** | **0** | **5** | **204** | **11.8** | **6** | **552** | **55.1** | **18:03** | **23** | **11** | **5** | **16** | **4** | **2** | **0** | **2** | **19:06** |
| **2001-02** | **Colorado** | **NHL** | **82** | **21** | **25** | **46** | **38** | **5** | **0** | **6** | **236** | **8.9** | **1** | **1139** | **53.2** | **17:57** | **21** | **5** | **7** | **12** | **10** | **1** | **0** | **3** | **17:01** |
| | United States | Olympics | 6 | 0 | 0 | 0 | 0 | .... | .... | .... | .... | .... | .... | .... | .... | .... | .... | .... | .... | .... | .... | .... | .... | .... | .... |
| **2002-03** | **Calgary** | **NHL** | **80** | **23** | **30** | **53** | **33** | **5** | **1** | **5** | **224** | **10.3** | **-9** | **942** | **53.8** | **18:33** | .... | .... | .... | .... | .... | .... | .... | .... | .... |
| **2003-04** | **Buffalo** | **NHL** | **76** | **18** | **35** | **53** | **68** | **5** | **1** | **2** | **152** | **11.8** | **8** | **1491** | **54.9** | **18:04** | .... | .... | .... | .... | .... | .... | .... | .... | .... |
| 2004-05 | | DID NOT PLAY | | | | | | | | | | | | | | | | | | | | | | | |
| **2005-06** | **Buffalo** | **NHL** | **81** | **30** | **37** | **67** | **32** | **16** | **2** | **5** | **172** | **17.4** | **-11** | **1641** | **55.5** | **18:06** | **18** | **9** | **9** | **18** | **10** | **5** | **1** | **1** | **19:20** |
| | United States | Olympics | 6 | 0 | 3 | 3 | 2 | .... | .... | .... | .... | .... | .... | .... | .... | .... | .... | .... | .... | .... | .... | .... | .... | .... | .... |
| **2006-07** | **Buffalo** | **NHL** | **77** | **37** | **32** | **69** | **30** | **17** | **3** | **9** | **199** | **18.6** | **1** | **1613** | **58.8** | **18:47** | **16** | **8** | **5** | **13** | **2** | **3** | **0** | **3** | **20:45** |
| **2007-08** | **NY Rangers** | **NHL** | **82** | **25** | **33** | **58** | **45** | **12** | **0** | **7** | **220** | **11.4** | **-3** | **1359** | **54.9** | **19:48** | **10** | **3** | **3** | **6** | **8** | **0** | **0** | **1** | **18:27** |
| **2008-09** | **NY Rangers** | **NHL** | **81** | **22** | **34** | **56** | **32** | **10** | **1** | **2** | **219** | **10.0** | **-8** | **1183** | **51.0** | **20:15** | **6** | **1** | **0** | **1** | **2** | **0** | **0** | **1** | **13:32** |
| | **NHL Totals** | | **791** | **240** | **338** | **578** | **429** | **94** | **8** | **46** | **1977** | **12.1** | | **11659** | **54.4** | **18:09** | **130** | **47** | **41** | **88** | **44** | **12** | **1** | **17** | **17:30** |

Hockey East Second All-Star Team (1996, 1997) • NCAA East Second All-American Team (1996) • Hockey East Player of the Year (1997, 1998) • NCAA East First All-American Team (1997, 1998) • NCAA Championship All-Tournament Team (1997) • Hockey East First All-Star Team (1998) • Hobey Baker Memorial Award (Top U.S. Collegiate Player) (1998) • NHL All-Rookie Team (1999) • Calder Memorial Trophy (1999)

• Rights transferred to **Colorado** after **Quebec** franchise relocated, June 21, 1995. Traded to **Calgary** by **Colorado** with Stephane Yelle for Derek Morris, Jeff Shantz and Dean McAmmond, October 1, 2002. Traded to **Buffalo** by **Calgary** with Steve Begin for Steve Reinprecht and Rhett Warrener, July 3, 2003. Signed as a free agent by **NY Rangers**, July 1, 2007.

## DUBINSKY, Brandon
(DOO-bihn-skee, BRAN-duhn) **NYR**

Center. Shoots left. 6'1", 205 lbs. Born, Anchorage, AK, April 29, 1986. NY Rangers' 6th choice, 60th overall, in 2004 Entry Draft.

| | | | Regular Season | | | | | | | | | | | | | | Playoffs | | | | | | | | |
|---|---|---|---|---|---|---|---|---|---|---|---|---|---|---|---|---|---|---|---|---|---|---|---|---|---|
| Season | Club | League | GP | G | A | Pts | PIM | PP | SH | GW | S | % | +/- | TF | F% | Min | GP | G | A | Pts | PIM | PP | SH | GW | Min |
| 2001-02 | Alaska All-Stars | AASHA | 37 | 14 | 24 | 38 | | .... | .... | .... | .... | .... | .... | .... | .... | .... | .... | .... | .... | .... | .... | .... | .... | .... | .... |
| 2002-03 | Portland | WHL | 44 | 8 | 18 | 26 | 35 | .... | .... | .... | .... | .... | .... | .... | .... | .... | 7 | 2 | 2 | 4 | 10 | .... | .... | .... | .... |
| 2003-04 | Portland | WHL | 71 | 30 | 48 | 78 | 137 | .... | .... | .... | .... | .... | .... | .... | .... | .... | 5 | 0 | 2 | 2 | 6 | .... | .... | .... | .... |
| 2004-05 | Portland | WHL | 68 | 23 | 36 | 59 | 160 | .... | .... | .... | .... | .... | .... | .... | .... | .... | 7 | 4 | 5 | 9 | 8 | .... | .... | .... | .... |
| 2005-06 | Portland | WHL | 51 | 21 | 46 | 67 | 98 | .... | .... | .... | .... | .... | .... | .... | .... | .... | 12 | 5 | 10 | 15 | 24 | .... | .... | .... | .... |
| | Hartford | AHL | .... | .... | .... | .... | .... | .... | .... | .... | .... | .... | .... | .... | .... | .... | 11 | 5 | 5 | 10 | 14 | .... | .... | .... | .... |
| **2006-07** | **NY Rangers** | **NHL** | **6** | **0** | **0** | **0** | **2** | **0** | **0** | **0** | **9** | **0.0** | **0** | **26** | **46.2** | **8:10** | .... | .... | .... | .... | .... | .... | .... | .... | .... |
| | Hartford | AHL | 71 | 21 | 22 | 43 | 115 | .... | .... | .... | .... | .... | .... | .... | .... | .... | 7 | 1 | 3 | 4 | 12 | .... | .... | .... | .... |
| **2007-08** | **NY Rangers** | **NHL** | **82** | **14** | **26** | **40** | **79** | **1** | **0** | **0** | **157** | **8.9** | **8** | **995** | **51.5** | **14:30** | **10** | **4** | **4** | **8** | **12** | **2** | **0** | **0** | **18:59** |
| **2008-09** | **NY Rangers** | **NHL** | **82** | **13** | **28** | **41** | **112** | **3** | **1** | **7** | **188** | **6.9** | **-6** | **870** | **53.6** | **16:38** | **7** | **1** | **3** | **4** | **18** | **0** | **0** | **1** | **18:14** |
| | **NHL Totals** | | **170** | **27** | **54** | **81** | **193** | **4** | **1** | **7** | **354** | **7.6** | | **1891** | **52.4** | **15:18** | **17** | **5** | **7** | **12** | **30** | **2** | **0** | **1** | **18:41** |

WHL West Second All-Star Team (2004, 2006)

## DUMONT, J.P.
(DOO-mawnt, JAY-pee) **NSH.**

Right wing. Shoots left. 6'1", 219 lbs. Born, Montreal, Que., April 1, 1978. NY Islanders' 1st choice, 3rd overall, in 1996 Entry Draft.

| | | | Regular Season | | | | | | | | | | | | | | Playoffs | | | | | | | | |
|---|---|---|---|---|---|---|---|---|---|---|---|---|---|---|---|---|---|---|---|---|---|---|---|---|---|
| Season | Club | League | GP | G | A | Pts | PIM | PP | SH | GW | S | % | +/- | TF | F% | Min | GP | G | A | Pts | PIM | PP | SH | GW | Min |
| 1993-94 | Mtl-Bourassa | QAAA | 44 | 27 | 20 | 47 | 44 | .... | .... | .... | .... | .... | .... | .... | .... | .... | 4 | 2 | 3 | 5 | 4 | .... | .... | .... | .... |
| 1994-95 | Mtl-Bourassa | QAAA | 10 | 2 | 7 | 9 | 12 | .... | .... | .... | .... | .... | .... | .... | .... | .... | .... | .... | .... | .... | .... | .... | .... | .... | .... |
| | Val-d'Or Foreurs | QMJHL | 48 | 5 | 14 | 19 | 24 | .... | .... | .... | .... | .... | .... | .... | .... | .... | .... | .... | .... | .... | .... | .... | .... | .... | .... |
| 1995-96 | Val-d'Or Foreurs | QMJHL | 66 | 48 | 57 | 105 | 109 | .... | .... | .... | .... | .... | .... | .... | .... | .... | 13 | 12 | 8 | 20 | 22 | .... | .... | .... | .... |
| 1996-97 | Val-d'Or Foreurs | QMJHL | 62 | 44 | 64 | 108 | 86 | .... | .... | .... | .... | .... | .... | .... | .... | .... | 13 | 9 | 7 | 16 | 12 | .... | .... | .... | .... |
| 1997-98 | Val-d'Or Foreurs | QMJHL | 55 | 57 | 42 | 99 | 63 | .... | .... | .... | .... | .... | .... | .... | .... | .... | 19 | 31 | 15 | 46 | 18 | .... | .... | .... | .... |
| **1998-99** | **Chicago** | **NHL** | **25** | **9** | **6** | **15** | **10** | **0** | **0** | **2** | **42** | **21.4** | **7** | **10** | **50.0** | **14:14** | .... | .... | .... | .... | .... | .... | .... | .... | .... |
| | Portland Pirates | AHL | 50 | 32 | 14 | 46 | 39 | .... | .... | .... | .... | .... | .... | .... | .... | .... | .... | .... | .... | .... | .... | .... | .... | .... | .... |
| | Chicago Wolves | IHL | .... | .... | .... | .... | .... | .... | .... | .... | .... | .... | .... | .... | .... | .... | 10 | 4 | 1 | 5 | 6 | .... | .... | .... | .... |
| **99-2000** | **Chicago** | **NHL** | **47** | **10** | **8** | **18** | **18** | **0** | **0** | **1** | **86** | **11.6** | **-6** | **12** | **33.3** | **12:54** | .... | .... | .... | .... | .... | .... | .... | .... | .... |
| | Cleveland | IHL | 7 | 5 | 2 | 7 | 8 | .... | .... | .... | .... | .... | .... | .... | .... | .... | .... | .... | .... | .... | .... | .... | .... | .... | .... |
| | Rochester | AHL | 13 | 7 | 10 | 17 | 18 | .... | .... | .... | .... | .... | .... | .... | .... | .... | 21 | 14 | 7 | 21 | 32 | .... | .... | .... | .... |
| **2000-01** | **Buffalo** | **NHL** | **79** | **23** | **28** | **51** | **54** | **9** | **0** | **5** | **156** | **14.7** | **1** | **3** | **33.3** | **15:01** | **13** | **4** | **3** | **7** | **8** | **0** | **0** | **0** | **14:32** |
| **2001-02** | **Buffalo** | **NHL** | **76** | **23** | **21** | **44** | **42** | **7** | **0** | **3** | **154** | **14.9** | **-10** | **4** | **50.0** | **15:14** | .... | .... | .... | .... | .... | .... | .... | .... | .... |
| **2002-03** | **Buffalo** | **NHL** | **76** | **14** | **21** | **35** | **44** | **2** | **0** | **2** | **135** | **10.4** | **-14** | **15** | **20.0** | **15:04** | .... | .... | .... | .... | .... | .... | .... | .... | .... |
| **2003-04** | **Buffalo** | **NHL** | **77** | **22** | **31** | **53** | **40** | **10** | **0** | **1** | **156** | **14.1** | **-9** | **32** | **43.8** | **17:00** | .... | .... | .... | .... | .... | .... | .... | .... | .... |
| 2004-05 | SC Bern | Swiss | 3 | 2 | 2 | 4 | 6 | .... | .... | .... | .... | .... | .... | .... | .... | .... | 10 | 4 | 1 | 5 | 16 | .... | .... | .... | .... |
| **2005-06** | **Buffalo** | **NHL** | **54** | **20** | **20** | **40** | **38** | **9** | **0** | **4** | **116** | **17.2** | **-1** | **9** | **11.1** | **16:00** | **18** | **7** | **7** | **14** | **14** | **3** | **0** | **1** | **16:39** |
| **2006-07** | **Nashville** | **NHL** | **82** | **21** | **45** | **66** | **28** | **5** | **0** | **3** | **143** | **14.7** | **14** | **6** | **16.7** | **16:12** | **5** | **4** | **2** | **6** | **0** | **1** | **1** | **1** | **21:03** |
| **2007-08** | **Nashville** | **NHL** | **80** | **29** | **43** | **72** | **34** | **7** | **0** | **8** | **192** | **15.1** | **5** | **13** | **23.1** | **18:30** | **6** | **0** | **2** | **2** | **4** | **0** | **0** | **0** | **17:23** |
| **2008-09** | **Nashville** | **NHL** | **82** | **16** | **49** | **65** | **20** | **5** | **0** | **4** | **176** | **9.1** | **1** | **6** | **50.0** | **17:30** | .... | .... | .... | .... | .... | .... | .... | .... | .... |
| | **NHL Totals** | | **678** | **187** | **272** | **459** | **328** | **54** | **0** | **33** | **1356** | **13.8** | | **110** | **33.6** | **16:02** | **42** | **15** | **14** | **29** | **26** | **4** | **1** | **2** | **16:37** |

QMJHL Second All-Star Team (1997) • AHL All-Rookie Team (1999)

• Rights traded to **Chicago** by **NY Islanders** with NY Islanders' 5th round choice (later traded to Philadelphia – Philadelphia selected Francis Belanger) in 1998 Entry Draft for Dmitri Nabokov, May 30, 1998. Traded to **Buffalo** by **Chicago** with Doug Gilmour for Michal Grosek, March 10, 2000. Signed as a free agent by **Bern** (Swiss), February 9, 2005. Signed as a free agent by **Nashville**, August 29, 2006.

## DuPONT, Micki
(DOO-pawnt, MIH-kee)

Defense. Shoots right. 5'10", 186 lbs. Born, Calgary, Alta., April 15, 1980. Calgary's 9th choice, 270th overall, in 2000 Entry Draft.

| | | | Regular Season | | | | | | | | | | | | | | Playoffs | | | | | | | | |
|---|---|---|---|---|---|---|---|---|---|---|---|---|---|---|---|---|---|---|---|---|---|---|---|---|---|
| Season | Club | League | GP | G | A | Pts | PIM | PP | SH | GW | S | % | +/- | TF | F% | Min | GP | G | A | Pts | PIM | PP | SH | GW | Min |
| 1995-96 | Calgary Blazers | AMHL | 35 | 10 | 35 | 45 | 68 | .... | .... | .... | .... | .... | .... | .... | .... | .... | .... | .... | .... | .... | .... | .... | .... | .... | .... |
| 1996-97 | Kamloops Blazers | WHL | 59 | 8 | 27 | 35 | 39 | .... | .... | .... | .... | .... | .... | .... | .... | .... | 5 | 0 | 4 | 4 | 8 | .... | .... | .... | .... |
| 1997-98 | Kamloops Blazers | WHL | 71 | 13 | 41 | 54 | 91 | .... | .... | .... | .... | .... | .... | .... | .... | .... | 7 | 0 | 1 | 1 | 10 | .... | .... | .... | .... |
| 1998-99 | Kamloops Blazers | WHL | 59 | 8 | 27 | 35 | 110 | .... | .... | .... | .... | .... | .... | .... | .... | .... | 15 | 2 | 8 | 10 | 22 | .... | .... | .... | .... |
| 99-2000 | Kamloops Blazers | WHL | 70 | 26 | 62 | 88 | 156 | .... | .... | .... | .... | .... | .... | .... | .... | .... | 4 | 0 | 2 | 2 | 17 | .... | .... | .... | .... |
| | Long Beach | IHL | 1 | 0 | 0 | 0 | 0 | .... | .... | .... | .... | .... | .... | .... | .... | .... | .... | .... | .... | .... | .... | .... | .... | .... | .... |
| | San Diego Gulls | WCHL | .... | .... | .... | .... | .... | .... | .... | .... | .... | .... | .... | .... | .... | .... | 7 | 2 | 2 | 4 | 0 | .... | .... | .... | .... |
| 2000-01 | Saint John Flames | AHL | 67 | 8 | 21 | 29 | 28 | .... | .... | .... | .... | .... | .... | .... | .... | .... | 19 | 1 | 9 | 10 | 14 | .... | .... | .... | .... |
| **2001-02** | **Calgary** | **NHL** | **2** | **0** | **0** | **0** | **2** | **0** | **0** | **0** | **2** | **0.0** | **0** | **0** | **0.0** | **14:44** | .... | .... | .... | .... | .... | .... | .... | .... | .... |
| | Saint John Flames | AHL | 77 | 7 | 33 | 40 | 77 | .... | .... | .... | .... | .... | .... | .... | .... | .... | .... | .... | .... | .... | .... | .... | .... | .... | .... |
| **2002-03** | **Calgary** | **NHL** | **16** | **1** | **2** | **3** | **4** | **0** | **0** | **0** | **27** | **3.7** | **-5** | **0** | **0.0** | **16:45** | .... | .... | .... | .... | .... | .... | .... | .... | .... |
| | Saint John Flames | AHL | 44 | 12 | 21 | 33 | 73 | .... | .... | .... | .... | .... | .... | .... | .... | .... | .... | .... | .... | .... | .... | .... | .... | .... | .... |
| | Wilkes-Barre | AHL | 14 | 1 | 4 | 5 | 16 | .... | .... | .... | .... | .... | .... | .... | .... | .... | 6 | 3 | 0 | 3 | 21 | .... | .... | .... | .... |
| 2003-04 | Eisbaren Berlin | Germany | 45 | 10 | 22 | 32 | 76 | .... | .... | .... | .... | .... | .... | .... | .... | .... | 10 | 3 | 6 | 9 | 35 | .... | .... | .... | .... |
| 2004-05 | Eisbaren Berlin | Germany | 51 | 11 | 22 | 33 | 93 | .... | .... | .... | .... | .... | .... | .... | .... | .... | 11 | 2 | 5 | 7 | 41 | .... | .... | .... | .... |
| 2005-06 | Eisbaren Berlin | Germany | 52 | 11 | 21 | 32 | 78 | .... | .... | .... | .... | .... | .... | .... | .... | .... | 11 | 4 | 10 | *14 | 10 | .... | .... | .... | .... |
| **2006-07** | **Pittsburgh** | **NHL** | **3** | **0** | **1** | **1** | **4** | **0** | **0** | **0** | **6** | **0.0** | **-3** | **0** | **0.0** | **13:48** | .... | .... | .... | .... | .... | .... | .... | .... | .... |
| | Wilkes-Barre | AHL | 78 | 18 | 33 | 51 | 101 | .... | .... | .... | .... | .... | .... | .... | .... | .... | 11 | 5 | 9 | 14 | 16 | .... | .... | .... | .... |

| | | | Regular Season | | | | | | | | | | | | | | Playoffs | | | | | | | | |
|---|---|---|---|---|---|---|---|---|---|---|---|---|---|---|---|---|---|---|---|---|---|---|---|---|---|
| Season | Club | League | GP | G | A | Pts | PIM | PP | SH | GW | S | % | +/- | TF | F% | Min | GP | G | A | Pts | PIM | PP | SH | GW | Min |
| **2007-08** | **St. Louis** | **NHL** | **2** | **0** | **0** | **0** | **2** | **0** | **0** | **0** | **3** | **0.0** | **1** | **0** | **0.0** | **12:34** | | | | | | | | | |
| | Peoria Rivermen | AHL | 76 | 10 | 36 | 46 | 77 | | | | | | | | | | | | | | | | | | |
| 2008-09 | EV Zug | Swiss | 50 | 13 | 19 | 32 | 58 | | | | | | | | | | 10 | 2 | 3 | 5 | 4 | | | | |
| | **NHL Totals** | | **23** | **1** | **3** | **4** | **12** | **0** | **0** | **0** | **38** | **2.6** | | **0** | **0.0** | **15:49** | | | | | | | | | |

AHL All-Rookie Team (2001) • AHL First All-Star Team (2007)

Traded to **Pittsburgh** by **Calgary** with Mathias Johansson for Shean Donovan, March 11, 2003. Signed as a free agent by **Berlin** (Germany), August 6, 2003. Signed as a free agent by **St. Louis**, July 3, 2007.

## DUPUIS, Pascal

(doo-PWEE, pas-KAL) **PIT.**

Left wing. Shoots left. 6'1", 205 lbs. Born, Laval, Que., April 7, 1979.

| Season | Club | League | GP | G | A | Pts | PIM | PP | SH | GW | S | % | +/- | TF | F% | Min | GP | G | A | Pts | PIM | PP | SH | GW | Min |
|---|---|---|---|---|---|---|---|---|---|---|---|---|---|---|---|---|---|---|---|---|---|---|---|---|---|
| 1995-96 | Laval-Laurentides | QAAA | 41 | 10 | 15 | 25 | | | | | | | | | | | 14 | 11 | 11 | 22 | | | | | |
| 1996-97 | Rouyn-Noranda | QMJHL | 44 | 9 | 15 | 24 | 20 | | | | | | | | | | | | | | | | | | |
| 1997-98 | Rouyn-Noranda | QMJHL | 39 | 9 | 17 | 26 | 36 | | | | | | | | | | | | | | | | | | |
| | Shawinigan | QMJHL | 28 | 7 | 13 | 20 | 10 | | | | | | | | | | 6 | 2 | 0 | 2 | 4 | | | | |
| 1998-99 | Shawinigan | QMJHL | 57 | 30 | 42 | 72 | 118 | | | | | | | | | | 6 | 1 | 8 | 9 | 18 | | | | |
| 99-2000 | Shawinigan | QMJHL | 61 | 50 | 55 | 105 | 99 | | | | | | | | | | 13 | *15 | 7 | 22 | 4 | | | | |
| **2000-01** | **Minnesota** | **NHL** | **4** | **1** | **0** | **1** | **4** | **1** | **0** | **0** | **8** | **12.5** | **0** | **0** | **0.0** | **15:36** | | | | | | | | | |
| | Cleveland | IHL | 70 | 19 | 24 | 43 | 37 | | | | | | | | | | 4 | 0 | 0 | 0 | 0 | | | | |
| **2001-02** | **Minnesota** | **NHL** | **76** | **15** | **12** | **27** | **16** | **3** | **2** | **0** | **154** | **9.7** | **-10** | **40** | **32.5** | **15:08** | | | | | | | | | |
| **2002-03** | **Minnesota** | **NHL** | **80** | **20** | **28** | **48** | **44** | **6** | **0** | **4** | **183** | **10.9** | **17** | **186** | **40.9** | **17:30** | **16** | **4** | **4** | **8** | **8** | **2** | **0** | **1** | **16:58** |
| **2003-04** | **Minnesota** | **NHL** | **59** | **11** | **15** | **26** | **20** | **2** | **0** | **1** | **127** | **8.7** | **5** | **129** | **45.7** | **15:48** | | | | | | | | | |
| 2004-05 | HC Ajoie | Swiss-2 | 8 | 5 | 5 | 10 | 26 | | | | | | | | | | 6 | 6 | 8 | 14 | 8 | | | | |
| **2005-06** | **Minnesota** | **NHL** | **67** | **10** | **16** | **26** | **40** | **4** | **0** | **2** | **151** | **6.6** | **-10** | **93** | **29.0** | **16:30** | | | | | | | | | |
| **2006-07** | **Minnesota** | **NHL** | **48** | **10** | **3** | **13** | **38** | **2** | **2** | **0** | **106** | **9.4** | **-7** | **110** | **27.3** | **15:07** | | | | | | | | | |
| | **NY Rangers** | **NHL** | **6** | **1** | **0** | **1** | **0** | **0** | **0** | **0** | **10** | **10.0** | **-4** | **2** | **50.0** | **15:30** | | | | | | | | | |
| | **Atlanta** | **NHL** | **17** | **3** | **2** | **5** | **4** | **0** | **0** | **1** | **40** | **7.5** | **-6** | **19** | **52.6** | **16:44** | **4** | **1** | **2** | **3** | **4** | **0** | **0** | **0** | **20:28** |
| **2007-08** | **Atlanta** | **NHL** | **62** | **10** | **5** | **15** | **24** | **0** | **3** | **1** | **111** | **9.0** | **-4** | **13** | **38.5** | **14:46** | | | | | | | | | |
| | **Pittsburgh** | **NHL** | **16** | **2** | **10** | **12** | **8** | **0** | **0** | **0** | **32** | **6.3** | **4** | **3** | **0.0** | **16:50** | **20** | **2** | **5** | **7** | **18** | **0** | **0** | **0** | **16:14** |
| **2008-09♦** | **Pittsburgh** | **NHL** | **71** | **12** | **16** | **28** | **30** | **0** | **0** | **2** | **145** | **8.3** | **1** | **16** | **18.8** | **14:13** | **16** | **0** | **0** | **0** | **8** | **0** | **0** | **0** | **8:23** |
| | **NHL Totals** | | **506** | **95** | **107** | **202** | **228** | **18** | **7** | **11** | **1067** | **8.9** | | **611** | **36.7** | **15:42** | **56** | **7** | **11** | **18** | **38** | **2** | **0** | **1** | **14:30** |

Signed as a free agent by **Minnesota**, August 18, 2000. Signed as a free agent by **Ajoie** (Swiss-2), January 14, 2005. Traded to **NY Rangers** by **Minnesota** for Adam Hall, February 9, 2007. Traded to **Atlanta** by **NY Rangers** with NY Rangers' 3rd round choice (later traded to Pittsburgh - Pittsburgh selected Robert Bortuzzo) in 2007 Entry Draft for Alex Bourret, February 27, 2007. Traded to **Pittsburgh** by **Atlanta** with Marian Hossa for Colby Armstrong, Erik Christensen, Angelo Esposito and Pittsburgh's 1st round choice (Daulton Leveille) in 2008 Entry Draft, February 26, 2008.

## DUPUIS, Philippe

(doo-PWEE, fihl-EEP) **COL.**

Center. Shoots right. 6', 196 lbs. Born, Laval, Que., April 24, 1985. Columbus' 5th choice, 104th overall, in 2003 Entry Draft.

| Season | Club | League | GP | G | A | Pts | PIM | PP | SH | GW | S | % | +/- | TF | F% | Min | GP | G | A | Pts | PIM | PP | SH | GW | Min |
|---|---|---|---|---|---|---|---|---|---|---|---|---|---|---|---|---|---|---|---|---|---|---|---|---|---|
| 2000-01 | Laval-Laurentides | QAAA | 46 | 16 | 27 | 43 | 74 | | | | | | | | | | 8 | 1 | 5 | 6 | 30 | | | | |
| 2001-02 | Hull Olympiques | QMJHL | 67 | 7 | 14 | 21 | 59 | | | | | | | | | | 12 | 6 | 5 | 11 | 14 | | | | |
| 2002-03 | Hull Olympiques | QMJHL | 68 | 22 | 34 | 56 | 89 | | | | | | | | | | 20 | 2 | 4 | 6 | 22 | | | | |
| 2003-04 | Gatineau | QMJHL | 60 | 18 | 37 | 55 | 77 | | | | | | | | | | 15 | 6 | 10 | 16 | 14 | | | | |
| 2004-05 | Rouyn-Noranda | QMJHL | 62 | 34 | 50 | 84 | 60 | | | | | | | | | | 10 | 5 | 3 | 8 | 8 | | | | |
| 2005-06 | Moncton Wildcats | QMJHL | 56 | 32 | 76 | 108 | 52 | | | | | | | | | | 19 | 14 | 18 | 32 | 14 | | | | |
| 2006-07 | Syracuse Crunch | AHL | 51 | 11 | 11 | 22 | 18 | | | | | | | | | | | | | | | | | | |
| | Dayton Bombers | ECHL | 8 | 3 | 2 | 5 | 8 | | | | | | | | | | 19 | 6 | 9 | 15 | 28 | | | | |
| 2007-08 | Syracuse Crunch | AHL | 29 | 7 | 4 | 11 | 2 | | | | | | | | | | | | | | | | | | |
| | Lake Erie | AHL | 17 | 5 | 3 | 8 | 12 | | | | | | | | | | | | | | | | | | |
| **2008-09** | **Colorado** | **NHL** | **8** | **0** | **0** | **0** | **4** | **0** | **0** | **0** | **11** | **0.0** | **-1** | **50** | **52.0** | **9:34** | | | | | | | | | |
| | Lake Erie | AHL | 67 | 17 | 29 | 46 | 42 | | | | | | | | | | | | | | | | | | |
| | **NHL Totals** | | **8** | **0** | **0** | **0** | **4** | **0** | **0** | **0** | **11** | **0.0** | | **50** | **52.0** | **9:34** | | | | | | | | | |

Traded to **Colorado** by **Columbus** with Darcy Campbell for Mark Rycroft, January 22, 2008.

## DURNO, Chris

(DUHR-noh, KRIHS) **COL.**

Center. Shoots left. 6'4", 205 lbs. Born, Scarborough, Ont., October 31, 1980.

| Season | Club | League | GP | G | A | Pts | PIM | PP | SH | GW | S | % | +/- | TF | F% | Min | GP | G | A | Pts | PIM | PP | SH | GW | Min |
|---|---|---|---|---|---|---|---|---|---|---|---|---|---|---|---|---|---|---|---|---|---|---|---|---|---|
| 99-2000 | Michigan Tech | WCHA | 24 | 1 | 1 | 2 | 30 | | | | | | | | | | | | | | | | | | |
| 2000-01 | Michigan Tech | WCHA | 35 | 9 | 6 | 15 | 46 | | | | | | | | | | | | | | | | | | |
| 2001-02 | Michigan Tech | WCHA | 36 | 7 | 8 | 15 | 48 | | | | | | | | | | | | | | | | | | |
| 2002-03 | Michigan Tech | WCHA | 35 | 5 | 11 | 16 | 60 | | | | | | | | | | | | | | | | | | |
| 2003-04 | Gwinnett | ECHL | 68 | 20 | 26 | 46 | 46 | | | | | | | | | | 13 | 7 | 5 | 12 | 10 | | | | |
| 2004-05 | Gwinnett | ECHL | 66 | 20 | 36 | 56 | 101 | | | | | | | | | | 8 | 5 | 2 | 7 | 8 | | | | |
| 2005-06 | Gwinnett | ECHL | 13 | 12 | 10 | 22 | 19 | | | | | | | | | | | | | | | | | | |
| | Milwaukee | AHL | 57 | 20 | 20 | 40 | 52 | | | | | | | | | | 21 | 2 | 2 | 4 | 18 | | | | |
| 2006-07 | Norfolk Admirals | AHL | 22 | 4 | 1 | 5 | 61 | | | | | | | | | | | | | | | | | | |
| | Portland Pirates | AHL | 12 | 1 | 1 | 2 | 2 | | | | | | | | | | | | | | | | | | |
| | Milwaukee | AHL | 29 | 13 | 3 | 16 | 24 | | | | | | | | | | 4 | 1 | 2 | 3 | 10 | | | | |
| 2007-08 | San Antonio | AHL | 80 | 23 | 26 | 49 | 109 | | | | | | | | | | 7 | 0 | 2 | 2 | 26 | | | | |
| **2008-09** | **Colorado** | **NHL** | **2** | **0** | **0** | **0** | **0** | **0** | **0** | **0** | **3** | **0.0** | **0** | **0** | **0.0** | **6:02** | | | | | | | | | |
| | Lake Erie | AHL | 76 | 18 | 27 | 45 | 131 | | | | | | | | | | | | | | | | | | |
| | **NHL Totals** | | **2** | **0** | **0** | **0** | **0** | **0** | **0** | **0** | **3** | **0.0** | | **0** | **0.0** | **6:02** | | | | | | | | | |

Signed as a free agent by **Chicago**, September 25, 2006. Traded to **Anaheim** by **Chicago** with Sebastiien Caron and Matt Keith for P. A. Parenteau and Bruno St. Jacques, December 28, 2006. Traded to **Nashville** by **Anaheim** for Shane Endicott, January 26, 2007. Signed as a free agent by **Colorado**, July 3, 2008.

## DVORAK, Radek

(duh-VOHR-ak, RA-dehk) **FLA.**

Right wing. Shoots right. 6'2", 200 lbs. Born, Tabor, Czech., March 9, 1977. Florida's 1st choice, 10th overall, in 1995 Entry Draft.

| Season | Club | League | GP | G | A | Pts | PIM | PP | SH | GW | S | % | +/- | TF | F% | Min | GP | G | A | Pts | PIM | PP | SH | GW | Min |
|---|---|---|---|---|---|---|---|---|---|---|---|---|---|---|---|---|---|---|---|---|---|---|---|---|---|
| 1992-93 | C. Budejovice Jr. | Czech-Jr. | 35 | 44 | 46 | 90 | | | | | | | | | | | | | | | | | | | |
| 1993-94 | C. Budejovice Jr. | CzRep-Jr. | 20 | 17 | 18 | 35 | | | | | | | | | | | | | | | | | | | |
| | C. Budejovice | CzRep | 8 | 0 | 0 | 0 | 0 | | | | | | | | | | | | | | | | | | |
| 1994-95 | C. Budejovice | CzRep | 10 | 3 | 5 | 8 | 2 | | | | | | | | | | 9 | 5 | 1 | 6 | | | | | |
| **1995-96** | **Florida** | **NHL** | **77** | **13** | **14** | **27** | **20** | **0** | **0** | **4** | **126** | **10.3** | **5** | | | | **16** | **1** | **3** | **4** | **0** | **0** | **0** | **0** | |
| **1996-97** | **Florida** | **NHL** | **78** | **18** | **21** | **39** | **30** | **2** | **0** | **1** | **139** | **12.9** | **-2** | | | | **3** | **0** | **0** | **0** | **0** | **0** | **0** | **0** | |
| **1997-98** | **Florida** | **NHL** | **64** | **12** | **24** | **36** | **33** | **2** | **3** | **0** | **112** | **10.7** | **-1** | | | | | | | | | | | | |
| **1998-99** | **Florida** | **NHL** | **82** | **19** | **24** | **43** | **29** | **0** | **4** | **0** | **182** | **10.4** | **7** | **98** | **46.9** | **16:13** | | | | | | | | | |
| **99-2000** | **Florida** | **NHL** | **35** | **7** | **10** | **17** | **6** | **0** | **0** | **1** | **67** | **10.4** | **5** | **16** | **37.5** | **15:25** | | | | | | | | | |
| | **NY Rangers** | **NHL** | **46** | **11** | **22** | **33** | **10** | **2** | **1** | **0** | **90** | **12.2** | **0** | **34** | **35.3** | **18:24** | | | | | | | | | |
| **2000-01** | **NY Rangers** | **NHL** | **82** | **31** | **36** | **67** | **20** | **5** | **2** | **3** | **230** | **13.5** | **9** | **20** | **30.0** | **19:04** | | | | | | | | | |
| **2001-02** | **NY Rangers** | **NHL** | **65** | **17** | **20** | **37** | **14** | **3** | **3** | **1** | **210** | **8.1** | **-20** | **5** | **0.0** | **19:44** | | | | | | | | | |
| | Czech Republic | Olympics | 4 | 0 | 0 | 0 | 0 | | | | | | | | | | | | | | | | | | |
| **2002-03** | **NY Rangers** | **NHL** | **63** | **6** | **21** | **27** | **16** | **2** | **0** | **0** | **134** | **4.5** | **-3** | **9** | **44.4** | **15:42** | | | | | | | | | |
| | **Edmonton** | **NHL** | **12** | **4** | **4** | **8** | **14** | **1** | **0** | **0** | **32** | **12.5** | **-3** | **1** | **0.0** | **16:07** | **4** | **1** | **0** | **1** | **0** | **0** | **0** | **1** | **15:05** |
| **2003-04** | **Edmonton** | **NHL** | **78** | **15** | **35** | **50** | **26** | **6** | **0** | **0** | **188** | **8.0** | **18** | **24** | **29.2** | **16:56** | | | | | | | | | |
| 2004-05 | C. Budejovice | CzRep-2 | 32 | 23 | 35 | 58 | 18 | | | | | | | | | | 16 | 5 | 13 | 18 | 20 | | | | |
| **2005-06** | **Edmonton** | **NHL** | **64** | **8** | **20** | **28** | **26** | **2** | **0** | **2** | **131** | **6.1** | **-2** | **14** | **28.6** | **16:34** | **16** | **0** | **2** | **2** | **4** | **0** | **0** | **0** | **13:29** |
| **2006-07** | **St. Louis** | **NHL** | **82** | **10** | **27** | **37** | **48** | **1** | **1** | **1** | **139** | **7.2** | **-6** | **26** | **38.5** | **15:38** | | | | | | | | | |
| **2007-08** | **Florida** | **NHL** | **67** | **8** | **9** | **17** | **16** | **0** | **1** | **1** | **146** | **5.5** | **-1** | **12** | **16.7** | **15:07** | | | | | | | | | |
| **2008-09** | **Florida** | **NHL** | **81** | **15** | **21** | **36** | **42** | **0** | **4** | **3** | **136** | **11.0** | **0** | **17** | **35.3** | **16:26** | | | | | | | | | |
| | **NHL Totals** | | **976** | **194** | **308** | **502** | **350** | **26** | **19** | **17** | **2062** | **9.4** | | **276** | **37.3** | **16:51** | **39** | **2** | **5** | **7** | **4** | **0** | **0** | **1** | **13:48** |

Traded to **San Jose** by **Florida** for Mike Vernon and San Jose's 3rd round choice (Sean O'Connor) in 2000 Entry Draft, December 30, 1999. Traded to **NY Rangers** by **San Jose** for Todd Harvey and NY Rangers' 4th round choice (Dimitri Patzold) in 2001 Entry Draft, December 30, 1999. Traded to **Edmonton** by **NY Rangers** with Cory Cross for Anson Carter and Ales Pisa, March 11, 2003. Signed as a free agent by **Ceske Budejovice** (CzRep-2), September 15, 2004. Signed as a free agent by **St. Louis**, September 14, 2006. Signed as a free agent by **Florida**, July 1, 2007.

## DWYER, Patrick

(DWIGH-uhr, PAT-rihk) **CAR.**

Right wing. Shoots right. 5'11", 175 lbs. Born, Spokane, WA, June 22, 1983. Atlanta's 3rd choice, 116th overall, in 2002 Entry Draft.

| | | | Regular Season | | | | | | | | | | | | | | Playoffs | | | | | | | | |
|---|---|---|---|---|---|---|---|---|---|---|---|---|---|---|---|---|---|---|---|---|---|---|---|---|---|
| Season | Club | League | GP | G | A | Pts | PIM | PP | SH | GW | S | % | +/- | TF | F% | Min | GP | G | A | Pts | PIM | PP | SH | GW | Min |
| 2000-01 | Great Falls | NWJHL | 40 | 33 | 57 | 90 | 106 | .... | .... | .... | .... | .... | .... | .... | .... | .... | 12 | 10 | 12 | 22 | .... | .... | .... | .... | .... |
| 2001-02 | Western Mich. | CCHA | 38 | 17 | 17 | 34 | 26 | .... | .... | .... | .... | .... | .... | .... | .... | .... | .... | .... | .... | .... | .... | .... | .... | .... | .... |
| 2002-03 | Western Mich. | CCHA | 33 | 9 | 10 | 19 | 20 | .... | .... | .... | .... | .... | .... | .... | .... | .... | .... | .... | .... | .... | .... | .... | .... | .... | .... |
| 2003-04 | Western Mich. | CCHA | 35 | 13 | 13 | 26 | 22 | .... | .... | .... | .... | .... | .... | .... | .... | .... | .... | .... | .... | .... | .... | .... | .... | .... | .... |
| 2004-05 | Western Mich. | CCHA | 36 | 6 | 16 | 22 | 56 | .... | .... | .... | .... | .... | .... | .... | .... | .... | .... | .... | .... | .... | .... | .... | .... | .... | .... |
| 2005-06 | Chicago Wolves | AHL | 73 | 16 | 29 | 45 | 49 | .... | .... | .... | .... | .... | .... | .... | .... | .... | .... | .... | .... | .... | .... | .... | .... | .... | .... |
| 2006-07 | Albany River Rats | AHL | 79 | 16 | 25 | 41 | 39 | .... | .... | .... | .... | .... | .... | .... | .... | .... | 5 | 0 | 1 | 1 | 5 | .... | .... | .... | .... |
| 2007-08 | Albany River Rats | AHL | 59 | 13 | 12 | 25 | 29 | .... | .... | .... | .... | .... | .... | .... | .... | .... | 7 | 0 | 2 | 2 | 0 | .... | .... | .... | .... |
| **2008-09** | **Carolina** | **NHL** | **13** | **1** | **0** | **1** | **0** | **0** | **0** | **0** | **9** | **11.1** | **-2** | **12** | **41.7** | **8:34** | **2** | **0** | **1** | **1** | **0** | **0** | **0** | **0** | **4:48** |
| | Albany River Rats | AHL | 62 | 24 | 16 | 40 | 29 | .... | .... | .... | .... | .... | .... | .... | .... | .... | .... | .... | .... | .... | .... | .... | .... | .... | .... |
| | **NHL Totals** | | **13** | **1** | **0** | **1** | **0** | **0** | **0** | **0** | **9** | **11.1** | | **12** | **41.7** | **8:34** | **2** | **0** | **1** | **1** | **0** | **0** | **0** | **0** | **4:48** |

CCHA All-Rookie Team (2002) • CCHA Rookie of the Year (2002)

Signed as a free agent by **Carolina**, July 7, 2006.

## EAGER, Ben

(EE-guhr, BEHN) **CHI.**

Left wing. Shoots left. 6'2", 220 lbs. Born, Ottawa, Ont., January 22, 1984. Phoenix's 2nd choice, 23rd overall, in 2002 Entry Draft.

| | | | | | | | | | | | | | | | | | | | | | | | | | |
|---|---|---|---|---|---|---|---|---|---|---|---|---|---|---|---|---|---|---|---|---|---|---|---|---|---|
| 99-2000 | Ott. Jr. Senators | CJHL | 50 | 8 | 11 | 19 | 119 | .... | .... | .... | .... | .... | .... | .... | .... | .... | .... | .... | .... | .... | .... | .... | .... | .... | .... |
| 2000-01 | Oshawa Generals | OHL | 61 | 4 | 6 | 10 | 120 | .... | .... | .... | .... | .... | .... | .... | .... | .... | .... | .... | .... | .... | .... | .... | .... | .... | .... |
| 2001-02 | Oshawa Generals | OHL | 63 | 14 | 23 | 37 | 255 | .... | .... | .... | .... | .... | .... | .... | .... | .... | 5 | 0 | 1 | 1 | 13 | .... | .... | .... | .... |
| 2002-03 | Oshawa Generals | OHL | 58 | 16 | 24 | 40 | 216 | .... | .... | .... | .... | .... | .... | .... | .... | .... | 8 | 0 | 4 | 4 | 8 | .... | .... | .... | .... |
| 2003-04 | Oshawa Generals | OHL | 61 | 25 | 27 | 52 | 204 | .... | .... | .... | .... | .... | .... | .... | .... | .... | 7 | 2 | 3 | 5 | 31 | .... | .... | .... | .... |
| | Philadelphia | AHL | 5 | 0 | 0 | 0 | 0 | .... | .... | .... | .... | .... | .... | .... | .... | .... | 3 | 0 | 1 | 1 | 8 | .... | .... | .... | .... |
| 2004-05 | Philadelphia | AHL | 66 | 7 | 10 | 17 | 232 | .... | .... | .... | .... | .... | .... | .... | .... | .... | 16 | 1 | 1 | 2 | 71 | .... | .... | .... | .... |
| **2005-06** | **Philadelphia** | **NHL** | **25** | **3** | **5** | **8** | **18** | **0** | **0** | **0** | **21** | **14.3** | **0** | **0** | **0.0** | **7:24** | **2** | **0** | **0** | **0** | **26** | **0** | **0** | **0** | **7:06** |
| | Philadelphia | AHL | 49 | 6 | 12 | 18 | 256 | .... | .... | .... | .... | .... | .... | .... | .... | .... | .... | .... | .... | .... | .... | .... | .... | .... | .... |
| **2006-07** | **Philadelphia** | **NHL** | **63** | **6** | **5** | **11** | ***233** | **0** | **0** | **0** | **48** | **12.5** | **-13** | **1** | **100.0** | **8:14** | .... | .... | .... | .... | .... | .... | .... | .... | .... |
| | Philadelphia | AHL | 3 | 0 | 0 | 0 | 21 | .... | .... | .... | .... | .... | .... | .... | .... | .... | .... | .... | .... | .... | .... | .... | .... | .... | .... |
| **2007-08** | **Philadelphia** | **NHL** | **23** | **0** | **0** | **0** | **62** | **0** | **0** | **0** | **11** | **0.0** | **-8** | **5** | **20.0** | **5:29** | .... | .... | .... | .... | .... | .... | .... | .... | .... |
| | **Chicago** | **NHL** | **9** | **0** | **2** | **2** | **27** | **0** | **0** | **0** | **5** | **0.0** | **-1** | **0** | **0.0** | **6:37** | .... | .... | .... | .... | .... | .... | .... | .... | .... |
| **2008-09** | **Chicago** | **NHL** | **75** | **11** | **4** | **15** | **161** | **0** | **0** | **0** | **80** | **13.8** | **1** | **0** | **0.0** | **8:31** | **17** | **1** | **1** | **2** | ***61** | **0** | **0** | **1** | **8:32** |
| | **NHL Totals** | | **195** | **20** | **16** | **36** | **501** | **0** | **0** | **0** | **165** | **12.1** | | **6** | **33.3** | **7:50** | **19** | **1** | **1** | **2** | **87** | **0** | **0** | **1** | **8:23** |

Traded to **Philadelphia** by **Phoenix** with Sean Burke and Branko Radivojevic for Mike Comrie, February 9, 2004. Traded to **Chicago** by **Philadelphia** for Jim Vandermeer, December 18, 2007.

## EARL, Robbie

(UHRL, RAW-bee) **MIN.**

Left wing. Shoots left. 6', 195 lbs. Born, Chicago, IL, June 6, 1985. Toronto's 4th choice, 187th overall, in 2004 Entry Draft.

| | | | | | | | | | | | | | | | | | | | | | | | | | |
|---|---|---|---|---|---|---|---|---|---|---|---|---|---|---|---|---|---|---|---|---|---|---|---|---|---|
| 2000-01 | L.A. Jr. Kings | Minor-CA | 29 | 48 | 22 | 70 | .... | .... | .... | .... | .... | .... | .... | .... | .... | .... | .... | .... | .... | .... | .... | .... | .... | .... | .... |
| 2001-02 | USNTDP | U-17 | 15 | 8 | 9 | 17 | .... | .... | .... | .... | .... | .... | .... | .... | .... | .... | .... | .... | .... | .... | .... | .... | .... | .... | .... |
| | USNTDP | NAHL | 43 | 14 | 7 | 21 | 43 | .... | .... | .... | .... | .... | .... | .... | .... | .... | .... | .... | .... | .... | .... | .... | .... | .... | .... |
| 2002-03 | USNTDP | U-18 | 43 | 16 | 8 | 24 | 58 | .... | .... | .... | .... | .... | .... | .... | .... | .... | .... | .... | .... | .... | .... | .... | .... | .... | .... |
| | USNTDP | NAHL | 10 | 4 | 5 | 9 | 18 | .... | .... | .... | .... | .... | .... | .... | .... | .... | .... | .... | .... | .... | .... | .... | .... | .... | .... |
| 2003-04 | U. of Wisconsin | WCHA | 42 | 14 | 13 | 27 | 46 | .... | .... | .... | .... | .... | .... | .... | .... | .... | .... | .... | .... | .... | .... | .... | .... | .... | .... |
| 2004-05 | U. of Wisconsin | WCHA | 41 | 20 | 24 | 44 | 62 | .... | .... | .... | .... | .... | .... | .... | .... | .... | .... | .... | .... | .... | .... | .... | .... | .... | .... |
| 2005-06 | U. of Wisconsin | WCHA | 42 | 24 | 26 | 50 | 56 | .... | .... | .... | .... | .... | .... | .... | .... | .... | .... | .... | .... | .... | .... | .... | .... | .... | .... |
| | Toronto Marlies | AHL | 1 | 0 | 0 | 0 | 0 | .... | .... | .... | .... | .... | .... | .... | .... | .... | 3 | 0 | 0 | 0 | 0 | .... | .... | .... | .... |
| 2006-07 | Toronto Marlies | AHL | 67 | 12 | 18 | 30 | 50 | .... | .... | .... | .... | .... | .... | .... | .... | .... | .... | .... | .... | .... | .... | .... | .... | .... | .... |
| **2007-08** | **Toronto** | **NHL** | **9** | **0** | **1** | **1** | **0** | **0** | **0** | **0** | **9** | **0.0** | **-2** | **2** | **100.0** | **9:14** | .... | .... | .... | .... | .... | .... | .... | .... | .... |
| | Toronto Marlies | AHL | 66 | 14 | 33 | 47 | 56 | .... | .... | .... | .... | .... | .... | .... | .... | .... | .... | .... | .... | .... | .... | .... | .... | .... | .... |
| 2008-09 | Toronto Marlies | AHL | 36 | 2 | 8 | 10 | 28 | .... | .... | .... | .... | .... | .... | .... | .... | .... | .... | .... | .... | .... | .... | .... | .... | .... | .... |
| | Houston Aeros | AHL | 33 | 4 | 5 | 9 | 26 | .... | .... | .... | .... | .... | .... | .... | .... | .... | 20 | 5 | 4 | 9 | 14 | .... | .... | .... | .... |
| | **NHL Totals** | | **9** | **0** | **1** | **1** | **0** | **0** | **0** | **0** | **9** | **0.0** | | **2** | **100.0** | **9:14** | .... | .... | .... | .... | .... | .... | .... | .... | .... |

WCHA All-Rookie Team (2004) • WCHA Second All-Star Team (2005) • NCAA Championship All-Tournament Team (2006) • NCAA Championship Tournament MVP (2006)

Traded to **Minnesota** by **Toronto** for Ryan Hamilton, January 21, 2009.

## EATON, Mark

(EE-tohn, MAHRK) **PIT.**

Defense. Shoots left. 6'2", 204 lbs. Born, Wilmington, DE, May 6, 1977.

| | | | | | | | | | | | | | | | | | | | | | | | | | |
|---|---|---|---|---|---|---|---|---|---|---|---|---|---|---|---|---|---|---|---|---|---|---|---|---|---|
| 1995-96 | Waterloo | USHL | 50 | 4 | 21 | 25 | .... | .... | .... | .... | .... | .... | .... | .... | .... | .... | .... | .... | .... | .... | .... | .... | .... | .... | .... |
| 1996-97 | Waterloo | USHL | 50 | 6 | 32 | 38 | 62 | .... | .... | .... | .... | .... | .... | .... | .... | .... | .... | .... | .... | .... | .... | .... | .... | .... | .... |
| 1997-98 | U. of Notre Dame | CCHA | 41 | 12 | 17 | 29 | 32 | .... | .... | .... | .... | .... | .... | .... | .... | .... | .... | .... | .... | .... | .... | .... | .... | .... | .... |
| 1998-99 | Philadelphia | AHL | 74 | 9 | 27 | 36 | 38 | .... | .... | .... | .... | .... | .... | .... | .... | .... | 16 | 4 | 8 | 12 | 0 | .... | .... | .... | .... |
| **99-2000** | **Philadelphia** | **NHL** | **27** | **1** | **1** | **2** | **8** | **0** | **0** | **1** | **25** | **4.0** | **1** | **0** | **0.0** | **18:17** | **7** | **0** | **0** | **0** | **0** | **0** | **0** | **0** | **13:36** |
| | Philadelphia | AHL | 47 | 9 | 17 | 26 | 6 | .... | .... | .... | .... | .... | .... | .... | .... | .... | .... | .... | .... | .... | .... | .... | .... | .... | .... |
| **2000-01** | **Nashville** | **NHL** | **34** | **3** | **8** | **11** | **14** | **1** | **0** | **1** | **32** | **9.4** | **7** | **0** | **0.0** | **17:13** | .... | .... | .... | .... | .... | .... | .... | .... | .... |
| | Milwaukee | IHL | 34 | 3 | 12 | 15 | 27 | .... | .... | .... | .... | .... | .... | .... | .... | .... | .... | .... | .... | .... | .... | .... | .... | .... | .... |
| **2001-02** | **Nashville** | **NHL** | **58** | **3** | **5** | **8** | **24** | **0** | **0** | **0** | **52** | **5.8** | **-12** | **0** | **0.0** | **17:12** | .... | .... | .... | .... | .... | .... | .... | .... | .... |
| **2002-03** | **Nashville** | **NHL** | **50** | **2** | **7** | **9** | **22** | **0** | **0** | **0** | **52** | **3.8** | **1** | **0** | **0.0** | **15:45** | .... | .... | .... | .... | .... | .... | .... | .... | .... |
| | Milwaukee | AHL | 3 | 1 | 0 | 1 | 2 | .... | .... | .... | .... | .... | .... | .... | .... | .... | .... | .... | .... | .... | .... | .... | .... | .... | .... |
| **2003-04** | **Nashville** | **NHL** | **75** | **4** | **9** | **13** | **26** | **0** | **0** | **1** | **82** | **4.9** | **16** | **0** | **0.0** | **20:56** | **6** | **0** | **0** | **0** | **2** | **0** | **0** | **0** | **19:51** |
| 2004-05 | Grand Rapids | AHL | 29 | 3 | 3 | 6 | 21 | .... | .... | .... | .... | .... | .... | .... | .... | .... | .... | .... | .... | .... | .... | .... | .... | .... | .... |
| **2005-06** | **Nashville** | **NHL** | **69** | **3** | **1** | **4** | **44** | **0** | **0** | **0** | **28** | **10.7** | **-2** | **0** | **0.0** | **19:43** | **5** | **0** | **0** | **0** | **8** | **0** | **0** | **0** | **17:49** |
| **2006-07** | **Pittsburgh** | **NHL** | **35** | **0** | **3** | **3** | **16** | **0** | **0** | **0** | **22** | **0.0** | **-6** | **0** | **0.0** | **19:12** | **5** | **0** | **0** | **0** | **0** | **0** | **0** | **0** | **18:31** |
| **2007-08** | **Pittsburgh** | **NHL** | **36** | **0** | **3** | **3** | **4** | **0** | **0** | **0** | **28** | **0.0** | **6** | **0** | **0.0** | **19:40** | .... | .... | .... | .... | .... | .... | .... | .... | .... |
| **2008-09** ♦ | **Pittsburgh** | **NHL** | **68** | **4** | **5** | **9** | **36** | **1** | **0** | **0** | **34** | **11.8** | **3** | **1** | **100.0** | **17:46** | **24** | **4** | **3** | **7** | **10** | **1** | **0** | **0** | **18:07** |
| | **NHL Totals** | | **452** | **20** | **42** | **62** | **194** | **2** | **0** | **3** | **355** | **5.6** | | **1** | **100.0** | **18:33** | **47** | **4** | **3** | **7** | **20** | **1** | **0** | **0** | **17:41** |

USHL Second All-Star Team (1997) • Curt Hammer Award (USHL – Most Gentlemanly Player) (1997) • CCHA Rookie of the Year (1998)

Signed as a free agent by **Philadelphia**, August 4, 1998. Traded to **Nashville** by **Philadelphia** for Detroit's 3rd round choice (previously acquired, Philadelphia selected Patrick Sharp) in 2001 Entry Draft, September 29, 2000. Signed as a free agent by **Grand Rapids** (AHL), February 16, 2005. Signed as a free agent by **Pittsburgh**, July 3, 2006.

## EAVES, Patrick

(EEVZ, PAT-rihk) **DET.**

Right wing. Shoots right. 5'11", 190 lbs. Born, Calgary, Alta., May 1, 1984. Ottawa's 1st choice, 29th overall, in 2003 Entry Draft.

| | | | | | | | | | | | | | | | | | | | | | | | | | |
|---|---|---|---|---|---|---|---|---|---|---|---|---|---|---|---|---|---|---|---|---|---|---|---|---|---|
| 99-2000 | Shat.-St. Mary's | High-MN | 50 | 23 | 24 | 47 | .... | .... | .... | .... | .... | .... | .... | .... | .... | .... | .... | .... | .... | .... | .... | .... | .... | .... | .... |
| 2000-01 | USNTDP | U-17 | 13 | 7 | 8 | 15 | 3 | .... | .... | .... | .... | .... | .... | .... | .... | .... | .... | .... | .... | .... | .... | .... | .... | .... | .... |
| | USNTDP | NAHL | 34 | 12 | 11 | 23 | 75 | .... | .... | .... | .... | .... | .... | .... | .... | .... | .... | .... | .... | .... | .... | .... | .... | .... | .... |
| 2001-02 | USNTDP | U-18 | 32 | 19 | 21 | 40 | 87 | .... | .... | .... | .... | .... | .... | .... | .... | .... | .... | .... | .... | .... | .... | .... | .... | .... | .... |
| | USNTDP | USHL | 9 | 1 | 4 | 5 | 18 | .... | .... | .... | .... | .... | .... | .... | .... | .... | .... | .... | .... | .... | .... | .... | .... | .... | .... |
| | USNTDP | NAHL | 8 | 5 | 3 | 8 | 37 | .... | .... | .... | .... | .... | .... | .... | .... | .... | .... | .... | .... | .... | .... | .... | .... | .... | .... |
| 2002-03 | Boston College | H-East | 14 | 10 | 8 | 18 | 61 | .... | .... | .... | .... | .... | .... | .... | .... | .... | .... | .... | .... | .... | .... | .... | .... | .... | .... |
| 2003-04 | Boston College | H-East | 34 | 18 | 23 | 41 | 66 | .... | .... | .... | .... | .... | .... | .... | .... | .... | .... | .... | .... | .... | .... | .... | .... | .... | .... |
| 2004-05 | Boston College | H-East | 36 | 19 | 29 | 48 | 36 | .... | .... | .... | .... | .... | .... | .... | .... | .... | .... | .... | .... | .... | .... | .... | .... | .... | .... |
| **2005-06** | **Ottawa** | **NHL** | **58** | **20** | **9** | **29** | **22** | **5** | **1** | **4** | **100** | **20.0** | **7** | **14** | **21.4** | **12:29** | **10** | **1** | **0** | **1** | **10** | **0** | **0** | **0** | **11:40** |
| | Binghamton | AHL | 18 | 5 | 8 | 13 | 10 | .... | .... | .... | .... | .... | .... | .... | .... | .... | .... | .... | .... | .... | .... | .... | .... | .... | .... |
| **2006-07** | **Ottawa** | **NHL** | **73** | **14** | **18** | **32** | **36** | **3** | **1** | **1** | **130** | **10.8** | **1** | **9** | **11.1** | **12:13** | **7** | **0** | **2** | **2** | **2** | **0** | **0** | **0** | **7:23** |
| **2007-08** | **Ottawa** | **NHL** | **26** | **4** | **6** | **10** | **6** | **1** | **0** | **1** | **59** | **6.8** | **0** | **1** | **100.0** | **12:44** | .... | .... | .... | .... | .... | .... | .... | .... | .... |
| | **Carolina** | **NHL** | **11** | **1** | **4** | **5** | **4** | **1** | **0** | **0** | **22** | **4.5** | **-2** | **2** | **0.0** | **12:51** | .... | .... | .... | .... | .... | .... | .... | .... | .... |
| **2008-09** | **Carolina** | **NHL** | **74** | **6** | **8** | **14** | **31** | **1** | **1** | **1** | **115** | **5.2** | **7** | **12** | **41.7** | **11:15** | **18** | **1** | **2** | **3** | **13** | **0** | **0** | **0** | **9:29** |
| | **NHL Totals** | | **242** | **45** | **45** | **90** | **99** | **11** | **3** | **7** | **426** | **10.6** | | **38** | **26.3** | **12:04** | **35** | **2** | **4** | **6** | **25** | **0** | **0** | **0** | **9:41** |

Hockey East Second All-Star Team (2004) • NCAA East Second All-American Team (2004) • Hockey East First All-Star Team (2005) • NCAA East First All-American Team (2005)

• Missed majority of 2002-03 season recovering from neck injury suffered in game vs. University of Maine (Hockey East), December 7, 2002. Traded to **Carolina** by **Ottawa** with Joe Corvo for Cory Stillman and Mike Commodore, February 11, 2008. • Missed majority of 2007-08 season recovering from shoulder injury suffered in game at Buffalo, November 21, 2007. Traded to **Boston** by **Carolina** with Carolina's 4th round choice in 2010 Entry Draft for Aaron Ward, July 24, 2009. Signed as a free agent by **Detroit**, August 4, 2009.

| | | | Regular Season | | | | | | | | | | | | | | Playoffs | | | | | | | | |
|---|---|---|---|---|---|---|---|---|---|---|---|---|---|---|---|---|---|---|---|---|---|---|---|---|---|
| Season | Club | League | GP | G | A | Pts | PIM | PP | SH | GW | S | % | +/- | TF | F% | Min | GP | G | A | Pts | PIM | PP | SH | GW | Min |

## EBBETT, Andrew
(EH-beht, AN-droo) **ANA.**

Center. Shoots left. 5'9", 182 lbs. Born, Calgary, Alta., January 2, 1983.

| | | | | | | | | | | | | | | | | | | | | | | | | | |
|---|---|---|---|---|---|---|---|---|---|---|---|---|---|---|---|---|---|---|---|---|---|---|---|---|---|
| 2002-03 | U. of Michigan | CCHA | 43 | 9 | 18 | 27 | 22 | .... | .... | .... | .... | .... | .... | .... | .... | .... | .... | .... | .... | .... | .... | .... | .... | .... | .... |
| 2003-04 | U. of Michigan | CCHA | 43 | 9 | 28 | 37 | 56 | .... | .... | .... | .... | .... | .... | .... | .... | .... | .... | .... | .... | .... | .... | .... | .... | .... | .... |
| 2004-05 | U. of Michigan | CCHA | 40 | 6 | 31 | 37 | 28 | .... | .... | .... | .... | .... | .... | .... | .... | .... | .... | .... | .... | .... | .... | .... | .... | .... | .... |
| 2005-06 | U. of Michigan | CCHA | 41 | 14 | 28 | 42 | 25 | .... | .... | .... | .... | .... | .... | .... | .... | .... | .... | .... | .... | .... | .... | .... | .... | .... | .... |
| 2006-07 | Binghamton | AHL | 71 | 26 | 39 | 65 | 44 | .... | .... | .... | .... | .... | .... | .... | .... | .... | .... | .... | .... | .... | .... | .... | .... | .... | .... |
| **2007-08** | **Anaheim** | **NHL** | **3** | **0** | **0** | **0** | **2** | **0** | **0** | **0** | **3** | **0.0** | **3** | **29** | **58.6** | **13:18** | .... | .... | .... | .... | .... | .... | .... | .... | .... |
| | Portland Pirates | AHL | 74 | 18 | 54 | 72 | 66 | .... | .... | .... | .... | .... | .... | .... | .... | .... | 18 | 6 | 11 | 17 | 4 | .... | .... | .... | .... |
| **2008-09** | **Anaheim** | **NHL** | **48** | **8** | **24** | **32** | **24** | **6** | **0** | **0** | **100** | **8.0** | **8** | **455** | **48.6** | **13:52** | **13** | **1** | **2** | **3** | **8** | **0** | **0** | **0** | **13:11** |
| | Iowa Chops | AHL | 28 | 10 | 19 | 29 | 6 | .... | .... | .... | .... | .... | .... | .... | .... | .... | .... | .... | .... | .... | .... | .... | .... | .... | .... |
| | **NHL Totals** | | **51** | **8** | **24** | **32** | **26** | **6** | **0** | **0** | **103** | **7.8** | | **484** | **49.2** | **13:50** | **13** | **1** | **2** | **3** | **8** | **0** | **0** | **0** | **13:11** |

Signed as a free agent by **Anaheim**, May 16, 2007.

## EDLER, Alexander
(EHD-luhr, al-EHX-AN-duhr) **VAN.**

Defense. Shoots left. 6'3", 220 lbs. Born, Ostersund, Sweden, April 21, 1986. Vancouver's 2nd choice, 91st overall, in 2004 Entry Draft.

| | | | | | | | | | | | | | | | | | | | | | | | | | |
|---|---|---|---|---|---|---|---|---|---|---|---|---|---|---|---|---|---|---|---|---|---|---|---|---|---|
| 2001-02 | Jamtland | Exhib. | 8 | 0 | 1 | 1 | 2 | .... | .... | .... | .... | .... | .... | .... | .... | .... | .... | .... | .... | .... | .... | .... | .... | .... | .... |
| 2002-03 | Jamtland | Exhib. | 8 | 2 | 1 | 3 | 0 | .... | .... | .... | .... | .... | .... | .... | .... | .... | .... | .... | .... | .... | .... | .... | .... | .... | .... |
| 2003-04 | Jamtland Jr. | Swe-Jr. | 6 | 0 | 3 | 3 | 6 | .... | .... | .... | .... | .... | .... | .... | .... | .... | .... | .... | .... | .... | .... | .... | .... | .... | .... |
| | Jamtland | Sweden-3 | 24 | 3 | 6 | 9 | 20 | .... | .... | .... | .... | .... | .... | .... | .... | .... | .... | .... | .... | .... | .... | .... | .... | .... | .... |
| 2004-05 | MODO Jr. | Swe-Jr. | 33 | 8 | 15 | 23 | 40 | .... | .... | .... | .... | .... | .... | .... | .... | .... | 5 | 1 | 0 | 1 | 6 | .... | .... | .... | .... |
| 2005-06 | Kelowna Rockets | WHL | 62 | 13 | 40 | 53 | 44 | .... | .... | .... | .... | .... | .... | .... | .... | .... | 12 | 3 | 5 | 8 | 12 | .... | .... | .... | .... |
| **2006-07** | **Vancouver** | **NHL** | **22** | **1** | **2** | **3** | **6** | **0** | **0** | **0** | **10** | **10.0** | **3** | **0** | **0.0** | **11:27** | **3** | **0** | **0** | **0** | **2** | **0** | **0** | **0** | **11:51** |
| | Manitoba Moose | AHL | 49 | 5 | 21 | 26 | 28 | .... | .... | .... | .... | .... | .... | .... | .... | .... | 8 | 0 | 0 | 0 | 2 | .... | .... | .... | .... |
| **2007-08** | **Vancouver** | **NHL** | **75** | **8** | **12** | **20** | **42** | **4** | **0** | **0** | **124** | **6.5** | **6** | **1** | **100.0** | **21:20** | .... | .... | .... | .... | .... | .... | .... | .... | .... |
| | Manitoba Moose | AHL | 2 | 0 | 1 | 1 | 0 | .... | .... | .... | .... | .... | .... | .... | .... | .... | .... | .... | .... | .... | .... | .... | .... | .... | .... |
| **2008-09** | **Vancouver** | **NHL** | **80** | **10** | **27** | **37** | **54** | **5** | **0** | **1** | **145** | **6.9** | **11** | **1** | **100.0** | **21:08** | **10** | **1** | **7** | **8** | **6** | **1** | **0** | **0** | **22:09** |
| | **NHL Totals** | | **177** | **19** | **41** | **60** | **102** | **9** | **0** | **1** | **279** | **6.8** | | **2** | **100.0** | **20:01** | **13** | **1** | **7** | **8** | **8** | **1** | **0** | **0** | **19:46** |

## EHRHOFF, Christian
(AIR-hawf, KRIHS-tyehn) **S.J.**

Defense. Shoots left. 6'2", 205 lbs. Born, Moers, West Germany, July 6, 1982. San Jose's 2nd choice, 106th overall, in 2001 Entry Draft.

| | | | | | | | | | | | | | | | | | | | | | | | | | |
|---|---|---|---|---|---|---|---|---|---|---|---|---|---|---|---|---|---|---|---|---|---|---|---|---|---|
| 1998-99 | Krefelder EV Jr. | Ger-Jr. | 22 | 10 | 14 | 24 | 46 | .... | .... | .... | .... | .... | .... | .... | .... | .... | .... | .... | .... | .... | .... | .... | .... | .... | .... |
| 99-2000 | EV Duisburg | German-3 | 41 | 3 | 12 | 15 | 50 | .... | .... | .... | .... | .... | .... | .... | .... | .... | .... | .... | .... | .... | .... | .... | .... | .... | .... |
| | Krefeld Pinguine | Germany | 9 | 1 | 0 | 1 | 6 | .... | .... | .... | .... | .... | .... | .... | .... | .... | 3 | 0 | 0 | 0 | 0 | .... | .... | .... | .... |
| 2000-01 | EV Duisburg | German-3 | 6 | 1 | 2 | 3 | 12 | .... | .... | .... | .... | .... | .... | .... | .... | .... | .... | .... | .... | .... | .... | .... | .... | .... | .... |
| | Krefeld Pinguine | Germany | 58 | 3 | 11 | 14 | 73 | .... | .... | .... | .... | .... | .... | .... | .... | .... | .... | .... | .... | .... | .... | .... | .... | .... | .... |
| 2001-02 | Krefeld Pinguine | Germany | 46 | 7 | 17 | 24 | 81 | .... | .... | .... | .... | .... | .... | .... | .... | .... | 3 | 0 | 0 | 0 | 2 | .... | .... | .... | .... |
| | Germany | Olympics | 7 | 0 | 0 | 0 | 8 | .... | .... | .... | .... | .... | .... | .... | .... | .... | .... | .... | .... | .... | .... | .... | .... | .... | .... |
| 2002-03 | Krefeld Pinguine | Germany | 48 | 10 | 17 | 27 | 54 | .... | .... | .... | .... | .... | .... | .... | .... | .... | 14 | 3 | 6 | 9 | 24 | .... | .... | .... | .... |
| **2003-04** | **San Jose** | **NHL** | **41** | **1** | **11** | **12** | **14** | **0** | **0** | **1** | **58** | **1.7** | **4** | **0** | **0.0** | **15:23** | .... | .... | .... | .... | .... | .... | .... | .... | .... |
| | Cleveland Barons | AHL | 27 | 4 | 10 | 14 | 43 | .... | .... | .... | .... | .... | .... | .... | .... | .... | 9 | 2 | 6 | 8 | 11 | .... | .... | .... | .... |
| 2004-05 | Cleveland Barons | AHL | 79 | 12 | 23 | 35 | 103 | .... | .... | .... | .... | .... | .... | .... | .... | .... | .... | .... | .... | .... | .... | .... | .... | .... | .... |
| **2005-06** | **San Jose** | **NHL** | **64** | **5** | **18** | **23** | **32** | **2** | **0** | **2** | **124** | **4.0** | **10** | **0** | **0.0** | **17:48** | **11** | **2** | **6** | **8** | **18** | **1** | **0** | **1** | **19:47** |
| | Germany | Olympics | 5 | 1 | 1 | 2 | 4 | .... | .... | .... | .... | .... | .... | .... | .... | .... | .... | .... | .... | .... | .... | .... | .... | .... | .... |
| **2006-07** | **San Jose** | **NHL** | **82** | **10** | **23** | **33** | **63** | **6** | **0** | **2** | **164** | **6.1** | **8** | **1** | **0.0** | **18:34** | **11** | **0** | **2** | **2** | **6** | **0** | **0** | **0** | **17:47** |
| **2007-08** | **San Jose** | **NHL** | **77** | **1** | **21** | **22** | **72** | **1** | **0** | **1** | **97** | **1.0** | **9** | **0** | **0.0** | **21:44** | **10** | **0** | **5** | **5** | **14** | **0** | **0** | **0** | **23:04** |
| **2008-09** | **San Jose** | **NHL** | **77** | **8** | **34** | **42** | **63** | **5** | **0** | **2** | **165** | **4.8** | **-12** | **0** | **0.0** | **21:14** | **6** | **0** | **0** | **0** | **2** | **0** | **0** | **0** | **24:47** |
| | **NHL Totals** | | **341** | **25** | **107** | **132** | **244** | **14** | **0** | **8** | **608** | **4.1** | | **1** | **0.0** | **19:21** | **38** | **2** | **13** | **15** | **40** | **1** | **0** | **1** | **20:52** |

## ELIAS, Patrik
(ehl-EE-ahsh, PAT-rihk) **N.J.**

Left wing. Shoots left. 6'1", 195 lbs. Born, Trebic, Czech., April 13, 1976. New Jersey's 2nd choice, 51st overall, in 1994 Entry Draft.

| | | | | | | | | | | | | | | | | | | | | | | | | | |
|---|---|---|---|---|---|---|---|---|---|---|---|---|---|---|---|---|---|---|---|---|---|---|---|---|---|
| 1992-93 | Poldi Kladno | Czech | 2 | 0 | 0 | 0 | .... | .... | .... | .... | .... | .... | .... | .... | .... | .... | .... | .... | .... | .... | .... | .... | .... | .... | .... |
| 1993-94 | HC Kladno | CzRep | 15 | 1 | 2 | 3 | .... | .... | .... | .... | .... | .... | .... | .... | .... | .... | 11 | 2 | 2 | 4 | .... | .... | .... | .... | .... |
| 1994-95 | HC Kladno | CzRep | 28 | 4 | 3 | 7 | 37 | .... | .... | .... | .... | .... | .... | .... | .... | .... | 7 | 1 | 2 | 3 | 12 | .... | .... | .... | .... |
| **1995-96** | **New Jersey** | **NHL** | **1** | **0** | **0** | **0** | **0** | **0** | **0** | **0** | **2** | **0.0** | **-1** | .... | .... | .... | .... | .... | .... | .... | .... | .... | .... | .... | .... |
| | Albany River Rats | AHL | 74 | 27 | 36 | 63 | 83 | .... | .... | .... | .... | .... | .... | .... | .... | .... | 4 | 1 | 1 | 2 | 2 | .... | .... | .... | .... |
| **1996-97** | **New Jersey** | **NHL** | **17** | **2** | **3** | **5** | **2** | **0** | **0** | **0** | **23** | **8.7** | **-4** | .... | .... | .... | **8** | **2** | **3** | **5** | **4** | **1** | **0** | **0** | .... |
| | Albany River Rats | AHL | 57 | 24 | 43 | 67 | 76 | .... | .... | .... | .... | .... | .... | .... | .... | .... | 6 | 1 | 2 | 3 | 8 | .... | .... | .... | .... |
| **1997-98** | **New Jersey** | **NHL** | **74** | **18** | **19** | **37** | **28** | **5** | **0** | **6** | **147** | **12.2** | **18** | .... | .... | .... | **4** | **0** | **1** | **1** | **0** | **0** | **0** | **0** | .... |
| | Albany River Rats | AHL | 3 | 3 | 0 | 3 | 2 | .... | .... | .... | .... | .... | .... | .... | .... | .... | .... | .... | .... | .... | .... | .... | .... | .... | .... |
| **1998-99** | **New Jersey** | **NHL** | **74** | **17** | **33** | **50** | **34** | **3** | **0** | **2** | **157** | **10.8** | **19** | **99** | **38.4** | **15:50** | **7** | **0** | **5** | **5** | **6** | **0** | **0** | **0** | **18:07** |
| **99-2000** | Trebic | CzRep-2 | 2 | 2 | 1 | 3 | 2 | .... | .... | .... | .... | .... | .... | .... | .... | .... | .... | .... | .... | .... | .... | .... | .... | .... | .... |
| | Pardubice | CzRep | 5 | 1 | 4 | 5 | 31 | .... | .... | .... | .... | .... | .... | .... | .... | .... | .... | .... | .... | .... | .... | .... | .... | .... | .... |
| | **♦ New Jersey** | **NHL** | **72** | **35** | **37** | **72** | **58** | **9** | **0** | **9** | **183** | **19.1** | **16** | **134** | **45.5** | **17:28** | **23** | **7** | ***13** | **20** | **9** | **2** | **1** | **1** | **17:44** |
| **2000-01** | **New Jersey** | **NHL** | **82** | **40** | **56** | **96** | **51** | **8** | **3** | **6** | **220** | **18.2** | **45** | **155** | **41.3** | **18:44** | **25** | **9** | **14** | **23** | **10** | **3** | **1** | **2** | **18:14** |
| **2001-02** | **New Jersey** | **NHL** | **75** | **29** | **32** | **61** | **36** | **8** | **1** | **8** | **199** | **14.6** | **4** | **128** | **45.3** | **18:57** | **6** | **2** | **4** | **6** | **6** | **2** | **0** | **0** | **20:33** |
| | Czech Republic | Olympics | 4 | 1 | 1 | 2 | 0 | .... | .... | .... | .... | .... | .... | .... | .... | .... | .... | .... | .... | .... | .... | .... | .... | .... | .... |
| **2002-03** | **♦ New Jersey** | **NHL** | **81** | **28** | **29** | **57** | **22** | **6** | **0** | **4** | **255** | **11.0** | **17** | **427** | **43.8** | **18:05** | **24** | **5** | **8** | **13** | **26** | **2** | **0** | **2** | **17:14** |
| **2003-04** | **New Jersey** | **NHL** | **82** | **38** | **43** | **81** | **44** | **9** | **3** | **9** | **300** | **12.7** | **26** | **49** | **36.7** | **18:46** | **5** | **3** | **2** | **5** | **2** | **1** | **0** | **1** | **18:59** |
| 2004-05 | Znojmo | CzRep | 28 | 8 | 20 | 28 | 65 | .... | .... | .... | .... | .... | .... | .... | .... | .... | .... | .... | .... | .... | .... | .... | .... | .... | .... |
| | Magnitogorsk | Russia | 17 | 5 | 9 | 14 | 28 | .... | .... | .... | .... | .... | .... | .... | .... | .... | .... | .... | .... | .... | .... | .... | .... | .... | .... |
| **2005-06** | **New Jersey** | **NHL** | **38** | **16** | **29** | **45** | **20** | **6** | **0** | **3** | **142** | **11.3** | **11** | **10** | **20.0** | **18:34** | **9** | **6** | **10** | **16** | **4** | **4** | **0** | **0** | **18:43** |
| | Czech Republic | Olympics | 1 | 0 | 0 | 0 | 2 | .... | .... | .... | .... | .... | .... | .... | .... | .... | .... | .... | .... | .... | .... | .... | .... | .... | .... |
| **2006-07** | **New Jersey** | **NHL** | **75** | **21** | **48** | **69** | **38** | **8** | **0** | **5** | **267** | **7.9** | **1** | **18** | **38.9** | **18:37** | **10** | **1** | **9** | **10** | **4** | **1** | **0** | **0** | **19:13** |
| **2007-08** | **New Jersey** | **NHL** | **74** | **20** | **35** | **55** | **38** | **7** | **0** | **8** | **263** | **7.6** | **10** | **776** | **45.6** | **18:28** | **5** | **4** | **2** | **6** | **4** | **3** | **0** | **0** | **20:30** |
| **2008-09** | **New Jersey** | **NHL** | **77** | **31** | **47** | **78** | **32** | **12** | **2** | **6** | **247** | **12.6** | **18** | **87** | **29.9** | **18:34** | **7** | **1** | **2** | **3** | **2** | **0** | **0** | **0** | **17:53** |
| | **NHL Totals** | | **822** | **295** | **411** | **706** | **403** | **81** | **9** | **66** | **2405** | **12.3** | | **1883** | **43.3** | **18:12** | **133** | **40** | **73** | **113** | **77** | **19** | **2** | **6** | **18:16** |

NHL All-Rookie Team (1998) • NHL First All-Star Team (2001) • Bud Light Plus/Minus Award (2001) (tied with Joe Sakic)
Played in NHL All-Star Game (2000, 2002)
Signed as a free agent by **Znojmo** (CzRep), September 6, 2004. Signed as a free agent by **Magnitogorsk** (Russia), December 9, 2004. • Missed majority of 2005-06 season recovering from hepatitis-A.

## ELLIS, Matt
(EHL-ihs, MAT) **BUF.**

Left wing. Shoots left. 6', 212 lbs. Born, Welland, Ont., August 31, 1981.

| | | | | | | | | | | | | | | | | | | | | | | | | | |
|---|---|---|---|---|---|---|---|---|---|---|---|---|---|---|---|---|---|---|---|---|---|---|---|---|---|
| 1998-99 | St. Michael's | OHL | 47 | 10 | 8 | 18 | 6 | .... | .... | .... | .... | .... | .... | .... | .... | .... | .... | .... | .... | .... | .... | .... | .... | .... | .... |
| 99-2000 | St. Michael's | OHL | 59 | 15 | 20 | 35 | 20 | .... | .... | .... | .... | .... | .... | .... | .... | .... | .... | .... | .... | .... | .... | .... | .... | .... | .... |
| 2000-01 | St. Michael's | OHL | 68 | 21 | 24 | 45 | 19 | .... | .... | .... | .... | .... | .... | .... | .... | .... | 18 | 4 | 8 | 12 | 6 | .... | .... | .... | .... |
| 2001-02 | St. Michael's | OHL | 66 | 38 | 51 | 89 | 20 | .... | .... | .... | .... | .... | .... | .... | .... | .... | 15 | 8 | 6 | 14 | 6 | .... | .... | .... | .... |
| 2002-03 | Toledo Storm | ECHL | 71 | 27 | 32 | 59 | 34 | .... | .... | .... | .... | .... | .... | .... | .... | .... | 7 | 3 | 5 | 8 | 0 | .... | .... | .... | .... |
| 2003-04 | Grand Rapids | AHL | 64 | 5 | 10 | 15 | 23 | .... | .... | .... | .... | .... | .... | .... | .... | .... | 4 | 0 | 0 | 0 | 2 | .... | .... | .... | .... |
| 2004-05 | Grand Rapids | AHL | 79 | 18 | 23 | 41 | 59 | .... | .... | .... | .... | .... | .... | .... | .... | .... | .... | .... | .... | .... | .... | .... | .... | .... | .... |
| 2005-06 | Grand Rapids | AHL | 74 | 20 | 28 | 48 | 61 | .... | .... | .... | .... | .... | .... | .... | .... | .... | 16 | 4 | 1 | 5 | 20 | .... | .... | .... | .... |
| **2006-07** | **Detroit** | **NHL** | **16** | **0** | **0** | **0** | **6** | **0** | **0** | **0** | **22** | **0.0** | **-1** | **48** | **47.9** | **5:35** | .... | .... | .... | .... | .... | .... | .... | .... | .... |
| | Grand Rapids | AHL | 65 | 26 | 23 | 49 | 44 | .... | .... | .... | .... | .... | .... | .... | .... | .... | 7 | 4 | 3 | 7 | 4 | .... | .... | .... | .... |
| **2007-08** | **Detroit** | **NHL** | **35** | **2** | **4** | **6** | **12** | **0** | **0** | **1** | **28** | **7.1** | **1** | **87** | **49.4** | **5:23** | .... | .... | .... | .... | .... | .... | .... | .... | .... |
| | **Los Angeles** | **NHL** | **19** | **1** | **1** | **2** | **14** | **0** | **1** | **0** | **38** | **2.6** | **2** | **27** | **37.0** | **12:41** | .... | .... | .... | .... | .... | .... | .... | .... | .... |
| **2008-09** | **Buffalo** | **NHL** | **45** | **7** | **5** | **12** | **12** | **0** | **0** | **2** | **73** | **9.6** | **4** | **239** | **46.9** | **8:50** | .... | .... | .... | .... | .... | .... | .... | .... | .... |
| | Portland Pirates | AHL | 12 | 2 | 2 | 4 | 4 | .... | .... | .... | .... | .... | .... | .... | .... | .... | .... | .... | .... | .... | .... | .... | .... | .... | .... |
| | **NHL Totals** | | **115** | **10** | **10** | **20** | **44** | **0** | **1** | **3** | **161** | **6.2** | | **401** | **46.9** | **7:58** | .... | .... | .... | .... | .... | .... | .... | .... | .... |

Signed as a free agent by **Detroit**, May 10, 2002. Claimed on waivers by **Los Angeles** from **Detroit**, February 21, 2008. Claimed on waivers by **Buffalo** from **Los Angeles**, October 1, 2008.

## ELLISON, Matt

(EHL-ih-suhn, MAT) **NSH.**

Right wing. Shoots right. 6', 192 lbs. Born, Duncan, B.C., December 8, 1983. Chicago's 4th choice, 128th overall, in 2002 Entry Draft.

| | | | Regular Season | | | | | | | | | | | | | | Playoffs | | | | | | | | |
|---|---|---|---|---|---|---|---|---|---|---|---|---|---|---|---|---|---|---|---|---|---|---|---|---|---|
| Season | Club | League | GP | G | A | Pts | PIM | PP | SH | GW | S | % | +/- | TF | F% | Min | GP | G | A | Pts | PIM | PP | SH | GW | Min |
| 1997-98 | Cowichan Valley | Minor-BC | 24 | 27 | 31 | 58 | 10 | .... | .... | .... | .... | .... | .... | .... | .... | .... | .... | .... | .... | .... | .... | .... | .... | .... | .... |
| 1998-99 | Kerry Park | VIJHL | 38 | 40 | 47 | 87 | 110 | .... | .... | .... | .... | .... | .... | .... | .... | .... | .... | .... | .... | .... | .... | .... | .... | .... | .... |
| 99-2000 | Cowichan Valley | BCHL | 60 | 11 | 23 | 34 | 95 | .... | .... | .... | .... | .... | .... | .... | .... | .... | .... | .... | .... | .... | .... | .... | .... | .... | .... |
| 2000-01 | Cowichan Valley | BCHL | 60 | 22 | 44 | 66 | 102 | .... | .... | .... | .... | .... | .... | .... | .... | .... | .... | .... | .... | .... | .... | .... | .... | .... | .... |
| 2001-02 | Cowichan Valley | BCHL | 60 | 42 | *75 | *117 | 76 | .... | .... | .... | .... | .... | .... | .... | .... | .... | 10 | 5 | 6 | 11 | 8 | .... | .... | .... | .... |
| 2002-03 | Red Deer Rebels | WHL | 72 | 40 | 56 | 96 | 80 | .... | .... | .... | .... | .... | .... | .... | .... | .... | 22 | 7 | 13 | 20 | 28 | .... | .... | .... | .... |
| **2003-04** | **Chicago** | **NHL** | **10** | **0** | **1** | **1** | **0** | **0** | **0** | **0** | **4** | **0.0** | **–3** | **46** | **39.1** | **12:40** | .... | .... | .... | .... | .... | .... | .... | .... | .... |
| | Norfolk Admirals | AHL | 71 | 14 | 21 | 35 | 115 | .... | .... | .... | .... | .... | .... | .... | .... | .... | 7 | 0 | 1 | 1 | 4 | .... | .... | .... | .... |
| 2004-05 | Norfolk Admirals | AHL | 71 | 14 | 37 | 51 | 44 | .... | .... | .... | .... | .... | .... | .... | .... | .... | 5 | 0 | 1 | 1 | 2 | .... | .... | .... | .... |
| **2005-06** | **Chicago** | **NHL** | **26** | **3** | **9** | **12** | **17** | **1** | **0** | **0** | **47** | **6.4** | **–4** | **76** | **43.4** | **14:45** | .... | .... | .... | .... | .... | .... | .... | .... | .... |
| | **Philadelphia** | **NHL** | **5** | **0** | **1** | **1** | **2** | **0** | **0** | **0** | **2** | **0.0** | **2** | **10** | **50.0** | **6:28** | .... | .... | .... | .... | .... | .... | .... | .... | .... |
| | Philadelphia | AHL | 48 | 12 | 13 | 25 | 35 | .... | .... | .... | .... | .... | .... | .... | .... | .... | .... | .... | .... | .... | .... | .... | .... | .... | .... |
| **2006-07** | **Philadelphia** | **NHL** | **2** | **0** | **0** | **0** | **0** | **0** | **0** | **0** | **1** | **0.0** | **0** | **8** | **37.5** | **5:58** | .... | .... | .... | .... | .... | .... | .... | .... | .... |
| | Philadelphia | AHL | 62 | 12 | 27 | 39 | 43 | .... | .... | .... | .... | .... | .... | .... | .... | .... | .... | .... | .... | .... | .... | .... | .... | .... | .... |
| 2007-08 | Milwaukee | AHL | 75 | 26 | 32 | 58 | 55 | .... | .... | .... | .... | .... | .... | .... | .... | .... | 5 | 0 | 0 | 0 | 2 | .... | .... | .... | .... |
| 2008-09 | Dynamo Riga | Rus-KHL | 55 | 15 | 22 | 37 | 84 | .... | .... | .... | .... | .... | .... | .... | .... | .... | 3 | 0 | 1 | 1 | 0 | .... | .... | .... | .... |
| | **NHL Totals** | | **43** | **3** | **11** | **14** | **19** | **1** | **0** | **0** | **54** | **5.6** | | **140** | **42.1** | **12:53** | .... | .... | .... | .... | .... | .... | .... | .... | .... |

WHL East Second All-Star Team (2003) • WHL Rookie of the Year (2003) • Canadian Major Junior Rookie of the Year (2003)

Traded to **Philadelphia** by **Chicago** with Chicago's 3rd round choice (later traded to Montreal - Montreal selected Ryan White) in 2006 Entry Draft for Patrick Sharp and Eric Meloche, December 5, 2005. Traded to **Nashville** by **Philadlephia** for future considerations, June 4, 2007.

## EMINGER, Steve

(EH-mihn-juhr, STEEV)

Defense. Shoots right. 6'2", 212 lbs. Born, Woodbridge, Ont., October 31, 1983. Washington's 1st choice, 12th overall, in 2002 Entry Draft.

| | | | Regular Season | | | | | | | | | | | | | | Playoffs | | | | | | | | |
|---|---|---|---|---|---|---|---|---|---|---|---|---|---|---|---|---|---|---|---|---|---|---|---|---|---|
| Season | Club | League | GP | G | A | Pts | PIM | PP | SH | GW | S | % | +/- | TF | F% | Min | GP | G | A | Pts | PIM | PP | SH | GW | Min |
| 1998-99 | Bramalea Blues | OPJHL | 47 | 6 | 9 | 15 | 81 | .... | .... | .... | .... | .... | .... | .... | .... | .... | .... | .... | .... | .... | .... | .... | .... | .... | .... |
| 99-2000 | Kitchener Rangers | OHL | 50 | 2 | 14 | 16 | 74 | .... | .... | .... | .... | .... | .... | .... | .... | .... | 5 | 0 | 0 | 0 | 0 | .... | .... | .... | .... |
| 2000-01 | Kitchener Rangers | OHL | 54 | 6 | 26 | 32 | 66 | .... | .... | .... | .... | .... | .... | .... | .... | .... | .... | .... | .... | .... | .... | .... | .... | .... | .... |
| 2001-02 | Kitchener Rangers | OHL | 64 | 19 | 39 | 58 | 93 | .... | .... | .... | .... | .... | .... | .... | .... | .... | 4 | 0 | 2 | 2 | 10 | .... | .... | .... | .... |
| **2002-03** | **Washington** | **NHL** | **17** | **0** | **2** | **2** | **24** | **0** | **0** | **0** | **6** | **0.0** | **–3** | **0** | **0.0** | **10:08** | .... | .... | .... | .... | .... | .... | .... | .... | .... |
| | Kitchener Rangers | OHL | 23 | 2 | 27 | 29 | 40 | .... | .... | .... | .... | .... | .... | .... | .... | .... | 21 | 3 | 8 | 11 | 44 | .... | .... | .... | .... |
| **2003-04** | **Washington** | **NHL** | **41** | **0** | **4** | **4** | **45** | **0** | **0** | **0** | **12** | **0.0** | **–11** | **0** | **0.0** | **17:32** | .... | .... | .... | .... | .... | .... | .... | .... | .... |
| | Portland Pirates | AHL | 41 | 0 | 4 | 4 | 40 | .... | .... | .... | .... | .... | .... | .... | .... | .... | 7 | 0 | 1 | 1 | 2 | .... | .... | .... | .... |
| 2004-05 | Portland Pirates | AHL | 62 | 3 | 17 | 20 | 40 | .... | .... | .... | .... | .... | .... | .... | .... | .... | .... | .... | .... | .... | .... | .... | .... | .... | .... |
| **2005-06** | **Washington** | **NHL** | **66** | **5** | **13** | **18** | **81** | **1** | **0** | **0** | **50** | **10.0** | **–12** | **1** | **100.0** | **21:21** | .... | .... | .... | .... | .... | .... | .... | .... | .... |
| **2006-07** | **Washington** | **NHL** | **68** | **1** | **16** | **17** | **63** | **0** | **0** | **0** | **27** | **3.7** | **–14** | **1** | **100.0** | **18:56** | .... | .... | .... | .... | .... | .... | .... | .... | .... |
| **2007-08** | **Washington** | **NHL** | **20** | **0** | **2** | **2** | **8** | **0** | **0** | **0** | **14** | **0.0** | **–4** | **0** | **0.0** | **11:08** | **5** | **1** | **0** | **1** | **2** | **0** | **0** | **0** | **16:06** |
| **2008-09** | **Philadelphia** | **NHL** | **12** | **0** | **2** | **2** | **8** | **0** | **0** | **0** | **9** | **0.0** | **0** | **0** | **0.0** | **17:53** | .... | .... | .... | .... | .... | .... | .... | .... | .... |
| | **Tampa Bay** | **NHL** | **50** | **4** | **19** | **23** | **36** | **2** | **0** | **0** | **63** | **6.3** | **–4** | **1** | **0.0** | **23:33** | .... | .... | .... | .... | .... | .... | .... | .... | .... |
| | **Florida** | **NHL** | **9** | **1** | **0** | **1** | **6** | **0** | **0** | **1** | **13** | **7.7** | **1** | **0** | **0.0** | **15:49** | .... | .... | .... | .... | .... | .... | .... | .... | .... |
| | **NHL Totals** | | **283** | **11** | **58** | **69** | **271** | **3** | **0** | **1** | **194** | **5.7** | | **3** | **66.7** | **18:53** | **5** | **1** | **0** | **1** | **2** | **0** | **0** | **0** | **16:06** |

OHL Second All-Star Team (2002, 2003) • Canadian Major Junior Second All-Star Team (2002) • Memorial Cup Tournament All-Star Team (2003)

Traded to **Philadelphia** by **Washington** with Washington's 3rd round choice (Jacob Deserres) in 2008 Entry Draft for Philadelphia's 1st round choice (John Carlson) in 2008 Entry Draft, June 20, 2008. Traded to **Tampa Bay** by **Philadelphia** with Steve Downie and Tampa Bay's 4th round choice (previously acquired, Tampa Bay selected Alex Hutchings) in 2009 Entry Draft for Matt Carle and San Jose's 3rd round choice (previously acquired, Philadelphia selected Simon Bertilsson) in 2009 Entry Draft, November 7, 2008. Traded to **Florida** by **Tampa Bay** for Noah Welch and Florida's 3rd round choice (later traded to Detroit – Detroit selected Andrej Nestrasil) in 2009 Entry Draft, March 4, 2009.

## ENSTROM, Tobias

(EHN-struhm, toh-BYE-uhs) **ATL.**

Defense. Shoots left. 5'10", 180 lbs. Born, Nordingra, Sweden, November 5, 1984. Atlanta's 8th choice, 239th overall, in 2003 Entry Draft.

| | | | Regular Season | | | | | | | | | | | | | | Playoffs | | | | | | | | |
|---|---|---|---|---|---|---|---|---|---|---|---|---|---|---|---|---|---|---|---|---|---|---|---|---|---|
| Season | Club | League | GP | G | A | Pts | PIM | PP | SH | GW | S | % | +/- | TF | F% | Min | GP | G | A | Pts | PIM | PP | SH | GW | Min |
| 99-2000 | MoDo U18 | Swe-U18 | 3 | 0 | 0 | 0 | 0 | .... | .... | .... | .... | .... | .... | .... | .... | .... | .... | .... | .... | .... | .... | .... | .... | .... | .... |
| 2000-01 | MoDo U18 | Swe-U18 | 16 | 7 | 6 | 13 | 18 | .... | .... | .... | .... | .... | .... | .... | .... | .... | .... | .... | .... | .... | .... | .... | .... | .... | .... |
| | MoDo Jr. | Swe-Jr. | 1 | 0 | 0 | 0 | 0 | .... | .... | .... | .... | .... | .... | .... | .... | .... | .... | .... | .... | .... | .... | .... | .... | .... | .... |
| 2001-02 | MODO Jr. | Swe-Jr. | 21 | 1 | 7 | 8 | 10 | .... | .... | .... | .... | .... | .... | .... | .... | .... | 2 | 1 | 1 | 2 | 2 | .... | .... | .... | .... |
| 2002-03 | MODO Jr. | Swe-Jr. | 7 | 4 | 6 | 10 | 31 | .... | .... | .... | .... | .... | .... | .... | .... | .... | .... | .... | .... | .... | .... | .... | .... | .... | .... |
| | MODO | Sweden | 42 | 1 | 5 | 6 | 16 | .... | .... | .... | .... | .... | .... | .... | .... | .... | 6 | 0 | 1 | 1 | 4 | .... | .... | .... | .... |
| 2003-04 | MODO | Sweden | 33 | 1 | 4 | 5 | 6 | .... | .... | .... | .... | .... | .... | .... | .... | .... | 6 | 1 | 1 | 2 | 2 | .... | .... | .... | .... |
| 2004-05 | MODO | Sweden | 49 | 4 | 10 | 14 | 24 | .... | .... | .... | .... | .... | .... | .... | .... | .... | 2 | 0 | 0 | 0 | 0 | .... | .... | .... | .... |
| 2005-06 | MODO | Sweden | 47 | 4 | 7 | 11 | 48 | .... | .... | .... | .... | .... | .... | .... | .... | .... | 4 | 0 | 1 | 1 | 25 | .... | .... | .... | .... |
| 2006-07 | MODO | Sweden | 55 | 7 | 21 | 28 | 52 | .... | .... | .... | .... | .... | .... | .... | .... | .... | 20 | 1 | 11 | 12 | 37 | .... | .... | .... | .... |
| **2007-08** | **Atlanta** | **NHL** | **82** | **5** | **33** | **38** | **42** | **4** | **0** | **0** | **105** | **4.8** | **–5** | **0** | **0.0** | **24:28** | .... | .... | .... | .... | .... | .... | .... | .... | .... |
| **2008-09** | **Atlanta** | **NHL** | **82** | **5** | **27** | **32** | **52** | **2** | **1** | **1** | **86** | **5.8** | **14** | **2** | **50.0** | **23:32** | .... | .... | .... | .... | .... | .... | .... | .... | .... |
| | **NHL Totals** | | **164** | **10** | **60** | **70** | **94** | **6** | **1** | **1** | **191** | **5.2** | | **2** | **50.0** | **24:00** | .... | .... | .... | .... | .... | .... | .... | .... | .... |

NHL All-Rookie Team (2008)

## ERAT, Martin

(EE-rat, MAHR-tihn) **NSH.**

Right wing. Shoots left. 6', 203 lbs. Born, Trebic, Czech., August 29, 1981. Nashville's 12th choice, 191st overall, in 1999 Entry Draft.

| | | | Regular Season | | | | | | | | | | | | | | Playoffs | | | | | | | | |
|---|---|---|---|---|---|---|---|---|---|---|---|---|---|---|---|---|---|---|---|---|---|---|---|---|---|
| Season | Club | League | GP | G | A | Pts | PIM | PP | SH | GW | S | % | +/- | TF | F% | Min | GP | G | A | Pts | PIM | PP | SH | GW | Min |
| 1997-98 | HC ZPS Zlin Jr. | CzRep-Jr. | 46 | 35 | 30 | 65 | .... | .... | .... | .... | .... | .... | .... | .... | .... | .... | .... | .... | .... | .... | .... | .... | .... | .... | .... |
| 1998-99 | HC ZPS Zlin Jr. | CzRep-Jr. | 35 | 21 | 23 | 44 | .... | .... | .... | .... | .... | .... | .... | .... | .... | .... | .... | .... | .... | .... | .... | .... | .... | .... | .... |
| | Zlin | CzRep | 5 | 0 | 0 | 0 | 2 | .... | .... | .... | .... | .... | .... | .... | .... | .... | .... | .... | .... | .... | .... | .... | .... | .... | .... |
| 99-2000 | Saskatoon Blades | WHL | 66 | 27 | 26 | 53 | 82 | .... | .... | .... | .... | .... | .... | .... | .... | .... | 11 | 4 | 8 | 12 | 16 | .... | .... | .... | .... |
| 2000-01 | Saskatoon Blades | WHL | 31 | 19 | 35 | 54 | 48 | .... | .... | .... | .... | .... | .... | .... | .... | .... | .... | .... | .... | .... | .... | .... | .... | .... | .... |
| | Red Deer Rebels | WHL | 17 | 4 | 24 | 28 | 24 | .... | .... | .... | .... | .... | .... | .... | .... | .... | 22 | *15 | *21 | *36 | 32 | .... | .... | .... | .... |
| **2001-02** | **Nashville** | **NHL** | **80** | **9** | **24** | **33** | **32** | **2** | **0** | **2** | **84** | **10.7** | **–11** | **3** | **66.7** | **13:10** | .... | .... | .... | .... | .... | .... | .... | .... | .... |
| **2002-03** | **Nashville** | **NHL** | **27** | **1** | **7** | **8** | **14** | **1** | **0** | **0** | **39** | **2.6** | **–9** | **1** | **0.0** | **12:47** | .... | .... | .... | .... | .... | .... | .... | .... | .... |
| | Milwaukee | AHL | 45 | 10 | 22 | 32 | 41 | .... | .... | .... | .... | .... | .... | .... | .... | .... | 6 | 5 | 4 | 9 | 4 | .... | .... | .... | .... |
| **2003-04** | **Nashville** | **NHL** | **76** | **16** | **33** | **49** | **38** | **4** | **0** | **2** | **137** | **11.7** | **10** | **31** | **29.0** | **15:00** | **6** | **0** | **1** | **1** | **6** | **0** | **0** | **0** | **14:09** |
| 2004-05 | HC Hame Zlin | CzRep | 48 | 20 | 23 | 43 | 129 | .... | .... | .... | .... | .... | .... | .... | .... | .... | 16 | *7 | 5 | 12 | 12 | .... | .... | .... | .... |
| **2005-06** | **Nashville** | **NHL** | **80** | **20** | **29** | **49** | **76** | **5** | **0** | **1** | **143** | **14.0** | **0** | **25** | **16.0** | **14:45** | **5** | **1** | **1** | **2** | **6** | **1** | **0** | **0** | **19:31** |
| | Czech Republic | Olympics | 8 | 1 | 1 | 2 | 4 | .... | .... | .... | .... | .... | .... | .... | .... | .... | .... | .... | .... | .... | .... | .... | .... | .... | .... |
| **2006-07** | **Nashville** | **NHL** | **68** | **16** | **41** | **57** | **50** | **5** | **1** | **3** | **132** | **12.1** | **13** | **43** | **44.2** | **18:59** | **3** | **0** | **1** | **1** | **0** | **0** | **0** | **0** | **14:13** |
| **2007-08** | **Nashville** | **NHL** | **76** | **23** | **34** | **57** | **40** | **4** | **0** | **6** | **163** | **14.1** | **–3** | **41** | **36.6** | **18:39** | **6** | **1** | **3** | **4** | **8** | **0** | **0** | **0** | **20:56** |
| **2008-09** | **Nashville** | **NHL** | **71** | **17** | **33** | **50** | **48** | **3** | **0** | **3** | **149** | **11.4** | **–7** | **38** | **29.0** | **18:34** | .... | .... | .... | .... | .... | .... | .... | .... | .... |
| | **NHL Totals** | | **478** | **102** | **201** | **303** | **298** | **24** | **1** | **17** | **847** | **12.0** | | **182** | **33.0** | **16:12** | **20** | **2** | **6** | **8** | **20** | **1** | **0** | **0** | **17:32** |

Signed as a free agent by **Zlin** (CzRep), September 5, 2004.

## ERICSSON, Jonathan

(AIR-ihk-suhn, JAWN-ah-thuhn) **DET.**

Defense. Shoots left. 6'4", 206 lbs. Born, Karlskrona, Sweden, March 2, 1984. Detroit's 10th choice, 291st overall, in 2002 Entry Draft.

| | | | Regular Season | | | | | | | | | | | | | | Playoffs | | | | | | | | |
|---|---|---|---|---|---|---|---|---|---|---|---|---|---|---|---|---|---|---|---|---|---|---|---|---|---|
| Season | Club | League | GP | G | A | Pts | PIM | PP | SH | GW | S | % | +/- | TF | F% | Min | GP | G | A | Pts | PIM | PP | SH | GW | Min |
| 2001-02 | Hasten Jr. | Swe-Jr. | STATISTICS NOT AVAILABLE | | | | | | | | | | | | | | | | | | | | | | |
| 2002-03 | Vita Hasten | Sweden-3 | 40 | 2 | 4 | 6 | 36 | .... | .... | .... | .... | .... | .... | .... | .... | .... | .... | .... | .... | .... | .... | .... | .... | .... | .... |
| 2003-04 | Sodertalje SK | Sweden | 42 | 1 | 0 | 1 | 12 | .... | .... | .... | .... | .... | .... | .... | .... | .... | .... | .... | .... | .... | .... | .... | .... | .... | .... |
| 2004-05 | Sodertalje SK | Sweden | 15 | 0 | 0 | 0 | 4 | .... | .... | .... | .... | .... | .... | .... | .... | .... | 1 | 0 | 0 | 0 | 0 | .... | .... | .... | .... |
| 2005-06 | Sodertalje SK Jr. | Swe-Jr. | 1 | 0 | 0 | 0 | 2 | .... | .... | .... | .... | .... | .... | .... | .... | .... | .... | .... | .... | .... | .... | .... | .... | .... | .... |
| | Almtuna | Sweden-2 | 19 | 2 | 3 | 5 | 44 | .... | .... | .... | .... | .... | .... | .... | .... | .... | .... | .... | .... | .... | .... | .... | .... | .... | .... |
| | Sodertalje SK | Sweden | 24 | 0 | 0 | 0 | 20 | .... | .... | .... | .... | .... | .... | .... | .... | .... | .... | .... | .... | .... | .... | .... | .... | .... | .... |
| | Sodertalje SK | Sweden-Q | 7 | 0 | 1 | 1 | 4 | .... | .... | .... | .... | .... | .... | .... | .... | .... | .... | .... | .... | .... | .... | .... | .... | .... | .... |
| 2006-07 | Grand Rapids | AHL | 67 | 5 | 24 | 29 | 102 | .... | .... | .... | .... | .... | .... | .... | .... | .... | 7 | 0 | 0 | 0 | 8 | .... | .... | .... | .... |
| **2007-08** | **Detroit** | **NHL** | **8** | **1** | **0** | **1** | **4** | **1** | **0** | **0** | **19** | **5.3** | **–3** | **0** | **0.0** | **15:58** | .... | .... | .... | .... | .... | .... | .... | .... | .... |
| | Grand Rapids | AHL | 69 | 10 | 24 | 34 | 83 | .... | .... | .... | .... | .... | .... | .... | .... | .... | .... | .... | .... | .... | .... | .... | .... | .... | .... |
| **2008-09** | **Detroit** | **NHL** | **19** | **1** | **3** | **4** | **15** | **0** | **0** | **0** | **25** | **4.0** | **–1** | **0** | **0.0** | **17:40** | **22** | **4** | **4** | **8** | **25** | **0** | **0** | **1** | **18:44** |
| | Grand Rapids | AHL | 40 | 2 | 13 | 15 | 48 | .... | .... | .... | .... | .... | .... | .... | .... | .... | .... | .... | .... | .... | .... | .... | .... | .... | .... |
| | **NHL Totals** | | **27** | **2** | **3** | **5** | **19** | **1** | **0** | **0** | **44** | **4.5** | | **0** | **0.0** | **17:10** | **22** | **4** | **4** | **8** | **25** | **0** | **0** | **1** | **18:44** |

## ERIKSSON, Anders

(AIR-ihk-suhn, AND-uhrs)

Defense. Shoots left. 6'3", 224 lbs. Born, Bollnas, Sweden, January 9, 1975. Detroit's 1st choice, 22nd overall, in 1993 Entry Draft.

| Season | Club | League | GP | G | A | Pts | PIM | PP | SH | GW | S | % | +/- | TF | F% | Min | GP | G | A | Pts | PIM | PP | SH | GW | Min |
|---|---|---|---|---|---|---|---|---|---|---|---|---|---|---|---|---|---|---|---|---|---|---|---|---|---|
| | | | Regular Season | | | | | | | | | | | | | | Playoffs | | | | | | | | |
| 1992-93 | MoDo Jr. | Swe-Jr. | 10 | 5 | 3 | 8 | 14 | .... | .... | .... | .... | .... | .... | .... | .... | .... | .... | .... | .... | .... | .... | .... | .... | .... | .... |
| | MoDo | Sweden | 20 | 0 | 2 | 2 | 2 | .... | .... | .... | .... | .... | .... | .... | .... | .... | 1 | 0 | 0 | 0 | 0 | .... | .... | .... | .... |
| 1993-94 | MoDo | Sweden | 38 | 2 | 8 | 10 | 42 | .... | .... | .... | .... | .... | .... | .... | .... | .... | 11 | 0 | 0 | 0 | 8 | .... | .... | .... | .... |
| | MoDo Jr. | Swe-Jr. | 3 | 1 | 2 | 3 | 34 | .... | .... | .... | .... | .... | .... | .... | .... | .... | .... | .... | .... | .... | .... | .... | .... | .... | .... |
| 1994-95 | MoDo | Sweden | 39 | 3 | 6 | 9 | 54 | .... | .... | .... | .... | .... | .... | .... | .... | .... | .... | .... | .... | .... | .... | .... | .... | .... | .... |
| **1995-96** | **Detroit** | **NHL** | **1** | **0** | **0** | **0** | **2** | **0** | **0** | **0** | **0** | **0.0** | **1** | .... | .... | .... | **3** | **0** | **0** | **0** | **0** | **0** | **0** | **0** | .... |
| | Adirondack | AHL | 75 | 6 | 36 | 42 | 64 | .... | .... | .... | .... | .... | .... | .... | .... | .... | 3 | 0 | 0 | 0 | 0 | .... | .... | .... | .... |
| **1996-97** | **Detroit** | **NHL** | **23** | **0** | **6** | **6** | **10** | **0** | **0** | **0** | **27** | **0.0** | **5** | .... | .... | .... | .... | .... | .... | .... | .... | .... | .... | .... | .... |
| | Adirondack | AHL | 44 | 3 | 25 | 28 | 36 | .... | .... | .... | .... | .... | .... | .... | .... | .... | 4 | 0 | 1 | 1 | 4 | .... | .... | .... | .... |
| **1997-98**♦ | **Detroit** | **NHL** | **66** | **7** | **14** | **21** | **32** | **1** | **0** | **2** | **91** | **7.7** | **21** | .... | .... | .... | **18** | **0** | **5** | **5** | **16** | **0** | **0** | **0** | .... |
| **1998-99** | **Detroit** | **NHL** | **61** | **2** | **10** | **12** | **34** | **0** | **0** | **1** | **67** | **3.0** | **5** | **0** | **0.0** | **15:54** | .... | .... | .... | .... | .... | .... | .... | .... | .... |
| | **Chicago** | **NHL** | **11** | **0** | **8** | **8** | **0** | **0** | **0** | **0** | **12** | **0.0** | **6** | **0** | **0.0** | **22:51** | .... | .... | .... | .... | .... | .... | .... | .... | .... |
| **99-2000** | **Chicago** | **NHL** | **73** | **3** | **25** | **28** | **20** | **0** | **0** | **1** | **86** | **3.5** | **4** | **1** | **100.0** | **21:03** | .... | .... | .... | .... | .... | .... | .... | .... | .... |
| **2000-01** | **Chicago** | **NHL** | **13** | **2** | **3** | **5** | **2** | **1** | **0** | **0** | **19** | **10.5** | **-4** | **0** | **0.0** | **21:20** | .... | .... | .... | .... | .... | .... | .... | .... | .... |
| | **Florida** | **NHL** | **60** | **0** | **21** | **21** | **28** | **0** | **0** | **0** | **80** | **0.0** | **2** | **1** | **0.0** | **21:02** | .... | .... | .... | .... | .... | .... | .... | .... | .... |
| **2001-02** | **Toronto** | **NHL** | **34** | **0** | **2** | **2** | **12** | **0** | **0** | **0** | **31** | **0.0** | **-1** | **0** | **0.0** | **15:55** | **10** | **0** | **0** | **0** | **0** | **0** | **0** | **0** | **17:24** |
| | St. John's | AHL | 25 | 4 | 6 | 10 | 14 | .... | .... | .... | .... | .... | .... | .... | .... | .... | 11 | 0 | 5 | 5 | 6 | .... | .... | .... | .... |
| **2002-03** | **Toronto** | **NHL** | **4** | **0** | **0** | **0** | **0** | **0** | **0** | **0** | **7** | **0.0** | **1** | **0** | **0.0** | **19:02** | .... | .... | .... | .... | .... | .... | .... | .... | .... |
| | St. John's | AHL | 72 | 5 | 34 | 39 | 133 | .... | .... | .... | .... | .... | .... | .... | .... | .... | .... | .... | .... | .... | .... | .... | .... | .... | .... |
| **2003-04** | **Columbus** | **NHL** | **66** | **7** | **20** | **27** | **18** | **2** | **0** | **1** | **84** | **8.3** | **-6** | **0** | **0.0** | **20:42** | .... | .... | .... | .... | .... | .... | .... | .... | .... |
| | Syracuse Crunch | AHL | 9 | 1 | 3 | 4 | 12 | .... | .... | .... | .... | .... | .... | .... | .... | .... | .... | .... | .... | .... | .... | .... | .... | .... | .... |
| 2004-05 | HV 71 Jonkoping | Sweden | 32 | 1 | 9 | 10 | 54 | .... | .... | .... | .... | .... | .... | .... | .... | .... | .... | .... | .... | .... | .... | .... | .... | .... | .... |
| 2005-06 | Magnitogorsk | Russia | 17 | 2 | 7 | 9 | 10 | .... | .... | .... | .... | .... | .... | .... | .... | .... | 11 | 3 | 2 | 5 | 16 | .... | .... | .... | .... |
| | Springfield | AHL | 12 | 1 | 8 | 9 | 10 | .... | .... | .... | .... | .... | .... | .... | .... | .... | .... | .... | .... | .... | .... | .... | .... | .... | .... |
| **2006-07** | **Columbus** | **NHL** | **79** | **0** | **23** | **23** | **46** | **0** | **0** | **0** | **78** | **0.0** | **12** | **1** | **100.0** | **20:12** | .... | .... | .... | .... | .... | .... | .... | .... | .... |
| **2007-08** | **Calgary** | **NHL** | **61** | **1** | **17** | **18** | **36** | **1** | **0** | **0** | **50** | **2.0** | **-5** | **0** | **0.0** | **20:47** | **3** | **0** | **1** | **1** | **2** | **0** | **0** | **0** | **18:16** |
| **2008-09** | Quad City Flames | AHL | 64 | 4 | 45 | 49 | 60 | .... | .... | .... | .... | .... | .... | .... | .... | .... | .... | .... | .... | .... | .... | .... | .... | .... | .... |
| | **Calgary** | **NHL** | .... | .... | .... | .... | .... | .... | .... | .... | .... | .... | .... | .... | .... | .... | **2** | **0** | **0** | **0** | **0** | **0** | **0** | **0** | **18:42** |
| | **NHL Totals** | | **552** | **22** | **149** | **171** | **240** | **5** | **0** | **5** | **632** | **3.5** | | **3** | **66.7** | **19:48** | **36** | **0** | **6** | **6** | **18** | **0** | **0** | **0** | **17:45** |

Traded to **Chicago** by **Detroit** with Detroit's 1st round choices in 1999 (Steve McCarthy) and 2001 (Adam Munro) Entry Drafts for Chris Chelios, March 23, 1999. Traded to **Florida** by **Chicago** for Jaroslav Spacek, November 6, 2000. Signed as a free agent by **Toronto**, July 4, 2001. Signed as a free agent by **Columbus**, October 10, 2003. Signed as a free agent by **Calgary**, September 16, 2004. Signed as a free agent by **Jonkoping** (Sweden), October 29, 2004. Signed as a fee agent by **Columbus**, July 1, 2006. Signed as a free agent by **Calgary**, July 5, 2007.

## ERIKSSON, Loui

(AIR-ihk-suhn, LOO-ee) **DAL.**

Left wing. Shoots left. 6'1", 183 lbs. Born, Goteborg, Sweden, July 17, 1985. Dallas' 1st choice, 33rd overall, in 2003 Entry Draft.

| Season | Club | League | GP | G | A | Pts | PIM | PP | SH | GW | S | % | +/- | TF | F% | Min | GP | G | A | Pts | PIM | PP | SH | GW | Min |
|---|---|---|---|---|---|---|---|---|---|---|---|---|---|---|---|---|---|---|---|---|---|---|---|---|---|
| 2000-01 | V.Frolunda U18 | Swe-U18 | 9 | 5 | 3 | 8 | 4 | .... | .... | .... | .... | .... | .... | .... | .... | .... | .... | .... | .... | .... | .... | .... | .... | .... | .... |
| | V.Frolunda Jr. | Swe-Jr. | 1 | 0 | 0 | 0 | 0 | .... | .... | .... | .... | .... | .... | .... | .... | .... | .... | .... | .... | .... | .... | .... | .... | .... | .... |
| 2001-02 | V.Frolunda U18 | Swe-U18 | 1 | 1 | 0 | 1 | 0 | .... | .... | .... | .... | .... | .... | .... | .... | .... | .... | .... | .... | .... | .... | .... | .... | .... | .... |
| | V.Frolunda Jr. | Swe-Jr. | 35 | 7 | 15 | 22 | 2 | .... | .... | .... | .... | .... | .... | .... | .... | .... | 8 | 2 | 3 | 5 | 2 | .... | .... | .... | .... |
| 2002-03 | V.Frolunda Jr. | Swe-Jr. | 30 | 16 | 15 | 31 | 10 | .... | .... | .... | .... | .... | .... | .... | .... | .... | 8 | 4 | 6 | 10 | 4 | .... | .... | .... | .... |
| 2003-04 | V.Frolunda | Sweden | 46 | 8 | 5 | 13 | 4 | .... | .... | .... | .... | .... | .... | .... | .... | .... | 10 | 1 | 5 | 6 | 0 | .... | .... | .... | .... |
| 2004-05 | Frolunda | Sweden | 39 | 5 | 9 | 14 | 4 | .... | .... | .... | .... | .... | .... | .... | .... | .... | 12 | 0 | 0 | 0 | 0 | .... | .... | .... | .... |
| 2005-06 | Iowa Stars | AHL | 78 | 31 | 29 | 60 | 27 | .... | .... | .... | .... | .... | .... | .... | .... | .... | 7 | 2 | 5 | 7 | 0 | .... | .... | .... | .... |
| **2006-07** | **Dallas** | **NHL** | **59** | **6** | **13** | **19** | **18** | **2** | **0** | **0** | **78** | **7.7** | **-3** | **9** | **44.4** | **13:11** | **4** | **0** | **1** | **1** | **0** | **0** | **0** | **0** | **15:47** |
| | Iowa Stars | AHL | 15 | 5 | 3 | 8 | 13 | .... | .... | .... | .... | .... | .... | .... | .... | .... | 9 | 2 | 5 | 7 | 0 | .... | .... | .... | .... |
| **2007-08** | **Dallas** | **NHL** | **69** | **14** | **17** | **31** | **28** | **4** | **0** | **0** | **120** | **11.7** | **5** | **13** | **15.4** | **14:02** | **18** | **4** | **4** | **8** | **8** | **1** | **0** | **0** | **18:12** |
| | Iowa Stars | AHL | 2 | 1 | 2 | 3 | 2 | .... | .... | .... | .... | .... | .... | .... | .... | .... | .... | .... | .... | .... | .... | .... | .... | .... | .... |
| **2008-09** | **Dallas** | **NHL** | **82** | **36** | **27** | **63** | **14** | **7** | **1** | **4** | **178** | **20.2** | **14** | **11** | **18.2** | **19:50** | .... | .... | .... | .... | .... | .... | .... | .... | .... |
| | **NHL Totals** | | **210** | **56** | **57** | **113** | **60** | **13** | **1** | **4** | **376** | **14.9** | | **33** | **24.2** | **16:03** | **22** | **4** | **5** | **9** | **8** | **1** | **0** | **0** | **17:46** |

## ERSKINE, John

(AIR-skign, JAWN) **WSH.**

Defense. Shoots left. 6'4", 216 lbs. Born, Kingston, Ont., June 26, 1980. Dallas' 1st choice, 39th overall, in 1998 Entry Draft.

| Season | Club | League | GP | G | A | Pts | PIM | PP | SH | GW | S | % | +/- | TF | F% | Min | GP | G | A | Pts | PIM | PP | SH | GW | Min |
|---|---|---|---|---|---|---|---|---|---|---|---|---|---|---|---|---|---|---|---|---|---|---|---|---|---|
| 1996-97 | Quinte Hawks | MTJHL | 48 | 4 | 16 | 20 | 241 | .... | .... | .... | .... | .... | .... | .... | .... | .... | .... | .... | .... | .... | .... | .... | .... | .... | .... |
| 1997-98 | London Knights | OHL | 55 | 0 | 9 | 9 | 205 | .... | .... | .... | .... | .... | .... | .... | .... | .... | 16 | 0 | 5 | 5 | 25 | .... | .... | .... | .... |
| 1998-99 | London Knights | OHL | 57 | 8 | 12 | 20 | 208 | .... | .... | .... | .... | .... | .... | .... | .... | .... | 25 | 5 | 10 | 15 | 38 | .... | .... | .... | .... |
| 99-2000 | London Knights | OHL | 58 | 12 | 31 | 43 | 177 | .... | .... | .... | .... | .... | .... | .... | .... | .... | .... | .... | .... | .... | .... | .... | .... | .... | .... |
| 2000-01 | Utah Grizzlies | IHL | 77 | 1 | 8 | 9 | 284 | .... | .... | .... | .... | .... | .... | .... | .... | .... | .... | .... | .... | .... | .... | .... | .... | .... | .... |
| **2001-02** | **Dallas** | **NHL** | **33** | **0** | **1** | **1** | **62** | **0** | **0** | **0** | **16** | **0.0** | **-8** | **0** | **0.0** | **10:44** | .... | .... | .... | .... | .... | .... | .... | .... | .... |
| | Utah Grizzlies | AHL | 39 | 2 | 6 | 8 | 118 | .... | .... | .... | .... | .... | .... | .... | .... | .... | 3 | 0 | 0 | 0 | 10 | .... | .... | .... | .... |
| **2002-03** | **Dallas** | **NHL** | **16** | **2** | **0** | **2** | **29** | **0** | **0** | **0** | **12** | **16.7** | **1** | **0** | **0.0** | **10:45** | .... | .... | .... | .... | .... | .... | .... | .... | .... |
| | Utah Grizzlies | AHL | 52 | 2 | 8 | 10 | 274 | .... | .... | .... | .... | .... | .... | .... | .... | .... | 1 | 0 | 1 | 1 | 15 | .... | .... | .... | .... |
| **2003-04** | **Dallas** | **NHL** | **32** | **0** | **1** | **1** | **84** | **0** | **0** | **0** | **23** | **0.0** | **-9** | **0** | **0.0** | **12:36** | .... | .... | .... | .... | .... | .... | .... | .... | .... |
| | Utah Grizzlies | AHL | 5 | 0 | 0 | 0 | 18 | .... | .... | .... | .... | .... | .... | .... | .... | .... | .... | .... | .... | .... | .... | .... | .... | .... | .... |
| 2004-05 | Houston Aeros | AHL | 61 | 3 | 7 | 10 | 238 | .... | .... | .... | .... | .... | .... | .... | .... | .... | 5 | 0 | 1 | 1 | 20 | .... | .... | .... | .... |
| **2005-06** | **Dallas** | **NHL** | **26** | **0** | **0** | **0** | **62** | **0** | **0** | **0** | **9** | **0.0** | **-3** | **0** | **0.0** | **11:00** | .... | .... | .... | .... | .... | .... | .... | .... | .... |
| | **NY Islanders** | **NHL** | **34** | **1** | **0** | **1** | **99** | **0** | **0** | **0** | **23** | **4.3** | **-12** | **0** | **0.0** | **14:37** | .... | .... | .... | .... | .... | .... | .... | .... | .... |
| **2006-07** | **Washington** | **NHL** | **29** | **1** | **6** | **7** | **69** | **0** | **0** | **0** | **14** | **7.1** | **-13** | **0** | **0.0** | **18:03** | .... | .... | .... | .... | .... | .... | .... | .... | .... |
| | Hershey Bears | AHL | 4 | 0 | 2 | 2 | 9 | .... | .... | .... | .... | .... | .... | .... | .... | .... | .... | .... | .... | .... | .... | .... | .... | .... | .... |
| **2007-08** | **Washington** | **NHL** | **51** | **2** | **7** | **9** | **96** | **0** | **0** | **1** | **48** | **4.2** | **1** | **0** | **0.0** | **15:43** | **7** | **0** | **2** | **2** | **6** | **0** | **0** | **0** | **17:07** |
| **2008-09** | **Washington** | **NHL** | **52** | **0** | **4** | **4** | **63** | **0** | **0** | **0** | **50** | **0.0** | **1** | **0** | **0.0** | **16:48** | **12** | **0** | **1** | **1** | **16** | **0** | **0** | **0** | **19:06** |
| | **NHL Totals** | | **273** | **6** | **19** | **25** | **564** | **0** | **0** | **1** | **195** | **3.1** | | **0** | **0.0** | **14:19** | **19** | **0** | **3** | **3** | **22** | **0** | **0** | **0** | **18:22** |

OHL First All-Star Team (2000)

• Missed majority of 2003-04 season recovering from ankle (December 27, 2003 vs. Columbus) and hernia (January 24, 2004 vs. St. Louis) injuries. Traded to **NY Islanders** by **Dallas** with Dallas' 2nd round choice (Jesse Joensuu) in 2006 Entry Draft for Janne Niinimaa and NY Islanders' 5th round choice (Ondrej Roman) in 2007 Entry Draft, January 10, 2005. Signed as a free agent by **Washington**, September 14, 2006. • Missed majority of 2006-07 season recovering from foot (December 16, 2006 vs. Philadelphia) and thumb (March 9, 2007 vs. Carolina) injuries.

## EVANS, Brennan

(EH-vans, BREH-nuhn) **ANA.**

Defense. Shoots left. 6'3", 220 lbs. Born, North Battleford, Sask., January 6, 1982.

| Season | Club | League | GP | G | A | Pts | PIM | PP | SH | GW | S | % | +/- | TF | F% | Min | GP | G | A | Pts | PIM | PP | SH | GW | Min |
|---|---|---|---|---|---|---|---|---|---|---|---|---|---|---|---|---|---|---|---|---|---|---|---|---|---|
| 1998-99 | Camrose Kodiaks | AJHL | 47 | 1 | 6 | 7 | 98 | .... | .... | .... | .... | .... | .... | .... | .... | .... | 5 | 0 | 2 | 2 | 0 | .... | .... | .... | .... |
| | Seattle | WHL | .... | .... | .... | .... | .... | .... | .... | .... | .... | .... | .... | .... | .... | .... | 1 | 0 | 0 | 0 | 0 | .... | .... | .... | .... |
| 99-2000 | Seattle | WHL | 52 | 1 | 2 | 3 | 40 | .... | .... | .... | .... | .... | .... | .... | .... | .... | 1 | 0 | 0 | 0 | 0 | .... | .... | .... | .... |
| 2000-01 | Seattle | WHL | 11 | 1 | 0 | 1 | 25 | .... | .... | .... | .... | .... | .... | .... | .... | .... | .... | .... | .... | .... | .... | .... | .... | .... | .... |
| | Kootenay Ice | WHL | 55 | 2 | 7 | 9 | 105 | .... | .... | .... | .... | .... | .... | .... | .... | .... | 11 | 0 | 0 | 0 | 25 | .... | .... | .... | .... |
| 2001-02 | Kootenay Ice | WHL | 72 | 2 | 3 | 5 | 121 | .... | .... | .... | .... | .... | .... | .... | .... | .... | 22 | 0 | 6 | 6 | 38 | .... | .... | .... | .... |
| 2002-03 | Kootenay Ice | WHL | 67 | 6 | 17 | 23 | 182 | .... | .... | .... | .... | .... | .... | .... | .... | .... | 11 | 1 | 1 | 2 | 24 | .... | .... | .... | .... |
| **2003-04** | Lowell | AHL | 64 | 1 | 9 | 10 | 65 | .... | .... | .... | .... | .... | .... | .... | .... | .... | .... | .... | .... | .... | .... | .... | .... | .... | .... |
| | **Calgary** | **NHL** | .... | .... | .... | .... | .... | .... | .... | .... | .... | .... | .... | .... | .... | .... | **2** | **0** | **0** | **0** | **0** | **0** | **0** | **0** | **2:52** |
| 2004-05 | Lowell | AHL | 51 | 0 | 7 | 7 | 79 | .... | .... | .... | .... | .... | .... | .... | .... | .... | 5 | 0 | 0 | 0 | 2 | .... | .... | .... | .... |
| 2005-06 | Binghamton | AHL | 70 | 3 | 6 | 9 | 198 | .... | .... | .... | .... | .... | .... | .... | .... | .... | .... | .... | .... | .... | .... | .... | .... | .... | .... |
| 2006-07 | Worcester Sharks | AHL | 75 | 2 | 14 | 16 | 170 | .... | .... | .... | .... | .... | .... | .... | .... | .... | 5 | 0 | 1 | 1 | 21 | .... | .... | .... | .... |
| 2007-08 | Worcester Sharks | AHL | 80 | 1 | 13 | 14 | 211 | .... | .... | .... | .... | .... | .... | .... | .... | .... | .... | .... | .... | .... | .... | .... | .... | .... | .... |
| 2008-09 | Iowa Chops | AHL | 75 | 1 | 14 | 15 | 189 | .... | .... | .... | .... | .... | .... | .... | .... | .... | .... | .... | .... | .... | .... | .... | .... | .... | .... |
| | **NHL Totals** | | .... | .... | .... | .... | .... | .... | .... | .... | .... | .... | .... | .... | .... | .... | **2** | **0** | **0** | **0** | **0** | **0** | **0** | **0** | **2:52** |

Signed as a free agent by **Calgary**, September 30, 2003. Signed as a free agent by **San Jose**, July 18, 2007. Signed as a free agent by **Anaheim**, July 11, 2008.

## EXELBY, Garnet

(EHX-uhl-bee, GAHR-neht) **TOR.**

Defense. Shoots left. 6'1", 215 lbs. Born, Ste. Anne, Man., August 16, 1981. Atlanta's 9th choice, 217th overall, in 1999 Entry Draft.

| Season | Club | League | GP | G | A | Pts | PIM | PP | SH | GW | S | % | +/- | TF | F% | Min | GP | G | A | Pts | PIM | PP | SH | GW | Min |
|---|---|---|---|---|---|---|---|---|---|---|---|---|---|---|---|---|---|---|---|---|---|---|---|---|---|
| 1997-98 | Winnipeg South | MJHL | 46 | 5 | 11 | 16 | 110 | .... | .... | .... | .... | .... | .... | .... | .... | .... | .... | .... | .... | .... | .... | .... | .... | .... | .... |
| 1998-99 | Saskatoon Blades | WHL | 61 | 5 | 3 | 8 | 91 | .... | .... | .... | .... | .... | .... | .... | .... | .... | .... | .... | .... | .... | .... | .... | .... | .... | .... |
| 99-2000 | Saskatoon Blades | WHL | 63 | 1 | 8 | 9 | 79 | .... | .... | .... | .... | .... | .... | .... | .... | .... | 11 | 0 | 2 | 2 | 21 | .... | .... | .... | .... |
| 2000-01 | Saskatoon Blades | WHL | 43 | 5 | 10 | 15 | 110 | .... | .... | .... | .... | .... | .... | .... | .... | .... | .... | .... | .... | .... | .... | .... | .... | .... | .... |
| | Regina Pats | WHL | 22 | 2 | 8 | 10 | 51 | .... | .... | .... | .... | .... | .... | .... | .... | .... | 6 | 0 | 2 | 2 | 2 | .... | .... | .... | .... |
| 2001-02 | Chicago Wolves | AHL | 75 | 3 | 4 | 7 | 257 | .... | .... | .... | .... | .... | .... | .... | .... | .... | 25 | 0 | 4 | 4 | 49 | .... | .... | .... | .... |

| | | | Regular Season | | | | | | | | | | | | | | Playoffs | | | | | | | | |
|---|---|---|---|---|---|---|---|---|---|---|---|---|---|---|---|---|---|---|---|---|---|---|---|---|---|
| Season | Club | League | GP | G | A | Pts | PIM | PP | SH | GW | S | % | +/- | TF | F% | Min | GP | G | A | Pts | PIM | PP | SH | GW | Min |
| **2002-03** | **Atlanta** | **NHL** | **15** | **0** | **2** | **2** | **41** | **0** | **0** | **0** | **9** | **0.0** | **0** | **0** | **0.0** | **18:04** | .... | .... | .... | .... | .... | .... | .... | .... | .... |
| | Chicago Wolves | AHL | 53 | 3 | 6 | 9 | 140 | .... | .... | .... | .... | .... | .... | .... | .... | .... | 9 | 0 | 1 | 1 | 27 | .... | .... | .... | .... |
| **2003-04** | **Atlanta** | **NHL** | **71** | **1** | **9** | **10** | **134** | **0** | **0** | **0** | **42** | **2.4** | **–10** | **0** | **0.0** | **19:32** | .... | .... | .... | .... | .... | .... | .... | .... | .... |
| 2004-05 | | | DID NOT PLAY | | | | | | | | | | | | | | | | | | | | | | |
| **2005-06** | **Atlanta** | **NHL** | **75** | **1** | **9** | **10** | **75** | **0** | **0** | **0** | **44** | **2.3** | **11** | **0** | **0.0** | **15:41** | .... | .... | .... | .... | .... | .... | .... | .... | .... |
| **2006-07** | **Atlanta** | **NHL** | **58** | **2** | **8** | **10** | **56** | **0** | **1** | **0** | **57** | **3.5** | **2** | **0** | **0.0** | **18:00** | **4** | **0** | **0** | **0** | **6** | **0** | **0** | **0** | **15:38** |
| **2007-08** | **Atlanta** | **NHL** | **79** | **2** | **5** | **7** | **85** | **0** | **0** | **0** | **37** | **5.4** | **–21** | **0** | **0.0** | **18:53** | .... | .... | .... | .... | .... | .... | .... | .... | .... |
| **2008-09** | **Atlanta** | **NHL** | **59** | **0** | **7** | **7** | **120** | **0** | **0** | **0** | **42** | **0.0** | **–2** | **0** | **0.0** | **16:43** | .... | .... | .... | .... | .... | .... | .... | .... | .... |
| | **NHL Totals** | | **357** | **6** | **40** | **46** | **511** | **0** | **1** | **0** | **231** | **2.6** | | **0** | **0.0** | **17:48** | **4** | **0** | **0** | **0** | **6** | **0** | **0** | **0** | **15:38** |

Traded to **Toronto** by **Atlanta** with Colin Stuart for Pavel Kubina and Tim Stapleton, July 1, 2009.

## FAHEY, Jim

(FA-hee, JIHM)

Defense. Shoots right. 6', 205 lbs. Born, Boston, MA, May 11, 1979. San Jose's 9th choice, 212th overall, in 1998 Entry Draft.

| | | | | | | | | | | | | | | | | | | | | | | | | | |
|---|---|---|---|---|---|---|---|---|---|---|---|---|---|---|---|---|---|---|---|---|---|---|---|---|---|
| 1997-98 | Catholic Memorial | High-MA | 24 | 12 | 32 | 44 | 28 | .... | .... | .... | .... | .... | .... | .... | .... | .... | .... | .... | .... | .... | .... | .... | .... | .... | .... |
| 1998-99 | Northeastern | H-East | 32 | 5 | 13 | 18 | 34 | .... | .... | .... | .... | .... | .... | .... | .... | .... | .... | .... | .... | .... | .... | .... | .... | .... | .... |
| 99-2000 | Northeastern | H-East | 36 | 3 | 17 | 20 | 62 | .... | .... | .... | .... | .... | .... | .... | .... | .... | .... | .... | .... | .... | .... | .... | .... | .... | .... |
| 2000-01 | Northeastern | H-East | 36 | 4 | 23 | 27 | 48 | .... | .... | .... | .... | .... | .... | .... | .... | .... | .... | .... | .... | .... | .... | .... | .... | .... | .... |
| 2001-02 | Northeastern | H-East | 39 | 14 | 32 | 46 | 50 | .... | .... | .... | .... | .... | .... | .... | .... | .... | .... | .... | .... | .... | .... | .... | .... | .... | .... |
| **2002-03** | **San Jose** | **NHL** | **43** | **1** | **19** | **20** | **33** | **0** | **0** | **0** | **66** | **1.5** | **–3** | **1** | **100.0** | **18:20** | .... | .... | .... | .... | .... | .... | .... | .... | .... |
| | Cleveland Barons | AHL | 25 | 3 | 14 | 17 | 42 | .... | .... | .... | .... | .... | .... | .... | .... | .... | .... | .... | .... | .... | .... | .... | .... | .... | .... |
| **2003-04** | **San Jose** | **NHL** | **15** | **0** | **2** | **2** | **18** | **0** | **0** | **0** | **19** | **0.0** | **–2** | **0** | **0.0** | **16:54** | **2** | **0** | **0** | **0** | **0** | **0** | **0** | **0** | **4:41** |
| | Cleveland Barons | AHL | 32 | 1 | 18 | 19 | 64 | .... | .... | .... | .... | .... | .... | .... | .... | .... | .... | .... | .... | .... | .... | .... | .... | .... | .... |
| 2004-05 | Cleveland Barons | AHL | 69 | 4 | 22 | 26 | 146 | .... | .... | .... | .... | .... | .... | .... | .... | .... | .... | .... | .... | .... | .... | .... | .... | .... | .... |
| **2005-06** | **San Jose** | **NHL** | **21** | **0** | **2** | **2** | **14** | **0** | **0** | **0** | **22** | **0.0** | **–11** | **0** | **0.0** | **12:39** | .... | .... | .... | .... | .... | .... | .... | .... | .... |
| **2006-07** | **New Jersey** | **NHL** | **13** | **0** | **1** | **1** | **2** | **0** | **0** | **0** | **7** | **0.0** | **0** | **0** | **0.0** | **10:47** | .... | .... | .... | .... | .... | .... | .... | .... | .... |
| | Lowell Devils | AHL | 28 | 0 | 9 | 9 | 37 | .... | .... | .... | .... | .... | .... | .... | .... | .... | .... | .... | .... | .... | .... | .... | .... | .... | .... |
| 2007-08 | Rockford IceHogs | AHL | 65 | 0 | 12 | 12 | 109 | .... | .... | .... | .... | .... | .... | .... | .... | .... | 12 | 1 | 3 | 4 | 18 | .... | .... | .... | .... |
| 2008-09 | Krefeld Pinguine | Germany | 47 | 5 | 16 | 21 | 83 | .... | .... | .... | .... | .... | .... | .... | .... | .... | 7 | 1 | 1 | 2 | 6 | .... | .... | .... | .... |
| | **NHL Totals** | | **92** | **1** | **24** | **25** | **67** | **0** | **0** | **0** | **114** | **0.9** | | **1** | **100.0** | **15:44** | **2** | **0** | **0** | **0** | **0** | **0** | **0** | **0** | **4:41** |

Hockey East Second All-Star Team (2001) • Hockey East First All-Star Team (2002)

• Spent majority of the 2005-06 season serving as a healthy reserve. Traded to **New Jersey** by **San Jose** with Alexander Korolyuk for Vladimir Malakhov and New Jersey's 1st round choice (later traded to St. Louis - St. Louis selected David Perron) in 2007 Entry Draft, October 1, 2006. Signed as a free agent by **Chicago**, July 27, 2007.

## FATA, Drew

(FA-tuh, DROO) **BOS.**

Defense. Shoots left. 6'1", 220 lbs. Born, Sault Ste. Marie, Ont., July 28, 1983. Pittsburgh's 3rd choice, 86th overall, in 2001 Entry Draft.

| | | | | | | | | | | | | | | | | | | | | | | | | | |
|---|---|---|---|---|---|---|---|---|---|---|---|---|---|---|---|---|---|---|---|---|---|---|---|---|---|
| 1998-99 | S.S. Marie AA | NOHA | 46 | 4 | 16 | 20 | 55 | .... | .... | .... | .... | .... | .... | .... | .... | .... | .... | .... | .... | .... | .... | .... | .... | .... | .... |
| 99-2000 | St. Mike's B's | OPJHL | 49 | 9 | 18 | 27 | 144 | .... | .... | .... | .... | .... | .... | .... | .... | .... | .... | .... | .... | .... | .... | .... | .... | .... | .... |
| 2000-01 | St. Michael's | OHL | 58 | 5 | 15 | 20 | 134 | .... | .... | .... | .... | .... | .... | .... | .... | .... | 18 | 1 | 3 | 4 | 26 | .... | .... | .... | .... |
| 2001-02 | St. Michael's | OHL | 67 | 7 | 21 | 28 | 175 | .... | .... | .... | .... | .... | .... | .... | .... | .... | 15 | 1 | 9 | 10 | 38 | .... | .... | .... | .... |
| 2002-03 | St. Michael's | OHL | 35 | 6 | 13 | 19 | 66 | .... | .... | .... | .... | .... | .... | .... | .... | .... | .... | .... | .... | .... | .... | .... | .... | .... | .... |
| | Kingston | OHL | 34 | 2 | 17 | 19 | 64 | .... | .... | .... | .... | .... | .... | .... | .... | .... | .... | .... | .... | .... | .... | .... | .... | .... | .... |
| 2003-04 | Wilkes-Barre | AHL | 23 | 1 | 2 | 3 | 26 | .... | .... | .... | .... | .... | .... | .... | .... | .... | 4 | 0 | 0 | 0 | 8 | .... | .... | .... | .... |
| | Wheeling Nailers | ECHL | 28 | 6 | 10 | 16 | 61 | .... | .... | .... | .... | .... | .... | .... | .... | .... | 5 | 0 | 1 | 1 | 37 | .... | .... | .... | .... |
| 2004-05 | Wilkes-Barre | AHL | 32 | 1 | 1 | 2 | 88 | .... | .... | .... | .... | .... | .... | .... | .... | .... | .... | .... | .... | .... | .... | .... | .... | .... | .... |
| | Wheeling Nailers | ECHL | 22 | 0 | 1 | 1 | 55 | .... | .... | .... | .... | .... | .... | .... | .... | .... | .... | .... | .... | .... | .... | .... | .... | .... | .... |
| 2005-06 | Wilkes-Barre | AHL | 28 | 1 | 12 | 13 | 98 | .... | .... | .... | .... | .... | .... | .... | .... | .... | 11 | 0 | 0 | 0 | 16 | .... | .... | .... | .... |
| | Wheeling Nailers | ECHL | 34 | 10 | 8 | 18 | 145 | .... | .... | .... | .... | .... | .... | .... | .... | .... | .... | .... | .... | .... | .... | .... | .... | .... | .... |
| **2006-07** | Bridgeport | AHL | 64 | 3 | 7 | 10 | 185 | .... | .... | .... | .... | .... | .... | .... | .... | .... | .... | .... | .... | .... | .... | .... | .... | .... | .... |
| | **NY Islanders** | **NHL** | **3** | **1** | **0** | **1** | **5** | **0** | **0** | **0** | **1** | **100.0** | **–2** | **0** | **0.0** | **10:17** | **1** | **0** | **0** | **0** | **0** | **0** | **0** | **0** | **6:04** |
| **2007-08** | **NY Islanders** | **NHL** | **5** | **0** | **1** | **1** | **4** | **0** | **0** | **0** | **4** | **0.0** | **–1** | **0** | **0.0** | **17:30** | .... | .... | .... | .... | .... | .... | .... | .... | .... |
| | Bridgeport | AHL | 71 | 3 | 11 | 14 | 197 | .... | .... | .... | .... | .... | .... | .... | .... | .... | .... | .... | .... | .... | .... | .... | .... | .... | .... |
| 2008-09 | San Antonio | AHL | 7 | 0 | 0 | 0 | 6 | .... | .... | .... | .... | .... | .... | .... | .... | .... | .... | .... | .... | .... | .... | .... | .... | .... | .... |
| | Binghamton | AHL | 68 | 7 | 9 | 16 | 135 | .... | .... | .... | .... | .... | .... | .... | .... | .... | .... | .... | .... | .... | .... | .... | .... | .... | .... |
| | **NHL Totals** | | **8** | **1** | **1** | **2** | **9** | **0** | **0** | **0** | **5** | **20.0** | | **0** | **0.0** | **14:48** | **1** | **0** | **0** | **0** | **0** | **0** | **0** | **0** | **6:04** |

Signed as a free agent by **NY Islanders**, December 21, 2006. Signed as a free agent by **Phoenix**, July 2, 2008. Traded to **Ottawa** by **Phoenix** for Alexander Nikulin, November 3, 2008. Signed as a free agent by **Boston**, July 7, 2009.

## FEDOROV, Sergei

(FEH-duh-rahf, SAIR-gay)

Center. Shoots left. 6'2", 207 lbs. Born, Pskov, USSR, December 13, 1969. Detroit's 4th choice, 74th overall, in 1989 Entry Draft.

| | | | | | | | | | | | | | | | | | | | | | | | | | |
|---|---|---|---|---|---|---|---|---|---|---|---|---|---|---|---|---|---|---|---|---|---|---|---|---|---|
| 1985-86 | Dynamo Minsk | USSR-2 | 15 | 6 | 1 | 7 | 10 | .... | .... | .... | .... | .... | .... | .... | .... | .... | .... | .... | .... | .... | .... | .... | .... | .... | .... |
| 1986-87 | CSKA Moscow | USSR | 29 | 6 | 6 | 12 | 12 | .... | .... | .... | .... | .... | .... | .... | .... | .... | .... | .... | .... | .... | .... | .... | .... | .... | .... |
| 1987-88 | CSKA Moscow | USSR | 48 | 7 | 9 | 16 | 20 | .... | .... | .... | .... | .... | .... | .... | .... | .... | .... | .... | .... | .... | .... | .... | .... | .... | .... |
| 1988-89 | CSKA Moscow | USSR | 44 | 9 | 8 | 17 | 35 | .... | .... | .... | .... | .... | .... | .... | .... | .... | .... | .... | .... | .... | .... | .... | .... | .... | .... |
| 1989-90 | CSKA Moscow | USSR | 48 | 19 | 10 | 29 | 22 | .... | .... | .... | .... | .... | .... | .... | .... | .... | .... | .... | .... | .... | .... | .... | .... | .... | .... |
| | CSKA Moscow | Super-S | 5 | 2 | 2 | 4 | 11 | .... | .... | .... | .... | .... | .... | .... | .... | .... | .... | .... | .... | .... | .... | .... | .... | .... | .... |
| **1990-91** | **Detroit** | **NHL** | **77** | **31** | **48** | **79** | **66** | **11** | **3** | **5** | **259** | **12.0** | **11** | .... | .... | .... | **7** | **1** | **5** | **6** | **4** | **0** | **0** | **1** | .... |
| **1991-92** | **Detroit** | **NHL** | **80** | **32** | **54** | **86** | **72** | **7** | **2** | **5** | **249** | **12.9** | **26** | .... | .... | .... | **11** | **5** | **5** | **10** | **8** | **1** | **2** | **1** | .... |
| **1992-93** | **Detroit** | **NHL** | **73** | **34** | **53** | **87** | **72** | **13** | **4** | **3** | **217** | **15.7** | **33** | .... | .... | .... | **7** | **3** | **6** | **9** | **23** | **1** | **1** | **0** | .... |
| **1993-94** | **Detroit** | **NHL** | **82** | **56** | **64** | **120** | **34** | **13** | **4** | **10** | **337** | **16.6** | **48** | .... | .... | .... | **7** | **1** | **7** | **8** | **6** | **0** | **0** | **0** | .... |
| **1994-95** | **Detroit** | **NHL** | **42** | **20** | **30** | **50** | **24** | **7** | **3** | **5** | **147** | **13.6** | **6** | .... | .... | .... | **17** | **7** | ***17** | ***24** | **6** | **3** | **0** | **0** | .... |
| **1995-96** | **Detroit** | **NHL** | **78** | **39** | **68** | **107** | **48** | **11** | **3** | **11** | **306** | **12.7** | **49** | .... | .... | .... | **19** | **2** | ***18** | **20** | **10** | **0** | **0** | **2** | .... |
| **1996-97** ♦ | **Detroit** | **NHL** | **74** | **30** | **33** | **63** | **30** | **9** | **2** | **4** | **273** | **11.0** | **29** | .... | .... | .... | **20** | **8** | **12** | **20** | **12** | **3** | **0** | **4** | .... |
| **1997-98** | Russia | Olympics | 6 | 1 | 5 | 6 | 8 | .... | .... | .... | .... | .... | .... | .... | .... | .... | .... | .... | .... | .... | .... | .... | .... | .... | .... |
| | ♦ **Detroit** | **NHL** | **21** | **6** | **11** | **17** | **25** | **2** | **0** | **2** | **68** | **8.8** | **10** | .... | .... | .... | **22** | ***10** | **10** | **20** | **12** | **2** | **1** | **1** | .... |
| **1998-99** | **Detroit** | **NHL** | **77** | **26** | **37** | **63** | **66** | **6** | **2** | **3** | **224** | **11.6** | **9** | **1414** | **51.7** | **19:21** | **10** | **1** | **8** | **9** | **8** | **0** | **0** | **0** | **19:54** |
| **99-2000** | **Detroit** | **NHL** | **68** | **27** | **35** | **62** | **22** | **4** | **4** | **7** | **263** | **10.3** | **8** | **1274** | **53.8** | **20:05** | **9** | **4** | **4** | **8** | **4** | **2** | **0** | **1** | **20:48** |
| **2000-01** | **Detroit** | **NHL** | **75** | **32** | **37** | **69** | **40** | **14** | **2** | **7** | **268** | **11.9** | **12** | **1601** | **55.8** | **21:05** | **6** | **2** | **5** | **7** | **0** | **1** | **0** | **1** | **22:19** |
| **2001-02** ♦ | **Detroit** | **NHL** | **81** | **31** | **37** | **68** | **36** | **10** | **0** | **6** | **256** | **12.1** | **20** | **1160** | **51.7** | **19:33** | **23** | **5** | **14** | **19** | **20** | **2** | **1** | **0** | **22:20** |
| | Russia | Olympics | 6 | 2 | 2 | 4 | 4 | .... | .... | .... | .... | .... | .... | .... | .... | .... | .... | .... | .... | .... | .... | .... | .... | .... | .... |
| **2002-03** | **Detroit** | **NHL** | **80** | **36** | **47** | **83** | **52** | **10** | **2** | **11** | **281** | **12.8** | **15** | **1580** | **53.4** | **21:11** | **4** | **1** | **2** | **3** | **0** | **0** | **0** | **0** | **22:07** |
| **2003-04** | **Anaheim** | **NHL** | **80** | **31** | **34** | **65** | **42** | **9** | **2** | **6** | **268** | **11.6** | **–5** | **1558** | **56.6** | **21:05** | .... | .... | .... | .... | .... | .... | .... | .... | .... |
| 2004-05 | | | DID NOT PLAY | | | | | | | | | | | | | | | | | | | | | | |
| **2005-06** | **Anaheim** | **NHL** | **5** | **0** | **1** | **1** | **2** | **0** | **0** | **0** | **18** | **0.0** | **–1** | **80** | **55.0** | **20:17** | .... | .... | .... | .... | .... | .... | .... | .... | .... |
| | **Columbus** | **NHL** | **62** | **12** | **31** | **43** | **64** | **3** | **1** | **2** | **142** | **8.5** | **–1** | **1169** | **51.8** | **21:06** | .... | .... | .... | .... | .... | .... | .... | .... | .... |
| **2006-07** | **Columbus** | **NHL** | **73** | **18** | **24** | **42** | **56** | **7** | **2** | **2** | **163** | **11.0** | **–7** | **680** | **52.4** | **19:56** | .... | .... | .... | .... | .... | .... | .... | .... | .... |
| **2007-08** | **Columbus** | **NHL** | **50** | **9** | **19** | **28** | **30** | **5** | **0** | **1** | **94** | **9.6** | **–3** | **685** | **54.5** | **17:28** | .... | .... | .... | .... | .... | .... | .... | .... | .... |
| | **Washington** | **NHL** | **18** | **2** | **11** | **13** | **8** | **1** | **0** | **1** | **34** | **5.9** | **–2** | **326** | **58.0** | **18:16** | **7** | **1** | **4** | **5** | **8** | **0** | **0** | **0** | **21:38** |
| **2008-09** | **Washington** | **NHL** | **52** | **11** | **22** | **33** | **50** | **2** | **0** | **2** | **118** | **9.3** | **4** | **655** | **56.2** | **16:31** | **14** | **1** | **7** | **8** | **12** | **0** | **0** | **1** | **16:40** |
| | **NHL Totals** | | **1248** | **483** | **696** | **1179** | **839** | **144** | **36** | **93** | **3985** | **12.1** | | **12182** | **53.9** | **19:52** | **183** | **52** | **124** | **176** | **133** | **15** | **5** | **12** | **20:38** |

NHL All-Rookie Team (1991) • NHL First All-Star Team (1994) • Frank J. Selke Trophy (1994, 1996) • Lester B. Pearson Award (1994) • Hart Memorial Trophy (1994)

Played in NHL All-Star Game (1992, 1994, 1996, 2001, 2002, 2003)

• Missed majority of 1997-98 season after failing to come to contract terms with **Detroit**. Signed as a free agent by **Anaheim**, July 19, 2003. Traded to **Columbus** by **Anaheim** with Anaheim's 5th round choice (Maxime Frechette) in 2006 Entry Draft for Tyler Wright and Francois Beauchemin, November 15, 2005. Traded to **Washington** by **Columbus** for Ted Ruth, February 26, 2008. Signed as a free agent by **Magnitogorsk** (Rus-KHL), June 25, 2009.

## FEDORUK, Todd

(FEH-duh-ruhk, TAWD) **T.B.**

Left wing. Shoots left. 6'2", 240 lbs. Born, Redwater, Alta., February 13, 1979. Philadelphia's 6th choice, 164th overall, in 1997 Entry Draft.

| | | | | | | | | | | | | | | | | | | | | | | | | | |
|---|---|---|---|---|---|---|---|---|---|---|---|---|---|---|---|---|---|---|---|---|---|---|---|---|---|
| 1994-95 | Ft. Saskatchewan | AMHL | STATISTICS NOT AVAILABLE | | | | | | | | | | | | | | | | | | | | | | |
| 1995-96 | Kelowna Rockets | WHL | 44 | 1 | 1 | 2 | 83 | .... | .... | .... | .... | .... | .... | .... | .... | .... | 4 | 0 | 0 | 0 | 6 | .... | .... | .... | .... |
| 1996-97 | Kelowna Rockets | WHL | 31 | 1 | 5 | 6 | 87 | .... | .... | .... | .... | .... | .... | .... | .... | .... | 6 | 0 | 0 | 0 | 13 | .... | .... | .... | .... |
| 1997-98 | Kelowna Rockets | WHL | 31 | 3 | 5 | 8 | 120 | .... | .... | .... | .... | .... | .... | .... | .... | .... | .... | .... | .... | .... | .... | .... | .... | .... | .... |
| | Regina Pats | WHL | 21 | 4 | 3 | 7 | 80 | .... | .... | .... | .... | .... | .... | .... | .... | .... | 9 | 1 | 2 | 3 | 23 | .... | .... | .... | .... |
| 1998-99 | Regina Pats | WHL | 39 | 12 | 12 | 24 | 107 | .... | .... | .... | .... | .... | .... | .... | .... | .... | .... | .... | .... | .... | .... | .... | .... | .... | .... |
| | Prince Albert | WHL | 28 | 6 | 4 | 10 | 75 | .... | .... | .... | .... | .... | .... | .... | .... | .... | 13 | 1 | 6 | 7 | 49 | .... | .... | .... | .... |
| 99-2000 | Trenton Titans | ECHL | 18 | 2 | 5 | 7 | 118 | .... | .... | .... | .... | .... | .... | .... | .... | .... | .... | .... | .... | .... | .... | .... | .... | .... | .... |
| | Philadelphia | AHL | 19 | 1 | 2 | 3 | 40 | .... | .... | .... | .... | .... | .... | .... | .... | .... | 5 | 0 | 1 | 1 | 2 | .... | .... | .... | .... |

| Season | Club | League | GP | G | A | Pts | PIM | PP | SH | GW | S | % | +/- | TF | F% | Min | GP | G | A | Pts | PIM | PP | SH | GW | Min |
|---|---|---|---|---|---|---|---|---|---|---|---|---|---|---|---|---|---|---|---|---|---|---|---|---|---|
| | | | Regular Season | | | | | | | | | | | | | | Playoffs | | | | | | | | |
| 2000-01 | Philadelphia | NHL | 53 | 5 | 5 | 10 | 109 | 0 | 0 | 0 | 28 | 17.9 | 0 | 0 | 0.0 | 7:02 | 2 | 0 | 0 | 0 | 20 | 0 | 0 | 0 | 5:57 |
| | Philadelphia | AHL | 14 | 0 | 1 | 1 | 49 | .... | .... | .... | .... | .... | .... | .... | .... | .... | .... | .... | .... | .... | .... | .... | .... | .... | .... |
| 2001-02 | Philadelphia | NHL | 55 | 3 | 4 | 7 | 141 | 0 | 0 | 0 | 21 | 14.3 | −2 | 5 | 0.0 | 6:21 | 3 | 0 | 0 | 0 | 0 | 0 | 0 | 0 | 2:46 |
| | Philadelphia | AHL | 7 | 0 | 1 | 1 | 54 | .... | .... | .... | .... | .... | .... | .... | .... | .... | .... | .... | .... | .... | .... | .... | .... | .... | .... |
| 2002-03 | Philadelphia | NHL | 63 | 1 | 5 | 6 | 105 | 0 | 0 | 0 | 33 | 3.0 | 1 | 1 | 0.0 | 6:30 | 1 | 0 | 0 | 0 | 0 | 0 | 0 | 0 | 4:52 |
| 2003-04 | Philadelphia | NHL | 49 | 1 | 4 | 5 | 136 | 0 | 0 | 1 | 33 | 3.0 | −4 | 0 | 0.0 | 6:47 | 1 | 0 | 0 | 0 | 2 | 0 | 0 | 0 | 6:42 |
| | Philadelphia | AHL | 2 | 0 | 2 | 2 | 2 | .... | .... | .... | .... | .... | .... | .... | .... | .... | .... | .... | .... | .... | .... | .... | .... | .... | .... |
| 2004-05 | Philadelphia | AHL | 42 | 4 | 12 | 16 | 142 | .... | .... | .... | .... | .... | .... | .... | .... | .... | 16 | 2 | 2 | 4 | 33 | .... | .... | .... | .... |
| 2005-06 | Anaheim | NHL | 76 | 4 | 19 | 23 | 174 | 0 | 0 | 1 | 69 | 5.8 | 6 | 8 | 37.5 | 8:24 | 12 | 0 | 0 | 0 | 16 | 0 | 0 | 0 | 8:19 |
| 2006-07 | Anaheim | NHL | 10 | 0 | 3 | 3 | 36 | 0 | 0 | 0 | 2 | 0.0 | 2 | 1 | 0.0 | 7:30 | .... | .... | .... | .... | .... | .... | .... | .... | .... |
| | Philadelphia | NHL | 48 | 3 | 8 | 11 | 84 | 0 | 0 | 0 | 28 | 10.7 | −11 | 2 | 0.0 | 9:03 | .... | .... | .... | .... | .... | .... | .... | .... | .... |
| 2007-08 | Dallas | NHL | 11 | 0 | 2 | 2 | 33 | 0 | 0 | 0 | 6 | 0.0 | 2 | 0 | 0.0 | 6:50 | .... | .... | .... | .... | .... | .... | .... | .... | .... |
| | Minnesota | NHL | 58 | 6 | 5 | 11 | 106 | 2 | 0 | 0 | 51 | 11.8 | 0 | 4 | 0.0 | 10:59 | 6 | 1 | 1 | 2 | 16 | 1 | 0 | 0 | 13:38 |
| 2008-09 | Phoenix | NHL | 72 | 6 | 7 | 13 | 72 | 0 | 0 | 0 | 56 | 10.7 | −9 | 15 | 26.7 | 10:36 | .... | .... | .... | .... | .... | .... | .... | .... | .... |
| | NHL Totals | | 495 | 29 | 62 | 91 | 996 | 2 | 0 | 2 | 327 | 8.9 | | 36 | 19.4 | 8:15 | 25 | 1 | 1 | 2 | 54 | 1 | 0 | 0 | 8:32 |

Traded to **Anaheim** by **Philadelphia** for Anaheim's 2nd round choice (later traded to Phoenix - Phoenix selected Pier-Olivier Pelletier) in 2005 Entry Draft, July 29, 2005. Traded to **Philadelphia** by **Anaheim** for Philadelphia's 4th round choice (Justin Vaive) in 2007 Entry Draft, November 13, 2006. Signed as a free agent by **Dallas**, July 9, 2007. Claimed on waivers by **Minnesota** from **Dallas**, November 22, 2007. Signed as a free agent by **Phoenix**, July 1, 2008. Traded to **Tampa Bay** by **Phoenix** with David Hale for Radim Vrbata, July 21, 2009.

## FEDOTENKO, Ruslan

(feh-doh-TEHN-koh, roos-LAHN) **PIT.**

Left wing. Shoots left. 6'2", 195 lbs. Born, Kiev, USSR, January 18, 1979.

| | | | | | | | | | | | | | | | | | | | | | | | | | |
|---|---|---|---|---|---|---|---|---|---|---|---|---|---|---|---|---|---|---|---|---|---|---|---|---|---|
| 1995-96 | Kiev 2 | EEHL | 33 | 9 | 11 | 20 | 12 | .... | .... | .... | .... | .... | .... | .... | .... | .... | .... | .... | .... | .... | .... | .... | .... | .... | .... |
| | Sokol Kiev | CIS | 2 | 0 | 0 | 0 | 0 | .... | .... | .... | .... | .... | .... | .... | .... | .... | .... | .... | .... | .... | .... | .... | .... | .... | .... |
| 1996-97 | TPS Turku U18 | Fin-U18 | 3 | 3 | 2 | 5 | 2 | .... | .... | .... | .... | .... | .... | .... | .... | .... | .... | .... | .... | .... | .... | .... | .... | .... | .... |
| | TPS Turku Jr. | Fin-Jr. | 11 | 1 | 1 | 2 | 2 | .... | .... | .... | .... | .... | .... | .... | .... | .... | .... | .... | .... | .... | .... | .... | .... | .... | .... |
| | Kiekko-67 Turku | Finland-2 | 22 | 4 | 3 | 7 | 16 | .... | .... | .... | .... | .... | .... | .... | .... | .... | .... | .... | .... | .... | .... | .... | .... | .... | .... |
| | Kiekko Turku | Finland-3 | .... | .... | .... | .... | .... | .... | .... | .... | .... | .... | .... | .... | .... | .... | 3 | 1 | 0 | 1 | 2 | .... | .... | .... | .... |
| 1997-98 | Melfort Mustangs | SJHL | 68 | 35 | 31 | 66 | 55 | .... | .... | .... | .... | .... | .... | .... | .... | .... | .... | .... | .... | .... | .... | .... | .... | .... | .... |
| 1998-99 | Sioux City | USHL | 55 | 43 | 34 | 77 | 139 | .... | .... | .... | .... | .... | .... | .... | .... | .... | 5 | 5 | 1 | 6 | 9 | .... | .... | .... | .... |
| 99-2000 | Trenton Titans | ECHL | 8 | 5 | 3 | 8 | 9 | .... | .... | .... | .... | .... | .... | .... | .... | .... | .... | .... | .... | .... | .... | .... | .... | .... | .... |
| | Philadelphia | AHL | 67 | 16 | 34 | 50 | 42 | .... | .... | .... | .... | .... | .... | .... | .... | .... | 2 | 0 | 0 | 0 | 0 | .... | .... | .... | .... |
| 2000-01 | Philadelphia | NHL | 74 | 16 | 20 | 36 | 72 | 3 | 0 | 4 | 119 | 13.4 | 8 | 7 | 71.4 | 14:38 | 6 | 0 | 1 | 1 | 4 | 0 | 0 | 0 | 11:18 |
| | Philadelphia | AHL | 8 | 1 | 0 | 1 | 8 | .... | .... | .... | .... | .... | .... | .... | .... | .... | .... | .... | .... | .... | .... | .... | .... | .... | .... |
| 2001-02 | Philadelphia | NHL | 78 | 17 | 9 | 26 | 43 | 0 | 1 | 3 | 121 | 14.0 | 15 | 41 | 43.9 | 13:56 | 5 | 1 | 0 | 1 | 2 | 0 | 0 | 1 | 14:11 |
| | Ukraine | Olympics | 1 | 1 | 0 | 1 | 4 | .... | .... | .... | .... | .... | .... | .... | .... | .... | .... | .... | .... | .... | .... | .... | .... | .... | .... |
| 2002-03 | Tampa Bay | NHL | 76 | 19 | 13 | 32 | 44 | 6 | 0 | 6 | 114 | 16.7 | −7 | 90 | 48.9 | 16:01 | 11 | 0 | 1 | 1 | 2 | 0 | 0 | 0 | 13:58 |
| 2003-04♦ | Tampa Bay | NHL | 77 | 17 | 22 | 39 | 30 | 0 | 0 | 3 | 116 | 14.7 | 14 | 58 | 55.2 | 14:39 | 22 | 12 | 2 | 14 | 14 | 5 | 0 | 3 | 16:40 |
| 2004-05 | | | DID NOT PLAY | | | | | | | | | | | | | | | | | | | | | | |
| 2005-06 | Tampa Bay | NHL | 80 | 26 | 15 | 41 | 44 | 4 | 0 | 6 | 164 | 15.9 | −4 | 28 | 42.9 | 15:21 | 5 | 0 | 0 | 0 | 20 | 0 | 0 | 0 | 14:38 |
| 2006-07 | Tampa Bay | NHL | 80 | 12 | 20 | 32 | 52 | 2 | 0 | 1 | 154 | 7.8 | −3 | 8 | 25.0 | 16:15 | 4 | 0 | 0 | 0 | 4 | 0 | 0 | 0 | 17:27 |
| 2007-08 | NY Islanders | NHL | 67 | 16 | 17 | 33 | 40 | 8 | 0 | 2 | 121 | 13.2 | −9 | 28 | 39.3 | 16:42 | .... | .... | .... | .... | .... | .... | .... | .... | .... |
| 2008-09♦ | Pittsburgh | NHL | 65 | 16 | 23 | 39 | 44 | 1 | 0 | 3 | 117 | 13.7 | 18 | 18 | 22.2 | 14:06 | 24 | 7 | 7 | 14 | 4 | 0 | 0 | 0 | 14:31 |
| | NHL Totals | | 597 | 139 | 139 | 278 | 369 | 24 | 1 | 28 | 1026 | 13.5 | | 278 | 46.0 | 15:12 | 77 | 20 | 11 | 31 | 50 | 5 | 0 | 4 | 14:56 |

USHL First All-Star Team (1999)

Signed as a free agent by **Philadelphia**, August 3, 1999. Traded to **Tampa Bay** by **Philadelphia** with Tampa Bay's 2nd round choice (previously acquired, later traded to Dallas – Dallas selected Tobias Stephan) in 2002 Entry Draft and Phoenix's 2nd round choice (previously acquired, later traded to San Jose – San Jose selected Dan Spang) in 2002 Entry Draft for Tampa Bay's 1st round choice (Joni Pitkanen) in 2002 Entry Draft, June 21, 2002. Signed as a free agent by **NY Islanders**, July 4, 2007. Signed as a free agent by **Pittsburgh**, July 3, 2008.

## FEHR, Eric

(FAIR, AIR-ihk) **WSH.**

Right wing. Shoots right. 6'4", 212 lbs. Born, Winkler, Man., September 7, 1985. Washington's 1st choice, 18th overall, in 2003 Entry Draft.

| | | | | | | | | | | | | | | | | | | | | | | | | | |
|---|---|---|---|---|---|---|---|---|---|---|---|---|---|---|---|---|---|---|---|---|---|---|---|---|---|
| 2000-01 | Pembina Valley | MMMHL | 36 | 45 | 13 | 58 | 30 | .... | .... | .... | .... | .... | .... | .... | .... | .... | .... | .... | .... | .... | .... | .... | .... | .... | .... |
| | Brandon | WHL | 4 | 0 | 0 | 0 | 0 | .... | .... | .... | .... | .... | .... | .... | .... | .... | .... | .... | .... | .... | .... | .... | .... | .... | .... |
| 2001-02 | Brandon | WHL | 63 | 11 | 16 | 27 | 29 | .... | .... | .... | .... | .... | .... | .... | .... | .... | 12 | 1 | 1 | 2 | 0 | .... | .... | .... | .... |
| 2002-03 | Brandon | WHL | 70 | 26 | 29 | 55 | 76 | .... | .... | .... | .... | .... | .... | .... | .... | .... | 17 | 4 | 8 | 12 | 26 | .... | .... | .... | .... |
| 2003-04 | Brandon | WHL | 71 | 50 | 34 | 84 | 129 | .... | .... | .... | .... | .... | .... | .... | .... | .... | 7 | 5 | 0 | 5 | 16 | .... | .... | .... | .... |
| 2004-05 | Brandon | WHL | 71 | *59 | 52 | *111 | 91 | .... | .... | .... | .... | .... | .... | .... | .... | .... | 24 | 16 | 16 | *32 | 47 | .... | .... | .... | .... |
| 2005-06 | Washington | NHL | 11 | 0 | 0 | 0 | 2 | 0 | 0 | 0 | 10 | 0.0 | 0 | 4 | 25.0 | 5:45 | .... | .... | .... | .... | .... | .... | .... | .... | .... |
| | Hershey Bears | AHL | 70 | 25 | 28 | 53 | 70 | .... | .... | .... | .... | .... | .... | .... | .... | .... | 19 | 8 | 3 | 11 | 8 | .... | .... | .... | .... |
| 2006-07 | Washington | NHL | 14 | 2 | 1 | 3 | 8 | 0 | 0 | 1 | 25 | 8.0 | 3 | 6 | 16.7 | 10:43 | .... | .... | .... | .... | .... | .... | .... | .... | .... |
| | Hershey Bears | AHL | 40 | 22 | 19 | 41 | 63 | .... | .... | .... | .... | .... | .... | .... | .... | .... | .... | .... | .... | .... | .... | .... | .... | .... | .... |
| 2007-08 | Washington | NHL | 23 | 1 | 5 | 6 | 6 | 0 | 0 | 0 | 40 | 2.5 | 4 | 2 | 0.0 | 10:31 | 5 | 1 | 0 | 1 | 0 | 0 | 0 | 0 | 9:41 |
| | Hershey Bears | AHL | 11 | 3 | 4 | 7 | 4 | .... | .... | .... | .... | .... | .... | .... | .... | .... | 2 | 1 | 3 | 4 | 2 | .... | .... | .... | .... |
| 2008-09 | Washington | NHL | 61 | 12 | 13 | 25 | 22 | 1 | 0 | 2 | 134 | 9.0 | 8 | 3 | 33.3 | 11:15 | 9 | 0 | 0 | 0 | 0 | 0 | 0 | 0 | 7:22 |
| | NHL Totals | | 109 | 15 | 19 | 34 | 38 | 1 | 0 | 3 | 209 | 7.2 | | 15 | 20.0 | 10:28 | 14 | 1 | 0 | 1 | 0 | 0 | 0 | 0 | 8:12 |

WHL East First All-Star Team (2005) • WHL Player of the Year (2005) • Canadian Major Junior Second All-Star Team (2005)

## FERENCE, Andrew

(FAIR-ehns, AN-droo) **BOS.**

Defense. Shoots left. 5'11", 189 lbs. Born, Edmonton, Alta., March 17, 1979. Pittsburgh's 8th choice, 208th overall, in 1997 Entry Draft.

| | | | | | | | | | | | | | | | | | | | | | | | | | |
|---|---|---|---|---|---|---|---|---|---|---|---|---|---|---|---|---|---|---|---|---|---|---|---|---|---|
| 1994-95 | Sherwood Park | AMHL | 31 | 4 | 14 | 18 | 74 | .... | .... | .... | .... | .... | .... | .... | .... | .... | .... | .... | .... | .... | .... | .... | .... | .... | .... |
| | Portland | WHL | 2 | 0 | 0 | 0 | 4 | .... | .... | .... | .... | .... | .... | .... | .... | .... | .... | .... | .... | .... | .... | .... | .... | .... | .... |
| 1995-96 | Portland | WHL | 72 | 9 | 31 | 40 | 159 | .... | .... | .... | .... | .... | .... | .... | .... | .... | 7 | 1 | 3 | 4 | 12 | .... | .... | .... | .... |
| 1996-97 | Portland | WHL | 72 | 12 | 32 | 44 | 163 | .... | .... | .... | .... | .... | .... | .... | .... | .... | 6 | 1 | 2 | 3 | 12 | .... | .... | .... | .... |
| 1997-98 | Portland | WHL | 72 | 11 | 57 | 68 | 142 | .... | .... | .... | .... | .... | .... | .... | .... | .... | 16 | 2 | 18 | 20 | 28 | .... | .... | .... | .... |
| 1998-99 | Portland | WHL | 40 | 11 | 21 | 32 | 104 | .... | .... | .... | .... | .... | .... | .... | .... | .... | 4 | 1 | 4 | 5 | 10 | .... | .... | .... | .... |
| | Kansas City | IHL | 5 | 1 | 2 | 3 | 4 | .... | .... | .... | .... | .... | .... | .... | .... | .... | 3 | 0 | 0 | 0 | 9 | .... | .... | .... | .... |
| 99-2000 | Pittsburgh | NHL | 30 | 2 | 4 | 6 | 20 | 0 | 0 | 1 | 26 | 7.7 | 3 | 0 | 0.0 | 16:19 | .... | .... | .... | .... | .... | .... | .... | .... | .... |
| | Wilkes-Barre | AHL | 44 | 8 | 20 | 28 | 58 | .... | .... | .... | .... | .... | .... | .... | .... | .... | .... | .... | .... | .... | .... | .... | .... | .... | .... |
| 2000-01 | Pittsburgh | NHL | 36 | 4 | 11 | 15 | 28 | 1 | 0 | 1 | 47 | 8.5 | 6 | 0 | 0.0 | 18:51 | 18 | 3 | 7 | 10 | 16 | 1 | 0 | 1 | 22:02 |
| | Wilkes-Barre | AHL | 43 | 6 | 18 | 24 | 95 | .... | .... | .... | .... | .... | .... | .... | .... | .... | 3 | 1 | 0 | 1 | 12 | .... | .... | .... | .... |
| 2001-02 | Pittsburgh | NHL | 75 | 4 | 7 | 11 | 73 | 1 | 0 | 0 | 82 | 4.9 | −12 | 2 | 0.0 | 18:34 | .... | .... | .... | .... | .... | .... | .... | .... | .... |
| 2002-03 | Pittsburgh | NHL | 22 | 1 | 3 | 4 | 36 | 1 | 0 | 0 | 22 | 4.5 | −16 | 1 | 100.0 | 19:33 | .... | .... | .... | .... | .... | .... | .... | .... | .... |
| | Wilkes-Barre | AHL | 1 | 0 | 0 | 0 | 2 | .... | .... | .... | .... | .... | .... | .... | .... | .... | .... | .... | .... | .... | .... | .... | .... | .... | .... |
| | Calgary | NHL | 16 | 0 | 4 | 4 | 6 | 0 | 0 | 0 | 17 | 0.0 | 1 | 0 | 0.0 | 17:38 | .... | .... | .... | .... | .... | .... | .... | .... | .... |
| 2003-04 | Calgary | NHL | 72 | 4 | 12 | 16 | 53 | 1 | 0 | 0 | 86 | 4.7 | 5 | 0 | 0.0 | 18:40 | 26 | 0 | 3 | 3 | 25 | 0 | 0 | 0 | 24:13 |
| 2004-05 | C. Budejovice | CzRep-2 | 19 | 5 | 6 | 11 | 45 | .... | .... | .... | .... | .... | .... | .... | .... | .... | 12 | 2 | 7 | 9 | 10 | .... | .... | .... | .... |
| 2005-06 | Calgary | NHL | 82 | 4 | 27 | 31 | 85 | 2 | 0 | 0 | 111 | 3.6 | −12 | 1 | 0.0 | 20:08 | 7 | 0 | 4 | 4 | 12 | 0 | 0 | 0 | 23:09 |
| 2006-07 | Calgary | NHL | 54 | 2 | 10 | 12 | 66 | 1 | 0 | 0 | 51 | 3.9 | 7 | 3 | 33.3 | 18:29 | .... | .... | .... | .... | .... | .... | .... | .... | .... |
| | Boston | NHL | 26 | 1 | 2 | 3 | 31 | 0 | 0 | 0 | 29 | 3.4 | −2 | 0 | 0.0 | 22:22 | .... | .... | .... | .... | .... | .... | .... | .... | .... |
| 2007-08 | Boston | NHL | 59 | 1 | 14 | 15 | 50 | 0 | 0 | 0 | 71 | 1.4 | −14 | 1 | 100.0 | 22:15 | 7 | 0 | 4 | 4 | 6 | 0 | 0 | 0 | 21:39 |
| 2008-09 | Boston | NHL | 47 | 1 | 15 | 16 | 40 | 1 | 0 | 0 | 72 | 1.4 | 7 | 0 | 0.0 | 21:32 | 3 | 0 | 0 | 0 | 4 | 0 | 0 | 0 | 15:30 |
| | NHL Totals | | 519 | 24 | 109 | 133 | 488 | 8 | 0 | 2 | 614 | 3.9 | | 8 | 37.5 | 19:36 | 61 | 3 | 18 | 21 | 63 | 1 | 0 | 1 | 22:44 |

WHL West First All-Star Team (1998) • WHL West Second All-Star Team (1999)

• Missed majority of 2002-03 season recovering from groin (November 18, 2002 vs. Montreal) and ankle (March 20, 2003 vs. Los Angeles) injuries. Traded to **Calgary** by **Pittsburgh** for Calgary's 3rd round choice (Brian Gifford) in 2004 Entry Draft, February 9, 2003. Signed as a free agent by **Ceske Budejovice** (CzRep-2), December 1, 2004. Traded to **Boston** by **Calgary** with Chuck Kobasew for Brad Stuart, Wayne Primeau and Washington's 4th round choice (previously acquired, Calgary selected T.J. Brodie) in 2008 Entry Draft, February 10, 2007.

## FERLAND, Jonathan

(fair-LAWN, JAWN-ah-thuhn)

Right wing. Shoots right. 6'2", 212 lbs. Born, Ste-Marie-de-Beauce, Que., February 9, 1983. Montreal's 5th choice, 212th overall, in 2002 Entry Draft.

| | | | | | | | | | | | | | | | | | | | | | | | | | |
|---|---|---|---|---|---|---|---|---|---|---|---|---|---|---|---|---|---|---|---|---|---|---|---|---|---|
| 1998-99 | Laval-Laurentides | QAAA | 42 | 18 | 17 | 35 | 50 | .... | .... | .... | .... | .... | .... | .... | .... | .... | .... | .... | .... | .... | .... | .... | .... | .... | .... |
| 99-2000 | Moncton Wildcats | QMJHL | 52 | 3 | 6 | 9 | 21 | .... | .... | .... | .... | .... | .... | .... | .... | .... | 11 | 0 | 1 | 1 | 0 | .... | .... | .... | .... |
| 2000-01 | Acadie-Bathurst | QMJHL | 70 | 17 | 11 | 28 | 135 | .... | .... | .... | .... | .... | .... | .... | .... | .... | 13 | 0 | 4 | 4 | 47 | .... | .... | .... | .... |
| 2001-02 | Acadie-Bathurst | QMJHL | 55 | 28 | 46 | 74 | 104 | .... | .... | .... | .... | .... | .... | .... | .... | .... | 16 | 5 | 12 | 17 | 16 | .... | .... | .... | .... |
| 2002-03 | Acadie-Bathurst | QMJHL | 68 | 45 | 44 | 89 | 94 | .... | .... | .... | .... | .... | .... | .... | .... | .... | 11 | 4 | 5 | 9 | 16 | .... | .... | .... | .... |
| 2003-04 | Hamilton | AHL | 70 | 5 | 10 | 15 | 43 | .... | .... | .... | .... | .... | .... | .... | .... | .... | 10 | 0 | 0 | 0 | 6 | .... | .... | .... | .... |
| 2004-05 | Hamilton | AHL | 62 | 6 | 8 | 14 | 24 | .... | .... | .... | .... | .... | .... | .... | .... | .... | 4 | 0 | 0 | 0 | 4 | .... | .... | .... | .... |

| | | | | | | | | Regular Season | | | | | | | | | Playoffs | | | | | | | | |
|---|---|---|---|---|---|---|---|---|---|---|---|---|---|---|---|---|---|---|---|---|---|---|---|---|---|
| Season | Club | League | GP | G | A | Pts | PIM | PP | SH | GW | S | % | +/- | TF | F% | Min | GP | G | A | Pts | PIM | PP | SH | GW | Min |
| **2005-06** | **Montreal** | **NHL** | **7** | **1** | **0** | **1** | **2** | **0** | **0** | **0** | **9** | **11.1** | **–2** | **2** | **0.0** | **6:37** | .... | .... | .... | .... | .... | .... | .... | .... | .... |
| | Hamilton | AHL | 39 | 7 | 8 | 15 | 65 | .... | .... | .... | .... | .... | .... | .... | .... | .... | .... | .... | .... | .... | .... | .... | .... | .... | .... |
| 2006-07 | Hamilton | AHL | 78 | 23 | 14 | 37 | 87 | .... | .... | .... | .... | .... | .... | .... | .... | .... | 22 | 3 | 6 | 9 | 19 | .... | .... | .... | .... |
| 2007-08 | Hamilton | AHL | 80 | 16 | 24 | 40 | 97 | .... | .... | .... | .... | .... | .... | .... | .... | .... | .... | .... | .... | .... | .... | .... | .... | .... | .... |
| 2008-09 | EC VSV Villach | Austria | 53 | 20 | 28 | 48 | 110 | .... | .... | .... | .... | .... | .... | .... | .... | .... | 6 | 2 | 2 | 4 | 18 | .... | .... | .... | .... |
| | **NHL Totals** | | **7** | **1** | **0** | **1** | **2** | **0** | **0** | **0** | **9** | **11.1** | | **2** | **0.0** | **6:37** | .... | .... | .... | .... | .... | .... | .... | .... | .... |

## FESTERLING, Brett

(FEHS-tuhr-lihng, BREHT) **ANA.**

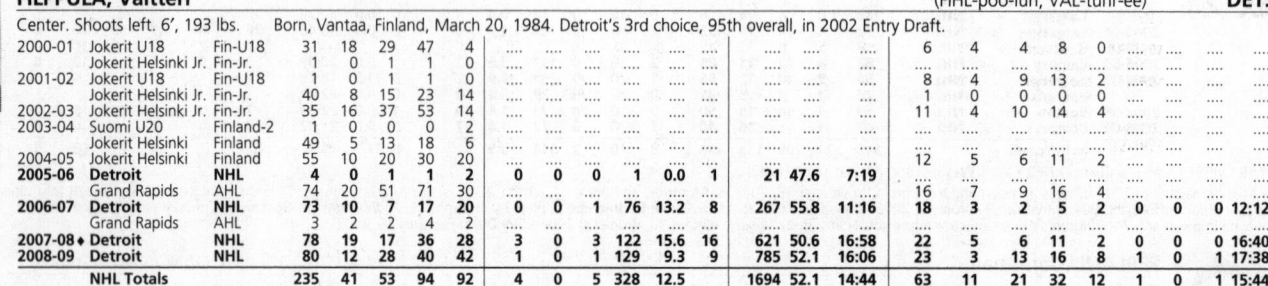

Defense. Shoots left. 6'1", 214 lbs. Born, Quesnel, B.C., March 3, 1986.

| Season | Club | League | GP | G | A | Pts | PIM | PP | SH | GW | S | % | +/- | TF | F% | Min | GP | G | A | Pts | PIM | PP | SH | GW | Min |
|---|---|---|---|---|---|---|---|---|---|---|---|---|---|---|---|---|---|---|---|---|---|---|---|---|---|
| 2001-02 | Quesnel Thunder | Minor-BC | 40 | 18 | 26 | 44 | 44 | .... | .... | .... | .... | .... | .... | .... | .... | .... | .... | .... | .... | .... | .... | .... | .... | .... | .... |
| | Quesnel | BCHL | 7 | 0 | 0 | 0 | 0 | .... | .... | .... | .... | .... | .... | .... | .... | .... | .... | .... | .... | .... | .... | .... | .... | .... | .... |
| | Tri-City | WHL | 3 | 0 | 0 | 0 | 0 | .... | .... | .... | .... | .... | .... | .... | .... | .... | .... | .... | .... | .... | .... | .... | .... | .... | .... |
| 2002-03 | Tri-City | WHL | 55 | 3 | 8 | 11 | 26 | .... | .... | .... | .... | .... | .... | .... | .... | .... | .... | .... | .... | .... | .... | .... | .... | .... | .... |
| 2003-04 | Tri-City | WHL | 54 | 1 | 9 | 10 | 34 | .... | .... | .... | .... | .... | .... | .... | .... | .... | 11 | 1 | 1 | 2 | 2 | .... | .... | .... | .... |
| 2004-05 | Tri-City | WHL | 33 | 3 | 11 | 14 | 20 | .... | .... | .... | .... | .... | .... | .... | .... | .... | .... | .... | .... | .... | .... | .... | .... | .... | .... |
| | Vancouver Giants | WHL | 32 | 2 | 4 | 6 | 10 | .... | .... | .... | .... | .... | .... | .... | .... | .... | 5 | 0 | 0 | 0 | 6 | .... | .... | .... | .... |
| 2005-06 | Vancouver Giants | WHL | 67 | 1 | 6 | 7 | 35 | .... | .... | .... | .... | .... | .... | .... | .... | .... | 18 | 0 | 1 | 1 | 10 | .... | .... | .... | .... |
| 2006-07 | Vancouver Giants | WHL | 70 | 5 | 16 | 21 | 80 | .... | .... | .... | .... | .... | .... | .... | .... | .... | 22 | 1 | 6 | 7 | 24 | .... | .... | .... | .... |
| 2007-08 | Portland Pirates | AHL | 74 | 3 | 11 | 14 | 64 | .... | .... | .... | .... | .... | .... | .... | .... | .... | 15 | 1 | 3 | 4 | 6 | .... | .... | .... | .... |
| **2008-09** | **Anaheim** | **NHL** | **40** | **0** | **5** | **5** | **18** | **0** | **0** | **0** | **15** | **0.0** | **5** | **0** | **0.0** | **16:40** | **1** | **0** | **0** | **0** | **0** | **0** | **0** | **0** | **14:34** |
| | Iowa Chops | AHL | 34 | 0 | 7 | 7 | 31 | .... | .... | .... | .... | .... | .... | .... | .... | .... | .... | .... | .... | .... | .... | .... | .... | .... | .... |
| | **NHL Totals** | | **40** | **0** | **5** | **5** | **18** | **0** | **0** | **0** | **15** | **0.0** | | **0** | **0.0** | **16:40** | **1** | **0** | **0** | **0** | **0** | **0** | **0** | **0** | **14:34** |

Signed as a free agent by **Anaheim**, September 14, 2005.

## FIDDLER, Vernon

(FIHD-luhr, VUHR-nuhn) **PHX.**

Center. Shoots left. 5'11", 201 lbs. Born, Edmonton, Alta., May 9, 1980.

| Season | Club | League | GP | G | A | Pts | PIM | PP | SH | GW | S | % | +/- | TF | F% | Min | GP | G | A | Pts | PIM | PP | SH | GW | Min |
|---|---|---|---|---|---|---|---|---|---|---|---|---|---|---|---|---|---|---|---|---|---|---|---|---|---|
| 1997-98 | Kelowna Rockets | WHL | 65 | 10 | 11 | 21 | 31 | .... | .... | .... | .... | .... | .... | .... | .... | .... | 7 | 0 | 1 | 1 | 4 | .... | .... | .... | .... |
| 1998-99 | Kelowna Rockets | WHL | 68 | 22 | 21 | 43 | 82 | .... | .... | .... | .... | .... | .... | .... | .... | .... | 6 | 2 | 0 | 2 | 8 | .... | .... | .... | .... |
| 99-2000 | Kelowna Rockets | WHL | 64 | 20 | 28 | 48 | 60 | .... | .... | .... | .... | .... | .... | .... | .... | .... | 5 | 1 | 3 | 4 | 4 | .... | .... | .... | .... |
| 2000-01 | Kelowna Rockets | WHL | 3 | 0 | 2 | 2 | 0 | .... | .... | .... | .... | .... | .... | .... | .... | .... | .... | .... | .... | .... | .... | .... | .... | .... | .... |
| | Medicine Hat | WHL | 67 | 33 | 38 | 71 | 100 | .... | .... | .... | .... | .... | .... | .... | .... | .... | .... | .... | .... | .... | .... | .... | .... | .... | .... |
| | Arkansas | ECHL | 3 | 0 | 1 | 1 | 2 | .... | .... | .... | .... | .... | .... | .... | .... | .... | 5 | 3 | 0 | 3 | 5 | .... | .... | .... | .... |
| 2001-02 | Roanoke Express | ECHL | 44 | 27 | 28 | 55 | 71 | .... | .... | .... | .... | .... | .... | .... | .... | .... | .... | .... | .... | .... | .... | .... | .... | .... | .... |
| | Norfolk Admirals | AHL | 38 | 8 | 5 | 13 | 28 | .... | .... | .... | .... | .... | .... | .... | .... | .... | 4 | 1 | 3 | 4 | 2 | .... | .... | .... | .... |
| **2002-03** | **Nashville** | **NHL** | **19** | **4** | **2** | **6** | **14** | **0** | **0** | **1** | **20** | **20.0** | **2** | **171** | **53.8** | **9:40** | .... | .... | .... | .... | .... | .... | .... | .... | .... |
| | Milwaukee | AHL | 54 | 8 | 16 | 24 | 70 | .... | .... | .... | .... | .... | .... | .... | .... | .... | 6 | 1 | 2 | 3 | 14 | .... | .... | .... | .... |
| **2003-04** | **Nashville** | **NHL** | **17** | **0** | **0** | **0** | **23** | **0** | **0** | **0** | **8** | **0.0** | **–6** | **123** | **49.6** | **8:06** | .... | .... | .... | .... | .... | .... | .... | .... | .... |
| | Milwaukee | AHL | 47 | 9 | 15 | 24 | 72 | .... | .... | .... | .... | .... | .... | .... | .... | .... | 22 | 5 | 3 | 8 | 36 | .... | .... | .... | .... |
| 2004-05 | Milwaukee | AHL | 73 | 20 | 22 | 42 | 70 | .... | .... | .... | .... | .... | .... | .... | .... | .... | 7 | 0 | 0 | 0 | 18 | .... | .... | .... | .... |
| **2005-06** | **Nashville** | **NHL** | **40** | **8** | **4** | **12** | **42** | **3** | **0** | **2** | **46** | **17.4** | **–2** | **464** | **52.6** | **13:49** | **2** | **0** | **1** | **1** | **0** | **0** | **0** | **0** | **8:48** |
| | Milwaukee | AHL | 11 | 1 | 6 | 7 | 20 | .... | .... | .... | .... | .... | .... | .... | .... | .... | .... | .... | .... | .... | .... | .... | .... | .... | .... |
| **2006-07** | **Nashville** | **NHL** | **72** | **11** | **15** | **26** | **40** | **0** | **1** | **1** | **90** | **12.2** | **11** | **680** | **51.6** | **13:38** | **5** | **1** | **1** | **2** | **4** | **0** | **0** | **0** | **12:21** |
| **2007-08** | **Nashville** | **NHL** | **79** | **11** | **21** | **32** | **47** | **2** | **1** | **1** | **97** | **11.3** | **–4** | **384** | **50.3** | **13:56** | **6** | **0** | **0** | **0** | **0** | **0** | **0** | **0** | **16:48** |
| **2008-09** | **Nashville** | **NHL** | **78** | **11** | **6** | **17** | **24** | **1** | **2** | **2** | **114** | **9.6** | **–13** | **612** | **54.1** | **13:58** | .... | .... | .... | .... | .... | .... | .... | .... | .... |
| | **NHL Totals** | | **305** | **45** | **48** | **93** | **190** | **6** | **4** | **7** | **375** | **12.0** | | **2434** | **52.3** | **13:16** | **13** | **1** | **2** | **3** | **4** | **0** | **0** | **0** | **13:51** |

ECHL All-Rookie Team (2002)

Signed as a free agent by **Arkansas** (ECHL), March 31, 2001. Traded to **Roanoke** (ECHL) by **Arkansas** (ECHL) for Calvin Elfring, August 11, 2001. Signed as a free agent by **Nashville**, May 6, 2002. Signed as a free agent by **Phoenix**, July 1, 2009.

## FILATOV, Nikita

(FIHL-uh-tawf, nih-KEE-ta) **CBJ**

Left wing. Shoots right. 6', 172 lbs. Born, Moscow, USSR, May 25, 1990. Columbus' 1st choice, 6th overall, in 2008 Entry Draft.

| Season | Club | League | GP | G | A | Pts | PIM | PP | SH | GW | S | % | +/- | TF | F% | Min | GP | G | A | Pts | PIM | PP | SH | GW | Min |
|---|---|---|---|---|---|---|---|---|---|---|---|---|---|---|---|---|---|---|---|---|---|---|---|---|---|
| 2005-06 | CSKA Moscow 2 | Russia-3 | STATISTICS NOT AVAILABLE | | | | | | | | | | | | | | | | | | | | | | |
| 2006-07 | CSKA Moscow 2 | Russia-3 | STATISTICS NOT AVAILABLE | | | | | | | | | | | | | | | | | | | | | | |
| 2007-08 | CSKA Moscow 2 | Russia-3 | 23 | 24 | 23 | 47 | 62 | .... | .... | .... | .... | .... | .... | .... | .... | .... | 11 | 14 | 9 | 23 | 28 | .... | .... | .... | .... |
| | CSKA Moscow | Russia | 5 | 0 | 0 | 0 | 0 | .... | .... | .... | .... | .... | .... | .... | .... | .... | .... | .... | .... | .... | .... | .... | .... | .... | .... |
| **2008-09** | **Columbus** | **NHL** | **8** | **4** | **0** | **4** | **0** | **0** | **0** | **1** | **10** | **40.0** | **3** | **0** | **0.0** | **8:08** | .... | .... | .... | .... | .... | .... | .... | .... | .... |
| | Syracuse Crunch | AHL | 39 | 16 | 16 | 32 | 24 | .... | .... | .... | .... | .... | .... | .... | .... | .... | .... | .... | .... | .... | .... | .... | .... | .... | .... |
| | **NHL Totals** | | **8** | **4** | **0** | **4** | **0** | **0** | **0** | **1** | **10** | **40.0** | | **0** | **0.0** | **8:08** | .... | .... | .... | .... | .... | .... | .... | .... | .... |

## FILEWICH, Jonathan

(FIGHL-uh-which, JAWN-ah-thuhn) **ST.L.**

Right wing. Shoots right. 6'2", 208 lbs. Born, Kelowna, B.C., October 2, 1984. Pittsburgh's 3rd choice, 70th overall, in 2003 Entry Draft.

| Season | Club | League | GP | G | A | Pts | PIM | PP | SH | GW | S | % | +/- | TF | F% | Min | GP | G | A | Pts | PIM | PP | SH | GW | Min |
|---|---|---|---|---|---|---|---|---|---|---|---|---|---|---|---|---|---|---|---|---|---|---|---|---|---|
| 1998-99 | Sherwood Park | AMBHL | 36 | 29 | 43 | 72 | 90 | .... | .... | .... | .... | .... | .... | .... | .... | .... | .... | .... | .... | .... | .... | .... | .... | .... | .... |
| 99-2000 | Sherwood Park | AMHL | 33 | 28 | 20 | 48 | 59 | .... | .... | .... | .... | .... | .... | .... | .... | .... | .... | .... | .... | .... | .... | .... | .... | .... | .... |
| | Prince George | WHL | 3 | 0 | 0 | 0 | 0 | .... | .... | .... | .... | .... | .... | .... | .... | .... | .... | .... | .... | .... | .... | .... | .... | .... | .... |
| 2000-01 | Prince George | WHL | 61 | 9 | 16 | 25 | 32 | .... | .... | .... | .... | .... | .... | .... | .... | .... | .... | .... | .... | .... | .... | .... | .... | .... | .... |
| 2001-02 | Prince George | WHL | 66 | 13 | 19 | 32 | 23 | .... | .... | .... | .... | .... | .... | .... | .... | .... | 7 | 2 | 0 | 2 | 2 | .... | .... | .... | .... |
| 2002-03 | Prince George | WHL | 51 | 27 | 27 | 54 | 45 | .... | .... | .... | .... | .... | .... | .... | .... | .... | 5 | 1 | 1 | 2 | 2 | .... | .... | .... | .... |
| 2003-04 | Prince George | WHL | 72 | 30 | 25 | 55 | 52 | .... | .... | .... | .... | .... | .... | .... | .... | .... | .... | .... | .... | .... | .... | .... | .... | .... | .... |
| 2004-05 | Lethbridge | WHL | 68 | 42 | 38 | 80 | 26 | .... | .... | .... | .... | .... | .... | .... | .... | .... | 5 | 1 | 1 | 2 | 2 | .... | .... | .... | .... |
| 2005-06 | Wilkes-Barre | AHL | 73 | 22 | 14 | 36 | 40 | .... | .... | .... | .... | .... | .... | .... | .... | .... | 11 | 6 | 4 | 10 | 6 | .... | .... | .... | .... |
| 2006-07 | Wilkes-Barre | AHL | 80 | 30 | 26 | 56 | 38 | .... | .... | .... | .... | .... | .... | .... | .... | .... | 11 | 4 | 2 | 6 | 8 | .... | .... | .... | .... |
| **2007-08** | **Pittsburgh** | **NHL** | **5** | **0** | **0** | **0** | **0** | **0** | **0** | **0** | **3** | **0.0** | **–2** | **0** | **0.0** | **8:42** | .... | .... | .... | .... | .... | .... | .... | .... | .... |
| | Wilkes-Barre | AHL | 71 | 10 | 21 | 31 | 44 | .... | .... | .... | .... | .... | .... | .... | .... | .... | 14 | 1 | 2 | 3 | 2 | .... | .... | .... | .... |
| 2008-09 | Wilkes-Barre | AHL | 19 | 2 | 2 | 4 | 6 | .... | .... | .... | .... | .... | .... | .... | .... | .... | .... | .... | .... | .... | .... | .... | .... | .... | .... |
| | Peoria Rivermen | AHL | 49 | 5 | 10 | 15 | 12 | .... | .... | .... | .... | .... | .... | .... | .... | .... | 7 | 2 | 1 | 3 | 6 | .... | .... | .... | .... |
| | **NHL Totals** | | **5** | **0** | **0** | **0** | **0** | **0** | **0** | **0** | **3** | **0.0** | | **0** | **0.0** | **8:42** | .... | .... | .... | .... | .... | .... | .... | .... | .... |

Traded to **St. Louis** by **Pittsburgh** for future considerations, December 19, 2008.

## FILPPULA, Valtteri

(FIHL-poo-luh, VAL-tuhr-ee) **DET.**

Center. Shoots left. 6', 193 lbs. Born, Vantaa, Finland, March 20, 1984. Detroit's 3rd choice, 95th overall, in 2002 Entry Draft.

| Season | Club | League | GP | G | A | Pts | PIM | PP | SH | GW | S | % | +/- | TF | F% | Min | GP | G | A | Pts | PIM | PP | SH | GW | Min |
|---|---|---|---|---|---|---|---|---|---|---|---|---|---|---|---|---|---|---|---|---|---|---|---|---|---|
| 2000-01 | Jokerit U18 | Fin-U18 | 31 | 18 | 29 | 47 | 4 | .... | .... | .... | .... | .... | .... | .... | .... | .... | 6 | 4 | 4 | 8 | 0 | .... | .... | .... | .... |
| | Jokerit Helsinki Jr. | Fin-Jr. | 1 | 0 | 1 | 1 | 0 | .... | .... | .... | .... | .... | .... | .... | .... | .... | .... | .... | .... | .... | .... | .... | .... | .... | .... |
| 2001-02 | Jokerit U18 | Fin-U18 | 1 | 0 | 1 | 1 | 0 | .... | .... | .... | .... | .... | .... | .... | .... | .... | 8 | 4 | 9 | 13 | 2 | .... | .... | .... | .... |
| | Jokerit Helsinki Jr. | Fin-Jr. | 40 | 8 | 15 | 23 | 14 | .... | .... | .... | .... | .... | .... | .... | .... | .... | 1 | 0 | 0 | 0 | 0 | .... | .... | .... | .... |
| 2002-03 | Jokerit Helsinki Jr. | Fin-Jr. | 35 | 16 | 37 | 53 | 14 | .... | .... | .... | .... | .... | .... | .... | .... | .... | 11 | 4 | 10 | 14 | 4 | .... | .... | .... | .... |
| 2003-04 | Suomi U20 | Finland-2 | 1 | 0 | 0 | 0 | 2 | .... | .... | .... | .... | .... | .... | .... | .... | .... | .... | .... | .... | .... | .... | .... | .... | .... | .... |
| | Jokerit Helsinki | Finland | 49 | 5 | 13 | 18 | 6 | .... | .... | .... | .... | .... | .... | .... | .... | .... | .... | .... | .... | .... | .... | .... | .... | .... | .... |
| 2004-05 | Jokerit Helsinki | Finland | 55 | 10 | 20 | 30 | 20 | .... | .... | .... | .... | .... | .... | .... | .... | .... | 12 | 5 | 6 | 11 | 2 | .... | .... | .... | .... |
| **2005-06** | **Detroit** | **NHL** | **4** | **0** | **1** | **1** | **2** | **0** | **0** | **0** | **1** | **0.0** | **1** | **21** | **47.6** | **7:19** | .... | .... | .... | .... | .... | .... | .... | .... | .... |
| | Grand Rapids | AHL | 74 | 20 | 51 | 71 | 30 | .... | .... | .... | .... | .... | .... | .... | .... | .... | 16 | 7 | 9 | 16 | 4 | .... | .... | .... | .... |
| **2006-07** | **Detroit** | **NHL** | **73** | **10** | **7** | **17** | **20** | **0** | **0** | **1** | **76** | **13.2** | **8** | **267** | **55.8** | **11:16** | **18** | **3** | **2** | **5** | **2** | **0** | **0** | **0** | **12:12** |
| | Grand Rapids | AHL | 3 | 2 | 2 | 4 | 2 | .... | .... | .... | .... | .... | .... | .... | .... | .... | .... | .... | .... | .... | .... | .... | .... | .... | .... |
| **2007-08**♦ | **Detroit** | **NHL** | **78** | **19** | **17** | **36** | **28** | **3** | **0** | **3** | **122** | **15.6** | **16** | **621** | **50.6** | **16:58** | **22** | **5** | **6** | **11** | **2** | **0** | **0** | **0** | **16:40** |
| **2008-09** | **Detroit** | **NHL** | **80** | **12** | **28** | **40** | **42** | **1** | **0** | **1** | **129** | **9.3** | **9** | **785** | **52.1** | **16:06** | **23** | **3** | **13** | **16** | **8** | **1** | **0** | **1** | **17:38** |
| | **NHL Totals** | | **235** | **41** | **53** | **94** | **92** | **4** | **0** | **5** | **328** | **12.5** | | **1694** | **52.1** | **14:44** | **63** | **11** | **21** | **32** | **12** | **1** | **0** | **1** | **15:44** |

## FINGER, Jeff

(FIHN-guhr, JEHF) **TOR.**

Defense. Shoots right. 6'1", 205 lbs. Born, Hancock, MI, December 18, 1979. Colorado's 11th choice, 240th overall, in 1999 Entry Draft.

| Season | Club | League | Regular Season GP | G | A | Pts | PIM | PP | SH | GW | S | % | +/- | TF | F% | Min | Playoffs GP | G | A | Pts | PIM | PP | SH | GW | Min |
|---|---|---|---|---|---|---|---|---|---|---|---|---|---|---|---|---|---|---|---|---|---|---|---|---|---|
| 1997-98 | Green Bay | USHL | 51 | 5 | 9 | 14 | 208 | .... | .... | .... | .... | .... | .... | .... | .... | .... | 4 | 0 | 0 | 0 | 18 | .... | .... | .... | .... |
| 1998-99 | Green Bay | USHL | 54 | 11 | 28 | 39 | 199 | .... | .... | .... | .... | .... | .... | .... | .... | .... | 6 | 0 | 3 | 3 | 14 | .... | .... | .... | .... |
| 99-2000 | Green Bay | USHL | 55 | 13 | 35 | 48 | 15 | .... | .... | .... | .... | .... | .... | .... | .... | .... | 14 | 3 | 11 | 14 | 40 | .... | .... | .... | .... |
| 2000-01 | St. Cloud State | WCHA | 41 | 4 | 5 | 9 | 84 | .... | .... | .... | .... | .... | .... | .... | .... | .... | .... | .... | .... | .... | .... | .... | .... | .... | .... |
| 2001-02 | St. Cloud State | WCHA | 42 | 6 | 20 | 26 | 105 | .... | .... | .... | .... | .... | .... | .... | .... | .... | .... | .... | .... | .... | .... | .... | .... | .... | .... |
| 2002-03 | St. Cloud State | WCHA | 24 | 5 | 8 | 13 | 46 | .... | .... | .... | .... | .... | .... | .... | .... | .... | .... | .... | .... | .... | .... | .... | .... | .... | .... |
| 2003-04 | Reading Royals | ECHL | 10 | 2 | 5 | 7 | 24 | .... | .... | .... | .... | .... | .... | .... | .... | .... | .... | .... | .... | .... | .... | .... | .... | .... | .... |
| | Hershey Bears | AHL | 63 | 2 | 9 | 11 | 88 | .... | .... | .... | .... | .... | .... | .... | .... | .... | .... | .... | .... | .... | .... | .... | .... | .... | .... |
| 2004-05 | Hershey Bears | AHL | 75 | 4 | 12 | 16 | 125 | .... | .... | .... | .... | .... | .... | .... | .... | .... | .... | .... | .... | .... | .... | .... | .... | .... | .... |
| 2005-06 | Lowell | AHL | 70 | 3 | 20 | 23 | 116 | .... | .... | .... | .... | .... | .... | .... | .... | .... | .... | .... | .... | .... | .... | .... | .... | .... | .... |
| **2006-07** | **Colorado** | **NHL** | 22 | 1 | 4 | 5 | 11 | 0 | 0 | 0 | 16 | 6.3 | 10 | 0 | 0.0 | 13:48 | .... | .... | .... | .... | .... | .... | .... | .... | .... |
| | Albany River Rats | AHL | 44 | 3 | 10 | 13 | 65 | .... | .... | .... | .... | .... | .... | .... | .... | .... | 5 | 1 | 1 | 2 | 4 | .... | .... | .... | .... |
| **2007-08** | **Colorado** | **NHL** | 72 | 8 | 11 | 19 | 40 | 1 | 1 | 1 | 93 | 8.6 | 12 | 1 | 100.0 | 19:57 | 5 | 0 | 2 | 2 | 4 | 0 | 0 | 0 | 22:05 |
| **2008-09** | **Toronto** | **NHL** | 66 | 6 | 17 | 23 | 43 | 0 | 0 | 0 | 68 | 8.8 | -7 | 0 | 0.0 | 20:29 | .... | .... | .... | .... | .... | .... | .... | .... | .... |
| | **NHL Totals** | | 160 | 15 | 32 | 47 | 94 | 1 | 1 | 1 | 177 | 8.5 | | 1 | 100.0 | 19:20 | 5 | 0 | 2 | 2 | 4 | 0 | 0 | 0 | 22:05 |

USHL Defenseman of the Year (2000)

Signed as a free agent by **Toronto**, July 1, 2008.

## FISHER, Mike

(FIH-shuhr, MIGHK) **OTT.**

Center. Shoots right. 6'1", 213 lbs. Born, Peterborough, Ont., June 5, 1980. Ottawa's 2nd choice, 44th overall, in 1998 Entry Draft.

| Season | Club | League | Regular Season GP | G | A | Pts | PIM | PP | SH | GW | S | % | +/- | TF | F% | Min | Playoffs GP | G | A | Pts | PIM | PP | SH | GW | Min |
|---|---|---|---|---|---|---|---|---|---|---|---|---|---|---|---|---|---|---|---|---|---|---|---|---|---|
| 1996-97 | Peterborough | OPJHL | 51 | 26 | 30 | 56 | 35 | .... | .... | .... | .... | .... | .... | .... | .... | .... | .... | .... | .... | .... | .... | .... | .... | .... | .... |
| 1997-98 | Sudbury Wolves | OHL | 66 | 24 | 25 | 49 | 65 | .... | .... | .... | .... | .... | .... | .... | .... | .... | 9 | 2 | 2 | 4 | 13 | .... | .... | .... | .... |
| 1998-99 | Sudbury Wolves | OHL | 68 | 41 | 65 | 106 | 55 | .... | .... | .... | .... | .... | .... | .... | .... | .... | 4 | 2 | 1 | 3 | 4 | .... | .... | .... | .... |
| **99-2000** | **Ottawa** | **NHL** | 32 | 4 | 5 | 9 | 15 | 0 | 0 | 1 | 49 | 8.2 | -6 | 356 | 47.8 | 12:57 | .... | .... | .... | .... | .... | .... | .... | .... | .... |
| **2000-01** | **Ottawa** | **NHL** | 60 | 7 | 12 | 19 | 46 | 0 | 0 | 3 | 83 | 8.4 | -1 | 709 | 50.2 | 11:38 | 4 | 0 | 1 | 1 | 4 | 0 | 0 | 0 | 13:41 |
| **2001-02** | **Ottawa** | **NHL** | 58 | 15 | 9 | 24 | 55 | 0 | 3 | 4 | 123 | 12.2 | 8 | 848 | 48.7 | 14:05 | 10 | 2 | 1 | 3 | 0 | 0 | 0 | 0 | 16:17 |
| **2002-03** | **Ottawa** | **NHL** | 74 | 18 | 20 | 38 | 54 | 5 | 1 | 3 | 142 | 12.7 | 13 | 1077 | 48.1 | 15:59 | 18 | 2 | 2 | 4 | 16 | 0 | 1 | 1 | 16:58 |
| **2003-04** | **Ottawa** | **NHL** | 24 | 4 | 6 | 10 | 39 | 1 | 0 | 0 | 47 | 8.5 | -3 | 357 | 42.0 | 17:26 | 7 | 1 | 0 | 1 | 4 | 0 | 0 | 1 | 16:11 |
| 2004-05 | EV Zug | Swiss | 21 | 9 | 18 | 27 | 34 | .... | .... | .... | .... | .... | .... | .... | .... | .... | 9 | 2 | 3 | 5 | 10 | .... | .... | .... | .... |
| **2005-06** | **Ottawa** | **NHL** | 68 | 22 | 22 | 44 | 64 | 2 | 4 | 3 | 150 | 14.7 | 23 | 883 | 50.3 | 17:09 | 10 | 2 | 2 | 4 | 12 | 0 | 1 | 0 | 18:50 |
| **2006-07** | **Ottawa** | **NHL** | 68 | 22 | 26 | 48 | 41 | 7 | 2 | 3 | 193 | 11.4 | 15 | 1191 | 52.1 | 18:25 | 20 | 5 | 5 | 10 | 24 | 2 | 1 | 1 | 17:43 |
| **2007-08** | **Ottawa** | **NHL** | 79 | 23 | 24 | 47 | 82 | 6 | 2 | 4 | 215 | 10.7 | -10 | 1230 | 50.2 | 19:46 | .... | .... | .... | .... | .... | .... | .... | .... | .... |
| **2008-09** | **Ottawa** | **NHL** | 78 | 13 | 19 | 32 | 66 | 1 | 2 | 3 | 182 | 7.1 | 0 | 1044 | 51.3 | 18:30 | .... | .... | .... | .... | .... | .... | .... | .... | .... |
| | **NHL Totals** | | 541 | 128 | 143 | 271 | 462 | 22 | 14 | 24 | 1184 | 10.8 | | 7695 | 49.7 | 16:33 | 69 | 12 | 11 | 23 | 60 | 2 | 3 | 3 | 17:05 |

• Missed majority of 1999-2000 season recovering from knee injury suffered in game vs. Boston, December 30, 1999. • Missed majority of 2003-04 season recovering from elbow injury suffered in practice, October 4, 2003. Signed as a free agent by **Zug** (Swiss), November 1, 2004.

## FISTRIC, Mark

(FIHST-rihc, MAHRK) **DAL.**

Defense. Shoots left. 6'2", 232 lbs. Born, Edmonton, Alta., June 1, 1986. Dallas' 1st choice, 28th overall, in 2004 Entry Draft.

| Season | Club | League | Regular Season GP | G | A | Pts | PIM | PP | SH | GW | S | % | +/- | TF | F% | Min | Playoffs GP | G | A | Pts | PIM | PP | SH | GW | Min |
|---|---|---|---|---|---|---|---|---|---|---|---|---|---|---|---|---|---|---|---|---|---|---|---|---|---|
| 2000-01 | Edmonton MLAC | AMBHL | 34 | 13 | 13 | 26 | 144 | .... | .... | .... | .... | .... | .... | .... | .... | .... | .... | .... | .... | .... | .... | .... | .... | .... | .... |
| 2001-02 | Edmonton MLAC | AMHL | 30 | 8 | 10 | 18 | 85 | .... | .... | .... | .... | .... | .... | .... | .... | .... | .... | .... | .... | .... | .... | .... | .... | .... | .... |
| | Vancouver Giants | WHL | 4 | 0 | 2 | 2 | 0 | .... | .... | .... | .... | .... | .... | .... | .... | .... | .... | .... | .... | .... | .... | .... | .... | .... | .... |
| 2002-03 | Vancouver Giants | WHL | 63 | 2 | 7 | 9 | 81 | .... | .... | .... | .... | .... | .... | .... | .... | .... | 4 | 0 | 0 | 0 | 8 | .... | .... | .... | .... |
| 2003-04 | Vancouver Giants | WHL | 72 | 1 | 11 | 12 | 192 | .... | .... | .... | .... | .... | .... | .... | .... | .... | 11 | 0 | 2 | 2 | 10 | .... | .... | .... | .... |
| 2004-05 | Vancouver Giants | WHL | 15 | 1 | 5 | 6 | 32 | .... | .... | .... | .... | .... | .... | .... | .... | .... | 6 | 1 | 1 | 2 | 16 | .... | .... | .... | .... |
| 2005-06 | Vancouver Giants | WHL | 60 | 7 | 22 | 29 | 148 | .... | .... | .... | .... | .... | .... | .... | .... | .... | 18 | 1 | 9 | 10 | 30 | .... | .... | .... | .... |
| 2006-07 | Iowa Stars | AHL | 80 | 2 | 22 | 24 | 83 | .... | .... | .... | .... | .... | .... | .... | .... | .... | 12 | 0 | 0 | 0 | 16 | .... | .... | .... | .... |
| **2007-08** | **Dallas** | **NHL** | 37 | 0 | 2 | 2 | 24 | 0 | 0 | 0 | 17 | 0.0 | 3 | 0 | 0.0 | 12:44 | 9 | 0 | 0 | 0 | 6 | 0 | 0 | 0 | 14:51 |
| | Iowa Stars | AHL | 30 | 1 | 4 | 5 | 48 | .... | .... | .... | .... | .... | .... | .... | .... | .... | .... | .... | .... | .... | .... | .... | .... | .... | .... |
| **2008-09** | **Dallas** | **NHL** | 36 | 0 | 4 | 4 | 42 | 0 | 0 | 0 | 35 | 0.0 | -1 | 0 | 0.0 | 15:57 | .... | .... | .... | .... | .... | .... | .... | .... | .... |
| | Manitoba Moose | AHL | 35 | 0 | 8 | 8 | 26 | .... | .... | .... | .... | .... | .... | .... | .... | .... | 22 | 2 | 5 | 7 | 26 | .... | .... | .... | .... |
| | **NHL Totals** | | 73 | 0 | 6 | 6 | 66 | 0 | 0 | 0 | 52 | 0.0 | | 0 | 0.0 | 14:19 | 9 | 0 | 0 | 0 | 6 | 0 | 0 | 0 | 14:51 |

## FITZGERALD, Zach

(fihtz-JAIR-uhld, ZAK) **CAR.**

Defense. Shoots left. 6'2", 214 lbs. Born, Two Harbors, MN, June 16, 1985. St. Louis' 4th choice, 88th overall, in 2003 Entry Draft.

| Season | Club | League | Regular Season GP | G | A | Pts | PIM | PP | SH | GW | S | % | +/- | TF | F% | Min | Playoffs GP | G | A | Pts | PIM | PP | SH | GW | Min |
|---|---|---|---|---|---|---|---|---|---|---|---|---|---|---|---|---|---|---|---|---|---|---|---|---|---|
| 2000-01 | Duluth East | High-MN | 26 | 1 | 7 | 8 | 44 | .... | .... | .... | .... | .... | .... | .... | .... | .... | .... | .... | .... | .... | .... | .... | .... | .... | .... |
| 2001-02 | Seattle | WHL | 61 | 3 | 7 | 10 | 214 | .... | .... | .... | .... | .... | .... | .... | .... | .... | 10 | 0 | 2 | 2 | 19 | .... | .... | .... | .... |
| 2002-03 | Seattle | WHL | 64 | 8 | 14 | 22 | 232 | .... | .... | .... | .... | .... | .... | .... | .... | .... | 15 | 0 | 4 | 4 | 33 | .... | .... | .... | .... |
| 2003-04 | Seattle | WHL | 58 | 4 | 15 | 19 | 163 | .... | .... | .... | .... | .... | .... | .... | .... | .... | .... | .... | .... | .... | .... | .... | .... | .... | .... |
| 2004-05 | Seattle | WHL | 65 | 7 | 18 | 25 | *244 | .... | .... | .... | .... | .... | .... | .... | .... | .... | 9 | 0 | 3 | 3 | 24 | .... | .... | .... | .... |
| 2005-06 | Peoria Rivermen | AHL | 13 | 1 | 1 | 2 | 47 | .... | .... | .... | .... | .... | .... | .... | .... | .... | .... | .... | .... | .... | .... | .... | .... | .... | .... |
| | Alaska Aces | ECHL | 12 | 1 | 1 | 2 | 108 | .... | .... | .... | .... | .... | .... | .... | .... | .... | .... | .... | .... | .... | .... | .... | .... | .... | .... |
| 2006-07 | Peoria Rivermen | AHL | 29 | 0 | 2 | 2 | 86 | .... | .... | .... | .... | .... | .... | .... | .... | .... | .... | .... | .... | .... | .... | .... | .... | .... | .... |
| | Alaska Aces | ECHL | 10 | 0 | 1 | 1 | 48 | .... | .... | .... | .... | .... | .... | .... | .... | .... | 14 | 2 | 3 | 5 | *82 | .... | .... | .... | .... |
| **2007-08** | **Vancouver** | **NHL** | 1 | 0 | 0 | 0 | 0 | 0 | 0 | 0 | 1 | 0.0 | 0 | 0 | 0.0 | 13:20 | .... | .... | .... | .... | .... | .... | .... | .... | .... |
| | Manitoba Moose | AHL | 48 | 5 | 3 | 8 | 158 | .... | .... | .... | .... | .... | .... | .... | .... | .... | 3 | 0 | 0 | 0 | 14 | .... | .... | .... | .... |
| 2008-09 | Manitoba Moose | AHL | 56 | 0 | 8 | 8 | 209 | .... | .... | .... | .... | .... | .... | .... | .... | .... | 16 | 0 | 1 | 1 | 14 | .... | .... | .... | .... |
| | **NHL Totals** | | 1 | 0 | 0 | 0 | 0 | 0 | 0 | 0 | 1 | 0.0 | | 0 | 0.0 | 13:20 | .... | .... | .... | .... | .... | .... | .... | .... | .... |

Traded to **Vancouver** by **St. Louis** for Francois-Pierre Guenette, August 1, 2007. Signed as a free agent by **Carolina**, July 15, 2009.

## FITZPATRICK, Rory

(FIHTZ-pa-trihk, ROHR-ee) **FLA.**

Defense. Shoots right. 6'2", 208 lbs. Born, Rochester, NY, January 11, 1975. Montreal's 2nd choice, 47th overall, in 1993 Entry Draft.

| Season | Club | League | Regular Season GP | G | A | Pts | PIM | PP | SH | GW | S | % | +/- | TF | F% | Min | Playoffs GP | G | A | Pts | PIM | PP | SH | GW | Min |
|---|---|---|---|---|---|---|---|---|---|---|---|---|---|---|---|---|---|---|---|---|---|---|---|---|---|
| 1990-91 | Rochester | EmJHL | 40 | 0 | 5 | 5 | .... | .... | .... | .... | .... | .... | .... | .... | .... | .... | .... | .... | .... | .... | .... | .... | .... | .... | .... |
| 1991-92 | Rochester | EmJHL | 28 | 8 | 28 | 36 | 141 | .... | .... | .... | .... | .... | .... | .... | .... | .... | .... | .... | .... | .... | .... | .... | .... | .... | .... |
| 1992-93 | Sudbury Wolves | OHL | 58 | 4 | 20 | 24 | 68 | .... | .... | .... | .... | .... | .... | .... | .... | .... | 14 | 0 | 0 | 0 | 17 | .... | .... | .... | .... |
| 1993-94 | Sudbury Wolves | OHL | 65 | 12 | 34 | 46 | 112 | .... | .... | .... | .... | .... | .... | .... | .... | .... | 10 | 2 | 5 | 7 | 10 | .... | .... | .... | .... |
| 1994-95 | Sudbury Wolves | OHL | 56 | 12 | 36 | 48 | 72 | .... | .... | .... | .... | .... | .... | .... | .... | .... | 18 | 3 | 15 | 18 | 21 | .... | .... | .... | .... |
| | Fredericton | AHL | .... | .... | .... | .... | .... | .... | .... | .... | .... | .... | .... | .... | .... | .... | 10 | 1 | 2 | 3 | 5 | .... | .... | .... | .... |
| **1995-96** | **Montreal** | **NHL** | 42 | 0 | 2 | 2 | 18 | 0 | 0 | 0 | 31 | 0.0 | -7 | .... | .... | .... | 6 | 1 | 1 | 2 | 0 | 0 | 0 | 0 | .... |
| | Fredericton | AHL | 18 | 4 | 6 | 10 | 36 | .... | .... | .... | .... | .... | .... | .... | .... | .... | .... | .... | .... | .... | .... | .... | .... | .... | .... |
| **1996-97** | **Montreal** | **NHL** | 6 | 0 | 1 | 1 | 6 | 0 | 0 | 0 | 5 | 0.0 | -2 | .... | .... | .... | .... | .... | .... | .... | .... | .... | .... | .... | .... |
| | **St. Louis** | **NHL** | 2 | 0 | 0 | 0 | 2 | 0 | 0 | 0 | 1 | 0.0 | -2 | .... | .... | .... | .... | .... | .... | .... | .... | .... | .... | .... | .... |
| | Worcester IceCats | AHL | 49 | 4 | 13 | 17 | 78 | .... | .... | .... | .... | .... | .... | .... | .... | .... | 5 | 1 | 2 | 3 | 0 | .... | .... | .... | .... |
| 1997-98 | Worcester IceCats | AHL | 62 | 8 | 22 | 30 | 111 | .... | .... | .... | .... | .... | .... | .... | .... | .... | 11 | 0 | 3 | 3 | 26 | .... | .... | .... | .... |
| **1998-99** | **St. Louis** | **NHL** | 1 | 0 | 0 | 0 | 2 | 0 | 0 | 0 | 0 | 0.0 | -3 | 0 | 0.0 | 4:49 | .... | .... | .... | .... | .... | .... | .... | .... | .... |
| | Worcester IceCats | AHL | 53 | 5 | 16 | 21 | 82 | .... | .... | .... | .... | .... | .... | .... | .... | .... | 4 | 0 | 1 | 1 | 17 | .... | .... | .... | .... |
| 99-2000 | Worcester IceCats | AHL | 28 | 0 | 5 | 5 | 48 | .... | .... | .... | .... | .... | .... | .... | .... | .... | .... | .... | .... | .... | .... | .... | .... | .... | .... |
| | Milwaukee | IHL | 27 | 2 | 1 | 3 | 27 | .... | .... | .... | .... | .... | .... | .... | .... | .... | 3 | 0 | 2 | 2 | 2 | .... | .... | .... | .... |
| **2000-01** | **Nashville** | **NHL** | 2 | 0 | 0 | 0 | 2 | 0 | 0 | 0 | 0 | 0.0 | -2 | 0 | 0.0 | 9:47 | .... | .... | .... | .... | .... | .... | .... | .... | .... |
| | Milwaukee | IHL | 22 | 0 | 2 | 2 | 32 | .... | .... | .... | .... | .... | .... | .... | .... | .... | .... | .... | .... | .... | .... | .... | .... | .... | .... |
| | Hamilton | AHL | 34 | 3 | 17 | 20 | 29 | .... | .... | .... | .... | .... | .... | .... | .... | .... | .... | .... | .... | .... | .... | .... | .... | .... | .... |
| **2001-02** | **Buffalo** | **NHL** | 5 | 0 | 0 | 0 | 4 | 0 | 0 | 0 | 2 | 0.0 | -2 | 0 | 0.0 | 11:54 | .... | .... | .... | .... | .... | .... | .... | .... | .... |
| | Rochester | AHL | 60 | 4 | 8 | 12 | 83 | .... | .... | .... | .... | .... | .... | .... | .... | .... | 2 | 0 | 1 | 1 | 0 | .... | .... | .... | .... |
| **2002-03** | **Buffalo** | **NHL** | 36 | 1 | 3 | 4 | 16 | 0 | 0 | 0 | 29 | 3.4 | -7 | 0 | 0.0 | 17:02 | .... | .... | .... | .... | .... | .... | .... | .... | .... |
| | Rochester | AHL | 41 | 5 | 11 | 16 | 65 | .... | .... | .... | .... | .... | .... | .... | .... | .... | .... | .... | .... | .... | .... | .... | .... | .... | .... |
| **2003-04** | **Buffalo** | **NHL** | 60 | 4 | 7 | 11 | 44 | 2 | 0 | 2 | 78 | 5.1 | -5 | 1 | 100.0 | 19:02 | .... | .... | .... | .... | .... | .... | .... | .... | .... |
| 2004-05 | Rochester | AHL | 20 | 1 | 1 | 2 | 18 | .... | .... | .... | .... | .... | .... | .... | .... | .... | 9 | 0 | 1 | 1 | 12 | .... | .... | .... | .... |
| **2005-06** | **Buffalo** | **NHL** | 56 | 4 | 5 | 9 | 50 | 2 | 0 | 1 | 45 | 8.9 | -18 | 1 | 0.0 | 16:22 | 11 | 0 | 4 | 4 | 16 | 0 | 0 | 0 | 17:12 |
| **2006-07** | **Vancouver** | **NHL** | 58 | 1 | 6 | 7 | 46 | 0 | 0 | 1 | 41 | 2.4 | 12 | 1 | 100.0 | 14:06 | 3 | 0 | 0 | 0 | 6 | 0 | 0 | 0 | 21:08 |

| | | | Regular Season | | | | | | | | | | | | | | Playoffs | | | | | | | | |
|---|---|---|---|---|---|---|---|---|---|---|---|---|---|---|---|---|---|---|---|---|---|---|---|---|---|
| Season | Club | League | GP | G | A | Pts | PIM | PP | SH | GW | S | % | +/- | TF | F% | Min | GP | G | A | Pts | PIM | PP | SH | GW | Min |
| **2007-08** | **Philadelphia** | **NHL** | **19** | **0** | **1** | **1** | **11** | **0** | **0** | **0** | **10** | **0.0** | **–12** | **0** | **0.0** | **12:44** | .... | .... | .... | .... | .... | .... | .... | .... | .... |
| | Philadelphia | AHL | 19 | 1 | 4 | 5 | 24 | .... | .... | .... | .... | .... | .... | .... | .... | .... | 12 | 0 | 2 | 2 | 11 | .... | .... | .... | .... |
| 2008-09 | Rochester | AHL | 46 | 4 | 10 | 14 | 37 | .... | .... | .... | .... | .... | .... | .... | .... | .... | .... | .... | .... | .... | .... | .... | .... | .... | .... |
| | **NHL Totals** | | **287** | **10** | **25** | **35** | **201** | **4** | **0** | **4** | **242** | **4.1** | | **3** | **66.7** | **16:06** | **20** | **1** | **5** | **6** | **22** | **0** | **0** | **0** | **18:02** |

OHL All-Rookie Team (1993)

Traded to **St. Louis** by **Montreal** with Pierre Turgeon and Craig Conroy for Murray Baron, Shayne Corson and St. Louis' 5th round choice (Gennady Razin) in 1997 Entry Draft, October 29, 1996. Claimed by **Boston** from **St. Louis** in Waiver Draft, October 5, 1998. Claimed on waivers by **St. Louis** from **Boston**, October 7, 1998. Traded to **Nashville** by **St. Louis** for Dan Keczmer, February 9, 2000. Traded to **Edmonton** by **Nashville** for future considerations, January 12, 2001. Signed as a free agent by **Buffalo**, August 14, 2001. Signed as a free agent by **Rochester** (AHL), March 2, 2005. Signed as a free agent by **Vancouver**, August 18, 2006. Signed as a free agent by **Philadelphia**, October 9, 2007. Signed as a free agent by **Florida**, July 3, 2008.

## FLEISCHMANN, Tomas (FLIGHSH-muhn, TAW-mahsh) WSH.

Left wing. Shoots left. 6'1", 190 lbs. Born, Koprivnice, Czech., May 16, 1984. Detroit's 2nd choice, 63rd overall, in 2002 Entry Draft.

| | | | | | | | | | | | | | | | | | | | | | | | | | |
|---|---|---|---|---|---|---|---|---|---|---|---|---|---|---|---|---|---|---|---|---|---|---|---|---|---|
| 99-2000 | HC Vitkovice Jr. | CzRep-Jr. | 46 | 9 | 13 | 22 | 6 | .... | .... | .... | .... | .... | .... | .... | .... | .... | .... | .... | .... | .... | .... | .... | .... | .... | .... |
| 2000-01 | HC Vitkovice U17 | CzR-U17 | 30 | 28 | 34 | 62 | 8 | .... | .... | .... | .... | .... | .... | .... | .... | .... | .... | .... | .... | .... | .... | .... | .... | .... | .... |
| | HC Vitkovice Jr. | CzRep-Jr. | 21 | 4 | 9 | 13 | 8 | .... | .... | .... | .... | .... | .... | .... | .... | .... | .... | .... | .... | .... | .... | .... | .... | .... | .... |
| 2001-02 | HC Vitkovice Jr. | CzRep-Jr. | 46 | 26 | 35 | 51 | 16 | .... | .... | .... | .... | .... | .... | .... | .... | .... | .... | .... | .... | .... | .... | .... | .... | .... | .... |
| | TJ Novy Jicin | CzRep-3 | 8 | 3 | 2 | 5 | 8 | .... | .... | .... | .... | .... | .... | .... | .... | .... | 7 | 3 | 4 | 7 | 35 | .... | .... | .... | .... |
| 2002-03 | Moose Jaw | WHL | 65 | 21 | 50 | 71 | 36 | .... | .... | .... | .... | .... | .... | .... | .... | .... | 12 | 4 | 11 | 15 | 6 | .... | .... | .... | .... |
| 2003-04 | Moose Jaw | WHL | 60 | 33 | 42 | 75 | 32 | .... | .... | .... | .... | .... | .... | .... | .... | .... | 10 | 3 | 4 | 7 | 10 | .... | .... | .... | .... |
| 2004-05 | Portland Pirates | AHL | 53 | 7 | 12 | 19 | 14 | .... | .... | .... | .... | .... | .... | .... | .... | .... | .... | .... | .... | .... | .... | .... | .... | .... | .... |
| **2005-06** | **Washington** | **NHL** | **14** | **0** | **2** | **2** | **0** | **0** | **0** | **0** | **11** | **0.0** | **–7** | **5** | **40.0** | **6:45** | .... | .... | .... | .... | .... | .... | .... | .... | .... |
| | Hershey Bears | AHL | 57 | 30 | 33 | 63 | 32 | .... | .... | .... | .... | .... | .... | .... | .... | .... | 20 | 11 | *21 | 32 | 15 | .... | .... | .... | .... |
| **2006-07** | **Washington** | **NHL** | **29** | **4** | **4** | **8** | **8** | **1** | **0** | **1** | **52** | **7.7** | **–6** | **14** | **35.7** | **11:38** | .... | .... | .... | .... | .... | .... | .... | .... | .... |
| | Hershey Bears | AHL | 45 | 22 | 29 | 51 | 22 | .... | .... | .... | .... | .... | .... | .... | .... | .... | 19 | 5 | 16 | 21 | 10 | .... | .... | .... | .... |
| **2007-08** | **Washington** | **NHL** | **75** | **10** | **20** | **30** | **18** | **1** | **0** | **1** | **107** | **9.3** | **–7** | **30** | **50.0** | **12:37** | **2** | **0** | **0** | **0** | **0** | **0** | **0** | **0** | **9:49** |
| **2008-09** | **Washington** | **NHL** | **73** | **19** | **18** | **37** | **20** | **7** | **0** | **4** | **131** | **14.5** | **–3** | **34** | **26.5** | **15:05** | **14** | **3** | **1** | **4** | **4** | **1** | **0** | **1** | **14:19** |
| | **NHL Totals** | | **191** | **33** | **44** | **77** | **46** | **9** | **0** | **6** | **301** | **11.0** | | **83** | **37.3** | **12:59** | **16** | **3** | **1** | **4** | **4** | **1** | **0** | **1** | **13:45** |

WHL East Second All-Star Team (2004)

Traded to **Washington** by **Detroit** with Detroit's 1st round choice (Mike Green) in 2004 Entry Draft and Detroit's 4th round choice (Luke Lynes) in 2006 Entry Draft for Robert Lang, February 27, 2004.

## FLINN, Ryan (FLIHN, RIGH-yan)

Left wing. Shoots left. 6'5", 248 lbs. Born, Halifax, N.S., April 20, 1980. New Jersey's 8th choice, 143rd overall, in 1998 Entry Draft.

| | | | | | | | | | | | | | | | | | | | | | | | | | |
|---|---|---|---|---|---|---|---|---|---|---|---|---|---|---|---|---|---|---|---|---|---|---|---|---|---|
| 1996-97 | Laval Titan | QMJHL | 23 | 3 | 2 | 5 | 56 | .... | .... | .... | .... | .... | .... | .... | .... | .... | 2 | 0 | 0 | 0 | 0 | .... | .... | .... | .... |
| 1997-98 | Laval Titan | QMJHL | 59 | 4 | 12 | 16 | 217 | .... | .... | .... | .... | .... | .... | .... | .... | .... | 15 | 1 | 0 | 1 | 63 | .... | .... | .... | .... |
| 1998-99 | Acadie-Bathurst | QMJHL | 44 | 3 | 4 | 7 | 195 | .... | .... | .... | .... | .... | .... | .... | .... | .... | 23 | 2 | 0 | 2 | 37 | .... | .... | .... | .... |
| 99-2000 | Halifax | QMJHL | 67 | 14 | 19 | 33 | 365 | .... | .... | .... | .... | .... | .... | .... | .... | .... | .... | .... | .... | .... | .... | .... | .... | .... | .... |
| 2000-01 | Cape Breton | QMJHL | 57 | 16 | 17 | 33 | 280 | .... | .... | .... | .... | .... | .... | .... | .... | .... | 9 | 1 | 1 | 2 | 43 | .... | .... | .... | .... |
| **2001-02** | Reading Royals | ECHL | 20 | 1 | 3 | 4 | 130 | .... | .... | .... | .... | .... | .... | .... | .... | .... | .... | .... | .... | .... | .... | .... | .... | .... | .... |
| | **Los Angeles** | **NHL** | **10** | **0** | **0** | **0** | **51** | **0** | **0** | **0** | **2** | **0.0** | **0** | **0** | **0.0** | **3:29** | .... | .... | .... | .... | .... | .... | .... | .... | .... |
| | Manchester | AHL | 37 | 0 | 1 | 1 | 113 | .... | .... | .... | .... | .... | .... | .... | .... | .... | 1 | 0 | 0 | 0 | 0 | .... | .... | .... | .... |
| **2002-03** | **Los Angeles** | **NHL** | **19** | **1** | **0** | **1** | **28** | **0** | **0** | **0** | **13** | **7.7** | **0** | **0** | **0.0** | **5:28** | .... | .... | .... | .... | .... | .... | .... | .... | .... |
| | Manchester | AHL | 27 | 2 | 2 | 4 | 95 | .... | .... | .... | .... | .... | .... | .... | .... | .... | .... | .... | .... | .... | .... | .... | .... | .... | .... |
| 2003-04 | Manchester | AHL | 59 | 3 | 5 | 8 | 164 | .... | .... | .... | .... | .... | .... | .... | .... | .... | 6 | 0 | 0 | 0 | 4 | .... | .... | .... | .... |
| 2004-05 | Manchester | AHL | 14 | 1 | 1 | 2 | 112 | .... | .... | .... | .... | .... | .... | .... | .... | .... | .... | .... | .... | .... | .... | .... | .... | .... | .... |
| **2005-06** | **Los Angeles** | **NHL** | **2** | **0** | **0** | **0** | **5** | **0** | **0** | **0** | **0** | **0.0** | **0** | **0** | **0.0** | **0:25** | .... | .... | .... | .... | .... | .... | .... | .... | .... |
| | Manchester | AHL | 6 | 0 | 1 | 1 | 38 | .... | .... | .... | .... | .... | .... | .... | .... | .... | .... | .... | .... | .... | .... | .... | .... | .... | .... |
| 2006-07 | San Antonio | AHL | 61 | 2 | 4 | 6 | 166 | .... | .... | .... | .... | .... | .... | .... | .... | .... | .... | .... | .... | .... | .... | .... | .... | .... | .... |
| 2007-08 | Springfield | AHL | 24 | 0 | 1 | 1 | 82 | .... | .... | .... | .... | .... | .... | .... | .... | .... | .... | .... | .... | .... | .... | .... | .... | .... | .... |
| | Hershey Bears | AHL | 17 | 3 | 0 | 3 | 53 | .... | .... | .... | .... | .... | .... | .... | .... | .... | 2 | 0 | 0 | 0 | 2 | .... | .... | .... | .... |
| 2008-09 | Hamilton | AHL | 52 | 2 | 2 | 4 | 122 | .... | .... | .... | .... | .... | .... | .... | .... | .... | 4 | 0 | 0 | 0 | 0 | .... | .... | .... | .... |
| | **NHL Totals** | | **31** | **1** | **0** | **1** | **84** | **0** | **0** | **0** | **15** | **6.7** | | **0** | **0.0** | **4:30** | .... | .... | .... | .... | .... | .... | .... | .... | .... |

Signed as a free agent by **Los Angeles**, January 8, 2002. • Missed majority of 2004-05 season recovering from foot and leg injuries. • Missed majority of 2005-06 season recovering from head injury suffered in game vs. Chicago, November 26, 2005. Signed as a free agent by **Edmonton**, July 17, 2007. Signed as a free agent by **Montreal**, July 7, 2008.

## FOLIGNO, Nick (foh-LEE-noh, NIHK) OTT.

Left wing. Shoots left. 6', 205 lbs. Born, Buffalo, NY, October 31, 1987. Ottawa's 1st choice, 28th overall, in 2006 Entry Draft.

| | | | | | | | | | | | | | | | | | | | | | | | | | |
|---|---|---|---|---|---|---|---|---|---|---|---|---|---|---|---|---|---|---|---|---|---|---|---|---|---|
| 2003-04 | USNTDP | U-17 | 18 | 7 | 9 | 16 | 28 | .... | .... | .... | .... | .... | .... | .... | .... | .... | .... | .... | .... | .... | .... | .... | .... | .... | .... |
| | USNTDP | NAHL | 43 | 8 | 12 | 20 | 44 | .... | .... | .... | .... | .... | .... | .... | .... | .... | 7 | 2 | 1 | 3 | 8 | .... | .... | .... | .... |
| 2004-05 | USNTDP | U-18 | 4 | 2 | 1 | 3 | 0 | .... | .... | .... | .... | .... | .... | .... | .... | .... | .... | .... | .... | .... | .... | .... | .... | .... | .... |
| | Sudbury Wolves | OHL | 65 | 10 | 28 | 38 | 111 | .... | .... | .... | .... | .... | .... | .... | .... | .... | 12 | 5 | 5 | 10 | 16 | .... | .... | .... | .... |
| 2005-06 | Sudbury Wolves | OHL | 65 | 24 | 46 | 70 | 146 | .... | .... | .... | .... | .... | .... | .... | .... | .... | 10 | 1 | 3 | 4 | 28 | .... | .... | .... | .... |
| 2006-07 | Sudbury Wolves | OHL | 66 | 31 | 57 | 88 | 135 | .... | .... | .... | .... | .... | .... | .... | .... | .... | 21 | 12 | 17 | 29 | 36 | .... | .... | .... | .... |
| **2007-08** | **Ottawa** | **NHL** | **45** | **6** | **3** | **9** | **20** | **0** | **0** | **0** | **44** | **13.6** | **0** | **49** | **44.9** | **9:10** | **4** | **1** | **0** | **1** | **2** | **0** | **0** | **0** | **12:50** |
| | Binghamton | AHL | 28 | 6 | 13 | 19 | 16 | .... | .... | .... | .... | .... | .... | .... | .... | .... | .... | .... | .... | .... | .... | .... | .... | .... | .... |
| **2008-09** | **Ottawa** | **NHL** | **81** | **17** | **15** | **32** | **59** | **7** | **0** | **2** | **145** | **11.7** | **–10** | **47** | **44.7** | **13:41** | .... | .... | .... | .... | .... | .... | .... | .... | .... |
| | **NHL Totals** | | **126** | **23** | **18** | **41** | **79** | **7** | **0** | **2** | **189** | **12.2** | | **96** | **44.8** | **12:04** | **4** | **1** | **0** | **1** | **2** | **0** | **0** | **0** | **12:50** |

## FOOTE, Adam (FUT, A-duhm) COL.

Defense. Shoots right. 6'2", 220 lbs. Born, Toronto, Ont., July 10, 1971. Quebec's 2nd choice, 22nd overall, in 1989 Entry Draft.

| | | | | | | | | | | | | | | | | | | | | | | | | | |
|---|---|---|---|---|---|---|---|---|---|---|---|---|---|---|---|---|---|---|---|---|---|---|---|---|---|
| 1987-88 | Whitby Midgets | Minor-ON | 65 | 25 | 43 | 68 | 108 | .... | .... | .... | .... | .... | .... | .... | .... | .... | .... | .... | .... | .... | .... | .... | .... | .... | .... |
| 1988-89 | Sault Ste. Marie | OHL | 66 | 7 | 32 | 39 | 120 | .... | .... | .... | .... | .... | .... | .... | .... | .... | .... | .... | .... | .... | .... | .... | .... | .... | .... |
| 1989-90 | Sault Ste. Marie | OHL | 61 | 12 | 43 | 55 | 199 | .... | .... | .... | .... | .... | .... | .... | .... | .... | .... | .... | .... | .... | .... | .... | .... | .... | .... |
| 1990-91 | Sault Ste. Marie | OHL | 59 | 18 | 51 | 69 | 93 | .... | .... | .... | .... | .... | .... | .... | .... | .... | 14 | 5 | 12 | 17 | 28 | .... | .... | .... | .... |
| **1991-92** | **Quebec** | **NHL** | **46** | **2** | **5** | **7** | **44** | **0** | **0** | **0** | **55** | **3.6** | **–4** | .... | .... | .... | .... | .... | .... | .... | .... | .... | .... | .... | .... |
| | Halifax Citadels | AHL | 6 | 0 | 1 | 1 | 2 | .... | .... | .... | .... | .... | .... | .... | .... | .... | .... | .... | .... | .... | .... | .... | .... | .... | .... |
| **1992-93** | **Quebec** | **NHL** | **81** | **4** | **12** | **16** | **168** | **0** | **1** | **0** | **54** | **7.4** | **6** | .... | .... | .... | **6** | **0** | **1** | **1** | **2** | **0** | **0** | **0** | .... |
| **1993-94** | **Quebec** | **NHL** | **45** | **2** | **6** | **8** | **67** | **0** | **0** | **0** | **42** | **4.8** | **3** | .... | .... | .... | .... | .... | .... | .... | .... | .... | .... | .... | .... |
| **1994-95** | **Quebec** | **NHL** | **35** | **0** | **7** | **7** | **52** | **0** | **0** | **0** | **24** | **0.0** | **17** | .... | .... | .... | **6** | **0** | **1** | **1** | **14** | **0** | **0** | **0** | .... |
| **1995-96♦** | **Colorado** | **NHL** | **73** | **5** | **11** | **16** | **88** | **1** | **0** | **1** | **49** | **10.2** | **27** | .... | .... | .... | **22** | **1** | **3** | **4** | **36** | **0** | **0** | **0** | .... |
| **1996-97** | **Colorado** | **NHL** | **78** | **2** | **19** | **21** | **135** | **0** | **0** | **0** | **60** | **3.3** | **16** | .... | .... | .... | **17** | **0** | **4** | **4** | **62** | **0** | **0** | **0** | .... |
| **1997-98** | **Colorado** | **NHL** | **77** | **3** | **14** | **17** | **124** | **0** | **0** | **1** | **64** | **4.7** | **–3** | .... | .... | .... | **7** | **0** | **0** | **0** | **23** | **0** | **0** | **0** | .... |
| | Canada | Olympics | 6 | 0 | 1 | 1 | 4 | .... | .... | .... | .... | .... | .... | .... | .... | .... | .... | .... | .... | .... | .... | .... | .... | .... | .... |
| **1998-99** | **Colorado** | **NHL** | **64** | **5** | **16** | **21** | **92** | **3** | **0** | **0** | **83** | **6.0** | **20** | **0** | **0.0** | **24:50** | **19** | **2** | **3** | **5** | **24** | **1** | **0** | **0** | **28:34** |
| **99-2000** | **Colorado** | **NHL** | **59** | **5** | **13** | **18** | **98** | **1** | **0** | **2** | **63** | **7.9** | **5** | **0** | **0.0** | **25:51** | **16** | **0** | **7** | **7** | **28** | **0** | **0** | **0** | **26:05** |
| **2000-01♦** | **Colorado** | **NHL** | **35** | **3** | **12** | **15** | **42** | **1** | **1** | **1** | **59** | **5.1** | **6** | **0** | **0.0** | **25:22** | **23** | **3** | **4** | **7** | ***47** | **1** | **0** | **1** | **28:22** |
| **2001-02** | **Colorado** | **NHL** | **55** | **5** | **22** | **27** | **55** | **1** | **1** | **0** | **85** | **5.9** | **7** | **0** | **0.0** | **25:59** | **21** | **1** | **6** | **7** | **28** | **0** | **0** | **0** | **27:46** |
| | Canada | Olympics | 6 | 1 | 0 | 1 | 2 | .... | .... | .... | .... | .... | .... | .... | .... | .... | .... | .... | .... | .... | .... | .... | .... | .... | .... |
| **2002-03** | **Colorado** | **NHL** | **78** | **11** | **20** | **31** | **88** | **3** | **0** | **2** | **106** | **10.4** | **30** | **0** | **0.0** | **25:43** | **6** | **0** | **1** | **1** | **8** | **0** | **0** | **0** | **24:12** |
| **2003-04** | **Colorado** | **NHL** | **73** | **8** | **22** | **30** | **87** | **5** | **0** | **1** | **105** | **7.6** | **13** | **0** | **0.0** | **24:03** | **11** | **0** | **4** | **4** | **10** | **0** | **0** | **0** | **25:06** |
| 2004-05 | | | DID NOT PLAY | | | | | | | | | | | | | | | | | | | | | | |
| **2005-06** | **Columbus** | **NHL** | **65** | **6** | **16** | **22** | **89** | **2** | **2** | **1** | **67** | **9.0** | **–16** | **0** | **0.0** | **24:34** | .... | .... | .... | .... | .... | .... | .... | .... | .... |
| | Canada | Olympics | 6 | 0 | 1 | 1 | 6 | .... | .... | .... | .... | .... | .... | .... | .... | .... | .... | .... | .... | .... | .... | .... | .... | .... | .... |
| **2006-07** | **Columbus** | **NHL** | **59** | **3** | **9** | **12** | **71** | **2** | **0** | **0** | **78** | **3.8** | **–17** | **0** | **0.0** | **24:44** | .... | .... | .... | .... | .... | .... | .... | .... | .... |
| **2007-08** | **Columbus** | **NHL** | **63** | **1** | **14** | **15** | **95** | **0** | **1** | **0** | **57** | **1.8** | **3** | **0** | **0.0** | **24:02** | .... | .... | .... | .... | .... | .... | .... | .... | .... |
| | **Colorado** | **NHL** | **12** | **0** | **1** | **1** | **12** | **0** | **0** | **0** | **9** | **0.0** | **–1** | **0** | **0.0** | **20:01** | **10** | **0** | **0** | **0** | **6** | **0** | **0** | **0** | **21:14** |
| **2008-09** | **Colorado** | **NHL** | **42** | **1** | **6** | **7** | **30** | **0** | **0** | **1** | **19** | **5.3** | **–12** | **0** | **0.0** | **19:41** | .... | .... | .... | .... | .... | .... | .... | .... | .... |
| | **NHL Totals** | | **1040** | **66** | **225** | **291** | **1437** | **19** | **6** | **10** | **1079** | **6.1** | | **0** | **0.0** | **24:31** | **164** | **7** | **34** | **41** | **288** | **2** | **0** | **1** | **26:41** |

OHL First All-Star Team (1991)

• Transferred to **Colorado** after **Quebec** franchise relocated, June 21, 1995. • Missed majority of 2000-01 season recovering from shoulder injury suffered in game vs. Carolina, January 6, 2001. Signed as a free agent by **Columbus**, August 2, 2005. Traded to **Colorado** by **Columbus** for Colorado's 1st round choice (later traded to Philadelphia - Philadelphia selected Luca Sbisa) in 2008 Entry Draft and Colorado's 4th round choice (David Savard) in 2009 Entry Draft, February 26, 2008.

## FOSTER, Alex

(FAW-stuhr, AL-ehx) **TOR.**

Center. Shoots left. 6'1", 195 lbs. Born, Canton, MI, August 26, 1984.

| Season | Club | League | GP | G | A | Pts | PIM | PP | SH | GW | S | % | +/- | TF | F% | Min | Playoffs GP | G | A | Pts | PIM | PP | SH | GW | Min |
|---|---|---|---|---|---|---|---|---|---|---|---|---|---|---|---|---|---|---|---|---|---|---|---|---|---|
| 2002-03 | Sioux Falls | USHL | 57 | 6 | 15 | 21 | 72 | .... | .... | .... | .... | .... | .... | .... | .... | .... | 3 | 0 | 1 | 1 | 8 | .... | .... | .... | .... |
| 2003-04 | Sioux Falls | USHL | 5 | 0 | 1 | 1 | 0 | .... | .... | .... | .... | .... | .... | .... | .... | .... | .... | .... | .... | .... | .... | .... | .... | .... | .... |
| | Danville Wings | USHL | 55 | 23 | 30 | 53 | 91 | .... | .... | .... | .... | .... | .... | .... | .... | .... | 6 | 1 | 2 | 3 | 6 | .... | .... | .... | .... |
| 2004-05 | Bowling Green | CCHA | 34 | 8 | 23 | 31 | 31 | .... | .... | .... | .... | .... | .... | .... | .... | .... | .... | .... | .... | .... | .... | .... | .... | .... | .... |
| 2005-06 | Bowling Green | CCHA | 38 | 11 | 40 | 51 | 40 | .... | .... | .... | .... | .... | .... | .... | .... | .... | .... | .... | .... | .... | .... | .... | .... | .... | .... |
| 2006-07 | Toronto Marlies | AHL | 57 | 8 | 9 | 17 | 31 | .... | .... | .... | .... | .... | .... | .... | .... | .... | .... | .... | .... | .... | .... | .... | .... | .... | .... |
| | Columbia Inferno | ECHL | 9 | 1 | 10 | 11 | 6 | .... | .... | .... | .... | .... | .... | .... | .... | .... | .... | .... | .... | .... | .... | .... | .... | .... | .... |
| **2007-08** | **Toronto** | **NHL** | **3** | **0** | **0** | **0** | **0** | **0** | **0** | **0** | **1** | **0.0** | **0** | **1** | **0.0** | **3:32** | .... | .... | .... | .... | .... | .... | .... | .... | .... |
| | Toronto Marlies | AHL | 67 | 18 | 28 | 46 | 30 | .... | .... | .... | .... | .... | .... | .... | .... | .... | 19 | 2 | 6 | 8 | 12 | .... | .... | .... | .... |
| 2008-09 | Toronto Marlies | AHL | 80 | 12 | 23 | 35 | 88 | .... | .... | .... | .... | .... | .... | .... | .... | .... | 6 | 2 | 3 | 5 | 8 | .... | .... | .... | .... |
| | **NHL Totals** | | **3** | **0** | **0** | **0** | **0** | **0** | **0** | **0** | **1** | **0.0** | | **1** | **0.0** | **3:32** | .... | .... | .... | .... | .... | .... | .... | .... | .... |

CCHA Second All-Star Team (2006)

Signed as a free agent by **Toronto**, March 8, 2006.

## FOSTER, Kurtis

(FAW-stuhr, KUHR-this) **T.B.**

Defense. Shoots right. 6'5", 220 lbs. Born, Carp, Ont., November 24, 1981. Calgary's 2nd choice, 40th overall, in 2000 Entry Draft.

| Season | Club | League | GP | G | A | Pts | PIM | PP | SH | GW | S | % | +/- | TF | F% | Min | Playoffs GP | G | A | Pts | PIM | PP | SH | GW | Min |
|---|---|---|---|---|---|---|---|---|---|---|---|---|---|---|---|---|---|---|---|---|---|---|---|---|---|
| 1996-97 | Ottawa Valley | ODMHA | 36 | 7 | 18 | 25 | 88 | .... | .... | .... | .... | .... | .... | .... | .... | .... | .... | .... | .... | .... | .... | .... | .... | .... | .... |
| 1997-98 | Peterborough | OHL | 39 | 1 | 1 | 2 | 45 | .... | .... | .... | .... | .... | .... | .... | .... | .... | 4 | 0 | 0 | 0 | 2 | .... | .... | .... | .... |
| 1998-99 | Peterborough | OHL | 54 | 2 | 13 | 15 | 59 | .... | .... | .... | .... | .... | .... | .... | .... | .... | 5 | 0 | 0 | 0 | 6 | .... | .... | .... | .... |
| 99-2000 | Peterborough | OHL | 68 | 6 | 18 | 24 | 116 | .... | .... | .... | .... | .... | .... | .... | .... | .... | 5 | 1 | 2 | 3 | 4 | .... | .... | .... | .... |
| 2000-01 | Peterborough | OHL | 62 | 17 | 24 | 41 | 78 | .... | .... | .... | .... | .... | .... | .... | .... | .... | 7 | 1 | 1 | 2 | 10 | .... | .... | .... | .... |
| 2001-02 | Peterborough | OHL | 33 | 10 | 4 | 14 | 58 | .... | .... | .... | .... | .... | .... | .... | .... | .... | .... | .... | .... | .... | .... | .... | .... | .... | .... |
| | Chicago Wolves | AHL | 39 | 6 | 9 | 15 | 59 | .... | .... | .... | .... | .... | .... | .... | .... | .... | 14 | 1 | 1 | 2 | 21 | .... | .... | .... | .... |
| **2002-03** | **Atlanta** | **NHL** | **2** | **0** | **0** | **0** | **0** | **0** | **0** | **0** | **1** | **0.0** | **–2** | **0** | **0.0** | **11:06** | .... | .... | .... | .... | .... | .... | .... | .... | .... |
| | Chicago Wolves | AHL | 75 | 15 | 27 | 42 | 159 | .... | .... | .... | .... | .... | .... | .... | .... | .... | 9 | 1 | 3 | 4 | 14 | .... | .... | .... | .... |
| **2003-04** | **Atlanta** | **NHL** | **3** | **0** | **1** | **1** | **0** | **0** | **0** | **0** | **1** | **0.0** | **0** | **0** | **0.0** | **6:58** | .... | .... | .... | .... | .... | .... | .... | .... | .... |
| | Chicago Wolves | AHL | 67 | 11 | 19 | 30 | 95 | .... | .... | .... | .... | .... | .... | .... | .... | .... | 10 | 0 | 3 | 3 | 12 | .... | .... | .... | .... |
| 2004-05 | Cincinnati | AHL | 78 | 17 | 25 | 42 | 71 | .... | .... | .... | .... | .... | .... | .... | .... | .... | 9 | 2 | 3 | 5 | 28 | .... | .... | .... | .... |
| **2005-06** | **Minnesota** | **NHL** | **58** | **10** | **18** | **28** | **60** | **6** | **0** | **2** | **124** | **8.1** | **–3** | **0** | **0.0** | **19:13** | .... | .... | .... | .... | .... | .... | .... | .... | .... |
| | Houston Aeros | AHL | 19 | 4 | 11 | 15 | 32 | .... | .... | .... | .... | .... | .... | .... | .... | .... | .... | .... | .... | .... | .... | .... | .... | .... | .... |
| **2006-07** | **Minnesota** | **NHL** | **57** | **3** | **20** | **23** | **52** | **0** | **0** | **0** | **135** | **2.2** | **–3** | **1** | **100.0** | **17:59** | .... | .... | .... | .... | .... | .... | .... | .... | .... |
| **2007-08** | **Minnesota** | **NHL** | **56** | **7** | **12** | **19** | **37** | **3** | **0** | **2** | **118** | **5.9** | **0** | **3** | **66.7** | **16:24** | **3** | **0** | **2** | **2** | **0** | **0** | **0** | **0** | **18:38** |
| **2008-09** | **Minnesota** | **NHL** | **10** | **1** | **5** | **6** | **6** | **0** | **0** | **0** | **10** | **10.0** | **7** | **0** | **0.0** | **13:35** | .... | .... | .... | .... | .... | .... | .... | .... | .... |
| | Houston Aeros | AHL | 6 | 1 | 5 | 6 | 6 | .... | .... | .... | .... | .... | .... | .... | .... | .... | .... | .... | .... | .... | .... | .... | .... | .... | .... |
| | **NHL Totals** | | **186** | **21** | **56** | **77** | **155** | **9** | **0** | **4** | **389** | **5.4** | | **4** | **75.0** | **17:24** | **3** | **0** | **2** | **2** | **0** | **0** | **0** | **0** | **18:38** |

Yanick Dupre Memorial Award (AHL - Outstanding Humanitarian Contribution) (2004)

• Rights traded to **Atlanta** by **Calgary** with Jeff Cowan for Petr Buzek and Atlanta's 6th round choice (Adam Pardy) in 2004 Entry Draft, December 18, 2001. Traded to **Anaheim** by **Atlanta** for Niclas Havelid, June 26, 2004. Signed as a free agent by **Minnesota**, August 4, 2005. • Missed majority of 2008-09 season recovering from leg injury suffered in game vs. San Jose, March 20, 2008. Signed as a free agent by **Tampa Bay**, July 8, 2009.

## FOY, Matt

(FOI, MAT)

Right wing. Shoots right. 6'2", 228 lbs. Born, Oakville, Ont., May 18, 1983. Minnesota's 6th choice, 175th overall, in 2002 Entry Draft.

| Season | Club | League | GP | G | A | Pts | PIM | PP | SH | GW | S | % | +/- | TF | F% | Min | Playoffs GP | G | A | Pts | PIM | PP | SH | GW | Min |
|---|---|---|---|---|---|---|---|---|---|---|---|---|---|---|---|---|---|---|---|---|---|---|---|---|---|
| 2000-01 | Wexford Raiders | OPJHL | 47 | 43 | 49 | 92 | 30 | .... | .... | .... | .... | .... | .... | .... | .... | .... | .... | .... | .... | .... | .... | .... | .... | .... | .... |
| 2001-02 | Merrimack | H-East | 31 | 7 | 17 | 24 | 48 | .... | .... | .... | .... | .... | .... | .... | .... | .... | .... | .... | .... | .... | .... | .... | .... | .... | .... |
| 2002-03 | Ottawa 67's | OHL | 68 | 61 | 71 | 132 | 112 | .... | .... | .... | .... | .... | .... | .... | .... | .... | 21 | 11 | 20 | 31 | 47 | .... | .... | .... | .... |
| 2003-04 | Houston Aeros | AHL | 51 | 11 | 13 | 24 | 74 | .... | .... | .... | .... | .... | .... | .... | .... | .... | 1 | 0 | 0 | 0 | 0 | .... | .... | .... | .... |
| 2004-05 | Houston Aeros | AHL | 69 | 12 | 13 | 25 | 78 | .... | .... | .... | .... | .... | .... | .... | .... | .... | 5 | 1 | 2 | 3 | 6 | .... | .... | .... | .... |
| **2005-06** | **Minnesota** | **NHL** | **19** | **2** | **3** | **5** | **16** | **1** | **0** | **0** | **21** | **9.5** | **–4** | **1** | **0.0** | **10:59** | .... | .... | .... | .... | .... | .... | .... | .... | .... |
| | Houston Aeros | AHL | 51 | 15 | 25 | 40 | 122 | .... | .... | .... | .... | .... | .... | .... | .... | .... | 8 | 5 | 3 | 8 | 29 | .... | .... | .... | .... |
| **2006-07** | **Minnesota** | **NHL** | **9** | **0** | **0** | **0** | **4** | **0** | **0** | **0** | **6** | **0.0** | **–1** | **0** | **0.0** | **7:11** | .... | .... | .... | .... | .... | .... | .... | .... | .... |
| | Houston Aeros | AHL | 62 | 27 | 23 | 50 | 121 | .... | .... | .... | .... | .... | .... | .... | .... | .... | .... | .... | .... | .... | .... | .... | .... | .... | .... |
| **2007-08** | **Minnesota** | **NHL** | **28** | **4** | **4** | **8** | **28** | **0** | **0** | **1** | **38** | **10.5** | **–1** | **7** | **28.6** | **7:50** | **1** | **0** | **0** | **0** | **0** | **0** | **0** | **0** | **6:49** |
| 2008-09 | Peoria Rivermen | AHL | 4 | 0 | 2 | 2 | 33 | .... | .... | .... | .... | .... | .... | .... | .... | .... | .... | .... | .... | .... | .... | .... | .... | .... | .... |
| | **NHL Totals** | | **56** | **6** | **7** | **13** | **48** | **1** | **0** | **1** | **65** | **9.2** | | **8** | **25.0** | **8:48** | **1** | **0** | **0** | **0** | **0** | **0** | **0** | **0** | **6:49** |

OHL First All-Star Team (2003) • Canadian Major Junior Second All-Star Team (2003)

• Officially announced intention to withdraw from **Merrimack College** (Hockey East) for academic reasons, May 30, 2002. • Spent majority of 2007-08 season serving as a healthy reserve. Signed as a free agent by **St. Louis**, July 14, 2008.. • Missed majority of 2008-09 season recovering from sports hernia injury suffered in training camp.

## FRANZEN, Johan

(FRAN-zehn, YOH-han) **DET.**

Left wing. Shoots left. 6'3", 220 lbs. Born, Landsbro, Sweden, December 23, 1979. Detroit's 1st choice, 97th overall, in 2004 Entry Draft.

| Season | Club | League | GP | G | A | Pts | PIM | PP | SH | GW | S | % | +/- | TF | F% | Min | Playoffs GP | G | A | Pts | PIM | PP | SH | GW | Min |
|---|---|---|---|---|---|---|---|---|---|---|---|---|---|---|---|---|---|---|---|---|---|---|---|---|---|
| 2001-02 | Linkopings HC | Sweden | 36 | 2 | 6 | 8 | 64 | .... | .... | .... | .... | .... | .... | .... | .... | .... | .... | .... | .... | .... | .... | .... | .... | .... | .... |
| 2002-03 | Linkopings HC | Sweden | 37 | 2 | 4 | 6 | 14 | .... | .... | .... | .... | .... | .... | .... | .... | .... | .... | .... | .... | .... | .... | .... | .... | .... | .... |
| 2003-04 | Linkopings HC | Sweden | 49 | 12 | 18 | 30 | 26 | .... | .... | .... | .... | .... | .... | .... | .... | .... | 5 | 0 | 1 | 1 | 8 | .... | .... | .... | .... |
| 2004-05 | Linkopings HC | Sweden | 43 | 7 | 7 | 14 | 45 | .... | .... | .... | .... | .... | .... | .... | .... | .... | 6 | 2 | 0 | 2 | 16 | .... | .... | .... | .... |
| **2005-06** | **Detroit** | **NHL** | **80** | **12** | **4** | **16** | **36** | **0** | **2** | **2** | **119** | **10.1** | **4** | **171** | **41.5** | **12:27** | **6** | **1** | **2** | **3** | **4** | **0** | **0** | **0** | **12:00** |
| **2006-07** | **Detroit** | **NHL** | **69** | **10** | **20** | **30** | **37** | **0** | **1** | **2** | **151** | **6.6** | **20** | **45** | **40.0** | **15:35** | **18** | **3** | **4** | **7** | **10** | **0** | **0** | **2** | **16:47** |
| **2007-08**♦ | **Detroit** | **NHL** | **72** | **27** | **11** | **38** | **51** | **14** | **0** | **8** | **199** | **13.6** | **12** | **390** | **48.5** | **17:44** | **16** | ***13** | **5** | **18** | **14** | **6** | **2** | **5** | **18:49** |
| **2008-09** | **Detroit** | **NHL** | **71** | **34** | **25** | **59** | **44** | **11** | **1** | **8** | **246** | **13.8** | **21** | **241** | **56.0** | **18:06** | **23** | **12** | **11** | **23** | **12** | **4** | **0** | **3** | **19:41** |
| | **NHL Totals** | | **292** | **83** | **60** | **143** | **168** | **25** | **4** | **20** | **715** | **11.6** | | **847** | **48.8** | **15:52** | **63** | **29** | **22** | **51** | **40** | **10** | **2** | **10** | **17:54** |

## FRASER, Colin

(FRAY-zuhr, KAW-lihn) **CHI.**

Center. Shoots left. 6'1", 188 lbs. Born, Surrey, B.C., January 28, 1985. Philadelphia's 3rd choice, 69th overall, in 2003 Entry Draft.

| Season | Club | League | GP | G | A | Pts | PIM | PP | SH | GW | S | % | +/- | TF | F% | Min | Playoffs GP | G | A | Pts | PIM | PP | SH | GW | Min |
|---|---|---|---|---|---|---|---|---|---|---|---|---|---|---|---|---|---|---|---|---|---|---|---|---|---|
| 2000-01 | Port Coquitlam | PIJHL | 38 | 16 | 24 | 40 | 90 | .... | .... | .... | .... | .... | .... | .... | .... | .... | 8 | 2 | 2 | 4 | 21 | .... | .... | .... | .... |
| 2001-02 | Red Deer Rebels | WHL | 67 | 11 | 31 | 42 | 126 | .... | .... | .... | .... | .... | .... | .... | .... | .... | 23 | 2 | 1 | 3 | 39 | .... | .... | .... | .... |
| 2002-03 | Red Deer Rebels | WHL | 69 | 15 | 37 | 52 | 192 | .... | .... | .... | .... | .... | .... | .... | .... | .... | 22 | 7 | 6 | 13 | 40 | .... | .... | .... | .... |
| 2003-04 | Red Deer Rebels | WHL | 70 | 24 | 29 | 53 | 174 | .... | .... | .... | .... | .... | .... | .... | .... | .... | 19 | 5 | 9 | 14 | 24 | .... | .... | .... | .... |
| 2004-05 | Red Deer Rebels | WHL | 63 | 24 | 43 | 67 | 148 | .... | .... | .... | .... | .... | .... | .... | .... | .... | 7 | 2 | 5 | 7 | 8 | .... | .... | .... | .... |
| | Norfolk Admirals | AHL | 3 | 0 | 0 | 0 | 20 | .... | .... | .... | .... | .... | .... | .... | .... | .... | 6 | 1 | 0 | 1 | 2 | .... | .... | .... | .... |
| 2005-06 | Norfolk Admirals | AHL | 75 | 12 | 13 | 25 | 145 | .... | .... | .... | .... | .... | .... | .... | .... | .... | 4 | 0 | 0 | 0 | 7 | .... | .... | .... | .... |
| **2006-07** | **Chicago** | **NHL** | **1** | **0** | **0** | **0** | **2** | **0** | **0** | **0** | **0** | **0.0** | **–1** | **2** | **0.0** | **3:18** | .... | .... | .... | .... | .... | .... | .... | .... | .... |
| | Norfolk Admirals | AHL | 67 | 12 | 24 | 36 | 158 | .... | .... | .... | .... | .... | .... | .... | .... | .... | 6 | 1 | 0 | 1 | 21 | .... | .... | .... | .... |
| **2007-08** | **Chicago** | **NHL** | **5** | **0** | **0** | **0** | **7** | **0** | **0** | **0** | **4** | **0.0** | **–2** | **38** | **36.8** | **10:19** | .... | .... | .... | .... | .... | .... | .... | .... | .... |
| | Rockford IceHogs | AHL | 75 | 17 | 24 | 41 | 165 | .... | .... | .... | .... | .... | .... | .... | .... | .... | 12 | 1 | 2 | 3 | 28 | .... | .... | .... | .... |
| **2008-09** | **Chicago** | **NHL** | **81** | **6** | **11** | **17** | **55** | **0** | **1** | **0** | **67** | **9.0** | **3** | **787** | **47.8** | **10:54** | **2** | **0** | **0** | **0** | **2** | **0** | **0** | **0** | **11:31** |
| | **NHL Totals** | | **87** | **6** | **11** | **17** | **64** | **0** | **1** | **0** | **71** | **8.5** | | **827** | **47.2** | **10:47** | **2** | **0** | **0** | **0** | **2** | **0** | **0** | **0** | **11:31** |

Canadian Major Junior Humanitarian Player of the Year (2005)

Traded to **Chicago** by **Philadelphia** with Jim Vandermeer and Los Angeles' 2nd round choice (previously acquired, Chicago selected Bryan Bickell) in 2004 Entry Draft for Alex Zhamnov and Washington's 4th round choice (previously acquired, Philadelphia selected R.J. Anderson) in 2004 Entry Draft, February 19, 2004.

## FRASER, Jamie

(FRAY-zuhr, JAY-mee) **MIN.**

Defense. Shoots left. 6'1", 200 lbs. Born, Sarnia, Ont., November 17, 1985.

| Season | Club | League | GP | G | A | Pts | PIM | PP | SH | GW | S | % | +/- | TF | F% | Min | Playoffs GP | G | A | Pts | PIM | PP | SH | GW | Min |
|---|---|---|---|---|---|---|---|---|---|---|---|---|---|---|---|---|---|---|---|---|---|---|---|---|---|
| 2002-03 | Brampton | OHL | 57 | 3 | 11 | 14 | 13 | .... | .... | .... | .... | .... | .... | .... | .... | .... | 10 | 0 | 2 | 2 | 2 | .... | .... | .... | .... |
| 2003-04 | Brampton | OHL | 61 | 4 | 13 | 17 | 36 | .... | .... | .... | .... | .... | .... | .... | .... | .... | 12 | 3 | 1 | 4 | 6 | .... | .... | .... | .... |
| 2004-05 | Sarnia Sting | OHL | 66 | 10 | 21 | 31 | 22 | .... | .... | .... | .... | .... | .... | .... | .... | .... | .... | .... | .... | .... | .... | .... | .... | .... | .... |
| 2005-06 | Sarnia Sting | OHL | 65 | 16 | 26 | 42 | 68 | .... | .... | .... | .... | .... | .... | .... | .... | .... | .... | .... | .... | .... | .... | .... | .... | .... | .... |
| | South Carolina | ECHL | 3 | 1 | 0 | 1 | 2 | .... | .... | .... | .... | .... | .... | .... | .... | .... | 6 | 1 | 1 | 2 | 2 | .... | .... | .... | .... |
| 2006-07 | Syracuse Crunch | AHL | 2 | 0 | 0 | 0 | 0 | .... | .... | .... | .... | .... | .... | .... | .... | .... | .... | .... | .... | .... | .... | .... | .... | .... | .... |
| | South Carolina | ECHL | 27 | 5 | 23 | 28 | 6 | .... | .... | .... | .... | .... | .... | .... | .... | .... | .... | .... | .... | .... | .... | .... | .... | .... | .... |
| | Bridgeport | AHL | 43 | 3 | 11 | 14 | 16 | .... | .... | .... | .... | .... | .... | .... | .... | .... | .... | .... | .... | .... | .... | .... | .... | .... | .... |
| 2007-08 | Bridgeport | AHL | 70 | 11 | 13 | 24 | 20 | .... | .... | .... | .... | .... | .... | .... | .... | .... | .... | .... | .... | .... | .... | .... | .... | .... | .... |

| | | | Regular Season | | | | | | | | | | | | | | Playoffs | | | | | | | | |
|---|---|---|---|---|---|---|---|---|---|---|---|---|---|---|---|---|---|---|---|---|---|---|---|---|---|
| Season | Club | League | GP | G | A | Pts | PIM | PP | SH | GW | S | % | +/- | TF | F% | Min | GP | G | A | Pts | PIM | PP | SH | GW | Min |
| **2008-09** | **NY Islanders** | **NHL** | **1** | **0** | **0** | **0** | **0** | **0** | **0** | **0** | **0** | **0.0** | **0** | **0** | **0.0** | **11:00** | .... | .... | .... | .... | .... | .... | .... | .... | .... |
| | Bridgeport | AHL | 66 | 7 | 14 | 21 | 30 | .... | .... | .... | .... | .... | .... | .... | .... | .... | .... | .... | .... | .... | .... | .... | .... | .... | .... |
| | **NHL Totals** | | **1** | **0** | **0** | **0** | **0** | **0** | **0** | **0** | **0** | **0.0** | | **0** | **0.0** | **11:00** | .... | .... | .... | .... | .... | .... | .... | .... | .... |

Signed as a free agent by **NY Islanders**, February 22, 2007. Signed as a free agent by **Minnesota**, July 8, 2009.

## FRASER, Mark

(FRAY-zuhr, MAHRK) **N.J.**

Defense. Shoots left. 6'3", 215 lbs. Born, Ottawa, Ont., September 29, 1986. New Jersey's 3rd choice, 84th overall, in 2005 Entry Draft.

| | | | | | | | | | | | | | | | | | | | | | | | | | |
|---|---|---|---|---|---|---|---|---|---|---|---|---|---|---|---|---|---|---|---|---|---|---|---|---|---|
| 2004-05 | Gloucester | CJHL | STATISTICS NOT AVAILABLE | | | | | | | | | | | | | | | | | | | | | | |
| | Kitchener Rangers | OHL | 58 | 0 | 8 | 8 | 96 | .... | .... | .... | .... | .... | .... | .... | .... | .... | 15 | 0 | 3 | 3 | 26 | .... | .... | .... | .... |
| 2005-06 | Kitchener Rangers | OHL | 59 | 0 | 5 | 5 | 129 | .... | .... | .... | .... | .... | .... | .... | .... | .... | 5 | 0 | 1 | 1 | 4 | .... | .... | .... | .... |
| | Albany River Rats | AHL | 4 | 0 | 0 | 0 | 2 | .... | .... | .... | .... | .... | .... | .... | .... | .... | .... | .... | .... | .... | .... | .... | .... | .... | .... |
| **2006-07** | **New Jersey** | **NHL** | **7** | **0** | **0** | **0** | **7** | **0** | **0** | **0** | **1** | **0.0** | **–1** | **0** | **0.0** | **3:34** | .... | .... | .... | .... | .... | .... | .... | .... | .... |
| | Lowell Devils | AHL | 71 | 1 | 8 | 9 | 73 | .... | .... | .... | .... | .... | .... | .... | .... | .... | .... | .... | .... | .... | .... | .... | .... | .... | .... |
| 2007-08 | Lowell Devils | AHL | 79 | 1 | 17 | 18 | 96 | .... | .... | .... | .... | .... | .... | .... | .... | .... | .... | .... | .... | .... | .... | .... | .... | .... | .... |
| 2008-09 | Lowell Devils | AHL | 74 | 3 | 14 | 17 | 152 | .... | .... | .... | .... | .... | .... | .... | .... | .... | .... | .... | .... | .... | .... | .... | .... | .... | .... |
| | **NHL Totals** | | **7** | **0** | **0** | **0** | **7** | **0** | **0** | **0** | **1** | **0.0** | | **0** | **0.0** | **3:34** | .... | .... | .... | .... | .... | .... | .... | .... | .... |

## FRITSCH, Jamie

(FRIHCH, JAY-mee)

Defense. Shoots left. 6'2", 195 lbs. Born, Odenton, MD, February 25, 1985.

| | | | | | | | | | | | | | | | | | | | | | | | | | |
|---|---|---|---|---|---|---|---|---|---|---|---|---|---|---|---|---|---|---|---|---|---|---|---|---|---|
| 2005-06 | New Hampshire | H-East | 32 | 4 | 6 | 10 | 24 | .... | .... | .... | .... | .... | .... | .... | .... | .... | .... | .... | .... | .... | .... | .... | .... | .... | .... |
| 2006-07 | New Hampshire | H-East | 39 | 2 | 9 | 11 | 50 | .... | .... | .... | .... | .... | .... | .... | .... | .... | .... | .... | .... | .... | .... | .... | .... | .... | .... |
| 2007-08 | New Hampshire | H-East | 37 | 4 | 6 | 10 | 49 | .... | .... | .... | .... | .... | .... | .... | .... | .... | .... | .... | .... | .... | .... | .... | .... | .... | .... |
| **2008-09** | New Hampshire | H-East | 38 | 1 | 7 | 8 | 48 | .... | .... | .... | .... | .... | .... | .... | .... | .... | .... | .... | .... | .... | .... | .... | .... | .... | .... |
| | **Philadelphia** | **NHL** | **1** | **0** | **0** | **0** | **0** | **0** | **0** | **0** | **0** | **0.0** | **1** | **0** | **0.0** | **4:34** | .... | .... | .... | .... | .... | .... | .... | .... | .... |
| | **NHL Totals** | | **1** | **0** | **0** | **0** | **0** | **0** | **0** | **0** | **0** | **0.0** | | **0** | **0.0** | **4:34** | .... | .... | .... | .... | .... | .... | .... | .... | .... |

Signed to an ATO (tryout) contract by **Philadelphia**, April 12, 2009.

## FRITSCHE, Dan

(FRIH-tchee, DAN)

Center. Shoots right. 6'1", 204 lbs. Born, Parma, OH, July 13, 1985. Columbus' 2nd choice, 46th overall, in 2003 Entry Draft.

| | | | | | | | | | | | | | | | | | | | | | | | | | |
|---|---|---|---|---|---|---|---|---|---|---|---|---|---|---|---|---|---|---|---|---|---|---|---|---|---|
| 2000-01 | Cleveland Barons | NAHL | 49 | 23 | 29 | 52 | 47 | .... | .... | .... | .... | .... | .... | .... | .... | .... | 1 | 1 | 1 | 2 | 0 | .... | .... | .... | .... |
| 2001-02 | Sarnia Sting | OHL | 17 | 5 | 13 | 18 | 20 | .... | .... | .... | .... | .... | .... | .... | .... | .... | .... | .... | .... | .... | .... | .... | .... | .... | .... |
| 2002-03 | Sarnia Sting | OHL | 61 | 32 | 39 | 71 | 79 | .... | .... | .... | .... | .... | .... | .... | .... | .... | 5 | 2 | 2 | 4 | 4 | .... | .... | .... | .... |
| **2003-04** | Sarnia Sting | OHL | 27 | 16 | 13 | 29 | 26 | .... | .... | .... | .... | .... | .... | .... | .... | .... | 5 | 1 | 5 | 6 | 0 | .... | .... | .... | .... |
| | **Columbus** | **NHL** | **19** | **1** | **0** | **1** | **12** | **0** | **0** | **0** | **19** | **5.3** | **–5** | **139** | **38.1** | **8:24** | .... | .... | .... | .... | .... | .... | .... | .... | .... |
| | Syracuse Crunch | AHL | 4 | 2 | 0 | 2 | 0 | .... | .... | .... | .... | .... | .... | .... | .... | .... | 4 | 0 | 1 | 1 | 4 | .... | .... | .... | .... |
| 2004-05 | Sarnia Sting | OHL | 2 | 1 | 1 | 2 | 0 | .... | .... | .... | .... | .... | .... | .... | .... | .... | .... | .... | .... | .... | .... | .... | .... | .... | .... |
| | London Knights | OHL | 28 | 17 | 18 | 35 | 18 | .... | .... | .... | .... | .... | .... | .... | .... | .... | 17 | 9 | 13 | 22 | 12 | .... | .... | .... | .... |
| **2005-06** | **Columbus** | **NHL** | **59** | **6** | **7** | **13** | **22** | **0** | **0** | **0** | **93** | **6.5** | **–14** | **270** | **48.9** | **10:17** | .... | .... | .... | .... | .... | .... | .... | .... | .... |
| | Syracuse Crunch | AHL | 19 | 5 | 4 | 9 | 12 | .... | .... | .... | .... | .... | .... | .... | .... | .... | 6 | 2 | 2 | 4 | 8 | .... | .... | .... | .... |
| **2006-07** | **Columbus** | **NHL** | **59** | **12** | **15** | **27** | **35** | **5** | **1** | **4** | **81** | **14.8** | **3** | **296** | **49.3** | **14:02** | .... | .... | .... | .... | .... | .... | .... | .... | .... |
| **2007-08** | **Columbus** | **NHL** | **69** | **10** | **12** | **22** | **22** | **1** | **1** | **4** | **109** | **9.2** | **2** | **121** | **48.8** | **12:21** | .... | .... | .... | .... | .... | .... | .... | .... | .... |
| **2008-09** | **NY Rangers** | **NHL** | **16** | **1** | **3** | **4** | **2** | **0** | **0** | **0** | **20** | **5.0** | **–2** | **7** | **71.4** | **9:33** | .... | .... | .... | .... | .... | .... | .... | .... | .... |
| | **Minnesota** | **NHL** | **34** | **4** | **5** | **9** | **10** | **1** | **1** | **0** | **34** | **11.8** | **–3** | **87** | **41.4** | **11:09** | .... | .... | .... | .... | .... | .... | .... | .... | .... |
| | **NHL Totals** | | **256** | **34** | **42** | **76** | **103** | **7** | **3** | **8** | **356** | **9.6** | | **920** | **46.8** | **11:38** | .... | .... | .... | .... | .... | .... | .... | .... | .... |

Memorial Cup Tournament All-Star Team (2005)

• Missed majority of 2001-02 season recovering from shoulder surgery, December 12, 2001. Traded to **NY Rangers** by **Columbus** with Nikolai Zherdev for Fedor Tyutin and Christian Backman, July 2, 2008. Traded to **Minnesota** by **NY Rangers** for Erik Reitz, January 29, 2009.

## FRITZ, Mitch

(FRIHTZ, MIHTCH)

Left wing. Shoots left. 6'8", 258 lbs. Born, Osoyoos, B.C., November 24, 1980.

| | | | | | | | | | | | | | | | | | | | | | | | | | |
|---|---|---|---|---|---|---|---|---|---|---|---|---|---|---|---|---|---|---|---|---|---|---|---|---|---|
| 1998-99 | Kelowna Rockets | WHL | 52 | 9 | 0 | 9 | 156 | .... | .... | .... | .... | .... | .... | .... | .... | .... | 2 | 0 | 0 | 0 | 0 | .... | .... | .... | .... |
| 99-2000 | Kelowna Rockets | WHL | 58 | 4 | 2 | 6 | 204 | .... | .... | .... | .... | .... | .... | .... | .... | .... | 5 | 0 | 0 | 0 | 0 | .... | .... | .... | .... |
| 2000-01 | Lowell | AHL | 5 | 0 | 0 | 0 | 20 | .... | .... | .... | .... | .... | .... | .... | .... | .... | .... | .... | .... | .... | .... | .... | .... | .... | .... |
| | Tallahassee | ECHL | 42 | 5 | 3 | 8 | 79 | .... | .... | .... | .... | .... | .... | .... | .... | .... | .... | .... | .... | .... | .... | .... | .... | .... | .... |
| 2001-02 | Hamilton | AHL | 13 | 0 | 0 | 0 | 37 | .... | .... | .... | .... | .... | .... | .... | .... | .... | .... | .... | .... | .... | .... | .... | .... | .... | .... |
| | Saint John Flames | AHL | 11 | 0 | 0 | 0 | 34 | .... | .... | .... | .... | .... | .... | .... | .... | .... | .... | .... | .... | .... | .... | .... | .... | .... | .... |
| | Columbus | ECHL | 45 | 3 | 7 | 10 | 284 | .... | .... | .... | .... | .... | .... | .... | .... | .... | .... | .... | .... | .... | .... | .... | .... | .... | .... |
| 2002-03 | Milwaukee | AHL | 13 | 1 | 2 | 3 | 33 | .... | .... | .... | .... | .... | .... | .... | .... | .... | .... | .... | .... | .... | .... | .... | .... | .... | .... |
| | Columbus | ECHL | 33 | 2 | 4 | 6 | 144 | .... | .... | .... | .... | .... | .... | .... | .... | .... | .... | .... | .... | .... | .... | .... | .... | .... | .... |
| 2003-04 | Worcester IceCats | AHL | 4 | 0 | 0 | 0 | 10 | .... | .... | .... | .... | .... | .... | .... | .... | .... | 4 | 0 | 0 | 0 | 4 | .... | .... | .... | .... |
| | Columbus | ECHL | 64 | 3 | 9 | 12 | 149 | .... | .... | .... | .... | .... | .... | .... | .... | .... | .... | .... | .... | .... | .... | .... | .... | .... | .... |
| 2004-05 | Springfield | AHL | 45 | 3 | 1 | 4 | 179 | .... | .... | .... | .... | .... | .... | .... | .... | .... | .... | .... | .... | .... | .... | .... | .... | .... | .... |
| 2005-06 | Springfield | AHL | 69 | 6 | 5 | 11 | 212 | .... | .... | .... | .... | .... | .... | .... | .... | .... | .... | .... | .... | .... | .... | .... | .... | .... | .... |
| 2006-07 | Springfield | AHL | 63 | 0 | 1 | 1 | 144 | .... | .... | .... | .... | .... | .... | .... | .... | .... | .... | .... | .... | .... | .... | .... | .... | .... | .... |
| 2007-08 | Hartford | AHL | 11 | 1 | 4 | 5 | 34 | .... | .... | .... | .... | .... | .... | .... | .... | .... | 2 | 0 | 0 | 0 | 4 | .... | .... | .... | .... |
| **2008-09** | **NY Islanders** | **NHL** | **20** | **0** | **0** | **0** | **42** | **0** | **0** | **0** | **2** | **0.0** | **–4** | **1** | **100.0** | **2:41** | .... | .... | .... | .... | .... | .... | .... | .... | .... |
| | Bridgeport | AHL | 36 | 0 | 2 | 2 | 58 | .... | .... | .... | .... | .... | .... | .... | .... | .... | .... | .... | .... | .... | .... | .... | .... | .... | .... |
| | **NHL Totals** | | **20** | **0** | **0** | **0** | **42** | **0** | **0** | **0** | **2** | **0.0** | | **1** | **100.0** | **2:41** | .... | .... | .... | .... | .... | .... | .... | .... | .... |

Yanick Dupre Memorial Award (AHL - Outstanding Humanitarian Contribution) (2006)

Signed as a free agent by **Tampa Bay**, August 5, 2005. • Rights traded to **NY Rangers** by **Tampa Bay** for the rights to Bryce Lampman, July 4, 2007. • Missed majority of 2007-08 season recovering from shoulder surgery. Signed as a free agent by **NY Islanders**, July 3, 2008.

## FROGREN, Jonas

(FREW-grehn, YOH-nuhs) **TOR.**

Defense. Shoots left. 6'2", 194 lbs. Born, Falun, Sweden, August 28, 1980. Calgary's 8th choice, 206th overall, in 1998 Entry Draft.

| | | | | | | | | | | | | | | | | | | | | | | | | | |
|---|---|---|---|---|---|---|---|---|---|---|---|---|---|---|---|---|---|---|---|---|---|---|---|---|---|
| 1996-97 | Farjestad Jr. | Swe-Jr. | 20 | 2 | 7 | 9 | 4 | .... | .... | .... | .... | .... | .... | .... | .... | .... | .... | .... | .... | .... | .... | .... | .... | .... | .... |
| 1997-98 | Farjestad Jr. | Swe-Jr. | 28 | 5 | 6 | 11 | 12 | .... | .... | .... | .... | .... | .... | .... | .... | .... | 2 | 1 | 0 | 1 | 0 | .... | .... | .... | .... |
| 1998-99 | Farjestad Jr. | Swe-Jr. | 28 | 10 | 8 | 18 | 16 | .... | .... | .... | .... | .... | .... | .... | .... | .... | 6 | 0 | 2 | 2 | 10 | .... | .... | .... | .... |
| | Farjestad | Sweden | 22 | 0 | 0 | 0 | 2 | .... | .... | .... | .... | .... | .... | .... | .... | .... | .... | .... | .... | .... | .... | .... | .... | .... | .... |
| | Farjestad | EuroHL | 5 | 0 | 0 | 0 | 0 | .... | .... | .... | .... | .... | .... | .... | .... | .... | 2 | 0 | 0 | 0 | 0 | .... | .... | .... | .... |
| 99-2000 | Bofors | Sweden-2 | 43 | 2 | 7 | 9 | 40 | .... | .... | .... | .... | .... | .... | .... | .... | .... | .... | .... | .... | .... | .... | .... | .... | .... | .... |
| 2000-01 | Farjestad | Sweden | 49 | 3 | 0 | 3 | 10 | .... | .... | .... | .... | .... | .... | .... | .... | .... | 16 | 0 | 0 | 0 | 4 | .... | .... | .... | .... |
| | Farjestad Jr. | Swe-Jr. | 1 | 0 | 0 | 0 | 0 | .... | .... | .... | .... | .... | .... | .... | .... | .... | .... | .... | .... | .... | .... | .... | .... | .... | .... |
| 2001-02 | Farjestad | Sweden | 50 | 3 | 6 | 9 | 18 | .... | .... | .... | .... | .... | .... | .... | .... | .... | 10 | 0 | 0 | 0 | 4 | .... | .... | .... | .... |
| 2002-03 | Farjestad | Sweden | 50 | 1 | 7 | 8 | 48 | .... | .... | .... | .... | .... | .... | .... | .... | .... | 14 | 0 | 0 | 0 | 16 | .... | .... | .... | .... |
| 2003-04 | Farjestad | Sweden | 47 | 5 | 5 | 10 | 38 | .... | .... | .... | .... | .... | .... | .... | .... | .... | 17 | 2 | 0 | 2 | 6 | .... | .... | .... | .... |
| 2004-05 | Farjestad | Sweden | 34 | 1 | 0 | 1 | 26 | .... | .... | .... | .... | .... | .... | .... | .... | .... | 15 | 0 | 2 | 2 | 2 | .... | .... | .... | .... |
| 2005-06 | Farjestad | Sweden | 46 | 3 | 3 | 6 | 84 | .... | .... | .... | .... | .... | .... | .... | .... | .... | 17 | 1 | 1 | 2 | 6 | .... | .... | .... | .... |
| 2006-07 | Farjestad | Sweden | 53 | 4 | 4 | 8 | 40 | .... | .... | .... | .... | .... | .... | .... | .... | .... | 7 | 1 | 0 | 1 | 0 | .... | .... | .... | .... |
| 2007-08 | Farjestad | Sweden | 47 | 0 | 1 | 1 | 38 | .... | .... | .... | .... | .... | .... | .... | .... | .... | 12 | 0 | 1 | 1 | 12 | .... | .... | .... | .... |
| **2008-09** | **Toronto** | **NHL** | **41** | **1** | **6** | **7** | **28** | **0** | **0** | **0** | **12** | **8.3** | **0** | **1** | **0.0** | **13:26** | .... | .... | .... | .... | .... | .... | .... | .... | .... |
| | Toronto Marlies | AHL | .... | .... | .... | .... | .... | .... | .... | .... | .... | .... | .... | .... | .... | .... | 3 | 0 | 0 | 0 | 0 | .... | .... | .... | .... |
| | **NHL Totals** | | **41** | **1** | **6** | **7** | **28** | **0** | **0** | **0** | **12** | **8.3** | | **1** | **0.0** | **13:26** | .... | .... | .... | .... | .... | .... | .... | .... | .... |

Signed as a free agent by **Toronto**, July 9, 2008.

## FROLIK, Michael

(FROH-lihk, MIGH-kuhl) **FLA.**

Center. Shoots left. 6'1", 185 lbs. Born, Kladno, Czech., February 17, 1988. Florida's 1st choice, 10th overall, in 2006 Entry Draft.

| | | | | | | | | | | | | | | | | | | | | | | | | | |
|---|---|---|---|---|---|---|---|---|---|---|---|---|---|---|---|---|---|---|---|---|---|---|---|---|---|
| 2002-03 | HC Kladno U17 | CzR-U17 | 46 | 37 | 21 | 58 | 36 | .... | .... | .... | .... | .... | .... | .... | .... | .... | 9 | 9 | 1 | 10 | 18 | .... | .... | .... | .... |
| | HC Kladno Jr. | CzRep-Jr. | .... | .... | .... | .... | .... | .... | .... | .... | .... | .... | .... | .... | .... | .... | 1 | 0 | 0 | 0 | 2 | .... | .... | .... | .... |
| 2003-04 | HC Kladno U17 | CzR-U17 | 1 | 0 | 1 | 1 | 2 | .... | .... | .... | .... | .... | .... | .... | .... | .... | .... | .... | .... | .... | .... | .... | .... | .... | .... |
| | HC Kladno Jr. | CzRep-Jr. | 53 | 21 | 23 | 44 | 22 | .... | .... | .... | .... | .... | .... | .... | .... | .... | 7 | 3 | 1 | 4 | 6 | .... | .... | .... | .... |

| | | | Regular Season | | | | | | | | | | | | | | Playoffs | | | | | | | | |
|---|---|---|---|---|---|---|---|---|---|---|---|---|---|---|---|---|---|---|---|---|---|---|---|---|---|
| **Season** | **Club** | **League** | **GP** | **G** | **A** | **Pts** | **PIM** | **PP** | **SH** | **GW** | **S** | **%** | **+/-** | **TF** | **F%** | **Min** | **GP** | **G** | **A** | **Pts** | **PIM** | **PP** | **SH** | **GW** | **Min** |
| 2004-05 | HC Kladno U17 | CzR-U17 | .... | .... | .... | .... | .... | .... | .... | .... | .... | .... | .... | .... | .... | .... | 1 | 1 | 0 | 1 | 0 | .... | .... | .... | .... |
| | HC Kladno Jr. | CzRep-Jr. | 15 | 9 | 11 | 20 | 18 | .... | .... | .... | .... | .... | .... | .... | .... | .... | 5 | 1 | 0 | 1 | 0 | .... | .... | .... | .... |
| | HC Rabat Kladno | CzRep | 27 | 3 | 1 | 4 | 6 | .... | .... | .... | .... | .... | .... | .... | .... | .... | 1 | 0 | 0 | 0 | 0 | .... | .... | .... | .... |
| 2005-06 | HC Kladno Jr. | CzRep-Jr. | 3 | 1 | 2 | 3 | 0 | .... | .... | .... | .... | .... | .... | .... | .... | .... | 6 | 3 | 9 | 12 | 6 | .... | .... | .... | .... |
| | HC Rabat Kladno | CzRep | 48 | 2 | 7 | 9 | 32 | .... | .... | .... | .... | .... | .... | .... | .... | .... | .... | .... | .... | .... | .... | .... | .... | .... | .... |
| 2006-07 | Rimouski Oceanic | QMJHL | 52 | 31 | 42 | 73 | 40 | .... | .... | .... | .... | .... | .... | .... | .... | .... | .... | .... | .... | .... | .... | .... | .... | .... | .... |
| 2007-08 | Rimouski Oceanic | QMJHL | 45 | 24 | 41 | 65 | 22 | .... | .... | .... | .... | .... | .... | .... | .... | .... | 9 | 2 | 4 | 6 | 12 | .... | .... | .... | .... |
| **2008-09** | **Florida** | **NHL** | **79** | **21** | **24** | **45** | **22** | **1** | **0** | **2** | **158** | **13.3** | **10** | **67** | **40.3** | **14:48** | .... | .... | .... | .... | .... | .... | .... | .... | .... |
| | **NHL Totals** | | **79** | **21** | **24** | **45** | **22** | **1** | **0** | **2** | **158** | **13.3** | | **67** | **40.3** | **14:48** | .... | .... | .... | .... | .... | .... | .... | .... | .... |

QMJHL All-Rookie Team (2007)

## FROLOV, Alexander

(FROH-lawf, Alehx-AN-duhr) **L.A.**

Left wing. Shoots right. 6'2", 204 lbs. Born, Moscow, USSR, June 19, 1982. Los Angeles' 1st choice, 20th overall, in 2000 Entry Draft.

| | | | | | | | | | | | | | | | | | | | | | | | | | |
|---|---|---|---|---|---|---|---|---|---|---|---|---|---|---|---|---|---|---|---|---|---|---|---|---|---|
| 1998-99 | Spartak Moscow | Russia | 1 | 0 | 0 | 0 | 0 | .... | .... | .... | .... | .... | .... | .... | .... | .... | .... | .... | .... | .... | .... | .... | .... | .... | .... |
| 99-2000 | Yaroslavl 2 | Russia-3 | 36 | 27 | 13 | 40 | 30 | .... | .... | .... | .... | .... | .... | .... | .... | .... | .... | .... | .... | .... | .... | .... | .... | .... | .... |
| 2000-01 | Krylja Sovetov | Russia-2 | 44 | 20 | 19 | 39 | 8 | .... | .... | .... | .... | .... | .... | .... | .... | .... | .... | .... | .... | .... | .... | .... | .... | .... | .... |
| 2001-02 | Krylja Sovetov | Russia | 43 | 18 | 12 | 30 | 16 | .... | .... | .... | .... | .... | .... | .... | .... | .... | 3 | 1 | 0 | 1 | 0 | .... | .... | .... | .... |
| | Krylja Sovetov 2 | Russia-3 | 2 | 0 | 0 | 0 | 4 | .... | .... | .... | .... | .... | .... | .... | .... | .... | .... | .... | .... | .... | .... | .... | .... | .... | .... |
| **2002-03** | **Los Angeles** | **NHL** | **79** | **14** | **17** | **31** | **34** | **1** | **0** | **3** | **141** | **9.9** | **12** | **9** | **22.2** | **14:23** | .... | .... | .... | .... | .... | .... | .... | .... | .... |
| **2003-04** | **Los Angeles** | **NHL** | **77** | **24** | **24** | **48** | **24** | **5** | **2** | **3** | **168** | **14.3** | **8** | **34** | **32.4** | **17:13** | .... | .... | .... | .... | .... | .... | .... | .... | .... |
| | Nizhny Novgorod | Russia | 1 | 0 | 0 | 0 | 0 | .... | .... | .... | .... | .... | .... | .... | .... | .... | .... | .... | .... | .... | .... | .... | .... | .... | .... |
| 2004-05 | CSKA Moscow | Russia | 42 | 20 | 17 | 37 | 10 | .... | .... | .... | .... | .... | .... | .... | .... | .... | .... | .... | .... | .... | .... | .... | .... | .... | .... |
| | Dynamo Moscow | Russia | 6 | 2 | 1 | 3 | 2 | .... | .... | .... | .... | .... | .... | .... | .... | .... | 6 | 2 | 1 | 3 | 0 | .... | .... | .... | .... |
| **2005-06** | **Los Angeles** | **NHL** | **69** | **21** | **33** | **54** | **40** | **4** | **3** | **4** | **174** | **12.1** | **17** | **4** | **50.0** | **19:18** | .... | .... | .... | .... | .... | .... | .... | .... | .... |
| | Russia | Olympics | 3 | 0 | 1 | 1 | 0 | .... | .... | .... | .... | .... | .... | .... | .... | .... | .... | .... | .... | .... | .... | .... | .... | .... | .... |
| **2006-07** | **Los Angeles** | **NHL** | **82** | **35** | **36** | **71** | **34** | **10** | **1** | **6** | **195** | **17.9** | **–8** | **19** | **36.8** | **19:56** | .... | .... | .... | .... | .... | .... | .... | .... | .... |
| **2007-08** | **Los Angeles** | **NHL** | **71** | **23** | **44** | **67** | **22** | **5** | **0** | **7** | **160** | **14.4** | **1** | **11** | **18.2** | **18:48** | .... | .... | .... | .... | .... | .... | .... | .... | .... |
| **2008-09** | **Los Angeles** | **NHL** | **77** | **32** | **27** | **59** | **30** | **12** | **1** | **1** | **176** | **18.2** | **–6** | **11** | **45.5** | **19:55** | .... | .... | .... | .... | .... | .... | .... | .... | .... |
| | **NHL Totals** | | **455** | **149** | **181** | **330** | **184** | **37** | **7** | **24** | **1014** | **14.7** | | **88** | **33.0** | **18:14** | .... | .... | .... | .... | .... | .... | .... | .... | .... |

Signed as a free agent by **CSKA Moscow** (Russia), July 14, 2004. Signed as a free agent by **Dynamo Moscow** (Russia), February 17, 2005.

## FUNK, Michael

(FUHNK, MIGH-kuhl) **VAN.**

Defense. Shoots left. 6'4", 199 lbs. Born, Abbotsford, B.C., August 15, 1986. Buffalo's 2nd choice, 43rd overall, in 2004 Entry Draft.

| | | | | | | | | | | | | | | | | | | | | | | | | | |
|---|---|---|---|---|---|---|---|---|---|---|---|---|---|---|---|---|---|---|---|---|---|---|---|---|---|
| 2001-02 | Abbotsford | Minor-BC | 72 | 9 | 24 | 33 | 84 | .... | .... | .... | .... | .... | .... | .... | .... | .... | .... | .... | .... | .... | .... | .... | .... | .... | .... |
| 2002-03 | Portland | WHL | 68 | 1 | 15 | 16 | 54 | .... | .... | .... | .... | .... | .... | .... | .... | .... | 7 | 0 | 1 | 1 | 15 | .... | .... | .... | .... |
| 2003-04 | Portland | WHL | 71 | 3 | 25 | 28 | 86 | .... | .... | .... | .... | .... | .... | .... | .... | .... | 5 | 0 | 1 | 1 | 6 | .... | .... | .... | .... |
| 2004-05 | Portland | WHL | 71 | 8 | 22 | 30 | 84 | .... | .... | .... | .... | .... | .... | .... | .... | .... | 7 | 1 | 1 | 2 | 4 | .... | .... | .... | .... |
| 2005-06 | Portland | WHL | 70 | 11 | 36 | 47 | 88 | .... | .... | .... | .... | .... | .... | .... | .... | .... | 5 | 0 | 0 | 0 | 8 | .... | .... | .... | .... |
| **2006-07** | **Buffalo** | **NHL** | **5** | **0** | **2** | **2** | **0** | **0** | **0** | **0** | **1** | **0.0** | **2** | **0** | **0.0** | **3:26** | .... | .... | .... | .... | .... | .... | .... | .... | .... |
| | Rochester | AHL | 61 | 2 | 5 | 7 | 57 | .... | .... | .... | .... | .... | .... | .... | .... | .... | 6 | 0 | 1 | 1 | 4 | .... | .... | .... | .... |
| **2007-08** | **Buffalo** | **NHL** | **4** | **0** | **0** | **0** | **0** | **0** | **0** | **0** | **1** | **0.0** | **–3** | **0** | **0.0** | **11:37** | .... | .... | .... | .... | .... | .... | .... | .... | .... |
| | Rochester | AHL | 58 | 0 | 10 | 10 | 104 | .... | .... | .... | .... | .... | .... | .... | .... | .... | .... | .... | .... | .... | .... | .... | .... | .... | .... |
| 2008-09 | Portland Pirates | AHL | 13 | 1 | 2 | 3 | 8 | .... | .... | .... | .... | .... | .... | .... | .... | .... | .... | .... | .... | .... | .... | .... | .... | .... | .... |
| | **NHL Totals** | | **9** | **0** | **2** | **2** | **0** | **0** | **0** | **0** | **2** | **0.0** | | **0** | **0.0** | **7:04** | .... | .... | .... | .... | .... | .... | .... | .... | .... |

• Missed majority of 2008-09 season recovering from head injury suffered during training camp, September, 2008. Signed as a free agent by **Vancouver**, July 22, 2009.

## GABORIK, Marian

(GAB-rihk, MAIR-ee-uhn) **NYR**

Right wing. Shoots left. 6'1", 199 lbs. Born, Trencin, Czech., February 14, 1982. Minnesota's 1st choice, 3rd overall, in 2000 Entry Draft.

| | | | | | | | | | | | | | | | | | | | | | | | | | |
|---|---|---|---|---|---|---|---|---|---|---|---|---|---|---|---|---|---|---|---|---|---|---|---|---|---|
| 1997-98 | Dukla Trencin Jr. | Slovak-Jr. | 36 | 37 | 22 | 59 | 28 | .... | .... | .... | .... | .... | .... | .... | .... | .... | .... | .... | .... | .... | .... | .... | .... | .... | .... |
| | Dukla Trencin | Slovakia | 1 | 1 | 0 | 1 | 0 | .... | .... | .... | .... | .... | .... | .... | .... | .... | .... | .... | .... | .... | .... | .... | .... | .... | .... |
| 1998-99 | Dukla Trencin | Slovakia | 33 | 11 | 9 | 20 | 6 | .... | .... | .... | .... | .... | .... | .... | .... | .... | 3 | 1 | 0 | 1 | 2 | .... | .... | .... | .... |
| 99-2000 | Dukla Trencin | Slovakia | 50 | 25 | 21 | 46 | 34 | .... | .... | .... | .... | .... | .... | .... | .... | .... | 5 | 1 | 2 | 3 | 2 | .... | .... | .... | .... |
| **2000-01** | **Minnesota** | **NHL** | **71** | **18** | **18** | **36** | **32** | **6** | **0** | **3** | **179** | **10.1** | **–6** | **3** | **33.3** | **15:26** | .... | .... | .... | .... | .... | .... | .... | .... | .... |
| **2001-02** | **Minnesota** | **NHL** | **78** | **30** | **37** | **67** | **34** | **10** | **0** | **4** | **221** | **13.6** | **0** | **4** | **25.0** | **16:47** | .... | .... | .... | .... | .... | .... | .... | .... | .... |
| **2002-03** | **Minnesota** | **NHL** | **81** | **30** | **35** | **65** | **46** | **5** | **1** | **8** | **280** | **10.7** | **12** | **16** | **25.0** | **17:24** | **18** | **9** | **8** | **17** | **6** | **4** | **0** | **0** | **18:12** |
| **2003-04** | Dukla Trencin | Slovakia | 9 | 10 | 3 | 13 | 10 | .... | .... | .... | .... | .... | .... | .... | .... | .... | .... | .... | .... | .... | .... | .... | .... | .... | .... |
| | **Minnesota** | **NHL** | **65** | **18** | **22** | **40** | **20** | **3** | **0** | **4** | **220** | **8.2** | **10** | **11** | **45.5** | **18:17** | .... | .... | .... | .... | .... | .... | .... | .... | .... |
| 2004-05 | Dukla Trencin | Slovakia | 29 | 25 | 27 | 52 | 46 | .... | .... | .... | .... | .... | .... | .... | .... | .... | 12 | 8 | 9 | 17 | 26 | .... | .... | .... | .... |
| | Farjestad | Sweden | 12 | 6 | 4 | 10 | 45 | .... | .... | .... | .... | .... | .... | .... | .... | .... | .... | .... | .... | .... | .... | .... | .... | .... | .... |
| **2005-06** | **Minnesota** | **NHL** | **65** | **38** | **28** | **66** | **64** | **10** | **2** | **7** | **252** | **15.1** | **6** | **11** | **27.3** | **18:26** | .... | .... | .... | .... | .... | .... | .... | .... | .... |
| | Slovakia | Olympics | 6 | 3 | 4 | 7 | 4 | .... | .... | .... | .... | .... | .... | .... | .... | .... | .... | .... | .... | .... | .... | .... | .... | .... | .... |
| **2006-07** | **Minnesota** | **NHL** | **48** | **30** | **27** | **57** | **40** | **12** | **1** | **7** | **196** | **15.3** | **12** | **4** | **0.0** | **19:38** | **5** | **3** | **1** | **4** | **8** | **1** | **1** | **1** | **19:32** |
| **2007-08** | **Minnesota** | **NHL** | **77** | **42** | **41** | **83** | **63** | **11** | **1** | **8** | **278** | **15.1** | **17** | **21** | **28.6** | **19:36** | **6** | **0** | **1** | **1** | **4** | **0** | **0** | **0** | **21:51** |
| **2008-09** | **Minnesota** | **NHL** | **17** | **13** | **10** | **23** | **2** | **2** | **1** | **2** | **68** | **19.1** | **3** | **5** | **0.0** | **20:00** | .... | .... | .... | .... | .... | .... | .... | .... | .... |
| | **NHL Totals** | | **502** | **219** | **218** | **437** | **301** | **59** | **6** | **43** | **1694** | **12.9** | | **75** | **26.7** | **17:55** | **29** | **12** | **10** | **22** | **18** | **5** | **1** | **1** | **19:11** |

Played in NHL All-Star Game (2003, 2008)

Signed as a free agent by **Trencin** (Slovakia), July 5, 2004. Signed as a free agent by **Farjestad** (Sweden), December 21, 2004. • Missed majority of 2008-09 season recovering from hip surgery, January 5, 2009. Signed as a free agent by **NY Rangers**, July 1, 2009.

## GAGNE, Simon

(gah-N'YAY, see-MOHN) **PHI.**

Left wing. Shoots left. 6', 195 lbs. Born, Ste-Foy, Que., February 29, 1980. Philadelphia's 1st choice, 22nd overall, in 1998 Entry Draft.

| | | | | | | | | | | | | | | | | | | | | | | | | | |
|---|---|---|---|---|---|---|---|---|---|---|---|---|---|---|---|---|---|---|---|---|---|---|---|---|---|
| 1995-96 | Ste-Foy | QAAA | 27 | 13 | 9 | 22 | 18 | .... | .... | .... | .... | .... | .... | .... | .... | .... | 15 | 7 | 8 | 15 | 8 | .... | .... | .... | .... |
| 1996-97 | Beauport | QMJHL | 51 | 9 | 22 | 31 | 49 | .... | .... | .... | .... | .... | .... | .... | .... | .... | .... | .... | .... | .... | .... | .... | .... | .... | .... |
| 1997-98 | Quebec Remparts | QMJHL | 53 | 30 | 39 | 69 | 26 | .... | .... | .... | .... | .... | .... | .... | .... | .... | 12 | 11 | 5 | 16 | 23 | .... | .... | .... | .... |
| 1998-99 | Quebec Remparts | QMJHL | 61 | 50 | *70 | *120 | 42 | .... | .... | .... | .... | .... | .... | .... | .... | .... | 13 | 9 | 8 | 17 | 4 | .... | .... | .... | .... |
| **99-2000** | **Philadelphia** | **NHL** | **80** | **20** | **28** | **48** | **22** | **8** | **1** | **4** | **159** | **12.6** | **11** | **443** | **42.2** | **14:59** | **17** | **5** | **5** | **10** | **2** | **2** | **0** | **1** | **16:46** |
| **2000-01** | **Philadelphia** | **NHL** | **69** | **27** | **32** | **59** | **18** | **6** | **0** | **7** | **191** | **14.1** | **24** | **21** | **28.6** | **18:05** | **6** | **3** | **0** | **3** | **0** | **2** | **0** | **0** | **19:09** |
| **2001-02** | **Philadelphia** | **NHL** | **79** | **33** | **33** | **66** | **32** | **4** | **1** | **7** | **199** | **16.6** | **31** | **6** | **83.3** | **18:09** | **5** | **0** | **0** | **0** | **2** | **0** | **0** | **0** | **19:16** |
| | Canada | Olympics | 6 | 1 | 3 | 4 | 0 | .... | .... | .... | .... | .... | .... | .... | .... | .... | .... | .... | .... | .... | .... | .... | .... | .... | .... |
| **2002-03** | **Philadelphia** | **NHL** | **46** | **9** | **18** | **27** | **16** | **1** | **1** | **3** | **115** | **7.8** | **20** | **70** | **42.9** | **17:24** | **13** | **4** | **1** | **5** | **6** | **0** | **1** | **1** | **18:13** |
| **2003-04** | **Philadelphia** | **NHL** | **80** | **24** | **21** | **45** | **29** | **6** | **0** | **6** | **211** | **11.4** | **12** | **104** | **39.4** | **16:27** | **18** | **5** | **4** | **9** | **12** | **0** | **0** | **1** | **16:48** |
| 2004-05 | | | DID NOT PLAY | | | | | | | | | | | | | | | | | | | | | | |
| **2005-06** | **Philadelphia** | **NHL** | **72** | **47** | **32** | **79** | **38** | **12** | **2** | **7** | **334** | **14.1** | **31** | **18** | **38.9** | **20:46** | **6** | **3** | **1** | **4** | **2** | **1** | **0** | **0** | **21:45** |
| | Canada | Olympics | 6 | 1 | 2 | 3 | 6 | .... | .... | .... | .... | .... | .... | .... | .... | .... | .... | .... | .... | .... | .... | .... | .... | .... | .... |
| **2006-07** | **Philadelphia** | **NHL** | **76** | **41** | **27** | **68** | **30** | **13** | **2** | **4** | **291** | **14.1** | **2** | **49** | **42.9** | **21:02** | .... | .... | .... | .... | .... | .... | .... | .... | .... |
| **2007-08** | **Philadelphia** | **NHL** | **25** | **7** | **11** | **18** | **4** | **5** | **0** | **2** | **76** | **9.2** | **–8** | **2** | **50.0** | **18:09** | .... | .... | .... | .... | .... | .... | .... | .... | .... |
| **2008-09** | **Philadelphia** | **NHL** | **79** | **34** | **40** | **74** | **42** | **12** | **4** | **3** | **221** | **15.4** | **21** | **10** | **30.0** | **19:01** | **6** | **3** | **1** | **4** | **2** | **1** | **1** | **1** | **20:29** |
| | **NHL Totals** | | **606** | **242** | **242** | **484** | **231** | **67** | **11** | **43** | **1797** | **13.5** | | **723** | **41.6** | **18:14** | **71** | **23** | **12** | **35** | **26** | **6** | **2** | **4** | **18:09** |

QMJHL Second All-Star Team (1999) • NHL All-Rookie Team (2000)

Played in NHL ALL-Star Game (2001, 2007)

• Missed majority of 2007-08 season recovering from head injury suffered in game at Pittsburgh, February 10, 2008.

## GAGNER, Sam

(GAH-n'yay, SAM) **EDM.**

Center/Wing. Shoots right. 5'11", 191 lbs. Born, London, Ont., August 10, 1989. Edmonton's 1st choice, 6th overall, in 2007 Entry Draft.

| | | | | | | | | | | | | | | | | | | | | | | | | | |
|---|---|---|---|---|---|---|---|---|---|---|---|---|---|---|---|---|---|---|---|---|---|---|---|---|---|
| 2001-02 | Tor. Marlboros | GTHL | 68 | 56 | 61 | 117 | 42 | .... | .... | .... | .... | .... | .... | .... | .... | .... | .... | .... | .... | .... | .... | .... | .... | .... | .... |
| 2002-03 | Tor. Marlboros | GTHL | 72 | 68 | 86 | 154 | 35 | .... | .... | .... | .... | .... | .... | .... | .... | .... | .... | .... | .... | .... | .... | .... | .... | .... | .... |
| 2003-04 | Tor. Marlboros | GTHL | 85 | 64 | 108 | 171 | 36 | .... | .... | .... | .... | .... | .... | .... | .... | .... | .... | .... | .... | .... | .... | .... | .... | .... | .... |
| 2004-05 | Tor. Marlboros | GTHL | 70 | 62 | 118 | 180 | 56 | .... | .... | .... | .... | .... | .... | .... | .... | .... | .... | .... | .... | .... | .... | .... | .... | .... | .... |
| | Milton Icehawks | OPJHL | 13 | 5 | 10 | 15 | 10 | .... | .... | .... | .... | .... | .... | .... | .... | .... | .... | .... | .... | .... | .... | .... | .... | .... | .... |
| 2005-06 | Sioux City | USHL | 56 | 11 | 35 | 46 | 60 | .... | .... | .... | .... | .... | .... | .... | .... | .... | .... | .... | .... | .... | .... | .... | .... | .... | .... |
| 2006-07 | London Knights | OHL | 53 | 35 | 83 | 118 | 36 | .... | .... | .... | .... | .... | .... | .... | .... | .... | 16 | 7 | *22 | 29 | 22 | .... | .... | .... | .... |

| | | | Regular Season | | | | | | | | | | | | | | Playoffs | | | | | | | | |
|---|---|---|---|---|---|---|---|---|---|---|---|---|---|---|---|---|---|---|---|---|---|---|---|---|---|
| Season | Club | League | GP | G | A | Pts | PIM | PP | SH | GW | S | % | +/- | TF | F% | Min | GP | G | A | Pts | PIM | PP | SH | GW | Min |
| **2007-08** | **Edmonton** | **NHL** | **79** | **13** | **36** | **49** | **23** | **4** | **0** | **1** | **135** | **9.6** | **–21** | **299** | **41.8** | **15:41** | .... | .... | .... | .... | .... | .... | .... | .... | .... |
| **2008-09** | **Edmonton** | **NHL** | **76** | **16** | **25** | **41** | **51** | **6** | **0** | **1** | **156** | **10.3** | **–1** | **690** | **42.0** | **16:46** | .... | .... | .... | .... | .... | .... | .... | .... | .... |
| | **NHL Totals** | | **155** | **29** | **61** | **90** | **74** | **10** | **0** | **2** | **291** | **10.0** | | **989** | **42.0** | **16:12** | .... | .... | .... | .... | .... | .... | .... | .... | .... |

USHL All-Rookie Team (2006) • OHL All-Rookie Team (2007)

## GALIARDI, T.J. (gal-ee-AR-dee, TEE-JAY) COL.

Left wing. Shoots left. 6'2", 190 lbs. Born, Calgary, Alta., April 22, 1988. Colorado's 4th choice, 55th overall, in 2007 Entry Draft.

| | | | | | | | | | | | | | | | | | | | | | | | | | |
|---|---|---|---|---|---|---|---|---|---|---|---|---|---|---|---|---|---|---|---|---|---|---|---|---|---|
| 2004-05 | Cgy. North Stars | AMHL | 36 | 14 | 16 | 30 | 32 | .... | .... | .... | .... | .... | .... | .... | .... | .... | .... | .... | .... | .... | .... | .... | .... | .... | .... |
| 2005-06 | Calgary Royals | AJHL | 56 | 19 | 37 | 56 | 60 | .... | .... | .... | .... | .... | .... | .... | .... | .... | .... | .... | .... | .... | .... | .... | .... | .... | .... |
| 2006-07 | Dartmouth | ECAC | 33 | 14 | 17 | 31 | 30 | .... | .... | .... | .... | .... | .... | .... | .... | .... | .... | .... | .... | .... | .... | .... | .... | .... | .... |
| 2007-08 | Calgary Hitmen | WHL | 72 | 18 | 52 | 70 | 77 | .... | .... | .... | .... | .... | .... | .... | .... | .... | 16 | 5 | *19 | *24 | 20 | .... | .... | .... | .... |
| **2008-09** | **Colorado** | **NHL** | **11** | **3** | **1** | **4** | **6** | **0** | **0** | **0** | **14** | **21.4** | **–4** | **133** | **42.1** | **16:21** | .... | .... | .... | .... | .... | .... | .... | .... | .... |
| | Lake Erie | AHL | 66 | 10 | 17 | 27 | 32 | .... | .... | .... | .... | .... | .... | .... | .... | .... | .... | .... | .... | .... | .... | .... | .... | .... | .... |
| | **NHL Totals** | | **11** | **3** | **1** | **4** | **6** | **0** | **0** | **0** | **14** | **21.4** | | **133** | **42.1** | **16:21** | .... | .... | .... | .... | .... | .... | .... | .... | .... |

ECAC All-Rookie Team (2007)

## GARRISON, Jason FLA.

Defense. Shoots left. 6'2", 220 lbs. Born, White Rock, B.C., November 13, 1984.

| | | | | | | | | | | | | | | | | | | | | | | | | | |
|---|---|---|---|---|---|---|---|---|---|---|---|---|---|---|---|---|---|---|---|---|---|---|---|---|---|
| 2003-04 | Nanaimo Clippers | BCHL | 52 | 7 | 20 | 27 | 31 | .... | .... | .... | .... | .... | .... | .... | .... | .... | 24 | 3 | 10 | 13 | 12 | .... | .... | .... | .... |
| 2004-05 | Nanaimo Clippers | BCHL | 57 | 22 | 40 | 62 | 42 | .... | .... | .... | .... | .... | .... | .... | .... | .... | .... | .... | .... | .... | .... | .... | .... | .... | .... |
| 2005-06 | U. Minn-Duluth | WCHA | 40 | 3 | 9 | 12 | 26 | .... | .... | .... | .... | .... | .... | .... | .... | .... | .... | .... | .... | .... | .... | .... | .... | .... | .... |
| 2006-07 | U. Minn-Duluth | WCHA | 21 | 1 | 2 | 3 | 16 | .... | .... | .... | .... | .... | .... | .... | .... | .... | .... | .... | .... | .... | .... | .... | .... | .... | .... |
| 2007-08 | U. Minn-Duluth | WCHA | 26 | 5 | 9 | 14 | 26 | .... | .... | .... | .... | .... | .... | .... | .... | .... | .... | .... | .... | .... | .... | .... | .... | .... | .... |
| **2008-09** | **Florida** | **NHL** | **1** | **0** | **0** | **0** | **0** | **0** | **0** | **0** | **0** | **0.0** | **0** | **0** | **0.0** | **11:57** | .... | .... | .... | .... | .... | .... | .... | .... | .... |
| | Rochester | AHL | 75 | 8 | 27 | 35 | 68 | .... | .... | .... | .... | .... | .... | .... | .... | .... | .... | .... | .... | .... | .... | .... | .... | .... | .... |
| | **NHL Totals** | | **1** | **0** | **0** | **0** | **0** | **0** | **0** | **0** | **0** | **0.0** | | **0** | **0.0** | **11:57** | .... | .... | .... | .... | .... | .... | .... | .... | .... |

Signed as a free agent by **Florida**, April 2, 2008.

## GAUSTAD, Paul (GAW-stad, PAWL) BUF.

Center. Shoots left. 6'5", 225 lbs. Born, Fargo, ND, February 3, 1982. Buffalo's 6th choice, 220th overall, in 2000 Entry Draft.

| | | | | | | | | | | | | | | | | | | | | | | | | | |
|---|---|---|---|---|---|---|---|---|---|---|---|---|---|---|---|---|---|---|---|---|---|---|---|---|---|
| 1998-99 | Portland Hawks | USAHA | 45 | 47 | 53 | 100 | 81 | .... | .... | .... | .... | .... | .... | .... | .... | .... | .... | .... | .... | .... | .... | .... | .... | .... | .... |
| 99-2000 | Portland | WHL | 56 | 6 | 8 | 14 | 110 | .... | .... | .... | .... | .... | .... | .... | .... | .... | .... | .... | .... | .... | .... | .... | .... | .... | .... |
| 2000-01 | Portland | WHL | 70 | 11 | 30 | 41 | 168 | .... | .... | .... | .... | .... | .... | .... | .... | .... | 16 | 10 | 6 | 16 | 59 | .... | .... | .... | .... |
| 2001-02 | Portland | WHL | 72 | 36 | 44 | 80 | 202 | .... | .... | .... | .... | .... | .... | .... | .... | .... | 6 | 3 | 1 | 4 | 16 | .... | .... | .... | .... |
| **2002-03** | **Buffalo** | **NHL** | **1** | **0** | **0** | **0** | **0** | **0** | **0** | **0** | **0** | **0.0** | **0** | **7** | **42.9** | **5:48** | .... | .... | .... | .... | .... | .... | .... | .... | .... |
| | Rochester | AHL | 80 | 14 | 39 | 53 | 137 | .... | .... | .... | .... | .... | .... | .... | .... | .... | 3 | 0 | 0 | 0 | 4 | .... | .... | .... | .... |
| 2003-04 | Rochester | AHL | 78 | 9 | 22 | 31 | 169 | .... | .... | .... | .... | .... | .... | .... | .... | .... | 16 | 3 | 10 | 13 | 30 | .... | .... | .... | .... |
| 2004-05 | Rochester | AHL | 76 | 18 | 25 | 43 | 192 | .... | .... | .... | .... | .... | .... | .... | .... | .... | 9 | 6 | 5 | 11 | 16 | .... | .... | .... | .... |
| **2005-06** | **Buffalo** | **NHL** | **78** | **9** | **15** | **24** | **65** | **0** | **0** | **0** | **113** | **8.0** | **4** | **829** | **52.2** | **12:08** | **18** | **0** | **4** | **4** | **14** | **0** | **0** | **0** | **12:21** |
| **2006-07** | **Buffalo** | **NHL** | **54** | **9** | **13** | **22** | **74** | **3** | **0** | **0** | **75** | **12.0** | **11** | **386** | **52.9** | **13:19** | **7** | **0** | **1** | **1** | **2** | **0** | **0** | **0** | **11:00** |
| **2007-08** | **Buffalo** | **NHL** | **82** | **10** | **26** | **36** | **85** | **5** | **0** | **2** | **136** | **7.4** | **–4** | **1165** | **54.9** | **17:10** | .... | .... | .... | .... | .... | .... | .... | .... | .... |
| **2008-09** | **Buffalo** | **NHL** | **62** | **12** | **17** | **29** | **108** | **3** | **1** | **1** | **122** | **9.8** | **4** | **858** | **52.7** | **16:06** | .... | .... | .... | .... | .... | .... | .... | .... | .... |
| | **NHL Totals** | | **277** | **40** | **71** | **111** | **332** | **11** | **1** | **3** | **446** | **9.0** | | **3245** | **53.4** | **14:43** | **25** | **0** | **5** | **5** | **16** | **0** | **0** | **0** | **11:58** |

## GAUTHIER, Denis (GOH-tyay, DEH-nihs)

Defense. Shoots left. 6'2", 220 lbs. Born, Montreal, Que., October 1, 1976. Calgary's 1st choice, 20th overall, in 1995 Entry Draft.

| | | | | | | | | | | | | | | | | | | | | | | | | | |
|---|---|---|---|---|---|---|---|---|---|---|---|---|---|---|---|---|---|---|---|---|---|---|---|---|---|
| 1991-92 | Richelieu AA | QAHA | STATISTICS NOT AVAILABLE | | | | | | | | | | | | | | | | | | | | | | |
| 1992-93 | Drummondville | QMJHL | 61 | 1 | 7 | 8 | 136 | .... | .... | .... | .... | .... | .... | .... | .... | .... | 10 | 0 | 5 | 5 | 40 | .... | .... | .... | .... |
| 1993-94 | Drummondville | QMJHL | 60 | 0 | 7 | 7 | 176 | .... | .... | .... | .... | .... | .... | .... | .... | .... | 9 | 2 | 0 | 2 | 41 | .... | .... | .... | .... |
| 1994-95 | Drummondville | QMJHL | 64 | 9 | 31 | 40 | 190 | .... | .... | .... | .... | .... | .... | .... | .... | .... | 4 | 0 | 5 | 5 | 12 | .... | .... | .... | .... |
| 1995-96 | Drummondville | QMJHL | 53 | 25 | 49 | 74 | 140 | .... | .... | .... | .... | .... | .... | .... | .... | .... | 6 | 4 | 4 | 8 | 32 | .... | .... | .... | .... |
| | Saint John Flames | AHL | 5 | 2 | 0 | 2 | 8 | .... | .... | .... | .... | .... | .... | .... | .... | .... | 16 | 1 | 6 | 7 | 20 | .... | .... | .... | .... |
| 1996-97 | Saint John Flames | AHL | 73 | 3 | 28 | 31 | 74 | .... | .... | .... | .... | .... | .... | .... | .... | .... | 5 | 0 | 0 | 0 | 6 | .... | .... | .... | .... |
| **1997-98** | **Calgary** | **NHL** | **10** | **0** | **0** | **0** | **16** | **0** | **0** | **0** | **3** | **0.0** | **–5** | .... | .... | .... | .... | .... | .... | .... | .... | .... | .... | .... | .... |
| | Saint John Flames | AHL | 68 | 4 | 20 | 24 | 154 | .... | .... | .... | .... | .... | .... | .... | .... | .... | 21 | 0 | 4 | 4 | 83 | .... | .... | .... | .... |
| **1998-99** | **Calgary** | **NHL** | **55** | **3** | **4** | **7** | **68** | **0** | **0** | **0** | **40** | **7.5** | **3** | **0** | **0.0** | **12:41** | .... | .... | .... | .... | .... | .... | .... | .... | .... |
| | Saint John Flames | AHL | 16 | 0 | 3 | 3 | 31 | .... | .... | .... | .... | .... | .... | .... | .... | .... | .... | .... | .... | .... | .... | .... | .... | .... | .... |
| **99-2000** | **Calgary** | **NHL** | **39** | **1** | **1** | **2** | **50** | **0** | **0** | **0** | **29** | **3.4** | **–4** | **0** | **0.0** | **19:21** | .... | .... | .... | .... | .... | .... | .... | .... | .... |
| **2000-01** | **Calgary** | **NHL** | **62** | **2** | **6** | **8** | **78** | **0** | **0** | **0** | **33** | **6.1** | **3** | **0** | **0.0** | **16:37** | .... | .... | .... | .... | .... | .... | .... | .... | .... |
| **2001-02** | **Calgary** | **NHL** | **66** | **5** | **8** | **13** | **91** | **0** | **1** | **2** | **76** | **6.6** | **9** | **0** | **0.0** | **19:19** | .... | .... | .... | .... | .... | .... | .... | .... | .... |
| **2002-03** | **Calgary** | **NHL** | **72** | **1** | **11** | **12** | **99** | **0** | **0** | **1** | **50** | **2.0** | **5** | **0** | **0.0** | **19:52** | .... | .... | .... | .... | .... | .... | .... | .... | .... |
| **2003-04** | **Calgary** | **NHL** | **80** | **1** | **15** | **16** | **113** | **0** | **0** | **0** | **90** | **1.1** | **4** | **0** | **0.0** | **18:43** | **6** | **0** | **1** | **1** | **4** | **0** | **0** | **0** | **18:33** |
| 2004-05 | | | DID NOT PLAY | | | | | | | | | | | | | | | | | | | | | | |
| **2005-06** | **Phoenix** | **NHL** | **45** | **2** | **9** | **11** | **61** | **0** | **0** | **0** | **43** | **4.7** | **–4** | **0** | **0.0** | **16:58** | .... | .... | .... | .... | .... | .... | .... | .... | .... |
| | **Philadelphia** | **NHL** | **17** | **0** | **0** | **0** | **37** | **0** | **0** | **0** | **13** | **0.0** | **6** | **0** | **0.0** | **15:21** | **6** | **0** | **1** | **1** | **19** | **0** | **0** | **0** | **18:21** |
| **2006-07** | **Philadelphia** | **NHL** | **43** | **0** | **4** | **4** | **45** | **0** | **0** | **0** | **23** | **0.0** | **–11** | **0** | **0.0** | **16:39** | .... | .... | .... | .... | .... | .... | .... | .... | .... |
| 2007-08 | Philadelphia | AHL | 78 | 3 | 15 | 18 | 80 | .... | .... | .... | .... | .... | .... | .... | .... | .... | 11 | 0 | 1 | 1 | 17 | .... | .... | .... | .... |
| **2008-09** | **Los Angeles** | **NHL** | **65** | **2** | **2** | **4** | **90** | **0** | **0** | **0** | **36** | **5.6** | **–11** | **0** | **0.0** | **14:32** | .... | .... | .... | .... | .... | .... | .... | .... | .... |
| | **NHL Totals** | | **554** | **17** | **60** | **77** | **748** | **0** | **1** | **3** | **436** | **3.9** | | **0** | **0.0** | **17:14** | **12** | **0** | **2** | **2** | **23** | **0** | **0** | **0** | **18:27** |

QMJHL First All-Star Team (1996) • Canadian Major Junior First All-Star Team (1996)

• Missed majority of 1999-2000 season recovering from hip injury suffered in game vs. St. Louis, February 1, 2000. Traded to **Phoenix** by **Calgary** with Oleg Saprykin for Daymond Langkow, August 26, 2004. Traded to **Philadelphia** by **Phoenix** for Josh Gratton, Florida's 2nd round choice (previously acquired, later traded to Detroit - Detroit selected Cory Emerton) in 2006 Entry Draft and Tampa Bay's 2nd round choice (previously acquired, later traded to Detroit - Detroit selected Shawn Matthias) in 2006 Entry Draft, March 9, 2006. Traded to **Los Angeles** by **Philadelphia** with Philadelphia's 2nd round choice in 2010 Entry Draft for Patrik Hersley and Ned Lukacevic, July 1, 2008.

## GAUTHIER, Gabe (GOH-tyay, GAYB) L.A.

Left wing. Shoots left. 5'9", 204 lbs. Born, Torrance, CA, January 20, 1984.

| | | | | | | | | | | | | | | | | | | | | | | | | | |
|---|---|---|---|---|---|---|---|---|---|---|---|---|---|---|---|---|---|---|---|---|---|---|---|---|---|
| 2002-03 | U. of Denver | WCHA | 41 | 8 | 8 | 16 | 30 | .... | .... | .... | .... | .... | .... | .... | .... | .... | .... | .... | .... | .... | .... | .... | .... | .... | .... |
| 2003-04 | U. of Denver | WCHA | 42 | 18 | 25 | 43 | 32 | .... | .... | .... | .... | .... | .... | .... | .... | .... | .... | .... | .... | .... | .... | .... | .... | .... | .... |
| 2004-05 | U. of Denver | WCHA | 41 | 23 | 29 | 52 | 44 | .... | .... | .... | .... | .... | .... | .... | .... | .... | .... | .... | .... | .... | .... | .... | .... | .... | .... |
| 2005-06 | U. of Denver | WCHA | 38 | 15 | 24 | 39 | 35 | .... | .... | .... | .... | .... | .... | .... | .... | .... | .... | .... | .... | .... | .... | .... | .... | .... | .... |
| **2006-07** | **Los Angeles** | **NHL** | **5** | **0** | **0** | **0** | **2** | **0** | **0** | **0** | **6** | **0.0** | **–1** | **23** | **47.8** | **9:57** | .... | .... | .... | .... | .... | .... | .... | .... | .... |
| | Manchester | AHL | 69 | 14 | 28 | 42 | 54 | .... | .... | .... | .... | .... | .... | .... | .... | .... | 16 | 1 | 4 | 5 | 14 | .... | .... | .... | .... |
| **2007-08** | **Los Angeles** | **NHL** | **3** | **0** | **0** | **0** | **0** | **0** | **0** | **0** | **2** | **0.0** | **0** | **17** | **47.1** | **7:08** | .... | .... | .... | .... | .... | .... | .... | .... | .... |
| | Manchester | AHL | 61 | 23 | 37 | 60 | 43 | .... | .... | .... | .... | .... | .... | .... | .... | .... | 3 | 0 | 0 | 0 | 4 | .... | .... | .... | .... |
| 2008-09 | Manchester | AHL | 69 | 12 | 30 | 42 | 32 | .... | .... | .... | .... | .... | .... | .... | .... | .... | .... | .... | .... | .... | .... | .... | .... | .... | .... |
| | **NHL Totals** | | **8** | **0** | **0** | **0** | **2** | **0** | **0** | **0** | **8** | **0.0** | | **40** | **47.5** | **8:53** | .... | .... | .... | .... | .... | .... | .... | .... | .... |

NCAA Championship All-Tournament Team (2005)

Signed as a free agent by **Los Angeles**, July 12, 2006.

## GERBE, Nathan (GUHR-bee, NAY-thuhn) BUF.

Center. Shoots left. 5'6", 160 lbs. Born, Oxford, MI, July 24, 1987. Buffalo's 5th choice, 142nd overall, in 2005 Entry Draft.

| | | | | | | | | | | | | | | | | | | | | | | | | | |
|---|---|---|---|---|---|---|---|---|---|---|---|---|---|---|---|---|---|---|---|---|---|---|---|---|---|
| 2002-03 | River City Lancers | USHL | 25 | 3 | 3 | 6 | 49 | .... | .... | .... | .... | .... | .... | .... | .... | .... | 7 | 1 | 1 | 2 | 2 | .... | .... | .... | .... |
| 2003-04 | USNTDP | U-17 | 32 | 14 | 12 | 26 | 66 | .... | .... | .... | .... | .... | .... | .... | .... | .... | .... | .... | .... | .... | .... | .... | .... | .... | .... |
| | USNTDP | NAHL | 26 | 11 | 7 | 18 | 87 | .... | .... | .... | .... | .... | .... | .... | .... | .... | .... | .... | .... | .... | .... | .... | .... | .... | .... |
| 2004-05 | USNTDP | U-18 | 26 | 6 | 11 | 17 | 48 | .... | .... | .... | .... | .... | .... | .... | .... | .... | .... | .... | .... | .... | .... | .... | .... | .... | .... |
| | USNTDP | NAHL | 12 | 7 | 5 | 12 | 25 | .... | .... | .... | .... | .... | .... | .... | .... | .... | .... | .... | .... | .... | .... | .... | .... | .... | .... |
| 2005-06 | Boston College | H-East | 39 | 11 | 7 | 18 | 75 | .... | .... | .... | .... | .... | .... | .... | .... | .... | .... | .... | .... | .... | .... | .... | .... | .... | .... |
| 2006-07 | Boston College | H-East | 41 | *25 | 22 | 47 | 76 | .... | .... | .... | .... | .... | .... | .... | .... | .... | .... | .... | .... | .... | .... | .... | .... | .... | .... |
| 2007-08 | Boston College | H-East | 43 | *35 | 33 | *68 | 65 | .... | .... | .... | .... | .... | .... | .... | .... | .... | .... | .... | .... | .... | .... | .... | .... | .... | .... |

| | | | Regular Season | | | | | | | | | | | | | | Playoffs | | | | | | | | |
|---|---|---|---|---|---|---|---|---|---|---|---|---|---|---|---|---|---|---|---|---|---|---|---|---|---|
| Season | Club | League | GP | G | A | Pts | PIM | PP | SH | GW | S | % | +/- | TF | F% | Min | GP | G | A | Pts | PIM | PP | SH | GW | Min |
| 2008-09 | Buffalo | NHL | 10 | 0 | 1 | 1 | 4 | 0 | 0 | 0 | 24 | 0.0 | 3 | 1 | 100.0 | 13:37 | .... | .... | .... | .... | .... | .... | .... | .... | .... |
| | Portland Pirates | AHL | 57 | 30 | 26 | 56 | 63 | .... | .... | .... | .... | .... | .... | .... | .... | .... | 5 | 0 | 0 | 0 | 4 | .... | .... | .... | .... |
| | NHL Totals | | 10 | 0 | 1 | 1 | 4 | 0 | 0 | 0 | 24 | 0.0 | | 1 | 100.0 | 13:37 | .... | .... | .... | .... | .... | .... | .... | .... | .... |

Hockey East Second Alll-Star Team (2007) • NCAA Championship All-Tournament Team (2007, 2008) • Hockey East First All-Star Team (2008) • NCAA East First All-American Team (2008) • NCAA Championship Tournament MVP (2008) • AHL All-Rookie Team (2009) • Dudley "Red" Garrett Memorial Award (AHL – Rookie of the Year) (2009)

## GERMYN, Carsen

(JUHR-mihn, KAHR-sehn) **CGY.**

Right wing. Shoots right. 5'11", 190 lbs. Born, Campbell River, B.C., February 22, 1982.

| Season | Club | League | GP | G | A | Pts | PIM | PP | SH | GW | S | % | +/- | TF | F% | Min | GP | G | A | Pts | PIM | PP | SH | GW | Min |
|---|---|---|---|---|---|---|---|---|---|---|---|---|---|---|---|---|---|---|---|---|---|---|---|---|---|
| 1998-99 | Kelowna Rockets | WHL | 59 | 6 | 10 | 16 | 61 | .... | .... | .... | .... | .... | .... | .... | .... | .... | 5 | 0 | 0 | 0 | 2 | .... | .... | .... | .... |
| 99-2000 | Kelowna Rockets | WHL | 71 | 16 | 29 | 45 | 111 | .... | .... | .... | .... | .... | .... | .... | .... | .... | 5 | 3 | 3 | 6 | 4 | .... | .... | .... | .... |
| 2000-01 | Kelowna Rockets | WHL | 71 | 35 | 52 | 87 | 102 | .... | .... | .... | .... | .... | .... | .... | .... | .... | 6 | 2 | 6 | 8 | 10 | .... | .... | .... | .... |
| 2001-02 | Kelowna Rockets | WHL | 23 | 10 | 18 | 28 | 43 | .... | .... | .... | .... | .... | .... | .... | .... | .... | .... | .... | .... | .... | .... | .... | .... | .... | .... |
| | Red Deer Rebels | WHL | 37 | 23 | 25 | 48 | 83 | .... | .... | .... | .... | .... | .... | .... | .... | .... | 23 | 4 | 12 | 16 | 24 | .... | .... | .... | .... |
| 2002-03 | Red Deer Rebels | WHL | 63 | 26 | 33 | 59 | 108 | .... | .... | .... | .... | .... | .... | .... | .... | .... | 23 | 4 | 9 | 13 | 25 | .... | .... | .... | .... |
| 2003-04 | Norfolk Admirals | AHL | 77 | 11 | 16 | 27 | 104 | .... | .... | .... | .... | .... | .... | .... | .... | .... | 6 | 1 | 0 | 1 | 2 | .... | .... | .... | .... |
| 2004-05 | Lowell | AHL | 60 | 9 | 11 | 20 | 115 | .... | .... | .... | .... | .... | .... | .... | .... | .... | 10 | 0 | 0 | 0 | 25 | .... | .... | .... | .... |
| 2005-06 | Calgary | NHL | 2 | 0 | 0 | 0 | 0 | 0 | 0 | 0 | 2 | 0.0 | –1 | 0 | 0.0 | 5:00 | .... | .... | .... | .... | .... | .... | .... | .... | .... |
| | Omaha | AHL | 77 | 24 | 31 | 55 | 127 | .... | .... | .... | .... | .... | .... | .... | .... | .... | .... | .... | .... | .... | .... | .... | .... | .... | .... |
| 2006-07 | Calgary | NHL | 2 | 0 | 0 | 0 | 0 | 0 | 0 | 0 | 3 | 0.0 | 0 | 2 | 50.0 | 8:26 | .... | .... | .... | .... | .... | .... | .... | .... | .... |
| | Omaha | AHL | 77 | 28 | 32 | 60 | 124 | .... | .... | .... | .... | .... | .... | .... | .... | .... | 6 | 1 | 1 | 2 | 2 | .... | .... | .... | .... |
| 2007-08 | Quad City Flames | AHL | 77 | 19 | 29 | 48 | 133 | .... | .... | .... | .... | .... | .... | .... | .... | .... | .... | .... | .... | .... | .... | .... | .... | .... | .... |
| 2008-09 | Quad City Flames | AHL | 75 | 13 | 47 | 60 | 57 | .... | .... | .... | .... | .... | .... | .... | .... | .... | .... | .... | .... | .... | .... | .... | .... | .... | .... |
| | NHL Totals | | 4 | 0 | 0 | 0 | 0 | 0 | 0 | 0 | 5 | 0.0 | | 2 | 50.0 | 6:43 | .... | .... | .... | .... | .... | .... | .... | .... | .... |

Signed as a free agent by **Calgary**, July 6, 2004.

## GERVAIS, Bruno

(ZHUR-vay, BROO-noh) **NYI**

Defense. Shoots right. 6'1", 205 lbs. Born, Longueuil, Que., October 3, 1984. NY Islanders' 6th choice, 182nd overall, in 2003 Entry Draft.

| Season | Club | League | GP | G | A | Pts | PIM | PP | SH | GW | S | % | +/- | TF | F% | Min | GP | G | A | Pts | PIM | PP | SH | GW | Min |
|---|---|---|---|---|---|---|---|---|---|---|---|---|---|---|---|---|---|---|---|---|---|---|---|---|---|
| 99-2000 | Antoine-Girouard | QAAA | 6 | 0 | 0 | 0 | 0 | .... | .... | .... | .... | .... | .... | .... | .... | .... | 4 | 0 | 0 | 0 | 0 | .... | .... | .... | .... |
| 2000-01 | Antoine-Girouard | QAAA | 40 | 8 | 27 | 35 | 46 | .... | .... | .... | .... | .... | .... | .... | .... | .... | 7 | 4 | 2 | 6 | 8 | .... | .... | .... | .... |
| 2001-02 | Acadie-Bathurst | QMJHL | 65 | 4 | 12 | 16 | 42 | .... | .... | .... | .... | .... | .... | .... | .... | .... | 16 | 3 | 1 | 4 | 8 | .... | .... | .... | .... |
| 2002-03 | Acadie-Bathurst | QMJHL | 72 | 22 | 28 | 50 | 73 | .... | .... | .... | .... | .... | .... | .... | .... | .... | 11 | 3 | 5 | 8 | 14 | .... | .... | .... | .... |
| 2003-04 | Acadie-Bathurst | QMJHL | 23 | 4 | 6 | 10 | 28 | .... | .... | .... | .... | .... | .... | .... | .... | .... | .... | .... | .... | .... | .... | .... | .... | .... | .... |
| 2004-05 | Bridgeport | AHL | 76 | 8 | 22 | 30 | 58 | .... | .... | .... | .... | .... | .... | .... | .... | .... | .... | .... | .... | .... | .... | .... | .... | .... | .... |
| 2005-06 | NY Islanders | NHL | 27 | 3 | 4 | 7 | 8 | 1 | 0 | 0 | 21 | 14.3 | –1 | 0 | 0.0 | 16:47 | .... | .... | .... | .... | .... | .... | .... | .... | .... |
| | Bridgeport | AHL | 55 | 17 | 25 | 42 | 70 | .... | .... | .... | .... | .... | .... | .... | .... | .... | 7 | 1 | 2 | 3 | 0 | .... | .... | .... | .... |
| 2006-07 | NY Islanders | NHL | 51 | 0 | 6 | 6 | 28 | 0 | 0 | 0 | 47 | 0.0 | –10 | 0 | 0.0 | 15:23 | 5 | 1 | 1 | 2 | 2 | 0 | 0 | 0 | 15:36 |
| | Bridgeport | AHL | 3 | 0 | 0 | 0 | 6 | .... | .... | .... | .... | .... | .... | .... | .... | .... | .... | .... | .... | .... | .... | .... | .... | .... | .... |
| 2007-08 | NY Islanders | NHL | 60 | 0 | 13 | 13 | 34 | 0 | 0 | 0 | 59 | 0.0 | –5 | 0 | 0.0 | 20:00 | .... | .... | .... | .... | .... | .... | .... | .... | .... |
| 2008-09 | NY Islanders | NHL | 69 | 3 | 16 | 19 | 33 | 0 | 0 | 1 | 82 | 3.7 | –15 | 1 | 0.0 | 21:36 | .... | .... | .... | .... | .... | .... | .... | .... | .... |
| | NHL Totals | | 207 | 6 | 39 | 45 | 103 | 1 | 0 | 1 | 209 | 2.9 | | 1 | 0.0 | 18:59 | 5 | 1 | 1 | 2 | 2 | 0 | 0 | 0 | 15:36 |

QMJHL Second All-Star Team (2003)

• Missed majority of 2003-04 season recovering from knee injury suffered during Team Canada Jr. training camp, December 12, 2003.

## GETZLAF, Ryan

(GEHTZ-laf, RIGH-uhn) **ANA.**

Center. Shoots right. 6'4", 221 lbs. Born, Regina, Sask., May 10, 1985. Anaheim's 1st choice, 19th overall, in 2003 Entry Draft.

| Season | Club | League | GP | G | A | Pts | PIM | PP | SH | GW | S | % | +/- | TF | F% | Min | GP | G | A | Pts | PIM | PP | SH | GW | Min |
|---|---|---|---|---|---|---|---|---|---|---|---|---|---|---|---|---|---|---|---|---|---|---|---|---|---|
| 2000-01 | Regina Rangers | SBHL | 41 | 33 | 41 | 74 | 189 | .... | .... | .... | .... | .... | .... | .... | .... | .... | .... | .... | .... | .... | .... | .... | .... | .... | .... |
| | Reg. Pat Cdns. | SMHL | 8 | 4 | 3 | 7 | 8 | .... | .... | .... | .... | .... | .... | .... | .... | .... | .... | .... | .... | .... | .... | .... | .... | .... | .... |
| 2001-02 | Calgary Hitmen | WHL | 63 | 9 | 9 | 18 | 34 | .... | .... | .... | .... | .... | .... | .... | .... | .... | 7 | 2 | 1 | 3 | 4 | .... | .... | .... | .... |
| 2002-03 | Calgary Hitmen | WHL | 70 | 29 | 39 | 68 | 121 | .... | .... | .... | .... | .... | .... | .... | .... | .... | 5 | 1 | 1 | 2 | 6 | .... | .... | .... | .... |
| 2003-04 | Calgary Hitmen | WHL | 49 | 28 | 47 | 75 | 97 | .... | .... | .... | .... | .... | .... | .... | .... | .... | 7 | 5 | 1 | 6 | 12 | .... | .... | .... | .... |
| 2004-05 | Calgary Hitmen | WHL | 51 | 29 | 25 | 54 | 102 | .... | .... | .... | .... | .... | .... | .... | .... | .... | 12 | 4 | 13 | 17 | 18 | .... | .... | .... | .... |
| | Cincinnati | AHL | .... | .... | .... | .... | .... | .... | .... | .... | .... | .... | .... | .... | .... | .... | 10 | 1 | 4 | 5 | 4 | .... | .... | .... | .... |
| 2005-06 | Anaheim | NHL | 57 | 14 | 25 | 39 | 22 | 10 | 0 | 1 | 116 | 12.1 | 6 | 534 | 44.0 | 12:35 | 16 | 3 | 4 | 7 | 13 | 2 | 0 | 1 | 15:49 |
| | Portland Pirates | AHL | 17 | 8 | 25 | 33 | 36 | .... | .... | .... | .... | .... | .... | .... | .... | .... | 1 | 0 | 0 | 0 | 4 | .... | .... | .... | .... |
| 2006-07♦ | Anaheim | NHL | 82 | 25 | 33 | 58 | 66 | 11 | 1 | 6 | 203 | 12.3 | 17 | 888 | 49.4 | 15:04 | 21 | 7 | 10 | 17 | 32 | 3 | 1 | 3 | 21:43 |
| 2007-08 | Anaheim | NHL | 77 | 24 | 58 | 82 | 94 | 4 | 1 | 2 | 185 | 13.0 | 32 | 1152 | 47.3 | 19:39 | 6 | 2 | 3 | 5 | 6 | 1 | 0 | 0 | 20:29 |
| 2008-09 | Anaheim | NHL | 81 | 25 | 66 | 91 | 121 | 9 | 0 | 2 | 227 | 11.0 | 5 | 1128 | 50.2 | 20:08 | 13 | 4 | 14 | 18 | 25 | 1 | 0 | 0 | 24:08 |
| | NHL Totals | | 297 | 88 | 182 | 270 | 303 | 34 | 2 | 11 | 731 | 12.0 | | 3702 | 48.2 | 17:09 | 56 | 16 | 31 | 47 | 76 | 7 | 1 | 4 | 20:28 |

WHL East First All-Star Team (2004) • WHL East Second All-Star Team (2005)

Played in NHL All-Star Game (2008, 2009)

## GILBERT, Tom

(GIHL-buhrt, TAWM) **EDM.**

Defense. Shoots right. 6'3", 206 lbs. Born, Minneapolis, MN, January 10, 1983. Colorado's 5th choice, 129th overall, in 2002 Entry Draft.

| Season | Club | League | GP | G | A | Pts | PIM | PP | SH | GW | S | % | +/- | TF | F% | Min | GP | G | A | Pts | PIM | PP | SH | GW | Min |
|---|---|---|---|---|---|---|---|---|---|---|---|---|---|---|---|---|---|---|---|---|---|---|---|---|---|
| 99-2000 | Bloomington-Jeff. | High-MN | 18 | 7 | 18 | 25 | .... | .... | .... | .... | .... | .... | .... | .... | .... | .... | .... | .... | .... | .... | .... | .... | .... | .... | .... |
| 2000-01 | Bloomington-Jeff. | High-MN | 23 | 20 | 18 | 38 | .... | .... | .... | .... | .... | .... | .... | .... | .... | .... | .... | .... | .... | .... | .... | .... | .... | .... | .... |
| | Chicago Steel | USHL | 1 | 0 | 0 | 0 | 0 | .... | .... | .... | .... | .... | .... | .... | .... | .... | .... | .... | .... | .... | .... | .... | .... | .... | .... |
| 2001-02 | Chicago Steel | USHL | 57 | 13 | 15 | 28 | 62 | .... | .... | .... | .... | .... | .... | .... | .... | .... | 4 | 0 | 0 | 0 | 4 | .... | .... | .... | .... |
| 2002-03 | U. of Wisconsin | WCHA | 39 | 7 | 13 | 20 | 36 | .... | .... | .... | .... | .... | .... | .... | .... | .... | .... | .... | .... | .... | .... | .... | .... | .... | .... |
| 2003-04 | U. of Wisconsin | WCHA | 39 | 6 | 15 | 21 | 36 | .... | .... | .... | .... | .... | .... | .... | .... | .... | .... | .... | .... | .... | .... | .... | .... | .... | .... |
| 2004-05 | U. of Wisconsin | WCHA | 41 | 8 | 9 | 17 | 48 | .... | .... | .... | .... | .... | .... | .... | .... | .... | .... | .... | .... | .... | .... | .... | .... | .... | .... |
| 2005-06 | U. of Wisconsin | WCHA | 43 | 12 | 19 | 31 | 32 | .... | .... | .... | .... | .... | .... | .... | .... | .... | .... | .... | .... | .... | .... | .... | .... | .... | .... |
| 2006-07 | Edmonton | NHL | 12 | 1 | 5 | 6 | 0 | 0 | 0 | 0 | 13 | 7.7 | –1 | 0 | 0.0 | 20:05 | .... | .... | .... | .... | .... | .... | .... | .... | .... |
| | Wilkes-Barre | AHL | 48 | 4 | 26 | 30 | 32 | .... | .... | .... | .... | .... | .... | .... | .... | .... | 10 | 1 | 7 | *8 | 10 | .... | .... | .... | .... |
| 2007-08 | Edmonton | NHL | 82 | 13 | 20 | 33 | 20 | 3 | 0 | 1 | 98 | 13.3 | –6 | 0 | 0.0 | 22:12 | .... | .... | .... | .... | .... | .... | .... | .... | .... |
| 2008-09 | Edmonton | NHL | 82 | 5 | 40 | 45 | 26 | 2 | 0 | 1 | 107 | 4.7 | 6 | 0 | 0.0 | 21:58 | .... | .... | .... | .... | .... | .... | .... | .... | .... |
| | NHL Totals | | 176 | 19 | 65 | 84 | 46 | 5 | 0 | 2 | 218 | 8.7 | | 0 | 0.0 | 21:57 | .... | .... | .... | .... | .... | .... | .... | .... | .... |

WCHA First All-Star Team (2006) • NCAA West Second All-American Team (2006) • NCAA Championship All-Tournament Team (2006) • NHL All-Rookie Team (2008)

Traded to **Edmonton** by **Colorado** for Tommy Salo and Edmonton's 6th round choice (Justin Mercier) in 2005 Entry Draft, March 8, 2004.

## GILL, Hal

(GIHL, HAL) **MTL.**

Defense. Shoots left. 6'7", 250 lbs. Born, Concord, MA, April 6, 1975. Boston's 8th choice, 207th overall, in 1993 Entry Draft.

| Season | Club | League | GP | G | A | Pts | PIM | PP | SH | GW | S | % | +/- | TF | F% | Min | GP | G | A | Pts | PIM | PP | SH | GW | Min |
|---|---|---|---|---|---|---|---|---|---|---|---|---|---|---|---|---|---|---|---|---|---|---|---|---|---|
| 1992-93 | Nashoba | High-MA | 20 | 25 | 25 | 50 | .... | .... | .... | .... | .... | .... | .... | .... | .... | .... | .... | .... | .... | .... | .... | .... | .... | .... | .... |
| 1993-94 | Providence | H-East | 31 | 1 | 2 | 3 | 26 | .... | .... | .... | .... | .... | .... | .... | .... | .... | .... | .... | .... | .... | .... | .... | .... | .... | .... |
| 1994-95 | Providence | H-East | 26 | 1 | 3 | 4 | 22 | .... | .... | .... | .... | .... | .... | .... | .... | .... | .... | .... | .... | .... | .... | .... | .... | .... | .... |
| 1995-96 | Providence | H-East | 39 | 5 | 12 | 17 | 54 | .... | .... | .... | .... | .... | .... | .... | .... | .... | .... | .... | .... | .... | .... | .... | .... | .... | .... |
| 1996-97 | Providence | H-East | 35 | 5 | 16 | 21 | 52 | .... | .... | .... | .... | .... | .... | .... | .... | .... | .... | .... | .... | .... | .... | .... | .... | .... | .... |
| 1997-98 | Boston | NHL | 68 | 2 | 4 | 6 | 47 | 0 | 0 | 0 | 56 | 3.6 | 4 | | | | 6 | 0 | 0 | 0 | 4 | 0 | 0 | 0 | |
| | Providence Bruins | AHL | 4 | 1 | 0 | 1 | 23 | .... | .... | .... | .... | .... | .... | .... | .... | .... | .... | .... | .... | .... | .... | .... | .... | .... | .... |
| 1998-99 | Boston | NHL | 80 | 3 | 7 | 10 | 63 | 0 | 0 | 2 | 102 | 2.9 | –10 | 1 | 100.0 | 20:54 | 12 | 0 | 0 | 0 | 14 | 0 | 0 | 0 | 20:41 |
| 99-2000 | Boston | NHL | 81 | 3 | 9 | 12 | 51 | 0 | 0 | 0 | 120 | 2.5 | 0 | 0 | 0.0 | 17:15 | .... | .... | .... | .... | .... | .... | .... | .... | .... |
| 2000-01 | Boston | NHL | 80 | 1 | 10 | 11 | 71 | 0 | 0 | 0 | 79 | 1.3 | –2 | 0 | 0.0 | 18:21 | .... | .... | .... | .... | .... | .... | .... | .... | .... |
| 2001-02 | Boston | NHL | 79 | 4 | 18 | 22 | 77 | 0 | 0 | 0 | 137 | 2.9 | 16 | 0 | 0.0 | 24:13 | 6 | 0 | 1 | 1 | 2 | 0 | 0 | 0 | 23:04 |
| 2002-03 | Boston | NHL | 76 | 4 | 13 | 17 | 56 | 0 | 0 | 0 | 114 | 3.5 | 21 | 0 | 0.0 | 20:42 | 5 | 0 | 0 | 0 | 4 | 0 | 0 | 0 | 20:19 |
| 2003-04 | Boston | NHL | 82 | 2 | 7 | 9 | 99 | 0 | 0 | 0 | 104 | 1.9 | 16 | 0 | 0.0 | 18:24 | 7 | 0 | 1 | 1 | 4 | 0 | 0 | 0 | 19:03 |
| 2004-05 | Lukko Rauma | Finland | 31 | 2 | 8 | 10 | 110 | .... | .... | .... | .... | .... | .... | .... | .... | .... | 8 | 0 | 0 | 0 | *57 | .... | .... | .... | .... |
| 2005-06 | Boston | NHL | 80 | 1 | 9 | 10 | 124 | 0 | 0 | 0 | 68 | 1.5 | –4 | 0 | 0.0 | 18:37 | .... | .... | .... | .... | .... | .... | .... | .... | .... |
| 2006-07 | Toronto | NHL | 82 | 6 | 14 | 20 | 91 | 0 | 0 | 1 | 79 | 7.6 | 11 | 1 | 0.0 | 18:53 | .... | .... | .... | .... | .... | .... | .... | .... | .... |

| | | | Regular Season | | | | | | | | | | | | | | Playoffs | | | | | | | | |
|---|---|---|---|---|---|---|---|---|---|---|---|---|---|---|---|---|---|---|---|---|---|---|---|---|---|
| Season | Club | League | GP | G | A | Pts | PIM | PP | SH | GW | S | % | +/- | TF | F% | Min | GP | G | A | Pts | PIM | PP | SH | GW | Min |
| 2007-08 | Toronto | NHL | 63 | 2 | 18 | 20 | 52 | 0 | 0 | 0 | 69 | 2.9 | 0 | 0 | 0.0 | 20:42 | .... | .... | .... | .... | .... | .... | .... | .... | .... |
| | Pittsburgh | NHL | 18 | 1 | 3 | 4 | 16 | 0 | 0 | 0 | 17 | 5.9 | 6 | 0 | 0.0 | 17:31 | 20 | 0 | 1 | 1 | 12 | 0 | 0 | 0 | 19:17 |
| 2008-09 ♦ | Pittsburgh | NHL | 62 | 2 | 8 | 10 | 53 | 0 | 0 | 0 | 40 | 5.0 | 11 | 0 | 0.0 | 17:54 | 24 | 0 | 2 | 2 | 6 | 0 | 0 | 0 | 19:26 |
| | NHL Totals | | 851 | 31 | 120 | 151 | 800 | 0 | 0 | 3 | 985 | 3.1 | | 2 | 50.0 | 19:32 | 80 | 0 | 5 | 5 | 46 | 0 | 0 | 0 | 19:55 |

Signed as a free agent by **Rauma** (Finland), November 25, 2004. Signed as a free agent by **Toronto**, July 1, 2006. Traded to **Pittsburgh** by **Toronto** for Pittsburgh's 2nd round choice (Jimmy Hayes) in 2008 Entry Draft and Pittsburgh's 5th round choice (later traded to NY Rangers – later traded back to Pittsburgh – Pittsburgh selected Andy Bathgate) in 2009 Entry Draft, February 26, 2008. Signed as a free agent by **Montreal**, July 1, 2009.

## GILLIES, Colton

(GIHL-eez, KOHL-tuhn) **MIN.**

Center. Shoots left. 6'4", 189 lbs. Born, White Rock, B.C., February 12, 1989. Minnesota's 1st choice, 16th overall, in 2007 Entry Draft.

| Season | Club | League | GP | G | A | Pts | PIM | PP | SH | GW | S | % | +/- | TF | F% | Min | GP | G | A | Pts | PIM | PP | SH | GW | Min |
|---|---|---|---|---|---|---|---|---|---|---|---|---|---|---|---|---|---|---|---|---|---|---|---|---|---|
| 2004-05 | North Delta Flyers | PIJHL | 44 | 9 | 17 | 26 | .... | .... | .... | .... | .... | .... | .... | .... | .... | .... | 6 | 2 | 1 | 3 | .... | .... | .... | .... | .... |
| | South Surrey | BCHL | 3 | 1 | 0 | 1 | 0 | .... | .... | .... | .... | .... | .... | .... | .... | .... | .... | .... | .... | .... | .... | .... | .... | .... | .... |
| | Saskatoon Blades | WHL | 9 | 1 | 1 | 2 | 8 | .... | .... | .... | .... | .... | .... | .... | .... | .... | 2 | 0 | 0 | 0 | 0 | .... | .... | .... | .... |
| 2005-06 | Saskatoon Blades | WHL | 63 | 6 | 6 | 12 | 57 | .... | .... | .... | .... | .... | .... | .... | .... | .... | 8 | 0 | 0 | 0 | 4 | .... | .... | .... | .... |
| 2006-07 | Saskatoon Blades | WHL | 65 | 13 | 17 | 30 | 148 | .... | .... | .... | .... | .... | .... | .... | .... | .... | .... | .... | .... | .... | .... | .... | .... | .... | .... |
| 2007-08 | Saskatoon Blades | WHL | 58 | 24 | 23 | 47 | 97 | .... | .... | .... | .... | .... | .... | .... | .... | .... | .... | .... | .... | .... | .... | .... | .... | .... | .... |
| | Houston Aeros | AHL | 11 | 1 | 7 | 8 | 4 | .... | .... | .... | .... | .... | .... | .... | .... | .... | 5 | 0 | 0 | 0 | 2 | .... | .... | .... | .... |
| 2008-09 | Minnesota | NHL | 45 | 2 | 5 | 7 | 18 | 0 | 0 | 1 | 22 | 9.1 | –2 | 2 | 50.0 | 8:14 | .... | .... | .... | .... | .... | .... | .... | .... | .... |
| | NHL Totals | | 45 | 2 | 5 | 7 | 18 | 0 | 0 | 1 | 22 | 9.1 | | 2 | 50.0 | 8:14 | .... | .... | .... | .... | .... | .... | .... | .... | .... |

## GILLIES, Trevor

(GIHL-eez, TREH-vuhr)

Left wing. Shoots left. 6'3", 215 lbs. Born, Cambridge, Ont., January 30, 1979.

| Season | Club | League | GP | G | A | Pts | PIM | PP | SH | GW | S | % | +/- | TF | F% | Min | GP | G | A | Pts | PIM | PP | SH | GW | Min |
|---|---|---|---|---|---|---|---|---|---|---|---|---|---|---|---|---|---|---|---|---|---|---|---|---|---|
| 1996-97 | North Bay | OHL | 26 | 0 | 3 | 3 | 72 | .... | .... | .... | .... | .... | .... | .... | .... | .... | .... | .... | .... | .... | .... | .... | .... | .... | .... |
| 1997-98 | North Bay | OHL | 2 | 0 | 0 | 0 | 4 | .... | .... | .... | .... | .... | .... | .... | .... | .... | .... | .... | .... | .... | .... | .... | .... | .... | .... |
| | Sarnia Sting | OHL | 17 | 0 | 1 | 1 | 33 | .... | .... | .... | .... | .... | .... | .... | .... | .... | .... | .... | .... | .... | .... | .... | .... | .... | .... |
| | Oshawa Generals | OHL | 45 | 1 | 2 | 3 | 184 | .... | .... | .... | .... | .... | .... | .... | .... | .... | 7 | 0 | 1 | 1 | 12 | .... | .... | .... | .... |
| 1998-99 | Oshawa Generals | OHL | 66 | 6 | 9 | 15 | 270 | .... | .... | .... | .... | .... | .... | .... | .... | .... | 11 | 0 | 2 | 2 | 28 | .... | .... | .... | .... |
| 99-2000 | Lowell | AHL | 8 | 0 | 0 | 0 | 38 | .... | .... | .... | .... | .... | .... | .... | .... | .... | .... | .... | .... | .... | .... | .... | .... | .... | .... |
| | Mississippi | ECHL | 53 | 0 | 6 | 6 | 202 | .... | .... | .... | .... | .... | .... | .... | .... | .... | .... | .... | .... | .... | .... | .... | .... | .... | .... |
| 2000-01 | Greensboro | ECHL | 63 | 1 | 6 | 7 | 303 | .... | .... | .... | .... | .... | .... | .... | .... | .... | .... | .... | .... | .... | .... | .... | .... | .... | .... |
| | Worcester IceCats | AHL | .... | .... | .... | .... | .... | .... | .... | .... | .... | .... | .... | .... | .... | .... | 6 | 0 | 0 | 0 | 24 | .... | .... | .... | .... |
| 2001-02 | Providence Bruins | AHL | 5 | 0 | 0 | 0 | 21 | .... | .... | .... | .... | .... | .... | .... | .... | .... | .... | .... | .... | .... | .... | .... | .... | .... | .... |
| | Augusta Lynx | ECHL | 46 | 0 | 1 | 1 | *269 | .... | .... | .... | .... | .... | .... | .... | .... | .... | .... | .... | .... | .... | .... | .... | .... | .... | .... |
| | Richmond | ECHL | 18 | 0 | 1 | 1 | *51 | .... | .... | .... | .... | .... | .... | .... | .... | .... | .... | .... | .... | .... | .... | .... | .... | .... | .... |
| 2002-03 | Lowell | AHL | 25 | 0 | 1 | 1 | 132 | .... | .... | .... | .... | .... | .... | .... | .... | .... | .... | .... | .... | .... | .... | .... | .... | .... | .... |
| | Richmond | ECHL | 6 | 0 | 0 | 0 | 20 | .... | .... | .... | .... | .... | .... | .... | .... | .... | .... | .... | .... | .... | .... | .... | .... | .... | .... |
| | Peoria Rivermen | ECHL | 24 | 0 | 1 | 1 | 180 | .... | .... | .... | .... | .... | .... | .... | .... | .... | .... | .... | .... | .... | .... | .... | .... | .... | .... |
| 2003-04 | Springfield | AHL | 61 | 2 | 1 | 3 | 277 | .... | .... | .... | .... | .... | .... | .... | .... | .... | .... | .... | .... | .... | .... | .... | .... | .... | .... |
| 2004-05 | Hartford | AHL | 49 | 0 | 2 | 2 | 277 | .... | .... | .... | .... | .... | .... | .... | .... | .... | .... | .... | .... | .... | .... | .... | .... | .... | .... |
| 2005-06 | Anaheim | NHL | 1 | 0 | 0 | 0 | 21 | 0 | 0 | 0 | 1 | 0.0 | 0 | 0 | 0.0 | 2:40 | .... | .... | .... | .... | .... | .... | .... | .... | .... |
| | Portland Pirates | AHL | 50 | 2 | 3 | 5 | 169 | .... | .... | .... | .... | .... | .... | .... | .... | .... | 4 | 0 | 0 | 0 | 0 | .... | .... | .... | .... |
| 2006-07 | Portland Pirates | AHL | 51 | 1 | 6 | 7 | 151 | .... | .... | .... | .... | .... | .... | .... | .... | .... | .... | .... | .... | .... | .... | .... | .... | .... | .... |
| | Augusta Lynx | ECHL | 7 | 0 | 2 | 2 | 23 | .... | .... | .... | .... | .... | .... | .... | .... | .... | .... | .... | .... | .... | .... | .... | .... | .... | .... |
| 2007-08 | Albany River Rats | AHL | 51 | 1 | 1 | 2 | 112 | .... | .... | .... | .... | .... | .... | .... | .... | .... | 7 | 0 | 0 | 0 | 19 | .... | .... | .... | .... |
| 2008-09 | Albany River Rats | AHL | 30 | 0 | 0 | 0 | 125 | .... | .... | .... | .... | .... | .... | .... | .... | .... | .... | .... | .... | .... | .... | .... | .... | .... | .... |
| | NHL Totals | | 1 | 0 | 0 | 0 | 21 | 0 | 0 | 0 | 1 | 0.0 | | 0 | 0.0 | 2:40 | .... | .... | .... | .... | .... | .... | .... | .... | .... |

Signed as a free agent by **NY Rangers**, July 20, 2004. Traded to **Anaheim** by **NY Rangers** with NY Rangers' 4th round choice (later traded back to NY Rangers - later traded to Washington - Washington selected Brett Bruneteau) in 2007 Entry Draft for Steve Rucchin, August 23, 2005. Signed as a free agent by **Carolina**, July 2, 2007. • Missed majority of 2008-09 season recovering from injury sufferd in game at Wilkes-Barre (AHL), December 20, 2008.

## GIONTA, Brian

(jee-OHN-tuh, BRIGH-uhn) **MTL.**

Right wing. Shoots right. 5'7", 175 lbs. Born, Rochester, NY, January 18, 1979. New Jersey's 4th choice, 82nd overall, in 1998 Entry Draft.

| Season | Club | League | GP | G | A | Pts | PIM | PP | SH | GW | S | % | +/- | TF | F% | Min | GP | G | A | Pts | PIM | PP | SH | GW | Min |
|---|---|---|---|---|---|---|---|---|---|---|---|---|---|---|---|---|---|---|---|---|---|---|---|---|---|
| 1994-95 | Rochester | EmJHL | 28 | *52 | 37 | *89 | .... | .... | .... | .... | .... | .... | .... | .... | .... | .... | .... | .... | .... | .... | .... | .... | .... | .... | .... |
| 1995-96 | Niagara Scenic | MTJHL | 51 | 47 | 44 | 91 | 59 | .... | .... | .... | .... | .... | .... | .... | .... | .... | .... | .... | .... | .... | .... | .... | .... | .... | .... |
| 1996-97 | Niagara Scenic | MTJHL | 50 | 57 | 70 | 127 | 101 | .... | .... | .... | .... | .... | .... | .... | .... | .... | 6 | 6 | 11 | 17 | 21 | .... | .... | .... | .... |
| 1997-98 | Boston College | H-East | 40 | 30 | 32 | 62 | 44 | .... | .... | .... | .... | .... | .... | .... | .... | .... | .... | .... | .... | .... | .... | .... | .... | .... | .... |
| 1998-99 | Boston College | H-East | 39 | 27 | 33 | 60 | 46 | .... | .... | .... | .... | .... | .... | .... | .... | .... | .... | .... | .... | .... | .... | .... | .... | .... | .... |
| 99-2000 | Boston College | H-East | 42 | *33 | 23 | 56 | 66 | .... | .... | .... | .... | .... | .... | .... | .... | .... | .... | .... | .... | .... | .... | .... | .... | .... | .... |
| 2000-01 | Boston College | H-East | 43 | *33 | 21 | *54 | 47 | .... | .... | .... | .... | .... | .... | .... | .... | .... | .... | .... | .... | .... | .... | .... | .... | .... | .... |
| 2001-02 | New Jersey | NHL | 33 | 4 | 7 | 11 | 8 | 0 | 0 | 0 | 58 | 6.9 | 10 | 36 | 44.4 | 13:25 | 6 | 2 | 2 | 4 | 0 | 0 | 1 | 2 | 17:08 |
| | Albany River Rats | AHL | 37 | 9 | 16 | 25 | 18 | .... | .... | .... | .... | .... | .... | .... | .... | .... | .... | .... | .... | .... | .... | .... | .... | .... | .... |
| 2002-03 ♦ | New Jersey | NHL | 58 | 12 | 13 | 25 | 23 | 2 | 0 | 3 | 129 | 9.3 | 5 | 14 | 57.1 | 14:48 | 24 | 1 | 8 | 9 | 6 | 0 | 0 | 0 | 14:31 |
| 2003-04 | New Jersey | NHL | 75 | 21 | 8 | 29 | 36 | 0 | 0 | 8 | 174 | 12.1 | 19 | 60 | 58.3 | 14:44 | 5 | 2 | 3 | 5 | 0 | 1 | 0 | 0 | 15:41 |
| 2004-05 | Albany River Rats | AHL | 15 | 5 | 7 | 12 | 10 | .... | .... | .... | .... | .... | .... | .... | .... | .... | .... | .... | .... | .... | .... | .... | .... | .... | .... |
| 2005-06 | New Jersey | NHL | 82 | 48 | 41 | 89 | 46 | 24 | 1 | 10 | 291 | 16.5 | 18 | 73 | 38.4 | 19:49 | 9 | 3 | 4 | 7 | 2 | 1 | 1 | 2 | 20:06 |
| | United States | Olympics | 6 | 4 | 0 | 4 | 2 | .... | .... | .... | .... | .... | .... | .... | .... | .... | .... | .... | .... | .... | .... | .... | .... | .... | .... |
| 2006-07 | New Jersey | NHL | 62 | 25 | 20 | 45 | 36 | 11 | 0 | 4 | 194 | 12.9 | –3 | 31 | 38.7 | 18:49 | 11 | 8 | 1 | 9 | 4 | 3 | 0 | 1 | 19:15 |
| 2007-08 | New Jersey | NHL | 82 | 22 | 31 | 53 | 46 | 8 | 1 | 4 | 257 | 8.6 | 1 | 55 | 54.6 | 18:16 | 5 | 1 | 0 | 1 | 2 | 0 | 0 | 0 | 17:52 |
| 2008-09 | New Jersey | NHL | 81 | 20 | 40 | 60 | 32 | 3 | 3 | 1 | 248 | 8.1 | 12 | 132 | 38.6 | 16:58 | 7 | 2 | 3 | 5 | 4 | 0 | 0 | 0 | 17:49 |
| | NHL Totals | | 473 | 152 | 160 | 312 | 227 | 48 | 5 | 30 | 1351 | 11.3 | | 401 | 44.9 | 17:04 | 67 | 19 | 21 | 40 | 18 | 5 | 2 | 5 | 16:58 |

Hockey East Rookie of the Year (1998) • Hockey East Second All-Star Team (1998) • NCAA East Second All-American Team (1998) • Hockey East First All-Star Team (1999, 2000, 2001) • NCAA East First All-American Team (1999, 2000, 2001) • Hockey East Player of the Year (2001)

Signed as a free agent by **Montreal**, July 1, 2009.

## GIORDANO, Mark

(jee-ohr-DAN-oh, MAHRK) **CGY.**

Defense. Shoots left. 6', 203 lbs. Born, Toronto, Ont., October 3, 1983.

| Season | Club | League | GP | G | A | Pts | PIM | PP | SH | GW | S | % | +/- | TF | F% | Min | GP | G | A | Pts | PIM | PP | SH | GW | Min |
|---|---|---|---|---|---|---|---|---|---|---|---|---|---|---|---|---|---|---|---|---|---|---|---|---|---|
| 2002-03 | Owen Sound | OHL | 68 | 18 | 30 | 48 | 109 | .... | .... | .... | .... | .... | .... | .... | .... | .... | 4 | 1 | 3 | 4 | 2 | .... | .... | .... | .... |
| 2003-04 | Owen Sound | OHL | 65 | 14 | 35 | 49 | 72 | .... | .... | .... | .... | .... | .... | .... | .... | .... | 7 | 1 | 3 | 4 | 5 | .... | .... | .... | .... |
| 2004-05 | Lowell | AHL | 66 | 6 | 10 | 16 | 85 | .... | .... | .... | .... | .... | .... | .... | .... | .... | 11 | 0 | 1 | 1 | 41 | .... | .... | .... | .... |
| 2005-06 | Calgary | NHL | 7 | 0 | 1 | 1 | 8 | 0 | 0 | 0 | 5 | 0.0 | 2 | 0 | 0.0 | 12:05 | .... | .... | .... | .... | .... | .... | .... | .... | .... |
| | Omaha | AHL | 73 | 16 | 42 | 58 | 141 | .... | .... | .... | .... | .... | .... | .... | .... | .... | .... | .... | .... | .... | .... | .... | .... | .... | .... |
| 2006-07 | Calgary | NHL | 48 | 7 | 8 | 15 | 36 | 3 | 0 | 2 | 49 | 14.3 | 7 | 0 | 0.0 | 13:27 | 4 | 1 | 0 | 1 | 0 | 1 | 0 | 0 | 12:16 |
| | Omaha | AHL | 5 | 0 | 2 | 2 | 8 | .... | .... | .... | .... | .... | .... | .... | .... | .... | 3 | 0 | 1 | 1 | 2 | .... | .... | .... | .... |
| 2007-08 | Dynamo Moscow | Russia | 50 | 4 | 8 | 12 | 89 | .... | .... | .... | .... | .... | .... | .... | .... | .... | 9 | 1 | 5 | 6 | 35 | .... | .... | .... | .... |
| 2008-09 | Calgary | NHL | 58 | 2 | 17 | 19 | 59 | 2 | 0 | 0 | 82 | 2.4 | 2 | 0 | 0.0 | 16:13 | .... | .... | .... | .... | .... | .... | .... | .... | .... |
| | NHL Totals | | 113 | 9 | 26 | 35 | 103 | 5 | 0 | 2 | 136 | 6.6 | | 0 | 0.0 | 14:47 | 4 | 1 | 0 | 1 | 0 | 1 | 0 | 0 | 12:16 |

Signed as a free agent by **Calgary**, July 6, 2004. Signed as a free agent by **Dynamo Moscow** (Russia) August 28, 2007. Signed as a free agent by **Calgary**, July 1, 2008.

## GIRARDI, Dan

(jih-RAHR-dee, DAN) **NYR**

Defense. Shoots right. 6'2", 210 lbs. Born, Welland, Ont., April 29, 1984.

| Season | Club | League | GP | G | A | Pts | PIM | PP | SH | GW | S | % | +/- | TF | F% | Min | GP | G | A | Pts | PIM | PP | SH | GW | Min |
|---|---|---|---|---|---|---|---|---|---|---|---|---|---|---|---|---|---|---|---|---|---|---|---|---|---|
| 2000-01 | Barrie Colts | OHL | 6 | 0 | 0 | 0 | 0 | .... | .... | .... | .... | .... | .... | .... | .... | .... | .... | .... | .... | .... | .... | .... | .... | .... | .... |
| 2001-02 | Barrie Colts | OHL | 21 | 0 | 1 | 1 | 0 | .... | .... | .... | .... | .... | .... | .... | .... | .... | 20 | 0 | 0 | 0 | 0 | .... | .... | .... | .... |
| 2002-03 | Barrie Colts | OHL | 31 | 3 | 13 | 16 | 24 | .... | .... | .... | .... | .... | .... | .... | .... | .... | .... | .... | .... | .... | .... | .... | .... | .... | .... |
| | Guelph Storm | OHL | 36 | 1 | 13 | 14 | 20 | .... | .... | .... | .... | .... | .... | .... | .... | .... | 11 | 0 | 9 | 9 | 14 | .... | .... | .... | .... |
| 2003-04 | Guelph Storm | OHL | 68 | 8 | 39 | 47 | 55 | .... | .... | .... | .... | .... | .... | .... | .... | .... | 22 | 2 | 17 | 19 | 10 | .... | .... | .... | .... |
| 2004-05 | Guelph Storm | OHL | 38 | 5 | 20 | 25 | 24 | .... | .... | .... | .... | .... | .... | .... | .... | .... | .... | .... | .... | .... | .... | .... | .... | .... | .... |
| | London Knights | OHL | 31 | 4 | 10 | 14 | 14 | .... | .... | .... | .... | .... | .... | .... | .... | .... | 18 | 0 | 6 | 6 | 10 | .... | .... | .... | .... |
| 2005-06 | Hartford | AHL | 66 | 8 | 31 | 39 | 44 | .... | .... | .... | .... | .... | .... | .... | .... | .... | 13 | 4 | 5 | 9 | 8 | .... | .... | .... | .... |
| | Charlotte | ECHL | 7 | 1 | 4 | 5 | 6 | .... | .... | .... | .... | .... | .... | .... | .... | .... | .... | .... | .... | .... | .... | .... | .... | .... | .... |
| 2006-07 | NY Rangers | NHL | 34 | 0 | 6 | 6 | 8 | 0 | 0 | 0 | 33 | 0.0 | 7 | 0 | 0.0 | 15:50 | 10 | 0 | 0 | 0 | 4 | 0 | 0 | 0 | 19:52 |
| | Hartford | AHL | 45 | 2 | 22 | 24 | 16 | .... | .... | .... | .... | .... | .... | .... | .... | .... | .... | .... | .... | .... | .... | .... | .... | .... | .... |

| Season | Club | League | Regular Season GP | G | A | Pts | PIM | PP | SH | GW | S | % | +/- | TF | F% | Min | Playoffs GP | G | A | Pts | PIM | PP | SH | GW | Min |
|---|---|---|---|---|---|---|---|---|---|---|---|---|---|---|---|---|---|---|---|---|---|---|---|---|---|
| **2007-08** | **NY Rangers** | **NHL** | **82** | **10** | **18** | **28** | **14** | **5** | **0** | **1** | **147** | **6.8** | **0** | **1** | **0.0** | **21:12** | **10** | **0** | **3** | **3** | **6** | **0** | **0** | **0** | **20:42** |
| **2008-09** | **NY Rangers** | **NHL** | **82** | **4** | **18** | **22** | **53** | **2** | **0** | **1** | **122** | **3.3** | **–14** | **0** | **0.0** | **21:32** | **7** | **0** | **0** | **0** | **6** | **0** | **0** | **0** | **21:04** |
| | **NHL Totals** | | **198** | **14** | **42** | **56** | **75** | **7** | **0** | **2** | **302** | **4.6** | | **1** | **0.0** | **20:25** | **27** | **0** | **3** | **3** | **16** | **0** | **0** | **0** | **20:29** |

AHL All-Rookie Team (2006)
Signed as a free agent by **NY Rangers**, July 1, 2006.

## GIROUX, Alexandre

(ZHIH-roo, al-ehx-AHN-druh) **WSH.**

Center/Left wing. Shoots left. 6'3", 190 lbs. Born, Quebec City, Que., June 16, 1981. Ottawa's 9th choice, 213th overall, in 1999 Entry Draft.

| | | | | | | | | | | | | | | | | | | | | | | | | | |
|---|---|---|---|---|---|---|---|---|---|---|---|---|---|---|---|---|---|---|---|---|---|---|---|---|---|
| 1997-98 | Ste-Foy | QAAA | 42 | 28 | 30 | 58 | 96 | .... | .... | .... | .... | .... | .... | .... | .... | .... | .... | .... | .... | .... | .... | .... | .... | .... | .... |
| 1998-99 | Hull Olympiques | QMJHL | 67 | 15 | 22 | 37 | 124 | .... | .... | .... | .... | .... | .... | .... | .... | .... | 22 | 2 | 2 | 4 | 8 | .... | .... | .... | .... |
| 99-2000 | Hull Olympiques | QMJHL | 72 | 52 | 47 | 99 | 117 | .... | .... | .... | .... | .... | .... | .... | .... | .... | 15 | 12 | 6 | 18 | 30 | .... | .... | .... | .... |
| 2000-01 | Hull Olympiques | QMJHL | 38 | 31 | 32 | 63 | 62 | .... | .... | .... | .... | .... | .... | .... | .... | .... | .... | .... | .... | .... | .... | .... | .... | .... | .... |
| | Rouyn-Noranda | QMJHL | 25 | 13 | 14 | 27 | 56 | .... | .... | .... | .... | .... | .... | .... | .... | .... | 9 | 2 | 6 | 8 | 22 | .... | .... | .... | .... |
| 2001-02 | Grand Rapids | AHL | 70 | 11 | 16 | 27 | 74 | .... | .... | .... | .... | .... | .... | .... | .... | .... | .... | .... | .... | .... | .... | .... | .... | .... | .... |
| 2002-03 | Binghamton | AHL | 67 | 19 | 16 | 35 | 101 | .... | .... | .... | .... | .... | .... | .... | .... | .... | 10 | 1 | 0 | 1 | 10 | .... | .... | .... | .... |
| 2003-04 | Binghamton | AHL | 59 | 19 | 23 | 42 | 79 | .... | .... | .... | .... | .... | .... | .... | .... | .... | .... | .... | .... | .... | .... | .... | .... | .... | .... |
| | Hartford | AHL | 16 | 6 | 3 | 9 | 13 | .... | .... | .... | .... | .... | .... | .... | .... | .... | 16 | 3 | 4 | 7 | 28 | .... | .... | .... | .... |
| 2004-05 | Hartford | AHL | 78 | 32 | 22 | 54 | 128 | .... | .... | .... | .... | .... | .... | .... | .... | .... | 6 | 3 | 3 | 6 | 23 | .... | .... | .... | .... |
| **2005-06** | **NY Rangers** | **NHL** | **1** | **0** | **0** | **0** | **0** | **0** | **0** | **0** | **0** | **0.0** | **–1** | **0** | **0.0** | **2:50** | .... | .... | .... | .... | .... | .... | .... | .... | .... |
| | Hartford | AHL | 73 | 36 | 31 | 67 | 102 | .... | .... | .... | .... | .... | .... | .... | .... | .... | 13 | 7 | 9 | 16 | 17 | .... | .... | .... | .... |
| **2006-07** | **Washington** | **NHL** | **9** | **2** | **2** | **4** | **2** | **0** | **0** | **0** | **11** | **18.2** | **–4** | **2** | **50.0** | **10:11** | .... | .... | .... | .... | .... | .... | .... | .... | .... |
| | Hershey Bears | AHL | 67 | 42 | 28 | 70 | 82 | .... | .... | .... | .... | .... | .... | .... | .... | .... | 19 | 4 | 7 | 11 | 27 | .... | .... | .... | .... |
| 2007-08 | Chicago Wolves | AHL | 44 | 19 | 22 | 41 | 47 | .... | .... | .... | .... | .... | .... | .... | .... | .... | .... | .... | .... | .... | .... | .... | .... | .... | .... |
| | Hershey Bears | AHL | 24 | 14 | 13 | 27 | 30 | .... | .... | .... | .... | .... | .... | .... | .... | .... | 5 | 3 | 1 | 4 | 2 | .... | .... | .... | .... |
| **2008-09** | **Washington** | **NHL** | **12** | **1** | **1** | **2** | **10** | **0** | **0** | **1** | **20** | **5.0** | **4** | **1** | **0.0** | **10:34** | .... | .... | .... | .... | .... | .... | .... | .... | .... |
| | Hershey Bears | AHL | 69 | *60 | 37 | *97 | 84 | .... | .... | .... | .... | .... | .... | .... | .... | .... | 22 | *15 | 13 | *28 | 22 | .... | .... | .... | .... |
| | **NHL Totals** | | **22** | **3** | **3** | **6** | **12** | **0** | **0** | **1** | **31** | **9.7** | | **3** | **33.3** | **10:04** | .... | .... | .... | .... | .... | .... | .... | .... | .... |

AHL First All-Star Team (2009) • Willie Marshall Award (AHL – Top Goal-scorer) (2009) • John B. Sollenberger Trophy (AHL – Leading Scorer) (2009) • Les Cunningham Award (AHL – MVP) (2009)
Traded to **NY Rangers** by **Ottawa** with Karel Rachunek for Greg De Vries, March 9, 2004. Signed as a free agent by **Washington**, July 14, 2006. Signed as a free agent by **Atlanta**, July 13, 2007. Traded to **Washington** by **Atlanta** for Joe Motzko, February 26, 2008.

## GIROUX, Claude

(zhih-ROO, KLOHD) **PHI.**

Right wing. Shoots right. 5'11", 172 lbs. Born, Hearst, Ont., January 12, 1988. Philadelphia's 1st choice, 22nd overall, in 2006 Entry Draft.

| | | | | | | | | | | | | | | | | | | | | | | | | | |
|---|---|---|---|---|---|---|---|---|---|---|---|---|---|---|---|---|---|---|---|---|---|---|---|---|---|
| 2004-05 | Cumberland | CJHL | 48 | 13 | 27 | 40 | 30 | .... | .... | .... | .... | .... | .... | .... | .... | .... | .... | .... | .... | .... | .... | .... | .... | .... | .... |
| 2005-06 | Gatineau | QMJHL | 69 | 39 | 64 | 103 | 64 | .... | .... | .... | .... | .... | .... | .... | .... | .... | 17 | 5 | 15 | 20 | 24 | .... | .... | .... | .... |
| 2006-07 | Gatineau | QMJHL | 63 | 48 | 64 | 112 | 49 | .... | .... | .... | .... | .... | .... | .... | .... | .... | 5 | 2 | 5 | 7 | 2 | .... | .... | .... | .... |
| | Philadelphia | AHL | 5 | 1 | 1 | 2 | 6 | .... | .... | .... | .... | .... | .... | .... | .... | .... | .... | .... | .... | .... | .... | .... | .... | .... | .... |
| **2007-08** | **Philadelphia** | **NHL** | **2** | **0** | **0** | **0** | **0** | **0** | **0** | **0** | **2** | **0.0** | **–2** | **0** | **0.0** | **9:35** | .... | .... | .... | .... | .... | .... | .... | .... | .... |
| | Gatineau | QMJHL | 55 | 38 | 68 | 106 | 37 | .... | .... | .... | .... | .... | .... | .... | .... | .... | 19 | 17 | *34 | *51 | 6 | .... | .... | .... | .... |
| **2008-09** | **Philadelphia** | **NHL** | **42** | **9** | **18** | **27** | **14** | **2** | **0** | **0** | **67** | **13.4** | **10** | **309** | **47.3** | **15:10** | **6** | **2** | **3** | **5** | **6** | **0** | **0** | **0** | **15:57** |
| | Philadelphia | AHL | 33 | 17 | 17 | 34 | 22 | .... | .... | .... | .... | .... | .... | .... | .... | .... | .... | .... | .... | .... | .... | .... | .... | .... | .... |
| | **NHL Totals** | | **44** | **9** | **18** | **27** | **14** | **2** | **0** | **0** | **69** | **13.0** | | **309** | **47.2** | **14:54** | **6** | **2** | **3** | **5** | **6** | **0** | **0** | **0** | **15:57** |

QMJHL All-Rookie Team (2006) • QMJHL First All-Star Team (2008) • Canadian Major Junior First All-Star Team (2008)

## GIULIANO, Jeff

(JOO-lee-A-noh, JEHF)

Left wing. Shoots left. 5'9", 205 lbs. Born, Nashua, NH, June 20, 1979.

| | | | | | | | | | | | | | | | | | | | | | | | | | |
|---|---|---|---|---|---|---|---|---|---|---|---|---|---|---|---|---|---|---|---|---|---|---|---|---|---|
| 1998-99 | Boston College | H-East | 43 | 5 | 15 | 20 | 10 | .... | .... | .... | .... | .... | .... | .... | .... | .... | .... | .... | .... | .... | .... | .... | .... | .... | .... |
| 99-2000 | Boston College | H-East | 42 | 10 | 13 | 23 | 16 | .... | .... | .... | .... | .... | .... | .... | .... | .... | .... | .... | .... | .... | .... | .... | .... | .... | .... |
| 2000-01 | Boston College | H-East | 43 | 14 | 22 | 36 | 28 | .... | .... | .... | .... | .... | .... | .... | .... | .... | .... | .... | .... | .... | .... | .... | .... | .... | .... |
| 2001-02 | Boston College | H-East | 38 | 11 | 24 | 35 | 14 | .... | .... | .... | .... | .... | .... | .... | .... | .... | .... | .... | .... | .... | .... | .... | .... | .... | .... |
| 2002-03 | Manchester | AHL | 47 | 4 | 11 | 15 | 8 | .... | .... | .... | .... | .... | .... | .... | .... | .... | 3 | 1 | 0 | 1 | 0 | .... | .... | .... | .... |
| | Reading Royals | ECHL | 38 | 7 | 23 | 30 | 6 | .... | .... | .... | .... | .... | .... | .... | .... | .... | .... | .... | .... | .... | .... | .... | .... | .... | .... |
| 2003-04 | Manchester | AHL | 80 | 6 | 14 | 20 | 16 | .... | .... | .... | .... | .... | .... | .... | .... | .... | 1 | 0 | 0 | 0 | 0 | .... | .... | .... | .... |
| 2004-05 | Manchester | AHL | 69 | 8 | 16 | 24 | 21 | .... | .... | .... | .... | .... | .... | .... | .... | .... | 2 | 0 | 0 | 0 | 0 | .... | .... | .... | .... |
| **2005-06** | **Los Angeles** | **NHL** | **48** | **3** | **4** | **7** | **26** | **0** | **0** | **2** | **32** | **9.4** | **0** | **252** | **46.0** | **9:45** | .... | .... | .... | .... | .... | .... | .... | .... | .... |
| | Manchester | AHL | 19 | 5 | 6 | 11 | 17 | .... | .... | .... | .... | .... | .... | .... | .... | .... | 7 | 3 | 1 | 4 | 2 | .... | .... | .... | .... |
| 2006-07 | Manchester | AHL | 35 | 4 | 10 | 14 | 27 | .... | .... | .... | .... | .... | .... | .... | .... | .... | 16 | 3 | 3 | 6 | 12 | .... | .... | .... | .... |
| **2007-08** | **Los Angeles** | **NHL** | **53** | **0** | **6** | **6** | **14** | **0** | **0** | **0** | **30** | **0.0** | **–9** | **239** | **45.2** | **11:49** | .... | .... | .... | .... | .... | .... | .... | .... | .... |
| | Manchester | AHL | 23 | 3 | 1 | 4 | 14 | .... | .... | .... | .... | .... | .... | .... | .... | .... | .... | .... | .... | .... | .... | .... | .... | .... | .... |
| 2008-09 | Dynamo Minsk | Rus-KHL | 46 | 1 | 4 | 5 | 30 | .... | .... | .... | .... | .... | .... | .... | .... | .... | .... | .... | .... | .... | .... | .... | .... | .... | .... |
| | **NHL Totals** | | **101** | **3** | **10** | **13** | **40** | **0** | **0** | **2** | **62** | **4.8** | | **491** | **45.6** | **10:50** | .... | .... | .... | .... | .... | .... | .... | .... | .... |

Signed as a free agent by **Los Angeles**, August 12, 2005. • Missed majority of 2006-07 season recovering from recurring abdominal injury.

## GLASS, Tanner

(GLAS, TA-nuhr) **VAN.**

Forward. Shoots left. 6', 196 lbs. Born, Regina, Sask., November 29, 1983. Florida's 13th choice, 265th overall, in 2003 Entry Draft.

| | | | | | | | | | | | | | | | | | | | | | | | | | |
|---|---|---|---|---|---|---|---|---|---|---|---|---|---|---|---|---|---|---|---|---|---|---|---|---|---|
| 2000-01 | Yorkton Mallers | SMHL | 39 | 31 | 29 | 60 | 120 | .... | .... | .... | .... | .... | .... | .... | .... | .... | 4 | 3 | 1 | 4 | 10 | .... | .... | .... | .... |
| 2001-02 | Penticton | BCHL | 57 | 11 | 28 | 39 | 171 | .... | .... | .... | .... | .... | .... | .... | .... | .... | .... | .... | .... | .... | .... | .... | .... | .... | .... |
| 2002-03 | Penticton | BCHL | 32 | 15 | 25 | 40 | 108 | .... | .... | .... | .... | .... | .... | .... | .... | .... | .... | .... | .... | .... | .... | .... | .... | .... | .... |
| | Nanaimo Clippers | BCHL | 18 | 8 | 14 | 22 | 46 | .... | .... | .... | .... | .... | .... | .... | .... | .... | .... | .... | .... | .... | .... | .... | .... | .... | .... |
| 2003-04 | Dartmouth | ECAC | 26 | 4 | 7 | 11 | 18 | .... | .... | .... | .... | .... | .... | .... | .... | .... | .... | .... | .... | .... | .... | .... | .... | .... | .... |
| 2004-05 | Dartmouth | ECAC | 33 | 7 | 8 | 15 | 32 | .... | .... | .... | .... | .... | .... | .... | .... | .... | .... | .... | .... | .... | .... | .... | .... | .... | .... |
| 2005-06 | Dartmouth | ECAC | 33 | 12 | 16 | 28 | 56 | .... | .... | .... | .... | .... | .... | .... | .... | .... | .... | .... | .... | .... | .... | .... | .... | .... | .... |
| 2006-07 | Dartmouth | ECAC | 32 | 8 | 20 | 28 | 92 | .... | .... | .... | .... | .... | .... | .... | .... | .... | .... | .... | .... | .... | .... | .... | .... | .... | .... |
| | Rochester | AHL | 4 | 0 | 1 | 1 | 5 | .... | .... | .... | .... | .... | .... | .... | .... | .... | .... | .... | .... | .... | .... | .... | .... | .... | .... |
| **2007-08** | **Florida** | **NHL** | **41** | **1** | **1** | **2** | **39** | **0** | **0** | **0** | **11** | **9.1** | **–5** | **2** | **0.0** | **4:25** | .... | .... | .... | .... | .... | .... | .... | .... | .... |
| | Rochester | AHL | 43 | 6 | 5 | 11 | 84 | .... | .... | .... | .... | .... | .... | .... | .... | .... | .... | .... | .... | .... | .... | .... | .... | .... | .... |
| **2008-09** | **Florida** | **NHL** | **3** | **0** | **0** | **0** | **7** | **0** | **0** | **0** | **1** | **0.0** | **0** | **1** | **100.0** | **6:45** | .... | .... | .... | .... | .... | .... | .... | .... | .... |
| | Rochester | AHL | 44 | 4 | 9 | 13 | 100 | .... | .... | .... | .... | .... | .... | .... | .... | .... | .... | .... | .... | .... | .... | .... | .... | .... | .... |
| | **NHL Totals** | | **44** | **1** | **1** | **2** | **46** | **0** | **0** | **0** | **12** | **8.3** | | **3** | **33.3** | **4:35** | .... | .... | .... | .... | .... | .... | .... | .... | .... |

Signed as a free aget by **Vancouver**, July 22, 2009.

## GLEASON, Tim

(GLEE-suhn, TIHM) **CAR.**

Defense. Shoots left. 6', 217 lbs. Born, Clawson, MI, January 29, 1983. Ottawa's 2nd choice, 23rd overall, in 2001 Entry Draft.

| | | | | | | | | | | | | | | | | | | | | | | | | | |
|---|---|---|---|---|---|---|---|---|---|---|---|---|---|---|---|---|---|---|---|---|---|---|---|---|---|
| 1998-99 | Leamington Flyers | OHA-B | 52 | 5 | 26 | 31 | 76 | .... | .... | .... | .... | .... | .... | .... | .... | .... | .... | .... | .... | .... | .... | .... | .... | .... | .... |
| 99-2000 | Windsor Spitfires | OHL | 55 | 5 | 13 | 18 | 101 | .... | .... | .... | .... | .... | .... | .... | .... | .... | 12 | 2 | 4 | 6 | 14 | .... | .... | .... | .... |
| 2000-01 | Windsor Spitfires | OHL | 47 | 8 | 28 | 36 | 124 | .... | .... | .... | .... | .... | .... | .... | .... | .... | 9 | 1 | 2 | 3 | 23 | .... | .... | .... | .... |
| 2001-02 | Windsor Spitfires | OHL | 67 | 17 | 42 | 59 | 109 | .... | .... | .... | .... | .... | .... | .... | .... | .... | 16 | 7 | 13 | 20 | 40 | .... | .... | .... | .... |
| 2002-03 | Windsor Spitfires | OHL | 45 | 7 | 31 | 38 | 75 | .... | .... | .... | .... | .... | .... | .... | .... | .... | 7 | 5 | 2 | 7 | 17 | .... | .... | .... | .... |
| **2003-04** | **Los Angeles** | **NHL** | **47** | **0** | **7** | **7** | **21** | **0** | **0** | **0** | **45** | **0.0** | **1** | **0** | **0.0** | **14:59** | .... | .... | .... | .... | .... | .... | .... | .... | .... |
| | Manchester | AHL | 22 | 0 | 8 | 8 | 19 | .... | .... | .... | .... | .... | .... | .... | .... | .... | 6 | 0 | 1 | 1 | 4 | .... | .... | .... | .... |
| 2004-05 | Manchester | AHL | 67 | 10 | 14 | 24 | 112 | .... | .... | .... | .... | .... | .... | .... | .... | .... | 5 | 0 | 0 | 0 | 4 | .... | .... | .... | .... |
| **2005-06** | **Los Angeles** | **NHL** | **78** | **2** | **19** | **21** | **77** | **0** | **0** | **0** | **72** | **2.8** | **0** | **0** | **0.0** | **17:41** | .... | .... | .... | .... | .... | .... | .... | .... | .... |
| **2006-07** | **Carolina** | **NHL** | **57** | **2** | **4** | **6** | **57** | **1** | **0** | **0** | **72** | **2.8** | **–10** | **0** | **0.0** | **18:53** | .... | .... | .... | .... | .... | .... | .... | .... | .... |
| **2007-08** | **Carolina** | **NHL** | **80** | **3** | **16** | **19** | **84** | **0** | **0** | **0** | **98** | **3.1** | **5** | **0** | **0.0** | **18:38** | .... | .... | .... | .... | .... | .... | .... | .... | .... |
| **2008-09** | **Carolina** | **NHL** | **70** | **0** | **12** | **12** | **68** | **0** | **0** | **0** | **61** | **0.0** | **3** | **0** | **0.0** | **20:40** | **18** | **1** | **4** | **5** | **32** | **0** | **0** | **1** | **20:29** |
| | **NHL Totals** | | **332** | **7** | **58** | **65** | **307** | **1** | **0** | **0** | **348** | **2.0** | | **0** | **0.0** | **18:22** | **18** | **1** | **4** | **5** | **32** | **0** | **0** | **1** | **20:29** |

• Rights traded to **Los Angeles** by **Ottawa** for Bryan Smolinski, March 11, 2003. Traded to **Carolina** by **Los Angeles** with Eric Belanger for Oleg Tverdovsky and Jack Johnson, September 29, 2006.

| | | | Regular Season | | | | | | | | | | | | | | Playoffs | | | | | | | | |
|---|---|---|---|---|---|---|---|---|---|---|---|---|---|---|---|---|---|---|---|---|---|---|---|---|---|
| Season | Club | League | GP | G | A | Pts | PIM | PP | SH | GW | S | % | +/- | TF | F% | Min | GP | G | A | Pts | PIM | PP | SH | GW | Min |

## GLENCROSS, Curtis

(GLEHN-kraws, KUHR-tihs) **CGY.**

Center. Shoots left. 6'1", 195 lbs. Born, Kindersley, Sask., December 28, 1982.

| Season | Club | League | GP | G | A | Pts | PIM | PP | SH | GW | S | % | +/- | TF | F% | Min | GP | G | A | Pts | PIM | PP | SH | GW | Min |
|---|---|---|---|---|---|---|---|---|---|---|---|---|---|---|---|---|---|---|---|---|---|---|---|---|---|
| 2001-02 | Brooks Bandits | AJHL | .... | 42 | 26 | 68 | .... | .... | .... | .... | .... | .... | .... | .... | .... | .... | .... | .... | .... | .... | .... | .... | .... | .... | .... |
| 2002-03 | Alaska Anchorage | WCHA | 35 | 11 | 12 | 23 | 79 | .... | .... | .... | .... | .... | .... | .... | .... | .... | .... | .... | .... | .... | .... | .... | .... | .... | .... |
| 2003-04 | Alaska Anchorage | WCHA | 37 | 21 | 13 | 34 | 79 | .... | .... | .... | .... | .... | .... | .... | .... | .... | .... | .... | .... | .... | .... | .... | .... | .... | .... |
| | Cincinnati | AHL | 7 | 2 | 1 | 3 | 6 | .... | .... | .... | .... | .... | .... | .... | .... | .... | 9 | 1 | 6 | 7 | 10 | .... | .... | .... | .... |
| 2004-05 | Cincinnati | AHL | 51 | 6 | 3 | 9 | 63 | .... | .... | .... | .... | .... | .... | .... | .... | .... | 12 | 2 | 0 | 2 | 10 | .... | .... | .... | .... |
| 2005-06 | Portland Pirates | AHL | 41 | 15 | 10 | 25 | 85 | .... | .... | .... | .... | .... | .... | .... | .... | .... | 19 | 4 | 6 | 10 | 37 | .... | .... | .... | .... |
| **2006-07** | **Anaheim** | **NHL** | 2 | 1 | 0 | 1 | 2 | 0 | 0 | 0 | 5 | 20.0 | –1 | 0 | 0.0 | 10:43 | .... | .... | .... | .... | .... | .... | .... | .... | .... |
| | Portland Pirates | AHL | 31 | 6 | 10 | 16 | 74 | .... | .... | .... | .... | .... | .... | .... | .... | .... | .... | .... | .... | .... | .... | .... | .... | .... | .... |
| | **Columbus** | **NHL** | 7 | 0 | 0 | 0 | 0 | 0 | 0 | 0 | 3 | 0.0 | –4 | 2 | 0.0 | 8:43 | .... | .... | .... | .... | .... | .... | .... | .... | .... |
| | Syracuse Crunch | AHL | 29 | 19 | 16 | 35 | 53 | .... | .... | .... | .... | .... | .... | .... | .... | .... | .... | .... | .... | .... | .... | .... | .... | .... | .... |
| **2007-08** | **Columbus** | **NHL** | 36 | 6 | 6 | 12 | 25 | 1 | 0 | 1 | 63 | 9.5 | 3 | 14 | 57.1 | 12:07 | .... | .... | .... | .... | .... | .... | .... | .... | .... |
| | **Edmonton** | **NHL** | 26 | 9 | 4 | 13 | 28 | 0 | 0 | 0 | 41 | 22.0 | 5 | 11 | 45.5 | 10:19 | .... | .... | .... | .... | .... | .... | .... | .... | .... |
| **2008-09** | **Calgary** | **NHL** | 74 | 13 | 27 | 40 | 42 | 1 | 1 | 3 | 152 | 8.6 | 14 | 62 | 48.4 | 14:41 | 6 | 0 | 3 | 3 | 12 | 0 | 0 | 0 | 15:00 |
| | **NHL Totals** | | 145 | 29 | 37 | 66 | 97 | 2 | 1 | 4 | 264 | 11.0 | | 89 | 48.3 | 12:55 | 6 | 0 | 3 | 3 | 12 | 0 | 0 | 0 | 15:00 |

Signed as a free agent by **Anaheim**, March 25, 2004. Traded to **Columbus** by **Anaheim** with Zenon Konopka and Anaheim's 7th round choice (Trent Vogelhuber) in 2007 Entry Draft for Mark Hartigan, Joe Motzko and Columbus' 4th round choice (Sebastian Stefaniszin) in 2007 Entry Draft, January 26, 2007. Traded to **Edmonton** by **Columbus** for Dick Tarnstrom, February 1, 2008. Signed as a free agent by **Calgary**, July 2, 2008.

## GLOBKE, Rob

(GLAWB-kee, RAWB)

Center. Shoots right. 6'2", 208 lbs. Born, Farmington, MI, October 24, 1982. Florida's 3rd choice, 40th overall, in 2002 Entry Draft.

| Season | Club | League | GP | G | A | Pts | PIM | PP | SH | GW | S | % | +/- | TF | F% | Min | GP | G | A | Pts | PIM | PP | SH | GW | Min |
|---|---|---|---|---|---|---|---|---|---|---|---|---|---|---|---|---|---|---|---|---|---|---|---|---|---|
| 1998-99 | Det. Compuware | NAHL | 55 | 8 | 14 | 22 | 111 | .... | .... | .... | .... | .... | .... | .... | .... | .... | 7 | 1 | 2 | 3 | 2 | .... | .... | .... | .... |
| 99-2000 | USNTDP | U-18 | 6 | 4 | 2 | 6 | 6 | .... | .... | .... | .... | .... | .... | .... | .... | .... | .... | .... | .... | .... | .... | .... | .... | .... | .... |
| | USNTDP | USHL | 54 | 15 | 21 | 36 | 68 | .... | .... | .... | .... | .... | .... | .... | .... | .... | .... | .... | .... | .... | .... | .... | .... | .... | .... |
| 2000-01 | U. of Notre Dame | CCHA | 33 | 17 | 9 | 26 | 74 | .... | .... | .... | .... | .... | .... | .... | .... | .... | .... | .... | .... | .... | .... | .... | .... | .... | .... |
| 2001-02 | U. of Notre Dame | CCHA | 33 | 11 | 11 | 22 | 79 | .... | .... | .... | .... | .... | .... | .... | .... | .... | .... | .... | .... | .... | .... | .... | .... | .... | .... |
| 2002-03 | U. of Notre Dame | CCHA | 40 | 21 | 15 | 36 | 44 | .... | .... | .... | .... | .... | .... | .... | .... | .... | .... | .... | .... | .... | .... | .... | .... | .... | .... |
| 2003-04 | U. of Notre Dame | CCHA | 39 | 19 | 21 | 40 | 42 | .... | .... | .... | .... | .... | .... | .... | .... | .... | .... | .... | .... | .... | .... | .... | .... | .... | .... |
| 2004-05 | San Antonio | AHL | 63 | 6 | 6 | 12 | 21 | .... | .... | .... | .... | .... | .... | .... | .... | .... | .... | .... | .... | .... | .... | .... | .... | .... | .... |
| | Texas Wildcatters | ECHL | 10 | 8 | 4 | 12 | 13 | .... | .... | .... | .... | .... | .... | .... | .... | .... | .... | .... | .... | .... | .... | .... | .... | .... | .... |
| **2005-06** | **Florida** | **NHL** | 18 | 1 | 0 | 1 | 6 | 0 | 0 | 0 | 18 | 5.6 | 0 | 1 | 0.0 | 7:17 | .... | .... | .... | .... | .... | .... | .... | .... | .... |
| | Rochester | AHL | 52 | 6 | 9 | 15 | 54 | .... | .... | .... | .... | .... | .... | .... | .... | .... | .... | .... | .... | .... | .... | .... | .... | .... | .... |
| **2006-07** | **Florida** | **NHL** | 19 | 0 | 1 | 1 | 0 | 0 | 0 | 0 | 15 | 0.0 | –3 | 0 | 0.0 | 6:04 | .... | .... | .... | .... | .... | .... | .... | .... | .... |
| | Rochester | AHL | 48 | 7 | 11 | 18 | 37 | .... | .... | .... | .... | .... | .... | .... | .... | .... | 4 | 0 | 0 | 0 | 0 | .... | .... | .... | .... |
| **2007-08** | **Florida** | **NHL** | 9 | 0 | 0 | 0 | 2 | 0 | 0 | 0 | 4 | 0.0 | –3 | 1 | 0.0 | 7:44 | .... | .... | .... | .... | .... | .... | .... | .... | .... |
| | Rochester | AHL | 64 | 9 | 12 | 21 | 42 | .... | .... | .... | .... | .... | .... | .... | .... | .... | .... | .... | .... | .... | .... | .... | .... | .... | .... |
| 2008-09 | Frederikshavn | Denmark | 28 | 11 | 11 | 22 | 92 | .... | .... | .... | .... | .... | .... | .... | .... | .... | 7 | 3 | 1 | 4 | 16 | .... | .... | .... | .... |
| | **NHL Totals** | | 46 | 1 | 1 | 2 | 8 | 0 | 0 | 0 | 37 | 2.7 | | 2 | 0.0 | 6:52 | .... | .... | .... | .... | .... | .... | .... | .... | .... |

CCHA Second All-Star Team (2004)

Signed as a free agent by **Frederikshavn** (Denmark), October 31, 2008.

## GLUMAC, Mike

(GLOO-kmak, MIGHK) **MTL.**

Right wing. Shoots right. 6'2", 200 lbs. Born, Niagara Falls, Ont., April 5, 1980.

| Season | Club | League | GP | G | A | Pts | PIM | PP | SH | GW | S | % | +/- | TF | F% | Min | GP | G | A | Pts | PIM | PP | SH | GW | Min |
|---|---|---|---|---|---|---|---|---|---|---|---|---|---|---|---|---|---|---|---|---|---|---|---|---|---|
| 1996-97 | St. Mike's B's | OPJHL | 50 | 13 | 25 | 38 | 33 | .... | .... | .... | .... | .... | .... | .... | .... | .... | 6 | 1 | 0 | 1 | 2 | .... | .... | .... | .... |
| 1997-98 | Newmarket | OPJHL | 36 | 16 | 16 | 32 | 57 | .... | .... | .... | .... | .... | .... | .... | .... | .... | .... | .... | .... | .... | .... | .... | .... | .... | .... |
| 1998-99 | Miami U. | CCHA | 35 | 2 | 0 | 2 | 44 | .... | .... | .... | .... | .... | .... | .... | .... | .... | .... | .... | .... | .... | .... | .... | .... | .... | .... |
| 99-2000 | Miami U. | CCHA | 36 | 8 | 5 | 13 | 52 | .... | .... | .... | .... | .... | .... | .... | .... | .... | .... | .... | .... | .... | .... | .... | .... | .... | .... |
| 2000-01 | Miami U. | CCHA | 37 | 9 | 10 | 19 | 46 | .... | .... | .... | .... | .... | .... | .... | .... | .... | .... | .... | .... | .... | .... | .... | .... | .... | .... |
| 2001-02 | Miami U. | CCHA | 36 | 15 | 8 | 23 | 28 | .... | .... | .... | .... | .... | .... | .... | .... | .... | .... | .... | .... | .... | .... | .... | .... | .... | .... |
| 2002-03 | Pee Dee Pride | ECHL | 69 | 37 | 32 | 69 | 49 | .... | .... | .... | .... | .... | .... | .... | .... | .... | .... | .... | .... | .... | .... | .... | .... | .... | .... |
| | Cleveland Barons | AHL | 2 | 0 | 0 | 0 | 0 | .... | .... | .... | .... | .... | .... | .... | .... | .... | .... | .... | .... | .... | .... | .... | .... | .... | .... |
| 2003-04 | Worcester IceCats | AHL | 80 | 28 | 24 | 52 | 74 | .... | .... | .... | .... | .... | .... | .... | .... | .... | 10 | 3 | 3 | 6 | 11 | .... | .... | .... | .... |
| 2004-05 | Worcester IceCats | AHL | 45 | 12 | 17 | 29 | 27 | .... | .... | .... | .... | .... | .... | .... | .... | .... | .... | .... | .... | .... | .... | .... | .... | .... | .... |
| **2005-06** | **St. Louis** | **NHL** | 33 | 7 | 5 | 12 | 33 | 5 | 0 | 0 | 55 | 12.7 | –8 | 5 | 40.0 | 12:25 | .... | .... | .... | .... | .... | .... | .... | .... | .... |
| | Peoria Rivermen | AHL | 49 | 25 | 32 | 57 | 64 | .... | .... | .... | .... | .... | .... | .... | .... | .... | 4 | 1 | 1 | 2 | 5 | .... | .... | .... | .... |
| **2006-07** | **St. Louis** | **NHL** | 3 | 0 | 1 | 1 | 0 | 0 | 0 | 0 | 4 | 0.0 | 1 | 0 | 0.0 | 8:24 | .... | .... | .... | .... | .... | .... | .... | .... | .... |
| | Peoria Rivermen | AHL | 72 | 27 | 30 | 57 | 115 | .... | .... | .... | .... | .... | .... | .... | .... | .... | .... | .... | .... | .... | .... | .... | .... | .... | .... |
| **2007-08** | **St. Louis** | **NHL** | 4 | 0 | 0 | 0 | 5 | 0 | 0 | 0 | 3 | 0.0 | –1 | 3 | 33.3 | 10:08 | .... | .... | .... | .... | .... | .... | .... | .... | .... |
| | Peoria Rivermen | AHL | 75 | 21 | 28 | 49 | 99 | .... | .... | .... | .... | .... | .... | .... | .... | .... | .... | .... | .... | .... | .... | .... | .... | .... | .... |
| 2008-09 | Hamilton | AHL | 66 | 33 | 19 | 52 | 60 | .... | .... | .... | .... | .... | .... | .... | .... | .... | 6 | 1 | 3 | 4 | 4 | .... | .... | .... | .... |
| | **NHL Totals** | | 40 | 7 | 6 | 13 | 38 | 5 | 0 | 0 | 62 | 11.3 | | 8 | 37.5 | 11:53 | .... | .... | .... | .... | .... | .... | .... | .... | .... |

ECHL All-Rookie Team (2003)

Signed as a free agent by **Pee Dee** (ECHL), August 28, 2002. Signed as a free agent by **Worcester** (AHL), October 6, 2003. Signed as a free agent by **St. Louis**, June 29, 2004. Signed as a free agent by **Montreal**, July 16, 2008.

## GOC, Marcel

(GAWCH, MAHR-sehl)

Center. Shoots left. 6', 200 lbs. Born, Calw, West Germany, August 24, 1983. San Jose's 1st choice, 20th overall, in 2001 Entry Draft.

| Season | Club | League | GP | G | A | Pts | PIM | PP | SH | GW | S | % | +/- | TF | F% | Min | GP | G | A | Pts | PIM | PP | SH | GW | Min |
|---|---|---|---|---|---|---|---|---|---|---|---|---|---|---|---|---|---|---|---|---|---|---|---|---|---|
| 1998-99 | Schwenningen Jr. | Ger-Jr. | 12 | 23 | 10 | 33 | 12 | .... | .... | .... | .... | .... | .... | .... | .... | .... | .... | .... | .... | .... | .... | .... | .... | .... | .... |
| 99-2000 | Schwenningen | Germany | 51 | 0 | 3 | 3 | 4 | .... | .... | .... | .... | .... | .... | .... | .... | .... | 11 | 1 | 1 | 2 | 2 | .... | .... | .... | .... |
| 2000-01 | Schwenningen | Germany | 58 | 13 | 28 | 41 | 12 | .... | .... | .... | .... | .... | .... | .... | .... | .... | .... | .... | .... | .... | .... | .... | .... | .... | .... |
| 2001-02 | Schwenningen | Germany | 45 | 8 | 9 | 17 | 24 | .... | .... | .... | .... | .... | .... | .... | .... | .... | .... | .... | .... | .... | .... | .... | .... | .... | .... |
| | Adler Mannheim | Germany | 8 | 0 | 2 | 2 | 0 | .... | .... | .... | .... | .... | .... | .... | .... | .... | .... | .... | .... | .... | .... | .... | .... | .... | .... |
| 2002-03 | Adler Mannheim | Germany | 36 | 6 | 14 | 20 | 16 | .... | .... | .... | .... | .... | .... | .... | .... | .... | 8 | 1 | 2 | 3 | 0 | .... | .... | .... | .... |
| **2003-04** | Cleveland Barons | AHL | 78 | 16 | 21 | 37 | 24 | .... | .... | .... | .... | .... | .... | .... | .... | .... | .... | .... | .... | .... | .... | .... | .... | .... | .... |
| | **San Jose** | **NHL** | .... | .... | .... | .... | .... | .... | .... | .... | .... | .... | .... | .... | .... | .... | 5 | 1 | 1 | 2 | 0 | 0 | 0 | 1 | 7:08 |
| 2004-05 | Cleveland Barons | AHL | 76 | 16 | 34 | 50 | 28 | .... | .... | .... | .... | .... | .... | .... | .... | .... | .... | .... | .... | .... | .... | .... | .... | .... | .... |
| **2005-06** | **San Jose** | **NHL** | 81 | 8 | 14 | 22 | 22 | 2 | 0 | 2 | 96 | 8.3 | –7 | 808 | 47.9 | 11:42 | 11 | 0 | 3 | 3 | 0 | 0 | 0 | 0 | 12:38 |
| | Germany | Olympics | 5 | 1 | 0 | 1 | 0 | .... | .... | .... | .... | .... | .... | .... | .... | .... | .... | .... | .... | .... | .... | .... | .... | .... | .... |
| **2006-07** | **San Jose** | **NHL** | 78 | 5 | 8 | 13 | 24 | 0 | 1 | 0 | 96 | 5.2 | –2 | 659 | 55.2 | 12:01 | 11 | 2 | 1 | 3 | 4 | 0 | 0 | 0 | 14:49 |
| **2007-08** | **San Jose** | **NHL** | 51 | 5 | 3 | 8 | 12 | 0 | 0 | 0 | 87 | 5.7 | –15 | 208 | 51.4 | 10:41 | 4 | 0 | 0 | 0 | 2 | 0 | 0 | 0 | 8:03 |
| **2008-09** | **San Jose** | **NHL** | 55 | 2 | 9 | 11 | 18 | 0 | 0 | 1 | 104 | 1.9 | –6 | 570 | 58.3 | 13:55 | 6 | 0 | 0 | 0 | 2 | 0 | 0 | 0 | 10:33 |
| | **NHL Totals** | | 265 | 20 | 34 | 54 | 76 | 2 | 1 | 3 | 383 | 5.2 | | 2245 | 53.0 | 12:04 | 37 | 3 | 5 | 8 | 8 | 0 | 0 | 1 | 11:42 |

## GODARD, Eric

(GAW-duhrd, AIR-ihk) **PIT.**

Right wing. Shoots right. 6'4", 214 lbs. Born, Vernon, B.C., March 7, 1980.

| Season | Club | League | GP | G | A | Pts | PIM | PP | SH | GW | S | % | +/- | TF | F% | Min | GP | G | A | Pts | PIM | PP | SH | GW | Min |
|---|---|---|---|---|---|---|---|---|---|---|---|---|---|---|---|---|---|---|---|---|---|---|---|---|---|
| 1997-98 | Lethbridge | WHL | 7 | 0 | 0 | 0 | 26 | .... | .... | .... | .... | .... | .... | .... | .... | .... | 2 | 0 | 0 | 0 | 0 | .... | .... | .... | .... |
| 1998-99 | Lethbridge | WHL | 66 | 2 | 5 | 7 | 213 | .... | .... | .... | .... | .... | .... | .... | .... | .... | 4 | 0 | 0 | 0 | 14 | .... | .... | .... | .... |
| 99-2000 | Lethbridge | WHL | 60 | 3 | 5 | 8 | *310 | .... | .... | .... | .... | .... | .... | .... | .... | .... | .... | .... | .... | .... | .... | .... | .... | .... | .... |
| | Louisville Panthers | AHL | 4 | 0 | 1 | 1 | 16 | .... | .... | .... | .... | .... | .... | .... | .... | .... | .... | .... | .... | .... | .... | .... | .... | .... | .... |
| 2000-01 | Louisville Panthers | AHL | 45 | 0 | 0 | 0 | 132 | .... | .... | .... | .... | .... | .... | .... | .... | .... | .... | .... | .... | .... | .... | .... | .... | .... | .... |
| 2001-02 | Bridgeport | AHL | 67 | 1 | 4 | 5 | 198 | .... | .... | .... | .... | .... | .... | .... | .... | .... | 20 | 0 | 4 | 4 | 30 | .... | .... | .... | .... |
| **2002-03** | **NY Islanders** | **NHL** | 19 | 0 | 0 | 0 | 48 | 0 | 0 | 0 | 6 | 0.0 | –3 | 0 | 0.0 | 4:32 | 2 | 0 | 1 | 1 | 4 | 0 | 0 | 0 | 1:09 |
| | Bridgeport | AHL | 46 | 2 | 2 | 4 | 199 | .... | .... | .... | .... | .... | .... | .... | .... | .... | 6 | 0 | 0 | 0 | 16 | .... | .... | .... | .... |
| **2003-04** | **NY Islanders** | **NHL** | 31 | 0 | 1 | 1 | 97 | 0 | 0 | 0 | 5 | 0.0 | –2 | 1 | 0.0 | 3:46 | .... | .... | .... | .... | .... | .... | .... | .... | .... |
| | Bridgeport | AHL | 7 | 0 | 0 | 0 | 13 | .... | .... | .... | .... | .... | .... | .... | .... | .... | .... | .... | .... | .... | .... | .... | .... | .... | .... |
| 2004-05 | Bridgeport | AHL | 75 | 7 | 11 | 18 | 295 | .... | .... | .... | .... | .... | .... | .... | .... | .... | .... | .... | .... | .... | .... | .... | .... | .... | .... |
| **2005-06** | **NY Islanders** | **NHL** | 57 | 2 | 2 | 4 | 115 | 0 | 0 | 0 | 17 | 11.8 | –2 | 1 | 0.0 | 3:34 | .... | .... | .... | .... | .... | .... | .... | .... | .... |
| **2006-07** | **Calgary** | **NHL** | 19 | 0 | 1 | 1 | 50 | 0 | 0 | 0 | 3 | 0.0 | 0 | 0 | 0.0 | 3:47 | .... | .... | .... | .... | .... | .... | .... | .... | .... |
| | Omaha | AHL | 36 | 5 | 4 | 9 | 94 | .... | .... | .... | .... | .... | .... | .... | .... | .... | .... | .... | .... | .... | .... | .... | .... | .... | .... |

| Season | Club | League | GP | G | A | Pts | PIM | PP | SH | GW | S | % | +/- | TF | F% | Min | GP | G | A | Pts | PIM | PP | SH | GW | Min |
|---|---|---|---|---|---|---|---|---|---|---|---|---|---|---|---|---|---|---|---|---|---|---|---|---|---|
| | | | Regular Season | | | | | | | | | | | | | | Playoffs | | | | | | | | |
| 2007-08 | Calgary | NHL | 74 | 1 | 1 | 2 | 171 | 0 | 0 | 1 | 14 | 7.1 | –8 | 1 | 0.0 | 4:43 | 5 | 0 | 0 | 0 | 2 | 0 | 0 | 0 | 3:31 |
| 2008-09 ♦ | Pittsburgh | NHL | 71 | 2 | 2 | 4 | 171 | 0 | 0 | 0 | 20 | 10.0 | –3 | 1 | 100.0 | 4:04 | .... | .... | .... | .... | .... | .... | .... | .... | .... |
| | NHL Totals | | 271 | 5 | 7 | 12 | 652 | 0 | 0 | 1 | 65 | 7.7 | | 4 | 25.0 | 4:07 | 7 | 0 | 1 | 1 | 6 | 0 | 0 | 0 | 2:50 |

Signed as a free agent by **Florida**, September 24, 1999. Traded to **NY Islanders** by **Florida** for Florida's 3rd round choice (previously acquired, Florida selected Gregory Campbell) in 2002 Entry Draft, June 22, 2002. • Spent majority of 2003-04 season serving as a healthy reserve. Signed as a free agent by **Calgary**, August 14, 2006. Signed as a free agent by **Pittsburgh**, July 1, 2008.

## GOERTZEN, Steven (GUHRT-sehn, STEE-vehn) CAR.

Right wing. Shoots right. 6'2", 216 lbs. Born, Stony Plain, Alta., May 26, 1984. Columbus' 11th choice, 225th overall, in 2002 Entry Draft.

| Season | Club | League | GP | G | A | Pts | PIM | PP | SH | GW | S | % | +/- | TF | F% | Min | GP | G | A | Pts | PIM | PP | SH | GW | Min |
|---|---|---|---|---|---|---|---|---|---|---|---|---|---|---|---|---|---|---|---|---|---|---|---|---|---|
| 99-2000 | Spruce Grove | AMBHL | 36 | 16 | 17 | 33 | 30 | .... | .... | .... | .... | .... | .... | .... | .... | .... | .... | .... | .... | .... | .... | .... | .... | .... | .... |
| 2000-01 | St. Albert Raiders | AMHL | 34 | 11 | 19 | 30 | 70 | .... | .... | .... | .... | .... | .... | .... | .... | .... | .... | .... | .... | .... | .... | .... | .... | .... | .... |
| | St. Albert Saints | AJHL | 1 | 0 | 0 | 0 | 0 | .... | .... | .... | .... | .... | .... | .... | .... | .... | .... | .... | .... | .... | .... | .... | .... | .... | .... |
| 2001-02 | Seattle | WHL | 66 | 6 | 9 | 15 | 45 | .... | .... | .... | .... | .... | .... | .... | .... | .... | 11 | 2 | 0 | 2 | 4 | .... | .... | .... | .... |
| 2002-03 | Seattle | WHL | 71 | 12 | 19 | 31 | 95 | .... | .... | .... | .... | .... | .... | .... | .... | .... | 14 | 4 | 3 | 7 | 9 | .... | .... | .... | .... |
| 2003-04 | Seattle | WHL | 69 | 15 | 18 | 33 | 115 | .... | .... | .... | .... | .... | .... | .... | .... | .... | .... | .... | .... | .... | .... | .... | .... | .... | .... |
| | Syracuse Crunch | AHL | 8 | 0 | 3 | 3 | 4 | .... | .... | .... | .... | .... | .... | .... | .... | .... | 1 | 0 | 0 | 0 | 0 | .... | .... | .... | .... |
| 2004-05 | Syracuse Crunch | AHL | 57 | 2 | 7 | 9 | 100 | .... | .... | .... | .... | .... | .... | .... | .... | .... | .... | .... | .... | .... | .... | .... | .... | .... | .... |
| | Dayton Bombers | ECHL | 11 | 0 | 3 | 3 | 2 | .... | .... | .... | .... | .... | .... | .... | .... | .... | .... | .... | .... | .... | .... | .... | .... | .... | .... |
| **2005-06** | **Columbus** | **NHL** | **39** | **0** | **0** | **0** | **44** | **0** | **0** | **0** | **23** | **0.0** | **–17** | **11** | **54.6** | **8:32** | .... | .... | .... | .... | .... | .... | .... | .... | .... |
| | Syracuse Crunch | AHL | 40 | 7 | 8 | 15 | 55 | .... | .... | .... | .... | .... | .... | .... | .... | .... | 6 | 0 | 1 | 1 | 34 | .... | .... | .... | .... |
| **2006-07** | **Columbus** | **NHL** | **7** | **0** | **0** | **0** | **10** | **0** | **0** | **0** | **1** | **0.0** | **0** | **0** | **0.0** | **5:21** | .... | .... | .... | .... | .... | .... | .... | .... | .... |
| | Syracuse Crunch | AHL | 60 | 9 | 7 | 16 | 120 | .... | .... | .... | .... | .... | .... | .... | .... | .... | .... | .... | .... | .... | .... | .... | .... | .... | .... |
| 2007-08 | Syracuse Crunch | AHL | 59 | 8 | 5 | 13 | 72 | .... | .... | .... | .... | .... | .... | .... | .... | .... | .... | .... | .... | .... | .... | .... | .... | .... | .... |
| | San Antonio | AHL | 22 | 1 | 3 | 4 | 34 | .... | .... | .... | .... | .... | .... | .... | .... | .... | 7 | 1 | 0 | 1 | 5 | .... | .... | .... | .... |
| **2008-09** | **Phoenix** | **NHL** | **16** | **2** | **2** | **4** | **24** | **0** | **0** | **0** | **18** | **11.1** | **–2** | **2** | **50.0** | **9:42** | .... | .... | .... | .... | .... | .... | .... | .... | .... |
| | San Antonio | AHL | 57 | 6 | 8 | 14 | 90 | .... | .... | .... | .... | .... | .... | .... | .... | .... | .... | .... | .... | .... | .... | .... | .... | .... | .... |
| | **NHL Totals** | | **62** | **2** | **2** | **4** | **78** | **0** | **0** | **0** | **42** | **4.8** | | **13** | **53.8** | **8:28** | .... | .... | .... | .... | .... | .... | .... | .... | .... |

Traded to **Phoenix** by **Columbus** for Nat DiCasmirro, February 28, 2008. Signed as a free agent by **Carolina**, July 8, 2009.

## GOLIGOSKI, Alex (goh-lih-GAW-skee, AL-ehx) PIT.

Defense. Shoots left. 5'11", 180 lbs. Born, Grand Rapids, MN, July 30, 1985. Pittsburgh's 3rd choice, 61st overall, in 2004 Entry Draft.

| Season | Club | League | GP | G | A | Pts | PIM | PP | SH | GW | S | % | +/- | TF | F% | Min | GP | G | A | Pts | PIM | PP | SH | GW | Min |
|---|---|---|---|---|---|---|---|---|---|---|---|---|---|---|---|---|---|---|---|---|---|---|---|---|---|
| 2002-03 | Grand Rapids | High-MN | 28 | 14 | 20 | 34 | 22 | .... | .... | .... | .... | .... | .... | .... | .... | .... | .... | .... | .... | .... | .... | .... | .... | .... | .... |
| 2003-04 | Grand Rapids | High-MN | 26 | 25 | 31 | 56 | 16 | .... | .... | .... | .... | .... | .... | .... | .... | .... | .... | .... | .... | .... | .... | .... | .... | .... | .... |
| | Sioux Falls | USHL | 10 | 0 | 2 | 2 | 6 | .... | .... | .... | .... | .... | .... | .... | .... | .... | .... | .... | .... | .... | .... | .... | .... | .... | .... |
| 2004-05 | U. of Minnesota | WCHA | 33 | 5 | 15 | 20 | 44 | .... | .... | .... | .... | .... | .... | .... | .... | .... | .... | .... | .... | .... | .... | .... | .... | .... | .... |
| 2005-06 | U. of Minnesota | WCHA | 41 | 11 | 28 | 39 | 63 | .... | .... | .... | .... | .... | .... | .... | .... | .... | .... | .... | .... | .... | .... | .... | .... | .... | .... |
| 2006-07 | U. of Minnesota | WCHA | 44 | 9 | 30 | 39 | 51 | .... | .... | .... | .... | .... | .... | .... | .... | .... | .... | .... | .... | .... | .... | .... | .... | .... | .... |
| **2007-08** | **Pittsburgh** | **NHL** | **3** | **0** | **2** | **2** | **2** | **0** | **0** | **0** | **2** | **0.0** | **2** | **0** | **0.0** | **13:56** | .... | .... | .... | .... | .... | .... | .... | .... | .... |
| | Wilkes-Barre | AHL | 70 | 10 | 28 | 38 | 53 | .... | .... | .... | .... | .... | .... | .... | .... | .... | 23 | 4 | 24 | 28 | 18 | .... | .... | .... | .... |
| **2008-09 ♦** | **Pittsburgh** | **NHL** | **45** | **6** | **14** | **20** | **16** | **4** | **0** | **0** | **61** | **9.8** | **5** | **0** | **0.0** | **18:18** | **2** | **0** | **1** | **1** | **0** | **0** | **0** | **0** | **10:22** |
| | Wilkes-Barre | AHL | 26 | 2 | 16 | 18 | 16 | .... | .... | .... | .... | .... | .... | .... | .... | .... | 9 | 1 | 5 | 6 | 10 | .... | .... | .... | .... |
| | **NHL Totals** | | **48** | **6** | **16** | **22** | **18** | **4** | **0** | **0** | **63** | **9.5** | | **0** | **0.0** | **18:02** | **2** | **0** | **1** | **1** | **0** | **0** | **0** | **0** | **10:22** |

WCHA All-Rookie Team (2005) • WCHA Second All-Star Team (2006) • WCHA First All-Star Team (2007) • NCAA West First All-American Team (2007)

## GOMEZ, Scott (GOH-mehz, SKAWT) MTL.

Center. Shoots left. 5'11", 200 lbs. Born, Anchorage, AK, December 23, 1979. New Jersey's 2nd choice, 27th overall, in 1998 Entry Draft.

| Season | Club | League | GP | G | A | Pts | PIM | PP | SH | GW | S | % | +/- | TF | F% | Min | GP | G | A | Pts | PIM | PP | SH | GW | Min |
|---|---|---|---|---|---|---|---|---|---|---|---|---|---|---|---|---|---|---|---|---|---|---|---|---|---|
| 1994-95 | East High | High-AK | 28 | 30 | 48 | 78 | .... | .... | .... | .... | .... | .... | .... | .... | .... | .... | .... | .... | .... | .... | .... | .... | .... | .... | .... |
| 1995-96 | East High | High-AK | 27 | *56 | 49 | *101 | .... | .... | .... | .... | .... | .... | .... | .... | .... | .... | .... | .... | .... | .... | .... | .... | .... | .... | .... |
| | Anchorage | AAHL | 40 | *70 | *67 | *137 | 44 | .... | .... | .... | .... | .... | .... | .... | .... | .... | .... | .... | .... | .... | .... | .... | .... | .... | .... |
| 1996-97 | South Surrey | BCHL | 56 | 48 | 76 | 124 | 94 | .... | .... | .... | .... | .... | .... | .... | .... | .... | 21 | 18 | 23 | 41 | 57 | .... | .... | .... | .... |
| 1997-98 | Tri-City | WHL | 45 | 12 | 37 | 49 | 57 | .... | .... | .... | .... | .... | .... | .... | .... | .... | .... | .... | .... | .... | .... | .... | .... | .... | .... |
| 1998-99 | Tri-City | WHL | 58 | 30 | *78 | 108 | 55 | .... | .... | .... | .... | .... | .... | .... | .... | .... | 10 | 6 | 13 | 19 | 31 | .... | .... | .... | .... |
| **99-2000 ♦** | **New Jersey** | **NHL** | **82** | **19** | **51** | **70** | **78** | **7** | **0** | **1** | **204** | **9.3** | **14** | **341** | **44.6** | **16:21** | **23** | **4** | **6** | **10** | **4** | **1** | **0** | **2** | **14:08** |
| **2000-01** | **New Jersey** | **NHL** | **76** | **14** | **49** | **63** | **46** | **2** | **0** | **4** | **155** | **9.0** | **–1** | **1010** | **44.6** | **15:46** | **25** | **5** | **9** | **14** | **24** | **0** | **0** | **0** | **16:06** |
| **2001-02** | **New Jersey** | **NHL** | **76** | **10** | **38** | **48** | **36** | **1** | **0** | **1** | **156** | **6.4** | **–4** | **628** | **48.7** | **16:46** | .... | .... | .... | .... | .... | .... | .... | .... | .... |
| **2002-03 ♦** | **New Jersey** | **NHL** | **80** | **13** | **42** | **55** | **48** | **2** | **0** | **4** | **205** | **6.3** | **17** | **864** | **47.5** | **16:01** | **24** | **3** | **9** | **12** | **2** | **0** | **0** | **0** | **13:45** |
| **2003-04** | **New Jersey** | **NHL** | **80** | **14** | ***56** | **70** | **70** | **3** | **0** | **1** | **189** | **7.4** | **18** | **1129** | **46.2** | **16:00** | **5** | **0** | **6** | **6** | **0** | **0** | **0** | **0** | **17:14** |
| 2004-05 | Alaska Aces | ECHL | 61 | 13 | *73 | *86 | 69 | .... | .... | .... | .... | .... | .... | .... | .... | .... | 4 | 1 | 3 | 4 | 4 | .... | .... | .... | .... |
| **2005-06** | **New Jersey** | **NHL** | **82** | **33** | **51** | **84** | **42** | **9** | **0** | **5** | **244** | **13.5** | **8** | **1434** | **52.6** | **18:47** | **9** | **5** | **4** | **9** | **6** | **4** | **0** | **1** | **18:14** |
| | United States | Olympics | 6 | 1 | 4 | 5 | 10 | .... | .... | .... | .... | .... | .... | .... | .... | .... | .... | .... | .... | .... | .... | .... | .... | .... | .... |
| **2006-07** | **New Jersey** | **NHL** | **72** | **13** | **47** | **60** | **42** | **4** | **0** | **1** | **248** | **5.2** | **7** | **1204** | **52.2** | **18:56** | **11** | **4** | **10** | **14** | **14** | **0** | **0** | **1** | **20:01** |
| **2007-08** | **NY Rangers** | **NHL** | **81** | **16** | **54** | **70** | **36** | **7** | **0** | **3** | **242** | **6.6** | **3** | **1165** | **52.5** | **19:54** | **10** | **4** | **7** | **11** | **8** | **1** | **0** | **0** | **20:53** |
| **2008-09** | **NY Rangers** | **NHL** | **77** | **16** | **42** | **58** | **60** | **3** | **1** | **7** | **271** | **5.9** | **–2** | **1312** | **52.4** | **21:04** | **7** | **2** | **3** | **5** | **4** | **1** | **0** | **0** | **19:58** |
| | **NHL Totals** | | **706** | **148** | **430** | **578** | **458** | **38** | **1** | **27** | **1914** | **7.7** | | **9087** | **49.7** | **17:43** | **114** | **27** | **54** | **81** | **62** | **7** | **0** | **4** | **16:28** |

WHL West First All-Star Team (1999) • NHL All-Rookie Team (2000) • Calder Memorial Trophy (2000) • ECHL First All-Star Team (2005) • ECHL MVP (2005)

Played in NHL All-Star Game (2000, 2008)

Signed as a free agent by **Alaska** (ECHL), October 25, 2004. Signed as a free agent by **NY Rangers**, July 1, 2007. Traded to **Montreal** by **NY Rangers** with Tom Pyatt and Mike Busto for Chris Higgins, Ryan McDonagh and Pavel Valentenko, June 30, 2009.

## GONCHAR, Sergei (gohn-CHAR, SAIR-gay) PIT.

Defense. Shoots left. 6'2", 211 lbs. Born, Chelyabinsk, USSR, April 13, 1974. Washington's 1st choice, 14th overall, in 1992 Entry Draft.

| Season | Club | League | GP | G | A | Pts | PIM | PP | SH | GW | S | % | +/- | TF | F% | Min | GP | G | A | Pts | PIM | PP | SH | GW | Min |
|---|---|---|---|---|---|---|---|---|---|---|---|---|---|---|---|---|---|---|---|---|---|---|---|---|---|
| 1990-91 | Mechel | USSR-2 | 2 | 0 | 0 | 0 | 0 | .... | .... | .... | .... | .... | .... | .... | .... | .... | .... | .... | .... | .... | .... | .... | .... | .... | .... |
| | Chelyabinsk | USSR-Q | 11 | 0 | 0 | 0 | 4 | .... | .... | .... | .... | .... | .... | .... | .... | .... | .... | .... | .... | .... | .... | .... | .... | .... | .... |
| 1991-92 | Chelyabinsk | CIS | 31 | 1 | 0 | 1 | 6 | .... | .... | .... | .... | .... | .... | .... | .... | .... | .... | .... | .... | .... | .... | .... | .... | .... | .... |
| 1992-93 | Dynamo Moscow | CIS | 31 | 1 | 3 | 4 | 70 | .... | .... | .... | .... | .... | .... | .... | .... | .... | 10 | 0 | 0 | 0 | 12 | .... | .... | .... | .... |
| 1993-94 | Dynamo Moscow | CIS | 44 | 4 | 5 | 9 | 36 | .... | .... | .... | .... | .... | .... | .... | .... | .... | .... | .... | .... | .... | .... | .... | .... | .... | .... |
| | Portland Pirates | AHL | .... | .... | .... | .... | .... | .... | .... | .... | .... | .... | .... | .... | .... | .... | 2 | 0 | 0 | 0 | 0 | .... | .... | .... | .... |
| **1994-95** | Portland Pirates | AHL | 61 | 10 | 32 | 42 | 67 | .... | .... | .... | .... | .... | .... | .... | .... | .... | .... | .... | .... | .... | .... | .... | .... | .... | .... |
| | **Washington** | **NHL** | **31** | **2** | **5** | **7** | **22** | **0** | **0** | **0** | **38** | **5.3** | **4** | .... | .... | .... | **7** | **2** | **2** | **4** | **2** | **0** | **0** | **1** | .... |
| **1995-96** | **Washington** | **NHL** | **78** | **15** | **26** | **41** | **60** | **4** | **0** | **4** | **139** | **10.8** | **25** | .... | .... | .... | **6** | **2** | **4** | **6** | **4** | **1** | **0** | **0** | .... |
| **1996-97** | **Washington** | **NHL** | **57** | **13** | **17** | **30** | **36** | **3** | **0** | **3** | **129** | **10.1** | **–11** | .... | .... | .... | .... | .... | .... | .... | .... | .... | .... | .... | .... |
| **1997-98** | Lada Togliatti | Russia | 7 | 3 | 2 | 5 | 4 | .... | .... | .... | .... | .... | .... | .... | .... | .... | .... | .... | .... | .... | .... | .... | .... | .... | .... |
| | **Washington** | **NHL** | **72** | **5** | **16** | **21** | **66** | **2** | **0** | **0** | **134** | **3.7** | **2** | .... | .... | .... | **21** | **7** | **4** | **11** | **30** | **3** | **1** | **2** | .... |
| | Russia | Olympics | 6 | 0 | 2 | 2 | 0 | .... | .... | .... | .... | .... | .... | .... | .... | .... | .... | .... | .... | .... | .... | .... | .... | .... | .... |
| **1998-99** | **Washington** | **NHL** | **53** | **21** | **10** | **31** | **57** | **13** | **1** | **3** | **180** | **11.7** | **1** | **0** | **0.0** | **23:55** | .... | .... | .... | .... | .... | .... | .... | .... | .... |
| **99-2000** | **Washington** | **NHL** | **73** | **18** | **36** | **54** | **52** | **5** | **0** | **3** | **181** | **9.9** | **26** | **0** | **0.0** | **21:46** | **5** | **1** | **0** | **1** | **6** | **0** | **0** | **0** | **19:58** |
| **2000-01** | **Washington** | **NHL** | **76** | **19** | **38** | **57** | **70** | **8** | **0** | **2** | **241** | **7.9** | **12** | **1** | **100.0** | **22:26** | **6** | **1** | **3** | **4** | **2** | **1** | **0** | **0** | **19:45** |
| **2001-02** | **Washington** | **NHL** | **76** | **26** | **33** | **59** | **58** | **7** | **0** | **2** | **216** | **12.0** | **–1** | **1** | **100.0** | **23:51** | .... | .... | .... | .... | .... | .... | .... | .... | .... |
| | Russia | Olympics | 6 | 0 | 0 | 0 | 2 | .... | .... | .... | .... | .... | .... | .... | .... | .... | .... | .... | .... | .... | .... | .... | .... | .... | .... |
| **2002-03** | **Washington** | **NHL** | **82** | **18** | **49** | **67** | **52** | **7** | **0** | **2** | **224** | **8.0** | **13** | **0** | **0.0** | **26:35** | **6** | **0** | **5** | **5** | **4** | **0** | **0** | **0** | **29:00** |
| **2003-04** | **Washington** | **NHL** | **56** | **7** | **42** | **49** | **44** | **4** | **0** | **0** | **127** | **5.5** | **–20** | **0** | **0.0** | **27:57** | .... | .... | .... | .... | .... | .... | .... | .... | .... |
| | **Boston** | **NHL** | **15** | **4** | **5** | **9** | **12** | **2** | **0** | **0** | **34** | **11.8** | **6** | **0** | **0.0** | **25:32** | **7** | **1** | **4** | **5** | **4** | **1** | **0** | **1** | **27:51** |
| 2004-05 | Magnitogorsk | Russia | 40 | 2 | 17 | 19 | 54 | .... | .... | .... | .... | .... | .... | .... | .... | .... | 4 | 1 | 1 | 2 | 6 | .... | .... | .... | .... |
| **2005-06** | **Pittsburgh** | **NHL** | **75** | **12** | **46** | **58** | **100** | **8** | **0** | **2** | **192** | **6.3** | **–13** | **0** | **0.0** | **24:40** | .... | .... | .... | .... | .... | .... | .... | .... | .... |
| | Russia | Olympics | 8 | 0 | 2 | 2 | 8 | .... | .... | .... | .... | .... | .... | .... | .... | .... | .... | .... | .... | .... | .... | .... | .... | .... | .... |
| **2006-07** | **Pittsburgh** | **NHL** | **82** | **13** | **54** | **67** | **72** | **10** | **1** | **3** | **191** | **6.8** | **–5** | **0** | **0.0** | **26:34** | **5** | **1** | **3** | **4** | **2** | **1** | **0** | **0** | **26:53** |
| **2007-08** | **Pittsburgh** | **NHL** | **78** | **12** | **53** | **65** | **66** | **8** | **0** | **2** | **173** | **6.9** | **13** | **0** | **0.0** | **25:55** | **20** | **1** | **13** | **14** | **8** | **1** | **0** | **0** | **25:13** |
| **2008-09 ♦** | **Pittsburgh** | **NHL** | **25** | **6** | **13** | **19** | **26** | **5** | **0** | **1** | **71** | **8.5** | **6** | **0** | **0.0** | **25:11** | **22** | **3** | **11** | **14** | **12** | **2** | **0** | **2** | **23:03** |
| | **NHL Totals** | | **929** | **191** | **443** | **634** | **793** | **86** | **2** | **27** | **2270** | **8.4** | | **2** | **100.0** | **24:52** | **105** | **19** | **49** | **68** | **74** | **10** | **1** | **6** | **24:24** |

NHL Second All-Star Team (2002, 2003)

Played in NHL All-Star Game (2001, 2002, 2003, 2008)

Traded to **Boston** by **Washington** for Shaonne Morrisonn and Boston's 1st (Jeff Schultz) and 2nd (Michail Yunkov) round choices in 2004 Entry Draft, March 3, 2004. Signed as a free agent by **Magnitogorsk** (Russia), September 21, 2004. Signed as a free agent by **Pittsburgh**, August 3, 2005.

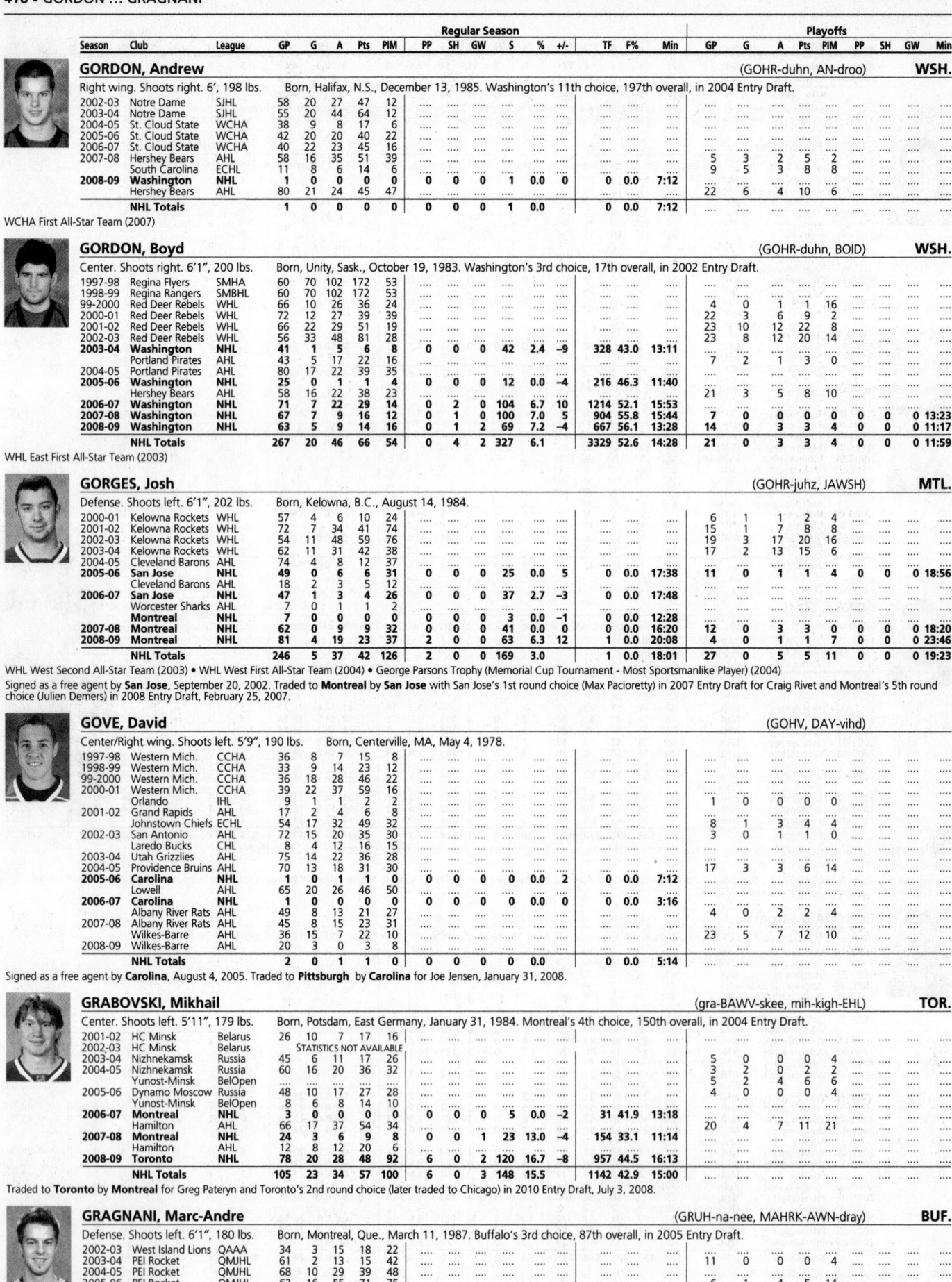

## GORDON, Andrew
(GOHR-duhn, AN-droo) **WSH.**

Right wing. Shoots right. 6', 198 lbs. Born, Halifax, N.S., December 13, 1985. Washington's 11th choice, 197th overall, in 2004 Entry Draft.

| Season | Club | League | GP | G | A | Pts | PIM | PP | SH | GW | S | % | +/- | TF | F% | Min | Playoffs GP | G | A | Pts | PIM | PP | SH | GW | Min |
|---|---|---|---|---|---|---|---|---|---|---|---|---|---|---|---|---|---|---|---|---|---|---|---|---|---|
| 2002-03 | Notre Dame | SJHL | 58 | 20 | 27 | 47 | 12 | | | | | | | | | | | | | | | | | | |
| 2003-04 | Notre Dame | SJHL | 55 | 20 | 44 | 64 | 12 | | | | | | | | | | | | | | | | | | |
| 2004-05 | St. Cloud State | WCHA | 38 | 9 | 8 | 17 | 6 | | | | | | | | | | | | | | | | | | |
| 2005-06 | St. Cloud State | WCHA | 42 | 20 | 20 | 40 | 22 | | | | | | | | | | | | | | | | | | |
| 2006-07 | St. Cloud State | WCHA | 40 | 22 | 23 | 45 | 16 | | | | | | | | | | | | | | | | | | |
| 2007-08 | Hershey Bears | AHL | 58 | 16 | 35 | 51 | 39 | | | | | | | | | | 5 | 3 | 2 | 5 | 2 | | | | |
| | South Carolina | ECHL | 11 | 8 | 6 | 14 | 6 | | | | | | | | | | 9 | 5 | 3 | 8 | 8 | | | | |
| **2008-09** | **Washington** | **NHL** | **1** | **0** | **0** | **0** | **0** | **0** | **0** | **0** | **1** | **0.0** | **0** | **0** | **0.0** | **7:12** | | | | | | | | | |
| | Hershey Bears | AHL | 80 | 21 | 24 | 45 | 47 | | | | | | | | | | 22 | 6 | 4 | 10 | 6 | | | | |
| | **NHL Totals** | | **1** | **0** | **0** | **0** | **0** | **0** | **0** | **0** | **1** | **0.0** | | **0** | **0.0** | **7:12** | | | | | | | | | |

WCHA First All-Star Team (2007)

## GORDON, Boyd
(GOHR-duhn, BOID) **WSH.**

Center. Shoots right. 6'1", 200 lbs. Born, Unity, Sask., October 19, 1983. Washington's 3rd choice, 17th overall, in 2002 Entry Draft.

| Season | Club | League | GP | G | A | Pts | PIM | PP | SH | GW | S | % | +/- | TF | F% | Min | Playoffs GP | G | A | Pts | PIM | PP | SH | GW | Min |
|---|---|---|---|---|---|---|---|---|---|---|---|---|---|---|---|---|---|---|---|---|---|---|---|---|---|
| 1997-98 | Regina Flyers | SMHA | 60 | 70 | 102 | 172 | 53 | | | | | | | | | | | | | | | | | | |
| 1998-99 | Regina Rangers | SMBHL | 60 | 70 | 102 | 172 | 53 | | | | | | | | | | | | | | | | | | |
| 99-2000 | Red Deer Rebels | WHL | 66 | 10 | 26 | 36 | 24 | | | | | | | | | | 4 | 0 | 1 | 1 | 16 | | | | |
| 2000-01 | Red Deer Rebels | WHL | 72 | 12 | 27 | 39 | 39 | | | | | | | | | | 22 | 3 | 6 | 9 | 2 | | | | |
| 2001-02 | Red Deer Rebels | WHL | 66 | 22 | 29 | 51 | 19 | | | | | | | | | | 23 | 10 | 12 | 22 | 8 | | | | |
| 2002-03 | Red Deer Rebels | WHL | 56 | 33 | 48 | 81 | 28 | | | | | | | | | | 23 | 8 | 12 | 20 | 14 | | | | |
| **2003-04** | **Washington** | **NHL** | **41** | **1** | **5** | **6** | **8** | **0** | **0** | **0** | **42** | **2.4** | **–9** | **328** | **43.0** | **13:11** | | | | | | | | | |
| | Portland Pirates | AHL | 43 | 5 | 17 | 22 | 16 | | | | | | | | | | 7 | 2 | 1 | 3 | 0 | | | | |
| 2004-05 | Portland Pirates | AHL | 80 | 17 | 22 | 39 | 35 | | | | | | | | | | | | | | | | | | |
| **2005-06** | **Washington** | **NHL** | **25** | **0** | **1** | **1** | **4** | **0** | **0** | **0** | **12** | **0.0** | **–4** | **216** | **46.3** | **11:40** | | | | | | | | | |
| | Hershey Bears | AHL | 58 | 16 | 22 | 38 | 23 | | | | | | | | | | 21 | 3 | 5 | 8 | 10 | | | | |
| **2006-07** | **Washington** | **NHL** | **71** | **7** | **22** | **29** | **14** | **0** | **2** | **0** | **104** | **6.7** | **10** | **1214** | **52.1** | **15:53** | | | | | | | | | |
| **2007-08** | **Washington** | **NHL** | **67** | **7** | **9** | **16** | **12** | **0** | **1** | **0** | **100** | **7.0** | **5** | **904** | **55.8** | **15:44** | **7** | **0** | **0** | **0** | **0** | **0** | **0** | **0** | **13:23** |
| **2008-09** | **Washington** | **NHL** | **63** | **5** | **9** | **14** | **16** | **0** | **1** | **2** | **69** | **7.2** | **–4** | **667** | **56.1** | **13:28** | **14** | **0** | **3** | **3** | **4** | **0** | **0** | **0** | **11:17** |
| | **NHL Totals** | | **267** | **20** | **46** | **66** | **54** | **0** | **4** | **2** | **327** | **6.1** | | **3329** | **52.6** | **14:28** | **21** | **0** | **3** | **3** | **4** | **0** | **0** | **0** | **11:59** |

WHL East First All-Star Team (2003)

## GORGES, Josh
(GOHR-juhz, JAWSH) **MTL.**

Defense. Shoots left. 6'1", 202 lbs. Born, Kelowna, B.C., August 14, 1984.

| Season | Club | League | GP | G | A | Pts | PIM | PP | SH | GW | S | % | +/- | TF | F% | Min | Playoffs GP | G | A | Pts | PIM | PP | SH | GW | Min |
|---|---|---|---|---|---|---|---|---|---|---|---|---|---|---|---|---|---|---|---|---|---|---|---|---|---|
| 2000-01 | Kelowna Rockets | WHL | 57 | 4 | 6 | 10 | 24 | | | | | | | | | | 6 | 1 | 1 | 2 | 4 | | | | |
| 2001-02 | Kelowna Rockets | WHL | 72 | 7 | 34 | 41 | 74 | | | | | | | | | | 15 | 1 | 7 | 8 | 8 | | | | |
| 2002-03 | Kelowna Rockets | WHL | 54 | 11 | 48 | 59 | 76 | | | | | | | | | | 19 | 3 | 17 | 20 | 16 | | | | |
| 2003-04 | Kelowna Rockets | WHL | 62 | 11 | 31 | 42 | 38 | | | | | | | | | | 17 | 2 | 13 | 15 | 6 | | | | |
| 2004-05 | Cleveland Barons | AHL | 74 | 4 | 8 | 12 | 37 | | | | | | | | | | | | | | | | | | |
| **2005-06** | **San Jose** | **NHL** | **49** | **0** | **6** | **6** | **31** | **0** | **0** | **0** | **25** | **0.0** | **5** | **0** | **0.0** | **17:38** | **11** | **0** | **1** | **1** | **4** | **0** | **0** | **0** | **18:56** |
| | Cleveland Barons | AHL | 18 | 2 | 3 | 5 | 12 | | | | | | | | | | | | | | | | | | |
| **2006-07** | **San Jose** | **NHL** | **47** | **1** | **3** | **4** | **26** | **0** | **0** | **0** | **37** | **2.7** | **–3** | **0** | **0.0** | **17:48** | | | | | | | | | |
| | Worcester Sharks | AHL | 7 | 0 | 1 | 1 | 2 | | | | | | | | | | | | | | | | | | |
| | **Montreal** | **NHL** | **7** | **0** | **0** | **0** | **0** | **0** | **0** | **0** | **3** | **0.0** | **–1** | **0** | **0.0** | **12:28** | | | | | | | | | |
| **2007-08** | **Montreal** | **NHL** | **62** | **0** | **9** | **9** | **32** | **0** | **0** | **0** | **41** | **0.0** | **0** | **0** | **0.0** | **16:20** | **12** | **0** | **3** | **3** | **0** | **0** | **0** | **0** | **18:20** |
| **2008-09** | **Montreal** | **NHL** | **81** | **4** | **19** | **23** | **37** | **2** | **0** | **0** | **63** | **6.3** | **12** | **1** | **0.0** | **20:08** | **4** | **0** | **1** | **1** | **7** | **0** | **0** | **0** | **23:46** |
| | **NHL Totals** | | **246** | **5** | **37** | **42** | **126** | **2** | **0** | **0** | **169** | **3.0** | | **1** | **0.0** | **18:01** | **27** | **0** | **5** | **5** | **11** | **0** | **0** | **0** | **19:23** |

WHL West Second All-Star Team (2003) • WHL West First All-Star Team (2004) • George Parsons Trophy (Memorial Cup Tournament - Most Sportsmanlike Player) (2004)

Signed as a free agent by **San Jose**, September 20, 2002. Traded to **Montreal** by **San Jose** with San Jose's 1st round choice (Max Pacioretty) in 2007 Entry Draft for Craig Rivet and Montreal's 5th round choice (Julien Demers) in 2008 Entry Draft, February 25, 2007.

## GOVE, David
(GOHV, DAY-vihd)

Center/Right wing. Shoots left. 5'9", 190 lbs. Born, Centerville, MA, May 4, 1978.

| Season | Club | League | GP | G | A | Pts | PIM | PP | SH | GW | S | % | +/- | TF | F% | Min | Playoffs GP | G | A | Pts | PIM | PP | SH | GW | Min |
|---|---|---|---|---|---|---|---|---|---|---|---|---|---|---|---|---|---|---|---|---|---|---|---|---|---|
| 1997-98 | Western Mich. | CCHA | 36 | 8 | 7 | 15 | 8 | | | | | | | | | | | | | | | | | | |
| 1998-99 | Western Mich. | CCHA | 33 | 9 | 14 | 23 | 12 | | | | | | | | | | | | | | | | | | |
| 99-2000 | Western Mich. | CCHA | 36 | 18 | 28 | 46 | 22 | | | | | | | | | | | | | | | | | | |
| 2000-01 | Western Mich. | CCHA | 39 | 22 | 37 | 59 | 16 | | | | | | | | | | | | | | | | | | |
| | Orlando | IHL | 9 | 1 | 1 | 2 | 2 | | | | | | | | | | 1 | 0 | 0 | 0 | 0 | | | | |
| 2001-02 | Grand Rapids | AHL | 17 | 2 | 4 | 6 | 8 | | | | | | | | | | | | | | | | | | |
| | Johnstown Chiefs | ECHL | 54 | 17 | 32 | 49 | 32 | | | | | | | | | | 8 | 1 | 3 | 4 | 4 | | | | |
| 2002-03 | San Antonio | AHL | 72 | 15 | 20 | 35 | 30 | | | | | | | | | | 3 | 0 | 1 | 1 | 0 | | | | |
| | Laredo Bucks | CHL | 8 | 4 | 12 | 16 | 15 | | | | | | | | | | | | | | | | | | |
| 2003-04 | Utah Grizzlies | AHL | 75 | 14 | 22 | 36 | 28 | | | | | | | | | | | | | | | | | | |
| 2004-05 | Providence Bruins | AHL | 70 | 13 | 18 | 31 | 30 | | | | | | | | | | 17 | 3 | 3 | 6 | 14 | | | | |
| **2005-06** | **Carolina** | **NHL** | **1** | **0** | **1** | **1** | **0** | **0** | **0** | **0** | **0** | **0.0** | **2** | **0** | **0.0** | **7:12** | | | | | | | | | |
| | Lowell | AHL | 65 | 20 | 26 | 46 | 50 | | | | | | | | | | | | | | | | | | |
| **2006-07** | **Carolina** | **NHL** | **1** | **0** | **0** | **0** | **0** | **0** | **0** | **0** | **0** | **0.0** | **0** | **0** | **0.0** | **3:16** | | | | | | | | | |
| | Albany River Rats | AHL | 49 | 8 | 13 | 21 | 27 | | | | | | | | | | 4 | 0 | 2 | 2 | 4 | | | | |
| 2007-08 | Albany River Rats | AHL | 45 | 8 | 15 | 23 | 31 | | | | | | | | | | | | | | | | | | |
| | Wilkes-Barre | AHL | 36 | 15 | 7 | 22 | 10 | | | | | | | | | | 23 | 5 | 7 | 12 | 10 | | | | |
| 2008-09 | Wilkes-Barre | AHL | 20 | 3 | 0 | 3 | 8 | | | | | | | | | | | | | | | | | | |
| | **NHL Totals** | | **2** | **0** | **1** | **1** | **0** | **0** | **0** | **0** | **0** | **0.0** | | **0** | **0.0** | **5:14** | | | | | | | | | |

Signed as a free agent by **Carolina**, August 4, 2005. Traded to **Pittsburgh** by **Carolina** for Joe Jensen, January 31, 2008.

## GRABOVSKI, Mikhail
(gra-BAWV-skee, mih-kigh-EHL) **TOR.**

Center. Shoots left. 5'11", 179 lbs. Born, Potsdam, East Germany, January 31, 1984. Montreal's 4th choice, 150th overall, in 2004 Entry Draft.

| Season | Club | League | GP | G | A | Pts | PIM | PP | SH | GW | S | % | +/- | TF | F% | Min | Playoffs GP | G | A | Pts | PIM | PP | SH | GW | Min |
|---|---|---|---|---|---|---|---|---|---|---|---|---|---|---|---|---|---|---|---|---|---|---|---|---|---|
| 2001-02 | HC Minsk | Belarus | 26 | 10 | 7 | 17 | 16 | | | | | | | | | | | | | | | | | | |
| 2002-03 | HC Minsk | Belarus | STATISTICS NOT AVAILABLE | | | | | | | | | | | | | | | | | | | | | | |
| 2003-04 | Nizhnekamsk | Russia | 45 | 6 | 11 | 17 | 26 | | | | | | | | | | 5 | 0 | 0 | 0 | 4 | | | | |
| 2004-05 | Nizhnekamsk | Russia | 60 | 16 | 20 | 36 | 32 | | | | | | | | | | 3 | 2 | 0 | 2 | 2 | | | | |
| | Yunost-Minsk | BelOpen | | | | | | | | | | | | | | | 5 | 2 | 4 | 6 | 6 | | | | |
| 2005-06 | Dynamo Moscow | Russia | 48 | 10 | 17 | 27 | 28 | | | | | | | | | | 4 | 0 | 0 | 0 | 4 | | | | |
| | Yunost-Minsk | BelOpen | 8 | 6 | 8 | 14 | 10 | | | | | | | | | | | | | | | | | | |
| **2006-07** | **Montreal** | **NHL** | **3** | **0** | **0** | **0** | **0** | **0** | **0** | **0** | **5** | **0.0** | **–2** | **31** | **41.9** | **13:18** | | | | | | | | | |
| | Hamilton | AHL | 66 | 17 | 37 | 54 | 34 | | | | | | | | | | 20 | 4 | 7 | 11 | 21 | | | | |
| **2007-08** | **Montreal** | **NHL** | **24** | **3** | **6** | **9** | **8** | **0** | **0** | **1** | **23** | **13.0** | **–4** | **154** | **33.1** | **11:14** | | | | | | | | | |
| | Hamilton | AHL | 12 | 8 | 12 | 20 | 6 | | | | | | | | | | | | | | | | | | |
| **2008-09** | **Toronto** | **NHL** | **78** | **20** | **28** | **48** | **92** | **6** | **0** | **2** | **120** | **16.7** | **–8** | **957** | **44.5** | **16:13** | | | | | | | | | |
| | **NHL Totals** | | **105** | **23** | **34** | **57** | **100** | **6** | **0** | **3** | **148** | **15.5** | | **1142** | **42.9** | **15:00** | | | | | | | | | |

Traded to **Toronto** by **Montreal** for Greg Pateryn and Toronto's 2nd round choice (later traded to Chicago) in 2010 Entry Draft, July 3, 2008.

## GRAGNANI, Marc-Andre
(GRUH-na-nee, MAHRK-AWN-dray) **BUF.**

Defense. Shoots left. 6'1", 180 lbs. Born, Montreal, Que., March 11, 1987. Buffalo's 3rd choice, 87th overall, in 2005 Entry Draft.

| Season | Club | League | GP | G | A | Pts | PIM | PP | SH | GW | S | % | +/- | TF | F% | Min | Playoffs GP | G | A | Pts | PIM | PP | SH | GW | Min |
|---|---|---|---|---|---|---|---|---|---|---|---|---|---|---|---|---|---|---|---|---|---|---|---|---|---|
| 2002-03 | West Island Lions | QAAA | 34 | 3 | 15 | 18 | 22 | | | | | | | | | | | | | | | | | | |
| 2003-04 | PEI Rocket | QMJHL | 61 | 2 | 13 | 15 | 42 | | | | | | | | | | 11 | 0 | 0 | 0 | 4 | | | | |
| 2004-05 | PEI Rocket | QMJHL | 68 | 10 | 29 | 39 | 48 | | | | | | | | | | | | | | | | | | |
| 2005-06 | PEI Rocket | QMJHL | 62 | 16 | 55 | 71 | 75 | | | | | | | | | | 6 | 1 | 4 | 5 | 14 | | | | |
| 2006-07 | PEI Rocket | QMJHL | 65 | 22 | 46 | 68 | 58 | | | | | | | | | | 7 | 5 | 8 | 13 | 4 | | | | |
| **2007-08** | **Buffalo** | **NHL** | **2** | **0** | **0** | **0** | **4** | **0** | **0** | **0** | **1** | **0.0** | **–2** | **0** | **0.0** | **6:18** | | | | | | | | | |
| | Rochester | AHL | 78 | 14 | 38 | 52 | 38 | | | | | | | | | | | | | | | | | | |

| | | | Regular Season | | | | | | | | | | | | | | Playoffs | | | | | | | | |
|---|---|---|---|---|---|---|---|---|---|---|---|---|---|---|---|---|---|---|---|---|---|---|---|---|---|
| Season | Club | League | GP | G | A | Pts | PIM | PP | SH | GW | S | % | +/- | TF | F% | Min | GP | G | A | Pts | PIM | PP | SH | GW | Min |
| **2008-09** | **Buffalo** | **NHL** | **4** | **0** | **0** | **0** | **2** | **0** | **0** | **0** | **3** | **0.0** | **2** | **0** | **0.0** | **15:23** | .... | .... | .... | .... | .... | .... | .... | .... | .... |
| | Portland Pirates | AHL | 76 | 9 | 42 | 51 | 59 | .... | .... | .... | .... | .... | .... | .... | .... | .... | 5 | 0 | 2 | 2 | 4 | .... | .... | .... | .... |
| | **NHL Totals** | | **6** | **0** | **0** | **0** | **6** | **0** | **0** | **0** | **4** | **0.0** | | **0** | **0.0** | **12:21** | .... | .... | .... | .... | .... | .... | .... | .... | .... |

## GRANT, Triston

(GRANT, TRIHS-tuhn) **NSH.**

Left wing. Shoots left. 6'1", 210 lbs. Born, Neepawa, Man., February 2, 1984. Philadelphia's 10th choice, 286th overall, in 2004 Entry Draft.

| Season | Club | League | GP | G | A | Pts | PIM | PP | SH | GW | S | % | +/- | TF | F% | Min | GP | G | A | Pts | PIM | PP | SH | GW | Min |
|---|---|---|---|---|---|---|---|---|---|---|---|---|---|---|---|---|---|---|---|---|---|---|---|---|---|
| 2000-01 | Neepawa Natives | MJHL | STATISTICS NOT AVAILABLE | | | | | | | | | | | | | | | | | | | | | | |
| | Lethbridge | WHL | 23 | 2 | 0 | 2 | 75 | .... | .... | .... | .... | .... | .... | .... | .... | .... | 5 | 0 | 0 | 0 | 11 | .... | .... | .... | .... |
| 2001-02 | Lethbridge | WHL | 36 | 8 | 1 | 9 | 110 | .... | .... | .... | .... | .... | .... | .... | .... | .... | .... | .... | .... | .... | .... | .... | .... | .... | .... |
| | Vancouver Giants | WHL | 21 | 2 | 4 | 6 | 53 | .... | .... | .... | .... | .... | .... | .... | .... | .... | .... | .... | .... | .... | .... | .... | .... | .... | .... |
| 2002-03 | Vancouver Giants | WHL | 72 | 10 | 10 | 20 | 200 | .... | .... | .... | .... | .... | .... | .... | .... | .... | 4 | 0 | 0 | 0 | 10 | .... | .... | .... | .... |
| 2003-04 | Vancouver Giants | WHL | 69 | 10 | 8 | 18 | 267 | .... | .... | .... | .... | .... | .... | .... | .... | .... | 11 | 1 | 1 | 2 | 33 | .... | .... | .... | .... |
| 2004-05 | Vancouver Giants | WHL | 70 | 20 | 12 | 32 | 193 | .... | .... | .... | .... | .... | .... | .... | .... | .... | 6 | 1 | 0 | 1 | 8 | .... | .... | .... | .... |
| 2005-06 | Philadelphia | AHL | 64 | 2 | 3 | 5 | 190 | .... | .... | .... | .... | .... | .... | .... | .... | .... | .... | .... | .... | .... | .... | .... | .... | .... | .... |
| **2006-07** | **Philadelphia** | **NHL** | **8** | **0** | **1** | **1** | **10** | **0** | **0** | **0** | **3** | **0.0** | **–1** | **0** | **0.0** | **4:32** | .... | .... | .... | .... | .... | .... | .... | .... | .... |
| | Philadelphia | AHL | 61 | 5 | 6 | 11 | 199 | .... | .... | .... | .... | .... | .... | .... | .... | .... | .... | .... | .... | .... | .... | .... | .... | .... | .... |
| 2007-08 | Philadelphia | AHL | 72 | 10 | 11 | 21 | 181 | .... | .... | .... | .... | .... | .... | .... | .... | .... | 12 | 0 | 2 | 2 | 34 | .... | .... | .... | .... |
| 2008-09 | Milwaukee | AHL | 55 | 3 | 8 | 11 | 153 | .... | .... | .... | .... | .... | .... | .... | .... | .... | 11 | 1 | 1 | 2 | 12 | .... | .... | .... | .... |
| | **NHL Totals** | | **8** | **0** | **1** | **1** | **10** | **0** | **0** | **0** | **3** | **0.0** | | **0** | **0.0** | **4:32** | .... | .... | .... | .... | .... | .... | .... | .... | .... |

Traded to **Nashville** by **Philadelphia** with Philadelphia's 7th round choice (later traded to St. Louis – St. Louis selected Maxwell Tardy) in 2009 Entry Draft for Janne Niskala, June 24, 2008.

## GRATTON, Chris

(GRAHT-uhn, KRIHS)

Center. Shoots left. 6'4", 226 lbs. Born, Brantford, Ont., July 5, 1975. Tampa Bay's 1st choice, 3rd overall, in 1993 Entry Draft.

| Season | Club | League | GP | G | A | Pts | PIM | PP | SH | GW | S | % | +/- | TF | F% | Min | GP | G | A | Pts | PIM | PP | SH | GW | Min |
|---|---|---|---|---|---|---|---|---|---|---|---|---|---|---|---|---|---|---|---|---|---|---|---|---|---|
| 1989-90 | Brantford Classics | OHA-B | 1 | 0 | 2 | 2 | 2 | .... | .... | .... | .... | .... | .... | .... | .... | .... | .... | .... | .... | .... | .... | .... | .... | .... | .... |
| 1990-91 | Brantford Classics | OHA-B | 31 | 30 | 30 | 60 | 28 | .... | .... | .... | .... | .... | .... | .... | .... | .... | .... | .... | .... | .... | .... | .... | .... | .... | .... |
| 1991-92 | Kingston | OHL | 62 | 27 | 39 | 66 | 37 | .... | .... | .... | .... | .... | .... | .... | .... | .... | .... | .... | .... | .... | .... | .... | .... | .... | .... |
| 1992-93 | Kingston | OHL | 58 | 55 | 54 | 109 | 125 | .... | .... | .... | .... | .... | .... | .... | .... | .... | 16 | 11 | 18 | 29 | 42 | .... | .... | .... | .... |
| **1993-94** | **Tampa Bay** | **NHL** | **84** | **13** | **29** | **42** | **123** | **5** | **1** | **2** | **161** | **8.1** | **–25** | .... | .... | .... | .... | .... | .... | .... | .... | .... | .... | .... | .... |
| **1994-95** | **Tampa Bay** | **NHL** | **46** | **7** | **20** | **27** | **89** | **2** | **0** | **0** | **91** | **7.7** | **–2** | .... | .... | .... | .... | .... | .... | .... | .... | .... | .... | .... | .... |
| **1995-96** | **Tampa Bay** | **NHL** | **82** | **17** | **21** | **38** | **105** | **7** | **0** | **3** | **183** | **9.3** | **–13** | .... | .... | .... | **6** | **0** | **2** | **2** | **27** | **0** | **0** | **0** | .... |
| **1996-97** | **Tampa Bay** | **NHL** | **82** | **30** | **32** | **62** | **201** | **9** | **0** | **4** | **230** | **13.0** | **–28** | .... | .... | .... | .... | .... | .... | .... | .... | .... | .... | .... | .... |
| **1997-98** | **Philadelphia** | **NHL** | **82** | **22** | **40** | **62** | **159** | **5** | **0** | **2** | **182** | **12.1** | **11** | .... | .... | .... | **5** | **2** | **0** | **2** | **10** | **0** | **0** | **0** | .... |
| **1998-99** | **Philadelphia** | **NHL** | **26** | **1** | **7** | **8** | **41** | **0** | **0** | **0** | **54** | **1.9** | **–8** | **38** | **42.1** | **14:25** | .... | .... | .... | .... | .... | .... | .... | .... | .... |
| | **Tampa Bay** | **NHL** | **52** | **7** | **19** | **26** | **102** | **1** | **0** | **1** | **127** | **5.5** | **–20** | **1032** | **53.9** | **18:20** | .... | .... | .... | .... | .... | .... | .... | .... | .... |
| **99-2000** | **Tampa Bay** | **NHL** | **58** | **14** | **27** | **41** | **121** | **4** | **0** | **1** | **168** | **8.3** | **–24** | **1341** | **55.9** | **20:03** | .... | .... | .... | .... | .... | .... | .... | .... | .... |
| | **Buffalo** | **NHL** | **14** | **1** | **7** | **8** | **15** | **0** | **0** | **0** | **34** | **2.9** | **1** | **256** | **54.3** | **16:40** | **5** | **0** | **1** | **1** | **4** | **0** | **0** | **0** | **14:56** |
| **2000-01** | **Buffalo** | **NHL** | **82** | **19** | **21** | **40** | **102** | **5** | **0** | **5** | **156** | **12.2** | **0** | **1161** | **57.3** | **14:37** | **13** | **6** | **4** | **10** | **14** | **2** | **0** | **1** | **12:33** |
| **2001-02** | **Buffalo** | **NHL** | **82** | **15** | **24** | **39** | **75** | **1** | **0** | **5** | **139** | **10.8** | **0** | **1297** | **53.8** | **14:57** | .... | .... | .... | .... | .... | .... | .... | .... | .... |
| **2002-03** | **Buffalo** | **NHL** | **66** | **15** | **29** | **44** | **86** | **4** | **0** | **2** | **187** | **8.0** | **–5** | **1099** | **58.9** | **16:26** | .... | .... | .... | .... | .... | .... | .... | .... | .... |
| | **Phoenix** | **NHL** | **14** | **0** | **1** | **1** | **21** | **0** | **0** | **0** | **28** | **0.0** | **–11** | **231** | **57.1** | **17:12** | .... | .... | .... | .... | .... | .... | .... | .... | .... |
| **2003-04** | **Phoenix** | **NHL** | **68** | **11** | **18** | **29** | **93** | **3** | **0** | **1** | **122** | **9.0** | **–19** | **1090** | **55.3** | **14:40** | .... | .... | .... | .... | .... | .... | .... | .... | .... |
| | **Colorado** | **NHL** | **13** | **2** | **1** | **3** | **18** | **0** | **0** | **0** | **28** | **7.1** | **1** | **252** | **57.5** | **16:55** | **11** | **0** | **0** | **0** | **27** | **0** | **0** | **0** | **12:14** |
| 2004-05 | | | DID NOT PLAY | | | | | | | | | | | | | | | | | | | | | | |
| **2005-06** | **Florida** | **NHL** | **76** | **17** | **22** | **39** | **104** | **4** | **1** | **2** | **135** | **12.6** | **6** | **960** | **51.3** | **15:43** | .... | .... | .... | .... | .... | .... | .... | .... | .... |
| **2006-07** | **Florida** | **NHL** | **81** | **13** | **22** | **35** | **94** | **1** | **0** | **1** | **131** | **9.9** | **1** | **517** | **56.7** | **12:06** | .... | .... | .... | .... | .... | .... | .... | .... | .... |
| **2007-08** | **Tampa Bay** | **NHL** | **60** | **10** | **11** | **21** | **77** | **1** | **0** | **1** | **92** | **10.9** | **–7** | **618** | **54.5** | **12:42** | .... | .... | .... | .... | .... | .... | .... | .... | .... |
| **2008-09** | **Tampa Bay** | **NHL** | **18** | **0** | **2** | **2** | **10** | **0** | **0** | **0** | **16** | **0.0** | **–3** | **180** | **62.2** | **10:48** | .... | .... | .... | .... | .... | .... | .... | .... | .... |
| | Norfolk Admirals | AHL | 24 | 3 | 12 | 15 | 8 | .... | .... | .... | .... | .... | .... | .... | .... | .... | .... | .... | .... | .... | .... | .... | .... | .... | .... |
| | **Columbus** | **NHL** | **6** | **0** | **1** | **1** | **2** | **0** | **0** | **0** | **4** | **0.0** | **2** | **49** | **44.9** | **9:46** | .... | .... | .... | .... | .... | .... | .... | .... | .... |
| | **NHL Totals** | | **1092** | **214** | **354** | **568** | **1638** | **52** | **2** | **30** | **2268** | **9.4** | | **10121** | **55.4** | **15:12** | **40** | **8** | **7** | **15** | **82** | **2** | **0** | **1** | **12:50** |

OHL All-Rookie Team (1992) • OHL Rookie of the Year (1992)

Signed as a free agent by **Philadelphia**, August 14, 1997. Traded to **Tampa Bay** by **Philadelphia** with Mike Sillinger for Mikael Renberg and Daymond Langkow, December 12, 1998. Traded to **Buffalo** by **Tampa Bay** with Tampa Bay's 2nd round choice (Derek Roy) in 2001 Entry Draft for Cory Sarich, Wayne Primeau, Brian Holzinger and Buffalo's 3rd round choice (Alexander Kharitonov) in 2000 Entry Draft, March 9, 2000. Traded to **Phoenix** by **Buffalo** with Buffalo's 4th round choice (later traded to Edmonton – Edmonton selected Liam Reddox) in 2004 Entry Draft for Daniel Briere and Phoenix's 3rd round choice (Andrej Sekera) in 2004 Entry Draft, March 10, 2003. Traded to **Colorado** by **Phoenix** with Ossi Vaananen and Phoenix's 2nd round choice (Paul Stastny) in 2005 Entry Draft for Derek Morris and Keith Ballard, March 9, 2004. Signed as a free agent by **Florida**, August 12, 2005. Traded to **Tampa Bay** by **Florida** for Tampa Bay's 2nd round choice (Jacob Markstrom) in 2008 Entry Draft, June 13, 2007. Claimed on waivers by **Columbus** from **Tampa Bay**, February 21, 2009.

## GRATTON, Josh

(GRAHT-uhn, JAWSH) **ATL.**

Left wing. Shoots left. 6'2", 215 lbs. Born, Brantford, Ont., September 9, 1982.

| Season | Club | League | GP | G | A | Pts | PIM | PP | SH | GW | S | % | +/- | TF | F% | Min | GP | G | A | Pts | PIM | PP | SH | GW | Min |
|---|---|---|---|---|---|---|---|---|---|---|---|---|---|---|---|---|---|---|---|---|---|---|---|---|---|
| 2000-01 | Sudbury Wolves | OHL | 44 | 5 | 13 | 18 | 110 | .... | .... | .... | .... | .... | .... | .... | .... | .... | 9 | 1 | 1 | 2 | 25 | .... | .... | .... | .... |
| 2001-02 | Sudbury Wolves | OHL | 14 | 5 | 4 | 9 | 47 | .... | .... | .... | .... | .... | .... | .... | .... | .... | .... | .... | .... | .... | .... | .... | .... | .... | .... |
| | Kingston | OHL | 46 | 14 | 14 | 28 | 140 | .... | .... | .... | .... | .... | .... | .... | .... | .... | 1 | 1 | 0 | 1 | 7 | .... | .... | .... | .... |
| 2002-03 | Windsor Spitfires | OHL | 62 | 26 | 30 | 56 | 192 | .... | .... | .... | .... | .... | .... | .... | .... | .... | 6 | 2 | 1 | 3 | 8 | .... | .... | .... | .... |
| 2003-04 | Cincinnati | AHL | 21 | 2 | 2 | 4 | 69 | .... | .... | .... | .... | .... | .... | .... | .... | .... | 8 | 0 | 0 | 0 | 35 | .... | .... | .... | .... |
| | San Diego Gulls | ECHL | 30 | 4 | 6 | 10 | 239 | .... | .... | .... | .... | .... | .... | .... | .... | .... | .... | .... | .... | .... | .... | .... | .... | .... | .... |
| 2004-05 | Philadelphia | AHL | 57 | 9 | 5 | 14 | 246 | .... | .... | .... | .... | .... | .... | .... | .... | .... | 21 | 3 | 3 | 6 | 78 | .... | .... | .... | .... |
| | Trenton Titans | ECHL | 1 | 0 | 0 | 0 | 0 | .... | .... | .... | .... | .... | .... | .... | .... | .... | .... | .... | .... | .... | .... | .... | .... | .... | .... |
| **2005-06** | **Philadelphia** | **NHL** | **3** | **0** | **0** | **0** | **14** | **0** | **0** | **0** | **3** | **0.0** | **0** | **0** | **0.0** | **5:00** | .... | .... | .... | .... | .... | .... | .... | .... | .... |
| | Philadelphia | AHL | 53 | 9 | 10 | 19 | 265 | .... | .... | .... | .... | .... | .... | .... | .... | .... | .... | .... | .... | .... | .... | .... | .... | .... | .... |
| | **Phoenix** | **NHL** | **11** | **1** | **0** | **1** | **30** | **0** | **0** | **0** | **14** | **7.1** | **–3** | **0** | **0.0** | **8:00** | .... | .... | .... | .... | .... | .... | .... | .... | .... |
| **2006-07** | **Phoenix** | **NHL** | **52** | **1** | **1** | **2** | **188** | **0** | **0** | **0** | **29** | **3.4** | **–9** | **1** | **0.0** | **5:54** | .... | .... | .... | .... | .... | .... | .... | .... | .... |
| | San Antonio | AHL | 3 | 1 | 1 | 2 | 8 | .... | .... | .... | .... | .... | .... | .... | .... | .... | .... | .... | .... | .... | .... | .... | .... | .... | .... |
| **2007-08** | **Phoenix** | **NHL** | **1** | **0** | **0** | **0** | **5** | **0** | **0** | **0** | **0** | **0.0** | **1** | **0** | **0.0** | **9:40** | .... | .... | .... | .... | .... | .... | .... | .... | .... |
| | San Antonio | AHL | 38 | 5 | 9 | 14 | 124 | .... | .... | .... | .... | .... | .... | .... | .... | .... | .... | .... | .... | .... | .... | .... | .... | .... | .... |
| | Hartford | AHL | 20 | 6 | 6 | 12 | 72 | .... | .... | .... | .... | .... | .... | .... | .... | .... | 4 | 0 | 1 | 1 | 11 | .... | .... | .... | .... |
| **2008-09** | Milwaukee | AHL | 7 | 2 | 3 | 5 | 10 | .... | .... | .... | .... | .... | .... | .... | .... | .... | .... | .... | .... | .... | .... | .... | .... | .... | .... |
| | **Philadelphia** | **NHL** | **19** | **1** | **2** | **3** | **57** | **0** | **0** | **0** | **14** | **7.1** | **–2** | **0** | **0.0** | **6:14** | .... | .... | .... | .... | .... | .... | .... | .... | .... |
| | Philadelphia | AHL | 14 | 1 | 0 | 1 | 46 | .... | .... | .... | .... | .... | .... | .... | .... | .... | 2 | 0 | 0 | 0 | 2 | .... | .... | .... | .... |
| | **NHL Totals** | | **86** | **3** | **3** | **6** | **294** | **0** | **0** | **0** | **60** | **5.0** | | **1** | **0.0** | **6:16** | .... | .... | .... | .... | .... | .... | .... | .... | .... |

Signed as a free agent by **Philadelphia**, July 27, 2004. Traded to **Phoenix** by **Philadelphia** with Florida's 2nd round choice (previously acquired, later traded to Detroit - Detroit selected Cory Emerton) in 2006 Entry Draft and Tampa Bay's 2nd round choice (previously acquired, later traded to Detroit - Detroit selected Shawn Matthias) in 2006 Entry Draft for Denis Gauthier, March 9, 2006. Traded to **NY Rangers** by **Phoenix** with David LeNeveu, Fredrik Sjostrom and Phoenix's 5th round choice (Roman Horak) in 2009 Entry Draft for Marcel Hossa and Al Montoya, February 26, 2008. Signed as a free agent by **Nashville**, July 9, 2008. Traded to **Philadelphia** by **Nashville** for Tim Ramholt, October 31, 2008. Signed as a free agent by **Atlanta**, July 30, 2009.

## GREBESHKOV, Denis

(greh-behsh-KAHV, DEH-nihs) **EDM.**

Defense. Shoots left. 6', 209 lbs. Born, Yaroslavl, USSR, October 11, 1983. Los Angeles' 1st choice, 18th overall, in 2002 Entry Draft.

| Season | Club | League | GP | G | A | Pts | PIM | PP | SH | GW | S | % | +/- | TF | F% | Min | GP | G | A | Pts | PIM | PP | SH | GW | Min |
|---|---|---|---|---|---|---|---|---|---|---|---|---|---|---|---|---|---|---|---|---|---|---|---|---|---|
| 99-2000 | Yaroslavl 2 | Russia-3 | 42 | 2 | 1 | 3 | 12 | .... | .... | .... | .... | .... | .... | .... | .... | .... | 6 | 0 | 0 | 0 | 2 | .... | .... | .... | .... |
| 2000-01 | Yaroslavl 2 | Russia-3 | 34 | 7 | 2 | 9 | 20 | .... | .... | .... | .... | .... | .... | .... | .... | .... | .... | .... | .... | .... | .... | .... | .... | .... | .... |
| 2001-02 | Yaroslavl 2 | Russia-3 | 7 | 1 | 1 | 2 | 2 | .... | .... | .... | .... | .... | .... | .... | .... | .... | .... | .... | .... | .... | .... | .... | .... | .... | .... |
| | Yaroslavl | Russia | 27 | 1 | 2 | 3 | 10 | .... | .... | .... | .... | .... | .... | .... | .... | .... | .... | .... | .... | .... | .... | .... | .... | .... | .... |
| 2002-03 | Yaroslavl | Russia | 48 | 0 | 7 | 7 | 26 | .... | .... | .... | .... | .... | .... | .... | .... | .... | 10 | 0 | 1 | 1 | 2 | .... | .... | .... | .... |
| **2003-04** | **Los Angeles** | **NHL** | **4** | **0** | **1** | **1** | **0** | **0** | **0** | **0** | **5** | **0.0** | **–4** | **0** | **0.0** | **18:29** | .... | .... | .... | .... | .... | .... | .... | .... | .... |
| | Manchester | AHL | 43 | 2 | 7 | 9 | 34 | .... | .... | .... | .... | .... | .... | .... | .... | .... | 6 | 0 | 1 | 1 | 6 | .... | .... | .... | .... |
| 2004-05 | Manchester | AHL | 75 | 5 | 44 | 49 | 87 | .... | .... | .... | .... | .... | .... | .... | .... | .... | 6 | 0 | 4 | 4 | 2 | .... | .... | .... | .... |
| **2005-06** | **Los Angeles** | **NHL** | **8** | **0** | **2** | **2** | **12** | **0** | **0** | **0** | **10** | **0.0** | **–4** | **0** | **0.0** | **15:16** | .... | .... | .... | .... | .... | .... | .... | .... | .... |
| | Manchester | AHL | 48 | 2 | 25 | 27 | 59 | .... | .... | .... | .... | .... | .... | .... | .... | .... | .... | .... | .... | .... | .... | .... | .... | .... | .... |
| | **NY Islanders** | **NHL** | **21** | **0** | **3** | **3** | **8** | **0** | **0** | **0** | **14** | **0.0** | **–8** | **0** | **0.0** | **17:11** | .... | .... | .... | .... | .... | .... | .... | .... | .... |
| | Bridgeport | AHL | .... | .... | .... | .... | .... | .... | .... | .... | .... | .... | .... | .... | .... | .... | 7 | 1 | 1 | 2 | 8 | .... | .... | .... | .... |
| 2006-07 | Yaroslavl | Russia | 47 | 8 | 9 | 17 | 79 | .... | .... | .... | .... | .... | .... | .... | .... | .... | 7 | 0 | 2 | 2 | 6 | .... | .... | .... | .... |
| **2007-08** | **Edmonton** | **NHL** | **71** | **3** | **15** | **18** | **22** | **1** | **0** | **0** | **34** | **8.8** | **2** | **0** | **0.0** | **16:53** | .... | .... | .... | .... | .... | .... | .... | .... | .... |
| **2008-09** | **Edmonton** | **NHL** | **72** | **7** | **32** | **39** | **38** | **2** | **0** | **0** | **62** | **11.3** | **12** | **0** | **0.0** | **21:10** | .... | .... | .... | .... | .... | .... | .... | .... | .... |
| | **NHL Totals** | | **176** | **10** | **53** | **63** | **80** | **3** | **0** | **0** | **125** | **8.0** | | **0** | **0.0** | **18:38** | .... | .... | .... | .... | .... | .... | .... | .... | .... |

Traded to **NY Islanders** by **Los Angeles** with Jeff Tambellini for Mark Parrish and Brent Sopel, March 8, 2006. Signed as a free agent by **Yaroslavl** (Russia), July 10, 2006. Traded to **Edmonton** by **NY Islanders** for Marc-Andre Bergeron and Edmonton's 3rd round choice (later traded back to Edmonton - later traded to Anaheim - later traded back to NY Islanders - NY Islanders selected Kirill Petrov) in 2008 Entry Draft, February 18, 2007.

## GREEN, Josh
(GREEN, JAWSH)

Left wing. Shoots left. 6'4", 225 lbs. Born, Camrose, Alta., November 16, 1977. Los Angeles' 1st choice, 30th overall, in 1996 Entry Draft.

| | | | Regular Season | | | | | | | | | | | | | | Playoffs | | | | | | | | |
|---|---|---|---|---|---|---|---|---|---|---|---|---|---|---|---|---|---|---|---|---|---|---|---|---|---|
| Season | Club | League | GP | G | A | Pts | PIM | PP | SH | GW | S | % | +/- | TF | F% | Min | GP | G | A | Pts | PIM | PP | SH | GW | Min |
| 1992-93 | Camrose Kodiaks | ABHL | 60 | 55 | 45 | 100 | 80 | | | | | | | | | | | | | | | | | | |
| 1993-94 | Medicine Hat | WHL | 63 | 22 | 22 | 44 | 43 | | | | | | | | | | 3 | 0 | 0 | 0 | 4 | | | | |
| 1994-95 | Medicine Hat | WHL | 68 | 32 | 23 | 55 | 64 | | | | | | | | | | 5 | 5 | 1 | 6 | 2 | | | | |
| 1995-96 | Medicine Hat | WHL | 46 | 18 | 25 | 43 | 55 | | | | | | | | | | 5 | 2 | 2 | 4 | 4 | | | | |
| 1996-97 | Medicine Hat | WHL | 51 | 25 | 32 | 57 | 61 | | | | | | | | | | | | | | | | | | |
| | Swift Current | WHL | 23 | 10 | 15 | 25 | 33 | | | | | | | | | | 10 | 9 | 7 | 16 | 19 | | | | |
| 1997-98 | Swift Current | WHL | 5 | 9 | 1 | 10 | 9 | | | | | | | | | | | | | | | | | | |
| | Portland | WHL | 26 | 26 | 18 | 44 | 27 | | | | | | | | | | | | | | | | | | |
| | Fredericton | AHL | 43 | 16 | 15 | 31 | 14 | | | | | | | | | | 4 | 1 | 3 | 4 | 6 | | | | |
| **1998-99** | **Los Angeles** | **NHL** | **27** | **1** | **3** | **4** | **8** | **1** | **0** | **0** | **35** | **2.9** | **–5** | **2** | **50.0** | **11:44** | | | | | | | | | |
| | Springfield | AHL | 41 | 15 | 15 | 30 | 29 | | | | | | | | | | | | | | | | | | |
| **99-2000** | **NY Islanders** | **NHL** | **49** | **12** | **14** | **26** | **41** | **2** | **0** | **3** | **109** | **11.0** | **–7** | **12** | **50.0** | **13:36** | | | | | | | | | |
| | Lowell | AHL | 17 | 6 | 2 | 8 | 19 | | | | | | | | | | | | | | | | | | |
| 2000-01 | Hamilton | AHL | 2 | 2 | 0 | 2 | 2 | | | | | | | | | | | | | | | | | | |
| | **Edmonton** | **NHL** | | | | | | | | | | | | | | | **3** | **0** | **0** | **0** | **0** | **0** | **0** | **0** | **7:55** |
| **2001-02** | **Edmonton** | **NHL** | **61** | **10** | **5** | **15** | **52** | **1** | **0** | **1** | **78** | **12.8** | **9** | **18** | **38.9** | **10:05** | | | | | | | | | |
| **2002-03** | **Edmonton** | **NHL** | **20** | **0** | **2** | **2** | **12** | **0** | **0** | **0** | **20** | **0.0** | **–3** | **5** | **0.0** | **10:22** | | | | | | | | | |
| | **NY Rangers** | **NHL** | **4** | **0** | **0** | **0** | **2** | **0** | **0** | **0** | **3** | **0.0** | **–1** | **0** | **0.0** | **9:07** | | | | | | | | | |
| | **Washington** | **NHL** | **21** | **1** | **2** | **3** | **7** | **0** | **0** | **0** | **20** | **5.0** | **1** | **3** | **0.0** | **8:07** | | | | | | | | | |
| **2003-04** | **Calgary** | **NHL** | **36** | **2** | **4** | **6** | **24** | **0** | **0** | **0** | **47** | **4.3** | **–3** | **39** | **30.8** | **11:18** | | | | | | | | | |
| | Lowell | AHL | 22 | 6 | 9 | 15 | 46 | | | | | | | | | | | | | | | | | | |
| | **NY Rangers** | **NHL** | **14** | **3** | **2** | **5** | **8** | **0** | **0** | **1** | **29** | **10.3** | **0** | **9** | **55.6** | **14:16** | | | | | | | | | |
| 2004-05 | Manitoba Moose | AHL | 67 | 21 | 19 | 40 | 72 | | | | | | | | | | 14 | 9 | 5 | 14 | 26 | | | | |
| **2005-06** | **Vancouver** | **NHL** | **33** | **4** | **2** | **6** | **14** | **0** | **0** | **0** | **35** | **11.4** | **2** | **146** | **40.4** | **8:35** | | | | | | | | | |
| | Manitoba Moose | AHL | 35 | 7 | 24 | 31 | 33 | | | | | | | | | | 10 | 5 | 5 | 10 | 23 | | | | |
| **2006-07** | **Vancouver** | **NHL** | **57** | **2** | **5** | **7** | **25** | **0** | **0** | **2** | **74** | **2.7** | **0** | **266** | **40.6** | **11:25** | **9** | **0** | **1** | **1** | **12** | **0** | **0** | **0** | **10:13** |
| 2007-08 | Salzburg | Austria | 43 | 20 | 22 | 42 | 100 | | | | | | | | | | | | | | | | | | |
| **2008-09** | Iowa Chops | AHL | 39 | 10 | 14 | 24 | 52 | | | | | | | | | | | | | | | | | | |
| | **Anaheim** | **NHL** | | | | | | | | | | | | | | | **5** | **0** | **0** | **0** | **0** | **0** | **0** | **0** | **5:53** |
| | **NHL Totals** | | **322** | **35** | **39** | **74** | **193** | **4** | **0** | **7** | **450** | **7.8** | | **500** | **39.6** | **11:02** | **17** | **0** | **1** | **1** | **12** | **0** | **0** | **0** | **8:32** |

Traded to **NY Islanders** by **Los Angeles** with Olli Jokinen, Mathieu Biron and Los Angeles' 1st round choice (Taylor Pyatt) in 1999 Entry Draft for Ziggy Palffy, Brian Smolinski, Marcel Cousineau and New Jersey's 4th round choice (previously acquired, Los Angeles selected Daniel Johansson) in 1999 Entry Draft, June 20, 1999. Traded to **Edmonton** by **NY Islanders** with Eric Brewer and NY Islanders' 2nd round choice (Brad Winchester) in 2000 Entry Draft for Roman Hamrlik, June 24, 2000. • Missed majority of 2000-01 season recovering from shoulder injury suffered in game vs. Detroit, October 10, 2000. Traded to **NY Rangers** by **Edmonton** for future considerations, December 12, 2002. Claimed on waivers by **Washington** from **NY Rangers**, January 15, 2003. Signed as a free agent by **Calgary**, July 17, 2003. Claimed on waivers by **NY Rangers** from **Calgary**, March 6, 2004. Signed to a PTO (tryout) contract by **Manitoba** (AHL), September 27, 2004. Signed as a free agent by **Vancouver**, August 23, 2005. Signed as a free agent by **Salzburg** (Austria), July 30, 2007. Signed as a free agent by **Anaheim**, July 22, 2008.

## GREEN, Mike
(GREEN, MIGHK) **WSH.**

Defense. Shoots right. 6'1", 208 lbs. Born, Calgary, Alta., October 12, 1985. Washington's 3rd choice, 29th overall, in 2004 Entry Draft.

| Season | Club | League | GP | G | A | Pts | PIM | PP | SH | GW | S | % | +/- | TF | F% | Min | GP | G | A | Pts | PIM | PP | SH | GW | Min |
|---|---|---|---|---|---|---|---|---|---|---|---|---|---|---|---|---|---|---|---|---|---|---|---|---|---|
| 2000-01 | Cgy. North Stars | AMHL | 36 | 4 | 23 | 27 | 34 | | | | | | | | | | | | | | | | | | |
| | Saskatoon Blades | WHL | 7 | 0 | 2 | 2 | 0 | | | | | | | | | | | | | | | | | | |
| 2001-02 | Saskatoon Blades | WHL | 62 | 3 | 20 | 23 | 57 | | | | | | | | | | 7 | 0 | 1 | 1 | 2 | | | | |
| 2002-03 | Saskatoon Blades | WHL | 72 | 6 | 36 | 42 | 70 | | | | | | | | | | 6 | 0 | 2 | 2 | 6 | | | | |
| 2003-04 | Saskatoon Blades | WHL | 59 | 14 | 25 | 39 | 92 | | | | | | | | | | | | | | | | | | |
| 2004-05 | Saskatoon Blades | WHL | 67 | 14 | 52 | 66 | 105 | | | | | | | | | | 4 | 0 | 0 | 0 | 6 | | | | |
| **2005-06** | **Washington** | **NHL** | **22** | **1** | **2** | **3** | **18** | **0** | **0** | **0** | **13** | **7.7** | **–8** | **0** | **0.0** | **14:54** | | | | | | | | | |
| | Hershey Bears | AHL | 56 | 9 | 34 | 43 | 79 | | | | | | | | | | 21 | 3 | 15 | 18 | 30 | | | | |
| **2006-07** | **Washington** | **NHL** | **70** | **2** | **10** | **12** | **36** | **0** | **0** | **0** | **68** | **2.9** | **–10** | **0** | **0.0** | **15:29** | | | | | | | | | |
| **2007-08** | **Washington** | **NHL** | **82** | **18** | **38** | **56** | **62** | **8** | **0** | **4** | **234** | **7.7** | **6** | **1** | **0.0** | **23:38** | **7** | **3** | **4** | **7** | **15** | **2** | **0** | **0** | **26:59** |
| **2008-09** | **Washington** | **NHL** | **68** | **31** | **42** | **73** | **68** | **18** | **1** | **4** | **243** | **12.8** | **24** | **0** | **0.0** | **25:46** | **14** | **1** | **8** | **9** | **12** | **1** | **0** | **0** | **24:59** |
| | **NHL Totals** | | **242** | **52** | **92** | **144** | **184** | **26** | **1** | **8** | **558** | **9.3** | | **1** | **0.0** | **21:05** | **21** | **4** | **12** | **16** | **27** | **3** | **0** | **0** | **25:39** |

WHL East First All-Star Team (2005) • AHL All-Rookie Team (2006) • NHL First All-Star Team (2009)

## GREENE, Andy
(GREEN, AN-dee) **N.J.**

Defense. Shoots left. 5'11", 190 lbs. Born, Trenton, MI, October 30, 1982.

| Season | Club | League | GP | G | A | Pts | PIM | PP | SH | GW | S | % | +/- | TF | F% | Min | GP | G | A | Pts | PIM | PP | SH | GW | Min |
|---|---|---|---|---|---|---|---|---|---|---|---|---|---|---|---|---|---|---|---|---|---|---|---|---|---|
| 2002-03 | Miami U. | CCHA | 41 | 4 | 19 | 23 | 64 | | | | | | | | | | | | | | | | | | |
| 2003-04 | Miami U. | CCHA | 41 | 7 | 19 | 26 | 78 | | | | | | | | | | | | | | | | | | |
| 2004-05 | Miami U. | CCHA | 38 | 7 | 27 | 34 | 66 | | | | | | | | | | | | | | | | | | |
| 2005-06 | Miami U. | CCHA | 39 | 9 | 22 | 31 | 48 | | | | | | | | | | | | | | | | | | |
| **2006-07** | **New Jersey** | **NHL** | **23** | **1** | **5** | **6** | **6** | **1** | **0** | **0** | **23** | **4.3** | **–1** | **0** | **0.0** | **14:15** | **11** | **2** | **1** | **3** | **2** | **0** | **0** | **1** | **17:04** |
| | Lowell Devils | AHL | 52 | 5 | 16 | 21 | 28 | | | | | | | | | | | | | | | | | | |
| **2007-08** | **New Jersey** | **NHL** | **59** | **2** | **8** | **10** | **22** | **2** | **0** | **0** | **50** | **4.0** | **0** | **0** | **0.0** | **19:30** | **2** | **0** | **0** | **0** | **0** | **0** | **0** | **0** | **15:11** |
| **2008-09** | **New Jersey** | **NHL** | **49** | **2** | **7** | **9** | **22** | **0** | **0** | **0** | **38** | **5.3** | **3** | **0** | **0.0** | **16:17** | **3** | **0** | **1** | **1** | **0** | **0** | **0** | **0** | **15:18** |
| | **NHL Totals** | | **131** | **5** | **20** | **25** | **50** | **3** | **0** | **0** | **111** | **4.5** | | **0** | **0.0** | **17:23** | **16** | **2** | **2** | **4** | **2** | **0** | **0** | **1** | **16:30** |

CCHA All-Rookie Team (2003) • CCHA First All-Star Team (2004, 2005, 2006) • NCAA West First All-American Team (2006)

Signed as a free agent by **New Jersey**, April 4, 2006.

## GREENE, Matt
(GREEN, MAT) **L.A.**

Defense. Shoots right. 6'4", 234 lbs. Born, Grand Ledge, MI, May 13, 1983. Edmonton's 4th choice, 44th overall, in 2002 Entry Draft.

| Season | Club | League | GP | G | A | Pts | PIM | PP | SH | GW | S | % | +/- | TF | F% | Min | GP | G | A | Pts | PIM | PP | SH | GW | Min |
|---|---|---|---|---|---|---|---|---|---|---|---|---|---|---|---|---|---|---|---|---|---|---|---|---|---|
| 2000-01 | USNTDP | U-18 | 34 | 0 | 9 | 9 | 8 | | | | | | | | | | | | | | | | | | |
| | USNTDP | USHL | 20 | 0 | 1 | 1 | 51 | | | | | | | | | | | | | | | | | | |
| 2001-02 | Green Bay | USHL | 55 | 4 | 20 | 24 | 150 | | | | | | | | | | 7 | 0 | 1 | 1 | 31 | | | | |
| 2002-03 | North Dakota | WCHA | 39 | 0 | 4 | 4 | *135 | | | | | | | | | | | | | | | | | | |
| 2003-04 | North Dakota | WCHA | 40 | 1 | 16 | 17 | 86 | | | | | | | | | | | | | | | | | | |
| 2004-05 | North Dakota | WCHA | 43 | 2 | 8 | 10 | *126 | | | | | | | | | | | | | | | | | | |
| **2005-06** | **Edmonton** | **NHL** | **27** | **0** | **2** | **2** | **43** | **0** | **0** | **0** | **10** | **0.0** | **–6** | **0** | **0.0** | **11:13** | **18** | **0** | **1** | **1** | **34** | **0** | **0** | **0** | **10:03** |
| | Iowa Stars | AHL | 26 | 2 | 5 | 7 | 47 | | | | | | | | | | | | | | | | | | |
| **2006-07** | **Edmonton** | **NHL** | **78** | **1** | **9** | **10** | **109** | **0** | **0** | **0** | **52** | **1.9** | **–22** | **0** | **0.0** | **17:36** | | | | | | | | | |
| **2007-08** | **Edmonton** | **NHL** | **46** | **0** | **1** | **1** | **53** | **0** | **0** | **0** | **28** | **0.0** | **–3** | **0** | **0.0** | **16:42** | | | | | | | | | |
| **2008-09** | **Los Angeles** | **NHL** | **82** | **2** | **12** | **14** | **111** | **0** | **0** | **0** | **76** | **2.6** | **1** | **1** | **100.0** | **19:44** | | | | | | | | | |
| | **NHL Totals** | | **233** | **3** | **24** | **27** | **316** | **0** | **0** | **0** | **166** | **1.8** | | **1** | **100.0** | **17:26** | **18** | **0** | **1** | **1** | **34** | **0** | **0** | **0** | **10:03** |

USHL Second All-Star Team (2002)

Traded to **Los Angeles** by **Edmonton** with Jarret Stoll for Lubomir Visnovsky, June 29, 2008.

## GREENTREE, Kyle
(GREEN-TREE, KIGHL) **CGY.**

Left wing. Shoots left. 6'3", 215 lbs. Born, Victoria, B.C., November 15, 1983.

| Season | Club | League | GP | G | A | Pts | PIM | PP | SH | GW | S | % | +/- | TF | F% | Min | GP | G | A | Pts | PIM | PP | SH | GW | Min |
|---|---|---|---|---|---|---|---|---|---|---|---|---|---|---|---|---|---|---|---|---|---|---|---|---|---|
| 99-2000 | Victoria Salsa | BCHL | 28 | 7 | 6 | 13 | 11 | | | | | | | | | | | | | | | | | | |
| 2000-01 | Victoria Salsa | BCHL | 59 | 27 | 38 | 65 | 50 | | | | | | | | | | | | | | | | | | |
| 2001-02 | Victoria Salsa | BCHL | 57 | 42 | 43 | 85 | 125 | | | | | | | | | | | | | | | | | | |
| 2002-03 | Victoria Salsa | BCHL | 52 | 46 | 53 | 99 | 110 | | | | | | | | | | | | | | | | | | |
| 2003-04 | Victoria Salsa | BCHL | 59 | 62 | 53 | 115 | 170 | | | | | | | | | | 5 | 4 | 5 | 9 | 29 | | | | |
| 2004-05 | Alaska | CCHA | 37 | 12 | 20 | 32 | 31 | | | | | | | | | | | | | | | | | | |
| 2005-06 | Alaska | CCHA | 39 | 8 | 19 | 27 | 58 | | | | | | | | | | | | | | | | | | |
| 2006-07 | Alaska | CCHA | 39 | 21 | 21 | 42 | 78 | | | | | | | | | | | | | | | | | | |
| | Philadelphia | AHL | 8 | 2 | 0 | 2 | 2 | | | | | | | | | | | | | | | | | | |
| **2007-08** | **Philadelphia** | **NHL** | **2** | **0** | **0** | **0** | **0** | **0** | **0** | **0** | **3** | **0.0** | **–1** | **0** | **0.0** | **9:12** | | | | | | | | | |
| | Philadelphia | AHL | 72 | 24 | 24 | 48 | 83 | | | | | | | | | | 12 | 1 | 3 | 4 | 11 | | | | |
| **2008-09** | **Calgary** | **NHL** | **2** | **0** | **0** | **0** | **0** | **0** | **0** | **0** | **3** | **0.0** | **–1** | **0** | **0.0** | **9:18** | | | | | | | | | |
| | Quad City Flames | AHL | 79 | 39 | 37 | 76 | 63 | | | | | | | | | | | | | | | | | | |
| | **NHL Totals** | | **4** | **0** | **0** | **0** | **0** | **0** | **0** | **0** | **6** | **0.0** | | **0** | **0.0** | **9:15** | | | | | | | | | |

Signed as a free agent by **Philadelphia**, March 14, 2007. Traded to **Calgary** by **Philadelphia** for Tim Ramholt, June 30, 2008.

## GRIER, Mike

(GREER, MIGHK) **BUF.**

Right wing. Shoots right. 6'1", 225 lbs. Born, Detroit, MI, January 5, 1975. St. Louis' 7th choice, 219th overall, in 1993 Entry Draft.

| | | | Regular Season | | | | | | | | | | | | | | Playoffs | | | | | | | | |
|---|---|---|---|---|---|---|---|---|---|---|---|---|---|---|---|---|---|---|---|---|---|---|---|---|---|
| Season | Club | League | GP | G | A | Pts | PIM | PP | SH | GW | S | % | +/- | TF | F% | Min | GP | G | A | Pts | PIM | PP | SH | GW | Min |
| 1992-93 | St. Sebastian's | High-MA | 22 | 16 | 27 | 43 | 32 | .... | .... | .... | .... | .... | .... | .... | .... | .... | .... | .... | .... | .... | .... | .... | .... | .... | .... |
| 1993-94 | Boston University | H-East | 39 | 9 | 9 | 18 | 56 | .... | .... | .... | .... | .... | .... | .... | .... | .... | .... | .... | .... | .... | .... | .... | .... | .... | .... |
| 1994-95 | Boston University | H-East | 37 | *29 | 26 | 55 | 85 | .... | .... | .... | .... | .... | .... | .... | .... | .... | .... | .... | .... | .... | .... | .... | .... | .... | .... |
| 1995-96 | Boston University | H-East | 38 | 21 | 25 | 46 | 82 | .... | .... | .... | .... | .... | .... | .... | .... | .... | .... | .... | .... | .... | .... | .... | .... | .... | .... |
| 1996-97 | Edmonton | NHL | 79 | 15 | 17 | 32 | 45 | 4 | 0 | 2 | 89 | 16.9 | 7 | .... | .... | .... | 12 | 3 | 1 | 4 | 4 | 1 | 0 | 1 | .... |
| 1997-98 | Edmonton | NHL | 66 | 9 | 6 | 15 | 73 | 1 | 0 | 1 | 90 | 10.0 | –3 | .... | .... | .... | 12 | 2 | 2 | 4 | 13 | 0 | 0 | 1 | .... |
| 1998-99 | Edmonton | NHL | 82 | 20 | 24 | 44 | 54 | 3 | 2 | 1 | 143 | 14.0 | 5 | 34 | 20.6 | 15:57 | 4 | 1 | 1 | 2 | 6 | 0 | 0 | 0 | 23:26 |
| 99-2000 | Edmonton | NHL | 65 | 9 | 22 | 31 | 68 | 0 | 3 | 2 | 115 | 7.8 | 9 | 32 | 46.8 | 15:45 | .... | .... | .... | .... | .... | .... | .... | .... | .... |
| 2000-01 | Edmonton | NHL | 74 | 20 | 16 | 36 | 20 | 2 | 3 | 2 | 124 | 16.1 | 11 | 36 | 38.9 | 16:44 | 6 | 0 | 0 | 0 | 8 | 0 | 0 | 0 | 21:23 |
| 2001-02 | Edmonton | NHL | 82 | 8 | 17 | 25 | 32 | 0 | 2 | 3 | 112 | 7.1 | 1 | 38 | 47.4 | 15:01 | .... | .... | .... | .... | .... | .... | .... | .... | .... |
| 2002-03 | Washington | NHL | 82 | 15 | 17 | 32 | 36 | 2 | 2 | 2 | 133 | 11.3 | –14 | 98 | 43.9 | 17:48 | 6 | 1 | 1 | 2 | 2 | 0 | 0 | 0 | 17:59 |
| 2003-04 | Washington | NHL | 68 | 8 | 12 | 20 | 32 | 1 | 1 | 0 | 115 | 7.0 | –19 | 54 | 44.4 | 17:25 | .... | .... | .... | .... | .... | .... | .... | .... | .... |
| | Buffalo | NHL | 14 | 1 | 8 | 9 | 4 | 0 | 0 | 0 | 18 | 5.6 | 10 | 11 | 63.6 | 17:29 | .... | .... | .... | .... | .... | .... | .... | .... | .... |
| 2004-05 | | | DID NOT PLAY | | | | | | | | | | | | | | | | | | | | | | |
| 2005-06 | Buffalo | NHL | 81 | 7 | 16 | 23 | 28 | 0 | 0 | 4 | 109 | 6.4 | –7 | 9 | 22.2 | 14:22 | 18 | 3 | 5 | 8 | 2 | 0 | 1 | 0 | 16:17 |
| 2006-07 | San Jose | NHL | 81 | 16 | 17 | 33 | 43 | 2 | 3 | 1 | 125 | 12.8 | –5 | 46 | 41.3 | 16:26 | 11 | 2 | 2 | 4 | 27 | 0 | 0 | 0 | 17:16 |
| 2007-08 | San Jose | NHL | 78 | 9 | 13 | 22 | 24 | 1 | 3 | 4 | 132 | 6.8 | –8 | 86 | 25.6 | 16:13 | 13 | 0 | 1 | 1 | 2 | 0 | 0 | 0 | 15:20 |
| 2008-09 | San Jose | NHL | 62 | 10 | 13 | 23 | 25 | 0 | 1 | 2 | 108 | 9.3 | 8 | 43 | 34.9 | 15:00 | 6 | 0 | 0 | 0 | 6 | 0 | 0 | 0 | 10:33 |
| | NHL Totals | | 914 | 147 | 198 | 345 | 484 | 16 | 20 | 24 | 1413 | 10.4 | | 487 | 38.2 | 16:06 | 88 | 12 | 13 | 25 | 70 | 1 | 1 | 2 | 16:48 |

Hockey East First All-Star Team (1995) • NCAA East First All-American Team (1995)

• Rights traded to **Edmonton** by **St. Louis** with Curtis Joseph for St. Louis' 1st round choices in 1996 (previously acquired, St. Louis selected Marty Reasoner) and 1997 (previously acquired, later traded to Los Angeles – Los Angeles selected Matt Zultek) Entry Drafts, August 4, 1995. Traded to **Washington** by **Edmonton** for Washington's 2nd round choice (later traded to NY Islanders – NY Islanders selected Evgeni Tunik) in 2003 Entry Draft and Vancouver's 3rd round choice (previously acquired, Edmonton selected Zachery Stortini) in 2003 Entry Draft, October 7, 2002. Traded to **Buffalo** by **Washington** for Jakub Klepis, March 9, 2004. Signed as a free agent by **San Jose**, July 3, 2006. Signed as a free agent by **Buffalo**, August 10, 2009.

## GROSSMAN, Nicklas

(GROHS-man, NIHK-luhs) **DAL.**

Defense. Shoots left. 6'3", 206 lbs. Born, Stockholm, Sweden, January 22, 1985. Dallas' 4th choice, 56th overall, in 2004 Entry Draft.

| Season | Club | League | GP | G | A | Pts | PIM | PP | SH | GW | S | % | +/- | TF | F% | Min | GP | G | A | Pts | PIM | PP | SH | GW | Min |
|---|---|---|---|---|---|---|---|---|---|---|---|---|---|---|---|---|---|---|---|---|---|---|---|---|---|
| 2002-03 | Sodertalje SK Jr. | Swe-Jr. | 34 | 1 | 1 | 2 | 32 | .... | .... | .... | .... | .... | .... | .... | .... | .... | .... | .... | .... | .... | .... | .... | .... | .... | .... |
| 2003-04 | Sodertalje SK Jr. | Swe-Jr. | 33 | 1 | 2 | 3 | 32 | .... | .... | .... | .... | .... | .... | .... | .... | .... | 2 | 0 | 0 | 0 | 0 | .... | .... | .... | .... |
| | Sodertalje SK | Sweden | 1 | 0 | 0 | 0 | 0 | .... | .... | .... | .... | .... | .... | .... | .... | .... | .... | .... | .... | .... | .... | .... | .... | .... | .... |
| 2004-05 | Sodertalje SK Jr. | Swe-Jr. | 12 | 3 | 6 | 9 | 8 | .... | .... | .... | .... | .... | .... | .... | .... | .... | 1 | 0 | 0 | 0 | 0 | .... | .... | .... | .... |
| | Sodertalje SK | Sweden | 31 | 0 | 2 | 2 | 14 | .... | .... | .... | .... | .... | .... | .... | .... | .... | 9 | 0 | 0 | 0 | 0 | .... | .... | .... | .... |
| 2005-06 | Iowa Stars | AHL | 61 | 2 | 3 | 5 | 49 | .... | .... | .... | .... | .... | .... | .... | .... | .... | 7 | 0 | 1 | 1 | 4 | .... | .... | .... | .... |
| 2006-07 | Dallas | NHL | 8 | 0 | 0 | 0 | 4 | 0 | 0 | 0 | 8 | 0.0 | –1 | 0 | 0.0 | 12:49 | .... | .... | .... | .... | .... | .... | .... | .... | .... |
| | Iowa Stars | AHL | 67 | 2 | 8 | 10 | 40 | .... | .... | .... | .... | .... | .... | .... | .... | .... | 8 | 0 | 0 | 0 | 10 | .... | .... | .... | .... |
| 2007-08 | Dallas | NHL | 62 | 0 | 7 | 7 | 22 | 0 | 0 | 0 | 34 | 0.0 | 10 | 0 | 0.0 | 15:33 | 18 | 1 | 1 | 2 | 6 | 0 | 0 | 0 | 18:37 |
| | Iowa Stars | AHL | 10 | 0 | 0 | 0 | 10 | .... | .... | .... | .... | .... | .... | .... | .... | .... | .... | .... | .... | .... | .... | .... | .... | .... | .... |
| 2008-09 | Dallas | NHL | 81 | 2 | 10 | 12 | 51 | 0 | 0 | 1 | 60 | 3.3 | –8 | 0 | 0.0 | 17:39 | .... | .... | .... | .... | .... | .... | .... | .... | .... |
| | NHL Totals | | 151 | 2 | 17 | 19 | 77 | 0 | 0 | 1 | 102 | 2.0 | | 0 | 0.0 | 16:32 | 18 | 1 | 1 | 2 | 6 | 0 | 0 | 0 | 18:37 |

## GUENIN, Nate

(GEH-nihn, NAYT) **PIT.**

Defense. Shoots right. 6'2", 210 lbs. Born, Sewickley, PA, December 10, 1982. NY Rangers' 3rd choice, 127th overall, in 2002 Entry Draft.

| Season | Club | League | GP | G | A | Pts | PIM | PP | SH | GW | S | % | +/- | TF | F% | Min | GP | G | A | Pts | PIM | PP | SH | GW | Min |
|---|---|---|---|---|---|---|---|---|---|---|---|---|---|---|---|---|---|---|---|---|---|---|---|---|---|
| 99-2000 | Pittsburgh | AAHA | 40 | 3 | 10 | 13 | 122 | .... | .... | .... | .... | .... | .... | .... | .... | .... | .... | .... | .... | .... | .... | .... | .... | .... | .... |
| 2000-01 | Green Bay | USHL | 54 | 2 | 11 | 13 | 70 | .... | .... | .... | .... | .... | .... | .... | .... | .... | 4 | 1 | 1 | 2 | 6 | .... | .... | .... | .... |
| 2001-02 | Green Bay | USHL | 56 | 4 | 11 | 15 | 150 | .... | .... | .... | .... | .... | .... | .... | .... | .... | 7 | 3 | 3 | 6 | 10 | .... | .... | .... | .... |
| 2002-03 | Ohio State | CCHA | 42 | 2 | 9 | 11 | 85 | .... | .... | .... | .... | .... | .... | .... | .... | .... | .... | .... | .... | .... | .... | .... | .... | .... | .... |
| 2003-04 | Ohio State | CCHA | 29 | 2 | 15 | 17 | 92 | .... | .... | .... | .... | .... | .... | .... | .... | .... | .... | .... | .... | .... | .... | .... | .... | .... | .... |
| 2004-05 | Ohio State | CCHA | 41 | 2 | 12 | 14 | 136 | .... | .... | .... | .... | .... | .... | .... | .... | .... | .... | .... | .... | .... | .... | .... | .... | .... | .... |
| 2005-06 | Ohio State | CCHA | 39 | 0 | 11 | 11 | 87 | .... | .... | .... | .... | .... | .... | .... | .... | .... | .... | .... | .... | .... | .... | .... | .... | .... | .... |
| 2006-07 | Philadelphia | NHL | 9 | 0 | 2 | 2 | 4 | 0 | 0 | 0 | 0 | 0.0 | 0 | 0 | 0.0 | 8:40 | .... | .... | .... | .... | .... | .... | .... | .... | .... |
| | Philadelphia | AHL | 68 | 3 | 9 | 12 | 92 | .... | .... | .... | .... | .... | .... | .... | .... | .... | .... | .... | .... | .... | .... | .... | .... | .... | .... |
| 2007-08 | Philadelphia | NHL | 2 | 0 | 0 | 0 | 2 | 0 | 0 | 0 | 0 | 0.0 | 2 | 0 | 0.0 | 9:57 | .... | .... | .... | .... | .... | .... | .... | .... | .... |
| | Philadelphia | AHL | 77 | 4 | 13 | 17 | 146 | .... | .... | .... | .... | .... | .... | .... | .... | .... | 12 | 0 | 1 | 1 | 18 | .... | .... | .... | .... |
| 2008-09 | Philadelphia | NHL | 1 | 0 | 0 | 0 | 0 | 0 | 0 | 0 | 0 | 0.0 | 0 | 0 | 0.0 | 13:25 | .... | .... | .... | .... | .... | .... | .... | .... | .... |
| | Philadelphia | AHL | 62 | 0 | 14 | 14 | 95 | .... | .... | .... | .... | .... | .... | .... | .... | .... | 4 | 0 | 0 | 0 | 10 | .... | .... | .... | .... |
| | NHL Totals | | 12 | 0 | 2 | 2 | 6 | 0 | 0 | 0 | 0 | 0.0 | | 0 | 0.0 | 9:17 | .... | .... | .... | .... | .... | .... | .... | .... | .... |

USHL All-Rookie Team (2001) • CCHA Second All-Star Team (2005)

Signed as a free agent by **Philadelphia**, August 16, 2006. Signed as a free agent by **Pittsburgh**, July 3, 2009.

## GUERIN, Bill

(GAIR-ihn, BIHL) **PIT.**

Right wing. Shoots right. 6'2", 220 lbs. Born, Worcester, MA, November 9, 1970. New Jersey's 1st choice, 5th overall, in 1989 Entry Draft.

| Season | Club | League | GP | G | A | Pts | PIM | PP | SH | GW | S | % | +/- | TF | F% | Min | GP | G | A | Pts | PIM | PP | SH | GW | Min |
|---|---|---|---|---|---|---|---|---|---|---|---|---|---|---|---|---|---|---|---|---|---|---|---|---|---|
| 1985-86 | Spring. Olympics | NEJHL | 48 | 26 | 19 | 45 | 71 | .... | .... | .... | .... | .... | .... | .... | .... | .... | .... | .... | .... | .... | .... | .... | .... | .... | .... |
| 1986-87 | Spring. Olympics | NEJHL | 32 | 34 | 20 | 54 | 40 | .... | .... | .... | .... | .... | .... | .... | .... | .... | .... | .... | .... | .... | .... | .... | .... | .... | .... |
| 1987-88 | Spring. Olympics | NEJHL | 38 | 31 | 44 | 75 | 146 | .... | .... | .... | .... | .... | .... | .... | .... | .... | .... | .... | .... | .... | .... | .... | .... | .... | .... |
| 1988-89 | Spring. Olympics | NEJHL | 31 | 32 | 35 | 67 | 90 | .... | .... | .... | .... | .... | .... | .... | .... | .... | .... | .... | .... | .... | .... | .... | .... | .... | .... |
| 1989-90 | Boston College | H-East | 39 | 14 | 11 | 25 | 54 | .... | .... | .... | .... | .... | .... | .... | .... | .... | .... | .... | .... | .... | .... | .... | .... | .... | .... |
| 1990-91 | Boston College | H-East | 38 | 26 | 19 | 45 | 102 | .... | .... | .... | .... | .... | .... | .... | .... | .... | .... | .... | .... | .... | .... | .... | .... | .... | .... |
| 1991-92 | United States | Nat-Tm | 46 | 12 | 15 | 27 | 67 | .... | .... | .... | .... | .... | .... | .... | .... | .... | .... | .... | .... | .... | .... | .... | .... | .... | .... |
| | New Jersey | NHL | 5 | 0 | 1 | 1 | 9 | 0 | 0 | 0 | 8 | 0.0 | 1 | .... | .... | .... | 6 | 3 | 0 | 3 | 4 | 0 | 0 | 0 | .... |
| | Utica Devils | AHL | 22 | 13 | 10 | 23 | 6 | .... | .... | .... | .... | .... | .... | .... | .... | .... | 4 | 1 | 3 | 4 | 14 | .... | .... | .... | .... |
| 1992-93 | New Jersey | NHL | 65 | 14 | 20 | 34 | 63 | 0 | 0 | 2 | 123 | 11.4 | 14 | .... | .... | .... | 5 | 1 | 1 | 2 | 4 | 0 | 0 | 0 | .... |
| | Utica Devils | AHL | 18 | 10 | 7 | 17 | 47 | .... | .... | .... | .... | .... | .... | .... | .... | .... | .... | .... | .... | .... | .... | .... | .... | .... | .... |
| 1993-94 | New Jersey | NHL | 81 | 25 | 19 | 44 | 101 | 2 | 0 | 3 | 195 | 12.8 | 14 | .... | .... | .... | 17 | 2 | 1 | 3 | 35 | 0 | 0 | 1 | .... |
| 1994-95 ♦ | New Jersey | NHL | 48 | 12 | 13 | 25 | 72 | 4 | 0 | 3 | 96 | 12.5 | 6 | .... | .... | .... | 20 | 3 | 8 | 11 | 30 | 1 | 0 | 0 | .... |
| 1995-96 | New Jersey | NHL | 80 | 23 | 30 | 53 | 116 | 8 | 0 | 6 | 216 | 10.6 | 7 | .... | .... | .... | .... | .... | .... | .... | .... | .... | .... | .... | .... |
| 1996-97 | New Jersey | NHL | 82 | 29 | 18 | 47 | 95 | 7 | 0 | 9 | 177 | 16.4 | –2 | .... | .... | .... | 8 | 2 | 1 | 3 | 18 | 1 | 0 | 1 | .... |
| 1997-98 | New Jersey | NHL | 19 | 5 | 5 | 10 | 13 | 1 | 0 | 2 | 48 | 10.4 | 0 | .... | .... | .... | .... | .... | .... | .... | .... | .... | .... | .... | .... |
| | Edmonton | NHL | 40 | 13 | 16 | 29 | 80 | 8 | 0 | 2 | 130 | 10.0 | 1 | .... | .... | .... | 12 | 7 | 1 | 8 | 17 | 4 | 0 | 0 | .... |
| | United States | Olympics | 4 | 0 | 3 | 3 | 2 | .... | .... | .... | .... | .... | .... | .... | .... | .... | .... | .... | .... | .... | .... | .... | .... | .... | .... |
| 1998-99 | Edmonton | NHL | 80 | 30 | 34 | 64 | 133 | 13 | 0 | 2 | 261 | 11.5 | 7 | 74 | 40.5 | 19:42 | 3 | 0 | 2 | 2 | 2 | 0 | 0 | 0 | 26:14 |
| 99-2000 | Edmonton | NHL | 70 | 24 | 22 | 46 | 123 | 11 | 0 | 2 | 188 | 12.8 | 4 | 13 | 46.2 | 18:01 | 5 | 3 | 2 | 5 | 9 | 1 | 0 | 0 | 17:55 |
| 2000-01 | Edmonton | NHL | 21 | 12 | 10 | 22 | 18 | 4 | 0 | 1 | 64 | 18.8 | 11 | 0 | 0.0 | 19:49 | .... | .... | .... | .... | .... | .... | .... | .... | .... |
| | Boston | NHL | 64 | 28 | 35 | 63 | 122 | 7 | 1 | 4 | 225 | 12.4 | –4 | 36 | 41.7 | 22:43 | .... | .... | .... | .... | .... | .... | .... | .... | .... |
| 2001-02 | Boston | NHL | 78 | 41 | 25 | 66 | 91 | 10 | 1 | 7 | 355 | 11.5 | –1 | 17 | 52.9 | 20:45 | 6 | 4 | 2 | 6 | 6 | 3 | 0 | 0 | 21:17 |
| | United States | Olympics | 6 | 4 | 0 | 4 | 4 | .... | .... | .... | .... | .... | .... | .... | .... | .... | .... | .... | .... | .... | .... | .... | .... | .... | .... |
| 2002-03 | Dallas | NHL | 64 | 25 | 25 | 50 | 113 | 11 | 0 | 2 | 229 | 10.9 | 5 | 20 | 25.0 | 18:33 | 4 | 0 | 0 | 0 | 4 | 0 | 0 | 0 | 8:34 |
| 2003-04 | Dallas | NHL | 82 | 34 | 35 | 69 | 109 | 9 | 0 | 10 | 263 | 12.9 | 14 | 16 | 18.8 | 18:42 | 5 | 0 | 1 | 1 | 4 | 0 | 0 | 0 | 20:09 |
| 2004-05 | | | DID NOT PLAY | | | | | | | | | | | | | | | | | | | | | | |
| 2005-06 | Dallas | NHL | 70 | 13 | 27 | 40 | 115 | 3 | 0 | 2 | 210 | 6.2 | 0 | 16 | 50.0 | 16:25 | 5 | 3 | 1 | 4 | 0 | 1 | 0 | 0 | 16:14 |
| | United States | Olympics | 6 | 1 | 0 | 1 | 0 | .... | .... | .... | .... | .... | .... | .... | .... | .... | .... | .... | .... | .... | .... | .... | .... | .... | .... |
| 2006-07 | St. Louis | NHL | 61 | 28 | 19 | 47 | 52 | 7 | 0 | 6 | 189 | 14.8 | 8 | 10 | 50.0 | 17:26 | .... | .... | .... | .... | .... | .... | .... | .... | .... |
| | San Jose | NHL | 16 | 8 | 1 | 9 | 14 | 2 | 0 | 1 | 36 | 22.2 | 2 | 2 | 50.0 | 15:22 | 9 | 0 | 2 | 2 | 12 | 0 | 0 | 0 | 17:06 |
| 2007-08 | NY Islanders | NHL | 81 | 23 | 21 | 44 | 65 | 7 | 0 | 5 | 227 | 10.1 | –15 | 18 | 66.7 | 17:23 | .... | .... | .... | .... | .... | .... | .... | .... | .... |
| 2008-09 | NY Islanders | NHL | 61 | 16 | 20 | 36 | 63 | 5 | 0 | 3 | 181 | 8.8 | –15 | 61 | 44.3 | 17:13 | .... | .... | .... | .... | .... | .... | .... | .... | .... |
| | ♦ Pittsburgh | NHL | 17 | 5 | 7 | 12 | 18 | 0 | 0 | 1 | 45 | 11.1 | 3 | 3 | 100.0 | 14:44 | 24 | 7 | 8 | 15 | 15 | 2 | 0 | 2 | 17:01 |
| | NHL Totals | | 1185 | 408 | 403 | 811 | 1585 | 119 | 2 | 73 | 3466 | 11.8 | | 286 | 43.4 | 18:35 | 129 | 35 | 30 | 65 | 160 | 13 | 0 | 4 | 17:37 |

NHL Second All-Star Team (2002)

Played in NHL All-Star Game (2001, 2003, 2004, 2007)

Traded to **Edmonton** by **New Jersey** with Valeri Zelepukin for Jason Arnott and Bryan Muir, January 4, 1998. Traded to **Boston** by **Edmonton** for Anson Carter, Boston's 1st (Ales Hemsky) and 2nd (Doug Lynch) round choices in 2001 Entry Draft and future considerations, November 15, 2000. Signed as a free agent by **Dallas**, July 3, 2002. Signed as a free agent by **St. Louis**, July 3, 2006. Traded to **San Jose** by **St. Louis** for Ville Nieminen, Jay Barriball and New Jersey's 1st round choice (previously acquired, St. Louis selected David Perron) in 2007 Entry Draft, February 27, 2007. Signed as a free agent by **NY Islanders**, July 5, 2007. Traded to **Pittsburgh** by **NY Islanders** for Pittsburgh's 3rd round choice (later traded to Phoenix – Phoenix selected Michael Lee) in 2009 Entry Draft, March 4, 2009.

## GUITE, Ben

(GEE-tay, BEHN) **NSH.**

Right wing. Shoots right. 6'1", 211 lbs. Born, Montreal, Que., July 17, 1978. Montreal's 8th choice, 172nd overall, in 1997 Entry Draft.

| Season | Club | League | Regular Season GP | G | A | Pts | PIM | PP | SH | GW | S | % | +/- | TF | F% | Min | Playoffs GP | G | A | Pts | PIM | PP | SH | GW | Min |
|---|---|---|---|---|---|---|---|---|---|---|---|---|---|---|---|---|---|---|---|---|---|---|---|---|---|
| 1994-95 | Lac St-Louis Lions | QAAA | 40 | 9 | 12 | 21 | | | | | | | | | | | 4 | 0 | 0 | 0 | 0 | | | | |
| 1995-96 | Capital District | Exhib. | STATISTICS NOT AVAILABLE | | | | | | | | | | | | | | | | | | | | | | |
| 1996-97 | U. of Maine | H-East | 34 | 7 | 7 | 14 | 21 | | | | | | | | | | | | | | | | | | |
| 1997-98 | U. of Maine | H-East | 32 | 6 | 12 | 18 | 20 | | | | | | | | | | | | | | | | | | |
| 1998-99 | U. of Maine | H-East | 40 | 12 | 16 | 28 | 30 | | | | | | | | | | | | | | | | | | |
| 99-2000 | U. of Maine | H-East | 40 | 22 | 14 | 36 | 36 | | | | | | | | | | | | | | | | | | |
| 2000-01 | Tallahassee | ECHL | 68 | 11 | 18 | 29 | 34 | | | | | | | | | | | | | | | | | | |
| 2001-02 | Bridgeport | AHL | 68 | 12 | 18 | 30 | 39 | | | | | | | | | | | | | | | | | | |
| | Cincinnati | AHL | 10 | 2 | 5 | 7 | 4 | | | | | | | | | | 3 | 0 | 0 | 0 | 2 | | | | |
| 2002-03 | Cincinnati | AHL | 80 | 13 | 16 | 29 | 44 | | | | | | | | | | | | | | | | | | |
| 2003-04 | Bridgeport | AHL | 79 | 6 | 18 | 24 | 73 | | | | | | | | | | 7 | 0 | 0 | 0 | 6 | | | | |
| 2004-05 | Providence Bruins | AHL | 77 | 9 | 15 | 24 | 69 | | | | | | | | | | 17 | 3 | 4 | 7 | 34 | | | | |
| **2005-06** | **Boston** | **NHL** | **1** | **0** | **0** | **0** | **0** | **0** | **0** | **0** | **2** | **0.0** | **0** | **11** | **18.2** | **8:53** | | | | | | | | | |
| | Providence Bruins | AHL | 73 | 22 | 30 | 52 | 87 | | | | | | | | | | 6 | 1 | 3 | 4 | 14 | | | | |
| **2006-07** | **Colorado** | **NHL** | **39** | **3** | **8** | **11** | **16** | **0** | **1** | **1** | **63** | **4.8** | **-4** | **388** | **49.5** | **12:17** | | | | | | | | | |
| | Albany River Rats | AHL | 36 | 10 | 19 | 29 | 22 | | | | | | | | | | | | | | | | | | |
| **2007-08** | **Colorado** | **NHL** | **79** | **11** | **11** | **22** | **47** | **0** | **0** | **2** | **103** | **10.7** | **1** | **805** | **48.0** | **13:05** | **10** | **1** | **0** | **1** | **14** | **0** | **1** | **0** | **12:02** |
| **2008-09** | **Colorado** | **NHL** | **50** | **5** | **7** | **12** | **30** | **0** | **0** | **1** | **63** | **7.9** | **2** | **555** | **51.5** | **12:43** | | | | | | | | | |
| | **NHL Totals** | | **169** | **19** | **26** | **45** | **93** | **0** | **1** | **4** | **231** | **8.2** | | **1759** | **49.2** | **12:46** | **10** | **1** | **0** | **1** | **14** | **0** | **1** | **0** | **12:02** |

Signed as a free agent by **NY Islanders**, August, 2001. Traded to **Anaheim** by **NY Islanders** with the rights to Bjorn Mellin for Dave Roche, March 19, 2002. Signed as a free agent by **NY Rangers**, September 16, 2003. Signed as a free agent by **Bridgeport** (AHL), October 10, 2003. Signed to a PTO (tryout) contract by **Providence** (AHL), September 28, 2004. Signed as a free agent by **Boston**, August 15, 2005. Signed as a free agent by **Colorado**, July 12, 2006. Signed as a free agent by **Nashville**, July 14, 2009.

## HAGMAN, Niklas

(HAG-muhn, NIHK-luhs) **TOR.**

Left wing. Shoots left. 6', 205 lbs. Born, Espoo, Finland, December 5, 1979. Florida's 3rd choice, 70th overall, in 1999 Entry Draft.

| Season | Club | League | Regular Season GP | G | A | Pts | PIM | PP | SH | GW | S | % | +/- | TF | F% | Min | Playoffs GP | G | A | Pts | PIM | PP | SH | GW | Min |
|---|---|---|---|---|---|---|---|---|---|---|---|---|---|---|---|---|---|---|---|---|---|---|---|---|---|
| 1995-96 | HIFK Helsinki U18 | Fin-U18 | 26 | 12 | 21 | 33 | 32 | | | | | | | | | | 4 | 3 | 0 | 3 | 2 | | | | |
| | HIFK Helsinki Jr. | Fin-Jr. | 12 | 3 | 1 | 4 | 0 | | | | | | | | | | | | | | | | | | |
| 1996-97 | HIFK Helsinki Jr. | Fin-Jr. | 30 | 13 | 12 | 25 | 30 | | | | | | | | | | | | | | | | | | |
| | HIFK Helsinki U18 | Fin-U18 | 21 | 19 | 12 | 31 | 46 | | | | | | | | | | 4 | 1 | 1 | 2 | 0 | | | | |
| 1997-98 | HIFK Helsinki U18 | Fin-U18 | 1 | 0 | 1 | 1 | 0 | | | | | | | | | | | | | | | | | | |
| | HIFK Helsinki Jr. | Fin-Jr. | 26 | 9 | 5 | 14 | 16 | | | | | | | | | | | | | | | | | | |
| | HIFK Helsinki | Finland | 8 | 1 | 0 | 1 | 0 | | | | | | | | | | | | | | | | | | |
| 1998-99 | HIFK Helsinki | Finland | 17 | 1 | 1 | 2 | 14 | | | | | | | | | | | | | | | | | | |
| | HIFK Helsinki Jr. | Fin-Jr. | 15 | 4 | 10 | 14 | 43 | | | | | | | | | | | | | | | | | | |
| | HIFK Helsinki | EuroHL | 1 | 0 | 1 | 1 | 0 | | | | | | | | | | | | | | | | | | |
| | Blues Espoo | Finland | 14 | 1 | 1 | 2 | 2 | | | | | | | | | | 4 | 1 | 0 | 1 | 0 | | | | |
| 99-2000 | Karpat Oulu Jr. | Fin-Jr. | 4 | 7 | 3 | 10 | 0 | | | | | | | | | | | | | | | | | | |
| | Karpat Oulu | Finland-2 | 41 | 17 | 18 | 35 | 12 | | | | | | | | | | 7 | 4 | 2 | 6 | 0 | | | | |
| 2000-01 | Karpat Oulu | Finland | 56 | 28 | 18 | 46 | 32 | | | | | | | | | | 8 | 3 | 1 | 4 | 0 | | | | |
| **2001-02** | **Florida** | **NHL** | **78** | **10** | **18** | **28** | **8** | **0** | **1** | **2** | **134** | **7.5** | **-6** | **32** | **28.1** | **13:50** | | | | | | | | | |
| | Finland | Olympics | 4 | 1 | 2 | 3 | 0 | | | | | | | | | | | | | | | | | | |
| **2002-03** | **Florida** | **NHL** | **80** | **8** | **15** | **23** | **20** | **2** | **0** | **0** | **132** | **6.1** | **-8** | **17** | **11.8** | **13:31** | | | | | | | | | |
| **2003-04** | **Florida** | **NHL** | **75** | **10** | **13** | **23** | **22** | **0** | **1** | **2** | **122** | **8.2** | **-5** | **19** | **21.1** | **14:47** | | | | | | | | | |
| 2004-05 | HC Davos | Swiss | 44 | 17 | 22 | 39 | 20 | | | | | | | | | | 15 | 10 | 7 | 17 | 6 | | | | |
| **2005-06** | **Florida** | **NHL** | **30** | **2** | **4** | **6** | **2** | **0** | **0** | **0** | **52** | **3.8** | **-8** | **10** | **10.0** | **14:00** | | | | | | | | | |
| | **Dallas** | **NHL** | **54** | **6** | **9** | **15** | **16** | **0** | **1** | **0** | **74** | **8.1** | **-2** | **6** | **66.7** | **11:17** | **5** | **2** | **1** | **3** | **4** | **0** | **0** | **1** | **10:50** |
| | Finland | Olympics | 8 | 0 | 1 | 1 | 2 | | | | | | | | | | | | | | | | | | |
| **2006-07** | **Dallas** | **NHL** | **82** | **17** | **12** | **29** | **34** | **2** | **1** | **2** | **152** | **11.2** | **3** | **15** | **20.0** | **14:26** | **7** | **0** | **1** | **1** | **10** | **0** | **0** | **0** | **16:26** |
| **2007-08** | **Dallas** | **NHL** | **82** | **27** | **14** | **41** | **51** | **4** | **4** | **8** | **178** | **15.2** | **4** | **19** | **10.5** | **15:36** | **18** | **2** | **1** | **3** | **14** | **0** | **0** | **0** | **13:25** |
| **2008-09** | **Toronto** | **NHL** | **65** | **22** | **20** | **42** | **4** | **6** | **0** | **3** | **168** | **13.1** | **-5** | **1** | **0.0** | **17:05** | | | | | | | | | |
| | **NHL Totals** | | **546** | **102** | **105** | **207** | **157** | **14** | **8** | **17** | **1012** | **10.1** | | **119** | **21.0** | **14:25** | **30** | **4** | **3** | **7** | **28** | **0** | **0** | **1** | **13:41** |

Signed as a free agent by **Davos** (Swiss), July 23, 2004. Traded to **Dallas** by **Florida** for Dallas' 7th round choice (Sergei Gayduchenko) in 2007 Entry Draft, December 12, 2005. Signed as a free agent by **Toronto**, July 1, 2008.

## HAINSEY, Ron

(HAYN-zee, RAWN) **ATL.**

Defense. Shoots left. 6'3", 205 lbs. Born, Bolton, CT, March 24, 1981. Montreal's 1st choice, 13th overall, in 2000 Entry Draft.

| Season | Club | League | Regular Season GP | G | A | Pts | PIM | PP | SH | GW | S | % | +/- | TF | F% | Min | Playoffs GP | G | A | Pts | PIM | PP | SH | GW | Min |
|---|---|---|---|---|---|---|---|---|---|---|---|---|---|---|---|---|---|---|---|---|---|---|---|---|---|
| 1997-98 | USNTDP | U-17 | 18 | 2 | 7 | 9 | 28 | | | | | | | | | | | | | | | | | | |
| | USNTDP | USHL | 3 | 0 | 0 | 0 | 0 | | | | | | | | | | | | | | | | | | |
| | USNTDP | NAHL | 40 | 4 | 7 | 11 | 16 | | | | | | | | | | 5 | 0 | 1 | 1 | 0 | | | | |
| 1998-99 | USNTDP | USHL | 48 | 5 | 12 | 17 | 45 | | | | | | | | | | | | | | | | | | |
| 99-2000 | U. Mass-Lowell | H-East | 30 | 3 | 8 | 11 | 20 | | | | | | | | | | | | | | | | | | |
| 2000-01 | U. Mass-Lowell | H-East | 33 | 10 | 26 | 36 | 51 | | | | | | | | | | | | | | | | | | |
| | Quebec Citadelles | AHL | 4 | 1 | 0 | 1 | 0 | | | | | | | | | | 1 | 0 | 0 | 0 | 0 | | | | |
| 2001-02 | Quebec Citadelles | AHL | 63 | 7 | 24 | 31 | 26 | | | | | | | | | | 3 | 0 | 0 | 0 | 0 | | | | |
| **2002-03** | **Montreal** | **NHL** | **21** | **0** | **0** | **0** | **2** | **0** | **0** | **0** | **12** | **0.0** | **-1** | **0** | **0.0** | **12:25** | | | | | | | | | |
| | Hamilton | AHL | 33 | 2 | 11 | 13 | 26 | | | | | | | | | | 23 | 1 | 10 | 11 | 20 | | | | |
| **2003-04** | **Montreal** | **NHL** | **11** | **1** | **1** | **2** | **4** | **0** | **0** | **0** | **11** | **9.1** | **3** | **0** | **0.0** | **13:15** | | | | | | | | | |
| | Hamilton | AHL | 54 | 7 | 24 | 31 | 35 | | | | | | | | | | 10 | 0 | 5 | 5 | 6 | | | | |
| 2004-05 | Hamilton | AHL | 68 | 9 | 14 | 23 | 45 | | | | | | | | | | 4 | 1 | 1 | 2 | 0 | | | | |
| **2005-06** | Hamilton | AHL | 22 | 3 | 14 | 17 | 19 | | | | | | | | | | | | | | | | | | |
| | **Columbus** | **NHL** | **55** | **2** | **15** | **17** | **43** | **1** | **0** | **0** | **81** | **2.5** | **13** | **1** | **0.0** | **17:47** | | | | | | | | | |
| **2006-07** | **Columbus** | **NHL** | **80** | **9** | **25** | **34** | **69** | **7** | **0** | **0** | **136** | **6.6** | **-19** | **2** | **50.0** | **22:53** | | | | | | | | | |
| **2007-08** | **Columbus** | **NHL** | **78** | **8** | **24** | **32** | **25** | **8** | **0** | **0** | **161** | **5.0** | **-7** | **0** | **0.0** | **22:34** | | | | | | | | | |
| **2008-09** | **Atlanta** | **NHL** | **81** | **6** | **33** | **39** | **32** | **4** | **0** | **0** | **148** | **4.1** | **-16** | **0** | **0.0** | **22:22** | | | | | | | | | |
| | **NHL Totals** | | **326** | **26** | **98** | **124** | **175** | **20** | **0** | **0** | **549** | **4.7** | | **3** | **33.3** | **20:49** | | | | | | | | | |

Hockey East First All-Star Team (2001) • NCAA East Second All-American Team (2001) • AHL All-Rookie Team (2002)

Claimed on waivers by **Columbus** from **Montreal**, November 29, 2005. Signed as a free agent by **Atlanta**, July 2, 2008.

## HALE, David

(HAYL, DAY-vihd) **T.B.**

Defense. Shoots left. 6'2", 213 lbs. Born, Colorado Springs, CO, June 18, 1981. New Jersey's 1st choice, 22nd overall, in 2000 Entry Draft.

| Season | Club | League | Regular Season GP | G | A | Pts | PIM | PP | SH | GW | S | % | +/- | TF | F% | Min | Playoffs GP | G | A | Pts | PIM | PP | SH | GW | Min |
|---|---|---|---|---|---|---|---|---|---|---|---|---|---|---|---|---|---|---|---|---|---|---|---|---|---|
| 1997-98 | Colorado North | High-CO | 25 | 11 | 33 | 44 | 154 | | | | | | | | | | | | | | | | | | |
| 1998-99 | Sioux City | USHL | 56 | 3 | 15 | 18 | 127 | | | | | | | | | | 5 | 0 | 0 | 0 | 18 | | | | |
| 99-2000 | Sioux City | USHL | 54 | 6 | 18 | 24 | 187 | | | | | | | | | | 5 | 0 | 2 | 2 | 6 | | | | |
| 2000-01 | North Dakota | WCHA | 44 | 4 | 5 | 9 | 79 | | | | | | | | | | | | | | | | | | |
| 2001-02 | North Dakota | WCHA | 34 | 4 | 5 | 9 | 63 | | | | | | | | | | | | | | | | | | |
| 2002-03 | North Dakota | WCHA | 26 | 2 | 6 | 8 | 49 | | | | | | | | | | | | | | | | | | |
| **2003-04** | **New Jersey** | **NHL** | **65** | **0** | **4** | **4** | **72** | **0** | **0** | **0** | **45** | **0.0** | **12** | **0** | **0.0** | **15:01** | **1** | **0** | **0** | **0** | **0** | **0** | **0** | **0** | **8:59** |
| 2004-05 | Albany River Rats | AHL | 30 | 2 | 3 | 5 | 39 | | | | | | | | | | | | | | | | | | |
| **2005-06** | **New Jersey** | **NHL** | **38** | **0** | **4** | **4** | **21** | **0** | **0** | **0** | **19** | **0.0** | **5** | **0** | **0.0** | **12:03** | **8** | **0** | **2** | **2** | **12** | **0** | **0** | **0** | **12:06** |
| | Albany River Rats | AHL | 30 | 2 | 5 | 7 | 64 | | | | | | | | | | | | | | | | | | |
| **2006-07** | **New Jersey** | **NHL** | **43** | **0** | **1** | **1** | **26** | **0** | **0** | **0** | **21** | **0.0** | **2** | **0** | **0.0** | **9:41** | | | | | | | | | |
| | Lowell Devils | AHL | 2 | 0 | 1 | 1 | 0 | | | | | | | | | | | | | | | | | | |
| | **Calgary** | **NHL** | **11** | **0** | **0** | **0** | **10** | **0** | **0** | **0** | **12** | **0.0** | **-2** | **0** | **0.0** | **15:47** | **2** | **0** | **0** | **0** | **6** | **0** | **0** | **0** | **12:42** |
| **2007-08** | **Calgary** | **NHL** | **58** | **0** | **2** | **2** | **46** | **0** | **0** | **0** | **35** | **0.0** | **0** | **0** | **0.0** | **13:53** | **6** | **0** | **0** | **0** | **2** | **0** | **0** | **0** | **12:48** |
| **2008-09** | **Phoenix** | **NHL** | **48** | **3** | **6** | **9** | **36** | **0** | **0** | **0** | **22** | **13.6** | **-11** | **0** | **0.0** | **15:08** | | | | | | | | | |
| | **NHL Totals** | | **263** | **3** | **17** | **20** | **211** | **0** | **0** | **0** | **154** | **1.9** | | **0** | **0.0** | **13:31** | **17** | **0** | **2** | **2** | **20** | **0** | **0** | **0** | **12:14** |

USHL First All-Star Team (2000)

Traded to **Calgary** by **New Jersey** with New Jersey's 5th round choice (later traded to Buffalo - Buffalo selected Jean-Simon Allard) in 2007 Entry Draft for Calgary's 3rd round choice (Nick Palmieri) in 2007 Entry Draft, February 27, 2007. Signed as a free agent by **Phoenix**, July 3, 2008. Traded to **Tampa Bay** by **Phoenix** with Todd Fedoruk for Radim Vrbata, July 21, 2009.

## HALISCHUK, Matt

(huh-LIHS-chuhk, MAT) **N.J.**

Right wing. Shoots right. 5'11", 180 lbs. Born, Toronto, Ont., June 1, 1988. New Jersey's 4th choice, 117th overall, in 2007 Entry Draft.

| | | | Regular Season | | | | | | | | | | | | | | Playoffs | | | | | | | | |
|---|---|---|---|---|---|---|---|---|---|---|---|---|---|---|---|---|---|---|---|---|---|---|---|---|---|
| Season | Club | League | GP | G | A | Pts | PIM | PP | SH | GW | S | % | +/- | TF | F% | Min | GP | G | A | Pts | PIM | PP | SH | GW | Min |
| 2003-04 | Tor. Jr. Canadiens | GTHL | 53 | 37 | 48 | 85 | 27 | .... | .... | .... | .... | .... | .... | .... | .... | .... | .... | .... | .... | .... | .... | .... | .... | .... | .... |
| 2004-05 | St. Michael's | OHL | 30 | 3 | 3 | 6 | 4 | .... | .... | .... | .... | .... | .... | .... | .... | .... | .... | .... | .... | .... | .... | .... | .... | .... | .... |
| | St. Mike's B's | OPJHL | 17 | 5 | 11 | 16 | 8 | .... | .... | .... | .... | .... | .... | .... | .... | .... | 32 | 10 | 15 | 25 | 4 | .... | .... | .... | .... |
| 2005-06 | St. Michael's | OHL | 61 | 13 | 18 | 31 | 16 | .... | .... | .... | .... | .... | .... | .... | .... | .... | 4 | 1 | 1 | 2 | 0 | .... | .... | .... | .... |
| 2006-07 | Kitchener Rangers | OHL | 67 | 33 | 33 | 66 | 20 | .... | .... | .... | .... | .... | .... | .... | .... | .... | 9 | 4 | 1 | 5 | 10 | .... | .... | .... | .... |
| 2007-08 | Kitchener Rangers | OHL | 40 | 13 | 46 | 59 | 16 | .... | .... | .... | .... | .... | .... | .... | .... | .... | 20 | *16 | 16 | 32 | 0 | .... | .... | .... | .... |
| **2008-09** | **New Jersey** | **NHL** | **1** | **0** | **1** | **1** | **0** | **0** | **0** | **0** | **0** | **0.0** | **–1** | **0** | **0.0** | **9:47** | .... | .... | .... | .... | .... | .... | .... | .... | .... |
| | Lowell Devils | AHL | 47 | 14 | 15 | 29 | 10 | .... | .... | .... | .... | .... | .... | .... | .... | .... | .... | .... | .... | .... | .... | .... | .... | .... | .... |
| | **NHL Totals** | | **1** | **0** | **1** | **1** | **0** | **0** | **0** | **0** | **0** | **0.0** | | **0** | **0.0** | **9:47** | .... | .... | .... | .... | .... | .... | .... | .... | .... |

OHL First All-Star Team (2008) • George Parsons Trophy (Memorial Cup Tournament - Most Sportsmanlike Player) (2008)

## HALL, Adam

(HAWL, A-duhm) **T.B.**

Right wing. Shoots right. 6'3", 206 lbs. Born, Kalamazoo, MI, August 14, 1980. Nashville's 3rd choice, 52nd overall, in 1999 Entry Draft.

| | | | Regular Season | | | | | | | | | | | | | | Playoffs | | | | | | | | |
|---|---|---|---|---|---|---|---|---|---|---|---|---|---|---|---|---|---|---|---|---|---|---|---|---|---|
| Season | Club | League | GP | G | A | Pts | PIM | PP | SH | GW | S | % | +/- | TF | F% | Min | GP | G | A | Pts | PIM | PP | SH | GW | Min |
| 1996-97 | Bramalea Blues | OPJHL | 43 | 9 | 14 | 23 | 92 | .... | .... | .... | .... | .... | .... | .... | .... | .... | .... | .... | .... | .... | .... | .... | .... | .... | .... |
| 1997-98 | USNTDP | U-18 | 29 | 18 | 9 | 27 | 19 | .... | .... | .... | .... | .... | .... | .... | .... | .... | .... | .... | .... | .... | .... | .... | .... | .... | .... |
| | USNTDP | USHL | 21 | 9 | 11 | 20 | 20 | .... | .... | .... | .... | .... | .... | .... | .... | .... | .... | .... | .... | .... | .... | .... | .... | .... | .... |
| | USNTDP | NAHL | 15 | 12 | 1 | 13 | 20 | .... | .... | .... | .... | .... | .... | .... | .... | .... | 6 | 3 | 2 | 5 | 4 | .... | .... | .... | .... |
| 1998-99 | Michigan State | CCHA | 36 | 16 | 7 | 23 | 74 | .... | .... | .... | .... | .... | .... | .... | .... | .... | .... | .... | .... | .... | .... | .... | .... | .... | .... |
| 99-2000 | Michigan State | CCHA | 40 | *26 | 13 | 39 | 38 | .... | .... | .... | .... | .... | .... | .... | .... | .... | .... | .... | .... | .... | .... | .... | .... | .... | .... |
| 2000-01 | Michigan State | CCHA | 42 | 18 | 12 | 30 | 42 | .... | .... | .... | .... | .... | .... | .... | .... | .... | .... | .... | .... | .... | .... | .... | .... | .... | .... |
| **2001-02** | Michigan State | CCHA | 41 | 19 | 15 | 34 | 36 | .... | .... | .... | .... | .... | .... | .... | .... | .... | .... | .... | .... | .... | .... | .... | .... | .... | .... |
| | **Nashville** | **NHL** | **1** | **0** | **1** | **1** | **0** | **0** | **0** | **0** | **2** | **0.0** | **0** | **0** | **0.0** | **14:04** | .... | .... | .... | .... | .... | .... | .... | .... | .... |
| | Milwaukee | AHL | 6 | 2 | 2 | 4 | 4 | .... | .... | .... | .... | .... | .... | .... | .... | .... | .... | .... | .... | .... | .... | .... | .... | .... | .... |
| **2002-03** | **Nashville** | **NHL** | **79** | **16** | **12** | **28** | **31** | **8** | **0** | **2** | **146** | **11.0** | **–8** | **17** | **52.9** | **14:09** | .... | .... | .... | .... | .... | .... | .... | .... | .... |
| | Milwaukee | AHL | 1 | 0 | 0 | 0 | 2 | .... | .... | .... | .... | .... | .... | .... | .... | .... | .... | .... | .... | .... | .... | .... | .... | .... | .... |
| **2003-04** | **Nashville** | **NHL** | **79** | **13** | **14** | **27** | **37** | **6** | **0** | **1** | **151** | **8.6** | **–8** | **348** | **56.3** | **16:14** | **6** | **2** | **1** | **3** | **2** | **0** | **0** | **1** | **18:29** |
| 2004-05 | KalPa Kuopio | Finland-2 | 36 | 23 | 17 | 40 | 28 | .... | .... | .... | .... | .... | .... | .... | .... | .... | 9 | 2 | 3 | 5 | 4 | .... | .... | .... | .... |
| **2005-06** | **Nashville** | **NHL** | **75** | **14** | **15** | **29** | **40** | **10** | **0** | **5** | **122** | **11.5** | **0** | **470** | **48.9** | **16:47** | **5** | **1** | **0** | **1** | **0** | **1** | **0** | **1** | **12:10** |
| **2006-07** | **NY Rangers** | **NHL** | **49** | **4** | **8** | **12** | **18** | **3** | **0** | **0** | **61** | **6.6** | **–13** | **59** | **45.8** | **12:27** | .... | .... | .... | .... | .... | .... | .... | .... | .... |
| | **Minnesota** | **NHL** | **23** | **2** | **3** | **5** | **8** | **0** | **0** | **0** | **42** | **4.8** | **2** | **11** | **72.7** | **12:13** | **3** | **0** | **0** | **0** | **7** | **0** | **0** | **0** | **10:06** |
| **2007-08** | **Pittsburgh** | **NHL** | **46** | **2** | **4** | **6** | **24** | **0** | **0** | **0** | **39** | **5.1** | **–2** | **290** | **50.3** | **11:52** | **17** | **3** | **1** | **4** | **8** | **0** | **0** | **1** | **10:59** |
| **2008-09** | **Tampa Bay** | **NHL** | **74** | **5** | **5** | **10** | **29** | **1** | **0** | **0** | **90** | **5.6** | **–9** | **338** | **50.0** | **11:12** | .... | .... | .... | .... | .... | .... | .... | .... | .... |
| | **NHL Totals** | | **426** | **56** | **62** | **118** | **187** | **28** | **0** | **8** | **653** | **8.6** | | **1533** | **51.2** | **13:56** | **31** | **6** | **2** | **8** | **17** | **1** | **0** | **3** | **12:32** |

CCHA Second All-Star Team (2000)

Signed as a free agent by **Kuopio** (Finland-2), October 11, 2004. Traded to **NY Rangers** by **Nashville** for Dominic Moore, July 19, 2006. Traded to **Minnesota** by **NY Rangers** for Pascal Dupuis, February 9, 2007. Signed as a free agent by **Pittsburgh**, October 1, 2007. Signed as a free agent by **Tampa Bay**, July 1, 2008.

## HALPERN, Jeff

(HAL-pehrn, JEHF) **T.B.**

Center. Shoots right. 6', 203 lbs. Born, Potomac, MD, May 3, 1976.

| | | | Regular Season | | | | | | | | | | | | | | Playoffs | | | | | | | | |
|---|---|---|---|---|---|---|---|---|---|---|---|---|---|---|---|---|---|---|---|---|---|---|---|---|---|
| Season | Club | League | GP | G | A | Pts | PIM | PP | SH | GW | S | % | +/- | TF | F% | Min | GP | G | A | Pts | PIM | PP | SH | GW | Min |
| 1994-95 | Stratford Cullitons | OHA-B | 44 | 29 | 54 | 83 | 43 | .... | .... | .... | .... | .... | .... | .... | .... | .... | .... | .... | .... | .... | .... | .... | .... | .... | .... |
| 1995-96 | Princeton | ECAC | 29 | 3 | 11 | 14 | 30 | .... | .... | .... | .... | .... | .... | .... | .... | .... | .... | .... | .... | .... | .... | .... | .... | .... | .... |
| 1996-97 | Princeton | ECAC | 33 | 7 | 24 | 31 | 35 | .... | .... | .... | .... | .... | .... | .... | .... | .... | .... | .... | .... | .... | .... | .... | .... | .... | .... |
| 1997-98 | Princeton | ECAC | 36 | *28 | 25 | *53 | 46 | .... | .... | .... | .... | .... | .... | .... | .... | .... | .... | .... | .... | .... | .... | .... | .... | .... | .... |
| 1998-99 | Princeton | ECAC | 33 | *22 | 22 | 44 | 32 | .... | .... | .... | .... | .... | .... | .... | .... | .... | .... | .... | .... | .... | .... | .... | .... | .... | .... |
| | Portland Pirates | AHL | 6 | 2 | 1 | 3 | 4 | .... | .... | .... | .... | .... | .... | .... | .... | .... | .... | .... | .... | .... | .... | .... | .... | .... | .... |
| **99-2000** | **Washington** | **NHL** | **79** | **18** | **11** | **29** | **39** | **4** | **4** | **1** | **108** | **16.7** | **21** | **812** | **51.1** | **13:14** | **5** | **2** | **1** | **3** | **0** | **1** | **0** | **1** | **15:16** |
| **2000-01** | **Washington** | **NHL** | **80** | **21** | **21** | **42** | **60** | **2** | **1** | **5** | **110** | **19.1** | **13** | **1293** | **52.4** | **16:08** | **6** | **2** | **3** | **5** | **17** | **1** | **0** | **1** | **20:02** |
| **2001-02** | **Washington** | **NHL** | **48** | **5** | **14** | **19** | **29** | **0** | **0** | **4** | **74** | **6.8** | **–9** | **661** | **56.0** | **15:19** | .... | .... | .... | .... | .... | .... | .... | .... | .... |
| **2002-03** | **Washington** | **NHL** | **82** | **13** | **21** | **34** | **88** | **1** | **2** | **2** | **126** | **10.3** | **6** | **1492** | **54.1** | **17:25** | **6** | **0** | **1** | **1** | **2** | **0** | **0** | **0** | **19:59** |
| **2003-04** | **Washington** | **NHL** | **79** | **19** | **27** | **46** | **56** | **7** | **0** | **2** | **114** | **16.7** | **–21** | **1509** | **54.3** | **19:03** | .... | .... | .... | .... | .... | .... | .... | .... | .... |
| 2004-05 | HC Ajoie | Swiss-2 | 15 | 5 | 12 | 17 | 52 | .... | .... | .... | .... | .... | .... | .... | .... | .... | .... | .... | .... | .... | .... | .... | .... | .... | .... |
| | Kloten Flyers | Swiss | 9 | 7 | 4 | 11 | 6 | .... | .... | .... | .... | .... | .... | .... | .... | .... | .... | .... | .... | .... | .... | .... | .... | .... | .... |
| **2005-06** | **Washington** | **NHL** | **70** | **11** | **33** | **44** | **79** | **6** | **0** | **1** | **151** | **7.3** | **–8** | **1454** | **55.2** | **20:00** | .... | .... | .... | .... | .... | .... | .... | .... | .... |
| **2006-07** | **Dallas** | **NHL** | **76** | **8** | **17** | **25** | **78** | **1** | **0** | **4** | **106** | **7.5** | **–7** | **1135** | **51.8** | **16:48** | **7** | **2** | **1** | **3** | **4** | **0** | **0** | **1** | **18:57** |
| **2007-08** | **Dallas** | **NHL** | **64** | **10** | **14** | **24** | **40** | **1** | **1** | **0** | **86** | **11.6** | **–2** | **548** | **54.0** | **16:21** | .... | .... | .... | .... | .... | .... | .... | .... | .... |
| | **Tampa Bay** | **NHL** | **19** | **10** | **8** | **18** | **14** | **3** | **0** | **2** | **46** | **21.7** | **2** | **185** | **46.0** | **18:12** | .... | .... | .... | .... | .... | .... | .... | .... | .... |
| **2008-09** | **Tampa Bay** | **NHL** | **52** | **7** | **9** | **16** | **32** | **1** | **1** | **1** | **60** | **11.7** | **–13** | **822** | **52.8** | **17:01** | .... | .... | .... | .... | .... | .... | .... | .... | .... |
| | **NHL Totals** | | **649** | **122** | **175** | **297** | **515** | **26** | **9** | **22** | **981** | **12.4** | | **9911** | **53.4** | **16:53** | **24** | **6** | **6** | **12** | **23** | **2** | **0** | **3** | **18:43** |

ECAC Second All-Star Team (1998, 1999)

Signed as a free agent by **Washington**, March 29, 1999. Signed as a free agent by **Ajoie** (Swiss-2), October 8, 2004. Signed as a free agent by **Kloten** (Swiss), December 30, 2004. Signed as a free agent by **Dallas**, July 5, 2006. Traded to **Tampa Bay** by **Dallas** with Jussi Jokinen, Mike Smith and Dallas' 4th round choice (later traded to Minnesota – later traded to Edmonton – Edmonton selected Kyle Bigos) in 2009 Entry Draft for Brad Richards and Johan Holmqvist, February 26, 2008.

## HAMEL, Denis

(ha-MEHL, deh-NEE)

Left wing. Shoots left. 6'1", 201 lbs. Born, Lachute, Que., May 10, 1977. St. Louis' 5th choice, 153rd overall, in 1995 Entry Draft.

| | | | Regular Season | | | | | | | | | | | | | | Playoffs | | | | | | | | |
|---|---|---|---|---|---|---|---|---|---|---|---|---|---|---|---|---|---|---|---|---|---|---|---|---|---|
| Season | Club | League | GP | G | A | Pts | PIM | PP | SH | GW | S | % | +/- | TF | F% | Min | GP | G | A | Pts | PIM | PP | SH | GW | Min |
| 1992-93 | Lachute Regents | QAAA | 32 | 18 | 24 | 42 | .... | .... | .... | .... | .... | .... | .... | .... | .... | .... | .... | .... | .... | .... | .... | .... | .... | .... | .... |
| 1993-94 | Lac St-Louis Lions | QAAA | 28 | 10 | 11 | 21 | 50 | .... | .... | .... | .... | .... | .... | .... | .... | .... | .... | .... | .... | .... | .... | .... | .... | .... | .... |
| | Abitibi Forestiers | QAAA | 15 | 5 | 7 | 12 | 29 | .... | .... | .... | .... | .... | .... | .... | .... | .... | 5 | 0 | 3 | 3 | 16 | .... | .... | .... | .... |
| 1994-95 | Chicoutimi | QMJHL | 66 | 15 | 12 | 27 | 155 | .... | .... | .... | .... | .... | .... | .... | .... | .... | 12 | 2 | 0 | 2 | 27 | .... | .... | .... | .... |
| 1995-96 | Chicoutimi | QMJHL | 65 | 40 | 49 | 89 | 199 | .... | .... | .... | .... | .... | .... | .... | .... | .... | 17 | 10 | 14 | 24 | 64 | .... | .... | .... | .... |
| 1996-97 | Chicoutimi | QMJHL | 70 | 50 | 50 | 100 | 357 | .... | .... | .... | .... | .... | .... | .... | .... | .... | 20 | 15 | 10 | 25 | 58 | .... | .... | .... | .... |
| 1997-98 | Rochester | AHL | 74 | 10 | 15 | 25 | 98 | .... | .... | .... | .... | .... | .... | .... | .... | .... | 4 | 1 | 2 | 3 | 0 | .... | .... | .... | .... |
| 1998-99 | Rochester | AHL | 74 | 16 | 17 | 33 | 121 | .... | .... | .... | .... | .... | .... | .... | .... | .... | 20 | 3 | 4 | 7 | 10 | .... | .... | .... | .... |
| **99-2000** | **Buffalo** | **NHL** | **3** | **1** | **0** | **1** | **0** | **0** | **0** | **0** | **3** | **33.3** | **–1** | **0** | **0.0** | **9:45** | .... | .... | .... | .... | .... | .... | .... | .... | .... |
| | Rochester | AHL | 76 | 34 | 24 | 58 | 122 | .... | .... | .... | .... | .... | .... | .... | .... | .... | 21 | 6 | 7 | 13 | 49 | .... | .... | .... | .... |
| **2000-01** | **Buffalo** | **NHL** | **41** | **8** | **3** | **11** | **22** | **1** | **1** | **3** | **55** | **14.5** | **–2** | **171** | **33.9** | **10:58** | .... | .... | .... | .... | .... | .... | .... | .... | .... |
| **2001-02** | **Buffalo** | **NHL** | **61** | **2** | **6** | **8** | **28** | **0** | **0** | **0** | **80** | **2.5** | **–1** | **94** | **39.4** | **11:00** | .... | .... | .... | .... | .... | .... | .... | .... | .... |
| **2002-03** | **Buffalo** | **NHL** | **25** | **2** | **0** | **2** | **17** | **0** | **0** | **1** | **41** | **4.9** | **–4** | **4** | **25.0** | **12:40** | .... | .... | .... | .... | .... | .... | .... | .... | .... |
| | Rochester | AHL | 48 | 27 | 20 | 47 | 64 | .... | .... | .... | .... | .... | .... | .... | .... | .... | 3 | 3 | 2 | 5 | 4 | .... | .... | .... | .... |
| **2003-04** | **Ottawa** | **NHL** | **5** | **0** | **0** | **0** | **0** | **0** | **0** | **0** | **6** | **0.0** | **–3** | **1** | **100.0** | **6:16** | .... | .... | .... | .... | .... | .... | .... | .... | .... |
| | Binghamton | AHL | 78 | 29 | 38 | 67 | 116 | .... | .... | .... | .... | .... | .... | .... | .... | .... | 2 | 0 | 0 | 0 | 2 | .... | .... | .... | .... |
| 2004-05 | Binghamton | AHL | 80 | 39 | 39 | 78 | 75 | .... | .... | .... | .... | .... | .... | .... | .... | .... | 5 | 1 | 0 | 1 | 4 | .... | .... | .... | .... |
| **2005-06** | **Ottawa** | **NHL** | **4** | **1** | **0** | **1** | **0** | **0** | **0** | **0** | **9** | **11.1** | **1** | **1** | **0.0** | **9:10** | .... | .... | .... | .... | .... | .... | .... | .... | .... |
| | Binghamton | AHL | 77 | *56 | 35 | 91 | 65 | .... | .... | .... | .... | .... | .... | .... | .... | .... | .... | .... | .... | .... | .... | .... | .... | .... | .... |
| **2006-07** | **Ottawa** | **NHL** | **43** | **4** | **3** | **7** | **10** | **0** | **0** | **0** | **36** | **11.1** | **4** | **9** | **33.3** | **5:38** | .... | .... | .... | .... | .... | .... | .... | .... | .... |
| | **Atlanta** | **NHL** | **3** | **1** | **0** | **1** | **0** | **0** | **0** | **0** | **3** | **33.3** | **0** | **2** | **0.0** | **10:25** | .... | .... | .... | .... | .... | .... | .... | .... | .... |
| | **Philadelphia** | **NHL** | **7** | **0** | **0** | **0** | **0** | **0** | **0** | **0** | **3** | **0.0** | **–4** | **0** | **0.0** | **6:58** | .... | .... | .... | .... | .... | .... | .... | .... | .... |
| 2007-08 | Binghamton | AHL | 67 | 32 | 23 | 55 | 60 | .... | .... | .... | .... | .... | .... | .... | .... | .... | .... | .... | .... | .... | .... | .... | .... | .... | .... |
| 2008-09 | Binghamton | AHL | 63 | 25 | 25 | 50 | 36 | .... | .... | .... | .... | .... | .... | .... | .... | .... | .... | .... | .... | .... | .... | .... | .... | .... | .... |
| | **NHL Totals** | | **192** | **19** | **12** | **31** | **77** | **1** | **1** | **4** | **236** | **8.1** | | **282** | **35.5** | **9:40** | .... | .... | .... | .... | .... | .... | .... | .... | .... |

QMJHL All-Rookie Team (1995) • AHL First All-Star Team (2004) • Willie Marshall Award (AHL - Top Goal-scorer) (2006) (tied with Don MacLean) • Yanick Dupre Memorial Award (AHL - Outstanding Humanitarian Contribution) (2008)

Traded to **Buffalo** by **St. Louis** for Charlie Huddy and Buffalo's 7th round choice (Daniel Corso) in 1996 Entry Draft, March 19, 1996. • Missed majority of 2000-01 season recovering from knee injury suffered in game vs. NY Islanders, January 27, 2001. Signed as a free agent by **Ottawa**, July 5, 2003. Claimed by **Washington** from **Ottawa** in Waiver Draft, October 3, 2003. Traded to **Ottawa** by **Washington** for future considerations, October 5, 2003. Claimed on waivers by **Atlanta** from **Ottawa**, February 10, 2007. Claimed on waivers by **Philadelphia** from **Atlanta**, February 27, 2007. Signed as a free agent by **Ottawa** , July 6, 2007.

## HAMHUIS, Dan

(HAM-HOOS, DAN) **NSH.**

Defense. Shoots left. 6'1", 203 lbs. Born, Smithers, B.C., December 13, 1982. Nashville's 1st choice, 12th overall, in 2001 Entry Draft.

| | | | Regular Season | | | | | | | | | | | | | | Playoffs | | | | | | | | |
|---|---|---|---|---|---|---|---|---|---|---|---|---|---|---|---|---|---|---|---|---|---|---|---|---|---|
| Season | Club | League | GP | G | A | Pts | PIM | PP | SH | GW | S | % | +/- | TF | F% | Min | GP | G | A | Pts | PIM | PP | SH | GW | Min |
| 1997-98 | Smithers A's | Minor-BC | 59 | 59 | 72 | 131 | 59 | .... | .... | .... | .... | .... | .... | .... | .... | .... | .... | .... | .... | .... | .... | .... | .... | .... | .... |
| 1998-99 | Prince George | WHL | 56 | 1 | 3 | 4 | 45 | .... | .... | .... | .... | .... | .... | .... | .... | .... | 7 | 1 | 2 | 3 | 8 | .... | .... | .... | .... |
| 99-2000 | Prince George | WHL | 70 | 10 | 23 | 33 | 140 | .... | .... | .... | .... | .... | .... | .... | .... | .... | 13 | 2 | 3 | 5 | 35 | .... | .... | .... | .... |
| 2000-01 | Prince George | WHL | 62 | 13 | 47 | 60 | 125 | .... | .... | .... | .... | .... | .... | .... | .... | .... | 6 | 2 | 3 | 5 | 15 | .... | .... | .... | .... |
| 2001-02 | Prince George | WHL | 59 | 10 | 50 | 60 | 135 | .... | .... | .... | .... | .... | .... | .... | .... | .... | 7 | 0 | 5 | 5 | 16 | .... | .... | .... | .... |
| 2002-03 | Milwaukee | AHL | 68 | 6 | 21 | 27 | 81 | .... | .... | .... | .... | .... | .... | .... | .... | .... | 6 | 0 | 3 | 3 | 2 | .... | .... | .... | .... |
| **2003-04** | **Nashville** | **NHL** | **80** | **7** | **19** | **26** | **57** | **2** | **0** | **4** | **115** | **6.1** | **–12** | **0** | **0.0** | **22:08** | **6** | **0** | **2** | **2** | **6** | **0** | **0** | **0** | **20:29** |
| 2004-05 | Milwaukee | AHL | 76 | 13 | 38 | 51 | 85 | .... | .... | .... | .... | .... | .... | .... | .... | .... | 7 | 0 | 2 | 2 | 10 | .... | .... | .... | .... |
| **2005-06** | **Nashville** | **NHL** | **82** | **7** | **31** | **38** | **70** | **4** | **1** | **1** | **135** | **5.2** | **11** | **0** | **0.0** | **22:34** | **5** | **0** | **2** | **2** | **2** | **0** | **0** | **0** | **19:41** |
| **2006-07** | **Nashville** | **NHL** | **81** | **6** | **14** | **20** | **66** | **0** | **0** | **1** | **84** | **7.1** | **8** | **1** | **0.0** | **21:20** | **5** | **0** | **1** | **1** | **2** | **0** | **0** | **0** | **21:36** |
| **2007-08** | **Nashville** | **NHL** | **80** | **4** | **23** | **27** | **66** | **1** | **0** | **1** | **127** | **3.1** | **–4** | **0** | **0.0** | **22:44** | **6** | **1** | **1** | **2** | **6** | **1** | **0** | **0** | **22:47** |
| **2008-09** | **Nashville** | **NHL** | **82** | **3** | **23** | **26** | **67** | **1** | **1** | **1** | **135** | **2.2** | **–4** | **0** | **0.0** | **22:50** | .... | .... | .... | .... | .... | .... | .... | .... | .... |
| | **NHL Totals** | | **405** | **27** | **110** | **137** | **326** | **8** | **2** | **8** | **596** | **4.5** | | **1** | **0.0** | **22:19** | **22** | **1** | **6** | **7** | **16** | **1** | **0** | **0** | **21:11** |

WHL West First All-Star Team (2001, 2002) • WHL Player of the Year (2002) • Canadian Major Junior First All-Star Team (2002) • Canadian Major Junior Defenseman of the Year (2002) • AHL Second All-Star Team (2005)

## HAMILTON, Jeff

(HAM-ihl-tuhn, JEHF)

Center. Shoots right. 5'10", 185 lbs. Born, Englewood, OH, September 4, 1977.

| | | | Regular Season | | | | | | | | | | | | | | Playoffs | | | | | | | | |
|---|---|---|---|---|---|---|---|---|---|---|---|---|---|---|---|---|---|---|---|---|---|---|---|---|---|
| Season | Club | League | GP | G | A | Pts | PIM | PP | SH | GW | S | % | +/- | TF | F% | Min | GP | G | A | Pts | PIM | PP | SH | GW | Min |
| 1995-96 | Avon Old Farms | High-CT | 24 | 29 | 23 | 52 | .... | .... | .... | .... | .... | .... | .... | .... | .... | .... | .... | .... | .... | .... | .... | .... | .... | .... | .... |
| 1996-97 | Yale | ECAC | 31 | 10 | 13 | 23 | 26 | .... | .... | .... | .... | .... | .... | .... | .... | .... | .... | .... | .... | .... | .... | .... | .... | .... | .... |
| 1997-98 | Yale | ECAC | 33 | 27 | 20 | 47 | 28 | .... | .... | .... | .... | .... | .... | .... | .... | .... | .... | .... | .... | .... | .... | .... | .... | .... | .... |
| 1998-99 | Yale | ECAC | 30 | 20 | 28 | 48 | 51 | .... | .... | .... | .... | .... | .... | .... | .... | .... | .... | .... | .... | .... | .... | .... | .... | .... | .... |
| 99-2000 | Yale | ECAC | 2 | 0 | 1 | 1 | 0 | .... | .... | .... | .... | .... | .... | .... | .... | .... | .... | .... | .... | .... | .... | .... | .... | .... | .... |
| 2000-01 | Yale | ECAC | 31 | 23 | 32 | 55 | 39 | .... | .... | .... | .... | .... | .... | .... | .... | .... | .... | .... | .... | .... | .... | .... | .... | .... | .... |
| 2001-02 | Karpat Oulu | Finland | 39 | 18 | 15 | 33 | 16 | .... | .... | .... | .... | .... | .... | .... | .... | .... | 3 | 0 | 0 | 0 | 0 | .... | .... | .... | .... |
| 2002-03 | Bridgeport | AHL | 67 | 22 | 16 | 38 | 35 | .... | .... | .... | .... | .... | .... | .... | .... | .... | 9 | 3 | 3 | 6 | 0 | .... | .... | .... | .... |
| **2003-04** | **NY Islanders** | **NHL** | **1** | **0** | **0** | **0** | **0** | **0** | **0** | **0** | **1** | **0.0** | **0** | **0** | **0.0** | **10:00** | .... | .... | .... | .... | .... | .... | .... | .... | .... |
| | Bridgeport | AHL | 67 | *43 | 25 | 68 | 26 | .... | .... | .... | .... | .... | .... | .... | .... | .... | 7 | 4 | 0 | 4 | 4 | .... | .... | .... | .... |
| 2004-05 | Hartford | AHL | 60 | 23 | 30 | 53 | 32 | .... | .... | .... | .... | .... | .... | .... | .... | .... | 6 | 4 | 3 | 7 | 0 | .... | .... | .... | .... |
| **2005-06** | Ak Bars Kazan | Russia | 8 | 0 | 1 | 1 | 16 | .... | .... | .... | .... | .... | .... | .... | .... | .... | .... | .... | .... | .... | .... | .... | .... | .... | .... |
| | **NY Islanders** | **NHL** | **13** | **2** | **6** | **8** | **8** | **1** | **0** | **0** | **29** | **6.9** | **0** | **6** | **16.7** | **10:33** | .... | .... | .... | .... | .... | .... | .... | .... | .... |
| | Bridgeport | AHL | 39 | 24 | 26 | 50 | 28 | .... | .... | .... | .... | .... | .... | .... | .... | .... | .... | .... | .... | .... | .... | .... | .... | .... | .... |
| **2006-07** | **Chicago** | **NHL** | **70** | **18** | **21** | **39** | **22** | **3** | **0** | **4** | **138** | **13.0** | **–4** | **55** | **36.4** | **12:56** | .... | .... | .... | .... | .... | .... | .... | .... | .... |
| **2007-08** | **Carolina** | **NHL** | **58** | **9** | **15** | **24** | **10** | **7** | **0** | **1** | **116** | **7.8** | **–8** | **79** | **48.1** | **10:48** | .... | .... | .... | .... | .... | .... | .... | .... | .... |
| | Albany River Rats | AHL | 9 | 3 | 6 | 9 | 6 | .... | .... | .... | .... | .... | .... | .... | .... | .... | .... | .... | .... | .... | .... | .... | .... | .... | .... |
| **2008-09** | Chicago Wolves | AHL | 50 | 16 | 37 | 53 | 18 | .... | .... | .... | .... | .... | .... | .... | .... | .... | .... | .... | .... | .... | .... | .... | .... | .... | .... |
| | **Toronto** | **NHL** | **15** | **3** | **3** | **6** | **4** | **0** | **0** | **1** | **30** | **10.0** | **2** | **11** | **27.3** | **12:57** | .... | .... | .... | .... | .... | .... | .... | .... | .... |
| | **NHL Totals** | | **157** | **32** | **45** | **77** | **44** | **11** | **0** | **6** | **314** | **10.2** | | **151** | **41.1** | **11:56** | .... | .... | .... | .... | .... | .... | .... | .... | .... |

ECAC All-Rookie Team (1997) • ECAC First All-Star Team (1998, 1999, 2001) • NCAA East Second All-American Team (1998, 1999) • NCAA East First All-American Team (2001) • AHL First All-Star Team (2004) • Willie Marshall Award (AHL - Top Goal-scorer) (2004)

• Missed majority of 1999-2000 season recovering from abdominal injury originally suffered in game vs. University of Michigan (CCHA), October 30, 1999. Signed as a free agent by **Oulu** (Finland), October 4, 2001. Signed as a free agent by **NY Islanders**, August 6, 2002. Signed as a free agent by **Hartford** (AHL), October 10, 2004. Signed as a free agent by **Kazan** (Russia), September 5, 2005. Signed as a free agent by **Chicago**, September 29, 2006. Signed as a free agent by **Carolina**, July 1, 2007. Signed as a free agent by **Toronto**, March 5, 2009.

## HAMRLIK, Roman

(HAHM-reh-lik, ROH-muhn) **MTL.**

Defense. Shoots left. 6'2", 209 lbs. Born, Zlin, Czech., April 12, 1974. Tampa Bay's 1st choice, 1st overall, in 1992 Entry Draft.

| | | | Regular Season | | | | | | | | | | | | | | Playoffs | | | | | | | | |
|---|---|---|---|---|---|---|---|---|---|---|---|---|---|---|---|---|---|---|---|---|---|---|---|---|---|
| Season | Club | League | GP | G | A | Pts | PIM | PP | SH | GW | S | % | +/- | TF | F% | Min | GP | G | A | Pts | PIM | PP | SH | GW | Min |
| 1990-91 | AC ZPS Zlin | Czech | 14 | 2 | 2 | 4 | 18 | .... | .... | .... | .... | .... | .... | .... | .... | .... | .... | .... | .... | .... | .... | .... | .... | .... | .... |
| 1991-92 | AC ZPS Zlin | Czech | 34 | 5 | 5 | 10 | 50 | .... | .... | .... | .... | .... | .... | .... | .... | .... | .... | .... | .... | .... | .... | .... | .... | .... | .... |
| **1992-93** | **Tampa Bay** | **NHL** | **67** | **6** | **15** | **21** | **71** | **1** | **0** | **1** | **113** | **5.3** | **–21** | .... | .... | .... | .... | .... | .... | .... | .... | .... | .... | .... | .... |
| | Atlanta Knights | IHL | 2 | 1 | 1 | 2 | 2 | .... | .... | .... | .... | .... | .... | .... | .... | .... | .... | .... | .... | .... | .... | .... | .... | .... | .... |
| **1993-94** | **Tampa Bay** | **NHL** | **64** | **3** | **18** | **21** | **135** | **0** | **0** | **0** | **158** | **1.9** | **–14** | .... | .... | .... | .... | .... | .... | .... | .... | .... | .... | .... | .... |
| **1994-95** | AC ZPS Zlin | CzRep | 2 | 1 | 0 | 1 | 10 | .... | .... | .... | .... | .... | .... | .... | .... | .... | .... | .... | .... | .... | .... | .... | .... | .... | .... |
| | **Tampa Bay** | **NHL** | **48** | **12** | **11** | **23** | **86** | **7** | **1** | **2** | **134** | **9.0** | **–18** | .... | .... | .... | .... | .... | .... | .... | .... | .... | .... | .... | .... |
| **1995-96** | **Tampa Bay** | **NHL** | **82** | **16** | **49** | **65** | **103** | **12** | **0** | **2** | **281** | **5.7** | **–24** | .... | .... | .... | **5** | **0** | **1** | **1** | **4** | **0** | **0** | **0** | .... |
| **1996-97** | **Tampa Bay** | **NHL** | **79** | **12** | **28** | **40** | **57** | **6** | **0** | **0** | **238** | **5.0** | **–29** | .... | .... | .... | .... | .... | .... | .... | .... | .... | .... | .... | .... |
| **1997-98** | **Tampa Bay** | **NHL** | **37** | **3** | **12** | **15** | **22** | **1** | **0** | **0** | **86** | **3.5** | **–18** | .... | .... | .... | .... | .... | .... | .... | .... | .... | .... | .... | .... |
| | **Edmonton** | **NHL** | **41** | **6** | **20** | **26** | **48** | **4** | **1** | **3** | **112** | **5.4** | **3** | .... | .... | .... | **12** | **0** | **6** | **6** | **12** | **0** | **0** | **0** | .... |
| | Czech Republic | Olympics | 6 | 1 | 0 | 1 | 2 | .... | .... | .... | .... | .... | .... | .... | .... | .... | .... | .... | .... | .... | .... | .... | .... | .... | .... |
| **1998-99** | **Edmonton** | **NHL** | **75** | **8** | **24** | **32** | **70** | **3** | **0** | **0** | **172** | **4.7** | **9** | **0** | **0.0** | **23:49** | **3** | **0** | **0** | **0** | **2** | **0** | **0** | **0** | **16:23** |
| **99-2000** | Zlin | CzRep | 6 | 0 | 3 | 3 | 4 | .... | .... | .... | .... | .... | .... | .... | .... | .... | .... | .... | .... | .... | .... | .... | .... | .... | .... |
| | **Edmonton** | **NHL** | **80** | **8** | **37** | **45** | **68** | **5** | **0** | **0** | **180** | **4.4** | **1** | **0** | **0.0** | **25:18** | **5** | **0** | **1** | **1** | **4** | **0** | **0** | **0** | **24:44** |
| **2000-01** | **NY Islanders** | **NHL** | **76** | **16** | **30** | **46** | **92** | **5** | **1** | **4** | **232** | **6.9** | **–20** | **1** | **100.0** | **25:12** | .... | .... | .... | .... | .... | .... | .... | .... | .... |
| **2001-02** | **NY Islanders** | **NHL** | **70** | **11** | **26** | **37** | **78** | **4** | **1** | **1** | **169** | **6.5** | **7** | **1** | **0.0** | **25:32** | **7** | **1** | **6** | **7** | **6** | **0** | **0** | **0** | **29:09** |
| | Czech Republic | Olympics | 4 | 0 | 1 | 1 | 2 | .... | .... | .... | .... | .... | .... | .... | .... | .... | .... | .... | .... | .... | .... | .... | .... | .... | .... |
| **2002-03** | **NY Islanders** | **NHL** | **73** | **9** | **32** | **41** | **87** | **3** | **0** | **2** | **151** | **6.0** | **21** | **0** | **0.0** | **26:34** | **5** | **0** | **2** | **2** | **2** | **0** | **0** | **0** | **29:24** |
| **2003-04** | **NY Islanders** | **NHL** | **81** | **7** | **22** | **29** | **68** | **2** | **0** | **2** | **182** | **3.8** | **2** | **0** | **0.0** | **24:35** | **5** | **0** | **1** | **1** | **2** | **0** | **0** | **0** | **25:30** |
| 2004-05 | HC Hame Zlin | CzRep | 45 | 2 | 14 | 16 | 70 | .... | .... | .... | .... | .... | .... | .... | .... | .... | 17 | 1 | 3 | 4 | 24 | .... | .... | .... | .... |
| **2005-06** | **Calgary** | **NHL** | **51** | **7** | **19** | **26** | **56** | **1** | **1** | **0** | **89** | **7.9** | **8** | **0** | **0.0** | **21:51** | **7** | **0** | **2** | **2** | **2** | **0** | **0** | **0** | **19:44** |
| **2006-07** | **Calgary** | **NHL** | **75** | **7** | **31** | **38** | **88** | **1** | **0** | **1** | **125** | **5.6** | **22** | **0** | **0.0** | **24:52** | **6** | **0** | **1** | **1** | **8** | **0** | **0** | **0** | **26:53** |
| **2007-08** | **Montreal** | **NHL** | **77** | **5** | **21** | **26** | **38** | **3** | **0** | **3** | **129** | **3.9** | **7** | **0** | **0.0** | **23:08** | **12** | **1** | **2** | **3** | **8** | **0** | **0** | **0** | **22:55** |
| **2008-09** | **Montreal** | **NHL** | **81** | **6** | **27** | **33** | **62** | **0** | **0** | **0** | **143** | **4.2** | **4** | **0** | **0.0** | **21:55** | **4** | **0** | **0** | **0** | **2** | **0** | **0** | **0** | **25:19** |
| | **NHL Totals** | | **1157** | **142** | **422** | **564** | **1229** | **58** | **5** | **21** | **2694** | **5.3** | | **2** | **50.0** | **24:20** | **71** | **2** | **22** | **24** | **52** | **0** | **0** | **0** | **24:34** |

Played in NHL All-Star Game (1996, 1999, 2003)

Traded to **Edmonton** by **Tampa Bay** with Paul Comrie for Bryan Marchment, Steve Kelly and Jason Bonsignore, December 30, 1997. Traded to **NY Islanders** by **Edmonton** for Eric Brewer, Josh Green and NY Islanders' 2nd round choice (Brad Winchester) in 2000 Entry Draft, June 24, 2000. Signed as a free agent by **Zlin** (CzRep), August 4, 2004. Signed as a free agent by **Calgary**, August 14, 2005 Signed as a free agent by **Montreal**, July 2, 2007.

## HANDZUS, Michal

(HAHND-zoos, MIGH-kuhl) **L.A.**

Center. Shoots left. 6'4", 218 lbs. Born, Banska Bystrica, Czech., March 11, 1977. St. Louis' 3rd choice, 101st overall, in 1995 Entry Draft.

| | | | Regular Season | | | | | | | | | | | | | | Playoffs | | | | | | | | |
|---|---|---|---|---|---|---|---|---|---|---|---|---|---|---|---|---|---|---|---|---|---|---|---|---|---|
| Season | Club | League | GP | G | A | Pts | PIM | PP | SH | GW | S | % | +/- | TF | F% | Min | GP | G | A | Pts | PIM | PP | SH | GW | Min |
| 1993-94 | B. Bystrica Jr. | Slovak-Jr. | 40 | 23 | 36 | 59 | .... | .... | .... | .... | .... | .... | .... | .... | .... | .... | .... | .... | .... | .... | .... | .... | .... | .... | .... |
| 1994-95 | B. Bystrica | Slovak-2 | 22 | 15 | 14 | 29 | 10 | .... | .... | .... | .... | .... | .... | .... | .... | .... | .... | .... | .... | .... | .... | .... | .... | .... | .... |
| 1995-96 | B. Bystrica | Slovakia | 19 | 3 | 1 | 4 | 8 | .... | .... | .... | .... | .... | .... | .... | .... | .... | .... | .... | .... | .... | .... | .... | .... | .... | .... |
| 1996-97 | HC SKP PS Poprad | Slovakia | 44 | 15 | 18 | 33 | .... | .... | .... | .... | .... | .... | .... | .... | .... | .... | .... | .... | .... | .... | .... | .... | .... | .... | .... |
| 1997-98 | Worcester IceCats | AHL | 69 | 27 | 36 | 63 | 54 | .... | .... | .... | .... | .... | .... | .... | .... | .... | 11 | 2 | 6 | 8 | 10 | .... | .... | .... | .... |
| **1998-99** | **St. Louis** | **NHL** | **66** | **4** | **12** | **16** | **30** | **0** | **0** | **0** | **78** | **5.1** | **–9** | **794** | **49.9** | **14:48** | **11** | **0** | **2** | **2** | **8** | **0** | **0** | **0** | **16:52** |
| **99-2000** | **St. Louis** | **NHL** | **81** | **25** | **28** | **53** | **44** | **3** | **4** | **5** | **166** | **15.1** | **19** | **1243** | **51.5** | **17:43** | **7** | **0** | **3** | **3** | **6** | **0** | **0** | **0** | **16:35** |
| **2000-01** | **St. Louis** | **NHL** | **36** | **10** | **14** | **24** | **12** | **3** | **2** | **2** | **58** | **17.2** | **11** | **581** | **50.6** | **18:00** | .... | .... | .... | .... | .... | .... | .... | .... | .... |
| | **Phoenix** | **NHL** | **10** | **4** | **4** | **8** | **21** | **0** | **1** | **0** | **14** | **28.6** | **5** | **111** | **60.4** | **15:26** | .... | .... | .... | .... | .... | .... | .... | .... | .... |
| **2001-02** | **Phoenix** | **NHL** | **79** | **15** | **30** | **45** | **34** | **3** | **1** | **1** | **94** | **16.0** | **–8** | **1227** | **48.7** | **16:09** | **5** | **0** | **0** | **0** | **2** | **0** | **0** | **0** | **15:01** |
| | Slovakia | Olympics | 2 | 1 | 0 | 1 | 6 | .... | .... | .... | .... | .... | .... | .... | .... | .... | .... | .... | .... | .... | .... | .... | .... | .... | .... |
| **2002-03** | **Philadelphia** | **NHL** | **82** | **23** | **21** | **44** | **46** | **1** | **1** | **9** | **133** | **17.3** | **13** | **1350** | **52.3** | **17:33** | **13** | **2** | **6** | **8** | **6** | **0** | **0** | **1** | **18:23** |
| **2003-04** | **Philadelphia** | **NHL** | **82** | **20** | **38** | **58** | **82** | **7** | **1** | **2** | **135** | **14.8** | **18** | **1457** | **49.9** | **18:43** | **18** | **5** | **5** | **10** | **10** | **0** | **0** | **0** | **18:33** |
| 2004-05 | HKm Zvolen | Slovakia | 33 | 14 | 24 | 38 | 34 | .... | .... | .... | .... | .... | .... | .... | .... | .... | 17 | 5 | 10 | 15 | 6 | .... | .... | .... | .... |
| **2005-06** | **Philadelphia** | **NHL** | **73** | **11** | **33** | **44** | **38** | **2** | **1** | **1** | **113** | **9.7** | **–2** | **1143** | **53.2** | **18:28** | **6** | **0** | **2** | **2** | **2** | **0** | **0** | **0** | **15:56** |
| **2006-07** | **Chicago** | **NHL** | **8** | **3** | **5** | **8** | **6** | **1** | **0** | **0** | **9** | **33.3** | **4** | **173** | **51.5** | **20:59** | .... | .... | .... | .... | .... | .... | .... | .... | .... |
| **2007-08** | **Los Angeles** | **NHL** | **82** | **7** | **14** | **21** | **45** | **0** | **3** | **0** | **89** | **7.9** | **–21** | **1167** | **45.6** | **15:14** | .... | .... | .... | .... | .... | .... | .... | .... | .... |
| **2008-09** | **Los Angeles** | **NHL** | **82** | **18** | **24** | **42** | **32** | **7** | **1** | **4** | **143** | **12.6** | **–7** | **1320** | **54.5** | **18:54** | .... | .... | .... | .... | .... | .... | .... | .... | .... |
| | **NHL Totals** | | **681** | **140** | **223** | **363** | **390** | **27** | **15** | **24** | **1032** | **13.6** | | **10566** | **50.9** | **17:18** | **60** | **7** | **18** | **25** | **34** | **0** | **0** | **1** | **17:25** |

Traded to **Phoenix** by **St. Louis** with Ladislav Nagy, the rights to Jeff Taffe and St. Louis' 1st round choice (Ben Eager) in 2002 Entry Draft for Keith Tkachuk, March 13, 2001. Traded to **Philadelphia** by **Phoenix** with Robert Esche for Brian Boucher and Nashville's 3rd round choice (previously acquired, Phoenix selected Joe Callahan) in 2002 Entry Draft, June 12, 2002. Signed as a free agent by **Zvolen** (Slovakia), October 27, 2004. Traded to **Chicago** by **Philadelphia** for Kyle Calder, August 4, 2006. • Missed remainder of 2006-07 season recovering from knee injury suffered in game vs. St. Louis, October 21, 2006. Signed as a free agent by **Los Angeles**, July 2, 2007.

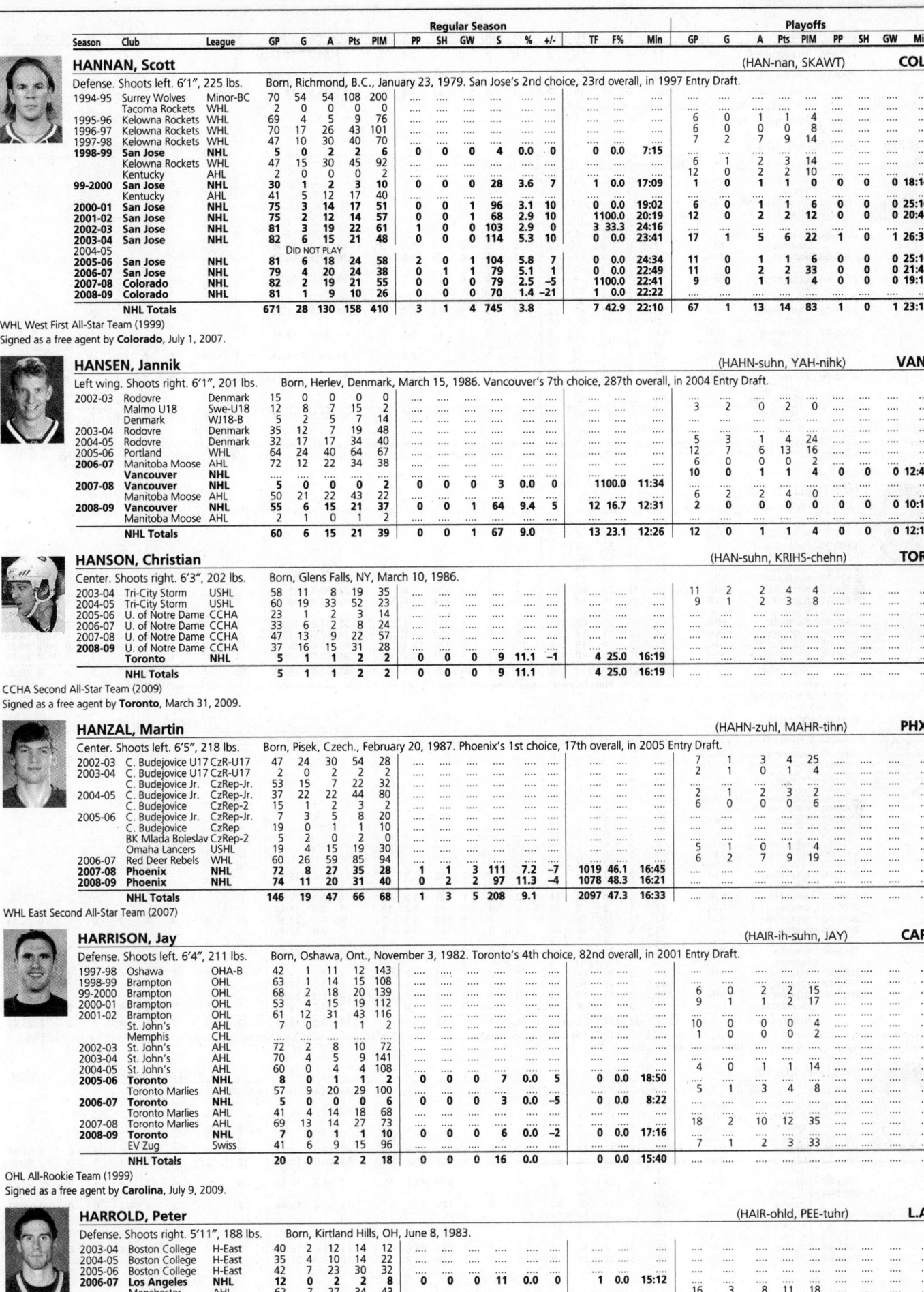

## HANNAN, Scott (HAN-nan, SKAWT) COL.

Defense. Shoots left. 6'1", 225 lbs. Born, Richmond, B.C., January 23, 1979. San Jose's 2nd choice, 23rd overall, in 1997 Entry Draft.

| | | | Regular Season | | | | | | | | | | | | | | Playoffs | | | | | | | | |
|---|---|---|---|---|---|---|---|---|---|---|---|---|---|---|---|---|---|---|---|---|---|---|---|---|---|
| Season | Club | League | GP | G | A | Pts | PIM | PP | SH | GW | S | % | +/- | TF | F% | Min | GP | G | A | Pts | PIM | PP | SH | GW | Min |
| 1994-95 | Surrey Wolves | Minor-BC | 70 | 54 | 54 | 108 | 200 | .... | .... | .... | .... | .... | .... | .... | .... | .... | .... | .... | .... | .... | .... | .... | .... | .... | .... |
| | Tacoma Rockets | WHL | 2 | 0 | 0 | 0 | 0 | .... | .... | .... | .... | .... | .... | .... | .... | .... | .... | .... | .... | .... | .... | .... | .... | .... | .... |
| 1995-96 | Kelowna Rockets | WHL | 69 | 4 | 5 | 9 | 76 | .... | .... | .... | .... | .... | .... | .... | .... | .... | 6 | 0 | 1 | 1 | 4 | .... | .... | .... | .... |
| 1996-97 | Kelowna Rockets | WHL | 70 | 17 | 26 | 43 | 101 | .... | .... | .... | .... | .... | .... | .... | .... | .... | 6 | 0 | 0 | 0 | 8 | .... | .... | .... | .... |
| 1997-98 | Kelowna Rockets | WHL | 47 | 10 | 30 | 40 | 70 | .... | .... | .... | .... | .... | .... | .... | .... | .... | 7 | 2 | 7 | 9 | 14 | .... | .... | .... | .... |
| **1998-99** | **San Jose** | **NHL** | **5** | **0** | **2** | **2** | **6** | **0** | **0** | **0** | **4** | **0.0** | **0** | **0** | **0.0** | **7:15** | .... | .... | .... | .... | .... | .... | .... | .... | .... |
| | Kelowna Rockets | WHL | 47 | 15 | 30 | 45 | 92 | .... | .... | .... | .... | .... | .... | .... | .... | .... | 6 | 1 | 2 | 3 | 14 | .... | .... | .... | .... |
| | Kentucky | AHL | 2 | 0 | 0 | 0 | 2 | .... | .... | .... | .... | .... | .... | .... | .... | .... | 12 | 0 | 2 | 2 | 10 | .... | .... | .... | .... |
| **99-2000** | **San Jose** | **NHL** | **30** | **1** | **2** | **3** | **10** | **0** | **0** | **0** | **28** | **3.6** | **7** | **1** | **0.0** | **17:09** | **1** | **0** | **1** | **1** | **0** | **0** | **0** | **0** | **18:14** |
| | Kentucky | AHL | 41 | 5 | 12 | 17 | 40 | .... | .... | .... | .... | .... | .... | .... | .... | .... | .... | .... | .... | .... | .... | .... | .... | .... | .... |
| **2000-01** | **San Jose** | **NHL** | **75** | **3** | **14** | **17** | **51** | **0** | **0** | **1** | **96** | **3.1** | **10** | **0** | **0.0** | **19:02** | **6** | **0** | **1** | **1** | **6** | **0** | **0** | **0** | **25:10** |
| **2001-02** | **San Jose** | **NHL** | **75** | **2** | **12** | **14** | **57** | **0** | **0** | **1** | **68** | **2.9** | **10** | **1** | **100.0** | **20:19** | **12** | **0** | **2** | **2** | **12** | **0** | **0** | **0** | **20:46** |
| **2002-03** | **San Jose** | **NHL** | **81** | **3** | **19** | **22** | **61** | **1** | **0** | **0** | **103** | **2.9** | **0** | **3** | **33.3** | **24:16** | .... | .... | .... | .... | .... | .... | .... | .... | .... |
| **2003-04** | **San Jose** | **NHL** | **82** | **6** | **15** | **21** | **48** | **0** | **0** | **0** | **114** | **5.3** | **10** | **0** | **0.0** | **23:41** | **17** | **1** | **5** | **6** | **22** | **1** | **0** | **1** | **26:38** |
| 2004-05 | | | DID NOT PLAY | | | | | | | | | | | | | | | | | | | | | | |
| **2005-06** | **San Jose** | **NHL** | **81** | **6** | **18** | **24** | **58** | **2** | **0** | **1** | **104** | **5.8** | **7** | **0** | **0.0** | **24:34** | **11** | **0** | **1** | **1** | **6** | **0** | **0** | **0** | **25:16** |
| **2006-07** | **San Jose** | **NHL** | **79** | **4** | **20** | **24** | **38** | **0** | **1** | **1** | **79** | **5.1** | **1** | **0** | **0.0** | **22:49** | **11** | **0** | **2** | **2** | **33** | **0** | **0** | **0** | **21:42** |
| **2007-08** | **Colorado** | **NHL** | **82** | **2** | **19** | **21** | **55** | **0** | **0** | **0** | **79** | **2.5** | **–5** | **1** | **100.0** | **22:41** | **9** | **0** | **1** | **1** | **4** | **0** | **0** | **0** | **19:15** |
| **2008-09** | **Colorado** | **NHL** | **81** | **1** | **9** | **10** | **26** | **0** | **0** | **0** | **70** | **1.4** | **–21** | **1** | **0.0** | **22:22** | .... | .... | .... | .... | .... | .... | .... | .... | .... |
| | **NHL Totals** | | **671** | **28** | **130** | **158** | **410** | **3** | **1** | **4** | **745** | **3.8** | | **7** | **42.9** | **22:10** | **67** | **1** | **13** | **14** | **83** | **1** | **0** | **1** | **23:18** |

WHL West First All-Star Team (1999)
Signed as a free agent by **Colorado**, July 1, 2007.

## HANSEN, Jannik (HAHN-suhn, YAH-nihk) VAN.

Left wing. Shoots right. 6'1", 201 lbs. Born, Herlev, Denmark, March 15, 1986. Vancouver's 7th choice, 287th overall, in 2004 Entry Draft.

| Season | Club | League | GP | G | A | Pts | PIM | PP | SH | GW | S | % | +/- | TF | F% | Min | GP | G | A | Pts | PIM | PP | SH | GW | Min |
|---|---|---|---|---|---|---|---|---|---|---|---|---|---|---|---|---|---|---|---|---|---|---|---|---|---|
| 2002-03 | Rodovre | Denmark | 15 | 0 | 0 | 0 | 0 | .... | .... | .... | .... | .... | .... | .... | .... | .... | .... | .... | .... | .... | .... | .... | .... | .... | .... |
| | Malmo U18 | Swe-U18 | 12 | 8 | 7 | 15 | 2 | .... | .... | .... | .... | .... | .... | .... | .... | .... | 3 | 2 | 0 | 2 | 0 | .... | .... | .... | .... |
| | Denmark | WJ18-B | 5 | 2 | 5 | 7 | 14 | .... | .... | .... | .... | .... | .... | .... | .... | .... | .... | .... | .... | .... | .... | .... | .... | .... | .... |
| 2003-04 | Rodovre | Denmark | 35 | 12 | 7 | 19 | 48 | .... | .... | .... | .... | .... | .... | .... | .... | .... | .... | .... | .... | .... | .... | .... | .... | .... | .... |
| 2004-05 | Rodovre | Denmark | 32 | 17 | 17 | 34 | 40 | .... | .... | .... | .... | .... | .... | .... | .... | .... | 5 | 3 | 1 | 4 | 24 | .... | .... | .... | .... |
| 2005-06 | Portland | WHL | 64 | 24 | 40 | 64 | 67 | .... | .... | .... | .... | .... | .... | .... | .... | .... | 12 | 7 | 6 | 13 | 16 | .... | .... | .... | .... |
| **2006-07** | Manitoba Moose | AHL | 72 | 12 | 22 | 34 | 38 | .... | .... | .... | .... | .... | .... | .... | .... | .... | 6 | 0 | 0 | 0 | 2 | .... | .... | .... | .... |
| | **Vancouver** | **NHL** | .... | .... | .... | .... | .... | .... | .... | .... | .... | .... | .... | .... | .... | .... | **10** | **0** | **1** | **1** | **4** | **0** | **0** | **0** | **12:41** |
| **2007-08** | **Vancouver** | **NHL** | **5** | **0** | **0** | **0** | **2** | **0** | **0** | **0** | **3** | **0.0** | **0** | **1** | **100.0** | **11:34** | .... | .... | .... | .... | .... | .... | .... | .... | .... |
| | Manitoba Moose | AHL | 50 | 21 | 22 | 43 | 22 | .... | .... | .... | .... | .... | .... | .... | .... | .... | 6 | 2 | 2 | 4 | 0 | .... | .... | .... | .... |
| **2008-09** | **Vancouver** | **NHL** | **55** | **6** | **15** | **21** | **37** | **0** | **0** | **1** | **64** | **9.4** | **5** | **12** | **16.7** | **12:31** | **2** | **0** | **0** | **0** | **0** | **0** | **0** | **0** | **10:16** |
| | Manitoba Moose | AHL | 2 | 1 | 0 | 1 | 2 | .... | .... | .... | .... | .... | .... | .... | .... | .... | .... | .... | .... | .... | .... | .... | .... | .... | .... |
| | **NHL Totals** | | **60** | **6** | **15** | **21** | **39** | **0** | **0** | **1** | **67** | **9.0** | | **13** | **23.1** | **12:26** | **12** | **0** | **1** | **1** | **4** | **0** | **0** | **0** | **12:17** |

## HANSON, Christian (HAN-suhn, KRIHS-chehn) TOR.

Center. Shoots right. 6'3", 202 lbs. Born, Glens Falls, NY, March 10, 1986.

| Season | Club | League | GP | G | A | Pts | PIM | PP | SH | GW | S | % | +/- | TF | F% | Min | GP | G | A | Pts | PIM | PP | SH | GW | Min |
|---|---|---|---|---|---|---|---|---|---|---|---|---|---|---|---|---|---|---|---|---|---|---|---|---|---|
| 2003-04 | Tri-City Storm | USHL | 58 | 11 | 8 | 19 | 35 | .... | .... | .... | .... | .... | .... | .... | .... | .... | 11 | 2 | 2 | 4 | 4 | .... | .... | .... | .... |
| 2004-05 | Tri-City Storm | USHL | 60 | 19 | 33 | 52 | 23 | .... | .... | .... | .... | .... | .... | .... | .... | .... | 9 | 1 | 2 | 3 | 8 | .... | .... | .... | .... |
| 2005-06 | U. of Notre Dame | CCHA | 23 | 1 | 2 | 3 | 14 | .... | .... | .... | .... | .... | .... | .... | .... | .... | .... | .... | .... | .... | .... | .... | .... | .... | .... |
| 2006-07 | U. of Notre Dame | CCHA | 33 | 6 | 2 | 8 | 24 | .... | .... | .... | .... | .... | .... | .... | .... | .... | .... | .... | .... | .... | .... | .... | .... | .... | .... |
| 2007-08 | U. of Notre Dame | CCHA | 47 | 13 | 9 | 22 | 57 | .... | .... | .... | .... | .... | .... | .... | .... | .... | .... | .... | .... | .... | .... | .... | .... | .... | .... |
| **2008-09** | U. of Notre Dame | CCHA | 37 | 16 | 15 | 31 | 28 | .... | .... | .... | .... | .... | .... | .... | .... | .... | .... | .... | .... | .... | .... | .... | .... | .... | .... |
| | **Toronto** | **NHL** | **5** | **1** | **1** | **2** | **2** | **0** | **0** | **0** | **9** | **11.1** | **–1** | **4** | **25.0** | **16:19** | .... | .... | .... | .... | .... | .... | .... | .... | .... |
| | **NHL Totals** | | **5** | **1** | **1** | **2** | **2** | **0** | **0** | **0** | **9** | **11.1** | | **4** | **25.0** | **16:19** | .... | .... | .... | .... | .... | .... | .... | .... | .... |

CCHA Second All-Star Team (2009)
Signed as a free agent by **Toronto**, March 31, 2009.

## HANZAL, Martin (HAHN-zuhl, MAHR-tihn) PHX.

Center. Shoots left. 6'5", 218 lbs. Born, Pisek, Czech., February 20, 1987. Phoenix's 1st choice, 17th overall, in 2005 Entry Draft.

| Season | Club | League | GP | G | A | Pts | PIM | PP | SH | GW | S | % | +/- | TF | F% | Min | GP | G | A | Pts | PIM | PP | SH | GW | Min |
|---|---|---|---|---|---|---|---|---|---|---|---|---|---|---|---|---|---|---|---|---|---|---|---|---|---|
| 2002-03 | C. Budejovice U17 | CzR-U17 | 47 | 24 | 30 | 54 | 28 | .... | .... | .... | .... | .... | .... | .... | .... | .... | 7 | 1 | 3 | 4 | 25 | .... | .... | .... | .... |
| 2003-04 | C. Budejovice U17 | CzR-U17 | 2 | 0 | 2 | 2 | 2 | .... | .... | .... | .... | .... | .... | .... | .... | .... | 2 | 1 | 0 | 1 | 4 | .... | .... | .... | .... |
| | C. Budejovice Jr. | CzRep-Jr. | 53 | 15 | 7 | 22 | 32 | .... | .... | .... | .... | .... | .... | .... | .... | .... | .... | .... | .... | .... | .... | .... | .... | .... | .... |
| 2004-05 | C. Budejovice Jr. | CzRep-Jr. | 37 | 22 | 22 | 44 | 80 | .... | .... | .... | .... | .... | .... | .... | .... | .... | 2 | 1 | 2 | 3 | 2 | .... | .... | .... | .... |
| | C. Budejovice | CzRep-2 | 15 | 1 | 2 | 3 | 2 | .... | .... | .... | .... | .... | .... | .... | .... | .... | 6 | 0 | 0 | 0 | 6 | .... | .... | .... | .... |
| 2005-06 | C. Budejovice Jr. | CzRep-Jr. | 7 | 3 | 5 | 8 | 20 | .... | .... | .... | .... | .... | .... | .... | .... | .... | .... | .... | .... | .... | .... | .... | .... | .... | .... |
| | C. Budejovice | CzRep | 19 | 0 | 1 | 1 | 10 | .... | .... | .... | .... | .... | .... | .... | .... | .... | .... | .... | .... | .... | .... | .... | .... | .... | .... |
| | BK Mlada Boleslav | CzRep-2 | 5 | 2 | 0 | 2 | 0 | .... | .... | .... | .... | .... | .... | .... | .... | .... | .... | .... | .... | .... | .... | .... | .... | .... | .... |
| | Omaha Lancers | USHL | 19 | 4 | 15 | 19 | 30 | .... | .... | .... | .... | .... | .... | .... | .... | .... | 5 | 1 | 0 | 1 | 4 | .... | .... | .... | .... |
| 2006-07 | Red Deer Rebels | WHL | 60 | 26 | 59 | 85 | 94 | .... | .... | .... | .... | .... | .... | .... | .... | .... | 6 | 2 | 7 | 9 | 19 | .... | .... | .... | .... |
| **2007-08** | **Phoenix** | **NHL** | **72** | **8** | **27** | **35** | **28** | **1** | **1** | **3** | **111** | **7.2** | **–7** | **1019** | **46.1** | **16:45** | .... | .... | .... | .... | .... | .... | .... | .... | .... |
| **2008-09** | **Phoenix** | **NHL** | **74** | **11** | **20** | **31** | **40** | **0** | **2** | **2** | **97** | **11.3** | **–4** | **1078** | **48.3** | **16:21** | .... | .... | .... | .... | .... | .... | .... | .... | .... |
| | **NHL Totals** | | **146** | **19** | **47** | **66** | **68** | **1** | **3** | **5** | **208** | **9.1** | | **2097** | **47.3** | **16:33** | .... | .... | .... | .... | .... | .... | .... | .... | .... |

WHL East Second All-Star Team (2007)

## HARRISON, Jay (HAIR-ih-suhn, JAY) CAR.

Defense. Shoots left. 6'4", 211 lbs. Born, Oshawa, Ont., November 3, 1982. Toronto's 4th choice, 82nd overall, in 2001 Entry Draft.

| Season | Club | League | GP | G | A | Pts | PIM | PP | SH | GW | S | % | +/- | TF | F% | Min | GP | G | A | Pts | PIM | PP | SH | GW | Min |
|---|---|---|---|---|---|---|---|---|---|---|---|---|---|---|---|---|---|---|---|---|---|---|---|---|---|
| 1997-98 | Oshawa | OHA-B | 42 | 1 | 11 | 12 | 143 | .... | .... | .... | .... | .... | .... | .... | .... | .... | .... | .... | .... | .... | .... | .... | .... | .... | .... |
| 1998-99 | Brampton | OHL | 63 | 1 | 14 | 15 | 108 | .... | .... | .... | .... | .... | .... | .... | .... | .... | .... | .... | .... | .... | .... | .... | .... | .... | .... |
| 99-2000 | Brampton | OHL | 68 | 2 | 18 | 20 | 139 | .... | .... | .... | .... | .... | .... | .... | .... | .... | 6 | 0 | 2 | 2 | 15 | .... | .... | .... | .... |
| 2000-01 | Brampton | OHL | 53 | 4 | 15 | 19 | 112 | .... | .... | .... | .... | .... | .... | .... | .... | .... | 9 | 1 | 1 | 2 | 17 | .... | .... | .... | .... |
| 2001-02 | Brampton | OHL | 61 | 12 | 31 | 43 | 116 | .... | .... | .... | .... | .... | .... | .... | .... | .... | .... | .... | .... | .... | .... | .... | .... | .... | .... |
| | St. John's | AHL | 7 | 0 | 1 | 1 | 2 | .... | .... | .... | .... | .... | .... | .... | .... | .... | 10 | 0 | 0 | 0 | 4 | .... | .... | .... | .... |
| | Memphis | CHL | .... | .... | .... | .... | .... | .... | .... | .... | .... | .... | .... | .... | .... | .... | 1 | 0 | 0 | 0 | 2 | .... | .... | .... | .... |
| 2002-03 | St. John's | AHL | 72 | 2 | 8 | 10 | 72 | .... | .... | .... | .... | .... | .... | .... | .... | .... | .... | .... | .... | .... | .... | .... | .... | .... | .... |
| 2003-04 | St. John's | AHL | 70 | 4 | 5 | 9 | 141 | .... | .... | .... | .... | .... | .... | .... | .... | .... | .... | .... | .... | .... | .... | .... | .... | .... | .... |
| 2004-05 | St. John's | AHL | 60 | 0 | 4 | 4 | 108 | .... | .... | .... | .... | .... | .... | .... | .... | .... | 4 | 0 | 1 | 1 | 14 | .... | .... | .... | .... |
| **2005-06** | **Toronto** | **NHL** | **8** | **0** | **1** | **1** | **2** | **0** | **0** | **0** | **7** | **0.0** | **5** | **0** | **0.0** | **18:50** | .... | .... | .... | .... | .... | .... | .... | .... | .... |
| | Toronto Marlies | AHL | 57 | 9 | 20 | 29 | 100 | .... | .... | .... | .... | .... | .... | .... | .... | .... | 5 | 1 | 3 | 4 | 8 | .... | .... | .... | .... |
| **2006-07** | **Toronto** | **NHL** | **5** | **0** | **0** | **0** | **6** | **0** | **0** | **0** | **3** | **0.0** | **–5** | **0** | **0.0** | **8:22** | .... | .... | .... | .... | .... | .... | .... | .... | .... |
| | Toronto Marlies | AHL | 41 | 4 | 14 | 18 | 68 | .... | .... | .... | .... | .... | .... | .... | .... | .... | .... | .... | .... | .... | .... | .... | .... | .... | .... |
| 2007-08 | Toronto Marlies | AHL | 69 | 13 | 14 | 27 | 73 | .... | .... | .... | .... | .... | .... | .... | .... | .... | 18 | 2 | 10 | 12 | 35 | .... | .... | .... | .... |
| **2008-09** | **Toronto** | **NHL** | **7** | **0** | **1** | **1** | **10** | **0** | **0** | **0** | **6** | **0.0** | **–2** | **0** | **0.0** | **17:16** | .... | .... | .... | .... | .... | .... | .... | .... | .... |
| | EV Zug | Swiss | 41 | 6 | 9 | 15 | 96 | .... | .... | .... | .... | .... | .... | .... | .... | .... | 7 | 1 | 2 | 3 | 33 | .... | .... | .... | .... |
| | **NHL Totals** | | **20** | **0** | **2** | **2** | **18** | **0** | **0** | **0** | **16** | **0.0** | | **0** | **0.0** | **15:40** | .... | .... | .... | .... | .... | .... | .... | .... | .... |

OHL All-Rookie Team (1999)
Signed as a free agent by **Carolina**, July 9, 2009.

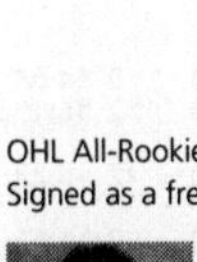

## HARROLD, Peter (HAIR-ohld, PEE-tuhr) L.A.

Defense. Shoots right. 5'11", 188 lbs. Born, Kirtland Hills, OH, June 8, 1983.

| Season | Club | League | GP | G | A | Pts | PIM | PP | SH | GW | S | % | +/- | TF | F% | Min | GP | G | A | Pts | PIM | PP | SH | GW | Min |
|---|---|---|---|---|---|---|---|---|---|---|---|---|---|---|---|---|---|---|---|---|---|---|---|---|---|
| 2003-04 | Boston College | H-East | 40 | 2 | 12 | 14 | 12 | .... | .... | .... | .... | .... | .... | .... | .... | .... | .... | .... | .... | .... | .... | .... | .... | .... | .... |
| 2004-05 | Boston College | H-East | 35 | 4 | 10 | 14 | 22 | .... | .... | .... | .... | .... | .... | .... | .... | .... | .... | .... | .... | .... | .... | .... | .... | .... | .... |
| 2005-06 | Boston College | H-East | 42 | 7 | 23 | 30 | 32 | .... | .... | .... | .... | .... | .... | .... | .... | .... | .... | .... | .... | .... | .... | .... | .... | .... | .... |
| **2006-07** | **Los Angeles** | **NHL** | **12** | **0** | **2** | **2** | **8** | **0** | **0** | **0** | **11** | **0.0** | **0** | **1** | **0.0** | **15:12** | .... | .... | .... | .... | .... | .... | .... | .... | .... |
| | Manchester | AHL | 62 | 7 | 27 | 34 | 43 | .... | .... | .... | .... | .... | .... | .... | .... | .... | 16 | 3 | 8 | 11 | 18 | .... | .... | .... | .... |

| | | | Regular Season | | | | | | | | | | | | | | Playoffs | | | | | | | | |
|---|---|---|---|---|---|---|---|---|---|---|---|---|---|---|---|---|---|---|---|---|---|---|---|---|---|
| Season | Club | League | GP | G | A | Pts | PIM | PP | SH | GW | S | % | +/- | TF | F% | Min | GP | G | A | Pts | PIM | PP | SH | GW | Min |
| 2007-08 | Los Angeles | NHL | 25 | 2 | 3 | 5 | 2 | 0 | 0 | 0 | 16 | 12.5 | 3 | 2 | 50.0 | 16:23 | | | | | | | | | |
| | Manchester | AHL | 49 | 7 | 36 | 43 | 25 | | | | | | | | | | 4 | 0 | 1 | 1 | 4 | | | | |
| 2008-09 | Los Angeles | NHL | 69 | 4 | 8 | 12 | 28 | 1 | 0 | 1 | 95 | 4.2 | –13 | 16 | 37.5 | 13:10 | | | | | | | | | |
| | NHL Totals | | 106 | 6 | 13 | 19 | 38 | 1 | 0 | 1 | 122 | 4.9 | | 19 | 36.8 | 14:10 | | | | | | | | | |

Hockey East First All-Star Team (2006) • NCAA East First All-American Team (2006)

Signed as a free agent by **Los Angeles**, April 12, 2006.

## HARTIGAN, Mark

(HAHR-tih-guhn, MAHRK)

Center. Shoots left. 6', 200 lbs. Born, Fort St. John, B.C., October 15, 1977.

| Season | Club | League | GP | G | A | Pts | PIM | PP | SH | GW | S | % | +/- | TF | F% | Min | GP | G | A | Pts | PIM | PP | SH | GW | Min |
|---|---|---|---|---|---|---|---|---|---|---|---|---|---|---|---|---|---|---|---|---|---|---|---|---|---|
| 1996-97 | Weyburn | SJHL | 52 | 44 | 32 | 76 | .... | | | | | | | | | | | | | | | | | | |
| 1997-98 | Weyburn | SJHL | 62 | *59 | 46 | *105 | 81 | | | | | | | | | | 23 | 17 | 21 | 38 | 10 | | | | |
| 1998-99 | St. Cloud State | WCHA | DID NOT PLAY – FRESHMAN | | | | | | | | | | | | | | | | | | | | | | |
| 99-2000 | St. Cloud State | WCHA | 37 | 22 | 20 | 42 | 24 | | | | | | | | | | | | | | | | | | |
| 2000-01 | St. Cloud State | WCHA | 40 | 27 | 21 | 48 | 20 | | | | | | | | | | | | | | | | | | |
| 2001-02 | St. Cloud State | WCHA | 42 | *37 | 38 | 75 | 42 | | | | | | | | | | | | | | | | | | |
| | Atlanta | NHL | 2 | 0 | 0 | 0 | 2 | 0 | 0 | 0 | 3 | 0.0 | –2 | 18 | 38.9 | 13:16 | | | | | | | | | |
| 2002-03 | Atlanta | NHL | 23 | 5 | 2 | 7 | 6 | 1 | 0 | 0 | 25 | 20.0 | –8 | 220 | 47.3 | 10:52 | | | | | | | | | |
| | Chicago Wolves | AHL | 55 | 15 | 31 | 46 | 43 | | | | | | | | | | 9 | 1 | 2 | 3 | 10 | | | | |
| 2003-04 | Columbus | NHL | 9 | 1 | 3 | 4 | 6 | 1 | 0 | 0 | 15 | 6.7 | –2 | 138 | 40.6 | 16:19 | | | | | | | | | |
| | Syracuse Crunch | AHL | 69 | 23 | 23 | 46 | 86 | | | | | | | | | | 7 | 1 | 4 | 5 | 8 | | | | |
| 2004-05 | Syracuse Crunch | AHL | 69 | 31 | 28 | 59 | 105 | | | | | | | | | | | | | | | | | | |
| 2005-06 | Columbus | NHL | 33 | 9 | 3 | 12 | 22 | 3 | 0 | 1 | 54 | 16.7 | –1 | 194 | 44.9 | 11:39 | | | | | | | | | |
| | Syracuse Crunch | AHL | 49 | 34 | 41 | 75 | 48 | | | | | | | | | | 6 | 1 | 2 | 3 | 33 | | | | |
| 2006-07 | Columbus | NHL | 6 | 1 | 2 | 3 | 2 | 1 | 0 | 0 | 11 | 9.1 | 2 | 83 | 45.8 | 13:51 | | | | | | | | | |
| | Syracuse Crunch | AHL | 34 | 19 | 13 | 32 | 51 | | | | | | | | | | | | | | | | | | |
| | ♦ Anaheim | NHL | 6 | 0 | 0 | 0 | 4 | 0 | 0 | 0 | 4 | 0.0 | –1 | 23 | 26.1 | 7:41 | 1 | 0 | 0 | 0 | 0 | 0 | 0 | 0 | 3:34 |
| | Portland Pirates | AHL | 25 | 9 | 16 | 25 | 20 | | | | | | | | | | | | | | | | | | |
| 2007-08 | Detroit | NHL | 23 | 3 | 1 | 4 | 16 | 0 | 0 | 0 | 19 | 15.8 | –2 | 114 | 52.6 | 7:09 | 4 | 0 | 1 | 1 | 4 | 0 | 0 | 0 | 5:21 |
| | Grand Rapids | AHL | 48 | 23 | 19 | 42 | 76 | | | | | | | | | | | | | | | | | | |
| 2008-09 | Dynamo Riga | Rus-KHL | 55 | 20 | 18 | 38 | 115 | | | | | | | | | | 3 | 1 | 0 | 1 | 10 | | | | |
| | NHL Totals | | 102 | 19 | 11 | 30 | 58 | 6 | 0 | 1 | 131 | 14.5 | | 790 | 45.3 | 10:48 | 5 | 0 | 1 | 1 | 4 | 0 | 0 | 0 | 5:00 |

WCHA First All-Star Team (2002) • WCHA Player of the Year (2002)

Signed as a free agent by **Atlanta**, March 27, 2002. Signed as a free agent by **Columbus**, July 15, 2003. Traded to **Anaheim** by **Columbus** with Joe Motzko and Columbus'4th round choice (Sebastian Stefaniszin) in 2007 Entry Draft for Zenon Konopka, Curtis Glencross and Anaheim's 7th round choice (Trent Vogelhuber) in 2007 Entry Draft, January 26, 2007. Signed as a free agent by **Detroit**, July 16, 2007.

## HARTNELL, Scott

(HAHRT-nuhl, SKAWT) **PHI.**

Left wing. Shoots left. 6'2", 210 lbs. Born, Regina, Sask., April 18, 1982. Nashville's 1st choice, 6th overall, in 2000 Entry Draft.

| Season | Club | League | GP | G | A | Pts | PIM | PP | SH | GW | S | % | +/- | TF | F% | Min | GP | G | A | Pts | PIM | PP | SH | GW | Min |
|---|---|---|---|---|---|---|---|---|---|---|---|---|---|---|---|---|---|---|---|---|---|---|---|---|---|
| 1997-98 | Lloydminster | AJHL | 56 | 9 | 25 | 34 | 82 | | | | | | | | | | 4 | 2 | 1 | 3 | 8 | | | | |
| | Prince Albert | WHL | 1 | 0 | 1 | 1 | 2 | | | | | | | | | | | | | | | | | | |
| 1998-99 | Prince Albert | WHL | 65 | 10 | 34 | 44 | 104 | | | | | | | | | | 14 | 0 | 5 | 5 | 22 | | | | |
| 99-2000 | Prince Albert | WHL | 62 | 27 | 55 | 82 | 124 | | | | | | | | | | 6 | 3 | 2 | 5 | 6 | | | | |
| 2000-01 | Nashville | NHL | 75 | 2 | 14 | 16 | 48 | 0 | 0 | 0 | 92 | 2.2 | –8 | 3 | 33.3 | 10:54 | | | | | | | | | |
| 2001-02 | Nashville | NHL | 75 | 14 | 27 | 41 | 111 | 3 | 0 | 4 | 162 | 8.6 | 5 | 12 | 25.0 | 16:58 | | | | | | | | | |
| 2002-03 | Nashville | NHL | 82 | 12 | 22 | 34 | 101 | 2 | 0 | 2 | 221 | 5.4 | –3 | 23 | 30.4 | 15:17 | | | | | | | | | |
| 2003-04 | Nashville | NHL | 59 | 18 | 15 | 33 | 87 | 5 | 0 | 3 | 154 | 11.7 | –5 | 48 | 37.5 | 16:16 | 6 | 1 | 2 | 3 | 2 | 0 | 0 | 0 | 15:37 |
| 2004-05 | Valerengen IF Oslo | Norway | 28 | 17 | 12 | 29 | 103 | | | | | | | | | | 11 | 12 | 7 | 19 | 24 | | | | |
| 2005-06 | Nashville | NHL | 81 | 25 | 23 | 48 | 101 | 10 | 2 | 8 | 211 | 11.8 | 8 | 58 | 37.9 | 16:05 | 5 | 1 | 0 | 1 | 4 | 0 | 0 | 0 | 12:12 |
| 2006-07 | Nashville | NHL | 64 | 22 | 17 | 39 | 96 | 10 | 0 | 2 | 150 | 14.7 | 19 | 134 | 47.0 | 15:43 | 5 | 1 | 1 | 2 | 28 | 1 | 0 | 0 | 14:23 |
| 2007-08 | Philadelphia | NHL | 80 | 24 | 19 | 43 | 159 | 10 | 1 | 6 | 176 | 13.6 | 2 | 32 | 40.6 | 16:11 | 17 | 3 | 4 | 7 | 20 | 0 | 0 | 0 | 15:28 |
| 2008-09 | Philadelphia | NHL | 82 | 30 | 30 | 60 | 143 | 6 | 1 | 5 | 210 | 14.3 | 14 | 36 | 50.0 | 17:48 | 6 | 1 | 1 | 2 | 23 | 1 | 0 | 0 | 18:36 |
| | NHL Totals | | 598 | 147 | 167 | 314 | 846 | 46 | 4 | 30 | 1376 | 10.7 | | 346 | 41.9 | 15:40 | 39 | 7 | 8 | 15 | 77 | 2 | 0 | 0 | 15:25 |

Signed as a free agent by **Oslo** (Norway), October 21, 2004. Traded to **Philadelphia** by **Nashville** with Kimmo Timmonen for Nashville's 1st round choice (previously acquired, Nashville selected Jonathon Blum) in 2007 Entry Draft, June 18, 2007.

## HAVELID, Niclas

(HAHV-lihd, NIHK-luhs)

Defense. Shoots left. 6', 200 lbs. Born, Stockholm, Sweden, April 12, 1973. Anaheim's 2nd choice, 83rd overall, in 1999 Entry Draft.

| Season | Club | League | GP | G | A | Pts | PIM | PP | SH | GW | S | % | +/- | TF | F% | Min | GP | G | A | Pts | PIM | PP | SH | GW | Min |
|---|---|---|---|---|---|---|---|---|---|---|---|---|---|---|---|---|---|---|---|---|---|---|---|---|---|
| 1988-89 | Enkopings SK | Sweden-3 | 7 | 0 | 1 | 1 | 0 | | | | | | | | | | | | | | | | | | |
| 1989-90 | Enkopings SK | Sweden-3 | 24 | 1 | 2 | 3 | 28 | | | | | | | | | | | | | | | | | | |
| 1990-91 | Arlanda | Sweden-2 | 30 | 2 | 3 | 5 | 22 | | | | | | | | | | | | | | | | | | |
| 1991-92 | AIK Solna | Sweden | 10 | 0 | 0 | 0 | 2 | | | | | | | | | | | | | | | | | | |
| 1992-93 | AIK Solna | Sweden | 30 | 1 | 2 | 3 | 22 | | | | | | | | | | 3 | 0 | 0 | 0 | 2 | | | | |
| 1993-94 | AIK Solna | Sweden-2 | 22 | 3 | 9 | 12 | 14 | | | | | | | | | | | | | | | | | | |
| 1994-95 | AIK Solna | Sweden | 40 | 3 | 7 | 10 | 38 | | | | | | | | | | | | | | | | | | |
| 1995-96 | AIK Solna | Sweden | 40 | 5 | 6 | 11 | 30 | | | | | | | | | | | | | | | | | | |
| 1996-97 | AIK Solna | Sweden | 49 | 3 | 6 | 9 | 42 | | | | | | | | | | 7 | 1 | 2 | 3 | 8 | | | | |
| 1997-98 | AIK Solna | Sweden | 43 | 8 | 4 | 12 | 42 | | | | | | | | | | 10 | 1 | 3 | 4 | 39 | | | | |
| 1998-99 | Malmo | Sweden | 50 | 10 | 12 | 22 | 42 | | | | | | | | | | 8 | 0 | 4 | 4 | 10 | | | | |
| 99-2000 | Anaheim | NHL | 50 | 2 | 7 | 9 | 20 | 0 | 0 | 2 | 70 | 2.9 | 0 | 1 | 0.0 | 19:10 | | | | | | | | | |
| | Cincinnati | AHL | 2 | 0 | 0 | 0 | 0 | | | | | | | | | | | | | | | | | | |
| 2000-01 | Anaheim | NHL | 47 | 4 | 10 | 14 | 34 | 2 | 0 | 1 | 69 | 5.8 | –6 | 4 | 0.0 | 21:51 | | | | | | | | | |
| 2001-02 | Anaheim | NHL | 52 | 1 | 2 | 3 | 40 | 0 | 0 | 0 | 45 | 2.2 | –13 | 1 | 0.0 | 17:01 | | | | | | | | | |
| 2002-03 | Anaheim | NHL | 82 | 11 | 22 | 33 | 30 | 4 | 0 | 5 | 169 | 6.5 | 5 | 3 | 0.0 | 22:30 | 21 | 0 | 4 | 4 | 2 | 0 | 0 | 0 | 25:41 |
| 2003-04 | Anaheim | NHL | 79 | 6 | 20 | 26 | 28 | 5 | 0 | 3 | 122 | 4.9 | –28 | 0 | 0.0 | 22:39 | | | | | | | | | |
| 2004-05 | Sodertalje SK | Sweden | 46 | 2 | 2 | 4 | 60 | | | | | | | | | | 10 | 1 | 1 | 2 | 18 | | | | |
| 2005-06 | Atlanta | NHL | 82 | 4 | 28 | 32 | 48 | 2 | 0 | 0 | 84 | 4.8 | 9 | 0 | 0.0 | 24:25 | | | | | | | | | |
| | Sweden | Olympics | 7 | 0 | 0 | 0 | 4 | | | | | | | | | | | | | | | | | | |
| 2006-07 | Atlanta | NHL | 77 | 3 | 18 | 21 | 52 | 1 | 0 | 1 | 82 | 3.7 | –2 | 1 | 0.0 | 25:16 | 4 | 0 | 2 | 2 | 0 | 0 | 0 | 0 | 24:14 |
| 2007-08 | Atlanta | NHL | 81 | 1 | 13 | 14 | 42 | 0 | 0 | 0 | 54 | 1.9 | 2 | 0 | 0.0 | 20:30 | | | | | | | | | |
| 2008-09 | Atlanta | NHL | 63 | 2 | 13 | 15 | 42 | 0 | 1 | 0 | 41 | 4.9 | 4 | 0 | 0.0 | 20:54 | | | | | | | | | |
| | New Jersey | NHL | 15 | 0 | 4 | 4 | 6 | 0 | 0 | 0 | 15 | 0.0 | –2 | 0 | 0.0 | 19:43 | 7 | 0 | 1 | 1 | 2 | 0 | 0 | 0 | 17:31 |
| | NHL Totals | | 628 | 34 | 137 | 171 | 342 | 14 | 1 | 12 | 751 | 4.5 | | 10 | 0.0 | 21:51 | 32 | 0 | 7 | 7 | 4 | 0 | 0 | 0 | 23:43 |

Traded to **Atlanta** by **Anaheim** for Kurtis Foster, June 26, 2004. Signed as a free agent by **Sodertalje** (Sweden), August 9, 2004. Traded to **New Jersey** by **Atlanta** with Myles Stoesz for Anssi Salmela, March 1, 2009. Signed as a free agent by **Linkoping** (Sweden), May 15, 2009.

## HAVLAT, Martin

(HAV-lat, MAHR-tihn) **MIN.**

Right wing. Shoots left. 6'2", 217 lbs. Born, Mlada Boleslav, Czech., April 19, 1981. Ottawa's 1st choice, 26th overall, in 1999 Entry Draft.

| Season | Club | League | GP | G | A | Pts | PIM | PP | SH | GW | S | % | +/- | TF | F% | Min | GP | G | A | Pts | PIM | PP | SH | GW | Min |
|---|---|---|---|---|---|---|---|---|---|---|---|---|---|---|---|---|---|---|---|---|---|---|---|---|---|
| 1997-98 | Ytong Brno Jr. | CzRep-Jr. | 32 | 38 | 29 | 67 | .... | | | | | | | | | | | | | | | | | | |
| 1998-99 | HC Trinec Jr. | CzRep-Jr. | 31 | 28 | 23 | 51 | .... | | | | | | | | | | | | | | | | | | |
| | Trinec | CzRep | 24 | 2 | 3 | 5 | 4 | | | | | | | | | | 8 | 0 | 0 | 0 | | | | | |
| 99-2000 | HC Ocelari Trinec | CzRep | 46 | 13 | 29 | 42 | 42 | | | | | | | | | | 4 | 0 | 2 | 2 | 8 | | | | |
| 2000-01 | Ottawa | NHL | 73 | 19 | 23 | 42 | 20 | 7 | 0 | 5 | 133 | 14.3 | 8 | 40 | 30.0 | 13:47 | 4 | 0 | 0 | 0 | 2 | 0 | 0 | 0 | 14:04 |
| 2001-02 | Ottawa | NHL | 72 | 22 | 28 | 50 | 66 | 9 | 0 | 6 | 145 | 15.2 | –7 | 15 | 40.0 | 14:46 | 12 | 2 | 5 | 7 | 14 | 2 | 0 | 2 | 16:19 |
| | Czech Republic | Olympics | 4 | 3 | 1 | 4 | 27 | | | | | | | | | | | | | | | | | | |
| 2002-03 | Ottawa | NHL | 67 | 24 | 35 | 59 | 30 | 9 | 0 | 4 | 179 | 13.4 | 20 | 7 | 14.3 | 16:27 | 18 | 5 | 6 | 11 | 14 | 1 | 0 | 2 | 16:27 |
| 2003-04 | HC Sparta Praha | CzRep | 5 | 1 | 3 | 4 | 8 | | | | | | | | | | | | | | | | | | |
| | Ottawa | NHL | 68 | 31 | 37 | 68 | 46 | 13 | 0 | 7 | 175 | 17.7 | 12 | 11 | 36.4 | 16:44 | 7 | 0 | 3 | 3 | 2 | 0 | 0 | 0 | 16:10 |
| 2004-05 | Znojmo | CzRep | 12 | 10 | 4 | 14 | 16 | | | | | | | | | | | | | | | | | | |
| | Dynamo Moscow | Russia | 10 | 2 | 0 | 2 | 14 | | | | | | | | | | | | | | | | | | |
| | HC Sparta Praha | CzRep | 9 | 5 | 4 | 9 | 37 | | | | | | | | | | 5 | 0 | 0 | 0 | 20 | | | | |
| 2005-06 | Ottawa | NHL | 18 | 9 | 7 | 16 | 4 | 2 | 1 | 1 | 57 | 15.8 | 6 | 25 | 36.0 | 18:11 | 10 | 7 | 6 | 13 | 4 | 3 | 0 | 1 | 17:13 |
| 2006-07 | Chicago | NHL | 56 | 25 | 32 | 57 | 28 | 5 | 0 | 1 | 176 | 14.2 | 15 | 12 | 33.3 | 21:24 | | | | | | | | | |

| | | | Regular Season | | | | | | | | | | | | | | Playoffs | | | | | | | | |
|---|---|---|---|---|---|---|---|---|---|---|---|---|---|---|---|---|---|---|---|---|---|---|---|---|---|
| Season | Club | League | GP | G | A | Pts | PIM | PP | SH | GW | S | % | +/- | TF | F% | Min | GP | G | A | Pts | PIM | PP | SH | GW | Min |
| **2007-08** | **Chicago** | **NHL** | **35** | **10** | **17** | **27** | **22** | **3** | **0** | **2** | **87** | **11.5** | **4** | **3** | **0.0** | **18:35** | .... | .... | .... | .... | .... | .... | .... | .... | .... |
| **2008-09** | **Chicago** | **NHL** | **81** | **29** | **48** | **77** | **30** | **5** | **0** | **5** | **249** | **11.6** | **29** | **8** | **25.0** | **17:25** | **16** | **5** | **10** | **15** | **8** | **0** | **0** | **1** | **15:34** |
| | **NHL Totals** | | **470** | **169** | **227** | **396** | **246** | **53** | **1** | **31** | **1201** | **14.1** | | **121** | **31.4** | **16:48** | **67** | **19** | **30** | **49** | **44** | **6** | **0** | **6** | **16:10** |

NHL All-Rookie Team (2001)

Played in NHL All-Star Game (2007)

Signed as a free agent by **Znojmo** (CzRep), September 24, 2004. Signed as a free agent by **Dynamo Moscow** (Russia), November 10, 2004. Signed as a free agent by **Sparta Praha** (CzRep), January 31, 2005. • Missed majority of 2005-06 season recovering from shoulder injury suffered in game vs. Montreal, November 29, 2005. Traded to **Chicago** by **Ottawa** with Bryan Smolinski for Tom Preissing, Josh Hennessy, Michal Barinka and Chicago's 2nd round choice (Patrick Wiercioch) in 2008 Entry Draft, July 10, 2006. • Missed majority of 2007-08 season recovering from shoulder (October 4, 2007 at Minnesota) and groin (December 22, 2007 at Ottawa) injuries. Signed as a free agent by **Minnesota**, July 1, 2009.

## HAYDAR, Darren

(HAY-duhr, DAIR-ehn) **COL.**

Right wing. Shoots right. 5'9", 170 lbs. Born, Toronto, Ont., October 22, 1979. Nashville's 15th choice, 248th overall, in 1999 Entry Draft.

| | | | | | | | | | | | | | | | | | | | | | | | | | |
|---|---|---|---|---|---|---|---|---|---|---|---|---|---|---|---|---|---|---|---|---|---|---|---|---|---|
| 1995-96 | Milton Merchants | OPJHL | 6 | 1 | 2 | 3 | 4 | .... | .... | .... | .... | .... | .... | .... | .... | .... | .... | .... | .... | .... | .... | .... | .... | .... | .... |
| 1996-97 | Milton Merchants | OPJHL | 51 | 32 | 68 | 100 | 68 | .... | .... | .... | .... | .... | .... | .... | .... | .... | .... | .... | .... | .... | .... | .... | .... | .... | .... |
| 1997-98 | Milton Merchants | OPJHL | 51 | *71 | *69 | *140 | 65 | .... | .... | .... | .... | .... | .... | .... | .... | .... | .... | .... | .... | .... | .... | .... | .... | .... | .... |
| 1998-99 | New Hampshire | H-East | 41 | 31 | 30 | 61 | 34 | .... | .... | .... | .... | .... | .... | .... | .... | .... | .... | .... | .... | .... | .... | .... | .... | .... | .... |
| 99-2000 | New Hampshire | H-East | 38 | 22 | 19 | 41 | 42 | .... | .... | .... | .... | .... | .... | .... | .... | .... | .... | .... | .... | .... | .... | .... | .... | .... | .... |
| 2000-01 | New Hampshire | H-East | 39 | 18 | 23 | 41 | 38 | .... | .... | .... | .... | .... | .... | .... | .... | .... | .... | .... | .... | .... | .... | .... | .... | .... | .... |
| 2001-02 | New Hampshire | H-East | 40 | 31 | *45 | *76 | 28 | .... | .... | .... | .... | .... | .... | .... | .... | .... | .... | .... | .... | .... | .... | .... | .... | .... | .... |
| **2002-03** | **Nashville** | **NHL** | **2** | **0** | **0** | **0** | **0** | **0** | **0** | **0** | **1** | **0.0** | **–1** | **0** | **0.0** | **8:54** | .... | .... | .... | .... | .... | .... | .... | .... | .... |
| | Milwaukee | AHL | 75 | 29 | 46 | 75 | 36 | .... | .... | .... | .... | .... | .... | .... | .... | .... | 6 | 1 | 4 | 5 | 2 | .... | .... | .... | .... |
| 2003-04 | Milwaukee | AHL | 79 | 22 | 37 | 59 | 35 | .... | .... | .... | .... | .... | .... | .... | .... | .... | 22 | *11 | 15 | *26 | 10 | .... | .... | .... | .... |
| 2004-05 | Milwaukee | AHL | 59 | 24 | 26 | 50 | 42 | .... | .... | .... | .... | .... | .... | .... | .... | .... | 7 | 3 | 4 | 7 | 14 | .... | .... | .... | .... |
| 2005-06 | Milwaukee | AHL | 80 | 35 | 57 | 92 | 50 | .... | .... | .... | .... | .... | .... | .... | .... | .... | 21 | *18 | 17 | *35 | 18 | .... | .... | .... | .... |
| **2006-07** | **Atlanta** | **NHL** | **4** | **0** | **0** | **0** | **0** | **0** | **0** | **0** | **4** | **0.0** | **0** | **3** | **66.7** | **8:01** | .... | .... | .... | .... | .... | .... | .... | .... | .... |
| | Chicago Wolves | AHL | 73 | 41 | *81 | *122 | 55 | .... | .... | .... | .... | .... | .... | .... | .... | .... | 15 | *10 | *14 | *24 | 14 | .... | .... | .... | .... |
| **2007-08** | **Atlanta** | **NHL** | **16** | **1** | **7** | **8** | **2** | **0** | **0** | **0** | **14** | **7.1** | **4** | **2** | **0.0** | **11:46** | .... | .... | .... | .... | .... | .... | .... | .... | .... |
| | Chicago Wolves | AHL | 51 | 19 | 39 | 58 | 52 | .... | .... | .... | .... | .... | .... | .... | .... | .... | 24 | *12 | 15 | 27 | 8 | .... | .... | .... | .... |
| 2008-09 | Grand Rapids | AHL | 79 | 31 | 49 | 80 | 26 | .... | .... | .... | .... | .... | .... | .... | .... | .... | 10 | 4 | 7 | 11 | 4 | .... | .... | .... | .... |
| | **NHL Totals** | | **22** | **1** | **7** | **8** | **2** | **0** | **0** | **0** | **19** | **5.3** | | **5** | **40.0** | **10:49** | .... | .... | .... | .... | .... | .... | .... | .... | .... |

Hockey East Second All-Star Team (1999, 2000) • Hockey East Rookie of the Year (1999) • Hockey East First All-Star Team (2002) • Hockey East Player of the Year (2002) • AHL All-Rookie Team (2003) • Dudley "Red" Garrett Memorial Award (AHL – Rookie of the Year) (2003) • AHL First All-Star Team (2007) • John P. Sollenberger Trophy (AHL - Top Scorer) (2007) • Les Cunningham Award (AHL - MVP) (2007) • AHL Second All-Star Team (2009)

Signed as a free agent by **Atlanta**, July 4, 2006. Signed as a free agent by **Detroit**, July 23, 2008. Signed as a free agent by **Colorado**, July 6, 2009.

## HEATLEY, Dany

(HEET-lee, DA-nee) **OTT.**

Left wing. Shoots left. 6'4", 221 lbs. Born, Freiburg, West Germany, January 21, 1981. Atlanta's 1st choice, 2nd overall, in 2000 Entry Draft.

| | | | | | | | | | | | | | | | | | | | | | | | | | |
|---|---|---|---|---|---|---|---|---|---|---|---|---|---|---|---|---|---|---|---|---|---|---|---|---|---|
| 1996-97 | Calgary Blazers | AMHL | 25 | 30 | 42 | 72 | 26 | .... | .... | .... | .... | .... | .... | .... | .... | .... | .... | .... | .... | .... | .... | .... | .... | .... | .... |
| 1997-98 | Calgary Buffaloes | AMHL | 36 | 39 | 42 | *81 | 34 | .... | .... | .... | .... | .... | .... | .... | .... | .... | 10 | 10 | 12 | *22 | 30 | .... | .... | .... | .... |
| 1998-99 | Calgary Canucks | AJHL | 60 | *70 | 56 | *126 | 91 | .... | .... | .... | .... | .... | .... | .... | .... | .... | 13 | *22 | 13 | *35 | 6 | .... | .... | .... | .... |
| 99-2000 | U. of Wisconsin | WCHA | 38 | 28 | 28 | 56 | 32 | .... | .... | .... | .... | .... | .... | .... | .... | .... | .... | .... | .... | .... | .... | .... | .... | .... | .... |
| 2000-01 | U. of Wisconsin | WCHA | 39 | 24 | 33 | 57 | 74 | .... | .... | .... | .... | .... | .... | .... | .... | .... | .... | .... | .... | .... | .... | .... | .... | .... | .... |
| **2001-02** | **Atlanta** | **NHL** | **82** | **26** | **41** | **67** | **56** | **7** | **0** | **4** | **202** | **12.9** | **–19** | **116** | **32.8** | **19:53** | .... | .... | .... | .... | .... | .... | .... | .... | .... |
| **2002-03** | **Atlanta** | **NHL** | **77** | **41** | **48** | **89** | **58** | **19** | **1** | **6** | **252** | **16.3** | **–8** | **49** | **36.7** | **21:57** | .... | .... | .... | .... | .... | .... | .... | .... | .... |
| **2003-04** | **Atlanta** | **NHL** | **31** | **13** | **12** | **25** | **18** | **5** | **0** | **3** | **83** | **15.7** | **–8** | **41** | **24.4** | **19:53** | .... | .... | .... | .... | .... | .... | .... | .... | .... |
| 2004-05 | SC Bern | Swiss | 16 | 14 | 10 | 24 | 58 | .... | .... | .... | .... | .... | .... | .... | .... | .... | .... | .... | .... | .... | .... | .... | .... | .... | .... |
| | Ak Bars Kazan | Russia | 11 | 3 | 1 | 4 | 22 | .... | .... | .... | .... | .... | .... | .... | .... | .... | 4 | 2 | 1 | 3 | 4 | .... | .... | .... | .... |
| **2005-06** | **Ottawa** | **NHL** | **82** | **50** | **53** | **103** | **86** | **23** | **2** | **7** | **300** | **16.7** | **29** | **166** | **53.6** | **21:09** | **10** | **3** | **9** | **12** | **11** | **3** | **0** | **1** | **18:56** |
| | Canada | Olympics | 6 | 2 | 1 | 3 | 8 | .... | .... | .... | .... | .... | .... | .... | .... | .... | .... | .... | .... | .... | .... | .... | .... | .... | .... |
| **2006-07** | **Ottawa** | **NHL** | **82** | **50** | **55** | **105** | **74** | **17** | **3** | **10** | **310** | **16.1** | **31** | **60** | **38.3** | **21:02** | **20** | **7** | ***15** | ***22** | **14** | **2** | **0** | **2** | **21:18** |
| **2007-08** | **Ottawa** | **NHL** | **71** | **41** | **41** | **82** | **76** | **13** | **0** | **8** | **224** | **18.3** | **33** | **26** | **57.7** | **21:44** | **4** | **0** | **1** | **1** | **6** | **0** | **0** | **0** | **21:41** |
| **2008-09** | **Ottawa** | **NHL** | **82** | **39** | **33** | **72** | **88** | **15** | **0** | **6** | **258** | **15.1** | **–11** | **30** | **46.7** | **20:07** | .... | .... | .... | .... | .... | .... | .... | .... | .... |
| | **NHL Totals** | | **507** | **260** | **283** | **543** | **456** | **99** | **6** | **44** | **1629** | **16.0** | | **488** | **42.4** | **20:53** | **34** | **10** | **25** | **35** | **31** | **5** | **0** | **3** | **20:39** |

WCHA First All-Star Team (2000) • WCHA Rookie of the Year (2000) • NCAA West Second All-American Team (2000) • WCHA Second All-Star Team (2001) • NCAA West First All-American Team (2001) • NHL All-Rookie Team (2002) • Calder Memorial Trophy (2002) • NHL Second All-Star Team (2006) • NHL First All-Star Team (2007)

Played in NHL All-Star Game (2003, 2007, 2009)

• Missed majority of 2003-04 season recovering from injuries suffered in automobile accident, September 29, 2003. Signed as a free agent by **Bern** (Swiss), October 13, 2004. Signed as a free agent by **Kazan** (Russia), February 9, 2005. Traded to **Ottawa** by **Atlanta** for Marian Hossa and Greg de Vries, August 23, 2005.

## HECHT, Jochen

(HEHSHT, YOH-khehn) **BUF.**

Left wing. Shoots left. 6'1", 199 lbs. Born, Mannheim, West Germany, June 21, 1977. St. Louis' 1st choice, 49th overall, in 1995 Entry Draft.

| | | | | | | | | | | | | | | | | | | | | | | | | | |
|---|---|---|---|---|---|---|---|---|---|---|---|---|---|---|---|---|---|---|---|---|---|---|---|---|---|
| 1993-94 | Mannheim Jr. | Ger-Jr. | 28 | 27 | 13 | 40 | 103 | .... | .... | .... | .... | .... | .... | .... | .... | .... | .... | .... | .... | .... | .... | .... | .... | .... | .... |
| 1994-95 | Adler Mannheim | Germany | 43 | 11 | 12 | 23 | 68 | .... | .... | .... | .... | .... | .... | .... | .... | .... | 10 | 5 | 4 | 9 | 12 | .... | .... | .... | .... |
| 1995-96 | Adler Mannheim | Germany | 44 | 12 | 16 | 28 | 68 | .... | .... | .... | .... | .... | .... | .... | .... | .... | 8 | 3 | 2 | 5 | 6 | .... | .... | .... | .... |
| 1996-97 | Adler Mannheim | Germany | 46 | 21 | 21 | 42 | 36 | .... | .... | .... | .... | .... | .... | .... | .... | .... | 9 | 3 | 3 | 6 | 4 | .... | .... | .... | .... |
| 1997-98 | Adler Mannheim | Germany | 44 | 7 | 19 | 26 | 42 | .... | .... | .... | .... | .... | .... | .... | .... | .... | 10 | 1 | 1 | 2 | 14 | .... | .... | .... | .... |
| | Adler Mannheim | EuroHL | 5 | 0 | 4 | 4 | 8 | .... | .... | .... | .... | .... | .... | .... | .... | .... | .... | .... | .... | .... | .... | .... | .... | .... | .... |
| | Germany | Olympics | 4 | 1 | 0 | 1 | 6 | .... | .... | .... | .... | .... | .... | .... | .... | .... | .... | .... | .... | .... | .... | .... | .... | .... | .... |
| **1998-99** | **St. Louis** | **NHL** | **3** | **0** | **0** | **0** | **0** | **0** | **0** | **0** | **4** | **0.0** | **–2** | **19** | **21.1** | **13:16** | **5** | **2** | **0** | **2** | **0** | **0** | **0** | **0** | **16:40** |
| | Worcester IceCats | AHL | 74 | 21 | 35 | 56 | 48 | .... | .... | .... | .... | .... | .... | .... | .... | .... | 4 | 1 | 1 | 2 | 2 | .... | .... | .... | .... |
| **99-2000** | **St. Louis** | **NHL** | **63** | **13** | **21** | **34** | **28** | **5** | **0** | **1** | **140** | **9.3** | **20** | **75** | **49.3** | **15:25** | **7** | **4** | **6** | **10** | **2** | **1** | **0** | **1** | **17:02** |
| **2000-01** | **St. Louis** | **NHL** | **72** | **19** | **25** | **44** | **48** | **8** | **3** | **1** | **208** | **9.1** | **11** | **160** | **43.8** | **17:56** | **15** | **2** | **4** | **6** | **4** | **0** | **0** | **0** | **17:19** |
| **2001-02** | **Edmonton** | **NHL** | **82** | **16** | **24** | **40** | **60** | **5** | **0** | **3** | **211** | **7.6** | **4** | **26** | **53.9** | **15:00** | .... | .... | .... | .... | .... | .... | .... | .... | .... |
| | Germany | Olympics | 4 | 1 | 1 | 2 | 2 | .... | .... | .... | .... | .... | .... | .... | .... | .... | .... | .... | .... | .... | .... | .... | .... | .... | .... |
| **2002-03** | **Buffalo** | **NHL** | **49** | **10** | **16** | **26** | **30** | **2** | **0** | **2** | **145** | **6.9** | **4** | **33** | **30.3** | **17:55** | .... | .... | .... | .... | .... | .... | .... | .... | .... |
| **2003-04** | **Buffalo** | **NHL** | **64** | **15** | **37** | **52** | **49** | **2** | **1** | **0** | **174** | **8.6** | **17** | **141** | **43.3** | **19:00** | .... | .... | .... | .... | .... | .... | .... | .... | .... |
| 2004-05 | Adler Mannheim | Germany | 48 | 16 | 34 | 50 | 151 | .... | .... | .... | .... | .... | .... | .... | .... | .... | 14 | 10 | 10 | *20 | 14 | .... | .... | .... | .... |
| **2005-06** | **Buffalo** | **NHL** | **64** | **18** | **24** | **42** | **34** | **4** | **2** | **4** | **179** | **10.1** | **10** | **156** | **39.7** | **18:07** | **15** | **2** | **6** | **8** | **8** | **0** | **0** | **1** | **17:29** |
| **2006-07** | **Buffalo** | **NHL** | **76** | **19** | **37** | **56** | **39** | **3** | **0** | **1** | **197** | **9.6** | **19** | **145** | **39.3** | **18:51** | **16** | **4** | **1** | **5** | **10** | **0** | **0** | **1** | **17:41** |
| **2007-08** | **Buffalo** | **NHL** | **75** | **22** | **27** | **49** | **38** | **3** | **1** | **2** | **229** | **9.6** | **1** | **905** | **42.0** | **19:19** | .... | .... | .... | .... | .... | .... | .... | .... | .... |
| **2008-09** | **Buffalo** | **NHL** | **70** | **12** | **15** | **27** | **33** | **3** | **1** | **1** | **173** | **6.9** | **–9** | **538** | **43.7** | **17:24** | .... | .... | .... | .... | .... | .... | .... | .... | .... |
| | **NHL Totals** | | **618** | **144** | **226** | **370** | **359** | **35** | **8** | **15** | **1660** | **8.7** | | **2198** | **42.3** | **17:37** | **58** | **14** | **17** | **31** | **24** | **1** | **0** | **3** | **17:22** |

Traded to **Edmonton** by **St. Louis** with Marty Reasoner and Jan Horacek for Doug Weight and Michel Riesen, July 1, 2001. Traded to **Buffalo** by **Edmonton** for Atlanta's 2nd round choice (previously acquired, Edmonton selected Jeff Deslauriers) in 2002 Entry Draft and Nashville's 2nd round choice (previously acquired, Edmonton selected Jarret Stoll) in 2002 Entry Draft, June 22, 2002. Signed as a free agent by **Mannheim** (Germany), August 2, 2004.

## HEDICAN, Bret

(HEH-dih-kan, BREHT)

Defense. Shoots left. 6'2", 210 lbs. Born, St. Paul, MN, August 10, 1970. St. Louis' 10th choice, 198th overall, in 1988 Entry Draft.

| | | | | | | | | | | | | | | | | | | | | | | | | | |
|---|---|---|---|---|---|---|---|---|---|---|---|---|---|---|---|---|---|---|---|---|---|---|---|---|---|
| 1987-88 | North St. Paul | High-MN | 23 | 15 | 19 | 34 | 16 | .... | .... | .... | .... | .... | .... | .... | .... | .... | .... | .... | .... | .... | .... | .... | .... | .... | .... |
| 1988-89 | St. Cloud State | NCAA-3 | 28 | 5 | 3 | 8 | 28 | .... | .... | .... | .... | .... | .... | .... | .... | .... | .... | .... | .... | .... | .... | .... | .... | .... | .... |
| 1989-90 | St. Cloud State | NCAA-3 | 36 | 4 | 17 | 21 | 37 | .... | .... | .... | .... | .... | .... | .... | .... | .... | .... | .... | .... | .... | .... | .... | .... | .... | .... |
| 1990-91 | St. Cloud State | WCHA | 41 | 21 | 26 | 47 | 26 | .... | .... | .... | .... | .... | .... | .... | .... | .... | .... | .... | .... | .... | .... | .... | .... | .... | .... |
| **1991-92** | United States | Nat-Tm | 54 | 1 | 8 | 9 | 59 | .... | .... | .... | .... | .... | .... | .... | .... | .... | .... | .... | .... | .... | .... | .... | .... | .... | .... |
| | United States | Olympics | 8 | 0 | 0 | 0 | 4 | .... | .... | .... | .... | .... | .... | .... | .... | .... | .... | .... | .... | .... | .... | .... | .... | .... | .... |
| | **St. Louis** | **NHL** | **4** | **1** | **0** | **1** | **0** | **0** | **0** | **0** | **1** | **100.0** | **1** | .... | .... | .... | **5** | **0** | **0** | **0** | **0** | **0** | **0** | **0** | .... |
| **1992-93** | **St. Louis** | **NHL** | **42** | **0** | **8** | **8** | **30** | **0** | **0** | **0** | **40** | **0.0** | **–2** | .... | .... | .... | **10** | **0** | **0** | **0** | **14** | **0** | **0** | **0** | .... |
| | Peoria Rivermen | IHL | 19 | 0 | 8 | 8 | 10 | .... | .... | .... | .... | .... | .... | .... | .... | .... | .... | .... | .... | .... | .... | .... | .... | .... | .... |
| **1993-94** | **St. Louis** | **NHL** | **61** | **0** | **11** | **11** | **64** | **0** | **0** | **0** | **78** | **0.0** | **–8** | .... | .... | .... | .... | .... | .... | .... | .... | .... | .... | .... | .... |
| | **Vancouver** | **NHL** | **8** | **0** | **1** | **1** | **0** | **0** | **0** | **0** | **10** | **0.0** | **1** | .... | .... | .... | **24** | **1** | **6** | **7** | **16** | **0** | **0** | **0** | .... |
| **1994-95** | **Vancouver** | **NHL** | **45** | **2** | **11** | **13** | **34** | **0** | **0** | **0** | **56** | **3.6** | **–3** | .... | .... | .... | **11** | **0** | **2** | **2** | **6** | **0** | **0** | **0** | .... |
| **1995-96** | **Vancouver** | **NHL** | **77** | **6** | **23** | **29** | **83** | **1** | **0** | **0** | **113** | **5.3** | **8** | .... | .... | .... | **6** | **0** | **1** | **1** | **10** | **0** | **0** | **0** | .... |
| **1996-97** | **Vancouver** | **NHL** | **67** | **4** | **15** | **19** | **51** | **2** | **0** | **1** | **93** | **4.3** | **–3** | .... | .... | .... | .... | .... | .... | .... | .... | .... | .... | .... | .... |
| **1997-98** | **Vancouver** | **NHL** | **71** | **3** | **24** | **27** | **79** | **1** | **0** | **0** | **84** | **3.6** | **3** | .... | .... | .... | .... | .... | .... | .... | .... | .... | .... | .... | .... |
| **1998-99** | **Vancouver** | **NHL** | **42** | **2** | **11** | **13** | **34** | **0** | **2** | **0** | **52** | **3.8** | **7** | **0** | **0.0** | **18:40** | .... | .... | .... | .... | .... | .... | .... | .... | .... |
| | **Florida** | **NHL** | **25** | **3** | **7** | **10** | **17** | **0** | **0** | **1** | **38** | **7.9** | **–2** | **0** | **0.0** | **22:24** | .... | .... | .... | .... | .... | .... | .... | .... | .... |

| | | | | | Regular Season | | | | | | | | | | | | Playoffs | | | | | | | | |
|---|---|---|---|---|---|---|---|---|---|---|---|---|---|---|---|---|---|---|---|---|---|---|---|---|---|
| Season | Club | League | GP | G | A | Pts | PIM | PP | SH | GW | S | % | +/- | TF | F% | Min | GP | G | A | Pts | PIM | PP | SH | GW | Min |
| **99-2000** | **Florida** | **NHL** | **76** | **6** | **19** | **25** | **68** | **2** | **0** | **1** | **58** | **10.3** | **4** | **0** | **0.0** | **19:36** | **4** | **0** | **0** | **0** | **0** | **0** | **0** | **0** | **20:42** |
| **2000-01** | **Florida** | **NHL** | **70** | **5** | **15** | **20** | **72** | **4** | **0** | **1** | **104** | **4.8** | **–7** | **0** | **0.0** | **21:49** | .... | .... | .... | .... | .... | .... | .... | .... | .... |
| **2001-02** | **Florida** | **NHL** | **31** | **3** | **7** | **10** | **12** | **0** | **0** | **0** | **46** | **6.5** | **–4** | **0** | **0.0** | **24:27** | .... | .... | .... | .... | .... | .... | .... | .... | .... |
| | **Carolina** | **NHL** | **26** | **2** | **4** | **6** | **10** | **0** | **0** | **1** | **39** | **5.1** | **3** | **0** | **0.0** | **22:56** | **23** | **1** | **4** | **5** | **20** | **0** | **0** | **0** | **23:52** |
| **2002-03** | **Carolina** | **NHL** | **72** | **3** | **14** | **17** | **75** | **1** | **0** | **1** | **113** | **2.7** | **–24** | **0** | **0.0** | **23:02** | .... | .... | .... | .... | .... | .... | .... | .... | .... |
| **2003-04** | **Carolina** | **NHL** | **81** | **7** | **17** | **24** | **64** | **2** | **0** | **3** | **112** | **6.3** | **–10** | **0** | **0.0** | **22:35** | .... | .... | .... | .... | .... | .... | .... | .... | .... |
| 2004-05 | DID NOT PLAY | | | | | | | | | | | | | | | | | | | | | | | | |
| **2005-06♦** | **Carolina** | **NHL** | **74** | **5** | **22** | **27** | **58** | **2** | **1** | **1** | **73** | **6.8** | **11** | **0** | **0.0** | **20:19** | **25** | **2** | **9** | **11** | **42** | **0** | **0** | **0** | **22:40** |
| | United States | Olympics | 6 | 0 | 1 | 1 | 6 | .... | .... | .... | .... | .... | .... | .... | .... | .... | .... | .... | .... | .... | .... | .... | .... | .... | .... |
| **2006-07** | **Carolina** | **NHL** | **50** | **0** | **10** | **10** | **36** | **0** | **0** | **0** | **44** | **0.0** | **–8** | **0** | **0.0** | **19:58** | .... | .... | .... | .... | .... | .... | .... | .... | .... |
| **2007-08** | **Carolina** | **NHL** | **66** | **2** | **15** | **17** | **70** | **0** | **0** | **0** | **80** | **2.5** | **17** | **0** | **0.0** | **19:18** | .... | .... | .... | .... | .... | .... | .... | .... | .... |
| **2008-09** | **Anaheim** | **NHL** | **51** | **1** | **5** | **6** | **36** | **0** | **0** | **0** | **40** | **2.5** | **–7** | **0** | **0.0** | **16:18** | .... | .... | .... | .... | .... | .... | .... | .... | .... |
| | **NHL Totals** | | **1039** | **55** | **239** | **294** | **893** | **15** | **3** | **10** | **1274** | **4.3** | | **0** | **0.0** | **20:48** | **108** | **4** | **22** | **26** | **108** | **0** | **0** | **0** | **23:03** |

WCHA First All-Star Team (1991)

Traded to **Vancouver** by **St. Louis** with Jeff Brown and Nathan LaFayette for Craig Janney, March 21, 1994. Traded to **Florida** by **Vancouver** with Pavel Bure, Brad Ference and Vancouver's 3rd round choice (Robert Fried) in 2000 Entry Draft for Ed Jovanovski, Dave Gagner, Mike Brown, Kevin Weekes and Florida's 1st round choice (Nathan Smith) in 2000 Entry Draft, January 17, 1999. Traded to **Carolina** by **Florida** with Kevyn Adams and Tomas Malec for Sandis Ozolinsh and Byron Ritchie, January 16, 2002. Signed as a free agent by **Anaheim**, October 23, 2008.

## HEJDA, Jan

(HAY-dah, YAHN) **CBJ**

Defense. Shoots left. 6'3", 218 lbs. Born, Prague, Czech., June 18, 1978. Buffalo's 4th choice, 106th overall, in 2003 Entry Draft.

| | | | | | | | | | | | | | | | | | | | | | | | | | |
|---|---|---|---|---|---|---|---|---|---|---|---|---|---|---|---|---|---|---|---|---|---|---|---|---|---|
| 1997-98 | HC Slavia Praha | CzRep | 44 | 2 | 5 | 7 | 51 | .... | .... | .... | .... | .... | .... | .... | .... | .... | 5 | 0 | 0 | 0 | 6 | .... | .... | .... | .... |
| 1998-99 | HC Slavia Praha | CzRep | 34 | 1 | 2 | 3 | 38 | .... | .... | .... | .... | .... | .... | .... | .... | .... | .... | .... | .... | .... | .... | .... | .... | .... | .... |
| 99-2000 | HC Slavia Praha | CzRep | 26 | 1 | 2 | 3 | 14 | .... | .... | .... | .... | .... | .... | .... | .... | .... | .... | .... | .... | .... | .... | .... | .... | .... | .... |
| | HC Femax Havirov | CzRep | 7 | 0 | 2 | 2 | 6 | .... | .... | .... | .... | .... | .... | .... | .... | .... | .... | .... | .... | .... | .... | .... | .... | .... | .... |
| | Liberec | CzRep-2 | 1 | 0 | 0 | 0 | 4 | .... | .... | .... | .... | .... | .... | .... | .... | .... | .... | .... | .... | .... | .... | .... | .... | .... | .... |
| 2000-01 | HC Slavia Praha | CzRep | 38 | 2 | 6 | 8 | 70 | .... | .... | .... | .... | .... | .... | .... | .... | .... | 11 | 3 | 0 | 3 | 12 | .... | .... | .... | .... |
| | SK Kadan | CzRep-2 | 8 | 1 | 0 | 1 | 6 | .... | .... | .... | .... | .... | .... | .... | .... | .... | .... | .... | .... | .... | .... | .... | .... | .... | .... |
| 2001-02 | HC Slavia Praha | CzRep | 42 | 9 | 8 | 17 | 52 | .... | .... | .... | .... | .... | .... | .... | .... | .... | 9 | 1 | 1 | 2 | 14 | .... | .... | .... | .... |
| 2002-03 | HC Slavia Praha | CzRep | 52 | 6 | 11 | 17 | 44 | .... | .... | .... | .... | .... | .... | .... | .... | .... | 17 | 5 | 8 | 13 | 12 | .... | .... | .... | .... |
| 2003-04 | CSKA Moscow | Russia | 60 | 1 | 5 | 6 | 26 | .... | .... | .... | .... | .... | .... | .... | .... | .... | .... | .... | .... | .... | .... | .... | .... | .... | .... |
| 2004-05 | CSKA Moscow | Russia | 60 | 2 | 11 | 13 | 59 | .... | .... | .... | .... | .... | .... | .... | .... | .... | .... | .... | .... | .... | .... | .... | .... | .... | .... |
| 2005-06 | Mytischi | Russia | 50 | 3 | 12 | 15 | 56 | .... | .... | .... | .... | .... | .... | .... | .... | .... | 9 | 2 | 3 | 5 | 24 | .... | .... | .... | .... |
| **2006-07** | **Edmonton** | **NHL** | **39** | **1** | **8** | **9** | **20** | **0** | **0** | **1** | **33** | **3.0** | **–6** | **0** | **0.0** | **20:23** | .... | .... | .... | .... | .... | .... | .... | .... | .... |
| | Hamilton | AHL | 5 | 0 | 3 | 3 | 21 | .... | .... | .... | .... | .... | .... | .... | .... | .... | .... | .... | .... | .... | .... | .... | .... | .... | .... |
| **2007-08** | **Columbus** | **NHL** | **81** | **0** | **13** | **13** | **61** | **0** | **0** | **0** | **71** | **0.0** | **20** | **0** | **0.0** | **21:08** | .... | .... | .... | .... | .... | .... | .... | .... | .... |
| **2008-09** | **Columbus** | **NHL** | **82** | **3** | **18** | **21** | **38** | **0** | **0** | **1** | **66** | **4.5** | **23** | **1** | **0.0** | **22:23** | **3** | **0** | **0** | **0** | **2** | **0** | **0** | **0** | **16:53** |
| | **NHL Totals** | | **202** | **4** | **39** | **43** | **119** | **0** | **0** | **2** | **170** | **2.4** | | **1** | **0.0** | **21:30** | **3** | **0** | **0** | **0** | **2** | **0** | **0** | **0** | **16:53** |

• Rights traded to **Edmonton** by **Buffalo** for Edmonton's 7th round choice (Nick Eno) in 2007 Entry Draft, July 10, 2006. Signed as a free agent by **Columbus**, July 5, 2007.

## HEJDUK, Milan

(HAY-dook, MEE-lan) **COL.**

Right wing. Shoots right. 6', 190 lbs. Born, Usti nad Labem, Czech., February 14, 1976. Quebec's 6th choice, 87th overall, in 1994 Entry Draft.

| | | | | | | | | | | | | | | | | | | | | | | | | | |
|---|---|---|---|---|---|---|---|---|---|---|---|---|---|---|---|---|---|---|---|---|---|---|---|---|---|
| 1993-94 | HC Pardubice | CzRep | 22 | 6 | 3 | 9 | .... | .... | .... | .... | .... | .... | .... | .... | .... | .... | 10 | 5 | 1 | 6 | .... | .... | .... | .... | .... |
| 1994-95 | HC Pardubice | CzRep | 43 | 11 | 13 | 24 | 6 | .... | .... | .... | .... | .... | .... | .... | .... | .... | 6 | 3 | 1 | 4 | 0 | .... | .... | .... | .... |
| 1995-96 | Pardubice | CzRep | 37 | 13 | 7 | 20 | .... | .... | .... | .... | .... | .... | .... | .... | .... | .... | .... | .... | .... | .... | .... | .... | .... | .... | .... |
| 1996-97 | Pardubice | CzRep | 51 | 27 | 11 | 38 | 10 | .... | .... | .... | .... | .... | .... | .... | .... | .... | 10 | 6 | 0 | 6 | 27 | .... | .... | .... | .... |
| 1997-98 | Pardubice | CzRep | 48 | 26 | 19 | 45 | 20 | .... | .... | .... | .... | .... | .... | .... | .... | .... | 3 | 0 | 0 | 0 | 2 | .... | .... | .... | .... |
| | Czech Republic | Olympics | 4 | 0 | 0 | 0 | 2 | .... | .... | .... | .... | .... | .... | .... | .... | .... | .... | .... | .... | .... | .... | .... | .... | .... | .... |
| **1998-99** | **Colorado** | **NHL** | **82** | **14** | **34** | **48** | **26** | **4** | **0** | **5** | **178** | **7.9** | **8** | **2** | **50.0** | **15:45** | **16** | **6** | **6** | **12** | **4** | **1** | **0** | **3** | **15:53** |
| **99-2000** | **Colorado** | **NHL** | **82** | **36** | **36** | **72** | **16** | **13** | **0** | **9** | **228** | **15.8** | **14** | **3** | **100.0** | **19:58** | **17** | **5** | **4** | **9** | **6** | **3** | **0** | **1** | **19:56** |
| **2000-01♦** | **Colorado** | **NHL** | **80** | **41** | **38** | **79** | **36** | **12** | **1** | **9** | **213** | **19.2** | **32** | **3** | **33.3** | **19:52** | **23** | **7** | ***16** | **23** | **6** | **4** | **0** | **1** | **21:33** |
| **2001-02** | **Colorado** | **NHL** | **62** | **21** | **23** | **44** | **24** | **7** | **1** | **5** | **139** | **15.1** | **0** | **5** | **40.0** | **20:11** | **16** | **3** | **3** | **6** | **4** | **1** | **0** | **0** | **18:24** |
| | Czech Republic | Olympics | 4 | 1 | 0 | 1 | 0 | .... | .... | .... | .... | .... | .... | .... | .... | .... | .... | .... | .... | .... | .... | .... | .... | .... | .... |
| **2002-03** | **Colorado** | **NHL** | **82** | ***50** | **48** | **98** | **32** | **18** | **0** | **4** | **244** | **20.5** | **52** | **43** | **44.2** | **19:50** | **7** | **2** | **2** | **4** | **2** | **1** | **0** | **0** | **20:42** |
| **2003-04** | **Colorado** | **NHL** | **82** | **35** | **40** | **75** | **20** | **16** | **0** | **6** | **237** | **14.8** | **19** | **69** | **47.8** | **18:46** | **11** | **5** | **2** | **7** | **0** | **2** | **0** | **0** | **18:40** |
| 2004-05 | Pardubice | CzRep | 48 | 25 | 26 | 51 | 14 | .... | .... | .... | .... | .... | .... | .... | .... | .... | 16 | 6 | 2 | 8 | 6 | .... | .... | .... | .... |
| **2005-06** | **Colorado** | **NHL** | **74** | **24** | **34** | **58** | **24** | **14** | **1** | **2** | **221** | **10.9** | **13** | **23** | **17.4** | **18:33** | **9** | **2** | **6** | **8** | **2** | **0** | **0** | **0** | **20:56** |
| | Czech Republic | Olympics | 8 | 2 | 1 | 3 | 2 | .... | .... | .... | .... | .... | .... | .... | .... | .... | .... | .... | .... | .... | .... | .... | .... | .... | .... |
| **2006-07** | **Colorado** | **NHL** | **80** | **35** | **35** | **70** | **44** | **12** | **1** | **6** | **257** | **13.6** | **10** | **109** | **45.0** | **17:53** | .... | .... | .... | .... | .... | .... | .... | .... | .... |
| **2007-08** | **Colorado** | **NHL** | **77** | **29** | **25** | **54** | **36** | **8** | **1** | **4** | **205** | **14.1** | **8** | **136** | **39.7** | **19:21** | **10** | **3** | **3** | **6** | **4** | **2** | **0** | **0** | **19:05** |
| **2008-09** | **Colorado** | **NHL** | **82** | **27** | **32** | **59** | **16** | **10** | **1** | **2** | **211** | **12.8** | **–19** | **160** | **45.0** | **19:56** | .... | .... | .... | .... | .... | .... | .... | .... | .... |
| | **NHL Totals** | | **783** | **312** | **345** | **657** | **274** | **114** | **6** | **52** | **2133** | **14.6** | | **553** | **43.0** | **18:59** | **109** | **33** | **42** | **75** | **28** | **14** | **0** | **5** | **19:23** |

NHL All-Rookie Team (1999) • NHL Second All-Star Team (2003) • Bud Light Plus/Minus Award (2003) (tied with Peter Forsberg) • Maurice "Rocket" Richard Trophy (2003)

Played in NHL All-Star Game (2000, 2001, 2009)

• Rights transferred to **Colorado** after **Quebec** franchise relocated, June 21, 1995. Signed as a free agent by **Pardubice** (CzRep), September 18, 2004.

## HELM, Darren

(HEHLM, DAIR-ehn) **DET.**

Center/Left wing. Shoots left. 5'11", 172 lbs. Born, Winnipeg, Man., January 21, 1987. Detroit's 5th choice, 132nd overall, in 2005 Entry Draft.

| | | | | | | | | | | | | | | | | | | | | | | | | | |
|---|---|---|---|---|---|---|---|---|---|---|---|---|---|---|---|---|---|---|---|---|---|---|---|---|---|
| 2003-04 | Selkirk Fishermen | MJBHL | 34 | 39 | 32 | 71 | 34 | .... | .... | .... | .... | .... | .... | .... | .... | .... | .... | .... | .... | .... | .... | .... | .... | .... | .... |
| 2004-05 | Medicine Hat | WHL | 72 | 10 | 14 | 24 | 27 | .... | .... | .... | .... | .... | .... | .... | .... | .... | 13 | 2 | 6 | 8 | 10 | .... | .... | .... | .... |
| 2005-06 | Medicine Hat | WHL | 70 | 41 | 38 | 79 | 37 | .... | .... | .... | .... | .... | .... | .... | .... | .... | 13 | 5 | 4 | 9 | 2 | .... | .... | .... | .... |
| 2006-07 | Medicine Hat | WHL | 59 | 25 | 39 | 64 | 53 | .... | .... | .... | .... | .... | .... | .... | .... | .... | 23 | 10 | 12 | 22 | 14 | .... | .... | .... | .... |
| **2007-08♦** | **Detroit** | **NHL** | **7** | **0** | **0** | **0** | **2** | **0** | **0** | **0** | **7** | **0.0** | **–2** | **23** | **21.7** | **7:00** | **18** | **2** | **2** | **4** | **2** | **0** | **0** | **0** | **7:30** |
| | Grand Rapids | AHL | 67 | 16 | 15 | 31 | 30 | .... | .... | .... | .... | .... | .... | .... | .... | .... | .... | .... | .... | .... | .... | .... | .... | .... | .... |
| **2008-09** | **Detroit** | **NHL** | **16** | **0** | **1** | **1** | **4** | **0** | **0** | **0** | **29** | **0.0** | **–7** | **132** | **56.1** | **12:26** | **23** | **4** | **1** | **5** | **4** | **0** | **0** | **1** | **12:06** |
| | Grand Rapids | AHL | 55 | 13 | 24 | 37 | 24 | .... | .... | .... | .... | .... | .... | .... | .... | .... | .... | .... | .... | .... | .... | .... | .... | .... | .... |
| | **NHL Totals** | | **23** | **0** | **1** | **1** | **6** | **0** | **0** | **0** | **36** | **0.0** | | **155** | **51.0** | **10:47** | **41** | **6** | **3** | **9** | **6** | **0** | **0** | **1** | **10:05** |

WHL East First All-Star Team (2006) • WHL East Second All-Star Team (2007) • Memorial Cup Tournament All-Star Team (2007)

## HELMER, Bryan

(HEHL-muhr, BRIGH-uhn)

Defense. Shoots right. 6'1", 208 lbs. Born, Sault Ste. Marie, Ont., July 15, 1972.

| | | | | | | | | | | | | | | | | | | | | | | | | | |
|---|---|---|---|---|---|---|---|---|---|---|---|---|---|---|---|---|---|---|---|---|---|---|---|---|---|
| 1989-90 | Wellington Dukes | OHA-B | 44 | 4 | 20 | 24 | 204 | .... | .... | .... | .... | .... | .... | .... | .... | .... | .... | .... | .... | .... | .... | .... | .... | .... | .... |
| | Belleville Bulls | OHL | 6 | 0 | 1 | 1 | 0 | .... | .... | .... | .... | .... | .... | .... | .... | .... | .... | .... | .... | .... | .... | .... | .... | .... | .... |
| 1990-91 | Wellington Dukes | OHA-B | 50 | 11 | 14 | 25 | 109 | .... | .... | .... | .... | .... | .... | .... | .... | .... | .... | .... | .... | .... | .... | .... | .... | .... | .... |
| 1991-92 | Wellington Dukes | MTJHL | 42 | 17 | 31 | 48 | 66 | .... | .... | .... | .... | .... | .... | .... | .... | .... | 3 | 2 | 1 | 3 | 0 | .... | .... | .... | .... |
| 1992-93 | Wellington Dukes | MTJHL | 48 | 21 | 54 | 75 | 84 | .... | .... | .... | .... | .... | .... | .... | .... | .... | 9 | 4 | 8 | 12 | 22 | .... | .... | .... | .... |
| 1993-94 | Albany River Rats | AHL | 65 | 4 | 19 | 23 | 79 | .... | .... | .... | .... | .... | .... | .... | .... | .... | 5 | 0 | 0 | 0 | 9 | .... | .... | .... | .... |
| 1994-95 | Albany River Rats | AHL | 77 | 7 | 36 | 43 | 101 | .... | .... | .... | .... | .... | .... | .... | .... | .... | 7 | 1 | 0 | 1 | 0 | .... | .... | .... | .... |
| 1995-96 | Albany River Rats | AHL | 80 | 14 | 30 | 44 | 107 | .... | .... | .... | .... | .... | .... | .... | .... | .... | 4 | 2 | 0 | 2 | 6 | .... | .... | .... | .... |
| 1996-97 | Albany River Rats | AHL | 77 | 12 | 27 | 39 | 113 | .... | .... | .... | .... | .... | .... | .... | .... | .... | 16 | 1 | 7 | 8 | 10 | .... | .... | .... | .... |
| 1997-98 | Albany River Rats | AHL | 80 | 14 | 49 | 63 | 101 | .... | .... | .... | .... | .... | .... | .... | .... | .... | 13 | 4 | 9 | 13 | 18 | .... | .... | .... | .... |
| **1998-99** | **Phoenix** | **NHL** | **11** | **0** | **0** | **0** | **23** | **0** | **0** | **0** | **11** | **0.0** | **2** | **0** | **0.0** | **7:43** | .... | .... | .... | .... | .... | .... | .... | .... | .... |
| | Las Vegas | IHL | 8 | 1 | 3 | 4 | 28 | .... | .... | .... | .... | .... | .... | .... | .... | .... | .... | .... | .... | .... | .... | .... | .... | .... | .... |
| | **St. Louis** | **NHL** | **29** | **0** | **4** | **4** | **19** | **0** | **0** | **0** | **38** | **0.0** | **3** | **1** | **100.0** | **19:08** | .... | .... | .... | .... | .... | .... | .... | .... | .... |
| | Worcester IceCats | AHL | 16 | 7 | 8 | 15 | 18 | .... | .... | .... | .... | .... | .... | .... | .... | .... | 4 | 0 | 0 | 0 | 12 | .... | .... | .... | .... |
| **99-2000** | **St. Louis** | **NHL** | **15** | **1** | **1** | **2** | **10** | **1** | **0** | **1** | **19** | **5.3** | **–3** | **0** | **0.0** | **16:15** | .... | .... | .... | .... | .... | .... | .... | .... | .... |
| | Worcester IceCats | AHL | 54 | 10 | 25 | 35 | 124 | .... | .... | .... | .... | .... | .... | .... | .... | .... | 9 | 1 | 4 | 5 | 10 | .... | .... | .... | .... |
| **2000-01** | **Vancouver** | **NHL** | **20** | **2** | **4** | **6** | **18** | **0** | **0** | **0** | **28** | **7.1** | **0** | **0** | **0.0** | **16:51** | .... | .... | .... | .... | .... | .... | .... | .... | .... |
| | Kansas City | IHL | 42 | 4 | 15 | 19 | 76 | .... | .... | .... | .... | .... | .... | .... | .... | .... | .... | .... | .... | .... | .... | .... | .... | .... | .... |
| **2001-02** | **Vancouver** | **NHL** | **40** | **5** | **5** | **10** | **53** | **2** | **0** | **1** | **43** | **11.6** | **10** | **0** | **0.0** | **12:04** | **6** | **0** | **0** | **0** | **0** | **0** | **0** | **0** | **9:09** |
| | Manitoba Moose | AHL | 34 | 6 | 18 | 24 | 69 | .... | .... | .... | .... | .... | .... | .... | .... | .... | .... | .... | .... | .... | .... | .... | .... | .... | .... |
| **2002-03** | **Vancouver** | **NHL** | **2** | **0** | **0** | **0** | **0** | **0** | **0** | **0** | **2** | **0.0** | **1** | **0** | **0.0** | **13:24** | .... | .... | .... | .... | .... | .... | .... | .... | .... |
| | Manitoba Moose | AHL | 60 | 7 | 24 | 31 | 82 | .... | .... | .... | .... | .... | .... | .... | .... | .... | 14 | 0 | 4 | 4 | 20 | .... | .... | .... | .... |
| **2003-04** | **Phoenix** | **NHL** | **17** | **0** | **1** | **1** | **10** | **0** | **0** | **0** | **10** | **0.0** | **–5** | **0** | **0.0** | **12:46** | .... | .... | .... | .... | .... | .... | .... | .... | .... |
| | Springfield | AHL | 9 | 1 | 6 | 7 | 6 | .... | .... | .... | .... | .... | .... | .... | .... | .... | .... | .... | .... | .... | .... | .... | .... | .... | .... |
| 2004-05 | Grand Rapids | AHL | 80 | 7 | 18 | 25 | 64 | .... | .... | .... | .... | .... | .... | .... | .... | .... | .... | .... | .... | .... | .... | .... | .... | .... | .... |
| 2005-06 | Grand Rapids | AHL | 80 | 12 | 44 | 56 | 138 | .... | .... | .... | .... | .... | .... | .... | .... | .... | 16 | 1 | 8 | 9 | 24 | .... | .... | .... | .... |

| Season | Club | League | Regular Season GP | G | A | Pts | PIM | PP | SH | GW | S | % | +/- | TF | F% | Min | Playoffs GP | G | A | Pts | PIM | PP | SH | GW | Min |
|---|---|---|---|---|---|---|---|---|---|---|---|---|---|---|---|---|---|---|---|---|---|---|---|---|---|
| 2006-07 | San Antonio | AHL | 70 | 6 | 23 | 29 | 81 | .... | .... | .... | .... | .... | .... | .... | .... | .... | .... | .... | .... | .... | .... | .... | .... | .... | .... |
| 2007-08 | San Antonio | AHL | 66 | 5 | 15 | 20 | 53 | .... | .... | .... | .... | .... | .... | .... | .... | .... | 7 | 0 | 0 | 0 | 6 | .... | .... | .... | .... |
| **2008-09** | **Washington** | **NHL** | **12** | **0** | **3** | **3** | **2** | **0** | **0** | **0** | **8** | **0.0** | **–1** | **0** | **0.0** | **16:36** | .... | .... | .... | .... | .... | .... | .... | .... | .... |
| | Hershey Bears | AHL | 63 | 2 | 25 | 27 | 59 | .... | .... | .... | .... | .... | .... | .... | .... | .... | 22 | 3 | 5 | 8 | 24 | .... | .... | .... | .... |
| | **NHL Totals** | | **146** | **8** | **18** | **26** | **135** | **3** | **0** | **2** | **159** | **5.0** | | **11** | **100.0** | **14:42** | **6** | **0** | **0** | **0** | **0** | **0** | **0** | **0** | **9:09** |

AHL First All-Star Team (1998) • AHL Second All-Star Team (2006)

Signed as a free agent by **New Jersey**, July 10, 1994. Signed as a free agent by **Phoenix**, July 17, 1998. Claimed on waivers by **St. Louis** from **Phoenix**, December 19, 1998. Signed as a free agent by **Vancouver**, August 21, 2000. Traded to **Phoenix** by **Vancouver** for Martin Grenier, July 25, 2003. • Missed majority of 2003-04 season recovering from shoulder injury suffered in training camp, September 29, 2003. Signed as a free agent by **Detroit**, July 21, 2004. Signed as a free agent by **Phoenix**, July 19, 2006. Signed as a free agent by **Washington**, November 28, 2008.

## HELMINEN, Dwight

(HEHL-mih-nehn, DWIGHT) **S.J.**

Center. Shoots left. 5'10", 190 lbs. Born, Hancock, MI, June 22, 1983. Edmonton's 12th choice, 244th overall, in 2002 Entry Draft.

| | | | | | | | | | | | | | | | | | | | | | | | | | |
|---|---|---|---|---|---|---|---|---|---|---|---|---|---|---|---|---|---|---|---|---|---|---|---|---|---|
| 1998-99 | Det. Compuware | MNHL | 32 | 9 | 7 | 16 | .... | .... | .... | .... | .... | .... | .... | .... | .... | .... | .... | .... | .... | .... | .... | .... | .... | .... | .... |
| 99-2000 | USNTDP | USHL | 30 | 5 | 7 | 12 | 10 | .... | .... | .... | .... | .... | .... | .... | .... | .... | .... | .... | .... | .... | .... | .... | .... | .... | .... |
| | USNTDP | NAHL | 30 | 7 | 10 | 17 | 8 | .... | .... | .... | .... | .... | .... | .... | .... | .... | .... | .... | .... | .... | .... | .... | .... | .... | .... |
| 2000-01 | USNTDP | U-18 | 42 | 9 | 36 | 45 | 20 | .... | .... | .... | .... | .... | .... | .... | .... | .... | .... | .... | .... | .... | .... | .... | .... | .... | .... |
| | USNTDP | USHL | 24 | 12 | 7 | 19 | 8 | .... | .... | .... | .... | .... | .... | .... | .... | .... | .... | .... | .... | .... | .... | .... | .... | .... | .... |
| | USNTDP | NAHL | 1 | 0 | 1 | 1 | 2 | .... | .... | .... | .... | .... | .... | .... | .... | .... | .... | .... | .... | .... | .... | .... | .... | .... | .... |
| 2001-02 | U. of Michigan | CCHA | 39 | 10 | 8 | 18 | 10 | .... | .... | .... | .... | .... | .... | .... | .... | .... | .... | .... | .... | .... | .... | .... | .... | .... | .... |
| 2002-03 | U. of Michigan | CCHA | 39 | 17 | 16 | 33 | 34 | .... | .... | .... | .... | .... | .... | .... | .... | .... | .... | .... | .... | .... | .... | .... | .... | .... | .... |
| 2003-04 | U. of Michigan | CCHA | 41 | 17 | 11 | 28 | 4 | .... | .... | .... | .... | .... | .... | .... | .... | .... | .... | .... | .... | .... | .... | .... | .... | .... | .... |
| 2004-05 | Hartford | AHL | 41 | 2 | 7 | 9 | 10 | .... | .... | .... | .... | .... | .... | .... | .... | .... | .... | .... | .... | .... | .... | .... | .... | .... | .... |
| | Charlotte | ECHL | 28 | 5 | 16 | 21 | 10 | .... | .... | .... | .... | .... | .... | .... | .... | .... | 15 | 7 | 3 | 10 | 2 | .... | .... | .... | .... |
| 2005-06 | Hartford | AHL | 77 | 32 | 24 | 56 | 40 | .... | .... | .... | .... | .... | .... | .... | .... | .... | 13 | 3 | 5 | 8 | 10 | .... | .... | .... | .... |
| 2006-07 | Hartford | AHL | 80 | 15 | 24 | 39 | 32 | .... | .... | .... | .... | .... | .... | .... | .... | .... | 7 | 1 | 1 | 2 | 2 | .... | .... | .... | .... |
| 2007-08 | JYP Jyvaskyla | Finland | 52 | 20 | 25 | 45 | 10 | .... | .... | .... | .... | .... | .... | .... | .... | .... | 6 | 3 | 3 | 6 | 0 | .... | .... | .... | .... |
| **2008-09** | **Carolina** | **NHL** | **23** | **1** | **1** | **2** | **0** | **0** | **0** | **0** | **15** | **6.7** | **–2** | **131** | **46.6** | **6:50** | **1** | **0** | **0** | **0** | **0** | **0** | **0** | **0** | **3:08** |
| | Albany River Rats | AHL | 54 | 15 | 15 | 30 | 26 | .... | .... | .... | .... | .... | .... | .... | .... | .... | .... | .... | .... | .... | .... | .... | .... | .... | .... |
| | **NHL Totals** | | **23** | **1** | **1** | **2** | **0** | **0** | **0** | **0** | **15** | **6.7** | | **131** | **46.6** | **6:50** | **1** | **0** | **0** | **0** | **0** | **0** | **0** | **0** | **3:08** |

Traded to **NY Rangers** by **Edmonton** with Steve Valiquette and Edmonton's 2nd round compensatory choice (Dane Byers) in 2004 Entry Draft for Petr Nedved and Jussi Markkanen, March 3, 2004. Signed as a free agent by **Jyvaskyla** (Finland), July 7, 2007. Signed as a free agent by **Carolina**, July 3, 2008. Signed as a free agent by **San Jose**, July 16, 2009.

## HEMSKY, Ales

(HEHM-skee, ahl-EHSH) **EDM.**

Right wing. Shoots right. 6', 192 lbs. Born, Pardubice, Czech., August 13, 1983. Edmonton's 1st choice, 13th overall, in 2001 Entry Draft.

| | | | | | | | | | | | | | | | | | | | | | | | | | |
|---|---|---|---|---|---|---|---|---|---|---|---|---|---|---|---|---|---|---|---|---|---|---|---|---|---|
| 99-2000 | HC Pardubice Jr. | CzRep-Jr. | 45 | 20 | 36 | 56 | 54 | .... | .... | .... | .... | .... | .... | .... | .... | .... | 7 | 4 | 14 | 18 | 36 | .... | .... | .... | .... |
| | Pardubice | CzRep | 4 | 0 | 1 | 1 | 0 | .... | .... | .... | .... | .... | .... | .... | .... | .... | .... | .... | .... | .... | .... | .... | .... | .... | .... |
| 2000-01 | Hull Olympiques | QMJHL | 68 | 36 | 64 | 100 | 67 | .... | .... | .... | .... | .... | .... | .... | .... | .... | 5 | 2 | 3 | 5 | 2 | .... | .... | .... | .... |
| 2001-02 | Hull Olympiques | QMJHL | 53 | 27 | 70 | 97 | 86 | .... | .... | .... | .... | .... | .... | .... | .... | .... | 10 | 6 | 10 | 16 | 6 | .... | .... | .... | .... |
| **2002-03** | **Edmonton** | **NHL** | **59** | **6** | **24** | **30** | **14** | **0** | **0** | **1** | **50** | **12.0** | **5** | **3** | **33.3** | **12:04** | **6** | **0** | **0** | **0** | **0** | **0** | **0** | **0** | **12:46** |
| **2003-04** | **Edmonton** | **NHL** | **71** | **12** | **22** | **34** | **14** | **4** | **0** | **3** | **87** | **13.8** | **–7** | **3** | **33.3** | **14:26** | .... | .... | .... | .... | .... | .... | .... | .... | .... |
| 2004-05 | Pardubice | CzRep | 47 | 13 | 18 | 31 | 28 | .... | .... | .... | .... | .... | .... | .... | .... | .... | 16 | 4 | *10 | *14 | 26 | .... | .... | .... | .... |
| **2005-06** | **Edmonton** | **NHL** | **81** | **19** | **58** | **77** | **64** | **7** | **1** | **4** | **178** | **10.7** | **–5** | **7** | **42.9** | **16:59** | **24** | **6** | **11** | **17** | **14** | **4** | **0** | **2** | **16:06** |
| | Czech Republic | Olympics | 8 | 1 | 2 | 3 | 2 | .... | .... | .... | .... | .... | .... | .... | .... | .... | .... | .... | .... | .... | .... | .... | .... | .... | .... |
| **2006-07** | **Edmonton** | **NHL** | **64** | **13** | **40** | **53** | **40** | **5** | **0** | **1** | **122** | **10.7** | **–7** | **10** | **30.0** | **16:59** | .... | .... | .... | .... | .... | .... | .... | .... | .... |
| **2007-08** | **Edmonton** | **NHL** | **74** | **20** | **51** | **71** | **34** | **8** | **0** | **2** | **184** | **10.9** | **–9** | **5** | **20.0** | **18:35** | .... | .... | .... | .... | .... | .... | .... | .... | .... |
| **2008-09** | **Edmonton** | **NHL** | **72** | **23** | **43** | **66** | **32** | **4** | **0** | **2** | **185** | **12.4** | **1** | **4** | **0.0** | **18:39** | .... | .... | .... | .... | .... | .... | .... | .... | .... |
| | **NHL Totals** | | **421** | **93** | **238** | **331** | **198** | **28** | **1** | **13** | **806** | **11.5** | | **32** | **28.1** | **16:26** | **30** | **6** | **11** | **17** | **14** | **4** | **0** | **2** | **15:26** |

QMJHL Second All-Star Team (2002)

Signed as a free agent by **Pardubice** (CzRep), September 18, 2004.

## HENDRICKS, Matt

(HEHN-drihks, MAT) **COL.**

Center. Shoots left. 6', 215 lbs. Born, Blaine, MN, June 17, 1981. Nashville's 5th choice, 131st overall, in 2000 Entry Draft.

| | | | | | | | | | | | | | | | | | | | | | | | | | |
|---|---|---|---|---|---|---|---|---|---|---|---|---|---|---|---|---|---|---|---|---|---|---|---|---|---|
| 1998-99 | Blaine Bengals | High-MN | 22 | 23 | 34 | 57 | 42 | .... | .... | .... | .... | .... | .... | .... | .... | .... | .... | .... | .... | .... | .... | .... | .... | .... | .... |
| 99-2000 | Blaine Bengals | High-MN | 21 | 23 | 30 | 53 | 28 | .... | .... | .... | .... | .... | .... | .... | .... | .... | .... | .... | .... | .... | .... | .... | .... | .... | .... |
| 2000-01 | St. Cloud State | WCHA | 37 | 3 | 9 | 12 | 23 | .... | .... | .... | .... | .... | .... | .... | .... | .... | .... | .... | .... | .... | .... | .... | .... | .... | .... |
| 2001-02 | St. Cloud State | WCHA | 42 | 19 | 20 | 39 | 74 | .... | .... | .... | .... | .... | .... | .... | .... | .... | .... | .... | .... | .... | .... | .... | .... | .... | .... |
| 2002-03 | St. Cloud State | WCHA | 37 | 18 | 18 | 36 | 64 | .... | .... | .... | .... | .... | .... | .... | .... | .... | .... | .... | .... | .... | .... | .... | .... | .... | .... |
| 2003-04 | St. Cloud State | WCHA | 36 | 13 | 11 | 24 | 32 | .... | .... | .... | .... | .... | .... | .... | .... | .... | .... | .... | .... | .... | .... | .... | .... | .... | .... |
| | Milwaukee | AHL | 1 | 0 | 0 | 0 | 2 | .... | .... | .... | .... | .... | .... | .... | .... | .... | .... | .... | .... | .... | .... | .... | .... | .... | .... |
| 2004-05 | Lowell | AHL | 15 | 1 | 2 | 3 | 10 | .... | .... | .... | .... | .... | .... | .... | .... | .... | .... | .... | .... | .... | .... | .... | .... | .... | .... |
| | Florida Everblades | ECHL | 54 | 24 | 26 | 50 | 94 | .... | .... | .... | .... | .... | .... | .... | .... | .... | 4 | 0 | 0 | 0 | 4 | .... | .... | .... | .... |
| 2005-06 | Rochester | AHL | 56 | 13 | 14 | 27 | 84 | .... | .... | .... | .... | .... | .... | .... | .... | .... | .... | .... | .... | .... | .... | .... | .... | .... | .... |
| 2006-07 | Hershey Bears | AHL | 65 | 18 | 26 | 44 | 105 | .... | .... | .... | .... | .... | .... | .... | .... | .... | 19 | 8 | 4 | 12 | 18 | .... | .... | .... | .... |
| 2007-08 | Providence Bruins | AHL | 67 | 22 | 30 | 52 | 121 | .... | .... | .... | .... | .... | .... | .... | .... | .... | 10 | 0 | 3 | 3 | 6 | .... | .... | .... | .... |
| **2008-09** | **Colorado** | **NHL** | **4** | **0** | **0** | **0** | **13** | **0** | **0** | **0** | **5** | **0.0** | **1** | **1** | **0.0** | **8:30** | .... | .... | .... | .... | .... | .... | .... | .... | .... |
| | Lake Erie | AHL | 43 | 14 | 15 | 29 | 71 | .... | .... | .... | .... | .... | .... | .... | .... | .... | .... | .... | .... | .... | .... | .... | .... | .... | .... |
| | **NHL Totals** | | **4** | **0** | **0** | **0** | **13** | **0** | **0** | **0** | **5** | **0.0** | | **1** | **0.0** | **8:30** | .... | .... | .... | .... | .... | .... | .... | .... | .... |

Signed as a free agent by **Boston**, July 9, 2007. Traded to **Colorado** by **Boston** for Johnny Boychuk, June 24, 2008.

## HENDRY, Jordan

(HEHN-dree, JOHR-dahn) **CHI.**

Defense. Shoots left. 6', 196 lbs. Born, Nokomis, Sask., February 23, 1984.

| | | | | | | | | | | | | | | | | | | | | | | | | | |
|---|---|---|---|---|---|---|---|---|---|---|---|---|---|---|---|---|---|---|---|---|---|---|---|---|---|
| 2002-03 | Alaska | CCHA | 35 | 3 | 5 | 8 | 10 | .... | .... | .... | .... | .... | .... | .... | .... | .... | .... | .... | .... | .... | .... | .... | .... | .... | .... |
| 2003-04 | Alaska | CCHA | 36 | 4 | 9 | 13 | 38 | .... | .... | .... | .... | .... | .... | .... | .... | .... | .... | .... | .... | .... | .... | .... | .... | .... | .... |
| 2004-05 | Alaska | CCHA | 3 | 0 | 1 | 1 | 21 | .... | .... | .... | .... | .... | .... | .... | .... | .... | .... | .... | .... | .... | .... | .... | .... | .... | .... |
| 2005-06 | Alaska | CCHA | 38 | 4 | 10 | 14 | 74 | .... | .... | .... | .... | .... | .... | .... | .... | .... | .... | .... | .... | .... | .... | .... | .... | .... | .... |
| | Norfolk Admirals | AHL | 13 | 1 | 4 | 5 | 13 | .... | .... | .... | .... | .... | .... | .... | .... | .... | 3 | 0 | 0 | 0 | 2 | .... | .... | .... | .... |
| 2006-07 | Norfolk Admirals | AHL | 80 | 4 | 12 | 16 | 84 | .... | .... | .... | .... | .... | .... | .... | .... | .... | 6 | 0 | 2 | 2 | 6 | .... | .... | .... | .... |
| **2007-08** | **Chicago** | **NHL** | **40** | **1** | **3** | **4** | **22** | **0** | **0** | **0** | **32** | **3.1** | **0** | **0** | **0.0** | **17:13** | .... | .... | .... | .... | .... | .... | .... | .... | .... |
| | Rockford IceHogs | AHL | 45 | 3 | 4 | 7 | 58 | .... | .... | .... | .... | .... | .... | .... | .... | .... | 1 | 0 | 0 | 0 | 2 | .... | .... | .... | .... |
| **2008-09** | **Chicago** | **NHL** | **9** | **0** | **0** | **0** | **4** | **0** | **0** | **0** | **1** | **0.0** | **–1** | **0** | **0.0** | **10:06** | .... | .... | .... | .... | .... | .... | .... | .... | .... |
| | Rockford IceHogs | AHL | 53 | 3 | 6 | 9 | 45 | .... | .... | .... | .... | .... | .... | .... | .... | .... | 4 | 0 | 0 | 0 | 2 | .... | .... | .... | .... |
| | **NHL Totals** | | **49** | **1** | **3** | **4** | **26** | **0** | **0** | **0** | **33** | **3.0** | | **0** | **0.0** | **15:55** | .... | .... | .... | .... | .... | .... | .... | .... | .... |

Signed as a free agent by **Chicago**, July 17, 2006.

## HENNESSY, Josh

(HEHN-eh-see, JAWSH) **OTT.**

Center. Shoots left. 6', 192 lbs. Born, Brockton, MA, February 7, 1985. San Jose's 3rd choice, 43rd overall, in 2003 Entry Draft.

| | | | | | | | | | | | | | | | | | | | | | | | | | |
|---|---|---|---|---|---|---|---|---|---|---|---|---|---|---|---|---|---|---|---|---|---|---|---|---|---|
| 2000-01 | Milton Academy | High-MA | 28 | 20 | 30 | 50 | 20 | .... | .... | .... | .... | .... | .... | .... | .... | .... | .... | .... | .... | .... | .... | .... | .... | .... | .... |
| 2001-02 | Quebec Remparts | QMJHL | 70 | 20 | 20 | 40 | 24 | .... | .... | .... | .... | .... | .... | .... | .... | .... | 9 | 3 | 9 | 12 | 8 | .... | .... | .... | .... |
| 2002-03 | Quebec Remparts | QMJHL | 72 | 33 | 51 | 84 | 44 | .... | .... | .... | .... | .... | .... | .... | .... | .... | 11 | 6 | 9 | 15 | 10 | .... | .... | .... | .... |
| 2003-04 | Quebec Remparts | QMJHL | 59 | 40 | 42 | 82 | 55 | .... | .... | .... | .... | .... | .... | .... | .... | .... | .... | .... | .... | .... | .... | .... | .... | .... | .... |
| 2004-05 | Quebec Remparts | QMJHL | 68 | 35 | 50 | 85 | 39 | .... | .... | .... | .... | .... | .... | .... | .... | .... | 12 | 2 | 9 | 11 | 6 | .... | .... | .... | .... |
| 2005-06 | Cleveland Barons | AHL | 80 | 24 | 39 | 63 | 60 | .... | .... | .... | .... | .... | .... | .... | .... | .... | .... | .... | .... | .... | .... | .... | .... | .... | .... |
| **2006-07** | **Ottawa** | **NHL** | **10** | **1** | **0** | **1** | **4** | **0** | **0** | **0** | **6** | **16.7** | **0** | **43** | **37.2** | **5:39** | .... | .... | .... | .... | .... | .... | .... | .... | .... |
| | Binghamton | AHL | 76 | 27 | 30 | 57 | 54 | .... | .... | .... | .... | .... | .... | .... | .... | .... | .... | .... | .... | .... | .... | .... | .... | .... | .... |
| **2007-08** | **Ottawa** | **NHL** | **5** | **0** | **0** | **0** | **0** | **0** | **0** | **0** | **2** | **0.0** | **–1** | **12** | **41.7** | **3:46** | .... | .... | .... | .... | .... | .... | .... | .... | .... |
| | Binghamton | AHL | 76 | 22 | 29 | 51 | 49 | .... | .... | .... | .... | .... | .... | .... | .... | .... | .... | .... | .... | .... | .... | .... | .... | .... | .... |
| **2008-09** | **Ottawa** | **NHL** | **1** | **0** | **0** | **0** | **0** | **0** | **0** | **0** | **0** | **0.0** | **0** | **7** | **28.6** | **13:40** | .... | .... | .... | .... | .... | .... | .... | .... | .... |
| | Binghamton | AHL | 59 | 20 | 17 | 37 | 26 | .... | .... | .... | .... | .... | .... | .... | .... | .... | .... | .... | .... | .... | .... | .... | .... | .... | .... |
| | **NHL Totals** | | **16** | **1** | **0** | **1** | **4** | **0** | **0** | **0** | **8** | **12.5** | | **62** | **37.1** | **5:34** | .... | .... | .... | .... | .... | .... | .... | .... | .... |

Traded to **Chicago** by **San Jose** with Tom Preissing for Mark Bell, July 9, 2006. Traded to **Ottawa** by **Chicago** with Tom Preissing, Michal Barinka and Chicago's 2nd round choice (Patrick Wiercioch) in 2008 Entry Draft for Martin Havlat and Bryan Smolinski, July 10, 2006.

## HENRY, Alex
(HEHN-ree, AL-ehx) **MTL.**

Defense. Shoots left. 6'6", 230 lbs. Born, Elliot Lake, Ont., October 18, 1979. Edmonton's 2nd choice, 67th overall, in 1998 Entry Draft.

| Season | Club | League | GP | G | A | Pts | PIM | PP | SH | GW | S | % | +/- | TF | F% | Min | Playoffs GP | G | A | Pts | PIM | PP | SH | GW | Min |
|---|---|---|---|---|---|---|---|---|---|---|---|---|---|---|---|---|---|---|---|---|---|---|---|---|---|
| 1995-96 | Timmins Majors | NOHA | 30 | 4 | 11 | 15 | 6 | | | | | | | | | | | | | | | | | | |
| | Timmins | NOJHA | 2 | 0 | 0 | 0 | 0 | | | | | | | | | | | | | | | | | | |
| 1996-97 | London Knights | OHL | 61 | 1 | 10 | 11 | 65 | | | | | | | | | | | | | | | | | | |
| 1997-98 | London Knights | OHL | 62 | 5 | 9 | 14 | 97 | | | | | | | | | | 16 | 0 | 3 | 3 | 14 | | | | |
| 1998-99 | London Knights | OHL | 68 | 5 | 23 | 28 | 105 | | | | | | | | | | 25 | 3 | 10 | 13 | 22 | | | | |
| 99-2000 | Hamilton | AHL | 60 | 1 | 0 | 1 | 69 | | | | | | | | | | | | | | | | | | |
| 2000-01 | Hamilton | AHL | 56 | 2 | 3 | 5 | 87 | | | | | | | | | | | | | | | | | | |
| 2001-02 | Hamilton | AHL | 69 | 4 | 8 | 12 | 143 | | | | | | | | | | 15 | 1 | 2 | 3 | 16 | | | | |
| **2002-03** | **Edmonton** | **NHL** | **3** | **0** | **0** | **0** | **0** | **0** | **0** | **0** | **0** | **0.0** | **–1** | **0** | **0.0** | **7:02** | | | | | | | | | |
| | **Washington** | **NHL** | **38** | **0** | **0** | **0** | **80** | **0** | **0** | **0** | **8** | **0.0** | **–4** | **1** | **0.0** | **3:39** | | | | | | | | | |
| | Portland Pirates | AHL | 3 | 0 | 1 | 1 | 0 | | | | | | | | | | | | | | | | | | |
| **2003-04** | **Minnesota** | **NHL** | **71** | **2** | **4** | **6** | **106** | **0** | **0** | **0** | **37** | **5.4** | **4** | **2** | **0.0** | **14:53** | | | | | | | | | |
| 2004-05 | ESV Kaufbeuren | German-2 | 26 | 6 | 6 | 12 | 32 | | | | | | | | | | | | | | | | | | |
| **2005-06** | **Minnesota** | **NHL** | **63** | **0** | **5** | **5** | **73** | **0** | **0** | **0** | **41** | **0.0** | **–4** | **2** | **50.0** | **11:26** | | | | | | | | | |
| 2006-07 | Milwaukee | AHL | 64 | 1 | 6 | 7 | 66 | | | | | | | | | | 2 | 0 | 0 | 0 | 7 | | | | |
| 2007-08 | Milwaukee | AHL | 80 | 3 | 13 | 16 | 142 | | | | | | | | | | 6 | 0 | 1 | 1 | 10 | | | | |
| **2008-09** | **Montreal** | **NHL** | **2** | **0** | **0** | **0** | **10** | **0** | **0** | **0** | **0** | **0.0** | **–2** | **0** | **0.0** | **6:34** | | | | | | | | | |
| | Hamilton | AHL | 79 | 3 | 7 | 10 | 127 | | | | | | | | | | 6 | 0 | 0 | 0 | 8 | | | | |
| | **NHL Totals** | | **177** | **2** | **9** | **11** | **269** | **0** | **0** | **0** | **86** | **2.3** | | **5** | **20.0** | **11:01** | | | | | | | | | |

Claimed on waivers by **Washington** from **Edmonton**, October 24, 2002. Claimed on waivers by **Minnesota** from **Washington**, October 9, 2003. Signed as a free agent by **Kaufbeuren** (German-2), January 15, 2005. Signed as a free agent by **Nashville**, August 22, 2006. Signed as a free agent by **Montreal**, July 3, 2008.

## HENSICK, T.J.
(HEHN-sihk, TEE-JAY) **COL.**

Center. Shoots right. 5'10", 185 lbs. Born, Lansing, MI, December 10, 1985. Colorado's 5th choice, 88th overall, in 2005 Entry Draft.

| Season | Club | League | GP | G | A | Pts | PIM | PP | SH | GW | S | % | +/- | TF | F% | Min | Playoffs GP | G | A | Pts | PIM | PP | SH | GW | Min |
|---|---|---|---|---|---|---|---|---|---|---|---|---|---|---|---|---|---|---|---|---|---|---|---|---|---|
| 2001-02 | USNTDP | U-17 | 17 | 10 | 5 | 15 | | | | | | | | | | | | | | | | | | | |
| | USNTDP | NAHL | 46 | 15 | 25 | 40 | 10 | | | | | | | | | | | | | | | | | | |
| 2002-03 | USNTDP | U-18 | 48 | 24 | 24 | 48 | 11 | | | | | | | | | | | | | | | | | | |
| | USNTDP | NAHL | 10 | 6 | 7 | 13 | 0 | | | | | | | | | | | | | | | | | | |
| 2003-04 | U. of Michigan | CCHA | 43 | 12 | *34 | 46 | 38 | | | | | | | | | | | | | | | | | | |
| 2004-05 | U. of Michigan | CCHA | 39 | 23 | 32 | 55 | 24 | | | | | | | | | | | | | | | | | | |
| 2005-06 | U. of Michigan | CCHA | 41 | 17 | 35 | 52 | 44 | | | | | | | | | | | | | | | | | | |
| 2006-07 | U. of Michigan | CCHA | 41 | 23 | *46 | *69 | 38 | | | | | | | | | | | | | | | | | | |
| **2007-08** | **Colorado** | **NHL** | **31** | **6** | **5** | **11** | **2** | **4** | **0** | **1** | **52** | **11.5** | **–4** | **256** | **42.2** | **11:59** | **2** | **0** | **1** | **1** | **0** | **0** | **0** | **0** | **15:29** |
| | Lake Erie | AHL | 50 | 12 | 33 | 45 | 18 | | | | | | | | | | | | | | | | | | |
| **2008-09** | **Colorado** | **NHL** | **61** | **4** | **17** | **21** | **14** | **1** | **0** | **0** | **116** | **3.4** | **–7** | **510** | **47.3** | **12:54** | | | | | | | | | |
| | Lake Erie | AHL | 12 | 7 | 9 | 16 | 2 | | | | | | | | | | | | | | | | | | |
| | **NHL Totals** | | **92** | **10** | **22** | **32** | **16** | **5** | **0** | **1** | **168** | **6.0** | | **766** | **45.6** | **12:36** | **2** | **0** | **1** | **1** | **0** | **0** | **0** | **0** | **15:29** |

CCHA All-Rookie Team (2004) • CCHA First All-Star Team (2004, 2005, 2007) • CCHA Rookie of the Year (2004) • NCAA West First All-American Team (2005, 2007) • CCHA Second All-Star Team (2006)

## HEWARD, Jamie
(HEW-uhrd, JAY-mee)

Defense. Shoots right. 6'2", 215 lbs. Born, Regina, Sask., March 30, 1971. Pittsburgh's 1st choice, 16th overall, in 1989 Entry Draft.

| Season | Club | League | GP | G | A | Pts | PIM | PP | SH | GW | S | % | +/- | TF | F% | Min | Playoffs GP | G | A | Pts | PIM | PP | SH | GW | Min |
|---|---|---|---|---|---|---|---|---|---|---|---|---|---|---|---|---|---|---|---|---|---|---|---|---|---|
| 1987-88 | Regina Pats | WHL | 68 | 10 | 17 | 27 | 17 | | | | | | | | | | 4 | 1 | 1 | 2 | 2 | | | | |
| 1988-89 | Regina Pats | WHL | 52 | 31 | 28 | 59 | 29 | | | | | | | | | | | | | | | | | | |
| 1989-90 | Regina Pats | WHL | 72 | 14 | 44 | 58 | 42 | | | | | | | | | | 11 | 2 | 2 | 4 | 10 | | | | |
| 1990-91 | Regina Pats | WHL | 71 | 23 | 61 | 84 | 41 | | | | | | | | | | 8 | 2 | 9 | 11 | 6 | | | | |
| 1991-92 | Muskegon | IHL | 54 | 6 | 21 | 27 | 37 | | | | | | | | | | 14 | 1 | 4 | 5 | 4 | | | | |
| 1992-93 | Cleveland | IHL | 58 | 9 | 18 | 27 | 64 | | | | | | | | | | | | | | | | | | |
| 1993-94 | Cleveland | IHL | 73 | 8 | 16 | 24 | 72 | | | | | | | | | | | | | | | | | | |
| 1994-95 | Canada | Nat-Tm | 51 | 11 | 35 | 46 | 32 | | | | | | | | | | | | | | | | | | |
| **1995-96** | **Toronto** | **NHL** | **5** | **0** | **0** | **0** | **0** | **0** | **0** | **0** | **8** | **0.0** | **–1** | | | | | | | | | | | | |
| | St. John's | AHL | 73 | 22 | 34 | 56 | 33 | | | | | | | | | | 3 | 1 | 1 | 2 | 6 | | | | |
| **1996-97** | **Toronto** | **NHL** | **20** | **1** | **4** | **5** | **6** | **0** | **0** | **0** | **23** | **4.3** | **–6** | | | | | | | | | | | | |
| | St. John's | AHL | 27 | 8 | 19 | 27 | 26 | | | | | | | | | | 9 | 1 | 3 | 4 | 6 | | | | |
| 1997-98 | Philadelphia | AHL | 72 | 17 | 48 | 65 | 54 | | | | | | | | | | 20 | 3 | 16 | 19 | 10 | | | | |
| **1998-99** | **Nashville** | **NHL** | **63** | **6** | **12** | **18** | **44** | **4** | **0** | **1** | **124** | **4.8** | **–24** | **0** | **0.0** | **16:12** | | | | | | | | | |
| **99-2000** | **NY Islanders** | **NHL** | **54** | **6** | **11** | **17** | **26** | **2** | **0** | **1** | **92** | **6.5** | **–9** | **0** | **0.0** | **19:58** | | | | | | | | | |
| **2000-01** | **Columbus** | **NHL** | **69** | **11** | **16** | **27** | **33** | **9** | **0** | **1** | **108** | **10.2** | **3** | **0** | **0.0** | **14:21** | | | | | | | | | |
| **2001-02** | **Columbus** | **NHL** | **28** | **1** | **2** | **3** | **7** | **0** | **0** | **0** | **38** | **2.6** | **–9** | **1** | **100.0** | **14:04** | | | | | | | | | |
| | Syracuse Crunch | AHL | 14 | 3 | 10 | 13 | 6 | | | | | | | | | | 10 | 0 | 4 | 4 | 6 | | | | |
| 2002-03 | Geneve | Swiss | 40 | 8 | 23 | 31 | 60 | | | | | | | | | | 6 | 1 | 1 | 2 | 22 | | | | |
| 2003-04 | ZSC Lions Zurich | Swiss | 25 | 5 | 9 | 14 | 57 | | | | | | | | | | 6 | 0 | 1 | 1 | 24 | | | | |
| 2004-05 | Langnau | Swiss | 44 | 3 | 14 | 17 | 91 | | | | | | | | | | 5 | 0 | 0 | 0 | 40 | | | | |
| **2005-06** | **Washington** | **NHL** | **71** | **7** | **21** | **28** | **54** | **4** | **0** | **2** | **140** | **5.0** | **–5** | **1** | **0.0** | **21:52** | | | | | | | | | |
| **2006-07** | **Washington** | **NHL** | **52** | **4** | **12** | **16** | **27** | **2** | **0** | **1** | **50** | **8.0** | **4** | **0** | **0.0** | **16:22** | | | | | | | | | |
| | **Los Angeles** | **NHL** | **19** | **2** | **6** | **8** | **20** | **1** | **0** | **0** | **25** | **8.0** | **–2** | **0** | **0.0** | **19:44** | | | | | | | | | |
| 2007-08 | St. Petersburg | Russia | 53 | 2 | 15 | 17 | 98 | | | | | | | | | | 9 | 2 | 0 | 2 | 10 | | | | |
| **2008-09** | **Tampa Bay** | **NHL** | **13** | **0** | **2** | **2** | **4** | **0** | **0** | **0** | **11** | **0.0** | **–1** | **0** | **0.0** | **11:49** | | | | | | | | | |
| | Norfolk Admirals | AHL | 20 | 6 | 8 | 14 | 25 | | | | | | | | | | | | | | | | | | |
| | **NHL Totals** | | **394** | **38** | **86** | **124** | **221** | **22** | **0** | **6** | **619** | **6.1** | | **2** | **50.0** | **17:23** | | | | | | | | | |

WHL East First All-Star Team (1991) • AHL First All-Star Team (1996, 1998) • Eddie Shore Award (AHL – Outstanding Defenseman) (1998)

Signed as a free agent by **Toronto**, May 4, 1995. Signed as a free agent by **Philadelphia**, July 31, 1997. Signed as a free agent by **Nashville**, August 10, 1998. Signed as a free agent by **NY Islanders**, July 27, 1999. Claimed on waivers by **Columbus** from **NY Islanders**, May 26, 2000. Signed as a free agent by **Geneve** (Swiss), April 17, 2000. Signed as a free agent by **Washington**, August 12, 2005. Traded to **Los Angeles** by **Washington** for future considerations, February 27, 2007. Signed as a free agent by **St. Petersburg** (Russia), August 13, 2007. Traded to **Toronto** by **Tampa Bay** with Olaf Kolzig, Andy Rogers and Carolina's 4th round choice (previously acquired – later forfeited) in 2009 Entry Draft for Richard Petiot, March 4, 2009.

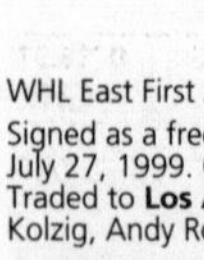

## HIGGINS, Christopher
(HIH-gihns, KRIHS-toh-fuhr) **NYR**

Center. Shoots left. 6', 203 lbs. Born, Smithtown, NY, June 2, 1983. Montreal's 1st choice, 14th overall, in 2002 Entry Draft.

| Season | Club | League | GP | G | A | Pts | PIM | PP | SH | GW | S | % | +/- | TF | F% | Min | Playoffs GP | G | A | Pts | PIM | PP | SH | GW | Min |
|---|---|---|---|---|---|---|---|---|---|---|---|---|---|---|---|---|---|---|---|---|---|---|---|---|---|
| 99-2000 | Avon Old Farms | High-CT | 27 | 19 | 20 | 39 | 10 | | | | | | | | | | | | | | | | | | |
| 2000-01 | Avon Old Farms | High-CT | 24 | 22 | 14 | 36 | 29 | | | | | | | | | | | | | | | | | | |
| 2001-02 | Yale | ECAC | 27 | 14 | 17 | 31 | 32 | | | | | | | | | | | | | | | | | | |
| 2002-03 | Yale | ECAC | 28 | 20 | 21 | 41 | 41 | | | | | | | | | | | | | | | | | | |
| **2003-04** | **Montreal** | **NHL** | **2** | **0** | **0** | **0** | **0** | **0** | **0** | **0** | **0** | **0.0** | **0** | **9** | **22.2** | **6:18** | | | | | | | | | |
| | Hamilton | AHL | 67 | 21 | 27 | 48 | 18 | | | | | | | | | | 10 | 3 | 2 | 5 | 0 | | | | |
| 2004-05 | Hamilton | AHL | 76 | 28 | 23 | 51 | 33 | | | | | | | | | | 4 | 3 | 3 | 6 | 4 | | | | |
| **2005-06** | **Montreal** | **NHL** | **80** | **23** | **15** | **38** | **26** | **7** | **3** | **3** | **148** | **15.5** | **–1** | **45** | **51.1** | **14:25** | **6** | **1** | **3** | **4** | **0** | **0** | **0** | **0** | **17:04** |
| **2006-07** | **Montreal** | **NHL** | **61** | **22** | **16** | **38** | **26** | **8** | **3** | **3** | **159** | **13.8** | **–11** | **53** | **34.0** | **17:54** | | | | | | | | | |
| **2007-08** | **Montreal** | **NHL** | **82** | **27** | **25** | **52** | **22** | **12** | **0** | **5** | **241** | **11.2** | **0** | **62** | **35.5** | **17:57** | **12** | **3** | **2** | **5** | **2** | **0** | **0** | **0** | **18:27** |
| **2008-09** | **Montreal** | **NHL** | **57** | **12** | **11** | **23** | **22** | **2** | **2** | **1** | **151** | **7.9** | **–1** | **57** | **50.9** | **17:00** | **4** | **2** | **0** | **2** | **2** | **0** | **0** | **0** | **17:35** |
| | **NHL Totals** | | **282** | **84** | **67** | **151** | **96** | **29** | **8** | **12** | **699** | **12.0** | | **226** | **41.6** | **16:40** | **22** | **6** | **5** | **11** | **4** | **0** | **0** | **0** | **17:55** |

ECAC All-Rookie Team (2002) • ECAC Second All-Star Team (2002) • ECAC Rookie of the Year (2002) • ECAC First All-Star Team (2003) • ECAC Player of the Year (2003) (co-winner - David LeNeveu) • NCAA East First All-American Team (2003)

Traded to **NY Rangers** by **Montreal** with Ryan McDonagh and Pavel Valentenko for Scott Gomez, Tom Pyatt and Mike Busto, June 30, 2009.

## HILBERT, Andy
(HIHL-buhrt, AN-dee)

Center/Left wing. Shoots left. 5'11", 194 lbs. Born, Lansing, MI, February 6, 1981. Boston's 3rd choice, 37th overall, in 2000 Entry Draft.

| Season | Club | League | GP | G | A | Pts | PIM | PP | SH | GW | S | % | +/- | TF | F% | Min | Playoffs GP | G | A | Pts | PIM | PP | SH | GW | Min |
|---|---|---|---|---|---|---|---|---|---|---|---|---|---|---|---|---|---|---|---|---|---|---|---|---|---|
| 1997-98 | USNTDP | U-17 | 29 | 14 | 10 | 24 | 34 | | | | | | | | | | | | | | | | | | |
| | USNTDP | NAHL | 39 | 19 | 16 | 35 | 102 | | | | | | | | | | 7 | 1 | 4 | 5 | 12 | | | | |
| 1998-99 | USNTDP | U-18 | 6 | 6 | 1 | 7 | 4 | | | | | | | | | | | | | | | | | | |
| | USNTDP | USHL | 46 | 23 | 35 | 58 | 140 | | | | | | | | | | | | | | | | | | |
| 99-2000 | U. of Michigan | CCHA | 35 | 17 | 15 | 32 | 39 | | | | | | | | | | | | | | | | | | |
| 2000-01 | U. of Michigan | CCHA | 42 | 26 | 38 | 64 | 72 | | | | | | | | | | | | | | | | | | |
| **2001-02** | **Boston** | **NHL** | **6** | **1** | **0** | **1** | **2** | **0** | **0** | **0** | **11** | **9.1** | **–2** | **4** | **50.0** | **11:34** | | | | | | | | | |
| | Providence Bruins | AHL | 72 | 26 | 27 | 53 | 74 | | | | | | | | | | 2 | 0 | 0 | 0 | 2 | | | | |

| | | | Regular Season | | | | | | | | | | | | | | Playoffs | | | | | | | | |
|---|---|---|---|---|---|---|---|---|---|---|---|---|---|---|---|---|---|---|---|---|---|---|---|---|---|
| Season | Club | League | GP | G | A | Pts | PIM | PP | SH | GW | S | % | +/- | TF | F% | Min | GP | G | A | Pts | PIM | PP | SH | GW | Min |
| **2002-03** | **Boston** | **NHL** | **14** | **0** | **3** | **3** | **7** | **0** | **0** | **0** | **22** | **0.0** | **-1** | **34** | **44.1** | **11:30** | .... | .... | .... | .... | .... | .... | .... | .... | .... |
| | Providence Bruins | AHL | 64 | 35 | 35 | 70 | 119 | .... | .... | .... | .... | .... | .... | .... | .... | .... | 4 | 0 | 1 | 1 | 4 | .... | .... | .... | .... |
| **2003-04** | **Boston** | **NHL** | **18** | **2** | **0** | **2** | **9** | **0** | **0** | **0** | **27** | **7.4** | **1** | **11** | **54.6** | **8:57** | **5** | **1** | **0** | **1** | **0** | **0** | **0** | **0** | **5:32** |
| | Providence Bruins | AHL | 19 | 3 | 5 | 8 | 20 | .... | .... | .... | .... | .... | .... | .... | .... | .... | .... | .... | .... | .... | .... | .... | .... | .... | .... |
| 2004-05 | Providence Bruins | AHL | 79 | 37 | 42 | 79 | 83 | .... | .... | .... | .... | .... | .... | .... | .... | .... | 17 | 7 | *14 | *21 | 27 | .... | .... | .... | .... |
| **2005-06** | **Chicago** | **NHL** | **28** | **5** | **4** | **9** | **22** | **0** | **0** | **1** | **50** | **10.0** | **-4** | **21** | **38.1** | **10:05** | .... | .... | .... | .... | .... | .... | .... | .... | .... |
| | Norfolk Admirals | AHL | 5 | 3 | 4 | 7 | 2 | .... | .... | .... | .... | .... | .... | .... | .... | .... | .... | .... | .... | .... | .... | .... | .... | .... | .... |
| | **Pittsburgh** | **NHL** | **19** | **7** | **11** | **18** | **16** | **3** | **0** | **1** | **51** | **13.7** | **8** | **146** | **38.4** | **17:27** | .... | .... | .... | .... | .... | .... | .... | .... | .... |
| **2006-07** | **NY Islanders** | **NHL** | **81** | **8** | **20** | **28** | **34** | **0** | **0** | **1** | **164** | **4.9** | **10** | **128** | **52.3** | **11:30** | **5** | **0** | **0** | **0** | **2** | **0** | **0** | **0** | **8:08** |
| **2007-08** | **NY Islanders** | **NHL** | **70** | **8** | **8** | **16** | **18** | **0** | **0** | **0** | **127** | **6.3** | **2** | **220** | **45.0** | **13:29** | .... | .... | .... | .... | .... | .... | .... | .... | .... |
| **2008-09** | **NY Islanders** | **NHL** | **67** | **11** | **16** | **27** | **22** | **1** | **1** | **0** | **167** | **6.6** | **-3** | **186** | **38.2** | **16:09** | .... | .... | .... | .... | .... | .... | .... | .... | .... |
| | **NHL Totals** | | **303** | **42** | **62** | **104** | **130** | **4** | **1** | **3** | **619** | **6.8** | | **750** | **43.2** | **13:05** | **10** | **1** | **0** | **1** | **2** | **0** | **0** | **0** | **6:50** |

CCHA First All-Star Team (2001) • NCAA West First All-American Team (2001) • AHL All-Rookie Team (2002) • AHL Second All-Star Team (2005)

• Missed majority of 2003-04 season recovering from groin injury suffered in pre-season game vs. Detroit, September 15, 2003. Traded to **Chicago** by **Boston** for Chicago's 5th round choice (later traded to NY Islanders - NY Islanders selected Shane Sims) in 2006 Entry Draft, November 6, 2005. Claimed on waivers by **Pittsburgh** from **Chicago**, March 9, 2006. Signed as a free agent by **NY Islanders**, July 4, 2006.

## HILLEN, Jack

(HIHL-uhn, JAK) **NYI**

Defense. Shoots left. 5'11", 200 lbs. Born, Minnetonka, MN, January 24, 1986.

| Season | Club | League | GP | G | A | Pts | PIM | PP | SH | GW | S | % | +/- | TF | F% | Min | GP | G | A | Pts | PIM | PP | SH | GW | Min |
|---|---|---|---|---|---|---|---|---|---|---|---|---|---|---|---|---|---|---|---|---|---|---|---|---|---|
| 2003-04 | Tri-City Storm | USHL | 31 | 12 | 32 | 44 | 18 | .... | .... | .... | .... | .... | .... | .... | .... | .... | .... | .... | .... | .... | .... | .... | .... | .... | .... |
| 2004-05 | Colorado College | WCHA | 30 | 2 | 9 | 11 | 20 | .... | .... | .... | .... | .... | .... | .... | .... | .... | .... | .... | .... | .... | .... | .... | .... | .... | .... |
| 2005-06 | Colorado College | WCHA | 42 | 4 | 9 | 13 | 48 | .... | .... | .... | .... | .... | .... | .... | .... | .... | .... | .... | .... | .... | .... | .... | .... | .... | .... |
| 2006-07 | Colorado College | WCHA | 38 | 7 | 8 | 15 | 38 | .... | .... | .... | .... | .... | .... | .... | .... | .... | .... | .... | .... | .... | .... | .... | .... | .... | .... |
| **2007-08** | Colorado College | WCHA | 41 | 6 | *31 | 37 | 60 | .... | .... | .... | .... | .... | .... | .... | .... | .... | .... | .... | .... | .... | .... | .... | .... | .... | .... |
| | **NY Islanders** | **NHL** | **2** | **0** | **1** | **1** | **4** | **0** | **0** | **0** | **3** | **0.0** | **1** | **0** | **0.0** | **15:32** | .... | .... | .... | .... | .... | .... | .... | .... | .... |
| **2008-09** | **NY Islanders** | **NHL** | **40** | **1** | **5** | **6** | **16** | **0** | **0** | **0** | **47** | **2.1** | **-9** | **0** | **0.0** | **15:13** | .... | .... | .... | .... | .... | .... | .... | .... | .... |
| | Bridgeport | AHL | 33 | 4 | 13 | 17 | 31 | .... | .... | .... | .... | .... | .... | .... | .... | .... | 5 | 0 | 2 | 2 | 2 | .... | .... | .... | .... |
| | **NHL Totals** | | **42** | **1** | **6** | **7** | **20** | **0** | **0** | **0** | **50** | **2.0** | | **0** | **0.0** | **15:14** | .... | .... | .... | .... | .... | .... | .... | .... | .... |

WCHA First All-Star Team (2008) • NCAA West First All-American Team (2008)

Signed as a free agent by **NY Islanders**, April 1, 2008.

## HINOTE, Dan

(HIGH-noht, DAN)

Right wing. Shoots right. 6', 187 lbs. Born, Leesburg, FL, January 30, 1977. Colorado's 9th choice, 167th overall, in 1996 Entry Draft.

| Season | Club | League | GP | G | A | Pts | PIM | PP | SH | GW | S | % | +/- | TF | F% | Min | GP | G | A | Pts | PIM | PP | SH | GW | Min |
|---|---|---|---|---|---|---|---|---|---|---|---|---|---|---|---|---|---|---|---|---|---|---|---|---|---|
| 1993-94 | Elk River Elks | High-MN | STATISTICS NOT AVAILABLE | | | | | | | | | | | | | | | | | | | | | | |
| 1994-95 | Army | NCAA | 33 | 20 | 24 | 44 | 20 | .... | .... | .... | .... | .... | .... | .... | .... | .... | .... | .... | .... | .... | .... | .... | .... | .... | .... |
| 1995-96 | Army | NCAA | 34 | 21 | 24 | 45 | 22 | .... | .... | .... | .... | .... | .... | .... | .... | .... | .... | .... | .... | .... | .... | .... | .... | .... | .... |
| 1996-97 | Oshawa Generals | OHL | 60 | 15 | 13 | 28 | 58 | .... | .... | .... | .... | .... | .... | .... | .... | .... | 18 | 4 | 5 | 9 | 8 | .... | .... | .... | .... |
| 1997-98 | Oshawa Generals | OHL | 35 | 12 | 15 | 27 | 39 | .... | .... | .... | .... | .... | .... | .... | .... | .... | 5 | 2 | 2 | 4 | 7 | .... | .... | .... | .... |
| | Hershey Bears | AHL | 24 | 1 | 4 | 5 | 25 | .... | .... | .... | .... | .... | .... | .... | .... | .... | .... | .... | .... | .... | .... | .... | .... | .... | .... |
| 1998-99 | Hershey Bears | AHL | 65 | 4 | 16 | 20 | 95 | .... | .... | .... | .... | .... | .... | .... | .... | .... | 5 | 3 | 1 | 4 | 6 | .... | .... | .... | .... |
| **99-2000** | **Colorado** | **NHL** | **27** | **1** | **3** | **4** | **10** | **0** | **0** | **0** | **14** | **7.1** | **0** | **132** | **51.5** | **7:51** | .... | .... | .... | .... | .... | .... | .... | .... | .... |
| | Hershey Bears | AHL | 55 | 28 | 31 | 59 | 96 | .... | .... | .... | .... | .... | .... | .... | .... | .... | 14 | 4 | 5 | 9 | 19 | .... | .... | .... | .... |
| **2000-01**♦ | **Colorado** | **NHL** | **76** | **5** | **10** | **15** | **51** | **1** | **0** | **1** | **69** | **7.2** | **1** | **506** | **49.8** | **10:21** | **23** | **2** | **4** | **6** | **21** | **0** | **0** | **0** | **8:22** |
| **2001-02** | **Colorado** | **NHL** | **58** | **6** | **6** | **12** | **39** | **0** | **1** | **3** | **75** | **8.0** | **8** | **267** | **51.3** | **12:27** | **19** | **1** | **2** | **3** | **9** | **0** | **0** | **0** | **10:46** |
| **2002-03** | **Colorado** | **NHL** | **60** | **6** | **4** | **10** | **49** | **0** | **0** | **3** | **65** | **9.2** | **4** | **218** | **46.8** | **10:36** | **7** | **1** | **2** | **3** | **2** | **0** | **0** | **0** | **14:19** |
| **2003-04** | **Colorado** | **NHL** | **59** | **4** | **7** | **11** | **57** | **0** | **2** | **0** | **53** | **7.5** | **-6** | **151** | **48.3** | **12:42** | **11** | **1** | **0** | **1** | **0** | **0** | **1** | **0** | **13:04** |
| 2004-05 | MODO | Sweden | 18 | 2 | 1 | 3 | 106 | .... | .... | .... | .... | .... | .... | .... | .... | .... | 5 | 0 | 0 | 0 | 56 | .... | .... | .... | .... |
| **2005-06** | **Colorado** | **NHL** | **73** | **5** | **8** | **13** | **48** | **0** | **1** | **2** | **70** | **7.1** | **-5** | **335** | **42.1** | **10:41** | **9** | **1** | **1** | **2** | **31** | **0** | **0** | **0** | **13:27** |
| **2006-07** | **St. Louis** | **NHL** | **41** | **5** | **5** | **10** | **23** | **0** | **0** | **1** | **37** | **13.5** | **-8** | **173** | **49.1** | **13:04** | .... | .... | .... | .... | .... | .... | .... | .... | .... |
| **2007-08** | **St. Louis** | **NHL** | **58** | **5** | **5** | **10** | **42** | **0** | **0** | **0** | **42** | **11.9** | **-3** | **33** | **42.4** | **10:31** | .... | .... | .... | .... | .... | .... | .... | .... | .... |
| **2008-09** | **St. Louis** | **NHL** | **51** | **1** | **4** | **5** | **64** | **0** | **0** | **0** | **24** | **4.2** | **-7** | **74** | **47.3** | **10:55** | **3** | **0** | **0** | **0** | **4** | **0** | **0** | **0** | **8:50** |
| | **NHL Totals** | | **503** | **38** | **52** | **90** | **383** | **1** | **4** | **10** | **449** | **8.5** | | **1889** | **48.0** | **11:07** | **72** | **6** | **9** | **15** | **67** | **0** | **1** | **0** | **10:57** |

Signed as a free agent by **MODO** (Sweden), December 22, 2004. Signed as a free agent by **St. Louis**, July 3, 2006.

## HJALMARSSON, Niklas

(JAHL-muhr-suhn, NIHK-luhs) **CHI.**

Defense. Shoots left. 6'2", 200 lbs. Born, Eksjo, Sweden, June 6, 1987. Chicago's 5th choice, 108th overall, in 2005 Entry Draft.

| Season | Club | League | GP | G | A | Pts | PIM | PP | SH | GW | S | % | +/- | TF | F% | Min | GP | G | A | Pts | PIM | PP | SH | GW | Min |
|---|---|---|---|---|---|---|---|---|---|---|---|---|---|---|---|---|---|---|---|---|---|---|---|---|---|
| 2003-04 | HV 71 Jr. | Swe-Jr. | 15 | 1 | 3 | 4 | 14 | .... | .... | .... | .... | .... | .... | .... | .... | .... | 2 | 0 | 0 | 0 | 8 | .... | .... | .... | .... |
| 2004-05 | HV 71 U18 | Swe-U18 | 3 | 0 | 2 | 2 | 4 | .... | .... | .... | .... | .... | .... | .... | .... | .... | .... | .... | .... | .... | .... | .... | .... | .... | .... |
| | HV 71 Jr. | Swe-Jr. | 31 | 4 | 11 | 15 | 87 | .... | .... | .... | .... | .... | .... | .... | .... | .... | .... | .... | .... | .... | .... | .... | .... | .... | .... |
| | HV 71 Jonkoping | Sweden | 14 | 0 | 0 | 0 | 0 | .... | .... | .... | .... | .... | .... | .... | .... | .... | .... | .... | .... | .... | .... | .... | .... | .... | .... |
| 2005-06 | HV 71 Jr. | Swe-Jr. | 7 | 3 | 2 | 5 | 12 | .... | .... | .... | .... | .... | .... | .... | .... | .... | .... | .... | .... | .... | .... | .... | .... | .... | .... |
| | HV 71 Jonkoping | Sweden | 4 | 1 | 2 | 3 | 0 | .... | .... | .... | .... | .... | .... | .... | .... | .... | 12 | 0 | 1 | 1 | 4 | .... | .... | .... | .... |
| 2006-07 | HV 71 Jonkoping | Sweden | 37 | 2 | 0 | 2 | 24 | .... | .... | .... | .... | .... | .... | .... | .... | .... | 14 | 1 | 1 | 2 | 0 | .... | .... | .... | .... |
| | HV 71 Jr. | Swe-Jr. | 7 | 0 | 2 | 2 | 14 | .... | .... | .... | .... | .... | .... | .... | .... | .... | .... | .... | .... | .... | .... | .... | .... | .... | .... |
| | IK Oskarshamn | Sweden-2 | 8 | 1 | 2 | 3 | 6 | .... | .... | .... | .... | .... | .... | .... | .... | .... | .... | .... | .... | .... | .... | .... | .... | .... | .... |
| **2007-08** | **Chicago** | **NHL** | **13** | **0** | **1** | **1** | **13** | **0** | **0** | **0** | **5** | **0.0** | **-2** | **0** | **0.0** | **13:37** | .... | .... | .... | .... | .... | .... | .... | .... | .... |
| | Rockford IceHogs | AHL | 47 | 4 | 9 | 13 | 31 | .... | .... | .... | .... | .... | .... | .... | .... | .... | 12 | 0 | 4 | 4 | 8 | .... | .... | .... | .... |
| **2008-09** | **Chicago** | **NHL** | **21** | **1** | **2** | **3** | **0** | **0** | **0** | **0** | **15** | **6.7** | **4** | **0** | **0.0** | **14:59** | **17** | **0** | **1** | **1** | **6** | **0** | **0** | **0** | **16:37** |
| | Rockford IceHogs | AHL | 52 | 2 | 16 | 18 | 53 | .... | .... | .... | .... | .... | .... | .... | .... | .... | .... | .... | .... | .... | .... | .... | .... | .... | .... |
| | **NHL Totals** | | **34** | **1** | **3** | **4** | **13** | **0** | **0** | **0** | **20** | **5.0** | | **0** | **0.0** | **14:28** | **17** | **0** | **1** | **1** | **6** | **0** | **0** | **0** | **16:37** |

## HLAVAC, Jan

(huh-LAH-vahch, YAHN)

Left wing. Shoots left. 6', 201 lbs. Born, Prague, Czech., September 20, 1976. NY Islanders' 2nd choice, 28th overall, in 1995 Entry Draft.

| Season | Club | League | GP | G | A | Pts | PIM | PP | SH | GW | S | % | +/- | TF | F% | Min | GP | G | A | Pts | PIM | PP | SH | GW | Min |
|---|---|---|---|---|---|---|---|---|---|---|---|---|---|---|---|---|---|---|---|---|---|---|---|---|---|
| 1993-94 | Sparta Jr. | CzRep-Jr. | 27 | 12 | 15 | 27 | .... | .... | .... | .... | .... | .... | .... | .... | .... | .... | .... | .... | .... | .... | .... | .... | .... | .... | .... |
| | HC Sparta Praha | CzRep | 9 | 1 | 1 | 2 | .... | .... | .... | .... | .... | .... | .... | .... | .... | .... | 5 | 0 | 2 | 2 | 0 | .... | .... | .... | .... |
| 1994-95 | HC Sparta Praha | CzRep | 38 | 7 | 6 | 13 | 18 | .... | .... | .... | .... | .... | .... | .... | .... | .... | 12 | 1 | 2 | 3 | .... | .... | .... | .... | .... |
| 1995-96 | HC Sparta Praha | CzRep | 34 | 8 | 5 | 13 | .... | .... | .... | .... | .... | .... | .... | .... | .... | .... | 10 | 5 | 2 | 7 | 2 | .... | .... | .... | .... |
| 1996-97 | HC Sparta Praha | CzRep | 38 | 8 | 13 | 21 | 24 | .... | .... | .... | .... | .... | .... | .... | .... | .... | .... | .... | .... | .... | .... | .... | .... | .... | .... |
| | HC Sparta Praha | EuroHL | 3 | 4 | 0 | 4 | 6 | .... | .... | .... | .... | .... | .... | .... | .... | .... | .... | .... | .... | .... | .... | .... | .... | .... | .... |
| 1997-98 | HC Sparta Praha | CzRep | 48 | 17 | 30 | 47 | 40 | .... | .... | .... | .... | .... | .... | .... | .... | .... | 5 | 1 | 0 | 1 | 2 | .... | .... | .... | .... |
| | HC Sparta Praha | EuroHL | 5 | 0 | 3 | 3 | 4 | .... | .... | .... | .... | .... | .... | .... | .... | .... | .... | .... | .... | .... | .... | .... | .... | .... | .... |
| 1998-99 | HC Sparta Praha | CzRep | 49 | *33 | 20 | 53 | 52 | .... | .... | .... | .... | .... | .... | .... | .... | .... | 6 | 1 | 3 | 4 | .... | .... | .... | .... | .... |
| | HC Sparta Praha | EuroHL | 5 | 4 | 2 | 6 | 0 | .... | .... | .... | .... | .... | .... | .... | .... | .... | 1 | 1 | 1 | 2 | 0 | .... | .... | .... | .... |
| **99-2000** | **NY Rangers** | **NHL** | **67** | **19** | **23** | **42** | **16** | **6** | **0** | **2** | **134** | **14.2** | **3** | **6** | **33.3** | **15:09** | .... | .... | .... | .... | .... | .... | .... | .... | .... |
| | Hartford | AHL | 3 | 1 | 0 | 1 | 0 | .... | .... | .... | .... | .... | .... | .... | .... | .... | .... | .... | .... | .... | .... | .... | .... | .... | .... |
| **2000-01** | **NY Rangers** | **NHL** | **79** | **28** | **36** | **64** | **20** | **5** | **0** | **6** | **195** | **14.4** | **3** | **0** | **0.0** | **16:38** | .... | .... | .... | .... | .... | .... | .... | .... | .... |
| **2001-02** | **Philadelphia** | **NHL** | **31** | **7** | **3** | **10** | **8** | **0** | **0** | **1** | **62** | **11.3** | **5** | **0** | **0.0** | **12:36** | .... | .... | .... | .... | .... | .... | .... | .... | .... |
| | **Vancouver** | **NHL** | **46** | **9** | **12** | **21** | **10** | **1** | **0** | **2** | **70** | **12.9** | **4** | **2** | **100.0** | **14:46** | **5** | **0** | **1** | **1** | **0** | **0** | **0** | **0** | **9:38** |
| **2002-03** | **Vancouver** | **NHL** | **9** | **1** | **1** | **2** | **6** | **0** | **0** | **0** | **7** | **14.3** | **-1** | **0** | **0.0** | **10:51** | .... | .... | .... | .... | .... | .... | .... | .... | .... |
| | **Carolina** | **NHL** | **52** | **9** | **15** | **24** | **22** | **6** | **0** | **1** | **116** | **7.8** | **-9** | **21** | **38.1** | **17:10** | .... | .... | .... | .... | .... | .... | .... | .... | .... |
| **2003-04** | **NY Rangers** | **NHL** | **72** | **5** | **21** | **26** | **16** | **2** | **0** | **0** | **125** | **4.0** | **-8** | **7** | **42.9** | **13:52** | .... | .... | .... | .... | .... | .... | .... | .... | .... |
| 2004-05 | HC Sparta Praha | CzRep | 48 | 10 | 28 | 38 | 34 | .... | .... | .... | .... | .... | .... | .... | .... | .... | 5 | 2 | 0 | 2 | 6 | .... | .... | .... | .... |
| 2005-06 | Geneve | Swiss | 42 | 12 | 22 | 34 | 28 | .... | .... | .... | .... | .... | .... | .... | .... | .... | 4 | 1 | 0 | 1 | 2 | .... | .... | .... | .... |
| 2006-07 | HC Sparta Praha | CzRep | 41 | 20 | 11 | 31 | 85 | .... | .... | .... | .... | .... | .... | .... | .... | .... | 16 | 8 | 2 | 10 | 16 | .... | .... | .... | .... |
| **2007-08** | **Tampa Bay** | **NHL** | **62** | **9** | **13** | **22** | **32** | **0** | **0** | **0** | **123** | **7.3** | **-10** | **2** | **50.0** | **14:46** | .... | .... | .... | .... | .... | .... | .... | .... | .... |
| | **Nashville** | **NHL** | **18** | **3** | **10** | **13** | **8** | **0** | **0** | **2** | **29** | **10.3** | **9** | **6** | **0.0** | **16:29** | **6** | **0** | **2** | **2** | **2** | **0** | **0** | **0** | **18:12** |
| 2008-09 | Linkopings HC | Sweden | 54 | 25 | 23 | 48 | 28 | .... | .... | .... | .... | .... | .... | .... | .... | .... | 5 | 3 | 1 | 4 | 0 | .... | .... | .... | .... |
| | **NHL Totals** | | **436** | **90** | **134** | **224** | **138** | **20** | **0** | **14** | **861** | **10.5** | | **44** | **36.4** | **15:08** | **11** | **0** | **3** | **3** | **2** | **0** | **0** | **0** | **14:19** |

Traded to **Calgary** by **NY Islanders** for Jorgen Jonsson, July 14, 1998. Rights traded to **NY Rangers** by **Calgary** with Calgary's 1st (Jamie Lundmark) and 3rd (later traded back to Calgary – Calgary selected Craig Andersson) round choices in 1999 Entry Draft for Marc Savard and NY Rangers' 1st round choice (Oleg Saprykin) in 1999 Entry Draft, June 26, 1999. Traded to **Philadelphia** by **NY Rangers** with Kim Johnsson, Pavel Brendl and NY Rangers' 3rd round choice (Stefan Ruzicka) in 2003 Entry Draft for Eric Lindros, August 20, 2001. Traded to **Vancouver** by **Philadelphia** with Tampa Bay's 3rd round choice (previously acquired, Vancouver selected Brett Skinner) in 2002 Entry Draft for Donald Brashear and Vancouver's 6th round choice (later traded to Columbus – Columbus selected Jaroslav Balastik) in 2002 Entry Draft, December 17, 2001. Traded to **Carolina** by **Vancouver** with Harold Druken for Darren Langdon and Marek Malik, November 1, 2002. Signed as a free agent by **NY Rangers**, August 28, 2003. Signed as a free agent by **Sparta Praha** (CzRep), August 9, 2004. Signed as a free agent by **Geneve** (Swiss), September, 2005. Signed as a free agent by **Sparta Praha** (CzRep), May 24, 2006. Signed as a free agent by **Tampa Bay**, June 14, 2007. Traded to **Nashville** by **Tampa Bay** for Nashville's 7th round choice (later traded to Philadelphia - Philadelphia selected Joacim Eriksson) in 2008 Entry Draft, February 26, 2008. Signed as a free agent by **Linkopings** (Sweden), August 7, 2009.

## HNIDY, Shane

(NIGH-dee, SHAYN) **MIN.**

Defense. Shoots right. 6'2", 204 lbs. Born, Neepawa, Man., November 8, 1975. Buffalo's 7th choice, 173rd overall, in 1994 Entry Draft.

| | | | Regular Season | | | | | | | | | | | | | | Playoffs | | | | | | | | |
|---|---|---|---|---|---|---|---|---|---|---|---|---|---|---|---|---|---|---|---|---|---|---|---|---|---|
| Season | Club | League | GP | G | A | Pts | PIM | PP | SH | GW | S | % | +/- | TF | F% | Min | GP | G | A | Pts | PIM | PP | SH | GW | Min |
| 1990-91 | Yellowhead | MMMHL | 36 | 9 | 11 | 20 | 92 | | | | | | | | | | | | | | | | | | |
| 1991-92 | Swift Current | WHL | 56 | 1 | 3 | 4 | 11 | | | | | | | | | | 4 | 0 | 0 | 0 | 0 | | | | |
| 1992-93 | Swift Current | WHL | 45 | 5 | 12 | 17 | 62 | | | | | | | | | | | | | | | | | | |
| | Prince Albert | WHL | 27 | 2 | 10 | 12 | 43 | | | | | | | | | | | | | | | | | | |
| 1993-94 | Prince Albert | WHL | 69 | 7 | 26 | 33 | 113 | | | | | | | | | | | | | | | | | | |
| 1994-95 | Prince Albert | WHL | 72 | 5 | 29 | 34 | 169 | | | | | | | | | | 15 | 4 | 7 | 11 | 29 | | | | |
| 1995-96 | Prince Albert | WHL | 58 | 11 | 42 | 53 | 100 | | | | | | | | | | 18 | 4 | 11 | 15 | 34 | | | | |
| 1996-97 | Baton Rouge | ECHL | 21 | 3 | 10 | 13 | 50 | | | | | | | | | | | | | | | | | | |
| | Saint John Flames | AHL | 44 | 2 | 12 | 14 | 112 | | | | | | | | | | | | | | | | | | |
| 1997-98 | Grand Rapids | IHL | 77 | 6 | 12 | 18 | 210 | | | | | | | | | | 3 | 0 | 2 | 2 | 23 | | | | |
| 1998-99 | Adirondack | AHL | 68 | 9 | 20 | 29 | 121 | | | | | | | | | | 3 | 0 | 1 | 1 | 0 | | | | |
| 99-2000 | Cincinnati | AHL | 68 | 9 | 19 | 28 | 153 | | | | | | | | | | | | | | | | | | |
| **2000-01** | **Ottawa** | **NHL** | **52** | **3** | **2** | **5** | **84** | **0** | **0** | **1** | **47** | **6.4** | **8** | **0** | **0.0** | **13:05** | **1** | **0** | **0** | **0** | **0** | **0** | **0** | **0** | **13:23** |
| | Grand Rapids | IHL | 2 | 0 | 0 | 0 | 2 | | | | | | | | | | | | | | | | | | |
| **2001-02** | **Ottawa** | **NHL** | **33** | **1** | **1** | **2** | **57** | **0** | **0** | **0** | **34** | **2.9** | **–10** | **0** | **0.0** | **16:56** | **12** | **1** | **1** | **2** | **12** | **0** | **0** | **0** | **16:00** |
| **2002-03** | **Ottawa** | **NHL** | **67** | **0** | **8** | **8** | **130** | **0** | **0** | **0** | **58** | **0.0** | **–1** | **1** | **0.0** | **13:55** | **1** | **0** | **0** | **0** | **0** | **0** | **0** | **0** | **9:38** |
| **2003-04** | **Ottawa** | **NHL** | **37** | **0** | **5** | **5** | **72** | **0** | **0** | **0** | **16** | **0.0** | **2** | **0** | **0.0** | **11:19** | | | | | | | | | |
| | **Nashville** | **NHL** | **9** | **0** | **2** | **2** | **10** | **0** | **0** | **0** | **12** | **0.0** | **3** | **0** | **0.0** | **18:11** | **5** | **0** | **0** | **0** | **6** | **0** | **0** | **0** | **12:31** |
| 2004-05 | Florida Everblades | ECHL | 19 | 1 | 4 | 5 | 56 | | | | | | | | | | 17 | 0 | 4 | 4 | 6 | | | | |
| **2005-06** | **Atlanta** | **NHL** | **66** | **0** | **3** | **3** | **33** | **0** | **0** | **0** | **50** | **0.0** | **1** | **0** | **0.0** | **10:14** | | | | | | | | | |
| **2006-07** | **Atlanta** | **NHL** | **72** | **5** | **7** | **12** | **63** | **0** | **1** | **1** | **86** | **5.8** | **15** | **0** | **0.0** | **15:38** | **4** | **1** | **0** | **1** | **0** | **0** | **0** | **0** | **15:48** |
| **2007-08** | **Anaheim** | **NHL** | **33** | **1** | **2** | **3** | **30** | **0** | **0** | **0** | **21** | **4.8** | **2** | **0** | **0.0** | **13:08** | | | | | | | | | |
| | **Boston** | **NHL** | **43** | **1** | **4** | **5** | **41** | **0** | **1** | **0** | **28** | **3.6** | **–4** | **0** | **0.0** | **14:42** | **7** | **1** | **1** | **2** | **9** | **0** | **0** | **0** | **17:11** |
| **2008-09** | **Boston** | **NHL** | **65** | **3** | **9** | **12** | **45** | **1** | **0** | **1** | **49** | **6.1** | **6** | **0** | **0.0** | **15:38** | **7** | **1** | **0** | **1** | **0** | **0** | **0** | **0** | **14:06** |
| | **NHL Totals** | | **477** | **14** | **43** | **57** | **565** | **1** | **2** | **3** | **401** | **3.5** | | **1** | **0.0** | **13:55** | **37** | **4** | **2** | **6** | **27** | **0** | **0** | **0** | **15:08** |

Signed as a free agent by **Detroit**, August 6, 1998. Traded to **Ottawa** by **Detroit** for Ottawa's 8th round choice (Todd Jackson) in 2000 Entry Draft, June 25, 2000. • Missed majority of 2001-02 season recovering from ankle injury suffered in game vs. Boston, December 26, 2001. Traded to **Nashville** by **Ottawa** for Colorado's 3rd round choice (previously acquired, Ottawa selected Peter Regin) in 2004 Entry Draft, March 9, 2004. Signed as a free agent by **Florida** (ECHL), December 6, 2004. Traded to **Atlanta** by **Nashville** for Atlanta's 4th round choice (Niko Snellman) in 2006 Entry Draft, July 30, 2005. Signed as a free agent by **Anaheim**, July 5, 2007. Traded to **Boston** by **Anaheim** with Anaheim's 6th round choice (Nicholas Tremblay) in 2008 Entry Draft for Brandon Bochenski, January 2, 2008. Signed as a free agent by **Minnesota**, July 3, 2009.

## HOGGAN, Jeff

(HOH-guhn, JEHF) **PHX.**

Left wing. Shoots left. 6'1", 188 lbs. Born, Hope, B.C., February 1, 1978.

| Season | Club | League | GP | G | A | Pts | PIM | PP | SH | GW | S | % | +/- | TF | F% | Min | GP | G | A | Pts | PIM | PP | SH | GW | Min |
|---|---|---|---|---|---|---|---|---|---|---|---|---|---|---|---|---|---|---|---|---|---|---|---|---|---|
| 1998-99 | Powell River Kings | BCHL | STATISTICS NOT AVAILABLE | | | | | | | | | | | | | | | | | | | | | | |
| 99-2000 | Nebraska-Omaha | CCHA | 34 | 16 | 9 | 25 | 82 | | | | | | | | | | | | | | | | | | |
| 2000-01 | Nebraska-Omaha | CCHA | 42 | 12 | 17 | 29 | 78 | | | | | | | | | | | | | | | | | | |
| 2001-02 | Nebraska-Omaha | CCHA | 41 | 24 | 21 | 45 | 92 | | | | | | | | | | | | | | | | | | |
| | Houston Aeros | AHL | | | | | | | | | | | | | | | 4 | 0 | 0 | 0 | 2 | | | | |
| 2002-03 | Houston Aeros | AHL | 65 | 6 | 5 | 11 | 45 | | | | | | | | | | 14 | 1 | 2 | 3 | 23 | | | | |
| 2003-04 | Houston Aeros | AHL | 77 | 21 | 15 | 36 | 88 | | | | | | | | | | 2 | 0 | 1 | 1 | 4 | | | | |
| 2004-05 | Worcester IceCats | AHL | 47 | 16 | 9 | 25 | 55 | | | | | | | | | | | | | | | | | | |
| **2005-06** | **St. Louis** | **NHL** | **52** | **2** | **6** | **8** | **34** | **0** | **0** | **0** | **60** | **3.3** | **–16** | **4** | **25.0** | **8:47** | | | | | | | | | |
| **2006-07** | **Boston** | **NHL** | **46** | **0** | **2** | **2** | **33** | **0** | **0** | **0** | **53** | **0.0** | **–8** | **3** | **33.3** | **7:04** | | | | | | | | | |
| | Providence Bruins | AHL | 22 | 4 | 7 | 11 | 27 | | | | | | | | | | 13 | 4 | 3 | 7 | 17 | | | | |
| **2007-08** | **Boston** | **NHL** | **1** | **0** | **0** | **0** | **0** | **0** | **0** | **0** | **0** | **0.0** | **0** | **0** | **0.0** | **7:57** | | | | | | | | | |
| | Providence Bruins | AHL | 71 | 29 | 31 | 60 | 59 | | | | | | | | | | 5 | 3 | 4 | 7 | 4 | | | | |
| **2008-09** | **Phoenix** | **NHL** | **4** | **0** | **1** | **1** | **7** | **0** | **0** | **0** | **7** | **0.0** | **–1** | **2** | **0.0** | **12:00** | | | | | | | | | |
| | San Antonio | AHL | 60 | 22 | 13 | 35 | 64 | | | | | | | | | | | | | | | | | | |
| | **NHL Totals** | | **103** | **2** | **9** | **11** | **74** | **0** | **0** | **0** | **120** | **1.7** | | **9** | **22.2** | **8:08** | | | | | | | | | |

CCHA First All-Star Team (2002) • NCAA West Second All-American Team (2002)

Signed to a PTO (tryout) contract by **Houston** (AHL), April 4, 2002. Signed as a free agent by **Minnesota**, August 20, 2002. Signed as a free agent by **Worcester** (AHL), September, 2004. Signed as a free agent by **St. Louis**, August 2, 2005. Signed as a free agent by **Boston**, July 21, 2006. Signed as a free agent by **Phoenix**, July 15, 2008.

## HOLIK, Bobby

(HOH-leek, BAW-bee)

Center. Shoots right. 6'4", 230 lbs. Born, Jihlava, Czech., January 1, 1971. Hartford's 1st choice, 10th overall, in 1989 Entry Draft.

| Season | Club | League | GP | G | A | Pts | PIM | PP | SH | GW | S | % | +/- | TF | F% | Min | GP | G | A | Pts | PIM | PP | SH | GW | Min |
|---|---|---|---|---|---|---|---|---|---|---|---|---|---|---|---|---|---|---|---|---|---|---|---|---|---|
| 1987-88 | Dukla Jihlava | Czech | 31 | 5 | 9 | 14 | 16 | | | | | | | | | | | | | | | | | | |
| 1988-89 | Dukla Jihlava | Czech | 24 | 7 | 10 | 17 | 32 | | | | | | | | | | | | | | | | | | |
| 1989-90 | Dukla Jihlava | Czech | 42 | 15 | 26 | 41 | | | | | | | | | | | | | | | | | | | |
| **1990-91** | **Hartford** | **NHL** | **78** | **21** | **22** | **43** | **113** | **8** | **0** | **3** | **173** | **12.1** | **–3** | | | | **6** | **0** | **0** | **0** | **7** | **0** | **0** | **0** | |
| **1991-92** | **Hartford** | **NHL** | **76** | **21** | **24** | **45** | **44** | **1** | **0** | **2** | **207** | **10.1** | **4** | | | | **7** | **0** | **1** | **1** | **6** | **0** | **0** | **0** | |
| **1992-93** | **New Jersey** | **NHL** | **61** | **20** | **19** | **39** | **76** | **7** | **0** | **4** | **180** | **11.1** | **–6** | | | | **5** | **1** | **1** | **2** | **6** | **0** | **0** | **0** | |
| | Utica Devils | AHL | 1 | 0 | 0 | 0 | 2 | | | | | | | | | | | | | | | | | | |
| **1993-94** | **New Jersey** | **NHL** | **70** | **13** | **20** | **33** | **72** | **2** | **0** | **3** | **130** | **10.0** | **28** | | | | **20** | **0** | **3** | **3** | **6** | **0** | **0** | **0** | |
| **1994-95** ♦ | **New Jersey** | **NHL** | **48** | **10** | **10** | **20** | **18** | **0** | **0** | **2** | **84** | **11.9** | **9** | | | | **20** | **4** | **4** | **8** | **22** | **2** | **0** | **1** | |
| **1995-96** | **New Jersey** | **NHL** | **63** | **13** | **17** | **30** | **58** | **1** | **0** | **1** | **157** | **8.3** | **9** | | | | | | | | | | | | |
| **1996-97** | **New Jersey** | **NHL** | **82** | **23** | **39** | **62** | **54** | **5** | **0** | **6** | **192** | **12.0** | **24** | | | | **10** | **2** | **3** | **5** | **4** | **1** | **0** | **0** | |
| **1997-98** | **New Jersey** | **NHL** | **82** | **29** | **36** | **65** | **100** | **8** | **0** | **8** | **238** | **12.2** | **23** | | | | **5** | **0** | **0** | **0** | **8** | **0** | **0** | **0** | |
| **1998-99** | **New Jersey** | **NHL** | **78** | **27** | **37** | **64** | **119** | **5** | **0** | **8** | **253** | **10.7** | **16** | **1350** | **53.6** | **17:34** | **7** | **0** | **7** | **7** | **6** | **0** | **0** | **0** | **18:14** |
| **99-2000** ♦ | **New Jersey** | **NHL** | **79** | **23** | **23** | **46** | **106** | **7** | **0** | **4** | **257** | **8.9** | **7** | **1390** | **55.6** | **16:53** | **23** | **3** | **7** | **10** | **14** | **0** | **0** | **1** | **17:29** |
| **2000-01** | **New Jersey** | **NHL** | **80** | **15** | **35** | **50** | **97** | **3** | **0** | **3** | **206** | **7.3** | **19** | **1365** | **56.0** | **15:49** | **25** | **6** | **10** | **16** | **37** | **1** | **0** | **3** | **16:05** |
| **2001-02** | **New Jersey** | **NHL** | **81** | **25** | **29** | **54** | **97** | **6** | **0** | **3** | **270** | **9.3** | **7** | **1594** | **54.5** | **17:42** | **6** | **4** | **1** | **5** | **2** | **1** | **0** | **0** | **17:53** |
| **2002-03** | **NY Rangers** | **NHL** | **64** | **16** | **19** | **35** | **52** | **3** | **0** | **2** | **213** | **7.5** | **–1** | **1390** | **58.2** | **18:07** | | | | | | | | | |
| **2003-04** | **NY Rangers** | **NHL** | **82** | **25** | **31** | **56** | **96** | **8** | **0** | **4** | **225** | **11.1** | **4** | **1664** | **54.2** | **18:34** | | | | | | | | | |
| 2004-05 | | | DID NOT PLAY | | | | | | | | | | | | | | | | | | | | | | |
| **2005-06** | **Atlanta** | **NHL** | **64** | **15** | **18** | **33** | **79** | **5** | **0** | **0** | **151** | **9.9** | **–6** | **1385** | **55.7** | **17:31** | | | | | | | | | |
| **2006-07** | **Atlanta** | **NHL** | **82** | **11** | **18** | **29** | **86** | **2** | **1** | **1** | **190** | **5.8** | **–3** | **1427** | **57.5** | **15:56** | **4** | **0** | **1** | **1** | **0** | **0** | **0** | **0** | **15:24** |
| **2007-08** | **Atlanta** | **NHL** | **82** | **15** | **19** | **34** | **90** | **3** | **0** | **3** | **140** | **10.7** | **–14** | **1502** | **58.4** | **15:58** | | | | | | | | | |
| **2008-09** | **New Jersey** | **NHL** | **62** | **4** | **5** | **9** | **66** | **0** | **0** | **1** | **79** | **5.1** | **–2** | **506** | **59.3** | **10:11** | **3** | **0** | **1** | **1** | **2** | **0** | **0** | **0** | **5:18** |
| | **NHL Totals** | | **1314** | **326** | **421** | **747** | **1423** | **74** | **1** | **58** | **3345** | **9.7** | | **13573** | **56.1** | **16:31** | **141** | **20** | **39** | **59** | **120** | **5** | **0** | **5** | **16:25** |

Played in NHL All-Star Game (1998, 1999)

Traded to **New Jersey** by **Hartford** with Hartford's 2nd round choice (Jay Pandolfo) in 1993 Entry Draft for Sean Burke and Eric Weinrich, August 28, 1992. Signed as a free agent by **NY Rangers**, July 1, 2002. Signed as a free agent by **Atlanta**, August 2, 2005. Signed as a free agent by **New Jersey**, July 1, 2008. • Officially announced his retirement, May 22, 2009.

## HOLLWEG, Ryan

(HOHL-wehg, RIGH-uhn)

Center. Shoots left. 5'11", 210 lbs. Born, Downey, CA, April 23, 1983. NY Rangers' 10th choice, 238th overall, in 2001 Entry Draft.

| Season | Club | League | GP | G | A | Pts | PIM | PP | SH | GW | S | % | +/- | TF | F% | Min | GP | G | A | Pts | PIM | PP | SH | GW | Min |
|---|---|---|---|---|---|---|---|---|---|---|---|---|---|---|---|---|---|---|---|---|---|---|---|---|---|
| 1998-99 | Langley Hornets | BCHL | 58 | 14 | 40 | 54 | 187 | | | | | | | | | | | | | | | | | | |
| 99-2000 | Medicine Hat | WHL | 54 | 19 | 27 | 46 | 107 | | | | | | | | | | | | | | | | | | |
| 2000-01 | Medicine Hat | WHL | 65 | 19 | 39 | 58 | 125 | | | | | | | | | | | | | | | | | | |
| 2001-02 | Medicine Hat | WHL | 58 | 30 | 40 | 70 | 121 | | | | | | | | | | | | | | | | | | |
| | Hartford | AHL | 8 | 1 | 1 | 2 | 2 | | | | | | | | | | 9 | 0 | 2 | 2 | 19 | | | | |
| 2002-03 | Medicine Hat | WHL | 4 | 1 | 1 | 2 | 8 | | | | | | | | | | | | | | | | | | |
| 2003-04 | Medicine Hat | WHL | 52 | 25 | 32 | 57 | 117 | | | | | | | | | | 20 | 6 | 9 | 15 | 22 | | | | |
| 2004-05 | Hartford | AHL | 73 | 8 | 6 | 14 | 239 | | | | | | | | | | 6 | 1 | 0 | 1 | 9 | | | | |
| **2005-06** | **NY Rangers** | **NHL** | **52** | **2** | **3** | **5** | **84** | **0** | **0** | **0** | **32** | **6.3** | **–3** | **19** | **57.9** | **7:15** | **4** | **0** | **1** | **1** | **19** | **0** | **0** | **0** | **10:26** |
| | Hartford | AHL | 7 | 2 | 1 | 3 | 11 | | | | | | | | | | | | | | | | | | |
| **2006-07** | **NY Rangers** | **NHL** | **78** | **1** | **2** | **3** | **131** | **0** | **0** | **0** | **63** | **1.6** | **–11** | **86** | **39.5** | **8:14** | **2** | **0** | **0** | **0** | **2** | **0** | **0** | **0** | **5:19** |
| **2007-08** | **NY Rangers** | **NHL** | **70** | **2** | **2** | **4** | **96** | **0** | **0** | **0** | **59** | **3.4** | **–12** | **39** | **46.2** | **8:18** | **8** | **0** | **0** | **0** | **2** | **0** | **0** | **0** | **4:50** |
| **2008-09** | **Toronto** | **NHL** | **25** | **0** | **2** | **2** | **38** | **0** | **0** | **0** | **12** | **0.0** | **–7** | **3** | **33.3** | **6:28** | | | | | | | | | |
| | Toronto Marlies | AHL | 28 | 2 | 1 | 3 | 34 | | | | | | | | | | 6 | 0 | 0 | 0 | 20 | | | | |
| | **NHL Totals** | | **225** | **5** | **9** | **14** | **349** | **0** | **0** | **0** | **166** | **3.0** | | **147** | **43.5** | **7:50** | **14** | **0** | **1** | **1** | **23** | **0** | **0** | **0** | **6:30** |

• Missed majority of 2002-03 season recovering from head injury suffered in game vs. Vancouver (WHL), October 8, 2002. Traded to **Toronto** by **NY Rangers** for Pittsburgh's 5th round choice (previously acquired, later traded back to Pittsburgh – Pittsburgh selected Andy Bathgate) in 2009 Entry Draft, July 14, 2008.

| | | | Regular Season | | | | | | | | | | | | | | Playoffs | | | | | | | | |
|---|---|---|---|---|---|---|---|---|---|---|---|---|---|---|---|---|---|---|---|---|---|---|---|---|---|
| Season | Club | League | GP | G | A | Pts | PIM | PP | SH | GW | S | % | +/- | TF | F% | Min | GP | G | A | Pts | PIM | PP | SH | GW | Min |

## HOLMSTROM, Tomas

(HOHLM-struhm, TAW-mas) **DET.**

Left wing. Shoots left. 6', 203 lbs. Born, Pitea, Sweden, January 23, 1973. Detroit's 9th choice, 257th overall, in 1994 Entry Draft.

| Season | Club | League | GP | G | A | Pts | PIM | PP | SH | GW | S | % | +/- | TF | F% | Min | GP | G | A | Pts | PIM | PP | SH | GW | Min |
|---|---|---|---|---|---|---|---|---|---|---|---|---|---|---|---|---|---|---|---|---|---|---|---|---|---|
| 1989-90 | Pitea HC | Sweden-2 | 9 | 1 | 0 | 1 | 4 | .... | .... | .... | .... | .... | .... | .... | .... | .... | .... | .... | .... | .... | .... | .... | .... | .... | .... |
| 1990-91 | Pitea HC | Sweden-2 | 26 | 5 | 4 | 9 | 16 | .... | .... | .... | .... | .... | .... | .... | .... | .... | .... | .... | .... | .... | .... | .... | .... | .... | .... |
| 1991-92 | Pitea HC | Sweden-2 | 31 | 15 | 12 | 27 | 44 | .... | .... | .... | .... | .... | .... | .... | .... | .... | .... | .... | .... | .... | .... | .... | .... | .... | .... |
| 1992-93 | Pitea HC | Sweden-2 | 32 | 17 | 15 | 32 | 30 | .... | .... | .... | .... | .... | .... | .... | .... | .... | .... | .... | .... | .... | .... | .... | .... | .... | .... |
| 1993-94 | Bodens IK | Sweden-2 | 34 | 23 | 16 | 39 | 86 | .... | .... | .... | .... | .... | .... | .... | .... | .... | 9 | 3 | 3 | 6 | 24 | .... | .... | .... | .... |
| 1994-95 | Lulea HF | Sweden | 40 | 14 | 14 | 28 | 56 | .... | .... | .... | .... | .... | .... | .... | .... | .... | 8 | 1 | 2 | 3 | 20 | .... | .... | .... | .... |
| 1995-96 | Lulea HF | Sweden | 34 | 12 | 11 | 23 | 78 | .... | .... | .... | .... | .... | .... | .... | .... | .... | 11 | 6 | 2 | 8 | 22 | .... | .... | .... | .... |
| 1996-97 ♦ | Detroit | NHL | 47 | 6 | 3 | 9 | 33 | 3 | 0 | 0 | 53 | 11.3 | –10 | .... | .... | .... | 1 | 0 | 0 | 0 | 0 | 0 | 0 | 0 | .... |
| | Adirondack | AHL | 6 | 3 | 1 | 4 | 7 | .... | .... | .... | .... | .... | .... | .... | .... | .... | .... | .... | .... | .... | .... | .... | .... | .... | .... |
| 1997-98 ♦ | Detroit | NHL | 57 | 5 | 17 | 22 | 44 | 1 | 0 | 1 | 48 | 10.4 | 6 | .... | .... | .... | 22 | 7 | 12 | 19 | 16 | 2 | 0 | 0 | .... |
| 1998-99 | Detroit | NHL | 82 | 13 | 21 | 34 | 69 | 5 | 0 | 4 | 100 | 13.0 | –11 | 0 | 0.0 | 12:22 | 10 | 4 | 3 | 7 | 4 | 2 | 0 | 1 | 12:32 |
| 99-2000 | Detroit | NHL | 72 | 13 | 22 | 35 | 43 | 4 | 0 | 1 | 71 | 18.3 | 4 | 0 | 0.0 | 12:06 | 9 | 3 | 1 | 4 | 16 | 1 | 0 | 1 | 11:42 |
| 2000-01 | Detroit | NHL | 73 | 16 | 24 | 40 | 40 | 9 | 0 | 2 | 74 | 21.6 | –12 | 2 | 50.0 | 11:41 | 6 | 1 | 3 | 4 | 8 | 1 | 0 | 0 | 14:23 |
| 2001-02 ♦ | Detroit | NHL | 69 | 8 | 18 | 26 | 58 | 6 | 0 | 1 | 79 | 10.1 | –12 | 2 | 0.0 | 12:23 | 23 | 8 | 3 | 11 | 8 | 3 | 0 | 2 | 11:31 |
| | Sweden | Olympics | 4 | 1 | 0 | 1 | 0 | .... | .... | .... | .... | .... | .... | .... | .... | .... | .... | .... | .... | .... | .... | .... | .... | .... | .... |
| 2002-03 | Detroit | NHL | 74 | 20 | 20 | 40 | 62 | 12 | 0 | 2 | 109 | 18.3 | 11 | 2 | 0.0 | 12:28 | 4 | 1 | 1 | 2 | 4 | 1 | 0 | 0 | 14:37 |
| 2003-04 | Detroit | NHL | 67 | 15 | 15 | 30 | 38 | 6 | 0 | 0 | 74 | 20.3 | 8 | 3 | 0.0 | 12:23 | 12 | 2 | 2 | 4 | 10 | 1 | 0 | 1 | 11:27 |
| 2004-05 | Lulea HF | Sweden | 47 | 14 | 16 | 30 | 50 | .... | .... | .... | .... | .... | .... | .... | .... | .... | 4 | 0 | 0 | 0 | 18 | .... | .... | .... | .... |
| 2005-06 | Detroit | NHL | 81 | 29 | 30 | 59 | 66 | 11 | 0 | 8 | 140 | 20.7 | 14 | 0 | 0.0 | 13:59 | 6 | 1 | 2 | 3 | 12 | 1 | 0 | 0 | 17:04 |
| | Sweden | Olympics | 8 | 1 | 3 | 4 | 10 | .... | .... | .... | .... | .... | .... | .... | .... | .... | .... | .... | .... | .... | .... | .... | .... | .... | .... |
| 2006-07 | Detroit | NHL | 77 | 30 | 22 | 52 | 58 | 13 | 0 | 5 | 176 | 17.0 | 13 | 0 | 0.0 | 15:13 | 15 | 5 | 3 | 8 | 14 | 4 | 0 | 1 | 16:15 |
| 2007-08 ♦ | Detroit | NHL | 59 | 20 | 20 | 40 | 58 | 11 | 0 | 5 | 137 | 14.6 | 9 | 1 | 0.0 | 17:33 | 21 | 4 | 8 | 12 | 26 | 1 | 0 | 0 | 17:10 |
| 2008-09 | Detroit | NHL | 53 | 14 | 23 | 37 | 38 | 8 | 0 | 1 | 75 | 18.7 | 18 | 8 | 37.5 | 15:16 | 23 | 2 | 5 | 7 | 22 | 0 | 0 | 0 | 13:45 |
| | NHL Totals | | 811 | 189 | 235 | 424 | 607 | 89 | 0 | 30 | 1136 | 16.6 | | 18 | 22.2 | 13:26 | 152 | 38 | 43 | 81 | 140 | 17 | 0 | 6 | 13:57 |

Signed as a free agent by **Lulea** (Sweden), September 16, 2004.

## HORCOFF, Shawn

(hohr-KAWF, SHAWN) **EDM.**

Center. Shoots left. 6'1", 208 lbs. Born, Trail, B.C., September 17, 1978. Edmonton's 3rd choice, 99th overall, in 1998 Entry Draft.

| Season | Club | League | GP | G | A | Pts | PIM | PP | SH | GW | S | % | +/- | TF | F% | Min | GP | G | A | Pts | PIM | PP | SH | GW | Min |
|---|---|---|---|---|---|---|---|---|---|---|---|---|---|---|---|---|---|---|---|---|---|---|---|---|---|
| 1994-95 | Trail Smokies | RMJHL | 47 | 50 | 46 | 96 | 26 | .... | .... | .... | .... | .... | .... | .... | .... | .... | .... | .... | .... | .... | .... | .... | .... | .... | .... |
| 1995-96 | Chilliwack Chiefs | BCHL | 58 | 49 | 96 | *145 | 44 | .... | .... | .... | .... | .... | .... | .... | .... | .... | 9 | 5 | 19 | 24 | 12 | .... | .... | .... | .... |
| 1996-97 | Michigan State | CCHA | 40 | 10 | 13 | 23 | 20 | .... | .... | .... | .... | .... | .... | .... | .... | .... | .... | .... | .... | .... | .... | .... | .... | .... | .... |
| 1997-98 | Michigan State | CCHA | 34 | 14 | 13 | 27 | 50 | .... | .... | .... | .... | .... | .... | .... | .... | .... | .... | .... | .... | .... | .... | .... | .... | .... | .... |
| 1998-99 | Michigan State | CCHA | 39 | 12 | 25 | 37 | 70 | .... | .... | .... | .... | .... | .... | .... | .... | .... | .... | .... | .... | .... | .... | .... | .... | .... | .... |
| 99-2000 | Michigan State | CCHA | 42 | 14 | *51 | *65 | 50 | .... | .... | .... | .... | .... | .... | .... | .... | .... | .... | .... | .... | .... | .... | .... | .... | .... | .... |
| 2000-01 | Edmonton | NHL | 49 | 9 | 7 | 16 | 10 | 0 | 0 | 2 | 42 | 21.4 | 8 | 122 | 41.8 | 9:14 | 5 | 0 | 0 | 0 | 0 | 0 | 0 | 0 | 6:31 |
| | Hamilton | AHL | 24 | 10 | 18 | 28 | 19 | .... | .... | .... | .... | .... | .... | .... | .... | .... | .... | .... | .... | .... | .... | .... | .... | .... | .... |
| 2001-02 | Edmonton | NHL | 61 | 8 | 14 | 22 | 18 | 0 | 0 | 0 | 57 | 14.0 | 3 | 454 | 46.3 | 11:20 | .... | .... | .... | .... | .... | .... | .... | .... | .... |
| | Hamilton | AHL | 2 | 1 | 2 | 3 | 6 | .... | .... | .... | .... | .... | .... | .... | .... | .... | .... | .... | .... | .... | .... | .... | .... | .... | .... |
| 2002-03 | Edmonton | NHL | 78 | 12 | 21 | 33 | 55 | 2 | 0 | 3 | 98 | 12.2 | 10 | 301 | 42.9 | 13:30 | 6 | 3 | 1 | 4 | 6 | 0 | 0 | 1 | 15:27 |
| 2003-04 | Edmonton | NHL | 80 | 15 | 25 | 40 | 73 | 0 | 2 | 3 | 110 | 13.6 | 0 | 1378 | 50.7 | 17:31 | .... | .... | .... | .... | .... | .... | .... | .... | .... |
| 2004-05 | Mora IK | Sweden | 50 | 19 | 27 | 46 | 117 | .... | .... | .... | .... | .... | .... | .... | .... | .... | .... | .... | .... | .... | .... | .... | .... | .... | .... |
| 2005-06 | Edmonton | NHL | 79 | 22 | 51 | 73 | 85 | 3 | 3 | 5 | 167 | 13.2 | 0 | 1421 | 52.7 | 19:59 | 24 | 7 | 12 | 19 | 12 | 1 | 1 | 2 | 21:37 |
| 2006-07 | Edmonton | NHL | 80 | 16 | 35 | 51 | 56 | 5 | 0 | 5 | 168 | 9.5 | –22 | 1422 | 50.6 | 20:50 | .... | .... | .... | .... | .... | .... | .... | .... | .... |
| 2007-08 | Edmonton | NHL | 53 | 21 | 29 | 50 | 30 | 6 | 0 | 2 | 115 | 18.3 | 1 | 963 | 50.6 | 22:13 | .... | .... | .... | .... | .... | .... | .... | .... | .... |
| 2008-09 | Edmonton | NHL | 80 | 17 | 36 | 53 | 39 | 8 | 0 | 2 | 178 | 9.6 | 7 | 1756 | 53.9 | 21:22 | .... | .... | .... | .... | .... | .... | .... | .... | .... |
| | NHL Totals | | 560 | 120 | 218 | 338 | 366 | 24 | 5 | 22 | 935 | 12.8 | | 7817 | 51.1 | 17:22 | 35 | 10 | 13 | 23 | 18 | 1 | 1 | 3 | 18:24 |

CCHA First All-Star Team (2000) • CCHA Player of the Year (2000) • NCAA West First All-American Team (2000)
Played in NHL All-Star Game (2008)
Signed as a free agent by **Mora** (Sweden), September 6, 2004.

## HORDICHUK, Darcy

(HOHR-dih-chuhk, DAHR-see) **VAN.**

Left wing. Shoots left. 6'1", 215 lbs. Born, Kamsack, Sask., August 10, 1980. Atlanta's 9th choice, 180th overall, in 2000 Entry Draft.

| Season | Club | League | GP | G | A | Pts | PIM | PP | SH | GW | S | % | +/- | TF | F% | Min | GP | G | A | Pts | PIM | PP | SH | GW | Min |
|---|---|---|---|---|---|---|---|---|---|---|---|---|---|---|---|---|---|---|---|---|---|---|---|---|---|
| 1996-97 | Yorkton Mallers | SMHL | 57 | 6 | 15 | 21 | 230 | .... | .... | .... | .... | .... | .... | .... | .... | .... | .... | .... | .... | .... | .... | .... | .... | .... | .... |
| | Calgary Hitmen | WHL | 3 | 0 | 0 | 0 | 2 | .... | .... | .... | .... | .... | .... | .... | .... | .... | .... | .... | .... | .... | .... | .... | .... | .... | .... |
| 1997-98 | Dauphin Kings | MJHL | 58 | 12 | 21 | 33 | 279 | .... | .... | .... | .... | .... | .... | .... | .... | .... | .... | .... | .... | .... | .... | .... | .... | .... | .... |
| 1998-99 | Saskatoon Blades | WHL | 66 | 3 | 2 | 5 | 246 | .... | .... | .... | .... | .... | .... | .... | .... | .... | .... | .... | .... | .... | .... | .... | .... | .... | .... |
| 99-2000 | Saskatoon Blades | WHL | 63 | 6 | 8 | 14 | 269 | .... | .... | .... | .... | .... | .... | .... | .... | .... | 11 | 4 | 2 | 6 | 43 | .... | .... | .... | .... |
| 2000-01 | Atlanta | NHL | 11 | 0 | 0 | 0 | 38 | 0 | 0 | 0 | 6 | 0.0 | –3 | 0 | 0.0 | 7:18 | .... | .... | .... | .... | .... | .... | .... | .... | .... |
| | Orlando | IHL | 69 | 7 | 3 | 10 | *369 | .... | .... | .... | .... | .... | .... | .... | .... | .... | 16 | 3 | 3 | 6 | *41 | .... | .... | .... | .... |
| 2001-02 | Atlanta | NHL | 33 | 1 | 1 | 2 | 127 | 0 | 0 | 0 | 8 | 12.5 | –5 | 4 | 25.0 | 6:03 | .... | .... | .... | .... | .... | .... | .... | .... | .... |
| | Chicago Wolves | AHL | 34 | 5 | 4 | 9 | 127 | .... | .... | .... | .... | .... | .... | .... | .... | .... | .... | .... | .... | .... | .... | .... | .... | .... | .... |
| | Phoenix | NHL | 1 | 0 | 0 | 0 | 14 | 0 | 0 | 0 | 0 | 0.0 | 0 | 0 | 0.0 | 7:18 | .... | .... | .... | .... | .... | .... | .... | .... | .... |
| 2002-03 | Phoenix | NHL | 25 | 0 | 0 | 0 | 82 | 0 | 0 | 0 | 5 | 0.0 | –1 | 0 | 0.0 | 4:47 | .... | .... | .... | .... | .... | .... | .... | .... | .... |
| | Springfield | AHL | 22 | 1 | 3 | 4 | 38 | .... | .... | .... | .... | .... | .... | .... | .... | .... | .... | .... | .... | .... | .... | .... | .... | .... | .... |
| | Florida | NHL | 3 | 0 | 0 | 0 | 15 | 0 | 0 | 0 | 2 | 0.0 | –1 | 0 | 0.0 | 9:45 | .... | .... | .... | .... | .... | .... | .... | .... | .... |
| 2003-04 | Florida | NHL | 57 | 3 | 1 | 4 | 158 | 0 | 0 | 1 | 27 | 11.1 | –10 | 4 | 50.0 | 6:46 | .... | .... | .... | .... | .... | .... | .... | .... | .... |
| 2004-05 | | | DID NOT PLAY | | | | | | | | | | | | | | | | | | | | | | |
| 2005-06 | Nashville | NHL | 74 | 7 | 6 | 13 | 163 | 0 | 0 | 1 | 52 | 13.5 | 9 | 1 | 0.0 | 6:09 | .... | .... | .... | .... | .... | .... | .... | .... | .... |
| 2006-07 | Nashville | NHL | 53 | 1 | 3 | 4 | 90 | 0 | 0 | 0 | 22 | 4.5 | –2 | 0 | 0.0 | 4:48 | 2 | 0 | 0 | 0 | 0 | 0 | 0 | 0 | 3:38 |
| 2007-08 | Nashville | NHL | 45 | 1 | 2 | 3 | 60 | 0 | 0 | 1 | 18 | 5.6 | –1 | 0 | 0.0 | 5:09 | 5 | 0 | 0 | 0 | 2 | 0 | 0 | 0 | 3:32 |
| 2008-09 | Vancouver | NHL | 73 | 4 | 1 | 5 | 109 | 0 | 0 | 0 | 26 | 15.4 | 1 | 1 | 100.0 | 5:32 | 10 | 1 | 0 | 1 | 14 | 0 | 0 | 0 | 5:20 |
| | NHL Totals | | 375 | 17 | 14 | 31 | 856 | 0 | 0 | 3 | 166 | 10.2 | | 10 | 40.0 | 5:47 | 17 | 1 | 0 | 1 | 16 | 0 | 0 | 0 | 4:36 |

Traded to **Phoenix** by **Atlanta** with Atlanta's 4th (Lance Monych) and 5th (John Zeiler) round choices in 2002 Entry Draft for Kiril Safronov, the rights to Ruslan Zainullin and Phoenix's 4th round choice (Patrick Dwyer) in 2002 Entry Draft, March 19, 2002. Traded to **Florida** by **Phoenix** with Phoenix's 2nd round choice (later traded to Tampa Bay – Tampa Bay selected Matt Smaby) in 2003 Entry Draft for Brad Ference, March 8, 2003. Traded to **Nashville** by **Florida** for Nashville's 4th round choice (Matt Duffy) in 2005 Entry Draft, July 27, 2005. Traded to **Carolina** by **Nashville** with Nashville's 5th round choice in 2010 Entry Draft for Carolina's 5th round choice (later traded to Tampa Bay – Tampa Bay selected Michael Zador) in 2009 Entry Draft, June 19, 2008. Signed as a free agent by **Vancouver**, July 1, 2008.

## HORNQVIST, Patric

(HOHRN-kwihst, PAT-rihk) **NSH.**

Right wing. Shoots left. 5'11", 186 lbs. Born, Sollentuna, Sweden, January 1, 1987. Nashville's 7th choice, 230th overall, in 2005 Entry Draft.

| Season | Club | League | GP | G | A | Pts | PIM | PP | SH | GW | S | % | +/- | TF | F% | Min | GP | G | A | Pts | PIM | PP | SH | GW | Min |
|---|---|---|---|---|---|---|---|---|---|---|---|---|---|---|---|---|---|---|---|---|---|---|---|---|---|
| 2003-04 | Vasby Jr. | Swe-Jr. | 10 | 7 | 10 | 17 | 30 | .... | .... | .... | .... | .... | .... | .... | .... | .... | .... | .... | .... | .... | .... | .... | .... | .... | .... |
| | Vasby | Sweden-3 | 32 | 8 | 5 | 13 | 26 | .... | .... | .... | .... | .... | .... | .... | .... | .... | .... | .... | .... | .... | .... | .... | .... | .... | .... |
| 2004-05 | Vasby | Sweden-3 | 28 | 12 | 12 | 24 | 36 | .... | .... | .... | .... | .... | .... | .... | .... | .... | .... | .... | .... | .... | .... | .... | .... | .... | .... |
| | Djurgarden Jr. | Swe-Jr. | 5 | 3 | 0 | 3 | 2 | .... | .... | .... | .... | .... | .... | .... | .... | .... | .... | .... | .... | .... | .... | .... | .... | .... | .... |
| 2005-06 | Djurgarden Jr. | Swe-Jr. | 4 | 2 | 1 | 3 | 2 | .... | .... | .... | .... | .... | .... | .... | .... | .... | 4 | 1 | 2 | 3 | 2 | .... | .... | .... | .... |
| | Djurgarden | Sweden | 47 | 5 | 2 | 7 | 36 | .... | .... | .... | .... | .... | .... | .... | .... | .... | .... | .... | .... | .... | .... | .... | .... | .... | .... |
| 2006-07 | Djurgarden | Sweden | 49 | 23 | 11 | 34 | 38 | .... | .... | .... | .... | .... | .... | .... | .... | .... | .... | .... | .... | .... | .... | .... | .... | .... | .... |
| | Djurgarden Jr. | Swe-Jr. | .... | .... | .... | .... | .... | .... | .... | .... | .... | .... | .... | .... | .... | .... | 7 | 2 | 5 | 7 | 14 | .... | .... | .... | .... |
| 2007-08 | Djurgarden | Sweden | 53 | 18 | 12 | 30 | 58 | .... | .... | .... | .... | .... | .... | .... | .... | .... | 5 | 0 | 1 | 1 | 6 | .... | .... | .... | .... |
| 2008-09 | Nashville | NHL | 28 | 2 | 5 | 7 | 16 | 0 | 0 | 0 | 54 | 3.7 | –3 | 5 | 20.0 | 11:24 | .... | .... | .... | .... | .... | .... | .... | .... | .... |
| | Milwaukee | AHL | 49 | 17 | 18 | 35 | 44 | .... | .... | .... | .... | .... | .... | .... | .... | .... | 11 | 4 | 4 | 8 | 6 | .... | .... | .... | .... |
| | NHL Totals | | 28 | 2 | 5 | 7 | 16 | 0 | 0 | 0 | 54 | 3.7 | | 5 | 20.0 | 11:24 | .... | .... | .... | .... | .... | .... | .... | .... | .... |

## HORTON, Nathan

(HOHR-tuhn, NAY-thuhn) **FLA.**

Center. Shoots right. 6'2", 229 lbs. Born, Welland, Ont., May 29, 1985. Florida's 1st choice, 3rd overall, in 2003 Entry Draft.

| Season | Club | League | GP | G | A | Pts | PIM | PP | SH | GW | S | % | +/- | TF | F% | Min | GP | G | A | Pts | PIM | PP | SH | GW | Min |
|---|---|---|---|---|---|---|---|---|---|---|---|---|---|---|---|---|---|---|---|---|---|---|---|---|---|
| 2000-01 | Thorold | OHA-B | 41 | 16 | 31 | 47 | 75 | .... | .... | .... | .... | .... | .... | .... | .... | .... | .... | .... | .... | .... | .... | .... | .... | .... | .... |
| 2001-02 | Oshawa Generals | OHL | 64 | 31 | 36 | 67 | 84 | .... | .... | .... | .... | .... | .... | .... | .... | .... | 5 | 1 | 2 | 3 | 10 | .... | .... | .... | .... |
| 2002-03 | Oshawa Generals | OHL | 54 | 33 | 35 | 68 | 111 | .... | .... | .... | .... | .... | .... | .... | .... | .... | 13 | 9 | 6 | 15 | 10 | .... | .... | .... | .... |
| 2003-04 | Florida | NHL | 55 | 14 | 8 | 22 | 57 | 6 | 1 | 0 | 81 | 17.3 | –5 | 270 | 41.9 | 13:20 | .... | .... | .... | .... | .... | .... | .... | .... | .... |
| 2004-05 | San Antonio | AHL | 21 | 5 | 4 | 9 | 21 | .... | .... | .... | .... | .... | .... | .... | .... | .... | .... | .... | .... | .... | .... | .... | .... | .... | .... |
| 2005-06 | Florida | NHL | 71 | 28 | 19 | 47 | 89 | 3 | 0 | 1 | 162 | 17.3 | 8 | 24 | 45.8 | 16:53 | .... | .... | .... | .... | .... | .... | .... | .... | .... |
| 2006-07 | Florida | NHL | 82 | 31 | 31 | 62 | 61 | 7 | 1 | 3 | 217 | 14.3 | 15 | 31 | 48.4 | 18:04 | .... | .... | .... | .... | .... | .... | .... | .... | .... |

| Season | Club | League | GP | G | A | Pts | PIM | PP | SH | GW | S | % | +/- | TF | F% | Min | GP | G | A | Pts | PIM | PP | SH | GW | Min |
|---|---|---|---|---|---|---|---|---|---|---|---|---|---|---|---|---|---|---|---|---|---|---|---|---|---|
| | | | Regular Season | | | | | | | | | | | | | | Playoffs | | | | | | | | |
| 2007-08 | Florida | NHL | 82 | 27 | 35 | 62 | 85 | 9 | 0 | 3 | 212 | 12.7 | 15 | 73 | 39.7 | 18:44 | .... | .... | .... | .... | .... | .... | .... | .... | .... |
| 2008-09 | Florida | NHL | 67 | 22 | 23 | 45 | 48 | 5 | 1 | 5 | 131 | 16.8 | –5 | 863 | 43.7 | 17:51 | .... | .... | .... | .... | .... | .... | .... | .... | .... |
| | NHL Totals | | 357 | 122 | 116 | 238 | 340 | 30 | 3 | 12 | 803 | 15.2 | | 1261 | 43.2 | 17:13 | .... | .... | .... | .... | .... | .... | .... | .... | .... |

OHL All-Rookie Team (2002)

Signed as a free agent by **San Antonio** (AHL), October 28, 2004.

## HOSSA, Marcel

(HOH-sa, MAHR-sehl)

Left wing. Shoots left. 6'3", 220 lbs. Born, Ilava, Czech., October 12, 1981. Montreal's 2nd choice, 16th overall, in 2000 Entry Draft.

| Season | Club | League | GP | G | A | Pts | PIM | PP | SH | GW | S | % | +/- | TF | F% | Min | GP | G | A | Pts | PIM | PP | SH | GW | Min |
|---|---|---|---|---|---|---|---|---|---|---|---|---|---|---|---|---|---|---|---|---|---|---|---|---|---|
| 1996-97 | Dukla Trencin Jr. | Slovak-Jr. | 45 | 30 | 21 | 51 | 30 | .... | .... | .... | .... | .... | .... | .... | .... | .... | .... | .... | .... | .... | .... | .... | .... | .... | .... |
| 1997-98 | Dukla Trencin Jr. | Slovak-Jr. | 39 | 11 | 38 | 49 | 44 | .... | .... | .... | .... | .... | .... | .... | .... | .... | .... | .... | .... | .... | .... | .... | .... | .... | .... |
| 1998-99 | Portland | WHL | 70 | 7 | 14 | 21 | 66 | .... | .... | .... | .... | .... | .... | .... | .... | .... | 2 | 0 | 0 | 0 | 2 | .... | .... | .... | .... |
| 99-2000 | Portland | WHL | 60 | 24 | 29 | 53 | 58 | .... | .... | .... | .... | .... | .... | .... | .... | .... | .... | .... | .... | .... | .... | .... | .... | .... | .... |
| 2000-01 | Portland | WHL | 58 | 34 | 56 | 90 | 58 | .... | .... | .... | .... | .... | .... | .... | .... | .... | 16 | 5 | 7 | 12 | 14 | .... | .... | .... | .... |
| 2001-02 | Montreal | NHL | 10 | 3 | 1 | 4 | 2 | 0 | 0 | 0 | 20 | 15.0 | 2 | 0 | 0.0 | 11:09 | .... | .... | .... | .... | .... | .... | .... | .... | .... |
| | Quebec Citadelles | AHL | 50 | 17 | 15 | 32 | 24 | .... | .... | .... | .... | .... | .... | .... | .... | .... | 3 | 0 | 0 | 0 | 4 | .... | .... | .... | .... |
| 2002-03 | Montreal | NHL | 34 | 6 | 7 | 13 | 14 | 2 | 0 | 1 | 51 | 11.8 | 3 | 4 | 50.0 | 13:58 | .... | .... | .... | .... | .... | .... | .... | .... | .... |
| | Hamilton | AHL | 37 | 19 | 13 | 32 | 18 | .... | .... | .... | .... | .... | .... | .... | .... | .... | 21 | 4 | 7 | 11 | 12 | .... | .... | .... | .... |
| 2003-04 | Montreal | NHL | 15 | 1 | 1 | 2 | 8 | 0 | 0 | 0 | 19 | 5.3 | –3 | 5 | 40.0 | 14:50 | .... | .... | .... | .... | .... | .... | .... | .... | .... |
| | Hamilton | AHL | 57 | 18 | 22 | 40 | 45 | .... | .... | .... | .... | .... | .... | .... | .... | .... | 10 | 2 | 3 | 5 | 8 | .... | .... | .... | .... |
| 2004-05 | Mora IK | Sweden | 48 | 18 | 6 | 24 | 69 | .... | .... | .... | .... | .... | .... | .... | .... | .... | .... | .... | .... | .... | .... | .... | .... | .... | .... |
| 2005-06 | NY Rangers | NHL | 64 | 10 | 6 | 16 | 28 | 3 | 0 | 0 | 105 | 9.5 | –6 | 7 | 28.6 | 10:45 | 4 | 0 | 0 | 0 | 6 | 0 | 0 | 0 | 13:18 |
| | Slovakia | Olympics | 6 | 0 | 0 | 0 | 0 | .... | .... | .... | .... | .... | .... | .... | .... | .... | .... | .... | .... | .... | .... | .... | .... | .... | .... |
| 2006-07 | NY Rangers | NHL | 64 | 10 | 8 | 18 | 26 | 3 | 0 | 2 | 83 | 12.0 | –4 | 18 | 16.7 | 12:27 | 10 | 2 | 2 | 4 | 4 | 0 | 0 | 0 | 15:58 |
| 2007-08 | NY Rangers | NHL | 36 | 1 | 7 | 8 | 24 | 0 | 0 | 0 | 54 | 1.9 | 8 | 5 | 20.0 | 14:36 | .... | .... | .... | .... | .... | .... | .... | .... | .... |
| | Hartford | AHL | 5 | 1 | 0 | 1 | 2 | .... | .... | .... | .... | .... | .... | .... | .... | .... | .... | .... | .... | .... | .... | .... | .... | .... | .... |
| | Phoenix | NHL | 14 | 0 | 0 | 0 | 4 | 0 | 0 | 0 | 12 | 0.0 | –6 | 10 | 20.0 | 11:39 | .... | .... | .... | .... | .... | .... | .... | .... | .... |
| 2008-09 | Dynamo Riga | Rus-KHL | 52 | 22 | 22 | 44 | 118 | .... | .... | .... | .... | .... | .... | .... | .... | .... | 3 | 2 | 0 | 2 | 0 | .... | .... | .... | .... |
| | NHL Totals | | 237 | 31 | 30 | 61 | 106 | 8 | 0 | 3 | 344 | 9.0 | | 49 | 24.5 | 12:35 | 14 | 2 | 2 | 4 | 10 | 0 | 0 | 0 | 15:12 |

WHL West Second All-Star Team (2001)

Signed as a free agent by **Mora** (Sweden), September 25, 2004. Traded to **NY Rangers** by **Montreal** for Garth Murray, September 30, 2005. Traded to **Phoenix** by **NY Rangers** with Al Montoya for Josh Gratton, David LeNeveu, Fredrik Sjostrom and Phoenix's 5th round choice (Roman Horak) in 2009 Entry Draft, February 26, 2008.

## HOSSA, Marian

(HOH-sa, MAIR-ee-uhn) **CHI.**

Right wing. Shoots left. 6'1", 210 lbs. Born, Stara Lubovna, Czech., January 12, 1979. Ottawa's 1st choice, 12th overall, in 1997 Entry Draft.

| Season | Club | League | GP | G | A | Pts | PIM | PP | SH | GW | S | % | +/- | TF | F% | Min | GP | G | A | Pts | PIM | PP | SH | GW | Min |
|---|---|---|---|---|---|---|---|---|---|---|---|---|---|---|---|---|---|---|---|---|---|---|---|---|---|
| 1995-96 | Dukla Trencin Jr. | Slovak-Jr. | 53 | 42 | 49 | 91 | 26 | .... | .... | .... | .... | .... | .... | .... | .... | .... | .... | .... | .... | .... | .... | .... | .... | .... | .... |
| 1996-97 | Dukla Trencin | Slovakia | 46 | 25 | 19 | 44 | 33 | .... | .... | .... | .... | .... | .... | .... | .... | .... | 7 | 5 | 5 | 10 | .... | .... | .... | .... | .... |
| 1997-98 | Portland | WHL | 53 | 45 | 40 | 85 | 50 | .... | .... | .... | .... | .... | .... | .... | .... | .... | 16 | 13 | 6 | 19 | 6 | .... | .... | .... | .... |
| | Ottawa | NHL | 7 | 0 | 1 | 1 | 0 | 0 | 0 | 0 | 10 | 0.0 | –1 | .... | .... | .... | .... | .... | .... | .... | .... | .... | .... | .... | .... |
| 1998-99 | Ottawa | NHL | 60 | 15 | 15 | 30 | 37 | 1 | 0 | 2 | 124 | 12.1 | 18 | 4 | 25.0 | 13:59 | 4 | 0 | 2 | 2 | 4 | 0 | 0 | 0 | 16:46 |
| 99-2000 | Ottawa | NHL | 78 | 29 | 27 | 56 | 32 | 5 | 0 | 4 | 240 | 12.1 | 5 | 7 | 57.1 | 17:12 | 6 | 0 | 0 | 0 | 2 | 0 | 0 | 0 | 15:22 |
| 2000-01 | Ottawa | NHL | 81 | 32 | 43 | 75 | 44 | 11 | 2 | 7 | 249 | 12.9 | 19 | 14 | 42.9 | 18:01 | 4 | 1 | 1 | 2 | 4 | 0 | 0 | 0 | 19:02 |
| 2001-02 | Dukla Trencin | Slovakia | 8 | 3 | 4 | 7 | 16 | .... | .... | .... | .... | .... | .... | .... | .... | .... | .... | .... | .... | .... | .... | .... | .... | .... | .... |
| | Ottawa | NHL | 80 | 31 | 35 | 66 | 50 | 9 | 1 | 4 | 278 | 11.2 | 11 | 12 | 33.3 | 18:29 | 12 | 4 | 6 | 10 | 2 | 1 | 0 | 0 | 19:04 |
| | Slovakia | Olympics | 2 | 4 | 2 | 6 | 0 | .... | .... | .... | .... | .... | .... | .... | .... | .... | .... | .... | .... | .... | .... | .... | .... | .... | .... |
| 2002-03 | Ottawa | NHL | 80 | 45 | 35 | 80 | 34 | 14 | 0 | 10 | 229 | 19.7 | 8 | 19 | 36.8 | 18:31 | 18 | 5 | 11 | 16 | 6 | 3 | 0 | 1 | 18:41 |
| 2003-04 | Ottawa | NHL | 81 | 36 | 46 | 82 | 46 | 14 | 1 | 5 | 233 | 15.5 | 4 | 25 | 40.0 | 18:37 | 7 | 3 | 1 | 4 | 0 | 1 | 0 | 2 | 21:24 |
| 2004-05 | Mora IK | Sweden | 24 | 18 | 14 | 32 | 22 | .... | .... | .... | .... | .... | .... | .... | .... | .... | .... | .... | .... | .... | .... | .... | .... | .... | .... |
| | Dukla Trencin | Slovakia | 25 | 22 | 20 | 42 | 38 | .... | .... | .... | .... | .... | .... | .... | .... | .... | 5 | 4 | 5 | 9 | 14 | .... | .... | .... | .... |
| 2005-06 | Atlanta | NHL | 80 | 39 | 53 | 92 | 67 | 14 | 7 | 7 | 341 | 11.4 | 17 | 15 | 26.7 | 21:41 | .... | .... | .... | .... | .... | .... | .... | .... | .... |
| | Slovakia | Olympics | 6 | 5 | 5 | 10 | 4 | .... | .... | .... | .... | .... | .... | .... | .... | .... | .... | .... | .... | .... | .... | .... | .... | .... | .... |
| 2006-07 | Atlanta | NHL | 82 | 43 | 57 | 100 | 49 | 17 | 3 | 5 | 340 | 12.6 | 18 | 18 | 22.2 | 21:41 | 4 | 0 | 1 | 1 | 6 | 0 | 0 | 0 | 18:55 |
| 2007-08 | Atlanta | NHL | 60 | 26 | 30 | 56 | 30 | 8 | 2 | 4 | 229 | 11.4 | –14 | 14 | 28.6 | 21:55 | .... | .... | .... | .... | .... | .... | .... | .... | .... |
| | Pittsburgh | NHL | 12 | 3 | 7 | 10 | 6 | 0 | 0 | 0 | 35 | 8.6 | 0 | 1 | 0.0 | 18:34 | 20 | 12 | 14 | 26 | 12 | 5 | 0 | 2 | 21:00 |
| 2008-09 | Detroit | NHL | 74 | 40 | 31 | 71 | 63 | 10 | 0 | 8 | 307 | 13.0 | 27 | 19 | 21.1 | 17:48 | 23 | 6 | 9 | 15 | 10 | 2 | 1 | 1 | 18:38 |
| | NHL Totals | | 775 | 339 | 380 | 719 | 458 | 103 | 16 | 56 | 2615 | 13.0 | | 148 | 32.4 | 18:51 | 98 | 31 | 45 | 76 | 46 | 12 | 1 | 6 | 19:08 |

WHL West First All-Star Team (1998) • WHL Rookie of the Year (1998) • Canadian Major Junior First All-Star Team (1998) • Memorial Cup Tournament All-Star Team (1998) • NHL All-Rookie Team (1999) • NHL Second All-Star Team (2009)

Played in NHL All-Star Game (2001, 2003, 2007, 2008)

Signed as a free agent by **Trencin** (Slovakia), September 16, 2004. Signed as a free agent by **Mora** (Sweden), November 11, 2004. Signed as a free agent by **Trencin** (Slovakia), January 31, 2005. Traded to **Atlanta** by **Ottawa** with Greg de Vries for Dany Heatley, August 23, 2005. Traded to **Pittsburgh** by **Atlanta** with Pascal Dupuis for Colby Armstrong, Erik Christensen, Angelo Esposito and Pittsburgh's 1st round choice (Daulton Leveille) in 2008 Entry Draft , February 26, 2008. Signed as a free agent by **Detroit**, July 2, 2008. Signed as a free agent by **Chicago**, July 1, 2009.

## HUDLER, Jiri

(HOOD-luhr, YIH-ree) **DET.**

Center. Shoots left. 5'10", 182 lbs. Born, Olomouc, Czech., January 4, 1984. Detroit's 1st choice, 58th overall, in 2002 Entry Draft.

| Season | Club | League | GP | G | A | Pts | PIM | PP | SH | GW | S | % | +/- | TF | F% | Min | GP | G | A | Pts | PIM | PP | SH | GW | Min |
|---|---|---|---|---|---|---|---|---|---|---|---|---|---|---|---|---|---|---|---|---|---|---|---|---|---|
| 1998-99 | HC Vsetin U17 | CzR-U17 | 46 | 57 | 57 | 114 | .... | .... | .... | .... | .... | .... | .... | .... | .... | .... | .... | .... | .... | .... | .... | .... | .... | .... | .... |
| 99-2000 | HC Vsetin Jr. | CzRep-Jr. | 53 | 29 | 31 | 60 | 75 | .... | .... | .... | .... | .... | .... | .... | .... | .... | .... | .... | .... | .... | .... | .... | .... | .... | .... |
| | Vsetin | CzRep | 2 | 0 | 1 | 1 | 0 | .... | .... | .... | .... | .... | .... | .... | .... | .... | .... | .... | .... | .... | .... | .... | .... | .... | .... |
| 2000-01 | HC Vsetin Jr. | CzRep-Jr. | 16 | 8 | 14 | 22 | 16 | .... | .... | .... | .... | .... | .... | .... | .... | .... | .... | .... | .... | .... | .... | .... | .... | .... | .... |
| | HC Slovnaft Vsetin | CzRep | 22 | 1 | 4 | 5 | 10 | .... | .... | .... | .... | .... | .... | .... | .... | .... | .... | .... | .... | .... | .... | .... | .... | .... | .... |
| | HC Femax Havirov | CzRep | 15 | 5 | 1 | 6 | 12 | .... | .... | .... | .... | .... | .... | .... | .... | .... | .... | .... | .... | .... | .... | .... | .... | .... | .... |
| 2001-02 | HC Vsetin | CzRep | 46 | 15 | 31 | 46 | 54 | .... | .... | .... | .... | .... | .... | .... | .... | .... | .... | .... | .... | .... | .... | .... | .... | .... | .... |
| | Liberec | CzRep-2 | 13 | 9 | 7 | 16 | 10 | .... | .... | .... | .... | .... | .... | .... | .... | .... | .... | .... | .... | .... | .... | .... | .... | .... | .... |
| | HC Olomouc | CzRep-3 | 1 | 0 | 2 | 2 | 4 | .... | .... | .... | .... | .... | .... | .... | .... | .... | .... | .... | .... | .... | .... | .... | .... | .... | .... |
| 2002-03 | HC Vsetin | CzRep | 30 | 19 | 27 | 46 | 22 | .... | .... | .... | .... | .... | .... | .... | .... | .... | .... | .... | .... | .... | .... | .... | .... | .... | .... |
| | Ak Bars Kazan | Russia | 11 | 1 | 5 | 6 | 12 | .... | .... | .... | .... | .... | .... | .... | .... | .... | 1 | 0 | 0 | 0 | 0 | .... | .... | .... | .... |
| 2003-04 | Detroit | NHL | 12 | 1 | 2 | 3 | 10 | 1 | 0 | 0 | 8 | 12.5 | –1 | 50 | 30.0 | 8:10 | .... | .... | .... | .... | .... | .... | .... | .... | .... |
| | Grand Rapids | AHL | 57 | 17 | 32 | 49 | 46 | .... | .... | .... | .... | .... | .... | .... | .... | .... | 4 | 1 | 5 | 6 | 2 | .... | .... | .... | .... |
| 2004-05 | Grand Rapids | AHL | 52 | 12 | 22 | 34 | 10 | .... | .... | .... | .... | .... | .... | .... | .... | .... | .... | .... | .... | .... | .... | .... | .... | .... | .... |
| | HC Vsetin | CzRep | 7 | 5 | 2 | 7 | 10 | .... | .... | .... | .... | .... | .... | .... | .... | .... | .... | .... | .... | .... | .... | .... | .... | .... | .... |
| 2005-06 | Detroit | NHL | 4 | 0 | 0 | 0 | 2 | 0 | 0 | 0 | 3 | 0.0 | 0 | 0 | 0.0 | 7:13 | .... | .... | .... | .... | .... | .... | .... | .... | .... |
| | Grand Rapids | AHL | 76 | 36 | 61 | 97 | 56 | .... | .... | .... | .... | .... | .... | .... | .... | .... | 16 | 6 | 16 | 22 | 20 | .... | .... | .... | .... |
| 2006-07 | Detroit | NHL | 76 | 15 | 10 | 25 | 36 | 3 | 0 | 4 | 107 | 14.0 | 16 | 20 | 30.0 | 10:02 | 6 | 0 | 2 | 2 | 4 | 0 | 0 | 0 | 9:09 |
| 2007-08 ♦ | Detroit | NHL | 81 | 13 | 29 | 42 | 26 | 3 | 0 | 2 | 131 | 9.9 | 11 | 26 | 38.5 | 13:10 | 22 | 5 | 9 | 14 | 14 | 2 | 0 | 2 | 11:36 |
| 2008-09 | Detroit | NHL | 82 | 23 | 34 | 57 | 16 | 6 | 0 | 2 | 155 | 14.8 | 7 | 29 | 44.8 | 13:39 | 23 | 4 | 8 | 12 | 6 | 2 | 0 | 1 | 13:28 |
| | NHL Totals | | 255 | 52 | 75 | 127 | 90 | 13 | 0 | 8 | 404 | 12.9 | | 125 | 35.2 | 12:04 | 51 | 9 | 19 | 28 | 24 | 4 | 0 | 3 | 12:09 |

AHL Second All-Star Team (2006)

Signed as a free agent by **Vsetin** (CzRep), December 2, 2004. Signed as a free agent by **Moscow Dynamo** (Rus-KHL) , July 10, 2009.

## HUNT, Jamie

(HUHNT, JAY-mee)

Defense. Shoots left. 6'2", 200 lbs. Born, Calgary, Alta., April 20, 1984.

| Season | Club | League | GP | G | A | Pts | PIM | PP | SH | GW | S | % | +/- | TF | F% | Min | GP | G | A | Pts | PIM | PP | SH | GW | Min |
|---|---|---|---|---|---|---|---|---|---|---|---|---|---|---|---|---|---|---|---|---|---|---|---|---|---|
| 2002-03 | Calgary Canucks | AJHL | 63 | 8 | 20 | 28 | 35 | .... | .... | .... | .... | .... | .... | .... | .... | .... | .... | .... | .... | .... | .... | .... | .... | .... | .... |
| 2003-04 | Mercyhurst | AH | 27 | 3 | 16 | 19 | 4 | .... | .... | .... | .... | .... | .... | .... | .... | .... | .... | .... | .... | .... | .... | .... | .... | .... | .... |
| 2004-05 | Mercyhurst | AH | 38 | 5 | 12 | 17 | 36 | .... | .... | .... | .... | .... | .... | .... | .... | .... | .... | .... | .... | .... | .... | .... | .... | .... | .... |
| 2005-06 | Mercyhurst | AH | 33 | 12 | 33 | 45 | 49 | .... | .... | .... | .... | .... | .... | .... | .... | .... | .... | .... | .... | .... | .... | .... | .... | .... | .... |
| 2006-07 | Washington | NHL | 1 | 0 | 0 | 0 | 0 | 0 | 0 | 0 | 0 | 0.0 | –1 | 0 | 0.0 | 6:01 | .... | .... | .... | .... | .... | .... | .... | .... | .... |
| | Hershey Bears | AHL | 36 | 2 | 10 | 12 | 33 | .... | .... | .... | .... | .... | .... | .... | .... | .... | .... | .... | .... | .... | .... | .... | .... | .... | .... |
| 2007-08 | Hershey Bears | AHL | 60 | 4 | 9 | 13 | 30 | .... | .... | .... | .... | .... | .... | .... | .... | .... | 4 | 0 | 0 | 0 | 0 | .... | .... | .... | .... |
| 2008-09 | Augsburg | Germany | 50 | 4 | 21 | 25 | 57 | .... | .... | .... | .... | .... | .... | .... | .... | .... | 4 | 1 | 0 | 1 | 4 | .... | .... | .... | .... |
| | NHL Totals | | 1 | 0 | 0 | 0 | 0 | 0 | 0 | 0 | 0 | 0.0 | | 0 | 0.0 | 6:01 | .... | .... | .... | .... | .... | .... | .... | .... | .... |

AH All-Rookie Team (2004) • AH First All-Star Team (2006)

Signed as a free agent by **Washington**, March 31, 2006. • Missed majority of 2006-07 season recovering from wrist injury suffered in game vs. Philadelphia (AHL), January 24, 2007.

| Season | Club | League | GP | G | A | Pts | PIM | PP | SH | GW | S | % | +/- | TF | F% | Min | GP | G | A | Pts | PIM | PP | SH | GW | Min |
|---|---|---|---|---|---|---|---|---|---|---|---|---|---|---|---|---|---|---|---|---|---|---|---|---|---|
| | | | Regular Season | | | | | | | | | | | | | | Playoffs | | | | | | | | |

## HUNTER, Trent

(HUHN-tuhr, TREHNT) **NYI**

Right wing. Shoots right. 6'3", 210 lbs. Born, Red Deer, Alta., July 5, 1980. Anaheim's 4th choice, 150th overall, in 1998 Entry Draft.

| Season | Club | League | GP | G | A | Pts | PIM | PP | SH | GW | S | % | +/- | TF | F% | Min | GP | G | A | Pts | PIM | PP | SH | GW | Min |
|---|---|---|---|---|---|---|---|---|---|---|---|---|---|---|---|---|---|---|---|---|---|---|---|---|---|
| 1996-97 | Red Deer | AMHL | 42 | 30 | 25 | 55 | 50 | .... | .... | .... | .... | .... | .... | .... | .... | .... | .... | .... | .... | .... | .... | .... | .... | .... | .... |
| 1997-98 | Prince George | WHL | 60 | 13 | 14 | 27 | 34 | .... | .... | .... | .... | .... | .... | .... | .... | .... | 8 | 1 | 0 | 1 | 4 | .... | .... | .... | .... |
| 1998-99 | Prince George | WHL | 50 | 18 | 20 | 38 | 34 | .... | .... | .... | .... | .... | .... | .... | .... | .... | 7 | 2 | 5 | 7 | 2 | .... | .... | .... | .... |
| 99-2000 | Prince George | WHL | 67 | 46 | 49 | 95 | 47 | .... | .... | .... | .... | .... | .... | .... | .... | .... | 13 | 7 | 15 | 22 | 6 | .... | .... | .... | .... |
| 2000-01 | Springfield | AHL | 57 | 18 | 17 | 35 | 14 | .... | .... | .... | .... | .... | .... | .... | .... | .... | .... | .... | .... | .... | .... | .... | .... | .... | .... |
| **2001-02** | Bridgeport | AHL | 80 | 30 | 35 | 65 | 30 | .... | .... | .... | .... | .... | .... | .... | .... | .... | 17 | 8 | 11 | 19 | 6 | .... | .... | .... | .... |
| | **NY Islanders** | **NHL** | .... | .... | .... | .... | .... | .... | .... | .... | .... | .... | .... | .... | .... | .... | **4** | **1** | **1** | **2** | **2** | **0** | **0** | **0** | **11:13** |
| **2002-03** | **NY Islanders** | **NHL** | **8** | **0** | **4** | **4** | **4** | **0** | **0** | **0** | **19** | **0.0** | **5** | **1** | **0.0** | **12:13** | .... | .... | .... | .... | .... | .... | .... | .... | .... |
| | Bridgeport | AHL | 70 | 30 | 41 | 71 | 39 | .... | .... | .... | .... | .... | .... | .... | .... | .... | 9 | 7 | 4 | 11 | 10 | .... | .... | .... | .... |
| **2003-04** | **NY Islanders** | **NHL** | **77** | **25** | **26** | **51** | **16** | **4** | **0** | **7** | **187** | **13.4** | **23** | **19** | **36.8** | **15:39** | **5** | **0** | **0** | **0** | **4** | **0** | **0** | **0** | **11:38** |
| 2004-05 | Nykoping | Sweden-2 | 33 | 13 | 12 | 25 | 73 | .... | .... | .... | .... | .... | .... | .... | .... | .... | 4 | 5 | 3 | 8 | 2 | .... | .... | .... | .... |
| **2005-06** | **NY Islanders** | **NHL** | **82** | **16** | **19** | **35** | **34** | **5** | **0** | **3** | **221** | **7.2** | **–9** | **32** | **28.1** | **17:50** | .... | .... | .... | .... | .... | .... | .... | .... | .... |
| **2006-07** | **NY Islanders** | **NHL** | **77** | **20** | **15** | **35** | **22** | **5** | **1** | **2** | **168** | **11.9** | **5** | **14** | **42.9** | **16:00** | **5** | **3** | **0** | **3** | **0** | **0** | **0** | **0** | **15:05** |
| **2007-08** | **NY Islanders** | **NHL** | **82** | **12** | **29** | **41** | **43** | **2** | **0** | **1** | **222** | **5.4** | **–17** | **29** | **20.7** | **18:13** | .... | .... | .... | .... | .... | .... | .... | .... | .... |
| **2008-09** | **NY Islanders** | **NHL** | **55** | **14** | **17** | **31** | **41** | **5** | **0** | **2** | **154** | **9.1** | **–8** | **20** | **25.0** | **16:23** | .... | .... | .... | .... | .... | .... | .... | .... | .... |
| | **NHL Totals** | | **381** | **87** | **110** | **197** | **160** | **21** | **1** | **15** | **971** | **9.0** | | **115** | **28.7** | **16:46** | **14** | **4** | **1** | **5** | **6** | **0** | **0** | **0** | **12:45** |

WHL West First All-Star Team (2000) • NHL All-Rookie Team (2004)

Traded to **NY Islanders** by **Anaheim** for Columbus' 4th round choice (previously acquired, Anaheim selected Jonas Ronnqvist) in 2000 Entry Draft, May 23, 2000. Signed as a free agent by **Nykoping** (Sweden-2), November 8, 2004.

## HUNWICK, Matt

(HUHN-wihk, MAT) **BOS.**

Defense. Shoots left. 5'11", 190 lbs. Born, Warren, MI, May 21, 1985. Boston's 6th choice, 224th overall, in 2004 Entry Draft.

| Season | Club | League | GP | G | A | Pts | PIM | PP | SH | GW | S | % | +/- | TF | F% | Min | GP | G | A | Pts | PIM | PP | SH | GW | Min |
|---|---|---|---|---|---|---|---|---|---|---|---|---|---|---|---|---|---|---|---|---|---|---|---|---|---|
| 2001-02 | USNTDP | U-17 | 14 | 3 | 4 | 7 | 6 | .... | .... | .... | .... | .... | .... | .... | .... | .... | .... | .... | .... | .... | .... | .... | .... | .... | .... |
| | USNTDP | NAHL | 29 | 2 | 1 | 3 | 30 | .... | .... | .... | .... | .... | .... | .... | .... | .... | .... | .... | .... | .... | .... | .... | .... | .... | .... |
| 2002-03 | USNTDP | U-18 | 40 | 6 | 16 | 22 | 40 | .... | .... | .... | .... | .... | .... | .... | .... | .... | .... | .... | .... | .... | .... | .... | .... | .... | .... |
| | USNTDP | NAHL | 8 | 2 | 2 | 4 | 23 | .... | .... | .... | .... | .... | .... | .... | .... | .... | .... | .... | .... | .... | .... | .... | .... | .... | .... |
| 2003-04 | U. of Michigan | CCHA | 41 | 1 | 14 | 15 | 62 | .... | .... | .... | .... | .... | .... | .... | .... | .... | .... | .... | .... | .... | .... | .... | .... | .... | .... |
| 2004-05 | U. of Michigan | CCHA | 40 | 6 | 19 | 25 | 60 | .... | .... | .... | .... | .... | .... | .... | .... | .... | .... | .... | .... | .... | .... | .... | .... | .... | .... |
| 2005-06 | U. of Michigan | CCHA | 41 | 11 | 19 | 30 | 70 | .... | .... | .... | .... | .... | .... | .... | .... | .... | .... | .... | .... | .... | .... | .... | .... | .... | .... |
| 2006-07 | U. of Michigan | CCHA | 41 | 6 | 21 | 27 | 64 | .... | .... | .... | .... | .... | .... | .... | .... | .... | .... | .... | .... | .... | .... | .... | .... | .... | .... |
| **2007-08** | **Boston** | **NHL** | **13** | **0** | **1** | **1** | **4** | **0** | **0** | **0** | **6** | **0.0** | **–1** | **0** | **0.0** | **10:36** | .... | .... | .... | .... | .... | .... | .... | .... | .... |
| | Providence Bruins | AHL | 55 | 2 | 21 | 23 | 49 | .... | .... | .... | .... | .... | .... | .... | .... | .... | 10 | 0 | 5 | 5 | 8 | .... | .... | .... | .... |
| **2008-09** | **Boston** | **NHL** | **53** | **6** | **21** | **27** | **31** | **0** | **0** | **1** | **58** | **10.3** | **15** | **0** | **0.0** | **16:59** | **1** | **0** | **0** | **0** | **0** | **0** | **0** | **0** | **15:59** |
| | Providence Bruins | AHL | 3 | 0 | 3 | 3 | 0 | .... | .... | .... | .... | .... | .... | .... | .... | .... | .... | .... | .... | .... | .... | .... | .... | .... | .... |
| | **NHL Totals** | | **66** | **6** | **22** | **28** | **35** | **0** | **0** | **1** | **64** | **9.4** | | **0** | **0.0** | **15:44** | **1** | **0** | **0** | **0** | **0** | **0** | **0** | **0** | **15:59** |

CCHA All-Rookie Team (2004) • CCHA Second All-Star Team (2005, 2006) • CCHA First All-Star Team (2007) • NCAA West Second All-American Team (2007)

## HUSELIUS, Kristian

(hoo-SAY-lee-uhs, KRIHST-yan) **CBJ**

Left wing. Shoots left. 6'1", 179 lbs. Born, Osterhaninge, Sweden, November 10, 1978. Florida's 2nd choice, 47th overall, in 1997 Entry Draft.

| Season | Club | League | GP | G | A | Pts | PIM | PP | SH | GW | S | % | +/- | TF | F% | Min | GP | G | A | Pts | PIM | PP | SH | GW | Min |
|---|---|---|---|---|---|---|---|---|---|---|---|---|---|---|---|---|---|---|---|---|---|---|---|---|---|
| 1994-95 | Hammarby Jr. | Swe-Jr. | 17 | 6 | 2 | 8 | 2 | .... | .... | .... | .... | .... | .... | .... | .... | .... | .... | .... | .... | .... | .... | .... | .... | .... | .... |
| 1995-96 | Hammarby Jr. | Swe-Jr. | 25 | 13 | 8 | 21 | 14 | .... | .... | .... | .... | .... | .... | .... | .... | .... | .... | .... | .... | .... | .... | .... | .... | .... | .... |
| | Hammarby | Sweden-2 | 6 | 1 | 0 | 1 | 0 | .... | .... | .... | .... | .... | .... | .... | .... | .... | .... | .... | .... | .... | .... | .... | .... | .... | .... |
| 1996-97 | Farjestad | Sweden | 13 | 2 | 0 | 2 | 4 | .... | .... | .... | .... | .... | .... | .... | .... | .... | 5 | 1 | 0 | 1 | 0 | .... | .... | .... | .... |
| 1997-98 | Farjestad | Sweden | 34 | 2 | 1 | 3 | 2 | .... | .... | .... | .... | .... | .... | .... | .... | .... | 11 | 0 | 0 | 0 | 0 | .... | .... | .... | .... |
| | Farjestad | EuroHL | 5 | 2 | 3 | 5 | 0 | .... | .... | .... | .... | .... | .... | .... | .... | .... | .... | .... | .... | .... | .... | .... | .... | .... | .... |
| 1998-99 | Farjestad | Sweden | 28 | 4 | 4 | 8 | 4 | .... | .... | .... | .... | .... | .... | .... | .... | .... | .... | .... | .... | .... | .... | .... | .... | .... | .... |
| | Farjestad | EuroHL | 6 | 2 | 2 | 4 | 8 | .... | .... | .... | .... | .... | .... | .... | .... | .... | 1 | 0 | 0 | 0 | 0 | .... | .... | .... | .... |
| | V.Frolunda | Sweden | 20 | 2 | 2 | 4 | 2 | .... | .... | .... | .... | .... | .... | .... | .... | .... | 4 | 1 | 0 | 1 | 0 | .... | .... | .... | .... |
| 99-2000 | V.Frolunda | Sweden | 50 | 21 | 23 | 44 | 20 | .... | .... | .... | .... | .... | .... | .... | .... | .... | 5 | 2 | 2 | 4 | 8 | .... | .... | .... | .... |
| 2000-01 | V.Frolunda | Sweden | 49 | *32 | *35 | *67 | 26 | .... | .... | .... | .... | .... | .... | .... | .... | .... | 5 | 4 | 5 | 9 | 14 | .... | .... | .... | .... |
| **2001-02** | **Florida** | **NHL** | **79** | **23** | **22** | **45** | **14** | **6** | **1** | **3** | **169** | **13.6** | **–4** | **14** | **21.4** | **16:55** | .... | .... | .... | .... | .... | .... | .... | .... | .... |
| **2002-03** | **Florida** | **NHL** | **78** | **20** | **23** | **43** | **20** | **3** | **0** | **3** | **187** | **10.7** | **–6** | **6** | **33.3** | **17:20** | .... | .... | .... | .... | .... | .... | .... | .... | .... |
| **2003-04** | **Florida** | **NHL** | **76** | **10** | **21** | **31** | **24** | **2** | **0** | **2** | **168** | **6.0** | **–6** | **185** | **37.8** | **14:14** | .... | .... | .... | .... | .... | .... | .... | .... | .... |
| 2004-05 | Linkopings HC | Sweden | 34 | 14 | *35 | 49 | 10 | .... | .... | .... | .... | .... | .... | .... | .... | .... | .... | .... | .... | .... | .... | .... | .... | .... | .... |
| | Rapperswil | Swiss | .... | .... | .... | .... | .... | .... | .... | .... | .... | .... | .... | .... | .... | .... | 4 | 1 | 3 | 4 | 2 | .... | .... | .... | .... |
| **2005-06** | **Florida** | **NHL** | **24** | **5** | **3** | **8** | **4** | **2** | **0** | **0** | **57** | **8.8** | **–11** | **3** | **66.7** | **14:44** | .... | .... | .... | .... | .... | .... | .... | .... | .... |
| | **Calgary** | **NHL** | **54** | **15** | **24** | **39** | **36** | **6** | **0** | **4** | **107** | **14.0** | **2** | **3** | **33.3** | **14:55** | **7** | **2** | **4** | **6** | **4** | **2** | **0** | **0** | **15:35** |
| **2006-07** | **Calgary** | **NHL** | **81** | **34** | **43** | **77** | **26** | **14** | **2** | **6** | **173** | **19.7** | **21** | **14** | **28.6** | **17:23** | **6** | **0** | **2** | **2** | **4** | **0** | **0** | **0** | **15:08** |
| **2007-08** | **Calgary** | **NHL** | **81** | **25** | **41** | **66** | **40** | **6** | **0** | **5** | **202** | **12.4** | **10** | **4** | **25.0** | **17:42** | **7** | **0** | **4** | **4** | **6** | **0** | **0** | **0** | **13:45** |
| **2008-09** | **Columbus** | **NHL** | **74** | **21** | **35** | **56** | **44** | **5** | **0** | **2** | **212** | **9.9** | **1** | **45** | **28.9** | **19:31** | **4** | **1** | **1** | **2** | **4** | **1** | **0** | **0** | **17:52** |
| | **NHL Totals** | | **547** | **153** | **212** | **365** | **208** | **44** | **3** | **25** | **1275** | **12.0** | | **274** | **35.0** | **16:51** | **24** | **3** | **11** | **14** | **18** | **3** | **0** | **0** | **15:19** |

NHL All-Rookie Team (2002)

Signed as a free agent by **Linkopings** (Sweden), July 29, 2004. Signed as a free agent by **Rapperswil** (Swiss), February 23, 2005. Traded to **Calgary** by **Florida** for Steve Montador and Dustin Johner, December 2, 2005. Signed as a free agent by **Columbus**, July 2, 2008.

## HUSKINS, Kent

(HUHS-kihnz, KEHNT) **S.J.**

Defense. Shoots left. 6'4", 205 lbs. Born, Ottawa, Ont., May 4, 1979. Chicago's 3rd choice, 156th overall, in 1998 Entry Draft.

| Season | Club | League | GP | G | A | Pts | PIM | PP | SH | GW | S | % | +/- | TF | F% | Min | GP | G | A | Pts | PIM | PP | SH | GW | Min |
|---|---|---|---|---|---|---|---|---|---|---|---|---|---|---|---|---|---|---|---|---|---|---|---|---|---|
| 1995-96 | Kanata Valley | CJHL | 49 | 6 | 21 | 27 | 18 | .... | .... | .... | .... | .... | .... | .... | .... | .... | .... | .... | .... | .... | .... | .... | .... | .... | .... |
| 1996-97 | Kanata Valley | CJHL | 53 | 11 | 36 | 47 | 89 | .... | .... | .... | .... | .... | .... | .... | .... | .... | .... | .... | .... | .... | .... | .... | .... | .... | .... |
| 1997-98 | Clarkson Knights | ECAC | 35 | 2 | 8 | 10 | 46 | .... | .... | .... | .... | .... | .... | .... | .... | .... | .... | .... | .... | .... | .... | .... | .... | .... | .... |
| 1998-99 | Clarkson Knights | ECAC | 37 | 5 | 11 | 16 | 28 | .... | .... | .... | .... | .... | .... | .... | .... | .... | .... | .... | .... | .... | .... | .... | .... | .... | .... |
| 99-2000 | Clarkson Knights | ECAC | 28 | 2 | 16 | 18 | 30 | .... | .... | .... | .... | .... | .... | .... | .... | .... | .... | .... | .... | .... | .... | .... | .... | .... | .... |
| 2000-01 | Clarkson Knights | ECAC | 35 | 6 | 28 | 34 | 22 | .... | .... | .... | .... | .... | .... | .... | .... | .... | .... | .... | .... | .... | .... | .... | .... | .... | .... |
| 2001-02 | Norfolk Admirals | AHL | 65 | 4 | 11 | 15 | 44 | .... | .... | .... | .... | .... | .... | .... | .... | .... | 4 | 0 | 1 | 1 | 0 | .... | .... | .... | .... |
| 2002-03 | Norfolk Admirals | AHL | 80 | 5 | 22 | 27 | 48 | .... | .... | .... | .... | .... | .... | .... | .... | .... | 9 | 2 | 2 | 4 | 4 | .... | .... | .... | .... |
| 2003-04 | San Antonio | AHL | 79 | 5 | 14 | 19 | 42 | .... | .... | .... | .... | .... | .... | .... | .... | .... | .... | .... | .... | .... | .... | .... | .... | .... | .... |
| 2004-05 | Manitoba Moose | AHL | 65 | 5 | 11 | 16 | 41 | .... | .... | .... | .... | .... | .... | .... | .... | .... | 14 | 0 | 2 | 2 | 12 | .... | .... | .... | .... |
| 2005-06 | Portland Pirates | AHL | 80 | 8 | 23 | 31 | 64 | .... | .... | .... | .... | .... | .... | .... | .... | .... | 18 | 3 | 6 | 9 | 14 | .... | .... | .... | .... |
| **2006-07** ♦ | **Anaheim** | **NHL** | **33** | **0** | **3** | **3** | **14** | **0** | **0** | **0** | **16** | **0.0** | **–3** | **0** | **0.0** | **14:04** | **21** | **0** | **1** | **1** | **11** | **0** | **0** | **0** | **11:45** |
| | Portland Pirates | AHL | 39 | 3 | 12 | 15 | 23 | .... | .... | .... | .... | .... | .... | .... | .... | .... | .... | .... | .... | .... | .... | .... | .... | .... | .... |
| **2007-08** | **Anaheim** | **NHL** | **76** | **4** | **15** | **19** | **59** | **1** | **0** | **2** | **46** | **8.7** | **23** | **0** | **0.0** | **16:05** | **6** | **0** | **1** | **1** | **2** | **0** | **0** | **0** | **14:35** |
| **2008-09** | **Anaheim** | **NHL** | **33** | **2** | **4** | **6** | **27** | **0** | **0** | **0** | **20** | **10.0** | **6** | **1** | **0.0** | **18:47** | .... | .... | .... | .... | .... | .... | .... | .... | .... |
| | **NHL Totals** | | **142** | **6** | **22** | **28** | **100** | **1** | **0** | **2** | **82** | **7.3** | | **1** | **0.0** | **16:15** | **27** | **0** | **2** | **2** | **13** | **0** | **0** | **0** | **12:23** |

ECAC First All-Star Team (2000, 2001) • NCAA East First All-American Team (2001)

Signed as a free agent by **Florida**, August 14, 2003. Signed as a free agent by **Manitoba** (AHL), September 16, 2004. Signed as a free agent by **Anaheim**, August 30, 2005. Traded to **San Jose** by **Anaheim** with Travis Moen for Timo Pielmeier, Nick Bonino and future considerations, March 4, 2009.

## HUTCHINSON, Andrew

(HUHT-chihn-suhn, AN-droo) **DAL.**

Defense. Shoots right. 6'2", 206 lbs. Born, Evanston, IL, March 24, 1980. Nashville's 4th choice, 54th overall, in 1999 Entry Draft.

| Season | Club | League | GP | G | A | Pts | PIM | PP | SH | GW | S | % | +/- | TF | F% | Min | GP | G | A | Pts | PIM | PP | SH | GW | Min |
|---|---|---|---|---|---|---|---|---|---|---|---|---|---|---|---|---|---|---|---|---|---|---|---|---|---|
| 1996-97 | Det. Caesars | MNHL | 82 | 15 | 41 | 56 | .... | .... | .... | .... | .... | .... | .... | .... | .... | .... | .... | .... | .... | .... | .... | .... | .... | .... | .... |
| 1997-98 | USNTDP | U-18 | 27 | 3 | 11 | 14 | 35 | .... | .... | .... | .... | .... | .... | .... | .... | .... | .... | .... | .... | .... | .... | .... | .... | .... | .... |
| | USNTDP | USHL | 15 | 0 | 7 | 7 | 8 | .... | .... | .... | .... | .... | .... | .... | .... | .... | .... | .... | .... | .... | .... | .... | .... | .... | .... |
| | USNTDP | NAHL | 12 | 2 | 0 | 2 | 8 | .... | .... | .... | .... | .... | .... | .... | .... | .... | 5 | 2 | 3 | 5 | 2 | .... | .... | .... | .... |
| 1998-99 | Michigan State | CCHA | 37 | 3 | 12 | 15 | 26 | .... | .... | .... | .... | .... | .... | .... | .... | .... | .... | .... | .... | .... | .... | .... | .... | .... | .... |
| 99-2000 | Michigan State | CCHA | 42 | 5 | 12 | 17 | 64 | .... | .... | .... | .... | .... | .... | .... | .... | .... | .... | .... | .... | .... | .... | .... | .... | .... | .... |
| 2000-01 | Michigan State | CCHA | 42 | 5 | 19 | 24 | 46 | .... | .... | .... | .... | .... | .... | .... | .... | .... | .... | .... | .... | .... | .... | .... | .... | .... | .... |
| 2001-02 | Michigan State | CCHA | 39 | 6 | 16 | 22 | 24 | .... | .... | .... | .... | .... | .... | .... | .... | .... | .... | .... | .... | .... | .... | .... | .... | .... | .... |
| | Milwaukee | AHL | 5 | 0 | 1 | 1 | 0 | .... | .... | .... | .... | .... | .... | .... | .... | .... | .... | .... | .... | .... | .... | .... | .... | .... | .... |
| 2002-03 | Milwaukee | AHL | 63 | 9 | 17 | 26 | 40 | .... | .... | .... | .... | .... | .... | .... | .... | .... | 3 | 1 | 0 | 1 | 0 | .... | .... | .... | .... |
| | Toledo Storm | ECHL | 10 | 2 | 5 | 7 | 4 | .... | .... | .... | .... | .... | .... | .... | .... | .... | .... | .... | .... | .... | .... | .... | .... | .... | .... |
| **2003-04** | **Nashville** | **NHL** | **18** | **4** | **4** | **8** | **4** | **2** | **0** | **1** | **24** | **16.7** | **1** | **0** | **0.0** | **16:43** | .... | .... | .... | .... | .... | .... | .... | .... | .... |
| | Milwaukee | AHL | 46 | 12 | 12 | 24 | 39 | .... | .... | .... | .... | .... | .... | .... | .... | .... | 22 | 5 | 11 | 16 | 33 | .... | .... | .... | .... |

| | | | Regular Season | | | | | | | | | | | | | | Playoffs | | | | | | | | |
|---|---|---|---|---|---|---|---|---|---|---|---|---|---|---|---|---|---|---|---|---|---|---|---|---|---|
| Season | Club | League | GP | G | A | Pts | PIM | PP | SH | GW | S | % | +/- | TF | F% | Min | GP | G | A | Pts | PIM | PP | SH | GW | Min |
| 2004-05 | Milwaukee | AHL | 76 | 10 | 35 | 45 | 79 | | | | | | | | | | 7 | 1 | 3 | 4 | 8 | | | | |
| 2005-06 ♦ | Carolina | NHL | 36 | 3 | 8 | 11 | 18 | 2 | 0 | 0 | 33 | 9.1 | –2 | 0 | 0.0 | 10:22 | | | | | | | | | |
| 2006-07 | Carolina | NHL | 41 | 3 | 11 | 14 | 30 | 2 | 0 | 0 | 45 | 6.7 | 0 | 0 | 0.0 | 12:13 | | | | | | | | | |
| 2007-08 | Hartford | AHL | 67 | 18 | 46 | 64 | 66 | | | | | | | | | | 5 | 2 | 2 | 4 | 4 | | | | |
| 2008-09 | Tampa Bay | NHL | 2 | 0 | 0 | 0 | 0 | 0 | 0 | 0 | 2 | 0.0 | –5 | 0 | 0.0 | 14:44 | | | | | | | | | |
| | Norfolk Admirals | AHL | 20 | 1 | 12 | 13 | 14 | | | | | | | | | | | | | | | | | | |
| | Dallas | NHL | 38 | 2 | 3 | 5 | 12 | 0 | 0 | 0 | 56 | 3.6 | –4 | 0 | 0.0 | 14:20 | | | | | | | | | |
| | NHL Totals | | 135 | 12 | 26 | 38 | 64 | 6 | 0 | 1 | 160 | 7.5 | | 0 | 0.0 | 12:58 | | | | | | | | | |

CCHA Second All-Star Team (2001, 2002) • NCAA West Second All-American Team (2002) • AHL First All-Star Team (2008) • Eddie Shore Award (AHL – Outstanding Defenseman) (2008)

Traded to **Carolina** by **Nashville** for Phoenix's 3rd round choice (previously acquired, Nashville selected Teemu Laakso) in 2005 Entry Draft, July 29, 2005. Traded to **NY Rangers** by **Carolina** with Joe Barnes and Carolina's 3rd round choice (Evgeny Grachev) in 2008 Entry Draft for Matt Cullen, July 17, 2007. Signed as a free agent by **Tampa Bay**, July 9, 2008. Traded to **Dallas** by **Tampa Bay** for Lauri Tukonen, November 30, 2008.

## IGGULDEN, Mike

(IHG-gul-den, MIGHK)

Right wing. Shoots right. 6'3", 215 lbs. Born, St. Catharines, Ont., November 9, 1982.

| | | | | | | | | | | | | | | | | | | | | | | | | | |
|---|---|---|---|---|---|---|---|---|---|---|---|---|---|---|---|---|---|---|---|---|---|---|---|---|---|
| 2001-02 | Cornell Big Red | ECAC | 30 | 1 | 3 | 4 | 6 | | | | | | | | | | | | | | | | | | |
| 2002-03 | Cornell Big Red | ECAC | 15 | 0 | 2 | 2 | 19 | | | | | | | | | | | | | | | | | | |
| 2003-04 | Cornell Big Red | ECAC | 30 | 2 | 8 | 10 | 10 | | | | | | | | | | | | | | | | | | |
| 2004-05 | Cornell Big Red | ECAC | 35 | 10 | 8 | 18 | 8 | | | | | | | | | | | | | | | | | | |
| | Rochester | AHL | 6 | 1 | 0 | 1 | 7 | | | | | | | | | | | | | | | | | | |
| 2005-06 | Cleveland Barons | AHL | 77 | 22 | 26 | 48 | 57 | | | | | | | | | | | | | | | | | | |
| 2006-07 | Worcester Sharks | AHL | 73 | 30 | 27 | 57 | 55 | | | | | | | | | | 6 | 3 | 3 | 6 | 0 | | | | |
| 2007-08 | San Jose | NHL | 1 | 0 | 0 | 0 | 0 | 0 | 0 | 0 | 1 | 0.0 | –1 | 0 | 0.0 | 6:40 | | | | | | | | | |
| | Worcester Sharks | AHL | 78 | 29 | 37 | 66 | 63 | | | | | | | | | | | | | | | | | | |
| 2008-09 | NY Islanders | NHL | 11 | 1 | 4 | 5 | 4 | 0 | 0 | 0 | 16 | 6.3 | –3 | 2 | 50.0 | 12:08 | | | | | | | | | |
| | Bridgeport | AHL | 72 | 25 | 40 | 65 | 42 | | | | | | | | | | 2 | 1 | 2 | 3 | 0 | | | | |
| | NHL Totals | | 12 | 1 | 4 | 5 | 4 | 0 | 0 | 0 | 17 | 5.9 | | 2 | 50.0 | 11:40 | | | | | | | | | |

Signed to an ATO (tryout) contract by **Rochester** (AHL), April 5, 2004. Signed to a PTO (tryout) contract by **Cleveland** (AHL), September 19, 2005. Signed as a free agent by **San Jose**, January 16, 2006. Signed as a free agent by **NY Islanders**, July 3, 2008.

## IGINLA, Jarome

(ih-GIHN-lah, jah-ROHM) **CGY.**

Right wing. Shoots right. 6'1", 207 lbs. Born, Edmonton, Alta., July 1, 1977. Dallas' 1st choice, 11th overall, in 1995 Entry Draft.

| | | | | | | | | | | | | | | | | | | | | | | | | | |
|---|---|---|---|---|---|---|---|---|---|---|---|---|---|---|---|---|---|---|---|---|---|---|---|---|---|
| 1991-92 | St. Albert Raiders | AMHL | 36 | 26 | 30 | 56 | 22 | | | | | | | | | | | | | | | | | | |
| 1992-93 | St. Albert Raiders | AMHL | 36 | 34 | 53 | *87 | 20 | | | | | | | | | | | | | | | | | | |
| 1993-94 | Kamloops Blazers | WHL | 48 | 6 | 23 | 29 | 33 | | | | | | | | | | 19 | 3 | 6 | 9 | 10 | | | | |
| 1994-95 | Kamloops Blazers | WHL | 72 | 33 | 38 | 71 | 111 | | | | | | | | | | 21 | 7 | 11 | 18 | 34 | | | | |
| 1995-96 | Kamloops Blazers | WHL | 63 | 63 | 73 | 136 | 120 | | | | | | | | | | 16 | 16 | 13 | 29 | 44 | | | | |
| | Calgary | NHL | | | | | | | | | | | | | | | 2 | 1 | 1 | 2 | 0 | 0 | 0 | 0 | |
| 1996-97 | Calgary | NHL | 82 | 21 | 29 | 50 | 37 | 8 | 1 | 3 | 169 | 12.4 | –4 | | | | | | | | | | | | |
| 1997-98 | Calgary | NHL | 70 | 13 | 19 | 32 | 29 | 0 | 2 | 1 | 154 | 8.4 | –10 | | | | | | | | | | | | |
| 1998-99 | Calgary | NHL | 82 | 28 | 23 | 51 | 58 | 7 | 0 | 4 | 211 | 13.3 | 1 | 111 | 51.4 | 16:30 | | | | | | | | | |
| 99-2000 | Calgary | NHL | 77 | 29 | 34 | 63 | 26 | 12 | 0 | 4 | 256 | 11.3 | 0 | 278 | 52.9 | 18:24 | | | | | | | | | |
| 2000-01 | Calgary | NHL | 77 | 31 | 40 | 71 | 62 | 10 | 0 | 4 | 229 | 13.5 | –2 | 638 | 51.7 | 19:58 | | | | | | | | | |
| 2001-02 | Calgary | NHL | 82 | *52 | 44 | *96 | 77 | 16 | 1 | 7 | 311 | 16.7 | 27 | 308 | 55.2 | 22:22 | | | | | | | | | |
| | Canada | Olympics | 6 | 3 | 1 | 4 | 0 | | | | | | | | | | | | | | | | | | |
| 2002-03 | Calgary | NHL | 75 | 35 | 32 | 67 | 49 | 11 | 3 | 6 | 316 | 11.1 | –10 | 90 | 43.3 | 21:26 | | | | | | | | | |
| 2003-04 | Calgary | NHL | 81 | *41 | 32 | 73 | 84 | 8 | 4 | 10 | 265 | 15.5 | 21 | 305 | 54.4 | 21:18 | 26 | *13 | 9 | 22 | 45 | 4 | 2 | 3 | 23:18 |
| 2004-05 | | | DID NOT PLAY | | | | | | | | | | | | | | | | | | | | | | |
| 2005-06 | Calgary | NHL | 82 | 35 | 32 | 67 | 86 | 17 | 1 | 6 | 293 | 11.9 | 5 | 541 | 54.2 | 21:42 | 7 | 5 | 3 | 8 | 11 | 1 | 1 | 1 | 24:14 |
| | Canada | Olympics | 6 | 2 | 1 | 3 | 4 | | | | | | | | | | | | | | | | | | |
| 2006-07 | Calgary | NHL | 70 | 39 | 55 | 94 | 40 | 13 | 1 | 7 | 264 | 14.8 | 12 | 406 | 53.0 | 22:04 | 6 | 2 | 2 | 4 | 12 | 0 | 0 | 1 | 23:45 |
| 2007-08 | Calgary | NHL | 82 | 50 | 48 | 98 | 83 | 15 | 0 | 9 | 338 | 14.8 | 27 | 445 | 55.1 | 21:26 | 7 | 4 | 5 | 9 | 2 | 3 | 0 | 0 | 22:43 |
| 2008-09 | Calgary | NHL | 82 | 35 | 54 | 89 | 37 | 10 | 0 | 4 | 289 | 12.1 | –2 | 501 | 52.5 | 21:37 | 6 | 3 | 1 | 4 | 0 | 2 | 0 | 0 | 20:56 |
| | NHL Totals | | 942 | 409 | 442 | 851 | 668 | 127 | 13 | 65 | 3095 | 13.2 | | 3623 | 53.1 | 20:40 | 54 | 28 | 21 | 49 | 70 | 10 | 3 | 5 | 23:08 |

George Parsons Trophy (Memorial Cup Tournament - Most Sportsmanlike Player) (1995) • WHL West First All-Star Team (1996) • WHL Player of the Year (1996) • Canadian Major Junior First All-Star Team (1996) • NHL All-Rookie Team (1997) • NHL First All-Star Team (2002, 2008, 2009) • Maurice "Rocket" Richard Trophy (2002) • Art Ross Trophy (2002) • Lester B. Pearson Award (2002) • NHL Second All-Star Team (2004) • King Clancy Memorial Trophy (2004) • Maurice "Rocket" Richard Trophy (2004) (tied with Ilya Kovalchuk and Rick Nash)

Played in NHL All-Star Game (2002, 2003, 2004, 2008, 2009)

Traded to **Calgary** by **Dallas** with Corey Millen for Joe Nieuwendyk, December 19, 1995.

## ISBISTER, Brad

(IHZ-bihs-tuhr, BRAD)

Left wing. Shoots right. 6'4", 225 lbs. Born, Edmonton, Alta., May 7, 1977. Winnipeg's 4th choice, 67th overall, in 1995 Entry Draft.

| | | | | | | | | | | | | | | | | | | | | | | | | | |
|---|---|---|---|---|---|---|---|---|---|---|---|---|---|---|---|---|---|---|---|---|---|---|---|---|---|
| 1992-93 | Calgary Canucks | ABHL | 35 | 24 | 25 | 49 | 74 | | | | | | | | | | | | | | | | | | |
| 1993-94 | Portland | WHL | 64 | 7 | 10 | 17 | 45 | | | | | | | | | | 10 | 0 | 2 | 2 | 0 | | | | |
| 1994-95 | Portland | WHL | 67 | 16 | 20 | 36 | 123 | | | | | | | | | | | | | | | | | | |
| 1995-96 | Portland | WHL | 71 | 45 | 44 | 89 | 184 | | | | | | | | | | 7 | 2 | 4 | 6 | 20 | | | | |
| 1996-97 | Portland | WHL | 24 | 15 | 18 | 33 | 45 | | | | | | | | | | 6 | 2 | 1 | 3 | 16 | | | | |
| | Springfield | AHL | 7 | 3 | 1 | 4 | 14 | | | | | | | | | | 9 | 1 | 2 | 3 | 10 | | | | |
| 1997-98 | Phoenix | NHL | 66 | 9 | 8 | 17 | 102 | 1 | 0 | 1 | 115 | 7.8 | 4 | | | | 5 | 0 | 0 | 0 | 2 | 0 | 0 | 0 | |
| | Springfield | AHL | 9 | 8 | 2 | 10 | 36 | | | | | | | | | | | | | | | | | | |
| 1998-99 | Phoenix | NHL | 32 | 4 | 4 | 8 | 46 | 0 | 0 | 2 | 48 | 8.3 | 1 | 3 | 0.0 | 11:33 | | | | | | | | | |
| | Springfield | AHL | 4 | 1 | 1 | 2 | 12 | | | | | | | | | | | | | | | | | | |
| | Las Vegas | IHL | 2 | 0 | 0 | 0 | 9 | | | | | | | | | | | | | | | | | | |
| 99-2000 | NY Islanders | NHL | 64 | 22 | 20 | 42 | 100 | 9 | 0 | 1 | 135 | 16.3 | –18 | 55 | 54.6 | 16:58 | | | | | | | | | |
| 2000-01 | NY Islanders | NHL | 51 | 18 | 14 | 32 | 59 | 7 | 1 | 4 | 129 | 14.0 | –19 | 255 | 45.9 | 19:26 | | | | | | | | | |
| 2001-02 | NY Islanders | NHL | 79 | 17 | 21 | 38 | 113 | 4 | 0 | 2 | 142 | 12.0 | 1 | 71 | 45.1 | 15:18 | 3 | 1 | 1 | 2 | 17 | 1 | 0 | 1 | 12:33 |
| 2002-03 | NY Islanders | NHL | 53 | 10 | 13 | 23 | 34 | 2 | 0 | 2 | 90 | 11.1 | –9 | 13 | 46.2 | 13:54 | | | | | | | | | |
| | Edmonton | NHL | 13 | 3 | 2 | 5 | 9 | 0 | 0 | 1 | 29 | 10.3 | 0 | 10 | 50.0 | 13:14 | 6 | 0 | 1 | 1 | 12 | 0 | 0 | 0 | 10:04 |
| 2003-04 | Edmonton | NHL | 51 | 10 | 8 | 18 | 54 | 1 | 0 | 2 | 80 | 12.5 | –2 | 55 | 56.4 | 12:46 | | | | | | | | | |
| 2004-05 | Innsbruck | Austria | 11 | 7 | 4 | 11 | 41 | | | | | | | | | | 5 | 3 | 1 | 4 | 6 | | | | |
| 2005-06 | Boston | NHL | 58 | 6 | 17 | 23 | 46 | 1 | 0 | 0 | 112 | 5.4 | –2 | 10 | 60.0 | 13:55 | | | | | | | | | |
| 2006-07 | Albany River Rats | AHL | 9 | 3 | 5 | 8 | 54 | | | | | | | | | | | | | | | | | | |
| | NY Rangers | NHL | 19 | 1 | 4 | 5 | 14 | 1 | 0 | 0 | 36 | 2.8 | 5 | 12 | 33.3 | 13:36 | 4 | 0 | 0 | 0 | 2 | 0 | 0 | 0 | 9:58 |
| | Hartford | AHL | 34 | 12 | 8 | 20 | 22 | | | | | | | | | | | | | | | | | | |
| 2007-08 | Vancouver | NHL | 55 | 6 | 5 | 11 | 38 | 0 | 0 | 1 | 71 | 8.5 | –4 | 17 | 47.1 | 10:49 | | | | | | | | | |
| 2008-09 | EV Zug | Swiss | 24 | 9 | 7 | 16 | 55 | | | | | | | | | | 3 | 1 | 1 | 2 | 12 | | | | |
| | NHL Totals | | 541 | 106 | 116 | 222 | 615 | 26 | 1 | 16 | 987 | 10.7 | | 501 | 47.7 | 14:29 | 18 | 1 | 2 | 3 | 33 | 1 | 0 | 1 | 10:36 |

WHL West Second All-Star Team (1997)

• Rights transferred to **Phoenix** after **Winnipeg** franchise relocated, July 1, 1996. Traded to **NY Islanders** by **Phoenix** with Phoenix's 3rd round choice (Brian Collins) in 1999 Entry Draft for Robert Reichel, NY Islanders' 3rd round choice (Jason Jaspers) in 1999 Entry Draft and Ottawa's 4th round choice (previously acquired, Phoenix selected Preston Mizzi) in 1999 Entry Draft, March 20, 1999. Traded to **Edmonton** by **NY Islanders** with Raffi Torres for Janne Niinimaa and Washington's 2nd round choice (previously acquired, NY Islanders selected Evgeni Tunik) in 2003 Entry Draft , March 11, 2003. Signed as a free agent by **Innsbruck** (Austria), February 12, 2005. Traded to **Boston** by **Edmonton** for Boston's 4th round choice (later traded back to Boston - later traded to San Jose - San Jose selected James Delory) in 2006 Entry Draft, August 1, 2005. Signed as a free agent by **Carolina**, August 30, 2006. Traded to **NY Rangers** by **Carolina** for Jakub Petruzalek and future considerations, November 21, 2006. Signed as a free agent by **Vancouver**, July 3, 2007. Signed as a free agent by **Ottawa**, September 4, 2008. Signed as a free agent by **Zug** (Swiss), October 13, 2008.

## IVANANS, Raitis

(EE-vahn-ahns, RIGHT-uhs) **L.A.**

Left wing. Shoots left. 6'4", 256 lbs. Born, Riga, Latvia, January 3, 1979.

| | | | | | | | | | | | | | | | | | | | | | | | | | |
|---|---|---|---|---|---|---|---|---|---|---|---|---|---|---|---|---|---|---|---|---|---|---|---|---|---|
| 1997-98 | Flint Generals | UHL | 18 | 0 | 1 | 1 | 20 | | | | | | | | | | | | | | | | | | |
| 1998-99 | Macon Whoopee | CHL | 16 | 1 | 1 | 2 | 20 | | | | | | | | | | | | | | | | | | |
| | Tulsa Oilers | CHL | 32 | 2 | 7 | 9 | 39 | | | | | | | | | | | | | | | | | | |
| 99-2000 | Pensacola | ECHL | 59 | 3 | 7 | 10 | 146 | | | | | | | | | | 2 | 0 | 0 | 0 | 0 | | | | |
| 2000-01 | Hershey Bears | AHL | 2 | 0 | 0 | 0 | 0 | | | | | | | | | | | | | | | | | | |
| | New Haven | UHL | 66 | 4 | 10 | 14 | 270 | | | | | | | | | | 8 | 1 | 0 | 1 | 4 | | | | |
| 2001-02 | Toledo Storm | ECHL | 16 | 2 | 2 | 4 | 59 | | | | | | | | | | | | | | | | | | |
| | Baton Rouge | ECHL | 40 | 4 | 5 | 9 | 180 | | | | | | | | | | | | | | | | | | |

| | | | Regular Season | | | | | | | | | | | | | | Playoffs | | | | | | | | |
|---|---|---|---|---|---|---|---|---|---|---|---|---|---|---|---|---|---|---|---|---|---|---|---|---|---|
| Season | Club | League | GP | G | A | Pts | PIM | PP | SH | GW | S | % | +/- | TF | F% | Min | GP | G | A | Pts | PIM | PP | SH | GW | Min |
| 2002-03 | Milwaukee | AHL | 17 | 0 | 0 | 0 | 38 | .... | .... | .... | .... | .... | .... | .... | .... | .... | 1 | 0 | 0 | 0 | 15 | .... | .... | .... | .... |
| | Rockford IceHogs | UHL | 50 | 4 | 2 | 6 | 208 | .... | .... | .... | .... | .... | .... | .... | .... | .... | .... | .... | .... | .... | .... | .... | .... | .... | .... |
| 2003-04 | Milwaukee | AHL | 54 | 1 | 7 | 8 | 166 | .... | .... | .... | .... | .... | .... | .... | .... | .... | 7 | 0 | 1 | 1 | 17 | .... | .... | .... | .... |
| | Rockford IceHogs | UHL | 1 | 0 | 0 | 0 | 0 | .... | .... | .... | .... | .... | .... | .... | .... | .... | .... | .... | .... | .... | .... | .... | .... | .... | .... |
| 2004-05 | Hamilton | AHL | 75 | 2 | 5 | 7 | 259 | .... | .... | .... | .... | .... | .... | .... | .... | .... | 2 | 0 | 1 | 1 | 0 | .... | .... | .... | .... |
| **2005-06** | **Montreal** | **NHL** | **4** | **0** | **0** | **0** | **9** | **0** | **0** | **0** | **0** | **0.0** | **–1** | **0** | **0.0** | **2:58** | .... | .... | .... | .... | .... | .... | .... | .... | .... |
| | Hamilton | AHL | 43 | 2 | 0 | 2 | 120 | .... | .... | .... | .... | .... | .... | .... | .... | .... | .... | .... | .... | .... | .... | .... | .... | .... | .... |
| **2006-07** | **Los Angeles** | **NHL** | **66** | **4** | **4** | **8** | **140** | **0** | **0** | **0** | **37** | **10.8** | **–12** | **1** | **0.0** | **6:59** | .... | .... | .... | .... | .... | .... | .... | .... | .... |
| **2007-08** | **Los Angeles** | **NHL** | **73** | **6** | **2** | **8** | **134** | **0** | **0** | **0** | **48** | **12.5** | **–10** | **1** | **0.0** | **7:30** | .... | .... | .... | .... | .... | .... | .... | .... | .... |
| **2008-09** | **Los Angeles** | **NHL** | **76** | **2** | **0** | **2** | **145** | **0** | **0** | **2** | **25** | **8.0** | **–8** | **0** | **0.0** | **6:22** | .... | .... | .... | .... | .... | .... | .... | .... | .... |
| | **NHL Totals** | | **219** | **12** | **6** | **18** | **428** | **0** | **0** | **2** | **110** | **10.9** | | **1** | **0.0** | **6:52** | .... | .... | .... | .... | .... | .... | .... | .... | .... |

Signed as a free agent by **Montreal**, July 16, 2004. Signed as a free agent by **Los Angeles**, July 13, 2006.

## JACKMAN, Barret

(JAK-man, BAIR-reht) **ST.L.**

Defense. Shoots left. 6', 203 lbs. Born, Trail, B.C., March 5, 1981. St. Louis' 1st choice, 17th overall, in 1999 Entry Draft.

| Season | Club | League | GP | G | A | Pts | PIM | PP | SH | GW | S | % | +/- | TF | F% | Min | GP | G | A | Pts | PIM | PP | SH | GW | Min |
|---|---|---|---|---|---|---|---|---|---|---|---|---|---|---|---|---|---|---|---|---|---|---|---|---|---|
| 1996-97 | Beaver Valley | VIJHL | 32 | 22 | 25 | 47 | 180 | .... | .... | .... | .... | .... | .... | .... | .... | .... | .... | .... | .... | .... | .... | .... | .... | .... | .... |
| 1997-98 | Regina Pats | WHL | 68 | 2 | 11 | 13 | 224 | .... | .... | .... | .... | .... | .... | .... | .... | .... | 9 | 0 | 3 | 3 | 32 | .... | .... | .... | .... |
| 1998-99 | Regina Pats | WHL | 70 | 8 | 36 | 44 | 259 | .... | .... | .... | .... | .... | .... | .... | .... | .... | .... | .... | .... | .... | .... | .... | .... | .... | .... |
| 99-2000 | Regina Pats | WHL | 53 | 9 | 37 | 46 | 175 | .... | .... | .... | .... | .... | .... | .... | .... | .... | 6 | 1 | 1 | 2 | 19 | .... | .... | .... | .... |
| | Worcester IceCats | AHL | .... | .... | .... | .... | .... | .... | .... | .... | .... | .... | .... | .... | .... | .... | 2 | 0 | 0 | 0 | 13 | .... | .... | .... | .... |
| 2000-01 | Regina Pats | WHL | 43 | 9 | 27 | 36 | 138 | .... | .... | .... | .... | .... | .... | .... | .... | .... | 6 | 0 | 3 | 3 | 8 | .... | .... | .... | .... |
| **2001-02** | **St. Louis** | **NHL** | **1** | **0** | **0** | **0** | **0** | **0** | **0** | **0** | **1** | **0.0** | **0** | **0** | **0.0** | **18:56** | **1** | **0** | **0** | **0** | **2** | **0** | **0** | **0** | **18:24** |
| | Worcester IceCats | AHL | 75 | 2 | 12 | 14 | 266 | .... | .... | .... | .... | .... | .... | .... | .... | .... | 3 | 0 | 1 | 1 | 4 | .... | .... | .... | .... |
| **2002-03** | **St. Louis** | **NHL** | **82** | **3** | **16** | **19** | **190** | **0** | **0** | **0** | **66** | **4.5** | **23** | **0** | **0.0** | **20:03** | **7** | **0** | **0** | **0** | **14** | **0** | **0** | **0** | **21:59** |
| **2003-04** | **St. Louis** | **NHL** | **15** | **1** | **2** | **3** | **41** | **0** | **0** | **0** | **11** | **9.1** | **–1** | **0** | **0.0** | **18:16** | .... | .... | .... | .... | .... | .... | .... | .... | .... |
| 2004-05 | Missouri | UHL | 28 | 3 | 17 | 20 | 61 | .... | .... | .... | .... | .... | .... | .... | .... | .... | 3 | 0 | 0 | 0 | 4 | .... | .... | .... | .... |
| **2005-06** | **St. Louis** | **NHL** | **63** | **4** | **6** | **10** | **156** | **0** | **0** | **2** | **56** | **7.1** | **–6** | **0** | **0.0** | **18:46** | .... | .... | .... | .... | .... | .... | .... | .... | .... |
| **2006-07** | **St. Louis** | **NHL** | **70** | **3** | **24** | **27** | **82** | **1** | **0** | **1** | **86** | **3.5** | **20** | **0** | **0.0** | **21:30** | .... | .... | .... | .... | .... | .... | .... | .... | .... |
| | Peoria Rivermen | AHL | 1 | 0 | 0 | 0 | 0 | .... | .... | .... | .... | .... | .... | .... | .... | .... | .... | .... | .... | .... | .... | .... | .... | .... | .... |
| **2007-08** | **St. Louis** | **NHL** | **78** | **2** | **14** | **16** | **93** | **1** | **0** | **0** | **80** | **2.5** | **–12** | **0** | **0.0** | **22:24** | .... | .... | .... | .... | .... | .... | .... | .... | .... |
| **2008-09** | **St. Louis** | **NHL** | **82** | **4** | **17** | **21** | **86** | **1** | **1** | **0** | **89** | **4.5** | **–17** | **0** | **0.0** | **23:26** | **4** | **0** | **1** | **1** | **5** | **0** | **0** | **0** | **25:18** |
| | **NHL Totals** | | **391** | **17** | **79** | **96** | **648** | **3** | **1** | **3** | **389** | **4.4** | | **0** | **0.0** | **21:13** | **12** | **0** | **1** | **1** | **21** | **0** | **0** | **0** | **22:47** |

WHL East Second All-Star Team (2000) • AHL All-Rookie Team (2002) • NHL All-Rookie Team (2003) • Calder Memorial Trophy (2003)

• Missed majority of 2003-04 season recovering from shoulder injury suffered in game vs. Vancouver, October 22, 2003. Signed as a free agent by **Missouri** (UHL), February 3, 2005.

## JACKMAN, Tim

(JAK-man, TIHM) **NYI**

Right wing. Shoots right. 6'4", 210 lbs. Born, Minot, ND, November 14, 1981. Columbus' 2nd choice, 38th overall, in 2001 Entry Draft.

| Season | Club | League | GP | G | A | Pts | PIM | PP | SH | GW | S | % | +/- | TF | F% | Min | GP | G | A | Pts | PIM | PP | SH | GW | Min |
|---|---|---|---|---|---|---|---|---|---|---|---|---|---|---|---|---|---|---|---|---|---|---|---|---|---|
| 1998-99 | Park Center | High-MN | 22 | 22 | 22 | 44 | .... | .... | .... | .... | .... | .... | .... | .... | .... | .... | .... | .... | .... | .... | .... | .... | .... | .... | .... |
| 99-2000 | Park Center | High-MN | 19 | 34 | 22 | 56 | .... | .... | .... | .... | .... | .... | .... | .... | .... | .... | .... | .... | .... | .... | .... | .... | .... | .... | .... |
| | Twin Cities | USHL | 25 | 11 | 9 | 20 | 58 | .... | .... | .... | .... | .... | .... | .... | .... | .... | 13 | 8 | 5 | 13 | 12 | .... | .... | .... | .... |
| 2000-01 | Minnesota State | WCHA | 37 | 11 | 14 | 25 | 92 | .... | .... | .... | .... | .... | .... | .... | .... | .... | .... | .... | .... | .... | .... | .... | .... | .... | .... |
| 2001-02 | Minnesota State | WCHA | 36 | 14 | 14 | 28 | 86 | .... | .... | .... | .... | .... | .... | .... | .... | .... | .... | .... | .... | .... | .... | .... | .... | .... | .... |
| 2002-03 | Syracuse Crunch | AHL | 77 | 9 | 7 | 16 | 48 | .... | .... | .... | .... | .... | .... | .... | .... | .... | .... | .... | .... | .... | .... | .... | .... | .... | .... |
| **2003-04** | **Columbus** | **NHL** | **19** | **1** | **2** | **3** | **16** | **0** | **0** | **0** | **18** | **5.6** | **–7** | **1** | **100.0** | **9:56** | .... | .... | .... | .... | .... | .... | .... | .... | .... |
| | Syracuse Crunch | AHL | 64 | 23 | 13 | 36 | 61 | .... | .... | .... | .... | .... | .... | .... | .... | .... | 7 | 2 | 3 | 5 | 12 | .... | .... | .... | .... |
| 2004-05 | Syracuse Crunch | AHL | 73 | 14 | 21 | 35 | 98 | .... | .... | .... | .... | .... | .... | .... | .... | .... | .... | .... | .... | .... | .... | .... | .... | .... | .... |
| **2005-06** | **Phoenix** | **NHL** | **8** | **0** | **0** | **0** | **21** | **0** | **0** | **0** | **4** | **0.0** | **1** | **1** | **0.0** | **7:13** | .... | .... | .... | .... | .... | .... | .... | .... | .... |
| | San Antonio | AHL | 50 | 7 | 13 | 20 | 127 | .... | .... | .... | .... | .... | .... | .... | .... | .... | .... | .... | .... | .... | .... | .... | .... | .... | .... |
| | Manchester | AHL | 18 | 2 | 3 | 5 | 33 | .... | .... | .... | .... | .... | .... | .... | .... | .... | 7 | 0 | 3 | 3 | 20 | .... | .... | .... | .... |
| **2006-07** | **Los Angeles** | **NHL** | **5** | **0** | **0** | **0** | **10** | **0** | **0** | **0** | **3** | **0.0** | **–1** | **0** | **0.0** | **6:36** | .... | .... | .... | .... | .... | .... | .... | .... | .... |
| | Manchester | AHL | 69 | 19 | 14 | 33 | 143 | .... | .... | .... | .... | .... | .... | .... | .... | .... | 16 | 3 | 3 | 6 | 26 | .... | .... | .... | .... |
| **2007-08** | **NY Islanders** | **NHL** | **36** | **1** | **3** | **4** | **57** | **0** | **0** | **0** | **36** | **2.8** | **–3** | **2** | **100.0** | **6:37** | .... | .... | .... | .... | .... | .... | .... | .... | .... |
| | Bridgeport | AHL | 44 | 15 | 21 | 36 | 67 | .... | .... | .... | .... | .... | .... | .... | .... | .... | .... | .... | .... | .... | .... | .... | .... | .... | .... |
| **2008-09** | **NY Islanders** | **NHL** | **69** | **5** | **7** | **12** | **155** | **0** | **1** | **0** | **99** | **5.1** | **–17** | **22** | **31.8** | **11:45** | .... | .... | .... | .... | .... | .... | .... | .... | .... |
| | Bridgeport | AHL | 12 | 6 | 1 | 7 | 35 | .... | .... | .... | .... | .... | .... | .... | .... | .... | .... | .... | .... | .... | .... | .... | .... | .... | .... |
| | **NHL Totals** | | **137** | **7** | **12** | **19** | **259** | **0** | **1** | **0** | **160** | **4.4** | | **26** | **38.5** | **9:42** | .... | .... | .... | .... | .... | .... | .... | .... | .... |

Traded to **Phoenix** by **Columbus** with Geoff Sanderson for Cale Hulse, Mike Rupp and Jason Chimera, October 8, 2005. Traded to **Los Angeles** by **Phoenix** for Yanick Lehoux, March 9, 2006. Signed as a free agent by **NY Islanders**, July 5, 2007.

## JACQUES, Jean-Francois

(ZHAWK, ZHAWN-fran-SWUH) **EDM.**

Left wing. Shoots left. 6'4", 217 lbs. Born, Montreal, Que., April 29, 1985. Edmonton's 3rd choice, 68th overall, in 2003 Entry Draft.

| Season | Club | League | GP | G | A | Pts | PIM | PP | SH | GW | S | % | +/- | TF | F% | Min | GP | G | A | Pts | PIM | PP | SH | GW | Min |
|---|---|---|---|---|---|---|---|---|---|---|---|---|---|---|---|---|---|---|---|---|---|---|---|---|---|
| 2000-01 | Cap-d-Madeleine | QAAA | 39 | 22 | 13 | 35 | 28 | .... | .... | .... | .... | .... | .... | .... | .... | .... | 10 | 5 | 8 | 13 | 14 | .... | .... | .... | .... |
| 2001-02 | Baie-Comeau | QMJHL | 66 | 10 | 14 | 24 | 136 | .... | .... | .... | .... | .... | .... | .... | .... | .... | 5 | 1 | 0 | 1 | 2 | .... | .... | .... | .... |
| 2002-03 | Baie-Comeau | QMJHL | 67 | 12 | 21 | 33 | 123 | .... | .... | .... | .... | .... | .... | .... | .... | .... | 12 | 4 | 2 | 6 | 13 | .... | .... | .... | .... |
| 2003-04 | Baie-Comeau | QMJHL | 59 | 20 | 24 | 44 | 70 | .... | .... | .... | .... | .... | .... | .... | .... | .... | 4 | 1 | 0 | 1 | 4 | .... | .... | .... | .... |
| 2004-05 | Baie-Comeau | QMJHL | 69 | 36 | 42 | 78 | 56 | .... | .... | .... | .... | .... | .... | .... | .... | .... | 6 | 3 | 5 | 8 | 6 | .... | .... | .... | .... |
| | Edmonton | AHL | 6 | 0 | 0 | 0 | 5 | .... | .... | .... | .... | .... | .... | .... | .... | .... | .... | .... | .... | .... | .... | .... | .... | .... | .... |
| **2005-06** | **Edmonton** | **NHL** | **7** | **0** | **0** | **0** | **0** | **0** | **0** | **0** | **8** | **0.0** | **–3** | **0** | **0.0** | **6:43** | .... | .... | .... | .... | .... | .... | .... | .... | .... |
| | Hamilton | AHL | 65 | 24 | 19 | 43 | 131 | .... | .... | .... | .... | .... | .... | .... | .... | .... | .... | .... | .... | .... | .... | .... | .... | .... | .... |
| **2006-07** | **Edmonton** | **NHL** | **37** | **0** | **0** | **0** | **33** | **0** | **0** | **0** | **23** | **0.0** | **–11** | **2** | **0.0** | **7:55** | .... | .... | .... | .... | .... | .... | .... | .... | .... |
| | Wilkes-Barre | AHL | 29 | 10 | 17 | 27 | 53 | .... | .... | .... | .... | .... | .... | .... | .... | .... | 11 | 1 | 2 | 3 | 43 | .... | .... | .... | .... |
| **2007-08** | **Edmonton** | **NHL** | **9** | **0** | **0** | **0** | **2** | **0** | **0** | **0** | **2** | **0.0** | **–3** | **0** | **0.0** | **6:10** | .... | .... | .... | .... | .... | .... | .... | .... | .... |
| | Springfield | AHL | 38 | 11 | 14 | 25 | 63 | .... | .... | .... | .... | .... | .... | .... | .... | .... | .... | .... | .... | .... | .... | .... | .... | .... | .... |
| **2008-09** | **Edmonton** | **NHL** | **7** | **1** | **0** | **1** | **9** | **0** | **0** | **0** | **3** | **33.3** | **0** | **0** | **0.0** | **7:22** | .... | .... | .... | .... | .... | .... | .... | .... | .... |
| | Springfield | AHL | 8 | 1 | 5 | 6 | 13 | .... | .... | .... | .... | .... | .... | .... | .... | .... | .... | .... | .... | .... | .... | .... | .... | .... | .... |
| | **NHL Totals** | | **60** | **1** | **0** | **1** | **44** | **0** | **0** | **0** | **36** | **2.8** | | **2** | **0.0** | **7:27** | .... | .... | .... | .... | .... | .... | .... | .... | .... |

• Missed majority of 2008-09 season recovering from off-season back surgery.

## JAFFRAY, Jason

(JAF-ray, JAY-suhn) **CGY.**

Left wing. Shoots left. 6'1", 195 lbs. Born, Rimbey, Alta., June 30, 1981.

| Season | Club | League | GP | G | A | Pts | PIM | PP | SH | GW | S | % | +/- | TF | F% | Min | GP | G | A | Pts | PIM | PP | SH | GW | Min |
|---|---|---|---|---|---|---|---|---|---|---|---|---|---|---|---|---|---|---|---|---|---|---|---|---|---|
| 1997-98 | Edmonton Ice | WHL | 6 | 0 | 1 | 1 | 0 | .... | .... | .... | .... | .... | .... | .... | .... | .... | .... | .... | .... | .... | .... | .... | .... | .... | .... |
| 1998-99 | Kootenay Ice | WHL | 57 | 14 | 12 | 26 | 50 | .... | .... | .... | .... | .... | .... | .... | .... | .... | 7 | 1 | 2 | 3 | 6 | .... | .... | .... | .... |
| 99-2000 | Kootenay Ice | WHL | 71 | 24 | 28 | 52 | 104 | .... | .... | .... | .... | .... | .... | .... | .... | .... | 21 | 10 | 9 | 19 | 17 | .... | .... | .... | .... |
| 2000-01 | Kootenay Ice | WHL | 70 | 31 | 42 | 73 | 108 | .... | .... | .... | .... | .... | .... | .... | .... | .... | 11 | 5 | 7 | 12 | 10 | .... | .... | .... | .... |
| 2001-02 | Kootenay Ice | WHL | 32 | 15 | 19 | 34 | 38 | .... | .... | .... | .... | .... | .... | .... | .... | .... | .... | .... | .... | .... | .... | .... | .... | .... | .... |
| | Swift Current | WHL | 41 | 23 | 26 | 49 | 44 | .... | .... | .... | .... | .... | .... | .... | .... | .... | 12 | 4 | 5 | 9 | 25 | .... | .... | .... | .... |
| 2002-03 | Norfolk Admirals | AHL | 2 | 0 | 0 | 0 | 0 | .... | .... | .... | .... | .... | .... | .... | .... | .... | .... | .... | .... | .... | .... | .... | .... | .... | .... |
| | Roanoke Express | ECHL | 64 | 34 | 51 | 85 | 89 | .... | .... | .... | .... | .... | .... | .... | .... | .... | 4 | 0 | 3 | 3 | 4 | .... | .... | .... | .... |
| 2003-04 | Wilkes-Barre | AHL | 5 | 0 | 1 | 1 | 0 | .... | .... | .... | .... | .... | .... | .... | .... | .... | .... | .... | .... | .... | .... | .... | .... | .... | .... |
| | Wheeling Nailers | ECHL | 54 | 37 | 37 | 74 | 81 | .... | .... | .... | .... | .... | .... | .... | .... | .... | 2 | 1 | 1 | 2 | 2 | .... | .... | .... | .... |
| 2004-05 | Cleveland Barons | AHL | 30 | 10 | 6 | 16 | 23 | .... | .... | .... | .... | .... | .... | .... | .... | .... | .... | .... | .... | .... | .... | .... | .... | .... | .... |
| | Manitoba Moose | AHL | 14 | 4 | 4 | 8 | 6 | .... | .... | .... | .... | .... | .... | .... | .... | .... | 1 | 0 | 0 | 0 | 0 | .... | .... | .... | .... |
| | Wheeling Nailers | ECHL | 23 | 6 | 6 | 12 | 22 | .... | .... | .... | .... | .... | .... | .... | .... | .... | .... | .... | .... | .... | .... | .... | .... | .... | .... |
| 2005-06 | Manitoba Moose | AHL | 73 | 12 | 35 | 47 | 58 | .... | .... | .... | .... | .... | .... | .... | .... | .... | 13 | 6 | 1 | 7 | 11 | .... | .... | .... | .... |
| 2006-07 | Manitoba Moose | AHL | 77 | 35 | 46 | 81 | 75 | .... | .... | .... | .... | .... | .... | .... | .... | .... | 13 | 6 | 7 | 13 | 6 | .... | .... | .... | .... |
| **2007-08** | **Vancouver** | **NHL** | **19** | **2** | **4** | **6** | **19** | **1** | **0** | **1** | **15** | **13.3** | **4** | **176** | **47.7** | **12:35** | .... | .... | .... | .... | .... | .... | .... | .... | .... |
| | Manitoba Moose | AHL | 43 | 21 | 27 | 48 | 51 | .... | .... | .... | .... | .... | .... | .... | .... | .... | 3 | 1 | 4 | 5 | 0 | .... | .... | .... | .... |
| **2008-09** | **Vancouver** | **NHL** | **14** | **2** | **2** | **4** | **14** | **0** | **0** | **2** | **11** | **18.2** | **–2** | **65** | **47.7** | **9:04** | .... | .... | .... | .... | .... | .... | .... | .... | .... |
| | Manitoba Moose | AHL | 56 | 23 | 26 | 49 | 52 | .... | .... | .... | .... | .... | .... | .... | .... | .... | 22 | 9 | 10 | 19 | 12 | .... | .... | .... | .... |
| | **NHL Totals** | | **33** | **4** | **6** | **10** | **33** | **1** | **0** | **3** | **26** | **15.4** | | **241** | **47.7** | **11:06** | .... | .... | .... | .... | .... | .... | .... | .... | .... |

AHL Second All-Star Team (2007)

Signed as a free agent by **Vancouver**, July 3, 2007. Signed as a free agent by **Calgary**, July 7, 2009.

| | | | Regular Season | | | | | | | | | | | | | | Playoffs | | | | | | | | |
|---|---|---|---|---|---|---|---|---|---|---|---|---|---|---|---|---|---|---|---|---|---|---|---|---|---|
| Season | Club | League | GP | G | A | Pts | PIM | PP | SH | GW | S | % | +/- | TF | F% | Min | GP | G | A | Pts | PIM | PP | SH | GW | Min |

## JAMES, Connor

(JAYMZ, KAW-nuhr)

Right wing. Shoots right. 5'10", 180 lbs. Born, Calgary, Alta., August 25, 1982. Los Angeles' 11th choice, 279th overall, in 2002 Entry Draft.

| | | | | | | | | | | | | | | | | | | | | | | | | | |
|---|---|---|---|---|---|---|---|---|---|---|---|---|---|---|---|---|---|---|---|---|---|---|---|---|---|
| 1998-99 | Calgary Buffaloes | AMHL | 36 | 33 | 53 | 86 | 20 | .... | .... | .... | .... | .... | .... | .... | .... | .... | .... | .... | .... | .... | .... | .... | .... | .... | .... |
| 99-2000 | Calgary Royals | AJHL | 64 | 36 | 57 | 93 | 41 | .... | .... | .... | .... | .... | .... | .... | .... | .... | .... | .... | .... | .... | .... | .... | .... | .... | .... |
| 2000-01 | U. of Denver | WCHA | 38 | 8 | 19 | 27 | 14 | .... | .... | .... | .... | .... | .... | .... | .... | .... | .... | .... | .... | .... | .... | .... | .... | .... | .... |
| 2001-02 | U. of Denver | WCHA | 41 | 16 | 26 | 42 | 18 | .... | .... | .... | .... | .... | .... | .... | .... | .... | .... | .... | .... | .... | .... | .... | .... | .... | .... |
| 2002-03 | U. of Denver | WCHA | 41 | 20 | 23 | 43 | 12 | .... | .... | .... | .... | .... | .... | .... | .... | .... | .... | .... | .... | .... | .... | .... | .... | .... | .... |
| 2003-04 | U. of Denver | WCHA | 40 | 13 | 25 | 38 | 16 | .... | .... | .... | .... | .... | .... | .... | .... | .... | .... | .... | .... | .... | .... | .... | .... | .... | .... |
| 2004-05 | Bakersfield | ECHL | 51 | 21 | 25 | 46 | 34 | .... | .... | .... | .... | .... | .... | .... | .... | .... | 5 | 3 | 1 | 4 | 0 | .... | .... | .... | .... |
| | Manchester | AHL | 14 | 2 | 1 | 3 | 10 | .... | .... | .... | .... | .... | .... | .... | .... | .... | 3 | 0 | 0 | 0 | 0 | .... | .... | .... | .... |
| **2005-06** | **Los Angeles** | **NHL** | **2** | **0** | **0** | **0** | **0** | **0** | **0** | **0** | **1** | **0.0** | **-1** | **6** | **33.3** | **7:19** | .... | .... | .... | .... | .... | .... | .... | .... | .... |
| | Manchester | AHL | 77 | 17 | 25 | 42 | 43 | .... | .... | .... | .... | .... | .... | .... | .... | .... | 7 | 0 | 0 | 0 | 2 | .... | .... | .... | .... |
| 2006-07 | Wilkes-Barre | AHL | 70 | 12 | 20 | 32 | 29 | .... | .... | .... | .... | .... | .... | .... | .... | .... | 11 | 4 | 4 | 8 | 8 | .... | .... | .... | .... |
| **2007-08** | **Pittsburgh** | **NHL** | **13** | **1** | **0** | **1** | **2** | **1** | **0** | **0** | **9** | **11.1** | **-2** | **0** | **0.0** | **7:26** | .... | .... | .... | .... | .... | .... | .... | .... | .... |
| | Wilkes-Barre | AHL | 64 | 9 | 28 | 37 | 30 | .... | .... | .... | .... | .... | .... | .... | .... | .... | 23 | 8 | 5 | 13 | 6 | .... | .... | .... | .... |
| **2008-09** | **Pittsburgh** | **NHL** | **1** | **0** | **0** | **0** | **0** | **0** | **0** | **0** | **0** | **0.0** | **0** | **0** | **0.0** | **8:15** | .... | .... | .... | .... | .... | .... | .... | .... | .... |
| | Wilkes-Barre | AHL | 76 | 19 | 30 | 49 | 24 | .... | .... | .... | .... | .... | .... | .... | .... | .... | 9 | 0 | 2 | 2 | 2 | .... | .... | .... | .... |
| | **NHL Totals** | | **16** | **1** | **0** | **1** | **2** | **1** | **0** | **0** | **10** | **10.0** | | **6** | **33.3** | **7:28** | .... | .... | .... | .... | .... | .... | .... | .... | .... |

NCAA Championship All-Tournament Team (2004)

Signed as a free agent by **Pittsburgh**, August 9, 2006.

## JANCEVSKI, Dan

(jan-SEHV-skee, DAN) **DAL.**

Defense. Shoots left. 6'3", 218 lbs. Born, Windsor, Ont., June 15, 1981. Dallas' 2nd choice, 66th overall, in 1999 Entry Draft.

| | | | | | | | | | | | | | | | | | | | | | | | | | |
|---|---|---|---|---|---|---|---|---|---|---|---|---|---|---|---|---|---|---|---|---|---|---|---|---|---|
| 1995-96 | Riverside Selects | Minor-ON | 59 | 9 | 22 | 31 | 67 | .... | .... | .... | .... | .... | .... | .... | .... | .... | .... | .... | .... | .... | .... | .... | .... | .... | .... |
| 1996-97 | Windsor Lions | Minor-ON | 47 | 6 | 20 | 26 | 99 | .... | .... | .... | .... | .... | .... | .... | .... | .... | .... | .... | .... | .... | .... | .... | .... | .... | .... |
| 1997-98 | Tecumseh | OHA-B | 49 | 3 | 11 | 14 | 145 | .... | .... | .... | .... | .... | .... | .... | .... | .... | .... | .... | .... | .... | .... | .... | .... | .... | .... |
| 1998-99 | London Knights | OHL | 68 | 2 | 12 | 14 | 115 | .... | .... | .... | .... | .... | .... | .... | .... | .... | 25 | 1 | 7 | 8 | 24 | .... | .... | .... | .... |
| 99-2000 | London Knights | OHL | 59 | 8 | 15 | 23 | 138 | .... | .... | .... | .... | .... | .... | .... | .... | .... | .... | .... | .... | .... | .... | .... | .... | .... | .... |
| 2000-01 | London Knights | OHL | 39 | 4 | 23 | 27 | 95 | .... | .... | .... | .... | .... | .... | .... | .... | .... | .... | .... | .... | .... | .... | .... | .... | .... | .... |
| | Sudbury Wolves | OHL | 31 | 3 | 14 | 17 | 42 | .... | .... | .... | .... | .... | .... | .... | .... | .... | 12 | 0 | 9 | 9 | 17 | .... | .... | .... | .... |
| 2001-02 | Utah Grizzlies | AHL | 77 | 0 | 13 | 13 | 147 | .... | .... | .... | .... | .... | .... | .... | .... | .... | 5 | 0 | 0 | 0 | 4 | .... | .... | .... | .... |
| 2002-03 | Utah Grizzlies | AHL | 76 | 1 | 10 | 11 | 172 | .... | .... | .... | .... | .... | .... | .... | .... | .... | 2 | 0 | 1 | 1 | 12 | .... | .... | .... | .... |
| 2003-04 | Utah Grizzlies | AHL | 80 | 5 | 17 | 22 | 171 | .... | .... | .... | .... | .... | .... | .... | .... | .... | .... | .... | .... | .... | .... | .... | .... | .... | .... |
| 2004-05 | Hamilton | AHL | 80 | 6 | 20 | 26 | 163 | .... | .... | .... | .... | .... | .... | .... | .... | .... | 4 | 0 | 0 | 0 | 2 | .... | .... | .... | .... |
| **2005-06** | **Dallas** | **NHL** | **2** | **0** | **0** | **0** | **0** | **0** | **0** | **0** | **0** | **0.0** | **1** | **0** | **0.0** | **9:13** | .... | .... | .... | .... | .... | .... | .... | .... | .... |
| | Iowa Stars | AHL | 77 | 9 | 29 | 38 | 91 | .... | .... | .... | .... | .... | .... | .... | .... | .... | 7 | 1 | 1 | 2 | 6 | .... | .... | .... | .... |
| 2006-07 | Hamilton | AHL | 80 | 7 | 24 | 31 | 87 | .... | .... | .... | .... | .... | .... | .... | .... | .... | 22 | 3 | 11 | 14 | 16 | .... | .... | .... | .... |
| **2007-08** | **Tampa Bay** | **NHL** | **2** | **0** | **0** | **0** | **2** | **0** | **0** | **0** | **0** | **0.0** | **-1** | **0** | **0.0** | **2:23** | .... | .... | .... | .... | .... | .... | .... | .... | .... |
| | Norfolk Admirals | AHL | 37 | 4 | 16 | 20 | 52 | .... | .... | .... | .... | .... | .... | .... | .... | .... | .... | .... | .... | .... | .... | .... | .... | .... | .... |
| | **Dallas** | **NHL** | **2** | **0** | **0** | **0** | **0** | **0** | **0** | **0** | **3** | **0.0** | **0** | **0** | **0.0** | **9:19** | .... | .... | .... | .... | .... | .... | .... | .... | .... |
| | Iowa Stars | AHL | 33 | 3 | 7 | 10 | 36 | .... | .... | .... | .... | .... | .... | .... | .... | .... | .... | .... | .... | .... | .... | .... | .... | .... | .... |
| **2008-09** | **Dallas** | **NHL** | **3** | **0** | **0** | **0** | **0** | **0** | **0** | **0** | **4** | **0.0** | **0** | **0** | **0.0** | **15:20** | .... | .... | .... | .... | .... | .... | .... | .... | .... |
| | Hamilton | AHL | 76 | 1 | 27 | 28 | 76 | .... | .... | .... | .... | .... | .... | .... | .... | .... | 6 | 0 | 3 | 3 | 6 | .... | .... | .... | .... |
| | **NHL Totals** | | **9** | **0** | **0** | **0** | **2** | **0** | **0** | **0** | **7** | **0.0** | | **0** | **0.0** | **9:45** | .... | .... | .... | .... | .... | .... | .... | .... | .... |

Signed as a free agent by **Montreal**, July 13, 2006. Signed as a free agent by **Tampa Bay**, July 6, 2007. Traded to **Dallas** by **Tampa Bay** for Junior Lessard, January 15, 2008.

## JANIK, Doug

(JAN-nihk, DUHG) **DET.**

Defense. Shoots left. 6'2", 209 lbs. Born, Agawam, MA, March 26, 1980. Buffalo's 3rd choice, 55th overall, in 1999 Entry Draft.

| | | | | | | | | | | | | | | | | | | | | | | | | | |
|---|---|---|---|---|---|---|---|---|---|---|---|---|---|---|---|---|---|---|---|---|---|---|---|---|---|
| 1995-96 | N.E. Jr. Whalers | EJHL | 48 | 16 | 38 | 54 | | .... | .... | .... | .... | .... | .... | .... | .... | .... | .... | .... | .... | .... | .... | .... | .... | .... | .... |
| 1996-97 | N.E. Jr. Whalers | EJHL | 39 | 12 | 24 | 36 | 22 | .... | .... | .... | .... | .... | .... | .... | .... | .... | 11 | 5 | 9 | 14 | 10 | .... | .... | .... | .... |
| 1997-98 | USNTDP | U-18 | 29 | 6 | 13 | 19 | 43 | .... | .... | .... | .... | .... | .... | .... | .... | .... | .... | .... | .... | .... | .... | .... | .... | .... | .... |
| | USNTDP | USHL | 19 | 1 | 6 | 7 | 34 | .... | .... | .... | .... | .... | .... | .... | .... | .... | .... | .... | .... | .... | .... | .... | .... | .... | .... |
| | USNTDP | NAHL | 10 | 0 | 4 | 4 | 10 | .... | .... | .... | .... | .... | .... | .... | .... | .... | 7 | 1 | 3 | 4 | 18 | .... | .... | .... | .... |
| 1998-99 | U. of Maine | H-East | 35 | 3 | 13 | 16 | 44 | .... | .... | .... | .... | .... | .... | .... | .... | .... | .... | .... | .... | .... | .... | .... | .... | .... | .... |
| 99-2000 | U. of Maine | H-East | 36 | 6 | 14 | 20 | 54 | .... | .... | .... | .... | .... | .... | .... | .... | .... | .... | .... | .... | .... | .... | .... | .... | .... | .... |
| 2000-01 | U. of Maine | H-East | 39 | 3 | 15 | 18 | 52 | .... | .... | .... | .... | .... | .... | .... | .... | .... | .... | .... | .... | .... | .... | .... | .... | .... | .... |
| 2001-02 | Rochester | AHL | 80 | 6 | 17 | 23 | 100 | .... | .... | .... | .... | .... | .... | .... | .... | .... | 2 | 0 | 0 | 0 | 0 | .... | .... | .... | .... |
| **2002-03** | **Buffalo** | **NHL** | **6** | **0** | **0** | **0** | **2** | **0** | **0** | **0** | **1** | **0.0** | **1** | **0** | **0.0** | **7:42** | .... | .... | .... | .... | .... | .... | .... | .... | .... |
| | Rochester | AHL | 75 | 3 | 13 | 16 | 120 | .... | .... | .... | .... | .... | .... | .... | .... | .... | 3 | 0 | 0 | 0 | 6 | .... | .... | .... | .... |
| **2003-04** | **Buffalo** | **NHL** | **4** | **0** | **0** | **0** | **19** | **0** | **0** | **0** | **3** | **0.0** | **0** | **0** | **0.0** | **8:26** | .... | .... | .... | .... | .... | .... | .... | .... | .... |
| | Rochester | AHL | 74 | 2 | 14 | 16 | 109 | .... | .... | .... | .... | .... | .... | .... | .... | .... | 16 | 1 | 2 | 3 | 22 | .... | .... | .... | .... |
| 2004-05 | Rochester | AHL | 76 | 2 | 10 | 12 | 196 | .... | .... | .... | .... | .... | .... | .... | .... | .... | 9 | 0 | 2 | 2 | 10 | .... | .... | .... | .... |
| 2005-06 | Rochester | AHL | 71 | 5 | 19 | 24 | 161 | .... | .... | .... | .... | .... | .... | .... | .... | .... | .... | .... | .... | .... | .... | .... | .... | .... | .... |
| | **Buffalo** | **NHL** | .... | .... | .... | .... | .... | .... | .... | .... | .... | .... | .... | .... | .... | .... | **5** | **1** | **0** | **1** | **2** | **0** | **0** | **0** | **10:30** |
| **2006-07** | **Tampa Bay** | **NHL** | **75** | **2** | **9** | **11** | **53** | **0** | **0** | **0** | **49** | **4.1** | **-11** | **0** | **0.0** | **14:28** | **1** | **0** | **0** | **0** | **0** | **0** | **0** | **0** | **3:42** |
| **2007-08** | **Tampa Bay** | **NHL** | **61** | **1** | **3** | **4** | **45** | **0** | **0** | **0** | **23** | **4.3** | **-3** | **0** | **0.0** | **9:20** | .... | .... | .... | .... | .... | .... | .... | .... | .... |
| **2008-09** | **Dallas** | **NHL** | **13** | **0** | **1** | **1** | **2** | **0** | **0** | **0** | **1** | **0.0** | **-2** | **0** | **0.0** | **9:45** | .... | .... | .... | .... | .... | .... | .... | .... | .... |
| | Rockford IceHogs | AHL | 4 | 0 | 2 | 2 | 4 | .... | .... | .... | .... | .... | .... | .... | .... | .... | .... | .... | .... | .... | .... | .... | .... | .... | .... |
| | **Montreal** | **NHL** | **2** | **0** | **0** | **0** | **2** | **0** | **0** | **0** | **0** | **0.0** | **-1** | **0** | **0.0** | **13:54** | .... | .... | .... | .... | .... | .... | .... | .... | .... |
| | Hamilton | AHL | 18 | 0 | 5 | 5 | 10 | .... | .... | .... | .... | .... | .... | .... | .... | .... | 6 | 0 | 0 | 0 | 7 | .... | .... | .... | .... |
| | **NHL Totals** | | **161** | **3** | **13** | **16** | **123** | **0** | **0** | **0** | **77** | **3.9** | | **0** | **0.0** | **11:44** | **6** | **1** | **0** | **1** | **2** | **0** | **0** | **0** | **9:22** |

Signed as a free agent by **Tampa Bay**, July 6, 2006. Signed as a free agent by **Chicago**, July 15, 2008. Claimed on waivers by **Dallas** from **Chicago**, October 2, 2008. Claimed on waivers by **Chicago** from **Dallas**, October 8, 2008. Traded to **Dallas** by **Chicago** for future considerations, October 8, 2008. Traded to **Montreal** by **Dallas** for Steve Begin, February 26, 2009. Signed as a free agent by **Detroit**, July 8, 2009.

## JANSSEN, Cam

(JAN-suhn, KAM) **ST.L.**

Right wing. Shoots right. 6', 218 lbs. Born, St. Louis, MO, April 15, 1984. New Jersey's 6th choice, 117th overall, in 2002 Entry Draft.

| | | | | | | | | | | | | | | | | | | | | | | | | | |
|---|---|---|---|---|---|---|---|---|---|---|---|---|---|---|---|---|---|---|---|---|---|---|---|---|---|
| 2000-01 | St. Louis Jr. Blues | CSJHL | 45 | 1 | 2 | 3 | 244 | .... | .... | .... | .... | .... | .... | .... | .... | .... | .... | .... | .... | .... | .... | .... | .... | .... | .... |
| 2001-02 | Windsor Spitfires | OHL | 64 | 5 | 17 | 22 | *268 | .... | .... | .... | .... | .... | .... | .... | .... | .... | 10 | 0 | 0 | 0 | 13 | .... | .... | .... | .... |
| 2002-03 | Windsor Spitfires | OHL | 50 | 1 | 12 | 13 | 211 | .... | .... | .... | .... | .... | .... | .... | .... | .... | 7 | 0 | 1 | 1 | 22 | .... | .... | .... | .... |
| 2003-04 | Windsor Spitfires | OHL | 35 | 4 | 9 | 13 | 144 | .... | .... | .... | .... | .... | .... | .... | .... | .... | .... | .... | .... | .... | .... | .... | .... | .... | .... |
| | Guelph Storm | OHL | 29 | 7 | 4 | 11 | 125 | .... | .... | .... | .... | .... | .... | .... | .... | .... | 22 | 3 | 3 | 6 | 49 | .... | .... | .... | .... |
| 2004-05 | Albany River Rats | AHL | 70 | 1 | 3 | 4 | 337 | .... | .... | .... | .... | .... | .... | .... | .... | .... | .... | .... | .... | .... | .... | .... | .... | .... | .... |
| **2005-06** | **New Jersey** | **NHL** | **47** | **0** | **0** | **0** | **91** | **0** | **0** | **0** | **10** | **0.0** | **-3** | **2** | **100.0** | **4:44** | **9** | **0** | **0** | **0** | **26** | **0** | **0** | **0** | **3:43** |
| | Albany River Rats | AHL | 26 | 1 | 3 | 4 | 117 | .... | .... | .... | .... | .... | .... | .... | .... | .... | .... | .... | .... | .... | .... | .... | .... | .... | .... |
| **2006-07** | **New Jersey** | **NHL** | **48** | **1** | **0** | **1** | **114** | **0** | **0** | **0** | **9** | **11.1** | **-2** | **1** | **100.0** | **4:06** | .... | .... | .... | .... | .... | .... | .... | .... | .... |
| | Lowell Devils | AHL | 9 | 0 | 1 | 1 | 29 | .... | .... | .... | .... | .... | .... | .... | .... | .... | .... | .... | .... | .... | .... | .... | .... | .... | .... |
| **2007-08** | **St. Louis** | **NHL** | **12** | **0** | **1** | **1** | **18** | **0** | **0** | **0** | **9** | **0.0** | **-1** | **0** | **0.0** | **7:07** | .... | .... | .... | .... | .... | .... | .... | .... | .... |
| | Lowell Devils | AHL | 3 | 0 | 0 | 0 | 4 | .... | .... | .... | .... | .... | .... | .... | .... | .... | .... | .... | .... | .... | .... | .... | .... | .... | .... |
| **2008-09** | **St. Louis** | **NHL** | **56** | **1** | **3** | **4** | **131** | **0** | **0** | **0** | **22** | **4.5** | **-5** | **2** | **0.0** | **5:01** | **1** | **0** | **0** | **0** | **0** | **0** | **0** | **0** | **3:59** |
| | **NHL Totals** | | **163** | **2** | **4** | **6** | **354** | **0** | **0** | **0** | **50** | **4.0** | | **5** | **60.0** | **4:49** | **10** | **0** | **0** | **0** | **26** | **0** | **0** | **0** | **3:45** |

Traded to **St. Louis** by **New Jersey** for Bryce Salvador, February 26, 2008.

## JEFFREY, Dustin

(JEHF-ree, DUHS-tihn) **PIT.**

Center. Shoots left. 6'1", 205 lbs. Born, Sarnia, Ont., February 27, 1988. Pittsburgh's 8th choice, 171st overall, in 2007 Entry Draft.

| | | | | | | | | | | | | | | | | | | | | | | | | | |
|---|---|---|---|---|---|---|---|---|---|---|---|---|---|---|---|---|---|---|---|---|---|---|---|---|---|
| 2003-04 | Lambton Sting | Minor-ON | 40 | 44 | 23 | 67 | 22 | .... | .... | .... | .... | .... | .... | .... | .... | .... | .... | .... | .... | .... | .... | .... | .... | .... | .... |
| 2004-05 | Mississauga | OHL | 53 | 10 | 15 | 25 | 20 | .... | .... | .... | .... | .... | .... | .... | .... | .... | .... | .... | .... | .... | .... | .... | .... | .... | .... |
| 2005-06 | Mississauga | OHL | 30 | 6 | 9 | 15 | 26 | .... | .... | .... | .... | .... | .... | .... | .... | .... | .... | .... | .... | .... | .... | .... | .... | .... | .... |
| | Sault Ste. Marie | OHL | 39 | 12 | 11 | 23 | 10 | .... | .... | .... | .... | .... | .... | .... | .... | .... | 4 | 1 | 2 | 3 | 2 | .... | .... | .... | .... |
| 2006-07 | Sault Ste. Marie | OHL | 68 | 34 | 58 | 92 | 40 | .... | .... | .... | .... | .... | .... | .... | .... | .... | 13 | 6 | 12 | 18 | 11 | .... | .... | .... | .... |
| 2007-08 | Sault Ste. Marie | OHL | 56 | 38 | 59 | 97 | 30 | .... | .... | .... | .... | .... | .... | .... | .... | .... | 14 | 3 | 8 | 11 | 12 | .... | .... | .... | .... |
| | Wilkes-Barre | AHL | .... | .... | .... | .... | .... | .... | .... | .... | .... | .... | .... | .... | .... | .... | 15 | 2 | 1 | 3 | 4 | .... | .... | .... | .... |
| **2008-09** | **Pittsburgh** | **NHL** | **14** | **1** | **2** | **3** | **0** | **0** | **0** | **0** | **18** | **5.6** | **4** | **103** | **41.8** | **10:47** | .... | .... | .... | .... | .... | .... | .... | .... | .... |
| | Wilkes-Barre | AHL | 63 | 11 | 26 | 37 | 31 | .... | .... | .... | .... | .... | .... | .... | .... | .... | 12 | 5 | 5 | 10 | 8 | .... | .... | .... | .... |
| | **NHL Totals** | | **14** | **1** | **2** | **3** | **0** | **0** | **0** | **0** | **18** | **5.6** | | **103** | **41.7** | **10:47** | .... | .... | .... | .... | .... | .... | .... | .... | .... |

## JENSEN, Joe

(JEHN-suhn, JOH)

Center. Shoots left. 5'11", 180 lbs. Born, Maple Grove, MN, February 6, 1983. Pittsburgh's 10th choice, 232nd overall, in 2003 Entry Draft.

| | | | Regular Season | | | | | | | | | | | | | | Playoffs | | | | | | | | |
|---|---|---|---|---|---|---|---|---|---|---|---|---|---|---|---|---|---|---|---|---|---|---|---|---|---|
| Season | Club | League | GP | G | A | Pts | PIM | PP | SH | GW | S | % | +/- | TF | F% | Min | GP | G | A | Pts | PIM | PP | SH | GW | Min |
| 2000-01 | Sioux City | USHL | 56 | 14 | 20 | 34 | 59 | .... | .... | .... | .... | .... | .... | .... | .... | .... | 8 | 2 | 4 | 6 | 12 | .... | .... | .... | .... |
| 2001-02 | Sioux City | USHL | 57 | 20 | 26 | 46 | 135 | .... | .... | .... | .... | .... | .... | .... | .... | .... | 3 | 0 | 0 | 0 | 6 | .... | .... | .... | .... |
| 2002-03 | St. Cloud State | WCHA | 37 | 9 | 9 | 18 | 14 | .... | .... | .... | .... | .... | .... | .... | .... | .... | .... | .... | .... | .... | .... | .... | .... | .... | .... |
| 2003-04 | St. Cloud State | WCHA | 38 | 10 | 14 | 24 | 42 | .... | .... | .... | .... | .... | .... | .... | .... | .... | .... | .... | .... | .... | .... | .... | .... | .... | .... |
| 2004-05 | St. Cloud State | WCHA | 40 | 12 | 14 | 26 | 36 | .... | .... | .... | .... | .... | .... | .... | .... | .... | .... | .... | .... | .... | .... | .... | .... | .... | .... |
| 2005-06 | St. Cloud State | WCHA | 38 | 14 | 18 | 32 | 14 | .... | .... | .... | .... | .... | .... | .... | .... | .... | .... | .... | .... | .... | .... | .... | .... | .... | .... |
| 2006-07 | Wilkes-Barre | AHL | 26 | 6 | 5 | 11 | 16 | .... | .... | .... | .... | .... | .... | .... | .... | .... | 7 | 2 | 1 | 3 | 6 | .... | .... | .... | .... |
| | Wheeling Nailers | ECHL | 28 | 11 | 18 | 29 | 45 | .... | .... | .... | .... | .... | .... | .... | .... | .... | .... | .... | .... | .... | .... | .... | .... | .... | .... |
| **2007-08** | Wilkes-Barre | AHL | 27 | 2 | 2 | 4 | 23 | .... | .... | .... | .... | .... | .... | .... | .... | .... | .... | .... | .... | .... | .... | .... | .... | .... | .... |
| | Wheeling Nailers | ECHL | 9 | 4 | 3 | 7 | 28 | .... | .... | .... | .... | .... | .... | .... | .... | .... | .... | .... | .... | .... | .... | .... | .... | .... | .... |
| | **Carolina** | **NHL** | **6** | **1** | **0** | **1** | **2** | **0** | **0** | **1** | **6** | **16.7** | **1** | **14** | **42.9** | **6:30** | .... | .... | .... | .... | .... | .... | .... | .... | .... |
| | Albany River Rats | AHL | 24 | 8 | 3 | 11 | 27 | .... | .... | .... | .... | .... | .... | .... | .... | .... | 7 | 1 | 0 | 1 | 8 | .... | .... | .... | .... |
| 2008-09 | Albany River Rats | AHL | 32 | 6 | 8 | 14 | 31 | .... | .... | .... | .... | .... | .... | .... | .... | .... | .... | .... | .... | .... | .... | .... | .... | .... | .... |
| | **NHL Totals** | | **6** | **1** | **0** | **1** | **2** | **0** | **0** | **1** | **6** | **16.7** | | **14** | **42.9** | **6:30** | .... | .... | .... | .... | .... | .... | .... | .... | .... |

Traded to **Carolina** by **Pittsburgh** for David Gove, January 31, 2008. • Missed majority of 2008-09 season recovering from various injuries.

## JILLSON, Jeff

(JIHL-suhn, JEHF)

Defense. Shoots right. 6'3", 215 lbs. Born, North Smithfield, RI, July 24, 1980. San Jose's 1st choice, 14th overall, in 1999 Entry Draft.

| Season | Club | League | GP | G | A | Pts | PIM | PP | SH | GW | S | % | +/- | TF | F% | Min | GP | G | A | Pts | PIM | PP | SH | GW | Min |
|---|---|---|---|---|---|---|---|---|---|---|---|---|---|---|---|---|---|---|---|---|---|---|---|---|---|
| 1995-96 | Mount St. Charles | High-RI | 15 | 8 | 7 | 15 | 15 | .... | .... | .... | .... | .... | .... | .... | .... | .... | 5 | 1 | 1 | 2 | 4 | .... | .... | .... | .... |
| 1996-97 | Mount St. Charles | High-RI | 15 | 16 | 14 | 30 | 20 | .... | .... | .... | .... | .... | .... | .... | .... | .... | 4 | 0 | 4 | 4 | 6 | .... | .... | .... | .... |
| 1997-98 | Mount St. Charles | High-RI | 15 | 10 | 13 | 23 | 32 | .... | .... | .... | .... | .... | .... | .... | .... | .... | 5 | 4 | 5 | 9 | 6 | .... | .... | .... | .... |
| 1998-99 | U. of Michigan | CCHA | 38 | 5 | 19 | 24 | 71 | .... | .... | .... | .... | .... | .... | .... | .... | .... | .... | .... | .... | .... | .... | .... | .... | .... | .... |
| 99-2000 | U. of Michigan | CCHA | 38 | 8 | 26 | 34 | 115 | .... | .... | .... | .... | .... | .... | .... | .... | .... | .... | .... | .... | .... | .... | .... | .... | .... | .... |
| 2000-01 | U. of Michigan | CCHA | 43 | 10 | 20 | 30 | 74 | .... | .... | .... | .... | .... | .... | .... | .... | .... | .... | .... | .... | .... | .... | .... | .... | .... | .... |
| **2001-02** | **San Jose** | **NHL** | **48** | **5** | **13** | **18** | **29** | **3** | **0** | **2** | **47** | **10.6** | **2** | **0** | **0.0** | **14:36** | **4** | **0** | **0** | **0** | **0** | **0** | **0** | **0** | **5:45** |
| | Cleveland Barons | AHL | 27 | 2 | 13 | 15 | 45 | .... | .... | .... | .... | .... | .... | .... | .... | .... | .... | .... | .... | .... | .... | .... | .... | .... | .... |
| **2002-03** | **San Jose** | **NHL** | **26** | **0** | **6** | **6** | **9** | **0** | **0** | **0** | **22** | **0.0** | **-7** | **0** | **0.0** | **13:45** | .... | .... | .... | .... | .... | .... | .... | .... | .... |
| | Cleveland Barons | AHL | 19 | 3 | 5 | 8 | 12 | .... | .... | .... | .... | .... | .... | .... | .... | .... | .... | .... | .... | .... | .... | .... | .... | .... | .... |
| | Providence Bruins | AHL | 30 | 4 | 11 | 15 | 26 | .... | .... | .... | .... | .... | .... | .... | .... | .... | 4 | 0 | 2 | 2 | 8 | .... | .... | .... | .... |
| **2003-04** | **Boston** | **NHL** | **50** | **4** | **10** | **14** | **35** | **1** | **0** | **1** | **80** | **5.0** | **-1** | **0** | **0.0** | **17:53** | .... | .... | .... | .... | .... | .... | .... | .... | .... |
| | **Buffalo** | **NHL** | **14** | **0** | **3** | **3** | **19** | **0** | **0** | **0** | **35** | **0.0** | **-3** | **0** | **0.0** | **18:21** | .... | .... | .... | .... | .... | .... | .... | .... | .... |
| 2004-05 | Rochester | AHL | 78 | 12 | 17 | 29 | 46 | .... | .... | .... | .... | .... | .... | .... | .... | .... | 9 | 1 | 1 | 2 | 12 | .... | .... | .... | .... |
| **2005-06** | **Buffalo** | **NHL** | **2** | **0** | **0** | **0** | **4** | **0** | **0** | **0** | **1** | **0.0** | **0** | **0** | **0.0** | **14:40** | **4** | **0** | **0** | **0** | **0** | **0** | **0** | **0** | **11:41** |
| | Rochester | AHL | 73 | 10 | 20 | 30 | 94 | .... | .... | .... | .... | .... | .... | .... | .... | .... | .... | .... | .... | .... | .... | .... | .... | .... | .... |
| 2006-07 | Eisbaren Berlin | Germany | 30 | 2 | 9 | 11 | 48 | .... | .... | .... | .... | .... | .... | .... | .... | .... | 1 | 0 | 0 | 0 | 2 | .... | .... | .... | .... |
| 2007-08 | Lake Erie | AHL | 70 | 3 | 19 | 22 | 46 | .... | .... | .... | .... | .... | .... | .... | .... | .... | .... | .... | .... | .... | .... | .... | .... | .... | .... |
| 2008-09 | MVD | Rus-KHL | 12 | 1 | 2 | 3 | 14 | .... | .... | .... | .... | .... | .... | .... | .... | .... | .... | .... | .... | .... | .... | .... | .... | .... | .... |
| | Lukko Rauma | Finland | 29 | 2 | 7 | 9 | 20 | .... | .... | .... | .... | .... | .... | .... | .... | .... | 7 | 0 | 1 | 1 | 4 | .... | .... | .... | .... |
| | **NHL Totals** | | **140** | **9** | **32** | **41** | **96** | **4** | **0** | **3** | **185** | **4.9** | | **0** | **0.0** | **15:59** | **8** | **0** | **0** | **0** | **0** | **0** | **0** | **0** | **8:43** |

CCHA All-Rookie Team (1999) • CCHA First All-Star Team (2000, 2001) • NCAA West First All-American Team (2000) • NCAA West Second All-American Team (2001)

Traded to **Boston** by **San Jose** with Jeff Hackett for Kyle McLaren and Boston's 4th round choice (Torrey Mitchell) in 2004 Entry Draft, January 23, 2003. Traded to **San Jose** by **Boston** for Brad Boyes, March 9, 2004. Traded to **Buffalo** by **San Jose** with San Jose's compensatory 7th round choice (Andrew Orpik) in 2005 Entry Draft for Curtis Brown and Andy Delmore, March 9, 2004. Signed as a free agent by **Berlin** (Germany), October 25, 2006. Signed as a free agent by **Colorado**, July 17, 2007.

## JOENSUU, Jesse

(YOH-ehn-soo, JEH-see) **NYI**

Wing. Shoots left. 6'4", 207 lbs. Born, Pori, Finland, October 5, 1987. NY Islanders' 2nd choice, 60th overall, in 2006 Entry Draft.

| Season | Club | League | GP | G | A | Pts | PIM | PP | SH | GW | S | % | +/- | TF | F% | Min | GP | G | A | Pts | PIM | PP | SH | GW | Min |
|---|---|---|---|---|---|---|---|---|---|---|---|---|---|---|---|---|---|---|---|---|---|---|---|---|---|
| 2002-03 | Assat Pori U18 | Fin-U18 | 26 | 8 | 10 | 18 | 53 | .... | .... | .... | .... | .... | .... | .... | .... | .... | 3 | 1 | 2 | 3 | 0 | .... | .... | .... | .... |
| | Assat Pori Jr. | Fin-Jr. | 3 | 0 | 1 | 1 | 2 | .... | .... | .... | .... | .... | .... | .... | .... | .... | .... | .... | .... | .... | .... | .... | .... | .... | .... |
| 2003-04 | Assat Pori U18 | Fin-U18 | 6 | 7 | 2 | 9 | 8 | .... | .... | .... | .... | .... | .... | .... | .... | .... | .... | .... | .... | .... | .... | .... | .... | .... | .... |
| | Assat Pori Jr. | Fin-Jr. | 28 | 7 | 9 | 16 | 18 | .... | .... | .... | .... | .... | .... | .... | .... | .... | 3 | 0 | 1 | 1 | 2 | .... | .... | .... | .... |
| | Assat Pori | Finland | 6 | 0 | 0 | 0 | 0 | .... | .... | .... | .... | .... | .... | .... | .... | .... | .... | .... | .... | .... | .... | .... | .... | .... | .... |
| 2004-05 | Assat Pori Jr. | Fin-Jr. | 17 | 7 | 13 | 20 | 20 | .... | .... | .... | .... | .... | .... | .... | .... | .... | 2 | 1 | 1 | 2 | 2 | .... | .... | .... | .... |
| | Assat Pori | Finland | 39 | 1 | 1 | 2 | 4 | .... | .... | .... | .... | .... | .... | .... | .... | .... | .... | .... | .... | .... | .... | .... | .... | .... | .... |
| 2005-06 | Suomi U20 | Finland-2 | 2 | 1 | 0 | 1 | 12 | .... | .... | .... | .... | .... | .... | .... | .... | .... | .... | .... | .... | .... | .... | .... | .... | .... | .... |
| | Assat Pori | Finland | 51 | 4 | 8 | 12 | 57 | .... | .... | .... | .... | .... | .... | .... | .... | .... | 14 | 0 | 2 | 2 | 12 | .... | .... | .... | .... |
| 2006-07 | Assat Pori Jr. | Fin-Jr. | 5 | 2 | 1 | 3 | 6 | .... | .... | .... | .... | .... | .... | .... | .... | .... | .... | .... | .... | .... | .... | .... | .... | .... | .... |
| | Suomi U20 | Finland-2 | 2 | 0 | 2 | 2 | 6 | .... | .... | .... | .... | .... | .... | .... | .... | .... | .... | .... | .... | .... | .... | .... | .... | .... | .... |
| | Assat Pori | Finland | 52 | 9 | 17 | 26 | 74 | .... | .... | .... | .... | .... | .... | .... | .... | .... | .... | .... | .... | .... | .... | .... | .... | .... | .... |
| 2007-08 | Assat Pori | Finland | 56 | 17 | 18 | 35 | 89 | .... | .... | .... | .... | .... | .... | .... | .... | .... | .... | .... | .... | .... | .... | .... | .... | .... | .... |
| | Bridgeport | AHL | 1 | 0 | 0 | 0 | 0 | .... | .... | .... | .... | .... | .... | .... | .... | .... | .... | .... | .... | .... | .... | .... | .... | .... | .... |
| **2008-09** | **NY Islanders** | **NHL** | **7** | **1** | **2** | **3** | **4** | **0** | **0** | **0** | **9** | **11.1** | **-1** | **0** | **0.0** | **12:06** | .... | .... | .... | .... | .... | .... | .... | .... | .... |
| | Bridgeport | AHL | 71 | 20 | 19 | 39 | 58 | .... | .... | .... | .... | .... | .... | .... | .... | .... | 5 | 2 | 1 | 3 | 4 | .... | .... | .... | .... |
| | **NHL Totals** | | **7** | **1** | **2** | **3** | **4** | **0** | **0** | **0** | **9** | **11.1** | | **0** | **0.0** | **12:06** | .... | .... | .... | .... | .... | .... | .... | .... | .... |

## JOHNSON, Aaron

(JAWN-suhn, AIR-ruhn) **CHI.**

Defense. Shoots left. 6'1", 211 lbs. Born, Port Hawkesbury, N.S., April 30, 1983. Columbus' 4th choice, 85th overall, in 2001 Entry Draft.

| Season | Club | League | GP | G | A | Pts | PIM | PP | SH | GW | S | % | +/- | TF | F% | Min | GP | G | A | Pts | PIM | PP | SH | GW | Min |
|---|---|---|---|---|---|---|---|---|---|---|---|---|---|---|---|---|---|---|---|---|---|---|---|---|---|
| 1998-99 | Cape Breton | NSAHA | 56 | 28 | 42 | 70 | 98 | .... | .... | .... | .... | .... | .... | .... | .... | .... | .... | .... | .... | .... | .... | .... | .... | .... | .... |
| 99-2000 | Rimouski Oceanic | QMJHL | 63 | 1 | 14 | 15 | 57 | .... | .... | .... | .... | .... | .... | .... | .... | .... | 8 | 0 | 0 | 0 | 0 | .... | .... | .... | .... |
| 2000-01 | Rimouski Oceanic | QMJHL | 64 | 12 | 41 | 53 | 128 | .... | .... | .... | .... | .... | .... | .... | .... | .... | 11 | 2 | 4 | 6 | 35 | .... | .... | .... | .... |
| 2001-02 | Rimouski Oceanic | QMJHL | 68 | 17 | 49 | 66 | 172 | .... | .... | .... | .... | .... | .... | .... | .... | .... | 7 | 1 | 2 | 3 | 12 | .... | .... | .... | .... |
| 2002-03 | Rimouski Oceanic | QMJHL | 25 | 4 | 20 | 24 | 41 | .... | .... | .... | .... | .... | .... | .... | .... | .... | .... | .... | .... | .... | .... | .... | .... | .... | .... |
| | Quebec Remparts | QMJHL | 32 | 6 | 31 | 37 | 41 | .... | .... | .... | .... | .... | .... | .... | .... | .... | 11 | 4 | 4 | 8 | 25 | .... | .... | .... | .... |
| **2003-04** | **Columbus** | **NHL** | **29** | **2** | **6** | **8** | **32** | **0** | **0** | **1** | **33** | **6.1** | **-2** | **0** | **0.0** | **15:02** | .... | .... | .... | .... | .... | .... | .... | .... | .... |
| | Syracuse Crunch | AHL | 49 | 6 | 15 | 21 | 83 | .... | .... | .... | .... | .... | .... | .... | .... | .... | 7 | 2 | 3 | 5 | 27 | .... | .... | .... | .... |
| 2004-05 | Syracuse Crunch | AHL | 77 | 6 | 17 | 23 | 140 | .... | .... | .... | .... | .... | .... | .... | .... | .... | .... | .... | .... | .... | .... | .... | .... | .... | .... |
| **2005-06** | **Columbus** | **NHL** | **26** | **2** | **6** | **8** | **23** | **1** | **0** | **1** | **28** | **7.1** | **9** | **0** | **0.0** | **14:12** | .... | .... | .... | .... | .... | .... | .... | .... | .... |
| | Syracuse Crunch | AHL | 49 | 5 | 24 | 29 | 122 | .... | .... | .... | .... | .... | .... | .... | .... | .... | 6 | 1 | 3 | 4 | 19 | .... | .... | .... | .... |
| **2006-07** | **Columbus** | **NHL** | **61** | **3** | **7** | **10** | **38** | **0** | **0** | **0** | **52** | **5.8** | **-9** | **0** | **0.0** | **12:44** | .... | .... | .... | .... | .... | .... | .... | .... | .... |
| **2007-08** | **NY Islanders** | **NHL** | **30** | **0** | **2** | **2** | **30** | **0** | **0** | **0** | **16** | **0.0** | **2** | **0** | **0.0** | **13:52** | .... | .... | .... | .... | .... | .... | .... | .... | .... |
| | Bridgeport | AHL | 2 | 0 | 0 | 0 | 0 | .... | .... | .... | .... | .... | .... | .... | .... | .... | .... | .... | .... | .... | .... | .... | .... | .... | .... |
| **2008-09** | **Chicago** | **NHL** | **38** | **3** | **5** | **8** | **33** | **0** | **0** | **1** | **27** | **11.1** | **19** | **0** | **0.0** | **14:09** | .... | .... | .... | .... | .... | .... | .... | .... | .... |
| | Rockford IceHogs | AHL | 2 | 0 | 1 | 1 | 4 | .... | .... | .... | .... | .... | .... | .... | .... | .... | .... | .... | .... | .... | .... | .... | .... | .... | .... |
| | **NHL Totals** | | **184** | **10** | **26** | **36** | **156** | **1** | **0** | **3** | **156** | **6.4** | | **0** | **0.0** | **13:46** | .... | .... | .... | .... | .... | .... | .... | .... | .... |

Signed as a free agent by **NY Islanders**, July 12, 2007. • Missed majority of 2007-08 season recovering from recurring knee injury and serving as a healthy reserve. Signed as a free agent by **Chicago**, July 15, 2008.

## JOHNSON, Erik

(JAWN-suhn, AIR-ihk) **ST.L.**

Defense. Shoots right. 6'4", 225 lbs. Born, Bloomington, MN, March 21, 1988. St. Louis' 1st choice, 1st overall, in 2006 Entry Draft.

| Season | Club | League | GP | G | A | Pts | PIM | PP | SH | GW | S | % | +/- | TF | F% | Min | GP | G | A | Pts | PIM | PP | SH | GW | Min |
|---|---|---|---|---|---|---|---|---|---|---|---|---|---|---|---|---|---|---|---|---|---|---|---|---|---|
| 2003-04 | Holy Angels | High-MN | 31 | 13 | 21 | 34 | .... | .... | .... | .... | .... | .... | .... | .... | .... | .... | .... | .... | .... | .... | .... | .... | .... | .... | .... |
| 2004-05 | USNTDP | U-17 | 26 | 5 | 9 | 14 | 14 | .... | .... | .... | .... | .... | .... | .... | .... | .... | .... | .... | .... | .... | .... | .... | .... | .... | .... |
| | USNTDP | NAHL | 31 | 6 | 6 | 12 | 12 | .... | .... | .... | .... | .... | .... | .... | .... | .... | .... | .... | .... | .... | .... | .... | .... | .... | .... |
| 2005-06 | USNTDP | U-18 | 36 | 12 | 22 | 34 | 78 | .... | .... | .... | .... | .... | .... | .... | .... | .... | .... | .... | .... | .... | .... | .... | .... | .... | .... |
| | USNTDP | NAHL | 11 | 4 | 11 | 15 | 10 | .... | .... | .... | .... | .... | .... | .... | .... | .... | .... | .... | .... | .... | .... | .... | .... | .... | .... |
| 2006-07 | U. of Minnesota | WCHA | 41 | 4 | 20 | 24 | 50 | .... | .... | .... | .... | .... | .... | .... | .... | .... | .... | .... | .... | .... | .... | .... | .... | .... | .... |
| **2007-08** | **St. Louis** | **NHL** | **69** | **5** | **28** | **33** | **28** | **4** | **0** | **3** | **105** | **4.8** | **-9** | **1** | **0.0** | **18:11** | .... | .... | .... | .... | .... | .... | .... | .... | .... |
| | Peoria Rivermen | AHL | 1 | 0 | 0 | 0 | 2 | .... | .... | .... | .... | .... | .... | .... | .... | .... | .... | .... | .... | .... | .... | .... | .... | .... | .... |
| **2008-09** | **St. Louis** | **NHL** | DID NOT PLAY – INJURED | | | | | | | | | | | | | | | | | | | | | | |
| | **NHL Totals** | | **69** | **5** | **28** | **33** | **28** | **4** | **0** | **3** | **105** | **4.8** | | **1** | **0.0** | **18:11** | .... | .... | .... | .... | .... | .... | .... | .... | .... |

WCHA All-Rookie Team (2007)

• Missed entire 2008-09 season recovering from off-ice knee injury, September 16, 2008 and resulting surgery, November 20, 2008.

**JOHNSON, Jack** (JAHN-suhn, JAK) **L.A.**

Defense. Shoots left. 6'1", 225 lbs. Born, Indianapolis, IN, January 13, 1987. Carolina's 1st choice, 3rd overall, in 2005 Entry Draft.

| | | | Regular Season | | | | | | | | | | | | | | Playoffs | | | | | | | | |
|---|---|---|---|---|---|---|---|---|---|---|---|---|---|---|---|---|---|---|---|---|---|---|---|---|---|
| Season | Club | League | GP | G | A | Pts | PIM | PP | SH | GW | S | % | +/- | TF | F% | Min | GP | G | A | Pts | PIM | PP | SH | GW | Min |
| 2002-03 | Shat.-St. Mary's | High-MN | 48 | 15 | 27 | 42 | .... | .... | .... | .... | .... | .... | .... | .... | .... | .... | .... | .... | .... | .... | .... | .... | .... | .... | .... |
| 2003-04 | USNTDP | U-17 | 31 | 12 | 9 | 21 | 78 | .... | .... | .... | .... | .... | .... | .... | .... | .... | .... | .... | .... | .... | .... | .... | .... | .... | .... |
| | USNTDP | NAHL | 29 | 3 | 12 | 15 | 93 | .... | .... | .... | .... | .... | .... | .... | .... | .... | .... | .... | .... | .... | .... | .... | .... | .... | .... |
| 2004-05 | USNTDP | U-18 | 26 | 5 | 9 | 14 | 86 | .... | .... | .... | .... | .... | .... | .... | .... | .... | .... | .... | .... | .... | .... | .... | .... | .... | .... |
| | USNTDP | NAHL | 12 | 7 | 10 | 17 | 57 | .... | .... | .... | .... | .... | .... | .... | .... | .... | .... | .... | .... | .... | .... | .... | .... | .... | .... |
| 2005-06 | U. of Michigan | CCHA | 38 | 10 | 22 | 32 | *149 | .... | .... | .... | .... | .... | .... | .... | .... | .... | .... | .... | .... | .... | .... | .... | .... | .... | .... |
| **2006-07** | U. of Michigan | CCHA | 36 | 16 | 23 | 39 | 87 | .... | .... | .... | .... | .... | .... | .... | .... | .... | .... | .... | .... | .... | .... | .... | .... | .... | .... |
| | **Los Angeles** | **NHL** | **5** | **0** | **0** | **0** | **18** | **0** | **0** | **0** | **5** | **0.0** | **–5** | **0** | **0.0** | **21:23** | .... | .... | .... | .... | .... | .... | .... | .... | .... |
| **2007-08** | **Los Angeles** | **NHL** | **74** | **3** | **8** | **11** | **76** | **0** | **0** | **0** | **81** | **3.7** | **–19** | **5** | **60.0** | **21:42** | .... | .... | .... | .... | .... | .... | .... | .... | .... |
| **2008-09** | **Los Angeles** | **NHL** | **41** | **6** | **5** | **11** | **46** | **3** | **0** | **0** | **50** | **12.0** | **–18** | **0** | **0.0** | **20:17** | .... | .... | .... | .... | .... | .... | .... | .... | .... |
| | **NHL Totals** | | **120** | **9** | **13** | **22** | **140** | **3** | **0** | **0** | **136** | **6.6** | | **5** | **60.0** | **21:12** | .... | .... | .... | .... | .... | .... | .... | .... | .... |

CCHA All-Rookie Team (2006) • CCHA First All-Star Team (2007) • NCAA West First All-American Team (2007)

Traded to **Los Angeles** by **Carolina** with Oleg Tverdovsky for Eric Belanger and Tim Gleason, September 29, 2006.

**JOHNSON, Ryan** (JAWN-suhn, RIGH-uhn) **VAN.**

Center. Shoots left. 6'1", 202 lbs. Born, Thunder Bay, Ont., June 14, 1976. Florida's 4th choice, 36th overall, in 1994 Entry Draft.

| | | | Regular Season | | | | | | | | | | | | | | Playoffs | | | | | | | | |
|---|---|---|---|---|---|---|---|---|---|---|---|---|---|---|---|---|---|---|---|---|---|---|---|---|---|
| Season | Club | League | GP | G | A | Pts | PIM | PP | SH | GW | S | % | +/- | TF | F% | Min | GP | G | A | Pts | PIM | PP | SH | GW | Min |
| 1992-93 | Thunder Bay | TBAHA | 60 | 25 | 33 | 58 | .... | .... | .... | .... | .... | .... | .... | .... | .... | .... | .... | .... | .... | .... | .... | .... | .... | .... | .... |
| 1993-94 | Thunder Bay | USHL | 48 | 14 | 36 | 50 | 28 | .... | .... | .... | .... | .... | .... | .... | .... | .... | .... | .... | .... | .... | .... | .... | .... | .... | .... |
| 1994-95 | North Dakota | WCHA | 38 | 6 | 22 | 28 | 39 | .... | .... | .... | .... | .... | .... | .... | .... | .... | .... | .... | .... | .... | .... | .... | .... | .... | .... |
| 1995-96 | North Dakota | WCHA | 21 | 2 | 17 | 19 | 14 | .... | .... | .... | .... | .... | .... | .... | .... | .... | .... | .... | .... | .... | .... | .... | .... | .... | .... |
| | Canada | Nat-Tm | 28 | 5 | 12 | 17 | 14 | .... | .... | .... | .... | .... | .... | .... | .... | .... | .... | .... | .... | .... | .... | .... | .... | .... | .... |
| 1996-97 | Carolina | AHL | 79 | 18 | 24 | 42 | 28 | .... | .... | .... | .... | .... | .... | .... | .... | .... | .... | .... | .... | .... | .... | .... | .... | .... | .... |
| **1997-98** | **Florida** | **NHL** | **10** | **0** | **2** | **2** | **0** | **0** | **0** | **0** | **6** | **0.0** | **–4** | .... | .... | .... | .... | .... | .... | .... | .... | .... | .... | .... | .... |
| | New Haven | AHL | 64 | 19 | 48 | 67 | 12 | .... | .... | .... | .... | .... | .... | .... | .... | .... | 3 | 0 | 1 | 1 | 0 | .... | .... | .... | .... |
| **1998-99** | **Florida** | **NHL** | **1** | **1** | **0** | **1** | **0** | **0** | **0** | **0** | **1** | **100.0** | **0** | **16** | **37.5** | **15:26** | .... | .... | .... | .... | .... | .... | .... | .... | .... |
| | New Haven | AHL | 37 | 8 | 19 | 27 | 18 | .... | .... | .... | .... | .... | .... | .... | .... | .... | .... | .... | .... | .... | .... | .... | .... | .... | .... |
| **99-2000** | **Florida** | **NHL** | **66** | **4** | **12** | **16** | **14** | **0** | **0** | **0** | **44** | **9.1** | **1** | **684** | **51.8** | **11:47** | .... | .... | .... | .... | .... | .... | .... | .... | .... |
| | **Tampa Bay** | **NHL** | **14** | **0** | **2** | **2** | **2** | **0** | **0** | **0** | **5** | **0.0** | **–9** | **117** | **53.0** | **11:02** | .... | .... | .... | .... | .... | .... | .... | .... | .... |
| **2000-01** | **Tampa Bay** | **NHL** | **80** | **7** | **14** | **21** | **44** | **1** | **0** | **0** | **71** | **9.9** | **–20** | **951** | **48.9** | **15:47** | .... | .... | .... | .... | .... | .... | .... | .... | .... |
| **2001-02** | **Florida** | **NHL** | **29** | **1** | **3** | **4** | **10** | **0** | **0** | **0** | **24** | **4.2** | **–5** | **336** | **47.9** | **13:00** | .... | .... | .... | .... | .... | .... | .... | .... | .... |
| **2002-03** | **Florida** | **NHL** | **58** | **2** | **5** | **7** | **26** | **0** | **0** | **0** | **54** | **3.7** | **–13** | **689** | **48.0** | **10:40** | .... | .... | .... | .... | .... | .... | .... | .... | .... |
| | **St. Louis** | **NHL** | **17** | **0** | **0** | **0** | **12** | **0** | **0** | **0** | **13** | **0.0** | **0** | **180** | **51.7** | **10:34** | **6** | **0** | **2** | **2** | **6** | **0** | **0** | **0** | **8:14** |
| **2003-04** | **St. Louis** | **NHL** | **69** | **4** | **7** | **11** | **8** | **0** | **1** | **1** | **36** | **11.1** | **–2** | **537** | **53.6** | **9:54** | **3** | **0** | **0** | **0** | **0** | **0** | **0** | **0** | **6:11** |
| 2004-05 | Missouri | UHL | 29 | 7 | 14 | 21 | 12 | .... | .... | .... | .... | .... | .... | .... | .... | .... | 6 | 1 | 0 | 1 | 13 | .... | .... | .... | .... |
| **2005-06** | **St. Louis** | **NHL** | **65** | **3** | **6** | **9** | **33** | **1** | **1** | **0** | **57** | **5.3** | **–21** | **569** | **55.9** | **11:24** | .... | .... | .... | .... | .... | .... | .... | .... | .... |
| **2006-07** | **St. Louis** | **NHL** | **59** | **7** | **4** | **11** | **47** | **0** | **2** | **0** | **50** | **14.0** | **–7** | **525** | **55.4** | **12:21** | .... | .... | .... | .... | .... | .... | .... | .... | .... |
| **2007-08** | **St. Louis** | **NHL** | **79** | **5** | **13** | **18** | **22** | **0** | **1** | **1** | **85** | **5.9** | **–2** | **803** | **54.6** | **14:22** | .... | .... | .... | .... | .... | .... | .... | .... | .... |
| **2008-09** | **Vancouver** | **NHL** | **62** | **2** | **7** | **9** | **12** | **0** | **0** | **1** | **22** | **9.1** | **1** | **565** | **48.5** | **11:01** | **10** | **1** | **1** | **2** | **2** | **0** | **0** | **0** | **11:52** |
| | **NHL Totals** | | **609** | **36** | **75** | **111** | **230** | **2** | **5** | **3** | **468** | **7.7** | | **5972** | **51.6** | **12:17** | **19** | **1** | **3** | **4** | **8** | **0** | **0** | **0** | **9:49** |

Traded to **Tampa Bay** by **Florida** with Dwayne Hay for Mike Sillinger, March 14, 2000. Traded to **Florida** by **Tampa Bay** with Tampa Bay's 6th round choice (later traded back to Tampa Bay – Tampa Bay selected Doug O'Brien) in 2003 Entry Draft for Vaclav Prospal, July 10, 2001. • Missed majority of 2001-02 season recovering from head injury suffered in game vs. St. Louis, December 22, 2001. Claimed on waivers by **St. Louis** from **Florida**, February 19, 2003. Signed as a free agent by **Missouri** (UHL), February 3, 2005. Signed as a free agent by **Vancouver**, July 2, 2008.

**JOHNSSON, Kim** (YAWN-suhn, KIHM) **MIN.**

Defense. Shoots left. 6'1", 193 lbs. Born, Malmo, Sweden, March 16, 1976. NY Rangers' 15th choice, 286th overall, in 1994 Entry Draft.

| | | | Regular Season | | | | | | | | | | | | | | Playoffs | | | | | | | | |
|---|---|---|---|---|---|---|---|---|---|---|---|---|---|---|---|---|---|---|---|---|---|---|---|---|---|
| Season | Club | League | GP | G | A | Pts | PIM | PP | SH | GW | S | % | +/- | TF | F% | Min | GP | G | A | Pts | PIM | PP | SH | GW | Min |
| 1993-94 | Malmo IF Jr. | Swe-Jr. | 14 | 5 | 3 | 8 | 14 | .... | .... | .... | .... | .... | .... | .... | .... | .... | .... | .... | .... | .... | .... | .... | .... | .... | .... |
| | Malmo IF | Sweden | 2 | 0 | 0 | 0 | 0 | .... | .... | .... | .... | .... | .... | .... | .... | .... | .... | .... | .... | .... | .... | .... | .... | .... | .... |
| 1994-95 | Malmo IF Jr. | Swe-Jr. | 29 | 6 | 15 | 21 | 40 | .... | .... | .... | .... | .... | .... | .... | .... | .... | .... | .... | .... | .... | .... | .... | .... | .... | .... |
| | Malmo IF | Sweden | 13 | 0 | 0 | 0 | 4 | .... | .... | .... | .... | .... | .... | .... | .... | .... | 1 | 0 | 0 | 0 | 0 | .... | .... | .... | .... |
| 1995-96 | Malmo IF | Sweden | 38 | 2 | 0 | 2 | 30 | .... | .... | .... | .... | .... | .... | .... | .... | .... | 4 | 0 | 1 | 1 | 8 | .... | .... | .... | .... |
| 1996-97 | Malmo | Sweden | 49 | 4 | 9 | 13 | 42 | .... | .... | .... | .... | .... | .... | .... | .... | .... | 4 | 0 | 0 | 0 | 2 | .... | .... | .... | .... |
| 1997-98 | Malmo | Sweden | 45 | 5 | 9 | 14 | 29 | .... | .... | .... | .... | .... | .... | .... | .... | .... | .... | .... | .... | .... | .... | .... | .... | .... | .... |
| 1998-99 | Malmo | Sweden | 49 | 9 | 8 | 17 | 76 | .... | .... | .... | .... | .... | .... | .... | .... | .... | 8 | 2 | 3 | 5 | 12 | .... | .... | .... | .... |
| **99-2000** | **NY Rangers** | **NHL** | **76** | **6** | **15** | **21** | **46** | **1** | **0** | **1** | **101** | **5.9** | **–13** | **0** | **0.0** | **18:06** | .... | .... | .... | .... | .... | .... | .... | .... | .... |
| **2000-01** | **NY Rangers** | **NHL** | **75** | **5** | **21** | **26** | **40** | **4** | **0** | **0** | **104** | **4.8** | **–3** | **0** | **0.0** | **21:16** | .... | .... | .... | .... | .... | .... | .... | .... | .... |
| **2001-02** | **Philadelphia** | **NHL** | **82** | **11** | **30** | **41** | **42** | **5** | **0** | **1** | **150** | **7.3** | **12** | **0** | **0.0** | **23:02** | **5** | **0** | **0** | **0** | **2** | **0** | **0** | **0** | **22:48** |
| | Sweden | Olympics | 4 | 1 | 1 | 2 | 0 | .... | .... | .... | .... | .... | .... | .... | .... | .... | .... | .... | .... | .... | .... | .... | .... | .... | .... |
| **2002-03** | **Philadelphia** | **NHL** | **82** | **10** | **29** | **39** | **38** | **5** | **0** | **2** | **159** | **6.3** | **11** | **0** | **0.0** | **24:05** | **13** | **0** | **3** | **3** | **8** | **0** | **0** | **0** | **26:07** |
| **2003-04** | **Philadelphia** | **NHL** | **80** | **13** | **29** | **42** | **26** | **4** | **0** | **3** | **189** | **6.9** | **16** | **0** | **0.0** | **24:27** | **15** | **2** | **6** | **8** | **8** | **0** | **0** | **1** | **26:11** |
| 2004-05 | HC Ambri-Piotta | Swiss | 24 | 4 | 10 | 14 | 61 | .... | .... | .... | .... | .... | .... | .... | .... | .... | .... | .... | .... | .... | .... | .... | .... | .... | .... |
| **2005-06** | **Philadelphia** | **NHL** | **47** | **6** | **19** | **25** | **34** | **3** | **0** | **0** | **97** | **6.2** | **5** | **0** | **0.0** | **23:17** | .... | .... | .... | .... | .... | .... | .... | .... | .... |
| | Sweden | Olympics | DID NOT PLAY | | | | | | | | | | | | | | | | | | | | | | |
| **2006-07** | **Minnesota** | **NHL** | **76** | **3** | **19** | **22** | **64** | **3** | **0** | **0** | **98** | **3.1** | **–4** | **0** | **0.0** | **23:33** | **4** | **0** | **0** | **0** | **2** | **0** | **0** | **0** | **23:06** |
| **2007-08** | **Minnesota** | **NHL** | **80** | **4** | **23** | **27** | **42** | **2** | **0** | **0** | **87** | **4.6** | **–4** | **0** | **0.0** | **23:27** | **6** | **0** | **1** | **1** | **18** | **0** | **0** | **0** | **28:08** |
| **2008-09** | **Minnesota** | **NHL** | **81** | **2** | **22** | **24** | **44** | **1** | **0** | **0** | **93** | **2.2** | **–3** | **0** | **0.0** | **24:32** | .... | .... | .... | .... | .... | .... | .... | .... | .... |
| | **NHL Totals** | | **679** | **60** | **207** | **267** | **376** | **28** | **0** | **7** | **1078** | **5.6** | | **0** | **0.0** | **22:53** | **43** | **2** | **10** | **12** | **38** | **0** | **0** | **1** | **25:45** |

Traded to **Philadelphia** by **NY Rangers** with Jan Hlavac, Pavel Brendl and NY Rangers' 3rd round choice (Stefan Ruzicka) in 2003 Entry Draft for Eric Lindros, August 20, 2001. Signed as a free agent by **Ambri-Piotta** (Swiss), September 18, 2004. Signed as a free agent by **Minnesota**, July 1, 2006.

**JOKINEN, Jussi** (YOH-kih-nihn, YEW-see) **CAR.**

Center. Shoots left. 5'11", 190 lbs. Born, Kalajoki, Finland, April 1, 1983. Dallas' 7th choice, 192nd overall, in 2001 Entry Draft.

| | | | Regular Season | | | | | | | | | | | | | | Playoffs | | | | | | | | |
|---|---|---|---|---|---|---|---|---|---|---|---|---|---|---|---|---|---|---|---|---|---|---|---|---|---|
| Season | Club | League | GP | G | A | Pts | PIM | PP | SH | GW | S | % | +/- | TF | F% | Min | GP | G | A | Pts | PIM | PP | SH | GW | Min |
| 99-2000 | Karpat Oulu U18 | Fin-U18 | 15 | 6 | 25 | 31 | 14 | .... | .... | .... | .... | .... | .... | .... | .... | .... | 6 | 2 | 3 | 5 | 0 | .... | .... | .... | .... |
| | Karpat Oulu Jr. | Fin-Jr. | 28 | 4 | 7 | 11 | 14 | .... | .... | .... | .... | .... | .... | .... | .... | .... | .... | .... | .... | .... | .... | .... | .... | .... | .... |
| 2000-01 | Karpat Oulu U18 | Fin-U18 | 1 | 2 | 1 | 3 | 0 | .... | .... | .... | .... | .... | .... | .... | .... | .... | .... | .... | .... | .... | .... | .... | .... | .... | .... |
| | Karpat Oulu Jr. | Fin-Jr. | 41 | 18 | 31 | 49 | 69 | .... | .... | .... | .... | .... | .... | .... | .... | .... | 6 | 2 | 1 | 3 | 0 | .... | .... | .... | .... |
| 2001-02 | Karpat Oulu Jr. | Fin-Jr. | 2 | 4 | 1 | 5 | 2 | .... | .... | .... | .... | .... | .... | .... | .... | .... | 1 | 1 | 1 | 2 | 0 | .... | .... | .... | .... |
| | Karpat Oulu | Finland | 54 | 10 | 6 | 16 | 38 | .... | .... | .... | .... | .... | .... | .... | .... | .... | 4 | 1 | 0 | 1 | 0 | .... | .... | .... | .... |
| 2002-03 | Karpat Oulu | Finland | 51 | 14 | 23 | 37 | 10 | .... | .... | .... | .... | .... | .... | .... | .... | .... | 15 | 2 | 1 | 3 | 33 | .... | .... | .... | .... |
| 2003-04 | Karpat Oulu | Finland | 55 | 15 | 23 | 38 | 20 | .... | .... | .... | .... | .... | .... | .... | .... | .... | 15 | 3 | 4 | 7 | 6 | .... | .... | .... | .... |
| 2004-05 | Karpat Oulu | Finland | 56 | 23 | 24 | 47 | 24 | .... | .... | .... | .... | .... | .... | .... | .... | .... | 12 | 3 | 4 | 7 | 2 | .... | .... | .... | .... |
| **2005-06** | **Dallas** | **NHL** | **81** | **17** | **38** | **55** | **30** | **8** | **0** | **2** | **107** | **15.9** | **2** | **23** | **30.4** | **13:34** | **5** | **2** | **1** | **3** | **0** | **1** | **0** | **0** | **13:40** |
| | Finland | Olympics | 8 | 1 | 3 | 4 | 2 | .... | .... | .... | .... | .... | .... | .... | .... | .... | .... | .... | .... | .... | .... | .... | .... | .... | .... |
| **2006-07** | **Dallas** | **NHL** | **82** | **14** | **34** | **48** | **18** | **6** | **0** | **1** | **121** | **11.6** | **8** | **278** | **52.2** | **13:54** | **4** | **0** | **1** | **1** | **0** | **0** | **0** | **0** | **13:22** |
| **2007-08** | **Dallas** | **NHL** | **52** | **14** | **14** | **28** | **14** | **5** | **0** | **2** | **93** | **15.1** | **2** | **295** | **53.2** | **12:44** | .... | .... | .... | .... | .... | .... | .... | .... | .... |
| | **Tampa Bay** | **NHL** | **20** | **2** | **12** | **14** | **4** | **1** | **0** | **0** | **38** | **5.3** | **–16** | **46** | **45.7** | **18:57** | .... | .... | .... | .... | .... | .... | .... | .... | .... |
| **2008-09** | **Tampa Bay** | **NHL** | **46** | **6** | **10** | **16** | **16** | **2** | **0** | **0** | **64** | **9.4** | **–8** | **510** | **52.2** | **15:38** | .... | .... | .... | .... | .... | .... | .... | .... | .... |
| | **Carolina** | **NHL** | **25** | **1** | **10** | **11** | **12** | **0** | **0** | **1** | **37** | **2.7** | **–2** | **163** | **58.3** | **14:43** | **18** | **7** | **4** | **11** | **2** | **2** | **0** | **3** | **15:35** |
| | **NHL Totals** | | **306** | **54** | **118** | **172** | **94** | **22** | **0** | **6** | **460** | **11.7** | | **1315** | **52.5** | **14:16** | **27** | **9** | **6** | **15** | **2** | **3** | **0** | **3** | **14:54** |

Traded to **Tampa Bay** by **Dallas** with Jeff Halpern, Mike Smith and Dallas' 4th round choice (later traded to Minnesota – later traded to Edmonton – Edmonton selected Kyle Bigos) in 2009 Entry Draft for Brad Richards and Johan Holmqvist, February 26, 2008. Traded to **Carolina** by **Tampa Bay** for Wade Brookbank, Josef Melichar and future considerations, February 7, 2009.

**JOKINEN, Olli** (YOH-kih-nihn, OH-lee) **CGY.**

Center. Shoots left. 6'3", 215 lbs. Born, Kuopio, Finland, December 5, 1978. Los Angeles' 1st choice, 3rd overall, in 1997 Entry Draft.

| | | | Regular Season | | | | | | | | | | | | | | Playoffs | | | | | | | | |
|---|---|---|---|---|---|---|---|---|---|---|---|---|---|---|---|---|---|---|---|---|---|---|---|---|---|
| Season | Club | League | GP | G | A | Pts | PIM | PP | SH | GW | S | % | +/- | TF | F% | Min | GP | G | A | Pts | PIM | PP | SH | GW | Min |
| 1994-95 | KalPa Kuopio U18 | Fin-U18 | 30 | 22 | 28 | 50 | 92 | .... | .... | .... | .... | .... | .... | .... | .... | .... | .... | .... | .... | .... | .... | .... | .... | .... | .... |
| | KalPa Kuopio Jr. | Fin-Jr. | 6 | 0 | 1 | 1 | 6 | .... | .... | .... | .... | .... | .... | .... | .... | .... | .... | .... | .... | .... | .... | .... | .... | .... | .... |
| 1995-96 | KalPa Kuopio U18 | Fin-U18 | 9 | 9 | 13 | 22 | 4 | .... | .... | .... | .... | .... | .... | .... | .... | .... | .... | .... | .... | .... | .... | .... | .... | .... | .... |
| | KalPa Kuopio Jr. | Fin-Jr. | 25 | 20 | 14 | 34 | 47 | .... | .... | .... | .... | .... | .... | .... | .... | .... | 7 | 4 | 4 | 8 | 20 | .... | .... | .... | .... |
| | KalPa Kuopio | Finland | 15 | 1 | 1 | 2 | 2 | .... | .... | .... | .... | .... | .... | .... | .... | .... | .... | .... | .... | .... | .... | .... | .... | .... | .... |
| 1996-97 | HIFK Helsinki Jr. | Fin-Jr. | 2 | 1 | 0 | 1 | 6 | .... | .... | .... | .... | .... | .... | .... | .... | .... | .... | .... | .... | .... | .... | .... | .... | .... | .... |
| | HIFK Helsinki | Finland | 50 | 14 | 27 | 41 | 88 | .... | .... | .... | .... | .... | .... | .... | .... | .... | .... | .... | .... | .... | .... | .... | .... | .... | .... |
| **1997-98** | **Los Angeles** | **NHL** | **8** | **0** | **0** | **0** | **6** | **0** | **0** | **0** | **12** | **0.0** | **–5** | .... | .... | .... | .... | .... | .... | .... | .... | .... | .... | .... | .... |
| | HIFK Helsinki | Finland | 30 | 11 | 28 | 39 | 32 | .... | .... | .... | .... | .... | .... | .... | .... | .... | 9 | 7 | 2 | 9 | 2 | .... | .... | .... | .... |

| | | | Regular Season | | | | | | | | | | | | | | Playoffs | | | | | | | | |
|---|---|---|---|---|---|---|---|---|---|---|---|---|---|---|---|---|---|---|---|---|---|---|---|---|---|
| Season | Club | League | GP | G | A | Pts | PIM | PP | SH | GW | S | % | +/- | TF | F% | Min | GP | G | A | Pts | PIM | PP | SH | GW | Min |
| **1998-99** | **Los Angeles** | **NHL** | **66** | **9** | **12** | **21** | **44** | **3** | **1** | **1** | **87** | **10.3** | **–10** | **779** | **43.9** | **14:42** | .... | .... | .... | .... | .... | .... | .... | .... | .... |
| | Springfield | AHL | 9 | 3 | 6 | 9 | 6 | .... | .... | .... | .... | .... | .... | .... | .... | .... | .... | .... | .... | .... | .... | .... | .... | .... | .... |
| **99-2000** | **NY Islanders** | **NHL** | **82** | **11** | **10** | **21** | **80** | **1** | **2** | **3** | **138** | **8.0** | **0** | **841** | **46.1** | **16:15** | .... | .... | .... | .... | .... | .... | .... | .... | .... |
| **2000-01** | **Florida** | **NHL** | **78** | **6** | **10** | **16** | **106** | **0** | **0** | **0** | **121** | **5.0** | **–22** | **638** | **42.3** | **13:23** | .... | .... | .... | .... | .... | .... | .... | .... | .... |
| **2001-02** | **Florida** | **NHL** | **80** | **9** | **20** | **29** | **98** | **3** | **1** | **0** | **153** | **5.9** | **–16** | **1222** | **45.2** | **18:05** | .... | .... | .... | .... | .... | .... | .... | .... | .... |
| | Finland | Olympics | 4 | 2 | 1 | 3 | 0 | .... | .... | .... | .... | .... | .... | .... | .... | .... | .... | .... | .... | .... | .... | .... | .... | .... | .... |
| **2002-03** | **Florida** | **NHL** | **81** | **36** | **29** | **65** | **79** | **13** | **3** | **6** | **240** | **15.0** | **–17** | **1925** | **46.7** | **22:02** | .... | .... | .... | .... | .... | .... | .... | .... | .... |
| **2003-04** | **Florida** | **NHL** | **82** | **26** | **32** | **58** | **81** | **8** | **2** | **8** | **280** | **9.3** | **–16** | **1986** | **47.1** | **22:35** | .... | .... | .... | .... | .... | .... | .... | .... | .... |
| 2004-05 | Kloten Flyers | Swiss | 8 | 6 | 1 | 7 | 14 | .... | .... | .... | .... | .... | .... | .... | .... | .... | .... | .... | .... | .... | .... | .... | .... | .... | .... |
| | Sodertalje SK | Sweden | 23 | 13 | 9 | 22 | 52 | .... | .... | .... | .... | .... | .... | .... | .... | .... | .... | .... | .... | .... | .... | .... | .... | .... | .... |
| | HIFK Helsinki | Finland | 14 | 9 | 8 | 17 | 10 | .... | .... | .... | .... | .... | .... | .... | .... | .... | 5 | 2 | 0 | 2 | 24 | .... | .... | .... | .... |
| **2005-06** | **Florida** | **NHL** | **82** | **38** | **51** | **89** | **88** | **14** | **1** | **9** | **351** | **10.8** | **14** | **955** | **46.9** | **20:29** | .... | .... | .... | .... | .... | .... | .... | .... | .... |
| | Finland | Olympics | 8 | 6 | 2 | 8 | 2 | .... | .... | .... | .... | .... | .... | .... | .... | .... | .... | .... | .... | .... | .... | .... | .... | .... | .... |
| **2006-07** | **Florida** | **NHL** | **82** | **39** | **52** | **91** | **78** | **9** | **1** | **8** | **351** | **11.1** | **18** | **1074** | **44.3** | **20:32** | .... | .... | .... | .... | .... | .... | .... | .... | .... |
| **2007-08** | **Florida** | **NHL** | **82** | **34** | **37** | **71** | **67** | **18** | **0** | **5** | **341** | **10.0** | **–19** | **938** | **43.1** | **19:54** | .... | .... | .... | .... | .... | .... | .... | .... | .... |
| **2008-09** | **Phoenix** | **NHL** | **57** | **21** | **21** | **42** | **49** | **6** | **2** | **2** | **169** | **12.4** | **–5** | **737** | **42.2** | **18:10** | .... | .... | .... | .... | .... | .... | .... | .... | .... |
| | **Calgary** | **NHL** | **19** | **8** | **7** | **15** | **18** | **3** | **0** | **1** | **67** | **11.9** | **–7** | **215** | **47.4** | **21:03** | **6** | **2** | **3** | **5** | **4** | **0** | **0** | **0** | **19:24** |
| | **NHL Totals** | | **799** | **237** | **281** | **518** | **794** | **78** | **13** | **43** | **2310** | **10.3** | | **11310** | **45.3** | **18:47** | **6** | **2** | **3** | **5** | **4** | **0** | **0** | **0** | **19:24** |

Played in NHL All-Star Game (2003)

Traded to **NY Islanders** by **Los Angeles** with Josh Green, Mathieu Biron and Los Angeles' 1st round choice (Taylor Pyatt) in 1999 Entry Draft for Ziggy Palffy, Bryan Smolinski, Marcel Cousineau and New Jersey's 4th round choice (previously acquired, Los Angeles selected Daniel Johansson) in 1999 Entry Draft, June 20, 1999. Traded to **Florida** by **NY Islanders** with Roberto Luongo for Mark Parrish and Oleg Kvasha, June 24, 2000. Signed as a free agent by **Kloten** (Swiss), September 15, 2004. Signed as a free agent by **Sodertalje** (Sweden), November, 2004. Signed as a free agent by **HIFK Helsinki** (Finland), January 30, 2005.Traded to **Phoenix** by **Florida** for Keith Ballard, Nick Boynton and Ottawa's 2nd round choice (previously acquired, later traded back to Phoenix - Phoenix selected Jared Staal) in 2008 Entry Draft, June 20, 2008. Traded to **Calgary** by **Phoenix** with Phoenix's 3rd round choice (later traded to Florida – Florida selected Josh Birkholz) in 2009 Entry Draft for Matthew Lombardi, Brandon Prust and Calgary's 1st round choice in 2010 Entry Draft, March 4, 2009.

## JONES, Blair

(JOHNZ, BLAYR) **T.B.**

Center. Shoots right. 6'3", 210 lbs. Born, Central Butte, Sask., September 27, 1986. Tampa Bay's 5th choice, 102nd overall, in 2005 Entry Draft.

| | | | | | | | | | | | | | | | | | | | | | | | | | |
|---|---|---|---|---|---|---|---|---|---|---|---|---|---|---|---|---|---|---|---|---|---|---|---|---|---|
| 2002-03 | Bethune | SBHL | STATISTICS NOT AVAILABLE | | | | | | | | | | | | | | | | | | | | | | |
| | Red Deer Rebels | WHL | 37 | 3 | 4 | 7 | 17 | .... | .... | .... | .... | .... | .... | .... | .... | .... | 10 | 1 | 0 | 1 | 0 | .... | .... | .... | .... |
| 2003-04 | Red Deer Rebels | WHL | 72 | 9 | 22 | 31 | 55 | .... | .... | .... | .... | .... | .... | .... | .... | .... | 19 | 1 | 5 | 6 | 24 | .... | .... | .... | .... |
| 2004-05 | Red Deer Rebels | WHL | 39 | 7 | 18 | 25 | 48 | .... | .... | .... | .... | .... | .... | .... | .... | .... | .... | .... | .... | .... | .... | .... | .... | .... | .... |
| | Moose Jaw | WHL | 29 | 7 | 18 | 25 | 30 | .... | .... | .... | .... | .... | .... | .... | .... | .... | 5 | 2 | 5 | 7 | 8 | .... | .... | .... | .... |
| 2005-06 | Moose Jaw | WHL | 72 | 35 | 50 | 85 | 85 | .... | .... | .... | .... | .... | .... | .... | .... | .... | 22 | 9 | 12 | 21 | 45 | .... | .... | .... | .... |
| **2006-07** | **Tampa Bay** | **NHL** | **20** | **1** | **2** | **3** | **2** | **0** | **0** | **0** | **6** | **16.7** | **0** | **65** | **41.5** | **5:46** | .... | .... | .... | .... | .... | .... | .... | .... | .... |
| | Springfield | AHL | 45 | 5 | 16 | 21 | 36 | .... | .... | .... | .... | .... | .... | .... | .... | .... | .... | .... | .... | .... | .... | .... | .... | .... | .... |
| **2007-08** | **Tampa Bay** | **NHL** | **4** | **0** | **0** | **0** | **0** | **0** | **0** | **0** | **1** | **0.0** | **0** | **8** | **12.5** | **1:55** | .... | .... | .... | .... | .... | .... | .... | .... | .... |
| | Norfolk Admirals | AHL | 75 | 14 | 28 | 42 | 50 | .... | .... | .... | .... | .... | .... | .... | .... | .... | .... | .... | .... | .... | .... | .... | .... | .... | .... |
| 2008-09 | Norfolk Admirals | AHL | 80 | 20 | 34 | 54 | 61 | .... | .... | .... | .... | .... | .... | .... | .... | .... | .... | .... | .... | .... | .... | .... | .... | .... | .... |
| | **NHL Totals** | | **24** | **1** | **2** | **3** | **2** | **0** | **0** | **0** | **7** | **14.3** | | **73** | **38.4** | **5:08** | .... | .... | .... | .... | .... | .... | .... | .... | .... |

WHL East Second All-Star Team (2006)

## JONES, David

(JOHNZ, DAY-vihd) **COL.**

Right wing. Shoots right. 6'2", 210 lbs. Born, Guelph, Ont., August 10, 1984. Colorado's 8th choice, 288th overall, in 2003 Entry Draft.

| | | | | | | | | | | | | | | | | | | | | | | | | | |
|---|---|---|---|---|---|---|---|---|---|---|---|---|---|---|---|---|---|---|---|---|---|---|---|---|---|
| 2000-01 | Port Coquitlam | PIJHL | 40 | 18 | 11 | 29 | 33 | .... | .... | .... | .... | .... | .... | .... | .... | .... | .... | .... | .... | .... | .... | .... | .... | .... | .... |
| 2001-02 | Coquitlam | BCHL | 59 | 19 | 32 | 51 | 62 | .... | .... | .... | .... | .... | .... | .... | .... | .... | .... | .... | .... | .... | .... | .... | .... | .... | .... |
| 2002-03 | Coquitlam | BCHL | 35 | 9 | 19 | 28 | 55 | .... | .... | .... | .... | .... | .... | .... | .... | .... | 7 | 2 | 6 | 8 | 8 | .... | .... | .... | .... |
| 2003-04 | Coquitlam | BCHL | 53 | 33 | 60 | 93 | 78 | .... | .... | .... | .... | .... | .... | .... | .... | .... | 7 | 3 | 6 | 9 | 4 | .... | .... | .... | .... |
| 2004-05 | Dartmouth | ECAC | 34 | 9 | 5 | 14 | 26 | .... | .... | .... | .... | .... | .... | .... | .... | .... | .... | .... | .... | .... | .... | .... | .... | .... | .... |
| 2005-06 | Dartmouth | ECAC | 33 | 17 | 17 | 34 | 38 | .... | .... | .... | .... | .... | .... | .... | .... | .... | .... | .... | .... | .... | .... | .... | .... | .... | .... |
| 2006-07 | Dartmouth | ECAC | 33 | 18 | 26 | *44 | 22 | .... | .... | .... | .... | .... | .... | .... | .... | .... | .... | .... | .... | .... | .... | .... | .... | .... | .... |
| **2007-08** | **Colorado** | **NHL** | **27** | **2** | **4** | **6** | **8** | **1** | **0** | **0** | **37** | **5.4** | **–5** | **8** | **37.5** | **11:22** | **10** | **0** | **1** | **1** | **6** | **0** | **0** | **0** | **11:50** |
| | Lake Erie | AHL | 45 | 14 | 16 | 30 | 16 | .... | .... | .... | .... | .... | .... | .... | .... | .... | .... | .... | .... | .... | .... | .... | .... | .... | .... |
| **2008-09** | **Colorado** | **NHL** | **40** | **8** | **5** | **13** | **8** | **1** | **0** | **1** | **47** | **17.0** | **–8** | **8** | **50.0** | **12:44** | .... | .... | .... | .... | .... | .... | .... | .... | .... |
| | **NHL Totals** | | **67** | **10** | **9** | **19** | **16** | **2** | **0** | **1** | **84** | **11.9** | | **16** | **43.8** | **12:11** | **10** | **0** | **1** | **1** | **6** | **0** | **0** | **0** | **11:50** |

ECAC Second All-Star Team (2006) • ECAC First All-Star Tearm (2007) • NCAA East First All-American Team (2007)

• Missed majority of 2008-09 season recovering from shoulder injury suffered in game vs. San Jose, January 27, 2009.

## JONES, Matt

(JOHNZ, MAT) **PHX.**

Defense. Shoots left. 6', 215 lbs. Born, Downers Grove, IL, August 8, 1983. Phoenix's 5th choice, 80th overall, in 2002 Entry Draft.

| | | | | | | | | | | | | | | | | | | | | | | | | | |
|---|---|---|---|---|---|---|---|---|---|---|---|---|---|---|---|---|---|---|---|---|---|---|---|---|---|
| 99-2000 | Green Bay | USHL | 54 | 1 | 4 | 5 | 59 | .... | .... | .... | .... | .... | .... | .... | .... | .... | 13 | 0 | 0 | 0 | 2 | .... | .... | .... | .... |
| 2000-01 | Green Bay | USHL | 52 | 3 | 10 | 13 | 58 | .... | .... | .... | .... | .... | .... | .... | .... | .... | 4 | 0 | 0 | 0 | 2 | .... | .... | .... | .... |
| 2001-02 | North Dakota | WCHA | 37 | 2 | 5 | 7 | 20 | .... | .... | .... | .... | .... | .... | .... | .... | .... | .... | .... | .... | .... | .... | .... | .... | .... | .... |
| 2002-03 | North Dakota | WCHA | 39 | 1 | 6 | 7 | 26 | .... | .... | .... | .... | .... | .... | .... | .... | .... | .... | .... | .... | .... | .... | .... | .... | .... | .... |
| 2003-04 | North Dakota | WCHA | 41 | 7 | 14 | 21 | 40 | .... | .... | .... | .... | .... | .... | .... | .... | .... | .... | .... | .... | .... | .... | .... | .... | .... | .... |
| 2004-05 | North Dakota | WCHA | 45 | 6 | 11 | 17 | 66 | .... | .... | .... | .... | .... | .... | .... | .... | .... | .... | .... | .... | .... | .... | .... | .... | .... | .... |
| **2005-06** | **Phoenix** | **NHL** | **16** | **0** | **2** | **2** | **14** | **0** | **0** | **0** | **10** | **0.0** | **–2** | **0** | **0.0** | **11:35** | .... | .... | .... | .... | .... | .... | .... | .... | .... |
| | San Antonio | AHL | 59 | 2 | 11 | 13 | 46 | .... | .... | .... | .... | .... | .... | .... | .... | .... | .... | .... | .... | .... | .... | .... | .... | .... | .... |
| **2006-07** | **Phoenix** | **NHL** | **45** | **1** | **6** | **7** | **39** | **0** | **0** | **0** | **20** | **5.0** | **–12** | **0** | **0.0** | **16:23** | .... | .... | .... | .... | .... | .... | .... | .... | .... |
| | San Antonio | AHL | 24 | 0 | 2 | 2 | 23 | .... | .... | .... | .... | .... | .... | .... | .... | .... | .... | .... | .... | .... | .... | .... | .... | .... | .... |
| **2007-08** | **Phoenix** | **NHL** | **45** | **0** | **2** | **2** | **10** | **0** | **0** | **0** | **25** | **0.0** | **–13** | **0** | **0.0** | **14:34** | .... | .... | .... | .... | .... | .... | .... | .... | .... |
| | San Antonio | AHL | 5 | 0 | 0 | 0 | 0 | .... | .... | .... | .... | .... | .... | .... | .... | .... | .... | .... | .... | .... | .... | .... | .... | .... | .... |
| 2008-09 | San Antonio | AHL | 58 | 2 | 4 | 6 | 40 | .... | .... | .... | .... | .... | .... | .... | .... | .... | .... | .... | .... | .... | .... | .... | .... | .... | .... |
| | **NHL Totals** | | **106** | **1** | **10** | **11** | **63** | **0** | **0** | **0** | **55** | **1.8** | | **0** | **0.0** | **14:53** | .... | .... | .... | .... | .... | .... | .... | .... | .... |

WCHA Second All-Star Team (2004)

## JONES, Randy

(JOHNZ, RAN-dee) **PHI.**

Defense. Shoots left. 6'2", 200 lbs. Born, Quispamsis, N.B., July 23, 1981.

| | | | | | | | | | | | | | | | | | | | | | | | | | |
|---|---|---|---|---|---|---|---|---|---|---|---|---|---|---|---|---|---|---|---|---|---|---|---|---|---|
| 99-2000 | Cobourg Cougars | OPJHL | 44 | 20 | 36 | 56 | 51 | .... | .... | .... | .... | .... | .... | .... | .... | .... | .... | .... | .... | .... | .... | .... | .... | .... | .... |
| 2000-01 | Cobourg Cougars | OPJHL | 28 | 15 | 21 | 36 | 46 | .... | .... | .... | .... | .... | .... | .... | .... | .... | .... | .... | .... | .... | .... | .... | .... | .... | .... |
| 2001-02 | Clarkson Knights | ECAC | 34 | 9 | 11 | 20 | 32 | .... | .... | .... | .... | .... | .... | .... | .... | .... | .... | .... | .... | .... | .... | .... | .... | .... | .... |
| 2002-03 | Clarkson Knights | ECAC | 33 | 13 | 20 | 33 | 65 | .... | .... | .... | .... | .... | .... | .... | .... | .... | .... | .... | .... | .... | .... | .... | .... | .... | .... |
| **2003-04** | **Philadelphia** | **NHL** | **5** | **0** | **0** | **0** | **0** | **0** | **0** | **0** | **5** | **0.0** | **1** | **0** | **0.0** | **12:00** | .... | .... | .... | .... | .... | .... | .... | .... | .... |
| | Philadelphia | AHL | 55 | 8 | 24 | 32 | 63 | .... | .... | .... | .... | .... | .... | .... | .... | .... | 12 | 0 | 1 | 1 | 17 | .... | .... | .... | .... |
| 2004-05 | Philadelphia | AHL | 69 | 5 | 19 | 24 | 32 | .... | .... | .... | .... | .... | .... | .... | .... | .... | 18 | 0 | 5 | 5 | 10 | .... | .... | .... | .... |
| **2005-06** | **Philadelphia** | **NHL** | **28** | **0** | **8** | **8** | **16** | **0** | **0** | **0** | **21** | **0.0** | **–6** | **1** | **100.0** | **14:58** | .... | .... | .... | .... | .... | .... | .... | .... | .... |
| | Philadelphia | AHL | 21 | 2 | 3 | 5 | 53 | .... | .... | .... | .... | .... | .... | .... | .... | .... | .... | .... | .... | .... | .... | .... | .... | .... | .... |
| **2006-07** | **Philadelphia** | **NHL** | **66** | **4** | **18** | **22** | **38** | **0** | **0** | **0** | **67** | **6.0** | **–14** | **1** | **0.0** | **16:06** | .... | .... | .... | .... | .... | .... | .... | .... | .... |
| **2007-08** | **Philadelphia** | **NHL** | **71** | **5** | **26** | **31** | **58** | **1** | **0** | **0** | **103** | **4.9** | **8** | **0** | **0.0** | **19:24** | **16** | **0** | **2** | **2** | **4** | **0** | **0** | **0** | **21:24** |
| **2008-09** | **Philadelphia** | **NHL** | **47** | **4** | **4** | **8** | **22** | **1** | **0** | **2** | **45** | **8.9** | **8** | **0** | **0.0** | **19:07** | **6** | **0** | **1** | **1** | **0** | **0** | **0** | **0** | **14:38** |
| | Philadelphia | AHL | 2 | 0 | 2 | 2 | 0 | .... | .... | .... | .... | .... | .... | .... | .... | .... | .... | .... | .... | .... | .... | .... | .... | .... | .... |
| | **NHL Totals** | | **217** | **13** | **56** | **69** | **134** | **2** | **0** | **2** | **241** | **5.4** | | **2** | **50.0** | **17:35** | **22** | **0** | **3** | **3** | **4** | **0** | **0** | **0** | **19:33** |

ECAC First All-Star Team (2003)

Signed as a free agent by **Philadelphia**, July 24, 2003.

## JONES, Ryan

(JOHNZ, RIGH-uhn) **NSH.**

Right wing. Shoots left. 6'1", 206 lbs. Born, Chatham, Ont., June 14, 1984. Minnesota's 5th choice, 111th overall, in 2004 Entry Draft.

| | | | | | | | | | | | | | | | | | | | | | | | | | |
|---|---|---|---|---|---|---|---|---|---|---|---|---|---|---|---|---|---|---|---|---|---|---|---|---|---|
| 2002-03 | Chatham | OHA-B | 38 | 12 | 11 | 23 | 42 | .... | .... | .... | .... | .... | .... | .... | .... | .... | .... | .... | .... | .... | .... | .... | .... | .... | .... |
| 2003-04 | Chatham | OHA-B | 46 | 39 | 30 | 69 | 64 | .... | .... | .... | .... | .... | .... | .... | .... | .... | 17 | 17 | 9 | 26 | 25 | .... | .... | .... | .... |
| 2004-05 | Miami U. | CCHA | 38 | 8 | 7 | 15 | 79 | .... | .... | .... | .... | .... | .... | .... | .... | .... | .... | .... | .... | .... | .... | .... | .... | .... | .... |
| 2005-06 | Miami U. | CCHA | 39 | 22 | 13 | 35 | 72 | .... | .... | .... | .... | .... | .... | .... | .... | .... | .... | .... | .... | .... | .... | .... | .... | .... | .... |
| 2006-07 | Miami U. | CCHA | 42 | 29 | 19 | 48 | 88 | .... | .... | .... | .... | .... | .... | .... | .... | .... | .... | .... | .... | .... | .... | .... | .... | .... | .... |
| 2007-08 | Miami U. | CCHA | 42 | 31 | 18 | 49 | 83 | .... | .... | .... | .... | .... | .... | .... | .... | .... | .... | .... | .... | .... | .... | .... | .... | .... | .... |
| | Houston Aeros | AHL | 4 | 0 | 0 | 0 | 2 | .... | .... | .... | .... | .... | .... | .... | .... | .... | 4 | 1 | 1 | 2 | 2 | .... | .... | .... | .... |

| | | | Regular Season | | | | | | | | | | | | | | Playoffs | | | | | | | | |
|---|---|---|---|---|---|---|---|---|---|---|---|---|---|---|---|---|---|---|---|---|---|---|---|---|---|
| Season | Club | League | GP | G | A | Pts | PIM | PP | SH | GW | S | % | +/- | TF | F% | Min | GP | G | A | Pts | PIM | PP | SH | GW | Min |
| **2008-09** | **Nashville** | **NHL** | **46** | **7** | **10** | **17** | **22** | **2** | **0** | **1** | **63** | **11.1** | **1** | **10** | **10.0** | **11:26** | .... | .... | .... | .... | .... | .... | .... | .... | .... |
| | Milwaukee | AHL | 25 | 13 | 9 | 22 | 30 | .... | .... | .... | .... | .... | .... | .... | .... | .... | 11 | 4 | 3 | 7 | 10 | .... | .... | .... | .... |
| | **NHL Totals** | | **46** | **7** | **10** | **17** | **22** | **2** | **0** | **1** | **63** | **11.1** | | **10** | **10.0** | **11:26** | .... | .... | .... | .... | .... | .... | .... | .... | .... |

CCHA Second All-Star Team (2006, 2007) • CCHA First All-Star Team (2008) • NCAA West First All-American Team (2008)

Traded to **Nashville** by **Minnesota** with Minnesota's 2nd round choice (Charles-Olivier Roussel) in 2009 Entry Draft for Marek Zidlicky, July 1, 2008

## JOSLIN, Derek

(JAWS-lihn, DAIR-ihk) **S.J.**

Defense. Shoots left. 6'1", 205 lbs. Born, Richmond Hill, Ont., March 17, 1987. San Jose's 5th choice, 149th overall, in 2005 Entry Draft.

| Season | Club | League | GP | G | A | Pts | PIM | PP | SH | GW | S | % | +/- | TF | F% | Min | GP | G | A | Pts | PIM | PP | SH | GW | Min |
|---|---|---|---|---|---|---|---|---|---|---|---|---|---|---|---|---|---|---|---|---|---|---|---|---|---|
| 2002-03 | Vaughan | GTHL | 60 | 9 | 18 | 27 | 72 | .... | .... | .... | .... | .... | .... | .... | .... | .... | .... | .... | .... | .... | .... | .... | .... | .... | .... |
| 2003-04 | Aurora Tigers | OPJHL | 36 | 4 | 12 | 16 | .... | .... | .... | .... | .... | .... | .... | .... | .... | .... | .... | .... | .... | .... | .... | .... | .... | .... | .... |
| | Ottawa 67's | OHL | 7 | 0 | 0 | 0 | 4 | .... | .... | .... | .... | .... | .... | .... | .... | .... | .... | .... | .... | .... | .... | .... | .... | .... | .... |
| 2004-05 | Ottawa 67's | OHL | 68 | 6 | 24 | 30 | 44 | .... | .... | .... | .... | .... | .... | .... | .... | .... | 21 | 0 | 3 | 3 | 24 | .... | .... | .... | .... |
| 2005-06 | Ottawa 67's | OHL | 68 | 11 | 37 | 48 | 40 | .... | .... | .... | .... | .... | .... | .... | .... | .... | 6 | 1 | 5 | 6 | 10 | .... | .... | .... | .... |
| | Cleveland Barons | AHL | 2 | 0 | 0 | 0 | 0 | .... | .... | .... | .... | .... | .... | .... | .... | .... | .... | .... | .... | .... | .... | .... | .... | .... | .... |
| 2006-07 | Ottawa 67's | OHL | 68 | 11 | 38 | 49 | 66 | .... | .... | .... | .... | .... | .... | .... | .... | .... | 5 | 1 | 4 | 5 | 4 | .... | .... | .... | .... |
| | Worcester Sharks | AHL | 3 | 0 | 0 | 0 | 0 | .... | .... | .... | .... | .... | .... | .... | .... | .... | 4 | 0 | 0 | 0 | 2 | .... | .... | .... | .... |
| 2007-08 | Worcester Sharks | AHL | 80 | 10 | 24 | 34 | 44 | .... | .... | .... | .... | .... | .... | .... | .... | .... | .... | .... | .... | .... | .... | .... | .... | .... | .... |
| **2008-09** | **San Jose** | **NHL** | **12** | **0** | **0** | **0** | **6** | **0** | **0** | **0** | **9** | **0.0** | **-3** | **0** | **0.0** | **11:22** | .... | .... | .... | .... | .... | .... | .... | .... | .... |
| | Worcester Sharks | AHL | 63 | 11 | 19 | 30 | 40 | .... | .... | .... | .... | .... | .... | .... | .... | .... | 12 | 0 | 2 | 2 | 8 | .... | .... | .... | .... |
| | **NHL Totals** | | **12** | **0** | **0** | **0** | **6** | **0** | **0** | **0** | **9** | **0.0** | | **0** | **0.0** | **11:22** | .... | .... | .... | .... | .... | .... | .... | .... | .... |

## JOVANOVSKI, Ed

(joh-van-OHV-skee, EHD) **PHX.**

Defense. Shoots left. 6'2", 214 lbs. Born, Windsor, Ont., June 26, 1976. Florida's 1st choice, 1st overall, in 1994 Entry Draft.

| Season | Club | League | GP | G | A | Pts | PIM | PP | SH | GW | S | % | +/- | TF | F% | Min | GP | G | A | Pts | PIM | PP | SH | GW | Min |
|---|---|---|---|---|---|---|---|---|---|---|---|---|---|---|---|---|---|---|---|---|---|---|---|---|---|
| 1991-92 | Windsor | Minor-ON | 50 | 25 | 40 | 65 | 88 | .... | .... | .... | .... | .... | .... | .... | .... | .... | .... | .... | .... | .... | .... | .... | .... | .... | .... |
| 1992-93 | Windsor Bulldogs | OHA-B | 48 | 7 | 46 | 53 | 88 | .... | .... | .... | .... | .... | .... | .... | .... | .... | .... | .... | .... | .... | .... | .... | .... | .... | .... |
| 1993-94 | Windsor Spitfires | OHL | 62 | 15 | 36 | 51 | 221 | .... | .... | .... | .... | .... | .... | .... | .... | .... | 4 | 0 | 0 | 0 | 15 | .... | .... | .... | .... |
| 1994-95 | Windsor Spitfires | OHL | 50 | 23 | 42 | 65 | 198 | .... | .... | .... | .... | .... | .... | .... | .... | .... | 9 | 2 | 7 | 9 | 39 | .... | .... | .... | .... |
| **1995-96** | **Florida** | **NHL** | **70** | **10** | **11** | **21** | **137** | **2** | **0** | **2** | **116** | **8.6** | **-3** | .... | .... | .... | **22** | **1** | **8** | **9** | **52** | **0** | **0** | **0** | .... |
| **1996-97** | **Florida** | **NHL** | **61** | **7** | **16** | **23** | **172** | **3** | **0** | **1** | **80** | **8.8** | **-1** | .... | .... | .... | **5** | **0** | **0** | **0** | **4** | **0** | **0** | **0** | .... |
| **1997-98** | **Florida** | **NHL** | **81** | **9** | **14** | **23** | **158** | **2** | **1** | **3** | **142** | **6.3** | **-12** | .... | .... | .... | .... | .... | .... | .... | .... | .... | .... | .... | .... |
| **1998-99** | **Florida** | **NHL** | **41** | **3** | **13** | **16** | **82** | **1** | **0** | **1** | **68** | **4.4** | **-4** | **0** | **0.0** | **22:35** | .... | .... | .... | .... | .... | .... | .... | .... | .... |
| | **Vancouver** | **NHL** | **31** | **2** | **9** | **11** | **44** | **0** | **0** | **0** | **41** | **4.9** | **-5** | **0** | **0.0** | **21:16** | .... | .... | .... | .... | .... | .... | .... | .... | .... |
| **99-2000** | **Vancouver** | **NHL** | **75** | **5** | **21** | **26** | **54** | **1** | **0** | **1** | **109** | **4.6** | **-3** | **0** | **0.0** | **24:03** | .... | .... | .... | .... | .... | .... | .... | .... | .... |
| **2000-01** | **Vancouver** | **NHL** | **79** | **12** | **35** | **47** | **102** | **4** | **0** | **2** | **193** | **6.2** | **-1** | **0** | **0.0** | **24:57** | **4** | **1** | **1** | **2** | **0** | **0** | **0** | **0** | **25:54** |
| **2001-02** | **Vancouver** | **NHL** | **82** | **17** | **31** | **48** | **101** | **7** | **1** | **3** | **202** | **8.4** | **-7** | **0** | **0.0** | **25:11** | **6** | **1** | **4** | **5** | **8** | **1** | **0** | **0** | **25:48** |
| | Canada | Olympics | 6 | 0 | 3 | 3 | 4 | .... | .... | .... | .... | .... | .... | .... | .... | .... | .... | .... | .... | .... | .... | .... | .... | .... | .... |
| **2002-03** | **Vancouver** | **NHL** | **67** | **6** | **40** | **46** | **113** | **2** | **0** | **1** | **145** | **4.1** | **19** | **0** | **0.0** | **24:15** | **14** | **7** | **1** | **8** | **22** | **4** | **1** | **2** | **23:40** |
| **2003-04** | **Vancouver** | **NHL** | **56** | **7** | **16** | **23** | **64** | **2** | **0** | **1** | **143** | **4.9** | **2** | **0** | **0.0** | **23:11** | **7** | **0** | **4** | **4** | **6** | **0** | **0** | **0** | **26:36** |
| 2004-05 | | | DID NOT PLAY | | | | | | | | | | | | | | | | | | | | | | |
| **2005-06** | **Vancouver** | **NHL** | **44** | **8** | **25** | **33** | **58** | **6** | **0** | **2** | **87** | **9.2** | **-8** | **0** | **0.0** | **24:26** | .... | .... | .... | .... | .... | .... | .... | .... | .... |
| | Canada | Olympics | DID NOT PLAY – INJURED | | | | | | | | | | | | | | | | | | | | | | |
| **2006-07** | **Phoenix** | **NHL** | **54** | **11** | **18** | **29** | **63** | **6** | **0** | **1** | **135** | **8.1** | **-6** | **0** | **0.0** | **23:09** | .... | .... | .... | .... | .... | .... | .... | .... | .... |
| **2007-08** | **Phoenix** | **NHL** | **80** | **12** | **39** | **51** | **73** | **8** | **0** | **2** | **240** | **5.0** | **-13** | **0** | **0.0** | **22:33** | .... | .... | .... | .... | .... | .... | .... | .... | .... |
| **2008-09** | **Phoenix** | **NHL** | **82** | **9** | **27** | **36** | **106** | **6** | **0** | **3** | **194** | **4.6** | **-15** | **1** | **0.0** | **22:10** | .... | .... | .... | .... | .... | .... | .... | .... | .... |
| | **NHL Totals** | | **903** | **118** | **315** | **433** | **1327** | **50** | **2** | **23** | **1895** | **6.2** | | **1** | **0.0** | **23:35** | **58** | **10** | **18** | **28** | **92** | **5** | **1** | **2** | **25:02** |

OHL All-Rookie Team (1994) • OHL Second All-Star Team (1994) • OHL First All-Star Team (1995) • NHL All-Rookie Team (1996)

Played in NHL All-Star Game (2001, 2002, 2003, 2007, 2008)

Traded to **Vancouver** by **Florida** with Dave Gagner, Mike Brown, Kevin Weekes and Florida's 1st round choice (Nathan Smith) in 2000 Entry Draft for Pavel Bure, Bret Hedican, Brad Ference and Vancouver's 3rd round choice (Robert Fried) in 2000 Entry Draft, January 17, 1999. Signed as a free agent by **Phoenix**, July 1, 2006.

## JUNLAND, Jonas

(YUHN-land, YOH-nuhs) **ST.L.**

Defense. Shoots left. 6'2", 198 lbs. Born, Linkoping, Sweden, November 15, 1987. St. Louis' 4th choice, 64th overall, in 2006 Entry Draft.

| Season | Club | League | GP | G | A | Pts | PIM | PP | SH | GW | S | % | +/- | TF | F% | Min | GP | G | A | Pts | PIM | PP | SH | GW | Min |
|---|---|---|---|---|---|---|---|---|---|---|---|---|---|---|---|---|---|---|---|---|---|---|---|---|---|
| 2002-03 | Linkoping U18 | Swe-U18 | 7 | 0 | 0 | 0 | 6 | .... | .... | .... | .... | .... | .... | .... | .... | .... | .... | .... | .... | .... | .... | .... | .... | .... | .... |
| 2003-04 | Linkoping U18 | Swe-U18 | 4 | 0 | 0 | 0 | 4 | .... | .... | .... | .... | .... | .... | .... | .... | .... | .... | .... | .... | .... | .... | .... | .... | .... | .... |
| | Linkopings HC Jr. | Swe-Jr. | 19 | 1 | 0 | 1 | 12 | .... | .... | .... | .... | .... | .... | .... | .... | .... | .... | .... | .... | .... | .... | .... | .... | .... | .... |
| 2004-05 | Linkoping U18 | Swe-U18 | 11 | 6 | 5 | 11 | 35 | .... | .... | .... | .... | .... | .... | .... | .... | .... | .... | .... | .... | .... | .... | .... | .... | .... | .... |
| | Linkopings HC Jr. | Swe-Jr. | 32 | 3 | 5 | 8 | 96 | .... | .... | .... | .... | .... | .... | .... | .... | .... | .... | .... | .... | .... | .... | .... | .... | .... | .... |
| 2005-06 | Linkopings HC Jr. | Swe-Jr. | 32 | 17 | 23 | 40 | 44 | .... | .... | .... | .... | .... | .... | .... | .... | .... | .... | .... | .... | .... | .... | .... | .... | .... | .... |
| | Linkoping U18 | Swe-U18 | 1 | 5 | 0 | 5 | 2 | .... | .... | .... | .... | .... | .... | .... | .... | .... | .... | .... | .... | .... | .... | .... | .... | .... | .... |
| | Linkopings HC | Sweden | 4 | 0 | 0 | 0 | 0 | .... | .... | .... | .... | .... | .... | .... | .... | .... | .... | .... | .... | .... | .... | .... | .... | .... | .... |
| 2006-07 | Linkopings HC Jr. | Swe-Jr. | 9 | 6 | 7 | 13 | 26 | .... | .... | .... | .... | .... | .... | .... | .... | .... | .... | .... | .... | .... | .... | .... | .... | .... | .... |
| | IK Oskarshamn | Sweden-2 | 4 | 0 | 3 | 3 | 4 | .... | .... | .... | .... | .... | .... | .... | .... | .... | .... | .... | .... | .... | .... | .... | .... | .... | .... |
| | Linkopings HC | Sweden | 41 | 1 | 4 | 5 | 22 | .... | .... | .... | .... | .... | .... | .... | .... | .... | 15 | 0 | 5 | 5 | 20 | .... | .... | .... | .... |
| 2007-08 | Linkopings HC | Sweden | 52 | 3 | 17 | 20 | 42 | .... | .... | .... | .... | .... | .... | .... | .... | .... | 16 | 4 | 3 | 7 | 18 | .... | .... | .... | .... |
| **2008-09** | **St. Louis** | **NHL** | **1** | **0** | **0** | **0** | **2** | **0** | **0** | **0** | **0** | **0.0** | **0** | **0** | **0.0** | **12:28** | .... | .... | .... | .... | .... | .... | .... | .... | .... |
| | Peoria Rivermen | AHL | 70 | 13 | 18 | 31 | 52 | .... | .... | .... | .... | .... | .... | .... | .... | .... | 5 | 0 | 1 | 1 | 6 | .... | .... | .... | .... |
| | **NHL Totals** | | **1** | **0** | **0** | **0** | **2** | **0** | **0** | **0** | **0** | **0.0** | | **0** | **0.0** | **12:28** | .... | .... | .... | .... | .... | .... | .... | .... | .... |

## JURCINA, Milan

(YEWR-chee-nah, MEE-lan) **WSH.**

Defense. Shoots right. 6'4", 240 lbs. Born, Liptovsky Mikulas, Czech., June 7, 1983. Boston's 7th choice, 241st overall, in 2001 Entry Draft.

| Season | Club | League | GP | G | A | Pts | PIM | PP | SH | GW | S | % | +/- | TF | F% | Min | GP | G | A | Pts | PIM | PP | SH | GW | Min |
|---|---|---|---|---|---|---|---|---|---|---|---|---|---|---|---|---|---|---|---|---|---|---|---|---|---|
| 99-2000 | L. Mikulas Jr. | Slovak-Jr. | STATISTICS NOT AVAILABLE | | | | | | | | | | | | | | | | | | | | | | |
| 2000-01 | Halifax | QMJHL | 68 | 0 | 5 | 5 | 56 | .... | .... | .... | .... | .... | .... | .... | .... | .... | 6 | 0 | 2 | 2 | 12 | .... | .... | .... | .... |
| 2001-02 | Halifax | QMJHL | 61 | 4 | 16 | 20 | 58 | .... | .... | .... | .... | .... | .... | .... | .... | .... | 13 | 5 | 3 | 8 | 10 | .... | .... | .... | .... |
| 2002-03 | Halifax | QMJHL | 51 | 15 | 13 | 28 | 102 | .... | .... | .... | .... | .... | .... | .... | .... | .... | 25 | 6 | 6 | 12 | 40 | .... | .... | .... | .... |
| 2003-04 | Providence Bruins | AHL | 73 | 5 | 12 | 17 | 52 | .... | .... | .... | .... | .... | .... | .... | .... | .... | 2 | 0 | 1 | 1 | 2 | .... | .... | .... | .... |
| 2004-05 | Providence Bruins | AHL | 79 | 6 | 17 | 23 | 92 | .... | .... | .... | .... | .... | .... | .... | .... | .... | 17 | 1 | 3 | 4 | 30 | .... | .... | .... | .... |
| **2005-06** | **Boston** | **NHL** | **51** | **6** | **5** | **11** | **54** | **2** | **0** | **0** | **64** | **9.4** | **3** | **1** | **0.0** | **16:28** | .... | .... | .... | .... | .... | .... | .... | .... | .... |
| | Providence Bruins | AHL | 7 | 0 | 3 | 3 | 8 | .... | .... | .... | .... | .... | .... | .... | .... | .... | .... | .... | .... | .... | .... | .... | .... | .... | .... |
| | Slovakia | Olympics | 6 | 0 | 1 | 1 | 8 | .... | .... | .... | .... | .... | .... | .... | .... | .... | .... | .... | .... | .... | .... | .... | .... | .... | .... |
| **2006-07** | **Boston** | **NHL** | **40** | **2** | **1** | **3** | **20** | **0** | **0** | **1** | **29** | **6.9** | **-5** | **0** | **0.0** | **10:42** | .... | .... | .... | .... | .... | .... | .... | .... | .... |
| | **Washington** | **NHL** | **30** | **2** | **7** | **9** | **24** | **0** | **0** | **0** | **42** | **4.8** | **5** | **0** | **0.0** | **23:09** | .... | .... | .... | .... | .... | .... | .... | .... | .... |
| **2007-08** | **Washington** | **NHL** | **75** | **1** | **8** | **9** | **30** | **1** | **0** | **0** | **58** | **1.7** | **4** | **0** | **0.0** | **16:38** | **7** | **0** | **0** | **0** | **6** | **0** | **0** | **0** | **16:26** |
| **2008-09** | **Washington** | **NHL** | **79** | **3** | **11** | **14** | **68** | **0** | **0** | **1** | **95** | **3.2** | **1** | **0** | **0.0** | **16:09** | **14** | **2** | **0** | **2** | **12** | **0** | **1** | **0** | **16:46** |
| | **NHL Totals** | | **275** | **14** | **32** | **46** | **196** | **3** | **0** | **2** | **288** | **4.9** | | **1** | **0.0** | **16:19** | **21** | **2** | **0** | **2** | **18** | **0** | **1** | **0** | **16:40** |

Traded to **Washington** by **Boston** for Washington's 4th round choice (later traded to Calgary - Calgary selected T. J. Brodie) in 2008 Entry Draft, February 1, 2007.

## KABERLE, Frantisek

(KA-buhr-lay, FRAN-tih-sehk)

Defense. Shoots left. 6', 190 lbs. Born, Kladno, Czech., November 8, 1973. Los Angeles' 3rd choice, 76th overall, in 1999 Entry Draft.

| Season | Club | League | GP | G | A | Pts | PIM | PP | SH | GW | S | % | +/- | TF | F% | Min | GP | G | A | Pts | PIM | PP | SH | GW | Min |
|---|---|---|---|---|---|---|---|---|---|---|---|---|---|---|---|---|---|---|---|---|---|---|---|---|---|
| 1991-92 | Poldi Kladno | Czech | 37 | 1 | 4 | 5 | 8 | .... | .... | .... | .... | .... | .... | .... | .... | .... | 8 | 0 | 1 | 1 | 0 | .... | .... | .... | .... |
| 1992-93 | Poldi Kladno | Czech | 40 | 4 | 5 | 9 | .... | .... | .... | .... | .... | .... | .... | .... | .... | .... | 9 | 2 | 4 | 6 | .... | .... | .... | .... | .... |
| 1993-94 | HC Kladno | CzRep | 41 | 4 | 16 | 20 | .... | .... | .... | .... | .... | .... | .... | .... | .... | .... | 11 | 1 | 1 | 2 | .... | .... | .... | .... | .... |
| 1994-95 | HC Kladno | CzRep | 40 | 7 | 17 | 24 | 20 | .... | .... | .... | .... | .... | .... | .... | .... | .... | 8 | 0 | 3 | 3 | 12 | .... | .... | .... | .... |
| 1995-96 | MoDo | Sweden | 40 | 5 | 7 | 12 | 34 | .... | .... | .... | .... | .... | .... | .... | .... | .... | 8 | 0 | 1 | 1 | 0 | .... | .... | .... | .... |
| 1996-97 | MoDo | Sweden | 50 | 3 | 11 | 14 | 28 | .... | .... | .... | .... | .... | .... | .... | .... | .... | .... | .... | .... | .... | .... | .... | .... | .... | .... |
| 1997-98 | MoDo | Sweden | 46 | 5 | 4 | 9 | 22 | .... | .... | .... | .... | .... | .... | .... | .... | .... | 9 | 1 | 1 | 2 | 4 | .... | .... | .... | .... |
| 1998-99 | MoDo | Sweden | 45 | 15 | 18 | 33 | 4 | .... | .... | .... | .... | .... | .... | .... | .... | .... | 13 | 2 | 5 | 7 | 8 | .... | .... | .... | .... |
| **99-2000** | **Los Angeles** | **NHL** | **37** | **0** | **9** | **9** | **4** | **0** | **0** | **0** | **41** | **0.0** | **3** | **0** | **0.0** | **17:04** | .... | .... | .... | .... | .... | .... | .... | .... | .... |
| | Long Beach | IHL | 18 | 2 | 8 | 10 | 8 | .... | .... | .... | .... | .... | .... | .... | .... | .... | .... | .... | .... | .... | .... | .... | .... | .... | .... |
| | **Atlanta** | **NHL** | **14** | **1** | **6** | **7** | **6** | **0** | **1** | **0** | **35** | **2.9** | **-13** | **0** | **0.0** | **24:39** | .... | .... | .... | .... | .... | .... | .... | .... | .... |
| | Lowell | AHL | 4 | 0 | 2 | 2 | 0 | .... | .... | .... | .... | .... | .... | .... | .... | .... | .... | .... | .... | .... | .... | .... | .... | .... | .... |
| **2000-01** | **Atlanta** | **NHL** | **51** | **4** | **11** | **15** | **18** | **1** | **0** | **1** | **99** | **4.0** | **11** | **1** | **0.0** | **22:17** | .... | .... | .... | .... | .... | .... | .... | .... | .... |
| **2001-02** | **Atlanta** | **NHL** | **61** | **5** | **20** | **25** | **24** | **1** | **0** | **0** | **82** | **6.1** | **-11** | **0** | **0.0** | **21:35** | .... | .... | .... | .... | .... | .... | .... | .... | .... |
| **2002-03** | **Atlanta** | **NHL** | **79** | **7** | **19** | **26** | **32** | **3** | **1** | **2** | **105** | **6.7** | **-19** | **0** | **0.0** | **21:57** | .... | .... | .... | .... | .... | .... | .... | .... | .... |
| **2003-04** | **Atlanta** | **NHL** | **67** | **3** | **26** | **29** | **30** | **2** | **0** | **1** | **94** | **3.2** | **2** | **2** | **50.0** | **23:20** | .... | .... | .... | .... | .... | .... | .... | .... | .... |

| | | | Regular Season | | | | | | | | | | | | | | Playoffs | | | | | | | | |
|---|---|---|---|---|---|---|---|---|---|---|---|---|---|---|---|---|---|---|---|---|---|---|---|---|---|
| Season | Club | League | GP | G | A | Pts | PIM | PP | SH | GW | S | % | +/- | TF | F% | Min | GP | G | A | Pts | PIM | PP | SH | GW | Min |
| 2004-05 | HC Rabat Kladno | CzRep | 22 | 5 | 11 | 16 | 34 | .... | .... | .... | .... | .... | .... | .... | .... | .... | .... | .... | .... | .... | .... | .... | .... | .... | .... |
| | MODO | Sweden | 8 | 2 | 2 | 4 | 0 | .... | .... | .... | .... | .... | .... | .... | .... | .... | 6 | 1 | 0 | 1 | 27 | .... | .... | .... | .... |
| **2005-06♦** | **Carolina** | **NHL** | **77** | **6** | **38** | **44** | **46** | **1** | **0** | **3** | **126** | **4.8** | **8** | **0** | **0.0** | **19:37** | **25** | **4** | **9** | **13** | **8** | **3** | **0** | **1** | **18:25** |
| | Czech Republic | Olympics | 8 | 0 | 1 | 1 | 6 | .... | .... | .... | .... | .... | .... | .... | .... | .... | .... | .... | .... | .... | .... | .... | .... | .... | .... |
| **2006-07** | **Carolina** | **NHL** | **27** | **2** | **6** | **8** | **20** | **1** | **0** | **1** | **33** | **6.1** | **8** | **0** | **0.0** | **15:32** | .... | .... | .... | .... | .... | .... | .... | .... | .... |
| **2007-08** | **Carolina** | **NHL** | **80** | **0** | **22** | **22** | **30** | **0** | **0** | **0** | **89** | **0.0** | **–4** | **0** | **0.0** | **17:09** | .... | .... | .... | .... | .... | .... | .... | .... | .... |
| **2008-09** | **Carolina** | **NHL** | **30** | **1** | **7** | **8** | **8** | **1** | **0** | **0** | **28** | **3.6** | **–4** | **0** | **0.0** | **14:03** | **7** | **0** | **1** | **1** | **2** | **0** | **0** | **0** | **12:14** |
| | **NHL Totals** | | **523** | **29** | **164** | **193** | **218** | **10** | **2** | **8** | **732** | **4.0** | | **3** | **33.3** | **19:59** | **32** | **4** | **10** | **14** | **10** | **3** | **0** | **1** | **17:04** |

Traded to **Atlanta** by **Los Angeles** with Donald Audette for Kelly Buchberger and Nelson Emerson, March 13, 2000. Signed as a free agent by **Carolina**, July 15, 2004. Signed as a free agent by **Kladno** (CzRep), September 17, 2004. Signed as a free agent by **MODO** (Sweden), January 31, 2005. • Missed majority of 2006-07 season recovering from off-season shoulder surgery. • Missed majority of 2008-09 season recovering from various injuries.

## KABERLE, Tomas
(KA-buhr-lay, TAW-mas) **TOR.**

Defense. Shoots left. 6'1", 198 lbs. Born, Rakovnik, Czech., March 2, 1978. Toronto's 13th choice, 204th overall, in 1996 Entry Draft.

| | | | | | | | | | | | | | | | | | | | | | | | | | |
|---|---|---|---|---|---|---|---|---|---|---|---|---|---|---|---|---|---|---|---|---|---|---|---|---|---|
| 1994-95 | HC Kladno Jr. | CzRep-Jr. | 37 | 7 | 10 | 17 | .... | .... | .... | .... | .... | .... | .... | .... | .... | .... | .... | .... | .... | .... | .... | .... | .... | .... | .... |
| | HC Kladno | CzRep | 4 | 0 | 1 | 1 | 0 | .... | .... | .... | .... | .... | .... | .... | .... | .... | .... | .... | .... | .... | .... | .... | .... | .... | .... |
| 1995-96 | Kladno Jr. | CzRep-Jr. | 23 | 6 | 13 | 19 | .... | .... | .... | .... | .... | .... | .... | .... | .... | .... | .... | .... | .... | .... | .... | .... | .... | .... | .... |
| | HC Poldi Kladno | CzRep | 23 | 0 | 1 | 1 | 2 | .... | .... | .... | .... | .... | .... | .... | .... | .... | 2 | 0 | 0 | 0 | 0 | .... | .... | .... | .... |
| 1996-97 | HC Poldi Kladno | CzRep | 49 | 0 | 5 | 5 | 26 | .... | .... | .... | .... | .... | .... | .... | .... | .... | 3 | 0 | 0 | 0 | 0 | .... | .... | .... | .... |
| 1997-98 | Kladno | CzRep | 47 | 4 | 19 | 23 | 12 | .... | .... | .... | .... | .... | .... | .... | .... | .... | .... | .... | .... | .... | .... | .... | .... | .... | .... |
| | St. John's | AHL | 2 | 0 | 0 | 0 | 0 | .... | .... | .... | .... | .... | .... | .... | .... | .... | .... | .... | .... | .... | .... | .... | .... | .... | .... |
| **1998-99** | **Toronto** | **NHL** | **57** | **4** | **18** | **22** | **12** | **0** | **0** | **2** | **71** | **5.6** | **3** | **0** | **0.0** | **18:42** | **14** | **0** | **3** | **3** | **2** | **0** | **0** | **0** | **17:10** |
| **99-2000** | **Toronto** | **NHL** | **82** | **7** | **33** | **40** | **24** | **2** | **0** | **0** | **82** | **8.5** | **3** | **0** | **0.0** | **22:55** | **12** | **1** | **4** | **5** | **0** | **0** | **0** | **1** | **23:01** |
| **2000-01** | **Toronto** | **NHL** | **82** | **6** | **39** | **45** | **24** | **0** | **0** | **1** | **96** | **6.3** | **10** | **2** | **0.0** | **22:41** | **11** | **1** | **3** | **4** | **0** | **0** | **0** | **1** | **21:33** |
| **2001-02** | Kladno | CzRep | 9 | 1 | 7 | 8 | 4 | .... | .... | .... | .... | .... | .... | .... | .... | .... | .... | .... | .... | .... | .... | .... | .... | .... | .... |
| | **Toronto** | **NHL** | **69** | **10** | **29** | **39** | **2** | **5** | **0** | **3** | **85** | **11.8** | **5** | **2** | **100.0** | **25:00** | **20** | **2** | **8** | **10** | **16** | **0** | **0** | **0** | **28:40** |
| | Czech Republic | Olympics | 4 | 0 | 1 | 1 | 2 | .... | .... | .... | .... | .... | .... | .... | .... | .... | .... | .... | .... | .... | .... | .... | .... | .... | .... |
| **2002-03** | **Toronto** | **NHL** | **82** | **11** | **36** | **47** | **30** | **4** | **1** | **2** | **119** | **9.2** | **20** | **3** | **66.7** | **24:50** | **7** | **2** | **1** | **3** | **0** | **1** | **0** | **1** | **30:04** |
| **2003-04** | **Toronto** | **NHL** | **71** | **3** | **28** | **31** | **18** | **0** | **0** | **1** | **88** | **3.4** | **16** | **2** | **0.0** | **23:12** | **13** | **0** | **3** | **3** | **6** | **0** | **0** | **0** | **20:16** |
| 2004-05 | HC Rabat Kladno | CzRep | 49 | 8 | 31 | 39 | 38 | .... | .... | .... | .... | .... | .... | .... | .... | .... | 7 | 1 | 0 | 1 | 0 | .... | .... | .... | .... |
| **2005-06** | **Toronto** | **NHL** | **82** | **9** | **58** | **67** | **46** | **6** | **0** | **2** | **163** | **5.5** | **–1** | **0** | **0.0** | **28:10** | .... | .... | .... | .... | .... | .... | .... | .... | .... |
| | Czech Republic | Olympics | 8 | 2 | 2 | 4 | 2 | .... | .... | .... | .... | .... | .... | .... | .... | .... | .... | .... | .... | .... | .... | .... | .... | .... | .... |
| **2006-07** | **Toronto** | **NHL** | **74** | **11** | **47** | **58** | **20** | **2** | **0** | **1** | **128** | **8.6** | **3** | **0** | **0.0** | **25:52** | .... | .... | .... | .... | .... | .... | .... | .... | .... |
| **2007-08** | **Toronto** | **NHL** | **82** | **8** | **45** | **53** | **22** | **6** | **0** | **1** | **155** | **5.2** | **–8** | **2** | **50.0** | **24:52** | .... | .... | .... | .... | .... | .... | .... | .... | .... |
| **2008-09** | **Toronto** | **NHL** | **57** | **4** | **27** | **31** | **8** | **3** | **0** | **1** | **93** | **4.3** | **–8** | **0** | **0.0** | **23:28** | .... | .... | .... | .... | .... | .... | .... | .... | .... |
| | **NHL Totals** | | **738** | **73** | **360** | **433** | **206** | **28** | **1** | **14** | **1080** | **6.8** | | **11** | **45.5** | **24:08** | **77** | **6** | **22** | **28** | **24** | **1** | **0** | **3** | **23:23** |

Played in NHL All-Star Game (2002, 2007, 2008, 2009)

Signed as a restricted free agent by **Kladno** (CzRep) with **Toronto** retaining NHL rights, September 29, 2001. Signed as a free agent by **Kladno** (CzRep), September 17, 2004.

## KAIGORODOV, Alexei
(kay-goh-ROH-dahv, al-EHX-ay) **PHX.**

Center. Shoots left. 6'1", 194 lbs. Born, Magnitogorsk, USSR, July 29, 1983. Ottawa's 2nd choice, 47th overall, in 2002 Entry Draft.

| | | | | | | | | | | | | | | | | | | | | | | | | | |
|---|---|---|---|---|---|---|---|---|---|---|---|---|---|---|---|---|---|---|---|---|---|---|---|---|---|
| 1998-99 | Magnitogorsk 2 | Russia-4 | 10 | 6 | 4 | 10 | 2 | .... | .... | .... | .... | .... | .... | .... | .... | .... | .... | .... | .... | .... | .... | .... | .... | .... | .... |
| 99-2000 | Magnitogorsk 2 | Russia-3 | 19 | 2 | 3 | 5 | 8 | .... | .... | .... | .... | .... | .... | .... | .... | .... | .... | .... | .... | .... | .... | .... | .... | .... | .... |
| 2000-01 | Magnitogorsk 2 | Russia-3 | 45 | 12 | 30 | 42 | 26 | .... | .... | .... | .... | .... | .... | .... | .... | .... | .... | .... | .... | .... | .... | .... | .... | .... | .... |
| 2001-02 | Magnitogorsk | Russia | 46 | 4 | 12 | 16 | 20 | .... | .... | .... | .... | .... | .... | .... | .... | .... | 9 | 0 | 3 | 3 | 2 | .... | .... | .... | .... |
| 2002-03 | Magnitogorsk | Russia | 46 | 8 | 14 | 22 | 20 | .... | .... | .... | .... | .... | .... | .... | .... | .... | 3 | 0 | 1 | 1 | 0 | .... | .... | .... | .... |
| 2003-04 | Magnitogorsk | Russia | 49 | 4 | 12 | 16 | 24 | .... | .... | .... | .... | .... | .... | .... | .... | .... | 14 | 2 | 2 | 4 | 4 | .... | .... | .... | .... |
| 2004-05 | Magnitogorsk | Russia | 57 | 15 | 34 | 49 | 40 | .... | .... | .... | .... | .... | .... | .... | .... | .... | 5 | 0 | 3 | 3 | 2 | .... | .... | .... | .... |
| 2005-06 | Magnitogorsk | Russia | 50 | 9 | 21 | 30 | 42 | .... | .... | .... | .... | .... | .... | .... | .... | .... | 11 | 0 | 1 | 1 | 6 | .... | .... | .... | .... |
| **2006-07** | **Ottawa** | **NHL** | **6** | **0** | **1** | **1** | **0** | **0** | **0** | **0** | **3** | **0.0** | **1** | **24** | **20.8** | **4:53** | .... | .... | .... | .... | .... | .... | .... | .... | .... |
| | Magnitogorsk | Russia | 32 | 6 | 12 | 18 | 18 | .... | .... | .... | .... | .... | .... | .... | .... | .... | 15 | 2 | 8 | 10 | 14 | .... | .... | .... | .... |
| 2007-08 | Magnitogorsk | Russia | 56 | 6 | 33 | 39 | 30 | .... | .... | .... | .... | .... | .... | .... | .... | .... | 13 | 1 | 4 | 5 | 4 | .... | .... | .... | .... |
| 2008-09 | Magnitogorsk | Rus-KHL | 56 | 10 | 29 | 39 | 26 | .... | .... | .... | .... | .... | .... | .... | .... | .... | 12 | 4 | 4 | 8 | 10 | .... | .... | .... | .... |
| | **NHL Totals** | | **6** | **0** | **1** | **1** | **0** | **0** | **0** | **0** | **3** | **0.0** | | **24** | **20.8** | **4:53** | .... | .... | .... | .... | .... | .... | .... | .... | .... |

Traded to **Phoenix** by **Ottawa** for Mike Comrie, January 3, 2007.

## KALETA, Patrick
(ka-LEH-tuh, PAT-rihk) **BUF.**

Right wing. Shoots right. 5'11", 198 lbs. Born, Buffalo, NY, June 8, 1986. Buffalo's 5th choice, 176th overall, in 2004 Entry Draft.

| | | | | | | | | | | | | | | | | | | | | | | | | | |
|---|---|---|---|---|---|---|---|---|---|---|---|---|---|---|---|---|---|---|---|---|---|---|---|---|---|
| 2002-03 | Peterborough | OHL | 67 | 7 | 9 | 16 | 67 | .... | .... | .... | .... | .... | .... | .... | .... | .... | 7 | 0 | 0 | 0 | 6 | .... | .... | .... | .... |
| 2003-04 | Peterborough | OHL | 67 | 14 | 14 | 28 | 124 | .... | .... | .... | .... | .... | .... | .... | .... | .... | .... | .... | .... | .... | .... | .... | .... | .... | .... |
| 2004-05 | Peterborough | OHL | 62 | 24 | 28 | 52 | 146 | .... | .... | .... | .... | .... | .... | .... | .... | .... | 14 | 3 | 3 | 6 | 30 | .... | .... | .... | .... |
| 2005-06 | Peterborough | OHL | 68 | 16 | 35 | 51 | 121 | .... | .... | .... | .... | .... | .... | .... | .... | .... | 19 | 8 | 10 | 18 | 43 | .... | .... | .... | .... |
| **2006-07** | **Buffalo** | **NHL** | **7** | **0** | **2** | **2** | **21** | **0** | **0** | **0** | **6** | **0.0** | **3** | **0** | **0.0** | **6:49** | .... | .... | .... | .... | .... | .... | .... | .... | .... |
| | Rochester | AHL | 58 | 5 | 10 | 15 | 133 | .... | .... | .... | .... | .... | .... | .... | .... | .... | 5 | 0 | 0 | 0 | 12 | .... | .... | .... | .... |
| **2007-08** | **Buffalo** | **NHL** | **40** | **3** | **2** | **5** | **41** | **0** | **0** | **0** | **26** | **11.5** | **1** | **6** | **16.7** | **6:19** | .... | .... | .... | .... | .... | .... | .... | .... | .... |
| | Rochester | AHL | 29 | 1 | 3 | 4 | 109 | .... | .... | .... | .... | .... | .... | .... | .... | .... | .... | .... | .... | .... | .... | .... | .... | .... | .... |
| **2008-09** | **Buffalo** | **NHL** | **51** | **4** | **5** | **9** | **89** | **0** | **0** | **0** | **35** | **11.4** | **1** | **5** | **20.0** | **8:55** | .... | .... | .... | .... | .... | .... | .... | .... | .... |
| | **NHL Totals** | | **98** | **7** | **9** | **16** | **151** | **0** | **0** | **0** | **67** | **10.4** | | **11** | **18.2** | **7:43** | .... | .... | .... | .... | .... | .... | .... | .... | .... |

## KALININ, Dmitri
(kah-LIHN-ihn, dih-MEE-tree)

Defense. Shoots left. 6'3", 210 lbs. Born, Chelyabinsk, USSR, July 22, 1980. Buffalo's 1st choice, 18th overall, in 1998 Entry Draft.

| | | | | | | | | | | | | | | | | | | | | | | | | | |
|---|---|---|---|---|---|---|---|---|---|---|---|---|---|---|---|---|---|---|---|---|---|---|---|---|---|
| 1995-96 | Chelyabinsk | CIS | 20 | 0 | 3 | 3 | 10 | .... | .... | .... | .... | .... | .... | .... | .... | .... | .... | .... | .... | .... | .... | .... | .... | .... | .... |
| 1996-97 | Yunior-T Kurgan | Russia-3 | 20 | 0 | 0 | 0 | 10 | .... | .... | .... | .... | .... | .... | .... | .... | .... | .... | .... | .... | .... | .... | .... | .... | .... | .... |
| | Chelyabinsk | Russia | 2 | 0 | 0 | 0 | 0 | .... | .... | .... | .... | .... | .... | .... | .... | .... | 2 | 0 | 0 | 0 | 0 | .... | .... | .... | .... |
| 1997-98 | Chelyabinsk | Russia | 26 | 0 | 2 | 2 | 24 | .... | .... | .... | .... | .... | .... | .... | .... | .... | .... | .... | .... | .... | .... | .... | .... | .... | .... |
| 1998-99 | Moncton Wildcats | QMJHL | 39 | 7 | 18 | 25 | 44 | .... | .... | .... | .... | .... | .... | .... | .... | .... | 4 | 1 | 1 | 2 | 0 | .... | .... | .... | .... |
| | Rochester | AHL | 3 | 0 | 1 | 1 | 14 | .... | .... | .... | .... | .... | .... | .... | .... | .... | 7 | 0 | 0 | 0 | 6 | .... | .... | .... | .... |
| **99-2000** | **Buffalo** | **NHL** | **4** | **0** | **0** | **0** | **4** | **0** | **0** | **0** | **3** | **0.0** | **0** | **0** | **0.0** | **16:53** | .... | .... | .... | .... | .... | .... | .... | .... | .... |
| | Rochester | AHL | 75 | 2 | 19 | 21 | 52 | .... | .... | .... | .... | .... | .... | .... | .... | .... | 21 | 2 | 9 | 11 | 8 | .... | .... | .... | .... |
| **2000-01** | **Buffalo** | **NHL** | **79** | **4** | **18** | **22** | **38** | **2** | **0** | **0** | **88** | **4.5** | **–2** | **1** | **100.0** | **19:50** | **13** | **0** | **2** | **2** | **4** | **0** | **0** | **0** | **20:05** |
| **2001-02** | **Buffalo** | **NHL** | **58** | **2** | **11** | **13** | **26** | **0** | **0** | **0** | **67** | **3.0** | **–6** | **0** | **0.0** | **18:03** | .... | .... | .... | .... | .... | .... | .... | .... | .... |
| **2002-03** | **Buffalo** | **NHL** | **65** | **8** | **13** | **21** | **57** | **3** | **1** | **0** | **83** | **9.6** | **–7** | **0** | **0.0** | **21:41** | .... | .... | .... | .... | .... | .... | .... | .... | .... |
| | Rochester | AHL | 1 | 0 | 0 | 0 | 0 | .... | .... | .... | .... | .... | .... | .... | .... | .... | .... | .... | .... | .... | .... | .... | .... | .... | .... |
| **2003-04** | **Buffalo** | **NHL** | **77** | **10** | **24** | **34** | **42** | **2** | **1** | **4** | **118** | **8.5** | **0** | **0** | **0.0** | **23:06** | .... | .... | .... | .... | .... | .... | .... | .... | .... |
| 2004-05 | Magnitogorsk | Russia | 48 | 2 | 8 | 10 | 14 | .... | .... | .... | .... | .... | .... | .... | .... | .... | 5 | 0 | 0 | 0 | 2 | .... | .... | .... | .... |
| **2005-06** | **Buffalo** | **NHL** | **55** | **2** | **16** | **18** | **54** | **0** | **0** | **0** | **47** | **4.3** | **14** | **0** | **0.0** | **16:45** | **8** | **0** | **2** | **2** | **2** | **0** | **0** | **0** | **16:53** |
| **2006-07** | **Buffalo** | **NHL** | **82** | **7** | **22** | **29** | **36** | **0** | **1** | **0** | **86** | **8.1** | **19** | **1** | **100.0** | **19:31** | **16** | **2** | **3** | **5** | **14** | **0** | **0** | **0** | **18:11** |
| **2007-08** | **Buffalo** | **NHL** | **46** | **1** | **7** | **8** | **32** | **1** | **0** | **0** | **60** | **1.7** | **–7** | **0** | **0.0** | **17:20** | .... | .... | .... | .... | .... | .... | .... | .... | .... |
| **2008-09** | **NY Rangers** | **NHL** | **58** | **1** | **12** | **13** | **26** | **0** | **0** | **0** | **51** | **2.0** | **–7** | **0** | **0.0** | **17:01** | .... | .... | .... | .... | .... | .... | .... | .... | .... |
| | **Phoenix** | **NHL** | **15** | **1** | **3** | **4** | **6** | **1** | **0** | **0** | **16** | **6.3** | **–2** | **0** | **0.0** | **20:12** | .... | .... | .... | .... | .... | .... | .... | .... | .... |
| | **NHL Totals** | | **539** | **36** | **126** | **162** | **321** | **9** | **3** | **4** | **619** | **5.8** | | **2** | **100.0** | **19:26** | **37** | **2** | **7** | **9** | **20** | **0** | **0** | **0** | **18:34** |

AHL All-Rookie Team (2000)

Signed as a free agent by **Magnitogorsk** (Russia), September 25, 2004. Signed as a free agent by **NY Rangers**, July 3, 2008. Traded to **Phoenix** by **NY Rangers** with Nigel Dawes and Petr Prucha for Derek Morris, March 4, 2009. Signed as a free agent by **Ufa** (Rus-KHL), July 21, 2009.

## KALINSKI, Jon
(kuh-LIHN-skee, JAWN) **PHI.**

Left wing. Shoots left. 6'1", 180 lbs. Born, Bonnyville, Alta., May 25, 1987. Philadelphia's 5th choice, 152nd overall, in 2007 Entry Draft.

| | | | | | | | | | | | | | | | | | | | | | | | | | |
|---|---|---|---|---|---|---|---|---|---|---|---|---|---|---|---|---|---|---|---|---|---|---|---|---|---|
| 2003-04 | Bonnyville | AJHL | 52 | 13 | 13 | 26 | 68 | .... | .... | .... | .... | .... | .... | .... | .... | .... | 5 | 0 | 0 | 0 | 8 | .... | .... | .... | .... |
| 2004-05 | Bonnyville | AJHL | 58 | 16 | 25 | 41 | 195 | .... | .... | .... | .... | .... | .... | .... | .... | .... | 4 | 2 | 0 | 2 | 6 | .... | .... | .... | .... |
| 2005-06 | Minnesota State | WCHA | 30 | 4 | 7 | 11 | 73 | .... | .... | .... | .... | .... | .... | .... | .... | .... | .... | .... | .... | .... | .... | .... | .... | .... | .... |
| 2006-07 | Minnesota State | WCHA | 37 | 17 | 10 | 27 | 74 | .... | .... | .... | .... | .... | .... | .... | .... | .... | .... | .... | .... | .... | .... | .... | .... | .... | .... |
| 2007-08 | Minnesota State | WCHA | 39 | 8 | 10 | 18 | 56 | .... | .... | .... | .... | .... | .... | .... | .... | .... | .... | .... | .... | .... | .... | .... | .... | .... | .... |
| | Philadelphia | AHL | 5 | 0 | 3 | 3 | 4 | .... | .... | .... | .... | .... | .... | .... | .... | .... | 10 | 1 | 2 | 3 | 14 | .... | .... | .... | .... |

| | | | Regular Season | | | | | | | | | | | | | | Playoffs | | | | | | | | |
|---|---|---|---|---|---|---|---|---|---|---|---|---|---|---|---|---|---|---|---|---|---|---|---|---|---|
| Season | Club | League | GP | G | A | Pts | PIM | PP | SH | GW | S | % | +/- | TF | F% | Min | GP | G | A | Pts | PIM | PP | SH | GW | Min |
| **2008-09** | **Philadelphia** | **NHL** | **12** | **1** | **2** | **3** | **0** | **0** | **0** | **1** | **7** | **14.3** | **–2** | **46** | **45.7** | **7:37** | | | | | | | | | |
| | Philadelphia | AHL | 46 | 10 | 7 | 17 | 49 | | | | | | | | | | 4 | 1 | 2 | 3 | 4 | | | | |
| | **NHL Totals** | | **12** | **1** | **2** | **3** | **0** | **0** | **0** | **1** | **7** | **14.3** | | **46** | **45.7** | **7:37** | | | | | | | | | |

## KALUS, Petr

(KAY-lihs, PEE-tuhr) **MIN.**

Left wing. Shoots left. 6'1", 201 lbs. Born, Ostrava, Czech., June 29, 1987. Boston's 2nd choice, 39th overall, in 2005 Entry Draft.

| Season | Club | League | GP | G | A | Pts | PIM | PP | SH | GW | S | % | +/- | TF | F% | Min | GP | G | A | Pts | PIM | PP | SH | GW | Min |
|---|---|---|---|---|---|---|---|---|---|---|---|---|---|---|---|---|---|---|---|---|---|---|---|---|---|
| 2002-03 | HC Ostrava U17 | CzR-U17 | 18 | 3 | 19 | 22 | 14 | | | | | | | | | | | | | | | | | | |
| | HC Vitkovice U17 | CzR-U17 | 10 | 3 | 1 | 4 | 37 | | | | | | | | | | | | | | | | | | |
| | HC Vitkovice Jr. | CzRep-Jr. | 11 | 0 | 0 | 0 | 4 | | | | | | | | | | | | | | | | | | |
| 2003-04 | HC Vitkovice U17 | CzR-U17 | 9 | 7 | 5 | 12 | 60 | | | | | | | | | | 7 | 3 | 5 | 8 | 2 | | | | |
| | HC Vitkovice Jr. | CzRep-Jr. | 41 | 8 | 8 | 16 | 67 | | | | | | | | | | | | | | | | | | |
| 2004-05 | HC Vitkovice Jr. | CzRep-Jr. | 39 | 20 | 11 | 31 | 161 | | | | | | | | | | 2 | 2 | 0 | 2 | 25 | | | | |
| | Vitkovice | CzRep | 1 | 0 | 0 | 0 | 0 | | | | | | | | | | | | | | | | | | |
| 2005-06 | Regina Pats | WHL | 60 | 36 | 22 | 58 | 87 | | | | | | | | | | 6 | 4 | 1 | 5 | 6 | | | | |
| **2006-07** | **Boston** | **NHL** | **9** | **4** | **1** | **5** | **6** | **1** | **0** | **0** | **8** | **50.0** | **0** | **0** | **0.0** | **11:16** | | | | | | | | | |
| | Providence Bruins | AHL | 43 | 13 | 17 | 30 | 110 | | | | | | | | | | 9 | 1 | 0 | 1 | 12 | | | | |
| 2007-08 | Houston Aeros | AHL | 58 | 8 | 10 | 18 | 57 | | | | | | | | | | | | | | | | | | |
| 2008-09 | MVD | Rus-KHL | 17 | 0 | 2 | 2 | 106 | | | | | | | | | | | | | | | | | | |
| | Houston Aeros | AHL | 2 | 0 | 0 | 0 | 0 | | | | | | | | | | | | | | | | | | |
| | **NHL Totals** | | **9** | **4** | **1** | **5** | **6** | **1** | **0** | **0** | **8** | **50.0** | | **0** | **0.0** | **11:16** | | | | | | | | | |

Traded to **Minnesota** by **Boston** with Boston's 4th round choice (Alexander Fallstrom) in 2009 Entry Draft for Manny Fernandez, July 1, 2007.

## KANE, Boyd

(KAYN, BOID) **WSH.**

Left wing. Shoots left. 6'2", 220 lbs. Born, Swift Current, Sask., April 18, 1978. NY Rangers' 4th choice, 114th overall, in 1998 Entry Draft.

| Season | Club | League | GP | G | A | Pts | PIM | PP | SH | GW | S | % | +/- | TF | F% | Min | GP | G | A | Pts | PIM | PP | SH | GW | Min |
|---|---|---|---|---|---|---|---|---|---|---|---|---|---|---|---|---|---|---|---|---|---|---|---|---|---|
| 1994-95 | Regina Pats | WHL | 25 | 6 | 5 | 11 | 6 | | | | | | | | | | 4 | 0 | 0 | 0 | 0 | | | | |
| 1995-96 | Regina Pats | WHL | 72 | 21 | 42 | 63 | 155 | | | | | | | | | | 11 | 5 | 7 | 12 | 12 | | | | |
| 1996-97 | Regina Pats | WHL | 66 | 25 | 50 | 75 | 154 | | | | | | | | | | 5 | 1 | 1 | 2 | 15 | | | | |
| 1997-98 | Regina Pats | WHL | 68 | 48 | 45 | 93 | 133 | | | | | | | | | | 9 | 5 | 7 | 12 | 29 | | | | |
| 1998-99 | Hartford | AHL | 56 | 3 | 5 | 8 | 23 | | | | | | | | | | | | | | | | | | |
| | Charlotte | ECHL | 12 | 5 | 6 | 11 | 14 | | | | | | | | | | | | | | | | | | |
| 99-2000 | Hartford | AHL | 8 | 0 | 0 | 0 | 9 | | | | | | | | | | | | | | | | | | |
| | Charlotte | ECHL | 47 | 10 | 19 | 29 | 110 | | | | | | | | | | | | | | | | | | |
| | Binghamton | UHL | 3 | 0 | 2 | 2 | 4 | | | | | | | | | | 1 | 0 | 0 | 0 | 0 | | | | |
| 2000-01 | Charlotte | ECHL | 12 | 9 | 8 | 17 | 6 | | | | | | | | | | | | | | | | | | |
| | Hartford | AHL | 56 | 11 | 17 | 28 | 81 | | | | | | | | | | 5 | 2 | 0 | 2 | 2 | | | | |
| 2001-02 | Hartford | AHL | 78 | 17 | 22 | 39 | 193 | | | | | | | | | | 10 | 1 | 2 | 3 | 50 | | | | |
| 2002-03 | Springfield | AHL | 72 | 15 | 22 | 37 | 121 | | | | | | | | | | 6 | 3 | 1 | 4 | 8 | | | | |
| **2003-04** | **Philadelphia** | **NHL** | **7** | **0** | **0** | **0** | **7** | **0** | **0** | **0** | **6** | **0.0** | **–4** | **3** | **33.3** | **9:56** | | | | | | | | | |
| | Philadelphia | AHL | 73 | 13 | 22 | 35 | 177 | | | | | | | | | | 12 | 0 | 1 | 1 | 39 | | | | |
| 2004-05 | Philadelphia | AHL | 58 | 9 | 15 | 24 | 112 | | | | | | | | | | 21 | 0 | 7 | 7 | 28 | | | | |
| **2005-06** | **Washington** | **NHL** | **5** | **0** | **1** | **1** | **2** | **0** | **0** | **0** | **1** | **0.0** | **1** | **0** | **0.0** | **4:04** | | | | | | | | | |
| | Hershey Bears | AHL | 74 | 20 | 29 | 49 | 185 | | | | | | | | | | 21 | 4 | 9 | 13 | 14 | | | | |
| **2006-07** | **Philadelphia** | **NHL** | **15** | **0** | **2** | **2** | **28** | **0** | **0** | **0** | **7** | **0.0** | **–4** | **4** | **25.0** | **6:58** | | | | | | | | | |
| | Philadelphia | AHL | 57 | 10 | 22 | 32 | 98 | | | | | | | | | | | | | | | | | | |
| 2007-08 | Philadelphia | AHL | 57 | 18 | 26 | 44 | 102 | | | | | | | | | | 12 | 4 | 4 | 8 | 25 | | | | |
| **2008-09** | **Philadelphia** | **NHL** | **1** | **0** | **0** | **0** | **0** | **0** | **0** | **0** | **0** | **0.0** | **0** | **0** | **0.0** | **8:12** | | | | | | | | | |
| | Philadelphia | AHL | 58 | 17 | 26 | 43 | 74 | | | | | | | | | | 4 | 1 | 1 | 2 | 6 | | | | |
| | **NHL Totals** | | **28** | **0** | **3** | **3** | **37** | **0** | **0** | **0** | **14** | **0.0** | | **7** | **28.6** | **7:14** | | | | | | | | | |

• Re-entered NHL Entry Draft. Originally Pittsburgh's 3rd choice, 72nd overall, in 1996 Entry Draft.

Traded to **Tampa Bay** by **NY Rangers** for Gordie Dwyer, October 10, 2002. Signed as a free agent by **Philadelphia**, July 14, 2003. Signed as a free agent by **Washington**, August 12, 2005. Signed as a free agent by **Philadelphia**, July 13, 2006. Signed as a free agent by **Washington**, July 13, 2009.

## KANE, Patrick

(KAYN, PAT-rihk) **CHI.**

Right wing. Shoots left. 5'10", 175 lbs. Born, Buffalo, NY, November 19, 1988. Chicago's 1st choice, 1st overall, in 2007 Entry Draft.

| Season | Club | League | GP | G | A | Pts | PIM | PP | SH | GW | S | % | +/- | TF | F% | Min | GP | G | A | Pts | PIM | PP | SH | GW | Min |
|---|---|---|---|---|---|---|---|---|---|---|---|---|---|---|---|---|---|---|---|---|---|---|---|---|---|
| 2003-04 | Det. Honeybaked | MWEHL | 70 | 83 | 77 | 160 | | | | | | | | | | | | | | | | | | | |
| 2004-05 | USNTDP | U-17 | 23 | 16 | 17 | 33 | 8 | | | | | | | | | | | | | | | | | | |
| | USNTDP | NAHL | 40 | 16 | 21 | 37 | 8 | | | | | | | | | | 9 | 7 | 8 | 15 | 2 | | | | |
| 2005-06 | USNTDP | U-18 | 43 | 35 | 33 | 68 | 10 | | | | | | | | | | | | | | | | | | |
| | USNTDP | NAHL | 15 | 17 | 17 | 34 | 12 | | | | | | | | | | | | | | | | | | |
| 2006-07 | London Knights | OHL | 58 | 62 | 83 | *145 | 52 | | | | | | | | | | 16 | 10 | 21 | *31 | 16 | | | | |
| **2007-08** | **Chicago** | **NHL** | **82** | **21** | **51** | **72** | **52** | **7** | **0** | **4** | **191** | **11.0** | **–5** | **26** | **61.5** | **18:22** | | | | | | | | | |
| **2008-09** | **Chicago** | **NHL** | **80** | **25** | **45** | **70** | **42** | **13** | **0** | **4** | **254** | **9.8** | **–2** | **31** | **41.9** | **18:40** | **16** | **9** | **5** | **14** | **12** | **2** | **0** | **0** | **16:36** |
| | **NHL Totals** | | **162** | **46** | **96** | **142** | **94** | **20** | **0** | **8** | **445** | **10.3** | | **57** | **50.9** | **18:31** | **16** | **9** | **5** | **14** | **12** | **2** | **0** | **0** | **16:36** |

OHL All-Rookie Team (2007) • OHL First All-Star Team (2007) • OHL Rookie of the Year (2007) • Canadian Major Junior First All-Star Team (2007) • Canadian Major Junior Rookie of the Year (2007) • NHL All-Rookie Team (2008) • Calder Memorial Trophy (2008)

Played in NHL All-Star Game (2009)

## KAPANEN, Niko

(KA-pah-nehn, NEE-KOH)

Center. Shoots left. 5'9", 180 lbs. Born, Hameenlinna, Finland, April 29, 1978. Dallas' 5th choice, 173rd overall, in 1998 Entry Draft.

| Season | Club | League | GP | G | A | Pts | PIM | PP | SH | GW | S | % | +/- | TF | F% | Min | GP | G | A | Pts | PIM | PP | SH | GW | Min |
|---|---|---|---|---|---|---|---|---|---|---|---|---|---|---|---|---|---|---|---|---|---|---|---|---|---|
| 1993-94 | HPK U18 | Fin-U18 | 31 | 17 | 33 | 50 | 34 | | | | | | | | | | | | | | | | | | |
| 1994-95 | HPK U18 | Fin-U18 | 31 | 16 | 39 | 55 | 40 | | | | | | | | | | | | | | | | | | |
| | HPK Jr. | Fin-Jr. | 6 | 3 | 5 | 8 | 0 | | | | | | | | | | | | | | | | | | |
| 1995-96 | HPK U18 | Fin-U18 | 10 | 6 | 6 | 12 | 8 | | | | | | | | | | | | | | | | | | |
| | HPK Jr. | Fin-Jr. | 26 | 15 | 22 | 37 | 34 | | | | | | | | | | | | | | | | | | |
| | HPK Hameenlinna | Finland | 7 | 1 | 0 | 1 | 0 | | | | | | | | | | | | | | | | | | |
| 1996-97 | HPK Jr. | Fin-Jr. | 5 | 1 | 7 | 8 | 2 | | | | | | | | | | 2 | 0 | 1 | 1 | 2 | | | | |
| | HPK Hameenlinna | Finland | 41 | 6 | 9 | 15 | 12 | | | | | | | | | | 10 | 4 | 5 | 9 | 2 | | | | |
| | HPK Hameenlinna | EuroHL | 6 | 3 | 0 | 3 | 4 | | | | | | | | | | 1 | 0 | 0 | 0 | 0 | | | | |
| 1997-98 | HPK Jr. | Fin-Jr. | 2 | 1 | 1 | 2 | 0 | | | | | | | | | | | | | | | | | | |
| | HPK Hameenlinna | Finland | 48 | 8 | 18 | 26 | 44 | | | | | | | | | | | | | | | | | | |
| 1998-99 | HPK Jr. | Fin-Jr. | 5 | 3 | 1 | 4 | 0 | | | | | | | | | | 1 | 0 | 2 | 2 | 0 | | | | |
| | HPK Hameenlinna | Finland | 53 | 14 | 29 | 43 | 49 | | | | | | | | | | 8 | 3 | 4 | 7 | 4 | | | | |
| 99-2000 | HPK Hameenlinna | Finland | 53 | 20 | 28 | 48 | 38 | | | | | | | | | | 8 | 1 | 9 | 10 | 4 | | | | |
| 2000-01 | TPS Turku | Finland | 56 | 11 | 22 | 33 | 20 | | | | | | | | | | 10 | 2 | 1 | 3 | 4 | | | | |
| **2001-02** | **Dallas** | **NHL** | **9** | **0** | **1** | **1** | **2** | **0** | **0** | **0** | **3** | **0.0** | **–1** | **59** | **40.7** | **9:44** | | | | | | | | | |
| | Utah Grizzlies | AHL | 59 | 13 | 28 | 41 | 40 | | | | | | | | | | 5 | 2 | 1 | 3 | 0 | | | | |
| **2002-03** | **Dallas** | **NHL** | **82** | **5** | **29** | **34** | **44** | **0** | **1** | **1** | **80** | **6.3** | **25** | **1111** | **47.5** | **14:39** | **12** | **4** | **3** | **7** | **12** | **0** | **1** | **0** | **16:03** |
| **2003-04** | **Dallas** | **NHL** | **67** | **1** | **5** | **6** | **16** | **0** | **0** | **0** | **57** | **1.8** | **–15** | **619** | **47.7** | **11:30** | **1** | **1** | **0** | **1** | **0** | **0** | **0** | **0** | **6:51** |
| 2004-05 | EV Zug | Swiss | 44 | 10 | 33 | 43 | 24 | | | | | | | | | | 9 | 2 | 5 | 7 | 35 | | | | |
| **2005-06** | **Dallas** | **NHL** | **81** | **14** | **21** | **35** | **36** | **5** | **2** | **4** | **97** | **14.4** | **–10** | **798** | **49.9** | **14:13** | **5** | **0** | **1** | **1** | **10** | **0** | **0** | **0** | **14:52** |
| | Finland | Olympics | 8 | 2 | 1 | 3 | 2 | | | | | | | | | | | | | | | | | | |
| **2006-07** | **Atlanta** | **NHL** | **60** | **4** | **9** | **13** | **20** | **1** | **0** | **0** | **51** | **7.8** | **–12** | **527** | **54.1** | **10:45** | | | | | | | | | |
| | **Phoenix** | **NHL** | **19** | **2** | **7** | **9** | **8** | **1** | **0** | **1** | **28** | **7.1** | **–11** | **279** | **54.1** | **17:36** | | | | | | | | | |
| **2007-08** | **Phoenix** | **NHL** | **79** | **10** | **18** | **28** | **34** | **5** | **0** | **5** | **85** | **11.8** | **–1** | **806** | **52.1** | **13:49** | | | | | | | | | |
| 2008-09 | Ak Bars Kazan | Rus-KHL | 53 | 12 | 19 | 31 | 22 | | | | | | | | | | 21 | 1 | 9 | 10 | 16 | | | | |
| | **NHL Totals** | | **397** | **36** | **90** | **126** | **160** | **12** | **3** | **11** | **401** | **9.0** | | **4199** | **50.0** | **13:18** | **18** | **5** | **4** | **9** | **22** | **0** | **1** | **0** | **15:13** |

Signed as a free agent by **Zug** (Swiss), June 9, 2004. Traded to **Atlanta** by **Dallas** with Dallas' 7th round choice (Will O'Neill) in 2006 Entry Draft for Patrik Stefan and Jaroslav Modry, June 24, 2006. Claimed on waivers by **Phoenix** from **Atlanta**, February 27, 2007.

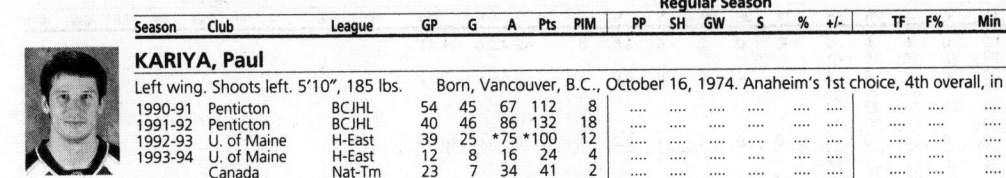

| | | | Regular Season | | | | | | | | | | | | | Playoffs | | | | | | | | |
|---|---|---|---|---|---|---|---|---|---|---|---|---|---|---|---|---|---|---|---|---|---|---|---|---|
| Season | Club | League | GP | G | A | Pts | PIM | PP | SH | GW | S | % | +/- | TF | F% | Min | GP | G | A | Pts | PIM | PP | SH | GW | Min |

## KARIYA, Paul

(kah-REE-ah, PAWL) **ST.L.**

Left wing. Shoots left. 5'10", 185 lbs. Born, Vancouver, B.C., October 16, 1974. Anaheim's 1st choice, 4th overall, in 1993 Entry Draft.

| Season | Club | League | GP | G | A | Pts | PIM | PP | SH | GW | S | % | +/- | TF | F% | Min | GP | G | A | Pts | PIM | PP | SH | GW | Min |
|---|---|---|---|---|---|---|---|---|---|---|---|---|---|---|---|---|---|---|---|---|---|---|---|---|---|
| 1990-91 | Penticton | BCJHL | 54 | 45 | 67 | 112 | 8 | .... | .... | .... | .... | .... | .... | .... | .... | .... | .... | .... | .... | .... | .... | .... | .... | .... | .... |
| 1991-92 | Penticton | BCJHL | 40 | 46 | 86 | 132 | 18 | .... | .... | .... | .... | .... | .... | .... | .... | .... | .... | .... | .... | .... | .... | .... | .... | .... | .... |
| 1992-93 | U. of Maine | H-East | 39 | 25 | *75 | *100 | 12 | .... | .... | .... | .... | .... | .... | .... | .... | .... | .... | .... | .... | .... | .... | .... | .... | .... | .... |
| 1993-94 | U. of Maine | H-East | 12 | 8 | 16 | 24 | 4 | .... | .... | .... | .... | .... | .... | .... | .... | .... | .... | .... | .... | .... | .... | .... | .... | .... | .... |
| | Canada | Nat-Tm | 23 | 7 | 34 | 41 | 2 | .... | .... | .... | .... | .... | .... | .... | .... | .... | .... | .... | .... | .... | .... | .... | .... | .... | .... |
| | Canada | Olympics | 8 | 3 | 4 | 7 | 2 | .... | .... | .... | .... | .... | .... | .... | .... | .... | .... | .... | .... | .... | .... | .... | .... | .... | .... |
| **1994-95** | **Anaheim** | **NHL** | **47** | **18** | **21** | **39** | **4** | **7** | **1** | **3** | **134** | **13.4** | **-17** | .... | .... | .... | .... | .... | .... | .... | .... | .... | .... | .... | .... |
| **1995-96** | **Anaheim** | **NHL** | **82** | **50** | **58** | **108** | **20** | **20** | **3** | **9** | **349** | **14.3** | **9** | .... | .... | .... | .... | .... | .... | .... | .... | .... | .... | .... | .... |
| **1996-97** | **Anaheim** | **NHL** | **69** | **44** | **55** | **99** | **6** | **15** | **3** | **10** | **340** | **12.9** | **36** | .... | .... | .... | **11** | **7** | **6** | **13** | **4** | **4** | **0** | **1** | .... |
| **1997-98** | **Anaheim** | **NHL** | **22** | **17** | **14** | **31** | **23** | **3** | **0** | **2** | **103** | **16.5** | **12** | .... | .... | .... | .... | .... | .... | .... | .... | .... | .... | .... | .... |
| **1998-99** | **Anaheim** | **NHL** | **82** | **39** | **62** | **101** | **40** | **11** | **2** | **4** | **429** | **9.1** | **17** | **91** | **48.4** | **25:32** | **3** | **1** | **3** | **4** | **0** | **0** | **0** | **0** | **26:03** |
| **99-2000** | **Anaheim** | **NHL** | **74** | **42** | **44** | **86** | **24** | **11** | **3** | **3** | **324** | **13.0** | **22** | **99** | **39.4** | **24:22** | .... | .... | .... | .... | .... | .... | .... | .... | .... |
| **2000-01** | **Anaheim** | **NHL** | **66** | **33** | **34** | **67** | **20** | **18** | **3** | **3** | **230** | **14.3** | **-9** | **149** | **44.3** | **23:02** | .... | .... | .... | .... | .... | .... | .... | .... | .... |
| **2001-02** | **Anaheim** | **NHL** | **82** | **32** | **25** | **57** | **28** | **11** | **0** | **8** | **289** | **11.1** | **-15** | **94** | **41.5** | **22:13** | .... | .... | .... | .... | .... | .... | .... | .... | .... |
| | Canada | Olympics | 6 | 3 | 1 | 4 | 0 | .... | .... | .... | .... | .... | .... | .... | .... | .... | .... | .... | .... | .... | .... | .... | .... | .... | .... |
| **2002-03** | **Anaheim** | **NHL** | **82** | **25** | **56** | **81** | **48** | **11** | **1** | **2** | **257** | **9.7** | **-3** | **39** | **30.8** | **20:17** | **21** | **6** | **6** | **12** | **6** | **0** | **0** | **1** | **21:15** |
| **2003-04** | **Colorado** | **NHL** | **51** | **11** | **25** | **36** | **22** | **5** | **1** | **1** | **110** | **10.0** | **-5** | **18** | **27.8** | **18:37** | **1** | **0** | **1** | **1** | **0** | **0** | **0** | **0** | **16:00** |
| 2004-05 | | | DID NOT PLAY | | | | | | | | | | | | | | | | | | | | | | |
| **2005-06** | **Nashville** | **NHL** | **82** | **31** | **54** | **85** | **40** | **14** | **0** | **3** | **245** | **12.7** | **-6** | **9** | **11.1** | **19:05** | **5** | **2** | **5** | **7** | **0** | **2** | **0** | **0** | **20:47** |
| **2006-07** | **Nashville** | **NHL** | **82** | **24** | **52** | **76** | **36** | **5** | **0** | **2** | **224** | **10.7** | **6** | **3** | **0.0** | **20:23** | **5** | **0** | **2** | **2** | **2** | **0** | **0** | **0** | **19:36** |
| **2007-08** | **St. Louis** | **NHL** | **82** | **16** | **49** | **65** | **50** | **5** | **0** | **1** | **223** | **7.2** | **-10** | **6** | **0.0** | **18:44** | .... | .... | .... | .... | .... | .... | .... | .... | .... |
| **2008-09** | **St. Louis** | **NHL** | **11** | **2** | **13** | **15** | **2** | **0** | **0** | **0** | **31** | **6.5** | **1** | **0** | **0.0** | **18:06** | .... | .... | .... | .... | .... | .... | .... | .... | .... |
| | **NHL Totals** | | **914** | **384** | **562** | **946** | **363** | **136** | **17** | **51** | **3288** | **11.7** | | **508** | **40.6** | **21:21** | **46** | **16** | **23** | **39** | **12** | **6** | **0** | **2** | **21:12** |

Hockey East First All-Star Team (1993) • Hockey East Rookie of the Year (1993) • Hockey East Player of the Year (1993) • NCAA East First All-American Team (1993) • NCAA Championship All-Tournament Team (1993) • Hobey Baker Memorial Award (Top U.S. Collegiate Player) (1993) • NHL All-Rookie Team (1995) • Lady Byng Memorial Trophy (1996, 1997) • NHL First All-Star Team (1996, 1997, 1999) • NHL Second All-Star Team (2000, 2003)

Played in NHL All-Star Game (1996, 1997, 1999, 2000, 2001, 2002, 2003)

• Missed majority of 1997-98 season after failing to come to contract terms with **Anaheim** and recovering from head injury suffered in game vs. San Jose, February 1, 1998. Signed as a free agent by **Colorado**, July 3, 2003. Signed as a free agent by **Nashville**, August 5, 2005. Signed as a free agent by **St. Louis**, July 1, 2007. • Missed majority of 2008-09 season recovering from lower body injury suffered in game at Anaheim, November 5, 2008.

## KARSUMS, Martins

(KAHR-suhmz, MAHR-tihnsh) **T.B.**

Right wing. Shoots right. 5'10", 198 lbs. Born, Riga, Latvia, February 26, 1986. Boston's 2nd choice, 64th overall, in 2004 Entry Draft.

| Season | Club | League | GP | G | A | Pts | PIM | PP | SH | GW | S | % | +/- | TF | F% | Min | GP | G | A | Pts | PIM | PP | SH | GW | Min |
|---|---|---|---|---|---|---|---|---|---|---|---|---|---|---|---|---|---|---|---|---|---|---|---|---|---|
| 2000-01 | Prizma '83 Riga Jr. | Latvia-Jr. | 2 | 0 | 0 | 0 | 0 | .... | .... | .... | .... | .... | .... | .... | .... | .... | .... | .... | .... | .... | .... | | | | |
| | Lido Nafta Jr. | Latvia-Jr. | 18 | 8 | 6 | 14 | .... | .... | .... | .... | .... | .... | .... | .... | .... | .... | .... | .... | .... | .... | .... | | | | |
| 2001-02 | Prizma '83 Riga | EEHL-B | 16 | 7 | 8 | 15 | 4 | .... | .... | .... | .... | .... | .... | .... | .... | .... | .... | .... | .... | .... | .... | | | | |
| | Prizma '83 Riga | Latvia | 6 | 4 | 1 | 5 | 4 | .... | .... | .... | .... | .... | .... | .... | .... | .... | .... | .... | .... | .... | .... | | | | |
| 2002-03 | HK Riga 2000 | EEHL | 2 | 0 | 0 | 0 | 0 | .... | .... | .... | .... | .... | .... | .... | .... | .... | .... | .... | .... | .... | .... | | | | |
| | Vilki Riga | Latvia | .... | 7 | 5 | 12 | 14 | .... | .... | .... | .... | .... | .... | .... | .... | .... | .... | .... | .... | .... | .... | | | | |
| 2003-04 | Moncton Wildcats | QMJHL | 60 | 30 | 23 | 53 | 76 | .... | .... | .... | .... | .... | .... | .... | .... | .... | 20 | 8 | 9 | 17 | 14 | | | | |
| 2004-05 | Moncton Wildcats | QMJHL | 30 | 14 | 12 | 26 | 31 | .... | .... | .... | .... | .... | .... | .... | .... | .... | 2 | 0 | 0 | 0 | 0 | | | | |
| 2005-06 | Moncton Wildcats | QMJHL | 49 | 34 | 31 | 65 | 89 | .... | .... | .... | .... | .... | .... | .... | .... | .... | 21 | 15 | 11 | 26 | 22 | | | | |
| 2006-07 | Providence Bruins | AHL | 54 | 13 | 22 | 35 | 41 | .... | .... | .... | .... | .... | .... | .... | .... | .... | 12 | 3 | 1 | 4 | 2 | | | | |
| 2007-08 | Providence Bruins | AHL | 79 | 20 | 43 | 63 | 57 | .... | .... | .... | .... | .... | .... | .... | .... | .... | 10 | 7 | 3 | 10 | 6 | | | | |
| **2008-09** | **Boston** | **NHL** | **6** | **0** | **1** | **1** | **0** | **0** | **0** | **0** | **6** | **0.0** | **-3** | **1** | **0.0** | **9:45** | .... | .... | .... | .... | .... | .... | .... | .... | .... |
| | Providence Bruins | AHL | 43 | 17 | 24 | 41 | 20 | .... | .... | .... | .... | .... | .... | .... | .... | .... | .... | .... | .... | .... | .... | | | | |
| | **Tampa Bay** | **NHL** | **18** | **1** | **4** | **5** | **6** | **0** | **0** | **0** | **22** | **4.5** | **-5** | **2** | **100.0** | **11:40** | .... | .... | .... | .... | .... | .... | .... | .... | .... |
| | **NHL Totals** | | **24** | **1** | **5** | **6** | **6** | **0** | **0** | **0** | **28** | **3.6** | | **3** | **66.7** | **11:11** | .... | .... | .... | .... | .... | .... | .... | .... | .... |

QMJHL All-Rookie Team (2004)

Traded to **Tampa Bay** by **Boston** with Matt Lashoff for Mark Recchi and Tampa Bay's 2nd round choice in 2010 Entry Draft, March 4, 2009.

## KASPAR, Lukas

(kash-PAR, LOO-kahsh) **PHI.**

Right wing. Shoots left. 6'2", 220 lbs. Born, Most, Czech., September 23, 1985. San Jose's 1st choice, 22nd overall, in 2004 Entry Draft.

| Season | Club | League | GP | G | A | Pts | PIM | PP | SH | GW | S | % | +/- | TF | F% | Min | GP | G | A | Pts | PIM | PP | SH | GW | Min |
|---|---|---|---|---|---|---|---|---|---|---|---|---|---|---|---|---|---|---|---|---|---|---|---|---|---|
| 2000-01 | Litvinov U17 | CzR-U17 | 48 | 27 | 19 | 46 | 64 | .... | .... | .... | .... | .... | .... | .... | .... | .... | 6 | 2 | 3 | 5 | 0 | | | | |
| 2001-02 | Litvinov U17 | CzR-U17 | 48 | 35 | 41 | 76 | 143 | .... | .... | .... | .... | .... | .... | .... | .... | .... | 2 | 1 | 1 | 2 | 0 | | | | |
| 2002-03 | Litvinov Jr. | CzRep-Jr. | 26 | 14 | 14 | 28 | 40 | .... | .... | .... | .... | .... | .... | .... | .... | .... | .... | .... | .... | .... | .... | | | | |
| | Litvinov | CzRep | 9 | 1 | 1 | 2 | 2 | .... | .... | .... | .... | .... | .... | .... | .... | .... | .... | .... | .... | .... | .... | | | | |
| 2003-04 | Litvinov Jr. | CzRep-Jr. | 23 | 21 | 14 | 35 | 56 | .... | .... | .... | .... | .... | .... | .... | .... | .... | 1 | 0 | 0 | 0 | 0 | | | | |
| | Litvinov | CzRep | 37 | 4 | 2 | 6 | 10 | .... | .... | .... | .... | .... | .... | .... | .... | .... | .... | .... | .... | .... | .... | | | | |
| | Usti n. L. | CzRep-2 | 1 | 1 | 0 | 1 | 0 | .... | .... | .... | .... | .... | .... | .... | .... | .... | .... | .... | .... | .... | .... | | | | |
| | Most | CzRep-3 | | | | | | .... | .... | .... | .... | .... | .... | .... | .... | .... | 1 | 0 | 0 | 0 | 2 | | | | |
| 2004-05 | Ottawa 67's | OHL | 59 | 21 | 30 | 51 | 45 | .... | .... | .... | .... | .... | .... | .... | .... | .... | 21 | 6 | 14 | 20 | 8 | | | | |
| 2005-06 | Cleveland Barons | AHL | 76 | 14 | 22 | 36 | 88 | .... | .... | .... | .... | .... | .... | .... | .... | .... | .... | .... | .... | .... | .... | | | | |
| 2006-07 | Worcester Sharks | AHL | 78 | 12 | 28 | 40 | 64 | .... | .... | .... | .... | .... | .... | .... | .... | .... | 6 | 0 | 2 | 2 | 6 | | | | |
| **2007-08** | **San Jose** | **NHL** | **3** | **0** | **0** | **0** | **0** | **0** | **0** | **0** | **5** | **0.0** | **-2** | **1** | **0.0** | **12:15** | .... | .... | .... | .... | .... | .... | .... | .... | .... |
| | Worcester Sharks | AHL | 73 | 17 | 24 | 41 | 44 | .... | .... | .... | .... | .... | .... | .... | .... | .... | .... | .... | .... | .... | .... | | | | |
| **2008-09** | **San Jose** | **NHL** | **13** | **2** | **2** | **4** | **8** | **0** | **0** | **1** | **14** | **14.3** | **0** | **4** | **0.0** | **9:08** | .... | .... | .... | .... | .... | .... | .... | .... | .... |
| | Worcester Sharks | AHL | 65 | 17 | 27 | 44 | 40 | .... | .... | .... | .... | .... | .... | .... | .... | .... | 12 | 2 | 2 | 4 | 0 | | | | |
| | **NHL Totals** | | **16** | **2** | **2** | **4** | **8** | **0** | **0** | **1** | **19** | **10.5** | | **5** | **0.0** | **9:43** | .... | .... | .... | .... | .... | .... | .... | .... | .... |

Signed as a free agent by **Philadelphia**, July 23, 2009.

## KEITH, Duncan

(KEETH, DUHN-kuhn) **CHI.**

Defense. Shoots left. 6'1", 194 lbs. Born, Winnipeg, Man., July 16, 1983. Chicago's 2nd choice, 54th overall, in 2002 Entry Draft.

| Season | Club | League | GP | G | A | Pts | PIM | PP | SH | GW | S | % | +/- | TF | F% | Min | GP | G | A | Pts | PIM | PP | SH | GW | Min |
|---|---|---|---|---|---|---|---|---|---|---|---|---|---|---|---|---|---|---|---|---|---|---|---|---|---|
| 1998-99 | Penticton | Minor-BC | 44 | 51 | 57 | 108 | 45 | .... | .... | .... | .... | .... | .... | .... | .... | .... | .... | .... | .... | .... | .... | | | | |
| 99-2000 | Penticton | BCHL | 59 | 9 | 27 | 36 | 37 | .... | .... | .... | .... | .... | .... | .... | .... | .... | .... | .... | .... | .... | .... | | | | |
| 2000-01 | Penticton | BCHL | 60 | 18 | 64 | 82 | 61 | .... | .... | .... | .... | .... | .... | .... | .... | .... | 9 | 4 | 6 | 10 | 18 | | | | |
| 2001-02 | Michigan State | CCHA | 41 | 3 | 12 | 15 | 18 | .... | .... | .... | .... | .... | .... | .... | .... | .... | .... | .... | .... | .... | .... | | | | |
| 2002-03 | Michigan State | CCHA | 15 | 3 | 6 | 9 | 8 | .... | .... | .... | .... | .... | .... | .... | .... | .... | .... | .... | .... | .... | .... | | | | |
| | Kelowna Rockets | WHL | 37 | 11 | 35 | 46 | 60 | .... | .... | .... | .... | .... | .... | .... | .... | .... | 19 | 3 | 11 | 14 | 12 | | | | |
| 2003-04 | Norfolk Admirals | AHL | 75 | 7 | 18 | 25 | 44 | .... | .... | .... | .... | .... | .... | .... | .... | .... | 8 | 1 | 1 | 2 | 6 | | | | |
| 2004-05 | Norfolk Admirals | AHL | 79 | 9 | 17 | 26 | 78 | .... | .... | .... | .... | .... | .... | .... | .... | .... | 6 | 0 | 0 | 0 | 14 | | | | |
| **2005-06** | **Chicago** | **NHL** | **81** | **9** | **12** | **21** | **79** | **1** | **1** | **0** | **134** | **6.7** | **-11** | **0** | **0.0** | **23:26** | .... | .... | .... | .... | .... | .... | .... | .... | .... |
| **2006-07** | **Chicago** | **NHL** | **82** | **2** | **29** | **31** | **76** | **0** | **0** | **0** | **122** | **1.6** | **0** | **0** | **0.0** | **23:36** | .... | .... | .... | .... | .... | .... | .... | .... | .... |
| **2007-08** | **Chicago** | **NHL** | **82** | **12** | **20** | **32** | **56** | **1** | **1** | **0** | **148** | **8.1** | **30** | **0** | **0.0** | **25:34** | .... | .... | .... | .... | .... | .... | .... | .... | .... |
| **2008-09** | **Chicago** | **NHL** | **77** | **8** | **36** | **44** | **60** | **2** | **1** | **1** | **173** | **4.6** | **33** | **0** | **0.0** | **25:34** | **17** | **0** | **6** | **6** | **10** | **0** | **0** | **0** | **24:39** |
| | **NHL Totals** | | **322** | **31** | **97** | **128** | **271** | **4** | **3** | **1** | **577** | **5.4** | | **0** | **0.0** | **24:32** | **17** | **0** | **6** | **6** | **10** | **0** | **0** | **0** | **24:39** |

Played in NHL All-Star Game (2008)

• Left **Michigan State** (CCHA) and signed as a free agent by **Kelowna** (WHL), December 27, 2002.

## KEITH, Matt

(KEETH, MAT)

Right wing. Shoots right. 6'2", 200 lbs. Born, Edmonton, Alta., April 11, 1983. Chicago's 3rd choice, 59th overall, in 2001 Entry Draft.

| Season | Club | League | GP | G | A | Pts | PIM | PP | SH | GW | S | % | +/- | TF | F% | Min | GP | G | A | Pts | PIM | PP | SH | GW | Min |
|---|---|---|---|---|---|---|---|---|---|---|---|---|---|---|---|---|---|---|---|---|---|---|---|---|---|
| 1998-99 | Banff Icemen | HJHL | STATISTICS NOT AVAILABLE | | | | | | | | | | | | | | | | | | | | | | |
| | Spokane Chiefs | WHL | 7 | 1 | 0 | 1 | 4 | .... | .... | .... | .... | .... | .... | .... | .... | .... | .... | .... | .... | .... | .... | | | | |
| 99-2000 | Spokane Chiefs | WHL | 39 | 1 | 3 | 4 | 37 | .... | .... | .... | .... | .... | .... | .... | .... | .... | 15 | 1 | 2 | 3 | 11 | | | | |
| 2000-01 | Spokane Chiefs | WHL | 33 | 13 | 14 | 27 | 63 | .... | .... | .... | .... | .... | .... | .... | .... | .... | 12 | 1 | 3 | 4 | 14 | | | | |
| 2001-02 | Spokane Chiefs | WHL | 68 | 34 | 33 | 67 | 71 | .... | .... | .... | .... | .... | .... | .... | .... | .... | 11 | 5 | 5 | 10 | 16 | | | | |
| 2002-03 | Spokane Chiefs | WHL | 7 | 2 | 2 | 4 | 11 | .... | .... | .... | .... | .... | .... | .... | .... | .... | .... | .... | .... | .... | .... | | | | |
| | Red Deer Rebels | WHL | 49 | 25 | 26 | 51 | 32 | .... | .... | .... | .... | .... | .... | .... | .... | .... | 23 | 6 | 7 | 13 | 30 | | | | |
| **2003-04** | **Chicago** | **NHL** | **20** | **2** | **3** | **5** | **10** | **1** | **0** | **0** | **21** | **9.5** | **-5** | **2** | **100.0** | **11:58** | .... | .... | .... | .... | .... | .... | .... | .... | .... |
| | Norfolk Admirals | AHL | 66 | 13 | 13 | 26 | 57 | .... | .... | .... | .... | .... | .... | .... | .... | .... | 8 | 1 | 2 | 3 | 10 | | | | |
| 2004-05 | Norfolk Admirals | AHL | 80 | 18 | 31 | 49 | 74 | .... | .... | .... | .... | .... | .... | .... | .... | .... | 6 | 0 | 1 | 1 | 0 | | | | |

| | | | Regular Season | | | | | | | | | | | | | | Playoffs | | | | | | | | |
|---|---|---|---|---|---|---|---|---|---|---|---|---|---|---|---|---|---|---|---|---|---|---|---|---|---|
| Season | Club | League | GP | G | A | Pts | PIM | PP | SH | GW | S | % | +/- | TF | F% | Min | GP | G | A | Pts | PIM | PP | SH | GW | Min |
| 2005-06 | Chicago | NHL | 2 | 0 | 0 | 0 | 0 | 0 | 0 | 0 | 6 | 0.0 | 0 | 0 | 0.0 | 11:42 | .... | .... | .... | .... | .... | .... | .... | .... | .... |
| | Norfolk Admirals | AHL | 72 | 26 | 19 | 45 | 61 | .... | .... | .... | .... | .... | .... | .... | .... | .... | 3 | 0 | 1 | 1 | 0 | .... | .... | .... | .... |
| 2006-07 | Chicago | NHL | 2 | 0 | 0 | 0 | 4 | 0 | 0 | 0 | 0 | 0.0 | –2 | 0 | 0.0 | 9:33 | .... | .... | .... | .... | .... | .... | .... | .... | .... |
| | Norfolk Admirals | AHL | 19 | 2 | 8 | 10 | 15 | .... | .... | .... | .... | .... | .... | .... | .... | .... | .... | .... | .... | .... | .... | .... | .... | .... | .... |
| | Portland Pirates | AHL | 44 | 10 | 12 | 22 | 22 | .... | .... | .... | .... | .... | .... | .... | .... | .... | .... | .... | .... | .... | .... | .... | .... | .... | .... |
| 2007-08 | Portland Pirates | AHL | 34 | 5 | 5 | 10 | 13 | .... | .... | .... | .... | .... | .... | .... | .... | .... | .... | .... | .... | .... | .... | .... | .... | .... | .... |
| | NY Islanders | NHL | 3 | 0 | 0 | 0 | 0 | 0 | 0 | 0 | 3 | 0.0 | –1 | 0 | 0.0 | 10:41 | .... | .... | .... | .... | .... | .... | .... | .... | .... |
| | Bridgeport | AHL | 42 | 8 | 9 | 17 | 22 | .... | .... | .... | .... | .... | .... | .... | .... | .... | .... | .... | .... | .... | .... | .... | .... | .... | .... |
| 2008-09 | ERC Ingolstadt | Germany | 46 | 15 | 13 | 28 | 60 | .... | .... | .... | .... | .... | .... | .... | .... | .... | .... | .... | .... | .... | .... | .... | .... | .... | .... |
| | NHL Totals | | 27 | 2 | 3 | 5 | 14 | 1 | 0 | 0 | 30 | 6.7 | | 2100.0 | | 11:37 | .... | .... | .... | .... | .... | .... | .... | .... | .... |

• Missed majority of 2000-01 season recovering from shoulder injury suffered in game vs. Tri-City (WHL), September 22, 2000. Traded to **Anaheim** by **Chicago** with Sebastien Caron and Chris Durno for P.A. Parenteau and Bruno St. Jacques, December 28, 2006. Traded to **NY Islanders** by **Anaheim** for Darryl Bootland, January 9, 2008.

## KELLY, Chris

(KEHL-lee, KRIHS) **OTT.**

Center/Left wing. Shoots left. 6', 198 lbs. Born, Toronto, Ont., November 11, 1980. Ottawa's 4th choice, 94th overall, in 1999 Entry Draft.

| | | | | | | | | | | | | | | | | | | | | | | | | | |
|---|---|---|---|---|---|---|---|---|---|---|---|---|---|---|---|---|---|---|---|---|---|---|---|---|---|
| 1995-96 | Toronto Marlies | MTHL | 42 | 25 | 45 | 70 | 25 | .... | .... | .... | .... | .... | .... | .... | .... | .... | .... | .... | .... | .... | .... | .... | .... | .... | .... |
| 1996-97 | Aurora Tigers | MTJHL | 49 | 14 | 20 | 34 | 11 | .... | .... | .... | .... | .... | .... | .... | .... | .... | .... | .... | .... | .... | .... | .... | .... | .... | .... |
| 1997-98 | London Knights | OHL | 54 | 15 | 14 | 29 | 4 | .... | .... | .... | .... | .... | .... | .... | .... | .... | 16 | 4 | 5 | 9 | 12 | .... | .... | .... | .... |
| 1998-99 | London Knights | OHL | 68 | 36 | 41 | 77 | 60 | .... | .... | .... | .... | .... | .... | .... | .... | .... | 25 | 9 | 17 | 26 | 22 | .... | .... | .... | .... |
| 99-2000 | London Knights | OHL | 63 | 29 | 43 | 72 | 57 | .... | .... | .... | .... | .... | .... | .... | .... | .... | .... | .... | .... | .... | .... | .... | .... | .... | .... |
| 2000-01 | London Knights | OHL | 31 | 21 | 34 | 55 | 46 | .... | .... | .... | .... | .... | .... | .... | .... | .... | .... | .... | .... | .... | .... | .... | .... | .... | .... |
| | Sudbury Wolves | OHL | 19 | 5 | 16 | 21 | 17 | .... | .... | .... | .... | .... | .... | .... | .... | .... | 12 | 11 | 5 | 16 | 14 | .... | .... | .... | .... |
| 2001-02 | Grand Rapids | AHL | 31 | 3 | 3 | 6 | 20 | .... | .... | .... | .... | .... | .... | .... | .... | .... | 5 | 1 | 1 | 2 | 5 | .... | .... | .... | .... |
| | Muskegon Fury | UHL | 4 | 1 | 2 | 3 | 0 | .... | .... | .... | .... | .... | .... | .... | .... | .... | .... | .... | .... | .... | .... | .... | .... | .... | .... |
| 2002-03 | Binghamton | AHL | 77 | 17 | 14 | 31 | 73 | .... | .... | .... | .... | .... | .... | .... | .... | .... | 14 | 2 | 3 | 5 | 8 | .... | .... | .... | .... |
| 2003-04 | Ottawa | NHL | 4 | 0 | 0 | 0 | 0 | 0 | 0 | 0 | 4 | 0.0 | –2 | 5 | 40.0 | 9:29 | .... | .... | .... | .... | .... | .... | .... | .... | .... |
| | Binghamton | AHL | 54 | 15 | 19 | 34 | 40 | .... | .... | .... | .... | .... | .... | .... | .... | .... | 2 | 0 | 0 | 0 | 4 | .... | .... | .... | .... |
| 2004-05 | Binghamton | AHL | 77 | 24 | 36 | 60 | 57 | .... | .... | .... | .... | .... | .... | .... | .... | .... | 6 | 1 | 2 | 3 | 11 | .... | .... | .... | .... |
| 2005-06 | Ottawa | NHL | 82 | 10 | 20 | 30 | 76 | 1 | 0 | 2 | 112 | 8.9 | 21 | 808 | 45.8 | 12:20 | 10 | 0 | 0 | 0 | 2 | 0 | 0 | 0 | 11:49 |
| 2006-07 | Ottawa | NHL | 82 | 15 | 23 | 38 | 40 | 1 | 2 | 0 | 131 | 11.5 | 28 | 564 | 49.8 | 15:18 | 20 | 3 | 4 | 7 | 4 | 0 | 0 | 0 | 15:28 |
| 2007-08 | Ottawa | NHL | 75 | 11 | 19 | 30 | 30 | 0 | 1 | 1 | 124 | 8.9 | 3 | 162 | 53.1 | 16:36 | .... | .... | .... | .... | .... | .... | .... | .... | .... |
| 2008-09 | Ottawa | NHL | 82 | 12 | 11 | 23 | 38 | 0 | 1 | 1 | 118 | 10.2 | –10 | 494 | 47.4 | 15:36 | .... | .... | .... | .... | .... | .... | .... | .... | .... |
| | NHL Totals | | 325 | 48 | 73 | 121 | 184 | 2 | 4 | 4 | 489 | 9.8 | | 2033 | 47.9 | 14:51 | 30 | 3 | 4 | 7 | 6 | 0 | 0 | 0 | 14:15 |

## KELLY, Steve

(KEHL-lee, STEEV)

Center. Shoots left. 6'2", 205 lbs. Born, Vancouver, B.C., October 26, 1976. Edmonton's 1st choice, 6th overall, in 1995 Entry Draft.

| | | | | | | | | | | | | | | | | | | | | | | | | | |
|---|---|---|---|---|---|---|---|---|---|---|---|---|---|---|---|---|---|---|---|---|---|---|---|---|---|
| 1991-92 | Westbank | Minor-BC | 30 | 25 | 60 | 85 | 75 | .... | .... | .... | .... | .... | .... | .... | .... | .... | .... | .... | .... | .... | .... | .... | .... | .... | .... |
| 1992-93 | Prince Albert | WHL | 65 | 11 | 9 | 20 | 75 | .... | .... | .... | .... | .... | .... | .... | .... | .... | .... | .... | .... | .... | .... | .... | .... | .... | .... |
| 1993-94 | Prince Albert | WHL | 65 | 19 | 42 | 61 | 106 | .... | .... | .... | .... | .... | .... | .... | .... | .... | .... | .... | .... | .... | .... | .... | .... | .... | .... |
| 1994-95 | Prince Albert | WHL | 68 | 31 | 41 | 72 | 153 | .... | .... | .... | .... | .... | .... | .... | .... | .... | 15 | 7 | 9 | 16 | 35 | .... | .... | .... | .... |
| 1995-96 | Prince Albert | WHL | 70 | 27 | 74 | 101 | 203 | .... | .... | .... | .... | .... | .... | .... | .... | .... | 18 | 13 | 18 | 31 | 47 | .... | .... | .... | .... |
| 1996-97 | Edmonton | NHL | 8 | 1 | 0 | 1 | 6 | 0 | 0 | 1 | 6 | 16.7 | –1 | .... | .... | .... | 6 | 0 | 0 | 0 | 2 | 0 | 0 | 0 | .... |
| | Hamilton | AHL | 48 | 9 | 29 | 38 | 111 | .... | .... | .... | .... | .... | .... | .... | .... | .... | 11 | 3 | 3 | 6 | 24 | .... | .... | .... | .... |
| 1997-98 | Edmonton | NHL | 19 | 0 | 2 | 2 | 8 | 0 | 0 | 0 | 5 | 0.0 | –4 | .... | .... | .... | .... | .... | .... | .... | .... | .... | .... | .... | .... |
| | Hamilton | AHL | 11 | 2 | 8 | 10 | 18 | .... | .... | .... | .... | .... | .... | .... | .... | .... | .... | .... | .... | .... | .... | .... | .... | .... | .... |
| | Tampa Bay | NHL | 24 | 2 | 1 | 3 | 15 | 1 | 0 | 0 | 17 | 11.8 | –9 | .... | .... | .... | .... | .... | .... | .... | .... | .... | .... | .... | .... |
| | Milwaukee | IHL | 5 | 0 | 1 | 1 | 19 | .... | .... | .... | .... | .... | .... | .... | .... | .... | .... | .... | .... | .... | .... | .... | .... | .... | .... |
| | Cleveland | IHL | 5 | 1 | 1 | 2 | 29 | .... | .... | .... | .... | .... | .... | .... | .... | .... | 1 | 0 | 1 | 1 | 0 | .... | .... | .... | .... |
| 1998-99 | Tampa Bay | NHL | 34 | 1 | 3 | 4 | 27 | 0 | 0 | 1 | 15 | 6.7 | –15 | 11 | 54.5 | 10:51 | .... | .... | .... | .... | .... | .... | .... | .... | .... |
| | Cleveland | IHL | 18 | 6 | 7 | 13 | 36 | .... | .... | .... | .... | .... | .... | .... | .... | .... | .... | .... | .... | .... | .... | .... | .... | .... | .... |
| 99-2000 | Detroit Vipers | IHL | 1 | 0 | 0 | 0 | 4 | .... | .... | .... | .... | .... | .... | .... | .... | .... | .... | .... | .... | .... | .... | .... | .... | .... | .... |
| | ◆ New Jersey | NHL | 1 | 0 | 0 | 0 | 0 | 0 | 0 | 0 | 0 | 0.0 | 0 | 0 | 0.0 | 4:28 | 10 | 0 | 0 | 0 | 4 | 0 | 0 | 0 | 11:32 |
| | Albany River Rats | AHL | 76 | 21 | 36 | 57 | 131 | .... | .... | .... | .... | .... | .... | .... | .... | .... | 3 | 1 | 1 | 2 | 2 | .... | .... | .... | .... |
| 2000-01 | New Jersey | NHL | 24 | 2 | 2 | 4 | 21 | 0 | 0 | 0 | 18 | 11.1 | 0 | 87 | 48.3 | 9:58 | .... | .... | .... | .... | .... | .... | .... | .... | .... |
| | Los Angeles | NHL | 11 | 1 | 0 | 1 | 4 | 0 | 0 | 0 | 4 | 25.0 | 0 | 51 | 39.2 | 6:44 | 8 | 0 | 0 | 0 | 2 | 0 | 0 | 0 | 5:23 |
| 2001-02 | Los Angeles | NHL | 8 | 0 | 1 | 1 | 2 | 0 | 0 | 0 | 0 | 0.0 | –1 | 44 | 36.4 | 6:52 | 1 | 0 | 0 | 0 | 0 | 0 | 0 | 0 | 5:54 |
| | Manchester | AHL | 49 | 10 | 21 | 31 | 88 | .... | .... | .... | .... | .... | .... | .... | .... | .... | 5 | 1 | 8 | 9 | 4 | .... | .... | .... | .... |
| 2002-03 | Los Angeles | NHL | 15 | 2 | 3 | 5 | 0 | 0 | 0 | 1 | 14 | 14.3 | –6 | 133 | 42.9 | 12:29 | .... | .... | .... | .... | .... | .... | .... | .... | .... |
| | Manchester | AHL | 54 | 19 | 44 | 63 | 144 | .... | .... | .... | .... | .... | .... | .... | .... | .... | 3 | 0 | 1 | 1 | 0 | .... | .... | .... | .... |
| 2003-04 | Los Angeles | NHL | 3 | 0 | 0 | 0 | 0 | 0 | 0 | 0 | 5 | 0.0 | 0 | 30 | 43.3 | 10:30 | .... | .... | .... | .... | .... | .... | .... | .... | .... |
| | Manchester | AHL | 59 | 21 | 49 | 70 | 117 | .... | .... | .... | .... | .... | .... | .... | .... | .... | 1 | 0 | 0 | 0 | 2 | .... | .... | .... | .... |
| 2004-05 | Adler Mannheim | Germany | 46 | 11 | 22 | 33 | *210 | .... | .... | .... | .... | .... | .... | .... | .... | .... | 12 | 1 | 4 | 5 | *72 | .... | .... | .... | .... |
| 2005-06 | Adler Mannheim | Germany | 19 | 4 | 17 | 21 | 44 | .... | .... | .... | .... | .... | .... | .... | .... | .... | .... | .... | .... | .... | .... | .... | .... | .... | .... |
| | Frankfurt Lions | Germany | 22 | 6 | 14 | 20 | 119 | .... | .... | .... | .... | .... | .... | .... | .... | .... | .... | .... | .... | .... | .... | .... | .... | .... | .... |
| 2006-07 | Frankfurt Lions | Germany | 47 | 9 | 29 | 38 | 209 | .... | .... | .... | .... | .... | .... | .... | .... | .... | 8 | 2 | 8 | 10 | 30 | .... | .... | .... | .... |
| 2007-08 | Minnesota | NHL | 2 | 0 | 0 | 0 | 0 | 0 | 0 | 0 | 1 | 0.0 | 0 | 3 | 66.7 | 3:44 | .... | .... | .... | .... | .... | .... | .... | .... | .... |
| | Houston Aeros | AHL | 48 | 10 | 18 | 28 | 81 | .... | .... | .... | .... | .... | .... | .... | .... | .... | 3 | 0 | 0 | 0 | 6 | .... | .... | .... | .... |
| 2008-09 | Syracuse Crunch | AHL | 45 | 10 | 12 | 22 | 74 | .... | .... | .... | .... | .... | .... | .... | .... | .... | .... | .... | .... | .... | .... | .... | .... | .... | .... |
| | NHL Totals | | 149 | 9 | 12 | 21 | 83 | 1 | 0 | 3 | 85 | 10.6 | | 359 | 43.5 | 9:53 | 25 | 0 | 0 | 0 | 8 | 0 | 0 | 0 | 8:39 |

Traded to **Tampa Bay** by **Edmonton** with Bryan Marchment and Jason Bonsignore for Roman Hamrlik and Paul Comrie, December 30, 1997. Traded to **New Jersey** by **Tampa Bay** for New Jersey's 7th round choice (Brian Eklund) in 2000 Entry Draft, October 7, 1999. Traded to **Los Angeles** by **New Jersey** to complete transaction that sent Bob Corkum to New Jersey (February 23, 2001), February 27, 2001. • Spent majority of 2000-01 season serving as a healthy reserve. Signed as a free agent by **Mannheim** (Germany), May 4, 2004. Signed as a free agent by **Minnesota**, July 2, 2007. Signed as a free agent by **Columbus**, July 16. 2008.

## KENNEDY, Tim

(KEH-nuh-dee, TIHM) **BUF.**

Left wing. Shoots left. 5'9", 176 lbs. Born, Buffalo, NY, April 30, 1986. Washington's 6th choice, 181st overall, in 2005 Entry Draft.

| | | | | | | | | | | | | | | | | | | | | | | | | | |
|---|---|---|---|---|---|---|---|---|---|---|---|---|---|---|---|---|---|---|---|---|---|---|---|---|---|
| 2003-04 | Sioux City | USHL | 56 | 9 | 10 | 19 | 42 | .... | .... | .... | .... | .... | .... | .... | .... | .... | 7 | 2 | 2 | 4 | 6 | .... | .... | .... | .... |
| 2004-05 | Sioux City | USHL | 54 | 30 | 31 | 61 | 112 | .... | .... | .... | .... | .... | .... | .... | .... | .... | 13 | *6 | *11 | *17 | 18 | .... | .... | .... | .... |
| 2005-06 | Michigan State | CCHA | 29 | 4 | 15 | 19 | 31 | .... | .... | .... | .... | .... | .... | .... | .... | .... | .... | .... | .... | .... | .... | .... | .... | .... | .... |
| 2006-07 | Michigan State | CCHA | 42 | 18 | 25 | 43 | 49 | .... | .... | .... | .... | .... | .... | .... | .... | .... | .... | .... | .... | .... | .... | .... | .... | .... | .... |
| 2007-08 | Michigan State | CCHA | 42 | 20 | 23 | 43 | 50 | .... | .... | .... | .... | .... | .... | .... | .... | .... | .... | .... | .... | .... | .... | .... | .... | .... | .... |
| 2008-09 | Buffalo | NHL | 1 | 0 | 0 | 0 | 0 | 0 | 0 | 0 | 1 | 0.0 | 0 | 1 | 0.0 | 11:04 | .... | .... | .... | .... | .... | .... | .... | .... | .... |
| | Portland Pirates | AHL | 73 | 18 | 49 | 67 | 51 | .... | .... | .... | .... | .... | .... | .... | .... | .... | 5 | 0 | 1 | 1 | 2 | .... | .... | .... | .... |
| | NHL Totals | | 1 | 0 | 0 | 0 | 0 | 0 | 0 | 0 | 1 | 0.0 | | 1 | 0.0 | 11:04 | .... | .... | .... | .... | .... | .... | .... | .... | .... |

USHL Second All-Star Team (2005) • NCAA Championship All-Tournament Team (2007) • CCHA Second All-Star Team (2008) • AHL All-Rookie Team (2009)

Traded to **Buffalo** by **Washington** for Buffalo's 6th round choice (Mathieu Perreault) in 2006 Entry Draft, July 30, 2005.

## KENNEDY, Tyler

(KEH-nuh-dee, TIGH-luhr) **PIT.**

Center. Shoots right. 5'11", 183 lbs. Born, Sault Ste. Marie, Ont., July 15, 1986. Pittsburgh's 6th choice, 99th overall, in 2004 Entry Draft.

| | | | | | | | | | | | | | | | | | | | | | | | | | |
|---|---|---|---|---|---|---|---|---|---|---|---|---|---|---|---|---|---|---|---|---|---|---|---|---|---|
| 2002-03 | Sault Ste. Marie | OHL | 61 | 5 | 10 | 15 | 28 | .... | .... | .... | .... | .... | .... | .... | .... | .... | 4 | 0 | 0 | 0 | 0 | .... | .... | .... | .... |
| 2003-04 | Sault Ste. Marie | OHL | 63 | 16 | 26 | 42 | 28 | .... | .... | .... | .... | .... | .... | .... | .... | .... | .... | .... | .... | .... | .... | .... | .... | .... | .... |
| 2004-05 | Sault Ste. Marie | OHL | 61 | 21 | 36 | 57 | 37 | .... | .... | .... | .... | .... | .... | .... | .... | .... | 4 | 1 | 3 | 4 | 4 | .... | .... | .... | .... |
| 2005-06 | Sault Ste. Marie | OHL | 64 | 22 | 48 | 70 | 60 | .... | .... | .... | .... | .... | .... | .... | .... | .... | 4 | 1 | 2 | 3 | 2 | .... | .... | .... | .... |
| 2006-07 | Wilkes-Barre | AHL | 40 | 12 | 25 | 37 | 20 | .... | .... | .... | .... | .... | .... | .... | .... | .... | .... | .... | .... | .... | .... | .... | .... | .... | .... |
| 2007-08 | Pittsburgh | NHL | 55 | 10 | 9 | 19 | 35 | 1 | 0 | 4 | 104 | 9.6 | 2 | 8 | 25.0 | 12:13 | 20 | 0 | 4 | 4 | 13 | 0 | 0 | 0 | 10:18 |
| | Wilkes-Barre | AHL | 10 | 5 | 4 | 9 | 10 | .... | .... | .... | .... | .... | .... | .... | .... | .... | .... | .... | .... | .... | .... | .... | .... | .... | .... |
| 2008-09 | ◆ Pittsburgh | NHL | 67 | 15 | 20 | 35 | 30 | 0 | 0 | 3 | 171 | 8.8 | 15 | 78 | 53.9 | 13:46 | 24 | 5 | 4 | 9 | 4 | 0 | 0 | 3 | 13:40 |
| | NHL Totals | | 122 | 25 | 29 | 54 | 65 | 1 | 0 | 7 | 275 | 9.1 | | 86 | 51.2 | 13:04 | 44 | 5 | 8 | 13 | 17 | 0 | 0 | 3 | 12:08 |

| Season | Club | League | GP | G | A | Pts | PIM | PP | SH | GW | S | % | +/- | TF | F% | Min | GP | G | A | Pts | PIM | PP | SH | GW | Min |
|---|---|---|---|---|---|---|---|---|---|---|---|---|---|---|---|---|---|---|---|---|---|---|---|---|---|
| | | | Regular Season | | | | | | | | | | | | | | Playoffs | | | | | | | | |

## KESLER, Ryan
(KEHZ-luhr, RIGH-uhn) **VAN.**

Center. Shoots right. 6'2", 205 lbs. Born, Livonia, MI, August 31, 1984. Vancouver's 1st choice, 23rd overall, in 2003 Entry Draft.

| Season | Club | League | GP | G | A | Pts | PIM | PP | SH | GW | S | % | +/- | TF | F% | Min | GP | G | A | Pts | PIM | PP | SH | GW | Min |
|---|---|---|---|---|---|---|---|---|---|---|---|---|---|---|---|---|---|---|---|---|---|---|---|---|---|
| 99-2000 | Det. Honeybaked | MWEHL | 72 | 44 | 73 | 117 | .... | .... | .... | .... | .... | .... | .... | .... | .... | .... | .... | .... | .... | .... | .... | .... | .... | .... | .... |
| 2000-01 | USNTDP | U-18 | 26 | 8 | 20 | 28 | 24 | .... | .... | .... | .... | .... | .... | .... | .... | .... | .... | .... | .... | .... | .... | .... | .... | .... | .... |
| | USNTDP | NAHL | 56 | 7 | 21 | 28 | 40 | .... | .... | .... | .... | .... | .... | .... | .... | .... | .... | .... | .... | .... | .... | .... | .... | .... | .... |
| 2001-02 | USNTDP | U-18 | 46 | 11 | 33 | 44 | 23 | .... | .... | .... | .... | .... | .... | .... | .... | .... | .... | .... | .... | .... | .... | .... | .... | .... | .... |
| | USNTDP | USHL | 13 | 5 | 5 | 10 | 10 | .... | .... | .... | .... | .... | .... | .... | .... | .... | .... | .... | .... | .... | .... | .... | .... | .... | .... |
| | USNTDP | NAHL | 10 | 5 | 6 | 11 | 4 | .... | .... | .... | .... | .... | .... | .... | .... | .... | .... | .... | .... | .... | .... | .... | .... | .... | .... |
| 2002-03 | Ohio State | CCHA | 40 | 11 | 20 | 31 | 44 | .... | .... | .... | .... | .... | .... | .... | .... | .... | .... | .... | .... | .... | .... | .... | .... | .... | .... |
| **2003-04** | **Vancouver** | **NHL** | **28** | **2** | **3** | **5** | **16** | **0** | **0** | **0** | **23** | **8.7** | **-2** | **194** | **40.2** | **10:42** | .... | .... | .... | .... | .... | .... | .... | .... | .... |
| | Manitoba Moose | AHL | 33 | 3 | 8 | 11 | 29 | .... | .... | .... | .... | .... | .... | .... | .... | .... | .... | .... | .... | .... | .... | .... | .... | .... | .... |
| 2004-05 | Manitoba Moose | AHL | 78 | 30 | 27 | 57 | 105 | .... | .... | .... | .... | .... | .... | .... | .... | .... | 14 | 4 | 5 | 9 | 8 | .... | .... | .... | .... |
| **2005-06** | **Vancouver** | **NHL** | **82** | **10** | **13** | **23** | **79** | **1** | **0** | **2** | **119** | **8.4** | **1** | **984** | **46.8** | **14:03** | .... | .... | .... | .... | .... | .... | .... | .... | .... |
| **2006-07** | **Vancouver** | **NHL** | **48** | **6** | **10** | **16** | **40** | **0** | **0** | **0** | **88** | **6.8** | **1** | **690** | **46.1** | **16:26** | **1** | **0** | **0** | **0** | **0** | **0** | **0** | **0** | **27:51** |
| **2007-08** | **Vancouver** | **NHL** | **80** | **21** | **16** | **37** | **79** | **4** | **2** | **2** | **177** | **11.9** | **1** | **1358** | **53.0** | **19:03** | .... | .... | .... | .... | .... | .... | .... | .... | .... |
| **2008-09** | **Vancouver** | **NHL** | **82** | **26** | **33** | **59** | **61** | **10** | **2** | **2** | **179** | **14.5** | **8** | **976** | **54.0** | **19:28** | **10** | **2** | **2** | **4** | **14** | **1** | **0** | **0** | **20:29** |
| | **NHL Totals** | | **320** | **65** | **75** | **140** | **275** | **15** | **4** | **6** | **586** | **11.1** | | **4202** | **50.0** | **16:45** | **11** | **2** | **2** | **4** | **14** | **1** | **0** | **0** | **21:09** |

## KESSEL, Phil
(KEH-suhl, FIHL) **BOS.**

Center. Shoots right. 5'11", 180 lbs. Born, Madison, WI, October 2, 1987. Boston's 1st choice, 5th overall, in 2006 Entry Draft.

| Season | Club | League | GP | G | A | Pts | PIM | PP | SH | GW | S | % | +/- | TF | F% | Min | GP | G | A | Pts | PIM | PP | SH | GW | Min |
|---|---|---|---|---|---|---|---|---|---|---|---|---|---|---|---|---|---|---|---|---|---|---|---|---|---|
| 2003-04 | USNTDP | U-17 | 32 | 31 | 18 | 49 | 8 | .... | .... | .... | .... | .... | .... | .... | .... | .... | .... | .... | .... | .... | .... | .... | .... | .... | .... |
| | USNTDP | NAHL | 30 | 21 | 12 | 33 | 18 | .... | .... | .... | .... | .... | .... | .... | .... | .... | .... | .... | .... | .... | .... | .... | .... | .... | .... |
| 2004-05 | USNTDP | U-18 | 31 | 41 | 32 | 73 | 16 | .... | .... | .... | .... | .... | .... | .... | .... | .... | .... | .... | .... | .... | .... | .... | .... | .... | .... |
| | USNTDP | NAHL | 14 | 11 | 14 | 25 | 21 | .... | .... | .... | .... | .... | .... | .... | .... | .... | .... | .... | .... | .... | .... | .... | .... | .... | .... |
| 2005-06 | U. of Minnesota | WCHA | 39 | 18 | 33 | 51 | 28 | .... | .... | .... | .... | .... | .... | .... | .... | .... | .... | .... | .... | .... | .... | .... | .... | .... | .... |
| **2006-07** | **Boston** | **NHL** | **70** | **11** | **18** | **29** | **12** | **1** | **0** | **0** | **170** | **6.5** | **-12** | **373** | **40.8** | **14:04** | .... | .... | .... | .... | .... | .... | .... | .... | .... |
| | Providence Bruins | AHL | 2 | 1 | 0 | 1 | 2 | .... | .... | .... | .... | .... | .... | .... | .... | .... | .... | .... | .... | .... | .... | .... | .... | .... | .... |
| **2007-08** | **Boston** | **NHL** | **82** | **19** | **18** | **37** | **28** | **5** | **0** | **3** | **213** | **8.9** | **-6** | **326** | **42.3** | **15:14** | **4** | **3** | **1** | **4** | **2** | **1** | **0** | **0** | **14:31** |
| **2008-09** | **Boston** | **NHL** | **70** | **36** | **24** | **60** | **16** | **8** | **0** | **6** | **232** | **15.5** | **23** | **87** | **48.3** | **16:34** | **11** | **6** | **5** | **11** | **4** | **0** | **0** | **0** | **15:55** |
| | **NHL Totals** | | **222** | **66** | **60** | **126** | **56** | **14** | **0** | **9** | **615** | **10.7** | | **786** | **42.2** | **15:17** | **15** | **9** | **6** | **15** | **6** | **1** | **0** | **0** | **15:33** |

WCHA All-Rookie Team (2006) • WCHA Rookie of the Year (2006) • Bill Masterton Memorial Trophy (2007)

## KING, D.J.
(KIHNG, DEE-JAY) **ST.L.**

Center. Shoots left. 6'3", 229 lbs. Born, Meadow Lake, Sask., January 27, 1984. St. Louis' 6th choice, 191st overall, in 2002 Entry Draft.

| Season | Club | League | GP | G | A | Pts | PIM | PP | SH | GW | S | % | +/- | TF | F% | Min | GP | G | A | Pts | PIM | PP | SH | GW | Min |
|---|---|---|---|---|---|---|---|---|---|---|---|---|---|---|---|---|---|---|---|---|---|---|---|---|---|
| 2000-01 | Beardy's | SMHL | 52 | 30 | 28 | 58 | 120 | .... | .... | .... | .... | .... | .... | .... | .... | .... | .... | .... | .... | .... | .... | .... | .... | .... | .... |
| 2001-02 | Lethbridge | WHL | 65 | 10 | 14 | 24 | 104 | .... | .... | .... | .... | .... | .... | .... | .... | .... | .... | .... | .... | .... | .... | .... | .... | .... | .... |
| 2002-03 | Lethbridge | WHL | 55 | 15 | 17 | 32 | 139 | .... | .... | .... | .... | .... | .... | .... | .... | .... | .... | .... | .... | .... | .... | .... | .... | .... | .... |
| 2003-04 | Lethbridge | WHL | 35 | 8 | 15 | 23 | 102 | .... | .... | .... | .... | .... | .... | .... | .... | .... | .... | .... | .... | .... | .... | .... | .... | .... | .... |
| | Kelowna Rockets | WHL | 28 | 5 | 2 | 7 | 80 | .... | .... | .... | .... | .... | .... | .... | .... | .... | 17 | 1 | 6 | 7 | 16 | .... | .... | .... | .... |
| 2004-05 | Worcester IceCats | AHL | 74 | 6 | 8 | 14 | 178 | .... | .... | .... | .... | .... | .... | .... | .... | .... | .... | .... | .... | .... | .... | .... | .... | .... | .... |
| 2005-06 | Peoria Rivermen | AHL | 67 | 5 | 6 | 11 | 160 | .... | .... | .... | .... | .... | .... | .... | .... | .... | 2 | 0 | 0 | 0 | 2 | .... | .... | .... | .... |
| | Alaska Aces | ECHL | 5 | 0 | 4 | 4 | 4 | .... | .... | .... | .... | .... | .... | .... | .... | .... | .... | .... | .... | .... | .... | .... | .... | .... | .... |
| **2006-07** | **St. Louis** | **NHL** | **27** | **1** | **1** | **2** | **52** | **0** | **0** | **0** | **12** | **8.3** | **-3** | **2** | **50.0** | **5:31** | .... | .... | .... | .... | .... | .... | .... | .... | .... |
| | Peoria Rivermen | AHL | 38 | 5 | 4 | 9 | 102 | .... | .... | .... | .... | .... | .... | .... | .... | .... | .... | .... | .... | .... | .... | .... | .... | .... | .... |
| **2007-08** | **St. Louis** | **NHL** | **61** | **3** | **3** | **6** | **100** | **0** | **0** | **1** | **36** | **8.3** | **-4** | **7** | **28.6** | **5:36** | .... | .... | .... | .... | .... | .... | .... | .... | .... |
| **2008-09** | **St. Louis** | **NHL** | **1** | **0** | **1** | **1** | **0** | **0** | **0** | **0** | **0** | **0.0** | **0** | **0** | **0.0** | **8:20** | .... | .... | .... | .... | .... | .... | .... | .... | .... |
| | **NHL Totals** | | **89** | **4** | **5** | **9** | **152** | **0** | **0** | **1** | **48** | **8.3** | | **9** | **33.3** | **5:37** | .... | .... | .... | .... | .... | .... | .... | .... | .... |

• Missed majority of 2008-09 season recovering from shoulder injury.

## KING, Jason
(KIHNG, JAY-suhn)

Center. Shoots left. 6'1", 195 lbs. Born, Corner Brook, Nfld., September 14, 1981. Vancouver's 5th choice, 212th overall, in 2001 Entry Draft.

| Season | Club | League | GP | G | A | Pts | PIM | PP | SH | GW | S | % | +/- | TF | F% | Min | GP | G | A | Pts | PIM | PP | SH | GW | Min |
|---|---|---|---|---|---|---|---|---|---|---|---|---|---|---|---|---|---|---|---|---|---|---|---|---|---|
| 99-2000 | Halifax | QMJHL | 53 | 3 | 7 | 10 | 8 | .... | .... | .... | .... | .... | .... | .... | .... | .... | 10 | 0 | 0 | 0 | 2 | .... | .... | .... | .... |
| 2000-01 | Halifax | QMJHL | 72 | 48 | 41 | 89 | 78 | .... | .... | .... | .... | .... | .... | .... | .... | .... | 6 | 3 | 2 | 5 | 16 | .... | .... | .... | .... |
| 2001-02 | Halifax | QMJHL | 61 | *63 | 36 | 99 | 39 | .... | .... | .... | .... | .... | .... | .... | .... | .... | 13 | 9 | 8 | 17 | 13 | .... | .... | .... | .... |
| **2002-03** | **Vancouver** | **NHL** | **8** | **0** | **2** | **2** | **0** | **0** | **0** | **0** | **12** | **0.0** | **0** | **0** | **0.0** | **11:17** | .... | .... | .... | .... | .... | .... | .... | .... | .... |
| | Manitoba Moose | AHL | 67 | 20 | 20 | 40 | 15 | .... | .... | .... | .... | .... | .... | .... | .... | .... | 14 | 4 | 3 | 7 | 14 | .... | .... | .... | .... |
| **2003-04** | **Vancouver** | **NHL** | **47** | **12** | **9** | **21** | **8** | **6** | **0** | **1** | **107** | **11.2** | **0** | **3** | **66.7** | **12:43** | **1** | **0** | **0** | **0** | **0** | **0** | **0** | **0** | **6:21** |
| | Manitoba Moose | AHL | 29 | 12 | 11 | 23 | 6 | .... | .... | .... | .... | .... | .... | .... | .... | .... | .... | .... | .... | .... | .... | .... | .... | .... | .... |
| 2004-05 | Manitoba Moose | AHL | 59 | 26 | 27 | 53 | 22 | .... | .... | .... | .... | .... | .... | .... | .... | .... | .... | .... | .... | .... | .... | .... | .... | .... | .... |
| 2005-06 | Manitoba Moose | AHL | 36 | 20 | 14 | 34 | 34 | .... | .... | .... | .... | .... | .... | .... | .... | .... | 13 | 3 | 4 | 7 | 8 | .... | .... | .... | .... |
| 2006-07 | Skelleftea AIK HK | Sweden | 55 | 15 | 4 | 19 | 20 | .... | .... | .... | .... | .... | .... | .... | .... | .... | .... | .... | .... | .... | .... | .... | .... | .... | .... |
| | Skelleftea AIK HK | Sweden-Q | 9 | 3 | 2 | 5 | 6 | .... | .... | .... | .... | .... | .... | .... | .... | .... | .... | .... | .... | .... | .... | .... | .... | .... | .... |
| **2007-08** | **Anaheim** | **NHL** | **4** | **0** | **0** | **0** | **0** | **0** | **0** | **0** | **2** | **0.0** | **-3** | **1** | **100.0** | **10:57** | .... | .... | .... | .... | .... | .... | .... | .... | .... |
| | Portland Pirates | AHL | 65 | 29 | 30 | 59 | 42 | .... | .... | .... | .... | .... | .... | .... | .... | .... | 13 | 6 | 3 | 9 | 12 | .... | .... | .... | .... |
| 2008-09 | Adler Mannheim | Germany | 37 | 7 | 10 | 17 | 70 | .... | .... | .... | .... | .... | .... | .... | .... | .... | 7 | 3 | 1 | 4 | 2 | .... | .... | .... | .... |
| | **NHL Totals** | | **59** | **12** | **11** | **23** | **8** | **6** | **0** | **1** | **121** | **9.9** | | **4** | **75.0** | **12:24** | **1** | **0** | **0** | **0** | **0** | **0** | **0** | **0** | **6:21** |

QMJHL Second All-Star Team (2001)

• Missed majority of 2005-06 season recovering from head injury suffered in game vs. Grand Rapids (AHL), March 9, 2005. Traded to **Anaheim** by **Vancouver** for Ryan Shannon and future considerations, June 23, 2007. Signed as a free agent by **Skelleftea** (Sweden), September 13, 2006. Signed as a free agent by **Hamburg** (Germany), May 15, 2009.

## KINRADE, Geoff
(KIHN-rayd, JEHF) **OTT.**

Defense. Shoots left. 6', 188 lbs. Born, Nelson, B.C., July 29, 1985.

| Season | Club | League | GP | G | A | Pts | PIM | PP | SH | GW | S | % | +/- | TF | F% | Min | GP | G | A | Pts | PIM | PP | SH | GW | Min |
|---|---|---|---|---|---|---|---|---|---|---|---|---|---|---|---|---|---|---|---|---|---|---|---|---|---|
| 2003-04 | Cowichan Valley | BCHL | 48 | 2 | 3 | 5 | 34 | .... | .... | .... | .... | .... | .... | .... | .... | .... | .... | .... | .... | .... | .... | .... | .... | .... | .... |
| 2004-05 | Cowichan Valley | BCHL | 60 | 13 | 21 | 34 | 49 | .... | .... | .... | .... | .... | .... | .... | .... | .... | 6 | 1 | 2 | 3 | 4 | .... | .... | .... | .... |
| 2005-06 | Michigan Tech | WCHA | 33 | 1 | 6 | 7 | 46 | .... | .... | .... | .... | .... | .... | .... | .... | .... | .... | .... | .... | .... | .... | .... | .... | .... | .... |
| 2006-07 | Michigan Tech | WCHA | 40 | 5 | 14 | 19 | 30 | .... | .... | .... | .... | .... | .... | .... | .... | .... | .... | .... | .... | .... | .... | .... | .... | .... | .... |
| 2007-08 | Michigan Tech | WCHA | 39 | 5 | 14 | 19 | 30 | .... | .... | .... | .... | .... | .... | .... | .... | .... | .... | .... | .... | .... | .... | .... | .... | .... | .... |
| **2008-09** | Michigan Tech | WCHA | 38 | 3 | 13 | 16 | 18 | .... | .... | .... | .... | .... | .... | .... | .... | .... | .... | .... | .... | .... | .... | .... | .... | .... | .... |
| | **Tampa Bay** | **NHL** | **1** | **0** | **0** | **0** | **0** | **0** | **0** | **0** | **1** | **0.0** | **-1** | **0** | **0.0** | **17:32** | .... | .... | .... | .... | .... | .... | .... | .... | .... |
| | Norfolk Admirals | AHL | 10 | 1 | 4 | 5 | 12 | .... | .... | .... | .... | .... | .... | .... | .... | .... | .... | .... | .... | .... | .... | .... | .... | .... | .... |
| | **NHL Totals** | | **1** | **0** | **0** | **0** | **0** | **0** | **0** | **0** | **1** | **0.0** | | **0** | **0.0** | **17:32** | .... | .... | .... | .... | .... | .... | .... | .... | .... |

Signed to an ATO (tryout) contract by **Tampa Bay**, April 9, 2009. Signed as a free agent by **Ottawa**, July 10, 2009.

## KLEE, Ken
(KLEE, KEHN)

Defense. Shoots right. 6'1", 210 lbs. Born, Indianapolis, IN, April 24, 1971. Washington's 11th choice, 177th overall, in 1990 Entry Draft.

| Season | Club | League | GP | G | A | Pts | PIM | PP | SH | GW | S | % | +/- | TF | F% | Min | GP | G | A | Pts | PIM | PP | SH | GW | Min |
|---|---|---|---|---|---|---|---|---|---|---|---|---|---|---|---|---|---|---|---|---|---|---|---|---|---|
| 1988-89 | St. Mike's B's | OHA-B | 40 | 9 | 23 | 32 | 64 | .... | .... | .... | .... | .... | .... | .... | .... | .... | 27 | 5 | 12 | 17 | 54 | .... | .... | .... | .... |
| 1989-90 | Bowling Green | CCHA | 39 | 0 | 5 | 5 | 52 | .... | .... | .... | .... | .... | .... | .... | .... | .... | .... | .... | .... | .... | .... | .... | .... | .... | .... |
| 1990-91 | Bowling Green | CCHA | 37 | 7 | 28 | 35 | 50 | .... | .... | .... | .... | .... | .... | .... | .... | .... | .... | .... | .... | .... | .... | .... | .... | .... | .... |
| 1991-92 | Bowling Green | CCHA | 10 | 0 | 1 | 1 | 14 | .... | .... | .... | .... | .... | .... | .... | .... | .... | .... | .... | .... | .... | .... | .... | .... | .... | .... |
| 1992-93 | Baltimore | AHL | 77 | 4 | 14 | 18 | 93 | .... | .... | .... | .... | .... | .... | .... | .... | .... | 7 | 0 | 1 | 1 | 15 | .... | .... | .... | .... |
| 1993-94 | Portland Pirates | AHL | 65 | 2 | 9 | 11 | 87 | .... | .... | .... | .... | .... | .... | .... | .... | .... | 17 | 1 | 2 | 3 | 14 | .... | .... | .... | .... |
| **1994-95** | Portland Pirates | AHL | 49 | 5 | 7 | 12 | 89 | .... | .... | .... | .... | .... | .... | .... | .... | .... | .... | .... | .... | .... | .... | .... | .... | .... | .... |
| | **Washington** | **NHL** | **23** | **3** | **1** | **4** | **41** | **0** | **0** | **0** | **18** | **16.7** | **2** | .... | .... | .... | **7** | **0** | **0** | **0** | **4** | **0** | **0** | **0** | .... |
| **1995-96** | **Washington** | **NHL** | **66** | **8** | **3** | **11** | **60** | **0** | **1** | **2** | **76** | **10.5** | **-1** | .... | .... | .... | **1** | **0** | **0** | **0** | **0** | **0** | **0** | **0** | .... |
| **1996-97** | **Washington** | **NHL** | **80** | **3** | **8** | **11** | **115** | **0** | **0** | **2** | **108** | **2.8** | **-5** | .... | .... | .... | .... | .... | .... | .... | .... | .... | .... | .... | .... |
| **1997-98** | **Washington** | **NHL** | **51** | **4** | **2** | **6** | **46** | **0** | **0** | **1** | **44** | **9.1** | **-3** | .... | .... | .... | **9** | **1** | **0** | **1** | **10** | **0** | **0** | **0** | .... |
| **1998-99** | **Washington** | **NHL** | **78** | **7** | **13** | **20** | **80** | **0** | **0** | **1** | **132** | **5.3** | **-9** | **0** | **0.0** | **19:07** | .... | .... | .... | .... | .... | .... | .... | .... | .... |
| **99-2000** | **Washington** | **NHL** | **80** | **7** | **13** | **20** | **79** | **0** | **0** | **2** | **113** | **6.2** | **8** | **0** | **0.0** | **20:29** | **5** | **0** | **1** | **1** | **10** | **0** | **0** | **0** | **21:38** |
| **2000-01** | **Washington** | **NHL** | **54** | **2** | **4** | **6** | **60** | **0** | **0** | **0** | **58** | **3.4** | **-5** | **0** | **0.0** | **17:15** | **6** | **0** | **1** | **1** | **8** | **0** | **0** | **0** | **13:47** |
| **2001-02** | **Washington** | **NHL** | **68** | **8** | **8** | **16** | **38** | **2** | **0** | **3** | **85** | **9.4** | **4** | **2** | **0.0** | **19:24** | .... | .... | .... | .... | .... | .... | .... | .... | .... |
| **2002-03** | **Washington** | **NHL** | **70** | **1** | **16** | **17** | **89** | **0** | **0** | **0** | **67** | **1.5** | **22** | **0** | **0.0** | **21:49** | **6** | **0** | **0** | **0** | **6** | **0** | **0** | **0** | **23:11** |
| **2003-04** | **Toronto** | **NHL** | **66** | **4** | **25** | **29** | **36** | **3** | **0** | **1** | **85** | **4.7** | **-1** | **1** | **100.0** | **22:08** | **11** | **0** | **0** | **0** | **6** | **0** | **0** | **0** | **18:45** |

| Season | Club | League | GP | G | A | Pts | PIM | PP | SH | GW | S | % | +/- | TF | F% | Min | Playoffs GP | G | A | Pts | PIM | PP | SH | GW | Min |
|---|---|---|---|---|---|---|---|---|---|---|---|---|---|---|---|---|---|---|---|---|---|---|---|---|---|
| | | | Regular Season | | | | | | | | | | | | | | | | | | | | | | |
| 2004-05 | | | Did not play | | | | | | | | | | | | | | | | | | | | | | |
| **2005-06** | **Toronto** | **NHL** | **56** | **3** | **12** | **15** | **66** | **1** | **0** | **1** | **65** | **4.6** | **−1** | **0** | **0.0** | **20:02** | .... | .... | .... | .... | .... | .... | .... | .... | .... |
| | **New Jersey** | **NHL** | **18** | **0** | **0** | **0** | **14** | **0** | **0** | **0** | **5** | **0.0** | **−3** | **0** | **0.0** | **15:03** | **6** | **1** | **0** | **1** | **6** | **0** | **0** | **0** | **12:05** |
| **2006-07** | **Colorado** | **NHL** | **81** | **3** | **16** | **19** | **68** | **0** | **0** | **0** | **90** | **3.3** | **18** | **0** | **0.0** | **20:38** | .... | .... | .... | .... | .... | .... | .... | .... | .... |
| **2007-08** | **Atlanta** | **NHL** | **72** | **1** | **9** | **10** | **60** | **0** | **0** | **0** | **56** | **1.8** | **−5** | **0** | **0.0** | **20:03** | .... | .... | .... | .... | .... | .... | .... | .... | .... |
| **2008-09** | **Anaheim** | **NHL** | **3** | **0** | **0** | **0** | **4** | **0** | **0** | **0** | **4** | **0.0** | **0** | **0** | **0.0** | **16:57** | .... | .... | .... | .... | .... | .... | .... | .... | .... |
| | **Phoenix** | **NHL** | **68** | **1** | **10** | **11** | **24** | **0** | **0** | **0** | **47** | **2.1** | **9** | **0** | **0.0** | **15:22** | .... | .... | .... | .... | .... | .... | .... | .... | .... |
| | **NHL Totals** | | **934** | **55** | **140** | **195** | **880** | **6** | **1** | **13** | **1053** | **5.2** | | **3** | **33.3** | **19:34** | **51** | **2** | **2** | **4** | **50** | **0** | **0** | **0** | **17:54** |

Signed as a free agent by **Toronto**, September 27, 2003. Traded to **New Jersey** by **Toronto** for Alexander Suglobov, March 8, 2006. Signed as a free agent by **Colorado**, July 24, 2006. Signed as a free agent by **Atlanta**, July 2, 2007. Traded to **Anaheim** by **Atlanta** with Brad Larsen and Chad Painchaud for Mathieu Schneider, September 26, 2008. Claimed on waivers by **Phoenix** from **Anaheim**, October 28, 2008.

## KLEIN, Kevin

(KLIGHN, KEH-vihn) **NSH.**

Defense. Shoots right. 6'1", 203 lbs. Born, Kitchener, Ont., December 13, 1984. Nashville's 3rd choice, 37th overall, in 2003 Entry Draft.

| Season | Club | League | GP | G | A | Pts | PIM | PP | SH | GW | S | % | +/- | TF | F% | Min | Playoffs GP | G | A | Pts | PIM | PP | SH | GW | Min |
|---|---|---|---|---|---|---|---|---|---|---|---|---|---|---|---|---|---|---|---|---|---|---|---|---|---|
| 99-2000 | Kitchener Midgets | Minor-ON | 54 | 12 | 29 | 41 | 40 | .... | .... | .... | .... | .... | .... | .... | .... | .... | .... | .... | .... | .... | .... | .... | .... | .... | .... |
| 2000-01 | St. Michael's | OHL | 58 | 3 | 16 | 19 | 21 | .... | .... | .... | .... | .... | .... | .... | .... | .... | 18 | 0 | 5 | 5 | 17 | .... | .... | .... | .... |
| 2001-02 | St. Michael's | OHL | 68 | 5 | 22 | 27 | 35 | .... | .... | .... | .... | .... | .... | .... | .... | .... | 15 | 2 | 7 | 9 | 12 | .... | .... | .... | .... |
| 2002-03 | St. Michael's | OHL | 67 | 11 | 33 | 44 | 88 | .... | .... | .... | .... | .... | .... | .... | .... | .... | 17 | 1 | 9 | 10 | 8 | .... | .... | .... | .... |
| 2003-04 | St. Michael's | OHL | 5 | 0 | 1 | 1 | 2 | .... | .... | .... | .... | .... | .... | .... | .... | .... | .... | .... | .... | .... | .... | .... | .... | .... | .... |
| | Guelph Storm | OHL | 46 | 6 | 23 | 29 | 40 | .... | .... | .... | .... | .... | .... | .... | .... | .... | 22 | 10 | 11 | 21 | 12 | .... | .... | .... | .... |
| 2004-05 | Milwaukee | AHL | 65 | 4 | 12 | 16 | 22 | .... | .... | .... | .... | .... | .... | .... | .... | .... | 7 | 0 | 0 | 0 | 11 | .... | .... | .... | .... |
| | Rockford IceHogs | UHL | 3 | 2 | 1 | 3 | 0 | .... | .... | .... | .... | .... | .... | .... | .... | .... | .... | .... | .... | .... | .... | .... | .... | .... | .... |
| **2005-06** | **Nashville** | **NHL** | **2** | **0** | **0** | **0** | **0** | **0** | **0** | **0** | **0** | **0.0** | **−1** | **0** | **0.0** | **13:40** | .... | .... | .... | .... | .... | .... | .... | .... | .... |
| | Milwaukee | AHL | 76 | 10 | 33 | 43 | 31 | .... | .... | .... | .... | .... | .... | .... | .... | .... | 21 | 3 | 7 | 10 | 31 | .... | .... | .... | .... |
| **2006-07** | **Nashville** | **NHL** | **3** | **1** | **0** | **1** | **0** | **0** | **0** | **0** | **2** | **50.0** | **3** | **0** | **0.0** | **16:37** | .... | .... | .... | .... | .... | .... | .... | .... | .... |
| | Milwaukee | AHL | 70 | 5 | 15 | 20 | 67 | .... | .... | .... | .... | .... | .... | .... | .... | .... | 4 | 1 | 0 | 1 | 0 | .... | .... | .... | .... |
| **2007-08** | **Nashville** | **NHL** | **13** | **0** | **2** | **2** | **6** | **0** | **0** | **0** | **14** | **0.0** | **−3** | **0** | **0.0** | **14:24** | .... | .... | .... | .... | .... | .... | .... | .... | .... |
| | Milwaukee | AHL | 9 | 0 | 3 | 3 | 2 | .... | .... | .... | .... | .... | .... | .... | .... | .... | .... | .... | .... | .... | .... | .... | .... | .... | .... |
| **2008-09** | **Nashville** | **NHL** | **63** | **4** | **8** | **12** | **19** | **1** | **0** | **0** | **41** | **9.8** | **−2** | **0** | **0.0** | **12:40** | .... | .... | .... | .... | .... | .... | .... | .... | .... |
| | **NHL Totals** | | **81** | **5** | **10** | **15** | **25** | **1** | **0** | **0** | **57** | **8.8** | | **0** | **0.0** | **13:07** | .... | .... | .... | .... | .... | .... | .... | .... | .... |

## KLEPIS, Jakub

(KLEH-pihsh, YA-kuhb) **WSH.**

Center. Shoots right. 6'1", 198 lbs. Born, Prague, Czech., June 5, 1984. Ottawa's 1st choice, 16th overall, in 2002 Entry Draft.

| Season | Club | League | GP | G | A | Pts | PIM | PP | SH | GW | S | % | +/- | TF | F% | Min | Playoffs GP | G | A | Pts | PIM | PP | SH | GW | Min |
|---|---|---|---|---|---|---|---|---|---|---|---|---|---|---|---|---|---|---|---|---|---|---|---|---|---|
| 99-2000 | Slavia Jr. | CzRep-Jr. | 48 | 14 | 26 | 40 | 30 | .... | .... | .... | .... | .... | .... | .... | .... | .... | .... | .... | .... | .... | .... | .... | .... | .... | .... |
| 2000-01 | Slavia Jr. | CzRep-Jr. | 52 | 21 | 25 | 46 | 82 | .... | .... | .... | .... | .... | .... | .... | .... | .... | .... | .... | .... | .... | .... | .... | .... | .... | .... |
| 2001-02 | Portland | WHL | 70 | 14 | 50 | 64 | 111 | .... | .... | .... | .... | .... | .... | .... | .... | .... | 7 | 0 | 3 | 3 | 22 | .... | .... | .... | .... |
| 2002-03 | HC Slavia Praha | CzRep | 38 | 2 | 6 | 8 | 22 | .... | .... | .... | .... | .... | .... | .... | .... | .... | 4 | 0 | 0 | 0 | 6 | .... | .... | .... | .... |
| | Slavia Jr. | CzRep-Jr. | 11 | 4 | 5 | 9 | 59 | .... | .... | .... | .... | .... | .... | .... | .... | .... | 3 | 0 | 3 | 3 | 4 | .... | .... | .... | .... |
| 2003-04 | HC Slavia Praha | CzRep | 44 | 4 | 9 | 13 | 43 | .... | .... | .... | .... | .... | .... | .... | .... | .... | 17 | 5 | 3 | 8 | 10 | .... | .... | .... | .... |
| 2004-05 | Portland Pirates | AHL | 78 | 13 | 14 | 27 | 76 | .... | .... | .... | .... | .... | .... | .... | .... | .... | .... | .... | .... | .... | .... | .... | .... | .... | .... |
| **2005-06** | **Washington** | **NHL** | **25** | **1** | **3** | **4** | **8** | **0** | **0** | **0** | **26** | **3.8** | **−11** | **22** | **40.9** | **7:25** | .... | .... | .... | .... | .... | .... | .... | .... | .... |
| | Hershey Bears | AHL | 54 | 11 | 20 | 31 | 49 | .... | .... | .... | .... | .... | .... | .... | .... | .... | 15 | 2 | 6 | 8 | 4 | .... | .... | .... | .... |
| **2006-07** | **Washington** | **NHL** | **41** | **3** | **7** | **10** | **28** | **0** | **0** | **0** | **38** | **7.9** | **−2** | **184** | **41.3** | **9:58** | .... | .... | .... | .... | .... | .... | .... | .... | .... |
| | Hershey Bears | AHL | 31 | 6 | 26 | 32 | 24 | .... | .... | .... | .... | .... | .... | .... | .... | .... | 19 | 7 | 7 | 14 | 14 | .... | .... | .... | .... |
| 2007-08 | Hershey Bears | AHL | 19 | 5 | 6 | 11 | 9 | .... | .... | .... | .... | .... | .... | .... | .... | .... | .... | .... | .... | .... | .... | .... | .... | .... | .... |
| | HC Slavia Praha | CzRep | 24 | 5 | 7 | 12 | 22 | .... | .... | .... | .... | .... | .... | .... | .... | .... | 19 | *10 | 7 | 17 | 24 | .... | .... | .... | .... |
| 2008-09 | Omsk | Rus-KHL | 55 | 18 | 17 | 35 | 51 | .... | .... | .... | .... | .... | .... | .... | .... | .... | 9 | 2 | 4 | 6 | 0 | .... | .... | .... | .... |
| | **NHL Totals** | | **66** | **4** | **10** | **14** | **36** | **0** | **0** | **0** | **64** | **6.3** | | **206** | **41.3** | **9:00** | .... | .... | .... | .... | .... | .... | .... | .... | .... |

Traded to **Buffalo** by **Ottawa** for Vaclav Varada and Buffalo's 5th round choice (Tim Cook) in 2003 Entry Draft, February 25, 2003. Traded to **Washington** by **Buffalo** for Mike Grier, March 9, 2004.

## KLESLA, Rostislav

(KLEHS-luh, RAHS-tih-slav) **CBJ**

Defense. Shoots left. 6'3", 220 lbs. Born, Novy Jicin, Czech., March 21, 1982. Columbus' 1st choice, 4th overall, in 2000 Entry Draft.

| Season | Club | League | GP | G | A | Pts | PIM | PP | SH | GW | S | % | +/- | TF | F% | Min | Playoffs GP | G | A | Pts | PIM | PP | SH | GW | Min |
|---|---|---|---|---|---|---|---|---|---|---|---|---|---|---|---|---|---|---|---|---|---|---|---|---|---|
| 1997-98 | HC Opava Jr. | CzRep-Jr. | 38 | 11 | 18 | 29 | 87 | .... | .... | .... | .... | .... | .... | .... | .... | .... | 8 | 2 | 2 | 4 | 0 | .... | .... | .... | .... |
| 1998-99 | Sioux City | USHL | 54 | 4 | 12 | 16 | 100 | .... | .... | .... | .... | .... | .... | .... | .... | .... | 5 | 2 | 0 | 2 | 2 | .... | .... | .... | .... |
| 99-2000 | Brampton | OHL | 67 | 16 | 29 | 45 | 174 | .... | .... | .... | .... | .... | .... | .... | .... | .... | 6 | 1 | 1 | 2 | 21 | .... | .... | .... | .... |
| **2000-01** | **Columbus** | **NHL** | **8** | **2** | **0** | **2** | **6** | **0** | **0** | **0** | **10** | **20.0** | **−1** | **0** | **0.0** | **18:25** | .... | .... | .... | .... | .... | .... | .... | .... | .... |
| | Brampton | OHL | 45 | 18 | 36 | 54 | 59 | .... | .... | .... | .... | .... | .... | .... | .... | .... | 9 | 2 | 9 | 11 | 26 | .... | .... | .... | .... |
| **2001-02** | **Columbus** | **NHL** | **75** | **8** | **8** | **16** | **74** | **1** | **0** | **0** | **102** | **7.8** | **−6** | **0** | **0.0** | **18:52** | .... | .... | .... | .... | .... | .... | .... | .... | .... |
| **2002-03** | **Columbus** | **NHL** | **72** | **2** | **14** | **16** | **71** | **0** | **0** | **0** | **89** | **2.2** | **−22** | **0** | **0.0** | **18:45** | .... | .... | .... | .... | .... | .... | .... | .... | .... |
| **2003-04** | **Columbus** | **NHL** | **47** | **2** | **11** | **13** | **27** | **0** | **0** | **1** | **74** | **2.7** | **−16** | **0** | **0.0** | **18:19** | .... | .... | .... | .... | .... | .... | .... | .... | .... |
| 2004-05 | HC Vsetin | CzRep | 41 | 7 | 17 | 24 | 136 | .... | .... | .... | .... | .... | .... | .... | .... | .... | .... | .... | .... | .... | .... | .... | .... | .... | .... |
| | HPK Hameenlinna | Finland | 9 | 1 | 2 | 3 | 12 | .... | .... | .... | .... | .... | .... | .... | .... | .... | 10 | 0 | 2 | 2 | 12 | .... | .... | .... | .... |
| **2005-06** | **Columbus** | **NHL** | **51** | **6** | **13** | **19** | **75** | **2** | **0** | **1** | **84** | **7.1** | **−4** | **2** | **100.0** | **21:27** | .... | .... | .... | .... | .... | .... | .... | .... | .... |
| **2006-07** | **Columbus** | **NHL** | **75** | **9** | **13** | **22** | **105** | **2** | **0** | **0** | **159** | **5.7** | **−13** | **0** | **0.0** | **22:54** | .... | .... | .... | .... | .... | .... | .... | .... | .... |
| **2007-08** | **Columbus** | **NHL** | **82** | **6** | **12** | **18** | **60** | **3** | **0** | **1** | **130** | **4.6** | **7** | **5** | **80.0** | **23:13** | .... | .... | .... | .... | .... | .... | .... | .... | .... |
| **2008-09** | **Columbus** | **NHL** | **34** | **1** | **8** | **9** | **38** | **0** | **0** | **0** | **30** | **3.3** | **2** | **1** | **0.0** | **20:59** | **4** | **0** | **1** | **1** | **0** | **0** | **0** | **0** | **21:22** |
| | **NHL Totals** | | **444** | **36** | **79** | **115** | **456** | **8** | **0** | **3** | **678** | **5.3** | | **8** | **75.0** | **20:44** | **4** | **0** | **1** | **1** | **0** | **0** | **0** | **0** | **21:22** |

OHL All-Rookie Team (2000) • Canadian Major Junior All-Rookie Team (2000) • OHL First All-Star Team (2001) • NHL All-Rookie Team (2002)

Signed as a free agent by **Vsetin** (CzRep), September 17, 2004. Signed as a free agent by **Hameenlinna** (Finland), January 29, 2005. • Missed majority of 2008-09 season recovering from various injuries.

## KNUBLE, Mike

(kuh-NOO-buhl, MIGHK) **WSH.**

Right wing. Shoots right. 6'3", 230 lbs. Born, Toronto, Ont., July 4, 1972. Detroit's 4th choice, 76th overall, in 1991 Entry Draft.

| Season | Club | League | GP | G | A | Pts | PIM | PP | SH | GW | S | % | +/- | TF | F% | Min | Playoffs GP | G | A | Pts | PIM | PP | SH | GW | Min |
|---|---|---|---|---|---|---|---|---|---|---|---|---|---|---|---|---|---|---|---|---|---|---|---|---|---|
| 1988-89 | East Kentwood | High-MI | 28 | 52 | 37 | 89 | 60 | .... | .... | .... | .... | .... | .... | .... | .... | .... | .... | .... | .... | .... | .... | .... | .... | .... | .... |
| 1989-90 | East Kentwood | High-MI | 29 | 63 | 40 | 103 | 40 | .... | .... | .... | .... | .... | .... | .... | .... | .... | .... | .... | .... | .... | .... | .... | .... | .... | .... |
| 1990-91 | Kalamazoo | NAHL | 36 | 18 | 24 | 42 | 30 | .... | .... | .... | .... | .... | .... | .... | .... | .... | .... | .... | .... | .... | .... | .... | .... | .... | .... |
| 1991-92 | U. of Michigan | CCHA | 43 | 7 | 8 | 15 | 48 | .... | .... | .... | .... | .... | .... | .... | .... | .... | .... | .... | .... | .... | .... | .... | .... | .... | .... |
| 1992-93 | U. of Michigan | CCHA | 39 | 26 | 16 | 42 | 57 | .... | .... | .... | .... | .... | .... | .... | .... | .... | .... | .... | .... | .... | .... | .... | .... | .... | .... |
| 1993-94 | U. of Michigan | CCHA | 41 | 32 | 26 | 58 | 71 | .... | .... | .... | .... | .... | .... | .... | .... | .... | .... | .... | .... | .... | .... | .... | .... | .... | .... |
| 1994-95 | U. of Michigan | CCHA | 34 | *38 | 22 | 60 | 62 | .... | .... | .... | .... | .... | .... | .... | .... | .... | .... | .... | .... | .... | .... | .... | .... | .... | .... |
| | Adirondack | AHL | .... | .... | .... | .... | .... | .... | .... | .... | .... | .... | .... | .... | .... | .... | 3 | 0 | 0 | 0 | 0 | .... | .... | .... | .... |
| 1995-96 | Adirondack | AHL | 80 | 22 | 23 | 45 | 59 | .... | .... | .... | .... | .... | .... | .... | .... | .... | 3 | 1 | 0 | 1 | 0 | .... | .... | .... | .... |
| **1996-97** | **Detroit** | **NHL** | **9** | **1** | **0** | **1** | **0** | **0** | **0** | **0** | **10** | **10.0** | **−1** | .... | .... | .... | .... | .... | .... | .... | .... | .... | .... | .... | .... |
| | Adirondack | AHL | 68 | 28 | 35 | 63 | 54 | .... | .... | .... | .... | .... | .... | .... | .... | .... | .... | .... | .... | .... | .... | .... | .... | .... | .... |
| **1997-98** ♦ | **Detroit** | **NHL** | **53** | **7** | **6** | **13** | **16** | **0** | **0** | **0** | **54** | **13.0** | **2** | .... | .... | .... | **3** | **0** | **1** | **1** | **0** | **0** | **0** | **0** | .... |
| **1998-99** | **NY Rangers** | **NHL** | **82** | **15** | **20** | **35** | **26** | **3** | **0** | **1** | **113** | **13.3** | **−7** | **1** | **100.0** | **14:52** | .... | .... | .... | .... | .... | .... | .... | .... | .... |
| **99-2000** | **NY Rangers** | **NHL** | **59** | **9** | **5** | **14** | **18** | **1** | **0** | **1** | **50** | **18.0** | **−5** | **9** | **55.6** | **10:39** | .... | .... | .... | .... | .... | .... | .... | .... | .... |
| | **Boston** | **NHL** | **14** | **3** | **3** | **6** | **8** | **1** | **0** | **1** | **28** | **10.7** | **−2** | **3** | **0.0** | **19:29** | .... | .... | .... | .... | .... | .... | .... | .... | .... |
| **2000-01** | **Boston** | **NHL** | **82** | **7** | **13** | **20** | **37** | **0** | **1** | **1** | **92** | **7.6** | **0** | **115** | **31.3** | **10:34** | .... | .... | .... | .... | .... | .... | .... | .... | .... |
| **2001-02** | **Boston** | **NHL** | **54** | **8** | **6** | **14** | **42** | **0** | **0** | **2** | **77** | **10.4** | **9** | **27** | **44.4** | **9:45** | **2** | **0** | **0** | **0** | **0** | **0** | **0** | **0** | **3:30** |
| **2002-03** | **Boston** | **NHL** | **75** | **30** | **29** | **59** | **45** | **9** | **0** | **4** | **185** | **16.2** | **18** | **34** | **44.1** | **17:24** | **5** | **0** | **2** | **2** | **2** | **0** | **0** | **0** | **17:35** |
| **2003-04** | **Boston** | **NHL** | **82** | **21** | **25** | **46** | **32** | **4** | **0** | **3** | **192** | **10.9** | **19** | **54** | **31.5** | **18:47** | **7** | **2** | **0** | **2** | **0** | **1** | **0** | **0** | **19:45** |
| 2004-05 | Linkopings HC | Sweden | 49 | *26 | 13 | 39 | 40 | .... | .... | .... | .... | .... | .... | .... | .... | .... | 6 | 0 | 1 | 1 | 2 | .... | .... | .... | .... |
| **2005-06** | **Philadelphia** | **NHL** | **82** | **34** | **31** | **65** | **80** | **13** | **2** | **6** | **217** | **15.7** | **25** | **161** | **32.3** | **20:21** | **6** | **1** | **3** | **4** | **8** | **0** | **0** | **0** | **19:17** |
| | United States | Olympics | 6 | 1 | 1 | 2 | 4 | .... | .... | .... | .... | .... | .... | .... | .... | .... | .... | .... | .... | .... | .... | .... | .... | .... | .... |
| **2006-07** | **Philadelphia** | **NHL** | **64** | **24** | **30** | **54** | **56** | **10** | **0** | **1** | **160** | **15.0** | **2** | **62** | **37.1** | **19:38** | .... | .... | .... | .... | .... | .... | .... | .... | .... |
| **2007-08** | **Philadelphia** | **NHL** | **82** | **29** | **26** | **55** | **72** | **15** | **1** | **3** | **177** | **16.4** | **−3** | **25** | **40.0** | **18:55** | **12** | **3** | **4** | **7** | **6** | **0** | **0** | **1** | **18:34** |
| **2008-09** | **Philadelphia** | **NHL** | **82** | **27** | **20** | **47** | **62** | **11** | **0** | **6** | **173** | **15.6** | **5** | **51** | **35.3** | **18:10** | **6** | **2** | **1** | **3** | **2** | **0** | **0** | **0** | **18:26** |
| | **NHL Totals** | | **820** | **215** | **214** | **429** | **494** | **67** | **4** | **29** | **1528** | **14.1** | | **542** | **34.9** | **16:16** | **41** | **8** | **11** | **19** | **18** | **1** | **0** | **1** | **17:57** |

CCHA Second All-Star Team (1994, 1995) • NCAA West Second All-American Team (1995)

Traded to **NY Rangers** by **Detroit** for NY Rangers' 2nd round choice (Tomas Kopecky) in 2000 Entry Draft, October 1, 1998. Traded to **Boston** by **NY Rangers** for Rob DiMaio, March 10, 2000. Signed as a free agent by **Philadelphia**, July 3, 2004. Signed as a free agent by **Linkopings** (Sweden), August 2, 2004. Signed as a free agent by **Washington**, July 1, 2009.

## KOBASEW, Chuck

(KOH-buh-soo, CHUHK) **BOS.**

Center. Shoots left. 5'11", 192 lbs. Born, Vancouver, B.C., April 17, 1982. Calgary's 1st choice, 14th overall, in 2001 Entry Draft.

| | | | Regular Season | | | | | | | | | | | | | | Playoffs | | | | | | | | |
|---|---|---|---|---|---|---|---|---|---|---|---|---|---|---|---|---|---|---|---|---|---|---|---|---|---|
| Season | Club | League | GP | G | A | Pts | PIM | PP | SH | GW | S | % | +/- | TF | F% | Min | GP | G | A | Pts | PIM | PP | SH | GW | Min |
| 1997-98 | Osoyoos Heat | KIJHL | 6 | 2 | 2 | 4 | 2 | .... | .... | .... | .... | .... | .... | .... | .... | .... | .... | .... | .... | .... | .... | .... | .... | .... | .... |
| 1998-99 | Osoyoos Heat | KIJHL | 23 | 25 | 24 | 49 | .... | .... | .... | .... | .... | .... | .... | .... | .... | .... | .... | .... | .... | .... | .... | .... | .... | .... | .... |
| | Penticton | BCHL | 30 | 11 | 17 | 28 | 18 | .... | .... | .... | .... | .... | .... | .... | .... | .... | .... | .... | .... | .... | .... | .... | .... | .... | .... |
| 99-2000 | Penticton | BCHL | 58 | *54 | 52 | 106 | 83 | .... | .... | .... | .... | .... | .... | .... | .... | .... | .... | .... | .... | .... | .... | .... | .... | .... | .... |
| 2000-01 | Boston College | H-East | 43 | 27 | 22 | 49 | 38 | .... | .... | .... | .... | .... | .... | .... | .... | .... | .... | .... | .... | .... | .... | .... | .... | .... | .... |
| 2001-02 | Kelowna Rockets | WHL | 55 | 41 | 21 | 62 | 114 | .... | .... | .... | .... | .... | .... | .... | .... | .... | 15 | 10 | 5 | 15 | 22 | .... | .... | .... | .... |
| **2002-03** | **Calgary** | **NHL** | **23** | **4** | **2** | **6** | **8** | **1** | **0** | **1** | **29** | **13.8** | **-3** | **5** | **0.0** | **11:48** | .... | .... | .... | .... | .... | .... | .... | .... | .... |
| | Saint John Flames | AHL | 48 | 21 | 12 | 33 | 61 | .... | .... | .... | .... | .... | .... | .... | .... | .... | .... | .... | .... | .... | .... | .... | .... | .... | .... |
| **2003-04** | **Calgary** | **NHL** | **70** | **6** | **11** | **17** | **51** | **3** | **0** | **0** | **78** | **7.7** | **-12** | **91** | **42.9** | **10:22** | **26** | **0** | **1** | **1** | **24** | **0** | **0** | **0** | **9:02** |
| 2004-05 | Lowell | AHL | 79 | 38 | 37 | 75 | 110 | .... | .... | .... | .... | .... | .... | .... | .... | .... | 11 | 6 | 3 | 9 | 27 | .... | .... | .... | .... |
| **2005-06** | **Calgary** | **NHL** | **77** | **20** | **11** | **31** | **64** | **10** | **0** | **4** | **143** | **14.0** | **-10** | **47** | **25.5** | **12:16** | **7** | **1** | **0** | **1** | **0** | **0** | **0** | **1** | **12:29** |
| **2006-07** | **Calgary** | **NHL** | **40** | **4** | **13** | **17** | **37** | **1** | **0** | **1** | **69** | **5.8** | **7** | **26** | **30.8** | **13:13** | .... | .... | .... | .... | .... | .... | .... | .... | .... |
| | **Boston** | **NHL** | **10** | **1** | **1** | **2** | **25** | **1** | **0** | **0** | **24** | **4.2** | **-6** | **6** | **16.7** | **18:51** | .... | .... | .... | .... | .... | .... | .... | .... | .... |
| **2007-08** | **Boston** | **NHL** | **73** | **22** | **17** | **39** | **29** | **6** | **3** | **3** | **147** | **15.0** | **6** | **70** | **40.0** | **17:41** | .... | .... | .... | .... | .... | .... | .... | .... | .... |
| **2008-09** | **Boston** | **NHL** | **68** | **21** | **21** | **42** | **56** | **6** | **0** | **3** | **129** | **16.3** | **5** | **26** | **23.1** | **14:41** | **11** | **3** | **3** | **6** | **14** | **0** | **0** | **1** | **16:09** |
| | **NHL Totals** | | **361** | **78** | **76** | **154** | **270** | **28** | **3** | **12** | **619** | **12.6** | | **271** | **34.7** | **13:42** | **44** | **4** | **4** | **8** | **38** | **0** | **0** | **2** | **11:21** |

Hockey East Second All-Star Team (2001) • Hockey East Rookie of the Year (2001) • NCAA Championship All-Tournament Team (2001) • NCAA Championship Tournament MVP (2001) • AHL First All-Star Team (2005)

• Left **Boston College** (Hockey East) and signed with **Kelowna** (WHL), August 13, 2001. Traded to **Boston** by **Calgary** with Andrew Ference for Brad Stuart, Wayne Primeau and Washington's 4th round choice (previously acquired, Calgary selected T.J. Brodie) in 2008 Entry Draft, February 10, 2007.

## KOCI, David

(KOH-chee, DAY-vihd) **COL.**

Left wing. Shoots left. 6'6", 238 lbs. Born, Prague, Czech., May 12, 1981. Pittsburgh's 5th choice, 146th overall, in 2000 Entry Draft.

| | | | Regular Season | | | | | | | | | | | | | | Playoffs | | | | | | | | |
|---|---|---|---|---|---|---|---|---|---|---|---|---|---|---|---|---|---|---|---|---|---|---|---|---|---|
| Season | Club | League | GP | G | A | Pts | PIM | PP | SH | GW | S | % | +/- | TF | F% | Min | GP | G | A | Pts | PIM | PP | SH | GW | Min |
| 1997-98 | Sparta Jr. | CzRep-Jr. | 41 | 2 | 9 | 11 | 105 | .... | .... | .... | .... | .... | .... | .... | .... | .... | .... | .... | .... | .... | .... | .... | .... | .... | .... |
| 1998-99 | Hvezda Praha Jr. | CzRep-Jr. | 22 | 1 | 3 | 4 | 36 | .... | .... | .... | .... | .... | .... | .... | .... | .... | .... | .... | .... | .... | .... | .... | .... | .... | .... |
| | Sparta Jr. | CzRep-Jr. | 7 | 0 | 0 | 0 | 4 | .... | .... | .... | .... | .... | .... | .... | .... | .... | .... | .... | .... | .... | .... | .... | .... | .... | .... |
| 99-2000 | Sparta Jr. | CzRep-Jr. | 47 | 0 | 6 | 6 | 124 | .... | .... | .... | .... | .... | .... | .... | .... | .... | .... | .... | .... | .... | .... | .... | .... | .... | .... |
| 2000-01 | Prince George | WHL | 70 | 2 | 7 | 9 | 155 | .... | .... | .... | .... | .... | .... | .... | .... | .... | 6 | 0 | 0 | 0 | 20 | .... | .... | .... | .... |
| 2001-02 | Wilkes-Barre | AHL | 26 | 1 | 3 | 4 | 98 | .... | .... | .... | .... | .... | .... | .... | .... | .... | .... | .... | .... | .... | .... | .... | .... | .... | .... |
| | Wheeling Nailers | ECHL | 33 | 2 | 4 | 6 | 105 | .... | .... | .... | .... | .... | .... | .... | .... | .... | .... | .... | .... | .... | .... | .... | .... | .... | .... |
| 2002-03 | Wilkes-Barre | AHL | 9 | 0 | 0 | 0 | 4 | .... | .... | .... | .... | .... | .... | .... | .... | .... | .... | .... | .... | .... | .... | .... | .... | .... | .... |
| | Wheeling Nailers | ECHL | 48 | 0 | 1 | 1 | 103 | .... | .... | .... | .... | .... | .... | .... | .... | .... | .... | .... | .... | .... | .... | .... | .... | .... | .... |
| 2003-04 | Wilkes-Barre | AHL | 78 | 1 | 7 | 8 | 298 | .... | .... | .... | .... | .... | .... | .... | .... | .... | 10 | 0 | 0 | 0 | 24 | .... | .... | .... | .... |
| 2004-05 | Wilkes-Barre | AHL | 68 | 1 | 8 | 9 | 311 | .... | .... | .... | .... | .... | .... | .... | .... | .... | .... | .... | .... | .... | .... | .... | .... | .... | .... |
| 2005-06 | Wilkes-Barre | AHL | 13 | 0 | 0 | 0 | 59 | .... | .... | .... | .... | .... | .... | .... | .... | .... | .... | .... | .... | .... | .... | .... | .... | .... | .... |
| **2006-07** | **Chicago** | **NHL** | **9** | **0** | **0** | **0** | **88** | **0** | **0** | **0** | **3** | **0.0** | **-3** | **0** | **0.0** | **4:44** | .... | .... | .... | .... | .... | .... | .... | .... | .... |
| | Norfolk Admirals | AHL | 44 | 0 | 1 | 1 | 223 | .... | .... | .... | .... | .... | .... | .... | .... | .... | .... | .... | .... | .... | .... | .... | .... | .... | .... |
| **2007-08** | **Chicago** | **NHL** | **18** | **0** | **0** | **0** | **68** | **0** | **0** | **0** | **2** | **0.0** | **-4** | **0** | **0.0** | **3:38** | .... | .... | .... | .... | .... | .... | .... | .... | .... |
| | Rockford IceHogs | AHL | 7 | 0 | 0 | 0 | 25 | .... | .... | .... | .... | .... | .... | .... | .... | .... | .... | .... | .... | .... | .... | .... | .... | .... | .... |
| | Norfolk Admirals | AHL | 21 | 0 | 2 | 2 | 57 | .... | .... | .... | .... | .... | .... | .... | .... | .... | .... | .... | .... | .... | .... | .... | .... | .... | .... |
| **2008-09** | **Tampa Bay** | **NHL** | **33** | **1** | **1** | **2** | **132** | **0** | **0** | **0** | **8** | **12.5** | **3** | **0** | **0.0** | **6:14** | .... | .... | .... | .... | .... | .... | .... | .... | .... |
| | **St. Louis** | **NHL** | **4** | **0** | **0** | **0** | **9** | **0** | **0** | **0** | **5** | **0.0** | **-2** | **0** | **0.0** | **3:37** | .... | .... | .... | .... | .... | .... | .... | .... | .... |
| | **NHL Totals** | | **64** | **1** | **1** | **2** | **297** | **0** | **0** | **0** | **18** | **5.6** | | **0** | **0.0** | **5:08** | .... | .... | .... | .... | .... | .... | .... | .... | .... |

• Missed majority of 2005-06 season recovering from knee injury, November, 2006. Signed as a free agent by **Chicago**, July 17, 2006. Signed as a free agent by **Tampa Bay**, July 3, 2008. Claimed on waivers by **St. Louis** from **Tampa Bay**, October 21, 2008. Claimed on waivers by **Tampa Bay** from **St. Louis**, November 20, 2008. Signed as a free agent by **Colorado**, July 1, 2009.

## KOISTINEN, Ville

(KOIS-tih-nehn, VIHL-ee) **FLA.**

Defense. Shoots left. 5'11", 187 lbs. Born, Oulu, Finland, June 17, 1982.

| | | | Regular Season | | | | | | | | | | | | | | Playoffs | | | | | | | | |
|---|---|---|---|---|---|---|---|---|---|---|---|---|---|---|---|---|---|---|---|---|---|---|---|---|---|
| Season | Club | League | GP | G | A | Pts | PIM | PP | SH | GW | S | % | +/- | TF | F% | Min | GP | G | A | Pts | PIM | PP | SH | GW | Min |
| 1998-99 | Ilves Tampere U18 | Fin-U18 | 34 | 4 | 10 | 14 | 86 | .... | .... | .... | .... | .... | .... | .... | .... | .... | .... | .... | .... | .... | .... | .... | .... | .... | .... |
| | Ilves Tampere Jr. | Fin-Jr. | 1 | 0 | 0 | 0 | 2 | .... | .... | .... | .... | .... | .... | .... | .... | .... | .... | .... | .... | .... | .... | .... | .... | .... | .... |
| 99-2000 | Ilves Tampere U18 | Fin-U18 | 14 | 4 | 6 | 10 | 69 | .... | .... | .... | .... | .... | .... | .... | .... | .... | .... | .... | .... | .... | .... | .... | .... | .... | .... |
| | Ilves Tampere Jr. | Fin-Jr. | 34 | 4 | 2 | 6 | 40 | .... | .... | .... | .... | .... | .... | .... | .... | .... | .... | .... | .... | .... | .... | .... | .... | .... | .... |
| 2000-01 | Ilves Tampere | Finland | 6 | 0 | 0 | 0 | 0 | .... | .... | .... | .... | .... | .... | .... | .... | .... | 5 | 0 | 1 | 1 | 0 | .... | .... | .... | .... |
| | Ilves Tampere Jr. | Fin-Jr. | 26 | 1 | 8 | 9 | 101 | .... | .... | .... | .... | .... | .... | .... | .... | .... | .... | .... | .... | .... | .... | .... | .... | .... | .... |
| 2001-02 | Ilves Tampere | Finland | 53 | 1 | 8 | 9 | 42 | .... | .... | .... | .... | .... | .... | .... | .... | .... | .... | .... | .... | .... | .... | .... | .... | .... | .... |
| | Ilves Tampere Jr. | Fin-Jr. | 6 | 2 | 2 | 4 | 16 | .... | .... | .... | .... | .... | .... | .... | .... | .... | .... | .... | .... | .... | .... | .... | .... | .... | .... |
| 2002-03 | Ilves Tampere | Finland | 18 | 4 | 1 | 5 | 8 | .... | .... | .... | .... | .... | .... | .... | .... | .... | .... | .... | .... | .... | .... | .... | .... | .... | .... |
| | Ilves Tampere Jr. | Fin-Jr. | 1 | 0 | 0 | 0 | 10 | .... | .... | .... | .... | .... | .... | .... | .... | .... | .... | .... | .... | .... | .... | .... | .... | .... | .... |
| 2003-04 | Ilves Tampere | Finland | 54 | 7 | 16 | 23 | 51 | .... | .... | .... | .... | .... | .... | .... | .... | .... | 7 | 0 | 2 | 2 | 0 | .... | .... | .... | .... |
| 2004-05 | Ilves Tampere | Finland | 52 | 6 | 14 | 20 | 69 | .... | .... | .... | .... | .... | .... | .... | .... | .... | 3 | 0 | 0 | 0 | 0 | .... | .... | .... | .... |
| 2005-06 | Ilves Tampere | Finland | 56 | 8 | 26 | 34 | 70 | .... | .... | .... | .... | .... | .... | .... | .... | .... | 4 | 0 | 1 | 1 | 2 | .... | .... | .... | .... |
| 2006-07 | Milwaukee | AHL | 59 | 9 | 32 | 41 | 44 | .... | .... | .... | .... | .... | .... | .... | .... | .... | 4 | 0 | 2 | 2 | 4 | .... | .... | .... | .... |
| **2007-08** | **Nashville** | **NHL** | **48** | **4** | **13** | **17** | **18** | **2** | **0** | **1** | **60** | **6.7** | **13** | **0** | **0.0** | **16:48** | .... | .... | .... | .... | .... | .... | .... | .... | .... |
| **2008-09** | **Nashville** | **NHL** | **38** | **3** | **8** | **11** | **14** | **1** | **0** | **2** | **42** | **7.1** | **0** | **1** | **0.0** | **14:42** | .... | .... | .... | .... | .... | .... | .... | .... | .... |
| | **NHL Totals** | | **86** | **7** | **21** | **28** | **32** | **3** | **0** | **3** | **102** | **6.9** | | **1** | **0.0** | **15:52** | .... | .... | .... | .... | .... | .... | .... | .... | .... |

Signed as a free agent by **Nashville**, May 11, 2006. • Spent majority of 2008-09 season serving as a healthy reserve.

## KOIVU, Mikko

(KOI-voo, MEE-koh) **MIN.**

Center. Shoots left. 6'2", 200 lbs. Born, Turku, Finland, March 12, 1983. Minnesota's 1st choice, 6th overall, in 2001 Entry Draft.

| | | | Regular Season | | | | | | | | | | | | | | Playoffs | | | | | | | | |
|---|---|---|---|---|---|---|---|---|---|---|---|---|---|---|---|---|---|---|---|---|---|---|---|---|---|
| Season | Club | League | GP | G | A | Pts | PIM | PP | SH | GW | S | % | +/- | TF | F% | Min | GP | G | A | Pts | PIM | PP | SH | GW | Min |
| 99-2000 | TPS Turku U18 | Fin-U18 | 11 | 4 | 9 | 13 | 18 | .... | .... | .... | .... | .... | .... | .... | .... | .... | .... | .... | .... | .... | .... | .... | .... | .... | .... |
| | TPS Turku Jr. | Fin-Jr. | 30 | 4 | 8 | 12 | 22 | .... | .... | .... | .... | .... | .... | .... | .... | .... | 13 | 1 | 4 | 5 | 8 | .... | .... | .... | .... |
| 2000-01 | TPS Turku U18 | Fin-U18 | .... | .... | .... | .... | .... | .... | .... | .... | .... | .... | .... | .... | .... | .... | 7 | 2 | 10 | 12 | 2 | .... | .... | .... | .... |
| | TPS Turku Jr. | Fin-Jr. | 26 | 9 | 36 | 45 | 26 | .... | .... | .... | .... | .... | .... | .... | .... | .... | 3 | 1 | 1 | 2 | 6 | .... | .... | .... | .... |
| | TPS Turku | Finland | 21 | 0 | 1 | 1 | 2 | .... | .... | .... | .... | .... | .... | .... | .... | .... | .... | .... | .... | .... | .... | .... | .... | .... | .... |
| 2001-02 | TPS Turku Jr. | Fin-Jr. | 2 | 0 | 1 | 1 | 12 | .... | .... | .... | .... | .... | .... | .... | .... | .... | .... | .... | .... | .... | .... | .... | .... | .... | .... |
| | TPS Turku | Finland | 48 | 4 | 3 | 7 | 34 | .... | .... | .... | .... | .... | .... | .... | .... | .... | 8 | 0 | 3 | 3 | 4 | .... | .... | .... | .... |
| 2002-03 | TPS Turku | Finland | 37 | 7 | 13 | 20 | 20 | .... | .... | .... | .... | .... | .... | .... | .... | .... | 7 | 2 | 2 | 4 | 6 | .... | .... | .... | .... |
| 2003-04 | TPS Turku | Finland | 45 | 6 | 24 | 30 | 36 | .... | .... | .... | .... | .... | .... | .... | .... | .... | 13 | 1 | 7 | 8 | 8 | .... | .... | .... | .... |
| 2004-05 | Houston Aeros | AHL | 67 | 20 | 28 | 48 | 47 | .... | .... | .... | .... | .... | .... | .... | .... | .... | 5 | 1 | 0 | 1 | 2 | .... | .... | .... | .... |
| **2005-06** | **Minnesota** | **NHL** | **64** | **6** | **15** | **21** | **40** | **3** | **0** | **0** | **96** | **6.3** | **-9** | **724** | **47.4** | **13:17** | .... | .... | .... | .... | .... | .... | .... | .... | .... |
| | Finland | Olympics | 8 | 0 | 0 | 0 | 6 | .... | .... | .... | .... | .... | .... | .... | .... | .... | .... | .... | .... | .... | .... | .... | .... | .... | .... |
| **2006-07** | **Minnesota** | **NHL** | **82** | **20** | **34** | **54** | **58** | **9** | **2** | **2** | **162** | **12.3** | **6** | **1165** | **50.9** | **17:29** | **5** | **1** | **0** | **1** | **4** | **0** | **0** | **0** | **17:43** |
| **2007-08** | **Minnesota** | **NHL** | **57** | **11** | **31** | **42** | **42** | **2** | **0** | **2** | **144** | **7.6** | **13** | **1032** | **52.5** | **20:53** | **6** | **4** | **1** | **5** | **4** | **0** | **1** | **0** | **21:56** |
| **2008-09** | **Minnesota** | **NHL** | **79** | **20** | **47** | **67** | **66** | **5** | **4** | **3** | **236** | **8.5** | **2** | **1625** | **52.7** | **21:29** | .... | .... | .... | .... | .... | .... | .... | .... | .... |
| | **NHL Totals** | | **282** | **57** | **127** | **184** | **206** | **19** | **6** | **7** | **638** | **8.9** | | **4546** | **51.4** | **18:20** | **11** | **5** | **1** | **6** | **8** | **0** | **1** | **0** | **20:01** |

## KOIVU, Saku

(KOI-voo, SA-koo) **ANA.**

Center. Shoots left. 5'10", 182 lbs. Born, Turku, Finland, November 23, 1974. Montreal's 1st choice, 21st overall, in 1993 Entry Draft.

| | | | Regular Season | | | | | | | | | | | | | | Playoffs | | | | | | | | |
|---|---|---|---|---|---|---|---|---|---|---|---|---|---|---|---|---|---|---|---|---|---|---|---|---|---|
| Season | Club | League | GP | G | A | Pts | PIM | PP | SH | GW | S | % | +/- | TF | F% | Min | GP | G | A | Pts | PIM | PP | SH | GW | Min |
| 1990-91 | TPS Turku U18 | Fin-U18 | 24 | 20 | 28 | 48 | 26 | .... | .... | .... | .... | .... | .... | .... | .... | .... | .... | .... | .... | .... | .... | .... | .... | .... | .... |
| | TPS Turku Jr. | Fin-Jr. | 13 | 3 | 7 | 10 | 6 | .... | .... | .... | .... | .... | .... | .... | .... | .... | .... | .... | .... | .... | .... | .... | .... | .... | .... |
| 1991-92 | TPS Turku U18 | Fin-U18 | 12 | 3 | 7 | 10 | 6 | .... | .... | .... | .... | .... | .... | .... | .... | .... | .... | .... | .... | .... | .... | .... | .... | .... | .... |
| | TPS Turku Jr. | Fin-Jr. | 34 | 25 | 28 | 53 | 57 | .... | .... | .... | .... | .... | .... | .... | .... | .... | 8 | 5 | 9 | 14 | 6 | .... | .... | .... | .... |
| 1992-93 | TPS Turku | Finland | 46 | 3 | 7 | 10 | 28 | .... | .... | .... | .... | .... | .... | .... | .... | .... | 11 | 3 | 2 | 5 | 2 | .... | .... | .... | .... |
| 1993-94 | TPS Turku | Finland | 47 | 23 | 30 | 53 | 42 | .... | .... | .... | .... | .... | .... | .... | .... | .... | 11 | 4 | 8 | 12 | 16 | .... | .... | .... | .... |
| | Finland | Olympics | 8 | 4 | 3 | 7 | 12 | .... | .... | .... | .... | .... | .... | .... | .... | .... | .... | .... | .... | .... | .... | .... | .... | .... | .... |
| 1994-95 | TPS Turku | Finland | 45 | 27 | 47 | 74 | 73 | .... | .... | .... | .... | .... | .... | .... | .... | .... | 13 | 7 | 10 | 17 | 16 | .... | .... | .... | .... |
| **1995-96** | **Montreal** | **NHL** | **82** | **20** | **25** | **45** | **40** | **8** | **3** | **2** | **136** | **14.7** | **-7** | .... | .... | .... | **6** | **3** | **1** | **4** | **8** | **0** | **0** | **0** | .... |
| **1996-97** | **Montreal** | **NHL** | **50** | **17** | **39** | **56** | **38** | **5** | **0** | **3** | **135** | **12.6** | **7** | .... | .... | .... | **5** | **1** | **3** | **4** | **10** | **0** | **0** | **0** | .... |
| **1997-98** | **Montreal** | **NHL** | **69** | **14** | **43** | **57** | **48** | **2** | **2** | **3** | **145** | **9.7** | **8** | .... | .... | .... | **6** | **2** | **3** | **5** | **2** | **1** | **0** | **0** | .... |
| | Finland | Olympics | 6 | 2 | 8 | 10 | 4 | .... | .... | .... | .... | .... | .... | .... | .... | .... | .... | .... | .... | .... | .... | .... | .... | .... | .... |
| **1998-99** | **Montreal** | **NHL** | **65** | **14** | **30** | **44** | **38** | **4** | **2** | **0** | **145** | **9.7** | **-7** | **1427** | **52.6** | **20:02** | .... | .... | .... | .... | .... | .... | .... | .... | .... |
| **99-2000** | **Montreal** | **NHL** | **24** | **3** | **18** | **21** | **14** | **1** | **0** | **0** | **53** | **5.7** | **7** | **495** | **52.9** | **19:13** | .... | .... | .... | .... | .... | .... | .... | .... | .... |
| **2000-01** | **Montreal** | **NHL** | **54** | **17** | **30** | **47** | **40** | **7** | **0** | **3** | **113** | **15.0** | **2** | **1092** | **47.6** | **21:23** | .... | .... | .... | .... | .... | .... | .... | .... | .... |

| | | | Regular Season | | | | | | | | | | | | | | Playoffs | | | | | | | | |
|---|---|---|---|---|---|---|---|---|---|---|---|---|---|---|---|---|---|---|---|---|---|---|---|---|---|
| Season | Club | League | GP | G | A | Pts | PIM | PP | SH | GW | S | % | +/- | TF | F% | Min | GP | G | A | Pts | PIM | PP | SH | GW | Min |
| **2001-02** | **Montreal** | **NHL** | **3** | **0** | **2** | **2** | **0** | **0** | **0** | **0** | **2** | **0.0** | **0** | **13** | **61.5** | **13:57** | **12** | **4** | **6** | **10** | **4** | **1** | **0** | **1** | **15:54** |
| **2002-03** | **Montreal** | **NHL** | **82** | **21** | **50** | **71** | **72** | **5** | **1** | **5** | **147** | **14.3** | **5** | **1566** | **49.6** | **19:14** | .... | .... | .... | .... | .... | .... | .... | .... | .... |
| **2003-04** | **Montreal** | **NHL** | **68** | **14** | **41** | **55** | **52** | **5** | **0** | **3** | **112** | **12.5** | **-5** | **1194** | **53.9** | **19:18** | **11** | **3** | **8** | **11** | **10** | **2** | **0** | **0** | **20:34** |
| 2004-05 | TPS Turku | Finland | 20 | 8 | 8 | 16 | 28 | .... | .... | .... | .... | .... | .... | .... | .... | .... | 6 | 3 | 2 | 5 | 30 | .... | .... | .... | .... |
| **2005-06** | **Montreal** | **NHL** | **72** | **17** | **45** | **62** | **70** | **5** | **0** | **4** | **138** | **12.3** | **1** | **1412** | **53.8** | **18:31** | **3** | **0** | **2** | **2** | **2** | **0** | **0** | **0** | **14:24** |
| | Finland | Olympics | 8 | 3 | *8 | *11 | 12 | .... | .... | .... | .... | .... | .... | .... | .... | .... | .... | .... | .... | .... | .... | .... | .... | .... | .... |
| **2006-07** | **Montreal** | **NHL** | **81** | **22** | **53** | **75** | **74** | **11** | **1** | **4** | **154** | **14.3** | **-21** | **1453** | **54.9** | **18:07** | .... | .... | .... | .... | .... | .... | .... | .... | .... |
| **2007-08** | **Montreal** | **NHL** | **77** | **16** | **40** | **56** | **93** | **8** | **0** | **3** | **150** | **10.7** | **-4** | **1341** | **52.3** | **18:07** | **7** | **3** | **6** | **9** | **4** | **2** | **0** | **0** | **19:33** |
| **2008-09** | **Montreal** | **NHL** | **65** | **16** | **34** | **50** | **44** | **5** | **0** | **5** | **123** | **13.0** | **4** | **1122** | **54.1** | **17:03** | **4** | **0** | **3** | **3** | **2** | **0** | **0** | **0** | **17:45** |
| | **NHL Totals** | | **792** | **191** | **450** | **641** | **623** | **66** | **9** | **35** | **1553** | **12.3** | | **11115** | **52.4** | **18:52** | **54** | **16** | **32** | **48** | **42** | **6** | **0** | **1** | **18:03** |

Bill Masterton Memorial Trophy (2002) • Olympic Tournament All-Star Team (2006) • King Clancy Memorial Trophy (2007)

Played in NHL All-Star Game (1998)

• Missed majority of 1999-2000 season recovering from shoulder injury suffered in game vs. NY Rangers, October 30, 1999. • Missed majority of 2001-02 season recovering from non-Hodgkin 's lymphoma, September 6, 2001. Signed as a free agent by **Turku** (Finland), October 21, 2004. Signed as a free agent by **Anaheim**, July 8, 2009.

## KOLANOS, Krys

(koh-LA-nohs, KRIHS) **PHI.**

Center. Shoots right. 6'3", 206 lbs. Born, Calgary, Alta., July 27, 1981. Phoenix's 1st choice, 19th overall, in 2000 Entry Draft.

| | | | | | | | | | | | | | | | | | | | | | | | | | |
|---|---|---|---|---|---|---|---|---|---|---|---|---|---|---|---|---|---|---|---|---|---|---|---|---|---|
| 1996-97 | Calgary Flames | AAHA | 24 | 24 | 35 | 59 | .... | .... | .... | .... | .... | .... | .... | .... | .... | .... | .... | .... | .... | .... | .... | .... | .... | .... | .... |
| 1997-98 | Calgary Buffaloes | AMHL | 34 | 34 | 43 | 77 | 29 | .... | .... | .... | .... | .... | .... | .... | .... | .... | .... | .... | .... | .... | .... | .... | .... | .... | .... |
| 1998-99 | Calgary Royals | AJHL | 58 | 43 | 67 | 110 | 98 | .... | .... | .... | .... | .... | .... | .... | .... | .... | .... | .... | .... | .... | .... | .... | .... | .... | .... |
| 99-2000 | Boston College | H-East | 42 | 16 | 16 | 32 | 48 | .... | .... | .... | .... | .... | .... | .... | .... | .... | .... | .... | .... | .... | .... | .... | .... | .... | .... |
| 2000-01 | Boston College | H-East | 41 | 25 | 25 | 50 | 54 | .... | .... | .... | .... | .... | .... | .... | .... | .... | .... | .... | .... | .... | .... | .... | .... | .... | .... |
| **2001-02** | **Phoenix** | **NHL** | **57** | **11** | **11** | **22** | **48** | **0** | **0** | **5** | **81** | **13.6** | **6** | **703** | **46.4** | **13:05** | **2** | **0** | **0** | **0** | **6** | **0** | **0** | **0** | **11:12** |
| **2002-03** | **Phoenix** | **NHL** | **2** | **0** | **0** | **0** | **0** | **0** | **0** | **0** | **8** | **0.0** | **0** | **16** | **31.3** | **14:06** | .... | .... | .... | .... | .... | .... | .... | .... | .... |
| **2003-04** | **Phoenix** | **NHL** | **41** | **4** | **6** | **10** | **24** | **1** | **0** | **1** | **61** | **6.6** | **-9** | **283** | **43.8** | **13:31** | .... | .... | .... | .... | .... | .... | .... | .... | .... |
| | Springfield | AHL | 32 | 10 | 11 | 21 | 38 | .... | .... | .... | .... | .... | .... | .... | .... | .... | .... | .... | .... | .... | .... | .... | .... | .... | .... |
| 2004-05 | Blues Espoo | Finland | 15 | 7 | 9 | 16 | 40 | .... | .... | .... | .... | .... | .... | .... | .... | .... | .... | .... | .... | .... | .... | .... | .... | .... | .... |
| | Krefeld Pinguine | Germany | 7 | 3 | 2 | 5 | 16 | .... | .... | .... | .... | .... | .... | .... | .... | .... | .... | .... | .... | .... | .... | .... | .... | .... | .... |
| **2005-06** | **Phoenix** | **NHL** | **9** | **2** | **1** | **3** | **2** | **1** | **0** | **0** | **15** | **13.3** | **2** | **75** | **53.3** | **11:30** | .... | .... | .... | .... | .... | .... | .... | .... | .... |
| | San Antonio | AHL | 3 | 0 | 1 | 1 | 0 | .... | .... | .... | .... | .... | .... | .... | .... | .... | .... | .... | .... | .... | .... | .... | .... | .... | .... |
| | **Edmonton** | **NHL** | **6** | **0** | **0** | **0** | **2** | **0** | **0** | **0** | **7** | **0.0** | **-1** | **32** | **50.0** | **7:39** | .... | .... | .... | .... | .... | .... | .... | .... | .... |
| | Lowell | AHL | 19 | 10 | 11 | 21 | 40 | .... | .... | .... | .... | .... | .... | .... | .... | .... | .... | .... | .... | .... | .... | .... | .... | .... | .... |
| | Wilkes-Barre | AHL | 18 | 10 | 8 | 18 | 19 | .... | .... | .... | .... | .... | .... | .... | .... | .... | 11 | 2 | 0 | 2 | 16 | .... | .... | .... | .... |
| 2006-07 | Grand Rapids | AHL | 17 | 6 | 6 | 12 | 8 | .... | .... | .... | .... | .... | .... | .... | .... | .... | .... | .... | .... | .... | .... | .... | .... | .... | .... |
| | Langnau | Swiss | 14 | 2 | 9 | 11 | 48 | .... | .... | .... | .... | .... | .... | .... | .... | .... | .... | .... | .... | .... | .... | .... | .... | .... | .... |
| | EV Zug | Swiss | .... | .... | .... | .... | .... | .... | .... | .... | .... | .... | .... | .... | .... | .... | 8 | 6 | 0 | 6 | 8 | .... | .... | .... | .... |
| 2007-08 | Quad City Flames | AHL | 65 | 30 | 33 | 63 | 84 | .... | .... | .... | .... | .... | .... | .... | .... | .... | .... | .... | .... | .... | .... | .... | .... | .... | .... |
| **2008-09** | **Minnesota** | **NHL** | **21** | **3** | **3** | **6** | **16** | **1** | **0** | **0** | **30** | **10.0** | **3** | **115** | **51.3** | **10:36** | .... | .... | .... | .... | .... | .... | .... | .... | .... |
| | Houston Aeros | AHL | 45 | 31 | 20 | 51 | 42 | .... | .... | .... | .... | .... | .... | .... | .... | .... | 18 | 6 | 8 | 14 | 18 | .... | .... | .... | .... |
| | **NHL Totals** | | **136** | **20** | **21** | **41** | **92** | **3** | **0** | **6** | **202** | **9.9** | | **1224** | **46.6** | **12:30** | **2** | **0** | **0** | **0** | **6** | **0** | **0** | **0** | **11:12** |

Hockey East All-Rookie Team (2000) • Hockey East Second All-Star Team (2001) • NCAA East Second All-American Team (2001) • NCAA Championship All-Tournament Team (2001)

• Missed majority of 2002-03 season recovering from head injury suffered in game vs. Pittsburgh, March 20, 2002. Signed as a free agent by **Espoo** (Finland), October 25, 2004. Signed as a free agent by **Krefeld** (Germany), February 16, 2005. Claimed on waivers by **Edmonton** from **Phoenix**, November 11, 2005. Claimed on waivers by **Phoenix** from **Edmonton**, December 19, 2005. Traded to **Carolina** by **Phoenix** for Pavel Brendl, December 28, 2005. Traded to **Pittsburgh** by **Carolina** with Niklas Nordgren and Carolina's 2nd round choice (later traded to San Jose - later traded to Philadelphia - Philadelphia selected Kevin Marshall) in 2007 Entry Draft for Mark Recchi, March 9, 2006. Signed as a free agent by **Detroit**, July 15, 2006. Signed as a free agent by **Minnesota**, July 11, 2008. Signed as a free agent by **Philadelphia**, July 23, 2009.

## KOMISAREK, Mike

(koh-mih-SAIR-ehk, MIGHK) **TOR.**

Defense. Shoots right. 6'4", 243 lbs. Born, West Islip, NY, January 19, 1982. Montreal's 1st choice, 7th overall, in 2001 Entry Draft.

| | | | | | | | | | | | | | | | | | | | | | | | | | |
|---|---|---|---|---|---|---|---|---|---|---|---|---|---|---|---|---|---|---|---|---|---|---|---|---|---|
| 1998-99 | N.E. Jr. Coyotes | EJHL | 53 | 17 | 24 | 51 | .... | .... | .... | .... | .... | .... | .... | .... | .... | .... | .... | .... | .... | .... | .... | .... | .... | .... | .... |
| 99-2000 | USNTDP | U-18 | 6 | 0 | 0 | 0 | 12 | .... | .... | .... | .... | .... | .... | .... | .... | .... | .... | .... | .... | .... | .... | .... | .... | .... | .... |
| | USNTDP | USHL | 51 | 5 | 8 | 13 | 124 | .... | .... | .... | .... | .... | .... | .... | .... | .... | .... | .... | .... | .... | .... | .... | .... | .... | .... |
| | USNTDP | NAHL | 1 | 0 | 0 | 0 | 16 | .... | .... | .... | .... | .... | .... | .... | .... | .... | .... | .... | .... | .... | .... | .... | .... | .... | .... |
| 2000-01 | U. of Michigan | CCHA | 41 | 4 | 12 | 16 | 77 | .... | .... | .... | .... | .... | .... | .... | .... | .... | .... | .... | .... | .... | .... | .... | .... | .... | .... |
| 2001-02 | U. of Michigan | CCHA | 40 | 11 | 19 | 30 | 70 | .... | .... | .... | .... | .... | .... | .... | .... | .... | .... | .... | .... | .... | .... | .... | .... | .... | .... |
| **2002-03** | **Montreal** | **NHL** | **21** | **0** | **1** | **1** | **28** | **0** | **0** | **0** | **26** | **0.0** | **-6** | **0** | **0.0** | **16:42** | .... | .... | .... | .... | .... | .... | .... | .... | .... |
| | Hamilton | AHL | 56 | 5 | 25 | 30 | 79 | .... | .... | .... | .... | .... | .... | .... | .... | .... | 23 | 1 | 5 | 6 | 60 | .... | .... | .... | .... |
| **2003-04** | **Montreal** | **NHL** | **46** | **0** | **4** | **4** | **34** | **0** | **0** | **0** | **40** | **0.0** | **4** | **0** | **0.0** | **12:00** | **7** | **0** | **0** | **0** | **8** | **0** | **0** | **0** | **14:09** |
| | Hamilton | AHL | 18 | 2 | 7 | 9 | 47 | .... | .... | .... | .... | .... | .... | .... | .... | .... | .... | .... | .... | .... | .... | .... | .... | .... | .... |
| 2004-05 | Hamilton | AHL | 20 | 1 | 4 | 5 | 49 | .... | .... | .... | .... | .... | .... | .... | .... | .... | 4 | 0 | 1 | 1 | 8 | .... | .... | .... | .... |
| **2005-06** | **Montreal** | **NHL** | **71** | **2** | **4** | **6** | **116** | **0** | **0** | **0** | **66** | **3.0** | **-1** | **0** | **0.0** | **14:40** | **6** | **0** | **0** | **0** | **10** | **0** | **0** | **0** | **18:35** |
| **2006-07** | **Montreal** | **NHL** | **82** | **4** | **15** | **19** | **96** | **0** | **2** | **1** | **78** | **5.1** | **7** | **0** | **0.0** | **19:16** | .... | .... | .... | .... | .... | .... | .... | .... | .... |
| **2007-08** | **Montreal** | **NHL** | **75** | **4** | **13** | **17** | **101** | **0** | **0** | **1** | **75** | **5.3** | **9** | **1** | **0.0** | **21:09** | **12** | **1** | **2** | **3** | **18** | **0** | **0** | **1** | **20:02** |
| **2008-09** | **Montreal** | **NHL** | **66** | **2** | **9** | **11** | **121** | **0** | **0** | **0** | **56** | **3.6** | **0** | **0** | **0.0** | **20:37** | **4** | **0** | **0** | **0** | **20** | **0** | **0** | **0** | **19:00** |
| | **NHL Totals** | | **361** | **12** | **46** | **58** | **496** | **0** | **2** | **2** | **341** | **3.5** | | **1** | **0.0** | **17:56** | **29** | **1** | **2** | **3** | **56** | **0** | **0** | **1** | **18:10** |

CCHA First All-Star Team (2002) • NCAA West First All-American Team (2002) • AHL All-Rookie Team (2003)

Played in NHL All-Star Game (2009)

Signed as a free agent by **Toronto**, July 1, 2009.

## KONOPKA, Zenon

(kuh-NOHP-kah, ZEH-nohn) **T.B.**

Center. Shoots left. 6'1", 213 lbs. Born, Niagara Falls, Ont., January 2, 1981.

| | | | | | | | | | | | | | | | | | | | | | | | | | |
|---|---|---|---|---|---|---|---|---|---|---|---|---|---|---|---|---|---|---|---|---|---|---|---|---|---|
| 1998-99 | Ottawa 67's | OHL | 56 | 7 | 8 | 15 | 62 | .... | .... | .... | .... | .... | .... | .... | .... | .... | 7 | 0 | 0 | 0 | 2 | .... | .... | .... | .... |
| 99-2000 | Ottawa 67's | OHL | 59 | 8 | 11 | 19 | 107 | .... | .... | .... | .... | .... | .... | .... | .... | .... | 11 | 1 | 2 | 3 | 8 | .... | .... | .... | .... |
| 2000-01 | Ottawa 67's | OHL | 66 | 20 | 45 | 65 | 120 | .... | .... | .... | .... | .... | .... | .... | .... | .... | 20 | 7 | 13 | 20 | 47 | .... | .... | .... | .... |
| 2001-02 | Ottawa 67's | OHL | 61 | 18 | 68 | 86 | 100 | .... | .... | .... | .... | .... | .... | .... | .... | .... | 13 | 8 | 6 | 14 | 49 | .... | .... | .... | .... |
| 2002-03 | Wilkes-Barre | AHL | 4 | 0 | 1 | 1 | 9 | .... | .... | .... | .... | .... | .... | .... | .... | .... | .... | .... | .... | .... | .... | .... | .... | .... | .... |
| | Wheeling Nailers | ECHL | 68 | 22 | 48 | 70 | 231 | .... | .... | .... | .... | .... | .... | .... | .... | .... | .... | .... | .... | .... | .... | .... | .... | .... | .... |
| 2003-04 | Utah Grizzlies | AHL | 43 | 7 | 4 | 11 | 198 | .... | .... | .... | .... | .... | .... | .... | .... | .... | .... | .... | .... | .... | .... | .... | .... | .... | .... |
| | Idaho Steelheads | ECHL | 23 | 6 | 22 | 28 | 82 | .... | .... | .... | .... | .... | .... | .... | .... | .... | 17 | 9 | 8 | 17 | 30 | .... | .... | .... | .... |
| 2004-05 | Cincinnati | AHL | 75 | 17 | 29 | 46 | 212 | .... | .... | .... | .... | .... | .... | .... | .... | .... | 12 | 3 | 3 | 6 | 26 | .... | .... | .... | .... |
| **2005-06** | **Anaheim** | **NHL** | **23** | **4** | **3** | **7** | **48** | **2** | **0** | **0** | **18** | **22.2** | **-4** | **142** | **53.5** | **7:19** | .... | .... | .... | .... | .... | .... | .... | .... | .... |
| | Portland Pirates | AHL | 34 | 18 | 26 | 44 | 57 | .... | .... | .... | .... | .... | .... | .... | .... | .... | 19 | 11 | 18 | 29 | 46 | .... | .... | .... | .... |
| **2006-07** | Lada Togliatti | Russia | 4 | 0 | 0 | 0 | 8 | .... | .... | .... | .... | .... | .... | .... | .... | .... | .... | .... | .... | .... | .... | .... | .... | .... | .... |
| | **Columbus** | **NHL** | **6** | **0** | **0** | **0** | **20** | **0** | **0** | **0** | **2** | **0.0** | **-2** | **22** | **63.6** | **5:00** | .... | .... | .... | .... | .... | .... | .... | .... | .... |
| | Portland Pirates | AHL | 42 | 11 | 24 | 35 | 97 | .... | .... | .... | .... | .... | .... | .... | .... | .... | .... | .... | .... | .... | .... | .... | .... | .... | .... |
| | Syracuse Crunch | AHL | 20 | 9 | 11 | 20 | 70 | .... | .... | .... | .... | .... | .... | .... | .... | .... | .... | .... | .... | .... | .... | .... | .... | .... | .... |
| **2007-08** | **Columbus** | **NHL** | **3** | **0** | **0** | **0** | **15** | **0** | **0** | **0** | **4** | **0.0** | **0** | **21** | **52.4** | **7:54** | .... | .... | .... | .... | .... | .... | .... | .... | .... |
| | Syracuse Crunch | AHL | 62 | 24 | 31 | 55 | 194 | .... | .... | .... | .... | .... | .... | .... | .... | .... | 13 | 3 | 7 | 10 | 42 | .... | .... | .... | .... |
| **2008-09** | **Tampa Bay** | **NHL** | **7** | **0** | **1** | **1** | **29** | **0** | **0** | **0** | **6** | **0.0** | **-1** | **25** | **68.0** | **7:01** | .... | .... | .... | .... | .... | .... | .... | .... | .... |
| | Norfolk Admirals | AHL | 70 | 17 | 40 | 57 | 186 | .... | .... | .... | .... | .... | .... | .... | .... | .... | .... | .... | .... | .... | .... | .... | .... | .... | .... |
| | **NHL Totals** | | **39** | **4** | **4** | **8** | **112** | **2** | **0** | **0** | **30** | **13.3** | | **210** | **56.2** | **6:57** | .... | .... | .... | .... | .... | .... | .... | .... | .... |

ECHL All-Rookie Team (2003)

Signed as a free agent by **Utah** (AHL), September 10, 2003. Signed as a free agent by **Anaheim**, September 1, 2004. Signed as a free agent by **Togliatti** (Russia), July 26, 2006. Traded to **Columbus** by **Anaheim** with Curtis Glencross and Anaheim's 7th round choice (Trent Vogelhuber) in 2007 Entry Draft for Mark Hartigan, Joe Motzko and Columbus' 4th round choice (Sebastian Stefaniszin) in 2007 Entry Draft, January 26, 2007. Signed as a free agent by **Tampa Bay**, July 10, 2008.

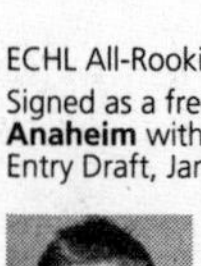

## KONTIOLA, Petri

(KAWN-tee-oh-la, PEH-tree) **ANA.**

Center. Shoots right. 6', 204 lbs. Born, Seinajoki, Finland, October 4, 1984. Chicago's 12th choice, 196th overall, in 2004 Entry Draft.

| | | | | | | | | | | | | | | | | | | | | | | | | | |
|---|---|---|---|---|---|---|---|---|---|---|---|---|---|---|---|---|---|---|---|---|---|---|---|---|---|
| 2001-02 | Tappara U18 | Fin-U18 | 22 | 5 | 3 | 8 | 8 | .... | .... | .... | .... | .... | .... | .... | .... | .... | 2 | 1 | 0 | 1 | 2 | .... | .... | .... | .... |
| 2002-03 | Tappara Jr. | Fin-Jr. | 36 | 7 | 10 | 17 | 12 | .... | .... | .... | .... | .... | .... | .... | .... | .... | 8 | 3 | 3 | 6 | 0 | .... | .... | .... | .... |
| 2003-04 | Suomi U20 | Finland-2 | 6 | 1 | 1 | 2 | 4 | .... | .... | .... | .... | .... | .... | .... | .... | .... | .... | .... | .... | .... | .... | .... | .... | .... | .... |
| | Tappara Jr. | Fin-Jr. | 12 | 3 | 12 | 15 | 8 | .... | .... | .... | .... | .... | .... | .... | .... | .... | 10 | 4 | 4 | 8 | 10 | .... | .... | .... | .... |
| | Tappara Tampere | Finland | 39 | 4 | 9 | 13 | 29 | .... | .... | .... | .... | .... | .... | .... | .... | .... | 3 | 1 | 1 | 2 | 0 | .... | .... | .... | .... |
| 2004-05 | Tappara Jr. | Fin-Jr. | 1 | 1 | 0 | 1 | 0 | .... | .... | .... | .... | .... | .... | .... | .... | .... | .... | .... | .... | .... | .... | .... | .... | .... | .... |
| | Tappara Tampere | Finland | 54 | 8 | 17 | 25 | 24 | .... | .... | .... | .... | .... | .... | .... | .... | .... | 8 | 2 | 2 | 4 | 2 | .... | .... | .... | .... |

| | | | | | | | | Regular Season | | | | | | | | | Playoffs | | | | | | | | |
|---|---|---|---|---|---|---|---|---|---|---|---|---|---|---|---|---|---|---|---|---|---|---|---|---|---|
| **Season** | **Club** | **League** | **GP** | **G** | **A** | **Pts** | **PIM** | **PP** | **SH** | **GW** | **S** | **%** | **+/-** | **TF** | **F%** | **Min** | **GP** | **G** | **A** | **Pts** | **PIM** | **PP** | **SH** | **GW** | **Min** |
| 2005-06 | Tappara Tampere | Finland | 56 | 9 | *35 | 44 | 55 | .... | .... | .... | .... | .... | .... | .... | .... | .... | 6 | 1 | 3 | 4 | 0 | .... | .... | .... | .... |
| 2006-07 | Tappara Tampere | Finland | 51 | 12 | 35 | 47 | 50 | .... | .... | .... | .... | .... | .... | .... | .... | .... | 5 | 1 | 3 | 4 | 8 | .... | .... | .... | .... |
| **2007-08** | **Chicago** | **NHL** | **12** | **0** | **5** | **5** | **6** | **0** | **0** | **0** | **13** | **0.0** | **5** | **45** | **68.9** | **14:33** | .... | .... | .... | .... | .... | .... | .... | .... | .... |
| | Rockford IceHogs | AHL | 66 | 18 | 50 | 68 | 32 | .... | .... | .... | .... | .... | .... | .... | .... | .... | 12 | 5 | 5 | 10 | 4 | .... | .... | .... | .... |
| 2008-09 | Rockford IceHogs | AHL | 61 | 15 | 38 | 53 | 22 | .... | .... | .... | .... | .... | .... | .... | .... | .... | .... | .... | .... | .... | .... | .... | .... | .... | .... |
| | Iowa Chops | AHL | 20 | 4 | 5 | 9 | 8 | .... | .... | .... | .... | .... | .... | .... | .... | .... | .... | .... | .... | .... | .... | .... | .... | .... | .... |
| | **NHL Totals** | | **12** | **0** | **5** | **5** | **6** | **0** | **0** | **0** | **13** | **0.0** | | **45** | **68.9** | **14:33** | .... | .... | .... | .... | .... | .... | .... | .... | .... |

Traded to **Anaheim** by **Chicago** with James Wisniewski for Samuel Pahlsson, Logan Stephenson and future considerations, March 4, 2009.

## KOPECKY, Tomas

(koh-PEHTS-kee, TAW-mahsh) **CHI.**

Center. Shoots left. 6'3", 200 lbs. Born, Ilava, Czech., February 5, 1982. Detroit's 2nd choice, 38th overall, in 2000 Entry Draft.

| Season | Club | League | GP | G | A | Pts | PIM | PP | SH | GW | S | % | +/- | TF | F% | Min | GP | G | A | Pts | PIM | PP | SH | GW | Min |
|---|---|---|---|---|---|---|---|---|---|---|---|---|---|---|---|---|---|---|---|---|---|---|---|---|---|
| 1997-98 | Dukla Trencin Jr. | Slovak-Jr. | 41 | 19 | 22 | 41 | .... | .... | .... | .... | .... | .... | .... | .... | .... | .... | .... | .... | .... | .... | .... | .... | .... | .... | .... |
| 1998-99 | Dukla Trencin Jr. | Slovak-Jr. | 44 | 13 | 16 | 29 | 18 | .... | .... | .... | .... | .... | .... | .... | .... | .... | .... | .... | .... | .... | .... | .... | .... | .... | .... |
| 99-2000 | Dukla Trencin Jr. | Slovak-Jr. | 14 | 8 | 9 | 17 | 36 | .... | .... | .... | .... | .... | .... | .... | .... | .... | .... | .... | .... | .... | .... | .... | .... | .... | .... |
| | Dukla Trencin | Slovakia | 52 | 3 | 4 | 7 | 24 | .... | .... | .... | .... | .... | .... | .... | .... | .... | 5 | 0 | 0 | 0 | 0 | .... | .... | .... | .... |
| 2000-01 | Lethbridge | WHL | 49 | 22 | 28 | 50 | 52 | .... | .... | .... | .... | .... | .... | .... | .... | .... | 5 | 1 | 1 | 2 | 6 | .... | .... | .... | .... |
| | Cincinnati | AHL | 1 | 0 | 0 | 0 | 0 | .... | .... | .... | .... | .... | .... | .... | .... | .... | .... | .... | .... | .... | .... | .... | .... | .... | .... |
| 2001-02 | Lethbridge | WHL | 60 | 34 | 42 | 76 | 94 | .... | .... | .... | .... | .... | .... | .... | .... | .... | 4 | 2 | 1 | 3 | 15 | .... | .... | .... | .... |
| | Cincinnati | AHL | 2 | 1 | 1 | 2 | 6 | .... | .... | .... | .... | .... | .... | .... | .... | .... | 2 | 0 | 0 | 0 | 0 | .... | .... | .... | .... |
| 2002-03 | Grand Rapids | AHL | 70 | 17 | 21 | 38 | 32 | .... | .... | .... | .... | .... | .... | .... | .... | .... | 14 | 0 | 0 | 0 | 6 | .... | .... | .... | .... |
| 2003-04 | Grand Rapids | AHL | 48 | 6 | 6 | 12 | 28 | .... | .... | .... | .... | .... | .... | .... | .... | .... | 1 | 0 | 0 | 0 | 2 | .... | .... | .... | .... |
| 2004-05 | Grand Rapids | AHL | 48 | 8 | 8 | 16 | 35 | .... | .... | .... | .... | .... | .... | .... | .... | .... | .... | .... | .... | .... | .... | .... | .... | .... | .... |
| **2005-06** | **Detroit** | **NHL** | **1** | **0** | **0** | **0** | **2** | **0** | **0** | **0** | **1** | **0.0** | **1** | **0** | **0.0** | **9:41** | .... | .... | .... | .... | .... | .... | .... | .... | .... |
| | Grand Rapids | AHL | 77 | 32 | 37 | 69 | 108 | .... | .... | .... | .... | .... | .... | .... | .... | .... | 16 | 3 | 4 | 7 | 25 | .... | .... | .... | .... |
| **2006-07** | **Detroit** | **NHL** | **26** | **1** | **0** | **1** | **22** | **0** | **0** | **0** | **27** | **3.7** | **–2** | **5** | **40.0** | **7:15** | **4** | **0** | **0** | **0** | **6** | **0** | **0** | **0** | **3:38** |
| **2007-08 ♦** | **Detroit** | **NHL** | **77** | **5** | **7** | **12** | **43** | **0** | **0** | **1** | **87** | **5.7** | **2** | **109** | **40.4** | **9:37** | .... | .... | .... | .... | .... | .... | .... | .... | .... |
| **2008-09** | **Detroit** | **NHL** | **79** | **6** | **13** | **19** | **46** | **1** | **1** | **2** | **110** | **5.5** | **–7** | **79** | **45.6** | **10:25** | **8** | **0** | **1** | **1** | **7** | **0** | **0** | **0** | **9:32** |
| | **NHL Totals** | | **183** | **12** | **20** | **32** | **113** | **1** | **1** | **3** | **225** | **5.3** | | **193** | **42.5** | **9:37** | **12** | **0** | **1** | **1** | **13** | **0** | **0** | **0** | **7:34** |

• Missed majority of 2006-07 season recovering from broken collarbone suffered in game vs. Chicago, December 14, 2006. Signed as a free agent by **Chicago**, July 1, 2009.

## KOPITAR, Anze

(KOH-pih-tahr, AHN-zheh) **L.A.**

Center. Shoots left. 6'3", 219 lbs. Born, Jesenice, Yugoslavia, August 24, 1987. Los Angeles' 1st choice, 11th overall, in 2005 Entry Draft.

| Season | Club | League | GP | G | A | Pts | PIM | PP | SH | GW | S | % | +/- | TF | F% | Min | GP | G | A | Pts | PIM | PP | SH | GW | Min |
|---|---|---|---|---|---|---|---|---|---|---|---|---|---|---|---|---|---|---|---|---|---|---|---|---|---|
| 2002-03 | Jesenice U18 | Sloven-U18 | 14 | 38 | 38 | 76 | 10 | .... | .... | .... | .... | .... | .... | .... | .... | .... | .... | .... | .... | .... | .... | .... | .... | .... | .... |
| | Jesenice Jr. | Sloven-Jr. | 20 | 15 | 12 | 27 | 8 | .... | .... | .... | .... | .... | .... | .... | .... | .... | .... | .... | .... | .... | .... | .... | .... | .... | .... |
| | Kranjska Gora | Slovenia | 11 | 4 | 4 | 8 | 4 | .... | .... | .... | .... | .... | .... | .... | .... | .... | .... | .... | .... | .... | .... | .... | .... | .... | .... |
| 2003-04 | Jesenice Jr. | Sloven-Jr. | 25 | 32 | 28 | 60 | 16 | .... | .... | .... | .... | .... | .... | .... | .... | .... | .... | .... | .... | .... | .... | .... | .... | .... | .... |
| | Kranjska Gora | Slovenia | 21 | 14 | 11 | 25 | 10 | .... | .... | .... | .... | .... | .... | .... | .... | .... | 4 | 1 | 1 | 2 | 0 | .... | .... | .... | .... |
| 2004-05 | Sodertalje SK U18 | Swe-U18 | 1 | 1 | 2 | 3 | 0 | .... | .... | .... | .... | .... | .... | .... | .... | .... | 1 | 0 | 0 | 0 | 2 | .... | .... | .... | .... |
| | Sodertalje SK Jr. | Swe-Jr. | 30 | 28 | 21 | 49 | 26 | .... | .... | .... | .... | .... | .... | .... | .... | .... | 2 | 1 | 1 | 2 | 0 | .... | .... | .... | .... |
| | Sodertalje SK | Sweden | 5 | 0 | 0 | 0 | 0 | .... | .... | .... | .... | .... | .... | .... | .... | .... | 10 | 0 | 0 | 0 | 0 | .... | .... | .... | .... |
| 2005-06 | Sodertalje SK | Sweden | 47 | 8 | 12 | 20 | 28 | .... | .... | .... | .... | .... | .... | .... | .... | .... | .... | .... | .... | .... | .... | .... | .... | .... | .... |
| | Sodertalje SK | Sweden-Q | 10 | 7 | 4 | 11 | 6 | .... | .... | .... | .... | .... | .... | .... | .... | .... | .... | .... | .... | .... | .... | .... | .... | .... | .... |
| **2006-07** | **Los Angeles** | **NHL** | **72** | **20** | **41** | **61** | **24** | **7** | **2** | **1** | **193** | **10.4** | **–12** | **1204** | **46.1** | **20:32** | .... | .... | .... | .... | .... | .... | .... | .... | .... |
| **2007-08** | **Los Angeles** | **NHL** | **82** | **32** | **45** | **77** | **22** | **12** | **2** | **3** | **201** | **15.9** | **–15** | **1150** | **49.2** | **20:41** | .... | .... | .... | .... | .... | .... | .... | .... | .... |
| **2008-09** | **Los Angeles** | **NHL** | **82** | **27** | **39** | **66** | **32** | **7** | **1** | **3** | **234** | **11.5** | **–17** | **1355** | **49.5** | **20:27** | .... | .... | .... | .... | .... | .... | .... | .... | .... |
| | **NHL Totals** | | **236** | **79** | **125** | **204** | **78** | **26** | **5** | **7** | **628** | **12.6** | | **3709** | **48.3** | **20:34** | .... | .... | .... | .... | .... | .... | .... | .... | .... |

Played in NHL All-Star Game (2008)

## KORPIKOSKI, Lauri

(kohr-pih-KAWS-kee, LOW-ree) **PHX.**

Left wing. Shoots left. 6'1", 195 lbs. Born, Turku, Finland, July 28, 1986. NY Rangers' 2nd choice, 19th overall, in 2004 Entry Draft.

| Season | Club | League | GP | G | A | Pts | PIM | PP | SH | GW | S | % | +/- | TF | F% | Min | GP | G | A | Pts | PIM | PP | SH | GW | Min |
|---|---|---|---|---|---|---|---|---|---|---|---|---|---|---|---|---|---|---|---|---|---|---|---|---|---|
| 2002-03 | TPS Turku U18 | Fin-U18 | 21 | 7 | 4 | 11 | 10 | .... | .... | .... | .... | .... | .... | .... | .... | .... | .... | .... | .... | .... | .... | .... | .... | .... | .... |
| 2003-04 | TPS Turku U18 | Fin-U18 | .... | .... | .... | .... | .... | .... | .... | .... | .... | .... | .... | .... | .... | .... | 4 | 5 | 3 | 8 | 16 | .... | .... | .... | .... |
| | TPS Turku Jr. | Fin-Jr. | 36 | 12 | 8 | 20 | 20 | .... | .... | .... | .... | .... | .... | .... | .... | .... | 4 | 0 | 2 | 2 | 4 | .... | .... | .... | .... |
| 2004-05 | TPS Turku Jr. | Fin-Jr. | 3 | 3 | 0 | 3 | 0 | .... | .... | .... | .... | .... | .... | .... | .... | .... | .... | .... | .... | .... | .... | .... | .... | .... | .... |
| | TPS Turku | Finland | 41 | 0 | 6 | 6 | 12 | .... | .... | .... | .... | .... | .... | .... | .... | .... | 6 | 1 | 0 | 1 | 0 | .... | .... | .... | .... |
| 2005-06 | TPS Turku Jr. | Fin-Jr. | 1 | 1 | 0 | 1 | 2 | .... | .... | .... | .... | .... | .... | .... | .... | .... | .... | .... | .... | .... | .... | .... | .... | .... | .... |
| | Suomi U20 | Finland-2 | 3 | 1 | 3 | 4 | 0 | .... | .... | .... | .... | .... | .... | .... | .... | .... | .... | .... | .... | .... | .... | .... | .... | .... | .... |
| | TPS Turku | Finland | 51 | 3 | 4 | 7 | 16 | .... | .... | .... | .... | .... | .... | .... | .... | .... | 2 | 0 | 1 | 1 | 0 | .... | .... | .... | .... |
| | Hartford | AHL | 5 | 2 | 1 | 3 | 0 | .... | .... | .... | .... | .... | .... | .... | .... | .... | 11 | 1 | 0 | 1 | 2 | .... | .... | .... | .... |
| 2006-07 | Hartford | AHL | 78 | 11 | 27 | 38 | 23 | .... | .... | .... | .... | .... | .... | .... | .... | .... | 7 | 0 | 0 | 0 | 0 | .... | .... | .... | .... |
| **2007-08** | Hartford | AHL | 79 | 23 | 27 | 50 | 71 | .... | .... | .... | .... | .... | .... | .... | .... | .... | 5 | 1 | 1 | 2 | 0 | .... | .... | .... | .... |
| | **NY Rangers** | **NHL** | .... | .... | .... | .... | .... | .... | .... | .... | .... | .... | .... | .... | .... | .... | **1** | **1** | **0** | **1** | **0** | **0** | **0** | **0** | **7:14** |
| **2008-09** | **NY Rangers** | **NHL** | **68** | **6** | **8** | **14** | **14** | **0** | **0** | **1** | **63** | **9.5** | **–10** | **220** | **40.0** | **10:55** | **7** | **0** | **2** | **2** | **0** | **0** | **0** | **0** | **13:10** |
| | Hartford | AHL | 4 | 4 | 2 | 6 | 0 | .... | .... | .... | .... | .... | .... | .... | .... | .... | .... | .... | .... | .... | .... | .... | .... | .... | .... |
| | **NHL Totals** | | **68** | **6** | **8** | **14** | **14** | **0** | **0** | **1** | **63** | **9.5** | | **220** | **40.0** | **10:55** | **8** | **1** | **2** | **3** | **0** | **0** | **0** | **0** | **12:25** |

Traded to **Phoenix** by **NY Rangers** for Enver Lisin, Julky 13, 2009.

## KOSTITSYN, Andrei

(kaws-TIHT-sihn, AWN-dray) **MTL.**

Left wing. Shoots left. 6', 208 lbs. Born, Novopolotsk, USSR, February 3, 1985. Montreal's 1st choice, 10th overall, in 2003 Entry Draft.

| Season | Club | League | GP | G | A | Pts | PIM | PP | SH | GW | S | % | +/- | TF | F% | Min | GP | G | A | Pts | PIM | PP | SH | GW | Min |
|---|---|---|---|---|---|---|---|---|---|---|---|---|---|---|---|---|---|---|---|---|---|---|---|---|---|
| 99-2000 | Belarus | WJ18-A | 6 | 0 | 0 | 0 | 4 | .... | .... | .... | .... | .... | .... | .... | .... | .... | .... | .... | .... | .... | .... | .... | .... | .... | .... |
| 2000-01 | Novopolotsk | Belarus | 1 | 2 | 1 | 3 | 2 | .... | .... | .... | .... | .... | .... | .... | .... | .... | .... | .... | .... | .... | .... | .... | .... | .... | .... |
| | Novopolotsk | EEHL | 5 | 1 | 0 | 1 | 0 | .... | .... | .... | .... | .... | .... | .... | .... | .... | .... | .... | .... | .... | .... | .... | .... | .... | .... |
| | Yunost Minsk | Belarus | 3 | 1 | 4 | 5 | 8 | .... | .... | .... | .... | .... | .... | .... | .... | .... | .... | .... | .... | .... | .... | .... | .... | .... | .... |
| | HC Vitebsk | Belarus | 17 | 17 | 6 | 23 | 42 | .... | .... | .... | .... | .... | .... | .... | .... | .... | .... | .... | .... | .... | .... | .... | .... | .... | .... |
| | Belarus | WJ18-B | 5 | 7 | 7 | *14 | 8 | .... | .... | .... | .... | .... | .... | .... | .... | .... | .... | .... | .... | .... | .... | .... | .... | .... | .... |
| 2001-02 | Novopolotsk | Belarus | 17 | 9 | 6 | 15 | 28 | .... | .... | .... | .... | .... | .... | .... | .... | .... | .... | .... | .... | .... | .... | .... | .... | .... | .... |
| | Novopolotsk | EEHL | 29 | 9 | 8 | 17 | 16 | .... | .... | .... | .... | .... | .... | .... | .... | .... | .... | .... | .... | .... | .... | .... | .... | .... | .... |
| | Yunost Minsk | Belarus | 6 | 2 | 0 | 2 | 8 | .... | .... | .... | .... | .... | .... | .... | .... | .... | .... | .... | .... | .... | .... | .... | .... | .... | .... |
| 2002-03 | CSKA Moscow | Russia | 6 | 0 | 0 | 0 | 2 | .... | .... | .... | .... | .... | .... | .... | .... | .... | .... | .... | .... | .... | .... | .... | .... | .... | .... |
| | Voskresensk | Russia-2 | 2 | 1 | 1 | 2 | 0 | .... | .... | .... | .... | .... | .... | .... | .... | .... | .... | .... | .... | .... | .... | .... | .... | .... | .... |
| | Yunost Minsk | Belarus | 4 | 6 | 4 | 10 | 43 | .... | .... | .... | .... | .... | .... | .... | .... | .... | .... | .... | .... | .... | .... | .... | .... | .... | .... |
| | CSKA Moscow 2 | Russia-3 | 3 | 2 | 2 | 4 | 25 | .... | .... | .... | .... | .... | .... | .... | .... | .... | .... | .... | .... | .... | .... | .... | .... | .... | .... |
| | Belarus | WC-A | 2 | 1 | 0 | 1 | 2 | .... | .... | .... | .... | .... | .... | .... | .... | .... | .... | .... | .... | .... | .... | .... | .... | .... | .... |
| 2003-04 | CSKA Moscow 2 | Russia-3 | STATISTICS NOT AVAILABLE | | | | | | | | | | | | | | | | | | | | | | |
| | CSKA Moscow | Russia | 12 | 0 | 1 | 1 | 2 | .... | .... | .... | .... | .... | .... | .... | .... | .... | .... | .... | .... | .... | .... | .... | .... | .... | .... |
| | Yunost Minsk | Belarus | STATISTICS NOT AVAILABLE | | | | | | | | | | | | | | | | | | | | | | |
| 2004-05 | Hamilton | AHL | 66 | 12 | 11 | 23 | 24 | .... | .... | .... | .... | .... | .... | .... | .... | .... | 3 | 0 | 0 | 0 | 0 | .... | .... | .... | .... |
| **2005-06** | **Montreal** | **NHL** | **12** | **2** | **1** | **3** | **2** | **0** | **0** | **0** | **9** | **22.2** | **1** | **1** | **0.0** | **7:32** | .... | .... | .... | .... | .... | .... | .... | .... | .... |
| | Hamilton | AHL | 64 | 18 | 29 | 47 | 76 | .... | .... | .... | .... | .... | .... | .... | .... | .... | .... | .... | .... | .... | .... | .... | .... | .... | .... |
| **2006-07** | **Montreal** | **NHL** | **22** | **1** | **10** | **11** | **6** | **0** | **0** | **0** | **38** | **2.6** | **3** | **1** | **0.0** | **13:17** | .... | .... | .... | .... | .... | .... | .... | .... | .... |
| | Hamilton | AHL | 50 | 21 | 31 | 52 | 50 | .... | .... | .... | .... | .... | .... | .... | .... | .... | .... | .... | .... | .... | .... | .... | .... | .... | .... |
| **2007-08** | **Montreal** | **NHL** | **78** | **26** | **27** | **53** | **29** | **12** | **0** | **5** | **156** | **16.7** | **15** | **6** | **66.7** | **15:41** | **12** | **5** | **3** | **8** | **2** | **1** | **0** | **1** | **16:01** |
| **2008-09** | **Montreal** | **NHL** | **74** | **23** | **18** | **41** | **50** | **6** | **0** | **2** | **169** | **13.6** | **–7** | **6** | **50.0** | **15:35** | **4** | **1** | **0** | **1** | **2** | **0** | **0** | **0** | **14:15** |
| | **NHL Totals** | | **186** | **52** | **56** | **108** | **87** | **18** | **0** | **7** | **372** | **14.0** | | **14** | **50.0** | **14:50** | **16** | **6** | **3** | **9** | **4** | **1** | **0** | **1** | **15:34** |



## KOSTITSYN, Sergei

(kaws-TIHT-sihn, SAIR-gay) **MTL.**

Left wing. Shoots left. 6', 204 lbs. Born, Novopolotsk, USSR, March 20, 1987. Montreal's 6th choice, 200th overall, in 2005 Entry Draft.

| Season | Club | League | GP | G | A | Pts | PIM | PP | SH | GW | S | % | +/- | TF | F% | Min | GP | G | A | Pts | PIM | PP | SH | GW | Min |
|---|---|---|---|---|---|---|---|---|---|---|---|---|---|---|---|---|---|---|---|---|---|---|---|---|---|
| 2003-04 | HK Gomel | EEHL | 6 | 0 | 1 | 1 | 0 | .... | .... | .... | .... | .... | .... | .... | .... | .... | .... | .... | .... | .... | .... | .... | .... | .... | .... |
| | HK Gomel 2 | EEHL-B | 6 | 7 | 2 | 9 | 14 | .... | .... | .... | .... | .... | .... | .... | .... | .... | .... | .... | .... | .... | .... | .... | .... | .... | .... |
| | Yunior Minsk | EEHL-B | STATISTICS NOT AVAILABLE | | | | | | | | | | | | | | | | | | | | | | |
| | Yunior Minsk | Belarus | 3 | 0 | 0 | 0 | 0 | .... | .... | .... | .... | .... | .... | .... | .... | .... | .... | .... | .... | .... | .... | .... | .... | .... | .... |
| | HK Gomel | Belarus | 22 | 5 | 4 | 9 | 4 | .... | .... | .... | .... | .... | .... | .... | .... | .... | 11 | 1 | 2 | 3 | 8 | .... | .... | .... | .... |
| 2004-05 | HK Gomel | BelOpen | 40 | 4 | 10 | 14 | 24 | .... | .... | .... | .... | .... | .... | .... | .... | .... | 4 | 2 | 0 | 2 | 12 | .... | .... | .... | .... |
| 2005-06 | London Knights | OHL | 63 | 26 | 52 | 78 | 78 | .... | .... | .... | .... | .... | .... | .... | .... | .... | 19 | 13 | 24 | 37 | *44 | .... | .... | .... | .... |
| 2006-07 | London Knights | OHL | 59 | 40 | *91 | 131 | 76 | .... | .... | .... | .... | .... | .... | .... | .... | .... | 16 | 9 | 12 | 21 | 39 | .... | .... | .... | .... |

| | | | Regular Season | | | | | | | | | | | | | | Playoffs | | | | | | | | |
|---|---|---|---|---|---|---|---|---|---|---|---|---|---|---|---|---|---|---|---|---|---|---|---|---|---|
| Season | Club | League | GP | G | A | Pts | PIM | PP | SH | GW | S | % | +/- | TF | F% | Min | GP | G | A | Pts | PIM | PP | SH | GW | Min |
| **2007-08** | **Montreal** | **NHL** | **52** | **9** | **18** | **27** | **51** | **3** | **1** | **0** | **49** | **18.4** | **9** | **23** | **34.8** | **14:21** | **12** | **3** | **5** | **8** | **14** | **0** | **0** | **0** | **15:09** |
| | Hamilton | AHL | 22 | 6 | 16 | 22 | 18 | .... | .... | .... | .... | .... | .... | .... | .... | .... | .... | .... | .... | .... | .... | .... | .... | .... | .... |
| **2008-09** | **Montreal** | **NHL** | **56** | **8** | **15** | **23** | **64** | **5** | **0** | **1** | **74** | **10.8** | **–3** | **9** | **33.3** | **14:08** | **1** | **0** | **0** | **0** | **2** | **0** | **0** | **0** | **12:10** |
| | Hamilton | AHL | 16 | 5 | 8 | 13 | 18 | .... | .... | .... | .... | .... | .... | .... | .... | .... | .... | .... | .... | .... | .... | .... | .... | .... | .... |
| | **NHL Totals** | | **108** | **17** | **33** | **50** | **115** | **8** | **1** | **1** | **123** | **13.8** | | **32** | **34.4** | **14:15** | **13** | **3** | **5** | **8** | **16** | **0** | **0** | **0** | **14:55** |

## KOSTOPOULOS, Tom

(kaw-STAWP-oh-lihs, TAWM) **CAR.**

Right wing. Shoots right. 6', 201 lbs. Born, Mississauga, Ont., January 24, 1979. Pittsburgh's 9th choice, 204th overall, in 1999 Entry Draft.

| | | | | | | | | | | | | | | | | | | | | | | | | | |
|---|---|---|---|---|---|---|---|---|---|---|---|---|---|---|---|---|---|---|---|---|---|---|---|---|---|
| 1995-96 | Brampton | OPJHL | 24 | 9 | 9 | 18 | 28 | .... | .... | .... | .... | .... | .... | .... | .... | .... | .... | .... | .... | .... | .... | .... | .... | .... | .... |
| 1996-97 | London Knights | OHL | 64 | 13 | 12 | 25 | 67 | .... | .... | .... | .... | .... | .... | .... | .... | .... | .... | .... | .... | .... | .... | .... | .... | .... | .... |
| 1997-98 | London Knights | OHL | 66 | 24 | 26 | 50 | 108 | .... | .... | .... | .... | .... | .... | .... | .... | .... | 16 | 6 | 4 | 10 | 26 | .... | .... | .... | .... |
| 1998-99 | London Knights | OHL | 66 | 27 | 60 | 87 | 114 | .... | .... | .... | .... | .... | .... | .... | .... | .... | 25 | 19 | 16 | 35 | 32 | .... | .... | .... | .... |
| 99-2000 | Wilkes-Barre | AHL | 76 | 26 | 32 | 58 | 121 | .... | .... | .... | .... | .... | .... | .... | .... | .... | .... | .... | .... | .... | .... | .... | .... | .... | .... |
| 2000-01 | Wilkes-Barre | AHL | 80 | 16 | 36 | 52 | 120 | .... | .... | .... | .... | .... | .... | .... | .... | .... | 21 | 3 | 9 | 12 | 6 | .... | .... | .... | .... |
| **2001-02** | **Pittsburgh** | **NHL** | **11** | **1** | **2** | **3** | **9** | **0** | **0** | **0** | **8** | **12.5** | **–1** | **0** | **0.0** | **12:03** | .... | .... | .... | .... | .... | .... | .... | .... | .... |
| | Wilkes-Barre | AHL | 70 | 27 | 26 | 53 | 112 | .... | .... | .... | .... | .... | .... | .... | .... | .... | .... | .... | .... | .... | .... | .... | .... | .... | .... |
| **2002-03** | **Pittsburgh** | **NHL** | **8** | **0** | **1** | **1** | **0** | **0** | **0** | **0** | **6** | **0.0** | **–4** | **2** | **0.0** | **4:33** | .... | .... | .... | .... | .... | .... | .... | .... | .... |
| | Wilkes-Barre | AHL | 71 | 21 | 42 | 63 | 131 | .... | .... | .... | .... | .... | .... | .... | .... | .... | 6 | 1 | 2 | 3 | 7 | .... | .... | .... | .... |
| **2003-04** | **Pittsburgh** | **NHL** | **60** | **9** | **13** | **22** | **67** | **2** | **1** | **1** | **101** | **8.9** | **–14** | **10** | **30.0** | **14:26** | .... | .... | .... | .... | .... | .... | .... | .... | .... |
| | Wilkes-Barre | AHL | 21 | 7 | 13 | 20 | 43 | .... | .... | .... | .... | .... | .... | .... | .... | .... | 24 | 7 | 16 | 23 | 32 | .... | .... | .... | .... |
| 2004-05 | Manchester | AHL | 64 | 25 | 46 | 71 | 99 | .... | .... | .... | .... | .... | .... | .... | .... | .... | 6 | 0 | 7 | 7 | 10 | .... | .... | .... | .... |
| **2005-06** | **Los Angeles** | **NHL** | **76** | **8** | **14** | **22** | **100** | **0** | **0** | **1** | **74** | **10.8** | **–8** | **30** | **36.7** | **12:56** | .... | .... | .... | .... | .... | .... | .... | .... | .... |
| **2006-07** | **Los Angeles** | **NHL** | **76** | **7** | **15** | **22** | **73** | **0** | **0** | **0** | **90** | **7.8** | **–2** | **62** | **29.0** | **11:34** | .... | .... | .... | .... | .... | .... | .... | .... | .... |
| **2007-08** | **Montreal** | **NHL** | **67** | **7** | **6** | **13** | **113** | **0** | **3** | **1** | **98** | **7.1** | **–3** | **28** | **28.6** | **11:16** | **12** | **3** | **1** | **4** | **6** | **0** | **0** | **1** | **13:35** |
| **2008-09** | **Montreal** | **NHL** | **78** | **8** | **14** | **22** | **106** | **0** | **1** | **0** | **121** | **6.6** | **–1** | **16** | **31.3** | **14:09** | **4** | **0** | **1** | **1** | **4** | **0** | **0** | **0** | **14:01** |
| | **NHL Totals** | | **376** | **40** | **65** | **105** | **468** | **2** | **5** | **3** | **498** | **8.0** | | **148** | **30.4** | **12:39** | **16** | **3** | **2** | **5** | **10** | **0** | **0** | **1** | **13:41** |

Signed as a free agent by **Manchester** (AHL), July 12, 2004. Signed as a free agent by **Los Angeles**, August 1, 2005. Signed as a free agent by **Montreal**, July 4, 2007. Signed as a free agent by **Carolina**, July 14, 2009.

## KOTALIK, Ales

(KOH-tahl-eek, ahl-EHSH) **NYR**

Right wing. Shoots right. 6'1", 227 lbs. Born, Jindrichuv Hradec, Czech., December 23, 1978. Buffalo's 7th choice, 164th overall, in 1998 Entry Draft.

| | | | | | | | | | | | | | | | | | | | | | | | | | |
|---|---|---|---|---|---|---|---|---|---|---|---|---|---|---|---|---|---|---|---|---|---|---|---|---|---|
| 1993-94 | C. Budejovice Jr. | CzRep-Jr. | 28 | 12 | 12 | 24 | .... | .... | .... | .... | .... | .... | .... | .... | .... | .... | .... | .... | .... | .... | .... | .... | .... | .... | .... |
| 1994-95 | C. Budejovice Jr. | CzRep-Jr. | 36 | 26 | 17 | 43 | .... | .... | .... | .... | .... | .... | .... | .... | .... | .... | .... | .... | .... | .... | .... | .... | .... | .... | .... |
| 1995-96 | C. Budejovice Jr. | CzRep-Jr. | 28 | 6 | 7 | 13 | .... | .... | .... | .... | .... | .... | .... | .... | .... | .... | .... | .... | .... | .... | .... | .... | .... | .... | .... |
| 1996-97 | C. Budejovice Jr. | CzRep-Jr. | 36 | 15 | 16 | 31 | 24 | .... | .... | .... | .... | .... | .... | .... | .... | .... | .... | .... | .... | .... | .... | .... | .... | .... | .... |
| 1997-98 | C. Budejovice | CzRep | 47 | 9 | 7 | 16 | 14 | .... | .... | .... | .... | .... | .... | .... | .... | .... | .... | .... | .... | .... | .... | .... | .... | .... | .... |
| 1998-99 | C. Budejovice | CzRep | 41 | 8 | 13 | 21 | 16 | .... | .... | .... | .... | .... | .... | .... | .... | .... | 3 | 0 | 0 | 0 | .... | .... | .... | .... | .... |
| 99-2000 | C. Budejovice | CzRep | 43 | 7 | 12 | 19 | 34 | .... | .... | .... | .... | .... | .... | .... | .... | .... | 3 | 0 | 1 | 1 | 6 | .... | .... | .... | .... |
| 2000-01 | C. Budejovice | CzRep | 52 | 19 | 29 | 48 | 54 | .... | .... | .... | .... | .... | .... | .... | .... | .... | .... | .... | .... | .... | .... | .... | .... | .... | .... |
| **2001-02** | **Buffalo** | **NHL** | **13** | **1** | **3** | **4** | **2** | **0** | **0** | **0** | **21** | **4.8** | **–1** | **11** | **27.3** | **12:35** | .... | .... | .... | .... | .... | .... | .... | .... | .... |
| | Rochester | AHL | 68 | 18 | 25 | 43 | 55 | .... | .... | .... | .... | .... | .... | .... | .... | .... | 1 | 0 | 0 | 0 | 0 | .... | .... | .... | .... |
| **2002-03** | **Buffalo** | **NHL** | **68** | **21** | **14** | **35** | **30** | **4** | **0** | **2** | **138** | **15.2** | **–2** | **37** | **51.4** | **15:15** | .... | .... | .... | .... | .... | .... | .... | .... | .... |
| | Rochester | AHL | 8 | 0 | 2 | 2 | 4 | .... | .... | .... | .... | .... | .... | .... | .... | .... | .... | .... | .... | .... | .... | .... | .... | .... | .... |
| **2003-04** | **Buffalo** | **NHL** | **62** | **15** | **11** | **26** | **41** | **2** | **0** | **3** | **142** | **10.6** | **–1** | **14** | **50.0** | **15:11** | .... | .... | .... | .... | .... | .... | .... | .... | .... |
| 2004-05 | Liberec | CzRep | 25 | 8 | 8 | 16 | 46 | .... | .... | .... | .... | .... | .... | .... | .... | .... | 12 | 2 | 5 | 7 | 12 | .... | .... | .... | .... |
| **2005-06** | **Buffalo** | **NHL** | **82** | **25** | **37** | **62** | **62** | **10** | **0** | **5** | **261** | **9.6** | **–3** | **29** | **41.4** | **15:34** | **18** | **4** | **7** | **11** | **8** | **0** | **0** | **3** | **15:15** |
| | Czech Republic | Olympics | 4 | 0 | 0 | 0 | 0 | .... | .... | .... | .... | .... | .... | .... | .... | .... | .... | .... | .... | .... | .... | .... | .... | .... | .... |
| **2006-07** | **Buffalo** | **NHL** | **66** | **16** | **22** | **38** | **46** | **3** | **0** | **4** | **162** | **9.9** | **–5** | **35** | **48.6** | **14:31** | **16** | **2** | **2** | **4** | **8** | **0** | **0** | **0** | **12:29** |
| **2007-08** | **Buffalo** | **NHL** | **79** | **23** | **20** | **43** | **58** | **12** | **0** | **1** | **207** | **11.1** | **–5** | **220** | **44.6** | **15:21** | .... | .... | .... | .... | .... | .... | .... | .... | .... |
| **2008-09** | **Buffalo** | **NHL** | **56** | **13** | **19** | **32** | **28** | **8** | **0** | **1** | **153** | **8.5** | **–7** | **77** | **39.0** | **15:14** | .... | .... | .... | .... | .... | .... | .... | .... | .... |
| | **Edmonton** | **NHL** | **19** | **7** | **4** | **11** | **6** | **1** | **0** | **0** | **55** | **12.7** | **2** | **8** | **75.0** | **16:06** | .... | .... | .... | .... | .... | .... | .... | .... | .... |
| | **NHL Totals** | | **445** | **121** | **130** | **251** | **273** | **40** | **0** | **16** | **1139** | **10.6** | | **431** | **44.5** | **15:10** | **34** | **6** | **9** | **15** | **16** | **0** | **0** | **3** | **13:57** |

Signed as a free agent by **Liberec** (CzRep), September 6, 2004. Traded to **Edmonton** by **Buffalo** for Carolina's 2nd round choice (previously acquired, later traded to Toronto – Toronto selected Jesse Blacker) in 2009 Entry Draft, March 4, 2009. Signed as a free agent by **NY Rangers**, July 9, 2009.

## KOVALCHUK, Ilya

(koh-vuhl-CHUHK, IHL-yah) **ATL.**

Left wing. Shoots right. 6'1", 230 lbs. Born, Tver, USSR, April 15, 1983. Atlanta's 1st choice, 1st overall, in 2001 Entry Draft.

| | | | | | | | | | | | | | | | | | | | | | | | | | |
|---|---|---|---|---|---|---|---|---|---|---|---|---|---|---|---|---|---|---|---|---|---|---|---|---|---|
| 99-2000 | Spartak Moscow | Russia-2 | 49 | 12 | 5 | 17 | 75 | .... | .... | .... | .... | .... | .... | .... | .... | .... | .... | .... | .... | .... | .... | .... | .... | .... | .... |
| | Spartak 2 | Russia-3 | 2 | 2 | 1 | 3 | 14 | .... | .... | .... | .... | .... | .... | .... | .... | .... | .... | .... | .... | .... | .... | .... | .... | .... | .... |
| 2000-01 | Spartak Moscow | Russia-2 | 40 | 28 | 18 | 46 | 78 | .... | .... | .... | .... | .... | .... | .... | .... | .... | 12 | 14 | 4 | 18 | 38 | .... | .... | .... | .... |
| **2001-02** | **Atlanta** | **NHL** | **65** | **29** | **22** | **51** | **28** | **7** | **0** | **4** | **184** | **15.8** | **–19** | **6** | **16.7** | **18:32** | .... | .... | .... | .... | .... | .... | .... | .... | .... |
| | Russia | Olympics | 6 | 1 | 2 | 3 | 14 | .... | .... | .... | .... | .... | .... | .... | .... | .... | .... | .... | .... | .... | .... | .... | .... | .... | .... |
| **2002-03** | **Atlanta** | **NHL** | **81** | **38** | **29** | **67** | **57** | **9** | **0** | **3** | **257** | **14.8** | **–24** | **15** | **40.0** | **19:27** | .... | .... | .... | .... | .... | .... | .... | .... | .... |
| **2003-04** | **Atlanta** | **NHL** | **81** | ***41** | **46** | **87** | **63** | **16** | **1** | **6** | **341** | **12.0** | **–10** | **28** | **32.1** | **23:41** | .... | .... | .... | .... | .... | .... | .... | .... | .... |
| 2004-05 | Ak Bars Kazan | Russia | 53 | 19 | 23 | 42 | 72 | .... | .... | .... | .... | .... | .... | .... | .... | .... | 4 | 0 | 1 | 1 | 0 | .... | .... | .... | .... |
| **2005-06** | **Atlanta** | **NHL** | **78** | **52** | **46** | **98** | **68** | **27** | **0** | **7** | **323** | **16.1** | **–6** | **47** | **40.4** | **22:23** | .... | .... | .... | .... | .... | .... | .... | .... | .... |
| | Russia | Olympics | 8 | 4 | 1 | 5 | 31 | .... | .... | .... | .... | .... | .... | .... | .... | .... | .... | .... | .... | .... | .... | .... | .... | .... | .... |
| **2006-07** | **Atlanta** | **NHL** | **82** | **42** | **34** | **76** | **66** | **18** | **0** | **7** | **336** | **12.5** | **–2** | **66** | **39.4** | **21:32** | **4** | **1** | **1** | **2** | **19** | **0** | **0** | **0** | **18:42** |
| **2007-08** | **Atlanta** | **NHL** | **79** | **52** | **35** | **87** | **52** | **16** | **2** | **4** | **283** | **18.4** | **–12** | **32** | **43.8** | **21:30** | .... | .... | .... | .... | .... | .... | .... | .... | .... |
| **2008-09** | **Atlanta** | **NHL** | **79** | **43** | **48** | **91** | **50** | **12** | **0** | **6** | **275** | **15.6** | **–12** | **14** | **35.7** | **21:48** | .... | .... | .... | .... | .... | .... | .... | .... | .... |
| | **NHL Totals** | | **545** | **297** | **260** | **557** | **384** | **105** | **3** | **37** | **1999** | **14.9** | | **208** | **38.5** | **21:21** | **4** | **1** | **1** | **2** | **19** | **0** | **0** | **0** | **18:42** |

NHL All-Rookie Team (2002) • NHL Second All-Star Team (2004) • Maurice "Rocket" Richard Trophy (2004) (tied with Jarome Iginla and Rick Nash)

Played in NHL All-Star Game (2004, 2008, 2009)

Signed as a free agent by **Kazan** (Russia) August 22, 2004.

## KOVALEV, Alex

(koh-VAH-lehv, AL-ehx) **OTT.**

Right wing. Shoots left. 6'1", 215 lbs. Born, Togliatti, USSR, February 24, 1973. NY Rangers' 1st choice, 15th overall, in 1991 Entry Draft.

| | | | | | | | | | | | | | | | | | | | | | | | | | |
|---|---|---|---|---|---|---|---|---|---|---|---|---|---|---|---|---|---|---|---|---|---|---|---|---|---|
| 1989-90 | Dynamo Moscow | USSR | 1 | 0 | 0 | 0 | 0 | .... | .... | .... | .... | .... | .... | .... | .... | .... | .... | .... | .... | .... | .... | .... | .... | .... | .... |
| 1990-91 | Dyn'o Moscow 2 | USSR-3 | 21 | 16 | .... | .... | .... | .... | .... | .... | .... | .... | .... | .... | .... | .... | .... | .... | .... | .... | .... | .... | .... | .... | .... |
| | Dynamo Moscow | USSR | 18 | 1 | 2 | 3 | 4 | .... | .... | .... | .... | .... | .... | .... | .... | .... | .... | .... | .... | .... | .... | .... | .... | .... | .... |
| | Dynamo Moscow | Super-S | 1 | 0 | 0 | 0 | 0 | .... | .... | .... | .... | .... | .... | .... | .... | .... | .... | .... | .... | .... | .... | .... | .... | .... | .... |
| 1991-92 | Dynamo Moscow | CIS | 33 | 16 | 9 | 25 | 20 | .... | .... | .... | .... | .... | .... | .... | .... | .... | .... | .... | .... | .... | .... | .... | .... | .... | .... |
| | Dyn'o Moscow 2 | CIS-3 | 4 | 5 | 0 | 5 | 12 | .... | .... | .... | .... | .... | .... | .... | .... | .... | .... | .... | .... | .... | .... | .... | .... | .... | .... |
| | Russia | Olympics | 8 | 1 | 2 | 3 | 14 | .... | .... | .... | .... | .... | .... | .... | .... | .... | .... | .... | .... | .... | .... | .... | .... | .... | .... |
| **1992-93** | **NY Rangers** | **NHL** | **65** | **20** | **18** | **38** | **79** | **3** | **0** | **3** | **134** | **14.9** | **–10** | .... | .... | .... | .... | .... | .... | .... | .... | .... | .... | .... | .... |
| | Binghamton | AHL | 13 | 13 | 11 | 24 | 35 | .... | .... | .... | .... | .... | .... | .... | .... | .... | 9 | 3 | 5 | 8 | 14 | .... | .... | .... | .... |
| **1993-94**♦ | **NY Rangers** | **NHL** | **76** | **23** | **33** | **56** | **154** | **7** | **0** | **3** | **184** | **12.5** | **18** | .... | .... | .... | **23** | **9** | **12** | **21** | **18** | **5** | **0** | **2** | .... |
| **1994-95** | Lada Togliatti | CIS | 12 | 8 | 8 | 16 | 49 | .... | .... | .... | .... | .... | .... | .... | .... | .... | .... | .... | .... | .... | .... | .... | .... | .... | .... |
| | **NY Rangers** | **NHL** | **48** | **13** | **15** | **28** | **30** | **1** | **1** | **1** | **103** | **12.6** | **–6** | .... | .... | .... | **10** | **4** | **7** | **11** | **10** | **0** | **0** | **0** | .... |
| **1995-96** | **NY Rangers** | **NHL** | **81** | **24** | **34** | **58** | **98** | **8** | **1** | **7** | **206** | **11.7** | **5** | .... | .... | .... | **11** | **3** | **4** | **7** | **14** | **0** | **0** | **1** | .... |
| **1996-97** | **NY Rangers** | **NHL** | **45** | **13** | **22** | **35** | **42** | **1** | **0** | **0** | **110** | **11.8** | **11** | .... | .... | .... | .... | .... | .... | .... | .... | .... | .... | .... | .... |
| **1997-98** | **NY Rangers** | **NHL** | **73** | **23** | **30** | **53** | **44** | **8** | **0** | **3** | **173** | **13.3** | **–22** | .... | .... | .... | .... | .... | .... | .... | .... | .... | .... | .... | .... |
| **1998-99** | **NY Rangers** | **NHL** | **14** | **3** | **4** | **7** | **12** | **1** | **0** | **1** | **35** | **8.6** | **–6** | **18** | **44.4** | **19:53** | .... | .... | .... | .... | .... | .... | .... | .... | .... |
| | **Pittsburgh** | **NHL** | **63** | **20** | **26** | **46** | **37** | **5** | **1** | **4** | **156** | **12.8** | **8** | **226** | **43.4** | **20:30** | **10** | **5** | **7** | **12** | **14** | **0** | **0** | **1** | **20:24** |
| **99-2000** | **Pittsburgh** | **NHL** | **82** | **26** | **40** | **66** | **94** | **9** | **2** | **4** | **254** | **10.2** | **–3** | **306** | **47.4** | **22:53** | **11** | **1** | **5** | **6** | **10** | **0** | **0** | **0** | **26:35** |
| **2000-01** | **Pittsburgh** | **NHL** | **79** | **44** | **51** | **95** | **96** | **12** | **2** | **9** | **307** | **14.3** | **12** | **255** | **40.0** | **23:35** | **18** | **5** | **5** | **10** | **16** | **1** | **0** | **0** | **20:57** |
| **2001-02** | **Pittsburgh** | **NHL** | **67** | **32** | **44** | **76** | **80** | **8** | **1** | **3** | **266** | **12.0** | **2** | **179** | **45.3** | **24:03** | .... | .... | .... | .... | .... | .... | .... | .... | .... |
| | Russia | Olympics | 6 | 3 | 1 | 4 | 4 | .... | .... | .... | .... | .... | .... | .... | .... | .... | .... | .... | .... | .... | .... | .... | .... | .... | .... |
| **2002-03** | **Pittsburgh** | **NHL** | **54** | **27** | **37** | **64** | **50** | **8** | **0** | **1** | **212** | **12.7** | **–11** | **19** | **31.6** | **24:03** | .... | .... | .... | .... | .... | .... | .... | .... | .... |
| | **NY Rangers** | **NHL** | **24** | **10** | **3** | **13** | **20** | **3** | **0** | **2** | **59** | **16.9** | **2** | **19** | **42.1** | **20:09** | .... | .... | .... | .... | .... | .... | .... | .... | .... |
| **2003-04** | **NY Rangers** | **NHL** | **66** | **13** | **29** | **42** | **54** | **3** | **0** | **0** | **178** | **7.3** | **–5** | **29** | **48.3** | **19:37** | .... | .... | .... | .... | .... | .... | .... | .... | .... |
| | **Montreal** | **NHL** | **12** | **1** | **2** | **3** | **12** | **0** | **0** | **1** | **29** | **3.4** | **–4** | **2** | **50.0** | **15:36** | **11** | **6** | **4** | **10** | **8** | **1** | **0** | **1** | **20:11** |
| 2004-05 | Ak Bars Kazan | Russia | 35 | 10 | 12 | 22 | 80 | .... | .... | .... | .... | .... | .... | .... | .... | .... | 4 | 0 | 0 | 0 | 8 | .... | .... | .... | .... |
| **2005-06** | **Montreal** | **NHL** | **69** | **23** | **42** | **65** | **76** | **9** | **0** | **5** | **206** | **11.2** | **–1** | **47** | **48.9** | **19:28** | **6** | **4** | **3** | **7** | **4** | **1** | **0** | **0** | **19:21** |
| | Russia | Olympics | 8 | 4 | 2 | 6 | 4 | .... | .... | .... | .... | .... | .... | .... | .... | .... | .... | .... | .... | .... | .... | .... | .... | .... | .... |
| **2006-07** | **Montreal** | **NHL** | **73** | **18** | **29** | **47** | **78** | **8** | **0** | **5** | **197** | **9.1** | **–19** | **162** | **46.3** | **18:15** | .... | .... | .... | .... | .... | .... | .... | .... | .... |

| Season | Club | League | GP | G | A | Pts | PIM | PP | SH | GW | S | % | +/- | TF | F% | Min | GP | G | A | Pts | PIM | PP | SH | GW | Min |
|---|---|---|---|---|---|---|---|---|---|---|---|---|---|---|---|---|---|---|---|---|---|---|---|---|---|
| | | | Regular Season | | | | | | | | | | | | | | Playoffs | | | | | | | | |
| **2007-08** | **Montreal** | **NHL** | 82 | 35 | 49 | 84 | 70 | 17 | 0 | 5 | 230 | 15.2 | 18 | 58 | 55.2 | 19:33 | 12 | 5 | 6 | 11 | 8 | 2 | 1 | 1 | 21:41 |
| **2008-09** | **Montreal** | **NHL** | 78 | 26 | 39 | 65 | 74 | 11 | 1 | 4 | 209 | 12.4 | -5 | 50 | 32.0 | 19:26 | 4 | 2 | 1 | 3 | 2 | 0 | 0 | 0 | 19:54 |
| | **NHL Totals** | | 1151 | 394 | 547 | 941 | 1200 | 122 | 9 | 61 | 3248 | 12.1 | | 1370 | 44.5 | 20:57 | 116 | 44 | 54 | 98 | 104 | 10 | 1 | 6 | 21:33 |

NHL Second All-Star Team (2008)

Played in NHL All-Star Game (2001, 2003, 2009)

Traded to **Pittsburgh** by **NY Rangers** with Harry York for Petr Nedved, Chris Tamer and Sean Pronger, November 25, 1998. Traded to **NY Rangers** by **Pittsburgh** with Mike Wilson, Janne Laukkanen and Dan LaCouture for Joel Bouchard, Richard Lintner, Rico Fata and Mikael Samuelsson, February 10, 2003. Traded to **Montreal** by **NY Rangers** for Jozef Balej and Montreal's 2nd round choice (Bruce Graham) in 2004 Entry Draft, March 2, 2004. Signed as a free agent by **Kazan** (Russia), November 3, 2004. Signed as a free agent by **Ottawa**, July 6, 2009.

## KOZLOV, Viktor

(KAWZ-lahf, VIHK-tohr)

Center. Shoots right. 6'4", 232 lbs. Born, Togliatti, USSR, February 14, 1975. San Jose's 1st choice, 6th overall, in 1993 Entry Draft.

| Season | Club | League | GP | G | A | Pts | PIM | PP | SH | GW | S | % | +/- | TF | F% | Min | GP | G | A | Pts | PIM | PP | SH | GW | Min |
|---|---|---|---|---|---|---|---|---|---|---|---|---|---|---|---|---|---|---|---|---|---|---|---|---|---|
| 1990-91 | Lada Togliatti | USSR-2 | 2 | 2 | 0 | 2 | 0 | .... | .... | .... | .... | .... | .... | .... | .... | .... | .... | .... | .... | .... | .... | .... | .... | .... | .... |
| 1991-92 | Lada Togliatti | CIS | 3 | 0 | 0 | 0 | 0 | .... | .... | .... | .... | .... | .... | .... | .... | .... | .... | .... | .... | .... | .... | .... | .... | .... | .... |
| 1992-93 | Dynamo Moscow | CIS | 30 | 6 | 5 | 11 | 4 | .... | .... | .... | .... | .... | .... | .... | .... | .... | 10 | 3 | 0 | 3 | 0 | .... | .... | .... | .... |
| 1993-94 | Dynamo Moscow | CIS | 42 | 16 | 9 | 25 | 14 | .... | .... | .... | .... | .... | .... | .... | .... | .... | .... | .... | .... | .... | .... | .... | .... | .... | .... |
| **1994-95** | Dynamo Moscow | CIS | 3 | 1 | 1 | 2 | 2 | .... | .... | .... | .... | .... | .... | .... | .... | .... | .... | .... | .... | .... | .... | .... | .... | .... | .... |
| | **San Jose** | **NHL** | 16 | 2 | 0 | 2 | 2 | 0 | 0 | 0 | 23 | 8.7 | -5 | .... | .... | .... | .... | .... | .... | .... | .... | .... | .... | .... | .... |
| | Kansas City | IHL | 4 | 1 | 1 | 2 | 0 | .... | .... | .... | .... | .... | .... | .... | .... | .... | 13 | 4 | 5 | 9 | 12 | .... | .... | .... | .... |
| **1995-96** | **San Jose** | **NHL** | 62 | 6 | 13 | 19 | 6 | 1 | 0 | 0 | 107 | 5.6 | -15 | .... | .... | .... | .... | .... | .... | .... | .... | .... | .... | .... | .... |
| | Kansas City | IHL | 15 | 4 | 7 | 11 | 12 | .... | .... | .... | .... | .... | .... | .... | .... | .... | .... | .... | .... | .... | .... | .... | .... | .... | .... |
| **1996-97** | **San Jose** | **NHL** | 78 | 16 | 25 | 41 | 40 | 4 | 0 | 4 | 184 | 8.7 | -16 | .... | .... | .... | .... | .... | .... | .... | .... | .... | .... | .... | .... |
| **1997-98** | **San Jose** | **NHL** | 18 | 5 | 2 | 7 | 2 | 2 | 0 | 0 | 51 | 9.8 | -2 | .... | .... | .... | .... | .... | .... | .... | .... | .... | .... | .... | .... |
| | **Florida** | **NHL** | 46 | 12 | 11 | 23 | 14 | 3 | 2 | 0 | 114 | 10.5 | -1 | .... | .... | .... | .... | .... | .... | .... | .... | .... | .... | .... | .... |
| **1998-99** | **Florida** | **NHL** | 65 | 16 | 35 | 51 | 24 | 5 | 1 | 1 | 209 | 7.7 | 13 | 985 | 41.2 | 19:03 | .... | .... | .... | .... | .... | .... | .... | .... | .... |
| **99-2000** | **Florida** | **NHL** | 80 | 17 | 53 | 70 | 16 | 6 | 0 | 2 | 223 | 7.6 | 24 | 1616 | 42.9 | 19:27 | 4 | 0 | 1 | 1 | 0 | 0 | 0 | 0 | 16:06 |
| **2000-01** | **Florida** | **NHL** | 51 | 14 | 23 | 37 | 10 | 6 | 0 | 2 | 139 | 10.1 | -4 | 817 | 41.6 | 18:23 | .... | .... | .... | .... | .... | .... | .... | .... | .... |
| **2001-02** | **Florida** | **NHL** | 50 | 9 | 18 | 27 | 20 | 6 | 0 | 1 | 143 | 6.3 | -16 | 840 | 43.1 | 19:54 | .... | .... | .... | .... | .... | .... | .... | .... | .... |
| **2002-03** | **Florida** | **NHL** | 74 | 22 | 34 | 56 | 18 | 7 | 1 | 1 | 232 | 9.5 | -8 | 404 | 42.8 | 22:35 | .... | .... | .... | .... | .... | .... | .... | .... | .... |
| **2003-04** | **Florida** | **NHL** | 48 | 11 | 16 | 27 | 16 | 3 | 1 | 1 | 117 | 9.4 | -4 | 200 | 49.0 | 19:30 | .... | .... | .... | .... | .... | .... | .... | .... | .... |
| | **New Jersey** | **NHL** | 11 | 2 | 4 | 6 | 2 | 0 | 0 | 0 | 26 | 7.7 | 0 | 112 | 56.3 | 13:26 | 2 | 0 | 0 | 0 | 0 | 0 | 0 | 0 | 8:55 |
| 2004-05 | Lada Togliatti | Russia | 52 | 15 | 22 | 37 | 22 | .... | .... | .... | .... | .... | .... | .... | .... | .... | 10 | 3 | 3 | 6 | 6 | .... | .... | .... | .... |
| **2005-06** | **New Jersey** | **NHL** | 69 | 12 | 13 | 25 | 16 | 2 | 0 | 1 | 122 | 9.8 | 0 | 185 | 47.0 | 13:32 | 3 | 0 | 0 | 0 | 0 | 0 | 0 | 0 | 14:05 |
| | Russia | Olympics | 8 | 2 | 3 | 5 | 2 | .... | .... | .... | .... | .... | .... | .... | .... | .... | .... | .... | .... | .... | .... | .... | .... | .... | .... |
| **2006-07** | **NY Islanders** | **NHL** | 81 | 25 | 26 | 51 | 28 | 5 | 0 | 4 | 165 | 15.2 | 12 | 462 | 39.0 | 16:25 | 5 | 0 | 2 | 2 | 2 | 0 | 0 | 0 | 16:34 |
| **2007-08** | **Washington** | **NHL** | 81 | 16 | 38 | 54 | 18 | 2 | 0 | 2 | 219 | 7.3 | 28 | 442 | 45.9 | 17:35 | 7 | 0 | 3 | 3 | 2 | 0 | 0 | 0 | 17:58 |
| **2008-09** | **Washington** | **NHL** | 67 | 13 | 28 | 41 | 16 | 2 | 0 | 0 | 153 | 8.5 | -9 | 33 | 30.3 | 15:40 | 14 | 4 | 2 | 6 | 6 | 0 | 0 | 1 | 15:54 |
| | **NHL Totals** | | 897 | 198 | 339 | 537 | 248 | 54 | 5 | 19 | 2227 | 8.9 | | 6096 | 42.9 | 18:03 | 35 | 4 | 8 | 12 | 10 | 0 | 0 | 1 | 15:52 |

Played in NHL All-Star Game (2000)

Traded to **Florida** by **San Jose** with Florida's 5th round choice (previously acquired, Florida selected Jaroslav Spacek) in 1998 Entry Draft for Dave Lowry and Florida's 1st round choice (later traded to Tampa Bay – Tampa Bay selected Vincent Lecavalier) in 1998 Entry Draft, November 13, 1997. Traded to **New Jersey** by **Florida** for Christian Berglund and Victor Uchevatov, March 1, 2004. Signed as a free agent by **Togliatti** (Russia), July 11, 2004. Signed as a free agent by **NY Islanders**, September 13, 2006. Signed as a free agent by **Washington**, July 1, 2007. Signed as a free agent by **Ufa** (Rus-KHL), May 26, 2009.

## KOZLOV, Vyacheslav

(KAWZ-lahf, V'YTACH-ih-slav) **ATL.**

Left wing. Shoots left. 5'10", 190 lbs. Born, Voskresensk, USSR, May 3, 1972. Detroit's 2nd choice, 45th overall, in 1990 Entry Draft.

| Season | Club | League | GP | G | A | Pts | PIM | PP | SH | GW | S | % | +/- | TF | F% | Min | GP | G | A | Pts | PIM | PP | SH | GW | Min |
|---|---|---|---|---|---|---|---|---|---|---|---|---|---|---|---|---|---|---|---|---|---|---|---|---|---|
| 1987-88 | Voskresensk | USSR | 2 | 0 | 0 | 0 | 0 | .... | .... | .... | .... | .... | .... | .... | .... | .... | .... | .... | .... | .... | .... | .... | .... | .... | .... |
| 1988-89 | Voskresensk | USSR | 14 | 0 | 1 | 1 | 2 | .... | .... | .... | .... | .... | .... | .... | .... | .... | .... | .... | .... | .... | .... | .... | .... | .... | .... |
| 1989-90 | Voskresensk | USSR | 45 | 14 | 12 | 26 | 38 | .... | .... | .... | .... | .... | .... | .... | .... | .... | .... | .... | .... | .... | .... | .... | .... | .... | .... |
| 1990-91 | Voskresensk | USSR | 45 | 11 | 13 | 24 | 46 | .... | .... | .... | .... | .... | .... | .... | .... | .... | .... | .... | .... | .... | .... | .... | .... | .... | .... |
| **1991-92** | CSKA Moscow | CIS | 11 | 6 | 5 | 11 | 12 | .... | .... | .... | .... | .... | .... | .... | .... | .... | .... | .... | .... | .... | .... | .... | .... | .... | .... |
| | **Detroit** | **NHL** | 7 | 0 | 2 | 2 | 2 | 0 | 0 | 0 | 9 | 0.0 | -2 | .... | .... | .... | .... | .... | .... | .... | .... | .... | .... | .... | .... |
| **1992-93** | **Detroit** | **NHL** | 17 | 4 | 1 | 5 | 14 | 0 | 0 | 0 | 26 | 15.4 | -1 | .... | .... | .... | 4 | 0 | 2 | 2 | 2 | 0 | 0 | 0 | .... |
| | Adirondack | AHL | 45 | 23 | 36 | 59 | 54 | .... | .... | .... | .... | .... | .... | .... | .... | .... | 4 | 1 | 1 | 2 | 4 | .... | .... | .... | .... |
| **1993-94** | **Detroit** | **NHL** | 77 | 34 | 39 | 73 | 50 | 8 | 2 | 6 | 202 | 16.8 | 27 | .... | .... | .... | 7 | 2 | 5 | 7 | 12 | 0 | 0 | 0 | .... |
| | Adirondack | AHL | 3 | 0 | 1 | 1 | 15 | .... | .... | .... | .... | .... | .... | .... | .... | .... | .... | .... | .... | .... | .... | .... | .... | .... | .... |
| **1994-95** | CSKA Moscow | CIS | 10 | 3 | 4 | 7 | 14 | .... | .... | .... | .... | .... | .... | .... | .... | .... | .... | .... | .... | .... | .... | .... | .... | .... | .... |
| | **Detroit** | **NHL** | 46 | 13 | 20 | 33 | 45 | 5 | 0 | 3 | 97 | 13.4 | 12 | .... | .... | .... | 18 | 9 | 7 | 16 | 10 | 1 | 0 | 4 | .... |
| **1995-96** | **Detroit** | **NHL** | 82 | 36 | 37 | 73 | 70 | 9 | 0 | 7 | 237 | 15.2 | 33 | .... | .... | .... | 19 | 5 | 7 | 12 | 10 | 2 | 0 | 1 | .... |
| **1996-97♦** | **Detroit** | **NHL** | 75 | 23 | 22 | 45 | 46 | 3 | 0 | 6 | 211 | 10.9 | 21 | .... | .... | .... | 20 | 8 | 5 | 13 | 14 | 4 | 0 | 2 | .... |
| **1997-98♦** | **Detroit** | **NHL** | 80 | 25 | 27 | 52 | 46 | 6 | 0 | 1 | 221 | 11.3 | 14 | .... | .... | .... | 22 | 6 | 8 | 14 | 10 | 1 | 0 | 4 | .... |
| **1998-99** | **Detroit** | **NHL** | 79 | 29 | 29 | 58 | 45 | 6 | 1 | 4 | 209 | 13.9 | 10 | 38 | 36.8 | 16:02 | 10 | 6 | 1 | 7 | 4 | 3 | 0 | 0 | 14:44 |
| **99-2000** | **Detroit** | **NHL** | 72 | 18 | 18 | 36 | 28 | 4 | 0 | 3 | 165 | 10.9 | 11 | 28 | 35.7 | 15:30 | 8 | 2 | 1 | 3 | 12 | 1 | 0 | 1 | 12:20 |
| **2000-01** | **Detroit** | **NHL** | 72 | 20 | 18 | 38 | 30 | 4 | 0 | 5 | 187 | 10.7 | 9 | 51 | 47.1 | 14:43 | 6 | 4 | 1 | 5 | 2 | 2 | 0 | 0 | 16:27 |
| **2001-02** | **Buffalo** | **NHL** | 38 | 9 | 13 | 22 | 16 | 3 | 0 | 1 | 68 | 13.2 | 0 | 24 | 41.7 | 16:31 | .... | .... | .... | .... | .... | .... | .... | .... | .... |
| **2002-03** | **Atlanta** | **NHL** | 79 | 21 | 49 | 70 | 66 | 9 | 1 | 2 | 185 | 11.4 | -10 | 67 | 34.3 | 20:01 | .... | .... | .... | .... | .... | .... | .... | .... | .... |
| **2003-04** | **Atlanta** | **NHL** | 76 | 20 | 32 | 52 | 74 | 6 | 0 | 1 | 191 | 10.5 | -12 | 164 | 32.3 | 20:20 | .... | .... | .... | .... | .... | .... | .... | .... | .... |
| 2004-05 | Voskresensk | Russia | 38 | 12 | 18 | 30 | 69 | .... | .... | .... | .... | .... | .... | .... | .... | .... | .... | .... | .... | .... | .... | .... | .... | .... | .... |
| | Ak Bars Kazan | Russia | 8 | 2 | 4 | 6 | 0 | .... | .... | .... | .... | .... | .... | .... | .... | .... | 4 | 1 | 0 | 1 | 8 | .... | .... | .... | .... |
| **2005-06** | **Atlanta** | **NHL** | 82 | 25 | 46 | 71 | 33 | 8 | 0 | 1 | 206 | 12.1 | 14 | 317 | 39.8 | 17:47 | .... | .... | .... | .... | .... | .... | .... | .... | .... |
| **2006-07** | **Atlanta** | **NHL** | 81 | 28 | 52 | 80 | 36 | 8 | 0 | 8 | 190 | 14.7 | 9 | 326 | 46.9 | 20:29 | 4 | 0 | 0 | 0 | 6 | 0 | 0 | 0 | 17:33 |
| **2007-08** | **Atlanta** | **NHL** | 82 | 17 | 24 | 41 | 26 | 5 | 0 | 4 | 161 | 10.6 | -10 | 68 | 45.6 | 15:56 | .... | .... | .... | .... | .... | .... | .... | .... | .... |
| **2008-09** | **Atlanta** | **NHL** | 82 | 26 | 50 | 76 | 44 | 12 | 0 | 3 | 165 | 15.8 | -14 | 8 | 37.5 | 17:14 | .... | .... | .... | .... | .... | .... | .... | .... | .... |
| | **NHL Totals** | | 1127 | 348 | 479 | 827 | 671 | 96 | 4 | 55 | 2730 | 12.7 | | 1091 | 41.0 | 17:33 | 118 | 42 | 37 | 79 | 82 | 14 | 0 | 12 | 14:49 |

Traded to **Buffalo** by **Detroit** with Detroit's 1st round choice (later traded to Columbus – later traded to Atlanta – Atlanta selected Jim Slater) in 2002 Entry Draft for Dominik Hasek, July 1, 2001. • Missed majority of 2001-02 season recovering from Achilles tendon injury suffered in game vs. Columbus, December 31, 2001. Traded to **Atlanta** by **Buffalo** with Buffalo's 2nd round choice (later traded to Columbus – Columbus selected Joakim Lindstrom) in 2003 Entry Draft for Atlanta's 2nd round choice (later traded to Edmonton – Edmonton selected Jeff Deslauriers) in 2003 Entry Draft and Vancouver's 3rd round choice (previously acquired, Buffalo selected John Adams) in 2003 Entry Draft, June 22, 2002. Signed as a free agent by **Voskresensk** (Russia), September 15, 2004. Signed as a free agent by **Kazan** (Russia), February 17, 2005.

## KRAJICEK, Lukas

(KRIGH-ee-chehk, LOO-kahsh) **T.B.**

Defense. Shoots left. 6'2", 196 lbs. Born, Prostejov, Czech., March 11, 1983. Florida's 2nd choice, 24th overall, in 2001 Entry Draft.

| Season | Club | League | GP | G | A | Pts | PIM | PP | SH | GW | S | % | +/- | TF | F% | Min | GP | G | A | Pts | PIM | PP | SH | GW | Min |
|---|---|---|---|---|---|---|---|---|---|---|---|---|---|---|---|---|---|---|---|---|---|---|---|---|---|
| 1998-99 | HC ZPS Zlin Jr. | CzRep-Jr. | 48 | 8 | 18 | 26 | 40 | .... | .... | .... | .... | .... | .... | .... | .... | .... | .... | .... | .... | .... | .... | .... | .... | .... | .... |
| 99-2000 | Det. Compuware | NAHL | 53 | 5 | 22 | 27 | 61 | .... | .... | .... | .... | .... | .... | .... | .... | .... | 5 | 0 | 1 | 1 | 18 | .... | .... | .... | .... |
| 2000-01 | Peterborough | OHL | 61 | 8 | 27 | 35 | 53 | .... | .... | .... | .... | .... | .... | .... | .... | .... | 7 | 0 | 5 | 5 | 0 | .... | .... | .... | .... |
| **2001-02** | **Florida** | **NHL** | 5 | 0 | 0 | 0 | 0 | 0 | 0 | 0 | 3 | 0.0 | 0 | 0 | 0.0 | 13:23 | .... | .... | .... | .... | .... | .... | .... | .... | .... |
| | Peterborough | OHL | 55 | 10 | 32 | 42 | 56 | .... | .... | .... | .... | .... | .... | .... | .... | .... | 6 | 0 | 5 | 5 | 6 | .... | .... | .... | .... |
| 2002-03 | Peterborough | OHL | 52 | 11 | 42 | 53 | 42 | .... | .... | .... | .... | .... | .... | .... | .... | .... | 7 | 0 | 3 | 3 | 0 | .... | .... | .... | .... |
| | San Antonio | AHL | 3 | 0 | 1 | 1 | 0 | .... | .... | .... | .... | .... | .... | .... | .... | .... | 3 | 0 | 0 | 0 | 0 | .... | .... | .... | .... |
| **2003-04** | **Florida** | **NHL** | 18 | 1 | 6 | 7 | 12 | 1 | 0 | 0 | 16 | 6.3 | -2 | 0 | 0.0 | 13:32 | .... | .... | .... | .... | .... | .... | .... | .... | .... |
| | San Antonio | AHL | 54 | 5 | 12 | 17 | 24 | .... | .... | .... | .... | .... | .... | .... | .... | .... | .... | .... | .... | .... | .... | .... | .... | .... | .... |
| 2004-05 | San Antonio | AHL | 78 | 2 | 22 | 24 | 57 | .... | .... | .... | .... | .... | .... | .... | .... | .... | .... | .... | .... | .... | .... | .... | .... | .... | .... |
| **2005-06** | **Florida** | **NHL** | 67 | 2 | 14 | 16 | 50 | 2 | 0 | 0 | 89 | 2.2 | 1 | 0 | 0.0 | 18:30 | .... | .... | .... | .... | .... | .... | .... | .... | .... |
| **2006-07** | **Vancouver** | **NHL** | 78 | 3 | 13 | 16 | 64 | 1 | 0 | 2 | 105 | 2.9 | -4 | 0 | 0.0 | 18:31 | 12 | 0 | 2 | 2 | 12 | 0 | 0 | 0 | 18:50 |
| **2007-08** | **Vancouver** | **NHL** | 39 | 2 | 9 | 11 | 36 | 1 | 0 | 0 | 28 | 7.1 | -3 | 0 | 0.0 | 18:10 | .... | .... | .... | .... | .... | .... | .... | .... | .... |
| **2008-09** | **Tampa Bay** | **NHL** | 71 | 2 | 17 | 19 | 48 | 0 | 0 | 0 | 66 | 3.0 | -8 | 0 | 0.0 | 19:37 | .... | .... | .... | .... | .... | .... | .... | .... | .... |
| | **NHL Totals** | | 278 | 10 | 59 | 69 | 210 | 5 | 0 | 2 | 307 | 3.3 | | 0 | 0.0 | 18:20 | 12 | 0 | 2 | 2 | 12 | 0 | 0 | 0 | 18:50 |

OHL All-Rookie Team (2001) • OHL First All-Star Team (2003) • Canadian Major Junior Second All-Star Team (2003)

Traded to **Vancouver** by **Florida** with Roberto Luongo and Florida's 6th round choice (Sergei Shirokov) in 2006 Entry Draft for Todd Bertuzzi, Bryan Allen and Alex Auld, June 23, 2006. Traded to **Tampa Bay** by **Vancouver** with Juraj Simek for Shane O'Brien and Michel Ouellet, October 6, 2008.

## KREJCI, David

(KRAY-chee, DAY-vihd) **BOS.**

Center. Shoots right. 6', 177 lbs. Born, Sternberk, Czech., April 28, 1986. Boston's 1st choice, 63rd overall, in 2004 Entry Draft.

| | | | Regular Season | | | | | | | | | | | | | | Playoffs | | | | | | | | |
|---|---|---|---|---|---|---|---|---|---|---|---|---|---|---|---|---|---|---|---|---|---|---|---|---|---|
| Season | Club | League | GP | G | A | Pts | PIM | PP | SH | GW | S | % | +/- | TF | F% | Min | GP | G | A | Pts | PIM | PP | SH | GW | Min |
| 2000-01 | HC Olomouc U17 | CzR-U17 | 26 | 2 | 6 | 8 | 4 | .... | .... | .... | .... | .... | .... | .... | .... | .... | 3 | 1 | 1 | 2 | 0 | .... | .... | .... | .... |
| 2001-02 | HC Trinec U17 | CzR-U17 | 48 | 32 | 27 | 59 | 30 | .... | .... | .... | .... | .... | .... | .... | .... | .... | 6 | 2 | 4 | 6 | 2 | .... | .... | .... | .... |
| 2002-03 | HC Trinec U17 | CzR-U17 | 22 | 12 | 24 | 36 | 42 | .... | .... | .... | .... | .... | .... | .... | .... | .... | .... | .... | .... | .... | .... | .... | .... | .... | .... |
| | HC Trinec Jr. | CzRep-Jr. | 12 | 4 | 5 | 9 | 2 | .... | .... | .... | .... | .... | .... | .... | .... | .... | 12 | 5 | 5 | 10 | 8 | .... | .... | .... | .... |
| 2003-04 | HC Kladno Jr. | CzRep-Jr. | 50 | 23 | 37 | 60 | 37 | .... | .... | .... | .... | .... | .... | .... | .... | .... | 7 | 3 | 6 | 9 | 4 | .... | .... | .... | .... |
| 2004-05 | Gatineau | QMJHL | 62 | 22 | 41 | 63 | 31 | .... | .... | .... | .... | .... | .... | .... | .... | .... | 10 | 2 | 7 | 9 | 10 | .... | .... | .... | .... |
| 2005-06 | Gatineau | QMJHL | 55 | 27 | 54 | 81 | 54 | .... | .... | .... | .... | .... | .... | .... | .... | .... | 17 | 10 | 22 | 32 | 24 | .... | .... | .... | .... |
| **2006-07** | **Boston** | **NHL** | **6** | **0** | **0** | **0** | **2** | **0** | **0** | **0** | **2** | **0.0** | **–3** | **14** | **28.6** | **4:24** | .... | .... | .... | .... | .... | .... | .... | .... | .... |
| | Providence Bruins | AHL | 69 | 31 | 43 | 74 | 47 | .... | .... | .... | .... | .... | .... | .... | .... | .... | 13 | 3 | 13 | 16 | 22 | .... | .... | .... | .... |
| **2007-08** | **Boston** | **NHL** | **56** | **6** | **21** | **27** | **20** | **1** | **1** | **0** | **73** | **8.2** | **–3** | **635** | **48.2** | **14:55** | **7** | **1** | **4** | **5** | **2** | **1** | **0** | **0** | **19:09** |
| | Providence Bruins | AHL | 25 | 7 | 21 | 28 | 19 | .... | .... | .... | .... | .... | .... | .... | .... | .... | .... | .... | .... | .... | .... | .... | .... | .... | .... |
| **2008-09** | **Boston** | **NHL** | **82** | **22** | **51** | **73** | **26** | **5** | **2** | **6** | **146** | **15.1** | **37** | **1048** | **50.3** | **16:52** | **11** | **2** | **6** | **8** | **2** | **0** | **0** | **1** | **17:18** |
| | **NHL Totals** | | **144** | **28** | **72** | **100** | **48** | **6** | **3** | **6** | **221** | **12.7** | | **1697** | **49.3** | **15:35** | **18** | **3** | **10** | **13** | **4** | **1** | **0** | **1** | **18:01** |

## KREPS, Kamil

(KREHPS, KA-mihl) **FLA.**

Center. Shoots right. 6'2", 194 lbs. Born, Litomerice, Czech., November 18, 1984. Florida's 3rd choice, 38th overall, in 2003 Entry Draft.

| Season | Club | League | GP | G | A | Pts | PIM | PP | SH | GW | S | % | +/- | TF | F% | Min | GP | G | A | Pts | PIM | PP | SH | GW | Min |
|---|---|---|---|---|---|---|---|---|---|---|---|---|---|---|---|---|---|---|---|---|---|---|---|---|---|
| 99-2000 | Litvinov Jr. | CzRep-Jr. | 48 | 18 | 16 | 34 | 10 | .... | .... | .... | .... | .... | .... | .... | .... | .... | .... | .... | .... | .... | .... | .... | .... | .... | .... |
| 2000-01 | Litvinov Jr. | CzRep-Jr. | 47 | 16 | 23 | 39 | 6 | .... | .... | .... | .... | .... | .... | .... | .... | .... | 6 | 2 | 6 | 8 | 10 | .... | .... | .... | .... |
| 2001-02 | Brampton | OHL | 68 | 19 | 24 | 43 | 14 | .... | .... | .... | .... | .... | .... | .... | .... | .... | .... | .... | .... | .... | .... | .... | .... | .... | .... |
| 2002-03 | Brampton | OHL | 53 | 19 | 42 | 61 | 12 | .... | .... | .... | .... | .... | .... | .... | .... | .... | 11 | 3 | 5 | 8 | 4 | .... | .... | .... | .... |
| 2003-04 | Brampton | OHL | 57 | 19 | 27 | 46 | 19 | .... | .... | .... | .... | .... | .... | .... | .... | .... | 12 | 7 | 8 | 15 | 2 | .... | .... | .... | .... |
| 2004-05 | San Antonio | AHL | 58 | 5 | 6 | 11 | 11 | .... | .... | .... | .... | .... | .... | .... | .... | .... | .... | .... | .... | .... | .... | .... | .... | .... | .... |
| | Texas Wildcatters | ECHL | 12 | 5 | 6 | 11 | 6 | .... | .... | .... | .... | .... | .... | .... | .... | .... | .... | .... | .... | .... | .... | .... | .... | .... | .... |
| 2005-06 | Rochester | AHL | 61 | 13 | 19 | 32 | 20 | .... | .... | .... | .... | .... | .... | .... | .... | .... | .... | .... | .... | .... | .... | .... | .... | .... | .... |
| **2006-07** | **Florida** | **NHL** | **14** | **1** | **1** | **2** | **6** | **0** | **0** | **0** | **20** | **5.0** | **–1** | **113** | **48.7** | **11:13** | .... | .... | .... | .... | .... | .... | .... | .... | .... |
| | Rochester | AHL | 50 | 14 | 21 | 35 | 16 | .... | .... | .... | .... | .... | .... | .... | .... | .... | 6 | 1 | 0 | 1 | 0 | .... | .... | .... | .... |
| **2007-08** | **Florida** | **NHL** | **76** | **8** | **17** | **25** | **29** | **1** | **0** | **2** | **99** | **8.1** | **10** | **763** | **53.9** | **12:59** | .... | .... | .... | .... | .... | .... | .... | .... | .... |
| | Rochester | AHL | 6 | 1 | 5 | 6 | 6 | .... | .... | .... | .... | .... | .... | .... | .... | .... | .... | .... | .... | .... | .... | .... | .... | .... | .... |
| **2008-09** | **Florida** | **NHL** | **66** | **4** | **15** | **19** | **18** | **0** | **1** | **1** | **77** | **5.2** | **2** | **870** | **50.5** | **13:58** | .... | .... | .... | .... | .... | .... | .... | .... | .... |
| | **NHL Totals** | | **156** | **13** | **33** | **46** | **53** | **1** | **1** | **3** | **196** | **6.6** | | **1746** | **51.8** | **13:15** | .... | .... | .... | .... | .... | .... | .... | .... | .... |

## KROG, Jason

(KROHG, JAY-suhn) **ATL.**

Center. Shoots right. 5'11", 185 lbs. Born, Fernie, B.C., October 9, 1975.

| Season | Club | League | GP | G | A | Pts | PIM | PP | SH | GW | S | % | +/- | TF | F% | Min | GP | G | A | Pts | PIM | PP | SH | GW | Min |
|---|---|---|---|---|---|---|---|---|---|---|---|---|---|---|---|---|---|---|---|---|---|---|---|---|---|
| 1992-93 | Chilliwack Chiefs | BCJHL | 52 | 30 | 27 | 57 | 52 | .... | .... | .... | .... | .... | .... | .... | .... | .... | .... | .... | .... | .... | .... | .... | .... | .... | .... |
| 1993-94 | Chilliwack Chiefs | BCJHL | 42 | 19 | 36 | 55 | 20 | .... | .... | .... | .... | .... | .... | .... | .... | .... | .... | .... | .... | .... | .... | .... | .... | .... | .... |
| 1994-95 | Chilliwack Chiefs | BCJHL | 60 | 47 | 81 | 128 | 36 | .... | .... | .... | .... | .... | .... | .... | .... | .... | .... | .... | .... | .... | .... | .... | .... | .... | .... |
| 1995-96 | New Hampshire | H-East | 34 | 4 | 16 | 20 | 20 | .... | .... | .... | .... | .... | .... | .... | .... | .... | .... | .... | .... | .... | .... | .... | .... | .... | .... |
| 1996-97 | New Hampshire | H-East | 39 | 23 | *44 | *67 | 28 | .... | .... | .... | .... | .... | .... | .... | .... | .... | .... | .... | .... | .... | .... | .... | .... | .... | .... |
| 1997-98 | New Hampshire | H-East | 38 | *33 | 33 | 66 | 44 | .... | .... | .... | .... | .... | .... | .... | .... | .... | .... | .... | .... | .... | .... | .... | .... | .... | .... |
| 1998-99 | New Hampshire | H-East | 41 | *34 | *51 | *85 | 38 | .... | .... | .... | .... | .... | .... | .... | .... | .... | .... | .... | .... | .... | .... | .... | .... | .... | .... |
| **99-2000** | **NY Islanders** | **NHL** | **17** | **2** | **4** | **6** | **6** | **1** | **0** | **0** | **22** | **9.1** | **–1** | **81** | **53.1** | **10:03** | .... | .... | .... | .... | .... | .... | .... | .... | .... |
| | Lowell | AHL | 45 | 6 | 21 | 27 | 22 | .... | .... | .... | .... | .... | .... | .... | .... | .... | .... | .... | .... | .... | .... | .... | .... | .... | .... |
| | Providence Bruins | AHL | 11 | 9 | 8 | 17 | 4 | .... | .... | .... | .... | .... | .... | .... | .... | .... | 6 | 2 | 2 | 4 | 0 | .... | .... | .... | .... |
| **2000-01** | **NY Islanders** | **NHL** | **9** | **0** | **3** | **3** | **0** | **0** | **0** | **0** | **7** | **0.0** | **4** | **60** | **48.3** | **10:32** | .... | .... | .... | .... | .... | .... | .... | .... | .... |
| | Lowell | AHL | 26 | 11 | 16 | 27 | 6 | .... | .... | .... | .... | .... | .... | .... | .... | .... | .... | .... | .... | .... | .... | .... | .... | .... | .... |
| | Springfield | AHL | 24 | 7 | 23 | 30 | 4 | .... | .... | .... | .... | .... | .... | .... | .... | .... | .... | .... | .... | .... | .... | .... | .... | .... | .... |
| **2001-02** | **NY Islanders** | **NHL** | **2** | **0** | **0** | **0** | **0** | **0** | **0** | **0** | **0** | **0.0** | **0** | **13** | **46.2** | **6:40** | .... | .... | .... | .... | .... | .... | .... | .... | .... |
| | Bridgeport | AHL | 64 | 26 | 36 | 62 | 13 | .... | .... | .... | .... | .... | .... | .... | .... | .... | 20 | 10 | 13 | 23 | 8 | .... | .... | .... | .... |
| **2002-03** | **Anaheim** | **NHL** | **67** | **10** | **15** | **25** | **12** | **0** | **1** | **1** | **92** | **10.9** | **1** | **634** | **60.4** | **13:47** | **21** | **3** | **1** | **4** | **4** | **0** | **0** | **0** | **12:10** |
| | Cincinnati | AHL | 9 | 3 | 4 | 7 | 6 | .... | .... | .... | .... | .... | .... | .... | .... | .... | .... | .... | .... | .... | .... | .... | .... | .... | .... |
| **2003-04** | **Anaheim** | **NHL** | **80** | **6** | **12** | **18** | **16** | **1** | **0** | **1** | **111** | **5.4** | **–4** | **769** | **58.5** | **11:58** | .... | .... | .... | .... | .... | .... | .... | .... | .... |
| 2004-05 | EC Villacher SV | Austria | 48 | 27 | 33 | 60 | 38 | .... | .... | .... | .... | .... | .... | .... | .... | .... | 3 | 0 | 1 | 1 | 4 | .... | .... | .... | .... |
| 2005-06 | Geneve | Swiss | 29 | 15 | 14 | 29 | 32 | .... | .... | .... | .... | .... | .... | .... | .... | .... | .... | .... | .... | .... | .... | .... | .... | .... | .... |
| | Frolunda | Sweden | 7 | 5 | 1 | 6 | 6 | .... | .... | .... | .... | .... | .... | .... | .... | .... | 17 | 5 | 3 | 8 | 10 | .... | .... | .... | .... |
| **2006-07** | **Atlanta** | **NHL** | **14** | **1** | **3** | **4** | **6** | **0** | **0** | **0** | **14** | **7.1** | **3** | **165** | **55.2** | **13:58** | .... | .... | .... | .... | .... | .... | .... | .... | .... |
| | Chicago Wolves | AHL | 44 | 26 | 54 | 80 | 20 | .... | .... | .... | .... | .... | .... | .... | .... | .... | 15 | 5 | 14 | 19 | 17 | .... | .... | .... | .... |
| | **NY Rangers** | **NHL** | **9** | **2** | **0** | **2** | **4** | **0** | **0** | **1** | **8** | **25.0** | **2** | **66** | **56.1** | **9:58** | .... | .... | .... | .... | .... | .... | .... | .... | .... |
| 2007-08 | Chicago Wolves | AHL | 80 | *39 | *73 | *112 | 30 | .... | .... | .... | .... | .... | .... | .... | .... | .... | 24 | *12 | *26 | *38 | 2 | .... | .... | .... | .... |
| **2008-09** | **Vancouver** | **NHL** | **4** | **1** | **0** | **1** | **2** | **1** | **0** | **0** | **5** | **20.0** | **0** | **24** | **58.3** | **10:14** | .... | .... | .... | .... | .... | .... | .... | .... | .... |
| | Manitoba Moose | AHL | 74 | 30 | 56 | 86 | 30 | .... | .... | .... | .... | .... | .... | .... | .... | .... | 22 | 8 | 15 | 23 | 0 | .... | .... | .... | .... |
| | **NHL Totals** | | **202** | **22** | **37** | **59** | **46** | **3** | **1** | **3** | **259** | **8.5** | | **1812** | **58.1** | **12:19** | **21** | **3** | **1** | **4** | **4** | **0** | **0** | **0** | **12:10** |

Hockey East First All-Star Team (1997, 1998, 1999) • NCAA East Second All-American Team (1997) • Hockey East Player of the Year (1999) • NCAA East First All-American Team (1999) • NCAA Championship All-Tournament Team (1999) • Hobey Baker Memorial Award (Top U.S. Collegiate Player) (1999) • AHL First All-Star Team (2008) • Willie Marshall Award (AHL – Top Goal-scorer) (2008) • John B. Sollenberger Trophy (AHL – Leading Scorer) (2008) • Les Cunningham Award (AHL – MVP) (2008) • AHL Second All-Star Team (2009)

Signed as a free agent by **NY Islanders**, May 14, 1999. • Loaned to **Providence** (AHL) by **NY Islanders**, March 1, 2000. Signed as a free agent by **Anaheim**, July 17, 2002. Signed as a free agent by **Villacher** (Austria), August 24, 2004. Signed as a free agent by **Geneve** (Swiss), May 19, 2005. Signed as a free agent by **Frolunda** (Sweden), January 31, 2006. Signed as a free agent by **Atlanta**, July 4, 2006. Claimed on waivers by **NY Rangers** from **Atlanta**, January 12, 2007. Claimed on waivers by **Atlanta** from **NY Rangers**, February 27, 2007. Signed as a free agent by **Vancouver**, July 14, 2008. Signed as a free agent by **Atlanta**, July 6, 2009.

## KRONWALL, Niklas

(KRAWN-wahl, NIHK-luhs) **DET.**

Defense. Shoots left. 6', 189 lbs. Born, Stockholm, Sweden, January 12, 1981. Detroit's 1st choice, 29th overall, in 2000 Entry Draft.

| Season | Club | League | GP | G | A | Pts | PIM | PP | SH | GW | S | % | +/- | TF | F% | Min | GP | G | A | Pts | PIM | PP | SH | GW | Min |
|---|---|---|---|---|---|---|---|---|---|---|---|---|---|---|---|---|---|---|---|---|---|---|---|---|---|
| 1996-97 | Djurgarden Jr. | Swe-Jr. | 1 | 0 | 0 | 0 | 0 | .... | .... | .... | .... | .... | .... | .... | .... | .... | .... | .... | .... | .... | .... | .... | .... | .... | .... |
| 1997-98 | Djurgarden Jr. | Swe-Jr. | 27 | 4 | 3 | 7 | 71 | .... | .... | .... | .... | .... | .... | .... | .... | .... | 2 | 0 | 0 | 0 | 2 | .... | .... | .... | .... |
| 1998-99 | Huddinge IK | Sweden-2 | 14 | 0 | 1 | 1 | 10 | .... | .... | .... | .... | .... | .... | .... | .... | .... | .... | .... | .... | .... | .... | .... | .... | .... | .... |
| | Huddinge IK Jr. | Swe-Jr. | 2 | 0 | 0 | 0 | 6 | .... | .... | .... | .... | .... | .... | .... | .... | .... | .... | .... | .... | .... | .... | .... | .... | .... | .... |
| 99-2000 | Djurgarden | Sweden | 37 | 1 | 4 | 5 | 16 | .... | .... | .... | .... | .... | .... | .... | .... | .... | 8 | 0 | 0 | 0 | 8 | .... | .... | .... | .... |
| 2000-01 | Djurgarden | Sweden | 31 | 1 | 9 | 10 | 32 | .... | .... | .... | .... | .... | .... | .... | .... | .... | 15 | 0 | 1 | 1 | 8 | .... | .... | .... | .... |
| 2001-02 | Djurgarden | Sweden | 48 | 5 | 7 | 12 | 34 | .... | .... | .... | .... | .... | .... | .... | .... | .... | 5 | 0 | 0 | 0 | 0 | .... | .... | .... | .... |
| 2002-03 | Djurgarden | Sweden | 50 | 5 | 13 | 18 | 46 | .... | .... | .... | .... | .... | .... | .... | .... | .... | 12 | 3 | 2 | 5 | 18 | .... | .... | .... | .... |
| **2003-04** | **Detroit** | **NHL** | **20** | **1** | **4** | **5** | **16** | **0** | **0** | **1** | **18** | **5.6** | **5** | **0** | **0.0** | **13:51** | .... | .... | .... | .... | .... | .... | .... | .... | .... |
| | Grand Rapids | AHL | 25 | 2 | 11 | 13 | 20 | .... | .... | .... | .... | .... | .... | .... | .... | .... | .... | .... | .... | .... | .... | .... | .... | .... | .... |
| 2004-05 | Grand Rapids | AHL | 76 | 13 | 40 | 53 | 53 | .... | .... | .... | .... | .... | .... | .... | .... | .... | .... | .... | .... | .... | .... | .... | .... | .... | .... |
| **2005-06** | **Detroit** | **NHL** | **27** | **1** | **8** | **9** | **28** | **1** | **0** | **0** | **28** | **3.6** | **11** | **0** | **0.0** | **20:31** | **6** | **0** | **3** | **3** | **2** | **0** | **0** | **0** | **22:43** |
| | Grand Rapids | AHL | 1 | 0 | 0 | 0 | 0 | .... | .... | .... | .... | .... | .... | .... | .... | .... | .... | .... | .... | .... | .... | .... | .... | .... | .... |
| | Sweden | Olympics | 2 | 1 | 1 | 2 | 8 | .... | .... | .... | .... | .... | .... | .... | .... | .... | .... | .... | .... | .... | .... | .... | .... | .... | .... |
| **2006-07** | **Detroit** | **NHL** | **68** | **1** | **21** | **22** | **54** | **1** | **0** | **0** | **104** | **1.0** | **0** | **0** | **0.0** | **20:39** | .... | .... | .... | .... | .... | .... | .... | .... | .... |
| **2007-08** ♦ | **Detroit** | **NHL** | **65** | **7** | **28** | **35** | **44** | **0** | **0** | **0** | **108** | **6.5** | **25** | **0** | **0.0** | **21:06** | **22** | **0** | **15** | **15** | **18** | **0** | **0** | **0** | **23:20** |
| **2008-09** | **Detroit** | **NHL** | **80** | **6** | **45** | **51** | **50** | **4** | **0** | **1** | **121** | **5.0** | **2** | **1** | **100.0** | **22:54** | **23** | **2** | **7** | **9** | **33** | **2** | **0** | **0** | **23:24** |
| | **NHL Totals** | | **260** | **16** | **106** | **122** | **192** | **6** | **0** | **2** | **379** | **4.2** | | **1** | **100.0** | **20:55** | **51** | **2** | **25** | **27** | **53** | **2** | **0** | **0** | **23:17** |

AHL First All-Star Team (2005) • Eddie Shore Award (AHL – Outstanding Defenseman) (2005)

• Missed majority of 2005-06 season recovering from knee surgery.

## KRONWALL, Staffan

(KRAWN-wahl, STAH-fuhn) **CGY.**

Defense. Shoots left. 6'4", 209 lbs. Born, Jarfalla, Sweden, September 10, 1982. Toronto's 9th choice, 285th overall, in 2002 Entry Draft.

| Season | Club | League | GP | G | A | Pts | PIM | PP | SH | GW | S | % | +/- | TF | F% | Min | GP | G | A | Pts | PIM | PP | SH | GW | Min |
|---|---|---|---|---|---|---|---|---|---|---|---|---|---|---|---|---|---|---|---|---|---|---|---|---|---|
| 99-2000 | Huddinge IK Jr. | Swe-Jr. | 34 | 2 | 0 | 2 | 38 | .... | .... | .... | .... | .... | .... | .... | .... | .... | .... | .... | .... | .... | .... | .... | .... | .... | .... |
| | Huddinge IK U18 | Swe-U18 | 7 | 0 | 3 | 3 | 0 | .... | .... | .... | .... | .... | .... | .... | .... | .... | .... | .... | .... | .... | .... | .... | .... | .... | .... |
| 2000-01 | Huddinge IK Jr. | Swe-Jr. | 23 | 6 | 1 | 7 | 16 | .... | .... | .... | .... | .... | .... | .... | .... | .... | .... | .... | .... | .... | .... | .... | .... | .... | .... |
| | Huddinge IK | Sweden-3 | 1 | 0 | 0 | 0 | 0 | .... | .... | .... | .... | .... | .... | .... | .... | .... | .... | .... | .... | .... | .... | .... | .... | .... | .... |
| 2001-02 | Huddinge IK | Sweden-2 | 42 | 4 | 7 | 11 | 30 | .... | .... | .... | .... | .... | .... | .... | .... | .... | .... | .... | .... | .... | .... | .... | .... | .... | .... |
| | Huddinge IK Jr. | Swe-Jr. | 1 | 0 | 0 | 0 | 0 | .... | .... | .... | .... | .... | .... | .... | .... | .... | 4 | 2 | 1 | 3 | 27 | .... | .... | .... | .... |
| 2002-03 | Djurgarden | Sweden | 48 | 4 | 6 | 10 | 65 | .... | .... | .... | .... | .... | .... | .... | .... | .... | 12 | 1 | 1 | 2 | 8 | .... | .... | .... | .... |
| 2003-04 | Djurgarden | Sweden | 44 | 1 | 5 | 6 | 54 | .... | .... | .... | .... | .... | .... | .... | .... | .... | 4 | 0 | 1 | 1 | 2 | .... | .... | .... | .... |

| Season | Club | League | Regular Season | | | | | | | | | | | | | | Playoffs | | | | | | | | |
|---|---|---|---|---|---|---|---|---|---|---|---|---|---|---|---|---|---|---|---|---|---|---|---|---|---|
| | | | GP | G | A | Pts | PIM | PP | SH | GW | S | % | +/- | TF | F% | Min | GP | G | A | Pts | PIM | PP | SH | GW | Min |
| 2004-05 | Brynas IF Gavle | Sweden | 3 | 0 | 1 | 1 | 4 | .... | .... | .... | .... | .... | .... | .... | .... | .... | .... | .... | .... | .... | .... | .... | .... | .... | .... |
| | Djurgarden Jr. | Swe-Jr. | 5 | 2 | 4 | 6 | 0 | .... | .... | .... | .... | .... | .... | .... | .... | .... | .... | .... | .... | .... | .... | .... | .... | .... | .... |
| | Djurgarden | Sweden | 35 | 1 | 4 | 5 | 43 | .... | .... | .... | .... | .... | .... | .... | .... | .... | 12 | 2 | 0 | 2 | 10 | .... | .... | .... | .... |
| **2005-06** | **Toronto** | **NHL** | **34** | **0** | **1** | **1** | **14** | **0** | **0** | **0** | **18** | **0.0** | **–3** | **0** | **0.0** | **12:57** | .... | .... | .... | .... | .... | .... | .... | .... | .... |
| | Toronto Marlies | AHL | 16 | 1 | 10 | 11 | 12 | .... | .... | .... | .... | .... | .... | .... | .... | .... | 4 | 0 | 2 | 2 | 2 | .... | .... | .... | .... |
| 2006-07 | Toronto Marlies | AHL | 47 | 3 | 14 | 17 | 32 | .... | .... | .... | .... | .... | .... | .... | .... | .... | .... | .... | .... | .... | .... | .... | .... | .... | .... |
| **2007-08** | **Toronto** | **NHL** | **18** | **0** | **0** | **0** | **7** | **0** | **0** | **0** | **9** | **0.0** | **–2** | **0** | **0.0** | **11:07** | .... | .... | .... | .... | .... | .... | .... | .... | .... |
| | Toronto Marlies | AHL | 26 | 3 | 7 | 10 | 14 | .... | .... | .... | .... | .... | .... | .... | .... | .... | 19 | 1 | 1 | 2 | 11 | .... | .... | .... | .... |
| **2008-09** | Toronto Marlies | AHL | 42 | 7 | 18 | 25 | 46 | .... | .... | .... | .... | .... | .... | .... | .... | .... | .... | .... | .... | .... | .... | .... | .... | .... | .... |
| | **Washington** | **NHL** | **3** | **0** | **0** | **0** | **0** | **0** | **0** | **0** | **4** | **0.0** | **–1** | **0** | **0.0** | **13:13** | .... | .... | .... | .... | .... | .... | .... | .... | .... |
| | Hershey Bears | AHL | 17 | 2 | 7 | 9 | 13 | .... | .... | .... | .... | .... | .... | .... | .... | .... | 21 | 3 | 9 | 12 | 6 | .... | .... | .... | .... |
| | **NHL Totals** | | **55** | **0** | **1** | **1** | **21** | **0** | **0** | **0** | **31** | **0.0** | | **0** | **0.0** | **12:22** | .... | .... | .... | .... | .... | .... | .... | .... | .... |

Claimed on waivers by **Washington** from **Toronto**, February 6, 2009. Signed as a free agent by **Calgary**, July 14, 2009.

## KUBA, Filip

(KOO-bah, FIHL-ihp) **OTT.**

Defense. Shoots left. 6'4", 226 lbs. Born, Ostrava, Czech., December 29, 1976. Florida's 8th choice, 192nd overall, in 1995 Entry Draft.

| Season | Club | League | GP | G | A | Pts | PIM | PP | SH | GW | S | % | +/- | TF | F% | Min | GP | G | A | Pts | PIM | PP | SH | GW | Min |
|---|---|---|---|---|---|---|---|---|---|---|---|---|---|---|---|---|---|---|---|---|---|---|---|---|---|
| 1994-95 | HC Vitkovice Jr. | CzRep-Jr. | 35 | 10 | 15 | 25 | .... | .... | .... | .... | .... | .... | .... | .... | .... | .... | .... | .... | .... | .... | .... | .... | .... | .... | .... |
| | HC Vitkovice | CzRep | .... | .... | .... | .... | .... | .... | .... | .... | .... | .... | .... | .... | .... | .... | 4 | 0 | 0 | 0 | 2 | .... | .... | .... | .... |
| 1995-96 | HC Vitkovice | CzRep | 19 | 0 | 1 | 1 | .... | .... | .... | .... | .... | .... | .... | .... | .... | .... | .... | .... | .... | .... | .... | .... | .... | .... | .... |
| 1996-97 | Carolina | AHL | 51 | 0 | 12 | 12 | 38 | .... | .... | .... | .... | .... | .... | .... | .... | .... | .... | .... | .... | .... | .... | .... | .... | .... | .... |
| 1997-98 | New Haven | AHL | 77 | 4 | 13 | 17 | 58 | .... | .... | .... | .... | .... | .... | .... | .... | .... | 3 | 1 | 1 | 2 | 0 | .... | .... | .... | .... |
| **1998-99** | **Florida** | **NHL** | **5** | **0** | **1** | **1** | **0** | **0** | **0** | **0** | **5** | **0.0** | **2** | **0** | **0.0** | **22:29** | .... | .... | .... | .... | .... | .... | .... | .... | .... |
| | Kentucky | AHL | 45 | 2 | 8 | 10 | 33 | .... | .... | .... | .... | .... | .... | .... | .... | .... | 10 | 0 | 1 | 1 | 4 | .... | .... | .... | .... |
| **99-2000** | **Florida** | **NHL** | **13** | **1** | **5** | **6** | **2** | **1** | **0** | **1** | **16** | **6.3** | **–3** | **0** | **0.0** | **13:52** | .... | .... | .... | .... | .... | .... | .... | .... | .... |
| | Houston Aeros | IHL | 27 | 3 | 6 | 9 | 13 | .... | .... | .... | .... | .... | .... | .... | .... | .... | 11 | 1 | 2 | 3 | 4 | .... | .... | .... | .... |
| **2000-01** | **Minnesota** | **NHL** | **75** | **9** | **21** | **30** | **28** | **4** | **0** | **4** | **141** | **6.4** | **–6** | **1** | **0.0** | **24:16** | .... | .... | .... | .... | .... | .... | .... | .... | .... |
| **2001-02** | **Minnesota** | **NHL** | **62** | **5** | **19** | **24** | **32** | **3** | **0** | **1** | **101** | **5.0** | **–6** | **0** | **0.0** | **25:30** | .... | .... | .... | .... | .... | .... | .... | .... | .... |
| **2002-03** | **Minnesota** | **NHL** | **78** | **8** | **21** | **29** | **29** | **4** | **2** | **1** | **129** | **6.2** | **0** | **1** | **0.0** | **23:56** | **18** | **3** | **5** | **8** | **24** | **3** | **0** | **0** | **26:46** |
| **2003-04** | **Minnesota** | **NHL** | **77** | **5** | **19** | **24** | **28** | **2** | **1** | **2** | **114** | **4.4** | **–7** | **2** | **0.0** | **24:06** | .... | .... | .... | .... | .... | .... | .... | .... | .... |
| 2004-05 | | | DID NOT PLAY | | | | | | | | | | | | | | | | | | | | | | |
| **2005-06** | **Minnesota** | **NHL** | **65** | **6** | **19** | **25** | **44** | **1** | **1** | **1** | **69** | **8.7** | **0** | **2** | **0.0** | **21:46** | .... | .... | .... | .... | .... | .... | .... | .... | .... |
| | Czech Republic | Olympics | 8 | 1 | 0 | 1 | 0 | .... | .... | .... | .... | .... | .... | .... | .... | .... | .... | .... | .... | .... | .... | .... | .... | .... | .... |
| **2006-07** | **Tampa Bay** | **NHL** | **81** | **15** | **22** | **37** | **36** | **5** | **1** | **2** | **106** | **14.2** | **–9** | **0** | **0.0** | **20:12** | **6** | **1** | **4** | **5** | **4** | **0** | **1** | **0** | **20:47** |
| **2007-08** | **Tampa Bay** | **NHL** | **75** | **6** | **25** | **31** | **40** | **2** | **0** | **0** | **113** | **5.3** | **–8** | **2** | **0.0** | **24:57** | .... | .... | .... | .... | .... | .... | .... | .... | .... |
| **2008-09** | **Ottawa** | **NHL** | **71** | **3** | **37** | **40** | **28** | **2** | **0** | **0** | **111** | **2.7** | **4** | **0** | **0.0** | **23:17** | .... | .... | .... | .... | .... | .... | .... | .... | .... |
| | **NHL Totals** | | **602** | **58** | **189** | **247** | **267** | **24** | **5** | **12** | **905** | **6.4** | | **8** | **0.0** | **23:15** | **24** | **4** | **9** | **13** | **28** | **3** | **1** | **0** | **25:16** |

Played in NHL All-Star Game (2004)

Traded to **Calgary** by **Florida** for Rocky Thompson, March 16, 2000. Claimed by **Minnesota** from **Calgary** in Expansion Draft, June 23, 2000. Signed as a free agent by **Tampa Bay**, July 1, 2006. Traded to **Ottawa** by **Tampa Bay** with Alexandre Picard and San Jose's 1st round choice (previously acquired, later traded to NY Islanders, later traded to Columbus, later traded to Anaheim - Anaheim selected Kyle Palmieri) in 2009 Entry Draft for Andrej Meszaros, August 29, 2008.

## KUBINA, Pavel

(koo-BEE-nuh, PAH-vehl) **ATL.**

Defense. Shoots right. 6'4", 245 lbs. Born, Celadna, Czech., April 15, 1977. Tampa Bay's 6th choice, 179th overall, in 1996 Entry Draft.

| Season | Club | League | GP | G | A | Pts | PIM | PP | SH | GW | S | % | +/- | TF | F% | Min | GP | G | A | Pts | PIM | PP | SH | GW | Min |
|---|---|---|---|---|---|---|---|---|---|---|---|---|---|---|---|---|---|---|---|---|---|---|---|---|---|
| 1993-94 | HC Vitkovice Jr. | CzRep-Jr. | 35 | 4 | 3 | 7 | .... | .... | .... | .... | .... | .... | .... | .... | .... | .... | .... | .... | .... | .... | .... | .... | .... | .... | .... |
| | HC Vitkovice | CzRep | 1 | 0 | 0 | 0 | .... | .... | .... | .... | .... | .... | .... | .... | .... | .... | .... | .... | .... | .... | .... | .... | .... | .... | .... |
| 1994-95 | HC Vitkovice Jr. | CzRep-Jr. | 20 | 6 | 10 | 16 | .... | .... | .... | .... | .... | .... | .... | .... | .... | .... | .... | .... | .... | .... | .... | .... | .... | .... | .... |
| | HC Vitkovice | CzRep | 8 | 2 | 0 | 2 | 10 | .... | .... | .... | .... | .... | .... | .... | .... | .... | 4 | 0 | 0 | 0 | 0 | .... | .... | .... | .... |
| 1995-96 | HC Vitkovice Jr. | CzRep-Jr. | 16 | 5 | 10 | 15 | .... | .... | .... | .... | .... | .... | .... | .... | .... | .... | .... | .... | .... | .... | .... | .... | .... | .... | .... |
| | HC Vitkovice | CzRep | 33 | 3 | 4 | 7 | 32 | .... | .... | .... | .... | .... | .... | .... | .... | .... | 4 | 0 | 0 | 0 | 0 | .... | .... | .... | .... |
| 1996-97 | HC Vitkovice | CzRep | 1 | 0 | 0 | 0 | 0 | .... | .... | .... | .... | .... | .... | .... | .... | .... | .... | .... | .... | .... | .... | .... | .... | .... | .... |
| | Moose Jaw | WHL | 61 | 12 | 32 | 44 | 116 | .... | .... | .... | .... | .... | .... | .... | .... | .... | 11 | 2 | 5 | 7 | 27 | .... | .... | .... | .... |
| **1997-98** | **Tampa Bay** | **NHL** | **10** | **1** | **2** | **3** | **22** | **0** | **0** | **0** | **8** | **12.5** | **–1** | .... | .... | .... | .... | .... | .... | .... | .... | .... | .... | .... | .... |
| | Adirondack | AHL | 55 | 4 | 8 | 12 | 86 | .... | .... | .... | .... | .... | .... | .... | .... | .... | 1 | 1 | 0 | 1 | 14 | .... | .... | .... | .... |
| **1998-99** | **Tampa Bay** | **NHL** | **68** | **9** | **12** | **21** | **80** | **3** | **1** | **1** | **119** | **7.6** | **–33** | **2** | **0.0** | **22:47** | .... | .... | .... | .... | .... | .... | .... | .... | .... |
| | Cleveland | IHL | 6 | 2 | 2 | 4 | 16 | .... | .... | .... | .... | .... | .... | .... | .... | .... | .... | .... | .... | .... | .... | .... | .... | .... | .... |
| **99-2000** | **Tampa Bay** | **NHL** | **69** | **8** | **18** | **26** | **93** | **6** | **0** | **3** | **128** | **6.3** | **–19** | **0** | **0.0** | **22:32** | .... | .... | .... | .... | .... | .... | .... | .... | .... |
| **2000-01** | **Tampa Bay** | **NHL** | **70** | **11** | **19** | **30** | **103** | **6** | **1** | **1** | **128** | **8.6** | **–14** | **2** | **0.0** | **24:06** | .... | .... | .... | .... | .... | .... | .... | .... | .... |
| **2001-02** | **Tampa Bay** | **NHL** | **82** | **11** | **23** | **34** | **106** | **5** | **2** | **3** | **189** | **5.8** | **–22** | **1** | **100.0** | **23:39** | .... | .... | .... | .... | .... | .... | .... | .... | .... |
| | Czech Republic | Olympics | 4 | 0 | 1 | 1 | 0 | .... | .... | .... | .... | .... | .... | .... | .... | .... | .... | .... | .... | .... | .... | .... | .... | .... | .... |
| **2002-03** | **Tampa Bay** | **NHL** | **75** | **3** | **19** | **22** | **78** | **0** | **0** | **0** | **139** | **2.2** | **–7** | **1** | **0.0** | **21:24** | **11** | **0** | **0** | **0** | **12** | **0** | **0** | **0** | **24:52** |
| **2003-04♦** | **Tampa Bay** | **NHL** | **81** | **17** | **18** | **35** | **85** | **8** | **1** | **4** | **153** | **11.1** | **9** | **1** | **0.0** | **21:09** | **22** | **0** | **4** | **4** | **50** | **0** | **0** | **0** | **22:54** |
| 2004-05 | Vitkovice | CzRep | 28 | 6 | 5 | 11 | 46 | .... | .... | .... | .... | .... | .... | .... | .... | .... | 12 | 4 | 6 | 10 | 34 | .... | .... | .... | .... |
| **2005-06** | **Tampa Bay** | **NHL** | **76** | **5** | **33** | **38** | **96** | **4** | **0** | **3** | **155** | **3.2** | **–12** | **2** | **0.0** | **22:25** | **5** | **1** | **1** | **2** | **26** | **1** | **0** | **0** | **20:09** |
| | Czech Republic | Olympics | 8 | 1 | 1 | 2 | 12 | .... | .... | .... | .... | .... | .... | .... | .... | .... | .... | .... | .... | .... | .... | .... | .... | .... | .... |
| **2006-07** | **Toronto** | **NHL** | **61** | **7** | **14** | **21** | **48** | **4** | **0** | **1** | **97** | **7.2** | **7** | **0** | **0.0** | **21:19** | .... | .... | .... | .... | .... | .... | .... | .... | .... |
| **2007-08** | **Toronto** | **NHL** | **72** | **11** | **29** | **40** | **116** | **6** | **0** | **4** | **136** | **8.1** | **5** | **1** | **0.0** | **23:55** | .... | .... | .... | .... | .... | .... | .... | .... | .... |
| **2008-09** | **Toronto** | **NHL** | **82** | **14** | **26** | **40** | **94** | **9** | **0** | **4** | **184** | **7.6** | **–15** | **0** | **0.0** | **22:03** | .... | .... | .... | .... | .... | .... | .... | .... | .... |
| | **NHL Totals** | | **746** | **97** | **213** | **310** | **921** | **51** | **5** | **24** | **1436** | **6.8** | | **10** | **10.0** | **22:32** | **38** | **1** | **5** | **6** | **88** | **1** | **0** | **0** | **23:06** |

Played in NHL All-Star Game (2004)

Signed as a free agent by **Vitkovice** (CzRep), September 17, 2004. Signed as a free agent by **Toronto**, July 1, 2006. Traded to **Atlanta** by **Toronto** with Tim Stapleton for Garnet Exelby and Colin Stuart, July 1, 2009.

## KUKKONEN, Lasse

(koo-KOH-nuhn, LAH-say)

Defense. Shoots left. 6'1", 190 lbs. Born, Oulu, Finland, September 18, 1981. Chicago's 4th choice, 151st overall, in 2003 Entry Draft.

| Season | Club | League | GP | G | A | Pts | PIM | PP | SH | GW | S | % | +/- | TF | F% | Min | GP | G | A | Pts | PIM | PP | SH | GW | Min |
|---|---|---|---|---|---|---|---|---|---|---|---|---|---|---|---|---|---|---|---|---|---|---|---|---|---|
| 1997-98 | Karpat Oulu U18 | Fin-U18 | 36 | 5 | 16 | 21 | 46 | .... | .... | .... | .... | .... | .... | .... | .... | .... | .... | .... | .... | .... | .... | .... | .... | .... | .... |
| 1998-99 | Karpat Oulu U18 | Fin-U18 | 2 | 1 | 2 | 3 | 0 | .... | .... | .... | .... | .... | .... | .... | .... | .... | .... | .... | .... | .... | .... | .... | .... | .... | .... |
| | Karpat Oulu Jr. | Fin-Jr. | 34 | 2 | 13 | 15 | 24 | .... | .... | .... | .... | .... | .... | .... | .... | .... | .... | .... | .... | .... | .... | .... | .... | .... | .... |
| 99-2000 | Karpat Oulu Jr. | Fin-Jr. | 27 | 9 | 11 | 20 | 26 | .... | .... | .... | .... | .... | .... | .... | .... | .... | .... | .... | .... | .... | .... | .... | .... | .... | .... |
| | Karpat Oulu | Finland-2 | 22 | 0 | 4 | 4 | 14 | .... | .... | .... | .... | .... | .... | .... | .... | .... | .... | .... | .... | .... | .... | .... | .... | .... | .... |
| 2000-01 | Karpat Oulu | Finland | 47 | 1 | 5 | 6 | 46 | .... | .... | .... | .... | .... | .... | .... | .... | .... | 9 | 0 | 2 | 2 | 4 | .... | .... | .... | .... |
| 2001-02 | Karpat Oulu | Finland | 55 | 2 | 6 | 8 | 42 | .... | .... | .... | .... | .... | .... | .... | .... | .... | 4 | 0 | 3 | 3 | 4 | .... | .... | .... | .... |
| | Karpat Oulu Jr. | Fin-Jr. | .... | .... | .... | .... | .... | .... | .... | .... | .... | .... | .... | .... | .... | .... | 1 | 1 | 0 | 1 | 0 | .... | .... | .... | .... |
| 2002-03 | Karpat Oulu | Finland | 56 | 6 | 12 | 18 | 67 | .... | .... | .... | .... | .... | .... | .... | .... | .... | 15 | 1 | 4 | 5 | 16 | .... | .... | .... | .... |
| **2003-04** | **Chicago** | **NHL** | **10** | **0** | **1** | **1** | **4** | **0** | **0** | **0** | **9** | **0.0** | **–2** | **0** | **0.0** | **13:37** | .... | .... | .... | .... | .... | .... | .... | .... | .... |
| | Norfolk Admirals | AHL | 59 | 3 | 11 | 14 | 58 | .... | .... | .... | .... | .... | .... | .... | .... | .... | 8 | 0 | 0 | 0 | 8 | .... | .... | .... | .... |
| 2004-05 | Karpat Oulu | Finland | 55 | 5 | 13 | 18 | 68 | .... | .... | .... | .... | .... | .... | .... | .... | .... | 12 | 0 | 2 | 2 | 6 | .... | .... | .... | .... |
| 2005-06 | Karpat Oulu | Finland | 56 | 11 | 16 | 27 | 38 | .... | .... | .... | .... | .... | .... | .... | .... | .... | 11 | 5 | 7 | 12 | 8 | .... | .... | .... | .... |
| | Finland | Olympics | 2 | 0 | 0 | 0 | 0 | .... | .... | .... | .... | .... | .... | .... | .... | .... | .... | .... | .... | .... | .... | .... | .... | .... | .... |
| **2006-07** | **Chicago** | **NHL** | **54** | **5** | **9** | **14** | **30** | **1** | **0** | **2** | **45** | **11.1** | **5** | **0** | **0.0** | **16:35** | .... | .... | .... | .... | .... | .... | .... | .... | .... |
| | **Philadelphia** | **NHL** | **20** | **0** | **0** | **0** | **8** | **0** | **0** | **0** | **9** | **0.0** | **–1** | **0** | **0.0** | **18:29** | .... | .... | .... | .... | .... | .... | .... | .... | .... |
| **2007-08** | **Philadelphia** | **NHL** | **53** | **1** | **4** | **5** | **38** | **0** | **0** | **0** | **31** | **3.2** | **3** | **0** | **0.0** | **15:44** | **14** | **0** | **2** | **2** | **6** | **0** | **0** | **0** | **15:22** |
| **2008-09** | **Philadelphia** | **NHL** | **22** | **0** | **2** | **2** | **10** | **0** | **0** | **0** | **10** | **0.0** | **–2** | **1** | **0.0** | **10:43** | .... | .... | .... | .... | .... | .... | .... | .... | .... |
| | Philadelphia | AHL | 26 | 0 | 11 | 11 | 20 | .... | .... | .... | .... | .... | .... | .... | .... | .... | 4 | 2 | 0 | 2 | 6 | .... | .... | .... | .... |
| | **NHL Totals** | | **159** | **6** | **16** | **22** | **90** | **1** | **0** | **2** | **104** | **5.8** | | **1** | **0.0** | **15:33** | **14** | **0** | **2** | **2** | **6** | **0** | **0** | **0** | **15:22** |

Signed as a free agent by **Oulu** (Finland), September 11, 2004. Traded to **Philadelphia** by **Chicago** with Chicago's 3rd round choice (Garrett Klotz) in 2007 Entry Draft for Kyle Calder, February 26, 2007.

## KULEMIN, Nikolai

(KOOL-ay-mihn, NIH-koh-ligh) **TOR.**

Wing. Shoots left. 6'1", 183 lbs. Born, Magnitogorsk, USSR, July 14, 1986. Toronto's 2nd choice, 44th overall, in 2006 Entry Draft.

| Season | Club | League | GP | G | A | Pts | PIM | PP | SH | GW | S | % | +/- | TF | F% | Min | GP | G | A | Pts | PIM | PP | SH | GW | Min |
|---|---|---|---|---|---|---|---|---|---|---|---|---|---|---|---|---|---|---|---|---|---|---|---|---|---|
| 2003-04 | Magnitogorsk 2 | Russia-3 | 43 | 8 | 18 | 26 | 91 | .... | .... | .... | .... | .... | .... | .... | .... | .... | .... | .... | .... | .... | .... | .... | .... | .... | .... |
| 2004-05 | Magnitogorsk 2 | Russia-3 | 43 | 9 | 13 | 22 | 44 | .... | .... | .... | .... | .... | .... | .... | .... | .... | .... | .... | .... | .... | .... | .... | .... | .... | .... |
| 2005-06 | Magnitogorsk 2 | Russia-3 | 4 | 3 | 1 | 4 | 6 | .... | .... | .... | .... | .... | .... | .... | .... | .... | .... | .... | .... | .... | .... | .... | .... | .... | .... |
| | Magnitogorsk | Russia | 31 | 5 | 7 | 12 | 8 | .... | .... | .... | .... | .... | .... | .... | .... | .... | 11 | 2 | 4 | 6 | 6 | .... | .... | .... | .... |
| 2006-07 | Magnitogorsk | Russia | 54 | 27 | 12 | 39 | 42 | .... | .... | .... | .... | .... | .... | .... | .... | .... | 15 | 10 | 1 | 11 | 10 | .... | .... | .... | .... |
| 2007-08 | Magnitogorsk | Russia | 57 | 21 | 12 | 33 | 63 | .... | .... | .... | .... | .... | .... | .... | .... | .... | 11 | 2 | 2 | 4 | 29 | .... | .... | .... | .... |

| Season | Club | League | Regular Season GP | G | A | Pts | PIM | PP | SH | GW | S | % | +/- | TF | F% | Min | Playoffs GP | G | A | Pts | PIM | PP | SH | GW | Min |
|---|---|---|---|---|---|---|---|---|---|---|---|---|---|---|---|---|---|---|---|---|---|---|---|---|---|
| **2008-09** | **Toronto** | **NHL** | **73** | **15** | **16** | **31** | **18** | **2** | **0** | **1** | **129** | **11.6** | **-8** | **66** | **53.0** | **13:48** | .... | .... | .... | .... | .... | .... | .... | .... | .... |
| | Toronto Marlies | AHL | 5 | 0 | 0 | 0 | 0 | .... | .... | .... | .... | .... | .... | .... | .... | .... | .... | .... | .... | .... | .... | .... | .... | .... | .... |
| | **NHL Totals** | | **73** | **15** | **16** | **31** | **18** | **2** | **0** | **1** | **129** | **11.6** | | **66** | **53.0** | **13:48** | .... | .... | .... | .... | .... | .... | .... | .... | .... |

### KUNITZ, Chris (KOO-nihtz, KRIHS) PIT.

Left wing. Shoots left. 6', 193 lbs. Born, Regina, Sask., September 26, 1979.

| | | | | | | | | | | | | | | | | | | | | | | | | | |
|---|---|---|---|---|---|---|---|---|---|---|---|---|---|---|---|---|---|---|---|---|---|---|---|---|---|
| 1996-97 | Yorkton Mallers | SMHL | 64 | 38 | 38 | 76 | 233 | .... | .... | .... | .... | .... | .... | .... | .... | .... | .... | .... | .... | .... | .... | .... | .... | .... | .... |
| 1997-98 | Melville | SJHL | STATISTICS NOT AVAILABLE | | | | | | | | | | | | | | | | | | | | | | |
| 1998-99 | Melville | SJHL | 63 | 57 | 32 | 89 | 222 | .... | .... | .... | .... | .... | .... | .... | .... | .... | .... | .... | .... | .... | .... | .... | .... | .... | .... |
| 99-2000 | Ferris State | CCHA | 38 | 20 | 9 | 29 | 70 | .... | .... | .... | .... | .... | .... | .... | .... | .... | .... | .... | .... | .... | .... | .... | .... | .... | .... |
| 2000-01 | Ferris State | CCHA | 37 | 16 | 13 | 29 | 81 | .... | .... | .... | .... | .... | .... | .... | .... | .... | .... | .... | .... | .... | .... | .... | .... | .... | .... |
| 2001-02 | Ferris State | CCHA | 35 | *28 | 10 | 38 | 68 | .... | .... | .... | .... | .... | .... | .... | .... | .... | .... | .... | .... | .... | .... | .... | .... | .... | .... |
| 2002-03 | Ferris State | CCHA | 42 | *35 | *44 | *79 | 56 | .... | .... | .... | .... | .... | .... | .... | .... | .... | .... | .... | .... | .... | .... | .... | .... | .... | .... |
| **2003-04** | **Anaheim** | **NHL** | **21** | **0** | **6** | **6** | **12** | **0** | **0** | **0** | **31** | **0.0** | **1** | **7** | **14.3** | **9:07** | .... | .... | .... | .... | .... | .... | .... | .... | .... |
| | Cincinnati | AHL | 59 | 19 | 25 | 44 | 101 | .... | .... | .... | .... | .... | .... | .... | .... | .... | 9 | 3 | 2 | 5 | 24 | .... | .... | .... | .... |
| 2004-05 | Cincinnati | AHL | 54 | 22 | 17 | 39 | 71 | .... | .... | .... | .... | .... | .... | .... | .... | .... | 12 | 1 | 7 | 8 | 20 | .... | .... | .... | .... |
| **2005-06** | **Atlanta** | **NHL** | **2** | **0** | **0** | **0** | **2** | **0** | **0** | **0** | **0** | **0.0** | **-3** | **0** | **0.0** | **5:43** | .... | .... | .... | .... | .... | .... | .... | .... | .... |
| | **Anaheim** | **NHL** | **67** | **19** | **22** | **41** | **69** | **5** | **1** | **2** | **149** | **12.8** | **19** | **15** | **46.7** | **14:08** | **16** | **3** | **5** | **8** | **8** | **0** | **0** | **0** | **12:30** |
| | Portland Pirates | AHL | 5 | 0 | 4 | 4 | 12 | .... | .... | .... | .... | .... | .... | .... | .... | .... | .... | .... | .... | .... | .... | .... | .... | .... | .... |
| **2006-07♦** | **Anaheim** | **NHL** | **81** | **25** | **35** | **60** | **81** | **11** | **0** | **5** | **180** | **13.9** | **23** | **13** | **30.8** | **17:03** | **13** | **1** | **5** | **6** | **19** | **0** | **0** | **0** | **17:47** |
| **2007-08** | **Anaheim** | **NHL** | **82** | **21** | **29** | **50** | **80** | **7** | **1** | **6** | **196** | **10.7** | **8** | **49** | **32.7** | **16:54** | **6** | **0** | **2** | **2** | **8** | **0** | **0** | **0** | **18:30** |
| **2008-09** | **Anaheim** | **NHL** | **62** | **16** | **19** | **35** | **55** | **3** | **0** | **2** | **139** | **11.5** | **9** | **22** | **45.5** | **16:29** | .... | .... | .... | .... | .... | .... | .... | .... | .... |
| | **♦ Pittsburgh** | **NHL** | **20** | **7** | **11** | **18** | **16** | **3** | **0** | **1** | **39** | **17.9** | **3** | **5** | **60.0** | **16:17** | **24** | **1** | **13** | **14** | **19** | **0** | **0** | **0** | **16:55** |
| | **NHL Totals** | | **335** | **88** | **122** | **210** | **315** | **29** | **2** | **16** | **734** | **12.0** | | **111** | **36.9** | **15:43** | **59** | **5** | **25** | **30** | **54** | **0** | **0** | **0** | **16:04** |

CCHA First All-Star Team (2002, 2003) • CCHA Player of the Year (2003) • NCAA West First All-American Team (2003)

Signed as a free agent by **Anaheim**, April 1, 2003. Claimed on waivers by **Atlanta** from **Anaheim**, October 4, 2005. Claimed on waivers by **Anaheim** from **Atlanta**, October 18, 2005. Traded to **Pittsburgh** by **Anaheim** with Eric Tangradi for Ryan Whitney, February 26, 2009.

### KWIATKOWSKI, Joel (KWEE-at-KOW-skee, JOHL)

Defense. Shoots left. 6'2", 210 lbs. Born, Kindersley, Sask., March 22, 1977. Dallas' 7th choice, 194th overall, in 1996 Entry Draft.

| | | | | | | | | | | | | | | | | | | | | | | | | | |
|---|---|---|---|---|---|---|---|---|---|---|---|---|---|---|---|---|---|---|---|---|---|---|---|---|---|
| 1994-95 | Tacoma Rockets | WHL | 70 | 4 | 13 | 17 | 66 | .... | .... | .... | .... | .... | .... | .... | .... | .... | 4 | 0 | 0 | 0 | 2 | .... | .... | .... | .... |
| 1995-96 | Kelowna Rockets | WHL | 40 | 6 | 17 | 23 | 85 | .... | .... | .... | .... | .... | .... | .... | .... | .... | .... | .... | .... | .... | .... | .... | .... | .... | .... |
| | Prince George | WHL | 32 | 6 | 11 | 17 | 48 | .... | .... | .... | .... | .... | .... | .... | .... | .... | .... | .... | .... | .... | .... | .... | .... | .... | .... |
| 1996-97 | Prince George | WHL | 72 | 15 | 37 | 52 | 94 | .... | .... | .... | .... | .... | .... | .... | .... | .... | 15 | 4 | 2 | 6 | 24 | .... | .... | .... | .... |
| 1997-98 | Prince George | WHL | 62 | 21 | 43 | 64 | 65 | .... | .... | .... | .... | .... | .... | .... | .... | .... | 11 | 3 | 6 | 9 | 6 | .... | .... | .... | .... |
| 1998-99 | Cincinnati | AHL | 80 | 12 | 21 | 33 | 48 | .... | .... | .... | .... | .... | .... | .... | .... | .... | 3 | 2 | 0 | 2 | 0 | .... | .... | .... | .... |
| 99-2000 | Cincinnati | AHL | 70 | 4 | 22 | 26 | 28 | .... | .... | .... | .... | .... | .... | .... | .... | .... | .... | .... | .... | .... | .... | .... | .... | .... | .... |
| **2000-01** | **Ottawa** | **NHL** | **4** | **1** | **0** | **1** | **0** | **0** | **0** | **0** | **2** | **50.0** | **1** | **0** | **0.0** | **12:04** | .... | .... | .... | .... | .... | .... | .... | .... | .... |
| | Grand Rapids | IHL | 77 | 4 | 17 | 21 | 58 | .... | .... | .... | .... | .... | .... | .... | .... | .... | 10 | 1 | 0 | 1 | 4 | .... | .... | .... | .... |
| **2001-02** | **Ottawa** | **NHL** | **11** | **0** | **0** | **0** | **12** | **0** | **0** | **0** | **9** | **0.0** | **5** | **0** | **0.0** | **13:41** | .... | .... | .... | .... | .... | .... | .... | .... | .... |
| | Grand Rapids | AHL | 65 | 8 | 21 | 29 | 94 | .... | .... | .... | .... | .... | .... | .... | .... | .... | 5 | 1 | 2 | 3 | 12 | .... | .... | .... | .... |
| **2002-03** | **Ottawa** | **NHL** | **20** | **0** | **2** | **2** | **6** | **0** | **0** | **0** | **28** | **0.0** | **2** | **2** | **0.0** | **12:13** | .... | .... | .... | .... | .... | .... | .... | .... | .... |
| | Binghamton | AHL | 1 | 0 | 0 | 0 | 2 | .... | .... | .... | .... | .... | .... | .... | .... | .... | .... | .... | .... | .... | .... | .... | .... | .... | .... |
| | **Washington** | **NHL** | **34** | **0** | **3** | **3** | **12** | **0** | **0** | **0** | **28** | **0.0** | **1** | **2** | **0.0** | **15:32** | **6** | **0** | **0** | **0** | **2** | **0** | **0** | **0** | **17:48** |
| **2003-04** | **Washington** | **NHL** | **80** | **6** | **6** | **12** | **89** | **2** | **0** | **0** | **90** | **6.7** | **-28** | **0** | **0.0** | **21:16** | .... | .... | .... | .... | .... | .... | .... | .... | .... |
| 2004-05 | San Antonio | AHL | 64 | 13 | 19 | 32 | 76 | .... | .... | .... | .... | .... | .... | .... | .... | .... | .... | .... | .... | .... | .... | .... | .... | .... | .... |
| | St. John's | AHL | 17 | 7 | 6 | 13 | 16 | .... | .... | .... | .... | .... | .... | .... | .... | .... | 5 | 0 | 4 | 4 | 23 | .... | .... | .... | .... |
| **2005-06** | **Florida** | **NHL** | **73** | **4** | **8** | **12** | **86** | **1** | **0** | **1** | **87** | **4.6** | **3** | **0** | **0.0** | **16:21** | .... | .... | .... | .... | .... | .... | .... | .... | .... |
| **2006-07** | **Florida** | **NHL** | **41** | **5** | **5** | **10** | **20** | **1** | **0** | **2** | **46** | **10.9** | **-5** | **1** | **100.0** | **9:46** | .... | .... | .... | .... | .... | .... | .... | .... | .... |
| | **Pittsburgh** | **NHL** | **1** | **0** | **0** | **0** | **0** | **0** | **0** | **0** | **0** | **0.0** | **-1** | **0** | **0.0** | **11:59** | .... | .... | .... | .... | .... | .... | .... | .... | .... |
| **2007-08** | **Atlanta** | **NHL** | **18** | **0** | **5** | **5** | **20** | **0** | **0** | **0** | **24** | **0.0** | **-5** | **0** | **0.0** | **16:44** | .... | .... | .... | .... | .... | .... | .... | .... | .... |
| | Chicago Wolves | AHL | 59 | 21 | 29 | 50 | 119 | .... | .... | .... | .... | .... | .... | .... | .... | .... | 24 | 10 | 15 | 25 | 30 | .... | .... | .... | .... |
| 2008-09 | Cherepovets | Rus-KHL | 52 | 13 | 12 | 25 | 64 | .... | .... | .... | .... | .... | .... | .... | .... | .... | .... | .... | .... | .... | .... | .... | .... | .... | .... |
| | **NHL Totals** | | **282** | **16** | **29** | **45** | **245** | **4** | **0** | **3** | **314** | **5.1** | | **5** | **20.0** | **16:14** | **6** | **0** | **0** | **0** | **2** | **0** | **0** | **0** | **17:48** |

WHL West Second All-Star Team (1997) • WHL West First All-Star Team (1998) • AHL Second All-Star Team (2008)

Signed as a free agent by **Anaheim**, June 18, 1998. Traded to **Ottawa** by **Anaheim** for Patrick Traverse, June 12, 2000. Traded to **Washington** by **Ottawa** for Washington's 9th round choice (later traded back to Washington – Washington selected Mark Olafson) in 2003 Entry Draft, January 15, 2003. Signed as a free agent by **Florida**, July 16, 2004. • Loaned to **St. John's** (AHL) by **Florida** (San Antonio-AHL) for cash, March 11, 2005. Traded to **Pittsburgh** by **Florida** for Florida's 4th round choice (previously acquired, Florida selected Matt Rust) in 2007 Entry Draft, February 27, 2007. Signed as a free agent by **Atlanta**, August 30, 2007. Signed as a free agent by **Cherepovets** (Rus-KHL), June 11, 2008. Signed as a free agent by **Atlanta**, July 6, 2009.

### LaCOUTURE, Dan (LA-koo-TUHR, DAN)

Left wing. Shoots left. 6'2", 215 lbs. Born, Hyannis, MA, April 18, 1977. NY Islanders' 2nd choice, 29th overall, in 1996 Entry Draft.

| | | | | | | | | | | | | | | | | | | | | | | | | | |
|---|---|---|---|---|---|---|---|---|---|---|---|---|---|---|---|---|---|---|---|---|---|---|---|---|---|
| 1992-93 | Natick Redmen | High-MA | 20 | 38 | 34 | 72 | 46 | .... | .... | .... | .... | .... | .... | .... | .... | .... | .... | .... | .... | .... | .... | .... | .... | .... | .... |
| 1993-94 | Natick Redmen | High-MA | 21 | 52 | 49 | 101 | 58 | .... | .... | .... | .... | .... | .... | .... | .... | .... | .... | .... | .... | .... | .... | .... | .... | .... | .... |
| 1994-95 | Spring. Olympics | NEJHL | 52 | 44 | 56 | 100 | 98 | .... | .... | .... | .... | .... | .... | .... | .... | .... | .... | .... | .... | .... | .... | .... | .... | .... | .... |
| 1995-96 | Spring. Olympics | NEJHL | 29 | 24 | 35 | 59 | 79 | .... | .... | .... | .... | .... | .... | .... | .... | .... | 13 | 12 | 13 | 25 | 23 | .... | .... | .... | .... |
| 1996-97 | Boston University | H-East | 31 | 13 | 12 | 25 | 18 | .... | .... | .... | .... | .... | .... | .... | .... | .... | .... | .... | .... | .... | .... | .... | .... | .... | .... |
| 1997-98 | Hamilton | AHL | 77 | 15 | 10 | 25 | 31 | .... | .... | .... | .... | .... | .... | .... | .... | .... | 5 | 1 | 0 | 1 | 0 | .... | .... | .... | .... |
| **1998-99** | **Edmonton** | **NHL** | **3** | **0** | **0** | **0** | **0** | **0** | **0** | **0** | **0** | **0.0** | **1** | **0** | **0.0** | **6:30** | .... | .... | .... | .... | .... | .... | .... | .... | .... |
| | Hamilton | AHL | 72 | 17 | 14 | 31 | 73 | .... | .... | .... | .... | .... | .... | .... | .... | .... | 9 | 2 | 1 | 3 | 2 | .... | .... | .... | .... |
| **99-2000** | **Edmonton** | **NHL** | **5** | **0** | **0** | **0** | **10** | **0** | **0** | **0** | **2** | **0.0** | **0** | **0** | **0.0** | **7:02** | **1** | **0** | **0** | **0** | **0** | **0** | **0** | **0** | **2:05** |
| | Hamilton | AHL | 70 | 23 | 17 | 40 | 85 | .... | .... | .... | .... | .... | .... | .... | .... | .... | 6 | 2 | 1 | 3 | 0 | .... | .... | .... | .... |
| **2000-01** | **Edmonton** | **NHL** | **37** | **2** | **4** | **6** | **29** | **0** | **0** | **1** | **22** | **9.1** | **-2** | **5** | **20.0** | **7:06** | .... | .... | .... | .... | .... | .... | .... | .... | .... |
| | **Pittsburgh** | **NHL** | **11** | **0** | **0** | **0** | **14** | **0** | **0** | **0** | **1** | **0.0** | **0** | **1** | **100.0** | **5:57** | **5** | **0** | **0** | **0** | **2** | **0** | **0** | **0** | **5:46** |
| **2001-02** | **Pittsburgh** | **NHL** | **82** | **6** | **11** | **17** | **71** | **0** | **1** | **0** | **77** | **7.8** | **-19** | **21** | **38.1** | **13:16** | .... | .... | .... | .... | .... | .... | .... | .... | .... |
| **2002-03** | **Pittsburgh** | **NHL** | **44** | **2** | **2** | **4** | **72** | **0** | **0** | **0** | **30** | **6.7** | **-8** | **5** | **80.0** | **9:13** | .... | .... | .... | .... | .... | .... | .... | .... | .... |
| | **NY Rangers** | **NHL** | **24** | **1** | **4** | **5** | **0** | **0** | **0** | **0** | **17** | **5.9** | **4** | **1** | **0.0** | **10:18** | .... | .... | .... | .... | .... | .... | .... | .... | .... |
| **2003-04** | **NY Rangers** | **NHL** | **59** | **5** | **2** | **7** | **82** | **1** | **0** | **1** | **39** | **12.8** | **-13** | **8** | **50.0** | **9:29** | .... | .... | .... | .... | .... | .... | .... | .... | .... |
| 2004-05 | Providence Bruins | AHL | 64 | 12 | 15 | 27 | 52 | .... | .... | .... | .... | .... | .... | .... | .... | .... | 6 | 1 | 1 | 2 | 4 | .... | .... | .... | .... |
| **2005-06** | HC Davos | Swiss | 4 | 2 | 1 | 3 | 4 | .... | .... | .... | .... | .... | .... | .... | .... | .... | .... | .... | .... | .... | .... | .... | .... | .... | .... |
| | **Boston** | **NHL** | **55** | **2** | **2** | **4** | **53** | **0** | **1** | **0** | **37** | **5.4** | **-6** | **0** | **0.0** | **6:15** | .... | .... | .... | .... | .... | .... | .... | .... | .... |
| **2006-07** | **New Jersey** | **NHL** | **6** | **0** | **0** | **0** | **7** | **0** | **0** | **0** | **0** | **0.0** | **0** | **0** | **0.0** | **4:57** | .... | .... | .... | .... | .... | .... | .... | .... | .... |
| | Lowell Devils | AHL | 39 | 8 | 3 | 11 | 33 | .... | .... | .... | .... | .... | .... | .... | .... | .... | .... | .... | .... | .... | .... | .... | .... | .... | .... |
| 2007-08 | HC Lugano | Swiss | 15 | 1 | 1 | 2 | 18 | .... | .... | .... | .... | .... | .... | .... | .... | .... | .... | .... | .... | .... | .... | .... | .... | .... | .... |
| **2008-09** | **Carolina** | **NHL** | **11** | **2** | **0** | **2** | **10** | **0** | **0** | **1** | **4** | **50.0** | **-1** | **10** | **40.0** | **4:16** | .... | .... | .... | .... | .... | .... | .... | .... | .... |
| | Albany River Rats | AHL | 12 | 1 | 5 | 6 | 4 | .... | .... | .... | .... | .... | .... | .... | .... | .... | .... | .... | .... | .... | .... | .... | .... | .... | .... |
| | **NHL Totals** | | **337** | **20** | **25** | **45** | **348** | **1** | **2** | **3** | **229** | **8.7** | | **51** | **43.1** | **9:13** | **6** | **0** | **0** | **0** | **2** | **0** | **0** | **0** | **5:09** |

Traded to **Edmonton** by **NY Islanders** for Mariusz Czerkawski, August 25, 1997. Traded to **Pittsburgh** by **Edmonton** for Sven Butenschon, March 13, 2001. Traded to **NY Rangers** by **Pittsburgh** with Mike Wilson, Alex Kovalev and Janne Laukkanen for Joel Bouchard, Richard Lintner, Rico Fata and Mikael Samuelsson, February 10, 2003. Signed to a PTO (tryout) contract by **Providence** (AHL), November 2, 2004. Signed as a free agent by **Boston**, November 24, 2005. Signed as a free agent by **New Jersey**, October 4, 2006. Signed as a free agent by **Anaheim**, July 18, 2007. Signed as a free agent by **Carolina**, October 6, 2008.

### LADD, Andrew (LAD, AN-droo) CHI.

Left wing. Shoots left. 6'2", 198 lbs. Born, Maple Ridge, B.C., December 12, 1985. Carolina's 1st choice, 4th overall, in 2004 Entry Draft.

| | | | | | | | | | | | | | | | | | | | | | | | | | |
|---|---|---|---|---|---|---|---|---|---|---|---|---|---|---|---|---|---|---|---|---|---|---|---|---|---|
| 2000-01 | Okanagan Chiefs | Minor-BC | 6 | 4 | 8 | 12 | 10 | .... | .... | .... | .... | .... | .... | .... | .... | .... | .... | .... | .... | .... | .... | .... | .... | .... | .... |
| 2001-02 | Port Coquitlam | Minor-BC | 50 | 50 | 41 | 91 | 49 | .... | .... | .... | .... | .... | .... | .... | .... | .... | .... | .... | .... | .... | .... | .... | .... | .... | .... |
| | Vancouver Giants | WHL | 1 | 0 | 0 | 0 | 0 | .... | .... | .... | .... | .... | .... | .... | .... | .... | .... | .... | .... | .... | .... | .... | .... | .... | .... |
| 2002-03 | Coquitlam | BCHL | 58 | 15 | 40 | 55 | 61 | .... | .... | .... | .... | .... | .... | .... | .... | .... | .... | .... | .... | .... | .... | .... | .... | .... | .... |
| 2003-04 | Calgary Hitmen | WHL | 71 | 30 | 45 | 75 | 119 | .... | .... | .... | .... | .... | .... | .... | .... | .... | 7 | 1 | 6 | 7 | 10 | .... | .... | .... | .... |
| 2004-05 | Calgary Hitmen | WHL | 65 | 19 | 26 | 45 | 167 | .... | .... | .... | .... | .... | .... | .... | .... | .... | 12 | 7 | 4 | 11 | 18 | .... | .... | .... | .... |
| **2005-06♦** | **Carolina** | **NHL** | **29** | **6** | **5** | **11** | **4** | **3** | **0** | **0** | **43** | **14.0** | **0** | **0** | **0.0** | **11:10** | **17** | **2** | **3** | **5** | **4** | **0** | **0** | **1** | **9:27** |
| | Lowell | AHL | 25 | 11 | 8 | 19 | 28 | .... | .... | .... | .... | .... | .... | .... | .... | .... | .... | .... | .... | .... | .... | .... | .... | .... | .... |
| **2006-07** | **Carolina** | **NHL** | **65** | **11** | **10** | **21** | **46** | **2** | **0** | **3** | **109** | **10.1** | **1** | **1** | **0.0** | **11:12** | .... | .... | .... | .... | .... | .... | .... | .... | .... |

| | | | Regular Season | | | | | | | | | | | | | | Playoffs | | | | | | | | |
|---|---|---|---|---|---|---|---|---|---|---|---|---|---|---|---|---|---|---|---|---|---|---|---|---|---|
| Season | Club | League | GP | G | A | Pts | PIM | PP | SH | GW | S | % | +/- | TF | F% | Min | GP | G | A | Pts | PIM | PP | SH | GW | Min |
| **2007-08** | **Carolina** | **NHL** | **43** | **9** | **9** | **18** | **31** | **0** | **0** | **1** | **76** | **11.8** | **9** | **5** | **60.0** | **11:45** | .... | .... | .... | .... | .... | .... | .... | .... | .... |
| | Albany River Rats | AHL | 2 | 1 | 0 | 1 | 4 | .... | .... | .... | .... | .... | .... | .... | .... | .... | .... | .... | .... | .... | .... | .... | .... | .... | .... |
| | **Chicago** | **NHL** | **20** | **5** | **7** | **12** | **4** | **1** | **0** | **0** | **55** | **9.1** | **4** | **3** | **33.3** | **14:58** | .... | .... | .... | .... | .... | .... | .... | .... | .... |
| **2008-09** | **Chicago** | **NHL** | **82** | **15** | **34** | **49** | **28** | **0** | **0** | **2** | **195** | **7.7** | **26** | **42** | **23.8** | **14:24** | **17** | **3** | **1** | **4** | **12** | **0** | **0** | **1** | **12:55** |
| | **NHL Totals** | | **239** | **46** | **65** | **111** | **113** | **6** | **0** | **6** | **478** | **9.6** | | **51** | **27.5** | **12:42** | **34** | **5** | **4** | **9** | **16** | **0** | **0** | **2** | **11:11** |

Traded to **Chicago** by **Carolina** for Tuomo Ruutu, February 26, 2008.

## LAICH, Brooks

(LIGHK, BRUKS) **WSH.**

Center. Shoots left. 6'2", 200 lbs. Born, Wawota, Sask., June 23, 1983. Ottawa's 7th choice, 193rd overall, in 2001 Entry Draft.

| Season | Club | League | GP | G | A | Pts | PIM | PP | SH | GW | S | % | +/- | TF | F% | Min | GP | G | A | Pts | PIM | PP | SH | GW | Min |
|---|---|---|---|---|---|---|---|---|---|---|---|---|---|---|---|---|---|---|---|---|---|---|---|---|---|
| 99-2000 | Tisdale Trojans | SMHL | 57 | 51 | 52 | 103 | .... | .... | .... | .... | .... | .... | .... | .... | .... | .... | .... | .... | .... | .... | .... | .... | .... | .... | .... |
| 2000-01 | Moose Jaw | WHL | 71 | 9 | 21 | 30 | 28 | .... | .... | .... | .... | .... | .... | .... | .... | .... | 4 | 0 | 0 | 0 | 5 | .... | .... | .... | .... |
| 2001-02 | Moose Jaw | WHL | 28 | 6 | 14 | 20 | 12 | .... | .... | .... | .... | .... | .... | .... | .... | .... | .... | .... | .... | .... | .... | .... | .... | .... | .... |
| | Seattle | WHL | 47 | 22 | 36 | 58 | 42 | .... | .... | .... | .... | .... | .... | .... | .... | .... | 11 | 5 | 3 | 8 | 11 | .... | .... | .... | .... |
| 2002-03 | Seattle | WHL | 60 | 41 | 53 | 94 | 65 | .... | .... | .... | .... | .... | .... | .... | .... | .... | 15 | 5 | 14 | 19 | 24 | .... | .... | .... | .... |
| **2003-04** | **Ottawa** | **NHL** | **1** | **0** | **0** | **0** | **2** | **0** | **0** | **0** | **1** | **0.0** | **0** | **7** | **42.9** | **9:34** | .... | .... | .... | .... | .... | .... | .... | .... | .... |
| | Binghamton | AHL | 44 | 15 | 18 | 33 | 16 | .... | .... | .... | .... | .... | .... | .... | .... | .... | .... | .... | .... | .... | .... | .... | .... | .... | .... |
| | **Washington** | **NHL** | **4** | **0** | **1** | **1** | **0** | **0** | **0** | **0** | **2** | **0.0** | **–1** | **49** | **51.0** | **10:50** | .... | .... | .... | .... | .... | .... | .... | .... | .... |
| | Portland Pirates | AHL | 22 | 1 | 3 | 4 | 12 | .... | .... | .... | .... | .... | .... | .... | .... | .... | 6 | 0 | 0 | 0 | 0 | .... | .... | .... | .... |
| 2004-05 | Portland Pirates | AHL | 68 | 16 | 10 | 26 | 33 | .... | .... | .... | .... | .... | .... | .... | .... | .... | .... | .... | .... | .... | .... | .... | .... | .... | .... |
| **2005-06** | **Washington** | **NHL** | **73** | **7** | **14** | **21** | **26** | **1** | **0** | **1** | **118** | **5.9** | **–9** | **666** | **49.7** | **11:13** | .... | .... | .... | .... | .... | .... | .... | .... | .... |
| | Hershey Bears | AHL | 10 | 7 | 6 | 13 | 8 | .... | .... | .... | .... | .... | .... | .... | .... | .... | 21 | 8 | 7 | 15 | 29 | .... | .... | .... | .... |
| **2006-07** | **Washington** | **NHL** | **73** | **8** | **10** | **18** | **29** | **2** | **3** | **0** | **119** | **6.7** | **–2** | **563** | **51.9** | **13:36** | .... | .... | .... | .... | .... | .... | .... | .... | .... |
| **2007-08** | **Washington** | **NHL** | **82** | **21** | **16** | **37** | **35** | **8** | **2** | **4** | **122** | **17.2** | **–3** | **596** | **47.2** | **14:03** | **7** | **1** | **5** | **6** | **4** | **0** | **0** | **0** | **18:37** |
| **2008-09** | **Washington** | **NHL** | **82** | **23** | **30** | **53** | **31** | **9** | **1** | **3** | **185** | **12.4** | **–1** | **511** | **51.1** | **17:17** | **14** | **3** | **4** | **7** | **10** | **2** | **0** | **0** | **17:27** |
| | **NHL Totals** | | **315** | **59** | **71** | **130** | **123** | **20** | **6** | **8** | **547** | **10.8** | | **2392** | **49.9** | **14:04** | **21** | **4** | **9** | **13** | **14** | **2** | **0** | **0** | **17:50** |

WHL West First All-Star Team (2003)

Traded to **Washington** by **Ottawa** with Ottawa's 2nd round choice (later traded to Colorado - Colorado selected Chris Durand) in 2005 Entry Draft for Peter Bondra, February 18, 2004.

## LAING, Quintin

(LANG, QUIHN-tihn) **WSH.**

Left wing. Shoots left. 6'2", 200 lbs. Born, Rosetown, Sask., June 8, 1979. Detroit's 3rd choice, 102nd overall, in 1997 Entry Draft.

| Season | Club | League | GP | G | A | Pts | PIM | PP | SH | GW | S | % | +/- | TF | F% | Min | GP | G | A | Pts | PIM | PP | SH | GW | Min |
|---|---|---|---|---|---|---|---|---|---|---|---|---|---|---|---|---|---|---|---|---|---|---|---|---|---|
| 1993-94 | Delisle Contacts | SAHA | 30 | 25 | 50 | 75 | 25 | .... | .... | .... | .... | .... | .... | .... | .... | .... | .... | .... | .... | .... | .... | .... | .... | .... | .... |
| 1994-95 | Delisle Contacts | SAHA | 30 | 30 | 45 | 75 | 15 | .... | .... | .... | .... | .... | .... | .... | .... | .... | .... | .... | .... | .... | .... | .... | .... | .... | .... |
| 1995-96 | Sask. Contacts | SMHL | 44 | 18 | 12 | 30 | 20 | .... | .... | .... | .... | .... | .... | .... | .... | .... | .... | .... | .... | .... | .... | .... | .... | .... | .... |
| 1996-97 | Kelowna Rockets | WHL | 63 | 13 | 24 | 37 | 54 | .... | .... | .... | .... | .... | .... | .... | .... | .... | 1 | 0 | 0 | 0 | 0 | .... | .... | .... | .... |
| 1997-98 | Kelowna Rockets | WHL | 59 | 11 | 24 | 35 | 47 | .... | .... | .... | .... | .... | .... | .... | .... | .... | 7 | 0 | 1 | 1 | 8 | .... | .... | .... | .... |
| 1998-99 | Kelowna Rockets | WHL | 70 | 11 | 10 | 21 | 107 | .... | .... | .... | .... | .... | .... | .... | .... | .... | 6 | 3 | 0 | 3 | 0 | .... | .... | .... | .... |
| 99-2000 | Kelowna Rockets | WHL | 68 | 22 | 30 | 52 | 61 | .... | .... | .... | .... | .... | .... | .... | .... | .... | 5 | 1 | 1 | 2 | 8 | .... | .... | .... | .... |
| 2000-01 | Norfolk Admirals | AHL | 10 | 0 | 1 | 1 | 10 | .... | .... | .... | .... | .... | .... | .... | .... | .... | .... | .... | .... | .... | .... | .... | .... | .... | .... |
| | Jackson Bandits | ECHL | 60 | 13 | 24 | 37 | 39 | .... | .... | .... | .... | .... | .... | .... | .... | .... | 5 | 0 | 0 | 0 | 0 | .... | .... | .... | .... |
| 2001-02 | Jackson Bandits | ECHL | 16 | 4 | 6 | 10 | 12 | .... | .... | .... | .... | .... | .... | .... | .... | .... | .... | .... | .... | .... | .... | .... | .... | .... | .... |
| | Norfolk Admirals | AHL | 61 | 6 | 15 | 21 | 32 | .... | .... | .... | .... | .... | .... | .... | .... | .... | 4 | 0 | 0 | 0 | 2 | .... | .... | .... | .... |
| 2002-03 | Norfolk Admirals | AHL | 69 | 5 | 12 | 17 | 33 | .... | .... | .... | .... | .... | .... | .... | .... | .... | 8 | 2 | 2 | 4 | 0 | .... | .... | .... | .... |
| **2003-04** | **Chicago** | **NHL** | **3** | **0** | **1** | **1** | **0** | **0** | **0** | **0** | **3** | **0.0** | **1** | **0** | **0.0** | **11:57** | .... | .... | .... | .... | .... | .... | .... | .... | .... |
| | Norfolk Admirals | AHL | 78 | 12 | 10 | 22 | 74 | .... | .... | .... | .... | .... | .... | .... | .... | .... | 8 | 5 | 1 | 6 | 4 | .... | .... | .... | .... |
| 2004-05 | Norfolk Admirals | AHL | 66 | 10 | 13 | 23 | 54 | .... | .... | .... | .... | .... | .... | .... | .... | .... | 4 | 0 | 0 | 0 | 0 | .... | .... | .... | .... |
| 2005-06 | Norfolk Admirals | AHL | 73 | 14 | 31 | 45 | 70 | .... | .... | .... | .... | .... | .... | .... | .... | .... | 4 | 0 | 0 | 0 | 0 | .... | .... | .... | .... |
| 2006-07 | Hershey Bears | AHL | 75 | 15 | 28 | 43 | 44 | .... | .... | .... | .... | .... | .... | .... | .... | .... | 19 | 2 | 5 | 7 | 21 | .... | .... | .... | .... |
| **2007-08** | **Washington** | **NHL** | **39** | **1** | **5** | **6** | **10** | **0** | **0** | **1** | **48** | **2.1** | **4** | **6** | **33.3** | **11:33** | .... | .... | .... | .... | .... | .... | .... | .... | .... |
| | Hershey Bears | AHL | 20 | 2 | 6 | 8 | 28 | .... | .... | .... | .... | .... | .... | .... | .... | .... | .... | .... | .... | .... | .... | .... | .... | .... | .... |
| **2008-09** | **Washington** | **NHL** | **1** | **0** | **0** | **0** | **0** | **0** | **0** | **0** | **2** | **0.0** | **1** | **0** | **0.0** | **10:19** | .... | .... | .... | .... | .... | .... | .... | .... | .... |
| | Hershey Bears | AHL | 55 | 9 | 16 | 25 | 21 | .... | .... | .... | .... | .... | .... | .... | .... | .... | 9 | 2 | 2 | 4 | 0 | .... | .... | .... | .... |
| | **NHL Totals** | | **43** | **1** | **6** | **7** | **10** | **0** | **0** | **1** | **53** | **1.9** | | **6** | **33.3** | **11:33** | .... | .... | .... | .... | .... | .... | .... | .... | .... |

Signed as a free agent by **Chicago**, June 4, 2003. Signed as a free agent by **Washington**, July 18, 2006.

## LAMPMAN, Bryce

(LAMP-man, BRIGHS) **ST.L.**

Defense. Shoots left. 6'1", 199 lbs. Born, Rochester, MN, August 31, 1982. NY Rangers' 4th choice, 113th overall, in 2001 Entry Draft.

| Season | Club | League | GP | G | A | Pts | PIM | PP | SH | GW | S | % | +/- | TF | F% | Min | GP | G | A | Pts | PIM | PP | SH | GW | Min |
|---|---|---|---|---|---|---|---|---|---|---|---|---|---|---|---|---|---|---|---|---|---|---|---|---|---|
| 1998-99 | Rochester | USHL | 53 | 3 | 8 | 11 | 33 | .... | .... | .... | .... | .... | .... | .... | .... | .... | .... | .... | .... | .... | .... | .... | .... | .... | .... |
| 99-2000 | Rochester | USHL | 10 | 0 | 0 | 0 | 14 | .... | .... | .... | .... | .... | .... | .... | .... | .... | .... | .... | .... | .... | .... | .... | .... | .... | .... |
| | Omaha Lancers | USHL | 11 | 1 | 2 | 3 | 38 | .... | .... | .... | .... | .... | .... | .... | .... | .... | 4 | 0 | 0 | 0 | 0 | .... | .... | .... | .... |
| 2000-01 | Omaha Lancers | USHL | 55 | 10 | 11 | 21 | 77 | .... | .... | .... | .... | .... | .... | .... | .... | .... | 12 | 1 | 4 | 5 | 12 | .... | .... | .... | .... |
| 2001-02 | Nebraska-Omaha | CCHA | 26 | 0 | 4 | 4 | 28 | .... | .... | .... | .... | .... | .... | .... | .... | .... | .... | .... | .... | .... | .... | .... | .... | .... | .... |
| 2002-03 | Kamloops Blazers | WHL | 29 | 1 | 17 | 18 | 32 | .... | .... | .... | .... | .... | .... | .... | .... | .... | .... | .... | .... | .... | .... | .... | .... | .... | .... |
| | Hartford | AHL | 45 | 0 | 6 | 6 | 32 | .... | .... | .... | .... | .... | .... | .... | .... | .... | 2 | 0 | 1 | 1 | 0 | .... | .... | .... | .... |
| **2003-04** | **NY Rangers** | **NHL** | **8** | **0** | **0** | **0** | **0** | **0** | **0** | **0** | **7** | **0.0** | **–4** | **0** | **0.0** | **19:34** | .... | .... | .... | .... | .... | .... | .... | .... | .... |
| | Hartford | AHL | 68 | 4 | 11 | 15 | 50 | .... | .... | .... | .... | .... | .... | .... | .... | .... | 16 | 1 | 3 | 4 | 14 | .... | .... | .... | .... |
| 2004-05 | Hartford | AHL | 74 | 7 | 18 | 25 | 74 | .... | .... | .... | .... | .... | .... | .... | .... | .... | 4 | 0 | 0 | 0 | 4 | .... | .... | .... | .... |
| **2005-06** | **NY Rangers** | **NHL** | **1** | **0** | **0** | **0** | **2** | **0** | **0** | **0** | **1** | **0.0** | **–1** | **0** | **0.0** | **13:40** | .... | .... | .... | .... | .... | .... | .... | .... | .... |
| | Hartford | AHL | 11 | 2 | 3 | 5 | 16 | .... | .... | .... | .... | .... | .... | .... | .... | .... | .... | .... | .... | .... | .... | .... | .... | .... | .... |
| **2006-07** | **NY Rangers** | **NHL** | **1** | **0** | **0** | **0** | **0** | **0** | **0** | **0** | **0** | **0.0** | **0** | **0** | **0.0** | **12:08** | .... | .... | .... | .... | .... | .... | .... | .... | .... |
| | Hartford | AHL | 60 | 6 | 19 | 25 | 62 | .... | .... | .... | .... | .... | .... | .... | .... | .... | 7 | 2 | 0 | 2 | 2 | .... | .... | .... | .... |
| 2007-08 | Norfolk Admirals | AHL | 16 | 3 | 3 | 6 | 4 | .... | .... | .... | .... | .... | .... | .... | .... | .... | .... | .... | .... | .... | .... | .... | .... | .... | .... |
| | Iowa Stars | AHL | 53 | 4 | 11 | 15 | 32 | .... | .... | .... | .... | .... | .... | .... | .... | .... | .... | .... | .... | .... | .... | .... | .... | .... | .... |
| 2008-09 | Amur Khabarovsk | Rus-KHL | 9 | 0 | 0 | 0 | 4 | .... | .... | .... | .... | .... | .... | .... | .... | .... | .... | .... | .... | .... | .... | .... | .... | .... | .... |
| | **NHL Totals** | | **10** | **0** | **0** | **0** | **2** | **0** | **0** | **0** | **8** | **0.0** | | **0** | **0.0** | **18:14** | .... | .... | .... | .... | .... | .... | .... | .... | .... |

• Left **University of Nebraska-Omaha** (CCHA) and signed as a free agent by **Kamloops** (WHL), August 1, 2002. • Missed majority of 2005-06 season recovering from shoulder injury. • Rights traded to **Tampa Bay** by **NY Rangers** for the rights to Mitch Fritz, July 4, 2007. Traded to **Dallas** by **Tampa Bay** for Mario Scalzo, November 19, 2007. • Missed majority of 2008-09 season recovering from various injuries. Signed as a free agent by **St. Louis** July 29, 2009.

## LANG, Robert

(LANG, RAW-buhrt)

Center. Shoots right. 6'3", 217 lbs. Born, Teplice, Czech., December 19, 1970. Los Angeles' 6th choice, 133rd overall, in 1990 Entry Draft.

| Season | Club | League | GP | G | A | Pts | PIM | PP | SH | GW | S | % | +/- | TF | F% | Min | GP | G | A | Pts | PIM | PP | SH | GW | Min |
|---|---|---|---|---|---|---|---|---|---|---|---|---|---|---|---|---|---|---|---|---|---|---|---|---|---|
| 1988-89 | CHZ Litvinov | Czech | 7 | 3 | 2 | 5 | 0 | .... | .... | .... | .... | .... | .... | .... | .... | .... | .... | .... | .... | .... | .... | .... | .... | .... | .... |
| 1989-90 | CHZ Litvinov | Czech | 32 | 8 | 7 | 15 | .... | .... | .... | .... | .... | .... | .... | .... | .... | .... | 8 | 3 | 3 | 6 | .... | .... | .... | .... | .... |
| 1990-91 | HC CHZ Litvinov | Czech | 56 | 26 | 26 | 52 | 38 | .... | .... | .... | .... | .... | .... | .... | .... | .... | .... | .... | .... | .... | .... | .... | .... | .... | .... |
| 1991-92 | Litvinov | Czech | 43 | 12 | 31 | 43 | 34 | .... | .... | .... | .... | .... | .... | .... | .... | .... | .... | .... | .... | .... | .... | .... | .... | .... | .... |
| | Czechoslovakia | Olympics | 8 | 5 | 8 | 13 | 8 | .... | .... | .... | .... | .... | .... | .... | .... | .... | .... | .... | .... | .... | .... | .... | .... | .... | .... |
| **1992-93** | **Los Angeles** | **NHL** | **11** | **0** | **5** | **5** | **2** | **0** | **0** | **0** | **3** | **0.0** | **–3** | .... | .... | .... | .... | .... | .... | .... | .... | .... | .... | .... | .... |
| | Phoenix | IHL | 38 | 9 | 21 | 30 | 20 | .... | .... | .... | .... | .... | .... | .... | .... | .... | .... | .... | .... | .... | .... | .... | .... | .... | .... |
| **1993-94** | **Los Angeles** | **NHL** | **32** | **9** | **10** | **19** | **10** | **0** | **0** | **0** | **41** | **22.0** | **7** | .... | .... | .... | .... | .... | .... | .... | .... | .... | .... | .... | .... |
| | Phoenix | IHL | 44 | 11 | 24 | 35 | 34 | .... | .... | .... | .... | .... | .... | .... | .... | .... | .... | .... | .... | .... | .... | .... | .... | .... | .... |
| **1994-95** | Litvinov | CzRep | 16 | 4 | 19 | 23 | 28 | .... | .... | .... | .... | .... | .... | .... | .... | .... | .... | .... | .... | .... | .... | .... | .... | .... | .... |
| | **Los Angeles** | **NHL** | **36** | **4** | **8** | **12** | **4** | **0** | **0** | **0** | **38** | **10.5** | **–7** | .... | .... | .... | .... | .... | .... | .... | .... | .... | .... | .... | .... |
| **1995-96** | **Los Angeles** | **NHL** | **68** | **6** | **16** | **22** | **10** | **0** | **2** | **0** | **71** | **8.5** | **–15** | .... | .... | .... | .... | .... | .... | .... | .... | .... | .... | .... | .... |
| 1996-97 | HC Sparta Praha | CzRep | 38 | 14 | 27 | 41 | 30 | .... | .... | .... | .... | .... | .... | .... | .... | .... | 5 | 1 | 2 | 3 | 4 | .... | .... | .... | .... |
| | HC Sparta Praha | EuroHL | 4 | 2 | 2 | 4 | 0 | .... | .... | .... | .... | .... | .... | .... | .... | .... | 4 | 2 | 1 | 3 | 2 | .... | .... | .... | .... |
| **1997-98** | **Boston** | **NHL** | **3** | **0** | **0** | **0** | **2** | **0** | **0** | **0** | **2** | **0.0** | **1** | .... | .... | .... | .... | .... | .... | .... | .... | .... | .... | .... | .... |
| | **Pittsburgh** | **NHL** | **51** | **9** | **13** | **22** | **14** | **1** | **1** | **2** | **64** | **14.1** | **6** | .... | .... | .... | **6** | **0** | **3** | **3** | **2** | **0** | **0** | **0** | .... |
| | Czech Republic | Olympics | 6 | 0 | 3 | 3 | 0 | .... | .... | .... | .... | .... | .... | .... | .... | .... | .... | .... | .... | .... | .... | .... | .... | .... | .... |
| | Houston Aeros | IHL | 9 | 1 | 7 | 8 | 4 | .... | .... | .... | .... | .... | .... | .... | .... | .... | .... | .... | .... | .... | .... | .... | .... | .... | .... |
| **1998-99** | **Pittsburgh** | **NHL** | **72** | **21** | **23** | **44** | **24** | **7** | **0** | **3** | **137** | **15.3** | **–10** | .... | .... | .... | **12** | **0** | **2** | **2** | **0** | **0** | **0** | **0** | **13:58** |
| **99-2000** | **Pittsburgh** | **NHL** | **78** | **23** | **42** | **65** | **14** | **13** | **0** | **5** | **142** | **16.2** | **–9** | **964** | **44.8** | **16:24** | **11** | **3** | **3** | **6** | **0** | **2** | **0** | **0** | **21:42** |
| **2000-01** | **Pittsburgh** | **NHL** | **82** | **32** | **48** | **80** | **28** | **10** | **0** | **2** | **177** | **18.1** | **20** | **1433** | **50.7** | **19:22** | **16** | **4** | **4** | **8** | **4** | **0** | **0** | **0** | **19:21** |
| **2001-02** | **Pittsburgh** | **NHL** | **62** | **18** | **32** | **50** | **16** | **5** | **1** | **3** | **175** | **10.3** | **9** | **1348** | **43.9** | **20:24** | .... | .... | .... | .... | .... | .... | .... | .... | .... |
| | Czech Republic | Olympics | 4 | 1 | 2 | 3 | 2 | .... | .... | .... | .... | .... | .... | **1172** | **46.3** | **22:56** | .... | .... | .... | .... | .... | .... | .... | .... | .... |
| **2002-03** | **Washington** | **NHL** | **82** | **22** | **47** | **69** | **22** | **10** | **0** | **2** | **146** | **15.1** | **12** | **1069** | **45.9** | **18:47** | **6** | **2** | **1** | **3** | **2** | **0** | **0** | **1** | **21:55** |
| **2003-04** | **Washington** | **NHL** | **63** | **29** | **45** | **74** | **24** | **10** | **0** | **2** | **149** | **19.5** | **2** | **744** | **44.1** | **21:46** | .... | .... | .... | .... | .... | .... | .... | .... | .... |
| | **Detroit** | **NHL** | **6** | **1** | **4** | **5** | **0** | **0** | **0** | **1** | **14** | **7.1** | **2** | **96** | **57.3** | **16:20** | **12** | **4** | **5** | **9** | **6** | **0** | **0** | **0** | **18:10** |

| | | | Regular Season | | | | | | | | | | | | | | Playoffs | | | | | | | | |
|---|---|---|---|---|---|---|---|---|---|---|---|---|---|---|---|---|---|---|---|---|---|---|---|---|---|
| Season | Club | League | GP | G | A | Pts | PIM | PP | SH | GW | S | % | +/- | TF | F% | Min | GP | G | A | Pts | PIM | PP | SH | GW | Min |
| 2004-05 | | | DID NOT PLAY | | | | | | | | | | | | | | | | | | | | | | |
| **2005-06** | **Detroit** | **NHL** | **72** | **20** | **42** | **62** | **72** | **8** | **0** | **3** | **171** | **11.7** | **17** | **861** | **50.3** | **16:15** | **6** | **3** | **3** | **6** | **2** | **2** | **0** | **0** | **19:12** |
| | Czech Republic | Olympics | 8 | 0 | 4 | 4 | 4 | .... | .... | .... | .... | .... | .... | .... | .... | .... | .... | .... | .... | .... | .... | .... | .... | .... | .... |
| **2006-07** | **Detroit** | **NHL** | **81** | **19** | **33** | **52** | **66** | **6** | **0** | **4** | **166** | **11.4** | **12** | **812** | **49.4** | **16:49** | **18** | **2** | **6** | **8** | **8** | **0** | **0** | **0** | **15:10** |
| **2007-08** | **Chicago** | **NHL** | **76** | **21** | **33** | **54** | **50** | **7** | **0** | **3** | **172** | **12.2** | **9** | **1117** | **53.1** | **18:25** | .... | .... | .... | .... | .... | .... | .... | .... | .... |
| **2008-09** | **Montreal** | **NHL** | **50** | **18** | **21** | **39** | **36** | **8** | **1** | **3** | **101** | **17.8** | **6** | **768** | **48.8** | **16:53** | .... | .... | .... | .... | .... | .... | .... | .... | .... |
| | **NHL Totals** | | **925** | **252** | **422** | **674** | **394** | **85** | **5** | **33** | **1769** | **14.2** | | **10384** | **47.9** | **18:45** | **87** | **18** | **27** | **45** | **24** | **4** | **0** | **1** | **17:57** |

Played in NHL All-Star Game (2004)

Signed as a free agent by **Pittsburgh**, September 2, 1997. Claimed by **Boston** from **Pittsburgh** in Waiver Draft, September 28, 1997. Claimed on waivers by **Pittsburgh** from **Boston**, October 25, 1997. Signed as a free agent by **Washington**, July 1, 2002. Traded to **Detroit** by **Washington** for Tomas Fleischmann, Detroit's 1st round choice (Mike Green) in 2004 Entry Draft and Detroit's 4th round choice (Luke Lynes) in 2006 Entry Draft, February 27, 2004. Signed as a free agent by **Chicago**, July 2, 2007. Traded to **Montreal** by **Chicago** for Toronto's 2nd round choice (previously acquired) in 2010 Entry Draft, September 12, 2008.

## LANGENBRUNNER, Jamie

(lan-gehn-BRUH-nuhr, JAY-mee) **N.J.**

Right wing. Shoots right. 6'1", 205 lbs. Born, Cloquet, MN, July 24, 1975. Dallas' 2nd choice, 35th overall, in 1993 Entry Draft.

| Season | Club | League | GP | G | A | Pts | PIM | PP | SH | GW | S | % | +/- | TF | F% | Min | GP | G | A | Pts | PIM | PP | SH | GW | Min |
|---|---|---|---|---|---|---|---|---|---|---|---|---|---|---|---|---|---|---|---|---|---|---|---|---|---|
| 1990-91 | Cloquet | High-MN | 20 | 6 | 16 | 22 | 8 | .... | .... | .... | .... | .... | .... | .... | .... | .... | .... | .... | .... | .... | .... | .... | .... | .... | .... |
| 1991-92 | Cloquet | High-MN | 23 | 16 | 23 | 39 | 24 | .... | .... | .... | .... | .... | .... | .... | .... | .... | .... | .... | .... | .... | .... | .... | .... | .... | .... |
| 1992-93 | Cloquet | High-MN | 27 | 27 | 62 | 89 | 18 | .... | .... | .... | .... | .... | .... | .... | .... | .... | .... | .... | .... | .... | .... | .... | .... | .... | .... |
| 1993-94 | Peterborough | OHL | 62 | 33 | 58 | 91 | 53 | .... | .... | .... | .... | .... | .... | .... | .... | .... | 7 | 4 | 6 | 10 | 2 | .... | .... | .... | .... |
| **1994-95** | Peterborough | OHL | 62 | 42 | 57 | 99 | 84 | .... | .... | .... | .... | .... | .... | .... | .... | .... | 11 | 8 | 14 | 22 | 12 | .... | .... | .... | .... |
| | **Dallas** | **NHL** | **2** | **0** | **0** | **0** | **2** | **0** | **0** | **0** | **1** | **0.0** | **0** | .... | .... | .... | .... | .... | .... | .... | .... | .... | .... | .... | .... |
| | Kalamazoo Wings | IHL | .... | .... | .... | .... | .... | .... | .... | .... | .... | .... | .... | .... | .... | .... | 11 | 1 | 3 | 4 | 2 | .... | .... | .... | .... |
| **1995-96** | **Dallas** | **NHL** | **12** | **2** | **2** | **4** | **6** | **1** | **0** | **0** | **15** | **13.3** | **–2** | .... | .... | .... | .... | .... | .... | .... | .... | .... | .... | .... | .... |
| | Michigan | IHL | 59 | 25 | 40 | 65 | 129 | .... | .... | .... | .... | .... | .... | .... | .... | .... | 10 | 3 | 10 | 13 | 8 | .... | .... | .... | .... |
| **1996-97** | **Dallas** | **NHL** | **76** | **13** | **26** | **39** | **51** | **3** | **0** | **3** | **112** | **11.6** | **–2** | .... | .... | .... | **5** | **1** | **1** | **2** | **14** | **0** | **0** | **1** | .... |
| **1997-98** | **Dallas** | **NHL** | **81** | **23** | **29** | **52** | **61** | **8** | **0** | **6** | **159** | **14.5** | **9** | .... | .... | .... | **16** | **1** | **4** | **5** | **14** | **0** | **0** | **1** | .... |
| | United States | Olympics | 3 | 0 | 0 | 0 | 4 | .... | .... | .... | .... | .... | .... | .... | .... | .... | .... | .... | .... | .... | .... | .... | .... | .... | .... |
| **1998-99♦** | **Dallas** | **NHL** | **75** | **12** | **33** | **45** | **62** | **4** | **0** | **1** | **145** | **8.3** | **10** | **217** | **46.1** | **15:51** | **23** | **10** | **7** | **17** | **16** | **4** | **0** | **3** | **17:43** |
| **99-2000** | **Dallas** | **NHL** | **65** | **18** | **21** | **39** | **68** | **4** | **2** | **6** | **153** | **11.8** | **16** | **40** | **50.0** | **17:33** | **15** | **1** | **7** | **8** | **18** | **1** | **0** | **0** | **15:28** |
| **2000-01** | **Dallas** | **NHL** | **53** | **12** | **18** | **30** | **57** | **3** | **2** | **4** | **104** | **11.5** | **4** | **316** | **45.3** | **16:30** | **10** | **2** | **2** | **4** | **6** | **0** | **0** | **1** | **19:26** |
| **2001-02** | **Dallas** | **NHL** | **68** | **10** | **16** | **26** | **54** | **0** | **1** | **2** | **132** | **7.6** | **–11** | **120** | **45.0** | **15:45** | .... | .... | .... | .... | .... | .... | .... | .... | .... |
| | **New Jersey** | **NHL** | **14** | **3** | **3** | **6** | **23** | **0** | **0** | **2** | **31** | **9.7** | **2** | **2** | **50.0** | **15:27** | **5** | **0** | **1** | **1** | **8** | **0** | **0** | **0** | **14:57** |
| **2002-03♦** | **New Jersey** | **NHL** | **78** | **22** | **33** | **55** | **65** | **5** | **1** | **5** | **197** | **11.2** | **17** | **72** | **47.2** | **17:48** | **24** | ***11** | **7** | ***18** | **16** | **1** | **0** | **4** | **17:34** |
| **2003-04** | **New Jersey** | **NHL** | **53** | **10** | **16** | **26** | **43** | **1** | **2** | **2** | **130** | **7.7** | **9** | **31** | **51.6** | **16:01** | **5** | **0** | **2** | **2** | **2** | **0** | **0** | **0** | **15:04** |
| 2004-05 | ERC Ingolstadt | Germany | 11 | 2 | 2 | 4 | 22 | .... | .... | .... | .... | .... | .... | .... | .... | .... | 11 | 1 | 6 | 7 | 6 | .... | .... | .... | .... |
| **2005-06** | **New Jersey** | **NHL** | **80** | **19** | **34** | **53** | **74** | **8** | **1** | **1** | **243** | **7.8** | **–1** | **41** | **43.9** | **18:36** | **9** | **3** | **10** | **13** | **16** | **1** | **0** | **1** | **19:46** |
| **2006-07** | **New Jersey** | **NHL** | **82** | **23** | **37** | **60** | **64** | **12** | **0** | **7** | **243** | **9.5** | **–9** | **23** | **34.8** | **18:33** | **11** | **2** | **6** | **8** | **7** | **1** | **0** | **1** | **19:16** |
| **2007-08** | **New Jersey** | **NHL** | **64** | **13** | **28** | **41** | **30** | **5** | **1** | **2** | **152** | **8.6** | **–1** | **18** | **55.6** | **18:18** | **5** | **0** | **4** | **4** | **4** | **0** | **0** | **0** | **18:30** |
| **2008-09** | **New Jersey** | **NHL** | **81** | **29** | **40** | **69** | **56** | **6** | **3** | **7** | **229** | **12.7** | **25** | **25** | **40.0** | **18:06** | **4** | **2** | **1** | **3** | **2** | **0** | **0** | **0** | **16:13** |
| | **NHL Totals** | | **884** | **209** | **336** | **545** | **716** | **60** | **13** | **48** | **2046** | **10.2** | | **905** | **45.7** | **17:21** | **132** | **33** | **52** | **85** | **123** | **8** | **0** | **12** | **17:35** |

Traded to **New Jersey** by **Dallas** with Joe Nieuwendyk for Jason Arnott, Randy McKay and New Jersey's 1st round choice (later traded to Columbus – later traded to Buffalo – Buffalo selected Daniel Paille) in 2002 Entry Draft, March 19, 2002. Signed as a free agent by **Ingolstadt** (Germany), January 24, 2005.

## LANGFELD, Josh

(LANG-fehld, JAWSH)

Right wing. Shoots right. 6'3", 216 lbs. Born, Fridley, MN, July 17, 1977. Ottawa's 3rd choice, 66th overall, in 1997 Entry Draft.

| Season | Club | League | GP | G | A | Pts | PIM | PP | SH | GW | S | % | +/- | TF | F% | Min | GP | G | A | Pts | PIM | PP | SH | GW | Min |
|---|---|---|---|---|---|---|---|---|---|---|---|---|---|---|---|---|---|---|---|---|---|---|---|---|---|
| 1995-96 | Great Falls | AFHL | 45 | 45 | 40 | 85 | 105 | .... | .... | .... | .... | .... | .... | .... | .... | .... | .... | .... | .... | .... | .... | .... | .... | .... | .... |
| 1996-97 | Lincoln Stars | USHL | 38 | 35 | 23 | 58 | 100 | .... | .... | .... | .... | .... | .... | .... | .... | .... | 14 | 8 | *13 | *21 | 42 | .... | .... | .... | .... |
| 1997-98 | U. of Michigan | CCHA | 46 | 19 | 17 | 36 | 66 | .... | .... | .... | .... | .... | .... | .... | .... | .... | .... | .... | .... | .... | .... | .... | .... | .... | .... |
| 1998-99 | U. of Michigan | CCHA | 41 | 21 | 14 | 35 | 84 | .... | .... | .... | .... | .... | .... | .... | .... | .... | .... | .... | .... | .... | .... | .... | .... | .... | .... |
| 99-2000 | U. of Michigan | CCHA | 39 | 9 | 21 | 30 | 56 | .... | .... | .... | .... | .... | .... | .... | .... | .... | .... | .... | .... | .... | .... | .... | .... | .... | .... |
| 2000-01 | U. of Michigan | CCHA | 42 | 16 | 12 | 28 | 44 | .... | .... | .... | .... | .... | .... | .... | .... | .... | .... | .... | .... | .... | .... | .... | .... | .... | .... |
| **2001-02** | **Ottawa** | **NHL** | **1** | **0** | **0** | **0** | **2** | **0** | **0** | **0** | **5** | **0.0** | **0** | **0** | **0.0** | **8:15** | .... | .... | .... | .... | .... | .... | .... | .... | .... |
| | Grand Rapids | AHL | 68 | 21 | 16 | 37 | 29 | .... | .... | .... | .... | .... | .... | .... | .... | .... | 5 | 2 | 0 | 2 | 0 | .... | .... | .... | .... |
| **2002-03** | **Ottawa** | **NHL** | **12** | **0** | **1** | **1** | **4** | **0** | **0** | **0** | **16** | **0.0** | **2** | **0** | **0.0** | **11:11** | .... | .... | .... | .... | .... | .... | .... | .... | .... |
| | Binghamton | AHL | 59 | 14 | 21 | 35 | 38 | .... | .... | .... | .... | .... | .... | .... | .... | .... | 13 | 5 | 3 | 8 | 8 | .... | .... | .... | .... |
| **2003-04** | **Ottawa** | **NHL** | **38** | **7** | **10** | **17** | **16** | **2** | **0** | **2** | **59** | **11.9** | **6** | **5** | **80.0** | **10:53** | .... | .... | .... | .... | .... | .... | .... | .... | .... |
| | Binghamton | AHL | 30 | 13 | 14 | 27 | 25 | .... | .... | .... | .... | .... | .... | .... | .... | .... | 2 | 0 | 0 | 0 | 0 | .... | .... | .... | .... |
| 2004-05 | Binghamton | AHL | 74 | 32 | 25 | 57 | 75 | .... | .... | .... | .... | .... | .... | .... | .... | .... | 6 | 2 | 2 | 4 | 2 | .... | .... | .... | .... |
| **2005-06** | **San Jose** | **NHL** | **39** | **2** | **9** | **11** | **16** | **0** | **1** | **0** | **53** | **3.8** | **4** | **8** | **12.5** | **11:46** | .... | .... | .... | .... | .... | .... | .... | .... | .... |
| | **Boston** | **NHL** | **18** | **0** | **1** | **1** | **10** | **0** | **0** | **0** | **32** | **0.0** | **–6** | **6** | **16.7** | **9:24** | .... | .... | .... | .... | .... | .... | .... | .... | .... |
| **2006-07** | **Detroit** | **NHL** | **33** | **0** | **2** | **2** | **12** | **0** | **0** | **0** | **37** | **0.0** | **2** | **1** | **100.0** | **5:33** | .... | .... | .... | .... | .... | .... | .... | .... | .... |
| | Grand Rapids | AHL | 38 | 13 | 19 | 32 | 44 | .... | .... | .... | .... | .... | .... | .... | .... | .... | .... | .... | .... | .... | .... | .... | .... | .... | .... |
| **2007-08** | **Nashville** | **NHL** | **2** | **0** | **0** | **0** | **0** | **0** | **0** | **0** | **5** | **0.0** | **0** | **0** | **0.0** | **9:48** | **1** | **0** | **0** | **0** | **0** | **0** | **0** | **0** | **6:30** |
| | Milwaukee | AHL | 44 | 22 | 7 | 29 | 34 | .... | .... | .... | .... | .... | .... | .... | .... | .... | 5 | 5 | 1 | 6 | 6 | .... | .... | .... | .... |
| 2008-09 | Frankfurt Lions | Germany | 45 | 21 | 16 | 37 | 63 | .... | .... | .... | .... | .... | .... | .... | .... | .... | 4 | 0 | 0 | 0 | 2 | .... | .... | .... | .... |
| | **NHL Totals** | | **143** | **9** | **23** | **32** | **60** | **2** | **1** | **2** | **207** | **4.3** | | **20** | **35.0** | **9:42** | **1** | **0** | **0** | **0** | **0** | **0** | **0** | **0** | **6:30** |

NCAA Championship All-Tournament Team (1998)

Signed as a free agent by **San Jose**, September 12, 2005. Claimed on waivers by **Boston** from **San Jose**, January 31, 2006. Signed as a free agent by **Detroit**, July 14, 2006. Signed as a free agent by **Nashville**, September 4, 2007.

## LANGKOW, Daymond

(LANG-kow, DAY-muhn) **CGY.**

Center. Shoots left. 5'10", 183 lbs. Born, Edmonton, Alta., September 27, 1976. Tampa Bay's 1st choice, 5th overall, in 1995 Entry Draft.

| Season | Club | League | GP | G | A | Pts | PIM | PP | SH | GW | S | % | +/- | TF | F% | Min | GP | G | A | Pts | PIM | PP | SH | GW | Min |
|---|---|---|---|---|---|---|---|---|---|---|---|---|---|---|---|---|---|---|---|---|---|---|---|---|---|
| 1991-92 | Edmonton Pats | AMHL | 35 | 36 | 45 | 81 | 100 | .... | .... | .... | .... | .... | .... | .... | .... | .... | .... | .... | .... | .... | .... | .... | .... | .... | .... |
| | Tri-City | WHL | 1 | 0 | 0 | 0 | 0 | .... | .... | .... | .... | .... | .... | .... | .... | .... | .... | .... | .... | .... | .... | .... | .... | .... | .... |
| 1992-93 | Tri-City | WHL | 64 | 22 | 42 | 64 | 100 | .... | .... | .... | .... | .... | .... | .... | .... | .... | 4 | 1 | 0 | 1 | 4 | .... | .... | .... | .... |
| 1993-94 | Tri-City | WHL | 61 | 40 | 43 | 83 | 174 | .... | .... | .... | .... | .... | .... | .... | .... | .... | 4 | 2 | 2 | 4 | 15 | .... | .... | .... | .... |
| 1994-95 | Tri-City | WHL | 72 | *67 | 73 | *140 | 142 | .... | .... | .... | .... | .... | .... | .... | .... | .... | 17 | 12 | 15 | 27 | 52 | .... | .... | .... | .... |
| **1995-96** | Tri-City | WHL | 48 | 30 | 61 | 91 | 103 | .... | .... | .... | .... | .... | .... | .... | .... | .... | 11 | 14 | 13 | 27 | 20 | .... | .... | .... | .... |
| | **Tampa Bay** | **NHL** | **4** | **0** | **1** | **1** | **0** | **0** | **0** | **0** | **4** | **0.0** | **–1** | .... | .... | .... | .... | .... | .... | .... | .... | .... | .... | .... | .... |
| **1996-97** | **Tampa Bay** | **NHL** | **79** | **15** | **13** | **28** | **35** | **3** | **1** | **1** | **170** | **8.8** | **1** | .... | .... | .... | .... | .... | .... | .... | .... | .... | .... | .... | .... |
| | Adirondack | AHL | 2 | 1 | 1 | 2 | 0 | .... | .... | .... | .... | .... | .... | .... | .... | .... | .... | .... | .... | .... | .... | .... | .... | .... | .... |
| **1997-98** | **Tampa Bay** | **NHL** | **68** | **8** | **14** | **22** | **62** | **2** | **0** | **1** | **156** | **5.1** | **–9** | .... | .... | .... | .... | .... | .... | .... | .... | .... | .... | .... | .... |
| **1998-99** | **Tampa Bay** | **NHL** | **22** | **4** | **6** | **10** | **15** | **1** | **0** | **1** | **40** | **10.0** | **0** | **399** | **48.4** | **17:10** | .... | .... | .... | .... | .... | .... | .... | .... | .... |
| | Cleveland | IHL | 4 | 1 | 1 | 2 | 18 | .... | .... | .... | .... | .... | .... | .... | .... | .... | .... | .... | .... | .... | .... | .... | .... | .... | .... |
| | **Philadelphia** | **NHL** | **56** | **10** | **13** | **23** | **24** | **3** | **1** | **1** | **109** | **9.2** | **–8** | **738** | **48.0** | **15:12** | **6** | **0** | **2** | **2** | **2** | **0** | **0** | **0** | **16:50** |
| **99-2000** | **Philadelphia** | **NHL** | **82** | **18** | **32** | **50** | **56** | **5** | **0** | **7** | **222** | **8.1** | **1** | **1263** | **45.1** | **16:57** | **16** | **5** | **5** | **10** | **23** | **1** | **1** | **2** | **20:03** |
| **2000-01** | **Philadelphia** | **NHL** | **71** | **13** | **41** | **54** | **50** | **3** | **0** | **2** | **190** | **6.8** | **12** | **1181** | **47.2** | **18:38** | **6** | **2** | **4** | **6** | **2** | **1** | **0** | **0** | **20:17** |
| **2001-02** | **Phoenix** | **NHL** | **80** | **27** | **35** | **62** | **36** | **6** | **3** | **2** | **171** | **15.8** | **18** | **1379** | **46.2** | **19:11** | **5** | **1** | **0** | **1** | **0** | **0** | **0** | **0** | **21:06** |
| **2002-03** | **Phoenix** | **NHL** | **82** | **20** | **32** | **52** | **56** | **4** | **2** | **2** | **196** | **10.2** | **20** | **1972** | **46.5** | **21:00** | .... | .... | .... | .... | .... | .... | .... | .... | .... |
| **2003-04** | **Phoenix** | **NHL** | **81** | **21** | **31** | **52** | **40** | **4** | **1** | **2** | **174** | **12.1** | **4** | **1472** | **43.1** | **21:07** | .... | .... | .... | .... | .... | .... | .... | .... | .... |
| 2004-05 | | | DID NOT PLAY | | | | | | | | | | | | | | | | | | | | | | |
| **2005-06** | **Calgary** | **NHL** | **82** | **25** | **34** | **59** | **46** | **11** | **0** | **7** | **171** | **14.6** | **2** | **1130** | **47.4** | **18:07** | **7** | **1** | **5** | **6** | **6** | **1** | **0** | **0** | **19:42** |
| **2006-07** | **Calgary** | **NHL** | **81** | **33** | **44** | **77** | **44** | **10** | **1** | **6** | **247** | **13.4** | **23** | **1173** | **45.9** | **20:07** | **6** | **2** | **2** | **4** | **4** | **2** | **0** | **1** | **20:06** |
| **2007-08** | **Calgary** | **NHL** | **80** | **30** | **35** | **65** | **19** | **14** | **1** | **4** | **201** | **14.9** | **16** | **817** | **43.7** | **18:50** | **7** | **3** | **2** | **5** | **0** | **2** | **0** | **0** | **18:21** |
| **2008-09** | **Calgary** | **NHL** | **73** | **21** | **28** | **49** | **20** | **4** | **0** | **3** | **161** | **13.0** | **1** | **753** | **46.9** | **17:11** | **6** | **0** | **3** | **3** | **2** | **0** | **0** | **0** | **17:06** |
| | **NHL Totals** | | **941** | **245** | **359** | **604** | **503** | **70** | **10** | **39** | **2212** | **11.1** | | **12277** | **46.0** | **18:43** | **59** | **14** | **23** | **37** | **39** | **7** | **1** | **3** | **19:18** |

WHL West First All-Star Team (1995) • Canadian Major Junior First All-Star Team (1995) • WHL West Second All-Star Team (1996)

Traded to **Philadelphia** by **Tampa Bay** with Mikael Renberg for Chris Gratton and Mike Sillinger, December 12, 1998. Traded to **Phoenix** by **Philadelphia** for Phoenix's 2nd round choice (later traded to Tampa Bay – later traded to San Jose – San Jose selected Dan Spang) in 2002 Entry Draft and Phoenix's 1st round choice (Jeff Carter) in 2003 Entry Draft, July 2, 2001. Traded to **Calgary** by **Phoenix** for Denis Gauthier and Oleg Saprykin, August 26, 2004.

## LAPERRIERE, Ian
(luh-PAIR-ee-YAIR, EE-an) **PHI.**

Right wing. Shoots right. 6'1", 200 lbs. Born, Montreal, Que., January 19, 1974. St. Louis' 6th choice, 158th overall, in 1992 Entry Draft.

| | | | Regular Season | | | | | | | | | | | | | | Playoffs | | | | | | | | |
|---|---|---|---|---|---|---|---|---|---|---|---|---|---|---|---|---|---|---|---|---|---|---|---|---|---|
| Season | Club | League | GP | G | A | Pts | PIM | PP | SH | GW | S | % | +/- | TF | F% | Min | GP | G | A | Pts | PIM | PP | SH | GW | Min |
| 1989-90 | Mtl-Bourassa | QAAA | 22 | 4 | 10 | 14 | 10 | .... | .... | .... | .... | .... | .... | .... | .... | .... | 3 | 0 | 1 | 1 | 6 | .... | .... | .... | .... |
| 1990-91 | Drummondville | QMJHL | 65 | 19 | 29 | 48 | 117 | .... | .... | .... | .... | .... | .... | .... | .... | .... | 14 | 2 | 9 | 11 | 48 | .... | .... | .... | .... |
| 1991-92 | Drummondville | QMJHL | 70 | 28 | 49 | 77 | 160 | .... | .... | .... | .... | .... | .... | .... | .... | .... | 4 | 2 | 2 | 4 | 9 | .... | .... | .... | .... |
| 1992-93 | Drummondville | QMJHL | 60 | 44 | *96 | 140 | 188 | .... | .... | .... | .... | .... | .... | .... | .... | .... | 10 | 6 | 13 | 19 | 20 | .... | .... | .... | .... |
| **1993-94** | Drummondville | QMJHL | 62 | 41 | 72 | 113 | 150 | .... | .... | .... | .... | .... | .... | .... | .... | .... | 9 | 4 | 6 | 10 | 35 | .... | .... | .... | .... |
| | **St. Louis** | **NHL** | **1** | **0** | **0** | **0** | **0** | **0** | **0** | **0** | **1** | **0.0** | **0** | .... | .... | .... | .... | .... | .... | .... | .... | .... | .... | .... | .... |
| | Peoria Rivermen | IHL | .... | .... | .... | .... | .... | .... | .... | .... | .... | .... | .... | .... | .... | .... | 5 | 1 | 3 | 4 | 2 | .... | .... | .... | .... |
| **1994-95** | Peoria Rivermen | IHL | 51 | 16 | 32 | 48 | 111 | .... | .... | .... | .... | .... | .... | .... | .... | .... | .... | .... | .... | .... | .... | .... | .... | .... | .... |
| | **St. Louis** | **NHL** | **37** | **13** | **14** | **27** | **85** | **1** | **0** | **1** | **53** | **24.5** | **12** | .... | .... | .... | **7** | **0** | **4** | **4** | **21** | **0** | **0** | **0** | .... |
| **1995-96** | **St. Louis** | **NHL** | **33** | **3** | **6** | **9** | **87** | **1** | **0** | **1** | **31** | **9.7** | **-4** | .... | .... | .... | .... | .... | .... | .... | .... | .... | .... | .... | .... |
| | Worcester IceCats | AHL | 3 | 2 | 1 | 3 | 22 | .... | .... | .... | .... | .... | .... | .... | .... | .... | .... | .... | .... | .... | .... | .... | .... | .... | .... |
| | **NY Rangers** | **NHL** | **28** | **1** | **2** | **3** | **53** | **0** | **0** | **0** | **21** | **4.8** | **-5** | .... | .... | .... | .... | .... | .... | .... | .... | .... | .... | .... | .... |
| | **Los Angeles** | **NHL** | **10** | **2** | **3** | **5** | **15** | **0** | **0** | **0** | **18** | **11.1** | **-2** | .... | .... | .... | .... | .... | .... | .... | .... | .... | .... | .... | .... |
| **1996-97** | **Los Angeles** | **NHL** | **62** | **8** | **15** | **23** | **102** | **0** | **1** | **2** | **84** | **9.5** | **-25** | .... | .... | .... | .... | .... | .... | .... | .... | .... | .... | .... | .... |
| **1997-98** | **Los Angeles** | **NHL** | **77** | **6** | **15** | **21** | **131** | **0** | **1** | **1** | **74** | **8.1** | **0** | .... | .... | .... | **4** | **1** | **0** | **1** | **6** | **0** | **0** | **0** | .... |
| **1998-99** | **Los Angeles** | **NHL** | **72** | **3** | **10** | **13** | **138** | **0** | **0** | **1** | **62** | **4.8** | **-5** | **643** | **47.3** | **11:47** | .... | .... | .... | .... | .... | .... | .... | .... | .... |
| **99-2000** | **Los Angeles** | **NHL** | **79** | **9** | **13** | **22** | **185** | **0** | **0** | **1** | **87** | **10.3** | **-14** | **1111** | **53.7** | **13:15** | **4** | **0** | **0** | **0** | **2** | **0** | **0** | **0** | **10:22** |
| **2000-01** | **Los Angeles** | **NHL** | **79** | **8** | **10** | **18** | **141** | **0** | **0** | **0** | **60** | **13.3** | **5** | **297** | **51.9** | **12:02** | **13** | **1** | **2** | **3** | **12** | **0** | **0** | **0** | **14:01** |
| **2001-02** | **Los Angeles** | **NHL** | **81** | **8** | **14** | **22** | **125** | **0** | **0** | **3** | **89** | **9.0** | **5** | **134** | **49.3** | **13:45** | **7** | **0** | **1** | **1** | **9** | **0** | **0** | **0** | **14:18** |
| **2002-03** | **Los Angeles** | **NHL** | **73** | **7** | **12** | **19** | **122** | **1** | **1** | **1** | **85** | **8.2** | **-9** | **317** | **49.2** | **15:46** | .... | .... | .... | .... | .... | .... | .... | .... | .... |
| **2003-04** | **Los Angeles** | **NHL** | **62** | **10** | **12** | **22** | **58** | **1** | **0** | **3** | **59** | **16.9** | **-4** | **446** | **54.0** | **15:50** | .... | .... | .... | .... | .... | .... | .... | .... | .... |
| 2004-05 | | | DID NOT PLAY | | | | | | | | | | | | | | | | | | | | | | |
| **2005-06** | **Colorado** | **NHL** | **82** | **21** | **24** | **45** | **116** | **1** | **1** | **3** | **133** | **15.8** | **3** | **963** | **45.9** | **17:10** | **9** | **0** | **1** | **1** | **27** | **0** | **0** | **0** | **13:40** |
| **2006-07** | **Colorado** | **NHL** | **81** | **8** | **21** | **29** | **133** | **0** | **0** | **0** | **118** | **6.8** | **5** | **389** | **46.8** | **13:51** | .... | .... | .... | .... | .... | .... | .... | .... | .... |
| **2007-08** | **Colorado** | **NHL** | **70** | **4** | **15** | **19** | **140** | **0** | **0** | **1** | **68** | **5.9** | **-5** | **141** | **45.4** | **13:39** | **10** | **1** | **1** | **2** | **19** | **0** | **0** | **0** | **12:54** |
| **2008-09** | **Colorado** | **NHL** | **74** | **7** | **12** | **19** | **163** | **0** | **0** | **0** | **61** | **11.5** | **0** | **446** | **44.0** | **13:50** | .... | .... | .... | .... | .... | .... | .... | .... | .... |
| | **NHL Totals** | | **1001** | **118** | **198** | **316** | **1794** | **5** | **4** | **18** | **1104** | **10.7** | | **4887** | **49.1** | **14:05** | **54** | **3** | **9** | **12** | **96** | **0** | **0** | **0** | **13:23** |

QMJHL Second All-Star Team (1993)

Traded to **NY Rangers** by **St. Louis** for Stephane Matteau, December 28, 1995. Traded to **Los Angeles** by **NY Rangers** with Ray Ferraro, Mattias Norstrom, Nathan LaFayette and NY Rangers' 4th round choice (Sean Blanchard) in 1997 Entry Draft for Marty McSorley, Jari Kurri and Shane Churla, March 14, 1996. Signed as a free agent by **Colorado**, July 2, 2004. Signed as a free agent by **Philadelphia**, July 1, 2009.

## LAPIERRE, Maxim
(la-PEE-air, max-EEM) **MTL.**

Center. Shoots right. 6'2", 207 lbs. Born, St. Leonard, Que., March 29, 1985. Montreal's 3rd choice, 61st overall, in 2003 Entry Draft.

| | | | Regular Season | | | | | | | | | | | | | | Playoffs | | | | | | | | |
|---|---|---|---|---|---|---|---|---|---|---|---|---|---|---|---|---|---|---|---|---|---|---|---|---|---|
| Season | Club | League | GP | G | A | Pts | PIM | PP | SH | GW | S | % | +/- | TF | F% | Min | GP | G | A | Pts | PIM | PP | SH | GW | Min |
| 2001-02 | Cap-d-Madeleine | QAAA | 42 | 14 | 27 | 41 | 44 | .... | .... | .... | .... | .... | .... | .... | .... | .... | 10 | 3 | 5 | 8 | 16 | .... | .... | .... | .... |
| | Montreal Rocket | QMJHL | 9 | 2 | 0 | 2 | 2 | .... | .... | .... | .... | .... | .... | .... | .... | .... | .... | .... | .... | .... | .... | .... | .... | .... | .... |
| 2002-03 | Montreal Rocket | QMJHL | 72 | 22 | 21 | 43 | 55 | .... | .... | .... | .... | .... | .... | .... | .... | .... | 7 | 1 | 3 | 4 | 6 | .... | .... | .... | .... |
| 2003-04 | PEI Rocket | QMJHL | 67 | 25 | 36 | 61 | 138 | .... | .... | .... | .... | .... | .... | .... | .... | .... | 11 | 7 | 2 | 9 | 14 | .... | .... | .... | .... |
| 2004-05 | PEI Rocket | QMJHL | 69 | 25 | 27 | 52 | 139 | .... | .... | .... | .... | .... | .... | .... | .... | .... | .... | .... | .... | .... | .... | .... | .... | .... | .... |
| **2005-06** | **Montreal** | **NHL** | **1** | **0** | **0** | **0** | **0** | **0** | **0** | **0** | **0** | **0.0** | **-1** | **2** | **50.0** | **3:04** | .... | .... | .... | .... | .... | .... | .... | .... | .... |
| | Hamilton | AHL | 73 | 13 | 23 | 36 | 214 | .... | .... | .... | .... | .... | .... | .... | .... | .... | .... | .... | .... | .... | .... | .... | .... | .... | .... |
| **2006-07** | **Montreal** | **NHL** | **46** | **6** | **6** | **12** | **24** | **0** | **1** | **2** | **82** | **7.3** | **-7** | **425** | **45.2** | **11:25** | .... | .... | .... | .... | .... | .... | .... | .... | .... |
| | Hamilton | AHL | 37 | 11 | 13 | 24 | 59 | .... | .... | .... | .... | .... | .... | .... | .... | .... | 22 | 6 | 6 | 12 | 41 | .... | .... | .... | .... |
| **2007-08** | **Montreal** | **NHL** | **53** | **7** | **11** | **18** | **60** | **0** | **0** | **0** | **68** | **10.3** | **5** | **527** | **49.2** | **13:10** | **12** | **0** | **3** | **3** | **6** | **0** | **0** | **0** | **11:38** |
| | Hamilton | AHL | 19 | 7 | 7 | 14 | 63 | .... | .... | .... | .... | .... | .... | .... | .... | .... | .... | .... | .... | .... | .... | .... | .... | .... | .... |
| **2008-09** | **Montreal** | **NHL** | **79** | **15** | **13** | **28** | **76** | **1** | **2** | **2** | **165** | **9.1** | **9** | **987** | **53.2** | **14:48** | **4** | **0** | **0** | **0** | **26** | **0** | **0** | **0** | **14:56** |
| | **NHL Totals** | | **179** | **28** | **30** | **58** | **160** | **1** | **3** | **4** | **315** | **8.9** | | **1941** | **50.3** | **13:23** | **16** | **0** | **3** | **3** | **32** | **0** | **0** | **0** | **12:27** |

## LARAQUE, Georges
(luh-RAK, ZHAWRZH) **MTL.**

Right wing. Shoots right. 6'3", 253 lbs. Born, Montreal, Que., December 7, 1976. Edmonton's 2nd choice, 31st overall, in 1995 Entry Draft.

| | | | Regular Season | | | | | | | | | | | | | | Playoffs | | | | | | | | |
|---|---|---|---|---|---|---|---|---|---|---|---|---|---|---|---|---|---|---|---|---|---|---|---|---|---|
| Season | Club | League | GP | G | A | Pts | PIM | PP | SH | GW | S | % | +/- | TF | F% | Min | GP | G | A | Pts | PIM | PP | SH | GW | Min |
| 1991-92 | Mtl-Bourassa | QAHA | 28 | 20 | 20 | 40 | 30 | .... | .... | .... | .... | .... | .... | .... | .... | .... | .... | .... | .... | .... | .... | .... | .... | .... | .... |
| 1992-93 | Mtl-Bourassa | QAAA | 37 | 8 | 20 | 28 | 50 | .... | .... | .... | .... | .... | .... | .... | .... | .... | 3 | 1 | 2 | 3 | 2 | .... | .... | .... | .... |
| 1993-94 | St-Jean Lynx | QMJHL | 70 | 11 | 11 | 22 | 142 | .... | .... | .... | .... | .... | .... | .... | .... | .... | 4 | 0 | 0 | 0 | 7 | .... | .... | .... | .... |
| 1994-95 | St-Jean Lynx | QMJHL | 62 | 19 | 22 | 41 | 259 | .... | .... | .... | .... | .... | .... | .... | .... | .... | 7 | 1 | 1 | 2 | 42 | .... | .... | .... | .... |
| 1995-96 | Laval Titan | QMJHL | 11 | 8 | 13 | 21 | 76 | .... | .... | .... | .... | .... | .... | .... | .... | .... | .... | .... | .... | .... | .... | .... | .... | .... | .... |
| | St-Hyacinthe | QMJHL | 8 | 3 | 4 | 7 | 59 | .... | .... | .... | .... | .... | .... | .... | .... | .... | .... | .... | .... | .... | .... | .... | .... | .... | .... |
| | Granby | QMJHL | 22 | 9 | 7 | 16 | 125 | .... | .... | .... | .... | .... | .... | .... | .... | .... | 18 | 7 | 6 | 13 | 104 | .... | .... | .... | .... |
| 1996-97 | Hamilton | AHL | 73 | 14 | 20 | 34 | 179 | .... | .... | .... | .... | .... | .... | .... | .... | .... | 15 | 1 | 3 | 4 | 12 | .... | .... | .... | .... |
| **1997-98** | **Edmonton** | **NHL** | **11** | **0** | **0** | **0** | **59** | **0** | **0** | **0** | **4** | **0.0** | **-4** | .... | .... | .... | .... | .... | .... | .... | .... | .... | .... | .... | .... |
| | Hamilton | AHL | 46 | 10 | 20 | 30 | 154 | .... | .... | .... | .... | .... | .... | .... | .... | .... | 3 | 0 | 0 | 0 | 11 | .... | .... | .... | .... |
| **1998-99** | **Edmonton** | **NHL** | **39** | **3** | **2** | **5** | **57** | **0** | **0** | **0** | **17** | **17.6** | **-1** | **0** | **0.0** | **5:31** | **4** | **0** | **0** | **0** | **2** | **0** | **0** | **0** | **7:35** |
| | Hamilton | AHL | 25 | 6 | 8 | 14 | 93 | .... | .... | .... | .... | .... | .... | .... | .... | .... | .... | .... | .... | .... | .... | .... | .... | .... | .... |
| **99-2000** | **Edmonton** | **NHL** | **76** | **8** | **8** | **16** | **123** | **0** | **0** | **0** | **56** | **14.3** | **5** | **0** | **0.0** | **8:28** | **5** | **0** | **1** | **1** | **6** | **0** | **0** | **0** | **9:14** |
| **2000-01** | **Edmonton** | **NHL** | **82** | **13** | **16** | **29** | **148** | **1** | **0** | **1** | **73** | **17.8** | **5** | **0** | **0.0** | **9:03** | **6** | **1** | **1** | **2** | **8** | **0** | **0** | **0** | **9:54** |
| **2001-02** | **Edmonton** | **NHL** | **80** | **5** | **14** | **19** | **157** | **1** | **0** | **1** | **95** | **5.3** | **6** | **0** | **0.0** | **9:48** | .... | .... | .... | .... | .... | .... | .... | .... | .... |
| **2002-03** | **Edmonton** | **NHL** | **64** | **6** | **7** | **13** | **110** | **0** | **0** | **2** | **46** | **13.0** | **-4** | **0** | **0.0** | **9:15** | **6** | **1** | **3** | **4** | **4** | **0** | **0** | **0** | **12:11** |
| **2003-04** | **Edmonton** | **NHL** | **66** | **6** | **11** | **17** | **99** | **1** | **0** | **1** | **54** | **11.1** | **7** | **0** | **0.0** | **9:22** | .... | .... | .... | .... | .... | .... | .... | .... | .... |
| 2004-05 | AIK Solna | Sweden-3 | 16 | 11 | 5 | 16 | 24 | .... | .... | .... | .... | .... | .... | .... | .... | .... | .... | .... | .... | .... | .... | .... | .... | .... | .... |
| **2005-06** | **Edmonton** | **NHL** | **72** | **2** | **10** | **12** | **73** | **0** | **0** | **0** | **50** | **4.0** | **-5** | **3** | **33.3** | **6:35** | **15** | **1** | **1** | **2** | ***44** | **0** | **0** | **0** | **5:31** |
| **2006-07** | **Phoenix** | **NHL** | **56** | **5** | **17** | **22** | **52** | **1** | **0** | **0** | **34** | **14.7** | **7** | **14** | **28.6** | **10:17** | .... | .... | .... | .... | .... | .... | .... | .... | .... |
| | **Pittsburgh** | **NHL** | **17** | **0** | **2** | **2** | **18** | **0** | **0** | **0** | **10** | **0.0** | **-3** | **3** | **33.3** | **7:34** | **2** | **0** | **0** | **0** | **0** | **0** | **0** | **0** | **4:25** |
| **2007-08** | **Pittsburgh** | **NHL** | **71** | **4** | **9** | **13** | **141** | **0** | **0** | **2** | **29** | **13.8** | **0** | **1** | **0.0** | **7:42** | **15** | **1** | **2** | **3** | **4** | **0** | **0** | **0** | **6:02** |
| **2008-09** | **Montreal** | **NHL** | **33** | **0** | **2** | **2** | **61** | **0** | **0** | **0** | **15** | **0.0** | **-6** | **1** | **0.0** | **7:39** | **4** | **0** | **0** | **0** | **4** | **0** | **0** | **0** | **10:58** |
| | **NHL Totals** | | **667** | **52** | **98** | **150** | **1098** | **4** | **0** | **7** | **483** | **10.8** | | **22** | **27.3** | **8:30** | **57** | **4** | **8** | **12** | **72** | **0** | **0** | **0** | **7:38** |

Signed as a free agent by **Solna** (Sweden-3), January 31, 2005. Signed as a free agent by **Phoenix**, July 5, 2006. Traded to **Pittsburgh** by **Phoenix** for Daniel Carcillo and Pittsburgh's 3rd round choice (later traded to NY Rangers - NY Rangers selected Tomas Kundratek) in 2008 Entry Draft, February 27, 2007. Signed as a free agent by **Montreal**, July 3, 2008. • Missed majority of 2008-09 season recovering from various injuries and serving as a healthy reserve.

## LARMAN, Drew
(LAHR-man, DROO) **BOS.**

Center. Shoots right. 6'3", 195 lbs. Born, Canton, MI, May 15, 1985.

| | | | Regular Season | | | | | | | | | | | | | | Playoffs | | | | | | | | |
|---|---|---|---|---|---|---|---|---|---|---|---|---|---|---|---|---|---|---|---|---|---|---|---|---|---|
| Season | Club | League | GP | G | A | Pts | PIM | PP | SH | GW | S | % | +/- | TF | F% | Min | GP | G | A | Pts | PIM | PP | SH | GW | Min |
| 2002-03 | Sarnia Sting | OHL | 67 | 4 | 14 | 18 | 25 | .... | .... | .... | .... | .... | .... | .... | .... | .... | .... | .... | .... | .... | .... | .... | .... | .... | .... |
| 2003-04 | Sarnia Sting | OHL | 68 | 9 | 18 | 27 | 13 | .... | .... | .... | .... | .... | .... | .... | .... | .... | 5 | 0 | 1 | 1 | 0 | .... | .... | .... | .... |
| 2004-05 | Sarnia Sting | OHL | 12 | 2 | 0 | 2 | 6 | .... | .... | .... | .... | .... | .... | .... | .... | .... | .... | .... | .... | .... | .... | .... | .... | .... | .... |
| | London Knights | OHL | 58 | 11 | 10 | 21 | 28 | .... | .... | .... | .... | .... | .... | .... | .... | .... | 18 | 3 | 4 | 7 | 8 | .... | .... | .... | .... |
| 2005-06 | Rochester | AHL | 44 | 7 | 8 | 15 | 24 | .... | .... | .... | .... | .... | .... | .... | .... | .... | .... | .... | .... | .... | .... | .... | .... | .... | .... |
| | Florida Everblades | ECHL | 6 | 0 | 0 | 0 | 4 | .... | .... | .... | .... | .... | .... | .... | .... | .... | 8 | 4 | 2 | 6 | 4 | .... | .... | .... | .... |
| **2006-07** | **Florida** | **NHL** | **16** | **2** | **0** | **2** | **2** | **0** | **0** | **0** | **15** | **13.3** | **-3** | **97** | **46.4** | **7:23** | .... | .... | .... | .... | .... | .... | .... | .... | .... |
| | Rochester | AHL | 54 | 17 | 11 | 28 | 35 | .... | .... | .... | .... | .... | .... | .... | .... | .... | .... | .... | .... | .... | .... | .... | .... | .... | .... |
| **2007-08** | **Florida** | **NHL** | **6** | **0** | **1** | **1** | **2** | **0** | **0** | **0** | **1** | **0.0** | **1** | **26** | **38.5** | **6:00** | .... | .... | .... | .... | .... | .... | .... | .... | .... |
| | Rochester | AHL | 54 | 10 | 12 | 22 | 44 | .... | .... | .... | .... | .... | .... | .... | .... | .... | .... | .... | .... | .... | .... | .... | .... | .... | .... |
| 2008-09 | Rochester | AHL | 61 | 10 | 13 | 23 | 40 | .... | .... | .... | .... | .... | .... | .... | .... | .... | .... | .... | .... | .... | .... | .... | .... | .... | .... |
| | **NHL Totals** | | **22** | **2** | **1** | **3** | **4** | **0** | **0** | **0** | **16** | **12.5** | | **123** | **44.7** | **7:00** | .... | .... | .... | .... | .... | .... | .... | .... | .... |

Signed as a free agent by **Florida**, September 28, 2005. Signed as a free agent by **Boston** July 13, 2009.

## LaROSE, Chad
(lah-ROHZ, CHAD) **CAR.**

Right wing. Shoots right. 5'10", 181 lbs. Born, Fraser, MI, March 27, 1982.

| | | | Regular Season | | | | | | | | | | | | | | Playoffs | | | | | | | | |
|---|---|---|---|---|---|---|---|---|---|---|---|---|---|---|---|---|---|---|---|---|---|---|---|---|---|
| Season | Club | League | GP | G | A | Pts | PIM | PP | SH | GW | S | % | +/- | TF | F% | Min | GP | G | A | Pts | PIM | PP | SH | GW | Min |
| 99-2000 | Sioux Falls | USHL | 54 | 29 | 26 | 55 | 28 | .... | .... | .... | .... | .... | .... | .... | .... | .... | 3 | 0 | 1 | 1 | 0 | .... | .... | .... | .... |
| 2000-01 | Sioux Falls | USHL | 24 | 11 | 22 | 33 | 50 | .... | .... | .... | .... | .... | .... | .... | .... | .... | .... | .... | .... | .... | .... | .... | .... | .... | .... |
| | Plymouth Whalers | OHL | 32 | 18 | 7 | 25 | 24 | .... | .... | .... | .... | .... | .... | .... | .... | .... | 19 | 10 | 10 | 20 | 22 | .... | .... | .... | .... |
| 2001-02 | Plymouth Whalers | OHL | 53 | 32 | 27 | 59 | 40 | .... | .... | .... | .... | .... | .... | .... | .... | .... | 6 | 3 | 4 | 7 | 16 | .... | .... | .... | .... |
| 2002-03 | Plymouth Whalers | OHL | 67 | 61 | 56 | 117 | 52 | .... | .... | .... | .... | .... | .... | .... | .... | .... | 15 | 9 | 8 | 17 | 25 | .... | .... | .... | .... |
| 2003-04 | Lowell | AHL | 36 | 7 | 9 | 16 | 29 | .... | .... | .... | .... | .... | .... | .... | .... | .... | .... | .... | .... | .... | .... | .... | .... | .... | .... |
| | Florida Everblades | ECHL | 41 | 16 | 19 | 35 | 16 | .... | .... | .... | .... | .... | .... | .... | .... | .... | 14 | 3 | 4 | 7 | 20 | .... | .... | .... | .... |

| Season | Club | League | Regular Season | | | | | | | | | | | | | | Playoffs | | | | | | | | |
|---|---|---|---|---|---|---|---|---|---|---|---|---|---|---|---|---|---|---|---|---|---|---|---|---|---|
| Season | Club | League | GP | G | A | Pts | PIM | PP | SH | GW | S | % | +/- | TF | F% | Min | GP | G | A | Pts | PIM | PP | SH | GW | Min |
| 2004-05 | Lowell | AHL | 66 | 20 | 22 | 42 | 32 | .... | .... | .... | .... | .... | .... | .... | .... | .... | 11 | 3 | 5 | 8 | 10 | .... | .... | .... | .... |
| **2005-06**• | **Carolina** | **NHL** | **49** | **1** | **12** | **13** | **35** | **0** | **0** | **1** | **62** | **1.6** | **7** | **5** | **40.0** | **10:35** | **21** | **0** | **1** | **1** | **10** | **0** | **0** | **0** | **8:58** |
| | Lowell | AHL | 23 | 14 | 11 | 25 | 10 | .... | .... | .... | .... | .... | .... | .... | .... | .... | .... | .... | .... | .... | .... | .... | .... | .... | .... |
| **2006-07** | **Carolina** | **NHL** | **80** | **6** | **12** | **18** | **10** | **0** | **2** | **0** | **94** | **6.4** | **–2** | **50** | **30.0** | **10:13** | .... | .... | .... | .... | .... | .... | .... | .... | .... |
| **2007-08** | **Carolina** | **NHL** | **58** | **11** | **12** | **23** | **46** | **0** | **1** | **2** | **117** | **9.4** | **6** | **19** | **31.6** | **14:03** | .... | .... | .... | .... | .... | .... | .... | .... | .... |
| **2008-09** | **Carolina** | **NHL** | **81** | **19** | **12** | **31** | **35** | **0** | **2** | **4** | **171** | **11.1** | **6** | **18** | **27.8** | **15:08** | **18** | **4** | **7** | **11** | **16** | **0** | **0** | **0** | **17:48** |
| | **NHL Totals** | | **268** | **37** | **48** | **85** | **126** | **0** | **5** | **7** | **444** | **8.3** | | **92** | **30.4** | **12:36** | **39** | **4** | **8** | **12** | **26** | **0** | **0** | **0** | **13:02** |

OHL Second All-Star Team (2003)

Signed as a free agent by **Carolina**, August 6, 2003.

## LAROSE, Cory

(lah-ROHZ, KOH-ree)

Center. Shoots left. 6', 191 lbs. Born, Campbellton, N.B., May 14, 1975.

| Season | Club | League | GP | G | A | Pts | PIM | PP | SH | GW | S | % | +/- | TF | F% | Min | GP | G | A | Pts | PIM | PP | SH | GW | Min |
|---|---|---|---|---|---|---|---|---|---|---|---|---|---|---|---|---|---|---|---|---|---|---|---|---|---|
| 1993-94 | Kimball Union | High-NH | 21 | 18 | 11 | 29 | 14 | .... | .... | .... | .... | .... | .... | .... | .... | .... | .... | .... | .... | .... | .... | .... | .... | .... | .... |
| 1994-95 | Langley Thunder | BCJHL | STATISTICS NOT AVAILABLE | | | | | | | | | | | | | | | | | | | | | | |
| 1995-96 | Langley Thunder | BCJHL | 54 | 28 | 46 | 74 | 61 | .... | .... | .... | .... | .... | .... | .... | .... | .... | .... | .... | .... | .... | .... | .... | .... | .... | .... |
| 1996-97 | U. of Maine | H-East | 35 | 10 | 27 | 37 | 32 | .... | .... | .... | .... | .... | .... | .... | .... | .... | .... | .... | .... | .... | .... | .... | .... | .... | .... |
| 1997-98 | U. of Maine | H-East | 34 | 15 | 25 | 40 | 22 | .... | .... | .... | .... | .... | .... | .... | .... | .... | .... | .... | .... | .... | .... | .... | .... | .... | .... |
| 1998-99 | U. of Maine | H-East | 38 | 21 | 31 | 52 | 34 | .... | .... | .... | .... | .... | .... | .... | .... | .... | .... | .... | .... | .... | .... | .... | .... | .... | .... |
| 99-2000 | U. of Maine | H-East | 39 | 15 | *36 | 51 | 45 | .... | .... | .... | .... | .... | .... | .... | .... | .... | .... | .... | .... | .... | .... | .... | .... | .... | .... |
| 2000-01 | Cleveland | IHL | 4 | 1 | 1 | 2 | 6 | .... | .... | .... | .... | .... | .... | .... | .... | .... | .... | .... | .... | .... | .... | .... | .... | .... | .... |
| | Jackson Bandits | ECHL | 63 | 21 | 32 | 53 | 73 | .... | .... | .... | .... | .... | .... | .... | .... | .... | 5 | 2 | 2 | 4 | 12 | .... | .... | .... | .... |
| 2001-02 | Houston Aeros | AHL | 78 | 32 | 32 | 64 | 73 | .... | .... | .... | .... | .... | .... | .... | .... | .... | 14 | 6 | 8 | 14 | 15 | .... | .... | .... | .... |
| 2002-03 | Houston Aeros | AHL | 58 | 18 | 38 | 56 | 57 | .... | .... | .... | .... | .... | .... | .... | .... | .... | .... | .... | .... | .... | .... | .... | .... | .... | .... |
| | Hartford | AHL | 24 | 9 | 10 | 19 | 20 | .... | .... | .... | .... | .... | .... | .... | .... | .... | 2 | 0 | 1 | 1 | 0 | .... | .... | .... | .... |
| **2003-04** | **NY Rangers** | **NHL** | **7** | **0** | **1** | **1** | **4** | **0** | **0** | **0** | **10** | **0.0** | **–2** | **40** | **47.5** | **11:27** | .... | .... | .... | .... | .... | .... | .... | .... | .... |
| | Hartford | AHL | 69 | 13 | 36 | 49 | 66 | .... | .... | .... | .... | .... | .... | .... | .... | .... | 14 | 4 | 6 | 10 | 24 | .... | .... | .... | .... |
| 2004-05 | Chicago Wolves | AHL | 80 | 26 | 37 | 63 | 44 | .... | .... | .... | .... | .... | .... | .... | .... | .... | 18 | 6 | 6 | 12 | 29 | .... | .... | .... | .... |
| 2005-06 | Langnau | Swiss | 42 | 17 | 14 | 31 | 76 | .... | .... | .... | .... | .... | .... | .... | .... | .... | 6 | 4 | 3 | 7 | 6 | .... | .... | .... | .... |
| 2006-07 | Chicago Wolves | AHL | 63 | 22 | 61 | 83 | 75 | .... | .... | .... | .... | .... | .... | .... | .... | .... | 15 | 3 | 4 | 7 | 21 | .... | .... | .... | .... |
| 2007-08 | Ak Bars Kazan | Russia | 4 | 0 | 0 | 0 | 0 | .... | .... | .... | .... | .... | .... | .... | .... | .... | .... | .... | .... | .... | .... | .... | .... | .... | .... |
| | Lulea HF | Sweden | 47 | 10 | 18 | 28 | 83 | .... | .... | .... | .... | .... | .... | .... | .... | .... | .... | .... | .... | .... | .... | .... | .... | .... | .... |
| 2008-09 | Worcester Sharks | AHL | 53 | 19 | 21 | 40 | 38 | .... | .... | .... | .... | .... | .... | .... | .... | .... | 8 | 1 | 1 | 2 | 4 | .... | .... | .... | .... |
| | **NHL Totals** | | **7** | **0** | **1** | **1** | **4** | **0** | **0** | **0** | **10** | **0.0** | | **40** | **47.5** | **11:27** | .... | .... | .... | .... | .... | .... | .... | .... | .... |

Hockey East First All-Star Team (2000) • NCAA East Second All-American Team (2000) • AHL All-Rookie Team (2002)

Signed as a free agent by **Minnesota**, May 10, 2000. Traded to **NY Rangers** by **Minnesota** for Jay Henderson, February 20, 2003. Signed as a free agent by **Atlanta**, July 14, 2004. Signed as a free agent by **Langnau** (Swiss), May 5, 2005. Signed as a free agent by **Atlanta**, June 21, 2006. Signed as a free agent by **San Jose**, July 15, 2008.

## LARSEN, Brad

(LAR-suhn, BRAD)

Left wing. Shoots left. 6', 210 lbs. Born, Nakusp, B.C., June 28, 1977. Colorado's 5th choice, 87th overall, in 1997 Entry Draft.

| Season | Club | League | GP | G | A | Pts | PIM | PP | SH | GW | S | % | +/- | TF | F% | Min | GP | G | A | Pts | PIM | PP | SH | GW | Min |
|---|---|---|---|---|---|---|---|---|---|---|---|---|---|---|---|---|---|---|---|---|---|---|---|---|---|
| 1992-93 | Nelson | RMJHL | 42 | 31 | 37 | 68 | 164 | .... | .... | .... | .... | .... | .... | .... | .... | .... | .... | .... | .... | .... | .... | .... | .... | .... | .... |
| 1993-94 | Swift Current | WHL | 64 | 15 | 18 | 33 | 32 | .... | .... | .... | .... | .... | .... | .... | .... | .... | 7 | 1 | 2 | 3 | 4 | .... | .... | .... | .... |
| 1994-95 | Swift Current | WHL | 62 | 24 | 33 | 57 | 73 | .... | .... | .... | .... | .... | .... | .... | .... | .... | 6 | 0 | 1 | 1 | 2 | .... | .... | .... | .... |
| 1995-96 | Swift Current | WHL | 51 | 30 | 47 | 77 | 67 | .... | .... | .... | .... | .... | .... | .... | .... | .... | 6 | 3 | 2 | 5 | 13 | .... | .... | .... | .... |
| 1996-97 | Swift Current | WHL | 61 | 36 | 46 | 82 | 61 | .... | .... | .... | .... | .... | .... | .... | .... | .... | .... | .... | .... | .... | .... | .... | .... | .... | .... |
| **1997-98** | **Colorado** | **NHL** | **1** | **0** | **0** | **0** | **0** | **0** | **0** | **0** | **0** | **0.0** | **0** | .... | .... | .... | .... | .... | .... | .... | .... | .... | .... | .... | .... |
| | Hershey Bears | AHL | 65 | 12 | 10 | 22 | 80 | .... | .... | .... | .... | .... | .... | .... | .... | .... | 7 | 3 | 2 | 5 | 2 | .... | .... | .... | .... |
| 1998-99 | Hershey Bears | AHL | 18 | 3 | 4 | 7 | 11 | .... | .... | .... | .... | .... | .... | .... | .... | .... | 5 | 0 | 1 | 1 | 6 | .... | .... | .... | .... |
| 99-2000 | Hershey Bears | AHL | 52 | 13 | 26 | 39 | 66 | .... | .... | .... | .... | .... | .... | .... | .... | .... | 14 | 5 | 2 | 7 | 29 | .... | .... | .... | .... |
| **2000-01** | **Colorado** | **NHL** | **9** | **0** | **0** | **0** | **0** | **0** | **0** | **0** | **3** | **0.0** | **1** | **14** | **57.1** | **9:17** | .... | .... | .... | .... | .... | .... | .... | .... | .... |
| | Hershey Bears | AHL | 67 | 21 | 25 | 46 | 93 | .... | .... | .... | .... | .... | .... | .... | .... | .... | 10 | 1 | 3 | 4 | 6 | .... | .... | .... | .... |
| **2001-02** | **Colorado** | **NHL** | **50** | **2** | **7** | **9** | **47** | **1** | **0** | **0** | **38** | **5.3** | **4** | **71** | **54.9** | **8:07** | **21** | **1** | **1** | **2** | **13** | **0** | **0** | **0** | **7:07** |
| **2002-03** | **Colorado** | **NHL** | **6** | **0** | **3** | **3** | **2** | **0** | **0** | **0** | **6** | **0.0** | **3** | **31** | **41.9** | **8:17** | .... | .... | .... | .... | .... | .... | .... | .... | .... |
| | Hershey Bears | AHL | 25 | 3 | 6 | 9 | 25 | .... | .... | .... | .... | .... | .... | .... | .... | .... | 4 | 1 | 1 | 2 | 8 | .... | .... | .... | .... |
| **2003-04** | **Colorado** | **NHL** | **26** | **2** | **2** | **4** | **11** | **0** | **0** | **0** | **17** | **11.8** | **2** | **9** | **44.4** | **7:41** | .... | .... | .... | .... | .... | .... | .... | .... | .... |
| | Hershey Bears | AHL | 21 | 4 | 13 | 17 | 40 | .... | .... | .... | .... | .... | .... | .... | .... | .... | .... | .... | .... | .... | .... | .... | .... | .... | .... |
| | **Atlanta** | **NHL** | **6** | **0** | **0** | **0** | **2** | **0** | **0** | **0** | **6** | **0.0** | **–2** | **6** | **66.7** | **13:39** | .... | .... | .... | .... | .... | .... | .... | .... | .... |
| 2004-05 | Chicago Wolves | AHL | 75 | 26 | 23 | 49 | 112 | .... | .... | .... | .... | .... | .... | .... | .... | .... | 18 | 4 | 7 | 11 | 22 | .... | .... | .... | .... |
| **2005-06** | **Atlanta** | **NHL** | **62** | **7** | **8** | **15** | **21** | **0** | **3** | **1** | **48** | **14.6** | **–3** | **81** | **34.6** | **10:59** | .... | .... | .... | .... | .... | .... | .... | .... | .... |
| | Chicago Wolves | AHL | 6 | 1 | 0 | 1 | 8 | .... | .... | .... | .... | .... | .... | .... | .... | .... | .... | .... | .... | .... | .... | .... | .... | .... | .... |
| **2006-07** | **Atlanta** | **NHL** | **72** | **7** | **6** | **13** | **39** | **0** | **2** | **0** | **61** | **11.5** | **–11** | **82** | **39.0** | **12:22** | **4** | **0** | **2** | **2** | **0** | **0** | **0** | **0** | **16:57** |
| **2007-08** | **Atlanta** | **NHL** | **62** | **1** | **3** | **4** | **12** | **0** | **0** | **0** | **35** | **2.9** | **–17** | **81** | **42.0** | **9:02** | .... | .... | .... | .... | .... | .... | .... | .... | .... |
| **2008-09** | **Anaheim** | **NHL** | DID NOT PLAY – INJURED | | | | | | | | | | | | | | | | | | | | | | |
| | **NHL Totals** | | **294** | **19** | **29** | **48** | **134** | **1** | **5** | **1** | **214** | **8.9** | | **375** | **43.2** | **10:05** | **25** | **1** | **3** | **4** | **13** | **0** | **0** | **0** | **8:41** |

• Re-entered NHL Entry Draft. Originally Ottawa's 3rd choice, 53rd overall, in 1995 Entry Draft.

WHL East Second All-Star Team (1997)

• Rights traded to **Colorado** by **Ottawa** for Janne Laukkanen, January 26, 1996. • Missed majority of 1998-99 season recovering from abdominal injury suffered in game vs. Albany (AHL), November 20, 1998. • Missed majority of 2002-03 season recovering from groin (October 27, 2002 vs. Minnesota) and back (December 11, 2002 vs. Vancouver) injuries. Claimed on waivers by **Atlanta** from **Colorado**, February 25, 2004. Traded to **Anaheim** by **Atlanta** with Ken Klee and Chad Painchaud for Mathieu Schneider, September 26, 2008. • Missed entire 2008-09 season recovering from surgery to repair sports hernia injury (October 3, 2008).

## LASHOFF, Matt

(LASH-awf, MAT) **T.B.**

Defense. Shoots left. 6'2", 204 lbs. Born, Albany, NY, September 29, 1986. Boston's 1st choice, 22nd overall, in 2005 Entry Draft.

| Season | Club | League | GP | G | A | Pts | PIM | PP | SH | GW | S | % | +/- | TF | F% | Min | GP | G | A | Pts | PIM | PP | SH | GW | Min |
|---|---|---|---|---|---|---|---|---|---|---|---|---|---|---|---|---|---|---|---|---|---|---|---|---|---|
| 2002-03 | USNTDP | U-17 | 16 | 1 | 3 | 4 | 14 | .... | .... | .... | .... | .... | .... | .... | .... | .... | .... | .... | .... | .... | .... | .... | .... | .... | .... |
| | USNTDP | NAHL | 46 | 2 | 5 | 7 | 53 | .... | .... | .... | .... | .... | .... | .... | .... | .... | .... | .... | .... | .... | .... | .... | .... | .... | .... |
| 2003-04 | Kitchener Rangers | OHL | 62 | 5 | 19 | 24 | 94 | .... | .... | .... | .... | .... | .... | .... | .... | .... | 5 | 0 | 1 | 1 | 0 | .... | .... | .... | .... |
| 2004-05 | Kitchener Rangers | OHL | 44 | 4 | 18 | 22 | 44 | .... | .... | .... | .... | .... | .... | .... | .... | .... | 13 | 0 | 3 | 3 | 18 | .... | .... | .... | .... |
| 2005-06 | Kitchener Rangers | OHL | 56 | 7 | 40 | 47 | 146 | .... | .... | .... | .... | .... | .... | .... | .... | .... | 5 | 1 | 1 | 2 | 12 | .... | .... | .... | .... |
| | Providence Bruins | AHL | 7 | 1 | 1 | 2 | 6 | .... | .... | .... | .... | .... | .... | .... | .... | .... | 6 | 0 | 0 | 0 | 6 | .... | .... | .... | .... |
| **2006-07** | **Boston** | **NHL** | **12** | **0** | **2** | **2** | **12** | **0** | **0** | **0** | **8** | **0.0** | **–6** | **0** | **0.0** | **14:55** | .... | .... | .... | .... | .... | .... | .... | .... | .... |
| | Providence Bruins | AHL | 64 | 11 | 26 | 37 | 60 | .... | .... | .... | .... | .... | .... | .... | .... | .... | .... | .... | .... | .... | .... | .... | .... | .... | .... |
| **2007-08** | **Boston** | **NHL** | **18** | **1** | **4** | **5** | **0** | **1** | **0** | **0** | **11** | **9.1** | **–2** | **0** | **0.0** | **13:35** | .... | .... | .... | .... | .... | .... | .... | .... | .... |
| | Providence Bruins | AHL | 60 | 9 | 27 | 36 | 79 | .... | .... | .... | .... | .... | .... | .... | .... | .... | 9 | 0 | 4 | 4 | 6 | .... | .... | .... | .... |
| **2008-09** | **Boston** | **NHL** | **16** | **0** | **1** | **1** | **10** | **0** | **0** | **0** | **6** | **0.0** | **1** | **0** | **0.0** | **13:07** | .... | .... | .... | .... | .... | .... | .... | .... | .... |
| | Providence Bruins | AHL | 33 | 5 | 16 | 21 | 36 | .... | .... | .... | .... | .... | .... | .... | .... | .... | .... | .... | .... | .... | .... | .... | .... | .... | .... |
| | **Tampa Bay** | **NHL** | **12** | **0** | **7** | **7** | **10** | **0** | **0** | **0** | **19** | **0.0** | **–7** | **0** | **0.0** | **23:46** | .... | .... | .... | .... | .... | .... | .... | .... | .... |
| | Norfolk Admirals | AHL | 2 | 0 | 0 | 0 | 2 | .... | .... | .... | .... | .... | .... | .... | .... | .... | .... | .... | .... | .... | .... | .... | .... | .... | .... |
| | **NHL Totals** | | **58** | **1** | **14** | **15** | **32** | **1** | **0** | **0** | **44** | **2.3** | | **0** | **0.0** | **15:50** | .... | .... | .... | .... | .... | .... | .... | .... | .... |

AHL All-Rookie Team (2007)

Traded to **Tampa Bay** by **Boston** with Martins Karsums for Mark Recchi and Tampa Bay's 2nd round choice in 2010 Entry Draft, March 4, 2009.

## LATENDRESSE, Guillaume

(lah-TEHN-drehs, GEE-OHM) **MTL.**

Left wing. Shoots left. 6'2", 230 lbs. Born, Ste-Catherine, Que., May 24, 1987. Montreal's 2nd choice, 45th overall, in 2005 Entry Draft.

| Season | Club | League | GP | G | A | Pts | PIM | PP | SH | GW | S | % | +/- | TF | F% | Min | GP | G | A | Pts | PIM | PP | SH | GW | Min |
|---|---|---|---|---|---|---|---|---|---|---|---|---|---|---|---|---|---|---|---|---|---|---|---|---|---|
| 2003-04 | Drummondville | QMJHL | 53 | 24 | 25 | 49 | 66 | .... | .... | .... | .... | .... | .... | .... | .... | .... | .... | .... | .... | .... | .... | .... | .... | .... | .... |
| 2004-05 | Drummondville | QMJHL | 65 | 29 | 49 | 78 | 76 | .... | .... | .... | .... | .... | .... | .... | .... | .... | 6 | 6 | 4 | 10 | 7 | .... | .... | .... | .... |
| 2005-06 | Drummondville | QMJHL | 51 | 43 | 40 | 83 | 105 | .... | .... | .... | .... | .... | .... | .... | .... | .... | 5 | 3 | 2 | 5 | 8 | .... | .... | .... | .... |
| **2006-07** | **Montreal** | **NHL** | **80** | **16** | **13** | **29** | **47** | **5** | **0** | **3** | **121** | **13.2** | **–20** | **16** | **12.5** | **12:36** | .... | .... | .... | .... | .... | .... | .... | .... | .... |
| **2007-08** | **Montreal** | **NHL** | **73** | **16** | **11** | **27** | **41** | **2** | **0** | **3** | **116** | **13.8** | **–2** | **8** | **25.0** | **12:15** | **8** | **0** | **1** | **1** | **19** | **0** | **0** | **0** | **10:43** |
| **2008-09** | **Montreal** | **NHL** | **56** | **14** | **12** | **26** | **45** | **1** | **0** | **2** | **117** | **12.0** | **4** | **2** | **50.0** | **13:37** | **4** | **0** | **0** | **0** | **12** | **0** | **0** | **0** | **11:44** |
| | **NHL Totals** | | **209** | **46** | **36** | **82** | **133** | **8** | **0** | **8** | **354** | **13.0** | | **26** | **19.2** | **12:45** | **12** | **0** | **1** | **1** | **31** | **0** | **0** | **0** | **11:03** |

QMJHL All-Rookie Team (2004)

## LaVALLEE, Jordan

(LA-VA-lee, JOHR-dahn) **ATL.**

Left wing. Shoots left. 6'3", 225 lbs. Born, Corvallis, OR, May 11, 1986. Atlanta's 5th choice, 116th overall, in 2005 Entry Draft.

| | | | Regular Season | | | | | | | | | | | | | | Playoffs | | | | | | | | |
|---|---|---|---|---|---|---|---|---|---|---|---|---|---|---|---|---|---|---|---|---|---|---|---|---|---|
| Season | Club | League | GP | G | A | Pts | PIM | PP | SH | GW | S | % | +/- | TF | F% | Min | GP | G | A | Pts | PIM | PP | SH | GW | Min |
| 2002-03 | Quebec Remparts | QMJHL | 55 | 3 | 6 | 9 | 54 | .... | .... | .... | .... | .... | .... | .... | .... | .... | 11 | 0 | 1 | 1 | 0 | .... | .... | .... | .... |
| 2003-04 | Quebec Remparts | QMJHL | 69 | 11 | 16 | 27 | 111 | .... | .... | .... | .... | .... | .... | .... | .... | .... | 5 | 2 | 0 | 2 | 6 | .... | .... | .... | .... |
| 2004-05 | Quebec Remparts | QMJHL | 64 | 40 | 26 | 66 | 108 | .... | .... | .... | .... | .... | .... | .... | .... | .... | 13 | 5 | 2 | 7 | 26 | .... | .... | .... | .... |
| 2005-06 | Quebec Remparts | QMJHL | 37 | 18 | 19 | 37 | 34 | .... | .... | .... | .... | .... | .... | .... | .... | .... | 23 | 7 | 8 | 15 | 30 | .... | .... | .... | .... |
| 2006-07 | Chicago Wolves | AHL | 79 | 16 | 18 | 34 | 90 | .... | .... | .... | .... | .... | .... | .... | .... | .... | 14 | 7 | 1 | 8 | 8 | .... | .... | .... | .... |
| **2007-08** | **Atlanta** | **NHL** | **2** | **1** | **1** | **2** | **0** | **0** | **0** | **0** | **1** | **100.0** | **2** | **0** | **0.0** | **11:28** | .... | .... | .... | .... | .... | .... | .... | .... | .... |
| | Chicago Wolves | AHL | 76 | 20 | 22 | 42 | 73 | .... | .... | .... | .... | .... | .... | .... | .... | .... | 24 | 3 | 5 | 8 | 16 | .... | .... | .... | .... |
| **2008-09** | **Atlanta** | **NHL** | **2** | **0** | **0** | **0** | **0** | **0** | **0** | **0** | **1** | **0.0** | **–1** | **0** | **0.0** | **6:40** | .... | .... | .... | .... | .... | .... | .... | .... | .... |
| | Chicago Wolves | AHL | 64 | 19 | 12 | 31 | 94 | .... | .... | .... | .... | .... | .... | .... | .... | .... | .... | .... | .... | .... | .... | .... | .... | .... | .... |
| | **NHL Totals** | | **4** | **1** | **1** | **2** | **0** | **0** | **0** | **0** | **2** | **50.0** | | **0** | **0.0** | **9:04** | .... | .... | .... | .... | .... | .... | .... | .... | .... |

## LEACH, Jay

(LEECH, JAY) **N.J.**

Defense. Shoots left. 6'5", 225 lbs. Born, Syracuse, NY, September 2, 1979. Phoenix's 5th choice, 115th overall, in 1998 Entry Draft.

| Season | Club | League | GP | G | A | Pts | PIM | PP | SH | GW | S | % | +/- | TF | F% | Min | GP | G | A | Pts | PIM | PP | SH | GW | Min |
|---|---|---|---|---|---|---|---|---|---|---|---|---|---|---|---|---|---|---|---|---|---|---|---|---|---|
| 1994-95 | John Marshall | High-MN | 10 | 0 | 0 | 0 | 14 | .... | .... | .... | .... | .... | .... | .... | .... | .... | .... | .... | .... | .... | .... | .... | .... | .... | .... |
| 1995-96 | John Marshall | High-MN | 11 | 1 | 2 | 3 | 8 | .... | .... | .... | .... | .... | .... | .... | .... | .... | 4 | 0 | 0 | 0 | 0 | .... | .... | .... | .... |
| | Capital District | Exhib. | 53 | 3 | 8 | 11 | 33 | .... | .... | .... | .... | .... | .... | .... | .... | .... | .... | .... | .... | .... | .... | .... | .... | .... | .... |
| 1996-97 | Capital District | Exhib. | 57 | 8 | 50 | 58 | 140 | .... | .... | .... | .... | .... | .... | .... | .... | .... | .... | .... | .... | .... | .... | .... | .... | .... | .... |
| 1997-98 | Providence | H-East | 32 | 0 | 8 | 8 | 29 | .... | .... | .... | .... | .... | .... | .... | .... | .... | .... | .... | .... | .... | .... | .... | .... | .... | .... |
| 1998-99 | Providence | H-East | 33 | 1 | 8 | 9 | 42 | .... | .... | .... | .... | .... | .... | .... | .... | .... | .... | .... | .... | .... | .... | .... | .... | .... | .... |
| 99-2000 | Providence | H-East | 37 | 1 | 9 | 10 | 101 | .... | .... | .... | .... | .... | .... | .... | .... | .... | .... | .... | .... | .... | .... | .... | .... | .... | .... |
| 2000-01 | Providence | H-East | 40 | 4 | 21 | 25 | 104 | .... | .... | .... | .... | .... | .... | .... | .... | .... | .... | .... | .... | .... | .... | .... | .... | .... | .... |
| 2001-02 | Mississippi | ECHL | 70 | 3 | 13 | 16 | 116 | .... | .... | .... | .... | .... | .... | .... | .... | .... | 10 | 1 | 1 | 2 | 8 | .... | .... | .... | .... |
| 2002-03 | Springfield | AHL | 9 | 0 | 0 | 0 | 0 | .... | .... | .... | .... | .... | .... | .... | .... | .... | .... | .... | .... | .... | .... | .... | .... | .... | .... |
| | Augusta Lynx | ECHL | 65 | 8 | 11 | 19 | 162 | .... | .... | .... | .... | .... | .... | .... | .... | .... | .... | .... | .... | .... | .... | .... | .... | .... | .... |
| 2003-04 | Providence Bruins | AHL | 3 | 0 | 0 | 0 | 4 | .... | .... | .... | .... | .... | .... | .... | .... | .... | .... | .... | .... | .... | .... | .... | .... | .... | .... |
| | Long Beach | ECHL | 3 | 0 | 1 | 1 | 4 | .... | .... | .... | .... | .... | .... | .... | .... | .... | .... | .... | .... | .... | .... | .... | .... | .... | .... |
| | Bridgeport | AHL | 23 | 0 | 1 | 1 | 33 | .... | .... | .... | .... | .... | .... | .... | .... | .... | 7 | 0 | 1 | 1 | 10 | .... | .... | .... | .... |
| | Trenton Titans | ECHL | 31 | 2 | 11 | 13 | 45 | .... | .... | .... | .... | .... | .... | .... | .... | .... | .... | .... | .... | .... | .... | .... | .... | .... | .... |
| 2004-05 | Providence Bruins | AHL | 62 | 4 | 5 | 9 | 92 | .... | .... | .... | .... | .... | .... | .... | .... | .... | 17 | 0 | 0 | 0 | 28 | .... | .... | .... | .... |
| | Trenton Titans | ECHL | 11 | 0 | 2 | 2 | 17 | .... | .... | .... | .... | .... | .... | .... | .... | .... | .... | .... | .... | .... | .... | .... | .... | .... | .... |
| **2005-06** | **Boston** | **NHL** | **2** | **0** | **0** | **0** | **7** | **0** | **0** | **0** | **0** | **0.0** | **1** | **0** | **0.0** | **6:20** | .... | .... | .... | .... | .... | .... | .... | .... | .... |
| | Providence Bruins | AHL | 72 | 5 | 11 | 16 | 100 | .... | .... | .... | .... | .... | .... | .... | .... | .... | 6 | 0 | 1 | 1 | 15 | .... | .... | .... | .... |
| 2006-07 | Providence Bruins | AHL | 73 | 2 | 5 | 7 | 128 | .... | .... | .... | .... | .... | .... | .... | .... | .... | 13 | 0 | 4 | 4 | 13 | .... | .... | .... | .... |
| **2007-08** | **Tampa Bay** | **NHL** | **2** | **0** | **0** | **0** | **0** | **0** | **0** | **0** | **0** | **0.0** | **–1** | **0** | **0.0** | **4:37** | .... | .... | .... | .... | .... | .... | .... | .... | .... |
| | Norfolk Admirals | AHL | 55 | 3 | 8 | 11 | 54 | .... | .... | .... | .... | .... | .... | .... | .... | .... | .... | .... | .... | .... | .... | .... | .... | .... | .... |
| | Portland Pirates | AHL | 20 | 3 | 6 | 9 | 30 | .... | .... | .... | .... | .... | .... | .... | .... | .... | 18 | 1 | 0 | 1 | 7 | .... | .... | .... | .... |
| **2008-09** | **New Jersey** | **NHL** | **24** | **0** | **1** | **1** | **21** | **0** | **0** | **0** | **5** | **0.0** | **0** | **0** | **0.0** | **14:50** | .... | .... | .... | .... | .... | .... | .... | .... | .... |
| | Lowell Devils | AHL | 24 | 2 | 4 | 6 | 29 | .... | .... | .... | .... | .... | .... | .... | .... | .... | .... | .... | .... | .... | .... | .... | .... | .... | .... |
| | **NHL Totals** | | **28** | **0** | **1** | **1** | **28** | **0** | **0** | **0** | **5** | **0.0** | | **0** | **0.0** | **13:30** | .... | .... | .... | .... | .... | .... | .... | .... | .... |

Signed as a free agent by **Boston**, September 26, 2003. Signed as a free agent by **Tampa Bay**, July 3, 2007. Traded to **Anaheim** by **Tampa Bay** for Brandon Segal and Anaheim's 7th round choice (David Carle) in 2008 Entry Draft, February 26, 2008. Signed as a free agent by **New Jersey**, July 17, 2008.

## LEBDA, Brett

(LEHB-dah, BREHT) **DET.**

Defense. Shoots left. 5'9", 195 lbs. Born, Buffalo Grove, IL, January 15, 1982.

| Season | Club | League | GP | G | A | Pts | PIM | PP | SH | GW | S | % | +/- | TF | F% | Min | GP | G | A | Pts | PIM | PP | SH | GW | Min |
|---|---|---|---|---|---|---|---|---|---|---|---|---|---|---|---|---|---|---|---|---|---|---|---|---|---|
| 1998-99 | USNTDP | U-17 | 11 | 1 | 7 | 8 | 4 | .... | .... | .... | .... | .... | .... | .... | .... | .... | .... | .... | .... | .... | .... | .... | .... | .... | .... |
| | USNTDP | USHL | 3 | 0 | 0 | 0 | 0 | .... | .... | .... | .... | .... | .... | .... | .... | .... | .... | .... | .... | .... | .... | .... | .... | .... | .... |
| | USNTDP | NAHL | 52 | 11 | 17 | 28 | 56 | .... | .... | .... | .... | .... | .... | .... | .... | .... | .... | .... | .... | .... | .... | .... | .... | .... | .... |
| 99-2000 | USNTDP | U-18 | 4 | 0 | 0 | 0 | 6 | .... | .... | .... | .... | .... | .... | .... | .... | .... | .... | .... | .... | .... | .... | .... | .... | .... | .... |
| | USNTDP | USHL | 22 | 6 | 7 | 13 | 28 | .... | .... | .... | .... | .... | .... | .... | .... | .... | .... | .... | .... | .... | .... | .... | .... | .... | .... |
| 2000-01 | U. of Notre Dame | CCHA | 39 | 7 | 19 | 26 | 109 | .... | .... | .... | .... | .... | .... | .... | .... | .... | .... | .... | .... | .... | .... | .... | .... | .... | .... |
| 2001-02 | U. of Notre Dame | CCHA | 34 | 6 | 8 | 14 | 54 | .... | .... | .... | .... | .... | .... | .... | .... | .... | .... | .... | .... | .... | .... | .... | .... | .... | .... |
| 2002-03 | U. of Notre Dame | CCHA | 40 | 7 | 14 | 21 | 48 | .... | .... | .... | .... | .... | .... | .... | .... | .... | .... | .... | .... | .... | .... | .... | .... | .... | .... |
| 2003-04 | U. of Notre Dame | CCHA | 39 | 6 | 18 | 24 | 42 | .... | .... | .... | .... | .... | .... | .... | .... | .... | .... | .... | .... | .... | .... | .... | .... | .... | .... |
| | Grand Rapids | AHL | 6 | 0 | 1 | 1 | 0 | .... | .... | .... | .... | .... | .... | .... | .... | .... | 4 | 0 | 0 | 0 | 2 | .... | .... | .... | .... |
| 2004-05 | Grand Rapids | AHL | 80 | 2 | 10 | 12 | 34 | .... | .... | .... | .... | .... | .... | .... | .... | .... | .... | .... | .... | .... | .... | .... | .... | .... | .... |
| **2005-06** | **Detroit** | **NHL** | **46** | **3** | **9** | **12** | **20** | **1** | **0** | **1** | **50** | **6.0** | **9** | **2** | **0.0** | **12:38** | **6** | **0** | **0** | **0** | **4** | **0** | **0** | **0** | **13:09** |
| | Grand Rapids | AHL | 25 | 4 | 14 | 18 | 42 | .... | .... | .... | .... | .... | .... | .... | .... | .... | 11 | 1 | 4 | 5 | 8 | .... | .... | .... | .... |
| **2006-07** | **Detroit** | **NHL** | **74** | **5** | **13** | **18** | **61** | **1** | **0** | **2** | **107** | **4.7** | **16** | **0** | **0.0** | **14:54** | **12** | **0** | **2** | **2** | **8** | **0** | **0** | **0** | **16:23** |
| **2007-08** ♦ | **Detroit** | **NHL** | **78** | **3** | **11** | **14** | **48** | **0** | **0** | **1** | **110** | **2.7** | **–1** | **1** | **0.0** | **16:29** | **19** | **0** | **2** | **2** | **6** | **0** | **0** | **0** | **12:33** |
| **2008-09** | **Detroit** | **NHL** | **65** | **6** | **10** | **16** | **48** | **0** | **0** | **1** | **69** | **8.7** | **9** | **1** | **100.0** | **13:39** | **23** | **0** | **6** | **6** | **22** | **0** | **0** | **0** | **13:21** |
| | **NHL Totals** | | **263** | **17** | **43** | **60** | **177** | **2** | **0** | **5** | **336** | **5.1** | | **4** | **25.0** | **14:40** | **60** | **0** | **10** | **10** | **40** | **0** | **0** | **0** | **13:41** |

CCHA All-Rookie Team (2001) • CCHA Second All-Star Team (2004)

Signed as a free agent by **Detroit**, April 1, 2004.

## LECAVALIER, Vincent

(luh-KAV-uhl-YAY, VIHN-sihnt) **T.B.**

Center. Shoots left. 6'4", 219 lbs. Born, Ile Bizard, Que., April 21, 1980. Tampa Bay's 1st choice, 1st overall, in 1998 Entry Draft.

| Season | Club | League | GP | G | A | Pts | PIM | PP | SH | GW | S | % | +/- | TF | F% | Min | GP | G | A | Pts | PIM | PP | SH | GW | Min |
|---|---|---|---|---|---|---|---|---|---|---|---|---|---|---|---|---|---|---|---|---|---|---|---|---|---|
| 1995-96 | Notre Dame | SMHL | 22 | 52 | 52 | 104 | .... | .... | .... | .... | .... | .... | .... | .... | .... | .... | .... | .... | .... | .... | .... | .... | .... | .... | .... |
| 1996-97 | Rimouski Oceanic | QMJHL | 64 | 42 | 61 | 103 | 38 | .... | .... | .... | .... | .... | .... | .... | .... | .... | 4 | 4 | 3 | 7 | 2 | .... | .... | .... | .... |
| 1997-98 | Rimouski Oceanic | QMJHL | 58 | 44 | 71 | 115 | 117 | .... | .... | .... | .... | .... | .... | .... | .... | .... | 18 | *15 | *26 | *41 | 46 | .... | .... | .... | .... |
| **1998-99** | **Tampa Bay** | **NHL** | **82** | **13** | **15** | **28** | **23** | **2** | **0** | **2** | **125** | **10.4** | **–19** | **953** | **40.3** | **13:40** | .... | .... | .... | .... | .... | .... | .... | .... | .... |
| **99-2000** | **Tampa Bay** | **NHL** | **80** | **25** | **42** | **67** | **43** | **6** | **0** | **3** | **166** | **15.1** | **–25** | **1288** | **44.4** | **19:18** | .... | .... | .... | .... | .... | .... | .... | .... | .... |
| **2000-01** | **Tampa Bay** | **NHL** | **68** | **23** | **28** | **51** | **66** | **7** | **0** | **3** | **165** | **13.9** | **–26** | **1278** | **44.9** | **19:57** | .... | .... | .... | .... | .... | .... | .... | .... | .... |
| **2001-02** | **Tampa Bay** | **NHL** | **76** | **20** | **17** | **37** | **61** | **5** | **0** | **3** | **164** | **12.2** | **–18** | **931** | **41.5** | **17:09** | .... | .... | .... | .... | .... | .... | .... | .... | .... |
| **2002-03** | **Tampa Bay** | **NHL** | **80** | **33** | **45** | **78** | **39** | **11** | **2** | **3** | **274** | **12.0** | **0** | **1200** | **43.9** | **19:33** | **11** | **3** | **3** | **6** | **22** | **1** | **0** | **1** | **22:36** |
| **2003-04** ♦ | **Tampa Bay** | **NHL** | **81** | **32** | **34** | **66** | **52** | **5** | **2** | **6** | **242** | **13.2** | **24** | **1119** | **41.4** | **18:04** | **23** | **9** | **7** | **16** | **25** | **2** | **0** | **0** | **19:39** |
| 2004-05 | Ak Bars Kazan | Russia | 30 | 7 | 9 | 16 | 78 | .... | .... | .... | .... | .... | .... | .... | .... | .... | 4 | 1 | 0 | 1 | 6 | .... | .... | .... | .... |
| **2005-06** | **Tampa Bay** | **NHL** | **80** | **35** | **40** | **75** | **90** | **13** | **2** | **7** | **309** | **11.3** | **0** | **1366** | **51.2** | **20:08** | **5** | **1** | **3** | **4** | **7** | **1** | **0** | **0** | **22:17** |
| | Canada | Olympics | 6 | 0 | 3 | 3 | 16 | .... | .... | .... | .... | .... | .... | .... | .... | .... | .... | .... | .... | .... | .... | .... | .... | .... | .... |
| **2006-07** | **Tampa Bay** | **NHL** | **82** | ***52** | **56** | **108** | **44** | **16** | **5** | **7** | **339** | **15.3** | **2** | **1653** | **46.6** | **22:36** | **6** | **5** | **2** | **7** | **10** | **1** | **0** | **1** | **26:29** |
| **2007-08** | **Tampa Bay** | **NHL** | **81** | **40** | **52** | **92** | **89** | **10** | **1** | **7** | **318** | **12.6** | **–17** | **1671** | **48.8** | **22:57** | .... | .... | .... | .... | .... | .... | .... | .... | .... |
| **2008-09** | **Tampa Bay** | **NHL** | **77** | **29** | **38** | **67** | **54** | **10** | **1** | **6** | **291** | **10.0** | **–9** | **1395** | **50.9** | **20:15** | .... | .... | .... | .... | .... | .... | .... | .... | .... |
| | **NHL Totals** | | **787** | **302** | **367** | **669** | **561** | **85** | **13** | **47** | **2393** | **12.6** | | **12854** | **45.9** | **19:21** | **45** | **18** | **15** | **33** | **64** | **5** | **0** | **2** | **21:34** |

QMJHL All-Rookie Team (1997) • QMJHL Offensive Rookie of the Year (1997) • Canadian Major Junior Rookie of the Year (1997) • QMJHL First All-Star Team (1998) • Canadian Major Junior First All-Star Team (1998) • NHL Second All-Star Team (2007) • Maurice "Rocket" Richard Trophy (2007) • King Clancy Memorial Trophy (2008)

Played in NHL All-Star Game (2003, 2007, 2008, 2009)

Signed as a free agent by **Kazan** (Russia), November 4, 2004.

## LEDIN, Per

(lay-DEEN, PAIR)

Left wing. Shoots left. 6', 194 lbs. Born, Lulea, Sweden, September 14, 1978.

| Season | Club | League | GP | G | A | Pts | PIM | PP | SH | GW | S | % | +/- | TF | F% | Min | GP | G | A | Pts | PIM | PP | SH | GW | Min |
|---|---|---|---|---|---|---|---|---|---|---|---|---|---|---|---|---|---|---|---|---|---|---|---|---|---|
| 1996-97 | Bjorkloven Jr. | Swe-Jr. | 27 | 19 | 11 | 30 | .... | .... | .... | .... | .... | .... | .... | .... | .... | .... | .... | .... | .... | .... | .... | .... | .... | .... | .... |
| | Bjorkloven | Sweden-2 | 6 | 0 | 0 | 0 | 2 | .... | .... | .... | .... | .... | .... | .... | .... | .... | .... | .... | .... | .... | .... | .... | .... | .... | .... |
| 1997-98 | Bjorkloven Jr. | Swe-Jr. | 11 | 8 | 4 | 12 | 44 | .... | .... | .... | .... | .... | .... | .... | .... | .... | .... | .... | .... | .... | .... | .... | .... | .... | .... |
| | Bjorkloven | Sweden-2 | 44 | 14 | 15 | 29 | 30 | .... | .... | .... | .... | .... | .... | .... | .... | .... | .... | .... | .... | .... | .... | .... | .... | .... | .... |
| 1998-99 | Bjorkloven | Sweden | 46 | 6 | 4 | 10 | 32 | .... | .... | .... | .... | .... | .... | .... | .... | .... | .... | .... | .... | .... | .... | .... | .... | .... | .... |
| | Bjorkloven | Sweden-Q | 9 | 1 | 0 | 1 | 29 | .... | .... | .... | .... | .... | .... | .... | .... | .... | .... | .... | .... | .... | .... | .... | .... | .... | .... |
| 99-2000 | Bjorkloven | Sweden-2 | 47 | 14 | 7 | 21 | 69 | .... | .... | .... | .... | .... | .... | .... | .... | .... | .... | .... | .... | .... | .... | .... | .... | .... | .... |
| 2000-01 | Baton Rouge | ECHL | 27 | 4 | 8 | 12 | 37 | .... | .... | .... | .... | .... | .... | .... | .... | .... | .... | .... | .... | .... | .... | .... | .... | .... | .... |
| | Lulea HF | Sweden | 18 | 1 | 0 | 1 | 14 | .... | .... | .... | .... | .... | .... | .... | .... | .... | 12 | 0 | 0 | 0 | 6 | .... | .... | .... | .... |
| 2001-02 | Lulea HF Jr. | Swe-Jr. | 4 | 5 | 2 | 7 | 4 | .... | .... | .... | .... | .... | .... | .... | .... | .... | .... | .... | .... | .... | .... | .... | .... | .... | .... |
| | Lulea HF | Sweden | 50 | 0 | 5 | 5 | 47 | .... | .... | .... | .... | .... | .... | .... | .... | .... | 6 | 0 | 0 | 0 | 8 | .... | .... | .... | .... |
| 2002-03 | Lulea HF Jr. | Swe-Jr. | 1 | 2 | 0 | 2 | 0 | .... | .... | .... | .... | .... | .... | .... | .... | .... | .... | .... | .... | .... | .... | .... | .... | .... | .... |
| | Lulea HF | Sweden | 50 | 8 | 7 | 15 | 72 | .... | .... | .... | .... | .... | .... | .... | .... | .... | 4 | 0 | 0 | 0 | 6 | .... | .... | .... | .... |
| 2003-04 | Lulea HF | Sweden | 50 | 6 | 9 | 15 | 112 | .... | .... | .... | .... | .... | .... | .... | .... | .... | 5 | 1 | 1 | 2 | 8 | .... | .... | .... | .... |

| | | | Regular Season | | | | | | | | | | | | | | Playoffs | | | | | | | | |
|---|---|---|---|---|---|---|---|---|---|---|---|---|---|---|---|---|---|---|---|---|---|---|---|---|---|
| Season | Club | League | GP | G | A | Pts | PIM | PP | SH | GW | S | % | +/- | TF | F% | Min | GP | G | A | Pts | PIM | PP | SH | GW | Min |
| 2004-05 | Lulea HF | Sweden | 46 | 16 | 20 | 36 | 94 | .... | .... | .... | .... | .... | .... | .... | .... | .... | 4 | 0 | 1 | 1 | 37 | .... | .... | .... | .... |
| 2005-06 | Farjestad | Sweden | 46 | 8 | 15 | 23 | 123 | .... | .... | .... | .... | .... | .... | .... | .... | .... | 18 | 3 | 7 | 10 | 55 | .... | .... | .... | .... |
| 2006-07 | Farjestad | Sweden | 55 | 9 | 15 | 24 | 148 | .... | .... | .... | .... | .... | .... | .... | .... | .... | .... | .... | .... | .... | .... | .... | .... | .... | .... |
| 2007-08 | HV 71 Jonkoping | Sweden | 52 | 16 | 17 | 33 | 137 | .... | .... | .... | .... | .... | .... | .... | .... | .... | 17 | 2 | 5 | 7 | 63 | .... | .... | .... | .... |
| **2008-09** | **Colorado** | **NHL** | **3** | **0** | **0** | **0** | **2** | **0** | **0** | **0** | **2** | **0.0** | **–1** | **0** | **0.0** | **9:56** | .... | .... | .... | .... | .... | .... | .... | .... | .... |
| | Lake Erie | AHL | 58 | 11 | 12 | 23 | 55 | .... | .... | .... | .... | .... | .... | .... | .... | .... | .... | .... | .... | .... | .... | .... | .... | .... | .... |
| | **NHL Totals** | | **3** | **0** | **0** | **0** | **2** | **0** | **0** | **0** | **2** | **0.0** | | **0** | **0.0** | **9:56** | .... | .... | .... | .... | .... | .... | .... | .... | .... |

Signed as a free agent by **Colorado**, July 1, 2008. Signed as a free agent by **Jonkoping** (Sweden), April 30, 2009.

## LEE, Brian

(LEE, BRIGH-uhn) **OTT.**

Defense. Shoots right. 6'2", 202 lbs. Born, Fargo, ND, March 26, 1987. Ottawa's 1st choice, 9th overall, in 2005 Entry Draft.

| Season | Club | League | GP | G | A | Pts | PIM | PP | SH | GW | S | % | +/- | TF | F% | Min | GP | G | A | Pts | PIM | PP | SH | GW | Min |
|---|---|---|---|---|---|---|---|---|---|---|---|---|---|---|---|---|---|---|---|---|---|---|---|---|---|
| 2003-04 | Moorhead Spuds | High-MN | 29 | 10 | 38 | 48 | .... | .... | .... | .... | .... | .... | .... | .... | .... | .... | .... | .... | .... | .... | .... | .... | .... | .... | .... |
| 2004-05 | Moorhead Spuds | High-MN | 25 | 12 | 26 | 38 | .... | .... | .... | .... | .... | .... | .... | .... | .... | .... | .... | .... | .... | .... | .... | .... | .... | .... | .... |
| | Lincoln Stars | USHL | 12 | 0 | 3 | 3 | 4 | .... | .... | .... | .... | .... | .... | .... | .... | .... | 4 | 2 | 3 | 5 | 2 | .... | .... | .... | .... |
| 2005-06 | North Dakota | WCHA | 44 | 4 | 23 | 27 | 44 | .... | .... | .... | .... | .... | .... | .... | .... | .... | .... | .... | .... | .... | .... | .... | .... | .... | .... |
| 2006-07 | North Dakota | WCHA | 38 | 2 | 24 | 26 | 69 | .... | .... | .... | .... | .... | .... | .... | .... | .... | .... | .... | .... | .... | .... | .... | .... | .... | .... |
| **2007-08** | **Ottawa** | **NHL** | **6** | **0** | **1** | **1** | **4** | **0** | **0** | **0** | **6** | **0.0** | **1** | **0** | **0.0** | **16:49** | **4** | **0** | **0** | **0** | **2** | **0** | **0** | **0** | **14:31** |
| | Binghamton | AHL | 55 | 3 | 22 | 25 | 51 | .... | .... | .... | .... | .... | .... | .... | .... | .... | .... | .... | .... | .... | .... | .... | .... | .... | .... |
| **2008-09** | **Ottawa** | **NHL** | **53** | **2** | **11** | **13** | **33** | **1** | **0** | **1** | **51** | **3.9** | **–2** | **0** | **0.0** | **18:53** | .... | .... | .... | .... | .... | .... | .... | .... | .... |
| | Binghamton | AHL | 27 | 2 | 10 | 12 | 41 | .... | .... | .... | .... | .... | .... | .... | .... | .... | .... | .... | .... | .... | .... | .... | .... | .... | .... |
| | **NHL Totals** | | **59** | **2** | **12** | **14** | **37** | **1** | **0** | **1** | **57** | **3.5** | | **0** | **0.0** | **18:41** | **4** | **0** | **0** | **0** | **2** | **0** | **0** | **0** | **14:31** |

WCHA All-Rookie Team (2006)

## LEGWAND, David

(LEHG-wawnd, DAY-vihd) **NSH.**

Center. Shoots left. 6'2", 202 lbs. Born, Detroit, MI, August 17, 1980. Nashville's 1st choice, 2nd overall, in 1998 Entry Draft.

| Season | Club | League | GP | G | A | Pts | PIM | PP | SH | GW | S | % | +/- | TF | F% | Min | GP | G | A | Pts | PIM | PP | SH | GW | Min |
|---|---|---|---|---|---|---|---|---|---|---|---|---|---|---|---|---|---|---|---|---|---|---|---|---|---|
| 1996-97 | Det. Compuware | MNHL | 44 | 21 | 41 | 62 | 58 | .... | .... | .... | .... | .... | .... | .... | .... | .... | .... | .... | .... | .... | .... | .... | .... | .... | .... |
| 1997-98 | Plymouth Whalers | OHL | 59 | 54 | 51 | 105 | 56 | .... | .... | .... | .... | .... | .... | .... | .... | .... | 15 | 8 | 12 | 20 | 24 | .... | .... | .... | .... |
| **1998-99** | Plymouth Whalers | OHL | 55 | 31 | 49 | 80 | 65 | .... | .... | .... | .... | .... | .... | .... | .... | .... | 11 | 3 | 8 | 11 | 8 | .... | .... | .... | .... |
| | **Nashville** | **NHL** | **1** | **0** | **0** | **0** | **0** | **0** | **0** | **0** | **2** | **0.0** | **0** | **9** | **55.6** | **12:50** | .... | .... | .... | .... | .... | .... | .... | .... | .... |
| **99-2000** | **Nashville** | **NHL** | **71** | **13** | **15** | **28** | **30** | **4** | **0** | **2** | **111** | **11.7** | **–6** | **637** | **41.6** | **14:43** | .... | .... | .... | .... | .... | .... | .... | .... | .... |
| **2000-01** | **Nashville** | **NHL** | **81** | **13** | **28** | **41** | **38** | **3** | **0** | **3** | **172** | **7.6** | **1** | **888** | **40.3** | **15:14** | .... | .... | .... | .... | .... | .... | .... | .... | .... |
| **2001-02** | **Nashville** | **NHL** | **63** | **11** | **19** | **30** | **54** | **1** | **1** | **1** | **121** | **9.1** | **1** | **843** | **40.5** | **16:25** | .... | .... | .... | .... | .... | .... | .... | .... | .... |
| **2002-03** | **Nashville** | **NHL** | **64** | **17** | **31** | **48** | **34** | **3** | **1** | **4** | **167** | **10.2** | **–2** | **1095** | **46.6** | **19:14** | .... | .... | .... | .... | .... | .... | .... | .... | .... |
| **2003-04** | **Nashville** | **NHL** | **82** | **18** | **29** | **47** | **46** | **5** | **1** | **5** | **165** | **10.9** | **9** | **1109** | **45.1** | **17:17** | **6** | **1** | **0** | **1** | **8** | **0** | **1** | **0** | **15:41** |
| 2004-05 | EHC Basel | Swiss-2 | 3 | 6 | 2 | 8 | 2 | .... | .... | .... | .... | .... | .... | .... | .... | .... | 19 | 16 | 23 | 39 | 20 | .... | .... | .... | .... |
| **2005-06** | **Nashville** | **NHL** | **44** | **7** | **19** | **26** | **34** | **0** | **0** | **5** | **109** | **6.4** | **3** | **580** | **44.7** | **16:50** | **5** | **0** | **1** | **1** | **8** | **0** | **0** | **0** | **17:21** |
| | Milwaukee | AHL | 3 | 0 | 0 | 0 | 0 | .... | .... | .... | .... | .... | .... | .... | .... | .... | .... | .... | .... | .... | .... | .... | .... | .... | .... |
| **2006-07** | **Nashville** | **NHL** | **78** | **27** | **36** | **63** | **44** | **3** | **1** | **7** | **153** | **17.6** | **23** | **1108** | **45.3** | **18:22** | **5** | **0** | **3** | **3** | **2** | **0** | **0** | **0** | **22:23** |
| **2007-08** | **Nashville** | **NHL** | **65** | **15** | **29** | **44** | **38** | **4** | **0** | **1** | **144** | **10.4** | **–4** | **700** | **43.6** | **18:01** | **3** | **1** | **0** | **1** | **2** | **0** | **0** | **0** | **18:15** |
| **2008-09** | **Nashville** | **NHL** | **73** | **20** | **22** | **42** | **32** | **1** | **3** | **1** | **175** | **11.4** | **–3** | **1023** | **49.8** | **19:27** | .... | .... | .... | .... | .... | .... | .... | .... | .... |
| | **NHL Totals** | | **622** | **141** | **228** | **369** | **350** | **24** | **7** | **29** | **1319** | **10.7** | | **7992** | **44.5** | **17:16** | **19** | **2** | **4** | **6** | **20** | **0** | **1** | **0** | **18:18** |

OHL All-Rookie Team (1998) • OHL First All-Star Team (1998) • OHL Rookie of the Year (1998) • OHL MVP (1998) • Canadian Major Junior Rookie of the Year (1998)

Signed as a free agent by **Basel** (Swiss-2), January 27, 2005.

## LEHMAN, Scott

(LAY-man, SKAWT) **ATL.**

Defense. Shoots left. 6'1", 200 lbs. Born, Fort McMurray, Alta., January 6, 1986. Atlanta's 3rd choice, 76th overall, in 2004 Entry Draft.

| Season | Club | League | GP | G | A | Pts | PIM | PP | SH | GW | S | % | +/- | TF | F% | Min | GP | G | A | Pts | PIM | PP | SH | GW | Min |
|---|---|---|---|---|---|---|---|---|---|---|---|---|---|---|---|---|---|---|---|---|---|---|---|---|---|
| 2002-03 | St. Michael's | OHL | 53 | 3 | 10 | 13 | 50 | .... | .... | .... | .... | .... | .... | .... | .... | .... | 19 | 1 | 3 | 4 | 34 | .... | .... | .... | .... |
| 2003-04 | St. Michael's | OHL | 66 | 5 | 27 | 32 | 189 | .... | .... | .... | .... | .... | .... | .... | .... | .... | 18 | 2 | 2 | 4 | 38 | .... | .... | .... | .... |
| 2004-05 | St. Michael's | OHL | 57 | 2 | 19 | 21 | 189 | .... | .... | .... | .... | .... | .... | .... | .... | .... | 10 | 2 | 2 | 4 | 31 | .... | .... | .... | .... |
| 2005-06 | St. Michael's | OHL | 68 | 5 | 50 | 55 | 175 | .... | .... | .... | .... | .... | .... | .... | .... | .... | 4 | 0 | 2 | 2 | 15 | .... | .... | .... | .... |
| 2006-07 | Chicago Wolves | AHL | 3 | 0 | 0 | 0 | 14 | .... | .... | .... | .... | .... | .... | .... | .... | .... | .... | .... | .... | .... | .... | .... | .... | .... | .... |
| | Gwinnett | ECHL | 72 | 2 | 12 | 14 | 86 | .... | .... | .... | .... | .... | .... | .... | .... | .... | 4 | 0 | 0 | 0 | 11 | .... | .... | .... | .... |
| 2007-08 | Chicago Wolves | AHL | 40 | 2 | 5 | 7 | 109 | .... | .... | .... | .... | .... | .... | .... | .... | .... | .... | .... | .... | .... | .... | .... | .... | .... | .... |
| | Gwinnett | ECHL | 6 | 0 | 2 | 2 | 18 | .... | .... | .... | .... | .... | .... | .... | .... | .... | .... | .... | .... | .... | .... | .... | .... | .... | .... |
| **2008-09** | **Atlanta** | **NHL** | **1** | **0** | **0** | **0** | **0** | **0** | **0** | **0** | **0** | **0.0** | **0** | **0** | **0.0** | **3:03** | .... | .... | .... | .... | .... | .... | .... | .... | .... |
| | Chicago Wolves | AHL | 50 | 2 | 3 | 5 | 86 | .... | .... | .... | .... | .... | .... | .... | .... | .... | .... | .... | .... | .... | .... | .... | .... | .... | .... |
| | **NHL Totals** | | **1** | **0** | **0** | **0** | **0** | **0** | **0** | **0** | **0** | **0.0** | | **0** | **0.0** | **3:03** | .... | .... | .... | .... | .... | .... | .... | .... | .... |

## LEHOUX, Yanick

(luh-HOO, YAH-nihk)

Center. Shoots right. 6'1", 200 lbs. Born, Montreal, Que., April 8, 1982. Los Angeles' 3rd choice, 86th overall, in 2000 Entry Draft.

| Season | Club | League | GP | G | A | Pts | PIM | PP | SH | GW | S | % | +/- | TF | F% | Min | GP | G | A | Pts | PIM | PP | SH | GW | Min |
|---|---|---|---|---|---|---|---|---|---|---|---|---|---|---|---|---|---|---|---|---|---|---|---|---|---|
| 1997-98 | Cap-d-Madeleine | QAAA | 42 | 29 | 50 | 79 | 26 | .... | .... | .... | .... | .... | .... | .... | .... | .... | .... | .... | .... | .... | .... | .... | .... | .... | .... |
| 1998-99 | Baie-Comeau | QMJHL | 63 | 10 | 20 | 30 | 31 | .... | .... | .... | .... | .... | .... | .... | .... | .... | .... | .... | .... | .... | .... | .... | .... | .... | .... |
| 99-2000 | Baie-Comeau | QMJHL | 67 | 31 | 61 | 92 | 14 | .... | .... | .... | .... | .... | .... | .... | .... | .... | 6 | 1 | 2 | 3 | 2 | .... | .... | .... | .... |
| 2000-01 | Baie-Comeau | QMJHL | 70 | 67 | 68 | 135 | 62 | .... | .... | .... | .... | .... | .... | .... | .... | .... | 11 | 8 | 16 | 24 | 0 | .... | .... | .... | .... |
| 2001-02 | Baie-Comeau | QMJHL | 66 | 56 | 69 | 125 | 63 | .... | .... | .... | .... | .... | .... | .... | .... | .... | 5 | 5 | 4 | 9 | 0 | .... | .... | .... | .... |
| | Manchester | AHL | .... | .... | .... | .... | .... | .... | .... | .... | .... | .... | .... | .... | .... | .... | 1 | 0 | 0 | 0 | 0 | .... | .... | .... | .... |
| 2002-03 | Manchester | AHL | 78 | 16 | 21 | 37 | 26 | .... | .... | .... | .... | .... | .... | .... | .... | .... | 1 | 0 | 0 | 0 | 0 | .... | .... | .... | .... |
| 2003-04 | Manchester | AHL | 66 | 14 | 28 | 42 | 22 | .... | .... | .... | .... | .... | .... | .... | .... | .... | 5 | 2 | 3 | 5 | 16 | .... | .... | .... | .... |
| 2004-05 | Manchester | AHL | 38 | 23 | 31 | 54 | 16 | .... | .... | .... | .... | .... | .... | .... | .... | .... | .... | .... | .... | .... | .... | .... | .... | .... | .... |
| **2005-06** | Geneve | Swiss | 7 | 5 | 2 | 7 | 6 | .... | .... | .... | .... | .... | .... | .... | .... | .... | .... | .... | .... | .... | .... | .... | .... | .... | .... |
| | EHC Basel | Swiss | 4 | 0 | 2 | 2 | 4 | .... | .... | .... | .... | .... | .... | .... | .... | .... | .... | .... | .... | .... | .... | .... | .... | .... | .... |
| | **Phoenix** | **NHL** | **3** | **1** | **0** | **1** | **2** | **0** | **0** | **0** | **5** | **20.0** | **1** | **24** | **33.3** | **9:50** | .... | .... | .... | .... | .... | .... | .... | .... | .... |
| | San Antonio | AHL | 23 | 8 | 6 | 14 | 13 | .... | .... | .... | .... | .... | .... | .... | .... | .... | .... | .... | .... | .... | .... | .... | .... | .... | .... |
| | Manchester | AHL | 31 | 10 | 6 | 16 | 23 | .... | .... | .... | .... | .... | .... | .... | .... | .... | .... | .... | .... | .... | .... | .... | .... | .... | .... |
| **2006-07** | **Phoenix** | **NHL** | **7** | **1** | **2** | **3** | **4** | **1** | **0** | **0** | **10** | **10.0** | **–1** | **10** | **60.0** | **12:32** | .... | .... | .... | .... | .... | .... | .... | .... | .... |
| | San Antonio | AHL | 72 | 31 | 42 | 73 | 26 | .... | .... | .... | .... | .... | .... | .... | .... | .... | .... | .... | .... | .... | .... | .... | .... | .... | .... |
| 2007-08 | San Antonio | AHL | 7 | 1 | 3 | 4 | 2 | .... | .... | .... | .... | .... | .... | .... | .... | .... | .... | .... | .... | .... | .... | .... | .... | .... | .... |
| | Mytischi | Russia | 17 | 2 | 5 | 7 | 8 | .... | .... | .... | .... | .... | .... | .... | .... | .... | .... | .... | .... | .... | .... | .... | .... | .... | .... |
| 2008-09 | Hamilton | AHL | 80 | 19 | 41 | 60 | 38 | .... | .... | .... | .... | .... | .... | .... | .... | .... | 6 | 1 | 1 | 2 | 4 | .... | .... | .... | .... |
| | **NHL Totals** | | **10** | **2** | **2** | **4** | **6** | **1** | **0** | **0** | **15** | **13.3** | | **34** | **41.2** | **11:44** | .... | .... | .... | .... | .... | .... | .... | .... | .... |

QMJHL Second All-Star Team (2002)

Signed as a free agent by **Geneve** (Swiss), September 5 2005. Claimed on waivers by **Phoenix** from **Los Angeles**, November 5, 2005. Claimed on waivers by **Los Angeles** from **Phoenix**, November 25, 2005. Traded to **Phoenix** by **Los Angeles** for Tim Jackman, March 9, 2006. Signed as a free agent by **Mytischi** (Russia), November 10, 2007. Signed as a free agent by **Montreal**, July 25, 2008.

## LEHTINEN, Jere

(LEH-tih-nehn, YUH-ree) **DAL.**

Right wing. Shoots right. 6', 192 lbs. Born, Espoo, Finland, June 24, 1973. Minnesota's 3rd choice, 88th overall, in 1992 Entry Draft.

| Season | Club | League | GP | G | A | Pts | PIM | PP | SH | GW | S | % | +/- | TF | F% | Min | GP | G | A | Pts | PIM | PP | SH | GW | Min |
|---|---|---|---|---|---|---|---|---|---|---|---|---|---|---|---|---|---|---|---|---|---|---|---|---|---|
| 1989-90 | Kiekko-Espoo Jr. | Fin-Jr. | 32 | 23 | 23 | 46 | 6 | .... | .... | .... | .... | .... | .... | .... | .... | .... | 5 | 0 | 3 | 3 | 0 | .... | .... | .... | .... |
| 1990-91 | K-Espoo U18 | Fin-U18 | 11 | 18 | 14 | 32 | 0 | .... | .... | .... | .... | .... | .... | .... | .... | .... | .... | .... | .... | .... | .... | .... | .... | .... | .... |
| | Kiekko-Espoo Jr. | Fin-Jr. | 10 | 8 | 6 | 14 | 4 | .... | .... | .... | .... | .... | .... | .... | .... | .... | .... | .... | .... | .... | .... | .... | .... | .... | .... |
| | Kiekko-Espoo | Finland-2 | 32 | 15 | 9 | 24 | 12 | .... | .... | .... | .... | .... | .... | .... | .... | .... | .... | .... | .... | .... | .... | .... | .... | .... | .... |
| 1991-92 | Kiekko-Espoo Jr. | Fin-Jr. | 8 | 5 | 4 | 9 | 2 | .... | .... | .... | .... | .... | .... | .... | .... | .... | .... | .... | .... | .... | .... | .... | .... | .... | .... |
| | Kiekko-Espoo | Finland-2 | 43 | 32 | 17 | 49 | 6 | .... | .... | .... | .... | .... | .... | .... | .... | .... | 5 | 2 | 4 | 6 | 2 | .... | .... | .... | .... |
| 1992-93 | Kiekko-Espoo Jr. | Fin-Jr. | 4 | 5 | 3 | 8 | 8 | .... | .... | .... | .... | .... | .... | .... | .... | .... | .... | .... | .... | .... | .... | .... | .... | .... | .... |
| | Kiekko-Espoo | Finland | 45 | 13 | 14 | 27 | 6 | .... | .... | .... | .... | .... | .... | .... | .... | .... | .... | .... | .... | .... | .... | .... | .... | .... | .... |
| 1993-94 | TPS Turku | Finland | 42 | 19 | 20 | 39 | 6 | .... | .... | .... | .... | .... | .... | .... | .... | .... | 11 | 11 | 2 | 13 | 2 | .... | .... | .... | .... |
| | Finland | Olympics | 8 | 3 | 0 | 3 | 0 | .... | .... | .... | .... | .... | .... | .... | .... | .... | .... | .... | .... | .... | .... | .... | .... | .... | .... |
| 1994-95 | TPS Turku | Finland | 39 | 19 | 23 | 42 | 33 | .... | .... | .... | .... | .... | .... | .... | .... | .... | 13 | 8 | 6 | 14 | 4 | .... | .... | .... | .... |
| **1995-96** | **Dallas** | **NHL** | **57** | **6** | **22** | **28** | **16** | **0** | **0** | **1** | **109** | **5.5** | **5** | .... | .... | .... | .... | .... | .... | .... | .... | .... | .... | .... | .... |
| | Michigan | IHL | 1 | 1 | 0 | 1 | 0 | .... | .... | .... | .... | .... | .... | .... | .... | .... | .... | .... | .... | .... | .... | .... | .... | .... | .... |
| **1996-97** | **Dallas** | **NHL** | **63** | **16** | **27** | **43** | **2** | **3** | **1** | **2** | **134** | **11.9** | **26** | .... | .... | .... | **7** | **2** | **2** | **4** | **0** | **0** | **0** | **0** | .... |
| **1997-98** | **Dallas** | **NHL** | **72** | **23** | **19** | **42** | **20** | **7** | **2** | **6** | **201** | **11.4** | **19** | .... | .... | .... | **12** | **3** | **5** | **8** | **2** | **1** | **0** | **0** | .... |
| | Finland | Olympics | 6 | 4 | 2 | 6 | 2 | .... | .... | .... | .... | .... | .... | .... | .... | .... | .... | .... | .... | .... | .... | .... | .... | .... | .... |
| **1998-99** ♦ | **Dallas** | **NHL** | **74** | **20** | **32** | **52** | **18** | **7** | **1** | **2** | **173** | **11.6** | **29** | **9** | **33.3** | **19:36** | **23** | **10** | **3** | **13** | **2** | **1** | **1** | **0** | **21:09** |
| **99-2000** | **Dallas** | **NHL** | **17** | **3** | **5** | **8** | **0** | **0** | **0** | **1** | **29** | **10.3** | **1** | **0** | **0.0** | **17:31** | **13** | **1** | **5** | **6** | **2** | **0** | **0** | **0** | **21:15** |

| | | | Regular Season | | | | | | | | | | | | | | Playoffs | | | | | | | | |
|---|---|---|---|---|---|---|---|---|---|---|---|---|---|---|---|---|---|---|---|---|---|---|---|---|---|
| Season | Club | League | GP | G | A | Pts | PIM | PP | SH | GW | S | % | +/- | TF | F% | Min | GP | G | A | Pts | PIM | PP | SH | GW | Min |
| **2000-01** | **Dallas** | **NHL** | **74** | **20** | **25** | **45** | **24** | **7** | **0** | **1** | **148** | **13.5** | **14** | **7** | **28.6** | **19:17** | **10** | **1** | **0** | **1** | **2** | **0** | **0** | **0** | **20:13** |
| **2001-02** | **Dallas** | **NHL** | **73** | **25** | **24** | **49** | **14** | **7** | **1** | **4** | **198** | **12.6** | **27** | **18** | **22.2** | **19:50** | .... | .... | .... | .... | .... | .... | .... | .... | .... |
| | Finland | Olympics | 4 | 1 | 2 | 3 | 2 | .... | .... | .... | .... | .... | .... | .... | .... | .... | .... | .... | .... | .... | .... | .... | .... | .... | .... |
| **2002-03** | **Dallas** | **NHL** | **80** | **31** | **17** | **48** | **20** | **5** | **0** | **3** | **238** | **13.0** | **39** | **36** | **22.2** | **18:47** | **12** | **3** | **2** | **5** | **0** | **1** | **0** | **1** | **21:12** |
| **2003-04** | **Dallas** | **NHL** | **58** | **13** | **13** | **26** | **20** | **4** | **1** | **4** | **138** | **9.4** | **0** | **10** | **40.0** | **19:27** | **5** | **0** | **0** | **0** | **0** | **0** | **0** | **0** | **19:19** |
| 2004-05 | | | DID NOT PLAY | | | | | | | | | | | | | | | | | | | | | | |
| **2005-06** | **Dallas** | **NHL** | **80** | **33** | **19** | **52** | **30** | **14** | **1** | **6** | **216** | **15.3** | **9** | **28** | **21.4** | **18:42** | **5** | **3** | **1** | **4** | **0** | **1** | **0** | **0** | **22:10** |
| | Finland | Olympics | 8 | 3 | 5 | 8 | 0 | .... | .... | .... | .... | .... | .... | .... | .... | .... | .... | .... | .... | .... | .... | .... | .... | .... | .... |
| **2006-07** | **Dallas** | **NHL** | **73** | **26** | **17** | **43** | **16** | **11** | **1** | **5** | **194** | **13.4** | **5** | **36** | **13.9** | **19:26** | **7** | **0** | **0** | **0** | **2** | **0** | **0** | **0** | **24:02** |
| **2007-08** | **Dallas** | **NHL** | **48** | **15** | **22** | **37** | **14** | **9** | **0** | **1** | **118** | **12.7** | **9** | **11** | **9.1** | **18:55** | **14** | **4** | **4** | **8** | **2** | **3** | **0** | **0** | **20:34** |
| **2008-09** | **Dallas** | **NHL** | **48** | **8** | **16** | **24** | **8** | **2** | **0** | **1** | **119** | **6.7** | **1** | **7** | **28.6** | **19:00** | .... | .... | .... | .... | .... | .... | .... | .... | .... |
| | **NHL Totals** | | **817** | **239** | **258** | **497** | **202** | **76** | **8** | **37** | **2015** | **11.9** | | **162** | **21.6** | **19:11** | **108** | **27** | **22** | **49** | **12** | **7** | **1** | **1** | **21:09** |

Frank J. Selke Trophy (1998, 1999, 2003)

Played in NHL All-Star Game (1998)

• Rights transferred to **Dallas** after **Minnesota** franchise relocated, June 9, 1993. • Missed majority of 1999-2000 season recovering from leg injury suffered in game vs. Nashville, October 16, 1999.

## LEHTONEN, Mikko

(LEH-tuh-nehn, MEE-koh) **BOS.**

Right wing. Shoots right. 6'5", 203 lbs. Born, Espoo, Finland, April 1, 1987. Boston's 3rd choice, 83rd overall, in 2005 Entry Draft.

| Season | Club | League | GP | G | A | Pts | PIM | PP | SH | GW | S | % | +/- | TF | F% | Min | GP | G | A | Pts | PIM | PP | SH | GW | Min |
|---|---|---|---|---|---|---|---|---|---|---|---|---|---|---|---|---|---|---|---|---|---|---|---|---|---|
| 2002-03 | Blues Espoo U18 | Fin-U18 | 11 | 1 | 3 | 4 | 2 | .... | .... | .... | .... | .... | .... | .... | .... | .... | 1 | 0 | 0 | 0 | 0 | .... | .... | .... | .... |
| 2003-04 | Blues Espoo U18 | Fin-U18 | 20 | 8 | 7 | 15 | 22 | .... | .... | .... | .... | .... | .... | .... | .... | .... | .... | .... | .... | .... | .... | .... | .... | .... | .... |
| | Blues Espoo Jr. | Fin-Jr. | 19 | 3 | 0 | 3 | 0 | .... | .... | .... | .... | .... | .... | .... | .... | .... | 5 | 0 | 0 | 0 | 0 | .... | .... | .... | .... |
| 2004-05 | Blues Espoo U18 | Fin-U18 | 2 | 0 | 2 | 2 | 0 | .... | .... | .... | .... | .... | .... | .... | .... | .... | .... | .... | .... | .... | .... | .... | .... | .... | .... |
| | Blues Espoo Jr. | Fin-Jr. | 37 | 6 | 9 | 15 | 38 | .... | .... | .... | .... | .... | .... | .... | .... | .... | 6 | 3 | 1 | 4 | 0 | .... | .... | .... | .... |
| | Blues Espoo | Finland | 1 | 0 | 0 | 0 | 0 | .... | .... | .... | .... | .... | .... | .... | .... | .... | .... | .... | .... | .... | .... | .... | .... | .... | .... |
| 2005-06 | Blues Espoo Jr. | Fin-Jr. | 15 | 3 | 4 | 7 | 12 | .... | .... | .... | .... | .... | .... | .... | .... | .... | 10 | 5 | 2 | 7 | 6 | .... | .... | .... | .... |
| | Suomi U20 | Finland-2 | 3 | 1 | 0 | 1 | 2 | .... | .... | .... | .... | .... | .... | .... | .... | .... | .... | .... | .... | .... | .... | .... | .... | .... | .... |
| | Blues Espoo | Finland | 25 | 4 | 0 | 4 | 0 | .... | .... | .... | .... | .... | .... | .... | .... | .... | .... | .... | .... | .... | .... | .... | .... | .... | .... |
| 2006-07 | Suomi U20 | Finland-2 | 3 | 0 | 3 | 3 | 0 | .... | .... | .... | .... | .... | .... | .... | .... | .... | .... | .... | .... | .... | .... | .... | .... | .... | .... |
| | Blues Espoo | Finland | 39 | 6 | 9 | 15 | 24 | .... | .... | .... | .... | .... | .... | .... | .... | .... | 9 | 1 | 1 | 2 | 4 | .... | .... | .... | .... |
| 2007-08 | Blues Espoo | Finland | 42 | 8 | 12 | 20 | 12 | .... | .... | .... | .... | .... | .... | .... | .... | .... | 17 | 1 | 8 | 9 | 4 | .... | .... | .... | .... |
| **2008-09** | **Boston** | **NHL** | **1** | **0** | **0** | **0** | **0** | **0** | **0** | **0** | **1** | **0.0** | **0** | **0** | **0.0** | **16:14** | .... | .... | .... | .... | .... | .... | .... | .... | .... |
| | Providence Bruins | AHL | 72 | 28 | 25 | 53 | 39 | .... | .... | .... | .... | .... | .... | .... | .... | .... | 14 | 2 | 5 | 7 | 4 | .... | .... | .... | .... |
| | **NHL Totals** | | **1** | **0** | **0** | **0** | **0** | **0** | **0** | **0** | **1** | **0.0** | | **0** | **0.0** | **16:14** | .... | .... | .... | .... | .... | .... | .... | .... | .... |

## LEINO, Ville

(LAY-noh, VIHL-ee) **DET.**

Left wing. Shoots left. 6', 182 lbs. Born, Savonlinna, Finland, October 6, 1983.

| Season | Club | League | GP | G | A | Pts | PIM | PP | SH | GW | S | % | +/- | TF | F% | Min | GP | G | A | Pts | PIM | PP | SH | GW | Min |
|---|---|---|---|---|---|---|---|---|---|---|---|---|---|---|---|---|---|---|---|---|---|---|---|---|---|
| 2002-03 | Ilves Tampere Jr. | Fin-Jr. | 26 | 14 | 21 | 35 | 24 | .... | .... | .... | .... | .... | .... | .... | .... | .... | .... | .... | .... | .... | .... | .... | .... | .... | .... |
| | Ilves Tampere | Finland | 23 | 1 | 1 | 2 | 0 | .... | .... | .... | .... | .... | .... | .... | .... | .... | .... | .... | .... | .... | .... | .... | .... | .... | .... |
| 2003-04 | Ilves Tampere Jr. | Fin-Jr. | 5 | 4 | 6 | 10 | 6 | .... | .... | .... | .... | .... | .... | .... | .... | .... | .... | .... | .... | .... | .... | .... | .... | .... | .... |
| | Ilves Tampere | Finland | 54 | 9 | 15 | 24 | 26 | .... | .... | .... | .... | .... | .... | .... | .... | .... | 7 | 1 | 1 | 2 | 4 | .... | .... | .... | .... |
| 2004-05 | Ilves Tampere | Finland | 56 | 8 | 11 | 19 | 32 | .... | .... | .... | .... | .... | .... | .... | .... | .... | 7 | 1 | 0 | 1 | 2 | .... | .... | .... | .... |
| 2005-06 | HPK Hameenlinna | Finland | 56 | 12 | 31 | 43 | 65 | .... | .... | .... | .... | .... | .... | .... | .... | .... | 13 | 3 | *9 | 12 | 4 | .... | .... | .... | .... |
| 2006-07 | HPK Hameenlinna | Finland | 50 | 11 | 29 | 40 | 73 | .... | .... | .... | .... | .... | .... | .... | .... | .... | 8 | 1 | 9 | 10 | 31 | .... | .... | .... | .... |
| 2007-08 | Jokerit Helsinki | Finland | 55 | 28 | *49 | 77 | 18 | .... | .... | .... | .... | .... | .... | .... | .... | .... | 14 | 8 | 11 | 19 | 8 | .... | .... | .... | .... |
| **2008-09** | **Detroit** | **NHL** | **13** | **5** | **4** | **9** | **6** | **0** | **0** | **1** | **17** | **29.4** | **5** | **12** | **58.3** | **12:42** | **7** | **0** | **2** | **2** | **0** | **0** | **0** | **0** | **8:44** |
| | Grand Rapids | AHL | 57 | 15 | 31 | 46 | 18 | .... | .... | .... | .... | .... | .... | .... | .... | .... | 10 | 3 | 10 | 13 | 10 | .... | .... | .... | .... |
| | **NHL Totals** | | **13** | **5** | **4** | **9** | **6** | **0** | **0** | **1** | **17** | **29.4** | | **12** | **58.3** | **12:42** | **7** | **0** | **2** | **2** | **0** | **0** | **0** | **0** | **8:44** |

Signed as a free agent by **Detroit**, May 10, 2008.

## LEMIEUX, Claude

(leh-M'YOO, KLOHD)

Right wing. Shoots right. 6'1", 215 lbs. Born, Buckingham, Que., July 16, 1965. Montreal's 2nd choice, 26th overall, in 1983 Entry Draft.

| Season | Club | League | GP | G | A | Pts | PIM | PP | SH | GW | S | % | +/- | TF | F% | Min | GP | G | A | Pts | PIM | PP | SH | GW | Min |
|---|---|---|---|---|---|---|---|---|---|---|---|---|---|---|---|---|---|---|---|---|---|---|---|---|---|
| 1981-82 | Richelieu Riverains | QAAA | 48 | 24 | 48 | 72 | 96 | .... | .... | .... | .... | .... | .... | .... | .... | .... | 8 | 10 | 13 | 23 | 14 | .... | .... | .... | .... |
| 1982-83 | Trois-Rivieres | QMJHL | 62 | 28 | 38 | 66 | 187 | .... | .... | .... | .... | .... | .... | .... | .... | .... | 4 | 1 | 0 | 1 | 30 | .... | .... | .... | .... |
| **1983-84** | Verdun Juniors | QMJHL | 51 | 41 | 45 | 86 | 225 | .... | .... | .... | .... | .... | .... | .... | .... | .... | 9 | 8 | 12 | 20 | 63 | .... | .... | .... | .... |
| | **Montreal** | **NHL** | **8** | **1** | **1** | **2** | **12** | **0** | **0** | **0** | **7** | **14.3** | **–2** | .... | .... | .... | .... | .... | .... | .... | .... | .... | .... | .... | .... |
| | Nova Scotia | AHL | .... | .... | .... | .... | .... | .... | .... | .... | .... | .... | .... | .... | .... | .... | 2 | 1 | 0 | 1 | 0 | .... | .... | .... | .... |
| **1984-85** | Verdun | QMJHL | 52 | 58 | 66 | 124 | 152 | .... | .... | .... | .... | .... | .... | .... | .... | .... | 14 | 23 | 17 | 40 | 38 | .... | .... | .... | .... |
| | **Montreal** | **NHL** | **1** | **0** | **1** | **1** | **7** | **0** | **0** | **0** | **0** | **0.0** | **1** | .... | .... | .... | .... | .... | .... | .... | .... | .... | .... | .... | .... |
| **1985-86 ♦** | **Montreal** | **NHL** | **10** | **1** | **2** | **3** | **22** | **1** | **0** | **0** | **16** | **6.3** | **–6** | .... | .... | .... | **20** | **10** | **6** | **16** | **68** | **4** | **0** | **4** | |
| | Sherbrooke | AHL | 58 | 21 | 32 | 53 | 145 | .... | .... | .... | .... | .... | .... | .... | .... | .... | .... | .... | .... | .... | .... | .... | .... | .... | .... |
| **1986-87** | **Montreal** | **NHL** | **76** | **27** | **26** | **53** | **156** | **5** | **0** | **1** | **184** | **14.7** | **0** | .... | .... | .... | **17** | **4** | **9** | **13** | **41** | **2** | **0** | **0** | .... |
| **1987-88** | **Montreal** | **NHL** | **78** | **31** | **30** | **61** | **137** | **6** | **0** | **3** | **241** | **12.9** | **16** | .... | .... | .... | **11** | **3** | **2** | **5** | **20** | **0** | **0** | **2** | .... |
| **1988-89** | **Montreal** | **NHL** | **69** | **29** | **22** | **51** | **136** | **7** | **0** | **3** | **220** | **13.2** | **14** | .... | .... | .... | **18** | **4** | **3** | **7** | **58** | **0** | **0** | **1** | .... |
| **1989-90** | **Montreal** | **NHL** | **39** | **8** | **10** | **18** | **106** | **3** | **0** | **1** | **104** | **7.7** | **–8** | .... | .... | .... | **11** | **1** | **3** | **4** | **38** | **0** | **0** | **1** | .... |
| **1990-91** | **New Jersey** | **NHL** | **78** | **30** | **17** | **47** | **105** | **10** | **0** | **2** | **271** | **11.1** | **–8** | .... | .... | .... | **7** | **4** | **0** | **4** | **34** | **2** | **0** | **1** | .... |
| **1991-92** | **New Jersey** | **NHL** | **74** | **41** | **27** | **68** | **109** | **13** | **1** | **8** | **296** | **13.9** | **9** | .... | .... | .... | **7** | **4** | **3** | **7** | **26** | **1** | **0** | **0** | .... |
| **1992-93** | **New Jersey** | **NHL** | **77** | **30** | **51** | **81** | **155** | **13** | **0** | **3** | **311** | **9.6** | **3** | .... | .... | .... | **5** | **2** | **0** | **2** | **19** | **1** | **0** | **0** | .... |
| **1993-94** | **New Jersey** | **NHL** | **79** | **18** | **26** | **44** | **86** | **5** | **0** | **5** | **181** | **9.9** | **13** | .... | .... | .... | **20** | **7** | **11** | **18** | **44** | **0** | **0** | **2** | .... |
| **1994-95 ♦** | **New Jersey** | **NHL** | **45** | **6** | **13** | **19** | **86** | **1** | **0** | **1** | **117** | **5.1** | **2** | .... | .... | .... | **20** | ***13** | **3** | **16** | **20** | **0** | **0** | **3** | .... |
| **1995-96 ♦** | **Colorado** | **NHL** | **79** | **39** | **32** | **71** | **117** | **9** | **2** | **10** | **315** | **12.4** | **14** | .... | .... | .... | **19** | **5** | **7** | **12** | **55** | **3** | **0** | **0** | .... |
| **1996-97** | **Colorado** | **NHL** | **45** | **11** | **17** | **28** | **43** | **5** | **0** | **4** | **168** | **6.5** | **–4** | .... | .... | .... | **17** | ***13** | **10** | **23** | **32** | **4** | **0** | **4** | .... |
| **1997-98** | **Colorado** | **NHL** | **78** | **26** | **27** | **53** | **115** | **11** | **1** | **1** | **261** | **10.0** | **–7** | .... | .... | .... | **7** | **3** | **3** | **6** | **8** | **1** | **0** | **1** | .... |
| **1998-99** | **Colorado** | **NHL** | **82** | **27** | **24** | **51** | **102** | **11** | **0** | **8** | **292** | **9.2** | **0** | **43** | **41.9** | **21:14** | **19** | **3** | **11** | **14** | **26** | **1** | **0** | **0** | **19:28** |
| **99-2000** | **Colorado** | **NHL** | **13** | **3** | **6** | **9** | **4** | **0** | **0** | **0** | **36** | **8.3** | **0** | **2** | **50.0** | **18:40** | .... | .... | .... | .... | .... | .... | .... | .... | .... |
| | **♦ New Jersey** | **NHL** | **70** | **17** | **21** | **38** | **86** | **7** | **0** | **3** | **221** | **7.7** | **–3** | **49** | **28.6** | **17:55** | **23** | **4** | **6** | **10** | **28** | **1** | **0** | **0** | **18:59** |
| **2000-01** | **Phoenix** | **NHL** | **46** | **10** | **16** | **26** | **58** | **2** | **0** | **1** | **99** | **10.1** | **1** | **28** | **21.4** | **17:12** | .... | .... | .... | .... | .... | .... | .... | .... | .... |
| **2001-02** | **Phoenix** | **NHL** | **82** | **16** | **25** | **41** | **70** | **4** | **1** | **3** | **174** | **9.2** | **–5** | **49** | **28.6** | **17:12** | **5** | **0** | **0** | **0** | **2** | **0** | **0** | **0** | **16:58** |
| **2002-03** | **Phoenix** | **NHL** | **36** | **6** | **8** | **14** | **30** | **1** | **1** | **0** | **74** | **8.1** | **–3** | **295** | **46.8** | **14:02** | .... | .... | .... | .... | .... | .... | .... | .... | .... |
| | **Dallas** | **NHL** | **32** | **2** | **4** | **6** | **14** | **0** | **0** | **0** | **45** | **4.4** | **–9** | **35** | **48.6** | **13:14** | **7** | **0** | **1** | **1** | **10** | **0** | **0** | **0** | **11:24** |
| 2003-04 | EV Zug | Swiss | 7 | 2 | 3 | 5 | 4 | .... | .... | .... | .... | .... | .... | .... | .... | .... | 5 | 1 | 3 | 4 | 8 | .... | .... | .... | .... |
| 2004-05 | | | OUT OF HOCKEY – RETIRED | | | | | | | | | | | | | | | | | | | | | | |
| 2005-06 | | | OUT OF HOCKEY – RETIRED | | | | | | | | | | | | | | | | | | | | | | |
| 2006-07 | | | OUT OF HOCKEY – RETIRED | | | | | | | | | | | | | | | | | | | | | | |
| 2007-08 | | | OUT OF HOCKEY – RETIRED | | | | | | | | | | | | | | | | | | | | | | |
| **2008-09** | China Sharks | ALIH | 2 | 0 | 1 | 1 | 4 | .... | .... | .... | .... | .... | .... | .... | .... | .... | .... | .... | .... | .... | .... | .... | .... | .... | .... |
| | Worcester Sharks | AHL | 23 | 3 | 8 | 11 | 24 | .... | .... | .... | .... | .... | .... | .... | .... | .... | .... | .... | .... | .... | .... | .... | .... | .... | .... |
| | **San Jose** | **NHL** | **18** | **0** | **1** | **1** | **21** | **0** | **0** | **0** | **17** | **0.0** | **–5** | **14** | **21.4** | **7:40** | **1** | **0** | **0** | **0** | **0** | **0** | **0** | **0** | **5:07** |
| | **NHL Totals** | | **1215** | **379** | **407** | **786** | **1777** | **114** | **6** | **57** | **3650** | **10.4** | | **515** | **41.0** | **17:10** | **234** | **80** | **78** | **158** | **529** | **20** | **0** | **19** | **17:45** |

QMJHL Second All-Star Team (1984) • QMJHL First All-Star Team (1985) • Conn Smythe Trophy (1995)

• Missed majority of 1989-90 season recovering from abdominal injury suffered in game vs. Boston, October 9, 1989. Traded to **New Jersey** by **Montreal** for Sylvain Turgeon, September 4, 1990. Traded to **NY Islanders** by **New Jersey** for Steve Thomas, October 3, 1995. Traded to **Colorado** by **NY Islanders** for Wendel Clark, October 3, 1995. Traded to **New Jersey** by **Colorado** with Colorado's 1st (David Hale) and 2nd (Matt DeMarchi) round choices in 2000 Entry Draft for Brian Rolston and New Jersey's 1st round choice (later traded to Boston – Boston selected Martin Samuelsson) in 2000 Entry Draft, November 3, 1999. Signed as a free agent by **Phoenix**, December 5, 2000. Traded to **Dallas** by **Phoenix** for Scott Pellerin and Dallas' 4th round choice (Kevin Porter) in 2004 Entry Draft, January 16, 2003. Signed as a free agent by **Zug** (Swiss), February 9, 2004. Signed as a free agent by **China** (ALIH), November 15, 2008. Signed as a free agent by **Worcester** (AHL), November 25, 2008. Signed as a free agent by **San Jose**, December 29, 2008. • Officially announced his retirement, July 8, 2009.

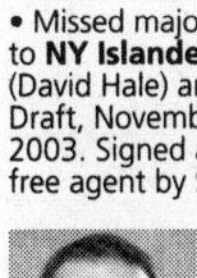

## LEOPOLD, Jordan

(LEE-oh-pohld, JOHR-dahn) **FLA.**

Defense. Shoots left. 6'1", 200 lbs. Born, Golden Valley, MN, August 3, 1980. Anaheim's 1st choice, 44th overall, in 1999 Entry Draft.

| Season | Club | League | GP | G | A | Pts | PIM | PP | SH | GW | S | % | +/- | TF | F% | Min | GP | G | A | Pts | PIM | PP | SH | GW | Min |
|---|---|---|---|---|---|---|---|---|---|---|---|---|---|---|---|---|---|---|---|---|---|---|---|---|---|
| 1995-96 | Armstrong | High-MN | 19 | 11 | 14 | 25 | 30 | .... | .... | .... | .... | .... | .... | .... | .... | .... | .... | .... | .... | .... | .... | .... | .... | .... | .... |
| 1996-97 | Armstrong | High-MN | 30 | 24 | 36 | 60 | .... | .... | .... | .... | .... | .... | .... | .... | .... | .... | .... | .... | .... | .... | .... | .... | .... | .... | .... |
| 1997-98 | USNTDP | U-18 | 25 | 7 | 3 | 10 | 2 | .... | .... | .... | .... | .... | .... | .... | .... | .... | .... | .... | .... | .... | .... | .... | .... | .... | .... |
| | USNTDP | USHL | 19 | 2 | 4 | 6 | 6 | .... | .... | .... | .... | .... | .... | .... | .... | .... | .... | .... | .... | .... | .... | .... | .... | .... | .... |
| | USNTDP | NAHL | 16 | 2 | 5 | 7 | 8 | .... | .... | .... | .... | .... | .... | .... | .... | .... | .... | .... | .... | .... | .... | .... | .... | .... | .... |
| 1998-99 | U. of Minnesota | WCHA | 39 | 7 | 16 | 23 | 20 | .... | .... | .... | .... | .... | .... | .... | .... | .... | .... | .... | .... | .... | .... | .... | .... | .... | .... |
| 99-2000 | U. of Minnesota | WCHA | 39 | 6 | 18 | 24 | 20 | .... | .... | .... | .... | .... | .... | .... | .... | .... | .... | .... | .... | .... | .... | .... | .... | .... | .... |
| 2000-01 | U. of Minnesota | WCHA | 42 | 12 | 37 | 49 | 38 | .... | .... | .... | .... | .... | .... | .... | .... | .... | .... | .... | .... | .... | .... | .... | .... | .... | .... |

| | | | Regular Season | | | | | | | | | | | | | | Playoffs | | | | | | | | |
|---|---|---|---|---|---|---|---|---|---|---|---|---|---|---|---|---|---|---|---|---|---|---|---|---|---|
| Season | Club | League | GP | G | A | Pts | PIM | PP | SH | GW | S | % | +/- | TF | F% | Min | GP | G | A | Pts | PIM | PP | SH | GW | Min |
| 2001-02 | U. of Minnesota | WCHA | 44 | 20 | 28 | 48 | 28 | .... | .... | .... | .... | .... | .... | .... | .... | .... | .... | .... | .... | .... | .... | .... | .... | .... | .... |
| **2002-03** | **Calgary** | **NHL** | **58** | **4** | **10** | **14** | **12** | **3** | **0** | **0** | **78** | **5.1** | **–15** | **0** | **0.0** | **20:36** | .... | .... | .... | .... | .... | .... | .... | .... | .... |
| | Saint John Flames | AHL | 3 | 1 | 2 | 3 | 0 | .... | .... | .... | .... | .... | .... | .... | .... | .... | .... | .... | .... | .... | .... | .... | .... | .... | .... |
| **2003-04** | **Calgary** | **NHL** | **82** | **9** | **24** | **33** | **24** | **6** | **0** | **1** | **138** | **6.5** | **8** | **0** | **0.0** | **22:14** | **26** | **0** | **10** | **10** | **6** | **0** | **0** | **0** | **25:41** |
| 2004-05 | | | DID NOT PLAY | | | | | | | | | | | | | | | | | | | | | | |
| **2005-06** | **Calgary** | **NHL** | **74** | **2** | **18** | **20** | **68** | **2** | **0** | **1** | **87** | **2.3** | **6** | **0** | **0.0** | **22:20** | **7** | **0** | **1** | **1** | **4** | **0** | **0** | **0** | **19:13** |
| | United States | Olympics | 6 | 1 | 0 | 1 | 4 | .... | .... | .... | .... | .... | .... | .... | .... | .... | .... | .... | .... | .... | .... | .... | .... | .... | .... |
| **2006-07** | **Colorado** | **NHL** | **15** | **2** | **3** | **5** | **14** | **1** | **1** | **0** | **19** | **10.5** | **–4** | **0** | **0.0** | **19:47** | .... | .... | .... | .... | .... | .... | .... | .... | .... |
| **2007-08** | **Colorado** | **NHL** | **43** | **5** | **8** | **13** | **20** | **2** | **0** | **1** | **35** | **14.3** | **5** | **0** | **0.0** | **15:59** | **7** | **0** | **3** | **3** | **0** | **0** | **0** | **0** | **17:00** |
| **2008-09** | **Colorado** | **NHL** | **64** | **6** | **14** | **20** | **18** | **1** | **0** | **1** | **82** | **7.3** | **–10** | **0** | **0.0** | **18:10** | .... | .... | .... | .... | .... | .... | .... | .... | .... |
| | **Calgary** | **NHL** | **19** | **1** | **3** | **4** | **6** | **0** | **0** | **0** | **25** | **4.0** | **–5** | **0** | **0.0** | **20:58** | **6** | **0** | **1** | **1** | **8** | **0** | **0** | **0** | **23:10** |
| | **NHL Totals** | | **355** | **29** | **80** | **109** | **162** | **15** | **1** | **4** | **464** | **6.3** | | **0** | **0.0** | **20:19** | **46** | **0** | **15** | **15** | **18** | **0** | **0** | **0** | **23:03** |

WCHA All-Rookie Team (1999) • WCHA Second All-Star Team (2000) • WCHA First All-Star Team (2001, 2002) • NCAA West First All-American Team (2001) • Hobey Baker Memorial Award (Top U.S. Collegiate Player) (2002)

Traded to **Calgary** by **Anaheim** for Andrei Nazarov and Calgary's 2nd round choice (later traded to Phoenix – later traded back to Calgary – Calgary selected Andrei Taratukhin) in 2001 Entry Draft, September 26, 2000. Traded to **Colorado** by **Calgary** with Calgary's 2nd round choice (Codey Burki) in 2006 Entry Draft and Calgary's 2nd round choice (Trevor Cann) in 2007 Entry Draft for Alex Tanguay, June 24, 2006. • Missed majority of 2006-07 season recovering from off-season hernia surgery, groin injury and wrist injury suffered in game vs. Calgary, February 15, 2007. Traded to **Calgary** by **Colorado** for Ryan Wilson, Lawrence Nycholat and Montreal's 2nd round choice (previously acquired, Colorado selected Stefan Elliott) in 2009 Entry Draft, March 4, 2009. Traded to **Florida** by **Calgary** with Phoenix's 3rd round choice (previously acquired, Florida selected Josh Birkholz) in 2009 Entry Draft for Jay Bouwmeester, June 27, 2009.

## LEPISTO, Sami

(LEH-pihs-toh, SA-mee) **PHX.**

Defense. Shoots left. 6'1", 195 lbs. Born, Espoo, Finland, October 17, 1984. Washington's 6th choice, 66th overall, in 2004 Entry Draft.

| Season | Club | League | GP | G | A | Pts | PIM | PP | SH | GW | S | % | +/- | TF | F% | Min | GP | G | A | Pts | PIM | PP | SH | GW | Min |
|---|---|---|---|---|---|---|---|---|---|---|---|---|---|---|---|---|---|---|---|---|---|---|---|---|---|
| 2001-02 | Jokerit U18 | Fin-U18 | 20 | 8 | 14 | 22 | 36 | .... | .... | .... | .... | .... | .... | .... | .... | .... | 8 | 4 | 8 | 12 | 12 | .... | .... | .... | .... |
| | Jokerit Helsinki Jr. | Fin-Jr. | 14 | 0 | 5 | 5 | 2 | .... | .... | .... | .... | .... | .... | .... | .... | .... | .... | .... | .... | .... | .... | .... | .... | .... | .... |
| 2002-03 | Jokerit Helsinki Jr. | Fin-Jr. | 36 | 5 | 14 | 19 | 34 | .... | .... | .... | .... | .... | .... | .... | .... | .... | 11 | 1 | 5 | 6 | 8 | .... | .... | .... | .... |
| 2003-04 | Suomi U20 | Finland-2 | 1 | 0 | 0 | 0 | 0 | .... | .... | .... | .... | .... | .... | .... | .... | .... | .... | .... | .... | .... | .... | .... | .... | .... | .... |
| | Jokerit Helsinki | Finland | 53 | 3 | 4 | 7 | 20 | .... | .... | .... | .... | .... | .... | .... | .... | .... | 8 | 0 | 1 | 1 | 4 | .... | .... | .... | .... |
| 2004-05 | Jokerit Helsinki | Finland | 55 | 7 | 18 | 25 | 44 | .... | .... | .... | .... | .... | .... | .... | .... | .... | 12 | 1 | 7 | 8 | 12 | .... | .... | .... | .... |
| 2005-06 | Jokerit Helsinki | Finland | 56 | 8 | 21 | 29 | 68 | .... | .... | .... | .... | .... | .... | .... | .... | .... | .... | .... | .... | .... | .... | .... | .... | .... | .... |
| 2006-07 | Jokerit Helsinki | Finland | 26 | 1 | 9 | 10 | 32 | .... | .... | .... | .... | .... | .... | .... | .... | .... | 10 | 2 | 2 | 4 | 4 | .... | .... | .... | .... |
| **2007-08** | **Washington** | **NHL** | **7** | **0** | **1** | **1** | **12** | **0** | **0** | **0** | **8** | **0.0** | **–1** | **0** | **0.0** | **13:17** | .... | .... | .... | .... | .... | .... | .... | .... | .... |
| | Hershey Bears | AHL | 55 | 4 | 41 | 45 | 51 | .... | .... | .... | .... | .... | .... | .... | .... | .... | 5 | 0 | 1 | 1 | 4 | .... | .... | .... | .... |
| **2008-09** | **Washington** | **NHL** | **7** | **0** | **4** | **4** | **6** | **0** | **0** | **0** | **7** | **0.0** | **–3** | **0** | **0.0** | **19:36** | .... | .... | .... | .... | .... | .... | .... | .... | .... |
| | Hershey Bears | AHL | 70 | 4 | 38 | 42 | 80 | .... | .... | .... | .... | .... | .... | .... | .... | .... | .... | .... | .... | .... | .... | .... | .... | .... | .... |
| | **NHL Totals** | | **14** | **0** | **5** | **5** | **18** | **0** | **0** | **0** | **15** | **0.0** | | **0** | **0.0** | **16:27** | .... | .... | .... | .... | .... | .... | .... | .... | .... |

Traded to **Phoenix** by **Washington** for Phoenix's 5th round choice in 2010 Entry Draft, June 27, 2009.

## LESSARD, Francis

(leh-SAHR, FRAN-sihs) **PHX.**

Right wing. Shoots right. 6'3", 225 lbs. Born, Montreal, Que., May 30, 1979. Carolina's 3rd choice, 80th overall, in 1997 Entry Draft.

| Season | Club | League | GP | G | A | Pts | PIM | PP | SH | GW | S | % | +/- | TF | F% | Min | GP | G | A | Pts | PIM | PP | SH | GW | Min |
|---|---|---|---|---|---|---|---|---|---|---|---|---|---|---|---|---|---|---|---|---|---|---|---|---|---|
| 1994-95 | Laval-Laurentides | QAAA | 1 | 0 | 0 | 0 | 0 | .... | .... | .... | .... | .... | .... | .... | .... | .... | .... | .... | .... | .... | .... | .... | .... | .... | .... |
| 1995-96 | Laval-Laurentides | QAAA | 41 | 5 | 7 | 12 | 73 | .... | .... | .... | .... | .... | .... | .... | .... | .... | 13 | 1 | 3 | 4 | | .... | .... | .... | .... |
| 1996-97 | Val-d'Or Foreurs | QMJHL | 66 | 1 | 9 | 10 | 287 | .... | .... | .... | .... | .... | .... | .... | .... | .... | .... | .... | .... | .... | .... | .... | .... | .... | .... |
| 1997-98 | Val-d'Or Foreurs | QMJHL | 63 | 3 | 20 | 23 | 338 | .... | .... | .... | .... | .... | .... | .... | .... | .... | 19 | 1 | 6 | 7 | *101 | .... | .... | .... | .... |
| 1998-99 | Drummondville | QMJHL | 53 | 12 | 36 | 48 | 295 | .... | .... | .... | .... | .... | .... | .... | .... | .... | .... | .... | .... | .... | .... | .... | .... | .... | .... |
| 99-2000 | Philadelphia | AHL | 78 | 4 | 8 | 12 | 416 | .... | .... | .... | .... | .... | .... | .... | .... | .... | 5 | 0 | 1 | 1 | 7 | .... | .... | .... | .... |
| 2000-01 | Philadelphia | AHL | 64 | 3 | 7 | 10 | 330 | .... | .... | .... | .... | .... | .... | .... | .... | .... | 10 | 0 | 0 | 0 | 33 | .... | .... | .... | .... |
| **2001-02** | Philadelphia | AHL | 60 | 0 | 6 | 6 | 251 | .... | .... | .... | .... | .... | .... | .... | .... | .... | .... | .... | .... | .... | .... | .... | .... | .... | .... |
| | **Atlanta** | **NHL** | **5** | **0** | **0** | **0** | **26** | **0** | **0** | **0** | **2** | **0.0** | **0** | **0** | **0.0** | **12:45** | .... | .... | .... | .... | .... | .... | .... | .... | .... |
| | Chicago Wolves | AHL | 7 | 2 | 1 | 3 | 34 | .... | .... | .... | .... | .... | .... | .... | .... | .... | 15 | 0 | 1 | 1 | 40 | .... | .... | .... | .... |
| **2002-03** | **Atlanta** | **NHL** | **18** | **0** | **2** | **2** | **61** | **0** | **0** | **0** | **7** | **0.0** | **1** | **0** | **0.0** | **5:40** | .... | .... | .... | .... | .... | .... | .... | .... | .... |
| | Chicago Wolves | AHL | 50 | 2 | 5 | 7 | 194 | .... | .... | .... | .... | .... | .... | .... | .... | .... | 1 | 0 | 0 | 0 | 0 | .... | .... | .... | .... |
| **2003-04** | **Atlanta** | **NHL** | **62** | **1** | **1** | **2** | **181** | **0** | **0** | **0** | **19** | **5.3** | **–5** | **1** | **0.0** | **4:28** | .... | .... | .... | .... | .... | .... | .... | .... | .... |
| 2004-05 | | | DID NOT PLAY | | | | | | | | | | | | | | | | | | | | | | |
| **2005-06** | **Atlanta** | **NHL** | **6** | **0** | **0** | **0** | **0** | **0** | **0** | **0** | **0** | **0.0** | **–2** | **0** | **0.0** | **2:33** | .... | .... | .... | .... | .... | .... | .... | .... | .... |
| | Chicago Wolves | AHL | 36 | 2 | 3 | 5 | 163 | .... | .... | .... | .... | .... | .... | .... | .... | .... | .... | .... | .... | .... | .... | .... | .... | .... | .... |
| 2006-07 | Hartford | AHL | 58 | 3 | 6 | 9 | *309 | .... | .... | .... | .... | .... | .... | .... | .... | .... | .... | .... | .... | .... | .... | .... | .... | .... | .... |
| 2007-08 | Hartford | AHL | 14 | 4 | 1 | 5 | 49 | .... | .... | .... | .... | .... | .... | .... | .... | .... | .... | .... | .... | .... | .... | .... | .... | .... | .... |
| 2008-09 | San Antonio | AHL | 59 | 2 | 2 | 4 | *324 | .... | .... | .... | .... | .... | .... | .... | .... | .... | .... | .... | .... | .... | .... | .... | .... | .... | .... |
| | **NHL Totals** | | **91** | **1** | **3** | **4** | **268** | **0** | **0** | **0** | **28** | **3.6** | | **1** | **0.0** | **5:02** | .... | .... | .... | .... | .... | .... | .... | .... | .... |

Memorial Cup Tournament All-Star Team (1998)

Traded to **Philadelphia** by **Carolina** for Philadelphia's 8th round choice (Antti Jokella) in 1999 Entry Draft, May 25, 1999. Traded to **Atlanta** by **Philadelphia** for David Harlock and Atlanta's 3rd (later traded to Phoenix – Phoenix selected Tyler Redenbach) and 7th (later traded to San Jose – San Jose selected Joe Pavelski) round choices in 2003 Entry Draft, March 15, 2002. Signed as a free agent by **Phoenix**, July 31, 2008.

## LESSARD, Junior

(leh-SAHR, JEW-nyuhr)

Right wing/Center. Shoots right. 5'11", 200 lbs. Born, St-Joseph-de-Beauce, Que., May 26, 1980.

| Season | Club | League | GP | G | A | Pts | PIM | PP | SH | GW | S | % | +/- | TF | F% | Min | GP | G | A | Pts | PIM | PP | SH | GW | Min |
|---|---|---|---|---|---|---|---|---|---|---|---|---|---|---|---|---|---|---|---|---|---|---|---|---|---|
| 99-2000 | Portage Terriers | MJHL | 60 | 60 | 48 | 108 | 61 | .... | .... | .... | .... | .... | .... | .... | .... | .... | .... | .... | .... | .... | .... | .... | .... | .... | .... |
| 2000-01 | U. Minn-Duluth | WCHA | 36 | 4 | 8 | 12 | 12 | .... | .... | .... | .... | .... | .... | .... | .... | .... | .... | .... | .... | .... | .... | .... | .... | .... | .... |
| 2001-02 | U. Minn-Duluth | WCHA | 39 | 17 | 13 | 30 | 50 | .... | .... | .... | .... | .... | .... | .... | .... | .... | .... | .... | .... | .... | .... | .... | .... | .... | .... |
| 2002-03 | U. Minn-Duluth | WCHA | 40 | 21 | 16 | 37 | 20 | .... | .... | .... | .... | .... | .... | .... | .... | .... | .... | .... | .... | .... | .... | .... | .... | .... | .... |
| 2003-04 | U. Minn-Duluth | WCHA | 45 | *32 | 31 | *63 | 34 | .... | .... | .... | .... | .... | .... | .... | .... | .... | .... | .... | .... | .... | .... | .... | .... | .... | .... |
| 2004-05 | Houston Aeros | AHL | 71 | 11 | 11 | 22 | 25 | .... | .... | .... | .... | .... | .... | .... | .... | .... | 5 | 1 | 0 | 1 | 0 | .... | .... | .... | .... |
| **2005-06** | **Dallas** | **NHL** | **5** | **1** | **0** | **1** | **12** | **0** | **0** | **0** | **6** | **16.7** | **0** | **0** | **0.0** | **7:23** | .... | .... | .... | .... | .... | .... | .... | .... | .... |
| | Iowa Stars | AHL | 66 | 26 | 31 | 57 | 30 | .... | .... | .... | .... | .... | .... | .... | .... | .... | 7 | 3 | 4 | 7 | 4 | .... | .... | .... | .... |
| **2006-07** | **Dallas** | **NHL** | **1** | **1** | **0** | **1** | **0** | **1** | **0** | **0** | **3** | **33.3** | **1** | **0** | **0.0** | **11:56** | .... | .... | .... | .... | .... | .... | .... | .... | .... |
| | Iowa Stars | AHL | 65 | 27 | 25 | 52 | 32 | .... | .... | .... | .... | .... | .... | .... | .... | .... | 12 | 4 | 5 | 9 | 4 | .... | .... | .... | .... |
| **2007-08** | **Dallas** | **NHL** | **2** | **0** | **0** | **0** | **2** | **0** | **0** | **0** | **3** | **0.0** | **–1** | **0** | **0.0** | **12:05** | .... | .... | .... | .... | .... | .... | .... | .... | .... |
| | Iowa Stars | AHL | 36 | 10 | 11 | 21 | 15 | .... | .... | .... | .... | .... | .... | .... | .... | .... | .... | .... | .... | .... | .... | .... | .... | .... | .... |
| | **Tampa Bay** | **NHL** | **19** | **1** | **1** | **2** | **9** | **0** | **0** | **0** | **18** | **5.6** | **–5** | **0** | **0.0** | **9:38** | .... | .... | .... | .... | .... | .... | .... | .... | .... |
| | Norfolk Admirals | AHL | 19 | 6 | 9 | 15 | 4 | .... | .... | .... | .... | .... | .... | .... | .... | .... | .... | .... | .... | .... | .... | .... | .... | .... | .... |
| 2008-09 | Chicago Wolves | AHL | 41 | 6 | 5 | 11 | 10 | .... | .... | .... | .... | .... | .... | .... | .... | .... | .... | .... | .... | .... | .... | .... | .... | .... | .... |
| | Bridgeport | AHL | 21 | 7 | 6 | 13 | 2 | .... | .... | .... | .... | .... | .... | .... | .... | .... | 1 | 0 | 1 | 1 | 0 | .... | .... | .... | .... |
| | **NHL Totals** | | **27** | **3** | **1** | **4** | **23** | **1** | **0** | **0** | **30** | **10.0** | | **0** | **0.0** | **9:29** | .... | .... | .... | .... | .... | .... | .... | .... | .... |

WCHA First All-Star Team (2004) • WCHA Player of the Year (2004) • NCAA West First All-American Team (2004) • NCAA Championship All-Tournament Team (2004) • Hobey Baker Memorial Award (Top U.S. Collegiate Player) (2004)

Signed as a free agent by **Dallas**, April 15, 2004. Traded to **Tampa Bay** by **Dallas** for Dan Jancevski, January 15, 2008. Signed as a free agent by **Atlanta**, July 9, 2008. Traded to **NY Islanders** by **Atlanta** for Brett Skinner, January 13, 2009.

## LETANG, Kris

(leh-TANG, KRIHS) **PIT.**

Defense. Shoots right. 6', 201 lbs. Born, Montreal, Que., April 24, 1987. Pittsburgh's 3rd choice, 62nd overall, in 2005 Entry Draft.

| Season | Club | League | GP | G | A | Pts | PIM | PP | SH | GW | S | % | +/- | TF | F% | Min | GP | G | A | Pts | PIM | PP | SH | GW | Min |
|---|---|---|---|---|---|---|---|---|---|---|---|---|---|---|---|---|---|---|---|---|---|---|---|---|---|
| 2002-03 | Antoine-Girouard | QAAA | 42 | 2 | 10 | 12 | 34 | .... | .... | .... | .... | .... | .... | .... | .... | .... | .... | .... | .... | .... | .... | .... | .... | .... | .... |
| 2003-04 | Antoine-Girouard | QAAA | 39 | 12 | 41 | 53 | 94 | .... | .... | .... | .... | .... | .... | .... | .... | .... | 13 | 7 | 9 | 16 | 38 | .... | .... | .... | .... |
| 2004-05 | Val-d'Or Foreurs | QMJHL | 70 | 13 | 19 | 32 | 79 | .... | .... | .... | .... | .... | .... | .... | .... | .... | .... | .... | .... | .... | .... | .... | .... | .... | .... |
| 2005-06 | Val-d'Or Foreurs | QMJHL | 60 | 25 | 43 | 68 | 156 | .... | .... | .... | .... | .... | .... | .... | .... | .... | 5 | 1 | 5 | 6 | 20 | .... | .... | .... | .... |
| **2006-07** | **Pittsburgh** | **NHL** | **7** | **2** | **0** | **2** | **4** | **2** | **0** | **0** | **8** | **25.0** | **–3** | **0** | **0.0** | **11:33** | .... | .... | .... | .... | .... | .... | .... | .... | .... |
| | Val-d'Or Foreurs | QMJHL | 40 | 14 | 38 | 52 | 74 | .... | .... | .... | .... | .... | .... | .... | .... | .... | 19 | 12 | 19 | 31 | 48 | .... | .... | .... | .... |
| | Wilkes-Barre | AHL | .... | .... | .... | .... | .... | .... | .... | .... | .... | .... | .... | .... | .... | .... | 1 | 0 | 1 | 1 | 2 | .... | .... | .... | .... |
| **2007-08** | **Pittsburgh** | **NHL** | **63** | **6** | **11** | **17** | **23** | **1** | **0** | **3** | **68** | **8.8** | **–1** | **0** | **0.0** | **18:10** | **16** | **0** | **2** | **2** | **12** | **0** | **0** | **0** | **17:07** |
| | Wilkes-Barre | AHL | 10 | 1 | 6 | 7 | 4 | .... | .... | .... | .... | .... | .... | .... | .... | .... | .... | .... | .... | .... | .... | .... | .... | .... | .... |
| **2008-09**♦ | **Pittsburgh** | **NHL** | **74** | **10** | **23** | **33** | **24** | **4** | **1** | **3** | **138** | **7.2** | **–7** | **1** | **0.0** | **21:09** | **23** | **4** | **9** | **13** | **26** | **2** | **0** | **1** | **19:18** |
| | **NHL Totals** | | **144** | **18** | **34** | **52** | **51** | **7** | **1** | **6** | **214** | **8.4** | | **1** | **0.0** | **19:22** | **39** | **4** | **11** | **15** | **38** | **2** | **0** | **1** | **18:24** |

QMJHL All-Rookie Team (2005) • Canadian Major Junior All-Rookie Team (2005) • QMJHL First All-Star Team (2006, 2007) • Canadian Major Junior Second All-Star Team (2006. 2007)

## LETOURNEAU-LEBLOND, Pierre-Luc

(leh-TOOR-noh-leh-BLAWN) **N.J.**

Left wing. Shoots left. 6'2", 210 lbs. Born, Levis, Que., June 4, 1985. New Jersey's 4th choice, 216th overall, in 2004 Entry Draft.

| Season | Club | League | Regular Season GP | G | A | Pts | PIM | PP | SH | GW | S | % | +/- | TF | F% | Min | Playoffs GP | G | A | Pts | PIM | PP | SH | GW | Min |
|---|---|---|---|---|---|---|---|---|---|---|---|---|---|---|---|---|---|---|---|---|---|---|---|---|---|
| 2003-04 | Baie-Comeau | QMJHL | 62 | 2 | 3 | 5 | 198 | | | | | | | | | | 4 | 0 | 0 | 0 | 6 | | | | |
| 2004-05 | Baie-Comeau | QMJHL | 67 | 1 | 6 | 7 | 229 | | | | | | | | | | 6 | 0 | 1 | 1 | 10 | | | | |
| 2005-06 | Albany River Rats | AHL | 27 | 1 | 1 | 2 | 130 | | | | | | | | | | | | | | | | | | |
| | Adirondack | UHL | 31 | 3 | 6 | 9 | 165 | | | | | | | | | | 6 | 0 | 1 | 1 | 29 | | | | |
| 2006-07 | Trenton Titans | ECHL | 52 | 4 | 9 | 13 | 183 | | | | | | | | | | 4 | 0 | 0 | 0 | 15 | | | | |
| 2007-08 | Lowell Devils | AHL | 36 | 3 | 3 | 6 | 98 | | | | | | | | | | | | | | | | | | |
| | Trenton Devils | ECHL | 6 | 0 | 1 | 1 | 46 | | | | | | | | | | | | | | | | | | |
| **2008-09** | **New Jersey** | **NHL** | **8** | **0** | **1** | **1** | **22** | **0** | **0** | **0** | **3** | **0.0** | **3** | **0** | **0.0** | **4:51** | | | | | | | | | |
| | Lowell Devils | AHL | 60 | 5 | 5 | 10 | 216 | | | | | | | | | | | | | | | | | | |
| | **NHL Totals** | | **8** | **0** | **1** | **1** | **22** | **0** | **0** | **0** | **3** | **0.0** | | **0** | **0.0** | **4:51** | | | | | | | | | |

## LETOWSKI, Trevor

(leh-TOW-skee, TREH-vuhr)

Right wing. Shoots right. 5'10", 180 lbs. Born, Thunder Bay, Ont., April 5, 1977. Phoenix's 6th choice, 174th overall, in 1996 Entry Draft.

| Season | Club | League | Regular Season GP | G | A | Pts | PIM | PP | SH | GW | S | % | +/- | TF | F% | Min | Playoffs GP | G | A | Pts | PIM | PP | SH | GW | Min |
|---|---|---|---|---|---|---|---|---|---|---|---|---|---|---|---|---|---|---|---|---|---|---|---|---|---|
| 1993-94 | T. Bay Kings | TBMHL | 64 | 41 | 60 | 101 | 48 | | | | | | | | | | | | | | | | | | |
| 1994-95 | Sarnia Sting | OHL | 66 | 22 | 19 | 41 | 33 | | | | | | | | | | 4 | 0 | 1 | 1 | 9 | | | | |
| 1995-96 | Sarnia Sting | OHL | 66 | 36 | 63 | 99 | 66 | | | | | | | | | | 10 | 9 | 5 | 14 | 10 | | | | |
| 1996-97 | Sarnia Sting | OHL | 55 | 35 | 73 | 108 | 51 | | | | | | | | | | 12 | 9 | 12 | 21 | 20 | | | | |
| 1997-98 | Springfield | AHL | 75 | 11 | 20 | 31 | 26 | | | | | | | | | | 4 | 1 | 0 | 1 | 2 | | | | |
| **1998-99** | **Phoenix** | **NHL** | **14** | **2** | **2** | **4** | **2** | **0** | **0** | **0** | **8** | **25.0** | **1** | **49** | **55.1** | **6:01** | | | | | | | | | |
| | Springfield | AHL | 67 | 32 | 35 | 67 | 46 | | | | | | | | | | 3 | 1 | 0 | 1 | 2 | | | | |
| **99-2000** | **Phoenix** | **NHL** | **82** | **19** | **20** | **39** | **20** | **3** | **4** | **3** | **125** | **15.2** | **2** | **692** | **47.7** | **16:03** | **5** | **1** | **1** | **2** | **4** | **0** | **0** | **0** | **15:52** |
| **2000-01** | **Phoenix** | **NHL** | **77** | **7** | **15** | **22** | **32** | **0** | **1** | **3** | **110** | **6.4** | **−2** | **726** | **46.1** | **16:20** | | | | | | | | | |
| **2001-02** | **Phoenix** | **NHL** | **33** | **2** | **6** | **8** | **4** | **0** | **0** | **0** | **43** | **4.7** | **2** | **250** | **52.4** | **14:27** | | | | | | | | | |
| | **Vancouver** | **NHL** | **42** | **7** | **10** | **17** | **15** | **1** | **0** | **0** | **65** | **10.8** | **2** | **111** | **44.1** | **12:47** | **6** | **0** | **1** | **1** | **8** | **0** | **0** | **0** | **11:50** |
| **2002-03** | **Vancouver** | **NHL** | **78** | **11** | **14** | **25** | **36** | **1** | **1** | **2** | **136** | **8.1** | **8** | **70** | **41.4** | **12:26** | **6** | **0** | **1** | **1** | **0** | **0** | **0** | **0** | **9:40** |
| **2003-04** | **Columbus** | **NHL** | **73** | **15** | **17** | **32** | **16** | **4** | **0** | **1** | **126** | **11.9** | **−12** | **146** | **43.8** | **16:19** | | | | | | | | | |
| 2004-05 | Fribourg | Swiss | 9 | 4 | 5 | 9 | 6 | | | | | | | | | | 11 | 7 | 9 | 16 | 8 | | | | |
| **2005-06** | **Columbus** | **NHL** | **81** | **10** | **18** | **28** | **36** | **1** | **1** | **1** | **135** | **7.4** | **−2** | **284** | **45.8** | **16:32** | | | | | | | | | |
| **2006-07** | **Carolina** | **NHL** | **61** | **2** | **6** | **8** | **18** | **0** | **0** | **0** | **69** | **2.9** | **−8** | **208** | **48.6** | **9:41** | | | | | | | | | |
| **2007-08** | **Carolina** | **NHL** | **75** | **9** | **9** | **18** | **30** | **0** | **1** | **1** | **67** | **13.4** | **−10** | **602** | **44.7** | **10:16** | | | | | | | | | |
| 2008-09 | Barys Astana | Rus-KHL | 37 | 9 | 7 | 16 | 30 | | | | | | | | | | 3 | 1 | 0 | 1 | 2 | | | | |
| | **NHL Totals** | | **616** | **84** | **117** | **201** | **209** | **10** | **8** | **11** | **884** | **9.5** | | **3138** | **46.7** | **13:51** | **17** | **1** | **3** | **4** | **12** | **0** | **0** | **0** | **12:15** |

Traded to **Vancouver** by **Phoenix** with Todd Warriner, Tyler Bouck and Phoenix's 3rd round choice (later traded back to Phoenix – Phoenix selected Dimitri Pestunov) in 2003 Entry Draft for Drake Berehowsky and Denis Pederson, December 28, 2001. Signed as a free agent by **Columbus**, July 3, 2003. Signed as a free agent by **Fribourg** (Swiss), January 7, 2005. Signed as a free agent by **Carolina**, July 6, 2006.

## LEWIS, Grant

(LOO-ihs, GRANT) **ATL.**

Defense. Shoots right. 6'3", 205 lbs. Born, Pittsburgh, PA, January 20, 1985. Atlanta's 2nd choice, 40th overall, in 2004 Entry Draft.

| Season | Club | League | Regular Season GP | G | A | Pts | PIM | PP | SH | GW | S | % | +/- | TF | F% | Min | Playoffs GP | G | A | Pts | PIM | PP | SH | GW | Min |
|---|---|---|---|---|---|---|---|---|---|---|---|---|---|---|---|---|---|---|---|---|---|---|---|---|---|
| 2002-03 | Pittsburgh Forge | NAHL | 50 | 2 | 7 | 9 | 59 | | | | | | | | | | | | | | | | | | |
| 2003-04 | Dartmouth | ECAC | 34 | 3 | 22 | 25 | 57 | | | | | | | | | | | | | | | | | | |
| 2004-05 | Dartmouth | ECAC | 33 | 5 | 17 | 22 | 32 | | | | | | | | | | | | | | | | | | |
| 2005-06 | Dartmouth | ECAC | 29 | 4 | 11 | 15 | 53 | | | | | | | | | | | | | | | | | | |
| 2006-07 | Dartmouth | ECAC | 24 | 1 | 14 | 15 | 30 | | | | | | | | | | | | | | | | | | |
| 2007-08 | Chicago Wolves | AHL | 43 | 2 | 14 | 16 | 44 | | | | | | | | | | 2 | 0 | 0 | 0 | 2 | | | | |
| **2008-09** | **Atlanta** | **NHL** | **1** | **0** | **0** | **0** | **0** | **0** | **0** | **0** | **1** | **0.0** | **0** | **0** | **0.0** | **15:29** | | | | | | | | | |
| | Chicago Wolves | AHL | 54 | 0 | 22 | 22 | 72 | | | | | | | | | | | | | | | | | | |
| | **NHL Totals** | | **1** | **0** | **0** | **0** | **0** | **0** | **0** | **0** | **1** | **0.0** | | **0** | **0.0** | **15:29** | | | | | | | | | |

ECAC All-Rookie Team (2004) • ECAC First All-Star Team (2004) • ECAC Second All-Star Team (2006)

## LEWIS, Trevor

(LOO-ihs, TREH-vuhr) **L.A.**

Center. Shoots right. 6'1", 204 lbs. Born, Salt Lake City, UT, January 8, 1987. Los Angeles' 2nd choice, 17th overall, in 2006 Entry Draft.

| Season | Club | League | Regular Season GP | G | A | Pts | PIM | PP | SH | GW | S | % | +/- | TF | F% | Min | Playoffs GP | G | A | Pts | PIM | PP | SH | GW | Min |
|---|---|---|---|---|---|---|---|---|---|---|---|---|---|---|---|---|---|---|---|---|---|---|---|---|---|
| 2004-05 | Des Moines | USHL | 52 | 10 | 12 | 22 | 70 | | | | | | | | | | | | | | | | | | |
| 2005-06 | Des Moines | USHL | 56 | 35 | 40 | 75 | 69 | | | | | | | | | | 11 | 3 | *13 | *16 | 16 | | | | |
| 2006-07 | Owen Sound | OHL | 62 | 29 | 44 | 73 | 51 | | | | | | | | | | 4 | 1 | 2 | 3 | 0 | | | | |
| | Manchester | AHL | 8 | 4 | 2 | 6 | 2 | | | | | | | | | | 2 | 0 | 0 | 0 | 0 | | | | |
| 2007-08 | Manchester | AHL | 76 | 12 | 16 | 28 | 43 | | | | | | | | | | 4 | 0 | 0 | 0 | 2 | | | | |
| **2008-09** | **Los Angeles** | **NHL** | **6** | **1** | **2** | **3** | **0** | **0** | **0** | **0** | **10** | **10.0** | **0** | **4** | **25.0** | **11:36** | | | | | | | | | |
| | Manchester | AHL | 75 | 20 | 31 | 51 | 30 | | | | | | | | | | | | | | | | | | |
| | **NHL Totals** | | **6** | **1** | **2** | **3** | **0** | **0** | **0** | **0** | **10** | **10.0** | | **4** | **25.0** | **11:36** | | | | | | | | | |

USHL Player of the Year (2006)

## LIDSTROM, Nicklas

(LID-struhm, NIHK-luhs) **DET.**

Defense. Shoots left. 6'1", 189 lbs. Born, Vasteras, Sweden, April 28, 1970. Detroit's 3rd choice, 53rd overall, in 1989 Entry Draft.

| Season | Club | League | Regular Season GP | G | A | Pts | PIM | PP | SH | GW | S | % | +/- | TF | F% | Min | Playoffs GP | G | A | Pts | PIM | PP | SH | GW | Min |
|---|---|---|---|---|---|---|---|---|---|---|---|---|---|---|---|---|---|---|---|---|---|---|---|---|---|
| 1987-88 | Vasteras | Sweden-2 | 3 | 0 | 0 | 0 | 0 | | | | | | | | | | 5 | 0 | 0 | 0 | 6 | | | | |
| 1988-89 | Vasteras IK | Sweden | 34 | 1 | 6 | 7 | 4 | | | | | | | | | | 5 | 0 | 2 | 2 | 0 | | | | |
| 1989-90 | Vasteras IK | Sweden | 39 | 8 | 8 | 16 | 14 | | | | | | | | | | 2 | 0 | 1 | 1 | 2 | | | | |
| 1990-91 | Vasteras IK | Sweden | 38 | 4 | 19 | 23 | 2 | | | | | | | | | | 4 | 0 | 0 | 0 | 4 | | | | |
| **1991-92** | **Detroit** | **NHL** | **80** | **11** | **49** | **60** | **22** | **5** | **0** | **1** | **168** | **6.5** | **36** | | | | **11** | **1** | **2** | **3** | **0** | **1** | **0** | **0** | |
| **1992-93** | **Detroit** | **NHL** | **84** | **7** | **34** | **41** | **28** | **3** | **0** | **2** | **156** | **4.5** | **7** | | | | **7** | **1** | **0** | **1** | **0** | **1** | **0** | **0** | |
| **1993-94** | **Detroit** | **NHL** | **84** | **10** | **46** | **56** | **26** | **4** | **0** | **3** | **200** | **5.0** | **43** | | | | **7** | **3** | **2** | **5** | **0** | **1** | **1** | **0** | |
| 1994-95 | Vasteras IK | Sweden | 13 | 2 | 10 | 12 | 4 | | | | | | | | | | | | | | | | | | |
| | **Detroit** | **NHL** | **43** | **10** | **16** | **26** | **6** | **7** | **0** | **0** | **90** | **11.1** | **15** | | | | **18** | **4** | **12** | **16** | **8** | **3** | **0** | **2** | |
| **1995-96** | **Detroit** | **NHL** | **81** | **17** | **50** | **67** | **20** | **8** | **1** | **1** | **211** | **8.1** | **29** | | | | **19** | **5** | **9** | **14** | **10** | **1** | **0** | **0** | |
| **1996-97♦** | **Detroit** | **NHL** | **79** | **15** | **42** | **57** | **30** | **8** | **0** | **1** | **214** | **7.0** | **11** | | | | **20** | **2** | **6** | **8** | **2** | **0** | **0** | **0** | |
| **1997-98♦** | **Detroit** | **NHL** | **80** | **17** | **42** | **59** | **18** | **7** | **1** | **1** | **205** | **8.3** | **22** | | | | **22** | **6** | **13** | **19** | **8** | **2** | **0** | **2** | |
| | Sweden | Olympics | 4 | 1 | 1 | 2 | 2 | | | | | | | | | | | | | | | | | | |
| **1998-99** | **Detroit** | **NHL** | **81** | **14** | **43** | **57** | **14** | **6** | **2** | **3** | **205** | **6.8** | **14** | **0** | **0.0** | **26:31** | **10** | **2** | **9** | **11** | **4** | **2** | **0** | **0** | **30:21** |
| **99-2000** | **Detroit** | **NHL** | **81** | **20** | **53** | **73** | **18** | **9** | **4** | **3** | **218** | **9.2** | **19** | **0** | **0.0** | **28:45** | **9** | **2** | **4** | **6** | **4** | **1** | **0** | **0** | **30:28** |
| **2000-01** | **Detroit** | **NHL** | **82** | **15** | **56** | **71** | **18** | **8** | **0** | **0** | **272** | **5.5** | **9** | **0** | **0.0** | **28:27** | **6** | **1** | **7** | **8** | **0** | **0** | **0** | **0** | **29:17** |
| **2001-02♦** | **Detroit** | **NHL** | **78** | **9** | **50** | **59** | **20** | **6** | **0** | **0** | **215** | **4.2** | **13** | **0** | **0.0** | **28:49** | **23** | **5** | **11** | **16** | **2** | **2** | **1** | **2** | **31:10** |
| | Sweden | Olympics | 4 | 1 | 5 | 6 | 0 | | | | | | | | | | | | | | | | | | |
| **2002-03** | **Detroit** | **NHL** | **82** | **18** | **44** | **62** | **38** | **8** | **1** | **4** | **175** | **10.3** | **40** | **0** | **0.0** | **29:20** | **4** | **0** | **2** | **2** | **0** | **0** | **0** | **0** | **33:35** |
| **2003-04** | **Detroit** | **NHL** | **81** | **10** | **28** | **38** | **18** | **3** | **1** | **3** | **194** | **5.2** | **19** | **0** | **0.0** | **27:39** | **12** | **2** | **5** | **7** | **4** | **2** | **0** | **0** | **27:01** |
| 2004-05 | | | Did not play | | | | | | | | | | | | | | | | | | | | | | |
| **2005-06** | **Detroit** | **NHL** | **80** | **16** | **64** | **80** | **50** | **9** | **0** | **2** | **243** | **6.6** | **21** | **0** | **0.0** | **28:07** | **6** | **1** | **1** | **2** | **2** | **1** | **0** | **1** | **31:55** |
| | Sweden | Olympics | 8 | 2 | 4 | 6 | 2 | | | | | | | | | | | | | | | | | | |
| **2006-07** | **Detroit** | **NHL** | **80** | **13** | **49** | **62** | **46** | **10** | **0** | **1** | **224** | **5.8** | **40** | **0** | **0.0** | **27:29** | **18** | **4** | **14** | **18** | **6** | **4** | **0** | **2** | **30:37** |
| **2007-08♦** | **Detroit** | **NHL** | **76** | **10** | **60** | **70** | **40** | **5** | **0** | **4** | **188** | **5.3** | **40** | **0** | **0.0** | **26:43** | **22** | **3** | **10** | **13** | **14** | **1** | **1** | **1** | **26:49** |
| **2008-09** | **Detroit** | **NHL** | **78** | **16** | **43** | **59** | **30** | **10** | **0** | **4** | **180** | **8.9** | **31** | **0** | **0.0** | **24:49** | **21** | **4** | **12** | **16** | **6** | **3** | **0** | **1** | **25:39** |
| | **NHL Totals** | | **1330** | **228** | **769** | **997** | **442** | **116** | **10** | **33** | **3358** | **6.8** | | **0** | **0.0** | **27:41** | **235** | **46** | **119** | **165** | **70** | **25** | **3** | **11** | **29:01** |

NHL All-Rookie Team (1992) • NHL First All-Star Team (1998, 1999, 2000, 2001, 2002, 2003, 2006, 2007, 2008) • James Norris Memorial Trophy (2001, 2002, 2003, 2006, 2007, 2008) • Conn Smythe Trophy (2002) • Olympic Tournament All-Star Team (2006) • NHL Second All-Star Team (2009)

Played in NHL All-Star Game (1996, 1998, 1999, 2000, 2001, 2002, 2003, 2004, 2007, 2008)

## LILES, John-Michael

(LIGH-uhls, JAWN-MIGHK-uhl) **COL.**

Defense. Shoots left. 5'10", 185 lbs. Born, Indianapolis, IN, November 25, 1980. Colorado's 8th choice, 159th overall, in 2000 Entry Draft.

| | | | Regular Season | | | | | | | | | | | | | | Playoffs | | | | | | | | |
|---|---|---|---|---|---|---|---|---|---|---|---|---|---|---|---|---|---|---|---|---|---|---|---|---|---|
| Season | Club | League | GP | G | A | Pts | PIM | PP | SH | GW | S | % | +/- | TF | F% | Min | GP | G | A | Pts | PIM | PP | SH | GW | Min |
| 1997-98 | USNTDP | U-17 | 15 | 0 | 6 | 6 | 4 | .... | .... | .... | .... | .... | .... | .... | .... | .... | .... | .... | .... | .... | .... | .... | .... | .... | .... |
| | USNTDP | USHL | 5 | 0 | 1 | 1 | 0 | .... | .... | .... | .... | .... | .... | .... | .... | .... | .... | .... | .... | .... | .... | .... | .... | .... | .... |
| | USNTDP | NAHL | 42 | 4 | 7 | 11 | 40 | .... | .... | .... | .... | .... | .... | .... | .... | .... | 5 | 2 | 0 | 2 | 0 | .... | .... | .... | .... |
| 1998-99 | USNTDP | USHL | 46 | 4 | 14 | 18 | 47 | .... | .... | .... | .... | .... | .... | .... | .... | .... | .... | .... | .... | .... | .... | .... | .... | .... | .... |
| | USNTDP | NAHL | 13 | 2 | 5 | 7 | 6 | .... | .... | .... | .... | .... | .... | .... | .... | .... | .... | .... | .... | .... | .... | .... | .... | .... | .... |
| 99-2000 | Michigan State | CCHA | 40 | 8 | 20 | 28 | 26 | .... | .... | .... | .... | .... | .... | .... | .... | .... | .... | .... | .... | .... | .... | .... | .... | .... | .... |
| 2000-01 | Michigan State | CCHA | 42 | 7 | 18 | 25 | 28 | .... | .... | .... | .... | .... | .... | .... | .... | .... | .... | .... | .... | .... | .... | .... | .... | .... | .... |
| 2001-02 | Michigan State | CCHA | 41 | 13 | 22 | 35 | 18 | .... | .... | .... | .... | .... | .... | .... | .... | .... | .... | .... | .... | .... | .... | .... | .... | .... | .... |
| 2002-03 | Michigan State | CCHA | 39 | 16 | 34 | 50 | 46 | .... | .... | .... | .... | .... | .... | .... | .... | .... | .... | .... | .... | .... | .... | .... | .... | .... | .... |
| | Hershey Bears | AHL | 5 | 0 | 1 | 1 | 4 | .... | .... | .... | .... | .... | .... | .... | .... | .... | 5 | 0 | 0 | 0 | 2 | .... | .... | .... | .... |
| **2003-04** | **Colorado** | **NHL** | **79** | **10** | **24** | **34** | **28** | **2** | **0** | **1** | **115** | **8.7** | **7** | **0** | **0.0** | **16:14** | **11** | **0** | **1** | **1** | **4** | **0** | **0** | **0** | **16:41** |
| 2004-05 | Iserlohn Roosters | Germany | 17 | 5 | 6 | 11 | 24 | .... | .... | .... | .... | .... | .... | .... | .... | .... | .... | .... | .... | .... | .... | .... | .... | .... | .... |
| **2005-06** | **Colorado** | **NHL** | **82** | **14** | **35** | **49** | **44** | **6** | **0** | **1** | **154** | **9.1** | **5** | **1** | **100.0** | **18:31** | **9** | **1** | **2** | **3** | **6** | **1** | **0** | **0** | **17:35** |
| | United States | Olympics | 6 | 0 | 2 | 2 | 2 | .... | .... | .... | .... | .... | .... | .... | .... | .... | .... | .... | .... | .... | .... | .... | .... | .... | .... |
| **2006-07** | **Colorado** | **NHL** | **71** | **14** | **30** | **44** | **24** | **8** | **0** | **3** | **128** | **10.9** | **0** | **0** | **0.0** | **17:46** | .... | .... | .... | .... | .... | .... | .... | .... | .... |
| **2007-08** | **Colorado** | **NHL** | **81** | **6** | **26** | **32** | **26** | **5** | **0** | **1** | **163** | **3.7** | **2** | **0** | **0.0** | **19:40** | **10** | **2** | **3** | **5** | **2** | **1** | **0** | **0** | **19:08** |
| **2008-09** | **Colorado** | **NHL** | **75** | **12** | **27** | **39** | **31** | **6** | **0** | **1** | **146** | **8.2** | **–19** | **0** | **0.0** | **21:33** | .... | .... | .... | .... | .... | .... | .... | .... | .... |
| | **NHL Totals** | | **388** | **56** | **142** | **198** | **153** | **27** | **0** | **7** | **706** | **7.9** | | **1** | **100.0** | **18:44** | **30** | **3** | **6** | **9** | **12** | **2** | **0** | **0** | **17:46** |

CCHA Second All-Star Team (2001) • CCHA First All-Star Team (2002, 2003) • NCAA West Second All-American Team (2002) • NCAA West First All-American Team (2003) • NHL All-Rookie Team (2004)

Signed as a free agent by **Iserlohn** (Germany), December 29, 2004.

## LILJA, Andreas

(LIHL-yuh, awn-DRAY-uhs) **DET.**

Defense. Shoots left. 6'3", 220 lbs. Born, Helsingborg, Sweden, July 13, 1975. Los Angeles' 2nd choice, 54th overall, in 2000 Entry Draft.

| Season | Club | League | GP | G | A | Pts | PIM | PP | SH | GW | S | % | +/- | TF | F% | Min | GP | G | A | Pts | PIM | PP | SH | GW | Min |
|---|---|---|---|---|---|---|---|---|---|---|---|---|---|---|---|---|---|---|---|---|---|---|---|---|---|
| 1993-94 | Malmo IF Jr. | Swe-Jr. | 14 | 3 | 7 | 10 | 38 | .... | .... | .... | .... | .... | .... | .... | .... | .... | .... | .... | .... | .... | .... | .... | .... | .... | .... |
| 1994-95 | Malmo IF Jr. | Swe-Jr. | 30 | 7 | 13 | 20 | 82 | .... | .... | .... | .... | .... | .... | .... | .... | .... | .... | .... | .... | .... | .... | .... | .... | .... | .... |
| | Malmo IF | Sweden | 3 | 0 | 0 | 0 | 2 | .... | .... | .... | .... | .... | .... | .... | .... | .... | .... | .... | .... | .... | .... | .... | .... | .... | .... |
| 1995-96 | Malmo IF Jr. | Swe-Jr. | 3 | 0 | 1 | 1 | 6 | .... | .... | .... | .... | .... | .... | .... | .... | .... | .... | .... | .... | .... | .... | .... | .... | .... | .... |
| | Malmo IF | Sweden | 40 | 1 | 5 | 6 | 63 | .... | .... | .... | .... | .... | .... | .... | .... | .... | 5 | 0 | 1 | 1 | 2 | .... | .... | .... | .... |
| 1996-97 | Malmo | Sweden | 47 | 1 | 0 | 1 | 22 | .... | .... | .... | .... | .... | .... | .... | .... | .... | 4 | 0 | 0 | 0 | 10 | .... | .... | .... | .... |
| 1997-98 | Malmo | Sweden | 10 | 0 | 0 | 0 | 0 | .... | .... | .... | .... | .... | .... | .... | .... | .... | .... | .... | .... | .... | .... | .... | .... | .... | .... |
| | Mora IK | Sweden-2 | 13 | 1 | 4 | 5 | 30 | .... | .... | .... | .... | .... | .... | .... | .... | .... | 4 | 1 | 0 | 1 | 14 | .... | .... | .... | .... |
| 1998-99 | Malmo | Sweden | 41 | 0 | 3 | 3 | 44 | .... | .... | .... | .... | .... | .... | .... | .... | .... | 1 | 0 | 0 | 0 | 4 | .... | .... | .... | .... |
| 99-2000 | Malmo | Sweden | 49 | 8 | 11 | 19 | 88 | .... | .... | .... | .... | .... | .... | .... | .... | .... | 6 | 0 | 0 | 0 | 8 | .... | .... | .... | .... |
| **2000-01** | **Los Angeles** | **NHL** | **2** | **0** | **0** | **0** | **4** | **0** | **0** | **0** | **1** | **0.0** | **–2** | **0** | **0.0** | **12:22** | **1** | **0** | **0** | **0** | **0** | **0** | **0** | **0** | **6:56** |
| | Lowell | AHL | 61 | 7 | 29 | 36 | 149 | .... | .... | .... | .... | .... | .... | .... | .... | .... | 4 | 0 | 6 | 6 | 6 | .... | .... | .... | .... |
| **2001-02** | **Los Angeles** | **NHL** | **26** | **1** | **4** | **5** | **22** | **1** | **0** | **0** | **12** | **8.3** | **3** | **0** | **0.0** | **11:27** | **5** | **0** | **0** | **0** | **6** | **0** | **0** | **0** | **10:26** |
| | Manchester | AHL | 4 | 0 | 1 | 1 | 4 | .... | .... | .... | .... | .... | .... | .... | .... | .... | .... | .... | .... | .... | .... | .... | .... | .... | .... |
| **2002-03** | **Los Angeles** | **NHL** | **17** | **0** | **3** | **3** | **14** | **0** | **0** | **0** | **13** | **0.0** | **5** | **0** | **0.0** | **20:04** | .... | .... | .... | .... | .... | .... | .... | .... | .... |
| | **Florida** | **NHL** | **56** | **4** | **8** | **12** | **56** | **0** | **0** | **0** | **59** | **6.8** | **8** | **0** | **0.0** | **19:11** | .... | .... | .... | .... | .... | .... | .... | .... | .... |
| **2003-04** | **Florida** | **NHL** | **79** | **3** | **4** | **7** | **90** | **0** | **0** | **0** | **79** | **3.8** | **–8** | **1** | **0.0** | **19:34** | .... | .... | .... | .... | .... | .... | .... | .... | .... |
| 2004-05 | Mora IK | Sweden | 44 | 3 | 8 | 11 | 67 | .... | .... | .... | .... | .... | .... | .... | .... | .... | .... | .... | .... | .... | .... | .... | .... | .... | .... |
| | HC Ambri-Piotta | Swiss | .... | .... | .... | .... | .... | .... | .... | .... | .... | .... | .... | .... | .... | .... | 5 | 0 | 2 | 2 | 6 | .... | .... | .... | .... |
| **2005-06** | **Detroit** | **NHL** | **82** | **2** | **13** | **15** | **98** | **0** | **0** | **1** | **78** | **2.6** | **18** | **1** | **0.0** | **19:01** | **6** | **0** | **1** | **1** | **6** | **0** | **0** | **0** | **19:21** |
| **2006-07** | **Detroit** | **NHL** | **57** | **0** | **5** | **5** | **54** | **0** | **0** | **0** | **37** | **0.0** | **6** | **1** | **0.0** | **15:25** | **18** | **1** | **0** | **1** | **10** | **0** | **0** | **0** | **19:02** |
| **2007-08 ♦** | **Detroit** | **NHL** | **79** | **2** | **10** | **12** | **93** | **0** | **0** | **2** | **72** | **2.8** | **–2** | **1** | **0.0** | **18:14** | **12** | **0** | **1** | **1** | **16** | **0** | **0** | **0** | **14:05** |
| **2008-09** | **Detroit** | **NHL** | **60** | **2** | **11** | **13** | **66** | **0** | **0** | **0** | **60** | **3.3** | **13** | **1** | **0.0** | **17:00** | .... | .... | .... | .... | .... | .... | .... | .... | .... |
| | **NHL Totals** | | **458** | **14** | **58** | **72** | **497** | **1** | **0** | **3** | **411** | **3.4** | | **5** | **0.0** | **17:52** | **42** | **1** | **2** | **3** | **38** | **0** | **0** | **0** | **16:21** |

• Spent majority of 2001-02 season serving as a healthy reserve. Traded to **Florida** by **Los Angeles** with Jaroslav Bednar for Dmitry Yushkevich and Florida's 5th round choice (previously acquired, Los Angeles selected Brady Murray) in 2003 Entry Draft, November 26, 2002. Signed as a free agent by **Nashville**, July 26, 2004. Signed as a free agent by **Mora** (Sweden), September 15, 2004. Signed as a free agent by **Ambri-Piotta** (Swiss), February 25, 2005. Signed as a free agent by **Detroit**, August 24, 2005.

## LINDSTROM, Joakim

(LIHND-struhm, YOH-ah-kihm)

Center. Shoots left. 6', 187 lbs. Born, Skelleftea, Sweden, December 5, 1983. Columbus' 2nd choice, 41st overall, in 2002 Entry Draft.

| Season | Club | League | GP | G | A | Pts | PIM | PP | SH | GW | S | % | +/- | TF | F% | Min | GP | G | A | Pts | PIM | PP | SH | GW | Min |
|---|---|---|---|---|---|---|---|---|---|---|---|---|---|---|---|---|---|---|---|---|---|---|---|---|---|
| 99-2000 | MoDo U18 | Swe-U18 | 17 | 6 | *14 | 20 | 32 | .... | .... | .... | .... | .... | .... | .... | .... | .... | .... | .... | .... | .... | .... | .... | .... | .... | .... |
| | Malmo Jr. | Swe-Jr. | 10 | 4 | 4 | 8 | 2 | .... | .... | .... | .... | .... | .... | .... | .... | .... | 4 | 2 | 3 | 5 | 24 | .... | .... | .... | .... |
| 2000-01 | Malmo Jr. | Swe-Jr. | 12 | 7 | 14 | 21 | 46 | .... | .... | .... | .... | .... | .... | .... | .... | .... | 7 | 0 | 1 | 1 | 0 | .... | .... | .... | .... |
| | MoDo | Sweden | 10 | 2 | 3 | 5 | 2 | .... | .... | .... | .... | .... | .... | .... | .... | .... | .... | .... | .... | .... | .... | .... | .... | .... | .... |
| 2001-02 | Malmo Jr. | Swe-Jr. | 10 | 9 | 6 | 15 | 67 | .... | .... | .... | .... | .... | .... | .... | .... | .... | .... | .... | .... | .... | .... | .... | .... | .... | .... |
| | IF Troja-Ljungby | Sweden-2 | 3 | 0 | 0 | 0 | 12 | .... | .... | .... | .... | .... | .... | .... | .... | .... | .... | .... | .... | .... | .... | .... | .... | .... | .... |
| | MODO | Sweden | 42 | 4 | 3 | 7 | 20 | .... | .... | .... | .... | .... | .... | .... | .... | .... | 14 | 3 | 5 | 8 | 8 | .... | .... | .... | .... |
| 2002-03 | MODO | Sweden | 29 | 4 | 2 | 6 | 14 | .... | .... | .... | .... | .... | .... | .... | .... | .... | 6 | 1 | 1 | 2 | 2 | .... | .... | .... | .... |
| | Malmo Jr. | Swe-Jr. | 2 | 5 | 1 | 6 | 8 | .... | .... | .... | .... | .... | .... | .... | .... | .... | .... | .... | .... | .... | .... | .... | .... | .... | .... |
| | Ornskoldsviks SK | Sweden-2 | 2 | 1 | 1 | 2 | 4 | .... | .... | .... | .... | .... | .... | .... | .... | .... | .... | .... | .... | .... | .... | .... | .... | .... | .... |
| 2003-04 | MODO | Sweden | 15 | 0 | 2 | 2 | 0 | .... | .... | .... | .... | .... | .... | .... | .... | .... | .... | .... | .... | .... | .... | .... | .... | .... | .... |
| | Sundsvall | Sweden-2 | 2 | 0 | 5 | 5 | 0 | .... | .... | .... | .... | .... | .... | .... | .... | .... | .... | .... | .... | .... | .... | .... | .... | .... | .... |
| 2004-05 | MODO Jr. | Swe-Jr. | 2 | 4 | 1 | 5 | 0 | .... | .... | .... | .... | .... | .... | .... | .... | .... | .... | .... | .... | .... | .... | .... | .... | .... | .... |
| | MODO | Sweden | 37 | 2 | 3 | 5 | 24 | .... | .... | .... | .... | .... | .... | .... | .... | .... | .... | .... | .... | .... | .... | .... | .... | .... | .... |
| | Syracuse Crunch | AHL | 13 | 4 | 4 | 8 | 0 | .... | .... | .... | .... | .... | .... | .... | .... | .... | .... | .... | .... | .... | .... | .... | .... | .... | .... |
| **2005-06** | **Columbus** | **NHL** | **3** | **0** | **0** | **0** | **0** | **0** | **0** | **0** | **4** | **0.0** | **0** | **0** | **0.0** | **5:11** | .... | .... | .... | .... | .... | .... | .... | .... | .... |
| | Syracuse Crunch | AHL | 64 | 14 | 29 | 43 | 52 | .... | .... | .... | .... | .... | .... | .... | .... | .... | 6 | 1 | 1 | 2 | 0 | .... | .... | .... | .... |
| **2006-07** | **Columbus** | **NHL** | **9** | **1** | **0** | **1** | **4** | **0** | **0** | **0** | **9** | **11.1** | **–3** | **0** | **0.0** | **8:28** | .... | .... | .... | .... | .... | .... | .... | .... | .... |
| | Syracuse Crunch | AHL | 50 | 22 | 26 | 48 | 34 | .... | .... | .... | .... | .... | .... | .... | .... | .... | .... | .... | .... | .... | .... | .... | .... | .... | .... |
| **2007-08** | **Columbus** | **NHL** | **25** | **3** | **4** | **7** | **14** | **2** | **0** | **1** | **25** | **12.0** | **0** | **7** | **28.6** | **9:26** | .... | .... | .... | .... | .... | .... | .... | .... | .... |
| | Syracuse Crunch | AHL | 49 | 25 | 35 | 60 | 68 | .... | .... | .... | .... | .... | .... | .... | .... | .... | 13 | 4 | 3 | 7 | 6 | .... | .... | .... | .... |
| 2008-09 | Iowa Chops | AHL | 21 | 7 | 14 | 21 | 33 | .... | .... | .... | .... | .... | .... | .... | .... | .... | .... | .... | .... | .... | .... | .... | .... | .... | .... |
| | **Phoenix** | **NHL** | **44** | **9** | **11** | **20** | **28** | **3** | **0** | **2** | **77** | **11.7** | **–6** | **14** | **35.7** | **14:52** | .... | .... | .... | .... | .... | .... | .... | .... | .... |
| | San Antonio | AHL | 3 | 1 | 1 | 2 | 2 | .... | .... | .... | .... | .... | .... | .... | .... | .... | .... | .... | .... | .... | .... | .... | .... | .... | .... |
| | **NHL Totals** | | **81** | **13** | **15** | **28** | **46** | **5** | **0** | **3** | **115** | **11.3** | | **21** | **33.3** | **12:07** | .... | .... | .... | .... | .... | .... | .... | .... | .... |

Traded to **Anaheim** by **Columbus** for future considerations, July 15, 2008. Claimed on waivers by **Chicago** from **Anaheim**, October 3, 2008. Claimed on waivers by **Anaheim** from **Chicago**, October 7, 2008. Traded to **Phoenix** by **Anaheim** for Logan Stephenson, December 3, 2008.

## LISIN, Enver

(LEE-sihn, EHN-vuhr) **NYR**

Right wing. Shoots left. 6'1", 190 lbs. Born, Moscow, USSR, April 22, 1986. Phoenix's 3rd choice, 50th overall, in 2004 Entry Draft.

| Season | Club | League | GP | G | A | Pts | PIM | PP | SH | GW | S | % | +/- | TF | F% | Min | GP | G | A | Pts | PIM | PP | SH | GW | Min |
|---|---|---|---|---|---|---|---|---|---|---|---|---|---|---|---|---|---|---|---|---|---|---|---|---|---|
| 2001-02 | Dyn'o Moscow 2 | Russia-3 | 6 | 3 | 0 | 3 | 14 | .... | .... | .... | .... | .... | .... | .... | .... | .... | .... | .... | .... | .... | .... | .... | .... | .... | .... |
| 2002-03 | Dyn'o Moscow 2 | Russia-3 | STATISTICS NOT AVAILABLE | | | | | | | | | | | | | | | | | | | | | | |
| 2003-04 | Dyn'o Moscow 2 | Russia-3 | STATISTICS NOT AVAILABLE | | | | | | | | | | | | | | | | | | | | | | |
| | Kristall Saratov | Russia-2 | 35 | 10 | 6 | 16 | 30 | .... | .... | .... | .... | .... | .... | .... | .... | .... | 4 | 1 | 0 | 1 | 0 | .... | .... | .... | .... |
| 2004-05 | Ak Bars Kazan 2 | Russia-3 | .... | 4 | 3 | 7 | .... | .... | .... | .... | .... | .... | .... | .... | .... | .... | .... | .... | .... | .... | .... | .... | .... | .... | .... |
| | Ak Bars Kazan | Russia | 53 | 8 | 4 | 12 | 4 | .... | .... | .... | .... | .... | .... | .... | .... | .... | 3 | 0 | 0 | 0 | 0 | .... | .... | .... | .... |
| 2005-06 | Ak Bars Kazan | Russia | 43 | 7 | 5 | 12 | 26 | .... | .... | .... | .... | .... | .... | .... | .... | .... | 13 | 3 | 1 | 4 | 6 | .... | .... | .... | .... |
| **2006-07** | **Phoenix** | **NHL** | **17** | **1** | **1** | **2** | **16** | **1** | **0** | **0** | **35** | **2.9** | **–18** | **7** | **28.6** | **15:02** | .... | .... | .... | .... | .... | .... | .... | .... | .... |
| | San Antonio | AHL | 2 | 2 | 0 | 2 | 4 | .... | .... | .... | .... | .... | .... | .... | .... | .... | .... | .... | .... | .... | .... | .... | .... | .... | .... |
| | Ak Bars Kazan | Russia | 20 | 6 | 2 | 8 | 18 | .... | .... | .... | .... | .... | .... | .... | .... | .... | 1 | 0 | 0 | 0 | 0 | .... | .... | .... | .... |
| **2007-08** | **Phoenix** | **NHL** | **13** | **4** | **1** | **5** | **6** | **1** | **0** | **0** | **27** | **14.8** | **–5** | **2** | **50.0** | **14:27** | .... | .... | .... | .... | .... | .... | .... | .... | .... |
| | San Antonio | AHL | 58 | 16 | 19 | 35 | 26 | .... | .... | .... | .... | .... | .... | .... | .... | .... | 6 | 1 | 2 | 3 | 0 | .... | .... | .... | .... |
| **2008-09** | **Phoenix** | **NHL** | **48** | **13** | **8** | **21** | **24** | **1** | **0** | **2** | **105** | **12.4** | **–13** | **6** | **33.3** | **14:50** | .... | .... | .... | .... | .... | .... | .... | .... | .... |
| | San Antonio | AHL | 10 | 2 | 4 | 6 | 6 | .... | .... | .... | .... | .... | .... | .... | .... | .... | .... | .... | .... | .... | .... | .... | .... | .... | .... |
| | **NHL Totals** | | **78** | **18** | **10** | **28** | **46** | **3** | **0** | **2** | **167** | **10.8** | | **15** | **33.3** | **14:49** | .... | .... | .... | .... | .... | .... | .... | .... | .... |

Traded to **NY Rangers** by **Phoenix** for Lauri Korpikoski, July 13, 2009.

## LITTLE, Bryan

(LIH-tuhl, BRIGH-uhn) **ATL.**

Center. Shoots right. 5'11", 185 lbs. Born, Edmonton, Alta., November 12, 1987. Atlanta's 1st choice, 12th overall, in 2006 Entry Draft.

| | | | Regular Season | | | | | | | | | | | | | | Playoffs | | | | | | | | |
|---|---|---|---|---|---|---|---|---|---|---|---|---|---|---|---|---|---|---|---|---|---|---|---|---|---|
| Season | Club | League | GP | G | A | Pts | PIM | PP | SH | GW | S | % | +/- | TF | F% | Min | GP | G | A | Pts | PIM | PP | SH | GW | Min |
| 2003-04 | Barrie Colts | OHL | 64 | 34 | 24 | 58 | 18 | .... | .... | .... | .... | .... | .... | .... | .... | .... | 12 | 5 | 5 | 10 | 7 | .... | .... | .... | .... |
| 2004-05 | Barrie Colts | OHL | 62 | 36 | 32 | 68 | 34 | .... | .... | .... | .... | .... | .... | .... | .... | .... | 4 | 5 | 1 | 6 | 2 | .... | .... | .... | .... |
| 2005-06 | Barrie Colts | OHL | 64 | 42 | 67 | 109 | 99 | .... | .... | .... | .... | .... | .... | .... | .... | .... | 14 | 8 | 15 | 23 | 19 | .... | .... | .... | .... |
| 2006-07 | Barrie Colts | OHL | 57 | 41 | 66 | 107 | 77 | .... | .... | .... | .... | .... | .... | .... | .... | .... | 8 | 4 | 5 | 9 | 8 | .... | .... | .... | .... |
| | Chicago Wolves | AHL | .... | .... | .... | .... | .... | .... | .... | .... | .... | .... | .... | .... | .... | .... | 2 | 0 | 0 | 0 | 0 | .... | .... | .... | .... |
| **2007-08** | **Atlanta** | **NHL** | **48** | **6** | **10** | **16** | **18** | **2** | **0** | **1** | **76** | **7.9** | **–2** | **505** | **45.2** | **15:37** | .... | .... | .... | .... | .... | .... | .... | .... | .... |
| | Chicago Wolves | AHL | 34 | 9 | 16 | 25 | 10 | .... | .... | .... | .... | .... | .... | .... | .... | .... | 24 | 8 | 5 | 13 | 10 | .... | .... | .... | .... |
| **2008-09** | **Atlanta** | **NHL** | **79** | **31** | **20** | **51** | **24** | **12** | **0** | **4** | **172** | **18.0** | **–5** | **214** | **43.5** | **16:55** | .... | .... | .... | .... | .... | .... | .... | .... | .... |
| | **NHL Totals** | | **127** | **37** | **30** | **67** | **42** | **14** | **0** | **5** | **248** | **14.9** | | **719** | **44.6** | **16:26** | .... | .... | .... | .... | .... | .... | .... | .... | .... |

OHL Second All-Star Team (2007)

## LOCKE, Corey

(LAWK, KOH-ree) **NYR**

Center. Shoots left. 5'9", 168 lbs. Born, Toronto, Ont., May 8, 1984. Montreal's 5th choice, 113th overall, in 2003 Entry Draft.

| Season | Club | League | GP | G | A | Pts | PIM | PP | SH | GW | S | % | +/- | TF | F% | Min | GP | G | A | Pts | PIM | PP | SH | GW | Min |
|---|---|---|---|---|---|---|---|---|---|---|---|---|---|---|---|---|---|---|---|---|---|---|---|---|---|
| 2000-01 | Newmarket | OPJHL | 49 | 34 | 51 | 85 | 16 | .... | .... | .... | .... | .... | .... | .... | .... | .... | 16 | 10 | 12 | 22 | 14 | .... | .... | .... | .... |
| 2001-02 | Ottawa 67's | OHL | 55 | 18 | 25 | 43 | 18 | .... | .... | .... | .... | .... | .... | .... | .... | .... | 13 | 6 | 7 | 13 | 10 | .... | .... | .... | .... |
| 2002-03 | Ottawa 67's | OHL | 66 | *63 | *88 | *151 | 83 | .... | .... | .... | .... | .... | .... | .... | .... | .... | 23 | *19 | 19 | *38 | 30 | .... | .... | .... | .... |
| 2003-04 | Ottawa 67's | OHL | 65 | *51 | 67 | *118 | 82 | .... | .... | .... | .... | .... | .... | .... | .... | .... | 7 | 7 | 3 | 10 | 10 | .... | .... | .... | .... |
| 2004-05 | Hamilton | AHL | 78 | 16 | 27 | 43 | 20 | .... | .... | .... | .... | .... | .... | .... | .... | .... | 4 | 0 | 0 | 0 | 2 | .... | .... | .... | .... |
| 2005-06 | Hamilton | AHL | 77 | 19 | 40 | 59 | 67 | .... | .... | .... | .... | .... | .... | .... | .... | .... | .... | .... | .... | .... | .... | .... | .... | .... | .... |
| 2006-07 | Hamilton | AHL | 80 | 20 | 35 | 55 | 54 | .... | .... | .... | .... | .... | .... | .... | .... | .... | 22 | *10 | 12 | 22 | 10 | .... | .... | .... | .... |
| **2007-08** | **Montreal** | **NHL** | **1** | **0** | **0** | **0** | **0** | **0** | **0** | **0** | **1** | **0.0** | **–1** | **5** | **40.0** | **5:59** | .... | .... | .... | .... | .... | .... | .... | .... | .... |
| | Hamilton | AHL | 78 | 30 | 42 | 72 | 50 | .... | .... | .... | .... | .... | .... | .... | .... | .... | .... | .... | .... | .... | .... | .... | .... | .... | .... |
| 2008-09 | Houston Aeros | AHL | 77 | 25 | 54 | 79 | 60 | .... | .... | .... | .... | .... | .... | .... | .... | .... | 20 | 12 | 11 | 23 | 32 | .... | .... | .... | .... |
| | **NHL Totals** | | **1** | **0** | **0** | **0** | **0** | **0** | **0** | **0** | **1** | **0.0** | | **5** | **40.0** | **5:59** | .... | .... | .... | .... | .... | .... | .... | .... | .... |

OHL First All-Star Team (2003, 2004) • OHL Player of the Year (2003, 2004) • Canadian Major Junior First All-Star Team (2003, 2004) • Canadian Major Junior Player of the Year (2003)

Traded to **Minnesota** by **Montreal** for Shawn Belle, July 11, 2008. Signed as a free agent by **NY Rangers**, July 3, 2009.

## LOJEK, Martin

(LOI-yehk, MAHR-tihn) **FLA.**

Defense. Shoots right. 6'4", 220 lbs. Born, Brno, Czech., August 19, 1985. Florida's 5th choice, 105th overall, in 2003 Entry Draft.

| Season | Club | League | GP | G | A | Pts | PIM | PP | SH | GW | S | % | +/- | TF | F% | Min | GP | G | A | Pts | PIM | PP | SH | GW | Min |
|---|---|---|---|---|---|---|---|---|---|---|---|---|---|---|---|---|---|---|---|---|---|---|---|---|---|
| 2000-01 | HC Pardubice Jr. | CzRep-Jr. | 48 | 2 | 2 | 4 | 42 | .... | .... | .... | .... | .... | .... | .... | .... | .... | 7 | 0 | 0 | 0 | 6 | .... | .... | .... | .... |
| 2001-02 | HC Pardubice Jr. | CzRep-Jr. | 40 | 2 | 4 | 6 | 24 | .... | .... | .... | .... | .... | .... | .... | .... | .... | 7 | 1 | 0 | 1 | 2 | .... | .... | .... | .... |
| 2002-03 | Brampton | OHL | 65 | 1 | 13 | 14 | 47 | .... | .... | .... | .... | .... | .... | .... | .... | .... | 11 | 0 | 1 | 1 | 6 | .... | .... | .... | .... |
| 2003-04 | Brampton | OHL | 68 | 3 | 17 | 20 | 37 | .... | .... | .... | .... | .... | .... | .... | .... | .... | 12 | 0 | 4 | 4 | 2 | .... | .... | .... | .... |
| 2004-05 | Brampton | OHL | 58 | 1 | 12 | 13 | 58 | .... | .... | .... | .... | .... | .... | .... | .... | .... | 6 | 0 | 0 | 0 | 6 | .... | .... | .... | .... |
| 2005-06 | Rochester | AHL | 15 | 1 | 1 | 2 | 16 | .... | .... | .... | .... | .... | .... | .... | .... | .... | .... | .... | .... | .... | .... | .... | .... | .... | .... |
| | Florida Everblades | ECHL | 45 | 3 | 11 | 14 | 40 | .... | .... | .... | .... | .... | .... | .... | .... | .... | 2 | 0 | 0 | 0 | 0 | .... | .... | .... | .... |
| **2006-07** | **Florida** | **NHL** | **3** | **0** | **1** | **1** | **0** | **0** | **0** | **0** | **0** | **0.0** | **2** | **0** | **0.0** | **8:23** | .... | .... | .... | .... | .... | .... | .... | .... | .... |
| | Rochester | AHL | 69 | 6 | 13 | 19 | 87 | .... | .... | .... | .... | .... | .... | .... | .... | .... | .... | .... | .... | .... | .... | .... | .... | .... | .... |
| **2007-08** | **Florida** | **NHL** | **2** | **0** | **0** | **0** | **0** | **0** | **0** | **0** | **2** | **0.0** | **–1** | **0** | **0.0** | **6:08** | .... | .... | .... | .... | .... | .... | .... | .... | .... |
| | Rochester | AHL | 72 | 6 | 5 | 11 | 97 | .... | .... | .... | .... | .... | .... | .... | .... | .... | .... | .... | .... | .... | .... | .... | .... | .... | .... |
| 2008-09 | HC Ocelari Trinec | CzRep | 9 | 0 | 1 | 1 | 6 | .... | .... | .... | .... | .... | .... | .... | .... | .... | .... | .... | .... | .... | .... | .... | .... | .... | .... |
| | Pardubice | CzRep | 12 | 0 | 0 | 0 | 0 | .... | .... | .... | .... | .... | .... | .... | .... | .... | 7 | 2 | 1 | 3 | 4 | .... | .... | .... | .... |
| | **NHL Totals** | | **5** | **0** | **1** | **1** | **0** | **0** | **0** | **0** | **2** | **0.0** | | **0** | **0.0** | **7:29** | .... | .... | .... | .... | .... | .... | .... | .... | .... |

## LOMBARDI, Matthew

(lawm-BAHR-dee, MA-thew) **PHX.**

Center. Shoots left. 6', 198 lbs. Born, Montreal, Que., March 18, 1982. Calgary's 3rd choice, 90th overall, in 2002 Entry Draft.

| Season | Club | League | GP | G | A | Pts | PIM | PP | SH | GW | S | % | +/- | TF | F% | Min | GP | G | A | Pts | PIM | PP | SH | GW | Min |
|---|---|---|---|---|---|---|---|---|---|---|---|---|---|---|---|---|---|---|---|---|---|---|---|---|---|
| 1997-98 | Gatineau | QAAA | 42 | 10 | 13 | 23 | .... | .... | .... | .... | .... | .... | .... | .... | .... | .... | 13 | 4 | 7 | 11 | .... | .... | .... | .... | .... |
| 1998-99 | Victoriaville Tigres | QMJHL | 47 | 6 | 10 | 16 | 8 | .... | .... | .... | .... | .... | .... | .... | .... | .... | 5 | 0 | 0 | 0 | 0 | .... | .... | .... | .... |
| 99-2000 | Victoriaville Tigres | QMJHL | 65 | 18 | 26 | 44 | 28 | .... | .... | .... | .... | .... | .... | .... | .... | .... | 6 | 0 | 0 | 0 | 6 | .... | .... | .... | .... |
| 2000-01 | Victoriaville Tigres | QMJHL | 72 | 28 | 39 | 67 | 66 | .... | .... | .... | .... | .... | .... | .... | .... | .... | 13 | 12 | 6 | 18 | 10 | .... | .... | .... | .... |
| 2001-02 | Victoriaville Tigres | QMJHL | 66 | 57 | 73 | 130 | 70 | .... | .... | .... | .... | .... | .... | .... | .... | .... | 22 | *17 | 18 | 35 | 18 | .... | .... | .... | .... |
| 2002-03 | Saint John Flames | AHL | 76 | 25 | 21 | 46 | 41 | .... | .... | .... | .... | .... | .... | .... | .... | .... | .... | .... | .... | .... | .... | .... | .... | .... | .... |
| **2003-04** | **Calgary** | **NHL** | **79** | **16** | **13** | **29** | **32** | **3** | **2** | **4** | **130** | **12.3** | **4** | **992** | **47.9** | **14:26** | **13** | **1** | **5** | **6** | **4** | **0** | **0** | **1** | **14:46** |
| 2004-05 | Lowell | AHL | 9 | 3 | 1 | 4 | 9 | .... | .... | .... | .... | .... | .... | .... | .... | .... | 11 | 0 | 3 | 3 | 16 | .... | .... | .... | .... |
| **2005-06** | **Calgary** | **NHL** | **55** | **6** | **20** | **26** | **48** | **1** | **2** | **2** | **72** | **8.3** | **–1** | **499** | **52.9** | **14:09** | **7** | **0** | **2** | **2** | **2** | **0** | **0** | **0** | **15:51** |
| | Omaha | AHL | 1 | 1 | 1 | 2 | 0 | .... | .... | .... | .... | .... | .... | .... | .... | .... | .... | .... | .... | .... | .... | .... | .... | .... | .... |
| **2006-07** | **Calgary** | **NHL** | **81** | **20** | **26** | **46** | **48** | **5** | **4** | **5** | **176** | **11.4** | **10** | **965** | **49.1** | **16:22** | **6** | **1** | **1** | **2** | **0** | **1** | **0** | **0** | **15:19** |
| **2007-08** | **Calgary** | **NHL** | **82** | **14** | **22** | **36** | **67** | **2** | **2** | **4** | **181** | **7.7** | **–6** | **955** | **47.6** | **17:19** | **7** | **0** | **0** | **0** | **4** | **0** | **0** | **0** | **17:14** |
| **2008-09** | **Calgary** | **NHL** | **50** | **9** | **21** | **30** | **30** | **0** | **1** | **2** | **119** | **7.6** | **11** | **459** | **53.4** | **16:27** | .... | .... | .... | .... | .... | .... | .... | .... | .... |
| | **Phoenix** | **NHL** | **19** | **5** | **11** | **16** | **14** | **1** | **0** | **0** | **58** | **8.6** | **2** | **384** | **50.3** | **20:54** | .... | .... | .... | .... | .... | .... | .... | .... | .... |
| | **NHL Totals** | | **366** | **70** | **113** | **183** | **239** | **12** | **11** | **17** | **736** | **9.5** | | **4254** | **49.5** | **16:05** | **33** | **2** | **8** | **10** | **10** | **1** | **0** | **1** | **15:37** |

• Re-entered NHL Entry Draft. Originally Edmonton's 7th choice, 215th overall, in 2000 Entry Draft.

Memorial Cup Tournament All-Star Team (2002) • Ed Chynoweth Trophy (Memorial Cup Tournament - Leading Scorer) (2002)

Traded to **Phoenix** by **Calgary** with Brandon Prust and Calgary's 1st round choice in 2010 Entry Draft for Olli Jokinen and Phoenix's 3rd round choice (later traded to Florida – Florida selected Josh Birkholz) in 2009 Entry Draft, March 4, 2009.

## LOVEJOY, Ben

(LUHV-joi, BEHN) **PIT.**

Defense. Shoots right. 6'2", 215 lbs. Born, Concord, NH, February 20, 1984.

| Season | Club | League | GP | G | A | Pts | PIM | PP | SH | GW | S | % | +/- | TF | F% | Min | GP | G | A | Pts | PIM | PP | SH | GW | Min |
|---|---|---|---|---|---|---|---|---|---|---|---|---|---|---|---|---|---|---|---|---|---|---|---|---|---|
| 2002-03 | Boston College | H-East | 22 | 0 | 6 | 6 | 6 | .... | .... | .... | .... | .... | .... | .... | .... | .... | .... | .... | .... | .... | .... | .... | .... | .... | .... |
| 2003-04 | Dartmouth | ECAC | DID NOT PLAY – TRANSFERRED COLLEGES | | | | | | | | | | | | | | | | | | | | | | |
| 2004-05 | Dartmouth | ECAC | 32 | 2 | 11 | 13 | 28 | .... | .... | .... | .... | .... | .... | .... | .... | .... | .... | .... | .... | .... | .... | .... | .... | .... | .... |
| 2005-06 | Dartmouth | ECAC | 32 | 2 | 16 | 18 | 24 | .... | .... | .... | .... | .... | .... | .... | .... | .... | .... | .... | .... | .... | .... | .... | .... | .... | .... |
| 2006-07 | Dartmouth | ECAC | 32 | 7 | 16 | 23 | 28 | .... | .... | .... | .... | .... | .... | .... | .... | .... | .... | .... | .... | .... | .... | .... | .... | .... | .... |
| | Norfolk Admirals | AHL | 5 | 0 | 0 | 0 | 6 | .... | .... | .... | .... | .... | .... | .... | .... | .... | .... | .... | .... | .... | .... | .... | .... | .... | .... |
| 2007-08 | Wilkes-Barre | AHL | 72 | 2 | 18 | 20 | 63 | .... | .... | .... | .... | .... | .... | .... | .... | .... | 23 | 2 | 8 | 10 | 18 | .... | .... | .... | .... |
| **2008-09** | **Pittsburgh** | **NHL** | **2** | **0** | **0** | **0** | **0** | **0** | **0** | **0** | **1** | **0.0** | **0** | **0** | **0.0** | **11:53** | .... | .... | .... | .... | .... | .... | .... | .... | .... |
| | Wilkes-Barre | AHL | 76 | 7 | 24 | 31 | 84 | .... | .... | .... | .... | .... | .... | .... | .... | .... | 12 | 1 | 1 | 2 | 14 | .... | .... | .... | .... |
| | **NHL Totals** | | **2** | **0** | **0** | **0** | **0** | **0** | **0** | **0** | **1** | **0.0** | | **0** | **0.0** | **11:53** | .... | .... | .... | .... | .... | .... | .... | .... | .... |

AHL Second All-Star Team (2009)

Signed as a free agent by **Wilkes-Barre** (AHL), June 14, 2007. Signed as a free agent by **Pittsburgh**, July 7, 2008.

## LUCIC, Milan

(LOO-cheech, MEE-lahn) **BOS.**

Left wing. Shoots left. 6'3", 228 lbs. Born, Vancouver, B.C., June 7, 1988. Boston's 3rd choice, 50th overall, in 2006 Entry Draft.

| Season | Club | League | GP | G | A | Pts | PIM | PP | SH | GW | S | % | +/- | TF | F% | Min | GP | G | A | Pts | PIM | PP | SH | GW | Min |
|---|---|---|---|---|---|---|---|---|---|---|---|---|---|---|---|---|---|---|---|---|---|---|---|---|---|
| 2004-05 | Coquitlam | BCHL | 50 | 9 | 14 | 23 | 100 | .... | .... | .... | .... | .... | .... | .... | .... | .... | .... | .... | .... | .... | .... | .... | .... | .... | .... |
| | Vancouver Giants | WHL | 1 | 0 | 0 | 0 | 2 | .... | .... | .... | .... | .... | .... | .... | .... | .... | 2 | 0 | 0 | 0 | 0 | .... | .... | .... | .... |
| 2005-06 | Vancouver Giants | WHL | 62 | 9 | 10 | 19 | 149 | .... | .... | .... | .... | .... | .... | .... | .... | .... | 18 | 3 | 4 | 7 | 23 | .... | .... | .... | .... |
| 2006-07 | Vancouver Giants | WHL | 70 | 30 | 38 | 68 | 147 | .... | .... | .... | .... | .... | .... | .... | .... | .... | 22 | 7 | 12 | 19 | 26 | .... | .... | .... | .... |
| **2007-08** | **Boston** | **NHL** | **77** | **8** | **19** | **27** | **89** | **1** | **0** | **4** | **88** | **9.1** | **–2** | **8** | **50.0** | **12:07** | **7** | **2** | **0** | **2** | **4** | **0** | **0** | **0** | **16:24** |
| **2008-09** | **Boston** | **NHL** | **72** | **17** | **25** | **42** | **136** | **2** | **0** | **3** | **97** | **17.5** | **17** | **10** | **60.0** | **14:57** | **10** | **3** | **6** | **9** | **43** | **0** | **0** | **0** | **15:14** |
| | **NHL Totals** | | **149** | **25** | **44** | **69** | **225** | **3** | **0** | **7** | **185** | **13.5** | | **18** | **55.6** | **13:29** | **17** | **5** | **6** | **11** | **47** | **0** | **0** | **0** | **15:43** |

Memorial Cup Tournament All-Star Team (2007) • Stafford Smythe Memorial Trophy (Memorial Cup Tournament - MVP) (2007)

## LUKOWICH, Brad

(loo-KUH-which, BRAD) **S.J.**

Defense. Shoots left. 6'1", 200 lbs. Born, Cranbrook, B.C., August 12, 1976. NY Islanders' 4th choice, 90th overall, in 1994 Entry Draft.

| | | | Regular Season | | | | | | | | | | | | | | Playoffs | | | | | | | | |
|---|---|---|---|---|---|---|---|---|---|---|---|---|---|---|---|---|---|---|---|---|---|---|---|---|---|
| Season | Club | League | GP | G | A | Pts | PIM | PP | SH | GW | S | % | +/- | TF | F% | Min | GP | G | A | Pts | PIM | PP | SH | GW | Min |
| 1992-93 | Cranbrook Colts | RMJHL | 54 | 21 | 41 | 62 | 162 | | | | | | | | | | | | | | | | | | |
| | Kamloops Blazers | WHL | 1 | 0 | 0 | 0 | 0 | | | | | | | | | | | | | | | | | | |
| 1993-94 | Kamloops Blazers | WHL | 42 | 5 | 11 | 16 | 166 | | | | | | | | | | 16 | 0 | 1 | 1 | 35 | | | | |
| 1994-95 | Kamloops Blazers | WHL | 63 | 10 | 35 | 45 | 125 | | | | | | | | | | 18 | 0 | 7 | 7 | 21 | | | | |
| 1995-96 | Kamloops Blazers | WHL | 65 | 14 | 55 | 69 | 114 | | | | | | | | | | 13 | 2 | 10 | 12 | 29 | | | | |
| 1996-97 | Michigan | IHL | 69 | 2 | 6 | 8 | 77 | | | | | | | | | | 4 | 0 | 1 | 1 | 2 | | | | |
| **1997-98** | **Dallas** | **NHL** | **4** | **0** | **1** | **1** | **2** | **0** | **0** | **0** | **2** | **0.0** | **–2** | | | | | | | | | | | | |
| | Michigan | IHL | 60 | 6 | 27 | 33 | 104 | | | | | | | | | | 4 | 0 | 4 | 4 | 14 | | | | |
| **1998-99** | **Dallas** | **NHL** | **14** | **1** | **2** | **3** | **19** | **0** | **0** | **0** | **8** | **12.5** | **3** | **0** | **0.0** | **16:18** | **8** | **0** | **1** | **1** | **4** | **0** | **0** | **0** | **10:00** |
| | Michigan | IHL | 67 | 8 | 21 | 29 | 95 | | | | | | | | | | | | | | | | | | |
| **99-2000** | **Dallas** | **NHL** | **60** | **3** | **1** | **4** | **50** | **0** | **0** | **1** | **33** | **9.1** | **–14** | **1** | **0.0** | **11:44** | | | | | | | | | |
| **2000-01** | **Dallas** | **NHL** | **80** | **4** | **10** | **14** | **76** | **0** | **0** | **2** | **43** | **9.3** | **28** | **1** | **100.0** | **14:48** | **10** | **1** | **0** | **1** | **4** | **0** | **0** | **0** | **17:28** |
| **2001-02** | **Dallas** | **NHL** | **66** | **1** | **6** | **7** | **40** | **0** | **0** | **0** | **56** | **1.8** | **–1** | **0** | **0.0** | **13:14** | | | | | | | | | |
| **2002-03** | **Tampa Bay** | **NHL** | **70** | **1** | **14** | **15** | **46** | **0** | **0** | **0** | **52** | **1.9** | **4** | **1** | **0.0** | **17:34** | **9** | **0** | **1** | **1** | **2** | **0** | **0** | **0** | **17:48** |
| **2003-04♦** | **Tampa Bay** | **NHL** | **79** | **5** | **14** | **19** | **24** | **0** | **0** | **1** | **86** | **5.8** | **29** | **3** | **0.0** | **18:45** | **18** | **0** | **2** | **2** | **6** | **0** | **0** | **0** | **15:51** |
| 2004-05 | Fort Worth | CHL | 16 | 3 | 5 | 8 | 33 | | | | | | | | | | | | | | | | | | |
| **2005-06** | **NY Islanders** | **NHL** | **57** | **1** | **12** | **13** | **32** | **0** | **0** | **1** | **36** | **2.8** | **–3** | **0** | **0.0** | **19:15** | | | | | | | | | |
| | **New Jersey** | **NHL** | **18** | **1** | **7** | **8** | **8** | **0** | **0** | **0** | **13** | **7.7** | **3** | **0** | **0.0** | **19:11** | **9** | **0** | **0** | **0** | **4** | **0** | **0** | **0** | **21:28** |
| **2006-07** | **New Jersey** | **NHL** | **75** | **4** | **8** | **12** | **36** | **0** | **1** | **2** | **50** | **8.0** | **1** | **0** | **0.0** | **20:13** | **11** | **0** | **1** | **1** | **2** | **0** | **0** | **0** | **19:57** |
| **2007-08** | **Tampa Bay** | **NHL** | **59** | **1** | **6** | **7** | **20** | **0** | **0** | **0** | **28** | **3.6** | **–15** | **0** | **0.0** | **16:36** | | | | | | | | | |
| **2008-09** | **San Jose** | **NHL** | **58** | **0** | **8** | **8** | **12** | **0** | **0** | **0** | **43** | **0.0** | **5** | **0** | **0.0** | **16:13** | **6** | **0** | **0** | **0** | **0** | **0** | **0** | **0** | **14:30** |
| | **NHL Totals** | | **640** | **22** | **89** | **111** | **365** | **0** | **1** | **7** | **450** | **4.9** | | **6** | **16.7** | **16:38** | **71** | **1** | **5** | **6** | **22** | **0** | **0** | **0** | **16:54** |

Traded to **Dallas** by **NY Islanders** for Dallas' 3rd round choice (Robert Schnabel) in 1997 Entry Draft, June 1, 1996. Traded to **Minnesota** by **Dallas** with Manny Fernandez for Minnesota's 3rd round choice (Joel Lundqvist) in 2000 Entry Draft and Minnesota's 4th round choice (later traded back to Minnesota – later traded to Los Angeles – Los Angeles selected Aaron Rome) in 2002 Entry Draft, June 12, 2000. Traded to **Dallas** by **Minnesota** with Minnesota's 3rd (Yared Hagos) and 9th (Dale Sullivan) round choices in 2001 Entry Draft for Aaron Gavey, Pavel Patera, Dallas' 8th round choice (Eric Johansson) in 2000 Entry Draft and Minnesota's 4th round choice (previously acquired, later traded to Los Angeles – Los Angeles selected Aaron Rome) in 2002 Entry Draft, June 25, 2000. Traded to **Tampa Bay** by **Dallas** with Dallas' 7th round choice (Jay Rosehill) in 2003 Entry Draft for Tampa Bay's 2nd round choice (previously acquired, later traded back to Tampa Bay – later traded to Dallas – Dallas selected Tobias Stephan) in 2002 Entry Draft, June 22, 2002. Signed as a free agent by **Fort Worth** (CHL), September 21, 2004. Signed as a free agent by **NY Islanders**, August 11, 2005. Traded to **New Jersey** by **NY Islanders** for New Jersey's 3rd round choice (later traded to Phoenix - Phoenix selected Jonas Ahnelov) in 2006 Entry Draft, March 9, 2006. Signed as a free agent by **Tampa Bay**, July 3, 2007. Traded to **San Jose** by **Tampa Bay** with Dan Boyle for Matt Carle, Ty Wishart, San Jose's 1st round choice (later traded to Ottawa, later traded to NY Islanders, later traded to Columbus, later traded to Anaheim - Anaheim selected Kyle Palmieri) in 2009 Entry Draft and San Jose's 4th round choice in 2010 Entry Draft, July 4, 2008.

## LUNDIN, Mike

(LUHN-dihn, MIGHK) **T.B.**

Defense. Shoots left. 6'2", 188 lbs. Born, Burnsville, MN, September 24, 1984. Tampa Bay's 3rd choice, 102nd overall, in 2004 Entry Draft.

| Season | Club | League | GP | G | A | Pts | PIM | PP | SH | GW | S | % | +/- | TF | F% | Min | GP | G | A | Pts | PIM | PP | SH | GW | Min |
|---|---|---|---|---|---|---|---|---|---|---|---|---|---|---|---|---|---|---|---|---|---|---|---|---|---|
| 2002-03 | Apple Valley | High-MN | 27 | 8 | 20 | 27 | | | | | | | | | | | | | | | | | | | |
| 2003-04 | U. of Maine | H-East | 44 | 3 | 16 | 19 | 34 | | | | | | | | | | | | | | | | | | |
| 2004-05 | U. of Maine | H-East | 40 | 1 | 13 | 14 | 2 | | | | | | | | | | | | | | | | | | |
| 2005-06 | U. of Maine | H-East | 36 | 3 | 13 | 16 | 4 | | | | | | | | | | | | | | | | | | |
| 2006-07 | U. of Maine | H-East | 40 | 6 | 14 | 20 | 2 | | | | | | | | | | | | | | | | | | |
| **2007-08** | **Tampa Bay** | **NHL** | **81** | **0** | **6** | **6** | **16** | **0** | **0** | **0** | **33** | **0.0** | **3** | **0** | **0.0** | **13:48** | | | | | | | | | |
| **2008-09** | **Tampa Bay** | **NHL** | **25** | **0** | **2** | **2** | **4** | **0** | **0** | **0** | **8** | **0.0** | **–4** | **1** | **0.0** | **16:39** | | | | | | | | | |
| | Norfolk Admirals | AHL | 51 | 4 | 25 | 29 | 18 | | | | | | | | | | | | | | | | | | |
| | **NHL Totals** | | **106** | **0** | **8** | **8** | **20** | **0** | **0** | **0** | **41** | **0.0** | | **1** | **0.0** | **14:28** | | | | | | | | | |

Hockey East Second All-Star Team (2007)

## LUNDMARK, Jamie

(LUHND-mahrk, JAY-mee) **CGY.**

Center. Shoots right. 6', 197 lbs. Born, Edmonton, Alta., January 16, 1981. NY Rangers' 2nd choice, 9th overall, in 1999 Entry Draft.

| Season | Club | League | GP | G | A | Pts | PIM | PP | SH | GW | S | % | +/- | TF | F% | Min | GP | G | A | Pts | PIM | PP | SH | GW | Min |
|---|---|---|---|---|---|---|---|---|---|---|---|---|---|---|---|---|---|---|---|---|---|---|---|---|---|
| 1996-97 | St. Albert Saints | AJHL | 35 | 10 | 9 | 19 | 8 | | | | | | | | | | | | | | | | | | |
| 1997-98 | St. Albert Saints | AJHL | 57 | 33 | 58 | 91 | 171 | | | | | | | | | | 19 | 13 | 18 | 31 | 5 | | | | |
| 1998-99 | Moose Jaw | WHL | 70 | 40 | 51 | 91 | 121 | | | | | | | | | | 11 | 5 | 4 | 9 | 24 | | | | |
| 99-2000 | Moose Jaw | WHL | 37 | 21 | 27 | 48 | 33 | | | | | | | | | | | | | | | | | | |
| 2000-01 | Seattle | WHL | 52 | 35 | 42 | 77 | 49 | | | | | | | | | | 9 | 4 | 4 | 8 | 16 | | | | |
| 2001-02 | Hartford | AHL | 79 | 27 | 32 | 59 | 56 | | | | | | | | | | 10 | 3 | 4 | 7 | 16 | | | | |
| **2002-03** | **NY Rangers** | **NHL** | **55** | **8** | **11** | **19** | **16** | **0** | **0** | **0** | **78** | **10.3** | **–3** | **62** | **43.6** | **12:04** | | | | | | | | | |
| | Hartford | AHL | 22 | 9 | 9 | 18 | 18 | | | | | | | | | | 2 | 0 | 0 | 0 | 0 | | | | |
| **2003-04** | **NY Rangers** | **NHL** | **56** | **2** | **8** | **10** | **33** | **0** | **0** | **1** | **68** | **2.9** | **–8** | **379** | **40.4** | **12:46** | | | | | | | | | |
| 2004-05 | HC Forst Bolzano | Italy | 14 | 9 | 9 | 18 | 22 | | | | | | | | | | | | | | | | | | |
| | Hartford | AHL | 64 | 14 | 27 | 41 | 146 | | | | | | | | | | 6 | 2 | 4 | 6 | 8 | | | | |
| **2005-06** | **NY Rangers** | **NHL** | **3** | **1** | **0** | **1** | **6** | **0** | **0** | **0** | **1** | **100.0** | **–2** | **2** | **0.0** | **9:49** | | | | | | | | | |
| | **Phoenix** | **NHL** | **38** | **5** | **13** | **18** | **36** | **1** | **0** | **0** | **61** | **8.2** | **–1** | **366** | **58.7** | **12:37** | | | | | | | | | |
| | San Antonio | AHL | 4 | 1 | 2 | 3 | 2 | | | | | | | | | | | | | | | | | | |
| | **Calgary** | **NHL** | **12** | **4** | **6** | **10** | **20** | **1** | **0** | **1** | **16** | **25.0** | **2** | **103** | **53.4** | **12:32** | **4** | **0** | **1** | **1** | **7** | **0** | **0** | **0** | **9:44** |
| **2006-07** | **Calgary** | **NHL** | **39** | **0** | **4** | **4** | **31** | **0** | **0** | **0** | **28** | **0.0** | **–4** | **233** | **55.4** | **8:37** | | | | | | | | | |
| | **Los Angeles** | **NHL** | **29** | **7** | **2** | **9** | **25** | **0** | **0** | **0** | **53** | **13.2** | **–8** | **410** | **47.6** | **16:03** | | | | | | | | | |
| 2007-08 | Dynamo Moscow | Russia | 17 | 2 | 1 | 3 | 31 | | | | | | | | | | | | | | | | | | |
| | Lake Erie | AHL | 51 | 13 | 20 | 33 | 71 | | | | | | | | | | | | | | | | | | |
| **2008-09** | **Calgary** | **NHL** | **27** | **8** | **8** | **16** | **17** | **0** | **0** | **0** | **50** | **16.0** | **2** | **120** | **51.7** | **13:59** | **2** | **0** | **0** | **0** | **0** | **0** | **0** | **0** | **7:06** |
| | Quad City Flames | AHL | 54 | 15 | 37 | 52 | 31 | | | | | | | | | | | | | | | | | | |
| | **NHL Totals** | | **259** | **35** | **52** | **87** | **184** | **2** | **0** | **2** | **355** | **9.9** | | **1675** | **49.9** | **12:25** | **6** | **0** | **1** | **1** | **7** | **0** | **0** | **0** | **8:51** |

WHL All-Rookie Team (1999) • WHL East Second All-Star Team (1999) • WHL West First All-Star Team (2001)

Signed as a free agent by **Bolzano** (Italy), September 21, 2004. Signed as a free agent by **Hartford** (AHL), November 16, 2004. Traded to **Phoenix** by **NY Rangers** for Jeff Taffe, October 18, 2005. Traded to **Calgary** by **Phoenix** for Calgary's 4th round choice (later traded to NY Islanders - NY Islanders selected Doug Rogers) in 2006 Entry Draft, March 9, 2006. Traded to **Los Angeles** by **Calgary** with Calgary's 4th round choice (Dwight King) in 2007 Entry Draft and Calgary's 2nd round choice (later traded back to Calgary - Calgary selected Mitch Wahl) in 2008 Entry Draft for Craig Conroy, January 29, 2007. Signed as a free agent by **Calgary**, July 16, 2008.

## LUNDQVIST, Joel

(LUHND-kvihst, JOHL)

Center. Shoots left. 6'1", 194 lbs. Born, Are, Sweden, March 2, 1982. Dallas' 3rd choice, 68th overall, in 2000 Entry Draft.

| Season | Club | League | GP | G | A | Pts | PIM | PP | SH | GW | S | % | +/- | TF | F% | Min | GP | G | A | Pts | PIM | PP | SH | GW | Min |
|---|---|---|---|---|---|---|---|---|---|---|---|---|---|---|---|---|---|---|---|---|---|---|---|---|---|
| 1997-98 | Rogle Jr. | Swe-Jr. | 59 | 36 | 40 | 76 | | | | | | | | | | | | | | | | | | | |
| 1998-99 | V.Frölunda U18 | Swe-U18 | 32 | 26 | 38 | 64 | 37 | | | | | | | | | | 4 | 3 | 1 | 4 | 2 | | | | |
| 99-2000 | V.Frolunda U18 | Swe-U18 | 4 | 2 | 4 | 6 | 4 | | | | | | | | | | | | | | | | | | |
| | V.Frolunda Jr. | Swe-Jr. | 25 | 7 | 12 | 19 | 2 | | | | | | | | | | 6 | 2 | 3 | 5 | 2 | | | | |
| 2000-01 | V.Frolunda Jr. | Swe-Jr. | 18 | 14 | 27 | 41 | 12 | | | | | | | | | | | | | | | | | | |
| | Molndal | Sweden-2 | 26 | 18 | 13 | 31 | 22 | | | | | | | | | | | | | | | | | | |
| | V.Frolunda | Sweden | 9 | 0 | 0 | 0 | 0 | | | | | | | | | | | | | | | | | | |
| 2001-02 | V.Frolunda | Sweden | 46 | 12 | 14 | 26 | 28 | | | | | | | | | | 10 | 1 | 3 | 4 | 8 | | | | |
| | V.Frolunda Jr. | Swe-Jr. | | | | | | | | | | | | | | | 1 | 0 | 0 | 0 | 0 | | | | |
| 2002-03 | V.Frolunda | Sweden | 50 | 17 | 20 | 37 | 113 | | | | | | | | | | 16 | 6 | 3 | 9 | 12 | | | | |
| 2003-04 | V.Frolunda | Sweden | 49 | 9 | 14 | 23 | 48 | | | | | | | | | | 10 | 2 | 2 | 4 | 8 | | | | |
| 2004-05 | Frolunda | Sweden | 50 | 7 | 12 | 19 | 38 | | | | | | | | | | 13 | 2 | 5 | 7 | 57 | | | | |
| 2005-06 | Frolunda | Sweden | 49 | 10 | 22 | 32 | 87 | | | | | | | | | | 17 | 3 | 4 | 7 | 34 | | | | |
| **2006-07** | **Dallas** | **NHL** | **36** | **3** | **3** | **6** | **14** | **0** | **0** | **0** | **36** | **8.3** | **–5** | **91** | **62.6** | **11:20** | **7** | **2** | **0** | **2** | **6** | **0** | **0** | **0** | **13:58** |
| | Iowa Stars | AHL | 40 | 16 | 22 | 38 | 30 | | | | | | | | | | 9 | 6 | 4 | 10 | 10 | | | | |
| **2007-08** | **Dallas** | **NHL** | **55** | **3** | **11** | **14** | **22** | **0** | **0** | **0** | **48** | **6.3** | **–3** | **224** | **47.8** | **10:52** | **18** | **2** | **5** | **7** | **8** | **0** | **0** | **1** | **14:07** |
| | Iowa Stars | AHL | 8 | 2 | 4 | 6 | 2 | | | | | | | | | | | | | | | | | | |
| **2008-09** | **Dallas** | **NHL** | **43** | **1** | **5** | **6** | **20** | **0** | **0** | **1** | **32** | **3.1** | **–9** | **76** | **38.2** | **10:49** | | | | | | | | | |
| | **NHL Totals** | | **134** | **7** | **19** | **26** | **56** | **0** | **0** | **1** | **116** | **6.0** | | **391** | **49.4** | **10:59** | **25** | **4** | **5** | **9** | **14** | **0** | **0** | **1** | **14:04** |

| Season | Club | League | GP | G | A | Pts | PIM | PP | SH | GW | S | % | +/- | TF | F% | Min | GP | G | A | Pts | PIM | PP | SH | GW | Min |
|---|---|---|---|---|---|---|---|---|---|---|---|---|---|---|---|---|---|---|---|---|---|---|---|---|---|
| | | | Regular Season | | | | | | | | | | | | | | Playoffs | | | | | | | | |

## LUPUL, Joffrey

(LOO-puhl, JAWF-ree) **ANA.**

Right wing. Shoots right. 6'1", 205 lbs. Born, Fort Saskatchewan, Alta., September 23, 1983. Anaheim's 1st choice, 7th overall, in 2002 Entry Draft.

| Season | Club | League | GP | G | A | Pts | PIM | PP | SH | GW | S | % | +/- | TF | F% | Min | GP | G | A | Pts | PIM | PP | SH | GW | Min |
|---|---|---|---|---|---|---|---|---|---|---|---|---|---|---|---|---|---|---|---|---|---|---|---|---|---|
| 1998-99 | Ft. Saskatchewan | ABHL | 36 | 40 | 50 | 90 | 40 | .... | .... | .... | .... | .... | .... | .... | .... | .... | .... | .... | .... | .... | .... | .... | .... | .... | .... |
| 99-2000 | Ft. Saskatchewan | AMHL | 34 | 43 | 30 | *73 | 47 | .... | .... | .... | .... | .... | .... | .... | .... | .... | 4 | 0 | 1 | 1 | 2 | .... | .... | .... | .... |
| 2000-01 | Medicine Hat | WHL | 69 | 30 | 26 | 56 | 39 | .... | .... | .... | .... | .... | .... | .... | .... | .... | 22 | 3 | 6 | 9 | 2 | .... | .... | .... | .... |
| 2001-02 | Medicine Hat | WHL | 72 | *56 | 50 | 106 | 95 | .... | .... | .... | .... | .... | .... | .... | .... | .... | .... | .... | .... | .... | .... | .... | .... | .... | .... |
| 2002-03 | Medicine Hat | WHL | 50 | 41 | 37 | 78 | 82 | .... | .... | .... | .... | .... | .... | .... | .... | .... | 11 | 4 | 11 | 15 | 20 | .... | .... | .... | .... |
| **2003-04** | **Anaheim** | **NHL** | **75** | **13** | **21** | **34** | **28** | **4** | **0** | **2** | **137** | **9.5** | **–6** | **11** | **9.1** | **13:37** | .... | .... | .... | .... | .... | .... | .... | .... | .... |
| | Cincinnati | AHL | 3 | 3 | 2 | 5 | 2 | .... | .... | .... | .... | .... | .... | .... | .... | .... | .... | .... | .... | .... | .... | .... | .... | .... | .... |
| 2004-05 | Cincinnati | AHL | 65 | 30 | 26 | 56 | 58 | .... | .... | .... | .... | .... | .... | .... | .... | .... | 12 | 3 | 9 | 12 | 27 | .... | .... | .... | .... |
| **2005-06** | **Anaheim** | **NHL** | **81** | **28** | **25** | **53** | **48** | **12** | **2** | **2** | **296** | **9.5** | **–13** | **101** | **37.6** | **16:38** | **16** | **9** | **2** | **11** | **31** | **1** | **0** | **1** | **16:43** |
| **2006-07** | **Edmonton** | **NHL** | **81** | **16** | **12** | **28** | **45** | **5** | **0** | **1** | **172** | **9.3** | **–29** | **14** | **35.7** | **15:36** | .... | .... | .... | .... | .... | .... | .... | .... | .... |
| **2007-08** | **Philadelphia** | **NHL** | **56** | **20** | **26** | **46** | **35** | **7** | **0** | **3** | **176** | **11.4** | **2** | **4** | **75.0** | **18:13** | **17** | **4** | **6** | **10** | **2** | **2** | **0** | **1** | **16:13** |
| **2008-09** | **Philadelphia** | **NHL** | **79** | **25** | **25** | **50** | **58** | **6** | **0** | **4** | **194** | **12.9** | **1** | **21** | **47.6** | **15:41** | **6** | **1** | **1** | **2** | **2** | **0** | **0** | **0** | **17:07** |
| | **NHL Totals** | | **372** | **102** | **109** | **211** | **214** | **34** | **2** | **12** | **975** | **10.5** | | **151** | **37.7** | **15:50** | **39** | **14** | **9** | **23** | **35** | **3** | **0** | **2** | **16:34** |

WHL East First All-Star Team (2002) • Canadian Major Junior First All-Star Team (2002)

Traded to **Edmonton** by **Anaheim** with Ladislav Smid, Anaheim's 1st round choice (later traded to Phoenix - Phoenix selected Nick Ross) in 2007 Entry Draft and Anaheim's 1st (Jordan Eberle) and 2nd (later traded to NY Islanders - NY Islanders selected Travis Hamonic) round choices in 2008 Entry Draft for Chris Pronger, July 3, 2006. Traded to **Philadelphia** by **Edmonton** with Jason Smith for Joni Pitkanen, Geoff Sanderson and Philadelphia's 3rd round choice (Cameron Abney) in 2009 Entry Draft, July 1, 2007. Traded to **Anaheim** by **Philadelphia** with Luca Sbisa, Philadelphia's 1st round choices in 2009 (later traded to Columbus - Columbus selected John Moore) and 2010 Entry Drafts and future considerations for Chris Pronger and Ryan Dingle, June 26, 2009.

## LYDMAN, Toni

(LEWD-man, TOH-nee) **BUF.**

Defense. Shoots left. 6'1", 210 lbs. Born, Lahti, Finland, September 25, 1977. Calgary's 5th choice, 89th overall, in 1996 Entry Draft.

| Season | Club | League | GP | G | A | Pts | PIM | PP | SH | GW | S | % | +/- | TF | F% | Min | GP | G | A | Pts | PIM | PP | SH | GW | Min |
|---|---|---|---|---|---|---|---|---|---|---|---|---|---|---|---|---|---|---|---|---|---|---|---|---|---|
| 1993-94 | K-Reipas U18 | Fin-U18 | 9 | 3 | 1 | 4 | 4 | .... | .... | .... | .... | .... | .... | .... | .... | .... | .... | .... | .... | .... | .... | .... | .... | .... | .... |
| | K-Reipas Jr. | Fin-Jr. | 1 | 0 | 0 | 0 | 0 | .... | .... | .... | .... | .... | .... | .... | .... | .... | .... | .... | .... | .... | .... | .... | .... | .... | .... |
| 1994-95 | K-Reipas U18 | Fin-U18 | 9 | 7 | 4 | 11 | 12 | .... | .... | .... | .... | .... | .... | .... | .... | .... | .... | .... | .... | .... | .... | .... | .... | .... | .... |
| | K-Reipas Jr. | Fin-Jr. | 26 | 6 | 4 | 10 | 10 | .... | .... | .... | .... | .... | .... | .... | .... | .... | .... | .... | .... | .... | .... | .... | .... | .... | .... |
| 1995-96 | Reipas Lahti Jr. | Fin-Jr. | 9 | 2 | 2 | 4 | 6 | .... | .... | .... | .... | .... | .... | .... | .... | .... | .... | .... | .... | .... | .... | .... | .... | .... | .... |
| | Reipas Lahti | Finland-2 | 39 | 5 | 2 | 7 | 30 | .... | .... | .... | .... | .... | .... | .... | .... | .... | 3 | 0 | 1 | 1 | 0 | .... | .... | .... | .... |
| 1996-97 | Tappara Tampere | Finland | 49 | 1 | 2 | 3 | 65 | .... | .... | .... | .... | .... | .... | .... | .... | .... | 3 | 0 | 0 | 0 | 6 | .... | .... | .... | .... |
| 1997-98 | Tappara Tampere | Finland | 48 | 4 | 10 | 14 | 48 | .... | .... | .... | .... | .... | .... | .... | .... | .... | 4 | 0 | 2 | 2 | 0 | .... | .... | .... | .... |
| 1998-99 | HIFK Helsinki | Finland | 42 | 4 | 7 | 11 | 36 | .... | .... | .... | .... | .... | .... | .... | .... | .... | 11 | 0 | 3 | 3 | 2 | .... | .... | .... | .... |
| | HIFK Helsinki | EuroHL | 6 | 0 | 2 | 2 | 29 | .... | .... | .... | .... | .... | .... | .... | .... | .... | 4 | 1 | .... | .... | .... | .... | .... | .... | .... |
| 99-2000 | HIFK Helsinki | Finland | 46 | 4 | 18 | 22 | 36 | .... | .... | .... | .... | .... | .... | .... | .... | .... | 9 | 0 | 4 | 4 | 6 | .... | .... | .... | .... |
| **2000-01** | **Calgary** | **NHL** | **62** | **3** | **16** | **19** | **30** | **1** | **0** | **0** | **80** | **3.8** | **–7** | **0** | **0.0** | **20:36** | .... | .... | .... | .... | .... | .... | .... | .... | .... |
| **2001-02** | **Calgary** | **NHL** | **79** | **6** | **22** | **28** | **52** | **1** | **0** | **0** | **126** | **4.8** | **–8** | **0** | **0.0** | **21:10** | .... | .... | .... | .... | .... | .... | .... | .... | .... |
| **2002-03** | **Calgary** | **NHL** | **81** | **6** | **20** | **26** | **28** | **3** | **0** | **0** | **143** | **4.2** | **–7** | **0** | **0.0** | **25:47** | .... | .... | .... | .... | .... | .... | .... | .... | .... |
| **2003-04** | **Calgary** | **NHL** | **67** | **4** | **16** | **20** | **30** | **2** | **0** | **1** | **93** | **4.3** | **6** | **0** | **0.0** | **21:13** | **6** | **0** | **1** | **1** | **2** | **0** | **0** | **0** | **14:30** |
| 2004-05 | HIFK Helsinki | Finland | 8 | 1 | 2 | 3 | 2 | .... | .... | .... | .... | .... | .... | .... | .... | .... | 5 | 0 | 3 | 3 | 0 | .... | .... | .... | .... |
| **2005-06** | **Buffalo** | **NHL** | **75** | **1** | **16** | **17** | **82** | **0** | **0** | **0** | **68** | **1.5** | **9** | **0** | **0.0** | **21:38** | **18** | **1** | **4** | **5** | **18** | **0** | **0** | **0** | **23:03** |
| | Finland | Olympics | 8 | 1 | 0 | 1 | 10 | .... | .... | .... | .... | .... | .... | .... | .... | .... | .... | .... | .... | .... | .... | .... | .... | .... | .... |
| **2006-07** | **Buffalo** | **NHL** | **67** | **2** | **17** | **19** | **55** | **0** | **0** | **1** | **44** | **4.5** | **10** | **0** | **0.0** | **20:36** | **16** | **2** | **2** | **4** | **14** | **0** | **0** | **0** | **23:41** |
| **2007-08** | **Buffalo** | **NHL** | **82** | **4** | **22** | **26** | **74** | **3** | **0** | **0** | **86** | **4.7** | **1** | **1** | **0.0** | **21:40** | .... | .... | .... | .... | .... | .... | .... | .... | .... |
| **2008-09** | **Buffalo** | **NHL** | **80** | **3** | **20** | **23** | **70** | **0** | **0** | **0** | **99** | **3.0** | **0** | **0** | **0.0** | **21:47** | .... | .... | .... | .... | .... | .... | .... | .... | .... |
| | **NHL Totals** | | **593** | **29** | **149** | **178** | **421** | **10** | **0** | **2** | **739** | **3.9** | | **1** | **0.0** | **21:53** | **40** | **3** | **7** | **10** | **34** | **0** | **0** | **0** | **22:01** |

Signed as a free agent by **HIFK Helsinki** (Finland), January 31, 2005. Traded to **Buffalo** by **Calgary** for Buffalo's 3rd round choice (John Armstrong) in 2006 Entry Draft, August 25, 2005.

## MacARTHUR, Clarke

(muh-KAR-thuhr, KLAHRK) **BUF.**

Left wing. Shoots left. 5'11", 191 lbs. Born, Lloydminster, Alta., April 6, 1985. Buffalo's 3rd choice, 74th overall, in 2003 Entry Draft.

| Season | Club | League | GP | G | A | Pts | PIM | PP | SH | GW | S | % | +/- | TF | F% | Min | GP | G | A | Pts | PIM | PP | SH | GW | Min |
|---|---|---|---|---|---|---|---|---|---|---|---|---|---|---|---|---|---|---|---|---|---|---|---|---|---|
| 99-2000 | Lloydminster | CABHL | 24 | 19 | 45 | 64 | 51 | .... | .... | .... | .... | .... | .... | .... | .... | .... | 5 | 9 | 6 | 15 | 4 | .... | .... | .... | .... |
| 2000-01 | Strathcona | AMBHL | 38 | 36 | 63 | 99 | 44 | .... | .... | .... | .... | .... | .... | .... | .... | .... | 8 | 6 | 2 | 8 | 10 | .... | .... | .... | .... |
| 2001-02 | Drayton Valley | AJHL | 61 | 22 | 40 | 62 | 33 | .... | .... | .... | .... | .... | .... | .... | .... | .... | 16 | 5 | 8 | 13 | 34 | .... | .... | .... | .... |
| 2002-03 | Medicine Hat | WHL | 70 | 23 | 52 | 75 | 104 | .... | .... | .... | .... | .... | .... | .... | .... | .... | 11 | 3 | 6 | 9 | 8 | .... | .... | .... | .... |
| 2003-04 | Medicine Hat | WHL | 62 | 35 | 40 | 75 | 93 | .... | .... | .... | .... | .... | .... | .... | .... | .... | 20 | 8 | 10 | 18 | 16 | .... | .... | .... | .... |
| 2004-05 | Medicine Hat | WHL | 58 | 30 | 44 | 74 | 100 | .... | .... | .... | .... | .... | .... | .... | .... | .... | 13 | 3 | 8 | 11 | 18 | .... | .... | .... | .... |
| | Rochester | AHL | .... | .... | .... | .... | .... | .... | .... | .... | .... | .... | .... | .... | .... | .... | 3 | 0 | 1 | 1 | 0 | .... | .... | .... | .... |
| 2005-06 | Rochester | AHL | 69 | 21 | 32 | 53 | 71 | .... | .... | .... | .... | .... | .... | .... | .... | .... | .... | .... | .... | .... | .... | .... | .... | .... | .... |
| **2006-07** | **Buffalo** | **NHL** | **19** | **3** | **4** | **7** | **4** | **0** | **0** | **0** | **16** | **18.8** | **4** | **50** | **46.0** | **8:54** | .... | .... | .... | .... | .... | .... | .... | .... | .... |
| | Rochester | AHL | 51 | 21 | 42 | 63 | 57 | .... | .... | .... | .... | .... | .... | .... | .... | .... | 6 | 2 | 4 | 6 | 4 | .... | .... | .... | .... |
| **2007-08** | **Buffalo** | **NHL** | **37** | **8** | **7** | **15** | **20** | **0** | **0** | **1** | **51** | **15.7** | **3** | **14** | **28.6** | **14:34** | .... | .... | .... | .... | .... | .... | .... | .... | .... |
| | Rochester | AHL | 43 | 14 | 28 | 42 | 26 | .... | .... | .... | .... | .... | .... | .... | .... | .... | .... | .... | .... | .... | .... | .... | .... | .... | .... |
| **2008-09** | **Buffalo** | **NHL** | **71** | **17** | **14** | **31** | **56** | **5** | **0** | **0** | **108** | **15.7** | **–4** | **218** | **34.9** | **13:50** | .... | .... | .... | .... | .... | .... | .... | .... | .... |
| | **NHL Totals** | | **127** | **28** | **25** | **53** | **80** | **5** | **0** | **1** | **175** | **16.0** | | **282** | **36.5** | **13:18** | .... | .... | .... | .... | .... | .... | .... | .... | .... |

Memorial Cup Tournament All-Star Team (2004) • WHL East First All-Star Team (2005)

## MacDONALD, Andrew

(MAK-DAWN-uhld, AN-droo) **NYI**

Defense. Shoots left. 6'1", 188 lbs. Born, Judique, N.S., September 7, 1986. NY Islanders' 10th choice, 160th overall, in 2006 Entry Draft.

| Season | Club | League | GP | G | A | Pts | PIM | PP | SH | GW | S | % | +/- | TF | F% | Min | GP | G | A | Pts | PIM | PP | SH | GW | Min |
|---|---|---|---|---|---|---|---|---|---|---|---|---|---|---|---|---|---|---|---|---|---|---|---|---|---|
| 2003-04 | Truro Bearcats | MJrHL | 50 | 8 | 20 | 28 | 43 | .... | .... | .... | .... | .... | .... | .... | .... | .... | 10 | 0 | 0 | 0 | .... | .... | .... | .... | .... |
| 2004-05 | Truro Bearcats | MJrHL | 56 | 11 | 22 | 33 | 60 | .... | .... | .... | .... | .... | .... | .... | .... | .... | 17 | 6 | 7 | 13 | .... | .... | .... | .... | .... |
| 2005-06 | Moncton Wildcats | QMJHL | 68 | 6 | 40 | 46 | 62 | .... | .... | .... | .... | .... | .... | .... | .... | .... | 21 | 2 | 11 | 13 | 10 | .... | .... | .... | .... |
| 2006-07 | Moncton Wildcats | QMJHL | 65 | 14 | 44 | 58 | 81 | .... | .... | .... | .... | .... | .... | .... | .... | .... | 7 | 1 | 5 | 6 | 4 | .... | .... | .... | .... |
| | Bridgeport | AHL | 3 | 0 | 0 | 0 | 0 | .... | .... | .... | .... | .... | .... | .... | .... | .... | .... | .... | .... | .... | .... | .... | .... | .... | .... |
| 2007-08 | Bridgeport | AHL | 21 | 2 | 3 | 5 | 10 | .... | .... | .... | .... | .... | .... | .... | .... | .... | .... | .... | .... | .... | .... | .... | .... | .... | .... |
| | Utah Grizzlies | ECHL | 37 | 1 | 11 | 12 | 39 | .... | .... | .... | .... | .... | .... | .... | .... | .... | 15 | 3 | 9 | 12 | 12 | .... | .... | .... | .... |
| **2008-09** | **NY Islanders** | **NHL** | **3** | **0** | **0** | **0** | **2** | **0** | **0** | **0** | **1** | **0.0** | **2** | **0** | **0.0** | **10:10** | .... | .... | .... | .... | .... | .... | .... | .... | .... |
| | Bridgeport | AHL | 69 | 9 | 24 | 33 | 46 | .... | .... | .... | .... | .... | .... | .... | .... | .... | 5 | 1 | 1 | 2 | 4 | .... | .... | .... | .... |
| | **NHL Totals** | | **3** | **0** | **0** | **0** | **2** | **0** | **0** | **0** | **1** | **0.0** | | **0** | **0.0** | **10:10** | .... | .... | .... | .... | .... | .... | .... | .... | .... |

QMJHL First All-Star Team (2007)

## MacDONALD, Craig

(MAK-DAWN-uhld, KRAYG)

Left wing. Shoots left. 6'1", 201 lbs. Born, Antigonish, N.S., April 7, 1977. Hartford's 3rd choice, 88th overall, in 1996 Entry Draft.

| Season | Club | League | GP | G | A | Pts | PIM | PP | SH | GW | S | % | +/- | TF | F% | Min | GP | G | A | Pts | PIM | PP | SH | GW | Min |
|---|---|---|---|---|---|---|---|---|---|---|---|---|---|---|---|---|---|---|---|---|---|---|---|---|---|
| 1994-95 | Lawrence | High-MA | 30 | 25 | 52 | 77 | 10 | .... | .... | .... | .... | .... | .... | .... | .... | .... | .... | .... | .... | .... | .... | .... | .... | .... | .... |
| 1995-96 | Harvard Crimson | ECAC | 34 | 7 | 10 | 17 | 10 | .... | .... | .... | .... | .... | .... | .... | .... | .... | .... | .... | .... | .... | .... | .... | .... | .... | .... |
| 1996-97 | Harvard Crimson | ECAC | 32 | 6 | 10 | 16 | 20 | .... | .... | .... | .... | .... | .... | .... | .... | .... | .... | .... | .... | .... | .... | .... | .... | .... | .... |
| 1997-98 | Canada | Nat-Tm | 58 | 18 | 29 | 47 | 38 | .... | .... | .... | .... | .... | .... | .... | .... | .... | .... | .... | .... | .... | .... | .... | .... | .... | .... |
| **1998-99** | **Carolina** | **NHL** | **11** | **0** | **0** | **0** | **0** | **0** | **0** | **0** | **5** | **0.0** | **0** | **2** | **100.0** | **2:29** | **1** | **0** | **0** | **0** | **0** | **0** | **0** | **0** | **2:46** |
| | New Haven | AHL | 62 | 17 | 31 | 48 | 77 | .... | .... | .... | .... | .... | .... | .... | .... | .... | .... | .... | .... | .... | .... | .... | .... | .... | .... |
| 99-2000 | Cincinnati | IHL | 78 | 12 | 24 | 36 | 76 | .... | .... | .... | .... | .... | .... | .... | .... | .... | 11 | 4 | 1 | 5 | 8 | .... | .... | .... | .... |
| 2000-01 | Cincinnati | IHL | 82 | 20 | 28 | 48 | 104 | .... | .... | .... | .... | .... | .... | .... | .... | .... | 5 | 0 | 1 | 1 | 6 | .... | .... | .... | .... |
| **2001-02** | **Carolina** | **NHL** | **12** | **1** | **1** | **2** | **0** | **0** | **0** | **0** | **15** | **6.7** | **–1** | **19** | **47.4** | **10:11** | **4** | **0** | **0** | **0** | **2** | **0** | **0** | **0** | **4:42** |
| | Lowell | AHL | 64 | 19 | 22 | 41 | 61 | .... | .... | .... | .... | .... | .... | .... | .... | .... | .... | .... | .... | .... | .... | .... | .... | .... | .... |
| **2002-03** | **Carolina** | **NHL** | **35** | **1** | **3** | **4** | **20** | **0** | **0** | **0** | **43** | **2.3** | **–3** | **72** | **55.6** | **9:21** | .... | .... | .... | .... | .... | .... | .... | .... | .... |
| | Lowell | AHL | 27 | 7 | 20 | 27 | 38 | .... | .... | .... | .... | .... | .... | .... | .... | .... | .... | .... | .... | .... | .... | .... | .... | .... | .... |
| **2003-04** | **Florida** | **NHL** | **34** | **0** | **3** | **3** | **25** | **0** | **0** | **0** | **42** | **0.0** | **–5** | **398** | **45.7** | **12:31** | .... | .... | .... | .... | .... | .... | .... | .... | .... |
| | San Antonio | AHL | 2 | 0 | 0 | 0 | 4 | .... | .... | .... | .... | .... | .... | .... | .... | .... | .... | .... | .... | .... | .... | .... | .... | .... | .... |
| | **Boston** | **NHL** | **18** | **0** | **3** | **3** | **8** | **0** | **0** | **0** | **17** | **0.0** | **0** | **155** | **47.1** | **8:42** | **1** | **0** | **0** | **0** | **0** | **0** | **0** | **0** | **2:11** |
| 2004-05 | Lowell | AHL | 71 | 10 | 18 | 28 | 104 | .... | .... | .... | .... | .... | .... | .... | .... | .... | 2 | 0 | 0 | 0 | 0 | .... | .... | .... | .... |
| **2005-06** | **Calgary** | **NHL** | **25** | **3** | **2** | **5** | **8** | **1** | **0** | **0** | **27** | **11.1** | **5** | **33** | **45.5** | **10:16** | **1** | **0** | **0** | **0** | **0** | **0** | **0** | **0** | **7:50** |
| | Omaha | AHL | 37 | 8 | 19 | 27 | 57 | .... | .... | .... | .... | .... | .... | .... | .... | .... | .... | .... | .... | .... | .... | .... | .... | .... | .... |
| **2006-07** | **Chicago** | **NHL** | **25** | **3** | **2** | **5** | **14** | **0** | **1** | **0** | **30** | **10.0** | **–2** | **178** | **47.8** | **11:12** | .... | .... | .... | .... | .... | .... | .... | .... | .... |
| | Norfolk Admirals | AHL | 50 | 15 | 25 | 40 | 45 | .... | .... | .... | .... | .... | .... | .... | .... | .... | 6 | 2 | 3 | 5 | 8 | .... | .... | .... | .... |
| **2007-08** | **Tampa Bay** | **NHL** | **65** | **2** | **9** | **11** | **16** | **0** | **0** | **0** | **84** | **2.4** | **–10** | **406** | **49.8** | **10:52** | .... | .... | .... | .... | .... | .... | .... | .... | .... |
| | Norfolk Admirals | AHL | 7 | 3 | 8 | 11 | 8 | .... | .... | .... | .... | .... | .... | .... | .... | .... | .... | .... | .... | .... | .... | .... | .... | .... | .... |

| | | | Regular Season | | | | | | | | | | | | | | Playoffs | | | | | | | | |
|---|---|---|---|---|---|---|---|---|---|---|---|---|---|---|---|---|---|---|---|---|---|---|---|---|---|
| Season | Club | League | GP | G | A | Pts | PIM | PP | SH | GW | S | % | +/- | TF | F% | Min | GP | G | A | Pts | PIM | PP | SH | GW | Min |
| **2008-09** | **Columbus** | **NHL** | **8** | **1** | **1** | **2** | **0** | **0** | **0** | **1** | **6** | **16.7** | **1** | **11** | **36.4** | **10:39** | .... | .... | .... | .... | .... | .... | .... | .... | .... |
| | Syracuse Crunch | AHL | 70 | 15 | 25 | 40 | 71 | .... | .... | .... | .... | .... | .... | .... | .... | .... | .... | .... | .... | .... | .... | .... | .... | .... | .... |
| | **NHL Totals** | | **233** | **11** | **24** | **35** | **91** | **1** | **1** | **1** | **269** | **4.1** | | **1274** | **48.0** | **10:15** | **7** | **0** | **0** | **0** | **2** | **0** | **0** | **0** | **4:31** |

• Rights transferred to **Carolina** after **Hartford** franchise relocated, June 25, 1997. Signed as a free agent by **Florida**, August 14, 2003. Claimed on waivers by **Boston** from **Florida**, January 20, 2004. Signed as a free agent by **Calgary**, August 11, 2005. Signed as a free agent by **Chicago**, August 1, 2006. Signed as a free agent by **Tampa Bay**, July 2, 2007. Signed as a free agent by **Columbus**, July 14, 2008.

## MACHACEK, Spencer (muh-HA-chehk, SPEHN-suhr) ATL.

Right wing. Shoots right. 6'1", 185 lbs. Born, Lethbridge, Alta., October 14, 1988. Atlanta's 1st choice, 67th overall, in 2007 Entry Draft.

| Season | Club | League | GP | G | A | Pts | PIM | PP | SH | GW | S | % | +/- | TF | F% | Min | GP | G | A | Pts | PIM | PP | SH | GW | Min |
|---|---|---|---|---|---|---|---|---|---|---|---|---|---|---|---|---|---|---|---|---|---|---|---|---|---|
| 2004-05 | Brooks Bandits | AJHL | 59 | 16 | 20 | 36 | 41 | .... | .... | .... | .... | .... | .... | .... | .... | .... | 10 | 2 | 2 | 4 | 8 | .... | .... | .... | .... |
| 2005-06 | Vancouver Giants | WHL | 70 | 23 | 22 | 45 | 53 | .... | .... | .... | .... | .... | .... | .... | .... | .... | 18 | 6 | 8 | 14 | 8 | .... | .... | .... | .... |
| 2006-07 | Vancouver Giants | WHL | 63 | 21 | 24 | 45 | 32 | .... | .... | .... | .... | .... | .... | .... | .... | .... | 22 | 9 | 11 | 20 | 14 | .... | .... | .... | .... |
| 2007-08 | Vancouver Giants | WHL | 70 | 33 | 45 | 78 | 69 | .... | .... | .... | .... | .... | .... | .... | .... | .... | 10 | 5 | 2 | 7 | 6 | .... | .... | .... | .... |
| **2008-09** | **Atlanta** | **NHL** | **2** | **0** | **0** | **0** | **0** | **0** | **0** | **0** | **1** | **0.0** | **0** | **0** | **0.0** | **8:12** | .... | .... | .... | .... | .... | .... | .... | .... | .... |
| | Chicago Wolves | AHL | 77 | 23 | 25 | 48 | 23 | .... | .... | .... | .... | .... | .... | .... | .... | .... | .... | .... | .... | .... | .... | .... | .... | .... | .... |
| | **NHL Totals** | | **2** | **0** | **0** | **0** | **0** | **0** | **0** | **0** | **1** | **0.0** | | **0** | **0.0** | **8:12** | .... | .... | .... | .... | .... | .... | .... | .... | .... |

## MACIAS, Ray (mah-CHEE-ahs, RAY) COL.

Defense. Shoots right. 6'2", 195 lbs. Born, Long Beach, CA, September 18, 1986. Colorado's 6th choice, 124th overall, in 2005 Entry Draft.

| Season | Club | League | GP | G | A | Pts | PIM | PP | SH | GW | S | % | +/- | TF | F% | Min | GP | G | A | Pts | PIM | PP | SH | GW | Min |
|---|---|---|---|---|---|---|---|---|---|---|---|---|---|---|---|---|---|---|---|---|---|---|---|---|---|
| 2002-03 | L.A. Jr. Kings | Minor-CA | 49 | 37 | 26 | 63 | 100 | .... | .... | .... | .... | .... | .... | .... | .... | .... | .... | .... | .... | .... | .... | .... | .... | .... | .... |
| | Kamloops Blazers | WHL | 4 | 0 | 0 | 0 | 0 | .... | .... | .... | .... | .... | .... | .... | .... | .... | 2 | 0 | 0 | 0 | 0 | .... | .... | .... | .... |
| 2003-04 | Kamloops Blazers | WHL | 69 | 12 | 17 | 29 | 14 | .... | .... | .... | .... | .... | .... | .... | .... | .... | 5 | 2 | 0 | 2 | 0 | .... | .... | .... | .... |
| 2004-05 | Kamloops Blazers | WHL | 69 | 12 | 35 | 47 | 18 | .... | .... | .... | .... | .... | .... | .... | .... | .... | 2 | 0 | 0 | 0 | 0 | .... | .... | .... | .... |
| 2005-06 | Kamloops Blazers | WHL | 68 | 12 | 26 | 38 | 34 | .... | .... | .... | .... | .... | .... | .... | .... | .... | .... | .... | .... | .... | .... | .... | .... | .... | .... |
| 2006-07 | Kamloops Blazers | WHL | 70 | 30 | 40 | 70 | 58 | .... | .... | .... | .... | .... | .... | .... | .... | .... | .... | .... | .... | .... | .... | .... | .... | .... | .... |
| 2007-08 | Lake Erie | AHL | 42 | 4 | 9 | 13 | 18 | .... | .... | .... | .... | .... | .... | .... | .... | .... | .... | .... | .... | .... | .... | .... | .... | .... | .... |
| | Johnstown Chiefs | ECHL | 5 | 0 | 5 | 5 | 0 | .... | .... | .... | .... | .... | .... | .... | .... | .... | 6 | 1 | 3 | 4 | 2 | .... | .... | .... | .... |
| **2008-09** | **Colorado** | **NHL** | **6** | **0** | **1** | **1** | **0** | **0** | **0** | **0** | **4** | **0.0** | **0** | **0** | **0.0** | **17:59** | .... | .... | .... | .... | .... | .... | .... | .... | .... |
| | Lake Erie | AHL | 36 | 3 | 15 | 18 | 20 | .... | .... | .... | .... | .... | .... | .... | .... | .... | .... | .... | .... | .... | .... | .... | .... | .... | .... |
| | Johnstown Chiefs | ECHL | 8 | 1 | 5 | 6 | 4 | .... | .... | .... | .... | .... | .... | .... | .... | .... | .... | .... | .... | .... | .... | .... | .... | .... | .... |
| | **NHL Totals** | | **6** | **0** | **1** | **1** | **0** | **0** | **0** | **0** | **4** | **0.0** | | **0** | **0.0** | **17:59** | .... | .... | .... | .... | .... | .... | .... | .... | .... |

WHL West First All-Star Team (2007)

## MacINTYRE, Steve (MAK-ihn-tighr, STEEV) EDM.

Left wing. Shoots left. 6'5", 250 lbs. Born, Brock, Sask., August 8, 1980.

| Season | Club | League | GP | G | A | Pts | PIM | PP | SH | GW | S | % | +/- | TF | F% | Min | GP | G | A | Pts | PIM | PP | SH | GW | Min |
|---|---|---|---|---|---|---|---|---|---|---|---|---|---|---|---|---|---|---|---|---|---|---|---|---|---|
| 2002-03 | St. Jean Mission | QSPHL | 10 | 1 | 1 | 2 | 68 | .... | .... | .... | .... | .... | .... | .... | .... | .... | .... | .... | .... | .... | .... | .... | .... | .... | .... |
| | Muskegon Fury | UHL | 54 | 2 | 1 | 3 | 279 | .... | .... | .... | .... | .... | .... | .... | .... | .... | 5 | 0 | 0 | 0 | 24 | .... | .... | .... | .... |
| 2003-04 | Hartford | AHL | 3 | 0 | 0 | 0 | 0 | .... | .... | .... | .... | .... | .... | .... | .... | .... | .... | .... | .... | .... | .... | .... | .... | .... | .... |
| | Charlotte | ECHL | 61 | 1 | 4 | 5 | 217 | .... | .... | .... | .... | .... | .... | .... | .... | .... | .... | .... | .... | .... | .... | .... | .... | .... | .... |
| | Jacksonville | WHA2 | 6 | 0 | 2 | 2 | 18 | .... | .... | .... | .... | .... | .... | .... | .... | .... | 5 | 0 | 1 | 1 | 17 | .... | .... | .... | .... |
| 2004-05 | Hartford | AHL | 27 | 1 | 1 | 2 | 207 | .... | .... | .... | .... | .... | .... | .... | .... | .... | .... | .... | .... | .... | .... | .... | .... | .... | .... |
| | Charlotte | ECHL | 46 | 1 | 4 | 5 | 214 | .... | .... | .... | .... | .... | .... | .... | .... | .... | 11 | 0 | 4 | 4 | 17 | .... | .... | .... | .... |
| 2005-06 | Charlotte | ECHL | 61 | 3 | 2 | 5 | 238 | .... | .... | .... | .... | .... | .... | .... | .... | .... | 1 | 0 | 0 | 0 | 4 | .... | .... | .... | .... |
| 2006-07 | Quad City | UHL | 46 | 2 | 1 | 3 | 168 | .... | .... | .... | .... | .... | .... | .... | .... | .... | 5 | 0 | 0 | 0 | 6 | .... | .... | .... | .... |
| 2007-08 | Providence Bruins | AHL | 62 | 2 | 3 | 5 | 213 | .... | .... | .... | .... | .... | .... | .... | .... | .... | 5 | 0 | 0 | 0 | 9 | .... | .... | .... | .... |
| **2008-09** | **Edmonton** | **NHL** | **22** | **2** | **0** | **2** | **40** | **0** | **0** | **1** | **6** | **33.3** | **–2** | **0** | **0.0** | **3:55** | .... | .... | .... | .... | .... | .... | .... | .... | .... |
| | **NHL Totals** | | **22** | **2** | **0** | **2** | **40** | **0** | **0** | **1** | **6** | **33.3** | | **0** | **0.0** | **3:55** | .... | .... | .... | .... | .... | .... | .... | .... | .... |

Signed as a free agent by **NY Rangers**, August 15, 2005. Signed as a free agent by **Quad City** (UHL), August 24, 2006. Signed as a free agent by **Florida**, July 3, 2008. Claimed on waivers by **Edmonton** from **Florida**, September 30, 2008. • Missed majority of 2008-09 season recovering from facial injury and serving as a healthy reserve.

## MacKENZIE, Aaron (muh-KEHN-zee, AIR-ruhn)

Defense. Shoots left. 6'1", 195 lbs. Born, Terrace Bay, Ont., March 7, 1981.

| Season | Club | League | GP | G | A | Pts | PIM | PP | SH | GW | S | % | +/- | TF | F% | Min | GP | G | A | Pts | PIM | PP | SH | GW | Min |
|---|---|---|---|---|---|---|---|---|---|---|---|---|---|---|---|---|---|---|---|---|---|---|---|---|---|
| 1998-99 | Thunder Bay | USHL | 49 | 8 | 12 | 20 | 123 | .... | .... | .... | .... | .... | .... | .... | .... | .... | 3 | 0 | 1 | 1 | 0 | .... | .... | .... | .... |
| 99-2000 | U. of Denver | WCHA | 40 | 1 | 9 | 10 | 56 | .... | .... | .... | .... | .... | .... | .... | .... | .... | .... | .... | .... | .... | .... | .... | .... | .... | .... |
| 2000-01 | U. of Denver | WCHA | 37 | 2 | 6 | 8 | 45 | .... | .... | .... | .... | .... | .... | .... | .... | .... | .... | .... | .... | .... | .... | .... | .... | .... | .... |
| 2001-02 | U. of Denver | WCHA | 39 | 5 | 18 | 23 | 30 | .... | .... | .... | .... | .... | .... | .... | .... | .... | .... | .... | .... | .... | .... | .... | .... | .... | .... |
| 2002-03 | U. of Denver | WCHA | 41 | 11 | 21 | 32 | 33 | .... | .... | .... | .... | .... | .... | .... | .... | .... | .... | .... | .... | .... | .... | .... | .... | .... | .... |
| 2003-04 | Worcester IceCats | AHL | 66 | 5 | 9 | 14 | 108 | .... | .... | .... | .... | .... | .... | .... | .... | .... | 10 | 0 | 2 | 2 | 10 | .... | .... | .... | .... |
| 2004-05 | Worcester IceCats | AHL | 75 | 2 | 13 | 15 | 106 | .... | .... | .... | .... | .... | .... | .... | .... | .... | .... | .... | .... | .... | .... | .... | .... | .... | .... |
| 2005-06 | Peoria Rivermen | AHL | 51 | 2 | 7 | 9 | 35 | .... | .... | .... | .... | .... | .... | .... | .... | .... | 4 | 0 | 0 | 0 | 6 | .... | .... | .... | .... |
| 2006-07 | Peoria Rivermen | AHL | 67 | 1 | 6 | 7 | 46 | .... | .... | .... | .... | .... | .... | .... | .... | .... | .... | .... | .... | .... | .... | .... | .... | .... | .... |
| 2007-08 | Peoria Rivermen | AHL | 55 | 0 | 5 | 5 | 20 | .... | .... | .... | .... | .... | .... | .... | .... | .... | .... | .... | .... | .... | .... | .... | .... | .... | .... |
| **2008-09** | **Colorado** | **NHL** | **5** | **0** | **0** | **0** | **0** | **0** | **0** | **0** | **3** | **0.0** | **1** | **0** | **0.0** | **14:38** | .... | .... | .... | .... | .... | .... | .... | .... | .... |
| | Lake Erie | AHL | 52 | 3 | 9 | 12 | 50 | .... | .... | .... | .... | .... | .... | .... | .... | .... | .... | .... | .... | .... | .... | .... | .... | .... | .... |
| | **NHL Totals** | | **5** | **0** | **0** | **0** | **0** | **0** | **0** | **0** | **3** | **0.0** | | **0** | **0.0** | **14:38** | .... | .... | .... | .... | .... | .... | .... | .... | .... |

WCHA First All-Star Team (2003)

Signed as a free agent by **Worcester** (AHL), October 6, 2003. Signed as a free agent by **St. Louis**, June 29, 2004. Signed as a free agent by **Peoria** (AHL), August 24, 2007. Signed as a free agent by **Colorado**, July 14, 2008.

## MacKENZIE, Derek (muh-KEHN-zee, DAIR-ihk) CBJ

Center. Shoots left. 5'11", 185 lbs. Born, Sudbury, Ont., June 11, 1981. Atlanta's 6th choice, 128th overall, in 1999 Entry Draft.

| Season | Club | League | GP | G | A | Pts | PIM | PP | SH | GW | S | % | +/- | TF | F% | Min | GP | G | A | Pts | PIM | PP | SH | GW | Min |
|---|---|---|---|---|---|---|---|---|---|---|---|---|---|---|---|---|---|---|---|---|---|---|---|---|---|
| 1996-97 | Rayside-Balfour | NOJHA | 40 | 23 | 32 | 55 | 40 | .... | .... | .... | .... | .... | .... | .... | .... | .... | .... | .... | .... | .... | .... | .... | .... | .... | .... |
| 1997-98 | Sudbury Wolves | OHL | 59 | 9 | 11 | 20 | 26 | .... | .... | .... | .... | .... | .... | .... | .... | .... | .... | .... | .... | .... | .... | .... | .... | .... | .... |
| 1998-99 | Sudbury Wolves | OHL | 68 | 22 | 65 | 87 | 74 | .... | .... | .... | .... | .... | .... | .... | .... | .... | 4 | 2 | 4 | 6 | 2 | .... | .... | .... | .... |
| 99-2000 | Sudbury Wolves | OHL | 68 | 24 | 33 | 57 | 110 | .... | .... | .... | .... | .... | .... | .... | .... | .... | 12 | 5 | 9 | 14 | 16 | .... | .... | .... | .... |
| 2000-01 | Sudbury Wolves | OHL | 62 | 40 | 49 | 89 | 89 | .... | .... | .... | .... | .... | .... | .... | .... | .... | 12 | 6 | 8 | 14 | 16 | .... | .... | .... | .... |
| **2001-02** | **Atlanta** | **NHL** | **1** | **0** | **0** | **0** | **2** | **0** | **0** | **0** | **1** | **0.0** | **–1** | **16** | **56.3** | **13:51** | .... | .... | .... | .... | .... | .... | .... | .... | .... |
| | Chicago Wolves | AHL | 68 | 13 | 12 | 25 | 80 | .... | .... | .... | .... | .... | .... | .... | .... | .... | 25 | 4 | 2 | 6 | 20 | .... | .... | .... | .... |
| 2002-03 | Chicago Wolves | AHL | 80 | 14 | 18 | 32 | 97 | .... | .... | .... | .... | .... | .... | .... | .... | .... | 9 | 0 | 0 | 0 | 4 | .... | .... | .... | .... |
| **2003-04** | **Atlanta** | **NHL** | **12** | **0** | **1** | **1** | **10** | **0** | **0** | **0** | **7** | **0.0** | **0** | **63** | **46.0** | **6:38** | .... | .... | .... | .... | .... | .... | .... | .... | .... |
| | Chicago Wolves | AHL | 63 | 19 | 16 | 35 | 67 | .... | .... | .... | .... | .... | .... | .... | .... | .... | 10 | 7 | 1 | 8 | 13 | .... | .... | .... | .... |
| 2004-05 | Chicago Wolves | AHL | 78 | 13 | 20 | 33 | 87 | .... | .... | .... | .... | .... | .... | .... | .... | .... | 18 | 5 | 6 | 11 | 33 | .... | .... | .... | .... |
| **2005-06** | **Atlanta** | **NHL** | **11** | **0** | **1** | **1** | **8** | **0** | **0** | **0** | **11** | **0.0** | **0** | **59** | **55.9** | **6:33** | .... | .... | .... | .... | .... | .... | .... | .... | .... |
| | Chicago Wolves | AHL | 36 | 10 | 12 | 22 | 48 | .... | .... | .... | .... | .... | .... | .... | .... | .... | .... | .... | .... | .... | .... | .... | .... | .... | .... |
| **2006-07** | **Atlanta** | **NHL** | **4** | **0** | **0** | **0** | **0** | **0** | **0** | **0** | **3** | **0.0** | **1** | **16** | **56.3** | **5:00** | .... | .... | .... | .... | .... | .... | .... | .... | .... |
| | Chicago Wolves | AHL | 52 | 14 | 23 | 37 | 62 | .... | .... | .... | .... | .... | .... | .... | .... | .... | .... | .... | .... | .... | .... | .... | .... | .... | .... |
| **2007-08** | **Columbus** | **NHL** | **17** | **2** | **0** | **2** | **8** | **0** | **0** | **0** | **19** | **10.5** | **–2** | **73** | **34.3** | **7:47** | .... | .... | .... | .... | .... | .... | .... | .... | .... |
| | Syracuse Crunch | AHL | 62 | 25 | 24 | 49 | 46 | .... | .... | .... | .... | .... | .... | .... | .... | .... | 13 | 6 | 8 | 14 | 22 | .... | .... | .... | .... |
| **2008-09** | **Columbus** | **NHL** | **1** | **0** | **0** | **0** | **2** | **0** | **0** | **0** | **1** | **0.0** | **–1** | **4** | **50.0** | **7:15** | .... | .... | .... | .... | .... | .... | .... | .... | .... |
| | Syracuse Crunch | AHL | 64 | 22 | 30 | 52 | 50 | .... | .... | .... | .... | .... | .... | .... | .... | .... | .... | .... | .... | .... | .... | .... | .... | .... | .... |
| | **NHL Totals** | | **46** | **2** | **2** | **4** | **30** | **0** | **0** | **0** | **42** | **4.8** | | **231** | **46.3** | **7:04** | .... | .... | .... | .... | .... | .... | .... | .... | .... |

Signed as a free agent by **Columbus**, July 11, 2007.

## MADDEN, John (MA-dehn, JAWN) CHI.

Center. Shoots left. 5'11", 190 lbs. Born, Barrie, Ont., May 4, 1973.

| Season | Club | League | GP | G | A | Pts | PIM | PP | SH | GW | S | % | +/- | TF | F% | Min | GP | G | A | Pts | PIM | PP | SH | GW | Min |
|---|---|---|---|---|---|---|---|---|---|---|---|---|---|---|---|---|---|---|---|---|---|---|---|---|---|
| 1989-90 | Alliston Hornets | OHA-C | 31 | 24 | 25 | 49 | 26 | .... | .... | .... | .... | .... | .... | .... | .... | .... | .... | .... | .... | .... | .... | .... | .... | .... | .... |
| 1990-91 | Alliston Hornets | OHA-C | 14 | 15 | 21 | 36 | 10 | .... | .... | .... | .... | .... | .... | .... | .... | .... | .... | .... | .... | .... | .... | .... | .... | .... | .... |
| | Barrie Colts | OHA-B | 1 | 0 | 0 | 0 | 0 | .... | .... | .... | .... | .... | .... | .... | .... | .... | .... | .... | .... | .... | .... | .... | .... | .... | .... |
| 1991-92 | Barrie Colts | OHA-B | 42 | 50 | 54 | 104 | 46 | .... | .... | .... | .... | .... | .... | .... | .... | .... | 13 | 10 | 9 | 19 | 14 | .... | .... | .... | .... |
| 1992-93 | Barrie Colts | COJHL | 43 | 49 | 75 | 124 | 62 | .... | .... | .... | .... | .... | .... | .... | .... | .... | .... | .... | .... | .... | .... | .... | .... | .... | .... |
| 1993-94 | U. of Michigan | CCHA | 36 | 6 | 11 | 17 | 14 | .... | .... | .... | .... | .... | .... | .... | .... | .... | .... | .... | .... | .... | .... | .... | .... | .... | .... |
| 1994-95 | U. of Michigan | CCHA | 39 | 21 | 22 | 43 | 8 | .... | .... | .... | .... | .... | .... | .... | .... | .... | .... | .... | .... | .... | .... | .... | .... | .... | .... |
| 1995-96 | U. of Michigan | CCHA | 43 | 27 | 30 | 57 | 45 | .... | .... | .... | .... | .... | .... | .... | .... | .... | .... | .... | .... | .... | .... | .... | .... | .... | .... |

| Season | Club | League | GP | G | A | Pts | PIM | PP | SH | GW | S | % | +/- | TF | F% | Min | GP | G | A | Pts | PIM | PP | SH | GW | Min |
|---|---|---|---|---|---|---|---|---|---|---|---|---|---|---|---|---|---|---|---|---|---|---|---|---|---|
| | | | Regular Season | | | | | | | | | | | | | | Playoffs | | | | | | | | |
| 1996-97 | U. of Michigan | CCHA | 42 | 26 | 37 | 63 | 56 | .... | .... | .... | .... | .... | .... | .... | .... | .... | .... | .... | .... | .... | .... | .... | .... | .... | .... |
| 1997-98 | Albany River Rats | AHL | 74 | 20 | 36 | 56 | 40 | .... | .... | .... | .... | .... | .... | .... | .... | .... | 13 | 3 | 13 | 16 | 14 | .... | .... | .... | .... |
| **1998-99** | **New Jersey** | **NHL** | **4** | **0** | **1** | **1** | **0** | **0** | **0** | **0** | **4** | **0.0** | **–2** | **0** | **0.0** | **9:13** | .... | .... | .... | .... | .... | .... | .... | .... | .... |
| | Albany River Rats | AHL | 75 | 38 | 60 | 98 | 44 | .... | .... | .... | .... | .... | .... | .... | .... | .... | 5 | 2 | 2 | 4 | 6 | .... | .... | .... | .... |
| **99-2000♦** | **New Jersey** | **NHL** | **74** | **16** | **9** | **25** | **6** | **0** | **6** | **3** | **115** | **13.9** | **7** | **770** | **47.5** | **11:40** | **20** | **3** | **4** | **7** | **0** | **0** | **1** | **2** | **15:30** |
| **2000-01** | **New Jersey** | **NHL** | **80** | **23** | **15** | **38** | **12** | **0** | **3** | **4** | **163** | **14.1** | **24** | **974** | **46.6** | **15:35** | **25** | **4** | **3** | **7** | **6** | **0** | **0** | **0** | **15:15** |
| **2001-02** | **New Jersey** | **NHL** | **82** | **15** | **8** | **23** | **25** | **0** | **0** | **2** | **170** | **8.8** | **6** | **1001** | **47.0** | **15:36** | **6** | **0** | **0** | **0** | **0** | **0** | **0** | **0** | **17:25** |
| **2002-03♦** | **New Jersey** | **NHL** | **80** | **19** | **22** | **41** | **26** | **2** | **2** | **3** | **207** | **9.2** | **13** | **1502** | **50.9** | **18:18** | **24** | **6** | **10** | **16** | **2** | **2** | **1** | **1** | **19:38** |
| **2003-04** | **New Jersey** | **NHL** | **80** | **12** | **23** | **35** | **22** | **1** | **1** | **1** | **210** | **5.7** | **7** | **1377** | **53.3** | **17:17** | **5** | **0** | **0** | **0** | **0** | **0** | **0** | **0** | **14:51** |
| 2004-05 | HIFK Helsinki | Finland | 3 | 0 | 0 | 0 | 0 | .... | .... | .... | .... | .... | .... | .... | .... | .... | .... | .... | .... | .... | .... | .... | .... | .... | .... |
| **2005-06** | **New Jersey** | **NHL** | **82** | **16** | **20** | **36** | **36** | **0** | **1** | **0** | **194** | **8.2** | **–7** | **1613** | **51.5** | **18:59** | **9** | **4** | **1** | **5** | **8** | **0** | **2** | **0** | **18:56** |
| **2006-07** | **New Jersey** | **NHL** | **74** | **12** | **20** | **32** | **14** | **0** | **0** | **1** | **153** | **7.8** | **–7** | **1366** | **49.8** | **18:53** | **11** | **1** | **1** | **2** | **2** | **0** | **0** | **0** | **21:17** |
| **2007-08** | **New Jersey** | **NHL** | **80** | **20** | **23** | **43** | **26** | **3** | **3** | **3** | **185** | **10.8** | **1** | **1463** | **53.7** | **19:27** | **5** | **2** | **1** | **3** | **2** | **0** | **0** | **1** | **21:18** |
| **2008-09** | **New Jersey** | **NHL** | **76** | **7** | **16** | **23** | **26** | **0** | **1** | **2** | **132** | **5.3** | **–7** | **1160** | **51.6** | **16:25** | **7** | **0** | **1** | **1** | **4** | **0** | **0** | **0** | **18:24** |
| | **NHL Totals** | | **712** | **140** | **157** | **297** | **193** | **6** | **17** | **19** | **1533** | **9.1** | | **11226** | **50.6** | **16:54** | **112** | **20** | **21** | **41** | **24** | **2** | **4** | **4** | **17:41** |

CCHA First All-Star Team (1997) • NCAA West First All-American Team (1997) • Frank J. Selke Trophy (2001)

Signed as a free agent by **New Jersey**, June 26, 1997. Signed as a free agent by **HIFK Helsinki** (Finland), November 29, 2004. Signed as a free agent by **Chicago**, July 2, 2009.

## MAIR, Adam

(MAIR, A-duhm) **BUF.**

Center. Shoots right. 6'1", 208 lbs. Born, Hamilton, Ont., February 15, 1979. Toronto's 2nd choice, 84th overall, in 1997 Entry Draft.

| Season | Club | League | GP | G | A | Pts | PIM | PP | SH | GW | S | % | +/- | TF | F% | Min | GP | G | A | Pts | PIM | PP | SH | GW | Min |
|---|---|---|---|---|---|---|---|---|---|---|---|---|---|---|---|---|---|---|---|---|---|---|---|---|---|
| 1994-95 | Ohsweken | OHA-B | 39 | 21 | 23 | 44 | 91 | .... | .... | .... | .... | .... | .... | .... | .... | .... | .... | .... | .... | .... | .... | .... | .... | .... | .... |
| 1995-96 | Owen Sound | OHL | 62 | 12 | 15 | 27 | 63 | .... | .... | .... | .... | .... | .... | .... | .... | .... | 6 | 0 | 0 | 0 | 2 | .... | .... | .... | .... |
| 1996-97 | Owen Sound | OHL | 65 | 16 | 35 | 51 | 113 | .... | .... | .... | .... | .... | .... | .... | .... | .... | 4 | 1 | 0 | 1 | 2 | .... | .... | .... | .... |
| 1997-98 | Owen Sound | OHL | 56 | 25 | 27 | 52 | 179 | .... | .... | .... | .... | .... | .... | .... | .... | .... | 11 | 6 | 3 | 9 | 31 | .... | .... | .... | .... |
| **1998-99** | Owen Sound | OHL | 43 | 23 | 41 | 64 | 109 | .... | .... | .... | .... | .... | .... | .... | .... | .... | 16 | 10 | 10 | 20 | *47 | .... | .... | .... | .... |
| | **Toronto** | **NHL** | .... | .... | .... | .... | .... | .... | .... | .... | .... | .... | .... | .... | .... | .... | **5** | **1** | **0** | **1** | **14** | **0** | **0** | **0** | **5:37** |
| | St. John's | AHL | .... | .... | .... | .... | .... | .... | .... | .... | .... | .... | .... | .... | .... | .... | 3 | 1 | 0 | 1 | 6 | .... | .... | .... | .... |
| **99-2000** | **Toronto** | **NHL** | **8** | **1** | **0** | **1** | **6** | **0** | **0** | **0** | **7** | **14.3** | **–1** | **9** | **33.3** | **11:33** | **5** | **0** | **0** | **0** | **8** | **0** | **0** | **0** | **10:15** |
| | St. John's | AHL | 66 | 22 | 27 | 49 | 124 | .... | .... | .... | .... | .... | .... | .... | .... | .... | .... | .... | .... | .... | .... | .... | .... | .... | .... |
| **2000-01** | **Toronto** | **NHL** | **16** | **0** | **2** | **2** | **14** | **0** | **0** | **0** | **17** | **0.0** | **3** | **56** | **51.8** | **9:01** | .... | .... | .... | .... | .... | .... | .... | .... | .... |
| | St. John's | AHL | 47 | 18 | 27 | 45 | 69 | .... | .... | .... | .... | .... | .... | .... | .... | .... | .... | .... | .... | .... | .... | .... | .... | .... | .... |
| | **Los Angeles** | **NHL** | **10** | **0** | **0** | **0** | **6** | **0** | **0** | **0** | **5** | **0.0** | **–3** | **21** | **61.9** | **6:14** | .... | .... | .... | .... | .... | .... | .... | .... | .... |
| **2001-02** | **Los Angeles** | **NHL** | **18** | **1** | **1** | **2** | **57** | **0** | **0** | **0** | **10** | **10.0** | **1** | **31** | **58.1** | **7:11** | .... | .... | .... | .... | .... | .... | .... | .... | .... |
| | Manchester | AHL | 27 | 10 | 9 | 19 | 48 | .... | .... | .... | .... | .... | .... | .... | .... | .... | 5 | 5 | 1 | 6 | 10 | .... | .... | .... | .... |
| **2002-03** | **Buffalo** | **NHL** | **79** | **6** | **11** | **17** | **146** | **0** | **1** | **1** | **83** | **7.2** | **–4** | **572** | **51.2** | **10:37** | .... | .... | .... | .... | .... | .... | .... | .... | .... |
| **2003-04** | **Buffalo** | **NHL** | **81** | **6** | **14** | **20** | **146** | **1** | **0** | **1** | **82** | **7.3** | **–3** | **340** | **45.9** | **9:38** | .... | .... | .... | .... | .... | .... | .... | .... | .... |
| 2004-05 | | | | DID NOT PLAY | | | | | | | | | | | | | | | | | | | | | |
| **2005-06** | **Buffalo** | **NHL** | **40** | **2** | **5** | **7** | **47** | **0** | **0** | **0** | **40** | **5.0** | **–2** | **12** | **41.7** | **7:59** | **3** | **0** | **0** | **0** | **0** | **0** | **0** | **0** | **9:17** |
| **2006-07** | **Buffalo** | **NHL** | **82** | **2** | **9** | **11** | **128** | **0** | **0** | **0** | **73** | **2.7** | **–1** | **130** | **46.2** | **7:33** | **16** | **1** | **4** | **5** | **10** | **0** | **0** | **0** | **7:33** |
| **2007-08** | **Buffalo** | **NHL** | **72** | **5** | **12** | **17** | **66** | **0** | **0** | **2** | **62** | **8.1** | **–2** | **361** | **45.4** | **8:52** | .... | .... | .... | .... | .... | .... | .... | .... | .... |
| **2008-09** | **Buffalo** | **NHL** | **75** | **8** | **11** | **19** | **95** | **0** | **0** | **1** | **75** | **10.7** | **4** | **414** | **48.3** | **10:35** | .... | .... | .... | .... | .... | .... | .... | .... | .... |
| | **NHL Totals** | | **481** | **31** | **65** | **96** | **711** | **1** | **1** | **5** | **454** | **6.8** | | **1946** | **48.4** | **9:11** | **29** | **2** | **4** | **6** | **32** | **0** | **0** | **0** | **7:52** |

Traded to **Los Angeles** by **Toronto** with Toronto's 2nd round choice (Michael Cammalleri) in 2001 Entry Draft for Aki Berg, March 13, 2001. Traded to **Buffalo** by **Los Angeles** with Los Angeles' 5th round choice (Thomas Morrow) in 2003 Entry Draft for Erik Rasmussen, July 24, 2002. • Missed majority of 2005-06 season recovering from groin (training camp) and head (January 12, 2006 vs. Phoenix) injuries.

## MAKI, Tomi

(MA-kee, TAW-mee) **CGY.**

Right wing. Shoots left. 5'11", 193 lbs. Born, Helsinki, Finland, August 19, 1983. Calgary's 4th choice, 108th overall, in 2001 Entry Draft.

| Season | Club | League | GP | G | A | Pts | PIM | PP | SH | GW | S | % | +/- | TF | F% | Min | GP | G | A | Pts | PIM | PP | SH | GW | Min |
|---|---|---|---|---|---|---|---|---|---|---|---|---|---|---|---|---|---|---|---|---|---|---|---|---|---|
| 99-2000 | Jokerit Helsinki Jr. | Fin-Jr. | 33 | 6 | 1 | 7 | 12 | .... | .... | .... | .... | .... | .... | .... | .... | .... | 3 | 0 | 0 | 0 | 0 | .... | .... | .... | .... |
| 2000-01 | Jokerit U18 | Fin-U18 | 10 | 4 | 10 | 14 | 4 | .... | .... | .... | .... | .... | .... | .... | .... | .... | 6 | 4 | 3 | 7 | 0 | .... | .... | .... | .... |
| | Jokerit Helsinki Jr. | Fin-Jr. | 39 | 7 | 8 | 15 | 10 | .... | .... | .... | .... | .... | .... | .... | .... | .... | 2 | 0 | 0 | 0 | 2 | .... | .... | .... | .... |
| 2001-02 | Jokerit Helsinki Jr. | Fin-Jr. | 29 | 12 | 13 | 25 | 12 | .... | .... | .... | .... | .... | .... | .... | .... | .... | 1 | 0 | 0 | 0 | 2 | .... | .... | .... | .... |
| | Kiekko-Vantaa | Finland-2 | 5 | 0 | 0 | 0 | 0 | .... | .... | .... | .... | .... | .... | .... | .... | .... | .... | .... | .... | .... | .... | .... | .... | .... | .... |
| | Jokerit Helsinki | Finland | 8 | 0 | 1 | 1 | 2 | .... | .... | .... | .... | .... | .... | .... | .... | .... | .... | .... | .... | .... | .... | .... | .... | .... | .... |
| 2002-03 | Jokerit Helsinki Jr. | Fin-Jr. | 14 | 4 | 4 | 8 | 12 | .... | .... | .... | .... | .... | .... | .... | .... | .... | 11 | 3 | 3 | 6 | 4 | .... | .... | .... | .... |
| | Kiekko-Vantaa | Finland-2 | 3 | 1 | 0 | 1 | 4 | .... | .... | .... | .... | .... | .... | .... | .... | .... | .... | .... | .... | .... | .... | .... | .... | .... | .... |
| | Jokerit Helsinki | Finland | 18 | 2 | 2 | 4 | 4 | .... | .... | .... | .... | .... | .... | .... | .... | .... | 1 | 0 | 0 | 0 | 0 | .... | .... | .... | .... |
| 2003-04 | Jokerit Helsinki | Finland | 50 | 5 | 5 | 10 | 14 | .... | .... | .... | .... | .... | .... | .... | .... | .... | 8 | 0 | 0 | 0 | 0 | .... | .... | .... | .... |
| 2004-05 | Jokerit Helsinki | Finland | 51 | 1 | 4 | 5 | 14 | .... | .... | .... | .... | .... | .... | .... | .... | .... | 12 | 1 | 1 | 2 | 2 | .... | .... | .... | .... |
| 2005-06 | Omaha | AHL | 80 | 12 | 17 | 29 | 33 | .... | .... | .... | .... | .... | .... | .... | .... | .... | .... | .... | .... | .... | .... | .... | .... | .... | .... |
| **2006-07** | **Calgary** | **NHL** | **1** | **0** | **0** | **0** | **0** | **0** | **0** | **0** | **0** | **0.0** | **0** | **0** | **0.0** | **10:56** | .... | .... | .... | .... | .... | .... | .... | .... | .... |
| | Omaha | AHL | 67 | 4 | 11 | 15 | 20 | .... | .... | .... | .... | .... | .... | .... | .... | .... | 6 | 1 | 1 | 2 | 2 | .... | .... | .... | .... |
| 2007-08 | Quad City Flames | AHL | 78 | 8 | 5 | 13 | 38 | .... | .... | .... | .... | .... | .... | .... | .... | .... | .... | .... | .... | .... | .... | .... | .... | .... | .... |
| 2008-09 | Jokerit Helsinki | Finland | 57 | 7 | 9 | 16 | 49 | .... | .... | .... | .... | .... | .... | .... | .... | .... | 5 | 0 | 0 | 0 | 6 | .... | .... | .... | .... |
| | **NHL Totals** | | **1** | **0** | **0** | **0** | **0** | **0** | **0** | **0** | **0** | **0.0** | | **0** | **0.0** | **10:56** | .... | .... | .... | .... | .... | .... | .... | .... | .... |

## MALHOTRA, Manny

(mal-HOH-truh, MAN-ee)

Center. Shoots left. 6'2", 217 lbs. Born, Mississauga, Ont., May 18, 1980. NY Rangers' 1st choice, 7th overall, in 1998 Entry Draft.

| Season | Club | League | GP | G | A | Pts | PIM | PP | SH | GW | S | % | +/- | TF | F% | Min | GP | G | A | Pts | PIM | PP | SH | GW | Min |
|---|---|---|---|---|---|---|---|---|---|---|---|---|---|---|---|---|---|---|---|---|---|---|---|---|---|
| 1995-96 | Mississauga Reps | MTHL | 54 | 27 | 44 | 71 | 62 | .... | .... | .... | .... | .... | .... | .... | .... | .... | .... | .... | .... | .... | .... | .... | .... | .... | .... |
| 1996-97 | Guelph Storm | OHL | 61 | 16 | 28 | 44 | 26 | .... | .... | .... | .... | .... | .... | .... | .... | .... | 18 | 7 | 7 | 14 | 11 | .... | .... | .... | .... |
| 1997-98 | Guelph Storm | OHL | 57 | 16 | 35 | 51 | 29 | .... | .... | .... | .... | .... | .... | .... | .... | .... | 12 | 7 | 6 | 13 | 8 | .... | .... | .... | .... |
| **1998-99** | **NY Rangers** | **NHL** | **73** | **8** | **8** | **16** | **13** | **1** | **0** | **2** | **61** | **13.1** | **–2** | **588** | **43.9** | **8:36** | .... | .... | .... | .... | .... | .... | .... | .... | .... |
| **99-2000** | **NY Rangers** | **NHL** | **27** | **0** | **0** | **0** | **4** | **0** | **0** | **0** | **18** | **0.0** | **–6** | **132** | **44.7** | **6:42** | .... | .... | .... | .... | .... | .... | .... | .... | .... |
| | Guelph Storm | OHL | 5 | 2 | 2 | 4 | 4 | .... | .... | .... | .... | .... | .... | .... | .... | .... | 6 | 0 | 2 | 2 | 4 | .... | .... | .... | .... |
| | Hartford | AHL | 12 | 1 | 5 | 6 | 2 | .... | .... | .... | .... | .... | .... | .... | .... | .... | 23 | 1 | 2 | 3 | 10 | .... | .... | .... | .... |
| **2000-01** | **NY Rangers** | **NHL** | **50** | **4** | **8** | **12** | **31** | **0** | **0** | **2** | **46** | **8.7** | **–10** | **248** | **44.4** | **9:03** | .... | .... | .... | .... | .... | .... | .... | .... | .... |
| | Hartford | AHL | 28 | 5 | 6 | 11 | 69 | .... | .... | .... | .... | .... | .... | .... | .... | .... | 5 | 0 | 0 | 0 | 0 | .... | .... | .... | .... |
| **2001-02** | **NY Rangers** | **NHL** | **56** | **7** | **6** | **13** | **42** | **0** | **1** | **1** | **41** | **17.1** | **–1** | **310** | **42.9** | **10:14** | .... | .... | .... | .... | .... | .... | .... | .... | .... |
| | **Dallas** | **NHL** | **16** | **1** | **0** | **1** | **5** | **0** | **0** | **0** | **19** | **5.3** | **–3** | **121** | **48.8** | **10:37** | .... | .... | .... | .... | .... | .... | .... | .... | .... |
| **2002-03** | **Dallas** | **NHL** | **59** | **3** | **7** | **10** | **42** | **0** | **0** | **1** | **62** | **4.8** | **–2** | **447** | **47.0** | **9:22** | **5** | **1** | **0** | **1** | **0** | **0** | **0** | **0** | **8:13** |
| **2003-04** | **Dallas** | **NHL** | **9** | **0** | **0** | **0** | **4** | **0** | **0** | **0** | **4** | **0.0** | **–2** | **13** | **61.5** | **7:48** | .... | .... | .... | .... | .... | .... | .... | .... | .... |
| | **Columbus** | **NHL** | **56** | **12** | **13** | **25** | **24** | **1** | **0** | **2** | **103** | **11.7** | **–5** | **840** | **53.8** | **14:47** | .... | .... | .... | .... | .... | .... | .... | .... | .... |
| 2004-05 | Ljubljana | Slovenia | 13 | 6 | 7 | 13 | 20 | .... | .... | .... | .... | .... | .... | .... | .... | .... | .... | .... | .... | .... | .... | .... | .... | .... | .... |
| | Ljubljana | Interliga | 13 | 7 | 7 | 14 | 16 | .... | .... | .... | .... | .... | .... | .... | .... | .... | .... | .... | .... | .... | .... | .... | .... | .... | .... |
| | HV 71 Jonkoping | Sweden | 20 | 5 | 2 | 7 | 16 | .... | .... | .... | .... | .... | .... | .... | .... | .... | .... | .... | .... | .... | .... | .... | .... | .... | .... |
| **2005-06** | **Columbus** | **NHL** | **58** | **10** | **21** | **31** | **41** | **1** | **1** | **0** | **102** | **9.8** | **1** | **827** | **56.4** | **16:21** | .... | .... | .... | .... | .... | .... | .... | .... | .... |
| **2006-07** | **Columbus** | **NHL** | **82** | **9** | **16** | **25** | **76** | **2** | **0** | **3** | **109** | **8.3** | **–8** | **1127** | **55.1** | **14:48** | .... | .... | .... | .... | .... | .... | .... | .... | .... |
| **2007-08** | **Columbus** | **NHL** | **71** | **11** | **18** | **29** | **34** | **2** | **0** | **2** | **112** | **9.8** | **–3** | **1158** | **59.0** | **16:28** | .... | .... | .... | .... | .... | .... | .... | .... | .... |
| **2008-09** | **Columbus** | **NHL** | **77** | **11** | **24** | **35** | **28** | **0** | **0** | **3** | **116** | **9.5** | **9** | **1380** | **58.0** | **18:01** | **4** | **0** | **0** | **0** | **0** | **0** | **0** | **0** | **17:54** |
| | **NHL Totals** | | **634** | **76** | **121** | **197** | **344** | **7** | **2** | **16** | **793** | **9.6** | | **7191** | **53.7** | **12:53** | **9** | **1** | **0** | **1** | **0** | **0** | **0** | **0** | **12:31** |

Memorial Cup Tournament All-Star Team (1998) • George Parsons Trophy (Memorial Cup Tournament - Most Sportsmanlike Player) (1998)

Traded to **Dallas** by **NY Rangers** with Barrett Heisten for Martin Rucinsky and Roman Lyashenko, March 12, 2002. Claimed on waivers by **Columbus** from **Dallas**, November 21, 2003. Signed as a free agent by **Ljubljana** (Slovenia), October 8, 2004. Signed as a free agent by **Jonkoping** (Sweden), December 20, 2004.

## MALIK, Marek

(MAW-leck, MAIR-ehk)

Defense. Shoots left. 6'6", 235 lbs. Born, Ostrava, Czech., June 24, 1975. Hartford's 2nd choice, 72nd overall, in 1993 Entry Draft.

| Season | Club | League | GP | G | A | Pts | PIM | PP | SH | GW | S | % | +/- | TF | F% | Min | GP | G | A | Pts | PIM | PP | SH | GW | Min |
|---|---|---|---|---|---|---|---|---|---|---|---|---|---|---|---|---|---|---|---|---|---|---|---|---|---|
| 1992-93 | TJ Vitkovice Jr. | Czech-Jr. | 20 | 5 | 10 | 15 | 16 | .... | .... | .... | .... | .... | .... | .... | .... | .... | .... | .... | .... | .... | .... | .... | .... | .... | .... |
| 1993-94 | HC Vitkovice | CzRep | 38 | 3 | 3 | 6 | 0 | .... | .... | .... | .... | .... | .... | .... | .... | .... | 3 | 0 | 1 | 1 | 0 | .... | .... | .... | .... |
| **1994-95** | Springfield | AHL | 58 | 11 | 30 | 41 | 91 | .... | .... | .... | .... | .... | .... | .... | .... | .... | .... | .... | .... | .... | .... | .... | .... | .... | .... |
| | **Hartford** | **NHL** | **1** | **0** | **1** | **1** | **0** | **0** | **0** | **0** | **0** | **0.0** | **1** | .... | .... | .... | .... | .... | .... | .... | .... | .... | .... | .... | .... |
| **1995-96** | **Hartford** | **NHL** | **7** | **0** | **0** | **0** | **4** | **0** | **0** | **0** | **2** | **0.0** | **–3** | .... | .... | .... | .... | .... | .... | .... | .... | .... | .... | .... | .... |
| | Springfield | AHL | 68 | 8 | 14 | 22 | 135 | .... | .... | .... | .... | .... | .... | .... | .... | .... | 8 | 1 | 3 | 4 | 20 | .... | .... | .... | .... |
| **1996-97** | **Hartford** | **NHL** | **47** | **1** | **5** | **6** | **50** | **0** | **0** | **1** | **33** | **3.0** | **5** | .... | .... | .... | .... | .... | .... | .... | .... | .... | .... | .... | .... |
| | Springfield | AHL | 3 | 0 | 3 | 3 | 4 | .... | .... | .... | .... | .... | .... | .... | .... | .... | .... | .... | .... | .... | .... | .... | .... | .... | .... |
| 1997-98 | Malmo | Sweden | 37 | 1 | 5 | 6 | 21 | .... | .... | .... | .... | .... | .... | .... | .... | .... | .... | .... | .... | .... | .... | .... | .... | .... | .... |

| | | | Regular Season | | | | | | | | | | | | | | Playoffs | | | | | | | | |
|---|---|---|---|---|---|---|---|---|---|---|---|---|---|---|---|---|---|---|---|---|---|---|---|---|---|
| Season | Club | League | GP | G | A | Pts | PIM | PP | SH | GW | S | % | +/- | TF | F% | Min | GP | G | A | Pts | PIM | PP | SH | GW | Min |
| 1998-99 | HC Vitkovice | CzRep | 1 | 1 | 0 | 1 | 6 | .... | .... | .... | .... | .... | .... | .... | .... | .... | .... | .... | .... | .... | .... | .... | .... | .... | .... |
| | **Carolina** | **NHL** | **52** | **2** | **9** | **11** | **36** | **1** | **0** | **0** | **36** | **5.6** | **–6** | **0** | **0.0** | **21:14** | **4** | **0** | **0** | **0** | **4** | **0** | **0** | **0** | **11:26** |
| | New Haven | AHL | 21 | 2 | 8 | 10 | 28 | .... | .... | .... | .... | .... | .... | .... | .... | .... | .... | .... | .... | .... | .... | .... | .... | .... | .... |
| **99-2000** | **Carolina** | **NHL** | **57** | **4** | **10** | **14** | **63** | **0** | **0** | **1** | **57** | **7.0** | **13** | **0** | **0.0** | **18:00** | .... | .... | .... | .... | .... | .... | .... | .... | .... |
| **2000-01** | **Carolina** | **NHL** | **61** | **6** | **14** | **20** | **34** | **1** | **0** | **1** | **72** | **8.3** | **–4** | **0** | **0.0** | **19:36** | **3** | **0** | **0** | **0** | **6** | **0** | **0** | **0** | **19:37** |
| **2001-02** | **Carolina** | **NHL** | **82** | **4** | **19** | **23** | **88** | **0** | **0** | **0** | **91** | **4.4** | **8** | **0** | **0.0** | **20:29** | **23** | **0** | **3** | **3** | **18** | **0** | **0** | **0** | **18:09** |
| **2002-03** | **Carolina** | **NHL** | **10** | **0** | **2** | **2** | **16** | **0** | **0** | **0** | **9** | **0.0** | **–3** | **0** | **0.0** | **17:02** | .... | .... | .... | .... | .... | .... | .... | .... | .... |
| | **Vancouver** | **NHL** | **69** | **7** | **11** | **18** | **52** | **1** | **1** | **2** | **68** | **10.3** | **23** | **1** | **0.0** | **18:06** | **14** | **1** | **1** | **2** | **10** | **1** | **0** | **0** | **16:06** |
| **2003-04** | **Vancouver** | **NHL** | **78** | **3** | **16** | **19** | **45** | **0** | **0** | **0** | **61** | **4.9** | **35** | **1** | **0.0** | **18:05** | **7** | **0** | **0** | **0** | **10** | **0** | **0** | **0** | **20:03** |
| 2004-05 | Vitkovice | CzRep | 42 | 1 | 9 | 10 | 50 | .... | .... | .... | .... | .... | .... | .... | .... | .... | 7 | 0 | 0 | 0 | 37 | .... | .... | .... | .... |
| **2005-06** | **NY Rangers** | **NHL** | **74** | **2** | **16** | **18** | **78** | **0** | **0** | **2** | **70** | **2.9** | **28** | **0** | **0.0** | **20:26** | **4** | **0** | **1** | **1** | **6** | **0** | **0** | **0** | **20:43** |
| | Czech Republic | Olympics | 8 | 0 | 0 | 0 | 8 | .... | .... | .... | .... | .... | .... | .... | .... | .... | .... | .... | .... | .... | .... | .... | .... | .... | .... |
| **2006-07** | **NY Rangers** | **NHL** | **69** | **2** | **19** | **21** | **70** | **0** | **0** | **0** | **57** | **3.5** | **32** | **2** | **0.0** | **19:16** | **10** | **1** | **3** | **4** | **10** | **0** | **0** | **0** | **21:25** |
| **2007-08** | **NY Rangers** | **NHL** | **42** | **2** | **8** | **10** | **48** | **0** | **0** | **0** | **34** | **5.9** | **7** | **0** | **0.0** | **19:14** | .... | .... | .... | .... | .... | .... | .... | .... | .... |
| **2008-09** | **Tampa Bay** | **NHL** | **42** | **0** | **5** | **5** | **36** | **0** | **0** | **0** | **22** | **0.0** | **–3** | **0** | **0.0** | **19:10** | .... | .... | .... | .... | .... | .... | .... | .... | .... |
| | **NHL Totals** | | **691** | **33** | **135** | **168** | **620** | **3** | **1** | **7** | **612** | **5.4** | | **4** | **0.0** | **19:19** | **65** | **2** | **8** | **10** | **64** | **1** | **0** | **0** | **18:14** |

• Transferred to **Carolina** after **Hartford** franchise relocated, June 25, 1997. Traded to **Vancouver** by **Carolina** with Darren Langdon for Jan Hlavac and Harold Druken, November 1, 2002. Signed as a free agent by **Vitkovice** (CzRep), September 17, 2004. Signed as a free agent by **NY Rangers**, August 2, 2005. Signed as a free agent by **Tampa Bay**, October 23, 2008.

## MALKIN, Evgeni

(MAHL-kihn, ehv-GEH-nee) **PIT.**

Center. Shoots left. 6'3", 195 lbs. Born, Magnitogorsk, USSR, July 31, 1986. Pittsburgh's 1st choice, 2nd overall, in 2004 Entry Draft.

| Season | Club | League | GP | G | A | Pts | PIM | PP | SH | GW | S | % | +/- | TF | F% | Min | GP | G | A | Pts | PIM | PP | SH | GW | Min |
|---|---|---|---|---|---|---|---|---|---|---|---|---|---|---|---|---|---|---|---|---|---|---|---|---|---|
| 2003-04 | Magnitogorsk 2 | Russia-3 | 2 | 1 | 0 | 1 | 8 | .... | .... | .... | .... | .... | .... | .... | .... | .... | .... | .... | .... | .... | .... | .... | .... | .... | .... |
| | Magnitogorsk | Russia | 34 | 3 | 9 | 12 | 12 | .... | .... | .... | .... | .... | .... | .... | .... | .... | .... | .... | .... | .... | .... | .... | .... | .... | .... |
| 2004-05 | Magnitogorsk 2 | Russia-3 | 2 | 1 | 1 | 2 | 2 | .... | .... | .... | .... | .... | .... | .... | .... | .... | .... | .... | .... | .... | .... | .... | .... | .... | .... |
| | Magnitogorsk | Russia | 52 | 12 | 20 | 32 | 24 | .... | .... | .... | .... | .... | .... | .... | .... | .... | 5 | 0 | 4 | 4 | 0 | .... | .... | .... | .... |
| 2005-06 | Magnitogorsk | Russia | 46 | 21 | 26 | 47 | 46 | .... | .... | .... | .... | .... | .... | .... | .... | .... | 11 | 5 | 10 | 15 | 41 | .... | .... | .... | .... |
| | Russia | Olympics | 7 | 2 | 4 | 6 | 31 | .... | .... | .... | .... | .... | .... | .... | .... | .... | .... | .... | .... | .... | .... | .... | .... | .... | .... |
| **2006-07** | **Pittsburgh** | **NHL** | **78** | **33** | **52** | **85** | **80** | **16** | **0** | **6** | **242** | **13.6** | **2** | **728** | **43.3** | **19:10** | **5** | **0** | **4** | **4** | **8** | **0** | **0** | **0** | **19:34** |
| **2007-08** | **Pittsburgh** | **NHL** | **82** | **47** | **59** | **106** | **78** | **17** | **0** | **5** | **272** | **17.3** | **16** | **890** | **39.3** | **21:19** | **20** | **10** | **12** | **22** | **24** | **5** | **1** | **3** | **20:48** |
| **2008-09♦** | **Pittsburgh** | **NHL** | **82** | **35** | ***78** | ***113** | **80** | **14** | **2** | **4** | **290** | **12.1** | **17** | **668** | **42.4** | **22:31** | **24** | **14** | ***22** | ***36** | **51** | **7** | **0** | **3** | **20:57** |
| | **NHL Totals** | | **242** | **115** | **189** | **304** | **238** | **47** | **2** | **15** | **804** | **14.3** | | **2286** | **41.5** | **21:02** | **49** | **24** | **38** | **62** | **83** | **12** | **1** | **6** | **20:45** |

NHL All-Rookie Team (2007) • Calder Memorial Trophy (2007) • NHL First All-Star Team (2008, 2009) • Art Ross Trophy (2009) • Conn Smythe Trophy (2009)
Played in NHL All-Star Game (2008, 2009)

## MALONE, Ryan

(MA-lohn, RIGH-uhn) **T.B.**

Left wing. Shoots left. 6'4", 224 lbs. Born, Pittsburgh, PA, December 1, 1979. Pittsburgh's 5th choice, 115th overall, in 1999 Entry Draft.

| Season | Club | League | GP | G | A | Pts | PIM | PP | SH | GW | S | % | +/- | TF | F% | Min | GP | G | A | Pts | PIM | PP | SH | GW | Min |
|---|---|---|---|---|---|---|---|---|---|---|---|---|---|---|---|---|---|---|---|---|---|---|---|---|---|
| 1997-98 | Shat.-St. Mary's | High-MN | 50 | 41 | 44 | 85 | 69 | .... | .... | .... | .... | .... | .... | .... | .... | .... | .... | .... | .... | .... | .... | .... | .... | .... | .... |
| 1998-99 | Omaha Lancers | USHL | 51 | 14 | 22 | 36 | 81 | .... | .... | .... | .... | .... | .... | .... | .... | .... | 12 | 2 | 4 | 6 | 23 | .... | .... | .... | .... |
| 99-2000 | St. Cloud State | WCHA | 38 | 9 | 21 | 30 | 68 | .... | .... | .... | .... | .... | .... | .... | .... | .... | .... | .... | .... | .... | .... | .... | .... | .... | .... |
| 2000-01 | St. Cloud State | WCHA | 36 | 7 | 18 | 25 | 52 | .... | .... | .... | .... | .... | .... | .... | .... | .... | .... | .... | .... | .... | .... | .... | .... | .... | .... |
| 2001-02 | St. Cloud State | WCHA | 41 | 24 | 25 | 49 | 76 | .... | .... | .... | .... | .... | .... | .... | .... | .... | .... | .... | .... | .... | .... | .... | .... | .... | .... |
| 2002-03 | St. Cloud State | WCHA | 27 | 16 | 20 | 36 | 85 | .... | .... | .... | .... | .... | .... | .... | .... | .... | .... | .... | .... | .... | .... | .... | .... | .... | .... |
| | Wilkes-Barre | AHL | 3 | 0 | 1 | 1 | 2 | .... | .... | .... | .... | .... | .... | .... | .... | .... | .... | .... | .... | .... | .... | .... | .... | .... | .... |
| **2003-04** | **Pittsburgh** | **NHL** | **81** | **22** | **21** | **43** | **64** | **5** | **3** | **4** | **139** | **15.8** | **–23** | **230** | **27.4** | **18:54** | .... | .... | .... | .... | .... | .... | .... | .... | .... |
| 2004-05 | Blues Espoo | Finland | 9 | 2 | 1 | 3 | 36 | .... | .... | .... | .... | .... | .... | .... | .... | .... | .... | .... | .... | .... | .... | .... | .... | .... | .... |
| | SV Renon | Italy | 10 | 6 | 2 | 8 | 20 | .... | .... | .... | .... | .... | .... | .... | .... | .... | 6 | 4 | 4 | 8 | 36 | .... | .... | .... | .... |
| | HC Ambri-Piotta | Swiss | .... | .... | .... | .... | .... | .... | .... | .... | .... | .... | .... | .... | .... | .... | 1 | 0 | 0 | 0 | 2 | .... | .... | .... | .... |
| **2005-06** | **Pittsburgh** | **NHL** | **77** | **22** | **22** | **44** | **63** | **10** | **5** | **1** | **153** | **14.4** | **–22** | **728** | **39.6** | **18:06** | .... | .... | .... | .... | .... | .... | .... | .... | .... |
| **2006-07** | **Pittsburgh** | **NHL** | **64** | **16** | **15** | **31** | **71** | **1** | **1** | **0** | **125** | **12.8** | **4** | **109** | **44.0** | **16:15** | **5** | **0** | **0** | **0** | **0** | **0** | **0** | **0** | **13:48** |
| **2007-08** | **Pittsburgh** | **NHL** | **77** | **27** | **24** | **51** | **103** | **11** | **2** | **6** | **159** | **17.0** | **14** | **38** | **31.6** | **19:05** | **20** | **6** | **10** | **16** | **25** | **3** | **0** | **2** | **18:43** |
| **2008-09** | **Tampa Bay** | **NHL** | **70** | **26** | **19** | **45** | **98** | **7** | **0** | **3** | **124** | **21.0** | **4** | **47** | **29.8** | **17:45** | .... | .... | .... | .... | .... | .... | .... | .... | .... |
| | **NHL Totals** | | **369** | **113** | **101** | **214** | **399** | **34** | **11** | **14** | **700** | **16.1** | | **1152** | **36.9** | **18:05** | **25** | **6** | **10** | **16** | **25** | **3** | **0** | **2** | **17:44** |

NHL All-Rookie Team (2004)
Signed as a free agent by **Espoo** (Finland), September 29, 2004. Signed as a free agent by **Renon** (Italy), January 3, 2005. Signed as a free agent by **Ambri-Piotta** (Swiss), February 25, 2005. Traded to **Tampa Bay** by **Pittsburgh** with Gary Roberts for Tampa Bay's 3rd round choice (Ben Hanowski) in 2009 Entry Draft, June 28, 2008.

## MALTBY, Kirk

(MAHLT-bee, KUHRK) **DET.**

Right wing. Shoots right. 6', 193 lbs. Born, Guelph, Ont., December 22, 1972. Edmonton's 4th choice, 65th overall, in 1992 Entry Draft.

| Season | Club | League | GP | G | A | Pts | PIM | PP | SH | GW | S | % | +/- | TF | F% | Min | GP | G | A | Pts | PIM | PP | SH | GW | Min |
|---|---|---|---|---|---|---|---|---|---|---|---|---|---|---|---|---|---|---|---|---|---|---|---|---|---|
| 1988-89 | Cambridge | OHA-B | 48 | 28 | 18 | 46 | 138 | .... | .... | .... | .... | .... | .... | .... | .... | .... | .... | .... | .... | .... | .... | .... | .... | .... | .... |
| 1989-90 | Owen Sound | OHL | 61 | 12 | 15 | 27 | 90 | .... | .... | .... | .... | .... | .... | .... | .... | .... | 12 | 1 | 6 | 7 | 15 | .... | .... | .... | .... |
| 1990-91 | Owen Sound | OHL | 66 | 34 | 32 | 66 | 100 | .... | .... | .... | .... | .... | .... | .... | .... | .... | .... | .... | .... | .... | .... | .... | .... | .... | .... |
| 1991-92 | Owen Sound | OHL | 66 | 50 | 41 | 91 | 99 | .... | .... | .... | .... | .... | .... | .... | .... | .... | 5 | 3 | 3 | 6 | 18 | .... | .... | .... | .... |
| 1992-93 | Cape Breton | AHL | 73 | 22 | 23 | 45 | 130 | .... | .... | .... | .... | .... | .... | .... | .... | .... | 16 | 3 | 3 | 6 | 45 | .... | .... | .... | .... |
| **1993-94** | **Edmonton** | **NHL** | **68** | **11** | **8** | **19** | **74** | **0** | **1** | **1** | **89** | **12.4** | **–2** | .... | .... | .... | .... | .... | .... | .... | .... | .... | .... | .... | .... |
| **1994-95** | **Edmonton** | **NHL** | **47** | **8** | **3** | **11** | **49** | **0** | **2** | **1** | **73** | **11.0** | **–11** | .... | .... | .... | .... | .... | .... | .... | .... | .... | .... | .... | .... |
| **1995-96** | **Edmonton** | **NHL** | **49** | **2** | **6** | **8** | **61** | **0** | **0** | **1** | **51** | **3.9** | **–16** | .... | .... | .... | .... | .... | .... | .... | .... | .... | .... | .... | .... |
| | Cape Breton | AHL | 4 | 1 | 2 | 3 | 6 | .... | .... | .... | .... | .... | .... | .... | .... | .... | .... | .... | .... | .... | .... | .... | .... | .... | .... |
| | **Detroit** | **NHL** | **6** | **1** | **0** | **1** | **6** | **0** | **0** | **0** | **4** | **25.0** | **0** | .... | .... | .... | **8** | **0** | **1** | **1** | **4** | **0** | **0** | **0** | .... |
| **1996-97♦** | **Detroit** | **NHL** | **66** | **3** | **5** | **8** | **75** | **0** | **0** | **0** | **62** | **4.8** | **3** | .... | .... | .... | **20** | **5** | **2** | **7** | **24** | **0** | **1** | **1** | .... |
| **1997-98♦** | **Detroit** | **NHL** | **65** | **14** | **9** | **23** | **89** | **2** | **1** | **3** | **106** | **13.2** | **11** | .... | .... | .... | **22** | **3** | **1** | **4** | **30** | **0** | **1** | **0** | .... |
| **1998-99** | **Detroit** | **NHL** | **53** | **8** | **6** | **14** | **34** | **0** | **1** | **2** | **76** | **10.5** | **–6** | **10** | **40.0** | **13:13** | **10** | **1** | **0** | **1** | **8** | **0** | **0** | **1** | **11:32** |
| **99-2000** | **Detroit** | **NHL** | **41** | **6** | **8** | **14** | **24** | **0** | **2** | **1** | **71** | **8.5** | **1** | **2** | **50.0** | **13:30** | **8** | **0** | **1** | **1** | **4** | **0** | **0** | **0** | **13:45** |
| **2000-01** | **Detroit** | **NHL** | **79** | **12** | **7** | **19** | **22** | **1** | **3** | **3** | **119** | **10.1** | **16** | **14** | **35.7** | **14:17** | **6** | **0** | **0** | **0** | **6** | **0** | **0** | **0** | **15:23** |
| **2001-02♦** | **Detroit** | **NHL** | **82** | **9** | **15** | **24** | **40** | **0** | **1** | **5** | **108** | **8.3** | **15** | **38** | **47.4** | **13:23** | **23** | **3** | **3** | **6** | **32** | **0** | **2** | **0** | **16:34** |
| **2002-03** | **Detroit** | **NHL** | **82** | **14** | **23** | **37** | **91** | **0** | **4** | **1** | **116** | **12.1** | **17** | **43** | **37.2** | **16:10** | **4** | **0** | **0** | **0** | **4** | **0** | **0** | **0** | **17:18** |
| **2003-04** | **Detroit** | **NHL** | **79** | **14** | **19** | **33** | **80** | **1** | **4** | **4** | **123** | **11.4** | **24** | **30** | **43.3** | **16:16** | **12** | **1** | **3** | **4** | **11** | **0** | **0** | **0** | **17:34** |
| 2004-05 | | | DID NOT PLAY | | | | | | | | | | | | | | | | | | | | | | |
| **2005-06** | **Detroit** | **NHL** | **82** | **5** | **6** | **11** | **80** | **0** | **1** | **0** | **115** | **4.3** | **–9** | **22** | **50.0** | **13:44** | **6** | **2** | **1** | **3** | **4** | **0** | **0** | **1** | **13:02** |
| **2006-07** | **Detroit** | **NHL** | **82** | **6** | **5** | **11** | **50** | **0** | **0** | **0** | **113** | **5.3** | **–9** | **14** | **28.6** | **13:11** | **18** | **1** | **1** | **2** | **10** | **0** | **1** | **0** | **10:46** |
| **2007-08♦** | **Detroit** | **NHL** | **61** | **6** | **4** | **10** | **32** | **0** | **0** | **1** | **70** | **8.6** | **–8** | **7** | **42.9** | **12:04** | **12** | **0** | **1** | **1** | **10** | **0** | **0** | **0** | **9:47** |
| **2008-09** | **Detroit** | **NHL** | **78** | **5** | **6** | **11** | **28** | **0** | **0** | **1** | **58** | **8.6** | **–9** | **10** | **40.0** | **9:08** | **20** | **0** | **1** | **1** | **2** | **0** | **0** | **0** | **9:07** |
| | **NHL Totals** | | **1020** | **124** | **130** | **254** | **835** | **4** | **20** | **24** | **1354** | **9.2** | | **190** | **41.6** | **13:33** | **169** | **16** | **15** | **31** | **149** | **0** | **5** | **3** | **13:02** |

Traded to **Detroit** by **Edmonton** for Dan McGillis, March 20, 1996. • Missed majority of 1999-2000 season recovering from hernia injury suffered in game vs. Dallas, October 5, 1999.

## MANCARI, Mark

(man-KAH-ree, MAHRK) **BUF.**

Right wing. Shoots right. 6'3", 225 lbs. Born, London, Ont., July 11, 1985. Buffalo's 6th choice, 207th overall, in 2004 Entry Draft.

| Season | Club | League | GP | G | A | Pts | PIM | PP | SH | GW | S | % | +/- | TF | F% | Min | GP | G | A | Pts | PIM | PP | SH | GW | Min |
|---|---|---|---|---|---|---|---|---|---|---|---|---|---|---|---|---|---|---|---|---|---|---|---|---|---|
| 2001-02 | Ottawa 67's | OHL | 34 | 3 | 3 | 6 | 10 | .... | .... | .... | .... | .... | .... | .... | .... | .... | 2 | 0 | 1 | 1 | 0 | .... | .... | .... | .... |
| 2002-03 | Ottawa 67's | OHL | 61 | 8 | 11 | 19 | 20 | .... | .... | .... | .... | .... | .... | .... | .... | .... | 11 | 2 | 1 | 3 | 2 | .... | .... | .... | .... |
| 2003-04 | Ottawa 67's | OHL | 67 | 29 | 36 | 65 | 56 | .... | .... | .... | .... | .... | .... | .... | .... | .... | 7 | 5 | 3 | 8 | 11 | .... | .... | .... | .... |
| 2004-05 | Ottawa 67's | OHL | 64 | 36 | 32 | 68 | 86 | .... | .... | .... | .... | .... | .... | .... | .... | .... | 21 | *14 | 10 | 24 | 24 | .... | .... | .... | .... |
| 2005-06 | Rochester | AHL | 71 | 18 | 24 | 42 | 80 | .... | .... | .... | .... | .... | .... | .... | .... | .... | .... | .... | .... | .... | .... | .... | .... | .... | .... |
| **2006-07** | **Buffalo** | **NHL** | **3** | **0** | **1** | **1** | **2** | **0** | **0** | **0** | **1** | **0.0** | **–1** | **0** | **0.0** | **6:12** | .... | .... | .... | .... | .... | .... | .... | .... | .... |
| | Rochester | AHL | 64 | 23 | 34 | 57 | 49 | .... | .... | .... | .... | .... | .... | .... | .... | .... | 6 | 1 | 5 | 6 | 6 | .... | .... | .... | .... |
| 2007-08 | Rochester | AHL | 80 | 21 | 36 | 57 | 78 | .... | .... | .... | .... | .... | .... | .... | .... | .... | .... | .... | .... | .... | .... | .... | .... | .... | .... |
| **2008-09** | **Buffalo** | **NHL** | **7** | **1** | **1** | **2** | **4** | **0** | **0** | **0** | **21** | **4.8** | **–4** | **7** | **57.1** | **13:16** | .... | .... | .... | .... | .... | .... | .... | .... | .... |
| | Portland Pirates | AHL | 73 | 29 | 38 | 67 | 61 | .... | .... | .... | .... | .... | .... | .... | .... | .... | 5 | 1 | 2 | 3 | 2 | .... | .... | .... | .... |
| | **NHL Totals** | | **10** | **1** | **2** | **3** | **6** | **0** | **0** | **0** | **22** | **4.5** | | **7** | **57.1** | **11:09** | .... | .... | .... | .... | .... | .... | .... | .... | .... |

## MARA, Paul

(MAIR-uh, PAWL) **MTL.**

Defense. Shoots left. 6'4", 212 lbs. Born, Ridgewood, NJ, September 7, 1979. Tampa Bay's 1st choice, 7th overall, in 1997 Entry Draft.

| Season | Club | League | GP | G | A | Pts | PIM | PP | SH | GW | S | % | +/- | TF | F% | Min | GP | G | A | Pts | PIM | PP | SH | GW | Min |
|---|---|---|---|---|---|---|---|---|---|---|---|---|---|---|---|---|---|---|---|---|---|---|---|---|---|
| | | | Regular Season | | | | | | | | | | | | | | Playoffs | | | | | | | | |
| 1994-95 | Belmont Hill | High-MA | 28 | 5 | 17 | 22 | 28 | .... | .... | .... | .... | .... | .... | .... | .... | .... | .... | .... | .... | .... | .... | .... | .... | .... | .... |
| 1995-96 | Belmont Hill | High-MA | 28 | 18 | 20 | 38 | 40 | .... | .... | .... | .... | .... | .... | .... | .... | .... | .... | .... | .... | .... | .... | .... | .... | .... | .... |
| 1996-97 | Sudbury Wolves | OHL | 44 | 9 | 34 | 43 | 61 | .... | .... | .... | .... | .... | .... | .... | .... | .... | .... | .... | .... | .... | .... | .... | .... | .... | .... |
| 1997-98 | Sudbury Wolves | OHL | 25 | 8 | 18 | 26 | 79 | .... | .... | .... | .... | .... | .... | .... | .... | .... | .... | .... | .... | .... | .... | .... | .... | .... | .... |
| | Plymouth Whalers | OHL | 25 | 8 | 15 | 23 | 30 | .... | .... | .... | .... | .... | .... | .... | .... | .... | 15 | 3 | 14 | 17 | 30 | .... | .... | .... | .... |
| 1998-99 | Plymouth Whalers | OHL | 52 | 13 | 41 | 54 | 95 | .... | .... | .... | .... | .... | .... | .... | .... | .... | 11 | 5 | 7 | 12 | 28 | .... | .... | .... | .... |
| | Tampa Bay | NHL | 1 | 1 | 1 | 2 | 0 | 1 | 0 | 0 | 1 | 100.0 | -3 | 0 | 0.0 | 19:34 | .... | .... | .... | .... | .... | .... | .... | .... | .... |
| 99-2000 | Tampa Bay | NHL | 54 | 7 | 11 | 18 | 73 | 4 | 0 | 1 | 78 | 9.0 | -27 | 0 | 0.0 | 22:13 | .... | .... | .... | .... | .... | .... | .... | .... | .... |
| | Detroit Vipers | IHL | 15 | 3 | 5 | 8 | 22 | .... | .... | .... | .... | .... | .... | .... | .... | .... | .... | .... | .... | .... | .... | .... | .... | .... | .... |
| 2000-01 | Tampa Bay | NHL | 46 | 6 | 10 | 16 | 40 | 2 | 0 | 1 | 58 | 10.3 | -17 | 0 | 0.0 | 23:06 | .... | .... | .... | .... | .... | .... | .... | .... | .... |
| | Detroit Vipers | IHL | 10 | 3 | 3 | 6 | 22 | .... | .... | .... | .... | .... | .... | .... | .... | .... | .... | .... | .... | .... | .... | .... | .... | .... | .... |
| | Phoenix | NHL | 16 | 0 | 4 | 4 | 14 | 0 | 0 | 0 | 20 | 0.0 | 1 | 0 | 0.0 | 19:22 | .... | .... | .... | .... | .... | .... | .... | .... | .... |
| 2001-02 | Phoenix | NHL | 75 | 7 | 17 | 24 | 58 | 2 | 0 | 0 | 112 | 6.3 | -6 | 2 | 100.0 | 21:34 | 5 | 0 | 0 | 0 | 4 | 0 | 0 | 0 | 22:57 |
| 2002-03 | Phoenix | NHL | 73 | 10 | 15 | 25 | 78 | 1 | 0 | 0 | 95 | 10.5 | -7 | 1 | 0.0 | 21:06 | .... | .... | .... | .... | .... | .... | .... | .... | .... |
| 2003-04 | Phoenix | NHL | 81 | 6 | 36 | 42 | 48 | 1 | 0 | 0 | 140 | 4.3 | -11 | 2 | 0.0 | 23:37 | .... | .... | .... | .... | .... | .... | .... | .... | .... |
| 2004-05 | Hannover | Germany | 35 | 5 | 13 | 18 | 89 | .... | .... | .... | .... | .... | .... | .... | .... | .... | .... | .... | .... | .... | .... | .... | .... | .... | .... |
| 2005-06 | Phoenix | NHL | 78 | 15 | 32 | 47 | 70 | 8 | 0 | 0 | 157 | 9.6 | -12 | 1 | 0.0 | 21:29 | .... | .... | .... | .... | .... | .... | .... | .... | .... |
| 2006-07 | Boston | NHL | 59 | 3 | 15 | 18 | 95 | 0 | 0 | 0 | 60 | 5.0 | -22 | 0 | 0.0 | 21:53 | .... | .... | .... | .... | .... | .... | .... | .... | .... |
| | NY Rangers | NHL | 19 | 2 | 3 | 5 | 18 | 1 | 0 | 0 | 40 | 5.0 | 6 | 0 | 0.0 | 22:56 | 10 | 2 | 2 | 4 | 18 | 2 | 0 | 0 | 19:43 |
| 2007-08 | NY Rangers | NHL | 61 | 1 | 16 | 17 | 52 | 0 | 0 | 0 | 80 | 1.3 | 1 | 1 | 0.0 | 17:53 | 10 | 0 | 1 | 1 | 20 | 0 | 0 | 0 | 17:48 |
| 2008-09 | NY Rangers | NHL | 76 | 5 | 16 | 21 | 94 | 1 | 0 | 0 | 102 | 4.9 | 2 | 2 | 50.0 | 18:58 | 7 | 1 | 1 | 2 | 8 | 0 | 0 | 0 | 14:43 |
| | NHL Totals | | 639 | 63 | 176 | 239 | 640 | 21 | 0 | 2 | 943 | 6.7 | | 9 | 33.3 | 21:17 | 32 | 3 | 4 | 7 | 50 | 2 | 0 | 0 | 18:32 |

Traded to **Phoenix** by **Tampa Bay** with Mike Johnson, Ruslan Zainullin and NY Islanders' 2nd round choice (previously acquired, Phoenix selected Matthew Spiller) in 2001 Entry Draft for Nikolai Khabibulin and Stan Neckar, March 5, 2001. Signed as a free agent by **Hannover** (Germany), October 29, 2004. Traded to **Boston** by **Phoenix** with Phoenix's 3rd round choice (later traded to Anaheim - Anaheim selected Maxime Macenauer) in 2007 Entry Draft for Nick Boynton and Boston's 4th round choice (later traded to Toronto - Toronto selected Matt Frattin) in 2007 Entry Draft, June 26, 2006. Traded to **NY Rangers** by **Boston** for Aaron Ward, February 27, 2007. Signed as a free agent by **Montreal**, July 10, 2009.

## MARCHANT, Todd

(mahr-SHAHNT, TAWD) **ANA.**

Center. Shoots left. 5'10", 182 lbs. Born, Buffalo, NY, August 12, 1973. NY Rangers' 8th choice, 164th overall, in 1993 Entry Draft.

| Season | Club | League | GP | G | A | Pts | PIM | PP | SH | GW | S | % | +/- | TF | F% | Min | GP | G | A | Pts | PIM | PP | SH | GW | Min |
|---|---|---|---|---|---|---|---|---|---|---|---|---|---|---|---|---|---|---|---|---|---|---|---|---|---|
| 1990-91 | Niagara Scenics | NAHL | 37 | 31 | 47 | 78 | .... | .... | .... | .... | .... | .... | .... | .... | .... | .... | .... | .... | .... | .... | .... | .... | .... | .... | .... |
| 1991-92 | Clarkson Knights | ECAC | 32 | 20 | 12 | 32 | 32 | .... | .... | .... | .... | .... | .... | .... | .... | .... | .... | .... | .... | .... | .... | .... | .... | .... | .... |
| 1992-93 | Clarkson Knights | ECAC | 33 | 18 | 28 | 46 | 38 | .... | .... | .... | .... | .... | .... | .... | .... | .... | .... | .... | .... | .... | .... | .... | .... | .... | .... |
| 1993-94 | United States | Nat-Tm | 59 | 28 | 39 | 67 | 48 | .... | .... | .... | .... | .... | .... | .... | .... | .... | .... | .... | .... | .... | .... | .... | .... | .... | .... |
| | United States | Olympics | 8 | 1 | 1 | 2 | 6 | .... | .... | .... | .... | .... | .... | .... | .... | .... | .... | .... | .... | .... | .... | .... | .... | .... | .... |
| | NY Rangers | NHL | 1 | 0 | 0 | 0 | 0 | 0 | 0 | 0 | 1 | 0.0 | -1 | .... | .... | .... | .... | .... | .... | .... | .... | .... | .... | .... | .... |
| | Binghamton | AHL | 8 | 2 | 7 | 9 | 6 | .... | .... | .... | .... | .... | .... | .... | .... | .... | .... | .... | .... | .... | .... | .... | .... | .... | .... |
| | Edmonton | NHL | 3 | 0 | 1 | 1 | 2 | 0 | 0 | 0 | 5 | 0.0 | -1 | .... | .... | .... | .... | .... | .... | .... | .... | .... | .... | .... | .... |
| | Cape Breton | AHL | 3 | 1 | 4 | 5 | 2 | .... | .... | .... | .... | .... | .... | .... | .... | .... | 5 | 1 | 1 | 2 | 0 | .... | .... | .... | .... |
| 1994-95 | Cape Breton | AHL | 38 | 22 | 25 | 47 | 25 | .... | .... | .... | .... | .... | .... | .... | .... | .... | .... | .... | .... | .... | .... | .... | .... | .... | .... |
| | Edmonton | NHL | 45 | 13 | 14 | 27 | 32 | 3 | 2 | 2 | 95 | 13.7 | -3 | .... | .... | .... | .... | .... | .... | .... | .... | .... | .... | .... | .... |
| 1995-96 | Edmonton | NHL | 81 | 19 | 19 | 38 | 66 | 2 | 3 | 2 | 221 | 8.6 | -19 | .... | .... | .... | .... | .... | .... | .... | .... | .... | .... | .... | .... |
| 1996-97 | Edmonton | NHL | 79 | 14 | 19 | 33 | 44 | 0 | 4 | 3 | 202 | 6.9 | 11 | .... | .... | .... | 12 | 4 | 2 | 6 | 12 | 0 | 3 | 1 | .... |
| 1997-98 | Edmonton | NHL | 76 | 14 | 21 | 35 | 71 | 2 | 1 | 3 | 194 | 7.2 | 9 | .... | .... | .... | 12 | 1 | 1 | 2 | 10 | 0 | 0 | 0 | .... |
| 1998-99 | Edmonton | NHL | 82 | 14 | 22 | 36 | 65 | 3 | 1 | 2 | 183 | 7.7 | 3 | 1449 | 50.0 | 16:47 | 4 | 1 | 1 | 2 | 12 | 0 | 0 | 0 | 24:21 |
| 99-2000 | Edmonton | NHL | 82 | 17 | 23 | 40 | 70 | 0 | 1 | 0 | 170 | 10.0 | 7 | 1593 | 52.9 | 17:08 | 3 | 1 | 0 | 1 | 2 | 0 | 0 | 0 | 18:07 |
| 2000-01 | Edmonton | NHL | 71 | 13 | 26 | 39 | 51 | 0 | 4 | 2 | 113 | 11.5 | 1 | 1549 | 53.8 | 17:54 | 6 | 0 | 0 | 0 | 4 | 0 | 0 | 0 | 22:57 |
| 2001-02 | Edmonton | NHL | 82 | 12 | 22 | 34 | 41 | 0 | 3 | 1 | 124 | 9.7 | 7 | 1523 | 52.4 | 16:58 | .... | .... | .... | .... | .... | .... | .... | .... | .... |
| 2002-03 | Edmonton | NHL | 77 | 20 | 40 | 60 | 48 | 7 | 1 | 3 | 146 | 13.7 | 13 | 1336 | 58.0 | 19:54 | 6 | 0 | 2 | 2 | 2 | 0 | 0 | 0 | 20:03 |
| 2003-04 | Columbus | NHL | 77 | 9 | 25 | 34 | 34 | 4 | 0 | 2 | 163 | 5.5 | -17 | 1412 | 50.9 | 20:39 | .... | .... | .... | .... | .... | .... | .... | .... | .... |
| 2004-05 | DID NOT PLAY | | | | | | | | | | | | | | | | | | | | | | | | |
| 2005-06 | Columbus | NHL | 18 | 3 | 6 | 9 | 20 | 0 | 0 | 0 | 42 | 7.1 | -1 | 289 | 50.2 | 20:05 | .... | .... | .... | .... | .... | .... | .... | .... | .... |
| | Anaheim | NHL | 61 | 6 | 19 | 25 | 46 | 0 | 0 | 0 | 90 | 6.7 | 3 | 743 | 51.7 | 16:25 | 16 | 3 | 10 | 13 | 14 | 0 | 0 | 0 | 17:34 |
| 2006-07♦ | Anaheim | NHL | 56 | 8 | 15 | 23 | 44 | 0 | 3 | 2 | 115 | 7.0 | 7 | 647 | 54.3 | 15:10 | 11 | 0 | 3 | 3 | 12 | 0 | 0 | 0 | 15:44 |
| 2007-08 | Anaheim | NHL | 75 | 9 | 7 | 16 | 48 | 0 | 0 | 0 | 93 | 9.7 | -3 | 673 | 49.2 | 14:49 | 6 | 2 | 0 | 2 | 0 | 0 | 0 | 0 | 17:40 |
| 2008-09 | Anaheim | NHL | 72 | 5 | 13 | 18 | 34 | 0 | 2 | 0 | 101 | 5.0 | -2 | 593 | 50.3 | 14:32 | 13 | 1 | 1 | 2 | 16 | 0 | 0 | 1 | 19:56 |
| | NHL Totals | | 1038 | 176 | 292 | 468 | 716 | 21 | 25 | 22 | 2058 | 8.6 | | 11807 | 52.5 | 17:11 | 89 | 13 | 20 | 33 | 84 | 0 | 3 | 2 | 18:54 |

ECAC Second All-Star Team (1993)

Traded to **Edmonton** by **NY Rangers** for Craig MacTavish, March 21, 1994. Signed as a free agent by **Columbus**, July 3, 2003. Claimed on waivers by **Anaheim** from **Columbus**, November 21, 2005.

## MARKOV, Andrei

(MAHR-kahf, AHN-dray) **MTL.**

Defense. Shoots left. 6', 209 lbs. Born, Voskresensk, USSR, December 20, 1978. Montreal's 6th choice, 162nd overall, in 1998 Entry Draft.

| Season | Club | League | GP | G | A | Pts | PIM | PP | SH | GW | S | % | +/- | TF | F% | Min | GP | G | A | Pts | PIM | PP | SH | GW | Min |
|---|---|---|---|---|---|---|---|---|---|---|---|---|---|---|---|---|---|---|---|---|---|---|---|---|---|
| 1995-96 | Voskresensk | CIS | 38 | 0 | 0 | 0 | 14 | .... | .... | .... | .... | .... | .... | .... | .... | .... | .... | .... | .... | .... | .... | .... | .... | .... | .... |
| 1996-97 | Voskresensk | Russia | 43 | 8 | 4 | 12 | 32 | .... | .... | .... | .... | .... | .... | .... | .... | .... | 2 | 1 | 1 | 2 | 0 | .... | .... | .... | .... |
| 1997-98 | Voskresensk | Russia | 43 | 10 | 5 | 15 | 83 | .... | .... | .... | .... | .... | .... | .... | .... | .... | .... | .... | .... | .... | .... | .... | .... | .... | .... |
| 1998-99 | Dynamo Moscow | Russia | 38 | 10 | 11 | 21 | 32 | .... | .... | .... | .... | .... | .... | .... | .... | .... | 16 | 3 | 6 | 9 | 6 | .... | .... | .... | .... |
| | Dynamo Moscow | EuroHL | 12 | 7 | 5 | 12 | 12 | .... | .... | .... | .... | .... | .... | .... | .... | .... | 6 | 2 | 2 | 4 | 4 | .... | .... | .... | .... |
| 99-2000 | Dynamo Moscow | Russia | 29 | 11 | 12 | 23 | 28 | .... | .... | .... | .... | .... | .... | .... | .... | .... | 17 | 4 | 3 | 7 | 8 | .... | .... | .... | .... |
| 2000-01 | Montreal | NHL | 63 | 6 | 17 | 23 | 18 | 2 | 0 | 0 | 82 | 7.3 | -6 | 2 | 50.0 | 16:53 | .... | .... | .... | .... | .... | .... | .... | .... | .... |
| | Quebec Citadelles | AHL | 14 | 0 | 5 | 5 | 4 | .... | .... | .... | .... | .... | .... | .... | .... | .... | 7 | 1 | 1 | 2 | 2 | .... | .... | .... | .... |
| 2001-02 | Montreal | NHL | 56 | 5 | 19 | 24 | 24 | 2 | 0 | 1 | 73 | 6.8 | -1 | 0 | 0.0 | 17:15 | 12 | 1 | 3 | 4 | 8 | 0 | 0 | 1 | 15:53 |
| | Quebec Citadelles | AHL | 12 | 4 | 6 | 10 | 7 | .... | .... | .... | .... | .... | .... | .... | .... | .... | .... | .... | .... | .... | .... | .... | .... | .... | .... |
| 2002-03 | Montreal | NHL | 79 | 13 | 24 | 37 | 34 | 3 | 0 | 2 | 159 | 8.2 | 13 | 1 | 0.0 | 23:17 | .... | .... | .... | .... | .... | .... | .... | .... | .... |
| 2003-04 | Montreal | NHL | 69 | 6 | 22 | 28 | 20 | 2 | 0 | 0 | 105 | 5.7 | -2 | 2 | 50.0 | 21:29 | 11 | 1 | 4 | 5 | 8 | 0 | 0 | 1 | 22:52 |
| 2004-05 | Dynamo Moscow | Russia | 42 | 7 | 16 | 23 | 76 | .... | .... | .... | .... | .... | .... | .... | .... | .... | 10 | 2 | 0 | 2 | 22 | .... | .... | .... | .... |
| 2005-06 | Montreal | NHL | 67 | 10 | 36 | 46 | 74 | 6 | 1 | 1 | 88 | 11.4 | 13 | 1 | 0.0 | 23:33 | 6 | 0 | 1 | 1 | 4 | 0 | 0 | 0 | 25:29 |
| | Russia | Olympics | 8 | 1 | 2 | 3 | 6 | .... | .... | .... | .... | .... | .... | .... | .... | .... | .... | .... | .... | .... | .... | .... | .... | .... | .... |
| 2006-07 | Montreal | NHL | 77 | 6 | 43 | 49 | 56 | 5 | 0 | 2 | 128 | 4.7 | 2 | 1 | 0.0 | 24:29 | .... | .... | .... | .... | .... | .... | .... | .... | .... |
| 2007-08 | Montreal | NHL | 82 | 16 | 42 | 58 | 63 | 10 | 1 | 2 | 145 | 11.0 | 1 | 0 | 0.0 | 24:58 | 12 | 1 | 3 | 4 | 8 | 0 | 0 | 0 | 24:54 |
| 2008-09 | Montreal | NHL | 78 | 12 | 52 | 64 | 36 | 7 | 0 | 3 | 165 | 7.3 | -2 | 0 | 0.0 | 24:38 | .... | .... | .... | .... | .... | .... | .... | .... | .... |
| | NHL Totals | | 571 | 74 | 255 | 329 | 325 | 37 | 2 | 11 | 945 | 7.8 | | 7 | 28.6 | 22:23 | 41 | 3 | 11 | 14 | 28 | 0 | 0 | 2 | 21:48 |

Played in NHL All-Star Game (2008, 2009)

Signed as a free agent by **Dynamo Moscow** (Russia), June 19, 2004.

## MARLEAU, Patrick

(mahr-LOH, PAT-rihk) **S.J.**

Center. Shoots left. 6'2", 220 lbs. Born, Aneroid, Sask., September 15, 1979. San Jose's 1st choice, 2nd overall, in 1997 Entry Draft.

| Season | Club | League | GP | G | A | Pts | PIM | PP | SH | GW | S | % | +/- | TF | F% | Min | GP | G | A | Pts | PIM | PP | SH | GW | Min |
|---|---|---|---|---|---|---|---|---|---|---|---|---|---|---|---|---|---|---|---|---|---|---|---|---|---|
| 1993-94 | Swift Current | SMHL | 53 | 72 | 95 | 167 | .... | .... | .... | .... | .... | .... | .... | .... | .... | .... | .... | .... | .... | .... | .... | .... | .... | .... | .... |
| 1994-95 | Swift Current | SMHL | 31 | 30 | 22 | 52 | 18 | .... | .... | .... | .... | .... | .... | .... | .... | .... | .... | .... | .... | .... | .... | .... | .... | .... | .... |
| 1995-96 | Seattle | WHL | 72 | 32 | 42 | 74 | 22 | .... | .... | .... | .... | .... | .... | .... | .... | .... | 5 | 3 | 4 | 7 | 4 | .... | .... | .... | .... |
| 1996-97 | Seattle | WHL | 71 | 51 | 74 | 125 | 37 | .... | .... | .... | .... | .... | .... | .... | .... | .... | 15 | 7 | 16 | 23 | 12 | .... | .... | .... | .... |
| 1997-98 | San Jose | NHL | 74 | 13 | 19 | 32 | 14 | 1 | 0 | 2 | 90 | 14.4 | 5 | .... | .... | .... | 5 | 0 | 1 | 1 | 0 | 0 | 0 | 0 | .... |
| 1998-99 | San Jose | NHL | 81 | 21 | 24 | 45 | 24 | 4 | 0 | 4 | 134 | 15.7 | 10 | 1121 | 43.4 | 15:11 | 6 | 2 | 1 | 3 | 4 | 2 | 0 | 0 | 11:08 |
| 99-2000 | San Jose | NHL | 81 | 17 | 23 | 40 | 36 | 3 | 0 | 3 | 161 | 10.6 | -9 | 851 | 42.0 | 14:11 | 5 | 1 | 1 | 2 | 2 | 1 | 0 | 0 | 11:51 |
| 2000-01 | San Jose | NHL | 81 | 25 | 27 | 52 | 22 | 5 | 0 | 6 | 146 | 17.1 | 7 | 1088 | 44.8 | 16:17 | 6 | 2 | 0 | 2 | 4 | 0 | 0 | 0 | 14:50 |
| 2001-02 | San Jose | NHL | 79 | 21 | 23 | 44 | 40 | 3 | 0 | 5 | 121 | 17.4 | 9 | 897 | 47.3 | 14:04 | 12 | 6 | 5 | 11 | 6 | 1 | 0 | 3 | 15:50 |
| 2002-03 | San Jose | NHL | 82 | 28 | 29 | 57 | 33 | 8 | 1 | 3 | 172 | 16.3 | -10 | 1403 | 47.3 | 18:31 | .... | .... | .... | .... | .... | .... | .... | .... | .... |
| 2003-04 | San Jose | NHL | 80 | 28 | 29 | 57 | 24 | 9 | 0 | 5 | 220 | 12.7 | -5 | 1014 | 41.6 | 18:12 | 17 | 8 | 4 | 12 | 6 | 4 | 1 | 2 | 19:16 |
| 2004-05 | DID NOT PLAY | | | | | | | | | | | | | | | | | | | | | | | | |
| 2005-06 | San Jose | NHL | 82 | 34 | 52 | 86 | 26 | 20 | 1 | 4 | 260 | 13.1 | -12 | 1216 | 46.8 | 19:56 | 11 | 9 | 5 | 14 | 8 | 4 | 0 | 2 | 21:07 |
| 2006-07 | San Jose | NHL | 77 | 32 | 46 | 78 | 33 | 14 | 0 | 9 | 180 | 17.8 | 9 | 693 | 50.5 | 18:34 | 11 | 3 | 3 | 6 | 2 | 1 | 0 | 1 | 18:59 |
| 2007-08 | San Jose | NHL | 78 | 19 | 29 | 48 | 33 | 7 | 0 | 2 | 185 | 10.3 | -19 | 605 | 52.4 | 18:14 | 13 | 4 | 4 | 8 | 2 | 0 | 2 | 0 | 23:04 |
| 2008-09 | San Jose | NHL | 76 | 38 | 33 | 71 | 18 | 11 | 5 | 10 | 251 | 15.1 | 16 | 591 | 52.5 | 21:21 | 6 | 2 | 1 | 3 | 8 | 1 | 0 | 2 | 20:29 |
| | NHL Totals | | 871 | 276 | 334 | 610 | 303 | 85 | 7 | 53 | 1920 | 14.4 | | 9479 | 46.3 | 17:26 | 92 | 37 | 25 | 62 | 42 | 14 | 3 | 10 | 18:21 |

WHL West First All-Star Team (1997)

Played in NHL All-Star Game (2004, 2007, 2009)

## MARTIN, Paul
(MAHR-tihn, PAWL) **N.J.**

Defense. Shoots left. 6'1", 200 lbs. Born, Minneapolis, MN, March 5, 1981. New Jersey's 5th choice, 62nd overall, in 2000 Entry Draft.

| | | | Regular Season | | | | | | | | | | | | | | Playoffs | | | | | | | | |
|---|---|---|---|---|---|---|---|---|---|---|---|---|---|---|---|---|---|---|---|---|---|---|---|---|---|
| Season | Club | League | GP | G | A | Pts | PIM | PP | SH | GW | S | % | +/- | TF | F% | Min | GP | G | A | Pts | PIM | PP | SH | GW | Min |
| 1998-99 | Elk River Elks | High-MN | 24 | 9 | 11 | 20 | | | | | | | | | | | | | | | | | | | |
| 99-2000 | Elk River Elks | High-MN | 24 | 15 | 35 | 50 | 26 | | | | | | | | | | | | | | | | | | |
| 2000-01 | U. of Minnesota | WCHA | 38 | 3 | 17 | 20 | 8 | | | | | | | | | | | | | | | | | | |
| 2001-02 | U. of Minnesota | WCHA | 44 | 8 | 30 | 38 | 22 | | | | | | | | | | | | | | | | | | |
| 2002-03 | U. of Minnesota | WCHA | 45 | 9 | 30 | 39 | 32 | | | | | | | | | | | | | | | | | | |
| **2003-04** | **New Jersey** | **NHL** | **70** | **6** | **18** | **24** | **4** | **2** | **0** | **2** | **82** | **7.3** | **12** | **0** | **0.0** | **20:08** | **5** | **1** | **1** | **2** | **4** | **1** | **0** | **0** | **23:40** |
| 2004-05 | Fribourg | Swiss | 11 | 3 | 4 | 7 | 2 | | | | | | | | | | | | | | | | | | |
| **2005-06** | **New Jersey** | **NHL** | **80** | **5** | **32** | **37** | **32** | **3** | **0** | **0** | **97** | **5.2** | **1** | **0** | **0.0** | **23:37** | **9** | **0** | **3** | **3** | **4** | **0** | **0** | **0** | **24:17** |
| | United States | Olympics | DID NOT PLAY | | | | | | | | | | | | | | | | | | | | | | |
| **2006-07** | **New Jersey** | **NHL** | **82** | **3** | **23** | **26** | **18** | **1** | **0** | **0** | **84** | **3.6** | **–9** | **0** | **0.0** | **25:13** | **11** | **0** | **4** | **4** | **6** | **0** | **0** | **0** | **25:09** |
| **2007-08** | **New Jersey** | **NHL** | **73** | **5** | **27** | **32** | **22** | **2** | **0** | **2** | **93** | **5.4** | **20** | **0** | **0.0** | **23:53** | **5** | **1** | **2** | **3** | **2** | **1** | **0** | **0** | **25:35** |
| **2008-09** | **New Jersey** | **NHL** | **73** | **5** | **28** | **33** | **36** | **2** | **0** | **1** | **107** | **4.7** | **21** | **0** | **0.0** | **24:22** | **7** | **0** | **4** | **4** | **2** | **0** | **0** | **0** | **26:20** |
| | **NHL Totals** | | **378** | **24** | **128** | **152** | **112** | **10** | **0** | **5** | **463** | **5.2** | | **0** | **0.0** | **23:31** | **37** | **2** | **14** | **16** | **18** | **2** | **0** | **0** | **25:01** |

Minnesota High School Player of the Year (1999) • WCHA All-Rookie Team (2001) • WCHA Second All-Star Team (2002, 2003) • NCAA West Second All-American Team (2003) • NCAA Championship All-Tournament Team (2003)

Signed as a free agent by **Fribourg** (Swiss), November 4, 2004.

## MARTINEK, Radek
(MAHR-tee-nihk, RA-dehk) **NYI**

Defense. Shoots right. 6'1", 203 lbs. Born, Havlickuv Brod, Czech., August 31, 1976. NY Islanders' 12th choice, 228th overall, in 1999 Entry Draft.

| Season | Club | League | GP | G | A | Pts | PIM | PP | SH | GW | S | % | +/- | TF | F% | Min | GP | G | A | Pts | PIM | PP | SH | GW | Min |
|---|---|---|---|---|---|---|---|---|---|---|---|---|---|---|---|---|---|---|---|---|---|---|---|---|---|
| 1996-97 | C. Budejovice | CzRep | 52 | 3 | 5 | 8 | 40 | | | | | | | | | | 5 | 0 | 1 | 1 | 2 | | | | |
| | C. Budejovice | EuroHL | 6 | 0 | 0 | 0 | 0 | | | | | | | | | | 2 | 0 | 0 | 0 | 0 | | | | |
| 1997-98 | C. Budejovice | CzRep | 42 | 2 | 7 | 9 | 36 | | | | | | | | | | | | | | | | | | |
| 1998-99 | C. Budejovice | CzRep | 52 | 12 | 13 | 25 | 50 | | | | | | | | | | 3 | 0 | 2 | 2 | | | | | |
| 99-2000 | C. Budejovice | CzRep | 45 | 5 | 18 | 23 | 24 | | | | | | | | | | 3 | 0 | 0 | 0 | 6 | | | | |
| 2000-01 | C. Budejovice | CzRep | 44 | 8 | 10 | 18 | 45 | | | | | | | | | | | | | | | | | | |
| **2001-02** | **NY Islanders** | **NHL** | **23** | **1** | **4** | **5** | **16** | **0** | **0** | **1** | **25** | **4.0** | **5** | **0** | **0.0** | **21:07** | | | | | | | | | |
| **2002-03** | **NY Islanders** | **NHL** | **66** | **2** | **11** | **13** | **26** | **0** | **0** | **1** | **67** | **3.0** | **15** | **0** | **0.0** | **17:15** | **4** | **0** | **0** | **0** | **4** | **0** | **0** | **0** | **10:16** |
| | Bridgeport | AHL | 3 | 0 | 3 | 3 | 2 | | | | | | | | | | | | | | | | | | |
| **2003-04** | **NY Islanders** | **NHL** | **47** | **4** | **3** | **7** | **43** | **0** | **0** | **1** | **48** | **8.3** | **–9** | **0** | **0.0** | **13:03** | **5** | **0** | **1** | **1** | **0** | **0** | **0** | **0** | **12:12** |
| 2004-05 | C. Budejovice | CzRep-2 | 30 | 12 | 18 | 30 | 80 | | | | | | | | | | 12 | 2 | 3 | 5 | 6 | | | | |
| **2005-06** | **NY Islanders** | **NHL** | **74** | **1** | **16** | **17** | **32** | **0** | **0** | **0** | **79** | **1.3** | **–9** | **1** | **0.0** | **18:16** | | | | | | | | | |
| **2006-07** | **NY Islanders** | **NHL** | **43** | **2** | **15** | **17** | **40** | **0** | **0** | **0** | **44** | **4.5** | **19** | **1** | **100.0** | **19:54** | | | | | | | | | |
| **2007-08** | **NY Islanders** | **NHL** | **69** | **0** | **15** | **15** | **40** | **0** | **0** | **0** | **98** | **0.0** | **–9** | **0** | **0.0** | **22:52** | | | | | | | | | |
| **2008-09** | **NY Islanders** | **NHL** | **51** | **6** | **4** | **10** | **28** | **1** | **0** | **1** | **54** | **11.1** | **–16** | **0** | **0.0** | **21:34** | | | | | | | | | |
| | **NHL Totals** | | **373** | **16** | **68** | **84** | **225** | **1** | **0** | **4** | **415** | **3.9** | | **2** | **50.0** | **19:06** | **9** | **0** | **1** | **1** | **4** | **0** | **0** | **0** | **11:20** |

• Missed majority of 2001-02 season recovering from knee injury suffered in game vs. NY Rangers, November 11, 2001. Signed as a free agent by **Ceske Budejovice** (CzRep-2), September 17, 2004.

## MATTHIAS, Shawn
(muh-TIGH-uhs, SHAWN) **FLA.**

Center. Shoots left. 6'3", 211 lbs. Born, Mississauga, Ont., February 19, 1988. Detroit's 2nd choice, 47th overall, in 2006 Entry Draft.

| Season | Club | League | GP | G | A | Pts | PIM | PP | SH | GW | S | % | +/- | TF | F% | Min | GP | G | A | Pts | PIM | PP | SH | GW | Min |
|---|---|---|---|---|---|---|---|---|---|---|---|---|---|---|---|---|---|---|---|---|---|---|---|---|---|
| 2004-05 | Belleville Bulls | OHL | 37 | 1 | 1 | 2 | 15 | | | | | | | | | | 3 | 0 | 0 | 0 | 0 | | | | |
| 2005-06 | Belleville Bulls | OHL | 67 | 13 | 21 | 34 | 42 | | | | | | | | | | 6 | 3 | 0 | 3 | 2 | | | | |
| 2006-07 | Belleville Bulls | OHL | 64 | 38 | 35 | 73 | 61 | | | | | | | | | | 15 | 13 | 5 | 18 | 10 | | | | |
| **2007-08** | **Florida** | **NHL** | **4** | **2** | **0** | **2** | **2** | **1** | **0** | **0** | **5** | **40.0** | **–2** | **38** | **44.7** | **13:08** | | | | | | | | | |
| | Belleville Bulls | OHL | 53 | 32 | 47 | 79 | 50 | | | | | | | | | | 1 | 1 | 0 | 1 | 0 | | | | |
| **2008-09** | **Florida** | **NHL** | **16** | **0** | **2** | **2** | **2** | **0** | **0** | **0** | **11** | **0.0** | **–3** | **91** | **50.6** | **9:10** | | | | | | | | | |
| | Rochester | AHL | 61 | 10 | 10 | 20 | 16 | | | | | | | | | | | | | | | | | | |
| | **NHL Totals** | | **20** | **2** | **2** | **4** | **4** | **1** | **0** | **0** | **16** | **12.5** | | **129** | **48.8** | **9:57** | | | | | | | | | |

Traded to **Florida** by **Detroit** with Detroit's 2nd round choice (later traded to Nashville - Nashville selected Nick Spaling) in 2007 Entry Draft for Todd Bertuzzi, February 27, 2007.

## MAULDIN, Greg
(MAWL-dihn, GREHG) **NYI**

Center. Shoots right. 5'10", 198 lbs. Born, Boston, MA, June 10, 1982. Columbus' 10th choice, 199th overall, in 2002 Entry Draft.

| Season | Club | League | GP | G | A | Pts | PIM | PP | SH | GW | S | % | +/- | TF | F% | Min | GP | G | A | Pts | PIM | PP | SH | GW | Min |
|---|---|---|---|---|---|---|---|---|---|---|---|---|---|---|---|---|---|---|---|---|---|---|---|---|---|
| 99-2000 | Bos. Jr. Bruins | EJHL | 58 | 45 | 42 | 87 | 14 | | | | | | | | | | | | | | | | | | |
| 2000-01 | Bos. Jr. Bruins | EJHL | 53 | 48 | 58 | 106 | 73 | | | | | | | | | | | | | | | | | | |
| 2001-02 | Massachusetts | H-East | 33 | 12 | 12 | 24 | 10 | | | | | | | | | | | | | | | | | | |
| 2002-03 | Massachusetts | H-East | 36 | 21 | 20 | 41 | 26 | | | | | | | | | | | | | | | | | | |
| **2003-04** | Massachusetts | H-East | 29 | 15 | 14 | 29 | 15 | | | | | | | | | | | | | | | | | | |
| | **Columbus** | **NHL** | **6** | **0** | **0** | **0** | **4** | **0** | **0** | **0** | **6** | **0.0** | **–2** | **0** | **0.0** | **8:47** | | | | | | | | | |
| | Syracuse Crunch | AHL | 2 | 0 | 0 | 0 | 0 | | | | | | | | | | 1 | 0 | 0 | 0 | 0 | | | | |
| 2004-05 | Syracuse Crunch | AHL | 66 | 7 | 20 | 27 | 49 | | | | | | | | | | | | | | | | | | |
| 2005-06 | Syracuse Crunch | AHL | 56 | 12 | 17 | 29 | 53 | | | | | | | | | | | | | | | | | | |
| | Houston Aeros | AHL | 11 | 1 | 3 | 4 | 0 | | | | | | | | | | 8 | 1 | 1 | 2 | 2 | | | | |
| 2006-07 | Bloomington | UHL | 2 | 0 | 0 | 0 | 2 | | | | | | | | | | | | | | | | | | |
| | Huddinge IK | Sweden-2 | 6 | 1 | 2 | 3 | 0 | | | | | | | | | | | | | | | | | | |
| | IK Oskarshamn | Sweden-2 | 26 | 5 | 8 | 13 | 31 | | | | | | | | | | | | | | | | | | |
| 2007-08 | Binghamton | AHL | 71 | 15 | 18 | 33 | 37 | | | | | | | | | | | | | | | | | | |
| 2008-09 | Binghamton | AHL | 80 | 24 | 27 | 51 | 41 | | | | | | | | | | | | | | | | | | |
| | **NHL Totals** | | **6** | **0** | **0** | **0** | **4** | **0** | **0** | **0** | **6** | **0.0** | | **0** | **0.0** | **8:47** | | | | | | | | | |

EJHL First All-Star Team (2000, 2001) • EJHL MVP (2000)

Signed as a free agent by **Oskarshamn** (Sweden-2), October 23, 2006. Signed as a free agent by **Binghamton** (AHL), August 9, 2007. Signed as a free agent by **Ottawa**, July 7, 2008. Signed as a free agent by **NY Islanders**, July 6, 2009.

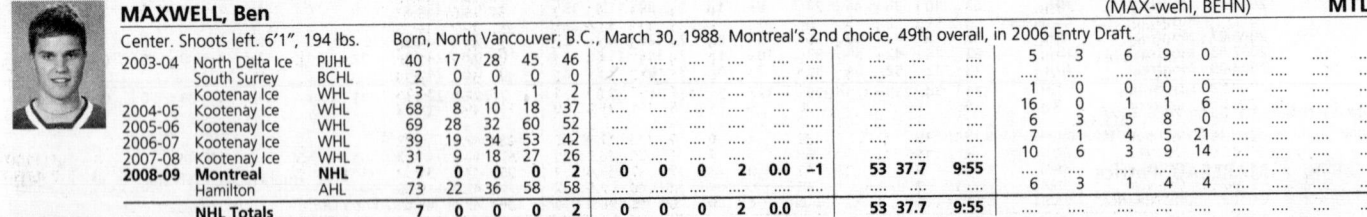

## MAXWELL, Ben
(MAX-wehl, BEHN) **MTL.**

Center. Shoots left. 6'1", 194 lbs. Born, North Vancouver, B.C., March 30, 1988. Montreal's 2nd choice, 49th overall, in 2006 Entry Draft.

| Season | Club | League | GP | G | A | Pts | PIM | PP | SH | GW | S | % | +/- | TF | F% | Min | GP | G | A | Pts | PIM | PP | SH | GW | Min |
|---|---|---|---|---|---|---|---|---|---|---|---|---|---|---|---|---|---|---|---|---|---|---|---|---|---|
| 2003-04 | North Delta Ice | PIJHL | 40 | 17 | 28 | 45 | 46 | | | | | | | | | | 5 | 3 | 6 | 9 | 0 | | | | |
| | South Surrey | BCHL | 2 | 0 | 0 | 0 | 0 | | | | | | | | | | | | | | | | | | |
| | Kootenay Ice | WHL | 3 | 0 | 1 | 1 | 2 | | | | | | | | | | 1 | 0 | 0 | 0 | 0 | | | | |
| 2004-05 | Kootenay Ice | WHL | 68 | 8 | 10 | 18 | 37 | | | | | | | | | | 16 | 0 | 1 | 1 | 6 | | | | |
| 2005-06 | Kootenay Ice | WHL | 69 | 28 | 32 | 60 | 52 | | | | | | | | | | 6 | 3 | 5 | 8 | 0 | | | | |
| 2006-07 | Kootenay Ice | WHL | 39 | 19 | 34 | 53 | 42 | | | | | | | | | | 7 | 1 | 4 | 5 | 21 | | | | |
| 2007-08 | Kootenay Ice | WHL | 31 | 9 | 18 | 27 | 26 | | | | | | | | | | 10 | 6 | 3 | 9 | 14 | | | | |
| **2008-09** | **Montreal** | **NHL** | **7** | **0** | **0** | **0** | **2** | **0** | **0** | **0** | **2** | **0.0** | **–1** | **53** | **37.7** | **9:55** | | | | | | | | | |
| | Hamilton | AHL | 73 | 22 | 36 | 58 | 58 | | | | | | | | | | 6 | 3 | 1 | 4 | 4 | | | | |
| | **NHL Totals** | | **7** | **0** | **0** | **0** | **2** | **0** | **0** | **0** | **2** | **0.0** | | **53** | **37.7** | **9:55** | | | | | | | | | |

## MAY, Brad
(MAY, BRAD)

Left wing. Shoots left. 6'1", 213 lbs. Born, Toronto, Ont., November 29, 1971. Buffalo's 1st choice, 14th overall, in 1990 Entry Draft.

| Season | Club | League | GP | G | A | Pts | PIM | PP | SH | GW | S | % | +/- | TF | F% | Min | GP | G | A | Pts | PIM | PP | SH | GW | Min |
|---|---|---|---|---|---|---|---|---|---|---|---|---|---|---|---|---|---|---|---|---|---|---|---|---|---|
| 1987-88 | Markham | Minor-ON | 31 | 22 | 37 | 59 | 58 | | | | | | | | | | | | | | | | | | |
| | Markham | OHA-B | 6 | 1 | 1 | 2 | 21 | | | | | | | | | | | | | | | | | | |
| 1988-89 | Niagara Falls | OHL | 65 | 8 | 14 | 22 | 304 | | | | | | | | | | 17 | 0 | 1 | 1 | 55 | | | | |
| 1989-90 | Niagara Falls | OHL | 61 | 32 | 58 | 90 | 223 | | | | | | | | | | 16 | 9 | 13 | 22 | 64 | | | | |
| 1990-91 | Niagara Falls | OHL | 34 | 37 | 32 | 69 | 93 | | | | | | | | | | 14 | 11 | 14 | 25 | 53 | | | | |
| **1991-92** | **Buffalo** | **NHL** | **69** | **11** | **6** | **17** | **309** | **1** | **0** | **3** | **82** | **13.4** | **–12** | | | | **7** | **1** | **4** | **5** | **2** | **0** | **0** | **1** | |
| **1992-93** | **Buffalo** | **NHL** | **82** | **13** | **13** | **26** | **242** | **0** | **0** | **1** | **114** | **11.4** | **3** | | | | **8** | **1** | **1** | **2** | **14** | **0** | **0** | **1** | |
| **1993-94** | **Buffalo** | **NHL** | **84** | **18** | **27** | **45** | **171** | **3** | **0** | **3** | **166** | **10.8** | **–6** | | | | **7** | **0** | **2** | **2** | **9** | **0** | **0** | **0** | |
| **1994-95** | **Buffalo** | **NHL** | **33** | **3** | **3** | **6** | **87** | **1** | **0** | **0** | **42** | **7.1** | **5** | | | | **4** | **0** | **0** | **0** | **2** | **0** | **0** | **0** | |
| **1995-96** | **Buffalo** | **NHL** | **79** | **15** | **29** | **44** | **295** | **3** | **0** | **4** | **168** | **8.9** | **6** | | | | | | | | | | | | |
| **1996-97** | **Buffalo** | **NHL** | **42** | **3** | **4** | **7** | **106** | **1** | **0** | **1** | **75** | **4.0** | **–8** | | | | **10** | **1** | **1** | **2** | **32** | **0** | **0** | **0** | |
| **1997-98** | **Buffalo** | **NHL** | **36** | **4** | **7** | **11** | **113** | **0** | **0** | **0** | **41** | **9.8** | **2** | | | | | | | | | | | | |
| | **Vancouver** | **NHL** | **27** | **9** | **3** | **12** | **41** | **4** | **0** | **2** | **56** | **16.1** | **0** | | | | | | | | | | | | |
| **1998-99** | **Vancouver** | **NHL** | **66** | **6** | **11** | **17** | **102** | **1** | **0** | **1** | **91** | **6.6** | **–14** | **8** | **12.5** | **13:04** | | | | | | | | | |
| **99-2000** | **Vancouver** | **NHL** | **59** | **9** | **7** | **16** | **90** | **0** | **0** | **3** | **66** | **13.6** | **–2** | **3** | **0.0** | **10:24** | | | | | | | | | |

| | | | Regular Season | | | | | | | | | | | | | | Playoffs | | | | | | | | |
|---|---|---|---|---|---|---|---|---|---|---|---|---|---|---|---|---|---|---|---|---|---|---|---|---|---|
| Season | Club | League | GP | G | A | Pts | PIM | PP | SH | GW | S | % | +/- | TF | F% | Min | GP | G | A | Pts | PIM | PP | SH | GW | Min |
| 2000-01 | Phoenix | NHL | 62 | 11 | 14 | 25 | 107 | 0 | 0 | 0 | 83 | 13.3 | 10 | 3 | 33.3 | 11:11 | .... | .... | .... | .... | .... | .... | .... | .... | .... |
| 2001-02 | Phoenix | NHL | 72 | 10 | 12 | 22 | 95 | 1 | 0 | 3 | 105 | 9.5 | 11 | 3 | 0.0 | 12:04 | 5 | 0 | 0 | 0 | 0 | 0 | 0 | 0 | 10:19 |
| 2002-03 | Phoenix | NHL | 20 | 3 | 4 | 7 | 32 | 0 | 0 | 0 | 24 | 12.5 | 3 | 0 | 0.0 | 9:56 | .... | .... | .... | .... | .... | .... | .... | .... | .... |
| | Vancouver | NHL | 3 | 0 | 0 | 0 | 10 | 0 | 0 | 0 | 1 | 0.0 | 1 | 0 | 0.0 | 7:48 | 14 | 0 | 0 | 0 | 15 | 0 | 0 | 0 | 7:25 |
| 2003-04 | Vancouver | NHL | 70 | 5 | 6 | 11 | 137 | 0 | 0 | 0 | 75 | 6.7 | –2 | 8 | 50.0 | 8:56 | 6 | 1 | 0 | 1 | 6 | 0 | 0 | 0 | 7:07 |
| 2004-05 | | | DID NOT PLAY | | | | | | | | | | | | | | | | | | | | | | |
| 2005-06 | Colorado | NHL | 54 | 3 | 3 | 6 | 82 | 0 | 0 | 0 | 55 | 5.5 | –14 | 6 | 33.3 | 8:23 | 3 | 0 | 0 | 0 | 0 | 0 | 0 | 0 | 9:21 |
| 2006-07 | Colorado | NHL | 10 | 0 | 3 | 3 | 8 | 0 | 0 | 0 | 11 | 0.0 | 0 | 0 | 0.0 | 11:28 | .... | .... | .... | .... | .... | .... | .... | .... | .... |
| | ♦ Anaheim | NHL | 14 | 0 | 1 | 1 | 13 | 0 | 0 | 0 | 11 | 0.0 | –1 | 0 | 0.0 | 8:39 | 18 | 0 | 1 | 1 | 28 | 0 | 0 | 0 | 7:21 |
| 2007-08 | Anaheim | NHL | 61 | 3 | 1 | 4 | 53 | 0 | 0 | 2 | 34 | 8.8 | 2 | 3 | 0.0 | 6:37 | 6 | 0 | 0 | 0 | 4 | 0 | 0 | 0 | 6:56 |
| 2008-09 | Anaheim | NHL | 20 | 0 | 5 | 5 | 28 | 0 | 0 | 0 | 5 | 0.0 | 5 | 3 | 33.3 | 6:22 | .... | .... | .... | .... | .... | .... | .... | .... | .... |
| | Toronto | NHL | 38 | 1 | 1 | 2 | 61 | 0 | 0 | 0 | 27 | 3.7 | –5 | 1 | 0.0 | 7:44 | .... | .... | .... | .... | .... | .... | .... | .... | .... |
| | NHL Totals | | 1001 | 127 | 160 | 287 | 2182 | 15 | 0 | 23 | 1332 | 9.5 | | 38 | 23.7 | 9:50 | 88 | 4 | 9 | 13 | 112 | 0 | 0 | 2 | 7:42 |

OHL Second All-Star Team (1990, 1991)

• Missed majority of 1990-91 season recovering from knee injury suffered at Team Canada Juniors evaluation camp, August 21, 1990. Traded to **Vancouver** by **Buffalo** with Buffalo's 3rd round choice (later traded to Tampa Bay – Tampa Bay selected Jimmie Olvestad) in 1999 Entry Draft for Geoff Sanderson, February 4, 1998. Traded to **Phoenix** by **Vancouver** for future considerations, June 24, 2000. • Missed majority of 2002-03 season recovering from shoulder injury suffered in pre-season game vs. Detroit, October 6, 2002. Traded to **Vancouver** by **Phoenix** for Phoenix's 3rd round choice (previously acquired, Phoenix selected Dimitri Pestunov) in 2003 Entry Draft, March 11, 2003. Signed as a free agent by **Colorado**, August 5, 2005. Traded to **Anaheim** by **Colorado** for Michael Wall, February 27, 2007. • Missed majority of 2006-07 season recovering from shoulder injury suffered in pre-season game vs. Detroit, September 25, 2006. Traded to **Toronto** by **Anaheim** for future considerations, January 7, 2009.

## MAYERS, Jamal

(MAI-uhrz, JUH-MAHL) **TOR.**

Right wing. Shoots right. 6'1", 214 lbs. Born, Toronto, Ont., October 24, 1974. St. Louis' 3rd choice, 89th overall, in 1993 Entry Draft.

| | | | | | | | | | | | | | | | | | | | | | | | | | |
|---|---|---|---|---|---|---|---|---|---|---|---|---|---|---|---|---|---|---|---|---|---|---|---|---|---|
| 1990-91 | Thornhill | MTJHL | 44 | 12 | 24 | 36 | 78 | .... | .... | .... | .... | .... | .... | .... | .... | .... | .... | .... | .... | .... | .... | .... | .... | .... | .... |
| 1991-92 | Thornhill | MTJHL | 56 | 38 | 69 | 107 | 36 | .... | .... | .... | .... | .... | .... | .... | .... | .... | .... | .... | .... | .... | .... | .... | .... | .... | .... |
| 1992-93 | Western Mich. | CCHA | 38 | 8 | 17 | 25 | 26 | .... | .... | .... | .... | .... | .... | .... | .... | .... | .... | .... | .... | .... | .... | .... | .... | .... | .... |
| 1993-94 | Western Mich. | CCHA | 40 | 17 | 32 | 49 | 40 | .... | .... | .... | .... | .... | .... | .... | .... | .... | .... | .... | .... | .... | .... | .... | .... | .... | .... |
| 1994-95 | Western Mich. | CCHA | 39 | 13 | 32 | 45 | 40 | .... | .... | .... | .... | .... | .... | .... | .... | .... | .... | .... | .... | .... | .... | .... | .... | .... | .... |
| 1995-96 | Western Mich. | CCHA | 38 | 17 | 22 | 39 | 75 | .... | .... | .... | .... | .... | .... | .... | .... | .... | .... | .... | .... | .... | .... | .... | .... | .... | .... |
| 1996-97 | St. Louis | NHL | 6 | 0 | 1 | 1 | 2 | 0 | 0 | 0 | 7 | 0.0 | –3 | .... | .... | .... | .... | .... | .... | .... | .... | .... | .... | .... | .... |
| | Worcester IceCats | AHL | 62 | 12 | 14 | 26 | 104 | .... | .... | .... | .... | .... | .... | .... | .... | .... | 5 | 4 | 5 | 9 | 4 | .... | .... | .... | .... |
| 1997-98 | Worcester IceCats | AHL | 61 | 19 | 24 | 43 | 117 | .... | .... | .... | .... | .... | .... | .... | .... | .... | 11 | 3 | 4 | 7 | 10 | .... | .... | .... | .... |
| 1998-99 | St. Louis | NHL | 34 | 4 | 5 | 9 | 40 | 0 | 0 | 0 | 48 | 8.3 | –3 | 2 | 50.0 | 8:08 | 11 | 0 | 1 | 1 | 8 | 0 | 0 | 0 | 8:34 |
| | Worcester IceCats | AHL | 20 | 9 | 7 | 16 | 34 | .... | .... | .... | .... | .... | .... | .... | .... | .... | .... | .... | .... | .... | .... | .... | .... | .... | .... |
| 99-2000 | St. Louis | NHL | 79 | 7 | 10 | 17 | 90 | 0 | 0 | 0 | 99 | 7.1 | 0 | 77 | 52.0 | 9:46 | 7 | 0 | 4 | 4 | 2 | 0 | 0 | 0 | 10:42 |
| 2000-01 | St. Louis | NHL | 77 | 8 | 13 | 21 | 117 | 0 | 0 | 0 | 132 | 6.1 | –3 | 273 | 51.3 | 11:04 | 15 | 2 | 3 | 5 | 8 | 0 | 0 | 0 | 11:28 |
| 2001-02 | St. Louis | NHL | 77 | 9 | 8 | 17 | 99 | 0 | 1 | 0 | 105 | 8.6 | 9 | 761 | 52.6 | 11:36 | 10 | 3 | 0 | 3 | 2 | 0 | 0 | 2 | 11:14 |
| 2002-03 | St. Louis | NHL | 15 | 2 | 5 | 7 | 8 | 0 | 0 | 0 | 26 | 7.7 | 1 | 111 | 51.4 | 14:21 | .... | .... | .... | .... | .... | .... | .... | .... | .... |
| 2003-04 | St. Louis | NHL | 80 | 6 | 5 | 11 | 91 | 0 | 1 | 3 | 130 | 4.6 | –19 | 681 | 48.6 | 13:01 | 5 | 0 | 0 | 0 | 0 | 0 | 0 | 0 | 12:55 |
| 2004-05 | Hammarby | Sweden-2 | 19 | 9 | 13 | 22 | 36 | .... | .... | .... | .... | .... | .... | .... | .... | .... | .... | .... | .... | .... | .... | .... | .... | .... | .... |
| | Missouri | UHL | 13 | 5 | 2 | 7 | 68 | .... | .... | .... | .... | .... | .... | .... | .... | .... | .... | .... | .... | .... | .... | .... | .... | .... | .... |
| 2005-06 | St. Louis | NHL | 67 | 15 | 11 | 26 | 129 | 0 | 2 | 1 | 111 | 13.5 | –22 | 363 | 48.5 | 15:07 | .... | .... | .... | .... | .... | .... | .... | .... | .... |
| 2006-07 | St. Louis | NHL | 80 | 8 | 14 | 22 | 89 | 0 | 2 | 0 | 129 | 6.2 | –19 | 432 | 57.4 | 14:37 | .... | .... | .... | .... | .... | .... | .... | .... | .... |
| 2007-08 | St. Louis | NHL | 80 | 12 | 15 | 27 | 91 | 0 | 1 | 3 | 153 | 7.8 | –19 | 683 | 56.2 | 15:56 | .... | .... | .... | .... | .... | .... | .... | .... | .... |
| 2008-09 | Toronto | NHL | 71 | 7 | 9 | 16 | 82 | 0 | 0 | 1 | 72 | 9.7 | –7 | 429 | 57.3 | 10:33 | .... | .... | .... | .... | .... | .... | .... | .... | .... |
| | NHL Totals | | 666 | 78 | 96 | 174 | 838 | 0 | 7 | 8 | 1012 | 7.7 | | 3812 | 53.1 | 12:30 | 48 | 5 | 8 | 13 | 20 | 0 | 0 | 2 | 10:47 |

• Missed majority of 2002-03 season recovering from knee injury suffered in game vs. Calgary, November 16, 2002. Signed as a free agent by **Hammarby** (Sweden-2), November 16, 2004. Signed as a free agent by **Missouri** (UHL), March 11, 2005. Traded to **Toronto** by **St. Louis** for Florida's 3rd round choice (previously acquired, St. Louis selected James Livingston) in 2008 Entry Draft, June 19, 2008.

## MAYOROV, Maksim

(may-YOHR-ahv, mahx-EEM) **CBJ**

Left wing. Shoots left. 6'2", 213 lbs. Born, Andizhan, USSR, March 26, 1989. Columbus' 5th choice, 94th overall, in 2007 Entry Draft.

| | | | | | | | | | | | | | | | | | | | | | | | | | |
|---|---|---|---|---|---|---|---|---|---|---|---|---|---|---|---|---|---|---|---|---|---|---|---|---|---|
| 2005-06 | Ak Bars Kazan 2 | Russia-3 | STATISTICS NOT AVAILABLE | | | | | | | | | | | | | | | | | | | | | | |
| 2006-07 | Leninogorsk | Russia-2 | 28 | 6 | 4 | 10 | 6 | .... | .... | .... | .... | .... | .... | .... | .... | .... | .... | .... | .... | .... | .... | .... | .... | .... | .... |
| | Almetjevsk | Russia-2 | 6 | 1 | 1 | 2 | 0 | .... | .... | .... | .... | .... | .... | .... | .... | .... | 4 | 0 | 0 | 0 | 2 | .... | .... | .... | .... |
| 2007-08 | Ak Bars Kazan | Russia | 11 | 1 | 0 | 1 | 16 | .... | .... | .... | .... | .... | .... | .... | .... | .... | .... | .... | .... | .... | .... | .... | .... | .... | .... |
| 2008-09 | Columbus | NHL | 3 | 0 | 0 | 0 | 0 | 0 | 0 | 0 | 1 | 0.0 | 0 | 0 | 0.0 | 5:44 | .... | .... | .... | .... | .... | .... | .... | .... | .... |
| | Syracuse Crunch | AHL | 71 | 17 | 14 | 31 | 30 | .... | .... | .... | .... | .... | .... | .... | .... | .... | .... | .... | .... | .... | .... | .... | .... | .... | .... |
| | NHL Totals | | 3 | 0 | 0 | 0 | 0 | 0 | 0 | 0 | 1 | 0.0 | | 0 | 0.0 | 5:44 | .... | .... | .... | .... | .... | .... | .... | .... | .... |

## McAMMOND, Dean

(muhK-AM-uhnd, DEEN)

Center. Shoots left. 5'11", 193 lbs. Born, Grand Cache, Alta., June 15, 1973. Chicago's 1st choice, 22nd overall, in 1991 Entry Draft.

| | | | | | | | | | | | | | | | | | | | | | | | | | |
|---|---|---|---|---|---|---|---|---|---|---|---|---|---|---|---|---|---|---|---|---|---|---|---|---|---|
| 1988-89 | St. Albert Raiders | AMHL | 36 | 33 | 44 | 77 | 132 | .... | .... | .... | .... | .... | .... | .... | .... | .... | .... | .... | .... | .... | .... | .... | .... | .... | .... |
| 1989-90 | Prince Albert | WHL | 53 | 11 | 11 | 22 | 49 | .... | .... | .... | .... | .... | .... | .... | .... | .... | 14 | 2 | 3 | 5 | 18 | .... | .... | .... | .... |
| 1990-91 | Prince Albert | WHL | 71 | 33 | 35 | 68 | 108 | .... | .... | .... | .... | .... | .... | .... | .... | .... | 2 | 0 | 1 | 1 | 6 | .... | .... | .... | .... |
| 1991-92 | Prince Albert | WHL | 63 | 37 | 54 | 91 | 189 | .... | .... | .... | .... | .... | .... | .... | .... | .... | 10 | 12 | 11 | 23 | 26 | .... | .... | .... | .... |
| | Chicago | NHL | 5 | 0 | 2 | 2 | 0 | 0 | 0 | 0 | 4 | 0.0 | –2 | .... | .... | .... | 3 | 0 | 0 | 0 | 2 | 0 | 0 | 0 | .... |
| 1992-93 | Prince Albert | WHL | 30 | 19 | 29 | 48 | 44 | .... | .... | .... | .... | .... | .... | .... | .... | .... | .... | .... | .... | .... | .... | .... | .... | .... | .... |
| | Swift Current | WHL | 18 | 10 | 13 | 23 | 24 | .... | .... | .... | .... | .... | .... | .... | .... | .... | 17 | *16 | 19 | 35 | 20 | .... | .... | .... | .... |
| 1993-94 | Edmonton | NHL | 45 | 6 | 21 | 27 | 16 | 2 | 0 | 0 | 52 | 11.5 | 12 | .... | .... | .... | .... | .... | .... | .... | .... | .... | .... | .... | .... |
| | Cape Breton | AHL | 28 | 9 | 12 | 21 | 38 | .... | .... | .... | .... | .... | .... | .... | .... | .... | .... | .... | .... | .... | .... | .... | .... | .... | .... |
| 1994-95 | Edmonton | NHL | 6 | 0 | 0 | 0 | 0 | 0 | 0 | 0 | 3 | 0.0 | –1 | .... | .... | .... | .... | .... | .... | .... | .... | .... | .... | .... | .... |
| 1995-96 | Edmonton | NHL | 53 | 15 | 15 | 30 | 23 | 4 | 0 | 0 | 79 | 19.0 | 6 | .... | .... | .... | .... | .... | .... | .... | .... | .... | .... | .... | .... |
| | Cape Breton | AHL | 22 | 9 | 15 | 24 | 55 | .... | .... | .... | .... | .... | .... | .... | .... | .... | .... | .... | .... | .... | .... | .... | .... | .... | .... |
| 1996-97 | Edmonton | NHL | 57 | 12 | 17 | 29 | 28 | 4 | 0 | 6 | 106 | 11.3 | –15 | .... | .... | .... | .... | .... | .... | .... | .... | .... | .... | .... | .... |
| 1997-98 | Edmonton | NHL | 77 | 19 | 31 | 50 | 46 | 8 | 0 | 3 | 128 | 14.8 | 9 | .... | .... | .... | 12 | 1 | 4 | 5 | 12 | 0 | 0 | 0 | .... |
| 1998-99 | Edmonton | NHL | 65 | 9 | 16 | 25 | 36 | 1 | 0 | 0 | 122 | 7.4 | 5 | 26 | 38.5 | 14:15 | .... | .... | .... | .... | .... | .... | .... | .... | .... |
| | Chicago | NHL | 12 | 1 | 4 | 5 | 2 | 0 | 0 | 1 | 16 | 6.3 | 3 | 37 | 48.6 | 15:43 | .... | .... | .... | .... | .... | .... | .... | .... | .... |
| 99-2000 | Chicago | NHL | 76 | 14 | 18 | 32 | 72 | 1 | 0 | 1 | 118 | 11.9 | 11 | 257 | 39.7 | 16:25 | .... | .... | .... | .... | .... | .... | .... | .... | .... |
| 2000-01 | Chicago | NHL | 61 | 10 | 16 | 26 | 43 | 1 | 0 | 1 | 95 | 10.5 | 4 | 23 | 43.5 | 15:30 | .... | .... | .... | .... | .... | .... | .... | .... | .... |
| | Philadelphia | NHL | 10 | 1 | 1 | 2 | 0 | 1 | 0 | 0 | 17 | 5.9 | –1 | 65 | 46.2 | 12:00 | 4 | 0 | 0 | 0 | 2 | 0 | 0 | 0 | 9:25 |
| 2001-02 | Calgary | NHL | 73 | 21 | 30 | 51 | 60 | 7 | 0 | 4 | 152 | 13.8 | 2 | 143 | 55.2 | 18:56 | .... | .... | .... | .... | .... | .... | .... | .... | .... |
| 2002-03 | Colorado | NHL | 41 | 10 | 8 | 18 | 10 | 2 | 0 | 2 | 72 | 13.9 | 1 | 9 | 55.6 | 14:24 | .... | .... | .... | .... | .... | .... | .... | .... | .... |
| 2003-04 | Calgary | NHL | 64 | 17 | 13 | 30 | 18 | 4 | 1 | 5 | 101 | 16.8 | 9 | 768 | 49.1 | 16:52 | .... | .... | .... | .... | .... | .... | .... | .... | .... |
| 2004-05 | Albany River Rats | AHL | 79 | 19 | 42 | 61 | 72 | .... | .... | .... | .... | .... | .... | .... | .... | .... | .... | .... | .... | .... | .... | .... | .... | .... | .... |
| 2005-06 | St. Louis | NHL | 78 | 15 | 22 | 37 | 32 | 4 | 0 | 0 | 116 | 12.9 | –25 | 289 | 47.4 | 16:02 | .... | .... | .... | .... | .... | .... | .... | .... | .... |
| 2006-07 | Ottawa | NHL | 81 | 14 | 15 | 29 | 28 | 0 | 2 | 1 | 86 | 16.3 | 11 | 677 | 44.2 | 11:08 | 18 | 5 | 3 | 8 | 11 | 0 | 1 | 1 | 11:27 |
| 2007-08 | Ottawa | NHL | 68 | 9 | 13 | 22 | 12 | 0 | 3 | 1 | 67 | 13.4 | 1 | 259 | 43.2 | 11:32 | 4 | 0 | 0 | 0 | 4 | 0 | 0 | 0 | 13:30 |
| 2008-09 | Ottawa | NHL | 44 | 3 | 4 | 7 | 16 | 0 | 1 | 2 | 40 | 7.5 | 2 | 276 | 42.0 | 9:40 | .... | .... | .... | .... | .... | .... | .... | .... | .... |
| | NY Islanders | NHL | 18 | 2 | 7 | 9 | 8 | 0 | 0 | 0 | 19 | 10.5 | 5 | 267 | 47.2 | 15:09 | .... | .... | .... | .... | .... | .... | .... | .... | .... |
| | NHL Totals | | 934 | 178 | 253 | 431 | 450 | 39 | 7 | 27 | 1393 | 12.8 | | 3096 | 45.9 | 14:38 | 41 | 6 | 7 | 13 | 31 | 0 | 1 | 1 | 11:27 |

Traded to **Edmonton** by **Chicago** with Igor Kravchuk for Joe Murphy, February 24, 1993. Traded to **Chicago** by **Edmonton** with Boris Mironov and Jonas Elofsson for Chad Kilger, Daniel Cleary, Ethan Moreau and Christian Laflamme, March 20, 1999. Traded to **Philadelphia** by **Chicago** for Philadelphia's 3rd round choice (later traded to Toronto – Toronto selected Nicolas Corbeil) in 2001 Entry Draft, March 13, 2001. Traded to **Calgary** by **Philadelphia** for Calgary's 4th round choice (Rosario Ruggeri) in 2002 Entry Draft, June 24, 2001. Traded to **Colorado** by **Calgary** with Derek Morris and Jeff Shantz for Chris Drury and Stephane Yelle, October 1, 2002. Traded to **Calgary** by **Colorado** for Calgary's 5th round choice (Mark McCutcheon) in 2003 Entry Draft, March 11, 2003. • Ruled ineligible to play remainder of 2002-03 season by NHL due to transaction violation by Calgary, March 15, 2003. Signed as a free agent by **New Jersey**, October 5, 2004. Signed as a free agent by **St. Louis**, August 9, 2005. Signed as a free agent by **Ottawa**, August 2, 2006. Traded to **NY Islanders** by **Ottawa** with San Jose's 1st round choice (previously acquired, later traded to Columbus, later traded to Anaheim – Anaheim selected Kyle Palmieri) in 2009 Entry Draft for Mike Comrie and Chris Campoli, February 20. 2009.

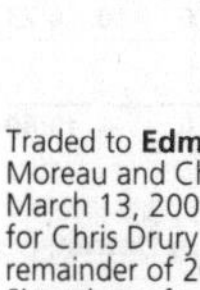

## McARDLE, Kenndal

(muh-KAHR-duhl, KEHN-dahl) **FLA.**

Left wing. Shoots left. 5'11", 190 lbs. Born, Toronto, Ont., January 4, 1987. Florida's 1st choice, 20th overall, in 2005 Entry Draft.

| | | | | | | | | | | | | | | | | | | | | | | | | | |
|---|---|---|---|---|---|---|---|---|---|---|---|---|---|---|---|---|---|---|---|---|---|---|---|---|---|
| 2002-03 | Burnaby W.C. | Minor-BC | 30 | 1 | 9 | 10 | 131 | .... | .... | .... | .... | .... | .... | .... | .... | .... | .... | .... | .... | .... | .... | .... | .... | .... | .... |
| | Moose Jaw | WHL | 2 | 0 | 0 | 0 | 0 | .... | .... | .... | .... | .... | .... | .... | .... | .... | .... | .... | .... | .... | .... | .... | .... | .... | .... |
| 2003-04 | Moose Jaw | WHL | 54 | 8 | 8 | 16 | 57 | .... | .... | .... | .... | .... | .... | .... | .... | .... | 10 | 3 | 2 | 5 | 6 | .... | .... | .... | .... |
| 2004-05 | Moose Jaw | WHL | 70 | 37 | 37 | 74 | 122 | .... | .... | .... | .... | .... | .... | .... | .... | .... | 5 | 1 | 0 | 1 | 16 | .... | .... | .... | .... |
| 2005-06 | Moose Jaw | WHL | 72 | 28 | 43 | 71 | 135 | .... | .... | .... | .... | .... | .... | .... | .... | .... | 22 | 6 | 10 | 16 | 43 | .... | .... | .... | .... |
| 2006-07 | Moose Jaw | WHL | 26 | 10 | 10 | 20 | 75 | .... | .... | .... | .... | .... | .... | .... | .... | .... | .... | .... | .... | .... | .... | .... | .... | .... | .... |
| | Vancouver Giants | WHL | 37 | 9 | 13 | 22 | 54 | .... | .... | .... | .... | .... | .... | .... | .... | .... | 22 | *11 | 9 | 20 | 49 | .... | .... | .... | .... |

| | | | Regular Season | | | | | | | | | | | | | | Playoffs | | | | | | | | |
|---|---|---|---|---|---|---|---|---|---|---|---|---|---|---|---|---|---|---|---|---|---|---|---|---|---|
| Season | Club | League | GP | G | A | Pts | PIM | PP | SH | GW | S | % | +/- | TF | F% | Min | GP | G | A | Pts | PIM | PP | SH | GW | Min |
| 2007-08 | Rochester | AHL | 36 | 5 | 5 | 10 | 31 | | | | | | | | | | | | | | | | | | |
| | Florida Everblades | ECHL | 6 | 3 | 1 | 4 | 26 | | | | | | | | | | 3 | 0 | 0 | 0 | 2 | | | | |
| **2008-09** | **Florida** | **NHL** | **3** | **0** | **0** | **0** | **2** | **0** | **0** | **0** | **1** | **0.0** | **–1** | **0** | **0.0** | **7:30** | | | | | | | | | |
| | Rochester | AHL | 58 | 12 | 12 | 24 | 79 | | | | | | | | | | | | | | | | | | |
| | **NHL Totals** | | **3** | **0** | **0** | **0** | **2** | **0** | **0** | **0** | **1** | **0.0** | | **0** | **0.0** | **7:30** | | | | | | | | | |

(muh-KAYB, BRIGH-uhn) **FLA.**

## McCABE, Bryan

Defense. Shoots left. 6'2", 220 lbs. Born, St. Catharines, Ont., June 8, 1975. NY Islanders' 2nd choice, 40th overall, in 1993 Entry Draft.

| Season | Club | League | GP | G | A | Pts | PIM | PP | SH | GW | S | % | +/- | TF | F% | Min | GP | G | A | Pts | PIM | PP | SH | GW | Min |
|---|---|---|---|---|---|---|---|---|---|---|---|---|---|---|---|---|---|---|---|---|---|---|---|---|---|
| 1990-91 | Calgary Canucks | AMHL | 33 | 14 | 34 | 48 | 55 | | | | | | | | | | | | | | | | | | |
| 1991-92 | Medicine Hat | WHL | 68 | 6 | 24 | 30 | 157 | | | | | | | | | | 4 | 0 | 0 | 0 | 6 | | | | |
| 1992-93 | Medicine Hat | WHL | 14 | 0 | 13 | 13 | 83 | | | | | | | | | | | | | | | | | | |
| | Spokane Chiefs | WHL | 46 | 3 | 44 | 47 | 134 | | | | | | | | | | 6 | 1 | 5 | 6 | 28 | | | | |
| 1993-94 | Spokane Chiefs | WHL | 64 | 22 | 62 | 84 | 218 | | | | | | | | | | 3 | 0 | 4 | 4 | 4 | | | | |
| 1994-95 | Spokane Chiefs | WHL | 42 | 14 | 39 | 53 | 115 | | | | | | | | | | | | | | | | | | |
| | Brandon | WHL | 20 | 6 | 10 | 16 | 38 | | | | | | | | | | 18 | 4 | 13 | 17 | 59 | | | | |
| **1995-96** | **NY Islanders** | **NHL** | **82** | **7** | **16** | **23** | **156** | **3** | **0** | **1** | **130** | **5.4** | **–24** | | | | | | | | | | | | |
| **1996-97** | **NY Islanders** | **NHL** | **82** | **8** | **20** | **28** | **165** | **2** | **1** | **2** | **117** | **6.8** | **–2** | | | | | | | | | | | | |
| **1997-98** | **NY Islanders** | **NHL** | **56** | **3** | **9** | **12** | **145** | **1** | **0** | **0** | **81** | **3.7** | **9** | | | | | | | | | | | | |
| | **Vancouver** | **NHL** | **26** | **1** | **11** | **12** | **64** | **0** | **1** | **0** | **42** | **2.4** | **10** | | | | | | | | | | | | |
| **1998-99** | **Vancouver** | **NHL** | **69** | **7** | **14** | **21** | **120** | **1** | **2** | **0** | **98** | **7.1** | **–11** | **1** | **0.0** | **24:13** | | | | | | | | | |
| **99-2000** | **Chicago** | **NHL** | **79** | **6** | **19** | **25** | **139** | **2** | **0** | **2** | **119** | **5.0** | **–8** | **1** | **0.0** | **23:23** | | | | | | | | | |
| **2000-01** | **Toronto** | **NHL** | **82** | **5** | **24** | **29** | **123** | **3** | **0** | **2** | **159** | **3.1** | **16** | **0** | **0.0** | **23:49** | **11** | **2** | **3** | **5** | **16** | **1** | **0** | **0** | **23:56** |
| **2001-02** | **Toronto** | **NHL** | **82** | **17** | **26** | **43** | **129** | **8** | **0** | **1** | **157** | **10.8** | **16** | **1** | **0.0** | **24:34** | **20** | **5** | **5** | **10** | **30** | **3** | **0** | **1** | **29:33** |
| **2002-03** | **Toronto** | **NHL** | **75** | **6** | **18** | **24** | **135** | **3** | **0** | **1** | **149** | **4.0** | **9** | **1** | **0.0** | **23:39** | **7** | **0** | **3** | **3** | **10** | **0** | **0** | **0** | **27:28** |
| **2003-04** | **Toronto** | **NHL** | **75** | **16** | **37** | **53** | **86** | **8** | **0** | **2** | **168** | **9.5** | **22** | **2** | **50.0** | **25:44** | **13** | **3** | **5** | **8** | **14** | **2** | **0** | **0** | **28:47** |
| 2004-05 | HV 71 Jonkoping | Sweden | 10 | 1 | 0 | 1 | 30 | | | | | | | | | | | | | | | | | | |
| **2005-06** | **Toronto** | **NHL** | **73** | **19** | **49** | **68** | **116** | **13** | **0** | **6** | **207** | **9.2** | **–1** | **1** | **0.0** | **28:18** | | | | | | | | | |
| | Canada | Olympics | 6 | 0 | 0 | 0 | 18 | | | | | | | | | | | | | | | | | | |
| **2006-07** | **Toronto** | **NHL** | **82** | **15** | **42** | **57** | **115** | **11** | **0** | **1** | **207** | **7.2** | **3** | **0** | **0.0** | **26:50** | | | | | | | | | |
| **2007-08** | **Toronto** | **NHL** | **54** | **5** | **18** | **23** | **81** | **4** | **0** | **2** | **107** | **4.7** | **–2** | **0** | **0.0** | **25:55** | | | | | | | | | |
| **2008-09** | **Florida** | **NHL** | **69** | **15** | **24** | **39** | **41** | **8** | **0** | **3** | **153** | **9.8** | **–1** | **0** | **0.0** | **23:08** | | | | | | | | | |
| | **NHL Totals** | | **986** | **130** | **327** | **457** | **1615** | **67** | **4** | **23** | **1894** | **6.9** | | **7** | **14.3** | **24:56** | **51** | **10** | **16** | **26** | **70** | **6** | **0** | **1** | **27:51** |

WHL West Second All-Star Team (1993) • WHL West First All-Star Team (1994) • WHL East First All-Star Team (1995) • Memorial Cup Tournament All-Star Team (1995) • NHL Second All-Star Team (2004)

Traded to **Vancouver** by **NY Islanders** with Todd Bertuzzi and NY Islanders' 3rd round choice (Jarkko Ruutu) in 1998 Entry Draft for Trevor Linden, February 6, 1998. Traded to **Chicago** by **Vancouver** with Vancouver's 1st round choice (Pavel Vorobiev) in 2000 Entry Draft for Chicago's 1st round choice (later traded to Tampa Bay – later traded to NY Rangers – NY Rangers selected Pavel Brendl) in 1999 Entry Draft, June 25, 1999. Traded to **Toronto** by **Chicago** for Alexander Karpovtsev and Toronto's 4th round choice (Vladimir Gusev) in 2001 Entry Draft, October 2, 2000. Signed as a free agent by **Jonkoping** (Sweden), October 29, 2004. Traded to **Florida** by **Toronto** with Toronto's 4th round choice in 2010 Entry Draft for Mike Van Ryn, September 2, 2008.

(muh-KAHR-thee, STEEV) **ANA.**

## McCARTHY, Steve

Defense. Shoots left. 6'1", 210 lbs. Born, Trail, B.C., February 3, 1981. Chicago's 1st choice, 23rd overall, in 1999 Entry Draft.

| Season | Club | League | GP | G | A | Pts | PIM | PP | SH | GW | S | % | +/- | TF | F% | Min | GP | G | A | Pts | PIM | PP | SH | GW | Min |
|---|---|---|---|---|---|---|---|---|---|---|---|---|---|---|---|---|---|---|---|---|---|---|---|---|---|
| 1996-97 | Trail | BCHL | 57 | 25 | 52 | 77 | 81 | | | | | | | | | | | | | | | | | | |
| | Edmonton Ice | WHL | 2 | 0 | 0 | 0 | 0 | | | | | | | | | | | | | | | | | | |
| 1997-98 | Edmonton Ice | WHL | 58 | 11 | 29 | 40 | 59 | | | | | | | | | | | | | | | | | | |
| 1998-99 | Kootenay Ice | WHL | 57 | 19 | 33 | 52 | 79 | | | | | | | | | | 6 | 0 | 5 | 5 | 8 | | | | |
| **99-2000** | **Chicago** | **NHL** | **5** | **1** | **1** | **2** | **4** | **1** | **0** | **0** | **4** | **25.0** | **0** | **0** | **0.0** | **15:09** | | | | | | | | | |
| | Kootenay Ice | WHL | 37 | 13 | 23 | 36 | 36 | | | | | | | | | | | | | | | | | | |
| **2000-01** | **Chicago** | **NHL** | **44** | **0** | **5** | **5** | **8** | **0** | **0** | **0** | **32** | **0.0** | **–7** | **0** | **0.0** | **14:47** | | | | | | | | | |
| | Norfolk Admirals | AHL | 7 | 0 | 4 | 4 | 2 | | | | | | | | | | | | | | | | | | |
| **2001-02** | **Chicago** | **NHL** | **3** | **0** | **0** | **0** | **2** | **0** | **0** | **0** | **2** | **0.0** | **–1** | **0** | **0.0** | **11:48** | | | | | | | | | |
| | Norfolk Admirals | AHL | 77 | 7 | 21 | 28 | 37 | | | | | | | | | | 2 | 0 | 3 | 3 | 2 | | | | |
| **2002-03** | **Chicago** | **NHL** | **57** | **1** | **4** | **5** | **23** | **0** | **0** | **0** | **55** | **1.8** | **–1** | **0** | **0.0** | **16:25** | | | | | | | | | |
| | Norfolk Admirals | AHL | 19 | 1 | 6 | 7 | 14 | | | | | | | | | | 9 | 0 | 4 | 4 | 0 | | | | |
| **2003-04** | **Chicago** | **NHL** | **25** | **1** | **3** | **4** | **8** | **0** | **0** | **0** | **29** | **3.4** | **–9** | **0** | **0.0** | **19:21** | | | | | | | | | |
| 2004-05 | | | DID NOT PLAY | | | | | | | | | | | | | | | | | | | | | | |
| **2005-06** | **Vancouver** | **NHL** | **51** | **2** | **4** | **6** | **43** | **0** | **0** | **0** | **46** | **4.3** | **3** | **0** | **0.0** | **13:17** | | | | | | | | | |
| | **Atlanta** | **NHL** | **16** | **7** | **3** | **10** | **8** | **2** | **0** | **0** | **20** | **35.0** | **0** | **0** | **0.0** | **16:44** | | | | | | | | | |
| **2006-07** | **Atlanta** | **NHL** | **46** | **4** | **12** | **16** | **24** | **3** | **0** | **0** | **51** | **7.8** | **4** | **0** | **0.0** | **15:17** | | | | | | | | | |
| **2007-08** | **Atlanta** | **NHL** | **55** | **1** | **6** | **7** | **48** | **0** | **0** | **0** | **41** | **2.4** | **–23** | **0** | **0.0** | **15:47** | | | | | | | | | |
| 2008-09 | Ufa | Rus-KHL | 18 | 0 | 0 | 0 | 16 | | | | | | | | | | | | | | | | | | |
| | **NHL Totals** | | **302** | **17** | **38** | **55** | **168** | **6** | **0** | **0** | **280** | **6.1** | | **0** | **0.0** | **15:33** | | | | | | | | | |

• Missed majority of 2003-04 season recovering from groin injury suffered in game vs. Calgary, November 22, 2003. Traded to **Vancouver** by **Chicago** for Vancouver's 3rd round choice (Josh Unice) in 2007 Entry Draft, August 22, 2005. Traded to **Atlanta** by **Vancouver** for Atlanta's 4th round choice (later traded back to Atlanta - Atlanta selected Niklas Lucenius) in 2007 Entry Draft, March 9, 2006. Signed as a free agent by **Anaheim**, July 10, 2009.

(muh-KAHR-tee, DAIR-ehn)

## McCARTY, Darren

Right wing. Shoots right. 6'1", 210 lbs. Born, Burnaby, B.C., April 1, 1972. Detroit's 2nd choice, 46th overall, in 1992 Entry Draft.

| Season | Club | League | GP | G | A | Pts | PIM | PP | SH | GW | S | % | +/- | TF | F% | Min | GP | G | A | Pts | PIM | PP | SH | GW | Min |
|---|---|---|---|---|---|---|---|---|---|---|---|---|---|---|---|---|---|---|---|---|---|---|---|---|---|
| 1988-89 | Peterborough | OHA-B | 34 | 18 | 17 | 35 | 135 | | | | | | | | | | | | | | | | | | |
| 1989-90 | Belleville Bulls | OHL | 63 | 12 | 15 | 27 | 142 | | | | | | | | | | 11 | 1 | 1 | 2 | 21 | | | | |
| 1990-91 | Belleville Bulls | OHL | 60 | 30 | 37 | 67 | 151 | | | | | | | | | | 6 | 2 | 2 | 4 | 13 | | | | |
| 1991-92 | Belleville Bulls | OHL | 65 | *55 | 72 | 127 | 177 | | | | | | | | | | 5 | 1 | 4 | 5 | 13 | | | | |
| 1992-93 | Adirondack | AHL | 73 | 17 | 19 | 36 | 278 | | | | | | | | | | 11 | 0 | 1 | 1 | 33 | | | | |
| **1993-94** | **Detroit** | **NHL** | **67** | **9** | **17** | **26** | **181** | **0** | **0** | **2** | **81** | **11.1** | **12** | | | | **7** | **2** | **2** | **4** | **8** | **0** | **0** | **0** | |
| **1994-95** | **Detroit** | **NHL** | **31** | **5** | **8** | **13** | **88** | **1** | **0** | **2** | **27** | **18.5** | **5** | | | | **18** | **3** | **2** | **5** | **14** | **0** | **0** | **0** | |
| **1995-96** | **Detroit** | **NHL** | **63** | **15** | **14** | **29** | **158** | **8** | **0** | **1** | **102** | **14.7** | **14** | | | | **19** | **3** | **2** | **5** | **20** | **0** | **0** | **1** | |
| **1996-97♦** | **Detroit** | **NHL** | **68** | **19** | **30** | **49** | **126** | **5** | **0** | **6** | **171** | **11.1** | **14** | | | | **20** | **3** | **4** | **7** | **34** | **0** | **0** | **2** | |
| **1997-98♦** | **Detroit** | **NHL** | **71** | **15** | **22** | **37** | **157** | **5** | **1** | **2** | **166** | **9.0** | **0** | | | | **22** | **3** | **8** | **11** | **34** | **0** | **0** | **1** | |
| **1998-99** | **Detroit** | **NHL** | **69** | **14** | **26** | **40** | **108** | **6** | **0** | **1** | **140** | **10.0** | **10** | **15** | **33.3** | **17:04** | **10** | **1** | **1** | **2** | **23** | **0** | **0** | **0** | **13:04** |
| **99-2000** | **Detroit** | **NHL** | **24** | **6** | **6** | **12** | **48** | **0** | **0** | **1** | **40** | **15.0** | **1** | **1** | **0.0** | **13:40** | **9** | **0** | **1** | **1** | **12** | **0** | **0** | **0** | **14:09** |
| **2000-01** | **Detroit** | **NHL** | **72** | **12** | **10** | **22** | **123** | **1** | **1** | **3** | **118** | **10.2** | **–5** | **26** | **53.9** | **13:26** | **6** | **1** | **0** | **1** | **2** | **0** | **0** | **0** | **13:11** |
| **2001-02♦** | **Detroit** | **NHL** | **62** | **5** | **7** | **12** | **98** | **0** | **0** | **1** | **74** | **6.8** | **2** | **26** | **38.5** | **11:47** | **23** | **4** | **4** | **8** | **34** | **0** | **0** | **1** | **13:33** |
| **2002-03** | **Detroit** | **NHL** | **73** | **13** | **9** | **22** | **138** | **1** | **0** | **2** | **129** | **10.1** | **10** | **320** | **57.8** | **13:18** | **4** | **0** | **0** | **0** | **6** | **0** | **0** | **0** | **15:45** |
| **2003-04** | **Detroit** | **NHL** | **43** | **6** | **5** | **11** | **50** | **1** | **0** | **0** | **61** | **9.8** | **2** | **141** | **50.4** | **12:20** | **12** | **0** | **1** | **1** | **7** | **0** | **0** | **0** | **11:30** |
| 2004-05 | | | DID NOT PLAY | | | | | | | | | | | | | | | | | | | | | | |
| **2005-06** | **Calgary** | **NHL** | **67** | **7** | **6** | **13** | **117** | **1** | **0** | **0** | **67** | **10.4** | **–1** | **234** | **50.0** | **11:43** | **7** | **2** | **0** | **2** | **15** | **0** | **0** | **1** | **9:50** |
| **2006-07** | **Calgary** | **NHL** | **32** | **0** | **0** | **0** | **58** | **0** | **0** | **0** | **15** | **0.0** | **–3** | **6** | **83.3** | **5:24** | | | | | | | | | |
| **2007-08** | Flint Generals | IHL | 11 | 3 | 3 | 6 | 30 | | | | | | | | | | | | | | | | | | |
| | Grand Rapids | AHL | 13 | 5 | 5 | 10 | 21 | | | | | | | | | | | | | | | | | | |
| | **♦ Detroit** | **NHL** | **3** | **0** | **1** | **1** | **2** | **0** | **0** | **0** | **3** | **0.0** | **2** | **0** | **0.0** | **7:47** | **17** | **1** | **1** | **2** | **19** | **0** | **0** | **0** | **6:23** |
| **2008-09** | **Detroit** | **NHL** | **13** | **1** | **0** | **1** | **25** | **0** | **0** | **0** | **6** | **16.7** | **–2** | **5** | **40.0** | **5:17** | | | | | | | | | |
| | Grand Rapids | AHL | 19 | 5 | 6 | 11 | 21 | | | | | | | | | | 10 | 3 | 1 | 4 | 8 | | | | |
| | **NHL Totals** | | **758** | **127** | **161** | **288** | **1477** | **29** | **2** | **21** | **1200** | **10.6** | | **774** | **52.8** | **12:34** | **174** | **23** | **26** | **49** | **228** | **0** | **0** | **6** | **11:40** |

OHL First All-Star Team (1992)

• Missed majority of 1999-2000 season recovering from hernia injury suffered in game vs. Dallas, November 10, 1999. Signed as a free agent by **Calgary**, August 2, 2005. • Missed majority of 2006-07 season recovering from recurring hernia injury. Signed as a free agent by **Flint** (IHL), January 9, 2008. Signed as a free agent by **Grand Rapids** (AHL), February 4, 2008. Signed as a free agent by **Detroit**, February 25, 2008. • Missed majority of 2008-09 season recovering from recurring hernia injury.

(muh-KLEHM-ehnt, JAY) **ST.L.**

## McCLEMENT, Jay

Center. Shoots left. 6'1", 201 lbs. Born, Kingston, Ont., March 2, 1983. St. Louis' 1st choice, 57th overall, in 2001 Entry Draft.

| Season | Club | League | GP | G | A | Pts | PIM | PP | SH | GW | S | % | +/- | TF | F% | Min | GP | G | A | Pts | PIM | PP | SH | GW | Min |
|---|---|---|---|---|---|---|---|---|---|---|---|---|---|---|---|---|---|---|---|---|---|---|---|---|---|
| 1997-98 | Kingston | OPJHL | 48 | 3 | 8 | 11 | 15 | | | | | | | | | | | | | | | | | | |
| 1998-99 | Kingston | OPJHL | 51 | 25 | 28 | 53 | 34 | | | | | | | | | | | | | | | | | | |
| 99-2000 | Brampton | OHL | 63 | 13 | 16 | 29 | 34 | | | | | | | | | | 6 | 0 | 4 | 4 | 8 | | | | |
| 2000-01 | Brampton | OHL | 66 | 30 | 19 | 49 | 61 | | | | | | | | | | 9 | 4 | 2 | 6 | 10 | | | | |
| 2001-02 | Brampton | OHL | 61 | 26 | 29 | 55 | 43 | | | | | | | | | | | | | | | | | | |
| 2002-03 | Brampton | OHL | 45 | 22 | 27 | 49 | 37 | | | | | | | | | | 11 | 3 | 4 | 7 | 11 | | | | |
| | Worcester IceCats | AHL | | | | | | | | | | | | | | | 1 | 0 | 0 | 0 | 0 | | | | |
| 2003-04 | Worcester IceCats | AHL | 69 | 12 | 13 | 25 | 20 | | | | | | | | | | 10 | 0 | 3 | 3 | 0 | | | | |

| Season | Club | League | GP | G | A | Pts | PIM | PP | SH | GW | S | % | +/- | TF | F% | Min | GP | G | A | Pts | PIM | PP | SH | GW | Min |
|---|---|---|---|---|---|---|---|---|---|---|---|---|---|---|---|---|---|---|---|---|---|---|---|---|---|
| | | | Regular Season | | | | | | | | | | | | | | Playoffs | | | | | | | | |
| 2004-05 | Worcester IceCats | AHL | 79 | 17 | 34 | 51 | 45 | .... | .... | .... | .... | .... | .... | .... | .... | .... | .... | .... | .... | .... | .... | .... | .... | .... | .... |
| **2005-06** | **St. Louis** | **NHL** | **67** | **6** | **21** | **27** | **30** | **1** | **0** | **2** | **76** | **7.9** | **–23** | **691** | **46.9** | **13:56** | .... | .... | .... | .... | .... | .... | .... | .... | .... |
| | Peoria Rivermen | AHL | 11 | 4 | 5 | 9 | 4 | .... | .... | .... | .... | .... | .... | .... | .... | .... | 4 | 0 | 2 | 2 | 2 | .... | .... | .... | .... |
| **2006-07** | **St. Louis** | **NHL** | **81** | **8** | **28** | **36** | **55** | **0** | **0** | **0** | **104** | **7.7** | **3** | **839** | **52.7** | **13:53** | .... | .... | .... | .... | .... | .... | .... | .... | .... |
| **2007-08** | **St. Louis** | **NHL** | **81** | **9** | **13** | **22** | **26** | **0** | **0** | **2** | **110** | **8.2** | **–17** | **700** | **52.3** | **13:55** | .... | .... | .... | .... | .... | .... | .... | .... | .... |
| **2008-09** | **St. Louis** | **NHL** | **82** | **12** | **14** | **26** | **29** | **0** | **3** | **3** | **137** | **8.8** | **–10** | **1451** | **52.1** | **16:36** | **4** | **0** | **0** | **0** | **4** | **0** | **0** | **0** | **16:28** |
| | **NHL Totals** | | **311** | **35** | **76** | **111** | **140** | **1** | **3** | **7** | **427** | **8.2** | | **3681** | **51.3** | **14:37** | **4** | **0** | **0** | **0** | **4** | **0** | **0** | **0** | **16:28** |

## McCORMICK, Cody

(muh-KOHR-mihk, KOH-dee) **BUF.**

Center/Right wing. Shoots right. 6'3", 215 lbs. Born, London, Ont., April 18, 1983. Colorado's 5th choice, 144th overall, in 2001 Entry Draft.

| Season | Club | League | GP | G | A | Pts | PIM | PP | SH | GW | S | % | +/- | TF | F% | Min | GP | G | A | Pts | PIM | PP | SH | GW | Min |
|---|---|---|---|---|---|---|---|---|---|---|---|---|---|---|---|---|---|---|---|---|---|---|---|---|---|
| 1998-99 | Elgin-Middlesex | MHAO | 58 | 22 | 40 | 62 | 81 | .... | .... | .... | .... | .... | .... | .... | .... | .... | .... | .... | .... | .... | .... | .... | .... | .... | .... |
| 99-2000 | Belleville Bulls | OHL | 45 | 3 | 4 | 7 | 42 | .... | .... | .... | .... | .... | .... | .... | .... | .... | 9 | 1 | 0 | 1 | 10 | .... | .... | .... | .... |
| 2000-01 | Belleville Bulls | OHL | 66 | 7 | 16 | 23 | 135 | .... | .... | .... | .... | .... | .... | .... | .... | .... | 10 | 1 | 1 | 2 | 23 | .... | .... | .... | .... |
| 2001-02 | Belleville Bulls | OHL | 63 | 10 | 17 | 27 | 118 | .... | .... | .... | .... | .... | .... | .... | .... | .... | 11 | 2 | 4 | 6 | 24 | .... | .... | .... | .... |
| 2002-03 | Belleville Bulls | OHL | 61 | 36 | 33 | 69 | 166 | .... | .... | .... | .... | .... | .... | .... | .... | .... | 7 | 4 | 7 | 11 | 11 | .... | .... | .... | .... |
| **2003-04** | **Colorado** | **NHL** | **44** | **2** | **3** | **5** | **73** | **0** | **0** | **1** | **33** | **6.1** | **–4** | **110** | **32.7** | **8:07** | .... | .... | .... | .... | .... | .... | .... | .... | .... |
| | Hershey Bears | AHL | 32 | 3 | 6 | 9 | 60 | .... | .... | .... | .... | .... | .... | .... | .... | .... | .... | .... | .... | .... | .... | .... | .... | .... | .... |
| 2004-05 | Hershey Bears | AHL | 40 | 5 | 6 | 11 | 68 | .... | .... | .... | .... | .... | .... | .... | .... | .... | .... | .... | .... | .... | .... | .... | .... | .... | .... |
| **2005-06** | **Colorado** | **NHL** | **45** | **4** | **4** | **8** | **29** | **0** | **0** | **1** | **43** | **9.3** | **1** | **16** | **25.0** | **7:42** | .... | .... | .... | .... | .... | .... | .... | .... | .... |
| | Lowell | AHL | 13 | 1 | 6 | 7 | 34 | .... | .... | .... | .... | .... | .... | .... | .... | .... | .... | .... | .... | .... | .... | .... | .... | .... | .... |
| **2006-07** | **Colorado** | **NHL** | **6** | **0** | **1** | **1** | **6** | **0** | **0** | **0** | **6** | **0.0** | **1** | **3** | **33.3** | **6:44** | .... | .... | .... | .... | .... | .... | .... | .... | .... |
| | Albany River Rats | AHL | 42 | 8 | 8 | 16 | 64 | .... | .... | .... | .... | .... | .... | .... | .... | .... | 5 | 1 | 0 | 1 | 4 | .... | .... | .... | .... |
| **2007-08** | **Colorado** | **NHL** | **40** | **2** | **2** | **4** | **50** | **0** | **0** | **1** | **45** | **4.4** | **5** | **17** | **35.3** | **10:58** | **4** | **0** | **1** | **1** | **7** | **0** | **0** | **0** | **11:53** |
| | Lake Erie | AHL | 13 | 2 | 4 | 6 | 16 | .... | .... | .... | .... | .... | .... | .... | .... | .... | .... | .... | .... | .... | .... | .... | .... | .... | .... |
| **2008-09** | **Colorado** | **NHL** | **55** | **1** | **11** | **12** | **92** | **0** | **0** | **0** | **66** | **1.5** | **–5** | **107** | **35.5** | **9:36** | .... | .... | .... | .... | .... | .... | .... | .... | .... |
| | **NHL Totals** | | **190** | **9** | **21** | **30** | **250** | **0** | **0** | **3** | **193** | **4.7** | | **253** | **33.6** | **9:00** | **4** | **0** | **1** | **1** | **7** | **0** | **0** | **0** | **11:53** |

OHL First All-Star Team (2003)

Signed as a free agent by **Buffalo**, August 1, 2009.

## McDONALD, Andy

(muhk-DAWN-uhld, AN-dee) **ST.L.**

Center. Shoots left. 5'10", 190 lbs. Born, Strathroy, Ont., August 25, 1977.

| Season | Club | League | GP | G | A | Pts | PIM | PP | SH | GW | S | % | +/- | TF | F% | Min | GP | G | A | Pts | PIM | PP | SH | GW | Min |
|---|---|---|---|---|---|---|---|---|---|---|---|---|---|---|---|---|---|---|---|---|---|---|---|---|---|
| 1993-94 | Strathroy Rockets | OHA-B | 7 | 2 | 2 | 4 | 0 | .... | .... | .... | .... | .... | .... | .... | .... | .... | .... | .... | .... | .... | .... | .... | .... | .... | .... |
| 1994-95 | Strathroy Rockets | OHA-B | 50 | 32 | 41 | 73 | 24 | .... | .... | .... | .... | .... | .... | .... | .... | .... | .... | .... | .... | .... | .... | .... | .... | .... | .... |
| 1995-96 | Strathroy Rockets | OHA-B | 52 | 31 | 56 | 87 | 103 | .... | .... | .... | .... | .... | .... | .... | .... | .... | .... | .... | .... | .... | .... | .... | .... | .... | .... |
| 1996-97 | Colgate | ECAC | 33 | 9 | 10 | 19 | 16 | .... | .... | .... | .... | .... | .... | .... | .... | .... | .... | .... | .... | .... | .... | .... | .... | .... | .... |
| 1997-98 | Colgate | ECAC | 35 | 13 | 19 | 32 | 26 | .... | .... | .... | .... | .... | .... | .... | .... | .... | .... | .... | .... | .... | .... | .... | .... | .... | .... |
| 1998-99 | Colgate | ECAC | 35 | 20 | 26 | 46 | 42 | .... | .... | .... | .... | .... | .... | .... | .... | .... | .... | .... | .... | .... | .... | .... | .... | .... | .... |
| 99-2000 | Colgate | ECAC | 34 | 25 | *33 | *58 | 49 | .... | .... | .... | .... | .... | .... | .... | .... | .... | .... | .... | .... | .... | .... | .... | .... | .... | .... |
| **2000-01** | **Anaheim** | **NHL** | **16** | **1** | **0** | **1** | **6** | **0** | **0** | **0** | **21** | **4.8** | **0** | **139** | **48.9** | **11:11** | .... | .... | .... | .... | .... | .... | .... | .... | .... |
| | Cincinnati | AHL | 46 | 15 | 25 | 40 | 21 | .... | .... | .... | .... | .... | .... | .... | .... | .... | 3 | 0 | 1 | 1 | 2 | .... | .... | .... | .... |
| **2001-02** | **Anaheim** | **NHL** | **53** | **7** | **21** | **28** | **10** | **2** | **0** | **3** | **79** | **8.9** | **2** | **818** | **53.7** | **15:59** | .... | .... | .... | .... | .... | .... | .... | .... | .... |
| | Cincinnati | AHL | 21 | 7 | 25 | 32 | 6 | .... | .... | .... | .... | .... | .... | .... | .... | .... | .... | .... | .... | .... | .... | .... | .... | .... | .... |
| **2002-03** | **Anaheim** | **NHL** | **46** | **10** | **11** | **21** | **14** | **3** | **0** | **1** | **92** | **10.9** | **–1** | **604** | **56.0** | **18:31** | .... | .... | .... | .... | .... | .... | .... | .... | .... |
| **2003-04** | **Anaheim** | **NHL** | **79** | **9** | **21** | **30** | **24** | **2** | **1** | **1** | **162** | **5.6** | **–13** | **282** | **54.3** | **16:34** | .... | .... | .... | .... | .... | .... | .... | .... | .... |
| 2004-05 | ERC Ingolstadt | Germany | 36 | 13 | 17 | 30 | 26 | .... | .... | .... | .... | .... | .... | .... | .... | .... | 10 | 5 | 2 | 7 | 35 | .... | .... | .... | .... |
| **2005-06** | **Anaheim** | **NHL** | **82** | **34** | **51** | **85** | **32** | **13** | **0** | **7** | **229** | **14.8** | **24** | **1095** | **56.3** | **16:48** | **16** | **2** | **7** | **9** | **10** | **2** | **0** | **0** | **16:33** |
| **2006-07♦** | **Anaheim** | **NHL** | **82** | **27** | **51** | **78** | **46** | **8** | **0** | **3** | **252** | **10.7** | **16** | **908** | **55.4** | **17:35** | **21** | **10** | **4** | **14** | **10** | **5** | **0** | **0** | **18:37** |
| **2007-08** | **Anaheim** | **NHL** | **33** | **4** | **12** | **16** | **30** | **0** | **0** | **0** | **79** | **5.1** | **–4** | **392** | **55.4** | **16:41** | .... | .... | .... | .... | .... | .... | .... | .... | .... |
| | **St. Louis** | **NHL** | **49** | **14** | **22** | **36** | **32** | **3** | **0** | **1** | **103** | **13.6** | **–17** | **556** | **55.8** | **18:40** | .... | .... | .... | .... | .... | .... | .... | .... | .... |
| **2008-09** | **St. Louis** | **NHL** | **46** | **15** | **29** | **44** | **24** | **6** | **1** | **1** | **128** | **11.7** | **–13** | **367** | **58.0** | **19:05** | **4** | **1** | **3** | **4** | **0** | **0** | **0** | **0** | **23:35** |
| | **NHL Totals** | | **486** | **121** | **218** | **339** | **218** | **37** | **2** | **17** | **1145** | **10.6** | | **5161** | **55.4** | **17:11** | **41** | **13** | **14** | **27** | **20** | **7** | **0** | **0** | **18:18** |

ECAC Second All-Star Team (1999) • ECAC First All-Star Team (2000) • ECAC Player of the Year (2000) • NCAA East First All-American Team (2000)

Played in NHL All-Star Game (2007)

Signed as a free agent by **Anaheim**, April 3, 2000. Signed as a free agent by **Ingolstadt** (Germany), September 17, 2004. Traded to **St. Louis** by **Anaheim** for Doug Weight, Michal Birner and St. Louis' 7th round choice (later traded to Los Angeles - later traded back to St. Louis - St. Louis selected Paul Karpowich) in 2008 Entry Draft, December 14, 2007.

## McGINN, Jamie

(muh-GIHN, JAY-mee) **S.J.**

Left wing. Shoots left. 6', 200 lbs. Born, Fergus, Ont., August 5, 1988. San Jose's 2nd choice, 36th overall, in 2006 Entry Draft.

| Season | Club | League | GP | G | A | Pts | PIM | PP | SH | GW | S | % | +/- | TF | F% | Min | GP | G | A | Pts | PIM | PP | SH | GW | Min |
|---|---|---|---|---|---|---|---|---|---|---|---|---|---|---|---|---|---|---|---|---|---|---|---|---|---|
| 2003-04 | Tor. Jr. Canadiens | GTHL | 31 | .... | .... | 48 | .... | .... | .... | .... | .... | .... | .... | .... | .... | .... | 18 | 14 | 18 | 32 | .... | .... | .... | .... | .... |
| 2004-05 | Ottawa 67's | OHL | 59 | 10 | 12 | 22 | 35 | .... | .... | .... | .... | .... | .... | .... | .... | .... | 18 | 4 | 7 | 11 | 0 | .... | .... | .... | .... |
| 2005-06 | Ottawa 67's | OHL | 65 | 26 | 31 | 57 | 113 | .... | .... | .... | .... | .... | .... | .... | .... | .... | 6 | 2 | 2 | 4 | 4 | .... | .... | .... | .... |
| 2006-07 | Ottawa 67's | OHL | 68 | 46 | 43 | 89 | 49 | .... | .... | .... | .... | .... | .... | .... | .... | .... | 5 | 5 | 1 | 6 | 2 | .... | .... | .... | .... |
| | Worcester Sharks | AHL | 4 | 1 | 1 | 2 | 4 | .... | .... | .... | .... | .... | .... | .... | .... | .... | 6 | 0 | 0 | 0 | 8 | .... | .... | .... | .... |
| 2007-08 | Ottawa 67's | OHL | 51 | 29 | 29 | 58 | 54 | .... | .... | .... | .... | .... | .... | .... | .... | .... | 4 | 2 | 2 | 4 | 4 | .... | .... | .... | .... |
| | Worcester Sharks | AHL | 8 | 0 | 2 | 2 | 0 | .... | .... | .... | .... | .... | .... | .... | .... | .... | .... | .... | .... | .... | .... | .... | .... | .... | .... |
| **2008-09** | **San Jose** | **NHL** | **35** | **4** | **2** | **6** | **2** | **1** | **0** | **1** | **27** | **14.8** | **–6** | **7** | **85.7** | **8:55** | .... | .... | .... | .... | .... | .... | .... | .... | .... |
| | Worcester Sharks | AHL | 47 | 19 | 11 | 30 | 52 | .... | .... | .... | .... | .... | .... | .... | .... | .... | 6 | 4 | 0 | 4 | 19 | .... | .... | .... | .... |
| | **NHL Totals** | | **35** | **4** | **2** | **6** | **2** | **1** | **0** | **1** | **27** | **14.8** | | **7** | **85.7** | **8:55** | .... | .... | .... | .... | .... | .... | .... | .... | .... |

## McGRATTAN, Brian

(muh-GRA-tuhn, BRIGH-uhn) **CGY.**

Right wing. Shoots right. 6'4", 235 lbs. Born, Hamilton, Ont., September 2, 1981. Los Angeles' 5th choice, 104th overall, in 1999 Entry Draft.

| Season | Club | League | GP | G | A | Pts | PIM | PP | SH | GW | S | % | +/- | TF | F% | Min | GP | G | A | Pts | PIM | PP | SH | GW | Min |
|---|---|---|---|---|---|---|---|---|---|---|---|---|---|---|---|---|---|---|---|---|---|---|---|---|---|
| 1997-98 | Guelph Fire | OHA-B | 15 | 4 | 3 | 7 | 94 | .... | .... | .... | .... | .... | .... | .... | .... | .... | .... | .... | .... | .... | .... | .... | .... | .... | .... |
| | Guelph Storm | OHL | 25 | 3 | 2 | 5 | 11 | .... | .... | .... | .... | .... | .... | .... | .... | .... | .... | .... | .... | .... | .... | .... | .... | .... | .... |
| 1998-99 | Guelph Storm | OHL | 6 | 1 | 3 | 4 | 15 | .... | .... | .... | .... | .... | .... | .... | .... | .... | .... | .... | .... | .... | .... | .... | .... | .... | .... |
| | Sudbury Wolves | OHL | 53 | 7 | 10 | 17 | 153 | .... | .... | .... | .... | .... | .... | .... | .... | .... | 4 | 0 | 0 | 0 | 8 | .... | .... | .... | .... |
| 99-2000 | Sudbury Wolves | OHL | 25 | 2 | 8 | 10 | 79 | .... | .... | .... | .... | .... | .... | .... | .... | .... | .... | .... | .... | .... | .... | .... | .... | .... | .... |
| | Mississauga | OHL | 42 | 9 | 13 | 22 | 166 | .... | .... | .... | .... | .... | .... | .... | .... | .... | .... | .... | .... | .... | .... | .... | .... | .... | .... |
| 2000-01 | Mississauga | OHL | 31 | 20 | 9 | 29 | 83 | .... | .... | .... | .... | .... | .... | .... | .... | .... | .... | .... | .... | .... | .... | .... | .... | .... | .... |
| 2001-02 | Mississauga | OHL | 7 | 2 | 3 | 5 | 16 | .... | .... | .... | .... | .... | .... | .... | .... | .... | .... | .... | .... | .... | .... | .... | .... | .... | .... |
| | Owen Sound | OHL | 2 | 0 | 0 | 0 | 0 | .... | .... | .... | .... | .... | .... | .... | .... | .... | .... | .... | .... | .... | .... | .... | .... | .... | .... |
| | Oshawa Generals | OHL | 25 | 10 | 5 | 15 | 72 | .... | .... | .... | .... | .... | .... | .... | .... | .... | .... | .... | .... | .... | .... | .... | .... | .... | .... |
| | Sault Ste. Marie | OHL | 26 | 8 | 7 | 15 | 71 | .... | .... | .... | .... | .... | .... | .... | .... | .... | 6 | 2 | 0 | 2 | 20 | .... | .... | .... | .... |
| 2002-03 | Binghamton | AHL | 59 | 9 | 10 | 19 | 173 | .... | .... | .... | .... | .... | .... | .... | .... | .... | 1 | 0 | 0 | 0 | 0 | .... | .... | .... | .... |
| 2003-04 | Binghamton | AHL | 66 | 9 | 11 | 20 | 327 | .... | .... | .... | .... | .... | .... | .... | .... | .... | 1 | 0 | 0 | 0 | 0 | .... | .... | .... | .... |
| 2004-05 | Binghamton | AHL | 71 | 7 | 1 | 8 | *551 | .... | .... | .... | .... | .... | .... | .... | .... | .... | 6 | 0 | 2 | 2 | 28 | .... | .... | .... | .... |
| **2005-06** | **Ottawa** | **NHL** | **60** | **2** | **3** | **5** | **141** | **0** | **0** | **0** | **36** | **5.6** | **0** | **0** | **0.0** | **4:14** | .... | .... | .... | .... | .... | .... | .... | .... | .... |
| **2006-07** | **Ottawa** | **NHL** | **45** | **0** | **2** | **2** | **100** | **0** | **0** | **0** | **22** | **0.0** | **–1** | **1** | **100.0** | **3:51** | .... | .... | .... | .... | .... | .... | .... | .... | .... |
| **2007-08** | **Ottawa** | **NHL** | **38** | **0** | **3** | **3** | **46** | **0** | **0** | **0** | **11** | **0.0** | **0** | **0** | **0.0** | **2:52** | .... | .... | .... | .... | .... | .... | .... | .... | .... |
| **2008-09** | **Phoenix** | **NHL** | **5** | **0** | **0** | **0** | **22** | **0** | **0** | **0** | **2** | **0.0** | **–2** | **0** | **0.0** | **5:31** | .... | .... | .... | .... | .... | .... | .... | .... | .... |
| | San Antonio | AHL | 1 | 0 | 0 | 0 | 2 | .... | .... | .... | .... | .... | .... | .... | .... | .... | .... | .... | .... | .... | .... | .... | .... | .... | .... |
| | **NHL Totals** | | **148** | **2** | **8** | **10** | **309** | **0** | **0** | **0** | **71** | **2.8** | | **1** | **100.0** | **3:49** | .... | .... | .... | .... | .... | .... | .... | .... | .... |

• Missed majority of 2000-01 season recovering from knee injury suffered in game vs. Kingston (OHL), January 1, 2001. Signed as a free agent by **Ottawa**, June 2, 2002. • Missed majority of 2007-08 season serving as a healthy reserve. Traded to **Phoenix** by **Ottawa** for Boston's 5th round choice (previously acquired, Ottawa selected Jeff Costello) in 2009 Entry Draft, June 25, 2008. Signed as a free agent by **Calgary**, July 11, 2009.

## McIVER, Nathan

(muh-KEE-vuhr, NAY-thuhn) **VAN.**

Defense. Shoots left. 6'2", 206 lbs. Born, Kinkora, P.E.I., January 6, 1985. Vancouver's 9th choice, 254th overall, in 2003 Entry Draft.

| Season | Club | League | GP | G | A | Pts | PIM | PP | SH | GW | S | % | +/- | TF | F% | Min | GP | G | A | Pts | PIM | PP | SH | GW | Min |
|---|---|---|---|---|---|---|---|---|---|---|---|---|---|---|---|---|---|---|---|---|---|---|---|---|---|
| 2001-02 | Summerside | MJrHL | 47 | 4 | 4 | 8 | 91 | .... | .... | .... | .... | .... | .... | .... | .... | .... | 5 | 0 | 0 | 0 | 9 | .... | .... | .... | .... |
| 2002-03 | St. Michael's | OHL | 68 | 5 | 10 | 15 | 121 | .... | .... | .... | .... | .... | .... | .... | .... | .... | 19 | 0 | 4 | 4 | 41 | .... | .... | .... | .... |
| 2003-04 | St. Michael's | OHL | 57 | 4 | 11 | 15 | 183 | .... | .... | .... | .... | .... | .... | .... | .... | .... | 16 | 0 | 1 | 1 | 22 | .... | .... | .... | .... |
| 2004-05 | St. Michael's | OHL | 67 | 4 | 22 | 26 | 160 | .... | .... | .... | .... | .... | .... | .... | .... | .... | 3 | 0 | 1 | 1 | 13 | .... | .... | .... | .... |
| 2005-06 | Manitoba Moose | AHL | 66 | 1 | 6 | 7 | 155 | .... | .... | .... | .... | .... | .... | .... | .... | .... | 12 | 0 | 0 | 0 | 28 | .... | .... | .... | .... |
| **2006-07** | **Vancouver** | **NHL** | **1** | **0** | **0** | **0** | **7** | **0** | **0** | **0** | **0** | **0.0** | **–3** | **0** | **0.0** | **11:20** | .... | .... | .... | .... | .... | .... | .... | .... | .... |
| | Manitoba Moose | AHL | 63 | 1 | 2 | 3 | 139 | .... | .... | .... | .... | .... | .... | .... | .... | .... | 2 | 0 | 0 | 0 | 0 | .... | .... | .... | .... |

| | | | Regular Season | | | | | | | | | | | | | | Playoffs | | | | | | | | |
|---|---|---|---|---|---|---|---|---|---|---|---|---|---|---|---|---|---|---|---|---|---|---|---|---|---|
| Season | Club | League | GP | G | A | Pts | PIM | PP | SH | GW | S | % | +/- | TF | F% | Min | GP | G | A | Pts | PIM | PP | SH | GW | Min |
| 2007-08 | Vancouver | NHL | 17 | 0 | 0 | 0 | 52 | 0 | 0 | 0 | 9 | 0.0 | –8 | 0 | 0.0 | 10:28 | | | | | | | | | |
| | Manitoba Moose | AHL | 43 | 3 | 3 | 6 | 108 | | | | | | | | | | 6 | 0 | 1 | 1 | 11 | | | | |
| 2008-09 | Anaheim | NHL | 18 | 0 | 1 | 1 | 36 | 0 | 0 | 0 | 5 | 0.0 | 2 | 0 | 0.0 | 9:24 | | | | | | | | | |
| | Manitoba Moose | AHL | 28 | 0 | 2 | 2 | 59 | | | | | | | | | | 10 | 0 | 0 | 0 | 10 | | | | |
| | NHL Totals | | 36 | 0 | 1 | 1 | 95 | 0 | 0 | 0 | 14 | 0.0 | | 0 | 0.0 | 9:57 | | | | | | | | | |

Claimed on waivers by **Anaheim** from **Vancouver**, October 4, 2008. Traded to **Vancouver** by **Anaheim** for Mike Brown, February 4, 2009.

## McKEE, Jay

(muh-KEE, JAY) **PIT.**

Defense. Shoots left. 6'4", 203 lbs. Born, Kingston, Ont., September 8, 1977. Buffalo's 1st choice, 14th overall, in 1995 Entry Draft.

| Season | Club | League | GP | G | A | Pts | PIM | PP | SH | GW | S | % | +/- | TF | F% | Min | GP | G | A | Pts | PIM | PP | SH | GW | Min |
|---|---|---|---|---|---|---|---|---|---|---|---|---|---|---|---|---|---|---|---|---|---|---|---|---|---|
| 1992-93 | Ernestown Jets | OHA-C | 36 | 0 | 17 | 17 | 37 | | | | | | | | | | | | | | | | | | |
| | Kingston | MTJHL | 2 | 0 | 0 | 0 | 0 | | | | | | | | | | | | | | | | | | |
| 1993-94 | Sudbury Wolves | OHL | 51 | 0 | 1 | 1 | 51 | | | | | | | | | | 3 | 0 | 0 | 0 | 0 | | | | |
| 1994-95 | Sudbury Wolves | OHL | 39 | 6 | 6 | 12 | 91 | | | | | | | | | | | | | | | | | | |
| | Niagara Falls | OHL | 26 | 3 | 13 | 16 | 60 | | | | | | | | | | 6 | 2 | 3 | 5 | 10 | | | | |
| 1995-96 | Niagara Falls | OHL | 64 | 5 | 41 | 46 | 129 | | | | | | | | | | 10 | 1 | 5 | 6 | 16 | | | | |
| | Buffalo | NHL | 1 | 0 | 1 | 1 | 2 | 0 | 0 | 0 | 2 | 0.0 | 1 | | | | | | | | | | | | |
| | Rochester | AHL | 4 | 0 | 1 | 1 | 15 | | | | | | | | | | | | | | | | | | |
| 1996-97 | Buffalo | NHL | 43 | 1 | 9 | 10 | 35 | 0 | 0 | 0 | 29 | 3.4 | 3 | | | | 3 | 0 | 0 | 0 | 0 | 0 | 0 | 0 | |
| | Rochester | AHL | 7 | 2 | 5 | 7 | 4 | | | | | | | | | | | | | | | | | | |
| 1997-98 | Buffalo | NHL | 56 | 1 | 13 | 14 | 42 | 0 | 0 | 0 | 55 | 1.8 | –1 | | | | 1 | 0 | 0 | 0 | 0 | 0 | 0 | 0 | |
| | Rochester | AHL | 13 | 1 | 7 | 8 | 11 | | | | | | | | | | | | | | | | | | |
| 1998-99 | Buffalo | NHL | 72 | 0 | 6 | 6 | 75 | 0 | 0 | 0 | 57 | 0.0 | 20 | 0 | 0.0 | 20:28 | 21 | 0 | 3 | 3 | 24 | 0 | 0 | 0 | 22:31 |
| 99-2000 | Buffalo | NHL | 78 | 5 | 12 | 17 | 50 | 1 | 0 | 1 | 84 | 6.0 | 5 | 0 | 0.0 | 20:58 | 1 | 0 | 0 | 0 | 0 | 0 | 0 | 0 | 17:57 |
| 2000-01 | Buffalo | NHL | 74 | 1 | 10 | 11 | 76 | 0 | 0 | 0 | 62 | 1.6 | 9 | 2 | 0.0 | 19:24 | 8 | 1 | 0 | 1 | 6 | 0 | 0 | 1 | 19:23 |
| 2001-02 | Buffalo | NHL | 81 | 2 | 11 | 13 | 43 | 0 | 0 | 1 | 50 | 4.0 | 18 | 0 | 0.0 | 19:26 | | | | | | | | | |
| 2002-03 | Buffalo | NHL | 59 | 0 | 5 | 5 | 49 | 0 | 0 | 0 | 44 | 0.0 | –16 | 0 | 0.0 | 18:45 | | | | | | | | | |
| 2003-04 | Buffalo | NHL | 43 | 2 | 3 | 5 | 41 | 0 | 0 | 1 | 29 | 6.9 | 6 | 0 | 0.0 | 17:44 | | | | | | | | | |
| 2004-05 | | | DID NOT PLAY | | | | | | | | | | | | | | | | | | | | | | |
| 2005-06 | Buffalo | NHL | 75 | 5 | 11 | 16 | 57 | 0 | 1 | 0 | 50 | 10.0 | 0 | 1 | 0.0 | 18:03 | 17 | 2 | 3 | 5 | 30 | 0 | 0 | 1 | 20:17 |
| 2006-07 | St. Louis | NHL | 23 | 0 | 0 | 0 | 12 | 0 | 0 | 0 | 19 | 0.0 | –9 | 0 | 0.0 | 20:14 | | | | | | | | | |
| 2007-08 | St. Louis | NHL | 66 | 2 | 7 | 9 | 42 | 0 | 0 | 2 | 42 | 4.8 | 2 | 0 | 0.0 | 17:54 | | | | | | | | | |
| 2008-09 | St. Louis | NHL | 69 | 1 | 7 | 8 | 44 | 0 | 0 | 1 | 43 | 2.3 | 11 | 2 | 0.0 | 17:19 | 4 | 0 | 0 | 0 | 4 | 0 | 0 | 0 | 14:56 |
| | NHL Totals | | 740 | 20 | 95 | 115 | 568 | 1 | 1 | 6 | 566 | 3.5 | | 5 | 0.0 | 19:02 | 55 | 3 | 6 | 9 | 64 | 0 | 0 | 2 | 20:36 |

OHL Second All-Star Team (1996)

Signed as a free agent by **St. Louis**, July 1, 2006. • Missed majority of 2006-07 season recovering from hand injury suffered in game vs. Vancouver, October 20, 2006. Signed as a free agent by **Pittsburgh**, July 10, 2009.

## McLAREN, Kyle

(muh-KLAIR-uhn, KIGHL)

Defense. Shoots left. 6'4", 235 lbs. Born, Humboldt, Sask., June 18, 1977. Boston's 1st choice, 9th overall, in 1995 Entry Draft.

| Season | Club | League | GP | G | A | Pts | PIM | PP | SH | GW | S | % | +/- | TF | F% | Min | GP | G | A | Pts | PIM | PP | SH | GW | Min |
|---|---|---|---|---|---|---|---|---|---|---|---|---|---|---|---|---|---|---|---|---|---|---|---|---|---|
| 1992-93 | Lethbridge | AMHL | 60 | 28 | 28 | 56 | 84 | | | | | | | | | | | | | | | | | | |
| 1993-94 | Tacoma Rockets | WHL | 62 | 1 | 9 | 10 | 53 | | | | | | | | | | 6 | 1 | 4 | 5 | 6 | | | | |
| 1994-95 | Tacoma Rockets | WHL | 47 | 13 | 19 | 32 | 68 | | | | | | | | | | 4 | 1 | 1 | 2 | 4 | | | | |
| 1995-96 | Boston | NHL | 74 | 5 | 12 | 17 | 73 | 0 | 0 | 0 | 74 | 6.8 | 16 | | | | 5 | 0 | 0 | 0 | 14 | 0 | 0 | 0 | |
| 1996-97 | Boston | NHL | 58 | 5 | 9 | 14 | 54 | 0 | 0 | 1 | 68 | 7.4 | –9 | | | | | | | | | | | | |
| 1997-98 | Boston | NHL | 66 | 5 | 20 | 25 | 56 | 2 | 0 | 0 | 101 | 5.0 | 13 | | | | 6 | 1 | 0 | 1 | 4 | 1 | 0 | 0 | |
| 1998-99 | Boston | NHL | 52 | 6 | 18 | 24 | 48 | 3 | 0 | 0 | 97 | 6.2 | 1 | 0 | 0.0 | 23:25 | 12 | 0 | 3 | 3 | 10 | 0 | 0 | 0 | 26:45 |
| 99-2000 | Boston | NHL | 71 | 8 | 11 | 19 | 67 | 2 | 0 | 3 | 142 | 5.6 | –4 | 5 | 40.0 | 23:18 | | | | | | | | | |
| 2000-01 | Boston | NHL | 58 | 5 | 12 | 17 | 53 | 2 | 0 | 0 | 91 | 5.5 | –5 | 4 | 50.0 | 24:14 | | | | | | | | | |
| 2001-02 | Boston | NHL | 38 | 0 | 8 | 8 | 19 | 0 | 0 | 0 | 57 | 0.0 | –4 | 1 | 0.0 | 19:21 | 4 | 0 | 0 | 0 | 20 | 0 | 0 | 0 | 18:37 |
| 2002-03 | San Jose | NHL | 33 | 0 | 8 | 8 | 30 | 0 | 0 | 0 | 43 | 0.0 | –10 | 0 | 0.0 | 22:40 | | | | | | | | | |
| 2003-04 | San Jose | NHL | 64 | 2 | 22 | 24 | 60 | 0 | 1 | 0 | 67 | 3.0 | 10 | 1 | 0.0 | 21:01 | 16 | 0 | 3 | 3 | 10 | 0 | 0 | 0 | 24:09 |
| 2004-05 | | | DID NOT PLAY | | | | | | | | | | | | | | | | | | | | | | |
| 2005-06 | San Jose | NHL | 77 | 2 | 21 | 23 | 66 | 0 | 0 | 1 | 67 | 3.0 | 6 | 0 | 0.0 | 22:52 | 11 | 0 | 3 | 3 | 4 | 0 | 0 | 0 | 20:42 |
| 2006-07 | San Jose | NHL | 67 | 5 | 12 | 17 | 61 | 1 | 0 | 0 | 43 | 11.6 | 10 | 0 | 0.0 | 21:25 | 11 | 0 | 4 | 4 | 10 | 0 | 0 | 0 | 22:47 |
| 2007-08 | San Jose | NHL | 61 | 3 | 8 | 11 | 84 | 0 | 0 | 0 | 39 | 7.7 | 3 | 0 | 0.0 | 18:21 | 5 | 0 | 0 | 0 | 6 | 0 | 0 | 0 | 9:45 |
| 2008-09 | Worcester Sharks | AHL | 22 | 1 | 6 | 7 | 19 | | | | | | | | | | 7 | 0 | 1 | 1 | 2 | | | | |
| | NHL Totals | | 719 | 46 | 161 | 207 | 671 | 10 | 1 | 5 | 889 | 5.2 | | 11 | 36.4 | 21:55 | 70 | 1 | 13 | 14 | 78 | 1 | 0 | 0 | 22:11 |

NHL All-Rookie Team (1996)

• Missed majority of 2001-02 season recovering from chest (October 10, 2001 vs. Minnesota) and wrist (December 26, 2001 vs. Ottawa) injuries. • Missed majority of 2002-03 season in contract dispute with Boston. Traded to **San Jose** by **Boston** with Boston's 4th round choice (Torrey Mitchell) in 2004 Entry Draft for Jeff Hackett and Jeff Jillson, January 23, 2003. • Missed majority of 2008-09 season recovering from head injury suffered in game vs. Springfield (AHL), December 10., 2008.

## McLEAN, Brett

(muh-KLAYN, BREHT)

Center. Shoots left. 5'11", 185 lbs. Born, Comox, B.C., August 14, 1978. Dallas' 9th choice, 242nd overall, in 1997 Entry Draft.

| Season | Club | League | GP | G | A | Pts | PIM | PP | SH | GW | S | % | +/- | TF | F% | Min | GP | G | A | Pts | PIM | PP | SH | GW | Min |
|---|---|---|---|---|---|---|---|---|---|---|---|---|---|---|---|---|---|---|---|---|---|---|---|---|---|
| 1993-94 | Notre Dame | SMBHL | 71 | 109 | 124 | 233 | 70 | | | | | | | | | | | | | | | | | | |
| 1994-95 | Tacoma Rockets | WHL | 67 | 11 | 23 | 34 | 33 | | | | | | | | | | 4 | 0 | 1 | 1 | 0 | | | | |
| 1995-96 | Kelowna Rockets | WHL | 71 | 37 | 42 | 79 | 60 | | | | | | | | | | 6 | 2 | 2 | 4 | 6 | | | | |
| 1996-97 | Kelowna Rockets | WHL | 72 | 44 | 60 | 104 | 98 | | | | | | | | | | 6 | 4 | 2 | 6 | 12 | | | | |
| 1997-98 | Kelowna Rockets | WHL | 54 | 42 | 45 | 87 | 91 | | | | | | | | | | 7 | 4 | 5 | 9 | 17 | | | | |
| 1998-99 | Kelowna Rockets | WHL | 44 | 32 | 38 | 70 | 46 | | | | | | | | | | | | | | | | | | |
| | Brandon | WHL | 21 | 15 | 16 | 31 | 20 | | | | | | | | | | 5 | 1 | 6 | 7 | 8 | | | | |
| | Cincinnati | AHL | 7 | 0 | 3 | 3 | 6 | | | | | | | | | | | | | | | | | | |
| 99-2000 | Johnstown Chiefs | ECHL | 8 | 4 | 7 | 11 | 6 | | | | | | | | | | | | | | | | | | |
| | Saint John Flames | AHL | 72 | 15 | 23 | 38 | 115 | | | | | | | | | | 3 | 0 | 1 | 1 | 2 | | | | |
| 2000-01 | Cleveland | IHL | 74 | 20 | 24 | 44 | 54 | | | | | | | | | | 4 | 0 | 0 | 0 | 18 | | | | |
| 2001-02 | Houston Aeros | AHL | 78 | 24 | 21 | 45 | 71 | | | | | | | | | | 14 | 1 | 6 | 7 | 12 | | | | |
| 2002-03 | Chicago | NHL | 2 | 0 | 0 | 0 | 0 | 0 | 0 | 0 | 1 | 0.0 | –1 | 19 | 26.3 | 10:47 | | | | | | | | | |
| | Norfolk Admirals | AHL | 77 | 23 | 38 | 61 | 60 | | | | | | | | | | 9 | 2 | 6 | 8 | 9 | | | | |
| 2003-04 | Chicago | NHL | 76 | 11 | 20 | 31 | 54 | 5 | 1 | 0 | 125 | 8.8 | –11 | 1135 | 51.1 | 17:33 | | | | | | | | | |
| | Norfolk Admirals | AHL | 4 | 3 | 3 | 6 | 6 | | | | | | | | | | | | | | | | | | |
| 2004-05 | Malmo | Sweden | 38 | 7 | 6 | 13 | 102 | | | | | | | | | | | | | | | | | | |
| | Malmo | Sweden-Q | 9 | 1 | 1 | 2 | 16 | | | | | | | | | | | | | | | | | | |
| 2005-06 | Colorado | NHL | 82 | 9 | 31 | 40 | 51 | 1 | 0 | 0 | 115 | 7.8 | –7 | 770 | 50.7 | 12:12 | 8 | 0 | 1 | 1 | 4 | 0 | 0 | 0 | 10:40 |
| 2006-07 | Colorado | NHL | 78 | 15 | 20 | 35 | 36 | 0 | 0 | 3 | 134 | 11.2 | 8 | 413 | 50.1 | 13:38 | | | | | | | | | |
| 2007-08 | Florida | NHL | 67 | 14 | 23 | 37 | 34 | 3 | 1 | 1 | 140 | 10.0 | –5 | 624 | 47.4 | 16:14 | | | | | | | | | |
| 2008-09 | Florida | NHL | 80 | 7 | 12 | 19 | 29 | 0 | 0 | 2 | 114 | 6.1 | –12 | 456 | 43.2 | 12:26 | | | | | | | | | |
| | NHL Totals | | 385 | 56 | 106 | 162 | 204 | 9 | 2 | 6 | 629 | 8.9 | | 3417 | 49.0 | 14:17 | 8 | 0 | 1 | 1 | 4 | 0 | 0 | 0 | 10:40 |

WHL West Second All-Star Team (1998)

Signed as a free agent by **Calgary**, September, 1999. Signed as a free agent by **Minnesota**, July 13, 2000. Signed as a free agent by **Chicago**, July 23, 2002. Signed as a free agent by **Colorado**, July 22, 2004. Signed as a free agent by **Malmo** (Sweden), September 24, 2004. Signed as a free agent by **Florida**, July 1, 2007.

## McLEAN, Kurtis

(muh-KLAYN, KUHR-this)

Center. Shoots right. 5'11", 175 lbs. Born, Kirkland Lake, Ont., November 2, 1980.

| Season | Club | League | GP | G | A | Pts | PIM | PP | SH | GW | S | % | +/- | TF | F% | Min | GP | G | A | Pts | PIM | PP | SH | GW | Min |
|---|---|---|---|---|---|---|---|---|---|---|---|---|---|---|---|---|---|---|---|---|---|---|---|---|---|
| 2005-06 | Wilkes-Barre | AHL | 32 | 4 | 11 | 15 | 8 | | | | | | | | | | | | | | | | | | |
| | Wheeling Nailers | ECHL | 41 | 31 | 25 | 56 | 32 | | | | | | | | | | 5 | 4 | 4 | 8 | 4 | | | | |
| 2006-07 | Wilkes-Barre | AHL | 55 | 16 | 16 | 32 | 24 | | | | | | | | | | 10 | 4 | 3 | 7 | 4 | | | | |
| | Wheeling Nailers | ECHL | 16 | 11 | 12 | 23 | 21 | | | | | | | | | | | | | | | | | | |
| 2007-08 | Wilkes-Barre | AHL | 76 | 22 | 32 | 54 | 58 | | | | | | | | | | 23 | 4 | 15 | 19 | 8 | | | | |
| 2008-09 | NY Islanders | NHL | 4 | 1 | 0 | 1 | 0 | 0 | 0 | 1 | 5 | 20.0 | 1 | 1 | 0.0 | 10:34 | | | | | | | | | |
| | Bridgeport | AHL | 62 | 15 | 37 | 52 | 30 | | | | | | | | | | | | | | | | | | |
| | NHL Totals | | 4 | 1 | 0 | 1 | 0 | 0 | 0 | 1 | 5 | 20.0 | | 1 | 0.0 | 10:34 | | | | | | | | | |

Signed as a free agent by **Wilkes-Barre** (AHL), September 29, 2005. Signed as a free agent by **Pittsburgh**, September 7, 2006. Signed as a free agent by **NY Islanders**, July 3, 2008. Signed as a free agent by **Lukko Rauma** (Finland), May 29, 2009.

| | | | Regular Season | | | | | | | | | | | | | | Playoffs | | | | | | | | |
|---|---|---|---|---|---|---|---|---|---|---|---|---|---|---|---|---|---|---|---|---|---|---|---|---|---|
| Season | Club | League | GP | G | A | Pts | PIM | PP | SH | GW | S | % | +/- | TF | F% | Min | GP | G | A | Pts | PIM | PP | SH | GW | Min |

## McLEOD, Cody
(muh-KLOWD, KOH-dee) **COL.**

Left wing. Shoots left. 6'2", 210 lbs. Born, Binscarth, Man., June 26, 1984.

| Season | Club | League | GP | G | A | Pts | PIM | PP | SH | GW | S | % | +/- | TF | F% | Min | GP | G | A | Pts | PIM | PP | SH | GW | Min |
|---|---|---|---|---|---|---|---|---|---|---|---|---|---|---|---|---|---|---|---|---|---|---|---|---|---|
| 2001-02 | Portland | WHL | 47 | 10 | 3 | 13 | 86 | .... | .... | .... | .... | .... | .... | .... | .... | .... | 5 | 0 | 0 | 0 | 0 | .... | .... | .... | .... |
| 2002-03 | Portland | WHL | 71 | 15 | 18 | 33 | 153 | .... | .... | .... | .... | .... | .... | .... | .... | .... | 7 | 1 | 1 | 2 | 13 | .... | .... | .... | .... |
| 2003-04 | Portland | WHL | 69 | 13 | 18 | 31 | 227 | .... | .... | .... | .... | .... | .... | .... | .... | .... | 5 | 2 | 2 | 4 | 6 | .... | .... | .... | .... |
| 2004-05 | Portland | WHL | 70 | 31 | 29 | 60 | 195 | .... | .... | .... | .... | .... | .... | .... | .... | .... | 7 | 0 | 3 | 3 | 8 | .... | .... | .... | .... |
| | Adirondack | UHL | 1 | 0 | 0 | 0 | 0 | .... | .... | .... | .... | .... | .... | .... | .... | .... | 5 | 0 | 0 | 0 | 11 | .... | .... | .... | .... |
| 2005-06 | Lowell | AHL | 33 | 4 | 5 | 9 | 87 | .... | .... | .... | .... | .... | .... | .... | .... | .... | .... | .... | .... | .... | .... | .... | .... | .... | .... |
| | San Diego Gulls | ECHL | 16 | 4 | 5 | 9 | 48 | .... | .... | .... | .... | .... | .... | .... | .... | .... | 2 | 2 | 1 | 3 | 14 | .... | .... | .... | .... |
| 2006-07 | Albany River Rats | AHL | 73 | 11 | 8 | 19 | 180 | .... | .... | .... | .... | .... | .... | .... | .... | .... | 5 | 0 | 0 | 0 | 4 | .... | .... | .... | .... |
| **2007-08** | **Colorado** | **NHL** | **49** | **4** | **5** | **9** | **120** | **0** | **0** | **0** | **60** | **6.7** | **–6** | **3** | **0.0** | **10:07** | **10** | **1** | **1** | **2** | **26** | **0** | **0** | **0** | **12:23** |
| | Lake Erie | AHL | 27 | 6 | 7 | 13 | 101 | .... | .... | .... | .... | .... | .... | .... | .... | .... | .... | .... | .... | .... | .... | .... | .... | .... | .... |
| **2008-09** | **Colorado** | **NHL** | **79** | **15** | **5** | **20** | **162** | **0** | **0** | **3** | **118** | **12.7** | **–11** | **5** | **40.0** | **11:35** | .... | .... | .... | .... | .... | .... | .... | .... | .... |
| | **NHL Totals** | | **128** | **19** | **10** | **29** | **282** | **0** | **0** | **3** | **178** | **10.7** | | **8** | **25.0** | **11:01** | **10** | **1** | **1** | **2** | **26** | **0** | **0** | **0** | **12:23** |

Signed as a free agent by **Colorado**, July 6, 2006.

## MEECH, Derek
(MEECH, DAIR-ihk) **DET.**

Defense. Shoots left. 5'11", 197 lbs. Born, Winnipeg, Man., April 21, 1984. Detroit's 7th choice, 229th overall, in 2002 Entry Draft.

| Season | Club | League | GP | G | A | Pts | PIM | PP | SH | GW | S | % | +/- | TF | F% | Min | GP | G | A | Pts | PIM | PP | SH | GW | Min |
|---|---|---|---|---|---|---|---|---|---|---|---|---|---|---|---|---|---|---|---|---|---|---|---|---|---|
| 99-2000 | Wpg. Warriors | MMMHL | 36 | 15 | 40 | 55 | 24 | .... | .... | .... | .... | .... | .... | .... | .... | .... | .... | .... | .... | .... | .... | .... | .... | .... | .... |
| | Red Deer Rebels | WHL | 5 | 1 | 0 | 1 | 2 | .... | .... | .... | .... | .... | .... | .... | .... | .... | .... | .... | .... | .... | .... | .... | .... | .... | .... |
| 2000-01 | Red Deer Rebels | WHL | 60 | 2 | 7 | 9 | 40 | .... | .... | .... | .... | .... | .... | .... | .... | .... | 22 | 0 | 0 | 0 | 9 | .... | .... | .... | .... |
| 2001-02 | Red Deer Rebels | WHL | 71 | 8 | 19 | 27 | 33 | .... | .... | .... | .... | .... | .... | .... | .... | .... | 13 | 1 | 1 | 2 | 6 | .... | .... | .... | .... |
| 2002-03 | Red Deer Rebels | WHL | 65 | 6 | 16 | 22 | 53 | .... | .... | .... | .... | .... | .... | .... | .... | .... | 12 | 1 | 1 | 2 | 12 | .... | .... | .... | .... |
| 2003-04 | Red Deer Rebels | WHL | 62 | 10 | 28 | 38 | 40 | .... | .... | .... | .... | .... | .... | .... | .... | .... | 19 | 4 | 7 | 11 | 10 | .... | .... | .... | .... |
| 2004-05 | Grand Rapids | AHL | 78 | 6 | 8 | 14 | 40 | .... | .... | .... | .... | .... | .... | .... | .... | .... | .... | .... | .... | .... | .... | .... | .... | .... | .... |
| 2005-06 | Grand Rapids | AHL | 79 | 4 | 16 | 20 | 85 | .... | .... | .... | .... | .... | .... | .... | .... | .... | 16 | 0 | 2 | 2 | 4 | .... | .... | .... | .... |
| **2006-07** | **Detroit** | **NHL** | **4** | **0** | **0** | **0** | **2** | **0** | **0** | **0** | **3** | **0.0** | **1** | **0** | **0.0** | **5:47** | .... | .... | .... | .... | .... | .... | .... | .... | .... |
| | Grand Rapids | AHL | 67 | 6 | 23 | 29 | 40 | .... | .... | .... | .... | .... | .... | .... | .... | .... | 7 | 0 | 1 | 1 | 4 | .... | .... | .... | .... |
| **2007-08** | **Detroit** | **NHL** | **32** | **0** | **3** | **3** | **6** | **0** | **0** | **0** | **44** | **0.0** | **–5** | **0** | **0.0** | **12:08** | .... | .... | .... | .... | .... | .... | .... | .... | .... |
| | Grand Rapids | AHL | 6 | 1 | 1 | 2 | 0 | .... | .... | .... | .... | .... | .... | .... | .... | .... | .... | .... | .... | .... | .... | .... | .... | .... | .... |
| **2008-09** | **Detroit** | **NHL** | **41** | **2** | **5** | **7** | **12** | **0** | **0** | **0** | **44** | **4.5** | **–12** | **2** | **0.0** | **10:03** | **2** | **0** | **0** | **0** | **0** | **0** | **0** | **0** | **4:04** |
| | **NHL Totals** | | **77** | **2** | **8** | **10** | **20** | **0** | **0** | **0** | **91** | **2.2** | | **2** | **0.0** | **10:42** | **2** | **0** | **0** | **0** | **0** | **0** | **0** | **0** | **4:04** |

WHL East Second All-Star Team (2004)

• Spent majority of 2007-08 season serving as a healthy reserve.

## MELICHAR, Josef
(mehl-ee-KHAHR, YOH-sehf)

Defense. Shoots left. 6'2", 220 lbs. Born, Ceske Budejovice, Czech., January 20, 1979. Pittsburgh's 3rd choice, 71st overall, in 1997 Entry Draft.

| Season | Club | League | GP | G | A | Pts | PIM | PP | SH | GW | S | % | +/- | TF | F% | Min | GP | G | A | Pts | PIM | PP | SH | GW | Min |
|---|---|---|---|---|---|---|---|---|---|---|---|---|---|---|---|---|---|---|---|---|---|---|---|---|---|
| 1995-96 | C. Budejovice Jr. | CzRep-Jr. | 38 | 3 | 4 | 7 | .... | .... | .... | .... | .... | .... | .... | .... | .... | .... | .... | .... | .... | .... | .... | .... | .... | .... | .... |
| 1996-97 | C. Budejovice Jr. | CzRep-Jr. | 41 | 2 | 3 | 5 | 10 | .... | .... | .... | .... | .... | .... | .... | .... | .... | .... | .... | .... | .... | .... | .... | .... | .... | .... |
| 1997-98 | Tri-City | WHL | 67 | 9 | 24 | 33 | 154 | .... | .... | .... | .... | .... | .... | .... | .... | .... | .... | .... | .... | .... | .... | .... | .... | .... | .... |
| 1998-99 | Tri-City | WHL | 65 | 8 | 28 | 36 | 125 | .... | .... | .... | .... | .... | .... | .... | .... | .... | 11 | 1 | 0 | 1 | 15 | .... | .... | .... | .... |
| 99-2000 | Wilkes-Barre | AHL | 80 | 3 | 9 | 12 | 126 | .... | .... | .... | .... | .... | .... | .... | .... | .... | .... | .... | .... | .... | .... | .... | .... | .... | .... |
| **2000-01** | **Pittsburgh** | **NHL** | **18** | **0** | **2** | **2** | **21** | **0** | **0** | **0** | **9** | **0.0** | **–5** | **0** | **0.0** | **14:54** | .... | .... | .... | .... | .... | .... | .... | .... | .... |
| | Wilkes-Barre | AHL | 46 | 2 | 5 | 7 | 69 | .... | .... | .... | .... | .... | .... | .... | .... | .... | 21 | 0 | 5 | 5 | 6 | .... | .... | .... | .... |
| **2001-02** | **Pittsburgh** | **NHL** | **60** | **0** | **3** | **3** | **68** | **0** | **0** | **0** | **46** | **0.0** | **–1** | **0** | **0.0** | **16:46** | .... | .... | .... | .... | .... | .... | .... | .... | .... |
| **2002-03** | **Pittsburgh** | **NHL** | **8** | **0** | **0** | **0** | **2** | **0** | **0** | **0** | **6** | **0.0** | **–2** | **0** | **0.0** | **15:19** | .... | .... | .... | .... | .... | .... | .... | .... | .... |
| **2003-04** | **Pittsburgh** | **NHL** | **82** | **3** | **5** | **8** | **62** | **0** | **0** | **0** | **78** | **3.8** | **–17** | **0** | **0.0** | **19:01** | .... | .... | .... | .... | .... | .... | .... | .... | .... |
| 2004-05 | HC Sparta Praha | CzRep | 13 | 0 | 4 | 4 | 8 | .... | .... | .... | .... | .... | .... | .... | .... | .... | 5 | 0 | 0 | 0 | 6 | .... | .... | .... | .... |
| **2005-06** | **Pittsburgh** | **NHL** | **72** | **3** | **12** | **15** | **66** | **0** | **1** | **0** | **53** | **5.7** | **–2** | **0** | **0.0** | **17:26** | .... | .... | .... | .... | .... | .... | .... | .... | .... |
| **2006-07** | **Pittsburgh** | **NHL** | **70** | **1** | **11** | **12** | **44** | **0** | **0** | **0** | **57** | **1.8** | **1** | **0** | **0.0** | **18:49** | **5** | **0** | **0** | **0** | **2** | **0** | **0** | **0** | **17:21** |
| 2007-08 | C. Budejovice | CzRep | 6 | 0 | 0 | 0 | 4 | .... | .... | .... | .... | .... | .... | .... | .... | .... | .... | .... | .... | .... | .... | .... | .... | .... | .... |
| | Linkopings HC | Sweden | 50 | 0 | 8 | 8 | 74 | .... | .... | .... | .... | .... | .... | .... | .... | .... | 16 | 1 | 1 | 2 | 39 | .... | .... | .... | .... |
| **2008-09** | **Carolina** | **NHL** | **15** | **0** | **4** | **4** | **8** | **0** | **0** | **0** | **3** | **0.0** | **–1** | **0** | **0.0** | **8:40** | .... | .... | .... | .... | .... | .... | .... | .... | .... |
| | Albany River Rats | AHL | 25 | 1 | 4 | 5 | 35 | .... | .... | .... | .... | .... | .... | .... | .... | .... | .... | .... | .... | .... | .... | .... | .... | .... | .... |
| | **Tampa Bay** | **NHL** | **24** | **0** | **5** | **5** | **29** | **0** | **0** | **0** | **16** | **0.0** | **1** | **0** | **0.0** | **16:58** | .... | .... | .... | .... | .... | .... | .... | .... | .... |
| | Norfolk Admirals | AHL | 1 | 0 | 0 | 0 | 0 | .... | .... | .... | .... | .... | .... | .... | .... | .... | .... | .... | .... | .... | .... | .... | .... | .... | .... |
| | **NHL Totals** | | **349** | **7** | **42** | **49** | **300** | **0** | **1** | **0** | **268** | **2.6** | | **0** | **0.0** | **17:23** | **5** | **0** | **0** | **0** | **2** | **0** | **0** | **0** | **17:21** |

• Missed majority of 2002-03 season recovering from shoulder injury suffered in game vs. Boston, October 13, 2002. Signed as a free agent by **Sparta Praha** (CzRep), September 17, 2004. Signed as a free agent by **Linkopings** (Sweden), October 3, 2007. Signed as a free agent by **Carolina**, July 2, 2008. Traded to **Tampa Bay** by **Carolina** with Wade Brookbank and future considerations for Jussi Jokinen, February 7, 2009.

## MESZAROS, Andrej
(MEHT-zahr-ohsh, AWN-dray) **T.B.**

Defense. Shoots left. 6'2", 218 lbs. Born, Povazska Bystrica, Czech., October 13, 1985. Ottawa's 1st choice, 23rd overall, in 2004 Entry Draft.

| Season | Club | League | GP | G | A | Pts | PIM | PP | SH | GW | S | % | +/- | TF | F% | Min | GP | G | A | Pts | PIM | PP | SH | GW | Min |
|---|---|---|---|---|---|---|---|---|---|---|---|---|---|---|---|---|---|---|---|---|---|---|---|---|---|
| 2002-03 | Dukla Trencin Jr. | Slovak-Jr. | 33 | 6 | 10 | 16 | 12 | .... | .... | .... | .... | .... | .... | .... | .... | .... | .... | .... | .... | .... | .... | .... | .... | .... | .... |
| | Dukla Trencin | Slovakia | 23 | 0 | 1 | 1 | 4 | .... | .... | .... | .... | .... | .... | .... | .... | .... | .... | .... | .... | .... | .... | .... | .... | .... | .... |
| 2003-04 | Dukla Trencin | Slovakia | 44 | 3 | 3 | 6 | 8 | .... | .... | .... | .... | .... | .... | .... | .... | .... | 14 | 3 | 1 | 4 | 2 | .... | .... | .... | .... |
| | Dukla Trencin Jr. | Slovak-Jr. | 5 | 2 | 2 | 4 | 0 | .... | .... | .... | .... | .... | .... | .... | .... | .... | .... | .... | .... | .... | .... | .... | .... | .... | .... |
| 2004-05 | Vancouver Giants | WHL | 59 | 11 | 30 | 41 | 94 | .... | .... | .... | .... | .... | .... | .... | .... | .... | 6 | 1 | 3 | 4 | 14 | .... | .... | .... | .... |
| **2005-06** | **Ottawa** | **NHL** | **82** | **10** | **29** | **39** | **61** | **5** | **0** | **2** | **137** | **7.3** | **34** | **1** | **0.0** | **18:11** | **10** | **1** | **0** | **1** | **18** | **0** | **0** | **0** | **17:50** |
| | Slovakia | Olympics | 6 | 0 | 2 | 2 | 4 | .... | .... | .... | .... | .... | .... | .... | .... | .... | .... | .... | .... | .... | .... | .... | .... | .... | .... |
| **2006-07** | **Ottawa** | **NHL** | **82** | **7** | **28** | **35** | **102** | **0** | **0** | **1** | **147** | **4.8** | **–15** | **0** | **0.0** | **21:41** | **20** | **1** | **6** | **7** | **12** | **0** | **0** | **0** | **20:29** |
| **2007-08** | **Ottawa** | **NHL** | **82** | **9** | **27** | **36** | **50** | **6** | **1** | **1** | **160** | **5.6** | **5** | **1** | **0.0** | **21:02** | **4** | **0** | **1** | **1** | **6** | **0** | **0** | **0** | **18:59** |
| **2008-09** | **Tampa Bay** | **NHL** | **52** | **2** | **14** | **16** | **36** | **1** | **0** | **1** | **87** | **2.3** | **–4** | **1** | **0.0** | **24:11** | .... | .... | .... | .... | .... | .... | .... | .... | .... |
| | **NHL Totals** | | **298** | **28** | **98** | **126** | **249** | **12** | **1** | **5** | **531** | **5.3** | | **3** | **0.0** | **20:59** | **34** | **2** | **7** | **9** | **36** | **0** | **0** | **0** | **19:32** |

WHL West Second All-Star Team (2005) • NHL All-Rookie Team (2006)

Traded to **Tampa Bay** by **Ottawa** for Filip Kuba, Alexandre Picard and San Jose's 1st round choice (previously acquired, later traded to NY Islanders, later traded to Columbus, later traded to Anahaim - Anaheim selected Kyle Palmieri) in 2009 Entry Draft, August 29, 2008.

## METHOT, Marc
(meh-THAWT, MAHRK) **CBJ**

Defense. Shoots left. 6'3", 224 lbs. Born, Ottawa, Ont., June 21, 1985. Columbus' 7th choice, 168th overall, in 2003 Entry Draft.

| Season | Club | League | GP | G | A | Pts | PIM | PP | SH | GW | S | % | +/- | TF | F% | Min | GP | G | A | Pts | PIM | PP | SH | GW | Min |
|---|---|---|---|---|---|---|---|---|---|---|---|---|---|---|---|---|---|---|---|---|---|---|---|---|---|
| 2001-02 | Kanata Laser | CJHL | 50 | 3 | 10 | 13 | 22 | .... | .... | .... | .... | .... | .... | .... | .... | .... | .... | .... | .... | .... | .... | .... | .... | .... | .... |
| 2002-03 | London Knights | OHL | 68 | 2 | 13 | 15 | 46 | .... | .... | .... | .... | .... | .... | .... | .... | .... | 14 | 2 | 4 | 6 | 6 | .... | .... | .... | .... |
| 2003-04 | London Knights | OHL | 63 | 2 | 9 | 11 | 66 | .... | .... | .... | .... | .... | .... | .... | .... | .... | 15 | 0 | 3 | 3 | 18 | .... | .... | .... | .... |
| 2004-05 | London Knights | OHL | 67 | 4 | 12 | 16 | 88 | .... | .... | .... | .... | .... | .... | .... | .... | .... | 18 | 2 | 1 | 3 | 32 | .... | .... | .... | .... |
| 2005-06 | Syracuse Crunch | AHL | 70 | 1 | 12 | 13 | 75 | .... | .... | .... | .... | .... | .... | .... | .... | .... | 5 | 0 | 0 | 0 | 8 | .... | .... | .... | .... |
| **2006-07** | **Columbus** | **NHL** | **20** | **0** | **4** | **4** | **12** | **0** | **0** | **0** | **11** | **0.0** | **5** | **0** | **0.0** | **14:38** | .... | .... | .... | .... | .... | .... | .... | .... | .... |
| | Syracuse Crunch | AHL | 59 | 1 | 15 | 16 | 58 | .... | .... | .... | .... | .... | .... | .... | .... | .... | .... | .... | .... | .... | .... | .... | .... | .... | .... |
| **2007-08** | **Columbus** | **NHL** | **9** | **0** | **0** | **0** | **8** | **0** | **0** | **0** | **9** | **0.0** | **–1** | **0** | **0.0** | **14:14** | .... | .... | .... | .... | .... | .... | .... | .... | .... |
| | Syracuse Crunch | AHL | 66 | 7 | 6 | 13 | 130 | .... | .... | .... | .... | .... | .... | .... | .... | .... | 13 | 0 | 6 | 6 | 14 | .... | .... | .... | .... |
| **2008-09** | **Columbus** | **NHL** | **66** | **4** | **13** | **17** | **55** | **0** | **0** | **0** | **58** | **6.9** | **7** | **0** | **0.0** | **17:57** | **4** | **0** | **0** | **0** | **2** | **0** | **0** | **0** | **16:15** |
| | **NHL Totals** | | **95** | **4** | **17** | **21** | **75** | **0** | **0** | **0** | **78** | **5.1** | | **0** | **0.0** | **16:54** | **4** | **0** | **0** | **0** | **2** | **0** | **0** | **0** | **16:15** |

## METROPOLIT, Glen
(meh-troh-PAW-liht, GLEHN) **MTL.**

Center. Shoots right. 5'10", 195 lbs. Born, Toronto, Ont., June 25, 1974.

| Season | Club | League | GP | G | A | Pts | PIM | PP | SH | GW | S | % | +/- | TF | F% | Min | GP | G | A | Pts | PIM | PP | SH | GW | Min |
|---|---|---|---|---|---|---|---|---|---|---|---|---|---|---|---|---|---|---|---|---|---|---|---|---|---|
| 1992-93 | Richmond Hill | MTJHL | 43 | 27 | 36 | 63 | 36 | .... | .... | .... | .... | .... | .... | .... | .... | .... | .... | .... | .... | .... | .... | .... | .... | .... | .... |
| 1993-94 | Richmond Hill | MTJHL | 49 | 38 | 62 | 100 | 83 | .... | .... | .... | .... | .... | .... | .... | .... | .... | .... | .... | .... | .... | .... | .... | .... | .... | .... |
| 1994-95 | Vernon Vipers | BCJHL | 60 | 43 | 74 | 117 | 92 | .... | .... | .... | .... | .... | .... | .... | .... | .... | .... | .... | .... | .... | .... | .... | .... | .... | .... |
| 1995-96 | Nashville Knights | ECHL | 58 | 30 | 31 | 61 | 62 | .... | .... | .... | .... | .... | .... | .... | .... | .... | 5 | 3 | 8 | 11 | 2 | .... | .... | .... | .... |
| | Atlanta Knights | IHL | 1 | 0 | 0 | 0 | 0 | .... | .... | .... | .... | .... | .... | .... | .... | .... | .... | .... | .... | .... | .... | .... | .... | .... | .... |
| 1996-97 | Pensacola | ECHL | 54 | 35 | 47 | 82 | 45 | .... | .... | .... | .... | .... | .... | .... | .... | .... | 12 | 9 | 16 | 25 | 28 | .... | .... | .... | .... |
| | Quebec Rafales | IHL | 22 | 5 | 4 | 9 | 14 | .... | .... | .... | .... | .... | .... | .... | .... | .... | 5 | 0 | 0 | 0 | 2 | .... | .... | .... | .... |
| 1997-98 | Grand Rapids | IHL | 79 | 20 | 35 | 55 | 90 | .... | .... | .... | .... | .... | .... | .... | .... | .... | 3 | 1 | 1 | 2 | 0 | .... | .... | .... | .... |
| 1998-99 | Grand Rapids | IHL | 77 | 28 | 53 | 81 | 92 | .... | .... | .... | .... | .... | .... | .... | .... | .... | .... | .... | .... | .... | .... | .... | .... | .... | .... |

| | | | Regular Season | | | | | | | | | | | | | | Playoffs | | | | | | | | |
|---|---|---|---|---|---|---|---|---|---|---|---|---|---|---|---|---|---|---|---|---|---|---|---|---|---|
| Season | Club | League | GP | G | A | Pts | PIM | PP | SH | GW | S | % | +/- | TF | F% | Min | GP | G | A | Pts | PIM | PP | SH | GW | Min |
| **99-2000** | **Washington** | **NHL** | **30** | **6** | **13** | **19** | **4** | **1** | **0** | **1** | **57** | **10.5** | **5** | **37** | **46.0** | **13:17** | **2** | **0** | **0** | **0** | **2** | **0** | **0** | **0** | **7:07** |
| | Portland Pirates | AHL | 48 | 18 | 42 | 60 | 73 | .... | .... | .... | .... | .... | .... | .... | .... | .... | 1 | 1 | 0 | 1 | 0 | .... | .... | .... | .... |
| **2000-01** | **Washington** | **NHL** | **15** | **1** | **5** | **6** | **10** | **0** | **0** | **0** | **20** | **5.0** | **–2** | **3** | **33.3** | **11:50** | **1** | **0** | **0** | **0** | **0** | **0** | **0** | **0** | **7:03** |
| | Portland Pirates | AHL | 51 | 25 | 42 | 67 | 59 | .... | .... | .... | .... | .... | .... | .... | .... | .... | .... | .... | .... | .... | .... | .... | .... | .... | .... |
| **2001-02** | **Tampa Bay** | **NHL** | **2** | **0** | **0** | **0** | **0** | **0** | **0** | **0** | **1** | **0.0** | **–2** | **2** | **50.0** | **10:26** | .... | .... | .... | .... | .... | .... | .... | .... | .... |
| | **Washington** | **NHL** | **33** | **1** | **16** | **17** | **6** | **0** | **0** | **0** | **51** | **2.0** | **3** | **145** | **49.7** | **14:24** | .... | .... | .... | .... | .... | .... | .... | .... | .... |
| | Portland Pirates | AHL | 32 | 17 | 22 | 39 | 20 | .... | .... | .... | .... | .... | .... | .... | .... | .... | .... | .... | .... | .... | .... | .... | .... | .... | .... |
| **2002-03** | **Washington** | **NHL** | **23** | **2** | **3** | **5** | **6** | **0** | **0** | **1** | **22** | **9.1** | **4** | **99** | **49.5** | **10:07** | .... | .... | .... | .... | .... | .... | .... | .... | .... |
| | Portland Pirates | AHL | 33 | 7 | 23 | 30 | 23 | .... | .... | .... | .... | .... | .... | .... | .... | .... | 3 | 1 | 1 | 2 | 0 | .... | .... | .... | .... |
| 2003-04 | Jokerit Helsinki | Finland | 55 | 15 | 35 | 50 | 77 | .... | .... | .... | .... | .... | .... | .... | .... | .... | 7 | 6 | 1 | 7 | 33 | .... | .... | .... | .... |
| 2004-05 | Jokerit Helsinki | Finland | 51 | 16 | 31 | 47 | 42 | .... | .... | .... | .... | .... | .... | .... | .... | .... | 12 | 5 | 6 | 11 | 20 | .... | .... | .... | .... |
| 2005-06 | HC Lugano | Swiss | 44 | 24 | *39 | *63 | 60 | .... | .... | .... | .... | .... | .... | .... | .... | .... | 17 | 9 | 18 | 27 | 8 | .... | .... | .... | .... |
| **2006-07** | **Atlanta** | **NHL** | **57** | **12** | **16** | **28** | **20** | **4** | **0** | **2** | **92** | **13.0** | **9** | **206** | **49.0** | **11:47** | .... | .... | .... | .... | .... | .... | .... | .... | .... |
| | **St. Louis** | **NHL** | **20** | **2** | **3** | **5** | **14** | **1** | **0** | **0** | **31** | **6.5** | **0** | **154** | **50.0** | **12:58** | .... | .... | .... | .... | .... | .... | .... | .... | .... |
| **2007-08** | **Boston** | **NHL** | **82** | **11** | **22** | **33** | **36** | **1** | **0** | **5** | **141** | **7.8** | **–3** | **1242** | **49.4** | **16:26** | **7** | **1** | **0** | **1** | **4** | **0** | **0** | **1** | **16:27** |
| **2008-09** | **Philadelphia** | **NHL** | **55** | **4** | **10** | **14** | **15** | **1** | **0** | **0** | **63** | **6.3** | **–1** | **562** | **50.2** | **12:59** | .... | .... | .... | .... | .... | .... | .... | .... | .... |
| | **Montreal** | **NHL** | **21** | **2** | **1** | **3** | **13** | **0** | **0** | **0** | **19** | **10.5** | **–4** | **215** | **46.5** | **11:37** | **4** | **0** | **2** | **2** | **2** | **0** | **0** | **0** | **16:04** |
| | **NHL Totals** | | **338** | **41** | **89** | **130** | **124** | **8** | **0** | **9** | **497** | **8.2** | | **2665** | **49.3** | **13:26** | **14** | **1** | **2** | **3** | **8** | **0** | **0** | **1** | **14:20** |

Signed as a free agent by **Washington**, July 19, 1999. Claimed by **Tampa Bay** from **Washington** in Waiver Draft, September 28, 2001. Claimed on waivers by **Washington** from **Tampa Bay**, October 20, 2001. Signed as a free agent by **Jokerit Helsinki** (Finland), April 22, 2003. Claimed by **Ottawa** from **Washington** in Waiver Draft, October 3, 2003. Signed as a free agent by **Atlanta**, July 3, 2006. Traded to **St. Louis** by **Atlanta** with Atlanta's 1st (later traded to Calgary - Calgary selected Mikael Backlund) and 3rd (Brett Sonne) round choices in 2007 Entry Draft and Atlanta's 1st (later traded back to Atlanta - Atlanta selected Zach Bogosian) and 2nd (Philip McRae) round choices in 2008 Entry Draft for Keith Tkachuk, February 25, 2007. Signed as a free agent by **Boston**, October 3, 2007. Signed as a free agent by **Philadelphia**, July 1, 2008. Claimed on waivers by **Montreal** from **Philadelphia**, February 27, 2009.

## MEYER, Freddy

(MAY-uhr, FREHD) **NYI**

Defense. Shoots left. 5'10", 192 lbs. Born, Sanbornville, NH, January 4, 1981.

| | | | | | | | | | | | | | | | | | | | | | | | | | |
|---|---|---|---|---|---|---|---|---|---|---|---|---|---|---|---|---|---|---|---|---|---|---|---|---|---|
| 1996-97 | Cardigan Mtn. | High-NH | STATISTICS NOT AVAILABLE | | | | | | | | | | | | | | | | | | | | | | |
| 1997-98 | USNTDP | NAHL | .... | .... | .... | .... | .... | .... | .... | .... | .... | .... | .... | .... | .... | .... | 2 | 1 | 0 | 1 | 37 | .... | .... | .... | .... |
| 1998-99 | USNTDP | U-18 | 6 | 1 | 4 | 5 | 8 | .... | .... | .... | .... | .... | .... | .... | .... | .... | .... | .... | .... | .... | .... | .... | .... | .... | .... |
| | USNTDP | USHL | 54 | 10 | 23 | 33 | 151 | .... | .... | .... | .... | .... | .... | .... | .... | .... | .... | .... | .... | .... | .... | .... | .... | .... | .... |
| 99-2000 | USNTDP | USHL | 28 | 3 | 8 | 11 | 60 | .... | .... | .... | .... | .... | .... | .... | .... | .... | .... | .... | .... | .... | .... | .... | .... | .... | .... |
| | USNTDP | NAHL | 3 | 0 | 2 | 2 | 0 | .... | .... | .... | .... | .... | .... | .... | .... | .... | .... | .... | .... | .... | .... | .... | .... | .... | .... |
| | Boston University | H-East | 25 | 1 | 11 | 12 | 52 | .... | .... | .... | .... | .... | .... | .... | .... | .... | .... | .... | .... | .... | .... | .... | .... | .... | .... |
| 2000-01 | Boston University | H-East | 28 | 6 | 13 | 19 | 82 | .... | .... | .... | .... | .... | .... | .... | .... | .... | .... | .... | .... | .... | .... | .... | .... | .... | .... |
| 2001-02 | Boston University | H-East | 37 | 5 | 15 | 20 | 78 | .... | .... | .... | .... | .... | .... | .... | .... | .... | .... | .... | .... | .... | .... | .... | .... | .... | .... |
| 2002-03 | Boston University | H-East | 36 | 5 | 16 | 21 | 76 | .... | .... | .... | .... | .... | .... | .... | .... | .... | .... | .... | .... | .... | .... | .... | .... | .... | .... |
| **2003-04** | **Philadelphia** | **NHL** | **1** | **0** | **0** | **0** | **0** | **0** | **0** | **0** | **1** | **0.0** | **0** | **0** | **0.0** | **15:24** | .... | .... | .... | .... | .... | .... | .... | .... | .... |
| | Philadelphia | AHL | 59 | 14 | 14 | 28 | 50 | .... | .... | .... | .... | .... | .... | .... | .... | .... | 12 | 0 | 3 | 3 | 8 | .... | .... | .... | .... |
| 2004-05 | Philadelphia | AHL | 59 | 6 | 9 | 15 | 71 | .... | .... | .... | .... | .... | .... | .... | .... | .... | 21 | 3 | 9 | 12 | 34 | .... | .... | .... | .... |
| **2005-06** | **Philadelphia** | **NHL** | **57** | **6** | **21** | **27** | **33** | **2** | **0** | **0** | **68** | **8.8** | **10** | **0** | **0.0** | **17:56** | **6** | **0** | **1** | **1** | **8** | **0** | **0** | **0** | **18:23** |
| | Philadelphia | AHL | 11 | 3 | 3 | 6 | 22 | .... | .... | .... | .... | .... | .... | .... | .... | .... | .... | .... | .... | .... | .... | .... | .... | .... | .... |
| **2006-07** | **Philadelphia** | **NHL** | **25** | **2** | **3** | **5** | **14** | **1** | **0** | **0** | **27** | **7.4** | **–4** | **0** | **0.0** | **18:36** | .... | .... | .... | .... | .... | .... | .... | .... | .... |
| | **NY Islanders** | **NHL** | **35** | **0** | **3** | **3** | **24** | **0** | **0** | **0** | **14** | **0.0** | **0** | **0** | **0.0** | **16:39** | .... | .... | .... | .... | .... | .... | .... | .... | .... |
| **2007-08** | **Phoenix** | **NHL** | **5** | **0** | **0** | **0** | **0** | **0** | **0** | **0** | **2** | **0.0** | **–4** | **0** | **0.0** | **6:43** | .... | .... | .... | .... | .... | .... | .... | .... | .... |
| | San Antonio | AHL | 8 | 0 | 2 | 2 | 12 | .... | .... | .... | .... | .... | .... | .... | .... | .... | .... | .... | .... | .... | .... | .... | .... | .... | .... |
| | **NY Islanders** | **NHL** | **52** | **3** | **9** | **12** | **22** | **0** | **0** | **2** | **49** | **6.1** | **6** | **0** | **0.0** | **19:54** | .... | .... | .... | .... | .... | .... | .... | .... | .... |
| **2008-09** | **NY Islanders** | **NHL** | **27** | **4** | **5** | **9** | **14** | **0** | **0** | **1** | **36** | **11.1** | **–19** | **0** | **0.0** | **21:00** | .... | .... | .... | .... | .... | .... | .... | .... | .... |
| | **NHL Totals** | | **202** | **15** | **41** | **56** | **107** | **3** | **0** | **3** | **197** | **7.6** | | **0** | **0.0** | **18:25** | **6** | **0** | **1** | **1** | **8** | **0** | **0** | **0** | **18:23** |

Hockey East All-Rookie Team (2000) • Hockey East First All-Star Team (2003) • NCAA East First All-American Team (2003)

Signed as a free agent by **Philadelphia**, May 21, 2003. Traded to **NY Islanders** by **Philadelphia** with Philadelphia's 3rd round choice (Mark Katic) in 2007 Entry Draft for Alexei Zhitnik, December 16, 2006. Claimed on waivers by **Phoenix** from **NY Islanders**, October 8, 2007. Claimed on waivers by **NY Islanders** from **Phoenix**, November 10, 2007. • Missed majority of 2008-09 season recovering from abdominal and groin injuries.

## MEYER, Stefan

(MAY-uhr, STEH-fan) **PHX.**

Left wing. Shoots left. 6'2", 194 lbs. Born, Medicine Hat, Alta., July 20, 1985. Florida's 4th choice, 55th overall, in 2003 Entry Draft.

| | | | | | | | | | | | | | | | | | | | | | | | | | |
|---|---|---|---|---|---|---|---|---|---|---|---|---|---|---|---|---|---|---|---|---|---|---|---|---|---|
| 2000-01 | Notre Dame | SBHL | 50 | 36 | 52 | 88 | 71 | .... | .... | .... | .... | .... | .... | .... | .... | .... | .... | .... | .... | .... | .... | .... | .... | .... | .... |
| 2001-02 | Medicine Hat | WHL | 67 | 18 | 22 | 40 | 48 | .... | .... | .... | .... | .... | .... | .... | .... | .... | .... | .... | .... | .... | .... | .... | .... | .... | .... |
| 2002-03 | Medicine Hat | WHL | 70 | 36 | 16 | 52 | 90 | .... | .... | .... | .... | .... | .... | .... | .... | .... | 11 | 3 | 3 | 6 | 14 | .... | .... | .... | .... |
| 2003-04 | Medicine Hat | WHL | 72 | 34 | 41 | 75 | 69 | .... | .... | .... | .... | .... | .... | .... | .... | .... | 19 | 7 | 10 | 17 | 27 | .... | .... | .... | .... |
| 2004-05 | Medicine Hat | WHL | 69 | 34 | 43 | 77 | 104 | .... | .... | .... | .... | .... | .... | .... | .... | .... | 13 | 2 | 4 | 6 | 8 | .... | .... | .... | .... |
| 2005-06 | Rochester | AHL | 68 | 12 | 16 | 28 | 139 | .... | .... | .... | .... | .... | .... | .... | .... | .... | .... | .... | .... | .... | .... | .... | .... | .... | .... |
| 2006-07 | Rochester | AHL | 63 | 13 | 9 | 22 | 90 | .... | .... | .... | .... | .... | .... | .... | .... | .... | 6 | 0 | 2 | 2 | 8 | .... | .... | .... | .... |
| **2007-08** | **Florida** | **NHL** | **4** | **0** | **0** | **0** | **0** | **0** | **0** | **0** | **0** | **0.0** | **–1** | **6** | **50.0** | **2:26** | .... | .... | .... | .... | .... | .... | .... | .... | .... |
| | Rochester | AHL | 70 | 21 | 19 | 40 | 77 | .... | .... | .... | .... | .... | .... | .... | .... | .... | .... | .... | .... | .... | .... | .... | .... | .... | .... |
| 2008-09 | Rochester | AHL | 65 | 18 | 22 | 40 | 57 | .... | .... | .... | .... | .... | .... | .... | .... | .... | .... | .... | .... | .... | .... | .... | .... | .... | .... |
| | **NHL Totals** | | **4** | **0** | **0** | **0** | **0** | **0** | **0** | **0** | **0** | **0.0** | | **6** | **50.0** | **2:26** | .... | .... | .... | .... | .... | .... | .... | .... | .... |

Traded to **Phoenix** by **Florida** for Steve Reinprecht, June 19, 2009.

## MEZEI, Branislav

(MEH-tzay, BRAN-ih-slav)

Defense. Shoots left. 6'4", 235 lbs. Born, Nitra, Czech., October 8, 1980. NY Islanders' 3rd choice, 10th overall, in 1999 Entry Draft.

| | | | | | | | | | | | | | | | | | | | | | | | | | |
|---|---|---|---|---|---|---|---|---|---|---|---|---|---|---|---|---|---|---|---|---|---|---|---|---|---|
| 1996-97 | Nitra Jr. | Slovak-Jr. | 40 | 8 | 17 | 25 | 42 | .... | .... | .... | .... | .... | .... | .... | .... | .... | .... | .... | .... | .... | .... | .... | .... | .... | .... |
| 1997-98 | Belleville Bulls | OHL | 53 | 3 | 5 | 8 | 58 | .... | .... | .... | .... | .... | .... | .... | .... | .... | 8 | 0 | 2 | 2 | 8 | .... | .... | .... | .... |
| 1998-99 | Belleville Bulls | OHL | 60 | 5 | 18 | 23 | 90 | .... | .... | .... | .... | .... | .... | .... | .... | .... | 18 | 0 | 4 | 4 | 29 | .... | .... | .... | .... |
| 99-2000 | Belleville Bulls | OHL | 58 | 7 | 21 | 28 | 99 | .... | .... | .... | .... | .... | .... | .... | .... | .... | 6 | 0 | 3 | 3 | 10 | .... | .... | .... | .... |
| **2000-01** | **NY Islanders** | **NHL** | **42** | **1** | **4** | **5** | **53** | **0** | **0** | **0** | **29** | **3.4** | **–5** | **0** | **0.0** | **14:48** | .... | .... | .... | .... | .... | .... | .... | .... | .... |
| | Lowell | AHL | 20 | 0 | 3 | 3 | 28 | .... | .... | .... | .... | .... | .... | .... | .... | .... | .... | .... | .... | .... | .... | .... | .... | .... | .... |
| **2001-02** | **NY Islanders** | **NHL** | **24** | **0** | **2** | **2** | **12** | **0** | **0** | **0** | **4** | **0.0** | **2** | **0** | **0.0** | **8:28** | .... | .... | .... | .... | .... | .... | .... | .... | .... |
| | Bridgeport | AHL | 59 | 1 | 9 | 10 | 137 | .... | .... | .... | .... | .... | .... | .... | .... | .... | 20 | 0 | 1 | 1 | 48 | .... | .... | .... | .... |
| **2002-03** | **Florida** | **NHL** | **11** | **2** | **0** | **2** | **10** | **0** | **0** | **1** | **10** | **20.0** | **–2** | **0** | **0.0** | **18:22** | .... | .... | .... | .... | .... | .... | .... | .... | .... |
| | San Antonio | AHL | 1 | 0 | 0 | 0 | 0 | .... | .... | .... | .... | .... | .... | .... | .... | .... | 3 | 0 | 0 | 0 | 0 | .... | .... | .... | .... |
| **2003-04** | **Florida** | **NHL** | **45** | **0** | **7** | **7** | **80** | **0** | **0** | **0** | **26** | **0.0** | **–4** | **0** | **0.0** | **17:43** | .... | .... | .... | .... | .... | .... | .... | .... | .... |
| 2004-05 | HC Ocelari Trinec | CzRep | 41 | 1 | 2 | 3 | 68 | .... | .... | .... | .... | .... | .... | .... | .... | .... | .... | .... | .... | .... | .... | .... | .... | .... | .... |
| | Dukla Trencin | Slovakia | 10 | 1 | 1 | 2 | 16 | .... | .... | .... | .... | .... | .... | .... | .... | .... | 12 | 1 | 2 | 3 | 38 | .... | .... | .... | .... |
| **2005-06** | **Florida** | **NHL** | **16** | **0** | **1** | **1** | **37** | **0** | **0** | **0** | **13** | **0.0** | **3** | **0** | **0.0** | **19:17** | .... | .... | .... | .... | .... | .... | .... | .... | .... |
| **2006-07** | **Florida** | **NHL** | **45** | **0** | **3** | **3** | **55** | **0** | **0** | **0** | **24** | **0.0** | **5** | **1** | **100.0** | **15:58** | .... | .... | .... | .... | .... | .... | .... | .... | .... |
| **2007-08** | **Florida** | **NHL** | **57** | **2** | **2** | **4** | **64** | **0** | **0** | **0** | **38** | **5.3** | **–13** | **0** | **0.0** | **14:28** | .... | .... | .... | .... | .... | .... | .... | .... | .... |
| 2008-09 | Barys Astana | Rus-KHL | 56 | 5 | 5 | 10 | 151 | .... | .... | .... | .... | .... | .... | .... | .... | .... | 3 | 0 | 1 | 1 | 6 | .... | .... | .... | .... |
| | **NHL Totals** | | **240** | **5** | **19** | **24** | **311** | **0** | **0** | **1** | **144** | **3.5** | | **1** | **100.0** | **15:19** | .... | .... | .... | .... | .... | .... | .... | .... | .... |

OHL First All-Star Team (2000)

Traded to **Florida** by **NY Islanders** for Jason Wiemer, July 3, 2002. • Missed majority of 2002-03 season recovering from ankle (October 12, 2002 vs. Atlanta) and foot (January 1, 2003 vs. New Jersey) injuries. Signed as a free agent by **Trinec** (CzRep), September 25, 2004. Signed as a free agent by **Trencin** (Slovakia), January 30, 2005. • Missed remainder of 2005-06 season recovering from knee injury suffered in game vs. NY Rangers, November 9, 2005.

## MICHALEK, Milan

(mih-KHAL-ihk, MEE-lan) **S.J.**

Right wing. Shoots left. 6'2", 225 lbs. Born, Jindrichuv Hradec, Czech., December 7, 1984. San Jose's 1st choice, 6th overall, in 2003 Entry Draft.

| | | | | | | | | | | | | | | | | | | | | | | | | | |
|---|---|---|---|---|---|---|---|---|---|---|---|---|---|---|---|---|---|---|---|---|---|---|---|---|---|
| 99-2000 | C. Budejovice Jr. | CzRep-Jr. | 48 | 16 | 26 | 42 | 42 | .... | .... | .... | .... | .... | .... | .... | .... | .... | 6 | 3 | 1 | 4 | 4 | .... | .... | .... | .... |
| 2000-01 | C. Budejovice Jr. | CzRep-Jr. | 30 | 10 | 13 | 23 | 30 | .... | .... | .... | .... | .... | .... | .... | .... | .... | 4 | 1 | 3 | 4 | 2 | .... | .... | .... | .... |
| | C. Budejovice | CzRep | 5 | 0 | 0 | 0 | 0 | .... | .... | .... | .... | .... | .... | .... | .... | .... | .... | .... | .... | .... | .... | .... | .... | .... | .... |
| 2001-02 | C. Budejovice | CzRep | 47 | 6 | 11 | 17 | 12 | .... | .... | .... | .... | .... | .... | .... | .... | .... | .... | .... | .... | .... | .... | .... | .... | .... | .... |
| | C. Budejovice Jr. | CzRep-Jr. | 5 | 3 | 2 | 5 | 4 | .... | .... | .... | .... | .... | .... | .... | .... | .... | 7 | 5 | 4 | 9 | 14 | .... | .... | .... | .... |
| 2002-03 | C. Budejovice | CzRep | 46 | 3 | 5 | 8 | 14 | .... | .... | .... | .... | .... | .... | .... | .... | .... | 4 | 1 | 0 | 1 | 2 | .... | .... | .... | .... |
| | Kladno | CzRep-2 | .... | .... | .... | .... | .... | .... | .... | .... | .... | .... | .... | .... | .... | .... | 6 | 2 | 2 | 4 | 16 | .... | .... | .... | .... |
| **2003-04** | **San Jose** | **NHL** | **2** | **1** | **0** | **1** | **4** | **0** | **0** | **0** | **1** | **100.0** | **1** | **0** | **0.0** | **9:05** | .... | .... | .... | .... | .... | .... | .... | .... | .... |
| | Cleveland Barons | AHL | 7 | 2 | 2 | 4 | 4 | .... | .... | .... | .... | .... | .... | .... | .... | .... | .... | .... | .... | .... | .... | .... | .... | .... | .... |
| 2004-05 | | | DID NOT PLAY | | | | | | | | | | | | | | | | | | | | | | |
| **2005-06** | **San Jose** | **NHL** | **81** | **17** | **18** | **35** | **45** | **4** | **0** | **2** | **159** | **10.7** | **1** | **4** | **0.0** | **15:46** | **9** | **1** | **4** | **5** | **8** | **1** | **0** | **0** | **15:11** |

| Season | Club | League | GP | G | A | Pts | PIM | PP | SH | GW | S | % | +/- | TF | F% | Min | GP | G | A | Pts | PIM | PP | SH | GW | Min |
|---|---|---|---|---|---|---|---|---|---|---|---|---|---|---|---|---|---|---|---|---|---|---|---|---|---|
| | | | Regular Season | | | | | | | | | | | | | | Playoffs | | | | | | | | |
| 2006-07 | San Jose | NHL | 78 | 26 | 40 | 66 | 36 | 11 | 0 | 9 | 191 | 13.6 | 17 | 11 | 18.2 | 16:46 | 11 | 4 | 2 | 6 | 4 | 0 | 0 | 1 | 18:50 |
| 2007-08 | San Jose | NHL | 79 | 24 | 31 | 55 | 47 | 5 | 1 | 8 | 233 | 10.3 | 19 | 10 | 60.0 | 18:05 | 13 | 4 | 0 | 4 | 4 | 1 | 0 | 1 | 17:34 |
| 2008-09 | San Jose | NHL | 77 | 23 | 34 | 57 | 52 | 6 | 0 | 6 | 179 | 12.8 | 11 | 30 | 46.7 | 18:27 | 6 | 1 | 0 | 1 | 2 | 1 | 0 | 0 | 19:22 |
| | NHL Totals | | 317 | 91 | 123 | 214 | 184 | 26 | 1 | 25 | 763 | 11.9 | | 55 | 40.0 | 17:12 | 39 | 10 | 6 | 16 | 18 | 3 | 0 | 2 | 17:39 |

• Missed majority of 2003-04 season recovering from knee injury suffered in game vs. Calgary, October 11, 2003.

## MICHALEK, Zbynek

(mih-KHAL-ihk, z'BIGH-nehk) **PHX.**

Defense. Shoots right. 6'2", 210 lbs. Born, Jindrichuv Hradec, Czech., December 23, 1982.

| Season | Club | League | GP | G | A | Pts | PIM | PP | SH | GW | S | % | +/- | TF | F% | Min | GP | G | A | Pts | PIM | PP | SH | GW | Min |
|---|---|---|---|---|---|---|---|---|---|---|---|---|---|---|---|---|---|---|---|---|---|---|---|---|---|
| 99-2000 | Karlovy Vary Jr. | CzRep-Jr. | 40 | 2 | 10 | 12 | 20 | .... | .... | .... | .... | .... | .... | .... | .... | .... | .... | .... | .... | .... | .... | .... | .... | .... | .... |
| 2000-01 | Shawinigan | QMJHL | 69 | 10 | 29 | 39 | 52 | .... | .... | .... | .... | .... | .... | .... | .... | .... | 3 | 0 | 0 | 0 | 0 | .... | .... | .... | .... |
| 2001-02 | Shawinigan | QMJHL | 68 | 16 | 35 | 51 | 54 | .... | .... | .... | .... | .... | .... | .... | .... | .... | 12 | 8 | 9 | 17 | 17 | .... | .... | .... | .... |
| 2002-03 | Houston Aeros | AHL | 62 | 4 | 10 | 14 | 26 | .... | .... | .... | .... | .... | .... | .... | .... | .... | 23 | 1 | 1 | 2 | 6 | .... | .... | .... | .... |
| **2003-04** | **Minnesota** | **NHL** | **22** | **1** | **1** | **2** | **4** | **0** | **0** | **0** | **17** | **5.9** | **-7** | **0** | **0.0** | **14:13** | .... | .... | .... | .... | .... | .... | .... | .... | .... |
| | Houston Aeros | AHL | 55 | 5 | 16 | 21 | 32 | .... | .... | .... | .... | .... | .... | .... | .... | .... | 2 | 1 | 0 | 1 | 0 | .... | .... | .... | .... |
| 2004-05 | Houston Aeros | AHL | 76 | 7 | 17 | 24 | 48 | .... | .... | .... | .... | .... | .... | .... | .... | .... | 5 | 1 | 2 | 3 | 4 | .... | .... | .... | .... |
| **2005-06** | **Phoenix** | **NHL** | **82** | **9** | **15** | **24** | **62** | **5** | **0** | **2** | **105** | **8.6** | **4** | **0** | **0.0** | **22:50** | .... | .... | .... | .... | .... | .... | .... | .... | .... |
| **2006-07** | **Phoenix** | **NHL** | **82** | **4** | **24** | **28** | **34** | **3** | **0** | **0** | **144** | **2.8** | **-20** | **1** | **100.0** | **23:40** | .... | .... | .... | .... | .... | .... | .... | .... | .... |
| **2007-08** | **Phoenix** | **NHL** | **75** | **4** | **13** | **17** | **34** | **0** | **0** | **2** | **92** | **4.3** | **9** | **0** | **0.0** | **21:36** | .... | .... | .... | .... | .... | .... | .... | .... | .... |
| **2008-09** | **Phoenix** | **NHL** | **82** | **6** | **21** | **27** | **28** | **0** | **0** | **0** | **106** | **5.7** | **-13** | **0** | **0.0** | **22:43** | .... | .... | .... | .... | .... | .... | .... | .... | .... |
| | **NHL Totals** | | **343** | **24** | **74** | **98** | **162** | **8** | **0** | **4** | **464** | **5.2** | | **1** | **100.0** | **22:11** | .... | .... | .... | .... | .... | .... | .... | .... | .... |

Signed as a free agent by **Minnesota**, September 29, 2001. Traded to **Phoenix** by **Minnesota** for Erik Westrum and Dustin Wood, August 26, 2005.

## MIETTINEN, Antti

(mih-EHT-tih-nehn, AN-tee) **MIN.**

Right wing. Shoots right. 6', 190 lbs. Born, Hameenlinna, Finland, July 3, 1980. Dallas' 10th choice, 224th overall, in 2000 Entry Draft.

| Season | Club | League | GP | G | A | Pts | PIM | PP | SH | GW | S | % | +/- | TF | F% | Min | GP | G | A | Pts | PIM | PP | SH | GW | Min |
|---|---|---|---|---|---|---|---|---|---|---|---|---|---|---|---|---|---|---|---|---|---|---|---|---|---|
| 1996-97 | HPK U18 | Fin-U18 | 36 | 24 | 29 | 53 | 34 | .... | .... | .... | .... | .... | .... | .... | .... | .... | .... | .... | .... | .... | .... | .... | .... | .... | .... |
| 1997-98 | HPK U18 | Fin-U18 | 34 | 13 | 28 | 41 | 63 | .... | .... | .... | .... | .... | .... | .... | .... | .... | .... | .... | .... | .... | .... | .... | .... | .... | .... |
| | HPK Jr. | Fin-Jr. | 8 | 1 | 0 | 1 | 2 | .... | .... | .... | .... | .... | .... | .... | .... | .... | .... | .... | .... | .... | .... | .... | .... | .... | .... |
| 1998-99 | HPK Jr. | Fin-Jr. | 35 | 17 | 22 | 39 | 28 | .... | .... | .... | .... | .... | .... | .... | .... | .... | 3 | 2 | 3 | 5 | 2 | .... | .... | .... | .... |
| | FPS Forssa | Finland-2 | 4 | 3 | 1 | 4 | 6 | .... | .... | .... | .... | .... | .... | .... | .... | .... | .... | .... | .... | .... | .... | .... | .... | .... | .... |
| | HPK Hameenlinna | Finland | 13 | 0 | 0 | 0 | 2 | .... | .... | .... | .... | .... | .... | .... | .... | .... | 4 | 0 | 0 | 0 | 0 | .... | .... | .... | .... |
| 99-2000 | HPK Jr. | Fin-Jr. | 31 | 24 | 53 | 77 | 28 | .... | .... | .... | .... | .... | .... | .... | .... | .... | 2 | 1 | 6 | 7 | 2 | .... | .... | .... | .... |
| | HPK Hameenlinna | Finland | 39 | 2 | 1 | 3 | 8 | .... | .... | .... | .... | .... | .... | .... | .... | .... | 7 | 1 | 0 | 1 | 0 | .... | .... | .... | .... |
| 2000-01 | HPK Jr. | Fin-Jr. | 4 | 3 | 10 | 13 | 2 | .... | .... | .... | .... | .... | .... | .... | .... | .... | .... | .... | .... | .... | .... | .... | .... | .... | .... |
| | HPK Hameenlinna | Finland | 55 | 13 | 11 | 24 | 20 | .... | .... | .... | .... | .... | .... | .... | .... | .... | .... | .... | .... | .... | .... | .... | .... | .... | .... |
| 2001-02 | HPK Hameenlinna | Finland | 56 | 19 | 37 | 56 | 50 | .... | .... | .... | .... | .... | .... | .... | .... | .... | 8 | 2 | 4 | 6 | 8 | .... | .... | .... | .... |
| 2002-03 | HPK Hameenlinna | Finland | 53 | 25 | 25 | 50 | 54 | .... | .... | .... | .... | .... | .... | .... | .... | .... | 10 | 1 | 7 | 8 | 29 | .... | .... | .... | .... |
| **2003-04** | **Dallas** | **NHL** | **16** | **1** | **0** | **1** | **0** | **0** | **0** | **1** | **17** | **5.9** | **-9** | **1** | **0.0** | **9:51** | .... | .... | .... | .... | .... | .... | .... | .... | .... |
| | Utah Grizzlies | AHL | 48 | 7 | 23 | 30 | 20 | .... | .... | .... | .... | .... | .... | .... | .... | .... | .... | .... | .... | .... | .... | .... | .... | .... | .... |
| 2004-05 | Hamilton | AHL | 35 | 8 | 20 | 28 | 21 | .... | .... | .... | .... | .... | .... | .... | .... | .... | 4 | 1 | 1 | 2 | 6 | .... | .... | .... | .... |
| **2005-06** | **Dallas** | **NHL** | **79** | **11** | **20** | **31** | **46** | **4** | **0** | **1** | **107** | **10.3** | **0** | **1** | **100.0** | **12:06** | **5** | **0** | **1** | **1** | **8** | **0** | **0** | **0** | **12:10** |
| **2006-07** | **Dallas** | **NHL** | **74** | **11** | **14** | **25** | **38** | **6** | **0** | **1** | **141** | **7.8** | **-5** | **11** | **18.2** | **14:20** | **4** | **1** | **1** | **2** | **2** | **0** | **0** | **0** | **12:16** |
| **2007-08** | **Dallas** | **NHL** | **69** | **15** | **19** | **34** | **34** | **5** | **0** | **3** | **136** | **11.0** | **4** | **23** | **60.9** | **13:59** | **15** | **1** | **1** | **2** | **0** | **0** | **0** | **0** | **9:33** |
| **2008-09** | **Minnesota** | **NHL** | **82** | **15** | **29** | **44** | **32** | **4** | **2** | **3** | **186** | **8.1** | **-1** | **60** | **46.7** | **18:17** | .... | .... | .... | .... | .... | .... | .... | .... | .... |
| | **NHL Totals** | | **320** | **53** | **82** | **135** | **150** | **19** | **2** | **9** | **587** | **9.0** | | **96** | **46.9** | **14:30** | **24** | **2** | **3** | **5** | **10** | **0** | **0** | **0** | **10:33** |

Signed as a free agent by **Minnesota**, July 3, 2008.

## MIHALIK, Vladimir

(mih-HAHL-ihk, vla-DIH-meer) **T.B.**

Defense. Shoots left. 6'7", 222 lbs. Born, Presov, Czech., January 29, 1987. Tampa Bay's 1st choice, 30th overall, in 2005 Entry Draft.

| Season | Club | League | GP | G | A | Pts | PIM | PP | SH | GW | S | % | +/- | TF | F% | Min | GP | G | A | Pts | PIM | PP | SH | GW | Min |
|---|---|---|---|---|---|---|---|---|---|---|---|---|---|---|---|---|---|---|---|---|---|---|---|---|---|
| 2003-04 | Presov | Svk-U18 | 6 | 4 | 4 | 8 | 4 | .... | .... | .... | .... | .... | .... | .... | .... | .... | .... | .... | .... | .... | .... | .... | .... | .... | .... |
| | Presov Jr. | Slovak-Jr. | 23 | 6 | 10 | 16 | 44 | .... | .... | .... | .... | .... | .... | .... | .... | .... | .... | .... | .... | .... | .... | .... | .... | .... | .... |
| 2004-05 | PHK Presov Jr. | Slovak-Jr. | 23 | 6 | 10 | 16 | 44 | .... | .... | .... | .... | .... | .... | .... | .... | .... | .... | .... | .... | .... | .... | .... | .... | .... | .... |
| | PHK Presov | Slovak-2 | 32 | 3 | 1 | 4 | 24 | .... | .... | .... | .... | .... | .... | .... | .... | .... | .... | .... | .... | .... | .... | .... | .... | .... | .... |
| 2005-06 | Red Deer Rebels | WHL | 62 | 3 | 9 | 12 | 86 | .... | .... | .... | .... | .... | .... | .... | .... | .... | 6 | 0 | 1 | 1 | 2 | .... | .... | .... | .... |
| 2006-07 | Prince George | WHL | 53 | 7 | 19 | 26 | 91 | .... | .... | .... | .... | .... | .... | .... | .... | .... | 15 | 1 | 2 | 3 | 17 | .... | .... | .... | .... |
| 2007-08 | Norfolk Admirals | AHL | 68 | 1 | 15 | 16 | 68 | .... | .... | .... | .... | .... | .... | .... | .... | .... | .... | .... | .... | .... | .... | .... | .... | .... | .... |
| **2008-09** | **Tampa Bay** | **NHL** | **11** | **0** | **3** | **3** | **6** | **0** | **0** | **0** | **7** | **0.0** | **-3** | **0** | **0.0** | **13:24** | .... | .... | .... | .... | .... | .... | .... | .... | .... |
| | Norfolk Admirals | AHL | 61 | 2 | 13 | 15 | 58 | .... | .... | .... | .... | .... | .... | .... | .... | .... | .... | .... | .... | .... | .... | .... | .... | .... | .... |
| | **NHL Totals** | | **11** | **0** | **3** | **3** | **6** | **0** | **0** | **0** | **7** | **0.0** | | **0** | **0.0** | **13:24** | .... | .... | .... | .... | .... | .... | .... | .... | .... |

## MIKHNOV, Alexei

(MIHKH-nahf, al-EHX-ay) **EDM.**

Left wing. Shoots left. 6'5", 200 lbs. Born, Kiev, USSR, August 31, 1982. Edmonton's 1st choice, 17th overall, in 2000 Entry Draft.

| Season | Club | League | GP | G | A | Pts | PIM | PP | SH | GW | S | % | +/- | TF | F% | Min | GP | G | A | Pts | PIM | PP | SH | GW | Min |
|---|---|---|---|---|---|---|---|---|---|---|---|---|---|---|---|---|---|---|---|---|---|---|---|---|---|
| 1997-98 | Yaroslavl | Russia | 6 | 0 | 0 | 0 | 0 | .... | .... | .... | .... | .... | .... | .... | .... | .... | .... | .... | .... | .... | .... | .... | .... | .... | .... |
| 1998-99 | Yaroslavl 2 | Russia-3 | 14 | 2 | 2 | 4 | 4 | .... | .... | .... | .... | .... | .... | .... | .... | .... | .... | .... | .... | .... | .... | .... | .... | .... | .... |
| 99-2000 | Yaroslavl 2 | Russia-3 | 53 | 24 | 17 | 41 | 10 | .... | .... | .... | .... | .... | .... | .... | .... | .... | .... | .... | .... | .... | .... | .... | .... | .... | .... |
| 2000-01 | HK Moscow | Russia-2 | 4 | 0 | 0 | 0 | 2 | .... | .... | .... | .... | .... | .... | .... | .... | .... | .... | .... | .... | .... | .... | .... | .... | .... | .... |
| | THK Tver | Russia-2 | 22 | 5 | 11 | 16 | 6 | .... | .... | .... | .... | .... | .... | .... | .... | .... | .... | .... | .... | .... | .... | .... | .... | .... | .... |
| 2001-02 | Dyn'o Moscow 2 | Russia-3 | 8 | 8 | 6 | 14 | 0 | .... | .... | .... | .... | .... | .... | .... | .... | .... | .... | .... | .... | .... | .... | .... | .... | .... | .... |
| | Dynamo Moscow | Russia | 35 | 2 | 1 | 3 | 4 | .... | .... | .... | .... | .... | .... | .... | .... | .... | 3 | 0 | 0 | 0 | 2 | .... | .... | .... | .... |
| | Ufa | Russia | 1 | 0 | 0 | 0 | 0 | .... | .... | .... | .... | .... | .... | .... | .... | .... | .... | .... | .... | .... | .... | .... | .... | .... | .... |
| 2002-03 | Sibir Novosibirsk | Russia | 51 | 7 | 9 | 16 | 10 | .... | .... | .... | .... | .... | .... | .... | .... | .... | .... | .... | .... | .... | .... | .... | .... | .... | .... |
| 2003-04 | Sibir Novosibirsk | Russia | 58 | 14 | 8 | 22 | 22 | .... | .... | .... | .... | .... | .... | .... | .... | .... | .... | .... | .... | .... | .... | .... | .... | .... | .... |
| 2004-05 | Sibir Novosibirsk | Russia | 26 | 2 | 3 | 5 | 12 | .... | .... | .... | .... | .... | .... | .... | .... | .... | .... | .... | .... | .... | .... | .... | .... | .... | .... |
| | Yaroslavl 2 | Russia-3 | 2 | 1 | 0 | 1 | 0 | .... | .... | .... | .... | .... | .... | .... | .... | .... | .... | .... | .... | .... | .... | .... | .... | .... | .... |
| | Yaroslavl | Russia | 18 | 0 | 9 | 9 | 4 | .... | .... | .... | .... | .... | .... | .... | .... | .... | 7 | 0 | 0 | 0 | 4 | .... | .... | .... | .... |
| 2005-06 | Yaroslavl | Russia | 40 | 14 | 7 | 21 | 18 | .... | .... | .... | .... | .... | .... | .... | .... | .... | 11 | 4 | 4 | 8 | 4 | .... | .... | .... | .... |
| **2006-07** | **Edmonton** | **NHL** | **2** | **0** | **0** | **0** | **0** | **0** | **0** | **0** | **0** | **0.0** | **0** | **0** | **0.0** | **6:52** | .... | .... | .... | .... | .... | .... | .... | .... | .... |
| | Wilkes-Barre | AHL | 27 | 6 | 12 | 18 | 22 | .... | .... | .... | .... | .... | .... | .... | .... | .... | .... | .... | .... | .... | .... | .... | .... | .... | .... |
| | Yaroslavl | Russia | 11 | 5 | 3 | 8 | 6 | .... | .... | .... | .... | .... | .... | .... | .... | .... | 7 | 2 | 3 | 5 | 4 | .... | .... | .... | .... |
| 2007-08 | Yaroslavl | Russia | 52 | 14 | 20 | 34 | 50 | .... | .... | .... | .... | .... | .... | .... | .... | .... | 16 | 3 | 5 | 8 | 14 | .... | .... | .... | .... |
| 2008-09 | Yaroslavl | Rus-KHL | 52 | 16 | 17 | 33 | 57 | .... | .... | .... | .... | .... | .... | .... | .... | .... | 19 | 8 | 4 | 12 | 10 | .... | .... | .... | .... |
| | **NHL Totals** | | **2** | **0** | **0** | **0** | **0** | **0** | **0** | **0** | **0** | **0.0** | | **0** | **0.0** | **6:52** | .... | .... | .... | .... | .... | .... | .... | .... | .... |

## MIKKELSON, Brendan

(MIGHK-ehl-sohn, BREHN-duhn) **ANA.**

Defense. Shoots left. 6'3", 210 lbs. Born, Regina, Sask., June 22, 1987. Anaheim's 2nd choice, 31st overall, in 2005 Entry Draft.

| Season | Club | League | GP | G | A | Pts | PIM | PP | SH | GW | S | % | +/- | TF | F% | Min | GP | G | A | Pts | PIM | PP | SH | GW | Min |
|---|---|---|---|---|---|---|---|---|---|---|---|---|---|---|---|---|---|---|---|---|---|---|---|---|---|
| 2003-04 | Portland | WHL | 65 | 3 | 12 | 15 | 43 | .... | .... | .... | .... | .... | .... | .... | .... | .... | 5 | 1 | 0 | 1 | 0 | .... | .... | .... | .... |
| 2004-05 | Portland | WHL | 70 | 5 | 10 | 15 | 60 | .... | .... | .... | .... | .... | .... | .... | .... | .... | 7 | 1 | 2 | 3 | 0 | .... | .... | .... | .... |
| 2005-06 | Portland | WHL | 3 | 1 | 1 | 2 | 4 | .... | .... | .... | .... | .... | .... | .... | .... | .... | .... | .... | .... | .... | .... | .... | .... | .... | .... |
| | Vancouver Giants | WHL | 19 | 1 | 8 | 9 | 37 | .... | .... | .... | .... | .... | .... | .... | .... | .... | .... | .... | .... | .... | .... | .... | .... | .... | .... |
| 2006-07 | Vancouver Giants | WHL | 69 | 6 | 23 | 29 | 60 | .... | .... | .... | .... | .... | .... | .... | .... | .... | 21 | 3 | 7 | 10 | 10 | .... | .... | .... | .... |
| 2007-08 | Portland Pirates | AHL | 66 | 6 | 10 | 16 | 50 | .... | .... | .... | .... | .... | .... | .... | .... | .... | 14 | 2 | 6 | 8 | 2 | .... | .... | .... | .... |
| **2008-09** | **Anaheim** | **NHL** | **34** | **0** | **2** | **2** | **17** | **0** | **0** | **0** | **19** | **0.0** | **0** | **0** | **0.0** | **13:56** | .... | .... | .... | .... | .... | .... | .... | .... | .... |
| | Iowa Chops | AHL | 31 | 2 | 8 | 10 | 18 | .... | .... | .... | .... | .... | .... | .... | .... | .... | .... | .... | .... | .... | .... | .... | .... | .... | .... |
| | **NHL Totals** | | **34** | **0** | **2** | **2** | **17** | **0** | **0** | **0** | **19** | **0.0** | | **0** | **0.0** | **13:56** | .... | .... | .... | .... | .... | .... | .... | .... | .... |

Memorial Cup Tournament All-Star Team (2007)

• Missed majority of 2005-06 season recovering from shoulder and knee injuries.

(MIHL-luhr, DROO) **ANA.**

## MILLER, Drew

Left wing. Shoots left. 6'2", 185 lbs. Born, Dover, NJ, February 17, 1984. Anaheim's 6th choice, 186th overall, in 2003 Entry Draft.

| Season | Club | League | GP | G | A | Pts | PIM | PP | SH | GW | S | % | +/- | TF | F% | Min | Playoffs GP | G | A | Pts | PIM | PP | SH | GW | Min |
|---|---|---|---|---|---|---|---|---|---|---|---|---|---|---|---|---|---|---|---|---|---|---|---|---|---|
| 2000-01 | Capital Centre | NAHL | 37 | 4 | 3 | 7 | 22 | .... | .... | .... | .... | .... | .... | .... | .... | .... | .... | .... | .... | .... | .... | .... | .... | .... | .... |
| 2001-02 | Capital Centre | NAHL | 54 | 18 | 16 | 34 | 56 | .... | .... | .... | .... | .... | .... | .... | .... | .... | .... | .... | .... | .... | .... | .... | .... | .... | .... |
| 2002-03 | Capital Centre | NAHL | 11 | 10 | 9 | 19 | .... | .... | .... | .... | .... | .... | .... | .... | .... | .... | .... | .... | .... | .... | .... | .... | .... | .... | .... |
| | River City Lancers | USHL | 49 | 14 | 11 | 25 | 22 | .... | .... | .... | .... | .... | .... | .... | .... | .... | 11 | 5 | 4 | 9 | 6 | .... | .... | .... | .... |
| 2003-04 | Michigan State | CCHA | 41 | 4 | 6 | 10 | 39 | .... | .... | .... | .... | .... | .... | .... | .... | .... | .... | .... | .... | .... | .... | .... | .... | .... | .... |
| 2004-05 | Michigan State | CCHA | 40 | 17 | 16 | 33 | 20 | .... | .... | .... | .... | .... | .... | .... | .... | .... | .... | .... | .... | .... | .... | .... | .... | .... | .... |
| 2005-06 | Michigan State | CCHA | 44 | 18 | 25 | 43 | 30 | .... | .... | .... | .... | .... | .... | .... | .... | .... | .... | .... | .... | .... | .... | .... | .... | .... | .... |
| **2006-07** | Portland Pirates | AHL | 79 | 16 | 20 | 36 | 51 | .... | .... | .... | .... | .... | .... | .... | .... | .... | .... | .... | .... | .... | .... | .... | .... | .... | .... |
| | ♦ **Anaheim** | **NHL** | .... | .... | .... | .... | .... | .... | .... | .... | .... | .... | .... | .... | .... | .... | **3** | **0** | **0** | **0** | **2** | **0** | **0** | **0** | **7:00** |
| **2007-08** | **Anaheim** | **NHL** | **26** | **2** | **3** | **5** | **6** | **0** | **0** | **0** | **30** | **6.7** | **–1** | **9** | **33.3** | **11:11** | .... | .... | .... | .... | .... | .... | .... | .... | .... |
| | Portland Pirates | AHL | 31 | 16 | 20 | 36 | 12 | .... | .... | .... | .... | .... | .... | .... | .... | .... | 16 | 1 | 7 | 8 | 12 | .... | .... | .... | .... |
| **2008-09** | **Anaheim** | **NHL** | **27** | **4** | **6** | **10** | **17** | **0** | **0** | **0** | **45** | **8.9** | **0** | **14** | **21.4** | **12:59** | **13** | **2** | **1** | **3** | **2** | **0** | **0** | **1** | **16:09** |
| | Iowa Chops | AHL | 53 | 23 | 15 | 38 | 10 | .... | .... | .... | .... | .... | .... | .... | .... | .... | .... | .... | .... | .... | .... | .... | .... | .... | .... |
| | **NHL Totals** | | **53** | **6** | **9** | **15** | **23** | **0** | **0** | **0** | **75** | **8.0** | | **23** | **26.1** | **12:06** | **16** | **2** | **1** | **3** | **4** | **0** | **0** | **1** | **14:26** |

(MIHL-roi, DUHN-kuhn) **MIN.**

## MILROY, Duncan

Right wing. Shoots right. 6', 195 lbs. Born, Edmonton, Alta., February 8, 1983. Montreal's 3rd choice, 37th overall, in 2001 Entry Draft.

| Season | Club | League | GP | G | A | Pts | PIM | PP | SH | GW | S | % | +/- | TF | F% | Min | Playoffs GP | G | A | Pts | PIM | PP | SH | GW | Min |
|---|---|---|---|---|---|---|---|---|---|---|---|---|---|---|---|---|---|---|---|---|---|---|---|---|---|
| 1998-99 | Edm. Maple Leafs | AMHL | 34 | 34 | 36 | 70 | 73 | .... | .... | .... | .... | .... | .... | .... | .... | .... | .... | .... | .... | .... | .... | .... | .... | .... | .... |
| | Swift Current | WHL | 3 | 0 | 0 | 0 | 0 | .... | .... | .... | .... | .... | .... | .... | .... | .... | .... | .... | .... | .... | .... | .... | .... | .... | .... |
| 99-2000 | Swift Current | WHL | 68 | 15 | 15 | 30 | 20 | .... | .... | .... | .... | .... | .... | .... | .... | .... | 12 | 3 | 5 | 8 | 12 | .... | .... | .... | .... |
| 2000-01 | Swift Current | WHL | 68 | 38 | 54 | 92 | 51 | .... | .... | .... | .... | .... | .... | .... | .... | .... | 19 | 9 | 12 | 21 | 6 | .... | .... | .... | .... |
| 2001-02 | Swift Current | WHL | 26 | 20 | 11 | 31 | 20 | .... | .... | .... | .... | .... | .... | .... | .... | .... | .... | .... | .... | .... | .... | .... | .... | .... | .... |
| | Kootenay Ice | WHL | 38 | 25 | 31 | 56 | 24 | .... | .... | .... | .... | .... | .... | .... | .... | .... | 22 | *17 | *20 | *37 | 26 | .... | .... | .... | .... |
| 2002-03 | Kootenay Ice | WHL | 61 | 34 | 44 | 78 | 40 | .... | .... | .... | .... | .... | .... | .... | .... | .... | 11 | 5 | 3 | 8 | 8 | .... | .... | .... | .... |
| 2003-04 | Hamilton | AHL | 50 | 4 | 10 | 14 | 14 | .... | .... | .... | .... | .... | .... | .... | .... | .... | 10 | 3 | 1 | 4 | 4 | .... | .... | .... | .... |
| 2004-05 | Hamilton | AHL | 76 | 15 | 18 | 33 | 18 | .... | .... | .... | .... | .... | .... | .... | .... | .... | 3 | 0 | 0 | 0 | 2 | .... | .... | .... | .... |
| 2005-06 | Hamilton | AHL | 77 | 16 | 19 | 35 | 63 | .... | .... | .... | .... | .... | .... | .... | .... | .... | .... | .... | .... | .... | .... | .... | .... | .... | .... |
| **2006-07** | **Montreal** | **NHL** | **5** | **0** | **1** | **1** | **0** | **0** | **0** | **0** | **6** | **0.0** | **–2** | **1** | **0.0** | **12:56** | .... | .... | .... | .... | .... | .... | .... | .... | .... |
| | Hamilton | AHL | 64 | 25 | 33 | 58 | 24 | .... | .... | .... | .... | .... | .... | .... | .... | .... | 22 | 2 | 11 | 13 | 10 | .... | .... | .... | .... |
| 2007-08 | Hamilton | AHL | 79 | 15 | 24 | 39 | 37 | .... | .... | .... | .... | .... | .... | .... | .... | .... | .... | .... | .... | .... | .... | .... | .... | .... | .... |
| 2008-09 | ERC Ingolstadt | Germany | 49 | 14 | 34 | 48 | 16 | .... | .... | .... | .... | .... | .... | .... | .... | .... | .... | .... | .... | .... | .... | .... | .... | .... | .... |
| | **NHL Totals** | | **5** | **0** | **1** | **1** | **0** | **0** | **0** | **0** | **6** | **0.0** | | **1** | **0.0** | **12:56** | .... | .... | .... | .... | .... | .... | .... | .... | .... |

Yanick Dupre Memorial Award (AHL - Outstanding Humanitarian Contribution) (2005)

(mih-NAHRD, KRIHS) **EDM.**

## MINARD, Chris

Center. Shoots left. 6'1", 190 lbs. Born, Thompson, Man., November 18, 1981.

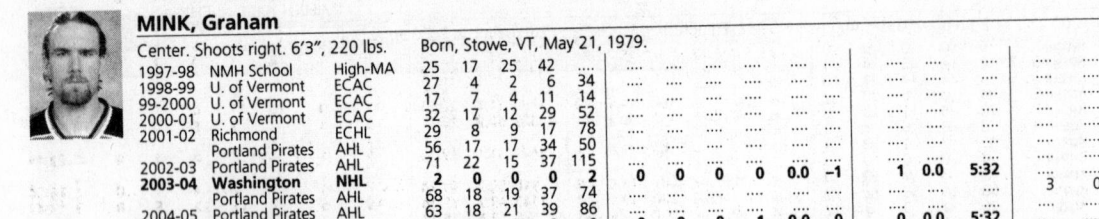

| Season | Club | League | GP | G | A | Pts | PIM | PP | SH | GW | S | % | +/- | TF | F% | Min | Playoffs GP | G | A | Pts | PIM | PP | SH | GW | Min |
|---|---|---|---|---|---|---|---|---|---|---|---|---|---|---|---|---|---|---|---|---|---|---|---|---|---|
| 1997-98 | Owen Sound | OHL | 9 | 0 | 1 | 1 | 1 | .... | .... | .... | .... | .... | .... | .... | .... | .... | 1 | 0 | 0 | 0 | 2 | .... | .... | .... | .... |
| 1998-99 | Owen Sound | OHL | 43 | 6 | 9 | 15 | 18 | .... | .... | .... | .... | .... | .... | .... | .... | .... | .... | .... | .... | .... | .... | .... | .... | .... | .... |
| 99-2000 | Owen Sound | OHL | 38 | 12 | 14 | 26 | 39 | .... | .... | .... | .... | .... | .... | .... | .... | .... | .... | .... | .... | .... | .... | .... | .... | .... | .... |
| | St. Michael's | OHL | 28 | 5 | 14 | 19 | 6 | .... | .... | .... | .... | .... | .... | .... | .... | .... | .... | .... | .... | .... | .... | .... | .... | .... | .... |
| 2000-01 | St. Michael's | OHL | 40 | 11 | 8 | 19 | 28 | .... | .... | .... | .... | .... | .... | .... | .... | .... | .... | .... | .... | .... | .... | .... | .... | .... | .... |
| | Oshawa Generals | OHL | 28 | 12 | 12 | 24 | 18 | .... | .... | .... | .... | .... | .... | .... | .... | .... | .... | .... | .... | .... | .... | .... | .... | .... | .... |
| 2001-02 | Oshawa Generals | OHL | 67 | 36 | 35 | 71 | 20 | .... | .... | .... | .... | .... | .... | .... | .... | .... | 5 | 2 | 3 | 5 | 6 | .... | .... | .... | .... |
| 2002-03 | Pensacola | ECHL | 72 | 15 | 17 | 32 | 71 | .... | .... | .... | .... | .... | .... | .... | .... | .... | 4 | 0 | 0 | 0 | 6 | .... | .... | .... | .... |
| 2003-04 | San Angelo Saints | CHL | 64 | 39 | 36 | 75 | 51 | .... | .... | .... | .... | .... | .... | .... | .... | .... | 5 | 1 | 1 | 2 | 2 | .... | .... | .... | .... |
| 2004-05 | Alaska Aces | ECHL | 69 | *49 | 29 | 78 | 54 | .... | .... | .... | .... | .... | .... | .... | .... | .... | 15 | 4 | 4 | 8 | 12 | .... | .... | .... | .... |
| | Milwaukee | AHL | 1 | 0 | 0 | 0 | 0 | .... | .... | .... | .... | .... | .... | .... | .... | .... | .... | .... | .... | .... | .... | .... | .... | .... | .... |
| 2005-06 | Albany River Rats | AHL | 37 | 7 | 12 | 19 | 26 | .... | .... | .... | .... | .... | .... | .... | .... | .... | .... | .... | .... | .... | .... | .... | .... | .... | .... |
| | Alaska Aces | ECHL | 33 | 26 | 16 | 42 | 38 | .... | .... | .... | .... | .... | .... | .... | .... | .... | 22 | *14 | 5 | 19 | *54 | .... | .... | .... | .... |
| 2006-07 | Lowell Devils | AHL | 65 | 32 | 17 | 49 | 30 | .... | .... | .... | .... | .... | .... | .... | .... | .... | .... | .... | .... | .... | .... | .... | .... | .... | .... |
| **2007-08** | **Pittsburgh** | **NHL** | **15** | **1** | **1** | **2** | **10** | **0** | **0** | **0** | **9** | **11.1** | **–1** | **0** | **0.0** | **3:53** | .... | .... | .... | .... | .... | .... | .... | .... | .... |
| | Wilkes-Barre | AHL | 56 | 25 | 17 | 42 | 33 | .... | .... | .... | .... | .... | .... | .... | .... | .... | 23 | 11 | 6 | 17 | 10 | .... | .... | .... | .... |
| **2008-09** | **Pittsburgh** | **NHL** | **20** | **1** | **2** | **3** | **4** | **0** | **0** | **1** | **33** | **3.0** | **0** | **2** | **100.0** | **9:25** | .... | .... | .... | .... | .... | .... | .... | .... | .... |
| | Wilkes-Barre | AHL | 54 | 34 | 23 | 57 | 38 | .... | .... | .... | .... | .... | .... | .... | .... | .... | 12 | 6 | 3 | 9 | 12 | .... | .... | .... | .... |
| | **NHL Totals** | | **35** | **2** | **3** | **5** | **14** | **0** | **0** | **1** | **42** | **4.8** | | **2** | **100.0** | **7:02** | .... | .... | .... | .... | .... | .... | .... | .... | .... |

Signed as a free agent by **Albany** (AHL), August 16, 2005. Signed as a free agent by **Pittsburgh**, July 12, 2007. Signed as a free agent by **Edmonton**, July 13, 2009.

(MIHNK, GRAY-uhm) **FLA.**

## MINK, Graham

Center. Shoots right. 6'3", 220 lbs. Born, Stowe, VT, May 21, 1979.

| Season | Club | League | GP | G | A | Pts | PIM | PP | SH | GW | S | % | +/- | TF | F% | Min | Playoffs GP | G | A | Pts | PIM | PP | SH | GW | Min |
|---|---|---|---|---|---|---|---|---|---|---|---|---|---|---|---|---|---|---|---|---|---|---|---|---|---|
| 1997-98 | NMH School | High-MA | 25 | 17 | 25 | 42 | .... | .... | .... | .... | .... | .... | .... | .... | .... | .... | .... | .... | .... | .... | .... | .... | .... | .... | .... |
| 1998-99 | U. of Vermont | ECAC | 27 | 4 | 2 | 6 | 34 | .... | .... | .... | .... | .... | .... | .... | .... | .... | .... | .... | .... | .... | .... | .... | .... | .... | .... |
| 99-2000 | U. of Vermont | ECAC | 17 | 7 | 4 | 11 | 14 | .... | .... | .... | .... | .... | .... | .... | .... | .... | .... | .... | .... | .... | .... | .... | .... | .... | .... |
| 2000-01 | U. of Vermont | ECAC | 32 | 17 | 12 | 29 | 52 | .... | .... | .... | .... | .... | .... | .... | .... | .... | .... | .... | .... | .... | .... | .... | .... | .... | .... |
| 2001-02 | Richmond | ECHL | 29 | 8 | 9 | 17 | 78 | .... | .... | .... | .... | .... | .... | .... | .... | .... | .... | .... | .... | .... | .... | .... | .... | .... | .... |
| | Portland Pirates | AHL | 56 | 17 | 17 | 34 | 50 | .... | .... | .... | .... | .... | .... | .... | .... | .... | .... | .... | .... | .... | .... | .... | .... | .... | .... |
| 2002-03 | Portland Pirates | AHL | 71 | 22 | 15 | 37 | 115 | .... | .... | .... | .... | .... | .... | .... | .... | .... | .... | .... | .... | .... | .... | .... | .... | .... | .... |
| **2003-04** | **Washington** | **NHL** | **2** | **0** | **0** | **0** | **2** | **0** | **0** | **0** | **0** | **0.0** | **–1** | **1** | **0.0** | **5:32** | .... | .... | .... | .... | .... | .... | .... | .... | .... |
| | Portland Pirates | AHL | 68 | 18 | 19 | 37 | 74 | .... | .... | .... | .... | .... | .... | .... | .... | .... | 3 | 0 | 1 | 1 | 4 | .... | .... | .... | .... |
| 2004-05 | Portland Pirates | AHL | 63 | 18 | 21 | 39 | 86 | .... | .... | .... | .... | .... | .... | .... | .... | .... | .... | .... | .... | .... | .... | .... | .... | .... | .... |
| **2005-06** | **Washington** | **NHL** | **3** | **0** | **0** | **0** | **0** | **0** | **0** | **0** | **1** | **0.0** | **0** | **0** | **0.0** | **5:32** | .... | .... | .... | .... | .... | .... | .... | .... | .... |
| | Hershey Bears | AHL | 43 | 21 | 19 | 40 | 50 | .... | .... | .... | .... | .... | .... | .... | .... | .... | 21 | 8 | 13 | 21 | 29 | .... | .... | .... | .... |
| 2006-07 | Worcester Sharks | AHL | 61 | 31 | 32 | 63 | 52 | .... | .... | .... | .... | .... | .... | .... | .... | .... | 6 | 1 | 5 | 6 | 8 | .... | .... | .... | .... |
| 2007-08 | Worcester Sharks | AHL | 71 | 24 | 31 | 55 | 67 | .... | .... | .... | .... | .... | .... | .... | .... | .... | .... | .... | .... | .... | .... | .... | .... | .... | .... |
| **2008-09** | **Washington** | **NHL** | **2** | **0** | **0** | **0** | **0** | **0** | **0** | **0** | **4** | **0.0** | **0** | **0** | **0.0** | **8:03** | .... | .... | .... | .... | .... | .... | .... | .... | .... |
| | Hershey Bears | AHL | 68 | 32 | 27 | 59 | 101 | .... | .... | .... | .... | .... | .... | .... | .... | .... | 22 | 7 | 8 | 15 | 16 | .... | .... | .... | .... |
| | **NHL Totals** | | **7** | **0** | **0** | **0** | **2** | **0** | **0** | **0** | **5** | **0.0** | | **1** | **0.0** | **6:15** | .... | .... | .... | .... | .... | .... | .... | .... | .... |

Signed as a free agent by **Portland** (AHL), September 30, 2001. Signed as a free agent by **Washington**, April 9, 2002. Signed as a free agent by **San Jose**, July 14, 2006. Signed as a free agent by **Washington**, July 2, 2008.

(MIH-chuhl, JAWN) **TOR.**

## MITCHELL, John

Center. Shoots left. 6'1", 182 lbs. Born, Waterloo, Ont., January 22, 1985. Toronto's 4th choice, 158th overall, in 2003 Entry Draft.

| Season | Club | League | GP | G | A | Pts | PIM | PP | SH | GW | S | % | +/- | TF | F% | Min | Playoffs GP | G | A | Pts | PIM | PP | SH | GW | Min |
|---|---|---|---|---|---|---|---|---|---|---|---|---|---|---|---|---|---|---|---|---|---|---|---|---|---|
| 2000-01 | Waterloo Siskens | OPJHL | 47 | 15 | 29 | 44 | 33 | .... | .... | .... | .... | .... | .... | .... | .... | .... | .... | .... | .... | .... | .... | .... | .... | .... | .... |
| 2001-02 | Plymouth Whalers | OHL | 62 | 9 | 9 | 18 | 23 | .... | .... | .... | .... | .... | .... | .... | .... | .... | 6 | 1 | 0 | 1 | 4 | .... | .... | .... | .... |
| 2002-03 | Plymouth Whalers | OHL | 68 | 18 | 37 | 55 | 31 | .... | .... | .... | .... | .... | .... | .... | .... | .... | 18 | 2 | 10 | 12 | 8 | .... | .... | .... | .... |
| 2003-04 | Plymouth Whalers | OHL | 65 | 28 | 54 | 82 | 45 | .... | .... | .... | .... | .... | .... | .... | .... | .... | 9 | 6 | 6 | 12 | 6 | .... | .... | .... | .... |
| 2004-05 | Plymouth Whalers | OHL | 63 | 25 | 50 | 75 | 59 | .... | .... | .... | .... | .... | .... | .... | .... | .... | 4 | 1 | 1 | 2 | 0 | .... | .... | .... | .... |
| | St. John's | AHL | 2 | 0 | 0 | 0 | 0 | .... | .... | .... | .... | .... | .... | .... | .... | .... | .... | .... | .... | .... | .... | .... | .... | .... | .... |
| 2005-06 | Toronto Marlies | AHL | 51 | 5 | 12 | 17 | 22 | .... | .... | .... | .... | .... | .... | .... | .... | .... | 2 | 0 | 0 | 0 | 0 | .... | .... | .... | .... |
| 2006-07 | Toronto Marlies | AHL | 73 | 16 | 20 | 36 | 46 | .... | .... | .... | .... | .... | .... | .... | .... | .... | .... | .... | .... | .... | .... | .... | .... | .... | .... |
| 2007-08 | Toronto Marlies | AHL | 79 | 20 | 31 | 51 | 56 | .... | .... | .... | .... | .... | .... | .... | .... | .... | 19 | 8 | 4 | 12 | 12 | .... | .... | .... | .... |
| **2008-09** | **Toronto** | **NHL** | **76** | **12** | **17** | **29** | **33** | **2** | **0** | **0** | **98** | **12.2** | **–16** | **669** | **48.7** | **13:48** | .... | .... | .... | .... | .... | .... | .... | .... | .... |
| | **NHL Totals** | | **76** | **12** | **17** | **29** | **33** | **2** | **0** | **0** | **98** | **12.2** | | **669** | **48.7** | **13:48** | .... | .... | .... | .... | .... | .... | .... | .... | .... |

## MITCHELL, Torrey
(MIH-chuhl, TOH-ree) **S.J.**

Center. Shoots right. 5'11", 190 lbs. Born, Montreal, Que., January 30, 1985. San Jose's 3rd choice, 126th overall, in 2004 Entry Draft.

| Season | Club | League | GP | G | A | Pts | PIM | PP | SH | GW | S | % | +/- | TF | F% | Min | GP | G | A | Pts | PIM | PP | SH | GW | Min |
|---|---|---|---|---|---|---|---|---|---|---|---|---|---|---|---|---|---|---|---|---|---|---|---|---|---|
| | | | Regular Season | | | | | | | | | | | | | | Playoffs | | | | | | | | |
| 2002-03 | Hotchkiss | High-CT | 26 | 19 | 30 | 49 | 33 | | | | | | | | | | | | | | | | | | |
| 2003-04 | Hotchkiss | High-CT | 25 | 25 | 37 | 62 | 42 | | | | | | | | | | | | | | | | | | |
| 2004-05 | U. of Vermont | ECAC | 38 | 11 | 19 | 30 | 74 | | | | | | | | | | | | | | | | | | |
| 2005-06 | U. of Vermont | H-East | 38 | 12 | 28 | 40 | 34 | | | | | | | | | | | | | | | | | | |
| 2006-07 | U. of Vermont | H-East | 39 | 12 | 23 | 35 | 46 | | | | | | | | | | | | | | | | | | |
| | Worcester Sharks | AHL | 11 | 2 | 5 | 7 | 27 | | | | | | | | | | 6 | 1 | 1 | 2 | 15 | | | | |
| **2007-08** | **San Jose** | **NHL** | **82** | **10** | **10** | **20** | **50** | **1** | **2** | **0** | **110** | **9.1** | **-3** | **692** | **49.4** | **14:19** | **13** | **1** | **2** | **3** | **10** | **1** | **0** | **0** | **14:00** |
| **2008-09** | Worcester Sharks | AHL | 2 | 1 | 0 | 1 | 0 | | | | | | | | | | | | | | | | | | |
| | **San Jose** | **NHL** | | | | | | | | | | | | | | | **4** | **0** | **0** | **0** | **2** | **0** | **0** | **0** | **9:38** |
| | **NHL Totals** | | **82** | **10** | **10** | **20** | **50** | **1** | **2** | **0** | **110** | **9.1** | | **692** | **49.4** | **14:19** | **17** | **1** | **2** | **3** | **12** | **1** | **0** | **0** | **12:58** |

ECAC All-Rookie Team (2005)

• Missed majority of season recovering from broken leg suffered during practice at training camp, September 18, 2008.

## MITCHELL, Willie
(MIH-chuhl, WIHL-lee) **VAN.**

Defense. Shoots left. 6'3", 210 lbs. Born, Port McNeill, B.C., April 23, 1977. New Jersey's 12th choice, 199th overall, in 1996 Entry Draft.

| Season | Club | League | GP | G | A | Pts | PIM | PP | SH | GW | S | % | +/- | TF | F% | Min | GP | G | A | Pts | PIM | PP | SH | GW | Min |
|---|---|---|---|---|---|---|---|---|---|---|---|---|---|---|---|---|---|---|---|---|---|---|---|---|---|
| | | | Regular Season | | | | | | | | | | | | | | Playoffs | | | | | | | | |
| 1993-94 | Notre Dame | SMHL | 31 | 4 | 11 | 15 | 81 | | | | | | | | | | | | | | | | | | |
| 1994-95 | Kelowna Spartans | BCHL | 42 | 3 | 8 | 11 | 71 | | | | | | | | | | | | | | | | | | |
| 1995-96 | Melfort Mustangs | SJHL | 19 | 2 | 6 | 8 | | | | | | | | | | | 14 | 0 | 2 | 2 | 12 | | | | |
| 1996-97 | Melfort Mustangs | SJHL | 64 | 14 | 42 | 56 | 227 | | | | | | | | | | 4 | 0 | 1 | 1 | 23 | | | | |
| 1997-98 | Clarkson Knights | ECAC | 34 | 9 | 17 | 26 | 105 | | | | | | | | | | | | | | | | | | |
| 1998-99 | Clarkson Knights | ECAC | 34 | 10 | 19 | 29 | 40 | | | | | | | | | | | | | | | | | | |
| | Albany River Rats | AHL | 6 | 1 | 3 | 4 | 29 | | | | | | | | | | | | | | | | | | |
| **99-2000** | **New Jersey** | **NHL** | **2** | **0** | **0** | **0** | **0** | **0** | **0** | **0** | **2** | **0.0** | **1** | **0** | **0.0** | **16:04** | | | | | | | | | |
| | Albany River Rats | AHL | 63 | 5 | 14 | 19 | 71 | | | | | | | | | | 5 | 1 | 2 | 3 | 4 | | | | |
| **2000-01** | **New Jersey** | **NHL** | **16** | **0** | **2** | **2** | **29** | **0** | **0** | **0** | **14** | **0.0** | **0** | **0** | **0.0** | **14:52** | | | | | | | | | |
| | Albany River Rats | AHL | 41 | 3 | 13 | 16 | 94 | | | | | | | | | | | | | | | | | | |
| | **Minnesota** | **NHL** | **17** | **1** | **7** | **8** | **11** | **0** | **0** | **0** | **16** | **6.3** | **4** | **0** | **0.0** | **20:49** | | | | | | | | | |
| **2001-02** | **Minnesota** | **NHL** | **68** | **3** | **10** | **13** | **68** | **0** | **0** | **1** | **67** | **4.5** | **-16** | **0** | **0.0** | **21:25** | | | | | | | | | |
| **2002-03** | **Minnesota** | **NHL** | **69** | **2** | **12** | **14** | **84** | **0** | **1** | **1** | **67** | **3.0** | **13** | **0** | **0.0** | **22:13** | **18** | **1** | **3** | **4** | **14** | **0** | **0** | **0** | **24:48** |
| **2003-04** | **Minnesota** | **NHL** | **70** | **1** | **13** | **14** | **83** | **0** | **0** | **0** | **58** | **1.7** | **12** | **2** | **50.0** | **22:36** | | | | | | | | | |
| 2004-05 | | | DID NOT PLAY | | | | | | | | | | | | | | | | | | | | | | |
| **2005-06** | **Minnesota** | **NHL** | **64** | **2** | **6** | **8** | **87** | **0** | **0** | **0** | **48** | **4.2** | **15** | **0** | **0.0** | **20:52** | | | | | | | | | |
| | **Dallas** | **NHL** | **16** | **0** | **2** | **2** | **26** | **0** | **0** | **0** | **10** | **0.0** | **4** | **0** | **0.0** | **20:46** | **5** | **0** | **0** | **0** | **2** | **0** | **0** | **0** | **23:21** |
| **2006-07** | **Vancouver** | **NHL** | **62** | **1** | **10** | **11** | **45** | **0** | **0** | **0** | **54** | **1.9** | **1** | **0** | **0.0** | **22:13** | **12** | **0** | **1** | **1** | **12** | **0** | **0** | **0** | **27:14** |
| **2007-08** | **Vancouver** | **NHL** | **72** | **2** | **10** | **12** | **81** | **0** | **0** | **1** | **65** | **3.1** | **6** | **0** | **0.0** | **23:12** | | | | | | | | | |
| **2008-09** | **Vancouver** | **NHL** | **82** | **3** | **20** | **23** | **59** | **0** | **0** | **1** | **88** | **3.4** | **29** | **1** | **0.0** | **22:55** | **10** | **0** | **2** | **2** | **22** | **0** | **0** | **0** | **24:13** |
| | **NHL Totals** | | **538** | **15** | **92** | **107** | **573** | **0** | **1** | **4** | **489** | **3.1** | | **3** | **33.3** | **21:49** | **45** | **1** | **6** | **7** | **50** | **0** | **0** | **0** | **25:09** |

SJHL First All-Star Team (1997) • SJHL Top Defenseman Award (1997) • ECAC Second All-Star Team (1998) • ECAC Rookie of the Year (1998) (co-winner - Erik Cole) • ECAC First All-Star Team (1999) • NCAA East Second All-American Team (1999)

Traded to **Minnesota** by **New Jersey** for Sean O'Donnell, March 4, 2001. Traded to **Dallas** by **Minnesota** with Minnesota's 2nd round choice (Nico Sacchetti) in 2007 Entry Draft for Martin Skoula and Shawn Belle, March 9, 2006. Signed as a free agent by **Vancouver**, July 1, 2006.

## MODANO, Mike
(moh-DA-noh, MIGHK) **DAL.**

Center. Shoots left. 6'3", 210 lbs. Born, Livonia, MI, June 7, 1970. Minnesota's 1st choice, 1st overall, in 1988 Entry Draft.

| Season | Club | League | GP | G | A | Pts | PIM | PP | SH | GW | S | % | +/- | TF | F% | Min | GP | G | A | Pts | PIM | PP | SH | GW | Min |
|---|---|---|---|---|---|---|---|---|---|---|---|---|---|---|---|---|---|---|---|---|---|---|---|---|---|
| | | | Regular Season | | | | | | | | | | | | | | Playoffs | | | | | | | | |
| 1985-86 | Det. Compuware | MNHL | 69 | 66 | 65 | 131 | 32 | | | | | | | | | | | | | | | | | | |
| 1986-87 | Prince Albert | WHL | 70 | 32 | 30 | 62 | 96 | | | | | | | | | | 8 | 1 | 4 | 5 | 4 | | | | |
| 1987-88 | Prince Albert | WHL | 65 | 47 | 80 | 127 | 80 | | | | | | | | | | 9 | 7 | 11 | 18 | 18 | | | | |
| **1988-89** | Prince Albert | WHL | 41 | 39 | 66 | 105 | 74 | | | | | | | | | | | | | | | | | | |
| | **Minnesota** | **NHL** | | | | | | | | | | | | | | | **2** | **0** | **0** | **0** | **0** | **0** | **0** | **0** | |
| **1989-90** | **Minnesota** | **NHL** | **80** | **29** | **46** | **75** | **63** | **12** | **0** | **2** | **172** | **16.9** | **-7** | | | | **7** | **1** | **1** | **2** | **12** | **0** | **0** | **0** | |
| **1990-91** | **Minnesota** | **NHL** | **79** | **28** | **36** | **64** | **65** | **9** | **0** | **2** | **232** | **12.1** | **2** | | | | **23** | **8** | **12** | **20** | **16** | **3** | **0** | **1** | |
| **1991-92** | **Minnesota** | **NHL** | **76** | **33** | **44** | **77** | **46** | **5** | **0** | **8** | **256** | **12.9** | **-9** | | | | **7** | **3** | **2** | **5** | **4** | **1** | **0** | **0** | |
| **1992-93** | **Minnesota** | **NHL** | **82** | **33** | **60** | **93** | **83** | **9** | **0** | **7** | **307** | **10.7** | **-7** | | | | | | | | | | | | |
| **1993-94** | **Dallas** | **NHL** | **76** | **50** | **43** | **93** | **54** | **18** | **0** | **4** | **281** | **17.8** | **-8** | | | | **9** | **7** | **3** | **10** | **16** | **2** | **0** | **2** | |
| **1994-95** | **Dallas** | **NHL** | **30** | **12** | **17** | **29** | **8** | **4** | **1** | **0** | **100** | **12.0** | **7** | | | | | | | | | | | | |
| **1995-96** | **Dallas** | **NHL** | **78** | **36** | **45** | **81** | **63** | **8** | **4** | **4** | **320** | **11.3** | **-12** | | | | | | | | | | | | |
| **1996-97** | **Dallas** | **NHL** | **80** | **35** | **48** | **83** | **42** | **9** | **5** | **9** | **291** | **12.0** | **43** | | | | **7** | **4** | **1** | **5** | **0** | **1** | **1** | **2** | |
| **1997-98** | **Dallas** | **NHL** | **52** | **21** | **38** | **59** | **32** | **7** | **5** | **2** | **191** | **11.0** | **25** | | | | **17** | **4** | **10** | **14** | **12** | **1** | **0** | **1** | |
| | United States | Olympics | 4 | 2 | 0 | 2 | 0 | | | | | | | | | | | | | | | | | | |
| **1998-99♦** | **Dallas** | **NHL** | **77** | **34** | **47** | **81** | **44** | **6** | **4** | **7** | **224** | **15.2** | **29** | **1572** | **51.1** | **20:50** | **23** | **5** | ***18** | **23** | **16** | **1** | **1** | **1** | **24:40** |
| **99-2000** | **Dallas** | **NHL** | **77** | **38** | **43** | **81** | **48** | **11** | **1** | **8** | **188** | **20.2** | **0** | **1763** | **51.4** | **22:55** | **23** | **10** | ***13** | **23** | **10** | **4** | **0** | **2** | **25:26** |
| **2000-01** | **Dallas** | **NHL** | **81** | **33** | **51** | **84** | **52** | **8** | **3** | **7** | **208** | **15.9** | **26** | **1791** | **52.0** | **22:24** | **9** | **3** | **4** | **7** | **0** | **2** | **0** | **0** | **25:43** |
| **2001-02** | **Dallas** | **NHL** | **78** | **34** | **43** | **77** | **38** | **6** | **2** | **5** | **219** | **15.5** | **14** | **1710** | **53.7** | **22:27** | | | | | | | | | |
| | United States | Olympics | 6 | 0 | *6 | 6 | 4 | | | | | | | | | | | | | | | | | | |
| **2002-03** | **Dallas** | **NHL** | **79** | **28** | **57** | **85** | **30** | **5** | **2** | **6** | **193** | **14.5** | **34** | **1808** | **51.4** | **20:53** | **12** | **5** | **10** | **15** | **4** | **1** | **0** | **2** | **23:53** |
| **2003-04** | **Dallas** | **NHL** | **76** | **14** | **30** | **44** | **46** | **6** | **0** | **0** | **152** | **9.2** | **-21** | **1523** | **52.6** | **20:27** | **5** | **1** | **2** | **3** | **8** | **1** | **0** | **0** | **23:17** |
| 2004-05 | | | DID NOT PLAY | | | | | | | | | | | | | | | | | | | | | | |
| **2005-06** | **Dallas** | **NHL** | **78** | **27** | **50** | **77** | **58** | **12** | **1** | **4** | **207** | **13.0** | **23** | **1421** | **51.1** | **19:34** | **5** | **1** | **3** | **4** | **4** | **1** | **0** | **0** | **22:14** |
| | United States | Olympics | 6 | 2 | 0 | 2 | 6 | | | | | | | | | | | | | | | | | | |
| **2006-07** | **Dallas** | **NHL** | **59** | **22** | **21** | **43** | **34** | **9** | **0** | **7** | **141** | **15.6** | **9** | **918** | **52.2** | **18:24** | **7** | **1** | **1** | **2** | **4** | **1** | **0** | **1** | **26:14** |
| **2007-08** | **Dallas** | **NHL** | **82** | **21** | **36** | **57** | **48** | **5** | **1** | **4** | **200** | **10.5** | **-11** | **1145** | **49.2** | **19:14** | **18** | **5** | **7** | **12** | **22** | **5** | **0** | **3** | **19:42** |
| **2008-09** | **Dallas** | **NHL** | **80** | **15** | **31** | **46** | **46** | **4** | **0** | **4** | **197** | **7.6** | **-13** | **1176** | **52.5** | **18:18** | | | | | | | | | |
| | **NHL Totals** | | **1400** | **543** | **786** | **1329** | **900** | **153** | **29** | **90** | **4079** | **13.3** | | **14827** | **51.8** | **20:35** | **174** | **58** | **87** | **145** | **128** | **24** | **2** | **15** | **23:53** |

WHL East First All-Star Team (1989) • NHL All-Rookie Team (1990) • NHL Second All-Star Team (2000)

Played in NHL All-Star Game (1993, 1998, 1999, 2000, 2003, 2004, 2009)

• Transferred to **Dallas** after **Minnesota** franchise relocated, June 9, 1993.

## MODIN, Fredrik
(moh-DEEN, FREHD-rihk) **CBJ**

Left wing. Shoots left. 6'4", 218 lbs. Born, Sundsvall, Sweden, October 8, 1974. Toronto's 3rd choice, 64th overall, in 1994 Entry Draft.

| Season | Club | League | GP | G | A | Pts | PIM | PP | SH | GW | S | % | +/- | TF | F% | Min | GP | G | A | Pts | PIM | PP | SH | GW | Min |
|---|---|---|---|---|---|---|---|---|---|---|---|---|---|---|---|---|---|---|---|---|---|---|---|---|---|
| | | | Regular Season | | | | | | | | | | | | | | Playoffs | | | | | | | | |
| 1991-92 | Sundsvall/Timra | Sweden-2 | 11 | 1 | 0 | 1 | 0 | | | | | | | | | | | | | | | | | | |
| 1992-93 | Sundsvall/Timra | Sweden-2 | 30 | 5 | 7 | 12 | 12 | | | | | | | | | | 5 | 1 | 0 | 1 | 0 | | | | |
| 1993-94 | Sundsvall/Timra | Sweden-2 | 30 | 16 | 15 | 31 | 36 | | | | | | | | | | 2 | 0 | 1 | 1 | 6 | | | | |
| 1994-95 | Brynas IF Gavle | Sweden | 38 | 9 | 10 | 19 | 33 | | | | | | | | | | 14 | 4 | 4 | 8 | 6 | | | | |
| 1995-96 | Brynas IF Gavle | Sweden | 22 | 4 | 8 | 12 | 22 | | | | | | | | | | | | | | | | | | |
| **1996-97** | **Toronto** | **NHL** | **76** | **6** | **7** | **13** | **24** | **0** | **0** | **0** | **85** | **7.1** | **-14** | | | | | | | | | | | | |
| **1997-98** | **Toronto** | **NHL** | **74** | **16** | **16** | **32** | **32** | **1** | **0** | **4** | **137** | **11.7** | **-5** | | | | | | | | | | | | |
| **1998-99** | **Toronto** | **NHL** | **67** | **16** | **15** | **31** | **35** | **1** | **0** | **3** | **108** | **14.8** | **14** | **2** | **50.0** | **13:34** | **8** | **0** | **0** | **0** | **6** | **0** | **0** | **0** | **9:50** |
| **99-2000** | **Tampa Bay** | **NHL** | **80** | **22** | **26** | **48** | **18** | **3** | **0** | **5** | **167** | **13.2** | **-26** | **6** | **50.0** | **15:32** | | | | | | | | | |
| **2000-01** | **Tampa Bay** | **NHL** | **76** | **32** | **24** | **56** | **48** | **8** | **0** | **4** | **217** | **14.7** | **-1** | **21** | **42.9** | **17:15** | | | | | | | | | |
| **2001-02** | **Tampa Bay** | **NHL** | **54** | **14** | **17** | **31** | **27** | **2** | **0** | **4** | **141** | **9.9** | **0** | **25** | **40.0** | **19:05** | | | | | | | | | |
| **2002-03** | **Tampa Bay** | **NHL** | **76** | **17** | **23** | **40** | **43** | **2** | **1** | **4** | **179** | **9.5** | **7** | **35** | **28.6** | **17:35** | **11** | **2** | **0** | **2** | **18** | **0** | **0** | **0** | **19:18** |
| **2003-04♦** | **Tampa Bay** | **NHL** | **82** | **29** | **28** | **57** | **32** | **5** | **1** | **2** | **206** | **14.1** | **31** | **138** | **38.4** | **18:12** | **23** | **8** | **11** | **19** | **10** | **3** | **0** | **2** | **20:47** |
| 2004-05 | Timra IK | Sweden | 43 | 12 | 24 | 36 | 58 | | | | | | | | | | 7 | 1 | 1 | 2 | 8 | | | | |
| **2005-06** | **Tampa Bay** | **NHL** | **77** | **31** | **23** | **54** | **56** | **12** | **1** | **4** | **221** | **14.0** | **5** | **171** | **51.5** | **19:35** | **5** | **0** | **0** | **0** | **6** | **0** | **0** | **0** | **18:46** |
| | Sweden | Olympics | 8 | 2 | 1 | 3 | 6 | | | | | | | | | | | | | | | | | | |
| **2006-07** | **Columbus** | **NHL** | **79** | **22** | **20** | **42** | **50** | **6** | **0** | **4** | **220** | **10.0** | **-3** | **508** | **46.5** | **19:07** | | | | | | | | | |
| **2007-08** | **Columbus** | **NHL** | **23** | **6** | **6** | **12** | **20** | **2** | **0** | **1** | **41** | **14.6** | **1** | **103** | **44.7** | **16:51** | | | | | | | | | |
| **2008-09** | **Columbus** | **NHL** | **50** | **9** | **16** | **25** | **28** | **2** | **0** | **0** | **113** | **8.0** | **2** | **122** | **40.2** | **16:53** | **4** | **1** | **0** | **1** | **0** | **0** | **0** | **0** | **13:07** |
| | **NHL Totals** | | **814** | **220** | **221** | **441** | **413** | **44** | **3** | **35** | **1835** | **12.0** | | **1131** | **44.7** | **17:26** | **51** | **11** | **11** | **22** | **40** | **3** | **0** | **2** | **17:56** |

Played in NHL All-Star Game (2001)

Traded to **Tampa Bay** by **Toronto** for Cory Cross and Tampa Bay's 7th round choice (Ivan Kolozvary) in 2001 Entry Draft, October 1, 1999. Signed as a free agent by **Timra** (Sweden), October 5, 2004. Traded to **Columbus** by **Tampa Bay** with Fredrik Norrena for Marc Denis, June 30, 2006. • Missed majority of 2007-08 season recovering from shoulder injury suffered in game at Anaheim, November 1, 2007.

## MODRY, Jaroslav

(MOH-dree, YAHR-roh-slav)

Defense. Shoots left. 6'2", 220 lbs. Born, Ceske Budejovice, Czech., February 27, 1971. New Jersey's 11th choice, 179th overall, in 1990 Entry Draft.

| | | | Regular Season | | | | | | | | | | | | | | Playoffs | | | | | | | | |
|---|---|---|---|---|---|---|---|---|---|---|---|---|---|---|---|---|---|---|---|---|---|---|---|---|---|
| Season | Club | League | GP | G | A | Pts | PIM | PP | SH | GW | S | % | +/- | TF | F% | Min | GP | G | A | Pts | PIM | PP | SH | GW | Min |
| 1987-88 | C. Budejovice | Czech | 3 | 0 | 0 | 0 | 0 | .... | .... | .... | .... | .... | .... | .... | .... | .... | .... | .... | .... | .... | .... | .... | .... | .... | .... |
| 1988-89 | C. Budejovice | Czech | 28 | 0 | 1 | 1 | 8 | .... | .... | .... | .... | .... | .... | .... | .... | .... | .... | .... | .... | .... | .... | .... | .... | .... | .... |
| 1989-90 | C. Budejovice | Czech | 41 | 2 | 2 | 4 | .... | .... | .... | .... | .... | .... | .... | .... | .... | .... | .... | .... | .... | .... | .... | .... | .... | .... | .... |
| 1990-91 | Dukla Trencin | Czech | 33 | 1 | 9 | 10 | 6 | .... | .... | .... | .... | .... | .... | .... | .... | .... | .... | .... | .... | .... | .... | .... | .... | .... | .... |
| 1991-92 | C. Budejovice | Czech-2 | 14 | 4 | 10 | 14 | .... | .... | .... | .... | .... | .... | .... | .... | .... | .... | .... | .... | .... | .... | .... | .... | .... | .... | .... |
| | Dukla Trencin | Czech | 18 | 0 | 4 | 4 | 6 | .... | .... | .... | .... | .... | .... | .... | .... | .... | .... | .... | .... | .... | .... | .... | .... | .... | .... |
| 1992-93 | Utica Devils | AHL | 80 | 7 | 35 | 42 | 62 | .... | .... | .... | .... | .... | .... | .... | .... | .... | 5 | 0 | 2 | 2 | 2 | .... | .... | .... | .... |
| **1993-94** | **New Jersey** | **NHL** | **41** | **2** | **15** | **17** | **18** | **2** | **0** | **0** | **35** | **5.7** | **10** | .... | .... | .... | .... | .... | .... | .... | .... | .... | .... | .... | .... |
| | Albany River Rats | AHL | 19 | 1 | 5 | 6 | 25 | .... | .... | .... | .... | .... | .... | .... | .... | .... | .... | .... | .... | .... | .... | .... | .... | .... | .... |
| **1994-95** | C. Budejovice | CzRep | 19 | 1 | 3 | 4 | 30 | .... | .... | .... | .... | .... | .... | .... | .... | .... | .... | .... | .... | .... | .... | .... | .... | .... | .... |
| | **New Jersey** | **NHL** | **11** | **0** | **0** | **0** | **0** | **0** | **0** | **0** | **10** | **0.0** | **-1** | .... | .... | .... | .... | .... | .... | .... | .... | .... | .... | .... | .... |
| | Albany River Rats | AHL | 18 | 5 | 6 | 11 | 14 | .... | .... | .... | .... | .... | .... | .... | .... | .... | 14 | 3 | 3 | 6 | 4 | .... | .... | .... | .... |
| **1995-96** | **Ottawa** | **NHL** | **64** | **4** | **14** | **18** | **38** | **1** | **0** | **1** | **89** | **4.5** | **-17** | .... | .... | .... | .... | .... | .... | .... | .... | .... | .... | .... | .... |
| | **Los Angeles** | **NHL** | **9** | **0** | **3** | **3** | **6** | **0** | **0** | **0** | **17** | **0.0** | **-4** | .... | .... | .... | .... | .... | .... | .... | .... | .... | .... | .... | .... |
| **1996-97** | **Los Angeles** | **NHL** | **30** | **3** | **3** | **6** | **25** | **1** | **1** | **0** | **32** | **9.4** | **-13** | .... | .... | .... | .... | .... | .... | .... | .... | .... | .... | .... | .... |
| | Phoenix | IHL | 23 | 3 | 12 | 15 | 17 | .... | .... | .... | .... | .... | .... | .... | .... | .... | .... | .... | .... | .... | .... | .... | .... | .... | .... |
| | Utah Grizzlies | IHL | 11 | 1 | 4 | 5 | 20 | .... | .... | .... | .... | .... | .... | .... | .... | .... | 7 | 0 | 1 | 1 | 6 | .... | .... | .... | .... |
| 1997-98 | Utah Grizzlies | IHL | 74 | 12 | 21 | 33 | 72 | .... | .... | .... | .... | .... | .... | .... | .... | .... | 4 | 0 | 2 | 2 | 6 | .... | .... | .... | .... |
| **1998-99** | **Los Angeles** | **NHL** | **5** | **0** | **1** | **1** | **0** | **0** | **0** | **0** | **11** | **0.0** | **1** | **0** | **0.0** | **26:00** | .... | .... | .... | .... | .... | .... | .... | .... | .... |
| | Long Beach | IHL | 64 | 6 | 29 | 35 | 44 | .... | .... | .... | .... | .... | .... | .... | .... | .... | 8 | 4 | 2 | 6 | 4 | .... | .... | .... | .... |
| **99-2000** | **Los Angeles** | **NHL** | **26** | **5** | **4** | **9** | **18** | **5** | **0** | **1** | **32** | **15.6** | **-2** | **0** | **0.0** | **19:13** | **2** | **0** | **0** | **0** | **2** | **0** | **0** | **0** | **16:48** |
| | Long Beach | IHL | 11 | 2 | 4 | 6 | 8 | .... | .... | .... | .... | .... | .... | .... | .... | .... | .... | .... | .... | .... | .... | .... | .... | .... | .... |
| **2000-01** | **Los Angeles** | **NHL** | **63** | **4** | **15** | **19** | **48** | **0** | **0** | **0** | **72** | **5.6** | **16** | **0** | **0.0** | **18:22** | **10** | **1** | **0** | **1** | **4** | **1** | **0** | **1** | **16:08** |
| **2001-02** | **Los Angeles** | **NHL** | **80** | **4** | **38** | **42** | **65** | **4** | **0** | **0** | **119** | **3.4** | **-4** | **0** | **0.0** | **19:31** | **7** | **0** | **2** | **2** | **0** | **0** | **0** | **0** | **21:26** |
| **2002-03** | **Los Angeles** | **NHL** | **82** | **13** | **25** | **38** | **68** | **8** | **0** | **1** | **205** | **6.3** | **-13** | **1** | **0.0** | **22:39** | .... | .... | .... | .... | .... | .... | .... | .... | .... |
| **2003-04** | **Los Angeles** | **NHL** | **79** | **5** | **27** | **32** | **44** | **1** | **0** | **1** | **196** | **2.6** | **11** | **1** | **0.0** | **24:24** | .... | .... | .... | .... | .... | .... | .... | .... | .... |
| 2004-05 | Liberec | CzRep | 19 | 3 | 7 | 10 | 24 | .... | .... | .... | .... | .... | .... | .... | .... | .... | 12 | 0 | 4 | 4 | 22 | .... | .... | .... | .... |
| **2005-06** | **Atlanta** | **NHL** | **79** | **7** | **31** | **38** | **76** | **5** | **0** | **2** | **143** | **4.9** | **-9** | **0** | **0.0** | **20:48** | .... | .... | .... | .... | .... | .... | .... | .... | .... |
| **2006-07** | **Dallas** | **NHL** | **57** | **1** | **9** | **10** | **32** | **0** | **0** | **0** | **60** | **1.7** | **10** | **1** | **0.0** | **17:30** | .... | .... | .... | .... | .... | .... | .... | .... | .... |
| | **Los Angeles** | **NHL** | **19** | **0** | **8** | **8** | **22** | **0** | **0** | **0** | **29** | **0.0** | **1** | **0** | **0.0** | **22:57** | .... | .... | .... | .... | .... | .... | .... | .... | .... |
| **2007-08** | **Los Angeles** | **NHL** | **61** | **1** | **5** | **6** | **42** | **0** | **0** | **0** | **39** | **2.6** | **2** | **1** | **0.0** | **18:35** | .... | .... | .... | .... | .... | .... | .... | .... | .... |
| | **Philadelphia** | **NHL** | **19** | **0** | **3** | **3** | **8** | **0** | **0** | **0** | **17** | **0.0** | **-11** | **0** | **0.0** | **20:38** | **9** | **0** | **3** | **3** | **0** | **0** | **0** | **0** | **19:50** |
| 2008-09 | Liberec | CzRep | 52 | 3 | 14 | 17 | 48 | .... | .... | .... | .... | .... | .... | .... | .... | .... | 3 | 0 | 0 | 0 | 6 | .... | .... | .... | .... |
| | **NHL Totals** | | **725** | **49** | **201** | **250** | **510** | **27** | **1** | **6** | **1106** | **4.4** | | **4** | **0.0** | **20:35** | **28** | **1** | **5** | **6** | **6** | **1** | **0** | **1** | **18:42** |

Played in NHL All-Star Game (2002)

Traded to **Ottawa** by **New Jersey** for Ottawa's 4th round choice (Alyn McCauley) in 1995 Entry Draft, July 8, 1995. Traded to **Los Angeles** by **Ottawa** with Ottawa's 8th round choice (Stephen Valiquette) in 1996 Entry Draft for Kevin Brown, March 20, 1996. Signed as a free agent by **Atlanta**, July 1, 2004. Signed as a free agent by **Liberec** (CzRep), October 20, 2004. Traded to **Dallas** by **Atlanta** with Patrik Stefan for Niko Kapanen and Dallas's 7th round choice (Will O'Neill) in 2006 Entry Draft, June 24, 2006. Traded to **Los Angeles** by **Dallas** with the rights to Johan Fransson, Dallas' 2nd (Oscar Moller) and 3rd (Bryan Cameron) round choices in 2007 Entry Draft and Dallas' 1st round choice (later traded to Phoenix - Phoenix selected Viktor Tikhonov) in 2008 Entry Draft for Mattias Norstrom, Konstantin Pushkarev and Los Angeles' 3rd (Sergei Korostin) and 4th (later traded to Columbus - Columbus selected Maxim Mayorov) round choices in 2007 Entry Draft, February 27, 2007. Traded to **Philadelphia** by **Los Angeles** for Philadelphia's 3rd round choice (Geordie Wudrick) in 2008 Entry Draft, February 19, 2008. Signed as a free agent by **Liberec** (CzRep), July 31, 2008.

## MOEN, Travis

(MOH-ehn, TRA-vihs) **MTL.**

Left wing. Shoots left. 6'2", 215 lbs. Born, Stewart Valley, Sask., April 6, 1982. Calgary's 6th choice, 155th overall, in 2000 Entry Draft.

| | | | | | | | | | | | | | | | | | | | | | | | | | |
|---|---|---|---|---|---|---|---|---|---|---|---|---|---|---|---|---|---|---|---|---|---|---|---|---|---|
| 1998-99 | Swift Current | SMHL | STATISTICS NOT AVAILABLE | | | | | | | | | | | | | | | | | | | | | | |
| | Kelowna Rockets | WHL | 4 | 0 | 0 | 0 | 0 | .... | .... | .... | .... | .... | .... | .... | .... | .... | .... | .... | .... | .... | .... | .... | .... | .... | .... |
| 99-2000 | Kelowna Rockets | WHL | 66 | 9 | 6 | 15 | 96 | .... | .... | .... | .... | .... | .... | .... | .... | .... | 5 | 1 | 1 | 2 | 2 | .... | .... | .... | .... |
| 2000-01 | Kelowna Rockets | WHL | 40 | 8 | 8 | 16 | 106 | .... | .... | .... | .... | .... | .... | .... | .... | .... | .... | .... | .... | .... | .... | .... | .... | .... | .... |
| 2001-02 | Kelowna Rockets | WHL | 71 | 10 | 17 | 27 | 197 | .... | .... | .... | .... | .... | .... | .... | .... | .... | 13 | 1 | 0 | 1 | 28 | .... | .... | .... | .... |
| 2002-03 | Norfolk Admirals | AHL | 42 | 1 | 2 | 3 | 62 | .... | .... | .... | .... | .... | .... | .... | .... | .... | 9 | 0 | 0 | 0 | 20 | .... | .... | .... | .... |
| **2003-04** | **Chicago** | **NHL** | **82** | **4** | **2** | **6** | **142** | **0** | **0** | **2** | **51** | **7.8** | **-17** | **19** | **15.8** | **10:57** | .... | .... | .... | .... | .... | .... | .... | .... | .... |
| 2004-05 | Norfolk Admirals | AHL | 79 | 8 | 12 | 20 | 187 | .... | .... | .... | .... | .... | .... | .... | .... | .... | 6 | 0 | 1 | 1 | 6 | .... | .... | .... | .... |
| **2005-06** | **Anaheim** | **NHL** | **39** | **4** | **1** | **5** | **72** | **0** | **0** | **0** | **28** | **14.3** | **-3** | **8** | **12.5** | **11:03** | **9** | **1** | **0** | **1** | **10** | **0** | **0** | **0** | **8:25** |
| **2006-07 ♦** | **Anaheim** | **NHL** | **82** | **11** | **10** | **21** | **101** | **0** | **0** | **0** | **124** | **8.9** | **-4** | **10** | **30.0** | **14:48** | **21** | **7** | **5** | **12** | **22** | **0** | **0** | **3** | **17:19** |
| **2007-08** | **Anaheim** | **NHL** | **77** | **3** | **5** | **8** | **81** | **0** | **1** | **1** | **98** | **3.1** | **-10** | **25** | **32.0** | **15:50** | **6** | **1** | **1** | **2** | **2** | **0** | **0** | **0** | **14:09** |
| **2008-09** | **Anaheim** | **NHL** | **63** | **4** | **7** | **11** | **77** | **0** | **2** | **1** | **77** | **5.2** | **-17** | **7** | **28.6** | **14:53** | .... | .... | .... | .... | .... | .... | .... | .... | .... |
| | **San Jose** | **NHL** | **19** | **3** | **2** | **5** | **14** | **0** | **1** | **1** | **24** | **12.5** | **-1** | **11** | **18.2** | **15:21** | **6** | **0** | **0** | **0** | **2** | **0** | **0** | **0** | **12:54** |
| | **NHL Totals** | | **362** | **29** | **27** | **56** | **487** | **0** | **4** | **5** | **402** | **7.2** | | **80** | **23.8** | **13:47** | **42** | **9** | **6** | **15** | **36** | **0** | **0** | **3** | **14:19** |

Signed as a free agent by **Chicago**, October 21, 2002. Traded to **Anaheim** by **Chicago** for Michael Holmqvist, July 30, 2005. • Missed majority of 2005-06 season recovering from knee and shoulder injuries and serving as a healthy reserve. Traded to **San Jose** by **Anaheim** with Kent Huskins for Timo Pielmeier, Nick Bonino and future considerations, March 4, 2009. Signed as a free agent by **Montreal**, July 10, 2009.

## MOJZIS, Tomas

(moi-ZHEESH, TAW-mash)

Defense. Shoots left. 6'1", 192 lbs. Born, Kolin, Czech., May 2, 1982. Toronto's 11th choice, 246th overall, in 2001 Entry Draft.

| | | | | | | | | | | | | | | | | | | | | | | | | | |
|---|---|---|---|---|---|---|---|---|---|---|---|---|---|---|---|---|---|---|---|---|---|---|---|---|---|
| 99-2000 | HC Pardubice Jr. | CzRep-Jr. | 40 | 7 | 1 | 8 | .... | .... | .... | .... | .... | .... | .... | .... | .... | .... | .... | .... | .... | .... | .... | .... | .... | .... | .... |
| 2000-01 | Moose Jaw | WHL | 72 | 11 | 25 | 36 | 115 | .... | .... | .... | .... | .... | .... | .... | .... | .... | 4 | 0 | 1 | 1 | 8 | .... | .... | .... | .... |
| 2001-02 | Moose Jaw | WHL | 28 | 2 | 11 | 13 | 43 | .... | .... | .... | .... | .... | .... | .... | .... | .... | .... | .... | .... | .... | .... | .... | .... | .... | .... |
| | Seattle | WHL | 36 | 8 | 15 | 23 | 66 | .... | .... | .... | .... | .... | .... | .... | .... | .... | 11 | 1 | 3 | 4 | 20 | .... | .... | .... | .... |
| 2002-03 | Seattle | WHL | 62 | 21 | 49 | 70 | 126 | .... | .... | .... | .... | .... | .... | .... | .... | .... | 15 | 1 | 6 | 7 | 36 | .... | .... | .... | .... |
| 2003-04 | Manitoba Moose | AHL | 63 | 5 | 13 | 18 | 50 | .... | .... | .... | .... | .... | .... | .... | .... | .... | .... | .... | .... | .... | .... | .... | .... | .... | .... |
| 2004-05 | Manitoba Moose | AHL | 80 | 7 | 23 | 30 | 62 | .... | .... | .... | .... | .... | .... | .... | .... | .... | 14 | 0 | 2 | 2 | 28 | .... | .... | .... | .... |
| **2005-06** | **Vancouver** | **NHL** | **7** | **0** | **1** | **1** | **12** | **0** | **0** | **0** | **7** | **0.0** | **2** | **0** | **0.0** | **13:57** | .... | .... | .... | .... | .... | .... | .... | .... | .... |
| | Manitoba Moose | AHL | 37 | 5 | 13 | 18 | 52 | .... | .... | .... | .... | .... | .... | .... | .... | .... | .... | .... | .... | .... | .... | .... | .... | .... | .... |
| | Peoria Rivermen | AHL | 12 | 3 | 4 | 7 | 14 | .... | .... | .... | .... | .... | .... | .... | .... | .... | 1 | 0 | 0 | 0 | 0 | .... | .... | .... | .... |
| **2006-07** | **St. Louis** | **NHL** | **6** | **1** | **0** | **1** | **0** | **0** | **0** | **0** | **7** | **14.3** | **0** | **0** | **0.0** | **10:03** | .... | .... | .... | .... | .... | .... | .... | .... | .... |
| | Peoria Rivermen | AHL | 69 | 2 | 24 | 26 | 112 | .... | .... | .... | .... | .... | .... | .... | .... | .... | .... | .... | .... | .... | .... | .... | .... | .... | .... |
| 2007-08 | Sibir Novosibirsk | Russia | 28 | 2 | 2 | 4 | 38 | .... | .... | .... | .... | .... | .... | .... | .... | .... | .... | .... | .... | .... | .... | .... | .... | .... | .... |
| **2008-09** | **Minnesota** | **NHL** | **4** | **0** | **1** | **1** | **2** | **0** | **0** | **0** | **2** | **0.0** | **-1** | **0** | **0.0** | **7:15** | .... | .... | .... | .... | .... | .... | .... | .... | .... |
| | Houston Aeros | AHL | 46 | 7 | 15 | 22 | 51 | .... | .... | .... | .... | .... | .... | .... | .... | .... | 15 | 2 | 0 | 2 | 8 | .... | .... | .... | .... |
| | **NHL Totals** | | **17** | **1** | **2** | **3** | **14** | **0** | **0** | **0** | **16** | **6.3** | | **0** | **0.0** | **11:00** | .... | .... | .... | .... | .... | .... | .... | .... | .... |

WHL West First All-Star Team (2003) • Canadian Major Junior First All-Star Team (2003)

Traded to **Vancouver** by **Toronto** for Brad Leeb, September 4, 2002. Traded to **St. Louis** by **Vancouver** with Vancouver's 3rd round choice (later traded to New Jersey - New Jersey selected Vladimir Zharkov) in 2006 Entry Draft for Eric Weinrich, March 9, 2006. Signed as a free agent by **Novosibirsk** (Russia), May 21, 2007. Signed as a free agent by **Minesota**, July 7, 2008.

## MOLLER, Oscar

(MOH-luhr, AH-skuhr) **L.A.**

Center. Shoots right. 5'11", 180 lbs. Born, Stockholm, Sweden, January 22, 1989. Los Angeles' 2nd choice, 52nd overall, in 2007 Entry Draft.

| | | | | | | | | | | | | | | | | | | | | | | | | | |
|---|---|---|---|---|---|---|---|---|---|---|---|---|---|---|---|---|---|---|---|---|---|---|---|---|---|
| 2003-04 | Spanga U18 | Swe-U18 | 32 | 28 | 12 | 40 | 68 | .... | .... | .... | .... | .... | .... | .... | .... | .... | .... | .... | .... | .... | .... | .... | .... | .... | .... |
| 2004-05 | Spanga U18 | Swe-U18 | 24 | 28 | 16 | 44 | 52 | .... | .... | .... | .... | .... | .... | .... | .... | .... | .... | .... | .... | .... | .... | .... | .... | .... | .... |
| | Spanga Jr. | Swe-Jr. | 4 | 6 | 1 | 7 | 6 | .... | .... | .... | .... | .... | .... | .... | .... | .... | .... | .... | .... | .... | .... | .... | .... | .... | .... |
| | Spanga | Sweden-4 | 6 | 6 | 4 | 10 | 0 | .... | .... | .... | .... | .... | .... | .... | .... | .... | .... | .... | .... | .... | .... | .... | .... | .... | .... |
| 2005-06 | Djurgarden U18 | Swe-U18 | 8 | 8 | 5 | 13 | 6 | .... | .... | .... | .... | .... | .... | .... | .... | .... | 2 | 1 | 0 | 1 | 0 | .... | .... | .... | .... |
| | Djurgarden Jr. | Swe-Jr. | 25 | 8 | 5 | 13 | 41 | .... | .... | .... | .... | .... | .... | .... | .... | .... | 4 | 2 | 0 | 2 | 0 | .... | .... | .... | .... |
| 2006-07 | Chilliwack Bruins | WHL | 68 | 32 | 37 | 69 | 50 | .... | .... | .... | .... | .... | .... | .... | .... | .... | 5 | 0 | 3 | 3 | 6 | .... | .... | .... | .... |
| 2007-08 | Chilliwack Bruins | WHL | 63 | 39 | 43 | 82 | 42 | .... | .... | .... | .... | .... | .... | .... | .... | .... | 4 | 2 | 1 | 3 | 4 | .... | .... | .... | .... |
| | Manchester | AHL | .... | .... | .... | .... | .... | .... | .... | .... | .... | .... | .... | .... | .... | .... | 2 | 0 | 1 | 1 | 0 | .... | .... | .... | .... |
| **2008-09** | **Los Angeles** | **NHL** | **40** | **7** | **8** | **15** | **16** | **5** | **0** | **0** | **81** | **8.6** | **-3** | **86** | **43.0** | **13:22** | .... | .... | .... | .... | .... | .... | .... | .... | .... |
| | Manchester | AHL | 8 | 2 | 3 | 5 | 6 | .... | .... | .... | .... | .... | .... | .... | .... | .... | .... | .... | .... | .... | .... | .... | .... | .... | .... |
| | **NHL Totals** | | **40** | **7** | **8** | **15** | **16** | **5** | **0** | **0** | **81** | **8.6** | | **86** | **43.0** | **13:22** | .... | .... | .... | .... | .... | .... | .... | .... | .... |

WHL West First All-Star Team (2008)

## MONTADOR, Steve

(MAWN-tuh-dohr, STEEV) **BUF.**

Defense. Shoots right. 6', 210 lbs. Born, Vancouver, B.C., December 21, 1979.

| Season | Club | League | GP | G | A | Pts | PIM | PP | SH | GW | S | % | +/- | TF | F% | Min | GP | G | A | Pts | PIM | PP | SH | GW | Min |
|---|---|---|---|---|---|---|---|---|---|---|---|---|---|---|---|---|---|---|---|---|---|---|---|---|---|
| | | | Regular Season | | | | | | | | | | | | | | Playoffs | | | | | | | | |
| 1995-96 | St. Mike's B's | OPJHL | 46 | 3 | 16 | 19 | 145 | | | | | | | | | | 7 | 1 | 2 | 3 | 10 | | | | |
| 1996-97 | North Bay | OHL | 63 | 7 | 28 | 35 | 129 | | | | | | | | | | | | | | | | | | |
| 1997-98 | North Bay | OHL | 37 | 5 | 16 | 21 | 54 | | | | | | | | | | | | | | | | | | |
| | Erie Otters | OHL | 26 | 3 | 17 | 20 | 35 | | | | | | | | | | 7 | 1 | 1 | 2 | 9 | | | | |
| 1998-99 | Erie Otters | OHL | 61 | 9 | 33 | 42 | 114 | | | | | | | | | | 5 | 0 | 2 | 2 | 4 | | | | |
| 99-2000 | Peterborough | OHL | 64 | 14 | 42 | 56 | 97 | | | | | | | | | | 5 | 0 | 2 | 2 | 4 | | | | |
| | Saint John Flames | AHL | | | | | | | | | | | | | | | 2 | 0 | 0 | 0 | 0 | | | | |
| 2000-01 | Saint John Flames | AHL | 58 | 1 | 6 | 7 | 95 | | | | | | | | | | 19 | 0 | 8 | 8 | 13 | | | | |
| **2001-02** | **Calgary** | **NHL** | **11** | **1** | **2** | **3** | **26** | **0** | **0** | **0** | **10** | **10.0** | **–2** | **0** | **0.0** | **12:12** | | | | | | | | | |
| | Saint John Flames | AHL | 67 | 9 | 16 | 25 | 107 | | | | | | | | | | | | | | | | | | |
| **2002-03** | **Calgary** | **NHL** | **50** | **1** | **1** | **2** | **114** | **0** | **0** | **0** | **64** | **1.6** | **–9** | **0** | **0.0** | **15:11** | | | | | | | | | |
| | Saint John Flames | AHL | 11 | 1 | 7 | 8 | 20 | | | | | | | | | | | | | | | | | | |
| **2003-04** | **Calgary** | **NHL** | **26** | **1** | **2** | **3** | **50** | **0** | **0** | **1** | **31** | **3.2** | **–1** | **1** | **0.0** | **11:46** | **20** | **1** | **2** | **3** | **6** | **0** | **0** | **1** | **17:43** |
| 2004-05 | HC Mulhouse | France | 15 | 1 | 7 | 8 | 69 | | | | | | | | | | | | | | | | | | |
| **2005-06** | **Calgary** | **NHL** | **7** | **1** | **0** | **1** | **11** | **0** | **0** | **0** | **13** | **7.7** | **0** | **0** | **0.0** | **11:49** | | | | | | | | | |
| | **Florida** | **NHL** | **51** | **1** | **5** | **6** | **68** | **0** | **0** | **0** | **42** | **2.4** | **4** | **0** | **0.0** | **14:04** | | | | | | | | | |
| **2006-07** | **Florida** | **NHL** | **72** | **1** | **8** | **9** | **119** | **0** | **0** | **0** | **88** | **1.1** | **1** | **0** | **0.0** | **13:08** | | | | | | | | | |
| **2007-08** | **Florida** | **NHL** | **73** | **8** | **15** | **23** | **73** | **2** | **0** | **0** | **96** | **8.3** | **1** | **0** | **0.0** | **11:39** | | | | | | | | | |
| **2008-09** | **Anaheim** | **NHL** | **65** | **4** | **16** | **20** | **125** | **0** | **0** | **0** | **100** | **4.0** | **14** | **0** | **0.0** | **16:12** | | | | | | | | | |
| | **Boston** | **NHL** | **13** | **0** | **1** | **1** | **18** | **0** | **0** | **0** | **17** | **0.0** | **3** | **1** | **0.0** | **15:55** | **11** | **1** | **2** | **3** | **18** | **0** | **0** | **0** | **19:33** |
| | **NHL Totals** | | **368** | **18** | **50** | **68** | **604** | **2** | **0** | **1** | **461** | **3.9** | | **2** | **0.0** | **13:45** | **31** | **2** | **4** | **6** | **24** | **0** | **0** | **1** | **18:22** |

Signed as a free agent by **Calgary**, April 10, 2000. • Spent majority of 2003-04 season serving as a healthy reserve. Signed as a free agent by **Mulhouse** (France), September 17, 2004. Traded to **Florida** by **Calgary** with Dustin Johner for Kristian Huselius, December 2, 2005. Signed as a free agent by **Anaheim**, July 11, 2008. Traded to **Boston** by **Anaheim** for Petteri Nokelainen, March 4, 2009. Signed as a free agent by **Buffalo**, July 1, 2009.

## MOORE, Dominic

(MOOR, DOHM-ihn-ihk)

Center. Shoots left. 6', 188 lbs. Born, Sarnia, Ont., August 3, 1980. NY Rangers' 2nd choice, 95th overall, in 2000 Entry Draft.

| Season | Club | League | GP | G | A | Pts | PIM | PP | SH | GW | S | % | +/- | TF | F% | Min | GP | G | A | Pts | PIM | PP | SH | GW | Min |
|---|---|---|---|---|---|---|---|---|---|---|---|---|---|---|---|---|---|---|---|---|---|---|---|---|---|
| 1996-97 | Thornhill Islanders | MTJHL | 29 | 4 | 6 | 10 | 48 | | | | | | | | | | 1 | 0 | 1 | 1 | 0 | | | | |
| 1997-98 | Aurora Tigers | OPJHL | 51 | 10 | 15 | 25 | 16 | | | | | | | | | | | | | | | | | | |
| 1998-99 | Aurora Tigers | OPJHL | 51 | 34 | 53 | 87 | 70 | | | | | | | | | | | | | | | | | | |
| 99-2000 | Harvard Crimson | ECAC | 30 | 12 | 24 | 28 | 16 | | | | | | | | | | | | | | | | | | |
| 2000-01 | Harvard Crimson | ECAC | 32 | 15 | 28 | 43 | 40 | | | | | | | | | | | | | | | | | | |
| 2001-02 | Harvard Crimson | ECAC | 32 | 13 | 16 | 29 | 37 | | | | | | | | | | | | | | | | | | |
| 2002-03 | Harvard Crimson | ECAC | 34 | *24 | 27 | *51 | 30 | | | | | | | | | | | | | | | | | | |
| **2003-04** | **NY Rangers** | **NHL** | **5** | **0** | **3** | **3** | **0** | **0** | **0** | **0** | **3** | **0.0** | **0** | **36** | **30.6** | **9:18** | | | | | | | | | |
| | Hartford | AHL | 70 | 14 | 25 | 39 | 60 | | | | | | | | | | 16 | 3 | 3 | 6 | 8 | | | | |
| 2004-05 | Hartford | AHL | 78 | 19 | 31 | 50 | 78 | | | | | | | | | | 6 | 1 | 1 | 2 | 4 | | | | |
| **2005-06** | **NY Rangers** | **NHL** | **82** | **9** | **9** | **18** | **28** | **2** | **0** | **1** | **139** | **6.5** | **4** | **814** | **46.3** | **12:28** | **4** | **0** | **0** | **0** | **2** | **0** | **0** | **0** | **11:21** |
| **2006-07** | **Pittsburgh** | **NHL** | **59** | **6** | **9** | **15** | **46** | **0** | **0** | **0** | **100** | **6.0** | **1** | **678** | **51.6** | **13:04** | | | | | | | | | |
| | **Minnesota** | **NHL** | **10** | **2** | **0** | **2** | **10** | **0** | **0** | **1** | **11** | **18.2** | **3** | **66** | **62.1** | **10:12** | | | | | | | | | |
| **2007-08** | **Minnesota** | **NHL** | **30** | **1** | **2** | **3** | **10** | **0** | **0** | **0** | **28** | **3.6** | **–11** | **311** | **52.4** | **11:57** | | | | | | | | | |
| | **Toronto** | **NHL** | **38** | **4** | **10** | **14** | **14** | **1** | **0** | **0** | **72** | **5.6** | **7** | **393** | **50.6** | **14:21** | | | | | | | | | |
| **2008-09** | **Toronto** | **NHL** | **63** | **12** | **29** | **41** | **69** | **4** | **1** | **1** | **132** | **9.1** | **–1** | **1007** | **54.8** | **17:18** | | | | | | | | | |
| | **Buffalo** | **NHL** | **18** | **1** | **3** | **4** | **23** | **0** | **0** | **0** | **33** | **3.0** | **–1** | **237** | **51.1** | **15:12** | | | | | | | | | |
| | **NHL Totals** | | **305** | **35** | **65** | **100** | **200** | **7** | **1** | **3** | **518** | **6.8** | | **3542** | **51.2** | **13:48** | **4** | **0** | **0** | **0** | **2** | **0** | **0** | **0** | **11:21** |

ECAC All-Rookie Team (2000) • ECAC Second All-Star Team (2001) • ECAC First All-Star Team (2003) • NCAA East First All-American Team (2003)

Traded to **Nashville** by **NY Rangers** for Adam Hall, July 19, 2006. Traded to **Pittsburgh** by **Nashville** with Libor Pivko for Pittsburgh's 3rd round choice (Ryan Thang) in 2007 Entry Draft, July 19, 2006. Traded to **Minnesota** by **Pittsburgh** for Minnesota's 3rd round choice (Casey Pierro-Zabotel) in 2007 Entry Draft, February 27, 2007. Claimed on waivers by **Toronto** from **Minnesota**, January 11, 2008. Traded to **Buffalo** by **Toronto** for Carolina's 2nd round choice (previously acquired, Toronto selected Jesse Blacker) in 2009 Entry Draft, March 4, 2009.

## MOORE, Greg

(MOOR, GREHG) **NYI**

Right wing. Shoots right. 6'1", 210 lbs. Born, Lisbon, ME, March 26, 1984. Calgary's 5th choice, 143rd overall, in 2003 Entry Draft.

| Season | Club | League | GP | G | A | Pts | PIM | PP | SH | GW | S | % | +/- | TF | F% | Min | GP | G | A | Pts | PIM | PP | SH | GW | Min |
|---|---|---|---|---|---|---|---|---|---|---|---|---|---|---|---|---|---|---|---|---|---|---|---|---|---|
| 99-2000 | St. Dominic | High-ME | 31 | 32 | 40 | 72 | | | | | | | | | | | | | | | | | | | |
| 2000-01 | USNTDP | U-17 | 13 | 4 | 6 | 10 | 1 | | | | | | | | | | | | | | | | | | |
| | USNTDP | NAHL | 56 | 8 | 12 | 20 | 22 | | | | | | | | | | | | | | | | | | |
| 2001-02 | USNTDP | U-18 | 35 | 8 | 20 | 28 | 14 | | | | | | | | | | | | | | | | | | |
| | USNTDP | USHL | 12 | 2 | 2 | 4 | 4 | | | | | | | | | | | | | | | | | | |
| | USNTDP | NAHL | 6 | 3 | 2 | 5 | 2 | | | | | | | | | | | | | | | | | | |
| 2002-03 | U. of Maine | H-East | 33 | 9 | 7 | 16 | 10 | | | | | | | | | | | | | | | | | | |
| 2003-04 | U. of Maine | H-East | 39 | 15 | 8 | 23 | 44 | | | | | | | | | | | | | | | | | | |
| 2004-05 | U. of Maine | H-East | 40 | 14 | 9 | 23 | 16 | | | | | | | | | | | | | | | | | | |
| 2005-06 | U. of Maine | H-East | 42 | 28 | 17 | 45 | 47 | | | | | | | | | | | | | | | | | | |
| | Hartford | AHL | 2 | 1 | 1 | 2 | 2 | | | | | | | | | | 13 | 2 | 5 | 7 | 6 | | | | |
| 2006-07 | Hartford | AHL | 79 | 8 | 17 | 25 | 41 | | | | | | | | | | 7 | 0 | 1 | 1 | 4 | | | | |
| **2007-08** | **NY Rangers** | **NHL** | **6** | **0** | **0** | **0** | **0** | **0** | **0** | **0** | **13** | **0.0** | **–2** | **8** | **37.5** | **11:49** | | | | | | | | | |
| | Hartford | AHL | 72 | 26 | 40 | 66 | 31 | | | | | | | | | | 5 | 1 | 2 | 3 | 2 | | | | |
| 2008-09 | Hartford | AHL | 71 | 23 | 16 | 39 | 28 | | | | | | | | | | 6 | 0 | 2 | 2 | 0 | | | | |
| | **NHL Totals** | | **6** | **0** | **0** | **0** | **0** | **0** | **0** | **0** | **13** | **0.0** | | **8** | **37.5** | **11:49** | | | | | | | | | |

Hockey East First All-Star Team (2006) • NCAA East First All-American Team (2006)

Traded to **NY Rangers** by **Calgary** with Jamie McLennan and Blair Betts for Chris Simon and NY Rangers' 7th round choice (Matt Schneider) in 2004 Entry Draft, March 6, 2004. Signed as a free agent by **NY Islanders**, July 6, 2009.

## MOREAU, Ethan

(moh-ROH, EE-thuhn) **EDM.**

Left wing. Shoots left. 6'2", 220 lbs. Born, Huntsville, Ont., September 22, 1975. Chicago's 1st choice, 14th overall, in 1994 Entry Draft.

| Season | Club | League | GP | G | A | Pts | PIM | PP | SH | GW | S | % | +/- | TF | F% | Min | GP | G | A | Pts | PIM | PP | SH | GW | Min |
|---|---|---|---|---|---|---|---|---|---|---|---|---|---|---|---|---|---|---|---|---|---|---|---|---|---|
| 1990-91 | Orillia Terriers | OHA-B | 42 | 17 | 22 | 39 | 26 | | | | | | | | | | 12 | 6 | 6 | 12 | 18 | | | | |
| 1991-92 | Niagara Falls | OHL | 62 | 20 | 35 | 55 | 39 | | | | | | | | | | 17 | 4 | 6 | 10 | 4 | | | | |
| 1992-93 | Niagara Falls | OHL | 65 | 32 | 41 | 73 | 69 | | | | | | | | | | 4 | 0 | 3 | 3 | 4 | | | | |
| 1993-94 | Niagara Falls | OHL | 59 | 44 | 54 | 98 | 100 | | | | | | | | | | | | | | | | | | |
| 1994-95 | Niagara Falls | OHL | 39 | 25 | 41 | 66 | 69 | | | | | | | | | | | | | | | | | | |
| | Sudbury Wolves | OHL | 23 | 13 | 17 | 30 | 22 | | | | | | | | | | 18 | 6 | 12 | 18 | 26 | | | | |
| **1995-96** | **Chicago** | **NHL** | **8** | **0** | **1** | **1** | **4** | **0** | **0** | **0** | **1** | **0.0** | **1** | | | | | | | | | | | | |
| | Indianapolis Ice | IHL | 71 | 21 | 20 | 41 | 126 | | | | | | | | | | 5 | 4 | 0 | 4 | 8 | | | | |
| **1996-97** | **Chicago** | **NHL** | **82** | **15** | **16** | **31** | **123** | **0** | **0** | **1** | **114** | **13.2** | **13** | | | | **6** | **1** | **0** | **1** | **9** | **0** | **0** | **0** | |
| **1997-98** | **Chicago** | **NHL** | **54** | **9** | **9** | **18** | **73** | **2** | **0** | **0** | **87** | **10.3** | **0** | | | | | | | | | | | | |
| **1998-99** | **Chicago** | **NHL** | **66** | **9** | **6** | **15** | **84** | **0** | **0** | **1** | **80** | **11.3** | **–5** | **3** | **33.3** | **12:30** | | | | | | | | | |
| | **Edmonton** | **NHL** | **14** | **1** | **5** | **6** | **8** | **0** | **0** | **1** | **16** | **6.3** | **2** | **1** | **0.0** | **11:47** | **4** | **0** | **3** | **3** | **6** | **0** | **0** | **0** | **17:26** |
| **99-2000** | **Edmonton** | **NHL** | **73** | **17** | **10** | **27** | **62** | **1** | **0** | **3** | **106** | **16.0** | **8** | **8** | **62.5** | **15:07** | **5** | **0** | **1** | **1** | **0** | **0** | **0** | **0** | **15:46** |
| **2000-01** | **Edmonton** | **NHL** | **68** | **9** | **10** | **19** | **90** | **0** | **1** | **3** | **97** | **9.3** | **–6** | **2** | **0.0** | **14:11** | **4** | **0** | **0** | **0** | **2** | **0** | **0** | **0** | **10:35** |
| **2001-02** | **Edmonton** | **NHL** | **80** | **11** | **5** | **16** | **81** | **0** | **2** | **1** | **129** | **8.5** | **4** | **11** | **54.6** | **12:43** | | | | | | | | | |
| **2002-03** | **Edmonton** | **NHL** | **78** | **14** | **17** | **31** | **112** | **2** | **3** | **2** | **137** | **10.2** | **–7** | **25** | **12.0** | **13:30** | **6** | **0** | **1** | **1** | **16** | **0** | **0** | **0** | **12:23** |
| **2003-04** | **Edmonton** | **NHL** | **81** | **20** | **12** | **32** | **96** | **0** | **3** | **5** | **180** | **11.1** | **7** | **59** | **44.1** | **15:04** | | | | | | | | | |
| 2004-05 | EC Villacher SV | Austria | 16 | 10 | 6 | 16 | 73 | | | | | | | | | | 3 | 4 | 0 | 4 | 0 | | | | |
| **2005-06** | **Edmonton** | **NHL** | **74** | **11** | **16** | **27** | **87** | **2** | **4** | **4** | **151** | **7.3** | **6** | **29** | **48.3** | **15:59** | **21** | **2** | **1** | **3** | **19** | **0** | **0** | **0** | **14:35** |
| **2006-07** | **Edmonton** | **NHL** | **7** | **1** | **0** | **1** | **12** | **0** | **0** | **0** | **18** | **5.6** | **–4** | **20** | **50.0** | **15:08** | | | | | | | | | |
| **2007-08** | **Edmonton** | **NHL** | **25** | **5** | **4** | **9** | **39** | **1** | **0** | **0** | **54** | **9.3** | **–4** | **23** | **43.5** | **15:55** | | | | | | | | | |
| **2008-09** | **Edmonton** | **NHL** | **77** | **14** | **12** | **26** | **133** | **0** | **1** | **2** | **159** | **8.8** | **0** | **36** | **30.6** | **15:22** | | | | | | | | | |
| | **NHL Totals** | | **787** | **136** | **123** | **259** | **1004** | **8** | **14** | **23** | **1329** | **10.2** | | **217** | **39.6** | **14:20** | **46** | **3** | **6** | **9** | **52** | **0** | **0** | **0** | **14:17** |

OHL All-Rookie Team (1992) • King Clancy Memorial Trophy (2009)

Traded to **Edmonton** by **Chicago** with Daniel Cleary, Chad Kilger and Christian Laflamme for Boris Mironov, Dean McAmmond and Jonas Elofsson, March 20, 1999. Signed as a free agent by **Villacher** (Austria), December 20, 2004. • Missed majority of 2006-07 season recovering from shoulder injury suffered in game vs. Detroit, October 21, 2006. • Missed majority of 2007-08 season recovering from fractured left foot injury suffered in training camp.

## MORMINA, Joey

(mohr-MEE-nah, JOH-ee) **PHI.**

Defense. Shoots left. 6'6", 220 lbs. Born, Montreal, Que., June 29, 1982. Philadelphia's 6th choice, 193rd overall, in 2002 Entry Draft.

| | | | Regular Season | | | | | | | | | | | | | | Playoffs | | | | | | | | |
|---|---|---|---|---|---|---|---|---|---|---|---|---|---|---|---|---|---|---|---|---|---|---|---|---|---|
| Season | Club | League | GP | G | A | Pts | PIM | PP | SH | GW | S | % | +/- | TF | F% | Min | GP | G | A | Pts | PIM | PP | SH | GW | Min |
| 2000-01 | Holderness | High-NH | 29 | 15 | 15 | 30 | .... | .... | .... | .... | .... | .... | .... | .... | .... | .... | .... | .... | .... | .... | .... | .... | .... | .... | .... |
| 2001-02 | Colgate | ECAC | 34 | 2 | 13 | 15 | 28 | .... | .... | .... | .... | .... | .... | .... | .... | .... | .... | .... | .... | .... | .... | .... | .... | .... | .... |
| 2002-03 | Colgate | ECAC | 40 | 4 | 9 | 13 | 52 | .... | .... | .... | .... | .... | .... | .... | .... | .... | .... | .... | .... | .... | .... | .... | .... | .... | .... |
| 2003-04 | Colgate | ECAC | 28 | 2 | 10 | 12 | 26 | .... | .... | .... | .... | .... | .... | .... | .... | .... | .... | .... | .... | .... | .... | .... | .... | .... | .... |
| 2004-05 | Colgate | ECAC | 39 | 8 | 8 | 16 | 50 | .... | .... | .... | .... | .... | .... | .... | .... | .... | .... | .... | .... | .... | .... | .... | .... | .... | .... |
| 2005-06 | Manchester | AHL | 61 | 0 | 13 | 13 | 70 | .... | .... | .... | .... | .... | .... | .... | .... | .... | 7 | 0 | 0 | 0 | 4 | .... | .... | .... | .... |
| 2006-07 | Manchester | AHL | 62 | 2 | 9 | 11 | 108 | .... | .... | .... | .... | .... | .... | .... | .... | .... | 1 | 0 | 0 | 0 | 2 | .... | .... | .... | .... |
| **2007-08** | **Carolina** | **NHL** | **1** | **0** | **0** | **0** | **0** | **0** | **0** | **0** | **1** | **0.0** | **0** | **0** | **0.0** | **7:45** | .... | .... | .... | .... | .... | .... | .... | .... | .... |
| | Albany River Rats | AHL | 77 | 4 | 9 | 13 | 96 | .... | .... | .... | .... | .... | .... | .... | .... | .... | 7 | 0 | 0 | 0 | 4 | .... | .... | .... | .... |
| 2008-09 | Wilkes-Barre | AHL | 70 | 2 | 9 | 11 | 71 | .... | .... | .... | .... | .... | .... | .... | .... | .... | 12 | 0 | 0 | 0 | 12 | .... | .... | .... | .... |
| | **NHL Totals** | | **1** | **0** | **0** | **0** | **0** | **0** | **0** | **0** | **1** | **0.0** | | **0** | **0.0** | **7:45** | .... | .... | .... | .... | .... | .... | .... | .... | .... |

Signed as a free agent by **Los Angeles**, August 24, 2005. Signed as a free agent by **Carolina**, July 2, 2007. Signed as a free agent by **Pittsburgh**, July 10, 2008.

## MORRIS, Derek

(MOH-rihs, DAIR-ihk) **BOS.**

Defense. Shoots right. 6', 221 lbs. Born, Edmonton, Alta., August 24, 1978. Calgary's 1st choice, 13th overall, in 1996 Entry Draft.

| Season | Club | League | GP | G | A | Pts | PIM | PP | SH | GW | S | % | +/- | TF | F% | Min | GP | G | A | Pts | PIM | PP | SH | GW | Min |
|---|---|---|---|---|---|---|---|---|---|---|---|---|---|---|---|---|---|---|---|---|---|---|---|---|---|
| 1994-95 | Red Deer Vipers | AMHL | 31 | 6 | 35 | 41 | 74 | .... | .... | .... | .... | .... | .... | .... | .... | .... | .... | .... | .... | .... | .... | .... | .... | .... | .... |
| 1995-96 | Regina Pats | WHL | 67 | 8 | 44 | 52 | 70 | .... | .... | .... | .... | .... | .... | .... | .... | .... | 11 | 1 | 7 | 8 | 26 | .... | .... | .... | .... |
| 1996-97 | Regina Pats | WHL | 67 | 18 | 57 | 75 | 180 | .... | .... | .... | .... | .... | .... | .... | .... | .... | 5 | 0 | 3 | 3 | 9 | .... | .... | .... | .... |
| | Saint John Flames | AHL | 7 | 0 | 3 | 3 | 7 | .... | .... | .... | .... | .... | .... | .... | .... | .... | 5 | 0 | 3 | 3 | 7 | .... | .... | .... | .... |
| **1997-98** | **Calgary** | **NHL** | **82** | **9** | **20** | **29** | **88** | **5** | **1** | **1** | **120** | **7.5** | **1** | .... | .... | .... | .... | .... | .... | .... | .... | .... | .... | .... | .... |
| **1998-99** | **Calgary** | **NHL** | **71** | **7** | **27** | **34** | **73** | **3** | **0** | **2** | **150** | **4.7** | **4** | **0** | **0.0** | **20:44** | .... | .... | .... | .... | .... | .... | .... | .... | .... |
| **99-2000** | **Calgary** | **NHL** | **78** | **9** | **29** | **38** | **80** | **3** | **0** | **2** | **193** | **4.7** | **2** | **0** | **0.0** | **24:51** | .... | .... | .... | .... | .... | .... | .... | .... | .... |
| **2000-01** | **Calgary** | **NHL** | **51** | **5** | **23** | **28** | **56** | **3** | **1** | **4** | **142** | **3.5** | **–15** | **0** | **0.0** | **25:51** | .... | .... | .... | .... | .... | .... | .... | .... | .... |
| | Saint John Flames | AHL | 3 | 1 | 2 | 3 | 2 | .... | .... | .... | .... | .... | .... | .... | .... | .... | .... | .... | .... | .... | .... | .... | .... | .... | .... |
| **2001-02** | **Calgary** | **NHL** | **61** | **4** | **30** | **34** | **88** | **2** | **0** | **1** | **166** | **2.4** | **–4** | **1** | **100.0** | **24:40** | .... | .... | .... | .... | .... | .... | .... | .... | .... |
| **2002-03** | **Colorado** | **NHL** | **75** | **11** | **37** | **48** | **68** | **9** | **0** | **7** | **191** | **5.8** | **16** | **0** | **0.0** | **23:49** | **7** | **0** | **3** | **3** | **6** | **0** | **0** | **0** | **22:44** |
| **2003-04** | **Colorado** | **NHL** | **69** | **6** | **22** | **28** | **47** | **2** | **0** | **1** | **139** | **4.3** | **4** | **0** | **0.0** | **20:53** | .... | .... | .... | .... | .... | .... | .... | .... | .... |
| | **Phoenix** | **NHL** | **14** | **0** | **4** | **4** | **2** | **0** | **0** | **0** | **28** | **0.0** | **–5** | **0** | **0.0** | **25:02** | .... | .... | .... | .... | .... | .... | .... | .... | .... |
| 2004-05 | | | DID NOT PLAY | | | | | | | | | | | | | | | | | | | | | | |
| **2005-06** | **Phoenix** | **NHL** | **53** | **6** | **21** | **27** | **54** | **4** | **1** | **2** | **91** | **6.6** | **–7** | **1** | **0.0** | **20:52** | .... | .... | .... | .... | .... | .... | .... | .... | .... |
| **2006-07** | **Phoenix** | **NHL** | **82** | **6** | **19** | **25** | **115** | **2** | **0** | **1** | **129** | **4.7** | **–18** | **1** | **100.0** | **20:29** | .... | .... | .... | .... | .... | .... | .... | .... | .... |
| **2007-08** | **Phoenix** | **NHL** | **82** | **8** | **17** | **25** | **83** | **2** | **0** | **0** | **135** | **5.9** | **8** | **1** | **0.0** | **21:43** | .... | .... | .... | .... | .... | .... | .... | .... | .... |
| **2008-09** | **Phoenix** | **NHL** | **57** | **5** | **7** | **12** | **24** | **0** | **1** | **0** | **89** | **5.6** | **–13** | **0** | **0.0** | **21:16** | .... | .... | .... | .... | .... | .... | .... | .... | .... |
| | **NY Rangers** | **NHL** | **18** | **0** | **8** | **8** | **16** | **0** | **0** | **0** | **31** | **0.0** | **3** | **0** | **0.0** | **19:41** | **7** | **0** | **2** | **2** | **0** | **0** | **0** | **0** | **16:24** |
| | **NHL Totals** | | **793** | **76** | **264** | **340** | **794** | **35** | **4** | **21** | **1604** | **4.7** | | **4** | **50.0** | **22:25** | **14** | **0** | **5** | **5** | **6** | **0** | **0** | **0** | **19:34** |

WHL East First All-Star Team (1997) • NHL All-Rookie Team (1998)

Traded to **Colorado** by **Calgary** with Jeff Shantz and Dean McAmmond for Chris Drury and Stephane Yelle, October 1, 2002. Traded to **Phoenix** by **Colorado** with Keith Ballard for Ossi Vaananen, Chris Gratton and Phoenix's 2nd round choice (Paul Stastny) in 2005 Entry Draft, March 9, 2004. Traded to **NY Rangers** by **Phoenix** for Dmitri Kalinin, Nigel Dawes and Petr Prucha, March 4, 2009. Signed as a free agent by **Boston**, July 25, 2009.

## MORRISON, Brendan

(MOHR-ih-suhn, BREHN-duhn) **WSH.**

Center. Shoots left. 5'11", 181 lbs. Born, Pitt Meadows, B.C., August 15, 1975. New Jersey's 3rd choice, 39th overall, in 1993 Entry Draft.

| Season | Club | League | GP | G | A | Pts | PIM | PP | SH | GW | S | % | +/- | TF | F% | Min | GP | G | A | Pts | PIM | PP | SH | GW | Min |
|---|---|---|---|---|---|---|---|---|---|---|---|---|---|---|---|---|---|---|---|---|---|---|---|---|---|
| 1990-91 | Ridge Meadows | Minor-BC | 77 | 126 | 127 | 253 | 88 | .... | .... | .... | .... | .... | .... | .... | .... | .... | .... | .... | .... | .... | .... | .... | .... | .... | .... |
| 1991-92 | Ridge Meadows | Minor-BC | 55 | 56 | 111 | 167 | 56 | .... | .... | .... | .... | .... | .... | .... | .... | .... | .... | .... | .... | .... | .... | .... | .... | .... | .... |
| 1992-93 | Penticton | BCJHL | 56 | 35 | 59 | 94 | 45 | .... | .... | .... | .... | .... | .... | .... | .... | .... | .... | .... | .... | .... | .... | .... | .... | .... | .... |
| 1993-94 | U. of Michigan | CCHA | 38 | 20 | 28 | 48 | 24 | .... | .... | .... | .... | .... | .... | .... | .... | .... | .... | .... | .... | .... | .... | .... | .... | .... | .... |
| 1994-95 | U. of Michigan | CCHA | 39 | 23 | *53 | *76 | 42 | .... | .... | .... | .... | .... | .... | .... | .... | .... | .... | .... | .... | .... | .... | .... | .... | .... | .... |
| 1995-96 | U. of Michigan | CCHA | 35 | 28 | 44 | *72 | 41 | .... | .... | .... | .... | .... | .... | .... | .... | .... | .... | .... | .... | .... | .... | .... | .... | .... | .... |
| 1996-97 | U. of Michigan | CCHA | 43 | 31 | *57 | *88 | 52 | .... | .... | .... | .... | .... | .... | .... | .... | .... | .... | .... | .... | .... | .... | .... | .... | .... | .... |
| **1997-98** | **New Jersey** | **NHL** | **11** | **5** | **4** | **9** | **0** | **0** | **0** | **1** | **19** | **26.3** | **3** | .... | .... | .... | **3** | **0** | **1** | **1** | **0** | **0** | **0** | **0** | .... |
| | Albany River Rats | AHL | 72 | 35 | 49 | 84 | 44 | .... | .... | .... | .... | .... | .... | .... | .... | .... | 8 | 3 | 4 | 7 | 19 | .... | .... | .... | .... |
| **1998-99** | **New Jersey** | **NHL** | **76** | **13** | **33** | **46** | **18** | **5** | **0** | **2** | **111** | **11.7** | **–4** | **920** | **51.1** | **13:55** | **7** | **0** | **2** | **2** | **0** | **0** | **0** | **0** | **13:04** |
| 99-2000 | Trebic | CzRep-2 | 2 | 0 | 0 | 0 | 0 | .... | .... | .... | .... | .... | .... | .... | .... | .... | .... | .... | .... | .... | .... | .... | .... | .... | .... |
| | Pardubice | CzRep | 6 | 5 | 2 | 7 | 2 | .... | .... | .... | .... | .... | .... | .... | .... | .... | .... | .... | .... | .... | .... | .... | .... | .... | .... |
| | **New Jersey** | **NHL** | **44** | **5** | **21** | **26** | **8** | **2** | **0** | **1** | **79** | **6.3** | **8** | **572** | **51.1** | **16:09** | .... | .... | .... | .... | .... | .... | .... | .... | .... |
| | **Vancouver** | **NHL** | **12** | **2** | **7** | **9** | **10** | **0** | **0** | **0** | **17** | **11.8** | **4** | **48** | **54.2** | **14:41** | .... | .... | .... | .... | .... | .... | .... | .... | .... |
| **2000-01** | **Vancouver** | **NHL** | **82** | **16** | **38** | **54** | **42** | **3** | **2** | **3** | **179** | **8.9** | **2** | **1685** | **50.1** | **18:22** | **4** | **1** | **2** | **3** | **0** | **1** | **0** | **0** | **20:50** |
| **2001-02** | **Vancouver** | **NHL** | **82** | **23** | **44** | **67** | **26** | **6** | **0** | **4** | **183** | **12.6** | **18** | **1307** | **49.9** | **19:21** | **6** | **0** | **2** | **2** | **6** | **0** | **0** | **0** | **19:44** |
| **2002-03** | **Vancouver** | **NHL** | **82** | **25** | **46** | **71** | **36** | **6** | **2** | **8** | **167** | **15.0** | **18** | **1585** | **48.3** | **21:13** | **14** | **4** | **7** | **11** | **18** | **1** | **0** | **1** | **20:18** |
| **2003-04** | **Vancouver** | **NHL** | **82** | **22** | **38** | **60** | **50** | **5** | **1** | **4** | **161** | **13.7** | **16** | **1486** | **51.0** | **20:08** | **7** | **2** | **3** | **5** | **8** | **1** | **0** | **1** | **22:00** |
| 2004-05 | Linkopings HC | Sweden | 45 | 16 | 28 | 44 | 50 | .... | .... | .... | .... | .... | .... | .... | .... | .... | 6 | 0 | 2 | 2 | 10 | .... | .... | .... | .... |
| **2005-06** | **Vancouver** | **NHL** | **82** | **19** | **37** | **56** | **84** | **8** | **0** | **5** | **156** | **12.2** | **–1** | **1328** | **50.5** | **19:31** | .... | .... | .... | .... | .... | .... | .... | .... | .... |
| **2006-07** | **Vancouver** | **NHL** | **82** | **20** | **31** | **51** | **60** | **6** | **2** | **3** | **139** | **14.4** | **–9** | **1230** | **50.8** | **17:57** | **12** | **1** | **3** | **4** | **6** | **0** | **0** | **0** | **23:09** |
| **2007-08** | **Vancouver** | **NHL** | **39** | **9** | **16** | **25** | **18** | **3** | **0** | **3** | **54** | **16.7** | **–3** | **370** | **45.1** | **15:23** | .... | .... | .... | .... | .... | .... | .... | .... | .... |
| **2008-09** | **Anaheim** | **NHL** | **62** | **10** | **12** | **22** | **16** | **1** | **0** | **2** | **82** | **12.2** | **0** | **350** | **46.0** | **13:51** | .... | .... | .... | .... | .... | .... | .... | .... | .... |
| | **Dallas** | **NHL** | **19** | **6** | **3** | **9** | **16** | **2** | **0** | **2** | **29** | **20.7** | **3** | **100** | **43.0** | **15:23** | .... | .... | .... | .... | .... | .... | .... | .... | .... |
| | **NHL Totals** | | **755** | **175** | **330** | **505** | **384** | **47** | **7** | **38** | **1376** | **12.7** | | **10981** | **49.8** | **17:49** | **53** | **8** | **20** | **28** | **38** | **3** | **0** | **2** | **20:11** |

CCHA Rookie of the Year (1994) • CCHA First All-Star Team (1995, 1996, 1997) • NCAA West First All-American Team (1995, 1996, 1997) • CCHA Player of the Year (1996, 1997) • NCAA Championship All-Tournament Team (1996) • NCAA Championship Tournament MVP (1996) • Hobey Baker Memorial Award (Top U.S. Collegiate Player) (1997) • AHL All-Rookie Team (1998)

Traded to **Vancouver** by **New Jersey** with Denis Pederson for Alexander Mogilny, March 14, 2000. Signed as a free agent by **Linkopings** (Sweden), September, 2004. Signed as a free agent by **Anaheim**, July 8, 2008. Claimed on waivers by **Dallas** from **Anaheim**, March 4, 2009. Signed as a free agent by **Washington**, July 10, 2009.

## MORRISONN, Shaone

(MOHR-ih-suhn, SHAWN) **WSH.**

Defense. Shoots left. 6'4", 215 lbs. Born, Vancouver, B.C., December 23, 1982. Boston's 1st choice, 19th overall, in 2001 Entry Draft.

| Season | Club | League | GP | G | A | Pts | PIM | PP | SH | GW | S | % | +/- | TF | F% | Min | GP | G | A | Pts | PIM | PP | SH | GW | Min |
|---|---|---|---|---|---|---|---|---|---|---|---|---|---|---|---|---|---|---|---|---|---|---|---|---|---|
| 1997-98 | Vancouver T-Birds | Minor-BC | 45 | 16 | 44 | 60 | 75 | .... | .... | .... | .... | .... | .... | .... | .... | .... | .... | .... | .... | .... | .... | .... | .... | .... | .... |
| 1998-99 | South Surrey | BCHL | 19 | 0 | 2 | 2 | 13 | .... | .... | .... | .... | .... | .... | .... | .... | .... | .... | .... | .... | .... | .... | .... | .... | .... | .... |
| 99-2000 | Kamloops Blazers | WHL | 57 | 1 | 6 | 7 | 80 | .... | .... | .... | .... | .... | .... | .... | .... | .... | 4 | 0 | 0 | 0 | 6 | .... | .... | .... | .... |
| 2000-01 | Kamloops Blazers | WHL | 61 | 13 | 25 | 38 | 132 | .... | .... | .... | .... | .... | .... | .... | .... | .... | 4 | 0 | 0 | 0 | 6 | .... | .... | .... | .... |
| 2001-02 | Kamloops Blazers | WHL | 61 | 11 | 26 | 37 | 106 | .... | .... | .... | .... | .... | .... | .... | .... | .... | 4 | 0 | 2 | 2 | 2 | .... | .... | .... | .... |
| **2002-03** | **Boston** | **NHL** | **11** | **0** | **0** | **0** | **8** | **0** | **0** | **0** | **4** | **0.0** | **0** | **0** | **0.0** | **8:57** | .... | .... | .... | .... | .... | .... | .... | .... | .... |
| | Providence Bruins | AHL | 60 | 5 | 16 | 21 | 103 | .... | .... | .... | .... | .... | .... | .... | .... | .... | 4 | 0 | 0 | 0 | 6 | .... | .... | .... | .... |
| **2003-04** | **Boston** | **NHL** | **30** | **1** | **7** | **8** | **10** | **0** | **0** | **0** | **13** | **7.7** | **10** | **0** | **0.0** | **18:11** | .... | .... | .... | .... | .... | .... | .... | .... | .... |
| | Providence Bruins | AHL | 18 | 0 | 2 | 2 | 16 | .... | .... | .... | .... | .... | .... | .... | .... | .... | .... | .... | .... | .... | .... | .... | .... | .... | .... |
| | **Washington** | **NHL** | **3** | **0** | **0** | **0** | **0** | **0** | **0** | **0** | **1** | **0.0** | **0** | **0** | **0.0** | **18:52** | .... | .... | .... | .... | .... | .... | .... | .... | .... |
| | Portland Pirates | AHL | 13 | 1 | 4 | 5 | 10 | .... | .... | .... | .... | .... | .... | .... | .... | .... | 7 | 0 | 1 | 1 | 4 | .... | .... | .... | .... |
| 2004-05 | Portland Pirates | AHL | 71 | 4 | 14 | 18 | 63 | .... | .... | .... | .... | .... | .... | .... | .... | .... | .... | .... | .... | .... | .... | .... | .... | .... | .... |
| **2005-06** | **Washington** | **NHL** | **80** | **1** | **13** | **14** | **91** | **0** | **0** | **0** | **56** | **1.8** | **7** | **4** | **0.0** | **20:44** | .... | .... | .... | .... | .... | .... | .... | .... | .... |
| **2006-07** | **Washington** | **NHL** | **78** | **3** | **10** | **13** | **106** | **0** | **0** | **0** | **46** | **6.5** | **3** | **2** | **0.0** | **20:57** | .... | .... | .... | .... | .... | .... | .... | .... | .... |
| **2007-08** | **Washington** | **NHL** | **76** | **1** | **9** | **10** | **63** | **0** | **0** | **1** | **47** | **2.1** | **4** | **1** | **100.0** | **20:16** | **7** | **0** | **1** | **1** | **6** | **0** | **0** | **0** | **21:18** |
| **2008-09** | **Washington** | **NHL** | **72** | **3** | **10** | **13** | **77** | **0** | **0** | **1** | **50** | **6.0** | **4** | **0** | **0.0** | **17:59** | **14** | **0** | **1** | **1** | **8** | **0** | **0** | **0** | **18:03** |
| | **NHL Totals** | | **350** | **9** | **49** | **58** | **355** | **0** | **0** | **2** | **217** | **4.1** | | **7** | **14.3** | **19:31** | **21** | **0** | **2** | **2** | **14** | **0** | **0** | **0** | **19:08** |

Traded to **Washington** by **Boston** with Boston's 1st (Jeff Schultz) and 2nd (Michail Yunkov) round choices in 2004 Entry Draft for Sergei Gonchar, March 3, 2004.

## MORROW, Brenden

(MOHR-roh, BREHN-duhn) **DAL.**

Left wing. Shoots left. 5'11", 205 lbs. Born, Carlyle, Sask., January 16, 1979. Dallas' 1st choice, 25th overall, in 1997 Entry Draft.

| Season | Club | League | GP | G | A | Pts | PIM | PP | SH | GW | S | % | +/- | TF | F% | Min | GP | G | A | Pts | PIM | PP | SH | GW | Min |
|---|---|---|---|---|---|---|---|---|---|---|---|---|---|---|---|---|---|---|---|---|---|---|---|---|---|
| 1994-95 | Estevan | SMBHL | 60 | 117 | 72 | 189 | 45 | .... | .... | .... | .... | .... | .... | .... | .... | .... | .... | .... | .... | .... | .... | .... | .... | .... | .... |
| 1995-96 | Portland | WHL | 65 | 13 | 12 | 25 | 61 | .... | .... | .... | .... | .... | .... | .... | .... | .... | 7 | 0 | 0 | 0 | 8 | .... | .... | .... | .... |
| 1996-97 | Portland | WHL | 71 | 39 | 49 | 88 | 178 | .... | .... | .... | .... | .... | .... | .... | .... | .... | 6 | 2 | 1 | 3 | 4 | .... | .... | .... | .... |
| 1997-98 | Portland | WHL | 68 | 34 | 52 | 86 | 184 | .... | .... | .... | .... | .... | .... | .... | .... | .... | 16 | 10 | 8 | 18 | 65 | .... | .... | .... | .... |
| 1998-99 | Portland | WHL | 61 | 41 | 44 | 85 | 248 | .... | .... | .... | .... | .... | .... | .... | .... | .... | 4 | 0 | 4 | 4 | 18 | .... | .... | .... | .... |
| **99-2000** | **Dallas** | **NHL** | **64** | **14** | **19** | **33** | **81** | **3** | **0** | **3** | **113** | **12.4** | **8** | **25** | **48.0** | **15:51** | **21** | **2** | **4** | **6** | **22** | **1** | **0** | **0** | **15:04** |
| | Michigan | IHL | 9 | 2 | 0 | 2 | 18 | .... | .... | .... | .... | .... | .... | .... | .... | .... | .... | .... | .... | .... | .... | .... | .... | .... | .... |
| **2000-01** | **Dallas** | **NHL** | **82** | **20** | **24** | **44** | **128** | **7** | **0** | **6** | **121** | **16.5** | **18** | **22** | **45.5** | **15:29** | **10** | **0** | **3** | **3** | **12** | **0** | **0** | **0** | **17:00** |

| Season | Club | League | GP | G | A | Pts | PIM | PP | SH | GW | S | % | +/- | TF | F% | Min | GP | G | A | Pts | PIM | PP | SH | GW | Min |
|---|---|---|---|---|---|---|---|---|---|---|---|---|---|---|---|---|---|---|---|---|---|---|---|---|---|
| | | | Regular Season | | | | | | | | | | | | | | Playoffs | | | | | | | | |
| **2001-02** | **Dallas** | **NHL** | **72** | **17** | **18** | **35** | **109** | **4** | **0** | **3** | **102** | **16.7** | **12** | **39** | **41.0** | **16:52** | .... | .... | .... | .... | .... | .... | .... | .... | .... |
| **2002-03** | **Dallas** | **NHL** | **71** | **21** | **22** | **43** | **134** | **2** | **3** | **4** | **105** | **20.0** | **20** | **29** | **27.6** | **15:43** | **12** | **3** | **5** | **8** | **16** | **2** | **0** | **0** | **21:03** |
| **2003-04** | **Dallas** | **NHL** | **81** | **25** | **24** | **49** | **121** | **9** | **0** | **3** | **132** | **18.9** | **10** | **38** | **47.4** | **19:24** | **5** | **0** | **1** | **1** | **4** | **0** | **0** | **0** | **21:29** |
| 2004-05 | Oklahoma City | CHL | 19 | 8 | 14 | 22 | 31 | .... | .... | .... | .... | .... | .... | .... | .... | .... | .... | .... | .... | .... | .... | .... | .... | .... | .... |
| **2005-06** | **Dallas** | **NHL** | **81** | **23** | **42** | **65** | **183** | **8** | **1** | **4** | **146** | **15.8** | **30** | **32** | **37.5** | **19:15** | **5** | **1** | **5** | **6** | **6** | **0** | **0** | **0** | **21:57** |
| **2006-07** | **Dallas** | **NHL** | **40** | **16** | **15** | **31** | **33** | **8** | **0** | **3** | **101** | **15.8** | **-2** | **51** | **39.2** | **18:16** | **7** | **2** | **1** | **3** | **18** | **2** | **0** | **1** | **21:54** |
| **2007-08** | **Dallas** | **NHL** | **82** | **32** | **42** | **74** | **105** | **12** | **2** | **7** | **207** | **15.5** | **23** | **41** | **39.0** | **20:00** | **18** | **9** | **6** | **15** | **22** | **4** | **0** | **2** | **23:17** |
| **2008-09** | **Dallas** | **NHL** | **18** | **5** | **10** | **15** | **49** | **2** | **0** | **0** | **52** | **9.6** | **-4** | **9** | **33.3** | **21:21** | .... | .... | .... | .... | .... | .... | .... | .... | .... |
| | **NHL Totals** | | **591** | **173** | **216** | **389** | **943** | **55** | **6** | **33** | **1079** | **16.0** | | **286** | **40.2** | **17:46** | **78** | **17** | **25** | **42** | **100** | **9** | **0** | **3** | **19:36** |

WHL West First All-Star Team (1999)

Signed as a free agent by **Oklahoma City** (CHL), October 19, 2004. • Missed majority of 2006-07 season recovering from groin (November 22, 2006 vs. Nashville) and wrist (December 26, 2006 at Chicago) injuries. • Missed majority of 2008-09 recovering from knee injury suffered in game vs. Chicago, November 20, 2008.

## MOSS, Dave

(MAWS, DAYV) **CGY.**

Left wing. Shoots left. 6'3", 200 lbs. Born, Livonia, MI, December 28, 1981. Calgary's 9th choice, 220th overall, in 2001 Entry Draft.

| Season | Club | League | GP | G | A | Pts | PIM | PP | SH | GW | S | % | +/- | TF | F% | Min | GP | G | A | Pts | PIM | PP | SH | GW | Min |
|---|---|---|---|---|---|---|---|---|---|---|---|---|---|---|---|---|---|---|---|---|---|---|---|---|---|
| 99-2000 | Catholic Central | High-MI | 28 | 18 | 20 | 28 | 20 | .... | .... | .... | .... | .... | .... | .... | .... | .... | .... | .... | .... | .... | .... | .... | .... | .... | .... |
| 2000-01 | St. Louis Jr. Blues | CSJHL | 9 | 2 | 2 | 4 | 2 | .... | .... | .... | .... | .... | .... | .... | .... | .... | .... | .... | .... | .... | .... | .... | .... | .... | .... |
| | Cedar Rapids | USHL | 51 | 20 | 18 | 38 | 14 | .... | .... | .... | .... | .... | .... | .... | .... | .... | 4 | 0 | 1 | 1 | 2 | .... | .... | .... | .... |
| 2001-02 | U. of Michigan | CCHA | 43 | 4 | 9 | 13 | 10 | .... | .... | .... | .... | .... | .... | .... | .... | .... | .... | .... | .... | .... | .... | .... | .... | .... | .... |
| 2002-03 | U. of Michigan | CCHA | 43 | 14 | 17 | 31 | 37 | .... | .... | .... | .... | .... | .... | .... | .... | .... | .... | .... | .... | .... | .... | .... | .... | .... | .... |
| 2003-04 | U. of Michigan | CCHA | 38 | 8 | 12 | 20 | 18 | .... | .... | .... | .... | .... | .... | .... | .... | .... | .... | .... | .... | .... | .... | .... | .... | .... | .... |
| 2004-05 | U. of Michigan | CCHA | 38 | 10 | 20 | 30 | 26 | .... | .... | .... | .... | .... | .... | .... | .... | .... | .... | .... | .... | .... | .... | .... | .... | .... | .... |
| 2005-06 | Omaha | AHL | 63 | 21 | 27 | 48 | 28 | .... | .... | .... | .... | .... | .... | .... | .... | .... | .... | .... | .... | .... | .... | .... | .... | .... | .... |
| **2006-07** | **Calgary** | **NHL** | **41** | **10** | **8** | **18** | **12** | **3** | **0** | **1** | **70** | **14.3** | **5** | **11** | **36.4** | **11:13** | **6** | **0** | **1** | **1** | **0** | **0** | **0** | **0** | **10:30** |
| | Omaha | AHL | 28 | 9 | 12 | 21 | 22 | .... | .... | .... | .... | .... | .... | .... | .... | .... | .... | .... | .... | .... | .... | .... | .... | .... | .... |
| **2007-08** | **Calgary** | **NHL** | **41** | **4** | **7** | **11** | **10** | **0** | **0** | **0** | **60** | **6.7** | **-4** | **17** | **41.2** | **12:24** | **5** | **1** | **1** | **2** | **4** | **0** | **0** | **0** | **10:20** |
| **2008-09** | **Calgary** | **NHL** | **81** | **20** | **19** | **39** | **22** | **8** | **0** | **4** | **194** | **10.3** | **-5** | **46** | **50.0** | **13:36** | **6** | **3** | **0** | **3** | **0** | **0** | **0** | **1** | **12:50** |
| | **NHL Totals** | | **163** | **34** | **34** | **68** | **44** | **11** | **0** | **5** | **324** | **10.5** | | **74** | **45.9** | **12:42** | **17** | **4** | **2** | **6** | **4** | **0** | **0** | **1** | **11:16** |

## MOTTAU, Mike

(MAW-tuh, MIGHK) **N.J.**

Defense. Shoots left. 6', 190 lbs. Born, Quincy, MA, March 19, 1978. NY Rangers' 10th choice, 182nd overall, in 1997 Entry Draft.

| Season | Club | League | GP | G | A | Pts | PIM | PP | SH | GW | S | % | +/- | TF | F% | Min | GP | G | A | Pts | PIM | PP | SH | GW | Min |
|---|---|---|---|---|---|---|---|---|---|---|---|---|---|---|---|---|---|---|---|---|---|---|---|---|---|
| 1994-95 | Thayer Academy | High-MA | 29 | 7 | 19 | 26 | .... | .... | .... | .... | .... | .... | .... | .... | .... | .... | .... | .... | .... | .... | .... | .... | .... | .... | .... |
| 1995-96 | Thayer Academy | High-MA | 31 | 6 | 20 | 26 | 14 | .... | .... | .... | .... | .... | .... | .... | .... | .... | .... | .... | .... | .... | .... | .... | .... | .... | .... |
| 1996-97 | Boston College | H-East | 38 | 5 | 18 | 23 | 77 | .... | .... | .... | .... | .... | .... | .... | .... | .... | .... | .... | .... | .... | .... | .... | .... | .... | .... |
| 1997-98 | Boston College | H-East | 40 | 13 | 36 | 49 | 50 | .... | .... | .... | .... | .... | .... | .... | .... | .... | .... | .... | .... | .... | .... | .... | .... | .... | .... |
| 1998-99 | Boston College | H-East | 43 | 3 | 39 | 42 | 44 | .... | .... | .... | .... | .... | .... | .... | .... | .... | .... | .... | .... | .... | .... | .... | .... | .... | .... |
| 99-2000 | Boston College | H-East | 42 | 6 | 37 | 43 | 61 | .... | .... | .... | .... | .... | .... | .... | .... | .... | .... | .... | .... | .... | .... | .... | .... | .... | .... |
| **2000-01** | **NY Rangers** | **NHL** | **18** | **0** | **3** | **3** | **13** | **0** | **0** | **0** | **17** | **0.0** | **-6** | **0** | **0.0** | **15:18** | .... | .... | .... | .... | .... | .... | .... | .... | .... |
| | Hartford | AHL | 61 | 10 | 33 | 43 | 45 | .... | .... | .... | .... | .... | .... | .... | .... | .... | 5 | 0 | 1 | 1 | 19 | .... | .... | .... | .... |
| **2001-02** | **NY Rangers** | **NHL** | **1** | **0** | **0** | **0** | **0** | **0** | **0** | **0** | **0** | **0.0** | **0** | **0** | **0.0** | **6:20** | .... | .... | .... | .... | .... | .... | .... | .... | .... |
| | Hartford | AHL | 80 | 9 | 42 | 51 | 56 | .... | .... | .... | .... | .... | .... | .... | .... | .... | 10 | 0 | 5 | 5 | 4 | .... | .... | .... | .... |
| 2002-03 | Hartford | AHL | 29 | 1 | 18 | 19 | 24 | .... | .... | .... | .... | .... | .... | .... | .... | .... | .... | .... | .... | .... | .... | .... | .... | .... | .... |
| | **Calgary** | **NHL** | **4** | **0** | **0** | **0** | **0** | **0** | **0** | **0** | **0** | **0.0** | **-1** | **0** | **0.0** | **9:50** | .... | .... | .... | .... | .... | .... | .... | .... | .... |
| | Saint John Flames | AHL | 32 | 5 | 12 | 17 | 14 | .... | .... | .... | .... | .... | .... | .... | .... | .... | .... | .... | .... | .... | .... | .... | .... | .... | .... |
| 2003-04 | Cincinnati | AHL | 69 | 9 | 22 | 31 | 79 | .... | .... | .... | .... | .... | .... | .... | .... | .... | 9 | 1 | 2 | 3 | 8 | .... | .... | .... | .... |
| 2004-05 | Worcester IceCats | AHL | 73 | 4 | 31 | 35 | 23 | .... | .... | .... | .... | .... | .... | .... | .... | .... | .... | .... | .... | .... | .... | .... | .... | .... | .... |
| 2005-06 | Peoria Rivermen | AHL | 76 | 8 | 48 | 56 | 81 | .... | .... | .... | .... | .... | .... | .... | .... | .... | 4 | 0 | 1 | 1 | 6 | .... | .... | .... | .... |
| 2006-07 | Lowell Devils | AHL | 43 | 1 | 26 | 27 | 33 | .... | .... | .... | .... | .... | .... | .... | .... | .... | .... | .... | .... | .... | .... | .... | .... | .... | .... |
| **2007-08** | **New Jersey** | **NHL** | **76** | **4** | **13** | **17** | **48** | **1** | **0** | **1** | **68** | **5.9** | **-11** | **0** | **0.0** | **20:39** | **5** | **1** | **0** | **1** | **0** | **0** | **0** | **0** | **21:24** |
| **2008-09** | **New Jersey** | **NHL** | **80** | **1** | **14** | **15** | **35** | **0** | **0** | **0** | **71** | **1.4** | **24** | **0** | **0.0** | **17:47** | **7** | **1** | **1** | **2** | **0** | **0** | **0** | **0** | **17:59** |
| | **NHL Totals** | | **179** | **5** | **30** | **35** | **96** | **1** | **0** | **1** | **156** | **3.2** | | **0** | **0.0** | **18:31** | **12** | **2** | **1** | **3** | **0** | **0** | **0** | **0** | **19:25** |

Hockey East First All-Star Team (1998, 2000) • NCAA East Second All-American Team (1998) • NCAA Championship All-Tournament Team (1998, 2000) • Hockey East Second All-Star Team (1999) • NCAA East First All-American Team (1999, 2000) • Hockey East Player of the Year (2000) (co-winner - Ty Conklin) • Hobey Baker Memorial Award (Top U.S. Collegiate Player) (2000) • AHL All-Rookie Team (2001)

Traded to **Calgary** by **NY Rangers** for Calgary's 6th round choice (Ivan Dornic) in 2003 Entry Draft and future considerations, January 22, 2003. Signed as a free agent by **Anaheim**, July 25, 2003. Signed as a free agent by **Worcester** (AHL), September 30, 2004. Signed as a free agent by **New Jersey**, July 17, 2006.

## MOTZKO, Joe

(MAWTS-koh, JOH)

Right wing. Shoots right. 6', 184 lbs. Born, Bemidji, MN, March 14, 1980.

| Season | Club | League | GP | G | A | Pts | PIM | PP | SH | GW | S | % | +/- | TF | F% | Min | GP | G | A | Pts | PIM | PP | SH | GW | Min |
|---|---|---|---|---|---|---|---|---|---|---|---|---|---|---|---|---|---|---|---|---|---|---|---|---|---|
| 1997-98 | Bemidji Jacks | High-MN | 25 | 24 | 28 | 52 | .... | .... | .... | .... | .... | .... | .... | .... | .... | .... | .... | .... | .... | .... | .... | .... | .... | .... | .... |
| 1998-99 | Omaha Lancers | USHL | 51 | 15 | 21 | 36 | 60 | .... | .... | .... | .... | .... | .... | .... | .... | .... | 12 | 7 | 3 | 10 | 12 | .... | .... | .... | .... |
| 99-2000 | St. Cloud State | WCHA | 36 | 9 | 15 | 24 | 52 | .... | .... | .... | .... | .... | .... | .... | .... | .... | .... | .... | .... | .... | .... | .... | .... | .... | .... |
| 2000-01 | St. Cloud State | WCHA | 41 | 17 | 20 | 37 | 54 | .... | .... | .... | .... | .... | .... | .... | .... | .... | .... | .... | .... | .... | .... | .... | .... | .... | .... |
| 2001-02 | St. Cloud State | WCHA | 39 | 9 | 30 | 39 | 34 | .... | .... | .... | .... | .... | .... | .... | .... | .... | .... | .... | .... | .... | .... | .... | .... | .... | .... |
| 2002-03 | St. Cloud State | WCHA | 38 | 17 | 25 | 42 | 59 | .... | .... | .... | .... | .... | .... | .... | .... | .... | .... | .... | .... | .... | .... | .... | .... | .... | .... |
| | Syracuse Crunch | AHL | 2 | 0 | 0 | 0 | 0 | .... | .... | .... | .... | .... | .... | .... | .... | .... | .... | .... | .... | .... | .... | .... | .... | .... | .... |
| **2003-04** | **Columbus** | **NHL** | **2** | **0** | **0** | **0** | **0** | **0** | **0** | **0** | **1** | **0.0** | **0** | **0** | **0.0** | **7:16** | .... | .... | .... | .... | .... | .... | .... | .... | .... |
| | Syracuse Crunch | AHL | 70 | 17 | 24 | 41 | 38 | .... | .... | .... | .... | .... | .... | .... | .... | .... | 7 | 2 | 2 | 4 | 6 | .... | .... | .... | .... |
| 2004-05 | Syracuse Crunch | AHL | 79 | 28 | 38 | 66 | 72 | .... | .... | .... | .... | .... | .... | .... | .... | .... | .... | .... | .... | .... | .... | .... | .... | .... | .... |
| **2005-06** | **Columbus** | **NHL** | **2** | **0** | **0** | **0** | **0** | **0** | **0** | **0** | **3** | **0.0** | **-2** | **1** | **0.0** | **10:35** | .... | .... | .... | .... | .... | .... | .... | .... | .... |
| | Syracuse Crunch | AHL | 61 | 27 | 34 | 61 | 54 | .... | .... | .... | .... | .... | .... | .... | .... | .... | 3 | 0 | 0 | 0 | 0 | .... | .... | .... | .... |
| **2006-07** | **Columbus** | **NHL** | **7** | **1** | **0** | **1** | **0** | **0** | **0** | **0** | **10** | **10.0** | **0** | **1** | **0.0** | **6:27** | .... | .... | .... | .... | .... | .... | .... | .... | .... |
| | Syracuse Crunch | AHL | 33 | 13 | 23 | 36 | 29 | .... | .... | .... | .... | .... | .... | .... | .... | .... | .... | .... | .... | .... | .... | .... | .... | .... | .... |
| | Portland Pirates | AHL | 34 | 15 | 14 | 29 | 20 | .... | .... | .... | .... | .... | .... | .... | .... | .... | .... | .... | .... | .... | .... | .... | .... | .... | .... |
| | ♦ **Anaheim** | **NHL** | .... | .... | .... | .... | .... | .... | .... | .... | .... | .... | .... | .... | .... | .... | **3** | **0** | **0** | **0** | **2** | **0** | **0** | **0** | **3:55** |
| **2007-08** | **Washington** | **NHL** | **8** | **2** | **2** | **4** | **0** | **0** | **0** | **0** | **10** | **20.0** | **1** | **3** | **0.0** | **12:27** | .... | .... | .... | .... | .... | .... | .... | .... | .... |
| | Hershey Bears | AHL | 48 | 21 | 27 | 48 | 44 | .... | .... | .... | .... | .... | .... | .... | .... | .... | .... | .... | .... | .... | .... | .... | .... | .... | .... |
| | Chicago Wolves | AHL | 24 | 6 | 16 | 22 | 16 | .... | .... | .... | .... | .... | .... | .... | .... | .... | 16 | 2 | 9 | 11 | 12 | .... | .... | .... | .... |
| **2008-09** | **Atlanta** | **NHL** | **6** | **1** | **0** | **1** | **0** | **0** | **0** | **0** | **8** | **12.5** | **1** | **3** | **33.3** | **11:39** | .... | .... | .... | .... | .... | .... | .... | .... | .... |
| | Chicago Wolves | AHL | 73 | 29 | 27 | 56 | 82 | .... | .... | .... | .... | .... | .... | .... | .... | .... | .... | .... | .... | .... | .... | .... | .... | .... | .... |
| | **NHL Totals** | | **25** | **4** | **2** | **6** | **0** | **0** | **0** | **0** | **32** | **12.5** | | **8** | **12.5** | **10:01** | **3** | **0** | **0** | **0** | **2** | **0** | **0** | **0** | **3:55** |

Signed as a free agent by **Columbus**, May 15, 2003. Traded to **Anaheim** by **Columbus** with Mark Hartigan and Columbus' 4th round choice (Sebastian Stefaniszin) in 2007 Entry Draft for Zenon Konopka, Curtis Glencross and Anaheim's 7th round choice (Trent Vogelhuber) in 2007 Entry Draft, January 26, 2007. Signed as a free agent by **Washington**, July 9, 2007. Traded to **Atlanta** by **Washington** for Alexandre Giroux, February 26, 2008.

## MOULSON, Matt

(MOHL-suhn, MAT) **NYI**

Left wing. Shoots left. 6'1", 205 lbs. Born, North York, Ont., November 1, 1983. Pittsburgh's 11th choice, 263rd overall, in 2003 Entry Draft.

| Season | Club | League | GP | G | A | Pts | PIM | PP | SH | GW | S | % | +/- | TF | F% | Min | GP | G | A | Pts | PIM | PP | SH | GW | Min |
|---|---|---|---|---|---|---|---|---|---|---|---|---|---|---|---|---|---|---|---|---|---|---|---|---|---|
| 2001-02 | Guelph | OHA-B | 42 | 56 | 46 | 102 | 80 | .... | .... | .... | .... | .... | .... | .... | .... | .... | .... | .... | .... | .... | .... | .... | .... | .... | .... |
| 2002-03 | Cornell Big Red | ECAC | 33 | 13 | 10 | 23 | 22 | .... | .... | .... | .... | .... | .... | .... | .... | .... | .... | .... | .... | .... | .... | .... | .... | .... | .... |
| 2003-04 | Cornell Big Red | ECAC | 32 | 18 | 17 | 35 | 37 | .... | .... | .... | .... | .... | .... | .... | .... | .... | .... | .... | .... | .... | .... | .... | .... | .... | .... |
| 2004-05 | Cornell Big Red | ECAC | 34 | 22 | 20 | 42 | 33 | .... | .... | .... | .... | .... | .... | .... | .... | .... | .... | .... | .... | .... | .... | .... | .... | .... | .... |
| 2005-06 | Cornell Big Red | ECAC | 35 | 18 | 20 | 38 | 14 | .... | .... | .... | .... | .... | .... | .... | .... | .... | .... | .... | .... | .... | .... | .... | .... | .... | .... |
| 2006-07 | Manchester | AHL | 77 | 25 | 32 | 57 | 23 | .... | .... | .... | .... | .... | .... | .... | .... | .... | 16 | 2 | 3 | 5 | 8 | .... | .... | .... | .... |
| **2007-08** | **Los Angeles** | **NHL** | **22** | **5** | **4** | **9** | **4** | **0** | **0** | **0** | **35** | **14.3** | **2** | **4** | **25.0** | **12:05** | .... | .... | .... | .... | .... | .... | .... | .... | .... |
| | Manchester | AHL | 57 | 28 | 28 | 56 | 29 | .... | .... | .... | .... | .... | .... | .... | .... | .... | 4 | 2 | 0 | 2 | 4 | .... | .... | .... | .... |
| **2008-09** | **Los Angeles** | **NHL** | **7** | **1** | **0** | **1** | **2** | **0** | **0** | **1** | **6** | **16.7** | **-4** | **0** | **0.0** | **14:30** | .... | .... | .... | .... | .... | .... | .... | .... | .... |
| | Manchester | AHL | 54 | 21 | 26 | 47 | 35 | .... | .... | .... | .... | .... | .... | .... | .... | .... | .... | .... | .... | .... | .... | .... | .... | .... | .... |
| | **NHL Totals** | | **29** | **6** | **4** | **10** | **6** | **0** | **0** | **1** | **41** | **14.6** | | **4** | **25.0** | **12:40** | .... | .... | .... | .... | .... | .... | .... | .... | .... |

ECAC First All-Star Team (2005) • NCAA East Second All-American Team (2005) • ECAC Second All-Star Team (2006)

Signed as a free agent by **Los Angeles**, September 1, 2006. Signed as a free agent by **NY Islanders**, July 6, 2009.

## MOWERS, Mark

(MAH-wuhrs, MAHRK)

Center. Shoots right. 5'11", 174 lbs. Born, Decatur, GA, February 16, 1974.

| Season | Club | League | GP | G | A | Pts | PIM | PP | SH | GW | S | % | +/- | TF | F% | Min | GP | G | A | Pts | PIM | PP | SH | GW | Min |
|---|---|---|---|---|---|---|---|---|---|---|---|---|---|---|---|---|---|---|---|---|---|---|---|---|---|
| | | | Regular Season | | | | | | | | | | | | | | Playoffs | | | | | | | | |
| 1992-93 | Saginaw Jr. Gears | NAHL | 39 | 31 | 39 | 70 | .... | .... | .... | .... | .... | .... | .... | .... | .... | .... | .... | .... | .... | .... | .... | .... | .... | .... | .... |
| 1993-94 | Dubuque | USHL | 47 | 51 | 31 | 82 | 80 | .... | .... | .... | .... | .... | .... | .... | .... | .... | .... | .... | .... | .... | .... | .... | .... | .... | .... |
| 1994-95 | New Hampshire | H-East | 36 | 13 | 23 | 36 | 16 | .... | .... | .... | .... | .... | .... | .... | .... | .... | .... | .... | .... | .... | .... | .... | .... | .... | .... |
| 1995-96 | New Hampshire | H-East | 34 | 21 | 26 | 47 | 18 | .... | .... | .... | .... | .... | .... | .... | .... | .... | .... | .... | .... | .... | .... | .... | .... | .... | .... |
| 1996-97 | New Hampshire | H-East | 39 | 26 | 32 | 58 | 52 | .... | .... | .... | .... | .... | .... | .... | .... | .... | .... | .... | .... | .... | .... | .... | .... | .... | .... |
| 1997-98 | New Hampshire | H-East | 35 | 25 | 31 | 56 | 32 | .... | .... | .... | .... | .... | .... | .... | .... | .... | .... | .... | .... | .... | .... | .... | .... | .... | .... |
| **1998-99** | **Nashville** | **NHL** | **30** | **0** | **6** | **6** | **4** | **0** | **0** | **0** | **24** | **0.0** | **-4** | **241** | **49.0** | **9:22** | .... | .... | .... | .... | .... | .... | .... | .... | .... |
| | Milwaukee | IHL | 51 | 14 | 22 | 36 | 24 | .... | .... | .... | .... | .... | .... | .... | .... | .... | 1 | 0 | 0 | 0 | 0 | .... | .... | .... | .... |
| **99-2000** | **Nashville** | **NHL** | **41** | **4** | **5** | **9** | **10** | **0** | **0** | **0** | **50** | **8.0** | **0** | **312** | **45.2** | **10:58** | .... | .... | .... | .... | .... | .... | .... | .... | .... |
| | Milwaukee | IHL | 23 | 11 | 15 | 26 | 34 | .... | .... | .... | .... | .... | .... | .... | .... | .... | .... | .... | .... | .... | .... | .... | .... | .... | .... |
| 2000-01 | Milwaukee | IHL | 63 | 25 | 25 | 50 | 54 | .... | .... | .... | .... | .... | .... | .... | .... | .... | 5 | 1 | 2 | 3 | 2 | .... | .... | .... | .... |
| **2001-02** | **Nashville** | **NHL** | **14** | **1** | **2** | **3** | **2** | **0** | **0** | **0** | **5** | **20.0** | **-2** | **24** | **33.3** | **8:31** | .... | .... | .... | .... | .... | .... | .... | .... | .... |
| | Milwaukee | AHL | 45 | 19 | 20 | 39 | 34 | .... | .... | .... | .... | .... | .... | .... | .... | .... | .... | .... | .... | .... | .... | .... | .... | .... | .... |
| 2002-03 | Grand Rapids | AHL | 78 | 34 | 47 | 81 | 47 | .... | .... | .... | .... | .... | .... | .... | .... | .... | 15 | 3 | 4 | 7 | 4 | .... | .... | .... | .... |
| **2003-04** | **Detroit** | **NHL** | **52** | **3** | **8** | **11** | **4** | **1** | **0** | **1** | **48** | **6.3** | **3** | **400** | **47.8** | **10:27** | .... | .... | .... | .... | .... | .... | .... | .... | .... |
| | Grand Rapids | AHL | 16 | 8 | 6 | 14 | 4 | .... | .... | .... | .... | .... | .... | .... | .... | .... | .... | .... | .... | .... | .... | .... | .... | .... | .... |
| 2004-05 | Malmo | Sweden | 9 | 2 | 0 | 2 | 0 | .... | .... | .... | .... | .... | .... | .... | .... | .... | .... | .... | .... | .... | .... | .... | .... | .... | .... |
| | Fribourg | Swiss | 3 | 2 | 0 | 2 | 0 | .... | .... | .... | .... | .... | .... | .... | .... | .... | 9 | 9 | 8 | 17 | 12 | .... | .... | .... | .... |
| **2005-06** | **Detroit** | **NHL** | **46** | **4** | **11** | **15** | **16** | **0** | **0** | **0** | **65** | **6.2** | **13** | **100** | **52.0** | **8:18** | **3** | **0** | **0** | **0** | **0** | **0** | **0** | **0** | **9:27** |
| **2006-07** | **Boston** | **NHL** | **78** | **5** | **12** | **17** | **26** | **0** | **1** | **0** | **60** | **8.3** | **-10** | **593** | **45.0** | **12:00** | .... | .... | .... | .... | .... | .... | .... | .... | .... |
| **2007-08** | **Anaheim** | **NHL** | **17** | **1** | **0** | **1** | **8** | **0** | **0** | **0** | **6** | **16.7** | **0** | **45** | **48.9** | **9:02** | .... | .... | .... | .... | .... | .... | .... | .... | .... |
| | SC Bern | Swiss | 10 | 2 | 4 | 6 | 8 | .... | .... | .... | .... | .... | .... | .... | .... | .... | .... | .... | .... | .... | .... | .... | .... | .... | .... |
| 2008-09 | Fribourg | Swiss | 23 | 3 | 8 | 11 | 26 | .... | .... | .... | .... | .... | .... | .... | .... | .... | 5 | 2 | 2 | 4 | 4 | .... | .... | .... | .... |
| | **NHL Totals** | | **278** | **18** | **44** | **62** | **70** | **1** | **1** | **1** | **258** | **7.0** | | **1715** | **46.6** | **10:18** | **3** | **0** | **0** | **0** | **0** | **0** | **0** | **0** | **9:27** |

Hockey East Rookie of the Year (1995) • Hockey East Second All-Star Team (1998) • NCAA East First All-American Team (1998) • Ken McKenzie Trophy (IHL – U.S. - Born Rookie of the Year) (1999) • AHL Second All-Star Team (2003)

Signed as a free agent by **Nashville**, June 11, 1998. Signed as a free agent by **Detroit**, August 5, 2002. Signed as a free agent by **Malmo** (Sweden), December 21, 2004. Signed as a free agent by **Fribourg** (Swiss), February 4, 2005. Signed as a free agent by **Boston**, July 6, 2006. Traded to **Anaheim** by **Boston** for Nathan Saunders and Brett Skinner, September 24, 2007. • Assigned to **Bern** (Swiss) by **Anaheim**, December 1, 2007. • Spent majority of 2007-08 season serving as a healthy reserve.

## MUELLER, Peter

(MEW-luhr, PEE-tuhr) **PHX.**

Center. Shoots right. 6'2", 205 lbs. Born, Bloomington, MN, April 14, 1988. Phoenix's 1st choice, 8th overall, in 2006 Entry Draft.

| Season | Club | League | GP | G | A | Pts | PIM | PP | SH | GW | S | % | +/- | TF | F% | Min | GP | G | A | Pts | PIM | PP | SH | GW | Min |
|---|---|---|---|---|---|---|---|---|---|---|---|---|---|---|---|---|---|---|---|---|---|---|---|---|---|
| 2003-04 | USNTDP | U-17 | 17 | 4 | 9 | 13 | 25 | .... | .... | .... | .... | .... | .... | .... | .... | .... | .... | .... | .... | .... | .... | .... | .... | .... | .... |
| | USNTDP | NAHL | 43 | 10 | 16 | 26 | 26 | .... | .... | .... | .... | .... | .... | .... | .... | .... | 7 | 3 | 2 | 5 | 4 | .... | .... | .... | .... |
| 2004-05 | USNTDP | U-18 | 43 | 27 | 27 | 64 | 75 | .... | .... | .... | .... | .... | .... | .... | .... | .... | .... | .... | .... | .... | .... | .... | .... | .... | .... |
| | USNTDP | NAHL | 14 | 11 | 13 | 24 | 16 | .... | .... | .... | .... | .... | .... | .... | .... | .... | .... | .... | .... | .... | .... | .... | .... | .... | .... |
| 2005-06 | Everett Silvertips | WHL | 52 | 26 | 32 | 58 | 44 | .... | .... | .... | .... | .... | .... | .... | .... | .... | 15 | 7 | 6 | 13 | 10 | .... | .... | .... | .... |
| 2006-07 | Everett Silvertips | WHL | 51 | 21 | 57 | 78 | 45 | .... | .... | .... | .... | .... | .... | .... | .... | .... | 12 | 7 | 9 | 16 | 12 | .... | .... | .... | .... |
| **2007-08** | **Phoenix** | **NHL** | **81** | **22** | **32** | **54** | **32** | **7** | **0** | **3** | **201** | **10.9** | **-13** | **251** | **41.8** | **17:16** | .... | .... | .... | .... | .... | .... | .... | .... | .... |
| **2008-09** | **Phoenix** | **NHL** | **72** | **13** | **23** | **36** | **24** | **5** | **0** | **4** | **138** | **9.4** | **-7** | **92** | **44.6** | **16:05** | .... | .... | .... | .... | .... | .... | .... | .... | .... |
| | **NHL Totals** | | **153** | **35** | **55** | **90** | **56** | **12** | **0** | **7** | **339** | **10.3** | | **343** | **42.6** | **16:42** | .... | .... | .... | .... | .... | .... | .... | .... | .... |

WHL Rookie ot the Year (2006) • WHL West First All-Star Team (2007) • Canadian Major Junior Second All-Star Team (2007)

## MURLEY, Matt

(MUHR-lee, MAT)

Left wing. Shoots left. 6'1", 206 lbs. Born, Troy, NY, December 17, 1979. Pittsburgh's 2nd choice, 51st overall, in 1999 Entry Draft.

| Season | Club | League | GP | G | A | Pts | PIM | PP | SH | GW | S | % | +/- | TF | F% | Min | GP | G | A | Pts | PIM | PP | SH | GW | Min |
|---|---|---|---|---|---|---|---|---|---|---|---|---|---|---|---|---|---|---|---|---|---|---|---|---|---|
| 1996-97 | Syracuse | MTJHL | 48 | 52 | 58 | 110 | 111 | .... | .... | .... | .... | .... | .... | .... | .... | .... | .... | .... | .... | .... | .... | .... | .... | .... | .... |
| 1997-98 | Syracuse | MTJHL | 49 | 56 | 70 | 126 | 103 | .... | .... | .... | .... | .... | .... | .... | .... | .... | .... | .... | .... | .... | .... | .... | .... | .... | .... |
| 1998-99 | RPI Engineers | ECAC | 36 | 17 | 32 | 49 | 32 | .... | .... | .... | .... | .... | .... | .... | .... | .... | .... | .... | .... | .... | .... | .... | .... | .... | .... |
| 99-2000 | RPI Engineers | ECAC | 35 | 9 | 29 | 38 | 42 | .... | .... | .... | .... | .... | .... | .... | .... | .... | .... | .... | .... | .... | .... | .... | .... | .... | .... |
| 2000-01 | RPI Engineers | ECAC | 34 | *24 | 18 | 42 | 34 | .... | .... | .... | .... | .... | .... | .... | .... | .... | .... | .... | .... | .... | .... | .... | .... | .... | .... |
| 2001-02 | RPI Engineers | ECAC | 32 | *24 | 22 | 46 | 26 | .... | .... | .... | .... | .... | .... | .... | .... | .... | .... | .... | .... | .... | .... | .... | .... | .... | .... |
| 2002-03 | Wilkes-Barre | AHL | 73 | 21 | 37 | 58 | 45 | .... | .... | .... | .... | .... | .... | .... | .... | .... | 6 | 0 | 2 | 2 | 15 | .... | .... | .... | .... |
| **2003-04** | **Pittsburgh** | **NHL** | **18** | **1** | **1** | **2** | **14** | **0** | **0** | **0** | **20** | **5.0** | **-6** | **2** | **50.0** | **11:49** | .... | .... | .... | .... | .... | .... | .... | .... | .... |
| | Wilkes-Barre | AHL | 63 | 10 | 26 | 36 | 69 | .... | .... | .... | .... | .... | .... | .... | .... | .... | 24 | 7 | 6 | 13 | 17 | .... | .... | .... | .... |
| 2004-05 | Wilkes-Barre | AHL | 80 | 17 | 24 | 41 | 55 | .... | .... | .... | .... | .... | .... | .... | .... | .... | 11 | 3 | 0 | 3 | 0 | .... | .... | .... | .... |
| **2005-06** | **Pittsburgh** | **NHL** | **41** | **1** | **5** | **6** | **24** | **0** | **0** | **0** | **48** | **2.1** | **-9** | **11** | **36.4** | **11:29** | .... | .... | .... | .... | .... | .... | .... | .... | .... |
| 2006-07 | Albany River Rats | AHL | 61 | 23 | 32 | 55 | 18 | .... | .... | .... | .... | .... | .... | .... | .... | .... | 5 | 1 | 5 | 6 | 8 | .... | .... | .... | .... |
| **2007-08** | **Phoenix** | **NHL** | **3** | **0** | **1** | **1** | **0** | **0** | **0** | **0** | **3** | **0.0** | **1** | **3** | **66.7** | **11:44** | .... | .... | .... | .... | .... | .... | .... | .... | .... |
| | San Antonio | AHL | 76 | 21 | 41 | 62 | 43 | .... | .... | .... | .... | .... | .... | .... | .... | .... | 7 | 2 | 2 | 4 | 0 | .... | .... | .... | .... |
| 2008-09 | Amur Khabarovsk | Rus-KHL | 33 | 4 | 4 | 8 | 28 | .... | .... | .... | .... | .... | .... | .... | .... | .... | .... | .... | .... | .... | .... | .... | .... | .... | .... |
| | **NHL Totals** | | **62** | **2** | **7** | **9** | **38** | **0** | **0** | **0** | **71** | **2.8** | | **16** | **43.8** | **11:35** | .... | .... | .... | .... | .... | .... | .... | .... | .... |

ECAC First All-Star Team (2002)

Signed as a free agent by **Colorado**, July 12, 2006. Signed as a free agent by **Phoenix**, July 20, 2007. Signed as a free agent by **Carolina**, September 15, 2008.

## MURPHY, Cory

(MUHR-fee, KOH-ree) **N.J.**

Defense. Shoots left. 5'10", 185 lbs. Born, Kanata, Ont., February 13, 1978.

| Season | Club | League | GP | G | A | Pts | PIM | PP | SH | GW | S | % | +/- | TF | F% | Min | GP | G | A | Pts | PIM | PP | SH | GW | Min |
|---|---|---|---|---|---|---|---|---|---|---|---|---|---|---|---|---|---|---|---|---|---|---|---|---|---|
| 1997-98 | Colgate | ECAC | 35 | 8 | 19 | 27 | 38 | .... | .... | .... | .... | .... | .... | .... | .... | .... | .... | .... | .... | .... | .... | .... | .... | .... | .... |
| 1998-99 | Colgate | ECAC | 34 | 3 | 23 | 26 | 26 | .... | .... | .... | .... | .... | .... | .... | .... | .... | .... | .... | .... | .... | .... | .... | .... | .... | .... |
| 99-2000 | Colgate | ECAC | 35 | 10 | 19 | 29 | 26 | .... | .... | .... | .... | .... | .... | .... | .... | .... | .... | .... | .... | .... | .... | .... | .... | .... | .... |
| 2000-01 | Colgate | ECAC | 34 | 7 | 22 | 29 | 34 | .... | .... | .... | .... | .... | .... | .... | .... | .... | .... | .... | .... | .... | .... | .... | .... | .... | .... |
| 2001-02 | Blues Espoo | Finland | 46 | 9 | 15 | 24 | 38 | .... | .... | .... | .... | .... | .... | .... | .... | .... | 3 | 0 | 1 | 1 | 0 | .... | .... | .... | .... |
| 2002-03 | Blues Espoo | Finland | 45 | 11 | 4 | 15 | 49 | .... | .... | .... | .... | .... | .... | .... | .... | .... | 7 | 1 | 0 | 1 | 2 | .... | .... | .... | .... |
| 2003-04 | Ilves Tampere | Finland | 56 | 18 | 26 | 44 | 22 | .... | .... | .... | .... | .... | .... | .... | .... | .... | 7 | 1 | 2 | 3 | 2 | .... | .... | .... | .... |
| 2004-05 | Ilves Tampere | Finland | 56 | 12 | 23 | 35 | 36 | .... | .... | .... | .... | .... | .... | .... | .... | .... | 7 | 1 | 3 | 4 | 18 | .... | .... | .... | .... |
| 2005-06 | Fribourg | Swiss | 44 | 13 | 22 | 35 | 52 | .... | .... | .... | .... | .... | .... | .... | .... | .... | .... | .... | .... | .... | .... | .... | .... | .... | .... |
| 2006-07 | HIFK Helsinki | Finland | 45 | 13 | 37 | 50 | 46 | .... | .... | .... | .... | .... | .... | .... | .... | .... | 5 | 0 | 1 | 1 | 4 | .... | .... | .... | .... |
| **2007-08** | **Florida** | **NHL** | **47** | **2** | **15** | **17** | **22** | **1** | **0** | **0** | **65** | **3.1** | **0** | **0** | **0.0** | **15:23** | .... | .... | .... | .... | .... | .... | .... | .... | .... |
| **2008-09** | **Florida** | **NHL** | **7** | **0** | **1** | **1** | **2** | **0** | **0** | **0** | **8** | **0.0** | **-1** | **0** | **0.0** | **10:10** | .... | .... | .... | .... | .... | .... | .... | .... | .... |
| | Rochester | AHL | 5 | 2 | 4 | 6 | 2 | .... | .... | .... | .... | .... | .... | .... | .... | .... | .... | .... | .... | .... | .... | .... | .... | .... | .... |
| | **Tampa Bay** | **NHL** | **25** | **5** | **10** | **15** | **12** | **4** | **0** | **0** | **47** | **10.6** | **-3** | **0** | **0.0** | **20:08** | .... | .... | .... | .... | .... | .... | .... | .... | .... |
| | **NHL Totals** | | **79** | **7** | **26** | **33** | **36** | **5** | **0** | **0** | **120** | **5.8** | | **0** | **0.0** | **16:26** | .... | .... | .... | .... | .... | .... | .... | .... | .... |

ECAC First All-Star Team (2000) • ECAC Second All-Star Team (2001)

Signed as a free agent by **Florida**, March 26, 2007. Claimed on waivers by **Tampa Bay** from **Florida**, January 19, 2009. Signed as a free agent by **New Jersey**, July 17, 2009.

## MURRAY, Andrew

(MUHR-ree, AN-droo) **CBJ**

Center. Shoots left. 6'2", 216 lbs. Born, Selkirk, Man., November 6, 1981. Columbus' 11th choice, 242nd overall, in 2001 Entry Draft.

| Season | Club | League | GP | G | A | Pts | PIM | PP | SH | GW | S | % | +/- | TF | F% | Min | GP | G | A | Pts | PIM | PP | SH | GW | Min |
|---|---|---|---|---|---|---|---|---|---|---|---|---|---|---|---|---|---|---|---|---|---|---|---|---|---|
| 99-2000 | Selkirk Steelers | MJHL | 63 | 29 | 48 | 77 | .... | .... | .... | .... | .... | .... | .... | .... | .... | .... | .... | .... | .... | .... | .... | .... | .... | .... | .... |
| 2000-01 | Selkirk Steelers | MJHL | 64 | 46 | 56 | 102 | 72 | .... | .... | .... | .... | .... | .... | .... | .... | .... | 5 | 3 | 0 | 3 | 6 | .... | .... | .... | .... |
| 2001-02 | Bemidji State | CHA | 35 | 15 | 15 | 30 | 22 | .... | .... | .... | .... | .... | .... | .... | .... | .... | .... | .... | .... | .... | .... | .... | .... | .... | .... |
| 2002-03 | Bemidji State | CHA | 36 | 9 | 18 | 27 | 38 | .... | .... | .... | .... | .... | .... | .... | .... | .... | .... | .... | .... | .... | .... | .... | .... | .... | .... |
| 2003-04 | Bemidji State | CHA | 25 | 6 | 14 | 20 | 41 | .... | .... | .... | .... | .... | .... | .... | .... | .... | .... | .... | .... | .... | .... | .... | .... | .... | .... |
| 2004-05 | Bemidji State | CHA | 32 | 16 | 22 | 38 | 30 | .... | .... | .... | .... | .... | .... | .... | .... | .... | .... | .... | .... | .... | .... | .... | .... | .... | .... |
| 2005-06 | Syracuse Crunch | AHL | 77 | 13 | 16 | 29 | 73 | .... | .... | .... | .... | .... | .... | .... | .... | .... | 6 | 0 | 1 | 1 | 17 | .... | .... | .... | .... |
| 2006-07 | Syracuse Crunch | AHL | 72 | 10 | 12 | 22 | 62 | .... | .... | .... | .... | .... | .... | .... | .... | .... | .... | .... | .... | .... | .... | .... | .... | .... | .... |
| **2007-08** | **Columbus** | **NHL** | **39** | **6** | **4** | **10** | **12** | **0** | **0** | **0** | **45** | **13.3** | **0** | **32** | **46.9** | **11:42** | .... | .... | .... | .... | .... | .... | .... | .... | .... |
| | Syracuse Crunch | AHL | 34 | 13 | 2 | 15 | 15 | .... | .... | .... | .... | .... | .... | .... | .... | .... | .... | .... | .... | .... | .... | .... | .... | .... | .... |
| **2008-09** | **Columbus** | **NHL** | **67** | **8** | **3** | **11** | **10** | **1** | **0** | **3** | **89** | **9.0** | **-6** | **85** | **45.9** | **11:16** | .... | .... | .... | .... | .... | .... | .... | .... | .... |
| | **NHL Totals** | | **106** | **14** | **7** | **21** | **22** | **1** | **0** | **3** | **134** | **10.4** | | **117** | **46.2** | **11:26** | .... | .... | .... | .... | .... | .... | .... | .... | .... |

CHA All-Rookie Team (2002)

## MURRAY, Brady

(MUHR-ree, BRAY-dee) **L.A.**

Center. Shoots left. 5'9", 185 lbs. Born, Brandon, Man., August 17, 1984. Los Angeles' 6th choice, 152nd overall, in 2003 Entry Draft.

| | | | Regular Season | | | | | | | | | | | | | | Playoffs | | | | | | | | |
|---|---|---|---|---|---|---|---|---|---|---|---|---|---|---|---|---|---|---|---|---|---|---|---|---|---|
| **Season** | **Club** | **League** | **GP** | **G** | **A** | **Pts** | **PIM** | **PP** | **SH** | **GW** | **S** | **%** | **+/-** | **TF** | **F%** | **Min** | **GP** | **G** | **A** | **Pts** | **PIM** | **PP** | **SH** | **GW** | **Min** |
| 2001-02 | Shat.-St. Mary's | High-MN | 60 | 58 | 92 | 150 | 50 | .... | .... | .... | .... | .... | .... | .... | .... | .... | .... | .... | .... | .... | .... | .... | .... | .... | .... |
| 2002-03 | Salmon Arm | BCHL | 59 | 42 | 59 | 101 | 30 | .... | .... | .... | .... | .... | .... | .... | .... | .... | .... | .... | .... | .... | .... | .... | .... | .... | .... |
| 2003-04 | North Dakota | WCHA | 37 | 19 | 27 | 46 | 32 | .... | .... | .... | .... | .... | .... | .... | .... | .... | .... | .... | .... | .... | .... | .... | .... | .... | .... |
| 2004-05 | North Dakota | WCHA | 25 | 8 | 12 | 20 | 22 | .... | .... | .... | .... | .... | .... | .... | .... | .... | .... | .... | .... | .... | .... | .... | .... | .... | .... |
| 2005-06 | Rapperswil | Swiss | 36 | 3 | 9 | 12 | 28 | .... | .... | .... | .... | .... | .... | .... | .... | .... | 10 | 3 | 2 | 5 | 10 | .... | .... | .... | .... |
| 2006-07 | Rapperswil | Swiss | 38 | 12 | 20 | 32 | 38 | .... | .... | .... | .... | .... | .... | .... | .... | .... | 7 | 4 | 2 | 6 | 6 | .... | .... | .... | .... |
| **2007-08** | **Los Angeles** | **NHL** | **4** | **1** | **0** | **1** | **6** | **0** | **0** | **0** | **2** | **50.0** | **-2** | **31** | **51.6** | **11:18** | .... | .... | .... | .... | .... | .... | .... | .... | .... |
| | Manchester | AHL | 58 | 14 | 13 | 27 | 50 | .... | .... | .... | .... | .... | .... | .... | .... | .... | 4 | 1 | 0 | 1 | 2 | .... | .... | .... | .... |
| 2008-09 | HC Lugano | Swiss | 36 | *26 | 14 | 40 | 26 | .... | .... | .... | .... | .... | .... | .... | .... | .... | 7 | 1 | 4 | 5 | 0 | .... | .... | .... | .... |
| | **NHL Totals** | | **4** | **1** | **0** | **1** | **6** | **0** | **0** | **0** | **2** | **50.0** | | **31** | **51.6** | **11:18** | .... | .... | .... | .... | .... | .... | .... | .... | .... |

WCHA All-Rookie Team (2004) • WCHA Rookie of the Year (2004)

• Assigned to **Lugano** (Swiss) by **Los Angeles**, October 9, 2008.

## MURRAY, Douglas

(MUHR-ree, DUHG-luhs) **S.J.**

Defense. Shoots left. 6'3", 240 lbs. Born, Bromma, Sweden, March 12, 1980. San Jose's 6th choice, 241st overall, in 1999 Entry Draft.

| Season | Club | League | GP | G | A | Pts | PIM | PP | SH | GW | S | % | +/- | TF | F% | Min | GP | G | A | Pts | PIM | PP | SH | GW | Min |
|---|---|---|---|---|---|---|---|---|---|---|---|---|---|---|---|---|---|---|---|---|---|---|---|---|---|
| 1998-99 | NY Apple Core | EJHL | 60 | 17 | 47 | 64 | 62 | .... | .... | .... | .... | .... | .... | .... | .... | .... | .... | .... | .... | .... | .... | .... | .... | .... | .... |
| 99-2000 | Cornell Big Red | ECAC | 32 | 3 | 6 | 9 | 38 | .... | .... | .... | .... | .... | .... | .... | .... | .... | .... | .... | .... | .... | .... | .... | .... | .... | .... |
| 2000-01 | Cornell Big Red | ECAC | 25 | 5 | 13 | 18 | 39 | .... | .... | .... | .... | .... | .... | .... | .... | .... | .... | .... | .... | .... | .... | .... | .... | .... | .... |
| 2001-02 | Cornell Big Red | ECAC | 35 | 11 | 21 | 32 | 67 | .... | .... | .... | .... | .... | .... | .... | .... | .... | .... | .... | .... | .... | .... | .... | .... | .... | .... |
| 2002-03 | Cornell Big Red | ECAC | 35 | 5 | 20 | 25 | 30 | .... | .... | .... | .... | .... | .... | .... | .... | .... | .... | .... | .... | .... | .... | .... | .... | .... | .... |
| 2003-04 | Cleveland Barons | AHL | 72 | 10 | 12 | 22 | 75 | .... | .... | .... | .... | .... | .... | .... | .... | .... | 9 | 3 | 0 | 3 | 37 | .... | .... | .... | .... |
| 2004-05 | Cleveland Barons | AHL | 54 | 6 | 17 | 23 | 56 | .... | .... | .... | .... | .... | .... | .... | .... | .... | .... | .... | .... | .... | .... | .... | .... | .... | .... |
| **2005-06** | **San Jose** | **NHL** | **34** | **0** | **1** | **1** | **27** | **0** | **0** | **0** | **21** | **0.0** | **3** | **0** | **0.0** | **13:53** | .... | .... | .... | .... | .... | .... | .... | .... | .... |
| | Cleveland Barons | AHL | 20 | 1 | 7 | 8 | 37 | .... | .... | .... | .... | .... | .... | .... | .... | .... | .... | .... | .... | .... | .... | .... | .... | .... | .... |
| **2006-07** | **San Jose** | **NHL** | **35** | **0** | **3** | **3** | **31** | **0** | **0** | **0** | **18** | **0.0** | **0** | **0** | **0.0** | **10:46** | .... | .... | .... | .... | .... | .... | .... | .... | .... |
| | Worcester Sharks | AHL | 5 | 2 | 1 | 3 | 8 | .... | .... | .... | .... | .... | .... | .... | .... | .... | .... | .... | .... | .... | .... | .... | .... | .... | .... |
| **2007-08** | **San Jose** | **NHL** | **66** | **1** | **9** | **10** | **98** | **0** | **0** | **0** | **48** | **2.1** | **20** | **2** | **50.0** | **17:28** | **13** | **1** | **1** | **2** | **2** | **0** | **0** | **0** | **18:09** |
| **2008-09** | **San Jose** | **NHL** | **75** | **0** | **7** | **7** | **38** | **0** | **0** | **0** | **56** | **0.0** | **6** | **0** | **0.0** | **16:39** | **6** | **0** | **0** | **0** | **9** | **0** | **0** | **0** | **16:51** |
| | **NHL Totals** | | **210** | **1** | **20** | **21** | **194** | **0** | **0** | **0** | **143** | **0.7** | | **2** | **50.0** | **15:29** | **19** | **1** | **1** | **2** | **11** | **0** | **0** | **0** | **17:44** |

ECAC First All-Star Team (2002, 2003) • NCAA East First All-American Team (2003)

• Missed majority of 2006-07 season recovering from respiratory infection.

## MURRAY, Garth

(MUHR-ree, GARTH) **CGY.**

Center. Shoots left. 6'2", 215 lbs. Born, Regina, Sask., September 17, 1982. NY Rangers' 3rd choice, 79th overall, in 2001 Entry Draft.

| Season | Club | League | GP | G | A | Pts | PIM | PP | SH | GW | S | % | +/- | TF | F% | Min | GP | G | A | Pts | PIM | PP | SH | GW | Min |
|---|---|---|---|---|---|---|---|---|---|---|---|---|---|---|---|---|---|---|---|---|---|---|---|---|---|
| 1997-98 | Calgary Buffaloes | AMHL | 56 | 26 | 34 | 60 | 110 | .... | .... | .... | .... | .... | .... | .... | .... | .... | .... | .... | .... | .... | .... | .... | .... | .... | .... |
| | Regina Pats | WHL | 4 | 0 | 0 | 0 | 2 | .... | .... | .... | .... | .... | .... | .... | .... | .... | 2 | 0 | 0 | 0 | 0 | .... | .... | .... | .... |
| 1998-99 | Regina Pats | WHL | 60 | 3 | 5 | 8 | 101 | .... | .... | .... | .... | .... | .... | .... | .... | .... | .... | .... | .... | .... | .... | .... | .... | .... | .... |
| 99-2000 | Regina Pats | WHL | 68 | 14 | 26 | 40 | 155 | .... | .... | .... | .... | .... | .... | .... | .... | .... | 7 | 1 | 1 | 2 | 7 | .... | .... | .... | .... |
| 2000-01 | Regina Pats | WHL | 72 | 28 | 16 | 44 | 183 | .... | .... | .... | .... | .... | .... | .... | .... | .... | 6 | 1 | 1 | 2 | 10 | .... | .... | .... | .... |
| 2001-02 | Regina Pats | WHL | 62 | 33 | 30 | 63 | 154 | .... | .... | .... | .... | .... | .... | .... | .... | .... | 6 | 2 | 3 | 5 | 9 | .... | .... | .... | .... |
| | Hartford | AHL | 4 | 0 | 0 | 0 | 0 | .... | .... | .... | .... | .... | .... | .... | .... | .... | 9 | 1 | 3 | 4 | 6 | .... | .... | .... | .... |
| 2002-03 | Hartford | AHL | 64 | 10 | 14 | 24 | 121 | .... | .... | .... | .... | .... | .... | .... | .... | .... | 2 | 0 | 0 | 0 | 6 | .... | .... | .... | .... |
| **2003-04** | **NY Rangers** | **NHL** | **20** | **1** | **0** | **1** | **24** | **0** | **0** | **0** | **18** | **5.6** | **-5** | **5** | **20.0** | **9:16** | .... | .... | .... | .... | .... | .... | .... | .... | .... |
| | Hartford | AHL | 63 | 11 | 11 | 22 | 159 | .... | .... | .... | .... | .... | .... | .... | .... | .... | 16 | 0 | 4 | 4 | 29 | .... | .... | .... | .... |
| 2004-05 | Hartford | AHL | 55 | 4 | 5 | 9 | 182 | .... | .... | .... | .... | .... | .... | .... | .... | .... | 5 | 1 | 0 | 1 | 8 | .... | .... | .... | .... |
| **2005-06** | **Montreal** | **NHL** | **36** | **5** | **1** | **6** | **44** | **0** | **0** | **1** | **25** | **20.0** | **-2** | **99** | **46.5** | **9:15** | **6** | **0** | **0** | **0** | **0** | **0** | **0** | **0** | **12:39** |
| | Hamilton | AHL | 26 | 1 | 1 | 2 | 46 | .... | .... | .... | .... | .... | .... | .... | .... | .... | .... | .... | .... | .... | .... | .... | .... | .... | .... |
| **2006-07** | **Montreal** | **NHL** | **43** | **2** | **1** | **3** | **32** | **0** | **0** | **0** | **28** | **7.1** | **-10** | **107** | **42.1** | **8:23** | .... | .... | .... | .... | .... | .... | .... | .... | .... |
| **2007-08** | **Montreal** | **NHL** | **1** | **0** | **0** | **0** | **0** | **0** | **0** | **0** | **0** | **0.0** | **0** | **1** | **0.0** | **12:46** | .... | .... | .... | .... | .... | .... | .... | .... | .... |
| | **Florida** | **NHL** | **6** | **0** | **0** | **0** | **19** | **0** | **0** | **0** | **3** | **0.0** | **0** | **2** | **0.0** | **5:09** | .... | .... | .... | .... | .... | .... | .... | .... | .... |
| **2008-09** | **Phoenix** | **NHL** | **10** | **0** | **0** | **0** | **12** | **0** | **0** | **0** | **12** | **0.0** | **-2** | **80** | **45.0** | **9:20** | .... | .... | .... | .... | .... | .... | .... | .... | .... |
| | San Antonio | AHL | 64 | 11 | 10 | 21 | 146 | .... | .... | .... | .... | .... | .... | .... | .... | .... | .... | .... | .... | .... | .... | .... | .... | .... | .... |
| | **NHL Totals** | | **116** | **8** | **2** | **10** | **131** | **0** | **0** | **1** | **86** | **9.3** | | **294** | **43.5** | **8:45** | **6** | **0** | **0** | **0** | **0** | **0** | **0** | **0** | **12:39** |

Traded to **Montreal** by **NY Rangers** for Marcel Hossa, September 30, 2005. Claimed on waivers by **Florida** from **Montreal**, November 13, 2007. Signed as a free agent by **Phoenix**, July 18, 2008. Signed as a free agent by **Calgary**, July 2, 2009.

## MURRAY, Marty

(MUHR-ree, MAHR-tee)

Center. Shoots left. 5'9", 180 lbs. Born, Deloraine, Man., February 16, 1975. Calgary's 5th choice, 96th overall, in 1993 Entry Draft.

| Season | Club | League | GP | G | A | Pts | PIM | PP | SH | GW | S | % | +/- | TF | F% | Min | GP | G | A | Pts | PIM | PP | SH | GW | Min |
|---|---|---|---|---|---|---|---|---|---|---|---|---|---|---|---|---|---|---|---|---|---|---|---|---|---|
| 1990-91 | S-W Cougars | MMMHL | 36 | 46 | 47 | 93 | 50 | .... | .... | .... | .... | .... | .... | .... | .... | .... | .... | .... | .... | .... | .... | .... | .... | .... | .... |
| 1991-92 | Brandon | WHL | 68 | 20 | 36 | 56 | 22 | .... | .... | .... | .... | .... | .... | .... | .... | .... | .... | .... | .... | .... | .... | .... | .... | .... | .... |
| 1992-93 | Brandon | WHL | 67 | 29 | 65 | 94 | 50 | .... | .... | .... | .... | .... | .... | .... | .... | .... | 4 | 1 | 3 | 4 | 0 | .... | .... | .... | .... |
| 1993-94 | Brandon | WHL | 64 | 43 | 71 | 114 | 33 | .... | .... | .... | .... | .... | .... | .... | .... | .... | 14 | 6 | 14 | 20 | 14 | .... | .... | .... | .... |
| 1994-95 | Brandon | WHL | 65 | 40 | *88 | 128 | 53 | .... | .... | .... | .... | .... | .... | .... | .... | .... | 18 | 9 | *20 | 29 | 16 | .... | .... | .... | .... |
| **1995-96** | **Calgary** | **NHL** | **15** | **3** | **3** | **6** | **0** | **2** | **0** | **0** | **22** | **13.6** | **-4** | .... | .... | .... | .... | .... | .... | .... | .... | .... | .... | .... | .... |
| | Saint John Flames | AHL | 58 | 25 | 31 | 56 | 20 | .... | .... | .... | .... | .... | .... | .... | .... | .... | 14 | 2 | 4 | 6 | 4 | .... | .... | .... | .... |
| **1996-97** | **Calgary** | **NHL** | **2** | **0** | **0** | **0** | **4** | **0** | **0** | **0** | **2** | **0.0** | **0** | .... | .... | .... | .... | .... | .... | .... | .... | .... | .... | .... | .... |
| | Saint John Flames | AHL | 67 | 19 | 39 | 58 | 40 | .... | .... | .... | .... | .... | .... | .... | .... | .... | 5 | 2 | 3 | 5 | 4 | .... | .... | .... | .... |
| **1997-98** | **Calgary** | **NHL** | **2** | **0** | **0** | **0** | **2** | **0** | **0** | **0** | **2** | **0.0** | **1** | .... | .... | .... | .... | .... | .... | .... | .... | .... | .... | .... | .... |
| | Saint John Flames | AHL | 41 | 10 | 30 | 40 | 16 | .... | .... | .... | .... | .... | .... | .... | .... | .... | 21 | 10 | 10 | 20 | 12 | .... | .... | .... | .... |
| 1998-99 | EC Villacher SV | Alpenliga | 33 | 26 | 41 | 67 | 12 | .... | .... | .... | .... | .... | .... | .... | .... | .... | .... | .... | .... | .... | .... | .... | .... | .... | .... |
| | EC Villacher SV | Austria | 17 | 13 | 17 | 30 | 6 | .... | .... | .... | .... | .... | .... | .... | .... | .... | 6 | 1 | 4 | 5 | 0 | .... | .... | .... | .... |
| 99-2000 | Kolner Haie | Germany | 56 | 12 | 47 | 59 | 28 | .... | .... | .... | .... | .... | .... | .... | .... | .... | 10 | 4 | 3 | 7 | 2 | .... | .... | .... | .... |
| **2000-01** | **Calgary** | **NHL** | **7** | **0** | **0** | **0** | **0** | **0** | **0** | **0** | **6** | **0.0** | **-2** | **88** | **55.7** | **14:28** | .... | .... | .... | .... | .... | .... | .... | .... | .... |
| | Saint John Flames | AHL | 56 | 24 | 52 | 76 | 36 | .... | .... | .... | .... | .... | .... | .... | .... | .... | 19 | 4 | 16 | 20 | 18 | .... | .... | .... | .... |
| **2001-02** | **Philadelphia** | **NHL** | **74** | **12** | **15** | **27** | **10** | **1** | **1** | **2** | **109** | **11.0** | **10** | **913** | **50.7** | **13:56** | **5** | **0** | **1** | **1** | **0** | **0** | **0** | **0** | **13:14** |
| | Philadelphia | AHL | 3 | 0 | 3 | 3 | 2 | .... | .... | .... | .... | .... | .... | .... | .... | .... | .... | .... | .... | .... | .... | .... | .... | .... | .... |
| **2002-03** | **Philadelphia** | **NHL** | **76** | **11** | **15** | **26** | **13** | **1** | **1** | **0** | **105** | **10.5** | **-1** | **472** | **55.1** | **12:22** | **4** | **0** | **0** | **0** | **4** | **0** | **0** | **0** | **11:01** |
| **2003-04** | **Carolina** | **NHL** | **66** | **5** | **7** | **12** | **8** | **0** | **0** | **0** | **56** | **8.9** | **6** | **229** | **52.8** | **11:49** | .... | .... | .... | .... | .... | .... | .... | .... | .... |
| 2004-05 | | | DID NOT PLAY | | | | | | | | | | | | | | | | | | | | | | |
| 2005-06 | Hannover | Germany | 24 | 7 | 15 | 22 | 16 | .... | .... | .... | .... | .... | .... | .... | .... | .... | 9 | 4 | 3 | 7 | 35 | .... | .... | .... | .... |
| **2006-07** | Philadelphia | AHL | 11 | 2 | 13 | 15 | 4 | .... | .... | .... | .... | .... | .... | .... | .... | .... | .... | .... | .... | .... | .... | .... | .... | .... | .... |
| | **Los Angeles** | **NHL** | **19** | **0** | **2** | **2** | **4** | **0** | **0** | **0** | **4** | **0.0** | **-5** | **139** | **46.8** | **9:32** | .... | .... | .... | .... | .... | .... | .... | .... | .... |
| | Manchester | AHL | 34 | 12 | 28 | 40 | 24 | .... | .... | .... | .... | .... | .... | .... | .... | .... | 16 | 6 | 8 | 14 | 11 | .... | .... | .... | .... |
| 2007-08 | HC Lugano | Swiss | 49 | 7 | 25 | 32 | 22 | .... | .... | .... | .... | .... | .... | .... | .... | .... | 5 | 2 | 3 | 5 | 0 | .... | .... | .... | .... |
| 2008-09 | Manchester | AHL | 76 | 15 | 39 | 54 | 37 | .... | .... | .... | .... | .... | .... | .... | .... | .... | .... | .... | .... | .... | .... | .... | .... | .... | .... |
| | **NHL Totals** | | **261** | **31** | **42** | **73** | **41** | **4** | **2** | **2** | **306** | **10.1** | | **1841** | **52.0** | **12:32** | **9** | **0** | **1** | **1** | **4** | **0** | **0** | **0** | **12:15** |

WHL East First All-Star Team (1994, 1995) • Canadian Major Junior Second All-Star Team (1994) • WHL Player of the Year (1995)

Signed as a free agent by **Philadelphia**, July 9, 2001. Traded to **Carolina** by **Philadelphia** for Carolina's 6th round choice (Frederik Cabana) in 2004 Entry Draft, June 22, 2003. Signed as a free agent by **Hannover** (Germany), August 16, 2005. Signed as a free agent by **Philadelphia**, June 15, 2006. Claimed on waivers by **Los Angeles** from **Philadelphia**, November 11, 2006. Signed as a free agent by **Lugano** (Swiss), May 27, 2007.

## NAGY, Ladislav

(NA-gee, LA-dih-slahv)

Left wing. Shoots left. 5'11", 192 lbs. Born, Saca, Czech., June 1, 1979. St. Louis' 6th choice, 177th overall, in 1997 Entry Draft.

| Season | Club | League | GP | G | A | Pts | PIM | PP | SH | GW | S | % | +/- | TF | F% | Min | GP | G | A | Pts | PIM | PP | SH | GW | Min |
|---|---|---|---|---|---|---|---|---|---|---|---|---|---|---|---|---|---|---|---|---|---|---|---|---|---|
| 1995-96 | HK Dragon Presov | Slovakia | 11 | 6 | 5 | 11 | .... | .... | .... | .... | .... | .... | .... | .... | .... | .... | .... | .... | .... | .... | .... | .... | .... | .... | .... |
| 1996-97 | HC Kosice Jr. | Slovak-Jr. | 45 | 29 | 30 | 59 | 105 | .... | .... | .... | .... | .... | .... | .... | .... | .... | .... | .... | .... | .... | .... | .... | .... | .... | .... |
| 1997-98 | HC Kosice | Slovakia | 29 | 19 | 15 | 34 | 41 | .... | .... | .... | .... | .... | .... | .... | .... | .... | 11 | 2 | 4 | 6 | 6 | .... | .... | .... | .... |
| 1998-99 | Halifax | QMJHL | 63 | 71 | 55 | 126 | 148 | .... | .... | .... | .... | .... | .... | .... | .... | .... | 5 | 3 | 3 | 6 | 18 | .... | .... | .... | .... |
| | Worcester IceCats | AHL | .... | .... | .... | .... | .... | .... | .... | .... | .... | .... | .... | .... | .... | .... | 3 | 2 | 2 | 4 | 0 | .... | .... | .... | .... |
| **99-2000** | **St. Louis** | **NHL** | **11** | **2** | **4** | **6** | **2** | **1** | **0** | **0** | **15** | **13.3** | **2** | **6** | **33.3** | **12:19** | **6** | **1** | **1** | **2** | **0** | **0** | **0** | **0** | **13:29** |
| | Worcester IceCats | AHL | 69 | 23 | 28 | 51 | 67 | .... | .... | .... | .... | .... | .... | .... | .... | .... | 2 | 1 | 0 | 1 | 0 | .... | .... | .... | .... |

| | | | Regular Season | | | | | | | | | | | | | | Playoffs | | | | | | | | |
|---|---|---|---|---|---|---|---|---|---|---|---|---|---|---|---|---|---|---|---|---|---|---|---|---|---|
| Season | Club | League | GP | G | A | Pts | PIM | PP | SH | GW | S | % | +/- | TF | F% | Min | GP | G | A | Pts | PIM | PP | SH | GW | Min |
| **2000-01** | **St. Louis** | **NHL** | **40** | **8** | **8** | **16** | **20** | **2** | **0** | **2** | **59** | **13.6** | **-2** | **28** | **50.0** | **13:03** | .... | .... | .... | .... | .... | .... | .... | .... | .... |
| | Worcester IceCats | AHL | 20 | 6 | 14 | 20 | 36 | .... | .... | .... | .... | .... | .... | .... | .... | .... | .... | .... | .... | .... | .... | .... | .... | .... | .... |
| | **Phoenix** | **NHL** | **6** | **0** | **1** | **1** | **2** | **0** | **0** | **0** | **5** | **0.0** | **0** | **0** | **0.0** | **12:38** | .... | .... | .... | .... | .... | .... | .... | .... | .... |
| **2001-02** | **Phoenix** | **NHL** | **74** | **23** | **19** | **42** | **50** | **5** | **0** | **5** | **187** | **12.3** | **6** | **17** | **47.1** | **15:04** | **5** | **0** | **0** | **0** | **21** | **0** | **0** | **0** | **15:45** |
| **2002-03** | HC Kosice | Slovakia | 1 | 2 | 1 | 3 | 0 | .... | .... | .... | .... | .... | .... | .... | .... | .... | .... | .... | .... | .... | .... | .... | .... | .... | .... |
| | **Phoenix** | **NHL** | **80** | **22** | **35** | **57** | **92** | **8** | **0** | **6** | **209** | **10.5** | **17** | **41** | **34.2** | **17:28** | .... | .... | .... | .... | .... | .... | .... | .... | .... |
| **2003-04** | **Phoenix** | **NHL** | **55** | **24** | **28** | **52** | **46** | **11** | **0** | **6** | **160** | **15.0** | **11** | **33** | **42.4** | **18:10** | .... | .... | .... | .... | .... | .... | .... | .... | .... |
| 2004-05 | HC Kosice | Slovakia | 18 | 9 | 7 | 16 | 40 | .... | .... | .... | .... | .... | .... | .... | .... | .... | .... | .... | .... | .... | .... | .... | .... | .... | .... |
| | Mora IK | Sweden | 19 | 4 | 4 | 8 | 22 | .... | .... | .... | .... | .... | .... | .... | .... | .... | .... | .... | .... | .... | .... | .... | .... | .... | .... |
| **2005-06** | **Phoenix** | **NHL** | **51** | **15** | **41** | **56** | **74** | **7** | **1** | **4** | **132** | **11.4** | **8** | **72** | **40.3** | **18:53** | .... | .... | .... | .... | .... | .... | .... | .... | .... |
| **2006-07** | **Phoenix** | **NHL** | **55** | **8** | **33** | **41** | **48** | **2** | **0** | **0** | **113** | **7.1** | **-2** | **43** | **30.2** | **17:52** | .... | .... | .... | .... | .... | .... | .... | .... | .... |
| | **Dallas** | **NHL** | **25** | **4** | **10** | **14** | **6** | **2** | **0** | **1** | **33** | **12.1** | **-3** | **5** | **20.0** | **16:08** | **7** | **1** | **1** | **2** | **2** | **0** | **0** | **0** | **18:53** |
| **2007-08** | **Los Angeles** | **NHL** | **38** | **9** | **17** | **26** | **18** | **2** | **0** | **1** | **78** | **11.5** | **-2** | **83** | **53.0** | **13:48** | .... | .... | .... | .... | .... | .... | .... | .... | .... |
| 2008-09 | Cherepovets | Rus-KHL | 45 | 5 | 14 | 19 | 103 | .... | .... | .... | .... | .... | .... | .... | .... | .... | .... | .... | .... | .... | .... | .... | .... | .... | .... |
| | **NHL Totals** | | **435** | **115** | **196** | **311** | **358** | **40** | **1** | **25** | **991** | **11.6** | | **328** | **42.4** | **16:22** | **18** | **2** | **2** | **4** | **23** | **0** | **0** | **0** | **16:13** |

Traded to **Phoenix** by **St. Louis** with Michal Handzus, the rights to Jeff Taffe and St. Louis' 1st round choice (Ben Eager) in 2002 Entry Draft for Keith Tkachuk, March 13, 2001. Signed as a free agent by **Kosice** (Slovakia), September 17, 2004. Signed as a free agent by **Mora** (Sweden), December 17, 2004. Traded to **Dallas** by **Phoenix** for Mathias Tjarnqvist and Dallas' 1st round choice (later traded to Edmonton - Edmonton selected Riley Nash) in 2007 Entry Draft, February 12, 2007. Signed as a free agent by **Los Angeles**, July 2, 2007.• Misssed majority of 2007-08 season with a recurring neck injury.

## NASH, Rick

(NASH, RIHK) **CBJ**

Left wing. Shoots left. 6'4", 218 lbs. Born, Brampton, Ont., June 16, 1984. Columbus' 1st choice, 1st overall, in 2002 Entry Draft.

| Season | Club | League | GP | G | A | Pts | PIM | PP | SH | GW | S | % | +/- | TF | F% | Min | GP | G | A | Pts | PIM | PP | SH | GW | Min |
|---|---|---|---|---|---|---|---|---|---|---|---|---|---|---|---|---|---|---|---|---|---|---|---|---|---|
| 99-2000 | Tor. Marlboros | GTHL | 34 | 61 | 54 | 115 | 34 | .... | .... | .... | .... | .... | .... | .... | .... | .... | .... | .... | .... | .... | .... | .... | .... | .... | .... |
| 2000-01 | London Knights | OHL | 58 | 31 | 35 | 66 | 56 | .... | .... | .... | .... | .... | .... | .... | .... | .... | 4 | 3 | 3 | 6 | 8 | .... | .... | .... | .... |
| 2001-02 | London Knights | OHL | 54 | 32 | 40 | 72 | 88 | .... | .... | .... | .... | .... | .... | .... | .... | .... | 12 | 10 | 9 | 19 | 21 | .... | .... | .... | .... |
| **2002-03** | **Columbus** | **NHL** | **74** | **17** | **22** | **39** | **78** | **6** | **0** | **2** | **154** | **11.0** | **-27** | **14** | **35.7** | **13:57** | .... | .... | .... | .... | .... | .... | .... | .... | .... |
| **2003-04** | **Columbus** | **NHL** | **80** | ***41** | **16** | **57** | **87** | **19** | **0** | **7** | **269** | **15.2** | **-35** | **21** | **28.6** | **17:38** | .... | .... | .... | .... | .... | .... | .... | .... | .... |
| 2004-05 | HC Davos | Swiss | 44 | 26 | 20 | 46 | 83 | .... | .... | .... | .... | .... | .... | .... | .... | .... | 15 | 9 | 2 | 11 | 26 | .... | .... | .... | .... |
| **2005-06** | **Columbus** | **NHL** | **54** | **31** | **23** | **54** | **51** | **11** | **0** | **4** | **170** | **18.2** | **5** | **38** | **50.0** | **18:16** | .... | .... | .... | .... | .... | .... | .... | .... | .... |
| | Canada | Olympics | 6 | 0 | 1 | 1 | 10 | .... | .... | .... | .... | .... | .... | .... | .... | .... | .... | .... | .... | .... | .... | .... | .... | .... | .... |
| **2006-07** | **Columbus** | **NHL** | **75** | **27** | **30** | **57** | **73** | **9** | **1** | **5** | **228** | **11.8** | **-8** | **143** | **42.7** | **19:12** | .... | .... | .... | .... | .... | .... | .... | .... | .... |
| **2007-08** | **Columbus** | **NHL** | **80** | **38** | **31** | **69** | **95** | **10** | **4** | **6** | **329** | **11.6** | **2** | **44** | **31.8** | **20:29** | .... | .... | .... | .... | .... | .... | .... | .... | .... |
| **2008-09** | **Columbus** | **NHL** | **78** | **40** | **39** | **79** | **52** | **6** | **5** | **5** | **263** | **15.2** | **11** | **18** | **27.8** | **21:10** | **4** | **1** | **2** | **3** | **2** | **0** | **0** | **0** | **20:52** |
| | **NHL Totals** | | **441** | **194** | **161** | **355** | **436** | **61** | **10** | **29** | **1413** | **13.7** | | **278** | **39.6** | **18:30** | **4** | **1** | **2** | **3** | **2** | **0** | **0** | **0** | **20:52** |

OHL All-Rookie Team (2001) • OHL Rookie of the Year (2001) • CHL All-Rookie Team (2001) • NHL All-Rookie Team (2003) • Maurice "Rocket" Richard Trophy (2004) (tied with Jarome Iginla and Ilya Kovalchuk)

Played in NHL All-Star Game (2004, 2007, 2008, 2009)

Signed as a free agent by **Davos** (Swiss), August 3, 2004.

## NASLUND, Markus

(NAZ-luhnd, MAHR-kuhs)

Left wing. Shoots left. 6', 195 lbs. Born, Ornskoldsvik, Sweden, July 30, 1973. Pittsburgh's 1st choice, 16th overall, in 1991 Entry Draft.

| Season | Club | League | GP | G | A | Pts | PIM | PP | SH | GW | S | % | +/- | TF | F% | Min | GP | G | A | Pts | PIM | PP | SH | GW | Min |
|---|---|---|---|---|---|---|---|---|---|---|---|---|---|---|---|---|---|---|---|---|---|---|---|---|---|
| 1988-89 | Ornskoldsviks IF | Sweden-3 | 14 | 7 | 6 | 13 | .... | .... | .... | .... | .... | .... | .... | .... | .... | .... | .... | .... | .... | .... | .... | .... | .... | .... | .... |
| 1989-90 | MoDo Jr. | Swe-Jr. | 33 | 43 | 35 | 78 | 20 | .... | .... | .... | .... | .... | .... | .... | .... | .... | .... | .... | .... | .... | .... | .... | .... | .... | .... |
| 1990-91 | MoDo | Sweden | 32 | 10 | 9 | 19 | 14 | .... | .... | .... | .... | .... | .... | .... | .... | .... | .... | .... | .... | .... | .... | .... | .... | .... | .... |
| 1991-92 | MoDo | Sweden | 39 | 22 | 18 | 40 | 54 | .... | .... | .... | .... | .... | .... | .... | .... | .... | .... | .... | .... | .... | .... | .... | .... | .... | .... |
| 1992-93 | MoDo Jr. | Swe-Jr. | 2 | 4 | 1 | 5 | 2 | .... | .... | .... | .... | .... | .... | .... | .... | .... | .... | .... | .... | .... | .... | .... | .... | .... | .... |
| | MoDo | Sweden | 39 | 22 | 17 | 39 | 67 | .... | .... | .... | .... | .... | .... | .... | .... | .... | 3 | 3 | 2 | 5 | 0 | .... | .... | .... | .... |
| **1993-94** | **Pittsburgh** | **NHL** | **71** | **4** | **7** | **11** | **27** | **1** | **0** | **0** | **80** | **5.0** | **-3** | .... | .... | .... | .... | .... | .... | .... | .... | .... | .... | .... | .... |
| | Cleveland | IHL | 5 | 1 | 6 | 7 | 4 | .... | .... | .... | .... | .... | .... | .... | .... | .... | .... | .... | .... | .... | .... | .... | .... | .... | .... |
| **1994-95** | **Pittsburgh** | **NHL** | **14** | **2** | **2** | **4** | **2** | **0** | **0** | **0** | **13** | **15.4** | **0** | .... | .... | .... | .... | .... | .... | .... | .... | .... | .... | .... | .... |
| | Cleveland | IHL | 7 | 3 | 4 | 7 | 6 | .... | .... | .... | .... | .... | .... | .... | .... | .... | 4 | 1 | 3 | 4 | 8 | .... | .... | .... | .... |
| **1995-96** | **Pittsburgh** | **NHL** | **66** | **19** | **33** | **52** | **36** | **3** | **0** | **4** | **125** | **15.2** | **17** | .... | .... | .... | .... | .... | .... | .... | .... | .... | .... | .... | .... |
| | **Vancouver** | **NHL** | **10** | **3** | **0** | **3** | **6** | **1** | **0** | **1** | **19** | **15.8** | **3** | .... | .... | .... | **6** | **1** | **2** | **3** | **8** | **1** | **0** | **0** | .... |
| **1996-97** | **Vancouver** | **NHL** | **78** | **21** | **20** | **41** | **30** | **4** | **0** | **4** | **120** | **17.5** | **-15** | .... | .... | .... | .... | .... | .... | .... | .... | .... | .... | .... | .... |
| **1997-98** | **Vancouver** | **NHL** | **76** | **14** | **20** | **34** | **56** | **2** | **1** | **0** | **106** | **13.2** | **5** | .... | .... | .... | .... | .... | .... | .... | .... | .... | .... | .... | .... |
| **1998-99** | **Vancouver** | **NHL** | **80** | **36** | **30** | **66** | **74** | **15** | **2** | **3** | **205** | **17.6** | **-13** | **14** | **57.1** | **19:57** | .... | .... | .... | .... | .... | .... | .... | .... | .... |
| **99-2000** | **Vancouver** | **NHL** | **82** | **27** | **38** | **65** | **64** | **6** | **2** | **3** | **271** | **10.0** | **-5** | **13** | **46.2** | **20:13** | .... | .... | .... | .... | .... | .... | .... | .... | .... |
| **2000-01** | **Vancouver** | **NHL** | **72** | **41** | **34** | **75** | **58** | **18** | **1** | **5** | **277** | **14.8** | **-2** | **6** | **50.0** | **19:03** | .... | .... | .... | .... | .... | .... | .... | .... | .... |
| **2001-02** | **Vancouver** | **NHL** | **81** | **40** | **50** | **90** | **50** | **8** | **0** | **6** | **302** | **13.2** | **22** | **5** | **20.0** | **19:31** | **6** | **1** | **1** | **2** | **2** | **0** | **0** | **0** | **18:54** |
| | Sweden | Olympics | 4 | 2 | 1 | 3 | 0 | .... | .... | .... | .... | .... | .... | .... | .... | .... | .... | .... | .... | .... | .... | .... | .... | .... | .... |
| **2002-03** | **Vancouver** | **NHL** | **82** | **48** | **56** | **104** | **52** | **24** | **0** | **12** | **294** | **16.3** | **6** | **6** | **33.3** | **19:54** | **14** | **5** | **9** | **14** | **18** | **2** | **0** | **1** | **18:14** |
| **2003-04** | **Vancouver** | **NHL** | **78** | **35** | **49** | **84** | **58** | **5** | **0** | **6** | **296** | **11.8** | **24** | **14** | **35.7** | **19:23** | **7** | **2** | **7** | **9** | **2** | **2** | **0** | **0** | **19:21** |
| 2004-05 | MODO | Sweden | 13 | 8 | 9 | 17 | 8 | .... | .... | .... | .... | .... | .... | .... | .... | .... | 6 | 0 | 1 | 1 | 10 | .... | .... | .... | .... |
| **2005-06** | **Vancouver** | **NHL** | **81** | **32** | **47** | **79** | **66** | **13** | **0** | **2** | **264** | **12.1** | **-19** | **7** | **28.6** | **18:28** | .... | .... | .... | .... | .... | .... | .... | .... | .... |
| | Sweden | Olympics | DID NOT PLAY – INJURED | | | | | | | | | | | | | | | | | | | | | | |
| **2006-07** | **Vancouver** | **NHL** | **82** | **24** | **36** | **60** | **54** | **9** | **0** | **5** | **222** | **10.8** | **3** | **6** | **50.0** | **17:44** | **12** | **4** | **1** | **5** | **16** | **1** | **0** | **0** | **21:36** |
| **2007-08** | **Vancouver** | **NHL** | **82** | **25** | **30** | **55** | **46** | **9** | **0** | **2** | **237** | **10.5** | **-7** | **1** | **0.0** | **17:23** | .... | .... | .... | .... | .... | .... | .... | .... | .... |
| **2008-09** | **NY Rangers** | **NHL** | **82** | **24** | **22** | **46** | **57** | **8** | **0** | **0** | **215** | **11.2** | **-10** | **2** | **50.0** | **17:11** | **7** | **1** | **2** | **3** | **10** | **1** | **0** | **0** | **16:06** |
| | **NHL Totals** | | **1117** | **395** | **474** | **869** | **736** | **126** | **6** | **53** | **3046** | **13.0** | | **74** | **41.9** | **18:52** | **52** | **14** | **22** | **36** | **56** | **7** | **0** | **1** | **19:03** |

NHL First All-Star Team (2002, 2003, 2004) • Lester B. Pearson Award (2003)

Played in NHL All-Star Game (1999, 2001, 2002, 2003, 2004)

Traded to **Vancouver** by **Pittsburgh** for Alek Stojanov, March 20, 1996. Signed as a free agent by **MODO** (Sweden), December 20, 2004. Signed as a free agent by **NY Rangers**, July 3, 2008. • Officially announced his retirement, May 4, 2009.

## NEAL, James

(NEEL, JAYMS) **DAL.**

Left wing. Shoots left. 6'3", 206 lbs. Born, Whitby, Ont., September 3, 1987. Dallas' 2nd choice, 33rd overall, in 2005 Entry Draft.

| Season | Club | League | GP | G | A | Pts | PIM | PP | SH | GW | S | % | +/- | TF | F% | Min | GP | G | A | Pts | PIM | PP | SH | GW | Min |
|---|---|---|---|---|---|---|---|---|---|---|---|---|---|---|---|---|---|---|---|---|---|---|---|---|---|
| 2003-04 | Bowmanville | OPJHL | 43 | 28 | 27 | 55 | .... | .... | .... | .... | .... | .... | .... | .... | .... | .... | .... | .... | .... | .... | .... | .... | .... | .... | .... |
| | Plymouth Whalers | OHL | 9 | 2 | 4 | 6 | 0 | .... | .... | .... | .... | .... | .... | .... | .... | .... | .... | .... | .... | .... | .... | .... | .... | .... | .... |
| 2004-05 | Plymouth Whalers | OHL | 67 | 18 | 26 | 44 | 32 | .... | .... | .... | .... | .... | .... | .... | .... | .... | 4 | 1 | 1 | 2 | 6 | .... | .... | .... | .... |
| 2005-06 | Plymouth Whalers | OHL | 66 | 21 | 37 | 58 | 109 | .... | .... | .... | .... | .... | .... | .... | .... | .... | 13 | 9 | 7 | 16 | 33 | .... | .... | .... | .... |
| 2006-07 | Plymouth Whalers | OHL | 45 | 27 | 38 | 65 | 94 | .... | .... | .... | .... | .... | .... | .... | .... | .... | 20 | 13 | 12 | 25 | 54 | .... | .... | .... | .... |
| 2007-08 | Iowa Stars | AHL | 62 | 18 | 19 | 37 | 63 | .... | .... | .... | .... | .... | .... | .... | .... | .... | .... | .... | .... | .... | .... | .... | .... | .... | .... |
| **2008-09** | **Dallas** | **NHL** | **77** | **24** | **13** | **37** | **51** | **9** | **0** | **2** | **171** | **14.0** | **-11** | **31** | **35.5** | **15:52** | .... | .... | .... | .... | .... | .... | .... | .... | .... |
| | Manitoba Moose | AHL | 5 | 4 | 1 | 5 | 2 | .... | .... | .... | .... | .... | .... | .... | .... | .... | .... | .... | .... | .... | .... | .... | .... | .... | .... |
| | **NHL Totals** | | **77** | **24** | **13** | **37** | **51** | **9** | **0** | **2** | **171** | **14.0** | | **31** | **35.5** | **15:52** | .... | .... | .... | .... | .... | .... | .... | .... | .... |

OHL First All-Star Team (2007) • Canadian Major Junior Second All-Star Team (2007)

## NEGRIN, John

(NEH-grihn, JAWN) **CGY.**

Defense. Shoots left. 6'2", 195 lbs. Born, West Vancouver, B.C., March 25, 1989. Calgary's 2nd choice, 70th overall, in 2007 Entry Draft.

| Season | Club | League | GP | G | A | Pts | PIM | PP | SH | GW | S | % | +/- | TF | F% | Min | GP | G | A | Pts | PIM | PP | SH | GW | Min |
|---|---|---|---|---|---|---|---|---|---|---|---|---|---|---|---|---|---|---|---|---|---|---|---|---|---|
| 2004-05 | North Delta Flyers | PIJHL | 45 | 3 | 12 | 15 | 53 | .... | .... | .... | .... | .... | .... | .... | .... | .... | .... | .... | .... | .... | .... | .... | .... | .... | .... |
| | Kootenay Ice | WHL | 2 | 0 | 0 | 0 | 0 | .... | .... | .... | .... | .... | .... | .... | .... | .... | .... | .... | .... | .... | .... | .... | .... | .... | .... |
| 2005-06 | Kootenay Ice | WHL | 55 | 3 | 7 | 10 | 48 | .... | .... | .... | .... | .... | .... | .... | .... | .... | 6 | 0 | 0 | 0 | 6 | .... | .... | .... | .... |
| 2006-07 | Kootenay Ice | WHL | 44 | 1 | 15 | 16 | 57 | .... | .... | .... | .... | .... | .... | .... | .... | .... | 7 | 0 | 2 | 2 | 8 | .... | .... | .... | .... |
| 2007-08 | Kootenay Ice | WHL | 71 | 1 | 41 | 42 | 68 | .... | .... | .... | .... | .... | .... | .... | .... | .... | 10 | 1 | 1 | 2 | 8 | .... | .... | .... | .... |
| **2008-09** | Kootenay Ice | WHL | 38 | 5 | 26 | 31 | 27 | .... | .... | .... | .... | .... | .... | .... | .... | .... | .... | .... | .... | .... | .... | .... | .... | .... | .... |
| | Swift Current | WHL | 25 | 3 | 15 | 18 | 22 | .... | .... | .... | .... | .... | .... | .... | .... | .... | 7 | 2 | 4 | 6 | 8 | .... | .... | .... | .... |
| | **Calgary** | **NHL** | **3** | **0** | **1** | **1** | **2** | **0** | **0** | **0** | **3** | **0.0** | **-2** | **0** | **0.0** | **9:59** | .... | .... | .... | .... | .... | .... | .... | .... | .... |
| | **NHL Totals** | | **3** | **0** | **1** | **1** | **2** | **0** | **0** | **0** | **3** | **0.0** | | **0** | **0.0** | **9:59** | .... | .... | .... | .... | .... | .... | .... | .... | .... |

WHL East Second All-Star Team (2009)

## NEIL, Chris (NEEL, KRIHS) OTT.

Right wing. Shoots right. 6'1", 212 lbs. Born, Markdale, Ont., June 18, 1979. Ottawa's 7th choice, 161st overall, in 1998 Entry Draft.

| | | | Regular Season | | | | | | | | | | | | | | Playoffs | | | | | | | | |
|---|---|---|---|---|---|---|---|---|---|---|---|---|---|---|---|---|---|---|---|---|---|---|---|---|---|
| Season | Club | League | GP | G | A | Pts | PIM | PP | SH | GW | S | % | +/- | TF | F% | Min | GP | G | A | Pts | PIM | PP | SH | GW | Min |
| 1995-96 | Orangeville | OHA-B | 43 | 15 | 15 | 30 | 50 | .... | .... | .... | .... | .... | .... | .... | .... | .... | .... | .... | .... | .... | .... | .... | .... | .... | .... |
| 1996-97 | North Bay | OHL | 65 | 13 | 16 | 29 | 150 | .... | .... | .... | .... | .... | .... | .... | .... | .... | .... | .... | .... | .... | .... | .... | .... | .... | .... |
| 1997-98 | North Bay | OHL | 59 | 26 | 29 | 55 | 231 | .... | .... | .... | .... | .... | .... | .... | .... | .... | .... | .... | .... | .... | .... | .... | .... | .... | .... |
| 1998-99 | North Bay | OHL | 66 | 26 | 46 | 72 | 215 | .... | .... | .... | .... | .... | .... | .... | .... | .... | 4 | 1 | 0 | 1 | 15 | .... | .... | .... | .... |
| 99-2000 | Mobile Mysticks | ECHL | 4 | 0 | 2 | 2 | 39 | .... | .... | .... | .... | .... | .... | .... | .... | .... | .... | .... | .... | .... | .... | .... | .... | .... | .... |
| | Grand Rapids | IHL | 51 | 9 | 10 | 19 | 301 | .... | .... | .... | .... | .... | .... | .... | .... | .... | 8 | 0 | 2 | 2 | 24 | .... | .... | .... | .... |
| 2000-01 | Grand Rapids | IHL | 78 | 15 | 21 | 36 | 354 | .... | .... | .... | .... | .... | .... | .... | .... | .... | 10 | 2 | 2 | 4 | 22 | .... | .... | .... | .... |
| **2001-02** | **Ottawa** | **NHL** | **72** | **10** | **7** | **17** | **231** | **1** | **0** | **0** | **56** | **17.9** | **5** | **0** | **0.0** | **8:22** | **12** | **0** | **0** | **0** | **12** | **0** | **0** | **0** | **7:12** |
| **2002-03** | **Ottawa** | **NHL** | **68** | **6** | **4** | **10** | **147** | **0** | **0** | **0** | **62** | **9.7** | **8** | **5** | **60.0** | **7:40** | **15** | **1** | **0** | **1** | **24** | **0** | **0** | **0** | **7:57** |
| **2003-04** | **Ottawa** | **NHL** | **82** | **8** | **8** | **16** | **194** | **0** | **0** | **1** | **76** | **10.5** | **13** | **14** | **42.9** | **8:51** | **7** | **0** | **1** | **1** | **19** | **0** | **0** | **0** | **6:45** |
| 2004-05 | Binghamton | AHL | 22 | 4 | 6 | 10 | 132 | .... | .... | .... | .... | .... | .... | .... | .... | .... | 6 | 1 | 1 | 2 | 26 | .... | .... | .... | .... |
| **2005-06** | **Ottawa** | **NHL** | **79** | **16** | **17** | **33** | **204** | **8** | **0** | **0** | **126** | **12.7** | **9** | **9** | **22.2** | **12:18** | **10** | **1** | **0** | **1** | **14** | **0** | **0** | **0** | **6:58** |
| **2006-07** | **Ottawa** | **NHL** | **82** | **12** | **16** | **28** | **177** | **3** | **0** | **3** | **139** | **8.6** | **6** | **13** | **38.5** | **13:08** | **20** | **2** | **2** | **4** | **20** | **0** | **0** | **0** | **10:40** |
| **2007-08** | **Ottawa** | **NHL** | **68** | **6** | **14** | **20** | **199** | **0** | **0** | **1** | **78** | **7.7** | **–3** | **0** | **0.0** | **12:46** | **4** | **0** | **1** | **1** | **22** | **0** | **0** | **0** | **11:17** |
| **2008-09** | **Ottawa** | **NHL** | **60** | **3** | **7** | **10** | **146** | **0** | **0** | **0** | **59** | **5.1** | **–13** | **6** | **16.7** | **10:58** | .... | .... | .... | .... | .... | .... | .... | .... | .... |
| | **NHL Totals** | | **511** | **61** | **73** | **134** | **1298** | **12** | **0** | **5** | **596** | **10.2** | | **47** | **36.2** | **10:37** | **68** | **4** | **4** | **8** | **111** | **0** | **0** | **0** | **8:33** |

Signed as a free agent by **Binghamton** (AHL), March 2, 2005.

## NEWBURY, Kris (new-BUHR-ee, KRIHS) DET.

Center. Shoots left. 5'10", 200 lbs. Born, Brampton, Ont., February 19, 1982. San Jose's 4th choice, 139th overall, in 2002 Entry Draft.

| | | | Regular Season | | | | | | | | | | | | | | Playoffs | | | | | | | | |
|---|---|---|---|---|---|---|---|---|---|---|---|---|---|---|---|---|---|---|---|---|---|---|---|---|---|
| Season | Club | League | GP | G | A | Pts | PIM | PP | SH | GW | S | % | +/- | TF | F% | Min | GP | G | A | Pts | PIM | PP | SH | GW | Min |
| 1996-97 | Brampton | OPJHL | 28 | 9 | 4 | 13 | 36 | .... | .... | .... | .... | .... | .... | .... | .... | .... | .... | .... | .... | .... | .... | .... | .... | .... | .... |
| 1997-98 | Brampton | OPJHL | 46 | 11 | 21 | 32 | 161 | .... | .... | .... | .... | .... | .... | .... | .... | .... | .... | .... | .... | .... | .... | .... | .... | .... | .... |
| 1998-99 | Belleville Bulls | OHL | 51 | 6 | 8 | 14 | 89 | .... | .... | .... | .... | .... | .... | .... | .... | .... | .... | .... | .... | .... | .... | .... | .... | .... | .... |
| 99-2000 | Belleville Bulls | OHL | 34 | 6 | 18 | 24 | 72 | .... | .... | .... | .... | .... | .... | .... | .... | .... | .... | .... | .... | .... | .... | .... | .... | .... | .... |
| | Sarnia Sting | OHL | 27 | 6 | 8 | 14 | 44 | .... | .... | .... | .... | .... | .... | .... | .... | .... | 7 | 0 | 3 | 3 | 16 | .... | .... | .... | .... |
| 2000-01 | Sarnia Sting | OHL | 64 | 28 | 30 | 58 | 126 | .... | .... | .... | .... | .... | .... | .... | .... | .... | 4 | 1 | 3 | 4 | 20 | .... | .... | .... | .... |
| 2001-02 | Sarnia Sting | OHL | 66 | 42 | 62 | 104 | 141 | .... | .... | .... | .... | .... | .... | .... | .... | .... | 5 | 1 | 3 | 4 | 15 | .... | .... | .... | .... |
| 2002-03 | Sarnia Sting | OHL | 64 | 34 | 58 | 92 | 149 | .... | .... | .... | .... | .... | .... | .... | .... | .... | 6 | 4 | 4 | 8 | 16 | .... | .... | .... | .... |
| 2003-04 | St. John's | AHL | 72 | 5 | 15 | 20 | 153 | .... | .... | .... | .... | .... | .... | .... | .... | .... | .... | .... | .... | .... | .... | .... | .... | .... | .... |
| 2004-05 | St. John's | AHL | 55 | 4 | 9 | 13 | 103 | .... | .... | .... | .... | .... | .... | .... | .... | .... | 5 | 0 | 0 | 0 | 36 | .... | .... | .... | .... |
| | Pensacola | ECHL | 6 | 2 | 4 | 6 | 20 | .... | .... | .... | .... | .... | .... | .... | .... | .... | .... | .... | .... | .... | .... | .... | .... | .... | .... |
| 2005-06 | Toronto Marlies | AHL | 74 | 22 | 37 | 59 | 215 | .... | .... | .... | .... | .... | .... | .... | .... | .... | 5 | 0 | 1 | 1 | 12 | .... | .... | .... | .... |
| **2006-07** | **Toronto** | **NHL** | **15** | **2** | **2** | **4** | **26** | **0** | **0** | **0** | **30** | **6.7** | **4** | **20** | **45.0** | **7:42** | .... | .... | .... | .... | .... | .... | .... | .... | .... |
| | Toronto Marlies | AHL | 37 | 12 | 24 | 36 | 87 | .... | .... | .... | .... | .... | .... | .... | .... | .... | .... | .... | .... | .... | .... | .... | .... | .... | .... |
| **2007-08** | **Toronto** | **NHL** | **28** | **1** | **1** | **2** | **32** | **0** | **0** | **0** | **14** | **7.1** | **–7** | **55** | **40.0** | **4:22** | .... | .... | .... | .... | .... | .... | .... | .... | .... |
| | Toronto Marlies | AHL | 54 | 16 | 27 | 43 | 101 | .... | .... | .... | .... | .... | .... | .... | .... | .... | 19 | 4 | 9 | 13 | *73 | .... | .... | .... | .... |
| **2008-09** | **Toronto** | **NHL** | **1** | **0** | **0** | **0** | **2** | **0** | **0** | **0** | **0** | **0.0** | **0** | **3** | **33.3** | **4:55** | .... | .... | .... | .... | .... | .... | .... | .... | .... |
| | Toronto Marlies | AHL | 33 | 6 | 23 | 29 | 72 | .... | .... | .... | .... | .... | .... | .... | .... | .... | .... | .... | .... | .... | .... | .... | .... | .... | .... |
| | **NHL Totals** | | **44** | **3** | **3** | **6** | **60** | **0** | **0** | **0** | **44** | **6.8** | | **78** | **41.0** | **5:31** | .... | .... | .... | .... | .... | .... | .... | .... | .... |

OHL Second All-Star Team (2002)

Signed as a free agent by **St. John's** (AHL), October 2, 2003. Signed as a free agent by **Toronto**, July 17, 2006. Signed as a free agent by **Detroit**, July 7, 2009.

## NICHOL, Scott (NIH-KOHL, SKAWT) S.J.

Center. Shoots right. 5'9", 180 lbs. Born, Edmonton, Alta., December 31, 1974. Buffalo's 9th choice, 272nd overall, in 1993 Entry Draft.

| | | | Regular Season | | | | | | | | | | | | | | Playoffs | | | | | | | | |
|---|---|---|---|---|---|---|---|---|---|---|---|---|---|---|---|---|---|---|---|---|---|---|---|---|---|
| Season | Club | League | GP | G | A | Pts | PIM | PP | SH | GW | S | % | +/- | TF | F% | Min | GP | G | A | Pts | PIM | PP | SH | GW | Min |
| 1991-92 | Cgy. AAA Flames | AMHL | 23 | 26 | 16 | 42 | 132 | .... | .... | .... | .... | .... | .... | .... | .... | .... | .... | .... | .... | .... | .... | .... | .... | .... | .... |
| 1992-93 | Portland | WHL | 67 | 31 | 33 | 64 | 146 | .... | .... | .... | .... | .... | .... | .... | .... | .... | 16 | 8 | 8 | 16 | 41 | .... | .... | .... | .... |
| 1993-94 | Portland | WHL | 65 | 40 | 53 | 93 | 144 | .... | .... | .... | .... | .... | .... | .... | .... | .... | 10 | 3 | 8 | 11 | 16 | .... | .... | .... | .... |
| 1994-95 | Rochester | AHL | 71 | 11 | 16 | 27 | 136 | .... | .... | .... | .... | .... | .... | .... | .... | .... | 5 | 0 | 3 | 3 | 14 | .... | .... | .... | .... |
| **1995-96** | **Buffalo** | **NHL** | **2** | **0** | **0** | **0** | **10** | **0** | **0** | **0** | **4** | **0.0** | **0** | .... | .... | .... | .... | .... | .... | .... | .... | .... | .... | .... | .... |
| | Rochester | AHL | 62 | 14 | 18 | 32 | 170 | .... | .... | .... | .... | .... | .... | .... | .... | .... | 19 | 7 | 6 | 13 | 36 | .... | .... | .... | .... |
| 1996-97 | Rochester | AHL | 68 | 22 | 21 | 43 | 133 | .... | .... | .... | .... | .... | .... | .... | .... | .... | 10 | 2 | 1 | 3 | 26 | .... | .... | .... | .... |
| **1997-98** | **Buffalo** | **NHL** | **3** | **0** | **0** | **0** | **4** | **0** | **0** | **0** | **5** | **0.0** | **0** | .... | .... | .... | .... | .... | .... | .... | .... | .... | .... | .... | .... |
| | Rochester | AHL | 35 | 13 | 7 | 20 | 113 | .... | .... | .... | .... | .... | .... | .... | .... | .... | 17 | 0 | 6 | 6 | 18 | .... | .... | .... | .... |
| 1998-99 | Rochester | AHL | 52 | 13 | 20 | 33 | 120 | .... | .... | .... | .... | .... | .... | .... | .... | .... | .... | .... | .... | .... | .... | .... | .... | .... | .... |
| 99-2000 | Rochester | AHL | 37 | 7 | 11 | 18 | 141 | .... | .... | .... | .... | .... | .... | .... | .... | .... | 12 | 0 | 3 | 3 | 10 | .... | .... | .... | .... |
| 2000-01 | Detroit Vipers | IHL | 67 | 7 | 24 | 31 | 198 | .... | .... | .... | .... | .... | .... | .... | .... | .... | 11 | 1 | 1 | 2 | 12 | .... | .... | .... | .... |
| **2001-02** | **Calgary** | **NHL** | **60** | **8** | **9** | **17** | **107** | **2** | **1** | **0** | **49** | **16.3** | **–9** | **458** | **53.1** | **12:41** | .... | .... | .... | .... | .... | .... | .... | .... | .... |
| **2002-03** | **Calgary** | **NHL** | **68** | **5** | **5** | **10** | **149** | **0** | **1** | **0** | **66** | **7.6** | **–7** | **357** | **58.3** | **10:47** | .... | .... | .... | .... | .... | .... | .... | .... | .... |
| **2003-04** | **Chicago** | **NHL** | **75** | **7** | **11** | **18** | **145** | **0** | **0** | **1** | **112** | **6.3** | **–16** | **1178** | **57.4** | **15:46** | .... | .... | .... | .... | .... | .... | .... | .... | .... |
| 2004-05 | London Racers | Britain | 16 | 7 | 12 | 19 | 86 | .... | .... | .... | .... | .... | .... | .... | .... | .... | .... | .... | .... | .... | .... | .... | .... | .... | .... |
| **2005-06** | **Nashville** | **NHL** | **34** | **3** | **3** | **6** | **79** | **0** | **1** | **0** | **32** | **9.4** | **3** | **242** | **58.3** | **10:30** | **3** | **0** | **0** | **0** | **2** | **0** | **0** | **0** | **7:45** |
| | Milwaukee | AHL | 6 | 3 | 5 | 8 | 18 | .... | .... | .... | .... | .... | .... | .... | .... | .... | .... | .... | .... | .... | .... | .... | .... | .... | .... |
| **2006-07** | **Nashville** | **NHL** | **59** | **7** | **6** | **13** | **79** | **1** | **1** | **2** | **58** | **12.1** | **7** | **623** | **58.0** | **12:32** | **5** | **0** | **0** | **0** | **17** | **0** | **0** | **0** | **10:22** |
| **2007-08** | **Nashville** | **NHL** | **73** | **10** | **8** | **18** | **72** | **0** | **2** | **1** | **101** | **9.9** | **12** | **738** | **59.8** | **13:16** | **2** | **0** | **0** | **0** | **0** | **0** | **0** | **0** | **7:31** |
| **2008-09** | **Nashville** | **NHL** | **43** | **4** | **6** | **10** | **41** | **0** | **0** | **0** | **42** | **9.5** | **0** | **359** | **54.6** | **11:04** | .... | .... | .... | .... | .... | .... | .... | .... | .... |
| | **NHL Totals** | | **417** | **44** | **48** | **92** | **686** | **3** | **6** | **4** | **469** | **9.4** | | **3955** | **57.3** | **12:40** | **10** | **0** | **0** | **0** | **19** | **0** | **0** | **0** | **9:00** |

• Missed majority of 1999-2000 season recovering from a knee injury suffered in game vs. Saint John (AHL), February 16, 2000. Signed as a free agent by **Calgary**, July 1, 2001. Signed as a free agent by **Chicago**, July 1, 2003. Signed as a free agent by **London** (Britain), October 26, 2004. Signed as a free agent by **Nashville**, August 6, 2005. Signed as a free agent by **San Jose**, July 15, 2009.

## NIEDERMAYER, Rob (NEE-duhr-MIGH-uhr, RAWB)

Center. Shoots left. 6'2", 201 lbs. Born, Cassiar, B.C., December 28, 1974. Florida's 1st choice, 5th overall, in 1993 Entry Draft.

| | | | Regular Season | | | | | | | | | | | | | | Playoffs | | | | | | | | |
|---|---|---|---|---|---|---|---|---|---|---|---|---|---|---|---|---|---|---|---|---|---|---|---|---|---|
| Season | Club | League | GP | G | A | Pts | PIM | PP | SH | GW | S | % | +/- | TF | F% | Min | GP | G | A | Pts | PIM | PP | SH | GW | Min |
| 1989-90 | Cranbrook Blazers | Minor-BC | 35 | 42 | 40 | 82 | 30 | .... | .... | .... | .... | .... | .... | .... | .... | .... | .... | .... | .... | .... | .... | .... | .... | .... | .... |
| 1990-91 | Medicine Hat | WHL | 71 | 24 | 26 | 50 | 8 | .... | .... | .... | .... | .... | .... | .... | .... | .... | 12 | 3 | 7 | 10 | 2 | .... | .... | .... | .... |
| 1991-92 | Medicine Hat | WHL | 71 | 32 | 46 | 78 | 77 | .... | .... | .... | .... | .... | .... | .... | .... | .... | 4 | 2 | 3 | 5 | 2 | .... | .... | .... | .... |
| 1992-93 | Medicine Hat | WHL | 52 | 43 | 34 | 77 | 67 | .... | .... | .... | .... | .... | .... | .... | .... | .... | .... | .... | .... | .... | .... | .... | .... | .... | .... |
| **1993-94** | **Florida** | **NHL** | **65** | **9** | **17** | **26** | **51** | **3** | **0** | **2** | **67** | **13.4** | **–11** | | | | .... | .... | .... | .... | .... | .... | .... | .... | .... |
| 1994-95 | Medicine Hat | WHL | 13 | 9 | 15 | 24 | 14 | .... | .... | .... | .... | .... | .... | | | | .... | .... | .... | .... | .... | .... | .... | .... | .... |
| | **Florida** | **NHL** | **48** | **4** | **6** | **10** | **36** | **1** | **0** | **0** | **58** | **6.9** | **–13** | | | | .... | .... | .... | .... | .... | .... | .... | .... | .... |
| **1995-96** | **Florida** | **NHL** | **82** | **26** | **35** | **61** | **107** | **11** | **0** | **6** | **155** | **16.8** | **1** | | | | **22** | **5** | **3** | **8** | **12** | **2** | **0** | **2** | .... |
| **1996-97** | **Florida** | **NHL** | **60** | **14** | **24** | **38** | **54** | **3** | **0** | **2** | **136** | **10.3** | **4** | | | | **5** | **2** | **1** | **3** | **6** | **1** | **0** | **0** | .... |
| **1997-98** | **Florida** | **NHL** | **33** | **8** | **7** | **15** | **41** | **5** | **0** | **2** | **64** | **12.5** | **–9** | | | | .... | .... | .... | .... | .... | .... | .... | .... | .... |
| **1998-99** | **Florida** | **NHL** | **82** | **18** | **33** | **51** | **50** | **6** | **1** | **3** | **142** | **12.7** | **–13** | **1895** | **47.1** | **21:17** | .... | .... | .... | .... | .... | .... | .... | .... | .... |
| **99-2000** | **Florida** | **NHL** | **81** | **10** | **23** | **33** | **46** | **1** | **0** | **4** | **135** | **7.4** | **–5** | **1632** | **47.9** | **19:04** | **4** | **1** | **0** | **1** | **6** | **0** | **0** | **0** | **15:55** |
| **2000-01** | **Florida** | **NHL** | **67** | **12** | **20** | **32** | **50** | **3** | **1** | **0** | **115** | **10.4** | **–12** | **997** | **45.0** | **20:30** | .... | .... | .... | .... | .... | .... | .... | .... | .... |
| **2001-02** | **Calgary** | **NHL** | **57** | **6** | **14** | **20** | **49** | **1** | **2** | **1** | **87** | **6.9** | **–15** | **777** | **48.4** | **18:01** | .... | .... | .... | .... | .... | .... | .... | .... | .... |
| **2002-03** | **Calgary** | **NHL** | **54** | **8** | **10** | **18** | **42** | **2** | **0** | **1** | **104** | **7.7** | **–13** | **139** | **48.9** | **17:29** | .... | .... | .... | .... | .... | .... | .... | .... | .... |
| | **Anaheim** | **NHL** | **12** | **2** | **2** | **4** | **15** | **1** | **0** | **0** | **21** | **9.5** | **3** | **14** | **42.9** | **15:21** | **21** | **3** | **7** | **10** | **18** | **0** | **2** | **0** | **23:35** |
| **2003-04** | **Anaheim** | **NHL** | **55** | **12** | **16** | **28** | **34** | **6** | **0** | **2** | **111** | **10.8** | **–6** | **45** | **64.4** | **19:28** | .... | .... | .... | .... | .... | .... | .... | .... | .... |
| 2004-05 | Ferencvaros | Hungary | 5 | 2 | 1 | 3 | 14 | .... | .... | .... | .... | .... | .... | .... | .... | .... | .... | .... | .... | .... | .... | .... | .... | .... | .... |
| **2005-06** | **Anaheim** | **NHL** | **76** | **15** | **24** | **39** | **89** | **4** | **0** | **2** | **140** | **10.7** | **–5** | **447** | **45.6** | **17:52** | **16** | **1** | **3** | **4** | **10** | **1** | **0** | **0** | **19:36** |
| **2006-07**♦ | **Anaheim** | **NHL** | **82** | **5** | **11** | **16** | **77** | **0** | **0** | **0** | **106** | **4.7** | **–8** | **76** | **40.8** | **16:39** | **21** | **5** | **5** | **10** | **39** | **0** | **1** | **1** | **18:35** |
| **2007-08** | **Anaheim** | **NHL** | **78** | **8** | **8** | **16** | **54** | **0** | **1** | **1** | **111** | **7.2** | **1** | **69** | **33.3** | **17:43** | **2** | **0** | **0** | **0** | **0** | **0** | **0** | **0** | **13:47** |
| **2008-09** | **Anaheim** | **NHL** | **79** | **14** | **7** | **21** | **42** | **1** | **1** | **2** | **88** | **15.9** | **–17** | **68** | **38.2** | **15:34** | **13** | **0** | **3** | **3** | **12** | **0** | **0** | **0** | **16:13** |
| | **NHL Totals** | | **1011** | **171** | **257** | **428** | **837** | **48** | **7** | **28** | **1640** | **10.4** | | **6159** | **46.9** | **18:17** | **104** | **17** | **22** | **39** | **103** | **4** | **3** | **3** | **19:30** |

WHL East First All-Star Team (1993)

• Missed majority of 1997-98 season recovering from thumb (November 26, 1997 vs. Boston) and head (March 19, 1998 vs. Buffalo) injuries. Traded to **Calgary** by **Florida** with Philadelphia's 2nd round choice (previously acquired, Calgary selected Andrei Medvedev) in 2001 Entry Draft for Valeri Bure and Jason Wiemer, June 23, 2001. Traded to **Anaheim** by **Calgary** for Mike Commodore and Jean-Francois Damphousse, March 11, 2003. Signed as a free agent by **Ferencvaros** (Hungary), January 17, 2005.

## NIEDERMAYER, Scott (NEE-duhr-MIGH-uhr, SKAWT) ANA.

Defense. Shoots left. 6'1", 195 lbs. Born, Edmonton, Alta., August 31, 1973. New Jersey's 1st choice, 3rd overall, in 1991 Entry Draft.

| | | | Regular Season | | | | | | | | | | | | | | Playoffs | | | | | | | | |
|---|---|---|---|---|---|---|---|---|---|---|---|---|---|---|---|---|---|---|---|---|---|---|---|---|---|
| Season | Club | League | GP | G | A | Pts | PIM | PP | SH | GW | S | % | +/- | TF | F% | Min | GP | G | A | Pts | PIM | PP | SH | GW | Min |
| 1988-89 | Cranbrook Blazers | Minor-BC | 62 | 55 | 37 | 92 | 100 | .... | .... | .... | .... | .... | .... | .... | .... | .... | .... | .... | .... | .... | .... | .... | .... | .... | .... |
| 1989-90 | Kamloops Blazers | WHL | 64 | 14 | 55 | 69 | 64 | .... | .... | .... | .... | .... | .... | .... | .... | .... | 17 | 2 | 14 | 16 | 35 | .... | .... | .... | .... |
| 1990-91 | Kamloops Blazers | WHL | 57 | 26 | 56 | 82 | 52 | .... | .... | .... | .... | .... | .... | .... | .... | .... | .... | .... | .... | .... | .... | .... | .... | .... | .... |
| **1991-92** | Kamloops Blazers | WHL | 35 | 7 | 32 | 39 | 61 | .... | .... | .... | .... | .... | .... | .... | .... | .... | 17 | 9 | 14 | 23 | 28 | .... | .... | .... | .... |
| | **New Jersey** | **NHL** | **4** | **0** | **1** | **1** | **2** | **0** | **0** | **0** | **4** | **0.0** | **1** | .... | .... | .... | .... | .... | .... | .... | .... | .... | .... | .... | .... |
| **1992-93** | **New Jersey** | **NHL** | **80** | **11** | **29** | **40** | **47** | **5** | **0** | **0** | **131** | **8.4** | **8** | .... | .... | .... | **5** | **0** | **3** | **3** | **2** | **0** | **0** | **0** | .... |
| **1993-94** | **New Jersey** | **NHL** | **81** | **10** | **36** | **46** | **42** | **5** | **0** | **2** | **135** | **7.4** | **34** | .... | .... | .... | **20** | **2** | **2** | **4** | **8** | **1** | **0** | **0** | .... |
| **1994-95♦** | **New Jersey** | **NHL** | **48** | **4** | **15** | **19** | **18** | **4** | **0** | **0** | **52** | **7.7** | **19** | .... | .... | .... | **20** | **4** | **7** | **11** | **10** | **2** | **0** | **1** | .... |
| **1995-96** | **New Jersey** | **NHL** | **79** | **8** | **25** | **33** | **46** | **6** | **0** | **0** | **179** | **4.5** | **5** | .... | .... | .... | .... | .... | .... | .... | .... | .... | .... | .... | .... |
| **1996-97** | **New Jersey** | **NHL** | **81** | **5** | **30** | **35** | **64** | **3** | **0** | **3** | **159** | **3.1** | **-4** | .... | .... | .... | **10** | **2** | **4** | **6** | **6** | **2** | **0** | **1** | .... |
| **1997-98** | **New Jersey** | **NHL** | **81** | **14** | **43** | **57** | **27** | **11** | **0** | **1** | **175** | **8.0** | **5** | .... | .... | .... | **6** | **0** | **2** | **2** | **4** | **0** | **0** | **0** | .... |
| **1998-99** | Utah Grizzlies | IHL | 5 | 0 | 2 | 2 | 0 | .... | .... | .... | .... | .... | .... | .... | .... | .... | .... | .... | .... | .... | .... | .... | .... | .... | .... |
| | **New Jersey** | **NHL** | **72** | **11** | **35** | **46** | **26** | **1** | **1** | **3** | **161** | **6.8** | **16** | **13** | **15.4** | **24:40** | **7** | **1** | **3** | **4** | **18** | **1** | **0** | **0** | **25:30** |
| **99-2000♦** | **New Jersey** | **NHL** | **71** | **7** | **31** | **38** | **48** | **1** | **0** | **0** | **109** | **6.4** | **19** | **8** | **37.5** | **24:21** | **22** | **5** | **2** | **7** | **10** | **0** | **2** | **1** | **25:28** |
| **2000-01** | **New Jersey** | **NHL** | **57** | **6** | **29** | **35** | **22** | **1** | **0** | **5** | **87** | **6.9** | **14** | **5** | **0.0** | **23:19** | **21** | **0** | **6** | **6** | **14** | **0** | **0** | **0** | **23:53** |
| **2001-02** | **New Jersey** | **NHL** | **76** | **11** | **22** | **33** | **30** | **2** | **0** | **6** | **129** | **8.5** | **12** | **1** | **100.0** | **24:17** | **6** | **0** | **2** | **2** | **6** | **0** | **0** | **0** | **26:37** |
| | Canada | Olympics | 6 | 1 | 1 | 2 | 4 | .... | .... | .... | .... | .... | .... | .... | .... | .... | .... | .... | .... | .... | .... | .... | .... | .... | .... |
| **2002-03♦** | **New Jersey** | **NHL** | **81** | **11** | **28** | **39** | **62** | **3** | **0** | **3** | **164** | **6.7** | **23** | **1** | **0.0** | **24:30** | **24** | **2** | ***16** | ***18** | **16** | **1** | **0** | **0** | **26:07** |
| **2003-04** | **New Jersey** | **NHL** | **81** | **14** | **40** | **54** | **44** | **9** | **0** | **3** | **165** | **8.5** | **20** | **1** | **0.0** | **25:56** | **5** | **1** | **0** | **1** | **6** | **0** | **0** | **0** | **27:21** |
| 2004-05 | | | DID NOT PLAY | | | | | | | | | | | | | | | | | | | | | | |
| **2005-06** | **Anaheim** | **NHL** | **82** | **13** | **50** | **63** | **96** | **9** | **0** | **3** | **181** | **7.2** | **8** | **7** | **28.6** | **25:30** | **16** | **2** | **9** | **11** | **14** | **1** | **1** | **1** | **28:54** |
| | Canada | Olympics | DID NOT PLAY – INJURED | | | | | | | | | | | | | | | | | | | | | | |
| **2006-07♦** | **Anaheim** | **NHL** | **79** | **15** | **54** | **69** | **86** | **9** | **0** | **3** | **172** | **8.7** | **6** | **1** | **100.0** | **27:31** | **21** | **3** | **8** | **11** | **26** | **1** | **0** | **2** | **29:51** |
| **2007-08** | **Anaheim** | **NHL** | **48** | **8** | **17** | **25** | **16** | **7** | **0** | **3** | **87** | **9.2** | **-2** | **0** | **0.0** | **23:54** | **6** | **0** | **2** | **2** | **4** | **0** | **0** | **0** | **24:24** |
| **2008-09** | **Anaheim** | **NHL** | **82** | **14** | **45** | **59** | **70** | **9** | **0** | **2** | **178** | **7.9** | **-8** | **1** | **0.0** | **26:55** | **13** | **3** | **7** | **10** | **11** | **3** | **0** | **2** | **26:18** |
| | **NHL Totals** | | **1183** | **162** | **530** | **692** | **746** | **85** | **1** | **37** | **2268** | **7.1** | | **38** | **23.7** | **25:13** | **202** | **25** | **73** | **98** | **155** | **12** | **3** | **8** | **26:32** |

WHL West First All-Star Team (1991, 1992) • Canadian Major Junior Scholastic Player of the Year (1991) • Memorial Cup Tournament All-Star Team (1992) • Stafford Smythe Memorial Trophy (Memorial Cup Tournament - MVP) (1992) • NHL All-Rookie Team (1993) • NHL Second All-Star Team (1998) • NHL First All-Star Team (2004, 2006, 2007) • James Norris Memorial Trophy (2004) • Conn Smythe Trophy (2007)

Played in NHL All-Star Game (1998, 2001, 2004, 2008, 2009)

Signed to PTO (tryout) contract by **Utah** (IHL) with **New Jersey** retaining NHL rights, October 19, 1998. Signed as a free agent by **Anaheim**, August 4, 2005.

## NIELSEN, Frans (NEEL-sehn, FRAHNZ) NYI

Center. Shoots left. 5'11", 172 lbs. Born, Herning, Denmark, April 24, 1984. NY Islanders' 2nd choice, 87th overall, in 2002 Entry Draft.

| | | | Regular Season | | | | | | | | | | | | | | Playoffs | | | | | | | | |
|---|---|---|---|---|---|---|---|---|---|---|---|---|---|---|---|---|---|---|---|---|---|---|---|---|---|
| Season | Club | League | GP | G | A | Pts | PIM | PP | SH | GW | S | % | +/- | TF | F% | Min | GP | G | A | Pts | PIM | PP | SH | GW | Min |
| 99-2000 | Herning IK Jr. | Den-Jr. | 36 | 18 | 16 | 34 | 6 | .... | .... | .... | .... | .... | .... | .... | .... | .... | .... | .... | .... | .... | .... | .... | .... | .... | .... |
| | Denmark | WJ18-B | 5 | 3 | 4 | 7 | 0 | .... | .... | .... | .... | .... | .... | .... | .... | .... | .... | .... | .... | .... | .... | .... | .... | .... | .... |
| 2000-01 | Herning IK | Denmark | 38 | 18 | 19 | 37 | 6 | .... | .... | .... | .... | .... | .... | .... | .... | .... | .... | .... | .... | .... | .... | .... | .... | .... | .... |
| | Denmark | WJ18-B | 3 | 2 | 1 | 3 | 0 | .... | .... | .... | .... | .... | .... | .... | .... | .... | .... | .... | .... | .... | .... | .... | .... | .... | .... |
| 2001-02 | Malmo | Sweden | 20 | 0 | 1 | 1 | 0 | .... | .... | .... | .... | .... | .... | .... | .... | .... | .... | .... | .... | .... | .... | .... | .... | .... | .... |
| | Malmo Jr. | Swe-Jr. | 29 | 15 | 27 | 42 | 8 | .... | .... | .... | .... | .... | .... | .... | .... | .... | 7 | 3 | 7 | 10 | 2 | | | | |
| 2002-03 | Malmo | Sweden | 47 | 3 | 6 | 9 | 10 | .... | .... | .... | .... | .... | .... | .... | .... | .... | .... | .... | .... | .... | .... | .... | .... | .... | .... |
| | Malmo Jr. | Swe-Jr. | 2 | 1 | 3 | 4 | 0 | .... | .... | .... | .... | .... | .... | .... | .... | .... | .... | .... | .... | .... | .... | .... | .... | .... | .... |
| 2003-04 | Malmo | Sweden | 50 | 9 | 7 | 16 | 28 | .... | .... | .... | .... | .... | .... | .... | .... | .... | .... | .... | .... | .... | .... | .... | .... | .... | .... |
| | Malmo | Sweden-Q | 10 | 3 | 5 | 8 | 2 | .... | .... | .... | .... | .... | .... | .... | .... | .... | .... | .... | .... | .... | .... | .... | .... | .... | .... |
| 2004-05 | Malmo | Sweden | 49 | 8 | 7 | 15 | 6 | .... | .... | .... | .... | .... | .... | .... | .... | .... | .... | .... | .... | .... | .... | .... | .... | .... | .... |
| | Malmo | Sweden-Q | 10 | 7 | 2 | 9 | 0 | .... | .... | .... | .... | .... | .... | .... | .... | .... | .... | .... | .... | .... | .... | .... | .... | .... | .... |
| 2005-06 | Timra IK | Sweden | 50 | 5 | 13 | 18 | 22 | .... | .... | .... | .... | .... | .... | .... | .... | .... | .... | .... | .... | .... | .... | .... | .... | .... | .... |
| **2006-07** | **NY Islanders** | **NHL** | **15** | **1** | **1** | **2** | **0** | **0** | **0** | **1** | **16** | **6.3** | **-2** | **53** | **45.3** | **5:13** | .... | .... | .... | .... | .... | .... | .... | .... | .... |
| | Bridgeport | AHL | 54 | 20 | 24 | 44 | 10 | .... | .... | .... | .... | .... | .... | .... | .... | .... | .... | .... | .... | .... | .... | .... | .... | .... | .... |
| **2007-08** | **NY Islanders** | **NHL** | **16** | **2** | **1** | **3** | **0** | **0** | **0** | **0** | **17** | **11.8** | **1** | **111** | **48.7** | **8:42** | .... | .... | .... | .... | .... | .... | .... | .... | .... |
| | Bridgeport | AHL | 48 | 10 | 28 | 38 | 18 | .... | .... | .... | .... | .... | .... | .... | .... | .... | .... | .... | .... | .... | .... | .... | .... | .... | .... |
| **2008-09** | **NY Islanders** | **NHL** | **59** | **9** | **24** | **33** | **18** | **3** | **1** | **2** | **101** | **8.9** | **-4** | **758** | **47.2** | **16:32** | .... | .... | .... | .... | .... | .... | .... | .... | .... |
| | **NHL Totals** | | **90** | **12** | **26** | **38** | **18** | **3** | **1** | **3** | **134** | **9.0** | | **922** | **47.3** | **13:16** | .... | .... | .... | .... | .... | .... | .... | .... | .... |

## NIKULIN, Alexander (nih-KOO-lihn, al-EHX-AN-duhr) PHX.

Center. Shoots left. 6'1", 205 lbs. Born, Moscow, USSR, August 25, 1985. Ottawa's 6th choice, 122nd overall, in 2004 Entry Draft.

| | | | Regular Season | | | | | | | | | | | | | | Playoffs | | | | | | | | |
|---|---|---|---|---|---|---|---|---|---|---|---|---|---|---|---|---|---|---|---|---|---|---|---|---|---|
| Season | Club | League | GP | G | A | Pts | PIM | PP | SH | GW | S | % | +/- | TF | F% | Min | GP | G | A | Pts | PIM | PP | SH | GW | Min |
| 2002-03 | CSKA Moscow 2 | Russia-3 | 46 | 22 | 14 | 36 | .... | .... | .... | .... | .... | .... | .... | .... | .... | .... | .... | .... | .... | .... | .... | .... | .... | .... | .... |
| 2003-04 | CSKA Moscow 2 | Russia-3 | 47 | 21 | 20 | 41 | 46 | .... | .... | .... | .... | .... | .... | .... | .... | .... | .... | .... | .... | .... | .... | .... | .... | .... | .... |
| 2004-05 | CSKA Moscow | Russia | 16 | 3 | 3 | 6 | 0 | .... | .... | .... | .... | .... | .... | .... | .... | .... | .... | .... | .... | .... | .... | .... | .... | .... | .... |
| 2005-06 | CSKA Moscow | Russia | 51 | 10 | 12 | 22 | 22 | .... | .... | .... | .... | .... | .... | .... | .... | .... | 7 | 1 | 0 | 1 | 2 | .... | .... | .... | .... |
| 2006-07 | CSKA Moscow | Russia | 33 | 5 | 11 | 16 | 8 | .... | .... | .... | .... | .... | .... | .... | .... | .... | 12 | 4 | 2 | 6 | 4 | .... | .... | .... | .... |
| **2007-08** | **Ottawa** | **NHL** | **2** | **0** | **0** | **0** | **0** | **0** | **0** | **0** | **0** | **0.0** | **-2** | **1** | **100.0** | **4:56** | .... | .... | .... | .... | .... | .... | .... | .... | .... |
| | Binghamton | AHL | 71 | 14 | 36 | 50 | 34 | .... | .... | .... | .... | .... | .... | .... | .... | .... | .... | .... | .... | .... | .... | .... | .... | .... | .... |
| **2008-09** | Binghamton | AHL | 5 | 2 | 0 | 2 | 0 | .... | .... | .... | .... | .... | .... | .... | .... | .... | .... | .... | .... | .... | .... | .... | .... | .... | .... |
| | **Phoenix** | **NHL** | **1** | **0** | **0** | **0** | **0** | **0** | **0** | **0** | **1** | **0.0** | **-1** | **3** | **0.0** | **5:35** | .... | .... | .... | .... | .... | .... | .... | .... | .... |
| | San Antonio | AHL | 64 | 7 | 16 | 23 | 20 | .... | .... | .... | .... | .... | .... | .... | .... | .... | .... | .... | .... | .... | .... | .... | .... | .... | .... |
| | **NHL Totals** | | **3** | **0** | **0** | **0** | **0** | **0** | **0** | **0** | **1** | **0.0** | | **4** | **25.0** | **5:09** | .... | .... | .... | .... | .... | .... | .... | .... | .... |

Traded to **Phoenix** by **Ottawa** for Drew Fata, November 3, 2008.

## NILSON, Marcus (NIHL-suhn, MAHR-kuhs)

Left wing. Shoots right. 6'2", 189 lbs. Born, Balsta, Sweden, March 1, 1978. Florida's 1st choice, 20th overall, in 1996 Entry Draft.

| | | | Regular Season | | | | | | | | | | | | | | Playoffs | | | | | | | | |
|---|---|---|---|---|---|---|---|---|---|---|---|---|---|---|---|---|---|---|---|---|---|---|---|---|---|
| Season | Club | League | GP | G | A | Pts | PIM | PP | SH | GW | S | % | +/- | TF | F% | Min | GP | G | A | Pts | PIM | PP | SH | GW | Min |
| 1994-95 | Djurgarden Jr. | Swe-Jr. | 24 | 7 | 8 | 15 | 22 | .... | .... | .... | .... | .... | .... | .... | .... | .... | .... | .... | .... | .... | .... | .... | .... | .... | .... |
| 1995-96 | Djurgarden Jr. | Swe-Jr. | 25 | 19 | 17 | 36 | 46 | .... | .... | .... | .... | .... | .... | .... | .... | .... | 2 | 1 | 1 | 2 | 12 | .... | .... | .... | .... |
| | Djurgarden | Sweden | 12 | 0 | 0 | 0 | 0 | .... | .... | .... | .... | .... | .... | .... | .... | .... | 1 | 0 | 0 | 0 | 0 | .... | .... | .... | .... |
| 1996-97 | Djurgarden | Sweden | 37 | 0 | 3 | 3 | 33 | .... | .... | .... | .... | .... | .... | .... | .... | .... | 4 | 0 | 0 | 0 | 0 | .... | .... | .... | .... |
| 1997-98 | Djurgarden | Sweden | 41 | 4 | 7 | 11 | 18 | .... | .... | .... | .... | .... | .... | .... | .... | .... | 15 | 2 | 1 | 3 | 16 | .... | .... | .... | .... |
| **1998-99** | **Florida** | **NHL** | **8** | **1** | **1** | **2** | **5** | **0** | **0** | **1** | **7** | **14.3** | **2** | **6** | **50.0** | **12:24** | .... | .... | .... | .... | .... | .... | .... | .... | .... |
| | New Haven | AHL | 69 | 8 | 25 | 33 | 10 | .... | .... | .... | .... | .... | .... | .... | .... | .... | .... | .... | .... | .... | .... | .... | .... | .... | .... |
| **99-2000** | **Florida** | **NHL** | **9** | **0** | **2** | **2** | **2** | **0** | **0** | **0** | **6** | **0.0** | **2** | **14** | **64.3** | **7:56** | .... | .... | .... | .... | .... | .... | .... | .... | .... |
| | Louisville Panthers | AHL | 64 | 9 | 23 | 32 | 52 | .... | .... | .... | .... | .... | .... | .... | .... | .... | 4 | 0 | 0 | 0 | 2 | .... | .... | .... | .... |
| **2000-01** | **Florida** | **NHL** | **78** | **12** | **24** | **36** | **74** | **0** | **0** | **2** | **141** | **8.5** | **-3** | **169** | **40.8** | **15:46** | .... | .... | .... | .... | .... | .... | .... | .... | .... |
| **2001-02** | **Florida** | **NHL** | **81** | **14** | **19** | **33** | **55** | **6** | **1** | **2** | **147** | **9.5** | **-14** | **539** | **43.8** | **16:31** | .... | .... | .... | .... | .... | .... | .... | .... | .... |
| **2002-03** | **Florida** | **NHL** | **82** | **15** | **19** | **34** | **31** | **7** | **1** | **0** | **187** | **8.0** | **2** | **469** | **46.7** | **15:31** | .... | .... | .... | .... | .... | .... | .... | .... | .... |
| **2003-04** | **Florida** | **NHL** | **69** | **6** | **13** | **19** | **26** | **1** | **1** | **1** | **110** | **5.5** | **-9** | **151** | **44.4** | **15:30** | .... | .... | .... | .... | .... | .... | .... | .... | .... |
| | **Calgary** | **NHL** | **14** | **5** | **0** | **5** | **14** | **1** | **0** | **2** | **23** | **21.7** | **3** | **173** | **45.1** | **16:43** | **26** | **4** | **7** | **11** | **12** | **0** | **0** | **1** | **19:25** |
| 2004-05 | Djurgarden | Sweden | 48 | 17 | 22 | 39 | 110 | .... | .... | .... | .... | .... | .... | .... | .... | .... | 7 | 1 | 2 | 3 | 10 | .... | .... | .... | .... |
| **2005-06** | **Calgary** | **NHL** | **70** | **6** | **11** | **17** | **32** | **2** | **0** | **2** | **83** | **7.2** | **13** | **392** | **45.4** | **14:50** | .... | .... | .... | .... | .... | .... | .... | .... | .... |
| **2006-07** | **Calgary** | **NHL** | **63** | **5** | **10** | **15** | **27** | **0** | **0** | **1** | **69** | **7.2** | **7** | **119** | **31.9** | **13:07** | **6** | **0** | **0** | **0** | **2** | **0** | **0** | **0** | **13:32** |
| **2007-08** | **Calgary** | **NHL** | **47** | **3** | **2** | **5** | **4** | **0** | **0** | **0** | **47** | **6.4** | **2** | **41** | **51.2** | **9:49** | **2** | **0** | **0** | **0** | **0** | **0** | **0** | **0** | **4:50** |
| 2008-09 | Yaroslavl | Rus-KHL | 36 | 6 | 3 | 9 | 30 | .... | .... | .... | .... | .... | .... | .... | .... | .... | 15 | 3 | 1 | 4 | 28 | .... | .... | .... | .... |
| | **NHL Totals** | | **521** | **67** | **101** | **168** | **270** | **17** | **3** | **11** | **820** | **8.2** | | **2073** | **44.3** | **14:40** | **34** | **4** | **7** | **11** | **14** | **0** | **0** | **1** | **17:31** |

Traded to **Calgary** by **Florida** for Calgary's 2nd round choice (David Booth) in 2004 Entry Draft, March 8, 2004. Signed as a free agent by **Djurgarden** (Sweden), September 16, 2004. Signed as a free agent by **Yaroslavl** (Rus-KHL), September 19, 2008.

## NILSSON, Robert (NIHL-suhn, RAW-buhrt) EDM.

Center. Shoots left. 5'11", 185 lbs. Born, Calgary, Alta., January 10, 1985. NY Islanders' 1st choice, 15th overall, in 2003 Entry Draft.

| | | | Regular Season | | | | | | | | | | | | | | Playoffs | | | | | | | | |
|---|---|---|---|---|---|---|---|---|---|---|---|---|---|---|---|---|---|---|---|---|---|---|---|---|---|
| Season | Club | League | GP | G | A | Pts | PIM | PP | SH | GW | S | % | +/- | TF | F% | Min | GP | G | A | Pts | PIM | PP | SH | GW | Min |
| 2000-01 | Leksands IF Jr. | Swe-Jr. | 23 | 14 | 28 | 42 | 26 | .... | .... | .... | .... | .... | .... | .... | .... | .... | 2 | 0 | 0 | 0 | 2 | .... | .... | .... | .... |
| | Leksands IF U18 | Swe-U18 | 4 | 6 | 3 | 9 | 6 | .... | .... | .... | .... | .... | .... | .... | .... | .... | 2 | 0 | 2 | 2 | 2 | .... | .... | .... | .... |
| 2001-02 | Leksands IF Jr. | Swe-Jr. | 21 | 13 | 18 | 31 | 24 | .... | .... | .... | .... | .... | .... | .... | .... | .... | 5 | 0 | 5 | 5 | 8 | .... | .... | .... | .... |
| | Leksands IF | Sweden-2 | 14 | 1 | 4 | 5 | 8 | .... | .... | .... | .... | .... | .... | .... | .... | .... | .... | .... | .... | .... | .... | .... | .... | .... | .... |
| 2002-03 | Leksands IF | Sweden | 41 | 8 | 13 | 21 | 10 | .... | .... | .... | .... | .... | .... | .... | .... | .... | 5 | 0 | 1 | 1 | 2 | .... | .... | .... | .... |
| | Leksands IF Jr. | Swe-Jr. | .... | .... | .... | .... | .... | .... | .... | .... | .... | .... | .... | .... | .... | .... | 2 | 1 | 1 | 2 | 2 | .... | .... | .... | .... |

| | | | Regular Season | | | | | | | | | | | | | | Playoffs | | | | | | | | |
|---|---|---|---|---|---|---|---|---|---|---|---|---|---|---|---|---|---|---|---|---|---|---|---|---|---|
| Season | Club | League | GP | G | A | Pts | PIM | PP | SH | GW | S | % | +/- | TF | F% | Min | GP | G | A | Pts | PIM | PP | SH | GW | Min |
| 2003-04 | Leksands IF Jr. | Swe-Jr. | 4 | 2 | 8 | 10 | 4 | | | | | | | | | | | | | | | | | | |
| | Leksands IF | Sweden | 34 | 2 | 4 | 6 | 6 | | | | | | | | | | | | | | | | | | |
| | Fribourg | Swiss | 7 | 1 | 3 | 4 | 2 | | | | | | | | | | 4 | 1 | 0 | 1 | 2 | | | | |
| 2004-05 | Almtuna | Sweden-2 | 3 | 0 | 1 | 1 | 2 | | | | | | | | | | | | | | | | | | |
| | Hammarby | Sweden-2 | 7 | 0 | 4 | 4 | 4 | | | | | | | | | | | | | | | | | | |
| | Djurgarden Jr. | Swe-Jr. | 8 | 8 | 4 | 12 | 12 | | | | | | | | | | | | | | | | | | |
| | Djurgarden | Sweden | 23 | 2 | 4 | 6 | 6 | | | | | | | | | | 3 | 0 | 0 | 0 | 0 | | | | |
| **2005-06** | **NY Islanders** | **NHL** | **53** | **6** | **14** | **20** | **26** | **1** | **0** | **1** | **70** | **8.6** | **-6** | **31** | **29.0** | **11:52** | | | | | | | | | |
| | Bridgeport | AHL | 29 | 8 | 20 | 28 | 12 | | | | | | | | | | 7 | 1 | 4 | 5 | 0 | | | | |
| **2006-07** | Bridgeport | AHL | 50 | 12 | 34 | 46 | 34 | | | | | | | | | | | | | | | | | | |
| | **Edmonton** | **NHL** | **4** | **1** | **0** | **1** | **4** | **0** | **0** | **0** | **8** | **12.5** | **-1** | **2** | **50.0** | **17:21** | | | | | | | | | |
| | Wilkes-Barre | AHL | 19 | 6 | 14 | 20 | 14 | | | | | | | | | | 11 | 3 | 12 | 15 | 8 | | | | |
| **2007-08** | **Edmonton** | **NHL** | **71** | **10** | **31** | **41** | **22** | **3** | **0** | **0** | **102** | **9.8** | **8** | **15** | **46.7** | **13:56** | | | | | | | | | |
| | Springfield | AHL | 5 | 2 | 2 | 4 | 4 | | | | | | | | | | | | | | | | | | |
| **2008-09** | **Edmonton** | **NHL** | **64** | **9** | **20** | **29** | **26** | **4** | **0** | **1** | **77** | **11.7** | **1** | **10** | **40.0** | **15:11** | | | | | | | | | |
| | **NHL Totals** | | **192** | **26** | **65** | **91** | **78** | **8** | **0** | **2** | **257** | **10.1** | | **58** | **36.2** | **13:51** | | | | | | | | | |

Traded to **Edmonton** by **NY Islanders** with Ryan O'Marra and NY Islanders' 1st round choice (Alex Plante) in 2007 Entry Draft for Ryan Smyth, February 27, 2007.

## NISKALA, Janne

(NIHS-kah-lah, YAH-nee)

Defense. Shoots left. 5'11", 199 lbs. Born, Vasteras, Sweden, September 22, 1981. Nashville's 5th choice, 147th overall, in 2004 Entry Draft.

| | | | Regular Season | | | | | | | | | | | | | | Playoffs | | | | | | | | |
|---|---|---|---|---|---|---|---|---|---|---|---|---|---|---|---|---|---|---|---|---|---|---|---|---|---|
| Season | Club | League | GP | G | A | Pts | PIM | PP | SH | GW | S | % | +/- | TF | F% | Min | GP | G | A | Pts | PIM | PP | SH | GW | Min |
| 1997-98 | Lukko Rauma U18 | Fin-U18 | 34 | 7 | 16 | 23 | 40 | | | | | | | | | | | | | | | | | | |
| 1998-99 | Lukko Rauma U18 | Fin-U18 | 14 | 7 | 4 | 11 | 42 | | | | | | | | | | | | | | | | | | |
| | Lukko Rauma Jr. | Fin-Jr. | 2 | 0 | 0 | 0 | 12 | | | | | | | | | | | | | | | | | | |
| 99-2000 | Lukko Rauma Jr. | Fin-Jr. | 40 | 14 | 15 | 29 | 50 | | | | | | | | | | 8 | 0 | 2 | 2 | 8 | | | | |
| 2000-01 | Lukko Rauma Jr. | Fin-Jr. | 13 | 4 | 8 | 12 | 40 | | | | | | | | | | | | | | | | | | |
| | Lukko Rauma | Finland | 18 | 0 | 0 | 0 | 0 | | | | | | | | | | | | | | | | | | |
| | Jaa-Kotkat | Finland-2 | 13 | 4 | 1 | 5 | 43 | | | | | | | | | | | | | | | | | | |
| | Manchester Storm | Britain | 16 | 0 | 1 | 1 | 14 | | | | | | | | | | | | | | | | | | |
| 2001-02 | Lukko Rauma Jr. | Fin-Jr. | 3 | 1 | 1 | 2 | 2 | | | | | | | | | | | | | | | | | | |
| | Lukko Rauma | Finland | 55 | 7 | 13 | 20 | 81 | | | | | | | | | | | | | | | | | | |
| 2002-03 | Lukko Rauma | Finland | 46 | 4 | 5 | 9 | 40 | | | | | | | | | | | | | | | | | | |
| 2003-04 | Lukko Rauma | Finland | 55 | 21 | 15 | 36 | 73 | | | | | | | | | | 4 | 0 | 0 | 0 | 16 | | | | |
| 2004-05 | Lukko Rauma | Finland | 44 | 9 | 12 | 21 | 63 | | | | | | | | | | 9 | 5 | 2 | 7 | 4 | | | | |
| 2005-06 | EV Zug | Swiss | 43 | 12 | 17 | 29 | 50 | | | | | | | | | | 7 | 0 | 2 | 2 | 10 | | | | |
| 2006-07 | Farjestad | Sweden | 53 | 19 | 30 | 49 | 62 | | | | | | | | | | 9 | 3 | 3 | 6 | 14 | | | | |
| 2007-08 | Milwaukee | AHL | 80 | 19 | 25 | 44 | 81 | | | | | | | | | | 6 | 0 | 1 | 1 | 8 | | | | |
| **2008-09** | **Tampa Bay** | **NHL** | **6** | **1** | **2** | **3** | **6** | **1** | **0** | **0** | **10** | **10.0** | **0** | **0** | **0.0** | **13:42** | | | | | | | | | |
| | Frolunda | Sweden | 35 | 9 | 10 | 19 | 20 | | | | | | | | | | 11 | 3 | 3 | 6 | 8 | | | | |
| | **NHL Totals** | | **6** | **1** | **2** | **3** | **6** | **1** | **0** | **0** | **10** | **10.0** | | **0** | **0.0** | **13:42** | | | | | | | | | |

Traded to **Philadelphia** by **Nashville** for Triston Grant and Philadelphia's 7th round choice (later traded to St. Louis – St. Louis selected Maxwell Tardy) in 2009 Entry Draft, June 24, 2008. Traded to **Tampa Bay** by **Philadelphia** for Tampa Bay's 6th round choice (Dave Labrecque) in 2009 Entry Draft, June 30, 2008.

## NISKANEN, Matt

(NIHS-kah-nehn, MAT) **DAL.**

Defense. Shoots right. 6', 194 lbs. Born, Virginia, MN, December 6, 1986. Dallas' 1st choice, 28th overall, in 2005 Entry Draft.

| | | | Regular Season | | | | | | | | | | | | | | Playoffs | | | | | | | | |
|---|---|---|---|---|---|---|---|---|---|---|---|---|---|---|---|---|---|---|---|---|---|---|---|---|---|
| Season | Club | League | GP | G | A | Pts | PIM | PP | SH | GW | S | % | +/- | TF | F% | Min | GP | G | A | Pts | PIM | PP | SH | GW | Min |
| 2003-04 | Virginia | High-MN | | 24 | 37 | 61 | | | | | | | | | | | | | | | | | | | |
| 2004-05 | Virginia | High-MN | 29 | 27 | 38 | 65 | 34 | | | | | | | | | | | | | | | | | | |
| 2005-06 | U. Minn-Duluth | WCHA | 38 | 1 | 13 | 14 | 40 | | | | | | | | | | | | | | | | | | |
| 2006-07 | U. Minn-Duluth | WCHA | 39 | 9 | 22 | 31 | 42 | | | | | | | | | | | | | | | | | | |
| | Iowa Stars | AHL | 13 | 0 | 3 | 3 | 6 | | | | | | | | | | 12 | 2 | 5 | 7 | 10 | | | | |
| **2007-08** | **Dallas** | **NHL** | **78** | **7** | **19** | **26** | **36** | **2** | **0** | **0** | **99** | **7.1** | **22** | **0** | **0.0** | **20:30** | **16** | **0** | **3** | **3** | **10** | **0** | **0** | **0** | **16:23** |
| **2008-09** | **Dallas** | **NHL** | **80** | **6** | **29** | **35** | **52** | **2** | **0** | **0** | **111** | **5.4** | **-11** | **0** | **0.0** | **19:58** | | | | | | | | | |
| | **NHL Totals** | | **158** | **13** | **48** | **61** | **88** | **4** | **0** | **0** | **210** | **6.2** | | **0** | **0.0** | **20:14** | **16** | **0** | **3** | **3** | **10** | **0** | **0** | **0** | **16:23** |

WCHA First All-Star Team (2007)

## NODL, Andreas

(NOHD'L, awn-DRAY-uhs) **PHI.**

Right wing. Shoots left. 6'1", 190 lbs. Born, Vienna, Austria, February 28, 1987. Philadelphia's 2nd choice, 39th overall, in 2006 Entry Draft.

| | | | Regular Season | | | | | | | | | | | | | | Playoffs | | | | | | | | |
|---|---|---|---|---|---|---|---|---|---|---|---|---|---|---|---|---|---|---|---|---|---|---|---|---|---|
| Season | Club | League | GP | G | A | Pts | PIM | PP | SH | GW | S | % | +/- | TF | F% | Min | GP | G | A | Pts | PIM | PP | SH | GW | Min |
| 2001-02 | Wien Jr. | Austria-Jr. | 1 | 0 | 0 | 0 | 0 | | | | | | | | | | | | | | | | | | |
| 2002-03 | Wien Jr. | Austria-Jr. | STATISTICS NOT AVAILABLE | | | | | | | | | | | | | | | | | | | | | | |
| | Austria | WJ18-B | 5 | 2 | 2 | 4 | 4 | | | | | | | | | | | | | | | | | | |
| 2003-04 | Vienna Capitals | Austria | 25 | 15 | 22 | 37 | 26 | | | | | | | | | | | | | | | | | | |
| | Wien Jr. | Austria-Jr. | 15 | 11 | 10 | 21 | 47 | | | | | | | | | | | | | | | | | | |
| | Austria | WJ18-B | 5 | 2 | 3 | 5 | 26 | | | | | | | | | | | | | | | | | | |
| 2004-05 | Sioux Falls | USHL | 44 | 7 | 9 | 16 | 24 | | | | | | | | | | | | | | | | | | |
| | Sioux Falls | USHL | 44 | 7 | 9 | 16 | 24 | | | | | | | | | | | | | | | | | | |
| 2005-06 | Sioux Falls | USHL | 58 | 29 | 30 | 59 | 16 | | | | | | | | | | 14 | 6 | 9 | 15 | 6 | | | | |
| 2006-07 | St. Cloud State | WCHA | 40 | 18 | 28 | 46 | 32 | | | | | | | | | | | | | | | | | | |
| 2007-08 | St. Cloud State | WCHA | 40 | 18 | 26 | 44 | 22 | | | | | | | | | | | | | | | | | | |
| | Philadelphia | AHL | 3 | 1 | 0 | 1 | 0 | | | | | | | | | | 10 | 1 | 0 | 1 | 2 | | | | |
| **2008-09** | **Philadelphia** | **NHL** | **38** | **1** | **3** | **4** | **2** | **0** | **0** | **0** | **33** | **3.0** | **-15** | **0** | **0.0** | **11:09** | | | | | | | | | |
| | Philadelphia | AHL | 39 | 6 | 14 | 20 | 20 | | | | | | | | | | 4 | 0 | 1 | 1 | 2 | | | | |
| | **NHL Totals** | | **38** | **1** | **3** | **4** | **2** | **0** | **0** | **0** | **33** | **3.0** | | **0** | **0.0** | **11:09** | | | | | | | | | |

USHL First All-Star Team (2006) • WCHA All-Rookie Team (2007) • WCHA Rookie of the Year (2007) • WCHA Second All-Star Team (2008)

## NOKELAINEN, Petteri

(noh-kuh-LAY-nehn, PEH-tuh-ree) **ANA.**

Center. Shoots right. 6'1", 191 lbs. Born, Imatra, Finland, January 16, 1986. NY Islanders' 1st choice, 16th overall, in 2004 Entry Draft.

| | | | Regular Season | | | | | | | | | | | | | | Playoffs | | | | | | | | |
|---|---|---|---|---|---|---|---|---|---|---|---|---|---|---|---|---|---|---|---|---|---|---|---|---|---|
| Season | Club | League | GP | G | A | Pts | PIM | PP | SH | GW | S | % | +/- | TF | F% | Min | GP | G | A | Pts | PIM | PP | SH | GW | Min |
| 2001-02 | SaiPa U18 | Fin-U18 | 6 | 2 | 1 | 3 | 14 | | | | | | | | | | | | | | | | | | |
| 2002-03 | SaiPa U18 | Fin-U18 | 10 | 3 | 8 | 11 | 18 | | | | | | | | | | | | | | | | | | |
| | SaiPa Jr. | Fin-Jr. | 28 | 7 | 4 | 11 | 28 | | | | | | | | | | 3 | 1 | 0 | 1 | 4 | | | | |
| | SaiPa | Finland | 2 | 1 | 0 | 1 | 2 | | | | | | | | | | | | | | | | | | |
| 2003-04 | Suomi U20 | Finland-2 | 3 | 0 | 1 | 1 | 0 | | | | | | | | | | | | | | | | | | |
| | SaiPa Jr. | Fin-Jr. | 10 | 5 | 3 | 8 | 4 | | | | | | | | | | 4 | 0 | 1 | 1 | 0 | | | | |
| | SaiPa | Finland | 40 | 4 | 4 | 8 | 16 | | | | | | | | | | | | | | | | | | |
| 2004-05 | SaiPa | Finland | 52 | 15 | 5 | 20 | 34 | | | | | | | | | | | | | | | | | | |
| **2005-06** | **NY Islanders** | **NHL** | **15** | **1** | **1** | **2** | **4** | **0** | **0** | **1** | **13** | **7.7** | **-1** | **82** | **48.8** | **7:47** | | | | | | | | | |
| 2006-07 | Bridgeport | AHL | 60 | 6 | 10 | 16 | 51 | | | | | | | | | | | | | | | | | | |
| **2007-08** | **Boston** | **NHL** | **57** | **7** | **3** | **10** | **19** | **0** | **0** | **1** | **40** | **17.5** | **0** | **288** | **52.8** | **8:16** | **7** | **0** | **2** | **2** | **4** | **0** | **0** | **0** | **12:38** |
| | Providence Bruins | AHL | 8 | 3 | 5 | 8 | 4 | | | | | | | | | | 6 | 4 | 1 | 5 | 0 | | | | |
| **2008-09** | **Boston** | **NHL** | **33** | **0** | **3** | **3** | **10** | **0** | **0** | **0** | **30** | **0.0** | **-1** | **87** | **62.1** | **9:40** | | | | | | | | | |
| | **Anaheim** | **NHL** | **17** | **4** | **2** | **6** | **6** | **0** | **1** | **0** | **26** | **15.4** | **3** | **205** | **49.8** | **14:20** | **9** | **0** | **0** | **0** | **2** | **0** | **0** | **0** | **8:42** |
| | **NHL Totals** | | **122** | **12** | **9** | **21** | **39** | **0** | **1** | **2** | **109** | **11.0** | | **662** | **52.6** | **9:26** | **16** | **0** | **2** | **2** | **6** | **0** | **0** | **0** | **10:26** |

• Missed majority of 2005-06 season recovering from knee injury suffered in game vs. Pittsburgh, November 3, 2005. Traded to **Boston** by **NY Islanders** for Ben Walter and Boston's 2nd round choice (later traded to Columbus – Columbus selected Kevin Lynch) in 2009 Entry Draft, September 11, 2007. Traded to **Anaheim** by **Boston** for Steve Montador, March 4, 2009.

## NOLAN, Brandon

(NOH-lan, BRAN-duhn)

Center/Left wing. Shoots left. 5'10", 185 lbs. Born, Sault Ste. Marie, Ont., July 18, 1983. Vancouver's 3rd choice, 111th overall, in 2003 Entry Draft.

| | | | Regular Season | | | | | | | | | | | | | | Playoffs | | | | | | | | |
|---|---|---|---|---|---|---|---|---|---|---|---|---|---|---|---|---|---|---|---|---|---|---|---|---|---|
| Season | Club | League | GP | G | A | Pts | PIM | PP | SH | GW | S | % | +/- | TF | F% | Min | GP | G | A | Pts | PIM | PP | SH | GW | Min |
| 99-2000 | St. Catharines | OHA-B | 47 | 18 | 13 | 31 | 10 | | | | | | | | | | | | | | | | | | |
| 2000-01 | Oshawa Generals | OHL | 52 | 15 | 23 | 38 | 21 | | | | | | | | | | | | | | | | | | |
| 2001-02 | Oshawa Generals | OHL | 57 | 30 | 28 | 58 | 78 | | | | | | | | | | 5 | 2 | 4 | 6 | 4 | | | | |
| 2002-03 | Oshawa Generals | OHL | 68 | 36 | 52 | 88 | 57 | | | | | | | | | | 13 | 10 | 7 | 17 | 4 | | | | |
| 2003-04 | Manitoba Moose | AHL | 48 | 7 | 10 | 17 | 18 | | | | | | | | | | | | | | | | | | |
| | Columbia Inferno | ECHL | 19 | 5 | 10 | 15 | 38 | | | | | | | | | | 3 | 0 | 1 | 1 | 17 | | | | |
| 2004-05 | Manitoba Moose | AHL | 48 | 4 | 8 | 12 | 16 | | | | | | | | | | | | | | | | | | |
| 2005-06 | Manitoba Moose | AHL | 18 | 3 | 8 | 11 | 10 | | | | | | | | | | | | | | | | | | |
| | Columbia Inferno | ECHL | 43 | 20 | 31 | 51 | 94 | | | | | | | | | | | | | | | | | | |

| | | | Regular Season | | | | | | | | | | | | | | Playoffs | | | | | | | | |
|---|---|---|---|---|---|---|---|---|---|---|---|---|---|---|---|---|---|---|---|---|---|---|---|---|---|
| Season | Club | League | GP | G | A | Pts | PIM | PP | SH | GW | S | % | +/- | TF | F% | Min | GP | G | A | Pts | PIM | PP | SH | GW | Min |
| 2006-07 | Bridgeport | AHL | 40 | 9 | 13 | 22 | 59 | .... | .... | .... | .... | .... | .... | .... | .... | .... | .... | .... | .... | .... | .... | .... | .... | .... | .... |
| | Vaxjo Lakers HC | Sweden-2 | 19 | 6 | 10 | 16 | 44 | .... | .... | .... | .... | .... | .... | .... | .... | .... | .... | .... | .... | .... | .... | .... | .... | .... | .... |
| **2007-08** | **Carolina** | **NHL** | **6** | **0** | **1** | **1** | **0** | **0** | **0** | **0** | **2** | **0.0** | **–2** | **0** | **0.0** | **7:15** | .... | .... | .... | .... | .... | .... | .... | .... | .... |
| | Albany River Rats | AHL | 48 | 22 | 26 | 48 | 72 | .... | .... | .... | .... | .... | .... | .... | .... | .... | .... | .... | .... | .... | .... | .... | .... | .... | .... |
| 2008-09 | | | DID NOT PLAY – INJURED | | | | | | | | | | | | | | | | | | | | | | |
| | **NHL Totals** | | **6** | **0** | **1** | **1** | **0** | **0** | **0** | **0** | **2** | **0.0** | | **0** | **0.0** | **7:15** | .... | .... | .... | .... | .... | .... | .... | .... | .... |

• Re-entered NHL Entry Draft. Originally New Jersey's 6th choice, 72nd overall, in 2001 Entry Draft.
OHL Second All-Star Team (2003)
Signed as a free agent by **Carolina**, July 2, 2007. • Missed entire 2008-09 season recovering from head injury.

### NOLAN, Owen (NOH-lan, OH-wehn) MIN.

Right wing. Shoots right. 6'1", 214 lbs. Born, Belfast, N.Ireland, February 12, 1972. Quebec's 1st choice, 1st overall, in 1990 Entry Draft.

| Season | Club | League | GP | G | A | Pts | PIM | PP | SH | GW | S | % | +/- | TF | F% | Min | GP | G | A | Pts | PIM | PP | SH | GW | Min |
|---|---|---|---|---|---|---|---|---|---|---|---|---|---|---|---|---|---|---|---|---|---|---|---|---|---|
| 1987-88 | Thorold | Minor-ON | 28 | 53 | 32 | 85 | 24 | .... | .... | .... | .... | .... | .... | .... | .... | .... | .... | .... | .... | .... | .... | .... | .... | .... | .... |
| | Thorold | OHA-B | 3 | 1 | 0 | 1 | 2 | .... | .... | .... | .... | .... | .... | .... | .... | .... | .... | .... | .... | .... | .... | .... | .... | .... | .... |
| 1988-89 | Cornwall Royals | OHL | 62 | 34 | 25 | 59 | 213 | .... | .... | .... | .... | .... | .... | .... | .... | .... | 18 | 5 | 11 | 16 | 41 | .... | .... | .... | .... |
| 1989-90 | Cornwall Royals | OHL | 58 | 51 | 59 | 110 | 240 | .... | .... | .... | .... | .... | .... | .... | .... | .... | 6 | 7 | 5 | 12 | 26 | .... | .... | .... | .... |
| **1990-91** | **Quebec** | **NHL** | **59** | **3** | **10** | **13** | **109** | **0** | **0** | **0** | **54** | **5.6** | **–19** | .... | .... | .... | .... | .... | .... | .... | .... | .... | .... | .... | .... |
| | Halifax Citadels | AHL | 6 | 4 | 4 | 8 | 11 | .... | .... | .... | .... | .... | .... | .... | .... | .... | .... | .... | .... | .... | .... | .... | .... | .... | .... |
| **1991-92** | **Quebec** | **NHL** | **75** | **42** | **31** | **73** | **183** | **17** | **0** | **0** | **190** | **22.1** | **–9** | .... | .... | .... | .... | .... | .... | .... | .... | .... | .... | .... | .... |
| **1992-93** | **Quebec** | **NHL** | **73** | **36** | **41** | **77** | **185** | **15** | **0** | **4** | **241** | **14.9** | **–1** | .... | .... | .... | **5** | **1** | **0** | **1** | **2** | **0** | **0** | **0** | .... |
| **1993-94** | **Quebec** | **NHL** | **6** | **2** | **2** | **4** | **8** | **0** | **0** | **0** | **15** | **13.3** | **2** | .... | .... | .... | .... | .... | .... | .... | .... | .... | .... | .... | .... |
| **1994-95** | **Quebec** | **NHL** | **46** | **30** | **19** | **49** | **46** | **13** | **2** | **8** | **137** | **21.9** | **21** | .... | .... | .... | **6** | **2** | **3** | **5** | **6** | **0** | **0** | **0** | .... |
| **1995-96** | **Colorado** | **NHL** | **9** | **4** | **4** | **8** | **9** | **4** | **0** | **0** | **23** | **17.4** | **–3** | .... | .... | .... | .... | .... | .... | .... | .... | .... | .... | .... | .... |
| | **San Jose** | **NHL** | **72** | **29** | **32** | **61** | **137** | **12** | **1** | **2** | **184** | **15.8** | **–30** | .... | .... | .... | .... | .... | .... | .... | .... | .... | .... | .... | .... |
| **1996-97** | **San Jose** | **NHL** | **72** | **31** | **32** | **63** | **155** | **10** | **0** | **3** | **225** | **13.8** | **–19** | .... | .... | .... | .... | .... | .... | .... | .... | .... | .... | .... | .... |
| **1997-98** | **San Jose** | **NHL** | **75** | **14** | **27** | **41** | **144** | **3** | **1** | **1** | **192** | **7.3** | **–2** | .... | .... | .... | **6** | **2** | **2** | **4** | **26** | **2** | **0** | **1** | .... |
| **1998-99** | **San Jose** | **NHL** | **78** | **19** | **26** | **45** | **129** | **6** | **2** | **3** | **207** | **9.2** | **16** | **657** | **49.3** | **19:09** | **6** | **1** | **1** | **2** | **6** | **0** | **0** | **0** | **20:15** |
| **99-2000** | **San Jose** | **NHL** | **78** | **44** | **40** | **84** | **110** | **18** | **4** | **6** | **261** | **16.9** | **–1** | **357** | **50.7** | **21:07** | **10** | **8** | **2** | **10** | **6** | **2** | **2** | **3** | **22:14** |
| **2000-01** | **San Jose** | **NHL** | **57** | **24** | **25** | **49** | **75** | **10** | **1** | **4** | **191** | **12.6** | **0** | **407** | **46.9** | **21:49** | **6** | **1** | **1** | **2** | **8** | **0** | **0** | **1** | **22:45** |
| **2001-02** | **San Jose** | **NHL** | **75** | **23** | **43** | **66** | **93** | **8** | **2** | **2** | **217** | **10.6** | **7** | **545** | **47.0** | **19:23** | **12** | **3** | **6** | **9** | **8** | **0** | **0** | **0** | **19:46** |
| | Canada | Olympics | 6 | 0 | 3 | 3 | 2 | .... | .... | .... | .... | .... | .... | .... | .... | .... | .... | .... | .... | .... | .... | .... | .... | .... | .... |
| **2002-03** | **San Jose** | **NHL** | **61** | **22** | **20** | **42** | **91** | **8** | **3** | **4** | **192** | **11.5** | **–5** | **226** | **50.4** | **18:08** | .... | .... | .... | .... | .... | .... | .... | .... | .... |
| | **Toronto** | **NHL** | **14** | **7** | **5** | **12** | **16** | **5** | **0** | **1** | **29** | **24.1** | **2** | **56** | **48.2** | **17:00** | **7** | **0** | **2** | **2** | **2** | **0** | **0** | **0** | **23:19** |
| **2003-04** | **Toronto** | **NHL** | **65** | **19** | **29** | **48** | **110** | **7** | **2** | **3** | **154** | **12.3** | **4** | **242** | **53.3** | **17:57** | .... | .... | .... | .... | .... | .... | .... | .... | .... |
| 2004-05 | | | DID NOT PLAY | | | | | | | | | | | | | | | | | | | | | | |
| 2005-06 | | | DID NOT PLAY – INJURED | | | | | | | | | | | | | | | | | | | | | | |
| **2006-07** | **Phoenix** | **NHL** | **76** | **16** | **24** | **40** | **56** | **2** | **3** | **1** | **154** | **10.4** | **–2** | **238** | **52.5** | **15:25** | .... | .... | .... | .... | .... | .... | .... | .... | .... |
| **2007-08** | **Calgary** | **NHL** | **77** | **16** | **16** | **32** | **71** | **1** | **1** | **3** | **163** | **9.8** | **6** | **346** | **52.3** | **16:33** | **7** | **3** | **2** | **5** | **2** | **0** | **0** | **2** | **19:11** |
| **2008-09** | **Minnesota** | **NHL** | **59** | **25** | **20** | **45** | **26** | **12** | **0** | **5** | **148** | **16.9** | **5** | **161** | **46.6** | **16:24** | .... | .... | .... | .... | .... | .... | .... | .... | .... |
| | **NHL Totals** | | **1127** | **406** | **446** | **852** | **1753** | **151** | **22** | **50** | **2977** | **13.6** | | **3235** | **49.6** | **18:23** | **65** | **21** | **19** | **40** | **66** | **4** | **2** | **7** | **21:09** |

OHL Rookie of the Year (1989) • OHL First All-Star Team (1990)
Played in NHL All-Star Game (1992, 1996, 1997, 2000, 2002)
• Missed majority of 1993-94 season recovering from shoulder injury suffered in game vs. Tampa Bay, November 13, 1993. Transferred to **Colorado** after **Quebec** franchise relocated, June 21, 1995. Traded to **San Jose** by **Colorado** for Sandis Ozolinsh, October 26, 1995. Traded to **Toronto** by **San Jose** for Alyn McCauley, Brad Boyes and Toronto's 1st round choice (later traded to Boston – Boston selected Mark Stuart) in 2003 Entry Draft, March 5, 2003. • Missed entire 2005-06 seaon recovering from knee surgery, July, 2005. Signed as a free agent by **Phoenix**, August 16, 2006. Signed as a free agent by **Calgary**, July 3, 2007. Signed as a free agent by **Minnesota**, July 6, 2008.

### NOVOTNY, Jiri (nuh-VAWT-nee, YIH-ree)

Center. Shoots right. 6'3", 204 lbs. Born, Pelhrimov, Czech., August 12, 1983. Buffalo's 1st choice, 22nd overall, in 2001 Entry Draft.

| Season | Club | League | GP | G | A | Pts | PIM | PP | SH | GW | S | % | +/- | TF | F% | Min | GP | G | A | Pts | PIM | PP | SH | GW | Min |
|---|---|---|---|---|---|---|---|---|---|---|---|---|---|---|---|---|---|---|---|---|---|---|---|---|---|
| 99-2000 | C. Budejovice Jr. | CzRep-Jr. | 36 | 11 | 10 | 21 | 6 | .... | .... | .... | .... | .... | .... | .... | .... | .... | .... | .... | .... | .... | .... | .... | .... | .... | .... |
| | C. Budejovice U17 | CzR-U17 | 11 | 5 | 7 | 12 | 4 | .... | .... | .... | .... | .... | .... | .... | .... | .... | .... | .... | .... | .... | .... | .... | .... | .... | .... |
| | HC Slezan Opava | CzRep-2 | 17 | 2 | 2 | 4 | 6 | .... | .... | .... | .... | .... | .... | .... | .... | .... | .... | .... | .... | .... | .... | .... | .... | .... | .... |
| 2000-01 | C. Budejovice Jr. | CzRep-Jr. | 33 | 10 | 10 | 20 | .... | .... | .... | .... | .... | .... | .... | .... | .... | .... | .... | .... | .... | .... | .... | .... | .... | .... | .... |
| | Havl. Brod | CzRep-3 | 1 | 0 | 0 | 0 | 0 | .... | .... | .... | .... | .... | .... | .... | .... | .... | .... | .... | .... | .... | .... | .... | .... | .... | .... |
| 2001-02 | C. Budejovice Jr. | CzRep-Jr. | 7 | 4 | 4 | 8 | 4 | .... | .... | .... | .... | .... | .... | .... | .... | .... | .... | .... | .... | .... | .... | .... | .... | .... | .... |
| | Jind. Hradec | CzRep-3 | 3 | 1 | 3 | 4 | 0 | .... | .... | .... | .... | .... | .... | .... | .... | .... | .... | .... | .... | .... | .... | .... | .... | .... | .... |
| | C. Budejovice | CzRep | 41 | 8 | 6 | 14 | 6 | .... | .... | .... | .... | .... | .... | .... | .... | .... | .... | .... | .... | .... | .... | .... | .... | .... | .... |
| 2002-03 | Rochester | AHL | 43 | 2 | 9 | 11 | 14 | .... | .... | .... | .... | .... | .... | .... | .... | .... | 3 | 0 | 1 | 1 | 10 | .... | .... | .... | .... |
| 2003-04 | Rochester | AHL | 48 | 1 | 14 | 15 | 16 | .... | .... | .... | .... | .... | .... | .... | .... | .... | 13 | 0 | 1 | 1 | 10 | .... | .... | .... | .... |
| 2004-05 | Rochester | AHL | 61 | 5 | 20 | 25 | 36 | .... | .... | .... | .... | .... | .... | .... | .... | .... | 9 | 2 | 2 | 4 | 4 | .... | .... | .... | .... |
| **2005-06** | **Buffalo** | **NHL** | **14** | **2** | **1** | **3** | **0** | **0** | **1** | **0** | **15** | **13.3** | **–5** | **139** | **45.3** | **12:15** | **4** | **0** | **0** | **0** | **0** | **0** | **0** | **0** | **10:27** |
| | Rochester | AHL | 66 | 17 | 37 | 54 | 40 | .... | .... | .... | .... | .... | .... | .... | .... | .... | .... | .... | .... | .... | .... | .... | .... | .... | .... |
| **2006-07** | **Buffalo** | **NHL** | **50** | **6** | **7** | **13** | **26** | **0** | **0** | **0** | **60** | **10.0** | **–2** | **324** | **44.1** | **12:19** | .... | .... | .... | .... | .... | .... | .... | .... | .... |
| | **Washington** | **NHL** | **18** | **0** | **6** | **6** | **2** | **0** | **0** | **0** | **19** | **0.0** | **–2** | **202** | **51.5** | **14:36** | .... | .... | .... | .... | .... | .... | .... | .... | .... |
| **2007-08** | **Columbus** | **NHL** | **65** | **8** | **14** | **22** | **24** | **1** | **0** | **0** | **91** | **8.8** | **–10** | **791** | **47.4** | **17:43** | .... | .... | .... | .... | .... | .... | .... | .... | .... |
| **2008-09** | **Columbus** | **NHL** | **42** | **4** | **3** | **7** | **14** | **0** | **1** | **0** | **56** | **7.1** | **4** | **293** | **52.9** | **13:21** | .... | .... | .... | .... | .... | .... | .... | .... | .... |
| | **NHL Totals** | | **189** | **20** | **31** | **51** | **66** | **1** | **2** | **0** | **241** | **8.3** | | **1749** | **48.0** | **14:37** | **4** | **0** | **0** | **0** | **0** | **0** | **0** | **0** | **10:27** |

Traded to **Washington** by **Buffalo** with Buffalo's 1st round choice (later traded to San Jose - San Jose selected Nicholas Petrecki) in 2007 Entry Draft for Dainius Zubrus and Timo Helbling, February 27, 2007. Signed as a free agent by **Columbus**, July 3, 2007.

### NUMMINEN, Teppo (NOO-mih-nehn, TEH-poh)

Defense. Shoots right. 6'2", 198 lbs. Born, Tampere, Finland, July 3, 1968. Winnipeg's 2nd choice, 29th overall, in 1986 Entry Draft.

| Season | Club | League | GP | G | A | Pts | PIM | PP | SH | GW | S | % | +/- | TF | F% | Min | GP | G | A | Pts | PIM | PP | SH | GW | Min |
|---|---|---|---|---|---|---|---|---|---|---|---|---|---|---|---|---|---|---|---|---|---|---|---|---|---|
| 1984-85 | Whitby Lawmen | OJHL | 16 | 3 | 9 | 12 | 0 | .... | .... | .... | .... | .... | .... | .... | .... | .... | .... | .... | .... | .... | .... | .... | .... | .... | .... |
| 1985-86 | Tappara Jr. | Fin-Jr. | 2 | 0 | 0 | 0 | 0 | .... | .... | .... | .... | .... | .... | .... | .... | .... | 3 | 0 | 1 | 1 | 2 | .... | .... | .... | .... |
| | Tappara Tampere | Finland | 31 | 2 | 4 | 6 | 6 | .... | .... | .... | .... | .... | .... | .... | .... | .... | 8 | 0 | 0 | 0 | 0 | .... | .... | .... | .... |
| 1986-87 | Tappara Tampere | Finland | 44 | 9 | 9 | 18 | 16 | .... | .... | .... | .... | .... | .... | .... | .... | .... | 9 | 4 | 1 | 5 | 4 | .... | .... | .... | .... |
| 1987-88 | Tappara Tampere | Finland | 40 | 10 | 10 | 20 | 29 | .... | .... | .... | .... | .... | .... | .... | .... | .... | 10 | 6 | 6 | 12 | 6 | .... | .... | .... | .... |
| | Finland | Olympics | 6 | 1 | 4 | 5 | 0 | .... | .... | .... | .... | .... | .... | .... | .... | .... | .... | .... | .... | .... | .... | .... | .... | .... | .... |
| **1988-89** | **Winnipeg** | **NHL** | **69** | **1** | **14** | **15** | **36** | **0** | **1** | **0** | **85** | **1.2** | **–11** | .... | .... | .... | .... | .... | .... | .... | .... | .... | .... | .... | .... |
| **1989-90** | **Winnipeg** | **NHL** | **79** | **11** | **32** | **43** | **20** | **1** | **0** | **1** | **105** | **10.5** | **–4** | .... | .... | .... | **7** | **1** | **2** | **3** | **10** | **0** | **0** | **0** | .... |
| **1990-91** | **Winnipeg** | **NHL** | **80** | **8** | **25** | **33** | **28** | **3** | **0** | **0** | **151** | **5.3** | **–15** | .... | .... | .... | .... | .... | .... | .... | .... | .... | .... | .... | .... |
| **1991-92** | **Winnipeg** | **NHL** | **80** | **5** | **34** | **39** | **32** | **4** | **0** | **1** | **143** | **3.5** | **15** | .... | .... | .... | **7** | **0** | **0** | **0** | **0** | **0** | **0** | **0** | .... |
| **1992-93** | **Winnipeg** | **NHL** | **66** | **7** | **30** | **37** | **33** | **3** | **1** | **0** | **103** | **6.8** | **4** | .... | .... | .... | **6** | **1** | **1** | **2** | **2** | **1** | **0** | **0** | .... |
| **1993-94** | **Winnipeg** | **NHL** | **57** | **5** | **18** | **23** | **28** | **4** | **0** | **1** | **89** | **5.6** | **–23** | .... | .... | .... | .... | .... | .... | .... | .... | .... | .... | .... | .... |
| **1994-95** | TuTo Turku | Finland | 12 | 3 | 8 | 11 | 4 | .... | .... | .... | .... | .... | .... | .... | .... | .... | .... | .... | .... | .... | .... | .... | .... | .... | .... |
| | **Winnipeg** | **NHL** | **42** | **5** | **16** | **21** | **16** | **2** | **0** | **0** | **86** | **5.8** | **12** | .... | .... | .... | .... | .... | .... | .... | .... | .... | .... | .... | .... |
| **1995-96** | **Winnipeg** | **NHL** | **74** | **11** | **43** | **54** | **22** | **6** | **0** | **3** | **165** | **6.7** | **–4** | .... | .... | .... | **6** | **0** | **0** | **0** | **2** | **0** | **0** | **0** | .... |
| **1996-97** | **Phoenix** | **NHL** | **82** | **2** | **25** | **27** | **28** | **0** | **0** | **0** | **135** | **1.5** | **–3** | .... | .... | .... | **7** | **3** | **3** | **6** | **0** | **1** | **0** | **1** | .... |
| **1997-98** | **Phoenix** | **NHL** | **82** | **11** | **40** | **51** | **30** | **6** | **0** | **2** | **126** | **8.7** | **25** | .... | .... | .... | **1** | **0** | **0** | **0** | **0** | **0** | **0** | **0** | .... |
| | Finland | Olympics | 6 | 1 | 1 | 2 | 2 | .... | .... | .... | .... | .... | .... | .... | .... | .... | .... | .... | .... | .... | .... | .... | .... | .... | .... |
| **1998-99** | **Phoenix** | **NHL** | **82** | **10** | **30** | **40** | **30** | **1** | **0** | **0** | **156** | **6.4** | **3** | **2** | **0.0** | **24:26** | **7** | **2** | **1** | **3** | **4** | **2** | **0** | **0** | **26:09** |
| **99-2000** | **Phoenix** | **NHL** | **79** | **8** | **34** | **42** | **16** | **2** | **0** | **2** | **126** | **6.3** | **21** | **1** | **0.0** | **23:37** | **5** | **1** | **1** | **2** | **0** | **0** | **0** | **0** | **23:11** |
| **2000-01** | **Phoenix** | **NHL** | **72** | **5** | **26** | **31** | **36** | **1** | **0** | **2** | **109** | **4.6** | **9** | **0** | **0.0** | **24:28** | .... | .... | .... | .... | .... | .... | .... | .... | .... |
| **2001-02** | **Phoenix** | **NHL** | **76** | **13** | **35** | **48** | **20** | **4** | **0** | **6** | **117** | **11.1** | **13** | **0** | **0.0** | **23:51** | **4** | **0** | **0** | **0** | **2** | **0** | **0** | **0** | **25:33** |
| | Finland | Olympics | 4 | 0 | 1 | 1 | 0 | .... | .... | .... | .... | .... | .... | .... | .... | .... | .... | .... | .... | .... | .... | .... | .... | .... | .... |
| **2002-03** | **Phoenix** | **NHL** | **78** | **6** | **24** | **30** | **30** | **2** | **0** | **1** | **108** | **5.6** | **0** | **0** | **0.0** | **23:51** | .... | .... | .... | .... | .... | .... | .... | .... | .... |
| **2003-04** | **Dallas** | **NHL** | **62** | **3** | **14** | **17** | **18** | **0** | **0** | **0** | **83** | **3.6** | **–5** | **1** | **100.0** | **21:40** | **4** | **0** | **1** | **1** | **0** | **0** | **0** | **0** | **19:13** |
| 2004-05 | | | DID NOT PLAY | | | | | | | | | | | | | | | | | | | | | | |
| **2005-06** | **Buffalo** | **NHL** | **75** | **2** | **38** | **40** | **36** | **0** | **0** | **0** | **60** | **3.3** | **6** | **1** | **100.0** | **19:30** | **12** | **1** | **1** | **2** | **4** | **1** | **0** | **0** | **18:45** |
| | Finland | Olympics | 8 | 1 | 2 | 3 | 2 | .... | .... | .... | .... | .... | .... | .... | .... | .... | .... | .... | .... | .... | .... | .... | .... | .... | .... |
| **2006-07** | **Buffalo** | **NHL** | **79** | **2** | **27** | **29** | **32** | **0** | **0** | **0** | **69** | **2.9** | **17** | **0** | **0.0** | **20:48** | **16** | **0** | **4** | **4** | **4** | **0** | **0** | **0** | **19:33** |
| **2007-08** | **Buffalo** | **NHL** | **1** | **0** | **0** | **0** | **0** | **0** | **0** | **0** | **1** | **0.0** | **0** | **0** | **0.0** | **16:03** | .... | .... | .... | .... | .... | .... | .... | .... | .... |
| **2008-09** | **Buffalo** | **NHL** | **57** | **2** | **15** | **17** | **22** | **1** | **0** | **1** | **34** | **5.9** | **–4** | **0** | **0.0** | **17:30** | .... | .... | .... | .... | .... | .... | .... | .... | .... |
| | **NHL Totals** | | **1372** | **117** | **520** | **637** | **513** | **40** | **2** | **20** | **2051** | **5.7** | | **5** | **40.0** | **22:20** | **82** | **9** | **14** | **23** | **28** | **5** | **0** | **1** | **21:10** |

Played in NHL All-Star Game (1999, 2000, 2001)
• Transferred to **Phoenix** after **Winnipeg** franchise relocated, July 1, 1996. Traded to **Dallas** by **Phoenix** for Mike Sillinger, July 22, 2003. Signed as a free agent by **Buffalo**, August 4, 2005. • Missed majority of 2007-08 recovering from open heart surgery, September 20, 2007. • Officially announced his retirement, August 5, 2009.

## NYCHOLAT, Lawrence

(NIH-koh-lat, LAW-rehnts) **VAN.**

Defense. Shoots left. 6', 200 lbs. Born, Calgary, Alta., May 7, 1979.

| | | | Regular Season | | | | | | | | | | | | | | | Playoffs | | | | | | | | |
|---|---|---|---|---|---|---|---|---|---|---|---|---|---|---|---|---|---|---|---|---|---|---|---|---|---|
| Season | Club | League | GP | G | A | Pts | PIM | PP | SH | GW | S | % | +/- | TF | F% | Min | GP | G | A | Pts | PIM | PP | SH | GW | Min |
| 1995-96 | Notre Dame | SMHL | 42 | 10 | 36 | 46 | 66 | .... | .... | .... | .... | .... | .... | .... | .... | .... | .... | .... | .... | .... | .... | .... | .... | .... | .... |
| 1996-97 | Swift Current | WHL | 67 | 8 | 13 | 21 | 82 | .... | .... | .... | .... | .... | .... | .... | .... | .... | 10 | 0 | 0 | 0 | 24 | .... | .... | .... | .... |
| 1997-98 | Swift Current | WHL | 71 | 13 | 35 | 48 | 108 | .... | .... | .... | .... | .... | .... | .... | .... | .... | 1 | 0 | 0 | 0 | 0 | .... | .... | .... | .... |
| 1998-99 | Swift Current | WHL | 72 | 16 | 44 | 60 | 125 | .... | .... | .... | .... | .... | .... | .... | .... | .... | 6 | 2 | 2 | 4 | 12 | .... | .... | .... | .... |
| 99-2000 | Swift Current | WHL | 70 | 22 | 58 | 80 | 92 | .... | .... | .... | .... | .... | .... | .... | .... | .... | 2 | 0 | 0 | 0 | 0 | .... | .... | .... | .... |
| 2000-01 | Jackson Bandits | ECHL | 5 | 1 | 2 | 3 | 5 | .... | .... | .... | .... | .... | .... | .... | .... | .... | .... | .... | .... | .... | .... | .... | .... | .... | .... |
| | Cleveland | IHL | 42 | 3 | 7 | 10 | 69 | .... | .... | .... | .... | .... | .... | .... | .... | .... | 4 | 0 | 0 | 0 | 2 | .... | .... | .... | .... |
| 2001-02 | Houston Aeros | AHL | 72 | 3 | 11 | 14 | 92 | .... | .... | .... | .... | .... | .... | .... | .... | .... | 14 | 1 | 0 | 1 | 23 | .... | .... | .... | .... |
| 2002-03 | Houston Aeros | AHL | 66 | 11 | 28 | 39 | 155 | .... | .... | .... | .... | .... | .... | .... | .... | .... | .... | .... | .... | .... | .... | .... | .... | .... | .... |
| | Hartford | AHL | 15 | 2 | 9 | 11 | 6 | .... | .... | .... | .... | .... | .... | .... | .... | .... | 2 | 2 | 0 | 2 | 0 | .... | .... | .... | .... |
| **2003-04** | **NY Rangers** | **NHL** | **9** | **0** | **0** | **0** | **6** | **0** | **0** | **0** | **6** | **0.0** | **–2** | **0** | **0.0** | **17:09** | .... | .... | .... | .... | .... | .... | .... | .... | .... |
| | Hartford | AHL | 72 | 6 | 26 | 32 | 130 | .... | .... | .... | .... | .... | .... | .... | .... | .... | 16 | 0 | 5 | 5 | 28 | .... | .... | .... | .... |
| 2004-05 | Hartford | AHL | 79 | 5 | 38 | 43 | 132 | .... | .... | .... | .... | .... | .... | .... | .... | .... | 6 | 0 | 3 | 3 | 11 | .... | .... | .... | .... |
| 2005-06 | Hershey Bears | AHL | 73 | 13 | 44 | 57 | 94 | .... | .... | .... | .... | .... | .... | .... | .... | .... | 16 | 2 | 12 | 14 | 12 | .... | .... | .... | .... |
| **2006-07** | **Washington** | **NHL** | **18** | **2** | **6** | **8** | **12** | **0** | **0** | **0** | **22** | **9.1** | **–3** | **0** | **0.0** | **20:32** | .... | .... | .... | .... | .... | .... | .... | .... | .... |
| | Hershey Bears | AHL | 29 | 3 | 25 | 28 | 39 | .... | .... | .... | .... | .... | .... | .... | .... | .... | .... | .... | .... | .... | .... | .... | .... | .... | .... |
| | **Ottawa** | **NHL** | **1** | **0** | **0** | **0** | **0** | **0** | **0** | **0** | **3** | **0.0** | **0** | **0** | **0.0** | **12:48** | .... | .... | .... | .... | .... | .... | .... | .... | .... |
| **2007-08** | **Ottawa** | **NHL** | **3** | **0** | **0** | **0** | **0** | **0** | **0** | **0** | **4** | **0.0** | **1** | **0** | **0.0** | **11:57** | .... | .... | .... | .... | .... | .... | .... | .... | .... |
| | Binghamton | AHL | 77 | 12 | 37 | 49 | 74 | .... | .... | .... | .... | .... | .... | .... | .... | .... | .... | .... | .... | .... | .... | .... | .... | .... | .... |
| **2008-09** | **Vancouver** | **NHL** | **14** | **0** | **1** | **1** | **6** | **0** | **0** | **0** | **8** | **0.0** | **3** | **0** | **0.0** | **9:41** | .... | .... | .... | .... | .... | .... | .... | .... | .... |
| | Manitoba Moose | AHL | 3 | 0 | 3 | 3 | 4 | .... | .... | .... | .... | .... | .... | .... | .... | .... | .... | .... | .... | .... | .... | .... | .... | .... | .... |
| | **Colorado** | **NHL** | **5** | **0** | **0** | **0** | **0** | **0** | **0** | **0** | **1** | **0.0** | **–2** | **0** | **0.0** | **10:33** | .... | .... | .... | .... | .... | .... | .... | .... | .... |
| | **NHL Totals** | | **50** | **2** | **7** | **9** | **24** | **0** | **0** | **0** | **44** | **4.5** | | **0** | **0.0** | **15:13** | .... | .... | .... | .... | .... | .... | .... | .... | .... |

AHL First All-Star Team (2008)

Signed as a free agent by **Minnesota**, August 31, 2000. Traded to **NY Rangers** by **Minnesota** for Johan Holmqvist, March 11, 2003. Signed as a free agent by **Washington**, August 9, 2005. Traded to **Ottawa** by **Washington** for Andy Hedlund and Ottawa's 6th round choice (Justin Taylor) in 2007 Entry Draft, February 26, 2007. Traded to **Vancouver** by **Ottawa** for Ryan Shannon, September 2, 2008. Claimed on waivers by **Calgary** from **Vancouver**, March 3, 2009. Traded to **Colorado** by **Calgary** with Ryan Wilson and and Montreal's 2nd round choice (previously acquired, Colorado selected Stefan Elliott) in 2009 Entry Draft for Jordan Leopold, March 4, 2009. Signed as a free agent by **Vancouver**, July 2, 2009.

## NYLANDER, Michael

(NEE-lan-duhr, MIGH-kuhl) **WSH.**

Center. Shoots left. 6'1", 195 lbs. Born, Stockholm, Sweden, October 3, 1972. Hartford's 4th choice, 59th overall, in 1991 Entry Draft.

| | | | | | | | | | | | | | | | | | | | | | | | | | |
|---|---|---|---|---|---|---|---|---|---|---|---|---|---|---|---|---|---|---|---|---|---|---|---|---|---|
| 1989-90 | Huddinge IK | Sweden-2 | 31 | 7 | 15 | 22 | 4 | .... | .... | .... | .... | .... | .... | .... | .... | .... | 5 | 3 | 0 | 3 | 0 | .... | .... | .... | .... |
| 1990-91 | Huddinge IK | Sweden-2 | 33 | 14 | 20 | 34 | 10 | .... | .... | .... | .... | .... | .... | .... | .... | .... | 2 | 0 | 0 | 0 | 0 | .... | .... | .... | .... |
| 1991-92 | AIK Solna | Sweden | 40 | 11 | 17 | 28 | 30 | .... | .... | .... | .... | .... | .... | .... | .... | .... | 3 | 1 | 4 | 5 | 4 | .... | .... | .... | .... |
| **1992-93** | **Hartford** | **NHL** | **59** | **11** | **22** | **33** | **36** | **3** | **0** | **1** | **85** | **12.9** | **–7** | .... | .... | .... | .... | .... | .... | .... | .... | .... | .... | .... | .... |
| | Springfield | AHL | .... | .... | .... | .... | .... | .... | .... | .... | .... | .... | .... | .... | .... | .... | 3 | 3 | 3 | 6 | 2 | .... | .... | .... | .... |
| **1993-94** | **Hartford** | **NHL** | **58** | **11** | **33** | **44** | **24** | **4** | **0** | **1** | **74** | **14.9** | **–2** | .... | .... | .... | .... | .... | .... | .... | .... | .... | .... | .... | .... |
| | Springfield | AHL | 4 | 0 | 9 | 9 | 0 | .... | .... | .... | .... | .... | .... | .... | .... | .... | .... | .... | .... | .... | .... | .... | .... | .... | .... |
| | **Calgary** | **NHL** | **15** | **2** | **9** | **11** | **6** | **0** | **0** | **0** | **21** | **9.5** | **10** | .... | .... | .... | **3** | **0** | **0** | **0** | **0** | **0** | **0** | **0** | .... |
| **1994-95** | JYP HT Jyvaskyla | Finland | 16 | 11 | 19 | 30 | 63 | .... | .... | .... | .... | .... | .... | .... | .... | .... | .... | .... | .... | .... | .... | .... | .... | .... | .... |
| | **Calgary** | **NHL** | **6** | **0** | **1** | **1** | **2** | **0** | **0** | **0** | **2** | **0.0** | **1** | .... | .... | .... | **6** | **0** | **6** | **6** | **2** | **0** | **0** | **0** | .... |
| **1995-96** | **Calgary** | **NHL** | **73** | **17** | **38** | **55** | **20** | **4** | **0** | **6** | **163** | **10.4** | **0** | .... | .... | .... | **4** | **0** | **0** | **0** | **0** | **0** | **0** | **0** | .... |
| 1996-97 | HC Lugano | Swiss | 36 | 12 | 43 | 55 | 28 | .... | .... | .... | .... | .... | .... | .... | .... | .... | 8 | 3 | 8 | 11 | 8 | .... | .... | .... | .... |
| **1997-98** | **Calgary** | **NHL** | **65** | **13** | **23** | **36** | **24** | **0** | **0** | **2** | **117** | **11.1** | **10** | .... | .... | .... | .... | .... | .... | .... | .... | .... | .... | .... | .... |
| | Sweden | Olympics | 4 | 0 | 0 | 0 | 6 | .... | .... | .... | .... | .... | .... | .... | .... | .... | .... | .... | .... | .... | .... | .... | .... | .... | .... |
| **1998-99** | **Calgary** | **NHL** | **9** | **2** | **3** | **5** | **2** | **1** | **0** | **0** | **7** | **28.6** | **1** | **25** | **60.0** | **11:10** | .... | .... | .... | .... | .... | .... | .... | .... | .... |
| | **Tampa Bay** | **NHL** | **24** | **2** | **7** | **9** | **6** | **0** | **0** | **0** | **26** | **7.7** | **–10** | **75** | **44.0** | **13:29** | .... | .... | .... | .... | .... | .... | .... | .... | .... |
| **99-2000** | **Tampa Bay** | **NHL** | **11** | **1** | **2** | **3** | **4** | **1** | **0** | **0** | **10** | **10.0** | **–3** | **35** | **57.1** | **10:32** | .... | .... | .... | .... | .... | .... | .... | .... | .... |
| | **Chicago** | **NHL** | **66** | **23** | **28** | **51** | **26** | **4** | **0** | **2** | **112** | **20.5** | **9** | **561** | **46.9** | **16:39** | .... | .... | .... | .... | .... | .... | .... | .... | .... |
| **2000-01** | **Chicago** | **NHL** | **82** | **25** | **39** | **64** | **32** | **4** | **0** | **5** | **176** | **14.2** | **7** | **1036** | **48.3** | **18:52** | .... | .... | .... | .... | .... | .... | .... | .... | .... |
| **2001-02** | **Chicago** | **NHL** | **82** | **15** | **46** | **61** | **50** | **6** | **0** | **2** | **158** | **9.5** | **28** | **974** | **50.2** | **15:33** | **5** | **0** | **3** | **3** | **2** | **0** | **0** | **0** | **15:20** |
| | Sweden | Olympics | 4 | 1 | 2 | 3 | 0 | .... | .... | .... | .... | .... | .... | .... | .... | .... | .... | .... | .... | .... | .... | .... | .... | .... | .... |
| **2002-03** | **Chicago** | **NHL** | **9** | **0** | **4** | **4** | **4** | **0** | **0** | **0** | **20** | **0.0** | **0** | **86** | **48.8** | **15:19** | .... | .... | .... | .... | .... | .... | .... | .... | .... |
| | **Washington** | **NHL** | **71** | **17** | **39** | **56** | **36** | **7** | **0** | **2** | **141** | **12.1** | **3** | **1005** | **47.4** | **18:41** | **6** | **3** | **2** | **5** | **8** | **1** | **0** | **1** | **16:45** |
| **2003-04** | **Washington** | **NHL** | **3** | **0** | **2** | **2** | **8** | **0** | **0** | **0** | **1** | **0.0** | **1** | **22** | **54.6** | **14:57** | .... | .... | .... | .... | .... | .... | .... | .... | .... |
| | **Boston** | **NHL** | **15** | **1** | **11** | **12** | **14** | **0** | **0** | **1** | **29** | **3.4** | **3** | **128** | **46.1** | **15:43** | **6** | **3** | **3** | **6** | **0** | **0** | **0** | **0** | **18:57** |
| 2004-05 | Karpat Oulu | Finland | 23 | 5 | 15 | 20 | 22 | .... | .... | .... | .... | .... | .... | .... | .... | .... | .... | .... | .... | .... | .... | .... | .... | .... | .... |
| | St. Petersburg | Russia | 8 | 2 | 5 | 7 | 0 | .... | .... | .... | .... | .... | .... | .... | .... | .... | .... | .... | .... | .... | .... | .... | .... | .... | .... |
| | Ak Bars Kazan | Russia | 5 | 0 | 1 | 1 | 2 | .... | .... | .... | .... | .... | .... | .... | .... | .... | .... | .... | .... | .... | .... | .... | .... | .... | .... |
| **2005-06** | **NY Rangers** | **NHL** | **81** | **23** | **56** | **79** | **76** | **6** | **0** | **4** | **172** | **13.4** | **31** | **1143** | **46.5** | **19:20** | **4** | **0** | **1** | **1** | **0** | **0** | **0** | **0** | **20:33** |
| **2006-07** | **NY Rangers** | **NHL** | **79** | **26** | **57** | **83** | **42** | **14** | **0** | **4** | **193** | **13.5** | **12** | **1054** | **47.5** | **20:23** | **10** | **6** | **7** | **13** | **0** | **2** | **0** | **2** | **21:50** |
| **2007-08** | **Washington** | **NHL** | **40** | **11** | **26** | **37** | **24** | **5** | **0** | **1** | **77** | **14.3** | **–19** | **535** | **49.2** | **19:09** | .... | .... | .... | .... | .... | .... | .... | .... | .... |
| **2008-09** | **Washington** | **NHL** | **72** | **9** | **24** | **33** | **32** | **4** | **0** | **2** | **87** | **10.3** | **0** | **632** | **45.9** | **14:02** | **3** | **0** | **0** | **0** | **2** | **0** | **0** | **0** | **8:48** |
| | **NHL Totals** | | **920** | **209** | **470** | **679** | **468** | **63** | **0** | **33** | **1671** | **12.5** | | **7311** | **47.8** | **17:20** | **47** | **12** | **22** | **34** | **14** | **3** | **0** | **3** | **18:10** |

Traded to **Calgary** by **Hartford** with James Patrick and Zarley Zalapski for Gary Suter, Paul Ranheim and Ted Drury, March 10, 1994. • Missed majority of 1994-95 season recovering from wrist injury suffered in game vs. St. Louis, January 24, 1995. Traded to **Tampa Bay** by **Calgary** for Andrei Nazarov, January 19, 1999. Traded to **Chicago** by **Tampa Bay** for Bryan Muir and Reid Simpson, November 12, 1999. Traded to **Washington** by **Chicago** with Chicago's 3rd round choice (Stephen Werner) in 2003 Entry Draft and future considerations for Chris Simon and Andrei Nikolishin, November 1, 2002. • Missed majority of 2003-04 season recovering from leg injury suffered in practice, October 2, 2003. Traded to **Boston** by **Washington** for Boston's 4th round compensatory choice (Patrick McNeill) in 2005 Entry Draft and Boston's 2nd round choice (Francois Bouchard) in 2006 Entry Draft, March 4, 2004. Signed as a free agent by **NY Rangers**, August 10, 2004. Signed as a free agent by **Oulu** (Finland), September 25, 2004. Signed as a free agent by **St. Petersburg** (Russia), December 20, 2004. Signed as a free agent by **Kazan** (Russia), February 14, 2005. Signed as a free agent by **Washington**, July 2, 2007.

## NYSTROM, Eric

(NIGH-stuhm, AIR-ihk) **CGY.**

Left wing. Shoots left. 6'1", 193 lbs. Born, Syosset, NY, February 14, 1983. Calgary's 1st choice, 10th overall, in 2002 Entry Draft.

| | | | | | | | | | | | | | | | | | | | | | | | | | |
|---|---|---|---|---|---|---|---|---|---|---|---|---|---|---|---|---|---|---|---|---|---|---|---|---|---|
| 99-2000 | USNTDP | NAHL | 55 | 7 | 16 | 23 | 57 | .... | .... | .... | .... | .... | .... | .... | .... | .... | 3 | 0 | 0 | 0 | 0 | .... | .... | .... | .... |
| 2000-01 | USNTDP | U-18 | 43 | 10 | 12 | 22 | 52 | .... | .... | .... | .... | .... | .... | .... | .... | .... | .... | .... | .... | .... | .... | .... | .... | .... | .... |
| | USNTDP | USHL | 23 | 5 | 5 | 10 | 50 | .... | .... | .... | .... | .... | .... | .... | .... | .... | .... | .... | .... | .... | .... | .... | .... | .... | .... |
| 2001-02 | U. of Michigan | CCHA | 40 | 18 | 13 | 31 | 42 | .... | .... | .... | .... | .... | .... | .... | .... | .... | .... | .... | .... | .... | .... | .... | .... | .... | .... |
| 2002-03 | U. of Michigan | CCHA | 39 | 15 | 11 | 26 | 24 | .... | .... | .... | .... | .... | .... | .... | .... | .... | .... | .... | .... | .... | .... | .... | .... | .... | .... |
| 2003-04 | U. of Michigan | CCHA | 43 | 10 | 12 | 22 | 50 | .... | .... | .... | .... | .... | .... | .... | .... | .... | .... | .... | .... | .... | .... | .... | .... | .... | .... |
| 2004-05 | U. of Michigan | CCHA | 38 | 13 | 19 | 32 | 33 | .... | .... | .... | .... | .... | .... | .... | .... | .... | .... | .... | .... | .... | .... | .... | .... | .... | .... |
| **2005-06** | **Calgary** | **NHL** | **2** | **0** | **0** | **0** | **0** | **0** | **0** | **0** | **0** | **0.0** | **–1** | **5** | **60.0** | **12:01** | .... | .... | .... | .... | .... | .... | .... | .... | .... |
| | Omaha | AHL | 78 | 15 | 18 | 33 | 37 | .... | .... | .... | .... | .... | .... | .... | .... | .... | .... | .... | .... | .... | .... | .... | .... | .... | .... |
| 2006-07 | Omaha | AHL | 12 | 2 | 0 | 2 | 0 | .... | .... | .... | .... | .... | .... | .... | .... | .... | 5 | 0 | 0 | 0 | 2 | .... | .... | .... | .... |
| **2007-08** | **Calgary** | **NHL** | **44** | **3** | **7** | **10** | **48** | **0** | **0** | **0** | **42** | **7.1** | **–5** | **14** | **50.0** | **11:30** | **7** | **0** | **0** | **0** | **2** | **0** | **0** | **0** | **7:39** |
| | Quad City Flames | AHL | 18 | 4 | 3 | 7 | 15 | .... | .... | .... | .... | .... | .... | .... | .... | .... | .... | .... | .... | .... | .... | .... | .... | .... | .... |
| **2008-09** | **Calgary** | **NHL** | **76** | **5** | **5** | **10** | **89** | **0** | **1** | **3** | **83** | **6.0** | **–7** | **29** | **37.9** | **9:16** | **6** | **2** | **2** | **4** | **0** | **0** | **0** | **1** | **10:57** |
| | **NHL Totals** | | **122** | **8** | **12** | **20** | **137** | **0** | **1** | **3** | **125** | **6.4** | | **48** | **43.8** | **10:07** | **13** | **2** | **2** | **4** | **2** | **0** | **0** | **1** | **9:10** |

CCHA All-Rookie Team (2002)

• Missed majority of 2006-07 season recovering from shoulder injury.

## O'BRIEN, Doug

(oh-BRIGH-uhn, DUHG)

Defense. Shoots left. 6'1", 200 lbs. Born, St. John's, Nfld., February 16, 1984. Tampa Bay's 4th choice, 192nd overall, in 2003 Entry Draft.

| | | | | | | | | | | | | | | | | | | | | | | | | | |
|---|---|---|---|---|---|---|---|---|---|---|---|---|---|---|---|---|---|---|---|---|---|---|---|---|---|
| 2000-01 | Hull Olympiques | QMJHL | 47 | 1 | 6 | 7 | 16 | .... | .... | .... | .... | .... | .... | .... | .... | .... | 5 | 0 | 1 | 1 | 0 | .... | .... | .... | .... |
| 2001-02 | Hull Olympiques | QMJHL | 46 | 1 | 5 | 6 | 36 | .... | .... | .... | .... | .... | .... | .... | .... | .... | 12 | 0 | 0 | 0 | 14 | .... | .... | .... | .... |
| 2002-03 | Hull Olympiques | QMJHL | 71 | 10 | 34 | 44 | 102 | .... | .... | .... | .... | .... | .... | .... | .... | .... | 19 | 3 | 12 | 15 | 18 | .... | .... | .... | .... |
| 2003-04 | Gatineau | QMJHL | 66 | 17 | 46 | 63 | 146 | .... | .... | .... | .... | .... | .... | .... | .... | .... | 15 | 1 | 8 | 9 | 16 | .... | .... | .... | .... |
| 2004-05 | Springfield | AHL | 74 | 4 | 13 | 17 | 76 | .... | .... | .... | .... | .... | .... | .... | .... | .... | .... | .... | .... | .... | .... | .... | .... | .... | .... |
| | Johnstown Chiefs | ECHL | 3 | 0 | 0 | 0 | 2 | .... | .... | .... | .... | .... | .... | .... | .... | .... | .... | .... | .... | .... | .... | .... | .... | .... | .... |
| **2005-06** | **Tampa Bay** | **NHL** | **5** | **0** | **0** | **0** | **2** | **0** | **0** | **0** | **2** | **0.0** | **0** | **0** | **0.0** | **7:44** | .... | .... | .... | .... | .... | .... | .... | .... | .... |
| | Springfield | AHL | 74 | 7 | 25 | 32 | 70 | .... | .... | .... | .... | .... | .... | .... | .... | .... | .... | .... | .... | .... | .... | .... | .... | .... | .... |
| 2006-07 | Springfield | AHL | 53 | 6 | 13 | 19 | 34 | .... | .... | .... | .... | .... | .... | .... | .... | .... | .... | .... | .... | .... | .... | .... | .... | .... | .... |
| | Portland Pirates | AHL | 22 | 0 | 6 | 6 | 19 | .... | .... | .... | .... | .... | .... | .... | .... | .... | .... | .... | .... | .... | .... | .... | .... | .... | .... |
| 2007-08 | Lukko Rauma | Finland | 39 | 5 | 4 | 9 | 51 | .... | .... | .... | .... | .... | .... | .... | .... | .... | .... | .... | .... | .... | .... | .... | .... | .... | .... |

| | | | Regular Season | | | | | | | | | | | | | | Playoffs | | | | | | | | |
|---|---|---|---|---|---|---|---|---|---|---|---|---|---|---|---|---|---|---|---|---|---|---|---|---|---|
| Season | Club | League | GP | G | A | Pts | PIM | PP | SH | GW | S | % | +/- | TF | F% | Min | GP | G | A | Pts | PIM | PP | SH | GW | Min |
| 2008-09 | Rochester | AHL | 12 | 0 | 2 | 2 | 8 | | | | | | | | | | | | | | | | | | |
| | Florida Everblades | ECHL | 56 | 7 | 18 | 25 | 130 | | | | | | | | | | 9 | 2 | 6 | 8 | 12 | | | | |
| | **NHL Totals** | | 5 | 0 | 0 | 0 | 2 | 0 | 0 | 0 | 2 | 0.0 | | 0 | 0.0 | 7:44 | | | | | | | | | |

QMJHL First All-Star Team (2004) • Memorial Cup Tournament All-Star Team (2003, 2004) • Ed Chynoweth Trophy (Memorial Cup Tournament - Leading Scorer) (2004)

Traded to **Anaheim** by **Tampa Bay** for Joe Rullier, February 27, 2007.

## O'BRIEN, Shane

(oh-BRIGH-uhn, SHAYN) **VAN.**

Defense. Shoots left. 6'3", 224 lbs. Born, Port Hope, Ont., August 9, 1983. Anaheim's 8th choice, 250th overall, in 2003 Entry Draft.

| | | | | | | | | | | | | | | | | | | | | | | | | | |
|---|---|---|---|---|---|---|---|---|---|---|---|---|---|---|---|---|---|---|---|---|---|---|---|---|---|
| 99-2000 | Port Hope | OPJHL | 47 | 6 | 27 | 33 | 110 | | | | | | | | | | | | | | | | | | |
| 2000-01 | Kingston | OHL | 61 | 2 | 12 | 14 | 89 | | | | | | | | | | 4 | 0 | 1 | 1 | 6 | | | | |
| 2001-02 | Kingston | OHL | 67 | 10 | 23 | 33 | 132 | | | | | | | | | | 1 | 0 | 0 | 0 | 2 | | | | |
| 2002-03 | Kingston | OHL | 28 | 8 | 15 | 23 | 100 | | | | | | | | | | | | | | | | | | |
| | St. Michael's | OHL | 34 | 8 | 11 | 19 | 108 | | | | | | | | | | 19 | 4 | 10 | 14 | *79 | | | | |
| 2003-04 | Cincinnati | AHL | 60 | 2 | 8 | 10 | 163 | | | | | | | | | | 9 | 0 | 2 | 2 | 20 | | | | |
| 2004-05 | Cincinnati | AHL | 77 | 5 | 20 | 25 | 319 | | | | | | | | | | 12 | 1 | 3 | 4 | 57 | | | | |
| 2005-06 | Portland Pirates | AHL | 77 | 8 | 33 | 41 | 287 | | | | | | | | | | 19 | 6 | 16 | 22 | *81 | | | | |
| **2006-07** | **Anaheim** | **NHL** | **62** | **2** | **12** | **14** | **140** | **1** | **0** | **2** | **55** | **3.6** | **5** | **0** | **0.0** | **14:04** | | | | | | | | | |
| | **Tampa Bay** | **NHL** | **18** | **0** | **2** | **2** | **36** | **0** | **0** | **0** | **17** | **0.0** | **-8** | **0** | **0.0** | **18:08** | **6** | **0** | **0** | **0** | **12** | **0** | **0** | **0** | **17:12** |
| **2007-08** | **Tampa Bay** | **NHL** | **77** | **4** | **17** | **21** | **154** | **0** | **0** | **1** | **69** | **5.8** | **-2** | **0** | **0.0** | **21:13** | | | | | | | | | |
| **2008-09** | **Tampa Bay** | **NHL** | **1** | **0** | **0** | **0** | **0** | **0** | **0** | **0** | **0** | **0.0** | **-1** | **0** | **0.0** | **14:04** | | | | | | | | | |
| | **Vancouver** | **NHL** | **76** | **0** | **10** | **10** | **196** | **0** | **0** | **0** | **39** | **0.0** | **6** | **0** | **0.0** | **14:56** | **10** | **1** | **1** | **2** | **24** | **0** | **0** | **0** | **12:06** |
| | **NHL Totals** | | **234** | **6** | **41** | **47** | **526** | **1** | **0** | **3** | **180** | **3.3** | | **0** | **0.0** | **17:01** | **16** | **1** | **1** | **2** | **36** | **0** | **0** | **0** | **14:01** |

Traded to **Tampa Bay** by **Anaheim** with Colorado's 3rd round choice (previously acquired, Tampa Bay selected Luca Cunti) in 2007 Entry Draft for Gerald Coleman and Tampa Bay's 1st round choice (later traded to Minnesota - Minnesota selected Colton Gillies) in 2007 Entry Draft, February 24, 2007. Traded to **Vancouver** by **Tampa Bay** with Michel Ouellet for Lukas Krajicek and Juraj Simek, October 6, 2008.

## O'BYRNE, Ryan

(oh-BUHRN, RIGH-uhn) **MTL.**

Defense. Shoots right. 6'5", 228 lbs. Born, Victoria, B.C., July 19, 1984. Montreal's 4th choice, 79th overall, in 2003 Entry Draft.

| | | | | | | | | | | | | | | | | | | | | | | | | | |
|---|---|---|---|---|---|---|---|---|---|---|---|---|---|---|---|---|---|---|---|---|---|---|---|---|---|
| 2001-02 | Victoria Salsa | BCHL | 52 | 2 | 9 | 11 | 91 | | | | | | | | | | | | | | | | | | |
| 2002-03 | Victoria Salsa | BCHL | 32 | 3 | 6 | 9 | 94 | | | | | | | | | | | | | | | | | | |
| | Nanaimo Clippers | BCHL | 9 | 2 | 4 | 6 | 24 | | | | | | | | | | | | | | | | | | |
| 2003-04 | Cornell Big Red | ECAC | 31 | 0 | 2 | 2 | 71 | | | | | | | | | | | | | | | | | | |
| 2004-05 | Cornell Big Red | ECAC | 33 | 3 | 7 | 10 | 68 | | | | | | | | | | | | | | | | | | |
| 2005-06 | Cornell Big Red | ECAC | 28 | 7 | 6 | 13 | 69 | | | | | | | | | | | | | | | | | | |
| 2006-07 | Hamilton | AHL | 80 | 0 | 12 | 12 | 129 | | | | | | | | | | 22 | 2 | 5 | 7 | 32 | | | | |
| **2007-08** | **Montreal** | **NHL** | **33** | **1** | **6** | **7** | **45** | **0** | **0** | **0** | **10** | **10.0** | **7** | **0** | **0.0** | **13:24** | **4** | **0** | **0** | **0** | **0** | **0** | **0** | **0** | **10:46** |
| | Hamilton | AHL | 20 | 2 | 6 | 8 | 49 | | | | | | | | | | | | | | | | | | |
| **2008-09** | **Montreal** | **NHL** | **37** | **0** | **5** | **5** | **58** | **0** | **0** | **0** | **14** | **0.0** | **-7** | **0** | **0.0** | **15:06** | **2** | **0** | **0** | **0** | **2** | **0** | **0** | **0** | **13:04** |
| | Hamilton | AHL | 18 | 1 | 5 | 6 | 35 | | | | | | | | | | | | | | | | | | |
| | **NHL Totals** | | **70** | **1** | **11** | **12** | **103** | **0** | **0** | **0** | **24** | **4.2** | | **0** | **0.0** | **14:18** | **6** | **0** | **0** | **0** | **2** | **0** | **0** | **0** | **11:32** |

## O'DONNELL, Sean

(oh-DAHN-uhl, SHAWN) **L.A.**

Defense. Shoots left. 6'2", 230 lbs. Born, Ottawa, Ont., October 13, 1971. Buffalo's 6th choice, 123rd overall, in 1991 Entry Draft.

| | | | | | | | | | | | | | | | | | | | | | | | | | |
|---|---|---|---|---|---|---|---|---|---|---|---|---|---|---|---|---|---|---|---|---|---|---|---|---|---|
| 1987-88 | Kanata Valley | CJHL | 54 | 4 | 25 | 29 | 96 | | | | | | | | | | | | | | | | | | |
| 1988-89 | Sudbury Wolves | OHL | 56 | 1 | 9 | 10 | 49 | | | | | | | | | | 7 | 1 | 2 | 3 | 8 | | | | |
| 1989-90 | Sudbury Wolves | OHL | 64 | 7 | 19 | 26 | 84 | | | | | | | | | | 5 | 1 | 4 | 5 | 10 | | | | |
| 1990-91 | Sudbury Wolves | OHL | 66 | 8 | 23 | 31 | 114 | | | | | | | | | | 16 | 1 | 2 | 3 | 21 | | | | |
| 1991-92 | Rochester | AHL | 73 | 4 | 9 | 13 | 193 | | | | | | | | | | 17 | 1 | 6 | 7 | 38 | | | | |
| 1992-93 | Rochester | AHL | 74 | 3 | 18 | 21 | 203 | | | | | | | | | | 4 | 0 | 1 | 1 | 21 | | | | |
| 1993-94 | Rochester | AHL | 64 | 2 | 10 | 12 | 242 | | | | | | | | | | 9 | 0 | 1 | 1 | 21 | | | | |
| **1994-95** | Phoenix | IHL | 61 | 2 | 18 | 20 | 132 | | | | | | | | | | | | | | | | | | |
| | **Los Angeles** | **NHL** | **15** | **0** | **2** | **2** | **49** | **0** | **0** | **0** | **12** | **0.0** | **-2** | | | | | | | | | | | | |
| **1995-96** | **Los Angeles** | **NHL** | **71** | **2** | **5** | **7** | **127** | **0** | **0** | **0** | **65** | **3.1** | **3** | | | | | | | | | | | | |
| **1996-97** | **Los Angeles** | **NHL** | **55** | **5** | **12** | **17** | **144** | **2** | **0** | **0** | **68** | **7.4** | **-13** | | | | | | | | | | | | |
| **1997-98** | **Los Angeles** | **NHL** | **80** | **2** | **15** | **17** | **179** | **0** | **0** | **1** | **71** | **2.8** | **7** | | | | **4** | **1** | **0** | **1** | **36** | **0** | **0** | **0** | |
| **1998-99** | **Los Angeles** | **NHL** | **80** | **1** | **13** | **14** | **186** | **0** | **0** | **0** | **64** | **1.6** | **1** | **0** | **0.0** | **19:10** | | | | | | | | | |
| **99-2000** | **Los Angeles** | **NHL** | **80** | **2** | **12** | **14** | **114** | **0** | **0** | **1** | **51** | **3.9** | **4** | **0** | **0.0** | **17:41** | **4** | **1** | **0** | **1** | **4** | **0** | **0** | **0** | **16:26** |
| **2000-01** | **Minnesota** | **NHL** | **63** | **4** | **12** | **16** | **128** | **1** | **0** | **2** | **58** | **6.9** | **-2** | **12** | **50.0** | **23:00** | | | | | | | | | |
| | **New Jersey** | **NHL** | **17** | **0** | **1** | **1** | **33** | **0** | **0** | **0** | **9** | **0.0** | **2** | **0** | **0.0** | **16:27** | **23** | **1** | **2** | **3** | **41** | **0** | **0** | **0** | **16:21** |
| **2001-02** | **Boston** | **NHL** | **80** | **3** | **22** | **25** | **89** | **1** | **0** | **2** | **112** | **2.7** | **27** | **0** | **0.0** | **24:50** | **6** | **0** | **2** | **2** | **4** | **0** | **0** | **0** | **24:58** |
| **2002-03** | **Boston** | **NHL** | **70** | **1** | **15** | **16** | **76** | **0** | **0** | **1** | **61** | **1.6** | **8** | **1** | **0.0** | **22:05** | | | | | | | | | |
| **2003-04** | **Boston** | **NHL** | **82** | **1** | **10** | **11** | **110** | **0** | **0** | **0** | **72** | **1.4** | **10** | **3** | **33.3** | **20:36** | **7** | **0** | **0** | **0** | **0** | **0** | **0** | **0** | **19:53** |
| 2004-05 | | | DID NOT PLAY | | | | | | | | | | | | | | | | | | | | | | |
| **2005-06** | **Phoenix** | **NHL** | **57** | **1** | **7** | **8** | **121** | **0** | **0** | **0** | **23** | **4.3** | **3** | **0** | **0.0** | **16:18** | | | | | | | | | |
| | **Anaheim** | **NHL** | **21** | **1** | **2** | **3** | **26** | **0** | **0** | **0** | **10** | **10.0** | **3** | **0** | **0.0** | **17:13** | **16** | **2** | **3** | **5** | **23** | **0** | **0** | **1** | **16:44** |
| **2006-07** ♦ | **Anaheim** | **NHL** | **79** | **2** | **15** | **17** | **92** | **0** | **0** | **1** | **47** | **4.3** | **9** | **1** | **0.0** | **19:55** | **21** | **0** | **2** | **2** | **10** | **0** | **0** | **0** | **20:20** |
| **2007-08** | **Anaheim** | **NHL** | **82** | **2** | **7** | **9** | **84** | **0** | **1** | **0** | **25** | **8.0** | **9** | **2** | **100.0** | **17:14** | **6** | **1** | **1** | **2** | **2** | **0** | **0** | **0** | **15:32** |
| **2008-09** | **Los Angeles** | **NHL** | **82** | **0** | **12** | **12** | **71** | **0** | **0** | **0** | **32** | **0.0** | **2** | **1** | **0.0** | **20:29** | | | | | | | | | |
| | **NHL Totals** | | **1014** | **27** | **162** | **189** | **1629** | **4** | **1** | **8** | **780** | **3.5** | | **20** | **45.0** | **20:00** | **87** | **6** | **10** | **16** | **120** | **0** | **0** | **1** | **18:18** |

Traded to **Los Angeles** by **Buffalo** for Doug Houda, July 26, 1994. Claimed by **Minnesota** from **Los Angeles** in Expansion Draft, June 23, 2000. Traded to **New Jersey** by **Minnesota** for Willie Mitchell, March 4, 2001. Signed as a free agent by **Boston**, July 2, 2001. Signed as a free agent by **Phoenix**, July 6, 2004. Traded to **Anaheim** by **Phoenix** for Joel Perreault, March 9, 2006. Traded to **Los Angeles** by **Anaheim** for future considerations, September 30, 2008.

## ODUYA, Johnny

(oh-DOO-yuh, JAW-nee) **N.J.**

Defense. Shoots left. 6', 200 lbs. Born, Stockholm, Sweden, October 1, 1981. Washington's 6th choice, 221st overall, in 2001 Entry Draft.

| | | | | | | | | | | | | | | | | | | | | | | | | | |
|---|---|---|---|---|---|---|---|---|---|---|---|---|---|---|---|---|---|---|---|---|---|---|---|---|---|
| 1996-97 | Hammarby Jr. | Swe-Jr. | 13 | 0 | 0 | 0 | | | | | | | | | | | | | | | | | | | |
| 1997-98 | Hammarby Jr. | Swe-Jr. | 26 | 3 | 11 | 14 | 70 | | | | | | | | | | | | | | | | | | |
| 1998-99 | Hammarby Jr. | Swe-Jr. | 38 | 14 | 31 | 45 | 45 | | | | | | | | | | | | | | | | | | |
| 99-2000 | Hammarby Jr. | Swe-Jr. | 32 | 3 | 18 | 21 | 48 | | | | | | | | | | 6 | 1 | 2 | 3 | 4 | | | | |
| | Hammarby | Sweden-2 | 1 | 0 | 0 | 0 | 0 | | | | | | | | | | 1 | 0 | 0 | 0 | 0 | | | | |
| 2000-01 | Moncton Wildcats | QMJHL | 44 | 11 | 38 | 49 | 147 | | | | | | | | | | | | | | | | | | |
| | Victoriaville Tigres | QMJHL | 24 | 3 | 16 | 19 | 112 | | | | | | | | | | 13 | 4 | 9 | 13 | 10 | | | | |
| 2001-02 | Hammarby | Sweden-2 | 46 | 11 | 14 | 25 | 66 | | | | | | | | | | 2 | 1 | 0 | 1 | 4 | | | | |
| 2002-03 | Hammarby | Sweden-2 | 48 | 15 | 25 | 40 | 200 | | | | | | | | | | | | | | | | | | |
| 2003-04 | Djurgarden | Sweden | 42 | 4 | 4 | 8 | *173 | | | | | | | | | | 4 | 0 | 0 | 0 | 6 | | | | |
| 2004-05 | Djurgarden | Sweden | 49 | 2 | 4 | 6 | 139 | | | | | | | | | | 12 | 0 | 2 | 2 | 39 | | | | |
| 2005-06 | Frolunda | Sweden | 47 | 8 | 11 | 19 | 95 | | | | | | | | | | 17 | 1 | 2 | 3 | 16 | | | | |
| **2006-07** | **New Jersey** | **NHL** | **76** | **2** | **9** | **11** | **61** | **0** | **0** | **0** | **55** | **3.6** | **-5** | **0** | **0.0** | **18:31** | **6** | **0** | **1** | **1** | **6** | **0** | **0** | **0** | **12:59** |
| **2007-08** | **New Jersey** | **NHL** | **75** | **6** | **20** | **26** | **46** | **2** | **0** | **0** | **63** | **9.5** | **27** | **0** | **0.0** | **19:02** | **5** | **0** | **1** | **1** | **6** | **0** | **0** | **0** | **20:40** |
| **2008-09** | **New Jersey** | **NHL** | **82** | **7** | **22** | **29** | **30** | **1** | **1** | **4** | **108** | **6.5** | **21** | **0** | **0.0** | **20:52** | **7** | **0** | **0** | **0** | **2** | **0** | **0** | **0** | **20:19** |
| | **NHL Totals** | | **233** | **15** | **51** | **66** | **137** | **3** | **1** | **4** | **226** | **6.6** | | **0** | **0.0** | **19:31** | **18** | **0** | **2** | **2** | **14** | **0** | **0** | **0** | **17:58** |

Signed as a free agent by **New Jersey**, July 24, 2006.

## OHLUND, Mattias

(OH-luhnd, mat-TEE-uhs) **T.B.**

Defense. Shoots left. 6'3", 220 lbs. Born, Pitea, Sweden, September 9, 1976. Vancouver's 1st choice, 13th overall, in 1994 Entry Draft.

| | | | | | | | | | | | | | | | | | | | | | | | | | |
|---|---|---|---|---|---|---|---|---|---|---|---|---|---|---|---|---|---|---|---|---|---|---|---|---|---|
| 1992-93 | Pitea HC | Sweden-2 | 22 | 0 | 6 | 6 | 16 | | | | | | | | | | | | | | | | | | |
| 1993-94 | Pitea HC | Sweden-2 | 28 | 7 | 10 | 17 | 66 | | | | | | | | | | | | | | | | | | |
| 1994-95 | Lulea HF | Sweden | 34 | 6 | 10 | 16 | 34 | | | | | | | | | | 9 | 4 | 0 | 4 | 16 | | | | |
| 1995-96 | Lulea HF | Sweden | 38 | 4 | 10 | 14 | 26 | | | | | | | | | | 13 | 1 | 3 | 4 | 47 | | | | |
| 1996-97 | Lulea HF | Sweden | 47 | 7 | 9 | 16 | 38 | | | | | | | | | | 10 | 1 | 2 | 3 | 8 | | | | |
| | Lulea HF | EuroHL | 6 | 0 | 3 | 3 | 0 | | | | | | | | | | | | | | | | | | |
| **1997-98** | **Vancouver** | **NHL** | **77** | **7** | **23** | **30** | **76** | **1** | **0** | **0** | **172** | **4.1** | **3** | | | | | | | | | | | | |
| | Sweden | Olympics | 4 | 0 | 1 | 1 | 4 | | | | | | | | | | | | | | | | | | |
| **1998-99** | **Vancouver** | **NHL** | **74** | **9** | **26** | **35** | **83** | **2** | **1** | **1** | **129** | **7.0** | **-19** | **0** | **0.0** | **26:04** | | | | | | | | | |
| **99-2000** | **Vancouver** | **NHL** | **42** | **4** | **16** | **20** | **24** | **2** | **1** | **1** | **63** | **6.3** | **6** | **0** | **0.0** | **27:41** | | | | | | | | | |

| | | | Regular Season | | | | | | | | | | | | | | Playoffs | | | | | | | | |
|---|---|---|---|---|---|---|---|---|---|---|---|---|---|---|---|---|---|---|---|---|---|---|---|---|---|
| Season | Club | League | GP | G | A | Pts | PIM | PP | SH | GW | S | % | +/- | TF | F% | Min | GP | G | A | Pts | PIM | PP | SH | GW | Min |
| 2000-01 | Vancouver | NHL | 65 | 8 | 20 | 28 | 46 | 1 | 1 | 4 | 136 | 5.9 | –16 | 0 | 0.0 | 25:00 | 4 | 1 | 3 | 4 | 6 | 1 | 0 | 0 | 26:32 |
| 2001-02 | Vancouver | NHL | 81 | 10 | 26 | 36 | 56 | 4 | 1 | 3 | 193 | 5.2 | 16 | 0 | 0.0 | 25:17 | 6 | 1 | 1 | 2 | 6 | 0 | 0 | 0 | 28:48 |
| | Sweden | Olympics | 4 | 0 | 2 | 2 | 2 | .... | .... | .... | .... | .... | .... | .... | .... | .... | .... | .... | .... | .... | .... | .... | .... | .... | .... |
| 2002-03 | Vancouver | NHL | 59 | 2 | 27 | 29 | 42 | 0 | 0 | 0 | 100 | 2.0 | 1 | 0 | 0.0 | 25:23 | 13 | 3 | 4 | 7 | 12 | 0 | 0 | 0 | 24:01 |
| 2003-04 | Vancouver | NHL | 82 | 14 | 20 | 34 | 73 | 5 | 0 | 3 | 129 | 10.9 | 14 | 0 | 0.0 | 25:47 | 7 | 1 | 4 | 5 | 13 | 0 | 0 | 1 | 27:25 |
| 2004-05 | Lulea HF | Sweden | 2 | 1 | 0 | 1 | 4 | .... | .... | .... | .... | .... | .... | .... | .... | .... | .... | .... | .... | .... | .... | .... | .... | .... | .... |
| 2005-06 | Vancouver | NHL | 78 | 13 | 20 | 33 | 92 | 8 | 1 | 2 | 183 | 7.1 | –6 | 1 | 0.0 | 25:40 | .... | .... | .... | .... | .... | .... | .... | .... | .... |
| | Sweden | Olympics | 6 | 0 | 2 | 2 | 2 | .... | .... | .... | .... | .... | .... | .... | .... | .... | .... | .... | .... | .... | .... | .... | .... | .... | .... |
| 2006-07 | Vancouver | NHL | 77 | 11 | 20 | 31 | 80 | 6 | 0 | 2 | 170 | 6.5 | –3 | 1 | 0.0 | 24:47 | 12 | 2 | 5 | 7 | 12 | 1 | 0 | 0 | 28:18 |
| 2007-08 | Vancouver | NHL | 53 | 9 | 15 | 24 | 79 | 4 | 0 | 2 | 128 | 7.0 | –1 | 0 | 0.0 | 23:46 | .... | .... | .... | .... | .... | .... | .... | .... | .... |
| 2008-09 | Vancouver | NHL | 82 | 6 | 19 | 25 | 105 | 3 | 0 | 1 | 131 | 4.6 | 14 | 0 | 0.0 | 21:34 | 10 | 1 | 2 | 3 | 6 | 1 | 0 | 0 | 23:54 |
| | **NHL Totals** | | **770** | **93** | **232** | **325** | **756** | **36** | **5** | **19** | **1534** | **6.1** | | **2** | **0.0** | **24:59** | **52** | **9** | **19** | **28** | **55** | **3** | **0** | **1** | **26:11** |

NHL All-Rookie Team (1998)
Played in NHL All-Star Game (1999)
Signed as a free agent by **Lulea** (Sweden), December 21, 2004. Signed as a free agent by **Tampa Bay**, July 1, 2009.

## OKPOSO, Kyle
(OH-poh-soh, KIGHL) **NYI**

Right wing. Shoots right. 6'1", 200 lbs. Born, St. Paul, MN, April 16, 1988. NY Islanders' 1st choice, 7th overall, in 2006 Entry Draft.

| | | | | | | | | | | | | | | | | | | | | | | | | | |
|---|---|---|---|---|---|---|---|---|---|---|---|---|---|---|---|---|---|---|---|---|---|---|---|---|---|
| 2004-05 | Shat.-St. Mary's | High-MN | 65 | 47 | 45 | 92 | 72 | .... | .... | .... | .... | .... | .... | .... | .... | .... | .... | .... | .... | .... | .... | .... | .... | .... | .... |
| 2005-06 | Des Moines | USHL | 50 | 27 | 31 | 58 | 56 | .... | .... | .... | .... | .... | .... | .... | .... | .... | 11 | 5 | 11 | *16 | 8 | .... | .... | .... | .... |
| 2006-07 | U. of Minnesota | WCHA | 40 | 19 | 21 | 40 | 34 | .... | .... | .... | .... | .... | .... | .... | .... | .... | .... | .... | .... | .... | .... | .... | .... | .... | .... |
| 2007-08 | U. of Minnesota | WCHA | 18 | 7 | 4 | 11 | 6 | .... | .... | .... | .... | .... | .... | .... | .... | .... | .... | .... | .... | .... | .... | .... | .... | .... | .... |
| | **NY Islanders** | **NHL** | **9** | **2** | **3** | **5** | **2** | **1** | **0** | **1** | **15** | **13.3** | **3** | **0** | **0.0** | **16:28** | .... | .... | .... | .... | .... | .... | .... | .... | .... |
| | Bridgeport | AHL | 35 | 9 | 19 | 28 | 12 | .... | .... | .... | .... | .... | .... | .... | .... | .... | .... | .... | .... | .... | .... | .... | .... | .... | .... |
| 2008-09 | **NY Islanders** | **NHL** | **65** | **18** | **21** | **39** | **36** | **9** | **0** | **3** | **165** | **10.9** | **–6** | **15** | **33.3** | **18:01** | .... | .... | .... | .... | .... | .... | .... | .... | .... |
| | Bridgeport | AHL | .... | .... | .... | .... | .... | .... | .... | .... | .... | .... | .... | .... | .... | .... | 2 | 1 | 0 | 1 | 2 | .... | .... | .... | .... |
| | **NHL Totals** | | **74** | **20** | **24** | **44** | **38** | **10** | **0** | **4** | **180** | **11.1** | | **15** | **33.3** | **17:49** | .... | .... | .... | .... | .... | .... | .... | .... | .... |

USHL All-Rookie Team (2006) • USHL First All-Star Team (2006) • USHL Rookie of the Year (2006) • WCHA All-Rookie Team (2007) • WCHA Second All-Star Team (2007)

## OLESZ, Rostislav
(OH-lehsh, RAHS-tih-slav) **FLA.**

Center. Shoots left. 6'1", 214 lbs. Born, Bilovec, Czech., October 10, 1985. Florida's 1st choice, 7th overall, in 2004 Entry Draft.

| | | | | | | | | | | | | | | | | | | | | | | | | | |
|---|---|---|---|---|---|---|---|---|---|---|---|---|---|---|---|---|---|---|---|---|---|---|---|---|---|
| 2000-01 | HC Vitkovice Jr. | CzRep-Jr. | 15 | 10 | 3 | 13 | 14 | .... | .... | .... | .... | .... | .... | .... | .... | .... | .... | .... | .... | .... | .... | .... | .... | .... | .... |
| | HC Vitkovice | CzRep | 3 | 0 | 1 | 1 | 0 | .... | .... | .... | .... | .... | .... | .... | .... | .... | .... | .... | .... | .... | .... | .... | .... | .... | .... |
| 2001-02 | HC Vitkovice | CzRep | 11 | 1 | 2 | 3 | 0 | .... | .... | .... | .... | .... | .... | .... | .... | .... | .... | .... | .... | .... | .... | .... | .... | .... | .... |
| | HC Vitkovice Jr. | CzRep-Jr. | 34 | 19 | 20 | 39 | 81 | .... | .... | .... | .... | .... | .... | .... | .... | .... | 2 | 0 | 0 | 0 | 2 | .... | .... | .... | .... |
| 2002-03 | HC Vitkovice Jr. | CzRep-Jr. | 7 | 1 | 1 | 2 | 12 | .... | .... | .... | .... | .... | .... | .... | .... | .... | .... | .... | .... | .... | .... | .... | .... | .... | .... |
| | HC Vitkovice | CzRep | 40 | 6 | 3 | 9 | 41 | .... | .... | .... | .... | .... | .... | .... | .... | .... | 5 | 0 | 0 | 0 | 2 | .... | .... | .... | .... |
| | HC Slezan Opava | CzRep-2 | 1 | 0 | 0 | 0 | 0 | .... | .... | .... | .... | .... | .... | .... | .... | .... | .... | .... | .... | .... | .... | .... | .... | .... | .... |
| 2003-04 | HC Vitkovice Jr. | CzRep-Jr. | 3 | 2 | 0 | 2 | 0 | .... | .... | .... | .... | .... | .... | .... | .... | .... | .... | .... | .... | .... | .... | .... | .... | .... | .... |
| | HC Vitkovice | CzRep | 35 | 1 | 11 | 12 | 10 | .... | .... | .... | .... | .... | .... | .... | .... | .... | 6 | 2 | 1 | 3 | 4 | .... | .... | .... | .... |
| | HC Dukla Jihlava | CzRep-2 | 2 | 1 | 0 | 1 | 0 | .... | .... | .... | .... | .... | .... | .... | .... | .... | 1 | 0 | 0 | 0 | 0 | .... | .... | .... | .... |
| 2004-05 | HC Sparta Praha | CzRep | 47 | 6 | 7 | 13 | 12 | .... | .... | .... | .... | .... | .... | .... | .... | .... | 5 | 0 | 2 | 2 | 0 | .... | .... | .... | .... |
| | Sparta Jr. | CzRep-Jr. | .... | .... | .... | .... | .... | .... | .... | .... | .... | .... | .... | .... | .... | .... | 1 | 0 | 1 | 1 | 0 | .... | .... | .... | .... |
| **2005-06** | **Florida** | **NHL** | **59** | **8** | **13** | **21** | **24** | **0** | **1** | **3** | **105** | **7.6** | **–4** | **10** | **30.0** | **14:52** | .... | .... | .... | .... | .... | .... | .... | .... | .... |
| | Czech Republic | Olympics | 8 | 0 | 0 | 0 | 2 | .... | .... | .... | .... | .... | .... | .... | .... | .... | .... | .... | .... | .... | .... | .... | .... | .... | .... |
| **2006-07** | **Florida** | **NHL** | **75** | **11** | **19** | **30** | **28** | **2** | **0** | **2** | **164** | **6.7** | **2** | **12** | **58.3** | **15:30** | .... | .... | .... | .... | .... | .... | .... | .... | .... |
| | Rochester | AHL | 4 | 1 | 2 | 3 | 4 | .... | .... | .... | .... | .... | .... | .... | .... | .... | .... | .... | .... | .... | .... | .... | .... | .... | .... |
| **2007-08** | **Florida** | **NHL** | **56** | **14** | **12** | **26** | **16** | **5** | **0** | **2** | **139** | **10.1** | **3** | **10** | **70.0** | **17:04** | .... | .... | .... | .... | .... | .... | .... | .... | .... |
| **2008-09** | **Florida** | **NHL** | **37** | **4** | **5** | **9** | **8** | **0** | **0** | **0** | **69** | **5.8** | **–5** | **5** | **20.0** | **13:12** | .... | .... | .... | .... | .... | .... | .... | .... | .... |
| | **NHL Totals** | | **227** | **37** | **49** | **86** | **76** | **7** | **1** | **7** | **477** | **7.8** | | **37** | **48.6** | **15:21** | .... | .... | .... | .... | .... | .... | .... | .... | .... |

• Missed majority of 2008-09 season recovering from groin injury and resulting sports hernia surgery.

## OLVECKY, Peter
(ohl-VEHT-skee, PEE-tuhr) **NSH.**

Center. Shoots left. 6'2", 195 lbs. Born, Trencin, Czech., October 11, 1985. Minnesota's 3rd choice, 78th overall, in 2004 Entry Draft.

| | | | | | | | | | | | | | | | | | | | | | | | | | |
|---|---|---|---|---|---|---|---|---|---|---|---|---|---|---|---|---|---|---|---|---|---|---|---|---|---|
| 2003-04 | Dukla Trencin Jr. | Slovak-Jr. | 40 | 16 | 20 | 36 | 74 | .... | .... | .... | .... | .... | .... | .... | .... | .... | 2 | 0 | 0 | 0 | 12 | .... | .... | .... | .... |
| | Dukla Trencin | Slovakia | 16 | 0 | 0 | 0 | 18 | .... | .... | .... | .... | .... | .... | .... | .... | .... | .... | .... | .... | .... | .... | .... | .... | .... | .... |
| | Dukla Trencin U18 | Svk-U18 | 2 | 0 | 0 | 0 | 0 | .... | .... | .... | .... | .... | .... | .... | .... | .... | .... | .... | .... | .... | .... | .... | .... | .... | .... |
| 2004-05 | SHK 37 Piestany | Slovak-2 | 1 | 0 | 0 | 0 | 10 | .... | .... | .... | .... | .... | .... | .... | .... | .... | .... | .... | .... | .... | .... | .... | .... | .... | .... |
| | Dukla Trencin Jr. | Slovak-Jr. | 8 | 1 | 3 | 4 | 10 | .... | .... | .... | .... | .... | .... | .... | .... | .... | 2 | 1 | 4 | 5 | 4 | .... | .... | .... | .... |
| | Dukla Trencin | Slovakia | 45 | 10 | 9 | 19 | 49 | .... | .... | .... | .... | .... | .... | .... | .... | .... | 12 | 1 | 0 | 1 | 6 | .... | .... | .... | .... |
| 2005-06 | Houston Aeros | AHL | 67 | 14 | 18 | 32 | 56 | .... | .... | .... | .... | .... | .... | .... | .... | .... | 7 | 1 | 3 | 4 | 4 | .... | .... | .... | .... |
| 2006-07 | Houston Aeros | AHL | 69 | 12 | 15 | 27 | 46 | .... | .... | .... | .... | .... | .... | .... | .... | .... | .... | .... | .... | .... | .... | .... | .... | .... | .... |
| 2007-08 | Houston Aeros | AHL | 61 | 17 | 16 | 33 | 38 | .... | .... | .... | .... | .... | .... | .... | .... | .... | 5 | 1 | 1 | 2 | 4 | .... | .... | .... | .... |
| **2008-09** | **Minnesota** | **NHL** | **31** | **2** | **5** | **7** | **12** | **0** | **0** | **1** | **19** | **10.5** | **1** | **158** | **39.9** | **8:55** | .... | .... | .... | .... | .... | .... | .... | .... | .... |
| | Houston Aeros | AHL | 41 | 6 | 17 | 23 | 31 | .... | .... | .... | .... | .... | .... | .... | .... | .... | 3 | 1 | 1 | 2 | 6 | .... | .... | .... | .... |
| | **NHL Totals** | | **31** | **2** | **5** | **7** | **12** | **0** | **0** | **1** | **19** | **10.5** | | **158** | **39.9** | **8:55** | .... | .... | .... | .... | .... | .... | .... | .... | .... |

Signed as a free agent by **Nashville**, July 16, 2009.

## ONDRUS, Ben
(AWN-druhs, BEHN) **TOR.**

Right wing. Shoots right. 6', 194 lbs. Born, Sherwood Park, Alta., June 25, 1982.

| | | | | | | | | | | | | | | | | | | | | | | | | | |
|---|---|---|---|---|---|---|---|---|---|---|---|---|---|---|---|---|---|---|---|---|---|---|---|---|---|
| 1997-98 | Sherwood Park | AMBHL | .... | .... | .... | .... | .... | .... | .... | .... | .... | .... | .... | .... | .... | .... | .... | .... | .... | .... | .... | .... | .... | .... | .... |
| 1998-99 | Swift Current | WHL | 46 | 4 | 4 | 8 | 58 | .... | .... | .... | .... | .... | .... | .... | .... | .... | 6 | 0 | 1 | 1 | 8 | .... | .... | .... | .... |
| 99-2000 | Swift Current | WHL | 67 | 14 | 15 | 29 | 138 | .... | .... | .... | .... | .... | .... | .... | .... | .... | 12 | 1 | 0 | 1 | 22 | .... | .... | .... | .... |
| 2000-01 | Swift Current | WHL | 69 | 13 | 17 | 30 | 151 | .... | .... | .... | .... | .... | .... | .... | .... | .... | .... | .... | .... | .... | .... | .... | .... | .... | .... |
| 2001-02 | Swift Current | WHL | 67 | 30 | 41 | 71 | 153 | .... | .... | .... | .... | .... | .... | .... | .... | .... | 12 | 4 | 3 | 7 | 18 | .... | .... | .... | .... |
| 2002-03 | Swift Current | WHL | 67 | 33 | 36 | 69 | 98 | .... | .... | .... | .... | .... | .... | .... | .... | .... | 3 | 0 | 1 | 1 | 11 | .... | .... | .... | .... |
| | Idaho Steelheads | WCHL | 4 | 0 | 3 | 3 | 0 | .... | .... | .... | .... | .... | .... | .... | .... | .... | 5 | 0 | 1 | 1 | 6 | .... | .... | .... | .... |
| 2003-04 | St. John's | AHL | 60 | 6 | 11 | 17 | 102 | .... | .... | .... | .... | .... | .... | .... | .... | .... | .... | .... | .... | .... | .... | .... | .... | .... | .... |
| 2004-05 | St. John's | AHL | 78 | 7 | 11 | 18 | 137 | .... | .... | .... | .... | .... | .... | .... | .... | .... | 5 | 0 | 1 | 1 | 7 | .... | .... | .... | .... |
| **2005-06** | **Toronto** | **NHL** | **22** | **0** | **0** | **0** | **18** | **0** | **0** | **0** | **17** | **0.0** | **–10** | **28** | **50.0** | **10:07** | .... | .... | .... | .... | .... | .... | .... | .... | .... |
| | Toronto Marlies | AHL | 53 | 12 | 17 | 29 | 104 | .... | .... | .... | .... | .... | .... | .... | .... | .... | 5 | 1 | 2 | 3 | 4 | .... | .... | .... | .... |
| **2006-07** | **Toronto** | **NHL** | **16** | **0** | **2** | **2** | **20** | **0** | **0** | **0** | **7** | **0.0** | **–5** | **9** | **44.4** | **4:54** | .... | .... | .... | .... | .... | .... | .... | .... | .... |
| | Toronto Marlies | AHL | 29 | 8 | 3 | 11 | 35 | .... | .... | .... | .... | .... | .... | .... | .... | .... | .... | .... | .... | .... | .... | .... | .... | .... | .... |
| **2007-08** | **Toronto** | **NHL** | **3** | **0** | **0** | **0** | **5** | **0** | **0** | **0** | **4** | **0.0** | **–1** | **3** | **33.3** | **5:07** | .... | .... | .... | .... | .... | .... | .... | .... | .... |
| | Toronto Marlies | AHL | 59 | 14 | 12 | 26 | 63 | .... | .... | .... | .... | .... | .... | .... | .... | .... | 19 | 1 | 5 | 6 | 14 | .... | .... | .... | .... |
| **2008-09** | **Toronto** | **NHL** | **11** | **0** | **0** | **0** | **34** | **0** | **0** | **0** | **2** | **0.0** | **–4** | **27** | **44.4** | **9:27** | .... | .... | .... | .... | .... | .... | .... | .... | .... |
| | Toronto Marlies | AHL | 57 | 10 | 7 | 17 | 83 | .... | .... | .... | .... | .... | .... | .... | .... | .... | 6 | 0 | 0 | 0 | 2 | .... | .... | .... | .... |
| | **NHL Totals** | | **52** | **0** | **2** | **2** | **77** | **0** | **0** | **0** | **30** | **0.0** | | **67** | **46.3** | **8:05** | .... | .... | .... | .... | .... | .... | .... | .... | .... |

Signed as a free agent by **Idaho** (WCHL), March 23, 2003. Signed as a free agent by **St. John's** (AHL), September 1, 2003. Signed as a free agent by **Toronto**, May 27, 2004.

## O'NEILL, Wes
(oh-NEEL, WEHS) **COL.**

Defense. Shoots left. 6'4", 215 lbs. Born, Windsor, Ont., March 3, 1986. NY Islanders' 4th choice, 115th overall, in 2004 Entry Draft.

| | | | | | | | | | | | | | | | | | | | | | | | | | |
|---|---|---|---|---|---|---|---|---|---|---|---|---|---|---|---|---|---|---|---|---|---|---|---|---|---|
| 2000-01 | Chatham | OHA-B | 51 | 6 | 9 | 15 | 50 | .... | .... | .... | .... | .... | .... | .... | .... | .... | .... | .... | .... | .... | .... | .... | .... | .... | .... |
| 2001-02 | Chatham | OHA-B | 51 | 9 | 36 | 45 | .... | .... | .... | .... | .... | .... | .... | .... | .... | .... | .... | .... | .... | .... | .... | .... | .... | .... | .... |
| 2002-03 | Green Bay | USHL | 50 | 2 | 15 | 17 | 79 | .... | .... | .... | .... | .... | .... | .... | .... | .... | .... | .... | .... | .... | .... | .... | .... | .... | .... |
| 2003-04 | U. of Notre Dame | CCHA | 39 | 2 | 10 | 12 | 28 | .... | .... | .... | .... | .... | .... | .... | .... | .... | .... | .... | .... | .... | .... | .... | .... | .... | .... |
| 2004-05 | U. of Notre Dame | CCHA | 38 | 6 | 14 | 20 | 52 | .... | .... | .... | .... | .... | .... | .... | .... | .... | .... | .... | .... | .... | .... | .... | .... | .... | .... |
| 2005-06 | U. of Notre Dame | CCHA | 35 | 6 | 19 | 25 | 40 | .... | .... | .... | .... | .... | .... | .... | .... | .... | .... | .... | .... | .... | .... | .... | .... | .... | .... |
| 2006-07 | U. of Notre Dame | CCHA | 42 | 3 | 18 | 21 | 40 | .... | .... | .... | .... | .... | .... | .... | .... | .... | .... | .... | .... | .... | .... | .... | .... | .... | .... |
| 2007-08 | Lake Erie | AHL | 51 | 2 | 4 | 6 | 50 | .... | .... | .... | .... | .... | .... | .... | .... | .... | .... | .... | .... | .... | .... | .... | .... | .... | .... |
| | Johnstown Chiefs | ECHL | 6 | 0 | 1 | 1 | 2 | .... | .... | .... | .... | .... | .... | .... | .... | .... | 6 | 0 | 0 | 0 | 8 | .... | .... | .... | .... |

| | | | Regular Season | | | | | | | | | | | | | | Playoffs | | | | | | | | |
|---|---|---|---|---|---|---|---|---|---|---|---|---|---|---|---|---|---|---|---|---|---|---|---|---|---|
| Season | Club | League | GP | G | A | Pts | PIM | PP | SH | GW | S | % | +/- | TF | F% | Min | GP | G | A | Pts | PIM | PP | SH | GW | Min |
| **2008-09** | **Colorado** | **NHL** | **3** | **0** | **0** | **0** | **4** | **0** | **0** | **0** | **1** | **0.0** | **–2** | **0** | **0.0** | **10:52** | .... | .... | .... | .... | .... | .... | .... | .... | .... |
| | Lake Erie | AHL | 54 | 1 | 5 | 6 | 34 | .... | .... | .... | .... | .... | .... | .... | .... | .... | .... | .... | .... | .... | .... | .... | .... | .... | .... |
| | Johnstown Chiefs | ECHL | 6 | 0 | 1 | 1 | 0 | .... | .... | .... | .... | .... | .... | .... | .... | .... | .... | .... | .... | .... | .... | .... | .... | .... | .... |
| | **NHL Totals** | | **3** | **0** | **0** | **0** | **4** | **0** | **0** | **0** | **1** | **0.0** | | **0** | **0.0** | **10:52** | .... | .... | .... | .... | .... | .... | .... | .... | .... |

Signed as a free agent by **Colorado**, August 20, 2007.

## O'REILLY, Cal

(oh-RIGH-lee, KAL) **NSH.**

Center. Shoots left. 6', 187 lbs. Born, Toronto, Ont., September 30, 1986. Nashville's 4th choice, 150th overall, in 2005 Entry Draft.

| | | | | | | | | | | | | | | | | | | | | | | | | | |
|---|---|---|---|---|---|---|---|---|---|---|---|---|---|---|---|---|---|---|---|---|---|---|---|---|---|
| 2002-03 | St. Mary's Lincolns | OJHL-B | 46 | 11 | 19 | 30 | 2 | .... | .... | .... | .... | .... | .... | .... | .... | .... | .... | .... | .... | .... | .... | .... | .... | .... | .... |
| 2003-04 | Windsor Spitfires | OHL | 61 | 3 | 18 | 21 | 2 | .... | .... | .... | .... | .... | .... | .... | .... | .... | 3 | 0 | 1 | 1 | 0 | .... | .... | .... | .... |
| 2004-05 | Windsor Spitfires | OHL | 68 | 24 | 50 | 74 | 16 | .... | .... | .... | .... | .... | .... | .... | .... | .... | 11 | 4 | 5 | 9 | 4 | .... | .... | .... | .... |
| 2005-06 | Windsor Spitfires | OHL | 68 | 18 | 81 | 99 | 8 | .... | .... | .... | .... | .... | .... | .... | .... | .... | 7 | 3 | 8 | 11 | 0 | .... | .... | .... | .... |
| | Milwaukee | AHL | 2 | 0 | 0 | 0 | 0 | .... | .... | .... | .... | .... | .... | .... | .... | .... | 10 | 0 | 1 | 1 | 0 | .... | .... | .... | .... |
| 2006-07 | Milwaukee | AHL | 78 | 18 | 47 | 65 | 20 | .... | .... | .... | .... | .... | .... | .... | .... | .... | 4 | 1 | 2 | 3 | 0 | .... | .... | .... | .... |
| 2007-08 | Milwaukee | AHL | 80 | 16 | 63 | 79 | 22 | .... | .... | .... | .... | .... | .... | .... | .... | .... | 6 | 1 | 2 | 3 | 0 | .... | .... | .... | .... |
| **2008-09** | **Nashville** | **NHL** | **11** | **3** | **2** | **5** | **2** | **0** | **0** | **0** | **6** | **50.0** | **2** | **88** | **39.8** | **12:36** | .... | .... | .... | .... | .... | .... | .... | .... | .... |
| | Milwaukee | AHL | 67 | 13 | 56 | 69 | 20 | .... | .... | .... | .... | .... | .... | .... | .... | .... | 11 | 2 | 6 | 8 | 0 | .... | .... | .... | .... |
| | **NHL Totals** | | **11** | **3** | **2** | **5** | **2** | **0** | **0** | **0** | **6** | **50.0** | | **88** | **39.8** | **12:36** | .... | .... | .... | .... | .... | .... | .... | .... | .... |

## ORESKOVIC, Phil

(oh-rehs-KOH-vihch, FIHL) **TOR.**

Defense. Shoots right. 6'4", 217 lbs. Born, North York, Ont., January 26, 1987. Toronto's 2nd choice, 82nd overall, in 2005 Entry Draft.

| | | | | | | | | | | | | | | | | | | | | | | | | | |
|---|---|---|---|---|---|---|---|---|---|---|---|---|---|---|---|---|---|---|---|---|---|---|---|---|---|
| 2003-04 | Brampton | OHL | 66 | 0 | 7 | 7 | 64 | .... | .... | .... | .... | .... | .... | .... | .... | .... | 12 | 0 | 2 | 2 | 16 | .... | .... | .... | .... |
| 2004-05 | Brampton | OHL | 61 | 1 | 6 | 7 | 147 | .... | .... | .... | .... | .... | .... | .... | .... | .... | 6 | 0 | 0 | 0 | 4 | .... | .... | .... | .... |
| 2005-06 | Brampton | OHL | 65 | 3 | 9 | 12 | 202 | .... | .... | .... | .... | .... | .... | .... | .... | .... | 11 | 0 | 0 | 0 | 34 | .... | .... | .... | .... |
| 2006-07 | Brampton | OHL | 36 | 2 | 12 | 14 | 113 | .... | .... | .... | .... | .... | .... | .... | .... | .... | .... | .... | .... | .... | .... | .... | .... | .... | .... |
| | Owen Sound | OHL | 26 | 1 | 7 | 8 | 66 | .... | .... | .... | .... | .... | .... | .... | .... | .... | 4 | 0 | 0 | 0 | 2 | .... | .... | .... | .... |
| | Toronto Marlies | AHL | 3 | 0 | 1 | 1 | 2 | .... | .... | .... | .... | .... | .... | .... | .... | .... | .... | .... | .... | .... | .... | .... | .... | .... | .... |
| 2007-08 | Toronto Marlies | AHL | 54 | 1 | 9 | 10 | 68 | .... | .... | .... | .... | .... | .... | .... | .... | .... | 7 | 0 | 1 | 1 | 11 | .... | .... | .... | .... |
| | Columbia Inferno | ECHL | 13 | 0 | 4 | 4 | 19 | .... | .... | .... | .... | .... | .... | .... | .... | .... | .... | .... | .... | .... | .... | .... | .... | .... | .... |
| **2008-09** | **Toronto** | **NHL** | **10** | **1** | **1** | **2** | **21** | **0** | **0** | **0** | **12** | **8.3** | **–2** | **0** | **0.0** | **16:14** | .... | .... | .... | .... | .... | .... | .... | .... | .... |
| | Toronto Marlies | AHL | 65 | 1 | 10 | 11 | 103 | .... | .... | .... | .... | .... | .... | .... | .... | .... | 6 | 0 | 0 | 0 | 12 | .... | .... | .... | .... |
| | **NHL Totals** | | **10** | **1** | **1** | **2** | **21** | **0** | **0** | **0** | **12** | **8.3** | | **0** | **0.0** | **16:14** | .... | .... | .... | .... | .... | .... | .... | .... | .... |

## ORPIK, Brooks

(OHR-pihk, BRUKS) **PIT.**

Defense. Shoots left. 6'2", 219 lbs. Born, San Francisco, CA, September 26, 1980. Pittsburgh's 1st choice, 18th overall, in 2000 Entry Draft.

| | | | | | | | | | | | | | | | | | | | | | | | | | |
|---|---|---|---|---|---|---|---|---|---|---|---|---|---|---|---|---|---|---|---|---|---|---|---|---|---|
| 1996-97 | Thayer Academy | High-MA | 20 | 4 | 1 | 5 | .... | .... | .... | .... | .... | .... | .... | .... | .... | .... | .... | .... | .... | .... | .... | .... | .... | .... | .... |
| 1997-98 | Thayer Academy | High-MA | 22 | 0 | 7 | 7 | .... | .... | .... | .... | .... | .... | .... | .... | .... | .... | .... | .... | .... | .... | .... | .... | .... | .... | .... |
| 1998-99 | Boston College | H-East | 41 | 1 | 10 | 11 | *96 | .... | .... | .... | .... | .... | .... | .... | .... | .... | .... | .... | .... | .... | .... | .... | .... | .... | .... |
| 99-2000 | Boston College | H-East | 38 | 1 | 9 | 10 | 102 | .... | .... | .... | .... | .... | .... | .... | .... | .... | .... | .... | .... | .... | .... | .... | .... | .... | .... |
| 2000-01 | Boston College | H-East | 40 | 0 | 20 | 20 | *124 | .... | .... | .... | .... | .... | .... | .... | .... | .... | .... | .... | .... | .... | .... | .... | .... | .... | .... |
| 2001-02 | Wilkes-Barre | AHL | 78 | 2 | 18 | 20 | 99 | .... | .... | .... | .... | .... | .... | .... | .... | .... | .... | .... | .... | .... | .... | .... | .... | .... | .... |
| **2002-03** | **Pittsburgh** | **NHL** | **6** | **0** | **0** | **0** | **2** | **0** | **0** | **0** | **2** | **0.0** | **–5** | **0** | **0.0** | **18:19** | .... | .... | .... | .... | .... | .... | .... | .... | .... |
| | Wilkes-Barre | AHL | 71 | 4 | 14 | 18 | 105 | .... | .... | .... | .... | .... | .... | .... | .... | .... | 6 | 0 | 0 | 0 | 14 | .... | .... | .... | .... |
| **2003-04** | **Pittsburgh** | **NHL** | **79** | **1** | **9** | **10** | **127** | **0** | **0** | **0** | **56** | **1.8** | **–36** | **0** | **0.0** | **18:25** | .... | .... | .... | .... | .... | .... | .... | .... | .... |
| | Wilkes-Barre | AHL | 3 | 0 | 0 | 0 | 2 | .... | .... | .... | .... | .... | .... | .... | .... | .... | 24 | 0 | 4 | 4 | 53 | .... | .... | .... | .... |
| **2005-06** | **Pittsburgh** | **NHL** | **64** | **2** | **7** | **9** | **124** | **0** | **0** | **0** | **32** | **6.3** | **–3** | **0** | **0.0** | **18:50** | .... | .... | .... | .... | .... | .... | .... | .... | .... |
| **2006-07** | **Pittsburgh** | **NHL** | **70** | **0** | **6** | **6** | **82** | **0** | **0** | **0** | **59** | **0.0** | **4** | **0** | **0.0** | **16:37** | **5** | **0** | **0** | **0** | **8** | **0** | **0** | **0** | **15:43** |
| **2007-08** | **Pittsburgh** | **NHL** | **78** | **1** | **10** | **11** | **57** | **0** | **0** | **0** | **50** | **2.0** | **11** | **0** | **0.0** | **16:58** | **20** | **0** | **2** | **2** | **18** | **0** | **0** | **0** | **20:47** |
| **2008-09** ♦ | **Pittsburgh** | **NHL** | **79** | **2** | **17** | **19** | **73** | **1** | **0** | **0** | **39** | **5.1** | **10** | **0** | **0.0** | **20:20** | **24** | **0** | **4** | **4** | **22** | **0** | **0** | **0** | **20:04** |
| | **NHL Totals** | | **376** | **6** | **49** | **55** | **465** | **1** | **0** | **0** | **238** | **2.5** | | **0** | **0.0** | **18:15** | **49** | **0** | **6** | **6** | **48** | **0** | **0** | **0** | **19:55** |

## ORR, Colton

(OHR, KOHL-tuhn) **TOR.**

Right wing. Shoots right. 6'3", 222 lbs. Born, Winnipeg, Man., March 3, 1982.

| | | | | | | | | | | | | | | | | | | | | | | | | | |
|---|---|---|---|---|---|---|---|---|---|---|---|---|---|---|---|---|---|---|---|---|---|---|---|---|---|
| 1998-99 | St. Boniface | MJHL | STATISTICS NOT AVAILABLE | | | | | | | | | | | | | | | | | | | | | | |
| | Swift Current | WHL | 2 | 0 | 0 | 0 | 0 | .... | .... | .... | .... | .... | .... | .... | .... | .... | .... | .... | .... | .... | .... | .... | .... | .... | .... |
| 99-2000 | Swift Current | WHL | 61 | 3 | 2 | 5 | 130 | .... | .... | .... | .... | .... | .... | .... | .... | .... | 12 | 1 | 0 | 1 | 25 | .... | .... | .... | .... |
| 2000-01 | Swift Current | WHL | 19 | 0 | 4 | 4 | 67 | .... | .... | .... | .... | .... | .... | .... | .... | .... | .... | .... | .... | .... | .... | .... | .... | .... | .... |
| | Kamloops Blazers | WHL | 41 | 8 | 1 | 9 | 179 | .... | .... | .... | .... | .... | .... | .... | .... | .... | 3 | 0 | 0 | 0 | 20 | .... | .... | .... | .... |
| 2001-02 | Kamloops Blazers | WHL | 1 | 0 | 0 | 0 | 7 | .... | .... | .... | .... | .... | .... | .... | .... | .... | 2 | 0 | 0 | 0 | 2 | .... | .... | .... | .... |
| 2002-03 | Kamloops Blazers | WHL | 3 | 2 | 0 | 2 | 17 | .... | .... | .... | .... | .... | .... | .... | .... | .... | .... | .... | .... | .... | .... | .... | .... | .... | .... |
| | Regina Pats | WHL | 37 | 6 | 2 | 8 | 170 | .... | .... | .... | .... | .... | .... | .... | .... | .... | 3 | 0 | 0 | 0 | 19 | .... | .... | .... | .... |
| | Providence Bruins | AHL | 1 | 0 | 0 | 0 | 7 | .... | .... | .... | .... | .... | .... | .... | .... | .... | .... | .... | .... | .... | .... | .... | .... | .... | .... |
| **2003-04** | **Boston** | **NHL** | **1** | **0** | **0** | **0** | **0** | **0** | **0** | **0** | **0** | **0.0** | **–1** | **0** | **0.0** | **2:13** | .... | .... | .... | .... | .... | .... | .... | .... | .... |
| | Providence Bruins | AHL | 64 | 1 | 4 | 5 | 257 | .... | .... | .... | .... | .... | .... | .... | .... | .... | 2 | 0 | 0 | 0 | 9 | .... | .... | .... | .... |
| 2004-05 | Providence Bruins | AHL | 61 | 1 | 6 | 7 | 279 | .... | .... | .... | .... | .... | .... | .... | .... | .... | 17 | 1 | 0 | 1 | 44 | .... | .... | .... | .... |
| **2005-06** | **Boston** | **NHL** | **20** | **0** | **0** | **0** | **27** | **0** | **0** | **0** | **1** | **0.0** | **0** | **0** | **0.0** | **1:49** | .... | .... | .... | .... | .... | .... | .... | .... | .... |
| | **NY Rangers** | **NHL** | **15** | **0** | **1** | **1** | **44** | **0** | **0** | **0** | **0** | **0.0** | **1** | **0** | **0.0** | **4:19** | **1** | **0** | **0** | **0** | **2** | **0** | **0** | **0** | **4:17** |
| **2006-07** | **NY Rangers** | **NHL** | **53** | **2** | **1** | **3** | **126** | **0** | **0** | **1** | **23** | **8.7** | **–2** | **0** | **0.0** | **5:20** | **4** | **0** | **0** | **0** | **12** | **0** | **0** | **0** | **4:57** |
| **2007-08** | **NY Rangers** | **NHL** | **74** | **1** | **1** | **2** | **159** | **0** | **0** | **1** | **24** | **4.2** | **–13** | **2** | **50.0** | **7:49** | **2** | **0** | **0** | **0** | **0** | **0** | **0** | **0** | **4:26** |
| **2008-09** | **NY Rangers** | **NHL** | **82** | **1** | **4** | **5** | **193** | **0** | **0** | **0** | **40** | **2.5** | **–15** | **16** | **25.0** | **6:29** | **5** | **0** | **0** | **0** | **16** | **0** | **0** | **0** | **3:50** |
| | **NHL Totals** | | **245** | **4** | **7** | **11** | **549** | **0** | **0** | **2** | **88** | **4.5** | | **18** | **27.8** | **6:07** | **12** | **0** | **0** | **0** | **30** | **0** | **0** | **0** | **4:21** |

Signed as a free agent by **Boston**, September 19, 2001. • Missed majority of 2001-02 season recovering from wrist injury suffered in game vs. Red Deer (WHL), October 20, 2001. Claimed on waivers by **NY Rangers** from **Boston**, November 29, 2005. Signed as a free agent by **Toronto**, July 1, 2009.

## ORTMEYER, Jed

(OHRT-migh-uhr, JEHD) **S.J.**

Center. Shoots right. 6', 200 lbs. Born, Omaha, NE, September 3, 1978.

| | | | | | | | | | | | | | | | | | | | | | | | | | |
|---|---|---|---|---|---|---|---|---|---|---|---|---|---|---|---|---|---|---|---|---|---|---|---|---|---|
| 1997-98 | Omaha Lancers | USHL | 54 | 23 | 25 | 48 | 52 | .... | .... | .... | .... | .... | .... | .... | .... | .... | 14 | 3 | 4 | 7 | 31 | .... | .... | .... | .... |
| 1998-99 | Omaha Lancers | USHL | 52 | 23 | 36 | 59 | 81 | .... | .... | .... | .... | .... | .... | .... | .... | .... | 12 | 5 | 6 | 11 | 16 | .... | .... | .... | .... |
| 99-2000 | U. of Michigan | CCHA | 41 | 8 | 16 | 24 | 40 | .... | .... | .... | .... | .... | .... | .... | .... | .... | .... | .... | .... | .... | .... | .... | .... | .... | .... |
| 2000-01 | U. of Michigan | CCHA | 27 | 10 | 11 | 21 | 52 | .... | .... | .... | .... | .... | .... | .... | .... | .... | .... | .... | .... | .... | .... | .... | .... | .... | .... |
| 2001-02 | U. of Michigan | CCHA | 41 | 15 | 23 | 38 | 40 | .... | .... | .... | .... | .... | .... | .... | .... | .... | .... | .... | .... | .... | .... | .... | .... | .... | .... |
| 2002-03 | U. of Michigan | CCHA | 36 | 18 | 16 | 34 | 48 | .... | .... | .... | .... | .... | .... | .... | .... | .... | .... | .... | .... | .... | .... | .... | .... | .... | .... |
| **2003-04** | **NY Rangers** | **NHL** | **58** | **2** | **4** | **6** | **16** | **0** | **0** | **0** | **48** | **4.2** | **–10** | **16** | **31.3** | **9:52** | .... | .... | .... | .... | .... | .... | .... | .... | .... |
| | Hartford | AHL | 13 | 2 | 8 | 10 | 4 | .... | .... | .... | .... | .... | .... | .... | .... | .... | 16 | 5 | 2 | 7 | 6 | .... | .... | .... | .... |
| 2004-05 | Hartford | AHL | 61 | 7 | 20 | 27 | 63 | .... | .... | .... | .... | .... | .... | .... | .... | .... | 6 | 0 | 1 | 1 | 4 | .... | .... | .... | .... |
| **2005-06** | **NY Rangers** | **NHL** | **78** | **5** | **2** | **7** | **38** | **0** | **0** | **1** | **90** | **5.6** | **2** | **21** | **23.8** | **11:06** | **4** | **1** | **0** | **1** | **4** | **0** | **0** | **0** | **11:40** |
| **2006-07** | **NY Rangers** | **NHL** | **41** | **2** | **9** | **11** | **22** | **0** | **1** | **0** | **67** | **3.0** | **7** | **8** | **12.5** | **12:35** | **9** | **0** | **0** | **0** | **2** | **0** | **0** | **0** | **9:37** |
| | Hartford | AHL | 8 | 1 | 3 | 4 | 6 | .... | .... | .... | .... | .... | .... | .... | .... | .... | .... | .... | .... | .... | .... | .... | .... | .... | .... |
| **2007-08** | **Nashville** | **NHL** | **51** | **4** | **4** | **8** | **32** | **0** | **1** | **0** | **68** | **5.9** | **–8** | **12** | **50.0** | **12:27** | .... | .... | .... | .... | .... | .... | .... | .... | .... |
| **2008-09** | **Nashville** | **NHL** | **2** | **0** | **0** | **0** | **0** | **0** | **0** | **0** | **4** | **0.0** | **0** | **0** | **0.0** | **11:01** | .... | .... | .... | .... | .... | .... | .... | .... | .... |
| | Milwaukee | AHL | 55 | 10 | 13 | 23 | 51 | .... | .... | .... | .... | .... | .... | .... | .... | .... | 11 | 1 | 6 | 7 | 8 | .... | .... | .... | .... |
| | **NHL Totals** | | **230** | **13** | **19** | **32** | **108** | **0** | **2** | **1** | **277** | **4.7** | | **57** | **29.8** | **11:21** | **13** | **1** | **0** | **1** | **6** | **0** | **0** | **0** | **10:15** |

Signed as a free agent by **NY Rangers**, May 10, 2003. Signed as a free agent by **Nashville**, July 2, 2007. Signed as a free agent by **San Jose**, July 16, 2009.

## OSALA, Oskar

(OH-sa-la, AWZ-kuhr) **WSH.**

Left wing. Shoots left. 6'4", 225 lbs. Born, Vaasa, Finland, December 26, 1987. Washington's 6th choice, 97th overall, in 2006 Entry Draft.

| | | | | | | | | | | | | | | | | | | | | | | | | | |
|---|---|---|---|---|---|---|---|---|---|---|---|---|---|---|---|---|---|---|---|---|---|---|---|---|---|
| 2003-04 | Sport Vaasa U18 | Fin-U18 | 25 | 19 | 18 | 37 | 32 | .... | .... | .... | .... | .... | .... | .... | .... | .... | .... | .... | .... | .... | .... | .... | .... | .... | .... |
| | Sport Vaasa Jr. | Fin-Jr. | 2 | 0 | 0 | 0 | 4 | .... | .... | .... | .... | .... | .... | .... | .... | .... | .... | .... | .... | .... | .... | .... | .... | .... | .... |
| | Sport Vaasa | Finland-2 | 5 | 0 | 0 | 0 | 0 | .... | .... | .... | .... | .... | .... | .... | .... | .... | .... | .... | .... | .... | .... | .... | .... | .... | .... |
| 2004-05 | Sport Vaasa U18 | Fin-U18 | 4 | 4 | 2 | 6 | 16 | .... | .... | .... | .... | .... | .... | .... | .... | .... | .... | .... | .... | .... | .... | .... | .... | .... | .... |
| | Sport Vaasa Jr. | Fin-Jr. | 19 | 13 | 14 | 27 | 28 | .... | .... | .... | .... | .... | .... | .... | .... | .... | 2 | 0 | 0 | 0 | 2 | .... | .... | .... | .... |
| | Sport Vaasa | Finland-2 | 21 | 1 | 4 | 5 | 6 | .... | .... | .... | .... | .... | .... | .... | .... | .... | 7 | 0 | 0 | 0 | 6 | .... | .... | .... | .... |
| 2005-06 | Mississauga | OHL | 68 | 17 | 26 | 43 | 86 | .... | .... | .... | .... | .... | .... | .... | .... | .... | .... | .... | .... | .... | .... | .... | .... | .... | .... |

| | | | Regular Season | | | | | | | | | | | | | | Playoffs | | | | | | | | |
|---|---|---|---|---|---|---|---|---|---|---|---|---|---|---|---|---|---|---|---|---|---|---|---|---|---|
| Season | Club | League | GP | G | A | Pts | PIM | PP | SH | GW | S | % | +/- | TF | F% | Min | GP | G | A | Pts | PIM | PP | SH | GW | Min |
| 2006-07 | Mississauga | OHL | 54 | 22 | 22 | 44 | 81 | | | | | | | | | | 5 | 2 | 2 | 4 | 0 | | | | |
| | Suomi U20 | Finland-2 | 2 | 1 | 0 | 1 | 0 | | | | | | | | | | | | | | | | | | |
| 2007-08 | Blues Espoo | Finland | 53 | 18 | 17 | 35 | 62 | | | | | | | | | | 17 | 7 | 3 | 10 | 8 | | | | |
| 2008-09 | Washington | NHL | 2 | 0 | 0 | 0 | 0 | 0 | 0 | 0 | 1 | 0.0 | –1 | 0 | 0.0 | 8:44 | | | | | | | | | |
| | Hershey Bears | AHL | 75 | 23 | 14 | 37 | 47 | | | | | | | | | | 22 | 6 | 4 | 10 | 17 | | | | |
| | NHL Totals | | 2 | 0 | 0 | 0 | 0 | 0 | 0 | 0 | 1 | 0.0 | | 0 | 0.0 | 8:44 | | | | | | | | | |

Signed as a free agent by **Espoo** (Finland), July 23, 2007.

## OSHIE, T.J.

(OH-shee, TEE-JAY) **ST.L.**

Center. Shoots right. 5'11", 189 lbs. Born, Mt. Vernon, WA, December 23, 1986. St. Louis' 1st choice, 24th overall, in 2005 Entry Draft.

| Season | Club | League | GP | G | A | Pts | PIM | PP | SH | GW | S | % | +/- | TF | F% | Min | GP | G | A | Pts | PIM | PP | SH | GW | Min |
|---|---|---|---|---|---|---|---|---|---|---|---|---|---|---|---|---|---|---|---|---|---|---|---|---|---|
| 2004-05 | Warroad Warriors | High-MN | 31 | 37 | 62 | 99 | 22 | | | | | | | | | | | | | | | | | | |
| | Sioux Falls | USHL | 11 | 3 | 2 | 5 | 6 | | | | | | | | | | | | | | | | | | |
| 2005-06 | North Dakota | WCHA | 44 | 24 | 21 | 45 | 33 | | | | | | | | | | | | | | | | | | |
| 2006-07 | North Dakota | WCHA | 43 | 17 | *35 | 52 | 30 | | | | | | | | | | | | | | | | | | |
| 2007-08 | North Dakota | WCHA | 42 | 18 | 27 | 45 | 57 | | | | | | | | | | | | | | | | | | |
| 2008-09 | St. Louis | NHL | 57 | 14 | 25 | 39 | 30 | 6 | 1 | 1 | 101 | 13.9 | 16 | 109 | 43.1 | 16:35 | 4 | 0 | 0 | 0 | 2 | 0 | 0 | 0 | 19:01 |
| | NHL Totals | | 57 | 14 | 25 | 39 | 30 | 6 | 1 | 1 | 101 | 13.9 | | 109 | 43.1 | 16:35 | 4 | 0 | 0 | 0 | 2 | 0 | 0 | 0 | 19:01 |

WCHA All-Rookie Team (2006) • WCHA First All-Star Team (2008) • NCAA West First All-American Team (2008)

## O'SULLIVAN, Patrick

(Oh-SUHL-ih-vihn, PAT-rihk) **EDM.**

Center. Shoots left. 5'11", 190 lbs. Born, Toronto, Ont., February 1, 1985. Minnesota's 2nd choice, 56th overall, in 2003 Entry Draft.

| Season | Club | League | GP | G | A | Pts | PIM | PP | SH | GW | S | % | +/- | TF | F% | Min | GP | G | A | Pts | PIM | PP | SH | GW | Min |
|---|---|---|---|---|---|---|---|---|---|---|---|---|---|---|---|---|---|---|---|---|---|---|---|---|---|
| 99-2000 | Strathroy Rockets | OHA-B | 45 | 6 | 13 | 19 | 53 | | | | | | | | | | | | | | | | | | |
| 2000-01 | USNTDP | U-17 | 8 | 8 | 10 | 18 | 12 | | | | | | | | | | | | | | | | | | |
| | USNTDP | NAHL | 56 | 22 | 35 | 57 | 57 | | | | | | | | | | | | | | | | | | |
| 2001-02 | Mississauga | OHL | 68 | 34 | 58 | 92 | 61 | | | | | | | | | | | | | | | | | | |
| | USNTDP | USHL | 1 | 1 | 0 | 1 | 2 | | | | | | | | | | | | | | | | | | |
| 2002-03 | Mississauga | OHL | 56 | 40 | 41 | 81 | 57 | | | | | | | | | | 5 | 2 | 9 | 11 | 18 | | | | |
| 2003-04 | Mississauga | OHL | 53 | 43 | 39 | 82 | 32 | | | | | | | | | | 24 | 12 | 11 | 23 | 16 | | | | |
| 2004-05 | Mississauga | OHL | 57 | 31 | 59 | 90 | 63 | | | | | | | | | | 5 | 0 | 4 | 4 | 6 | | | | |
| 2005-06 | Houston Aeros | AHL | 78 | 47 | 46 | 93 | 64 | | | | | | | | | | 8 | 5 | 5 | 10 | 4 | | | | |
| 2006-07 | Los Angeles | NHL | 44 | 5 | 14 | 19 | 14 | 2 | 0 | 1 | 92 | 5.4 | –6 | 127 | 46.5 | 14:04 | | | | | | | | | |
| | Manchester | AHL | 41 | 18 | 21 | 39 | 12 | | | | | | | | | | 16 | 8 | 9 | 17 | 10 | | | | |
| 2007-08 | Los Angeles | NHL | 82 | 22 | 31 | 53 | 36 | 3 | 3 | 2 | 220 | 10.0 | –8 | 461 | 44.0 | 18:42 | | | | | | | | | |
| 2008-09 | Los Angeles | NHL | 62 | 14 | 23 | 37 | 16 | 2 | 1 | 1 | 200 | 7.0 | 1 | 39 | 46.2 | 19:26 | | | | | | | | | |
| | Edmonton | NHL | 19 | 2 | 4 | 6 | 12 | 0 | 0 | 0 | 59 | 3.4 | –7 | 60 | 38.3 | 18:14 | | | | | | | | | |
| | NHL Totals | | 207 | 43 | 72 | 115 | 78 | 7 | 4 | 4 | 571 | 7.5 | | 687 | 44.1 | 17:54 | | | | | | | | | |

Canadian Major Junior Rookie of the Year (2002) • AHL All-Rookie Team (2006) • Dudley "Red" Garrett Memorial Trophy (AHL - Top Rookie) (2006)

Traded to **Los Angeles** by **Minnesota** with Edmonton's 1st round choice (previously acquired, Los Angeles selected Trevor Lewis) in 2006 Entry Draft for Pavol Demitra, June 24, 2006. Traded to **Carolina** by **Los Angeles** with Calgary's 2nd round choice (previously acquired, Carolina selected Brian Dumoulin) in 2009 Entry Draft for Justin Williams, March 4, 2009. Traded to **Edmonton** by **Carolina** with Carolina's 2nd round choice (later traded to Buffalo – later traded to Toronto – Toronto selected Jesse Blacker) in 2009 Entry Draft for Erik Cole and Edmonton's 5th round choice (Matt Kennedy) in 2009 Entry Draft, March 4, 2009.

## OTT, Steve

(AWT, STEEV) **DAL.**

Center. Shoots left. 6', 193 lbs. Born, Summerside, P.E.I., August 19, 1982. Dallas' 1st choice, 25th overall, in 2000 Entry Draft.

| Season | Club | League | GP | G | A | Pts | PIM | PP | SH | GW | S | % | +/- | TF | F% | Min | GP | G | A | Pts | PIM | PP | SH | GW | Min |
|---|---|---|---|---|---|---|---|---|---|---|---|---|---|---|---|---|---|---|---|---|---|---|---|---|---|
| 1998-99 | Leamington Flyers | OHA-B | 48 | 14 | 30 | 44 | 110 | | | | | | | | | | | | | | | | | | |
| 99-2000 | Windsor Spitfires | OHL | 66 | 23 | 39 | 62 | 131 | | | | | | | | | | 12 | 3 | 5 | 8 | 21 | | | | |
| 2000-01 | Windsor Spitfires | OHL | 55 | 50 | 37 | 87 | 164 | | | | | | | | | | 9 | 3 | 8 | 11 | 27 | | | | |
| 2001-02 | Windsor Spitfires | OHL | 53 | 43 | 45 | 88 | 178 | | | | | | | | | | 14 | 6 | 10 | 16 | 49 | | | | |
| 2002-03 | Dallas | NHL | 26 | 3 | 4 | 7 | 31 | 0 | 0 | 0 | 25 | 12.0 | 6 | 4 | 50.0 | 8:46 | 1 | 0 | 0 | 0 | 0 | 0 | 0 | 0 | 6:57 |
| | Utah Grizzlies | AHL | 40 | 9 | 11 | 20 | 98 | | | | | | | | | | | | | | | | | | |
| 2003-04 | Dallas | NHL | 73 | 2 | 10 | 12 | 152 | 0 | 0 | 1 | 74 | 2.7 | –2 | 59 | 49.2 | 10:14 | 4 | 1 | 0 | 1 | 0 | 0 | 0 | 1 | 6:55 |
| 2004-05 | Hamilton | AHL | 67 | 18 | 21 | 39 | 279 | | | | | | | | | | 4 | 0 | 0 | 0 | 20 | | | | |
| 2005-06 | Dallas | NHL | 82 | 5 | 17 | 22 | 178 | 0 | 0 | 1 | 89 | 5.6 | 1 | 535 | 49.2 | 11:54 | 5 | 0 | 1 | 1 | 2 | 0 | 0 | 0 | 7:41 |
| 2006-07 | Dallas | NHL | 19 | 0 | 4 | 4 | 35 | 0 | 0 | 0 | 17 | 0.0 | –4 | 39 | 59.0 | 9:11 | 6 | 0 | 0 | 0 | 8 | 0 | 0 | 0 | 6:43 |
| | Iowa Stars | AHL | 3 | 0 | 0 | 0 | 8 | | | | | | | | | | | | | | | | | | |
| 2007-08 | Dallas | NHL | 73 | 11 | 11 | 22 | 147 | 0 | 1 | 2 | 89 | 12.4 | 2 | 311 | 58.8 | 14:28 | 18 | 2 | 1 | 3 | 22 | 1 | 0 | 1 | 13:46 |
| 2008-09 | Dallas | NHL | 64 | 19 | 27 | 46 | 135 | 5 | 0 | 0 | 132 | 14.4 | 3 | 172 | 46.5 | 17:35 | | | | | | | | | |
| | NHL Totals | | 337 | 40 | 73 | 113 | 678 | 5 | 1 | 4 | 426 | 9.4 | | 1120 | 51.8 | 12:47 | 34 | 3 | 2 | 5 | 32 | 1 | 0 | 2 | 10:37 |

Canadian Major Junior Second All-Star Team (2001) • OHL Second All-Star Team (2002)

• Missed majority of 2006-07 season recovering from ankle injury suffered in game vs. Los Angeles, October 28, 2006.

## OUELLET, Michel

(oo-LEHT, mee-SHEHL)

Right wing. Shoots right. 6'1", 193 lbs. Born, Rimouski, Que., March 5, 1982. Pittsburgh's 4th choice, 124th overall, in 2000 Entry Draft.

| Season | Club | League | GP | G | A | Pts | PIM | PP | SH | GW | S | % | +/- | TF | F% | Min | GP | G | A | Pts | PIM | PP | SH | GW | Min |
|---|---|---|---|---|---|---|---|---|---|---|---|---|---|---|---|---|---|---|---|---|---|---|---|---|---|
| 1997-98 | Jonquiere Elites | QAAA | 33 | 20 | 32 | 52 | 52 | | | | | | | | | | | | | | | | | | |
| 1998-99 | Rimouski Oceanic | QMJHL | 28 | 7 | 13 | 20 | 10 | | | | | | | | | | 11 | 0 | 1 | 1 | 6 | | | | |
| 99-2000 | Rimouski Oceanic | QMJHL | 72 | 36 | 53 | 89 | 38 | | | | | | | | | | 14 | 4 | 5 | 9 | 14 | | | | |
| 2000-01 | Rimouski Oceanic | QMJHL | 63 | 42 | 50 | 92 | 50 | | | | | | | | | | 11 | 6 | 7 | 13 | 8 | | | | |
| 2001-02 | Rimouski Oceanic | QMJHL | 61 | 40 | 58 | 98 | 66 | | | | | | | | | | 7 | 3 | 6 | 9 | 4 | | | | |
| 2002-03 | Wilkes-Barre | AHL | 4 | 0 | 2 | 2 | 0 | | | | | | | | | | | | | | | | | | |
| | Wheeling Nailers | ECHL | 55 | 20 | 26 | 46 | 40 | | | | | | | | | | | | | | | | | | |
| 2003-04 | Wilkes-Barre | AHL | 79 | 30 | 19 | 49 | 34 | | | | | | | | | | 22 | 2 | 10 | 12 | 6 | | | | |
| 2004-05 | Wilkes-Barre | AHL | 80 | 31 | 32 | 63 | 56 | | | | | | | | | | 11 | 2 | 3 | 5 | 6 | | | | |
| 2005-06 | Pittsburgh | NHL | 50 | 16 | 16 | 32 | 16 | 11 | 0 | 0 | 87 | 18.4 | –13 | 16 | 37.5 | 14:02 | | | | | | | | | |
| | Wilkes-Barre | AHL | 19 | 10 | 20 | 30 | 12 | | | | | | | | | | | | | | | | | | |
| 2006-07 | Pittsburgh | NHL | 73 | 19 | 29 | 48 | 30 | 11 | 0 | 2 | 148 | 12.8 | –3 | 8 | 37.5 | 13:20 | 5 | 0 | 2 | 2 | 6 | 0 | 0 | 0 | 12:54 |
| 2007-08 | Tampa Bay | NHL | 64 | 17 | 19 | 36 | 12 | 5 | 0 | 0 | 132 | 12.9 | 11 | 42 | 45.2 | 13:38 | | | | | | | | | |
| 2008-09 | Vancouver | NHL | 3 | 0 | 0 | 0 | 0 | 0 | 0 | 0 | 3 | 0.0 | 1 | 1 | 0.0 | 9:39 | | | | | | | | | |
| | Manitoba Moose | AHL | 46 | 13 | 27 | 40 | 30 | | | | | | | | | | | | | | | | | | |
| | NHL Totals | | 190 | 52 | 64 | 116 | 58 | 27 | 0 | 2 | 370 | 14.1 | | 67 | 41.8 | 13:33 | 5 | 0 | 2 | 2 | 6 | 0 | 0 | 0 | 12:54 |

AHL All-Rookie Team (2004)

Signed as a free agent by **Tampa Bay**, July 1, 2007. Traded to **Vancouver** by **Tampa Bay** with Shane O'Brien for Lukas Krajicek and Juraj Simek, October 6, 2008.

## OVECHKIN, Alex

(oh-VEHCH-kihn, AL-ehx) **WSH.**

Left wing. Shoots right. 6'2", 225 lbs. Born, Moscow, USSR, September 17, 1985. Washington's 1st choice, 1st overall, in 2004 Entry Draft.

| Season | Club | League | GP | G | A | Pts | PIM | PP | SH | GW | S | % | +/- | TF | F% | Min | GP | G | A | Pts | PIM | PP | SH | GW | Min |
|---|---|---|---|---|---|---|---|---|---|---|---|---|---|---|---|---|---|---|---|---|---|---|---|---|---|
| 2001-02 | Dyn'o Moscow 2 | Russia-3 | 19 | 18 | 8 | 26 | 20 | | | | | | | | | | | | | | | | | | |
| | Dynamo Moscow | Russia | 22 | 2 | 2 | 4 | 4 | | | | | | | | | | 3 | 0 | 0 | 0 | 0 | | | | |
| 2002-03 | Dynamo Moscow | Russia | 40 | 8 | 7 | 15 | 28 | | | | | | | | | | 5 | 0 | 0 | 0 | 2 | | | | |
| 2003-04 | Dynamo Moscow | Russia | 53 | 13 | 11 | 24 | 40 | | | | | | | | | | 3 | 0 | 0 | 0 | 2 | | | | |
| 2004-05 | Dynamo Moscow | Russia | 37 | 13 | 13 | 26 | 32 | | | | | | | | | | 10 | 2 | 4 | 6 | 31 | | | | |
| 2005-06 | Washington | NHL | 81 | 52 | 54 | 106 | 52 | 21 | 3 | 5 | 425 | 12.2 | 2 | 16 | 12.5 | 21:37 | | | | | | | | | |
| | Russia | Olympics | 8 | 5 | 0 | 5 | 8 | | | | | | | | | | | | | | | | | | |
| 2006-07 | Washington | NHL | 82 | 46 | 46 | 92 | 52 | 16 | 0 | 8 | 392 | 11.7 | –19 | 17 | 47.1 | 21:23 | | | | | | | | | |
| 2007-08 | Washington | NHL | 82 | *65 | 47 | *112 | 40 | 22 | 0 | 11 | 446 | 14.6 | 28 | 18 | 38.9 | 23:06 | 7 | 4 | 5 | 9 | 0 | 1 | 0 | 2 | 24:03 |
| 2008-09 | Washington | NHL | 79 | *56 | 54 | 110 | 72 | 19 | 1 | 10 | 528 | 10.6 | 8 | 32 | 25.0 | 23:00 | 14 | 11 | 10 | 21 | 8 | 3 | 0 | 1 | 23:21 |
| | NHL Totals | | 324 | 219 | 201 | 420 | 216 | 78 | 4 | 34 | 1791 | 12.2 | | 83 | 30.1 | 22:16 | 21 | 15 | 15 | 30 | 8 | 4 | 0 | 3 | 23:35 |

Olympic Tournament All-Star Team (2006) • NHL All-Rookie Team (2006) • NHL First All-Star Team (2006, 2007, 2008, 2009) • Calder Memorial Trophy (2006) • Maurice "Rocket" Richard Trophy (2008, 2009) • Art Ross Trophy (2008) • Lester B. Pearson Award (2008, 2009) • Hart Trophy (2008, 2009)

Played in NHL All-Star Game (2007, 2008, 2009)

## OYSTRICK, Nathan

(OI-strihk, NAY-thuhn) **ATL.**

Defense. Shoots left. 6', 210 lbs. Born, Regina, Sask., December 17, 1982. Atlanta's 7th choice, 198th overall, in 2002 Entry Draft.

| Season | Club | League | GP | G | A | Pts | PIM | PP | SH | GW | S | % | +/- | TF | F% | Min | Playoffs GP | G | A | Pts | PIM | PP | SH | GW | Min |
|---|---|---|---|---|---|---|---|---|---|---|---|---|---|---|---|---|---|---|---|---|---|---|---|---|---|
| 99-2000 | Reg. Pat Cdns. | SMHL | 43 | 6 | 22 | 28 | 214 | .... | .... | .... | .... | .... | .... | .... | .... | .... | .... | .... | .... | .... | .... | .... | .... | .... | .... |
| 2000-01 | South Surrey | BCHL | STATISTICS NOT AVAILABLE | | | | | .... | .... | .... | .... | .... | .... | .... | .... | .... | .... | .... | .... | .... | .... | .... | .... | .... | .... |
| 2001-02 | South Surrey | BCHL | 50 | 15 | 42 | 57 | 142 | .... | .... | .... | .... | .... | .... | .... | .... | .... | .... | .... | .... | .... | .... | .... | .... | .... | .... |
| 2002-03 | Northern Mich. | CCHA | 34 | 2 | 10 | 12 | 26 | .... | .... | .... | .... | .... | .... | .... | .... | .... | .... | .... | .... | .... | .... | .... | .... | .... | .... |
| 2003-04 | Northern Mich. | CCHA | 39 | 8 | 20 | 28 | 98 | .... | .... | .... | .... | .... | .... | .... | .... | .... | .... | .... | .... | .... | .... | .... | .... | .... | .... |
| 2004-05 | Northern Mich. | CCHA | 40 | 7 | 13 | 20 | 87 | .... | .... | .... | .... | .... | .... | .... | .... | .... | .... | .... | .... | .... | .... | .... | .... | .... | .... |
| 2005-06 | Northern Mich. | CCHA | 38 | 9 | 20 | 29 | 58 | .... | .... | .... | .... | .... | .... | .... | .... | .... | .... | .... | .... | .... | .... | .... | .... | .... | .... |
| | Chicago Wolves | AHL | 2 | 0 | 1 | 1 | 4 | .... | .... | .... | .... | .... | .... | .... | .... | .... | .... | .... | .... | .... | .... | .... | .... | .... | .... |
| 2006-07 | Chicago Wolves | AHL | 80 | 15 | 32 | 47 | 105 | .... | .... | .... | .... | .... | .... | .... | .... | .... | 15 | 0 | 6 | 6 | 16 | .... | .... | .... | .... |
| 2007-08 | Chicago Wolves | AHL | 80 | 15 | 28 | 43 | 112 | .... | .... | .... | .... | .... | .... | .... | .... | .... | 24 | 3 | 8 | 11 | 35 | .... | .... | .... | .... |
| **2008-09** | **Atlanta** | **NHL** | **53** | **4** | **8** | **12** | **50** | **0** | **0** | **0** | **43** | **9.3** | **–2** | **0** | **0.0** | **15:45** | .... | .... | .... | .... | .... | .... | .... | .... | .... |
| | **NHL Totals** | | **53** | **4** | **8** | **12** | **50** | **0** | **0** | **0** | **43** | **9.3** | | **0** | **0.0** | **15:45** | .... | .... | .... | .... | .... | .... | .... | .... | .... |

CCHA Second All-Star Team (2004) • CCHA First All-Star Team (2005, 2006) • NCAA West Second All-American Team (2006) • AHL All-Rookie Team (2007) • AHL Second All-Star Team (2007)

## PACIORETTY, Max

(pahk-OHR-eht-tee, MAX) **MTL.**

Left wing. Shoots left. 6'2", 192 lbs. Born, New Canaan, CT, November 20, 1988. Montreal's 2nd choice, 22nd overall, in 2007 Entry Draft.

| Season | Club | League | GP | G | A | Pts | PIM | PP | SH | GW | S | % | +/- | TF | F% | Min | Playoffs GP | G | A | Pts | PIM | PP | SH | GW | Min |
|---|---|---|---|---|---|---|---|---|---|---|---|---|---|---|---|---|---|---|---|---|---|---|---|---|---|
| 2004-05 | Taft Rhinos | High-CT | 23 | 5 | 14 | 19 | .... | .... | .... | .... | .... | .... | .... | .... | .... | .... | .... | .... | .... | .... | .... | .... | .... | .... | .... |
| 2005-06 | Taft Rhinos | High-CT | 26 | 7 | 26 | 33 | .... | .... | .... | .... | .... | .... | .... | .... | .... | .... | .... | .... | .... | .... | .... | .... | .... | .... | .... |
| 2006-07 | Sioux City | USHL | 60 | 21 | 42 | 63 | 119 | .... | .... | .... | .... | .... | .... | .... | .... | .... | 7 | 4 | 6 | 10 | 10 | .... | .... | .... | .... |
| 2007-08 | U. of Michigan | CCHA | 37 | 15 | 24 | 39 | 59 | .... | .... | .... | .... | .... | .... | .... | .... | .... | .... | .... | .... | .... | .... | .... | .... | .... | .... |
| **2008-09** | **Montreal** | **NHL** | **34** | **3** | **8** | **11** | **27** | **1** | **0** | **0** | **57** | **5.3** | **–3** | **2** | **50.0** | **12:37** | .... | .... | .... | .... | .... | .... | .... | .... | .... |
| | Hamilton | AHL | 37 | 6 | 23 | 29 | 43 | .... | .... | .... | .... | .... | .... | .... | .... | .... | .... | .... | .... | .... | .... | .... | .... | .... | .... |
| | **NHL Totals** | | **34** | **3** | **8** | **11** | **27** | **1** | **0** | **0** | **57** | **5.3** | | **2** | **50.0** | **12:37** | .... | .... | .... | .... | .... | .... | .... | .... | .... |

USHL All-Rookie Team (2007) • USHL Rookie of the Year (2007) • CCHA All-Rookie Team (2008) • CCHA Rookie of the Year (2008)

## PADDOCK, Cam

(PA-dawk, KAM) **ST.L.**

Center. Shoots right. 6'1", 191 lbs. Born, Vancouver, B.C., March 22, 1983. Pittsburgh's 6th choice, 137th overall, in 2002 Entry Draft.

| Season | Club | League | GP | G | A | Pts | PIM | PP | SH | GW | S | % | +/- | TF | F% | Min | Playoffs GP | G | A | Pts | PIM | PP | SH | GW | Min |
|---|---|---|---|---|---|---|---|---|---|---|---|---|---|---|---|---|---|---|---|---|---|---|---|---|---|
| 99-2000 | Kelowna Rockets | WHL | 46 | 5 | 5 | 10 | 42 | .... | .... | .... | .... | .... | .... | .... | .... | .... | 5 | 0 | 0 | 0 | 0 | .... | .... | .... | .... |
| 2000-01 | Kelowna Rockets | WHL | 72 | 14 | 10 | 24 | 110 | .... | .... | .... | .... | .... | .... | .... | .... | .... | 6 | 0 | 0 | 0 | 4 | .... | .... | .... | .... |
| 2001-02 | Kelowna Rockets | WHL | 72 | 38 | 35 | 73 | 122 | .... | .... | .... | .... | .... | .... | .... | .... | .... | 15 | 8 | 6 | 14 | 35 | .... | .... | .... | .... |
| 2002-03 | Kelowna Rockets | WHL | 71 | 33 | 26 | 59 | 107 | .... | .... | .... | .... | .... | .... | .... | .... | .... | 19 | 11 | 8 | 19 | 18 | .... | .... | .... | .... |
| 2003-04 | Wilkes-Barre | AHL | 1 | 0 | 0 | 0 | 2 | .... | .... | .... | .... | .... | .... | .... | .... | .... | .... | .... | .... | .... | .... | .... | .... | .... | .... |
| | Kelowna Rockets | WHL | 62 | 17 | 22 | 39 | 86 | .... | .... | .... | .... | .... | .... | .... | .... | .... | 16 | 3 | 4 | 7 | 22 | .... | .... | .... | .... |
| 2004-05 | Wilkes-Barre | AHL | 16 | 0 | 0 | 0 | 13 | .... | .... | .... | .... | .... | .... | .... | .... | .... | .... | .... | .... | .... | .... | .... | .... | .... | .... |
| | Wheeling Nailers | ECHL | 53 | 11 | 18 | 29 | 70 | .... | .... | .... | .... | .... | .... | .... | .... | .... | .... | .... | .... | .... | .... | .... | .... | .... | .... |
| 2005-06 | Wilkes-Barre | AHL | 4 | 0 | 0 | 0 | 2 | .... | .... | .... | .... | .... | .... | .... | .... | .... | .... | .... | .... | .... | .... | .... | .... | .... | .... |
| | Wheeling Nailers | ECHL | 61 | 14 | 24 | 38 | 90 | .... | .... | .... | .... | .... | .... | .... | .... | .... | 9 | 0 | 0 | 0 | 12 | .... | .... | .... | .... |
| 2006-07 | Phoenix | ECHL | 46 | 11 | 20 | 31 | 117 | .... | .... | .... | .... | .... | .... | .... | .... | .... | 3 | 2 | 0 | 2 | 9 | .... | .... | .... | .... |
| | San Antonio | AHL | 22 | 0 | 2 | 2 | 13 | .... | .... | .... | .... | .... | .... | .... | .... | .... | .... | .... | .... | .... | .... | .... | .... | .... | .... |
| 2007-08 | San Antonio | AHL | 78 | 12 | 13 | 25 | 107 | .... | .... | .... | .... | .... | .... | .... | .... | .... | 7 | 0 | 2 | 2 | 18 | .... | .... | .... | .... |
| **2008-09** | **St. Louis** | **NHL** | **16** | **2** | **1** | **3** | **0** | **0** | **0** | **0** | **17** | **11.8** | **–4** | **87** | **46.0** | **10:41** | .... | .... | .... | .... | .... | .... | .... | .... | .... |
| | Peoria Rivermen | AHL | 60 | 8 | 7 | 15 | 96 | .... | .... | .... | .... | .... | .... | .... | .... | .... | 7 | 2 | 2 | 4 | 0 | .... | .... | .... | .... |
| | **NHL Totals** | | **16** | **2** | **1** | **3** | **0** | **0** | **0** | **0** | **17** | **11.8** | | **87** | **46.0** | **10:41** | .... | .... | .... | .... | .... | .... | .... | .... | .... |

Signed as a free agent by **San Antonio** (AHL), December 26, 2006. Signed as a free agent by **St. Louis**, July 15, 2008.

## PAETSCH, Nathan

(PASH, NAY-thuhn) **BUF.**

Defense. Shoots left. 6'1", 198 lbs. Born, Humboldt, Sask., March 30, 1983. Buffalo's 8th choice, 202nd overall, in 2003 Entry Draft.

| Season | Club | League | GP | G | A | Pts | PIM | PP | SH | GW | S | % | +/- | TF | F% | Min | Playoffs GP | G | A | Pts | PIM | PP | SH | GW | Min |
|---|---|---|---|---|---|---|---|---|---|---|---|---|---|---|---|---|---|---|---|---|---|---|---|---|---|
| 1998-99 | Tisdale Trojans | SMHL | 74 | 20 | 55 | 75 | 120 | .... | .... | .... | .... | .... | .... | .... | .... | .... | .... | .... | .... | .... | .... | .... | .... | .... | .... |
| | Moose Jaw | WHL | 2 | 0 | 0 | 0 | 0 | .... | .... | .... | .... | .... | .... | .... | .... | .... | .... | .... | .... | .... | .... | .... | .... | .... | .... |
| 99-2000 | Moose Jaw | WHL | 68 | 9 | 35 | 44 | 49 | .... | .... | .... | .... | .... | .... | .... | .... | .... | 4 | 0 | 1 | 1 | 0 | .... | .... | .... | .... |
| 2000-01 | Moose Jaw | WHL | 70 | 8 | 54 | 62 | 118 | .... | .... | .... | .... | .... | .... | .... | .... | .... | 4 | 1 | 2 | 3 | 6 | .... | .... | .... | .... |
| 2001-02 | Moose Jaw | WHL | 59 | 16 | 36 | 52 | 86 | .... | .... | .... | .... | .... | .... | .... | .... | .... | 12 | 0 | 4 | 4 | 16 | .... | .... | .... | .... |
| 2002-03 | Moose Jaw | WHL | 59 | 15 | 39 | 54 | 81 | .... | .... | .... | .... | .... | .... | .... | .... | .... | 13 | 3 | 10 | 13 | 6 | .... | .... | .... | .... |
| 2003-04 | Rochester | AHL | 54 | 5 | 5 | 10 | 49 | .... | .... | .... | .... | .... | .... | .... | .... | .... | 16 | 1 | 1 | 2 | 28 | .... | .... | .... | .... |
| 2004-05 | Rochester | AHL | 80 | 4 | 19 | 23 | 150 | .... | .... | .... | .... | .... | .... | .... | .... | .... | 9 | 1 | 1 | 2 | 16 | .... | .... | .... | .... |
| **2005-06** | **Buffalo** | **NHL** | **1** | **0** | **1** | **1** | **0** | **0** | **0** | **0** | **0** | **0.0** | **–1** | **0** | **0.0** | **15:38** | **1** | **0** | **0** | **0** | **0** | **0** | **0** | **0** | **12:06** |
| | Rochester | AHL | 72 | 11 | 39 | 50 | 90 | .... | .... | .... | .... | .... | .... | .... | .... | .... | .... | .... | .... | .... | .... | .... | .... | .... | .... |
| **2006-07** | **Buffalo** | **NHL** | **63** | **2** | **22** | **24** | **50** | **0** | **0** | **0** | **62** | **3.2** | **10** | **0** | **0.0** | **15:15** | .... | .... | .... | .... | .... | .... | .... | .... | .... |
| **2007-08** | **Buffalo** | **NHL** | **59** | **2** | **7** | **9** | **27** | **0** | **0** | **0** | **49** | **4.1** | **3** | **0** | **0.0** | **13:38** | .... | .... | .... | .... | .... | .... | .... | .... | .... |
| **2008-09** | **Buffalo** | **NHL** | **23** | **2** | **4** | **6** | **25** | **0** | **0** | **0** | **21** | **9.5** | **3** | **0** | **0.0** | **12:11** | .... | .... | .... | .... | .... | .... | .... | .... | .... |
| | **NHL Totals** | | **146** | **6** | **34** | **40** | **102** | **0** | **0** | **0** | **132** | **4.5** | | **0** | **0.0** | **14:07** | **1** | **0** | **0** | **0** | **0** | **0** | **0** | **0** | **12:06** |

• Re-entered NHL Entry Draft. Originally Washington's 1st choice, 58th overall, in 2001 Entry Draft.
WHL East Second All-Star Team (2003)
• Spent majority of 2008-09 season serving as a healthy reserve.

## PAHLSSON, Samuel

(PAWL-suhn, SAM-ew-l) **CBJ**

Center. Shoots left. 6', 204 lbs. Born, Ange, Sweden, December 17, 1977. Colorado's 10th choice, 176th overall, in 1996 Entry Draft.

| Season | Club | League | GP | G | A | Pts | PIM | PP | SH | GW | S | % | +/- | TF | F% | Min | Playoffs GP | G | A | Pts | PIM | PP | SH | GW | Min |
|---|---|---|---|---|---|---|---|---|---|---|---|---|---|---|---|---|---|---|---|---|---|---|---|---|---|
| 1992-93 | Ange IK | Sweden-4 | 9 | 0 | 0 | 0 | 0 | .... | .... | .... | .... | .... | .... | .... | .... | .... | .... | .... | .... | .... | .... | .... | .... | .... | .... |
| 1993-94 | Ange IK | Sweden-4 | STATISTICS NOT AVAILABLE | | | | | .... | .... | .... | .... | .... | .... | .... | .... | .... | .... | .... | .... | .... | .... | .... | .... | .... | .... |
| 1994-95 | MoDo | Sweden | 1 | 0 | 0 | 0 | 0 | .... | .... | .... | .... | .... | .... | .... | .... | .... | .... | .... | .... | .... | .... | .... | .... | .... | .... |
| 1995-96 | MoDo Jr. | Swe-Jr. | 30 | 10 | 11 | 21 | 26 | .... | .... | .... | .... | .... | .... | .... | .... | .... | .... | .... | .... | .... | .... | .... | .... | .... | .... |
| | MoDo | Sweden | 36 | 1 | 3 | 4 | 8 | .... | .... | .... | .... | .... | .... | .... | .... | .... | 4 | 0 | 0 | 0 | 0 | .... | .... | .... | .... |
| 1996-97 | MoDo | Sweden | 49 | 8 | 9 | 17 | 83 | .... | .... | .... | .... | .... | .... | .... | .... | .... | .... | .... | .... | .... | .... | .... | .... | .... | .... |
| | MoDo Jr. | Swe-Jr. | 5 | 2 | 6 | 8 | 2 | .... | .... | .... | .... | .... | .... | .... | .... | .... | .... | .... | .... | .... | .... | .... | .... | .... | .... |
| 1997-98 | MoDo | Sweden | 23 | 6 | 11 | 17 | 24 | .... | .... | .... | .... | .... | .... | .... | .... | .... | 9 | 3 | 0 | 3 | 6 | .... | .... | .... | .... |
| 1998-99 | MoDo | Sweden | 50 | 17 | 17 | 34 | 44 | .... | .... | .... | .... | .... | .... | .... | .... | .... | 13 | 3 | 3 | 6 | 10 | .... | .... | .... | .... |
| 99-2000 | MoDo | Sweden | 47 | 16 | 11 | 27 | 67 | .... | .... | .... | .... | .... | .... | .... | .... | .... | 13 | 3 | 3 | 6 | 8 | .... | .... | .... | .... |
| | MoDo | EuroHL | 4 | 1 | 0 | 1 | 0 | .... | .... | .... | .... | .... | .... | .... | .... | .... | 3 | 1 | 1 | 2 | 2 | .... | .... | .... | .... |
| **2000-01** | **Boston** | **NHL** | **17** | **1** | **1** | **2** | **6** | **0** | **0** | **0** | **13** | **7.7** | **–5** | **239** | **40.2** | **14:19** | .... | .... | .... | .... | .... | .... | .... | .... | .... |
| | **Anaheim** | **NHL** | **59** | **3** | **4** | **7** | **14** | **1** | **1** | **1** | **46** | **6.5** | **–9** | **867** | **45.1** | **14:14** | .... | .... | .... | .... | .... | .... | .... | .... | .... |
| **2001-02** | **Anaheim** | **NHL** | **80** | **6** | **14** | **20** | **26** | **1** | **1** | **0** | **99** | **6.1** | **–16** | **1201** | **49.8** | **16:24** | .... | .... | .... | .... | .... | .... | .... | .... | .... |
| **2002-03** | **Anaheim** | **NHL** | **34** | **4** | **11** | **15** | **18** | **0** | **1** | **2** | **28** | **14.3** | **10** | **118** | **52.5** | **13:20** | **21** | **2** | **4** | **6** | **12** | **0** | **0** | **0** | **16:41** |
| | Cincinnati | AHL | 13 | 1 | 7 | 8 | 24 | .... | .... | .... | .... | .... | .... | .... | .... | .... | .... | .... | .... | .... | .... | .... | .... | .... | .... |
| **2003-04** | **Anaheim** | **NHL** | **82** | **8** | **14** | **22** | **52** | **1** | **0** | **2** | **134** | **6.0** | **–2** | **908** | **55.3** | **16:51** | .... | .... | .... | .... | .... | .... | .... | .... | .... |
| 2004-05 | Frolunda | Sweden | 48 | 6 | 18 | 24 | 56 | .... | .... | .... | .... | .... | .... | .... | .... | .... | 14 | 4 | 7 | 11 | 24 | .... | .... | .... | .... |
| **2005-06** | **Anaheim** | **NHL** | **82** | **11** | **10** | **21** | **34** | **0** | **3** | **1** | **116** | **9.5** | **–1** | **1517** | **52.8** | **16:30** | **16** | **2** | **3** | **5** | **18** | **0** | **0** | **2** | **17:06** |
| | Sweden | Olympics | 8 | 2 | 2 | 4 | 8 | .... | .... | .... | .... | .... | .... | .... | .... | .... | .... | .... | .... | .... | .... | .... | .... | .... | .... |
| **2006-07** ♦ | **Anaheim** | **NHL** | **82** | **8** | **18** | **26** | **42** | **0** | **0** | **1** | **111** | **7.2** | **–4** | **1523** | **52.7** | **17:22** | **21** | **3** | **9** | **12** | **20** | **0** | **0** | **2** | **19:25** |
| **2007-08** | **Anaheim** | **NHL** | **56** | **6** | **9** | **15** | **34** | **0** | **3** | **3** | **94** | **6.4** | **–2** | **1066** | **55.0** | **18:46** | **6** | **0** | **0** | **0** | **0** | **0** | **0** | **0** | **18:18** |
| **2008-09** | **Anaheim** | **NHL** | **52** | **5** | **10** | **15** | **32** | **1** | **0** | **1** | **74** | **6.8** | **–16** | **1064** | **53.5** | **18:31** | .... | .... | .... | .... | .... | .... | .... | .... | .... |
| | **Chicago** | **NHL** | **13** | **2** | **1** | **3** | **2** | **0** | **0** | **1** | **14** | **14.3** | **–1** | **173** | **53.8** | **17:25** | **17** | **2** | **3** | **5** | **4** | **1** | **0** | **0** | **16:38** |
| | **NHL Totals** | | **557** | **54** | **92** | **146** | **260** | **4** | **9** | **12** | **729** | **7.4** | | **8676** | **51.9** | **16:36** | **81** | **9** | **19** | **28** | **54** | **1** | **0** | **4** | **17:35** |

Traded to **Boston** by **Colorado** with Brian Rolston, Martin Grenier and New Jersey's 1st round choice (previously acquired, Boston selected Martin Samuelsson) in 2000 Entry Draft for Raymond Bourque and Dave Andreychuk, March 6, 2000. Traded to **Anaheim** by **Boston** for Patrick Traverse and Andrei Nazarov, November 18, 2000. Signed as a free agent by **Frolunda** (Sweden), September, 2004. Traded to **Chicago** by **Anaheim** with Logan Stephenson and future considerations for James Wisniewski and Petri Kontiola, March 4, 2009. Signed as a free agent by **Columbus**, July 1, 2009.

## PAILLE, Daniel
(PIGH-yay, DAN-yehl) **BUF.**

Left wing. Shoots left. 6', 200 lbs. Born, Welland, Ont., April 15, 1984. Buffalo's 2nd choice, 20th overall, in 2002 Entry Draft.

| | | | Regular Season | | | | | | | | | | | | | | Playoffs | | | | | | | | |
|---|---|---|---|---|---|---|---|---|---|---|---|---|---|---|---|---|---|---|---|---|---|---|---|---|---|
| Season | Club | League | GP | G | A | Pts | PIM | PP | SH | GW | S | % | +/- | TF | F% | Min | GP | G | A | Pts | PIM | PP | SH | GW | Min |
| 99-2000 | Welland Cougars | OHA-B | 42 | 14 | 17 | 31 | 19 | .... | .... | .... | .... | .... | .... | .... | .... | .... | 16 | 16 | 16 | 32 | .... | .... | .... | .... | .... |
| 2000-01 | Guelph Storm | OHL | 64 | 22 | 31 | 53 | 57 | .... | .... | .... | .... | .... | .... | .... | .... | .... | 4 | 2 | 0 | 2 | 2 | .... | .... | .... | .... |
| 2001-02 | Guelph Storm | OHL | 62 | 27 | 30 | 57 | 54 | .... | .... | .... | .... | .... | .... | .... | .... | .... | 9 | 5 | 2 | 7 | 9 | .... | .... | .... | .... |
| 2002-03 | Guelph Storm | OHL | 54 | 30 | 27 | 57 | 28 | .... | .... | .... | .... | .... | .... | .... | .... | .... | 11 | 8 | 6 | 14 | 6 | .... | .... | .... | .... |
| 2003-04 | Guelph Storm | OHL | 59 | 37 | 43 | 80 | 63 | .... | .... | .... | .... | .... | .... | .... | .... | .... | 22 | 9 | 9 | 18 | 14 | .... | .... | .... | .... |
| 2004-05 | Rochester | AHL | 79 | 14 | 15 | 29 | 54 | .... | .... | .... | .... | .... | .... | .... | .... | .... | 9 | 2 | 2 | 4 | 6 | .... | .... | .... | .... |
| **2005-06** | **Buffalo** | **NHL** | **14** | **1** | **2** | **3** | **2** | **0** | **0** | **0** | **15** | **6.7** | **5** | **4** | **25.0** | **10:24** | .... | .... | .... | .... | .... | .... | .... | .... | .... |
| | Rochester | AHL | 45 | 14 | 13 | 27 | 29 | .... | .... | .... | .... | .... | .... | .... | .... | .... | .... | .... | .... | .... | .... | .... | .... | .... | .... |
| **2006-07** | **Buffalo** | **NHL** | **29** | **3** | **8** | **11** | **18** | **0** | **0** | **0** | **45** | **6.7** | **5** | **6** | **33.3** | **12:47** | **1** | **0** | **0** | **0** | **0** | **0** | **0** | **0** | **4:52** |
| | Rochester | AHL | 29 | 7 | 14 | 21 | 12 | .... | .... | .... | .... | .... | .... | .... | .... | .... | .... | .... | .... | .... | .... | .... | .... | .... | .... |
| **2007-08** | **Buffalo** | **NHL** | **77** | **19** | **16** | **35** | **14** | **0** | **3** | **2** | **110** | **17.3** | **9** | **41** | **36.6** | **13:16** | .... | .... | .... | .... | .... | .... | .... | .... | .... |
| **2008-09** | **Buffalo** | **NHL** | **73** | **12** | **15** | **27** | **20** | **0** | **0** | **2** | **80** | **15.0** | **0** | **17** | **17.7** | **11:54** | .... | .... | .... | .... | .... | .... | .... | .... | .... |
| | **NHL Totals** | | **193** | **35** | **41** | **76** | **54** | **0** | **3** | **4** | **250** | **14.0** | | **68** | **30.9** | **12:28** | **1** | **0** | **0** | **0** | **0** | **0** | **0** | **0** | **4:52** |

## PANDOLFO, Jay
(pan-DAWL-foh, JAY) **N.J.**

Left wing. Shoots left. 6'1", 190 lbs. Born, Winchester, MA, December 27, 1974. New Jersey's 2nd choice, 32nd overall, in 1993 Entry Draft.

| Season | Club | League | GP | G | A | Pts | PIM | PP | SH | GW | S | % | +/- | TF | F% | Min | GP | G | A | Pts | PIM | PP | SH | GW | Min |
|---|---|---|---|---|---|---|---|---|---|---|---|---|---|---|---|---|---|---|---|---|---|---|---|---|---|
| 1989-90 | Burlington | High-MA | 23 | 33 | 30 | 63 | 18 | .... | .... | .... | .... | .... | .... | .... | .... | .... | .... | .... | .... | .... | .... | .... | .... | .... | .... |
| 1990-91 | Burlington | High-MA | 20 | 19 | 27 | 46 | 10 | .... | .... | .... | .... | .... | .... | .... | .... | .... | .... | .... | .... | .... | .... | .... | .... | .... | .... |
| 1991-92 | Burlington | High-MA | 20 | 35 | 34 | 69 | 14 | .... | .... | .... | .... | .... | .... | .... | .... | .... | .... | .... | .... | .... | .... | .... | .... | .... | .... |
| 1992-93 | Boston University | H-East | 37 | 16 | 22 | 38 | 16 | .... | .... | .... | .... | .... | .... | .... | .... | .... | .... | .... | .... | .... | .... | .... | .... | .... | .... |
| 1993-94 | Boston University | H-East | 37 | 17 | 25 | 42 | 27 | .... | .... | .... | .... | .... | .... | .... | .... | .... | .... | .... | .... | .... | .... | .... | .... | .... | .... |
| 1994-95 | Boston University | H-East | 20 | 7 | 13 | 20 | 6 | .... | .... | .... | .... | .... | .... | .... | .... | .... | .... | .... | .... | .... | .... | .... | .... | .... | .... |
| 1995-96 | Boston University | H-East | 39 | *38 | 29 | 67 | 6 | .... | .... | .... | .... | .... | .... | .... | .... | .... | .... | .... | .... | .... | .... | .... | .... | .... | .... |
| | Albany River Rats | AHL | 5 | 3 | 1 | 4 | 0 | .... | .... | .... | .... | .... | .... | .... | .... | .... | 3 | 0 | 0 | 0 | 0 | .... | .... | .... | .... |
| **1996-97** | **New Jersey** | **NHL** | **46** | **6** | **8** | **14** | **6** | **0** | **0** | **1** | **61** | **9.8** | **–1** | .... | .... | .... | **6** | **0** | **1** | **1** | **0** | **0** | **0** | **0** | .... |
| | Albany River Rats | AHL | 12 | 3 | 9 | 12 | 0 | .... | .... | .... | .... | .... | .... | .... | .... | .... | .... | .... | .... | .... | .... | .... | .... | .... | .... |
| **1997-98** | **New Jersey** | **NHL** | **23** | **1** | **3** | **4** | **4** | **0** | **0** | **0** | **23** | **4.3** | **–4** | .... | .... | .... | **3** | **0** | **2** | **2** | **0** | **0** | **0** | **0** | .... |
| | Albany River Rats | AHL | 51 | 18 | 19 | 37 | 24 | .... | .... | .... | .... | .... | .... | .... | .... | .... | .... | .... | .... | .... | .... | .... | .... | .... | .... |
| **1998-99** | **New Jersey** | **NHL** | **70** | **14** | **13** | **27** | **10** | **1** | **1** | **4** | **100** | **14.0** | **3** | **10** | **40.0** | **15:13** | **7** | **1** | **0** | **1** | **0** | **0** | **0** | **0** | **13:19** |
| **99-2000♦** | **New Jersey** | **NHL** | **71** | **7** | **8** | **15** | **4** | **0** | **0** | **0** | **86** | **8.1** | **0** | **19** | **47.4** | **13:25** | **23** | **0** | **5** | **5** | **0** | **0** | **0** | **0** | **15:35** |
| **2000-01** | **New Jersey** | **NHL** | **63** | **4** | **12** | **16** | **16** | **0** | **0** | **0** | **57** | **7.0** | **3** | **15** | **53.3** | **14:05** | **25** | **1** | **4** | **5** | **4** | **0** | **0** | **0** | **12:38** |
| **2001-02** | **New Jersey** | **NHL** | **65** | **4** | **10** | **14** | **15** | **0** | **1** | **0** | **72** | **5.6** | **12** | **12** | **41.7** | **13:59** | **6** | **0** | **0** | **0** | **0** | **0** | **0** | **0** | **16:11** |
| **2002-03♦** | **New Jersey** | **NHL** | **68** | **6** | **11** | **17** | **23** | **0** | **1** | **4** | **92** | **6.5** | **12** | **13** | **23.1** | **16:08** | **24** | **6** | **6** | **12** | **2** | **0** | **0** | **1** | **16:34** |
| **2003-04** | **New Jersey** | **NHL** | **82** | **13** | **13** | **26** | **14** | **1** | **2** | **4** | **140** | **9.3** | **5** | **25** | **44.0** | **16:00** | **5** | **0** | **0** | **0** | **0** | **0** | **0** | **0** | **13:41** |
| 2004-05 | Salzburg | Austria | 19 | 5 | 7 | 12 | 0 | .... | .... | .... | .... | .... | .... | .... | .... | .... | .... | .... | .... | .... | .... | .... | .... | .... | .... |
| **2005-06** | **New Jersey** | **NHL** | **82** | **10** | **10** | **20** | **16** | **0** | **0** | **0** | **116** | **8.6** | **2** | **13** | **30.8** | **18:03** | **9** | **1** | **4** | **5** | **0** | **0** | **1** | **1** | **18:37** |
| **2006-07** | **New Jersey** | **NHL** | **82** | **13** | **14** | **27** | **8** | **0** | **1** | **1** | **109** | **11.9** | **–5** | **16** | **6.3** | **18:37** | **11** | **1** | **0** | **1** | **4** | **0** | **0** | **0** | **19:39** |
| **2007-08** | **New Jersey** | **NHL** | **54** | **12** | **12** | **24** | **22** | **0** | **0** | **1** | **78** | **15.4** | **10** | **7** | **42.9** | **17:17** | **5** | **0** | **0** | **0** | **2** | **0** | **0** | **0** | **16:15** |
| **2008-09** | **New Jersey** | **NHL** | **61** | **5** | **5** | **10** | **10** | **0** | **1** | **1** | **63** | **7.9** | **–12** | **18** | **22.2** | **14:50** | **7** | **1** | **0** | **1** | **0** | **0** | **0** | **0** | **16:35** |
| | **NHL Totals** | | **767** | **95** | **119** | **214** | **148** | **2** | **7** | **16** | **997** | **9.5** | | **148** | **35.1** | **15:51** | **131** | **11** | **22** | **33** | **12** | **0** | **1** | **2** | **15:40** |

Hockey East First All-Star Team (1996) • Hockey East Player of the Year (1996) • NCAA East First All-American Team (1996)

Signed as a free agent by **Salzburg** (Austria), December 27, 2004.

## PARDY, Adam
(PAHR-dee, A-duhm) **CGY.**

Defense. Shoots left. 6'4", 206 lbs. Born, Bonavista, Nfld., March 29, 1984. Calgary's 6th choice, 173rd overall, in 2004 Entry Draft.

| Season | Club | League | GP | G | A | Pts | PIM | PP | SH | GW | S | % | +/- | TF | F% | Min | GP | G | A | Pts | PIM | PP | SH | GW | Min |
|---|---|---|---|---|---|---|---|---|---|---|---|---|---|---|---|---|---|---|---|---|---|---|---|---|---|
| 2002-03 | Yarmouth | MJrHL | 1 | 0 | 0 | 0 | 2 | .... | .... | .... | .... | .... | .... | .... | .... | .... | .... | .... | .... | .... | .... | .... | .... | .... | .... |
| | Antigonish | MJrHL | 31 | 5 | 16 | 21 | 42 | .... | .... | .... | .... | .... | .... | .... | .... | .... | .... | .... | .... | .... | .... | .... | .... | .... | .... |
| | Cape Breton | QMJHL | 7 | 0 | 1 | 1 | 2 | .... | .... | .... | .... | .... | .... | .... | .... | .... | 2 | 0 | 0 | 0 | 0 | .... | .... | .... | .... |
| 2003-04 | Cape Breton | QMJHL | 68 | 4 | 12 | 16 | 137 | .... | .... | .... | .... | .... | .... | .... | .... | .... | 5 | 0 | 1 | 1 | 8 | .... | .... | .... | .... |
| 2004-05 | Cape Breton | QMJHL | 69 | 12 | 27 | 39 | 163 | .... | .... | .... | .... | .... | .... | .... | .... | .... | 5 | 2 | 2 | 4 | 8 | .... | .... | .... | .... |
| 2005-06 | Omaha | AHL | 24 | 0 | 0 | 0 | 18 | .... | .... | .... | .... | .... | .... | .... | .... | .... | .... | .... | .... | .... | .... | .... | .... | .... | .... |
| | Las Vegas | ECHL | 41 | 1 | 11 | 12 | 55 | .... | .... | .... | .... | .... | .... | .... | .... | .... | 10 | 2 | 1 | 3 | 12 | .... | .... | .... | .... |
| 2006-07 | Omaha | AHL | 70 | 2 | 6 | 8 | 60 | .... | .... | .... | .... | .... | .... | .... | .... | .... | 6 | 1 | 1 | 2 | 0 | .... | .... | .... | .... |
| 2007-08 | Quad City Flames | AHL | 65 | 5 | 13 | 18 | 67 | .... | .... | .... | .... | .... | .... | .... | .... | .... | .... | .... | .... | .... | .... | .... | .... | .... | .... |
| **2008-09** | **Calgary** | **NHL** | **60** | **1** | **9** | **10** | **69** | **0** | **0** | **0** | **38** | **2.6** | **3** | **0** | **0.0** | **15:00** | **6** | **0** | **2** | **2** | **5** | **0** | **0** | **0** | **14:51** |
| | **NHL Totals** | | **60** | **1** | **9** | **10** | **69** | **0** | **0** | **0** | **38** | **2.6** | | **0** | **0.0** | **15:00** | **6** | **0** | **2** | **2** | **5** | **0** | **0** | **0** | **14:51** |

## PARENT, Ryan
(PAIR-ehnt, RIGH-uhn) **PHI.**

Defense. Shoots left. 6'3", 183 lbs. Born, Prince Albert, Sask., March 17, 1987. Nashville's 1st choice, 18th overall, in 2005 Entry Draft.

| Season | Club | League | GP | G | A | Pts | PIM | PP | SH | GW | S | % | +/- | TF | F% | Min | GP | G | A | Pts | PIM | PP | SH | GW | Min |
|---|---|---|---|---|---|---|---|---|---|---|---|---|---|---|---|---|---|---|---|---|---|---|---|---|---|
| 2002-03 | Waterloo Siskins | OHA-B | 41 | 2 | 8 | 10 | 35 | .... | .... | .... | .... | .... | .... | .... | .... | .... | .... | .... | .... | .... | .... | .... | .... | .... | .... |
| 2003-04 | Guelph Storm | OHL | 58 | 1 | 5 | 6 | 18 | .... | .... | .... | .... | .... | .... | .... | .... | .... | 22 | 0 | 0 | 0 | 2 | .... | .... | .... | .... |
| 2004-05 | Guelph Storm | OHL | 66 | 2 | 17 | 19 | 36 | .... | .... | .... | .... | .... | .... | .... | .... | .... | 4 | 0 | 1 | 1 | 4 | .... | .... | .... | .... |
| 2005-06 | Guelph Storm | OHL | 60 | 4 | 17 | 21 | 122 | .... | .... | .... | .... | .... | .... | .... | .... | .... | 15 | 1 | 4 | 5 | 24 | .... | .... | .... | .... |
| | Milwaukee | AHL | .... | .... | .... | .... | .... | .... | .... | .... | .... | .... | .... | .... | .... | .... | 10 | 0 | 0 | 0 | 4 | .... | .... | .... | .... |
| **2006-07** | **Philadelphia** | **NHL** | **1** | **0** | **0** | **0** | **0** | **0** | **0** | **0** | **1** | **0.0** | **0** | **0** | **0.0** | **14:10** | .... | .... | .... | .... | .... | .... | .... | .... | .... |
| | Philadelphia | AHL | 6 | 1 | 0 | 1 | 4 | .... | .... | .... | .... | .... | .... | .... | .... | .... | .... | .... | .... | .... | .... | .... | .... | .... | .... |
| | Guelph Storm | OHL | 43 | 3 | 7 | 10 | 86 | .... | .... | .... | .... | .... | .... | .... | .... | .... | 4 | 0 | 1 | 1 | 14 | .... | .... | .... | .... |
| **2007-08** | **Philadelphia** | **NHL** | **22** | **0** | **0** | **0** | **6** | **0** | **0** | **0** | **9** | **0.0** | **–4** | **0** | **0.0** | **14:59** | **4** | **0** | **1** | **1** | **0** | **0** | **0** | **0** | **16:36** |
| | Philadelphia | AHL | 53 | 1 | 7 | 8 | 42 | .... | .... | .... | .... | .... | .... | .... | .... | .... | .... | .... | .... | .... | .... | .... | .... | .... | .... |
| **2008-09** | **Philadelphia** | **NHL** | **31** | **0** | **4** | **4** | **10** | **0** | **0** | **0** | **9** | **0.0** | **3** | **0** | **0.0** | **18:12** | **6** | **0** | **0** | **0** | **6** | **0** | **0** | **0** | **18:52** |
| | Philadelphia | AHL | 15 | 0 | 1 | 1 | 18 | .... | .... | .... | .... | .... | .... | .... | .... | .... | .... | .... | .... | .... | .... | .... | .... | .... | .... |
| | **NHL Totals** | | **54** | **0** | **4** | **4** | **16** | **0** | **0** | **0** | **19** | **0.0** | | **0** | **0.0** | **16:49** | **10** | **0** | **1** | **1** | **6** | **0** | **0** | **0** | **17:58** |

OHL Second All-Star Team (2006, 2007)

Traded to **Philadelphia** by **Nashville** with Scottie Upshall and Nashville's 1st (later traded back to Nashville - Nashville selected Jonathon Blum) and 3rd (later traded to Washington - Washington selected Phil Desimone) round choices in 2007 Entry Draft for Peter Forsberg, February 15, 2007.

## PARENTEAU, P.A.
(pair-ehn-TOH, PEE- AY) **NYR**

Left wing. Shoots right. 5'11", 195 lbs. Born, Hull, Que., March 24, 1983. Anaheim's 11th choice, 264th overall, in 2001 Entry Draft.

| Season | Club | League | GP | G | A | Pts | PIM | PP | SH | GW | S | % | +/- | TF | F% | Min | GP | G | A | Pts | PIM | PP | SH | GW | Min |
|---|---|---|---|---|---|---|---|---|---|---|---|---|---|---|---|---|---|---|---|---|---|---|---|---|---|
| 99-2000 | Charles-Lemoyne | QAAA | 40 | 25 | 40 | 65 | 18 | .... | .... | .... | .... | .... | .... | .... | .... | .... | 16 | 4 | 9 | 13 | 8 | .... | .... | .... | .... |
| 2000-01 | Moncton Wildcats | QMJHL | 45 | 10 | 19 | 29 | 38 | .... | .... | .... | .... | .... | .... | .... | .... | .... | .... | .... | .... | .... | .... | .... | .... | .... | .... |
| | Chicoutimi | QMJHL | 28 | 10 | 13 | 23 | 14 | .... | .... | .... | .... | .... | .... | .... | .... | .... | 7 | 4 | 7 | 11 | 2 | .... | .... | .... | .... |
| 2001-02 | Chicoutimi | QMJHL | 68 | 51 | 67 | 118 | 120 | .... | .... | .... | .... | .... | .... | .... | .... | .... | 4 | 3 | 1 | 4 | 10 | .... | .... | .... | .... |
| 2002-03 | Chicoutimi | QMJHL | 31 | 20 | 35 | 55 | 56 | .... | .... | .... | .... | .... | .... | .... | .... | .... | .... | .... | .... | .... | .... | .... | .... | .... | .... |
| | Sherbrooke | QMJHL | 28 | 13 | 35 | 48 | 84 | .... | .... | .... | .... | .... | .... | .... | .... | .... | 12 | 8 | 11 | 19 | 6 | .... | .... | .... | .... |
| 2003-04 | Cincinnati | AHL | 66 | 14 | 16 | 30 | 20 | .... | .... | .... | .... | .... | .... | .... | .... | .... | 7 | 1 | 2 | 3 | 6 | .... | .... | .... | .... |
| 2004-05 | Cincinnati | AHL | 76 | 17 | 24 | 41 | 58 | .... | .... | .... | .... | .... | .... | .... | .... | .... | 9 | 2 | 0 | 2 | 8 | .... | .... | .... | .... |
| 2005-06 | Portland Pirates | AHL | 56 | 22 | 27 | 49 | 42 | .... | .... | .... | .... | .... | .... | .... | .... | .... | 19 | 5 | 17 | 22 | 24 | .... | .... | .... | .... |
| | Augusta Lynx | ECHL | 2 | 0 | 1 | 1 | 0 | .... | .... | .... | .... | .... | .... | .... | .... | .... | .... | .... | .... | .... | .... | .... | .... | .... | .... |
| **2006-07** | Portland Pirates | AHL | 28 | 15 | 13 | 28 | 35 | .... | .... | .... | .... | .... | .... | .... | .... | .... | .... | .... | .... | .... | .... | .... | .... | .... | .... |
| | **Chicago** | **NHL** | **5** | **0** | **1** | **1** | **2** | **0** | **0** | **0** | **7** | **0.0** | **–1** | **2** | **50.0** | **11:05** | .... | .... | .... | .... | .... | .... | .... | .... | .... |
| | Norfolk Admirals | AHL | 40 | 15 | 36 | 51 | 12 | .... | .... | .... | .... | .... | .... | .... | .... | .... | 6 | 2 | 1 | 3 | 2 | .... | .... | .... | .... |
| 2007-08 | Hartford | AHL | 75 | 34 | 47 | 81 | 81 | .... | .... | .... | .... | .... | .... | .... | .... | .... | 5 | 3 | 2 | 5 | 13 | .... | .... | .... | .... |
| 2008-09 | Hartford | AHL | 74 | 29 | 49 | 78 | 142 | .... | .... | .... | .... | .... | .... | .... | .... | .... | .... | .... | .... | .... | .... | .... | .... | .... | .... |
| | **NHL Totals** | | **5** | **0** | **1** | **1** | **2** | **0** | **0** | **0** | **7** | **0.0** | | **2** | **50.0** | **11:05** | .... | .... | .... | .... | .... | .... | .... | .... | .... |

AHL Second All-Star Team (2008) • AHL First All-Star Team (2009)

Traded to **Chicago** by **Anaheim** with Bruno St. Jacques for Sebastien Caron, Matt Keith and Chris Durno, December 28, 2006. Traded to **NY Rangers** by **Chicago** for future considerations, October 11, 2007.

## PARISE, Zach
(pah-REE-say, ZAK) **N.J.**

Left wing. Shoots left. 5'11", 190 lbs. Born, Minneapolis, MN, July 28, 1984. New Jersey's 1st choice, 17th overall, in 2003 Entry Draft.

| | | | Regular Season | | | | | | | | | | | | | | Playoffs | | | | | | | | |
|---|---|---|---|---|---|---|---|---|---|---|---|---|---|---|---|---|---|---|---|---|---|---|---|---|---|
| Season | Club | League | GP | G | A | Pts | PIM | PP | SH | GW | S | % | +/- | TF | F% | Min | GP | G | A | Pts | PIM | PP | SH | GW | Min |
| 2000-01 | Shat.-St. Mary's | High-MN | 58 | 69 | 93 | 162 | .... | .... | .... | .... | .... | .... | .... | .... | .... | .... | .... | .... | .... | .... | .... | .... | .... | .... | .... |
| 2001-02 | Shat.-St. Mary's | High-MN | 67 | 77 | 101 | 178 | 58 | .... | .... | .... | .... | .... | .... | .... | .... | .... | .... | .... | .... | .... | .... | .... | .... | .... | .... |
| | USNTDP | U-18 | 12 | 7 | 7 | 14 | 6 | .... | .... | .... | .... | .... | .... | .... | .... | .... | .... | .... | .... | .... | .... | .... | .... | .... | .... |
| 2002-03 | North Dakota | WCHA | 39 | 26 | 35 | 61 | 34 | .... | .... | .... | .... | .... | .... | .... | .... | .... | .... | .... | .... | .... | .... | .... | .... | .... | .... |
| 2003-04 | North Dakota | WCHA | 37 | 23 | 32 | 55 | 24 | .... | .... | .... | .... | .... | .... | .... | .... | .... | .... | .... | .... | .... | .... | .... | .... | .... | .... |
| 2004-05 | Albany River Rats | AHL | 73 | 18 | 40 | 58 | 56 | .... | .... | .... | .... | .... | .... | .... | .... | .... | .... | .... | .... | .... | .... | .... | .... | .... | .... |
| **2005-06** | **New Jersey** | **NHL** | **81** | **14** | **18** | **32** | **28** | **2** | **0** | **5** | **133** | **10.5** | **−1** | **162** | **42.6** | **13:08** | **9** | **1** | **2** | **3** | **2** | **0** | **0** | **0** | **15:03** |
| **2006-07** | **New Jersey** | **NHL** | **82** | **31** | **31** | **62** | **30** | **9** | **0** | **7** | **247** | **12.6** | **−3** | **52** | **44.2** | **17:32** | **11** | **7** | **3** | **10** | **8** | **2** | **0** | **1** | **19:08** |
| **2007-08** | **New Jersey** | **NHL** | **81** | **32** | **33** | **65** | **25** | **10** | **1** | **8** | **266** | **12.0** | **13** | **104** | **48.1** | **18:04** | **5** | **1** | **4** | **5** | **2** | **1** | **0** | **0** | **18:29** |
| **2008-09** | **New Jersey** | **NHL** | **82** | **45** | **49** | **94** | **24** | **14** | **0** | **8** | **364** | **12.4** | **30** | **121** | **44.6** | **18:45** | **7** | **3** | **3** | **6** | **2** | **1** | **0** | **1** | **19:02** |
| | **NHL Totals** | | **326** | **122** | **131** | **253** | **107** | **35** | **1** | **28** | **1010** | **12.1** | | **439** | **44.6** | **16:53** | **32** | **12** | **12** | **24** | **14** | **4** | **0** | **2** | **17:52** |

WCHA All-Rookie Team (2003) • WCHA First All-Star Team (2004) • NCAA West First All-American Team (2004) • NHL Second All-Star Team (2009)

Played in NHL All-Star Game (2009)

## PARK, Richard
(PAHRK, RIH-chuhrd) **NYI**

Right wing. Shoots right. 5'11", 190 lbs. Born, Seoul, South Korea, May 27, 1976. Pittsburgh's 2nd choice, 50th overall, in 1994 Entry Draft.

| Season | Club | League | GP | G | A | Pts | PIM | PP | SH | GW | S | % | +/- | TF | F% | Min | GP | G | A | Pts | PIM | PP | SH | GW | Min |
|---|---|---|---|---|---|---|---|---|---|---|---|---|---|---|---|---|---|---|---|---|---|---|---|---|---|
| 1991-92 | Tor. Young Nats | MTHL | 76 | 49 | 58 | 107 | 91 | .... | .... | .... | .... | .... | .... | .... | .... | .... | .... | .... | .... | .... | .... | .... | .... | .... | .... |
| 1992-93 | Belleville Bulls | OHL | 66 | 23 | 38 | 61 | 38 | .... | .... | .... | .... | .... | .... | .... | .... | .... | 5 | 0 | 0 | 0 | 14 | .... | .... | .... | .... |
| 1993-94 | Belleville Bulls | OHL | 59 | 27 | 49 | 76 | 70 | .... | .... | .... | .... | .... | .... | .... | .... | .... | 12 | 3 | 5 | 8 | 18 | .... | .... | .... | .... |
| **1994-95** | Belleville Bulls | OHL | 45 | 28 | 51 | 79 | 35 | .... | .... | .... | .... | .... | .... | .... | .... | .... | 16 | 9 | 18 | 27 | 12 | .... | .... | .... | .... |
| | **Pittsburgh** | **NHL** | **1** | **0** | **1** | **1** | **2** | **0** | **0** | **0** | **4** | **0.0** | **1** | .... | .... | .... | **3** | **0** | **0** | **0** | **2** | **0** | **0** | **0** | .... |
| **1995-96** | Belleville Bulls | OHL | 6 | 7 | 6 | 13 | 2 | .... | .... | .... | .... | .... | .... | .... | .... | .... | 14 | 18 | 12 | 30 | 10 | .... | .... | .... | .... |
| | **Pittsburgh** | **NHL** | **56** | **4** | **6** | **10** | **36** | **0** | **1** | **1** | **62** | **6.5** | **3** | .... | .... | .... | **1** | **0** | **0** | **0** | **0** | **0** | **0** | **0** | .... |
| **1996-97** | **Pittsburgh** | **NHL** | **1** | **0** | **0** | **0** | **0** | **0** | **0** | **0** | **1** | **0.0** | **−1** | .... | .... | .... | .... | .... | .... | .... | .... | .... | .... | .... | .... |
| | Cleveland | IHL | 50 | 12 | 15 | 27 | 30 | .... | .... | .... | .... | .... | .... | .... | .... | .... | .... | .... | .... | .... | .... | .... | .... | .... | .... |
| | **Anaheim** | **NHL** | **11** | **1** | **1** | **2** | **10** | **0** | **0** | **0** | **9** | **11.1** | **0** | .... | .... | .... | **11** | **0** | **1** | **1** | **2** | **0** | **0** | **0** | .... |
| **1997-98** | **Anaheim** | **NHL** | **15** | **0** | **2** | **2** | **8** | **0** | **0** | **0** | **14** | **0.0** | **−3** | .... | .... | .... | .... | .... | .... | .... | .... | .... | .... | .... | .... |
| | Cincinnati | AHL | 56 | 17 | 26 | 43 | 36 | .... | .... | .... | .... | .... | .... | .... | .... | .... | .... | .... | .... | .... | .... | .... | .... | .... | .... |
| **1998-99** | **Philadelphia** | **NHL** | **7** | **0** | **0** | **0** | **0** | **0** | **0** | **0** | **5** | **0.0** | **−1** | **15** | **53.3** | **9:21** | .... | .... | .... | .... | .... | .... | .... | .... | .... |
| | Philadelphia | AHL | 75 | 41 | 42 | 83 | 33 | .... | .... | .... | .... | .... | .... | .... | .... | .... | 16 | 9 | 6 | 15 | 4 | .... | .... | .... | .... |
| 99-2000 | Utah Grizzlies | IHL | 82 | 28 | 32 | 60 | 36 | .... | .... | .... | .... | .... | .... | .... | .... | .... | 5 | 1 | 0 | 1 | 0 | .... | .... | .... | .... |
| 2000-01 | Cleveland | IHL | 75 | 27 | 21 | 48 | 29 | .... | .... | .... | .... | .... | .... | .... | .... | .... | 4 | 0 | 2 | 2 | 4 | .... | .... | .... | .... |
| **2001-02** | **Minnesota** | **NHL** | **63** | **10** | **15** | **25** | **10** | **2** | **1** | **2** | **115** | **8.7** | **−1** | **79** | **41.8** | **16:28** | .... | .... | .... | .... | .... | .... | .... | .... | .... |
| | Houston Aeros | AHL | 13 | 4 | 10 | 14 | 6 | .... | .... | .... | .... | .... | .... | .... | .... | .... | .... | .... | .... | .... | .... | .... | .... | .... | .... |
| **2002-03** | **Minnesota** | **NHL** | **81** | **14** | **10** | **24** | **16** | **2** | **2** | **3** | **149** | **9.4** | **−3** | **178** | **48.9** | **16:36** | **18** | **3** | **3** | **6** | **4** | **0** | **0** | **1** | **17:03** |
| **2003-04** | **Minnesota** | **NHL** | **73** | **13** | **12** | **25** | **28** | **4** | **0** | **1** | **142** | **9.2** | **0** | **379** | **40.1** | **16:30** | .... | .... | .... | .... | .... | .... | .... | .... | .... |
| 2004-05 | Malmo | Sweden | 9 | 1 | 3 | 4 | 4 | .... | .... | .... | .... | .... | .... | .... | .... | .... | .... | .... | .... | .... | .... | .... | .... | .... | .... |
| | Langnau | Swiss | 10 | 3 | 0 | 3 | 8 | .... | .... | .... | .... | .... | .... | .... | .... | .... | 6 | 4 | 1 | 5 | 6 | .... | .... | .... | .... |
| **2005-06** | **Vancouver** | **NHL** | **60** | **8** | **10** | **18** | **29** | **0** | **1** | **2** | **97** | **8.2** | **−2** | **26** | **26.9** | **11:00** | .... | .... | .... | .... | .... | .... | .... | .... | .... |
| **2006-07** | **NY Islanders** | **NHL** | **82** | **10** | **16** | **26** | **33** | **0** | **2** | **2** | **93** | **10.8** | **4** | **218** | **39.0** | **11:39** | **5** | **0** | **1** | **1** | **2** | **0** | **0** | **0** | **9:16** |
| **2007-08** | **NY Islanders** | **NHL** | **82** | **12** | **20** | **32** | **20** | **1** | **4** | **2** | **132** | **9.1** | **−4** | **626** | **50.2** | **15:14** | .... | .... | .... | .... | .... | .... | .... | .... | .... |
| **2008-09** | **NY Islanders** | **NHL** | **71** | **14** | **17** | **31** | **34** | **4** | **2** | **1** | **138** | **10.1** | **−13** | **809** | **49.0** | **17:10** | .... | .... | .... | .... | .... | .... | .... | .... | .... |
| | **NHL Totals** | | **603** | **86** | **110** | **196** | **226** | **13** | **13** | **14** | **961** | **8.9** | | **2330** | **46.4** | **14:54** | **38** | **3** | **5** | **8** | **10** | **0** | **0** | **1** | **15:22** |

OHL All-Rookie Team (1993) • AHL Second All-Star Team (1999)

Traded to **Anaheim** by **Pittsburgh** for Roman Oksiuta, March 18, 1997. Signed as a free agent by **Philadelphia**, August 24, 1998. Signed as a free agent by **Utah** (IHL), September 22, 1999. Signed as a free agent by **Minnesota**, June 6, 2000. Signed as a free agent by **Malmo** (Sweden), November 8, 2004. Signed as a free agent by **Langnau** (Swiss), January 4, 2005. Signed as a free agent by **Vancouver**, August 8, 2005. Signed as a free agent by **NY Islanders**, October 2, 2006.

## PARRISH, Mark
(PAIR-ihsh, MAHRK)

Right wing. Shoots right. 5'11", 199 lbs. Born, Bloomington, MN, February 2, 1977. Colorado's 3rd choice, 79th overall, in 1996 Entry Draft.

| Season | Club | League | GP | G | A | Pts | PIM | PP | SH | GW | S | % | +/- | TF | F% | Min | GP | G | A | Pts | PIM | PP | SH | GW | Min |
|---|---|---|---|---|---|---|---|---|---|---|---|---|---|---|---|---|---|---|---|---|---|---|---|---|---|
| 1994-95 | Jefferson Jaguars | High-MN | 27 | 40 | 20 | 60 | 42 | .... | .... | .... | .... | .... | .... | .... | .... | .... | .... | .... | .... | .... | .... | .... | .... | .... | .... |
| 1995-96 | St. Cloud State | WCHA | 39 | 15 | 13 | 28 | 30 | .... | .... | .... | .... | .... | .... | .... | .... | .... | .... | .... | .... | .... | .... | .... | .... | .... | .... |
| 1996-97 | St. Cloud State | WCHA | 35 | *27 | 15 | 42 | 60 | .... | .... | .... | .... | .... | .... | .... | .... | .... | .... | .... | .... | .... | .... | .... | .... | .... | .... |
| 1997-98 | Seattle | WHL | 54 | 54 | 38 | 92 | 29 | .... | .... | .... | .... | .... | .... | .... | .... | .... | 5 | 2 | 3 | 5 | 2 | .... | .... | .... | .... |
| | New Haven | AHL | 1 | 1 | 0 | 1 | 2 | .... | .... | .... | .... | .... | .... | .... | .... | .... | .... | .... | .... | .... | .... | .... | .... | .... | .... |
| **1998-99** | **Florida** | **NHL** | **73** | **24** | **13** | **37** | **25** | **5** | **0** | **5** | **129** | **18.6** | **−6** | **1** | **0.0** | **13:59** | .... | .... | .... | .... | .... | .... | .... | .... | .... |
| | New Haven | AHL | 2 | 1 | 0 | 1 | 0 | .... | .... | .... | .... | .... | .... | .... | .... | .... | .... | .... | .... | .... | .... | .... | .... | .... | .... |
| **99-2000** | **Florida** | **NHL** | **81** | **26** | **18** | **44** | **39** | **6** | **0** | **3** | **152** | **17.1** | **1** | **8** | **75.0** | **14:04** | **4** | **0** | **1** | **1** | **0** | **0** | **0** | **0** | **12:37** |
| **2000-01** | **NY Islanders** | **NHL** | **70** | **17** | **13** | **30** | **28** | **6** | **0** | **3** | **123** | **13.8** | **−27** | **3** | **33.3** | **15:27** | .... | .... | .... | .... | .... | .... | .... | .... | .... |
| **2001-02** | **NY Islanders** | **NHL** | **78** | **30** | **30** | **60** | **32** | **9** | **1** | **6** | **162** | **18.5** | **10** | **10** | **40.0** | **16:48** | **7** | **2** | **1** | **3** | **6** | **2** | **0** | **0** | **17:27** |
| **2002-03** | **NY Islanders** | **NHL** | **81** | **23** | **25** | **48** | **28** | **9** | **0** | **5** | **147** | **15.6** | **−11** | **9** | **44.4** | **16:12** | **5** | **1** | **0** | **1** | **4** | **1** | **0** | **0** | **16:02** |
| **2003-04** | **NY Islanders** | **NHL** | **59** | **24** | **11** | **35** | **18** | **6** | **0** | **6** | **105** | **22.9** | **8** | **5** | **20.0** | **17:20** | **5** | **1** | **2** | **3** | **0** | **0** | **0** | **0** | **20:35** |
| 2004-05 | | | DID NOT PLAY | | | | | | | | | | | | | | | | | | | | | | |
| **2005-06** | **NY Islanders** | **NHL** | **57** | **24** | **17** | **41** | **16** | **13** | **0** | **5** | **102** | **23.5** | **−14** | **12** | **16.7** | **19:34** | .... | .... | .... | .... | .... | .... | .... | .... | .... |
| | **Los Angeles** | **NHL** | **19** | **5** | **3** | **8** | **4** | **3** | **0** | **0** | **35** | **14.3** | **−9** | **0** | **0.0** | **15:29** | .... | .... | .... | .... | .... | .... | .... | .... | .... |
| | United States | Olympics | 6 | 0 | 0 | 0 | 4 | .... | .... | .... | .... | .... | .... | .... | .... | .... | .... | .... | .... | .... | .... | .... | .... | .... | .... |
| **2006-07** | **Minnesota** | **NHL** | **76** | **19** | **20** | **39** | **18** | **5** | **0** | **4** | **141** | **13.5** | **9** | **13** | **30.8** | **14:20** | **5** | **1** | **0** | **1** | **0** | **0** | **0** | **0** | **15:46** |
| **2007-08** | **Minnesota** | **NHL** | **66** | **16** | **14** | **30** | **16** | **7** | **0** | **0** | **95** | **16.8** | **2** | **10** | **40.0** | **14:56** | **1** | **0** | **0** | **0** | **0** | **0** | **0** | **0** | **5:04** |
| **2008-09** | **Dallas** | **NHL** | **44** | **8** | **5** | **13** | **18** | **4** | **0** | **3** | **46** | **17.4** | **−3** | **5** | **20.0** | **11:16** | .... | .... | .... | .... | .... | .... | .... | .... | .... |
| | Bridgeport | AHL | 3 | 1 | 1 | 2 | 2 | .... | .... | .... | .... | .... | .... | .... | .... | .... | .... | .... | .... | .... | .... | .... | .... | .... | .... |
| | **NHL Totals** | | **704** | **216** | **169** | **385** | **242** | **73** | **1** | **40** | **1237** | **17.5** | | **76** | **35.5** | **15:26** | **27** | **5** | **4** | **9** | **10** | **3** | **0** | **0** | **16:17** |

NCAA West Second All-American Team (1997) • WHL West First All-Star Team (1998)

Played in NHL All-Star Game (2002)

• Rights traded to **Florida** by **Colorado** with Anaheim's 3rd round choice (previously acquired, Florida selected Lance Ward) in 1998 Entry Draft for Tom Fitzgerald, March 24, 1998. Traded to **NY Islanders** by **Florida** with Oleg Kvasha for Roberto Luongo and Olli Jokinen, June 24, 2000. Traded to **Los Angeles** by **NY Islanders** with Brent Sopel for Denis Grebeshkov and Jeff Tambellini, March 8, 2006. Signed as a free agent by **Minnesota**, July 1, 2006. Signed as a free agent by **Dallas**, November 5, 2008.

## PARROS, George
(PAIR-ohs, JOHRJ) **ANA.**

Right wing. Shoots right. 6'5", 231 lbs. Born, Washington, PA, December 29, 1979. Los Angeles' 9th choice, 222nd overall, in 1999 Entry Draft.

| Season | Club | League | GP | G | A | Pts | PIM | PP | SH | GW | S | % | +/- | TF | F% | Min | GP | G | A | Pts | PIM | PP | SH | GW | Min |
|---|---|---|---|---|---|---|---|---|---|---|---|---|---|---|---|---|---|---|---|---|---|---|---|---|---|
| 1996-97 | Delbarton | High-NJ | 14 | 15 | 8 | 23 | .... | .... | .... | .... | .... | .... | .... | .... | .... | .... | .... | .... | .... | .... | .... | .... | .... | .... | .... |
| 1997-98 | Delbarton | High-NJ | 15 | 22 | 17 | 39 | .... | .... | .... | .... | .... | .... | .... | .... | .... | .... | .... | .... | .... | .... | .... | .... | .... | .... | .... |
| 1998-99 | Chicago Freeze | NAHL | 54 | 30 | 20 | 50 | 126 | .... | .... | .... | .... | .... | .... | .... | .... | .... | .... | .... | .... | .... | .... | .... | .... | .... | .... |
| 99-2000 | Princeton | ECAC | 27 | 4 | 2 | 6 | 14 | .... | .... | .... | .... | .... | .... | .... | .... | .... | .... | .... | .... | .... | .... | .... | .... | .... | .... |
| 2000-01 | Princeton | ECAC | 31 | 7 | 10 | 17 | 38 | .... | .... | .... | .... | .... | .... | .... | .... | .... | .... | .... | .... | .... | .... | .... | .... | .... | .... |
| 2001-02 | Princeton | ECAC | 31 | 9 | 13 | 22 | 36 | .... | .... | .... | .... | .... | .... | .... | .... | .... | .... | .... | .... | .... | .... | .... | .... | .... | .... |
| 2002-03 | Princeton | ECAC | 22 | 0 | 7 | 7 | 29 | .... | .... | .... | .... | .... | .... | .... | .... | .... | .... | .... | .... | .... | .... | .... | .... | .... | .... |
| | Manchester | AHL | 9 | 0 | 1 | 1 | 7 | .... | .... | .... | .... | .... | .... | .... | .... | .... | .... | .... | .... | .... | .... | .... | .... | .... | .... |
| 2003-04 | Manchester | AHL | 57 | 3 | 6 | 9 | 126 | .... | .... | .... | .... | .... | .... | .... | .... | .... | 5 | 0 | 0 | 0 | 4 | .... | .... | .... | .... |
| 2004-05 | Manchester | AHL | 67 | 14 | 8 | 22 | 247 | .... | .... | .... | .... | .... | .... | .... | .... | .... | 6 | 1 | 1 | 2 | 27 | .... | .... | .... | .... |
| | Reading Royals | ECHL | 3 | 0 | 0 | 0 | 9 | .... | .... | .... | .... | .... | .... | .... | .... | .... | .... | .... | .... | .... | .... | .... | .... | .... | .... |
| **2005-06** | **Los Angeles** | **NHL** | **55** | **2** | **3** | **5** | **138** | **0** | **0** | **0** | **23** | **8.7** | **1** | **1** | **0.0** | **4:56** | .... | .... | .... | .... | .... | .... | .... | .... | .... |
| **2006-07** | **Colorado** | **NHL** | **2** | **0** | **0** | **0** | **0** | **0** | **0** | **0** | **1** | **0.0** | **−1** | **0** | **0.0** | **3:33** | .... | .... | .... | .... | .... | .... | .... | .... | .... |
| | ♦ **Anaheim** | **NHL** | **32** | **1** | **0** | **1** | **102** | **0** | **0** | **0** | **18** | **5.6** | **−2** | **0** | **0.0** | **5:09** | **5** | **0** | **0** | **0** | **10** | **0** | **0** | **0** | **3:49** |
| **2007-08** | **Anaheim** | **NHL** | **69** | **1** | **4** | **5** | **183** | **0** | **0** | **0** | **30** | **3.3** | **3** | **10** | **30.0** | **5:57** | **1** | **0** | **0** | **0** | **0** | **0** | **0** | **0** | **2:42** |
| **2008-09** | **Anaheim** | **NHL** | **74** | **5** | **5** | **10** | **135** | **0** | **0** | **0** | **47** | **10.6** | **8** | **3** | **0.0** | **6:16** | **7** | **0** | **0** | **0** | **9** | **0** | **0** | **0** | **5:33** |
| | **NHL Totals** | | **232** | **9** | **12** | **21** | **558** | **0** | **0** | **0** | **119** | **7.6** | | **14** | **21.4** | **5:41** | **13** | **0** | **0** | **0** | **19** | **0** | **0** | **0** | **4:40** |

Claimed on waivers by **Colorado** from **Los Angeles**, October 3, 2006. Traded to **Anaheim** by **Colorado** with Colorado's 3rd round choice (later traded to Tampa Bay - Tampa Bay selected Luca Cunti) in 2007 Entry Draft for Atlanta's 2nd round choice (previously acquired, Colorado selected T.J. Galiardi) in 2007 Entry Draft and Anaheim's 3rd round choice (later traded to San Jose - San Jose selected Tyson Sexsmith) in 2007 Entry Draft, November 13, 2006.

## PAVELSKI, Joe

(pah-VEHL-skee, JOH) **S.J.**

Center. Shoots left. 5'11", 195 lbs. Born, Plover, WI, July 11, 1984. San Jose's 7th choice, 205th overall, in 2003 Entry Draft.

| | | | Regular Season | | | | | | | | | | | | | | Playoffs | | | | | | | | |
|---|---|---|---|---|---|---|---|---|---|---|---|---|---|---|---|---|---|---|---|---|---|---|---|---|---|
| Season | Club | League | GP | G | A | Pts | PIM | PP | SH | GW | S | % | +/- | TF | F% | Min | GP | G | A | Pts | PIM | PP | SH | GW | Min |
| 2002-03 | Waterloo | USHL | 60 | 36 | 33 | 69 | 32 | .... | .... | .... | .... | .... | .... | .... | .... | .... | 7 | 5 | 7 | 12 | 8 | .... | .... | .... | .... |
| 2003-04 | Waterloo | USHL | 54 | 21 | 31 | 52 | 58 | .... | .... | .... | .... | .... | .... | .... | .... | .... | 12 | 6 | 6 | 12 | 10 | .... | .... | .... | .... |
| 2004-05 | U. of Wisconsin | WCHA | 41 | 16 | 29 | 45 | 26 | .... | .... | .... | .... | .... | .... | .... | .... | .... | .... | .... | .... | .... | .... | .... | .... | .... | .... |
| 2005-06 | U. of Wisconsin | WCHA | 43 | 23 | 33 | 56 | 34 | .... | .... | .... | .... | .... | .... | .... | .... | .... | .... | .... | .... | .... | .... | .... | .... | .... | .... |
| **2006-07** | **San Jose** | **NHL** | **46** | **14** | **14** | **28** | **18** | **5** | **0** | **3** | **111** | **12.6** | **4** | **389** | **48.6** | **15:02** | **6** | **1** | **0** | **1** | **0** | **0** | **0** | **0** | **10:27** |
| | Worcester Sharks | AHL | 16 | 8 | 18 | 26 | 8 | .... | .... | .... | .... | .... | .... | .... | .... | .... | .... | .... | .... | .... | .... | .... | .... | .... | .... |
| **2007-08** | **San Jose** | **NHL** | **82** | **19** | **21** | **40** | **28** | **8** | **1** | **4** | **207** | **9.2** | **1** | **501** | **53.5** | **14:07** | **13** | **5** | **4** | **9** | **0** | **2** | **0** | **3** | **22:03** |
| **2008-09** | **San Jose** | **NHL** | **80** | **25** | **34** | **59** | **46** | **8** | **3** | **3** | **266** | **9.4** | **5** | **1274** | **56.3** | **18:58** | **6** | **0** | **1** | **1** | **9** | **0** | **0** | **0** | **19:21** |
| | **NHL Totals** | | **208** | **58** | **69** | **127** | **92** | **21** | **4** | **10** | **584** | **9.9** | | **2164** | **54.3** | **16:11** | **25** | **6** | **5** | **11** | **9** | **2** | **0** | **3** | **18:37** |

USHL All-Rookie Team (2003) • USHL First All-Star Team (2003) • USHL Rookie of the Year (2003) • WCHA All-Rookie Team (2005) • WCHA Second All-Star Team (2006) • NCAA West Second All-American Team (2006)

## PAYER, Serge

(pie-YAY, SAIRZH)

Center. Shoots left. 6', 191 lbs. Born, Rockland, Ont., May 7, 1979.

| Season | Club | League | GP | G | A | Pts | PIM | PP | SH | GW | S | % | +/- | TF | F% | Min | GP | G | A | Pts | PIM | PP | SH | GW | Min |
|---|---|---|---|---|---|---|---|---|---|---|---|---|---|---|---|---|---|---|---|---|---|---|---|---|---|
| 1994-95 | Cumberland Colts | ODMHA | 42 | 37 | 46 | 83 | 55 | .... | .... | .... | .... | .... | .... | .... | .... | .... | .... | .... | .... | .... | .... | .... | .... | .... | .... |
| 1995-96 | Kitchener Rangers | OHL | 66 | 8 | 16 | 24 | 18 | .... | .... | .... | .... | .... | .... | .... | .... | .... | 12 | 0 | 2 | 2 | 2 | .... | .... | .... | .... |
| 1996-97 | Kitchener Rangers | OHL | 63 | 7 | 16 | 23 | 27 | .... | .... | .... | .... | .... | .... | .... | .... | .... | 13 | 1 | 3 | 4 | 2 | .... | .... | .... | .... |
| 1997-98 | Kitchener Rangers | OHL | 44 | 20 | 21 | 41 | 51 | .... | .... | .... | .... | .... | .... | .... | .... | .... | 6 | 3 | 0 | 3 | 7 | .... | .... | .... | .... |
| 1998-99 | Kitchener Rangers | OHL | 40 | 18 | 19 | 37 | 22 | .... | .... | .... | .... | .... | .... | .... | .... | .... | .... | .... | .... | .... | .... | .... | .... | .... | .... |
| 99-2000 | Kitchener Rangers | OHL | 44 | 10 | 26 | 36 | 53 | .... | .... | .... | .... | .... | .... | .... | .... | .... | 5 | 0 | 3 | 3 | 6 | .... | .... | .... | .... |
| **2000-01** | **Florida** | **NHL** | **43** | **5** | **1** | **6** | **21** | **0** | **1** | **0** | **34** | **14.7** | **0** | **97** | **42.3** | **7:27** | .... | .... | .... | .... | .... | .... | .... | .... | .... |
| | Louisville Panthers | AHL | 32 | 6 | 6 | 12 | 15 | .... | .... | .... | .... | .... | .... | .... | .... | .... | .... | .... | .... | .... | .... | .... | .... | .... | .... |
| 2001-02 | Utah Grizzlies | AHL | 20 | 6 | 2 | 8 | 9 | .... | .... | .... | .... | .... | .... | .... | .... | .... | .... | .... | .... | .... | .... | .... | .... | .... | .... |
| 2002-03 | San Antonio | AHL | 78 | 10 | 31 | 41 | 30 | .... | .... | .... | .... | .... | .... | .... | .... | .... | 1 | 0 | 0 | 0 | 2 | .... | .... | .... | .... |
| **2003-04** | **Ottawa** | **NHL** | **5** | **0** | **1** | **1** | **2** | **0** | **0** | **0** | **2** | **0.0** | **1** | **43** | **46.5** | **10:30** | .... | .... | .... | .... | .... | .... | .... | .... | .... |
| | Binghamton | AHL | 67 | 14 | 20 | 34 | 91 | .... | .... | .... | .... | .... | .... | .... | .... | .... | 2 | 0 | 0 | 0 | 0 | .... | .... | .... | .... |
| 2004-05 | San Antonio | AHL | 3 | 1 | 1 | 2 | 4 | .... | .... | .... | .... | .... | .... | .... | .... | .... | .... | .... | .... | .... | .... | .... | .... | .... | .... |
| **2005-06** | **Florida** | **NHL** | **71** | **2** | **4** | **6** | **26** | **0** | **0** | **0** | **70** | **2.9** | **–7** | **543** | **47.5** | **9:53** | .... | .... | .... | .... | .... | .... | .... | .... | .... |
| **2006-07** | **Ottawa** | **NHL** | **5** | **0** | **0** | **0** | **0** | **0** | **0** | **0** | **4** | **0.0** | **–1** | **13** | **61.5** | **7:01** | .... | .... | .... | .... | .... | .... | .... | .... | .... |
| | Binghamton | AHL | 43 | 6 | 12 | 18 | 31 | .... | .... | .... | .... | .... | .... | .... | .... | .... | .... | .... | .... | .... | .... | .... | .... | .... | .... |
| 2007-08 | Houston Aeros | AHL | 66 | 11 | 20 | 31 | 57 | .... | .... | .... | .... | .... | .... | .... | .... | .... | 5 | 0 | 1 | 1 | 4 | .... | .... | .... | .... |
| 2008-09 | Krefeld Pinguine | Germany | 44 | 8 | 18 | 26 | 40 | .... | .... | .... | .... | .... | .... | .... | .... | .... | 7 | 1 | 6 | 7 | 2 | .... | .... | .... | .... |
| | **NHL Totals** | | **124** | **7** | **6** | **13** | **49** | **0** | **1** | **0** | **110** | **6.4** | | **696** | **47.0** | **8:57** | .... | .... | .... | .... | .... | .... | .... | .... | .... |

Signed as a free agent by **Florida**, September 30, 1997. • Missed majority of 2001-02 season recovering from back injury suffered in training camp, September, 2001. Traded to **Ottawa** by **Florida** for Ottawa's 9th round choice (Luke Beaverson) in 2004 Entry Draft, September 10, 2003. Signed as a free agent by **Florida**, July 23, 2004. Signed as a free agent by **Ottawa**, August 2, 2006. Signed as a free agent by **Minnesota**, August 20, 2007.

## PECA, Michael

(PEH-kuh, MIGH-kuhl)

Center. Shoots right. 5'11", 183 lbs. Born, Toronto, Ont., March 26, 1974. Vancouver's 2nd choice, 40th overall, in 1992 Entry Draft.

| Season | Club | League | GP | G | A | Pts | PIM | PP | SH | GW | S | % | +/- | TF | F% | Min | GP | G | A | Pts | PIM | PP | SH | GW | Min |
|---|---|---|---|---|---|---|---|---|---|---|---|---|---|---|---|---|---|---|---|---|---|---|---|---|---|
| 1989-90 | Tor. Red Wings | MTHL | 39 | 42 | 53 | 95 | 40 | .... | .... | .... | .... | .... | .... | .... | .... | .... | .... | .... | .... | .... | .... | .... | .... | .... | .... |
| 1990-91 | Sudbury Wolves | OHL | 62 | 14 | 27 | 41 | 24 | .... | .... | .... | .... | .... | .... | .... | .... | .... | 5 | 1 | 0 | 1 | 7 | .... | .... | .... | .... |
| 1991-92 | Sudbury Wolves | OHL | 39 | 16 | 34 | 50 | 61 | .... | .... | .... | .... | .... | .... | .... | .... | .... | .... | .... | .... | .... | .... | .... | .... | .... | .... |
| | Ottawa 67's | OHL | 27 | 8 | 17 | 25 | 32 | .... | .... | .... | .... | .... | .... | .... | .... | .... | 11 | 6 | 10 | 16 | 6 | .... | .... | .... | .... |
| 1992-93 | Ottawa 67's | OHL | 55 | 38 | 64 | 102 | 80 | .... | .... | .... | .... | .... | .... | .... | .... | .... | .... | .... | .... | .... | .... | .... | .... | .... | .... |
| | Hamilton | AHL | 9 | 6 | 3 | 9 | 11 | .... | .... | .... | .... | .... | .... | .... | .... | .... | .... | .... | .... | .... | .... | .... | .... | .... | .... |
| **1993-94** | Ottawa 67's | OHL | 55 | 50 | 63 | 113 | 101 | .... | .... | .... | .... | .... | .... | .... | .... | .... | 17 | 7 | 22 | 29 | 30 | .... | .... | .... | .... |
| | **Vancouver** | **NHL** | **4** | **0** | **0** | **0** | **2** | **0** | **0** | **0** | **5** | **0.0** | **–1** | .... | .... | .... | .... | .... | .... | .... | .... | .... | .... | .... | .... |
| 1994-95 | Syracuse Crunch | AHL | 35 | 10 | 24 | 34 | 75 | .... | .... | .... | .... | .... | .... | .... | .... | .... | .... | .... | .... | .... | .... | .... | .... | .... | .... |
| | **Vancouver** | **NHL** | **33** | **6** | **6** | **12** | **30** | **2** | **0** | **1** | **46** | **13.0** | **–6** | .... | .... | .... | **5** | **0** | **1** | **1** | **8** | **0** | **0** | **0** | .... |
| **1995-96** | **Buffalo** | **NHL** | **68** | **11** | **20** | **31** | **67** | **4** | **3** | **1** | **109** | **10.1** | **–1** | .... | .... | .... | .... | .... | .... | .... | .... | .... | .... | .... | .... |
| **1996-97** | **Buffalo** | **NHL** | **79** | **20** | **29** | **49** | **80** | **5** | **6** | **4** | **137** | **14.6** | **26** | .... | .... | .... | **10** | **0** | **2** | **2** | **8** | **0** | **0** | **0** | .... |
| **1997-98** | **Buffalo** | **NHL** | **61** | **18** | **22** | **40** | **57** | **6** | **5** | **1** | **132** | **13.6** | **12** | .... | .... | .... | **13** | **3** | **2** | **5** | **8** | **0** | **0** | **1** | .... |
| **1998-99** | **Buffalo** | **NHL** | **82** | **27** | **29** | **56** | **81** | **10** | **0** | **8** | **199** | **13.6** | **7** | **1855** | **49.4** | **20:44** | **21** | **5** | **8** | **13** | **18** | **2** | **1** | **0** | **22:28** |
| **99-2000** | **Buffalo** | **NHL** | **73** | **20** | **21** | **41** | **67** | **2** | **0** | **3** | **144** | **13.9** | **6** | **1604** | **48.6** | **19:57** | **5** | **0** | **1** | **1** | **4** | **0** | **0** | **0** | **18:42** |
| 2000-01 | | | DID NOT PLAY | | | | | | | | | | | | | | | | | | | | | | |
| **2001-02** | **NY Islanders** | **NHL** | **80** | **25** | **35** | **60** | **62** | **3** | **6** | **5** | **168** | **14.9** | **19** | **1804** | **52.4** | **20:14** | **5** | **1** | **0** | **1** | **2** | **0** | **0** | **0** | **16:15** |
| | Canada | Olympics | 6 | 0 | 2 | 2 | 2 | .... | .... | .... | .... | .... | .... | .... | .... | .... | .... | .... | .... | .... | .... | .... | .... | .... | .... |
| **2002-03** | **NY Islanders** | **NHL** | **66** | **13** | **29** | **42** | **43** | **4** | **2** | **2** | **117** | **11.1** | **–4** | **1315** | **53.0** | **18:57** | **5** | **0** | **0** | **0** | **4** | **0** | **0** | **0** | **20:10** |
| **2003-04** | **NY Islanders** | **NHL** | **76** | **11** | **29** | **40** | **71** | **0** | **1** | **0** | **117** | **9.4** | **17** | **1674** | **53.1** | **19:02** | **5** | **0** | **0** | **0** | **6** | **0** | **0** | **0** | **23:01** |
| 2004-05 | | | DID NOT PLAY | | | | | | | | | | | | | | | | | | | | | | |
| **2005-06** | **Edmonton** | **NHL** | **71** | **9** | **14** | **23** | **56** | **2** | **2** | **1** | **108** | **8.3** | **–4** | **1048** | **54.9** | **16:39** | **24** | **6** | **5** | **11** | **20** | **0** | **1** | **1** | **19:06** |
| **2006-07** | **Toronto** | **NHL** | **35** | **4** | **11** | **15** | **60** | **0** | **0** | **2** | **42** | **9.5** | **2** | **615** | **49.9** | **17:25** | .... | .... | .... | .... | .... | .... | .... | .... | .... |
| **2007-08** | **Columbus** | **NHL** | **65** | **8** | **26** | **34** | **64** | **3** | **0** | **3** | **86** | **9.3** | **–1** | **1084** | **52.7** | **18:34** | .... | .... | .... | .... | .... | .... | .... | .... | .... |
| **2008-09** | **Columbus** | **NHL** | **71** | **4** | **18** | **22** | **58** | **0** | **0** | **2** | **74** | **5.4** | **–6** | **839** | **49.7** | **14:06** | **4** | **0** | **0** | **0** | **2** | **0** | **0** | **0** | **12:40** |
| | **NHL Totals** | | **864** | **176** | **289** | **465** | **798** | **41** | **25** | **33** | **1484** | **11.9** | | **11838** | **51.5** | **18:32** | **97** | **15** | **19** | **34** | **80** | **2** | **2** | **2** | **19:52** |

Frank J. Selke Trophy (1997, 2002)

Traded to **Buffalo** by **Vancouver** with Mike Wilson and Vancouver's 1st round choice (Jay McKee) in 1995 Entry Draft for Alexander Mogilny and Buffalo's 5th round choice (Todd Norman) in 1995 Entry Draft, July 8, 1995. • Missed entire 2000-01 season after failing to come to contract terms with **Buffalo**. • Rights traded to **NY Islanders** by **Buffalo** for Tim Connolly and Taylor Pyatt, June 24, 2001. Traded to **Edmonton** by **NY Islanders** for Mike York and Edmonton's 4th round choice (later traded to Colorado - Colorado selected Kevin Montgomery) in 2006 Entry Draft, August 3, 2005. Signed as a free agent by **Toronto**, July 18, 2006. • Missed remainder of 2006-07 season recovering from leg injury suffered in game vs. Chicago, December 22, 2006. Signed as a free agent by **Columbus**, August 21, 2007.

## PECKHAM, Theo

(PEHK-uhm, THEE-oh) **EDM.**

Defense. Shoots left. 6'2", 223 lbs. Born, Richmond Hill, Ont., November 10, 1987. Edmonton's 2nd choice, 75th overall, in 2006 Entry Draft.

| Season | Club | League | GP | G | A | Pts | PIM | PP | SH | GW | S | % | +/- | TF | F% | Min | GP | G | A | Pts | PIM | PP | SH | GW | Min |
|---|---|---|---|---|---|---|---|---|---|---|---|---|---|---|---|---|---|---|---|---|---|---|---|---|---|
| 2003-04 | North York | OPJHL | 29 | 1 | 4 | 5 | 46 | .... | .... | .... | .... | .... | .... | .... | .... | .... | .... | .... | .... | .... | .... | .... | .... | .... | .... |
| 2004-05 | Owen Sound | OHL | 61 | 1 | 9 | 10 | 209 | .... | .... | .... | .... | .... | .... | .... | .... | .... | 8 | 0 | 0 | 0 | 8 | .... | .... | .... | .... |
| 2005-06 | Owen Sound | OHL | 67 | 6 | 9 | 15 | 236 | .... | .... | .... | .... | .... | .... | .... | .... | .... | 11 | 1 | 6 | 7 | 32 | .... | .... | .... | .... |
| 2006-07 | Owen Sound | OHL | 53 | 10 | 25 | 35 | 173 | .... | .... | .... | .... | .... | .... | .... | .... | .... | 4 | 0 | 1 | 1 | 0 | .... | .... | .... | .... |
| **2007-08** | **Edmonton** | **NHL** | **1** | **0** | **0** | **0** | **2** | **0** | **0** | **0** | **0** | **0.0** | **0** | **0** | **0.0** | **13:22** | .... | .... | .... | .... | .... | .... | .... | .... | .... |
| | Springfield | AHL | 59 | 6 | 7 | 13 | 174 | .... | .... | .... | .... | .... | .... | .... | .... | .... | .... | .... | .... | .... | .... | .... | .... | .... | .... |
| **2008-09** | **Edmonton** | **NHL** | **15** | **0** | **0** | **0** | **59** | **0** | **0** | **0** | **8** | **0.0** | **–1** | **0** | **0.0** | **11:38** | .... | .... | .... | .... | .... | .... | .... | .... | .... |
| | Springfield | AHL | 47 | 6 | 13 | 19 | 107 | .... | .... | .... | .... | .... | .... | .... | .... | .... | .... | .... | .... | .... | .... | .... | .... | .... | .... |
| | **NHL Totals** | | **16** | **0** | **0** | **0** | **61** | **0** | **0** | **0** | **8** | **0.0** | | **0** | **0.0** | **11:44** | .... | .... | .... | .... | .... | .... | .... | .... | .... |

## PELECH, Matt

(PEH-lihk, MAT) **CGY.**

Defense. Shoots right. 6'4", 220 lbs. Born, Toronto, Ont., September 4, 1987. Calgary's 1st choice, 26th overall, in 2005 Entry Draft.

| Season | Club | League | GP | G | A | Pts | PIM | PP | SH | GW | S | % | +/- | TF | F% | Min | GP | G | A | Pts | PIM | PP | SH | GW | Min |
|---|---|---|---|---|---|---|---|---|---|---|---|---|---|---|---|---|---|---|---|---|---|---|---|---|---|
| 2002-03 | Vaughan | GTHL | 44 | 3 | 13 | 16 | 113 | .... | .... | .... | .... | .... | .... | .... | .... | .... | .... | .... | .... | .... | .... | .... | .... | .... | .... |
| 2003-04 | Sarnia Sting | OHL | 62 | 4 | 6 | 10 | 39 | .... | .... | .... | .... | .... | .... | .... | .... | .... | 5 | 0 | 1 | 1 | 12 | .... | .... | .... | .... |
| 2004-05 | Sarnia Sting | OHL | 31 | 1 | 5 | 6 | 74 | .... | .... | .... | .... | .... | .... | .... | .... | .... | .... | .... | .... | .... | .... | .... | .... | .... | .... |
| 2005-06 | Sarnia Sting | OHL | 18 | 0 | 2 | 2 | 59 | .... | .... | .... | .... | .... | .... | .... | .... | .... | .... | .... | .... | .... | .... | .... | .... | .... | .... |
| | London Knights | OHL | 34 | 1 | 7 | 8 | 80 | .... | .... | .... | .... | .... | .... | .... | .... | .... | 19 | 0 | 0 | 0 | 48 | .... | .... | .... | .... |
| 2006-07 | Belleville Bulls | OHL | 58 | 5 | 30 | 35 | 171 | .... | .... | .... | .... | .... | .... | .... | .... | .... | 12 | 0 | 3 | 3 | 22 | .... | .... | .... | .... |
| 2007-08 | Quad City Flames | AHL | 77 | 3 | 6 | 9 | 141 | .... | .... | .... | .... | .... | .... | .... | .... | .... | .... | .... | .... | .... | .... | .... | .... | .... | .... |
| **2008-09** | **Calgary** | **NHL** | **5** | **0** | **3** | **3** | **9** | **0** | **0** | **0** | **4** | **0.0** | **1** | **0** | **0.0** | **13:16** | .... | .... | .... | .... | .... | .... | .... | .... | .... |
| | Quad City Flames | AHL | 59 | 3 | 6 | 9 | 130 | .... | .... | .... | .... | .... | .... | .... | .... | .... | .... | .... | .... | .... | .... | .... | .... | .... | .... |
| | **NHL Totals** | | **5** | **0** | **3** | **3** | **9** | **0** | **0** | **0** | **4** | **0.0** | | **0** | **0.0** | **13:16** | .... | .... | .... | .... | .... | .... | .... | .... | .... |

## PELLETIER, Pascal
(PEHL-tyay, pas-KAL) **CBJ**

Right wing. Shoots right. 5'11", 197 lbs. Born, Labrador City, Nfld., June 16, 1983.

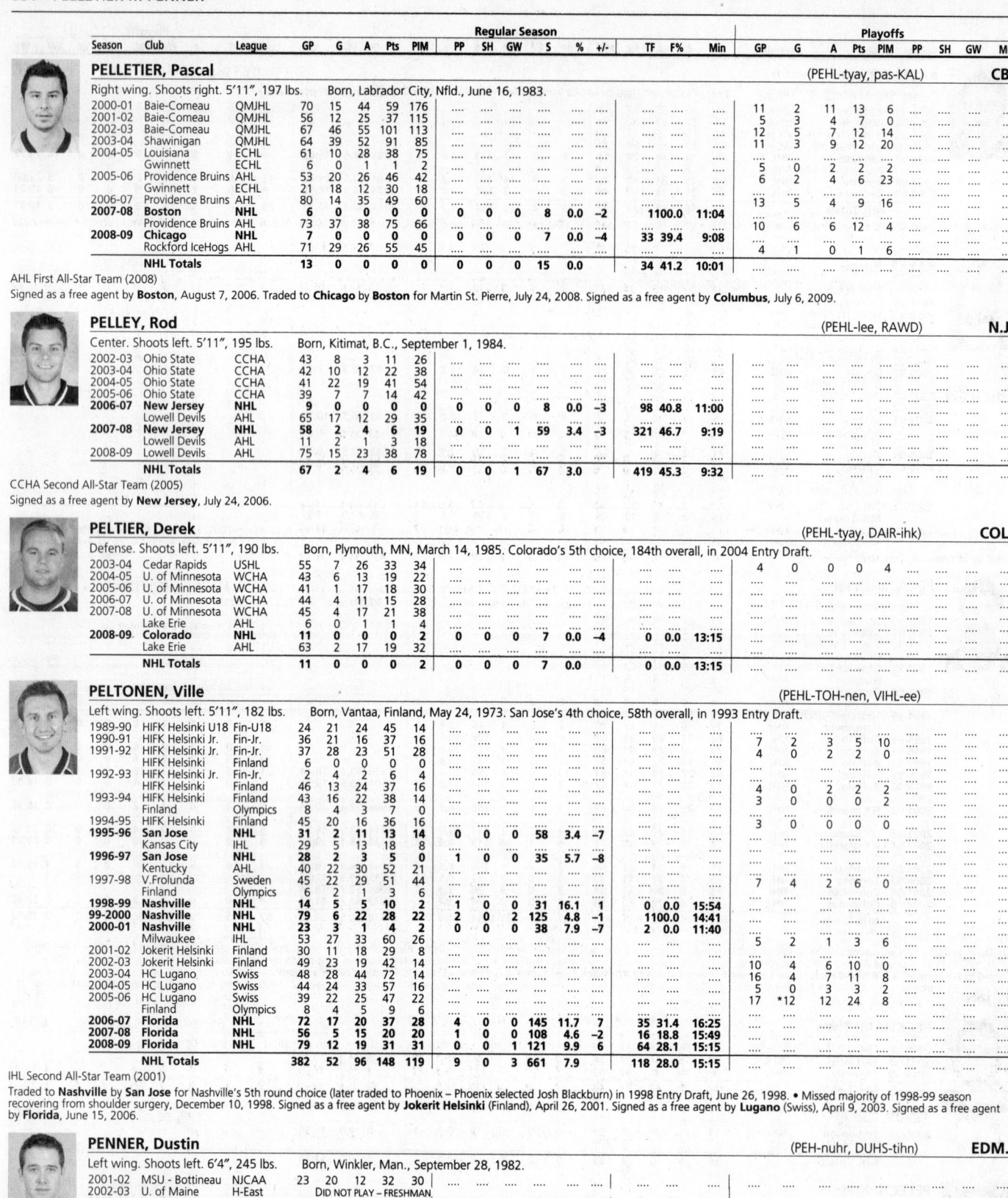

| | | | Regular Season | | | | | | | | | | | | | | Playoffs | | | | | | | | |
|---|---|---|---|---|---|---|---|---|---|---|---|---|---|---|---|---|---|---|---|---|---|---|---|---|---|
| Season | Club | League | GP | G | A | Pts | PIM | PP | SH | GW | S | % | +/- | TF | F% | Min | GP | G | A | Pts | PIM | PP | SH | GW | Min |
| 2000-01 | Baie-Comeau | QMJHL | 70 | 15 | 44 | 59 | 176 | .... | .... | .... | .... | .... | .... | .... | .... | .... | 11 | 2 | 11 | 13 | 6 | .... | .... | .... | .... |
| 2001-02 | Baie-Comeau | QMJHL | 56 | 12 | 25 | 37 | 115 | .... | .... | .... | .... | .... | .... | .... | .... | .... | 5 | 3 | 4 | 7 | 0 | .... | .... | .... | .... |
| 2002-03 | Baie-Comeau | QMJHL | 67 | 46 | 55 | 101 | 113 | .... | .... | .... | .... | .... | .... | .... | .... | .... | 12 | 5 | 7 | 12 | 14 | .... | .... | .... | .... |
| 2003-04 | Shawinigan | QMJHL | 64 | 39 | 52 | 91 | 85 | .... | .... | .... | .... | .... | .... | .... | .... | .... | 11 | 3 | 9 | 12 | 20 | .... | .... | .... | .... |
| 2004-05 | Louisiana | ECHL | 61 | 10 | 28 | 38 | 75 | .... | .... | .... | .... | .... | .... | .... | .... | .... | .... | .... | .... | .... | .... | .... | .... | .... | .... |
| | Gwinnett | ECHL | 6 | 0 | 1 | 1 | 2 | .... | .... | .... | .... | .... | .... | .... | .... | .... | 5 | 0 | 2 | 2 | 2 | .... | .... | .... | .... |
| 2005-06 | Providence Bruins | AHL | 53 | 20 | 26 | 46 | 42 | .... | .... | .... | .... | .... | .... | .... | .... | .... | 6 | 2 | 4 | 6 | 23 | .... | .... | .... | .... |
| | Gwinnett | ECHL | 21 | 18 | 12 | 30 | 18 | .... | .... | .... | .... | .... | .... | .... | .... | .... | .... | .... | .... | .... | .... | .... | .... | .... | .... |
| 2006-07 | Providence Bruins | AHL | 80 | 14 | 35 | 49 | 60 | .... | .... | .... | .... | .... | .... | .... | .... | .... | 13 | 5 | 4 | 9 | 16 | .... | .... | .... | .... |
| **2007-08** | **Boston** | **NHL** | 6 | 0 | 0 | 0 | 0 | 0 | 0 | 0 | 8 | 0.0 | –2 | 1 | 100.0 | 11:04 | .... | .... | .... | .... | .... | .... | .... | .... | .... |
| | Providence Bruins | AHL | 73 | 37 | 38 | 75 | 66 | .... | .... | .... | .... | .... | .... | .... | .... | .... | 10 | 6 | 6 | 12 | 4 | .... | .... | .... | .... |
| **2008-09** | **Chicago** | **NHL** | 7 | 0 | 0 | 0 | 0 | 0 | 0 | 0 | 7 | 0.0 | –4 | 33 | 39.4 | 9:08 | .... | .... | .... | .... | .... | .... | .... | .... | .... |
| | Rockford IceHogs | AHL | 71 | 29 | 26 | 55 | 45 | .... | .... | .... | .... | .... | .... | .... | .... | .... | 4 | 1 | 0 | 1 | 6 | .... | .... | .... | .... |
| | **NHL Totals** | | 13 | 0 | 0 | 0 | 0 | 0 | 0 | 0 | 15 | 0.0 | | 34 | 41.2 | 10:01 | .... | .... | .... | .... | .... | .... | .... | .... | .... |

AHL First All-Star Team (2008)

Signed as a free agent by **Boston**, August 7, 2006. Traded to **Chicago** by **Boston** for Martin St. Pierre, July 24, 2008. Signed as a free agent by **Columbus**, July 6, 2009.

## PELLEY, Rod
(PEHL-lee, RAWD) **N.J.**

Center. Shoots left. 5'11", 195 lbs. Born, Kitimat, B.C., September 1, 1984.

| Season | Club | League | GP | G | A | Pts | PIM | PP | SH | GW | S | % | +/- | TF | F% | Min | GP | G | A | Pts | PIM | PP | SH | GW | Min |
|---|---|---|---|---|---|---|---|---|---|---|---|---|---|---|---|---|---|---|---|---|---|---|---|---|---|
| 2002-03 | Ohio State | CCHA | 43 | 8 | 3 | 11 | 26 | .... | .... | .... | .... | .... | .... | .... | .... | .... | .... | .... | .... | .... | .... | .... | .... | .... | .... |
| 2003-04 | Ohio State | CCHA | 42 | 10 | 12 | 22 | 38 | .... | .... | .... | .... | .... | .... | .... | .... | .... | .... | .... | .... | .... | .... | .... | .... | .... | .... |
| 2004-05 | Ohio State | CCHA | 41 | 22 | 19 | 41 | 54 | .... | .... | .... | .... | .... | .... | .... | .... | .... | .... | .... | .... | .... | .... | .... | .... | .... | .... |
| 2005-06 | Ohio State | CCHA | 39 | 7 | 7 | 14 | 42 | .... | .... | .... | .... | .... | .... | .... | .... | .... | .... | .... | .... | .... | .... | .... | .... | .... | .... |
| **2006-07** | **New Jersey** | **NHL** | 9 | 0 | 0 | 0 | 0 | 0 | 0 | 0 | 8 | 0.0 | –3 | 98 | 40.8 | 11:00 | .... | .... | .... | .... | .... | .... | .... | .... | .... |
| | Lowell Devils | AHL | 65 | 17 | 12 | 29 | 35 | .... | .... | .... | .... | .... | .... | .... | .... | .... | .... | .... | .... | .... | .... | .... | .... | .... | .... |
| **2007-08** | **New Jersey** | **NHL** | 58 | 2 | 4 | 6 | 19 | 0 | 0 | 1 | 59 | 3.4 | –3 | 321 | 46.7 | 9:19 | .... | .... | .... | .... | .... | .... | .... | .... | .... |
| | Lowell Devils | AHL | 11 | 2 | 1 | 3 | 18 | .... | .... | .... | .... | .... | .... | .... | .... | .... | .... | .... | .... | .... | .... | .... | .... | .... | .... |
| 2008-09 | Lowell Devils | AHL | 75 | 15 | 23 | 38 | 78 | .... | .... | .... | .... | .... | .... | .... | .... | .... | .... | .... | .... | .... | .... | .... | .... | .... | .... |
| | **NHL Totals** | | 67 | 2 | 4 | 6 | 19 | 0 | 0 | 1 | 67 | 3.0 | | 419 | 45.3 | 9:32 | .... | .... | .... | .... | .... | .... | .... | .... | .... |

CCHA Second All-Star Team (2005)

Signed as a free agent by **New Jersey**, July 24, 2006.

## PELTIER, Derek
(PEHL-tyay, DAIR-ihk) **COL.**

Defense. Shoots left. 5'11", 190 lbs. Born, Plymouth, MN, March 14, 1985. Colorado's 5th choice, 184th overall, in 2004 Entry Draft.

| Season | Club | League | GP | G | A | Pts | PIM | PP | SH | GW | S | % | +/- | TF | F% | Min | GP | G | A | Pts | PIM | PP | SH | GW | Min |
|---|---|---|---|---|---|---|---|---|---|---|---|---|---|---|---|---|---|---|---|---|---|---|---|---|---|
| 2003-04 | Cedar Rapids | USHL | 55 | 7 | 26 | 33 | 34 | .... | .... | .... | .... | .... | .... | .... | .... | .... | 4 | 0 | 0 | 0 | 4 | .... | .... | .... | .... |
| 2004-05 | U. of Minnesota | WCHA | 43 | 6 | 13 | 19 | 22 | .... | .... | .... | .... | .... | .... | .... | .... | .... | .... | .... | .... | .... | .... | .... | .... | .... | .... |
| 2005-06 | U. of Minnesota | WCHA | 41 | 1 | 17 | 18 | 30 | .... | .... | .... | .... | .... | .... | .... | .... | .... | .... | .... | .... | .... | .... | .... | .... | .... | .... |
| 2006-07 | U. of Minnesota | WCHA | 44 | 4 | 11 | 15 | 28 | .... | .... | .... | .... | .... | .... | .... | .... | .... | .... | .... | .... | .... | .... | .... | .... | .... | .... |
| 2007-08 | U. of Minnesota | WCHA | 45 | 4 | 17 | 21 | 38 | .... | .... | .... | .... | .... | .... | .... | .... | .... | .... | .... | .... | .... | .... | .... | .... | .... | .... |
| | Lake Erie | AHL | 6 | 0 | 1 | 1 | 4 | .... | .... | .... | .... | .... | .... | .... | .... | .... | .... | .... | .... | .... | .... | .... | .... | .... | .... |
| **2008-09** | **Colorado** | **NHL** | 11 | 0 | 0 | 0 | 2 | 0 | 0 | 0 | 7 | 0.0 | –4 | 0 | 0.0 | 13:15 | .... | .... | .... | .... | .... | .... | .... | .... | .... |
| | Lake Erie | AHL | 63 | 2 | 17 | 19 | 32 | .... | .... | .... | .... | .... | .... | .... | .... | .... | .... | .... | .... | .... | .... | .... | .... | .... | .... |
| | **NHL Totals** | | 11 | 0 | 0 | 0 | 2 | 0 | 0 | 0 | 7 | 0.0 | | 0 | 0.0 | 13:15 | .... | .... | .... | .... | .... | .... | .... | .... | .... |

## PELTONEN, Ville
(PEHL-TOH-nen, VIHL-ee)

Left wing. Shoots left. 5'11", 182 lbs. Born, Vantaa, Finland, May 24, 1973. San Jose's 4th choice, 58th overall, in 1993 Entry Draft.

| Season | Club | League | GP | G | A | Pts | PIM | PP | SH | GW | S | % | +/- | TF | F% | Min | GP | G | A | Pts | PIM | PP | SH | GW | Min |
|---|---|---|---|---|---|---|---|---|---|---|---|---|---|---|---|---|---|---|---|---|---|---|---|---|---|
| 1989-90 | HIFK Helsinki U18 | Fin-U18 | 24 | 21 | 24 | 45 | 14 | .... | .... | .... | .... | .... | .... | .... | .... | .... | .... | .... | .... | .... | .... | .... | .... | .... | .... |
| 1990-91 | HIFK Helsinki Jr. | Fin-Jr. | 36 | 21 | 16 | 37 | 16 | .... | .... | .... | .... | .... | .... | .... | .... | .... | 7 | 2 | 3 | 5 | 10 | .... | .... | .... | .... |
| 1991-92 | HIFK Helsinki Jr. | Fin-Jr. | 37 | 28 | 23 | 51 | 28 | .... | .... | .... | .... | .... | .... | .... | .... | .... | 4 | 0 | 2 | 2 | 0 | .... | .... | .... | .... |
| | HIFK Helsinki | Finland | 6 | 0 | 0 | 0 | 0 | .... | .... | .... | .... | .... | .... | .... | .... | .... | .... | .... | .... | .... | .... | .... | .... | .... | .... |
| 1992-93 | HIFK Helsinki Jr. | Fin-Jr. | 2 | 4 | 2 | 6 | 4 | .... | .... | .... | .... | .... | .... | .... | .... | .... | .... | .... | .... | .... | .... | .... | .... | .... | .... |
| | HIFK Helsinki | Finland | 46 | 13 | 24 | 37 | 16 | .... | .... | .... | .... | .... | .... | .... | .... | .... | 4 | 0 | 2 | 2 | 2 | .... | .... | .... | .... |
| 1993-94 | HIFK Helsinki | Finland | 43 | 16 | 22 | 38 | 14 | .... | .... | .... | .... | .... | .... | .... | .... | .... | 3 | 0 | 0 | 0 | 2 | .... | .... | .... | .... |
| | Finland | Olympics | 8 | 4 | 3 | 7 | 0 | .... | .... | .... | .... | .... | .... | .... | .... | .... | .... | .... | .... | .... | .... | .... | .... | .... | .... |
| 1994-95 | HIFK Helsinki | Finland | 45 | 20 | 16 | 36 | 16 | .... | .... | .... | .... | .... | .... | .... | .... | .... | 3 | 0 | 0 | 0 | 0 | .... | .... | .... | .... |
| **1995-96** | **San Jose** | **NHL** | 31 | 2 | 11 | 13 | 14 | 0 | 0 | 0 | 58 | 3.4 | –7 | .... | .... | .... | .... | .... | .... | .... | .... | .... | .... | .... | .... |
| | Kansas City | IHL | 29 | 5 | 13 | 18 | 8 | .... | .... | .... | .... | .... | .... | .... | .... | .... | .... | .... | .... | .... | .... | .... | .... | .... | .... |
| **1996-97** | **San Jose** | **NHL** | 28 | 2 | 3 | 5 | 0 | 1 | 0 | 0 | 35 | 5.7 | –8 | .... | .... | .... | .... | .... | .... | .... | .... | .... | .... | .... | .... |
| | Kentucky | AHL | 40 | 22 | 30 | 52 | 21 | .... | .... | .... | .... | .... | .... | .... | .... | .... | .... | .... | .... | .... | .... | .... | .... | .... | .... |
| 1997-98 | V.Frolunda | Sweden | 45 | 22 | 29 | 51 | 44 | .... | .... | .... | .... | .... | .... | .... | .... | .... | 7 | 4 | 2 | 6 | 0 | .... | .... | .... | .... |
| | Finland | Olympics | 6 | 2 | 1 | 3 | 6 | .... | .... | .... | .... | .... | .... | .... | .... | .... | .... | .... | .... | .... | .... | .... | .... | .... | .... |
| **1998-99** | **Nashville** | **NHL** | 14 | 5 | 5 | 10 | 2 | 1 | 0 | 0 | 31 | 16.1 | 1 | 0 | 0.0 | 15:54 | .... | .... | .... | .... | .... | .... | .... | .... | .... |
| **99-2000** | **Nashville** | **NHL** | 79 | 6 | 22 | 28 | 22 | 2 | 0 | 2 | 125 | 4.8 | –1 | 1 | 100.0 | 14:41 | .... | .... | .... | .... | .... | .... | .... | .... | .... |
| **2000-01** | **Nashville** | **NHL** | 23 | 3 | 1 | 4 | 2 | 0 | 0 | 0 | 38 | 7.9 | –7 | 2 | 0.0 | 11:40 | .... | .... | .... | .... | .... | .... | .... | .... | .... |
| | Milwaukee | IHL | 53 | 27 | 33 | 60 | 26 | .... | .... | .... | .... | .... | .... | .... | .... | .... | 5 | 2 | 1 | 3 | 6 | .... | .... | .... | .... |
| 2001-02 | Jokerit Helsinki | Finland | 30 | 11 | 18 | 29 | 8 | .... | .... | .... | .... | .... | .... | .... | .... | .... | .... | .... | .... | .... | .... | .... | .... | .... | .... |
| 2002-03 | Jokerit Helsinki | Finland | 49 | 23 | 19 | 42 | 14 | .... | .... | .... | .... | .... | .... | .... | .... | .... | 10 | 4 | 6 | 10 | 0 | .... | .... | .... | .... |
| 2003-04 | HC Lugano | Swiss | 48 | 28 | 44 | 72 | 14 | .... | .... | .... | .... | .... | .... | .... | .... | .... | 16 | 4 | 7 | 11 | 8 | .... | .... | .... | .... |
| 2004-05 | HC Lugano | Swiss | 44 | 24 | 33 | 57 | 16 | .... | .... | .... | .... | .... | .... | .... | .... | .... | 5 | 0 | 3 | 3 | 2 | .... | .... | .... | .... |
| 2005-06 | HC Lugano | Swiss | 39 | 22 | 25 | 47 | 22 | .... | .... | .... | .... | .... | .... | .... | .... | .... | 17 | *12 | 12 | 24 | 8 | .... | .... | .... | .... |
| | Finland | Olympics | 8 | 4 | 5 | 9 | 6 | .... | .... | .... | .... | .... | .... | .... | .... | .... | .... | .... | .... | .... | .... | .... | .... | .... | .... |
| **2006-07** | **Florida** | **NHL** | 72 | 17 | 20 | 37 | 28 | 4 | 0 | 0 | 145 | 11.7 | 7 | 35 | 31.4 | 16:25 | .... | .... | .... | .... | .... | .... | .... | .... | .... |
| **2007-08** | **Florida** | **NHL** | 56 | 5 | 15 | 20 | 20 | 1 | 0 | 0 | 108 | 4.6 | –2 | 16 | 18.8 | 15:49 | .... | .... | .... | .... | .... | .... | .... | .... | .... |
| **2008-09** | **Florida** | **NHL** | 79 | 12 | 19 | 31 | 31 | 0 | 0 | 1 | 121 | 9.9 | 6 | 64 | 28.1 | 15:15 | .... | .... | .... | .... | .... | .... | .... | .... | .... |
| | **NHL Totals** | | 382 | 52 | 96 | 148 | 119 | 9 | 0 | 3 | 661 | 7.9 | | 118 | 28.0 | 15:15 | .... | .... | .... | .... | .... | .... | .... | .... | .... |

IHL Second All-Star Team (2001)

Traded to **Nashville** by **San Jose** for Nashville's 5th round choice (later traded to Phoenix – Phoenix selected Josh Blackburn) in 1998 Entry Draft, June 26, 1998. • Missed majority of 1998-99 season recovering from shoulder surgery, December 10, 1998. Signed as a free agent by **Jokerit Helsinki** (Finland), April 26, 2001. Signed as a free agent by **Lugano** (Swiss), April 9, 2003. Signed as a free agent by **Florida**, June 15, 2006.



## PENNER, Dustin
(PEH-nuhr, DUHS-tihn) **EDM.**

Left wing. Shoots left. 6'4", 245 lbs. Born, Winkler, Man., September 28, 1982.

| Season | Club | League | GP | G | A | Pts | PIM | PP | SH | GW | S | % | +/- | TF | F% | Min | GP | G | A | Pts | PIM | PP | SH | GW | Min |
|---|---|---|---|---|---|---|---|---|---|---|---|---|---|---|---|---|---|---|---|---|---|---|---|---|---|
| 2001-02 | MSU - Bottineau | NJCAA | 23 | 20 | 12 | 32 | 30 | .... | .... | .... | .... | .... | .... | .... | .... | .... | .... | .... | .... | .... | .... | .... | .... | .... | .... |
| 2002-03 | U. of Maine | H-East | DID NOT PLAY – FRESHMAN | | | | | | | | | | | | | | | | | | | | | | |
| 2003-04 | U. of Maine | H-East | 43 | 11 | 12 | 23 | 52 | .... | .... | .... | .... | .... | .... | .... | .... | .... | .... | .... | .... | .... | .... | .... | .... | .... | .... |
| 2004-05 | Cincinnati | AHL | 77 | 10 | 18 | 28 | 82 | .... | .... | .... | .... | .... | .... | .... | .... | .... | 9 | 2 | 3 | 5 | 13 | .... | .... | .... | .... |
| **2005-06** | **Anaheim** | **NHL** | 19 | 4 | 3 | 7 | 14 | 2 | 0 | 1 | 46 | 8.7 | 3 | 1 | 0.0 | 11:58 | 13 | 3 | 6 | 9 | 12 | 0 | 0 | 0 | 13:16 |
| | Portland Pirates | AHL | 57 | 39 | 45 | 84 | 68 | .... | .... | .... | .... | .... | .... | .... | .... | .... | 5 | 4 | 3 | 7 | 0 | .... | .... | .... | .... |
| **2006-07** ♦ | **Anaheim** | **NHL** | 82 | 29 | 16 | 45 | 58 | 9 | 0 | 5 | 204 | 14.2 | –2 | 58 | 46.6 | 13:59 | 21 | 3 | 5 | 8 | 2 | 0 | 0 | 2 | 14:05 |
| **2007-08** | **Edmonton** | **NHL** | 82 | 23 | 24 | 47 | 45 | 13 | 0 | 4 | 201 | 11.4 | –12 | 189 | 55.0 | 17:12 | .... | .... | .... | .... | .... | .... | .... | .... | .... |
| **2008-09** | **Edmonton** | **NHL** | 78 | 17 | 20 | 37 | 61 | 5 | 0 | 5 | 137 | 12.4 | 7 | 114 | 47.4 | 15:23 | .... | .... | .... | .... | .... | .... | .... | .... | .... |
| | **NHL Totals** | | 261 | 73 | 63 | 136 | 178 | 29 | 0 | 15 | 588 | 12.4 | | 362 | 51.1 | 15:16 | 34 | 6 | 11 | 17 | 14 | 0 | 0 | 2 | 13:46 |

NCAA Championship All-Tournament Team (2004) • AHL Second All-Star Team (2006)

Signed as a free agent by **Anaheim**, May 12, 2004. Signed as a free agent by **Edmonton**, August 2, 2007.

## PERREZHOGIN, Alexander

(pehr-eh-ZHOI-gihn, al-EHX-AN-duhr) **MTL.**

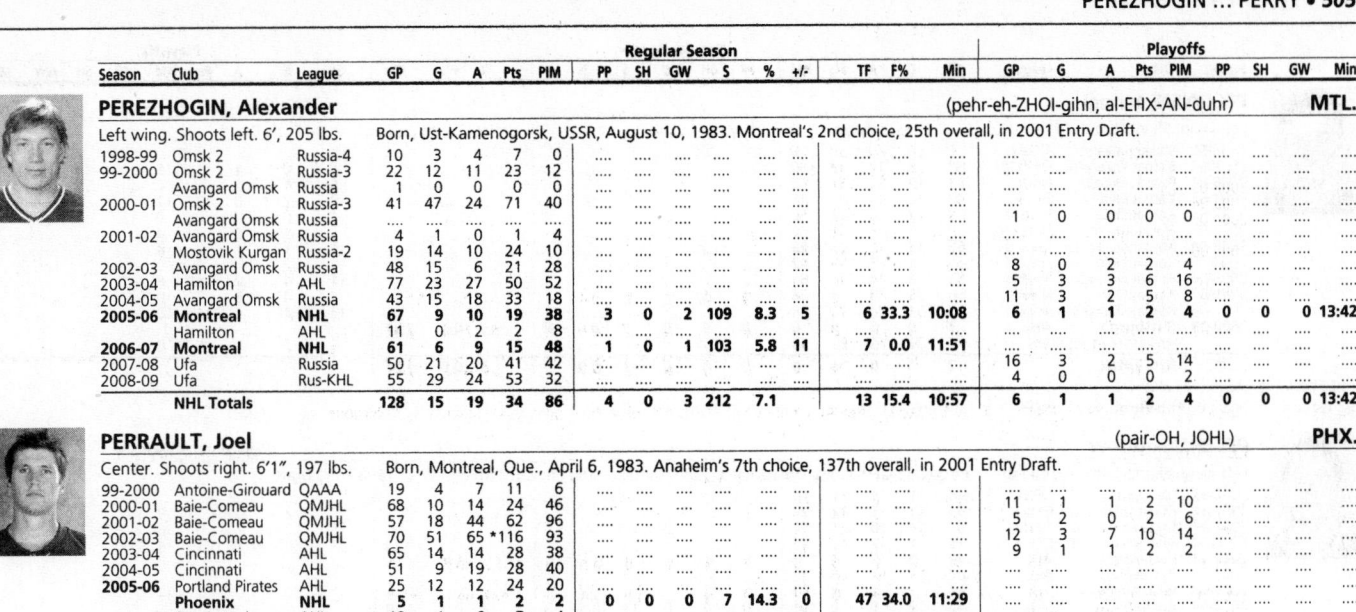

Left wing. Shoots left. 6', 205 lbs. Born, Ust-Kamenogorsk, USSR, August 10, 1983. Montreal's 2nd choice, 25th overall, in 2001 Entry Draft.

| | | | Regular Season | | | | | | | | | | | | | | Playoffs | | | | | | | | |
|---|---|---|---|---|---|---|---|---|---|---|---|---|---|---|---|---|---|---|---|---|---|---|---|---|---|
| Season | Club | League | GP | G | A | Pts | PIM | PP | SH | GW | S | % | +/- | TF | F% | Min | GP | G | A | Pts | PIM | PP | SH | GW | Min |
| 1998-99 | Omsk 2 | Russia-4 | 10 | 3 | 4 | 7 | 0 | | | | | | | | | | | | | | | | | | |
| 99-2000 | Omsk 2 | Russia-3 | 22 | 12 | 11 | 23 | 12 | | | | | | | | | | | | | | | | | | |
| | Avangard Omsk | Russia | 1 | 0 | 0 | 0 | 0 | | | | | | | | | | | | | | | | | | |
| 2000-01 | Omsk 2 | Russia-3 | 41 | 47 | 24 | 71 | 40 | | | | | | | | | | | | | | | | | | |
| | Avangard Omsk | Russia | | | | | | | | | | | | | | | 1 | 0 | 0 | 0 | 0 | | | | |
| 2001-02 | Avangard Omsk | Russia | 4 | 1 | 0 | 1 | 4 | | | | | | | | | | | | | | | | | | |
| | Mostovik Kurgan | Russia-2 | 19 | 14 | 10 | 24 | 10 | | | | | | | | | | | | | | | | | | |
| 2002-03 | Avangard Omsk | Russia | 48 | 15 | 6 | 21 | 28 | | | | | | | | | | 8 | 0 | 2 | 2 | 4 | | | | |
| 2003-04 | Hamilton | AHL | 77 | 23 | 27 | 50 | 52 | | | | | | | | | | 5 | 3 | 3 | 6 | 16 | | | | |
| 2004-05 | Avangard Omsk | Russia | 43 | 15 | 18 | 33 | 18 | | | | | | | | | | 11 | 3 | 2 | 5 | 8 | | | | |
| 2005-06 | Montreal | NHL | 67 | 9 | 10 | 19 | 38 | 3 | 0 | 2 | 109 | 8.3 | 5 | 6 | 33.3 | 10:08 | 6 | 1 | 1 | 2 | 4 | 0 | 0 | 0 | 13:42 |
| | Hamilton | AHL | 11 | 0 | 2 | 2 | 8 | | | | | | | | | | | | | | | | | | |
| 2006-07 | Montreal | NHL | 61 | 6 | 9 | 15 | 48 | 1 | 0 | 1 | 103 | 5.8 | 11 | 7 | 0.0 | 11:51 | | | | | | | | | |
| 2007-08 | Ufa | Russia | 50 | 21 | 20 | 41 | 42 | | | | | | | | | | 16 | 3 | 2 | 5 | 14 | | | | |
| 2008-09 | Ufa | Rus-KHL | 55 | 29 | 24 | 53 | 32 | | | | | | | | | | 4 | 0 | 0 | 0 | 2 | | | | |
| | NHL Totals | | 128 | 15 | 19 | 34 | 86 | 4 | 0 | 3 | 212 | 7.1 | | 13 | 15.4 | 10:57 | 6 | 1 | 1 | 2 | 4 | 0 | 0 | 0 | 13:42 |

## PERRAULT, Joel

(pair-OH, JOHL) **PHX.**

Center. Shoots right. 6'1", 197 lbs. Born, Montreal, Que., April 6, 1983. Anaheim's 7th choice, 137th overall, in 2001 Entry Draft.

| Season | Club | League | GP | G | A | Pts | PIM | PP | SH | GW | S | % | +/- | TF | F% | Min | GP | G | A | Pts | PIM | PP | SH | GW | Min |
|---|---|---|---|---|---|---|---|---|---|---|---|---|---|---|---|---|---|---|---|---|---|---|---|---|---|
| 99-2000 | Antoine-Girouard | QAAA | 19 | 4 | 7 | 11 | 6 | | | | | | | | | | | | | | | | | | |
| 2000-01 | Baie-Comeau | QMJHL | 68 | 10 | 14 | 24 | 46 | | | | | | | | | | 11 | 1 | 1 | 2 | 10 | | | | |
| 2001-02 | Baie-Comeau | QMJHL | 57 | 18 | 44 | 62 | 96 | | | | | | | | | | 5 | 2 | 0 | 2 | 6 | | | | |
| 2002-03 | Baie-Comeau | QMJHL | 70 | 51 | 65 | *116 | 93 | | | | | | | | | | 12 | 3 | 7 | 10 | 14 | | | | |
| 2003-04 | Cincinnati | AHL | 65 | 14 | 14 | 28 | 38 | | | | | | | | | | 9 | 1 | 1 | 2 | 2 | | | | |
| 2004-05 | Cincinnati | AHL | 51 | 9 | 19 | 28 | 40 | | | | | | | | | | | | | | | | | | |
| 2005-06 | Portland Pirates | AHL | 25 | 12 | 12 | 24 | 20 | | | | | | | | | | | | | | | | | | |
| | Phoenix | NHL | 5 | 1 | 1 | 2 | 2 | 0 | 0 | 0 | 7 | 14.3 | 0 | 47 | 34.0 | 11:29 | | | | | | | | | |
| | San Antonio | AHL | 12 | 1 | 6 | 7 | 4 | | | | | | | | | | | | | | | | | | |
| 2006-07 | Phoenix | NHL | 15 | 1 | 2 | 3 | 14 | 0 | 0 | 0 | 18 | 9.1 | -3 | 109 | 82.6 | 11:29 | | | | | | | | | |
| | St. Louis | NHL | 11 | 0 | 0 | 0 | 0 | 0 | 0 | 0 | 13 | 0.0 | -4 | 20 | 25.0 | 8:19 | | | | | | | | | |
| | Peoria Rivermen | AHL | 2 | 0 | 2 | 2 | 7 | | | | | | | | | | | | | | | | | | |
| | San Antonio | AHL | 21 | 10 | 4 | 14 | 8 | | | | | | | | | | | | | | | | | | |
| 2007-08 | Phoenix | NHL | 49 | 7 | 10 | 17 | 48 | 3 | 0 | 2 | 87 | 8.0 | -11 | 599 | 49.1 | 14:26 | | | | | | | | | |
| | San Antonio | AHL | 28 | 14 | 13 | 27 | 36 | | | | | | | | | | | | | | | | | | |
| 2008-09 | Phoenix | NHL | 7 | 2 | 1 | 3 | 4 | 0 | 0 | 0 | 15 | 13.3 | 2 | 76 | 44.7 | 12:52 | | | | | | | | | |
| | San Antonio | AHL | 46 | 18 | 31 | 49 | 46 | | | | | | | | | | | | | | | | | | |
| | NHL Totals | | 87 | 11 | 14 | 25 | 68 | 3 | 0 | 2 | 140 | 7.9 | | 851 | 51.6 | 12:51 | | | | | | | | | |

QMJHL First All-Star Team (2003) • Canadian Major Junior First All-Star Team (2003)

Traded to **Phoenix** by **Anaheim** for Sean O'Donnell, March 9, 2006. Claimed on waivers by **St. Louis** from **Phoenix**, October 31, 2006. Claimed on waivers by **Phoenix** from **St. Louis**, December 19, 2006.

## PERRIN, Eric

(peh-REHN, AIR-ihk)

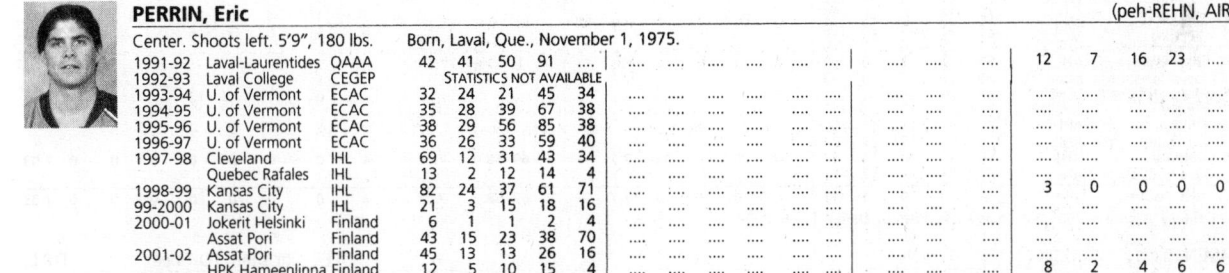

Center. Shoots left. 5'9", 180 lbs. Born, Laval, Que., November 1, 1975.

| Season | Club | League | GP | G | A | Pts | PIM | PP | SH | GW | S | % | +/- | TF | F% | Min | GP | G | A | Pts | PIM | PP | SH | GW | Min |
|---|---|---|---|---|---|---|---|---|---|---|---|---|---|---|---|---|---|---|---|---|---|---|---|---|---|
| 1991-92 | Laval-Laurentides | QAAA | 42 | 41 | 50 | 91 | | | | | | | | | | | 12 | 7 | 16 | 23 | | | | | |
| 1992-93 | Laval College | CEGEP | STATISTICS NOT AVAILABLE | | | | | | | | | | | | | | | | | | | | | | |
| 1993-94 | U. of Vermont | ECAC | 32 | 24 | 21 | 45 | 34 | | | | | | | | | | | | | | | | | | |
| 1994-95 | U. of Vermont | ECAC | 35 | 28 | 39 | 67 | 38 | | | | | | | | | | | | | | | | | | |
| 1995-96 | U. of Vermont | ECAC | 38 | 29 | 56 | 85 | 38 | | | | | | | | | | | | | | | | | | |
| 1996-97 | U. of Vermont | ECAC | 36 | 26 | 33 | 59 | 40 | | | | | | | | | | | | | | | | | | |
| 1997-98 | Cleveland | IHL | 69 | 12 | 31 | 43 | 34 | | | | | | | | | | | | | | | | | | |
| | Quebec Rafales | IHL | 13 | 2 | 12 | 14 | 4 | | | | | | | | | | | | | | | | | | |
| 1998-99 | Kansas City | IHL | 82 | 24 | 37 | 61 | 71 | | | | | | | | | | 3 | 0 | 0 | 0 | 0 | | | | |
| 99-2000 | Kansas City | IHL | 21 | 3 | 15 | 18 | 16 | | | | | | | | | | | | | | | | | | |
| 2000-01 | Jokerit Helsinki | Finland | 6 | 1 | 1 | 2 | 4 | | | | | | | | | | | | | | | | | | |
| | Assat Pori | Finland | 43 | 15 | 23 | 38 | 70 | | | | | | | | | | | | | | | | | | |
| 2001-02 | Assat Pori | Finland | 45 | 13 | 13 | 26 | 16 | | | | | | | | | | 8 | 2 | 4 | 6 | 6 | | | | |
| | HPK Hameenlinna | Finland | 12 | 5 | 10 | 15 | 4 | | | | | | | | | | | | | | | | | | |
| 2002-03 | JYP Jyvaskyla | Finland | 56 | 18 | 28 | 46 | 36 | | | | | | | | | | 7 | 4 | 6 | 10 | 8 | | | | |
| 2003-04♦ | Tampa Bay | NHL | 4 | 0 | 0 | 0 | 0 | 0 | 0 | 0 | 3 | 0.0 | -1 | 30 | 60.0 | 8:32 | 12 | 0 | 1 | 1 | 6 | 0 | 0 | 0 | 5:20 |
| | Hershey Bears | AHL | 71 | 21 | 54 | 75 | 49 | | | | | | | | | | | | | | | | | | |
| 2004-05 | Hershey Bears | AHL | 80 | 24 | 49 | 73 | 46 | | | | | | | | | | | | | | | | | | |
| 2005-06 | SC Bern | Swiss | 44 | 13 | 25 | 38 | 28 | | | | | | | | | | 6 | 2 | 4 | 6 | 8 | | | | |
| 2006-07 | Tampa Bay | NHL | 82 | 13 | 23 | 36 | 30 | 2 | 1 | 0 | 151 | 8.6 | -7 | 407 | 50.9 | 17:00 | 6 | 1 | 1 | 2 | 2 | 0 | 0 | 0 | 12:32 |
| 2007-08 | Atlanta | NHL | 81 | 12 | 33 | 45 | 26 | 2 | 2 | 0 | 121 | 9.9 | -5 | 717 | 53.0 | 17:50 | | | | | | | | | |
| 2008-09 | Atlanta | NHL | 78 | 7 | 16 | 23 | 36 | 1 | 1 | 0 | 109 | 6.4 | -2 | 213 | 52.1 | 14:11 | | | | | | | | | |
| | NHL Totals | | 245 | 32 | 72 | 104 | 92 | 5 | 4 | 0 | 384 | 8.3 | | 1367 | 52.4 | 16:14 | 18 | 1 | 2 | 3 | 8 | 0 | 0 | 0 | 7:44 |

ECAC All-Rookie Team (1994) • ECAC Rookie of the Year (1994) • ECAC First All-Star Team (1995, 1996) • ECAC Player of the Year (1996) • NCAA East First All-American Team (1996) • AHL First All-Star Team (2004)

Signed as a free agent by **Tampa Bay**, June 19, 2003. Signed as a free agent by **Bern** (Swiss), August 22, 2005. Signed as a free agent by **Atlanta**, July 1, 2007.

## PERRON, David

(peh-RAWN, DAY-vihd) **ST.L.**

Left wing. Shoots right. 5'11", 192 lbs. Born, Sherbrooke, Que., May 28, 1988. St. Louis' 3rd choice, 26th overall, in 2007 Entry Draft.

| Season | Club | League | GP | G | A | Pts | PIM | PP | SH | GW | S | % | +/- | TF | F% | Min | GP | G | A | Pts | PIM | PP | SH | GW | Min |
|---|---|---|---|---|---|---|---|---|---|---|---|---|---|---|---|---|---|---|---|---|---|---|---|---|---|
| 2005-06 | St-Jerome | QJHL | 51 | 24 | 45 | 69 | 92 | | | | | | | | | | 8 | 4 | 5 | 9 | 8 | | | | |
| 2006-07 | Lewiston | QMJHL | 70 | 39 | 44 | 83 | 75 | | | | | | | | | | 17 | 12 | 16 | 28 | 22 | | | | |
| 2007-08 | St. Louis | NHL | 62 | 13 | 14 | 27 | 38 | 3 | 0 | 1 | 68 | 19.1 | 16 | 14 | 35.7 | 12:33 | | | | | | | | | |
| 2008-09 | St. Louis | NHL | 81 | 15 | 35 | 50 | 50 | 4 | 0 | 3 | 161 | 9.3 | 13 | 6 | 16.7 | 14:32 | 4 | 1 | 1 | 2 | 4 | 0 | 0 | 0 | 17:12 |
| | NHL Totals | | 143 | 28 | 49 | 77 | 88 | 7 | 0 | 4 | 229 | 12.2 | | 20 | 30.0 | 13:40 | 4 | 1 | 1 | 2 | 4 | 0 | 0 | 0 | 17:12 |

## PERRY, Corey

(PAIR-ee, KOH-ree) **ANA.**

Right wing. Shoots right. 6'3", 209 lbs. Born, Peterborough, Ont., May 16, 1985. Anaheim's 2nd choice, 28th overall, in 2003 Entry Draft.

| Season | Club | League | GP | G | A | Pts | PIM | PP | SH | GW | S | % | +/- | TF | F% | Min | GP | G | A | Pts | PIM | PP | SH | GW | Min |
|---|---|---|---|---|---|---|---|---|---|---|---|---|---|---|---|---|---|---|---|---|---|---|---|---|---|
| 2000-01 | Peterborough | Minor-ON | 64 | 69 | 46 | 115 | 20 | | | | | | | | | | 3 | 3 | 0 | 3 | 0 | | | | |
| 2001-02 | London Knights | OHL | 67 | 28 | 31 | 59 | 56 | | | | | | | | | | 12 | 2 | 3 | 5 | 30 | | | | |
| 2002-03 | London Knights | OHL | 67 | 25 | 53 | 78 | 145 | | | | | | | | | | 14 | 7 | 16 | 23 | 27 | | | | |
| 2003-04 | London Knights | OHL | 66 | 40 | *73 | 113 | 98 | | | | | | | | | | 15 | 7 | 15 | 22 | 20 | | | | |
| | Cincinnati | AHL | | | | | | | | | | | | | | | 3 | 1 | 1 | 2 | 4 | | | | |
| 2004-05 | London Knights | OHL | 60 | *47 | *83 | *130 | 117 | | | | | | | | | | 18 | 11 | *27 | *38 | 46 | | | | |
| 2005-06 | Anaheim | NHL | 56 | 13 | 12 | 25 | 50 | 4 | 0 | 2 | 98 | 13.3 | 1 | 11 | 27.3 | 11:34 | 11 | 0 | 3 | 3 | 16 | 0 | 0 | 0 | 9:33 |
| | Portland Pirates | AHL | 19 | 16 | 18 | 34 | 32 | | | | | | | | | | 1 | 1 | 0 | 1 | 0 | | | | |
| 2006-07♦ | Anaheim | NHL | 82 | 17 | 27 | 44 | 55 | 4 | 0 | 3 | 194 | 8.8 | 12 | 21 | 42.9 | 12:28 | 21 | 6 | 9 | 15 | 37 | 1 | 0 | 1 | 16:30 |
| 2007-08 | Anaheim | NHL | 70 | 29 | 25 | 54 | 108 | 11 | 0 | 4 | 200 | 14.5 | 12 | 16 | 18.8 | 17:57 | 3 | 2 | 1 | 3 | 8 | 0 | 0 | 0 | 14:55 |
| 2008-09 | Anaheim | NHL | 78 | 32 | 40 | 72 | 109 | 10 | 0 | 8 | 283 | 11.3 | 10 | 31 | 29.0 | 18:36 | 13 | 8 | 6 | 14 | 36 | 2 | 0 | 1 | 22:00 |
| | NHL Totals | | 286 | 91 | 104 | 195 | 322 | 29 | 0 | 17 | 775 | 11.7 | | 79 | 30.4 | 15:18 | 48 | 16 | 19 | 35 | 97 | 3 | 0 | 2 | 16:18 |

OHL First All-Star Team (2004, 2005) • Canadian Major Junior Second All-Star Team (2004) • Canadian Major Junior First All-Star Team (2005) • Memorial Cup Tournament All-Star Team (2005) • Stafford Smythe Memorial Trophy (Memorial Cup Tournament - MVP) (2005)

Played in NHL All-Star Game (2008)

## PESONEN, Janne

(PEHS-oh-nihn, YAH-nee)

Left wing. Shoots left. 5'11", 180 lbs. Born, Suomussalmi, Finland, May 11, 1982. Anaheim's 8th choice, 269th overall, in 2004 Entry Draft.

| Season | Club | League | GP | G | A | Pts | PIM | PP | SH | GW | S | % | +/- | TF | F% | Min | GP | G | A | Pts | PIM | PP | SH | GW | Min |
|---|---|---|---|---|---|---|---|---|---|---|---|---|---|---|---|---|---|---|---|---|---|---|---|---|---|
| | | | Regular Season | | | | | | | | | | | | | | Playoffs | | | | | | | | |
| 1998-99 | Hokki Kajaani | Finland-3 | 2 | 0 | 0 | 0 | 0 | .... | .... | .... | .... | .... | .... | .... | .... | .... | .... | .... | .... | .... | .... | .... | .... | .... | .... |
| 99-2000 | Karpat Oulu U18 | Fin-U18 | 33 | 6 | 12 | 18 | 30 | .... | .... | .... | .... | .... | .... | .... | .... | .... | 3 | 0 | 1 | 1 | 0 | .... | .... | .... | .... |
| 2000-01 | Karpat Oulu Jr. | Fin-Jr. | 41 | 9 | 22 | 31 | 18 | .... | .... | .... | .... | .... | .... | .... | .... | .... | 6 | 1 | 1 | 2 | 0 | .... | .... | .... | .... |
| 2001-02 | Karpat Oulu Jr. | Fin-Jr. | 42 | 12 | 19 | 31 | 18 | .... | .... | .... | .... | .... | .... | .... | .... | .... | 3 | 2 | 0 | 2 | 2 | .... | .... | .... | .... |
| | Karpat Oulu | Finland | 9 | 2 | 0 | 2 | 0 | .... | .... | .... | .... | .... | .... | .... | .... | .... | 1 | 0 | 0 | 0 | 0 | .... | .... | .... | .... |
| 2002-03 | Hokki Kajaani | Finland-2 | 40 | 15 | 21 | 36 | 62 | .... | .... | .... | .... | .... | .... | .... | .... | .... | 3 | 2 | 0 | 2 | 4 | .... | .... | .... | .... |
| 2003-04 | Karpat Oulu | Finland | 56 | 17 | 13 | 30 | 28 | .... | .... | .... | .... | .... | .... | .... | .... | .... | 15 | 1 | 1 | 2 | 4 | .... | .... | .... | .... |
| 2004-05 | Karpat Oulu | Finland | 55 | 11 | 18 | 29 | 42 | .... | .... | .... | .... | .... | .... | .... | .... | .... | 12 | 2 | 0 | 2 | 0 | .... | .... | .... | .... |
| 2005-06 | Karpat Oulu | Finland | 53 | 8 | 14 | 22 | 34 | .... | .... | .... | .... | .... | .... | .... | .... | .... | 11 | 4 | 0 | 4 | 8 | .... | .... | .... | .... |
| 2006-07 | Karpat Oulu | Finland | 56 | 22 | 33 | 55 | 38 | .... | .... | .... | .... | .... | .... | .... | .... | .... | 9 | 4 | 3 | 7 | 10 | .... | .... | .... | .... |
| 2007-08 | Karpat Oulu | Finland | 56 | *34 | 44 | *78 | 58 | .... | .... | .... | .... | .... | .... | .... | .... | .... | 14 | 7 | 9 | 16 | 10 | .... | .... | .... | .... |
| **2008-09** | **Pittsburgh** | **NHL** | **7** | **0** | **0** | **0** | **0** | **0** | **0** | **0** | **3** | **0.0** | **-3** | **3** | **0.0** | **7:27** | .... | .... | .... | .... | .... | .... | .... | .... | .... |
| | Wilkes-Barre | AHL | 70 | 32 | 50 | 82 | 33 | .... | .... | .... | .... | .... | .... | .... | .... | .... | 5 | 1 | 5 | 6 | 0 | .... | .... | .... | .... |
| | **NHL Totals** | | **7** | **0** | **0** | **0** | **0** | **0** | **0** | **0** | **3** | **0.0** | | **3** | **0.0** | **7:27** | .... | .... | .... | .... | .... | .... | .... | .... | .... |

AHL Second All-Star Team (2009)

Signed as a free agent by **Pittsburgh**, July 7, 2008.

## PETERS, Andrew

(PEE-tuhrz, AN-droo)

Left wing. Shoots left. 6'4", 247 lbs. Born, St. Catharines, Ont., May 5, 1980. Buffalo's 2nd choice, 34th overall, in 1998 Entry Draft.

| Season | Club | League | GP | G | A | Pts | PIM | PP | SH | GW | S | % | +/- | TF | F% | Min | GP | G | A | Pts | PIM | PP | SH | GW | Min |
|---|---|---|---|---|---|---|---|---|---|---|---|---|---|---|---|---|---|---|---|---|---|---|---|---|---|
| 1996-97 | Georgetown | OPJHL | 46 | 11 | 16 | 27 | 65 | .... | .... | .... | .... | .... | .... | .... | .... | .... | .... | .... | .... | .... | .... | .... | .... | .... | .... |
| 1997-98 | Oshawa Generals | OHL | 60 | 11 | 7 | 18 | 220 | .... | .... | .... | .... | .... | .... | .... | .... | .... | 7 | 2 | 0 | 2 | 19 | .... | .... | .... | .... |
| 1998-99 | Oshawa Generals | OHL | 54 | 14 | 10 | 24 | 137 | .... | .... | .... | .... | .... | .... | .... | .... | .... | 15 | 2 | 7 | 9 | 36 | .... | .... | .... | .... |
| 99-2000 | Kitchener Rangers | OHL | 42 | 6 | 13 | 19 | 95 | .... | .... | .... | .... | .... | .... | .... | .... | .... | 4 | 0 | 1 | 1 | 14 | .... | .... | .... | .... |
| 2000-01 | Rochester | AHL | 49 | 0 | 4 | 4 | 118 | .... | .... | .... | .... | .... | .... | .... | .... | .... | .... | .... | .... | .... | .... | .... | .... | .... | .... |
| 2001-02 | Rochester | AHL | 67 | 4 | 1 | 5 | *388 | .... | .... | .... | .... | .... | .... | .... | .... | .... | .... | .... | .... | .... | .... | .... | .... | .... | .... |
| 2002-03 | Rochester | AHL | 57 | 3 | 0 | 3 | 223 | .... | .... | .... | .... | .... | .... | .... | .... | .... | 3 | 0 | 0 | 0 | 24 | .... | .... | .... | .... |
| **2003-04** | **Buffalo** | **NHL** | **42** | **2** | **0** | **2** | **151** | **0** | **0** | **0** | **19** | **10.5** | **-3** | **2** | **0.0** | **4:10** | .... | .... | .... | .... | .... | .... | .... | .... | .... |
| 2004-05 | Bodens IK | Sweden-2 | 22 | 2 | 4 | 6 | 195 | .... | .... | .... | .... | .... | .... | .... | .... | .... | .... | .... | .... | .... | .... | .... | .... | .... | .... |
| **2005-06** | **Buffalo** | **NHL** | **28** | **0** | **0** | **0** | **100** | **0** | **0** | **0** | **6** | **0.0** | **-2** | **2** | **100.0** | **3:16** | .... | .... | .... | .... | .... | .... | .... | .... | .... |
| **2006-07** | **Buffalo** | **NHL** | **58** | **1** | **1** | **2** | **125** | **0** | **0** | **0** | **19** | **5.3** | **-1** | **0** | **0.0** | **3:46** | .... | .... | .... | .... | .... | .... | .... | .... | .... |
| **2007-08** | **Buffalo** | **NHL** | **44** | **1** | **1** | **2** | **100** | **0** | **0** | **0** | **18** | **5.6** | **-4** | **1** | **0.0** | **3:09** | .... | .... | .... | .... | .... | .... | .... | .... | .... |
| **2008-09** | **Buffalo** | **NHL** | **28** | **0** | **1** | **1** | **81** | **0** | **0** | **0** | **10** | **0.0** | **-2** | **1** | **0.0** | **4:01** | .... | .... | .... | .... | .... | .... | .... | .... | .... |
| | **NHL Totals** | | **200** | **4** | **3** | **7** | **557** | **0** | **0** | **0** | **72** | **5.6** | | **6** | **33.3** | **3:41** | .... | .... | .... | .... | .... | .... | .... | .... | .... |

Signed as a free agent by **Bodens** (Sweden-2), August 20, 2004. • Spent majority of 2008-09 season serving as a healthy reserve.

## PETERS, Warren

(PEE-tuhrz, WAHR-ihn) **DAL.**

Center. Shoots left. 6', 198 lbs. Born, Saskatoon, Sask., July 10, 1982.

| Season | Club | League | GP | G | A | Pts | PIM | PP | SH | GW | S | % | +/- | TF | F% | Min | GP | G | A | Pts | PIM | PP | SH | GW | Min |
|---|---|---|---|---|---|---|---|---|---|---|---|---|---|---|---|---|---|---|---|---|---|---|---|---|---|
| 1998-99 | Saskatoon Blades | WHL | 53 | 8 | 6 | 14 | 111 | .... | .... | .... | .... | .... | .... | .... | .... | .... | .... | .... | .... | .... | .... | .... | .... | .... | .... |
| 99-2000 | Saskatoon Blades | WHL | 70 | 11 | 17 | 28 | 97 | .... | .... | .... | .... | .... | .... | .... | .... | .... | 10 | 1 | 2 | 3 | 13 | .... | .... | .... | .... |
| 2000-01 | Saskatoon Blades | WHL | 63 | 27 | 14 | 41 | 111 | .... | .... | .... | .... | .... | .... | .... | .... | .... | .... | .... | .... | .... | .... | .... | .... | .... | .... |
| 2001-02 | Saskatoon Blades | WHL | 72 | 34 | 26 | 60 | 115 | .... | .... | .... | .... | .... | .... | .... | .... | .... | 7 | 1 | 4 | 5 | 13 | .... | .... | .... | .... |
| 2002-03 | Saskatoon Blades | WHL | 71 | 31 | 44 | 75 | 108 | .... | .... | .... | .... | .... | .... | .... | .... | .... | 6 | 1 | 6 | 7 | 6 | .... | .... | .... | .... |
| | Portland Pirates | AHL | 1 | 0 | 0 | 0 | 0 | .... | .... | .... | .... | .... | .... | .... | .... | .... | .... | .... | .... | .... | .... | .... | .... | .... | .... |
| 2003-04 | Utah Grizzlies | AHL | 55 | 4 | 4 | 8 | 63 | .... | .... | .... | .... | .... | .... | .... | .... | .... | .... | .... | .... | .... | .... | .... | .... | .... | .... |
| | Idaho Steelheads | ECHL | 21 | 6 | 7 | 13 | 33 | .... | .... | .... | .... | .... | .... | .... | .... | .... | .... | .... | .... | .... | .... | .... | .... | .... | .... |
| 2004-05 | Idaho Steelheads | ECHL | 69 | 23 | 23 | 46 | 131 | .... | .... | .... | .... | .... | .... | .... | .... | .... | 4 | 0 | 1 | 1 | 12 | .... | .... | .... | .... |
| 2005-06 | Omaha | AHL | 77 | 15 | 10 | 25 | 133 | .... | .... | .... | .... | .... | .... | .... | .... | .... | .... | .... | .... | .... | .... | .... | .... | .... | .... |
| 2006-07 | Omaha | AHL | 79 | 17 | 16 | 33 | 95 | .... | .... | .... | .... | .... | .... | .... | .... | .... | 6 | 2 | 1 | 3 | 4 | .... | .... | .... | .... |
| 2007-08 | Quad City Flames | AHL | 75 | 11 | 13 | 24 | 74 | .... | .... | .... | .... | .... | .... | .... | .... | .... | .... | .... | .... | .... | .... | .... | .... | .... | .... |
| **2008-09** | **Calgary** | **NHL** | **16** | **1** | **0** | **1** | **12** | **0** | **0** | **0** | **13** | **7.7** | **-2** | **69** | **58.0** | **7:05** | **4** | **0** | **0** | **0** | **0** | **0** | **0** | **0** | **7:03** |
| | Quad City Flames | AHL | 62 | 11 | 6 | 17 | 51 | .... | .... | .... | .... | .... | .... | .... | .... | .... | .... | .... | .... | .... | .... | .... | .... | .... | .... |
| | **NHL Totals** | | **16** | **1** | **0** | **1** | **12** | **0** | **0** | **0** | **13** | **7.7** | | **69** | **58.0** | **7:05** | **4** | **0** | **0** | **0** | **0** | **0** | **0** | **0** | **7:03** |

Signed as a free agent by **Calgary**, August 5, 2005. Signed as a free agent by **Dallas**, July 6, 2009.

## PETERSEN, Toby

(PEE-tuhr-suhn, TOH-bee) **DAL.**

Center. Shoots left. 5'10", 197 lbs. Born, Minneapolis, MN, October 27, 1978. Pittsburgh's 9th choice, 244th overall, in 1998 Entry Draft.

| Season | Club | League | GP | G | A | Pts | PIM | PP | SH | GW | S | % | +/- | TF | F% | Min | GP | G | A | Pts | PIM | PP | SH | GW | Min |
|---|---|---|---|---|---|---|---|---|---|---|---|---|---|---|---|---|---|---|---|---|---|---|---|---|---|
| 1995-96 | Jefferson Jaguars | High-MN | 25 | 29 | 30 | 59 | .... | .... | .... | .... | .... | .... | .... | .... | .... | .... | .... | .... | .... | .... | .... | .... | .... | .... | .... |
| 1996-97 | Colorado College | WCHA | 40 | 17 | 21 | 38 | 18 | .... | .... | .... | .... | .... | .... | .... | .... | .... | .... | .... | .... | .... | .... | .... | .... | .... | .... |
| 1997-98 | Colorado College | WCHA | 40 | 16 | 17 | 33 | 34 | .... | .... | .... | .... | .... | .... | .... | .... | .... | .... | .... | .... | .... | .... | .... | .... | .... | .... |
| 1998-99 | Colorado College | WCHA | 21 | 12 | 12 | 24 | 2 | .... | .... | .... | .... | .... | .... | .... | .... | .... | .... | .... | .... | .... | .... | .... | .... | .... | .... |
| 99-2000 | Colorado College | WCHA | 37 | 14 | 19 | 33 | 8 | .... | .... | .... | .... | .... | .... | .... | .... | .... | .... | .... | .... | .... | .... | .... | .... | .... | .... |
| **2000-01** | **Pittsburgh** | **NHL** | **12** | **2** | **6** | **8** | **4** | **0** | **0** | **1** | **25** | **8.0** | **3** | **39** | **35.9** | **13:22** | .... | .... | .... | .... | .... | .... | .... | .... | .... |
| | Wilkes-Barre | AHL | 73 | 26 | 41 | 67 | 22 | .... | .... | .... | .... | .... | .... | .... | .... | .... | 21 | 7 | 6 | 13 | 4 | .... | .... | .... | .... |
| **2001-02** | **Pittsburgh** | **NHL** | **79** | **8** | **10** | **18** | **4** | **1** | **1** | **0** | **116** | **6.9** | **-15** | **338** | **45.6** | **12:16** | .... | .... | .... | .... | .... | .... | .... | .... | .... |
| 2002-03 | Wilkes-Barre | AHL | 80 | 31 | 35 | 66 | 24 | .... | .... | .... | .... | .... | .... | .... | .... | .... | 6 | 1 | 3 | 4 | 4 | .... | .... | .... | .... |
| 2003-04 | Wilkes-Barre | AHL | 62 | 15 | 29 | 44 | 4 | .... | .... | .... | .... | .... | .... | .... | .... | .... | 21 | 2 | 10 | 12 | 12 | .... | .... | .... | .... |
| 2004-05 | Edmonton | AHL | 78 | 14 | 15 | 29 | 21 | .... | .... | .... | .... | .... | .... | .... | .... | .... | .... | .... | .... | .... | .... | .... | .... | .... | .... |
| **2005-06** | **Edmonton** | **NHL** | .... | .... | .... | .... | .... | .... | .... | .... | .... | .... | .... | .... | .... | .... | **2** | **1** | **0** | **1** | **0** | **0** | **0** | **0** | **6:23** |
| | Iowa Stars | AHL | 79 | 26 | 47 | 73 | 48 | .... | .... | .... | .... | .... | .... | .... | .... | .... | 7 | 2 | 4 | 6 | 2 | .... | .... | .... | .... |
| **2006-07** | **Edmonton** | **NHL** | **64** | **6** | **9** | **15** | **4** | **0** | **2** | **1** | **92** | **6.5** | **-18** | **214** | **48.1** | **13:40** | .... | .... | .... | .... | .... | .... | .... | .... | .... |
| | Iowa Stars | AHL | 7 | 2 | 6 | 8 | 0 | .... | .... | .... | .... | .... | .... | .... | .... | .... | .... | .... | .... | .... | .... | .... | .... | .... | .... |
| **2007-08** | **Dallas** | **NHL** | **8** | **0** | **3** | **3** | **4** | **0** | **0** | **0** | **6** | **0.0** | **0** | **44** | **50.0** | **7:50** | **16** | **0** | **0** | **0** | **2** | **0** | **0** | **0** | **9:45** |
| | Iowa Stars | AHL | 63 | 21 | 30 | 51 | 24 | .... | .... | .... | .... | .... | .... | .... | .... | .... | .... | .... | .... | .... | .... | .... | .... | .... | .... |
| **2008-09** | **Dallas** | **NHL** | **57** | **4** | **7** | **11** | **14** | **0** | **0** | **0** | **80** | **5.0** | **1** | **283** | **45.2** | **11:25** | .... | .... | .... | .... | .... | .... | .... | .... | .... |
| | **NHL Totals** | | **220** | **20** | **35** | **55** | **30** | **1** | **3** | **2** | **319** | **6.3** | | **918** | **45.9** | **12:21** | **18** | **1** | **0** | **1** | **2** | **0** | **0** | **0** | **9:23** |

WCHA All-Rookie Team (1997) • AHL All-Rookie Team (2001)

Signed as a free agent by **Edmonton**, July 30, 2004. Signed as a free agent by **Dallas**, July 6, 2007.

## PETIOT, Richard

(PEH-tee-awt, RIH-chuhrd) **CHI.**

Defense. Shoots left. 6'2", 190 lbs. Born, Daysland, Alta., August 20, 1982. Los Angeles' 6th choice, 116th overall, in 2001 Entry Draft.

| Season | Club | League | GP | G | A | Pts | PIM | PP | SH | GW | S | % | +/- | TF | F% | Min | GP | G | A | Pts | PIM | PP | SH | GW | Min |
|---|---|---|---|---|---|---|---|---|---|---|---|---|---|---|---|---|---|---|---|---|---|---|---|---|---|
| 2000-01 | Camrose Kodiaks | AJHL | 55 | 8 | 16 | 24 | 81 | .... | .... | .... | .... | .... | .... | .... | .... | .... | 8 | 2 | 1 | 3 | 8 | .... | .... | .... | .... |
| 2001-02 | Colorado College | WCHA | 39 | 4 | 6 | 10 | 35 | .... | .... | .... | .... | .... | .... | .... | .... | .... | .... | .... | .... | .... | .... | .... | .... | .... | .... |
| 2002-03 | Colorado College | WCHA | 38 | 1 | 6 | 7 | 86 | .... | .... | .... | .... | .... | .... | .... | .... | .... | .... | .... | .... | .... | .... | .... | .... | .... | .... |
| 2003-04 | Colorado College | WCHA | 39 | 3 | 5 | 8 | 61 | .... | .... | .... | .... | .... | .... | .... | .... | .... | .... | .... | .... | .... | .... | .... | .... | .... | .... |
| 2004-05 | Colorado College | WCHA | 26 | 3 | 5 | 8 | 42 | .... | .... | .... | .... | .... | .... | .... | .... | .... | .... | .... | .... | .... | .... | .... | .... | .... | .... |
| **2005-06** | **Los Angeles** | **NHL** | **2** | **0** | **0** | **0** | **2** | **0** | **0** | **0** | **1** | **0.0** | **-2** | **0** | **0.0** | **4:47** | .... | .... | .... | .... | .... | .... | .... | .... | .... |
| | Manchester | AHL | 63 | 4 | 10 | 14 | 52 | .... | .... | .... | .... | .... | .... | .... | .... | .... | 7 | 1 | 0 | 1 | 6 | .... | .... | .... | .... |
| 2006-07 | Manchester | AHL | 13 | 1 | 1 | 2 | 25 | .... | .... | .... | .... | .... | .... | .... | .... | .... | 2 | 0 | 0 | 0 | 2 | .... | .... | .... | .... |
| 2007-08 | Manchester | AHL | 40 | 2 | 5 | 7 | 56 | .... | .... | .... | .... | .... | .... | .... | .... | .... | .... | .... | .... | .... | .... | .... | .... | .... | .... |
| **2008-09** | Toronto Marlies | AHL | 45 | 3 | 11 | 14 | 59 | .... | .... | .... | .... | .... | .... | .... | .... | .... | .... | .... | .... | .... | .... | .... | .... | .... | .... |
| | **Tampa Bay** | **NHL** | **11** | **0** | **3** | **3** | **21** | **0** | **0** | **0** | **10** | **0.0** | **5** | **0** | **0.0** | **20:37** | .... | .... | .... | .... | .... | .... | .... | .... | .... |
| | Norfolk Admirals | AHL | 1 | 0 | 0 | 0 | 0 | .... | .... | .... | .... | .... | .... | .... | .... | .... | .... | .... | .... | .... | .... | .... | .... | .... | .... |
| | **NHL Totals** | | **13** | **0** | **3** | **3** | **23** | **0** | **0** | **0** | **11** | **0.0** | | **0** | **0.0** | **18:11** | .... | .... | .... | .... | .... | .... | .... | .... | .... |

AJHL All-Rookie Team (2001) • AJHL South Second All-Star Team (2001)

• Missed majority of 2006-07 season recovering from knee injury suffered in rookie training camp and resulting surgery, October 6, 2006. Signed as a free agent by **Toronto**, July 15, 2008. Traded to **Tampa Bay** by **Toronto** for Olaf Kolzig, Jamie Heward, Andy Rogers and Carolina's 4th round choice (previously acquired – later forfeited) in 2009 Entry Draft, March 4, 2009. Signed as a free agent by **Chicago**, July 9, 2009.

## PETRUZALEK, Jakub

(peh-troo-ZAL-ehk, YA-kuhb)

Center/Right wing. Shoots right. 5'10", 176 lbs. Born, Most, Czech., April 24, 1985. NY Rangers' 13th choice, 266th overall, in 2004 Entry Draft.

| Season | Club | League | GP | G | A | Pts | PIM | PP | SH | GW | S | % | +/- | TF | F% | Min | GP | G | A | Pts | PIM | PP | SH | GW | Min |
|---|---|---|---|---|---|---|---|---|---|---|---|---|---|---|---|---|---|---|---|---|---|---|---|---|---|
| | | | Regular Season | | | | | | | | | | | | | | Playoffs | | | | | | | | |
| 2002-03 | Litvinov Jr. | CzRep-Jr. | 21 | 17 | 13 | 30 | 10 | .... | .... | .... | .... | .... | .... | .... | .... | .... | .... | .... | .... | .... | .... | .... | .... | .... | .... |
| | Litvinov | CzRep | 5 | 0 | 0 | 0 | 0 | .... | .... | .... | .... | .... | .... | .... | .... | .... | .... | .... | .... | .... | .... | .... | .... | .... | .... |
| 2003-04 | Litvinov Jr. | CzRep-Jr. | 53 | 38 | 51 | 89 | 110 | .... | .... | .... | .... | .... | .... | .... | .... | .... | 2 | 0 | 0 | 0 | 2 | .... | .... | .... | .... |
| | Litvinov | CzRep | 7 | 0 | 0 | 0 | 2 | .... | .... | .... | .... | .... | .... | .... | .... | .... | .... | .... | .... | .... | .... | .... | .... | .... | .... |
| | Most | CzRep-3 | 1 | 0 | 0 | 0 | 0 | .... | .... | .... | .... | .... | .... | .... | .... | .... | .... | .... | .... | .... | .... | .... | .... | .... | .... |
| 2004-05 | Ottawa 67's | OHL | 59 | 23 | 40 | 63 | 64 | .... | .... | .... | .... | .... | .... | .... | .... | .... | 21 | 8 | 10 | 18 | 30 | .... | .... | .... | .... |
| 2005-06 | Litvinov Jr. | CzRep-Jr. | 3 | 4 | 2 | 6 | 4 | .... | .... | .... | .... | .... | .... | .... | .... | .... | .... | .... | .... | .... | .... | .... | .... | .... | .... |
| | Litvinov | CzRep | 19 | 1 | 1 | 2 | 6 | .... | .... | .... | .... | .... | .... | .... | .... | .... | .... | .... | .... | .... | .... | .... | .... | .... | .... |
| | Barrie Colts | OHL | 24 | 11 | 20 | 31 | 28 | .... | .... | .... | .... | .... | .... | .... | .... | .... | 14 | 8 | 11 | 19 | 14 | .... | .... | .... | .... |
| 2006-07 | Hartford | AHL | 6 | 0 | 2 | 2 | 0 | .... | .... | .... | .... | .... | .... | .... | .... | .... | .... | .... | .... | .... | .... | .... | .... | .... | .... |
| | Charlotte | ECHL | 7 | 1 | 9 | 10 | 4 | .... | .... | .... | .... | .... | .... | .... | .... | .... | .... | .... | .... | .... | .... | .... | .... | .... | .... |
| | Albany River Rats | AHL | 54 | 10 | 18 | 28 | 16 | .... | .... | .... | .... | .... | .... | .... | .... | .... | 5 | 2 | 2 | 4 | 10 | .... | .... | .... | .... |
| 2007-08 | Albany River Rats | AHL | 78 | 14 | 31 | 45 | 52 | .... | .... | .... | .... | .... | .... | .... | .... | .... | 7 | 2 | 1 | 3 | 8 | .... | .... | .... | .... |
| **2008-09** | **Carolina** | **NHL** | **2** | **0** | **1** | **1** | **0** | **0** | **0** | **0** | **0** | **0.0** | **1** | **7** | **57.1** | **8:05** | .... | .... | .... | .... | .... | .... | .... | .... | .... |
| | Albany River Rats | AHL | 77 | 19 | 35 | 54 | 35 | .... | .... | .... | .... | .... | .... | .... | .... | .... | .... | .... | .... | .... | .... | .... | .... | .... | .... |
| | **NHL Totals** | | **2** | **0** | **1** | **1** | **0** | **0** | **0** | **0** | **0** | **0.0** | | **7** | **57.1** | **8:04** | .... | .... | .... | .... | .... | .... | .... | .... | .... |

Traded to **Carolina** by **NY Rangers** with future considerations for Brad Isbister, November 21, 2006. Signed as a free agent by **Lukko Rauma** (Finland), May 15, 2009.

## PETTINGER, Matt

(PEH-tihn-juhr, MAT)

Left wing. Shoots left. 6'1", 205 lbs. Born, Edmonton, Alta., October 22, 1980. Washington's 2nd choice, 43rd overall, in 2000 Entry Draft.

| Season | Club | League | GP | G | A | Pts | PIM | PP | SH | GW | S | % | +/- | TF | F% | Min | GP | G | A | Pts | PIM | PP | SH | GW | Min |
|---|---|---|---|---|---|---|---|---|---|---|---|---|---|---|---|---|---|---|---|---|---|---|---|---|---|
| 1994-95 | Victoria Racquet | Minor-BC | 55 | 52 | 48 | 100 | 41 | .... | .... | .... | .... | .... | .... | .... | .... | .... | .... | .... | .... | .... | .... | .... | .... | .... | .... |
| 1995-96 | Victoria Racquet | Minor-BC | 60 | 80 | 65 | 145 | 45 | .... | .... | .... | .... | .... | .... | .... | .... | .... | .... | .... | .... | .... | .... | .... | .... | .... | .... |
| 1996-97 | Victoria Salsa | BCHL | 49 | 22 | 14 | 36 | 31 | .... | .... | .... | .... | .... | .... | .... | .... | .... | .... | .... | .... | .... | .... | .... | .... | .... | .... |
| 1997-98 | Victoria Salsa | BCHL | 55 | 22 | 20 | 42 | 56 | .... | .... | .... | .... | .... | .... | .... | .... | .... | 7 | 5 | 1 | 6 | 8 | .... | .... | .... | .... |
| 1998-99 | U. of Denver | WCHA | 33 | 6 | 14 | 20 | 44 | .... | .... | .... | .... | .... | .... | .... | .... | .... | .... | .... | .... | .... | .... | .... | .... | .... | .... |
| 99-2000 | U. of Denver | WCHA | 19 | 2 | 6 | 8 | 49 | .... | .... | .... | .... | .... | .... | .... | .... | .... | .... | .... | .... | .... | .... | .... | .... | .... | .... |
| | Calgary Hitmen | WHL | 27 | 14 | 6 | 20 | 41 | .... | .... | .... | .... | .... | .... | .... | .... | .... | 11 | 2 | 6 | 8 | 30 | .... | .... | .... | .... |
| **2000-01** | **Washington** | **NHL** | **10** | **0** | **0** | **0** | **2** | **0** | **0** | **0** | **6** | **0.0** | **–1** | **2** | **50.0** | **7:47** | .... | .... | .... | .... | .... | .... | .... | .... | .... |
| | Portland Pirates | AHL | 64 | 19 | 17 | 36 | 92 | .... | .... | .... | .... | .... | .... | .... | .... | .... | 2 | 0 | 0 | 0 | 4 | .... | .... | .... | .... |
| **2001-02** | **Washington** | **NHL** | **61** | **7** | **3** | **10** | **44** | **1** | **0** | **1** | **73** | **9.6** | **–8** | **5** | **20.0** | **9:39** | .... | .... | .... | .... | .... | .... | .... | .... | .... |
| | Portland Pirates | AHL | 9 | 3 | 3 | 6 | 24 | .... | .... | .... | .... | .... | .... | .... | .... | .... | .... | .... | .... | .... | .... | .... | .... | .... | .... |
| **2002-03** | **Washington** | **NHL** | **1** | **0** | **0** | **0** | **0** | **0** | **0** | **0** | **0** | **0.0** | **0** | **1** | **0.0** | **3:30** | .... | .... | .... | .... | .... | .... | .... | .... | .... |
| | Portland Pirates | AHL | 69 | 14 | 13 | 27 | 72 | .... | .... | .... | .... | .... | .... | .... | .... | .... | 3 | 0 | 2 | 2 | 2 | .... | .... | .... | .... |
| **2003-04** | **Washington** | **NHL** | **71** | **7** | **5** | **12** | **37** | **1** | **0** | **1** | **92** | **7.6** | **–9** | **18** | **44.4** | **11:25** | .... | .... | .... | .... | .... | .... | .... | .... | .... |
| 2004-05 | Ljubljana | Slovenia | 1 | 0 | 1 | 1 | 0 | .... | .... | .... | .... | .... | .... | .... | .... | .... | .... | .... | .... | .... | .... | .... | .... | .... | .... |
| | Ljubljana | Interliga | 7 | 2 | 4 | 6 | 41 | .... | .... | .... | .... | .... | .... | .... | .... | .... | .... | .... | .... | .... | .... | .... | .... | .... | .... |
| **2005-06** | **Washington** | **NHL** | **71** | **20** | **18** | **38** | **39** | **4** | **5** | **2** | **134** | **14.9** | **–2** | **39** | **12.8** | **15:29** | .... | .... | .... | .... | .... | .... | .... | .... | .... |
| **2006-07** | **Washington** | **NHL** | **64** | **16** | **16** | **32** | **22** | **4** | **3** | **2** | **111** | **14.4** | **–13** | **23** | **30.4** | **16:53** | .... | .... | .... | .... | .... | .... | .... | .... | .... |
| **2007-08** | **Washington** | **NHL** | **56** | **2** | **5** | **7** | **25** | **1** | **0** | **1** | **98** | **2.0** | **–11** | **12** | **58.3** | **14:43** | .... | .... | .... | .... | .... | .... | .... | .... | .... |
| | **Vancouver** | **NHL** | **20** | **4** | **2** | **6** | **11** | **0** | **0** | **2** | **29** | **13.8** | **0** | **7** | **57.1** | **13:10** | .... | .... | .... | .... | .... | .... | .... | .... | .... |
| **2008-09** | Manitoba Moose | AHL | 2 | 3 | 0 | 3 | 0 | .... | .... | .... | .... | .... | .... | .... | .... | .... | .... | .... | .... | .... | .... | .... | .... | .... | .... |
| | **Tampa Bay** | **NHL** | **59** | **8** | **7** | **15** | **24** | **2** | **0** | **1** | **82** | **9.8** | **–14** | **18** | **16.7** | **12:19** | .... | .... | .... | .... | .... | .... | .... | .... | .... |
| | **NHL Totals** | | **413** | **64** | **56** | **120** | **204** | **13** | **8** | **10** | **625** | **10.2** | | **125** | **28.8** | **13:15** | .... | .... | .... | .... | .... | .... | .... | .... | .... |

• Left **University of Denver** (WCHA) and signed as a free agent with **Calgary** (WHL), January 10, 2000. Signed as a free agent by **Ljubljana** (Slovenia), December 6, 2004. Traded to **Vancouver** by **Washington** for Matt Cooke, February 26, 2008. Claimed on waivers by **Tampa Bay** from **Vancouver**, October 21, 2008.

## PEVERLEY, Rich

(PEH-vuhr-lee, RIHTCH) **ATL.**

Center. Shoots right. 6', 185 lbs. Born, Guelph, Ont., July 8, 1982.

| Season | Club | League | GP | G | A | Pts | PIM | PP | SH | GW | S | % | +/- | TF | F% | Min | GP | G | A | Pts | PIM | PP | SH | GW | Min |
|---|---|---|---|---|---|---|---|---|---|---|---|---|---|---|---|---|---|---|---|---|---|---|---|---|---|
| 2000-01 | St. Lawrence | ECAC | 29 | 2 | 4 | 6 | 4 | .... | .... | .... | .... | .... | .... | .... | .... | .... | .... | .... | .... | .... | .... | .... | .... | .... | .... |
| 2001-02 | St. Lawrence | ECAC | 34 | 10 | 21 | 31 | 18 | .... | .... | .... | .... | .... | .... | .... | .... | .... | .... | .... | .... | .... | .... | .... | .... | .... | .... |
| 2002-03 | St. Lawrence | ECAC | 34 | 15 | 23 | 38 | 12 | .... | .... | .... | .... | .... | .... | .... | .... | .... | .... | .... | .... | .... | .... | .... | .... | .... | .... |
| 2003-04 | St. Lawrence | ECAC | 41 | 17 | 25 | 42 | 34 | .... | .... | .... | .... | .... | .... | .... | .... | .... | .... | .... | .... | .... | .... | .... | .... | .... | .... |
| 2004-05 | Portland Pirates | AHL | 1 | 0 | 0 | 0 | 0 | .... | .... | .... | .... | .... | .... | .... | .... | .... | .... | .... | .... | .... | .... | .... | .... | .... | .... |
| | South Carolina | ECHL | 69 | 30 | 28 | 58 | 72 | .... | .... | .... | .... | .... | .... | .... | .... | .... | 4 | 2 | 2 | 4 | 6 | .... | .... | .... | .... |
| 2005-06 | Milwaukee | AHL | 65 | 12 | 34 | 46 | 44 | .... | .... | .... | .... | .... | .... | .... | .... | .... | 21 | 2 | 9 | 11 | 18 | .... | .... | .... | .... |
| | Reading Royals | ECHL | 11 | 4 | 11 | 15 | 4 | .... | .... | .... | .... | .... | .... | .... | .... | .... | .... | .... | .... | .... | .... | .... | .... | .... | .... |
| **2006-07** | Milwaukee | AHL | 66 | 30 | 38 | 68 | 62 | .... | .... | .... | .... | .... | .... | .... | .... | .... | 4 | 1 | 2 | 3 | 8 | .... | .... | .... | .... |
| | **Nashville** | **NHL** | **13** | **0** | **1** | **1** | **0** | **0** | **0** | **0** | **9** | **0.0** | **–1** | **45** | **48.9** | **7:31** | .... | .... | .... | .... | .... | .... | .... | .... | .... |
| **2007-08** | **Nashville** | **NHL** | **33** | **5** | **5** | **10** | **8** | **0** | **0** | **2** | **43** | **11.6** | **4** | **132** | **46.2** | **10:20** | **6** | **0** | **2** | **2** | **0** | **0** | **0** | **0** | **8:52** |
| | Milwaukee | AHL | 45 | 14 | 40 | 54 | 50 | .... | .... | .... | .... | .... | .... | .... | .... | .... | 3 | 1 | 0 | 1 | 0 | .... | .... | .... | .... |
| **2008-09** | **Nashville** | **NHL** | **27** | **2** | **7** | **9** | **15** | **0** | **0** | **0** | **42** | **4.8** | **–3** | **130** | **49.2** | **12:08** | .... | .... | .... | .... | .... | .... | .... | .... | .... |
| | **Atlanta** | **NHL** | **39** | **13** | **22** | **35** | **18** | **2** | **1** | **5** | **75** | **17.3** | **16** | **554** | **52.4** | **18:49** | .... | .... | .... | .... | .... | .... | .... | .... | .... |
| | **NHL Totals** | | **112** | **20** | **35** | **55** | **41** | **2** | **1** | **7** | **169** | **11.8** | | **861** | **50.8** | **13:24** | **6** | **0** | **2** | **2** | **0** | **0** | **0** | **0** | **8:52** |

Signed as a free agent by **Nashville**, January 18, 2007. Claimed on waivers by **Atlanta** from **Nashville**, January 10, 2009.

## PHANEUF, Dion

(fah-NOOF, DEE-awn) **CGY.**

Defense. Shoots left. 6'3", 214 lbs. Born, Edmonton, Alta., April 10, 1985. Calgary's 1st choice, 9th overall, in 2003 Entry Draft.

| Season | Club | League | GP | G | A | Pts | PIM | PP | SH | GW | S | % | +/- | TF | F% | Min | GP | G | A | Pts | PIM | PP | SH | GW | Min |
|---|---|---|---|---|---|---|---|---|---|---|---|---|---|---|---|---|---|---|---|---|---|---|---|---|---|
| 2000-01 | Southgate Lions | AMBHL | 35 | 15 | 50 | 65 | 208 | .... | .... | .... | .... | .... | .... | .... | .... | .... | 4 | 3 | 4 | 7 | 15 | .... | .... | .... | .... |
| 2001-02 | Red Deer Rebels | WHL | 67 | 5 | 12 | 17 | 170 | .... | .... | .... | .... | .... | .... | .... | .... | .... | 21 | 0 | 2 | 2 | 14 | .... | .... | .... | .... |
| 2002-03 | Red Deer Rebels | WHL | 71 | 16 | 14 | 30 | 185 | .... | .... | .... | .... | .... | .... | .... | .... | .... | 23 | 7 | 7 | 14 | 34 | .... | .... | .... | .... |
| 2003-04 | Red Deer Rebels | WHL | 62 | 19 | 24 | 43 | 126 | .... | .... | .... | .... | .... | .... | .... | .... | .... | 19 | 2 | 9 | 11 | 30 | .... | .... | .... | .... |
| 2004-05 | Red Deer Rebels | WHL | 55 | 24 | 32 | 56 | 73 | .... | .... | .... | .... | .... | .... | .... | .... | .... | 7 | 1 | 4 | 5 | 12 | .... | .... | .... | .... |
| **2005-06** | **Calgary** | **NHL** | **82** | **20** | **29** | **49** | **93** | **16** | **0** | **7** | **242** | **8.3** | **5** | **0** | **0.0** | **21:44** | **7** | **1** | **0** | **1** | **7** | **1** | **0** | **0** | **18:37** |
| **2006-07** | **Calgary** | **NHL** | **79** | **17** | **33** | **50** | **98** | **13** | **0** | **4** | **230** | **7.4** | **10** | **0** | **0.0** | **25:40** | **6** | **1** | **0** | **1** | **7** | **1** | **0** | **0** | **26:24** |
| **2007-08** | **Calgary** | **NHL** | **82** | **17** | **43** | **60** | **182** | **10** | **1** | **4** | **263** | **6.5** | **12** | **0** | **0.0** | **26:25** | **7** | **3** | **4** | **7** | **4** | **1** | **0** | **0** | **27:07** |
| **2008-09** | **Calgary** | **NHL** | **80** | **11** | **36** | **47** | **100** | **4** | **0** | **4** | **277** | **4.0** | **–11** | **0** | **0.0** | **26:32** | **5** | **0** | **3** | **3** | **4** | **0** | **0** | **0** | **24:48** |
| | **NHL Totals** | | **323** | **65** | **141** | **206** | **473** | **43** | **1** | **19** | **1012** | **6.4** | | **0** | **0.0** | **25:04** | **25** | **5** | **7** | **12** | **22** | **3** | **0** | **0** | **24:06** |

WHL East First All-Star Team (2004, 2005) • WHL Defenseman of the Year (2004, 2005) • Canadian Major Junior First All-Star Team (2004, 2005) • NHL All-Rookie Team (2006) • NHL First All-Star Team (2008)

Played in NHL All-Star Game (2007, 2008)

## PHILLIPS, Chris

(FIHL-ihps, KRIHS) **OTT.**

Defense. Shoots left. 6'3", 217 lbs. Born, Calgary, Alta., March 9, 1978. Ottawa's 1st choice, 1st overall, in 1996 Entry Draft.

| Season | Club | League | GP | G | A | Pts | PIM | PP | SH | GW | S | % | +/- | TF | F% | Min | GP | G | A | Pts | PIM | PP | SH | GW | Min |
|---|---|---|---|---|---|---|---|---|---|---|---|---|---|---|---|---|---|---|---|---|---|---|---|---|---|
| 1993-94 | Fort McMurray | AJHL | 56 | 6 | 16 | 22 | 72 | .... | .... | .... | .... | .... | .... | .... | .... | .... | 10 | 0 | 3 | 3 | 16 | .... | .... | .... | .... |
| 1994-95 | Fort McMurray | AJHL | 48 | 16 | 32 | 48 | 127 | .... | .... | .... | .... | .... | .... | .... | .... | .... | 11 | 4 | 2 | 6 | 10 | .... | .... | .... | .... |
| 1995-96 | Prince Albert | WHL | 61 | 10 | 30 | 40 | 97 | .... | .... | .... | .... | .... | .... | .... | .... | .... | 18 | 2 | 12 | 14 | 30 | .... | .... | .... | .... |
| 1996-97 | Prince Albert | WHL | 32 | 3 | 23 | 26 | 58 | .... | .... | .... | .... | .... | .... | .... | .... | .... | .... | .... | .... | .... | .... | .... | .... | .... | .... |
| | Lethbridge | WHL | 26 | 4 | 18 | 22 | 28 | .... | .... | .... | .... | .... | .... | .... | .... | .... | 19 | 4 | *21 | 25 | 20 | .... | .... | .... | .... |
| **1997-98** | **Ottawa** | **NHL** | **72** | **5** | **11** | **16** | **38** | **2** | **0** | **2** | **107** | **4.7** | **2** | .... | .... | .... | **11** | **0** | **2** | **2** | **2** | **0** | **0** | **0** | .... |
| **1998-99** | **Ottawa** | **NHL** | **34** | **3** | **3** | **6** | **32** | **2** | **0** | **0** | **51** | **5.9** | **–5** | **0** | **0.0** | **18:06** | **3** | **0** | **0** | **0** | **0** | **0** | **0** | **0** | **13:50** |
| **99-2000** | **Ottawa** | **NHL** | **65** | **5** | **14** | **19** | **39** | **0** | **0** | **1** | **96** | **5.2** | **12** | **0** | **0.0** | **16:50** | **6** | **0** | **1** | **1** | **4** | **0** | **0** | **0** | **18:17** |
| **2000-01** | **Ottawa** | **NHL** | **73** | **2** | **12** | **14** | **31** | **2** | **0** | **0** | **77** | **2.6** | **8** | **1** | **0.0** | **21:28** | **1** | **1** | **0** | **1** | **0** | **0** | **0** | **0** | **20:52** |
| **2001-02** | **Ottawa** | **NHL** | **63** | **6** | **16** | **22** | **29** | **1** | **0** | **1** | **103** | **5.8** | **5** | **0** | **0.0** | **19:31** | **12** | **0** | **0** | **0** | **12** | **0** | **0** | **0** | **21:44** |
| **2002-03** | **Ottawa** | **NHL** | **78** | **3** | **16** | **19** | **71** | **2** | **0** | **1** | **97** | **3.1** | **7** | **0** | **0.0** | **20:13** | **18** | **2** | **4** | **6** | **12** | **0** | **0** | **1** | **21:36** |
| **2003-04** | **Ottawa** | **NHL** | **82** | **7** | **16** | **23** | **46** | **0** | **0** | **1** | **93** | **7.5** | **15** | **1** | **100.0** | **20:50** | **7** | **1** | **0** | **1** | **12** | **1** | **0** | **0** | **20:26** |
| 2004-05 | Brynas IF Gavle | Sweden | 27 | 5 | 3 | 8 | 45 | .... | .... | .... | .... | .... | .... | .... | .... | .... | .... | .... | .... | .... | .... | .... | .... | .... | .... |
| | Brynas IF Gavle | Sweden-Q | 9 | 1 | 2 | 3 | 2 | .... | .... | .... | .... | .... | .... | .... | .... | .... | .... | .... | .... | .... | .... | .... | .... | .... | .... |
| **2005-06** | **Ottawa** | **NHL** | **69** | **1** | **18** | **19** | **90** | **0** | **0** | **0** | **79** | **1.3** | **19** | **0** | **0.0** | **20:52** | **9** | **2** | **0** | **2** | **6** | **0** | **0** | **0** | **21:41** |
| **2006-07** | **Ottawa** | **NHL** | **82** | **8** | **18** | **26** | **80** | **0** | **1** | **3** | **94** | **8.5** | **36** | **2** | **0.0** | **22:22** | **20** | **0** | **0** | **0** | **24** | **0** | **0** | **0** | **23:11** |

| | | | Regular Season | | | | | | | | | | | | | | Playoffs | | | | | | | | |
|---|---|---|---|---|---|---|---|---|---|---|---|---|---|---|---|---|---|---|---|---|---|---|---|---|---|
| Season | Club | League | GP | G | A | Pts | PIM | PP | SH | GW | S | % | +/- | TF | F% | Min | GP | G | A | Pts | PIM | PP | SH | GW | Min |
| **2007-08** | **Ottawa** | **NHL** | **81** | **5** | **13** | **18** | **56** | **1** | **0** | **1** | **80** | **6.3** | **15** | **1** | **0.0** | **22:29** | **4** | **0** | **0** | **0** | **4** | **0** | **0** | **0** | **22:00** |
| **2008-09** | **Ottawa** | **NHL** | **82** | **6** | **16** | **22** | **66** | **0** | **1** | **0** | **88** | **6.8** | **–14** | **0** | **0.0** | **21:52** | .... | .... | .... | .... | .... | .... | .... | .... | .... |
| | **NHL Totals** | | **781** | **51** | **153** | **204** | **578** | **10** | **2** | **10** | **965** | **5.3** | | **5** | **20.0** | **20:42** | **91** | **6** | **7** | **13** | **76** | **1** | **0** | **1** | **21:24** |

WHL Rookie of the Year (1996) • WHL East First All-Star Team (1997) • Canadian Major Junior First All-Star Team (1997) • Memorial Cup Tournament All-Star Team (1997)
• Missed majority of 1998-99 season recovering from ankle injury suffered in game vs. Buffalo, December 30, 1998. Signed as a free agent by **Gavle** (Sweden), November 2, 2004.

## PICARD, Alexandre

(pee-KAR, al-ehx-AHN-druh) **OTT.**

Defense. Shoots left. 6'2", 210 lbs. Born, Gatineau, Que., July 5, 1985. Philadelphia's 5th choice, 85th overall, in 2003 Entry Draft.

| Season | Club | League | GP | G | A | Pts | PIM | PP | SH | GW | S | % | +/- | TF | F% | Min | GP | G | A | Pts | PIM | PP | SH | GW | Min |
|---|---|---|---|---|---|---|---|---|---|---|---|---|---|---|---|---|---|---|---|---|---|---|---|---|---|
| 2000-01 | Gatineau | QAAA | 42 | 6 | 15 | 21 | 38 | .... | .... | .... | .... | .... | .... | .... | .... | .... | 11 | 0 | 1 | 1 | 8 | .... | .... | .... | .... |
| 2001-02 | Halifax | QMJHL | 59 | 2 | 12 | 14 | 28 | .... | .... | .... | .... | .... | .... | .... | .... | .... | 13 | 2 | 3 | 5 | 6 | .... | .... | .... | .... |
| 2002-03 | Halifax | QMJHL | 71 | 4 | 30 | 34 | 64 | .... | .... | .... | .... | .... | .... | .... | .... | .... | 25 | 1 | 5 | 6 | 14 | .... | .... | .... | .... |
| 2003-04 | Cape Breton | QMJHL | 57 | 10 | 26 | 36 | 44 | .... | .... | .... | .... | .... | .... | .... | .... | .... | 5 | 0 | 0 | 0 | 0 | .... | .... | .... | .... |
| 2004-05 | Halifax | QMJHL | 68 | 15 | 23 | 38 | 46 | .... | .... | .... | .... | .... | .... | .... | .... | .... | 13 | 1 | 5 | 6 | 14 | .... | .... | .... | .... |
| | Philadelphia | AHL | .... | .... | .... | .... | .... | .... | .... | .... | .... | .... | .... | .... | .... | .... | 2 | 0 | 0 | 0 | 0 | .... | .... | .... | .... |
| **2005-06** | **Philadelphia** | **NHL** | **6** | **0** | **0** | **0** | **4** | **0** | **0** | **0** | **9** | **0.0** | **–2** | **0** | **0.0** | **9:33** | .... | .... | .... | .... | .... | .... | .... | .... | .... |
| | Philadelphia | AHL | 75 | 7 | 26 | 33 | 82 | .... | .... | .... | .... | .... | .... | .... | .... | .... | .... | .... | .... | .... | .... | .... | .... | .... | .... |
| **2006-07** | **Philadelphia** | **NHL** | **62** | **3** | **19** | **22** | **17** | **1** | **0** | **0** | **56** | **5.4** | **–19** | **0** | **0.0** | **18:29** | .... | .... | .... | .... | .... | .... | .... | .... | .... |
| | Philadelphia | AHL | 6 | 1 | 2 | 3 | 2 | .... | .... | .... | .... | .... | .... | .... | .... | .... | .... | .... | .... | .... | .... | .... | .... | .... | .... |
| **2007-08** | **Philadelphia** | **NHL** | **4** | **0** | **0** | **0** | **2** | **0** | **0** | **0** | **3** | **0.0** | **–3** | **0** | **0.0** | **13:02** | .... | .... | .... | .... | .... | .... | .... | .... | .... |
| | Philadelphia | AHL | 53 | 8 | 30 | 38 | 31 | .... | .... | .... | .... | .... | .... | .... | .... | .... | .... | .... | .... | .... | .... | .... | .... | .... | .... |
| | **Tampa Bay** | **NHL** | **20** | **3** | **3** | **6** | **8** | **1** | **0** | **1** | **21** | **14.3** | **–9** | **0** | **0.0** | **21:54** | .... | .... | .... | .... | .... | .... | .... | .... | .... |
| | Norfolk Admirals | AHL | 1 | 0 | 0 | 0 | 0 | .... | .... | .... | .... | .... | .... | .... | .... | .... | .... | .... | .... | .... | .... | .... | .... | .... | .... |
| **2008-09** | **Ottawa** | **NHL** | **47** | **6** | **8** | **14** | **8** | **6** | **0** | **1** | **72** | **8.3** | **–2** | **0** | **0.0** | **18:52** | .... | .... | .... | .... | .... | .... | .... | .... | .... |
| | **NHL Totals** | | **139** | **12** | **30** | **42** | **39** | **8** | **0** | **2** | **161** | **7.5** | | **0** | **0.0** | **18:34** | .... | .... | .... | .... | .... | .... | .... | .... | .... |

QMJHL Second All-Star Team (2005)

Traded to **Tampa Bay** by **Philadelphia** with Philadelphia's 2nd round choice (Richard Panik) in 2009 Entry Draft for Vaclav Prospal, February 25, 2008. Traded to **Ottawa** by **Tampa Bay** with Filip Kuba and San Jose's 1st round choice (previously acquired, later traded to Columbus, later readed to NY Islanders, later traded to Anahaim - Anaheim selected Kyle Palmieri) in 2009 Entry Draft for Andrej Meszaros, August 29, 2008.

## PICARD, Alexandre

(pee-KARD, al-ehx-AHN-druh) **CBJ**

Left wing. Shoots left. 6'2", 206 lbs. Born, Les Saules, Que., October 9, 1985. Columbus' 1st choice, 8th overall, in 2004 Entry Draft.

| Season | Club | League | GP | G | A | Pts | PIM | PP | SH | GW | S | % | +/- | TF | F% | Min | GP | G | A | Pts | PIM | PP | SH | GW | Min |
|---|---|---|---|---|---|---|---|---|---|---|---|---|---|---|---|---|---|---|---|---|---|---|---|---|---|
| 2000-01 | St-Francois | QAAA | 5 | 1 | 1 | 2 | 0 | .... | .... | .... | .... | .... | .... | .... | .... | .... | .... | .... | .... | .... | .... | .... | .... | .... | .... |
| 2001-02 | St-Francois | QAAA | 41 | 21 | 30 | 51 | 48 | .... | .... | .... | .... | .... | .... | .... | .... | .... | 8 | 2 | 7 | 9 | 8 | .... | .... | .... | .... |
| | Sherbrooke | QMJHL | 6 | 0 | 3 | 3 | 0 | .... | .... | .... | .... | .... | .... | .... | .... | .... | .... | .... | .... | .... | .... | .... | .... | .... | .... |
| 2002-03 | Sherbrooke | QMJHL | 66 | 14 | 15 | 29 | 41 | .... | .... | .... | .... | .... | .... | .... | .... | .... | 12 | 4 | 0 | 4 | 10 | .... | .... | .... | .... |
| 2003-04 | Lewiston | QMJHL | 69 | 39 | 41 | 80 | 88 | .... | .... | .... | .... | .... | .... | .... | .... | .... | 7 | 7 | 4 | 11 | 6 | .... | .... | .... | .... |
| 2004-05 | Lewiston | QMJHL | 65 | 40 | 45 | 85 | 160 | .... | .... | .... | .... | .... | .... | .... | .... | .... | 8 | 5 | 2 | 7 | 18 | .... | .... | .... | .... |
| **2005-06** | **Columbus** | **NHL** | **17** | **0** | **0** | **0** | **14** | **0** | **0** | **0** | **10** | **0.0** | **–2** | **3** | **33.3** | **9:09** | .... | .... | .... | .... | .... | .... | .... | .... | .... |
| | Syracuse Crunch | AHL | 45 | 15 | 15 | 30 | 54 | .... | .... | .... | .... | .... | .... | .... | .... | .... | 6 | 1 | 0 | 1 | 19 | .... | .... | .... | .... |
| **2006-07** | **Columbus** | **NHL** | **23** | **0** | **1** | **1** | **6** | **0** | **0** | **0** | **20** | **0.0** | **–3** | **0** | **0.0** | **7:49** | .... | .... | .... | .... | .... | .... | .... | .... | .... |
| | Syracuse Crunch | AHL | 48 | 11 | 18 | 29 | 73 | .... | .... | .... | .... | .... | .... | .... | .... | .... | .... | .... | .... | .... | .... | .... | .... | .... | .... |
| **2007-08** | **Columbus** | **NHL** | **3** | **0** | **0** | **0** | **2** | **0** | **0** | **0** | **1** | **0.0** | **0** | **0** | **0.0** | **6:46** | .... | .... | .... | .... | .... | .... | .... | .... | .... |
| | Syracuse Crunch | AHL | 50 | 7 | 13 | 20 | 116 | .... | .... | .... | .... | .... | .... | .... | .... | .... | 13 | 2 | 1 | 3 | 14 | .... | .... | .... | .... |
| **2008-09** | **Columbus** | **NHL** | **15** | **0** | **1** | **1** | **26** | **0** | **0** | **0** | **10** | **0.0** | **–1** | **0** | **0.0** | **6:53** | .... | .... | .... | .... | .... | .... | .... | .... | .... |
| | Syracuse Crunch | AHL | 49 | 22 | 10 | 32 | 107 | .... | .... | .... | .... | .... | .... | .... | .... | .... | .... | .... | .... | .... | .... | .... | .... | .... | .... |
| | **NHL Totals** | | **58** | **0** | **2** | **2** | **48** | **0** | **0** | **0** | **41** | **0.0** | | **3** | **33.3** | **7:55** | .... | .... | .... | .... | .... | .... | .... | .... | .... |

QMJHL Second All-Star Team (2004)

## PIETRANGELO, Alex

(puh-TRAN-geh-loh, AL-ehx) **ST.L.**

Defense. Shoots right. 6'3", 204 lbs. Born, King City, Ont., January 18, 1990. St. Louis' 1st choice, 4th overall, in 2008 Entry Draft.

| Season | Club | League | GP | G | A | Pts | PIM | PP | SH | GW | S | % | +/- | TF | F% | Min | GP | G | A | Pts | PIM | PP | SH | GW | Min |
|---|---|---|---|---|---|---|---|---|---|---|---|---|---|---|---|---|---|---|---|---|---|---|---|---|---|
| 2005-06 | Tor. Jr. Canadiens | GTHL | 44 | 13 | 31 | 44 | 33 | .... | .... | .... | .... | .... | .... | .... | .... | .... | .... | .... | .... | .... | .... | .... | .... | .... | .... |
| 2006-07 | Mississauga | OHL | 59 | 7 | 45 | 52 | 45 | .... | .... | .... | .... | .... | .... | .... | .... | .... | 4 | 0 | 0 | 0 | 8 | .... | .... | .... | .... |
| 2007-08 | Niagara Ice Dogs | OHL | 60 | 13 | 40 | 53 | 94 | .... | .... | .... | .... | .... | .... | .... | .... | .... | 6 | 5 | 4 | 9 | 4 | .... | .... | .... | .... |
| **2008-09** | **St. Louis** | **NHL** | **8** | **0** | **1** | **1** | **2** | **0** | **0** | **0** | **7** | **0.0** | **0** | **0** | **0.0** | **16:31** | .... | .... | .... | .... | .... | .... | .... | .... | .... |
| | Niagara Ice Dogs | OHL | 36 | 8 | 21 | 29 | 32 | .... | .... | .... | .... | .... | .... | .... | .... | .... | 12 | 1 | 5 | 6 | 20 | .... | .... | .... | .... |
| | Peoria Rivermen | AHL | 1 | 0 | 0 | 0 | 4 | .... | .... | .... | .... | .... | .... | .... | .... | .... | 7 | 0 | 3 | 3 | 2 | .... | .... | .... | .... |
| | **NHL Totals** | | **8** | **0** | **1** | **1** | **2** | **0** | **0** | **0** | **7** | **0.0** | | **0** | **0.0** | **16:31** | .... | .... | .... | .... | .... | .... | .... | .... | .... |

## PIHLMAN, Tuomas

(PIHL-mahn, TAWH-muhs) **N.J.**

Left wing. Shoots left. 6'2", 215 lbs. Born, Espoo, Finland, November 13, 1982. New Jersey's 3rd choice, 48th overall, in 2001 Entry Draft.

| Season | Club | League | GP | G | A | Pts | PIM | PP | SH | GW | S | % | +/- | TF | F% | Min | GP | G | A | Pts | PIM | PP | SH | GW | Min |
|---|---|---|---|---|---|---|---|---|---|---|---|---|---|---|---|---|---|---|---|---|---|---|---|---|---|
| 1997-98 | JYP Jyvaskyla U18 | Fin-U18 | 30 | 2 | 5 | 7 | 18 | .... | .... | .... | .... | .... | .... | .... | .... | .... | 4 | 1 | 3 | 4 | 6 | .... | .... | .... | .... |
| 1998-99 | JYP Jyvaskyla U18 | Fin-U18 | 35 | 21 | 20 | 41 | 64 | .... | .... | .... | .... | .... | .... | .... | .... | .... | 6 | 1 | 1 | 2 | 12 | .... | .... | .... | .... |
| 99-2000 | JYP Jyvaskyla U18 | Fin-U18 | 3 | 3 | 0 | 3 | 0 | .... | .... | .... | .... | .... | .... | .... | .... | .... | .... | .... | .... | .... | .... | .... | .... | .... | .... |
| | JYP Jyvaskyla Jr. | Fin-Jr. | 20 | 4 | 4 | 8 | 54 | .... | .... | .... | .... | .... | .... | .... | .... | .... | 4 | 0 | 0 | 0 | 8 | .... | .... | .... | .... |
| | JYP Jyvaskyla | Finland | 17 | 0 | 0 | 0 | 18 | .... | .... | .... | .... | .... | .... | .... | .... | .... | .... | .... | .... | .... | .... | .... | .... | .... | .... |
| 2000-01 | JYP Jyvaskyla Jr. | Fin-Jr. | 1 | 1 | 0 | 1 | 2 | .... | .... | .... | .... | .... | .... | .... | .... | .... | 6 | 2 | 4 | 6 | 4 | .... | .... | .... | .... |
| | JYP Jyvaskyla | Finland | 47 | 3 | 6 | 9 | 59 | .... | .... | .... | .... | .... | .... | .... | .... | .... | .... | .... | .... | .... | .... | .... | .... | .... | .... |
| 2001-02 | JYP Jyvaskyla Jr. | Fin-Jr. | 3 | 1 | 1 | 2 | 4 | .... | .... | .... | .... | .... | .... | .... | .... | .... | .... | .... | .... | .... | .... | .... | .... | .... | .... |
| | JYP Jyvaskyla | Finland | 44 | 9 | 2 | 11 | 95 | .... | .... | .... | .... | .... | .... | .... | .... | .... | .... | .... | .... | .... | .... | .... | .... | .... | .... |
| 2002-03 | JYP Jyvaskyla | Finland | 53 | 19 | 15 | 34 | 58 | .... | .... | .... | .... | .... | .... | .... | .... | .... | 1 | 0 | 0 | 0 | 0 | .... | .... | .... | .... |
| **2003-04** | **New Jersey** | **NHL** | **2** | **0** | **0** | **0** | **2** | **0** | **0** | **0** | **1** | **0.0** | **0** | **0** | **0.0** | **6:56** | .... | .... | .... | .... | .... | .... | .... | .... | .... |
| | Albany River Rats | AHL | 73 | 10 | 19 | 29 | 59 | .... | .... | .... | .... | .... | .... | .... | .... | .... | .... | .... | .... | .... | .... | .... | .... | .... | .... |
| 2004-05 | Albany River Rats | AHL | 68 | 9 | 13 | 22 | 48 | .... | .... | .... | .... | .... | .... | .... | .... | .... | .... | .... | .... | .... | .... | .... | .... | .... | .... |
| **2005-06** | **New Jersey** | **NHL** | **11** | **1** | **1** | **2** | **10** | **0** | **0** | **0** | **14** | **7.1** | **–1** | **22** | **40.9** | **10:04** | .... | .... | .... | .... | .... | .... | .... | .... | .... |
| | Albany River Rats | AHL | 63 | 12 | 15 | 27 | 64 | .... | .... | .... | .... | .... | .... | .... | .... | .... | .... | .... | .... | .... | .... | .... | .... | .... | .... |
| **2006-07** | **New Jersey** | **NHL** | **2** | **0** | **0** | **0** | **0** | **0** | **0** | **0** | **0** | **0.0** | **0** | **0** | **0.0** | **6:32** | .... | .... | .... | .... | .... | .... | .... | .... | .... |
| | Lowell Devils | AHL | 67 | 8 | 18 | 26 | 34 | .... | .... | .... | .... | .... | .... | .... | .... | .... | .... | .... | .... | .... | .... | .... | .... | .... | .... |
| 2007-08 | JYP Jyvaskyla | Finland | 56 | 20 | 29 | 49 | 58 | .... | .... | .... | .... | .... | .... | .... | .... | .... | 6 | 4 | 0 | 4 | 10 | .... | .... | .... | .... |
| 2008-09 | JYP Jyvaskyla | Finland | 58 | 24 | 32 | 56 | 54 | .... | .... | .... | .... | .... | .... | .... | .... | .... | 15 | 6 | 5 | 11 | 16 | .... | .... | .... | .... |
| | **NHL Totals** | | **15** | **1** | **1** | **2** | **12** | **0** | **0** | **0** | **15** | **6.7** | | **22** | **40.9** | **9:11** | .... | .... | .... | .... | .... | .... | .... | .... | .... |

## PIHLSTROM, Antti

(PIHL-stuhm, AN-tee) **NSH.**

Left wing. Shoots left. 5'11", 190 lbs. Born, Vanntaa, Finland, October 22, 1984.

| Season | Club | League | GP | G | A | Pts | PIM | PP | SH | GW | S | % | +/- | TF | F% | Min | GP | G | A | Pts | PIM | PP | SH | GW | Min |
|---|---|---|---|---|---|---|---|---|---|---|---|---|---|---|---|---|---|---|---|---|---|---|---|---|---|
| 2001-02 | Jokerit U18 | Fin-U18 | 26 | 15 | 14 | 29 | 41 | .... | .... | .... | .... | .... | .... | .... | .... | .... | 8 | 0 | 5 | 5 | 18 | .... | .... | .... | .... |
| | Jokerit Helsinki Jr. | Fin-Jr. | 1 | 0 | 0 | 0 | 0 | .... | .... | .... | .... | .... | .... | .... | .... | .... | .... | .... | .... | .... | .... | .... | .... | .... | .... |
| 2002-03 | Blues Espoo Jr. | Fin-Jr. | 36 | 10 | 16 | 26 | 38 | .... | .... | .... | .... | .... | .... | .... | .... | .... | 10 | 1 | 1 | 2 | 8 | .... | .... | .... | .... |
| 2003-04 | Blues Espoo Jr. | Fin-Jr. | 23 | 9 | 19 | 28 | 42 | .... | .... | .... | .... | .... | .... | .... | .... | .... | 1 | 0 | 2 | 2 | 0 | .... | .... | .... | .... |
| | Suomi U20 | Finland-2 | 4 | 0 | 1 | 1 | 2 | .... | .... | .... | .... | .... | .... | .... | .... | .... | .... | .... | .... | .... | .... | .... | .... | .... | .... |
| | Blues Espoo | Finland | 49 | 1 | 3 | 4 | 18 | .... | .... | .... | .... | .... | .... | .... | .... | .... | 9 | 0 | 0 | 0 | 0 | .... | .... | .... | .... |
| 2004-05 | Blues Espoo | Finland | 53 | 4 | 3 | 7 | 30 | .... | .... | .... | .... | .... | .... | .... | .... | .... | .... | .... | .... | .... | .... | .... | .... | .... | .... |
| | Blues Espoo Jr. | Fin-Jr. | 11 | 7 | 3 | 10 | 36 | .... | .... | .... | .... | .... | .... | .... | .... | .... | 7 | 0 | 2 | 2 | 26 | .... | .... | .... | .... |
| 2005-06 | SaiPa | Finland | 54 | 10 | 11 | 21 | 60 | .... | .... | .... | .... | .... | .... | .... | .... | .... | 8 | 1 | 0 | 1 | 2 | .... | .... | .... | .... |
| 2006-07 | HPK Hameenlinna | Finland | 56 | 16 | 23 | 39 | 63 | .... | .... | .... | .... | .... | .... | .... | .... | .... | 9 | 3 | 5 | 8 | 4 | .... | .... | .... | .... |
| **2007-08** | **Nashville** | **NHL** | **1** | **0** | **0** | **0** | **0** | **0** | **0** | **0** | **1** | **0.0** | **–1** | **0** | **0.0** | **9:08** | .... | .... | .... | .... | .... | .... | .... | .... | .... |
| | Milwaukee | AHL | 78 | 27 | 18 | 45 | 62 | .... | .... | .... | .... | .... | .... | .... | .... | .... | 6 | 1 | 0 | 1 | 8 | .... | .... | .... | .... |
| **2008-09** | **Nashville** | **NHL** | **53** | **2** | **5** | **7** | **10** | **1** | **0** | **0** | **88** | **2.3** | **–1** | **1** | **0.0** | **11:27** | .... | .... | .... | .... | .... | .... | .... | .... | .... |
| | Milwaukee | AHL | 15 | 8 | 4 | 12 | 10 | .... | .... | .... | .... | .... | .... | .... | .... | .... | .... | .... | .... | .... | .... | .... | .... | .... | .... |
| | **NHL Totals** | | **54** | **2** | **5** | **7** | **10** | **1** | **0** | **0** | **89** | **2.2** | | **1** | **0.0** | **11:24** | .... | .... | .... | .... | .... | .... | .... | .... | .... |

Signed as a free agent by **Nashville**, June 1, 2007.

## PINEAULT, Adam

(PEE-noh, A-duhm)

Right wing. Shoots right. 6'1", 211 lbs. Born, Holyoke, MA, May 23, 1986. Columbus' 2nd choice, 46th overall, in 2004 Entry Draft.

| | | | Regular Season | | | | | | | | | | | | | | Playoffs | | | | | | | | |
|---|---|---|---|---|---|---|---|---|---|---|---|---|---|---|---|---|---|---|---|---|---|---|---|---|---|
| Season | Club | League | GP | G | A | Pts | PIM | PP | SH | GW | S | % | +/- | TF | F% | Min | GP | G | A | Pts | PIM | PP | SH | GW | Min |
| 2000-01 | Bos. Jr. Bruins | EJHL | 57 | 30 | 35 | 65 | 56 | .... | .... | .... | .... | .... | .... | .... | .... | .... | .... | .... | .... | .... | .... | .... | .... | .... | .... |
| 2001-02 | USNTDP | U-17 | 20 | 5 | 4 | 9 | 14 | .... | .... | .... | .... | .... | .... | .... | .... | .... | .... | .... | .... | .... | .... | .... | .... | .... | .... |
| | USNTDP | NAHL | 38 | 11 | 4 | 15 | 11 | .... | .... | .... | .... | .... | .... | .... | .... | .... | .... | .... | .... | .... | .... | .... | .... | .... | .... |
| 2002-03 | USNTDP | U-17 | 43 | 13 | 15 | 28 | 76 | .... | .... | .... | .... | .... | .... | .... | .... | .... | .... | .... | .... | .... | .... | .... | .... | .... | .... |
| | USNTDP | U-18 | 4 | 4 | 3 | 7 | 6 | .... | .... | .... | .... | .... | .... | .... | .... | .... | .... | .... | .... | .... | .... | .... | .... | .... | .... |
| | USNTDP | NAHL | 9 | 5 | 4 | 9 | 13 | .... | .... | .... | .... | .... | .... | .... | .... | .... | .... | .... | .... | .... | .... | .... | .... | .... | .... |
| 2003-04 | Boston College | H-East | 30 | 4 | 4 | 8 | 32 | .... | .... | .... | .... | .... | .... | .... | .... | .... | .... | .... | .... | .... | .... | .... | .... | .... | .... |
| 2004-05 | Moncton Wildcats | QMJHL | 61 | 26 | 20 | 46 | 64 | .... | .... | .... | .... | .... | .... | .... | .... | .... | 12 | 2 | 6 | 8 | 18 | .... | .... | .... | .... |
| 2005-06 | Moncton Wildcats | QMJHL | 55 | 29 | 30 | 59 | 94 | .... | .... | .... | .... | .... | .... | .... | .... | .... | 21 | 14 | 8 | 22 | 25 | .... | .... | .... | .... |
| 2006-07 | Syracuse Crunch | AHL | 57 | 12 | 16 | 28 | 66 | .... | .... | .... | .... | .... | .... | .... | .... | .... | .... | .... | .... | .... | .... | .... | .... | .... | .... |
| **2007-08** | **Columbus** | **NHL** | **3** | **0** | **0** | **0** | **0** | **0** | **0** | **0** | **5** | **0.0** | **-2** | **1** | **0.0** | **11:03** | .... | .... | .... | .... | .... | .... | .... | .... | .... |
| | Syracuse Crunch | AHL | 74 | 21 | 27 | 48 | 64 | .... | .... | .... | .... | .... | .... | .... | .... | .... | 8 | 0 | 2 | 2 | 2 | .... | .... | .... | .... |
| 2008-09 | Syracuse Crunch | AHL | 29 | 5 | 7 | 12 | 36 | .... | .... | .... | .... | .... | .... | .... | .... | .... | .... | .... | .... | .... | .... | .... | .... | .... | .... |
| | Rockford IceHogs | AHL | 41 | 5 | 9 | 14 | 16 | .... | .... | .... | .... | .... | .... | .... | .... | .... | 4 | 0 | 0 | 0 | 2 | .... | .... | .... | .... |
| | **NHL Totals** | | **3** | **0** | **0** | **0** | **0** | **0** | **0** | **0** | **5** | **0.0** | | **1** | **0.0** | **11:03** | .... | .... | .... | .... | .... | .... | .... | .... | .... |

Memorial Cup Tournament All-Star Team (2006)

Traded to **Chicago** by **Columbus** for Michael Blunden, January 10, 2009.

## PISANI, Fernando

(pih-ZAN-ee, FUHR-nan-DOH) **EDM.**

Right wing. Shoots left. 6'1", 205 lbs. Born, Edmonton, Alta., December 27, 1976. Edmonton's 9th choice, 195th overall, in 1996 Entry Draft.

| | | | Regular Season | | | | | | | | | | | | | | Playoffs | | | | | | | | |
|---|---|---|---|---|---|---|---|---|---|---|---|---|---|---|---|---|---|---|---|---|---|---|---|---|---|
| Season | Club | League | GP | G | A | Pts | PIM | PP | SH | GW | S | % | +/- | TF | F% | Min | GP | G | A | Pts | PIM | PP | SH | GW | Min |
| 1993-94 | St. Albert Saints | AJHL | 50 | 6 | 21 | 27 | 24 | .... | .... | .... | .... | .... | .... | .... | .... | .... | .... | .... | .... | .... | .... | .... | .... | .... | .... |
| 1994-95 | Bonnyville | AJHL | 16 | 4 | 34 | 37 | 97 | .... | .... | .... | .... | .... | .... | .... | .... | .... | .... | .... | .... | .... | .... | .... | .... | .... | .... |
| | St. Albert Saints | AJHL | 40 | 26 | 21 | 47 | 16 | .... | .... | .... | .... | .... | .... | .... | .... | .... | .... | .... | .... | .... | .... | .... | .... | .... | .... |
| 1995-96 | St. Albert Saints | AJHL | 58 | 40 | 63 | 103 | 134 | .... | .... | .... | .... | .... | .... | .... | .... | .... | 18 | 7 | 22 | 29 | 28 | .... | .... | .... | .... |
| 1996-97 | Providence | H-East | 35 | 12 | 18 | 30 | 36 | .... | .... | .... | .... | .... | .... | .... | .... | .... | .... | .... | .... | .... | .... | .... | .... | .... | .... |
| 1997-98 | Providence | H-East | 36 | 16 | 18 | 34 | 20 | .... | .... | .... | .... | .... | .... | .... | .... | .... | .... | .... | .... | .... | .... | .... | .... | .... | .... |
| 1998-99 | Providence | H-East | 38 | 14 | 37 | 51 | 42 | .... | .... | .... | .... | .... | .... | .... | .... | .... | .... | .... | .... | .... | .... | .... | .... | .... | .... |
| 99-2000 | Providence | H-East | 38 | 14 | 24 | 38 | 56 | .... | .... | .... | .... | .... | .... | .... | .... | .... | .... | .... | .... | .... | .... | .... | .... | .... | .... |
| 2000-01 | Hamilton | AHL | 52 | 12 | 13 | 25 | 28 | .... | .... | .... | .... | .... | .... | .... | .... | .... | .... | .... | .... | .... | .... | .... | .... | .... | .... |
| 2001-02 | Hamilton | AHL | 79 | 26 | 34 | 60 | 60 | .... | .... | .... | .... | .... | .... | .... | .... | .... | 15 | 4 | 6 | 10 | 4 | .... | .... | .... | .... |
| **2002-03** | **Edmonton** | **NHL** | **35** | **8** | **5** | **13** | **10** | **0** | **1** | **0** | **32** | **25.0** | **9** | **1** | **100.0** | **10:43** | **6** | **1** | **0** | **1** | **2** | **0** | **0** | **0** | **13:48** |
| | Hamilton | AHL | 41 | 17 | 15 | 32 | 24 | .... | .... | .... | .... | .... | .... | .... | .... | .... | .... | .... | .... | .... | .... | .... | .... | .... | .... |
| **2003-04** | **Edmonton** | **NHL** | **76** | **16** | **14** | **30** | **46** | **4** | **1** | **1** | **99** | **16.2** | **14** | **10** | **20.0** | **12:46** | .... | .... | .... | .... | .... | .... | .... | .... | .... |
| 2004-05 | Langnau | Swiss | 7 | 1 | 3 | 4 | 0 | .... | .... | .... | .... | .... | .... | .... | .... | .... | .... | .... | .... | .... | .... | .... | .... | .... | .... |
| | Asiago | Italy | 12 | 1 | 5 | 6 | 6 | .... | .... | .... | .... | .... | .... | .... | .... | .... | 9 | 4 | 6 | 10 | 0 | .... | .... | .... | .... |
| **2005-06** | **Edmonton** | **NHL** | **80** | **18** | **19** | **37** | **42** | **4** | **1** | **2** | **131** | **13.7** | **5** | **35** | **22.9** | **13:51** | **24** | ***14** | **4** | **18** | **10** | **3** | **1** | **5** | **17:12** |
| **2006-07** | **Edmonton** | **NHL** | **77** | **14** | **14** | **28** | **40** | **2** | **1** | **0** | **142** | **9.9** | **-1** | **20** | **40.0** | **16:54** | .... | .... | .... | .... | .... | .... | .... | .... | .... |
| **2007-08** | **Edmonton** | **NHL** | **56** | **13** | **9** | **22** | **28** | **4** | **0** | **3** | **96** | **13.5** | **-5** | **7** | **28.6** | **16:32** | .... | .... | .... | .... | .... | .... | .... | .... | .... |
| **2008-09** | **Edmonton** | **NHL** | **38** | **7** | **8** | **15** | **14** | **0** | **0** | **0** | **72** | **9.7** | **-1** | **123** | **40.7** | **15:19** | .... | .... | .... | .... | .... | .... | .... | .... | .... |
| | **NHL Totals** | | **362** | **76** | **69** | **145** | **180** | **14** | **4** | **6** | **572** | **13.3** | | **196** | **36.2** | **14:32** | **30** | **15** | **4** | **19** | **12** | **3** | **1** | **5** | **16:31** |

Signed as a free agent by **Langnau** (Swiss), October 24, 2004. Signed as a free agent by **Asiago** (Italy), December 23, 2004. • Missed majority of 2008-09 season recovering from broken ankle suffered in game at Detroit, November 17, 2008.

## PISKULA, Joe

(Pihs-KOO-luh, JOH) **L.A.**

Defense. Shoots left. 6'3", 212 lbs. Born, Antigo, WI, July 5, 1984.

| | | | Regular Season | | | | | | | | | | | | | | Playoffs | | | | | | | | |
|---|---|---|---|---|---|---|---|---|---|---|---|---|---|---|---|---|---|---|---|---|---|---|---|---|---|
| Season | Club | League | GP | G | A | Pts | PIM | PP | SH | GW | S | % | +/- | TF | F% | Min | GP | G | A | Pts | PIM | PP | SH | GW | Min |
| 2002-03 | Chicago Steel | USHL | 13 | 0 | 0 | 0 | 18 | .... | .... | .... | .... | .... | .... | .... | .... | .... | .... | .... | .... | .... | .... | .... | .... | .... | .... |
| | Des Moines | USHL | 32 | 2 | 6 | 8 | 18 | .... | .... | .... | .... | .... | .... | .... | .... | .... | 4 | 0 | 1 | 1 | 4 | .... | .... | .... | .... |
| 2003-04 | Des Moines | USHL | 58 | 2 | 4 | 6 | 68 | .... | .... | .... | .... | .... | .... | .... | .... | .... | 3 | 0 | 1 | 1 | 0 | .... | .... | .... | .... |
| 2004-05 | U. of Wisconsin | WCHA | 40 | 0 | 6 | 6 | 24 | .... | .... | .... | .... | .... | .... | .... | .... | .... | .... | .... | .... | .... | .... | .... | .... | .... | .... |
| 2005-06 | U. of Wisconsin | WCHA | 34 | 2 | 9 | 11 | 22 | .... | .... | .... | .... | .... | .... | .... | .... | .... | .... | .... | .... | .... | .... | .... | .... | .... | .... |
| **2006-07** | U. of Wisconsin | WCHA | 38 | 1 | 4 | 5 | 34 | .... | .... | .... | .... | .... | .... | .... | .... | .... | .... | .... | .... | .... | .... | .... | .... | .... | .... |
| | **Los Angeles** | **NHL** | **5** | **0** | **0** | **0** | **6** | **0** | **0** | **0** | **4** | **0.0** | **-3** | **0** | **0.0** | **9:59** | .... | .... | .... | .... | .... | .... | .... | .... | .... |
| 2007-08 | Manchester | AHL | 55 | 0 | 7 | 7 | 57 | .... | .... | .... | .... | .... | .... | .... | .... | .... | 4 | 0 | 0 | 0 | 4 | .... | .... | .... | .... |
| 2008-09 | Manchester | AHL | 67 | 0 | 12 | 12 | 40 | .... | .... | .... | .... | .... | .... | .... | .... | .... | .... | .... | .... | .... | .... | .... | .... | .... | .... |
| | **NHL Totals** | | **5** | **0** | **0** | **0** | **6** | **0** | **0** | **0** | **4** | **0.0** | | **0** | **0.0** | **9:59** | .... | .... | .... | .... | .... | .... | .... | .... | .... |

Signed as a free agent by **Los Angeles**, March 21, 2007.

## PITKANEN, Joni

(PIHT-ka-nuhn, YOH-nee) **CAR.**

Defense. Shoots left. 6'3", 210 lbs. Born, Oulu, Finland, September 19, 1983. Philadelphia's 1st choice, 4th overall, in 2002 Entry Draft.

| | | | Regular Season | | | | | | | | | | | | | | Playoffs | | | | | | | | |
|---|---|---|---|---|---|---|---|---|---|---|---|---|---|---|---|---|---|---|---|---|---|---|---|---|---|
| Season | Club | League | GP | G | A | Pts | PIM | PP | SH | GW | S | % | +/- | TF | F% | Min | GP | G | A | Pts | PIM | PP | SH | GW | Min |
| 1998-99 | Karpat Oulu U18 | Fin-U18 | 30 | 1 | 5 | 6 | 12 | .... | .... | .... | .... | .... | .... | .... | .... | .... | .... | .... | .... | .... | .... | .... | .... | .... | .... |
| 99-2000 | Karpat Oulu U18 | Fin-U18 | 36 | 12 | 14 | 26 | 26 | .... | .... | .... | .... | .... | .... | .... | .... | .... | 6 | 1 | 4 | 5 | 2 | .... | .... | .... | .... |
| | Karpat Oulu Jr. | Fin-Jr. | 2 | 0 | 0 | 0 | 0 | .... | .... | .... | .... | .... | .... | .... | .... | .... | .... | .... | .... | .... | .... | .... | .... | .... | .... |
| 2000-01 | Karpat Oulu Jr. | Fin-Jr. | 24 | 6 | 11 | 17 | 77 | .... | .... | .... | .... | .... | .... | .... | .... | .... | .... | .... | .... | .... | .... | .... | .... | .... | .... |
| | Karpat Oulu | Finland | 21 | 0 | 0 | 0 | 10 | .... | .... | .... | .... | .... | .... | .... | .... | .... | 2 | 0 | 0 | 0 | 2 | .... | .... | .... | .... |
| 2001-02 | Karpat Oulu Jr. | Fin-Jr. | .... | .... | .... | .... | .... | .... | .... | .... | .... | .... | .... | .... | .... | .... | 1 | 0 | 0 | 0 | 0 | .... | .... | .... | .... |
| | Karpat Oulu | Finland | 49 | 4 | 15 | 19 | 65 | .... | .... | .... | .... | .... | .... | .... | .... | .... | 4 | 0 | 0 | 0 | 12 | .... | .... | .... | .... |
| 2002-03 | Karpat Oulu | Finland | 35 | 5 | 15 | 20 | 38 | .... | .... | .... | .... | .... | .... | .... | .... | .... | .... | .... | .... | .... | .... | .... | .... | .... | .... |
| **2003-04** | **Philadelphia** | **NHL** | **71** | **8** | **19** | **27** | **44** | **5** | **0** | **2** | **133** | **6.0** | **15** | **0** | **0.0** | **16:35** | **15** | **0** | **3** | **3** | **6** | **0** | **0** | **0** | **12:13** |
| 2004-05 | Philadelphia | AHL | 76 | 6 | 35 | 41 | 105 | .... | .... | .... | .... | .... | .... | .... | .... | .... | 21 | 3 | 4 | 7 | 16 | .... | .... | .... | .... |
| **2005-06** | **Philadelphia** | **NHL** | **58** | **13** | **33** | **46** | **78** | **5** | **0** | **3** | **118** | **11.0** | **22** | **0** | **0.0** | **23:43** | **6** | **0** | **2** | **2** | **2** | **0** | **0** | **0** | **24:12** |
| | Finland | Olympics | DID NOT PLAY – INJURED | | | | | | | | | | | | | | | | | | | | | | |
| **2006-07** | **Philadelphia** | **NHL** | **77** | **4** | **39** | **43** | **88** | **1** | **0** | **0** | **137** | **2.9** | **-25** | **0** | **0.0** | **24:33** | .... | .... | .... | .... | .... | .... | .... | .... | .... |
| **2007-08** | **Edmonton** | **NHL** | **63** | **8** | **18** | **26** | **56** | **1** | **1** | **1** | **101** | **7.9** | **-5** | **0** | **0.0** | **24:07** | .... | .... | .... | .... | .... | .... | .... | .... | .... |
| **2008-09** | **Carolina** | **NHL** | **71** | **7** | **26** | **33** | **58** | **2** | **0** | **3** | **147** | **4.8** | **11** | **0** | **0.0** | **24:48** | **18** | **0** | **8** | **8** | **16** | **0** | **0** | **0** | **26:29** |
| | **NHL Totals** | | **340** | **40** | **135** | **175** | **324** | **14** | **1** | **9** | **636** | **6.3** | | **0** | **0.0** | **22:43** | **39** | **0** | **13** | **13** | **24** | **0** | **0** | **0** | **20:39** |

NHL All-Rookie Team (2004)

Traded to **Edmonton** by **Philadelphia** with Geoff Sanderson and Philadelphia's 3rd round choice (Cameron Abney) in 2009 Entry Draft for Joffrey Lupul and Jason Smith, July 1, 2007. Traded to **Carolina** by **Edmonton** for Erik Cole, July 1, 2008.

## PLATT, Geoff

(PLAT, JEHF) **ANA.**

Center. Shoots left. 5'9", 175 lbs. Born, Toronto, Ont., July 10, 1985.

| | | | Regular Season | | | | | | | | | | | | | | Playoffs | | | | | | | | |
|---|---|---|---|---|---|---|---|---|---|---|---|---|---|---|---|---|---|---|---|---|---|---|---|---|---|
| Season | Club | League | GP | G | A | Pts | PIM | PP | SH | GW | S | % | +/- | TF | F% | Min | GP | G | A | Pts | PIM | PP | SH | GW | Min |
| 2000-01 | St. Mike's B's | OPJHL | 6 | 2 | 0 | 2 | 4 | .... | .... | .... | .... | .... | .... | .... | .... | .... | .... | .... | .... | .... | .... | .... | .... | .... | .... |
| 2001-02 | North Bay | OHL | 63 | 4 | 6 | 10 | 34 | .... | .... | .... | .... | .... | .... | .... | .... | .... | 5 | 0 | 0 | 0 | 6 | .... | .... | .... | .... |
| 2002-03 | Saginaw Spirit | OHL | 62 | 32 | 22 | 54 | 81 | .... | .... | .... | .... | .... | .... | .... | .... | .... | .... | .... | .... | .... | .... | .... | .... | .... | .... |
| 2003-04 | Saginaw Spirit | OHL | 27 | 7 | 13 | 20 | 49 | .... | .... | .... | .... | .... | .... | .... | .... | .... | .... | .... | .... | .... | .... | .... | .... | .... | .... |
| | Erie Otters | OHL | 28 | 18 | 11 | 29 | 22 | .... | .... | .... | .... | .... | .... | .... | .... | .... | 9 | 9 | 1 | 10 | 22 | .... | .... | .... | .... |
| 2004-05 | Erie Otters | OHL | 68 | 45 | 34 | 79 | 84 | .... | .... | .... | .... | .... | .... | .... | .... | .... | 6 | 2 | 3 | 5 | 16 | .... | .... | .... | .... |
| | Atlantic City | ECHL | 2 | 0 | 2 | 2 | 0 | .... | .... | .... | .... | .... | .... | .... | .... | .... | 3 | 0 | 0 | 0 | 0 | .... | .... | .... | .... |
| **2005-06** | Syracuse Crunch | AHL | 66 | 31 | 34 | 65 | 58 | .... | .... | .... | .... | .... | .... | .... | .... | .... | 6 | 3 | 0 | 3 | 6 | .... | .... | .... | .... |
| | **Columbus** | **NHL** | **15** | **0** | **5** | **5** | **16** | **0** | **0** | **0** | **29** | **0.0** | **-4** | **53** | **45.3** | **11:12** | .... | .... | .... | .... | .... | .... | .... | .... | .... |
| **2006-07** | **Columbus** | **NHL** | **26** | **4** | **5** | **9** | **10** | **0** | **0** | **0** | **40** | **10.0** | **1** | **168** | **56.6** | **10:04** | .... | .... | .... | .... | .... | .... | .... | .... | .... |
| | Syracuse Crunch | AHL | 53 | 28 | 21 | 49 | 59 | .... | .... | .... | .... | .... | .... | .... | .... | .... | .... | .... | .... | .... | .... | .... | .... | .... | .... |
| **2007-08** | Syracuse Crunch | AHL | 15 | 4 | 3 | 7 | 6 | .... | .... | .... | .... | .... | .... | .... | .... | .... | .... | .... | .... | .... | .... | .... | .... | .... | .... |
| | **Anaheim** | **NHL** | **5** | **0** | **0** | **0** | **2** | **0** | **0** | **0** | **4** | **0.0** | **2** | **7** | **28.6** | **11:17** | .... | .... | .... | .... | .... | .... | .... | .... | .... |
| | Portland Pirates | AHL | 60 | 28 | 30 | 58 | 49 | .... | .... | .... | .... | .... | .... | .... | .... | .... | 18 | 8 | 9 | 17 | 24 | .... | .... | .... | .... |
| 2008-09 | Dynamo Minsk | Rus-KHL | 13 | 2 | 3 | 5 | 8 | .... | .... | .... | .... | .... | .... | .... | .... | .... | .... | .... | .... | .... | .... | .... | .... | .... | .... |
| | Ilves Tampere | Finland | 45 | 19 | 18 | 37 | 54 | .... | .... | .... | .... | .... | .... | .... | .... | .... | 3 | 1 | 0 | 1 | 4 | .... | .... | .... | .... |
| | **NHL Totals** | | **46** | **4** | **10** | **14** | **28** | **0** | **0** | **0** | **73** | **5.5** | | **228** | **53.1** | **10:34** | .... | .... | .... | .... | .... | .... | .... | .... | .... |

Signed as a free agent by **Syracuse** (AHL), September 23, 2005. Signed as a free agent by **Columbus**, November 25, 2005. Traded to **Anaheim** by **Columbus** for Aaron Rome and Clay Wilson, November 15, 2007. Signed as a free agent by **Minsk** (Rus-KHL), May 15, 2009.

## PLEKANEC, Tomas
(pleh-KA-nyehts, TAW-mahsh) **MTL.**

Left wing. Shoots left. 5'11", 197 lbs. Born, Kladno, Czech., October 31, 1982. Montreal's 4th choice, 71st overall, in 2001 Entry Draft.

| | | | Regular Season | | | | | | | | | | | | | | Playoffs | | | | | | | | |
|---|---|---|---|---|---|---|---|---|---|---|---|---|---|---|---|---|---|---|---|---|---|---|---|---|---|
| Season | Club | League | GP | G | A | Pts | PIM | PP | SH | GW | S | % | +/- | TF | F% | Min | GP | G | A | Pts | PIM | PP | SH | GW | Min |
| 1996-97 | Kladno U17 | CzR-U17 | 13 | 1 | 3 | 4 | .... | .... | .... | .... | .... | .... | .... | .... | .... | .... | .... | .... | .... | .... | .... | .... | .... | .... | .... |
| 1997-98 | HC Kladno U17 | CzR-U17 | 45 | 38 | 26 | 64 | .... | .... | .... | .... | .... | .... | .... | .... | .... | .... | .... | .... | .... | .... | .... | .... | .... | .... | .... |
| 1998-99 | HC Kladno Jr. | CzRep-Jr. | 53 | 22 | 20 | 42 | .... | .... | .... | .... | .... | .... | .... | .... | .... | .... | .... | .... | .... | .... | .... | .... | .... | .... | .... |
| 99-2000 | HC Kladno Jr. | CzRep-Jr. | 43 | 14 | 16 | 30 | .... | .... | .... | .... | .... | .... | .... | .... | .... | .... | .... | .... | .... | .... | .... | .... | .... | .... | .... |
| | Kralupy | CzRep-3 | 6 | 2 | 2 | 4 | 2 | .... | .... | .... | .... | .... | .... | .... | .... | .... | .... | .... | .... | .... | .... | .... | .... | .... | .... |
| | HC CKD Slany | CzRep-3 | 3 | 0 | 1 | 1 | 6 | .... | .... | .... | .... | .... | .... | .... | .... | .... | .... | .... | .... | .... | .... | .... | .... | .... | .... |
| 2000-01 | Kladno | CzRep | 47 | 9 | 9 | 18 | 24 | .... | .... | .... | .... | .... | .... | .... | .... | .... | .... | .... | .... | .... | .... | .... | .... | .... | .... |
| | HC Kladno Jr. | CzRep-Jr. | 9 | 6 | 4 | 10 | 4 | .... | .... | .... | .... | .... | .... | .... | .... | .... | .... | .... | .... | .... | .... | .... | .... | .... | .... |
| 2001-02 | Kladno | CzRep | 48 | 7 | 16 | 23 | 28 | .... | .... | .... | .... | .... | .... | .... | .... | .... | .... | .... | .... | .... | .... | .... | .... | .... | .... |
| | BK Mlada Boleslav | CzRep-3 | 6 | 6 | 3 | 9 | 14 | .... | .... | .... | .... | .... | .... | .... | .... | .... | .... | .... | .... | .... | .... | .... | .... | .... | .... |
| | Kladno | CzRep-Q | 5 | 0 | 1 | 1 | 0 | .... | .... | .... | .... | .... | .... | .... | .... | .... | .... | .... | .... | .... | .... | .... | .... | .... | .... |
| 2002-03 | Hamilton | AHL | 77 | 19 | 27 | 46 | 74 | .... | .... | .... | .... | .... | .... | .... | .... | .... | 13 | 3 | 2 | 5 | 8 | .... | .... | .... | .... |
| **2003-04** | **Montreal** | **NHL** | **2** | **0** | **0** | **0** | **0** | **0** | **0** | **0** | **0** | **0.0** | **0** | **11** | **45.5** | **9:02** | .... | .... | .... | .... | .... | .... | .... | .... | .... |
| | Hamilton | AHL | 74 | 23 | 43 | 66 | 90 | .... | .... | .... | .... | .... | .... | .... | .... | .... | 10 | 2 | 5 | 7 | 6 | .... | .... | .... | .... |
| 2004-05 | Hamilton | AHL | 80 | 29 | 35 | 64 | 68 | .... | .... | .... | .... | .... | .... | .... | .... | .... | 4 | 2 | 4 | 6 | 6 | .... | .... | .... | .... |
| **2005-06** | **Montreal** | **NHL** | **67** | **9** | **20** | **29** | **32** | **1** | **0** | **0** | **99** | **9.1** | **4** | **708** | **50.3** | **13:15** | **6** | **0** | **4** | **4** | **6** | **0** | **0** | **0** | **18:00** |
| | Hamilton | AHL | 2 | 0 | 0 | 0 | 2 | .... | .... | .... | .... | .... | .... | .... | .... | .... | .... | .... | .... | .... | .... | .... | .... | .... | .... |
| **2006-07** | **Montreal** | **NHL** | **81** | **20** | **27** | **47** | **36** | **5** | **2** | **1** | **150** | **13.3** | **10** | **1159** | **48.3** | **15:59** | .... | .... | .... | .... | .... | .... | .... | .... | .... |
| **2007-08** | **Montreal** | **NHL** | **81** | **29** | **40** | **69** | **42** | **12** | **2** | **6** | **186** | **15.6** | **15** | **1381** | **49.5** | **18:05** | **12** | **4** | **5** | **9** | **2** | **2** | **0** | **0** | **18:02** |
| **2008-09** | **Montreal** | **NHL** | **80** | **20** | **19** | **39** | **54** | **6** | **3** | **2** | **202** | **9.9** | **-9** | **1351** | **50.6** | **17:15** | **3** | **0** | **0** | **0** | **4** | **0** | **0** | **0** | **13:36** |
| | **NHL Totals** | | **311** | **78** | **106** | **184** | **164** | **24** | **7** | **9** | **637** | **12.2** | | **4610** | **49.6** | **16:13** | **21** | **4** | **9** | **13** | **12** | **2** | **0** | **0** | **17:24** |

## PLIHAL, Tomas
(PLEE-hahl, TOH-mahs)

Center. Shoots left. 6'1", 210 lbs. Born, Frydlant, Czech., March 28, 1983. San Jose's 4th choice, 140th overall, in 2001 Entry Draft.

| | | | Regular Season | | | | | | | | | | | | | | Playoffs | | | | | | | | |
|---|---|---|---|---|---|---|---|---|---|---|---|---|---|---|---|---|---|---|---|---|---|---|---|---|---|
| Season | Club | League | GP | G | A | Pts | PIM | PP | SH | GW | S | % | +/- | TF | F% | Min | GP | G | A | Pts | PIM | PP | SH | GW | Min |
| 99-2000 | Liberec U17 | CzR-U17 | 38 | 22 | 14 | 36 | .... | .... | .... | .... | .... | .... | .... | .... | .... | .... | .... | .... | .... | .... | .... | .... | .... | .... | .... |
| | Liberec Jr. | CzRep-Jr. | 2 | 0 | 0 | 0 | 0 | .... | .... | .... | .... | .... | .... | .... | .... | .... | .... | .... | .... | .... | .... | .... | .... | .... | .... |
| 2000-01 | HC Liberec U17 | CzR-U17 | 18 | 3 | 5 | 8 | .... | .... | .... | .... | .... | .... | .... | .... | .... | .... | .... | .... | .... | .... | .... | .... | .... | .... | .... |
| | HC Liberec Jr. | CzRep-Jr. | 33 | 16 | 12 | 28 | .... | .... | .... | .... | .... | .... | .... | .... | .... | .... | .... | .... | .... | .... | .... | .... | .... | .... | .... |
| 2001-02 | Kootenay Ice | WHL | 72 | 32 | 54 | 86 | 28 | .... | .... | .... | .... | .... | .... | .... | .... | .... | 22 | 4 | 10 | 14 | 14 | .... | .... | .... | .... |
| 2002-03 | Kootenay Ice | WHL | 67 | 35 | 42 | 77 | 113 | .... | .... | .... | .... | .... | .... | .... | .... | .... | 11 | 2 | 4 | 6 | 18 | .... | .... | .... | .... |
| 2003-04 | Cleveland Barons | AHL | 51 | 4 | 12 | 16 | 16 | .... | .... | .... | .... | .... | .... | .... | .... | .... | 6 | 0 | 3 | 3 | 2 | .... | .... | .... | .... |
| 2004-05 | Cleveland Barons | AHL | 62 | 17 | 11 | 28 | 26 | .... | .... | .... | .... | .... | .... | .... | .... | .... | .... | .... | .... | .... | .... | .... | .... | .... | .... |
| 2005-06 | Cleveland Barons | AHL | 74 | 11 | 19 | 30 | 53 | .... | .... | .... | .... | .... | .... | .... | .... | .... | .... | .... | .... | .... | .... | .... | .... | .... | .... |
| **2006-07** | **San Jose** | **NHL** | **3** | **0** | **0** | **0** | **0** | **0** | **0** | **0** | **10** | **0.0** | **0** | **8** | **75.0** | **9:44** | .... | .... | .... | .... | .... | .... | .... | .... | .... |
| | Worcester Sharks | AHL | 47 | 6 | 9 | 15 | 28 | .... | .... | .... | .... | .... | .... | .... | .... | .... | .... | .... | .... | .... | .... | .... | .... | .... | .... |
| **2007-08** | **San Jose** | **NHL** | **22** | **2** | **1** | **3** | **4** | **0** | **0** | **0** | **34** | **5.9** | **4** | **19** | **26.3** | **10:50** | **4** | **0** | **0** | **0** | **0** | **0** | **0** | **0** | **13:16** |
| | Worcester Sharks | AHL | 22 | 5 | 7 | 12 | 12 | .... | .... | .... | .... | .... | .... | .... | .... | .... | .... | .... | .... | .... | .... | .... | .... | .... | .... |
| **2008-09** | **San Jose** | **NHL** | **64** | **5** | **8** | **13** | **22** | **0** | **1** | **1** | **79** | **6.3** | **-4** | **248** | **52.8** | **10:08** | .... | .... | .... | .... | .... | .... | .... | .... | .... |
| | **NHL Totals** | | **89** | **7** | **9** | **16** | **26** | **0** | **1** | **1** | **123** | **5.7** | | **275** | **51.6** | **10:17** | **4** | **0** | **0** | **0** | **0** | **0** | **0** | **0** | **13:16** |

George Parsons Trophy (Memorial Cup Tournament - Most Sportsmanlike Player) (2002)

## POCK, Thomas
(POHK, TAW-muhs)

Defense. Shoots left. 6'1", 210 lbs. Born, Klagenfurt, Austria, December 2, 1981.

| | | | Regular Season | | | | | | | | | | | | | | Playoffs | | | | | | | | |
|---|---|---|---|---|---|---|---|---|---|---|---|---|---|---|---|---|---|---|---|---|---|---|---|---|---|
| Season | Club | League | GP | G | A | Pts | PIM | PP | SH | GW | S | % | +/- | TF | F% | Min | GP | G | A | Pts | PIM | PP | SH | GW | Min |
| 1998-99 | Klagenfurt Jr. | Austria-Jr. | 31 | 0 | 0 | 0 | 2 | .... | .... | .... | .... | .... | .... | .... | .... | .... | .... | .... | .... | .... | .... | .... | .... | .... | .... |
| 99-2000 | Klagenfurter AC | Austria | 15 | 3 | 8 | 11 | 14 | .... | .... | .... | .... | .... | .... | .... | .... | .... | .... | .... | .... | .... | .... | .... | .... | .... | .... |
| | Klagenfurt | Alpenliga | 33 | 4 | 11 | 15 | 48 | .... | .... | .... | .... | .... | .... | .... | .... | .... | .... | .... | .... | .... | .... | .... | .... | .... | .... |
| 2000-01 | Massachusetts | H-East | 33 | 6 | 6 | 12 | 59 | .... | .... | .... | .... | .... | .... | .... | .... | .... | .... | .... | .... | .... | .... | .... | .... | .... | .... |
| 2001-02 | Massachusetts | H-East | 23 | 5 | 7 | 12 | 26 | .... | .... | .... | .... | .... | .... | .... | .... | .... | .... | .... | .... | .... | .... | .... | .... | .... | .... |
| | Austria | Nat-Tm | 10 | 1 | 2 | 3 | 4 | .... | .... | .... | .... | .... | .... | .... | .... | .... | .... | .... | .... | .... | .... | .... | .... | .... | .... |
| | Austria | Olympics | 4 | 0 | 0 | 0 | 2 | .... | .... | .... | .... | .... | .... | .... | .... | .... | .... | .... | .... | .... | .... | .... | .... | .... | .... |
| 2002-03 | Massachusetts | H-East | 37 | 17 | 20 | 37 | 46 | .... | .... | .... | .... | .... | .... | .... | .... | .... | .... | .... | .... | .... | .... | .... | .... | .... | .... |
| | Austria | WC-A | 6 | 1 | 0 | 1 | 4 | .... | .... | .... | .... | .... | .... | .... | .... | .... | .... | .... | .... | .... | .... | .... | .... | .... | .... |
| **2003-04** | Massachusetts | H-East | 37 | 16 | 25 | 41 | 48 | .... | .... | .... | .... | .... | .... | .... | .... | .... | .... | .... | .... | .... | .... | .... | .... | .... | .... |
| | **NY Rangers** | **NHL** | **6** | **2** | **2** | **4** | **0** | **0** | **0** | **0** | **8** | **25.0** | **-4** | **0** | **0.0** | **18:38** | .... | .... | .... | .... | .... | .... | .... | .... | .... |
| 2004-05 | Hartford | AHL | 50 | 1 | 5 | 6 | 55 | .... | .... | .... | .... | .... | .... | .... | .... | .... | 6 | 0 | 1 | 1 | 8 | .... | .... | .... | .... |
| | Charlotte | ECHL | 3 | 0 | 2 | 2 | 2 | .... | .... | .... | .... | .... | .... | .... | .... | .... | .... | .... | .... | .... | .... | .... | .... | .... | .... |
| **2005-06** | **NY Rangers** | **NHL** | **8** | **1** | **1** | **2** | **4** | **0** | **0** | **0** | **15** | **6.7** | **-3** | **0** | **0.0** | **15:10** | .... | .... | .... | .... | .... | .... | .... | .... | .... |
| | Hartford | AHL | 67 | 15 | 46 | 61 | 99 | .... | .... | .... | .... | .... | .... | .... | .... | .... | 6 | 0 | 3 | 3 | 15 | .... | .... | .... | .... |
| **2006-07** | **NY Rangers** | **NHL** | **44** | **4** | **4** | **8** | **16** | **0** | **0** | **0** | **76** | **5.3** | **-4** | **0** | **0.0** | **16:14** | **4** | **0** | **3** | **3** | **4** | **0** | **0** | **0** | **13:29** |
| | Hartford | AHL | 4 | 0 | 1 | 1 | 2 | .... | .... | .... | .... | .... | .... | .... | .... | .... | .... | .... | .... | .... | .... | .... | .... | .... | .... |
| **2007-08** | **NY Rangers** | **NHL** | **1** | **0** | **0** | **0** | **0** | **0** | **0** | **0** | **2** | **0.0** | **-2** | **0** | **0.0** | **18:53** | .... | .... | .... | .... | .... | .... | .... | .... | .... |
| | Hartford | AHL | 74 | 7 | 37 | 44 | 63 | .... | .... | .... | .... | .... | .... | .... | .... | .... | 5 | 0 | 0 | 0 | 8 | .... | .... | .... | .... |
| **2008-09** | **NY Islanders** | **NHL** | **59** | **1** | **2** | **3** | **35** | **0** | **0** | **0** | **51** | **2.0** | **-17** | **0** | **0.0** | **12:42** | .... | .... | .... | .... | .... | .... | .... | .... | .... |
| | **NHL Totals** | | **118** | **8** | **9** | **17** | **55** | **0** | **0** | **0** | **152** | **5.3** | | **0** | **0.0** | **14:32** | **4** | **0** | **3** | **3** | **4** | **0** | **0** | **0** | **13:29** |

Hockey East Second All-Star Team (2003) • Hockey East First All-Star Team (2004) • NCAA East First All-American Team (2004) • AHL Second All-Star Team (2006)

Signed as a free agent by **NY Rangers**, March 23, 2004. Claimed on waivers by **NY Islanders** from **NY Rangers**, September 29, 2008.

## POHL, John
(PAWL, JAWN)

Center. Shoots right. 6'1", 196 lbs. Born, Rochester, MN, June 29, 1979. St. Louis' 8th choice, 255th overall, in 1998 Entry Draft.

| | | | Regular Season | | | | | | | | | | | | | | Playoffs | | | | | | | | |
|---|---|---|---|---|---|---|---|---|---|---|---|---|---|---|---|---|---|---|---|---|---|---|---|---|---|
| Season | Club | League | GP | G | A | Pts | PIM | PP | SH | GW | S | % | +/- | TF | F% | Min | GP | G | A | Pts | PIM | PP | SH | GW | Min |
| 1997-98 | Red Wing High | High-MN | 28 | 30 | 77 | 107 | 18 | .... | .... | .... | .... | .... | .... | .... | .... | .... | .... | .... | .... | .... | .... | .... | .... | .... | .... |
| | Twin Cities | USHL | 10 | 5 | 3 | 8 | 10 | .... | .... | .... | .... | .... | .... | .... | .... | .... | .... | .... | .... | .... | .... | .... | .... | .... | .... |
| 1998-99 | U. of Minnesota | WCHA | 42 | 7 | 10 | 17 | 18 | .... | .... | .... | .... | .... | .... | .... | .... | .... | .... | .... | .... | .... | .... | .... | .... | .... | .... |
| 99-2000 | U. of Minnesota | WCHA | 41 | 18 | 41 | 59 | 26 | .... | .... | .... | .... | .... | .... | .... | .... | .... | .... | .... | .... | .... | .... | .... | .... | .... | .... |
| 2000-01 | U. of Minnesota | WCHA | 38 | 19 | 26 | 45 | 24 | .... | .... | .... | .... | .... | .... | .... | .... | .... | .... | .... | .... | .... | .... | .... | .... | .... | .... |
| 2001-02 | U. of Minnesota | WCHA | 44 | 27 | *52 | *79 | 26 | .... | .... | .... | .... | .... | .... | .... | .... | .... | .... | .... | .... | .... | .... | .... | .... | .... | .... |
| 2002-03 | Worcester IceCats | AHL | 58 | 26 | 32 | 58 | 34 | .... | .... | .... | .... | .... | .... | .... | .... | .... | 3 | 0 | 1 | 1 | 6 | .... | .... | .... | .... |
| **2003-04** | **St. Louis** | **NHL** | **1** | **0** | **0** | **0** | **0** | **0** | **0** | **0** | **1** | **0.0** | **-2** | **9** | **55.6** | **8:18** | .... | .... | .... | .... | .... | .... | .... | .... | .... |
| | Worcester IceCats | AHL | 65 | 16 | 25 | 41 | 65 | .... | .... | .... | .... | .... | .... | .... | .... | .... | 3 | 0 | 1 | 1 | 2 | .... | .... | .... | .... |
| 2004-05 | Worcester IceCats | AHL | 13 | 3 | 6 | 9 | 2 | .... | .... | .... | .... | .... | .... | .... | .... | .... | .... | .... | .... | .... | .... | .... | .... | .... | .... |
| **2005-06** | **Toronto** | **NHL** | **7** | **3** | **1** | **4** | **4** | **1** | **0** | **0** | **17** | **17.6** | **2** | **41** | **53.7** | **12:47** | .... | .... | .... | .... | .... | .... | .... | .... | .... |
| | Toronto Marlies | AHL | 60 | 36 | 39 | 75 | 42 | .... | .... | .... | .... | .... | .... | .... | .... | .... | 5 | 1 | 5 | 6 | 10 | .... | .... | .... | .... |
| **2006-07** | **Toronto** | **NHL** | **74** | **13** | **16** | **29** | **10** | **3** | **0** | **1** | **105** | **12.4** | **-4** | **553** | **53.4** | **11:21** | .... | .... | .... | .... | .... | .... | .... | .... | .... |
| **2007-08** | **Toronto** | **NHL** | **33** | **1** | **4** | **5** | **10** | **0** | **0** | **1** | **23** | **4.3** | **-4** | **94** | **43.6** | **7:06** | .... | .... | .... | .... | .... | .... | .... | .... | .... |
| 2008-09 | Frolunda | Sweden | 12 | 5 | 7 | 12 | 6 | .... | .... | .... | .... | .... | .... | .... | .... | .... | 11 | 2 | 7 | 9 | 8 | .... | .... | .... | .... |
| | HC Lugano | Swiss | 22 | 3 | 22 | 25 | 26 | .... | .... | .... | .... | .... | .... | .... | .... | .... | .... | .... | .... | .... | .... | .... | .... | .... | .... |
| | **NHL Totals** | | **115** | **17** | **21** | **38** | **24** | **4** | **0** | **2** | **146** | **11.6** | | **697** | **52.1** | **10:11** | .... | .... | .... | .... | .... | .... | .... | .... | .... |

WCHA Second All-Star Team (2000) • WCHA First All-Star Team (2002) • NCAA Championship All-Tournament Team (2002)

Traded to **Toronto** by **St. Louis** for future considerations, August 24, 2005.

## POLAK, Roman
(POH-lahk, ROH-muhn) **ST.L.**

Defense. Shoots right. 6', 232 lbs. Born, Ostrava, Czech., April 28, 1986. St. Louis' 6th choice, 180th overall, in 2004 Entry Draft.

| | | | Regular Season | | | | | | | | | | | | | | Playoffs | | | | | | | | |
|---|---|---|---|---|---|---|---|---|---|---|---|---|---|---|---|---|---|---|---|---|---|---|---|---|---|
| Season | Club | League | GP | G | A | Pts | PIM | PP | SH | GW | S | % | +/- | TF | F% | Min | GP | G | A | Pts | PIM | PP | SH | GW | Min |
| 2001-02 | HC Ostrava Jr. | CzRep-Jr. | 46 | 4 | 9 | 13 | 84 | .... | .... | .... | .... | .... | .... | .... | .... | .... | .... | .... | .... | .... | .... | .... | .... | .... | .... |
| 2002-03 | HC Ostrava Jr. | CzRep-Jr. | 32 | 3 | 12 | 15 | 34 | .... | .... | .... | .... | .... | .... | .... | .... | .... | .... | .... | .... | .... | .... | .... | .... | .... | .... |
| 2003-04 | HC Vitkovice Jr. | CzRep-Jr. | 52 | 4 | 8 | 12 | 48 | .... | .... | .... | .... | .... | .... | .... | .... | .... | .... | .... | .... | .... | .... | .... | .... | .... | .... |
| 2004-05 | Kootenay Ice | WHL | 65 | 5 | 18 | 23 | 85 | .... | .... | .... | .... | .... | .... | .... | .... | .... | 9 | 0 | 0 | 0 | 6 | .... | .... | .... | .... |
| 2005-06 | HC Vitkovice Jr. | CzRep-Jr. | 1 | 0 | 0 | 0 | 4 | .... | .... | .... | .... | .... | .... | .... | .... | .... | .... | .... | .... | .... | .... | .... | .... | .... | .... |
| | Vitkovice | CzRep | 37 | 0 | 1 | 1 | 16 | .... | .... | .... | .... | .... | .... | .... | .... | .... | 6 | 0 | 0 | 0 | 6 | .... | .... | .... | .... |
| **2006-07** | **St. Louis** | **NHL** | **19** | **0** | **0** | **0** | **6** | **0** | **0** | **0** | **13** | **0.0** | **-3** | **0** | **0.0** | **13:38** | .... | .... | .... | .... | .... | .... | .... | .... | .... |
| | Peoria Rivermen | AHL | 53 | 4 | 8 | 12 | 66 | .... | .... | .... | .... | .... | .... | .... | .... | .... | .... | .... | .... | .... | .... | .... | .... | .... | .... |
| **2007-08** | **St. Louis** | **NHL** | **6** | **0** | **1** | **1** | **0** | **0** | **0** | **0** | **2** | **0.0** | **1** | **0** | **0.0** | **11:32** | .... | .... | .... | .... | .... | .... | .... | .... | .... |
| | Peoria Rivermen | AHL | 34 | 0 | 7 | 7 | 33 | .... | .... | .... | .... | .... | .... | .... | .... | .... | .... | .... | .... | .... | .... | .... | .... | .... | .... |
| **2008-09** | **St. Louis** | **NHL** | **69** | **1** | **14** | **15** | **45** | **0** | **0** | **1** | **73** | **1.4** | **-15** | **1** | **0.0** | **21:32** | **4** | **0** | **0** | **0** | **0** | **0** | **0** | **0** | **21:49** |
| | **NHL Totals** | | **94** | **1** | **15** | **16** | **51** | **0** | **0** | **1** | **88** | **1.1** | | **1** | **0.0** | **19:18** | **4** | **0** | **0** | **0** | **0** | **0** | **0** | **0** | **21:49** |

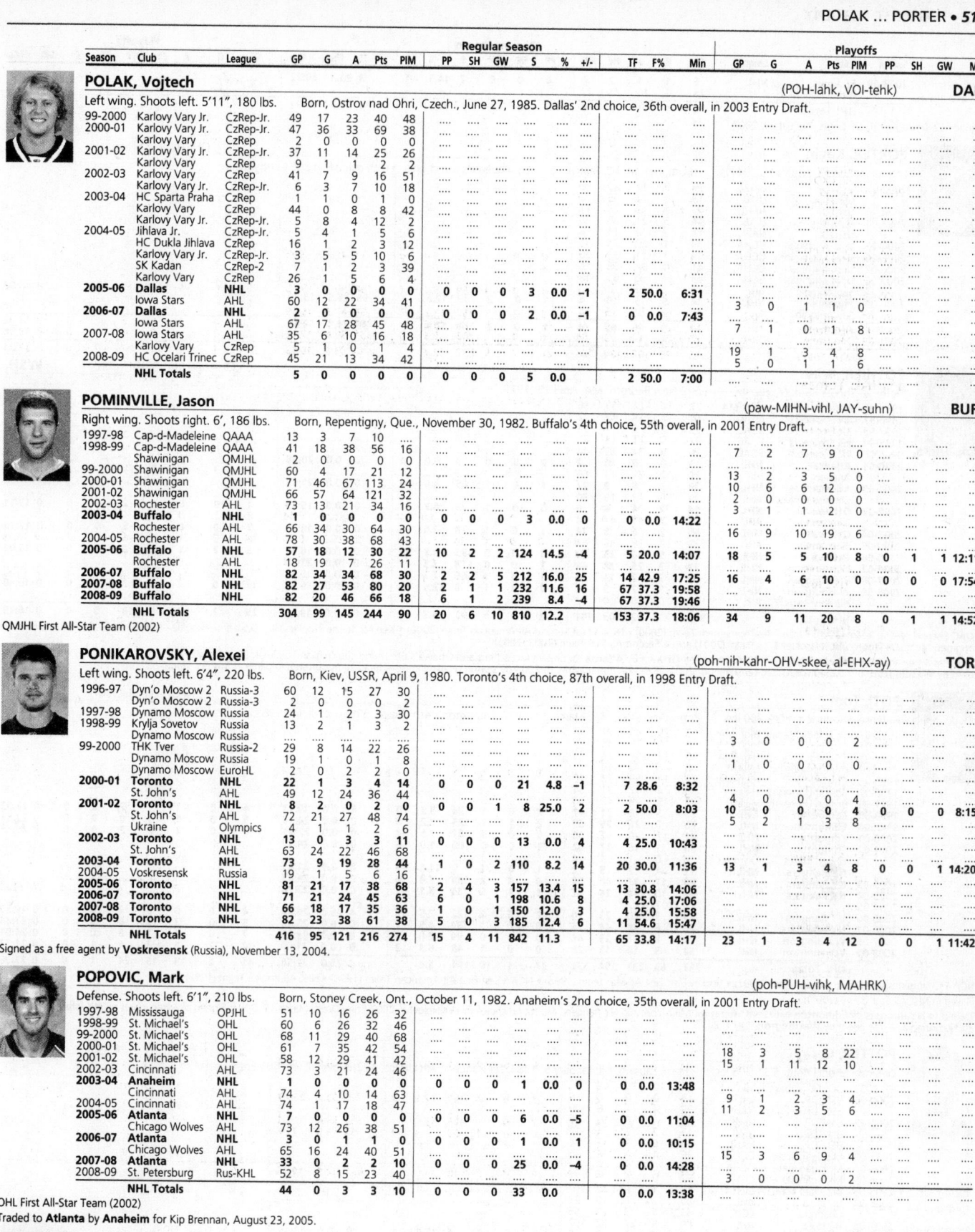

## POLAK, Vojtech

(POH-lahk, VOI-tehk) **DAL.**

Left wing. Shoots left. 5'11", 180 lbs. Born, Ostrov nad Ohri, Czech., June 27, 1985. Dallas' 2nd choice, 36th overall, in 2003 Entry Draft.

| | | | Regular Season | | | | | | | | | | | | | | Playoffs | | | | | | | | |
|---|---|---|---|---|---|---|---|---|---|---|---|---|---|---|---|---|---|---|---|---|---|---|---|---|---|
| Season | Club | League | GP | G | A | Pts | PIM | PP | SH | GW | S | % | +/- | TF | F% | Min | GP | G | A | Pts | PIM | PP | SH | GW | Min |
| 99-2000 | Karlovy Vary Jr. | CzRep-Jr. | 49 | 17 | 23 | 40 | 48 | .... | .... | .... | .... | .... | .... | .... | .... | .... | .... | .... | .... | .... | .... | .... | .... | .... | .... |
| 2000-01 | Karlovy Vary Jr. | CzRep-Jr. | 47 | 36 | 33 | 69 | 38 | .... | .... | .... | .... | .... | .... | .... | .... | .... | .... | .... | .... | .... | .... | .... | .... | .... | .... |
| | Karlovy Vary | CzRep | 2 | 0 | 0 | 0 | 0 | .... | .... | .... | .... | .... | .... | .... | .... | .... | .... | .... | .... | .... | .... | .... | .... | .... | .... |
| 2001-02 | Karlovy Vary Jr. | CzRep-Jr. | 37 | 11 | 14 | 25 | 26 | .... | .... | .... | .... | .... | .... | .... | .... | .... | .... | .... | .... | .... | .... | .... | .... | .... | .... |
| | Karlovy Vary | CzRep | 9 | 1 | 1 | 2 | 2 | .... | .... | .... | .... | .... | .... | .... | .... | .... | .... | .... | .... | .... | .... | .... | .... | .... | .... |
| 2002-03 | Karlovy Vary | CzRep | 41 | 7 | 9 | 16 | 51 | .... | .... | .... | .... | .... | .... | .... | .... | .... | .... | .... | .... | .... | .... | .... | .... | .... | .... |
| | Karlovy Vary Jr. | CzRep-Jr. | 6 | 3 | 7 | 10 | 18 | .... | .... | .... | .... | .... | .... | .... | .... | .... | .... | .... | .... | .... | .... | .... | .... | .... | .... |
| 2003-04 | HC Sparta Praha | CzRep | 1 | 1 | 0 | 1 | 0 | .... | .... | .... | .... | .... | .... | .... | .... | .... | .... | .... | .... | .... | .... | .... | .... | .... | .... |
| | Karlovy Vary | CzRep | 44 | 0 | 8 | 8 | 42 | .... | .... | .... | .... | .... | .... | .... | .... | .... | .... | .... | .... | .... | .... | .... | .... | .... | .... |
| | Karlovy Vary Jr. | CzRep-Jr. | 5 | 8 | 4 | 12 | 2 | .... | .... | .... | .... | .... | .... | .... | .... | .... | .... | .... | .... | .... | .... | .... | .... | .... | .... |
| 2004-05 | Jihlava Jr. | CzRep-Jr. | 5 | 4 | 1 | 5 | 6 | .... | .... | .... | .... | .... | .... | .... | .... | .... | .... | .... | .... | .... | .... | .... | .... | .... | .... |
| | HC Dukla Jihlava | CzRep | 16 | 1 | 2 | 3 | 12 | .... | .... | .... | .... | .... | .... | .... | .... | .... | .... | .... | .... | .... | .... | .... | .... | .... | .... |
| | Karlovy Vary Jr. | CzRep-Jr. | 3 | 5 | 5 | 10 | 6 | .... | .... | .... | .... | .... | .... | .... | .... | .... | .... | .... | .... | .... | .... | .... | .... | .... | .... |
| | SK Kadan | CzRep-2 | 7 | 1 | 2 | 3 | 39 | .... | .... | .... | .... | .... | .... | .... | .... | .... | .... | .... | .... | .... | .... | .... | .... | .... | .... |
| | Karlovy Vary | CzRep | 26 | 1 | 5 | 6 | 4 | .... | .... | .... | .... | .... | .... | .... | .... | .... | .... | .... | .... | .... | .... | .... | .... | .... | .... |
| **2005-06** | **Dallas** | **NHL** | **3** | **0** | **0** | **0** | **0** | **0** | **0** | **0** | **3** | **0.0** | **−1** | **2** | **50.0** | **6:31** | .... | .... | .... | .... | .... | .... | .... | .... | .... |
| | Iowa Stars | AHL | 60 | 12 | 22 | 34 | 41 | .... | .... | .... | .... | .... | .... | .... | .... | .... | 3 | 0 | 1 | 1 | 0 | .... | .... | .... | .... |
| **2006-07** | **Dallas** | **NHL** | **2** | **0** | **0** | **0** | **0** | **0** | **0** | **0** | **2** | **0.0** | **−1** | **0** | **0.0** | **7:43** | .... | .... | .... | .... | .... | .... | .... | .... | .... |
| | Iowa Stars | AHL | 67 | 17 | 28 | 45 | 48 | .... | .... | .... | .... | .... | .... | .... | .... | .... | 7 | 1 | 0 | 1 | 8 | .... | .... | .... | .... |
| 2007-08 | Iowa Stars | AHL | 35 | 6 | 10 | 16 | 18 | .... | .... | .... | .... | .... | .... | .... | .... | .... | .... | .... | .... | .... | .... | .... | .... | .... | .... |
| | Karlovy Vary | CzRep | 5 | 1 | 0 | 1 | 4 | .... | .... | .... | .... | .... | .... | .... | .... | .... | 19 | 1 | 3 | 4 | 8 | .... | .... | .... | .... |
| 2008-09 | HC Ocelari Trinec | CzRep | 45 | 21 | 13 | 34 | 42 | .... | .... | .... | .... | .... | .... | .... | .... | .... | 5 | 0 | 1 | 1 | 6 | .... | .... | .... | .... |
| | **NHL Totals** | | **5** | **0** | **0** | **0** | **0** | **0** | **0** | **0** | **5** | **0.0** | | **2** | **50.0** | **7:00** | .... | .... | .... | .... | .... | .... | .... | .... | .... |

## POMINVILLE, Jason

(paw-MIHN-vihl, JAY-suhn) **BUF.**

Right wing. Shoots right. 6', 186 lbs. Born, Repentigny, Que., November 30, 1982. Buffalo's 4th choice, 55th overall, in 2001 Entry Draft.

| Season | Club | League | GP | G | A | Pts | PIM | PP | SH | GW | S | % | +/- | TF | F% | Min | GP | G | A | Pts | PIM | PP | SH | GW | Min |
|---|---|---|---|---|---|---|---|---|---|---|---|---|---|---|---|---|---|---|---|---|---|---|---|---|---|
| 1997-98 | Cap-d-Madeleine | QAAA | 13 | 3 | 7 | 10 | .... | .... | .... | .... | .... | .... | .... | .... | .... | .... | .... | .... | .... | .... | .... | .... | .... | .... | .... |
| 1998-99 | Cap-d-Madeleine | QAAA | 41 | 18 | 38 | 56 | 16 | .... | .... | .... | .... | .... | .... | .... | .... | .... | 7 | 2 | 7 | 9 | 0 | .... | .... | .... | .... |
| | Shawinigan | QMJHL | 2 | 0 | 0 | 0 | 0 | .... | .... | .... | .... | .... | .... | .... | .... | .... | .... | .... | .... | .... | .... | .... | .... | .... | .... |
| 99-2000 | Shawinigan | QMJHL | 60 | 4 | 17 | 21 | 12 | .... | .... | .... | .... | .... | .... | .... | .... | .... | 13 | 2 | 3 | 5 | 0 | .... | .... | .... | .... |
| 2000-01 | Shawinigan | QMJHL | 71 | 46 | 67 | 113 | 24 | .... | .... | .... | .... | .... | .... | .... | .... | .... | 10 | 6 | 6 | 12 | 0 | .... | .... | .... | .... |
| 2001-02 | Shawinigan | QMJHL | 66 | 57 | 64 | 121 | 32 | .... | .... | .... | .... | .... | .... | .... | .... | .... | 2 | 0 | 0 | 0 | 0 | .... | .... | .... | .... |
| 2002-03 | Rochester | AHL | 73 | 13 | 21 | 34 | 16 | .... | .... | .... | .... | .... | .... | .... | .... | .... | 3 | 1 | 1 | 2 | 0 | .... | .... | .... | .... |
| **2003-04** | **Buffalo** | **NHL** | **1** | **0** | **0** | **0** | **0** | **0** | **0** | **0** | **3** | **0.0** | **0** | **0** | **0.0** | **14:22** | .... | .... | .... | .... | .... | .... | .... | .... | .... |
| | Rochester | AHL | 66 | 34 | 30 | 64 | 30 | .... | .... | .... | .... | .... | .... | .... | .... | .... | 16 | 9 | 10 | 19 | 6 | .... | .... | .... | .... |
| 2004-05 | Rochester | AHL | 78 | 30 | 38 | 68 | 43 | .... | .... | .... | .... | .... | .... | .... | .... | .... | .... | .... | .... | .... | .... | .... | .... | .... | .... |
| **2005-06** | **Buffalo** | **NHL** | **57** | **18** | **12** | **30** | **22** | **10** | **2** | **2** | **124** | **14.5** | **−4** | **5** | **20.0** | **14:07** | **18** | **5** | **5** | **10** | **8** | **0** | **1** | **1** | **12:11** |
| | Rochester | AHL | 18 | 19 | 7 | 26 | 11 | .... | .... | .... | .... | .... | .... | .... | .... | .... | .... | .... | .... | .... | .... | .... | .... | .... | .... |
| **2006-07** | **Buffalo** | **NHL** | **82** | **34** | **34** | **68** | **30** | **2** | **2** | **5** | **212** | **16.0** | **25** | **14** | **42.9** | **17:25** | **16** | **4** | **6** | **10** | **0** | **0** | **0** | **0** | **17:54** |
| **2007-08** | **Buffalo** | **NHL** | **82** | **27** | **53** | **80** | **20** | **2** | **1** | **1** | **232** | **11.6** | **16** | **67** | **37.3** | **19:58** | .... | .... | .... | .... | .... | .... | .... | .... | .... |
| **2008-09** | **Buffalo** | **NHL** | **82** | **20** | **46** | **66** | **18** | **6** | **1** | **2** | **239** | **8.4** | **−4** | **67** | **37.3** | **19:46** | .... | .... | .... | .... | .... | .... | .... | .... | .... |
| | **NHL Totals** | | **304** | **99** | **145** | **244** | **90** | **20** | **6** | **10** | **810** | **12.2** | | **153** | **37.3** | **18:06** | **34** | **9** | **11** | **20** | **8** | **0** | **1** | **1** | **14:52** |

QMJHL First All-Star Team (2002)

## PONIKAROVSKY, Alexei

(poh-nih-kahr-OHV-skee, al-EHX-ay) **TOR.**

Left wing. Shoots left. 6'4", 220 lbs. Born, Kiev, USSR, April 9, 1980. Toronto's 4th choice, 87th overall, in 1998 Entry Draft.

| Season | Club | League | GP | G | A | Pts | PIM | PP | SH | GW | S | % | +/- | TF | F% | Min | GP | G | A | Pts | PIM | PP | SH | GW | Min |
|---|---|---|---|---|---|---|---|---|---|---|---|---|---|---|---|---|---|---|---|---|---|---|---|---|---|
| 1996-97 | Dyn'o Moscow 2 | Russia-3 | 60 | 12 | 15 | 27 | 30 | .... | .... | .... | .... | .... | .... | .... | .... | .... | .... | .... | .... | .... | .... | .... | .... | .... | .... |
| | Dyn'o Moscow 2 | Russia-3 | 2 | 0 | 0 | 0 | 2 | .... | .... | .... | .... | .... | .... | .... | .... | .... | .... | .... | .... | .... | .... | .... | .... | .... | .... |
| 1997-98 | Dynamo Moscow | Russia | 24 | 1 | 2 | 3 | 30 | .... | .... | .... | .... | .... | .... | .... | .... | .... | .... | .... | .... | .... | .... | .... | .... | .... | .... |
| 1998-99 | Krylja Sovetov | Russia | 13 | 2 | 1 | 3 | 2 | .... | .... | .... | .... | .... | .... | .... | .... | .... | .... | .... | .... | .... | .... | .... | .... | .... | .... |
| | Dynamo Moscow | Russia | .... | .... | .... | .... | .... | .... | .... | .... | .... | .... | .... | .... | .... | .... | 3 | 0 | 0 | 0 | 2 | .... | .... | .... | .... |
| 99-2000 | THK Tver | Russia-2 | 29 | 8 | 14 | 22 | 26 | .... | .... | .... | .... | .... | .... | .... | .... | .... | .... | .... | .... | .... | .... | .... | .... | .... | .... |
| | Dynamo Moscow | Russia | 19 | 1 | 0 | 1 | 8 | .... | .... | .... | .... | .... | .... | .... | .... | .... | 1 | 0 | 0 | 0 | 0 | .... | .... | .... | .... |
| | Dynamo Moscow | EuroHL | 2 | 0 | 2 | 2 | 0 | .... | .... | .... | .... | .... | .... | .... | .... | .... | .... | .... | .... | .... | .... | .... | .... | .... | .... |
| **2000-01** | **Toronto** | **NHL** | **22** | **1** | **3** | **4** | **14** | **0** | **0** | **0** | **21** | **4.8** | **−1** | **7** | **28.6** | **8:32** | .... | .... | .... | .... | .... | .... | .... | .... | .... |
| | St. John's | AHL | 49 | 12 | 24 | 36 | 44 | .... | .... | .... | .... | .... | .... | .... | .... | .... | 4 | 0 | 0 | 0 | 4 | .... | .... | .... | .... |
| **2001-02** | **Toronto** | **NHL** | **8** | **2** | **0** | **2** | **0** | **0** | **0** | **1** | **8** | **25.0** | **2** | **2** | **50.0** | **8:03** | **10** | **0** | **0** | **0** | **4** | **0** | **0** | **0** | **8:15** |
| | St. John's | AHL | 72 | 21 | 27 | 48 | 74 | .... | .... | .... | .... | .... | .... | .... | .... | .... | 5 | 2 | 1 | 3 | 8 | .... | .... | .... | .... |
| | Ukraine | Olympics | 4 | 1 | 1 | 2 | 6 | .... | .... | .... | .... | .... | .... | .... | .... | .... | .... | .... | .... | .... | .... | .... | .... | .... | .... |
| **2002-03** | **Toronto** | **NHL** | **13** | **0** | **3** | **3** | **11** | **0** | **0** | **0** | **13** | **0.0** | **4** | **4** | **25.0** | **10:43** | .... | .... | .... | .... | .... | .... | .... | .... | .... |
| | St. John's | AHL | 63 | 24 | 22 | 46 | 68 | .... | .... | .... | .... | .... | .... | .... | .... | .... | .... | .... | .... | .... | .... | .... | .... | .... | .... |
| **2003-04** | **Toronto** | **NHL** | **73** | **9** | **19** | **28** | **44** | **1** | **0** | **2** | **110** | **8.2** | **14** | **20** | **30.0** | **11:36** | **13** | **1** | **3** | **4** | **8** | **0** | **0** | **1** | **14:20** |
| 2004-05 | Voskresensk | Russia | 19 | 1 | 5 | 6 | 16 | .... | .... | .... | .... | .... | .... | .... | .... | .... | .... | .... | .... | .... | .... | .... | .... | .... | .... |
| **2005-06** | **Toronto** | **NHL** | **81** | **21** | **17** | **38** | **68** | **2** | **4** | **3** | **157** | **13.4** | **15** | **13** | **30.8** | **14:06** | .... | .... | .... | .... | .... | .... | .... | .... | .... |
| **2006-07** | **Toronto** | **NHL** | **71** | **21** | **24** | **45** | **63** | **6** | **0** | **1** | **198** | **10.6** | **8** | **4** | **25.0** | **17:06** | .... | .... | .... | .... | .... | .... | .... | .... | .... |
| **2007-08** | **Toronto** | **NHL** | **66** | **18** | **17** | **35** | **36** | **1** | **0** | **1** | **150** | **12.0** | **3** | **4** | **25.0** | **15:58** | .... | .... | .... | .... | .... | .... | .... | .... | .... |
| **2008-09** | **Toronto** | **NHL** | **82** | **23** | **38** | **61** | **38** | **5** | **0** | **3** | **185** | **12.4** | **6** | **11** | **54.6** | **15:47** | .... | .... | .... | .... | .... | .... | .... | .... | .... |
| | **NHL Totals** | | **416** | **95** | **121** | **216** | **274** | **15** | **4** | **11** | **842** | **11.3** | | **65** | **33.8** | **14:17** | **23** | **1** | **3** | **4** | **12** | **0** | **0** | **1** | **11:42** |

Signed as a free agent by **Voskresensk** (Russia), November 13, 2004.

## POPOVIC, Mark

(poh-PUH-vihk, MAHRK)

Defense. Shoots left. 6'1", 210 lbs. Born, Stoney Creek, Ont., October 11, 1982. Anaheim's 2nd choice, 35th overall, in 2001 Entry Draft.

| Season | Club | League | GP | G | A | Pts | PIM | PP | SH | GW | S | % | +/- | TF | F% | Min | GP | G | A | Pts | PIM | PP | SH | GW | Min |
|---|---|---|---|---|---|---|---|---|---|---|---|---|---|---|---|---|---|---|---|---|---|---|---|---|---|
| 1997-98 | Mississauga | OPJHL | 51 | 10 | 16 | 26 | 32 | .... | .... | .... | .... | .... | .... | .... | .... | .... | .... | .... | .... | .... | .... | .... | .... | .... | .... |
| 1998-99 | St. Michael's | OHL | 60 | 6 | 26 | 32 | 46 | .... | .... | .... | .... | .... | .... | .... | .... | .... | .... | .... | .... | .... | .... | .... | .... | .... | .... |
| 99-2000 | St. Michael's | OHL | 68 | 11 | 29 | 40 | 68 | .... | .... | .... | .... | .... | .... | .... | .... | .... | .... | .... | .... | .... | .... | .... | .... | .... | .... |
| 2000-01 | St. Michael's | OHL | 61 | 7 | 35 | 42 | 54 | .... | .... | .... | .... | .... | .... | .... | .... | .... | 18 | 3 | 5 | 8 | 22 | .... | .... | .... | .... |
| 2001-02 | St. Michael's | OHL | 58 | 12 | 29 | 41 | 42 | .... | .... | .... | .... | .... | .... | .... | .... | .... | 15 | 1 | 11 | 12 | 10 | .... | .... | .... | .... |
| 2002-03 | Cincinnati | AHL | 73 | 3 | 21 | 24 | 46 | .... | .... | .... | .... | .... | .... | .... | .... | .... | .... | .... | .... | .... | .... | .... | .... | .... | .... |
| **2003-04** | **Anaheim** | **NHL** | **1** | **0** | **0** | **0** | **0** | **0** | **0** | **0** | **1** | **0.0** | **0** | **0** | **0.0** | **13:48** | .... | .... | .... | .... | .... | .... | .... | .... | .... |
| | Cincinnati | AHL | 74 | 4 | 10 | 14 | 63 | .... | .... | .... | .... | .... | .... | .... | .... | .... | 9 | 1 | 2 | 3 | 4 | .... | .... | .... | .... |
| 2004-05 | Cincinnati | AHL | 74 | 1 | 17 | 18 | 47 | .... | .... | .... | .... | .... | .... | .... | .... | .... | 11 | 2 | 3 | 5 | 6 | .... | .... | .... | .... |
| **2005-06** | **Atlanta** | **NHL** | **7** | **0** | **0** | **0** | **0** | **0** | **0** | **0** | **6** | **0.0** | **−5** | **0** | **0.0** | **11:04** | .... | .... | .... | .... | .... | .... | .... | .... | .... |
| | Chicago Wolves | AHL | 73 | 12 | 26 | 38 | 51 | .... | .... | .... | .... | .... | .... | .... | .... | .... | .... | .... | .... | .... | .... | .... | .... | .... | .... |
| **2006-07** | **Atlanta** | **NHL** | **3** | **0** | **1** | **1** | **0** | **0** | **0** | **0** | **1** | **0.0** | **1** | **0** | **0.0** | **10:15** | .... | .... | .... | .... | .... | .... | .... | .... | .... |
| | Chicago Wolves | AHL | 65 | 16 | 24 | 40 | 51 | .... | .... | .... | .... | .... | .... | .... | .... | .... | 15 | 3 | 6 | 9 | 4 | .... | .... | .... | .... |
| **2007-08** | **Atlanta** | **NHL** | **33** | **0** | **2** | **2** | **10** | **0** | **0** | **0** | **25** | **0.0** | **−4** | **0** | **0.0** | **14:28** | .... | .... | .... | .... | .... | .... | .... | .... | .... |
| 2008-09 | St. Petersburg | Rus-KHL | 52 | 8 | 15 | 23 | 40 | .... | .... | .... | .... | .... | .... | .... | .... | .... | 3 | 0 | 0 | 0 | 2 | .... | .... | .... | .... |
| | **NHL Totals** | | **44** | **0** | **3** | **3** | **10** | **0** | **0** | **0** | **33** | **0.0** | | **0** | **0.0** | **13:38** | .... | .... | .... | .... | .... | .... | .... | .... | .... |

OHL First All-Star Team (2002)

Traded to **Atlanta** by **Anaheim** for Kip Brennan, August 23, 2005.

## PORTER, Chris

(POHR-tuhr, KRIHS) **ST.L.**

Center. Shoots left. 6'1", 205 lbs. Born, Toronto, Ont., May 29, 1984. Chicago's 10th choice, 282nd overall, in 2003 Entry Draft.

| Season | Club | League | GP | G | A | Pts | PIM | PP | SH | GW | S | % | +/- | TF | F% | Min | GP | G | A | Pts | PIM | PP | SH | GW | Min |
|---|---|---|---|---|---|---|---|---|---|---|---|---|---|---|---|---|---|---|---|---|---|---|---|---|---|
| 2001-02 | Shat.-St. Mary's | High-MN | 75 | 10 | 25 | 35 | 32 | .... | .... | .... | .... | .... | .... | .... | .... | .... | .... | .... | .... | .... | .... | .... | .... | .... | .... |
| 2002-03 | Lincoln Stars | USHL | 59 | 13 | 22 | 35 | 74 | .... | .... | .... | .... | .... | .... | .... | .... | .... | 10 | 4 | 3 | 7 | 10 | .... | .... | .... | .... |
| 2003-04 | North Dakota | WCHA | 41 | 10 | 15 | 25 | 46 | .... | .... | .... | .... | .... | .... | .... | .... | .... | .... | .... | .... | .... | .... | .... | .... | .... | .... |
| 2004-05 | North Dakota | WCHA | 45 | 12 | 3 | 15 | 36 | .... | .... | .... | .... | .... | .... | .... | .... | .... | .... | .... | .... | .... | .... | .... | .... | .... | .... |
| 2005-06 | North Dakota | WCHA | 46 | 7 | 16 | 23 | 40 | .... | .... | .... | .... | .... | .... | .... | .... | .... | .... | .... | .... | .... | .... | .... | .... | .... | .... |
| 2006-07 | North Dakota | WCHA | 43 | 13 | 17 | 30 | 38 | .... | .... | .... | .... | .... | .... | .... | .... | .... | .... | .... | .... | .... | .... | .... | .... | .... | .... |
| 2007-08 | Peoria Rivermen | AHL | 80 | 12 | 25 | 37 | 72 | .... | .... | .... | .... | .... | .... | .... | .... | .... | .... | .... | .... | .... | .... | .... | .... | .... | .... |

| | | | Regular Season | | | | | | | | | | | | | | Playoffs | | | | | | | | |
|---|---|---|---|---|---|---|---|---|---|---|---|---|---|---|---|---|---|---|---|---|---|---|---|---|---|
| Season | Club | League | GP | G | A | Pts | PIM | PP | SH | GW | S | % | +/- | TF | F% | Min | GP | G | A | Pts | PIM | PP | SH | GW | Min |
| **2008-09** | **St. Louis** | **NHL** | **6** | **1** | **1** | **2** | **0** | **0** | **0** | **0** | **7** | **14.3** | **–1** | **3** | **33.3** | **10:32** | .... | .... | .... | .... | .... | .... | .... | .... | .... |
| | Peoria Rivermen | AHL | 74 | 7 | 16 | 23 | 72 | .... | .... | .... | .... | .... | .... | .... | .... | .... | 7 | 1 | 1 | 2 | 0 | .... | .... | .... | .... |
| | **NHL Totals** | | **6** | **1** | **1** | **2** | **0** | **0** | **0** | **0** | **7** | **14.3** | | **3** | **33.3** | **10:32** | .... | .... | .... | .... | .... | .... | .... | .... | .... |

Signed as a free agent by **St. Louis**, August 21, 2007.

## PORTER, Kevin

(POHR-tuhr, KEH-vihn) **PHX.**

Left wing. Shoots left. 5'11", 194 lbs. Born, Detroit, MI, March 12, 1986. Phoenix's 5th choice, 119th overall, in 2004 Entry Draft.

| Season | Club | League | GP | G | A | Pts | PIM | PP | SH | GW | S | % | +/- | TF | F% | Min | GP | G | A | Pts | PIM | PP | SH | GW | Min |
|---|---|---|---|---|---|---|---|---|---|---|---|---|---|---|---|---|---|---|---|---|---|---|---|---|---|
| 2002-03 | USNTDP | U-17 | 19 | 9 | 11 | 20 | 8 | .... | .... | .... | .... | .... | .... | .... | .... | .... | .... | .... | .... | .... | .... | .... | .... | .... | .... |
| | USNTDP | U-18 | 13 | 1 | 2 | 3 | 2 | .... | .... | .... | .... | .... | .... | .... | .... | .... | .... | .... | .... | .... | .... | .... | .... | .... | .... |
| | USNTDP | NAHL | 40 | 19 | 9 | 28 | 17 | .... | .... | .... | .... | .... | .... | .... | .... | .... | .... | .... | .... | .... | .... | .... | .... | .... | .... |
| 2003-04 | USNTDP | U-18 | 44 | 5 | 21 | 26 | 26 | .... | .... | .... | .... | .... | .... | .... | .... | .... | .... | .... | .... | .... | .... | .... | .... | .... | .... |
| | USNTDP | NAHL | 11 | 3 | 8 | 11 | 4 | .... | .... | .... | .... | .... | .... | .... | .... | .... | .... | .... | .... | .... | .... | .... | .... | .... | .... |
| 2004-05 | U. of Michigan | CCHA | 39 | 11 | 13 | 24 | 51 | .... | .... | .... | .... | .... | .... | .... | .... | .... | .... | .... | .... | .... | .... | .... | .... | .... | .... |
| 2005-06 | U. of Michigan | CCHA | 39 | 17 | 21 | 38 | 30 | .... | .... | .... | .... | .... | .... | .... | .... | .... | .... | .... | .... | .... | .... | .... | .... | .... | .... |
| 2006-07 | U. of Michigan | CCHA | 41 | 24 | 34 | 58 | 16 | .... | .... | .... | .... | .... | .... | .... | .... | .... | .... | .... | .... | .... | .... | .... | .... | .... | .... |
| 2007-08 | U. of Michigan | CCHA | 43 | *33 | 30 | *63 | 18 | .... | .... | .... | .... | .... | .... | .... | .... | .... | .... | .... | .... | .... | .... | .... | .... | .... | .... |
| | San Antonio | AHL | .... | .... | .... | .... | .... | .... | .... | .... | .... | .... | .... | .... | .... | .... | 7 | 0 | 4 | 4 | 0 | .... | .... | .... | .... |
| **2008-09** | **Phoenix** | **NHL** | **34** | **5** | **5** | **10** | **4** | **1** | **0** | **2** | **39** | **12.8** | **–2** | **95** | **29.5** | **13:38** | .... | .... | .... | .... | .... | .... | .... | .... | .... |
| | San Antonio | AHL | 42 | 13 | 22 | 35 | 14 | .... | .... | .... | .... | .... | .... | .... | .... | .... | .... | .... | .... | .... | .... | .... | .... | .... | .... |
| | **NHL Totals** | | **34** | **5** | **5** | **10** | **4** | **1** | **0** | **2** | **39** | **12.8** | | **95** | **29.5** | **13:38** | .... | .... | .... | .... | .... | .... | .... | .... | .... |

CCHA Second All-Star Team (2007) • CCHA First All-Star Team (2008) • CCHA Player of the Year (2008) • NCAA West First All-American Team (2008)

## POTHIER, Brian

(POH-thee-uhr, BRIGH-uhn) **WSH.**

Defense. Shoots right. 6', 200 lbs. Born, New Bedford, MA, April 15, 1977.

| Season | Club | League | GP | G | A | Pts | PIM | PP | SH | GW | S | % | +/- | TF | F% | Min | GP | G | A | Pts | PIM | PP | SH | GW | Min |
|---|---|---|---|---|---|---|---|---|---|---|---|---|---|---|---|---|---|---|---|---|---|---|---|---|---|
| 1995-96 | NMH School | High-MA | 27 | 11 | 22 | 33 | 36 | .... | .... | .... | .... | .... | .... | .... | .... | .... | .... | .... | .... | .... | .... | .... | .... | .... | .... |
| 1996-97 | RPI Engineers | ECAC | 34 | 1 | 11 | 12 | 42 | .... | .... | .... | .... | .... | .... | .... | .... | .... | .... | .... | .... | .... | .... | .... | .... | .... | .... |
| 1997-98 | RPI Engineers | ECAC | 35 | 2 | 9 | 11 | 28 | .... | .... | .... | .... | .... | .... | .... | .... | .... | .... | .... | .... | .... | .... | .... | .... | .... | .... |
| 1998-99 | RPI Engineers | ECAC | 37 | 5 | 13 | 18 | 36 | .... | .... | .... | .... | .... | .... | .... | .... | .... | .... | .... | .... | .... | .... | .... | .... | .... | .... |
| 99-2000 | RPI Engineers | ECAC | 36 | 9 | 24 | 33 | 44 | .... | .... | .... | .... | .... | .... | .... | .... | .... | .... | .... | .... | .... | .... | .... | .... | .... | .... |
| **2000-01** | **Atlanta** | **NHL** | **3** | **0** | **0** | **0** | **2** | **0** | **0** | **0** | **0** | **0.0** | **4** | **0** | **0.0** | **20:38** | .... | .... | .... | .... | .... | .... | .... | .... | .... |
| | Orlando | IHL | 76 | 12 | 29 | 41 | 69 | .... | .... | .... | .... | .... | .... | .... | .... | .... | 16 | 3 | 5 | 8 | 11 | .... | .... | .... | .... |
| **2001-02** | **Atlanta** | **NHL** | **33** | **3** | **6** | **9** | **22** | **1** | **0** | **1** | **65** | **4.6** | **–19** | **0** | **0.0** | **21:41** | .... | .... | .... | .... | .... | .... | .... | .... | .... |
| | Chicago Wolves | AHL | 39 | 6 | 13 | 19 | 30 | .... | .... | .... | .... | .... | .... | .... | .... | .... | .... | .... | .... | .... | .... | .... | .... | .... | .... |
| **2002-03** | **Ottawa** | **NHL** | **14** | **2** | **4** | **6** | **6** | **0** | **0** | **1** | **23** | **8.7** | **11** | **0** | **0.0** | **15:23** | **1** | **0** | **0** | **0** | **2** | **0** | **0** | **0** | **13:11** |
| | Binghamton | AHL | 68 | 7 | 40 | 47 | 58 | .... | .... | .... | .... | .... | .... | .... | .... | .... | 8 | 2 | 8 | 10 | 4 | .... | .... | .... | .... |
| **2003-04** | **Ottawa** | **NHL** | **55** | **2** | **6** | **8** | **24** | **1** | **0** | **1** | **78** | **2.6** | **6** | **0** | **0.0** | **16:43** | **7** | **0** | **0** | **0** | **6** | **0** | **0** | **0** | **17:15** |
| 2004-05 | Binghamton | AHL | 77 | 12 | 36 | 48 | 64 | .... | .... | .... | .... | .... | .... | .... | .... | .... | 6 | 0 | 1 | 1 | 6 | .... | .... | .... | .... |
| **2005-06** | **Ottawa** | **NHL** | **77** | **5** | **30** | **35** | **59** | **3** | **0** | **0** | **133** | **3.8** | **29** | **0** | **0.0** | **16:46** | **8** | **2** | **1** | **3** | **2** | **0** | **0** | **0** | **15:02** |
| **2006-07** | **Washington** | **NHL** | **72** | **3** | **25** | **28** | **44** | **2** | **0** | **0** | **118** | **2.5** | **–11** | **0** | **0.0** | **23:59** | .... | .... | .... | .... | .... | .... | .... | .... | .... |
| **2007-08** | **Washington** | **NHL** | **38** | **5** | **9** | **14** | **20** | **1** | **0** | **1** | **65** | **7.7** | **5** | **0** | **0.0** | **18:42** | .... | .... | .... | .... | .... | .... | .... | .... | .... |
| **2008-09** | **Washington** | **NHL** | **9** | **1** | **2** | **3** | **4** | **0** | **0** | **1** | **8** | **12.5** | **0** | **0** | **0.0** | **16:35** | **13** | **0** | **2** | **2** | **8** | **0** | **0** | **0** | **16:48** |
| | Hershey Bears | AHL | 4 | 0 | 0 | 0 | 2 | .... | .... | .... | .... | .... | .... | .... | .... | .... | .... | .... | .... | .... | .... | .... | .... | .... | .... |
| | **NHL Totals** | | **301** | **21** | **82** | **103** | **181** | **8** | **0** | **5** | **490** | **4.3** | | **0** | **0.0** | **19:14** | **29** | **2** | **3** | **5** | **18** | **0** | **0** | **0** | **16:18** |

ECAC Second All-Star Team (2000) • ECAC All-Tournament Team (2000) • NCAA East Second All-American Team (2000) • Ken McKenzie Trophy (IHL – U.S. - Born Rookie of the Year) (2001) • Garry F. Longman Memorial Trophy (IHL – Rookie of the Year) (2001) • AHL Second All-Star Team (2003, 2005)

Signed as a free agent by **Atlanta**, March 27, 2000. Traded to **Ottawa** by **Atlanta** for Shawn McEachern and Ottawa's 6th round choice (Dan Turple) in 2004 Entry Draft, June 29, 2002. Signed as a free agent by **Washington**, July 1, 2006. • Missed remainder of 2007-08 season and majority of 2008-09 season recovering from head injury suffered in game at Boston, January 3, 2008.

## POTI, Tom

(POH-tee, TAWM) **WSH.**

Defense. Shoots left. 6'3", 200 lbs. Born, Worcester, MA, March 22, 1977. Edmonton's 4th choice, 59th overall, in 1996 Entry Draft.

| Season | Club | League | GP | G | A | Pts | PIM | PP | SH | GW | S | % | +/- | TF | F% | Min | GP | G | A | Pts | PIM | PP | SH | GW | Min |
|---|---|---|---|---|---|---|---|---|---|---|---|---|---|---|---|---|---|---|---|---|---|---|---|---|---|
| 1992-93 | St. Peter's Marian | High-MA | 55 | 25 | 46 | 71 | .... | .... | .... | .... | .... | .... | .... | .... | .... | .... | .... | .... | .... | .... | .... | .... | .... | .... | .... |
| 1993-94 | Cushing | High-MA | 30 | 10 | 35 | 45 | | .... | .... | .... | .... | .... | .... | .... | .... | .... | .... | .... | .... | .... | .... | .... | .... | .... | .... |
| 1994-95 | Cushing | High-MA | 36 | 17 | 54 | 71 | 35 | .... | .... | .... | .... | .... | .... | .... | .... | .... | .... | .... | .... | .... | .... | .... | .... | .... | .... |
| | Central-Mass | MBAHL | 8 | 8 | 10 | 18 | .... | .... | .... | .... | .... | .... | .... | .... | .... | .... | .... | .... | .... | .... | .... | .... | .... | .... | .... |
| 1995-96 | Cushing | High-MA | 29 | 14 | 59 | 73 | 18 | .... | .... | .... | .... | .... | .... | .... | .... | .... | .... | .... | .... | .... | .... | .... | .... | .... | .... |
| 1996-97 | Boston University | H-East | 38 | 4 | 17 | 21 | 54 | .... | .... | .... | .... | .... | .... | .... | .... | .... | .... | .... | .... | .... | .... | .... | .... | .... | .... |
| 1997-98 | Boston University | H-East | 38 | 13 | 29 | 42 | 60 | .... | .... | .... | .... | .... | .... | .... | .... | .... | .... | .... | .... | .... | .... | .... | .... | .... | .... |
| **1998-99** | **Edmonton** | **NHL** | **73** | **5** | **16** | **21** | **42** | **2** | **0** | **3** | **94** | **5.3** | **10** | **0** | **0.0** | **19:33** | **4** | **0** | **1** | **1** | **2** | **0** | **0** | **0** | **28:02** |
| **99-2000** | **Edmonton** | **NHL** | **76** | **9** | **26** | **35** | **65** | **2** | **1** | **1** | **125** | **7.2** | **8** | **0** | **0.0** | **24:10** | **5** | **0** | **1** | **1** | **0** | **0** | **0** | **0** | **23:53** |
| **2000-01** | **Edmonton** | **NHL** | **81** | **12** | **20** | **32** | **60** | **6** | **0** | **3** | **161** | **7.5** | **–4** | **0** | **0.0** | **22:44** | **6** | **0** | **2** | **2** | **2** | **0** | **0** | **0** | **20:25** |
| **2001-02** | **Edmonton** | **NHL** | **55** | **1** | **16** | **17** | **42** | **1** | **0** | **0** | **100** | **1.0** | **–6** | **0** | **0.0** | **24:32** | .... | .... | .... | .... | .... | .... | .... | .... | .... |
| | United States | Olympics | 6 | 0 | 1 | 1 | 4 | .... | .... | .... | .... | .... | .... | .... | .... | .... | .... | .... | .... | .... | .... | .... | .... | .... | .... |
| | **NY Rangers** | **NHL** | **11** | **1** | **7** | **8** | **2** | **1** | **0** | **1** | **9** | **11.1** | **–4** | **0** | **0.0** | **21:45** | .... | .... | .... | .... | .... | .... | .... | .... | .... |
| **2002-03** | **NY Rangers** | **NHL** | **80** | **11** | **37** | **48** | **58** | **3** | **0** | **2** | **148** | **7.4** | **–6** | **0** | **0.0** | **24:43** | .... | .... | .... | .... | .... | .... | .... | .... | .... |
| **2003-04** | **NY Rangers** | **NHL** | **67** | **10** | **14** | **24** | **47** | **4** | **0** | **5** | **124** | **8.1** | **–1** | **0** | **0.0** | **22:28** | .... | .... | .... | .... | .... | .... | .... | .... | .... |
| 2004-05 | | | DID NOT PLAY | | | | | | | | | | | | | | | | | | | | | | |
| **2005-06** | **NY Rangers** | **NHL** | **73** | **3** | **20** | **23** | **70** | **2** | **0** | **2** | **122** | **2.5** | **16** | **4** | **25.0** | **20:46** | **4** | **0** | **0** | **0** | **2** | **0** | **0** | **0** | **19:39** |
| **2006-07** | **NY Islanders** | **NHL** | **78** | **6** | **38** | **44** | **74** | **6** | **0** | **1** | **134** | **4.5** | **–1** | **0** | **0.0** | **25:43** | **5** | **0** | **3** | **3** | **6** | **0** | **0** | **0** | **27:34** |
| **2007-08** | **Washington** | **NHL** | **71** | **2** | **27** | **29** | **46** | **0** | **0** | **0** | **99** | **2.0** | **9** | **0** | **0.0** | **23:29** | **7** | **0** | **1** | **1** | **8** | **0** | **0** | **0** | **24:01** |
| **2008-09** | **Washington** | **NHL** | **52** | **3** | **10** | **13** | **28** | **0** | **0** | **1** | **48** | **6.3** | **3** | **0** | **0.0** | **21:09** | **14** | **2** | **5** | **7** | **4** | **1** | **0** | **0** | **21:37** |
| | **NHL Totals** | | **717** | **63** | **231** | **294** | **534** | **27** | **1** | **19** | **1164** | **5.4** | | **4** | **25.0** | **22:58** | **45** | **2** | **13** | **15** | **24** | **1** | **0** | **0** | **23:08** |

NCAA Championship All-Tournament Team (1997) • Hockey East First All-Star Team (1998) • NCAA East First All-American Team (1998) • NHL All-Rookie Team (1999)

Played in NHL All-Star Game (2003)

Traded to **NY Rangers** by **Edmonton** with Rem Murray for Mike York and NY Rangers' 4th round choice (Ivan Koltsov) in 2002 Entry Draft, March 19, 2002. Signed as a free agent by **NY Islanders**, July 8, 2006. Signed as a free agent by **Washington**, July 1, 2007.

## POTTER, Corey

(PAW-tuhr, KOHR-ee) **NYR**

Defense. Shoots right. 6'3", 200 lbs. Born, Lansing, MI, January 5, 1984. NY Rangers' 4th choice, 122nd overall, in 2003 Entry Draft.

| Season | Club | League | GP | G | A | Pts | PIM | PP | SH | GW | S | % | +/- | TF | F% | Min | GP | G | A | Pts | PIM | PP | SH | GW | Min |
|---|---|---|---|---|---|---|---|---|---|---|---|---|---|---|---|---|---|---|---|---|---|---|---|---|---|
| 99-2000 | Det. Honeybaked | MWEHL | 58 | 10 | 38 | 48 | .... | .... | .... | .... | .... | .... | .... | .... | .... | .... | .... | .... | .... | .... | .... | .... | .... | .... | .... |
| 2000-01 | USNTDP | U-17 | 13 | 0 | 0 | 0 | 6 | .... | .... | .... | .... | .... | .... | .... | .... | .... | .... | .... | .... | .... | .... | .... | .... | .... | .... |
| | USNTDP | NAHL | 53 | 4 | 4 | 8 | 20 | .... | .... | .... | .... | .... | .... | .... | .... | .... | .... | .... | .... | .... | .... | .... | .... | .... | .... |
| 2001-02 | USNTDP | U-18 | 38 | 4 | 6 | 10 | 49 | .... | .... | .... | .... | .... | .... | .... | .... | .... | .... | .... | .... | .... | .... | .... | .... | .... | .... |
| | USNTDP | USHL | 13 | 2 | 2 | 4 | 12 | .... | .... | .... | .... | .... | .... | .... | .... | .... | .... | .... | .... | .... | .... | .... | .... | .... | .... |
| | USNTDP | NAHL | 10 | 0 | 3 | 3 | 4 | .... | .... | .... | .... | .... | .... | .... | .... | .... | .... | .... | .... | .... | .... | .... | .... | .... | .... |
| 2002-03 | Michigan State | CCHA | 35 | 4 | 4 | 8 | 30 | .... | .... | .... | .... | .... | .... | .... | .... | .... | .... | .... | .... | .... | .... | .... | .... | .... | .... |
| 2003-04 | Michigan State | CCHA | 38 | 0 | 8 | 8 | 63 | .... | .... | .... | .... | .... | .... | .... | .... | .... | .... | .... | .... | .... | .... | .... | .... | .... | .... |
| 2004-05 | Michigan State | CCHA | 32 | 0 | 6 | 6 | 73 | .... | .... | .... | .... | .... | .... | .... | .... | .... | .... | .... | .... | .... | .... | .... | .... | .... | .... |
| 2005-06 | Michigan State | CCHA | 45 | 4 | 18 | 22 | 117 | .... | .... | .... | .... | .... | .... | .... | .... | .... | .... | .... | .... | .... | .... | .... | .... | .... | .... |
| 2006-07 | Hartford | AHL | 30 | 2 | 8 | 10 | 21 | .... | .... | .... | .... | .... | .... | .... | .... | .... | 7 | 1 | 4 | 5 | 12 | .... | .... | .... | .... |
| | Charlotte | ECHL | 43 | 6 | 13 | 19 | 56 | .... | .... | .... | .... | .... | .... | .... | .... | .... | .... | .... | .... | .... | .... | .... | .... | .... | .... |
| 2007-08 | Hartford | AHL | 80 | 5 | 27 | 32 | 102 | .... | .... | .... | .... | .... | .... | .... | .... | .... | 5 | 0 | 1 | 1 | 14 | .... | .... | .... | .... |
| **2008-09** | **NY Rangers** | **NHL** | **5** | **1** | **1** | **2** | **0** | **0** | **0** | **0** | **4** | **25.0** | **–1** | **0** | **0.0** | **13:15** | .... | .... | .... | .... | .... | .... | .... | .... | .... |
| | Hartford | AHL | 67 | 10 | 22 | 32 | 82 | .... | .... | .... | .... | .... | .... | .... | .... | .... | 6 | 1 | 3 | 4 | 23 | .... | .... | .... | .... |
| | **NHL Totals** | | **5** | **1** | **1** | **2** | **0** | **0** | **0** | **0** | **4** | **25.0** | | **0** | **0.0** | **13:15** | .... | .... | .... | .... | .... | .... | .... | .... | .... |

## POTULNY, Ryan

(poh-TUHL-nee, RIGH-uhn) **EDM.**

Center. Shoots left. 6', 190 lbs. Born, Grand Forks, ND, September 5, 1984. Philadelphia's 6th choice, 87th overall, in 2003 Entry Draft.

| Season | Club | League | GP | G | A | Pts | PIM | PP | SH | GW | S | % | +/- | TF | F% | Min | GP | G | A | Pts | PIM | PP | SH | GW | Min |
|---|---|---|---|---|---|---|---|---|---|---|---|---|---|---|---|---|---|---|---|---|---|---|---|---|---|
| 2001-02 | Lincoln Stars | USHL | 60 | 23 | 34 | 57 | 65 | .... | .... | .... | .... | .... | .... | .... | .... | .... | 4 | 0 | 1 | 1 | 2 | .... | .... | .... | .... |
| 2002-03 | Lincoln Stars | USHL | 54 | 35 | *43 | *78 | 18 | .... | .... | .... | .... | .... | .... | .... | .... | .... | 10 | 6 | *11 | *17 | 8 | .... | .... | .... | .... |
| 2003-04 | U. of Minnesota | WCHA | 15 | 6 | 8 | 14 | 10 | .... | .... | .... | .... | .... | .... | .... | .... | .... | .... | .... | .... | .... | .... | .... | .... | .... | .... |
| 2004-05 | U. of Minnesota | WCHA | 44 | 24 | 17 | 41 | 20 | .... | .... | .... | .... | .... | .... | .... | .... | .... | .... | .... | .... | .... | .... | .... | .... | .... | .... |
| **2005-06** | U. of Minnesota | WCHA | 41 | *38 | 25 | *63 | 31 | .... | .... | .... | .... | .... | .... | .... | .... | .... | .... | .... | .... | .... | .... | .... | .... | .... | .... |
| | **Philadelphia** | **NHL** | **2** | **0** | **1** | **1** | **0** | **0** | **0** | **0** | **0** | **0.0** | **1** | **9** | **44.4** | **6:09** | | | | | | | | | |

| | | | Regular Season | | | | | | | | | | | | | | Playoffs | | | | | | | | |
|---|---|---|---|---|---|---|---|---|---|---|---|---|---|---|---|---|---|---|---|---|---|---|---|---|---|
| Season | Club | League | GP | G | A | Pts | PIM | PP | SH | GW | S | % | +/- | TF | F% | Min | GP | G | A | Pts | PIM | PP | SH | GW | Min |
| **2006-07** | **Philadelphia** | **NHL** | **35** | **7** | **5** | **12** | **22** | **0** | **0** | **2** | **56** | **12.5** | **1** | **278** | **43.5** | **11:00** | .... | .... | .... | .... | .... | .... | .... | .... | .... |
| | Philadelphia | AHL | 30 | 12 | 14 | 26 | 34 | .... | .... | .... | .... | .... | .... | .... | .... | .... | .... | .... | .... | .... | .... | .... | .... | .... | .... |
| **2007-08** | **Philadelphia** | **NHL** | **7** | **0** | **1** | **1** | **4** | **0** | **0** | **0** | **5** | **0.0** | **0** | **32** | **43.8** | **6:30** | .... | .... | .... | .... | .... | .... | .... | .... | .... |
| | Philadelphia | AHL | 58 | 21 | 26 | 47 | 51 | .... | .... | .... | .... | .... | .... | .... | .... | .... | 12 | 3 | 5 | 8 | 10 | .... | .... | .... | .... |
| **2008-09** | **Edmonton** | **NHL** | **8** | **0** | **3** | **3** | **0** | **0** | **0** | **0** | **9** | **0.0** | **2** | **10** | **10.0** | **10:29** | .... | .... | .... | .... | .... | .... | .... | .... | .... |
| | Springfield | AHL | 70 | 38 | 24 | 62 | 48 | .... | .... | .... | .... | .... | .... | .... | .... | .... | .... | .... | .... | .... | .... | .... | .... | .... | .... |
| | **NHL Totals** | | **52** | **7** | **10** | **17** | **26** | **0** | **0** | **2** | **70** | **10.0** | | **329** | **42.6** | **10:08** | .... | .... | .... | .... | .... | .... | .... | .... | .... |

USHL First All-Star Team (2003) • USHL Player of the Year (2003) • WCHA First All-Star Team (2006) • NCAA West First All-American Team (2006)

• Missed majority of 2003-04 season recovering from knee injury suffered in game vs. North Dakota (WCHA), November 7, 2003. Traded to **Edmonton** by **Philadelphia** for Danny Syvret, June 6, 2008.

## POULIOT, Benoit
(POO-lee-aht, BEHN-wah) **MIN.**

Left wing. Shoots Left. 6'3", 199 lbs. Born, Alfred, Ont., September 29, 1986. Minnesota's 1st choice, 4th overall, in 2005 Entry Draft.

| Season | Club | League | GP | G | A | Pts | PIM | PP | SH | GW | S | % | +/- | TF | F% | Min | GP | G | A | Pts | PIM | PP | SH | GW | Min |
|---|---|---|---|---|---|---|---|---|---|---|---|---|---|---|---|---|---|---|---|---|---|---|---|---|---|
| 2002-03 | Clarence Beavers | OHA-B | 38 | 13 | 17 | 30 | 86 | .... | .... | .... | .... | .... | .... | .... | .... | .... | 5 | 0 | 2 | 2 | 8 | .... | .... | .... | .... |
| | Hawkesbury | CJHL | 1 | 1 | 0 | 1 | 0 | .... | .... | .... | .... | .... | .... | .... | .... | .... | .... | .... | .... | .... | .... | .... | .... | .... | .... |
| 2003-04 | Hawkesbury | CJHL | 45 | 21 | 21 | 42 | 85 | .... | .... | .... | .... | .... | .... | .... | .... | .... | 6 | 3 | 7 | 10 | 10 | .... | .... | .... | .... |
| | Sudbury Wolves | OHL | 4 | 2 | 2 | 4 | 0 | .... | .... | .... | .... | .... | .... | .... | .... | .... | 4 | 2 | 1 | 3 | 0 | .... | .... | .... | .... |
| 2004-05 | Sudbury Wolves | OHL | 67 | 29 | 38 | 67 | 102 | .... | .... | .... | .... | .... | .... | .... | .... | .... | 12 | 6 | 8 | 14 | 20 | .... | .... | .... | .... |
| 2005-06 | Sudbury Wolves | OHL | 51 | 35 | 30 | 65 | 141 | .... | .... | .... | .... | .... | .... | .... | .... | .... | 8 | 8 | 3 | 11 | 16 | .... | .... | .... | .... |
| | Houston Aeros | AHL | .... | .... | .... | .... | .... | .... | .... | .... | .... | .... | .... | .... | .... | .... | 2 | 0 | 0 | 0 | 2 | .... | .... | .... | .... |
| **2006-07** | **Minnesota** | **NHL** | **3** | **0** | **0** | **0** | **0** | **0** | **0** | **0** | **1** | **0.0** | **–1** | **2** | **0.0** | **6:58** | .... | .... | .... | .... | .... | .... | .... | .... | .... |
| | Houston Aeros | AHL | 67 | 19 | 17 | 36 | 109 | .... | .... | .... | .... | .... | .... | .... | .... | .... | .... | .... | .... | .... | .... | .... | .... | .... | .... |
| **2007-08** | **Minnesota** | **NHL** | **11** | **2** | **1** | **3** | **0** | **0** | **0** | **0** | **10** | **20.0** | **–1** | **65** | **40.0** | **8:49** | **1** | **0** | **0** | **0** | **0** | **0** | **0** | **0** | **10:16** |
| | Houston Aeros | AHL | 46 | 10 | 14 | 24 | 67 | .... | .... | .... | .... | .... | .... | .... | .... | .... | 3 | 0 | 0 | 0 | 2 | .... | .... | .... | .... |
| **2008-09** | **Minnesota** | **NHL** | **37** | **5** | **6** | **11** | **18** | **2** | **0** | **1** | **34** | **14.7** | **1** | **217** | **42.9** | **11:51** | .... | .... | .... | .... | .... | .... | .... | .... | .... |
| | Houston Aeros | AHL | 30 | 9 | 15 | 24 | 20 | .... | .... | .... | .... | .... | .... | .... | .... | .... | 20 | 1 | 7 | 8 | 28 | .... | .... | .... | .... |
| | **NHL Totals** | | **51** | **7** | **7** | **14** | **18** | **2** | **0** | **1** | **45** | **15.6** | | **284** | **41.9** | **10:54** | **1** | **0** | **0** | **0** | **0** | **0** | **0** | **0** | **10:16** |

OHL First All-Star Team (2005) • OHL Rookie of the Year (2005) • Canadian Major Junior All-Rookie Team (2005) • Canadian Major Junior Rookie of the Year (2005)

## POULIOT, Marc-Antoine
(POO-lee-awt, MAHRK-AN-twahn) **EDM.**

Center. Shoots right. 6'1", 195 lbs. Born, Quebec City, Que., May 22, 1985. Edmonton's 1st choice, 22nd overall, in 2003 Entry Draft.

| Season | Club | League | GP | G | A | Pts | PIM | PP | SH | GW | S | % | +/- | TF | F% | Min | GP | G | A | Pts | PIM | PP | SH | GW | Min |
|---|---|---|---|---|---|---|---|---|---|---|---|---|---|---|---|---|---|---|---|---|---|---|---|---|---|
| 2000-01 | Ste-Foy | QAAA | 38 | 16 | 39 | 55 | 52 | .... | .... | .... | .... | .... | .... | .... | .... | .... | 16 | 8 | 12 | 20 | 16 | .... | .... | .... | .... |
| 2001-02 | Rimouski Oceanic | QMJHL | 28 | 9 | 14 | 23 | 32 | .... | .... | .... | .... | .... | .... | .... | .... | .... | 5 | 0 | 0 | 0 | 4 | .... | .... | .... | .... |
| 2002-03 | Rimouski Oceanic | QMJHL | 65 | 32 | 41 | 73 | 100 | .... | .... | .... | .... | .... | .... | .... | .... | .... | .... | .... | .... | .... | .... | .... | .... | .... | .... |
| 2003-04 | Rimouski Oceanic | QMJHL | 42 | 25 | 33 | 58 | 62 | .... | .... | .... | .... | .... | .... | .... | .... | .... | 9 | 5 | 7 | 12 | 12 | .... | .... | .... | .... |
| 2004-05 | Rimouski Oceanic | QMJHL | 70 | 45 | 69 | 114 | 83 | .... | .... | .... | .... | .... | .... | .... | .... | .... | 13 | 4 | 15 | 19 | 8 | .... | .... | .... | .... |
| **2005-06** | **Edmonton** | **NHL** | **8** | **1** | **0** | **1** | **0** | **0** | **0** | **0** | **5** | **20.0** | **1** | **56** | **55.4** | **8:30** | .... | .... | .... | .... | .... | .... | .... | .... | .... |
| | Hamilton | AHL | 65 | 15 | 31 | 46 | 63 | .... | .... | .... | .... | .... | .... | .... | .... | .... | .... | .... | .... | .... | .... | .... | .... | .... | .... |
| **2006-07** | **Edmonton** | **NHL** | **46** | **4** | **7** | **11** | **18** | **0** | **0** | **0** | **73** | **5.5** | **–2** | **353** | **48.7** | **13:03** | .... | .... | .... | .... | .... | .... | .... | .... | .... |
| | Wilkes-Barre | AHL | 33 | 14 | 17 | 31 | 20 | .... | .... | .... | .... | .... | .... | .... | .... | .... | 11 | 5 | 5 | 10 | 4 | .... | .... | .... | .... |
| **2007-08** | **Edmonton** | **NHL** | **24** | **1** | **6** | **7** | **12** | **0** | **0** | **0** | **32** | **3.1** | **–1** | **44** | **47.7** | **10:20** | .... | .... | .... | .... | .... | .... | .... | .... | .... |
| | Springfield | AHL | 55 | 21 | 26 | 47 | 47 | .... | .... | .... | .... | .... | .... | .... | .... | .... | .... | .... | .... | .... | .... | .... | .... | .... | .... |
| **2008-09** | **Edmonton** | **NHL** | **63** | **8** | **12** | **20** | **23** | **0** | **0** | **2** | **94** | **8.5** | **1** | **211** | **48.3** | **11:30** | .... | .... | .... | .... | .... | .... | .... | .... | .... |
| | **NHL Totals** | | **141** | **14** | **25** | **39** | **53** | **0** | **0** | **2** | **204** | **6.9** | | **664** | **49.1** | **11:38** | .... | .... | .... | .... | .... | .... | .... | .... | .... |

QMJHL First All-Star Team (2005) • George Parsons Trophy (Memorial Cup Tournament - Most Sportsmanlike Player) (2005)

## POWE, Darroll
(POW, DAIR-ohl) **PHI.**

Left wing. Shoots left. 5'11", 212 lbs. Born, Saskatoon, Sask., June 22, 1985.

| Season | Club | League | GP | G | A | Pts | PIM | PP | SH | GW | S | % | +/- | TF | F% | Min | GP | G | A | Pts | PIM | PP | SH | GW | Min |
|---|---|---|---|---|---|---|---|---|---|---|---|---|---|---|---|---|---|---|---|---|---|---|---|---|---|
| 2003-04 | Princeton | ECAC | 29 | 4 | 5 | 9 | 28 | .... | .... | .... | .... | .... | .... | .... | .... | .... | .... | .... | .... | .... | .... | .... | .... | .... | .... |
| 2004-05 | Princeton | ECAC | 30 | 5 | 2 | 7 | 41 | .... | .... | .... | .... | .... | .... | .... | .... | .... | .... | .... | .... | .... | .... | .... | .... | .... | .... |
| 2005-06 | Princeton | ECAC | 27 | 6 | 10 | 16 | 48 | .... | .... | .... | .... | .... | .... | .... | .... | .... | .... | .... | .... | .... | .... | .... | .... | .... | .... |
| 2006-07 | Princeton | ECAC | 34 | 13 | 15 | 28 | 63 | .... | .... | .... | .... | .... | .... | .... | .... | .... | .... | .... | .... | .... | .... | .... | .... | .... | .... |
| | Philadelphia | AHL | 11 | 2 | 2 | 4 | 20 | .... | .... | .... | .... | .... | .... | .... | .... | .... | .... | .... | .... | .... | .... | .... | .... | .... | .... |
| 2007-08 | Philadelphia | AHL | 76 | 9 | 14 | 23 | 133 | .... | .... | .... | .... | .... | .... | .... | .... | .... | 10 | 1 | 0 | 1 | 6 | .... | .... | .... | .... |
| **2008-09** | **Philadelphia** | **NHL** | **60** | **6** | **5** | **11** | **35** | **0** | **0** | **0** | **72** | **8.3** | **–8** | **263** | **48.7** | **10:32** | **6** | **1** | **2** | **3** | **7** | **0** | **0** | **0** | **14:02** |
| | Philadelphia | AHL | 8 | 4 | 3 | 7 | 20 | .... | .... | .... | .... | .... | .... | .... | .... | .... | .... | .... | .... | .... | .... | .... | .... | .... | .... |
| | **NHL Totals** | | **60** | **6** | **5** | **11** | **35** | **0** | **0** | **0** | **72** | **8.3** | | **263** | **48.7** | **10:32** | **6** | **1** | **2** | **3** | **7** | **0** | **0** | **0** | **14:02** |

Signed as a free agent by **Philadelphia**, April 17, 2008.

## PRATT, Nolan
(PRAT, NOH-luhn)

Defense. Shoots left. 6'3", 207 lbs. Born, Fort McMurray, Alta., August 14, 1975. Hartford's 4th choice, 115th overall, in 1993 Entry Draft.

| Season | Club | League | GP | G | A | Pts | PIM | PP | SH | GW | S | % | +/- | TF | F% | Min | GP | G | A | Pts | PIM | PP | SH | GW | Min |
|---|---|---|---|---|---|---|---|---|---|---|---|---|---|---|---|---|---|---|---|---|---|---|---|---|---|
| 1991-92 | Bonnyville | AJHL | 33 | 3 | 7 | 10 | 57 | .... | .... | .... | .... | .... | .... | .... | .... | .... | .... | .... | .... | .... | .... | .... | .... | .... | .... |
| | Portland | WHL | 22 | 2 | 9 | 11 | 13 | .... | .... | .... | .... | .... | .... | .... | .... | .... | 6 | 1 | 3 | 4 | 12 | .... | .... | .... | .... |
| 1992-93 | Portland | WHL | 70 | 4 | 19 | 23 | 97 | .... | .... | .... | .... | .... | .... | .... | .... | .... | 16 | 2 | 7 | 9 | 31 | .... | .... | .... | .... |
| 1993-94 | Portland | WHL | 72 | 4 | 32 | 36 | 105 | .... | .... | .... | .... | .... | .... | .... | .... | .... | 10 | 1 | 2 | 3 | 14 | .... | .... | .... | .... |
| 1994-95 | Portland | WHL | 72 | 6 | 37 | 43 | 196 | .... | .... | .... | .... | .... | .... | .... | .... | .... | 9 | 1 | 6 | 7 | 10 | .... | .... | .... | .... |
| 1995-96 | Springfield | AHL | 62 | 2 | 6 | 8 | 72 | .... | .... | .... | .... | .... | .... | .... | .... | .... | 2 | 0 | 0 | 0 | 0 | .... | .... | .... | .... |
| | Richmond | ECHL | 4 | 1 | 0 | 1 | 2 | .... | .... | .... | .... | .... | .... | .... | .... | .... | .... | .... | .... | .... | .... | .... | .... | .... | .... |
| **1996-97** | **Hartford** | **NHL** | **9** | **0** | **2** | **2** | **6** | **0** | **0** | **0** | **4** | **0.0** | **0** | | | | .... | .... | .... | .... | .... | .... | .... | .... | .... |
| | Springfield | AHL | 66 | 1 | 18 | 19 | 127 | .... | .... | .... | .... | .... | .... | .... | .... | .... | 17 | 0 | 3 | 3 | 18 | .... | .... | .... | .... |
| **1997-98** | **Carolina** | **NHL** | **23** | **0** | **2** | **2** | **44** | **0** | **0** | **0** | **11** | **0.0** | **–2** | | | | .... | .... | .... | .... | .... | .... | .... | .... | .... |
| | New Haven | AHL | 54 | 3 | 15 | 18 | 135 | .... | .... | .... | .... | .... | .... | .... | .... | .... | .... | .... | .... | .... | .... | .... | .... | .... | .... |
| **1998-99** | **Carolina** | **NHL** | **61** | **1** | **14** | **15** | **95** | **0** | **0** | **1** | **46** | **2.2** | **15** | **0** | **0.0** | **16:45** | **3** | **0** | **0** | **0** | **2** | **0** | **0** | **0** | **19:58** |
| **99-2000** | **Carolina** | **NHL** | **64** | **3** | **1** | **4** | **90** | **0** | **0** | **1** | **47** | **6.4** | **–22** | **0** | **0.0** | **19:10** | .... | .... | .... | .... | .... | .... | .... | .... | .... |
| **2000-01** | **Colorado** | **NHL** | **46** | **1** | **2** | **3** | **40** | **0** | **0** | **1** | **26** | **3.8** | **2** | **1** | **0.0** | **9:50** | .... | .... | .... | .... | .... | .... | .... | .... | .... |
| **2001-02** | **Tampa Bay** | **NHL** | **46** | **0** | **3** | **3** | **51** | **0** | **0** | **0** | **38** | **0.0** | **–4** | **1** | **0.0** | **18:25** | .... | .... | .... | .... | .... | .... | .... | .... | .... |
| **2002-03** | **Tampa Bay** | **NHL** | **67** | **1** | **7** | **8** | **35** | **0** | **0** | **0** | **38** | **2.6** | **–6** | **0** | **0.0** | **17:34** | **4** | **0** | **1** | **1** | **0** | **0** | **0** | **0** | **21:01** |
| **2003-04♦** | **Tampa Bay** | **NHL** | **58** | **1** | **3** | **4** | **42** | **0** | **0** | **0** | **35** | **2.9** | **11** | **0** | **0.0** | **16:25** | **20** | **0** | **0** | **0** | **8** | **0** | **0** | **0** | **18:06** |
| 2004-05 | EV Duisburg | German-2 | 10 | 2 | 2 | 4 | 14 | .... | .... | .... | .... | .... | .... | .... | .... | .... | 12 | 0 | 3 | 3 | 10 | .... | .... | .... | .... |
| **2005-06** | **Tampa Bay** | **NHL** | **82** | **0** | **9** | **9** | **60** | **0** | **0** | **0** | **26** | **0.0** | **7** | **0** | **0.0** | **17:59** | **5** | **0** | **0** | **0** | **7** | **0** | **0** | **0** | **15:30** |
| **2006-07** | **Tampa Bay** | **NHL** | **81** | **1** | **7** | **8** | **44** | **0** | **0** | **0** | **30** | **3.3** | **0** | **1** | **0.0** | **15:47** | **6** | **0** | **0** | **0** | **5** | **0** | **0** | **0** | **14:32** |
| **2007-08** | **Buffalo** | **NHL** | **55** | **1** | **6** | **7** | **30** | **0** | **0** | **0** | **21** | **4.8** | **1** | **0** | **0.0** | **13:31** | .... | .... | .... | .... | .... | .... | .... | .... | .... |
| 2008-09 | Amur Khabarovsk | Rus-KHL | 35 | 1 | 8 | 9 | 28 | .... | .... | .... | .... | .... | .... | .... | .... | .... | .... | .... | .... | .... | .... | .... | .... | .... | .... |
| | **NHL Totals** | | **592** | **9** | **56** | **65** | **537** | **0** | **0** | **3** | **322** | **2.8** | | **3** | **0.0** | **16:23** | **38** | **0** | **1** | **1** | **22** | **0** | **0** | **0** | **17:39** |

• Transferred to **Carolina** after **Hartford** franchise relocated, June 25, 1997. Traded to **Colorado** by **Carolina** with Carolina's 1st (Vaclav Nedorost) and 2nd (Jared Aulin) round choices in 2000 Entry Draft and Philadelphia's 2nd round choice (previously acquired, Colorado selected Agris Saviels) in 2000 Entry Draft for Sandis Ozolinsh and Columbus' 2nd round choice (previously acquired, Carolina selected Tomas Kurka) in 2000 Entry Draft, June 24, 2000. Traded to **Tampa Bay** by **Colorado** for Los Angeles' 6th round choice (previously acquired, Colorado selected Scott Horvath) in 2001 Entry Draft, June 24, 2001. Signed as a free agent by **Duisburg** (German-2), January 15, 2005. Signed as a free agent by **Buffalo**, November 1, 2007.

## PREISSING, Tom
(PRIGH-sihng, TAHM) **COL.**

Defense. Shoots right. 6', 198 lbs. Born, Arlington Heights, IL, December 3, 1978.

| Season | Club | League | GP | G | A | Pts | PIM | PP | SH | GW | S | % | +/- | TF | F% | Min | GP | G | A | Pts | PIM | PP | SH | GW | Min |
|---|---|---|---|---|---|---|---|---|---|---|---|---|---|---|---|---|---|---|---|---|---|---|---|---|---|
| 1997-98 | Green Bay | USHL | 56 | 8 | 13 | 21 | 30 | .... | .... | .... | .... | .... | .... | .... | .... | .... | 4 | 0 | 2 | 2 | 2 | .... | .... | .... | .... |
| 1998-99 | Green Bay | USHL | 53 | 18 | 37 | 55 | 40 | .... | .... | .... | .... | .... | .... | .... | .... | .... | 6 | 3 | 6 | 9 | 2 | .... | .... | .... | .... |
| 99-2000 | Colorado College | WCHA | 36 | 4 | 14 | 18 | 20 | .... | .... | .... | .... | .... | .... | .... | .... | .... | .... | .... | .... | .... | .... | .... | .... | .... | .... |
| 2000-01 | Colorado College | WCHA | 33 | 6 | 18 | 24 | 26 | .... | .... | .... | .... | .... | .... | .... | .... | .... | .... | .... | .... | .... | .... | .... | .... | .... | .... |
| 2001-02 | Colorado College | WCHA | 43 | 6 | 26 | 32 | 42 | .... | .... | .... | .... | .... | .... | .... | .... | .... | .... | .... | .... | .... | .... | .... | .... | .... | .... |
| 2002-03 | Colorado College | WCHA | 42 | 23 | 29 | 52 | 16 | .... | .... | .... | .... | .... | .... | .... | .... | .... | .... | .... | .... | .... | .... | .... | .... | .... | .... |
| **2003-04** | **San Jose** | **NHL** | **69** | **2** | **17** | **19** | **12** | **2** | **0** | **1** | **89** | **2.2** | **8** | **0** | **0.0** | **18:12** | **11** | **0** | **1** | **1** | **0** | **0** | **0** | **0** | **12:49** |
| 2004-05 | Krefeld Pinguine | Germany | 33 | 1 | 6 | 7 | 32 | .... | .... | .... | .... | .... | .... | .... | .... | .... | .... | .... | .... | .... | .... | .... | .... | .... | .... |
| **2005-06** | **San Jose** | **NHL** | **74** | **11** | **32** | **43** | **26** | **2** | **0** | **2** | **131** | **8.4** | **17** | **1** | **0.0** | **20:30** | **11** | **1** | **6** | **7** | **4** | **0** | **0** | **0** | **23:50** |
| **2006-07** | **Ottawa** | **NHL** | **80** | **7** | **31** | **38** | **18** | **3** | **0** | **0** | **94** | **7.4** | **40** | **0** | **0.0** | **15:15** | **20** | **2** | **5** | **7** | **10** | **1** | **0** | **1** | **15:02** |
| **2007-08** | **Los Angeles** | **NHL** | **77** | **8** | **16** | **24** | **16** | **6** | **0** | **1** | **93** | **8.6** | **–6** | **9** | **22.2** | **17:53** | .... | .... | .... | .... | .... | .... | .... | .... | .... |

| Season | Club | League | GP | G | A | Pts | PIM | PP | SH | GW | S | % | +/- | TF | F% | Min | GP | G | A | Pts | PIM | PP | SH | GW | Min |
|---|---|---|---|---|---|---|---|---|---|---|---|---|---|---|---|---|---|---|---|---|---|---|---|---|---|
| | | | Regular Season | | | | | | | | | | | | | | Playoffs | | | | | | | | |
| 2008-09 | Los Angeles | NHL | 22 | 3 | 4 | 7 | 6 | 2 | 0 | 0 | 40 | 7.5 | -7 | 0 | 0.0 | 16:45 | .... | .... | .... | .... | .... | .... | .... | .... | .... |
| | Manchester | AHL | 14 | 2 | 4 | 6 | 6 | .... | .... | .... | .... | .... | .... | .... | .... | .... | .... | .... | .... | .... | .... | .... | .... | .... | .... |
| | NHL Totals | | 322 | 31 | 100 | 131 | 78 | 15 | 0 | 4 | 447 | 6.9 | | 10 | 20.0 | 17:49 | 42 | 3 | 12 | 15 | 14 | 1 | 0 | 1 | 16:45 |

USHL First All-Star Team (1999) • USHL Defenseman of the Year (1999) • WCHA First All-Star Team (2003) • NCAA West First All-American Team (2003)

Signed as a free agent by **San Jose**, April 4, 2003. Signed as a free agent by **Krefeld** (Germany), November 15, 2004. Traded to **Chicago** by **San Jose** with Josh Hennessy for Mark Bell, July 9, 2006. Traded to **Ottawa** by **Chicago** with Josh Hennessy, Michal Barinka and Chicago's 2nd round choice (Patrick Wiercioch) in 2008 Entry Draft for Martin Havlat and Bryan Smolinski, July 10, 2006. Signed as a free agent by **Los Angeles**, July 2, 2007. Traded to **Colorado** by **Los Angeles** with Kyle Quincey and Los Angeles' 5th round choice in 2010 Entry Draft for Ryan Smyth, July 3, 2009.

## PRIMEAU, Wayne

(PREE-moh, WAYN) **TOR.**

Center. Shoots left. 6'4", 225 lbs. Born, Scarborough, Ont., June 4, 1976. Buffalo's 1st choice, 17th overall, in 1994 Entry Draft.

| Season | Club | League | GP | G | A | Pts | PIM | PP | SH | GW | S | % | +/- | TF | F% | Min | GP | G | A | Pts | PIM | PP | SH | GW | Min |
|---|---|---|---|---|---|---|---|---|---|---|---|---|---|---|---|---|---|---|---|---|---|---|---|---|---|
| 1991-92 | Whitby Flyers | Minor-ON | 63 | 36 | 50 | 86 | 96 | .... | .... | .... | .... | .... | .... | .... | .... | .... | .... | .... | .... | .... | .... | .... | .... | .... | .... |
| 1992-93 | Owen Sound | OHL | 66 | 10 | 27 | 37 | 108 | .... | .... | .... | .... | .... | .... | .... | .... | .... | 8 | 1 | 4 | 5 | 0 | .... | .... | .... | .... |
| 1993-94 | Owen Sound | OHL | 65 | 25 | 50 | 75 | 75 | .... | .... | .... | .... | .... | .... | .... | .... | .... | 9 | 1 | 6 | 7 | 8 | .... | .... | .... | .... |
| 1994-95 | Owen Sound | OHL | 66 | 34 | 62 | 96 | 84 | .... | .... | .... | .... | .... | .... | .... | .... | .... | 10 | 4 | 9 | 13 | 15 | .... | .... | .... | .... |
| | Buffalo | NHL | 1 | 1 | 0 | 1 | 0 | 0 | 0 | 1 | 2 | 50.0 | -2 | .... | .... | .... | .... | .... | .... | .... | .... | .... | .... | .... | .... |
| 1995-96 | Owen Sound | OHL | 28 | 15 | 29 | 44 | 52 | .... | .... | .... | .... | .... | .... | .... | .... | .... | .... | .... | .... | .... | .... | .... | .... | .... | .... |
| | Oshawa Generals | OHL | 24 | 12 | 13 | 25 | 33 | .... | .... | .... | .... | .... | .... | .... | .... | .... | 3 | 2 | 3 | 5 | 2 | .... | .... | .... | .... |
| | Buffalo | NHL | 2 | 0 | 0 | 0 | 0 | 0 | 0 | 0 | 0 | 0.0 | 0 | .... | .... | .... | .... | .... | .... | .... | .... | .... | .... | .... | .... |
| | Rochester | AHL | 8 | 2 | 3 | 5 | 6 | .... | .... | .... | .... | .... | .... | .... | .... | .... | 17 | 3 | 1 | 4 | 11 | .... | .... | .... | .... |
| 1996-97 | Buffalo | NHL | 45 | 2 | 4 | 6 | 64 | 1 | 0 | 0 | 25 | 8.0 | -2 | .... | .... | .... | 9 | 0 | 0 | 0 | 6 | 0 | 0 | 0 | .... |
| | Rochester | AHL | 24 | 9 | 5 | 14 | 27 | .... | .... | .... | .... | .... | .... | .... | .... | .... | 1 | 0 | 0 | 0 | 0 | .... | .... | .... | .... |
| 1997-98 | Buffalo | NHL | 69 | 6 | 6 | 12 | 87 | 2 | 0 | 1 | 51 | 11.8 | 9 | .... | .... | .... | 14 | 1 | 3 | 4 | 6 | 0 | 0 | 0 | .... |
| 1998-99 | Buffalo | NHL | 67 | 5 | 8 | 13 | 38 | 0 | 0 | 0 | 55 | 9.1 | -6 | 529 | 48.6 | 10:19 | 19 | 3 | 4 | 7 | 6 | 1 | 0 | 0 | 13:29 |
| 99-2000 | Buffalo | NHL | 41 | 5 | 7 | 12 | 38 | 2 | 0 | 1 | 40 | 12.5 | -8 | 430 | 45.6 | 11:03 | .... | .... | .... | .... | .... | .... | .... | .... | .... |
| | Tampa Bay | NHL | 17 | 2 | 3 | 5 | 25 | 0 | 0 | 0 | 35 | 5.7 | -4 | 290 | 45.5 | 14:21 | .... | .... | .... | .... | .... | .... | .... | .... | .... |
| 2000-01 | Tampa Bay | NHL | 47 | 2 | 13 | 15 | 77 | 0 | 0 | 0 | 47 | 4.3 | -17 | 630 | 52.2 | 14:11 | .... | .... | .... | .... | .... | .... | .... | .... | .... |
| | Pittsburgh | NHL | 28 | 1 | 6 | 7 | 54 | 0 | 0 | 0 | 30 | 3.3 | 0 | 318 | 51.3 | 12:45 | 18 | 1 | 3 | 4 | 2 | 0 | 0 | 0 | 15:06 |
| 2001-02 | Pittsburgh | NHL | 33 | 3 | 7 | 10 | 18 | 0 | 1 | 0 | 28 | 10.7 | -1 | 519 | 53.2 | 12:38 | .... | .... | .... | .... | .... | .... | .... | .... | .... |
| 2002-03 | Pittsburgh | NHL | 70 | 5 | 11 | 16 | 55 | 1 | 0 | 0 | 101 | 5.0 | -30 | 1240 | 50.4 | 16:17 | .... | .... | .... | .... | .... | .... | .... | .... | .... |
| | San Jose | NHL | 7 | 1 | 1 | 2 | 0 | 0 | 0 | 0 | 13 | 7.7 | 2 | 98 | 45.9 | 15:59 | .... | .... | .... | .... | .... | .... | .... | .... | .... |
| 2003-04 | San Jose | NHL | 72 | 9 | 20 | 29 | 90 | 0 | 1 | 1 | 142 | 6.3 | 4 | 867 | 46.6 | 15:28 | 17 | 1 | 2 | 3 | 4 | 0 | 0 | 0 | 15:41 |
| 2004-05 | | | DID NOT PLAY | | | | | | | | | | | | | | | | | | | | | | |
| 2005-06 | San Jose | NHL | 21 | 5 | 3 | 8 | 17 | 1 | 1 | 1 | 35 | 14.3 | -6 | 194 | 41.8 | 13:55 | .... | .... | .... | .... | .... | .... | .... | .... | .... |
| | Boston | NHL | 50 | 6 | 8 | 14 | 40 | 0 | 0 | 0 | 66 | 9.1 | -10 | 749 | 49.8 | 17:16 | .... | .... | .... | .... | .... | .... | .... | .... | .... |
| 2006-07 | Boston | NHL | 51 | 7 | 8 | 15 | 75 | 2 | 1 | 1 | 72 | 9.7 | -15 | 652 | 50.5 | 15:05 | .... | .... | .... | .... | .... | .... | .... | .... | .... |
| | Calgary | NHL | 27 | 3 | 4 | 7 | 36 | 0 | 1 | 2 | 35 | 8.6 | -2 | 199 | 46.2 | 10:38 | 6 | 0 | 2 | 2 | 14 | 0 | 0 | 0 | 13:29 |
| 2007-08 | Calgary | NHL | 43 | 3 | 7 | 10 | 26 | 0 | 0 | 0 | 39 | 7.7 | -3 | 94 | 54.3 | 11:03 | 7 | 1 | 0 | 1 | 4 | 0 | 0 | 0 | 10:35 |
| 2008-09 | Calgary | NHL | 24 | 0 | 4 | 4 | 14 | 0 | 0 | 0 | 22 | 0.0 | -3 | 217 | 53.0 | 10:23 | .... | .... | .... | .... | .... | .... | .... | .... | .... |
| | NHL Totals | | 715 | 66 | 120 | 186 | 754 | 9 | 5 | 8 | 838 | 7.9 | | 7026 | 49.4 | 13:36 | 90 | 7 | 14 | 21 | 42 | 1 | 0 | 0 | 14:11 |

Traded to **Tampa Bay** by **Buffalo** with Cory Sarich, Brian Holzinger and Buffalo's 3rd round choice (Alexander Kharitonov) in 2000 Entry Draft for Chris Gratton and Tampa Bay's 2nd round choice (Derek Roy) in 2001 Entry Draft, March 9, 2000. Traded to **Pittsburgh** by **Tampa Bay** for Matthew Barnaby, February 1, 2001. • Missed majority of 2001-02 season recovering from knee injury suffered in game vs. Buffalo, January 8, 2002. Traded to **San Jose** by **Pittsburgh** for Matt Bradley, March 11, 2003. Traded to **Boston** by **San Jose** with Brad Stuart and Marco Sturm for Joe Thornton, November 30, 2005. Traded to **Calgary** by **Boston** with Brad Stuart and Washington's 4th round choice (previously acquired, Calgary selected T.J. Brodie) in 2008 Entry Draft for Andrew Ference and Chuck Kobasew, February 10, 2007. • Missed remainder of 2008-09 season recovering from ankle injury suffered in game at St, Louis. December 5, 2008. Traded to **Toronto** by **Calgary** with Calgary's 2nd round choice in 2011 Entry Draft for Anton Stralman, Colin Stuart and Toronto's 7th round choice in 2012 Entry Draft, July 27, 2009.

## PRONGER, Chris

(PRAWN-guhr, KRIHS) **PHI.**

Defense. Shoots left. 6'6", 214 lbs. Born, Dryden, Ont., October 10, 1974. Hartford's 1st choice, 2nd overall, in 1993 Entry Draft.

| Season | Club | League | GP | G | A | Pts | PIM | PP | SH | GW | S | % | +/- | TF | F% | Min | GP | G | A | Pts | PIM | PP | SH | GW | Min |
|---|---|---|---|---|---|---|---|---|---|---|---|---|---|---|---|---|---|---|---|---|---|---|---|---|---|
| 1990-91 | Stratford Cullitons | OHA-B | 48 | 15 | 37 | 52 | 132 | .... | .... | .... | .... | .... | .... | .... | .... | .... | .... | .... | .... | .... | .... | .... | .... | .... | .... |
| 1991-92 | Peterborough | OHL | 63 | 17 | 45 | 62 | 90 | .... | .... | .... | .... | .... | .... | .... | .... | .... | 10 | 1 | 8 | 9 | 28 | .... | .... | .... | .... |
| 1992-93 | Peterborough | OHL | 61 | 15 | 62 | 77 | 108 | .... | .... | .... | .... | .... | .... | .... | .... | .... | 21 | 15 | 25 | 40 | 51 | .... | .... | .... | .... |
| 1993-94 | Hartford | NHL | 81 | 5 | 25 | 30 | 113 | 2 | 0 | 0 | 174 | 2.9 | -3 | .... | .... | .... | .... | .... | .... | .... | .... | .... | .... | .... | .... |
| 1994-95 | Hartford | NHL | 43 | 5 | 9 | 14 | 54 | 3 | 0 | 1 | 94 | 5.3 | -12 | .... | .... | .... | .... | .... | .... | .... | .... | .... | .... | .... | .... |
| 1995-96 | St. Louis | NHL | 78 | 7 | 18 | 25 | 110 | 3 | 1 | 1 | 138 | 5.1 | -18 | .... | .... | .... | 13 | 1 | 5 | 6 | 16 | 0 | 0 | 0 | .... |
| 1996-97 | St. Louis | NHL | 79 | 11 | 24 | 35 | 143 | 4 | 0 | 0 | 147 | 7.5 | 15 | .... | .... | .... | 6 | 1 | 1 | 2 | 22 | 0 | 0 | 0 | .... |
| 1997-98 | St. Louis | NHL | 81 | 9 | 27 | 36 | 180 | 1 | 0 | 2 | 145 | 6.2 | 47 | .... | .... | .... | 10 | 1 | 9 | 10 | 26 | 0 | 0 | 0 | .... |
| | Canada | Olympics | 6 | 0 | 0 | 0 | 4 | .... | .... | .... | .... | .... | .... | .... | .... | .... | .... | .... | .... | .... | .... | .... | .... | .... | .... |
| 1998-99 | St. Louis | NHL | 67 | 13 | 33 | 46 | 113 | 8 | 0 | 0 | 172 | 7.6 | 3 | 0 | 0.0 | 30:36 | 13 | 1 | 4 | 5 | 28 | 1 | 0 | 0 | 35:53 |
| 99-2000 | St. Louis | NHL | 79 | 14 | 48 | 62 | 92 | 8 | 0 | 3 | 192 | 7.3 | 52 | 1 | 0.0 | 30:14 | 7 | 3 | 4 | 7 | 32 | 2 | 0 | 2 | 30:14 |
| 2000-01 | St. Louis | NHL | 51 | 8 | 39 | 47 | 75 | 4 | 0 | 0 | 121 | 6.6 | 21 | 0 | 0.0 | 27:45 | 15 | 1 | 7 | 8 | 32 | 0 | 0 | 0 | 33:50 |
| 2001-02 | St. Louis | NHL | 78 | 7 | 40 | 47 | 120 | 4 | 1 | 3 | 204 | 3.4 | 23 | 0 | 0.0 | 29:28 | 9 | 1 | 7 | 8 | 24 | 0 | 0 | 0 | 27:51 |
| | Canada | Olympics | 6 | 0 | 1 | 1 | 2 | .... | .... | .... | .... | .... | .... | .... | .... | .... | .... | .... | .... | .... | .... | .... | .... | .... | .... |
| 2002-03 | St. Louis | NHL | 5 | 1 | 3 | 4 | 10 | 0 | 0 | 0 | 11 | 9.1 | -2 | 1 | 0.0 | 21:39 | 7 | 1 | 3 | 4 | 14 | 0 | 0 | 0 | 24:36 |
| 2003-04 | St. Louis | NHL | 80 | 14 | 40 | 54 | 88 | 7 | 0 | 3 | 203 | 6.9 | -1 | 2 | 0.0 | 27:28 | 5 | 0 | 1 | 1 | 16 | 0 | 0 | 0 | 27:54 |
| 2004-05 | | | DID NOT PLAY | | | | | | | | | | | | | | | | | | | | | | |
| 2005-06 | Edmonton | NHL | 80 | 12 | 44 | 56 | 74 | 10 | 0 | 3 | 155 | 7.7 | 2 | 1 | 0.0 | 27:59 | 24 | 5 | 16 | 21 | 26 | 3 | 0 | 0 | 30:57 |
| | Canada | Olympics | 6 | 1 | 2 | 3 | 16 | .... | .... | .... | .... | .... | .... | .... | .... | .... | .... | .... | .... | .... | .... | .... | .... | .... | .... |
| 2006-07 ♦ | Anaheim | NHL | 66 | 13 | 46 | 59 | 69 | 8 | 0 | 2 | 166 | 7.8 | 27 | 4 | 25.0 | 27:06 | 19 | 3 | 12 | 15 | 26 | 1 | 0 | 0 | 30:11 |
| 2007-08 | Anaheim | NHL | 72 | 12 | 31 | 43 | 128 | 8 | 0 | 4 | 182 | 6.6 | -1 | 7 | 57.1 | 26:00 | 6 | 2 | 3 | 5 | 12 | 2 | 0 | 1 | 24:14 |
| 2008-09 | Anaheim | NHL | 82 | 11 | 37 | 48 | 88 | 4 | 0 | 2 | 196 | 5.6 | 0 | 7 | 28.6 | 26:56 | 13 | 2 | 8 | 10 | 12 | 1 | 0 | 0 | 27:13 |
| | NHL Totals | | 1022 | 142 | 464 | 606 | 1457 | 74 | 2 | 24 | 2300 | 6.2 | | 23 | 30.4 | 28:08 | 147 | 22 | 80 | 102 | 286 | 10 | 0 | 3 | 30:12 |

OHL All-Rookie Team (1992) • OHL First All-Star Team (1993) • Canadian Major Junior First All-Star Team (1993) • Canadian Major Junior Defenseman of the Year (1993) • NHL All-Rookie Team (1994) • NHL Second All-Star Team (1998, 2004, 2007) • Bud Ice Plus/Minus Award (1998) • NHL First All-Star Team (2000) • Bud Light Plus/Minus Award (2000) • James Norris Memorial Trophy (2000) • Hart Memorial Trophy (2000)

Played in NHL All-Star Game (1999, 2000, 2002, 2004, 2008)

Traded to **St. Louis** by **Hartford** for Brendan Shanahan, July 27, 1995. • Missed majority of 2002-03 season recovering from wrist and knee surgery, September 10, 2002. Traded to **Edmonton** by **St. Louis** for Eric Brewer, Doug Lynch and Jeff Woywitka, August 2, 2005. Traded to **Anaheim** by **Edmonton** for Joffrey Lupul, Ladislav Smid, Anaheim's 1st round choice (later traded to Phoenix - Phoenix selected Nick Ross) in 2007 Entry Draft and Anaheim's 1st (Jordan Eberle) and 2nd (later traded to NY Islanders - NY Islanders selected Travis Hamonic) round choices in 2008 Entry Draft, July 3, 2006. Traded to **Philadelphia** by **Anaheim** with Ryan Dingle for Joffrey Lupul, Luca Sbisa, Philadelphia's 1st round choices in 2009 (later traded to Columbus - Columbus selected John Moore) and 2010 Entry Drafts and future considerations, June 26, 2009.

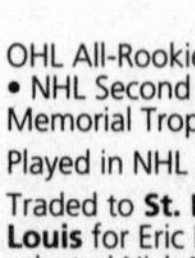

## PROSPAL, Vaclav

(PRAWS-puhl, VAT-slav)

Center. Shoots left. 6'2", 198 lbs. Born, Ceske Budejovice, Czech., February 17, 1975. Philadelphia's 2nd choice, 71st overall, in 1993 Entry Draft.

| Season | Club | League | GP | G | A | Pts | PIM | PP | SH | GW | S | % | +/- | TF | F% | Min | GP | G | A | Pts | PIM | PP | SH | GW | Min |
|---|---|---|---|---|---|---|---|---|---|---|---|---|---|---|---|---|---|---|---|---|---|---|---|---|---|
| 1991-92 | C. Budejovice Jr. | Czech-Jr. | 36 | 16 | 16 | 32 | 12 | .... | .... | .... | .... | .... | .... | .... | .... | .... | .... | .... | .... | .... | .... | .... | .... | .... | .... |
| 1992-93 | C. Budejovice Jr. | Czech-Jr. | 32 | 26 | 31 | 57 | 24 | .... | .... | .... | .... | .... | .... | .... | .... | .... | .... | .... | .... | .... | .... | .... | .... | .... | .... |
| 1993-94 | Hershey Bears | AHL | 55 | 14 | 21 | 35 | 38 | .... | .... | .... | .... | .... | .... | .... | .... | .... | 2 | 0 | 0 | 0 | 2 | .... | .... | .... | .... |
| 1994-95 | Hershey Bears | AHL | 69 | 13 | 32 | 45 | 36 | .... | .... | .... | .... | .... | .... | .... | .... | .... | 2 | 1 | 0 | 1 | 4 | .... | .... | .... | .... |
| 1995-96 | Hershey Bears | AHL | 68 | 15 | 36 | 51 | 59 | .... | .... | .... | .... | .... | .... | .... | .... | .... | 5 | 2 | 4 | 6 | 2 | .... | .... | .... | .... |
| 1996-97 | Philadelphia | NHL | 18 | 5 | 10 | 15 | 4 | 0 | 0 | 0 | 35 | 14.3 | 3 | .... | .... | .... | 5 | 1 | 3 | 4 | 4 | 0 | 0 | 0 | .... |
| | Philadelphia | AHL | 63 | 32 | 63 | 95 | 70 | .... | .... | .... | .... | .... | .... | .... | .... | .... | .... | .... | .... | .... | .... | .... | .... | .... | .... |
| 1997-98 | Philadelphia | NHL | 41 | 5 | 13 | 18 | 17 | 4 | 0 | 0 | 60 | 8.3 | -10 | .... | .... | .... | .... | .... | .... | .... | .... | .... | .... | .... | .... |
| | Ottawa | NHL | 15 | 1 | 6 | 7 | 4 | 0 | 0 | 0 | 28 | 3.6 | -1 | .... | .... | .... | 6 | 0 | 0 | 0 | 0 | 0 | 0 | 0 | .... |
| 1998-99 | Ottawa | NHL | 79 | 10 | 26 | 36 | 58 | 2 | 0 | 3 | 114 | 8.8 | 8 | 997 | 56.2 | 13:03 | 4 | 0 | 0 | 0 | 0 | 0 | 0 | 0 | 12:37 |
| 99-2000 | Ottawa | NHL | 79 | 22 | 33 | 55 | 40 | 5 | 0 | 4 | 204 | 10.8 | -2 | 1331 | 49.6 | 16:26 | 6 | 0 | 4 | 4 | 4 | 0 | 0 | 0 | 17:40 |
| 2000-01 | Ottawa | NHL | 40 | 1 | 12 | 13 | 12 | 0 | 0 | 0 | 68 | 1.5 | 1 | 501 | 50.1 | 12:57 | .... | .... | .... | .... | .... | .... | .... | .... | .... |
| | Florida | NHL | 34 | 4 | 12 | 16 | 10 | 1 | 0 | 0 | 68 | 5.9 | -2 | 487 | 54.6 | 16:36 | .... | .... | .... | .... | .... | .... | .... | .... | .... |
| 2001-02 | Tampa Bay | NHL | 81 | 18 | 37 | 55 | 38 | 7 | 0 | 2 | 166 | 10.8 | -11 | 555 | 52.8 | 17:31 | .... | .... | .... | .... | .... | .... | .... | .... | .... |
| 2002-03 | Tampa Bay | NHL | 80 | 22 | 57 | 79 | 53 | 9 | 0 | 4 | 134 | 16.4 | 9 | 161 | 51.6 | 18:39 | 11 | 4 | 2 | 6 | 8 | 2 | 0 | 0 | 21:15 |
| 2003-04 | Anaheim | NHL | 82 | 19 | 35 | 54 | 54 | 7 | 0 | 4 | 185 | 10.3 | -9 | 45 | 46.7 | 18:37 | .... | .... | .... | .... | .... | .... | .... | .... | .... |
| 2004-05 | C. Budejovice | CzRep-2 | 39 | 28 | 60 | 88 | 82 | .... | .... | .... | .... | .... | .... | .... | .... | .... | 16 | 15 | 15 | 30 | 32 | .... | .... | .... | .... |
| 2005-06 | Tampa Bay | NHL | 81 | 25 | 55 | 80 | 50 | 10 | 0 | 3 | 236 | 10.6 | -3 | 267 | 45.3 | 19:10 | 5 | 0 | 2 | 2 | 0 | 0 | 0 | 0 | 15:56 |
| | Czech Republic | Olympics | 8 | 4 | 2 | 6 | 2 | .... | .... | .... | .... | .... | .... | .... | .... | .... | .... | .... | .... | .... | .... | .... | .... | .... | .... |
| 2006-07 | Tampa Bay | NHL | 82 | 14 | 41 | 55 | 36 | 2 | 0 | 1 | 219 | 6.4 | -24 | 124 | 52.4 | 19:04 | 6 | 1 | 4 | 5 | 4 | 0 | 0 | 1 | 22:19 |

| | | | Regular Season | | | | | | | | | | | | | | Playoffs | | | | | | | | |
|---|---|---|---|---|---|---|---|---|---|---|---|---|---|---|---|---|---|---|---|---|---|---|---|---|---|
| Season | Club | League | GP | G | A | Pts | PIM | PP | SH | GW | S | % | +/- | TF | F% | Min | GP | G | A | Pts | PIM | PP | SH | GW | Min |
| 2007-08 | Tampa Bay | NHL | 62 | 29 | 28 | 57 | 39 | 9 | 0 | 4 | 175 | 16.6 | –7 | 176 | 54.6 | 20:00 | | | | | | | | | |
| | Philadelphia | NHL | 18 | 4 | 10 | 14 | 6 | 1 | 0 | 1 | 40 | 10.0 | 7 | 86 | 58.1 | 17:15 | 17 | 3 | 10 | 13 | 6 | 1 | 0 | 0 | 16:49 |
| 2008-09 | Tampa Bay | NHL | 82 | 19 | 26 | 45 | 52 | 7 | 0 | 2 | 194 | 9.8 | –20 | 202 | 53.0 | 17:41 | | | | | | | | | |
| | NHL Totals | | 874 | 198 | 401 | 599 | 473 | 64 | 0 | 28 | 1926 | 10.3 | | 4932 | 52.2 | 17:28 | 60 | 9 | 25 | 34 | 26 | 3 | 0 | 1 | 18:09 |

AHL First All-Star Team (1997)

Traded to **Ottawa** by **Philadelphia** with Pat Falloon and Dallas' 2nd round choice (previously acquired, Ottawa selected Chris Bala) in 1998 Entry Draft for Alexandre Daigle, January 17, 1998. Traded to **Florida** by **Ottawa** for future considerations, January 20, 2001. Traded to **Tampa Bay** by **Florida** for Ryan Johnson and Tampa Bay's 6th round choice (later traded back to Tampa Bay – Tampa Bay selected Doug O'Brien) in 2003 Entry Draft, July 10, 2001. Signed as a free agent by **Anaheim**, July 17, 2003. Traded to **Tampa Bay** by **Anaheim** for Tampa Bay's 2nd round choice (Brendan Mikkelson) in 2005 Entry Draft, August 16, 2004. Signed as a free agent by **Ceske Budejovice** (CzRep-2), September 17, 2004. Traded to **Philadelphia** by **Tampa Bay** for Alexandre Picard and Philadelphia's 2nd round choice (Richard Panik) in 2009 Entry Draft, February 25, 2008. Traded to **Tampa Bay** by **Philadelphia** for Nashville's 7th round choice (previously acquired, Philadelphia selected Joacim Eriksson) in 2008 Entry Draft and future considerations, June 18, 2008.

## PRUCHA, Petr
(PROO-khah, PEE-tuhr) **PHX.**

Right wing. Shoots right. 6', 175 lbs. Born, Chrudim, Czech., September 14, 1982. NY Rangers' 8th choice, 240th overall, in 2002 Entry Draft.

| Season | Club | League | GP | G | A | Pts | PIM | PP | SH | GW | S | % | +/- | TF | F% | Min | GP | G | A | Pts | PIM | PP | SH | GW | Min |
|---|---|---|---|---|---|---|---|---|---|---|---|---|---|---|---|---|---|---|---|---|---|---|---|---|---|
| 99-2000 | HC Chrudim Jr. | CzRep-Jr. | 43 | 35 | 27 | 62 | 62 | | | | | | | | | | | | | | | | | | |
| 2000-01 | HC Pardubice Jr. | CzRep-Jr. | 54 | 39 | 22 | 61 | 18 | | | | | | | | | | | | | | | | | | |
| 2001-02 | HC Pardubice Jr. | CzRep-Jr. | 28 | 38 | 28 | 66 | 18 | | | | | | | | | | 3 | 2 | 6 | 8 | 0 | | | | |
| | Sumperk | CzRep-2 | 8 | 6 | 4 | 10 | 0 | | | | | | | | | | | | | | | | | | |
| | Sumperk | CzRep-Q | 5 | 5 | 3 | 8 | 0 | | | | | | | | | | | | | | | | | | |
| | Pardubice | CzRep | 20 | 1 | 1 | 2 | 2 | | | | | | | | | | 5 | 0 | 0 | 0 | 0 | | | | |
| 2002-03 | Pardubice | CzRep | 49 | 7 | 9 | 16 | 12 | | | | | | | | | | 17 | 2 | 6 | 8 | 8 | | | | |
| | HC Pardubice Jr. | CzRep-Jr. | 4 | 5 | 4 | 9 | 25 | | | | | | | | | | | | | | | | | | |
| | Hr. Kralove | CzRep-2 | 11 | 3 | 5 | 8 | 35 | | | | | | | | | | | | | | | | | | |
| 2003-04 | Pardubice | CzRep | 48 | 11 | 13 | 24 | 24 | | | | | | | | | | 7 | 4 | 3 | 7 | 2 | | | | |
| | Hr. Kralove | CzRep-2 | 3 | 1 | 0 | 1 | 25 | | | | | | | | | | | | | | | | | | |
| 2004-05 | Pardubice | CzRep | 47 | 7 | 10 | 17 | 24 | | | | | | | | | | 16 | 6 | 7 | 13 | 2 | | | | |
| 2005-06 | NY Rangers | NHL | 68 | 30 | 17 | 47 | 32 | 16 | 0 | 2 | 130 | 23.1 | 3 | 150 | 52.0 | 13:42 | 4 | 1 | 0 | 1 | 0 | 1 | 0 | 0 | 14:13 |
| | Hartford | AHL | 2 | 2 | 1 | 3 | 0 | | | | | | | | | | | | | | | | | | |
| 2006-07 | NY Rangers | NHL | 79 | 22 | 18 | 40 | 30 | 8 | 0 | 2 | 136 | 16.2 | –7 | 70 | 50.0 | 13:00 | 10 | 0 | 1 | 1 | 4 | 0 | 0 | 0 | 13:35 |
| 2007-08 | NY Rangers | NHL | 62 | 7 | 10 | 17 | 22 | 2 | 0 | 1 | 89 | 7.9 | 3 | 3 | 66.7 | 11:38 | 3 | 0 | 0 | 0 | 0 | 0 | 0 | 0 | 8:13 |
| 2008-09 | NY Rangers | NHL | 28 | 4 | 5 | 9 | 16 | 0 | 0 | 0 | 44 | 9.1 | –2 | 0 | 0.0 | 12:09 | | | | | | | | | |
| | Phoenix | NHL | 19 | 2 | 8 | 10 | 6 | 1 | 0 | 1 | 23 | 8.7 | 1 | 8 | 12.5 | 18:26 | | | | | | | | | |
| | NHL Totals | | 256 | 65 | 58 | 123 | 106 | 27 | 0 | 6 | 422 | 15.4 | | 231 | 50.2 | 13:10 | 17 | 1 | 1 | 2 | 4 | 1 | 0 | 0 | 12:47 |

Traded to **Phoenix** by **NY Rangers** with Dmitri Kalinin and Nigel Dawes for Derek Morris, March 4, 2009.

## PRUST, Brandon
(PROOST, BRAN-duhn) **CGY.**

Center/Left wing. Shoots left. 5'11", 195 lbs. Born, London, Ont., March 16, 1984. Calgary's 2nd choice, 70th overall, in 2004 Entry Draft.

| Season | Club | League | GP | G | A | Pts | PIM | PP | SH | GW | S | % | +/- | TF | F% | Min | GP | G | A | Pts | PIM | PP | SH | GW | Min |
|---|---|---|---|---|---|---|---|---|---|---|---|---|---|---|---|---|---|---|---|---|---|---|---|---|---|
| 2001-02 | London Nationals | OHA-B | 52 | 17 | 35 | 52 | 38 | | | | | | | | | | | | | | | | | | |
| 2002-03 | London Knights | OHL | 65 | 12 | 17 | 29 | 94 | | | | | | | | | | 14 | 2 | 1 | 3 | 21 | | | | |
| 2003-04 | London Knights | OHL | 64 | 19 | 33 | 52 | 269 | | | | | | | | | | 15 | 7 | 13 | 20 | 33 | | | | |
| 2004-05 | London Knights | OHL | 48 | 10 | 20 | 30 | 174 | | | | | | | | | | 15 | 3 | 5 | 8 | *71 | | | | |
| 2005-06 | Omaha | AHL | 79 | 12 | 14 | 26 | 294 | | | | | | | | | | | | | | | | | | |
| 2006-07 | Calgary | NHL | 10 | 0 | 0 | 0 | 25 | 0 | 0 | 0 | 1 | 0.0 | 1 | 0 | 0.0 | 6:03 | | | | | | | | | |
| | Omaha | AHL | 63 | 17 | 10 | 27 | 211 | | | | | | | | | | 6 | 0 | 3 | 3 | 20 | | | | |
| 2007-08 | Quad City Flames | AHL | 79 | 10 | 27 | 37 | 248 | | | | | | | | | | | | | | | | | | |
| 2008-09 | Calgary | NHL | 25 | 1 | 1 | 2 | 79 | 0 | 0 | 1 | 15 | 6.7 | –4 | 15 | 53.3 | 6:21 | | | | | | | | | |
| | Phoenix | NHL | 11 | 0 | 1 | 1 | 29 | 0 | 0 | 0 | 8 | 0.0 | –4 | 16 | 56.3 | 9:59 | | | | | | | | | |
| | NHL Totals | | 46 | 1 | 2 | 3 | 133 | 0 | 0 | 1 | 24 | 4.2 | | 31 | 54.8 | 7:09 | | | | | | | | | |

Traded to **Phoenix** by **Calgary** with Matthew Lombardi and Calgary's 1st round choice in 2010 Entry Draft for Olli Jokinen and Phoenix's 3rd round choice (later traded to Florida – Florida selected Josh Birkholz) in 2009 Entry Draft, March 4, 2009. Traded to **Calgary** by **Phoenix** for Jim Vandermeer, June 27, 2009.

## PURCELL, Teddy
(PUHR-sihl, TEH-dee) **L.A.**

Right wing. Shoots right. 6'3", 202 lbs. Born, St. Johns, Nfld., September 8, 1985.

| Season | Club | League | GP | G | A | Pts | PIM | PP | SH | GW | S | % | +/- | TF | F% | Min | GP | G | A | Pts | PIM | PP | SH | GW | Min |
|---|---|---|---|---|---|---|---|---|---|---|---|---|---|---|---|---|---|---|---|---|---|---|---|---|---|
| 2003-04 | Notre Dame | SJHL | 51 | 21 | 25 | 46 | 8 | | | | | | | | | | | | | | | | | | |
| 2004-05 | Cedar Rapids | USHL | 58 | 20 | 47 | 67 | 22 | | | | | | | | | | 11 | 5 | 9 | 14 | 4 | | | | |
| 2005-06 | Cedar Rapids | USHL | 55 | 19 | 52 | 71 | 14 | | | | | | | | | | 8 | 3 | 8 | 11 | 4 | | | | |
| 2006-07 | U. of Maine | H-East | 40 | 16 | 27 | 43 | 34 | | | | | | | | | | | | | | | | | | |
| 2007-08 | Los Angeles | NHL | 10 | 1 | 2 | 3 | 0 | 0 | 0 | 0 | 10 | 10.0 | 2 | 0 | 0.0 | 11:59 | | | | | | | | | |
| | Manchester | AHL | 67 | 25 | 58 | 83 | 34 | | | | | | | | | | 4 | 0 | 3 | 3 | 0 | | | | |
| 2008-09 | Los Angeles | NHL | 40 | 4 | 12 | 16 | 4 | 2 | 0 | 1 | 68 | 5.9 | –4 | 29 | 17.2 | 13:31 | | | | | | | | | |
| | Manchester | AHL | 38 | 16 | 22 | 38 | 12 | | | | | | | | | | | | | | | | | | |
| | NHL Totals | | 50 | 5 | 14 | 19 | 4 | 2 | 0 | 1 | 78 | 6.4 | | 29 | 17.2 | 13:13 | | | | | | | | | |

AHL First All-Star Team (2008)

Signed as a free agent by **Los Angeles**, April 27, 2007.

## PUSHKAREV, Konstantin
(puhsh-KAR-ehv, KAWN-stan-tihn) **DAL.**

Right wing. Shoots left. 6', 180 lbs. Born, Ust-Kamenogorsk, USSR, February 12, 1985. Los Angeles' 4th choice, 44th overall, in 2003 Entry Draft.

| Season | Club | League | GP | G | A | Pts | PIM | PP | SH | GW | S | % | +/- | TF | F% | Min | GP | G | A | Pts | PIM | PP | SH | GW | Min |
|---|---|---|---|---|---|---|---|---|---|---|---|---|---|---|---|---|---|---|---|---|---|---|---|---|---|
| 2002-03 | Ust-Kam'gorsk 2 | Russia-3 | STATISTICS NOT AVAILABLE | | | | | | | | | | | | | | | | | | | | | | |
| | Ust-Kamenogorsk | Russia-2 | 4 | 0 | 0 | 0 | 4 | | | | | | | | | | | | | | | | | | |
| 2003-04 | Omsk 2 | Russia-3 | 34 | 17 | 11 | 28 | 64 | | | | | | | | | | | | | | | | | | |
| | Avangard Omsk | Russia | 5 | 1 | 0 | 1 | 0 | | | | | | | | | | | | | | | | | | |
| 2004-05 | Avangard Omsk | Russia | 1 | 0 | 0 | 0 | 0 | | | | | | | | | | | | | | | | | | |
| | Calgary Hitmen | WHL | 69 | 22 | 30 | 52 | 50 | | | | | | | | | | 12 | 2 | 5 | 7 | 4 | | | | |
| 2005-06 | Los Angeles | NHL | 1 | 0 | 1 | 1 | 0 | 0 | 0 | 0 | 0 | 0.0 | 0 | 0 | 0.0 | 9:33 | | | | | | | | | |
| | Manchester | AHL | 77 | 19 | 19 | 38 | 95 | | | | | | | | | | 7 | 1 | 1 | 2 | 4 | | | | |
| 2006-07 | Los Angeles | NHL | 16 | 2 | 2 | 4 | 8 | 0 | 0 | 0 | 10 | 20.0 | –2 | 1 | 0.0 | 9:10 | | | | | | | | | |
| | Manchester | AHL | 35 | 4 | 11 | 15 | 29 | | | | | | | | | | | | | | | | | | |
| | Iowa Stars | AHL | 15 | 2 | 5 | 7 | 25 | | | | | | | | | | 12 | 1 | 4 | 5 | 18 | | | | |
| 2007-08 | Iowa Stars | AHL | 49 | 13 | 27 | 40 | 52 | | | | | | | | | | | | | | | | | | |
| | CSKA Moscow | Russia | 5 | 0 | 1 | 1 | 2 | | | | | | | | | | | | | | | | | | |
| 2008-09 | Magnitogorsk | Rus-KHL | 30 | 5 | 1 | 6 | 14 | | | | | | | | | | 4 | 0 | 0 | 0 | 0 | | | | |
| | NHL Totals | | 17 | 2 | 3 | 5 | 8 | 0 | 0 | 0 | 10 | 20.0 | | 1 | 0.0 | 9:12 | | | | | | | | | |

Traded to **Dallas** by **Los Angeles** with Mattias Norstrom and Los Angeles' 3rd (Sergei Korostin) and 4th (later traded to Columbus - Columbus selected Maxim Mayorov) round choices in 2007 Entry Draft for Jaroslav Modry, the rights to Johan Fransson, Dallas' 2nd (Oscar Moller) and 3rd (Bryan Cameron) round choices in 2007 Entry Draft and Dallas' 1st round choice (later traded to Phoenix - Phoenix selected Viktor Tikhonov) in 2008 Entry Draft , February 27, 2007.

## PYATT, Taylor
(PIGH-at, TAY-luhr)

Left wing. Shoots left. 6'4", 230 lbs. Born, Thunder Bay, Ont., August 19, 1981. NY Islanders' 2nd choice, 8th overall, in 1999 Entry Draft.

| Season | Club | League | GP | G | A | Pts | PIM | PP | SH | GW | S | % | +/- | TF | F% | Min | GP | G | A | Pts | PIM | PP | SH | GW | Min |
|---|---|---|---|---|---|---|---|---|---|---|---|---|---|---|---|---|---|---|---|---|---|---|---|---|---|
| 1996-97 | Thunder Bay | TBAHA | 60 | 52 | 61 | 113 | 72 | | | | | | | | | | | | | | | | | | |
| 1997-98 | Sudbury Wolves | OHL | 58 | 14 | 17 | 31 | 104 | | | | | | | | | | 10 | 3 | 1 | 4 | 8 | | | | |
| 1998-99 | Sudbury Wolves | OHL | 68 | 37 | 38 | 75 | 95 | | | | | | | | | | 4 | 0 | 4 | 4 | 6 | | | | |
| 99-2000 | Sudbury Wolves | OHL | 68 | 40 | 49 | 89 | 98 | | | | | | | | | | 12 | 8 | 7 | 15 | 25 | | | | |
| 2000-01 | NY Islanders | NHL | 78 | 4 | 14 | 18 | 39 | 1 | 0 | 2 | 86 | 4.7 | –17 | 1 | 0.0 | 12:14 | | | | | | | | | |
| 2001-02 | Buffalo | NHL | 48 | 10 | 10 | 20 | 35 | 0 | 0 | 0 | 61 | 16.4 | 4 | 0 | 0.0 | 13:30 | | | | | | | | | |
| | Rochester | AHL | 27 | 6 | 4 | 10 | 36 | | | | | | | | | | | | | | | | | | |
| 2002-03 | Buffalo | NHL | 78 | 14 | 14 | 28 | 38 | 2 | 0 | 0 | 110 | 12.7 | –8 | 8 | 25.0 | 14:06 | | | | | | | | | |
| 2003-04 | Buffalo | NHL | 63 | 8 | 12 | 20 | 25 | 1 | 2 | 4 | 98 | 8.2 | –7 | 19 | 26.3 | 15:36 | | | | | | | | | |
| 2004-05 | Hammarby | Sweden-2 | 24 | 11 | 9 | 20 | 20 | | | | | | | | | | | | | | | | | | |
| 2005-06 | Buffalo | NHL | 41 | 6 | 6 | 12 | 33 | 0 | 0 | 1 | 62 | 9.7 | –1 | 11 | 18.2 | 11:14 | 14 | 0 | 5 | 5 | 10 | 0 | 0 | 0 | 11:08 |
| 2006-07 | Vancouver | NHL | 76 | 23 | 14 | 37 | 42 | 9 | 0 | 4 | 150 | 15.3 | 5 | 4 | 0.0 | 13:58 | 12 | 2 | 4 | 6 | 6 | 0 | 0 | 1 | 18:02 |

| Season | Club | League | GP | G | A | Pts | PIM | PP | SH | GW | S | % | +/- | TF | F% | Min | GP | G | A | Pts | PIM | PP | SH | GW | Min |
|---|---|---|---|---|---|---|---|---|---|---|---|---|---|---|---|---|---|---|---|---|---|---|---|---|---|
| | | | Regular Season | | | | | | | | | | | | | | Playoffs | | | | | | | | |
| **2007-08** | **Vancouver** | **NHL** | **79** | **16** | **21** | **37** | **60** | **7** | **0** | **2** | **167** | **9.6** | **9** | **36** | **33.3** | **15:47** | .... | .... | .... | .... | .... | .... | .... | .... | .... |
| **2008-09** | **Vancouver** | **NHL** | **69** | **10** | **9** | **19** | **43** | **0** | **0** | **1** | **99** | **10.1** | **0** | **33** | **48.5** | **14:43** | **4** | **0** | **0** | **0** | **2** | **0** | **0** | **0** | **14:13** |
| | **NHL Totals** | | **532** | **91** | **100** | **191** | **315** | **20** | **2** | **14** | **833** | **10.9** | | **112** | **33.0** | **14:02** | **30** | **2** | **9** | **11** | **18** | **0** | **0** | **1** | **14:18** |

OHL First All-Star Team (2000)

Traded to **Buffalo** by **NY Islanders** with Tim Connolly for Michael Peca, June 24, 2001. Signed as a free agent by **Hammarby** (Sweden-2), November 16, 2004. • Rights traded to **Vancouver** by **Buffalo** for Vancouver's 4th round choice (later traded to Calgary - Calgary selected Keith Aulie) in 2007 Entry Draft, July 14, 2006.

## QUICK, Kevin

(KWIHK, KEH-vihn) **T.B.**

Defense. Shoots left. 6', 175 lbs. Born, Buffalo, NY, March 29, 1988. Tampa Bay's 2nd choice, 78th overall, in 2006 Entry Draft.

| Season | Club | League | GP | G | A | Pts | PIM | PP | SH | GW | S | % | +/- | TF | F% | Min | GP | G | A | Pts | PIM | PP | SH | GW | Min |
|---|---|---|---|---|---|---|---|---|---|---|---|---|---|---|---|---|---|---|---|---|---|---|---|---|---|
| 2004-05 | Salisbury School | High-CT | 27 | 3 | 9 | 12 | 3 | .... | .... | .... | .... | .... | .... | .... | .... | .... | .... | .... | .... | .... | .... | .... | .... | .... | .... |
| 2005-06 | Salisbury School | High-CT | 28 | 3 | 20 | 23 | 6 | .... | .... | .... | .... | .... | .... | .... | .... | .... | .... | .... | .... | .... | .... | .... | .... | .... | .... |
| 2006-07 | Salisbury School | High-CT | 25 | 1 | 10 | 11 | 10 | .... | .... | .... | .... | .... | .... | .... | .... | .... | .... | .... | .... | .... | .... | .... | .... | .... | .... |
| 2007-08 | U. of Michigan | CCHA | 21 | 2 | 2 | 4 | 12 | .... | .... | .... | .... | .... | .... | .... | .... | .... | .... | .... | .... | .... | .... | .... | .... | .... | .... |
| | Norfolk Admirals | AHL | 18 | 0 | 4 | 4 | 6 | .... | .... | .... | .... | .... | .... | .... | .... | .... | .... | .... | .... | .... | .... | .... | .... | .... | .... |
| **2008-09** | **Tampa Bay** | **NHL** | **6** | **0** | **1** | **1** | **0** | **0** | **0** | **0** | **7** | **0.0** | **0** | **0** | **0.0** | **13:23** | .... | .... | .... | .... | .... | .... | .... | .... | .... |
| | Norfolk Admirals | AHL | 49 | 1 | 8 | 9 | 8 | .... | .... | .... | .... | .... | .... | .... | .... | .... | .... | .... | .... | .... | .... | .... | .... | .... | .... |
| | Elmira Jackals | ECHL | .... | .... | .... | .... | .... | .... | .... | .... | .... | .... | .... | .... | .... | .... | 9 | 0 | 1 | 1 | 0 | .... | .... | .... | .... |
| | **NHL Totals** | | **6** | **0** | **1** | **1** | **0** | **0** | **0** | **0** | **7** | **0.0** | | **0** | **0.0** | **13:23** | .... | .... | .... | .... | .... | .... | .... | .... | .... |

## QUINCEY, Kyle

(KWIHN-see, KIGHL) **COL.**

Defense. Shoots left. 6'2", 207 lbs. Born, Kitchener, Ont., August 12, 1985. Detroit's 2nd choice, 132nd overall, in 2003 Entry Draft.

| Season | Club | League | GP | G | A | Pts | PIM | PP | SH | GW | S | % | +/- | TF | F% | Min | GP | G | A | Pts | PIM | PP | SH | GW | Min |
|---|---|---|---|---|---|---|---|---|---|---|---|---|---|---|---|---|---|---|---|---|---|---|---|---|---|
| 2001-02 | Mississauga | OPJHL | 27 | 5 | 14 | 19 | 31 | .... | .... | .... | .... | .... | .... | .... | .... | .... | .... | .... | .... | .... | .... | .... | .... | .... | .... |
| 2002-03 | London Knights | OHL | 66 | 6 | 12 | 18 | 77 | .... | .... | .... | .... | .... | .... | .... | .... | .... | 14 | 3 | 4 | 7 | 11 | .... | .... | .... | .... |
| 2003-04 | London Knights | OHL | 3 | 0 | 2 | 2 | 4 | .... | .... | .... | .... | .... | .... | .... | .... | .... | .... | .... | .... | .... | .... | .... | .... | .... | .... |
| | Mississauga | OHL | 61 | 14 | 23 | 37 | 135 | .... | .... | .... | .... | .... | .... | .... | .... | .... | 24 | 3 | 13 | 16 | 32 | .... | .... | .... | .... |
| 2004-05 | Mississauga | OHL | 59 | 15 | 31 | 46 | 111 | .... | .... | .... | .... | .... | .... | .... | .... | .... | 5 | 0 | 3 | 3 | 4 | .... | .... | .... | .... |
| **2005-06** | **Detroit** | **NHL** | **1** | **0** | **0** | **0** | **0** | **0** | **0** | **0** | **1** | **0.0** | **0** | **0** | **0.0** | **11:37** | .... | .... | .... | .... | .... | .... | .... | .... | .... |
| | Grand Rapids | AHL | 70 | 7 | 26 | 33 | 107 | .... | .... | .... | .... | .... | .... | .... | .... | .... | 16 | 0 | 1 | 1 | 27 | .... | .... | .... | .... |
| **2006-07** | **Detroit** | **NHL** | **6** | **1** | **0** | **1** | **0** | **0** | **0** | **0** | **7** | **14.3** | **0** | **0** | **0.0** | **11:26** | **13** | **0** | **0** | **0** | **2** | **0** | **0** | **0** | **8:11** |
| | Grand Rapids | AHL | 65 | 4 | 18 | 22 | 126 | .... | .... | .... | .... | .... | .... | .... | .... | .... | 2 | 0 | 0 | 0 | 0 | .... | .... | .... | .... |
| **2007-08** | **Detroit** | **NHL** | **6** | **0** | **0** | **0** | **4** | **0** | **0** | **0** | **5** | **0.0** | **−3** | **0** | **0.0** | **13:58** | .... | .... | .... | .... | .... | .... | .... | .... | .... |
| | Grand Rapids | AHL | 66 | 5 | 15 | 20 | 149 | .... | .... | .... | .... | .... | .... | .... | .... | .... | .... | .... | .... | .... | .... | .... | .... | .... | .... |
| **2008-09** | **Los Angeles** | **NHL** | **72** | **4** | **34** | **38** | **63** | **2** | **0** | **2** | **150** | **2.7** | **−5** | **0** | **0.0** | **20:59** | .... | .... | .... | .... | .... | .... | .... | .... | .... |
| | **NHL Totals** | | **85** | **5** | **34** | **39** | **67** | **2** | **0** | **2** | **163** | **3.1** | | **0** | **0.0** | **19:42** | **13** | **0** | **0** | **0** | **2** | **0** | **0** | **0** | **8:11** |

OHL Second All-Star Team (2005)

Claimed on waivers by **Los Angeles** from **Detroit**, October 13, 2008. Traded to **Colorado** by **Los Angeles** with Tom Preissing and Los Angeles' 5th round choice in 2010 Entry Draft for Ryan Smyth, July 3, 2009.

## RACHUNEK, Karel

(ra-KHOO-nehk, KAH-rehl)

Defense. Shoots right. 6'2", 220 lbs. Born, Gottwaldov/Zlin, Czech., August 27, 1979. Ottawa's 8th choice, 229th overall, in 1997 Entry Draft.

| Season | Club | League | GP | G | A | Pts | PIM | PP | SH | GW | S | % | +/- | TF | F% | Min | GP | G | A | Pts | PIM | PP | SH | GW | Min |
|---|---|---|---|---|---|---|---|---|---|---|---|---|---|---|---|---|---|---|---|---|---|---|---|---|---|
| 1995-96 | AC ZPS Zlin Jr. | CzRep-Jr. | 38 | 8 | 11 | 19 | .... | .... | .... | .... | .... | .... | .... | .... | .... | .... | .... | .... | .... | .... | .... | .... | .... | .... | .... |
| 1996-97 | AC ZPS Zlin Jr. | CzRep-Jr. | 27 | 2 | 11 | 13 | .... | .... | .... | .... | .... | .... | .... | .... | .... | .... | .... | .... | .... | .... | .... | .... | .... | .... | .... |
| 1997-98 | Zlin | CzRep | 27 | 1 | 2 | 3 | 16 | .... | .... | .... | .... | .... | .... | .... | .... | .... | .... | .... | .... | .... | .... | .... | .... | .... | .... |
| 1998-99 | Zlin | CzRep | 39 | 3 | 9 | 12 | 88 | .... | .... | .... | .... | .... | .... | .... | .... | .... | 6 | 0 | 0 | 0 | .... | .... | .... | .... | .... |
| **99-2000** | **Ottawa** | **NHL** | **6** | **0** | **0** | **0** | **2** | **0** | **0** | **0** | **3** | **0.0** | **0** | **0** | **0.0** | **8:03** | .... | .... | .... | .... | .... | .... | .... | .... | .... |
| | Grand Rapids | IHL | 62 | 6 | 20 | 26 | 64 | .... | .... | .... | .... | .... | .... | .... | .... | .... | 9 | 0 | 5 | 5 | 6 | .... | .... | .... | .... |
| **2000-01** | **Ottawa** | **NHL** | **71** | **3** | **30** | **33** | **60** | **3** | **0** | **0** | **77** | **3.9** | **17** | **0** | **0.0** | **20:54** | **3** | **0** | **0** | **0** | **0** | **0** | **0** | **0** | **22:38** |
| **2001-02** | **Ottawa** | **NHL** | **51** | **3** | **15** | **18** | **24** | **1** | **0** | **2** | **55** | **5.5** | **7** | **2** | **0.0** | **19:19** | .... | .... | .... | .... | .... | .... | .... | .... | .... |
| **2002-03** | Yaroslavl | Russia | 9 | 3 | 0 | 3 | 8 | .... | .... | .... | .... | .... | .... | .... | .... | .... | .... | .... | .... | .... | .... | .... | .... | .... | .... |
| | **Ottawa** | **NHL** | **58** | **4** | **25** | **29** | **30** | **3** | **0** | **1** | **110** | **3.6** | **23** | **3** | **33.3** | **21:46** | **17** | **1** | **3** | **4** | **14** | **0** | **0** | **0** | **23:14** |
| | Binghamton | AHL | 6 | 0 | 2 | 2 | 10 | .... | .... | .... | .... | .... | .... | .... | .... | .... | .... | .... | .... | .... | .... | .... | .... | .... | .... |
| **2003-04** | **Ottawa** | **NHL** | **60** | **1** | **16** | **17** | **29** | **0** | **0** | **0** | **99** | **1.0** | **17** | **0** | **0.0** | **19:43** | .... | .... | .... | .... | .... | .... | .... | .... | .... |
| | **NY Rangers** | **NHL** | **12** | **1** | **3** | **4** | **4** | **1** | **0** | **0** | **21** | **4.8** | **−9** | **0** | **0.0** | **19:04** | .... | .... | .... | .... | .... | .... | .... | .... | .... |
| 2004-05 | Znojmo | CzRep | 21 | 5 | 6 | 11 | 55 | .... | .... | .... | .... | .... | .... | .... | .... | .... | .... | .... | .... | .... | .... | .... | .... | .... | .... |
| | Yaroslavl | Russia | 27 | 6 | 8 | 14 | 69 | .... | .... | .... | .... | .... | .... | .... | .... | .... | 9 | 2 | 0 | 2 | 6 | .... | .... | .... | .... |
| 2005-06 | Yaroslavl | Russia | 45 | 11 | 16 | 27 | 73 | .... | .... | .... | .... | .... | .... | .... | .... | .... | 2 | 0 | 0 | 0 | 29 | .... | .... | .... | .... |
| **2006-07** | **NY Rangers** | **NHL** | **66** | **6** | **20** | **26** | **38** | **4** | **1** | **1** | **99** | **6.1** | **−9** | **0** | **0.0** | **19:23** | **6** | **0** | **4** | **4** | **2** | **0** | **0** | **0** | **18:22** |
| **2007-08** | **New Jersey** | **NHL** | **47** | **4** | **9** | **13** | **40** | **0** | **0** | **0** | **68** | **5.9** | **3** | **0** | **0.0** | **19:23** | .... | .... | .... | .... | .... | .... | .... | .... | .... |
| 2008-09 | Dynamo Moscow | Rus-KHL | 50 | 9 | 23 | 32 | 85 | .... | .... | .... | .... | .... | .... | .... | .... | .... | 12 | 4 | 4 | 8 | 8 | .... | .... | .... | .... |
| | **NHL Totals** | | **371** | **22** | **118** | **140** | **227** | **12** | **1** | **4** | **532** | **4.1** | | **5** | **20.0** | **19:54** | **26** | **1** | **7** | **8** | **16** | **0** | **0** | **0** | **22:03** |

Traded to **NY Rangers** by **Ottawa** with Alexandre Giroux for Greg De Vries, March 9, 2004. Signed as a free agent by **Znojmo** (CzRep), September 6, 2004. Signed as a free agent by **Yaroslavl** (Russia), November 1, 2004. Signed as a free agent by **New Jersey**, July 3, 2007.

## RADIVOJEVIC, Branko

(ra-dih-VOI-uh-vihch, BRAN-koh)

Right wing. Shoots right. 6', 208 lbs. Born, Piestany, Czech., November 24, 1980. Colorado's 3rd choice, 93rd overall, in 1999 Entry Draft.

| Season | Club | League | GP | G | A | Pts | PIM | PP | SH | GW | S | % | +/- | TF | F% | Min | GP | G | A | Pts | PIM | PP | SH | GW | Min |
|---|---|---|---|---|---|---|---|---|---|---|---|---|---|---|---|---|---|---|---|---|---|---|---|---|---|
| 1997-98 | Dukla Trencin Jr. | Slovak-Jr. | 52 | 30 | 31 | 61 | 50 | .... | .... | .... | .... | .... | .... | .... | .... | .... | .... | .... | .... | .... | .... | .... | .... | .... | .... |
| | Dukla Trencin | Slovakia | 1 | 0 | 0 | 0 | 2 | .... | .... | .... | .... | .... | .... | .... | .... | .... | .... | .... | .... | .... | .... | .... | .... | .... | .... |
| 1998-99 | Belleville Bulls | OHL | 68 | 20 | 38 | 58 | 61 | .... | .... | .... | .... | .... | .... | .... | .... | .... | 21 | 7 | 17 | 24 | 18 | .... | .... | .... | .... |
| 99-2000 | Belleville Bulls | OHL | 59 | 23 | 49 | 72 | 86 | .... | .... | .... | .... | .... | .... | .... | .... | .... | 16 | 5 | 8 | 13 | 32 | .... | .... | .... | .... |
| 2000-01 | Belleville Bulls | OHL | 61 | 34 | 70 | 104 | 77 | .... | .... | .... | .... | .... | .... | .... | .... | .... | 10 | 6 | 10 | 16 | 18 | .... | .... | .... | .... |
| **2001-02** | **Phoenix** | **NHL** | **18** | **4** | **2** | **6** | **4** | **0** | **0** | **1** | **19** | **21.1** | **1** | **0** | **0.0** | **9:22** | **1** | **0** | **0** | **0** | **2** | **0** | **0** | **0** | **8:07** |
| | Springfield | AHL | 62 | 18 | 21 | 39 | 64 | .... | .... | .... | .... | .... | .... | .... | .... | .... | .... | .... | .... | .... | .... | .... | .... | .... | .... |
| **2002-03** | **Phoenix** | **NHL** | **79** | **12** | **15** | **27** | **63** | **1** | **0** | **3** | **109** | **11.0** | **−2** | **20** | **40.0** | **13:18** | .... | .... | .... | .... | .... | .... | .... | .... | .... |
| **2003-04** | **Phoenix** | **NHL** | **53** | **9** | **14** | **23** | **36** | **2** | **1** | **2** | **83** | **10.8** | **−5** | **30** | **30.0** | **16:27** | .... | .... | .... | .... | .... | .... | .... | .... | .... |
| | **Philadelphia** | **NHL** | **24** | **1** | **8** | **9** | **36** | **0** | **0** | **0** | **24** | **4.2** | **0** | **11** | **54.6** | **10:28** | **18** | **1** | **1** | **2** | **32** | **0** | **0** | **0** | **9:56** |
| 2004-05 | HC Vsetin | CzRep | 31 | 7 | 11 | 18 | 114 | .... | .... | .... | .... | .... | .... | .... | .... | .... | .... | .... | .... | .... | .... | .... | .... | .... | .... |
| | Lulea HF | Sweden | 10 | 6 | 5 | 11 | 8 | .... | .... | .... | .... | .... | .... | .... | .... | .... | 4 | 0 | 0 | 0 | 44 | .... | .... | .... | .... |
| **2005-06** | **Philadelphia** | **NHL** | **64** | **8** | **6** | **14** | **44** | **1** | **0** | **1** | **84** | **9.5** | **−6** | **14** | **42.9** | **12:46** | **5** | **1** | **0** | **1** | **0** | **0** | **0** | **0** | **10:34** |
| **2006-07** | **Minnesota** | **NHL** | **82** | **11** | **13** | **24** | **21** | **4** | **0** | **3** | **116** | **9.5** | **−9** | **18** | **50.0** | **12:59** | **5** | **0** | **0** | **0** | **2** | **0** | **0** | **0** | **14:14** |
| **2007-08** | **Minnesota** | **NHL** | **73** | **7** | **10** | **17** | **48** | **1** | **0** | **3** | **91** | **7.7** | **−14** | **39** | **38.5** | **14:55** | **2** | **0** | **0** | **0** | **0** | **0** | **0** | **0** | **14:35** |
| 2008-09 | Spartak Moscow | Rus-KHL | 49 | 17 | 26 | 43 | 86 | .... | .... | .... | .... | .... | .... | .... | .... | .... | 6 | 2 | 1 | 3 | 6 | .... | .... | .... | .... |
| | **NHL Totals** | | **393** | **52** | **68** | **120** | **252** | **9** | **1** | **13** | **526** | **9.9** | | **132** | **40.2** | **13:31** | **31** | **2** | **1** | **3** | **36** | **0** | **0** | **0** | **10:58** |

OHL First All-Star Team (2001)

Signed as a free agent by **Phoenix**, June 19, 2001. Traded to **Philadelphia** by **Phoenix** with Sean Burke and Ben Eager for Mike Comrie, February 9, 2004. Signed as a free agent by **Vsetin** (CzRep), September 17, 2004. Signed as a free agent by **Lulea** (Sweden), January 27, 2005. Signed as a free agent by **Minnesota**, July 6, 2006.

## RADULOV, Alexander

(ra-DEW-lahf, al-EHX-AN-duhr) **NSH.**

Right wing. Shoots left. 6'1", 188 lbs. Born, Nizhny Tagil, USSR, July 5, 1986. Nashville's 1st choice, 15th overall, in 2004 Entry Draft.

| Season | Club | League | GP | G | A | Pts | PIM | PP | SH | GW | S | % | +/- | TF | F% | Min | GP | G | A | Pts | PIM | PP | SH | GW | Min |
|---|---|---|---|---|---|---|---|---|---|---|---|---|---|---|---|---|---|---|---|---|---|---|---|---|---|
| 2002-03 | Dyn'o Moscow 2 | Russia-3 | STATISTICS NOT AVAILABLE | | | | | | | | | | | | | | | | | | | | | | |
| 2003-04 | Dyn'o Moscow 2 | Russia-3 | STATISTICS NOT AVAILABLE | | | | | | | | | | | | | | | | | | | | | | |
| | THK Tver | Russia-2 | 42 | 15 | 16 | 31 | 102 | .... | .... | .... | .... | .... | .... | .... | .... | .... | .... | .... | .... | .... | .... | .... | .... | .... | .... |
| | Dynamo Moscow | Russia | 1 | 0 | 0 | 0 | 2 | .... | .... | .... | .... | .... | .... | .... | .... | .... | .... | .... | .... | .... | .... | .... | .... | .... | .... |
| 2004-05 | Quebec Remparts | QMJHL | 65 | 32 | 43 | 75 | 64 | .... | .... | .... | .... | .... | .... | .... | .... | .... | 13 | 6 | 5 | 11 | 15 | .... | .... | .... | .... |
| 2005-06 | Quebec Remparts | QMJHL | 62 | 61 | *91 | *152 | 101 | .... | .... | .... | .... | .... | .... | .... | .... | .... | 23 | 21 | *34 | *55 | 30 | .... | .... | .... | .... |
| **2006-07** | **Nashville** | **NHL** | **64** | **18** | **19** | **37** | **26** | **5** | **0** | **4** | **96** | **18.8** | **19** | **0** | **0.0** | **11:38** | **4** | **3** | **1** | **4** | **19** | **0** | **0** | **0** | **13:10** |
| | Milwaukee | AHL | 11 | 6 | 12 | 18 | 26 | .... | .... | .... | .... | .... | .... | .... | .... | .... | .... | .... | .... | .... | .... | .... | .... | .... | .... |
| **2007-08** | **Nashville** | **NHL** | **81** | **26** | **32** | **58** | **44** | **4** | **0** | **2** | **183** | **14.2** | **7** | **1** | **0.0** | **16:24** | **6** | **2** | **2** | **4** | **6** | **1** | **0** | **0** | **15:59** |
| 2008-09 | Ufa | Rus-KHL | 52 | 22 | 26 | 48 | 92 | .... | .... | .... | .... | .... | .... | .... | .... | .... | 4 | 0 | 2 | 2 | 4 | .... | .... | .... | .... |
| | **NHL Totals** | | **145** | **44** | **51** | **95** | **70** | **9** | **0** | **6** | **279** | **15.8** | | **1** | **0.0** | **14:18** | **10** | **5** | **3** | **8** | **25** | **1** | **0** | **0** | **14:51** |

QMJHL All-Rookie Team (2005) • QMJHL First All-Star Team (2006) • QMJHL Player of the Year (2006) • Canadian Major Junior First All-Star Team (2006) • Canadian Major Junior Player of the Year (2006) • Memorial Cup Tournament All-Star Team (2006) • Stafford Smythe Memorial Trophy (Memorial Cup Tournament - MVP) (2006)

## RADUNS, Nate

(RAH-duhnz, NAYT)

Right wing. Shoots right. 6'3", 205 lbs. Born, Sauk Rapids, MN, May 17, 1984.

| | | | Regular Season | | | | | | | | | | | | | | Playoffs | | | | | | | | |
|---|---|---|---|---|---|---|---|---|---|---|---|---|---|---|---|---|---|---|---|---|---|---|---|---|---|
| Season | Club | League | GP | G | A | Pts | PIM | PP | SH | GW | S | % | +/- | TF | F% | Min | GP | G | A | Pts | PIM | PP | SH | GW | Min |
| 2001-02 | USNTDP | USHL | 13 | 3 | 3 | 6 | 14 | .... | .... | .... | .... | .... | .... | .... | .... | .... | .... | .... | .... | .... | .... | .... | .... | .... | .... |
| | USNTDP | NAHL | 10 | 0 | 4 | 4 | 7 | .... | .... | .... | .... | .... | .... | .... | .... | .... | .... | .... | .... | .... | .... | .... | .... | .... | .... |
| 2002-03 | River City Lancers | USHL | 48 | 5 | 17 | 22 | 50 | .... | .... | .... | .... | .... | .... | .... | .... | .... | 11 | 1 | 3 | 4 | 8 | .... | .... | .... | .... |
| 2003-04 | St. Cloud State | WCHA | 34 | 4 | 7 | 11 | 40 | .... | .... | .... | .... | .... | .... | .... | .... | .... | .... | .... | .... | .... | .... | .... | .... | .... | .... |
| 2004-05 | St. Cloud State | WCHA | 28 | 4 | 8 | 12 | 32 | .... | .... | .... | .... | .... | .... | .... | .... | .... | .... | .... | .... | .... | .... | .... | .... | .... | .... |
| 2005-06 | St. Cloud State | WCHA | 41 | 5 | 10 | 15 | 50 | .... | .... | .... | .... | .... | .... | .... | .... | .... | .... | .... | .... | .... | .... | .... | .... | .... | .... |
| 2006-07 | St. Cloud State | WCHA | 40 | 6 | 6 | 12 | 53 | .... | .... | .... | .... | .... | .... | .... | .... | .... | .... | .... | .... | .... | .... | .... | .... | .... | .... |
| 2007-08 | Worcester Sharks | AHL | 56 | 12 | 15 | 27 | 42 | .... | .... | .... | .... | .... | .... | .... | .... | .... | .... | .... | .... | .... | .... | .... | .... | .... | .... |
| **2008-09** | **Philadelphia** | **NHL** | **1** | **0** | **0** | **0** | **0** | **0** | **0** | **0** | **0** | **0.0** | **0** | **1** | **0.0** | **6:02** | .... | .... | .... | .... | .... | .... | .... | .... | .... |
| | Philadelphia | AHL | 70 | 5 | 9 | 14 | 71 | .... | .... | .... | .... | .... | .... | .... | .... | .... | 3 | 0 | 0 | 0 | 2 | .... | .... | .... | .... |
| | **NHL Totals** | | **1** | **0** | **0** | **0** | **0** | **0** | **0** | **0** | **0** | **0.0** | | **1** | **0.0** | **6:02** | .... | .... | .... | .... | .... | .... | .... | .... | .... |

Signed as a free agent by **Philadelphia**, July 1, 2008.

## RAFALSKI, Brian

(ra-FAWL-skee, BRIGH-uhn) **DET.**

Defense. Shoots right. 5'10", 191 lbs. Born, Dearborn, MI, September 28, 1973.

| | | | Regular Season | | | | | | | | | | | | | | Playoffs | | | | | | | | |
|---|---|---|---|---|---|---|---|---|---|---|---|---|---|---|---|---|---|---|---|---|---|---|---|---|---|
| Season | Club | League | GP | G | A | Pts | PIM | PP | SH | GW | S | % | +/- | TF | F% | Min | GP | G | A | Pts | PIM | PP | SH | GW | Min |
| 1990-91 | Madison Capitols | USHL | 47 | 12 | 11 | 23 | 28 | .... | .... | .... | .... | .... | .... | .... | .... | .... | .... | .... | .... | .... | .... | .... | .... | .... | .... |
| 1991-92 | U. of Wisconsin | WCHA | 34 | 3 | 14 | 17 | 34 | .... | .... | .... | .... | .... | .... | .... | .... | .... | .... | .... | .... | .... | .... | .... | .... | .... | .... |
| 1992-93 | U. of Wisconsin | WCHA | 32 | 0 | 13 | 13 | 10 | .... | .... | .... | .... | .... | .... | .... | .... | .... | .... | .... | .... | .... | .... | .... | .... | .... | .... |
| 1993-94 | U. of Wisconsin | WCHA | 37 | 6 | 17 | 23 | 26 | .... | .... | .... | .... | .... | .... | .... | .... | .... | .... | .... | .... | .... | .... | .... | .... | .... | .... |
| 1994-95 | U. of Wisconsin | WCHA | 43 | 11 | 34 | 45 | 48 | .... | .... | .... | .... | .... | .... | .... | .... | .... | .... | .... | .... | .... | .... | .... | .... | .... | .... |
| 1995-96 | Brynas IF Gavle | Sweden | 40 | 4 | 14 | 18 | 26 | .... | .... | .... | .... | .... | .... | .... | .... | .... | 9 | 0 | 1 | 1 | 2 | .... | .... | .... | .... |
| 1996-97 | HPK Hameenlinna | Finland | 49 | 11 | 24 | 35 | 26 | .... | .... | .... | .... | .... | .... | .... | .... | .... | 10 | 6 | 5 | 11 | 4 | .... | .... | .... | .... |
| 1997-98 | HIFK Helsinki | Finland | 40 | 13 | 10 | 23 | 20 | .... | .... | .... | .... | .... | .... | .... | .... | .... | 9 | 5 | 6 | 11 | 0 | .... | .... | .... | .... |
| 1998-99 | HIFK Helsinki | Finland | 53 | 19 | 34 | 53 | 18 | .... | .... | .... | .... | .... | .... | .... | .... | .... | 11 | 5 | *9 | *14 | 4 | .... | .... | .... | .... |
| | HIFK Helsinki | EuroHL | 6 | 4 | 6 | 10 | 10 | .... | .... | .... | .... | .... | .... | .... | .... | .... | 4 | 1 | 0 | 1 | 2 | .... | .... | .... | .... |
| **99-2000♦** | **New Jersey** | **NHL** | **75** | **5** | **27** | **32** | **28** | **1** | **0** | **1** | **128** | **3.9** | **21** | **1** | **0.0** | **18:51** | **23** | **2** | **6** | **8** | **8** | **0** | **0** | **1** | **21:25** |
| **2000-01** | **New Jersey** | **NHL** | **78** | **9** | **43** | **52** | **26** | **6** | **0** | **1** | **142** | **6.3** | **36** | **2** | **100.0** | **21:41** | **25** | **7** | **11** | **18** | **7** | **1** | **0** | **3** | **22:08** |
| **2001-02** | **New Jersey** | **NHL** | **76** | **7** | **40** | **47** | **18** | **2** | **0** | **4** | **125** | **5.6** | **15** | **0** | **0.0** | **22:08** | **6** | **3** | **2** | **5** | **4** | **3** | **0** | **0** | **21:45** |
| | United States | Olympics | 6 | 1 | 2 | 3 | 2 | .... | .... | .... | .... | .... | .... | .... | .... | .... | .... | .... | .... | .... | .... | .... | .... | .... | .... |
| **2002-03♦** | **New Jersey** | **NHL** | **79** | **3** | **37** | **40** | **14** | **2** | **0** | **0** | **178** | **1.7** | **18** | **1** | **0.0** | **23:09** | **23** | **2** | **9** | **11** | **8** | **2** | **0** | **0** | **25:46** |
| **2003-04** | **New Jersey** | **NHL** | **69** | **6** | **30** | **36** | **24** | **2** | **0** | **1** | **130** | **4.6** | **6** | **0** | **0.0** | **22:48** | **5** | **0** | **1** | **1** | **0** | **0** | **0** | **0** | **22:22** |
| 2004-05 | | | DID NOT PLAY | | | | | | | | | | | | | | | | | | | | | | |
| **2005-06** | **New Jersey** | **NHL** | **82** | **6** | **43** | **49** | **36** | **3** | **0** | **2** | **126** | **4.8** | **0** | **1** | **0.0** | **25:32** | **9** | **1** | **8** | **9** | **2** | **1** | **0** | **0** | **27:26** |
| | United States | Olympics | 5 | 0 | 2 | 2 | 0 | .... | .... | .... | .... | .... | .... | .... | .... | .... | .... | .... | .... | .... | .... | .... | .... | .... | .... |
| **2006-07** | **New Jersey** | **NHL** | **82** | **8** | **47** | **55** | **34** | **3** | **1** | **4** | **148** | **5.4** | **4** | **0** | **0.0** | **25:29** | **11** | **2** | **6** | **8** | **8** | **2** | **0** | **0** | **22:54** |
| **2007-08♦** | **Detroit** | **NHL** | **73** | **13** | **42** | **55** | **34** | **10** | **0** | **1** | **175** | **7.4** | **27** | **0** | **0.0** | **24:04** | **22** | **4** | **10** | **14** | **12** | **2** | **0** | **0** | **24:53** |
| **2008-09** | **Detroit** | **NHL** | **78** | **10** | **49** | **59** | **20** | **5** | **0** | **1** | **141** | **7.1** | **17** | **0** | **0.0** | **23:10** | **18** | **3** | **9** | **12** | **11** | **3** | **0** | **1** | **22:27** |
| | **NHL Totals** | | **692** | **67** | **358** | **425** | **234** | **34** | **1** | **15** | **1293** | **5.2** | | **5** | **40.0** | **23:02** | **142** | **24** | **62** | **86** | **60** | **14** | **0** | **5** | **23:28** |

WCHA First All-Star Team (1995) • NCAA West First All-American Team (1995) • NHL All-Rookie Team (2000)
Played in NHL All-Star Game (2004, 2007)
Signed as a free agent by **New Jersey**, June 18, 1999. Signed as a free agent by **Detroit**, July 1, 2007.

## RAMHOLT, Tim

(RAM-hohlt, TIHM)

Defense. Shoots left. 6'1", 194 lbs. Born, Zurich, Switz., November 2, 1984. Calgary's 2nd choice, 39th overall, in 2003 Entry Draft.

| | | | Regular Season | | | | | | | | | | | | | | Playoffs | | | | | | | | |
|---|---|---|---|---|---|---|---|---|---|---|---|---|---|---|---|---|---|---|---|---|---|---|---|---|---|
| Season | Club | League | GP | G | A | Pts | PIM | PP | SH | GW | S | % | +/- | TF | F% | Min | GP | G | A | Pts | PIM | PP | SH | GW | Min |
| 99-2000 | Zurich/Kusn Jr. | Swiss-Jr. | 35 | 2 | 9 | 11 | 26 | .... | .... | .... | .... | .... | .... | .... | .... | .... | 4 | 0 | 2 | 2 | 4 | .... | .... | .... | .... |
| | Grasshopper | Swiss-2 | 2 | 0 | 0 | 0 | 0 | .... | .... | .... | .... | .... | .... | .... | .... | .... | .... | .... | .... | .... | .... | .... | .... | .... | .... |
| 2000-01 | GC Zurich | Swiss-2 | 37 | 0 | 2 | 2 | 38 | .... | .... | .... | .... | .... | .... | .... | .... | .... | 3 | 0 | 0 | 0 | 4 | .... | .... | .... | .... |
| | GC Zurich Jr. | Swiss-Jr. | 17 | 3 | 6 | 9 | 10 | .... | .... | .... | .... | .... | .... | .... | .... | .... | .... | .... | .... | .... | .... | .... | .... | .... | .... |
| 2001-02 | ZSC Lions Zurich | Swiss | 37 | 3 | 0 | 3 | 14 | .... | .... | .... | .... | .... | .... | .... | .... | .... | 17 | 0 | 3 | 3 | 2 | .... | .... | .... | .... |
| | GCK/ZSC Zurich Jr. | | Swiss-Jr. | 5 | 2 | 2 | 4 | 4 | .... | .... | .... | .... | .... | .... | .... | .... | .... | .... | .... | .... | .... | .... | .... | .... |
| .... | | | | | | | | | | | | | | | | | | | | | | | | | |
| | GC Zurich | Swiss-2 | 3 | 0 | 0 | 0 | 0 | .... | .... | .... | .... | .... | .... | .... | .... | .... | .... | .... | .... | .... | .... | .... | .... | .... | .... |
| 2002-03 | ZSC Lions Zurich | Swiss | 30 | 2 | 0 | 2 | 12 | .... | .... | .... | .... | .... | .... | .... | .... | .... | 9 | 0 | 1 | 1 | 0 | .... | .... | .... | .... |
| | GC Zurich | Swiss-2 | 12 | 0 | 4 | 4 | 6 | .... | .... | .... | .... | .... | .... | .... | .... | .... | .... | .... | .... | .... | .... | .... | .... | .... | .... |
| 2003-04 | Cape Breton | QMJHL | 51 | 9 | 27 | 36 | 26 | .... | .... | .... | .... | .... | .... | .... | .... | .... | 5 | 0 | 1 | 1 | 4 | .... | .... | .... | .... |
| 2004-05 | ZSC Lions Zurich | Swiss | 41 | 1 | 3 | 4 | 38 | .... | .... | .... | .... | .... | .... | .... | .... | .... | 15 | 0 | 0 | 0 | 10 | .... | .... | .... | .... |
| 2005-06 | Kloten Flyers | Swiss | 42 | 0 | 1 | 1 | 48 | .... | .... | .... | .... | .... | .... | .... | .... | .... | 11 | 0 | 1 | 1 | 8 | .... | .... | .... | .... |
| 2006-07 | Omaha | AHL | 67 | 2 | 10 | 12 | 61 | .... | .... | .... | .... | .... | .... | .... | .... | .... | 6 | 0 | 1 | 1 | 10 | .... | .... | .... | .... |
| **2007-08** | **Calgary** | **NHL** | **1** | **0** | **0** | **0** | **0** | **0** | **0** | **0** | **0** | **0.0** | **–1** | **0** | **0.0** | **0:45** | .... | .... | .... | .... | .... | .... | .... | .... | .... |
| | Quad City Flames | AHL | 77 | 4 | 20 | 24 | 73 | .... | .... | .... | .... | .... | .... | .... | .... | .... | .... | .... | .... | .... | .... | .... | .... | .... | .... |
| 2008-09 | Philadelphia | AHL | 7 | 0 | 0 | 0 | 0 | .... | .... | .... | .... | .... | .... | .... | .... | .... | .... | .... | .... | .... | .... | .... | .... | .... | .... |
| | Milwaukee | AHL | 59 | 2 | 8 | 10 | 36 | .... | .... | .... | .... | .... | .... | .... | .... | .... | 8 | 0 | 1 | 1 | 8 | .... | .... | .... | .... |
| | **NHL Totals** | | **1** | **0** | **0** | **0** | **0** | **0** | **0** | **0** | **0** | **0.0** | | **0** | **0.0** | **0:45** | .... | .... | .... | .... | .... | .... | .... | .... | .... |

Traded to **Philadelphia** by **Calgary** for Kyle Greentree, June 30, 2008. Traded to **Nashville** by **Philadelphia** for Josh Gratton, October 30, 2008.

## RANGER, Paul

(RAIN-juhr, PAWL) **T.B.**

Defense. Shoots left. 6'3", 208 lbs. Born, Whitby, Ont., September 12, 1984. Tampa Bay's 7th choice, 183rd overall, in 2002 Entry Draft.

| | | | Regular Season | | | | | | | | | | | | | | Playoffs | | | | | | | | |
|---|---|---|---|---|---|---|---|---|---|---|---|---|---|---|---|---|---|---|---|---|---|---|---|---|---|
| Season | Club | League | GP | G | A | Pts | PIM | PP | SH | GW | S | % | +/- | TF | F% | Min | GP | G | A | Pts | PIM | PP | SH | GW | Min |
| 2000-01 | Oshawa Generals | OHL | 32 | 0 | 1 | 1 | 2 | .... | .... | .... | .... | .... | .... | .... | .... | .... | .... | .... | .... | .... | .... | .... | .... | .... | .... |
| 2001-02 | Oshawa Generals | OHL | 62 | 0 | 9 | 9 | 49 | .... | .... | .... | .... | .... | .... | .... | .... | .... | 5 | 0 | 0 | 0 | 4 | .... | .... | .... | .... |
| 2002-03 | Oshawa Generals | OHL | 68 | 10 | 28 | 38 | 70 | .... | .... | .... | .... | .... | .... | .... | .... | .... | 13 | 0 | 3 | 3 | 10 | .... | .... | .... | .... |
| 2003-04 | Oshawa Generals | OHL | 62 | 12 | 31 | 43 | 72 | .... | .... | .... | .... | .... | .... | .... | .... | .... | 7 | 0 | 1 | 1 | 10 | .... | .... | .... | .... |
| 2004-05 | Springfield | AHL | 69 | 3 | 8 | 11 | 46 | .... | .... | .... | .... | .... | .... | .... | .... | .... | .... | .... | .... | .... | .... | .... | .... | .... | .... |
| **2005-06** | **Tampa Bay** | **NHL** | **76** | **1** | **17** | **18** | **58** | **0** | **0** | **1** | **73** | **1.4** | **5** | **0** | **0.0** | **17:07** | **5** | **2** | **4** | **6** | **0** | **1** | **0** | **0** | **21:43** |
| | Springfield | AHL | 1 | 1 | 2 | 3 | 0 | .... | .... | .... | .... | .... | .... | .... | .... | .... | .... | .... | .... | .... | .... | .... | .... | .... | .... |
| **2006-07** | **Tampa Bay** | **NHL** | **72** | **4** | **24** | **28** | **42** | **0** | **0** | **2** | **90** | **4.4** | **5** | **0** | **0.0** | **20:19** | **6** | **0** | **1** | **1** | **4** | **0** | **0** | **0** | **21:22** |
| **2007-08** | **Tampa Bay** | **NHL** | **72** | **10** | **21** | **31** | **56** | **0** | **1** | **0** | **105** | **9.5** | **–13** | **0** | **0.0** | **25:13** | .... | .... | .... | .... | .... | .... | .... | .... | .... |
| **2008-09** | **Tampa Bay** | **NHL** | **42** | **2** | **11** | **13** | **56** | **0** | **0** | **0** | **69** | **2.9** | **–5** | **0** | **0.0** | **24:30** | .... | .... | .... | .... | .... | .... | .... | .... | .... |
| | **NHL Totals** | | **262** | **17** | **73** | **90** | **212** | **0** | **1** | **3** | **337** | **5.0** | | **0** | **0.0** | **21:24** | **11** | **2** | **5** | **7** | **4** | **1** | **0** | **0** | **21:31** |

## RASMUSSEN, Erik

(RAS-moo-suhn, AIR-ihk)

Left wing/Center. Shoots left. 6'1", 215 lbs. Born, Minneapolis, MN, March 28, 1977. Buffalo's 1st choice, 7th overall, in 1996 Entry Draft.

| | | | Regular Season | | | | | | | | | | | | | | Playoffs | | | | | | | | |
|---|---|---|---|---|---|---|---|---|---|---|---|---|---|---|---|---|---|---|---|---|---|---|---|---|---|
| Season | Club | League | GP | G | A | Pts | PIM | PP | SH | GW | S | % | +/- | TF | F% | Min | GP | G | A | Pts | PIM | PP | SH | GW | Min |
| 1992-93 | St. Louis Park | High-MN | 23 | 16 | 24 | 40 | 50 | .... | .... | .... | .... | .... | .... | .... | .... | .... | .... | .... | .... | .... | .... | .... | .... | .... | .... |
| 1993-94 | St. Louis Park | High-MN | 18 | 25 | 18 | 43 | 80 | .... | .... | .... | .... | .... | .... | .... | .... | .... | .... | .... | .... | .... | .... | .... | .... | .... | .... |
| 1994-95 | St. Louis Park | High-MN | 23 | 19 | 33 | 52 | 80 | .... | .... | .... | .... | .... | .... | .... | .... | .... | .... | .... | .... | .... | .... | .... | .... | .... | .... |
| 1995-96 | U. of Minnesota | WCHA | 40 | 16 | 32 | 48 | 55 | .... | .... | .... | .... | .... | .... | .... | .... | .... | .... | .... | .... | .... | .... | .... | .... | .... | .... |
| 1996-97 | U. of Minnesota | WCHA | 34 | 15 | 12 | 27 | *123 | .... | .... | .... | .... | .... | .... | .... | .... | .... | .... | .... | .... | .... | .... | .... | .... | .... | .... |
| **1997-98** | **Buffalo** | **NHL** | **21** | **2** | **3** | **5** | **14** | **0** | **0** | **0** | **28** | **7.1** | **2** | .... | .... | .... | .... | .... | .... | .... | .... | .... | .... | .... | .... |
| | Rochester | AHL | 53 | 9 | 14 | 23 | 83 | .... | .... | .... | .... | .... | .... | .... | .... | .... | 1 | 0 | 0 | 0 | 5 | .... | .... | .... | .... |
| **1998-99** | **Buffalo** | **NHL** | **42** | **3** | **7** | **10** | **37** | **0** | **0** | **0** | **40** | **7.5** | **6** | **67** | **40.3** | **12:22** | **21** | **2** | **4** | **6** | **18** | **0** | **0** | **1** | **12:51** |
| | Rochester | AHL | 37 | 12 | 14 | 26 | 47 | .... | .... | .... | .... | .... | .... | .... | .... | .... | .... | .... | .... | .... | .... | .... | .... | .... | .... |
| **99-2000** | **Buffalo** | **NHL** | **67** | **8** | **6** | **14** | **43** | **0** | **0** | **2** | **76** | **10.5** | **1** | **130** | **44.6** | **11:27** | **3** | **0** | **0** | **0** | **4** | **0** | **0** | **0** | **8:59** |
| **2000-01** | **Buffalo** | **NHL** | **82** | **12** | **19** | **31** | **51** | **1** | **0** | **3** | **95** | **12.6** | **0** | **565** | **43.7** | **13:47** | **3** | **0** | **1** | **1** | **0** | **0** | **0** | **0** | **16:26** |
| **2001-02** | **Buffalo** | **NHL** | **69** | **8** | **11** | **19** | **34** | **0** | **0** | **2** | **89** | **9.0** | **–1** | **236** | **39.8** | **13:03** | .... | .... | .... | .... | .... | .... | .... | .... | .... |
| **2002-03** | **Los Angeles** | **NHL** | **57** | **4** | **12** | **16** | **28** | **0** | **0** | **1** | **75** | **5.3** | **–1** | **278** | **44.6** | **13:39** | .... | .... | .... | .... | .... | .... | .... | .... | .... |
| **2003-04** | **New Jersey** | **NHL** | **69** | **7** | **6** | **13** | **41** | **0** | **0** | **0** | **68** | **10.3** | **5** | **423** | **44.4** | **11:34** | **5** | **0** | **2** | **2** | **2** | **0** | **0** | **0** | **14:44** |
| 2004-05 | | | DID NOT PLAY | | | | | | | | | | | | | | | | | | | | | | |
| **2005-06** | **New Jersey** | **NHL** | **67** | **5** | **5** | **10** | **32** | **1** | **0** | **0** | **45** | **11.1** | **–4** | **230** | **37.4** | **7:04** | **9** | **0** | **0** | **0** | **8** | **0** | **0** | **0** | **6:44** |
| **2006-07** | **New Jersey** | **NHL** | **71** | **3** | **7** | **10** | **25** | **0** | **0** | **0** | **80** | **3.8** | **–3** | **52** | **48.1** | **9:28** | **11** | **0** | **0** | **0** | **14** | **0** | **0** | **0** | **5:21** |
| 2007-08 | Lowell Devils | AHL | 26 | 2 | 3 | 5 | 14 | .... | .... | .... | .... | .... | .... | .... | .... | .... | .... | .... | .... | .... | .... | .... | .... | .... | .... |

| | | | Regular Season | | | | | | | | | | | | | | Playoffs | | | | | | | | |
|---|---|---|---|---|---|---|---|---|---|---|---|---|---|---|---|---|---|---|---|---|---|---|---|---|---|
| Season | Club | League | GP | G | A | Pts | PIM | PP | SH | GW | S | % | +/- | TF | F% | Min | GP | G | A | Pts | PIM | PP | SH | GW | Min |
| 2008-09 | Assat Pori | Finland | 31 | 1 | 8 | 9 | 60 | .... | .... | .... | .... | .... | .... | .... | .... | .... | 7 | 1 | 4 | 5 | 24 | .... | .... | .... | .... |
| | Assat Pori | Finland-Q | 6 | 3 | 1 | 4 | 14 | .... | .... | .... | .... | .... | .... | .... | .... | .... | .... | .... | .... | .... | .... | .... | .... | .... | .... |
| | **NHL Totals** | | **545** | **52** | **76** | **128** | **305** | **2** | **0** | **8** | **596** | **8.7** | | **1981** | **42.9** | **11:31** | **52** | **2** | **7** | **9** | **46** | **0** | **0** | **1** | **10:22** |

Minnesota High School Player of the Year (1995)
Traded to **Los Angeles** by **Buffalo** for Adam Mair and Los Angeles' 5th round choice (Thomas Morrow) in 2003 Entry Draft, July 24, 2002. Signed as a free agent by **New Jersey**, July 25, 2003.

## RAYMOND, Mason
(RAY-muhnd, MAY-sohn) **VAN.**

Left wing. Shoots left. 6', 182 lbs. Born, Cochrane, Alta., September 17, 1985. Vancouver's 2nd choice, 51st overall, in 2005 Entry Draft.

| | | | Regular Season | | | | | | | | | | | | | | Playoffs | | | | | | | | |
|---|---|---|---|---|---|---|---|---|---|---|---|---|---|---|---|---|---|---|---|---|---|---|---|---|---|
| Season | Club | League | GP | G | A | Pts | PIM | PP | SH | GW | S | % | +/- | TF | F% | Min | GP | G | A | Pts | PIM | PP | SH | GW | Min |
| 2003-04 | Camrose Kodiaks | AJHL | .... | 27 | 35 | 62 | | .... | .... | .... | .... | .... | .... | .... | .... | .... | .... | .... | .... | .... | .... | .... | .... | .... | .... |
| 2004-05 | Camrose Kodiaks | AJHL | 55 | *41 | 41 | 82 | 80 | .... | .... | .... | .... | .... | .... | .... | .... | .... | 15 | 8 | *12 | 20 | .... | .... | .... | .... | .... |
| 2005-06 | U. Minn-Duluth | WCHA | 40 | 11 | 17 | 28 | 30 | .... | .... | .... | .... | .... | .... | .... | .... | .... | .... | .... | .... | .... | .... | .... | .... | .... | .... |
| 2006-07 | U. Minn-Duluth | WCHA | 39 | 14 | 32 | 46 | 45 | .... | .... | .... | .... | .... | .... | .... | .... | .... | .... | .... | .... | .... | .... | .... | .... | .... | .... |
| | Manitoba Moose | AHL | 11 | 2 | 2 | 4 | 6 | .... | .... | .... | .... | .... | .... | .... | .... | .... | 13 | 0 | 1 | 1 | 0 | .... | .... | .... | .... |
| **2007-08** | **Vancouver** | **NHL** | **49** | **9** | **12** | **21** | **2** | **1** | **0** | **0** | **80** | **11.3** | **1** | **63** | **38.1** | **12:31** | .... | .... | .... | .... | .... | .... | .... | .... | .... |
| | Manitoba Moose | AHL | 20 | 7 | 10 | 17 | 6 | .... | .... | .... | .... | .... | .... | .... | .... | .... | .... | .... | .... | .... | .... | .... | .... | .... | .... |
| **2008-09** | **Vancouver** | **NHL** | **72** | **11** | **12** | **23** | **24** | **4** | **0** | **0** | **145** | **7.6** | **2** | **50** | **34.0** | **13:43** | **10** | **2** | **1** | **3** | **2** | **0** | **0** | **0** | **15:12** |
| | **NHL Totals** | | **121** | **20** | **24** | **44** | **26** | **5** | **0** | **0** | **225** | **8.9** | | **113** | **36.3** | **13:14** | **10** | **2** | **1** | **3** | **2** | **0** | **0** | **0** | **15:12** |

AJHL MVP (2005) • WCHA All-Rookie Team (2006) • WCHA First All-Star Team (2007)

## REASONER, Marty
(REE-suh-nuhr, MAHR-tee) **ATL.**

Center. Shoots left. 6'1", 205 lbs. Born, Honeoye Falls, NY, February 26, 1977. St. Louis' 1st choice, 14th overall, in 1996 Entry Draft.

| | | | Regular Season | | | | | | | | | | | | | | Playoffs | | | | | | | | |
|---|---|---|---|---|---|---|---|---|---|---|---|---|---|---|---|---|---|---|---|---|---|---|---|---|---|
| Season | Club | League | GP | G | A | Pts | PIM | PP | SH | GW | S | % | +/- | TF | F% | Min | GP | G | A | Pts | PIM | PP | SH | GW | Min |
| 1993-94 | Deerfield | High-MA | 22 | 27 | 25 | 52 | .... | .... | .... | .... | .... | .... | .... | .... | .... | .... | .... | .... | .... | .... | .... | .... | .... | .... | .... |
| 1994-95 | Deerfield | High-MA | 26 | 25 | 32 | 57 | 14 | .... | .... | .... | .... | .... | .... | .... | .... | .... | .... | .... | .... | .... | .... | .... | .... | .... | .... |
| 1995-96 | Boston College | H-East | 34 | 16 | 29 | 45 | 32 | .... | .... | .... | .... | .... | .... | .... | .... | .... | .... | .... | .... | .... | .... | .... | .... | .... | .... |
| 1996-97 | Boston College | H-East | 35 | 20 | 24 | 44 | 31 | .... | .... | .... | .... | .... | .... | .... | .... | .... | .... | .... | .... | .... | .... | .... | .... | .... | .... |
| 1997-98 | Boston College | H-East | 42 | *33 | 40 | *73 | 56 | .... | .... | .... | .... | .... | .... | .... | .... | .... | .... | .... | .... | .... | .... | .... | .... | .... | .... |
| **1998-99** | **St. Louis** | **NHL** | **22** | **3** | **7** | **10** | **8** | **1** | **0** | **0** | **33** | **9.1** | **2** | **224** | **53.6** | **13:55** | .... | .... | .... | .... | .... | .... | .... | .... | .... |
| | Worcester IceCats | AHL | 44 | 17 | 22 | 39 | 24 | .... | .... | .... | .... | .... | .... | .... | .... | .... | 4 | 2 | 1 | 3 | 6 | .... | .... | .... | .... |
| **99-2000** | **St. Louis** | **NHL** | **32** | **10** | **14** | **24** | **20** | **3** | **0** | **0** | **51** | **19.6** | **9** | **379** | **49.6** | **15:20** | **7** | **2** | **1** | **3** | **4** | **1** | **0** | **0** | **13:12** |
| | Worcester IceCats | AHL | 44 | 23 | 28 | 51 | 39 | .... | .... | .... | .... | .... | .... | .... | .... | .... | .... | .... | .... | .... | .... | .... | .... | .... | .... |
| **2000-01** | **St. Louis** | **NHL** | **41** | **4** | **9** | **13** | **14** | **0** | **0** | **0** | **65** | **6.2** | **-5** | **454** | **53.1** | **14:00** | **10** | **3** | **1** | **4** | **0** | **0** | **0** | **1** | **12:21** |
| | Worcester IceCats | AHL | 34 | 17 | 18 | 35 | 25 | .... | .... | .... | .... | .... | .... | .... | .... | .... | .... | .... | .... | .... | .... | .... | .... | .... | .... |
| **2001-02** | **Edmonton** | **NHL** | **52** | **6** | **5** | **11** | **41** | **3** | **0** | **2** | **66** | **9.1** | **0** | **470** | **55.5** | **11:44** | .... | .... | .... | .... | .... | .... | .... | .... | .... |
| **2002-03** | **Edmonton** | **NHL** | **70** | **11** | **20** | **31** | **28** | **2** | **2** | **0** | **102** | **10.8** | **19** | **968** | **53.5** | **14:50** | **6** | **1** | **0** | **1** | **2** | **1** | **0** | **0** | **14:22** |
| | Hamilton | AHL | 2 | 0 | 2 | 2 | 2 | .... | .... | .... | .... | .... | .... | .... | .... | .... | .... | .... | .... | .... | .... | .... | .... | .... | .... |
| **2003-04** | **Edmonton** | **NHL** | **17** | **2** | **6** | **8** | **10** | **0** | **1** | **0** | **28** | **7.1** | **5** | **321** | **52.7** | **16:30** | .... | .... | .... | .... | .... | .... | .... | .... | .... |
| 2004-05 | Salzburg | Austria | 11 | 5 | 4 | 9 | 12 | .... | .... | .... | .... | .... | .... | .... | .... | .... | .... | .... | .... | .... | .... | .... | .... | .... | .... |
| **2005-06** | **Edmonton** | **NHL** | **58** | **9** | **17** | **26** | **20** | **5** | **0** | **1** | **63** | **14.3** | **-12** | **524** | **52.5** | **12:45** | .... | .... | .... | .... | .... | .... | .... | .... | .... |
| | **Boston** | **NHL** | **19** | **2** | **6** | **8** | **8** | **1** | **0** | **0** | **39** | **5.1** | **-2** | **227** | **46.7** | **15:09** | .... | .... | .... | .... | .... | .... | .... | .... | .... |
| **2006-07** | **Edmonton** | **NHL** | **72** | **6** | **14** | **20** | **60** | **0** | **0** | **1** | **84** | **7.1** | **-15** | **765** | **54.6** | **13:52** | .... | .... | .... | .... | .... | .... | .... | .... | .... |
| **2007-08** | **Edmonton** | **NHL** | **82** | **11** | **14** | **25** | **50** | **0** | **0** | **0** | **113** | **9.7** | **-17** | **906** | **52.8** | **14:58** | .... | .... | .... | .... | .... | .... | .... | .... | .... |
| **2008-09** | **Atlanta** | **NHL** | **79** | **14** | **16** | **30** | **36** | **0** | **1** | **2** | **131** | **10.7** | **11** | **1141** | **52.9** | **15:19** | .... | .... | .... | .... | .... | .... | .... | .... | .... |
| | **NHL Totals** | | **544** | **78** | **128** | **206** | **295** | **15** | **4** | **6** | **775** | **10.1** | | **6379** | **52.9** | **14:16** | **23** | **6** | **2** | **8** | **6** | **2** | **0** | **1** | **13:08** |

Hockey East Rookie of the Year (1996) • Hockey East First All-Star Team (1997, 1998) • NCAA East First All-American Team (1998) • NCAA Championship All-Tournament Team (1998)
Traded to **Edmonton** by **St. Louis** with Jochen Hecht and Jan Horacek for Doug Weight and Michel Riesen, July 1, 2001. • Missed majority of 2003-04 season recovering from ankle (November 8, 2003 vs. Toronto) and knee (January 13, 2004 vs. Florida) injuries. Signed as a free agent by **Salzburg** (Austria), January 30, 2005. Traded to **Boston** by **Edmonton** with Yan Stastny and Edmonton's 2nd round choice (Milan Lucic) in 2006 Entry Draft for Sergei Samsonov, March 9, 2006. Signed as a free agent by **Edmonton**, July 4, 2006. Signed as a free agent by **Atlanta**, July 17, 2008.

## RECCHI, Mark
(REH-kee, MAHRK) **BOS.**

Right wing. Shoots left. 5'10", 195 lbs. Born, Kamloops, B.C., February 1, 1968. Pittsburgh's 4th choice, 67th overall, in 1988 Entry Draft.

| | | | Regular Season | | | | | | | | | | | | | | Playoffs | | | | | | | | |
|---|---|---|---|---|---|---|---|---|---|---|---|---|---|---|---|---|---|---|---|---|---|---|---|---|---|
| Season | Club | League | GP | G | A | Pts | PIM | PP | SH | GW | S | % | +/- | TF | F% | Min | GP | G | A | Pts | PIM | PP | SH | GW | Min |
| 1984-85 | Langley Eagles | BCJHL | 51 | 26 | 39 | 65 | 39 | .... | .... | .... | .... | .... | .... | .... | .... | .... | .... | .... | .... | .... | .... | .... | .... | .... | .... |
| | New Westminster | WHL | 4 | 1 | 0 | 1 | 0 | .... | .... | .... | .... | .... | .... | .... | .... | .... | .... | .... | .... | .... | .... | .... | .... | .... | .... |
| 1985-86 | New Westminster | WHL | 72 | 21 | 40 | 61 | 55 | .... | .... | .... | .... | .... | .... | .... | .... | .... | .... | .... | .... | .... | .... | .... | .... | .... | .... |
| 1986-87 | Kamloops Blazers | WHL | 40 | 26 | 50 | 76 | 63 | .... | .... | .... | .... | .... | .... | .... | .... | .... | 13 | 3 | 16 | 19 | 17 | .... | .... | .... | .... |
| 1987-88 | Kamloops Blazers | WHL | 62 | 61 | *93 | 154 | 75 | .... | .... | .... | .... | .... | .... | .... | .... | .... | 17 | 10 | *21 | *31 | 18 | .... | .... | .... | .... |
| **1988-89** | **Pittsburgh** | **NHL** | **15** | **1** | **1** | **2** | **0** | **0** | **0** | **0** | **11** | **9.1** | **-2** | .... | .... | .... | .... | .... | .... | .... | .... | .... | .... | .... | .... |
| | Muskegon | IHL | 63 | 50 | 49 | 99 | 86 | .... | .... | .... | .... | .... | .... | .... | .... | .... | 14 | 7 | *14 | *21 | 28 | .... | .... | .... | .... |
| **1989-90** | **Pittsburgh** | **NHL** | **74** | **30** | **37** | **67** | **44** | **6** | **2** | **4** | **143** | **21.0** | **6** | .... | .... | .... | .... | .... | .... | .... | .... | .... | .... | .... | .... |
| | Muskegon | IHL | 4 | 7 | 4 | 11 | 2 | .... | .... | .... | .... | .... | .... | .... | .... | .... | .... | .... | .... | .... | .... | .... | .... | .... | .... |
| **1990-91** ♦ | **Pittsburgh** | **NHL** | **78** | **40** | **73** | **113** | **48** | **12** | **0** | **9** | **184** | **21.7** | **0** | .... | .... | .... | **24** | **10** | **24** | **34** | **33** | **5** | **0** | **2** | .... |
| **1991-92** | **Pittsburgh** | **NHL** | **58** | **33** | **37** | **70** | **78** | **16** | **1** | **4** | **156** | **21.2** | **-16** | .... | .... | .... | .... | .... | .... | .... | .... | .... | .... | .... | .... |
| | **Philadelphia** | **NHL** | **22** | **10** | **17** | **27** | **18** | **4** | **0** | **1** | **54** | **18.5** | **-5** | .... | .... | .... | .... | .... | .... | .... | .... | .... | .... | .... | .... |
| **1992-93** | **Philadelphia** | **NHL** | **84** | **53** | **70** | **123** | **95** | **15** | **4** | **6** | **274** | **19.3** | **1** | .... | .... | .... | .... | .... | .... | .... | .... | .... | .... | .... | .... |
| **1993-94** | **Philadelphia** | **NHL** | **84** | **40** | **67** | **107** | **46** | **11** | **0** | **5** | **217** | **18.4** | **-2** | .... | .... | .... | .... | .... | .... | .... | .... | .... | .... | .... | .... |
| **1994-95** | **Philadelphia** | **NHL** | **10** | **2** | **3** | **5** | **12** | **1** | **0** | **2** | **17** | **11.8** | **-6** | .... | .... | .... | .... | .... | .... | .... | .... | .... | .... | .... | .... |
| | **Montreal** | **NHL** | **39** | **14** | **29** | **43** | **16** | **8** | **0** | **1** | **104** | **13.5** | **-3** | .... | .... | .... | .... | .... | .... | .... | .... | .... | .... | .... | .... |
| **1995-96** | **Montreal** | **NHL** | **82** | **28** | **50** | **78** | **69** | **11** | **2** | **6** | **191** | **14.7** | **20** | .... | .... | .... | **6** | **3** | **3** | **6** | **0** | **3** | **0** | **0** | .... |
| **1996-97** | **Montreal** | **NHL** | **82** | **34** | **46** | **80** | **58** | **7** | **2** | **3** | **202** | **16.8** | **-1** | .... | .... | .... | **5** | **4** | **2** | **6** | **2** | **0** | **0** | **0** | .... |
| **1997-98** | **Montreal** | **NHL** | **82** | **32** | **42** | **74** | **51** | **9** | **1** | **6** | **216** | **14.8** | **11** | .... | .... | .... | **10** | **4** | **8** | **12** | **6** | **0** | **0** | **2** | .... |
| | Canada | Olympics | 5 | 0 | 2 | 2 | 0 | .... | .... | .... | .... | .... | .... | .... | .... | .... | .... | .... | .... | .... | .... | .... | .... | .... | .... |
| **1998-99** | **Montreal** | **NHL** | **61** | **12** | **35** | **47** | **28** | **3** | **0** | **2** | **152** | **7.9** | **-4** | **239** | **44.8** | **20:37** | .... | .... | .... | .... | .... | .... | .... | .... | .... |
| | **Philadelphia** | **NHL** | **10** | **4** | **2** | **6** | **6** | **0** | **0** | **0** | **19** | **21.1** | **-3** | **4** | **25.0** | **19:30** | **6** | **0** | **1** | **1** | **2** | **0** | **0** | **0** | **19:35** |
| **99-2000** | **Philadelphia** | **NHL** | **82** | **28** | ***63** | **91** | **50** | **7** | **1** | **5** | **223** | **12.6** | **20** | **353** | **49.6** | **21:43** | **18** | **6** | **12** | **18** | **6** | **2** | **0** | **1** | **23:10** |
| **2000-01** | **Philadelphia** | **NHL** | **69** | **27** | **50** | **77** | **33** | **7** | **1** | **8** | **191** | **14.1** | **15** | **138** | **42.8** | **21:40** | **6** | **2** | **2** | **4** | **2** | **1** | **0** | **1** | **23:01** |
| **2001-02** | **Philadelphia** | **NHL** | **80** | **22** | **42** | **64** | **46** | **7** | **2** | **4** | **205** | **10.7** | **5** | **82** | **53.7** | **20:40** | **4** | **0** | **0** | **0** | **2** | **0** | **0** | **0** | **21:10** |
| **2002-03** | **Philadelphia** | **NHL** | **79** | **20** | **32** | **52** | **35** | **8** | **1** | **3** | **171** | **11.7** | **0** | **168** | **52.4** | **18:50** | **13** | **7** | **3** | **10** | **2** | **1** | **0** | **1** | **18:00** |
| **2003-04** | **Philadelphia** | **NHL** | **82** | **26** | **49** | **75** | **47** | **14** | **1** | **5** | **167** | **15.6** | **18** | **298** | **52.4** | **17:12** | **18** | **4** | **2** | **6** | **4** | **2** | **0** | **0** | **16:46** |
| 2004-05 | | | DID NOT PLAY | | | | | | | | | | | | | | | | | | | | | | |
| **2005-06** | **Pittsburgh** | **NHL** | **63** | **24** | **33** | **57** | **56** | **11** | **0** | **2** | **164** | **14.6** | **-28** | **387** | **48.3** | **21:17** | .... | .... | .... | .... | .... | .... | .... | .... | .... |
| | ♦ **Carolina** | **NHL** | **20** | **4** | **3** | **7** | **12** | **2** | **0** | **1** | **35** | **11.4** | **-8** | **6** | **33.3** | **17:37** | **25** | **7** | **9** | **16** | **18** | **2** | **0** | **2** | **16:34** |
| **2006-07** | **Pittsburgh** | **NHL** | **82** | **24** | **44** | **68** | **62** | **14** | **0** | **3** | **190** | **12.6** | **1** | **26** | **46.2** | **19:42** | **5** | **0** | **4** | **4** | **0** | **0** | **0** | **0** | **19:09** |
| **2007-08** | **Pittsburgh** | **NHL** | **19** | **2** | **6** | **8** | **12** | **2** | **0** | **0** | **36** | **5.6** | **-2** | **9** | **44.4** | **16:25** | .... | .... | .... | .... | .... | .... | .... | .... | .... |
| | **Atlanta** | **NHL** | **53** | **12** | **28** | **40** | **20** | **5** | **0** | **0** | **85** | **14.1** | **-16** | **49** | **46.9** | **18:23** | .... | .... | .... | .... | .... | .... | .... | .... | .... |
| **2008-09** | **Tampa Bay** | **NHL** | **62** | **13** | **32** | **45** | **20** | **2** | **0** | **1** | **97** | **13.4** | **-15** | **54** | **40.7** | **16:53** | .... | .... | .... | .... | .... | .... | .... | .... | .... |
| | **Boston** | **NHL** | **18** | **10** | **6** | **16** | **2** | **4** | **0** | **2** | **32** | **31.3** | **-3** | **2** | **100.0** | **16:22** | **11** | **3** | **3** | **6** | **2** | **1** | **0** | **1** | **16:57** |
| | **NHL Totals** | | **1490** | **545** | **897** | **1442** | **964** | **186** | **18** | **83** | **3536** | **15.4** | | **1815** | **48.6** | **19:31** | **151** | **50** | **73** | **123** | **79** | **17** | **0** | **10** | **18:46** |

WHL West First All-Star Team (1988) • IHL Second All-Star Team (1989) • NHL Second All-Star Team (1992)
Played in NHL All-Star Game (1991, 1993, 1994, 1997, 1998, 1999, 2000)
Traded to **Philadelphia** by **Pittsburgh** with Brian Benning and Los Angeles' 1st round choice (previously acquired, Philadelphia selected Jason Bowen) in 1992 Entry Draft for Rick Tocchet, Kjell Samuelsson, Ken Wregget and Philadelphia's 3rd round choice (Dave Roche) in 1993 Entry Draft, February 19, 1992. Traded to **Montreal** by **Philadelphia** with Philadelphia's 3rd round choice (Martin Hohenberger) in 1995 Entry Draft for Eric Desjardins, Gilbert Dionne and John LeClair, February 9, 1995. Traded to **Philadelphia** by **Montreal** for Danius Zubrus, Philadelphia's 2nd round choice (Matt Carkner) in 1999 Entry Draft and NY Islanders' 6th round choice (previously acquired, Montreal selected Scott Selig) in 2000 Entry Draft, March 10, 1999. Signed as a free agent by **Pittsburgh**, July 9, 2004. Traded to **Carolina** by **Pittsburgh** for Niklas Nordgren, Krys Kolanos and Carolina's 2nd round choice (later traded to San Jose - later traded to Philadelphia - Philadelphia selected Kevin Marshall) in 2007 Entry Draft, March 9, 2006. Signed as a free agent by **Pittsburgh**, July 25, 2006. Claimed on waivers by **Atlanta** from **Pittsburgh**, December 8, 2007. Signed as a free agent by **Tampa Bay**, July 8, 2008. Traded to **Boston** by **Tampa Bay** with Tampa Bay's 2nd round choice in 2010 Entry Draft for Matt Lashoff and Martins Karsums, March 4, 2009.

## RECHLICZ, Joel
(REHK-lihj, JOHL) **NYI**

Right wing. Shoots right. 6'4", 220 lbs. Born, Brookfield, WI, June 14, 1987.

| | | | Regular Season | | | | | | | | | | | | | | Playoffs | | | | | | | | |
|---|---|---|---|---|---|---|---|---|---|---|---|---|---|---|---|---|---|---|---|---|---|---|---|---|---|
| Season | Club | League | GP | G | A | Pts | PIM | PP | SH | GW | S | % | +/- | TF | F% | Min | GP | G | A | Pts | PIM | PP | SH | GW | Min |
| 2004-05 | Santa Fe | NAHL | 3 | 0 | 1 | 1 | 29 | .... | .... | .... | .... | .... | .... | .... | .... | .... | .... | .... | .... | .... | .... | .... | .... | .... | .... |
| 2005-06 | Des Moines | USHL | 2 | 0 | 0 | 0 | 4 | .... | .... | .... | .... | .... | .... | .... | .... | .... | .... | .... | .... | .... | .... | .... | .... | .... | .... |
| | Indiana Ice | USHL | 2 | 0 | 0 | 0 | 16 | .... | .... | .... | .... | .... | .... | .... | .... | .... | .... | .... | .... | .... | .... | .... | .... | .... | .... |
| | Gatineau | QMJHL | 3 | 0 | 0 | 0 | 17 | .... | .... | .... | .... | .... | .... | .... | .... | .... | .... | .... | .... | .... | .... | .... | .... | .... | .... |
| 2006-07 | Chicoutimi | QMJHL | 55 | 0 | 1 | 1 | 159 | .... | .... | .... | .... | .... | .... | .... | .... | .... | 1 | 0 | 0 | 0 | 2 | .... | .... | .... | .... |
| | Chicago Hounds | UHL | 2 | 0 | 0 | 0 | 9 | .... | .... | .... | .... | .... | .... | .... | .... | .... | .... | .... | .... | .... | .... | .... | .... | .... | .... |

| | | | Regular Season | | | | | | | | | | | | | | Playoffs | | | | | | | | |
|---|---|---|---|---|---|---|---|---|---|---|---|---|---|---|---|---|---|---|---|---|---|---|---|---|---|
| Season | Club | League | GP | G | A | Pts | PIM | PP | SH | GW | S | % | +/- | TF | F% | Min | GP | G | A | Pts | PIM | PP | SH | GW | Min |
| 2007-08 | Albany River Rats | AHL | 25 | 0 | 1 | 1 | 106 | | | | | | | | | | | | | | | | | | |
| | Kalamazoo Wings | IHL | 25 | 1 | 0 | 1 | 100 | | | | | | | | | | | | | | | | | | |
| 2008-09 | NY Islanders | NHL | 17 | 0 | 1 | 1 | 68 | 0 | 0 | 0 | 7 | 0.0 | -1 | 0 | 0.0 | 4:52 | | | | | | | | | |
| | Bridgeport | AHL | 4 | 0 | 0 | 0 | 12 | | | | | | | | | | | | | | | | | | |
| | Utah Grizzlies | ECHL | 45 | 0 | 1 | 1 | 110 | | | | | | | | | | | | | | | | | | |
| | NHL Totals | | 17 | 0 | 1 | 1 | 68 | 0 | 0 | 0 | 7 | 0.0 | | 0 | 0.0 | 4:52 | | | | | | | | | |

Signed as a free agent by **NY Islanders**, May 6, 2008.

## REDDEN, Wade
(REH-duhn, WAYD) **NYR**

Defense. Shoots left. 6'2", 212 lbs. Born, Lloydminster, Sask., June 12, 1977. NY Islanders' 1st choice, 2nd overall, in 1995 Entry Draft.

| Season | Club | League | GP | G | A | Pts | PIM | PP | SH | GW | S | % | +/- | TF | F% | Min | GP | G | A | Pts | PIM | PP | SH | GW | Min |
|---|---|---|---|---|---|---|---|---|---|---|---|---|---|---|---|---|---|---|---|---|---|---|---|---|---|
| 1992-93 | Lloydminster | AJHL | 34 | 4 | 11 | 15 | 64 | | | | | | | | | | | | | | | | | | |
| 1993-94 | Brandon | WHL | 63 | 4 | 35 | 39 | 98 | | | | | | | | | | 14 | 2 | 4 | 6 | 10 | | | | |
| 1994-95 | Brandon | WHL | 64 | 14 | 46 | 60 | 83 | | | | | | | | | | 18 | 5 | 10 | 15 | 8 | | | | |
| 1995-96 | Brandon | WHL | 51 | 9 | 45 | 54 | 55 | | | | | | | | | | 19 | 5 | 10 | 15 | 19 | | | | |
| 1996-97 | Ottawa | NHL | 82 | 6 | 24 | 30 | 41 | 2 | 0 | 1 | 102 | 5.9 | 1 | | | | 7 | 1 | 3 | 4 | 2 | 0 | 0 | 0 | |
| 1997-98 | Ottawa | NHL | 80 | 8 | 14 | 22 | 27 | 3 | 0 | 2 | 103 | 7.8 | 17 | | | | 9 | 0 | 2 | 2 | 2 | 0 | 0 | 0 | |
| 1998-99 | Ottawa | NHL | 72 | 8 | 21 | 29 | 54 | 3 | 0 | 1 | 127 | 6.3 | 7 | 0 | 0.0 | 23:27 | 4 | 1 | 2 | 3 | 2 | 1 | 0 | 0 | 26:39 |
| 99-2000 | Ottawa | NHL | 81 | 10 | 26 | 36 | 49 | 3 | 0 | 2 | 163 | 6.1 | -1 | 0 | 0.0 | 23:43 | | | | | | | | | |
| 2000-01 | Ottawa | NHL | 78 | 10 | 37 | 47 | 49 | 4 | 0 | 0 | 159 | 6.3 | 22 | 0 | 0.0 | 25:17 | 4 | 0 | 0 | 0 | 0 | 0 | 0 | 0 | 27:29 |
| 2001-02 | Ottawa | NHL | 79 | 9 | 25 | 34 | 48 | 4 | 1 | 1 | 156 | 5.8 | 22 | 1 | 0.0 | 25:06 | 12 | 3 | 2 | 5 | 6 | 1 | 0 | 1 | 27:56 |
| 2002-03 | Ottawa | NHL | 76 | 10 | 35 | 45 | 70 | 4 | 0 | 3 | 154 | 6.5 | 23 | 0 | 0.0 | 25:24 | 18 | 1 | 8 | 9 | 10 | 0 | 0 | 1 | 25:28 |
| 2003-04 | Ottawa | NHL | 81 | 17 | 26 | 43 | 65 | 12 | 0 | 3 | 175 | 9.7 | 21 | 0 | 0.0 | 24:54 | 7 | 1 | 0 | 1 | 2 | 1 | 0 | 0 | 26:47 |
| 2004-05 | | | DID NOT PLAY | | | | | | | | | | | | | | | | | | | | | | |
| 2005-06 | Ottawa | NHL | 65 | 10 | 40 | 50 | 63 | 8 | 0 | 4 | 153 | 6.5 | 35 | 1 | 100.0 | 23:28 | 9 | 2 | 8 | 10 | 10 | 2 | 0 | 1 | 25:06 |
| | Canada | Olympics | 6 | 1 | 0 | 1 | 0 | | | | | | | | | | | | | | | | | | |
| 2006-07 | Ottawa | NHL | 64 | 7 | 29 | 36 | 50 | 4 | 0 | 3 | 122 | 5.7 | 1 | 0 | 0.0 | 22:54 | 20 | 3 | 7 | 10 | 10 | 3 | 0 | 1 | 23:37 |
| 2007-08 | Ottawa | NHL | 80 | 6 | 32 | 38 | 60 | 4 | 0 | 1 | 136 | 4.4 | 11 | 0 | 0.0 | 22:13 | 4 | 0 | 1 | 1 | 11 | 0 | 0 | 0 | 19:21 |
| 2008-09 | NY Rangers | NHL | 81 | 3 | 23 | 26 | 51 | 2 | 0 | 0 | 161 | 1.9 | -5 | 0 | 0.0 | 22:20 | 7 | 0 | 2 | 2 | 0 | 0 | 0 | 0 | 23:24 |
| | NHL Totals | | 919 | 104 | 332 | 436 | 627 | 53 | 1 | 21 | 1711 | 6.1 | | 2 | 50.0 | 23:54 | 101 | 12 | 35 | 47 | 55 | 8 | 0 | 4 | 25:08 |

WHL Rookie of the Year (1994) • WHL East Second All-Star Team (1995) • WHL East First All-Star Team (1996) • Memorial Cup Tournament All-Star Team (1996)
Played in NHL All-Star Game (2002)
Traded to **Ottawa** by **NY Islanders** with Damian Rhodes for Don Beaupre, Martin Straka and Bryan Berard, January 23, 1996. Signed as a free agent by **NY Rangers**, July 1, 2008.

## REDDOX, Liam
(REH-dawks, LEE-uhm) **EDM.**

Left wing. Shoots left. 5'10", 180 lbs. Born, East York, Ont., January 27, 1986. Edmonton's 5th choice, 112th overall, in 2004 Entry Draft.

| Season | Club | League | GP | G | A | Pts | PIM | PP | SH | GW | S | % | +/- | TF | F% | Min | GP | G | A | Pts | PIM | PP | SH | GW | Min |
|---|---|---|---|---|---|---|---|---|---|---|---|---|---|---|---|---|---|---|---|---|---|---|---|---|---|
| 2002-03 | Wellington Dukes | OPJHL | 45 | 32 | 32 | 64 | 29 | | | | | | | | | | | | | | | | | | |
| | Peterborough | OHL | 4 | 0 | 0 | 0 | 0 | | | | | | | | | | | | | | | | | | |
| 2003-04 | Peterborough | OHL | 68 | 31 | 33 | 64 | 24 | | | | | | | | | | | | | | | | | | |
| 2004-05 | Peterborough | OHL | 68 | 36 | 46 | 82 | 38 | | | | | | | | | | 14 | 3 | 10 | 13 | 10 | | | | |
| 2005-06 | Peterborough | OHL | 68 | 19 | 45 | 64 | 74 | | | | | | | | | | 19 | 5 | 9 | 14 | 20 | | | | |
| 2006-07 | Stockton Thunder | ECHL | 70 | 8 | 18 | 26 | 49 | | | | | | | | | | 6 | 2 | 1 | 3 | 4 | | | | |
| 2007-08 | Edmonton | NHL | 1 | 0 | 0 | 0 | 0 | 0 | 0 | 0 | 1 | 0.0 | -1 | 0 | 0.0 | 5:55 | | | | | | | | | |
| | Springfield | AHL | 65 | 16 | 28 | 44 | 48 | | | | | | | | | | | | | | | | | | |
| 2008-09 | Edmonton | NHL | 46 | 5 | 7 | 12 | 10 | 1 | 0 | 0 | 39 | 12.8 | -6 | 25 | 44.0 | 10:28 | | | | | | | | | |
| | Springfield | AHL | 14 | 5 | 4 | 9 | 2 | | | | | | | | | | | | | | | | | | |
| | NHL Totals | | 47 | 5 | 7 | 12 | 10 | 1 | 0 | 0 | 40 | 12.5 | | 25 | 44.0 | 10:22 | | | | | | | | | |

OHL All-Rookie Team (2004)

## REGEHR, Robyn
(reh-GEER, RAW-bihn) **CGY.**

Defense. Shoots left. 6'3", 225 lbs. Born, Recife, Brazil, April 19, 1980. Colorado's 3rd choice, 19th overall, in 1998 Entry Draft.

| Season | Club | League | GP | G | A | Pts | PIM | PP | SH | GW | S | % | +/- | TF | F% | Min | GP | G | A | Pts | PIM | PP | SH | GW | Min |
|---|---|---|---|---|---|---|---|---|---|---|---|---|---|---|---|---|---|---|---|---|---|---|---|---|---|
| 1995-96 | Prince Albert | SMHL | 59 | 8 | 24 | 32 | 157 | | | | | | | | | | | | | | | | | | |
| 1996-97 | Kamloops Blazers | WHL | 64 | 4 | 19 | 23 | 96 | | | | | | | | | | 5 | 0 | 1 | 1 | 18 | | | | |
| 1997-98 | Kamloops Blazers | WHL | 65 | 4 | 10 | 14 | 120 | | | | | | | | | | 5 | 0 | 3 | 3 | 8 | | | | |
| 1998-99 | Kamloops Blazers | WHL | 54 | 12 | 20 | 32 | 130 | | | | | | | | | | 12 | 1 | 4 | 5 | 21 | | | | |
| 99-2000 | Calgary | NHL | 57 | 5 | 7 | 12 | 46 | 2 | 0 | 0 | 64 | 7.8 | -2 | 0 | 0.0 | 18:24 | | | | | | | | | |
| | Saint John Flames | AHL | 5 | 0 | 0 | 0 | 0 | | | | | | | | | | | | | | | | | | |
| 2000-01 | Calgary | NHL | 71 | 1 | 3 | 4 | 70 | 0 | 0 | 0 | 62 | 1.6 | -7 | 1 | 0.0 | 19:43 | | | | | | | | | |
| 2001-02 | Calgary | NHL | 77 | 2 | 6 | 8 | 93 | 0 | 0 | 0 | 82 | 2.4 | -24 | 0 | 0.0 | 20:54 | | | | | | | | | |
| 2002-03 | Calgary | NHL | 76 | 0 | 12 | 12 | 87 | 0 | 0 | 0 | 109 | 0.0 | -9 | 1 | 100.0 | 22:45 | | | | | | | | | |
| 2003-04 | Calgary | NHL | 82 | 4 | 14 | 18 | 74 | 2 | 0 | 1 | 106 | 3.8 | 14 | 2 | 50.0 | 22:21 | 26 | 2 | 7 | 9 | 20 | 0 | 0 | 0 | 26:27 |
| 2004-05 | | | DID NOT PLAY | | | | | | | | | | | | | | | | | | | | | | |
| 2005-06 | Calgary | NHL | 68 | 6 | 20 | 26 | 67 | 5 | 0 | 2 | 89 | 6.7 | 6 | 1 | 100.0 | 23:08 | 7 | 1 | 3 | 4 | 6 | 1 | 0 | 0 | 22:22 |
| | Canada | Olympics | 6 | 0 | 1 | 1 | 2 | | | | | | | | | | | | | | | | | | |
| 2006-07 | Calgary | NHL | 78 | 2 | 19 | 21 | 75 | 0 | 0 | 0 | 66 | 3.0 | 27 | 1 | 0.0 | 21:55 | 1 | 0 | 0 | 0 | 0 | 0 | 0 | 0 | 11:15 |
| 2007-08 | Calgary | NHL | 82 | 5 | 15 | 20 | 79 | 1 | 1 | 0 | 93 | 5.4 | 11 | 0 | 0.0 | 21:20 | 7 | 0 | 2 | 2 | 2 | 0 | 0 | 0 | 21:50 |
| 2008-09 | Calgary | NHL | 75 | 0 | 8 | 8 | 73 | 0 | 0 | 0 | 79 | 0.0 | 10 | 0 | 0.0 | 21:09 | | | | | | | | | |
| | NHL Totals | | 666 | 25 | 104 | 129 | 664 | 10 | 1 | 3 | 750 | 3.3 | | 6 | 50.0 | 21:23 | 41 | 3 | 12 | 15 | 28 | 1 | 0 | 0 | 24:36 |

WHL West First All-Star Team (1999)
Traded to **Calgary** by **Colorado** with Rene Corbet, Wade Belak and Colorado's 2nd round compensatory choice (Jarret Stoll) in 2000 Entry Draft for Theoren Fleury and Chris Dingman, February 28, 1999.

## REGIER, Steve
(reh-GEER, STEEV)

Left wing. Shoots left. 6'4", 194 lbs. Born, Edmonton, Alta., August 31, 1984. NY Islanders' 5th choice, 148th overall, in 2004 Entry Draft.

| Season | Club | League | GP | G | A | Pts | PIM | PP | SH | GW | S | % | +/- | TF | F% | Min | GP | G | A | Pts | PIM | PP | SH | GW | Min |
|---|---|---|---|---|---|---|---|---|---|---|---|---|---|---|---|---|---|---|---|---|---|---|---|---|---|
| 2000-01 | Leduc Oil Kings | AMHL | 35 | 22 | 39 | 61 | 135 | | | | | | | | | | | | | | | | | | |
| 2001-02 | Medicine Hat | WHL | 59 | 1 | 4 | 5 | 31 | | | | | | | | | | | | | | | | | | |
| 2002-03 | Medicine Hat | WHL | 61 | 11 | 10 | 21 | 114 | | | | | | | | | | 11 | 2 | 2 | 4 | 20 | | | | |
| 2003-04 | Medicine Hat | WHL | 72 | 25 | 35 | 60 | 111 | | | | | | | | | | 18 | 5 | 11 | 16 | 20 | | | | |
| 2004-05 | Bridgeport | AHL | 75 | 7 | 15 | 22 | 43 | | | | | | | | | | | | | | | | | | |
| 2005-06 | NY Islanders | NHL | 9 | 0 | 0 | 0 | 0 | 0 | 0 | 0 | 4 | 0.0 | -1 | 0 | 0.0 | 6:02 | | | | | | | | | |
| | Bridgeport | AHL | 73 | 16 | 21 | 37 | 54 | | | | | | | | | | 7 | 0 | 2 | 2 | 6 | | | | |
| 2006-07 | NY Islanders | NHL | 1 | 0 | 0 | 0 | 0 | 0 | 0 | 0 | 0 | 0.0 | 0 | 0 | 0.0 | 4:41 | | | | | | | | | |
| | Bridgeport | AHL | 77 | 19 | 27 | 46 | 77 | | | | | | | | | | | | | | | | | | |
| 2007-08 | NY Islanders | NHL | 8 | 0 | 0 | 0 | 4 | 0 | 0 | 0 | 7 | 0.0 | -1 | 1 | 0.0 | 7:59 | | | | | | | | | |
| | Bridgeport | AHL | 65 | 19 | 25 | 44 | 60 | | | | | | | | | | | | | | | | | | |
| 2008-09 | St. Louis | NHL | 8 | 3 | 1 | 4 | 4 | 2 | 0 | 0 | 11 | 27.3 | -1 | 7 | 42.9 | 10:59 | | | | | | | | | |
| | Peoria Rivermen | AHL | 73 | 22 | 28 | 50 | 61 | | | | | | | | | | 7 | 2 | 2 | 4 | 4 | | | | |
| | NHL Totals | | 26 | 3 | 1 | 4 | 8 | 2 | 0 | 0 | 22 | 13.6 | | 8 | 37.5 | 8:06 | | | | | | | | | |

Signed as a free agent by **St. Louis**, July 15, 2008.

## REGIN, Peter
(REE-gihn, PEE-tuhr) **OTT.**

Center. Shoots left. 6'2", 195 lbs. Born, Herning, Denmark, April 16, 1986. Ottawa's 4th choice, 87th overall, in 2004 Entry Draft.

| Season | Club | League | GP | G | A | Pts | PIM | PP | SH | GW | S | % | +/- | TF | F% | Min | GP | G | A | Pts | PIM | PP | SH | GW | Min |
|---|---|---|---|---|---|---|---|---|---|---|---|---|---|---|---|---|---|---|---|---|---|---|---|---|---|
| 2002-03 | Herning IK | Denmark | 24 | 0 | 1 | 1 | 4 | | | | | | | | | | 10 | 1 | 3 | 4 | 4 | | | | |
| 2003-04 | Herning IK | Denmark | 33 | 9 | 11 | 20 | 14 | | | | | | | | | | | | | | | | | | |
| 2004-05 | Herning Blue Fox | Denmark | 36 | 19 | 27 | 46 | 43 | | | | | | | | | | 16 | 5 | 8 | 13 | 2 | | | | |
| 2005-06 | Timra IK | Sweden | 44 | 4 | 7 | 11 | 14 | | | | | | | | | | | | | | | | | | |
| 2006-07 | Timra IK | Sweden | 51 | 9 | 7 | 16 | 16 | | | | | | | | | | 7 | 2 | 2 | 4 | 2 | | | | |
| 2007-08 | Timra IK | Sweden | 55 | 12 | 19 | 31 | 36 | | | | | | | | | | 11 | 2 | 7 | 9 | 2 | | | | |
| 2008-09 | Ottawa | NHL | 11 | 1 | 1 | 2 | 2 | 0 | 0 | 1 | 7 | 14.3 | 0 | 77 | 53.3 | 10:32 | | | | | | | | | |
| | Binghamton | AHL | 56 | 18 | 29 | 47 | 36 | | | | | | | | | | | | | | | | | | |
| | NHL Totals | | 11 | 1 | 1 | 2 | 2 | 0 | 0 | 1 | 7 | 14.3 | | 77 | 53.2 | 10:32 | | | | | | | | | |

Regular Season / Playoffs

## REICH, Jeremy

(REECH, JAIR-eh-mee) **NYI**

Left wing. Shoots left. 6'1", 203 lbs. Born, Craik, Sask., February 11, 1979. Chicago's 3rd choice, 39th overall, in 1997 Entry Draft.

| Season | Club | League | GP | G | A | Pts | PIM | PP | SH | GW | S | % | +/- | TF | F% | Min | GP | G | A | Pts | PIM | PP | SH | GW | Min |
|---|---|---|---|---|---|---|---|---|---|---|---|---|---|---|---|---|---|---|---|---|---|---|---|---|---|
| 1993-94 | Pilote Butte | SAHA | 80 | 70 | 65 | 135 | 120 | | | | | | | | | | | | | | | | | | |
| 1994-95 | Sask. Contacts | SMHL | 35 | 13 | 20 | 33 | 81 | | | | | | | | | | | | | | | | | | |
| 1995-96 | Seattle | WHL | 65 | 11 | 11 | 22 | 88 | | | | | | | | | | 5 | 0 | 1 | 1 | 10 | | | | |
| 1996-97 | Seattle | WHL | 62 | 19 | 31 | 50 | 134 | | | | | | | | | | 15 | 2 | 5 | 7 | 36 | | | | |
| 1997-98 | Seattle | WHL | 43 | 24 | 23 | 47 | 121 | | | | | | | | | | | | | | | | | | |
| | Swift Current | WHL | 22 | 8 | 8 | 16 | 47 | | | | | | | | | | 12 | 5 | 6 | 11 | 37 | | | | |
| 1998-99 | Swift Current | WHL | 67 | 21 | 28 | 49 | 220 | | | | | | | | | | 6 | 0 | 3 | 3 | 26 | | | | |
| 99-2000 | Swift Current | WHL | 72 | 33 | 58 | 91 | 167 | | | | | | | | | | 12 | 2 | 10 | 12 | 19 | | | | |
| 2000-01 | Syracuse Crunch | AHL | 56 | 6 | 9 | 15 | 108 | | | | | | | | | | 5 | 0 | 0 | 0 | 6 | | | | |
| 2001-02 | Syracuse Crunch | AHL | 59 | 9 | 7 | 16 | 178 | | | | | | | | | | 10 | 4 | 0 | 4 | 16 | | | | |
| 2002-03 | Syracuse Crunch | AHL | 78 | 14 | 13 | 27 | 195 | | | | | | | | | | | | | | | | | | |
| **2003-04** | **Columbus** | **NHL** | **9** | **0** | **1** | **1** | **20** | **0** | **0** | **0** | **3** | **0.0** | **–3** | **0** | **0.0** | **7:38** | | | | | | | | | |
| | Syracuse Crunch | AHL | 72 | 14 | 37 | 51 | 150 | | | | | | | | | | 6 | 1 | 1 | 2 | 13 | | | | |
| 2004-05 | Syracuse Crunch | AHL | 50 | 4 | 5 | 9 | 189 | | | | | | | | | | | | | | | | | | |
| | Houston Aeros | AHL | 18 | 3 | 4 | 7 | 34 | | | | | | | | | | 5 | 0 | 1 | 1 | 28 | | | | |
| 2005-06 | Providence Bruins | AHL | 77 | 8 | 15 | 23 | 235 | | | | | | | | | | 6 | 0 | 0 | 0 | 27 | | | | |
| **2006-07** | **Boston** | **NHL** | **32** | **0** | **1** | **1** | **63** | **0** | **0** | **0** | **27** | **0.0** | **–10** | **4** | **25.0** | **8:14** | | | | | | | | | |
| | Providence Bruins | AHL | 46 | 4 | 7 | 11 | 105 | | | | | | | | | | | | | | | | | | |
| **2007-08** | **Boston** | **NHL** | **58** | **2** | **2** | **4** | **78** | **0** | **0** | **1** | **39** | **5.1** | **–5** | **31** | **48.4** | **8:15** | **4** | **0** | **0** | **0** | **8** | **0** | **0** | **0** | **10:27** |
| 2008-09 | Providence Bruins | AHL | 76 | 21 | 13 | 34 | 139 | | | | | | | | | | 16 | 3 | 5 | 8 | 21 | | | | |
| | **NHL Totals** | | **99** | **2** | **4** | **6** | **161** | **0** | **0** | **1** | **69** | **2.9** | | **35** | **45.7** | **8:12** | **4** | **0** | **0** | **0** | **8** | **0** | **0** | **0** | **10:27** |

Signed as a free agent by **Columbus**, May 17, 2000. • Loaned to **Houston** (AHL) by **Syracuse** (AHL) for the loan of Jason Beckett, March 10, 2005. Signed as a free agent by **Boston**, September 7, 2005. Signed as a free agent by **NY Islanders**, July 2, 2009.

## REID, Darren

(REED, DAIR-ehn)

Right wing. Shoots right. 6'2", 205 lbs. Born, Lac La Biche, Alta., May 8, 1983. Tampa Bay's 11th choice, 256th overall, in 2002 Entry Draft.

| Season | Club | League | GP | G | A | Pts | PIM | PP | SH | GW | S | % | +/- | TF | F% | Min | GP | G | A | Pts | PIM | PP | SH | GW | Min |
|---|---|---|---|---|---|---|---|---|---|---|---|---|---|---|---|---|---|---|---|---|---|---|---|---|---|
| 2000-01 | Drayton Valley | AJHL | 55 | 8 | 18 | 26 | 116 | | | | | | | | | | | | | | | | | | |
| 2001-02 | Drayton Valley | AJHL | 31 | 9 | 12 | 21 | 195 | | | | | | | | | | | | | | | | | | |
| | Medicine Hat | WHL | 37 | 8 | 9 | 17 | 70 | | | | | | | | | | | | | | | | | | |
| 2002-03 | Medicine Hat | WHL | 63 | 14 | 30 | 44 | 163 | | | | | | | | | | 11 | 5 | 0 | 5 | 19 | | | | |
| 2003-04 | Medicine Hat | WHL | 67 | 33 | 48 | 81 | 194 | | | | | | | | | | 20 | *13 | 8 | 21 | 31 | | | | |
| 2004-05 | Springfield | AHL | 56 | 3 | 19 | 22 | 99 | | | | | | | | | | | | | | | | | | |
| **2005-06** | **Tampa Bay** | **NHL** | **7** | **0** | **1** | **1** | **0** | **0** | **0** | **0** | **3** | **0.0** | **–2** | **0** | **0.0** | **5:41** | | | | | | | | | |
| | Springfield | AHL | 50 | 8 | 9 | 17 | 59 | | | | | | | | | | | | | | | | | | |
| **2006-07** | Springfield | AHL | 10 | 1 | 0 | 1 | 5 | | | | | | | | | | | | | | | | | | |
| | **Philadelphia** | **NHL** | **14** | **0** | **0** | **0** | **18** | **0** | **0** | **0** | **8** | **0.0** | **–7** | **1** | **100.0** | **8:11** | | | | | | | | | |
| | Philadelphia | AHL | 43 | 16 | 14 | 30 | 20 | | | | | | | | | | | | | | | | | | |
| 2007-08 | Philadelphia | AHL | 41 | 8 | 13 | 21 | 37 | | | | | | | | | | 9 | 1 | 2 | 3 | 0 | | | | |
| 2008-09 | Hershey Bears | AHL | 38 | 2 | 3 | 5 | 61 | | | | | | | | | | 7 | 3 | 0 | 3 | 18 | | | | |
| | **NHL Totals** | | **21** | **0** | **1** | **1** | **18** | **0** | **0** | **0** | **11** | **0.0** | | **1** | **100.0** | **7:21** | | | | | | | | | |

Traded to **Philadelphia** by **Tampa Bay** for Daniel Corso, November 9, 2006.

## REINPRECHT, Steve

(REIGHN-prehkt, STEEV) **FLA.**

Center. Shoots left. 6', 195 lbs. Born, Edmonton, Alta., May 7, 1976.

| Season | Club | League | GP | G | A | Pts | PIM | PP | SH | GW | S | % | +/- | TF | F% | Min | GP | G | A | Pts | PIM | PP | SH | GW | Min |
|---|---|---|---|---|---|---|---|---|---|---|---|---|---|---|---|---|---|---|---|---|---|---|---|---|---|
| 1993-94 | Edmonton SSAC | AMHL | 71 | 48 | 77 | 125 | | | | | | | | | | | | | | | | | | | |
| 1994-95 | St. Albert Saints | AJHL | 56 | 35 | 44 | 79 | 14 | | | | | | | | | | | | | | | | | | |
| 1995-96 | St. Albert Saints | AJHL | 39 | 24 | 33 | 57 | 16 | | | | | | | | | | | | | | | | | | |
| 1996-97 | U. of Wisconsin | WCHA | 38 | 11 | 9 | 20 | 12 | | | | | | | | | | | | | | | | | | |
| 1997-98 | U. of Wisconsin | WCHA | 41 | 19 | 24 | 43 | 18 | | | | | | | | | | | | | | | | | | |
| 1998-99 | U. of Wisconsin | WCHA | 38 | 16 | 17 | 33 | 14 | | | | | | | | | | | | | | | | | | |
| **99-2000** | U. of Wisconsin | WCHA | 37 | 26 | 40 | *66 | 14 | | | | | | | | | | | | | | | | | | |
| | **Los Angeles** | **NHL** | **1** | **0** | **0** | **0** | **2** | **0** | **0** | **0** | **0** | **0.0** | **0** | **6** | **50.0** | **6:01** | | | | | | | | | |
| **2000-01** | **Los Angeles** | **NHL** | **59** | **12** | **17** | **29** | **12** | **3** | **2** | **3** | **72** | **16.7** | **11** | **676** | **41.4** | **12:39** | | | | | | | | | |
| | **♦ Colorado** | **NHL** | **21** | **3** | **4** | **7** | **2** | **0** | **0** | **0** | **28** | **10.7** | **–1** | **209** | **51.2** | **15:38** | **22** | **2** | **3** | **5** | **2** | **0** | **0** | **0** | **12:09** |
| **2001-02** | **Colorado** | **NHL** | **67** | **19** | **27** | **46** | **18** | **4** | **0** | **3** | **111** | **17.1** | **14** | **413** | **52.1** | **16:32** | **21** | **7** | **5** | **12** | **8** | **0** | **0** | **2** | **16:23** |
| **2002-03** | **Colorado** | **NHL** | **77** | **18** | **33** | **51** | **18** | **2** | **1** | **1** | **146** | **12.3** | **–6** | **928** | **46.4** | **17:22** | **7** | **1** | **2** | **3** | **0** | **0** | **0** | **0** | **15:32** |
| **2003-04** | **Calgary** | **NHL** | **44** | **7** | **22** | **29** | **4** | **3** | **0** | **1** | **68** | **10.3** | **1** | **120** | **40.0** | **17:05** | | | | | | | | | |
| 2004-05 | HC Mulhouse | France | 22 | 20 | 27 | 47 | 6 | | | | | | | | | | 10 | 7 | 6 | 13 | 2 | | | | |
| **2005-06** | **Calgary** | **NHL** | **52** | **10** | **19** | **29** | **24** | **5** | **0** | **1** | **72** | **13.9** | **10** | **340** | **49.4** | **14:49** | | | | | | | | | |
| | **Phoenix** | **NHL** | **28** | **12** | **11** | **23** | **8** | **4** | **1** | **2** | **58** | **20.7** | **1** | **526** | **47.3** | **19:06** | | | | | | | | | |
| **2006-07** | **Phoenix** | **NHL** | **49** | **9** | **24** | **33** | **28** | **2** | **0** | **1** | **71** | **12.7** | **–3** | **537** | **52.3** | **15:40** | | | | | | | | | |
| **2007-08** | **Phoenix** | **NHL** | **81** | **16** | **30** | **46** | **26** | **5** | **1** | **0** | **105** | **15.2** | **–3** | **1020** | **50.6** | **15:42** | | | | | | | | | |
| **2008-09** | **Phoenix** | **NHL** | **73** | **14** | **27** | **41** | **20** | **3** | **0** | **3** | **95** | **14.7** | **0** | **886** | **46.3** | **15:54** | | | | | | | | | |
| | **NHL Totals** | | **552** | **120** | **214** | **334** | **162** | **31** | **5** | **15** | **826** | **14.5** | | **5661** | **47.8** | **15:55** | **50** | **10** | **10** | **20** | **10** | **0** | **0** | **2** | **14:24** |

WCHA Second All-Star Team (1998) • WCHA First All-Star Team (2000) • WCHA Player of the Year (2000) • NCAA West First All-American Team (2000)

Signed as a free agent by **Los Angeles**, March 31, 2000. Traded to **Colorado** by **Los Angeles** with Rob Blake for Adam Deadmarsh, Aaron Miller, a player to be named later (Jared Aulin, March 22, 2001) and Colorado's 1st round choices in 2001 (Dave Steckel) and 2003 (Brian Boyle) Entry Drafts, February 21, 2001. Traded to **Buffalo** by **Colorado** for Keith Ballard, July 3, 2003. Traded to **Calgary** by **Buffalo** with Rhett Warrener for Chris Drury and Steve Begin, July 3, 2003. Signed as a free agent by **Mulhouse** (France), September 28, 2004. Traded to **Phoenix** by **Calgary** with Philippe Sauve for Brian Boucher and Mike Leclerc, February 2, 2006. Traded to **Florida** by **Phoenix** for Stefan Meyer, June 19, 2009.

## REITZ, Erik

(REETZ, AIR-ihk)

Defense. Shoots right. 6'1", 222 lbs. Born, Detroit, MI, July 29, 1982. Minnesota's 5th choice, 170th overall, in 2000 Entry Draft.

| Season | Club | League | GP | G | A | Pts | PIM | PP | SH | GW | S | % | +/- | TF | F% | Min | GP | G | A | Pts | PIM | PP | SH | GW | Min |
|---|---|---|---|---|---|---|---|---|---|---|---|---|---|---|---|---|---|---|---|---|---|---|---|---|---|
| 1998-99 | Leamington Flyers | OHA-B | 50 | 5 | 10 | 15 | 80 | | | | | | | | | | | | | | | | | | |
| 99-2000 | Barrie Colts | OHL | 63 | 2 | 10 | 12 | 85 | | | | | | | | | | 25 | 0 | 5 | 5 | 44 | | | | |
| 2000-01 | Barrie Colts | OHL | 68 | 5 | 21 | 26 | 178 | | | | | | | | | | 5 | 1 | 0 | 1 | 21 | | | | |
| 2001-02 | Barrie Colts | OHL | 61 | 13 | 27 | 40 | 153 | | | | | | | | | | 20 | 4 | 16 | 20 | 40 | | | | |
| 2002-03 | Houston Aeros | AHL | 62 | 6 | 13 | 19 | 112 | | | | | | | | | | 11 | 0 | 3 | 3 | 31 | | | | |
| 2003-04 | Houston Aeros | AHL | 69 | 5 | 19 | 24 | 148 | | | | | | | | | | 2 | 0 | 0 | 0 | 0 | | | | |
| 2004-05 | Houston Aeros | AHL | 38 | 2 | 12 | 14 | 91 | | | | | | | | | | | | | | | | | | |
| **2005-06** | **Minnesota** | **NHL** | **5** | **0** | **0** | **0** | **4** | **0** | **0** | **0** | **0** | **0.0** | **–2** | **0** | **0.0** | **13:09** | | | | | | | | | |
| | Houston Aeros | AHL | 72 | 5 | 23 | 28 | 139 | | | | | | | | | | 8 | 0 | 5 | 5 | 20 | | | | |
| **2006-07** | **Minnesota** | **NHL** | **1** | **0** | **0** | **0** | **0** | **0** | **0** | **0** | **0** | **0.0** | **1** | **0** | **0.0** | **10:36** | | | | | | | | | |
| | Houston Aeros | AHL | 73 | 9 | 25 | 34 | 132 | | | | | | | | | | | | | | | | | | |
| **2007-08** | Houston Aeros | AHL | 49 | 8 | 26 | 34 | 99 | | | | | | | | | | 3 | 0 | 0 | 0 | 2 | | | | |
| | **Minnesota** | **NHL** | | | | | | | | | | | | | | | **2** | **0** | **0** | **0** | **0** | **0** | **0** | **0** | **6:18** |
| **2008-09** | **Minnesota** | **NHL** | **31** | **1** | **1** | **2** | **41** | **0** | **0** | **0** | **15** | **6.7** | **–2** | **0** | **0.0** | **9:52** | | | | | | | | | |
| | **NY Rangers** | **NHL** | **11** | **0** | **0** | **0** | **24** | **0** | **0** | **0** | **7** | **0.0** | **–4** | **0** | **0.0** | **10:16** | | | | | | | | | |
| | **NHL Totals** | | **48** | **1** | **1** | **2** | **69** | **0** | **0** | **0** | **22** | **4.5** | | **0** | **0.0** | **10:19** | **2** | **0** | **0** | **0** | **0** | **0** | **0** | **0** | **6:18** |

Memorial Cup Tournament All-Star Team (2000) • OHL First All-Star Team (2002)

• Missed majority of 2004-05 season recovering from elbow injury suffered in game vs. Milwaukee (AHL), February 5, 2005. Traded to **NY Rangers** by **Minnesota** for Dan Fritsche, January 29, 2009. Claimed on waivers by **Toronto** from **NY Rangers**, March 4, 2009.

## REPIK, Michal

(REH-pihk, MEE-khahl) **FLA.**

Right wing. Shoots right. 5'10", 180 lbs. Born, Vlasim, Czech., December 31, 1988. Florida's 2nd choice, 40th overall, in 2007 Entry Draft.

| Season | Club | League | GP | G | A | Pts | PIM | PP | SH | GW | S | % | +/- | TF | F% | Min | GP | G | A | Pts | PIM | PP | SH | GW | Min |
|---|---|---|---|---|---|---|---|---|---|---|---|---|---|---|---|---|---|---|---|---|---|---|---|---|---|
| 2002-03 | Sparta U17 | CzR-U17 | 18 | 7 | 10 | 17 | 6 | | | | | | | | | | 2 | 0 | 0 | 0 | 0 | | | | |
| 2003-04 | Sparta U17 | CzR-U17 | 33 | 25 | 17 | 42 | 42 | | | | | | | | | | 3 | 0 | 0 | 0 | 0 | | | | |
| | Sparta Jr. | CzRep-Jr. | 23 | 12 | 5 | 17 | 10 | | | | | | | | | | | | | | | | | | |
| 2004-05 | Sparta U17 | CzR-U17 | 2 | 2 | 3 | 5 | 6 | | | | | | | | | | | | | | | | | | |
| | Sparta Jr. | CzRep-Jr. | 45 | 26 | 31 | 57 | 24 | | | | | | | | | | 8 | 2 | 4 | 6 | 10 | | | | |
| 2005-06 | Vancouver Giants | WHL | 69 | 24 | 28 | 52 | 55 | | | | | | | | | | 14 | 3 | 3 | 6 | 19 | | | | |
| 2006-07 | Vancouver Giants | WHL | 56 | 24 | 31 | 55 | 56 | | | | | | | | | | 22 | 10 | *16 | *26 | 24 | | | | |
| 2007-08 | Vancouver Giants | WHL | 51 | 27 | 34 | 61 | 62 | | | | | | | | | | 10 | 5 | 6 | 11 | 18 | | | | |

| Season | Club | League | GP | G | A | Pts | PIM | PP | SH | GW | S | % | +/- | TF | F% | Min | GP | G | A | Pts | PIM | PP | SH | GW | Min |
|---|---|---|---|---|---|---|---|---|---|---|---|---|---|---|---|---|---|---|---|---|---|---|---|---|---|
| | | | Regular Season | | | | | | | | | | | | | | Playoffs | | | | | | | | |
| **2008-09** | **Florida** | **NHL** | **5** | **2** | **0** | **2** | **2** | **0** | **0** | **0** | **7** | **28.6** | **1** | **1** | **100.0** | **7:32** | .... | .... | .... | .... | .... | .... | .... | .... | .... |
| | Rochester | AHL | 75 | 19 | 30 | 49 | 58 | .... | .... | .... | .... | .... | .... | .... | .... | .... | .... | .... | .... | .... | .... | .... | .... | .... | .... |
| | **NHL Totals** | | **5** | **2** | **0** | **2** | **2** | **0** | **0** | **0** | **7** | **28.6** | | **1** | **100.0** | **7:32** | .... | .... | .... | .... | .... | .... | .... | .... | .... |

Memorial Cup Tournament All-Star Team (2007) • Ed Chynoweth Trophy (Memorial Cup Tournament - Leading Scorer) (2007)

## RHEAUME, Pascal

(RAY-awm, pas-KAL)

Center. Shoots left. 6'1", 210 lbs. Born, Quebec City, Que., June 21, 1973.

| Season | Club | League | GP | G | A | Pts | PIM | PP | SH | GW | S | % | +/- | TF | F% | Min | GP | G | A | Pts | PIM | PP | SH | GW | Min |
|---|---|---|---|---|---|---|---|---|---|---|---|---|---|---|---|---|---|---|---|---|---|---|---|---|---|
| 1990-91 | Ste-Foy | QAAA | 37 | 20 | 38 | 58 | 25 | .... | .... | .... | .... | .... | .... | .... | .... | .... | 7 | 7 | 1 | 8 | 6 | .... | .... | .... | .... |
| 1991-92 | Trois-Rivieres | QMJHL | 65 | 17 | 20 | 37 | 84 | .... | .... | .... | .... | .... | .... | .... | .... | .... | 14 | 5 | 4 | 9 | 23 | .... | .... | .... | .... |
| 1992-93 | Sherbrooke | QMJHL | 65 | 28 | 34 | 62 | 88 | .... | .... | .... | .... | .... | .... | .... | .... | .... | 14 | 6 | 5 | 11 | 31 | .... | .... | .... | .... |
| 1993-94 | Albany River Rats | AHL | 55 | 17 | 18 | 35 | 43 | .... | .... | .... | .... | .... | .... | .... | .... | .... | 5 | 0 | 1 | 1 | 0 | .... | .... | .... | .... |
| 1994-95 | Albany River Rats | AHL | 78 | 19 | 25 | 44 | 46 | .... | .... | .... | .... | .... | .... | .... | .... | .... | 14 | 3 | 6 | 9 | 19 | .... | .... | .... | .... |
| 1995-96 | Albany River Rats | AHL | 68 | 26 | 42 | 68 | 50 | .... | .... | .... | .... | .... | .... | .... | .... | .... | 4 | 1 | 2 | 3 | 2 | .... | .... | .... | .... |
| **1996-97** | **New Jersey** | **NHL** | **2** | **1** | **0** | **1** | **0** | **0** | **0** | **0** | **5** | **20.0** | **1** | .... | .... | .... | .... | .... | .... | .... | .... | .... | .... | .... | .... |
| | Albany River Rats | AHL | 51 | 22 | 23 | 45 | 40 | .... | .... | .... | .... | .... | .... | .... | .... | .... | 16 | 2 | 8 | 10 | 16 | .... | .... | .... | .... |
| **1997-98** | **St. Louis** | **NHL** | **48** | **6** | **9** | **15** | **35** | **1** | **0** | **0** | **45** | **13.3** | **4** | .... | .... | .... | **10** | **1** | **3** | **4** | **8** | **1** | **0** | **0** | .... |
| **1998-99** | **St. Louis** | **NHL** | **60** | **9** | **18** | **27** | **24** | **2** | **0** | **0** | **85** | **10.6** | **10** | **21** | **71.4** | **13:19** | **5** | **1** | **0** | **1** | **4** | **0** | **0** | **0** | **11:36** |
| **99-2000** | **St. Louis** | **NHL** | **7** | **1** | **1** | **2** | **6** | **0** | **0** | **0** | **5** | **20.0** | **–2** | **2** | **0.0** | **10:08** | .... | .... | .... | .... | .... | .... | .... | .... | .... |
| | Worcester IceCats | AHL | 7 | 1 | 1 | 2 | 4 | .... | .... | .... | .... | .... | .... | .... | .... | .... | .... | .... | .... | .... | .... | .... | .... | .... | .... |
| **2000-01** | **St. Louis** | **NHL** | **8** | **2** | **0** | **2** | **5** | **2** | **0** | **0** | **16** | **12.5** | **–1** | **7** | **42.9** | **11:56** | **3** | **0** | **1** | **1** | **0** | **0** | **0** | **0** | **11:30** |
| | Worcester IceCats | AHL | 56 | 23 | 35 | 58 | 63 | .... | .... | .... | .... | .... | .... | .... | .... | .... | 11 | 2 | 4 | 6 | 2 | .... | .... | .... | .... |
| **2001-02** | **Chicago** | **NHL** | **19** | **0** | **2** | **2** | **4** | **0** | **0** | **0** | **19** | **0.0** | **–1** | **165** | **51.5** | **9:22** | .... | .... | .... | .... | .... | .... | .... | .... | .... |
| | **Atlanta** | **NHL** | **42** | **11** | **9** | **20** | **25** | **6** | **0** | **2** | **61** | **18.0** | **–3** | **510** | **45.9** | **14:27** | .... | .... | .... | .... | .... | .... | .... | .... | .... |
| **2002-03** | **Atlanta** | **NHL** | **56** | **4** | **9** | **13** | **24** | **0** | **2** | **1** | **70** | **5.7** | **–8** | **602** | **46.8** | **12:17** | .... | .... | .... | .... | .... | .... | .... | .... | .... |
| | **♦ New Jersey** | **NHL** | **21** | **4** | **1** | **5** | **8** | **0** | **1** | **1** | **23** | **17.4** | **3** | **248** | **51.6** | **11:50** | **24** | **1** | **2** | **3** | **13** | **0** | **0** | **0** | **13:32** |
| **2003-04** | **NY Rangers** | **NHL** | **17** | **0** | **0** | **0** | **5** | **0** | **0** | **0** | **15** | **0.0** | **–3** | **46** | **56.5** | **10:02** | .... | .... | .... | .... | .... | .... | .... | .... | .... |
| | Hartford | AHL | 3 | 1 | 0 | 1 | 0 | .... | .... | .... | .... | .... | .... | .... | .... | .... | .... | .... | .... | .... | .... | .... | .... | .... | .... |
| | **St. Louis** | **NHL** | **25** | **1** | **3** | **4** | **4** | **0** | **0** | **0** | **23** | **4.3** | **–3** | **26** | **38.5** | **10:19** | **3** | **0** | **0** | **0** | **2** | **0** | **0** | **0** | **6:55** |
| 2004-05 | Albany River Rats | AHL | 78 | 24 | 25 | 49 | 85 | .... | .... | .... | .... | .... | .... | .... | .... | .... | .... | .... | .... | .... | .... | .... | .... | .... | .... |
| **2005-06** | **New Jersey** | **NHL** | **12** | **0** | **0** | **0** | **4** | **0** | **0** | **0** | **11** | **0.0** | **–6** | **81** | **42.0** | **9:15** | .... | .... | .... | .... | .... | .... | .... | .... | .... |
| | Albany River Rats | AHL | 9 | 2 | 0 | 2 | 9 | .... | .... | .... | .... | .... | .... | .... | .... | .... | .... | .... | .... | .... | .... | .... | .... | .... | .... |
| | **Phoenix** | **NHL** | **1** | **0** | **0** | **0** | **0** | **0** | **0** | **0** | **0** | **0.0** | **–1** | **3** | **66.7** | **6:10** | .... | .... | .... | .... | .... | .... | .... | .... | .... |
| | San Antonio | AHL | 47 | 13 | 13 | 26 | 35 | .... | .... | .... | .... | .... | .... | .... | .... | .... | .... | .... | .... | .... | .... | .... | .... | .... | .... |
| 2006-07 | San Antonio | AHL | 79 | 15 | 32 | 47 | 63 | .... | .... | .... | .... | .... | .... | .... | .... | .... | .... | .... | .... | .... | .... | .... | .... | .... | .... |
| 2007-08 | Vienna Capitals | Austria | 35 | 11 | 18 | 29 | 30 | .... | .... | .... | .... | .... | .... | .... | .... | .... | 7 | 1 | 1 | 2 | 33 | .... | .... | .... | .... |
| 2008-09 | Lowell Devils | AHL | 56 | 11 | 19 | 30 | 44 | .... | .... | .... | .... | .... | .... | .... | .... | .... | .... | .... | .... | .... | .... | .... | .... | .... | .... |
| | **NHL Totals** | | **318** | **39** | **52** | **91** | **144** | **11** | **3** | **4** | **378** | **10.3** | | **1711** | **47.9** | **12:04** | **45** | **3** | **6** | **9** | **27** | **1** | **0** | **0** | **12:31** |

Signed as a free agent by **New Jersey**, October 1, 1993. Claimed by **St. Louis** from **New Jersey** in Waiver Draft, September 28, 1997. • Missed majority of 1999-2000 season recovering from shoulder surgery, August, 1999. Signed as a free agent by **Chicago**, July 31, 2001. Claimed on waivers by **Atlanta** from **Chicago**, November 14, 2001. Traded to **New Jersey** by **Atlanta** for future considerations, February 24, 2003. Signed as a free agent by **NY Rangers**, October 22, 2003. Claimed on waivers by **St. Louis** from **NY Rangers**, January 29, 2004. Signed as a free agent by **New Jersey**, August 13, 2004. Traded to **Phoenix** by **New Jersey** with Ray Schultz and Steven Spencer for Brad Ference, November 25, 2005. Signed as a free agent by **Vienna** (Austria), August 21, 2007. Signed as a free agent by **Lowell** (AHL), August 5, 2008.

## RIBEIRO, Mike

(rih-BAIR-roh, MIGHK) **DAL.**

Center. Shoots left. 6', 178 lbs. Born, Montreal, Que., February 10, 1980. Montreal's 2nd choice, 45th overall, in 1998 Entry Draft.

| Season | Club | League | GP | G | A | Pts | PIM | PP | SH | GW | S | % | +/- | TF | F% | Min | GP | G | A | Pts | PIM | PP | SH | GW | Min |
|---|---|---|---|---|---|---|---|---|---|---|---|---|---|---|---|---|---|---|---|---|---|---|---|---|---|
| 1996-97 | Mtl-Bourassa | QAAA | 43 | 32 | 57 | 89 | 48 | .... | .... | .... | .... | .... | .... | .... | .... | .... | 16 | 15 | 23 | 38 | 14 | .... | .... | .... | .... |
| 1997-98 | Rouyn-Noranda | QMJHL | 67 | 40 | *85 | 125 | 55 | .... | .... | .... | .... | .... | .... | .... | .... | .... | 6 | 3 | 1 | 4 | 0 | .... | .... | .... | .... |
| 1998-99 | Rouyn-Noranda | QMJHL | 69 | *67 | *100 | *167 | 137 | .... | .... | .... | .... | .... | .... | .... | .... | .... | 11 | 5 | 11 | 16 | 12 | .... | .... | .... | .... |
| | Fredericton | AHL | .... | .... | .... | .... | .... | .... | .... | .... | .... | .... | .... | .... | .... | .... | 5 | 0 | 1 | 1 | 2 | .... | .... | .... | .... |
| **99-2000** | **Montreal** | **NHL** | **19** | **1** | **1** | **2** | **2** | **1** | **0** | **0** | **18** | **5.6** | **–6** | **95** | **34.7** | **10:40** | .... | .... | .... | .... | .... | .... | .... | .... | .... |
| | Quebec Citadelles | AHL | 3 | 0 | 0 | 0 | 2 | .... | .... | .... | .... | .... | .... | .... | .... | .... | .... | .... | .... | .... | .... | .... | .... | .... | .... |
| | Rouyn-Noranda | QMJHL | 2 | 1 | 3 | 4 | 0 | .... | .... | .... | .... | .... | .... | .... | .... | .... | .... | .... | .... | .... | .... | .... | .... | .... | .... |
| | Quebec Remparts | QMJHL | 21 | 17 | 28 | 45 | 30 | .... | .... | .... | .... | .... | .... | .... | .... | .... | 11 | 3 | 20 | 23 | 38 | .... | .... | .... | .... |
| **2000-01** | **Montreal** | **NHL** | **2** | **0** | **0** | **0** | **2** | **0** | **0** | **0** | **3** | **0.0** | **0** | **11** | **18.2** | **10:38** | .... | .... | .... | .... | .... | .... | .... | .... | .... |
| | Quebec Citadelles | AHL | 74 | 26 | 40 | 66 | 44 | .... | .... | .... | .... | .... | .... | .... | .... | .... | 9 | 1 | 5 | 6 | 23 | .... | .... | .... | .... |
| **2001-02** | **Montreal** | **NHL** | **43** | **8** | **10** | **18** | **12** | **3** | **0** | **0** | **48** | **16.7** | **–11** | **141** | **44.0** | **13:55** | .... | .... | .... | .... | .... | .... | .... | .... | .... |
| | Quebec Citadelles | AHL | 23 | 9 | 14 | 23 | 36 | .... | .... | .... | .... | .... | .... | .... | .... | .... | 3 | 0 | 3 | 3 | 0 | .... | .... | .... | .... |
| **2002-03** | **Montreal** | **NHL** | **52** | **5** | **12** | **17** | **6** | **2** | **0** | **0** | **57** | **8.8** | **–3** | **358** | **50.3** | **11:07** | .... | .... | .... | .... | .... | .... | .... | .... | .... |
| | Hamilton | AHL | 3 | 0 | 1 | 1 | 0 | .... | .... | .... | .... | .... | .... | .... | .... | .... | .... | .... | .... | .... | .... | .... | .... | .... | .... |
| **2003-04** | **Montreal** | **NHL** | **81** | **20** | **45** | **65** | **34** | **7** | **0** | **5** | **103** | **19.4** | **15** | **913** | **44.8** | **17:05** | **11** | **2** | **1** | **3** | **18** | **0** | **0** | **0** | **16:31** |
| 2004-05 | Blues Espoo | Finland | 17 | 8 | 9 | 17 | 4 | .... | .... | .... | .... | .... | .... | .... | .... | .... | .... | .... | .... | .... | .... | .... | .... | .... | .... |
| **2005-06** | **Montreal** | **NHL** | **79** | **16** | **35** | **51** | **36** | **8** | **0** | **2** | **130** | **12.3** | **–6** | **843** | **44.7** | **16:35** | **6** | **0** | **2** | **2** | **0** | **0** | **0** | **0** | **18:22** |
| **2006-07** | **Dallas** | **NHL** | **81** | **18** | **41** | **59** | **22** | **6** | **0** | **3** | **111** | **16.2** | **3** | **678** | **46.6** | **14:56** | **7** | **0** | **3** | **3** | **4** | **0** | **0** | **0** | **18:28** |
| **2007-08** | **Dallas** | **NHL** | **76** | **27** | **56** | **83** | **46** | **7** | **0** | **5** | **107** | **25.2** | **21** | **883** | **45.0** | **18:26** | **18** | **3** | **14** | **17** | **16** | **0** | **0** | **0** | **21:45** |
| **2008-09** | **Dallas** | **NHL** | **82** | **22** | **56** | **78** | **52** | **7** | **0** | **1** | **163** | **13.5** | **–4** | **1240** | **45.5** | **20:57** | .... | .... | .... | .... | .... | .... | .... | .... | .... |
| | **NHL Totals** | | **515** | **117** | **256** | **373** | **212** | **41** | **0** | **16** | **740** | **15.8** | | **5162** | **45.3** | **16:21** | **42** | **5** | **20** | **25** | **38** | **0** | **0** | **0** | **19:21** |

QMJHL Second All-Star Team (1998) • QMJHL First All-Star Team (1999) • Canadian Major Junior First All-Star Team (1999)
Played in NHL All-Star Game (2008)

Signed as a free agent by **Espoo** (Finland), January 17, 2005. Traded to **Dallas** by **Montreal** with Montreal's 6th round choice (Matthew Tassone) in 2008 Entry Draft for Janne Niinimaa and Dallas' 5th round choice (Andrew Conboy) in 2007 Entry Draft, September 30, 2006.

## RICHARDS, Brad

(RIH-chuhrds, BRAD) **DAL.**

Center. Shoots left. 6', 192 lbs. Born, Murray Harbour, P.E.I., May 2, 1980. Tampa Bay's 2nd choice, 64th overall, in 1998 Entry Draft.

| Season | Club | League | GP | G | A | Pts | PIM | PP | SH | GW | S | % | +/- | TF | F% | Min | GP | G | A | Pts | PIM | PP | SH | GW | Min |
|---|---|---|---|---|---|---|---|---|---|---|---|---|---|---|---|---|---|---|---|---|---|---|---|---|---|
| 1996-97 | Notre Dame | SJHL | 63 | 39 | 48 | 87 | 73 | .... | .... | .... | .... | .... | .... | .... | .... | .... | .... | .... | .... | .... | .... | .... | .... | .... | .... |
| 1997-98 | Rimouski Oceanic | QMJHL | 68 | 33 | 82 | 115 | 44 | .... | .... | .... | .... | .... | .... | .... | .... | .... | 19 | 8 | 24 | 32 | 2 | .... | .... | .... | .... |
| 1998-99 | Rimouski Oceanic | QMJHL | 59 | 39 | 92 | 131 | 55 | .... | .... | .... | .... | .... | .... | .... | .... | .... | 11 | 9 | 12 | 21 | 6 | .... | .... | .... | .... |
| 99-2000 | Rimouski Oceanic | QMJHL | 63 | *71 | *115 | *186 | 69 | .... | .... | .... | .... | .... | .... | .... | .... | .... | 12 | 13 | *24 | *37 | 16 | .... | .... | .... | .... |
| **2000-01** | **Tampa Bay** | **NHL** | **82** | **21** | **41** | **62** | **14** | **7** | **0** | **3** | **179** | **11.7** | **–10** | **955** | **41.4** | **16:54** | .... | .... | .... | .... | .... | .... | .... | .... | .... |
| **2001-02** | **Tampa Bay** | **NHL** | **82** | **20** | **42** | **62** | **13** | **5** | **0** | **0** | **251** | **8.0** | **–18** | **911** | **41.2** | **19:48** | .... | .... | .... | .... | .... | .... | .... | .... | .... |
| **2002-03** | **Tampa Bay** | **NHL** | **80** | **17** | **57** | **74** | **24** | **4** | **0** | **2** | **277** | **6.1** | **3** | **1007** | **47.5** | **19:56** | **11** | **0** | **5** | **5** | **12** | **0** | **0** | **0** | **22:21** |
| **2003-04 ♦** | **Tampa Bay** | **NHL** | **82** | **26** | **53** | **79** | **12** | **5** | **1** | **6** | **244** | **10.7** | **13** | **1167** | **46.7** | **20:26** | **23** | **12** | **14** | ***26** | **4** | **7** | **0** | **7** | **23:28** |
| 2004-05 | Ak Bars Kazan | Russia | 6 | 2 | 5 | 7 | 16 | .... | .... | .... | .... | .... | .... | .... | .... | .... | .... | .... | .... | .... | .... | .... | .... | .... | .... |
| **2005-06** | **Tampa Bay** | **NHL** | **82** | **23** | **68** | **91** | **32** | **7** | **4** | **0** | **282** | **8.2** | **0** | **1288** | **50.2** | **22:45** | **5** | **3** | **5** | **8** | **6** | **0** | **0** | **0** | **24:11** |
| | Canada | Olympics | 6 | 2 | 2 | 4 | 6 | .... | .... | .... | .... | .... | .... | .... | .... | .... | .... | .... | .... | .... | .... | .... | .... | .... | .... |
| **2006-07** | **Tampa Bay** | **NHL** | **82** | **25** | **45** | **70** | **23** | **12** | **1** | **3** | **272** | **9.2** | **–19** | **1580** | **51.4** | **24:07** | **6** | **3** | **5** | **8** | **6** | **2** | **0** | **0** | **25:39** |
| **2007-08** | **Tampa Bay** | **NHL** | **62** | **18** | **33** | **51** | **15** | **9** | **1** | **4** | **228** | **7.9** | **–25** | **944** | **48.1** | **24:17** | .... | .... | .... | .... | .... | .... | .... | .... | .... |
| | **Dallas** | **NHL** | **12** | **2** | **9** | **11** | **0** | **0** | **1** | **0** | **21** | **9.5** | **–2** | **130** | **56.2** | **19:15** | **18** | **3** | **12** | **15** | **8** | **0** | **0** | **0** | **21:06** |
| **2008-09** | **Dallas** | **NHL** | **56** | **16** | **32** | **48** | **6** | **5** | **0** | **2** | **180** | **8.9** | **–4** | **911** | **50.6** | **20:29** | .... | .... | .... | .... | .... | .... | .... | .... | .... |
| | **NHL Totals** | | **620** | **168** | **380** | **548** | **139** | **54** | **8** | **20** | **1934** | **8.7** | | **8893** | **47.7** | **20:59** | **63** | **21** | **41** | **62** | **36** | **9** | **0** | **7** | **22:52** |

QMJHL First All-Star Team (2000) • Canadian Major Junior First All-Star Team (2000) • Canadian Major Junior Player of the Year (2000) • Memorial Cup Tournament All-Star Team (2000) • Stafford Smythe Memorial Trophy (Memorial Cup Tournament - MVP) (2000) • NHL All-Rookie Team (2001) • Lady Byng Memorial Trophy (2004) • Conn Smythe Trophy (2004)

Signed as a free agent by **Kazan** (Russia), November 8, 2004. Traded to **Dallas** by **Tampa Bay** with Johan Holmqvist for Jussi Jokinen, Jeff Halpern, Mike Smith and Dallas' 4th round choice (later traded to Minnesota – later traded to Edmonton – Edmonton selected Kyle Bigos) in 2009 Entry Draft, February 26, 2008.

## RICHARDS, Mike

(RIH-chuhrds, MIGHK) **PHI.**

Center. Shoots left. 5'11", 195 lbs. Born, Kenora, Ont., February 11, 1985. Philadelphia's 2nd choice, 24th overall, in 2003 Entry Draft.

| Season | Club | League | GP | G | A | Pts | PIM | PP | SH | GW | S | % | +/- | TF | F% | Min | GP | G | A | Pts | PIM | PP | SH | GW | Min |
|---|---|---|---|---|---|---|---|---|---|---|---|---|---|---|---|---|---|---|---|---|---|---|---|---|---|
| 2000-01 | Kenora Stars | NOHA | 85 | 76 | 73 | 149 | 20 | .... | .... | .... | .... | .... | .... | .... | .... | .... | .... | .... | .... | .... | .... | .... | .... | .... | .... |
| 2001-02 | Kitchener Rangers | OHL | 65 | 20 | 38 | 58 | 52 | .... | .... | .... | .... | .... | .... | .... | .... | .... | 4 | 0 | 1 | 1 | 6 | .... | .... | .... | .... |
| 2002-03 | Kitchener Rangers | OHL | 67 | 37 | 50 | 87 | 99 | .... | .... | .... | .... | .... | .... | .... | .... | .... | 21 | 9 | 18 | 27 | 24 | .... | .... | .... | .... |
| 2003-04 | Kitchener Rangers | OHL | 58 | 36 | 53 | 89 | 82 | .... | .... | .... | .... | .... | .... | .... | .... | .... | 1 | 0 | 0 | 0 | 0 | .... | .... | .... | .... |
| 2004-05 | Kitchener Rangers | OHL | 43 | 22 | 36 | 58 | 75 | .... | .... | .... | .... | .... | .... | .... | .... | .... | 15 | 11 | 17 | 28 | 36 | .... | .... | .... | .... |
| | Philadelphia | AHL | .... | .... | .... | .... | .... | .... | .... | .... | .... | .... | .... | .... | .... | .... | 14 | 7 | 8 | 15 | 28 | .... | .... | .... | .... |
| **2005-06** | **Philadelphia** | **NHL** | **79** | **11** | **23** | **34** | **65** | **1** | **3** | **1** | **168** | **6.5** | **6** | **914** | **45.7** | **15:23** | **6** | **0** | **1** | **1** | **0** | **0** | **0** | **0** | **15:41** |
| **2006-07** | **Philadelphia** | **NHL** | **59** | **10** | **22** | **32** | **52** | **1** | **4** | **3** | **130** | **7.7** | **–12** | **978** | **47.8** | **17:50** | .... | .... | .... | .... | .... | .... | .... | .... | .... |

| | | | Regular Season | | | | | | | | | | | | | | Playoffs | | | | | | | | |
|---|---|---|---|---|---|---|---|---|---|---|---|---|---|---|---|---|---|---|---|---|---|---|---|---|---|
| Season | Club | League | GP | G | A | Pts | PIM | PP | SH | GW | S | % | +/- | TF | F% | Min | GP | G | A | Pts | PIM | PP | SH | GW | Min |
| 2007-08 | Philadelphia | NHL | 73 | 28 | 47 | 75 | 76 | 8 | 5 | 6 | 212 | 13.2 | 14 | 1381 | 50.5 | 21:31 | 17 | 7 | 7 | 14 | 10 | 1 | 2 | 0 | 20:55 |
| 2008-09 | Philadelphia | NHL | 79 | 30 | 50 | 80 | 63 | 8 | 7 | 4 | 238 | 12.6 | 22 | 1660 | 49.0 | 21:44 | 6 | 1 | 4 | 5 | 6 | 1 | 0 | 0 | 22:58 |
| | NHL Totals | | 290 | 79 | 142 | 221 | 256 | 18 | 19 | 14 | 748 | 10.6 | | 4933 | 48.6 | 19:09 | 29 | 8 | 12 | 20 | 16 | 2 | 2 | 0 | 20:16 |

Memorial Cup Tournament All-Star Team (2003) • OHL Second All-Star Team (2005) • Canadian Major Junior Second All-Star Team (2005)
Played in NHL All-Star Game (2008)

## RICHARDSON, Brad

(RIHTCH-uhrd-suhn, BRAD) **L.A.**

Center. Shoots left. 5'11", 184 lbs. Born, Belleville, Ont., February 4, 1985. Colorado's 4th choice, 163rd overall, in 2003 Entry Draft.

| | | | | | | | | | | | | | | | | | | | | | | | | | |
|---|---|---|---|---|---|---|---|---|---|---|---|---|---|---|---|---|---|---|---|---|---|---|---|---|---|
| 2001-02 | Owen Sound | OHL | 58 | 12 | 21 | 33 | 20 | .... | .... | .... | .... | .... | .... | .... | .... | .... | .... | .... | .... | .... | .... | .... | .... | .... | .... |
| 2002-03 | Owen Sound | OHL | 67 | 27 | 40 | 67 | 54 | .... | .... | .... | .... | .... | .... | .... | .... | .... | 4 | 1 | 1 | 2 | 10 | .... | .... | .... | .... |
| 2003-04 | Owen Sound | OHL | 15 | 7 | 9 | 16 | 4 | .... | .... | .... | .... | .... | .... | .... | .... | .... | .... | .... | .... | .... | .... | .... | .... | .... | .... |
| 2004-05 | Owen Sound | OHL | 68 | 41 | 56 | 97 | 60 | .... | .... | .... | .... | .... | .... | .... | .... | .... | 8 | 6 | 4 | 10 | 8 | .... | .... | .... | .... |
| **2005-06** | **Colorado** | **NHL** | **41** | **3** | **10** | **13** | **12** | **1** | **0** | **0** | **51** | **5.9** | **0** | **305** | **41.0** | **10:44** | **9** | **1** | **0** | **1** | **6** | **0** | **0** | **0** | **11:41** |
| | Lowell | AHL | 29 | 4 | 13 | 17 | 20 | .... | .... | .... | .... | .... | .... | .... | .... | .... | .... | .... | .... | .... | .... | .... | .... | .... | .... |
| **2006-07** | **Colorado** | **NHL** | **73** | **14** | **8** | **22** | **28** | **0** | **3** | **3** | **129** | **10.9** | **4** | **358** | **40.8** | **13:10** | .... | .... | .... | .... | .... | .... | .... | .... | .... |
| | Albany River Rats | AHL | 3 | 0 | 1 | 1 | 2 | .... | .... | .... | .... | .... | .... | .... | .... | .... | .... | .... | .... | .... | .... | .... | .... | .... | .... |
| **2007-08** | **Colorado** | **NHL** | **22** | **2** | **3** | **5** | **8** | **0** | **0** | **0** | **32** | **6.3** | **–3** | **60** | **43.3** | **13:29** | .... | .... | .... | .... | .... | .... | .... | .... | .... |
| | Lake Erie | AHL | 38 | 14 | 26 | 40 | 18 | .... | .... | .... | .... | .... | .... | .... | .... | .... | .... | .... | .... | .... | .... | .... | .... | .... | .... |
| **2008-09** | **Los Angeles** | **NHL** | **31** | **0** | **5** | **5** | **11** | **0** | **0** | **0** | **37** | **0.0** | **–6** | **95** | **54.7** | **10:48** | .... | .... | .... | .... | .... | .... | .... | .... | .... |
| | Manchester | AHL | 3 | 1 | 2 | 3 | 0 | .... | .... | .... | .... | .... | .... | .... | .... | .... | .... | .... | .... | .... | .... | .... | .... | .... | .... |
| | **NHL Totals** | | **167** | **19** | **26** | **45** | **59** | **1** | **3** | **3** | **249** | **7.6** | | **818** | **42.7** | **12:10** | **9** | **1** | **0** | **1** | **6** | **0** | **0** | **0** | **11:41** |

Traded to **Los Angeles** by **Colorado** for Detroit's 2nd round choice (previously acquired, Colorado selected Peter Delmas) in 2008 Entry Draft, June 21, 2008.

## RICHARDSON, Luke

(RIH-chard-suhn, LEWK)

Defense. Shoots left. 6'3", 208 lbs. Born, Ottawa, Ont., March 26, 1969. Toronto's 1st choice, 7th overall, in 1987 Entry Draft.

| | | | | | | | | | | | | | | | | | | | | | | | | | |
|---|---|---|---|---|---|---|---|---|---|---|---|---|---|---|---|---|---|---|---|---|---|---|---|---|---|
| 1984-85 | Ottawa Knights | Minor-ON | 35 | 5 | 26 | 31 | 72 | .... | .... | .... | .... | .... | .... | .... | .... | .... | .... | .... | .... | .... | .... | .... | .... | .... | .... |
| 1985-86 | Peterborough | OHL | 63 | 6 | 18 | 24 | 57 | .... | .... | .... | .... | .... | .... | .... | .... | .... | 16 | 2 | 1 | 3 | 50 | .... | .... | .... | .... |
| 1986-87 | Peterborough | OHL | 59 | 13 | 32 | 45 | 70 | .... | .... | .... | .... | .... | .... | .... | .... | .... | 12 | 0 | 5 | 5 | 24 | .... | .... | .... | .... |
| **1987-88** | **Toronto** | **NHL** | **78** | **4** | **6** | **10** | **90** | **0** | **0** | **0** | **49** | **8.2** | **–25** | .... | .... | .... | **2** | **0** | **0** | **0** | **0** | **0** | **0** | **0** | .... |
| **1988-89** | **Toronto** | **NHL** | **55** | **2** | **7** | **9** | **106** | **0** | **0** | **0** | **59** | **3.4** | **–15** | .... | .... | .... | .... | .... | .... | .... | .... | .... | .... | .... | .... |
| **1989-90** | **Toronto** | **NHL** | **67** | **4** | **14** | **18** | **122** | **0** | **0** | **0** | **80** | **5.0** | **–1** | .... | .... | .... | **5** | **0** | **0** | **0** | **22** | **0** | **0** | **0** | .... |
| **1990-91** | **Toronto** | **NHL** | **78** | **1** | **9** | **10** | **238** | **0** | **0** | **0** | **68** | **1.5** | **–28** | .... | .... | .... | .... | .... | .... | .... | .... | .... | .... | .... | .... |
| **1991-92** | **Edmonton** | **NHL** | **75** | **2** | **19** | **21** | **118** | **0** | **0** | **0** | **85** | **2.4** | **–9** | .... | .... | .... | **16** | **0** | **5** | **5** | **45** | **0** | **0** | **0** | .... |
| **1992-93** | **Edmonton** | **NHL** | **82** | **3** | **10** | **13** | **142** | **0** | **2** | **0** | **78** | **3.8** | **–18** | .... | .... | .... | .... | .... | .... | .... | .... | .... | .... | .... | .... |
| **1993-94** | **Edmonton** | **NHL** | **69** | **2** | **6** | **8** | **131** | **0** | **0** | **0** | **92** | **2.2** | **–13** | .... | .... | .... | .... | .... | .... | .... | .... | .... | .... | .... | .... |
| **1994-95** | **Edmonton** | **NHL** | **46** | **3** | **10** | **13** | **40** | **1** | **1** | **1** | **51** | **5.9** | **–6** | .... | .... | .... | .... | .... | .... | .... | .... | .... | .... | .... | .... |
| **1995-96** | **Edmonton** | **NHL** | **82** | **2** | **9** | **11** | **108** | **0** | **0** | **0** | **61** | **3.3** | **–27** | .... | .... | .... | .... | .... | .... | .... | .... | .... | .... | .... | .... |
| **1996-97** | **Edmonton** | **NHL** | **82** | **1** | **11** | **12** | **91** | **0** | **0** | **0** | **67** | **1.5** | **9** | .... | .... | .... | **12** | **0** | **2** | **2** | **14** | **0** | **0** | **0** | .... |
| **1997-98** | **Philadelphia** | **NHL** | **81** | **2** | **3** | **5** | **139** | **2** | **0** | **0** | **57** | **3.5** | **7** | .... | .... | .... | **5** | **0** | **0** | **0** | **0** | **0** | **0** | **0** | .... |
| **1998-99** | **Philadelphia** | **NHL** | **78** | **0** | **6** | **6** | **106** | **0** | **0** | **0** | **49** | **0.0** | **–3** | **0** | **0.0** | **16:33** | .... | .... | .... | .... | .... | .... | .... | .... | .... |
| **99-2000** | **Philadelphia** | **NHL** | **74** | **2** | **5** | **7** | **140** | **0** | **0** | **1** | **50** | **4.0** | **14** | **0** | **0.0** | **16:11** | **18** | **0** | **1** | **1** | **41** | **0** | **0** | **0** | **21:58** |
| **2000-01** | **Philadelphia** | **NHL** | **82** | **2** | **6** | **8** | **131** | **0** | **1** | **0** | **75** | **2.7** | **23** | **1** | **0.0** | **20:42** | **6** | **0** | **0** | **0** | **4** | **0** | **0** | **0** | **24:39** |
| **2001-02** | **Philadelphia** | **NHL** | **72** | **1** | **8** | **9** | **102** | **0** | **0** | **0** | **65** | **1.5** | **18** | **0** | **0.0** | **18:17** | **5** | **0** | **0** | **0** | **4** | **0** | **0** | **0** | **19:18** |
| **2002-03** | **Columbus** | **NHL** | **82** | **0** | **13** | **13** | **73** | **0** | **0** | **0** | **56** | **0.0** | **–16** | **2** | **50.0** | **23:32** | .... | .... | .... | .... | .... | .... | .... | .... | .... |
| **2003-04** | **Columbus** | **NHL** | **64** | **1** | **5** | **6** | **48** | **0** | **0** | **1** | **34** | **2.9** | **–11** | **0** | **0.0** | **20:07** | .... | .... | .... | .... | .... | .... | .... | .... | .... |
| 2004-05 | | | DID NOT PLAY | | | | | | | | | | | | | | | | | | | | | | |
| **2005-06** | **Columbus** | **NHL** | **44** | **1** | **6** | **7** | **30** | **0** | **0** | **0** | **24** | **4.2** | **–18** | **0** | **0.0** | **15:15** | .... | .... | .... | .... | .... | .... | .... | .... | .... |
| | **Toronto** | **NHL** | **21** | **0** | **3** | **3** | **41** | **0** | **0** | **0** | **16** | **0.0** | **–1** | **0** | **0.0** | **18:48** | .... | .... | .... | .... | .... | .... | .... | .... | .... |
| **2006-07** | **Tampa Bay** | **NHL** | **27** | **0** | **3** | **3** | **16** | **0** | **0** | **0** | **3** | **0.0** | **3** | **0** | **0.0** | **7:07** | .... | .... | .... | .... | .... | .... | .... | .... | .... |
| **2007-08** | **Ottawa** | **NHL** | **76** | **2** | **7** | **9** | **41** | **0** | **0** | **0** | **41** | **4.9** | **1** | **0** | **0.0** | **12:19** | .... | .... | .... | .... | .... | .... | .... | .... | .... |
| **2008-09** | **Ottawa** | **NHL** | **2** | **0** | **0** | **0** | **2** | **0** | **0** | **0** | **0** | **0.0** | **–3** | **0** | **0.0** | **12:45** | .... | .... | .... | .... | .... | .... | .... | .... | .... |
| | **NHL Totals** | | **1417** | **35** | **166** | **201** | **2055** | **3** | **4** | **3** | **1160** | **3.0** | | **3** | **33.3** | **17:35** | **69** | **0** | **8** | **8** | **130** | **0** | **0** | **0** | **22:04** |

Traded to **Edmonton** by **Toronto** with Vincent Damphousse, Peter Ing and Scott Thornton for Grant Fuhr, Glenn Anderson and Craig Berube, September 19, 1991. Signed as a free agent by **Philadelphia**, July 23, 1997. Signed as a free agent by **Columbus**, July 4, 2002. Traded to **Toronto** by **Columbus** for Toronto's 5th round choice (Nick Sucharski) in 2006 Entry Draft, March 8, 2006. Signed as a free agent by **Tampa Bay**, July 11, 2006. • Spent majority of 2006-07 season serving as a healthy reserve. Signed as a free agent by **Ottawa**, August 8, 2007. • Officially announced his retirement, November 29, 2008.

## RICHMOND, Danny

(RIHCH-muhnd, DA-nee) **ST.L.**

Defense. Shoots left. 6', 192 lbs. Born, Chicago, IL, August 1, 1984. Carolina's 2nd choice, 31st overall, in 2003 Entry Draft.

| | | | | | | | | | | | | | | | | | | | | | | | | | |
|---|---|---|---|---|---|---|---|---|---|---|---|---|---|---|---|---|---|---|---|---|---|---|---|---|---|
| 2000-01 | Team Illinois | MWEHL | 79 | 25 | 40 | 65 | .... | .... | .... | .... | .... | .... | .... | .... | .... | .... | .... | .... | .... | .... | .... | .... | .... | .... | .... |
| 2001-02 | Chicago Steel | USHL | 56 | 8 | 45 | 53 | 129 | .... | .... | .... | .... | .... | .... | .... | .... | .... | 4 | 0 | 4 | 4 | 20 | .... | .... | .... | .... |
| 2002-03 | U. of Michigan | CCHA | 43 | 3 | 19 | 22 | 48 | .... | .... | .... | .... | .... | .... | .... | .... | .... | .... | .... | .... | .... | .... | .... | .... | .... | .... |
| 2003-04 | London Knights | OHL | 59 | 13 | 22 | 35 | 92 | .... | .... | .... | .... | .... | .... | .... | .... | .... | 15 | 5 | 6 | 11 | 10 | .... | .... | .... | .... |
| 2004-05 | Lowell | AHL | 63 | 4 | 9 | 13 | 139 | .... | .... | .... | .... | .... | .... | .... | .... | .... | 6 | 0 | 2 | 2 | 8 | .... | .... | .... | .... |
| **2005-06** | **Carolina** | **NHL** | **10** | **0** | **1** | **1** | **7** | **0** | **0** | **0** | **7** | **0.0** | **–3** | **0** | **0.0** | **9:00** | .... | .... | .... | .... | .... | .... | .... | .... | .... |
| | Lowell | AHL | 32 | 4 | 11 | 15 | 60 | .... | .... | .... | .... | .... | .... | .... | .... | .... | .... | .... | .... | .... | .... | .... | .... | .... | .... |
| | **Chicago** | **NHL** | **10** | **0** | **0** | **0** | **18** | **0** | **0** | **0** | **6** | **0.0** | **–3** | **0** | **0.0** | **13:36** | .... | .... | .... | .... | .... | .... | .... | .... | .... |
| | Norfolk Admirals | AHL | 31 | 4 | 8 | 12 | 42 | .... | .... | .... | .... | .... | .... | .... | .... | .... | 3 | 0 | 1 | 1 | 2 | .... | .... | .... | .... |
| **2006-07** | **Chicago** | **NHL** | **22** | **0** | **2** | **2** | **48** | **0** | **0** | **0** | **13** | **0.0** | **–1** | **0** | **0.0** | **12:20** | .... | .... | .... | .... | .... | .... | .... | .... | .... |
| | Norfolk Admirals | AHL | 57 | 10 | 24 | 34 | 144 | .... | .... | .... | .... | .... | .... | .... | .... | .... | 6 | 0 | 0 | 0 | 8 | .... | .... | .... | .... |
| **2007-08** | **Chicago** | **NHL** | **7** | **0** | **0** | **0** | **2** | **0** | **0** | **0** | **2** | **0.0** | **–5** | **0** | **0.0** | **9:24** | .... | .... | .... | .... | .... | .... | .... | .... | .... |
| | Rockford IceHogs | AHL | 40 | 2 | 12 | 14 | 156 | .... | .... | .... | .... | .... | .... | .... | .... | .... | .... | .... | .... | .... | .... | .... | .... | .... | .... |
| 2008-09 | Wilkes-Barre | AHL | 55 | 3 | 14 | 17 | 108 | .... | .... | .... | .... | .... | .... | .... | .... | .... | .... | .... | .... | .... | .... | .... | .... | .... | .... |
| | Peoria Rivermen | AHL | 18 | 1 | 4 | 5 | 21 | .... | .... | .... | .... | .... | .... | .... | .... | .... | 7 | 0 | 4 | 4 | 2 | .... | .... | .... | .... |
| | **NHL Totals** | | **49** | **0** | **3** | **3** | **75** | **0** | **0** | **0** | **28** | **0.0** | | **0** | **0.0** | **11:29** | .... | .... | .... | .... | .... | .... | .... | .... | .... |

USHL All-Rookie Team (2002) • USHL First All-Star Team (2002) • USHL Rookie of the Year (2002) • CCHA All-Rookie Team (2003)
• Left **University of Michigan** (CCHA) and signed with **London** (OHL), June 6, 2003. Traded to **Chicago** by **Carolina** with Columbus' 4th round choice (previously acquired, later traded to Toronto - Toronto selected James Reimer) in 2006 Entry Draft for Anton Babchuk and Chicago's 4th round choice (later traded to St. Louis - St. Louis selected Cade Fairchild) in 2007 Entry Draft, January 20, 2006. Traded to **Pittsburgh** by **Chicago** for Tim Brent, July 17, 2008. Traded to **St. Louis** by **Pittsburgh** for Andy Wozniewski, March 4, 2009.

## RISSMILLER, Patrick

(RIGHZ-mih-luhr, PAT-rihk) **NYR**

Left wing. Shoots left. 6'4", 220 lbs. Born, Belmont, MA, October 26, 1978.

| | | | | | | | | | | | | | | | | | | | | | | | | | |
|---|---|---|---|---|---|---|---|---|---|---|---|---|---|---|---|---|---|---|---|---|---|---|---|---|---|
| 1997-98 | The Hill School | High-PA | STATISTICS NOT AVAILABLE | | | | | .... | .... | .... | .... | .... | .... | .... | .... | .... | .... | .... | .... | .... | .... | .... | .... | .... | .... |
| 1998-99 | Holy Cross | MAAC | 34 | 13 | 28 | 41 | 23 | .... | .... | .... | .... | .... | .... | .... | .... | .... | .... | .... | .... | .... | .... | .... | .... | .... | .... |
| 99-2000 | Holy Cross | MAAC | 35 | 10 | 17 | 27 | 22 | .... | .... | .... | .... | .... | .... | .... | .... | .... | .... | .... | .... | .... | .... | .... | .... | .... | .... |
| 2000-01 | Holy Cross | MAAC | 29 | 14 | 15 | 29 | 40 | .... | .... | .... | .... | .... | .... | .... | .... | .... | .... | .... | .... | .... | .... | .... | .... | .... | .... |
| 2001-02 | Holy Cross | MAAC | 33 | 16 | *30 | *46 | 31 | .... | .... | .... | .... | .... | .... | .... | .... | .... | .... | .... | .... | .... | .... | .... | .... | .... | .... |
| 2002-03 | Cleveland Barons | AHL | 72 | 14 | 26 | 40 | 24 | .... | .... | .... | .... | .... | .... | .... | .... | .... | .... | .... | .... | .... | .... | .... | .... | .... | .... |
| | Cincinnati | ECHL | 2 | 2 | 2 | 4 | 0 | .... | .... | .... | .... | .... | .... | .... | .... | .... | .... | .... | .... | .... | .... | .... | .... | .... | .... |
| **2003-04** | **San Jose** | **NHL** | **4** | **0** | **0** | **0** | **0** | **0** | **0** | **0** | **2** | **0.0** | **0** | **26** | **53.9** | **7:07** | .... | .... | .... | .... | .... | .... | .... | .... | .... |
| | Cleveland Barons | AHL | 75 | 14 | 31 | 45 | 66 | .... | .... | .... | .... | .... | .... | .... | .... | .... | 9 | 0 | 1 | 1 | 8 | .... | .... | .... | .... |
| 2004-05 | Cleveland Barons | AHL | 69 | 21 | 23 | 44 | 50 | .... | .... | .... | .... | .... | .... | .... | .... | .... | .... | .... | .... | .... | .... | .... | .... | .... | .... |
| **2005-06** | **San Jose** | **NHL** | **18** | **3** | **3** | **6** | **8** | **1** | **0** | **1** | **26** | **11.5** | **1** | **3** | **0.0** | **9:22** | **11** | **2** | **1** | **3** | **6** | **0** | **0** | **0** | **8:06** |
| | Cleveland Barons | AHL | 68 | 15 | 37 | 52 | 30 | .... | .... | .... | .... | .... | .... | .... | .... | .... | .... | .... | .... | .... | .... | .... | .... | .... | .... |
| **2006-07** | **San Jose** | **NHL** | **79** | **7** | **15** | **22** | **22** | **1** | **0** | **0** | **100** | **7.0** | **1** | **25** | **36.0** | **12:10** | **11** | **1** | **3** | **4** | **0** | **0** | **0** | **1** | **12:40** |
| **2007-08** | **San Jose** | **NHL** | **79** | **8** | **9** | **17** | **30** | **0** | **0** | **2** | **119** | **6.7** | **–8** | **214** | **50.9** | **13:10** | **8** | **0** | **0** | **0** | **4** | **0** | **0** | **0** | **11:25** |
| **2008-09** | **NY Rangers** | **NHL** | **2** | **0** | **0** | **0** | **0** | **0** | **0** | **0** | **2** | **0.0** | **–2** | **0** | **0.0** | **9:13** | .... | .... | .... | .... | .... | .... | .... | .... | .... |
| | Hartford | AHL | 64 | 14 | 40 | 54 | 24 | .... | .... | .... | .... | .... | .... | .... | .... | .... | 6 | 0 | 1 | 1 | 6 | .... | .... | .... | .... |
| | **NHL Totals** | | **182** | **18** | **27** | **45** | **60** | **2** | **0** | **3** | **249** | **7.2** | | **268** | **49.3** | **12:11** | **30** | **3** | **4** | **7** | **10** | **0** | **0** | **1** | **10:40** |

MAAC All-Rookie Team (1999) • MAAC First All-Star Team (2002) • MAAC Offensive Player of the Year (2002)
Signed as a free agent by **Cleveland** (AHL), September 23, 2002. Signed as a free agent by **San Jose**, June 30, 2003. Signed as a free agent by **NY Rangers**, July 1, 2008.

| | | | Regular Season | | | | | | | | | | | | | | Playoffs | | | | | | | | |
|---|---|---|---|---|---|---|---|---|---|---|---|---|---|---|---|---|---|---|---|---|---|---|---|---|---|
| Season | Club | League | GP | G | A | Pts | PIM | PP | SH | GW | S | % | +/- | TF | F% | Min | GP | G | A | Pts | PIM | PP | SH | GW | Min |

## RITCHIE, Byron

(RIHT-chee, BIGH-rohn)

Center. Shoots left. 5'10", 190 lbs. Born, Burnaby, B.C., April 24, 1977. Hartford's 6th choice, 165th overall, in 1995 Entry Draft.

| | | | | | | | | | | | | | | | | | | | | | | | | | |
|---|---|---|---|---|---|---|---|---|---|---|---|---|---|---|---|---|---|---|---|---|---|---|---|---|---|
| 1992-93 | North Delta | Minor-BC | 60 | 102 | 151 | 253 | 147 | .... | .... | .... | .... | .... | .... | .... | .... | .... | .... | .... | .... | .... | .... | .... | .... | .... | .... |
| 1993-94 | Lethbridge | WHL | 44 | 4 | 11 | 15 | 44 | .... | .... | .... | .... | .... | .... | .... | .... | .... | 6 | 0 | 0 | 0 | 14 | .... | .... | .... | .... |
| 1994-95 | Lethbridge | WHL | 58 | 22 | 28 | 50 | 132 | .... | .... | .... | .... | .... | .... | .... | .... | .... | .... | .... | .... | .... | .... | .... | .... | .... | .... |
| 1995-96 | Lethbridge | WHL | 66 | 55 | 51 | 106 | 163 | .... | .... | .... | .... | .... | .... | .... | .... | .... | 4 | 0 | 2 | 2 | 4 | .... | .... | .... | .... |
| | Springfield | AHL | 6 | 2 | 1 | 3 | 4 | .... | .... | .... | .... | .... | .... | .... | .... | .... | 8 | 0 | 3 | 3 | 0 | .... | .... | .... | .... |
| 1996-97 | Lethbridge | WHL | 63 | 50 | 76 | 126 | 115 | .... | .... | .... | .... | .... | .... | .... | .... | .... | 18 | *16 | 12 | *28 | 28 | .... | .... | .... | .... |
| 1997-98 | New Haven | AHL | 65 | 13 | 18 | 31 | 97 | .... | .... | .... | .... | .... | .... | .... | .... | .... | .... | .... | .... | .... | .... | .... | .... | .... | .... |
| **1998-99** | **Carolina** | **NHL** | **3** | **0** | **0** | **0** | **0** | **0** | **0** | **0** | **0** | **0.0** | **0** | **5** | **20.0** | **3:25** | .... | .... | .... | .... | .... | .... | .... | .... | .... |
| | New Haven | AHL | 66 | 24 | 33 | 57 | 139 | .... | .... | .... | .... | .... | .... | .... | .... | .... | .... | .... | .... | .... | .... | .... | .... | .... | .... |
| **99-2000** | **Carolina** | **NHL** | **26** | **0** | **2** | **2** | **17** | **0** | **0** | **0** | **13** | **0.0** | **–10** | **155** | **49.7** | **7:24** | .... | .... | .... | .... | .... | .... | .... | .... | .... |
| | Cincinnati | IHL | 34 | 8 | 13 | 21 | 81 | .... | .... | .... | .... | .... | .... | .... | .... | .... | 10 | 1 | 6 | 7 | 32 | .... | .... | .... | .... |
| 2000-01 | Cincinnati | IHL | 77 | 31 | 35 | 66 | 166 | .... | .... | .... | .... | .... | .... | .... | .... | .... | 5 | 3 | 2 | 5 | 10 | .... | .... | .... | .... |
| **2001-02** | **Carolina** | **NHL** | **4** | **0** | **0** | **0** | **2** | **0** | **0** | **0** | **5** | **0.0** | **0** | **9** | **44.4** | **11:30** | .... | .... | .... | .... | .... | .... | .... | .... | .... |
| | Lowell | AHL | 43 | 25 | 30 | 55 | 38 | .... | .... | .... | .... | .... | .... | .... | .... | .... | .... | .... | .... | .... | .... | .... | .... | .... | .... |
| | **Florida** | **NHL** | **31** | **5** | **6** | **11** | **34** | **2** | **0** | **0** | **55** | **9.1** | **–2** | **324** | **50.9** | **12:26** | .... | .... | .... | .... | .... | .... | .... | .... | .... |
| **2002-03** | **Florida** | **NHL** | **30** | **0** | **3** | **3** | **19** | **0** | **0** | **0** | **29** | **0.0** | **–4** | **251** | **48.2** | **9:18** | .... | .... | .... | .... | .... | .... | .... | .... | .... |
| | San Antonio | AHL | 26 | 3 | 14 | 17 | 68 | .... | .... | .... | .... | .... | .... | .... | .... | .... | 3 | 1 | 0 | 1 | 0 | .... | .... | .... | .... |
| **2003-04** | **Florida** | **NHL** | **50** | **5** | **6** | **11** | **84** | **0** | **0** | **2** | **65** | **7.7** | **–10** | **168** | **48.8** | **13:54** | .... | .... | .... | .... | .... | .... | .... | .... | .... |
| 2004-05 | Rogle | Sweden-2 | 30 | 17 | 16 | 33 | 111 | .... | .... | .... | .... | .... | .... | .... | .... | .... | 2 | 0 | 0 | 0 | 4 | .... | .... | .... | .... |
| **2005-06** | **Calgary** | **NHL** | **45** | **4** | **2** | **6** | **69** | **0** | **0** | **0** | **34** | **11.8** | **–2** | **313** | **52.4** | **9:52** | **7** | **0** | **0** | **0** | **0** | **0** | **0** | **0** | **9:15** |
| **2006-07** | **Calgary** | **NHL** | **64** | **8** | **6** | **14** | **68** | **0** | **1** | **0** | **46** | **17.4** | **3** | **282** | **50.0** | **9:46** | **1** | **0** | **0** | **0** | **10** | **0** | **0** | **0** | **4:41** |
| **2007-08** | **Vancouver** | **NHL** | **71** | **3** | **8** | **11** | **80** | **0** | **0** | **0** | **73** | **4.1** | **–10** | **515** | **50.9** | **12:19** | .... | .... | .... | .... | .... | .... | .... | .... | .... |
| 2008-09 | Geneve | Swiss | 45 | 23 | 38 | 61 | 62 | .... | .... | .... | .... | .... | .... | .... | .... | .... | 3 | 0 | 0 | 0 | 14 | .... | .... | .... | .... |
| | **NHL Totals** | | **324** | **25** | **33** | **58** | **373** | **2** | **1** | **2** | **320** | **7.8** | | **2022** | **50.3** | **10:58** | **8** | **0** | **0** | **0** | **10** | **0** | **0** | **0** | **8:41** |

WHL East Second All-Star Team (1996, 1997) • Memorial Cup Tournament All-Star Team (1997)

• Rights transferred to **Carolina** after **Hartford** franchise relocated, June 25, 1997. Traded to **Florida** by **Carolina** with Sandis Ozolinsh for Bret Hedican, Kevyn Adams and Tomas Malec, January 16, 2002. Signed as a free agent by **Calgary**, July 2, 2004. Signed as a free agent by **Rogle** (Sweden-2) September 25, 2004. Signed as a free agent by **Vancouver**, July 3, 2007.

## RITOLA, Mattias

(RIH-toh-lah, mat-TEE-uhs) **DET.**

Right wing. Shoots left. 6', 192 lbs. Born, Borlange, Sweden, March 14, 1987. Detroit's 4th choice, 103rd overall, in 2005 Entry Draft.

| | | | | | | | | | | | | | | | | | | | | | | | | | |
|---|---|---|---|---|---|---|---|---|---|---|---|---|---|---|---|---|---|---|---|---|---|---|---|---|---|
| 2003-04 | V.Frolunda U18 | Swe-U18 | 11 | 4 | 11 | 15 | 35 | .... | .... | .... | .... | .... | .... | .... | .... | .... | 7 | 2 | 7 | 9 | 12 | .... | .... | .... | .... |
| | V.Frolunda Jr. | Swe-Jr. | 24 | 7 | 4 | 11 | 8 | .... | .... | .... | .... | .... | .... | .... | .... | .... | 5 | 0 | 1 | 1 | 0 | .... | .... | .... | .... |
| 2004-05 | Frolunda Jr. | Swe-Jr. | 9 | 2 | 6 | 8 | 6 | .... | .... | .... | .... | .... | .... | .... | .... | .... | .... | .... | .... | .... | .... | .... | .... | .... | .... |
| | Leksands IF U18 | Swe-U18 | STATISTICS NOT AVAILABLE | | | | | | | | | | | | | | | | | | | | | | |
| | Leksands IF Jr. | Swe-Jr. | 18 | 8 | 10 | 18 | 14 | .... | .... | .... | .... | .... | .... | .... | .... | .... | 5 | 1 | 1 | 2 | 2 | .... | .... | .... | .... |
| 2005-06 | Leksands IF Jr. | Swe-Jr. | 14 | 4 | 2 | 6 | 16 | .... | .... | .... | .... | .... | .... | .... | .... | .... | .... | .... | .... | .... | .... | .... | .... | .... | .... |
| | Leksands IF | Sweden | 30 | 0 | 3 | 3 | 10 | .... | .... | .... | .... | .... | .... | .... | .... | .... | .... | .... | .... | .... | .... | .... | .... | .... | .... |
| | Leksands IF | Sweden-Q | 8 | 0 | 0 | 0 | 4 | .... | .... | .... | .... | .... | .... | .... | .... | .... | .... | .... | .... | .... | .... | .... | .... | .... | .... |
| 2006-07 | Leksands IF Jr. | Swe-Jr. | 12 | 5 | 7 | 12 | 16 | .... | .... | .... | .... | .... | .... | .... | .... | .... | .... | .... | .... | .... | .... | .... | .... | .... | .... |
| | Leksands IF | Sweden-2 | 23 | 1 | 4 | 5 | 4 | .... | .... | .... | .... | .... | .... | .... | .... | .... | .... | .... | .... | .... | .... | .... | .... | .... | .... |
| | IFK Arboga IK | Sweden-2 | 3 | 1 | 0 | 1 | 2 | .... | .... | .... | .... | .... | .... | .... | .... | .... | .... | .... | .... | .... | .... | .... | .... | .... | .... |
| | Borlange HF | Sweden-3 | 11 | 4 | 6 | 10 | 14 | .... | .... | .... | .... | .... | .... | .... | .... | .... | .... | .... | .... | .... | .... | .... | .... | .... | .... |
| **2007-08** | **Detroit** | **NHL** | **2** | **0** | **1** | **1** | **0** | **0** | **0** | **0** | **2** | **0.0** | **0** | **0** | **0.0** | **5:47** | .... | .... | .... | .... | .... | .... | .... | .... | .... |
| | Grand Rapids | AHL | 72 | 7 | 15 | 22 | 62 | .... | .... | .... | .... | .... | .... | .... | .... | .... | .... | .... | .... | .... | .... | .... | .... | .... | .... |
| 2008-09 | Grand Rapids | AHL | 66 | 15 | 27 | 42 | 32 | .... | .... | .... | .... | .... | .... | .... | .... | .... | 8 | 0 | 2 | 2 | 0 | .... | .... | .... | .... |
| | **NHL Totals** | | **2** | **0** | **1** | **1** | **0** | **0** | **0** | **0** | **2** | **0.0** | | **0** | **0.0** | **5:47** | .... | .... | .... | .... | .... | .... | .... | .... | .... |

## RIVERS, Jamie

(RIH-vuhrs, JAY-mee)

Defense. Shoots left. 6'1", 206 lbs. Born, Ottawa, Ont., March 16, 1975. St. Louis' 2nd choice, 63rd overall, in 1993 Entry Draft.

| | | | | | | | | | | | | | | | | | | | | | | | | | |
|---|---|---|---|---|---|---|---|---|---|---|---|---|---|---|---|---|---|---|---|---|---|---|---|---|---|
| 1989-90 | Ottawa South | ODMHA | 50 | 26 | 46 | 72 | 46 | .... | .... | .... | .... | .... | .... | .... | .... | .... | .... | .... | .... | .... | .... | .... | .... | .... | .... |
| 1990-91 | Ott. Jr. Senators | CJHL | 55 | 4 | 30 | 34 | 74 | .... | .... | .... | .... | .... | .... | .... | .... | .... | .... | .... | .... | .... | .... | .... | .... | .... | .... |
| 1991-92 | Sudbury Wolves | OHL | 55 | 3 | 13 | 16 | 20 | .... | .... | .... | .... | .... | .... | .... | .... | .... | 8 | 0 | 0 | 0 | 0 | .... | .... | .... | .... |
| 1992-93 | Sudbury Wolves | OHL | 62 | 12 | 43 | 55 | 20 | .... | .... | .... | .... | .... | .... | .... | .... | .... | 14 | 7 | 19 | 26 | 4 | .... | .... | .... | .... |
| 1993-94 | Sudbury Wolves | OHL | 65 | 32 | *89 | 121 | 58 | .... | .... | .... | .... | .... | .... | .... | .... | .... | 10 | 1 | 9 | 10 | 14 | .... | .... | .... | .... |
| 1994-95 | Sudbury Wolves | OHL | 46 | 9 | 56 | 65 | 30 | .... | .... | .... | .... | .... | .... | .... | .... | .... | 18 | 7 | 26 | 33 | 22 | .... | .... | .... | .... |
| **1995-96** | **St. Louis** | **NHL** | **3** | **0** | **0** | **0** | **2** | **0** | **0** | **0** | **5** | **0.0** | **–1** | .... | .... | .... | .... | .... | .... | .... | .... | .... | .... | .... | .... |
| | Worcester IceCats | AHL | 75 | 7 | 45 | 52 | 130 | .... | .... | .... | .... | .... | .... | .... | .... | .... | 4 | 0 | 1 | 1 | 4 | .... | .... | .... | .... |
| **1996-97** | **St. Louis** | **NHL** | **15** | **2** | **5** | **7** | **6** | **1** | **0** | **0** | **9** | **22.2** | **–4** | .... | .... | .... | .... | .... | .... | .... | .... | .... | .... | .... | .... |
| | Worcester IceCats | AHL | 63 | 8 | 35 | 43 | 83 | .... | .... | .... | .... | .... | .... | .... | .... | .... | 5 | 1 | 2 | 3 | 14 | .... | .... | .... | .... |
| **1997-98** | **St. Louis** | **NHL** | **59** | **2** | **4** | **6** | **36** | **1** | **0** | **1** | **53** | **3.8** | **5** | .... | .... | .... | .... | .... | .... | .... | .... | .... | .... | .... | .... |
| **1998-99** | **St. Louis** | **NHL** | **76** | **2** | **5** | **7** | **47** | **1** | **0** | **0** | **78** | **2.6** | **–3** | **0** | **0.0** | **14:10** | **9** | **1** | **1** | **2** | **2** | **1** | **0** | **1** | **6:29** |
| **99-2000** | **NY Islanders** | **NHL** | **75** | **1** | **16** | **17** | **84** | **1** | **0** | **0** | **95** | **1.1** | **–4** | **0** | **0.0** | **19:39** | .... | .... | .... | .... | .... | .... | .... | .... | .... |
| **2000-01** | **Ottawa** | **NHL** | **45** | **2** | **4** | **6** | **44** | **0** | **0** | **0** | **41** | **4.9** | **6** | **0** | **0.0** | **14:01** | **1** | **0** | **0** | **0** | **4** | **0** | **0** | **0** | **12:45** |
| | Grand Rapids | IHL | 2 | 0 | 0 | 0 | 2 | .... | .... | .... | .... | .... | .... | .... | .... | .... | .... | .... | .... | .... | .... | .... | .... | .... | .... |
| **2001-02** | **Ottawa** | **NHL** | **2** | **0** | **0** | **0** | **4** | **0** | **0** | **0** | **3** | **0.0** | **–3** | **0** | **0.0** | **11:37** | .... | .... | .... | .... | .... | .... | .... | .... | .... |
| | **Boston** | **NHL** | **64** | **4** | **2** | **6** | **45** | **1** | **0** | **1** | **48** | **8.3** | **6** | **39** | **33.3** | **8:27** | **3** | **0** | **0** | **0** | **0** | **0** | **0** | **0** | **4:57** |
| **2002-03** | **Florida** | **NHL** | **1** | **0** | **0** | **0** | **2** | **0** | **0** | **0** | **2** | **0.0** | **–2** | **0** | **0.0** | **18:27** | .... | .... | .... | .... | .... | .... | .... | .... | .... |
| | San Antonio | AHL | 50 | 6 | 19 | 25 | 68 | .... | .... | .... | .... | .... | .... | .... | .... | .... | 3 | 0 | 1 | 1 | 10 | .... | .... | .... | .... |
| **2003-04** | **Detroit** | **NHL** | **50** | **3** | **4** | **7** | **41** | **0** | **0** | **0** | **31** | **9.7** | **9** | **1** | **0.0** | **10:14** | **2** | **0** | **0** | **0** | **2** | **0** | **0** | **0** | **5:40** |
| | Grand Rapids | AHL | 2 | 0 | 0 | 0 | 4 | .... | .... | .... | .... | .... | .... | .... | .... | .... | .... | .... | .... | .... | .... | .... | .... | .... | .... |
| 2004-05 | Hershey Bears | AHL | 50 | 7 | 13 | 20 | 46 | .... | .... | .... | .... | .... | .... | .... | .... | .... | .... | .... | .... | .... | .... | .... | .... | .... | .... |
| **2005-06** | **Detroit** | **NHL** | **15** | **0** | **1** | **1** | **12** | **0** | **0** | **0** | **4** | **0.0** | **0** | **0** | **0.0** | **8:51** | .... | .... | .... | .... | .... | .... | .... | .... | .... |
| | **Phoenix** | **NHL** | **18** | **0** | **5** | **5** | **26** | **0** | **0** | **0** | **32** | **0.0** | **2** | **0** | **0.0** | **20:06** | .... | .... | .... | .... | .... | .... | .... | .... | .... |
| **2006-07** | **St. Louis** | **NHL** | **31** | **1** | **3** | **4** | **36** | **1** | **0** | **0** | **17** | **5.9** | **–7** | **0** | **0.0** | **14:11** | .... | .... | .... | .... | .... | .... | .... | .... | .... |
| | Peoria Rivermen | AHL | 30 | 4 | 19 | 23 | 24 | .... | .... | .... | .... | .... | .... | .... | .... | .... | .... | .... | .... | .... | .... | .... | .... | .... | .... |
| 2007-08 | Spartak Moscow | Russia | 19 | 0 | 3 | 3 | 42 | .... | .... | .... | .... | .... | .... | .... | .... | .... | 4 | 0 | 0 | 0 | 8 | .... | .... | .... | .... |
| 2008-09 | Chicago Wolves | AHL | 69 | 4 | 24 | 28 | 72 | .... | .... | .... | .... | .... | .... | .... | .... | .... | .... | .... | .... | .... | .... | .... | .... | .... | .... |
| | **NHL Totals** | | **454** | **17** | **49** | **66** | **385** | **6** | **0** | **2** | **418** | **4.1** | | **40** | **32.5** | **13:49** | **15** | **1** | **1** | **2** | **8** | **1** | **0** | **1** | **6:29** |

OHL First All-Star Team (1994) • Canadian Major Junior Second All-Star Team (1994) • OHL Second All-Star Team (1995) • AHL Second All-Star Team (1997)

Claimed by **NY Islanders** from **St. Louis** in Waiver Draft, September 27, 1999. Signed as a free agent by **Ottawa**, November 30, 2000. Claimed on waivers by **Boston** from **Ottawa**, October 13, 2001. Signed as a free agent by **San Antonio** (AHL), November 2, 2002. Signed as a free agent by **Florida**, December 16, 2002. Signed as a free agent by **Detroit**, July 29, 2003. Signed as a free agent by **Hershey** (AHL), November 3, 2004. Traded to **Phoenix** by **Detroit** for Phoenix's 7th round choice (Nick Oslund) in 2006 Entry Draft, March 9, 2006. • Spent majority of 2005-06 season serving as a healthy reserve. Signed as a free agent by **St. Louis**, August 18, 2006. Signed as a free agent by **Montreal**, July 5, 2007.

## RIVET, Craig

(rih-VAY, KRAYG) **BUF.**

Defense. Shoots right. 6'2", 210 lbs. Born, North Bay, Ont., September 13, 1974. Montreal's 4th choice, 68th overall, in 1992 Entry Draft.

| | | | | | | | | | | | | | | | | | | | | | | | | | |
|---|---|---|---|---|---|---|---|---|---|---|---|---|---|---|---|---|---|---|---|---|---|---|---|---|---|
| 1990-91 | Barrie Colts | OHA-B | 42 | 9 | 17 | 26 | 55 | .... | .... | .... | .... | .... | .... | .... | .... | .... | .... | .... | .... | .... | .... | .... | .... | .... | .... |
| 1991-92 | Kingston | OHL | 66 | 5 | 21 | 26 | 97 | .... | .... | .... | .... | .... | .... | .... | .... | .... | .... | .... | .... | .... | .... | .... | .... | .... | .... |
| 1992-93 | Kingston | OHL | 64 | 19 | 55 | 74 | 117 | .... | .... | .... | .... | .... | .... | .... | .... | .... | 16 | 5 | 7 | 12 | 39 | .... | .... | .... | .... |
| 1993-94 | Kingston | OHL | 61 | 12 | 52 | 64 | 100 | .... | .... | .... | .... | .... | .... | .... | .... | .... | 6 | 0 | 3 | 3 | 6 | .... | .... | .... | .... |
| | Fredericton | AHL | 4 | 0 | 2 | 2 | 2 | .... | .... | .... | .... | .... | .... | .... | .... | .... | .... | .... | .... | .... | .... | .... | .... | .... | .... |
| **1994-95** | Fredericton | AHL | 78 | 5 | 27 | 32 | 126 | .... | .... | .... | .... | .... | .... | .... | .... | .... | 12 | 0 | 4 | 4 | 17 | .... | .... | .... | .... |
| | **Montreal** | **NHL** | **5** | **0** | **1** | **1** | **5** | **0** | **0** | **0** | **2** | **0.0** | **2** | .... | .... | .... | .... | .... | .... | .... | .... | .... | .... | .... | .... |
| **1995-96** | **Montreal** | **NHL** | **19** | **1** | **4** | **5** | **54** | **0** | **0** | **0** | **9** | **11.1** | **4** | .... | .... | .... | .... | .... | .... | .... | .... | .... | .... | .... | .... |
| | Fredericton | AHL | 49 | 5 | 18 | 23 | 189 | .... | .... | .... | .... | .... | .... | .... | .... | .... | 6 | 0 | 0 | 0 | 12 | .... | .... | .... | .... |
| **1996-97** | **Montreal** | **NHL** | **35** | **0** | **4** | **4** | **54** | **0** | **0** | **0** | **24** | **0.0** | **7** | .... | .... | .... | **5** | **0** | **1** | **1** | **14** | **0** | **0** | **0** | .... |
| | Fredericton | AHL | 23 | 3 | 12 | 15 | 99 | .... | .... | .... | .... | .... | .... | .... | .... | .... | .... | .... | .... | .... | .... | .... | .... | .... | .... |
| **1997-98** | **Montreal** | **NHL** | **61** | **0** | **2** | **2** | **93** | **0** | **0** | **0** | **26** | **0.0** | **–3** | .... | .... | .... | **5** | **0** | **0** | **0** | **2** | **0** | **0** | **0** | .... |
| **1998-99** | **Montreal** | **NHL** | **66** | **2** | **8** | **10** | **66** | **0** | **0** | **0** | **39** | **5.1** | **–3** | **0** | **0.0** | **14:20** | .... | .... | .... | .... | .... | .... | .... | .... | .... |
| **99-2000** | **Montreal** | **NHL** | **61** | **3** | **14** | **17** | **76** | **0** | **0** | **1** | **71** | **4.2** | **11** | **0** | **0.0** | **19:03** | .... | .... | .... | .... | .... | .... | .... | .... | .... |
| **2000-01** | **Montreal** | **NHL** | **26** | **1** | **2** | **3** | **36** | **0** | **0** | **0** | **22** | **4.5** | **–8** | **0** | **0.0** | **19:04** | .... | .... | .... | .... | .... | .... | .... | .... | .... |
| **2001-02** | **Montreal** | **NHL** | **82** | **8** | **17** | **25** | **76** | **0** | **0** | **0** | **90** | **8.9** | **1** | **1** | **0.0** | **19:00** | **12** | **0** | **3** | **3** | **4** | **0** | **0** | **0** | **21:26** |
| **2002-03** | **Montreal** | **NHL** | **82** | **7** | **15** | **22** | **71** | **3** | **0** | **2** | **118** | **5.9** | **1** | **0** | **0.0** | **22:00** | .... | .... | .... | .... | .... | .... | .... | .... | .... |
| **2003-04** | **Montreal** | **NHL** | **80** | **4** | **8** | **12** | **98** | **2** | **0** | **1** | **96** | **4.2** | **–1** | **0** | **0.0** | **19:28** | **11** | **1** | **4** | **5** | **2** | **1** | **0** | **0** | **24:07** |
| 2004-05 | TPS Turku | Finland | 18 | 3 | 1 | 4 | 28 | .... | .... | .... | .... | .... | .... | .... | .... | .... | 6 | 0 | 0 | 0 | 39 | .... | .... | .... | .... |

| Season | Club | League | GP | G | A | Pts | PIM | PP | SH | GW | S | % | +/- | TF | F% | Min | GP | G | A | Pts | PIM | PP | SH | GW | Min |
|---|---|---|---|---|---|---|---|---|---|---|---|---|---|---|---|---|---|---|---|---|---|---|---|---|---|
| | | | Regular Season | | | | | | | | | | | | | | Playoffs | | | | | | | | |
| 2005-06 | Montreal | NHL | 82 | 7 | 27 | 34 | 109 | 5 | 0 | 1 | 122 | 5.7 | –5 | 2 | 0.0 | 22:27 | 6 | 0 | 2 | 2 | 2 | 0 | 0 | 0 | 24:09 |
| 2006-07 | Montreal | NHL | 54 | 6 | 10 | 16 | 57 | 2 | 0 | 0 | 58 | 10.3 | –7 | 0 | 0.0 | 21:04 | .... | .... | .... | .... | .... | .... | .... | .... | .... |
| | San Jose | NHL | 17 | 1 | 7 | 8 | 12 | 0 | 0 | 0 | 31 | 3.2 | 8 | 0 | 0.0 | 23:31 | 11 | 2 | 3 | 5 | 18 | 1 | 0 | 0 | 25:18 |
| 2007-08 | San Jose | NHL | 74 | 5 | 30 | 35 | 104 | 2 | 0 | 0 | 105 | 4.8 | 3 | 0 | 0.0 | 21:12 | 13 | 0 | 6 | 6 | 16 | 0 | 0 | 0 | 23:01 |
| 2008-09 | Buffalo | NHL | 64 | 2 | 22 | 24 | 125 | 1 | 0 | 0 | 80 | 2.5 | 4 | 0 | 0.0 | 20:14 | .... | .... | .... | .... | .... | .... | .... | .... | .... |
| | NHL Totals | | 808 | 47 | 171 | 218 | 1036 | 15 | 0 | 5 | 893 | 5.3 | | 3 | 0.0 | 20:00 | 63 | 3 | 19 | 22 | 58 | 2 | 0 | 0 | 23:29 |

• Missed majority of 2000-01 season recovering from shoulder injury suffered in game vs. Vancouver, October 30, 2000. Signed as a free agent by **Turku** (Finland), January 11, 2005. Traded to **San Jose** by **Montreal** with Montreal's 5th round choice (Julien Demers) in 2008 Entry Draft for Josh Gorges and San Jose's 1st round choice (Max Pacioretty) in 2007 Entry Draft, February 25, 2007. Traded to **Buffalo** by **San Jose** with San Jose's 7th round choice in 2010 Entry Draft for Buffalo's 2nd round choices in 2009 (William Wrenn) and 2010 Entry Drafts, July 4, 2008.

## ROBERTS, Gary

(RAW-buhrts, GAIR-ree)

Left wing. Shoots left. 6'2", 215 lbs. Born, North York, Ont., May 23, 1966. Calgary's 1st choice, 12th overall, in 1984 Entry Draft.

| Season | Club | League | GP | G | A | Pts | PIM | PP | SH | GW | S | % | +/- | TF | F% | Min | GP | G | A | Pts | PIM | PP | SH | GW | Min |
|---|---|---|---|---|---|---|---|---|---|---|---|---|---|---|---|---|---|---|---|---|---|---|---|---|---|
| 1980-81 | Hamilton Kilty B's | OHA-B | 3 | 0 | 1 | 1 | 0 | .... | .... | .... | .... | .... | .... | .... | .... | .... | .... | .... | .... | .... | .... | .... | .... | .... | .... |
| 1981-82 | Whitby | Minor-ON | 44 | 55 | 31 | 86 | 133 | .... | .... | .... | .... | .... | .... | .... | .... | .... | .... | .... | .... | .... | .... | .... | .... | .... | .... |
| 1982-83 | Ottawa 67's | OHL | 53 | 12 | 8 | 20 | 83 | .... | .... | .... | .... | .... | .... | .... | .... | .... | 5 | 1 | 0 | 1 | 19 | .... | .... | .... | .... |
| 1983-84 | Ottawa 67's | OHL | 48 | 27 | 30 | 57 | 144 | .... | .... | .... | .... | .... | .... | .... | .... | .... | 13 | 10 | 7 | 17 | 62 | .... | .... | .... | .... |
| 1984-85 | Ottawa 67's | OHL | 59 | 44 | 62 | 106 | 186 | .... | .... | .... | .... | .... | .... | .... | .... | .... | 5 | 2 | 8 | 10 | 10 | .... | .... | .... | .... |
| | Moncton | AHL | 7 | 4 | 2 | 6 | 7 | .... | .... | .... | .... | .... | .... | .... | .... | .... | .... | .... | .... | .... | .... | .... | .... | .... | .... |
| 1985-86 | Ottawa 67's | OHL | 24 | 26 | 25 | 51 | 83 | .... | .... | .... | .... | .... | .... | .... | .... | .... | .... | .... | .... | .... | .... | .... | .... | .... | .... |
| | Guelph Platers | OHL | 23 | 18 | 15 | 33 | 65 | .... | .... | .... | .... | .... | .... | .... | .... | .... | 20 | 18 | 13 | 31 | 43 | .... | .... | .... | .... |
| 1986-87 | Calgary | NHL | 32 | 5 | 10 | 15 | 85 | 0 | 0 | 0 | 38 | 13.2 | 6 | .... | .... | .... | 2 | 0 | 0 | 0 | 4 | 0 | 0 | 0 | .... |
| | Moncton | AHL | 38 | 20 | 18 | 38 | 72 | .... | .... | .... | .... | .... | .... | .... | .... | .... | .... | .... | .... | .... | .... | .... | .... | .... | .... |
| 1987-88 | Calgary | NHL | 74 | 13 | 15 | 28 | 282 | 0 | 0 | 1 | 118 | 11.0 | 24 | .... | .... | .... | 9 | 2 | 3 | 5 | 29 | 0 | 0 | 0 | .... |
| 1988-89 ♦ | Calgary | NHL | 71 | 22 | 16 | 38 | 250 | 0 | 1 | 2 | 123 | 17.9 | 32 | .... | .... | .... | 22 | 5 | 7 | 12 | 57 | 0 | 0 | 0 | .... |
| 1989-90 | Calgary | NHL | 78 | 39 | 33 | 72 | 222 | 5 | 0 | 5 | 175 | 22.3 | 31 | .... | .... | .... | 6 | 2 | 5 | 7 | 41 | 0 | 0 | 0 | .... |
| 1990-91 | Calgary | NHL | 80 | 22 | 31 | 53 | 252 | 0 | 0 | 3 | 132 | 16.7 | 15 | .... | .... | .... | 7 | 1 | 3 | 4 | 18 | 0 | 0 | 0 | .... |
| 1991-92 | Calgary | NHL | 76 | 53 | 37 | 90 | 207 | 15 | 0 | 2 | 196 | 27.0 | 32 | .... | .... | .... | .... | .... | .... | .... | .... | .... | .... | .... | .... |
| 1992-93 | Calgary | NHL | 58 | 38 | 41 | 79 | 172 | 8 | 3 | 4 | 166 | 22.9 | 32 | .... | .... | .... | 5 | 1 | 6 | 7 | 43 | 1 | 0 | 0 | .... |
| 1993-94 | Calgary | NHL | 73 | 41 | 43 | 84 | 145 | 12 | 3 | 5 | 202 | 20.3 | 37 | .... | .... | .... | 7 | 2 | 6 | 8 | 24 | 1 | 0 | 1 | .... |
| 1994-95 | Calgary | NHL | 8 | 2 | 2 | 4 | 43 | 2 | 0 | 0 | 20 | 10.0 | 1 | .... | .... | .... | .... | .... | .... | .... | .... | .... | .... | .... | .... |
| 1995-96 | Calgary | NHL | 35 | 22 | 20 | 42 | 78 | 9 | 0 | 5 | 84 | 26.2 | 15 | .... | .... | .... | .... | .... | .... | .... | .... | .... | .... | .... | .... |
| 1996-97 | Calgary | NHL | DID NOT PLAY – INJURED | | | | | | | | | | | | | | | | | | | | | | |
| 1997-98 | Carolina | NHL | 61 | 20 | 29 | 49 | 103 | 4 | 0 | 2 | 106 | 18.9 | 3 | .... | .... | .... | .... | .... | .... | .... | .... | .... | .... | .... | .... |
| 1998-99 | Carolina | NHL | 77 | 14 | 28 | 42 | 178 | 1 | 1 | 4 | 138 | 10.1 | 2 | 15 | 46.7 | 19:36 | 6 | 1 | 1 | 2 | 8 | 0 | 0 | 0 | 21:01 |
| 99-2000 | Carolina | NHL | 69 | 23 | 30 | 53 | 62 | 12 | 0 | 1 | 150 | 15.3 | –10 | 7 | 28.6 | 18:31 | .... | .... | .... | .... | .... | .... | .... | .... | .... |
| 2000-01 | Toronto | NHL | 82 | 29 | 24 | 53 | 109 | 8 | 2 | 3 | 138 | 21.0 | 16 | 13 | 46.2 | 17:08 | 11 | 2 | 9 | 11 | 0 | 0 | 0 | 0 | 19:49 |
| 2001-02 | Toronto | NHL | 69 | 21 | 27 | 48 | 63 | 6 | 2 | 2 | 122 | 17.2 | –4 | 6 | 33.3 | 17:23 | 19 | 7 | 12 | 19 | 56 | 3 | 0 | 1 | 19:28 |
| 2002-03 | Toronto | NHL | 14 | 5 | 3 | 8 | 10 | 3 | 0 | 0 | 22 | 22.7 | –2 | 4 | 50.0 | 15:35 | 7 | 1 | 1 | 2 | 8 | 0 | 0 | 0 | 21:04 |
| 2003-04 | Toronto | NHL | 72 | 28 | 20 | 48 | 84 | 11 | 1 | 7 | 124 | 22.6 | 9 | 12 | 33.3 | 17:33 | 13 | 4 | 4 | 8 | 10 | 2 | 0 | 1 | 17:45 |
| 2004-05 | | | DID NOT PLAY | | | | | | | | | | | | | | | | | | | | | | |
| 2005-06 | Florida | NHL | 58 | 14 | 26 | 40 | 51 | 4 | 0 | 1 | 122 | 11.5 | 4 | 19 | 31.6 | 16:45 | .... | .... | .... | .... | .... | .... | .... | .... | .... |
| 2006-07 | Florida | NHL | 50 | 13 | 16 | 29 | 71 | 2 | 0 | 3 | 94 | 13.8 | 5 | 28 | 60.7 | 17:05 | .... | .... | .... | .... | .... | .... | .... | .... | .... |
| | Pittsburgh | NHL | 19 | 7 | 6 | 13 | 26 | 4 | 0 | 1 | 31 | 22.6 | –5 | 3 | 66.7 | 15:47 | 5 | 2 | 2 | 4 | 2 | 1 | 0 | 0 | 17:07 |
| 2007-08 | Pittsburgh | NHL | 38 | 3 | 12 | 15 | 40 | 1 | 0 | 0 | 41 | 7.3 | –3 | 7 | 71.4 | 13:20 | 11 | 2 | 2 | 4 | 32 | 1 | 0 | 1 | 10:16 |
| 2008-09 | Tampa Bay | NHL | 30 | 4 | 3 | 7 | 27 | 2 | 0 | 1 | 32 | 12.5 | –11 | 2 | 50.0 | 11:39 | .... | .... | .... | .... | .... | .... | .... | .... | .... |
| | NHL Totals | | 1224 | 438 | 472 | 910 | 2560 | 109 | 13 | 52 | 2374 | 18.4 | | 116 | 46.6 | 17:03 | 130 | 32 | 61 | 93 | 332 | 9 | 0 | 4 | 17:55 |

OHL Second All-Star Team (1985, 1986) • Bill Masterton Memorial Trophy (1996)

Played in NHL All-Star Game (1992, 1993, 2004)

• Missed remainder of 1994-95 season and majority of 1995-96 season recovering from neck injury suffered in game vs. Toronto, February 4, 1995. • Missed remainder of 1995-96 season and entire 1996-97 season recovering from neck injury suffered in game vs. Vancouver, April 3, 1996. Traded to **Carolina** by **Calgary** with Trevor Kidd for Andrew Cassels and Jean-Sebastien Giguere, August 25, 1997. Signed as a free agent by **Toronto**, July 4, 2000. • Missed majority of 2002-03 season recovering from off-season shoulder surgery, August 13, 2002. Signed as a free agent by **Florida**, August 1, 2005. Traded to **Pittsburgh** by **Florida** for Noah Welch, February 27, 2007. • Rights traded to **Tampa Bay** by **Pittsburgh** with Ryan Malone for Tampa Bay's 3rd round choice (Ben Hanowski) in 2009 Entry Draft, June 28, 2008. • Officially announced his retirement, March 10, 2009.

## ROBIDAS, Stephane

(ROH-bih-dah, STEH-fan) **DAL.**

Defense. Shoots right. 5'11", 190 lbs. Born, Sherbrooke, Que., March 3, 1977. Montreal's 7th choice, 164th overall, in 1995 Entry Draft.

| Season | Club | League | GP | G | A | Pts | PIM | PP | SH | GW | S | % | +/- | TF | F% | Min | GP | G | A | Pts | PIM | PP | SH | GW | Min |
|---|---|---|---|---|---|---|---|---|---|---|---|---|---|---|---|---|---|---|---|---|---|---|---|---|---|
| 1992-93 | Magog | QAAA | 41 | 3 | 12 | 15 | 16 | .... | .... | .... | .... | .... | .... | .... | .... | .... | 5 | 1 | 1 | 2 | 2 | .... | .... | .... | .... |
| 1993-94 | Shawinigan | QMJHL | 67 | 3 | 18 | 21 | 33 | .... | .... | .... | .... | .... | .... | .... | .... | .... | 1 | 0 | 0 | 0 | 0 | .... | .... | .... | .... |
| 1994-95 | Shawinigan | QMJHL | 71 | 13 | 56 | 69 | 44 | .... | .... | .... | .... | .... | .... | .... | .... | .... | 15 | 7 | 12 | 19 | 4 | .... | .... | .... | .... |
| 1995-96 | Shawinigan | QMJHL | 67 | 23 | 56 | 79 | 53 | .... | .... | .... | .... | .... | .... | .... | .... | .... | 6 | 1 | 5 | 6 | 10 | .... | .... | .... | .... |
| 1996-97 | Shawinigan | QMJHL | 67 | 24 | 51 | 75 | 59 | .... | .... | .... | .... | .... | .... | .... | .... | .... | 7 | 4 | 6 | 10 | 14 | .... | .... | .... | .... |
| 1997-98 | Fredericton | AHL | 79 | 10 | 21 | 31 | 50 | .... | .... | .... | .... | .... | .... | .... | .... | .... | 4 | 0 | 2 | 2 | 0 | .... | .... | .... | .... |
| 1998-99 | Fredericton | AHL | 79 | 8 | 33 | 41 | 59 | .... | .... | .... | .... | .... | .... | .... | .... | .... | 15 | 1 | 5 | 6 | 10 | .... | .... | .... | .... |
| 99-2000 | Montreal | NHL | 1 | 0 | 0 | 0 | 0 | 0 | 0 | 0 | 0 | 0.0 | 0 | 0 | 0.0 | 15:54 | .... | .... | .... | .... | .... | .... | .... | .... | .... |
| | Quebec Citadelles | AHL | 76 | 14 | 31 | 45 | 36 | .... | .... | .... | .... | .... | .... | .... | .... | .... | 3 | 0 | 1 | 1 | 0 | .... | .... | .... | .... |
| 2000-01 | Montreal | NHL | 65 | 6 | 6 | 12 | 14 | 1 | 0 | 0 | 77 | 7.8 | 0 | 1 | 100.0 | 20:44 | .... | .... | .... | .... | .... | .... | .... | .... | .... |
| 2001-02 | Montreal | NHL | 56 | 1 | 10 | 11 | 14 | 1 | 0 | 0 | 68 | 1.5 | –25 | 3 | 33.3 | 18:58 | 2 | 0 | 0 | 0 | 4 | 0 | 0 | 0 | 13:07 |
| 2002-03 | Dallas | NHL | 76 | 3 | 7 | 10 | 35 | 0 | 0 | 1 | 47 | 6.4 | 15 | 1 | 100.0 | 12:54 | 12 | 0 | 1 | 1 | 20 | 0 | 0 | 0 | 13:54 |
| 2003-04 | Dallas | NHL | 14 | 1 | 0 | 1 | 8 | 1 | 0 | 0 | 8 | 12.5 | –2 | 1 | 100.0 | 12:57 | .... | .... | .... | .... | .... | .... | .... | .... | .... |
| | Chicago | NHL | 45 | 2 | 10 | 12 | 33 | 0 | 1 | 1 | 55 | 3.6 | 6 | 0 | 0.0 | 20:56 | .... | .... | .... | .... | .... | .... | .... | .... | .... |
| 2004-05 | Frankfurt Lions | Germany | 51 | 15 | 32 | 47 | 64 | .... | .... | .... | .... | .... | .... | .... | .... | .... | 6 | 1 | 2 | 3 | 6 | .... | .... | .... | .... |
| 2005-06 | Dallas | NHL | 75 | 5 | 15 | 20 | 67 | 1 | 1 | 0 | 95 | 5.3 | 15 | 0 | 0.0 | 16:59 | 5 | 0 | 2 | 2 | 4 | 0 | 0 | 0 | 16:42 |
| 2006-07 | Dallas | NHL | 75 | 0 | 17 | 17 | 86 | 0 | 0 | 0 | 106 | 0.0 | –1 | 0 | 0.0 | 18:04 | 7 | 0 | 1 | 1 | 2 | 0 | 0 | 0 | 19:02 |
| 2007-08 | Dallas | NHL | 82 | 9 | 17 | 26 | 85 | 7 | 0 | 2 | 153 | 5.9 | 0 | 0 | 0.0 | 20:39 | 18 | 3 | 8 | 11 | 12 | 3 | 0 | 0 | 25:31 |
| 2008-09 | Dallas | NHL | 72 | 3 | 23 | 26 | 76 | 1 | 0 | 0 | 158 | 1.9 | 10 | 1 | 100.0 | 24:32 | .... | .... | .... | .... | .... | .... | .... | .... | .... |
| | NHL Totals | | 561 | 30 | 105 | 135 | 418 | 12 | 2 | 4 | 767 | 3.9 | | 7 | 71.4 | 18:56 | 44 | 3 | 12 | 15 | 42 | 3 | 0 | 0 | 19:45 |

QMJHL First All-Star Team (1996, 1997)

Played in NHL All-Star Game (2009)

Claimed by **Atlanta** from **Montreal** in Waiver Draft, October 4, 2002. Traded to **Dallas** by **Atlanta** for future considerations, October 4, 2002. Traded to **Chicago** by **Dallas** with Dallas' 2nd round choice (Jakub Sindel) in 2004 Entry Draft for Jon Klemm and NY Rangers' 4th round choice (previously acquired, Dallas selected Fredrik Naslund) in 2004 Entry Draft, November 17, 2003. Signed as a free agent by **Frankfurt** (Germany), September 17, 2004. Signed as a free agent by **Dallas**, August 6, 2005.

## ROBITAILLE, Randy

(ROH-buh-tigh, RAN-dee)

Center. Shoots left. 5'11", 200 lbs. Born, Ottawa, Ont., October 12, 1975.

| Season | Club | League | GP | G | A | Pts | PIM | PP | SH | GW | S | % | +/- | TF | F% | Min | GP | G | A | Pts | PIM | PP | SH | GW | Min |
|---|---|---|---|---|---|---|---|---|---|---|---|---|---|---|---|---|---|---|---|---|---|---|---|---|---|
| 1993-94 | Ott. Jr. Senators | CJHL | 57 | 33 | 55 | 88 | 31 | .... | .... | .... | .... | .... | .... | .... | .... | .... | .... | .... | .... | .... | .... | .... | .... | .... | .... |
| 1994-95 | Ott. Jr. Senators | CJHL | 54 | 48 | 77 | *125 | 111 | .... | .... | .... | .... | .... | .... | .... | .... | .... | .... | .... | .... | .... | .... | .... | .... | .... | .... |
| 1995-96 | Miami U. | CCHA | 36 | 14 | 31 | 45 | 26 | .... | .... | .... | .... | .... | .... | .... | .... | .... | .... | .... | .... | .... | .... | .... | .... | .... | .... |
| 1996-97 | Miami U. | CCHA | 39 | 27 | 34 | 61 | 44 | .... | .... | .... | .... | .... | .... | .... | .... | .... | .... | .... | .... | .... | .... | .... | .... | .... | .... |
| | Boston | NHL | 1 | 0 | 0 | 0 | 0 | 0 | 0 | 0 | 0 | 0.0 | 0 | .... | .... | .... | .... | .... | .... | .... | .... | .... | .... | .... | .... |
| 1997-98 | Boston | NHL | 4 | 0 | 0 | 0 | 0 | 0 | 0 | 0 | 5 | 0.0 | –2 | .... | .... | .... | .... | .... | .... | .... | .... | .... | .... | .... | .... |
| | Providence Bruins | AHL | 48 | 15 | 29 | 44 | 16 | .... | .... | .... | .... | .... | .... | .... | .... | .... | .... | .... | .... | .... | .... | .... | .... | .... | .... |
| 1998-99 | Boston | NHL | 4 | 0 | 2 | 2 | 0 | 0 | 0 | 0 | 5 | 0.0 | –1 | 24 | 25.0 | 10:11 | 1 | 0 | 0 | 0 | 0 | 0 | 0 | 0 | 7:14 |
| | Providence Bruins | AHL | 74 | 28 | *74 | 102 | 34 | .... | .... | .... | .... | .... | .... | .... | .... | .... | 19 | 6 | *14 | 20 | 20 | .... | .... | .... | .... |
| 99-2000 | Nashville | NHL | 69 | 11 | 14 | 25 | 10 | 2 | 0 | 1 | 113 | 9.7 | –13 | 528 | 51.5 | 12:52 | .... | .... | .... | .... | .... | .... | .... | .... | .... |
| 2000-01 | Nashville | NHL | 62 | 9 | 17 | 26 | 12 | 5 | 0 | 0 | 121 | 7.4 | –11 | 481 | 48.4 | 14:10 | .... | .... | .... | .... | .... | .... | .... | .... | .... |
| | Milwaukee | IHL | 19 | 10 | 23 | 33 | 4 | .... | .... | .... | .... | .... | .... | .... | .... | .... | .... | .... | .... | .... | .... | .... | .... | .... | .... |
| 2001-02 | Los Angeles | NHL | 18 | 4 | 3 | 7 | 17 | 2 | 0 | 0 | 30 | 13.3 | –9 | 60 | 65.0 | 12:54 | .... | .... | .... | .... | .... | .... | .... | .... | .... |
| | Manchester | AHL | 6 | 7 | 3 | 10 | 0 | .... | .... | .... | .... | .... | .... | .... | .... | .... | .... | .... | .... | .... | .... | .... | .... | .... | .... |
| | Pittsburgh | NHL | 40 | 10 | 20 | 30 | 16 | 3 | 0 | 1 | 91 | 11.0 | –14 | 599 | 51.4 | 18:08 | .... | .... | .... | .... | .... | .... | .... | .... | .... |
| 2002-03 | Pittsburgh | NHL | 41 | 5 | 12 | 17 | 8 | 1 | 0 | 2 | 61 | 8.2 | 5 | 429 | 55.9 | 13:58 | .... | .... | .... | .... | .... | .... | .... | .... | .... |
| | NY Islanders | NHL | 10 | 1 | 2 | 3 | 2 | 1 | 0 | 0 | 8 | 12.5 | 0 | 68 | 48.5 | 12:28 | 5 | 1 | 1 | 2 | 0 | 1 | 0 | 0 | 13:03 |
| 2003-04 | Atlanta | NHL | 69 | 11 | 26 | 37 | 20 | 5 | 0 | 2 | 121 | 9.1 | –12 | 1069 | 50.2 | 15:51 | .... | .... | .... | .... | .... | .... | .... | .... | .... |
| 2004-05 | ZSC Lions Zurich | Swiss | 36 | 22 | *45 | *67 | 56 | .... | .... | .... | .... | .... | .... | .... | .... | .... | 15 | 2 | 16 | 18 | 10 | .... | .... | .... | .... |
| 2005-06 | Minnesota | NHL | 67 | 12 | 28 | 40 | 54 | 7 | 0 | 2 | 112 | 10.7 | –5 | 381 | 51.4 | 14:44 | .... | .... | .... | .... | .... | .... | .... | .... | .... |
| 2006-07 | Philadelphia | NHL | 28 | 5 | 12 | 17 | 22 | 2 | 0 | 0 | 46 | 10.9 | –4 | 280 | 53.6 | 14:34 | .... | .... | .... | .... | .... | .... | .... | .... | .... |
| | NY Islanders | NHL | 50 | 6 | 17 | 23 | 22 | 1 | 0 | 1 | 74 | 8.1 | –2 | 519 | 53.2 | 13:54 | 5 | 0 | 2 | 2 | 8 | 0 | 0 | 0 | 14:12 |

| | | | Regular Season | | | | | | | | | | | | | | Playoffs | | | | | | | | |
|---|---|---|---|---|---|---|---|---|---|---|---|---|---|---|---|---|---|---|---|---|---|---|---|---|---|
| Season | Club | League | GP | G | A | Pts | PIM | PP | SH | GW | S | % | +/- | TF | F% | Min | GP | G | A | Pts | PIM | PP | SH | GW | Min |
| **2007-08** | Yaroslavl | Russia | 14 | 3 | 5 | 8 | 10 | | | | | | | | | | | | | | | | | | |
| | **Ottawa** | **NHL** | **68** | **10** | **19** | **29** | **18** | **1** | **0** | **1** | **99** | **10.1** | **4** | **142** | **57.8** | **13:34** | **2** | **0** | **1** | **1** | **0** | **0** | **0** | **0** | **11:33** |
| 2008-09 | HC Lugano | Swiss | 30 | 1 | 27 | 28 | 10 | | | | | | | | | | 7 | 2 | 2 | 4 | 22 | | | | |
| | **NHL Totals** | | **531** | **84** | **172** | **256** | **201** | **30** | **0** | **10** | **886** | **9.5** | | **4580** | **51.8** | **14:23** | **13** | **1** | **4** | **5** | **8** | **1** | **0** | **0** | **12:49** |

CCHA First All-Star Team (1997) • NCAA West First All-American Team (1997) • AHL First All-Star Team (1999) • Les Cunningham Award (AHL – MVP) (1999)

Signed as a free agent by **Boston**, March 27, 1997. Traded to **Atlanta** by **Boston** for Peter Ferraro, June 25, 1999. Traded to **Nashville** by **Atlanta** for Denny Lambert, August 16, 1999. Signed as a free agent by **Los Angeles**, July 6, 2001. Claimed on waivers by **Pittsburgh** from **Los Angeles**, January 4, 2002. Traded to **NY Islanders** by **Pittsburgh** for Philadelphia's 5th round choice (previously acquired, Pittsburgh selected Evgeni Isakov) in 2003 Entry Draft, March 9, 2003. Signed as a free agent by **Atlanta**, August 12, 2003. Signed as a free agent by **Zurich** (Swiss), April 26, 2004. Signed as a free agent by **Nashville**, August 19, 2005. Claimed on waivers by **Minnesota** from **Nashville**, October 4, 2005. Signed as a free agent by **Philadelphia**, July 4, 2006. Traded to **NY Islanders** by **Philadelphia** with Philadelphia's 5th round choice (Matthew Martin) in 2008 Entry Draft for Mike York, December 20, 2006. Signed as a free agent by **Yaroslavl** (Russia), May 18, 2007. Signed as a free agent by **Ottawa**, October 16, 2007.

## ROCHE, Travis

(ROHSH, TRA-vihs)

Defense. Shoots right. 6'1", 200 lbs. Born, Grand Cache, Alta., June 17, 1978.

| Season | Club | League | GP | G | A | Pts | PIM | PP | SH | GW | S | % | +/- | TF | F% | Min | GP | G | A | Pts | PIM | PP | SH | GW | Min |
|---|---|---|---|---|---|---|---|---|---|---|---|---|---|---|---|---|---|---|---|---|---|---|---|---|---|
| 1996-97 | Trail | BCHL | 49 | 17 | 40 | 57 | 159 | | | | | | | | | | | | | | | | | | |
| 1997-98 | Trail | BCHL | 38 | 11 | 31 | 42 | 104 | | | | | | | | | | 11 | 0 | 8 | 8 | 21 | | | | |
| 1998-99 | North Dakota | WCHA | DID NOT PLAY – FRESHMAN | | | | | | | | | | | | | | | | | | | | | | |
| 99-2000 | North Dakota | WCHA | 42 | 6 | 22 | 28 | 60 | | | | | | | | | | | | | | | | | | |
| **2000-01** | North Dakota | WCHA | 42 | 11 | 38 | 49 | 42 | | | | | | | | | | | | | | | | | | |
| | **Minnesota** | **NHL** | **1** | **0** | **0** | **0** | **0** | **0** | **0** | **0** | **0** | **0.0** | **0** | **0** | **0.0** | **15:22** | | | | | | | | | |
| **2001-02** | **Minnesota** | **NHL** | **4** | **0** | **0** | **0** | **2** | **0** | **0** | **0** | **1** | **0.0** | **–1** | **0** | **0.0** | **12:30** | | | | | | | | | |
| | Houston Aeros | AHL | 60 | 13 | 21 | 34 | 107 | | | | | | | | | | 12 | 2 | 3 | 5 | 6 | | | | |
| 2002-03 | Houston Aeros | AHL | 65 | 14 | 34 | 48 | 42 | | | | | | | | | | 23 | 3 | 5 | 8 | 26 | | | | |
| **2003-04** | **Minnesota** | **NHL** | **5** | **0** | **1** | **1** | **0** | **0** | **0** | **0** | **5** | **0.0** | **–3** | **0** | **0.0** | **16:07** | | | | | | | | | |
| | Houston Aeros | AHL | 60 | 8 | 30 | 38 | 18 | | | | | | | | | | 2 | 0 | 0 | 0 | 2 | | | | |
| 2004-05 | Chicago Wolves | AHL | 73 | 12 | 38 | 50 | 59 | | | | | | | | | | 18 | 1 | 6 | 7 | 18 | | | | |
| 2005-06 | Chicago Wolves | AHL | 59 | 8 | 31 | 39 | 73 | | | | | | | | | | | | | | | | | | |
| **2006-07** | **Phoenix** | **NHL** | **50** | **6** | **13** | **19** | **22** | **2** | **0** | **1** | **32** | **18.8** | **2** | **0** | **0.0** | **17:01** | | | | | | | | | |
| | San Antonio | AHL | 17 | 1 | 8 | 9 | 16 | | | | | | | | | | | | | | | | | | |
| 2007-08 | San Antonio | AHL | 71 | 6 | 35 | 41 | 65 | | | | | | | | | | 5 | 0 | 2 | 2 | 8 | | | | |
| 2008-09 | SC Bern | Swiss | 49 | 16 | 31 | 47 | 113 | | | | | | | | | | 4 | 0 | 3 | 3 | 6 | | | | |
| | **NHL Totals** | | **60** | **6** | **14** | **20** | **24** | **2** | **0** | **1** | **38** | **15.8** | | **0** | **0.0** | **16:37** | | | | | | | | | |

BCHL Second All-Star Team (1997) • BCHL Rookie of the Year Award (1997) • BCHL Playoff MVP Award (1997) • BCHL First All-Star Team (1998) • BCHL Best Defenseman Award (1998) • WCHA All-Rookie Team (2000) • WCHA First All-Star Team (2001) • NCAA West First All-American Team (2001) • NCAA Championship All-Tournament Team (2001) • Yanick Dupre Memorial Award (AHL - Outstanding Humanitarian Contribution) (2002) • AHL First All-Star Team (2005)

Signed as a free agent by **Minnesota**, April 8, 2001. Signed as a free agent by **Atlanta**, July 14, 2004. Signed as a free agent by **Phoenix**, July 20, 2006.

## RODNEY, Bryan

(ROHD-nee, BRIGH-uhn) **CAR.**

Defense. Shoots right. 6', 195 lbs. Born, London, Ont., April 22, 1984.

| Season | Club | League | GP | G | A | Pts | PIM | PP | SH | GW | S | % | +/- | TF | F% | Min | GP | G | A | Pts | PIM | PP | SH | GW | Min |
|---|---|---|---|---|---|---|---|---|---|---|---|---|---|---|---|---|---|---|---|---|---|---|---|---|---|
| 2000-01 | Ottawa 67's | OHL | 65 | 0 | 15 | 15 | 26 | | | | | | | | | | 20 | 1 | 4 | 5 | 20 | | | | |
| 2001-02 | Ottawa 67's | OHL | 30 | 3 | 8 | 11 | 14 | | | | | | | | | | | | | | | | | | |
| | Kingston | OHL | 18 | 2 | 8 | 10 | 8 | | | | | | | | | | 1 | 0 | 0 | 0 | 0 | | | | |
| 2002-03 | Kingston | OHL | 67 | 8 | 52 | 60 | 60 | | | | | | | | | | | | | | | | | | |
| 2003-04 | Kingston | OHL | 67 | 11 | 65 | 76 | 68 | | | | | | | | | | 5 | 1 | 4 | 5 | 8 | | | | |
| 2004-05 | London Knights | OHL | 64 | 23 | 39 | 62 | 48 | | | | | | | | | | 12 | 5 | 10 | 15 | 20 | | | | |
| 2005-06 | Hartford | AHL | 8 | 1 | 2 | 3 | 0 | | | | | | | | | | | | | | | | | | |
| | Charlotte | ECHL | 59 | 4 | 21 | 25 | 47 | | | | | | | | | | 3 | 0 | 1 | 1 | 0 | | | | |
| 2006-07 | Charlotte | ECHL | 31 | 2 | 19 | 21 | 14 | | | | | | | | | | | | | | | | | | |
| | Columbia Inferno | ECHL | 14 | 2 | 9 | 11 | 12 | | | | | | | | | | | | | | | | | | |
| 2007-08 | Albany River Rats | AHL | 42 | 4 | 11 | 15 | 22 | | | | | | | | | | 7 | 3 | 3 | 6 | 2 | | | | |
| | Columbia Inferno | ECHL | 17 | 2 | 9 | 11 | 10 | | | | | | | | | | | | | | | | | | |
| | Elmira Jackals | ECHL | 6 | 5 | 5 | 10 | 2 | | | | | | | | | | | | | | | | | | |
| **2008-09** | **Carolina** | **NHL** | **8** | **0** | **2** | **2** | **2** | **0** | **0** | **0** | **3** | **0.0** | **–3** | **0** | **0.0** | **12:38** | | | | | | | | | |
| | Albany River Rats | AHL | 58 | 3 | 33 | 36 | 28 | | | | | | | | | | | | | | | | | | |
| | **NHL Totals** | | **8** | **0** | **2** | **2** | **2** | **0** | **0** | **0** | **3** | **0.0** | | **0** | **0.0** | **12:38** | | | | | | | | | |

Signed as a free agent by **Charlotte** (ECHL), October 21, 2005. Signed as a free agent by **Albany** (AHL), December 16, 2007. Signed as a free agent by **Carolina**, May 12, 2008.

## ROENICK, Jeremy

(ROH-nihk, JAIR-eh-mee)

Center. Shoots right. 6'1", 205 lbs. Born, Boston, MA, January 17, 1970. Chicago's 1st choice, 8th overall, in 1988 Entry Draft.

| Season | Club | League | GP | G | A | Pts | PIM | PP | SH | GW | S | % | +/- | TF | F% | Min | GP | G | A | Pts | PIM | PP | SH | GW | Min |
|---|---|---|---|---|---|---|---|---|---|---|---|---|---|---|---|---|---|---|---|---|---|---|---|---|---|
| 1986-87 | Thayer Academy | High-MA | 24 | 31 | 34 | 65 | | | | | | | | | | | | | | | | | | | |
| 1987-88 | Thayer Academy | High-MA | 24 | 34 | 50 | 84 | | | | | | | | | | | | | | | | | | | |
| **1988-89** | Hull Olympiques | QMJHL | 28 | 34 | 36 | 70 | 14 | | | | | | | | | | | | | | | | | | |
| | **Chicago** | **NHL** | **20** | **9** | **9** | **18** | **4** | **2** | **0** | **0** | **52** | **17.3** | **4** | | | | **10** | **1** | **3** | **4** | **7** | **1** | **0** | **1** | |
| **1989-90** | **Chicago** | **NHL** | **78** | **26** | **40** | **66** | **54** | **6** | **0** | **4** | **173** | **15.0** | **2** | | | | **20** | **11** | **7** | **18** | **8** | **4** | **0** | **1** | |
| **1990-91** | **Chicago** | **NHL** | **79** | **41** | **53** | **94** | **80** | **15** | **4** | **10** | **194** | **21.1** | **38** | | | | **6** | **3** | **5** | **8** | **4** | **1** | **0** | **1** | |
| **1991-92** | **Chicago** | **NHL** | **80** | **53** | **50** | **103** | **98** | **22** | **3** | **13** | **234** | **22.6** | **23** | | | | **18** | **12** | **10** | **22** | **12** | **4** | **0** | **3** | |
| **1992-93** | **Chicago** | **NHL** | **84** | **50** | **57** | **107** | **86** | **22** | **3** | **3** | **255** | **19.6** | **15** | | | | **4** | **1** | **2** | **3** | **2** | **0** | **0** | **0** | |
| **1993-94** | **Chicago** | **NHL** | **84** | **46** | **61** | **107** | **125** | **24** | **5** | **5** | **281** | **16.4** | **21** | | | | **6** | **1** | **6** | **7** | **2** | **0** | **0** | **1** | |
| **1994-95** | Kolner Haie | Germany | 3 | 3 | 1 | 4 | 2 | | | | | | | | | | | | | | | | | | |
| | **Chicago** | **NHL** | **33** | **10** | **24** | **34** | **14** | **5** | **0** | **1** | **93** | **10.8** | **5** | | | | **8** | **1** | **2** | **3** | **16** | **0** | **0** | **0** | |
| **1995-96** | **Chicago** | **NHL** | **66** | **32** | **35** | **67** | **109** | **12** | **4** | **2** | **171** | **18.7** | **9** | | | | **10** | **5** | **7** | **12** | **2** | **1** | **0** | **1** | |
| **1996-97** | **Phoenix** | **NHL** | **72** | **29** | **40** | **69** | **115** | **10** | **3** | **7** | **228** | **12.7** | **–7** | | | | **6** | **2** | **4** | **6** | **4** | **0** | **0** | **0** | |
| **1997-98** | **Phoenix** | **NHL** | **79** | **24** | **32** | **56** | **103** | **6** | **1** | **3** | **182** | **13.2** | **5** | | | | **6** | **5** | **3** | **8** | **4** | **2** | **2** | **2** | |
| | United States | Olympics | 4 | 0 | 1 | 1 | 6 | | | | | | | | | | | | | | | | | | |
| **1998-99** | **Phoenix** | **NHL** | **78** | **24** | **48** | **72** | **130** | **4** | **0** | **3** | **203** | **11.8** | **7** | **956** | **47.6** | **20:10** | **1** | **0** | **0** | **0** | **0** | **0** | **0** | **0** | **26:55** |
| **99-2000** | **Phoenix** | **NHL** | **75** | **34** | **44** | **78** | **102** | **6** | **3** | **12** | **192** | **17.7** | **11** | **925** | **50.1** | **20:51** | **5** | **2** | **2** | **4** | **10** | **1** | **0** | **0** | **19:46** |
| **2000-01** | **Phoenix** | **NHL** | **80** | **30** | **46** | **76** | **114** | **13** | **0** | **7** | **192** | **15.6** | **–1** | **888** | **49.1** | **21:00** | | | | | | | | | |
| **2001-02** | **Philadelphia** | **NHL** | **75** | **21** | **46** | **67** | **74** | **5** | **0** | **3** | **167** | **12.6** | **32** | **1329** | **49.1** | **18:14** | **5** | **0** | **0** | **0** | **14** | **0** | **0** | **0** | **18:41** |
| | United States | Olympics | 6 | 1 | 4 | 5 | 2 | | | | | | | | | | | | | | | | | | |
| **2002-03** | **Philadelphia** | **NHL** | **79** | **27** | **32** | **59** | **75** | **8** | **1** | **6** | **197** | **13.7** | **20** | **1088** | **53.0** | **18:48** | **13** | **3** | **5** | **8** | **8** | **0** | **0** | **1** | **21:07** |
| **2003-04** | **Philadelphia** | **NHL** | **62** | **19** | **28** | **47** | **62** | **10** | **1** | **1** | **128** | **14.8** | **1** | **846** | **51.5** | **17:37** | **18** | **4** | **9** | **13** | **8** | **2** | **0** | **1** | **18:05** |
| 2004-05 | | | DID NOT PLAY | | | | | | | | | | | | | | | | | | | | | | |
| **2005-06** | **Los Angeles** | **NHL** | **58** | **9** | **13** | **22** | **36** | **2** | **0** | **1** | **111** | **8.1** | **–5** | **536** | **49.4** | **17:22** | | | | | | | | | |
| **2006-07** | **Phoenix** | **NHL** | **70** | **11** | **17** | **28** | **32** | **4** | **0** | **1** | **89** | **12.4** | **–18** | **595** | **51.4** | **13:54** | | | | | | | | | |
| **2007-08** | **San Jose** | **NHL** | **69** | **14** | **19** | **33** | **26** | **7** | **0** | **10** | **89** | **15.7** | **–8** | **188** | **44.2** | **13:45** | **12** | **2** | **3** | **5** | **2** | **1** | **0** | **0** | **14:30** |
| **2008-09** | **San Jose** | **NHL** | **42** | **4** | **9** | **13** | **24** | **1** | **0** | **0** | **50** | **8.0** | **–1** | **232** | **47.0** | **11:39** | **6** | **0** | **1** | **1** | **12** | **0** | **0** | **0** | **12:14** |
| | **NHL Totals** | | **1363** | **513** | **703** | **1216** | **1463** | **184** | **28** | **92** | **3281** | **15.6** | | **7583** | **49.9** | **17:42** | **154** | **53** | **69** | **122** | **115** | **17** | **2** | **12** | **17:46** |

QMJHL Second All-Star Team (1989)

Played in NHL All-Star Game (1991, 1992, 1993, 1994, 1999, 2000, 2002, 2003, 2004)

Traded to **Phoenix** by **Chicago** for Alex Zhamnov, Craig Mills and Phoenix's 1st round choice (Ty Jones) in 1997 Entry Draft, August 16, 1996. Signed as a free agent by **Philadelphia**, July 2, 2001. Traded to **Los Angeles** by **Philadelphia** with Nashville's 3rd round choice (previously acquired, Los Angeles selected Bud Holloway) in 2006 Entry Draft for future considerations, August 4, 2005. Signed as a free agent by **Phoenix**, July 4, 2006. Signed as a free agent by **San Jose**, September 4, 2007. • Officially announced his retirement, August 6, 2009.

## ROLSTON, Brian

(ROHL-stuhn, BRIGH-uhn) **N.J.**

Center. Shoots left. 6'2", 210 lbs. Born, Flint, MI, February 21, 1973. New Jersey's 2nd choice, 11th overall, in 1991 Entry Draft.

| Season | Club | League | GP | G | A | Pts | PIM | PP | SH | GW | S | % | +/- | TF | F% | Min | GP | G | A | Pts | PIM | PP | SH | GW | Min |
|---|---|---|---|---|---|---|---|---|---|---|---|---|---|---|---|---|---|---|---|---|---|---|---|---|---|
| 1989-90 | Det. Compuware | NAHL | 40 | 36 | 37 | 73 | 57 | | | | | | | | | | | | | | | | | | |
| 1990-91 | Det. Compuware | NAHL | 36 | 49 | 46 | 95 | 14 | | | | | | | | | | | | | | | | | | |
| 1991-92 | Lake Superior | CCHA | 37 | 14 | 23 | 37 | 14 | | | | | | | | | | | | | | | | | | |
| 1992-93 | Lake Superior | CCHA | 39 | 33 | 31 | 64 | 20 | | | | | | | | | | | | | | | | | | |
| 1993-94 | United States | Nat-Tm | 41 | 20 | 28 | 48 | 36 | | | | | | | | | | | | | | | | | | |
| | United States | Olympics | 8 | 7 | 0 | 7 | 8 | | | | | | | | | | | | | | | | | | |
| | Albany River Rats | AHL | 17 | 5 | 5 | 10 | 8 | | | | | | | | | | 5 | 1 | 2 | 3 | 0 | | | | |
| **1994-95** | Albany River Rats | AHL | 18 | 9 | 11 | 20 | 10 | | | | | | | | | | | | | | | | | | |
| | ♦ **New Jersey** | **NHL** | **40** | **7** | **11** | **18** | **17** | **2** | **0** | **3** | **92** | **7.6** | **5** | | | | **6** | **2** | **1** | **3** | **4** | **1** | **0** | **0** | |
| **1995-96** | **New Jersey** | **NHL** | **58** | **13** | **11** | **24** | **8** | **3** | **1** | **4** | **139** | **9.4** | **9** | | | | | | | | | | | | |

| | | | Regular Season | | | | | | | | | | | | | | Playoffs | | | | | | | | |
|---|---|---|---|---|---|---|---|---|---|---|---|---|---|---|---|---|---|---|---|---|---|---|---|---|---|
| Season | Club | League | GP | G | A | Pts | PIM | PP | SH | GW | S | % | +/- | TF | F% | Min | GP | G | A | Pts | PIM | PP | SH | GW | Min |
| 1996-97 | New Jersey | NHL | 81 | 18 | 27 | 45 | 20 | 2 | 2 | 3 | 237 | 7.6 | 6 | .... | .... | .... | 10 | 4 | 1 | 5 | 6 | 1 | 2 | 0 | .... |
| 1997-98 | New Jersey | NHL | 76 | 16 | 14 | 30 | 16 | 0 | 2 | 1 | 185 | 8.6 | 7 | .... | .... | .... | 6 | 1 | 0 | 1 | 2 | 0 | 1 | 0 | .... |
| 1998-99 | New Jersey | NHL | 82 | 24 | 33 | 57 | 14 | 5 | 5 | 3 | 210 | 11.4 | 11 | 51 | 45.1 | 18:49 | 7 | 1 | 0 | 1 | 2 | 0 | 1 | 0 | 17:36 |
| 99-2000 | New Jersey | NHL | 11 | 3 | 1 | 4 | 0 | 1 | 0 | 2 | 33 | 9.1 | –2 | 37 | 37.8 | 19:09 | .... | .... | .... | .... | .... | .... | .... | .... | .... |
| | Colorado | NHL | 50 | 8 | 10 | 18 | 12 | 1 | 0 | 3 | 107 | 7.5 | –6 | 65 | 41.5 | 16:18 | .... | .... | .... | .... | .... | .... | .... | .... | .... |
| | Boston | NHL | 16 | 5 | 4 | 9 | 6 | 3 | 0 | 1 | 66 | 7.6 | –4 | 265 | 41.1 | 22:13 | .... | .... | .... | .... | .... | .... | .... | .... | .... |
| 2000-01 | Boston | NHL | 77 | 19 | 39 | 58 | 28 | 5 | 0 | 4 | 286 | 6.6 | 6 | 666 | 45.7 | 19:19 | .... | .... | .... | .... | .... | .... | .... | .... | .... |
| 2001-02 | Boston | NHL | 82 | 31 | 31 | 62 | 30 | 6 | 9 | 7 | 331 | 9.4 | 11 | 1289 | 46.6 | 20:24 | 6 | 4 | 1 | 5 | 0 | 1 | 1 | 0 | 20:37 |
| | United States | Olympics | 6 | 0 | 3 | 3 | 0 | .... | .... | .... | .... | .... | .... | .... | .... | .... | .... | .... | .... | .... | .... | .... | .... | .... | .... |
| 2002-03 | Boston | NHL | 81 | 27 | 32 | 59 | 32 | 6 | 5 | 5 | 281 | 9.6 | 1 | 1148 | 47.6 | 20:28 | 5 | 0 | 2 | 2 | 0 | 0 | 0 | 0 | 18:39 |
| 2003-04 | Boston | NHL | 82 | 19 | 29 | 48 | 40 | 3 | 2 | 3 | 257 | 7.4 | 9 | 1205 | 50.7 | 19:38 | 7 | 1 | 0 | 1 | 8 | 0 | 0 | 0 | 16:33 |
| 2004-05 | | | DID NOT PLAY | | | | | | | | | | | | | | | | | | | | | | |
| 2005-06 | Minnesota | NHL | 82 | 34 | 45 | 79 | 50 | 15 | 5 | 7 | 293 | 11.6 | 14 | 403 | 46.4 | 20:21 | .... | .... | .... | .... | .... | .... | .... | .... | .... |
| | United States | Olympics | 6 | 3 | 1 | 4 | 4 | .... | .... | .... | .... | .... | .... | .... | .... | .... | .... | .... | .... | .... | .... | .... | .... | .... | .... |
| 2006-07 | Minnesota | NHL | 78 | 31 | 33 | 64 | 46 | 13 | 1 | 6 | 305 | 10.2 | 6 | 295 | 45.4 | 21:16 | 5 | 1 | 1 | 2 | 4 | 0 | 0 | 0 | 20:25 |
| 2007-08 | Minnesota | NHL | 81 | 31 | 28 | 59 | 53 | 11 | 1 | 8 | 289 | 10.7 | –1 | 165 | 40.6 | 20:04 | 6 | 2 | 4 | 6 | 8 | 0 | 1 | 0 | 22:27 |
| 2008-09 | New Jersey | NHL | 64 | 15 | 17 | 32 | 30 | 8 | 0 | 3 | 174 | 8.6 | 2 | 180 | 46.1 | 15:06 | 7 | 1 | 1 | 2 | 4 | 1 | 0 | 0 | 14:09 |
| | **NHL Totals** | | **1041** | **301** | **365** | **666** | **402** | **84** | **33** | **63** | **3285** | **9.2** | | **5769** | **46.9** | **19:26** | **65** | **17** | **11** | **28** | **38** | **4** | **6** | **0** | **18:25** |

NCAA Championship All-Tournament Team (1992, 1993) • CCHA First All-Star Team (1993) • NCAA West Second All-American Team (1993)

Played in NHL All-Star Game (2007)

Traded to **Colorado** by **New Jersey** with New Jersey's 1st round choice (later traded to Boston – Boston selected Martin Samuelsson) in 2000 Entry Draft for Claude Lemieux and Colorado's 1st (David Hale) and 2nd (Matt DeMarchi) round choices in 2000 Entry Draft, November 3, 1999. Traded to **Boston** by **Colorado** with Martin Grenier, Samuel Pahlsson and New Jersey's 1st round choice (previously acquired, Boston selected Martin Samuelsson) in 2000 Entry Draft for Raymond Bourque and Dave Andreychuk, March 6, 2000. Signed as a free agent by **Minnesota**, July 8, 2004. Traded to **Tampa Bay** by **Minnesota** for Dallas' 4th round choice (previously acquired, later traded to Edmonton – Edmonton selected Kyle Bigos) in 2009 Entry Draft, June 29, 2008. Signed as a free agent by **New Jersey**, July 1, 2008.

## ROME, Aaron

(ROHM, AIR-ruhn) **VAN.**

Defense. Shoots left. 6'1", 223 lbs. Born, Nesbitt, Man., September 27, 1983. Los Angeles' 4th choice, 104th overall, in 2002 Entry Draft.

| Season | Club | League | GP | G | A | Pts | PIM | PP | SH | GW | S | % | +/- | TF | F% | Min | GP | G | A | Pts | PIM | PP | SH | GW | Min |
|---|---|---|---|---|---|---|---|---|---|---|---|---|---|---|---|---|---|---|---|---|---|---|---|---|---|
| 1998-99 | Sask. Contacts | SMHL | STATISTICS NOT AVAILABLE | | | | | | | | | | | | | | | | | | | | | | |
| | Saskatoon Blades | WHL | 1 | 0 | 0 | 0 | 0 | .... | .... | .... | .... | .... | .... | .... | .... | .... | .... | .... | .... | .... | .... | .... | .... | .... | .... |
| 99-2000 | Saskatoon Blades | WHL | 47 | 0 | 6 | 6 | 22 | .... | .... | .... | .... | .... | .... | .... | .... | .... | 1 | 0 | 0 | 0 | 0 | .... | .... | .... | .... |
| 2000-01 | Saskatoon Blades | WHL | 3 | 0 | 0 | 0 | 2 | .... | .... | .... | .... | .... | .... | .... | .... | .... | .... | .... | .... | .... | .... | .... | .... | .... | .... |
| | Kootenay Ice | WHL | 53 | 2 | 8 | 10 | 43 | .... | .... | .... | .... | .... | .... | .... | .... | .... | 11 | 1 | 3 | 4 | 6 | .... | .... | .... | .... |
| 2001-02 | Kootenay Ice | WHL | 33 | 4 | 13 | 17 | 55 | .... | .... | .... | .... | .... | .... | .... | .... | .... | .... | .... | .... | .... | .... | .... | .... | .... | .... |
| | Swift Current | WHL | 37 | 3 | 11 | 14 | 113 | .... | .... | .... | .... | .... | .... | .... | .... | .... | 10 | 1 | 4 | 5 | 23 | .... | .... | .... | .... |
| 2002-03 | Swift Current | WHL | 61 | 12 | 44 | 56 | 201 | .... | .... | .... | .... | .... | .... | .... | .... | .... | 4 | 1 | 0 | 1 | 20 | .... | .... | .... | .... |
| 2003-04 | Swift Current | WHL | 41 | 7 | 26 | 33 | 122 | .... | .... | .... | .... | .... | .... | .... | .... | .... | .... | .... | .... | .... | .... | .... | .... | .... | .... |
| | Moose Jaw | WHL | 28 | 3 | 16 | 19 | 88 | .... | .... | .... | .... | .... | .... | .... | .... | .... | 8 | 0 | 6 | 6 | 17 | .... | .... | .... | .... |
| 2004-05 | Cincinnati | AHL | 75 | 2 | 14 | 16 | 130 | .... | .... | .... | .... | .... | .... | .... | .... | .... | 12 | 3 | 3 | 6 | 33 | .... | .... | .... | .... |
| 2005-06 | Portland Pirates | AHL | 64 | 5 | 19 | 24 | 87 | .... | .... | .... | .... | .... | .... | .... | .... | .... | 18 | 1 | 4 | 5 | 33 | .... | .... | .... | .... |
| **2006-07** ♦ | **Anaheim** | **NHL** | **1** | **0** | **0** | **0** | **0** | **0** | **0** | **0** | **1** | **0.0** | **–1** | **0** | **0.0** | **14:31** | **1** | **0** | **0** | **0** | **0** | **0** | **0** | **0** | **11:01** |
| | Portland Pirates | AHL | 76 | 8 | 17 | 25 | 139 | .... | .... | .... | .... | .... | .... | .... | .... | .... | .... | .... | .... | .... | .... | .... | .... | .... | .... |
| **2007-08** | **Columbus** | **NHL** | **17** | **1** | **1** | **2** | **33** | **0** | **0** | **0** | **15** | **6.7** | **–4** | **0** | **0.0** | **18:11** | .... | .... | .... | .... | .... | .... | .... | .... | .... |
| | Portland Pirates | AHL | 14 | 2 | 3 | 5 | 31 | .... | .... | .... | .... | .... | .... | .... | .... | .... | .... | .... | .... | .... | .... | .... | .... | .... | .... |
| | Syracuse Crunch | AHL | 41 | 3 | 21 | 24 | 126 | .... | .... | .... | .... | .... | .... | .... | .... | .... | .... | .... | .... | .... | .... | .... | .... | .... | .... |
| **2008-09** | **Columbus** | **NHL** | **8** | **0** | **1** | **1** | **0** | **0** | **0** | **0** | **7** | **0.0** | **1** | **0** | **0.0** | **15:28** | **1** | **0** | **1** | **1** | **0** | **0** | **0** | **0** | **15:24** |
| | Syracuse Crunch | AHL | 48 | 7 | 21 | 28 | 153 | .... | .... | .... | .... | .... | .... | .... | .... | .... | .... | .... | .... | .... | .... | .... | .... | .... | .... |
| | **NHL Totals** | | **26** | **1** | **2** | **3** | **33** | **0** | **0** | **0** | **23** | **4.3** | | **0** | **0.0** | **17:12** | **2** | **0** | **1** | **1** | **0** | **0** | **0** | **0** | **13:13** |

WHL East Second All-Star Team (2004)

Signed as a free agent by **Anaheim**, June 7, 2004. Traded to **Columbus** by **Anaheim** with Clay Wilson for Geoff Platt, November 15, 2007. Signed as a free agent by **Vancouver**, July 1, 2009.

## ROSS, Jared

(RAWS, JAIR-uhd) **PHI.**

Center. Shoots left. 5'9", 165 lbs. Born, Huntsville, AL, September 18, 1982.

| Season | Club | League | GP | G | A | Pts | PIM | PP | SH | GW | S | % | +/- | TF | F% | Min | GP | G | A | Pts | PIM | PP | SH | GW | Min |
|---|---|---|---|---|---|---|---|---|---|---|---|---|---|---|---|---|---|---|---|---|---|---|---|---|---|
| 2001-02 | AL-Huntsville | CHA | 37 | 11 | 17 | 28 | 8 | .... | .... | .... | .... | .... | .... | .... | .... | .... | .... | .... | .... | .... | .... | .... | .... | .... | .... |
| 2002-03 | AL-Huntsville | CHA | 35 | 20 | 20 | 40 | 30 | .... | .... | .... | .... | .... | .... | .... | .... | .... | .... | .... | .... | .... | .... | .... | .... | .... | .... |
| 2003-04 | AL-Huntsville | CHA | 31 | 19 | 31 | 50 | 46 | .... | .... | .... | .... | .... | .... | .... | .... | .... | .... | .... | .... | .... | .... | .... | .... | .... | .... |
| 2004-05 | AL-Huntsville | CHA | 30 | 22 | 18 | 40 | 53 | .... | .... | .... | .... | .... | .... | .... | .... | .... | .... | .... | .... | .... | .... | .... | .... | .... | .... |
| | Motor City | UHL | 12 | 3 | 5 | 8 | 2 | .... | .... | .... | .... | .... | .... | .... | .... | .... | .... | .... | .... | .... | .... | .... | .... | .... | .... |
| 2005-06 | Chicago Wolves | AHL | 62 | 10 | 27 | 37 | 37 | .... | .... | .... | .... | .... | .... | .... | .... | .... | .... | .... | .... | .... | .... | .... | .... | .... | .... |
| | Gwinnett | ECHL | 1 | 0 | 0 | 0 | 0 | .... | .... | .... | .... | .... | .... | .... | .... | .... | .... | .... | .... | .... | .... | .... | .... | .... | .... |
| 2006-07 | Chicago Wolves | AHL | 41 | 7 | 8 | 15 | 14 | .... | .... | .... | .... | .... | .... | .... | .... | .... | .... | .... | .... | .... | .... | .... | .... | .... | .... |
| | Philadelphia | AHL | 21 | 4 | 10 | 14 | 6 | .... | .... | .... | .... | .... | .... | .... | .... | .... | .... | .... | .... | .... | .... | .... | .... | .... | .... |
| 2007-08 | Philadelphia | AHL | 67 | 23 | 39 | 62 | 56 | .... | .... | .... | .... | .... | .... | .... | .... | .... | 12 | 5 | 4 | 9 | 4 | .... | .... | .... | .... |
| **2008-09** | **Philadelphia** | **NHL** | **10** | **0** | **0** | **0** | **2** | **0** | **0** | **0** | **12** | **0.0** | **–4** | **48** | **56.3** | **7:44** | **6** | **1** | **0** | **1** | **0** | **0** | **0** | **0** | **4:10** |
| | Philadelphia | AHL | 64 | 29 | 40 | 69 | 26 | .... | .... | .... | .... | .... | .... | .... | .... | .... | .... | .... | .... | .... | .... | .... | .... | .... | .... |
| | **NHL Totals** | | **10** | **0** | **0** | **0** | **2** | **0** | **0** | **0** | **12** | **0.0** | | **48** | **56.3** | **7:44** | **6** | **1** | **0** | **1** | **0** | **0** | **0** | **0** | **4:09** |

Traded to **Philadelphia** (AHL) by **Chicago** (AHL) for the loan of Niko Dimitrakos, March 1, 2007. Signed as a free agent by **Philadelphia**, April 8, 2008.

## ROURKE, Allan

(RAWRK, AL-lan)

Defense. Shoots left. 6'2", 215 lbs. Born, Mississauga, Ont., March 6, 1980. Toronto's 6th choice, 154th overall, in 1998 Entry Draft.

| Season | Club | League | GP | G | A | Pts | PIM | PP | SH | GW | S | % | +/- | TF | F% | Min | GP | G | A | Pts | PIM | PP | SH | GW | Min |
|---|---|---|---|---|---|---|---|---|---|---|---|---|---|---|---|---|---|---|---|---|---|---|---|---|---|
| 1995-96 | Mississauga Reps | MTHL | 38 | 15 | 25 | 40 | 173 | .... | .... | .... | .... | .... | .... | .... | .... | .... | .... | .... | .... | .... | .... | .... | .... | .... | .... |
| 1996-97 | Kitchener Rangers | OHL | 25 | 1 | 1 | 2 | 12 | .... | .... | .... | .... | .... | .... | .... | .... | .... | 6 | 0 | 0 | 0 | 0 | .... | .... | .... | .... |
| 1997-98 | Kitchener Rangers | OHL | 48 | 5 | 17 | 22 | 59 | .... | .... | .... | .... | .... | .... | .... | .... | .... | 6 | 1 | 1 | 2 | 6 | .... | .... | .... | .... |
| 1998-99 | Kitchener Rangers | OHL | 66 | 11 | 28 | 39 | 79 | .... | .... | .... | .... | .... | .... | .... | .... | .... | 1 | 0 | 0 | 0 | 2 | .... | .... | .... | .... |
| 99-2000 | Kitchener Rangers | OHL | 67 | 31 | 43 | 74 | 57 | .... | .... | .... | .... | .... | .... | .... | .... | .... | 5 | 0 | 6 | 6 | 13 | .... | .... | .... | .... |
| 2000-01 | St. John's | AHL | 64 | 9 | 19 | 28 | 36 | .... | .... | .... | .... | .... | .... | .... | .... | .... | .... | .... | .... | .... | .... | .... | .... | .... | .... |
| 2001-02 | St. John's | AHL | 62 | 2 | 9 | 11 | 48 | .... | .... | .... | .... | .... | .... | .... | .... | .... | 10 | 0 | 2 | 2 | 6 | .... | .... | .... | .... |
| 2002-03 | St. John's | AHL | 65 | 12 | 19 | 31 | 49 | .... | .... | .... | .... | .... | .... | .... | .... | .... | .... | .... | .... | .... | .... | .... | .... | .... | .... |
| **2003-04** | **Carolina** | **NHL** | **25** | **1** | **2** | **3** | **22** | **0** | **0** | **0** | **24** | **4.2** | **4** | **0** | **0.0** | **12:28** | .... | .... | .... | .... | .... | .... | .... | .... | .... |
| | Lowell | AHL | 45 | 5 | 9 | 14 | 45 | .... | .... | .... | .... | .... | .... | .... | .... | .... | .... | .... | .... | .... | .... | .... | .... | .... | .... |
| 2004-05 | Lowell | AHL | 60 | 7 | 9 | 16 | 75 | .... | .... | .... | .... | .... | .... | .... | .... | .... | 11 | 1 | 2 | 3 | 40 | .... | .... | .... | .... |
| **2005-06** | **NY Islanders** | **NHL** | **6** | **0** | **1** | **1** | **0** | **0** | **0** | **0** | **2** | **0.0** | **1** | **1** | **0.0** | **17:15** | .... | .... | .... | .... | .... | .... | .... | .... | .... |
| | Bridgeport | AHL | 58 | 9 | 21 | 30 | 42 | .... | .... | .... | .... | .... | .... | .... | .... | .... | 1 | 1 | 0 | 1 | 0 | .... | .... | .... | .... |
| **2006-07** | **NY Islanders** | **NHL** | **11** | **0** | **1** | **1** | **4** | **0** | **0** | **0** | **1** | **0.0** | **0** | **0** | **0.0** | **10:40** | .... | .... | .... | .... | .... | .... | .... | .... | .... |
| | Bridgeport | AHL | 60 | 5 | 15 | 20 | 60 | .... | .... | .... | .... | .... | .... | .... | .... | .... | .... | .... | .... | .... | .... | .... | .... | .... | .... |
| **2007-08** | **Edmonton** | **NHL** | **13** | **0** | **0** | **0** | **5** | **0** | **0** | **0** | **4** | **0.0** | **–1** | **0** | **0.0** | **10:56** | .... | .... | .... | .... | .... | .... | .... | .... | .... |
| | Springfield | AHL | 44 | 3 | 11 | 14 | 24 | .... | .... | .... | .... | .... | .... | .... | .... | .... | .... | .... | .... | .... | .... | .... | .... | .... | .... |
| 2008-09 | ERC Ingolstadt | Germany | 42 | 4 | 14 | 18 | 12 | .... | .... | .... | .... | .... | .... | .... | .... | .... | .... | .... | .... | .... | .... | .... | .... | .... | .... |
| | **NHL Totals** | | **55** | **1** | **4** | **5** | **31** | **0** | **0** | **0** | **31** | **3.2** | | **1** | **0.0** | **12:16** | .... | .... | .... | .... | .... | .... | .... | .... | .... |

OHL Second All-Star Team (2000)

Traded to **Carolina** by **Toronto** for Harold Druken, May 29, 2003. Signed as a free agent by **NY Islanders**, August 12, 2005. Traded to **Edmonton** by **NY Islanders** with Edmonton's 3rd round choice (previously acquired, later traded to Anaheim - later traded back to NY Islanders - NY Islanders selected Kiril Petrov) in 2008 Entry Draft for Anaheim's 2nd round choice (previously acquired, NY Islanders selected Travis Hamonic) in 2008 Entry Draft, July 5, 2007. Signed as a free agent by **Ingolstadt** (Germany), July 15, 2008.

## ROY, Andre

(WAH, AWN-dray)

Right wing. Shoots left. 6'4", 229 lbs. Born, Port Chester, NY, February 8, 1975. Boston's 5th choice, 151st overall, in 1994 Entry Draft.

| Season | Club | League | GP | G | A | Pts | PIM | PP | SH | GW | S | % | +/- | TF | F% | Min | GP | G | A | Pts | PIM | PP | SH | GW | Min |
|---|---|---|---|---|---|---|---|---|---|---|---|---|---|---|---|---|---|---|---|---|---|---|---|---|---|
| 1992-93 | Nord Selects | QAHA | STATISTICS NOT AVAILABLE | | | | | | | | | | | | | | | | | | | | | | |
| 1993-94 | Goulbourn Royals | OHA-C | 9 | 9 | 13 | 22 | 98 | .... | .... | .... | .... | .... | .... | .... | .... | .... | .... | .... | .... | .... | .... | .... | .... | .... | .... |
| | Beauport | QMJHL | 33 | 6 | 7 | 13 | 125 | .... | .... | .... | .... | .... | .... | .... | .... | .... | .... | .... | .... | .... | .... | .... | .... | .... | .... |
| | Chicoutimi | QMJHL | 32 | 4 | 14 | 18 | 152 | .... | .... | .... | .... | .... | .... | .... | .... | .... | 25 | 3 | 6 | 9 | 94 | .... | .... | .... | .... |
| 1994-95 | Chicoutimi | QMJHL | 20 | 15 | 8 | 23 | 90 | .... | .... | .... | .... | .... | .... | .... | .... | .... | .... | .... | .... | .... | .... | .... | .... | .... | .... |
| | Drummondville | QMJHL | 34 | 18 | 13 | 31 | 233 | .... | .... | .... | .... | .... | .... | .... | .... | .... | 4 | 2 | 0 | 2 | 34 | .... | .... | .... | .... |
| **1995-96** | **Boston** | **NHL** | **3** | **0** | **0** | **0** | **0** | **0** | **0** | **0** | **0** | **0.0** | **0** | .... | .... | .... | .... | .... | .... | .... | .... | .... | .... | .... | .... |
| | Providence Bruins | AHL | 58 | 7 | 8 | 15 | 167 | .... | .... | .... | .... | .... | .... | .... | .... | .... | 1 | 0 | 0 | 0 | 10 | .... | .... | .... | .... |
| **1996-97** | **Boston** | **NHL** | **10** | **0** | **2** | **2** | **12** | **0** | **0** | **0** | **12** | **0.0** | **–5** | .... | .... | .... | .... | .... | .... | .... | .... | .... | .... | .... | .... |
| | Providence Bruins | AHL | 50 | 17 | 11 | 28 | 234 | .... | .... | .... | .... | .... | .... | .... | .... | .... | .... | .... | .... | .... | .... | .... | .... | .... | .... |

| Season | Club | League | Regular Season | | | | | | | | | | | | | | Playoffs | | | | | | | | |
|---|---|---|---|---|---|---|---|---|---|---|---|---|---|---|---|---|---|---|---|---|---|---|---|---|---|
| | | | GP | G | A | Pts | PIM | PP | SH | GW | S | % | +/- | TF | F% | Min | GP | G | A | Pts | PIM | PP | SH | GW | Min |
| 1997-98 | Providence Bruins | AHL | 36 | 3 | 11 | 14 | 154 | .... | .... | .... | .... | .... | .... | .... | .... | .... | .... | .... | .... | .... | .... | .... | .... | .... | .... |
| | Charlotte | ECHL | 27 | 10 | 8 | 18 | 132 | .... | .... | .... | .... | .... | .... | .... | .... | .... | 7 | 2 | 3 | 5 | 34 | .... | .... | .... | .... |
| 1998-99 | Fort Wayne | IHL | 65 | 15 | 6 | 21 | *395 | .... | .... | .... | .... | .... | .... | .... | .... | .... | 2 | 0 | 0 | 0 | 11 | .... | .... | .... | .... |
| **99-2000** | **Ottawa** | **NHL** | **73** | **4** | **3** | **7** | **145** | **0** | **0** | **1** | **39** | **10.3** | **3** | **3** | **33.3** | **6:29** | **5** | **0** | **0** | **0** | **2** | **0** | **0** | **0** | **5:54** |
| **2000-01** | **Ottawa** | **NHL** | **64** | **3** | **5** | **8** | **169** | **0** | **0** | **0** | **33** | **9.1** | **1** | **2** | **50.0** | **4:36** | **2** | **0** | **0** | **0** | **16** | **0** | **0** | **0** | **4:16** |
| **2001-02** | **Ottawa** | **NHL** | **56** | **6** | **8** | **14** | **148** | **0** | **0** | **0** | **60** | **10.0** | **3** | **1** | **100.0** | **8:23** | .... | .... | .... | .... | .... | .... | .... | .... | .... |
| | **Tampa Bay** | **NHL** | **9** | **1** | **1** | **2** | **63** | **0** | **0** | **0** | **6** | **16.7** | **–5** | **0** | **0.0** | **8:58** | .... | .... | .... | .... | .... | .... | .... | .... | .... |
| **2002-03** | **Tampa Bay** | **NHL** | **62** | **10** | **7** | **17** | **119** | **0** | **0** | **2** | **85** | **11.8** | **0** | **7** | **57.1** | **10:46** | **5** | **0** | **1** | **1** | **2** | **0** | **0** | **0** | **12:31** |
| **2003-04♦** | **Tampa Bay** | **NHL** | **33** | **1** | **1** | **2** | **78** | **0** | **0** | **0** | **24** | **4.2** | **–5** | **2** | **50.0** | **7:52** | **21** | **1** | **2** | **3** | **61** | **0** | **0** | **1** | **6:11** |
| 2004-05 | | | Did not play | | | | | | | | | | | | | | | | | | | | | | |
| **2005-06** | **Pittsburgh** | **NHL** | **42** | **2** | **1** | **3** | **116** | **0** | **0** | **1** | **11** | **18.2** | **–3** | **1** | **100.0** | **5:03** | .... | .... | .... | .... | .... | .... | .... | .... | .... |
| **2006-07** | **Pittsburgh** | **NHL** | **5** | **0** | **0** | **0** | **12** | **0** | **0** | **0** | **1** | **0.0** | **–1** | **1** | **0.0** | **3:12** | .... | .... | .... | .... | .... | .... | .... | .... | .... |
| | **Tampa Bay** | **NHL** | **51** | **1** | **2** | **3** | **116** | **0** | **0** | **0** | **14** | **7.1** | **–3** | **2** | **0.0** | **4:35** | **6** | **0** | **0** | **0** | **17** | **0** | **0** | **0** | **2:31** |
| **2007-08** | **Tampa Bay** | **NHL** | **63** | **4** | **3** | **7** | **108** | **0** | **0** | **0** | **38** | **10.5** | **–1** | **0** | **0.0** | **5:28** | .... | .... | .... | .... | .... | .... | .... | .... | .... |
| **2008-09** | **Calgary** | **NHL** | **44** | **3** | **0** | **3** | **83** | **0** | **0** | **1** | **26** | **11.5** | **–1** | **1** | **100.0** | **5:29** | **2** | **0** | **0** | **0** | **0** | **0** | **0** | **0** | **4:05** |
| | **NHL Totals** | | **515** | **35** | **33** | **68** | **1169** | **0** | **0** | **5** | **349** | **10.0** | | **20** | **50.0** | **6:33** | **41** | **1** | **3** | **4** | **98** | **0** | **0** | **1** | **6:11** |

Signed as a free agent by **Ottawa**, April 28, 1999. Traded to **Tampa Bay** by **Ottawa** with Ottawa's 6th round choice (Paul Ranger) in 2002 Entry Draft for Juha Ylonen, March 15, 2002. • Spent majority of 2003-04 season serving as a healthy reserve. Signed as a free agent by **Pittsburgh**, August 4, 2005. Claimed on waivers by **Tampa Bay** from **Pittsburgh**, December 2, 2006. Signed as a free agent by **Calgary**, July 21, 2008.

## ROY, Derek

(ROI, DAIR-ihk) **BUF.**

Center. Shoots left. 5'9", 188 lbs. Born, Ottawa, Ont., May 4, 1983. Buffalo's 2nd choice, 32nd overall, in 2001 Entry Draft.

| Season | Club | League | GP | G | A | Pts | PIM | PP | SH | GW | S | % | +/- | TF | F% | Min | GP | G | A | Pts | PIM | PP | SH | GW | Min |
|---|---|---|---|---|---|---|---|---|---|---|---|---|---|---|---|---|---|---|---|---|---|---|---|---|---|
| 1998-99 | Ontario East | Minor-ON | 34 | 61 | 31 | 92 | 42 | .... | .... | .... | .... | .... | .... | .... | .... | .... | .... | .... | .... | .... | .... | .... | .... | .... | .... |
| 99-2000 | Kitchener Rangers | OHL | 66 | 34 | 53 | 87 | 44 | .... | .... | .... | .... | .... | .... | .... | .... | .... | 5 | 4 | 1 | 5 | 6 | .... | .... | .... | .... |
| 2000-01 | Kitchener Rangers | OHL | 65 | 42 | 39 | 81 | 114 | .... | .... | .... | .... | .... | .... | .... | .... | .... | .... | .... | .... | .... | .... | .... | .... | .... | .... |
| 2001-02 | Kitchener Rangers | OHL | 62 | 43 | 46 | 89 | 92 | .... | .... | .... | .... | .... | .... | .... | .... | .... | 4 | 1 | 2 | 3 | 2 | .... | .... | .... | .... |
| 2002-03 | Kitchener Rangers | OHL | 49 | 28 | 50 | 78 | 73 | .... | .... | .... | .... | .... | .... | .... | .... | .... | 21 | 9 | *23 | 32 | 14 | .... | .... | .... | .... |
| **2003-04** | **Buffalo** | **NHL** | **49** | **9** | **10** | **19** | **12** | **1** | **0** | **4** | **71** | **12.7** | **–8** | **715** | **47.4** | **15:19** | .... | .... | .... | .... | .... | .... | .... | .... | .... |
| | Rochester | AHL | 26 | 10 | 16 | 26 | 20 | .... | .... | .... | .... | .... | .... | .... | .... | .... | 16 | 6 | 8 | 14 | 18 | .... | .... | .... | .... |
| 2004-05 | Rochester | AHL | 67 | 16 | 45 | 61 | 60 | .... | .... | .... | .... | .... | .... | .... | .... | .... | 9 | 6 | 5 | 11 | 6 | .... | .... | .... | .... |
| **2005-06** | **Buffalo** | **NHL** | **70** | **18** | **28** | **46** | **57** | **5** | **1** | **1** | **151** | **11.9** | **1** | **807** | **48.0** | **17:02** | **18** | **5** | **10** | **15** | **16** | **1** | **1** | **0** | **17:03** |
| | Rochester | AHL | 8 | 7 | 13 | 20 | 10 | .... | .... | .... | .... | .... | .... | .... | .... | .... | .... | .... | .... | .... | .... | .... | .... | .... | .... |
| **2006-07** | **Buffalo** | **NHL** | **75** | **21** | **42** | **63** | **60** | **6** | **1** | **3** | **130** | **16.2** | **37** | **1129** | **48.5** | **18:28** | **16** | **2** | **5** | **7** | **14** | **0** | **0** | **0** | **18:03** |
| **2007-08** | **Buffalo** | **NHL** | **78** | **32** | **49** | **81** | **46** | **6** | **3** | **4** | **218** | **14.7** | **13** | **1393** | **51.2** | **20:58** | .... | .... | .... | .... | .... | .... | .... | .... | .... |
| **2008-09** | **Buffalo** | **NHL** | **82** | **28** | **42** | **70** | **38** | **9** | **1** | **9** | **221** | **12.7** | **–5** | **1469** | **50.7** | **21:12** | .... | .... | .... | .... | .... | .... | .... | .... | .... |
| | **NHL Totals** | | **354** | **108** | **171** | **279** | **213** | **27** | **6** | **21** | **791** | **13.7** | | **5513** | **49.6** | **18:56** | **34** | **7** | **15** | **22** | **30** | **1** | **1** | **0** | **17:31** |

OHL All-Rookie Team (2000) • OHL Rookie of the Year (2000) • CHL All-Rookie Team (2000) • CHL Plus/Minus Award (2000) • CHL Most Sportsmanlike Player (2000) • Memorial Cup Tournament All-Star Team (2003) • Stafford Smythe Memorial Trophy (Memorial Cup Tournament - MVP) (2003)

## ROY, Mathieu

(WAH, MA-tyew) **CBJ**

Defense. Shoots right. 6'2", 210 lbs. Born, St-Georges, Que., August 10, 1983. Edmonton's 10th choice, 215th overall, in 2003 Entry Draft.

| Season | Club | League | GP | G | A | Pts | PIM | PP | SH | GW | S | % | +/- | TF | F% | Min | GP | G | A | Pts | PIM | PP | SH | GW | Min |
|---|---|---|---|---|---|---|---|---|---|---|---|---|---|---|---|---|---|---|---|---|---|---|---|---|---|
| 1998-99 | Levis | QAAA | 11 | 4 | 1 | 5 | 16 | | | | | | | | | | | | | | | | | | |
| 99-2000 | Levis | QAAA | 24 | 3 | 4 | 7 | 88 | .... | .... | .... | .... | .... | .... | .... | .... | .... | .... | .... | .... | .... | .... | .... | .... | .... | .... |
| | Val-d'Or Foreurs | QMJHL | 48 | 1 | 4 | 5 | 66 | .... | .... | .... | .... | .... | .... | .... | .... | .... | 6 | 1 | 1 | 2 | 22 | .... | .... | .... | .... |
| 2000-01 | Val-d'Or Foreurs | QMJHL | 30 | 0 | 7 | 7 | 60 | .... | .... | .... | .... | .... | .... | .... | .... | .... | .... | .... | .... | .... | .... | .... | .... | .... | .... |
| 2001-02 | Val-d'Or Foreurs | QMJHL | 53 | 7 | 26 | 33 | 103 | .... | .... | .... | .... | .... | .... | .... | .... | .... | 17 | 0 | 0 | 0 | 4 | .... | .... | .... | .... |
| 2002-03 | Val-d'Or Foreurs | QMJHL | 52 | 11 | 21 | 32 | 164 | .... | .... | .... | .... | .... | .... | .... | .... | .... | 7 | 0 | 2 | 2 | 19 | .... | .... | .... | .... |
| 2003-04 | Toronto | AHL | 30 | 0 | 2 | 2 | 46 | .... | .... | .... | .... | .... | .... | .... | .... | .... | 7 | 1 | 0 | 1 | 8 | .... | .... | .... | .... |
| | Columbus | ECHL | 10 | 1 | 2 | 3 | 13 | .... | .... | .... | .... | .... | .... | .... | .... | .... | .... | .... | .... | .... | .... | .... | .... | .... | .... |
| 2004-05 | Edmonton | AHL | 51 | 3 | 22 | 25 | 68 | .... | .... | .... | .... | .... | .... | .... | .... | .... | .... | .... | .... | .... | .... | .... | .... | .... | .... |
| **2005-06** | **Edmonton** | **NHL** | **1** | **0** | **0** | **0** | **0** | **0** | **0** | **0** | **0** | **0.0** | **–1** | **0** | **0.0** | **13:00** | .... | .... | .... | .... | .... | .... | .... | .... | .... |
| | Hamilton | AHL | 50 | 3 | 16 | 19 | 82 | .... | .... | .... | .... | .... | .... | .... | .... | .... | .... | .... | .... | .... | .... | .... | .... | .... | .... |
| **2006-07** | **Edmonton** | **NHL** | **16** | **2** | **0** | **2** | **30** | **0** | **0** | **0** | **18** | **11.1** | **–7** | **0** | **0.0** | **14:06** | .... | .... | .... | .... | .... | .... | .... | .... | .... |
| | Hamilton | AHL | 31 | 6 | 12 | 18 | 40 | .... | .... | .... | .... | .... | .... | .... | .... | .... | .... | .... | .... | .... | .... | .... | .... | .... | .... |
| **2007-08** | **Edmonton** | **NHL** | **13** | **0** | **1** | **1** | **27** | **0** | **0** | **0** | **8** | **0.0** | **0** | **0** | **0.0** | **10:23** | .... | .... | .... | .... | .... | .... | .... | .... | .... |
| | Springfield | AHL | 20 | 2 | 8 | 10 | 34 | .... | .... | .... | .... | .... | .... | .... | .... | .... | .... | .... | .... | .... | .... | .... | .... | .... | .... |
| 2008-09 | Springfield | AHL | 59 | 2 | 15 | 17 | 120 | .... | .... | .... | .... | .... | .... | .... | .... | .... | .... | .... | .... | .... | .... | .... | .... | .... | .... |
| | **NHL Totals** | | **30** | **2** | **1** | **3** | **57** | **0** | **0** | **0** | **26** | **7.7** | | **0** | **0.0** | **12:28** | .... | .... | .... | .... | .... | .... | .... | .... | .... |

• Missed majority of 2007-08 season recovering from shoulder injury and serving as a healthy reserve. Signed as a free agent by **Columbus**, July 14, 2009.

## ROZSIVAL, Michal

(roh-ZIH-vahl, MEE-khahl) **NYR**

Defense. Shoots right. 6'2", 205 lbs. Born, Vlasim, Czech., September 3, 1978. Pittsburgh's 5th choice, 105th overall, in 1996 Entry Draft.

| Season | Club | League | GP | G | A | Pts | PIM | PP | SH | GW | S | % | +/- | TF | F% | Min | GP | G | A | Pts | PIM | PP | SH | GW | Min |
|---|---|---|---|---|---|---|---|---|---|---|---|---|---|---|---|---|---|---|---|---|---|---|---|---|---|
| 1994-95 | Jihlava Jr. | CzRep-Jr. | 31 | 8 | 13 | 21 | .... | .... | .... | .... | .... | .... | .... | .... | .... | .... | .... | .... | .... | .... | .... | .... | .... | .... | .... |
| 1995-96 | HC Dukla Jihlava | CzRep | 36 | 3 | 4 | 7 | .... | .... | .... | .... | .... | .... | .... | .... | .... | .... | .... | .... | .... | .... | .... | .... | .... | .... | .... |
| 1996-97 | Swift Current | WHL | 63 | 8 | 31 | 39 | 80 | .... | .... | .... | .... | .... | .... | .... | .... | .... | 10 | 0 | 6 | 6 | 15 | .... | .... | .... | .... |
| 1997-98 | Swift Current | WHL | 71 | 14 | 55 | 69 | 122 | .... | .... | .... | .... | .... | .... | .... | .... | .... | 12 | 0 | 5 | 5 | 33 | .... | .... | .... | .... |
| 1998-99 | Syracuse Crunch | AHL | 49 | 3 | 22 | 25 | 72 | .... | .... | .... | .... | .... | .... | .... | .... | .... | .... | .... | .... | .... | .... | .... | .... | .... | .... |
| **99-2000** | **Pittsburgh** | **NHL** | **75** | **4** | **17** | **21** | **48** | **1** | **0** | **1** | **73** | **5.5** | **11** | **1** | **0.0** | **19:01** | **2** | **0** | **0** | **0** | **4** | **0** | **0** | **0** | **30:56** |
| **2000-01** | **Pittsburgh** | **NHL** | **30** | **1** | **4** | **5** | **26** | **0** | **0** | **0** | **17** | **5.9** | **3** | **1** | **100.0** | **17:06** | .... | .... | .... | .... | .... | .... | .... | .... | .... |
| | Wilkes-Barre | AHL | 29 | 8 | 8 | 16 | 32 | .... | .... | .... | .... | .... | .... | .... | .... | .... | 21 | 3 | *19 | 22 | 23 | .... | .... | .... | .... |
| **2001-02** | **Pittsburgh** | **NHL** | **79** | **9** | **20** | **29** | **47** | **4** | **0** | **4** | **89** | **10.1** | **–6** | **0** | **0.0** | **20:01** | .... | .... | .... | .... | .... | .... | .... | .... | .... |
| **2002-03** | **Pittsburgh** | **NHL** | **53** | **4** | **6** | **10** | **40** | **1** | **0** | **0** | **61** | **6.6** | **–5** | **0** | **0.0** | **20:25** | .... | .... | .... | .... | .... | .... | .... | .... | .... |
| 2003-04 | Wilkes-Barre | AHL | 1 | 0 | 0 | 0 | 2 | .... | .... | .... | .... | .... | .... | .... | .... | .... | .... | .... | .... | .... | .... | .... | .... | .... | .... |
| 2004-05 | HC Ocelari Trinec | CzRep | 35 | 1 | 10 | 11 | 40 | .... | .... | .... | .... | .... | .... | .... | .... | .... | .... | .... | .... | .... | .... | .... | .... | .... | .... |
| | Pardubice | CzRep | 16 | 1 | 3 | 4 | 30 | .... | .... | .... | .... | .... | .... | .... | .... | .... | 16 | 1 | 2 | 3 | 34 | .... | .... | .... | .... |
| **2005-06** | **NY Rangers** | **NHL** | **82** | **5** | **25** | **30** | **90** | **3** | **0** | **3** | **115** | **4.3** | **35** | **1** | **0.0** | **22:27** | **4** | **0** | **1** | **1** | **8** | **0** | **0** | **0** | **24:31** |
| **2006-07** | **NY Rangers** | **NHL** | **80** | **10** | **30** | **40** | **52** | **7** | **0** | **3** | **104** | **9.6** | **10** | **3** | **0.0** | **23:46** | **10** | **3** | **4** | **7** | **10** | **2** | **0** | **1** | **24:45** |
| **2007-08** | **NY Rangers** | **NHL** | **80** | **13** | **25** | **38** | **80** | **6** | **2** | **0** | **127** | **10.2** | **0** | **0** | **0.0** | **24:33** | **10** | **1** | **5** | **6** | **10** | **0** | **0** | **0** | **25:05** |
| **2008-09** | **NY Rangers** | **NHL** | **76** | **8** | **22** | **30** | **52** | **3** | **0** | **2** | **120** | **6.7** | **–7** | **0** | **0.0** | **22:31** | **7** | **0** | **0** | **0** | **4** | **0** | **0** | **0** | **22:41** |
| | **NHL Totals** | | **555** | **54** | **149** | **203** | **435** | **25** | **2** | **13** | **706** | **7.6** | | **6** | **16.7** | **21:40** | **33** | **4** | **10** | **14** | **36** | **2** | **0** | **1** | **24:46** |

WHL East First All-Star Team (1998)

• Missed majority of 2003-04 season recovering from knee injury suffered in training camp, September 18, 2003. Signed as a free agent by **Trinec** (CzRep), September 17, 2004. Signed as a free agent by **Pardubice** (CzRep), January, 2005. Signed as a free agent by **NY Rangers**, August 29, 2005.

## RUPP, Mike

(RUHP, MIGHK) **PIT.**

Center. Shoots left. 6'5", 230 lbs. Born, Cleveland, OH, January 13, 1980. New Jersey's 7th choice, 76th overall, in 2000 Entry Draft.

| Season | Club | League | GP | G | A | Pts | PIM | PP | SH | GW | S | % | +/- | TF | F% | Min | GP | G | A | Pts | PIM | PP | SH | GW | Min |
|---|---|---|---|---|---|---|---|---|---|---|---|---|---|---|---|---|---|---|---|---|---|---|---|---|---|
| 1996-97 | St. Edward's | High-OH | 20 | 26 | 24 | 50 | | | | | | | | | | | | | | | | | | | |
| 1997-98 | Windsor Spitfires | OHL | 38 | 9 | 8 | 17 | 60 | .... | .... | .... | .... | .... | .... | .... | .... | .... | .... | .... | .... | .... | .... | .... | .... | .... | .... |
| | Erie Otters | OHL | 26 | 7 | 3 | 10 | 57 | .... | .... | .... | .... | .... | .... | .... | .... | .... | 7 | 3 | 1 | 4 | 6 | .... | .... | .... | .... |
| 1998-99 | Erie Otters | OHL | 63 | 22 | 25 | 47 | 102 | .... | .... | .... | .... | .... | .... | .... | .... | .... | 5 | 0 | 2 | 2 | 25 | .... | .... | .... | .... |
| 99-2000 | Erie Otters | OHL | 58 | 32 | 21 | 53 | 134 | .... | .... | .... | .... | .... | .... | .... | .... | .... | 13 | 5 | 5 | 10 | 22 | .... | .... | .... | .... |
| 2000-01 | Albany River Rats | AHL | 71 | 10 | 10 | 20 | 63 | .... | .... | .... | .... | .... | .... | .... | .... | .... | .... | .... | .... | .... | .... | .... | .... | .... | .... |
| 2001-02 | Albany River Rats | AHL | 78 | 13 | 17 | 30 | 90 | .... | .... | .... | .... | .... | .... | .... | .... | .... | .... | .... | .... | .... | .... | .... | .... | .... | .... |
| **2002-03♦** | **New Jersey** | **NHL** | **26** | **5** | **3** | **8** | **21** | **2** | **0** | **3** | **34** | **14.7** | **0** | **150** | **44.7** | **11:39** | **4** | **1** | **3** | **4** | **0** | **0** | **0** | **1** | **11:28** |
| | Albany River Rats | AHL | 47 | 8 | 11 | 19 | 74 | .... | .... | .... | .... | .... | .... | .... | .... | .... | .... | .... | .... | .... | .... | .... | .... | .... | .... |
| **2003-04** | **New Jersey** | **NHL** | **51** | **6** | **5** | **11** | **41** | **1** | **0** | **1** | **64** | **9.4** | **–1** | **386** | **47.9** | **10:38** | .... | .... | .... | .... | .... | .... | .... | .... | .... |
| | **Phoenix** | **NHL** | **6** | **0** | **1** | **1** | **6** | **0** | **0** | **0** | **12** | **0.0** | **–3** | **94** | **57.5** | **16:59** | .... | .... | .... | .... | .... | .... | .... | .... | .... |
| 2004-05 | Danbury Trashers | UHL | 14 | 5 | 5 | 10 | 30 | .... | .... | .... | .... | .... | .... | .... | .... | .... | 11 | 3 | 4 | 7 | 38 | .... | .... | .... | .... |
| **2005-06** | **Phoenix** | **NHL** | **1** | **0** | **0** | **0** | **0** | **0** | **0** | **0** | **1** | **0.0** | **0** | **1** | **0.0** | **6:30** | .... | .... | .... | .... | .... | .... | .... | .... | .... |
| | **Columbus** | **NHL** | **39** | **4** | **2** | **6** | **58** | **0** | **0** | **0** | **38** | **10.5** | **–3** | **264** | **48.1** | **9:04** | .... | .... | .... | .... | .... | .... | .... | .... | .... |
| | Syracuse Crunch | AHL | 3 | 1 | 2 | 3 | 12 | .... | .... | .... | .... | .... | .... | .... | .... | .... | .... | .... | .... | .... | .... | .... | .... | .... | .... |
| **2006-07** | **New Jersey** | **NHL** | **76** | **6** | **3** | **9** | **92** | **0** | **0** | **1** | **60** | **10.0** | **–10** | **33** | **45.5** | **6:27** | **9** | **0** | **1** | **1** | **7** | **0** | **0** | **0** | **2:46** |

| | | | Regular Season | | | | | | | | | | | | | | Playoffs | | | | | | | | |
|---|---|---|---|---|---|---|---|---|---|---|---|---|---|---|---|---|---|---|---|---|---|---|---|---|---|
| Season | Club | League | GP | G | A | Pts | PIM | PP | SH | GW | S | % | +/- | TF | F% | Min | GP | G | A | Pts | PIM | PP | SH | GW | Min |
| **2007-08** | **New Jersey** | **NHL** | 64 | 3 | 6 | 9 | 58 | 1 | 0 | 0 | 69 | 4.3 | –8 | 155 | 48.4 | 8:04 | 5 | 0 | 1 | 1 | 2 | 0 | 0 | 0 | 7:48 |
| **2008-09** | **New Jersey** | **NHL** | 72 | 3 | 6 | 9 | 136 | 0 | 0 | 0 | 76 | 3.9 | –2 | 90 | 51.1 | 8:44 | 7 | 0 | 0 | 0 | 14 | 0 | 0 | 0 | 6:55 |
| | **NHL Totals** | | 335 | 27 | 26 | 53 | 412 | 4 | 0 | 5 | 354 | 7.6 | | 1173 | 48.5 | 8:47 | 25 | 1 | 5 | 6 | 23 | 0 | 0 | 1 | 6:20 |

• Re-entered NHL Entry Draft. Originally NY Islanders' 1st choice, 9th overall, in 1998 Entry Draft.

Traded to **Phoenix** by **New Jersey** with New Jersey's 2nd round choice (later traded to Edmonton – Edmonton selected Geoff Paukovich) in 2004 Entry Draft for Jan Hrdina, March 5, 2004. Signed as a free agent by **Danbury** (UHL), February 10, 2005. Traded to **Columbus** by **Phoenix** with Cale Hulse and Jason Chimera for Geoff Sanderson and Tim Jackman, October 8, 2005. Signed as a free agent by **New Jersey**, July 10, 2006. Signed as a free agent by **Pittsburgh**, July 1, 2009.

## RUSSELL, Kris
(RUH-sehl, KRIHS) **CBJ**

Defense. Shoots left. 5'10", 180 lbs. Born, Red Deer, Alta., May 2, 1987. Columbus' 3rd choice, 67th overall, in 2005 Entry Draft.

| Season | Club | League | GP | G | A | Pts | PIM | PP | SH | GW | S | % | +/- | TF | F% | Min | GP | G | A | Pts | PIM | PP | SH | GW | Min |
|---|---|---|---|---|---|---|---|---|---|---|---|---|---|---|---|---|---|---|---|---|---|---|---|---|---|
| 2003-04 | Medicine Hat | WHL | 55 | 4 | 15 | 19 | 30 | .... | .... | .... | .... | .... | .... | .... | .... | .... | 20 | 3 | 2 | 5 | 4 | .... | .... | .... | .... |
| 2004-05 | Medicine Hat | WHL | 72 | 26 | 35 | 61 | 37 | .... | .... | .... | .... | .... | .... | .... | .... | .... | 10 | 2 | 1 | 3 | 4 | .... | .... | .... | .... |
| 2005-06 | Medicine Hat | WHL | 55 | 14 | 33 | 47 | 18 | .... | .... | .... | .... | .... | .... | .... | .... | .... | 13 | 4 | 8 | 12 | 11 | .... | .... | .... | .... |
| 2006-07 | Medicine Hat | WHL | 59 | 32 | 37 | 69 | 56 | .... | .... | .... | .... | .... | .... | .... | .... | .... | 23 | 4 | 15 | 19 | 24 | .... | .... | .... | .... |
| **2007-08** | **Columbus** | **NHL** | 67 | 2 | 8 | 10 | 14 | 1 | 0 | 1 | 90 | 2.2 | –12 | 0 | 0.0 | 14:47 | .... | .... | .... | .... | .... | .... | .... | .... | .... |
| **2008-09** | **Columbus** | **NHL** | 66 | 2 | 19 | 21 | 28 | 1 | 0 | 1 | 86 | 2.3 | –10 | 0 | 0.0 | 16:07 | 4 | 1 | 1 | 2 | 2 | 0 | 0 | 0 | 16:40 |
| | Syracuse Crunch | AHL | 14 | 3 | 5 | 8 | 0 | .... | .... | .... | .... | .... | .... | .... | .... | .... | .... | .... | .... | .... | .... | .... | .... | .... | .... |
| | **NHL Totals** | | 133 | 4 | 27 | 31 | 42 | 2 | 0 | 2 | 176 | 2.3 | | 0 | 0.0 | 15:27 | 4 | 1 | 1 | 2 | 2 | 0 | 0 | 0 | 16:40 |

WHL East Second All-Star Team (2005) • WHL East First All-Star Team (2006, 2007) • WHL Defenseman of the Year (2006, 2007) • Canadian Major Junior Second All-Star Team (2006) • Canadian Major Junior Sportsman of the Year (2006) • WHL Player of the Year (2007) • Canadian Major Junior First All-Star Team (2007) • Canadian Major Junior Defenseman of the Year (2007)

## RUUTU, Jarkko
(ROO-too, YAHR-koh) **OTT.**

Right wing. Shoots left. 6'1", 207 lbs. Born, Vantaa, Finland, August 23, 1975. Vancouver's 3rd choice, 68th overall, in 1998 Entry Draft.

| Season | Club | League | GP | G | A | Pts | PIM | PP | SH | GW | S | % | +/- | TF | F% | Min | GP | G | A | Pts | PIM | PP | SH | GW | Min |
|---|---|---|---|---|---|---|---|---|---|---|---|---|---|---|---|---|---|---|---|---|---|---|---|---|---|
| 1991-92 | HIFK Helsinki Jr. | Fin-Jr. | 1 | 0 | 0 | 0 | 0 | .... | .... | .... | .... | .... | .... | .... | .... | .... | .... | .... | .... | .... | .... | .... | .... | .... | .... |
| 1992-93 | HIFK Helsinki U18 | Fin-U18 | 33 | 26 | 21 | 47 | 53 | .... | .... | .... | .... | .... | .... | .... | .... | .... | .... | .... | .... | .... | .... | .... | .... | .... | .... |
| | HIFK Helsinki Jr. | Fin-Jr. | 1 | 0 | 0 | 0 | 0 | .... | .... | .... | .... | .... | .... | .... | .... | .... | .... | .... | .... | .... | .... | .... | .... | .... | .... |
| 1993-94 | HIFK Helsinki Jr. | Fin-Jr. | 19 | 9 | 12 | 21 | 44 | .... | .... | .... | .... | .... | .... | .... | .... | .... | .... | .... | .... | .... | .... | .... | .... | .... | .... |
| 1994-95 | HIFK Helsinki Jr. | Fin-Jr. | 35 | 26 | 22 | 48 | 117 | .... | .... | .... | .... | .... | .... | .... | .... | .... | .... | .... | .... | .... | .... | .... | .... | .... | .... |
| 1995-96 | Michigan Tech | WCHA | 39 | 12 | 10 | 22 | 96 | .... | .... | .... | .... | .... | .... | .... | .... | .... | .... | .... | .... | .... | .... | .... | .... | .... | .... |
| 1996-97 | HIFK Helsinki | Finland | 48 | 11 | 10 | 21 | 155 | .... | .... | .... | .... | .... | .... | .... | .... | .... | .... | .... | .... | .... | .... | .... | .... | .... | .... |
| 1997-98 | HIFK Helsinki | Finland | 37 | 10 | 10 | 20 | 166 | .... | .... | .... | .... | .... | .... | .... | .... | .... | 9 | 7 | 4 | 11 | 10 | .... | .... | .... | .... |
| 1998-99 | HIFK Helsinki | Finland | 25 | 10 | 4 | 14 | 136 | .... | .... | .... | .... | .... | .... | .... | .... | .... | 9 | 0 | 2 | 2 | 43 | .... | .... | .... | .... |
| | HIFK Helsinki | EuroHL | 5 | 1 | 2 | 3 | 8 | .... | .... | .... | .... | .... | .... | .... | .... | .... | .... | .... | .... | .... | .... | .... | .... | .... | .... |
| **99-2000** | **Vancouver** | **NHL** | 8 | 0 | 1 | 1 | 6 | 0 | 0 | 0 | 4 | 0.0 | –1 | 0 | 0.0 | 8:47 | .... | .... | .... | .... | .... | .... | .... | .... | .... |
| | Syracuse Crunch | AHL | 65 | 26 | 32 | 58 | 164 | .... | .... | .... | .... | .... | .... | .... | .... | .... | 4 | 3 | 1 | 4 | 8 | .... | .... | .... | .... |
| **2000-01** | **Vancouver** | **NHL** | 21 | 3 | 3 | 6 | 32 | 0 | 1 | 0 | 23 | 13.0 | 1 | 0 | 0.0 | 10:39 | 4 | 0 | 1 | 1 | 8 | 0 | 0 | 0 | 10:18 |
| | Kansas City | IHL | 46 | 11 | 18 | 29 | 111 | .... | .... | .... | .... | .... | .... | .... | .... | .... | .... | .... | .... | .... | .... | .... | .... | .... | .... |
| **2001-02** | **Vancouver** | **NHL** | 49 | 2 | 7 | 9 | 74 | 0 | 0 | 0 | 37 | 5.4 | –1 | 5 | 0.0 | 10:11 | 1 | 0 | 0 | 0 | 0 | 0 | 0 | 0 | 8:53 |
| | Finland | Olympics | 4 | 0 | 0 | 0 | 4 | .... | .... | .... | .... | .... | .... | .... | .... | .... | .... | .... | .... | .... | .... | .... | .... | .... | .... |
| **2002-03** | **Vancouver** | **NHL** | 36 | 2 | 2 | 4 | 66 | 0 | 0 | 1 | 36 | 5.6 | –7 | 6 | 16.7 | 8:58 | 13 | 0 | 2 | 2 | 14 | 0 | 0 | 0 | 11:59 |
| **2003-04** | **Vancouver** | **NHL** | 71 | 6 | 8 | 14 | 133 | 1 | 0 | 0 | 70 | 8.6 | –13 | 20 | 30.0 | 11:29 | 6 | 1 | 0 | 1 | 10 | 0 | 0 | 0 | 9:13 |
| 2004-05 | HIFK Helsinki | Finland | 50 | 10 | 18 | 28 | 215 | .... | .... | .... | .... | .... | .... | .... | .... | .... | 3 | 0 | 0 | 0 | 41 | .... | .... | .... | .... |
| **2005-06** | **Vancouver** | **NHL** | 82 | 10 | 7 | 17 | 142 | 2 | 0 | 2 | 85 | 11.8 | 1 | 11 | 0.0 | 11:42 | .... | .... | .... | .... | .... | .... | .... | .... | .... |
| | Finland | Olympics | 8 | 0 | 0 | 0 | 31 | .... | .... | .... | .... | .... | .... | .... | .... | .... | .... | .... | .... | .... | .... | .... | .... | .... | .... |
| **2006-07** | **Pittsburgh** | **NHL** | 81 | 7 | 9 | 16 | 125 | 0 | 0 | 2 | 63 | 11.1 | 0 | 3 | 100.0 | 9:20 | 5 | 0 | 0 | 0 | 10 | 0 | 0 | 0 | 6:38 |
| **2007-08** | **Pittsburgh** | **NHL** | 71 | 6 | 10 | 16 | 138 | 0 | 1 | 1 | 55 | 10.9 | 3 | 10 | 40.0 | 10:12 | 20 | 2 | 1 | 3 | 26 | 0 | 0 | 1 | 10:37 |
| **2008-09** | **Ottawa** | **NHL** | 78 | 7 | 14 | 21 | 144 | 0 | 1 | 0 | 89 | 7.9 | 0 | 8 | 25.0 | 11:43 | .... | .... | .... | .... | .... | .... | .... | .... | .... |
| | **NHL Totals** | | 497 | 43 | 61 | 104 | 860 | 3 | 3 | 6 | 462 | 9.3 | | 63 | 25.4 | 10:38 | 49 | 3 | 4 | 7 | 68 | 0 | 0 | 1 | 10:20 |

• Spent majority of 2002-03 season serving as a healthy reserve. Signed as a free agent by **HIFK Helsinki** (Finland), September 23, 2004. Signed as a free agent by **Pittsburgh**, July 4, 2006. Signed as a free agent by **Ottawa**, July 2, 2008.

## RUUTU, Tuomo
(ROO-too, TOO-oh-moh) **CAR.**

Center/Left wing. Shoots left. 6', 205 lbs. Born, Vantaa, Finland, February 16, 1983. Chicago's 1st choice, 9th overall, in 2001 Entry Draft.

| Season | Club | League | GP | G | A | Pts | PIM | PP | SH | GW | S | % | +/- | TF | F% | Min | GP | G | A | Pts | PIM | PP | SH | GW | Min |
|---|---|---|---|---|---|---|---|---|---|---|---|---|---|---|---|---|---|---|---|---|---|---|---|---|---|
| 1998-99 | HIFK Helsinki U18 | Fin-U18 | 25 | 9 | 11 | 20 | 88 | .... | .... | .... | .... | .... | .... | .... | .... | .... | 2 | 1 | 1 | 2 | 2 | .... | .... | .... | .... |
| 99-2000 | HIFK Helsinki U18 | Fin-U18 | 5 | 0 | 3 | 3 | 12 | .... | .... | .... | .... | .... | .... | .... | .... | .... | 3 | 1 | 2 | 3 | 2 | .... | .... | .... | .... |
| | HIFK Helsinki Jr. | Fin-Jr. | 35 | 11 | 16 | 27 | 32 | .... | .... | .... | .... | .... | .... | .... | .... | .... | 3 | 0 | 1 | 1 | 4 | .... | .... | .... | .... |
| | HIFK Helsinki | Finland | 1 | 0 | 0 | 0 | 2 | .... | .... | .... | .... | .... | .... | .... | .... | .... | .... | .... | .... | .... | .... | .... | .... | .... | .... |
| 2000-01 | Jokerit Helsinki Jr. | Fin-Jr. | 2 | 1 | 0 | 1 | 0 | .... | .... | .... | .... | .... | .... | .... | .... | .... | .... | .... | .... | .... | .... | .... | .... | .... | .... |
| | Jokerit Helsinki | Finland | 47 | 11 | 11 | 22 | 94 | .... | .... | .... | .... | .... | .... | .... | .... | .... | 5 | 0 | 0 | 0 | 4 | .... | .... | .... | .... |
| 2001-02 | Jokerit Helsinki | Finland | 51 | 7 | 16 | 23 | 69 | .... | .... | .... | .... | .... | .... | .... | .... | .... | 10 | 0 | 6 | 6 | 29 | .... | .... | .... | .... |
| 2002-03 | HIFK Helsinki | Finland | 30 | 12 | 15 | 27 | 24 | .... | .... | .... | .... | .... | .... | .... | .... | .... | .... | .... | .... | .... | .... | .... | .... | .... | .... |
| **2003-04** | **Chicago** | **NHL** | 82 | 23 | 21 | 44 | 58 | 10 | 0 | 3 | 174 | 13.2 | –31 | 317 | 46.4 | 16:24 | .... | .... | .... | .... | .... | .... | .... | .... | .... |
| 2004-05 | | | DID NOT PLAY | | | | | | | | | | | | | | | | | | | | | | |
| **2005-06** | **Chicago** | **NHL** | 15 | 2 | 3 | 5 | 31 | 1 | 0 | 0 | 30 | 6.7 | –7 | 90 | 46.7 | 14:43 | .... | .... | .... | .... | .... | .... | .... | .... | .... |
| **2006-07** | **Chicago** | **NHL** | 71 | 17 | 21 | 38 | 95 | 1 | 0 | 1 | 115 | 14.8 | 4 | 347 | 42.7 | 17:21 | .... | .... | .... | .... | .... | .... | .... | .... | .... |
| **2007-08** | **Chicago** | **NHL** | 60 | 6 | 15 | 21 | 75 | 1 | 0 | 1 | 71 | 8.5 | 3 | 49 | 53.1 | 15:35 | .... | .... | .... | .... | .... | .... | .... | .... | .... |
| | **Carolina** | **NHL** | 17 | 4 | 7 | 11 | 16 | 3 | 0 | 0 | 29 | 13.8 | 1 | 17 | 11.8 | 17:01 | .... | .... | .... | .... | .... | .... | .... | .... | .... |
| **2008-09** | **Carolina** | **NHL** | 79 | 26 | 28 | 54 | 79 | 10 | 0 | 4 | 190 | 13.7 | 0 | 37 | 51.4 | 18:19 | 16 | 1 | 3 | 4 | 8 | 0 | 0 | 0 | 14:16 |
| | **NHL Totals** | | 324 | 78 | 95 | 173 | 354 | 26 | 0 | 9 | 609 | 12.8 | | 857 | 44.8 | 16:53 | 16 | 1 | 3 | 4 | 8 | 0 | 0 | 0 | 14:16 |

• Missed majority of 2005-06 season recovering from back (October 15, 2005 at San Jose) and ankle (January 8, 2006 vs. Nashville) injuries. Traded to **Carolina** by **Chicago** for Andrew Ladd, February 26, 2008.

## RUZICKA, Stefan
(roo-ZHEECH-kuh, STEH-fan) **PHI.**

Right wing. Shoots right. 6', 205 lbs. Born, Nitra, Czech., February 17, 1985. Philadelphia's 4th choice, 81st overall, in 2003 Entry Draft.

| Season | Club | League | GP | G | A | Pts | PIM | PP | SH | GW | S | % | +/- | TF | F% | Min | GP | G | A | Pts | PIM | PP | SH | GW | Min |
|---|---|---|---|---|---|---|---|---|---|---|---|---|---|---|---|---|---|---|---|---|---|---|---|---|---|
| 2000-01 | Nitra Jr. | Slovak-Jr. | 38 | 30 | 15 | 45 | .... | .... | .... | .... | .... | .... | .... | .... | .... | .... | .... | .... | .... | .... | .... | .... | .... | .... | .... |
| 2001-02 | HKM Nitra Jr. | Slovak-Jr. | 29 | 27 | 25 | 52 | .... | .... | .... | .... | .... | .... | .... | .... | .... | .... | .... | .... | .... | .... | .... | .... | .... | .... | .... |
| | HKM Nitra | Slovakia | 19 | 0 | 5 | 5 | 29 | .... | .... | .... | .... | .... | .... | .... | .... | .... | .... | .... | .... | .... | .... | .... | .... | .... | .... |
| 2002-03 | HKM Nitra Jr. | Slovak-Jr. | 30 | 18 | 22 | 40 | 64 | .... | .... | .... | .... | .... | .... | .... | .... | .... | .... | .... | .... | .... | .... | .... | .... | .... | .... |
| | HKM Nitra | Slovak-2 | 17 | 5 | 7 | 12 | 4 | .... | .... | .... | .... | .... | .... | .... | .... | .... | .... | .... | .... | .... | .... | .... | .... | .... | .... |
| 2003-04 | Owen Sound | OHL | 62 | 34 | 38 | 72 | 63 | .... | .... | .... | .... | .... | .... | .... | .... | .... | 7 | 1 | 6 | 7 | 8 | .... | .... | .... | .... |
| | Philadelphia | AHL | 2 | 0 | 0 | 0 | 0 | .... | .... | .... | .... | .... | .... | .... | .... | .... | 3 | 1 | 0 | 1 | 2 | .... | .... | .... | .... |
| 2004-05 | Owen Sound | OHL | 62 | 37 | 33 | 70 | 61 | .... | .... | .... | .... | .... | .... | .... | .... | .... | 8 | 3 | 3 | 6 | 14 | .... | .... | .... | .... |
| **2005-06** | **Philadelphia** | **NHL** | 1 | 0 | 0 | 0 | 2 | 0 | 0 | 0 | 1 | 0.0 | 0 | 1 | 0.0 | 4:48 | .... | .... | .... | .... | .... | .... | .... | .... | .... |
| | Philadelphia | AHL | 73 | 16 | 32 | 48 | 88 | .... | .... | .... | .... | .... | .... | .... | .... | .... | .... | .... | .... | .... | .... | .... | .... | .... | .... |
| **2006-07** | **Philadelphia** | **NHL** | 40 | 3 | 10 | 13 | 18 | 1 | 0 | 0 | 75 | 4.0 | –6 | 3 | 0.0 | 12:44 | .... | .... | .... | .... | .... | .... | .... | .... | .... |
| | Philadelphia | AHL | 32 | 16 | 11 | 27 | 29 | .... | .... | .... | .... | .... | .... | .... | .... | .... | .... | .... | .... | .... | .... | .... | .... | .... | .... |
| **2007-08** | **Philadelphia** | **NHL** | 14 | 1 | 3 | 4 | 27 | 0 | 0 | 0 | 10 | 10.0 | 5 | 5 | 0.0 | 8:40 | .... | .... | .... | .... | .... | .... | .... | .... | .... |
| | Philadelphia | AHL | 59 | 19 | 31 | 50 | 105 | .... | .... | .... | .... | .... | .... | .... | .... | .... | 12 | 4 | 9 | 13 | 30 | .... | .... | .... | .... |
| 2008-09 | Spartak Moscow | Rus-KHL | 55 | 18 | 19 | 37 | 81 | .... | .... | .... | .... | .... | .... | .... | .... | .... | 6 | 3 | 4 | 7 | 6 | .... | .... | .... | .... |
| | **NHL Totals** | | 55 | 4 | 13 | 17 | 47 | 1 | 0 | 0 | 86 | 4.7 | | 9 | 0.0 | 11:33 | .... | .... | .... | .... | .... | .... | .... | .... | .... |

OHL All-Rookie Team (2004) • OHL Second All-Star Team (2004)

## RYAN, Bobby
(RIGH-uhn, BAW-bee) **ANA.**

Right wing. Shoots right. 6'2", 208 lbs. Born, Cherry Hill, NJ, March 17, 1987. Anaheim's 1st choice, 2nd overall, in 2005 Entry Draft.

| Season | Club | League | GP | G | A | Pts | PIM | PP | SH | GW | S | % | +/- | TF | F% | Min | GP | G | A | Pts | PIM | PP | SH | GW | Min |
|---|---|---|---|---|---|---|---|---|---|---|---|---|---|---|---|---|---|---|---|---|---|---|---|---|---|
| 2003-04 | Owen Sound | OHL | 65 | 22 | 17 | 39 | 52 | .... | .... | .... | .... | .... | .... | .... | .... | .... | 7 | 1 | 2 | 3 | 2 | .... | .... | .... | .... |
| 2004-05 | Owen Sound | OHL | 62 | 37 | 52 | 89 | 51 | .... | .... | .... | .... | .... | .... | .... | .... | .... | 8 | 2 | 7 | 9 | 8 | .... | .... | .... | .... |
| 2005-06 | Owen Sound | OHL | 59 | 31 | 64 | 95 | 44 | .... | .... | .... | .... | .... | .... | .... | .... | .... | 11 | 5 | 7 | 12 | 14 | .... | .... | .... | .... |
| | Portland Pirates | AHL | .... | .... | .... | .... | .... | .... | .... | .... | .... | .... | .... | .... | .... | .... | 19 | 1 | 7 | 8 | 22 | .... | .... | .... | .... |
| 2006-07 | Owen Sound | OHL | 63 | 43 | 59 | 102 | 63 | .... | .... | .... | .... | .... | .... | .... | .... | .... | 4 | 1 | 1 | 2 | 2 | .... | .... | .... | .... |
| | Portland Pirates | AHL | 8 | 3 | 6 | 9 | 6 | .... | .... | .... | .... | .... | .... | .... | .... | .... | .... | .... | .... | .... | .... | .... | .... | .... | .... |
| **2007-08** | **Anaheim** | **NHL** | 23 | 5 | 5 | 10 | 6 | 3 | 0 | 0 | 37 | 13.5 | –1 | 1 | 100.0 | 11:16 | 2 | 0 | 0 | 0 | 2 | 0 | 0 | 0 | 11:09 |
| | Portland Pirates | AHL | 48 | 21 | 28 | 49 | 38 | .... | .... | .... | .... | .... | .... | .... | .... | .... | 16 | 8 | 12 | 20 | 18 | .... | .... | .... | .... |

| | | | Regular Season | | | | | | | | | | | | | | Playoffs | | | | | | | | |
|---|---|---|---|---|---|---|---|---|---|---|---|---|---|---|---|---|---|---|---|---|---|---|---|---|---|
| Season | Club | League | GP | G | A | Pts | PIM | PP | SH | GW | S | % | +/- | TF | F% | Min | GP | G | A | Pts | PIM | PP | SH | GW | Min |
| **2008-09** | **Anaheim** | **NHL** | **64** | **31** | **26** | **57** | **33** | **12** | **0** | **3** | **174** | **17.8** | **13** | **13** | **46.2** | **15:26** | **13** | **5** | **2** | **7** | **0** | **2** | **0** | **1** | **19:41** |
| | Iowa Chops | AHL | 14 | 9 | 10 | 19 | 19 | | | | | | | | | | | | | | | | | | |
| | **NHL Totals** | | **87** | **36** | **31** | **67** | **39** | **15** | **0** | **3** | **211** | **17.1** | | **14** | **50.0** | **14:20** | **15** | **5** | **2** | **7** | **2** | **2** | **0** | **1** | **18:32** |

OHL First All-Star Team (2005) • NHL All-Rookie Team (2009)

## RYAN, Michael

(RIGH-uhn, MIGH-kuhl) **CAR.**

Center. Shoots left. 6'1", 188 lbs. Born, Boston, MA, May 16, 1980. Dallas' 1st choice, 32nd overall, in 1999 Entry Draft.

| Season | Club | League | GP | G | A | Pts | PIM | PP | SH | GW | S | % | +/- | TF | F% | Min | GP | G | A | Pts | PIM | PP | SH | GW | Min |
|---|---|---|---|---|---|---|---|---|---|---|---|---|---|---|---|---|---|---|---|---|---|---|---|---|---|
| 1997-98 | Bos. College High | High-MA | 23 | 22 | 14 | 36 | 28 | | | | | | | | | | | | | | | | | | |
| 1998-99 | Bos. College High | High-MA | 21 | 20 | 24 | 44 | 22 | | | | | | | | | | | | | | | | | | |
| 99-2000 | Northeastern | H-East | 32 | 4 | 9 | 13 | 47 | | | | | | | | | | | | | | | | | | |
| 2000-01 | Northeastern | H-East | 33 | 17 | 12 | 29 | 52 | | | | | | | | | | | | | | | | | | |
| 2001-02 | Northeastern | H-East | 36 | 24 | 15 | 39 | 54 | | | | | | | | | | | | | | | | | | |
| 2002-03 | Northeastern | H-East | 34 | 18 | 14 | 32 | 30 | | | | | | | | | | | | | | | | | | |
| 2003-04 | Rochester | AHL | 45 | 3 | 9 | 12 | 31 | | | | | | | | | | | | | | | | | | |
| 2004-05 | Rochester | AHL | 59 | 11 | 11 | 22 | 20 | | | | | | | | | | | | | | | | | | |
| 2005-06 | Rochester | AHL | 56 | 15 | 22 | 37 | 70 | | | | | | | | | | 5 | 0 | 1 | 1 | 4 | | | | |
| **2006-07** | **Buffalo** | **NHL** | **19** | **3** | **2** | **5** | **2** | **0** | **1** | **0** | **34** | **8.8** | **–8** | **2** | **0.0** | **13:40** | | | | | | | | | |
| | Rochester | AHL | 50 | 28 | 23 | 51 | 68 | | | | | | | | | | 6 | 4 | 0 | 4 | 4 | | | | |
| **2007-08** | **Buffalo** | **NHL** | **46** | **4** | **4** | **8** | **30** | **0** | **0** | **0** | **60** | **6.7** | **–4** | **2** | **0.0** | **9:53** | | | | | | | | | |
| **2008-09** | **Carolina** | **NHL** | **18** | **0** | **2** | **2** | **2** | **0** | **0** | **0** | **24** | **0.0** | **–3** | **6** | **16.7** | **8:12** | | | | | | | | | |
| | Albany River Rats | AHL | 40 | 25 | 17 | 42 | 34 | | | | | | | | | | | | | | | | | | |
| | **NHL Totals** | | **83** | **7** | **8** | **15** | **34** | **0** | **1** | **0** | **118** | **5.9** | | **10** | **10.0** | **10:23** | | | | | | | | | |

Traded to **Buffalo** by **Dallas** with Dallas's 2nd round choice (Branislav Fabry) in 2003 Entry Draft for Stu Barnes, March 10, 2003. Signed as a free agent by **Carolina**, October 31, 2008.

## RYDER, Michael

(RIGH-duhr, MIGH-kuhl) **BOS.**

Right wing. Shoots right. 6', 192 lbs. Born, St. John's, Nfld., March 31, 1980. Montreal's 9th choice, 216th overall, in 1998 Entry Draft.

| Season | Club | League | GP | G | A | Pts | PIM | PP | SH | GW | S | % | +/- | TF | F% | Min | GP | G | A | Pts | PIM | PP | SH | GW | Min |
|---|---|---|---|---|---|---|---|---|---|---|---|---|---|---|---|---|---|---|---|---|---|---|---|---|---|
| 1996-97 | Bonavista Saints | NFAHA | 23 | 31 | 17 | 48 | | | | | | | | | | | | | | | | | | | |
| 1997-98 | Hull Olympiques | QMJHL | 69 | 34 | 28 | 62 | 41 | | | | | | | | | | 10 | 4 | 2 | 6 | 4 | | | | |
| 1998-99 | Hull Olympiques | QMJHL | 69 | 44 | 43 | 87 | 65 | | | | | | | | | | 23 | *20 | 16 | 36 | 39 | | | | |
| 99-2000 | Hull Olympiques | QMJHL | 63 | 50 | 58 | 108 | 50 | | | | | | | | | | 15 | 11 | 17 | 28 | 28 | | | | |
| 2000-01 | Tallahassee | ECHL | 5 | 4 | 5 | 9 | 6 | | | | | | | | | | | | | | | | | | |
| | Quebec Citadelles | AHL | 61 | 6 | 9 | 15 | 14 | | | | | | | | | | | | | | | | | | |
| 2001-02 | Mississippi | ECHL | 20 | 14 | 13 | 27 | 2 | | | | | | | | | | | | | | | | | | |
| | Quebec Citadelles | AHL | 50 | 11 | 17 | 28 | 9 | | | | | | | | | | 3 | 0 | 1 | 1 | 2 | | | | |
| 2002-03 | Hamilton | AHL | 69 | 34 | 33 | 67 | 43 | | | | | | | | | | 23 | 11 | 6 | 17 | 8 | | | | |
| **2003-04** | **Montreal** | **NHL** | **81** | **25** | **38** | **63** | **26** | **10** | **0** | **4** | **215** | **11.6** | **10** | **25** | **24.0** | **16:00** | **11** | **1** | **2** | **3** | **4** | **0** | **0** | **0** | **16:52** |
| 2004-05 | Leksands IF | Sweden-2 | 42 | 34 | 27 | 61 | 32 | | | | | | | | | | | | | | | | | | |
| **2005-06** | **Montreal** | **NHL** | **81** | **30** | **25** | **55** | **40** | **18** | **0** | **6** | **243** | **12.3** | **–5** | **17** | **52.9** | **16:10** | **6** | **2** | **3** | **5** | **0** | **1** | **0** | **1** | **16:09** |
| **2006-07** | **Montreal** | **NHL** | **82** | **30** | **28** | **58** | **60** | **17** | **2** | **3** | **221** | **13.6** | **–25** | **28** | **42.9** | **16:17** | | | | | | | | | |
| **2007-08** | **Montreal** | **NHL** | **70** | **14** | **17** | **31** | **30** | **1** | **0** | **2** | **134** | **10.4** | **–4** | **19** | **26.3** | **13:15** | **4** | **0** | **0** | **0** | **2** | **0** | **0** | **0** | **10:46** |
| **2008-09** | **Boston** | **NHL** | **74** | **27** | **26** | **53** | **26** | **10** | **0** | **7** | **185** | **14.6** | **28** | **15** | **46.7** | **14:55** | **11** | **5** | **8** | **13** | **8** | **1** | **0** | **1** | **15:45** |
| | **NHL Totals** | | **388** | **126** | **134** | **260** | **182** | **56** | **2** | **22** | **998** | **12.6** | | **104** | **37.5** | **15:24** | **32** | **8** | **13** | **21** | **14** | **2** | **0** | **2** | **15:35** |

NHL All-Rookie Team (2004)

Signed as a free agent by **Leksands** (Sweden-2), September 19, 2004. Signed as a free agent by **Boston**, July 1, 2008.

## RYPIEN, Rick

(RIH-pihn, RIHK) **VAN.**

Center. Shoots right. 5'11", 170 lbs. Born, Coleman, Alta., May 16, 1984.

| Season | Club | League | GP | G | A | Pts | PIM | PP | SH | GW | S | % | +/- | TF | F% | Min | GP | G | A | Pts | PIM | PP | SH | GW | Min |
|---|---|---|---|---|---|---|---|---|---|---|---|---|---|---|---|---|---|---|---|---|---|---|---|---|---|
| 2001-02 | Crowsnest Pass | AJHL | 57 | 12 | 10 | 22 | 143 | | | | | | | | | | | | | | | | | | |
| | Regina Pats | WHL | 1 | 0 | 0 | 0 | 0 | | | | | | | | | | | | | | | | | | |
| 2002-03 | Regina Pats | WHL | 50 | 6 | 12 | 18 | 159 | | | | | | | | | | 5 | 1 | 1 | 2 | 21 | | | | |
| 2003-04 | Regina Pats | WHL | 65 | 19 | 26 | 45 | 186 | | | | | | | | | | 4 | 0 | 1 | 1 | 18 | | | | |
| 2004-05 | Regina Pats | WHL | 63 | 22 | 29 | 51 | 148 | | | | | | | | | | | | | | | | | | |
| | Manitoba Moose | AHL | 8 | 1 | 1 | 2 | 5 | | | | | | | | | | 14 | 0 | 0 | 0 | 35 | | | | |
| **2005-06** | Manitoba Moose | AHL | 49 | 9 | 6 | 15 | 122 | | | | | | | | | | 13 | 1 | 1 | 2 | 22 | | | | |
| | **Vancouver** | **NHL** | **5** | **1** | **0** | **1** | **4** | **0** | **0** | **0** | **6** | **16.7** | **1** | **22** | **36.4** | **6:19** | | | | | | | | | |
| **2006-07** | **Vancouver** | **NHL** | **2** | **0** | **0** | **0** | **5** | **0** | **0** | **0** | **0** | **0.0** | **0** | **6** | **66.7** | **4:46** | | | | | | | | | |
| | Manitoba Moose | AHL | 14 | 3 | 3 | 6 | 35 | | | | | | | | | | | | | | | | | | |
| **2007-08** | **Vancouver** | **NHL** | **22** | **1** | **2** | **3** | **41** | **0** | **0** | **0** | **8** | **12.5** | **–5** | **106** | **41.5** | **8:07** | | | | | | | | | |
| | Manitoba Moose | AHL | 34 | 3 | 11 | 14 | 81 | | | | | | | | | | 6 | 0 | 0 | 0 | 10 | | | | |
| **2008-09** | **Vancouver** | **NHL** | **12** | **3** | **0** | **3** | **19** | **0** | **1** | **0** | **16** | **18.8** | **–3** | **18** | **50.0** | **9:20** | **10** | **0** | **2** | **2** | **40** | **0** | **0** | **0** | **7:30** |
| | **NHL Totals** | | **41** | **5** | **2** | **7** | **69** | **0** | **1** | **0** | **30** | **16.7** | | **152** | **42.8** | **8:05** | **10** | **0** | **2** | **2** | **40** | **0** | **0** | **0** | **7:30** |

Signed to an ATO (tryout) contract by **Manitoba** (AHL), March 22, 2005. Signed as a free agent by **Vancouver**, November 9, 2005. • Missed majority of 2006-07 season recovering from recurring groin injury. • Missed majority of 2008-09 season recovering from viral infection.

## RYZNAR, Jason

(RIHZ-nuhr, JAY-suhn)

Left wing. Shoots left. 6'4", 205 lbs. Born, Anchorage, AK, February 19, 1983. New Jersey's 3rd choice, 64th overall, in 2002 Entry Draft.

| Season | Club | League | GP | G | A | Pts | PIM | PP | SH | GW | S | % | +/- | TF | F% | Min | GP | G | A | Pts | PIM | PP | SH | GW | Min |
|---|---|---|---|---|---|---|---|---|---|---|---|---|---|---|---|---|---|---|---|---|---|---|---|---|---|
| 99-2000 | USNTDP | NAHL | 52 | 5 | 10 | 15 | 22 | | | | | | | | | | 3 | 1 | 1 | 2 | 4 | | | | |
| 2000-01 | USNTDP | U-18 | 42 | 11 | 14 | 25 | 71 | | | | | | | | | | | | | | | | | | |
| | USNTDP | USHL | 24 | 4 | 3 | 7 | 31 | | | | | | | | | | | | | | | | | | |
| 2001-02 | U. of Michigan | CCHA | 40 | 9 | 7 | 16 | 22 | | | | | | | | | | | | | | | | | | |
| 2002-03 | U. of Michigan | CCHA | 34 | 7 | 9 | 16 | 24 | | | | | | | | | | | | | | | | | | |
| 2003-04 | U. of Michigan | CCHA | 36 | 6 | 11 | 17 | 28 | | | | | | | | | | | | | | | | | | |
| 2004-05 | U. of Michigan | CCHA | 36 | 6 | 17 | 23 | 46 | | | | | | | | | | | | | | | | | | |
| **2005-06** | **New Jersey** | **NHL** | **8** | **0** | **0** | **0** | **2** | **0** | **0** | **0** | **1** | **0.0** | **–1** | **0** | **0.0** | **5:19** | | | | | | | | | |
| | Albany River Rats | AHL | 59 | 7 | 18 | 25 | 52 | | | | | | | | | | | | | | | | | | |
| 2006-07 | Lowell Devils | AHL | 55 | 5 | 5 | 10 | 25 | | | | | | | | | | | | | | | | | | |
| 2007-08 | Lowell Devils | AHL | 55 | 10 | 8 | 18 | 38 | | | | | | | | | | | | | | | | | | |
| 2008-09 | Houston Aeros | AHL | 77 | 4 | 2 | 6 | 56 | | | | | | | | | | 10 | 0 | 2 | 2 | 2 | | | | |
| | **NHL Totals** | | **8** | **0** | **0** | **0** | **2** | **0** | **0** | **0** | **1** | **0.0** | | **0** | **0.0** | **5:19** | | | | | | | | | |

## ST. JACQUES, Bruno

(SAINT ZHAWK, BROO-noh)

Defense. Shoots left. 6'2", 216 lbs. Born, Montreal, Que., August 22, 1980. Philadelphia's 12th choice, 253rd overall, in 1998 Entry Draft.

| Season | Club | League | GP | G | A | Pts | PIM | PP | SH | GW | S | % | +/- | TF | F% | Min | GP | G | A | Pts | PIM | PP | SH | GW | Min |
|---|---|---|---|---|---|---|---|---|---|---|---|---|---|---|---|---|---|---|---|---|---|---|---|---|---|
| 1996-97 | Mtl-Bourassa | QAAA | 40 | 5 | 8 | 13 | | | | | | | | | | | 16 | 0 | 7 | 7 | | | | | |
| 1997-98 | Baie-Comeau | QMJHL | 63 | 1 | 11 | 12 | 140 | | | | | | | | | | | | | | | | | | |
| 1998-99 | Baie-Comeau | QMJHL | 49 | 8 | 13 | 21 | 85 | | | | | | | | | | | | | | | | | | |
| 99-2000 | Baie-Comeau | QMJHL | 60 | 8 | 28 | 36 | 120 | | | | | | | | | | 6 | 0 | 2 | 2 | 10 | | | | |
| | Philadelphia | AHL | 3 | 0 | 1 | 1 | 0 | | | | | | | | | | 1 | 0 | 0 | 0 | 0 | | | | |
| 2000-01 | Philadelphia | AHL | 45 | 1 | 16 | 17 | 83 | | | | | | | | | | 10 | 1 | 0 | 1 | 16 | | | | |
| **2001-02** | **Philadelphia** | **NHL** | **7** | **0** | **0** | **0** | **2** | **0** | **0** | **0** | **4** | **0.0** | **4** | **0** | **0.0** | **13:51** | | | | | | | | | |
| | Philadelphia | AHL | 55 | 3 | 11 | 14 | 59 | | | | | | | | | | 4 | 0 | 0 | 0 | 0 | | | | |
| **2002-03** | **Philadelphia** | **NHL** | **6** | **0** | **0** | **0** | **2** | **0** | **0** | **0** | **5** | **0.0** | **–1** | **0** | **0.0** | **14:35** | | | | | | | | | |
| | Philadelphia | AHL | 30 | 0 | 7 | 7 | 46 | | | | | | | | | | | | | | | | | | |
| | **Carolina** | **NHL** | **18** | **2** | **5** | **7** | **12** | **0** | **0** | **0** | **14** | **14.3** | **–3** | **0** | **0.0** | **18:15** | | | | | | | | | |
| | Lowell | AHL | 8 | 1 | 1 | 2 | 8 | | | | | | | | | | | | | | | | | | |
| **2003-04** | **Carolina** | **NHL** | **35** | **0** | **2** | **2** | **31** | **0** | **0** | **0** | **16** | **0.0** | **–7** | **0** | **0.0** | **11:50** | | | | | | | | | |
| | Lowell | AHL | 6 | 0 | 0 | 0 | 8 | | | | | | | | | | | | | | | | | | |
| 2004-05 | Lowell | AHL | 68 | 2 | 12 | 14 | 60 | | | | | | | | | | 11 | 1 | 4 | 5 | 4 | | | | |
| **2005-06** | **Anaheim** | **NHL** | **1** | **1** | **0** | **1** | **0** | **0** | **0** | **0** | **2** | **50.0** | **1** | **0** | **0.0** | **13:53** | | | | | | | | | |
| | Portland Pirates | AHL | 60 | 6 | 19 | 25 | 55 | | | | | | | | | | 14 | 3 | 4 | 7 | 18 | | | | |
| 2006-07 | Portland Pirates | AHL | 25 | 1 | 8 | 9 | 26 | | | | | | | | | | | | | | | | | | |
| | Norfolk Admirals | AHL | 37 | 4 | 8 | 12 | 33 | | | | | | | | | | 6 | 0 | 2 | 2 | 10 | | | | |

| | | | Regular Season | | | | | | | | | | | | | | Playoffs | | | | | | | | |
|---|---|---|---|---|---|---|---|---|---|---|---|---|---|---|---|---|---|---|---|---|---|---|---|---|---|
| Season | Club | League | GP | G | A | Pts | PIM | PP | SH | GW | S | % | +/- | TF | F% | Min | GP | G | A | Pts | PIM | PP | SH | GW | Min |
| 2007-08 | Syracuse Crunch | AHL | 13 | 0 | 8 | 8 | 16 | .... | .... | .... | .... | .... | .... | .... | .... | .... | .... | .... | .... | .... | .... | .... | .... | .... | .... |
| | Portland Pirates | AHL | 48 | 8 | 12 | 20 | 49 | .... | .... | .... | .... | .... | .... | .... | .... | .... | 6 | 0 | 3 | 3 | 17 | .... | .... | .... | .... |
| 2008-09 | ERC Ingolstadt | Germany | 41 | 9 | 16 | 25 | 68 | .... | .... | .... | .... | .... | .... | .... | .... | .... | .... | .... | .... | .... | .... | .... | .... | .... | .... |
| | **NHL Totals** | | **67** | **3** | **7** | **10** | **47** | **0** | **0** | **0** | **41** | **7.3** | | **0** | **0.0** | **14:03** | .... | .... | .... | .... | .... | .... | .... | .... | .... |

Traded to **Carolina** by **Philadelphia** with Pavel Brendl for Sami Kapanen and Ryan Bast, February 7, 2003. • Missed majority of 2003-04 season recovering from abdominal injury suffered in game vs. Philadelphia, November 28, 2003. Traded to **Anaheim** by **Carolina** for Craig Adams, October 3, 2005. Traded to **Chicago** by **Anaheim** with P.A. Parenteau for Sebastien Caron, Matt Keith and Chris Durno, December 28, 2006. Signed as a free agent by **Syracuse** (AHL), October 4, 2007. Traded to **Portland** (AHL) by **Syracuse** (AHL) for future considerations, November 15, 2007. Signed as a free agent by **Anaheim**, December 10, 2007.

## ST. LOUIS, Martin

(SAINT loo-EE, mahr-TEHN) **T.B.**

Right wing. Shoots left. 5'9", 177 lbs. Born, Laval, Que., June 18, 1975.

| | | | | | | | | | | | | | | | | | | | | | | | | | |
|---|---|---|---|---|---|---|---|---|---|---|---|---|---|---|---|---|---|---|---|---|---|---|---|---|---|
| 1991-92 | Laval-Laurentides | QAAA | 42 | 29 | *74 | *103 | 38 | .... | .... | .... | .... | .... | .... | .... | .... | .... | 12 | 7 | 15 | 22 | 16 | .... | .... | .... | .... |
| 1992-93 | Hawkesbury | CJHL | 31 | 37 | 50 | 87 | 70 | .... | .... | .... | .... | .... | .... | .... | .... | .... | .... | .... | .... | .... | .... | .... | .... | .... | .... |
| 1993-94 | U. of Vermont | ECAC | 33 | 15 | 36 | 51 | 24 | .... | .... | .... | .... | .... | .... | .... | .... | .... | .... | .... | .... | .... | .... | .... | .... | .... | .... |
| 1994-95 | U. of Vermont | ECAC | 35 | 23 | 48 | 71 | 36 | .... | .... | .... | .... | .... | .... | .... | .... | .... | .... | .... | .... | .... | .... | .... | .... | .... | .... |
| 1995-96 | U. of Vermont | ECAC | 35 | 29 | 56 | 85 | 38 | .... | .... | .... | .... | .... | .... | .... | .... | .... | .... | .... | .... | .... | .... | .... | .... | .... | .... |
| 1996-97 | U. of Vermont | ECAC | 36 | 24 | *36 | 60 | 65 | .... | .... | .... | .... | .... | .... | .... | .... | .... | .... | .... | .... | .... | .... | .... | .... | .... | .... |
| 1997-98 | Cleveland | IHL | 56 | 16 | 34 | 50 | 24 | .... | .... | .... | .... | .... | .... | .... | .... | .... | .... | .... | .... | .... | .... | .... | .... | .... | .... |
| | Saint John Flames | AHL | 25 | 15 | 11 | 26 | 20 | .... | .... | .... | .... | .... | .... | .... | .... | .... | 20 | 5 | 15 | 20 | 16 | .... | .... | .... | .... |
| **1998-99** | **Calgary** | **NHL** | **13** | **1** | **1** | **2** | **10** | **0** | **0** | **0** | **14** | **7.1** | **–2** | **0** | **0.0** | **8:15** | .... | .... | .... | .... | .... | .... | .... | .... | .... |
| | Saint John Flames | AHL | 53 | 28 | 34 | 62 | 30 | .... | .... | .... | .... | .... | .... | .... | .... | .... | 7 | 4 | 4 | 8 | 2 | .... | .... | .... | .... |
| **99-2000** | **Calgary** | **NHL** | **56** | **3** | **15** | **18** | **22** | **0** | **0** | **1** | **73** | **4.1** | **–5** | **3** | **0.0** | **14:41** | .... | .... | .... | .... | .... | .... | .... | .... | .... |
| | Saint John Flames | AHL | 17 | 15 | 11 | 26 | 14 | .... | .... | .... | .... | .... | .... | .... | .... | .... | .... | .... | .... | .... | .... | .... | .... | .... | .... |
| **2000-01** | **Tampa Bay** | **NHL** | **78** | **18** | **22** | **40** | **12** | **3** | **3** | **4** | **141** | **12.8** | **–4** | **48** | **41.7** | **15:14** | .... | .... | .... | .... | .... | .... | .... | .... | .... |
| **2001-02** | **Tampa Bay** | **NHL** | **53** | **16** | **19** | **35** | **20** | **6** | **1** | **2** | **105** | **15.2** | **4** | **33** | **39.4** | **18:41** | .... | .... | .... | .... | .... | .... | .... | .... | .... |
| **2002-03** | **Tampa Bay** | **NHL** | **82** | **33** | **37** | **70** | **32** | **12** | **3** | **5** | **201** | **16.4** | **10** | **37** | **37.8** | **19:43** | **11** | **7** | **5** | **12** | **0** | **1** | **2** | **3** | **22:21** |
| **2003-04♦** | **Tampa Bay** | **NHL** | **82** | **38** | ***56** | ***94** | **24** | **8** | **8** | **7** | **212** | **17.9** | **35** | **24** | **33.3** | **20:35** | **23** | **9** | ***15** | **24** | **14** | **3** | **1** | **3** | **22:52** |
| 2004-05 | Lausanne HC | Swiss | 23 | 9 | 16 | 25 | 16 | .... | .... | .... | .... | .... | .... | .... | .... | .... | .... | .... | .... | .... | .... | .... | .... | .... | .... |
| **2005-06** | **Tampa Bay** | **NHL** | **80** | **31** | **30** | **61** | **38** | **9** | **3** | **7** | **221** | **14.0** | **–3** | **13** | **23.1** | **20:59** | **5** | **4** | **0** | **4** | **2** | **1** | **0** | **1** | **22:53** |
| | Canada | Olympics | 6 | 2 | 1 | 3 | 0 | .... | .... | .... | .... | .... | .... | .... | .... | .... | .... | .... | .... | .... | .... | .... | .... | .... | .... |
| **2006-07** | **Tampa Bay** | **NHL** | **82** | **43** | **59** | **102** | **28** | **14** | **5** | **7** | **273** | **15.8** | **7** | **20** | **35.0** | **24:09** | **6** | **3** | **5** | **8** | **8** | **1** | **0** | **0** | **28:07** |
| **2007-08** | **Tampa Bay** | **NHL** | **82** | **25** | **58** | **83** | **26** | **10** | **2** | **5** | **241** | **10.4** | **–23** | **12** | **25.0** | **24:17** | .... | .... | .... | .... | .... | .... | .... | .... | .... |
| **2008-09** | **Tampa Bay** | **NHL** | **82** | **30** | **50** | **80** | **14** | **7** | **2** | **3** | **262** | **11.5** | **4** | **30** | **46.7** | **21:17** | .... | .... | .... | .... | .... | .... | .... | .... | .... |
| | **NHL Totals** | | **690** | **238** | **347** | **585** | **226** | **69** | **27** | **41** | **1743** | **13.7** | | **220** | **37.3** | **20:01** | **45** | **23** | **25** | **48** | **24** | **6** | **3** | **7** | **23:27** |

ECAC First All-Star Team (1995, 1996, 1997) • ECAC Player of the Year (1995) • NCAA East First All-American Team (1995, 1996, 1997) • NCAA Championship All-Tournament Team (1996) • NHL First All-Star Team (2004) • Art Ross Trophy (2004) • Lester B. Pearson Award (2004) • Hart Memorial Trophy (2004) • NHL Second All-Star Team (2007)

Played in NHL All-Star Game (2003, 2004, 2007, 2008, 2009)

Signed as a free agent by **Calgary**, February 19, 1998. Signed as a free agent by **Tampa Bay**, July 31, 2000. Signed as a free agent by **Lausanne** (Swiss), November 4, 2004.

## ST. PIERRE, Martin

(SAINT PEE-aihr, mahr-TEHN) **OTT.**

Center. Shoots left. 5'9", 185 lbs. Born, Ottawa, Ont., August 11, 1983.

| | | | | | | | | | | | | | | | | | | | | | | | | | |
|---|---|---|---|---|---|---|---|---|---|---|---|---|---|---|---|---|---|---|---|---|---|---|---|---|---|
| 2000-01 | Guelph Storm | OHL | 68 | 20 | 49 | 69 | 40 | .... | .... | .... | .... | .... | .... | .... | .... | .... | 4 | 0 | 0 | 0 | 4 | .... | .... | .... | .... |
| 2001-02 | Guelph Storm | OHL | 66 | 32 | 53 | 85 | 68 | .... | .... | .... | .... | .... | .... | .... | .... | .... | 9 | 3 | 9 | 12 | 12 | .... | .... | .... | .... |
| 2002-03 | Guelph Storm | OHL | 55 | 11 | 45 | 56 | 74 | .... | .... | .... | .... | .... | .... | .... | .... | .... | 11 | 5 | 11 | 16 | 4 | .... | .... | .... | .... |
| 2003-04 | Guelph Storm | OHL | 68 | 45 | 65 | 110 | 95 | .... | .... | .... | .... | .... | .... | .... | .... | .... | 22 | 8 | *27 | *35 | 20 | .... | .... | .... | .... |
| 2004-05 | Greenville | ECHL | 45 | 14 | 39 | 53 | 55 | .... | .... | .... | .... | .... | .... | .... | .... | .... | 7 | 2 | 5 | 7 | 6 | .... | .... | .... | .... |
| | Edmonton | AHL | 18 | 4 | 3 | 7 | 8 | .... | .... | .... | .... | .... | .... | .... | .... | .... | .... | .... | .... | .... | .... | .... | .... | .... | .... |
| **2005-06** | **Chicago** | **NHL** | **2** | **0** | **0** | **0** | **0** | **0** | **0** | **0** | **1** | **0.0** | **–1** | **15** | **33.3** | **12:02** | .... | .... | .... | .... | .... | .... | .... | .... | .... |
| | Norfolk Admirals | AHL | 77 | 23 | 50 | 73 | 98 | .... | .... | .... | .... | .... | .... | .... | .... | .... | 4 | 0 | 3 | 3 | 2 | .... | .... | .... | .... |
| **2006-07** | **Chicago** | **NHL** | **14** | **1** | **3** | **4** | **8** | **1** | **0** | **0** | **13** | **7.7** | **–3** | **129** | **48.1** | **12:29** | .... | .... | .... | .... | .... | .... | .... | .... | .... |
| | Norfolk Admirals | AHL | 65 | 27 | 72 | 99 | 100 | .... | .... | .... | .... | .... | .... | .... | .... | .... | 6 | 0 | 1 | 1 | 6 | .... | .... | .... | .... |
| **2007-08** | Mytischi | Russia | 14 | 1 | 6 | 7 | 16 | .... | .... | .... | .... | .... | .... | .... | .... | .... | .... | .... | .... | .... | .... | .... | .... | .... | .... |
| | **Chicago** | **NHL** | **5** | **0** | **0** | **0** | **0** | **0** | **0** | **0** | **2** | **0.0** | **–3** | **59** | **55.9** | **15:17** | .... | .... | .... | .... | .... | .... | .... | .... | .... |
| | Rockford IceHogs | AHL | 69 | 21 | 67 | 88 | 80 | .... | .... | .... | .... | .... | .... | .... | .... | .... | 12 | 2 | 12 | 14 | 12 | .... | .... | .... | .... |
| **2008-09** | **Boston** | **NHL** | **14** | **2** | **2** | **4** | **4** | **0** | **1** | **1** | **15** | **13.3** | **–1** | **101** | **42.6** | **11:24** | .... | .... | .... | .... | .... | .... | .... | .... | .... |
| | Providence Bruins | AHL | 61 | 15 | 51 | 66 | 58 | .... | .... | .... | .... | .... | .... | .... | .... | .... | 16 | 5 | 11 | 16 | 26 | .... | .... | .... | .... |
| | **NHL Totals** | | **35** | **3** | **5** | **8** | **12** | **1** | **1** | **1** | **31** | **9.7** | | **304** | **47.0** | **12:25** | .... | .... | .... | .... | .... | .... | .... | .... | .... |

AHL All-Rookie Team (2006) • AHL First All-Star Team (2007) • AHL Second All-Star Team (2008)

Signed as a free agent by **Chicago**, November 3, 2005. Signed as a free agent by **Mytischi** (Russia), June 22, 2007. Traded to **Boston** by **Chicago** for Pascal Pelletier, July 24, 2008. Signed as a free agent by **Ottawa**, July 1, 2009.

## SAKIC, Joe

(SAK-ihk, JOH)

Center. Shoots left. 5'11", 195 lbs. Born, Burnaby, B.C., July 7, 1969. Quebec's 2nd choice, 15th overall, in 1987 Entry Draft.

| | | | | | | | | | | | | | | | | | | | | | | | | | |
|---|---|---|---|---|---|---|---|---|---|---|---|---|---|---|---|---|---|---|---|---|---|---|---|---|---|
| 1985-86 | Burnaby | Minor-BC | 80 | 83 | 73 | 156 | 96 | .... | .... | .... | .... | .... | .... | .... | .... | .... | .... | .... | .... | .... | .... | .... | .... | .... | .... |
| | Lethbridge | WHL | 3 | 0 | 0 | 0 | 0 | .... | .... | .... | .... | .... | .... | .... | .... | .... | .... | .... | .... | .... | .... | .... | .... | .... | .... |
| 1986-87 | Swift Current | WHL | 72 | 60 | 73 | 133 | 31 | .... | .... | .... | .... | .... | .... | .... | .... | .... | 4 | 0 | 1 | 1 | 0 | .... | .... | .... | .... |
| 1987-88 | Swift Current | WHL | 64 | *78 | 82 | *160 | 64 | .... | .... | .... | .... | .... | .... | .... | .... | .... | 10 | 11 | 13 | 24 | 12 | .... | .... | .... | .... |
| **1988-89** | **Quebec** | **NHL** | **70** | **23** | **39** | **62** | **24** | **10** | **0** | **2** | **148** | **15.5** | **–36** | .... | .... | .... | .... | .... | .... | .... | .... | .... | .... | .... | .... |
| **1989-90** | **Quebec** | **NHL** | **80** | **39** | **63** | **102** | **27** | **8** | **1** | **2** | **234** | **16.7** | **–40** | .... | .... | .... | .... | .... | .... | .... | .... | .... | .... | .... | .... |
| **1990-91** | **Quebec** | **NHL** | **80** | **48** | **61** | **109** | **24** | **12** | **3** | **7** | **245** | **19.6** | **–26** | .... | .... | .... | .... | .... | .... | .... | .... | .... | .... | .... | .... |
| **1991-92** | **Quebec** | **NHL** | **69** | **29** | **65** | **94** | **20** | **6** | **3** | **1** | **217** | **13.4** | **5** | .... | .... | .... | .... | .... | .... | .... | .... | .... | .... | .... | .... |
| **1992-93** | **Quebec** | **NHL** | **78** | **48** | **57** | **105** | **40** | **20** | **2** | **4** | **264** | **18.2** | **–3** | .... | .... | .... | **6** | **3** | **3** | **6** | **2** | **1** | **0** | **0** | .... |
| **1993-94** | **Quebec** | **NHL** | **84** | **28** | **64** | **92** | **18** | **10** | **1** | **9** | **279** | **10.0** | **–8** | .... | .... | .... | .... | .... | .... | .... | .... | .... | .... | .... | .... |
| **1994-95** | **Quebec** | **NHL** | **47** | **19** | **43** | **62** | **30** | **3** | **2** | **5** | **157** | **12.1** | **7** | .... | .... | .... | **6** | **4** | **1** | **5** | **0** | **1** | **1** | **1** | .... |
| **1995-96♦** | **Colorado** | **NHL** | **82** | **51** | **69** | **120** | **44** | **17** | **6** | **7** | **339** | **15.0** | **14** | .... | .... | .... | **22** | ***18** | **16** | ***34** | **14** | **6** | **0** | **6** | .... |
| **1996-97** | **Colorado** | **NHL** | **65** | **22** | **52** | **74** | **34** | **10** | **2** | **5** | **261** | **8.4** | **–10** | .... | .... | .... | **17** | **8** | ***17** | **25** | **14** | **3** | **0** | **0** | .... |
| **1997-98** | **Colorado** | **NHL** | **64** | **27** | **36** | **63** | **50** | **12** | **1** | **2** | **254** | **10.6** | **0** | .... | .... | .... | **6** | **2** | **3** | **5** | **6** | **0** | **1** | **2** | .... |
| | Canada | Olympics | 4 | 1 | 2 | 3 | 4 | .... | .... | .... | .... | .... | .... | .... | .... | .... | .... | .... | .... | .... | .... | .... | .... | .... | .... |
| **1998-99** | **Colorado** | **NHL** | **73** | **41** | **55** | **96** | **29** | **12** | **5** | **6** | **255** | **16.1** | **23** | **1723** | **51.4** | **25:35** | **19** | **6** | **13** | **19** | **8** | **1** | **1** | **1** | **25:01** |
| **99-2000** | **Colorado** | **NHL** | **60** | **28** | **53** | **81** | **28** | **5** | **1** | **5** | **242** | **11.6** | **30** | **1392** | **53.8** | **23:16** | **17** | **2** | **7** | **9** | **8** | **2** | **0** | **0** | **23:50** |
| **2000-01♦** | **Colorado** | **NHL** | **82** | **54** | **64** | **118** | **30** | **19** | **3** | **12** | **332** | **16.3** | **45** | **2292** | **53.0** | **23:01** | **21** | ***13** | **13** | ***26** | **6** | **5** | **0** | **3** | **21:33** |
| **2001-02** | **Colorado** | **NHL** | **82** | **26** | **53** | **79** | **18** | **9** | **1** | **4** | **260** | **10.0** | **12** | **2148** | **52.2** | **22:01** | **21** | **9** | **10** | **19** | **4** | **4** | **0** | **1** | **22:44** |
| | Canada | Olympics | 6 | 4 | 3 | 7 | 0 | .... | .... | .... | .... | .... | .... | .... | .... | .... | .... | .... | .... | .... | .... | .... | .... | .... | .... |
| **2002-03** | **Colorado** | **NHL** | **58** | **26** | **32** | **58** | **24** | **8** | **0** | **1** | **190** | **13.7** | **4** | **1359** | **50.8** | **21:12** | **7** | **6** | **3** | **9** | **2** | **2** | **0** | **1** | **22:29** |
| **2003-04** | **Colorado** | **NHL** | **81** | **33** | **54** | **87** | **42** | **13** | **1** | **3** | **253** | **13.0** | **11** | **1705** | **52.6** | **20:16** | **11** | **7** | **5** | **12** | **8** | **1** | **1** | **2** | **21:15** |
| 2004-05 | | | DID NOT PLAY | | | | | | | | | | | | | | | | | | | | | | |
| **2005-06** | **Colorado** | **NHL** | **82** | **32** | **55** | **87** | **60** | **10** | **0** | **6** | **263** | **12.2** | **10** | **1669** | **52.5** | **19:55** | **9** | **4** | **5** | **9** | **6** | **1** | **0** | **1** | **21:38** |
| | Canada | Olympics | 6 | 1 | 2 | 3 | 0 | .... | .... | .... | .... | .... | .... | .... | .... | .... | .... | .... | .... | .... | .... | .... | .... | .... | .... |
| **2006-07** | **Colorado** | **NHL** | **82** | **36** | **64** | **100** | **46** | **16** | **0** | **4** | **258** | **14.0** | **2** | **1368** | **53.1** | **20:11** | .... | .... | .... | .... | .... | .... | .... | .... | .... |
| **2007-08** | **Colorado** | **NHL** | **44** | **13** | **27** | **40** | **20** | **5** | **0** | **1** | **124** | **10.5** | **–4** | **586** | **50.5** | **19:59** | **10** | **2** | **8** | **10** | **0** | **0** | **0** | **1** | **19:07** |
| **2008-09** | **Colorado** | **NHL** | **15** | **2** | **10** | **12** | **6** | **0** | **0** | **0** | **46** | **4.3** | **–6** | **216** | **54.2** | **18:07** | .... | .... | .... | .... | .... | .... | .... | .... | .... |
| | **NHL Totals** | | **1378** | **625** | **1016** | **1641** | **614** | **205** | **32** | **86** | **4621** | **13.5** | | **14458** | **52.4** | **21:39** | **172** | **84** | **104** | **188** | **78** | **27** | **4** | **19** | **22:30** |

WHL East Second All-Star Team (1987) • WHL East Rookie of the Year (1987) • WHL East Player of the Year (1987) • WHL East First All-Star Team (1988) • WHL Player of the Year (1988) • Canadian Major Junior Player of the Year (1988) • Conn Smythe Trophy (1996) • NHL First All-Star Team (2001, 2002, 2004) • Bud Light Plus/Minus Award (2001) (tied with Patrik Elias) • Lady Byng Memorial Trophy (2001) • Lester B. Pearson Award (2001) • Hart Memorial Trophy (2001) • Olympic Tournament - MVP (2002)

Played in NHL All-Star Game (1990, 1991, 1992, 1993, 1994, 1996, 1998, 2000, 2001, 2002, 2004, 2007)

• Transferred to **Colorado** after **Quebec** franchise relocated, June 21, 1995. • Missed majority of 2008-09 season recovering from recurring back injury and resulting back surgery to replace herniated disc, January 7, 2009. • Officially announced his retirement, July 9, 2009.

## SALCIDO, Brian

(sal-SEE-doh, BRIGH-uhn) **ANA.**

Defense. Shoots left. 6'2", 208 lbs. Born, Los Angeles, CA, April 14, 1985. Anaheim's 5th choice, 141st overall, in 2005 Entry Draft.

| | | | Regular Season | | | | | | | | | | | | | | Playoffs | | | | | | | | |
|---|---|---|---|---|---|---|---|---|---|---|---|---|---|---|---|---|---|---|---|---|---|---|---|---|---|
| Season | Club | League | GP | G | A | Pts | PIM | PP | SH | GW | S | % | +/- | TF | F% | Min | GP | G | A | Pts | PIM | PP | SH | GW | Min |
| 2002-03 | Shat.-St. Mary's | High-MN | 53 | 8 | 35 | 43 | .... | | | | | | | | | | | | | | | | | | |
| 2003-04 | Colorado College | WCHA | 12 | 1 | 0 | 1 | 48 | | | | | | | | | | | | | | | | | | |
| 2004-05 | Colorado College | WCHA | 38 | 7 | 23 | 30 | 52 | | | | | | | | | | | | | | | | | | |
| 2005-06 | Colorado College | WCHA | 42 | 8 | 32 | 40 | 69 | | | | | | | | | | | | | | | | | | |
| 2006-07 | Portland Pirates | AHL | 76 | 7 | 20 | 27 | 80 | | | | | | | | | | | | | | | | | | |
| 2007-08 | Portland Pirates | AHL | 71 | 11 | 42 | 53 | 58 | | | | | | | | | | 18 | 0 | 6 | 6 | 18 | | | | |
| 2008-09 | Anaheim | NHL | 2 | 0 | 1 | 1 | 0 | 0 | 0 | 0 | 1 | 0.0 | 2 | 0 | 0.0 | 12:18 | | | | | | | | | |
| | Iowa Chops | AHL | 76 | 10 | 33 | 43 | 108 | | | | | | | | | | | | | | | | | | |
| | NHL Totals | | 2 | 0 | 1 | 1 | 0 | 0 | 0 | 0 | 1 | 0.0 | | 0 | 0.0 | 12:18 | | | | | | | | | |

WCHA Second All-Star Team (2006) • AHL Second All-Star Team (2008)

## SALEI, Ruslan

(sah-LAY, roos-LAHN) **COL.**

Defense. Shoots left. 6'1", 212 lbs. Born, Minsk, USSR, November 2, 1974. Anaheim's 1st choice, 9th overall, in 1996 Entry Draft.

| Season | Club | League | GP | G | A | Pts | PIM | PP | SH | GW | S | % | +/- | TF | F% | Min | GP | G | A | Pts | PIM | PP | SH | GW | Min |
|---|---|---|---|---|---|---|---|---|---|---|---|---|---|---|---|---|---|---|---|---|---|---|---|---|---|
| 1992-93 | Dynamo Moscow | CIS | 9 | 1 | 0 | 1 | 10 | | | | | | | | | | | | | | | | | | |
| 1993-94 | Tivali Minsk | CIS | 39 | 2 | 3 | 5 | 50 | | | | | | | | | | | | | | | | | | |
| 1994-95 | Tivali Minsk | CIS | 51 | 4 | 2 | 6 | 44 | | | | | | | | | | | | | | | | | | |
| 1995-96 | Las Vegas | IHL | 76 | 7 | 23 | 30 | 123 | | | | | | | | | | 15 | 3 | 7 | 10 | 18 | | | | |
| 1996-97 | Anaheim | NHL | 30 | 0 | 1 | 1 | 37 | 0 | 0 | 0 | 14 | 0.0 | -8 | | | | | | | | | | | | |
| | Baltimore Bandits | AHL | 12 | 1 | 4 | 5 | 12 | | | | | | | | | | | | | | | | | | |
| | Las Vegas | IHL | 8 | 0 | 2 | 2 | 24 | | | | | | | | | | 3 | 2 | 1 | 3 | 6 | | | | |
| 1997-98 | Anaheim | NHL | 66 | 5 | 10 | 15 | 70 | 1 | 0 | 0 | 104 | 4.8 | 7 | | | | | | | | | | | | |
| | Cincinnati | AHL | 6 | 3 | 6 | 9 | 14 | | | | | | | | | | | | | | | | | | |
| | Belarus | Olympics | 7 | 1 | 0 | 1 | 4 | | | | | | | | | | | | | | | | | | |
| 1998-99 | Anaheim | NHL | 74 | 2 | 14 | 16 | 65 | 1 | 0 | 0 | 123 | 1.6 | 1 | 0 | 0.0 | 22:03 | 3 | 0 | 0 | 0 | 4 | 0 | 0 | 0 | 15:40 |
| 99-2000 | Anaheim | NHL | 71 | 5 | 5 | 10 | 94 | 1 | 0 | 0 | 116 | 4.3 | 3 | 0 | 0.0 | 20:21 | | | | | | | | | |
| 2000-01 | Anaheim | NHL | 50 | 1 | 5 | 6 | 70 | 0 | 0 | 0 | 73 | 1.4 | -14 | 0 | 0.0 | 20:40 | | | | | | | | | |
| 2001-02 | Anaheim | NHL | 82 | 4 | 7 | 11 | 97 | 0 | 0 | 1 | 96 | 4.2 | -10 | 0 | 0.0 | 21:25 | | | | | | | | | |
| | Belarus | Olympics | 6 | 2 | 1 | 3 | 4 | | | | | | | | | | | | | | | | | | |
| 2002-03 | Anaheim | NHL | 61 | 4 | 8 | 12 | 78 | 0 | 0 | 0 | 93 | 4.3 | 2 | 0 | 0.0 | 21:53 | 21 | 2 | 3 | 5 | 26 | 0 | 0 | 1 | 26:05 |
| 2003-04 | Anaheim | NHL | 82 | 4 | 11 | 15 | 110 | 0 | 1 | 2 | 145 | 2.8 | -1 | 0 | 0.0 | 23:42 | | | | | | | | | |
| 2004-05 | Ak Bars Kazan | Russia | 35 | 8 | 12 | 20 | 36 | | | | | | | | | | 4 | 0 | 0 | 0 | 2 | | | | |
| 2005-06 | Anaheim | NHL | 78 | 1 | 18 | 19 | 114 | 0 | 0 | 0 | 108 | 0.9 | 17 | 2 | 100.0 | 22:31 | 16 | 3 | 2 | 5 | 18 | 0 | 0 | 1 | 22:08 |
| 2006-07 | Florida | NHL | 82 | 6 | 26 | 32 | 102 | 2 | 0 | 0 | 148 | 4.1 | -13 | 0 | 0.0 | 23:20 | | | | | | | | | |
| 2007-08 | Florida | NHL | 65 | 3 | 20 | 23 | 75 | 1 | 0 | 0 | 81 | 3.7 | -5 | 1 | 0.0 | 23:17 | | | | | | | | | |
| | Colorado | NHL | 17 | 3 | 4 | 7 | 23 | 0 | 0 | 1 | 30 | 10.0 | 1 | 0 | 0.0 | 19:17 | 10 | 1 | 4 | 5 | 4 | 1 | 0 | 0 | 20:52 |
| 2008-09 | Colorado | NHL | 70 | 4 | 17 | 21 | 72 | 1 | 0 | 0 | 93 | 4.3 | -4 | 0 | 0.0 | 21:06 | | | | | | | | | |
| | NHL Totals | | 828 | 42 | 146 | 188 | 1007 | 7 | 1 | 4 | 1224 | 3.4 | | 3 | 66.7 | 22:02 | 50 | 6 | 9 | 15 | 52 | 1 | 0 | 2 | 23:09 |

Signed as a free agent by **Kazan** (Russia), October 20, 2004. Signed as a free agent by **Florida**, July 2, 2006. Traded to **Colorado** by **Florida** for Karlis Skrastins and Colorado's 3rd round choice (Adam Comrie) in 2008 Entry Draft, February 26, 2008.

## SALMELA, Anssi

(sahl-MEHL-ah, AN-see) **ATL.**

Defense. Shoots left. 6'1", 200 lbs. Born, Nokia, Finland, August 13, 1984.

| Season | Club | League | GP | G | A | Pts | PIM | PP | SH | GW | S | % | +/- | TF | F% | Min | GP | G | A | Pts | PIM | PP | SH | GW | Min |
|---|---|---|---|---|---|---|---|---|---|---|---|---|---|---|---|---|---|---|---|---|---|---|---|---|---|
| 2000-01 | Tappara U18 | Fin-U18 | 32 | 7 | 3 | 10 | 24 | | | | | | | | | | 2 | 0 | 1 | 1 | 4 | | | | |
| 2001-02 | Tappara U18 | Fin-U18 | 11 | 6 | 4 | 10 | 12 | | | | | | | | | | | | | | | | | | |
| | Tappara Jr. | Fin-Jr. | 26 | 3 | 4 | 7 | 22 | | | | | | | | | | 2 | 2 | 1 | 3 | 0 | | | | |
| 2002-03 | Tappara Jr. | Fin-Jr. | 23 | 5 | 9 | 14 | 22 | | | | | | | | | | | | | | | | | | |
| 2003-04 | Suomi U20 | Finland-2 | 5 | 2 | 2 | 4 | 0 | | | | | | | | | | | | | | | | | | |
| | Tappara Jr. | Fin-Jr. | 27 | 10 | 9 | 19 | 22 | | | | | | | | | | 12 | 5 | 3 | 8 | 4 | | | | |
| | Tappara Tampere | Finland | 10 | 0 | 0 | 0 | 2 | | | | | | | | | | 3 | 0 | 0 | 0 | 2 | | | | |
| 2004-05 | Tappara Jr. | Fin-Jr. | 10 | 2 | 4 | 6 | 6 | | | | | | | | | | 1 | 0 | 0 | 0 | 0 | | | | |
| | Tappara Tampere | Finland | 48 | 1 | 5 | 6 | 49 | | | | | | | | | | 8 | 0 | 0 | 0 | 0 | | | | |
| 2005-06 | Tappara Tampere | Finland | 8 | 0 | 1 | 1 | 0 | | | | | | | | | | | | | | | | | | |
| | Pelicans Lahti | Finland | 40 | 8 | 7 | 15 | 59 | | | | | | | | | | | | | | | | | | |
| 2006-07 | Pelicans Lahti | Finland | 56 | 11 | 12 | 23 | 58 | | | | | | | | | | 6 | 1 | 1 | 2 | 4 | | | | |
| 2007-08 | Tappara Tampere | Finland | 56 | 16 | 16 | 32 | 40 | | | | | | | | | | 11 | 0 | 6 | 6 | 14 | | | | |
| 2008-09 | New Jersey | NHL | 17 | 0 | 3 | 3 | 6 | 0 | 0 | 0 | 33 | 0.0 | 1 | 0 | 0.0 | 15:10 | | | | | | | | | |
| | Lowell Devils | AHL | 38 | 8 | 16 | 24 | 41 | | | | | | | | | | | | | | | | | | |
| | Atlanta | NHL | 9 | 1 | 2 | 3 | 2 | 1 | 0 | 0 | 8 | 12.5 | 0 | 0 | 0.0 | 17:31 | | | | | | | | | |
| | Chicago Wolves | AHL | 2 | 0 | 0 | 0 | 0 | | | | | | | | | | | | | | | | | | |
| | NHL Totals | | 26 | 1 | 5 | 6 | 8 | 1 | 0 | 0 | 41 | 2.4 | | 0 | 0.0 | 15:59 | | | | | | | | | |

Signed as a free agent by **New Jersey**, May 30, 2008. Traded to **Atlanta** by **New Jersey** for Niclas Havelid and Myles Stoesz, March 2, 2009.

## SALO, Sami

(SA-loh, SA-mee) **VAN.**

Defense. Shoots right. 6'3", 215 lbs. Born, Turku, Finland, September 2, 1974. Ottawa's 7th choice, 239th overall, in 1996 Entry Draft.

| Season | Club | League | GP | G | A | Pts | PIM | PP | SH | GW | S | % | +/- | TF | F% | Min | GP | G | A | Pts | PIM | PP | SH | GW | Min |
|---|---|---|---|---|---|---|---|---|---|---|---|---|---|---|---|---|---|---|---|---|---|---|---|---|---|
| 1991-92 | Kiekko-67 Jr. | Fin-Jr. | 23 | 4 | 5 | 9 | 26 | | | | | | | | | | | | | | | | | | |
| 1992-93 | Kiekko-67 Jr. | Fin-Jr. | 21 | 9 | 4 | 13 | 4 | | | | | | | | | | | | | | | | | | |
| 1993-94 | TPS Turku Jr. | Fin-Jr. | 36 | 7 | 13 | 20 | 16 | | | | | | | | | | 7 | 0 | 1 | 1 | 10 | | | | |
| 1994-95 | TPS Turku Jr. | Fin-Jr. | 14 | 1 | 3 | 4 | 6 | | | | | | | | | | | | | | | | | | |
| | Kiekko-67 Turku | Finland-2 | 19 | 4 | 2 | 6 | 4 | | | | | | | | | | | | | | | | | | |
| | TPS Turku | Finland | 7 | 1 | 2 | 3 | 6 | | | | | | | | | | 1 | 0 | 0 | 0 | 0 | | | | |
| 1995-96 | TPS Turku | Finland | 47 | 7 | 14 | 21 | 32 | | | | | | | | | | 11 | 1 | 3 | 4 | 8 | | | | |
| 1996-97 | TPS Turku | Finland | 48 | 9 | 6 | 15 | 10 | | | | | | | | | | 10 | 2 | 3 | 5 | 4 | | | | |
| | TPS Turku | EuroHL | 6 | 0 | 2 | 2 | 6 | | | | | | | | | | 2 | 0 | 0 | 0 | 2 | | | | |
| 1997-98 | Jokerit Helsinki | Finland | 35 | 3 | 5 | 8 | 24 | | | | | | | | | | 8 | 0 | 1 | 1 | 2 | | | | |
| | Jokerit Helsinki | EuroHL | 6 | 1 | 1 | 2 | 2 | | | | | | | | | | | | | | | | | | |
| 1998-99 | Ottawa | NHL | 61 | 7 | 12 | 19 | 24 | 2 | 0 | 1 | 106 | 6.6 | 20 | 0 | 0.0 | 19:42 | 4 | 0 | 0 | 0 | 0 | 0 | 0 | 0 | 21:32 |
| | Detroit Vipers | IHL | 5 | 0 | 2 | 2 | 0 | | | | | | | | | | | | | | | | | | |
| 99-2000 | Ottawa | NHL | 37 | 6 | 8 | 14 | 2 | 3 | 0 | 1 | 85 | 7.1 | 6 | 0 | 0.0 | 20:18 | 6 | 1 | 1 | 2 | 0 | 1 | 0 | 0 | 24:11 |
| 2000-01 | Ottawa | NHL | 31 | 2 | 16 | 18 | 10 | 1 | 0 | 0 | 61 | 3.3 | 9 | 0 | 0.0 | 19:44 | 4 | 0 | 0 | 0 | 0 | 0 | 0 | 0 | 22:30 |
| 2001-02 | Ottawa | NHL | 66 | 4 | 14 | 18 | 14 | 1 | 1 | 2 | 122 | 3.3 | 1 | 0 | 0.0 | 19:52 | 12 | 2 | 1 | 3 | 4 | 0 | 0 | 0 | 20:23 |
| | Finland | Olympics | 4 | 0 | 0 | 0 | 0 | | | | | | | | | | | | | | | | | | |
| 2002-03 | Vancouver | NHL | 79 | 9 | 21 | 30 | 10 | 4 | 0 | 1 | 126 | 7.1 | 9 | 0 | 0.0 | 20:08 | 12 | 1 | 3 | 4 | 0 | 0 | 0 | 0 | 20:52 |
| 2003-04 | Vancouver | NHL | 74 | 7 | 19 | 26 | 22 | 5 | 0 | 2 | 143 | 4.9 | 8 | 1 | 100.0 | 22:14 | 7 | 1 | 2 | 3 | 2 | 1 | 0 | 0 | 22:59 |
| 2004-05 | Frolunda | Sweden | 41 | 6 | 8 | 14 | 18 | | | | | | | | | | 14 | 1 | 6 | 7 | 2 | | | | |
| 2005-06 | Vancouver | NHL | 59 | 10 | 23 | 33 | 38 | 9 | 0 | 2 | 140 | 7.1 | 9 | 0 | 0.0 | 24:30 | | | | | | | | | |
| | Finland | Olympics | 6 | 1 | 3 | 4 | 0 | | | | | | | | | | | | | | | | | | |
| 2006-07 | Vancouver | NHL | 67 | 14 | 23 | 37 | 26 | 5 | 0 | 6 | 143 | 9.8 | 21 | 0 | 0.0 | 21:27 | 10 | 0 | 1 | 1 | 4 | 0 | 0 | 0 | 25:53 |
| 2007-08 | Vancouver | NHL | 63 | 8 | 17 | 25 | 38 | 6 | 0 | 1 | 122 | 6.6 | 8 | 0 | 0.0 | 23:39 | | | | | | | | | |
| 2008-09 | Vancouver | NHL | 60 | 5 | 20 | 25 | 26 | 5 | 0 | 2 | 110 | 4.5 | 5 | 0 | 0.0 | 20:11 | 7 | 3 | 4 | 7 | 2 | 2 | 0 | 2 | 18:36 |
| | NHL Totals | | 597 | 72 | 173 | 245 | 210 | 41 | 1 | 18 | 1158 | 6.2 | | 1 | 100.0 | 21:16 | 62 | 8 | 12 | 20 | 12 | 4 | 0 | 2 | 22:02 |

NHL All-Rookie Team (1999)

• Missed majority of 1999-2000 season recovering from wrist injury suffered in game vs. Philadelphia, November 28, 1999. • Missed majority of 2000-01 season recovering from shoulder injury suffered in game vs. Atlanta, December 14, 2000. Traded to **Vancouver** by **Ottawa** for Peter Schaefer, September 21, 2002. Signed as a free agent by **Frolunda** (Sweden), September 24, 2004.

## SALVADOR, Bryce

(SAL-vuh-dohr, BRIGHS) **N.J.**

Defense. Shoots left. 6'3", 215 lbs. Born, Brandon, Man., February 11, 1976. Tampa Bay's 6th choice, 138th overall, in 1994 Entry Draft.

| Season | Club | League | GP | G | A | Pts | PIM | PP | SH | GW | S | % | +/- | TF | F% | Min | GP | G | A | Pts | PIM | PP | SH | GW | Min |
|---|---|---|---|---|---|---|---|---|---|---|---|---|---|---|---|---|---|---|---|---|---|---|---|---|---|
| 1991-92 | Brandon | MAHA | 52 | 6 | 23 | 29 | 38 | | | | | | | | | | | | | | | | | | |
| 1992-93 | Lethbridge | WHL | 64 | 1 | 4 | 5 | 29 | | | | | | | | | | 4 | 0 | 0 | 0 | 0 | | | | |
| 1993-94 | Lethbridge | WHL | 61 | 4 | 14 | 18 | 36 | | | | | | | | | | 9 | 0 | 1 | 1 | 2 | | | | |
| 1994-95 | Lethbridge | WHL | 67 | 1 | 9 | 10 | 88 | | | | | | | | | | | | | | | | | | |
| 1995-96 | Lethbridge | WHL | 56 | 4 | 12 | 16 | 75 | | | | | | | | | | 3 | 0 | 1 | 1 | 2 | | | | |
| 1996-97 | Lethbridge | WHL | 63 | 8 | 32 | 40 | 81 | | | | | | | | | | 19 | 0 | 7 | 7 | 14 | | | | |
| 1997-98 | Worcester IceCats | AHL | 46 | 2 | 8 | 10 | 74 | | | | | | | | | | 11 | 0 | 1 | 1 | 45 | | | | |

| | | | Regular Season | | | | | | | | | | | | | | Playoffs | | | | | | | | |
|---|---|---|---|---|---|---|---|---|---|---|---|---|---|---|---|---|---|---|---|---|---|---|---|---|---|
| Season | Club | League | GP | G | A | Pts | PIM | PP | SH | GW | S | % | +/- | TF | F% | Min | GP | G | A | Pts | PIM | PP | SH | GW | Min |
| 1998-99 | Worcester IceCats | AHL | 69 | 5 | 13 | 18 | 129 | .... | .... | .... | .... | .... | .... | .... | .... | .... | 4 | 0 | 1 | 1 | 2 | .... | .... | .... | .... |
| 99-2000 | Worcester IceCats | AHL | 55 | 0 | 13 | 13 | 53 | .... | .... | .... | .... | .... | .... | .... | .... | .... | 9 | 0 | 1 | 1 | 2 | .... | .... | .... | .... |
| 2000-01 | St. Louis | NHL | 75 | 2 | 8 | 10 | 69 | 0 | 0 | 1 | 60 | 3.3 | –4 | 1 | 0.0 | 16:38 | 14 | 2 | 0 | 2 | 18 | 0 | 0 | 1 | 14:41 |
| 2001-02 | St. Louis | NHL | 66 | 5 | 7 | 12 | 78 | 1 | 0 | 2 | 37 | 13.5 | 3 | 0 | 0.0 | 16:55 | 10 | 0 | 1 | 1 | 4 | 0 | 0 | 0 | 12:34 |
| 2002-03 | St. Louis | NHL | 71 | 2 | 8 | 10 | 95 | 1 | 0 | 0 | 73 | 2.7 | 7 | 0 | 0.0 | 18:57 | 7 | 0 | 0 | 0 | 2 | 0 | 0 | 0 | 17:17 |
| 2003-04 | St. Louis | NHL | 69 | 3 | 5 | 8 | 47 | 0 | 0 | 1 | 60 | 5.0 | –4 | 0 | 0.0 | 17:29 | 5 | 0 | 0 | 0 | 2 | 0 | 0 | 0 | 14:31 |
| | Worcester IceCats | AHL | 2 | 0 | 1 | 1 | 0 | .... | .... | .... | .... | .... | .... | .... | .... | .... | .... | .... | .... | .... | .... | .... | .... | .... | .... |
| 2004-05 | Missouri | UHL | 7 | 0 | 0 | 0 | 16 | .... | .... | .... | .... | .... | .... | .... | .... | .... | 3 | 0 | 0 | 0 | 0 | .... | .... | .... | .... |
| 2005-06 | St. Louis | NHL | 46 | 1 | 4 | 5 | 26 | 0 | 0 | 0 | 23 | 4.3 | –24 | 1 | 0.0 | 19:48 | .... | .... | .... | .... | .... | .... | .... | .... | .... |
| 2006-07 | St. Louis | NHL | 64 | 2 | 5 | 7 | 55 | 0 | 0 | 0 | 40 | 5.0 | –5 | 0 | 0.0 | 19:44 | .... | .... | .... | .... | .... | .... | .... | .... | .... |
| 2007-08 | St. Louis | NHL | 56 | 1 | 10 | 11 | 43 | 0 | 0 | 1 | 29 | 3.4 | 12 | 1 | 0.0 | 19:38 | .... | .... | .... | .... | .... | .... | .... | .... | .... |
| | New Jersey | NHL | 8 | 0 | 0 | 0 | 11 | 0 | 0 | 0 | 0 | 0.0 | 0 | 0 | 0.0 | 20:54 | 5 | 1 | 0 | 1 | 2 | 0 | 0 | 0 | 17:55 |
| 2008-09 | New Jersey | NHL | 76 | 3 | 13 | 16 | 78 | 0 | 0 | 2 | 68 | 4.4 | –1 | 1 | 100.0 | 19:29 | 4 | 0 | 0 | 0 | 4 | 0 | 0 | 0 | 15:29 |
| | NHL Totals | | 531 | 19 | 60 | 79 | 502 | 2 | 0 | 7 | 390 | 4.9 | | 4 | 25.0 | 18:31 | 45 | 3 | 1 | 4 | 32 | 0 | 0 | 1 | 15:02 |

Signed as a free agent by **St. Louis**, December 16, 1996. Signed as a free agent by **Missouri** (UHL), March 11, 2005. Traded to **New Jersey** by **St. Louis** for Cam Janssen, February 26, 2008.

## SAMSONOV, Sergei

(sam-SAWN-nahf, SAIR-gay) **CAR.**

Left wing. Shoots right. 5'8", 188 lbs. Born, Moscow, USSR, October 27, 1978. Boston's 2nd choice, 8th overall, in 1997 Entry Draft.

| Season | Club | League | GP | G | A | Pts | PIM | PP | SH | GW | S | % | +/- | TF | F% | Min | GP | G | A | Pts | PIM | PP | SH | GW | Min |
|---|---|---|---|---|---|---|---|---|---|---|---|---|---|---|---|---|---|---|---|---|---|---|---|---|---|
| 1994-95 | CSKA Moscow 2 | CIS-2 | 50 | 110 | 72 | 182 | .... | .... | .... | .... | .... | .... | .... | .... | .... | .... | .... | .... | .... | .... | .... | .... | .... | .... | .... |
| | CSKA Moscow | CIS | 13 | 2 | 2 | 4 | 14 | .... | .... | .... | .... | .... | .... | .... | .... | .... | 2 | 0 | 0 | 0 | 0 | .... | .... | .... | .... |
| 1995-96 | CSKA Moscow | CIS | 51 | 21 | 17 | 38 | 12 | .... | .... | .... | .... | .... | .... | .... | .... | .... | 3 | 1 | 1 | 2 | 4 | .... | .... | .... | .... |
| 1996-97 | Detroit Vipers | IHL | 73 | 29 | 35 | 64 | 18 | .... | .... | .... | .... | .... | .... | .... | .... | .... | 19 | 8 | 4 | 12 | 12 | .... | .... | .... | .... |
| 1997-98 | Boston | NHL | 81 | 22 | 25 | 47 | 8 | 7 | 0 | 3 | 159 | 13.8 | 9 | .... | .... | .... | 6 | 2 | 5 | 7 | 0 | 0 | 0 | 1 | |
| 1998-99 | Boston | NHL | 79 | 25 | 26 | 51 | 18 | 6 | 0 | 8 | 160 | 15.6 | –6 | 0 | 0.0 | 16:23 | 11 | 3 | 1 | 4 | 0 | 0 | 0 | 0 | 16:11 |
| 99-2000 | Boston | NHL | 77 | 19 | 26 | 45 | 4 | 6 | 0 | 3 | 145 | 13.1 | –6 | 3 | 0.0 | 16:32 | .... | .... | .... | .... | .... | .... | .... | .... | .... |
| 2000-01 | Boston | NHL | 82 | 29 | 46 | 75 | 18 | 3 | 0 | 3 | 215 | 13.5 | 6 | 14 | 42.9 | 19:23 | .... | .... | .... | .... | .... | .... | .... | .... | .... |
| 2001-02 | Boston | NHL | 74 | 29 | 41 | 70 | 27 | 3 | 0 | 4 | 192 | 15.1 | 21 | 1 | 0.0 | 18:47 | 6 | 2 | 2 | 4 | 0 | 0 | 0 | 0 | 17:41 |
| | Russia | Olympics | 6 | 1 | 2 | 3 | 4 | .... | .... | .... | .... | .... | .... | .... | .... | .... | .... | .... | .... | .... | .... | .... | .... | .... | .... |
| 2002-03 | Boston | NHL | 8 | 5 | 6 | 11 | 2 | 1 | 0 | 3 | 23 | 21.7 | 8 | 0 | 0.0 | 20:20 | 5 | 0 | 2 | 2 | 0 | 0 | 0 | 0 | 17:07 |
| 2003-04 | Boston | NHL | 58 | 17 | 23 | 40 | 4 | 3 | 0 | 5 | 132 | 12.9 | 12 | 4 | 25.0 | 17:27 | 7 | 2 | 5 | 7 | 0 | 0 | 0 | 0 | 17:18 |
| 2004-05 | Dynamo Moscow | Russia | 3 | 1 | 0 | 1 | 0 | .... | .... | .... | .... | .... | .... | .... | .... | .... | 3 | 1 | 2 | 3 | 0 | .... | .... | .... | .... |
| 2005-06 | Boston | NHL | 55 | 18 | 19 | 37 | 22 | 6 | 0 | 1 | 107 | 16.8 | –3 | 1 | 100.0 | 16:53 | .... | .... | .... | .... | .... | .... | .... | .... | .... |
| | Edmonton | NHL | 19 | 5 | 11 | 16 | 6 | 4 | 0 | 0 | 36 | 13.9 | 0 | 2 | 0.0 | 15:26 | 24 | 4 | 11 | 15 | 14 | 1 | 0 | 0 | 14:30 |
| 2006-07 | Montreal | NHL | 63 | 9 | 17 | 26 | 10 | 0 | 0 | 0 | 114 | 7.9 | –4 | 14 | 14.3 | 13:59 | .... | .... | .... | .... | .... | .... | .... | .... | .... |
| 2007-08 | Chicago | NHL | 23 | 0 | 4 | 4 | 6 | 0 | 0 | 0 | 38 | 0.0 | –7 | 1 | 0.0 | 12:21 | .... | .... | .... | .... | .... | .... | .... | .... | .... |
| | Rockford IceHogs | AHL | 2 | 1 | 0 | 1 | 0 | .... | .... | .... | .... | .... | .... | .... | .... | .... | .... | .... | .... | .... | .... | .... | .... | .... | .... |
| | Carolina | NHL | 38 | 14 | 18 | 32 | 10 | 3 | 0 | 2 | 71 | 19.7 | 6 | 2 | 0.0 | 18:02 | .... | .... | .... | .... | .... | .... | .... | .... | .... |
| 2008-09 | Carolina | NHL | 81 | 16 | 32 | 48 | 28 | 3 | 0 | 3 | 155 | 10.3 | –8 | 7 | 57.1 | 17:19 | 17 | 5 | 3 | 8 | 6 | 0 | 0 | 0 | 15:48 |
| | NHL Totals | | 738 | 208 | 294 | 502 | 163 | 45 | 0 | 35 | 1547 | 13.4 | | 49 | 28.6 | 17:02 | 76 | 18 | 29 | 47 | 20 | 1 | 0 | 1 | 15:49 |

Garry F. Longman Memorial Trophy (IHL – Rookie of the Year) (1997) • NHL All-Rookie Team (1998) • Calder Memorial Trophy (1998)

Played in NHL All-Star Game (2001)

• Missed majority of 2002-03 season recovering from wrist injury suffered in game vs. Columbus, October 18, 2002. Signed as a free agent by **Dynamo Moscow** (Russia), February 2, 2005. Traded to **Edmonton** by **Boston** for Marty Reasoner, Yan Stastny and Edmonton's 2nd round choice (Milan Lucic) in 2006 Entry Draft, March 9, 2006. Signed as a free agent by **Montreal**, July 12, 2006. Traded to **Chicago** by **Montreal** for Jassen Cullimore and Tony Salmelainen, June 16, 2007. Claimed on waivers by **Carolina** from **Chicago**, January 8, 2008.

## SAMUELSSON, Mikael

(SAM-yuhl-suhn, MIH-kigh-ehl) **VAN.**

Right wing. Shoots right. 6'2", 213 lbs. Born, Mariefred, Sweden, December 23, 1976. San Jose's 7th choice, 145th overall, in 1998 Entry Draft.

| Season | Club | League | GP | G | A | Pts | PIM | PP | SH | GW | S | % | +/- | TF | F% | Min | GP | G | A | Pts | PIM | PP | SH | GW | Min |
|---|---|---|---|---|---|---|---|---|---|---|---|---|---|---|---|---|---|---|---|---|---|---|---|---|---|
| 1994-95 | Sodertalje SK Jr. | Swe-Jr. | 30 | 8 | 6 | 14 | 12 | .... | .... | .... | .... | .... | .... | .... | .... | .... | .... | .... | .... | .... | .... | .... | .... | .... | .... |
| 1995-96 | Sodertalje SK Jr. | Swe-Jr. | 22 | 13 | 12 | 25 | 20 | .... | .... | .... | .... | .... | .... | .... | .... | .... | .... | .... | .... | .... | .... | .... | .... | .... | .... |
| | Sodertalje SK | Sweden-2 | 18 | 5 | 1 | 6 | 0 | .... | .... | .... | .... | .... | .... | .... | .... | .... | 4 | 0 | 0 | 0 | 0 | .... | .... | .... | .... |
| 1996-97 | Sodertalje SK Jr. | Swe-Jr. | 2 | 2 | 1 | 3 | .... | .... | .... | .... | .... | .... | .... | .... | .... | .... | .... | .... | .... | .... | .... | .... | .... | .... | .... |
| | Sodertalje SK | Sweden | 29 | 3 | 2 | 5 | 10 | .... | .... | .... | .... | .... | .... | .... | .... | .... | 10 | 0 | 0 | 0 | 4 | .... | .... | .... | .... |
| 1997-98 | Nykoping | Sweden-2 | 10 | 5 | 1 | 6 | 14 | .... | .... | .... | .... | .... | .... | .... | .... | .... | .... | .... | .... | .... | .... | .... | .... | .... | .... |
| | Sodertalje SK | Sweden | 41 | 11 | 9 | 20 | 66 | .... | .... | .... | .... | .... | .... | .... | .... | .... | .... | .... | .... | .... | .... | .... | .... | .... | .... |
| 1998-99 | Sodertalje SK | Sweden-2 | 18 | 13 | 10 | 23 | 26 | .... | .... | .... | .... | .... | .... | .... | .... | .... | 10 | 2 | 2 | 4 | 12 | .... | .... | .... | .... |
| | V.Frolunda | Sweden | 27 | 0 | 5 | 5 | 10 | .... | .... | .... | .... | .... | .... | .... | .... | .... | .... | .... | .... | .... | .... | .... | .... | .... | .... |
| 99-2000 | Brynas IF Gavle | Sweden | 40 | 4 | 3 | 7 | 76 | .... | .... | .... | .... | .... | .... | .... | .... | .... | 11 | 7 | 2 | 9 | 6 | .... | .... | .... | .... |
| | Brynas IF Gavle | EuroHL | 4 | 0 | 2 | 2 | 4 | .... | .... | .... | .... | .... | .... | .... | .... | .... | .... | .... | .... | .... | .... | .... | .... | .... | .... |
| 2000-01 | San Jose | NHL | 4 | 0 | 0 | 0 | 0 | 0 | 0 | 0 | 3 | 0.0 | 0 | 0 | 0.0 | 4:41 | .... | .... | .... | .... | .... | .... | .... | .... | .... |
| | Kentucky | AHL | 66 | 32 | 46 | 78 | 58 | .... | .... | .... | .... | .... | .... | .... | .... | .... | 3 | 1 | 0 | 1 | 0 | .... | .... | .... | .... |
| 2001-02 | NY Rangers | NHL | 67 | 6 | 10 | 16 | 23 | 1 | 2 | 1 | 94 | 6.4 | 10 | 5 | 40.0 | 11:52 | .... | .... | .... | .... | .... | .... | .... | .... | .... |
| | Hartford | AHL | 8 | 3 | 6 | 9 | 12 | .... | .... | .... | .... | .... | .... | .... | .... | .... | .... | .... | .... | .... | .... | .... | .... | .... | .... |
| 2002-03 | NY Rangers | NHL | 58 | 8 | 14 | 22 | 32 | 1 | 1 | 2 | 118 | 6.8 | 0 | 35 | 42.9 | 15:32 | .... | .... | .... | .... | .... | .... | .... | .... | .... |
| | Pittsburgh | NHL | 22 | 2 | 0 | 2 | 8 | 1 | 0 | 0 | 36 | 5.6 | –21 | 8 | 75.0 | 14:04 | .... | .... | .... | .... | .... | .... | .... | .... | .... |
| 2003-04 | Florida | NHL | 37 | 3 | 6 | 9 | 35 | 0 | 0 | 1 | 50 | 6.0 | 0 | 28 | 28.6 | 12:15 | .... | .... | .... | .... | .... | .... | .... | .... | .... |
| 2004-05 | Geneve | Swiss | 12 | 2 | 4 | 6 | 14 | .... | .... | .... | .... | .... | .... | .... | .... | .... | .... | .... | .... | .... | .... | .... | .... | .... | .... |
| | Sodertalje SK | Sweden | 29 | 7 | 13 | 20 | 45 | .... | .... | .... | .... | .... | .... | .... | .... | .... | 10 | 3 | 3 | 6 | 24 | .... | .... | .... | .... |
| 2005-06 | Rapperswil | Swiss | 1 | 0 | 0 | 0 | 0 | .... | .... | .... | .... | .... | .... | .... | .... | .... | .... | .... | .... | .... | .... | .... | .... | .... | .... |
| | Detroit | NHL | 71 | 23 | 22 | 45 | 42 | 7 | 0 | 3 | 187 | 12.3 | 27 | 11 | 27.3 | 13:31 | 6 | 0 | 1 | 1 | 6 | 0 | 0 | 0 | 15:33 |
| | Sweden | Olympics | 8 | 1 | 3 | 4 | 2 | .... | .... | .... | .... | .... | .... | .... | .... | .... | .... | .... | .... | .... | .... | .... | .... | .... | .... |
| 2006-07 | Detroit | NHL | 53 | 14 | 20 | 34 | 28 | 6 | 0 | 2 | 189 | 7.4 | 1 | 3 | 66.7 | 15:09 | 18 | 3 | 8 | 11 | 14 | 1 | 0 | 1 | 15:27 |
| 2007-08 ♦ | Detroit | NHL | 73 | 11 | 29 | 40 | 26 | 3 | 0 | 1 | 249 | 4.4 | 21 | 14 | 42.9 | 16:16 | 22 | 5 | 8 | 13 | 8 | 0 | 0 | 1 | 15:56 |
| 2008-09 | Detroit | NHL | 81 | 19 | 21 | 40 | 50 | 7 | 0 | 1 | 257 | 7.4 | 0 | 8 | 25.0 | 15:22 | 23 | 5 | 5 | 10 | 6 | 0 | 0 | 2 | 15:08 |
| | NHL Totals | | 466 | 86 | 122 | 208 | 244 | 26 | 3 | 11 | 1183 | 7.3 | | 112 | 39.3 | 14:19 | 69 | 13 | 22 | 35 | 34 | 1 | 0 | 4 | 15:30 |

Traded to **NY Rangers** by **San Jose** with Christian Gosselin for Adam Graves and future considerations, June 24, 2001. Traded to **Pittsburgh** by **NY Rangers** with Joel Bouchard, Richard Lintner and Rico Fata for Mike Wilson, Alex Kovalev, Janne Laukkanen and Dan LaCouture, February 10, 2003. Traded to **Florida** by **Pittsburgh** with Pittsburgh's 1st round choice (Nathan Horton) and 2nd round compensatory choice (Stefan Meyer) in 2003 Entry Draft for Florida's 1st (Marc-Andre Fleury) and 3rd (Daniel Carcillo) round choices in 2003 Entry Draft, June 21, 2003. • Missed majority of 2003-04 season recovering from jaw (November 21, 2003 vs. Washington) and hand (January 21, 2004 vs. Columbus) injuries. Signed as a free agent by **Geneve** (Swiss), September 8, 2004. Signed as a free agent by **Sodertalje** (Sweden), October 26, 2004. Signed as a free agent by **Detroit**, September 17, 2005. Signed as a free agent by **Vancouver**, July 3, 2009.

## SANTORELLI, Mike

(san-toh-REHL-ee, MIGHK) **NSH.**

Center. Shoots right. 6', 189 lbs. Born, Vancouver, B.C., December 14, 1985. Nashville's 6th choice, 178th overall, in 2004 Entry Draft.

| Season | Club | League | GP | G | A | Pts | PIM | PP | SH | GW | S | % | +/- | TF | F% | Min | GP | G | A | Pts | PIM | PP | SH | GW | Min |
|---|---|---|---|---|---|---|---|---|---|---|---|---|---|---|---|---|---|---|---|---|---|---|---|---|---|
| 2003-04 | Vernon Vipers | BCHL | 60 | 43 | 53 | 96 | 26 | .... | .... | .... | .... | .... | .... | .... | .... | .... | 5 | 0 | 2 | 2 | 0 | .... | .... | .... | .... |
| 2004-05 | Northern Mich. | CCHA | 40 | 16 | 14 | 30 | 22 | .... | .... | .... | .... | .... | .... | .... | .... | .... | .... | .... | .... | .... | .... | .... | .... | .... | .... |
| 2005-06 | Northern Mich. | CCHA | 40 | 15 | 18 | 33 | 24 | .... | .... | .... | .... | .... | .... | .... | .... | .... | .... | .... | .... | .... | .... | .... | .... | .... | .... |
| 2006-07 | Northern Mich. | CCHA | 41 | *30 | 17 | 47 | 28 | .... | .... | .... | .... | .... | .... | .... | .... | .... | .... | .... | .... | .... | .... | .... | .... | .... | .... |
| 2007-08 | Milwaukee | AHL | 80 | 21 | 21 | 42 | 60 | .... | .... | .... | .... | .... | .... | .... | .... | .... | 6 | 0 | 0 | 0 | 2 | .... | .... | .... | .... |
| 2008-09 | Nashville | NHL | 7 | 0 | 0 | 0 | 2 | 0 | 0 | 0 | 11 | 0.0 | –5 | 47 | 44.7 | 12:15 | .... | .... | .... | .... | .... | .... | .... | .... | .... |
| | Milwaukee | AHL | 70 | 27 | 43 | 70 | 36 | .... | .... | .... | .... | .... | .... | .... | .... | .... | 11 | 6 | 5 | 11 | 6 | .... | .... | .... | .... |
| | NHL Totals | | 7 | 0 | 0 | 0 | 2 | 0 | 0 | 0 | 11 | 0.0 | | 47 | 44.7 | 12:15 | .... | .... | .... | .... | .... | .... | .... | .... | .... |

CCHA All-Rookie Team (2005) • CCHA First All-Star Team (2007) • NCAA West Second All-American Team (2007)

## SARICH, Cory

(SAHR-ihch, KOH-ree) **CGY.**

Defense. Shoots right. 6'4", 207 lbs. Born, Saskatoon, Sask., August 16, 1978. Buffalo's 2nd choice, 27th overall, in 1996 Entry Draft.

| Season | Club | League | GP | G | A | Pts | PIM | PP | SH | GW | S | % | +/- | TF | F% | Min | GP | G | A | Pts | PIM | PP | SH | GW | Min |
|---|---|---|---|---|---|---|---|---|---|---|---|---|---|---|---|---|---|---|---|---|---|---|---|---|---|
| 1994-95 | Sask. Contacts | SMHL | 31 | 5 | 22 | 27 | 99 | .... | .... | .... | .... | .... | .... | .... | .... | .... | .... | .... | .... | .... | .... | .... | .... | .... | .... |
| | Saskatoon Blades | WHL | 6 | 0 | 0 | 0 | 4 | .... | .... | .... | .... | .... | .... | .... | .... | .... | 3 | 0 | 1 | 1 | 0 | .... | .... | .... | .... |
| 1995-96 | Saskatoon Blades | WHL | 59 | 5 | 18 | 23 | 54 | .... | .... | .... | .... | .... | .... | .... | .... | .... | 3 | 0 | 0 | 0 | 4 | .... | .... | .... | .... |
| 1996-97 | Saskatoon Blades | WHL | 58 | 6 | 27 | 33 | 158 | .... | .... | .... | .... | .... | .... | .... | .... | .... | .... | .... | .... | .... | .... | .... | .... | .... | .... |
| 1997-98 | Saskatoon Blades | WHL | 33 | 5 | 24 | 29 | 90 | .... | .... | .... | .... | .... | .... | .... | .... | .... | .... | .... | .... | .... | .... | .... | .... | .... | .... |
| | Seattle | WHL | 13 | 3 | 16 | 19 | 47 | .... | .... | .... | .... | .... | .... | .... | .... | .... | .... | .... | .... | .... | .... | .... | .... | .... | .... |
| 1998-99 | Buffalo | NHL | 4 | 0 | 0 | 0 | 0 | 0 | 0 | 0 | 2 | 0.0 | 3 | 0 | 0.0 | 13:11 | .... | .... | .... | .... | .... | .... | .... | .... | .... |
| | Rochester | AHL | 77 | 3 | 26 | 29 | 82 | .... | .... | .... | .... | .... | .... | .... | .... | .... | 20 | 2 | 4 | 6 | 14 | .... | .... | .... | .... |
| 99-2000 | Buffalo | NHL | 42 | 0 | 4 | 4 | 35 | 0 | 0 | 0 | 49 | 0.0 | 2 | 0 | 0.0 | 17:42 | .... | .... | .... | .... | .... | .... | .... | .... | .... |
| | Rochester | AHL | 15 | 0 | 6 | 6 | 44 | .... | .... | .... | .... | .... | .... | .... | .... | .... | .... | .... | .... | .... | .... | .... | .... | .... | .... |
| | Tampa Bay | NHL | 17 | 0 | 2 | 2 | 42 | 0 | 0 | 0 | 20 | 0.0 | –8 | 0 | 0.0 | 20:42 | .... | .... | .... | .... | .... | .... | .... | .... | .... |

| Season | Club | League | Regular Season GP | G | A | Pts | PIM | PP | SH | GW | S | % | +/- | TF | F% | Min | Playoffs GP | G | A | Pts | PIM | PP | SH | GW | Min |
|---|---|---|---|---|---|---|---|---|---|---|---|---|---|---|---|---|---|---|---|---|---|---|---|---|---|
| **2000-01** | **Tampa Bay** | **NHL** | **73** | **1** | **8** | **9** | **106** | **0** | **0** | **1** | **66** | **1.5** | **–25** | **3** | **0.0** | **18:44** | .... | .... | .... | .... | .... | .... | .... | .... | .... |
| | Detroit Vipers | IHL | 3 | 0 | 2 | 2 | 2 | .... | .... | .... | .... | .... | .... | .... | .... | .... | .... | .... | .... | .... | .... | .... | .... | .... | .... |
| **2001-02** | **Tampa Bay** | **NHL** | **72** | **0** | **11** | **11** | **105** | **0** | **0** | **0** | **55** | **0.0** | **–4** | **2** | **50.0** | **16:06** | .... | .... | .... | .... | .... | .... | .... | .... | .... |
| | Springfield | AHL | 2 | 0 | 0 | 0 | 0 | .... | .... | .... | .... | .... | .... | .... | .... | .... | .... | .... | .... | .... | .... | .... | .... | .... | .... |
| **2002-03** | **Tampa Bay** | **NHL** | **82** | **5** | **9** | **14** | **63** | **0** | **0** | **2** | **79** | **6.3** | **–3** | **3** | **0.0** | **19:36** | **11** | **0** | **2** | **2** | **6** | **0** | **0** | **0** | **21:18** |
| **2003-04♦** | **Tampa Bay** | **NHL** | **82** | **3** | **16** | **19** | **89** | **0** | **1** | **1** | **93** | **3.2** | **5** | **1** | **0.0** | **18:31** | **23** | **0** | **2** | **2** | **25** | **0** | **0** | **0** | **19:11** |
| 2004-05 | | | DID NOT PLAY | | | | | | | | | | | | | | | | | | | | | | |
| **2005-06** | **Tampa Bay** | **NHL** | **82** | **1** | **14** | **15** | **79** | **0** | **0** | **0** | **88** | **1.1** | **–2** | **0** | **0.0** | **18:34** | **5** | **0** | **1** | **1** | **4** | **0** | **0** | **0** | **15:46** |
| **2006-07** | **Tampa Bay** | **NHL** | **82** | **0** | **15** | **15** | **70** | **0** | **0** | **0** | **64** | **0.0** | **–6** | **1** | **0.0** | **18:07** | **6** | **0** | **0** | **0** | **2** | **0** | **0** | **0** | **16:37** |
| **2007-08** | **Calgary** | **NHL** | **80** | **2** | **5** | **7** | **135** | **0** | **0** | **0** | **57** | **3.5** | **2** | **0** | **0.0** | **18:49** | **7** | **0** | **1** | **1** | **4** | **0** | **0** | **0** | **19:35** |
| **2008-09** | **Calgary** | **NHL** | **76** | **2** | **18** | **20** | **112** | **0** | **0** | **0** | **57** | **3.5** | **12** | **0** | **0.0** | **17:53** | **5** | **0** | **1** | **1** | **4** | **0** | **0** | **0** | **18:44** |
| | **NHL Totals** | | **692** | **14** | **102** | **116** | **836** | **0** | **1** | **4** | **630** | **2.2** | | **10** | **10.0** | **18:19** | **57** | **0** | **7** | **7** | **45** | **0** | **0** | **0** | **19:02** |

WHL West Second All-Star Team (1998) • AHL All-Rookie Team (1999)

Traded to **Tampa Bay** by **Buffalo** with Wayne Primeau, Brian Holzinger and Buffalo's 3rd round choice (Alexander Kharitonov) in 2000 Entry Draft for Chris Gratton and Tampa Bay's 2nd round choice (Derek Roy) in 2001 Entry Draft, March 9, 2000. Signed as a free agent by **Calgary**, July 1, 2007.

## SATAN, Miroslav

(shuh-TAN, MEER-oh-slav)

Left wing. Shoots left. 6'3", 191 lbs. Born, Topolcany, Czech., October 22, 1974. Edmonton's 6th choice, 111th overall, in 1993 Entry Draft.

| Season | Club | League | GP | G | A | Pts | PIM | PP | SH | GW | S | % | +/- | TF | F% | Min | GP | G | A | Pts | PIM | PP | SH | GW | Min |
|---|---|---|---|---|---|---|---|---|---|---|---|---|---|---|---|---|---|---|---|---|---|---|---|---|---|
| 1991-92 | Topolcany Jr. | Czech-Jr. | 31 | 30 | 22 | 52 | | .... | .... | .... | .... | .... | .... | .... | .... | .... | .... | .... | .... | .... | .... | .... | .... | .... | .... |
| | VTJ Topolcany | Czech-2 | 9 | 2 | 1 | 3 | 6 | .... | .... | .... | .... | .... | .... | .... | .... | .... | .... | .... | .... | .... | .... | .... | .... | .... | .... |
| 1992-93 | Dukla Trencin | Czech | 38 | 11 | 6 | 17 | | .... | .... | .... | .... | .... | .... | .... | .... | .... | .... | .... | .... | .... | .... | .... | .... | .... | .... |
| 1993-94 | Dukla Trencin | Slovakia | 30 | 32 | 16 | 48 | 16 | .... | .... | .... | .... | .... | .... | .... | .... | .... | .... | .... | .... | .... | .... | .... | .... | .... | .... |
| | Slovakia | Olympics | 8 | *9 | 0 | 9 | 0 | .... | .... | .... | .... | .... | .... | .... | .... | .... | .... | .... | .... | .... | .... | .... | .... | .... | .... |
| 1994-95 | Cape Breton | AHL | 25 | 24 | 16 | 40 | 15 | .... | .... | .... | .... | .... | .... | .... | .... | .... | .... | .... | .... | .... | .... | .... | .... | .... | .... |
| | Detroit Vipers | IHL | 8 | 1 | 3 | 4 | 4 | .... | .... | .... | .... | .... | .... | .... | .... | .... | .... | .... | .... | .... | .... | .... | .... | .... | .... |
| | San Diego Gulls | IHL | 6 | 0 | 2 | 2 | 6 | .... | .... | .... | .... | .... | .... | .... | .... | .... | .... | .... | .... | .... | .... | .... | .... | .... | .... |
| **1995-96** | **Edmonton** | **NHL** | **62** | **18** | **17** | **35** | **22** | **6** | **0** | **4** | **113** | **15.9** | **0** | .... | .... | .... | .... | .... | .... | .... | .... | .... | .... | .... | .... |
| **1996-97** | **Edmonton** | **NHL** | **64** | **17** | **11** | **28** | **22** | **5** | **0** | **2** | **90** | **18.9** | **–4** | .... | .... | .... | .... | .... | .... | .... | .... | .... | .... | .... | .... |
| | **Buffalo** | **NHL** | **12** | **8** | **2** | **10** | **4** | **2** | **0** | **1** | **29** | **27.6** | **1** | .... | .... | .... | **7** | **0** | **0** | **0** | **0** | **0** | **0** | **0** | .... |
| **1997-98** | **Buffalo** | **NHL** | **79** | **22** | **24** | **46** | **34** | **9** | **0** | **4** | **139** | **15.8** | **2** | .... | .... | .... | **14** | **5** | **4** | **9** | **4** | **4** | **0** | **1** | .... |
| **1998-99** | **Buffalo** | **NHL** | **81** | **40** | **26** | **66** | **44** | **13** | **3** | **6** | **208** | **19.2** | **24** | **9** | **55.6** | **20:49** | **12** | **3** | **5** | **8** | **2** | **1** | **0** | **1** | **21:18** |
| **99-2000** | Dukla Trencin | Slovakia | 3 | 2 | 8 | 10 | 2 | .... | .... | .... | .... | .... | .... | .... | .... | .... | .... | .... | .... | .... | .... | .... | .... | .... | .... |
| | **Buffalo** | **NHL** | **81** | **33** | **34** | **67** | **32** | **5** | **3** | **5** | **265** | **12.5** | **16** | **7** | **14.3** | **20:35** | **5** | **3** | **2** | **5** | **0** | **0** | **0** | **0** | **19:52** |
| **2000-01** | **Buffalo** | **NHL** | **82** | **29** | **33** | **62** | **36** | **8** | **2** | **4** | **206** | **14.1** | **5** | **11** | **36.4** | **19:56** | **13** | **3** | **10** | **13** | **8** | **1** | **0** | **0** | **21:18** |
| **2001-02** | **Buffalo** | **NHL** | **82** | **37** | **36** | **73** | **33** | **15** | **5** | **5** | **267** | **13.9** | **14** | **4** | **50.0** | **21:10** | .... | .... | .... | .... | .... | .... | .... | .... | .... |
| | Slovakia | Olympics | 2 | 0 | 1 | 1 | 0 | .... | .... | .... | .... | .... | .... | .... | .... | .... | .... | .... | .... | .... | .... | .... | .... | .... | .... |
| **2002-03** | **Buffalo** | **NHL** | **79** | **26** | **49** | **75** | **20** | **11** | **1** | **3** | **240** | **10.8** | **–3** | **10** | **20.0** | **21:23** | .... | .... | .... | .... | .... | .... | .... | .... | .... |
| **2003-04** | Bratislava | Slovakia | 7 | 6 | 4 | 10 | 41 | .... | .... | .... | .... | .... | .... | .... | .... | .... | .... | .... | .... | .... | .... | .... | .... | .... | .... |
| | **Buffalo** | **NHL** | **82** | **29** | **28** | **57** | **30** | **11** | **1** | **5** | **206** | **14.1** | **–15** | **9** | **22.2** | **20:02** | .... | .... | .... | .... | .... | .... | .... | .... | .... |
| 2004-05 | Bratislava | Slovakia | 18 | 11 | 9 | 20 | 14 | .... | .... | .... | .... | .... | .... | .... | .... | .... | 18 | *15 | 7 | *22 | 16 | .... | .... | .... | .... |
| **2005-06** | **NY Islanders** | **NHL** | **82** | **35** | **31** | **66** | **54** | **17** | **0** | **2** | **253** | **13.8** | **–8** | **342** | **53.2** | **19:10** | .... | .... | .... | .... | .... | .... | .... | .... | .... |
| | Slovakia | Olympics | 6 | 0 | 2 | 2 | 2 | .... | .... | .... | .... | .... | .... | .... | .... | .... | .... | .... | .... | .... | .... | .... | .... | .... | .... |
| **2006-07** | **NY Islanders** | **NHL** | **81** | **27** | **32** | **59** | **46** | **7** | **1** | **2** | **216** | **12.5** | **–12** | **164** | **55.5** | **18:35** | **5** | **1** | **2** | **3** | **0** | **0** | **0** | **0** | **15:15** |
| **2007-08** | **NY Islanders** | **NHL** | **80** | **16** | **25** | **41** | **39** | **5** | **0** | **4** | **171** | **9.4** | **–11** | **38** | **50.0** | **18:19** | .... | .... | .... | .... | .... | .... | .... | .... | .... |
| **2008-09♦** | **Pittsburgh** | **NHL** | **65** | **17** | **19** | **36** | **36** | **6** | **0** | **2** | **120** | **14.2** | **3** | **12** | **41.7** | **15:45** | **17** | **1** | **5** | **6** | **11** | **0** | **0** | **0** | **9:55** |
| | Wilkes-Barre | AHL | 10 | 3 | 6 | 9 | 4 | .... | .... | .... | .... | .... | .... | .... | .... | .... | .... | .... | .... | .... | .... | .... | .... | .... | .... |
| | **NHL Totals** | | **1012** | **354** | **367** | **721** | **452** | **120** | **16** | **49** | **2523** | **14.0** | | **606** | **51.7** | **19:39** | **73** | **16** | **28** | **44** | **25** | **6** | **0** | **2** | **16:51** |

Played in NHL All-Star Game (2000, 2003)

Traded to **Buffalo** by **Edmonton** for Barrie Moore and Craig Millar, March 18, 1997. Signed as a free agent by **Bratislava** (Slovakia), December 29, 2004. Signed as a free agent by **NY Islanders**, August 3, 2005. Signed as a free agent by **Pittsburgh**, July 3, 2008.

## SAUER, Kurt

(SAW-uhr, KUHRT) **PHX.**

Defense. Shoots left. 6'4", 220 lbs. Born, St. Cloud, MN, January 16, 1981. Colorado's 5th choice, 88th overall, in 2000 Entry Draft.

| Season | Club | League | GP | G | A | Pts | PIM | PP | SH | GW | S | % | +/- | TF | F% | Min | GP | G | A | Pts | PIM | PP | SH | GW | Min |
|---|---|---|---|---|---|---|---|---|---|---|---|---|---|---|---|---|---|---|---|---|---|---|---|---|---|
| 1998-99 | North Iowa | USHL | 52 | 1 | 4 | 5 | 67 | .... | .... | .... | .... | .... | .... | .... | .... | .... | .... | .... | .... | .... | .... | .... | .... | .... | .... |
| 99-2000 | Spokane Chiefs | WHL | 71 | 3 | 12 | 15 | 48 | .... | .... | .... | .... | .... | .... | .... | .... | .... | 15 | 2 | 1 | 3 | 8 | .... | .... | .... | .... |
| 2000-01 | Spokane Chiefs | WHL | 48 | 5 | 10 | 15 | 85 | .... | .... | .... | .... | .... | .... | .... | .... | .... | 3 | 1 | 0 | 1 | 2 | .... | .... | .... | .... |
| 2001-02 | Spokane Chiefs | WHL | 61 | 4 | 20 | 24 | 73 | .... | .... | .... | .... | .... | .... | .... | .... | .... | 11 | 0 | 3 | 3 | 12 | .... | .... | .... | .... |
| **2002-03** | **Anaheim** | **NHL** | **80** | **1** | **2** | **3** | **74** | **0** | **0** | **0** | **50** | **2.0** | **–23** | **0** | **0.0** | **18:33** | **21** | **1** | **1** | **2** | **6** | **0** | **1** | **1** | **20:45** |
| **2003-04** | **Anaheim** | **NHL** | **55** | **1** | **4** | **5** | **32** | **0** | **0** | **0** | **32** | **3.1** | **–8** | **0** | **0.0** | **16:54** | .... | .... | .... | .... | .... | .... | .... | .... | .... |
| | **Colorado** | **NHL** | **14** | **0** | **1** | **1** | **19** | **0** | **0** | **0** | **12** | **0.0** | **–3** | **0** | **0.0** | **15:04** | **3** | **0** | **0** | **0** | **0** | **0** | **0** | **0** | **11:56** |
| 2004-05 | | | DID NOT PLAY | | | | | | | | | | | | | | | | | | | | | | |
| **2005-06** | **Colorado** | **NHL** | **37** | **1** | **4** | **5** | **24** | **0** | **0** | **0** | **19** | **5.3** | **5** | **0** | **0.0** | **12:48** | **9** | **0** | **0** | **0** | **4** | **0** | **0** | **0** | **8:39** |
| | Lowell | AHL | 4 | 0 | 0 | 0 | 0 | .... | .... | .... | .... | .... | .... | .... | .... | .... | .... | .... | .... | .... | .... | .... | .... | .... | .... |
| **2006-07** | **Colorado** | **NHL** | **48** | **0** | **6** | **6** | **24** | **0** | **0** | **0** | **29** | **0.0** | **–3** | **0** | **0.0** | **18:20** | .... | .... | .... | .... | .... | .... | .... | .... | .... |
| **2007-08** | **Colorado** | **NHL** | **54** | **1** | **5** | **6** | **41** | **0** | **0** | **0** | **28** | **3.6** | **17** | **0** | **0.0** | **18:41** | **10** | **1** | **0** | **1** | **8** | **0** | **0** | **0** | **19:23** |
| **2008-09** | **Phoenix** | **NHL** | **68** | **1** | **6** | **7** | **36** | **0** | **0** | **0** | **33** | **3.0** | **–1** | **1** | **0.0** | **20:37** | .... | .... | .... | .... | .... | .... | .... | .... | .... |
| | **NHL Totals** | | **356** | **5** | **28** | **33** | **250** | **0** | **0** | **0** | **203** | **2.5** | | **1** | **0.0** | **17:57** | **43** | **2** | **1** | **3** | **18** | **0** | **1** | **1** | **17:17** |

WHL West First All-Star Team (2002)

Signed as a free agent by **Anaheim**, July 6, 2002. Traded to **Colorado** by **Anaheim** with Anaheim's 4th round choice (Raymond Macias) in 2005 Entry Draft for Martin Skoula, February 21, 2004. Signed as a free agent by **Phoenix**, July 1, 2008.

## SAUER, Michael

(SAW-uhr, MIGH-kuhl) **NYR**

Defense. Shoots right. 6'3", 215 lbs. Born, St. Cloud, MN, August 7, 1987. NY Rangers' 2nd choice, 40th overall, in 2005 Entry Draft.

| Season | Club | League | GP | G | A | Pts | PIM | PP | SH | GW | S | % | +/- | TF | F% | Min | GP | G | A | Pts | PIM | PP | SH | GW | Min |
|---|---|---|---|---|---|---|---|---|---|---|---|---|---|---|---|---|---|---|---|---|---|---|---|---|---|
| 2003-04 | St. Cloud Tech | High-MN | 18 | 12 | 16 | 28 | 34 | .... | .... | .... | .... | .... | .... | .... | .... | .... | .... | .... | .... | .... | .... | .... | .... | .... | .... |
| 2004-05 | Portland | WHL | 32 | 2 | 11 | 13 | 10 | .... | .... | .... | .... | .... | .... | .... | .... | .... | .... | .... | .... | .... | .... | .... | .... | .... | .... |
| 2005-06 | Portland | WHL | 59 | 8 | 23 | 31 | 68 | .... | .... | .... | .... | .... | .... | .... | .... | .... | 12 | 4 | 2 | 6 | 8 | .... | .... | .... | .... |
| 2006-07 | Portland | WHL | 33 | 4 | 8 | 12 | 46 | .... | .... | .... | .... | .... | .... | .... | .... | .... | .... | .... | .... | .... | .... | .... | .... | .... | .... |
| | Medicine Hat | WHL | 32 | 1 | 10 | 11 | 29 | .... | .... | .... | .... | .... | .... | .... | .... | .... | 23 | 1 | 5 | 6 | 34 | .... | .... | .... | .... |
| 2007-08 | Hartford | AHL | 71 | 4 | 7 | 11 | 80 | .... | .... | .... | .... | .... | .... | .... | .... | .... | 2 | 0 | 0 | 0 | 0 | .... | .... | .... | .... |
| **2008-09** | **NY Rangers** | **NHL** | **3** | **0** | **0** | **0** | **0** | **0** | **0** | **0** | **2** | **0.0** | **–1** | **0** | **0.0** | **9:21** | .... | .... | .... | .... | .... | .... | .... | .... | .... |
| | Hartford | AHL | 64 | 6 | 17 | 23 | 35 | .... | .... | .... | .... | .... | .... | .... | .... | .... | 6 | 0 | 0 | 0 | 10 | .... | .... | .... | .... |
| | **NHL Totals** | | **3** | **0** | **0** | **0** | **0** | **0** | **0** | **0** | **2** | **0.0** | | **0** | **0.0** | **9:21** | .... | .... | .... | .... | .... | .... | .... | .... | .... |

• Missed majority of 2004-05 season due to hip injury and resulting surgery.

## SAVARD, Marc

(suh-VAHRD, MAHRK) **BOS.**

Center. Shoots left. 5'10", 191 lbs. Born, Ottawa, Ont., July 17, 1977. NY Rangers' 3rd choice, 91st overall, in 1995 Entry Draft.

| Season | Club | League | GP | G | A | Pts | PIM | PP | SH | GW | S | % | +/- | TF | F% | Min | GP | G | A | Pts | PIM | PP | SH | GW | Min |
|---|---|---|---|---|---|---|---|---|---|---|---|---|---|---|---|---|---|---|---|---|---|---|---|---|---|
| 1992-93 | Metcalfe Jets | OHA-B | 36 | *44 | 55 | *99 | 38 | .... | .... | .... | .... | .... | .... | .... | .... | .... | .... | .... | .... | .... | .... | .... | .... | .... | .... |
| 1993-94 | Oshawa Generals | OHL | 61 | 18 | 39 | 57 | 20 | .... | .... | .... | .... | .... | .... | .... | .... | .... | 5 | 4 | 3 | 7 | 8 | .... | .... | .... | .... |
| 1994-95 | Oshawa Generals | OHL | 66 | 43 | 96 | *139 | 78 | .... | .... | .... | .... | .... | .... | .... | .... | .... | 7 | 5 | 6 | 11 | 8 | .... | .... | .... | .... |
| 1995-96 | Oshawa Generals | OHL | 48 | 28 | 59 | 87 | 77 | .... | .... | .... | .... | .... | .... | .... | .... | .... | 5 | 4 | 5 | 9 | 6 | .... | .... | .... | .... |
| 1996-97 | Oshawa Generals | OHL | 64 | 43 | *87 | *130 | 94 | .... | .... | .... | .... | .... | .... | .... | .... | .... | 18 | 13 | *24 | *37 | 20 | .... | .... | .... | .... |
| **1997-98** | **NY Rangers** | **NHL** | **28** | **1** | **5** | **6** | **4** | **0** | **0** | **0** | **32** | **3.1** | **–4** | .... | .... | .... | .... | .... | .... | .... | .... | .... | .... | .... | .... |
| | Hartford | AHL | 58 | 21 | 53 | 74 | 66 | .... | .... | .... | .... | .... | .... | .... | .... | .... | 15 | 8 | 19 | 27 | 24 | .... | .... | .... | .... |
| **1998-99** | **NY Rangers** | **NHL** | **70** | **9** | **36** | **45** | **38** | **4** | **0** | **1** | **116** | **7.8** | **–7** | **956** | **48.4** | **14:35** | .... | .... | .... | .... | .... | .... | .... | .... | .... |
| | Hartford | AHL | 9 | 3 | 10 | 13 | 16 | .... | .... | .... | .... | .... | .... | .... | .... | .... | 7 | 1 | 12 | 13 | 16 | .... | .... | .... | .... |
| **99-2000** | **Calgary** | **NHL** | **78** | **22** | **31** | **53** | **56** | **4** | **0** | **3** | **184** | **12.0** | **–2** | **1021** | **49.6** | **16:36** | .... | .... | .... | .... | .... | .... | .... | .... | .... |
| **2000-01** | **Calgary** | **NHL** | **77** | **23** | **42** | **65** | **46** | **10** | **1** | **5** | **197** | **11.7** | **–12** | **1050** | **53.1** | **19:13** | .... | .... | .... | .... | .... | .... | .... | .... | .... |
| **2001-02** | **Calgary** | **NHL** | **56** | **14** | **19** | **33** | **48** | **7** | **0** | **3** | **140** | **10.0** | **–18** | **577** | **54.8** | **17:20** | .... | .... | .... | .... | .... | .... | .... | .... | .... |
| **2002-03** | **Calgary** | **NHL** | **10** | **1** | **2** | **3** | **8** | **0** | **0** | **0** | **21** | **4.8** | **–3** | **89** | **52.8** | **14:41** | .... | .... | .... | .... | .... | .... | .... | .... | .... |
| | **Atlanta** | **NHL** | **57** | **16** | **31** | **47** | **77** | **6** | **0** | **4** | **127** | **12.6** | **–11** | **1247** | **50.9** | **19:50** | .... | .... | .... | .... | .... | .... | .... | .... | .... |
| **2003-04** | **Atlanta** | **NHL** | **45** | **19** | **33** | **52** | **85** | **6** | **1** | **3** | **133** | **14.3** | **–8** | **1083** | **49.9** | **22:19** | .... | .... | .... | .... | .... | .... | .... | .... | .... |
| 2004-05 | HC Thurgau | Swiss-2 | 13 | 9 | 19 | 28 | 10 | .... | .... | .... | .... | .... | .... | .... | .... | .... | .... | .... | .... | .... | .... | .... | .... | .... | .... |
| | SC Bern | Swiss | 5 | 1 | 2 | 3 | 0 | .... | .... | .... | .... | .... | .... | .... | .... | .... | .... | .... | .... | .... | .... | .... | .... | .... | .... |
| **2005-06** | **Atlanta** | **NHL** | **82** | **28** | **69** | **97** | **100** | **14** | **1** | **4** | **212** | **13.2** | **7** | **1529** | **51.6** | **20:30** | .... | .... | .... | .... | .... | .... | .... | .... | .... |
| **2006-07** | **Boston** | **NHL** | **82** | **22** | **74** | **96** | **96** | **10** | **1** | **3** | **221** | **10.0** | **–19** | **1420** | **50.1** | **20:13** | .... | .... | .... | .... | .... | .... | .... | .... | .... |

| | | | Regular Season | | | | | | | | | | | | | | Playoffs | | | | | | | | |
|---|---|---|---|---|---|---|---|---|---|---|---|---|---|---|---|---|---|---|---|---|---|---|---|---|---|
| Season | Club | League | GP | G | A | Pts | PIM | PP | SH | GW | S | % | +/- | TF | F% | Min | GP | G | A | Pts | PIM | PP | SH | GW | Min |
| 2007-08 | Boston | NHL | 74 | 15 | 63 | 78 | 66 | 4 | 0 | 2 | 196 | 7.7 | 3 | 1555 | 51.6 | 20:31 | 7 | 1 | 5 | 6 | 6 | 0 | 0 | 1 | 17:06 |
| 2008-09 | Boston | NHL | 82 | 25 | 63 | 88 | 70 | 9 | 0 | 5 | 213 | 11.7 | 25 | 1289 | 49.9 | 19:32 | 11 | 6 | 7 | 13 | 4 | 3 | 0 | 2 | 19:36 |
| | **NHL Totals** | | 741 | 195 | 468 | 663 | 694 | 74 | 4 | 33 | 1792 | 10.9 | | 11816 | 50.9 | 18:57 | 18 | 7 | 12 | 19 | 10 | 3 | 0 | 3 | 18:38 |

OHL Second All-Star Team (1995)

Played in NHL All-Star Game (2008, 2009)

Traded to **Calgary** by **NY Rangers** with NY Rangers 1st round choice (Oleg Saprykin) in 1999 Entry Draft for the rights to Jan Hlavac and Calgary's 1st (Jamie Lundmark) and 3rd (later traded back to Calgary – Calgary selected Craig Andersson) round choices in 1999 Entry Draft, June 26, 1999. Traded to **Atlanta** by **Calgary** for Ruslan Zainullin, November 15, 2002. Signed as a free agent by **Thurgau** (Swiss-2), October 11, 2004. Signed as a free agent by **Bern** (Swiss), November 23, 2004. Signed as a free agent by **Boston**, July 1, 2006.

## SAWADA, Raymond

(suh-WAW-duh, RAY-muhnd) **DAL.**

Right wing. Shoots right. 6'2", 195 lbs. Born, Richmond, B.C., February 19, 1985. Dallas' 3rd choice, 52nd overall, in 2004 Entry Draft.

| Season | Club | League | GP | G | A | Pts | PIM | PP | SH | GW | S | % | +/- | TF | F% | Min | GP | G | A | Pts | PIM | PP | SH | GW | Min |
|---|---|---|---|---|---|---|---|---|---|---|---|---|---|---|---|---|---|---|---|---|---|---|---|---|---|
| 2002-03 | Richmond | PIJHL | 36 | 7 | 17 | 24 | 155 | .... | .... | .... | .... | .... | .... | .... | .... | .... | .... | .... | .... | .... | .... | .... | .... | .... | .... |
| 2003-04 | Nanaimo Clippers | BCHL | 54 | 20 | 32 | 52 | 93 | .... | .... | .... | .... | .... | .... | .... | .... | .... | 25 | 6 | 16 | 22 | 22 | .... | .... | .... | .... |
| 2004-05 | Cornell Big Red | ECAC | 35 | 4 | 5 | 9 | 48 | .... | .... | .... | .... | .... | .... | .... | .... | .... | .... | .... | .... | .... | .... | .... | .... | .... | .... |
| 2005-06 | Cornell Big Red | ECAC | 35 | 7 | 13 | 20 | 20 | .... | .... | .... | .... | .... | .... | .... | .... | .... | .... | .... | .... | .... | .... | .... | .... | .... | .... |
| 2006-07 | Cornell Big Red | ECAC | 31 | 10 | 11 | 21 | 29 | .... | .... | .... | .... | .... | .... | .... | .... | .... | .... | .... | .... | .... | .... | .... | .... | .... | .... |
| 2007-08 | Cornell Big Red | ECAC | 36 | 10 | 16 | 26 | 34 | .... | .... | .... | .... | .... | .... | .... | .... | .... | .... | .... | .... | .... | .... | .... | .... | .... | .... |
| | Iowa Stars | AHL | 10 | 2 | 7 | 9 | 14 | .... | .... | .... | .... | .... | .... | .... | .... | .... | .... | .... | .... | .... | .... | .... | .... | .... | .... |
| **2008-09** | **Dallas** | **NHL** | **5** | **1** | **0** | **1** | **0** | **0** | **0** | **0** | **2** | **50.0** | **–1** | **0** | **0.0** | **8:42** | .... | .... | .... | .... | .... | .... | .... | .... | .... |
| | Manitoba Moose | AHL | 52 | 6 | 15 | 21 | 31 | .... | .... | .... | .... | .... | .... | .... | .... | .... | 22 | 4 | 4 | 8 | 4 | .... | .... | .... | .... |
| | **NHL Totals** | | 5 | 1 | 0 | 1 | 0 | 0 | 0 | 0 | 2 | 50.0 | | 0 | 0.0 | 8:42 | .... | .... | .... | .... | .... | .... | .... | .... | .... |

## SBISA, Luca

(S'BEE-za, LOO-ka) **ANA.**

Defense. Shoots left. 6'2", 195 lbs. Born, Ozieri, Italy, January 30, 1990. Philadelphia's 1st choice, 19th overall, in 2008 Entry Draft.

| Season | Club | League | GP | G | A | Pts | PIM | PP | SH | GW | S | % | +/- | TF | F% | Min | GP | G | A | Pts | PIM | PP | SH | GW | Min |
|---|---|---|---|---|---|---|---|---|---|---|---|---|---|---|---|---|---|---|---|---|---|---|---|---|---|
| 2005-06 | EV Zug Jr. | Swiss-Jr. | 18 | 0 | 3 | 3 | 18 | .... | .... | .... | .... | .... | .... | .... | .... | .... | .... | .... | .... | .... | .... | .... | .... | .... | .... |
| 2006-07 | EV Zug Jr. | Swiss-Jr. | STATISTICS NOT AVAILABLE | | | | | | | | | | | | | | | | | | | | | | |
| | EHC Seewen | Swiss-3 | 6 | 1 | 2 | 3 | 4 | .... | .... | .... | .... | .... | .... | .... | .... | .... | .... | .... | .... | .... | .... | .... | .... | .... | .... |
| | EV Zug | Swiss | 7 | 0 | 0 | 0 | 0 | .... | .... | .... | .... | .... | .... | .... | .... | .... | 1 | 0 | 0 | 0 | 0 | .... | .... | .... | .... |
| 2007-08 | Lethbridge | WHL | 62 | 6 | 27 | 33 | 63 | .... | .... | .... | .... | .... | .... | .... | .... | .... | 19 | 3 | 12 | 15 | 17 | .... | .... | .... | .... |
| **2008-09** | **Philadelphia** | **NHL** | **39** | **0** | **7** | **7** | **36** | **0** | **0** | **0** | **38** | **0.0** | **–6** | **0** | **0.0** | **17:29** | **1** | **0** | **0** | **0** | **2** | **0** | **0** | **0** | **5:37** |
| | Lethbridge | WHL | 18 | 4 | 11 | 15 | 19 | .... | .... | .... | .... | .... | .... | .... | .... | .... | 11 | 2 | 1 | 3 | 12 | .... | .... | .... | .... |
| | Philadelphia | AHL | 2 | 1 | 1 | 2 | 2 | .... | .... | .... | .... | .... | .... | .... | .... | .... | .... | .... | .... | .... | .... | .... | .... | .... | .... |
| | **NHL Totals** | | 39 | 0 | 7 | 7 | 36 | 0 | 0 | 0 | 38 | 0.0 | | 0 | 0.0 | 17:29 | 1 | 0 | 0 | 0 | 2 | 0 | 0 | 0 | 5:37 |

Traded to **Anaheim** by **Philadelphia** with Joffrey Lupul, Philadelphia's 1st round choices in 2009 (later traded to Columbus - Columbus selected John Moore) and 2010 Entry Drafts and future considerations for Chris Pronger and Ryan Dingle, June 26, 2009.

## SCHAEFER, Peter

(SHAY-fuhr, PEE-tuhr)

Left wing. Shoots left. 6'1", 200 lbs. Born, Regina, Sask., July 12, 1977. Vancouver's 3rd choice, 66th overall, in 1995 Entry Draft.

| Season | Club | League | GP | G | A | Pts | PIM | PP | SH | GW | S | % | +/- | TF | F% | Min | GP | G | A | Pts | PIM | PP | SH | GW | Min |
|---|---|---|---|---|---|---|---|---|---|---|---|---|---|---|---|---|---|---|---|---|---|---|---|---|---|
| 1993-94 | Yorkton Mallers | SMHL | 32 | 27 | 14 | 41 | 133 | .... | .... | .... | .... | .... | .... | .... | .... | .... | .... | .... | .... | .... | .... | .... | .... | .... | .... |
| | Brandon | WHL | 2 | 1 | 0 | 1 | 0 | .... | .... | .... | .... | .... | .... | .... | .... | .... | .... | .... | .... | .... | .... | .... | .... | .... | .... |
| 1994-95 | Brandon | WHL | 68 | 27 | 32 | 59 | 34 | .... | .... | .... | .... | .... | .... | .... | .... | .... | 18 | 5 | 3 | 8 | 18 | .... | .... | .... | .... |
| 1995-96 | Brandon | WHL | 69 | 47 | 61 | 108 | 53 | .... | .... | .... | .... | .... | .... | .... | .... | .... | 19 | 10 | 13 | 23 | 5 | .... | .... | .... | .... |
| 1996-97 | Brandon | WHL | 61 | 49 | 74 | 123 | 85 | .... | .... | .... | .... | .... | .... | .... | .... | .... | 6 | 1 | 4 | 5 | 4 | .... | .... | .... | .... |
| | Syracuse Crunch | AHL | 5 | 0 | 3 | 3 | 0 | .... | .... | .... | .... | .... | .... | .... | .... | .... | 3 | 1 | 3 | 4 | 14 | .... | .... | .... | .... |
| 1997-98 | Syracuse Crunch | AHL | 73 | 19 | 44 | 63 | 41 | .... | .... | .... | .... | .... | .... | .... | .... | .... | 5 | 2 | 1 | 3 | 2 | .... | .... | .... | .... |
| **1998-99** | **Vancouver** | **NHL** | **25** | **4** | **4** | **8** | **8** | **1** | **0** | **1** | **24** | **16.7** | **–1** | **6** | **0.0** | **13:21** | .... | .... | .... | .... | .... | .... | .... | .... | .... |
| | Syracuse Crunch | AHL | 41 | 10 | 19 | 29 | 66 | .... | .... | .... | .... | .... | .... | .... | .... | .... | .... | .... | .... | .... | .... | .... | .... | .... | .... |
| **99-2000** | **Vancouver** | **NHL** | **71** | **16** | **15** | **31** | **20** | **2** | **2** | **4** | **101** | **15.8** | **0** | **21** | **19.1** | **15:28** | .... | .... | .... | .... | .... | .... | .... | .... | .... |
| | Syracuse Crunch | AHL | 2 | 0 | 0 | 0 | 2 | .... | .... | .... | .... | .... | .... | .... | .... | .... | .... | .... | .... | .... | .... | .... | .... | .... | .... |
| **2000-01** | **Vancouver** | **NHL** | **82** | **16** | **20** | **36** | **22** | **3** | **4** | **2** | **163** | **9.8** | **4** | **25** | **32.0** | **16:18** | **3** | **0** | **0** | **0** | **0** | **0** | **0** | **0** | **13:08** |
| 2001-02 | TPS Turku | Finland | 33 | 16 | 15 | 31 | 93 | .... | .... | .... | .... | .... | .... | .... | .... | .... | 8 | 1 | 2 | 3 | 2 | .... | .... | .... | .... |
| **2002-03** | **Ottawa** | **NHL** | **75** | **6** | **17** | **23** | **32** | **0** | **0** | **1** | **93** | **6.5** | **11** | **44** | **20.5** | **14:59** | **16** | **2** | **3** | **5** | **6** | **0** | **1** | **0** | **11:51** |
| **2003-04** | **Ottawa** | **NHL** | **81** | **15** | **24** | **39** | **26** | **2** | **2** | **3** | **112** | **13.4** | **22** | **39** | **23.1** | **15:36** | **7** | **0** | **2** | **2** | **4** | **0** | **0** | **0** | **14:25** |
| 2004-05 | HC Forst Bolzano | Italy | 15 | 11 | 14 | 25 | 10 | .... | .... | .... | .... | .... | .... | .... | .... | .... | 10 | 1 | 7 | 8 | 12 | .... | .... | .... | .... |
| **2005-06** | **Ottawa** | **NHL** | **82** | **20** | **30** | **50** | **40** | **4** | **4** | **2** | **137** | **14.6** | **16** | **27** | **37.0** | **15:49** | **10** | **2** | **5** | **7** | **14** | **0** | **0** | **0** | **16:39** |
| **2006-07** | **Ottawa** | **NHL** | **77** | **12** | **34** | **46** | **32** | **5** | **0** | **2** | **132** | **9.1** | **7** | **7** | **28.6** | **16:44** | **20** | **1** | **5** | **6** | **10** | **0** | **0** | **0** | **14:32** |
| **2007-08** | **Boston** | **NHL** | **63** | **9** | **17** | **26** | **18** | **0** | **0** | **0** | **91** | **9.9** | **4** | **7** | **42.9** | **14:58** | **7** | **1** | **3** | **4** | **0** | **0** | **0** | **0** | **12:50** |
| 2008-09 | Providence Bruins | AHL | 47 | 7 | 19 | 26 | 10 | .... | .... | .... | .... | .... | .... | .... | .... | .... | 16 | 3 | 4 | 7 | 2 | .... | .... | .... | .... |
| | **NHL Totals** | | 556 | 98 | 161 | 259 | 198 | 17 | 12 | 15 | 853 | 11.5 | | 176 | 25.6 | 15:37 | 63 | 6 | 18 | 24 | 34 | 0 | 1 | 0 | 13:55 |

WHL East First All-Star Team (1996, 1997) • WHL Player of the Year (1997) • Canadian Major Junior First All-Star Team (1997)

Signed as a free agent by **Turku** (Finland), October 18, 2001. Traded to **Ottawa** by **Vancouver** for Sami Salo, September 21, 2002. Signed as a free agent by **Bolzano** (Italy), November 30, 2004. Traded to **Boston** by **Ottawa** for Shean Donovan, July 17, 2007.

## SCHENN, Luke

(SHEHN, LEWK) **TOR.**

Defense. Shoots right. 6'2", 216 lbs. Born, Saskatoon, Sask., November 2, 1989. Toronto's 1st choice, 5th overall, in 2008 Entry Draft.

| Season | Club | League | GP | G | A | Pts | PIM | PP | SH | GW | S | % | +/- | TF | F% | Min | GP | G | A | Pts | PIM | PP | SH | GW | Min |
|---|---|---|---|---|---|---|---|---|---|---|---|---|---|---|---|---|---|---|---|---|---|---|---|---|---|
| 2004-05 | Sask. Contacts | SMHL | 41 | 5 | 22 | 27 | 69 | .... | .... | .... | .... | .... | .... | .... | .... | .... | .... | .... | .... | .... | .... | .... | .... | .... | .... |
| 2005-06 | Kelowna Rockets | WHL | 60 | 3 | 8 | 11 | 86 | .... | .... | .... | .... | .... | .... | .... | .... | .... | 12 | 0 | 0 | 0 | 14 | .... | .... | .... | .... |
| 2006-07 | Kelowna Rockets | WHL | 72 | 2 | 27 | 29 | 139 | .... | .... | .... | .... | .... | .... | .... | .... | .... | .... | .... | .... | .... | .... | .... | .... | .... | .... |
| 2007-08 | Kelowna Rockets | WHL | 57 | 7 | 21 | 28 | 100 | .... | .... | .... | .... | .... | .... | .... | .... | .... | 7 | 2 | 2 | 4 | 6 | .... | .... | .... | .... |
| **2008-09** | **Toronto** | **NHL** | **70** | **2** | **12** | **14** | **71** | **1** | **0** | **0** | **102** | **2.0** | **–12** | **0** | **0.0** | **21:32** | .... | .... | .... | .... | .... | .... | .... | .... | .... |
| | **NHL Totals** | | 70 | 2 | 12 | 14 | 71 | 1 | 0 | 0 | 102 | 2.0 | | 0 | 0.0 | 21:32 | .... | .... | .... | .... | .... | .... | .... | .... | .... |

WHL West Second All-Star Team (2008) • NHL All-Rookie Team (2009)

## SCHLEMKO, David

(SHLEHM-koh, DAY-vihd) **PHX.**

Defense. Shoots left. 6'1", 195 lbs. Born, Edmonton, Alta., May 7, 1987.

| Season | Club | League | GP | G | A | Pts | PIM | PP | SH | GW | S | % | +/- | TF | F% | Min | GP | G | A | Pts | PIM | PP | SH | GW | Min |
|---|---|---|---|---|---|---|---|---|---|---|---|---|---|---|---|---|---|---|---|---|---|---|---|---|---|
| 2004-05 | Medicine Hat | WHL | 65 | 5 | 24 | 29 | 23 | .... | .... | .... | .... | .... | .... | .... | .... | .... | 13 | 0 | 3 | 3 | 10 | .... | .... | .... | .... |
| 2005-06 | Medicine Hat | WHL | 69 | 9 | 35 | 44 | 44 | .... | .... | .... | .... | .... | .... | .... | .... | .... | 13 | 2 | 5 | 7 | 15 | .... | .... | .... | .... |
| 2006-07 | Medicine Hat | WHL | 64 | 8 | 50 | 58 | 78 | .... | .... | .... | .... | .... | .... | .... | .... | .... | 23 | 3 | 13 | 16 | 12 | .... | .... | .... | .... |
| 2007-08 | San Antonio | AHL | 1 | 0 | 0 | 0 | 4 | .... | .... | .... | .... | .... | .... | .... | .... | .... | .... | .... | .... | .... | .... | .... | .... | .... | .... |
| | Arizona Sundogs | CHL | 58 | 10 | 29 | 39 | 24 | .... | .... | .... | .... | .... | .... | .... | .... | .... | 14 | 3 | 5 | 8 | 6 | .... | .... | .... | .... |
| **2008-09** | **Phoenix** | **NHL** | **3** | **0** | **1** | **1** | **0** | **0** | **0** | **0** | **3** | **0.0** | **–2** | **0** | **0.0** | **19:16** | .... | .... | .... | .... | .... | .... | .... | .... | .... |
| | San Antonio | AHL | 68 | 7 | 22 | 29 | 20 | .... | .... | .... | .... | .... | .... | .... | .... | .... | .... | .... | .... | .... | .... | .... | .... | .... | .... |
| | **NHL Totals** | | 3 | 0 | 1 | 1 | 0 | 0 | 0 | 0 | 3 | 0.0 | | 0 | 0.0 | 19:16 | .... | .... | .... | .... | .... | .... | .... | .... | .... |

WHL East Second All-Star Team (2007)

Signed as a free agent by **Phoenix**, July 19, 2007.

## SCHNEIDER, Mathieu

(SHNIGH-duhr, MA-thew)

Defense. Shoots left. 5'11", 195 lbs. Born, New York, NY, June 12, 1969. Montreal's 4th choice, 44th overall, in 1987 Entry Draft.

| Season | Club | League | GP | G | A | Pts | PIM | PP | SH | GW | S | % | +/- | TF | F% | Min | GP | G | A | Pts | PIM | PP | SH | GW | Min |
|---|---|---|---|---|---|---|---|---|---|---|---|---|---|---|---|---|---|---|---|---|---|---|---|---|---|
| 1985-86 | Mount St. Charles | High-RI | 19 | 3 | 27 | 30 | .... | .... | .... | .... | .... | .... | .... | .... | .... | .... | .... | .... | .... | .... | .... | .... | .... | .... | .... |
| 1986-87 | Cornwall Royals | OHL | 63 | 7 | 29 | 36 | 75 | .... | .... | .... | .... | .... | .... | .... | .... | .... | 5 | 0 | 0 | 0 | 22 | .... | .... | .... | .... |
| **1987-88** | Cornwall Royals | OHL | 48 | 21 | 40 | 61 | 83 | .... | .... | .... | .... | .... | .... | .... | .... | .... | 11 | 2 | 6 | 8 | 14 | .... | .... | .... | .... |
| | **Montreal** | **NHL** | **4** | **0** | **0** | **0** | **2** | **0** | **0** | **0** | **2** | **0.0** | **–1** | .... | .... | .... | .... | .... | .... | .... | .... | .... | .... | .... | .... |
| | Sherbrooke | AHL | .... | .... | .... | .... | .... | .... | .... | .... | .... | .... | .... | .... | .... | .... | 3 | 0 | 3 | 3 | 12 | .... | .... | .... | .... |
| 1988-89 | Cornwall Royals | OHL | 59 | 16 | 57 | 73 | 96 | .... | .... | .... | .... | .... | .... | .... | .... | .... | 18 | 7 | 20 | 27 | 30 | .... | .... | .... | .... |
| **1989-90** | **Montreal** | **NHL** | **44** | **7** | **14** | **21** | **25** | **5** | **0** | **1** | **84** | **8.3** | **2** | .... | .... | .... | **9** | **1** | **3** | **4** | **31** | **1** | **0** | **0** | .... |
| | Sherbrooke | AHL | 28 | 6 | 13 | 19 | 20 | .... | .... | .... | .... | .... | .... | .... | .... | .... | .... | .... | .... | .... | .... | .... | .... | .... | .... |
| **1990-91** | **Montreal** | **NHL** | **69** | **10** | **20** | **30** | **63** | **5** | **0** | **3** | **164** | **6.1** | **7** | .... | .... | .... | **13** | **2** | **7** | **9** | **18** | **1** | **0** | **0** | .... |
| **1991-92** | **Montreal** | **NHL** | **78** | **8** | **24** | **32** | **72** | **2** | **0** | **1** | **194** | **4.1** | **10** | .... | .... | .... | **10** | **1** | **4** | **5** | **6** | **1** | **0** | **0** | .... |
| **1992-93** ♦ | **Montreal** | **NHL** | **60** | **13** | **31** | **44** | **91** | **3** | **0** | **2** | **169** | **7.7** | **8** | .... | .... | .... | **11** | **1** | **2** | **3** | **16** | **0** | **0** | **0** | .... |
| **1993-94** | **Montreal** | **NHL** | **75** | **20** | **32** | **52** | **62** | **11** | **0** | **4** | **193** | **10.4** | **15** | .... | .... | .... | **1** | **0** | **0** | **0** | **0** | **0** | **0** | **0** | .... |

| Season | Club | League | GP | G | A | Pts | PIM | PP | SH | GW | S | % | +/- | TF | F% | Min | GP | G | A | Pts | PIM | PP | SH | GW | Min |
|---|---|---|---|---|---|---|---|---|---|---|---|---|---|---|---|---|---|---|---|---|---|---|---|---|---|
| | | | Regular Season | | | | | | | | | | | | | | Playoffs | | | | | | | | |
| **1994-95** | **Montreal** | **NHL** | **30** | **5** | **15** | **20** | **49** | **2** | **0** | **0** | **82** | **6.1** | **-3** | .... | .... | .... | .... | .... | .... | .... | .... | .... | .... | .... | .... |
| | **NY Islanders** | **NHL** | **13** | **3** | **6** | **9** | **30** | **1** | **0** | **2** | **36** | **8.3** | **-5** | .... | .... | .... | .... | .... | .... | .... | .... | .... | .... | .... | .... |
| **1995-96** | **NY Islanders** | **NHL** | **65** | **11** | **36** | **47** | **93** | **7** | **0** | **1** | **155** | **7.1** | **-18** | .... | .... | .... | .... | .... | .... | .... | .... | .... | .... | .... | .... |
| | **Toronto** | **NHL** | **13** | **2** | **5** | **7** | **10** | **0** | **0** | **0** | **36** | **5.6** | **-2** | .... | .... | .... | **6** | **0** | **4** | **4** | **8** | **0** | **0** | **0** | .... |
| **1996-97** | **Toronto** | **NHL** | **26** | **5** | **7** | **12** | **20** | **1** | **0** | **1** | **63** | **7.9** | **3** | .... | .... | .... | .... | .... | .... | .... | .... | .... | .... | .... | .... |
| **1997-98** | **Toronto** | **NHL** | **76** | **11** | **26** | **37** | **44** | **4** | **1** | **1** | **181** | **6.1** | **-12** | .... | .... | .... | .... | .... | .... | .... | .... | .... | .... | .... | .... |
| | United States | Olympics | 4 | 0 | 0 | 0 | 6 | .... | .... | .... | .... | .... | .... | .... | .... | .... | .... | .... | .... | .... | .... | .... | .... | .... | .... |
| **1998-99** | **NY Rangers** | **NHL** | **75** | **10** | **24** | **34** | **71** | **5** | **0** | **2** | **159** | **6.3** | **-19** | **0** | **0.0** | **24:35** | .... | .... | .... | .... | .... | .... | .... | .... | .... |
| **99-2000** | **NY Rangers** | **NHL** | **80** | **10** | **20** | **30** | **78** | **3** | **0** | **1** | **228** | **4.4** | **-6** | **0** | **0.0** | **22:31** | .... | .... | .... | .... | .... | .... | .... | .... | .... |
| **2000-01** | **Los Angeles** | **NHL** | **73** | **16** | **35** | **51** | **56** | **7** | **1** | **2** | **183** | **8.7** | **0** | **0** | **0.0** | **23:04** | **13** | **0** | **9** | **9** | **10** | **0** | **0** | **0** | **25:51** |
| **2001-02** | **Los Angeles** | **NHL** | **55** | **7** | **23** | **30** | **68** | **4** | **0** | **0** | **123** | **5.7** | **3** | **0** | **0.0** | **22:25** | **7** | **0** | **1** | **1** | **18** | **0** | **0** | **0** | **22:52** |
| **2002-03** | **Los Angeles** | **NHL** | **65** | **14** | **29** | **43** | **57** | **10** | **0** | **1** | **162** | **8.6** | **0** | **0** | **0.0** | **22:20** | .... | .... | .... | .... | .... | .... | .... | .... | .... |
| | **Detroit** | **NHL** | **13** | **2** | **5** | **7** | **16** | **1** | **0** | **0** | **37** | **5.4** | **2** | **0** | **0.0** | **22:42** | **4** | **0** | **0** | **0** | **6** | **0** | **0** | **0** | **28:16** |
| **2003-04** | **Detroit** | **NHL** | **78** | **14** | **32** | **46** | **56** | **4** | **1** | **4** | **165** | **8.5** | **22** | **4** | **0.0** | **24:29** | **12** | **1** | **2** | **3** | **8** | **1** | **0** | **1** | **26:30** |
| 2004-05 | | DID NOT PLAY | | | | | | | | | | | | | | | | | | | | | | | |
| **2005-06** | **Detroit** | **NHL** | **72** | **21** | **38** | **59** | **86** | **11** | **0** | **4** | **188** | **11.2** | **33** | **4** | **25.0** | **24:31** | **6** | **1** | **7** | **8** | **6** | **0** | **0** | **0** | **26:44** |
| | United States | Olympics | 6 | 1 | 2 | 3 | 16 | .... | .... | .... | .... | .... | .... | .... | .... | .... | .... | .... | .... | .... | .... | .... | .... | .... | .... |
| **2006-07** | **Detroit** | **NHL** | **68** | **11** | **41** | **52** | **66** | **2** | **1** | **2** | **184** | **6.0** | **12** | **0** | **0.0** | **23:35** | **11** | **2** | **4** | **6** | **16** | **1** | **0** | **1** | **23:35** |
| **2007-08** | **Anaheim** | **NHL** | **65** | **12** | **27** | **39** | **50** | **5** | **0** | **2** | **139** | **8.6** | **22** | **0** | **0.0** | **22:18** | **6** | **1** | **0** | **1** | **8** | **0** | **0** | **0** | **20:29** |
| **2008-09** | **Atlanta** | **NHL** | **44** | **4** | **11** | **15** | **50** | **1** | **0** | **0** | **82** | **4.9** | **-10** | **0** | **0.0** | **21:02** | .... | .... | .... | .... | .... | .... | .... | .... | .... |
| | **Montreal** | **NHL** | **23** | **5** | **12** | **17** | **14** | **5** | **0** | **2** | **46** | **10.9** | **-2** | **0** | **0.0** | **20:57** | **2** | **0** | **0** | **0** | **4** | **0** | **0** | **0** | **18:58** |
| | **NHL Totals** | | **1264** | **221** | **513** | **734** | **1229** | **99** | **4** | **36** | **3055** | **7.2** | | **8** | **12.5** | **23:08** | **111** | **10** | **43** | **53** | **155** | **5** | **0** | **2** | **24:43** |

OHL First All-Star Team (1988, 1989)

Played in NHL All-Star Game (1996, 2003)

Traded to **NY Islanders** by **Montreal** with Kirk Muller and Craig Darby for Pierre Turgeon and Vladimir Malakhov, April 5, 1995. Traded to **Toronto** by **NY Islanders** with Wendel Clark and D.J. Smith for Darby Hendrickson, Sean Haggerty, Kenny Jonsson and Toronto's 1st round choice (Roberto Luongo) in 1997 Entry Draft, March 13, 1996. • Missed majority of 1996-97 season recovering from groin injury suffered in game vs. St. Louis, December 27, 1996. • Rights traded to **NY Rangers** by **Toronto** for Alexander Karpovtsev and NY Rangers' 4th round choice (Mirko Murovic) in 1999 Entry Draft, October 14, 1998. Claimed by **Columbus** from **NY Rangers** in Expansion Draft, June 23, 2000. Signed as a free agent by **Los Angeles**, August 14, 2000. Traded to **Detroit** by **Los Angeles** for Sean Avery, Maxim Kuznetsov, Detroit's 1st round choice (Jeff Tambellini) in 2003 Entry Draft and Detroit's 2nd round choice (later traded to Boston – Boston selected Martins Karsums) in 2004 Entry Draft, March 11, 2003. Signed as a free agent by **Anaheim**, July 1, 2007. Traded to **Atlanta** by **Anaheim** for Ken Klee, Brad Larsen and Chad Painchaud, September 26, 2008. Traded to **Montreal** by **Atlanta** with Atlanta's 3rd round choice (Joonas Nattinen) in 2009 Entry Draft for Anaheim's 2nd round choice (previously acquired, Atlanta selected Jeremy Morin) in 2009 Entry Draft and Montreal's 3rd round choice in 2010 Entry Draft, February 16, 2009.

## SCHREMP, Rob

(SHREHMP, RAWB) **EDM.**

Center. Shoots left. 5'11", 200 lbs. Born, Syracuse, NY, July 1, 1986. Edmonton's 2nd choice, 25th overall, in 2004 Entry Draft.

| Season | Club | League | GP | G | A | Pts | PIM | PP | SH | GW | S | % | +/- | TF | F% | Min | GP | G | A | Pts | PIM | PP | SH | GW | Min |
|---|---|---|---|---|---|---|---|---|---|---|---|---|---|---|---|---|---|---|---|---|---|---|---|---|---|
| 2000-01 | Syracuse | OPJHL | 49 | 32 | 46 | 78 | .... | .... | .... | .... | .... | .... | .... | .... | .... | .... | .... | .... | .... | .... | .... | .... | .... | .... | .... |
| 2001-02 | Syracuse | OPJHL | 47 | 41 | 47 | 88 | 93 | .... | .... | .... | .... | .... | .... | .... | .... | .... | 1 | 1 | 2 | 3 | 0 | .... | .... | .... | .... |
| 2002-03 | Mississauga | OHL | 65 | 26 | 48 | 74 | 25 | .... | .... | .... | .... | .... | .... | .... | .... | .... | 2 | 1 | 0 | 1 | 0 | .... | .... | .... | .... |
| 2003-04 | USNTDP | U-18 | 2 | 0 | 0 | 0 | 8 | .... | .... | .... | .... | .... | .... | .... | .... | .... | .... | .... | .... | .... | .... | .... | .... | .... | .... |
| | Mississauga | OHL | 3 | 2 | 4 | 6 | 0 | .... | .... | .... | .... | .... | .... | .... | .... | .... | .... | .... | .... | .... | .... | .... | .... | .... | .... |
| | London Knights | OHL | 60 | 28 | 41 | 69 | 18 | .... | .... | .... | .... | .... | .... | .... | .... | .... | 15 | 7 | 6 | 13 | 2 | .... | .... | .... | .... |
| 2004-05 | London Knights | OHL | 62 | 41 | 49 | 90 | 54 | .... | .... | .... | .... | .... | .... | .... | .... | .... | 18 | 13 | 16 | 29 | 16 | .... | .... | .... | .... |
| 2005-06 | London Knights | OHL | 57 | *57 | *88 | *145 | 74 | .... | .... | .... | .... | .... | .... | .... | .... | .... | 19 | 10 | *37 | *47 | 35 | .... | .... | .... | .... |
| **2006-07** | **Edmonton** | **NHL** | **1** | **0** | **0** | **0** | **0** | **0** | **0** | **0** | **2** | **0.0** | **0** | **12** | **50.0** | **13:50** | .... | .... | .... | .... | .... | .... | .... | .... | .... |
| | Wilkes-Barre | AHL | 69 | 17 | 36 | 53 | 36 | .... | .... | .... | .... | .... | .... | .... | .... | .... | .... | .... | .... | .... | .... | .... | .... | .... | .... |
| **2007-08** | **Edmonton** | **NHL** | **2** | **0** | **0** | **0** | **0** | **0** | **0** | **0** | **3** | **0.0** | **-1** | **1** | **0.0** | **6:57** | .... | .... | .... | .... | .... | .... | .... | .... | .... |
| | Springfield | AHL | 78 | 23 | 53 | 76 | 64 | .... | .... | .... | .... | .... | .... | .... | .... | .... | .... | .... | .... | .... | .... | .... | .... | .... | .... |
| **2008-09** | **Edmonton** | **NHL** | **4** | **0** | **3** | **3** | **2** | **0** | **0** | **0** | **3** | **0.0** | **2** | **2** | **50.0** | **13:35** | .... | .... | .... | .... | .... | .... | .... | .... | .... |
| | Springfield | AHL | 69 | 7 | 35 | 42 | 50 | .... | .... | .... | .... | .... | .... | .... | .... | .... | .... | .... | .... | .... | .... | .... | .... | .... | .... |
| | **NHL Totals** | | **7** | **0** | **3** | **3** | **2** | **0** | **0** | **0** | **8** | **0.0** | | **15** | **46.7** | **11:43** | .... | .... | .... | .... | .... | .... | .... | .... | .... |

OPJHL Rookie of the Year (2001) • OHL All-Rookie Team (2003) • OHL Rookie of the Year (2003) • OHL First All-Star Team (2006) • Canadian Major Junior First All-Star Team (2006)

## SCHUBERT, Christoph

(SHOO-buhrt, KRIHS-tawf) **OTT.**

Defense. Shoots left. 6'3", 230 lbs. Born, Munich, West Germany, February 5, 1982. Ottawa's 5th choice, 127th overall, in 2001 Entry Draft.

| Season | Club | League | GP | G | A | Pts | PIM | PP | SH | GW | S | % | +/- | TF | F% | Min | GP | G | A | Pts | PIM | PP | SH | GW | Min |
|---|---|---|---|---|---|---|---|---|---|---|---|---|---|---|---|---|---|---|---|---|---|---|---|---|---|
| 1998-99 | EV Landshut Jr. | Ger-Jr. | 28 | 15 | 20 | 35 | 77 | .... | .... | .... | .... | .... | .... | .... | .... | .... | .... | .... | .... | .... | .... | .... | .... | .... | .... |
| 99-2000 | EV Landshut Jr. | Ger-Jr. | 11 | 14 | 11 | 25 | 51 | .... | .... | .... | .... | .... | .... | .... | .... | .... | .... | .... | .... | .... | .... | .... | .... | .... | .... |
| | EV Landshut | German-3 | 55 | 7 | 5 | 12 | 68 | .... | .... | .... | .... | .... | .... | .... | .... | .... | .... | .... | .... | .... | .... | .... | .... | .... | .... |
| 2000-01 | Munchen Barons | Germany | 55 | 6 | 3 | 9 | 80 | .... | .... | .... | .... | .... | .... | .... | .... | .... | 10 | 0 | 2 | 2 | 27 | .... | .... | .... | .... |
| 2001-02 | Munchen Barons | Germany | 50 | 5 | 11 | 16 | 125 | .... | .... | .... | .... | .... | .... | .... | .... | .... | 9 | 3 | 4 | 7 | 32 | .... | .... | .... | .... |
| 2002-03 | Binghamton | AHL | 70 | 2 | 8 | 10 | 102 | .... | .... | .... | .... | .... | .... | .... | .... | .... | 8 | 0 | 1 | 1 | 2 | .... | .... | .... | .... |
| 2003-04 | Binghamton | AHL | 70 | 2 | 10 | 12 | 69 | .... | .... | .... | .... | .... | .... | .... | .... | .... | 1 | 0 | 0 | 0 | 0 | .... | .... | .... | .... |
| 2004-05 | Binghamton | AHL | 76 | 10 | 22 | 32 | 110 | .... | .... | .... | .... | .... | .... | .... | .... | .... | 6 | 2 | 2 | 4 | 20 | .... | .... | .... | .... |
| **2005-06** | **Ottawa** | **NHL** | **56** | **4** | **6** | **10** | **48** | **0** | **1** | **0** | **72** | **5.6** | **4** | **5** | **0.0** | **11:06** | **7** | **0** | **1** | **1** | **4** | **0** | **0** | **0** | **7:53** |
| | Germany | Olympics | 5 | 0 | 1 | 1 | 2 | .... | .... | .... | .... | .... | .... | .... | .... | .... | .... | .... | .... | .... | .... | .... | .... | .... | .... |
| **2006-07** | **Ottawa** | **NHL** | **80** | **8** | **17** | **25** | **56** | **1** | **0** | **1** | **97** | **8.2** | **30** | **1** | **0.0** | **11:13** | **20** | **0** | **1** | **1** | **22** | **0** | **0** | **0** | **9:10** |
| **2007-08** | **Ottawa** | **NHL** | **82** | **8** | **16** | **24** | **64** | **1** | **0** | **0** | **137** | **5.8** | **7** | **4** | **25.0** | **13:34** | **4** | **0** | **0** | **0** | **8** | **0** | **0** | **0** | **11:58** |
| **2008-09** | **Ottawa** | **NHL** | **50** | **3** | **3** | **6** | **26** | **1** | **0** | **0** | **57** | **5.3** | **-8** | **0** | **0.0** | **13:36** | .... | .... | .... | .... | .... | .... | .... | .... | .... |
| | **NHL Totals** | | **268** | **23** | **42** | **65** | **194** | **3** | **1** | **1** | **363** | **6.3** | | **10** | **10.0** | **12:21** | **31** | **0** | **2** | **2** | **34** | **0** | **0** | **0** | **9:14** |

## SCHULTZ, Jeff

(SHUHLTZ, JEHF) **WSH.**

Defense. Shoots left. 6'6", 227 lbs. Born, Calgary, Alta., February 25, 1986. Washington's 2nd choice, 27th overall, in 2004 Entry Draft.

| Season | Club | League | GP | G | A | Pts | PIM | PP | SH | GW | S | % | +/- | TF | F% | Min | GP | G | A | Pts | PIM | PP | SH | GW | Min |
|---|---|---|---|---|---|---|---|---|---|---|---|---|---|---|---|---|---|---|---|---|---|---|---|---|---|
| 2000-01 | Calgary Hawks | CBHL | 27 | 7 | 8 | 15 | 20 | .... | .... | .... | .... | .... | .... | .... | .... | .... | .... | .... | .... | .... | .... | .... | .... | .... | .... |
| 2001-02 | Calgary Rangers | CBHL | 27 | 5 | 18 | 23 | 42 | .... | .... | .... | .... | .... | .... | .... | .... | .... | .... | .... | .... | .... | .... | .... | .... | .... | .... |
| 2002-03 | Calgary Hitmen | WHL | 50 | 2 | 1 | 3 | 4 | .... | .... | .... | .... | .... | .... | .... | .... | .... | 4 | 0 | 0 | 0 | 0 | .... | .... | .... | .... |
| 2003-04 | Calgary Hitmen | WHL | 72 | 11 | 24 | 35 | 33 | .... | .... | .... | .... | .... | .... | .... | .... | .... | 7 | 1 | 1 | 2 | 0 | .... | .... | .... | .... |
| 2004-05 | Calgary Hitmen | WHL | 72 | 2 | 27 | 29 | 31 | .... | .... | .... | .... | .... | .... | .... | .... | .... | 12 | 2 | 1 | 3 | 6 | .... | .... | .... | .... |
| 2005-06 | Calgary Hitmen | WHL | 68 | 7 | 33 | 40 | 36 | .... | .... | .... | .... | .... | .... | .... | .... | .... | 13 | 4 | 6 | 10 | 6 | .... | .... | .... | .... |
| | Hershey Bears | AHL | .... | .... | .... | .... | .... | .... | .... | .... | .... | .... | .... | .... | .... | .... | 7 | 1 | 3 | 4 | 4 | .... | .... | .... | .... |
| **2006-07** | **Washington** | **NHL** | **38** | **0** | **3** | **3** | **16** | **0** | **0** | **0** | **22** | **0.0** | **5** | **0** | **0.0** | **18:13** | .... | .... | .... | .... | .... | .... | .... | .... | .... |
| | Hershey Bears | AHL | 44 | 2 | 10 | 12 | 39 | .... | .... | .... | .... | .... | .... | .... | .... | .... | 19 | 0 | 1 | 1 | 18 | .... | .... | .... | .... |
| **2007-08** | **Washington** | **NHL** | **72** | **5** | **13** | **18** | **28** | **0** | **0** | **0** | **36** | **13.9** | **12** | **1** | **100.0** | **18:05** | **2** | **0** | **0** | **0** | **2** | **0** | **0** | **0** | **10:25** |
| | Hershey Bears | AHL | 1 | 0 | 0 | 0 | 0 | .... | .... | .... | .... | .... | .... | .... | .... | .... | .... | .... | .... | .... | .... | .... | .... | .... | .... |
| **2008-09** | **Washington** | **NHL** | **64** | **1** | **11** | **12** | **21** | **0** | **1** | **0** | **40** | **2.5** | **13** | **0** | **0.0** | **19:46** | **1** | **0** | **0** | **0** | **0** | **0** | **0** | **0** | **12:26** |
| | **NHL Totals** | | **174** | **6** | **27** | **33** | **65** | **0** | **1** | **0** | **98** | **6.1** | | **1** | **100.0** | **18:44** | **3** | **0** | **0** | **0** | **2** | **0** | **0** | **0** | **11:05** |

WHL East Second All-Star Team (2006)

## SCHULTZ, Jesse

(SHUHLTZ, JEH-see)

Right wing. Shoots right. 6'1", 195 lbs. Born, Strasbourg, Sask., September 28, 1982.

| Season | Club | League | GP | G | A | Pts | PIM | PP | SH | GW | S | % | +/- | TF | F% | Min | GP | G | A | Pts | PIM | PP | SH | GW | Min |
|---|---|---|---|---|---|---|---|---|---|---|---|---|---|---|---|---|---|---|---|---|---|---|---|---|---|
| 99-2000 | Tri-City | WHL | 62 | 10 | 6 | 16 | 34 | .... | .... | .... | .... | .... | .... | .... | .... | .... | 4 | 1 | 1 | 2 | 2 | .... | .... | .... | .... |
| 2000-01 | Tri-City | WHL | 30 | 5 | 8 | 13 | 16 | .... | .... | .... | .... | .... | .... | .... | .... | .... | .... | .... | .... | .... | .... | .... | .... | .... | .... |
| | Prince Albert | WHL | 35 | 14 | 18 | 32 | 14 | .... | .... | .... | .... | .... | .... | .... | .... | .... | .... | .... | .... | .... | .... | .... | .... | .... | .... |
| 2001-02 | Prince Albert | WHL | 45 | 18 | 24 | 42 | 16 | .... | .... | .... | .... | .... | .... | .... | .... | .... | .... | .... | .... | .... | .... | .... | .... | .... | .... |
| | Kelowna Rockets | WHL | 28 | 10 | 12 | 22 | 14 | .... | .... | .... | .... | .... | .... | .... | .... | .... | .... | .... | .... | .... | .... | .... | .... | .... | .... |
| 2002-03 | Kelowna Rockets | WHL | 72 | 53 | 51 | 104 | 47 | .... | .... | .... | .... | .... | .... | .... | .... | .... | 19 | *12 | 16 | *28 | 21 | .... | .... | .... | .... |
| 2003-04 | Manitoba Moose | AHL | 2 | 0 | 1 | 1 | 0 | .... | .... | .... | .... | .... | .... | .... | .... | .... | .... | .... | .... | .... | .... | .... | .... | .... | .... |
| | Columbia Inferno | ECHL | 52 | 27 | 21 | 48 | 72 | .... | .... | .... | .... | .... | .... | .... | .... | .... | 4 | 1 | 2 | 3 | 2 | .... | .... | .... | .... |
| 2004-05 | Manitoba Moose | AHL | 70 | 9 | 15 | 24 | 33 | .... | .... | .... | .... | .... | .... | .... | .... | .... | 14 | 3 | 2 | 5 | 2 | .... | .... | .... | .... |
| 2005-06 | Manitoba Moose | AHL | 80 | 37 | 30 | 67 | 63 | .... | .... | .... | .... | .... | .... | .... | .... | .... | 13 | 5 | 7 | 12 | 10 | .... | .... | .... | .... |
| **2006-07** | **Vancouver** | **NHL** | **2** | **0** | **0** | **0** | **0** | **0** | **0** | **0** | **6** | **0.0** | **0** | **0** | **0.0** | **10:09** | .... | .... | .... | .... | .... | .... | .... | .... | .... |
| | Manitoba Moose | AHL | 67 | 18 | 21 | 39 | 35 | .... | .... | .... | .... | .... | .... | .... | .... | .... | 7 | 0 | 0 | 0 | 2 | .... | .... | .... | .... |
| 2007-08 | Chicago Wolves | AHL | 80 | 26 | 40 | 66 | 43 | .... | .... | .... | .... | .... | .... | .... | .... | .... | 24 | 8 | 6 | 14 | 18 | .... | .... | .... | .... |
| 2008-09 | Houston Aeros | AHL | 76 | 22 | 33 | 55 | 51 | .... | .... | .... | .... | .... | .... | .... | .... | .... | 8 | 1 | 1 | 2 | 2 | .... | .... | .... | .... |
| | **NHL Totals** | | **2** | **0** | **0** | **0** | **0** | **0** | **0** | **0** | **6** | **0.0** | | **0** | **0.0** | **10:09** | .... | .... | .... | .... | .... | .... | .... | .... | .... |

WHL West First All-Star Team (2003)

Signed as a free agent by **Vancouver**, July 31, 2003. Traded to **Atlanta** by **Vancouver** for Jim Sharrow, June 23, 2007. Signed as a free agent by **Minnesota**, July 6, 2008.

| | | | Regular Season | | | | | | | | | | | | | | Playoffs | | | | | | | | |
|---|---|---|---|---|---|---|---|---|---|---|---|---|---|---|---|---|---|---|---|---|---|---|---|---|---|
| Season | Club | League | GP | G | A | Pts | PIM | PP | SH | GW | S | % | +/- | TF | F% | Min | GP | G | A | Pts | PIM | PP | SH | GW | Min |

## SCHULTZ, Nick

(SHUHLTZ, NIHK) **MIN.**

Defense. Shoots left. 6'1", 200 lbs. Born, Strasbourg, Sask., August 25, 1982. Minnesota's 2nd choice, 33rd overall, in 2000 Entry Draft.

| Season | Club | League | GP | G | A | Pts | PIM | PP | SH | GW | S | % | +/- | TF | F% | Min | GP | G | A | Pts | PIM | PP | SH | GW | Min |
|---|---|---|---|---|---|---|---|---|---|---|---|---|---|---|---|---|---|---|---|---|---|---|---|---|---|
| 1997-98 | Yorkton Mallers | SMHL | 59 | 10 | 30 | 40 | 74 | .... | .... | .... | .... | .... | .... | .... | .... | .... | .... | .... | .... | .... | .... | .... | .... | .... | .... |
| 1998-99 | Prince Albert | WHL | 58 | 5 | 18 | 23 | 37 | .... | .... | .... | .... | .... | .... | .... | .... | .... | 14 | 0 | 7 | 7 | 0 | .... | .... | .... | .... |
| 99-2000 | Prince Albert | WHL | 72 | 11 | 33 | 44 | 38 | .... | .... | .... | .... | .... | .... | .... | .... | .... | 6 | 0 | 3 | 3 | 2 | .... | .... | .... | .... |
| 2000-01 | Prince Albert | WHL | 59 | 17 | 30 | 47 | 120 | .... | .... | .... | .... | .... | .... | .... | .... | .... | .... | .... | .... | .... | .... | .... | .... | .... | .... |
| | Cleveland | IHL | 4 | 1 | 1 | 2 | 2 | .... | .... | .... | .... | .... | .... | .... | .... | .... | 3 | 0 | 1 | 1 | 0 | .... | .... | .... | .... |
| 2001-02 | Minnesota | NHL | 52 | 4 | 6 | 10 | 14 | 1 | 0 | 1 | 47 | 8.5 | 0 | 0 | 0.0 | 16:08 | .... | .... | .... | .... | .... | .... | .... | .... | .... |
| | Houston Aeros | AHL | .... | .... | .... | .... | .... | .... | .... | .... | .... | .... | .... | .... | .... | .... | 14 | 1 | 5 | 6 | 2 | .... | .... | .... | .... |
| 2002-03 | Minnesota | NHL | 75 | 3 | 7 | 10 | 23 | 0 | 0 | 1 | 70 | 4.3 | 11 | 0 | 0.0 | 18:28 | 18 | 0 | 1 | 1 | 10 | 0 | 0 | 0 | 19:39 |
| 2003-04 | Minnesota | NHL | 79 | 6 | 10 | 16 | 16 | 1 | 0 | 0 | 72 | 8.3 | 12 | 0 | 0.0 | 20:19 | .... | .... | .... | .... | .... | .... | .... | .... | .... |
| 2004-05 | Kassel Huskies | Germany | 46 | 7 | 15 | 22 | 26 | .... | .... | .... | .... | .... | .... | .... | .... | .... | 7 | 0 | 4 | 4 | 6 | .... | .... | .... | .... |
| 2005-06 | Minnesota | NHL | 79 | 2 | 12 | 14 | 43 | 0 | 0 | 0 | 45 | 4.4 | 2 | 0 | 0.0 | 17:58 | .... | .... | .... | .... | .... | .... | .... | .... | .... |
| 2006-07 | Minnesota | NHL | 82 | 2 | 10 | 12 | 42 | 0 | 0 | 1 | 69 | 2.9 | 0 | 0 | 0.0 | 20:13 | 5 | 0 | 1 | 1 | 0 | 0 | 0 | 0 | 18:06 |
| 2007-08 | Minnesota | NHL | 81 | 2 | 13 | 15 | 42 | 0 | 0 | 0 | 52 | 3.8 | 9 | 0 | 0.0 | 20:10 | 1 | 0 | 0 | 0 | 0 | 0 | 0 | 0 | 16:11 |
| 2008-09 | Minnesota | NHL | 79 | 2 | 9 | 11 | 31 | 0 | 0 | 0 | 48 | 4.2 | –4 | 1 | 0.0 | 20:33 | .... | .... | .... | .... | .... | .... | .... | .... | .... |
| | **NHL Totals** | | **527** | **21** | **67** | **88** | **211** | **2** | **0** | **3** | **403** | **5.2** | | **1** | **0.0** | **19:17** | **24** | **0** | **2** | **2** | **10** | **0** | **0** | **0** | **19:11** |

Signed as a free agent by **Kassel** (Germany), September 24, 2004.

## SCOTT, John

(SKAWT, JAWN) **MIN.**

Defense. Shoots left. 6'8", 258 lbs. Born, St. Catharines, Ont., September 26, 1982.

| Season | Club | League | GP | G | A | Pts | PIM | PP | SH | GW | S | % | +/- | TF | F% | Min | GP | G | A | Pts | PIM | PP | SH | GW | Min |
|---|---|---|---|---|---|---|---|---|---|---|---|---|---|---|---|---|---|---|---|---|---|---|---|---|---|
| 2002-03 | Michigan Tech | WCHA | 31 | 1 | 3 | 4 | 64 | .... | .... | .... | .... | .... | .... | .... | .... | .... | .... | .... | .... | .... | .... | .... | .... | .... | .... |
| 2003-04 | Michigan Tech | WCHA | 35 | 1 | 3 | 4 | 100 | .... | .... | .... | .... | .... | .... | .... | .... | .... | .... | .... | .... | .... | .... | .... | .... | .... | .... |
| 2004-05 | Michigan Tech | WCHA | 36 | 2 | 3 | 5 | 101 | .... | .... | .... | .... | .... | .... | .... | .... | .... | .... | .... | .... | .... | .... | .... | .... | .... | .... |
| 2005-06 | Michigan Tech | WCHA | 24 | 3 | 2 | 5 | 87 | .... | .... | .... | .... | .... | .... | .... | .... | .... | .... | .... | .... | .... | .... | .... | .... | .... | .... |
| 2006-07 | Houston Aeros | AHL | 65 | 1 | 5 | 6 | 107 | .... | .... | .... | .... | .... | .... | .... | .... | .... | .... | .... | .... | .... | .... | .... | .... | .... | .... |
| 2007-08 | Houston Aeros | AHL | 64 | 3 | 0 | 3 | 184 | .... | .... | .... | .... | .... | .... | .... | .... | .... | 5 | 0 | 0 | 0 | 13 | .... | .... | .... | .... |
| 2008-09 | Minnesota | NHL | 20 | 0 | 1 | 1 | 21 | 0 | 0 | 0 | 6 | 0.0 | –1 | 0 | 0.0 | 9:14 | .... | .... | .... | .... | .... | .... | .... | .... | .... |
| | Houston Aeros | AHL | 44 | 2 | 2 | 4 | 111 | .... | .... | .... | .... | .... | .... | .... | .... | .... | .... | .... | .... | .... | .... | .... | .... | .... | .... |
| | **NHL Totals** | | **20** | **0** | **1** | **1** | **21** | **0** | **0** | **0** | **6** | **0.0** | | **0** | **0.0** | **9:14** | .... | .... | .... | .... | .... | .... | .... | .... | .... |

Signed as a free agent by **Houston** (AHL), September 26, 2006. Signed as a free agent by **Minnesota**, December 31, 2006.

## SCUDERI, Rob

(SKUD-uh-ree, RAWB) **L.A.**

Defense. Shoots left. 6', 218 lbs. Born, Syosset, NY, December 30, 1978. Pittsburgh's 5th choice, 134th overall, in 1998 Entry Draft.

| Season | Club | League | GP | G | A | Pts | PIM | PP | SH | GW | S | % | +/- | TF | F% | Min | GP | G | A | Pts | PIM | PP | SH | GW | Min |
|---|---|---|---|---|---|---|---|---|---|---|---|---|---|---|---|---|---|---|---|---|---|---|---|---|---|
| 1995-96 | NY Apple Core | MtJHL | 76 | 18 | 60 | 78 | .... | .... | .... | .... | .... | .... | .... | .... | .... | .... | .... | .... | .... | .... | .... | .... | .... | .... | .... |
| 1996-97 | NY Apple Core | MtJHL | 82 | 42 | 70 | 112 | 64 | .... | .... | .... | .... | .... | .... | .... | .... | .... | .... | .... | .... | .... | .... | .... | .... | .... | .... |
| 1997-98 | Boston College | H-East | 42 | 0 | 24 | 24 | 12 | .... | .... | .... | .... | .... | .... | .... | .... | .... | .... | .... | .... | .... | .... | .... | .... | .... | .... |
| 1998-99 | Boston College | H-East | 41 | 2 | 8 | 10 | 20 | .... | .... | .... | .... | .... | .... | .... | .... | .... | .... | .... | .... | .... | .... | .... | .... | .... | .... |
| 99-2000 | Boston College | H-East | 42 | 1 | 12 | 13 | 22 | .... | .... | .... | .... | .... | .... | .... | .... | .... | .... | .... | .... | .... | .... | .... | .... | .... | .... |
| 2000-01 | Boston College | H-East | 43 | 4 | 19 | 23 | 42 | .... | .... | .... | .... | .... | .... | .... | .... | .... | .... | .... | .... | .... | .... | .... | .... | .... | .... |
| 2001-02 | Wilkes-Barre | AHL | 75 | 1 | 22 | 23 | 66 | .... | .... | .... | .... | .... | .... | .... | .... | .... | .... | .... | .... | .... | .... | .... | .... | .... | .... |
| 2002-03 | Wilkes-Barre | AHL | 74 | 4 | 17 | 21 | 44 | .... | .... | .... | .... | .... | .... | .... | .... | .... | 6 | 0 | 1 | 1 | 4 | .... | .... | .... | .... |
| 2003-04 | Pittsburgh | NHL | 13 | 1 | 2 | 3 | 4 | 0 | 0 | 0 | 4 | 25.0 | 2 | 0 | 0.0 | 20:06 | .... | .... | .... | .... | .... | .... | .... | .... | .... |
| | Wilkes-Barre | AHL | 64 | 1 | 15 | 16 | 54 | .... | .... | .... | .... | .... | .... | .... | .... | .... | 24 | 0 | 3 | 3 | 14 | .... | .... | .... | .... |
| 2004-05 | Wilkes-Barre | AHL | 79 | 2 | 18 | 20 | 34 | .... | .... | .... | .... | .... | .... | .... | .... | .... | 11 | 2 | 1 | 3 | 2 | .... | .... | .... | .... |
| 2005-06 | Pittsburgh | NHL | 57 | 0 | 4 | 4 | 36 | 0 | 0 | 0 | 28 | 0.0 | –18 | 0 | 0.0 | 20:15 | .... | .... | .... | .... | .... | .... | .... | .... | .... |
| | Wilkes-Barre | AHL | 13 | 0 | 8 | 8 | 8 | .... | .... | .... | .... | .... | .... | .... | .... | .... | .... | .... | .... | .... | .... | .... | .... | .... | .... |
| 2006-07 | Pittsburgh | NHL | 78 | 1 | 10 | 11 | 28 | 0 | 0 | 0 | 31 | 3.2 | 3 | 0 | 0.0 | 18:49 | 5 | 0 | 0 | 0 | 2 | 0 | 0 | 0 | 17:14 |
| 2007-08 | Pittsburgh | NHL | 71 | 0 | 5 | 5 | 26 | 0 | 0 | 0 | 28 | 0.0 | 3 | 0 | 0.0 | 18:45 | 20 | 0 | 3 | 3 | 2 | 0 | 0 | 0 | 19:02 |
| 2008-09 ♦ | Pittsburgh | NHL | 81 | 1 | 15 | 16 | 18 | 0 | 0 | 0 | 51 | 2.0 | 23 | 0 | 0.0 | 19:10 | 24 | 1 | 4 | 5 | 6 | 0 | 0 | 0 | 20:30 |
| | **NHL Totals** | | **300** | **3** | **36** | **39** | **112** | **0** | **0** | **0** | **142** | **2.1** | | **0** | **0.0** | **19:13** | **49** | **1** | **7** | **8** | **10** | **0** | **0** | **0** | **19:34** |

NCAA Championship All-Tournament Team (2001)

Signed as a free agent by **Los Angeles** July 2, 2009.

## SEABROOK, Brent

(SEE-bruk, BREHNT) **CHI.**

Defense. Shoots right. 6'3", 220 lbs. Born, Richmond, B.C., April 20, 1985. Chicago's 1st choice, 14th overall, in 2003 Entry Draft.

| Season | Club | League | GP | G | A | Pts | PIM | PP | SH | GW | S | % | +/- | TF | F% | Min | GP | G | A | Pts | PIM | PP | SH | GW | Min |
|---|---|---|---|---|---|---|---|---|---|---|---|---|---|---|---|---|---|---|---|---|---|---|---|---|---|
| 2000-01 | Delta Ice Hawks | PIJHL | 54 | 16 | 26 | 42 | 55 | .... | .... | .... | .... | .... | .... | .... | .... | .... | .... | .... | .... | .... | .... | .... | .... | .... | .... |
| | Lethbridge | WHL | 4 | 0 | 0 | 0 | 0 | .... | .... | .... | .... | .... | .... | .... | .... | .... | .... | .... | .... | .... | .... | .... | .... | .... | .... |
| 2001-02 | Lethbridge | WHL | 67 | 6 | 33 | 39 | 70 | .... | .... | .... | .... | .... | .... | .... | .... | .... | 4 | 1 | 1 | 2 | 2 | .... | .... | .... | .... |
| 2002-03 | Lethbridge | WHL | 69 | 9 | 33 | 42 | 113 | .... | .... | .... | .... | .... | .... | .... | .... | .... | .... | .... | .... | .... | .... | .... | .... | .... | .... |
| 2003-04 | Lethbridge | WHL | 61 | 12 | 29 | 41 | 107 | .... | .... | .... | .... | .... | .... | .... | .... | .... | .... | .... | .... | .... | .... | .... | .... | .... | .... |
| 2004-05 | Lethbridge | WHL | 63 | 12 | 42 | 54 | 107 | .... | .... | .... | .... | .... | .... | .... | .... | .... | 5 | 1 | 2 | 3 | 10 | .... | .... | .... | .... |
| | Norfolk Admirals | AHL | 3 | 0 | 0 | 0 | 2 | .... | .... | .... | .... | .... | .... | .... | .... | .... | 6 | 0 | 1 | 1 | 6 | .... | .... | .... | .... |
| 2005-06 | Chicago | NHL | 69 | 5 | 27 | 32 | 60 | 1 | 0 | 2 | 114 | 4.4 | 5 | 0 | 0.0 | 20:02 | .... | .... | .... | .... | .... | .... | .... | .... | .... |
| 2006-07 | Chicago | NHL | 81 | 4 | 20 | 24 | 104 | 0 | 0 | 0 | 144 | 2.8 | –6 | 2 | 50.0 | 20:46 | .... | .... | .... | .... | .... | .... | .... | .... | .... |
| 2007-08 | Chicago | NHL | 82 | 9 | 23 | 32 | 90 | 4 | 0 | 2 | 152 | 5.9 | 13 | 1 | 0.0 | 21:30 | .... | .... | .... | .... | .... | .... | .... | .... | .... |
| 2008-09 | Chicago | NHL | 82 | 8 | 18 | 26 | 62 | 3 | 1 | 1 | 132 | 6.1 | 23 | 0 | 0.0 | 23:19 | 17 | 1 | 11 | 12 | 14 | 1 | 0 | 0 | 26:00 |
| | **NHL Totals** | | **314** | **26** | **88** | **114** | **316** | **8** | **1** | **5** | **542** | **4.8** | | **3** | **33.3** | **21:28** | **17** | **1** | **11** | **12** | **14** | **1** | **0** | **0** | **26:00** |

WHL East Second All-Star Team (2005)

## SEDIN, Daniel

(suh-DEEN, DAN-yehl) **VAN.**

Left wing. Shoots left. 6'1", 185 lbs. Born, Ornskoldsvik, Sweden, September 26, 1980. Vancouver's 1st choice, 2nd overall, in 1999 Entry Draft.

| Season | Club | League | GP | G | A | Pts | PIM | PP | SH | GW | S | % | +/- | TF | F% | Min | GP | G | A | Pts | PIM | PP | SH | GW | Min |
|---|---|---|---|---|---|---|---|---|---|---|---|---|---|---|---|---|---|---|---|---|---|---|---|---|---|
| 1997-98 | Malmo Jr. | Swe-Jr. | 4 | 3 | 3 | 6 | 4 | .... | .... | .... | .... | .... | .... | .... | .... | .... | .... | .... | .... | .... | .... | .... | .... | .... | .... |
| | MoDo Jr. | Swe-Jr. | 26 | 26 | 14 | 40 | .... | .... | .... | .... | .... | .... | .... | .... | .... | .... | .... | .... | .... | .... | .... | .... | .... | .... | .... |
| | MoDo | Sweden | 45 | 4 | 8 | 12 | 26 | .... | .... | .... | .... | .... | .... | .... | .... | .... | 9 | 0 | 0 | 0 | 2 | .... | .... | .... | .... |
| 1998-99 | MoDo | Sweden | 50 | 21 | 21 | 42 | 20 | .... | .... | .... | .... | .... | .... | .... | .... | .... | 13 | 4 | 8 | 12 | 14 | .... | .... | .... | .... |
| 99-2000 | MoDo | Sweden | 50 | 19 | 26 | 45 | 28 | .... | .... | .... | .... | .... | .... | .... | .... | .... | 13 | *8 | 6 | 14 | 18 | .... | .... | .... | .... |
| | MoDo | EuroHL | 4 | 3 | 3 | 6 | 0 | .... | .... | .... | .... | .... | .... | .... | .... | .... | 2 | 0 | 0 | 0 | 0 | .... | .... | .... | .... |
| 2000-01 | Vancouver | NHL | 75 | 20 | 14 | 34 | 24 | 10 | 0 | 3 | 127 | 15.7 | –3 | 10 | 60.0 | 13:00 | 4 | 1 | 2 | 3 | 0 | 0 | 0 | 0 | 16:15 |
| 2001-02 | Vancouver | NHL | 79 | 9 | 23 | 32 | 32 | 4 | 0 | 2 | 117 | 7.7 | 1 | 18 | 33.3 | 12:22 | 6 | 0 | 1 | 1 | 0 | 0 | 0 | 0 | 10:44 |
| 2002-03 | Vancouver | NHL | 79 | 14 | 17 | 31 | 34 | 4 | 0 | 2 | 134 | 10.4 | 8 | 24 | 45.8 | 12:26 | 14 | 1 | 5 | 6 | 8 | 1 | 0 | 1 | 12:23 |
| 2003-04 | Vancouver | NHL | 82 | 18 | 36 | 54 | 18 | 1 | 0 | 3 | 153 | 11.8 | 18 | 71 | 47.9 | 13:33 | 7 | 1 | 2 | 3 | 0 | 1 | 0 | 0 | 16:03 |
| 2004-05 | MODO | Sweden | 49 | 13 | 20 | 33 | 40 | .... | .... | .... | .... | .... | .... | .... | .... | .... | 6 | 0 | 3 | 3 | 6 | .... | .... | .... | .... |
| 2005-06 | Vancouver | NHL | 82 | 22 | 49 | 71 | 34 | 11 | 0 | 4 | 204 | 10.8 | 7 | 49 | 42.9 | 16:40 | .... | .... | .... | .... | .... | .... | .... | .... | .... |
| | Sweden | Olympics | 8 | 1 | 3 | 4 | 2 | .... | .... | .... | .... | .... | .... | .... | .... | .... | .... | .... | .... | .... | .... | .... | .... | .... | .... |
| 2006-07 | Vancouver | NHL | 81 | 36 | 48 | 84 | 36 | 16 | 0 | 8 | 236 | 15.3 | 19 | 44 | 22.7 | 18:04 | 12 | 2 | 3 | 5 | 4 | 0 | 0 | 0 | 21:31 |
| 2007-08 | Vancouver | NHL | 82 | 29 | 45 | 74 | 50 | 12 | 0 | 7 | 247 | 11.7 | 6 | 38 | 44.7 | 19:03 | .... | .... | .... | .... | .... | .... | .... | .... | .... |
| 2008-09 | Vancouver | NHL | 82 | 31 | 51 | 82 | 36 | 9 | 0 | 7 | 285 | 10.9 | 24 | 35 | 40.0 | 18:48 | 10 | 4 | 6 | 10 | 8 | 2 | 0 | 0 | 18:37 |
| | **NHL Totals** | | **642** | **179** | **283** | **462** | **264** | **67** | **0** | **36** | **1503** | **11.9** | | **289** | **41.2** | **15:33** | **53** | **9** | **19** | **28** | **20** | **4** | **0** | **1** | **16:13** |

Signed as a free agent by **MODO** (Sweden), September 18, 2004.

## SEDIN, Henrik

(suh-DEEN, HEHN-rihk) **VAN.**

Center. Shoots left. 6'2", 190 lbs. Born, Ornskoldsvik, Sweden, September 26, 1980. Vancouver's 2nd choice, 3rd overall, in 1999 Entry Draft.

| Season | Club | League | GP | G | A | Pts | PIM | PP | SH | GW | S | % | +/- | TF | F% | Min | GP | G | A | Pts | PIM | PP | SH | GW | Min |
|---|---|---|---|---|---|---|---|---|---|---|---|---|---|---|---|---|---|---|---|---|---|---|---|---|---|
| 1997-98 | Malmo Jr. | Swe-Jr. | 8 | 4 | 7 | 11 | 6 | .... | .... | .... | .... | .... | .... | .... | .... | .... | .... | .... | .... | .... | .... | .... | .... | .... | .... |
| | MoDo Jr. | Swe-Jr. | 26 | 14 | 22 | 36 | .... | .... | .... | .... | .... | .... | .... | .... | .... | .... | .... | .... | .... | .... | .... | .... | .... | .... | .... |
| | MoDo | Sweden | 39 | 1 | 4 | 5 | 8 | .... | .... | .... | .... | .... | .... | .... | .... | .... | 7 | 0 | 0 | 0 | 0 | .... | .... | .... | .... |
| 1998-99 | MoDo | Sweden | 49 | 12 | 22 | 34 | 32 | .... | .... | .... | .... | .... | .... | .... | .... | .... | 13 | 2 | 8 | 10 | 6 | .... | .... | .... | .... |
| 99-2000 | MoDo | Sweden | 50 | 9 | 38 | 47 | 22 | .... | .... | .... | .... | .... | .... | .... | .... | .... | 13 | 5 | 9 | 14 | 2 | .... | .... | .... | .... |
| 2000-01 | Vancouver | NHL | 82 | 9 | 20 | 29 | 38 | 2 | 0 | 1 | 98 | 9.2 | –2 | 1020 | 44.1 | 13:31 | 4 | 0 | 4 | 4 | 0 | 0 | 0 | 0 | 16:31 |
| 2001-02 | Vancouver | NHL | 82 | 16 | 20 | 36 | 36 | 3 | 0 | 1 | 78 | 20.5 | 9 | 785 | 47.4 | 12:48 | 6 | 3 | 0 | 3 | 0 | 0 | 0 | 1 | 11:55 |
| 2002-03 | Vancouver | NHL | 78 | 8 | 31 | 39 | 38 | 4 | 1 | 1 | 81 | 9.9 | 9 | 995 | 48.2 | 13:58 | 14 | 3 | 2 | 5 | 8 | 1 | 0 | 0 | 13:01 |
| 2003-04 | Vancouver | NHL | 76 | 11 | 31 | 42 | 32 | 2 | 0 | 2 | 99 | 11.1 | 23 | 961 | 50.0 | 14:02 | 7 | 2 | 2 | 4 | 2 | 2 | 0 | 0 | 16:02 |
| 2004-05 | MODO | Sweden | 44 | 14 | 22 | 36 | 50 | .... | .... | .... | .... | .... | .... | .... | .... | .... | 6 | 1 | 3 | 4 | 6 | .... | .... | .... | .... |

| | | | Regular Season | | | | | | | | | | | | | | Playoffs | | | | | | | | |
|---|---|---|---|---|---|---|---|---|---|---|---|---|---|---|---|---|---|---|---|---|---|---|---|---|---|
| Season | Club | League | GP | G | A | Pts | PIM | PP | SH | GW | S | % | +/- | TF | F% | Min | GP | G | A | Pts | PIM | PP | SH | GW | Min |
| **2005-06** | **Vancouver** | **NHL** | **82** | **18** | **57** | **75** | **56** | **5** | **1** | **0** | **113** | **15.9** | **11** | **1238** | **50.7** | **16:54** | .... | .... | .... | .... | .... | .... | .... | .... | .... |
| | Sweden | Olympics | 8 | 3 | 1 | 4 | 2 | .... | .... | .... | .... | .... | .... | .... | .... | .... | .... | .... | .... | .... | .... | .... | .... | .... | .... |
| **2006-07** | **Vancouver** | **NHL** | **82** | **10** | **71** | **81** | **66** | **1** | **0** | **2** | **134** | **7.5** | **19** | **1220** | **52.5** | **18:26** | **12** | **2** | **2** | **4** | **14** | **1** | **0** | **1** | **22:12** |
| **2007-08** | **Vancouver** | **NHL** | **82** | **15** | **61** | **76** | **56** | **4** | **1** | **2** | **141** | **10.6** | **6** | **1369** | **47.0** | **19:31** | .... | .... | .... | .... | .... | .... | .... | .... | .... |
| **2008-09** | **Vancouver** | **NHL** | **82** | **22** | **60** | **82** | **48** | **4** | **0** | **8** | **143** | **15.4** | **22** | **1364** | **49.6** | **19:31** | **10** | **4** | **6** | **10** | **2** | **1** | **0** | **0** | **20:07** |
| | **NHL Totals** | | **646** | **109** | **351** | **460** | **370** | **25** | **3** | **17** | **887** | **12.3** | | **8952** | **48.8** | **16:07** | **53** | **14** | **16** | **30** | **26** | **5** | **0** | **2** | **16:58** |

Played in NHL All-Star Game (2008)

Signed as a free agent by **MODO** (Sweden), September 18, 2004.

## SEGAL, Brandon

(SEE-guhl, BRAN-duhn) **L.A.**

Right wing. Shoots right. 6'2", 214 lbs. Born, Richmond, B.C., July 12, 1983. Nashville's 2nd choice, 102nd overall, in 2002 Entry Draft.

| Season | Club | League | GP | G | A | Pts | PIM | PP | SH | GW | S | % | +/- | TF | F% | Min | GP | G | A | Pts | PIM | PP | SH | GW | Min |
|---|---|---|---|---|---|---|---|---|---|---|---|---|---|---|---|---|---|---|---|---|---|---|---|---|---|
| 99-2000 | Calgary Hitmen | WHL | 44 | 2 | 6 | 8 | 76 | .... | .... | .... | .... | .... | .... | .... | .... | .... | 13 | 1 | 1 | 2 | 13 | .... | .... | .... | .... |
| | Delta Ice Hawks | PIJHL | .... | .... | .... | .... | .... | .... | .... | .... | .... | .... | .... | .... | .... | .... | 3 | 0 | 1 | 1 | 2 | .... | .... | .... | .... |
| 2000-01 | Calgary Hitmen | WHL | 72 | 16 | 11 | 27 | 103 | .... | .... | .... | .... | .... | .... | .... | .... | .... | 12 | 1 | 1 | 2 | 17 | .... | .... | .... | .... |
| 2001-02 | Calgary Hitmen | WHL | 71 | 43 | 40 | 83 | 122 | .... | .... | .... | .... | .... | .... | .... | .... | .... | 7 | 1 | 4 | 5 | 16 | .... | .... | .... | .... |
| 2002-03 | Calgary Hitmen | WHL | 71 | 31 | 27 | 58 | 104 | .... | .... | .... | .... | .... | .... | .... | .... | .... | 5 | 2 | 2 | 4 | 4 | .... | .... | .... | .... |
| 2003-04 | Calgary Hitmen | WHL | 28 | 18 | 12 | 30 | 29 | .... | .... | .... | .... | .... | .... | .... | .... | .... | .... | .... | .... | .... | .... | .... | .... | .... | .... |
| | Milwaukee | AHL | 44 | 11 | 10 | 21 | 54 | .... | .... | .... | .... | .... | .... | .... | .... | .... | 13 | 2 | 1 | 3 | 21 | .... | .... | .... | .... |
| 2004-05 | Milwaukee | AHL | 59 | 7 | 8 | 15 | 45 | .... | .... | .... | .... | .... | .... | .... | .... | .... | 3 | 1 | 0 | 1 | 11 | .... | .... | .... | .... |
| | Rockford IceHogs | UHL | 10 | 5 | 4 | 9 | 27 | .... | .... | .... | .... | .... | .... | .... | .... | .... | 11 | 11 | 5 | 16 | 10 | .... | .... | .... | .... |
| 2005-06 | Milwaukee | AHL | 79 | 18 | 15 | 33 | 126 | .... | .... | .... | .... | .... | .... | .... | .... | .... | 21 | 1 | 2 | 3 | 16 | .... | .... | .... | .... |
| 2006-07 | Milwaukee | AHL | 77 | 20 | 9 | 29 | 84 | .... | .... | .... | .... | .... | .... | .... | .... | .... | 4 | 1 | 0 | 1 | 2 | .... | .... | .... | .... |
| 2007-08 | Portland Pirates | AHL | 54 | 5 | 9 | 14 | 46 | .... | .... | .... | .... | .... | .... | .... | .... | .... | .... | .... | .... | .... | .... | .... | .... | .... | .... |
| | Norfolk Admirals | AHL | 22 | 7 | 6 | 13 | 25 | .... | .... | .... | .... | .... | .... | .... | .... | .... | .... | .... | .... | .... | .... | .... | .... | .... | .... |
| **2008-09** | **Tampa Bay** | **NHL** | **2** | **0** | **0** | **0** | **0** | **0** | **0** | **0** | **2** | **0.0** | **0** | **0** | **0.0** | **13:48** | .... | .... | .... | .... | .... | .... | .... | .... | .... |
| | Norfolk Admirals | AHL | 69 | 26 | 26 | 52 | 95 | .... | .... | .... | .... | .... | .... | .... | .... | .... | .... | .... | .... | .... | .... | .... | .... | .... | .... |
| | **NHL Totals** | | **2** | **0** | **0** | **0** | **0** | **0** | **0** | **0** | **2** | **0.0** | | **0** | **0.0** | **13:48** | .... | .... | .... | .... | .... | .... | .... | .... | .... |

Traded to **Anaheim** by **Nashville** for future considerations, June 25, 2007. Traded to **Tampa Bay** by **Anaheim** with Anaheim's 7th round choice (David Carle) in 2008 Entry Draft for Jay Leach, February 26, 2008. Signed as a free agent by **Los Angeles**, July 13, 2009.

## SEIDENBERG, Dennis

(SIGH-dehn-buhrg, DEH-nihs)

Defense. Shoots left. 6'1", 210 lbs. Born, Schwenningen, West Germany, July 18, 1981. Philadelphia's 6th choice, 172nd overall, in 2001 Entry Draft.

| Season | Club | League | GP | G | A | Pts | PIM | PP | SH | GW | S | % | +/- | TF | F% | Min | GP | G | A | Pts | PIM | PP | SH | GW | Min |
|---|---|---|---|---|---|---|---|---|---|---|---|---|---|---|---|---|---|---|---|---|---|---|---|---|---|
| 99-2000 | Mannheim Jr. | Ger-Jr. | 52 | 12 | 28 | 40 | 28 | .... | .... | .... | .... | .... | .... | .... | .... | .... | .... | .... | .... | .... | .... | .... | .... | .... | .... |
| | Adler Mannheim | Germany | 3 | 0 | 0 | 0 | 0 | .... | .... | .... | .... | .... | .... | .... | .... | .... | .... | .... | .... | .... | .... | .... | .... | .... | .... |
| 2000-01 | Mannheim Jr. | Ger-Jr. | 9 | 3 | 8 | 11 | 20 | .... | .... | .... | .... | .... | .... | .... | .... | .... | .... | .... | .... | .... | .... | .... | .... | .... | .... |
| | Adler Mannheim | Germany | 55 | 2 | 5 | 7 | 6 | .... | .... | .... | .... | .... | .... | .... | .... | .... | 12 | 0 | 1 | 1 | 10 | .... | .... | .... | .... |
| 2001-02 | Adler Mannheim | Germany | 55 | 7 | 13 | 20 | 56 | .... | .... | .... | .... | .... | .... | .... | .... | .... | 8 | 0 | 0 | 0 | 2 | .... | .... | .... | .... |
| **2002-03** | **Philadelphia** | **NHL** | **58** | **4** | **9** | **13** | **20** | **1** | **0** | **0** | **123** | **3.3** | **8** | **1** | **0.0** | **16:50** | .... | .... | .... | .... | .... | .... | .... | .... | .... |
| | Philadelphia | AHL | 19 | 5 | 6 | 11 | 17 | .... | .... | .... | .... | .... | .... | .... | .... | .... | .... | .... | .... | .... | .... | .... | .... | .... | .... |
| **2003-04** | **Philadelphia** | **NHL** | **5** | **0** | **0** | **0** | **2** | **0** | **0** | **0** | **14** | **0.0** | **–4** | **0** | **0.0** | **17:20** | **3** | **0** | **0** | **0** | **0** | **0** | **0** | **0** | **7:36** |
| | Philadelphia | AHL | 33 | 7 | 12 | 19 | 31 | .... | .... | .... | .... | .... | .... | .... | .... | .... | 9 | 2 | 2 | 4 | 4 | .... | .... | .... | .... |
| 2004-05 | Philadelphia | AHL | 79 | 13 | 28 | 41 | 47 | .... | .... | .... | .... | .... | .... | .... | .... | .... | 18 | 2 | 8 | 10 | 19 | .... | .... | .... | .... |
| **2005-06** | **Philadelphia** | **NHL** | **29** | **2** | **5** | **7** | **4** | **1** | **0** | **0** | **34** | **5.9** | **–4** | **1** | **0.0** | **14:22** | .... | .... | .... | .... | .... | .... | .... | .... | .... |
| | **Phoenix** | **NHL** | **34** | **1** | **10** | **11** | **14** | **1** | **0** | **0** | **49** | **2.0** | **-9** | **0** | **0.0** | **19:13** | .... | .... | .... | .... | .... | .... | .... | .... | .... |
| | Germany | Olympics | 5 | 0 | 0 | 0 | 6 | .... | .... | .... | .... | .... | .... | .... | .... | .... | .... | .... | .... | .... | .... | .... | .... | .... | .... |
| **2006-07** | **Phoenix** | **NHL** | **32** | **1** | **1** | **2** | **16** | **0** | **0** | **0** | **36** | **2.8** | **–4** | **0** | **0.0** | **14:43** | .... | .... | .... | .... | .... | .... | .... | .... | .... |
| | **Carolina** | **NHL** | **20** | **1** | **5** | **6** | **2** | **0** | **0** | **0** | **47** | **2.1** | **–12** | **0** | **0.0** | **18:29** | .... | .... | .... | .... | .... | .... | .... | .... | .... |
| **2007-08** | **Carolina** | **NHL** | **47** | **0** | **15** | **15** | **18** | **0** | **0** | **0** | **80** | **0.0** | **6** | **1** | **100.0** | **18:50** | .... | .... | .... | .... | .... | .... | .... | .... | .... |
| **2008-09** | **Carolina** | **NHL** | **70** | **5** | **25** | **30** | **37** | **2** | **0** | **1** | **129** | **3.9** | **–9** | **0** | **0.0** | **22:20** | **16** | **1** | **5** | **6** | **16** | **0** | **0** | **0** | **22:25** |
| | **NHL Totals** | | **295** | **14** | **70** | **84** | **113** | **5** | **0** | **1** | **512** | **2.7** | | **3** | **33.3** | **18:23** | **19** | **1** | **5** | **6** | **16** | **0** | **0** | **0** | **20:05** |

• Missed majority of 2003-04 season recovering from leg injury suffered in game vs. Edmonton, January 10, 2004. Traded to **Phoenix** by **Philadelphia** with Philadelphia's 4th round choice (later traded to NY Islanders - NY Islanders selected Tomas Marcinko) in 2006 Entry Draft for Petr Nedved and Phoenix's 4th round choice (Joonas Lehtivuori) in 2006 Entry Draft, January 20, 2006. Traded to **Carolina** by **Phoenix** for Kevyn Adams, January 8, 2007.

## SEKERA, Andrej

(seh-KAIR-ah, AWN-dray) **BUF.**

Defense. Shoots left. 6', 197 lbs. Born, Bojnice, Czech., June 8, 1986. Buffalo's 3rd choice, 71st overall, in 2004 Entry Draft.

| Season | Club | League | GP | G | A | Pts | PIM | PP | SH | GW | S | % | +/- | TF | F% | Min | GP | G | A | Pts | PIM | PP | SH | GW | Min |
|---|---|---|---|---|---|---|---|---|---|---|---|---|---|---|---|---|---|---|---|---|---|---|---|---|---|
| 2001-02 | Dukla Trencin Jr. | Slovak-Jr. | 52 | 5 | 10 | 15 | 10 | .... | .... | .... | .... | .... | .... | .... | .... | .... | .... | .... | .... | .... | .... | .... | .... | .... | .... |
| 2002-03 | Dukla Trencin Jr. | Slovak-Jr. | 48 | 9 | 15 | 24 | 20 | .... | .... | .... | .... | .... | .... | .... | .... | .... | .... | .... | .... | .... | .... | .... | .... | .... | .... |
| 2003-04 | Dukla Trencin Jr. | Slovak-Jr. | 42 | 5 | 12 | 17 | 40 | .... | .... | .... | .... | .... | .... | .... | .... | .... | 2 | 0 | 1 | 1 | 4 | .... | .... | .... | .... |
| | Dukla Trencin | Slovakia | 3 | 0 | 0 | 0 | 2 | .... | .... | .... | .... | .... | .... | .... | .... | .... | .... | .... | .... | .... | .... | .... | .... | .... | .... |
| | Dukla Trencin U18 | Svk-U18 | 5 | 0 | 0 | 0 | 0 | .... | .... | .... | .... | .... | .... | .... | .... | .... | .... | .... | .... | .... | .... | .... | .... | .... | .... |
| 2004-05 | Owen Sound | OHL | 51 | 7 | 21 | 28 | 18 | .... | .... | .... | .... | .... | .... | .... | .... | .... | 6 | 0 | 4 | 4 | 4 | .... | .... | .... | .... |
| 2005-06 | Owen Sound | OHL | 51 | 21 | 34 | 55 | 54 | .... | .... | .... | .... | .... | .... | .... | .... | .... | 11 | 5 | 8 | 13 | 9 | .... | .... | .... | .... |
| **2006-07** | **Buffalo** | **NHL** | **2** | **0** | **0** | **0** | **2** | **0** | **0** | **0** | **0** | **0.0** | **1** | **0** | **0.0** | **7:31** | .... | .... | .... | .... | .... | .... | .... | .... | .... |
| | Rochester | AHL | 54 | 3 | 16 | 19 | 28 | .... | .... | .... | .... | .... | .... | .... | .... | .... | .... | .... | .... | .... | .... | .... | .... | .... | .... |
| **2007-08** | **Buffalo** | **NHL** | **37** | **2** | **6** | **8** | **16** | **0** | **0** | **1** | **28** | **7.1** | **5** | **0** | **0.0** | **19:37** | .... | .... | .... | .... | .... | .... | .... | .... | .... |
| | Rochester | AHL | 40 | 2 | 15 | 17 | 22 | .... | .... | .... | .... | .... | .... | .... | .... | .... | .... | .... | .... | .... | .... | .... | .... | .... | .... |
| **2008-09** | **Buffalo** | **NHL** | **69** | **3** | **16** | **19** | **22** | **1** | **0** | **1** | **84** | **3.6** | **–11** | **1** | **0.0** | **20:42** | .... | .... | .... | .... | .... | .... | .... | .... | .... |
| | **NHL Totals** | | **108** | **5** | **22** | **27** | **40** | **1** | **0** | **2** | **112** | **4.5** | | **1** | **0.0** | **20:05** | .... | .... | .... | .... | .... | .... | .... | .... | .... |

OHL All-Rookie Team (2005) • OHL First All-Star Team (2006)

## SELANNE, Teemu

(seh-LAH-nee, TEE-moo) **ANA.**

Right wing. Shoots right. 6', 200 lbs. Born, Helsinki, Finland, July 3, 1970. Winnipeg's 1st choice, 10th overall, in 1988 Entry Draft.

| Season | Club | League | GP | G | A | Pts | PIM | PP | SH | GW | S | % | +/- | TF | F% | Min | GP | G | A | Pts | PIM | PP | SH | GW | Min |
|---|---|---|---|---|---|---|---|---|---|---|---|---|---|---|---|---|---|---|---|---|---|---|---|---|---|
| 1986-87 | Jokerit U18 | Fin-U18 | .... | .... | .... | .... | .... | .... | .... | .... | .... | .... | .... | .... | .... | .... | 7 | 10 | 3 | 13 | 2 | .... | .... | .... | .... |
| | Jokerit Helsinki Jr. | Fin-Jr. | 33 | 10 | 12 | 22 | 8 | .... | .... | .... | .... | .... | .... | .... | .... | .... | .... | .... | .... | .... | .... | .... | .... | .... | .... |
| 1987-88 | Jokerit Helsinki Jr. | Fin-Jr. | 33 | 43 | 23 | 66 | 18 | .... | .... | .... | .... | .... | .... | .... | .... | .... | 5 | 4 | 3 | 7 | 2 | .... | .... | .... | .... |
| | Jokerit Helsinki | Finland-2 | 5 | 1 | 1 | 2 | 0 | .... | .... | .... | .... | .... | .... | .... | .... | .... | .... | .... | .... | .... | .... | .... | .... | .... | .... |
| 1988-89 | PvUK Lahti Jr. | Fin-Jr. | 3 | 3 | 1 | 4 | 2 | .... | .... | .... | .... | .... | .... | .... | .... | .... | .... | .... | .... | .... | .... | .... | .... | .... | .... |
| | Jokerit Helsinki Jr. | Fin-Jr. | 3 | 8 | 8 | 16 | 4 | .... | .... | .... | .... | .... | .... | .... | .... | .... | .... | .... | .... | .... | .... | .... | .... | .... | .... |
| | Jokerit Helsinki | Finland-2 | 35 | 36 | 33 | 69 | 14 | .... | .... | .... | .... | .... | .... | .... | .... | .... | 5 | 7 | 3 | 10 | 4 | .... | .... | .... | .... |
| 1989-90 | Jokerit Helsinki | Finland | 11 | 4 | 8 | 12 | 0 | .... | .... | .... | .... | .... | .... | .... | .... | .... | .... | .... | .... | .... | .... | .... | .... | .... | .... |
| 1990-91 | Jokerit Helsinki Jr. | Fin-Jr. | 4 | 3 | 2 | 5 | 10 | .... | .... | .... | .... | .... | .... | .... | .... | .... | .... | .... | .... | .... | .... | .... | .... | .... | .... |
| | Jokerit Helsinki | Finland | 42 | 33 | 25 | 58 | 12 | .... | .... | .... | .... | .... | .... | .... | .... | .... | .... | .... | .... | .... | .... | .... | .... | .... | .... |
| 1991-92 | Jokerit Helsinki | Finland | 44 | 39 | 23 | 62 | 20 | .... | .... | .... | .... | .... | .... | .... | .... | .... | 10 | 10 | 7 | 17 | 18 | .... | .... | .... | .... |
| | Finland | Olympics | 8 | 7 | 4 | 11 | 6 | .... | .... | .... | .... | .... | .... | .... | .... | .... | .... | .... | .... | .... | .... | .... | .... | .... | .... |
| **1992-93** | **Winnipeg** | **NHL** | **84** | ***76** | **56** | **132** | **45** | **24** | **0** | **7** | **387** | **19.6** | **8** | .... | .... | .... | **6** | **4** | **2** | **6** | **2** | **2** | **0** | **2** | .... |
| **1993-94** | **Winnipeg** | **NHL** | **51** | **25** | **29** | **54** | **22** | **11** | **0** | **2** | **191** | **13.1** | **–23** | .... | .... | .... | .... | .... | .... | .... | .... | .... | .... | .... | .... |
| **1994-95** | Jokerit Helsinki | Finland | 20 | 7 | 12 | 19 | 6 | .... | .... | .... | .... | .... | .... | .... | .... | .... | .... | .... | .... | .... | .... | .... | .... | .... | .... |
| | **Winnipeg** | **NHL** | **45** | **22** | **26** | **48** | **2** | **8** | **2** | **1** | **167** | **13.2** | **1** | .... | .... | .... | .... | .... | .... | .... | .... | .... | .... | .... | .... |
| **1995-96** | **Winnipeg** | **NHL** | **51** | **24** | **48** | **72** | **18** | **6** | **1** | **4** | **163** | **14.7** | **3** | .... | .... | .... | .... | .... | .... | .... | .... | .... | .... | .... | .... |
| | **Anaheim** | **NHL** | **28** | **16** | **20** | **36** | **4** | **3** | **0** | **1** | **104** | **15.4** | **2** | .... | .... | .... | .... | .... | .... | .... | .... | .... | .... | .... | .... |
| **1996-97** | **Anaheim** | **NHL** | **78** | **51** | **58** | **109** | **34** | **11** | **1** | **8** | **273** | **18.7** | **28** | .... | .... | .... | **11** | **7** | **3** | **10** | **4** | **3** | **0** | **1** | .... |
| **1997-98** | **Anaheim** | **NHL** | **73** | ***52** | **34** | **86** | **30** | **10** | **1** | **10** | **268** | **19.4** | **12** | .... | .... | .... | .... | .... | .... | .... | .... | .... | .... | .... | .... |
| | Finland | Olympics | 5 | 4 | 6 | 10 | 8 | .... | .... | .... | .... | .... | .... | .... | .... | .... | .... | .... | .... | .... | .... | .... | .... | .... | .... |
| **1998-99** | **Anaheim** | **NHL** | **75** | ***47** | **60** | **107** | **30** | **25** | **0** | **7** | **281** | **16.7** | **18** | **5** | **20.0** | **22:47** | **4** | **2** | **2** | **4** | **2** | **1** | **0** | **0** | **22:23** |
| **99-2000** | **Anaheim** | **NHL** | **79** | **33** | **52** | **85** | **12** | **8** | **0** | **6** | **236** | **14.0** | **6** | **13** | **23.1** | **22:44** | .... | .... | .... | .... | .... | .... | .... | .... | .... |
| **2000-01** | **Anaheim** | **NHL** | **61** | **26** | **33** | **59** | **36** | **10** | **0** | **5** | **202** | **12.9** | **–8** | **4** | **50.0** | **21:51** | .... | .... | .... | .... | .... | .... | .... | .... | .... |
| | **San Jose** | **NHL** | **12** | **7** | **6** | **13** | **0** | **2** | **0** | **2** | **31** | **22.6** | **1** | **4** | **75.0** | **18:14** | **6** | **0** | **2** | **2** | **2** | **0** | **0** | **0** | **17:13** |
| **2001-02** | **San Jose** | **NHL** | **82** | **29** | **25** | **54** | **40** | **9** | **1** | **8** | **202** | **14.4** | **–11** | **12** | **25.0** | **16:58** | **12** | **5** | **3** | **8** | **2** | **2** | **0** | **1** | **16:51** |
| | Finland | Olympics | 4 | 3 | 0 | 3 | 2 | .... | .... | .... | .... | .... | .... | .... | .... | .... | .... | .... | .... | .... | .... | .... | .... | .... | .... |
| **2002-03** | **San Jose** | **NHL** | **82** | **28** | **36** | **64** | **30** | **7** | **0** | **5** | **253** | **11.1** | **–6** | **107** | **42.1** | **19:14** | .... | .... | .... | .... | .... | .... | .... | .... | .... |
| **2003-04** | **Colorado** | **NHL** | **78** | **16** | **16** | **32** | **32** | **6** | **1** | **4** | **182** | **8.8** | **2** | **80** | **43.8** | **16:10** | **10** | **0** | **3** | **3** | **2** | **0** | **0** | **0** | **12:53** |
| 2004-05 | | | DID NOT PLAY | | | | | | | | | | | | | | | | | | | | | | |
| **2005-06** | **Anaheim** | **NHL** | **80** | **40** | **50** | **90** | **44** | **18** | **0** | **5** | **267** | **15.0** | **28** | **209** | **41.6** | **17:48** | **16** | **6** | **8** | **14** | **6** | **1** | **0** | **2** | **17:56** |
| | Finland | Olympics | 8 | *6 | 5 | *11 | 4 | .... | .... | .... | .... | .... | .... | .... | .... | .... | .... | .... | .... | .... | .... | .... | .... | .... | .... |
| **2006-07**♦ | **Anaheim** | **NHL** | **82** | **48** | **46** | **94** | **82** | **25** | **0** | **10** | **257** | **18.7** | **26** | **351** | **50.7** | **17:42** | **21** | **5** | **10** | **15** | **10** | **0** | **0** | **2** | **19:08** |

| | | | Regular Season | | | | | | | | | | | | | | Playoffs | | | | | | | | |
|---|---|---|---|---|---|---|---|---|---|---|---|---|---|---|---|---|---|---|---|---|---|---|---|---|---|
| Season | Club | League | GP | G | A | Pts | PIM | PP | SH | GW | S | % | +/- | TF | F% | Min | GP | G | A | Pts | PIM | PP | SH | GW | Min |
| 2007-08 | **Anaheim** | **NHL** | **26** | **12** | **11** | **23** | **8** | **7** | **0** | **2** | **87** | **13.8** | **5** | **67** | **50.8** | **18:07** | **6** | **2** | **2** | **4** | **6** | **2** | **0** | **1** | **19:35** |
| 2008-09 | **Anaheim** | **NHL** | **65** | **27** | **27** | **54** | **36** | **16** | **0** | **5** | **186** | **14.5** | **–3** | **224** | **49.1** | **16:29** | **13** | **4** | **2** | **6** | **4** | **2** | **0** | **1** | **15:08** |
| | **NHL Totals** | | **1132** | **579** | **633** | **1212** | **505** | **206** | **7** | **92** | **3737** | **15.5** | | **1076** | **46.6** | **18:59** | **105** | **35** | **37** | **72** | **40** | **13** | **0** | **10** | **17:21** |

NHL All-Rookie Team (1993) • NHL First All-Star Team (1993, 1997) • Calder Memorial Trophy (1993) • NHL Second All-Star Team (1998, 1999) • Maurice "Rocket" Richard Trophy (1999) • Olympic Tournament All-Star Team (2006) • Best Forward - Olympic Tournament (2006) • Bill Masterton Memorial Trophy (2006)

Played in NHL All-Star Game (1993, 1994, 1996, 1997, 1998, 1999, 2000, 2002, 2003, 2007)

• Missed majority of 1989-90 season recovering from leg injury suffered in game vs. HIFK Helsinki (Finland), October 19, 1989. Traded to **Anaheim** by **Winnipeg** with Marc Chouinard and Winnipeg's 4th round choice (later traded to Toronto – later traded to Montreal – Montreal selected Kim Staal) in 1996 Entry Draft for Chad Kilger, Oleg Tverdovsky and Anaheim's 3rd round choice (Per-Anton Lundstrom) in 1996 Entry Draft, February 7, 1996. Traded to **San Jose** by **Anaheim** for Jeff Friesen, Steve Shields and San Jose's 2nd round choice (later traded to Dallas – Dallas selected Vojtech Polak) in 2003 Entry Draft, March 5, 2001. Signed as a free agent by **Colorado**, July 3, 2003. Signed as a free agent by **Anaheim**, August 22, 2005. • Missed majority of 2007-08 season contemplating retirement.

## SEMENOV, Alexei

(seh-MEH-nahv, al-EHX-ay)

Defense. Shoots left. 6'6", 245 lbs. Born, Murmansk, USSR, April 10, 1981. Edmonton's 2nd choice, 36th overall, in 1999 Entry Draft.

| | | | | | | | | | | | | | | | | | | | | | | | | | |
|---|---|---|---|---|---|---|---|---|---|---|---|---|---|---|---|---|---|---|---|---|---|---|---|---|---|
| 1997-98 | Krylja Sovetov 2 | Russia-3 | 52 | 1 | 2 | 3 | 48 | .... | .... | .... | .... | .... | .... | .... | .... | .... | .... | .... | .... | .... | .... | .... | .... | .... | .... |
| 1998-99 | St. Petersburg 2 | Russia-4 | 19 | 0 | 1 | 1 | 20 | .... | .... | .... | .... | .... | .... | .... | .... | .... | .... | .... | .... | .... | .... | .... | .... | .... | .... |
| | Sudbury Wolves | OHL | 28 | 0 | 3 | 3 | 28 | .... | .... | .... | .... | .... | .... | .... | .... | .... | 2 | 0 | 0 | 0 | 4 | .... | .... | .... | .... |
| 99-2000 | Sudbury Wolves | OHL | 65 | 9 | 35 | 44 | 135 | .... | .... | .... | .... | .... | .... | .... | .... | .... | 12 | 1 | 3 | 4 | 23 | .... | .... | .... | .... |
| | Hamilton | AHL | .... | .... | .... | .... | .... | .... | .... | .... | .... | .... | .... | .... | .... | .... | 3 | 0 | 0 | 0 | 0 | .... | .... | .... | .... |
| 2000-01 | Sudbury Wolves | OHL | 65 | 21 | 42 | 63 | 106 | .... | .... | .... | .... | .... | .... | .... | .... | .... | 12 | 4 | 13 | 17 | 17 | .... | .... | .... | .... |
| 2001-02 | Hamilton | AHL | 78 | 5 | 11 | 16 | 67 | .... | .... | .... | .... | .... | .... | .... | .... | .... | .... | .... | .... | .... | .... | .... | .... | .... | .... |
| **2002-03** | **Edmonton** | **NHL** | **46** | **1** | **6** | **7** | **58** | **0** | **0** | **0** | **33** | **3.0** | **–7** | **0** | **0.0** | **19:41** | **6** | **0** | **0** | **0** | **0** | **0** | **0** | **0** | **13:05** |
| | Hamilton | AHL | 37 | 4 | 3 | 7 | 45 | .... | .... | .... | .... | .... | .... | .... | .... | .... | .... | .... | .... | .... | .... | .... | .... | .... | .... |
| **2003-04** | **Edmonton** | **NHL** | **46** | **2** | **3** | **5** | **32** | **1** | **0** | **0** | **36** | **5.6** | **8** | **0** | **0.0** | **17:16** | .... | .... | .... | .... | .... | .... | .... | .... | .... |
| 2004-05 | St. Petersburg | Russia | 50 | 0 | 8 | 8 | 26 | .... | .... | .... | .... | .... | .... | .... | .... | .... | .... | .... | .... | .... | .... | .... | .... | .... | .... |
| **2005-06** | Yaroslavl | Russia | 2 | 0 | 1 | 1 | 2 | .... | .... | .... | .... | .... | .... | .... | .... | .... | .... | .... | .... | .... | .... | .... | .... | .... | .... |
| | **Edmonton** | **NHL** | **11** | **1** | **1** | **2** | **17** | **0** | **0** | **0** | **3** | **33.3** | **–3** | **0** | **0.0** | **10:49** | .... | .... | .... | .... | .... | .... | .... | .... | .... |
| | **Florida** | **NHL** | **16** | **1** | **1** | **2** | **21** | **1** | **0** | **0** | **13** | **7.7** | **–1** | **0** | **0.0** | **12:33** | .... | .... | .... | .... | .... | .... | .... | .... | .... |
| | Rochester | AHL | 3 | 0 | 0 | 0 | 7 | .... | .... | .... | .... | .... | .... | .... | .... | .... | .... | .... | .... | .... | .... | .... | .... | .... | .... |
| **2006-07** | **Florida** | **NHL** | **23** | **0** | **5** | **5** | **28** | **0** | **0** | **0** | **23** | **0.0** | **9** | **1** | **0.0** | **12:22** | .... | .... | .... | .... | .... | .... | .... | .... | .... |
| | Rochester | AHL | 4 | 0 | 0 | 0 | 6 | .... | .... | .... | .... | .... | .... | .... | .... | .... | .... | .... | .... | .... | .... | .... | .... | .... | .... |
| | Ufa | Russia | 20 | 1 | 2 | 3 | 32 | .... | .... | .... | .... | .... | .... | .... | .... | .... | .... | .... | .... | .... | .... | .... | .... | .... | .... |
| **2007-08** | **San Jose** | **NHL** | **22** | **1** | **3** | **4** | **36** | **1** | **0** | **0** | **23** | **4.3** | **–8** | **0** | **0.0** | **15:15** | **2** | **0** | **0** | **0** | **2** | **0** | **0** | **0** | **11:15** |
| **2008-09** | **San Jose** | **NHL** | **47** | **1** | **7** | **8** | **57** | **0** | **0** | **0** | **28** | **3.6** | **3** | **1** | **0.0** | **13:03** | .... | .... | .... | .... | .... | .... | .... | .... | .... |
| | **NHL Totals** | | **211** | **7** | **26** | **33** | **249** | **3** | **0** | **0** | **159** | **4.4** | | **2** | **0.0** | **15:25** | **8** | **0** | **0** | **0** | **2** | **0** | **0** | **0** | **12:37** |

OHL First All-Star Team (2001)

Signed as a free agent by **St. Petersburg** (Russia), July 30, 2004. Traded to **Florida** by **Edmonton** for Florida's 5th round choice (Bryan Pitton) in 2006 Entry Draft, November 19, 2005. Signed as a free agent by **San Jose**, July 27, 2007.

## SEMIN, Alexander

(SEH-min, al-EHX-AN-duhr) **WSH.**

Left wing. Shoots left. 6'2", 205 lbs. Born, Krasnoyarsk, USSR, March 3, 1984. Washington's 2nd choice, 13th overall, in 2002 Entry Draft.

| | | | | | | | | | | | | | | | | | | | | | | | | | |
|---|---|---|---|---|---|---|---|---|---|---|---|---|---|---|---|---|---|---|---|---|---|---|---|---|---|
| 2001-02 | Chelyabinsk | Russia-2 | 46 | 13 | 8 | 21 | 52 | .... | .... | .... | .... | .... | .... | .... | .... | .... | 2 | 2 | 0 | 2 | 0 | .... | .... | .... | .... |
| 2002-03 | Lada Togliatti | Russia | 47 | 10 | 7 | 17 | 36 | .... | .... | .... | .... | .... | .... | .... | .... | .... | 10 | *5 | 3 | 8 | 10 | .... | .... | .... | .... |
| **2003-04** | **Washington** | **NHL** | **52** | **10** | **12** | **22** | **36** | **4** | **0** | **2** | **92** | **10.9** | **–2** | **6** | **50.0** | **12:37** | .... | .... | .... | .... | .... | .... | .... | .... | .... |
| | Portland Pirates | AHL | 4 | 3 | 1 | 4 | 6 | .... | .... | .... | .... | .... | .... | .... | .... | .... | 7 | 4 | 7 | 11 | 19 | .... | .... | .... | .... |
| 2004-05 | Lada Togliatti | Russia | 50 | 19 | 11 | 30 | 56 | .... | .... | .... | .... | .... | .... | .... | .... | .... | 10 | 1 | 1 | 2 | 0 | .... | .... | .... | .... |
| 2005-06 | Lada Togliatti | Russia | 16 | 5 | 4 | 9 | 52 | .... | .... | .... | .... | .... | .... | .... | .... | .... | .... | .... | .... | .... | .... | .... | .... | .... | .... |
| | Mytischi | Russia | 26 | 3 | 7 | 10 | 24 | .... | .... | .... | .... | .... | .... | .... | .... | .... | 8 | 3 | 2 | 5 | 6 | .... | .... | .... | .... |
| **2006-07** | **Washington** | **NHL** | **77** | **38** | **35** | **73** | **90** | **17** | **0** | **6** | **243** | **15.6** | **–7** | **44** | **27.3** | **18:24** | .... | .... | .... | .... | .... | .... | .... | .... | .... |
| **2007-08** | **Washington** | **NHL** | **63** | **26** | **16** | **42** | **54** | **10** | **0** | **2** | **185** | **14.1** | **–18** | **11** | **36.4** | **16:55** | **7** | **3** | **5** | **8** | **8** | **2** | **0** | **1** | **19:45** |
| **2008-09** | **Washington** | **NHL** | **62** | **34** | **45** | **79** | **77** | **8** | **0** | **8** | **223** | **15.2** | **25** | **24** | **50.0** | **19:14** | **14** | **5** | **9** | **14** | **16** | **1** | **0** | **1** | **19:58** |
| | **NHL Totals** | | **254** | **108** | **108** | **216** | **257** | **39** | **0** | **18** | **743** | **14.5** | | **85** | **36.5** | **17:03** | **21** | **8** | **14** | **22** | **24** | **3** | **0** | **2** | **19:54** |

Signed as a free agent by **Togliatti** (Russia), September 25, 2004. • Suspended by **Washington** for failing to report to **Portland** (AHL), September 28, 2004. Signed as a free agent by **Mytischi** (Russia), November 22, 2005.

## SESTITO, Tim

(sehs-TEE-toh, TIHM) **N.J.**

Center. Shoots left. 6', 195 lbs. Born, Rome, NY, August 28, 1984.

| | | | | | | | | | | | | | | | | | | | | | | | | | |
|---|---|---|---|---|---|---|---|---|---|---|---|---|---|---|---|---|---|---|---|---|---|---|---|---|---|
| 2001-02 | Plymouth Whalers | OHL | 51 | 10 | 11 | 21 | 40 | .... | .... | .... | .... | .... | .... | .... | .... | .... | 6 | 0 | 0 | 0 | 0 | .... | .... | .... | .... |
| 2002-03 | Plymouth Whalers | OHL | 61 | 11 | 7 | 18 | 49 | .... | .... | .... | .... | .... | .... | .... | .... | .... | 18 | 2 | 3 | 5 | 4 | .... | .... | .... | .... |
| 2003-04 | Plymouth Whalers | OHL | 57 | 10 | 20 | 30 | 68 | .... | .... | .... | .... | .... | .... | .... | .... | .... | 9 | 4 | 1 | 5 | 14 | .... | .... | .... | .... |
| 2004-05 | Plymouth Whalers | OHL | 67 | 14 | 18 | 32 | 93 | .... | .... | .... | .... | .... | .... | .... | .... | .... | 4 | 0 | 0 | 0 | 14 | .... | .... | .... | .... |
| | Bridgeport | AHL | 9 | 2 | 1 | 3 | 12 | .... | .... | .... | .... | .... | .... | .... | .... | .... | .... | .... | .... | .... | .... | .... | .... | .... | .... |
| 2005-06 | Greenville | ECHL | 72 | 21 | 23 | 44 | 127 | .... | .... | .... | .... | .... | .... | .... | .... | .... | 6 | 2 | 2 | 4 | 24 | .... | .... | .... | .... |
| 2006-07 | Wilkes-Barre | AHL | 4 | 0 | 0 | 0 | 6 | .... | .... | .... | .... | .... | .... | .... | .... | .... | .... | .... | .... | .... | .... | .... | .... | .... | .... |
| | Stockton Thunder | ECHL | 66 | 13 | 13 | 26 | 132 | .... | .... | .... | .... | .... | .... | .... | .... | .... | 6 | 2 | 1 | 3 | 6 | .... | .... | .... | .... |
| 2007-08 | Springfield | AHL | 77 | 7 | 10 | 17 | 175 | .... | .... | .... | .... | .... | .... | .... | .... | .... | .... | .... | .... | .... | .... | .... | .... | .... | .... |
| **2008-09** | **Edmonton** | **NHL** | **1** | **0** | **0** | **0** | **0** | **0** | **0** | **0** | **1** | **0.0** | **0** | **2** | **50.0** | **5:53** | .... | .... | .... | .... | .... | .... | .... | .... | .... |
| | Springfield | AHL | 51 | 5 | 3 | 8 | 77 | .... | .... | .... | .... | .... | .... | .... | .... | .... | .... | .... | .... | .... | .... | .... | .... | .... | .... |
| | **NHL Totals** | | **1** | **0** | **0** | **0** | **0** | **0** | **0** | **0** | **1** | **0.0** | | **2** | **50.0** | **5:53** | .... | .... | .... | .... | .... | .... | .... | .... | .... |

Signed as a free agent by **Edmonton**, August 28, 2006. Traded to **New Jersey** by **Edmonton** for future considerations, July 9, 2009.

## SESTITO, Tom

(sehs-TEE-toh, TAWM) **CBJ**

Left wing. Shoots left. 6'5", 226 lbs. Born, Utica, NY, September 28, 1987. Columbus' 3rd choice, 85th overall, in 2006 Entry Draft.

| | | | | | | | | | | | | | | | | | | | | | | | | | |
|---|---|---|---|---|---|---|---|---|---|---|---|---|---|---|---|---|---|---|---|---|---|---|---|---|---|
| 2003-04 | Syracuse Jr. Stars | EmJHL | 31 | 13 | 16 | 29 | 137 | .... | .... | .... | .... | .... | .... | .... | .... | .... | 6 | 5 | 6 | 11 | 32 | .... | .... | .... | .... |
| 2004-05 | Plymouth Whalers | OHL | 35 | 1 | 3 | 4 | 88 | .... | .... | .... | .... | .... | .... | .... | .... | .... | .... | .... | .... | .... | .... | .... | .... | .... | .... |
| 2005-06 | Plymouth Whalers | OHL | 57 | 10 | 10 | 20 | 176 | .... | .... | .... | .... | .... | .... | .... | .... | .... | 13 | 5 | 2 | 7 | 29 | .... | .... | .... | .... |
| 2006-07 | Plymouth Whalers | OHL | 60 | 42 | 22 | 64 | 135 | .... | .... | .... | .... | .... | .... | .... | .... | .... | 19 | 11 | 6 | 17 | 57 | .... | .... | .... | .... |
| **2007-08** | **Columbus** | **NHL** | **1** | **0** | **0** | **0** | **17** | **0** | **0** | **0** | **0** | **0.0** | **0** | **0** | **0.0** | **4:36** | .... | .... | .... | .... | .... | .... | .... | .... | .... |
| | Syracuse Crunch | AHL | 66 | 7 | 16 | 23 | 202 | .... | .... | .... | .... | .... | .... | .... | .... | .... | 9 | 3 | 0 | 3 | 57 | .... | .... | .... | .... |
| 2008-09 | Syracuse Crunch | AHL | 52 | 8 | 12 | 20 | 168 | .... | .... | .... | .... | .... | .... | .... | .... | .... | .... | .... | .... | .... | .... | .... | .... | .... | .... |
| | **NHL Totals** | | **1** | **0** | **0** | **0** | **17** | **0** | **0** | **0** | **0** | **0.0** | | **0** | **0.0** | **4:36** | .... | .... | .... | .... | .... | .... | .... | .... | .... |

## SETOGUCHI, Devin

(SEHT-oh-GOO-chee, DEH-vihn) **S.J.**

Right wing. Shoots right. 6', 200 lbs. Born, Taber, Alta., January 1, 1987. San Jose's 1st choice, 8th overall, in 2005 Entry Draft.

| | | | | | | | | | | | | | | | | | | | | | | | | | |
|---|---|---|---|---|---|---|---|---|---|---|---|---|---|---|---|---|---|---|---|---|---|---|---|---|---|
| 2003-04 | Saskatoon Blades | WHL | 66 | 13 | 18 | 31 | 53 | .... | .... | .... | .... | .... | .... | .... | .... | .... | .... | .... | .... | .... | .... | .... | .... | .... | .... |
| 2004-05 | Saskatoon Blades | WHL | 69 | 33 | 31 | 64 | 34 | .... | .... | .... | .... | .... | .... | .... | .... | .... | 4 | 0 | 1 | 1 | 0 | .... | .... | .... | .... |
| 2005-06 | Saskatoon Blades | WHL | 65 | 36 | 47 | 83 | 69 | .... | .... | .... | .... | .... | .... | .... | .... | .... | 10 | 8 | 4 | 12 | 8 | .... | .... | .... | .... |
| 2006-07 | Prince George | WHL | 55 | 36 | 29 | 65 | 55 | .... | .... | .... | .... | .... | .... | .... | .... | .... | 15 | *11 | 10 | 21 | 24 | .... | .... | .... | .... |
| **2007-08** | **San Jose** | **NHL** | **44** | **11** | **6** | **17** | **8** | **3** | **0** | **2** | **105** | **10.5** | **6** | **17** | **64.7** | **14:15** | **9** | **1** | **1** | **2** | **2** | **0** | **0** | **0** | **10:25** |
| | Worcester Sharks | AHL | 23 | 8 | 11 | 19 | 25 | .... | .... | .... | .... | .... | .... | .... | .... | .... | .... | .... | .... | .... | .... | .... | .... | .... | .... |
| **2008-09** | **San Jose** | **NHL** | **81** | **31** | **34** | **65** | **25** | **11** | **0** | **3** | **246** | **12.6** | **16** | **21** | **28.6** | **16:13** | **6** | **1** | **2** | **3** | **2** | **0** | **0** | **0** | **16:21** |
| | **NHL Totals** | | **125** | **42** | **40** | **82** | **33** | **14** | **0** | **5** | **351** | **12.0** | | **38** | **44.7** | **15:31** | **15** | **2** | **3** | **5** | **4** | **0** | **0** | **0** | **12:47** |

WHL East Second All-Star Team (2006)

## SHANAHAN, Brendan

(SHA-na-HAN, BREHN-duhn) **N.J.**

Left wing. Shoots right. 6'3", 220 lbs. Born, Mimico, Ont., January 23, 1969. New Jersey's 1st choice, 2nd overall, in 1987 Entry Draft.

| | | | | | | | | | | | | | | | | | | | | | | | | | |
|---|---|---|---|---|---|---|---|---|---|---|---|---|---|---|---|---|---|---|---|---|---|---|---|---|---|
| 1984-85 | Mississauga Reps | MTHL | 36 | 20 | 21 | 41 | 26 | .... | .... | .... | .... | .... | .... | .... | .... | .... | .... | .... | .... | .... | .... | .... | .... | .... | .... |
| | Dixie Beehives | OJHL | 1 | 0 | 0 | 0 | 0 | .... | .... | .... | .... | .... | .... | .... | .... | .... | .... | .... | .... | .... | .... | .... | .... | .... | .... |
| 1985-86 | London Knights | OHL | 59 | 28 | 34 | 62 | 70 | .... | .... | .... | .... | .... | .... | .... | .... | .... | 5 | 5 | 5 | 10 | 5 | .... | .... | .... | .... |
| 1986-87 | London Knights | OHL | 56 | 39 | 53 | 92 | 92 | .... | .... | .... | .... | .... | .... | .... | .... | .... | .... | .... | .... | .... | .... | .... | .... | .... | .... |
| **1987-88** | **New Jersey** | **NHL** | **65** | **7** | **19** | **26** | **131** | **2** | **0** | **2** | **72** | **9.7** | **–20** | .... | .... | .... | **12** | **2** | **1** | **3** | **44** | **1** | **0** | **0** | .... |
| **1988-89** | **New Jersey** | **NHL** | **68** | **22** | **28** | **50** | **115** | **9** | **0** | **0** | **152** | **14.5** | **2** | .... | .... | .... | .... | .... | .... | .... | .... | .... | .... | .... | .... |
| **1989-90** | **New Jersey** | **NHL** | **73** | **30** | **42** | **72** | **137** | **8** | **0** | **5** | **196** | **15.3** | **15** | .... | .... | .... | **6** | **3** | **3** | **6** | **20** | **1** | **0** | **1** | .... |

| | | | Regular Season | | | | | | | | | | | | | | Playoffs | | | | | | | | |
|---|---|---|---|---|---|---|---|---|---|---|---|---|---|---|---|---|---|---|---|---|---|---|---|---|---|
| Season | Club | League | GP | G | A | Pts | PIM | PP | SH | GW | S | % | +/- | TF | F% | Min | GP | G | A | Pts | PIM | PP | SH | GW | Min |
| 1990-91 | New Jersey | NHL | 75 | 29 | 37 | 66 | 141 | 7 | 0 | 2 | 195 | 14.9 | 4 | .... | .... | .... | 7 | 3 | 5 | 8 | 12 | 2 | 0 | 0 | .... |
| 1991-92 | St. Louis | NHL | 80 | 33 | 36 | 69 | 171 | 13 | 0 | 2 | 215 | 15.3 | –3 | .... | .... | .... | 6 | 2 | 3 | 5 | 14 | 1 | 0 | 0 | .... |
| 1992-93 | St. Louis | NHL | 71 | 51 | 43 | 94 | 174 | 18 | 0 | 8 | 232 | 22.0 | 10 | .... | .... | .... | 11 | 4 | 3 | 7 | 18 | 2 | 0 | 0 | .... |
| 1993-94 | St. Louis | NHL | 81 | 52 | 50 | 102 | 211 | 15 | 7 | 8 | 397 | 13.1 | –9 | .... | .... | .... | 4 | 2 | 5 | 7 | 4 | 0 | 0 | 0 | .... |
| 1994-95 | Dusseldorfer EG | Germany | 3 | 5 | 3 | 8 | 4 | .... | .... | .... | .... | .... | .... | .... | .... | .... | .... | .... | .... | .... | .... | .... | .... | .... | .... |
| | St. Louis | NHL | 45 | 20 | 21 | 41 | 136 | 6 | 2 | 6 | 153 | 13.1 | 7 | .... | .... | .... | 5 | 4 | 5 | 9 | 14 | 1 | 0 | 1 | .... |
| 1995-96 | Hartford | NHL | 74 | 44 | 34 | 78 | 125 | 17 | 2 | 6 | 280 | 15.7 | 2 | .... | .... | .... | .... | .... | .... | .... | .... | .... | .... | .... | .... |
| 1996-97 | Hartford | NHL | 2 | 1 | 0 | 1 | 0 | 0 | 1 | 0 | 13 | 7.7 | 1 | .... | .... | .... | .... | .... | .... | .... | .... | .... | .... | .... | .... |
| | ♦ Detroit | NHL | 79 | 46 | 41 | 87 | 131 | 20 | 2 | 7 | 323 | 14.2 | 31 | .... | .... | .... | 20 | 9 | 8 | 17 | 43 | 2 | 0 | 2 | .... |
| 1997-98 ♦ | Detroit | NHL | 75 | 28 | 29 | 57 | 154 | 15 | 1 | 9 | 266 | 10.5 | 6 | .... | .... | .... | 20 | 5 | 4 | 9 | 22 | 3 | 0 | 2 | .... |
| | Canada | Olympics | 6 | 2 | 0 | 2 | 0 | .... | .... | .... | .... | .... | .... | .... | .... | .... | .... | .... | .... | .... | .... | .... | .... | .... | .... |
| 1998-99 | Detroit | NHL | 81 | 31 | 27 | 58 | 123 | 5 | 0 | 5 | 288 | 10.8 | 2 | 18 | 44.4 | 17:31 | 10 | 3 | 7 | 10 | 6 | 1 | 0 | 1 | 18:31 |
| 99-2000 | Detroit | NHL | 78 | 41 | 37 | 78 | 105 | 13 | 1 | 9 | 283 | 14.5 | 24 | 24 | 50.0 | 18:35 | 9 | 3 | 2 | 5 | 10 | 0 | 0 | 0 | 17:36 |
| 2000-01 | Detroit | NHL | 81 | 31 | 45 | 76 | 81 | 15 | 1 | 7 | 278 | 11.2 | 9 | 115 | 43.5 | 18:22 | 2 | 2 | 2 | 4 | 0 | 0 | 0 | 1 | 21:02 |
| 2001-02 ♦ | Detroit | NHL | 80 | 37 | 38 | 75 | 118 | 12 | 3 | 7 | 277 | 13.4 | 23 | 70 | 47.1 | 18:55 | 23 | 8 | 11 | 19 | 20 | 1 | 0 | 2 | 19:06 |
| | Canada | Olympics | 6 | 0 | 1 | 1 | 0 | .... | .... | .... | .... | .... | .... | .... | .... | .... | .... | .... | .... | .... | .... | .... | .... | .... | .... |
| 2002-03 | Detroit | NHL | 78 | 30 | 38 | 68 | 103 | 13 | 0 | 6 | 260 | 11.5 | 5 | 28 | 60.7 | 18:38 | 4 | 1 | 1 | 2 | 4 | 1 | 0 | 0 | 22:03 |
| 2003-04 | Detroit | NHL | 82 | 25 | 28 | 53 | 117 | 8 | 0 | 7 | 280 | 8.9 | 15 | 32 | 46.9 | 18:05 | 12 | 1 | 5 | 6 | 20 | 0 | 1 | 0 | 16:49 |
| 2004-05 | | | DID NOT PLAY | | | | | | | | | | | | | | | | | | | | | | |
| 2005-06 | Detroit | NHL | 82 | 40 | 41 | 81 | 105 | 14 | 0 | 6 | 289 | 13.8 | 29 | 26 | 50.0 | 16:35 | 6 | 1 | 1 | 2 | 6 | 0 | 0 | 0 | 18:54 |
| 2006-07 | NY Rangers | NHL | 67 | 29 | 33 | 62 | 47 | 14 | 3 | 3 | 295 | 9.8 | 2 | 281 | 48.0 | 19:49 | 10 | 5 | 2 | 7 | 12 | 3 | 0 | 2 | 19:00 |
| 2007-08 | NY Rangers | NHL | 73 | 23 | 23 | 46 | 35 | 11 | 0 | 3 | 265 | 8.7 | –2 | 8 | 75.0 | 18:31 | 10 | 1 | 4 | 5 | 8 | 0 | 0 | 0 | 17:05 |
| 2008-09 | New Jersey | NHL | 34 | 6 | 8 | 14 | 29 | 2 | 0 | 1 | 77 | 7.8 | –2 | 27 | 44.4 | 14:54 | 7 | 1 | 2 | 3 | 2 | 0 | 0 | 0 | 16:46 |
| | **NHL Totals** | | **1524** | **656** | **698** | **1354** | **2489** | **237** | **23** | **109** | **5086** | **12.9** | | **629** | **47.9** | **18:08** | **184** | **60** | **74** | **134** | **279** | **19** | **1** | **12** | **18:21** |

NHL First All-Star Team (1994, 2000) • NHL Second All-Star Team (2002) • King Clancy Memorial Trophy (2003)

Played in NHL All-Star Game (1994, 1996, 1997, 1998, 1999, 2000, 2002, 2007)

Signed as a free agent by **St. Louis**, July 25, 1991. Traded to **Hartford** by **St. Louis** for Chris Pronger, July 27, 1995. Traded to **Detroit** by **Hartford** with Brian Glynn for Paul Coffey, Keith Primeau and Detroit's 1st round choice (Nikos Tselios) in 1997 Entry Draft, October 9, 1996. Signed as a free agent by **NY Rangers**, July 9, 2006. Signed as a free agent by **New Jersey**, January 15, 2009.

## SHANNON, Ryan

(SHA-nuhn, RIGH-uhn) **OTT.**

Center. Shoots right. 5'9", 171 lbs. Born, Darien, CT, March 2, 1983.

| | | | | | | | | | | | | | | | | | | | | | | | | | |
|---|---|---|---|---|---|---|---|---|---|---|---|---|---|---|---|---|---|---|---|---|---|---|---|---|---|
| 2001-02 | Boston College | H-East | 38 | 8 | 17 | 25 | 12 | .... | .... | .... | .... | .... | .... | .... | .... | .... | .... | .... | .... | .... | .... | .... | .... | .... | .... |
| 2002-03 | Boston College | H-East | 36 | 14 | 24 | 38 | 4 | .... | .... | .... | .... | .... | .... | .... | .... | .... | .... | .... | .... | .... | .... | .... | .... | .... | .... |
| 2003-04 | Boston College | H-East | 42 | 15 | 27 | 42 | 22 | .... | .... | .... | .... | .... | .... | .... | .... | .... | .... | .... | .... | .... | .... | .... | .... | .... | .... |
| 2004-05 | Boston College | H-East | 38 | 14 | 31 | 45 | 22 | .... | .... | .... | .... | .... | .... | .... | .... | .... | .... | .... | .... | .... | .... | .... | .... | .... | .... |
| | Cincinnati | AHL | 4 | 1 | 0 | 1 | 2 | .... | .... | .... | .... | .... | .... | .... | .... | .... | .... | .... | .... | .... | .... | .... | .... | .... | .... |
| 2005-06 | Portland Pirates | AHL | 71 | 27 | 59 | 86 | 44 | .... | .... | .... | .... | .... | .... | .... | .... | .... | 19 | 11 | 11 | 22 | 8 | .... | .... | .... | .... |
| 2006-07 ♦ | Anaheim | NHL | 53 | 2 | 9 | 11 | 10 | 0 | 0 | 0 | 77 | 2.6 | –2 | 25 | 52.0 | 10:39 | 11 | 0 | 0 | 0 | 6 | 0 | 0 | 0 | 4:04 |
| | Portland Pirates | AHL | 14 | 2 | 7 | 9 | 12 | .... | .... | .... | .... | .... | .... | .... | .... | .... | .... | .... | .... | .... | .... | .... | .... | .... | .... |
| 2007-08 | Vancouver | NHL | 27 | 5 | 8 | 13 | 24 | 4 | 0 | 0 | 34 | 14.7 | –1 | 82 | 39.0 | 12:53 | .... | .... | .... | .... | .... | .... | .... | .... | .... |
| | Manitoba Moose | AHL | 13 | 1 | 7 | 8 | 10 | .... | .... | .... | .... | .... | .... | .... | .... | .... | .... | .... | .... | .... | .... | .... | .... | .... | .... |
| 2008-09 | Ottawa | NHL | 35 | 8 | 12 | 20 | 2 | 3 | 0 | 1 | 61 | 13.1 | –1 | 6 | 33.3 | 15:04 | .... | .... | .... | .... | .... | .... | .... | .... | .... |
| | Binghamton | AHL | 36 | 10 | 25 | 35 | 16 | .... | .... | .... | .... | .... | .... | .... | .... | .... | .... | .... | .... | .... | .... | .... | .... | .... | .... |
| | **NHL Totals** | | **115** | **15** | **29** | **44** | **36** | **7** | **0** | **1** | **172** | **8.7** | | **113** | **41.6** | **12:31** | **11** | **0** | **0** | **0** | **6** | **0** | **0** | **0** | **4:04** |

Hockey East First All-Star Team (2004) • NCAA East Second All-American Team (2004) • AHL All-Rookie Team (2006)

Signed as a free agent by **Anaheim**, November 28, 2005. Traded to **Vancouver** by **Anaheim** for Jason King and future considerations, June 23, 2007. Traded to **Ottawa** by **Vancouver** for Lawrence Nycholat, September 2, 2008.

## SHARP, Patrick

(SHAHRP, PAT-rihk) **CHI.**

Center. Shoots right. 6'1", 197 lbs. Born, Winnipeg, Man., December 27, 1981. Philadelphia's 2nd choice, 95th overall, in 2001 Entry Draft.

| | | | | | | | | | | | | | | | | | | | | | | | | | |
|---|---|---|---|---|---|---|---|---|---|---|---|---|---|---|---|---|---|---|---|---|---|---|---|---|---|
| 1998-99 | Thunder Bay | USHL | 55 | 19 | 24 | 43 | 48 | .... | .... | .... | .... | .... | .... | .... | .... | .... | 3 | 1 | 1 | 2 | 0 | .... | .... | .... | .... |
| 99-2000 | Thunder Bay | USHL | 56 | 20 | 35 | 55 | 41 | .... | .... | .... | .... | .... | .... | .... | .... | .... | .... | .... | .... | .... | .... | .... | .... | .... | .... |
| 2000-01 | U. of Vermont | ECAC | 34 | 12 | 15 | 27 | 36 | .... | .... | .... | .... | .... | .... | .... | .... | .... | .... | .... | .... | .... | .... | .... | .... | .... | .... |
| 2001-02 | U. of Vermont | ECAC | 31 | 13 | 13 | 26 | 50 | .... | .... | .... | .... | .... | .... | .... | .... | .... | .... | .... | .... | .... | .... | .... | .... | .... | .... |
| 2002-03 | Philadelphia | NHL | 3 | 0 | 0 | 0 | 2 | 0 | 0 | 0 | 3 | 0.0 | 0 | 7 | 42.9 | 5:59 | .... | .... | .... | .... | .... | .... | .... | .... | .... |
| | Philadelphia | AHL | 53 | 14 | 19 | 33 | 39 | .... | .... | .... | .... | .... | .... | .... | .... | .... | .... | .... | .... | .... | .... | .... | .... | .... | .... |
| 2003-04 | Philadelphia | NHL | 41 | 5 | 2 | 7 | 55 | 0 | 0 | 1 | 44 | 11.4 | –3 | 272 | 46.7 | 9:56 | 12 | 1 | 0 | 1 | 2 | 0 | 0 | 0 | 6:12 |
| | Philadelphia | AHL | 35 | 15 | 14 | 29 | 45 | .... | .... | .... | .... | .... | .... | .... | .... | .... | 1 | 2 | 0 | 2 | 0 | .... | .... | .... | .... |
| 2004-05 | Philadelphia | AHL | 75 | 23 | 29 | 52 | 80 | .... | .... | .... | .... | .... | .... | .... | .... | .... | 21 | 8 | 13 | *21 | 20 | .... | .... | .... | .... |
| 2005-06 | Philadelphia | NHL | 22 | 5 | 3 | 8 | 10 | 1 | 0 | 3 | 33 | 15.2 | 4 | 38 | 52.6 | 7:43 | .... | .... | .... | .... | .... | .... | .... | .... | .... |
| | Chicago | NHL | 50 | 9 | 14 | 23 | 36 | 0 | 1 | 2 | 111 | 8.1 | 1 | 664 | 48.0 | 16:19 | .... | .... | .... | .... | .... | .... | .... | .... | .... |
| 2006-07 | Chicago | NHL | 80 | 20 | 15 | 35 | 74 | 5 | 3 | 1 | 160 | 12.5 | –15 | 1008 | 46.5 | 17:04 | .... | .... | .... | .... | .... | .... | .... | .... | .... |
| 2007-08 | Chicago | NHL | 80 | 36 | 26 | 62 | 55 | 9 | 7 | 7 | 209 | 17.2 | 23 | 594 | 51.4 | 18:47 | .... | .... | .... | .... | .... | .... | .... | .... | .... |
| 2008-09 | Chicago | NHL | 61 | 26 | 18 | 44 | 41 | 9 | 0 | 4 | 184 | 14.1 | 6 | 566 | 45.8 | 17:57 | 17 | 7 | 4 | 11 | 6 | 3 | 0 | 2 | 16:17 |
| | **NHL Totals** | | **337** | **101** | **78** | **179** | **273** | **24** | **11** | **18** | **744** | **13.6** | | **3149** | **47.7** | **15:57** | **29** | **8** | **4** | **12** | **8** | **3** | **0** | **2** | **12:07** |

Traded to **Chicago** by **Philadelphia** with Eric Meloche for Matt Ellison and Chicago's 3rd round choice (later traded to Montreal - Montreal selected Ryan White) in 2006 Entry Draft, December 5, 2005.

## SHELLEY, Jody

(SHEH-lee, JOH-dee) **S.J.**

Left wing. Shoots left. 6'3", 225 lbs. Born, Thompson, Man., February 7, 1976.

| | | | | | | | | | | | | | | | | | | | | | | | | | |
|---|---|---|---|---|---|---|---|---|---|---|---|---|---|---|---|---|---|---|---|---|---|---|---|---|---|
| 1994-95 | Halifax | QMJHL | 72 | 10 | 12 | 22 | 194 | .... | .... | .... | .... | .... | .... | .... | .... | .... | 7 | 0 | 1 | 1 | 12 | .... | .... | .... | .... |
| 1995-96 | Halifax | QMJHL | 50 | 13 | 19 | 32 | 319 | .... | .... | .... | .... | .... | .... | .... | .... | .... | 6 | 0 | 2 | 2 | 36 | .... | .... | .... | .... |
| 1996-97 | Halifax | QMJHL | 58 | 25 | 19 | 44 | *448 | .... | .... | .... | .... | .... | .... | .... | .... | .... | 17 | 6 | 6 | 12 | *123 | .... | .... | .... | .... |
| 1997-98 | Dalhousie | AUAA | 19 | 6 | 11 | 17 | 145 | .... | .... | .... | .... | .... | .... | .... | .... | .... | .... | .... | .... | .... | .... | .... | .... | .... | .... |
| | Saint John Flames | AHL | 18 | 1 | 1 | 2 | 50 | .... | .... | .... | .... | .... | .... | .... | .... | .... | .... | .... | .... | .... | .... | .... | .... | .... | .... |
| 1998-99 | Saint John Flames | AHL | 8 | 0 | 0 | 0 | 46 | .... | .... | .... | .... | .... | .... | .... | .... | .... | .... | .... | .... | .... | .... | .... | .... | .... | .... |
| | Johnstown Chiefs | ECHL | 52 | 12 | 17 | 29 | 325 | .... | .... | .... | .... | .... | .... | .... | .... | .... | .... | .... | .... | .... | .... | .... | .... | .... | .... |
| 99-2000 | Johnstown Chiefs | ECHL | 36 | 9 | 17 | 26 | 256 | .... | .... | .... | .... | .... | .... | .... | .... | .... | .... | .... | .... | .... | .... | .... | .... | .... | .... |
| | Saint John Flames | AHL | 22 | 1 | 4 | 5 | 93 | .... | .... | .... | .... | .... | .... | .... | .... | .... | 3 | 0 | 0 | 0 | 2 | .... | .... | .... | .... |
| 2000-01 | Syracuse Crunch | AHL | 69 | 1 | 7 | 8 | *357 | .... | .... | .... | .... | .... | .... | .... | .... | .... | 5 | 0 | 0 | 0 | 21 | .... | .... | .... | .... |
| | Columbus | NHL | 1 | 0 | 0 | 0 | 10 | 0 | 0 | 0 | 0 | 0.0 | 0 | 0 | 0.0 | 1:33 | .... | .... | .... | .... | .... | .... | .... | .... | .... |
| 2001-02 | Columbus | NHL | 52 | 3 | 3 | 6 | 206 | 0 | 0 | 0 | 35 | 8.6 | 1 | 0 | 0.0 | 6:32 | .... | .... | .... | .... | .... | .... | .... | .... | .... |
| | Syracuse Crunch | AHL | 22 | 3 | 5 | 8 | 165 | .... | .... | .... | .... | .... | .... | .... | .... | .... | .... | .... | .... | .... | .... | .... | .... | .... | .... |
| 2002-03 | Columbus | NHL | 68 | 1 | 4 | 5 | *249 | 0 | 0 | 0 | 39 | 2.6 | –5 | 1 | 0.0 | 6:08 | .... | .... | .... | .... | .... | .... | .... | .... | .... |
| 2003-04 | Columbus | NHL | 76 | 3 | 3 | 6 | 228 | 1 | 0 | 0 | 62 | 4.8 | –10 | 3 | 0.0 | 7:14 | .... | .... | .... | .... | .... | .... | .... | .... | .... |
| 2004-05 | JYP Jyvaskyla | Finland | 11 | 0 | 1 | 1 | 20 | .... | .... | .... | .... | .... | .... | .... | .... | .... | 3 | 0 | 0 | 0 | 25 | .... | .... | .... | .... |
| 2005-06 | Columbus | NHL | 80 | 3 | 7 | 10 | 163 | 0 | 0 | 1 | 39 | 7.7 | –4 | 7 | 14.3 | 5:58 | .... | .... | .... | .... | .... | .... | .... | .... | .... |
| 2006-07 | Columbus | NHL | 72 | 1 | 1 | 2 | 125 | 0 | 0 | 0 | 32 | 3.1 | –6 | 2 | 0.0 | 4:52 | .... | .... | .... | .... | .... | .... | .... | .... | .... |
| 2007-08 | Columbus | NHL | 31 | 0 | 0 | 0 | 44 | 0 | 0 | 0 | 10 | 0.0 | –2 | 1 | 0.0 | 4:20 | .... | .... | .... | .... | .... | .... | .... | .... | .... |
| | San Jose | NHL | 31 | 1 | 6 | 7 | 91 | 0 | 0 | 0 | 31 | 3.2 | –2 | 1 | 0.0 | 7:24 | 6 | 0 | 0 | 0 | 2 | 0 | 0 | 0 | 3:16 |
| 2008-09 | San Jose | NHL | 70 | 2 | 2 | 4 | 116 | 0 | 0 | 1 | 44 | 4.5 | –6 | 7 | 42.9 | 6:11 | 1 | 0 | 0 | 0 | 0 | 0 | 0 | 0 | 2:02 |
| | **NHL Totals** | | **481** | **14** | **26** | **40** | **1232** | **1** | **0** | **2** | **292** | **4.8** | | **22** | **18.2** | **6:06** | **7** | **0** | **0** | **0** | **2** | **0** | **0** | **0** | **3:05** |

Signed as a free agent by **Calgary**, September 1, 1998. Signed as a free agent by **Syracuse** (AHL), September 15, 2000. Signed as a free agent by **Columbus**, January 31, 2001. Signed as a free agent by **Jyvaskyla** (Finland), January 17, 2005. Traded to **San Jose** by **Columbus** for San Jose's 6th round choice (later traded to Atlanta – later traded to Chicago – Chicago selected David Pacan) in 2009 Entry Draft, January 29, 2008.

## SHEPPARD, James

(sheh-PUHRD, JAYMZ) **MIN.**

Center. Shoots left. 6'2", 210 lbs. Born, Halifax, N.S., April 25, 1988. Minnesota's 1st choice, 9th overall, in 2006 Entry Draft.

| | | | | | | | | | | | | | | | | | | | | | | | | | |
|---|---|---|---|---|---|---|---|---|---|---|---|---|---|---|---|---|---|---|---|---|---|---|---|---|---|
| 2003-04 | Dartmouth | NSMHL | 61 | 38 | 54 | 92 | 46 | .... | .... | .... | .... | .... | .... | .... | .... | .... | .... | .... | .... | .... | .... | .... | .... | .... | .... |
| 2004-05 | Cape Breton | QMJHL | 65 | 14 | 31 | 45 | 40 | .... | .... | .... | .... | .... | .... | .... | .... | .... | 5 | 1 | 3 | 4 | 2 | .... | .... | .... | .... |
| 2005-06 | Cape Breton | QMJHL | 66 | 30 | 54 | 84 | 78 | .... | .... | .... | .... | .... | .... | .... | .... | .... | 9 | 2 | 5 | 7 | 12 | .... | .... | .... | .... |
| 2006-07 | Cape Breton | QMJHL | 56 | 33 | 63 | 96 | 62 | .... | .... | .... | .... | .... | .... | .... | .... | .... | 16 | 8 | 12 | 20 | 14 | .... | .... | .... | .... |
| 2007-08 | Minnesota | NHL | 78 | 4 | 15 | 19 | 29 | 0 | 0 | 1 | 57 | 7.0 | 0 | 655 | 41.5 | 10:37 | 6 | 0 | 1 | 1 | 4 | 0 | 0 | 0 | 10:37 |
| 2008-09 | Minnesota | NHL | 82 | 5 | 19 | 24 | 41 | 0 | 0 | 1 | 88 | 5.7 | –14 | 870 | 41.5 | 15:11 | .... | .... | .... | .... | .... | .... | .... | .... | .... |
| | **NHL Totals** | | **160** | **9** | **34** | **43** | **70** | **0** | **0** | **2** | **145** | **6.2** | | **1525** | **41.5** | **12:57** | **6** | **0** | **1** | **1** | **4** | **0** | **0** | **0** | **10:37** |

QMJHL Second All-Star Team (2007)

## SIFERS, Jaime

(SIH-fuhrs, JAY-mee) **MIN.**

Defense. Shoots right. 5'11", 210 lbs. Born, Stratford, CT, January 18, 1983.

| | | | Regular Season | | | | | | | | | | | | | | Playoffs | | | | | | | | |
|---|---|---|---|---|---|---|---|---|---|---|---|---|---|---|---|---|---|---|---|---|---|---|---|---|---|
| Season | Club | League | GP | G | A | Pts | PIM | PP | SH | GW | S | % | +/- | TF | F% | Min | GP | G | A | Pts | PIM | PP | SH | GW | Min |
| 2002-03 | U. of Vermont | ECAC | 34 | 4 | 14 | 18 | 66 | .... | .... | .... | .... | .... | .... | .... | .... | .... | .... | .... | .... | .... | .... | .... | .... | .... | .... |
| 2003-04 | U. of Vermont | ECAC | 35 | 4 | 14 | 18 | 93 | .... | .... | .... | .... | .... | .... | .... | .... | .... | .... | .... | .... | .... | .... | .... | .... | .... | .... |
| 2004-05 | U. of Vermont | ECAC | 36 | 4 | 12 | 16 | 57 | .... | .... | .... | .... | .... | .... | .... | .... | .... | .... | .... | .... | .... | .... | .... | .... | .... | .... |
| 2005-06 | U. of Vermont | H-East | 38 | 3 | 15 | 18 | 60 | .... | .... | .... | .... | .... | .... | .... | .... | .... | .... | .... | .... | .... | .... | .... | .... | .... | .... |
| | Toronto Marlies | AHL | 2 | 0 | 0 | 0 | 2 | .... | .... | .... | .... | .... | .... | .... | .... | .... | .... | .... | .... | .... | .... | .... | .... | .... | .... |
| 2006-07 | Toronto Marlies | AHL | 80 | 7 | 18 | 25 | 75 | .... | .... | .... | .... | .... | .... | .... | .... | .... | .... | .... | .... | .... | .... | .... | .... | .... | .... |
| 2007-08 | Toronto Marlies | AHL | 80 | 3 | 10 | 13 | 57 | .... | .... | .... | .... | .... | .... | .... | .... | .... | 19 | 2 | 3 | 5 | 6 | .... | .... | .... | .... |
| **2008-09** | **Toronto** | **NHL** | **23** | **0** | **2** | **2** | **18** | **0** | **0** | **0** | **25** | **0.0** | **–4** | **0** | **0.0** | **12:50** | .... | .... | .... | .... | .... | .... | .... | .... | .... |
| | Toronto Marlies | AHL | 43 | 4 | 16 | 20 | 47 | .... | .... | .... | .... | .... | .... | .... | .... | .... | 4 | 0 | 1 | 1 | 4 | .... | .... | .... | .... |
| | **NHL Totals** | | **23** | **0** | **2** | **2** | **18** | **0** | **0** | **0** | **25** | **0.0** | | **0** | **0.0** | **12:50** | .... | .... | .... | .... | .... | .... | .... | .... | .... |

ECAC Second All-Star Team (2005)

Signed as a free agent by **Toronto**, July 20, 2006. Signed as a free agent by **Minnesota**, July 8, 2009.

## SIGALET, Jonathan

(SIH-ga-leht, JAWN-ah-thuhn) **CBJ**

Defense. Shoots left. 6'1", 199 lbs. Born, Vancouver, B.C., February 12, 1986. Boston's 4th choice, 100th overall, in 2005 Entry Draft.

| | | | Regular Season | | | | | | | | | | | | | | Playoffs | | | | | | | | |
|---|---|---|---|---|---|---|---|---|---|---|---|---|---|---|---|---|---|---|---|---|---|---|---|---|---|
| Season | Club | League | GP | G | A | Pts | PIM | PP | SH | GW | S | % | +/- | TF | F% | Min | GP | G | A | Pts | PIM | PP | SH | GW | Min |
| 2002-03 | Salmon Arm | BCHL | 52 | 13 | 39 | 52 | 34 | .... | .... | .... | .... | .... | .... | .... | .... | .... | .... | .... | .... | .... | .... | .... | .... | .... | .... |
| 2003-04 | Bowling Green | CCHA | 37 | 3 | 12 | 15 | 26 | .... | .... | .... | .... | .... | .... | .... | .... | .... | .... | .... | .... | .... | .... | .... | .... | .... | .... |
| 2004-05 | Bowling Green | CCHA | 35 | 3 | 13 | 16 | 36 | .... | .... | .... | .... | .... | .... | .... | .... | .... | .... | .... | .... | .... | .... | .... | .... | .... | .... |
| 2005-06 | Providence Bruins | AHL | 75 | 9 | 27 | 36 | 59 | .... | .... | .... | .... | .... | .... | .... | .... | .... | 6 | 2 | 1 | 3 | 9 | .... | .... | .... | .... |
| **2006-07** | **Boston** | **NHL** | **1** | **0** | **0** | **0** | **4** | **0** | **0** | **0** | **1** | **0.0** | **–2** | **0** | **0.0** | **14:41** | .... | .... | .... | .... | .... | .... | .... | .... | .... |
| | Providence Bruins | AHL | 50 | 9 | 13 | 22 | 37 | .... | .... | .... | .... | .... | .... | .... | .... | .... | .... | .... | .... | .... | .... | .... | .... | .... | .... |
| 2007-08 | Providence Bruins | AHL | 74 | 3 | 20 | 23 | 58 | .... | .... | .... | .... | .... | .... | .... | .... | .... | 10 | 0 | 3 | 3 | 12 | .... | .... | .... | .... |
| 2008-09 | Syracuse Crunch | AHL | 19 | 5 | 6 | 11 | 16 | .... | .... | .... | .... | .... | .... | .... | .... | .... | .... | .... | .... | .... | .... | .... | .... | .... | .... |
| | **NHL Totals** | | **1** | **0** | **0** | **0** | **4** | **0** | **0** | **0** | **1** | **0.0** | | **0** | **0.0** | **14:41** | .... | .... | .... | .... | .... | .... | .... | .... | .... |

Traded to **Columbus** by **Boston** for Matt Marquardt, May 27, 2008.

## SILLINGER, Mike

(SIHL-ihn-juhr, MIGHK)

Center. Shoots right. 5'11", 198 lbs. Born, Regina, Sask., June 29, 1971. Detroit's 1st choice, 11th overall, in 1989 Entry Draft.

| | | | Regular Season | | | | | | | | | | | | | | Playoffs | | | | | | | | |
|---|---|---|---|---|---|---|---|---|---|---|---|---|---|---|---|---|---|---|---|---|---|---|---|---|---|
| Season | Club | League | GP | G | A | Pts | PIM | PP | SH | GW | S | % | +/- | TF | F% | Min | GP | G | A | Pts | PIM | PP | SH | GW | Min |
| 1986-87 | Regina Kings | SMHL | 31 | 83 | 51 | 134 | .... | .... | .... | .... | .... | .... | .... | .... | .... | .... | .... | .... | .... | .... | .... | .... | .... | .... | .... |
| 1987-88 | Regina Pats | WHL | 67 | 18 | 25 | 43 | 17 | .... | .... | .... | .... | .... | .... | .... | .... | .... | 4 | 2 | 2 | 4 | 0 | .... | .... | .... | .... |
| 1988-89 | Regina Pats | WHL | 72 | 53 | 78 | 131 | 52 | .... | .... | .... | .... | .... | .... | .... | .... | .... | .... | .... | .... | .... | .... | .... | .... | .... | .... |
| 1989-90 | Regina Pats | WHL | 70 | 57 | 72 | 129 | 41 | .... | .... | .... | .... | .... | .... | .... | .... | .... | 11 | 12 | 10 | 22 | 2 | .... | .... | .... | .... |
| | Adirondack | AHL | .... | .... | .... | .... | .... | .... | .... | .... | .... | .... | .... | .... | .... | .... | 1 | 0 | 0 | 0 | 0 | .... | .... | .... | .... |
| **1990-91** | Regina Pats | WHL | 57 | 50 | 66 | 116 | 42 | .... | .... | .... | .... | .... | .... | .... | .... | .... | 8 | 6 | 9 | 15 | 4 | .... | .... | .... | .... |
| | **Detroit** | **NHL** | **3** | **0** | **1** | **1** | **0** | **0** | **0** | **0** | **6** | **0.0** | **–2** | .... | .... | .... | **3** | **0** | **1** | **1** | **0** | **0** | **0** | **0** | .... |
| **1991-92** | Adirondack | AHL | 64 | 25 | 41 | 66 | 26 | .... | .... | .... | .... | .... | .... | .... | .... | .... | 15 | 9 | *19 | *28 | 12 | .... | .... | .... | .... |
| | **Detroit** | **NHL** | .... | .... | .... | .... | .... | .... | .... | .... | .... | .... | .... | .... | .... | .... | **8** | **2** | **2** | **4** | **2** | **0** | **0** | **0** | .... |
| **1992-93** | **Detroit** | **NHL** | **51** | **4** | **17** | **21** | **16** | **0** | **0** | **0** | **47** | **8.5** | **0** | .... | .... | .... | .... | .... | .... | .... | .... | .... | .... | .... | .... |
| | Adirondack | AHL | 15 | 10 | 20 | 30 | 31 | .... | .... | .... | .... | .... | .... | .... | .... | .... | 11 | 5 | 13 | 18 | 10 | .... | .... | .... | .... |
| **1993-94** | **Detroit** | **NHL** | **62** | **8** | **21** | **29** | **10** | **0** | **1** | **1** | **91** | **8.8** | **2** | .... | .... | .... | .... | .... | .... | .... | .... | .... | .... | .... | .... |
| **1994-95** | CE Wien | Austria | 13 | 13 | 14 | 27 | 10 | .... | .... | .... | .... | .... | .... | .... | .... | .... | .... | .... | .... | .... | .... | .... | .... | .... | .... |
| | **Detroit** | **NHL** | **13** | **2** | **6** | **8** | **2** | **0** | **0** | **0** | **11** | **18.2** | **3** | .... | .... | .... | .... | .... | .... | .... | .... | .... | .... | .... | .... |
| | **Anaheim** | **NHL** | **15** | **2** | **5** | **7** | **6** | **2** | **0** | **0** | **28** | **7.1** | **1** | .... | .... | .... | .... | .... | .... | .... | .... | .... | .... | .... | .... |
| **1995-96** | **Anaheim** | **NHL** | **62** | **13** | **21** | **34** | **32** | **7** | **0** | **2** | **143** | **9.1** | **–20** | .... | .... | .... | .... | .... | .... | .... | .... | .... | .... | .... | .... |
| | **Vancouver** | **NHL** | **12** | **1** | **3** | **4** | **6** | **0** | **1** | **0** | **16** | **6.3** | **2** | .... | .... | .... | **6** | **0** | **0** | **0** | **2** | **0** | **0** | **0** | .... |
| **1996-97** | **Vancouver** | **NHL** | **78** | **17** | **20** | **37** | **25** | **3** | **3** | **2** | **112** | **15.2** | **–3** | .... | .... | .... | .... | .... | .... | .... | .... | .... | .... | .... | .... |
| **1997-98** | **Vancouver** | **NHL** | **48** | **10** | **9** | **19** | **34** | **1** | **2** | **1** | **56** | **17.9** | **–14** | .... | .... | .... | .... | .... | .... | .... | .... | .... | .... | .... | .... |
| | **Philadelphia** | **NHL** | **27** | **11** | **11** | **22** | **16** | **1** | **2** | **0** | **40** | **27.5** | **3** | .... | .... | .... | **3** | **1** | **0** | **1** | **0** | **0** | **0** | **0** | .... |
| **1998-99** | **Philadelphia** | **NHL** | **25** | **0** | **3** | **3** | **8** | **0** | **0** | **0** | **23** | **0.0** | **–9** | **229** | **62.9** | **10:42** | .... | .... | .... | .... | .... | .... | .... | .... | .... |
| | **Tampa Bay** | **NHL** | **54** | **8** | **2** | **10** | **28** | **0** | **2** | **0** | **69** | **11.6** | **–20** | **320** | **57.8** | **13:57** | .... | .... | .... | .... | .... | .... | .... | .... | .... |
| **99-2000** | **Tampa Bay** | **NHL** | **67** | **19** | **25** | **44** | **86** | **6** | **3** | **1** | **126** | **15.1** | **–29** | **493** | **56.0** | **19:42** | .... | .... | .... | .... | .... | .... | .... | .... | .... |
| | **Florida** | **NHL** | **13** | **4** | **4** | **8** | **16** | **2** | **0** | **1** | **20** | **20.0** | **–1** | **248** | **61.3** | **19:33** | **4** | **2** | **1** | **3** | **2** | **0** | **0** | **0** | **20:24** |
| **2000-01** | **Florida** | **NHL** | **55** | **13** | **21** | **34** | **44** | **1** | **0** | **2** | **100** | **13.0** | **–12** | **1028** | **59.7** | **18:52** | .... | .... | .... | .... | .... | .... | .... | .... | .... |
| | **Ottawa** | **NHL** | **13** | **3** | **4** | **7** | **4** | **0** | **0** | **0** | **19** | **15.8** | **1** | **215** | **63.3** | **14:31** | **4** | **0** | **0** | **0** | **2** | **0** | **0** | **0** | **13:40** |
| **2001-02** | **Columbus** | **NHL** | **80** | **20** | **23** | **43** | **54** | **8** | **0** | **5** | **150** | **13.3** | **–35** | **2024** | **57.0** | **20:51** | .... | .... | .... | .... | .... | .... | .... | .... | .... |
| **2002-03** | **Columbus** | **NHL** | **75** | **18** | **25** | **43** | **52** | **9** | **3** | **3** | **128** | **14.1** | **–21** | **1490** | **56.5** | **19:08** | .... | .... | .... | .... | .... | .... | .... | .... | .... |
| **2003-04** | **Phoenix** | **NHL** | **60** | **8** | **6** | **14** | **54** | **0** | **1** | **0** | **66** | **12.1** | **–14** | **771** | **56.3** | **15:22** | .... | .... | .... | .... | .... | .... | .... | .... | .... |
| | **St. Louis** | **NHL** | **16** | **5** | **5** | **10** | **14** | **0** | **1** | **0** | **40** | **12.5** | **4** | **351** | **57.8** | **20:08** | **5** | **3** | **1** | **4** | **6** | **0** | **1** | **0** | **22:17** |
| 2004-05 | | | DID NOT PLAY | | | | | | | | | | | | | | | | | | | | | | |
| **2005-06** | **St. Louis** | **NHL** | **48** | **22** | **19** | **41** | **49** | **11** | **1** | **1** | **131** | **16.8** | **–17** | **797** | **55.3** | **19:41** | .... | .... | .... | .... | .... | .... | .... | .... | .... |
| | **Nashville** | **NHL** | **31** | **10** | **12** | **22** | **14** | **3** | **0** | **1** | **80** | **12.5** | **0** | **542** | **56.6** | **18:34** | **5** | **2** | **1** | **3** | **12** | **1** | **0** | **0** | **17:09** |
| **2006-07** | **NY Islanders** | **NHL** | **82** | **26** | **33** | **59** | **46** | **11** | **2** | **3** | **152** | **17.1** | **5** | **1708** | **58.8** | **19:19** | **5** | **1** | **1** | **2** | **2** | **1** | **0** | **0** | **20:49** |
| **2007-08** | **NY Islanders** | **NHL** | **52** | **14** | **12** | **26** | **28** | **3** | **2** | **2** | **94** | **14.9** | **–10** | **1027** | **56.3** | **18:36** | .... | .... | .... | .... | .... | .... | .... | .... | .... |
| **2008-09** | **NY Islanders** | **NHL** | **7** | **2** | **0** | **2** | **0** | **1** | **0** | **0** | **14** | **14.3** | **–5** | **122** | **58.2** | **14:08** | .... | .... | .... | .... | .... | .... | .... | .... | .... |
| | Bridgeport | AHL | 3 | 1 | 3 | 4 | 2 | .... | .... | .... | .... | .... | .... | .... | .... | .... | .... | .... | .... | .... | .... | .... | .... | .... | .... |
| | **NHL Totals** | | **1049** | **240** | **308** | **548** | **644** | **69** | **24** | **25** | **1762** | **13.6** | | **11365** | **57.6** | **18:12** | **43** | **11** | **7** | **18** | **28** | **2** | **1** | **0** | **19:01** |

WHL East Second All-Star Team (1990) • WHL East First All-Star Team (1991)

Traded to **Anaheim** by **Detroit** with Jason York for Stu Grimson, Mark Ferner and Anaheim's 6th round choice (Magnus Nilsson) in 1996 Entry Draft, April 4, 1995. Traded to **Vancouver** by **Anaheim** for Roman Oksiuta, March 15, 1996. Traded to **Philadelphia** by **Vancouver** for Philadelphia's 5th round choice (later traded back to Philadelphia – Philadelphia selected Garrett Prosofsky) in 1998 Entry Draft, February 5, 1998. Traded to **Tampa Bay** by **Philadelphia** with Chris Gratton for Mikael Renberg and Daymond Langkow, December 12, 1998. Traded to **Florida** by **Tampa Bay** for Ryan Johnson and Dwayne Hay, March 14, 2000. Traded to **Ottawa** by **Florida** for future considerations, March 13, 2001. Signed as a free agent by **Columbus**, July 7, 2001. Traded to **Dallas** by **Columbus** with Columbus' 2nd round choice (Johan Fransson) in 2004 Entry Draft for Darryl Sydor, July 22, 2003. Traded to **Phoenix** by **Dallas** with future considerations for Teppo Numminen, July 22, 2003. Traded to **St. Louis** by **Phoenix** for Brent Johnson, March 4, 2004. Traded to **Nashville** by **St. Louis** for Timofei Shishkanov, January 30, 2006. Signed as a free agent by **NY Islanders**, July 2, 2006. • Missed majority of 2008-09 season recovering from hip resurfacing surgery, January 26, 2009.

## SIM, Jon

(SIHM, JAWN) **NYI**

Left wing. Shoots left. 5'10", 195 lbs. Born, New Glasgow, N.S., September 29, 1977. Dallas' 2nd choice, 70th overall, in 1996 Entry Draft.

| | | | Regular Season | | | | | | | | | | | | | | Playoffs | | | | | | | | |
|---|---|---|---|---|---|---|---|---|---|---|---|---|---|---|---|---|---|---|---|---|---|---|---|---|---|
| Season | Club | League | GP | G | A | Pts | PIM | PP | SH | GW | S | % | +/- | TF | F% | Min | GP | G | A | Pts | PIM | PP | SH | GW | Min |
| 1994-95 | Laval Titan | QMJHL | 9 | 0 | 1 | 1 | 6 | .... | .... | .... | .... | .... | .... | .... | .... | .... | .... | .... | .... | .... | .... | .... | .... | .... | .... |
| | Sarnia Sting | OHL | 25 | 9 | 12 | 21 | 19 | .... | .... | .... | .... | .... | .... | .... | .... | .... | 4 | 3 | 2 | 5 | 2 | .... | .... | .... | .... |
| 1995-96 | Sarnia Sting | OHL | 63 | 56 | 46 | 102 | 130 | .... | .... | .... | .... | .... | .... | .... | .... | .... | 10 | 8 | 7 | 15 | 26 | .... | .... | .... | .... |
| 1996-97 | Sarnia Sting | OHL | 64 | *56 | 39 | 95 | 109 | .... | .... | .... | .... | .... | .... | .... | .... | .... | 12 | 9 | 5 | 14 | 32 | .... | .... | .... | .... |
| 1997-98 | Sarnia Sting | OHL | 59 | 44 | 50 | 94 | 95 | .... | .... | .... | .... | .... | .... | .... | .... | .... | 5 | 1 | 4 | 5 | 14 | .... | .... | .... | .... |
| **1998-99** ♦ | **Dallas** | **NHL** | **7** | **1** | **0** | **1** | **12** | **0** | **0** | **0** | **8** | **12.5** | **1** | **6** | **50.0** | **11:26** | **4** | **0** | **0** | **0** | **0** | **0** | **0** | **0** | **6:27** |
| | Michigan | IHL | 68 | 24 | 27 | 51 | 91 | .... | .... | .... | .... | .... | .... | .... | .... | .... | 5 | 3 | 1 | 4 | 18 | .... | .... | .... | .... |
| **99-2000** | **Dallas** | **NHL** | **25** | **5** | **3** | **8** | **10** | **2** | **0** | **1** | **44** | **11.4** | **4** | **4** | **75.0** | **10:51** | **7** | **1** | **0** | **1** | **6** | **0** | **0** | **0** | **11:11** |
| | Michigan | IHL | 35 | 14 | 16 | 30 | 65 | .... | .... | .... | .... | .... | .... | .... | .... | .... | .... | .... | .... | .... | .... | .... | .... | .... | .... |
| **2000-01** | **Dallas** | **NHL** | **15** | **0** | **3** | **3** | **6** | **0** | **0** | **0** | **18** | **0.0** | **–2** | **1** | **100.0** | **8:47** | .... | .... | .... | .... | .... | .... | .... | .... | .... |
| | Utah Grizzlies | IHL | 39 | 16 | 13 | 29 | 44 | .... | .... | .... | .... | .... | .... | .... | .... | .... | .... | .... | .... | .... | .... | .... | .... | .... | .... |
| **2001-02** | **Dallas** | **NHL** | **26** | **3** | **0** | **3** | **10** | **1** | **0** | **0** | **43** | **7.0** | **–3** | **3** | **0.0** | **9:30** | .... | .... | .... | .... | .... | .... | .... | .... | .... |
| | Utah Grizzlies | AHL | 31 | 21 | 6 | 27 | 63 | .... | .... | .... | .... | .... | .... | .... | .... | .... | .... | .... | .... | .... | .... | .... | .... | .... | .... |
| **2002-03** | **Dallas** | **NHL** | **4** | **0** | **0** | **0** | **0** | **0** | **0** | **0** | **7** | **0.0** | **–1** | **2** | **50.0** | **9:10** | .... | .... | .... | .... | .... | .... | .... | .... | .... |
| | Utah Grizzlies | AHL | 42 | 16 | 31 | 47 | 85 | .... | .... | .... | .... | .... | .... | .... | .... | .... | .... | .... | .... | .... | .... | .... | .... | .... | .... |
| | **Nashville** | **NHL** | **4** | **1** | **0** | **1** | **0** | **0** | **0** | **0** | **3** | **33.3** | **0** | **14** | **35.7** | **9:18** | .... | .... | .... | .... | .... | .... | .... | .... | .... |
| | **Los Angeles** | **NHL** | **14** | **0** | **2** | **2** | **19** | **0** | **0** | **0** | **29** | **0.0** | **–3** | **3** | **33.3** | **12:05** | .... | .... | .... | .... | .... | .... | .... | .... | .... |
| **2003-04** | **Los Angeles** | **NHL** | **48** | **6** | **7** | **13** | **27** | **0** | **0** | **1** | **73** | **8.2** | **0** | **19** | **31.6** | **10:01** | .... | .... | .... | .... | .... | .... | .... | .... | .... |
| | **Pittsburgh** | **NHL** | **15** | **2** | **3** | **5** | **6** | **0** | **0** | **1** | **27** | **7.4** | **–4** | **0** | **0.0** | **13:39** | .... | .... | .... | .... | .... | .... | .... | .... | .... |
| 2004-05 | Utah Grizzlies | AHL | 10 | 2 | 2 | 4 | 12 | .... | .... | .... | .... | .... | .... | .... | .... | .... | .... | .... | .... | .... | .... | .... | .... | .... | .... |
| | Philadelphia | AHL | 63 | 35 | 26 | 61 | 66 | .... | .... | .... | .... | .... | .... | .... | .... | .... | 21 | *10 | 7 | 17 | 44 | .... | .... | .... | .... |
| **2005-06** | **Philadelphia** | **NHL** | **39** | **7** | **7** | **14** | **28** | **4** | **0** | **2** | **80** | **8.8** | **–6** | **1** | **0.0** | **10:59** | .... | .... | .... | .... | .... | .... | .... | .... | .... |
| | **Florida** | **NHL** | **33** | **10** | **8** | **18** | **26** | **4** | **0** | **3** | **92** | **10.9** | **–1** | **0** | **0.0** | **12:28** | .... | .... | .... | .... | .... | .... | .... | .... | .... |
| **2006-07** | **Atlanta** | **NHL** | **77** | **17** | **12** | **29** | **60** | **2** | **0** | **1** | **141** | **12.1** | **–1** | **9** | **22.2** | **11:45** | **4** | **0** | **0** | **0** | **0** | **0** | **0** | **0** | **5:29** |
| **2007-08** | **NY Islanders** | **NHL** | **2** | **0** | **1** | **1** | **2** | **0** | **0** | **0** | **8** | **0.0** | **–1** | **0** | **0.0** | **14:19** | .... | .... | .... | .... | .... | .... | .... | .... | .... |

| Season | Club | League | GP | G | A | Pts | PIM | PP | SH | GW | S | % | +/- | TF | F% | Min | Playoffs GP | G | A | Pts | PIM | PP | SH | GW | Min |
|---|---|---|---|---|---|---|---|---|---|---|---|---|---|---|---|---|---|---|---|---|---|---|---|---|---|
| **2008-09** | **NY Islanders** | **NHL** | **49** | **9** | **6** | **15** | **42** | **3** | **0** | **0** | **90** | **10.0** | **–12** | **6** | **16.7** | **12:10** | .... | .... | .... | .... | .... | .... | .... | .... | .... |
| | Bridgeport | AHL | 18 | 13 | 10 | 23 | 12 | .... | .... | .... | .... | .... | .... | .... | .... | .... | 5 | 2 | 3 | 5 | 10 | .... | .... | .... | .... |
| | **NHL Totals** | | **358** | **61** | **52** | **113** | **248** | **16** | **0** | **9** | **663** | **9.2** | | **68** | **33.8** | **11:15** | **15** | **1** | **0** | **1** | **6** | **0** | **0** | **0** | **8:24** |

(Regular Season: GP through Min; Playoffs: GP through Min)

OHL Second All-Star Team (1998)

Traded to **Nashville** by **Dallas** for Bubba Berenzweig and future considerations, February 17, 2003. Claimed on waivers by **Los Angeles** from **Nashville**, March 8, 2003. Claimed on waivers by **Pittsburgh** from **Los Angeles**, March 4, 2004. Signed as a free agent by **Phoenix**, September 2, 2004. • Loaned to **Philadelphia** (AHL) by **Phoenix** (Utah - AHL) for the loan of Peter White, November 14, 2004. Signed as a free agent by **Philadelphia**, August 2, 2005. Traded to **Florida** by **Philadelphia** for Florida's 6th round choice (Patrick Maroon) in 2007 Entry Draft, January 23, 2006. Signed as a free agent by **Atlanta**, July 14, 2006. Signed as a free agent by **NY Islanders**, July 1, 2007.

## SIMMONDS, Wayne
(SIHM-muhnds, WAYN) **L.A.**

Right wing. Shoots right. 6'2", 181 lbs. Born, Scarborough, Ont., August 26, 1988. Los Angeles' 3rd choice, 61st overall, in 2007 Entry Draft.

| Season | Club | League | GP | G | A | Pts | PIM | PP | SH | GW | S | % | +/- | TF | F% | Min | Playoffs GP | G | A | Pts | PIM | PP | SH | GW | Min |
|---|---|---|---|---|---|---|---|---|---|---|---|---|---|---|---|---|---|---|---|---|---|---|---|---|---|
| 2004-05 | Tor. Jr. Canadiens | GTHL | 67 | 32 | 40 | 72 | 97 | .... | .... | .... | .... | .... | .... | .... | .... | .... | .... | .... | .... | .... | .... | .... | .... | .... | .... |
| 2005-06 | Brockville Braves | CJHL | 49 | 24 | 19 | 43 | 127 | .... | .... | .... | .... | .... | .... | .... | .... | .... | 7 | 4 | 2 | 6 | 12 | .... | .... | .... | .... |
| 2006-07 | Owen Sound | OHL | 66 | 23 | 26 | 49 | 112 | .... | .... | .... | .... | .... | .... | .... | .... | .... | 4 | 1 | 1 | 2 | 4 | .... | .... | .... | .... |
| 2007-08 | Owen Sound | OHL | 29 | 17 | 22 | 39 | 43 | .... | .... | .... | .... | .... | .... | .... | .... | .... | .... | .... | .... | .... | .... | .... | .... | .... | .... |
| | Sault Ste. Marie | OHL | 31 | 16 | 20 | 36 | 68 | .... | .... | .... | .... | .... | .... | .... | .... | .... | 14 | 5 | 9 | 14 | 22 | .... | .... | .... | .... |
| **2008-09** | **Los Angeles** | **NHL** | **82** | **9** | **14** | **23** | **73** | **2** | **0** | **2** | **127** | **7.1** | **–8** | **25** | **36.0** | **13:50** | .... | .... | .... | .... | .... | .... | .... | .... | .... |
| | **NHL Totals** | | **82** | **9** | **14** | **23** | **73** | **2** | **0** | **2** | **127** | **7.1** | | **25** | **36.0** | **13:50** | .... | .... | .... | .... | .... | .... | .... | .... | .... |

## SIMON, Ben
(SIGH-muhn, BEHN)

Left wing. Shoots left. 6', 195 lbs. Born, Shaker Heights, OH, June 14, 1978. Chicago's 5th choice, 110th overall, in 1997 Entry Draft.

| Season | Club | League | GP | G | A | Pts | PIM | PP | SH | GW | S | % | +/- | TF | F% | Min | Playoffs GP | G | A | Pts | PIM | PP | SH | GW | Min |
|---|---|---|---|---|---|---|---|---|---|---|---|---|---|---|---|---|---|---|---|---|---|---|---|---|---|
| 1992-93 | Shaker Heights | High-OH | 25 | 15 | 21 | 36 | .... | .... | .... | .... | .... | .... | .... | .... | .... | .... | .... | .... | .... | .... | .... | .... | .... | .... | .... |
| 1993-94 | Shaker Heights | High-OH | 24 | 45 | 41 | 86 | .... | .... | .... | .... | .... | .... | .... | .... | .... | .... | .... | .... | .... | .... | .... | .... | .... | .... | .... |
| 1994-95 | Shaker Heights | High-OH | 25 | 61 | 68 | 129 | .... | .... | .... | .... | .... | .... | .... | .... | .... | .... | .... | .... | .... | .... | .... | .... | .... | .... | .... |
| 1995-96 | Cleveland Barons | NAHL | 45 | 38 | 33 | 71 | .... | .... | .... | .... | .... | .... | .... | .... | .... | .... | 5 | 7 | 13 | 20 | .... | .... | .... | .... | .... |
| 1996-97 | U. of Notre Dame | CCHA | 30 | 4 | 15 | 19 | 79 | .... | .... | .... | .... | .... | .... | .... | .... | .... | .... | .... | .... | .... | .... | .... | .... | .... | .... |
| 1997-98 | U. of Notre Dame | CCHA | 37 | 9 | 28 | 37 | 91 | .... | .... | .... | .... | .... | .... | .... | .... | .... | .... | .... | .... | .... | .... | .... | .... | .... | .... |
| 1998-99 | U. of Notre Dame | CCHA | 37 | 18 | 24 | 42 | 65 | .... | .... | .... | .... | .... | .... | .... | .... | .... | .... | .... | .... | .... | .... | .... | .... | .... | .... |
| 99-2000 | U. of Notre Dame | CCHA | 40 | 13 | 19 | 32 | 53 | .... | .... | .... | .... | .... | .... | .... | .... | .... | .... | .... | .... | .... | .... | .... | .... | .... | .... |
| 2000-01 | Orlando | IHL | 77 | 8 | 12 | 20 | 47 | .... | .... | .... | .... | .... | .... | .... | .... | .... | 16 | 6 | 5 | 11 | 20 | .... | .... | .... | .... |
| **2001-02** | **Atlanta** | **NHL** | **6** | **0** | **0** | **0** | **6** | **0** | **0** | **0** | **7** | **0.0** | **1** | **32** | **40.6** | **9:20** | .... | .... | .... | .... | .... | .... | .... | .... | .... |
| | Chicago Wolves | AHL | 74 | 11 | 23 | 34 | 56 | .... | .... | .... | .... | .... | .... | .... | .... | .... | 25 | 2 | 3 | 5 | 24 | .... | .... | .... | .... |
| **2002-03** | **Atlanta** | **NHL** | **10** | **0** | **1** | **1** | **9** | **0** | **0** | **0** | **7** | **0.0** | **0** | **54** | **31.5** | **9:25** | .... | .... | .... | .... | .... | .... | .... | .... | .... |
| | Chicago Wolves | AHL | 69 | 15 | 17 | 32 | 78 | .... | .... | .... | .... | .... | .... | .... | .... | .... | 9 | 0 | 0 | 0 | 6 | .... | .... | .... | .... |
| **2003-04** | Milwaukee | AHL | 18 | 1 | 3 | 4 | 6 | .... | .... | .... | .... | .... | .... | .... | .... | .... | .... | .... | .... | .... | .... | .... | .... | .... | .... |
| | **Atlanta** | **NHL** | **52** | **3** | **0** | **3** | **28** | **0** | **0** | **0** | **30** | **10.0** | **–10** | **203** | **33.0** | **6:05** | .... | .... | .... | .... | .... | .... | .... | .... | .... |
| 2004-05 | Chicago Wolves | AHL | 53 | 11 | 10 | 21 | 58 | .... | .... | .... | .... | .... | .... | .... | .... | .... | 18 | 1 | 5 | 6 | 44 | .... | .... | .... | .... |
| **2005-06** | **Columbus** | **NHL** | **13** | **0** | **0** | **0** | **4** | **0** | **0** | **0** | **7** | **0.0** | **–4** | **53** | **24.5** | **5:38** | .... | .... | .... | .... | .... | .... | .... | .... | .... |
| | Syracuse Crunch | AHL | 66 | 13 | 24 | 37 | 88 | .... | .... | .... | .... | .... | .... | .... | .... | .... | 3 | 0 | 1 | 1 | 2 | .... | .... | .... | .... |
| 2006-07 | Syracuse Crunch | AHL | 56 | 9 | 12 | 21 | 77 | .... | .... | .... | .... | .... | .... | .... | .... | .... | .... | .... | .... | .... | .... | .... | .... | .... | .... |
| | Grand Rapids | AHL | 21 | 4 | 5 | 9 | 28 | .... | .... | .... | .... | .... | .... | .... | .... | .... | 7 | 0 | 0 | 0 | 9 | .... | .... | .... | .... |
| 2007-08 | Springfield | AHL | 80 | 12 | 10 | 22 | 88 | .... | .... | .... | .... | .... | .... | .... | .... | .... | .... | .... | .... | .... | .... | .... | .... | .... | .... |
| 2008-09 | Iserlohn Roosters | Germany | 51 | 5 | 10 | 15 | 64 | .... | .... | .... | .... | .... | .... | .... | .... | .... | .... | .... | .... | .... | .... | .... | .... | .... | .... |
| | **NHL Totals** | | **81** | **3** | **1** | **4** | **47** | **0** | **0** | **0** | **51** | **5.9** | | **342** | **32.2** | **6:40** | .... | .... | .... | .... | .... | .... | .... | .... | .... |

CCHA Second All-Star Team (1999)

• Rights traded to **Atlanta** by **Chicago** for Atlanta's 9th round choice (Peter Flache) in 2000 Entry Draft, June 25, 2000. Signed as a free agent by **Nashville**, July 14, 2003. Traded to **Atlanta** by **Nashville** with Tomas Kloucek for Simon Gamache and Kirill Safronov, December 2, 2003. Signed as a free agent by **Columbus**, August 11, 2005.

## SJOSTROM, Fredrik
(SHAW-strahm, FREHD-rihk) **CGY.**

Right wing. Shoots left. 6'1", 218 lbs. Born, Fargelanda, Sweden, May 6, 1983. Phoenix's 1st choice, 11th overall, in 2001 Entry Draft.

| Season | Club | League | GP | G | A | Pts | PIM | PP | SH | GW | S | % | +/- | TF | F% | Min | Playoffs GP | G | A | Pts | PIM | PP | SH | GW | Min |
|---|---|---|---|---|---|---|---|---|---|---|---|---|---|---|---|---|---|---|---|---|---|---|---|---|---|
| 99-2000 | MoDo U18 | Swe-U18 | 4 | 0 | 2 | 2 | 6 | .... | .... | .... | .... | .... | .... | .... | .... | .... | .... | .... | .... | .... | .... | .... | .... | .... | .... |
| | Malmo Jr. | Swe-Jr. | 18 | 4 | 6 | 10 | 8 | .... | .... | .... | .... | .... | .... | .... | .... | .... | .... | .... | .... | .... | .... | .... | .... | .... | .... |
| 2000-01 | V.Frolunda Jr. | Swe-Jr. | 11 | 3 | 7 | 10 | 12 | .... | .... | .... | .... | .... | .... | .... | .... | .... | 4 | 1 | 2 | 3 | 6 | .... | .... | .... | .... |
| | V.Frolunda | Sweden | 31 | 3 | 2 | 5 | 6 | .... | .... | .... | .... | .... | .... | .... | .... | .... | 5 | 0 | 0 | 0 | 2 | .... | .... | .... | .... |
| 2001-02 | Calgary Hitmen | WHL | 58 | 19 | 31 | 50 | 51 | .... | .... | .... | .... | .... | .... | .... | .... | .... | 4 | 1 | 1 | 2 | 8 | .... | .... | .... | .... |
| 2002-03 | Calgary Hitmen | WHL | 63 | 34 | 43 | 77 | 95 | .... | .... | .... | .... | .... | .... | .... | .... | .... | 5 | 1 | 3 | 4 | 4 | .... | .... | .... | .... |
| | Springfield | AHL | 2 | 1 | 0 | 1 | 0 | .... | .... | .... | .... | .... | .... | .... | .... | .... | 6 | 2 | 0 | 2 | 12 | .... | .... | .... | .... |
| **2003-04** | **Phoenix** | **NHL** | **57** | **7** | **6** | **13** | **22** | **0** | **0** | **1** | **73** | **9.6** | **–7** | **7** | **28.6** | **11:35** | .... | .... | .... | .... | .... | .... | .... | .... | .... |
| | Springfield | AHL | 17 | 0 | 7 | 7 | 8 | .... | .... | .... | .... | .... | .... | .... | .... | .... | .... | .... | .... | .... | .... | .... | .... | .... | .... |
| 2004-05 | Utah Grizzlies | AHL | 80 | 14 | 24 | 38 | 57 | .... | .... | .... | .... | .... | .... | .... | .... | .... | .... | .... | .... | .... | .... | .... | .... | .... | .... |
| **2005-06** | **Phoenix** | **NHL** | **75** | **6** | **17** | **23** | **42** | **1** | **0** | **1** | **109** | **5.5** | **1** | **8** | **12.5** | **13:20** | .... | .... | .... | .... | .... | .... | .... | .... | .... |
| **2006-07** | **Phoenix** | **NHL** | **78** | **9** | **9** | **18** | **48** | **2** | **0** | **1** | **125** | **7.2** | **–11** | **15** | **13.3** | **14:07** | .... | .... | .... | .... | .... | .... | .... | .... | .... |
| **2007-08** | **Phoenix** | **NHL** | **51** | **10** | **9** | **19** | **14** | **2** | **2** | **1** | **84** | **11.9** | **–2** | **33** | **18.2** | **13:33** | .... | .... | .... | .... | .... | .... | .... | .... | .... |
| | **NY Rangers** | **NHL** | **18** | **2** | **0** | **2** | **8** | **0** | **0** | **1** | **26** | **7.7** | **0** | **3** | **0.0** | **8:05** | **10** | **0** | **1** | **1** | **2** | **0** | **0** | **0** | **6:28** |
| **2008-09** | **NY Rangers** | **NHL** | **79** | **7** | **6** | **13** | **30** | **0** | **2** | **0** | **95** | **7.4** | **–11** | **5** | **60.0** | **12:10** | **7** | **0** | **1** | **1** | **0** | **0** | **0** | **0** | **11:46** |
| | **NHL Totals** | | **358** | **41** | **47** | **88** | **164** | **5** | **4** | **5** | **512** | **8.0** | | **71** | **19.7** | **12:44** | **17** | **0** | **2** | **2** | **2** | **0** | **0** | **0** | **8:39** |

Traded to **NY Rangers** by **Phoenix** with Josh Gratton, David LeNeveu and Phoenix's 5th round choice (Roman Horak) in 2009 Entry Draft for Marcel Hossa and Al Montoya, February 26, 2008. Signed as a free agent by **Calgary**, July 1, 2009.

## SKILLE, Jack
(SKIH-lee, JAK) **CHI.**

Right wing. Shoots right. 6'1", 198 lbs. Born, Madison, WI, May 19, 1987. Chicago's 1st choice, 7th overall, in 2005 Entry Draft.

| Season | Club | League | GP | G | A | Pts | PIM | PP | SH | GW | S | % | +/- | TF | F% | Min | Playoffs GP | G | A | Pts | PIM | PP | SH | GW | Min |
|---|---|---|---|---|---|---|---|---|---|---|---|---|---|---|---|---|---|---|---|---|---|---|---|---|---|
| 2003-04 | USNTDP | U-17 | 33 | 14 | 10 | 24 | 30 | .... | .... | .... | .... | .... | .... | .... | .... | .... | .... | .... | .... | .... | .... | .... | .... | .... | .... |
| | USNTDP | NAHL | 28 | 11 | 9 | 20 | 31 | .... | .... | .... | .... | .... | .... | .... | .... | .... | .... | .... | .... | .... | .... | .... | .... | .... | .... |
| 2004-05 | USNTDP | U-18 | 26 | 9 | 11 | 20 | 36 | .... | .... | .... | .... | .... | .... | .... | .... | .... | .... | .... | .... | .... | .... | .... | .... | .... | .... |
| | USNTDP | NAHL | 16 | 6 | 11 | 17 | 20 | .... | .... | .... | .... | .... | .... | .... | .... | .... | .... | .... | .... | .... | .... | .... | .... | .... | .... |
| 2005-06 | U. of Wisconsin | WCHA | 41 | 13 | 8 | 21 | 37 | .... | .... | .... | .... | .... | .... | .... | .... | .... | .... | .... | .... | .... | .... | .... | .... | .... | .... |
| 2006-07 | U. of Wisconsin | WCHA | 26 | 8 | 10 | 18 | 12 | .... | .... | .... | .... | .... | .... | .... | .... | .... | .... | .... | .... | .... | .... | .... | .... | .... | .... |
| | Norfolk Admirals | AHL | 9 | 4 | 4 | 8 | 0 | .... | .... | .... | .... | .... | .... | .... | .... | .... | 3 | 0 | 0 | 0 | 2 | .... | .... | .... | .... |
| **2007-08** | **Chicago** | **NHL** | **16** | **3** | **2** | **5** | **0** | **0** | **0** | **0** | **23** | **13.0** | **1** | **4** | **50.0** | **11:59** | .... | .... | .... | .... | .... | .... | .... | .... | .... |
| | Rockford IceHogs | AHL | 59 | 16 | 18 | 34 | 44 | .... | .... | .... | .... | .... | .... | .... | .... | .... | 12 | 2 | 1 | 3 | 6 | .... | .... | .... | .... |
| **2008-09** | **Chicago** | **NHL** | **8** | **1** | **0** | **1** | **5** | **0** | **0** | **0** | **14** | **7.1** | **–3** | **0** | **0.0** | **9:26** | .... | .... | .... | .... | .... | .... | .... | .... | .... |
| | Rockford IceHogs | AHL | 58 | 20 | 25 | 45 | 56 | .... | .... | .... | .... | .... | .... | .... | .... | .... | .... | .... | .... | .... | .... | .... | .... | .... | .... |
| | **NHL Totals** | | **24** | **4** | **2** | **6** | **5** | **0** | **0** | **0** | **37** | **10.8** | | **4** | **50.0** | **11:08** | .... | .... | .... | .... | .... | .... | .... | .... | .... |

## SKINNER, Brett
(SKIH-nuhr, BREHT) **COL.**

Defense. Shoots left. 6'1", 183 lbs. Born, Brandon, Man., June 28, 1983. Vancouver's 3rd choice, 68th overall, in 2002 Entry Draft.

| Season | Club | League | GP | G | A | Pts | PIM | PP | SH | GW | S | % | +/- | TF | F% | Min | Playoffs GP | G | A | Pts | PIM | PP | SH | GW | Min |
|---|---|---|---|---|---|---|---|---|---|---|---|---|---|---|---|---|---|---|---|---|---|---|---|---|---|
| 1998-99 | Brandon Kings | MMBHL | 29 | 3 | 18 | 21 | 20 | .... | .... | .... | .... | .... | .... | .... | .... | .... | .... | .... | .... | .... | .... | .... | .... | .... | .... |
| 99-2000 | Brandon Kings | MMMHL | 40 | 8 | 27 | 35 | 48 | .... | .... | .... | .... | .... | .... | .... | .... | .... | .... | .... | .... | .... | .... | .... | .... | .... | .... |
| 2000-01 | Trail | BCHL | 59 | 11 | 24 | 35 | 43 | .... | .... | .... | .... | .... | .... | .... | .... | .... | .... | .... | .... | .... | .... | .... | .... | .... | .... |
| 2001-02 | Des Moines | USHL | 44 | 9 | 38 | 47 | 25 | .... | .... | .... | .... | .... | .... | .... | .... | .... | 3 | 0 | 1 | 1 | 0 | .... | .... | .... | .... |
| 2002-03 | U. of Denver | WCHA | 37 | 4 | 13 | 17 | 27 | .... | .... | .... | .... | .... | .... | .... | .... | .... | .... | .... | .... | .... | .... | .... | .... | .... | .... |
| 2003-04 | U. of Denver | WCHA | 44 | 7 | 23 | 30 | 32 | .... | .... | .... | .... | .... | .... | .... | .... | .... | .... | .... | .... | .... | .... | .... | .... | .... | .... |
| 2004-05 | U. of Denver | WCHA | 43 | 4 | 36 | 40 | 30 | .... | .... | .... | .... | .... | .... | .... | .... | .... | .... | .... | .... | .... | .... | .... | .... | .... | .... |
| 2005-06 | Manitoba Moose | AHL | 65 | 4 | 21 | 25 | 33 | .... | .... | .... | .... | .... | .... | .... | .... | .... | 13 | 0 | 4 | 4 | 19 | .... | .... | .... | .... |
| 2006-07 | Portland Pirates | AHL | 41 | 6 | 12 | 18 | 24 | .... | .... | .... | .... | .... | .... | .... | .... | .... | .... | .... | .... | .... | .... | .... | .... | .... | .... |
| | Augusta Lynx | ECHL | 5 | 1 | 3 | 4 | 8 | .... | .... | .... | .... | .... | .... | .... | .... | .... | .... | .... | .... | .... | .... | .... | .... | .... | .... |
| | Omaha | AHL | 21 | 0 | 6 | 6 | 2 | .... | .... | .... | .... | .... | .... | .... | .... | .... | 5 | 0 | 3 | 3 | 2 | .... | .... | .... | .... |
| 2007-08 | Providence Bruins | AHL | 68 | 7 | 40 | 47 | 47 | .... | .... | .... | .... | .... | .... | .... | .... | .... | 10 | 0 | 1 | 1 | 0 | .... | .... | .... | .... |

| | | | Regular Season | | | | | | | | | | | | | | Playoffs | | | | | | | | |
|---|---|---|---|---|---|---|---|---|---|---|---|---|---|---|---|---|---|---|---|---|---|---|---|---|---|
| Season | Club | League | GP | G | A | Pts | PIM | PP | SH | GW | S | % | +/- | TF | F% | Min | GP | G | A | Pts | PIM | PP | SH | GW | Min |
| **2008-09** | **NY Islanders** | **NHL** | **11** | **0** | **0** | **0** | **4** | **0** | **0** | **0** | **5** | **0.0** | **3** | **0** | **0.0** | **11:43** | .... | .... | .... | .... | .... | .... | .... | .... | .... |
| | Bridgeport | AHL | 24 | 1 | 11 | 12 | 10 | .... | .... | .... | .... | .... | .... | .... | .... | .... | .... | .... | .... | .... | .... | .... | .... | .... | .... |
| | Chicago Wolves | AHL | 37 | 3 | 20 | 23 | 4 | .... | .... | .... | .... | .... | .... | .... | .... | .... | .... | .... | .... | .... | .... | .... | .... | .... | .... |
| | **NHL Totals** | | **11** | **0** | **0** | **0** | **4** | **0** | **0** | **0** | **5** | **0.0** | | **0** | **0.0** | **11:43** | .... | .... | .... | .... | .... | .... | .... | .... | .... |

USHL First All-Star Team (2002) • USHL Defenseman of the Year (2002) • WCHA First All-Star Team (2005) • NCAA West Second All-American Team (2005) • NCAA Championship All-Tournament Team (2005)

Traded to **Anaheim** by **Vancouver** with NY Islanders' 2nd round choice (previously acquired, Anaheim selected Bryce Swan) in 2006 Entry Draft for Keith Carney and Juha Alen, March 9, 2006. Traded to **Boston** by **Anaheim** with Nathan Saunders for Mark Mowers, September 24, 2007. Signed as a free agent by **NY Islanders**, July 3, 2008. Traded to **Atlanta** by **NY Islanders** for Junior Lessard, January 13, 2009. Signed as a free agent by **Colorado**, July 8, 2009.

## SKOULA, Martin

(SHKOO-la, MAHR-tihn)

Defense. Shoots left. 6'3", 226 lbs. Born, Litomerice, Czech., October 28, 1979. Colorado's 2nd choice, 17th overall, in 1998 Entry Draft.

| Season | Club | League | GP | G | A | Pts | PIM | PP | SH | GW | S | % | +/- | TF | F% | Min | GP | G | A | Pts | PIM | PP | SH | GW | Min |
|---|---|---|---|---|---|---|---|---|---|---|---|---|---|---|---|---|---|---|---|---|---|---|---|---|---|
| 1995-96 | Litvinov Jr. | CzRep-Jr. | 38 | 0 | 4 | 4 | .... | .... | .... | .... | .... | .... | .... | .... | .... | .... | .... | .... | .... | .... | .... | .... | .... | .... | .... |
| | Litvinov | CzRep | .... | .... | .... | .... | .... | .... | .... | .... | .... | .... | .... | .... | .... | .... | 1 | 0 | 0 | 0 | 0 | .... | .... | .... | .... |
| 1996-97 | Litvinov Jr. | CzRep-Jr. | 38 | 2 | 9 | 11 | .... | .... | .... | .... | .... | .... | .... | .... | .... | .... | .... | .... | .... | .... | .... | .... | .... | .... | .... |
| | Litvinov | CzRep | 1 | 0 | 0 | 0 | 0 | .... | .... | .... | .... | .... | .... | .... | .... | .... | .... | .... | .... | .... | .... | .... | .... | .... | .... |
| 1997-98 | Barrie Colts | OHL | 66 | 8 | 36 | 44 | 36 | .... | .... | .... | .... | .... | .... | .... | .... | .... | 6 | 1 | 3 | 4 | 4 | .... | .... | .... | .... |
| 1998-99 | Barrie Colts | OHL | 67 | 13 | 46 | 59 | 46 | .... | .... | .... | .... | .... | .... | .... | .... | .... | 12 | 3 | 10 | 13 | 13 | .... | .... | .... | .... |
| | Hershey Bears | AHL | .... | .... | .... | .... | .... | .... | .... | .... | .... | .... | .... | .... | .... | .... | 1 | 0 | 0 | 0 | 0 | .... | .... | .... | .... |
| **99-2000** | **Colorado** | **NHL** | **80** | **3** | **13** | **16** | **20** | **2** | **0** | **0** | **66** | **4.5** | **5** | **0** | **0.0** | **18:15** | **17** | **0** | **2** | **2** | **4** | **0** | **0** | **0** | **18:45** |
| **2000-01**♦ | **Colorado** | **NHL** | **82** | **8** | **17** | **25** | **38** | **3** | **0** | **2** | **108** | **7.4** | **8** | **1** | **100.0** | **20:41** | **23** | **1** | **4** | **5** | **8** | **0** | **0** | **0** | **11:59** |
| **2001-02** | **Colorado** | **NHL** | **82** | **10** | **21** | **31** | **42** | **5** | **0** | **1** | **100** | **10.0** | **–3** | **0** | **0.0** | **22:18** | **21** | **0** | **6** | **6** | **2** | **0** | **0** | **0** | **14:37** |
| | Czech Republic | Olympics | 4 | 0 | 0 | 0 | 0 | .... | .... | .... | .... | .... | .... | .... | .... | .... | .... | .... | .... | .... | .... | .... | .... | .... | .... |
| **2002-03** | **Colorado** | **NHL** | **81** | **4** | **21** | **25** | **68** | **2** | **0** | **0** | **93** | **4.3** | **11** | **1** | **100.0** | **18:27** | **7** | **0** | **1** | **1** | **4** | **0** | **0** | **0** | **11:05** |
| **2003-04** | **Colorado** | **NHL** | **58** | **2** | **14** | **16** | **30** | **0** | **0** | **0** | **54** | **3.7** | **2** | **0** | **0.0** | **17:21** | .... | .... | .... | .... | .... | .... | .... | .... | .... |
| | **Anaheim** | **NHL** | **21** | **2** | **7** | **9** | **2** | **1** | **0** | **0** | **30** | **6.7** | **3** | **1** | **0.0** | **21:14** | .... | .... | .... | .... | .... | .... | .... | .... | .... |
| 2004-05 | Litvinov | CzRep | 47 | 4 | 15 | 19 | 101 | .... | .... | .... | .... | .... | .... | .... | .... | .... | 6 | 0 | 0 | 0 | 6 | .... | .... | .... | .... |
| **2005-06** | **Dallas** | **NHL** | **61** | **4** | **11** | **15** | **36** | **3** | **0** | **1** | **78** | **5.1** | **6** | **0** | **0.0** | **18:41** | .... | .... | .... | .... | .... | .... | .... | .... | .... |
| | **Minnesota** | **NHL** | **17** | **1** | **5** | **6** | **10** | **0** | **0** | **0** | **14** | **7.1** | **0** | **0** | **0.0** | **20:49** | .... | .... | .... | .... | .... | .... | .... | .... | .... |
| **2006-07** | **Minnesota** | **NHL** | **81** | **0** | **15** | **15** | **36** | **0** | **0** | **0** | **91** | **0.0** | **9** | **0** | **0.0** | **20:14** | **5** | **0** | **0** | **0** | **4** | **0** | **0** | **0** | **19:02** |
| **2007-08** | **Minnesota** | **NHL** | **80** | **3** | **8** | **11** | **26** | **0** | **0** | **1** | **63** | **4.8** | **–16** | **0** | **0.0** | **20:29** | **6** | **0** | **0** | **0** | **0** | **0** | **0** | **0** | **26:41** |
| **2008-09** | **Minnesota** | **NHL** | **81** | **4** | **12** | **16** | **10** | **0** | **0** | **0** | **55** | **7.3** | **–12** | **0** | **0.0** | **19:58** | .... | .... | .... | .... | .... | .... | .... | .... | .... |
| | **NHL Totals** | | **724** | **41** | **144** | **185** | **318** | **16** | **0** | **5** | **752** | **5.5** | | **3** | **66.7** | **19:47** | **79** | **1** | **13** | **14** | **22** | **0** | **0** | **0** | **15:37** |

OHL All-Rookie Team (1998) • OHL Second All-Star Team (1999)

Traded to **Anaheim** by **Colorado** for Kurt Sauer and Anaheim's 4th round choice (Raymond Macias) in 2005 Entry Draft, February 21, 2004. Signed as a free agent by **Litvinov** (CzRep), September 17, 2004. Signed as a free agent by **Dallas**, August 3, 2005. Traded to **Minnesota** by **Dallas** with Shawn Belle for Willie Mitchell and Minnesota's 2nd round choice (Nico Saccheti) in 2007 Entry Draft, March 8, 2006.

## SKRASTINS, Karlis

(SKRAS-tihnz, KAR-lihs) **DAL.**

Defense. Shoots left. 6'1", 210 lbs. Born, Riga, Latvia, July 9, 1974. Nashville's 8th choice, 230th overall, in 1998 Entry Draft.

| Season | Club | League | GP | G | A | Pts | PIM | PP | SH | GW | S | % | +/- | TF | F% | Min | GP | G | A | Pts | PIM | PP | SH | GW | Min |
|---|---|---|---|---|---|---|---|---|---|---|---|---|---|---|---|---|---|---|---|---|---|---|---|---|---|
| 1992-93 | Pardaugava Riga | CIS | 40 | 3 | 5 | 8 | 16 | .... | .... | .... | .... | .... | .... | .... | .... | .... | 2 | 0 | 0 | 0 | 0 | .... | .... | .... | .... |
| 1993-94 | Pardaugava Riga | CIS | 42 | 7 | 5 | 12 | 18 | .... | .... | .... | .... | .... | .... | .... | .... | .... | 2 | 1 | 0 | 1 | 4 | .... | .... | .... | .... |
| 1994-95 | Pardaugava Riga | CIS | 52 | 4 | 14 | 18 | 69 | .... | .... | .... | .... | .... | .... | .... | .... | .... | .... | .... | .... | .... | .... | .... | .... | .... | .... |
| 1995-96 | TPS Turku | Finland | 50 | 4 | 11 | 15 | 32 | .... | .... | .... | .... | .... | .... | .... | .... | .... | 11 | 2 | 2 | 4 | 10 | .... | .... | .... | .... |
| 1996-97 | TPS Turku | Finland | 50 | 2 | 8 | 10 | 20 | .... | .... | .... | .... | .... | .... | .... | .... | .... | 12 | 0 | 4 | 4 | 2 | .... | .... | .... | .... |
| | TPS Turku | EuroHL | 6 | 0 | 1 | 1 | 4 | .... | .... | .... | .... | .... | .... | .... | .... | .... | 4 | 0 | 0 | 0 | 14 | .... | .... | .... | .... |
| 1997-98 | TPS Turku | Finland | 48 | 4 | 15 | 19 | 67 | .... | .... | .... | .... | .... | .... | .... | .... | .... | 4 | 0 | 0 | 0 | 0 | .... | .... | .... | .... |
| | TPS Turku | EuroHL | 6 | 0 | 1 | 1 | 6 | .... | .... | .... | .... | .... | .... | .... | .... | .... | .... | .... | .... | .... | .... | .... | .... | .... | .... |
| **1998-99** | **Nashville** | **NHL** | **2** | **0** | **1** | **1** | **0** | **0** | **0** | **0** | **0** | **0.0** | **0** | **0** | **0.0** | **11:47** | .... | .... | .... | .... | .... | .... | .... | .... | .... |
| | Milwaukee | IHL | 75 | 8 | 36 | 44 | 47 | .... | .... | .... | .... | .... | .... | .... | .... | .... | 2 | 0 | 1 | 1 | 2 | .... | .... | .... | .... |
| **99-2000** | **Nashville** | **NHL** | **59** | **5** | **6** | **11** | **20** | **1** | **0** | **2** | **51** | **9.8** | **–7** | **0** | **0.0** | **20:51** | .... | .... | .... | .... | .... | .... | .... | .... | .... |
| | Milwaukee | IHL | 19 | 3 | 8 | 11 | 10 | .... | .... | .... | .... | .... | .... | .... | .... | .... | .... | .... | .... | .... | .... | .... | .... | .... | .... |
| **2000-01** | **Nashville** | **NHL** | **82** | **1** | **11** | **12** | **30** | **0** | **0** | **1** | **66** | **1.5** | **–12** | **0** | **0.0** | **19:12** | .... | .... | .... | .... | .... | .... | .... | .... | .... |
| **2001-02** | **Nashville** | **NHL** | **82** | **4** | **13** | **17** | **36** | **0** | **0** | **1** | **84** | **4.8** | **–12** | **0** | **0.0** | **20:29** | .... | .... | .... | .... | .... | .... | .... | .... | .... |
| | Latvia | Olympics | 1 | 0 | 0 | 0 | 0 | .... | .... | .... | .... | .... | .... | .... | .... | .... | .... | .... | .... | .... | .... | .... | .... | .... | .... |
| **2002-03** | **Nashville** | **NHL** | **82** | **3** | **10** | **13** | **44** | **0** | **1** | **0** | **86** | **3.5** | **–18** | **0** | **0.0** | **20:17** | .... | .... | .... | .... | .... | .... | .... | .... | .... |
| **2003-04** | **Colorado** | **NHL** | **82** | **5** | **8** | **13** | **26** | **0** | **1** | **1** | **102** | **4.9** | **18** | **0** | **0.0** | **21:49** | **11** | **0** | **2** | **2** | **2** | **0** | **0** | **0** | **23:07** |
| 2004-05 | HK Riga 2000 | Latvia | 4 | 0 | 4 | 4 | 0 | .... | .... | .... | .... | .... | .... | .... | .... | .... | 9 | 3 | 10 | 13 | 33 | .... | .... | .... | .... |
| | HK Riga 2000 | BelOpen | 34 | 8 | 17 | 25 | 30 | .... | .... | .... | .... | .... | .... | .... | .... | .... | 3 | 0 | 0 | 0 | 25 | .... | .... | .... | .... |
| **2005-06** | **Colorado** | **NHL** | **82** | **3** | **11** | **14** | **65** | **0** | **2** | **0** | **58** | **5.2** | **–7** | **0** | **0.0** | **21:49** | **9** | **0** | **1** | **1** | **10** | **0** | **0** | **0** | **23:24** |
| | Latvia | Olympics | 5 | 0 | 1 | 1 | 0 | .... | .... | .... | .... | .... | .... | .... | .... | .... | .... | .... | .... | .... | .... | .... | .... | .... | .... |
| **2006-07** | **Colorado** | **NHL** | **68** | **0** | **11** | **11** | **30** | **0** | **0** | **0** | **65** | **0.0** | **0** | **0** | **0.0** | **21:14** | .... | .... | .... | .... | .... | .... | .... | .... | .... |
| **2007-08** | **Colorado** | **NHL** | **43** | **1** | **3** | **4** | **20** | **0** | **0** | **0** | **34** | **2.9** | **–2** | **0** | **0.0** | **18:02** | .... | .... | .... | .... | .... | .... | .... | .... | .... |
| | **Florida** | **NHL** | **17** | **1** | **0** | **1** | **12** | **0** | **0** | **1** | **11** | **9.1** | **–9** | **0** | **0.0** | **20:03** | .... | .... | .... | .... | .... | .... | .... | .... | .... |
| **2008-09** | **Florida** | **NHL** | **80** | **4** | **14** | **18** | **30** | **0** | **0** | **0** | **55** | **7.3** | **9** | **0** | **0.0** | **20:34** | .... | .... | .... | .... | .... | .... | .... | .... | .... |
| | **NHL Totals** | | **679** | **27** | **88** | **115** | **313** | **1** | **4** | **6** | **612** | **4.4** | | **0** | **0.0** | **20:33** | **20** | **0** | **3** | **3** | **12** | **0** | **0** | **0** | **23:15** |

Traded to **Colorado** by **Nashville** for Colorado's 3rd round choice (later traded to Ottawa – Ottawa selected Peter Regin Jensen) in 2004 Entry Draft, June 30, 2003. Signed as a free agent by **Riga** (Latvia), September 25, 2004. Traded to **Florida** by **Colorado** with Colorado's 3rd round choice (Adam Comrie) in 2008 Entry Draft for Ruslan Salei, February 26, 2008. Signed as a free agent by **Dallas**, July 2, 2009.

## SLATER, Jim

(SLAY-tuhr, JIHM) **ATL.**

Center. Shoots left. 6', 200 lbs. Born, Petoskey, MI, December 9, 1982. Atlanta's 2nd choice, 30th overall, in 2002 Entry Draft.

| Season | Club | League | GP | G | A | Pts | PIM | PP | SH | GW | S | % | +/- | TF | F% | Min | GP | G | A | Pts | PIM | PP | SH | GW | Min |
|---|---|---|---|---|---|---|---|---|---|---|---|---|---|---|---|---|---|---|---|---|---|---|---|---|---|
| 1998-99 | USNTDP | U-18 | 3 | 0 | 1 | 1 | 0 | .... | .... | .... | .... | .... | .... | .... | .... | .... | .... | .... | .... | .... | .... | .... | .... | .... | .... |
| | Cleveland Barons | NAHL | 50 | 13 | 20 | 33 | 58 | .... | .... | .... | .... | .... | .... | .... | .... | .... | 2 | 0 | 0 | 0 | 2 | .... | .... | .... | .... |
| 99-2000 | Cleveland Barons | NAHL | 56 | 35 | 50 | 85 | 129 | .... | .... | .... | .... | .... | .... | .... | .... | .... | 3 | 1 | 3 | 4 | 4 | .... | .... | .... | .... |
| 2000-01 | Cleveland Barons | NAHL | 48 | 27 | 37 | 64 | 122 | .... | .... | .... | .... | .... | .... | .... | .... | .... | 6 | 6 | 6 | 12 | 6 | .... | .... | .... | .... |
| 2001-02 | Michigan State | CCHA | 37 | 11 | 21 | 32 | 50 | .... | .... | .... | .... | .... | .... | .... | .... | .... | .... | .... | .... | .... | .... | .... | .... | .... | .... |
| 2002-03 | Michigan State | CCHA | 37 | 18 | 26 | 44 | 26 | .... | .... | .... | .... | .... | .... | .... | .... | .... | .... | .... | .... | .... | .... | .... | .... | .... | .... |
| 2003-04 | Michigan State | CCHA | 42 | 19 | 29 | *48 | 38 | .... | .... | .... | .... | .... | .... | .... | .... | .... | .... | .... | .... | .... | .... | .... | .... | .... | .... |
| 2004-05 | Michigan State | CCHA | 41 | 16 | 32 | 48 | 30 | .... | .... | .... | .... | .... | .... | .... | .... | .... | .... | .... | .... | .... | .... | .... | .... | .... | .... |
| **2005-06** | **Atlanta** | **NHL** | **71** | **10** | **10** | **20** | **46** | **1** | **0** | **0** | **108** | **9.3** | **1** | **287** | **56.5** | **10:06** | .... | .... | .... | .... | .... | .... | .... | .... | .... |
| | Chicago Wolves | AHL | 4 | 0 | 2 | 2 | 2 | .... | .... | .... | .... | .... | .... | .... | .... | .... | .... | .... | .... | .... | .... | .... | .... | .... | .... |
| **2006-07** | **Atlanta** | **NHL** | **74** | **5** | **14** | **19** | **62** | **0** | **0** | **2** | **90** | **5.6** | **8** | **373** | **54.4** | **10:14** | **4** | **0** | **0** | **0** | **2** | **0** | **0** | **0** | **5:10** |
| **2007-08** | **Atlanta** | **NHL** | **69** | **8** | **5** | **13** | **41** | **0** | **2** | **0** | **95** | **8.4** | **–10** | **367** | **52.0** | **10:24** | .... | .... | .... | .... | .... | .... | .... | .... | .... |
| | Chicago Wolves | AHL | 3 | 0 | 0 | 0 | 0 | .... | .... | .... | .... | .... | .... | .... | .... | .... | .... | .... | .... | .... | .... | .... | .... | .... | .... |
| **2008-09** | **Atlanta** | **NHL** | **60** | **8** | **10** | **18** | **52** | **0** | **2** | **0** | **94** | **8.5** | **0** | **462** | **53.0** | **11:15** | .... | .... | .... | .... | .... | .... | .... | .... | .... |
| | **NHL Totals** | | **274** | **31** | **39** | **70** | **201** | **1** | **4** | **2** | **387** | **8.0** | | **1489** | **53.8** | **10:27** | **4** | **0** | **0** | **0** | **2** | **0** | **0** | **0** | **5:10** |

CCHA All-Rookie Team (2002) • CCHA First All-Star Team (2003, 2004) • NCAA West Second All-American Team (2004)

## SLOAN, Tyler

(SLOHN, TIGH-luhr) **WSH.**

Defense. Shoots left. 6'4", 203 lbs. Born, Calgary, Alta., March 15, 1981.

| Season | Club | League | GP | G | A | Pts | PIM | PP | SH | GW | S | % | +/- | TF | F% | Min | GP | G | A | Pts | PIM | PP | SH | GW | Min |
|---|---|---|---|---|---|---|---|---|---|---|---|---|---|---|---|---|---|---|---|---|---|---|---|---|---|
| 1997-98 | Calgary Buffaloes | AMHL | 36 | 2 | 11 | 13 | 24 | .... | .... | .... | .... | .... | .... | .... | .... | .... | 10 | 0 | 4 | 4 | 2 | .... | .... | .... | .... |
| 1998-99 | Calgary Royals | AJHL | STATISTICS NOT AVAILABLE | | | | | | | | | | | | | | | | | | | | | | |
| 99-2000 | Calgary Royals | AJHL | 45 | 5 | 26 | 31 | 80 | .... | .... | .... | .... | .... | .... | .... | .... | .... | .... | .... | .... | .... | .... | .... | .... | .... | .... |
| 2000-01 | Kamloops Blazers | WHL | 70 | 5 | 28 | 33 | 146 | .... | .... | .... | .... | .... | .... | .... | .... | .... | 4 | 0 | 0 | 0 | 4 | .... | .... | .... | .... |
| 2001-02 | Kamloops Blazers | WHL | 70 | 3 | 29 | 32 | 89 | .... | .... | .... | .... | .... | .... | .... | .... | .... | 4 | 0 | 0 | 0 | 15 | .... | .... | .... | .... |
| | Syracuse Crunch | AHL | 2 | 0 | 0 | 0 | 5 | .... | .... | .... | .... | .... | .... | .... | .... | .... | .... | .... | .... | .... | .... | .... | .... | .... | .... |
| 2002-03 | Syracuse Crunch | AHL | 39 | 2 | 1 | 3 | 46 | .... | .... | .... | .... | .... | .... | .... | .... | .... | .... | .... | .... | .... | .... | .... | .... | .... | .... |
| | Dayton Bombers | ECHL | 14 | 1 | 2 | 3 | 22 | .... | .... | .... | .... | .... | .... | .... | .... | .... | .... | .... | .... | .... | .... | .... | .... | .... | .... |
| 2003-04 | Syracuse Crunch | AHL | 69 | 2 | 4 | 6 | 50 | .... | .... | .... | .... | .... | .... | .... | .... | .... | 7 | 0 | 0 | 0 | 8 | .... | .... | .... | .... |
| 2004-05 | Syracuse Crunch | AHL | 14 | 0 | 2 | 2 | 18 | .... | .... | .... | .... | .... | .... | .... | .... | .... | .... | .... | .... | .... | .... | .... | .... | .... | .... |
| | Dayton Bombers | ECHL | 43 | 6 | 11 | 17 | 84 | .... | .... | .... | .... | .... | .... | .... | .... | .... | .... | .... | .... | .... | .... | .... | .... | .... | .... |
| 2005-06 | Las Vegas | ECHL | 48 | 4 | 16 | 20 | 71 | .... | .... | .... | .... | .... | .... | .... | .... | .... | 13 | 0 | 4 | 4 | 27 | .... | .... | .... | .... |
| | Manitoba Moose | AHL | 4 | 0 | 0 | 0 | 0 | .... | .... | .... | .... | .... | .... | .... | .... | .... | .... | .... | .... | .... | .... | .... | .... | .... | .... |
| | Hershey Bears | AHL | .... | .... | .... | .... | .... | .... | .... | .... | .... | .... | .... | .... | .... | .... | 2 | 0 | 1 | 1 | 2 | .... | .... | .... | .... |
| 2006-07 | Hershey Bears | AHL | 68 | 2 | 9 | 11 | 104 | .... | .... | .... | .... | .... | .... | .... | .... | .... | 17 | 0 | 7 | 7 | 30 | .... | .... | .... | .... |

| Season | Club | League | GP | G | A | Pts | PIM | PP | SH | GW | S | % | +/- | TF | F% | Min | Playoffs GP | G | A | Pts | PIM | PP | SH | GW | Min |
|---|---|---|---|---|---|---|---|---|---|---|---|---|---|---|---|---|---|---|---|---|---|---|---|---|---|
| 2007-08 | Hershey Bears | AHL | 56 | 1 | 7 | 8 | 90 | | | | | | | | | | 5 | 0 | 0 | 0 | 8 | | | | |
| **2008-09** | **Washington** | **NHL** | **26** | **1** | **4** | **5** | **14** | **0** | **0** | **0** | **8** | **12.5** | **4** | **0** | **0.0** | **16:39** | **2** | **0** | **1** | **1** | **0** | **0** | **0** | **0** | **18:24** |
| | Hershey Bears | AHL | 46 | 2 | 10 | 12 | 61 | | | | | | | | | | 16 | 0 | 5 | 5 | 14 | | | | |
| | **NHL Totals** | | **26** | **1** | **4** | **5** | **14** | **0** | **0** | **0** | **8** | **12.5** | | **0** | **0.0** | **16:39** | **2** | **0** | **1** | **1** | **0** | **0** | **0** | **0** | **18:23** |

Signed as a free agent by **Columbus**, September 24, 2000. Signed as a free agent by **Hershey** (AHL), August 15, 2007. Signed as a free agent by **Washington**, July 2, 2008.

## SLOANE, David

(SLOHN, DAY-vihd)

Right wing. Shoots right. 6'4", 220 lbs. Born, Philadelphia, PA, April 6, 1985.

| Season | Club | League | GP | G | A | Pts | PIM | PP | SH | GW | S | % | +/- | TF | F% | Min | Playoffs GP | G | A | Pts | PIM | PP | SH | GW | Min |
|---|---|---|---|---|---|---|---|---|---|---|---|---|---|---|---|---|---|---|---|---|---|---|---|---|---|
| 2004-05 | Chicago Steel | USHL | 17 | 0 | 1 | 1 | 12 | | | | | | | | | | | | | | | | | | |
| 2005-06 | Colgate | ECAC | 27 | 4 | 1 | 5 | 16 | | | | | | | | | | | | | | | | | | |
| 2006-07 | Colgate | ECAC | 35 | 4 | 5 | 9 | 27 | | | | | | | | | | | | | | | | | | |
| 2007-08 | Colgate | ECAC | 32 | 2 | 3 | 5 | 20 | | | | | | | | | | | | | | | | | | |
| **2008-09** | Colgate | ECAC | 35 | 0 | 4 | 4 | 37 | | | | | | | | | | | | | | | | | | |
| | **Philadelphia** | **NHL** | **1** | **0** | **0** | **0** | **0** | **0** | **0** | **0** | **0** | **0.0** | **0** | **0** | **0.0** | **6:44** | | | | | | | | | |
| | Philadelphia | AHL | 1 | 0 | 0 | 0 | 2 | | | | | | | | | | | | | | | | | | |
| | **NHL Totals** | | **1** | **0** | **0** | **0** | **0** | **0** | **0** | **0** | **0** | **0.0** | | **0** | **0.0** | **6:44** | | | | | | | | | |

Signed to an ATO (tryout) contract by **Philadelphia**, April 9, 2009.

## SMABY, Matt

(SMA-bee, MAT) **T.B.**

Defense. Shoots left. 6'5", 222 lbs. Born, Minneapolis, MN, October 14, 1984. Tampa Bay's 2nd choice, 41st overall, in 2003 Entry Draft.

| Season | Club | League | GP | G | A | Pts | PIM | PP | SH | GW | S | % | +/- | TF | F% | Min | Playoffs GP | G | A | Pts | PIM | PP | SH | GW | Min |
|---|---|---|---|---|---|---|---|---|---|---|---|---|---|---|---|---|---|---|---|---|---|---|---|---|---|
| 2001-02 | Shat.-St. Mary's | High-MN | 65 | 7 | 18 | 25 | 134 | | | | | | | | | | | | | | | | | | |
| 2002-03 | Shat.-St. Mary's | High-MN | 57 | 3 | 20 | 23 | 114 | | | | | | | | | | | | | | | | | | |
| 2003-04 | North Dakota | WCHA | 39 | 1 | 6 | 7 | 81 | | | | | | | | | | | | | | | | | | |
| 2004-05 | North Dakota | WCHA | 44 | 1 | 2 | 3 | 86 | | | | | | | | | | | | | | | | | | |
| 2005-06 | North Dakota | WCHA | 46 | 4 | 15 | 19 | *113 | | | | | | | | | | | | | | | | | | |
| 2006-07 | Springfield | AHL | 66 | 2 | 14 | 16 | 43 | | | | | | | | | | | | | | | | | | |
| **2007-08** | **Tampa Bay** | **NHL** | **14** | **0** | **0** | **0** | **12** | **0** | **0** | **0** | **7** | **0.0** | **–6** | **0** | **0.0** | **12:08** | | | | | | | | | |
| | Norfolk Admirals | AHL | 58 | 1 | 5 | 6 | 66 | | | | | | | | | | | | | | | | | | |
| **2008-09** | **Tampa Bay** | **NHL** | **43** | **0** | **4** | **4** | **50** | **0** | **0** | **0** | **28** | **0.0** | **–11** | **1** | **100.0** | **19:05** | | | | | | | | | |
| | Norfolk Admirals | AHL | 25 | 2 | 4 | 6 | 30 | | | | | | | | | | | | | | | | | | |
| | **NHL Totals** | | **57** | **0** | **4** | **4** | **62** | **0** | **0** | **0** | **35** | **0.0** | | **1** | **100.0** | **17:23** | | | | | | | | | |

## SMID, Ladislav

(SHMIHD, LA-dih-slahv) **EDM.**

Defense. Shoots left. 6'3", 226 lbs. Born, Frydlant V Cechach, Czech., February 1, 1986. Anaheim's 1st choice, 9th overall, in 2004 Entry Draft.

| Season | Club | League | GP | G | A | Pts | PIM | PP | SH | GW | S | % | +/- | TF | F% | Min | Playoffs GP | G | A | Pts | PIM | PP | SH | GW | Min |
|---|---|---|---|---|---|---|---|---|---|---|---|---|---|---|---|---|---|---|---|---|---|---|---|---|---|
| 2001-02 | HC Liberec Jr. | CzRep-Jr. | 43 | 6 | 10 | 16 | 87 | | | | | | | | | | | | | | | | | | |
| 2002-03 | HC Liberec Jr. | CzRep-Jr. | 32 | 1 | 14 | 15 | 12 | | | | | | | | | | 8 | 2 | 1 | 3 | 31 | | | | |
| | Liberec | CzRep | 4 | 0 | 0 | 0 | 0 | | | | | | | | | | | | | | | | | | |
| 2003-04 | HC Liberec Jr. | CzRep-Jr. | 14 | 4 | 10 | 14 | 38 | | | | | | | | | | 2 | 1 | 0 | 1 | 6 | | | | |
| | Liberec | CzRep | 45 | 1 | 1 | 2 | 51 | | | | | | | | | | | | | | | | | | |
| | Beroun | CzRep-2 | | | | | | | | | | | | | | | 3 | 1 | 1 | 2 | 4 | | | | |
| 2004-05 | HC Liberec Jr. | CzRep-Jr. | 3 | 0 | 1 | 1 | 4 | | | | | | | | | | | | | | | | | | |
| | Liberec | CzRep | 39 | 1 | 3 | 4 | 14 | | | | | | | | | | 12 | 0 | 0 | 0 | 6 | | | | |
| 2005-06 | Portland Pirates | AHL | 71 | 3 | 25 | 28 | 48 | | | | | | | | | | 16 | 0 | 1 | 1 | 16 | | | | |
| **2006-07** | **Edmonton** | **NHL** | **77** | **3** | **7** | **10** | **37** | **0** | **0** | **0** | **53** | **5.7** | **–16** | **0** | **0.0** | **19:14** | | | | | | | | | |
| **2007-08** | **Edmonton** | **NHL** | **65** | **0** | **4** | **4** | **58** | **0** | **0** | **0** | **45** | **0.0** | **–15** | **0** | **0.0** | **17:52** | | | | | | | | | |
| | Springfield | AHL | 8 | 1 | 4 | 5 | 15 | | | | | | | | | | | | | | | | | | |
| **2008-09** | **Edmonton** | **NHL** | **60** | **0** | **11** | **11** | **57** | **0** | **0** | **0** | **33** | **0.0** | **–6** | **0** | **0.0** | **14:57** | | | | | | | | | |
| | **NHL Totals** | | **202** | **3** | **22** | **25** | **152** | **0** | **0** | **0** | **131** | **2.3** | | **0** | **0.0** | **17:31** | | | | | | | | | |

Traded to **Edmonton** by **Anaheim** with Joffrey Lupul, Anaheim's 1st round choice (later traded to Phoenix - Phoenix selected Nick Ross) in 2007 Entry Draft and Anaheim's 1st (Jordan Eberle) and 2nd (later traded to NY Islanders - NY Islanders selected Travis Hamonic) round choices in 2008 Entry Draft for Chris Pronger, July 3, 2006.

## SMITH, Dan

(SMIHTH, DAN)

Defense. Shoots left. 6'2", 200 lbs. Born, Fernie, B.C., October 19, 1976. Colorado's 7th choice, 181st overall, in 1995 Entry Draft.

| Season | Club | League | GP | G | A | Pts | PIM | PP | SH | GW | S | % | +/- | TF | F% | Min | Playoffs GP | G | A | Pts | PIM | PP | SH | GW | Min |
|---|---|---|---|---|---|---|---|---|---|---|---|---|---|---|---|---|---|---|---|---|---|---|---|---|---|
| 1994-95 | U.B.C. | CWUAA | 28 | 1 | 3 | 4 | 26 | | | | | | | | | | | | | | | | | | |
| 1995-96 | Tri-City | WHL | 58 | 1 | 21 | 22 | 70 | | | | | | | | | | 11 | 1 | 3 | 4 | 14 | | | | |
| 1996-97 | Tri-City | WHL | 72 | 5 | 19 | 24 | 174 | | | | | | | | | | | | | | | | | | |
| | Hershey Bears | AHL | 8 | 0 | 1 | 1 | 6 | | | | | | | | | | 15 | 0 | 1 | 1 | 25 | | | | |
| 1997-98 | Hershey Bears | AHL | 50 | 1 | 2 | 3 | 71 | | | | | | | | | | 6 | 0 | 0 | 0 | 4 | | | | |
| **1998-99** | **Colorado** | **NHL** | **12** | **0** | **0** | **0** | **9** | **0** | **0** | **0** | **6** | **0.0** | **5** | **0** | **0.0** | **12:14** | | | | | | | | | |
| | Hershey Bears | AHL | 54 | 5 | 7 | 12 | 72 | | | | | | | | | | 5 | 0 | 1 | 1 | 0 | | | | |
| **99-2000** | **Colorado** | **NHL** | **3** | **0** | **0** | **0** | **0** | **0** | **0** | **0** | **0** | **0.0** | **2** | **0** | **0.0** | **11:03** | | | | | | | | | |
| | Hershey Bears | AHL | 49 | 7 | 15 | 22 | 56 | | | | | | | | | | | | | | | | | | |
| 2000-01 | Hershey Bears | AHL | 58 | 2 | 12 | 14 | 34 | | | | | | | | | | 12 | 0 | 1 | 1 | 4 | | | | |
| 2001-02 | Colorado | WCHL | 12 | 0 | 2 | 2 | 16 | | | | | | | | | | | | | | | | | | |
| | Lukko Rauma | Finland | 32 | 1 | 2 | 3 | 18 | | | | | | | | | | | | | | | | | | |
| 2002-03 | Springfield | AHL | 69 | 1 | 14 | 15 | 53 | | | | | | | | | | 6 | 0 | 2 | 2 | 0 | | | | |
| 2003-04 | Toronto | AHL | 66 | 4 | 9 | 13 | 41 | | | | | | | | | | | | | | | | | | |
| 2004-05 | Edmonton | AHL | 72 | 5 | 10 | 15 | 72 | | | | | | | | | | | | | | | | | | |
| **2005-06** | **Edmonton** | **NHL** | **7** | **0** | **0** | **0** | **7** | **0** | **0** | **0** | **1** | **0.0** | **1** | **0** | **0.0** | **11:21** | | | | | | | | | |
| | Hamilton | AHL | 69 | 0 | 15 | 15 | 61 | | | | | | | | | | | | | | | | | | |
| 2006-07 | Grand Rapids | AHL | 80 | 1 | 10 | 11 | 97 | | | | | | | | | | 7 | 0 | 1 | 1 | 8 | | | | |
| 2007-08 | Syracuse Crunch | AHL | 77 | 1 | 6 | 7 | 73 | | | | | | | | | | 10 | 0 | 1 | 1 | 17 | | | | |
| 2008-09 | Syracuse Crunch | AHL | 79 | 3 | 4 | 7 | 91 | | | | | | | | | | | | | | | | | | |
| | **NHL Totals** | | **22** | **0** | **0** | **0** | **16** | **0** | **0** | **0** | **7** | **0.0** | | **0** | **0.0** | **11:47** | | | | | | | | | |

Signed as a free agent by **Colorado** (WCHL), October 26, 2001. Signed as a free agent by **Rauma** (Finland) after receiving release from Colorado (WCHL), November 21, 2001. Signed as a free agent by **Edmonton**, August 21, 2003. Signed as a free agent by **Detroit**, July 13, 2006. Signed as a free agent by **Columbus**, July 11, 2007.

## SMITH, Jason

(SMIHTH, JAY-suhn) **OTT.**

Defense. Shoots right. 6'3", 220 lbs. Born, Calgary, Alta., November 2, 1973. New Jersey's 1st choice, 18th overall, in 1992 Entry Draft.

| Season | Club | League | GP | G | A | Pts | PIM | PP | SH | GW | S | % | +/- | TF | F% | Min | Playoffs GP | G | A | Pts | PIM | PP | SH | GW | Min |
|---|---|---|---|---|---|---|---|---|---|---|---|---|---|---|---|---|---|---|---|---|---|---|---|---|---|
| 1990-91 | Calgary Canucks | AJHL | 45 | 3 | 15 | 18 | 69 | | | | | | | | | | | | | | | | | | |
| | Regina Pats | WHL | 2 | 0 | 0 | 0 | 7 | | | | | | | | | | 4 | 0 | 0 | 0 | 2 | | | | |
| 1991-92 | Regina Pats | WHL | 62 | 9 | 29 | 38 | 138 | | | | | | | | | | | | | | | | | | |
| 1992-93 | Regina Pats | WHL | 64 | 14 | 52 | 66 | 175 | | | | | | | | | | 13 | 4 | 8 | 12 | 39 | | | | |
| | Utica Devils | AHL | | | | | | | | | | | | | | | 1 | 0 | 0 | 0 | 2 | | | | |
| **1993-94** | **New Jersey** | **NHL** | **41** | **0** | **5** | **5** | **43** | **0** | **0** | **0** | **47** | **0.0** | **7** | | | | **6** | **0** | **0** | **0** | **7** | **0** | **0** | **0** | |
| | Albany River Rats | AHL | 20 | 6 | 3 | 9 | 31 | | | | | | | | | | | | | | | | | | |
| **1994-95** | Albany River Rats | AHL | 7 | 0 | 2 | 2 | 15 | | | | | | | | | | 11 | 2 | 2 | 4 | 19 | | | | |
| | **New Jersey** | **NHL** | **2** | **0** | **0** | **0** | **0** | **0** | **0** | **0** | **5** | **0.0** | **–3** | | | | | | | | | | | | |
| **1995-96** | **New Jersey** | **NHL** | **64** | **2** | **1** | **3** | **86** | **0** | **0** | **0** | **52** | **3.8** | **5** | | | | | | | | | | | | |
| **1996-97** | **New Jersey** | **NHL** | **57** | **1** | **2** | **3** | **38** | **0** | **0** | **0** | **48** | **2.1** | **–8** | | | | | | | | | | | | |
| | **Toronto** | **NHL** | **21** | **0** | **5** | **5** | **16** | **0** | **0** | **0** | **26** | **0.0** | **–4** | | | | | | | | | | | | |
| **1997-98** | **Toronto** | **NHL** | **81** | **3** | **13** | **16** | **100** | **0** | **0** | **0** | **97** | **3.1** | **–5** | | | | | | | | | | | | |
| **1998-99** | **Toronto** | **NHL** | **60** | **2** | **11** | **13** | **40** | **0** | **0** | **0** | **53** | **3.8** | **–9** | **0** | **0.0** | **17:31** | | | | | | | | | |
| | **Edmonton** | **NHL** | **12** | **1** | **1** | **2** | **11** | **0** | **0** | **0** | **15** | **6.7** | **0** | **0** | **0.0** | **20:26** | **4** | **0** | **1** | **1** | **4** | **0** | **0** | **0** | **26:29** |
| **99-2000** | **Edmonton** | **NHL** | **80** | **3** | **11** | **14** | **60** | **0** | **0** | **1** | **96** | **3.1** | **16** | **1** | **100.0** | **21:15** | **5** | **0** | **1** | **1** | **4** | **0** | **0** | **0** | **21:56** |
| **2000-01** | **Edmonton** | **NHL** | **82** | **5** | **15** | **20** | **120** | **1** | **1** | **0** | **140** | **3.6** | **14** | **1** | **0.0** | **21:40** | **6** | **0** | **2** | **2** | **6** | **0** | **0** | **0** | **25:27** |
| **2001-02** | **Edmonton** | **NHL** | **74** | **5** | **13** | **18** | **103** | **0** | **1** | **1** | **85** | **5.9** | **14** | **0** | **0.0** | **21:00** | | | | | | | | | |
| **2002-03** | **Edmonton** | **NHL** | **68** | **4** | **8** | **12** | **64** | **0** | **0** | **1** | **93** | **4.3** | **5** | **0** | **0.0** | **21:46** | **6** | **0** | **0** | **0** | **19** | **0** | **0** | **0** | **21:17** |
| **2003-04** | **Edmonton** | **NHL** | **68** | **7** | **12** | **19** | **98** | **0** | **1** | **1** | **84** | **8.3** | **13** | **2** | **50.0** | **21:22** | | | | | | | | | |
| 2004-05 | | | DID NOT PLAY | | | | | | | | | | | | | | | | | | | | | | |
| **2005-06** | **Edmonton** | **NHL** | **76** | **4** | **13** | **17** | **84** | **0** | **0** | **0** | **79** | **5.1** | **1** | **0** | **0.0** | **19:39** | **24** | **1** | **4** | **5** | **16** | **0** | **0** | **1** | **22:29** |
| **2006-07** | **Edmonton** | **NHL** | **82** | **2** | **9** | **11** | **103** | **0** | **0** | **1** | **61** | **3.3** | **–13** | **1** | **0.0** | **21:08** | | | | | | | | | |

| | | | Regular Season | | | | | | | | | | | | | | Playoffs | | | | | | | | |
|---|---|---|---|---|---|---|---|---|---|---|---|---|---|---|---|---|---|---|---|---|---|---|---|---|---|
| Season | Club | League | GP | G | A | Pts | PIM | PP | SH | GW | S | % | +/- | TF | F% | Min | GP | G | A | Pts | PIM | PP | SH | GW | Min |
| 2007-08 | Philadelphia | NHL | 77 | 1 | 9 | 10 | 86 | 0 | 0 | 0 | 58 | 1.7 | -4 | 1 | 100.0 | 17:56 | 17 | 0 | 2 | 2 | 4 | 0 | 0 | 0 | 16:42 |
| 2008-09 | Ottawa | NHL | 63 | 1 | 0 | 1 | 47 | 0 | 0 | 1 | 53 | 1.9 | -3 | 1 | 0.0 | 17:32 | | | | | | | | | |
| | NHL Totals | | 1008 | 41 | 128 | 169 | 1099 | 1 | 3 | 6 | 1092 | 3.8 | | 7 | 28.6 | 20:11 | 68 | 1 | 10 | 11 | 60 | 0 | 0 | 1 | 21:17 |

WHL East First All-Star Team (1993) • Canadian Major Junior First All-Star Team (1993)

• Missed majority of 1994-95 season recovering from knee injury suffered in practice, November 5, 1994. Traded to **Toronto** by **New Jersey** with Steve Sullivan and the rights to Alyn McCauley for Doug Gilmour, Dave Ellett and New Jersey's 4th round choice (previously acquired, New Jersey selected Andre Lakos) in 1999 Entry Draft, February 25, 1997. Traded to **Edmonton** by **Toronto** for Edmonton's 4th round choice (Jonathon Zion) in 1999 Entry Draft and Edmonton's 2nd round choice (Kris Vernarsky) in 2000 Entry Draft, March 23, 1999. Traded to **Philadelphia** by **Edmonton** with Joffrey Lupul for Joni Pitkanen, Geoff Sanderson and Philadelphia's 3rd round choice (Cameron Abney) in 2009 Entry Draft, July 1, 2007. Signed as a free agent by **Ottawa**, July 8, 2008.

## SMITH, Mark

(SMIHTH, MAHRK)

Center. Shoots left. 5'10", 200 lbs. Born, Edmonton, Alta., October 24, 1977. San Jose's 7th choice, 219th overall, in 1997 Entry Draft.

| Season | Club | League | GP | G | A | Pts | PIM | PP | SH | GW | S | % | +/- | TF | F% | Min | GP | G | A | Pts | PIM | PP | SH | GW | Min |
|---|---|---|---|---|---|---|---|---|---|---|---|---|---|---|---|---|---|---|---|---|---|---|---|---|---|
| 1993-94 | Nipawin Hawks | SJHL | 62 | 14 | 12 | 26 | 44 | | | | | | | | | | | | | | | | | | |
| 1994-95 | Lethbridge | WHL | 49 | 3 | 4 | 7 | 25 | | | | | | | | | | | | | | | | | | |
| 1995-96 | Lethbridge | WHL | 71 | 11 | 24 | 35 | 59 | | | | | | | | | | 4 | 2 | 0 | 2 | 2 | | | | |
| 1996-97 | Lethbridge | WHL | 62 | 19 | 38 | 57 | 125 | | | | | | | | | | 19 | 7 | 13 | 20 | 51 | | | | |
| 1997-98 | Lethbridge | WHL | 70 | 42 | 67 | 109 | 206 | | | | | | | | | | 3 | 0 | 2 | 2 | 18 | | | | |
| | Kentucky | AHL | 2 | 0 | 0 | 0 | 0 | | | | | | | | | | | | | | | | | | |
| 1998-99 | Kentucky | AHL | 78 | 18 | 21 | 39 | 101 | | | | | | | | | | 12 | 2 | 7 | 9 | 16 | | | | |
| 99-2000 | Kentucky | AHL | 79 | 21 | 45 | 66 | 153 | | | | | | | | | | 9 | 0 | 5 | 5 | 22 | | | | |
| **2000-01** | **San Jose** | **NHL** | **42** | **2** | **2** | **4** | **51** | **0** | **0** | **0** | **39** | **5.1** | **2** | **308** | **52.9** | **8:48** | | | | | | | | | |
| | Kentucky | AHL | 6 | 2 | 6 | 8 | 23 | | | | | | | | | | | | | | | | | | |
| **2001-02** | **San Jose** | **NHL** | **49** | **3** | **3** | **6** | **72** | **0** | **0** | **1** | **40** | **7.5** | **-1** | **368** | **54.1** | **8:03** | | | | | | | | | |
| **2002-03** | **San Jose** | **NHL** | **75** | **4** | **11** | **15** | **64** | **0** | **0** | **0** | **68** | **5.9** | **1** | **632** | **57.0** | **9:21** | | | | | | | | | |
| **2003-04** | **San Jose** | **NHL** | **36** | **1** | **3** | **4** | **72** | **0** | **0** | **0** | **31** | **3.2** | **-5** | **207** | **50.2** | **8:22** | **10** | **1** | **0** | **1** | **11** | **0** | **0** | **1** | **7:44** |
| 2004-05 | Victoria | ECHL | 20 | 6 | 9 | 15 | 41 | | | | | | | | | | | | | | | | | | |
| **2005-06** | **San Jose** | **NHL** | **80** | **9** | **15** | **24** | **97** | **2** | **1** | **1** | **100** | **9.0** | **3** | **514** | **52.0** | **12:03** | **11** | **3** | **0** | **3** | **6** | **1** | **0** | **0** | **13:21** |
| **2006-07** | **San Jose** | **NHL** | **41** | **3** | **10** | **13** | **42** | **2** | **0** | **0** | **38** | **7.9** | **-4** | **79** | **59.5** | **10:25** | **3** | **0** | **0** | **0** | **4** | **0** | **0** | **0** | **8:28** |
| **2007-08** | **Calgary** | **NHL** | **54** | **1** | **3** | **4** | **59** | **0** | **0** | **0** | **27** | **3.7** | **-6** | **57** | **54.4** | **5:56** | | | | | | | | | |
| 2008-09 | DID NOT PLAY – INJURED | | | | | | | | | | | | | | | | | | | | | | | | |
| | **NHL Totals** | | **377** | **23** | **47** | **70** | **457** | **4** | **1** | **2** | **343** | **6.7** | | **2165** | **54.1** | **9:13** | **24** | **4** | **0** | **4** | **21** | **1** | **0** | **1** | **10:24** |

WHL East Second All-Star Team (1998)

• Missed majority of 2003-04 season serving as a healthy reserve. Signed as a free agent by **Victoria** (ECHL), January 21, 2005. Signed as a free agent by **Calgary**, September 29, 2007. • Missed entire 2008-09 season recovering from head injury.

## SMITH, Nathan

(SMIHTH, NAY-thun) **MIN.**

Center. Shoots left. 6'2", 206 lbs. Born, Edmonton, Alta., February 9, 1982. Vancouver's 1st choice, 23rd overall, in 2000 Entry Draft.

| Season | Club | League | GP | G | A | Pts | PIM | PP | SH | GW | S | % | +/- | TF | F% | Min | GP | G | A | Pts | PIM | PP | SH | GW | Min |
|---|---|---|---|---|---|---|---|---|---|---|---|---|---|---|---|---|---|---|---|---|---|---|---|---|---|
| 1997-98 | Sherwood Park | AMHL | 35 | 15 | 13 | 28 | 24 | | | | | | | | | | | | | | | | | | |
| 1998-99 | Swift Current | WHL | 47 | 5 | 8 | 13 | 26 | | | | | | | | | | | | | | | | | | |
| 99-2000 | Swift Current | WHL | 70 | 21 | 28 | 49 | 72 | | | | | | | | | | 12 | 1 | 6 | 7 | 4 | | | | |
| 2000-01 | Swift Current | WHL | 67 | 28 | 62 | 90 | 78 | | | | | | | | | | 19 | 4 | 3 | 7 | 20 | | | | |
| 2001-02 | Swift Current | WHL | 47 | 22 | 38 | 60 | 52 | | | | | | | | | | 12 | 3 | 6 | 9 | 18 | | | | |
| 2002-03 | Manitoba Moose | AHL | 53 | 9 | 8 | 17 | 30 | | | | | | | | | | 14 | 1 | 3 | 4 | 25 | | | | |
| **2003-04** | **Vancouver** | **NHL** | **2** | **0** | **0** | **0** | **0** | **0** | **0** | **0** | **1** | **0.0** | **-1** | **12** | **33.3** | **5:16** | | | | | | | | | |
| | Manitoba Moose | AHL | 76 | 4 | 16 | 20 | 71 | | | | | | | | | | | | | | | | | | |
| 2004-05 | Manitoba Moose | AHL | 72 | 7 | 9 | 16 | 67 | | | | | | | | | | 14 | 2 | 4 | 6 | 20 | | | | |
| **2005-06** | **Vancouver** | **NHL** | **1** | **0** | **0** | **0** | **0** | **0** | **0** | **0** | **2** | **0.0** | **0** | **9** | **33.3** | **10:52** | | | | | | | | | |
| | Manitoba Moose | AHL | 20 | 5 | 4 | 9 | 57 | | | | | | | | | | | | | | | | | | |
| **2006-07** | **Vancouver** | **NHL** | **1** | **0** | **0** | **0** | **0** | **0** | **0** | **0** | **0** | **0.0** | **0** | **9** | **66.7** | **8:45** | **4** | **0** | **0** | **0** | **0** | **0** | **0** | **0** | **6:57** |
| | Manitoba Moose | AHL | 72 | 19 | 21 | 40 | 76 | | | | | | | | | | 6 | 0 | 1 | 1 | 12 | | | | |
| **2007-08** | **Pittsburgh** | **NHL** | **13** | **0** | **0** | **0** | **2** | **0** | **0** | **0** | **3** | **0.0** | **0** | **75** | **53.3** | **7:41** | | | | | | | | | |
| | Wilkes-Barre | AHL | 68 | 22 | 28 | 50 | 61 | | | | | | | | | | 22 | 7 | 11 | 18 | 40 | | | | |
| 2008-09 | Lake Erie | AHL | 44 | 6 | 10 | 16 | 42 | | | | | | | | | | | | | | | | | | |
| | **NHL Totals** | | **17** | **0** | **0** | **0** | **2** | **0** | **0** | **0** | **6** | **0.0** | | **105** | **50.5** | **7:39** | **4** | **0** | **0** | **0** | **0** | **0** | **0** | **0** | **6:57** |

• Missed remainder of 2005-06 season recovering from knee injury suffered in game vs. Cleveland (AHL), November 27, 2005. Signed as a free agent by **Pittsburgh**, July 12, 2007. Signed as a free agent by **Colorado**, July 14, 2008. Signed as a free agent by **Minnesota**, July 22, 2009.

## SMITH, Trevor

(SMIHTH, TREH-vuhr) **NYI**

Left wing. Shoots left. 6'1", 195 lbs. Born, North Vancouver, B.C., February 8, 1985.

| Season | Club | League | GP | G | A | Pts | PIM | PP | SH | GW | S | % | +/- | TF | F% | Min | GP | G | A | Pts | PIM | PP | SH | GW | Min |
|---|---|---|---|---|---|---|---|---|---|---|---|---|---|---|---|---|---|---|---|---|---|---|---|---|---|
| 2003-04 | Quesnel | BCHL | 44 | 28 | 19 | 47 | 50 | | | | | | | | | | | | | | | | | | |
| 2004-05 | Omaha Lancers | USHL | 60 | 29 | 39 | 68 | 78 | | | | | | | | | | 5 | 3 | 1 | 4 | 2 | | | | |
| 2005-06 | New Hampshire | H-East | 39 | 10 | 10 | 20 | 34 | | | | | | | | | | | | | | | | | | |
| 2006-07 | New Hampshire | H-East | 39 | 21 | 22 | 43 | 39 | | | | | | | | | | | | | | | | | | |
| | Bridgeport | AHL | 8 | 1 | 2 | 3 | 2 | | | | | | | | | | | | | | | | | | |
| 2007-08 | Bridgeport | AHL | 53 | 20 | 17 | 37 | 16 | | | | | | | | | | | | | | | | | | |
| | Utah Grizzlies | ECHL | 22 | 11 | 14 | 25 | 28 | | | | | | | | | | | | | | | | | | |
| **2008-09** | **NY Islanders** | **NHL** | **7** | **1** | **0** | **1** | **0** | **0** | **0** | **0** | **7** | **14.3** | **-3** | **9** | **66.7** | **11:48** | | | | | | | | | |
| | Bridgeport | AHL | 76 | 30 | 32 | 62 | 40 | | | | | | | | | | 5 | 1 | 3 | 4 | 0 | | | | |
| | **NHL Totals** | | **7** | **1** | **0** | **1** | **0** | **0** | **0** | **0** | **7** | **14.3** | | **9** | **66.7** | **11:48** | | | | | | | | | |

NCAA East Second All-American Team (2007)

Signed as a free agent by **NY Islanders**, April 2, 2007.

## SMITH, Wyatt

(SMIHTH, WIGH-uht) **PIT.**

Center. Shoots left. 5'11", 205 lbs. Born, Thief River Falls, MN, February 13, 1977. Phoenix's 6th choice, 233rd overall, in 1997 Entry Draft.

| Season | Club | League | GP | G | A | Pts | PIM | PP | SH | GW | S | % | +/- | TF | F% | Min | GP | G | A | Pts | PIM | PP | SH | GW | Min |
|---|---|---|---|---|---|---|---|---|---|---|---|---|---|---|---|---|---|---|---|---|---|---|---|---|---|
| 1994-95 | Warroad Warriors | High-MN | 28 | 29 | 31 | 60 | 28 | | | | | | | | | | | | | | | | | | |
| 1995-96 | U. of Minnesota | WCHA | 32 | 4 | 5 | 9 | 32 | | | | | | | | | | | | | | | | | | |
| 1996-97 | U. of Minnesota | WCHA | 38 | 16 | 14 | 30 | 44 | | | | | | | | | | | | | | | | | | |
| 1997-98 | U. of Minnesota | WCHA | 39 | 24 | 23 | 47 | 62 | | | | | | | | | | | | | | | | | | |
| 1998-99 | U. of Minnesota | WCHA | 43 | 23 | 20 | 43 | 37 | | | | | | | | | | | | | | | | | | |
| **99-2000** | **Phoenix** | **NHL** | **2** | **0** | **0** | **0** | **0** | **0** | **0** | **0** | **0** | **0.0** | **-2** | **20** | **30.0** | **11:39** | | | | | | | | | |
| | Springfield | AHL | 60 | 14 | 26 | 40 | 26 | | | | | | | | | | 5 | 2 | 3 | 5 | 13 | | | | |
| **2000-01** | **Phoenix** | **NHL** | **42** | **3** | **7** | **10** | **13** | **0** | **1** | **0** | **40** | **7.5** | **7** | **335** | **40.9** | **12:20** | | | | | | | | | |
| | Springfield | AHL | 18 | 5 | 7 | 12 | 11 | | | | | | | | | | | | | | | | | | |
| **2001-02** | **Phoenix** | **NHL** | **10** | **0** | **0** | **0** | **0** | **0** | **0** | **0** | **4** | **0.0** | **-5** | **81** | **48.2** | **10:36** | | | | | | | | | |
| | Springfield | AHL | 69 | 23 | 32 | 55 | 69 | | | | | | | | | | | | | | | | | | |
| **2002-03** | **Nashville** | **NHL** | **11** | **1** | **0** | **1** | **0** | **0** | **0** | **0** | **8** | **12.5** | **-1** | **123** | **49.6** | **11:56** | | | | | | | | | |
| | Milwaukee | AHL | 56 | 24 | 27 | 51 | 89 | | | | | | | | | | 4 | 1 | 0 | 1 | 2 | | | | |
| **2003-04** | **Nashville** | **NHL** | **18** | **3** | **1** | **4** | **2** | **0** | **1** | **0** | **21** | **14.3** | **2** | **193** | **57.0** | **10:22** | | | | | | | | | |
| | Milwaukee | AHL | 40 | 9 | 7 | 16 | 40 | | | | | | | | | | 22 | 5 | 7 | 12 | 25 | | | | |
| 2004-05 | Milwaukee | AHL | 69 | 19 | 28 | 47 | 89 | | | | | | | | | | 7 | 1 | 4 | 5 | 10 | | | | |
| **2005-06** | **NY Islanders** | **NHL** | **42** | **0** | **8** | **8** | **26** | **0** | **0** | **0** | **37** | **0.0** | **-7** | **384** | **48.4** | **11:14** | | | | | | | | | |
| | Bridgeport | AHL | 39 | 13 | 16 | 29 | 40 | | | | | | | | | | | | | | | | | | |
| **2006-07** | **Minnesota** | **NHL** | **61** | **3** | **3** | **6** | **16** | **1** | **0** | **0** | **44** | **6.8** | **-8** | **508** | **43.5** | **9:31** | **4** | **0** | **0** | **0** | **0** | **0** | **0** | **0** | **11:02** |
| | Houston Aeros | AHL | 12 | 4 | 3 | 7 | 12 | | | | | | | | | | | | | | | | | | |
| **2007-08** | **Colorado** | **NHL** | **25** | **0** | **3** | **3** | **8** | **0** | **0** | **0** | **25** | **0.0** | **-4** | **108** | **50.9** | **11:38** | **1** | **0** | **0** | **0** | **0** | **0** | **0** | **0** | **10:47** |
| | Lake Erie | AHL | 40 | 17 | 18 | 35 | 34 | | | | | | | | | | | | | | | | | | |
| 2008-09 | Norfolk Admirals | AHL | 18 | 3 | 4 | 7 | 12 | | | | | | | | | | | | | | | | | | |
| | San Antonio | AHL | 53 | 16 | 24 | 40 | 59 | | | | | | | | | | | | | | | | | | |
| | **NHL Totals** | | **211** | **10** | **22** | **32** | **65** | **1** | **2** | **0** | **179** | **5.6** | | **1752** | **46.5** | **10:56** | **5** | **0** | **0** | **0** | **0** | **0** | **0** | **0** | **10:59** |

Signed as a free agent by **Nashville**, July 15, 2002. Signed as a free agent by **NY Islanders**, August 10, 2005. Signed as a free agent by **Minnesota**, July 19, 2006. Signed as a free agent by **Colorado** , August 20, 2007. Signed as a free agent by **Tampa Bay**, July 3, 2008. Traded to **Phoenix** by **Tampa Bay** for future consideratons, November 25, 2008. Signed as a free agent by **Pittsburgh**, July 31, 2009.

| Season | Club | League | GP | G | A | Pts | PIM | PP | SH | GW | S | % | +/- | TF | F% | Min | GP | G | A | Pts | PIM | PP | SH | GW | Min |
|---|---|---|---|---|---|---|---|---|---|---|---|---|---|---|---|---|---|---|---|---|---|---|---|---|---|
| | | | Regular Season | | | | | | | | | | | | | | Playoffs | | | | | | | | |

## SMITH, Zack

(SMIHTH, ZAK) **OTT.**

Center. Shoots left. 6'2", 209 lbs. Born, Medicine Hat, Alta., April 5, 1988. Ottawa's 3rd choice, 79th overall, in 2008 Entry Draft.

| Season | Club | League | GP | G | A | Pts | PIM | PP | SH | GW | S | % | +/- | TF | F% | Min | GP | G | A | Pts | PIM | PP | SH | GW | Min |
|---|---|---|---|---|---|---|---|---|---|---|---|---|---|---|---|---|---|---|---|---|---|---|---|---|---|
| 2004-05 | Swift Current | SMHL | 43 | 15 | 27 | 42 | 83 | .... | .... | .... | .... | .... | .... | .... | .... | .... | .... | .... | .... | .... | .... | .... | .... | .... | .... |
| | Swift Current | WHL | 14 | 1 | 1 | 2 | 0 | .... | .... | .... | .... | .... | .... | .... | .... | .... | .... | .... | .... | .... | .... | .... | .... | .... | .... |
| 2005-06 | Swift Current | WHL | 64 | 2 | 5 | 7 | 78 | .... | .... | .... | .... | .... | .... | .... | .... | .... | 3 | 0 | 0 | 0 | 9 | .... | .... | .... | .... |
| 2006-07 | Swift Current | WHL | 71 | 16 | 15 | 31 | 130 | .... | .... | .... | .... | .... | .... | .... | .... | .... | 6 | 0 | 2 | 2 | 11 | .... | .... | .... | .... |
| 2007-08 | Swift Current | WHL | 72 | 22 | 47 | 69 | 136 | .... | .... | .... | .... | .... | .... | .... | .... | .... | 12 | 5 | 5 | 10 | 29 | .... | .... | .... | .... |
| | Manitoba Moose | AHL | .... | .... | .... | .... | .... | .... | .... | .... | .... | .... | .... | .... | .... | .... | 6 | 0 | 1 | 1 | 0 | .... | .... | .... | .... |
| **2008-09** | **Ottawa** | **NHL** | **1** | **0** | **0** | **0** | **0** | **0** | **0** | **0** | **0** | **0.0** | **0** | **1** | **0.0** | **7:01** | .... | .... | .... | .... | .... | .... | .... | .... | .... |
| | Binghamton | AHL | 79 | 24 | 24 | 48 | 132 | .... | .... | .... | .... | .... | .... | .... | .... | .... | .... | .... | .... | .... | .... | .... | .... | .... | .... |
| | **NHL Totals** | | **1** | **0** | **0** | **0** | **0** | **0** | **0** | **0** | **0** | **0.0** | | **1** | **0.0** | **7:01** | .... | .... | .... | .... | .... | .... | .... | .... | .... |

## SMITHSON, Jerred

(SMIHTH-suhn, JEHR-rehd) **NSH.**

Center. Shoots right. 6'3", 204 lbs. Born, Vernon, B.C., February 4, 1979.

| Season | Club | League | GP | G | A | Pts | PIM | PP | SH | GW | S | % | +/- | TF | F% | Min | GP | G | A | Pts | PIM | PP | SH | GW | Min |
|---|---|---|---|---|---|---|---|---|---|---|---|---|---|---|---|---|---|---|---|---|---|---|---|---|---|
| 1994-95 | Vernon | Minor-BC | 64 | 39 | 46 | 85 | 120 | .... | .... | .... | .... | .... | .... | .... | .... | .... | .... | .... | .... | .... | .... | .... | .... | .... | .... |
| 1995-96 | Calgary Hitmen | WHL | 60 | 4 | 2 | 6 | 16 | .... | .... | .... | .... | .... | .... | .... | .... | .... | .... | .... | .... | .... | .... | .... | .... | .... | .... |
| 1996-97 | Calgary Hitmen | WHL | 65 | 3 | 6 | 9 | 49 | .... | .... | .... | .... | .... | .... | .... | .... | .... | .... | .... | .... | .... | .... | .... | .... | .... | .... |
| 1997-98 | Calgary Hitmen | WHL | 65 | 12 | 9 | 21 | 65 | .... | .... | .... | .... | .... | .... | .... | .... | .... | 18 | 0 | 2 | 2 | 25 | .... | .... | .... | .... |
| 1998-99 | Calgary Hitmen | WHL | 63 | 14 | 22 | 36 | 108 | .... | .... | .... | .... | .... | .... | .... | .... | .... | 21 | 3 | 7 | 10 | 17 | .... | .... | .... | .... |
| 99-2000 | Calgary Hitmen | WHL | 66 | 14 | 25 | 39 | 111 | .... | .... | .... | .... | .... | .... | .... | .... | .... | 10 | 1 | 1 | 2 | 16 | .... | .... | .... | .... |
| 2000-01 | Lowell | AHL | 24 | 1 | 1 | 2 | 10 | .... | .... | .... | .... | .... | .... | .... | .... | .... | 4 | 0 | 0 | 0 | 2 | .... | .... | .... | .... |
| | Trenton Titans | ECHL | 3 | 0 | 1 | 1 | 2 | .... | .... | .... | .... | .... | .... | .... | .... | .... | .... | .... | .... | .... | .... | .... | .... | .... | .... |
| 2001-02 | Manchester | AHL | 78 | 5 | 13 | 18 | 45 | .... | .... | .... | .... | .... | .... | .... | .... | .... | 5 | 0 | 1 | 1 | 4 | .... | .... | .... | .... |
| **2002-03** | **Los Angeles** | **NHL** | **22** | **0** | **2** | **2** | **21** | **0** | **0** | **0** | **9** | **0.0** | **-5** | **175** | **48.0** | **8:50** | .... | .... | .... | .... | .... | .... | .... | .... | .... |
| | Manchester | AHL | 38 | 4 | 21 | 25 | 60 | .... | .... | .... | .... | .... | .... | .... | .... | .... | 3 | 0 | 0 | 0 | 4 | .... | .... | .... | .... |
| **2003-04** | **Los Angeles** | **NHL** | **8** | **0** | **1** | **1** | **4** | **0** | **0** | **0** | **2** | **0.0** | **0** | **86** | **64.0** | **10:39** | .... | .... | .... | .... | .... | .... | .... | .... | .... |
| | Manchester | AHL | 66 | 7 | 13 | 20 | 51 | .... | .... | .... | .... | .... | .... | .... | .... | .... | 6 | 0 | 1 | 1 | 10 | .... | .... | .... | .... |
| 2004-05 | Milwaukee | AHL | 80 | 11 | 11 | 22 | 92 | .... | .... | .... | .... | .... | .... | .... | .... | .... | 5 | 0 | 0 | 0 | 4 | .... | .... | .... | .... |
| **2005-06** | **Nashville** | **NHL** | **66** | **5** | **9** | **14** | **54** | **0** | **0** | **1** | **50** | **10.0** | **9** | **613** | **54.3** | **11:50** | **3** | **0** | **0** | **0** | **4** | **0** | **0** | **0** | **9:26** |
| | Milwaukee | AHL | 8 | 0 | 0 | 0 | 12 | .... | .... | .... | .... | .... | .... | .... | .... | .... | .... | .... | .... | .... | .... | .... | .... | .... | .... |
| **2006-07** | **Nashville** | **NHL** | **64** | **5** | **7** | **12** | **42** | **1** | **1** | **2** | **47** | **10.6** | **-8** | **420** | **56.4** | **11:03** | **5** | **0** | **0** | **0** | **17** | **0** | **0** | **0** | **11:30** |
| **2007-08** | **Nashville** | **NHL** | **81** | **7** | **9** | **16** | **50** | **0** | **2** | **2** | **61** | **11.5** | **-9** | **572** | **52.1** | **12:05** | **6** | **0** | **0** | **0** | **2** | **0** | **0** | **0** | **11:52** |
| **2008-09** | **Nashville** | **NHL** | **82** | **4** | **9** | **13** | **49** | **0** | **0** | **0** | **74** | **5.4** | **-6** | **722** | **52.6** | **13:51** | .... | .... | .... | .... | .... | .... | .... | .... | .... |
| | **NHL Totals** | | **323** | **21** | **37** | **58** | **220** | **1** | **3** | **5** | **243** | **8.6** | | **2588** | **53.6** | **12:01** | **14** | **0** | **0** | **0** | **23** | **0** | **0** | **0** | **11:13** |

Signed as a free agent by **Los Angeles**, February 18, 2000. Signed as a free agent by **Nashville**, July 22, 2004.

## SMOLENAK, Radek

(SMOH-lehn-ahk, RA-dehk) **T.B.**

Left wing. Shoots left. 6'3", 180 lbs. Born, Prague, Czech., December 3, 1986. Tampa Bay's 2nd choice, 73rd overall, in 2005 Entry Draft.

| Season | Club | League | GP | G | A | Pts | PIM | PP | SH | GW | S | % | +/- | TF | F% | Min | GP | G | A | Pts | PIM | PP | SH | GW | Min |
|---|---|---|---|---|---|---|---|---|---|---|---|---|---|---|---|---|---|---|---|---|---|---|---|---|---|
| 2001-02 | HC Kladno U17 | CzR-U17 | 47 | 29 | 20 | 49 | 42 | .... | .... | .... | .... | .... | .... | .... | .... | .... | .... | .... | .... | .... | .... | .... | .... | .... | .... |
| 2002-03 | HC Kladno U17 | CzR-U17 | 41 | 39 | 27 | 66 | 52 | .... | .... | .... | .... | .... | .... | .... | .... | .... | 9 | 7 | 3 | 10 | 18 | .... | .... | .... | .... |
| | HC Kladno Jr. | CzRep-Jr. | 4 | 2 | 0 | 2 | 6 | .... | .... | .... | .... | .... | .... | .... | .... | .... | .... | .... | .... | .... | .... | .... | .... | .... | .... |
| 2003-04 | HC Kladno Jr. | CzRep-Jr. | 54 | 27 | 25 | 52 | 51 | .... | .... | .... | .... | .... | .... | .... | .... | .... | 7 | 3 | 4 | 7 | 0 | .... | .... | .... | .... |
| 2004-05 | Kingston | OHL | 67 | 32 | 28 | 60 | 58 | .... | .... | .... | .... | .... | .... | .... | .... | .... | .... | .... | .... | .... | .... | .... | .... | .... | .... |
| 2005-06 | Kingston | OHL | 65 | 42 | 42 | 84 | 109 | .... | .... | .... | .... | .... | .... | .... | .... | .... | 6 | 1 | 3 | 4 | 20 | .... | .... | .... | .... |
| 2006-07 | Springfield | AHL | 20 | 0 | 1 | 1 | 8 | .... | .... | .... | .... | .... | .... | .... | .... | .... | .... | .... | .... | .... | .... | .... | .... | .... | .... |
| | Johnstown Chiefs | ECHL | 43 | 15 | 20 | 35 | 35 | .... | .... | .... | .... | .... | .... | .... | .... | .... | 1 | 0 | 0 | 0 | 0 | .... | .... | .... | .... |
| 2007-08 | Norfolk Admirals | AHL | 56 | 15 | 11 | 26 | 108 | .... | .... | .... | .... | .... | .... | .... | .... | .... | .... | .... | .... | .... | .... | .... | .... | .... | .... |
| | Mississippi | ECHL | 19 | 7 | 8 | 15 | 14 | .... | .... | .... | .... | .... | .... | .... | .... | .... | .... | .... | .... | .... | .... | .... | .... | .... | .... |
| **2008-09** | **Tampa Bay** | **NHL** | **6** | **0** | **1** | **1** | **10** | **0** | **0** | **0** | **14** | **0.0** | **1** | **0** | **0.0** | **8:21** | .... | .... | .... | .... | .... | .... | .... | .... | .... |
| | Norfolk Admirals | AHL | 71 | 24 | 25 | 49 | 165 | .... | .... | .... | .... | .... | .... | .... | .... | .... | .... | .... | .... | .... | .... | .... | .... | .... | .... |
| | **NHL Totals** | | **6** | **0** | **1** | **1** | **10** | **0** | **0** | **0** | **14** | **0.0** | | **0** | **0.0** | **8:21** | .... | .... | .... | .... | .... | .... | .... | .... | .... |

## SMYTH, Ryan

(SMIHTH, RIGH-uhn) **L.A.**

Left wing. Shoots left. 6'1", 190 lbs. Born, Banff, Alta., February 21, 1976. Edmonton's 2nd choice, 6th overall, in 1994 Entry Draft.

| Season | Club | League | GP | G | A | Pts | PIM | PP | SH | GW | S | % | +/- | TF | F% | Min | GP | G | A | Pts | PIM | PP | SH | GW | Min |
|---|---|---|---|---|---|---|---|---|---|---|---|---|---|---|---|---|---|---|---|---|---|---|---|---|---|
| 1990-91 | Banff Blazers | ABHL | 25 | 100 | 50 | 150 | .... | .... | .... | .... | .... | .... | .... | .... | .... | .... | .... | .... | .... | .... | .... | .... | .... | .... | .... |
| | Lethbridge | AMHL | 34 | 8 | 21 | 29 | .... | .... | .... | .... | .... | .... | .... | .... | .... | .... | .... | .... | .... | .... | .... | .... | .... | .... | .... |
| 1991-92 | Caronport | SMHL | 35 | 55 | 61 | 116 | 98 | .... | .... | .... | .... | .... | .... | .... | .... | .... | .... | .... | .... | .... | .... | .... | .... | .... | .... |
| | Moose Jaw | WHL | 2 | 0 | 0 | 0 | 0 | .... | .... | .... | .... | .... | .... | .... | .... | .... | .... | .... | .... | .... | .... | .... | .... | .... | .... |
| 1992-93 | Moose Jaw | WHL | 64 | 19 | 14 | 33 | 59 | .... | .... | .... | .... | .... | .... | .... | .... | .... | .... | .... | .... | .... | .... | .... | .... | .... | .... |
| 1993-94 | Moose Jaw | WHL | 72 | 50 | 55 | 105 | 88 | .... | .... | .... | .... | .... | .... | .... | .... | .... | .... | .... | .... | .... | .... | .... | .... | .... | .... |
| **1994-95** | Moose Jaw | WHL | 50 | 41 | 45 | 86 | 66 | .... | .... | .... | .... | .... | .... | .... | .... | .... | 10 | 6 | 9 | 15 | 22 | .... | .... | .... | .... |
| | **Edmonton** | **NHL** | **3** | **0** | **0** | **0** | **0** | **0** | **0** | **0** | **2** | **0.0** | **-1** | .... | .... | .... | .... | .... | .... | .... | .... | .... | .... | .... | .... |
| **1995-96** | **Edmonton** | **NHL** | **48** | **2** | **9** | **11** | **28** | **1** | **0** | **0** | **65** | **3.1** | **-10** | .... | .... | .... | .... | .... | .... | .... | .... | .... | .... | .... | .... |
| | Cape Breton | AHL | 9 | 6 | 5 | 11 | 4 | .... | .... | .... | .... | .... | .... | .... | .... | .... | .... | .... | .... | .... | .... | .... | .... | .... | .... |
| **1996-97** | **Edmonton** | **NHL** | **82** | **39** | **22** | **61** | **76** | **20** | **0** | **4** | **265** | **14.7** | **-7** | .... | .... | .... | **12** | **5** | **5** | **10** | **12** | **1** | **0** | **2** | .... |
| **1997-98** | **Edmonton** | **NHL** | **65** | **20** | **13** | **33** | **44** | **10** | **0** | **2** | **205** | **9.8** | **-24** | .... | .... | .... | **12** | **1** | **3** | **4** | **16** | **1** | **0** | **0** | .... |
| **1998-99** | **Edmonton** | **NHL** | **71** | **13** | **18** | **31** | **62** | **6** | **0** | **2** | **161** | **8.1** | **0** | **5** | **20.0** | **14:26** | **3** | **3** | **0** | **3** | **2** | **2** | **0** | **0** | **24:35** |
| **99-2000** | **Edmonton** | **NHL** | **82** | **28** | **26** | **54** | **58** | **11** | **0** | **4** | **238** | **11.8** | **-2** | **24** | **54.2** | **19:12** | **5** | **1** | **0** | **1** | **6** | **0** | **1** | **0** | **19:18** |
| **2000-01** | **Edmonton** | **NHL** | **82** | **31** | **39** | **70** | **58** | **11** | **0** | **6** | **245** | **12.7** | **10** | **17** | **35.3** | **19:58** | **6** | **3** | **4** | **7** | **4** | **0** | **0** | **0** | **24:46** |
| **2001-02** | **Edmonton** | **NHL** | **61** | **15** | **35** | **50** | **48** | **7** | **1** | **5** | **150** | **10.0** | **7** | **12** | **41.7** | **19:27** | .... | .... | .... | .... | .... | .... | .... | .... | .... |
| | Canada | Olympics | 6 | 0 | 1 | 1 | 0 | .... | .... | .... | .... | .... | .... | .... | .... | .... | .... | .... | .... | .... | .... | .... | .... | .... | .... |
| **2002-03** | **Edmonton** | **NHL** | **66** | **27** | **34** | **61** | **67** | **10** | **0** | **3** | **199** | **13.6** | **5** | **42** | **42.9** | **19:21** | **6** | **2** | **0** | **2** | **16** | **0** | **1** | **0** | **17:39** |
| **2003-04** | **Edmonton** | **NHL** | **82** | **23** | **36** | **59** | **70** | **8** | **2** | **6** | **245** | **9.4** | **11** | **484** | **47.1** | **19:39** | .... | .... | .... | .... | .... | .... | .... | .... | .... |
| 2004-05 | | | DID NOT PLAY | | | | | | | | | | | | | | | | | | | | | | |
| **2005-06** | **Edmonton** | **NHL** | **75** | **36** | **30** | **66** | **58** | **19** | **2** | **3** | **230** | **15.7** | **-5** | **159** | **47.8** | **20:13** | **24** | **7** | **9** | **16** | **22** | **4** | **0** | **1** | **21:27** |
| | Canada | Olympics | 6 | 0 | 1 | 1 | 4 | .... | .... | .... | .... | .... | .... | .... | .... | .... | .... | .... | .... | .... | .... | .... | .... | .... | .... |
| **2006-07** | **Edmonton** | **NHL** | **53** | **31** | **22** | **53** | **38** | **14** | **1** | **5** | **161** | **19.3** | **2** | **63** | **47.6** | **20:09** | .... | .... | .... | .... | .... | .... | .... | .... | .... |
| | **NY Islanders** | **NHL** | **18** | **5** | **10** | **15** | **14** | **1** | **0** | **0** | **49** | **10.2** | **0** | **9** | **22.2** | **22:26** | **5** | **1** | **3** | **4** | **4** | **0** | **0** | **0** | **22:42** |
| **2007-08** | **Colorado** | **NHL** | **55** | **14** | **23** | **37** | **50** | **2** | **0** | **3** | **168** | **8.3** | **-4** | **33** | **39.4** | **19:37** | **8** | **2** | **3** | **5** | **2** | **1** | **0** | **1** | **17:29** |
| **2008-09** | **Colorado** | **NHL** | **77** | **26** | **33** | **59** | **62** | **10** | **1** | **3** | **257** | **10.1** | **-15** | **174** | **51.2** | **20:17** | .... | .... | .... | .... | .... | .... | .... | .... | .... |
| | **NHL Totals** | | **920** | **310** | **350** | **660** | **733** | **130** | **7** | **46** | **2640** | **11.7** | | **1022** | **47.1** | **19:18** | **81** | **25** | **27** | **52** | **82** | **9** | **2** | **4** | **20:56** |

WHL East Second All-Star Team (1995)
Played in NHL All-Star Game (2007)

Traded to **NY Islanders** by **Edmonton** for Ryan O'Marra, Robert Nilsson and NY Islanders' 1st round choice (Alex Plante) in 2007 Entry Draft, February 27, 2007. Signed as a free agent by **Colorado**, July 1, 2007. Traded to **Los Angeles** by **Colorado** for Kyle Quincey, Tom Preissing and Los Angeles' 5th round choice in 2010 Entry Draft, July 3, 2009.

## SOBOTKA, Vladimir

(suh-BOHT-kah, vla-DIH-meer) **BOS.**

Center. Shoots left. 5'11", 193 lbs. Born, Trebic, Czech., July 2, 1987. Boston's 5th choice, 106th overall, in 2005 Entry Draft.

| Season | Club | League | GP | G | A | Pts | PIM | PP | SH | GW | S | % | +/- | TF | F% | Min | GP | G | A | Pts | PIM | PP | SH | GW | Min |
|---|---|---|---|---|---|---|---|---|---|---|---|---|---|---|---|---|---|---|---|---|---|---|---|---|---|
| 2002-03 | Slavia U17 | CzR-U17 | 46 | 16 | 24 | 40 | 48 | .... | .... | .... | .... | .... | .... | .... | .... | .... | 8 | 1 | 1 | 2 | 29 | .... | .... | .... | .... |
| 2003-04 | Slavia U17 | CzR-U17 | 35 | 24 | 41 | 65 | 109 | .... | .... | .... | .... | .... | .... | .... | .... | .... | 7 | 7 | 12 | 19 | 8 | .... | .... | .... | .... |
| | Slavia Jr. | CzRep-Jr. | 18 | 6 | 6 | 12 | 16 | .... | .... | .... | .... | .... | .... | .... | .... | .... | .... | .... | .... | .... | .... | .... | .... | .... | .... |
| | HC Slavia Praha | CzRep | 1 | 0 | 0 | 0 | 0 | .... | .... | .... | .... | .... | .... | .... | .... | .... | .... | .... | .... | .... | .... | .... | .... | .... | .... |
| 2004-05 | Slavia Jr. | CzRep-Jr. | 27 | 12 | 21 | 33 | 93 | .... | .... | .... | .... | .... | .... | .... | .... | .... | .... | .... | .... | .... | .... | .... | .... | .... | .... |
| | HC Slavia Praha | CzRep | 18 | 0 | 1 | 1 | 8 | .... | .... | .... | .... | .... | .... | .... | .... | .... | .... | .... | .... | .... | .... | .... | .... | .... | .... |
| | Havl. Brod | CzRep-3 | 7 | 3 | 0 | 3 | 31 | .... | .... | .... | .... | .... | .... | .... | .... | .... | 7 | 1 | 5 | 6 | 0 | .... | .... | .... | .... |
| 2005-06 | Slavia Jr. | CzRep-Jr. | 8 | 10 | 4 | 14 | 42 | .... | .... | .... | .... | .... | .... | .... | .... | .... | .... | .... | .... | .... | .... | .... | .... | .... | .... |
| | HC Slavia Praha | CzRep | 33 | 1 | 9 | 10 | 28 | .... | .... | .... | .... | .... | .... | .... | .... | .... | 11 | 2 | 3 | 5 | 10 | .... | .... | .... | .... |
| 2006-07 | HC Slavia Praha | CzRep | 33 | 7 | 6 | 13 | 38 | .... | .... | .... | .... | .... | .... | .... | .... | .... | .... | .... | .... | .... | .... | .... | .... | .... | .... |
| **2007-08** | **Boston** | **NHL** | **48** | **1** | **6** | **7** | **24** | **0** | **0** | **1** | **40** | **2.5** | **1** | **247** | **48.6** | **8:50** | **6** | **2** | **0** | **2** | **0** | **0** | **0** | **0** | **8:37** |
| | Providence Bruins | AHL | 18 | 10 | 10 | 20 | 37 | .... | .... | .... | .... | .... | .... | .... | .... | .... | 6 | 0 | 4 | 4 | 0 | .... | .... | .... | .... |
| **2008-09** | **Boston** | **NHL** | **25** | **1** | **4** | **5** | **10** | **0** | **0** | **0** | **19** | **5.3** | **-10** | **52** | **57.7** | **10:33** | .... | .... | .... | .... | .... | .... | .... | .... | .... |
| | Providence Bruins | AHL | 44 | 20 | 24 | 44 | 83 | .... | .... | .... | .... | .... | .... | .... | .... | .... | 14 | 2 | 11 | 13 | 43 | .... | .... | .... | .... |
| | **NHL Totals** | | **73** | **2** | **10** | **12** | **34** | **0** | **0** | **1** | **59** | **3.4** | | **299** | **50.2** | **9:25** | **6** | **2** | **0** | **2** | **0** | **0** | **0** | **0** | **8:37** |

## SOPEL, Brent

(SOH-puhl, BREHNT) **CHI.**

Defense. Shoots right. 6'1", 211 lbs. Born, Calgary, Alta., January 7, 1977. Vancouver's 6th choice, 144th overall, in 1995 Entry Draft.

| | | | Regular Season | | | | | | | | | | | | | | Playoffs | | | | | | | | |
|---|---|---|---|---|---|---|---|---|---|---|---|---|---|---|---|---|---|---|---|---|---|---|---|---|---|
| Season | Club | League | GP | G | A | Pts | PIM | PP | SH | GW | S | % | +/- | TF | F% | Min | GP | G | A | Pts | PIM | PP | SH | GW | Min |
| 1992-93 | Sask. Legion | SMHL | 36 | 7 | 17 | 24 | 95 | .... | .... | .... | .... | .... | .... | .... | .... | .... | .... | .... | .... | .... | .... | .... | .... | .... | .... |
| 1993-94 | Saskatoon Blazers | SMHL | 34 | 9 | 30 | 39 | 180 | .... | .... | .... | .... | .... | .... | .... | .... | .... | .... | .... | .... | .... | .... | .... | .... | .... | .... |
| | Saskatoon Blades | WHL | 11 | 2 | 2 | 4 | 2 | .... | .... | .... | .... | .... | .... | .... | .... | .... | .... | .... | .... | .... | .... | .... | .... | .... | .... |
| 1994-95 | Saskatoon Blades | WHL | 22 | 1 | 10 | 11 | 31 | .... | .... | .... | .... | .... | .... | .... | .... | .... | .... | .... | .... | .... | .... | .... | .... | .... | .... |
| | Swift Current | WHL | 41 | 4 | 19 | 23 | 50 | .... | .... | .... | .... | .... | .... | .... | .... | .... | 3 | 0 | 3 | 3 | 0 | .... | .... | .... | .... |
| 1995-96 | Swift Current | WHL | 71 | 13 | 48 | 61 | 87 | .... | .... | .... | .... | .... | .... | .... | .... | .... | 6 | 1 | 2 | 3 | 4 | .... | .... | .... | .... |
| | Syracuse Crunch | AHL | 1 | 0 | 0 | 0 | 0 | .... | .... | .... | .... | .... | .... | .... | .... | .... | .... | .... | .... | .... | .... | .... | .... | .... | .... |
| 1996-97 | Swift Current | WHL | 62 | 15 | 41 | 56 | 109 | .... | .... | .... | .... | .... | .... | .... | .... | .... | 10 | 5 | 11 | 16 | 32 | .... | .... | .... | .... |
| | Syracuse Crunch | AHL | 2 | 0 | 0 | 0 | 0 | .... | .... | .... | .... | .... | .... | .... | .... | .... | 3 | 0 | 0 | 0 | 0 | .... | .... | .... | .... |
| 1997-98 | Syracuse Crunch | AHL | 76 | 10 | 33 | 43 | 70 | .... | .... | .... | .... | .... | .... | .... | .... | .... | 5 | 0 | 7 | 7 | 12 | .... | .... | .... | .... |
| **1998-99** | **Vancouver** | **NHL** | **5** | **1** | **0** | **1** | **4** | **1** | **0** | **0** | **5** | **20.0** | **−1** | **0** | **0.0** | **11:58** | .... | .... | .... | .... | .... | .... | .... | .... | .... |
| | Syracuse Crunch | AHL | 53 | 10 | 21 | 31 | 59 | .... | .... | .... | .... | .... | .... | .... | .... | .... | .... | .... | .... | .... | .... | .... | .... | .... | .... |
| **99-2000** | **Vancouver** | **NHL** | **18** | **2** | **4** | **6** | **12** | **0** | **0** | **1** | **11** | **18.2** | **9** | **0** | **0.0** | **10:31** | .... | .... | .... | .... | .... | .... | .... | .... | .... |
| | Syracuse Crunch | AHL | 50 | 6 | 25 | 31 | 67 | .... | .... | .... | .... | .... | .... | .... | .... | .... | 4 | 0 | 2 | 2 | 8 | .... | .... | .... | .... |
| **2000-01** | **Vancouver** | **NHL** | **52** | **4** | **10** | **14** | **10** | **0** | **0** | **1** | **57** | **7.0** | **4** | **0** | **0.0** | **16:01** | **4** | **0** | **0** | **0** | **2** | **0** | **0** | **0** | **19:05** |
| | Kansas City | IHL | 4 | 0 | 1 | 1 | 0 | .... | .... | .... | .... | .... | .... | .... | .... | .... | .... | .... | .... | .... | .... | .... | .... | .... | .... |
| **2001-02** | **Vancouver** | **NHL** | **66** | **8** | **17** | **25** | **44** | **1** | **0** | **3** | **116** | **6.9** | **21** | **0** | **0.0** | **19:01** | **6** | **0** | **2** | **2** | **2** | **0** | **0** | **0** | **24:45** |
| **2002-03** | **Vancouver** | **NHL** | **81** | **7** | **30** | **37** | **23** | **6** | **0** | **1** | **167** | **4.2** | **−15** | **0** | **0.0** | **21:42** | **14** | **2** | **6** | **8** | **4** | **1** | **0** | **1** | **22:33** |
| **2003-04** | **Vancouver** | **NHL** | **80** | **10** | **32** | **42** | **36** | **6** | **0** | **2** | **173** | **5.8** | **11** | **0** | **0.0** | **21:56** | **7** | **0** | **1** | **1** | **0** | **0** | **0** | **0** | **23:55** |
| 2004-05 | | | DID NOT PLAY | | | | | | | | | | | | | | | | | | | | | | |
| **2005-06** | **NY Islanders** | **NHL** | **57** | **2** | **25** | **27** | **64** | **2** | **0** | **0** | **121** | **1.7** | **−9** | **0** | **0.0** | **23:35** | .... | .... | .... | .... | .... | .... | .... | .... | .... |
| | **Los Angeles** | **NHL** | **11** | **0** | **1** | **1** | **6** | **0** | **0** | **0** | **12** | **0.0** | **−4** | **0** | **0.0** | **22:02** | .... | .... | .... | .... | .... | .... | .... | .... | .... |
| **2006-07** | **Los Angeles** | **NHL** | **44** | **4** | **19** | **23** | **14** | **2** | **0** | **2** | **104** | **3.8** | **2** | **3** | **33.3** | **21:06** | .... | .... | .... | .... | .... | .... | .... | .... | .... |
| | **Vancouver** | **NHL** | **20** | **1** | **4** | **5** | **10** | **0** | **0** | **0** | **27** | **3.7** | **0** | **0** | **0.0** | **18:25** | **11** | **0** | **0** | **0** | **2** | **0** | **0** | **0** | **19:44** |
| **2007-08** | **Chicago** | **NHL** | **58** | **1** | **19** | **20** | **28** | **0** | **0** | **0** | **56** | **1.8** | **9** | **0** | **0.0** | **20:18** | .... | .... | .... | .... | .... | .... | .... | .... | .... |
| **2008-09** | **Chicago** | **NHL** | **23** | **1** | **1** | **2** | **8** | **0** | **0** | **1** | **15** | **6.7** | **−4** | **0** | **0.0** | **13:49** | .... | .... | .... | .... | .... | .... | .... | .... | .... |
| | **NHL Totals** | | **515** | **41** | **162** | **203** | **259** | **18** | **0** | **11** | **864** | **4.7** | | **3** | **33.3** | **19:52** | **42** | **2** | **9** | **11** | **10** | **1** | **0** | **1** | **22:02** |

Traded to **NY Islanders** by **Vancouver** for NY Islanders' 2nd round choice (later traded to Anaheim - Anaheim selected Bryce Swan) in 2006 Entry Draft, August 3, 2005. Traded to **Los Angeles** by **NY Islanders** with Mark Parrish for Denis Grebeshkov and Jeff Tambellini, March 8, 2006. Traded to **Vancouver** by **Los Angeles** for Anaheim's 2nd round choice (previously acquired, Los Angeles selected Wayne Simmonds) in 2007 Entry Draft and and Vancouver's 4th round choice (later traded to Buffalo - Buffalo selected Justin Jokinen) in 2008 Entry Draft, February 26, 2006. Signed as a free agent by **Chicago**, October 3, 2007. • Missed majority of 2008-09 season recovering from recurring elbow injury.

## SOURAY, Sheldon

(SOO-ray, SHEHL-duhn) **EDM.**

Defense. Shoots left. 6'4", 233 lbs. Born, Elk Point, Alta., July 13, 1976. New Jersey's 3rd choice, 71st overall, in 1994 Entry Draft.

| | | | Regular Season | | | | | | | | | | | | | | Playoffs | | | | | | | | |
|---|---|---|---|---|---|---|---|---|---|---|---|---|---|---|---|---|---|---|---|---|---|---|---|---|---|
| Season | Club | League | GP | G | A | Pts | PIM | PP | SH | GW | S | % | +/- | TF | F% | Min | GP | G | A | Pts | PIM | PP | SH | GW | Min |
| 1990-91 | Bonnyville Sabres | AAHA | 30 | 15 | 20 | 35 | 100 | .... | .... | .... | .... | .... | .... | .... | .... | .... | .... | .... | .... | .... | .... | .... | .... | .... | .... |
| 1991-92 | Quesnel | Minor-BC | 20 | 5 | 15 | 20 | 200 | .... | .... | .... | .... | .... | .... | .... | .... | .... | .... | .... | .... | .... | .... | .... | .... | .... | .... |
| | Alberta Cycle | AMHL | 11 | 0 | 5 | 5 | 67 | .... | .... | .... | .... | .... | .... | .... | .... | .... | .... | .... | .... | .... | .... | .... | .... | .... | .... |
| 1992-93 | Ft. Saskatchewan | AJHL | 35 | 0 | 12 | 12 | 125 | .... | .... | .... | .... | .... | .... | .... | .... | .... | .... | .... | .... | .... | .... | .... | .... | .... | .... |
| | Tri-City | WHL | 2 | 0 | 0 | 0 | 0 | .... | .... | .... | .... | .... | .... | .... | .... | .... | .... | .... | .... | .... | .... | .... | .... | .... | .... |
| 1993-94 | Tri-City | WHL | 42 | 3 | 6 | 9 | 122 | .... | .... | .... | .... | .... | .... | .... | .... | .... | .... | .... | .... | .... | .... | .... | .... | .... | .... |
| 1994-95 | Tri-City | WHL | 40 | 2 | 24 | 26 | 140 | .... | .... | .... | .... | .... | .... | .... | .... | .... | .... | .... | .... | .... | .... | .... | .... | .... | .... |
| | Prince George | WHL | 11 | 2 | 3 | 5 | 23 | .... | .... | .... | .... | .... | .... | .... | .... | .... | .... | .... | .... | .... | .... | .... | .... | .... | .... |
| | Albany River Rats | AHL | 7 | 0 | 2 | 2 | 8 | .... | .... | .... | .... | .... | .... | .... | .... | .... | .... | .... | .... | .... | .... | .... | .... | .... | .... |
| 1995-96 | Prince George | WHL | 32 | 9 | 18 | 27 | 91 | .... | .... | .... | .... | .... | .... | .... | .... | .... | .... | .... | .... | .... | .... | .... | .... | .... | .... |
| | Kelowna Rockets | WHL | 27 | 7 | 20 | 27 | 94 | .... | .... | .... | .... | .... | .... | .... | .... | .... | 6 | 0 | 5 | 5 | 2 | .... | .... | .... | .... |
| | Albany River Rats | AHL | 6 | 0 | 2 | 2 | 12 | .... | .... | .... | .... | .... | .... | .... | .... | .... | 4 | 0 | 1 | 1 | 4 | .... | .... | .... | .... |
| 1996-97 | Albany River Rats | AHL | 70 | 2 | 11 | 13 | 160 | .... | .... | .... | .... | .... | .... | .... | .... | .... | 16 | 2 | 3 | 5 | 47 | .... | .... | .... | .... |
| **1997-98** | **New Jersey** | **NHL** | **60** | **3** | **7** | **10** | **85** | **0** | **0** | **1** | **74** | **4.1** | **18** | .... | .... | .... | **3** | **0** | **1** | **1** | **2** | **0** | **0** | **0** | .... |
| | Albany River Rats | AHL | 6 | 0 | 0 | 0 | 8 | .... | .... | .... | .... | .... | .... | .... | .... | .... | .... | .... | .... | .... | .... | .... | .... | .... | .... |
| **1998-99** | **New Jersey** | **NHL** | **70** | **1** | **7** | **8** | **110** | **0** | **0** | **0** | **101** | **1.0** | **5** | **0** | **0.0** | **14:56** | **2** | **0** | **1** | **1** | **0** | **0** | **0** | **0** | **12:57** |
| **99-2000** | **New Jersey** | **NHL** | **52** | **0** | **8** | **8** | **70** | **0** | **0** | **0** | **74** | **0.0** | **−6** | **0** | **0.0** | **17:12** | .... | .... | .... | .... | .... | .... | .... | .... | .... |
| | **Montreal** | **NHL** | **19** | **3** | **0** | **3** | **44** | **0** | **0** | **0** | **39** | **7.7** | **7** | **0** | **0.0** | **19:18** | .... | .... | .... | .... | .... | .... | .... | .... | .... |
| **2000-01** | **Montreal** | **NHL** | **52** | **3** | **8** | **11** | **95** | **0** | **0** | **2** | **103** | **2.9** | **−11** | **0** | **0.0** | **20:36** | .... | .... | .... | .... | .... | .... | .... | .... | .... |
| **2001-02** | **Montreal** | **NHL** | **34** | **3** | **5** | **8** | **62** | **1** | **0** | **0** | **56** | **5.4** | **−5** | **1** | **100.0** | **18:11** | **12** | **0** | **1** | **1** | **16** | **0** | **0** | **0** | **19:01** |
| **2002-03** | **Montreal** | **NHL** | DID NOT PLAY – INJURED | | | | | | | | | | | | | | | | | | | | | | |
| **2003-04** | **Montreal** | **NHL** | **63** | **15** | **20** | **35** | **104** | **6** | **1** | **3** | **186** | **8.1** | **4** | **0** | **0.0** | **23:26** | **11** | **0** | **2** | **2** | **39** | **0** | **0** | **0** | **23:55** |
| 2004-05 | Farjestad | Sweden | 39 | 9 | 8 | 17 | 117 | .... | .... | .... | .... | .... | .... | .... | .... | .... | 15 | 1 | 6 | 7 | 77 | .... | .... | .... | .... |
| **2005-06** | **Montreal** | **NHL** | **75** | **12** | **27** | **39** | **116** | **7** | **1** | **0** | **202** | **5.9** | **−11** | **0** | **0.0** | **22:15** | **6** | **3** | **2** | **5** | **8** | **2** | **0** | **0** | **18:47** |
| **2006-07** | **Montreal** | **NHL** | **81** | **26** | **38** | **64** | **135** | **19** | **1** | **6** | **224** | **11.6** | **−28** | **2** | **100.0** | **23:11** | .... | .... | .... | .... | .... | .... | .... | .... | .... |
| **2007-08** | **Edmonton** | **NHL** | **26** | **3** | **7** | **10** | **36** | **2** | **0** | **1** | **71** | **4.2** | **−7** | **0** | **0.0** | **24:21** | .... | .... | .... | .... | .... | .... | .... | .... | .... |
| **2008-09** | **Edmonton** | **NHL** | **81** | **23** | **30** | **53** | **98** | **12** | **1** | **5** | **268** | **8.6** | **1** | **0** | **0.0** | **24:51** | .... | .... | .... | .... | .... | .... | .... | .... | .... |
| | **NHL Totals** | | **613** | **92** | **157** | **249** | **955** | **47** | **4** | **18** | **1398** | **6.6** | | **3** | **100.0** | **21:06** | **34** | **3** | **7** | **10** | **65** | **2** | **0** | **0** | **20:19** |

WHL West Second All-Star Team (1996)

Played in NHL All-Star Game (2004, 2007, 2009)

Traded to **Montreal** by **New Jersey** with Josh DeWolf and New Jersey's 2nd round choice (later traded to Washington – later traded to Tampa Bay – Tampa Bay selected Andreas Holmqvist) in 2001 Entry Draft for Vladimir Malakhov, March 1, 2000. • Missed remainder of 2001-02 season and entire 2002-03 season recovering from wrist injury suffered in game vs. Tampa Bay, November 17, 2001. Signed as a free agent by **Farjestad** (Sweden), September 22, 2004. Signed as a free agent by **Edmonton**, July 12, 2007. • Missed majority of 2007-08 season recovering from shoulder injury suffered in game at Vancouver, October 13, 2007 and resulting surgery, February 8, 2008.

## SPACEK, Jaroslav

(SPAH-chehk, YAHR-roh-slav) **MTL.**

Defense. Shoots left. 5'11", 204 lbs. Born, Rokycany, Czech., February 11, 1974. Florida's 5th choice, 117th overall, in 1998 Entry Draft.

| | | | Regular Season | | | | | | | | | | | | | | Playoffs | | | | | | | | |
|---|---|---|---|---|---|---|---|---|---|---|---|---|---|---|---|---|---|---|---|---|---|---|---|---|---|
| Season | Club | League | GP | G | A | Pts | PIM | PP | SH | GW | S | % | +/- | TF | F% | Min | GP | G | A | Pts | PIM | PP | SH | GW | Min |
| 1992-93 | HC Skoda Plzen | Czech | 16 | 1 | 3 | 4 | .... | .... | .... | .... | .... | .... | .... | .... | .... | .... | .... | .... | .... | .... | .... | .... | .... | .... | .... |
| 1993-94 | HC Skoda Plzen | CzRep | 34 | 2 | 6 | 8 | .... | .... | .... | .... | .... | .... | .... | .... | .... | .... | .... | .... | .... | .... | .... | .... | .... | .... | .... |
| 1994-95 | Plzen | CzRep | 38 | 4 | 8 | 12 | 14 | .... | .... | .... | .... | .... | .... | .... | .... | .... | 3 | 1 | 0 | 1 | 2 | .... | .... | .... | .... |
| 1995-96 | HC ZKZ Plzen | CzRep | 40 | 3 | 10 | 13 | 42 | .... | .... | .... | .... | .... | .... | .... | .... | .... | 3 | 0 | 1 | 1 | 4 | .... | .... | .... | .... |
| 1996-97 | HC ZKZ Plzen | CzRep | 52 | 9 | 29 | 38 | 44 | .... | .... | .... | .... | .... | .... | .... | .... | .... | .... | .... | .... | .... | .... | .... | .... | .... | .... |
| 1997-98 | Farjestad | Sweden | 45 | 10 | 16 | 26 | 63 | .... | .... | .... | .... | .... | .... | .... | .... | .... | 12 | 2 | 5 | 7 | 14 | .... | .... | .... | .... |
| | Farjestad | EuroHL | 6 | 2 | 3 | 5 | 2 | .... | .... | .... | .... | .... | .... | .... | .... | .... | .... | .... | .... | .... | .... | .... | .... | .... | .... |
| **1998-99** | **Florida** | **NHL** | **63** | **3** | **12** | **15** | **28** | **2** | **1** | **0** | **92** | **3.3** | **15** | **1** | **100.0** | **19:27** | .... | .... | .... | .... | .... | .... | .... | .... | .... |
| | New Haven | AHL | 14 | 4 | 8 | 12 | 15 | .... | .... | .... | .... | .... | .... | .... | .... | .... | .... | .... | .... | .... | .... | .... | .... | .... | .... |
| **99-2000** | **Florida** | **NHL** | **82** | **10** | **26** | **36** | **53** | **4** | **0** | **1** | **111** | **9.0** | **7** | **1** | **0.0** | **22:40** | **4** | **0** | **0** | **0** | **0** | **0** | **0** | **0** | **20:29** |
| **2000-01** | **Florida** | **NHL** | **12** | **2** | **1** | **3** | **8** | **1** | **0** | **0** | **21** | **9.5** | **−4** | **0** | **0.0** | **19:12** | .... | .... | .... | .... | .... | .... | .... | .... | .... |
| | **Chicago** | **NHL** | **50** | **5** | **18** | **23** | **20** | **2** | **0** | **1** | **85** | **5.9** | **7** | **0** | **0.0** | **21:31** | .... | .... | .... | .... | .... | .... | .... | .... | .... |
| **2001-02** | **Chicago** | **NHL** | **60** | **3** | **10** | **13** | **29** | **0** | **0** | **1** | **64** | **4.7** | **5** | **0** | **0.0** | **16:25** | .... | .... | .... | .... | .... | .... | .... | .... | .... |
| | Czech Republic | Olympics | 4 | 0 | 0 | 0 | 0 | .... | .... | .... | .... | .... | .... | .... | .... | .... | .... | .... | .... | .... | .... | .... | .... | .... | .... |
| | **Columbus** | **NHL** | **14** | **2** | **3** | **5** | **24** | **1** | **1** | **1** | **29** | **6.9** | **−9** | **0** | **0.0** | **23:35** | .... | .... | .... | .... | .... | .... | .... | .... | .... |
| **2002-03** | **Columbus** | **NHL** | **81** | **9** | **36** | **45** | **70** | **5** | **0** | **1** | **166** | **5.4** | **−23** | **0** | **0.0** | **24:47** | .... | .... | .... | .... | .... | .... | .... | .... | .... |
| **2003-04** | **Columbus** | **NHL** | **58** | **5** | **17** | **22** | **45** | **2** | **1** | **2** | **108** | **4.6** | **−13** | **0** | **0.0** | **23:26** | .... | .... | .... | .... | .... | .... | .... | .... | .... |
| 2004-05 | Plzen | CzRep | 30 | 3 | 8 | 11 | 26 | .... | .... | .... | .... | .... | .... | .... | .... | .... | .... | .... | .... | .... | .... | .... | .... | .... | .... |
| | HC Slavia Praha | CzRep | 17 | 4 | 9 | 13 | 29 | .... | .... | .... | .... | .... | .... | .... | .... | .... | 7 | 0 | 2 | 2 | 8 | .... | .... | .... | .... |
| **2005-06** | **Chicago** | **NHL** | **45** | **7** | **17** | **24** | **72** | **1** | **0** | **0** | **80** | **8.8** | **8** | **0** | **0.0** | **23:00** | .... | .... | .... | .... | .... | .... | .... | .... | .... |
| | **Edmonton** | **NHL** | **31** | **5** | **14** | **19** | **24** | **3** | **0** | **0** | **70** | **7.1** | **3** | **0** | **0.0** | **24:37** | **24** | **3** | **11** | **14** | **24** | **2** | **0** | **0** | **25:53** |
| **2006-07** | **Buffalo** | **NHL** | **65** | **5** | **16** | **21** | **62** | **1** | **0** | **2** | **78** | **6.4** | **20** | **0** | **0.0** | **19:09** | **16** | **0** | **0** | **0** | **10** | **0** | **0** | **0** | **14:39** |
| **2007-08** | **Buffalo** | **NHL** | **60** | **9** | **23** | **32** | **42** | **7** | **0** | **1** | **95** | **9.5** | **7** | **0** | **0.0** | **22:59** | .... | .... | .... | .... | .... | .... | .... | .... | .... |
| **2008-09** | **Buffalo** | **NHL** | **80** | **8** | **37** | **45** | **38** | **4** | **0** | **0** | **130** | **6.2** | **2** | **0** | **0.0** | **22:17** | .... | .... | .... | .... | .... | .... | .... | .... | .... |
| | **NHL Totals** | | **701** | **73** | **230** | **303** | **515** | **33** | **3** | **10** | **1129** | **6.5** | | **2** | **50.0** | **21:48** | **44** | **3** | **11** | **14** | **34** | **2** | **0** | **0** | **21:18** |

Traded to **Chicago** by **Florida** for Anders Eriksson, November 6, 2000. Traded to **Columbus** by **Chicago** with Chicago's 2nd round choice (Dan Fritsche) in 2003 Entry Draft for Lyle Odelein, March 19, 2002. Signed as a free agent by **Plzen** (CzRep), September 17, 2004. Signed as a free agent by **Slavia Praha** (CzRep), January 4, 2005. Signed as a free agent by **Chicago**, August 3, 2005. Traded to **Edmonton** by **Chicago** for Tony Salmelainen, January 26, 2006. Signed as a free agent by **Buffalo**, July 5, 2006. Signed as a free agent by **Montreal**, July 1, 2009.

## SPEZZA, Jason

(SPEHT-zuh, JAY-suhn) **OTT.**

Center. Shoots right. 6'3", 215 lbs. Born, Mississauga, Ont., June 13, 1983. Ottawa's 1st choice, 2nd overall, in 2001 Entry Draft.

| | | | Regular Season | | | | | | | | | | | | | | Playoffs | | | | | | | | |
|---|---|---|---|---|---|---|---|---|---|---|---|---|---|---|---|---|---|---|---|---|---|---|---|---|---|
| Season | Club | League | GP | G | A | Pts | PIM | PP | SH | GW | S | % | +/- | TF | F% | Min | GP | G | A | Pts | PIM | PP | SH | GW | Min |
| 1997-98 | Toronto Marlies | MTHL | 54 | 53 | 61 | 114 | 42 | .... | .... | .... | .... | .... | .... | .... | .... | .... | .... | .... | .... | .... | .... | .... | .... | .... | .... |
| 1998-99 | Brampton | OHL | 67 | 22 | 49 | 71 | 18 | .... | .... | .... | .... | .... | .... | .... | .... | .... | .... | .... | .... | .... | .... | .... | .... | .... | .... |
| 99-2000 | Mississauga | OHL | 52 | 24 | 37 | 61 | 33 | .... | .... | .... | .... | .... | .... | .... | .... | .... | .... | .... | .... | .... | .... | .... | .... | .... | .... |
| 2000-01 | Mississauga | OHL | 15 | 7 | 23 | 30 | 11 | .... | .... | .... | .... | .... | .... | .... | .... | .... | .... | .... | .... | .... | .... | .... | .... | .... | .... |
| | Windsor Spitfires | OHL | 41 | 36 | 50 | 86 | 32 | .... | .... | .... | .... | .... | .... | .... | .... | .... | 9 | 4 | 5 | 9 | 10 | .... | .... | .... | .... |
| 2001-02 | Windsor Spitfires | OHL | 27 | 19 | 26 | 45 | 16 | .... | .... | .... | .... | .... | .... | .... | .... | .... | .... | .... | .... | .... | .... | .... | .... | .... | .... |
| | Belleville Bulls | OHL | 26 | 23 | 37 | 60 | 26 | .... | .... | .... | .... | .... | .... | .... | .... | .... | 11 | 5 | 6 | 11 | 18 | .... | .... | .... | .... |
| | Grand Rapids | AHL | .... | .... | .... | .... | .... | .... | .... | .... | .... | .... | .... | .... | .... | .... | 3 | 1 | 0 | 1 | 2 | .... | .... | .... | .... |
| **2002-03** | **Ottawa** | **NHL** | **33** | **7** | **14** | **21** | **8** | **3** | **0** | **0** | **65** | **10.8** | **-3** | **330** | **45.8** | **12:40** | **3** | **1** | **1** | **2** | **0** | **1** | **0** | **0** | **11:34** |
| | Binghamton | AHL | 43 | 22 | 32 | 54 | 71 | .... | .... | .... | .... | .... | .... | .... | .... | .... | 2 | 1 | 2 | 3 | 4 | .... | .... | .... | .... |
| **2003-04** | **Ottawa** | **NHL** | **78** | **22** | **33** | **55** | **71** | **5** | **0** | **3** | **142** | **15.5** | **22** | **956** | **47.7** | **14:38** | **3** | **0** | **0** | **0** | **2** | **0** | **0** | **0** | **9:44** |
| 2004-05 | Binghamton | AHL | 80 | 32 | *85 | *117 | 50 | .... | .... | .... | .... | .... | .... | .... | .... | .... | 6 | 1 | 3 | 4 | 6 | .... | .... | .... | .... |
| **2005-06** | **Ottawa** | **NHL** | **68** | **19** | **71** | **90** | **33** | **7** | **0** | **5** | **156** | **12.2** | **23** | **1220** | **52.6** | **19:00** | **10** | **5** | **9** | **14** | **2** | **3** | **0** | **1** | **17:59** |
| **2006-07** | **Ottawa** | **NHL** | **67** | **34** | **53** | **87** | **45** | **13** | **1** | **5** | **162** | **21.0** | **19** | **1261** | **53.0** | **19:17** | **20** | **7** | ***15** | ***22** | **10** | **3** | **0** | **0** | **20:58** |
| **2007-08** | **Ottawa** | **NHL** | **76** | **34** | **58** | **92** | **66** | **11** | **0** | **6** | **210** | **16.2** | **26** | **1445** | **50.5** | **20:40** | **4** | **0** | **1** | **1** | **0** | **0** | **0** | **0** | **19:45** |
| **2008-09** | **Ottawa** | **NHL** | **82** | **32** | **41** | **73** | **79** | **13** | **1** | **3** | **246** | **13.0** | **-14** | **1477** | **53.3** | **19:41** | .... | .... | .... | .... | .... | .... | .... | .... | .... |
| | **NHL Totals** | | **404** | **148** | **270** | **418** | **302** | **52** | **2** | **22** | **981** | **15.1** | | **6689** | **51.3** | **18:09** | **40** | **13** | **26** | **39** | **14** | **7** | **0** | **1** | **18:33** |

OHL All-Rookie Team (1999) • AHL All-Rookie Team (2003) • AHL First All-Star Team (2005) • John P. Sollenberger Trophy (AHL - Top Scorer) (2005) • Les Cunningham Award (AHL – MVP) (2005)
Played in NHL All-Star Game (2008)

## SPILLER, Matthew

(SPIHL-uhr, MA-thew)

Defense. Shoots left. 6'5", 235 lbs. Born, Daysland, Alta., February 7, 1983. Phoenix's 2nd choice, 31st overall, in 2001 Entry Draft.

| Season | Club | League | GP | G | A | Pts | PIM | PP | SH | GW | S | % | +/- | TF | F% | Min | GP | G | A | Pts | PIM | PP | SH | GW | Min |
|---|---|---|---|---|---|---|---|---|---|---|---|---|---|---|---|---|---|---|---|---|---|---|---|---|---|
| 1998-99 | East Central Chill | AMBHL | 36 | 8 | 19 | 27 | 140 | .... | .... | .... | .... | .... | .... | .... | .... | .... | .... | .... | .... | .... | .... | .... | .... | .... | .... |
| 99-2000 | Seattle | WHL | 60 | 1 | 10 | 11 | 108 | .... | .... | .... | .... | .... | .... | .... | .... | .... | 7 | 0 | 0 | 0 | 25 | .... | .... | .... | .... |
| 2000-01 | Seattle | WHL | 71 | 4 | 7 | 11 | 174 | .... | .... | .... | .... | .... | .... | .... | .... | .... | .... | .... | .... | .... | .... | .... | .... | .... | .... |
| 2001-02 | Seattle | WHL | 72 | 8 | 23 | 31 | 168 | .... | .... | .... | .... | .... | .... | .... | .... | .... | 1 | 0 | 0 | 0 | 4 | .... | .... | .... | .... |
| 2002-03 | Seattle | WHL | 68 | 11 | 24 | 35 | 198 | .... | .... | .... | .... | .... | .... | .... | .... | .... | 15 | 2 | 7 | 9 | 36 | .... | .... | .... | .... |
| **2003-04** | **Phoenix** | **NHL** | **51** | **0** | **0** | **0** | **54** | **0** | **0** | **0** | **22** | **0.0** | **-11** | **0** | **0.0** | **10:42** | .... | .... | .... | .... | .... | .... | .... | .... | .... |
| | Springfield | AHL | 21 | 1 | 2 | 3 | 32 | .... | .... | .... | .... | .... | .... | .... | .... | .... | .... | .... | .... | .... | .... | .... | .... | .... | .... |
| 2004-05 | Utah Grizzlies | AHL | 79 | 4 | 7 | 11 | 160 | .... | .... | .... | .... | .... | .... | .... | .... | .... | .... | .... | .... | .... | .... | .... | .... | .... | .... |
| **2005-06** | **Phoenix** | **NHL** | **8** | **0** | **1** | **1** | **13** | **0** | **0** | **0** | **3** | **0.0** | **-1** | **0** | **0.0** | **10:30** | .... | .... | .... | .... | .... | .... | .... | .... | .... |
| | San Antonio | AHL | 69 | 2 | 7 | 9 | 167 | .... | .... | .... | .... | .... | .... | .... | .... | .... | .... | .... | .... | .... | .... | .... | .... | .... | .... |
| 2006-07 | San Antonio | AHL | 80 | 1 | 7 | 8 | 187 | .... | .... | .... | .... | .... | .... | .... | .... | .... | .... | .... | .... | .... | .... | .... | .... | .... | .... |
| **2007-08** | **NY Islanders** | **NHL** | **9** | **0** | **1** | **1** | **7** | **0** | **0** | **0** | **6** | **0.0** | **-2** | **0** | **0.0** | **19:47** | .... | .... | .... | .... | .... | .... | .... | .... | .... |
| | Bridgeport | AHL | 75 | 1 | 6 | 7 | 177 | .... | .... | .... | .... | .... | .... | .... | .... | .... | .... | .... | .... | .... | .... | .... | .... | .... | .... |
| 2008-09 | Lowell Devils | AHL | 71 | 2 | 11 | 13 | 90 | .... | .... | .... | .... | .... | .... | .... | .... | .... | .... | .... | .... | .... | .... | .... | .... | .... | .... |
| | **NHL Totals** | | **68** | **0** | **2** | **2** | **74** | **0** | **0** | **0** | **31** | **0.0** | | **0** | **0.0** | **11:53** | .... | .... | .... | .... | .... | .... | .... | .... | .... |

Signed as a free agent by **NY Islanders**, July 3, 2007. Signed as a free agent by **New Jersey**, July, 2008.

## SPRUKTS, Janis

(SPRUKTS, YAN-ish)

Center. Shoots left. 6'3", 235 lbs. Born, Riga, Latvia, January 31, 1982. Florida's 7th choice, 234th overall, in 2000 Entry Draft.

| Season | Club | League | GP | G | A | Pts | PIM | PP | SH | GW | S | % | +/- | TF | F% | Min | GP | G | A | Pts | PIM | PP | SH | GW | Min |
|---|---|---|---|---|---|---|---|---|---|---|---|---|---|---|---|---|---|---|---|---|---|---|---|---|---|
| 99-2000 | Lukko Rauma Jr. | Fin-Jr. | 26 | 2 | 5 | 7 | 6 | .... | .... | .... | .... | .... | .... | .... | .... | .... | 3 | 0 | 0 | 0 | 0 | .... | .... | .... | .... |
| | HC Essamika Jr. | EEHL-2 | 2 | 4 | 4 | 8 | 0 | .... | .... | .... | .... | .... | .... | .... | .... | .... | .... | .... | .... | .... | .... | .... | .... | .... | .... |
| 2000-01 | Lukko Rauma Jr. | Fin-Jr. | 36 | 15 | 22 | 37 | 24 | .... | .... | .... | .... | .... | .... | .... | .... | .... | 3 | 0 | 0 | 0 | 0 | .... | .... | .... | .... |
| | Lukko Rauma | Finland | 9 | 0 | 0 | 0 | 2 | .... | .... | .... | .... | .... | .... | .... | .... | .... | .... | .... | .... | .... | .... | .... | .... | .... | .... |
| 2001-02 | Acadie-Bathurst | QMJHL | 63 | 35 | 44 | 79 | 46 | .... | .... | .... | .... | .... | .... | .... | .... | .... | 16 | 14 | 8 | 22 | 12 | .... | .... | .... | .... |
| 2002-03 | Sport Vaasa | Finland-2 | 21 | 5 | 6 | 11 | 8 | .... | .... | .... | .... | .... | .... | .... | .... | .... | .... | .... | .... | .... | .... | .... | .... | .... | .... |
| | Acadie-Bathurst | QMJHL | 30 | 9 | 29 | 38 | 12 | .... | .... | .... | .... | .... | .... | .... | .... | .... | 11 | 3 | 5 | 8 | 0 | .... | .... | .... | .... |
| 2003-04 | ASK Ogre | Latvia | 5 | 2 | 4 | 6 | 0 | .... | .... | .... | .... | .... | .... | .... | .... | .... | .... | .... | .... | .... | .... | .... | .... | .... | .... |
| | Odense IK | Denmark | 2 | 0 | 1 | 1 | 2 | .... | .... | .... | .... | .... | .... | .... | .... | .... | .... | .... | .... | .... | .... | .... | .... | .... | .... |
| 2004-05 | HK Riga 2000 | BelOpen | 21 | 7 | 9 | 16 | 10 | .... | .... | .... | .... | .... | .... | .... | .... | .... | 3 | 0 | 0 | 0 | 2 | .... | .... | .... | .... |
| | HK Riga 2000 | Latvia | 3 | 2 | 3 | 5 | 0 | .... | .... | .... | .... | .... | .... | .... | .... | .... | 9 | 3 | 4 | 7 | 2 | .... | .... | .... | .... |
| 2005-06 | HPK Hameenlinna | Finland | 35 | 18 | 10 | 28 | 14 | .... | .... | .... | .... | .... | .... | .... | .... | .... | 13 | 3 | 4 | 7 | 14 | .... | .... | .... | .... |
| **2006-07** | **Florida** | **NHL** | **13** | **1** | **2** | **3** | **2** | **0** | **0** | **0** | **10** | **10.0** | **1** | **61** | **44.3** | **6:19** | .... | .... | .... | .... | .... | .... | .... | .... | .... |
| | Rochester | AHL | 58 | 18 | 41 | 59 | 60 | .... | .... | .... | .... | .... | .... | .... | .... | .... | 6 | 1 | 3 | 4 | 4 | .... | .... | .... | .... |
| 2007-08 | Lukko Rauma | Finland | 53 | 12 | 17 | 29 | 20 | .... | .... | .... | .... | .... | .... | .... | .... | .... | 3 | 0 | 1 | 1 | 0 | .... | .... | .... | .... |
| **2008-09** | **Florida** | **NHL** | **1** | **0** | **0** | **0** | **0** | **0** | **0** | **0** | **1** | **0.0** | **0** | **0** | **0.0** | **12:19** | .... | .... | .... | .... | .... | .... | .... | .... | .... |
| | Rochester | AHL | 59 | 16 | 31 | 47 | 20 | .... | .... | .... | .... | .... | .... | .... | .... | .... | .... | .... | .... | .... | .... | .... | .... | .... | .... |
| | **NHL Totals** | | **14** | **1** | **2** | **3** | **2** | **0** | **0** | **0** | **11** | **9.1** | | **61** | **44.3** | **6:45** | .... | .... | .... | .... | .... | .... | .... | .... | .... |

• Released by **Vaasa** (Finland-2) and returned to **Acadie-Bathurst** (QMJHL), January 3, 2003.

## STAAL, Eric

(STAHL, AIR-ihk) **CAR.**

Center. Shoots left. 6'4", 205 lbs. Born, Thunder Bay, Ont., October 29, 1984. Carolina's 1st choice, 2nd overall, in 2003 Entry Draft.

| Season | Club | League | GP | G | A | Pts | PIM | PP | SH | GW | S | % | +/- | TF | F% | Min | GP | G | A | Pts | PIM | PP | SH | GW | Min |
|---|---|---|---|---|---|---|---|---|---|---|---|---|---|---|---|---|---|---|---|---|---|---|---|---|---|
| 99-2000 | Thunder Bay | Exhib. | 7 | 4 | 8 | 12 | 0 | .... | .... | .... | .... | .... | .... | .... | .... | .... | .... | .... | .... | .... | .... | .... | .... | .... | .... |
| 2000-01 | Peterborough | OHL | 63 | 19 | 30 | 49 | 23 | .... | .... | .... | .... | .... | .... | .... | .... | .... | 7 | 2 | 5 | 7 | 4 | .... | .... | .... | .... |
| 2001-02 | Peterborough | OHL | 56 | 23 | 39 | 62 | 40 | .... | .... | .... | .... | .... | .... | .... | .... | .... | 6 | 3 | 6 | 9 | 10 | .... | .... | .... | .... |
| 2002-03 | Peterborough | OHL | 66 | 39 | 59 | 98 | 36 | .... | .... | .... | .... | .... | .... | .... | .... | .... | 7 | 9 | 5 | 14 | 6 | .... | .... | .... | .... |
| **2003-04** | **Carolina** | **NHL** | **81** | **11** | **20** | **31** | **40** | **2** | **1** | **3** | **164** | **6.7** | **-6** | **669** | **43.1** | **16:40** | .... | .... | .... | .... | .... | .... | .... | .... | .... |
| 2004-05 | Lowell | AHL | 77 | 26 | 51 | 77 | 88 | .... | .... | .... | .... | .... | .... | .... | .... | .... | 11 | 2 | 8 | 10 | 12 | .... | .... | .... | .... |
| **2005-06** ♦ | **Carolina** | **NHL** | **82** | **45** | **55** | **100** | **81** | **19** | **4** | **4** | **279** | **16.1** | **-8** | **1309** | **42.6** | **19:39** | **25** | **9** | ***19** | ***28** | **8** | **7** | **0** | **1** | **19:48** |
| **2006-07** | **Carolina** | **NHL** | **82** | **30** | **40** | **70** | **68** | **12** | **1** | **1** | **288** | **10.4** | **-6** | **1238** | **45.2** | **20:08** | .... | .... | .... | .... | .... | .... | .... | .... | .... |
| **2007-08** | **Carolina** | **NHL** | **82** | **38** | **44** | **82** | **50** | **14** | **0** | **7** | **310** | **12.3** | **-2** | **1708** | **44.9** | **21:38** | .... | .... | .... | .... | .... | .... | .... | .... | .... |
| **2008-09** | **Carolina** | **NHL** | **82** | **40** | **35** | **75** | **50** | **14** | **1** | **8** | **372** | **10.8** | **15** | **1586** | **45.3** | **21:03** | **18** | **10** | **5** | **15** | **4** | **3** | **0** | **1** | **21:31** |
| | **NHL Totals** | | **409** | **164** | **194** | **358** | **289** | **61** | **7** | **23** | **1413** | **11.6** | | **6510** | **44.4** | **19:50** | **43** | **19** | **24** | **43** | **12** | **10** | **0** | **2** | **20:31** |

OHL Second All-Star Team (2003) • Canadian Major Junior First All-Star Team (2003) • NHL Second All-Star Team (2006)
Played in NHL All-Star Game (2007, 2008, 2009)

## STAAL, Jordan

(STAHL, JOHR-dahn) **PIT.**

Center. Shoots left. 6'4", 220 lbs. Born, Thunder Bay, Ont., September 10, 1988. Pittsburgh's 1st choice, 2nd overall, in 2006 Entry Draft.

| Season | Club | League | GP | G | A | Pts | PIM | PP | SH | GW | S | % | +/- | TF | F% | Min | GP | G | A | Pts | PIM | PP | SH | GW | Min |
|---|---|---|---|---|---|---|---|---|---|---|---|---|---|---|---|---|---|---|---|---|---|---|---|---|---|
| 2004-05 | Peterborough | OHL | 66 | 9 | 19 | 28 | 29 | .... | .... | .... | .... | .... | .... | .... | .... | .... | 14 | 5 | 5 | 10 | 16 | .... | .... | .... | .... |
| 2005-06 | Peterborough | OHL | 68 | 28 | 40 | 68 | 69 | .... | .... | .... | .... | .... | .... | .... | .... | .... | 19 | 10 | 6 | 16 | 16 | .... | .... | .... | .... |
| **2006-07** | **Pittsburgh** | **NHL** | **81** | **29** | **13** | **42** | **24** | **4** | **7** | **4** | **131** | **22.1** | **16** | **383** | **37.1** | **14:56** | **5** | **3** | **0** | **3** | **2** | **0** | **0** | **0** | **16:00** |
| **2007-08** | **Pittsburgh** | **NHL** | **82** | **12** | **16** | **28** | **55** | **3** | **0** | **4** | **183** | **6.6** | **-5** | **1202** | **42.2** | **18:16** | **20** | **6** | **1** | **7** | **14** | **1** | **0** | **1** | **18:16** |
| **2008-09** ♦ | **Pittsburgh** | **NHL** | **82** | **22** | **27** | **49** | **37** | **2** | **1** | **3** | **166** | **13.3** | **5** | **1206** | **47.0** | **19:51** | **24** | **4** | **5** | **9** | **8** | **0** | **1** | **0** | **19:13** |
| | **NHL Totals** | | **245** | **63** | **56** | **119** | **116** | **9** | **8** | **11** | **480** | **13.1** | | **2791** | **43.6** | **17:42** | **49** | **13** | **6** | **19** | **24** | **1** | **1** | **1** | **18:30** |

NHL All-Rookie Team (2007)

## STAAL, Marc

(STAHL, MAHRK) **NYR**

Defense. Shoots left. 6'4", 209 lbs. Born, Thunder Bay, Ont., January 13, 1987. NY Rangers' 1st choice, 12th overall, in 2005 Entry Draft.

| Season | Club | League | GP | G | A | Pts | PIM | PP | SH | GW | S | % | +/- | TF | F% | Min | GP | G | A | Pts | PIM | PP | SH | GW | Min |
|---|---|---|---|---|---|---|---|---|---|---|---|---|---|---|---|---|---|---|---|---|---|---|---|---|---|
| 2003-04 | Sudbury Wolves | OHL | 61 | 1 | 13 | 14 | 34 | .... | .... | .... | .... | .... | .... | .... | .... | .... | 7 | 1 | 2 | 3 | 2 | .... | .... | .... | .... |
| 2004-05 | Sudbury Wolves | OHL | 65 | 6 | 20 | 26 | 53 | .... | .... | .... | .... | .... | .... | .... | .... | .... | 12 | 0 | 4 | 4 | 15 | .... | .... | .... | .... |
| 2005-06 | Sudbury Wolves | OHL | 57 | 11 | 38 | 49 | 60 | .... | .... | .... | .... | .... | .... | .... | .... | .... | 10 | 0 | 8 | 8 | 8 | .... | .... | .... | .... |
| | Hartford | AHL | .... | .... | .... | .... | .... | .... | .... | .... | .... | .... | .... | .... | .... | .... | 12 | 0 | 2 | 2 | 8 | .... | .... | .... | .... |
| 2006-07 | Sudbury Wolves | OHL | 53 | 5 | 29 | 34 | 68 | .... | .... | .... | .... | .... | .... | .... | .... | .... | 21 | 5 | 15 | 20 | 22 | .... | .... | .... | .... |
| **2007-08** | **NY Rangers** | **NHL** | **80** | **2** | **8** | **10** | **42** | **0** | **0** | **0** | **78** | **2.6** | **2** | **0** | **0.0** | **18:48** | **10** | **1** | **2** | **3** | **8** | **0** | **0** | **1** | **22:21** |
| **2008-09** | **NY Rangers** | **NHL** | **82** | **3** | **12** | **15** | **64** | **0** | **0** | **1** | **96** | **3.1** | **-7** | **0** | **0.0** | **21:08** | **7** | **1** | **0** | **1** | **0** | **0** | **0** | **0** | **21:33** |
| | **NHL Totals** | | **162** | **5** | **20** | **25** | **106** | **0** | **0** | **1** | **174** | **2.9** | | **0** | **0.0** | **19:59** | **17** | **2** | **2** | **4** | **8** | **0** | **0** | **1** | **22:01** |

OHL First All-Star Team (2006, 2007) • Canadian Major Junior First All-Star Team (2006, 2007)

| Season | Club | League | Regular Season GP | G | A | Pts | PIM | PP | SH | GW | S | % | +/- | TF | F% | Min | Playoffs GP | G | A | Pts | PIM | PP | SH | GW | Min |
|---|---|---|---|---|---|---|---|---|---|---|---|---|---|---|---|---|---|---|---|---|---|---|---|---|---|

## STAFFORD, Drew

(STA-fuhrd, DROO) **BUF.**

Right wing. Shoots right. 6'2", 216 lbs. Born, Milwaukee, WI, October 30, 1985. Buffalo's 1st choice, 13th overall, in 2004 Entry Draft.

| Season | Club | League | GP | G | A | Pts | PIM | PP | SH | GW | S | % | +/- | TF | F% | Min | GP | G | A | Pts | PIM | PP | SH | GW | Min |
|---|---|---|---|---|---|---|---|---|---|---|---|---|---|---|---|---|---|---|---|---|---|---|---|---|---|
| 2001-02 | Shat.-St. Mary's | High-MN | 45 | 35 | 53 | 88 | 30 | .... | .... | .... | .... | .... | .... | .... | .... | .... | .... | .... | .... | .... | .... | .... | .... | .... | .... |
| 2002-03 | Shat.-St. Mary's | High-MN | 65 | 49 | 67 | 116 | .... | .... | .... | .... | .... | .... | .... | .... | .... | .... | .... | .... | .... | .... | .... | .... | .... | .... | .... |
| 2003-04 | North Dakota | WCHA | 36 | 11 | 21 | 32 | 30 | .... | .... | .... | .... | .... | .... | .... | .... | .... | .... | .... | .... | .... | .... | .... | .... | .... | .... |
| 2004-05 | North Dakota | WCHA | 42 | 13 | 25 | 38 | 34 | .... | .... | .... | .... | .... | .... | .... | .... | .... | .... | .... | .... | .... | .... | .... | .... | .... | .... |
| 2005-06 | North Dakota | WCHA | 42 | 24 | 24 | 48 | 63 | .... | .... | .... | .... | .... | .... | .... | .... | .... | .... | .... | .... | .... | .... | .... | .... | .... | .... |
| **2006-07** | **Buffalo** | **NHL** | **41** | **13** | **14** | **27** | **33** | **3** | **0** | **3** | **67** | **19.4** | **5** | **13** | **46.2** | **13:08** | **10** | **2** | **2** | **4** | **4** | **0** | **0** | **0** | **11:52** |
| | Rochester | AHL | 34 | 22 | 22 | 44 | 30 | .... | .... | .... | .... | .... | .... | .... | .... | .... | .... | .... | .... | .... | .... | .... | .... | .... | .... |
| **2007-08** | **Buffalo** | **NHL** | **64** | **16** | **22** | **38** | **51** | **1** | **0** | **5** | **103** | **15.5** | **3** | **21** | **38.1** | **13:32** | .... | .... | .... | .... | .... | .... | .... | .... | .... |
| **2008-09** | **Buffalo** | **NHL** | **79** | **20** | **25** | **45** | **29** | **9** | **0** | **0** | **183** | **10.9** | **3** | **20** | **20.0** | **15:38** | .... | .... | .... | .... | .... | .... | .... | .... | .... |
| | **NHL Totals** | | **184** | **49** | **61** | **110** | **113** | **13** | **0** | **8** | **353** | **13.9** | | **54** | **33.3** | **14:21** | **10** | **2** | **2** | **4** | **4** | **0** | **0** | **0** | **11:52** |

## STAFFORD, Garrett

(STA-fuhrd, GAIR-reht) **DAL.**

Defense. Shoots right. 6', 200 lbs. Born, Los Angeles, CA, January 28, 1980.

| Season | Club | League | GP | G | A | Pts | PIM | PP | SH | GW | S | % | +/- | TF | F% | Min | GP | G | A | Pts | PIM | PP | SH | GW | Min |
|---|---|---|---|---|---|---|---|---|---|---|---|---|---|---|---|---|---|---|---|---|---|---|---|---|---|
| 1996-97 | Des Moines | USHL | 37 | 1 | 10 | 11 | 40 | .... | .... | .... | .... | .... | .... | .... | .... | .... | 5 | 0 | 0 | 0 | 0 | .... | .... | .... | .... |
| 1997-98 | Des Moines | USHL | 53 | 6 | 17 | 23 | 89 | .... | .... | .... | .... | .... | .... | .... | .... | .... | 12 | 1 | 3 | 4 | 42 | .... | .... | .... | .... |
| 1998-99 | Des Moines | USHL | 56 | 8 | 33 | 41 | 54 | .... | .... | .... | .... | .... | .... | .... | .... | .... | 13 | 2 | 2 | 4 | 18 | .... | .... | .... | .... |
| 99-2000 | New Hampshire | H-East | 38 | 3 | 9 | 12 | 28 | .... | .... | .... | .... | .... | .... | .... | .... | .... | .... | .... | .... | .... | .... | .... | .... | .... | .... |
| 2000-01 | New Hampshire | H-East | 37 | 5 | 21 | 26 | 44 | .... | .... | .... | .... | .... | .... | .... | .... | .... | .... | .... | .... | .... | .... | .... | .... | .... | .... |
| 2001-02 | New Hampshire | H-East | 36 | 5 | 22 | 27 | 42 | .... | .... | .... | .... | .... | .... | .... | .... | .... | .... | .... | .... | .... | .... | .... | .... | .... | .... |
| 2002-03 | New Hampshire | H-East | 23 | 1 | 15 | 16 | 24 | .... | .... | .... | .... | .... | .... | .... | .... | .... | .... | .... | .... | .... | .... | .... | .... | .... | .... |
| 2003-04 | Cleveland Barons | AHL | 73 | 12 | 34 | 46 | 71 | .... | .... | .... | .... | .... | .... | .... | .... | .... | 6 | 0 | 0 | 0 | 6 | .... | .... | .... | .... |
| 2004-05 | Cleveland Barons | AHL | 68 | 6 | 18 | 24 | 55 | .... | .... | .... | .... | .... | .... | .... | .... | .... | .... | .... | .... | .... | .... | .... | .... | .... | .... |
| 2005-06 | Cleveland Barons | AHL | 80 | 11 | 28 | 39 | 86 | .... | .... | .... | .... | .... | .... | .... | .... | .... | .... | .... | .... | .... | .... | .... | .... | .... | .... |
| 2006-07 | Worcester Sharks | AHL | 77 | 11 | 30 | 41 | 58 | .... | .... | .... | .... | .... | .... | .... | .... | .... | 6 | 0 | 3 | 3 | 2 | .... | .... | .... | .... |
| **2007-08** | **Detroit** | **NHL** | **2** | **0** | **0** | **0** | **0** | **0** | **0** | **0** | **1** | **0.0** | **0** | **0** | **0.0** | **6:45** | .... | .... | .... | .... | .... | .... | .... | .... | .... |
| | Grand Rapids | AHL | 69 | 11 | 33 | 44 | 36 | .... | .... | .... | .... | .... | .... | .... | .... | .... | .... | .... | .... | .... | .... | .... | .... | .... | .... |
| **2008-09** | **Dallas** | **NHL** | **3** | **0** | **2** | **2** | **0** | **0** | **0** | **0** | **5** | **0.0** | **0** | **0** | **0.0** | **18:00** | .... | .... | .... | .... | .... | .... | .... | .... | .... |
| | Grand Rapids | AHL | 70 | 11 | 34 | 45 | 50 | .... | .... | .... | .... | .... | .... | .... | .... | .... | 10 | 0 | 5 | 5 | 4 | .... | .... | .... | .... |
| | **NHL Totals** | | **5** | **0** | **2** | **2** | **0** | **0** | **0** | **0** | **6** | **0.0** | | **0** | **0.0** | **13:30** | .... | .... | .... | .... | .... | .... | .... | .... | .... |

Hockey East Second All-Star Team (2002) • AHL All-Rookie Team (2004) • AHL Second All-Star Team (2004)

Signed as a free agent by **Cleveland** (AHL), October 10, 2003. Signed as a free agent by **San Jose**, December 9, 2003. Signed as a free agent by **Detroit**, July 16, 2007. Signed as a free agent by **Dallas**, July 3, 2008.

## STAIOS, Steve

(STAY-ohs, STEEV) **EDM.**

Defense. Shoots right. 6'1", 200 lbs. Born, Hamilton, Ont., July 28, 1973. St. Louis' 1st choice, 27th overall, in 1991 Entry Draft.

| Season | Club | League | GP | G | A | Pts | PIM | PP | SH | GW | S | % | +/- | TF | F% | Min | GP | G | A | Pts | PIM | PP | SH | GW | Min |
|---|---|---|---|---|---|---|---|---|---|---|---|---|---|---|---|---|---|---|---|---|---|---|---|---|---|
| 1988-89 | Hamilton Huskies | Minor-ON | 58 | 13 | 39 | 52 | 78 | .... | .... | .... | .... | .... | .... | .... | .... | .... | .... | .... | .... | .... | .... | .... | .... | .... | .... |
| 1989-90 | Hamilton Kilty B's | OHA-B | 40 | 9 | 27 | 36 | 66 | .... | .... | .... | .... | .... | .... | .... | .... | .... | .... | .... | .... | .... | .... | .... | .... | .... | .... |
| 1990-91 | Niagara Falls | OHL | 66 | 17 | 29 | 46 | 115 | .... | .... | .... | .... | .... | .... | .... | .... | .... | 12 | 2 | 3 | 5 | 10 | .... | .... | .... | .... |
| 1991-92 | Niagara Falls | OHL | 65 | 11 | 42 | 53 | 122 | .... | .... | .... | .... | .... | .... | .... | .... | .... | 17 | 7 | 8 | 15 | 27 | .... | .... | .... | .... |
| 1992-93 | Niagara Falls | OHL | 12 | 4 | 14 | 18 | 30 | .... | .... | .... | .... | .... | .... | .... | .... | .... | .... | .... | .... | .... | .... | .... | .... | .... | .... |
| | Sudbury Wolves | OHL | 53 | 13 | 44 | 57 | 67 | .... | .... | .... | .... | .... | .... | .... | .... | .... | 11 | 5 | 6 | 11 | 22 | .... | .... | .... | .... |
| 1993-94 | Peoria Rivermen | IHL | 38 | 3 | 9 | 12 | 42 | .... | .... | .... | .... | .... | .... | .... | .... | .... | .... | .... | .... | .... | .... | .... | .... | .... | .... |
| 1994-95 | Peoria Rivermen | IHL | 60 | 3 | 13 | 16 | 64 | .... | .... | .... | .... | .... | .... | .... | .... | .... | 6 | 0 | 0 | 0 | 10 | .... | .... | .... | .... |
| **1995-96** | Peoria Rivermen | IHL | 6 | 0 | 1 | 1 | 14 | .... | .... | .... | .... | .... | .... | .... | .... | .... | .... | .... | .... | .... | .... | .... | .... | .... | .... |
| | Worcester IceCats | AHL | 57 | 1 | 11 | 12 | 114 | .... | .... | .... | .... | .... | .... | .... | .... | .... | .... | .... | .... | .... | .... | .... | .... | .... | .... |
| | **Boston** | **NHL** | **12** | **0** | **0** | **0** | **4** | **0** | **0** | **0** | **4** | **0.0** | **–5** | .... | .... | .... | **3** | **0** | **0** | **0** | **0** | **0** | **0** | **0** | .... |
| | Providence Bruins | AHL | 7 | 1 | 4 | 5 | 8 | .... | .... | .... | .... | .... | .... | .... | .... | .... | .... | .... | .... | .... | .... | .... | .... | .... | .... |
| **1996-97** | **Boston** | **NHL** | **54** | **3** | **8** | **11** | **71** | **0** | **0** | **0** | **56** | **5.4** | **–26** | .... | .... | .... | .... | .... | .... | .... | .... | .... | .... | .... | .... |
| | **Vancouver** | **NHL** | **9** | **0** | **6** | **6** | **20** | **0** | **0** | **0** | **10** | **0.0** | **2** | .... | .... | .... | .... | .... | .... | .... | .... | .... | .... | .... | .... |
| **1997-98** | **Vancouver** | **NHL** | **77** | **3** | **4** | **7** | **134** | **0** | **0** | **1** | **45** | **6.7** | **–3** | .... | .... | .... | .... | .... | .... | .... | .... | .... | .... | .... | .... |
| **1998-99** | **Vancouver** | **NHL** | **57** | **0** | **2** | **2** | **54** | **0** | **0** | **0** | **33** | **0.0** | **–12** | **4** | **25.0** | **6:53** | .... | .... | .... | .... | .... | .... | .... | .... | .... |
| **99-2000** | **Atlanta** | **NHL** | **27** | **2** | **3** | **5** | **66** | **0** | **0** | **0** | **38** | **5.3** | **–5** | **2** | **50.0** | **13:01** | .... | .... | .... | .... | .... | .... | .... | .... | .... |
| **2000-01** | **Atlanta** | **NHL** | **70** | **9** | **13** | **22** | **137** | **4** | **0** | **0** | **156** | **5.8** | **–23** | **1** | **0.0** | **21:45** | .... | .... | .... | .... | .... | .... | .... | .... | .... |
| **2001-02** | **Edmonton** | **NHL** | **73** | **5** | **5** | **10** | **108** | **0** | **0** | **1** | **101** | **5.0** | **10** | **0** | **0.0** | **18:05** | .... | .... | .... | .... | .... | .... | .... | .... | .... |
| **2002-03** | **Edmonton** | **NHL** | **76** | **5** | **21** | **26** | **96** | **1** | **3** | **0** | **126** | **4.0** | **13** | **1** | **0.0** | **22:17** | **6** | **0** | **0** | **0** | **4** | **0** | **0** | **0** | **23:27** |
| **2003-04** | **Edmonton** | **NHL** | **82** | **6** | **22** | **28** | **86** | **1** | **0** | **1** | **153** | **3.9** | **17** | **0** | **0.0** | **23:03** | .... | .... | .... | .... | .... | .... | .... | .... | .... |
| 2004-05 | Lulea HF | Sweden | 7 | 2 | 1 | 3 | 12 | .... | .... | .... | .... | .... | .... | .... | .... | .... | .... | .... | .... | .... | .... | .... | .... | .... | .... |
| **2005-06** | **Edmonton** | **NHL** | **82** | **8** | **20** | **28** | **84** | **1** | **0** | **1** | **140** | **5.7** | **10** | **0** | **0.0** | **20:53** | **24** | **1** | **5** | **6** | **28** | **1** | **0** | **0** | **21:31** |
| **2006-07** | **Edmonton** | **NHL** | **58** | **2** | **15** | **17** | **97** | **0** | **0** | **0** | **71** | **2.8** | **–5** | **0** | **0.0** | **21:23** | .... | .... | .... | .... | .... | .... | .... | .... | .... |
| **2007-08** | **Edmonton** | **NHL** | **82** | **7** | **9** | **16** | **121** | **1** | **0** | **0** | **73** | **9.6** | **–14** | **1** | **100.0** | **22:01** | .... | .... | .... | .... | .... | .... | .... | .... | .... |
| **2008-09** | **Edmonton** | **NHL** | **80** | **2** | **12** | **14** | **92** | **0** | **0** | **0** | **78** | **2.6** | **–5** | **0** | **0.0** | **19:48** | .... | .... | .... | .... | .... | .... | .... | .... | .... |
| | **NHL Totals** | | **839** | **52** | **140** | **192** | **1170** | **8** | **3** | **4** | **1084** | **4.8** | | **9** | **33.3** | **19:40** | **33** | **1** | **5** | **6** | **32** | **1** | **0** | **0** | **21:54** |

Traded to **Boston** by **St. Louis** with Kevin Sawyer for Steve Leach, March 8, 1996. Claimed on waivers by **Vancouver** from **Boston**, March 18, 1997. Claimed by **Atlanta** from **Vancouver** in Expansion Draft, June 25, 1999. • Missed majority of 1999-2000 season recovering from knee injury suffered in game vs. Colorado, October 23, 1999. Traded to **New Jersey** by **Atlanta** for New Jersey's 9th round choice (Simon Gamache) in 2000 Entry Draft, June 12, 2000. Traded to **Atlanta** by **New Jersey** for future considerations, July 10, 2000. Signed as a free agent by **Edmonton**, July 12, 2001. Signed as a free agent by **Lulea** (Sweden), January 28, 2005.

## STAJAN, Matt

(STAY-juhn, MAHT) **TOR.**

Center. Shoots left. 6'1", 200 lbs. Born, Mississauga, Ont., December 19, 1983. Toronto's 2nd choice, 57th overall, in 2002 Entry Draft.

| Season | Club | League | GP | G | A | Pts | PIM | PP | SH | GW | S | % | +/- | TF | F% | Min | GP | G | A | Pts | PIM | PP | SH | GW | Min |
|---|---|---|---|---|---|---|---|---|---|---|---|---|---|---|---|---|---|---|---|---|---|---|---|---|---|
| 99-2000 | Miss. Senators | GTHL | STATISTICS NOT AVAILABLE | | | | | | | | | | | | | | | | | | | | | | |
| 2000-01 | Belleville Bulls | OHL | 57 | 9 | 18 | 27 | 27 | .... | .... | .... | .... | .... | .... | .... | .... | .... | 7 | 1 | 6 | 7 | 5 | .... | .... | .... | .... |
| 2001-02 | Belleville Bulls | OHL | 68 | 33 | 52 | 85 | 50 | .... | .... | .... | .... | .... | .... | .... | .... | .... | 11 | 3 | 8 | 11 | 14 | .... | .... | .... | .... |
| **2002-03** | Belleville Bulls | OHL | 57 | 34 | 60 | 94 | 75 | .... | .... | .... | .... | .... | .... | .... | .... | .... | 7 | 5 | 8 | 13 | 16 | .... | .... | .... | .... |
| | St. John's | AHL | 1 | 0 | 1 | 1 | 0 | .... | .... | .... | .... | .... | .... | .... | .... | .... | .... | .... | .... | .... | .... | .... | .... | .... | .... |
| | **Toronto** | **NHL** | **1** | **1** | **0** | **1** | **0** | **0** | **0** | **0** | **1** | **100.0** | **1** | **12** | **33.3** | **11:00** | .... | .... | .... | .... | .... | .... | .... | .... | .... |
| **2003-04** | **Toronto** | **NHL** | **69** | **14** | **13** | **27** | **22** | **0** | **0** | **0** | **63** | **22.2** | **7** | **450** | **38.9** | **11:00** | **3** | **0** | **0** | **0** | **2** | **0** | **0** | **0** | **11:13** |
| 2004-05 | St. John's | AHL | 80 | 23 | 43 | 66 | 43 | .... | .... | .... | .... | .... | .... | .... | .... | .... | 5 | 2 | 2 | 4 | 6 | .... | .... | .... | .... |
| **2005-06** | **Toronto** | **NHL** | **80** | **15** | **12** | **27** | **50** | **3** | **4** | **5** | **83** | **18.1** | **5** | **373** | **44.5** | **11:38** | .... | .... | .... | .... | .... | .... | .... | .... | .... |
| **2006-07** | **Toronto** | **NHL** | **82** | **10** | **29** | **39** | **44** | **1** | **1** | **1** | **132** | **7.6** | **3** | **985** | **46.1** | **16:09** | .... | .... | .... | .... | .... | .... | .... | .... | .... |
| **2007-08** | **Toronto** | **NHL** | **82** | **16** | **17** | **33** | **47** | **2** | **1** | **3** | **127** | **12.6** | **–11** | **1293** | **47.6** | **18:54** | .... | .... | .... | .... | .... | .... | .... | .... | .... |
| **2008-09** | **Toronto** | **NHL** | **76** | **15** | **40** | **55** | **54** | **5** | **1** | **1** | **114** | **13.2** | **–4** | **1177** | **51.4** | **16:56** | .... | .... | .... | .... | .... | .... | .... | .... | .... |
| | **NHL Totals** | | **390** | **71** | **111** | **182** | **217** | **11** | **7** | **10** | **520** | **13.7** | | **4290** | **47.1** | **15:02** | **3** | **0** | **0** | **0** | **2** | **0** | **0** | **0** | **11:13** |

• Scored a goal in his first NHL game (April 5, 2003 vs. Ottawa).

## STAMKOS, Steven

(STAM-kohs, STEE-vehn) **T.B.**

Center. Shoots right. 6'1", 196 lbs. Born, Markham, Ont., February 7, 1990. Tampa Bay's 1st choice, 1st overall, in 2008 Entry Draft.

| Season | Club | League | GP | G | A | Pts | PIM | PP | SH | GW | S | % | +/- | TF | F% | Min | GP | G | A | Pts | PIM | PP | SH | GW | Min |
|---|---|---|---|---|---|---|---|---|---|---|---|---|---|---|---|---|---|---|---|---|---|---|---|---|---|
| 2005-06 | Markham Waxers | Minor-ON | 66 | 105 | 92 | 197 | 87 | .... | .... | .... | .... | .... | .... | .... | .... | .... | .... | .... | .... | .... | .... | .... | .... | .... | .... |
| 2006-07 | Sarnia Sting | OHL | 63 | 42 | 50 | 92 | 56 | .... | .... | .... | .... | .... | .... | .... | .... | .... | 4 | 3 | 3 | 6 | 0 | .... | .... | .... | .... |
| 2007-08 | Sarnia Sting | OHL | 61 | 58 | 47 | 105 | 88 | .... | .... | .... | .... | .... | .... | .... | .... | .... | 9 | 11 | 0 | 11 | 20 | .... | .... | .... | .... |
| **2008-09** | **Tampa Bay** | **NHL** | **79** | **23** | **23** | **46** | **39** | **9** | **0** | **1** | **181** | **12.7** | **–13** | **557** | **45.4** | **14:56** | .... | .... | .... | .... | .... | .... | .... | .... | .... |
| | **NHL Totals** | | **79** | **23** | **23** | **46** | **39** | **9** | **0** | **1** | **181** | **12.7** | | **557** | **45.4** | **14:56** | .... | .... | .... | .... | .... | .... | .... | .... | .... |

OHL Second All-Star Team (2008) • Canadian Major Junior First All-Star Team (2008)

## STAPLETON, Tim

(STAY-puhl-TOHN, TIHM) **ATL.**

Center. Shoots right. 5'9", 160 lbs. Born, La Grange, IL, July 9, 1982.

| Season | Club | League | GP | G | A | Pts | PIM | PP | SH | GW | S | % | +/- | TF | F% | Min | GP | G | A | Pts | PIM | PP | SH | GW | Min |
|---|---|---|---|---|---|---|---|---|---|---|---|---|---|---|---|---|---|---|---|---|---|---|---|---|---|
| 2000-01 | Green Bay | USHL | 52 | 7 | 15 | 22 | 8 | .... | .... | .... | .... | .... | .... | .... | .... | .... | 4 | 1 | 2 | 3 | 4 | .... | .... | .... | .... |
| 2001-02 | Green Bay | USHL | 61 | 24 | 36 | 60 | 10 | .... | .... | .... | .... | .... | .... | .... | .... | .... | 7 | 4 | 7 | 11 | 0 | .... | .... | .... | .... |
| 2002-03 | U. Minn-Duluth | WCHA | 42 | 14 | 28 | 42 | 6 | .... | .... | .... | .... | .... | .... | .... | .... | .... | .... | .... | .... | .... | .... | .... | .... | .... | .... |
| 2003-04 | U. Minn-Duluth | WCHA | 43 | 16 | 25 | 41 | 18 | .... | .... | .... | .... | .... | .... | .... | .... | .... | .... | .... | .... | .... | .... | .... | .... | .... | .... |
| 2004-05 | U. Minn-Duluth | WCHA | 38 | 19 | 20 | 39 | 6 | .... | .... | .... | .... | .... | .... | .... | .... | .... | .... | .... | .... | .... | .... | .... | .... | .... | .... |

| Season | Club | League | Regular Season GP | G | A | Pts | PIM | PP | SH | GW | S | % | +/- | TF | F% | Min | Playoffs GP | G | A | Pts | PIM | PP | SH | GW | Min |
|---|---|---|---|---|---|---|---|---|---|---|---|---|---|---|---|---|---|---|---|---|---|---|---|---|---|
| 2005-06 | U. Minn-Duluth | WCHA | 39 | 14 | 16 | 30 | 4 | .... | .... | .... | .... | .... | .... | .... | .... | .... | .... | .... | .... | .... | .... | .... | .... | .... | .... |
| | Portland Pirates | AHL | 9 | 0 | 5 | 5 | 4 | .... | .... | .... | .... | .... | .... | .... | .... | .... | 4 | 0 | 0 | 0 | 2 | .... | .... | .... | .... |
| 2006-07 | Jokerit Helsinki | Finland | 56 | 19 | 29 | 48 | 24 | .... | .... | .... | .... | .... | .... | .... | .... | .... | 10 | 6 | 4 | 10 | 8 | .... | .... | .... | .... |
| 2007-08 | Jokerit Helsinki | Finland | 55 | 29 | 33 | 62 | 36 | .... | .... | .... | .... | .... | .... | .... | .... | .... | 14 | *9 | 8 | 17 | 8 | .... | .... | .... | .... |
| **2008-09** | **Toronto** | **NHL** | **4** | **1** | **0** | **1** | **0** | **0** | **0** | **0** | **9** | **11.1** | **-3** | **5** | **20.0** | **15:06** | .... | .... | .... | .... | .... | .... | .... | .... | .... |
| | Toronto Marlies | AHL | 70 | 28 | 51 | 79 | 26 | .... | .... | .... | .... | .... | .... | .... | .... | .... | 6 | 2 | 0 | 2 | 2 | .... | .... | .... | .... |
| | **NHL Totals** | | **4** | **1** | **0** | **1** | **0** | **0** | **0** | **0** | **9** | **11.1** | | **5** | **20.0** | **15:06** | .... | .... | .... | .... | .... | .... | .... | .... | .... |

Signed as a free agent by **Toronto**, June 6, 2008. Traded to **Atlanta** by **Toronto** with Pavel Kubina for Garnet Exelby and Colin Stuart, July 1, 2009.

## STASTNY, Paul

(STAS-nee, PAWL) **COL.**

Center. Shoots left. 6', 205 lbs. Born, Quebec City, Que., December 27, 1985. Colorado's 2nd choice, 44th overall, in 2005 Entry Draft.

| | | | | | | | | | | | | | | | | | | | | | | | | | |
|---|---|---|---|---|---|---|---|---|---|---|---|---|---|---|---|---|---|---|---|---|---|---|---|---|---|
| 2003-04 | River City Lancers | USHL | 56 | 30 | *47 | 77 | 46 | .... | .... | .... | .... | .... | .... | .... | .... | .... | 3 | 1 | 2 | 3 | 0 | .... | .... | .... | .... |
| 2004-05 | U. of Denver | WCHA | 42 | 17 | 28 | 45 | 30 | .... | .... | .... | .... | .... | .... | .... | .... | .... | .... | .... | .... | .... | .... | .... | .... | .... | .... |
| 2005-06 | U. of Denver | WCHA | 39 | 19 | 34 | 53 | 79 | .... | .... | .... | .... | .... | .... | .... | .... | .... | .... | .... | .... | .... | .... | .... | .... | .... | .... |
| **2006-07** | **Colorado** | **NHL** | **82** | **28** | **50** | **78** | **42** | **11** | **0** | **6** | **185** | **15.1** | **4** | **1226** | **48.5** | **18:10** | .... | .... | .... | .... | .... | .... | .... | .... | .... |
| **2007-08** | **Colorado** | **NHL** | **66** | **24** | **47** | **71** | **24** | **3** | **0** | **4** | **138** | **17.4** | **22** | **1101** | **51.0** | **21:05** | **9** | **2** | **1** | **3** | **6** | **0** | **0** | **1** | **19:56** |
| **2008-09** | **Colorado** | **NHL** | **45** | **11** | **25** | **36** | **22** | **7** | **0** | **2** | **118** | **9.3** | **-9** | **850** | **51.8** | **21:14** | .... | .... | .... | .... | .... | .... | .... | .... | .... |
| | **NHL Totals** | | **193** | **63** | **122** | **185** | **88** | **21** | **0** | **12** | **441** | **14.3** | | **3177** | **50.2** | **19:53** | **9** | **2** | **1** | **3** | **6** | **0** | **0** | **1** | **19:56** |

WCHA All-Rookie Team (2005) • WCHA Rookie of the Year (2005) • NCAA Championship All-Tournament Team (2005) • WCHA First All-Star Team (2006) • NCAA West Second All-American Team (2006) • NHL All-Rookie Team (2007)

## STASTNY, Yan

(STAS-nee, YAHN) **ST.L.**

Center. Shoots left. 5'10", 191 lbs. Born, Quebec City, Que., September 30, 1982. Boston's 6th choice, 259th overall, in 2002 Entry Draft.

| | | | | | | | | | | | | | | | | | | | | | | | | | |
|---|---|---|---|---|---|---|---|---|---|---|---|---|---|---|---|---|---|---|---|---|---|---|---|---|---|
| 99-2000 | St. Louis Sting | NAHL | 45 | 12 | 23 | 35 | 77 | .... | .... | .... | .... | .... | .... | .... | .... | .... | .... | .... | .... | .... | .... | .... | .... | .... | .... |
| 2000-01 | St. Louis Jr. Blues | CSJHL | 6 | 0 | 2 | 2 | 23 | .... | .... | .... | .... | .... | .... | .... | .... | .... | .... | .... | .... | .... | .... | .... | .... | .... | .... |
| | Omaha Lancers | USHL | 44 | 17 | 14 | 31 | 101 | .... | .... | .... | .... | .... | .... | .... | .... | .... | 11 | 6 | 6 | 12 | 12 | .... | .... | .... | .... |
| 2001-02 | U. of Notre Dame | CCHA | 33 | 6 | 11 | 17 | 38 | .... | .... | .... | .... | .... | .... | .... | .... | .... | .... | .... | .... | .... | .... | .... | .... | .... | .... |
| 2002-03 | U. of Notre Dame | CCHA | 39 | 14 | 9 | 23 | 44 | .... | .... | .... | .... | .... | .... | .... | .... | .... | .... | .... | .... | .... | .... | .... | .... | .... | .... |
| 2003-04 | Nurnberg | Germany | 44 | 9 | 20 | 29 | 83 | .... | .... | .... | .... | .... | .... | .... | .... | .... | 6 | 0 | 1 | 1 | 6 | .... | .... | .... | .... |
| 2004-05 | Nurnberg | Germany | 51 | 24 | 30 | 54 | 60 | .... | .... | .... | .... | .... | .... | .... | .... | .... | 6 | 2 | 1 | 3 | 8 | .... | .... | .... | .... |
| **2005-06** | **Edmonton** | **NHL** | **3** | **0** | **0** | **0** | **0** | **0** | **0** | **0** | **1** | **0.0** | **-2** | **17** | **41.2** | **6:53** | .... | .... | .... | .... | .... | .... | .... | .... | .... |
| | Iowa Stars | AHL | 51 | 14 | 17 | 31 | 42 | .... | .... | .... | .... | .... | .... | .... | .... | .... | .... | .... | .... | .... | .... | .... | .... | .... | .... |
| | **Boston** | **NHL** | **17** | **1** | **3** | **4** | **10** | **0** | **0** | **0** | **13** | **7.7** | **-2** | **122** | **42.6** | **10:16** | .... | .... | .... | .... | .... | .... | .... | .... | .... |
| | Providence Bruins | AHL | .... | .... | .... | .... | .... | .... | .... | .... | .... | .... | .... | .... | .... | .... | 6 | 0 | 5 | 5 | 12 | .... | .... | .... | .... |
| **2006-07** | **Boston** | **NHL** | **21** | **0** | **2** | **2** | **19** | **0** | **0** | **0** | **7** | **0.0** | **-3** | **51** | **45.1** | **7:28** | .... | .... | .... | .... | .... | .... | .... | .... | .... |
| | Providence Bruins | AHL | 11 | 3 | 9 | 12 | 12 | .... | .... | .... | .... | .... | .... | .... | .... | .... | .... | .... | .... | .... | .... | .... | .... | .... | .... |
| | Peoria Rivermen | AHL | 39 | 11 | 17 | 28 | 35 | .... | .... | .... | .... | .... | .... | .... | .... | .... | .... | .... | .... | .... | .... | .... | .... | .... | .... |
| **2007-08** | **St. Louis** | **NHL** | **12** | **1** | **1** | **2** | **9** | **0** | **0** | **0** | **10** | **10.0** | **0** | **61** | **44.3** | **10:59** | .... | .... | .... | .... | .... | .... | .... | .... | .... |
| | Peoria Rivermen | AHL | 43 | 13 | 11 | 24 | 69 | .... | .... | .... | .... | .... | .... | .... | .... | .... | .... | .... | .... | .... | .... | .... | .... | .... | .... |
| **2008-09** | **St. Louis** | **NHL** | **34** | **3** | **4** | **7** | **20** | **0** | **0** | **0** | **30** | **10.0** | **-14** | **102** | **45.1** | **12:45** | .... | .... | .... | .... | .... | .... | .... | .... | .... |
| | Peoria Rivermen | AHL | 30 | 12 | 7 | 19 | 21 | .... | .... | .... | .... | .... | .... | .... | .... | .... | 6 | 2 | 2 | 4 | 2 | .... | .... | .... | .... |
| | **NHL Totals** | | **87** | **5** | **10** | **15** | **58** | **0** | **0** | **0** | **61** | **8.2** | | **353** | **43.9** | **10:33** | .... | .... | .... | .... | .... | .... | .... | .... | .... |

Signed as a free agent by **Nurnberg** (Germany), September 18, 2003. Traded to **Edmonton** by **Boston** for Boston's 4th round choice (previously acquired, later traded to San Jose - San Jose selected James Delory) in 2006 Entry Draft, August 30, 2005. Traded to **Boston** by **Edmonton** with Marty Reasoner and Edmonton's 2nd round choice (Milan Lucic) in 2006 Entry Draft for Sergei Samsonov, March 9, 2006. Traded to **St. Louis** by **Boston** for St. Louis' 5th round choice (Denis Reul) in 2007 Entry Draft, January 16, 2006.

## STAUBITZ, Brad

(STAW-bihtz, BRAD) **S.J.**

Right wing. Shoots right. 6'1", 215 lbs. Born, Bright's Grove, Ont., July 28, 1984.

| | | | | | | | | | | | | | | | | | | | | | | | | | |
|---|---|---|---|---|---|---|---|---|---|---|---|---|---|---|---|---|---|---|---|---|---|---|---|---|---|
| 2001-02 | Sault Ste. Marie | OHL | 45 | 0 | 3 | 3 | 46 | .... | .... | .... | .... | .... | .... | .... | .... | .... | 3 | 0 | 0 | 0 | 2 | .... | .... | .... | .... |
| 2002-03 | Sault Ste. Marie | OHL | 55 | 2 | 6 | 8 | 116 | .... | .... | .... | .... | .... | .... | .... | .... | .... | 4 | 0 | 0 | 0 | 7 | .... | .... | .... | .... |
| 2003-04 | Sault Ste. Marie | OHL | 66 | 6 | 18 | 24 | 140 | .... | .... | .... | .... | .... | .... | .... | .... | .... | .... | .... | .... | .... | .... | .... | .... | .... | .... |
| 2004-05 | Sault Ste. Marie | OHL | 40 | 2 | 11 | 13 | 101 | .... | .... | .... | .... | .... | .... | .... | .... | .... | .... | .... | .... | .... | .... | .... | .... | .... | .... |
| | Ottawa 67's | OHL | 30 | 5 | 8 | 13 | 80 | .... | .... | .... | .... | .... | .... | .... | .... | .... | 21 | 4 | 16 | 20 | 70 | .... | .... | .... | .... |
| 2005-06 | Cleveland Barons | AHL | 71 | 0 | 6 | 6 | 245 | .... | .... | .... | .... | .... | .... | .... | .... | .... | .... | .... | .... | .... | .... | .... | .... | .... | .... |
| 2006-07 | Worcester Sharks | AHL | 51 | 1 | 4 | 5 | 137 | .... | .... | .... | .... | .... | .... | .... | .... | .... | 5 | 0 | 0 | 0 | 13 | .... | .... | .... | .... |
| 2007-08 | Worcester Sharks | AHL | 73 | 6 | 14 | 20 | 195 | .... | .... | .... | .... | .... | .... | .... | .... | .... | .... | .... | .... | .... | .... | .... | .... | .... | .... |
| **2008-09** | **San Jose** | **NHL** | **35** | **1** | **2** | **3** | **76** | **0** | **0** | **1** | **22** | **4.5** | **0** | **2** | **0.0** | **6:13** | .... | .... | .... | .... | .... | .... | .... | .... | .... |
| | Worcester Sharks | AHL | 38 | 0 | 5 | 5 | 130 | .... | .... | .... | .... | .... | .... | .... | .... | .... | 10 | 0 | 2 | 2 | 15 | .... | .... | .... | .... |
| | **NHL Totals** | | **35** | **1** | **2** | **3** | **76** | **0** | **0** | **1** | **22** | **4.5** | | **2** | **0.0** | **6:13** | .... | .... | .... | .... | .... | .... | .... | .... | .... |

Signed as a free agent by **San Jose**, September 19, 2005.

## STECKEL, David

(STEH-kuhl, DAY-vihd) **WSH.**

Center. Shoots left. 6'5", 222 lbs. Born, Westbend, WI, March 15, 1982. Los Angeles' 2nd choice, 30th overall, in 2001 Entry Draft.

| | | | | | | | | | | | | | | | | | | | | | | | | | |
|---|---|---|---|---|---|---|---|---|---|---|---|---|---|---|---|---|---|---|---|---|---|---|---|---|---|
| 1998-99 | USNTDP | USHL | 2 | 0 | 0 | 0 | 2 | .... | .... | .... | .... | .... | .... | .... | .... | .... | .... | .... | .... | .... | .... | .... | .... | .... | .... |
| | USNTDP | NAHL | 51 | 3 | 14 | 17 | 18 | .... | .... | .... | .... | .... | .... | .... | .... | .... | .... | .... | .... | .... | .... | .... | .... | .... | .... |
| 99-2000 | USNTDP | U-18 | 6 | 2 | 5 | 7 | 14 | .... | .... | .... | .... | .... | .... | .... | .... | .... | .... | .... | .... | .... | .... | .... | .... | .... | .... |
| | USNTDP | USHL | 52 | 13 | 13 | 26 | 94 | .... | .... | .... | .... | .... | .... | .... | .... | .... | .... | .... | .... | .... | .... | .... | .... | .... | .... |
| 2000-01 | Ohio State | CCHA | 33 | 17 | 18 | 35 | 80 | .... | .... | .... | .... | .... | .... | .... | .... | .... | .... | .... | .... | .... | .... | .... | .... | .... | .... |
| 2001-02 | Ohio State | CCHA | 36 | 6 | 16 | 22 | 75 | .... | .... | .... | .... | .... | .... | .... | .... | .... | .... | .... | .... | .... | .... | .... | .... | .... | .... |
| 2002-03 | Ohio State | CCHA | 36 | 10 | 8 | 18 | 50 | .... | .... | .... | .... | .... | .... | .... | .... | .... | .... | .... | .... | .... | .... | .... | .... | .... | .... |
| 2003-04 | Ohio State | CCHA | 41 | 17 | 13 | 30 | 44 | .... | .... | .... | .... | .... | .... | .... | .... | .... | .... | .... | .... | .... | .... | .... | .... | .... | .... |
| 2004-05 | Manchester | AHL | 63 | 10 | 7 | 17 | 26 | .... | .... | .... | .... | .... | .... | .... | .... | .... | 6 | 1 | 1 | 2 | 4 | .... | .... | .... | .... |
| **2005-06** | **Washington** | **NHL** | **7** | **0** | **0** | **0** | **0** | **0** | **0** | **0** | **6** | **0.0** | **1** | **48** | **35.4** | **7:39** | .... | .... | .... | .... | .... | .... | .... | .... | .... |
| | Hershey Bears | AHL | 74 | 14 | 20 | 34 | 58 | .... | .... | .... | .... | .... | .... | .... | .... | .... | 21 | 10 | 5 | 15 | 20 | .... | .... | .... | .... |
| **2006-07** | **Washington** | **NHL** | **5** | **0** | **0** | **0** | **2** | **0** | **0** | **0** | **4** | **0.0** | **-2** | **43** | **65.1** | **12:26** | .... | .... | .... | .... | .... | .... | .... | .... | .... |
| | Hershey Bears | AHL | 71 | 30 | 31 | 61 | 46 | .... | .... | .... | .... | .... | .... | .... | .... | .... | 19 | 6 | 9 | 15 | 16 | .... | .... | .... | .... |
| **2007-08** | **Washington** | **NHL** | **67** | **5** | **7** | **12** | **34** | **0** | **0** | **1** | **66** | **7.6** | **1** | **900** | **56.3** | **13:34** | **7** | **1** | **1** | **2** | **4** | **0** | **0** | **0** | **14:23** |
| **2008-09** | **Washington** | **NHL** | **76** | **8** | **11** | **19** | **34** | **0** | **2** | **1** | **103** | **7.8** | **2** | **886** | **57.9** | **13:49** | **14** | **3** | **2** | **5** | **4** | **0** | **0** | **1** | **16:03** |
| | **NHL Totals** | | **155** | **13** | **18** | **31** | **70** | **0** | **2** | **2** | **179** | **7.3** | | **1877** | **56.7** | **13:23** | **21** | **4** | **3** | **7** | **8** | **0** | **0** | **1** | **15:30** |

CCHA All-Rookie Team (2001)

Signed as a free agent by **Washington**, August 25, 2005.

## STEEN, Alex

(STEEN, AL-ehx) **ST.L.**

Center. Shoots left. 6'1", 205 lbs. Born, Winnipeg, Man., March 1, 1984. Toronto's 1st choice, 24th overall, in 2002 Entry Draft.

| | | | | | | | | | | | | | | | | | | | | | | | | | |
|---|---|---|---|---|---|---|---|---|---|---|---|---|---|---|---|---|---|---|---|---|---|---|---|---|---|
| 99-2000 | V.Frolunda Jr. | Swe-Jr. | 8 | 5 | 7 | 12 | 0 | .... | .... | .... | .... | .... | .... | .... | .... | .... | .... | .... | .... | .... | .... | .... | .... | .... | .... |
| | V.Frolunda U18 | Swe-U18 | 14 | 3 | 5 | 8 | 16 | .... | .... | .... | .... | .... | .... | .... | .... | .... | .... | .... | .... | .... | .... | .... | .... | .... | .... |
| 2000-01 | V.Frolunda Jr. | Swe-Jr. | 23 | 11 | 12 | 23 | 15 | .... | .... | .... | .... | .... | .... | .... | .... | .... | 3 | 1 | 0 | 1 | 2 | .... | .... | .... | .... |
| | V.Frolunda U18 | Swe-U18 | 6 | 3 | 3 | 6 | 9 | .... | .... | .... | .... | .... | .... | .... | .... | .... | .... | .... | .... | .... | .... | .... | .... | .... | .... |
| 2001-02 | V.Frolunda Jr. | Swe-Jr. | 23 | 21 | 17 | 38 | 47 | .... | .... | .... | .... | .... | .... | .... | .... | .... | 2 | 1 | 1 | 2 | 2 | .... | .... | .... | .... |
| | V.Frolunda | Sweden | 26 | 0 | 3 | 3 | 14 | .... | .... | .... | .... | .... | .... | .... | .... | .... | 10 | 1 | 2 | 3 | 0 | .... | .... | .... | .... |
| 2002-03 | V.Frolunda | Sweden | 45 | 5 | 10 | 15 | 18 | .... | .... | .... | .... | .... | .... | .... | .... | .... | 16 | 2 | 3 | 5 | 4 | .... | .... | .... | .... |
| | V.Frolunda Jr. | Swe-Jr. | 2 | 0 | 2 | 2 | 0 | .... | .... | .... | .... | .... | .... | .... | .... | .... | .... | .... | .... | .... | .... | .... | .... | .... | .... |
| 2003-04 | V.Frolunda | Sweden | 48 | 10 | 14 | 24 | 50 | .... | .... | .... | .... | .... | .... | .... | .... | .... | 10 | 4 | 6 | 10 | 14 | .... | .... | .... | .... |
| 2004-05 | MODO | Sweden | 50 | 9 | 8 | 17 | 26 | .... | .... | .... | .... | .... | .... | .... | .... | .... | 6 | 1 | 0 | 1 | 4 | .... | .... | .... | .... |
| **2005-06** | **Toronto** | **NHL** | **75** | **18** | **27** | **45** | **42** | **9** | **1** | **3** | **176** | **10.2** | **-9** | **29** | **24.1** | **17:37** | .... | .... | .... | .... | .... | .... | .... | .... | .... |
| **2006-07** | **Toronto** | **NHL** | **82** | **15** | **20** | **35** | **26** | **4** | **0** | **5** | **192** | **7.8** | **5** | **44** | **34.1** | **15:42** | .... | .... | .... | .... | .... | .... | .... | .... | .... |
| **2007-08** | **Toronto** | **NHL** | **76** | **15** | **27** | **42** | **32** | **2** | **1** | **2** | **169** | **8.9** | **0** | **179** | **33.0** | **18:05** | .... | .... | .... | .... | .... | .... | .... | .... | .... |
| **2008-09** | **Toronto** | **NHL** | **20** | **2** | **2** | **4** | **6** | **1** | **0** | **0** | **31** | **6.5** | **-4** | **82** | **52.4** | **15:38** | .... | .... | .... | .... | .... | .... | .... | .... | .... |
| | **St. Louis** | **NHL** | **61** | **6** | **18** | **24** | **24** | **2** | **1** | **0** | **117** | **5.1** | **-6** | **154** | **41.6** | **16:34** | **4** | **0** | **1** | **1** | **0** | **0** | **0** | **0** | **17:47** |
| | **NHL Totals** | | **314** | **56** | **94** | **150** | **130** | **18** | **3** | **10** | **685** | **8.2** | | **488** | **38.5** | **16:54** | **4** | **0** | **1** | **1** | **0** | **0** | **0** | **0** | **17:47** |

Traded to **St. Louis** by **Toronto** with Carlo Colaiacovo for Lee Stempniak, November 24, 2008.

## STEMPNIAK, Lee

(STEHMP-nee-ak, LEE) **TOR.**

Right wing. Shoots right. 6', 195 lbs. Born, Buffalo, NY, February 4, 1983. St. Louis' 7th choice, 148th overall, in 2003 Entry Draft.

| | | | Regular Season | | | | | | | | | | | | | | Playoffs | | | | | | | | |
|---|---|---|---|---|---|---|---|---|---|---|---|---|---|---|---|---|---|---|---|---|---|---|---|---|---|
| Season | Club | League | GP | G | A | Pts | PIM | PP | SH | GW | S | % | +/- | TF | F% | Min | GP | G | A | Pts | PIM | PP | SH | GW | Min |
| 2000-01 | Buffalo Lightning | OPJHL | 48 | 34 | 51 | 86 | 36 | .... | .... | .... | .... | .... | .... | .... | .... | .... | .... | .... | .... | .... | .... | .... | .... | .... | .... |
| 2001-02 | Dartmouth | ECAC | 32 | 12 | 9 | 21 | 8 | .... | .... | .... | .... | .... | .... | .... | .... | .... | .... | .... | .... | .... | .... | .... | .... | .... | .... |
| 2002-03 | Dartmouth | ECAC | 34 | 21 | 28 | 49 | 32 | .... | .... | .... | .... | .... | .... | .... | .... | .... | .... | .... | .... | .... | .... | .... | .... | .... | .... |
| 2003-04 | Dartmouth | ECAC | 34 | 16 | 22 | 38 | 42 | .... | .... | .... | .... | .... | .... | .... | .... | .... | .... | .... | .... | .... | .... | .... | .... | .... | .... |
| 2004-05 | Dartmouth | ECAC | 35 | 14 | *29 | 43 | 34 | .... | .... | .... | .... | .... | .... | .... | .... | .... | .... | .... | .... | .... | .... | .... | .... | .... | .... |
| **2005-06** | **St. Louis** | **NHL** | **57** | **14** | **13** | **27** | **22** | **5** | **0** | **2** | **100** | **14.0** | **–10** | **7** | **42.9** | **14:22** | .... | .... | .... | .... | .... | .... | .... | .... | .... |
| | Peoria Rivermen | AHL | 26 | 8 | 7 | 15 | 32 | .... | .... | .... | .... | .... | .... | .... | .... | .... | 3 | 0 | 3 | 3 | 2 | .... | .... | .... | .... |
| **2006-07** | **St. Louis** | **NHL** | **82** | **27** | **25** | **52** | **33** | **8** | **0** | **4** | **166** | **16.3** | **–2** | **7** | **14.3** | **14:43** | .... | .... | .... | .... | .... | .... | .... | .... | .... |
| **2007-08** | **St. Louis** | **NHL** | **80** | **13** | **25** | **38** | **40** | **3** | **0** | **2** | **162** | **8.0** | **0** | **11** | **36.4** | **15:53** | .... | .... | .... | .... | .... | .... | .... | .... | .... |
| **2008-09** | **St. Louis** | **NHL** | **14** | **3** | **10** | **13** | **2** | **0** | **0** | **1** | **43** | **7.0** | **–3** | **1** | **0.0** | **19:28** | .... | .... | .... | .... | .... | .... | .... | .... | .... |
| | **Toronto** | **NHL** | **61** | **11** | **20** | **31** | **31** | **3** | **0** | **0** | **128** | **8.6** | **–9** | **12** | **33.3** | **15:52** | .... | .... | .... | .... | .... | .... | .... | .... | .... |
| | **NHL Totals** | | **294** | **68** | **93** | **161** | **128** | **19** | **0** | **9** | **599** | **11.4** | | **38** | **31.6** | **15:26** | .... | .... | .... | .... | .... | .... | .... | .... | .... |

ECAC All-Rookie Team (2002) • ECAC First All-Star Team (2004, 2005) • NCAA East First All-American Team (2004) • NCAA East Second All-American Team (2005)
Traded to **Toronto** by **St. Louis** for Alex Steen and Carlo Colaiacovo, November 24, 2008.

## STERLING, Brett

(STUHR-lihng, BREHT) **ATL.**

Left wing. Shoots left. 5'7", 175 lbs. Born, Los Angeles, CA, April 24, 1984. Atlanta's 5th choice, 145th overall, in 2003 Entry Draft.

| Season | Club | League | GP | G | A | Pts | PIM | PP | SH | GW | S | % | +/- | TF | F% | Min | GP | G | A | Pts | PIM | PP | SH | GW | Min |
|---|---|---|---|---|---|---|---|---|---|---|---|---|---|---|---|---|---|---|---|---|---|---|---|---|---|
| 99-2000 | L.A. Jr. Kings | SCAHA | 35 | 45 | 25 | 70 | .... | .... | .... | .... | .... | .... | .... | .... | .... | .... | .... | .... | .... | .... | .... | .... | .... | .... | .... |
| 2000-01 | USNTDP | U-17 | 13 | .... | .... | .... | .... | .... | .... | .... | .... | .... | .... | .... | .... | .... | .... | .... | .... | .... | .... | .... | .... | .... | .... |
| | USNTDP | NAHL | 47 | 29 | 15 | 44 | 72 | .... | .... | .... | .... | .... | .... | .... | .... | .... | .... | .... | .... | .... | .... | .... | .... | .... | .... |
| 2001-02 | USNTDP | U-18 | 31 | 21 | 15 | 36 | 18 | .... | .... | .... | .... | .... | .... | .... | .... | .... | .... | .... | .... | .... | .... | .... | .... | .... | .... |
| | USNTDP | USHL | 10 | 6 | 3 | 9 | 8 | .... | .... | .... | .... | .... | .... | .... | .... | .... | .... | .... | .... | .... | .... | .... | .... | .... | .... |
| | USNTDP | NAHL | 9 | 2 | 1 | 3 | 10 | .... | .... | .... | .... | .... | .... | .... | .... | .... | .... | .... | .... | .... | .... | .... | .... | .... | .... |
| 2002-03 | Colorado College | WCHA | 36 | 27 | 11 | 38 | 30 | .... | .... | .... | .... | .... | .... | .... | .... | .... | .... | .... | .... | .... | .... | .... | .... | .... | .... |
| 2003-04 | Colorado College | WCHA | 30 | 16 | 12 | 28 | 40 | .... | .... | .... | .... | .... | .... | .... | .... | .... | .... | .... | .... | .... | .... | .... | .... | .... | .... |
| 2004-05 | Colorado College | WCHA | 43 | *34 | 29 | 63 | 74 | .... | .... | .... | .... | .... | .... | .... | .... | .... | .... | .... | .... | .... | .... | .... | .... | .... | .... |
| 2005-06 | Colorado College | WCHA | 42 | 31 | 24 | 55 | 66 | .... | .... | .... | .... | .... | .... | .... | .... | .... | .... | .... | .... | .... | .... | .... | .... | .... | .... |
| 2006-07 | Chicago Wolves | AHL | 77 | *55 | 42 | 97 | 96 | .... | .... | .... | .... | .... | .... | .... | .... | .... | 15 | 7 | 5 | 12 | 24 | .... | .... | .... | .... |
| **2007-08** | **Atlanta** | **NHL** | **13** | **1** | **2** | **3** | **14** | **0** | **0** | **0** | **14** | **7.1** | **–2** | **3** | **66.7** | **12:24** | .... | .... | .... | .... | .... | .... | .... | .... | .... |
| | Chicago Wolves | AHL | 70 | 38 | 33 | 71 | 116 | .... | .... | .... | .... | .... | .... | .... | .... | .... | 16 | 4 | 5 | 9 | 18 | .... | .... | .... | .... |
| **2008-09** | **Atlanta** | **NHL** | **6** | **1** | **0** | **1** | **2** | **0** | **0** | **0** | **11** | **9.1** | **–3** | **0** | **0.0** | **13:53** | .... | .... | .... | .... | .... | .... | .... | .... | .... |
| | Chicago Wolves | AHL | 52 | 16 | 23 | 39 | 84 | .... | .... | .... | .... | .... | .... | .... | .... | .... | .... | .... | .... | .... | .... | .... | .... | .... | .... |
| | **NHL Totals** | | **19** | **2** | **2** | **4** | **16** | **0** | **0** | **0** | **25** | **8.0** | | **3** | **66.7** | **12:52** | .... | .... | .... | .... | .... | .... | .... | .... | .... |

WCHA All-Rookie Team (2003) • WCHA First All-Star Team (2005, 2006) • NCAA West First All-American Team (2005, 2006) • AHL All-Rookie Team (2007) • AHL First All-Star Team (2007) • Dudley "Red" Garrett Memorial Award (AHL - Rookie of the Year) (2007) • Willie Marshall Award (AHL - Top Goal-scorer) (2007) • AHL Second All-Star Team (2008)

## STEVENSON, Grant

(STEE-vehn-suhn, GRANT)

Center. Shoots right. 5'11", 170 lbs. Born, Spruce Grove, Alta., October 15, 1981.

| Season | Club | League | GP | G | A | Pts | PIM | PP | SH | GW | S | % | +/- | TF | F% | Min | GP | G | A | Pts | PIM | PP | SH | GW | Min |
|---|---|---|---|---|---|---|---|---|---|---|---|---|---|---|---|---|---|---|---|---|---|---|---|---|---|
| 1998-99 | Spruce Grove | RAMHL | 26 | 15 | 32 | 47 | 90 | .... | .... | .... | .... | .... | .... | .... | .... | .... | 8 | 10 | 10 | 20 | 30 | .... | .... | .... | .... |
| 99-2000 | Bonnyville | AJHL | 63 | 20 | 38 | 58 | .... | .... | .... | .... | .... | .... | .... | .... | .... | .... | .... | .... | .... | .... | .... | .... | .... | .... | .... |
| 2000-01 | Grande Prairie | AJHL | 53 | 24 | 49 | 73 | 62 | .... | .... | .... | .... | .... | .... | .... | .... | .... | 15 | 7 | 2 | 9 | 38 | .... | .... | .... | .... |
| 2001-02 | Minnesota State | WCHA | 38 | 8 | 8 | 16 | 36 | .... | .... | .... | .... | .... | .... | .... | .... | .... | .... | .... | .... | .... | .... | .... | .... | .... | .... |
| 2002-03 | Minnesota State | WCHA | 38 | 27 | 36 | 63 | 38 | .... | .... | .... | .... | .... | .... | .... | .... | .... | .... | .... | .... | .... | .... | .... | .... | .... | .... |
| 2003-04 | Cleveland Barons | AHL | 71 | 13 | 26 | 39 | 45 | .... | .... | .... | .... | .... | .... | .... | .... | .... | 9 | 0 | 7 | 7 | 6 | .... | .... | .... | .... |
| 2004-05 | Cleveland Barons | AHL | 77 | 14 | 25 | 39 | 70 | .... | .... | .... | .... | .... | .... | .... | .... | .... | .... | .... | .... | .... | .... | .... | .... | .... | .... |
| | Johnstown Chiefs | ECHL | 2 | 1 | 0 | 1 | 2 | .... | .... | .... | .... | .... | .... | .... | .... | .... | .... | .... | .... | .... | .... | .... | .... | .... | .... |
| **2005-06** | **San Jose** | **NHL** | **47** | **10** | **12** | **22** | **14** | **5** | **0** | **2** | **67** | **14.9** | **–7** | **6** | **33.3** | **11:57** | **5** | **0** | **0** | **0** | **4** | **0** | **0** | **0** | **6:59** |
| | Cleveland Barons | AHL | 17 | 8 | 8 | 16 | 8 | .... | .... | .... | .... | .... | .... | .... | .... | .... | .... | .... | .... | .... | .... | .... | .... | .... | .... |
| 2006-07 | Worcester Sharks | AHL | 59 | 14 | 25 | 39 | 30 | .... | .... | .... | .... | .... | .... | .... | .... | .... | 6 | 2 | 0 | 2 | 2 | .... | .... | .... | .... |
| 2007-08 | Quad City Flames | AHL | 80 | 30 | 43 | 73 | 58 | .... | .... | .... | .... | .... | .... | .... | .... | .... | .... | .... | .... | .... | .... | .... | .... | .... | .... |
| 2008-09 | Chicago Wolves | AHL | 59 | 10 | 11 | 21 | 31 | .... | .... | .... | .... | .... | .... | .... | .... | .... | .... | .... | .... | .... | .... | .... | .... | .... | .... |
| | **NHL Totals** | | **47** | **10** | **12** | **22** | **14** | **5** | **0** | **2** | **67** | **14.9** | | **6** | **33.3** | **11:57** | **5** | **0** | **0** | **0** | **4** | **0** | **0** | **0** | **6:59** |

WCHA First All-Star Team (2003) • NCAA West Second All-American Team (2003)
Signed as a free agent by **San Jose**, April 18, 2003. Signed as a free agent by **Calgary**, July 4, 2007. Signed as a free agent by **Atlanta**, July 9, 2008. Signed as a free agent by **Kloten** (Swiss), June 25, 2009.

## STEWART, Anthony

(STEW-ahrt, AN-thu-nee) **ATL.**

Center. Shoots right. 6'2", 240 lbs. Born, LaSalle, Que., January 5, 1985. Florida's 2nd choice, 25th overall, in 2003 Entry Draft.

| Season | Club | League | GP | G | A | Pts | PIM | PP | SH | GW | S | % | +/- | TF | F% | Min | GP | G | A | Pts | PIM | PP | SH | GW | Min |
|---|---|---|---|---|---|---|---|---|---|---|---|---|---|---|---|---|---|---|---|---|---|---|---|---|---|
| 2000-01 | North York | MTHL | 34 | 30 | 70 | 100 | .... | .... | .... | .... | .... | .... | .... | .... | .... | .... | .... | .... | .... | .... | .... | .... | .... | .... | .... |
| | St. Mike's B's | OPJHL | 5 | 0 | 2 | 2 | 0 | .... | .... | .... | .... | .... | .... | .... | .... | .... | .... | .... | .... | .... | .... | .... | .... | .... | .... |
| 2001-02 | Kingston | OHL | 65 | 19 | 24 | 43 | 12 | .... | .... | .... | .... | .... | .... | .... | .... | .... | 1 | 0 | 0 | 0 | 0 | .... | .... | .... | .... |
| 2002-03 | Kingston | OHL | 68 | 32 | 38 | 70 | 47 | .... | .... | .... | .... | .... | .... | .... | .... | .... | .... | .... | .... | .... | .... | .... | .... | .... | .... |
| 2003-04 | Kingston | OHL | 53 | 35 | 23 | 58 | 76 | .... | .... | .... | .... | .... | .... | .... | .... | .... | 5 | 3 | 4 | 7 | 7 | .... | .... | .... | .... |
| 2004-05 | Kingston | OHL | 62 | 32 | 35 | 67 | 70 | .... | .... | .... | .... | .... | .... | .... | .... | .... | .... | .... | .... | .... | .... | .... | .... | .... | .... |
| | San Antonio | AHL | 10 | 1 | 2 | 3 | 14 | .... | .... | .... | .... | .... | .... | .... | .... | .... | .... | .... | .... | .... | .... | .... | .... | .... | .... |
| **2005-06** | **Florida** | **NHL** | **10** | **2** | **1** | **3** | **2** | **1** | **0** | **0** | **16** | **12.5** | **2** | **1** | **0.0** | **7:13** | .... | .... | .... | .... | .... | .... | .... | .... | .... |
| | Rochester | AHL | 4 | 2 | 3 | 5 | 0 | .... | .... | .... | .... | .... | .... | .... | .... | .... | .... | .... | .... | .... | .... | .... | .... | .... | .... |
| **2006-07** | **Florida** | **NHL** | **10** | **0** | **1** | **1** | **2** | **0** | **0** | **0** | **8** | **0.0** | **1** | **0** | **0.0** | **6:51** | .... | .... | .... | .... | .... | .... | .... | .... | .... |
| | Rochester | AHL | 62 | 13 | 14 | 27 | 64 | .... | .... | .... | .... | .... | .... | .... | .... | .... | 6 | 2 | 0 | 2 | 2 | .... | .... | .... | .... |
| **2007-08** | **Florida** | **NHL** | **26** | **0** | **1** | **1** | **0** | **0** | **0** | **0** | **21** | **0.0** | **–1** | **0** | **0.0** | **6:08** | .... | .... | .... | .... | .... | .... | .... | .... | .... |
| | Rochester | AHL | 54 | 13 | 18 | 31 | 61 | .... | .... | .... | .... | .... | .... | .... | .... | .... | .... | .... | .... | .... | .... | .... | .... | .... | .... |
| **2008-09** | **Florida** | **NHL** | **59** | **2** | **5** | **7** | **34** | **0** | **0** | **0** | **56** | **3.6** | **–6** | **3** | **33.3** | **7:39** | .... | .... | .... | .... | .... | .... | .... | .... | .... |
| | **NHL Totals** | | **105** | **4** | **8** | **12** | **38** | **1** | **0** | **0** | **101** | **4.0** | | **4** | **25.0** | **7:09** | .... | .... | .... | .... | .... | .... | .... | .... | .... |

• Missed remainder of 2005-06 season recovering from wrist injury suffered in game vs. Carolina, November 11, 2005. Signed as a free agent by **Atlanta**, July 13, 2009.

## STEWART, Chris

(STEW-ahrt, KRIHS) **COL.**

Right wing. Shoots right. 6'2", 228 lbs. Born, Toronto, Ont., October 30, 1987. Colorado's 1st choice, 18th overall, in 2006 Entry Draft.

| Season | Club | League | GP | G | A | Pts | PIM | PP | SH | GW | S | % | +/- | TF | F% | Min | GP | G | A | Pts | PIM | PP | SH | GW | Min |
|---|---|---|---|---|---|---|---|---|---|---|---|---|---|---|---|---|---|---|---|---|---|---|---|---|---|
| 2004-05 | Kingston | OHL | 64 | 18 | 12 | 30 | 45 | .... | .... | .... | .... | .... | .... | .... | .... | .... | .... | .... | .... | .... | .... | .... | .... | .... | .... |
| 2005-06 | Kingston | OHL | 62 | 37 | 50 | 87 | 118 | .... | .... | .... | .... | .... | .... | .... | .... | .... | 6 | 2 | 0 | 2 | 13 | .... | .... | .... | .... |
| 2006-07 | Kingston | OHL | 61 | 36 | 46 | 82 | 108 | .... | .... | .... | .... | .... | .... | .... | .... | .... | 5 | 4 | 2 | 6 | 6 | .... | .... | .... | .... |
| | Albany River Rats | AHL | 5 | 1 | 2 | 3 | 2 | .... | .... | .... | .... | .... | .... | .... | .... | .... | 1 | 0 | 0 | 0 | 0 | .... | .... | .... | .... |
| 2007-08 | Lake Erie | AHL | 77 | 25 | 19 | 44 | 93 | .... | .... | .... | .... | .... | .... | .... | .... | .... | .... | .... | .... | .... | .... | .... | .... | .... | .... |
| **2008-09** | **Colorado** | **NHL** | **53** | **11** | **8** | **19** | **54** | **1** | **1** | **1** | **98** | **11.2** | **–18** | **21** | **33.3** | **12:20** | .... | .... | .... | .... | .... | .... | .... | .... | .... |
| | Lake Erie | AHL | 19 | 5 | 6 | 11 | 23 | .... | .... | .... | .... | .... | .... | .... | .... | .... | .... | .... | .... | .... | .... | .... | .... | .... | .... |
| | **NHL Totals** | | **53** | **11** | **8** | **19** | **54** | **1** | **1** | **1** | **98** | **11.2** | | **21** | **33.3** | **12:20** | .... | .... | .... | .... | .... | .... | .... | .... | .... |

## STEWART, Greg

(STEW-ahrt, GREHG) **MTL.**

Left wing. Shoots left. 6'2", 200 lbs. Born, Kitchener, Ont., May 21, 1986. Montreal's 7th choice, 246th overall, in 2004 Entry Draft.

| Season | Club | League | GP | G | A | Pts | PIM | PP | SH | GW | S | % | +/- | TF | F% | Min | GP | G | A | Pts | PIM | PP | SH | GW | Min |
|---|---|---|---|---|---|---|---|---|---|---|---|---|---|---|---|---|---|---|---|---|---|---|---|---|---|
| 2003-04 | Peterborough | OHL | 58 | 4 | 6 | 10 | 76 | .... | .... | .... | .... | .... | .... | .... | .... | .... | .... | .... | .... | .... | .... | .... | .... | .... | .... |
| 2004-05 | Peterborough | OHL | 68 | 16 | 18 | 34 | 111 | .... | .... | .... | .... | .... | .... | .... | .... | .... | 14 | 3 | 3 | 6 | 20 | .... | .... | .... | .... |
| 2005-06 | Peterborough | OHL | 60 | 24 | 15 | 39 | 83 | .... | .... | .... | .... | .... | .... | .... | .... | .... | 19 | 1 | 6 | 7 | 30 | .... | .... | .... | .... |
| 2006-07 | Cincinnati | ECHL | 62 | 8 | 15 | 23 | 126 | .... | .... | .... | .... | .... | .... | .... | .... | .... | 10 | 5 | 2 | 7 | 36 | .... | .... | .... | .... |
| **2007-08** | **Montreal** | **NHL** | **1** | **0** | **0** | **0** | **5** | **0** | **0** | **0** | **2** | **0.0** | **0** | **0** | **0.0** | **11:26** | .... | .... | .... | .... | .... | .... | .... | .... | .... |
| | Hamilton | AHL | 69 | 10 | 7 | 17 | 137 | .... | .... | .... | .... | .... | .... | .... | .... | .... | .... | .... | .... | .... | .... | .... | .... | .... | .... |
| **2008-09** | **Montreal** | **NHL** | **20** | **0** | **1** | **1** | **32** | **0** | **0** | **0** | **16** | **0.0** | **–4** | **1** | **100.0** | **8:37** | **2** | **0** | **0** | **0** | **2** | **0** | **0** | **0** | **8:31** |
| | Hamilton | AHL | 51 | 7 | 10 | 17 | 170 | .... | .... | .... | .... | .... | .... | .... | .... | .... | 2 | 1 | 0 | 1 | 9 | .... | .... | .... | .... |
| | **NHL Totals** | | **21** | **0** | **1** | **1** | **37** | **0** | **0** | **0** | **18** | **0.0** | | **1** | **100.0** | **8:45** | **2** | **0** | **0** | **0** | **2** | **0** | **0** | **0** | **8:31** |

## STEWART, Karl

(STEW-ahrt, KAHRL)

Left wing. Shoots left. 5'11", 185 lbs. Born, Aurora, Ont., June 30, 1983.

| | | | Regular Season | | | | | | | | | | | | | | Playoffs | | | | | | | | |
|---|---|---|---|---|---|---|---|---|---|---|---|---|---|---|---|---|---|---|---|---|---|---|---|---|---|
| Season | Club | League | GP | G | A | Pts | PIM | PP | SH | GW | S | % | +/- | TF | F% | Min | GP | G | A | Pts | PIM | PP | SH | GW | Min |
| 99-2000 | Thornhill Rattlers | OPJHL | 49 | 15 | 19 | 34 | 61 | .... | .... | .... | .... | .... | .... | .... | .... | .... | .... | .... | .... | .... | .... | .... | .... | .... | .... |
| 2000-01 | Plymouth Whalers | OHL | 68 | 9 | 14 | 23 | 87 | .... | .... | .... | .... | .... | .... | .... | .... | .... | 19 | 3 | 4 | 7 | 14 | .... | .... | .... | .... |
| 2001-02 | Plymouth Whalers | OHL | 65 | 20 | 23 | 43 | 104 | .... | .... | .... | .... | .... | .... | .... | .... | .... | 6 | 0 | 2 | 2 | 21 | .... | .... | .... | .... |
| 2002-03 | Plymouth Whalers | OHL | 68 | 35 | 50 | 85 | 120 | .... | .... | .... | .... | .... | .... | .... | .... | .... | 17 | 7 | 10 | 17 | 31 | .... | .... | .... | .... |
| **2003-04** | **Atlanta** | **NHL** | **5** | **0** | **1** | **1** | **4** | **0** | **0** | **0** | **2** | **0.0** | **0** | **10** | **10.0** | **4:27** | .... | .... | .... | .... | .... | .... | .... | .... | .... |
| | Chicago Wolves | AHL | 72 | 10 | 32 | 42 | 186 | .... | .... | .... | .... | .... | .... | .... | .... | .... | 10 | 2 | 3 | 5 | 29 | .... | .... | .... | .... |
| 2004-05 | Chicago Wolves | AHL | 77 | 16 | 8 | 24 | 226 | .... | .... | .... | .... | .... | .... | .... | .... | .... | 12 | 4 | 2 | 6 | 32 | .... | .... | .... | .... |
| **2005-06** | **Atlanta** | **NHL** | **8** | **0** | **0** | **0** | **15** | **0** | **0** | **0** | **6** | **0.0** | **–3** | **3** | **100.0** | **5:40** | .... | .... | .... | .... | .... | .... | .... | .... | .... |
| | Chicago Wolves | AHL | 71 | 22 | 18 | 40 | 184 | .... | .... | .... | .... | .... | .... | .... | .... | .... | .... | .... | .... | .... | .... | .... | .... | .... | .... |
| **2006-07** | **Pittsburgh** | **NHL** | **3** | **0** | **0** | **0** | **2** | **0** | **0** | **0** | **0** | **0.0** | **–1** | **1** | **100.0** | **3:23** | .... | .... | .... | .... | .... | .... | .... | .... | .... |
| | **Chicago** | **NHL** | **37** | **2** | **3** | **5** | **43** | **0** | **1** | **0** | **19** | **10.5** | **–2** | **2** | **50.0** | **9:22** | .... | .... | .... | .... | .... | .... | .... | .... | .... |
| | **Tampa Bay** | **NHL** | **7** | **0** | **0** | **0** | **2** | **0** | **0** | **0** | **2** | **0.0** | **–2** | **0** | **0.0** | **7:10** | .... | .... | .... | .... | .... | .... | .... | .... | .... |
| **2007-08** | **Tampa Bay** | **NHL** | **9** | **0** | **0** | **0** | **2** | **0** | **0** | **0** | **2** | **0.0** | **–2** | **0** | **0.0** | **4:06** | .... | .... | .... | .... | .... | .... | .... | .... | .... |
| | Norfolk Admirals | AHL | 62 | 14 | 13 | 27 | 96 | .... | .... | .... | .... | .... | .... | .... | .... | .... | .... | .... | .... | .... | .... | .... | .... | .... | .... |
| 2008-09 | Rochester | AHL | 72 | 20 | 8 | 28 | 70 | .... | .... | .... | .... | .... | .... | .... | .... | .... | .... | .... | .... | .... | .... | .... | .... | .... | .... |
| | **NHL Totals** | | **69** | **2** | **4** | **6** | **68** | **0** | **1** | **0** | **31** | **6.5** | | **16** | **37.5** | **7:25** | .... | .... | .... | .... | .... | .... | .... | .... | .... |

Signed as a free agent by **Atlanta**, September 28, 2001. Traded to **Anaheim** by **Atlanta** with Atlanta's 2nd round choice (later traded to Colorado - Colorado selected T.J. Galiardi) in 2007 Entry Draft and future considerations for Vitaly Vishnevski, August 17, 2006. Claimed on waivers by **Pittsburgh** from **Anaheim**, September 27, 2006. Claimed on waivers by **Chicago** from **Pittsburgh**, October 26, 2006. Traded to **Tampa Bay** by **Chicago** with Florida's 6th round choice (previously acquired, Tampa Bay selected Luke Witkowski) in 2008 Entry Draft for Nikita Alexeev, February 27, 2007.

## STILLMAN, Cory

(STIHL-mahn, KOHR-ee) **FLA.**

Left wing. Shoots left. 6', 200 lbs. Born, Peterborough, Ont., December 20, 1973. Calgary's 1st choice, 6th overall, in 1992 Entry Draft.

| Season | Club | League | GP | G | A | Pts | PIM | PP | SH | GW | S | % | +/- | TF | F% | Min | GP | G | A | Pts | PIM | PP | SH | GW | Min |
|---|---|---|---|---|---|---|---|---|---|---|---|---|---|---|---|---|---|---|---|---|---|---|---|---|---|
| 1989-90 | Peterborough | OHA-B | 41 | 30 | *54 | 84 | 76 | .... | .... | .... | .... | .... | .... | .... | .... | .... | .... | .... | .... | .... | .... | .... | .... | .... | .... |
| 1990-91 | Windsor Spitfires | OHL | 64 | 31 | 70 | 101 | 31 | .... | .... | .... | .... | .... | .... | .... | .... | .... | 11 | 3 | 6 | 9 | 8 | .... | .... | .... | .... |
| 1991-92 | Windsor Spitfires | OHL | 53 | 29 | 61 | 90 | 59 | .... | .... | .... | .... | .... | .... | .... | .... | .... | 7 | 2 | 4 | 6 | 8 | .... | .... | .... | .... |
| 1992-93 | Peterborough | OHL | 61 | 25 | 55 | 80 | 55 | .... | .... | .... | .... | .... | .... | .... | .... | .... | 18 | 3 | 8 | 11 | 18 | .... | .... | .... | .... |
| 1993-94 | Saint John Flames | AHL | 79 | 35 | 48 | 83 | 52 | .... | .... | .... | .... | .... | .... | .... | .... | .... | 7 | 2 | 4 | 6 | 16 | .... | .... | .... | .... |
| **1994-95** | Saint John Flames | AHL | 63 | 28 | 53 | 81 | 70 | .... | .... | .... | .... | .... | .... | .... | .... | .... | 5 | 0 | 2 | 2 | 2 | .... | .... | .... | .... |
| | **Calgary** | **NHL** | **10** | **0** | **2** | **2** | **2** | **0** | **0** | **0** | **7** | **0.0** | **1** | .... | .... | .... | .... | .... | .... | .... | .... | .... | .... | .... | .... |
| **1995-96** | **Calgary** | **NHL** | **74** | **16** | **19** | **35** | **41** | **4** | **1** | **3** | **132** | **12.1** | **–5** | .... | .... | .... | **2** | **1** | **1** | **2** | **0** | **0** | **0** | **0** | .... |
| **1996-97** | **Calgary** | **NHL** | **58** | **6** | **20** | **26** | **14** | **2** | **0** | **0** | **112** | **5.4** | **–6** | .... | .... | .... | .... | .... | .... | .... | .... | .... | .... | .... | .... |
| **1997-98** | **Calgary** | **NHL** | **72** | **27** | **22** | **49** | **40** | **9** | **4** | **1** | **178** | **15.2** | **–9** | .... | .... | .... | .... | .... | .... | .... | .... | .... | .... | .... | .... |
| **1998-99** | **Calgary** | **NHL** | **76** | **27** | **30** | **57** | **38** | **9** | **3** | **5** | **175** | **15.4** | **7** | **535** | **46.5** | **16:19** | .... | .... | .... | .... | .... | .... | .... | .... | .... |
| **99-2000** | **Calgary** | **NHL** | **37** | **12** | **9** | **21** | **12** | **6** | **0** | **3** | **59** | **20.3** | **–9** | **283** | **54.4** | **17:45** | .... | .... | .... | .... | .... | .... | .... | .... | .... |
| **2000-01** | **Calgary** | **NHL** | **66** | **21** | **24** | **45** | **45** | **7** | **0** | **4** | **148** | **14.2** | **–6** | **346** | **43.9** | **18:50** | .... | .... | .... | .... | .... | .... | .... | .... | .... |
| | **St. Louis** | **NHL** | **12** | **3** | **4** | **7** | **6** | **3** | **0** | **0** | **26** | **11.5** | **–2** | **36** | **61.1** | **18:37** | **15** | **3** | **5** | **8** | **8** | **1** | **0** | **1** | **14:58** |
| **2001-02** | **St. Louis** | **NHL** | **80** | **23** | **22** | **45** | **36** | **6** | **0** | **4** | **140** | **16.4** | **8** | **196** | **46.4** | **15:03** | **9** | **0** | **2** | **2** | **2** | **0** | **0** | **0** | **12:46** |
| **2002-03** | **St. Louis** | **NHL** | **79** | **24** | **43** | **67** | **56** | **6** | **0** | **4** | **157** | **15.3** | **12** | **266** | **41.7** | **18:20** | **6** | **2** | **2** | **4** | **2** | **2** | **0** | **1** | **18:05** |
| **2003-04♦** | **Tampa Bay** | **NHL** | **81** | **25** | **55** | **80** | **36** | **11** | **1** | **6** | **178** | **14.0** | **18** | **38** | **31.6** | **19:32** | **21** | **2** | **5** | **7** | **15** | **0** | **1** | **0** | **17:22** |
| 2004-05 | | | DID NOT PLAY | | | | | | | | | | | | | | | | | | | | | | |
| **2005-06♦** | **Carolina** | **NHL** | **72** | **21** | **55** | **76** | **32** | **10** | **0** | **3** | **177** | **11.9** | **–9** | **11** | **27.3** | **18:40** | **25** | **9** | **17** | **26** | **14** | **4** | **0** | **3** | **18:42** |
| **2006-07** | **Carolina** | **NHL** | **43** | **5** | **22** | **27** | **24** | **1** | **0** | **0** | **85** | **5.9** | **–8** | **7** | **28.6** | **17:25** | .... | .... | .... | .... | .... | .... | .... | .... | .... |
| **2007-08** | **Carolina** | **NHL** | **55** | **21** | **25** | **46** | **14** | **10** | **0** | **6** | **124** | **16.9** | **–7** | **11** | **54.6** | **19:53** | .... | .... | .... | .... | .... | .... | .... | .... | .... |
| | **Ottawa** | **NHL** | **24** | **3** | **16** | **19** | **10** | **1** | **0** | **0** | **42** | **7.1** | **–8** | **6** | **16.7** | **16:54** | **4** | **2** | **0** | **2** | **2** | **1** | **0** | **0** | **18:26** |
| **2008-09** | **Florida** | **NHL** | **63** | **17** | **32** | **49** | **37** | **8** | **0** | **2** | **115** | **14.8** | **1** | **30** | **36.7** | **16:35** | .... | .... | .... | .... | .... | .... | .... | .... | .... |
| | **NHL Totals** | | **902** | **251** | **400** | **651** | **443** | **93** | **9** | **41** | **1855** | **13.5** | | **1765** | **46.1** | **17:47** | **82** | **19** | **32** | **51** | **43** | **8** | **1** | **5** | **16:55** |

OHL Rookie of the Year (1991)

• Missed majority of 1999-2000 season recovering from shoulder injury suffered in game vs. Philadelphia, December 27, 1999. Traded to **St. Louis by Calgary** for Craig Conroy and St. Louis' 7th round choice (David Moss) in 2001 Entry Draft, March 13, 2001. Traded to **Tampa Bay** by **St. Louis** for Tampa Bay's 2nd round choice (David Backes) in 2003 Entry Draft, June 21, 2003. Signed as a free agent by **Carolina**, August 2, 2005. Traded to **Ottawa** by **Carolina** with Mike Commodore for Joe Corvo and Patrick Eaves, February 11, 2008. Signed as a free agent by **Florida**, July 1, 2008.

## STOLL, Jarret

(STOHL, JAIR-iht) **L.A.**

Center. Shoots right. 6', 214 lbs. Born, Melville, Sask., June 25, 1982. Edmonton's 3rd choice, 36th overall, in 2002 Entry Draft.

| Season | Club | League | GP | G | A | Pts | PIM | PP | SH | GW | S | % | +/- | TF | F% | Min | GP | G | A | Pts | PIM | PP | SH | GW | Min |
|---|---|---|---|---|---|---|---|---|---|---|---|---|---|---|---|---|---|---|---|---|---|---|---|---|---|
| 1997-98 | Saskatoon Blazers | SMHL | 44 | 45 | 44 | *89 | 78 | .... | .... | .... | .... | .... | .... | .... | .... | .... | .... | .... | .... | .... | .... | .... | .... | .... | .... |
| | Edmonton Ice | WHL | 8 | 2 | 3 | 5 | 4 | .... | .... | .... | .... | .... | .... | .... | .... | .... | .... | .... | .... | .... | .... | .... | .... | .... | .... |
| 1998-99 | Kootenay Ice | WHL | 57 | 13 | 21 | 34 | 38 | .... | .... | .... | .... | .... | .... | .... | .... | .... | 4 | 0 | 0 | 0 | 2 | .... | .... | .... | .... |
| 99-2000 | Kootenay Ice | WHL | 71 | 37 | 38 | 75 | 64 | .... | .... | .... | .... | .... | .... | .... | .... | .... | 20 | 7 | 9 | 16 | 24 | .... | .... | .... | .... |
| 2000-01 | Kootenay Ice | WHL | 62 | 40 | 66 | 106 | 105 | .... | .... | .... | .... | .... | .... | .... | .... | .... | 11 | 5 | 9 | 14 | 22 | .... | .... | .... | .... |
| 2001-02 | Kootenay Ice | WHL | 47 | 32 | 34 | 66 | 64 | .... | .... | .... | .... | .... | .... | .... | .... | .... | 22 | 6 | 14 | 20 | 35 | .... | .... | .... | .... |
| **2002-03** | **Edmonton** | **NHL** | **4** | **0** | **1** | **1** | **0** | **0** | **0** | **0** | **5** | **0.0** | **–3** | **30** | **63.3** | **7:44** | .... | .... | .... | .... | .... | .... | .... | .... | .... |
| | Hamilton | AHL | 76 | 21 | 33 | 54 | 86 | .... | .... | .... | .... | .... | .... | .... | .... | .... | 23 | 5 | 8 | 13 | 25 | .... | .... | .... | .... |
| **2003-04** | **Edmonton** | **NHL** | **68** | **10** | **11** | **21** | **42** | **1** | **1** | **2** | **107** | **9.3** | **8** | **1019** | **54.1** | **13:54** | .... | .... | .... | .... | .... | .... | .... | .... | .... |
| 2004-05 | Edmonton | AHL | 66 | 21 | 17 | 38 | 92 | .... | .... | .... | .... | .... | .... | .... | .... | .... | .... | .... | .... | .... | .... | .... | .... | .... | .... |
| **2005-06** | **Edmonton** | **NHL** | **82** | **22** | **46** | **68** | **74** | **11** | **1** | **4** | **243** | **9.1** | **4** | **1348** | **56.8** | **18:23** | **24** | **4** | **6** | **10** | **24** | **2** | **0** | **1** | **17:06** |
| **2006-07** | **Edmonton** | **NHL** | **51** | **13** | **26** | **39** | **48** | **6** | **1** | **2** | **115** | **11.3** | **2** | **901** | **55.6** | **18:12** | .... | .... | .... | .... | .... | .... | .... | .... | .... |
| **2007-08** | **Edmonton** | **NHL** | **81** | **14** | **22** | **36** | **74** | **8** | **3** | **1** | **187** | **7.5** | **–23** | **1229** | **55.1** | **17:56** | .... | .... | .... | .... | .... | .... | .... | .... | .... |
| **2008-09** | **Los Angeles** | **NHL** | **74** | **18** | **23** | **41** | **68** | **10** | **0** | **1** | **155** | **11.6** | **–7** | **1047** | **57.2** | **17:05** | .... | .... | .... | .... | .... | .... | .... | .... | .... |
| | **NHL Totals** | | **360** | **77** | **129** | **206** | **306** | **36** | **6** | **10** | **812** | **9.5** | | **5574** | **55.8** | **17:01** | **24** | **4** | **6** | **10** | **24** | **2** | **0** | **1** | **17:06** |

• Re-entered NHL Entry Draft. Originally Calgary's 3rd choice, 46th overall, in 2000 Entry Draft.

WHL East First All-Star Team (2001) • Canadian Major Junior First All-Star Team (2001) • WHL West First All-Star Team (2002)

Traded to **Los Angeles** by **Edmonton** with Matt Greene for Lubomir Visnovsky, June 29, 2008.

## STONE, Ryan

(STOHN, RIGH-uhn) **EDM.**

Center. Shoots left. 6'2", 207 lbs. Born, Calgary, Alta., March 20, 1985. Pittsburgh's 2nd choice, 32nd overall, in 2003 Entry Draft.

| Season | Club | League | GP | G | A | Pts | PIM | PP | SH | GW | S | % | +/- | TF | F% | Min | GP | G | A | Pts | PIM | PP | SH | GW | Min |
|---|---|---|---|---|---|---|---|---|---|---|---|---|---|---|---|---|---|---|---|---|---|---|---|---|---|
| 2000-01 | Cgy. North Stars | AMHL | 34 | 37 | 28 | 55 | 90 | .... | .... | .... | .... | .... | .... | .... | .... | .... | .... | .... | .... | .... | .... | .... | .... | .... | .... |
| 2001-02 | Brandon | WHL | 65 | 11 | 27 | 38 | 128 | .... | .... | .... | .... | .... | .... | .... | .... | .... | 19 | 0 | 3 | 3 | 39 | .... | .... | .... | .... |
| 2002-03 | Brandon | WHL | 54 | 14 | 31 | 45 | 158 | .... | .... | .... | .... | .... | .... | .... | .... | .... | 12 | 4 | 2 | 6 | 20 | .... | .... | .... | .... |
| 2003-04 | Brandon | WHL | 50 | 20 | 38 | 58 | 125 | .... | .... | .... | .... | .... | .... | .... | .... | .... | 11 | 1 | 3 | 4 | 24 | .... | .... | .... | .... |
| 2004-05 | Brandon | WHL | 70 | 33 | *66 | 99 | 127 | .... | .... | .... | .... | .... | .... | .... | .... | .... | 24 | 4 | *23 | 27 | 48 | .... | .... | .... | .... |
| 2005-06 | Wilkes-Barre | AHL | 75 | 14 | 22 | 36 | 109 | .... | .... | .... | .... | .... | .... | .... | .... | .... | 11 | 4 | 7 | 11 | 12 | .... | .... | .... | .... |
| 2006-07 | Wilkes-Barre | AHL | 41 | 7 | 26 | 33 | 86 | .... | .... | .... | .... | .... | .... | .... | .... | .... | 10 | 2 | 3 | 5 | 21 | .... | .... | .... | .... |
| **2007-08** | **Pittsburgh** | **NHL** | **6** | **0** | **1** | **1** | **5** | **0** | **0** | **0** | **3** | **0.0** | **–1** | **5** | **60.0** | **6:25** | .... | .... | .... | .... | .... | .... | .... | .... | .... |
| | Wilkes-Barre | AHL | 65 | 11 | 28 | 39 | 129 | .... | .... | .... | .... | .... | .... | .... | .... | .... | 23 | 5 | 12 | 17 | 33 | .... | .... | .... | .... |
| **2008-09** | **Pittsburgh** | **NHL** | **2** | **0** | **0** | **0** | **2** | **0** | **0** | **0** | **5** | **0.0** | **1** | **0** | **0.0** | **10:20** | .... | .... | .... | .... | .... | .... | .... | .... | .... |
| | Wilkes-Barre | AHL | 38 | 9 | 19 | 28 | 53 | .... | .... | .... | .... | .... | .... | .... | .... | .... | .... | .... | .... | .... | .... | .... | .... | .... | .... |
| | Springfield | AHL | 39 | 8 | 21 | 29 | 64 | .... | .... | .... | .... | .... | .... | .... | .... | .... | .... | .... | .... | .... | .... | .... | .... | .... | .... |
| | **NHL Totals** | | **8** | **0** | **1** | **1** | **7** | **0** | **0** | **0** | **8** | **0.0** | | **5** | **60.0** | **7:24** | .... | .... | .... | .... | .... | .... | .... | .... | .... |

WHL East First All-Star Team (2005)

Traded to **Edmonton** by **Pittsburgh** with Dany Sabourin and Pittsburgh's 4th round choice in 2011 Entry Draft for Mathieu Garon, January 17, 2009.

## STORTINI, Zack

(stohr-TEE-nee, ZAK) **EDM.**

Right wing. Shoots right. 6'3", 228 lbs. Born, Elliot Lake, Ont., September 11, 1985. Edmonton's 5th choice, 94th overall, in 2003 Entry Draft.

| Season | Club | League | GP | G | A | Pts | PIM | PP | SH | GW | S | % | +/- | TF | F% | Min | GP | G | A | Pts | PIM | PP | SH | GW | Min |
|---|---|---|---|---|---|---|---|---|---|---|---|---|---|---|---|---|---|---|---|---|---|---|---|---|---|
| 2000-01 | Newmarket | OPJHL | 34 | 3 | 10 | 13 | 68 | .... | .... | .... | .... | .... | .... | .... | .... | .... | .... | .... | .... | .... | .... | .... | .... | .... | .... |
| 2001-02 | Sudbury Wolves | OHL | 65 | 8 | 6 | 14 | 187 | .... | .... | .... | .... | .... | .... | .... | .... | .... | 5 | 1 | 0 | 1 | 24 | .... | .... | .... | .... |
| 2002-03 | Sudbury Wolves | OHL | 62 | 13 | 16 | 29 | 222 | .... | .... | .... | .... | .... | .... | .... | .... | .... | .... | .... | .... | .... | .... | .... | .... | .... | .... |
| 2003-04 | Sudbury Wolves | OHL | 62 | 21 | 16 | 37 | 151 | .... | .... | .... | .... | .... | .... | .... | .... | .... | 7 | 1 | 1 | 2 | 14 | .... | .... | .... | .... |
| | Toronto | AHL | 2 | 0 | 0 | 0 | 7 | .... | .... | .... | .... | .... | .... | .... | .... | .... | 3 | 0 | 0 | 0 | 4 | .... | .... | .... | .... |
| 2004-05 | Sudbury Wolves | OHL | 58 | 13 | 27 | 40 | 186 | .... | .... | .... | .... | .... | .... | .... | .... | .... | 12 | 2 | 5 | 7 | 27 | .... | .... | .... | .... |
| 2005-06 | Iowa Stars | AHL | 27 | 2 | 1 | 3 | 108 | .... | .... | .... | .... | .... | .... | .... | .... | .... | .... | .... | .... | .... | .... | .... | .... | .... | .... |
| | Milwaukee | AHL | 37 | 0 | 7 | 7 | 153 | .... | .... | .... | .... | .... | .... | .... | .... | .... | .... | .... | .... | .... | .... | .... | .... | .... | .... |
| **2006-07** | **Edmonton** | **NHL** | **29** | **1** | **0** | **1** | **105** | **0** | **0** | **0** | **17** | **5.9** | **–7** | **3** | **100.0** | **7:09** | .... | .... | .... | .... | .... | .... | .... | .... | .... |
| | Hamilton | AHL | 47 | 9 | 6 | 15 | 195 | .... | .... | .... | .... | .... | .... | .... | .... | .... | 22 | 3 | 0 | 3 | *56 | .... | .... | .... | .... |

| | | | Regular Season | | | | | | | | | | | | | | Playoffs | | | | | | | | |
|---|---|---|---|---|---|---|---|---|---|---|---|---|---|---|---|---|---|---|---|---|---|---|---|---|---|
| Season | Club | League | GP | G | A | Pts | PIM | PP | SH | GW | S | % | +/- | TF | F% | Min | GP | G | A | Pts | PIM | PP | SH | GW | Min |
| **2007-08** | **Edmonton** | **NHL** | **66** | **3** | **9** | **12** | **201** | **0** | **0** | **0** | **38** | **7.9** | **3** | **7** | **42.9** | **8:10** | .... | .... | .... | .... | .... | .... | .... | .... | .... |
| | Springfield | AHL | 4 | 3 | 2 | 5 | 21 | .... | .... | .... | .... | .... | .... | .... | .... | .... | .... | .... | .... | .... | .... | .... | .... | .... | .... |
| **2008-09** | **Edmonton** | **NHL** | **52** | **6** | **5** | **11** | **181** | **0** | **0** | **0** | **23** | **26.1** | **–3** | **11** | **63.6** | **7:17** | .... | .... | .... | .... | .... | .... | .... | .... | .... |
| | **NHL Totals** | | **147** | **10** | **14** | **24** | **487** | **0** | **0** | **0** | **78** | **12.8** | | **21** | **61.9** | **7:40** | .... | .... | .... | .... | .... | .... | .... | .... | .... |

## STRACHAN, Tyson

(STRAWN, TIGH-suhn) **ST.L.**

Defense. Shoots right. 6'1", 212 lbs. Born, Melfort, Sask., October 30, 1984. Carolina's 6th choice, 137th overall, in 2003 Entry Draft.

| | | | | | | | | | | | | | | | | | | | | | | | | | |
|---|---|---|---|---|---|---|---|---|---|---|---|---|---|---|---|---|---|---|---|---|---|---|---|---|---|
| 2001-02 | Tisdale Trojans | SMHL | 42 | 5 | 18 | 23 | 70 | .... | .... | .... | .... | .... | .... | .... | .... | .... | .... | .... | .... | .... | .... | .... | .... | .... | .... |
| | Melville | SJHL | 2 | 0 | 0 | 0 | 0 | .... | .... | .... | .... | .... | .... | .... | .... | .... | .... | .... | .... | .... | .... | .... | .... | .... | .... |
| 2002-03 | Vernon Vipers | BCHL | 56 | 6 | 22 | 28 | 99 | .... | .... | .... | .... | .... | .... | .... | .... | .... | .... | .... | .... | .... | .... | .... | .... | .... | .... |
| 2003-04 | Ohio State | CCHA | 30 | 2 | 5 | 7 | 8 | .... | .... | .... | .... | .... | .... | .... | .... | .... | .... | .... | .... | .... | .... | .... | .... | .... | .... |
| 2004-05 | Ohio State | CCHA | 31 | 1 | 4 | 5 | 32 | .... | .... | .... | .... | .... | .... | .... | .... | .... | .... | .... | .... | .... | .... | .... | .... | .... | .... |
| 2005-06 | Ohio State | CCHA | 23 | 3 | 2 | 5 | 37 | .... | .... | .... | .... | .... | .... | .... | .... | .... | .... | .... | .... | .... | .... | .... | .... | .... | .... |
| 2006-07 | Ohio State | CCHA | 35 | 7 | 11 | 18 | 55 | .... | .... | .... | .... | .... | .... | .... | .... | .... | .... | .... | .... | .... | .... | .... | .... | .... | .... |
| | Albany River Rats | AHL | 1 | 0 | 0 | 0 | 0 | .... | .... | .... | .... | .... | .... | .... | .... | .... | .... | .... | .... | .... | .... | .... | .... | .... | .... |
| 2007-08 | Peoria Rivermen | AHL | 34 | 1 | 2 | 3 | 61 | .... | .... | .... | .... | .... | .... | .... | .... | .... | .... | .... | .... | .... | .... | .... | .... | .... | .... |
| | Las Vegas | ECHL | 25 | 2 | 7 | 9 | 68 | .... | .... | .... | .... | .... | .... | .... | .... | .... | 16 | 0 | 4 | 4 | 12 | .... | .... | .... | .... |
| **2008-09** | **St. Louis** | **NHL** | **30** | **0** | **3** | **3** | **39** | **0** | **0** | **0** | **21** | **0.0** | **8** | **0** | **0.0** | **13:26** | .... | .... | .... | .... | .... | .... | .... | .... | .... |
| | Peoria Rivermen | AHL | 29 | 2 | 3 | 5 | 67 | .... | .... | .... | .... | .... | .... | .... | .... | .... | 3 | 0 | 0 | 0 | 11 | .... | .... | .... | .... |
| | **NHL Totals** | | **30** | **0** | **3** | **3** | **39** | **0** | **0** | **0** | **21** | **0.0** | | **0** | **0.0** | **13:26** | .... | .... | .... | .... | .... | .... | .... | .... | .... |

Signed as a free agent by **St. Louis**, October 9, 2008.

## STRALMAN, Anton

(STROHL-muhn, AN-tawn) **CGY.**

Defense. Shoots right. 6'1", 200 lbs. Born, Tibro, Sweden, August 1, 1986. Toronto's 5th choice, 216th overall, in 2005 Entry Draft.

| | | | | | | | | | | | | | | | | | | | | | | | | | |
|---|---|---|---|---|---|---|---|---|---|---|---|---|---|---|---|---|---|---|---|---|---|---|---|---|---|
| 2002-03 | Skovde IK Jr. | Swe-Jr. | 46 | 20 | 9 | 29 | 38 | .... | .... | .... | .... | .... | .... | .... | .... | .... | .... | .... | .... | .... | .... | .... | .... | .... | .... |
| 2003-04 | Skovde IK | Sweden-3 | 27 | 4 | 8 | 12 | 18 | .... | .... | .... | .... | .... | .... | .... | .... | .... | .... | .... | .... | .... | .... | .... | .... | .... | .... |
| 2004-05 | Skovde IK | Sweden-2 | 50 | 10 | 11 | 21 | 40 | .... | .... | .... | .... | .... | .... | .... | .... | .... | .... | .... | .... | .... | .... | .... | .... | .... | .... |
| 2005-06 | Timra IK | Sweden | 45 | 1 | 4 | 5 | 28 | .... | .... | .... | .... | .... | .... | .... | .... | .... | .... | .... | .... | .... | .... | .... | .... | .... | .... |
| | Timra IK Jr. | Swe-Jr. | .... | .... | .... | .... | .... | .... | .... | .... | .... | .... | .... | .... | .... | .... | 3 | 0 | 0 | 0 | 4 | .... | .... | .... | .... |
| 2006-07 | Timra IK | Sweden | 53 | 10 | 11 | 21 | 34 | .... | .... | .... | .... | .... | .... | .... | .... | .... | 7 | 1 | 3 | 4 | 10 | .... | .... | .... | .... |
| **2007-08** | **Toronto** | **NHL** | **50** | **3** | **6** | **9** | **18** | **0** | **0** | **0** | **40** | **7.5** | **–10** | **0** | **0.0** | **12:49** | .... | .... | .... | .... | .... | .... | .... | .... | .... |
| | Toronto Marlies | AHL | 21 | 0 | 11 | 11 | 22 | .... | .... | .... | .... | .... | .... | .... | .... | .... | .... | .... | .... | .... | .... | .... | .... | .... | .... |
| **2008-09** | **Toronto** | **NHL** | **38** | **1** | **12** | **13** | **20** | **0** | **0** | **1** | **43** | **2.3** | **–2** | **1** | **100.0** | **15:34** | .... | .... | .... | .... | .... | .... | .... | .... | .... |
| | Toronto Marlies | AHL | 36 | 7 | 9 | 16 | 24 | .... | .... | .... | .... | .... | .... | .... | .... | .... | 6 | 1 | 2 | 3 | 0 | .... | .... | .... | .... |
| | **NHL Totals** | | **88** | **4** | **18** | **22** | **38** | **0** | **0** | **1** | **83** | **4.8** | | **1** | **100.0** | **14:00** | .... | .... | .... | .... | .... | .... | .... | .... | .... |

Traded to **Calgary** by **Toronto** with Colin Stuart and Toronto's 7th round choice in 2012 Entry Draft for Wayne Primeau and Calgary's 2nd round choice in 2011 Entry Draft, July 27, 2009.

## STREIT, Mark

(STRIGHT, MAHRK) **NYI**

Defense. Shoots left. 6', 197 lbs. Born, Englisberg, Switz., December 11, 1977. Montreal's 8th choice, 262nd overall, in 2004 Entry Draft.

| | | | | | | | | | | | | | | | | | | | | | | | | | |
|---|---|---|---|---|---|---|---|---|---|---|---|---|---|---|---|---|---|---|---|---|---|---|---|---|---|
| 1995-96 | Fribourg | Swiss | 34 | 2 | 2 | 4 | 6 | .... | .... | .... | .... | .... | .... | .... | .... | .... | 4 | 0 | 0 | 0 | 2 | .... | .... | .... | .... |
| 1996-97 | HC Davos | Swiss | 46 | 2 | 9 | 11 | 18 | .... | .... | .... | .... | .... | .... | .... | .... | .... | 6 | 0 | 0 | 0 | 0 | .... | .... | .... | .... |
| 1997-98 | HC Ambri-Piotta | Swiss | 2 | 0 | 0 | 0 | 0 | .... | .... | .... | .... | .... | .... | .... | .... | .... | .... | .... | .... | .... | .... | .... | .... | .... | .... |
| | HC Davos | Swiss | 38 | 4 | 10 | 14 | 14 | .... | .... | .... | .... | .... | .... | .... | .... | .... | 18 | 1 | 5 | 6 | 20 | .... | .... | .... | .... |
| 1998-99 | HC Davos | Swiss | 44 | 7 | 18 | 25 | 42 | .... | .... | .... | .... | .... | .... | .... | .... | .... | 6 | 3 | 3 | 6 | 8 | .... | .... | .... | .... |
| 99-2000 | Springfield | AHL | 43 | 3 | 12 | 15 | 18 | .... | .... | .... | .... | .... | .... | .... | .... | .... | 5 | 0 | 0 | 0 | 2 | .... | .... | .... | .... |
| | Utah Grizzlies | IHL | 1 | 0 | 1 | 1 | 2 | .... | .... | .... | .... | .... | .... | .... | .... | .... | .... | .... | .... | .... | .... | .... | .... | .... | .... |
| | Tallahassee | ECHL | 14 | 0 | 5 | 5 | 16 | .... | .... | .... | .... | .... | .... | .... | .... | .... | .... | .... | .... | .... | .... | .... | .... | .... | .... |
| 2000-01 | ZSC Lions Zurich | Swiss | 44 | 5 | 11 | 16 | 48 | .... | .... | .... | .... | .... | .... | .... | .... | .... | 16 | 2 | 5 | 7 | 37 | .... | .... | .... | .... |
| 2001-02 | ZSC Lions Zurich | Swiss | 28 | 6 | 17 | 23 | 36 | .... | .... | .... | .... | .... | .... | .... | .... | .... | 16 | 0 | 6 | 6 | 14 | .... | .... | .... | .... |
| | Switzerland | Olympics | 4 | 1 | 1 | 2 | 0 | .... | .... | .... | .... | .... | .... | .... | .... | .... | .... | .... | .... | .... | .... | .... | .... | .... | .... |
| 2002-03 | ZSC Lions Zurich | Swiss | 37 | 4 | 19 | 23 | 62 | .... | .... | .... | .... | .... | .... | .... | .... | .... | 12 | 1 | 7 | 8 | 2 | .... | .... | .... | .... |
| 2003-04 | ZSC Lions Zurich | Swiss | 48 | 12 | 24 | 36 | 78 | .... | .... | .... | .... | .... | .... | .... | .... | .... | 13 | 5 | 2 | 7 | 14 | .... | .... | .... | .... |
| 2004-05 | ZSC Lions Zurich | Swiss | 44 | 14 | 29 | 43 | 46 | .... | .... | .... | .... | .... | .... | .... | .... | .... | 15 | 4 | 11 | 15 | 20 | .... | .... | .... | .... |
| **2005-06** | **Montreal** | **NHL** | **48** | **2** | **9** | **11** | **28** | **2** | **0** | **0** | **52** | **3.8** | **–6** | **1** | **0.0** | **14:36** | **1** | **0** | **0** | **0** | **0** | **0** | **0** | **0** | **3:29** |
| | Switzerland | Olympics | 6 | 2 | 1 | 3 | 6 | .... | .... | .... | .... | .... | .... | .... | .... | .... | .... | .... | .... | .... | .... | .... | .... | .... | .... |
| **2006-07** | **Montreal** | **NHL** | **76** | **10** | **26** | **36** | **14** | **2** | **1** | **1** | **102** | **9.8** | **–5** | **12** | **33.3** | **14:01** | .... | .... | .... | .... | .... | .... | .... | .... | .... |
| **2007-08** | **Montreal** | **NHL** | **81** | **13** | **49** | **62** | **28** | **7** | **0** | **3** | **165** | **7.9** | **–6** | **1** | **0.0** | **17:31** | **11** | **1** | **3** | **4** | **8** | **0** | **0** | **0** | **14:48** |
| **2008-09** | **NY Islanders** | **NHL** | **74** | **16** | **40** | **56** | **62** | **10** | **1** | **1** | **150** | **10.7** | **5** | **0** | **0.0** | **25:13** | .... | .... | .... | .... | .... | .... | .... | .... | .... |
| | **NHL Totals** | | **279** | **41** | **124** | **165** | **132** | **21** | **2** | **5** | **469** | **8.7** | | **14** | **28.6** | **18:06** | **12** | **1** | **3** | **4** | **8** | **0** | **0** | **0** | **13:51** |

Played in NHL All-Star Game (2009)

Signed as a free agent by **NY Islanders**, July 1, 2008.

## STRUDWICK, Jason

(STRUHD-wihk, JAY-suhn) **EDM.**

Defense. Shoots left. 6'4", 225 lbs. Born, Edmonton, Alta., July 17, 1975. NY Islanders' 3rd choice, 63rd overall, in 1994 Entry Draft.

| | | | | | | | | | | | | | | | | | | | | | | | | | |
|---|---|---|---|---|---|---|---|---|---|---|---|---|---|---|---|---|---|---|---|---|---|---|---|---|---|
| 1991-92 | Edmonton Legion | AMHL | 35 | 3 | 8 | 11 | 67 | .... | .... | .... | .... | .... | .... | .... | .... | .... | .... | .... | .... | .... | .... | .... | .... | .... | .... |
| 1992-93 | Edmonton Pats | AMHL | 33 | 8 | 20 | 28 | 135 | .... | .... | .... | .... | .... | .... | .... | .... | .... | .... | .... | .... | .... | .... | .... | .... | .... | .... |
| 1993-94 | Kamloops Blazers | WHL | 61 | 6 | 8 | 14 | 118 | .... | .... | .... | .... | .... | .... | .... | .... | .... | 19 | 0 | 4 | 4 | 24 | .... | .... | .... | .... |
| 1994-95 | Kamloops Blazers | WHL | 72 | 3 | 11 | 14 | 183 | .... | .... | .... | .... | .... | .... | .... | .... | .... | 21 | 1 | 1 | 2 | 39 | .... | .... | .... | .... |
| **1995-96** | **NY Islanders** | **NHL** | **1** | **0** | **0** | **0** | **7** | **0** | **0** | **0** | **0** | **0.0** | **0** | .... | .... | .... | .... | .... | .... | .... | .... | .... | .... | .... | .... |
| | Worcester IceCats | AHL | 60 | 2 | 7 | 9 | 119 | .... | .... | .... | .... | .... | .... | .... | .... | .... | 4 | 0 | 1 | 1 | 0 | .... | .... | .... | .... |
| 1996-97 | Kentucky | AHL | 80 | 1 | 9 | 10 | 198 | .... | .... | .... | .... | .... | .... | .... | .... | .... | 4 | 0 | 0 | 0 | 0 | .... | .... | .... | .... |
| **1997-98** | **NY Islanders** | **NHL** | **17** | **0** | **1** | **1** | **36** | **0** | **0** | **0** | **3** | **0.0** | **1** | .... | .... | .... | .... | .... | .... | .... | .... | .... | .... | .... | .... |
| | Kentucky | AHL | 39 | 3 | 1 | 4 | 87 | .... | .... | .... | .... | .... | .... | .... | .... | .... | .... | .... | .... | .... | .... | .... | .... | .... | .... |
| | **Vancouver** | **NHL** | **11** | **0** | **1** | **1** | **29** | **0** | **0** | **0** | **5** | **0.0** | **–3** | .... | .... | .... | .... | .... | .... | .... | .... | .... | .... | .... | .... |
| | Syracuse Crunch | AHL | .... | .... | .... | .... | .... | .... | .... | .... | .... | .... | .... | .... | .... | .... | 3 | 0 | 0 | 0 | 6 | .... | .... | .... | .... |
| **1998-99** | **Vancouver** | **NHL** | **65** | **0** | **3** | **3** | **114** | **0** | **0** | **0** | **25** | **0.0** | **–19** | **0** | **0.0** | **12:49** | .... | .... | .... | .... | .... | .... | .... | .... | .... |
| **99-2000** | **Vancouver** | **NHL** | **63** | **1** | **3** | **4** | **64** | **0** | **0** | **0** | **18** | **5.6** | **–13** | **0** | **0.0** | **15:12** | .... | .... | .... | .... | .... | .... | .... | .... | .... |
| **2000-01** | **Vancouver** | **NHL** | **60** | **1** | **4** | **5** | **64** | **0** | **0** | **1** | **21** | **4.8** | **16** | **0** | **0.0** | **9:59** | **2** | **0** | **0** | **0** | **0** | **0** | **0** | **0** | **2:15** |
| **2001-02** | **Vancouver** | **NHL** | **44** | **2** | **4** | **6** | **96** | **0** | **0** | **0** | **13** | **15.4** | **4** | **0** | **0.0** | **9:45** | .... | .... | .... | .... | .... | .... | .... | .... | .... |
| **2002-03** | **Chicago** | **NHL** | **48** | **2** | **3** | **5** | **87** | **0** | **0** | **0** | **19** | **10.5** | **–4** | **3** | **0.0** | **8:32** | .... | .... | .... | .... | .... | .... | .... | .... | .... |
| **2003-04** | **Chicago** | **NHL** | **54** | **1** | **3** | **4** | **73** | **0** | **0** | **0** | **32** | **3.1** | **–16** | **1** | **0.0** | **14:55** | .... | .... | .... | .... | .... | .... | .... | .... | .... |
| 2004-05 | Ferencvaros | Hungary | 6 | 1 | 2 | 3 | 8 | .... | .... | .... | .... | .... | .... | .... | .... | .... | .... | .... | .... | .... | .... | .... | .... | .... | .... |
| **2005-06** | **NY Rangers** | **NHL** | **65** | **3** | **4** | **7** | **66** | **0** | **0** | **0** | **31** | **9.7** | **–10** | **3** | **33.3** | **15:31** | **3** | **0** | **0** | **0** | **0** | **0** | **0** | **0** | **13:35** |
| **2006-07** | **NY Rangers** | **NHL** | **8** | **0** | **0** | **0** | **2** | **0** | **0** | **0** | **3** | **0.0** | **0** | **0** | **0.0** | **13:40** | .... | .... | .... | .... | .... | .... | .... | .... | .... |
| | HC Lugano | Swiss | 34 | 2 | 3 | 5 | 28 | .... | .... | .... | .... | .... | .... | .... | .... | .... | 6 | 0 | 0 | 0 | 4 | .... | .... | .... | .... |
| **2007-08** | **NY Rangers** | **NHL** | **52** | **1** | **1** | **2** | **40** | **0** | **0** | **1** | **21** | **4.8** | **0** | **0** | **0.0** | **12:57** | **2** | **0** | **0** | **0** | **0** | **0** | **0** | **0** | **9:41** |
| **2008-09** | **Edmonton** | **NHL** | **71** | **2** | **7** | **9** | **60** | **0** | **0** | **0** | **32** | **6.3** | **–4** | **0** | **0.0** | **12:38** | .... | .... | .... | .... | .... | .... | .... | .... | .... |
| | **NHL Totals** | | **559** | **13** | **34** | **47** | **738** | **0** | **0** | **2** | **223** | **5.8** | | **7** | **14.3** | **12:41** | **7** | **0** | **0** | **0** | **0** | **0** | **0** | **0** | **9:14** |

Traded to **Vancouver** by **NY Islanders** for Gino Odjick, March 23, 1998. Signed as a free agent by **Chicago**, July 15, 2002. Signed as a free agent by **NY Rangers**, July 20, 2004. Signed as a free agent by **Ferencvaros** (Hungary), January 17, 2005. Signed as a free agent by **Edmonton**, July 10, 2008.

## STUART, Brad

(STEW-ahrt, BRAD) **DET.**

Defense. Shoots left. 6'2", 213 lbs. Born, Rocky Mountain House, Alta., November 6, 1979. San Jose's 1st choice, 3rd overall, in 1998 Entry Draft.

| | | | | | | | | | | | | | | | | | | | | | | | | | |
|---|---|---|---|---|---|---|---|---|---|---|---|---|---|---|---|---|---|---|---|---|---|---|---|---|---|
| 1995-96 | Red Deer | AMHL | 35 | 12 | 25 | 37 | 83 | .... | .... | .... | .... | .... | .... | .... | .... | .... | .... | .... | .... | .... | .... | .... | .... | .... | .... |
| | Regina Pats | WHL | 3 | 0 | 0 | 0 | 0 | .... | .... | .... | .... | .... | .... | .... | .... | .... | .... | .... | .... | .... | .... | .... | .... | .... | .... |
| 1996-97 | Regina Pats | WHL | 57 | 7 | 36 | 43 | 58 | .... | .... | .... | .... | .... | .... | .... | .... | .... | 5 | 0 | 4 | 4 | 14 | .... | .... | .... | .... |
| 1997-98 | Regina Pats | WHL | 72 | 20 | 45 | 65 | 82 | .... | .... | .... | .... | .... | .... | .... | .... | .... | 9 | 3 | 4 | 7 | 10 | .... | .... | .... | .... |
| 1998-99 | Regina Pats | WHL | 29 | 10 | 19 | 29 | 43 | .... | .... | .... | .... | .... | .... | .... | .... | .... | .... | .... | .... | .... | .... | .... | .... | .... | .... |
| | Calgary Hitmen | WHL | 30 | 11 | 22 | 33 | 26 | .... | .... | .... | .... | .... | .... | .... | .... | .... | 21 | 8 | 15 | 23 | 59 | .... | .... | .... | .... |
| **99-2000** | **San Jose** | **NHL** | **82** | **10** | **26** | **36** | **32** | **5** | **1** | **3** | **133** | **7.5** | **3** | **0** | **0.0** | **20:24** | **12** | **1** | **0** | **1** | **6** | **1** | **0** | **0** | **16:30** |
| **2000-01** | **San Jose** | **NHL** | **77** | **5** | **18** | **23** | **56** | **1** | **0** | **2** | **119** | **4.2** | **10** | **0** | **0.0** | **20:06** | **5** | **1** | **0** | **1** | **0** | **0** | **0** | **0** | **20:19** |
| **2001-02** | **San Jose** | **NHL** | **82** | **6** | **23** | **29** | **39** | **2** | **0** | **2** | **96** | **6.3** | **13** | **0** | **0.0** | **21:41** | **12** | **0** | **3** | **3** | **8** | **0** | **0** | **0** | **19:42** |
| **2002-03** | **San Jose** | **NHL** | **36** | **4** | **10** | **14** | **46** | **2** | **0** | **1** | **63** | **6.3** | **–6** | **0** | **0.0** | **20:53** | .... | .... | .... | .... | .... | .... | .... | .... | .... |
| **2003-04** | **San Jose** | **NHL** | **77** | **9** | **30** | **39** | **34** | **5** | **0** | **0** | **129** | **7.0** | **9** | **0** | **0.0** | **22:09** | **17** | **1** | **5** | **6** | **13** | **0** | **0** | **0** | **23:23** |

| Season | Club | League | GP | G | A | Pts | PIM | PP | SH | GW | S | % | +/- | TF | F% | Min | GP | G | A | Pts | PIM | PP | SH | GW | Min |
|---|---|---|---|---|---|---|---|---|---|---|---|---|---|---|---|---|---|---|---|---|---|---|---|---|---|
| | | | Regular Season | | | | | | | | | | | | | | Playoffs | | | | | | | | |
| 2004-05 | | | DID NOT PLAY | | | | | | | | | | | | | | | | | | | | | | |
| **2005-06** | **San Jose** | **NHL** | **23** | **2** | **10** | **12** | **14** | **1** | **0** | **0** | **41** | **4.9** | **-2** | **0** | **0.0** | **23:15** | .... | .... | .... | .... | .... | .... | .... | .... | .... |
| | **Boston** | **NHL** | **55** | **10** | **21** | **31** | **38** | **6** | **0** | **2** | **122** | **8.2** | **-6** | **0** | **0.0** | **25:40** | .... | .... | .... | .... | .... | .... | .... | .... | .... |
| **2006-07** | **Boston** | **NHL** | **48** | **7** | **10** | **17** | **26** | **1** | **0** | **2** | **74** | **9.5** | **-22** | **0** | **0.0** | **22:55** | .... | .... | .... | .... | .... | .... | .... | .... | .... |
| | **Calgary** | **NHL** | **27** | **0** | **5** | **5** | **18** | **0** | **0** | **0** | **35** | **0.0** | **12** | **0** | **0.0** | **22:48** | **6** | **0** | **1** | **1** | **6** | **0** | **0** | **0** | **25:16** |
| **2007-08** | **Los Angeles** | **NHL** | **63** | **5** | **16** | **21** | **67** | **2** | **0** | **1** | **111** | **4.5** | **-16** | **4** | **0.0** | **21:13** | .... | .... | .... | .... | .... | .... | .... | .... | .... |
| | **♦ Detroit** | **NHL** | **9** | **1** | **1** | **2** | **2** | **0** | **0** | **0** | **21** | **4.8** | **6** | **0** | **0.0** | **20:46** | **21** | **1** | **6** | **7** | **14** | **0** | **0** | **1** | **21:40** |
| **2008-09** | **Detroit** | **NHL** | **67** | **2** | **13** | **15** | **26** | **1** | **0** | **0** | **105** | **1.9** | **-3** | **0** | **0.0** | **20:13** | **23** | **3** | **6** | **9** | **12** | **1** | **0** | **0** | **24:09** |
| | **NHL Totals** | | **646** | **61** | **183** | **244** | **398** | **26** | **1** | **13** | **1049** | **5.8** | | **4** | **0.0** | **21:40** | **96** | **7** | **21** | **28** | **59** | **2** | **0** | **1** | **21:50** |

WHL East Second All-Star Team (1998) • WHL East First All-Star Team (1999) • Canadian Major Junior First All-Star Team (1999) • Canadian Major Junior Defenseman of the Year (1999) • NHL All-Rookie Team (2000)

• Missed majority of 2002-03 season recovering from ankle (January 4, 2003 vs. Los Angeles) and head (February 21, 2003 vs. Columbus) injuries. Traded to **Boston** by **San Jose** with Marco Sturm and Wayne Primeau for Joe Thornton, November 30, 2005. Traded to **Calgary** by **Boston** with Wayne Primeau and Washington's 4th round choice (previously acquired, Calgary selected T.J. Brodie) in 2008 Entry Draft for Andrew Ference and Chuck Kobasew, February 10, 2007. Signed as a free agent by **Los Angeles**, July 3, 2007. Traded to **Detroit** by **Los Angeles** for Detroit's 2nd round choice (later traded to Colorado – Colorado selected Peter Delmas) in 2008 Entry Draft and Detroit's 4th round choice (later traded to Atlanta – Atlanta selected Ben Chiarot) in 2009 Entry Draft, February 26, 2008.

## STUART, Colin
(STEW-ahrt, KAW-lihn) **CGY.**

Left wing. Shoots left. 6'2", 205 lbs. Born, Rochester, MN, July 8, 1982. Atlanta's 5th choice, 135th overall, in 2001 Entry Draft.

| Season | Club | League | GP | G | A | Pts | PIM | PP | SH | GW | S | % | +/- | TF | F% | Min | GP | G | A | Pts | PIM | PP | SH | GW | Min |
|---|---|---|---|---|---|---|---|---|---|---|---|---|---|---|---|---|---|---|---|---|---|---|---|---|---|
| 1998-99 | Roch. Lourdes | High-MN | 23 | 22 | 32 | 54 | .... | .... | .... | .... | .... | .... | .... | .... | .... | .... | .... | .... | .... | .... | .... | .... | .... | .... | .... |
| 99-2000 | Lincoln Stars | USHL | 53 | 18 | 19 | 37 | 38 | .... | .... | .... | .... | .... | .... | .... | .... | .... | 9 | 1 | 3 | 4 | 2 | .... | .... | .... | .... |
| 2000-01 | Colorado College | WCHA | 41 | 2 | 7 | 9 | 26 | .... | .... | .... | .... | .... | .... | .... | .... | .... | .... | .... | .... | .... | .... | .... | .... | .... | .... |
| 2001-02 | Colorado College | WCHA | 43 | 13 | 9 | 22 | 34 | .... | .... | .... | .... | .... | .... | .... | .... | .... | .... | .... | .... | .... | .... | .... | .... | .... | .... |
| 2002-03 | Colorado College | WCHA | 42 | 13 | 11 | 24 | 56 | .... | .... | .... | .... | .... | .... | .... | .... | .... | .... | .... | .... | .... | .... | .... | .... | .... | .... |
| 2003-04 | Colorado College | WCHA | 30 | 10 | 12 | 22 | 38 | .... | .... | .... | .... | .... | .... | .... | .... | .... | .... | .... | .... | .... | .... | .... | .... | .... | .... |
| 2004-05 | Chicago Wolves | AHL | 39 | 3 | 2 | 5 | 12 | .... | .... | .... | .... | .... | .... | .... | .... | .... | .... | .... | .... | .... | .... | .... | .... | .... | .... |
| | Gwinnett | ECHL | 5 | 1 | 3 | 4 | 4 | .... | .... | .... | .... | .... | .... | .... | .... | .... | .... | .... | .... | .... | .... | .... | .... | .... | .... |
| 2005-06 | Chicago Wolves | AHL | 78 | 13 | 14 | 27 | 65 | .... | .... | .... | .... | .... | .... | .... | .... | .... | .... | .... | .... | .... | .... | .... | .... | .... | .... |
| 2006-07 | Chicago Wolves | AHL | 67 | 18 | 11 | 29 | 75 | .... | .... | .... | .... | .... | .... | .... | .... | .... | 15 | 2 | 5 | 7 | 10 | .... | .... | .... | .... |
| **2007-08** | **Atlanta** | **NHL** | **18** | **3** | **2** | **5** | **6** | **0** | **1** | **1** | **19** | **15.8** | **2** | **7** | **57.1** | **12:20** | .... | .... | .... | .... | .... | .... | .... | .... | .... |
| | Chicago Wolves | AHL | 58 | 8 | 8 | 16 | 45 | .... | .... | .... | .... | .... | .... | .... | .... | .... | 24 | 3 | 3 | 6 | 18 | .... | .... | .... | .... |
| **2008-09** | **Atlanta** | **NHL** | **33** | **5** | **3** | **8** | **18** | **0** | **3** | **0** | **54** | **9.3** | **3** | **12** | **41.7** | **12:29** | .... | .... | .... | .... | .... | .... | .... | .... | .... |
| | Chicago Wolves | AHL | 42 | 9 | 6 | 15 | 38 | .... | .... | .... | .... | .... | .... | .... | .... | .... | .... | .... | .... | .... | .... | .... | .... | .... | .... |
| | **NHL Totals** | | **51** | **8** | **5** | **13** | **24** | **0** | **4** | **1** | **73** | **11.0** | | **19** | **47.4** | **12:26** | .... | .... | .... | .... | .... | .... | .... | .... | .... |

Traded to **Toronto** by **Atlanta** with Garnet Exelby for Pavel Kubina and Tim Stapleton, July 1, 2009. Traded to **Calgary** by **Toronto** with Anton Stralman and Toronto's 7th round choice in 2012 Entry Draft for Wayne Primeau and Calgary's 2nd round choice in 2011 Entry Draft, July 27, 2009.

## STUART, Mark
(STOO-uhrt, MAHRK) **BOS.**

Defense. Shoots left. 6'2", 213 lbs. Born, Rochester, MN, April 27, 1984. Boston's 1st choice, 21st overall, in 2003 Entry Draft.

| Season | Club | League | GP | G | A | Pts | PIM | PP | SH | GW | S | % | +/- | TF | F% | Min | GP | G | A | Pts | PIM | PP | SH | GW | Min |
|---|---|---|---|---|---|---|---|---|---|---|---|---|---|---|---|---|---|---|---|---|---|---|---|---|---|
| 99-2000 | Roch. Lourdes | High-MN | 28 | 19 | 22 | 41 | .... | .... | .... | .... | .... | .... | .... | .... | .... | .... | .... | .... | .... | .... | .... | .... | .... | .... | .... |
| 2000-01 | USNTDP | U-17 | 12 | 1 | 5 | 6 | 6 | .... | .... | .... | .... | .... | .... | .... | .... | .... | .... | .... | .... | .... | .... | .... | .... | .... | .... |
| | USNTDP | NAHL | 52 | 2 | 11 | 13 | 114 | .... | .... | .... | .... | .... | .... | .... | .... | .... | .... | .... | .... | .... | .... | .... | .... | .... | .... |
| 2001-02 | USNTDP | U-18 | 40 | 9 | 9 | 18 | .... | .... | .... | .... | .... | .... | .... | .... | .... | .... | .... | .... | .... | .... | .... | .... | .... | .... | .... |
| | USNTDP | USHL | 12 | 0 | 1 | 1 | 25 | .... | .... | .... | .... | .... | .... | .... | .... | .... | .... | .... | .... | .... | .... | .... | .... | .... | .... |
| | USNTDP | NAHL | 9 | 0 | 1 | 1 | 18 | .... | .... | .... | .... | .... | .... | .... | .... | .... | .... | .... | .... | .... | .... | .... | .... | .... | .... |
| 2002-03 | Colorado College | WCHA | 38 | 3 | 17 | 20 | 81 | .... | .... | .... | .... | .... | .... | .... | .... | .... | .... | .... | .... | .... | .... | .... | .... | .... | .... |
| 2003-04 | Colorado College | WCHA | 37 | 4 | 11 | 15 | 100 | .... | .... | .... | .... | .... | .... | .... | .... | .... | .... | .... | .... | .... | .... | .... | .... | .... | .... |
| 2004-05 | Colorado College | WCHA | 43 | 5 | 14 | 19 | 94 | .... | .... | .... | .... | .... | .... | .... | .... | .... | .... | .... | .... | .... | .... | .... | .... | .... | .... |
| **2005-06** | **Boston** | **NHL** | **17** | **1** | **1** | **2** | **10** | **0** | **0** | **0** | **9** | **11.1** | **-1** | **0** | **0.0** | **17:46** | .... | .... | .... | .... | .... | .... | .... | .... | .... |
| | Providence Bruins | AHL | 60 | 4 | 3 | 7 | 76 | .... | .... | .... | .... | .... | .... | .... | .... | .... | 6 | 0 | 0 | 0 | 25 | .... | .... | .... | .... |
| **2006-07** | **Boston** | **NHL** | **15** | **0** | **1** | **1** | **14** | **0** | **0** | **0** | **4** | **0.0** | **7** | **0** | **0.0** | **10:23** | .... | .... | .... | .... | .... | .... | .... | .... | .... |
| | Providence Bruins | AHL | 49 | 4 | 16 | 20 | 62 | .... | .... | .... | .... | .... | .... | .... | .... | .... | 3 | 0 | 1 | 1 | 9 | .... | .... | .... | .... |
| **2007-08** | **Boston** | **NHL** | **82** | **4** | **4** | **8** | **81** | **0** | **0** | **1** | **60** | **6.7** | **2** | **0** | **0.0** | **15:22** | **7** | **0** | **1** | **1** | **8** | **0** | **0** | **0** | **16:00** |
| **2008-09** | **Boston** | **NHL** | **82** | **5** | **12** | **17** | **76** | **0** | **0** | **1** | **61** | **8.2** | **20** | **0** | **0.0** | **15:25** | **11** | **0** | **1** | **1** | **7** | **0** | **0** | **0** | **17:57** |
| | **NHL Totals** | | **196** | **10** | **18** | **28** | **181** | **0** | **0** | **2** | **134** | **7.5** | | **0** | **0.0** | **15:13** | **18** | **0** | **2** | **2** | **15** | **0** | **0** | **0** | **17:11** |

WCHA All-Rookie Team (2003) • WCHA Second All-Star Team (2005) • NCAA West First All-American Team (2005)

## STURM, Marco
(STUHRM, MAHR-koh) **BOS.**

Left wing. Shoots left. 6', 194 lbs. Born, Dingolfing, West Germany, September 8, 1978. San Jose's 2nd choice, 21st overall, in 1996 Entry Draft.

| Season | Club | League | GP | G | A | Pts | PIM | PP | SH | GW | S | % | +/- | TF | F% | Min | GP | G | A | Pts | PIM | PP | SH | GW | Min |
|---|---|---|---|---|---|---|---|---|---|---|---|---|---|---|---|---|---|---|---|---|---|---|---|---|---|
| 1995-96 | EV Landshut | Germany | 47 | 12 | 20 | 32 | 50 | .... | .... | .... | .... | .... | .... | .... | .... | .... | 11 | 1 | 3 | 4 | 18 | .... | .... | .... | .... |
| 1996-97 | EV Landshut | Germany | 46 | 16 | 27 | 43 | 40 | .... | .... | .... | .... | .... | .... | .... | .... | .... | 7 | 1 | 4 | 5 | 6 | .... | .... | .... | .... |
| **1997-98** | **San Jose** | **NHL** | **74** | **10** | **20** | **30** | **40** | **2** | **0** | **3** | **118** | **8.5** | **-2** | .... | .... | .... | **2** | **0** | **0** | **0** | **0** | **0** | **0** | **0** | .... |
| | Germany | Olympics | 2 | 0 | 0 | 0 | 0 | .... | .... | .... | .... | .... | .... | .... | .... | .... | .... | .... | .... | .... | .... | .... | .... | .... | .... |
| **1998-99** | **San Jose** | **NHL** | **78** | **16** | **22** | **38** | **52** | **3** | **2** | **3** | **140** | **11.4** | **7** | **576** | **45.0** | **15:23** | **6** | **2** | **2** | **4** | **4** | **0** | **0** | **1** | **14:16** |
| **99-2000** | **San Jose** | **NHL** | **74** | **12** | **15** | **27** | **22** | **2** | **4** | **3** | **120** | **10.0** | **4** | **183** | **45.4** | **14:07** | **12** | **1** | **3** | **4** | **6** | **0** | **0** | **0** | **13:00** |
| **2000-01** | **San Jose** | **NHL** | **81** | **14** | **18** | **32** | **28** | **2** | **3** | **5** | **153** | **9.2** | **9** | **517** | **40.2** | **16:06** | **6** | **0** | **2** | **2** | **0** | **0** | **0** | **0** | **18:18** |
| **2001-02** | **San Jose** | **NHL** | **77** | **21** | **20** | **41** | **32** | **4** | **3** | **5** | **174** | **12.1** | **23** | **105** | **47.6** | **15:39** | **12** | **3** | **2** | **5** | **2** | **0** | **0** | **0** | **15:33** |
| | Germany | Olympics | 5 | 0 | 1 | 1 | 0 | .... | .... | .... | .... | .... | .... | .... | .... | .... | .... | .... | .... | .... | .... | .... | .... | .... | .... |
| **2002-03** | **San Jose** | **NHL** | **82** | **28** | **20** | **48** | **16** | **6** | **0** | **2** | **208** | **13.5** | **9** | **83** | **48.2** | **16:31** | .... | .... | .... | .... | .... | .... | .... | .... | .... |
| **2003-04** | **San Jose** | **NHL** | **64** | **21** | **20** | **41** | **36** | **10** | **2** | **6** | **158** | **13.3** | **0** | **7** | **42.9** | **16:25** | .... | .... | .... | .... | .... | .... | .... | .... | .... |
| 2004-05 | ERC Ingolstadt | Germany | 45 | 22 | 16 | 38 | 56 | .... | .... | .... | .... | .... | .... | .... | .... | .... | 11 | 3 | 4 | 7 | 12 | .... | .... | .... | .... |
| **2005-06** | **San Jose** | **NHL** | **23** | **6** | **10** | **16** | **16** | **3** | **0** | **0** | **48** | **12.5** | **-8** | **9** | **44.4** | **17:28** | .... | .... | .... | .... | .... | .... | .... | .... | .... |
| | **Boston** | **NHL** | **51** | **23** | **20** | **43** | **32** | **5** | **0** | **6** | **132** | **17.4** | **14** | **3** | **33.3** | **18:44** | .... | .... | .... | .... | .... | .... | .... | .... | .... |
| **2006-07** | **Boston** | **NHL** | **76** | **27** | **17** | **44** | **46** | **10** | **2** | **1** | **224** | **12.1** | **-24** | **13** | **61.5** | **18:36** | .... | .... | .... | .... | .... | .... | .... | .... | .... |
| **2007-08** | **Boston** | **NHL** | **80** | **27** | **29** | **56** | **40** | **10** | **1** | **5** | **229** | **11.8** | **11** | **34** | **29.4** | **18:00** | **7** | **2** | **2** | **4** | **6** | **0** | **1** | **1** | **18:20** |
| **2008-09** | **Boston** | **NHL** | **19** | **7** | **6** | **13** | **8** | **4** | **0** | **0** | **45** | **15.6** | **9** | **4** | **75.0** | **16:01** | .... | .... | .... | .... | .... | .... | .... | .... | .... |
| | **NHL Totals** | | **779** | **212** | **217** | **429** | **368** | **61** | **17** | **39** | **1749** | **12.1** | | **1534** | **43.6** | **16:33** | **45** | **8** | **11** | **19** | **18** | **0** | **1** | **2** | **15:29** |

Played in NHL All-Star Game (1999)

Signed as a free agent by **Ingolstadt** (Germany), August 8, 2004. Traded to **Boston** by **San Jose** with Brad Stuart and Wayne Primeau for Joe Thornton, November 30, 2005. • Missed majority of 2008-09 season recovering from knee injury suffered in game vs. Toronto, December 18, 2008.

## SULLIVAN, Steve
(SUHL-ih-vuhn, STEEV) **NSH.**

Right wing. Shoots right. 5'9", 173 lbs. Born, Timmins, Ont., July 6, 1974. New Jersey's 10th choice, 233rd overall, in 1994 Entry Draft.

| Season | Club | League | GP | G | A | Pts | PIM | PP | SH | GW | S | % | +/- | TF | F% | Min | GP | G | A | Pts | PIM | PP | SH | GW | Min |
|---|---|---|---|---|---|---|---|---|---|---|---|---|---|---|---|---|---|---|---|---|---|---|---|---|---|
| 1991-92 | Timmins | NOJHA | 47 | 66 | 55 | 121 | 141 | .... | .... | .... | .... | .... | .... | .... | .... | .... | .... | .... | .... | .... | .... | .... | .... | .... | .... |
| 1992-93 | Sault Ste. Marie | OHL | 62 | 36 | 27 | 63 | 44 | .... | .... | .... | .... | .... | .... | .... | .... | .... | 16 | 3 | 8 | 11 | 18 | .... | .... | .... | .... |
| 1993-94 | Sault Ste. Marie | OHL | 63 | 51 | 62 | 113 | 82 | .... | .... | .... | .... | .... | .... | .... | .... | .... | 14 | 9 | 16 | 25 | 22 | .... | .... | .... | .... |
| 1994-95 | Albany River Rats | AHL | 75 | 31 | 50 | 81 | 124 | .... | .... | .... | .... | .... | .... | .... | .... | .... | 14 | 4 | 7 | 11 | 10 | .... | .... | .... | .... |
| **1995-96** | **New Jersey** | **NHL** | **16** | **5** | **4** | **9** | **8** | **2** | **0** | **1** | **23** | **21.7** | **3** | .... | .... | .... | .... | .... | .... | .... | .... | .... | .... | .... | .... |
| | Albany River Rats | AHL | 53 | 33 | 42 | 75 | 127 | .... | .... | .... | .... | .... | .... | .... | .... | .... | 4 | 3 | 0 | 3 | 6 | .... | .... | .... | .... |
| **1996-97** | **New Jersey** | **NHL** | **33** | **8** | **14** | **22** | **14** | **2** | **0** | **2** | **63** | **12.7** | **9** | .... | .... | .... | .... | .... | .... | .... | .... | .... | .... | .... | .... |
| | Albany River Rats | AHL | 15 | 8 | 7 | 15 | 16 | .... | .... | .... | .... | .... | .... | .... | .... | .... | .... | .... | .... | .... | .... | .... | .... | .... | .... |
| | **Toronto** | **NHL** | **21** | **5** | **11** | **16** | **23** | **1** | **0** | **1** | **45** | **11.1** | **5** | .... | .... | .... | .... | .... | .... | .... | .... | .... | .... | .... | .... |
| **1997-98** | **Toronto** | **NHL** | **63** | **10** | **18** | **28** | **40** | **1** | **0** | **1** | **112** | **8.9** | **-8** | .... | .... | .... | .... | .... | .... | .... | .... | .... | .... | .... | .... |
| **1998-99** | **Toronto** | **NHL** | **63** | **20** | **20** | **40** | **28** | **4** | **0** | **5** | **110** | **18.2** | **12** | **685** | **44.4** | **14:12** | **13** | **3** | **3** | **6** | **14** | **2** | **0** | **0** | **16:20** |
| **99-2000** | **Toronto** | **NHL** | **7** | **0** | **1** | **1** | **4** | **0** | **0** | **0** | **11** | **0.0** | **-1** | **47** | **48.9** | **11:52** | .... | .... | .... | .... | .... | .... | .... | .... | .... |
| | **Chicago** | **NHL** | **73** | **22** | **42** | **64** | **52** | **2** | **1** | **6** | **169** | **13.0** | **20** | **692** | **48.0** | **18:05** | .... | .... | .... | .... | .... | .... | .... | .... | .... |
| **2000-01** | **Chicago** | **NHL** | **81** | **34** | **41** | **75** | **54** | **6** | **8** | **3** | **204** | **16.7** | **3** | **649** | **42.4** | **20:32** | .... | .... | .... | .... | .... | .... | .... | .... | .... |
| **2001-02** | **Chicago** | **NHL** | **78** | **21** | **39** | **60** | **67** | **3** | **0** | **8** | **155** | **13.5** | **23** | **758** | **48.9** | **19:10** | **5** | **1** | **0** | **1** | **2** | **0** | **0** | **0** | **18:04** |
| **2002-03** | **Chicago** | **NHL** | **82** | **26** | **35** | **61** | **42** | **4** | **2** | **3** | **190** | **13.7** | **15** | **382** | **46.1** | **19:15** | .... | .... | .... | .... | .... | .... | .... | .... | .... |
| **2003-04** | **Chicago** | **NHL** | **56** | **15** | **28** | **43** | **36** | **4** | **2** | **4** | **140** | **10.7** | **-7** | **103** | **44.7** | **21:19** | .... | .... | .... | .... | .... | .... | .... | .... | .... |
| | **Nashville** | **NHL** | **24** | **9** | **21** | **30** | **12** | **7** | **0** | **0** | **78** | **11.5** | **8** | **124** | **43.6** | **20:02** | **6** | **1** | **1** | **2** | **6** | **0** | **0** | **1** | **18:58** |
| 2004-05 | | | DID NOT PLAY | | | | | | | | | | | | | | | | | | | | | | |
| **2005-06** | **Nashville** | **NHL** | **69** | **31** | **37** | **68** | **50** | **13** | **4** | **5** | **192** | **16.1** | **2** | **42** | **52.4** | **19:06** | **5** | **0** | **2** | **2** | **0** | **0** | **0** | **0** | **17:02** |
| **2006-07** | **Nashville** | **NHL** | **57** | **22** | **38** | **60** | **20** | **6** | **3** | **4** | **122** | **18.0** | **16** | **39** | **38.5** | **19:25** | | | | | | | | | |

| | | | Regular Season | | | | | | | | | | | | | | Playoffs | | | | | | | | |
|---|---|---|---|---|---|---|---|---|---|---|---|---|---|---|---|---|---|---|---|---|---|---|---|---|---|
| Season | Club | League | GP | G | A | Pts | PIM | PP | SH | GW | S | % | +/- | TF | F% | Min | GP | G | A | Pts | PIM | PP | SH | GW | Min |
| 2007-08 | Nashville | NHL | DID NOT PLAY – INJURED | | | | | | | | | | | | | | | | | | | | | | |
| 2008-09 | Nashville | NHL | 41 | 11 | 21 | 32 | 30 | 3 | 0 | 2 | 83 | 13.3 | 2 | 4 | 0.0 | 18:29 | .... | .... | .... | .... | .... | .... | .... | .... | .... |
| | NHL Totals | | 764 | 239 | 370 | 609 | 480 | 58 | 20 | 45 | 1697 | 14.1 | | 3525 | 45.9 | 18:51 | 29 | 5 | 6 | 11 | 22 | 2 | 0 | 1 | 17:18 |

AHL First All-Star Team (1996) • Bill Masterton Memorial Trophy (2009)

Traded to **Toronto** by **New Jersey** with Jason Smith and the rights to Alyn McCauley for Doug Gilmour, Dave Ellett and New Jersey's 3rd round choice (previously acquired, New Jersey selected Andre Lakos) in 1999 Entry Draft, February 25, 1997. Claimed on waivers by **Chicago** from **Toronto**, October 23, 1999. Traded to **Nashville** by **Chicago** for Nashville's 2nd round choices in 2004 (Ryan Garlock) and 2005 (Michael Blunden) Entry Drafts, February 16, 2004. • Missed remainder of 2006-07 season, entire 2007-08 season and start of 2008-09 season recovering from back injury suffered in game vs. Montreal, February 22, 2006.

## SULZER, Alexander

(ZUHLT-suhr, al-EHX-AN-duhr) **NSH.**

Defense. Shoots left. 6'1", 196 lbs. Born, Kaufbeuren, West Germany, May 30, 1984. Nashville's 7th choice, 92nd overall, in 2003 Entry Draft.

| | | | | | | | | | | | | | | | | | | | | | | | | | |
|---|---|---|---|---|---|---|---|---|---|---|---|---|---|---|---|---|---|---|---|---|---|---|---|---|---|
| 2000-01 | ESV Kaufbeuren | German-3 | 38 | 3 | 6 | 9 | 20 | .... | .... | .... | .... | .... | .... | .... | .... | .... | .... | .... | .... | .... | .... | .... | .... | .... | .... |
| | Kaufbeuren Jr. | Ger-Jr. | 1 | 0 | 2 | 2 | 2 | .... | .... | .... | .... | .... | .... | .... | .... | .... | .... | .... | .... | .... | .... | .... | .... | .... | .... |
| 2001-02 | ESV Kaufbeuren | German-3 | 19 | 1 | 9 | 10 | 14 | .... | .... | .... | .... | .... | .... | .... | .... | .... | .... | .... | .... | .... | .... | .... | .... | .... | .... |
| | Kaufbeuren Jr. | Ger-Jr. | 1 | 0 | 0 | 0 | 4 | .... | .... | .... | .... | .... | .... | .... | .... | .... | .... | .... | .... | .... | .... | .... | .... | .... | .... |
| 2002-03 | ESV Kaufbeuren | German-2 | 26 | 5 | 3 | 8 | 38 | .... | .... | .... | .... | .... | .... | .... | .... | .... | 1 | 0 | 1 | 1 | 4 | .... | .... | .... | .... |
| | Hamburg Freezers | Germany | 18 | 0 | 1 | 1 | 18 | .... | .... | .... | .... | .... | .... | .... | .... | .... | 5 | 0 | 0 | 0 | 12 | .... | .... | .... | .... |
| 2003-04 | Dusseldorf | Germany | 46 | 4 | 1 | 5 | 56 | .... | .... | .... | .... | .... | .... | .... | .... | .... | 4 | 0 | 0 | 0 | 8 | .... | .... | .... | .... |
| 2004-05 | Dusseldorf | Germany | 42 | 5 | 6 | 11 | 68 | .... | .... | .... | .... | .... | .... | .... | .... | .... | .... | .... | .... | .... | .... | .... | .... | .... | .... |
| | EV Duisburg | German-2 | .... | .... | .... | .... | .... | .... | .... | .... | .... | .... | .... | .... | .... | .... | 7 | 0 | 3 | 3 | 6 | .... | .... | .... | .... |
| 2005-06 | Dusseldorf | Germany | 48 | 3 | 15 | 18 | 82 | .... | .... | .... | .... | .... | .... | .... | .... | .... | 13 | 3 | 6 | 9 | 22 | .... | .... | .... | .... |
| | Germany | Olympics | 5 | 0 | 1 | 1 | 2 | .... | .... | .... | .... | .... | .... | .... | .... | .... | .... | .... | .... | .... | .... | .... | .... | .... | .... |
| 2006-07 | Dusseldorf | Germany | 44 | 4 | 11 | 15 | 82 | .... | .... | .... | .... | .... | .... | .... | .... | .... | 9 | 2 | 1 | 3 | 20 | .... | .... | .... | .... |
| 2007-08 | Milwaukee | AHL | 61 | 7 | 25 | 32 | 47 | .... | .... | .... | .... | .... | .... | .... | .... | .... | .... | .... | .... | .... | .... | .... | .... | .... | .... |
| **2008-09** | **Nashville** | **NHL** | **2** | **0** | **0** | **0** | **0** | 0 | 0 | 0 | 0 | 0.0 | 0 | 0 | 0.0 | 6:34 | .... | .... | .... | .... | .... | .... | .... | .... | .... |
| | Milwaukee | AHL | 48 | 8 | 26 | 34 | 36 | .... | .... | .... | .... | .... | .... | .... | .... | .... | .... | .... | .... | .... | .... | .... | .... | .... | .... |
| | NHL Totals | | 2 | 0 | 0 | 0 | 0 | 0 | 0 | 0 | 0 | 0.0 | | 0 | 0.0 | 6:34 | .... | .... | .... | .... | .... | .... | .... | .... | .... |

## SUNDIN, Mats

(suhn-DEEN, MATS)

Center. Shoots right. 6'5", 231 lbs. Born, Bromma, Sweden, February 13, 1971. Quebec's 1st choice, 1st overall, in 1989 Entry Draft.

| | | | | | | | | | | | | | | | | | | | | | | | | | |
|---|---|---|---|---|---|---|---|---|---|---|---|---|---|---|---|---|---|---|---|---|---|---|---|---|---|
| 1988-89 | Nacka HK | Sweden-2 | 25 | 10 | 8 | 18 | 18 | .... | .... | .... | .... | .... | .... | .... | .... | .... | .... | .... | .... | .... | .... | .... | .... | .... | .... |
| 1989-90 | Djurgarden | Sweden | 34 | 10 | 8 | 18 | 16 | .... | .... | .... | .... | .... | .... | .... | .... | .... | 8 | 7 | 0 | 7 | 4 | .... | .... | .... | .... |
| **1990-91** | **Quebec** | **NHL** | 80 | 23 | 36 | 59 | 58 | 4 | 0 | 0 | 155 | 14.8 | -24 | .... | .... | .... | .... | .... | .... | .... | .... | .... | .... | .... | .... |
| **1991-92** | **Quebec** | **NHL** | 80 | 33 | 43 | 76 | 103 | 8 | 2 | 2 | 231 | 14.3 | -19 | .... | .... | .... | .... | .... | .... | .... | .... | .... | .... | .... | .... |
| **1992-93** | **Quebec** | **NHL** | 80 | 47 | 67 | 114 | 96 | 13 | 4 | 9 | 215 | 21.9 | 21 | .... | .... | .... | 6 | 3 | 1 | 4 | 6 | 1 | 0 | 0 | .... |
| **1993-94** | **Quebec** | **NHL** | 84 | 32 | 53 | 85 | 60 | 6 | 2 | 4 | 226 | 14.2 | 1 | .... | .... | .... | .... | .... | .... | .... | .... | .... | .... | .... | .... |
| 1994-95 | Djurgarden | Sweden | 12 | 7 | 2 | 9 | 14 | .... | .... | .... | .... | .... | .... | .... | .... | .... | .... | .... | .... | .... | .... | .... | .... | .... | .... |
| | **Toronto** | **NHL** | 47 | 23 | 24 | 47 | 14 | 9 | 0 | 4 | 173 | 13.3 | -5 | .... | .... | .... | 7 | 5 | 4 | 9 | 4 | 2 | 0 | 1 | .... |
| **1995-96** | **Toronto** | **NHL** | 76 | 33 | 50 | 83 | 46 | 7 | 6 | 7 | 301 | 11.0 | 8 | .... | .... | .... | 6 | 3 | 1 | 4 | 4 | 2 | 0 | 1 | .... |
| **1996-97** | **Toronto** | **NHL** | 82 | 41 | 53 | 94 | 59 | 7 | 4 | 8 | 281 | 14.6 | 6 | .... | .... | .... | .... | .... | .... | .... | .... | .... | .... | .... | .... |
| **1997-98** | **Toronto** | **NHL** | 82 | 33 | 41 | 74 | 49 | 9 | 1 | 5 | 219 | 15.1 | -3 | .... | .... | .... | .... | .... | .... | .... | .... | .... | .... | .... | .... |
| | Sweden | Olympics | 4 | 3 | 0 | 3 | 4 | .... | .... | .... | .... | .... | .... | .... | .... | .... | .... | .... | .... | .... | .... | .... | .... | .... | .... |
| **1998-99** | **Toronto** | **NHL** | 82 | 31 | 52 | 83 | 58 | 4 | 0 | 6 | 209 | 14.8 | 22 | 1993 | 57.3 | 20:41 | 17 | 8 | 8 | 16 | 16 | 3 | 0 | 2 | 22:46 |
| **99-2000** | **Toronto** | **NHL** | 73 | 32 | 41 | 73 | 46 | 10 | 2 | 7 | 184 | 17.4 | 16 | 1619 | 50.8 | 20:11 | 12 | 3 | 5 | 8 | 10 | 0 | 0 | 1 | 21:27 |
| **2000-01** | **Toronto** | **NHL** | 82 | 28 | 46 | 74 | 76 | 9 | 0 | 6 | 226 | 12.4 | 15 | 1870 | 56.6 | 19:21 | 11 | 6 | 7 | 13 | 14 | 2 | 1 | 1 | 20:12 |
| **2001-02** | **Toronto** | **NHL** | 82 | 41 | 39 | 80 | 94 | 10 | 2 | 9 | 262 | 15.6 | 6 | 1812 | 57.5 | 19:20 | 8 | 2 | 5 | 7 | 4 | 0 | 0 | 0 | 20:07 |
| | Sweden | Olympics | 4 | 5 | 4 | *9 | 10 | .... | .... | .... | .... | .... | .... | .... | .... | .... | .... | .... | .... | .... | .... | .... | .... | .... | .... |
| **2002-03** | **Toronto** | **NHL** | 75 | 37 | 35 | 72 | 58 | 16 | 3 | 8 | 223 | 16.6 | 1 | 1774 | 56.1 | 20:15 | 7 | 1 | 3 | 4 | 6 | 1 | 0 | 0 | 24:17 |
| **2003-04** | **Toronto** | **NHL** | 81 | 31 | 44 | 75 | 52 | 11 | 1 | 10 | 226 | 13.7 | 11 | 1705 | 53.0 | 19:52 | 9 | 4 | 5 | 9 | 8 | 0 | 0 | 1 | 18:24 |
| 2004-05 | | | DID NOT PLAY | | | | | | | | | | | | | | | | | | | | | | |
| **2005-06** | **Toronto** | **NHL** | 70 | 31 | 47 | 78 | 58 | 16 | 2 | 2 | 220 | 14.1 | 7 | 1557 | 54.0 | 19:59 | .... | .... | .... | .... | .... | .... | .... | .... | .... |
| | Sweden | Olympics | 8 | 3 | 5 | 8 | 4 | .... | .... | .... | .... | .... | .... | .... | .... | .... | .... | .... | .... | .... | .... | .... | .... | .... | .... |
| **2006-07** | **Toronto** | **NHL** | 75 | 27 | 49 | 76 | 62 | 6 | 1 | 3 | 321 | 8.4 | -2 | 1790 | 55.2 | 20:28 | .... | .... | .... | .... | .... | .... | .... | .... | .... |
| **2007-08** | **Toronto** | **NHL** | 74 | 32 | 46 | 78 | 76 | 10 | 1 | 4 | 259 | 12.4 | 17 | 1713 | 55.2 | 20:04 | .... | .... | .... | .... | .... | .... | .... | .... | .... |
| **2008-09** | **Vancouver** | **NHL** | 41 | 9 | 19 | 28 | 28 | 5 | 0 | 2 | 84 | 10.7 | -5 | 601 | 55.2 | 16:51 | 8 | 3 | 5 | 8 | 2 | 0 | 0 | 1 | 15:55 |
| | NHL Totals | | 1346 | 564 | 785 | 1349 | 1093 | 160 | 31 | 96 | 4015 | 14.0 | | 16434 | 55.2 | 19:50 | 91 | 38 | 44 | 82 | 74 | 11 | 1 | 8 | 20:42 |

NHL Second All-Star Team (2002, 2004)

Played in NHL All-Star Game (1996, 1997, 1998, 1999, 2000, 2001, 2002, 2004)

Traded to **Toronto** by **Quebec** with Garth Butcher, Todd Warriner and Philadelphia's 1st round choice (previously acquired, later traded to Washington – Washington selected Nolan Baumgartner) in 1994 Entry Draft for Wendel Clark, Sylvain Lefebvre, Landon Wilson and Toronto's 1st round choice (Jeffrey Kealty) in 1994 Entry Draft, June 28, 1994. Signed as a free agent by **Vancouver**, December 18, 2008.

## SUTER, Ryan

(SOO-tuhr, RIGH-uhn) **NSH.**

Defense. Shoots left. 6'1", 194 lbs. Born, Madison, WI, January 21, 1985. Nashville's 1st choice, 7th overall, in 2003 Entry Draft.

| | | | | | | | | | | | | | | | | | | | | | | | | | |
|---|---|---|---|---|---|---|---|---|---|---|---|---|---|---|---|---|---|---|---|---|---|---|---|---|---|
| 2000-01 | Culver Academy | High-IN | 26 | 13 | 32 | 45 | | .... | .... | .... | .... | .... | .... | .... | .... | .... | .... | .... | .... | .... | .... | .... | .... | .... | .... |
| 2001-02 | USNTDP | U-17 | 8 | 2 | 11 | 13 | 21 | .... | .... | .... | .... | .... | .... | .... | .... | .... | .... | .... | .... | .... | .... | .... | .... | .... | .... |
| | USNTDP | U-18 | 27 | 4 | 10 | 14 | 6 | .... | .... | .... | .... | .... | .... | .... | .... | .... | .... | .... | .... | .... | .... | .... | .... | .... | .... |
| | USNTDP | NAHL | 35 | 2 | 10 | 12 | 75 | .... | .... | .... | .... | .... | .... | .... | .... | .... | .... | .... | .... | .... | .... | .... | .... | .... | .... |
| 2002-03 | USNTDP | NAHL | 9 | 2 | 5 | 7 | 12 | .... | .... | .... | .... | .... | .... | .... | .... | .... | .... | .... | .... | .... | .... | .... | .... | .... | .... |
| | USNTDP | U-18 | 42 | 7 | 17 | 24 | 124 | .... | .... | .... | .... | .... | .... | .... | .... | .... | .... | .... | .... | .... | .... | .... | .... | .... | .... |
| 2003-04 | U. of Wisconsin | WCHA | 39 | 3 | 16 | 19 | 93 | .... | .... | .... | .... | .... | .... | .... | .... | .... | .... | .... | .... | .... | .... | .... | .... | .... | .... |
| 2004-05 | Milwaukee | AHL | 63 | 7 | 16 | 23 | 70 | .... | .... | .... | .... | .... | .... | .... | .... | .... | 7 | 1 | 5 | 6 | 16 | .... | .... | .... | .... |
| **2005-06** | **Nashville** | **NHL** | 71 | 1 | 15 | 16 | 66 | 0 | 0 | 0 | 84 | 1.2 | 7 | 0 | 0.0 | 17:21 | .... | .... | .... | .... | .... | .... | .... | .... | .... |
| **2006-07** | **Nashville** | **NHL** | 82 | 8 | 16 | 24 | 54 | 1 | 0 | 0 | 87 | 9.2 | 10 | 0 | 0.0 | 20:09 | 5 | 1 | 0 | 1 | 8 | 0 | 0 | 0 | 23:19 |
| **2007-08** | **Nashville** | **NHL** | 76 | 7 | 24 | 31 | 71 | 1 | 0 | 1 | 138 | 5.1 | 3 | 0 | 0.0 | 20:35 | 6 | 1 | 1 | 2 | 4 | 0 | 0 | 0 | 21:12 |
| **2008-09** | **Nashville** | **NHL** | 82 | 7 | 38 | 45 | 73 | 3 | 0 | 3 | 143 | 4.9 | -16 | 0 | 0.0 | 24:16 | .... | .... | .... | .... | .... | .... | .... | .... | .... |
| | NHL Totals | | 311 | 23 | 93 | 116 | 264 | 5 | 0 | 4 | 452 | 5.1 | | 0 | 0.0 | 20:42 | 11 | 2 | 1 | 3 | 12 | 0 | 0 | 0 | 22:10 |

WCHA All-Rookie Team (2004)

## SUTHERBY, Brian

(SUH-thur-bee, BRIGH-uhn) **DAL.**

Center. Shoots left. 6'3", 209 lbs. Born, Edmonton, Alta., March 1, 1982. Washington's 1st choice, 26th overall, in 2000 Entry Draft.

| | | | | | | | | | | | | | | | | | | | | | | | | | |
|---|---|---|---|---|---|---|---|---|---|---|---|---|---|---|---|---|---|---|---|---|---|---|---|---|---|
| 1997-98 | CAC Cement | AMHL | 36 | 36 | 23 | 59 | 60 | .... | .... | .... | .... | .... | .... | .... | .... | .... | .... | .... | .... | .... | .... | .... | .... | .... | .... |
| 1998-99 | Moose Jaw | WHL | 66 | 9 | 12 | 21 | 47 | .... | .... | .... | .... | .... | .... | .... | .... | .... | 11 | 0 | 1 | 1 | 0 | .... | .... | .... | .... |
| 99-2000 | Moose Jaw | WHL | 47 | 18 | 17 | 35 | 102 | .... | .... | .... | .... | .... | .... | .... | .... | .... | 4 | 1 | 1 | 2 | 12 | .... | .... | .... | .... |
| 2000-01 | Moose Jaw | WHL | 59 | 34 | 43 | 77 | 138 | .... | .... | .... | .... | .... | .... | .... | .... | .... | 4 | 2 | 1 | 3 | 10 | .... | .... | .... | .... |
| **2001-02** | **Washington** | **NHL** | 7 | 0 | 0 | 0 | 2 | 0 | 0 | 0 | 3 | 0.0 | -3 | 39 | 35.9 | 7:17 | .... | .... | .... | .... | .... | .... | .... | .... | .... |
| | Moose Jaw | WHL | 36 | 18 | 27 | 45 | 75 | .... | .... | .... | .... | .... | .... | .... | .... | .... | 12 | 7 | 5 | 12 | 33 | .... | .... | .... | .... |
| **2002-03** | **Washington** | **NHL** | 72 | 2 | 9 | 11 | 93 | 0 | 0 | 0 | 38 | 5.3 | 7 | 288 | 43.8 | 9:44 | 5 | 0 | 0 | 0 | 10 | 0 | 0 | 0 | 4:10 |
| | Portland Pirates | AHL | 5 | 0 | 5 | 5 | 11 | .... | .... | .... | .... | .... | .... | .... | .... | .... | .... | .... | .... | .... | .... | .... | .... | .... | .... |
| **2003-04** | **Washington** | **NHL** | 30 | 2 | 0 | 2 | 28 | 0 | 0 | 0 | 24 | 8.3 | -5 | 116 | 41.4 | 10:15 | .... | .... | .... | .... | .... | .... | .... | .... | .... |
| | Portland Pirates | AHL | 6 | 2 | 4 | 6 | 16 | .... | .... | .... | .... | .... | .... | .... | .... | .... | .... | .... | .... | .... | .... | .... | .... | .... | .... |
| 2004-05 | Portland Pirates | AHL | 53 | 10 | 19 | 29 | 115 | .... | .... | .... | .... | .... | .... | .... | .... | .... | .... | .... | .... | .... | .... | .... | .... | .... | .... |
| **2005-06** | **Washington** | **NHL** | 76 | 14 | 16 | 30 | 73 | 0 | 2 | 0 | 85 | 16.5 | -17 | 904 | 48.7 | 13:44 | .... | .... | .... | .... | .... | .... | .... | .... | .... |
| **2006-07** | **Washington** | **NHL** | 69 | 7 | 10 | 17 | 78 | 1 | 0 | 0 | 87 | 8.0 | -9 | 762 | 50.1 | 13:41 | .... | .... | .... | .... | .... | .... | .... | .... | .... |
| **2007-08** | **Washington** | **NHL** | 5 | 1 | 0 | 1 | 7 | 0 | 0 | 0 | 3 | 33.3 | -2 | 23 | 52.2 | 6:49 | .... | .... | .... | .... | .... | .... | .... | .... | .... |
| | **Anaheim** | **NHL** | 45 | 0 | 1 | 1 | 57 | 0 | 0 | 0 | 46 | 0.0 | -2 | 255 | 45.5 | 8:47 | 5 | 0 | 0 | 0 | 2 | 0 | 0 | 0 | 5:29 |
| **2008-09** | **Anaheim** | **NHL** | 17 | 3 | 3 | 6 | 19 | 0 | 0 | 0 | 17 | 17.6 | 6 | 45 | 48.9 | 7:12 | .... | .... | .... | .... | .... | .... | .... | .... | .... |
| | **Dallas** | **NHL** | 42 | 5 | 4 | 9 | 52 | 0 | 1 | 0 | 50 | 10.0 | -5 | 219 | 41.1 | 12:25 | .... | .... | .... | .... | .... | .... | .... | .... | .... |
| | NHL Totals | | 363 | 34 | 43 | 77 | 409 | 1 | 3 | 0 | 353 | 9.6 | | 2651 | 47.2 | 11:21 | 10 | 0 | 0 | 0 | 12 | 0 | 0 | 0 | 4:49 |

• Missed majority of 2003-04 season recovering from groin injury suffered in game vs. St. Louis, October 18, 2003. Traded to **Anaheim** by **Washington** for Anaheim's 2nd round choice (later traded to Montreal – later traded to Atlanta – Atlanta selected Jeremy Morin) in 2009 Entry Draft, November 19, 2007. Traded to **Dallas** by **Anaheim** for David McIntyre and future considerations, December 14, 2008.

| Season | Club | League | Regular Season GP | G | A | Pts | PIM | PP | SH | GW | S | % | +/- | TF | F% | Min | Playoffs GP | G | A | Pts | PIM | PP | SH | GW | Min |
|---|---|---|---|---|---|---|---|---|---|---|---|---|---|---|---|---|---|---|---|---|---|---|---|---|---|

## SUTTER, Brandon
(SUH-tuhr, BRAN-duhn) **CAR.**

Center/Right wing. Shoots right. 6'3", 183 lbs. Born, Huntington, NY, February 14, 1989. Carolina's 1st choice, 11th overall, in 2007 Entry Draft.

| Season | Club | League | GP | G | A | Pts | PIM | PP | SH | GW | S | % | +/- | TF | F% | Min | GP | G | A | Pts | PIM | PP | SH | GW | Min |
|---|---|---|---|---|---|---|---|---|---|---|---|---|---|---|---|---|---|---|---|---|---|---|---|---|---|
| 2003-04 | Red Deer Chiefs | AMBHL | 35 | 25 | 34 | 59 | 28 | .... | .... | .... | .... | .... | .... | .... | .... | .... | 11 | 5 | 4 | 9 | .... | .... | .... | .... | .... |
| 2004-05 | Red Deer | AMHL | 34 | 4 | 16 | 20 | 28 | .... | .... | .... | .... | .... | .... | .... | .... | .... | .... | .... | .... | .... | .... | .... | .... | .... | .... |
| | Red Deer Rebels | WHL | 7 | 0 | 2 | 2 | 8 | .... | .... | .... | .... | .... | .... | .... | .... | .... | 7 | 1 | 4 | 5 | 2 | .... | .... | .... | .... |
| 2005-06 | Red Deer Rebels | WHL | 68 | 22 | 24 | 46 | 36 | .... | .... | .... | .... | .... | .... | .... | .... | .... | .... | .... | .... | .... | .... | .... | .... | .... | .... |
| 2006-07 | Red Deer Rebels | WHL | 71 | 20 | 37 | 57 | 54 | .... | .... | .... | .... | .... | .... | .... | .... | .... | 7 | 0 | 3 | 3 | 14 | .... | .... | .... | .... |
| 2007-08 | Red Deer Rebels | WHL | 59 | 26 | 23 | 49 | 38 | .... | .... | .... | .... | .... | .... | .... | .... | .... | .... | .... | .... | .... | .... | .... | .... | .... | .... |
| | Albany River Rats | AHL | 7 | 1 | 1 | 2 | 2 | .... | .... | .... | .... | .... | .... | .... | .... | .... | 7 | 0 | 2 | 2 | 4 | .... | .... | .... | .... |
| **2008-09** | **Carolina** | **NHL** | **50** | **1** | **5** | **6** | **16** | **0** | **0** | **0** | **57** | **1.8** | **–1** | **332** | **38.6** | **8:50** | .... | .... | .... | .... | .... | .... | .... | .... | .... |
| | Albany River Rats | AHL | 22 | 4 | 8 | 12 | 6 | .... | .... | .... | .... | .... | .... | .... | .... | .... | .... | .... | .... | .... | .... | .... | .... | .... | .... |
| | **NHL Totals** | | **50** | **1** | **5** | **6** | **16** | **0** | **0** | **0** | **57** | **1.8** | | **332** | **38.6** | **8:50** | .... | .... | .... | .... | .... | .... | .... | .... | .... |

## SUTTER, Brett
(SUH-tuhr, BREHT) **CGY.**

Center/Left wing. Shoots left. 6', 195 lbs. Born, Viking, Alta., June 2, 1987. Calgary's 7th choice, 179th overall, in 2005 Entry Draft.

| Season | Club | League | GP | G | A | Pts | PIM | PP | SH | GW | S | % | +/- | TF | F% | Min | GP | G | A | Pts | PIM | PP | SH | GW | Min |
|---|---|---|---|---|---|---|---|---|---|---|---|---|---|---|---|---|---|---|---|---|---|---|---|---|---|
| 2003-04 | Kootenay Ice | WHL | 44 | 5 | 7 | 12 | 26 | .... | .... | .... | .... | .... | .... | .... | .... | .... | 4 | 0 | 0 | 0 | 4 | .... | .... | .... | .... |
| 2004-05 | Kootenay Ice | WHL | 70 | 8 | 11 | 19 | 70 | .... | .... | .... | .... | .... | .... | .... | .... | .... | 16 | 1 | 2 | 3 | 16 | .... | .... | .... | .... |
| 2005-06 | Kootenay Ice | WHL | 16 | 8 | 7 | 15 | 21 | .... | .... | .... | .... | .... | .... | .... | .... | .... | .... | .... | .... | .... | .... | .... | .... | .... | .... |
| | Red Deer Rebels | WHL | 57 | 9 | 26 | 35 | 80 | .... | .... | .... | .... | .... | .... | .... | .... | .... | .... | .... | .... | .... | .... | .... | .... | .... | .... |
| 2006-07 | Red Deer Rebels | WHL | 67 | 28 | 29 | 57 | 77 | .... | .... | .... | .... | .... | .... | .... | .... | .... | 7 | 3 | 4 | 7 | 11 | .... | .... | .... | .... |
| 2007-08 | Quad City Flames | AHL | 75 | 4 | 6 | 10 | 63 | .... | .... | .... | .... | .... | .... | .... | .... | .... | .... | .... | .... | .... | .... | .... | .... | .... | .... |
| **2008-09** | **Calgary** | **NHL** | **4** | **1** | **0** | **1** | **2** | **0** | **0** | **0** | **6** | **16.7** | **–2** | **1** | **0.0** | **8:04** | .... | .... | .... | .... | .... | .... | .... | .... | .... |
| | Quad City Flames | AHL | 71 | 10 | 15 | 25 | 50 | .... | .... | .... | .... | .... | .... | .... | .... | .... | .... | .... | .... | .... | .... | .... | .... | .... | .... |
| | **NHL Totals** | | **4** | **1** | **0** | **1** | **2** | **0** | **0** | **0** | **6** | **16.7** | | **1** | **0.0** | **8:04** | .... | .... | .... | .... | .... | .... | .... | .... | .... |

## SUTTON, Andy
(SUH-tuhn, AN-dee) **NYI**

Defense. Shoots left. 6'6", 245 lbs. Born, Kingston, Ont., March 10, 1975.

| Season | Club | League | GP | G | A | Pts | PIM | PP | SH | GW | S | % | +/- | TF | F% | Min | GP | G | A | Pts | PIM | PP | SH | GW | Min |
|---|---|---|---|---|---|---|---|---|---|---|---|---|---|---|---|---|---|---|---|---|---|---|---|---|---|
| 1991-92 | Gananoque | OHA-B | 36 | 11 | 9 | 20 | .... | .... | .... | .... | .... | .... | .... | .... | .... | .... | 14 | 9 | 21 | 30 | .... | .... | .... | .... | .... |
| 1992-93 | Gananoque | OHA-B | 38 | 14 | 9 | 23 | .... | .... | .... | .... | .... | .... | .... | .... | .... | .... | 12 | 16 | 13 | 29 | .... | .... | .... | .... | .... |
| 1993-94 | St. Mike's B's | MTJHL | 48 | 17 | 23 | 40 | 161 | .... | .... | .... | .... | .... | .... | .... | .... | .... | 3 | 0 | 0 | 0 | 20 | .... | .... | .... | .... |
| 1994-95 | Michigan Tech | WCHA | 19 | 2 | 1 | 3 | 42 | .... | .... | .... | .... | .... | .... | .... | .... | .... | .... | .... | .... | .... | .... | .... | .... | .... | .... |
| 1995-96 | Michigan Tech | WCHA | 33 | 2 | 2 | 4 | 58 | .... | .... | .... | .... | .... | .... | .... | .... | .... | .... | .... | .... | .... | .... | .... | .... | .... | .... |
| 1996-97 | Michigan Tech | WCHA | 32 | 2 | 7 | 9 | 73 | .... | .... | .... | .... | .... | .... | .... | .... | .... | .... | .... | .... | .... | .... | .... | .... | .... | .... |
| 1997-98 | Michigan Tech | WCHA | 38 | 16 | 24 | 40 | 97 | .... | .... | .... | .... | .... | .... | .... | .... | .... | .... | .... | .... | .... | .... | .... | .... | .... | .... |
| | Kentucky | AHL | 7 | 0 | 0 | 0 | 33 | .... | .... | .... | .... | .... | .... | .... | .... | .... | .... | .... | .... | .... | .... | .... | .... | .... | .... |
| **1998-99** | **San Jose** | **NHL** | **31** | **0** | **3** | **3** | **65** | **0** | **0** | **0** | **24** | **0.0** | **–4** | **0** | **0.0** | **12:58** | .... | .... | .... | .... | .... | .... | .... | .... | .... |
| | Kentucky | AHL | 21 | 5 | 10 | 15 | 53 | .... | .... | .... | .... | .... | .... | .... | .... | .... | 5 | 0 | 0 | 0 | 23 | .... | .... | .... | .... |
| **99-2000** | **San Jose** | **NHL** | **40** | **1** | **1** | **2** | **80** | **0** | **0** | **0** | **29** | **3.4** | **–5** | **0** | **0.0** | **12:57** | .... | .... | .... | .... | .... | .... | .... | .... | .... |
| | Kentucky | AHL | 3 | 0 | 1 | 1 | 0 | .... | .... | .... | .... | .... | .... | .... | .... | .... | .... | .... | .... | .... | .... | .... | .... | .... | .... |
| **2000-01** | **Minnesota** | **NHL** | **69** | **3** | **4** | **7** | **131** | **2** | **0** | **0** | **64** | **4.7** | **–11** | **3** | **33.3** | **12:55** | .... | .... | .... | .... | .... | .... | .... | .... | .... |
| **2001-02** | **Minnesota** | **NHL** | **19** | **2** | **4** | **6** | **35** | **1** | **0** | **0** | **21** | **9.5** | **–4** | **2** | **0.0** | **10:57** | .... | .... | .... | .... | .... | .... | .... | .... | .... |
| | **Atlanta** | **NHL** | **24** | **0** | **4** | **4** | **46** | **0** | **0** | **0** | **20** | **0.0** | **0** | **0** | **0.0** | **15:25** | .... | .... | .... | .... | .... | .... | .... | .... | .... |
| **2002-03** | **Atlanta** | **NHL** | **53** | **3** | **18** | **21** | **114** | **1** | **1** | **0** | **65** | **4.6** | **–8** | **3** | **33.3** | **18:00** | .... | .... | .... | .... | .... | .... | .... | .... | .... |
| **2003-04** | **Atlanta** | **NHL** | **65** | **8** | **13** | **21** | **94** | **7** | **1** | **1** | **102** | **7.8** | **0** | **1** | **0.0** | **23:21** | .... | .... | .... | .... | .... | .... | .... | .... | .... |
| 2004-05 | GCK Lions Zurich | Swiss-2 | 18 | 8 | 18 | 26 | 58 | .... | .... | .... | .... | .... | .... | .... | .... | .... | 6 | 2 | 4 | 6 | 16 | .... | .... | .... | .... |
| | ZSC Lions Zurich | Swiss | 8 | 2 | 2 | 4 | 32 | .... | .... | .... | .... | .... | .... | .... | .... | .... | 1 | 0 | 1 | 1 | 2 | .... | .... | .... | .... |
| **2005-06** | **Atlanta** | **NHL** | **76** | **8** | **17** | **25** | **144** | **2** | **1** | **3** | **86** | **9.3** | **13** | **1** | **0.0** | **21:05** | .... | .... | .... | .... | .... | .... | .... | .... | .... |
| **2006-07** | **Atlanta** | **NHL** | **55** | **2** | **14** | **16** | **76** | **0** | **1** | **0** | **51** | **3.9** | **6** | **0** | **0.0** | **19:28** | **4** | **0** | **0** | **0** | **10** | **0** | **0** | **0** | **17:34** |
| **2007-08** | **NY Islanders** | **NHL** | **58** | **1** | **7** | **8** | **86** | **0** | **0** | **1** | **57** | **1.8** | **–6** | **0** | **0.0** | **18:10** | .... | .... | .... | .... | .... | .... | .... | .... | .... |
| **2008-09** | **NY Islanders** | **NHL** | **23** | **2** | **8** | **10** | **40** | **0** | **0** | **0** | **19** | **10.5** | **3** | **0** | **0.0** | **20:14** | .... | .... | .... | .... | .... | .... | .... | .... | .... |
| | **NHL Totals** | | **513** | **30** | **93** | **123** | **911** | **13** | **4** | **5** | **538** | **5.6** | | **10** | **20.0** | **17:39** | **4** | **0** | **0** | **0** | **10** | **0** | **0** | **0** | **17:34** |

WCHA Second All-Star Team (1998)

Signed as a free agent by **San Jose**, March 20, 1998. Traded to **Minnesota** by **San Jose** with San Jose's 7th round choice (Peter Bartos) in 2000 Entry Draft and San Jose's 3rd round choice (later traded to Atlanta – later traded to Pittsburgh – later traded to Columbus – Columbus selected Aaron Johnson) in 2001 Entry Draft for Minnesota's 8th round choice (later traded to Calgary – Calgary selected Joe Campbell) in 2001 Entry Draft and future considerations, June 12, 2000. Traded to **Atlanta** by **Minnesota** for Hnat Domenichelli, January 22, 2002. Signed as a free agent by **GCK Zurich** (Swiss-2), September 24, 2004. Loaned to **ZSC Zurich** (Swiss) by **GCK Zurich** (Swiss-2), February 22, 2005. Signed as a free agent by **NY Islanders**, August 10, 2007. • Missed majority of 2008-09 season recovering from broken foot suffered in game at Minnesota, December 19, 2008.

## SVATOS, Marek
(SVA-tohs, MAIR-ehk) **COL.**

Right wing. Shoots right. 5'10", 185 lbs. Born, Kosice, Czech., June 17, 1982. Colorado's 10th choice, 227th overall, in 2001 Entry Draft.

| Season | Club | League | GP | G | A | Pts | PIM | PP | SH | GW | S | % | +/- | TF | F% | Min | GP | G | A | Pts | PIM | PP | SH | GW | Min |
|---|---|---|---|---|---|---|---|---|---|---|---|---|---|---|---|---|---|---|---|---|---|---|---|---|---|
| 99-2000 | HC VSZ Kosice Jr. | Slovak-Jr. | 39 | 43 | 30 | 73 | 28 | .... | .... | .... | .... | .... | .... | .... | .... | .... | .... | .... | .... | .... | .... | .... | .... | .... | .... |
| | HC VSZ Kosice | Slovakia | 19 | 2 | 2 | 4 | 0 | .... | .... | .... | .... | .... | .... | .... | .... | .... | .... | .... | .... | .... | .... | .... | .... | .... | .... |
| 2000-01 | Kootenay Ice | WHL | 39 | 23 | 18 | 41 | 47 | .... | .... | .... | .... | .... | .... | .... | .... | .... | 11 | 7 | 2 | 9 | 26 | .... | .... | .... | .... |
| 2001-02 | Kootenay Ice | WHL | 53 | 38 | 39 | 77 | 58 | .... | .... | .... | .... | .... | .... | .... | .... | .... | 21 | 12 | 6 | 18 | 40 | .... | .... | .... | .... |
| 2002-03 | Hershey Bears | AHL | 30 | 9 | 4 | 13 | 10 | .... | .... | .... | .... | .... | .... | .... | .... | .... | .... | .... | .... | .... | .... | .... | .... | .... | .... |
| **2003-04** | **Colorado** | **NHL** | **4** | **2** | **0** | **2** | **0** | **1** | **0** | **1** | **6** | **33.3** | **1** | **0** | **0.0** | **10:18** | **11** | **1** | **5** | **6** | **2** | **0** | **0** | **1** | **12:29** |
| 2004-05 | Hershey Bears | AHL | 72 | 18 | 28 | 46 | 69 | .... | .... | .... | .... | .... | .... | .... | .... | .... | .... | .... | .... | .... | .... | .... | .... | .... | .... |
| **2005-06** | **Colorado** | **NHL** | **61** | **32** | **18** | **50** | **60** | **12** | **0** | **9** | **165** | **19.4** | **0** | **5** | **20.0** | **13:45** | .... | .... | .... | .... | .... | .... | .... | .... | .... |
| | Slovakia | Olympics | 6 | 0 | 0 | 0 | 0 | .... | .... | .... | .... | .... | .... | .... | .... | .... | .... | .... | .... | .... | .... | .... | .... | .... | .... |
| **2006-07** | **Colorado** | **NHL** | **66** | **15** | **15** | **30** | **46** | **8** | **0** | **2** | **179** | **8.4** | **1** | **1** | **100.0** | **12:30** | .... | .... | .... | .... | .... | .... | .... | .... | .... |
| **2007-08** | **Colorado** | **NHL** | **62** | **26** | **11** | **37** | **32** | **3** | **0** | **6** | **140** | **18.6** | **13** | **3** | **33.3** | **13:39** | .... | .... | .... | .... | .... | .... | .... | .... | .... |
| **2008-09** | **Colorado** | **NHL** | **69** | **14** | **20** | **34** | **34** | **6** | **0** | **1** | **140** | **10.0** | **–6** | **3** | **0.0** | **13:06** | .... | .... | .... | .... | .... | .... | .... | .... | .... |
| | **NHL Totals** | | **262** | **89** | **64** | **153** | **172** | **30** | **0** | **19** | **630** | **14.1** | | **12** | **25.0** | **13:11** | **11** | **1** | **5** | **6** | **2** | **0** | **0** | **1** | **12:29** |

WHL West Second All-Star Team (2002)

• Missed majority of 2002-03 season recovering from shoulder injury that required surgery, January 28, 2003. • Missed majority of 2003-04 season recovering from shoulder injury suffered in game vs. St. Louis, October 12, 2003.

## SVITOV, Alexander
(SVEE-tawf, al-EHX-AN-duhr) **CBJ**

Center. Shoots left. 6'3", 231 lbs. Born, Omsk, USSR, November 3, 1982. Tampa Bay's 1st choice, 3rd overall, in 2001 Entry Draft.

| Season | Club | League | GP | G | A | Pts | PIM | PP | SH | GW | S | % | +/- | TF | F% | Min | GP | G | A | Pts | PIM | PP | SH | GW | Min |
|---|---|---|---|---|---|---|---|---|---|---|---|---|---|---|---|---|---|---|---|---|---|---|---|---|---|
| 1997-98 | Novokuznetsk 2 | Russia-3 | 4 | 0 | 0 | 0 | 0 | .... | .... | .... | .... | .... | .... | .... | .... | .... | .... | .... | .... | .... | .... | .... | .... | .... | .... |
| 1998-99 | Omsk 2 | Russia-4 | 27 | 15 | 8 | 23 | 20 | .... | .... | .... | .... | .... | .... | .... | .... | .... | .... | .... | .... | .... | .... | .... | .... | .... | .... |
| | Avangard Omsk | Russia | .... | .... | .... | .... | .... | .... | .... | .... | .... | .... | .... | .... | .... | .... | 1 | 0 | 0 | 0 | 0 | .... | .... | .... | .... |
| 99-2000 | Omsk 2 | Russia-3 | 14 | 13 | 9 | 22 | 62 | .... | .... | .... | .... | .... | .... | .... | .... | .... | .... | .... | .... | .... | .... | .... | .... | .... | .... |
| | Avangard Omsk | Russia | 18 | 3 | 3 | 6 | 45 | .... | .... | .... | .... | .... | .... | .... | .... | .... | 6 | 1 | 0 | 1 | 16 | .... | .... | .... | .... |
| 2000-01 | Avangard Omsk | Russia | 39 | 8 | 6 | 14 | 115 | .... | .... | .... | .... | .... | .... | .... | .... | .... | 14 | 2 | 1 | 3 | 34 | .... | .... | .... | .... |
| 2001-02 | CSKA Moscow 2 | Russia-3 | 2 | 1 | 0 | 1 | 2 | .... | .... | .... | .... | .... | .... | .... | .... | .... | .... | .... | .... | .... | .... | .... | .... | .... | .... |
| | Avangard Omsk | Russia | 2 | 0 | 1 | 1 | 2 | .... | .... | .... | .... | .... | .... | .... | .... | .... | .... | .... | .... | .... | .... | .... | .... | .... | .... |
| **2002-03** | **Tampa Bay** | **NHL** | **63** | **4** | **4** | **8** | **58** | **1** | **0** | **0** | **69** | **5.8** | **–4** | **395** | **42.8** | **8:50** | **7** | **0** | **0** | **0** | **6** | **0** | **0** | **0** | **7:19** |
| | Springfield | AHL | 11 | 4 | 5 | 9 | 17 | .... | .... | .... | .... | .... | .... | .... | .... | .... | .... | .... | .... | .... | .... | .... | .... | .... | .... |
| **2003-04** | **Tampa Bay** | **NHL** | **11** | **0** | **3** | **3** | **4** | **0** | **0** | **0** | **16** | **0.0** | **0** | **79** | **58.2** | **9:18** | .... | .... | .... | .... | .... | .... | .... | .... | .... |
| | Hamilton | AHL | 30 | 9 | 9 | 18 | 79 | .... | .... | .... | .... | .... | .... | .... | .... | .... | .... | .... | .... | .... | .... | .... | .... | .... | .... |
| | **Columbus** | **NHL** | **29** | **2** | **6** | **8** | **16** | **0** | **0** | **0** | **36** | **5.6** | **–8** | **293** | **43.0** | **12:39** | .... | .... | .... | .... | .... | .... | .... | .... | .... |
| 2004-05 | Syracuse Crunch | AHL | 69 | 19 | 23 | 42 | 200 | .... | .... | .... | .... | .... | .... | .... | .... | .... | .... | .... | .... | .... | .... | .... | .... | .... | .... |
| 2005-06 | Avangard Omsk | Russia | 32 | 3 | 6 | 9 | 142 | .... | .... | .... | .... | .... | .... | .... | .... | .... | 13 | 4 | 1 | 5 | 10 | .... | .... | .... | .... |
| **2006-07** | **Columbus** | **NHL** | **76** | **7** | **11** | **18** | **145** | **1** | **0** | **2** | **83** | **8.4** | **–10** | **928** | **50.9** | **13:47** | .... | .... | .... | .... | .... | .... | .... | .... | .... |
| 2007-08 | Avangard Omsk | Russia | 54 | 10 | 11 | 21 | 140 | .... | .... | .... | .... | .... | .... | .... | .... | .... | 4 | 0 | 3 | 3 | 10 | .... | .... | .... | .... |
| 2008-09 | Omsk | Rus-KHL | 32 | 8 | 8 | 16 | 86 | .... | .... | .... | .... | .... | .... | .... | .... | .... | 6 | 1 | 0 | 1 | 41 | .... | .... | .... | .... |
| | **NHL Totals** | | **179** | **13** | **24** | **37** | **223** | **2** | **0** | **2** | **204** | **6.4** | | **1695** | **48.0** | **11:35** | **7** | **0** | **0** | **0** | **6** | **0** | **0** | **0** | **7:19** |

Traded to **Columbus** by **Tampa Bay** with Tampa Bay's 3rd round choice (later traded to Calgary – Calgary selected Dustin Boyd) in 2004 Entry Draft for Darryl Sydor and Columbus' 4th round choice (Mike Lundin) in 2004 Entry Draft, January 27, 2004. Signed as a free agent by **Omsk** (Russia), August 17, 2007.

## SYDOR, Darryl
(sih-DOHR, DAIR-uhl)

Defense. Shoots left. 6'1", 211 lbs. Born, Edmonton, Alta., May 13, 1972. Los Angeles' 1st choice, 7th overall, in 1990 Entry Draft.

| | | | Regular Season | | | | | | | | | | | | | | Playoffs | | | | | | | | |
|---|---|---|---|---|---|---|---|---|---|---|---|---|---|---|---|---|---|---|---|---|---|---|---|---|---|
| Season | Club | League | GP | G | A | Pts | PIM | PP | SH | GW | S | % | +/- | TF | F% | Min | GP | G | A | Pts | PIM | PP | SH | GW | Min |
| 1985-86 | Genstar Cement | AAHA | 34 | 20 | 17 | 37 | 60 | .... | .... | .... | .... | .... | .... | .... | .... | .... | .... | .... | .... | .... | .... | .... | .... | .... | .... |
| 1986-87 | Genstar Cement | AAHA | 36 | 15 | 20 | 35 | 60 | .... | .... | .... | .... | .... | .... | .... | .... | .... | .... | .... | .... | .... | .... | .... | .... | .... | .... |
| 1987-88 | Edmonton Mets | AJHL | 38 | 10 | 11 | 21 | 54 | .... | .... | .... | .... | .... | .... | .... | .... | .... | .... | .... | .... | .... | .... | .... | .... | .... | .... |
| 1988-89 | Kamloops Blazers | WHL | 65 | 12 | 14 | 26 | 86 | .... | .... | .... | .... | .... | .... | .... | .... | .... | 15 | 1 | 4 | 5 | 19 | .... | .... | .... | .... |
| 1989-90 | Kamloops Blazers | WHL | 67 | 29 | 66 | 95 | 129 | .... | .... | .... | .... | .... | .... | .... | .... | .... | 17 | 2 | 9 | 11 | 28 | .... | .... | .... | .... |
| 1990-91 | Kamloops Blazers | WHL | 66 | 27 | 78 | 105 | 88 | .... | .... | .... | .... | .... | .... | .... | .... | .... | 12 | 3 | *22 | 25 | 10 | .... | .... | .... | .... |
| **1991-92** | Kamloops Blazers | WHL | 29 | 9 | 39 | 48 | 33 | .... | .... | .... | .... | .... | .... | .... | .... | .... | 17 | 3 | 15 | 18 | 18 | .... | .... | .... | .... |
| | **Los Angeles** | **NHL** | **18** | **1** | **5** | **6** | **22** | **0** | **0** | **0** | **18** | **5.6** | **−3** | .... | .... | .... | .... | .... | .... | .... | .... | .... | .... | .... | .... |
| **1992-93** | **Los Angeles** | **NHL** | **80** | **6** | **23** | **29** | **63** | **0** | **0** | **1** | **112** | **5.4** | **−2** | .... | .... | .... | **24** | **3** | **8** | **11** | **16** | **2** | **0** | **0** | .... |
| **1993-94** | **Los Angeles** | **NHL** | **84** | **8** | **27** | **35** | **94** | **1** | **0** | **0** | **146** | **5.5** | **−9** | .... | .... | .... | .... | .... | .... | .... | .... | .... | .... | .... | .... |
| **1994-95** | **Los Angeles** | **NHL** | **48** | **4** | **19** | **23** | **36** | **3** | **0** | **0** | **96** | **4.2** | **−2** | .... | .... | .... | .... | .... | .... | .... | .... | .... | .... | .... | .... |
| **1995-96** | **Los Angeles** | **NHL** | **58** | **1** | **11** | **12** | **34** | **1** | **0** | **0** | **84** | **1.2** | **−11** | .... | .... | .... | .... | .... | .... | .... | .... | .... | .... | .... | .... |
| | **Dallas** | **NHL** | **26** | **2** | **6** | **8** | **41** | **1** | **0** | **0** | **33** | **6.1** | **−1** | .... | .... | .... | .... | .... | .... | .... | .... | .... | .... | .... | .... |
| **1996-97** | **Dallas** | **NHL** | **82** | **8** | **40** | **48** | **51** | **2** | **0** | **2** | **142** | **5.6** | **37** | .... | .... | .... | **7** | **0** | **2** | **2** | **0** | **0** | **0** | **0** | .... |
| **1997-98** | **Dallas** | **NHL** | **79** | **11** | **35** | **46** | **51** | **4** | **1** | **1** | **166** | **6.6** | **17** | .... | .... | .... | **17** | **0** | **5** | **5** | **14** | **0** | **0** | **0** | .... |
| **1998-99** ♦ | **Dallas** | **NHL** | **74** | **14** | **34** | **48** | **50** | **9** | **0** | **2** | **163** | **8.6** | **−1** | **1** | **100.0** | **21:16** | **23** | **3** | **9** | **12** | **16** | **1** | **0** | **1** | **22:20** |
| **99-2000** | **Dallas** | **NHL** | **74** | **8** | **26** | **34** | **32** | **5** | **0** | **1** | **132** | **6.1** | **6** | **1** | **0.0** | **23:09** | **23** | **1** | **6** | **7** | **6** | **0** | **0** | **0** | **20:48** |
| **2000-01** | **Dallas** | **NHL** | **81** | **10** | **37** | **47** | **34** | **8** | **0** | **1** | **140** | **7.1** | **5** | **1** | **0.0** | **21:25** | **10** | **1** | **3** | **4** | **0** | **1** | **0** | **0** | **22:42** |
| **2001-02** | **Dallas** | **NHL** | **78** | **4** | **29** | **33** | **50** | **2** | **0** | **0** | **183** | **2.2** | **3** | **0** | **0.0** | **21:07** | .... | .... | .... | .... | .... | .... | .... | .... | .... |
| **2002-03** | **Dallas** | **NHL** | **81** | **5** | **31** | **36** | **40** | **2** | **0** | **1** | **132** | **3.8** | **22** | **0** | **0.0** | **18:19** | **12** | **0** | **6** | **6** | **6** | **0** | **0** | **0** | **19:14** |
| **2003-04** | **Columbus** | **NHL** | **49** | **2** | **13** | **15** | **26** | **1** | **0** | **0** | **80** | **2.5** | **−19** | **1** | **0.0** | **21:54** | .... | .... | .... | .... | .... | .... | .... | .... | .... |
| | ♦ **Tampa Bay** | **NHL** | **31** | **1** | **6** | **7** | **6** | **0** | **0** | **0** | **42** | **2.4** | **3** | **0** | **0.0** | **19:06** | **23** | **0** | **6** | **6** | **9** | **0** | **0** | **0** | **21:50** |
| 2004-05 | | | DID NOT PLAY | | | | | | | | | | | | | | | | | | | | | | |
| **2005-06** | **Tampa Bay** | **NHL** | **80** | **4** | **19** | **23** | **30** | **1** | **0** | **0** | **64** | **6.3** | **−18** | **1** | **0.0** | **19:06** | **5** | **0** | **1** | **1** | **0** | **0** | **0** | **0** | **17:54** |
| **2006-07** | **Dallas** | **NHL** | **74** | **5** | **16** | **21** | **36** | **2** | **0** | **1** | **75** | **6.7** | **−4** | **0** | **0.0** | **20:09** | **7** | **1** | **1** | **2** | **4** | **0** | **0** | **0** | **23:19** |
| **2007-08** | **Pittsburgh** | **NHL** | **74** | **1** | **12** | **13** | **26** | **1** | **0** | **0** | **59** | **1.7** | **1** | **0** | **0.0** | **17:33** | **4** | **0** | **0** | **0** | **2** | **0** | **0** | **0** | **16:20** |
| **2008-09** | **Pittsburgh** | **NHL** | **8** | **1** | **1** | **2** | **2** | **0** | **0** | **0** | **7** | **14.3** | **5** | **0** | **0.0** | **14:23** | .... | .... | .... | .... | .... | .... | .... | .... | .... |
| | **Dallas** | **NHL** | **65** | **2** | **11** | **13** | **16** | **0** | **0** | **0** | **66** | **3.0** | **−2** | **0** | **0.0** | **18:42** | .... | .... | .... | .... | .... | .... | .... | .... | .... |
| | **NHL Totals** | | **1244** | **98** | **401** | **499** | **740** | **43** | **1** | **10** | **1940** | **5.1** | | **5** | **20.0** | **20:07** | **155** | **9** | **47** | **56** | **73** | **4** | **0** | **1** | **21:13** |

WHL West First All-Star Team (1990, 1991, 1992)

Played in NHL All-Star Game (1998, 1999)

Traded to **Dallas** by **Los Angeles** with Los Angeles' 5th round choice (Ryan Christie) in 1996 Entry Draft for Shane Churla and Doug Zmolek, February 17, 1996. Traded to **Columbus** by **Dallas** for Mike Sillinger and Columbus' 2nd round choice (Johan Fransson) in 2004 Entry Draft, July 22, 2003. Traded to **Tampa Bay** by **Columbus** with Columbus' 4th round choice (Mike Lundin) in 2004 Entry Draft for Alexander Svitov and Tampa Bay's 3rd round choice (later traded to Calgary – Calgary selected Dustin Boyd) in 2004 Entry Draft, January 27, 2004. Traded to **Dallas** by **Tampa Bay** for Dallas' 4th round choice (later traded to Ottawa - Ottawa selected Derek Grant) in 2008 Entry Draft, July 2, 2006. Signed as a free agent by **Pittsburgh**, July 2, 2007. Traded to **Dallas** by **Pittsburgh** for Philippe Boucher, November 16, 2008.

## SYKORA, Petr
(sih-KOH-ra, PEE-tuhr)

Right wing. Shoots left. 6', 190 lbs. Born, Plzen, Czech., November 19, 1976. New Jersey's 1st choice, 18th overall, in 1995 Entry Draft.

| | | | Regular Season | | | | | | | | | | | | | | Playoffs | | | | | | | | |
|---|---|---|---|---|---|---|---|---|---|---|---|---|---|---|---|---|---|---|---|---|---|---|---|---|---|
| Season | Club | League | GP | G | A | Pts | PIM | PP | SH | GW | S | % | +/- | TF | F% | Min | GP | G | A | Pts | PIM | PP | SH | GW | Min |
| 1991-92 | Plzen Jr. | Czech-Jr. | 30 | 50 | 50 | 100 | .... | .... | .... | .... | .... | .... | .... | .... | .... | .... | .... | .... | .... | .... | .... | .... | .... | .... | .... |
| 1992-93 | HC Skoda Plzen | Czech | 19 | 12 | 5 | 17 | .... | .... | .... | .... | .... | .... | .... | .... | .... | .... | .... | .... | .... | .... | .... | .... | .... | .... | .... |
| 1993-94 | HC Skoda Plzen | CzRep | 37 | 10 | 16 | 26 | .... | .... | .... | .... | .... | .... | .... | .... | .... | .... | 4 | 0 | 1 | 1 | | .... | .... | .... | .... |
| | Cleveland | IHL | 13 | 4 | 5 | 9 | 8 | .... | .... | .... | .... | .... | .... | .... | .... | .... | .... | .... | .... | .... | .... | .... | .... | .... | .... |
| 1994-95 | Detroit Vipers | IHL | 29 | 12 | 17 | 29 | 16 | .... | .... | .... | .... | .... | .... | .... | .... | .... | .... | .... | .... | .... | .... | .... | .... | .... | .... |
| **1995-96** | **New Jersey** | **NHL** | **63** | **18** | **24** | **42** | **32** | **8** | **0** | **3** | **128** | **14.1** | **7** | .... | .... | .... | .... | .... | .... | .... | .... | .... | .... | .... | .... |
| | Albany River Rats | AHL | 5 | 4 | 1 | 5 | 0 | .... | .... | .... | .... | .... | .... | .... | .... | .... | .... | .... | .... | .... | .... | .... | .... | .... | .... |
| **1996-97** | **New Jersey** | **NHL** | **19** | **1** | **2** | **3** | **4** | **0** | **0** | **0** | **26** | **3.8** | **−8** | .... | .... | .... | **2** | **0** | **0** | **0** | **2** | **0** | **0** | **0** | .... |
| | Albany River Rats | AHL | 43 | 20 | 25 | 45 | 48 | .... | .... | .... | .... | .... | .... | .... | .... | .... | 4 | 1 | 4 | 5 | 2 | .... | .... | .... | .... |
| **1997-98** | **New Jersey** | **NHL** | **58** | **16** | **20** | **36** | **22** | **3** | **1** | **4** | **130** | **12.3** | **0** | .... | .... | .... | **2** | **0** | **0** | **0** | **0** | **0** | **0** | **0** | .... |
| | Albany River Rats | AHL | 2 | 4 | 1 | 5 | 0 | .... | .... | .... | .... | .... | .... | .... | .... | .... | .... | .... | .... | .... | .... | .... | .... | .... | .... |
| **1998-99** | **New Jersey** | **NHL** | **80** | **29** | **43** | **72** | **22** | **15** | **0** | **7** | **222** | **13.1** | **16** | **33** | **33.3** | **16:14** | **7** | **3** | **3** | **6** | **4** | **0** | **0** | **1** | **18:11** |
| **99-2000** ♦ | **New Jersey** | **NHL** | **79** | **25** | **43** | **68** | **26** | **5** | **1** | **4** | **222** | **11.3** | **24** | **47** | **61.7** | **17:06** | **23** | **9** | **8** | **17** | **10** | **1** | **0** | **3** | **15:20** |
| **2000-01** | **New Jersey** | **NHL** | **73** | **35** | **46** | **81** | **32** | **9** | **2** | **3** | **249** | **14.1** | **36** | **15** | **33.3** | **17:44** | **25** | **10** | **12** | **22** | **12** | **2** | **2** | **2** | **18:40** |
| **2001-02** | **New Jersey** | **NHL** | **73** | **21** | **27** | **48** | **44** | **4** | **0** | **4** | **194** | **10.8** | **12** | **1** | **0.0** | **17:51** | **4** | **0** | **1** | **1** | **0** | **0** | **0** | **0** | **17:57** |
| | Czech Republic | Olympics | 4 | 1 | 0 | 1 | 0 | .... | .... | .... | .... | .... | .... | .... | .... | .... | .... | .... | .... | .... | .... | .... | .... | .... | .... |
| **2002-03** | **Anaheim** | **NHL** | **82** | **34** | **25** | **59** | **24** | **15** | **1** | **5** | **299** | **11.4** | **−7** | **23** | **39.1** | **18:29** | **21** | **4** | **9** | **13** | **12** | **1** | **0** | **2** | **18:39** |
| **2003-04** | **Anaheim** | **NHL** | **81** | **23** | **29** | **52** | **34** | **6** | **0** | **2** | **277** | **8.3** | **−9** | **9** | **22.2** | **17:57** | .... | .... | .... | .... | .... | .... | .... | .... | .... |
| 2004-05 | Magnitogorsk | Russia | 45 | 18 | 13 | 31 | 46 | .... | .... | .... | .... | .... | .... | .... | .... | .... | 5 | 2 | 3 | 5 | 8 | .... | .... | .... | .... |
| **2005-06** | **Anaheim** | **NHL** | **34** | **7** | **13** | **20** | **28** | **1** | **0** | **0** | **118** | **5.9** | **1** | **5** | **40.0** | **17:11** | .... | .... | .... | .... | .... | .... | .... | .... | .... |
| | **NY Rangers** | **NHL** | **40** | **16** | **15** | **31** | **22** | **7** | **0** | **0** | **112** | **14.3** | **5** | **69** | **37.7** | **15:11** | **4** | **0** | **0** | **0** | **0** | **0** | **0** | **0** | **17:45** |
| **2006-07** | **Edmonton** | **NHL** | **82** | **22** | **31** | **53** | **40** | **6** | **0** | **6** | **206** | **10.7** | **−20** | **462** | **48.1** | **16:40** | .... | .... | .... | .... | .... | .... | .... | .... | .... |
| **2007-08** | **Pittsburgh** | **NHL** | **81** | **28** | **35** | **63** | **41** | **15** | **0** | **4** | **201** | **13.9** | **1** | **15** | **60.0** | **16:51** | **20** | **6** | **3** | **9** | **16** | **2** | **0** | **1** | **14:57** |
| **2008-09** ♦ | **Pittsburgh** | **NHL** | **76** | **25** | **21** | **46** | **36** | **13** | **0** | **10** | **180** | **13.9** | **3** | **12** | **41.7** | **16:17** | **7** | **0** | **1** | **1** | **0** | **0** | **0** | **0** | **11:55** |
| | **NHL Totals** | | **921** | **300** | **374** | **674** | **407** | **107** | **5** | **52** | **2564** | **11.7** | | **691** | **46.0** | **17:08** | **115** | **32** | **37** | **69** | **56** | **6** | **2** | **9** | **16:47** |

NHL All-Rookie Team (1996)

Traded to **Anaheim** by **New Jersey** with Mike Commodore, Jean-Francois Damphousse and Igor Pohanka for Jeff Friesen, Oleg Tverdovsky and Maxim Balmochnykh, July 6, 2002. Signed as a free agent by **Magnitogorsk** (Russia), August 12, 2004. Traded to **NY Rangers** by **Anaheim** with NY Rangers' 4th round choice (previously acquired, later traded to Washington - Washington selected Brett Bruneteau) in 2007 Entry Draft for Maxim Kondratiev, January 8, 2006. Signed as a free agent by **Edmonton**, August 11, 2006. Signed as a free agent by **Pittsburgh**, July 2, 2007.

## SYVRET, Danny
(SIHV-reht, DA-nee) **PHI.**

Defense. Shoots left. 5'11", 203 lbs. Born, Millgrove, Ont., June 13, 1985. Edmonton's 3rd choice, 81st overall, in 2005 Entry Draft.

| | | | Regular Season | | | | | | | | | | | | | | Playoffs | | | | | | | | |
|---|---|---|---|---|---|---|---|---|---|---|---|---|---|---|---|---|---|---|---|---|---|---|---|---|---|
| Season | Club | League | GP | G | A | Pts | PIM | PP | SH | GW | S | % | +/- | TF | F% | Min | GP | G | A | Pts | PIM | PP | SH | GW | Min |
| 2001-02 | Cambridge | OHA-B | 43 | 6 | 41 | 47 | 23 | .... | .... | .... | .... | .... | .... | .... | .... | .... | .... | .... | .... | .... | .... | .... | .... | .... | .... |
| | London Knights | OHL | 1 | 0 | 0 | 0 | 0 | .... | .... | .... | .... | .... | .... | .... | .... | .... | .... | .... | .... | .... | .... | .... | .... | .... | .... |
| 2002-03 | London Knights | OHL | 68 | 8 | 14 | 22 | 31 | .... | .... | .... | .... | .... | .... | .... | .... | .... | 14 | 1 | 6 | 7 | 11 | .... | .... | .... | .... |
| 2003-04 | London Knights | OHL | 68 | 3 | 28 | 31 | 32 | .... | .... | .... | .... | .... | .... | .... | .... | .... | 15 | 1 | 6 | 7 | 4 | .... | .... | .... | .... |
| 2004-05 | London Knights | OHL | 62 | 23 | 46 | 69 | 33 | .... | .... | .... | .... | .... | .... | .... | .... | .... | 18 | 5 | 15 | 20 | 4 | .... | .... | .... | .... |
| **2005-06** | **Edmonton** | **NHL** | **10** | **0** | **0** | **0** | **6** | **0** | **0** | **0** | **8** | **0.0** | **−1** | **0** | **0.0** | **12:19** | .... | .... | .... | .... | .... | .... | .... | .... | .... |
| | Hamilton | AHL | 62 | 0 | 21 | 21 | 38 | .... | .... | .... | .... | .... | .... | .... | .... | .... | .... | .... | .... | .... | .... | .... | .... | .... | .... |
| **2006-07** | **Edmonton** | **NHL** | **16** | **0** | **1** | **1** | **6** | **0** | **0** | **0** | **15** | **0.0** | **−10** | **0** | **0.0** | **18:28** | .... | .... | .... | .... | .... | .... | .... | .... | .... |
| | Grand Rapids | AHL | 57 | 4 | 16 | 20 | 16 | .... | .... | .... | .... | .... | .... | .... | .... | .... | .... | .... | .... | .... | .... | .... | .... | .... | .... |
| 2007-08 | Springfield | AHL | 36 | 1 | 7 | 8 | 14 | .... | .... | .... | .... | .... | .... | .... | .... | .... | .... | .... | .... | .... | .... | .... | .... | .... | .... |
| | Hershey Bears | AHL | 27 | 1 | 11 | 12 | 29 | .... | .... | .... | .... | .... | .... | .... | .... | .... | 5 | 0 | 0 | 0 | 0 | .... | .... | .... | .... |
| **2008-09** | **Philadelphia** | **NHL** | **2** | **0** | **0** | **0** | **0** | **0** | **0** | **0** | **0** | **0.0** | **−1** | **0** | **0.0** | **9:26** | .... | .... | .... | .... | .... | .... | .... | .... | .... |
| | Philadelphia | AHL | 76 | 12 | 45 | 57 | 44 | .... | .... | .... | .... | .... | .... | .... | .... | .... | 4 | 0 | 1 | 1 | 0 | .... | .... | .... | .... |
| | **NHL Totals** | | **28** | **0** | **1** | **1** | **12** | **0** | **0** | **0** | **23** | **0.0** | | **0** | **0.0** | **15:37** | .... | .... | .... | .... | .... | .... | .... | .... | .... |

OHL First All-Star Team (2005) • Canadian Major Junior Defenseman of the Year (2005) • Canadian Major Junior First All-Star Team (2005) • Memorial Cup Tournament All-Star Team (2005) • AHL First All-Star Team (2009)

Traded to **Philadelphia** by **Edmonton** for Ryan Potulny, June 6, 2008.

## SZCZECHURA, Paul
(sha-HUR-uh, PAWL) **T.B.**

Right wing. Shoots right. 5'11", 190 lbs. Born, Brantford, Ont., November 30, 1985.

| | | | Regular Season | | | | | | | | | | | | | | Playoffs | | | | | | | | |
|---|---|---|---|---|---|---|---|---|---|---|---|---|---|---|---|---|---|---|---|---|---|---|---|---|---|
| Season | Club | League | GP | G | A | Pts | PIM | PP | SH | GW | S | % | +/- | TF | F% | Min | GP | G | A | Pts | PIM | PP | SH | GW | Min |
| 2003-04 | Western Mich. | CCHA | 39 | 9 | 11 | 20 | 12 | .... | .... | .... | .... | .... | .... | .... | .... | .... | .... | .... | .... | .... | .... | .... | .... | .... | .... |
| 2004-05 | Western Mich. | CCHA | 37 | 6 | 23 | 29 | 22 | .... | .... | .... | .... | .... | .... | .... | .... | .... | .... | .... | .... | .... | .... | .... | .... | .... | .... |
| 2005-06 | Western Mich. | CCHA | 40 | 10 | 26 | 36 | 47 | .... | .... | .... | .... | .... | .... | .... | .... | .... | .... | .... | .... | .... | .... | .... | .... | .... | .... |
| 2006-07 | Western Mich. | CCHA | 37 | 19 | 26 | 45 | 26 | .... | .... | .... | .... | .... | .... | .... | .... | .... | .... | .... | .... | .... | .... | .... | .... | .... | .... |
| | Iowa Stars | AHL | 14 | 3 | 4 | 7 | 19 | .... | .... | .... | .... | .... | .... | .... | .... | .... | 10 | 3 | 1 | 4 | 8 | .... | .... | .... | .... |
| 2007-08 | Iowa Stars | AHL | 29 | 2 | 3 | 5 | 15 | .... | .... | .... | .... | .... | .... | .... | .... | .... | .... | .... | .... | .... | .... | .... | .... | .... | .... |
| | Norfolk Admirals | AHL | 24 | 14 | 12 | 26 | 16 | .... | .... | .... | .... | .... | .... | .... | .... | .... | .... | .... | .... | .... | .... | .... | .... | .... | .... |
| **2008-09** | **Tampa Bay** | **NHL** | **31** | **4** | **5** | **9** | **12** | **1** | **0** | **0** | **51** | **7.8** | **−1** | **232** | **40.5** | **13:33** | .... | .... | .... | .... | .... | .... | .... | .... | .... |
| | Norfolk Admirals | AHL | 33 | 13 | 16 | 29 | 26 | .... | .... | .... | .... | .... | .... | .... | .... | .... | .... | .... | .... | .... | .... | .... | .... | .... | .... |
| | **NHL Totals** | | **31** | **4** | **5** | **9** | **12** | **1** | **0** | **0** | **51** | **7.8** | | **232** | **40.5** | **13:33** | .... | .... | .... | .... | .... | .... | .... | .... | .... |

Signed as a free agent by **Tampa Bay**, April 24, 2008.

## TAFFE, Jeff

(TAYF, JEHF) **FLA.**

Center. Shoots left. 6'3", 207 lbs. Born, Hastings, MN, February 19, 1981. St. Louis' 1st choice, 30th overall, in 2000 Entry Draft.

| | | | Regular Season | | | | | | | | | | | | | | Playoffs | | | | | | | | |
|---|---|---|---|---|---|---|---|---|---|---|---|---|---|---|---|---|---|---|---|---|---|---|---|---|---|
| Season | Club | League | GP | G | A | Pts | PIM | PP | SH | GW | S | % | +/- | TF | F% | Min | GP | G | A | Pts | PIM | PP | SH | GW | Min |
| 1996-97 | Hastings Huskies | High-MN | 25 | 21 | 37 | 58 | .... | .... | .... | .... | .... | .... | .... | .... | .... | .... | .... | .... | .... | .... | .... | .... | .... | .... | .... |
| 1997-98 | Hastings Huskies | High-MN | 28 | 37 | 29 | 66 | .... | .... | .... | .... | .... | .... | .... | .... | .... | .... | .... | .... | .... | .... | .... | .... | .... | .... | .... |
| 1998-99 | Hastings Huskies | High-MN | 28 | 39 | 51 | 90 | .... | .... | .... | .... | .... | .... | .... | .... | .... | .... | .... | .... | .... | .... | .... | .... | .... | .... | .... |
| | Rochester | USHL | 17 | 12 | 9 | 21 | 26 | .... | .... | .... | .... | .... | .... | .... | .... | .... | .... | .... | .... | .... | .... | .... | .... | .... | .... |
| 99-2000 | U. of Minnesota | WCHA | 39 | 10 | 10 | 20 | 22 | .... | .... | .... | .... | .... | .... | .... | .... | .... | .... | .... | .... | .... | .... | .... | .... | .... | .... |
| 2000-01 | U. of Minnesota | WCHA | 38 | 12 | 23 | 35 | 56 | .... | .... | .... | .... | .... | .... | .... | .... | .... | .... | .... | .... | .... | .... | .... | .... | .... | .... |
| 2001-02 | U. of Minnesota | WCHA | 43 | 34 | 24 | 58 | 86 | .... | .... | .... | .... | .... | .... | .... | .... | .... | .... | .... | .... | .... | .... | .... | .... | .... | .... |
| **2002-03** | **Phoenix** | **NHL** | **20** | **3** | **1** | **4** | **4** | **1** | **0** | **1** | **18** | **16.7** | **–4** | **113** | **29.2** | **11:34** | .... | .... | .... | .... | .... | .... | .... | .... | .... |
| | Springfield | AHL | 57 | 23 | 26 | 49 | 44 | .... | .... | .... | .... | .... | .... | .... | .... | .... | 5 | 0 | 3 | 3 | 8 | .... | .... | .... | .... |
| **2003-04** | **Phoenix** | **NHL** | **59** | **8** | **10** | **18** | **20** | **5** | **0** | **0** | **67** | **11.9** | **–8** | **219** | **43.4** | **11:02** | .... | .... | .... | .... | .... | .... | .... | .... | .... |
| | Springfield | AHL | 15 | 10 | 6 | 16 | 19 | .... | .... | .... | .... | .... | .... | .... | .... | .... | .... | .... | .... | .... | .... | .... | .... | .... | .... |
| 2004-05 | Utah Grizzlies | AHL | 27 | 9 | 10 | 19 | 35 | .... | .... | .... | .... | .... | .... | .... | .... | .... | .... | .... | .... | .... | .... | .... | .... | .... | .... |
| **2005-06** | **NY Rangers** | **NHL** | **2** | **0** | **0** | **0** | **0** | **0** | **0** | **0** | **1** | **0.0** | **0** | **0** | **0.0** | **3:49** | .... | .... | .... | .... | .... | .... | .... | .... | .... |
| | Hartford | AHL | 36 | 6 | 16 | 22 | 34 | .... | .... | .... | .... | .... | .... | .... | .... | .... | .... | .... | .... | .... | .... | .... | .... | .... | .... |
| | **Phoenix** | **NHL** | **2** | **0** | **0** | **0** | **0** | **0** | **0** | **0** | **2** | **0.0** | **0** | **1** | **100.0** | **9:06** | .... | .... | .... | .... | .... | .... | .... | .... | .... |
| | San Antonio | AHL | 33 | 5 | 6 | 11 | 29 | .... | .... | .... | .... | .... | .... | .... | .... | .... | .... | .... | .... | .... | .... | .... | .... | .... | .... |
| **2006-07** | **Phoenix** | **NHL** | **17** | **4** | **2** | **6** | **2** | **1** | **0** | **0** | **34** | **11.8** | **–7** | **64** | **39.1** | **14:12** | .... | .... | .... | .... | .... | .... | .... | .... | .... |
| | San Antonio | AHL | 59 | 20 | 20 | 40 | 22 | .... | .... | .... | .... | .... | .... | .... | .... | .... | .... | .... | .... | .... | .... | .... | .... | .... | .... |
| **2007-08** | **Pittsburgh** | **NHL** | **45** | **5** | **7** | **12** | **8** | **1** | **0** | **1** | **56** | **8.9** | **2** | **152** | **48.7** | **9:35** | .... | .... | .... | .... | .... | .... | .... | .... | .... |
| | Wilkes-Barre | AHL | 27 | 11 | 10 | 21 | 22 | .... | .... | .... | .... | .... | .... | .... | .... | .... | .... | .... | .... | .... | .... | .... | .... | .... | .... |
| **2008-09** | **Pittsburgh** | **NHL** | **8** | **0** | **2** | **2** | **2** | **0** | **0** | **0** | **5** | **0.0** | **–4** | **40** | **52.5** | **8:30** | .... | .... | .... | .... | .... | .... | .... | .... | .... |
| | Wilkes-Barre | AHL | 74 | 25 | 50 | 75 | 65 | .... | .... | .... | .... | .... | .... | .... | .... | .... | 12 | 5 | 6 | 11 | 22 | .... | .... | .... | .... |
| | **NHL Totals** | | **153** | **20** | **22** | **42** | **36** | **8** | **0** | **2** | **183** | **10.9** | | **589** | **42.3** | **10:46** | .... | .... | .... | .... | .... | .... | .... | .... | .... |

• Rights traded to **Phoenix** by **St. Louis** with Michal Handzus, Ladislav Nagy and St. Louis' 1st round choice (Ben Eager) in 2002 Entry Draft for Keith Tkachuk, March 13, 2001. Traded to **NY Rangers** by **Phoenix** for Jamie Lundmark, October 18, 2005. Traded to **Phoenix** by **NY Rangers** for Martin Sonnenberg, January 24, 2006. Signed as a free agent by **Pittsburgh**, July 13, 2007. Signed as a free agent by **Florida**, July 6, 2009.

## TALBOT, Maxime

(TAL-buht, max-EEM) **PIT.**

Center. Shoots left. 5'11", 190 lbs. Born, Lemoyne, Que., February 11, 1984. Pittsburgh's 9th choice, 234th overall, in 2002 Entry Draft.

| Season | Club | League | GP | G | A | Pts | PIM | PP | SH | GW | S | % | +/- | TF | F% | Min | GP | G | A | Pts | PIM | PP | SH | GW | Min |
|---|---|---|---|---|---|---|---|---|---|---|---|---|---|---|---|---|---|---|---|---|---|---|---|---|---|
| 99-2000 | Antoine-Girouard | QAAA | 42 | 19 | 21 | 40 | 32 | .... | .... | .... | .... | .... | .... | .... | .... | .... | 7 | 3 | 6 | 9 | 0 | .... | .... | .... | .... |
| 2000-01 | Rouyn-Noranda | QMJHL | 40 | 9 | 15 | 24 | 78 | .... | .... | .... | .... | .... | .... | .... | .... | .... | .... | .... | .... | .... | .... | .... | .... | .... | .... |
| | Hull Olympiques | QMJHL | 24 | 6 | 7 | 13 | 60 | .... | .... | .... | .... | .... | .... | .... | .... | .... | 5 | 1 | 0 | 1 | 2 | .... | .... | .... | .... |
| 2001-02 | Hull Olympiques | QMJHL | 65 | 24 | 36 | 60 | 174 | .... | .... | .... | .... | .... | .... | .... | .... | .... | 12 | 4 | 6 | 10 | 51 | .... | .... | .... | .... |
| 2002-03 | Hull Olympiques | QMJHL | 69 | 46 | 58 | 104 | 130 | .... | .... | .... | .... | .... | .... | .... | .... | .... | 20 | 14 | *30 | *44 | 33 | .... | .... | .... | .... |
| 2003-04 | Gatineau | QMJHL | 51 | 25 | 73 | 98 | 41 | .... | .... | .... | .... | .... | .... | .... | .... | .... | 15 | *11 | *16 | *27 | 0 | .... | .... | .... | .... |
| 2004-05 | Wilkes-Barre | AHL | 75 | 7 | 12 | 19 | 62 | .... | .... | .... | .... | .... | .... | .... | .... | .... | 11 | 0 | 1 | 1 | 22 | .... | .... | .... | .... |
| **2005-06** | **Pittsburgh** | **NHL** | **48** | **5** | **3** | **8** | **59** | **0** | **2** | **1** | **45** | **11.1** | **–12** | **473** | **42.9** | **10:58** | .... | .... | .... | .... | .... | .... | .... | .... | .... |
| | Wilkes-Barre | AHL | 42 | 12 | 20 | 32 | 80 | .... | .... | .... | .... | .... | .... | .... | .... | .... | 11 | 3 | 6 | 9 | 16 | .... | .... | .... | .... |
| **2006-07** | **Pittsburgh** | **NHL** | **75** | **13** | **11** | **24** | **53** | **0** | **4** | **4** | **88** | **14.8** | **–2** | **903** | **44.4** | **13:54** | **5** | **0** | **1** | **1** | **7** | **0** | **0** | **0** | **15:51** |
| | Wilkes-Barre | AHL | 5 | 4 | 0 | 4 | 2 | .... | .... | .... | .... | .... | .... | .... | .... | .... | .... | .... | .... | .... | .... | .... | .... | .... | .... |
| **2007-08** | **Pittsburgh** | **NHL** | **63** | **12** | **14** | **26** | **53** | **0** | **2** | **1** | **80** | **15.0** | **8** | **513** | **45.0** | **15:28** | **17** | **3** | **6** | **9** | **36** | **0** | **0** | **1** | **14:27** |
| **2008-09♦** | **Pittsburgh** | **NHL** | **75** | **12** | **10** | **22** | **63** | **0** | **2** | **1** | **102** | **11.8** | **–9** | **542** | **51.1** | **14:08** | **24** | **8** | **5** | **13** | **19** | **0** | **0** | **2** | **15:14** |
| | **NHL Totals** | | **261** | **42** | **38** | **80** | **228** | **0** | **10** | **7** | **315** | **13.3** | | **2431** | **45.7** | **13:48** | **46** | **11** | **12** | **23** | **62** | **0** | **0** | **3** | **15:00** |

QMJHL Second All-Star Team (2003, 2004)

## TALLACKSON, Barry

(TAL-ak-suhn, BAIR-ee) **ST.L.**

Right wing. Shoots right. 6'5", 215 lbs. Born, Grafton, ND, April 14, 1983. New Jersey's 2nd choice, 53rd overall, in 2002 Entry Draft.

| Season | Club | League | GP | G | A | Pts | PIM | PP | SH | GW | S | % | +/- | TF | F% | Min | GP | G | A | Pts | PIM | PP | SH | GW | Min |
|---|---|---|---|---|---|---|---|---|---|---|---|---|---|---|---|---|---|---|---|---|---|---|---|---|---|
| 99-2000 | USNTDP | NAHL | 53 | 14 | 6 | 20 | 90 | .... | .... | .... | .... | .... | .... | .... | .... | .... | 3 | 1 | 0 | 1 | 8 | .... | .... | .... | .... |
| 2000-01 | USNTDP | U-18 | 40 | 16 | 17 | 33 | 45 | .... | .... | .... | .... | .... | .... | .... | .... | .... | .... | .... | .... | .... | .... | .... | .... | .... | .... |
| | USNTDP | USHL | 23 | 7 | 7 | 14 | 32 | .... | .... | .... | .... | .... | .... | .... | .... | .... | .... | .... | .... | .... | .... | .... | .... | .... | .... |
| 2001-02 | U. of Minnesota | WCHA | 44 | 13 | 10 | 23 | 44 | .... | .... | .... | .... | .... | .... | .... | .... | .... | .... | .... | .... | .... | .... | .... | .... | .... | .... |
| 2002-03 | U. of Minnesota | WCHA | 32 | 9 | 14 | 23 | 18 | .... | .... | .... | .... | .... | .... | .... | .... | .... | .... | .... | .... | .... | .... | .... | .... | .... | .... |
| 2003-04 | U. of Minnesota | WCHA | 44 | 10 | 15 | 25 | 46 | .... | .... | .... | .... | .... | .... | .... | .... | .... | .... | .... | .... | .... | .... | .... | .... | .... | .... |
| 2004-05 | U. of Minnesota | WCHA | 36 | 11 | 8 | 19 | 54 | .... | .... | .... | .... | .... | .... | .... | .... | .... | .... | .... | .... | .... | .... | .... | .... | .... | .... |
| | Albany River Rats | AHL | 4 | 1 | 1 | 2 | 0 | .... | .... | .... | .... | .... | .... | .... | .... | .... | .... | .... | .... | .... | .... | .... | .... | .... | .... |
| **2005-06** | **New Jersey** | **NHL** | **10** | **1** | **1** | **2** | **2** | **0** | **0** | **0** | **11** | **9.1** | **–2** | **2** | **0.0** | **8:04** | .... | .... | .... | .... | .... | .... | .... | .... | .... |
| | Albany River Rats | AHL | 60 | 14 | 23 | 37 | 62 | .... | .... | .... | .... | .... | .... | .... | .... | .... | .... | .... | .... | .... | .... | .... | .... | .... | .... |
| **2006-07** | **New Jersey** | **NHL** | **3** | **0** | **0** | **0** | **0** | **0** | **0** | **0** | **3** | **0.0** | **–1** | **0** | **0.0** | **12:06** | .... | .... | .... | .... | .... | .... | .... | .... | .... |
| | Lowell Devils | AHL | 58 | 10 | 24 | 34 | 33 | .... | .... | .... | .... | .... | .... | .... | .... | .... | .... | .... | .... | .... | .... | .... | .... | .... | .... |
| **2007-08** | **New Jersey** | **NHL** | **3** | **0** | **0** | **0** | **0** | **0** | **0** | **0** | **0** | **0.0** | **0** | **0** | **0.0** | **7:03** | .... | .... | .... | .... | .... | .... | .... | .... | .... |
| | Lowell Devils | AHL | 63 | 22 | 23 | 45 | 54 | .... | .... | .... | .... | .... | .... | .... | .... | .... | .... | .... | .... | .... | .... | .... | .... | .... | .... |
| **2008-09** | **New Jersey** | **NHL** | **4** | **0** | **0** | **0** | **0** | **0** | **0** | **0** | **2** | **0.0** | **–1** | **1** | **0.0** | **4:29** | .... | .... | .... | .... | .... | .... | .... | .... | .... |
| | Lowell Devils | AHL | 56 | 11 | 10 | 21 | 29 | .... | .... | .... | .... | .... | .... | .... | .... | .... | .... | .... | .... | .... | .... | .... | .... | .... | .... |
| | **NHL Totals** | | **20** | **1** | **1** | **2** | **2** | **0** | **0** | **0** | **16** | **6.3** | | **3** | **0.0** | **7:48** | .... | .... | .... | .... | .... | .... | .... | .... | .... |

Signed as a free agent by **St. Louis**, July 23, 2009.

## TALLINDER, Henrik

(tah-LIHN-duhr, HEHN-rihk) **BUF.**

Defense. Shoots left. 6'3", 214 lbs. Born, Stockholm, Sweden, January 10, 1979. Buffalo's 2nd choice, 48th overall, in 1997 Entry Draft.

| Season | Club | League | GP | G | A | Pts | PIM | PP | SH | GW | S | % | +/- | TF | F% | Min | GP | G | A | Pts | PIM | PP | SH | GW | Min |
|---|---|---|---|---|---|---|---|---|---|---|---|---|---|---|---|---|---|---|---|---|---|---|---|---|---|
| 1996-97 | AIK Solna Jr. | Swe-Jr. | 40 | 4 | 13 | 17 | 55 | .... | .... | .... | .... | .... | .... | .... | .... | .... | .... | .... | .... | .... | .... | .... | .... | .... | .... |
| | AIK Solna | Sweden | 1 | 0 | 0 | 0 | 0 | .... | .... | .... | .... | .... | .... | .... | .... | .... | .... | .... | .... | .... | .... | .... | .... | .... | .... |
| 1997-98 | AIK Solna | Sweden | 34 | 0 | 0 | 0 | 26 | .... | .... | .... | .... | .... | .... | .... | .... | .... | .... | .... | .... | .... | .... | .... | .... | .... | .... |
| 1998-99 | AIK Solna | Sweden | 36 | 0 | 0 | 0 | 30 | .... | .... | .... | .... | .... | .... | .... | .... | .... | .... | .... | .... | .... | .... | .... | .... | .... | .... |
| 99-2000 | AIK Solna | Sweden | 50 | 0 | 2 | 2 | 59 | .... | .... | .... | .... | .... | .... | .... | .... | .... | .... | .... | .... | .... | .... | .... | .... | .... | .... |
| 2000-01 | TPS Turku | Finland | 56 | 5 | 9 | 14 | 62 | .... | .... | .... | .... | .... | .... | .... | .... | .... | 10 | 2 | 1 | 3 | 8 | .... | .... | .... | .... |
| **2001-02** | **Buffalo** | **NHL** | **2** | **0** | **0** | **0** | **0** | **0** | **0** | **0** | **4** | **0.0** | **–1** | **0** | **0.0** | **18:10** | .... | .... | .... | .... | .... | .... | .... | .... | .... |
| | Rochester | AHL | 73 | 6 | 14 | 20 | 26 | .... | .... | .... | .... | .... | .... | .... | .... | .... | 2 | 0 | 0 | 0 | 0 | .... | .... | .... | .... |
| **2002-03** | **Buffalo** | **NHL** | **46** | **3** | **10** | **13** | **28** | **1** | **0** | **0** | **37** | **8.1** | **–3** | **0** | **0.0** | **19:53** | .... | .... | .... | .... | .... | .... | .... | .... | .... |
| **2003-04** | **Buffalo** | **NHL** | **72** | **1** | **9** | **10** | **26** | **0** | **0** | **0** | **63** | **1.6** | **5** | **1** | **0.0** | **18:23** | .... | .... | .... | .... | .... | .... | .... | .... | .... |
| 2004-05 | Linkopings HC | Sweden | 44 | 6 | 10 | 16 | 63 | .... | .... | .... | .... | .... | .... | .... | .... | .... | .... | .... | .... | .... | .... | .... | .... | .... | .... |
| | SC Bern | Swiss | .... | .... | .... | .... | .... | .... | .... | .... | .... | .... | .... | .... | .... | .... | 10 | 1 | 1 | 2 | 4 | .... | .... | .... | .... |
| **2005-06** | **Buffalo** | **NHL** | **82** | **6** | **15** | **21** | **74** | **0** | **1** | **1** | **79** | **7.6** | **10** | **0** | **0.0** | **20:21** | **14** | **2** | **6** | **8** | **16** | **0** | **0** | **0** | **22:16** |
| **2006-07** | **Buffalo** | **NHL** | **47** | **4** | **10** | **14** | **34** | **0** | **0** | **0** | **34** | **11.8** | **19** | **1** | **0.0** | **21:07** | **16** | **0** | **2** | **2** | **10** | **0** | **0** | **0** | **23:40** |
| **2007-08** | **Buffalo** | **NHL** | **71** | **1** | **17** | **18** | **48** | **0** | **0** | **0** | **70** | **1.4** | **5** | **0** | **0.0** | **21:02** | .... | .... | .... | .... | .... | .... | .... | .... | .... |
| **2008-09** | **Buffalo** | **NHL** | **66** | **1** | **11** | **12** | **36** | **0** | **0** | **1** | **35** | **2.9** | **–2** | **0** | **0.0** | **18:26** | .... | .... | .... | .... | .... | .... | .... | .... | .... |
| | **NHL Totals** | | **386** | **16** | **72** | **88** | **246** | **1** | **1** | **2** | **322** | **5.0** | | **2** | **0.0** | **19:48** | **30** | **2** | **8** | **10** | **26** | **0** | **0** | **0** | **23:01** |

Signed as a free agent by **Linkopings** (Sweden), September 9, 2004. Signed as a free agent by **Bern** (Swiss), February 22, 2005.

## TAMBELLINI, Jeff

(tam-buh-LEE-nee, JEHF) **NYI**

Left wing. Shoots left. 5'11", 186 lbs. Born, Calgary, Alta., April 13, 1984. Los Angeles' 3rd choice, 27th overall, in 2003 Entry Draft.

| Season | Club | League | GP | G | A | Pts | PIM | PP | SH | GW | S | % | +/- | TF | F% | Min | GP | G | A | Pts | PIM | PP | SH | GW | Min |
|---|---|---|---|---|---|---|---|---|---|---|---|---|---|---|---|---|---|---|---|---|---|---|---|---|---|
| 99-2000 | Port Coquitlam | PIJHL | 41 | 30 | 34 | 64 | .... | .... | .... | .... | .... | .... | .... | .... | .... | .... | .... | .... | .... | .... | .... | .... | .... | .... | .... |
| 2000-01 | Chilliwack Chiefs | BCHL | 54 | 21 | 30 | 51 | 13 | .... | .... | .... | .... | .... | .... | .... | .... | .... | .... | .... | .... | .... | .... | .... | .... | .... | .... |
| 2001-02 | Chilliwack Chiefs | BCHL | 34 | 46 | 71 | 117 | 23 | .... | .... | .... | .... | .... | .... | .... | .... | .... | 29 | 27 | 27 | 54 | .... | .... | .... | .... | .... |
| 2002-03 | U. of Michigan | CCHA | 43 | 26 | 19 | 45 | 24 | .... | .... | .... | .... | .... | .... | .... | .... | .... | .... | .... | .... | .... | .... | .... | .... | .... | .... |
| 2003-04 | U. of Michigan | CCHA | 39 | 15 | 12 | 27 | 18 | .... | .... | .... | .... | .... | .... | .... | .... | .... | .... | .... | .... | .... | .... | .... | .... | .... | .... |
| 2004-05 | U. of Michigan | CCHA | 42 | *24 | 33 | *57 | 32 | .... | .... | .... | .... | .... | .... | .... | .... | .... | .... | .... | .... | .... | .... | .... | .... | .... | .... |
| **2005-06** | **Los Angeles** | **NHL** | **4** | **0** | **0** | **0** | **2** | **0** | **0** | **0** | **6** | **0.0** | **–1** | **1** | **0.0** | **9:23** | .... | .... | .... | .... | .... | .... | .... | .... | .... |
| | Manchester | AHL | 56 | 25 | 31 | 56 | 26 | .... | .... | .... | .... | .... | .... | .... | .... | .... | .... | .... | .... | .... | .... | .... | .... | .... | .... |
| | **NY Islanders** | **NHL** | **21** | **1** | **3** | **4** | **8** | **0** | **0** | **0** | **11** | **9.1** | **2** | **3** | **33.3** | **9:54** | .... | .... | .... | .... | .... | .... | .... | .... | .... |
| | Bridgeport | AHL | .... | .... | .... | .... | .... | .... | .... | .... | .... | .... | .... | .... | .... | .... | 7 | 1 | 2 | 3 | 2 | .... | .... | .... | .... |
| **2006-07** | **NY Islanders** | **NHL** | **23** | **2** | **7** | **9** | **6** | **0** | **0** | **0** | **20** | **10.0** | **6** | **1** | **0.0** | **7:14** | .... | .... | .... | .... | .... | .... | .... | .... | .... |
| | Bridgeport | AHL | 50 | 30 | 29 | 59 | 46 | .... | .... | .... | .... | .... | .... | .... | .... | .... | .... | .... | .... | .... | .... | .... | .... | .... | .... |
| **2007-08** | **NY Islanders** | **NHL** | **31** | **1** | **3** | **4** | **8** | **0** | **0** | **0** | **43** | **2.3** | **–9** | **0** | **0.0** | **10:25** | .... | .... | .... | .... | .... | .... | .... | .... | .... |
| | Bridgeport | AHL | 57 | 38 | 38 | 76 | 38 | .... | .... | .... | .... | .... | .... | .... | .... | .... | .... | .... | .... | .... | .... | .... | .... | .... | .... |

| | | | Regular Season | | | | | | | | | | | | | | Playoffs | | | | | | | | |
|---|---|---|---|---|---|---|---|---|---|---|---|---|---|---|---|---|---|---|---|---|---|---|---|---|---|
| Season | Club | League | GP | G | A | Pts | PIM | PP | SH | GW | S | % | +/- | TF | F% | Min | GP | G | A | Pts | PIM | PP | SH | GW | Min |
| **2008-09** | **NY Islanders** | **NHL** | **65** | **7** | **8** | **15** | **32** | **0** | **0** | **0** | **98** | **7.1** | **-20** | **5** | **60.0** | **13:07** | .... | .... | .... | .... | .... | .... | .... | .... | .... |
| | Bridgeport | AHL | 6 | 3 | 0 | 3 | 2 | .... | .... | .... | .... | .... | .... | .... | .... | .... | .... | .... | .... | .... | .... | .... | .... | .... | .... |
| | **NHL Totals** | | **144** | **11** | **21** | **32** | **56** | **0** | **0** | **0** | **178** | **6.2** | | **10** | **40.0** | **11:01** | .... | .... | .... | .... | .... | .... | .... | .... | .... |

CCHA All-Rookie Team (2003) • CCHA Second All-Star Team (2003) • CCHA Rookie of the Year (2003) • CCHA First All-Star Team (2005) • NCAA West Second All-American Team (2005)

Traded to **NY Islanders** by **Los Angeles** with Denis Grebeshkov for Mark Parrish and Brent Sopel, March 8, 2006.

## TANGUAY, Alex
(TAHNG-ay, AL-ehx)

Left wing. Shoots left. 6'1", 189 lbs. Born, Ste-Justine, Que., November 21, 1979. Colorado's 1st choice, 12th overall, in 1998 Entry Draft.

| Season | Club | League | GP | G | A | Pts | PIM | PP | SH | GW | S | % | +/- | TF | F% | Min | GP | G | A | Pts | PIM | PP | SH | GW | Min |
|---|---|---|---|---|---|---|---|---|---|---|---|---|---|---|---|---|---|---|---|---|---|---|---|---|---|
| 1994-95 | Cap-d-Madeleine | QAAA | 1 | 0 | 1 | 1 | 0 | .... | .... | .... | .... | .... | .... | .... | .... | .... | .... | .... | .... | .... | .... | .... | .... | .... | .... |
| 1995-96 | Cap-d-Madeleine | QAAA | 44 | 29 | 34 | 63 | 64 | .... | .... | .... | .... | .... | .... | .... | .... | .... | 5 | 2 | 4 | 6 | 14 | .... | .... | .... | .... |
| 1996-97 | Halifax | QMJHL | 70 | 27 | 41 | 68 | 60 | .... | .... | .... | .... | .... | .... | .... | .... | .... | 12 | 5 | 8 | 13 | 8 | .... | .... | .... | .... |
| 1997-98 | Halifax | QMJHL | 51 | 47 | 38 | 85 | 32 | .... | .... | .... | .... | .... | .... | .... | .... | .... | 5 | 7 | 6 | 13 | 4 | .... | .... | .... | .... |
| 1998-99 | Halifax | QMJHL | 31 | 27 | 34 | 61 | 30 | .... | .... | .... | .... | .... | .... | .... | .... | .... | 5 | 1 | 2 | 3 | 2 | .... | .... | .... | .... |
| | Hershey Bears | AHL | 5 | 1 | 2 | 3 | 2 | .... | .... | .... | .... | .... | .... | .... | .... | .... | 5 | 0 | 2 | 2 | 0 | .... | .... | .... | .... |
| **99-2000** | **Colorado** | **NHL** | **76** | **17** | **34** | **51** | **22** | **5** | **0** | **3** | **74** | **23.0** | **6** | **11** | **45.5** | **15:38** | **17** | **2** | **1** | **3** | **2** | **1** | **0** | **1** | **10:49** |
| **2000-01♦** | **Colorado** | **NHL** | **82** | **27** | **50** | **77** | **37** | **7** | **1** | **3** | **135** | **20.0** | **35** | **30** | **43.3** | **17:51** | **23** | **6** | **15** | **21** | **8** | **1** | **0** | **2** | **19:18** |
| **2001-02** | **Colorado** | **NHL** | **70** | **13** | **35** | **48** | **36** | **7** | **0** | **2** | **90** | **14.4** | **8** | **37** | **40.5** | **18:20** | **19** | **5** | **8** | **13** | **0** | **3** | **0** | **0** | **17:25** |
| **2002-03** | **Colorado** | **NHL** | **82** | **26** | **41** | **67** | **36** | **3** | **0** | **5** | **142** | **18.3** | **34** | **123** | **39.0** | **17:48** | **7** | **1** | **2** | **3** | **4** | **0** | **0** | **1** | **19:06** |
| **2003-04** | **Colorado** | **NHL** | **69** | **25** | **54** | **79** | **42** | **7** | **0** | **5** | **117** | **21.4** | **30** | **71** | **40.9** | **18:21** | **8** | **2** | **2** | **4** | **2** | **1** | **0** | **1** | **15:46** |
| 2004-05 | HC Lugano | Swiss | 6 | 3 | 3 | 6 | 4 | .... | .... | .... | .... | .... | .... | .... | .... | .... | .... | .... | .... | .... | .... | .... | .... | .... | .... |
| **2005-06** | **Colorado** | **NHL** | **71** | **29** | **49** | **78** | **46** | **8** | **0** | **4** | **125** | **23.2** | **8** | **20** | **30.0** | **18:22** | **9** | **2** | **4** | **6** | **12** | **0** | **0** | **1** | **18:20** |
| **2006-07** | **Calgary** | **NHL** | **81** | **22** | **59** | **81** | **44** | **5** | **0** | **0** | **107** | **20.6** | **12** | **24** | **25.0** | **17:40** | **6** | **1** | **3** | **4** | **8** | **1** | **0** | **0** | **17:56** |
| **2007-08** | **Calgary** | **NHL** | **78** | **18** | **40** | **58** | **48** | **3** | **2** | **3** | **121** | **14.9** | **11** | **20** | **35.0** | **18:46** | **7** | **0** | **4** | **4** | **4** | **0** | **0** | **0** | **18:15** |
| **2008-09** | **Montreal** | **NHL** | **50** | **16** | **25** | **41** | **34** | **5** | **0** | **3** | **76** | **21.1** | **13** | **9** | **33.3** | **16:05** | **2** | **0** | **1** | **1** | **2** | **0** | **0** | **0** | **15:29** |
| | **NHL Totals** | | **659** | **193** | **387** | **580** | **345** | **50** | **3** | **28** | **987** | **19.6** | | **345** | **38.3** | **17:42** | **98** | **19** | **40** | **59** | **42** | **7** | **0** | **6** | **16:50** |

QMJHL All-Rookie Team (1997)

Played in NHL All-Star Game (2004)

Signed as a free agent by **Lugano** (Swiss), October 7, 2004. Traded to **Calgary** by **Colorado** for Jordan Leopold, Calgary's 2nd round choice (Codey Burki) in 2006 Entry Draft and Calgary's 2nd round choice (Trevor Cann) in 2007 Entry Draft, June 24, 2006. Traded to **Montreal** by **Calgary** with Calgary's 5th round choice (Maxim Trunev) in 2008 Entry Draft for Montreal's 1st round choice (Greg Nemisz) in 2008 Entry Draft and Montreal's 2nd round choice (later traded to Colorado – Colorado selected Stefan Elliott) in 2009 Entry Draft, June 20, 2008.

## TARNASKY, Nick
(tahr-NAS-kee, NIHK) **FLA.**

Center. Shoots left. 6'2", 224 lbs. Born, Rocky Mtn. House, Alta., November 25, 1984. Tampa Bay's 11th choice, 287th overall, in 2003 Entry Draft.

| Season | Club | League | GP | G | A | Pts | PIM | PP | SH | GW | S | % | +/- | TF | F% | Min | GP | G | A | Pts | PIM | PP | SH | GW | Min |
|---|---|---|---|---|---|---|---|---|---|---|---|---|---|---|---|---|---|---|---|---|---|---|---|---|---|
| 99-2000 | Leduc Oil Kings | AMBHL | 36 | 21 | 11 | 32 | 59 | .... | .... | .... | .... | .... | .... | .... | .... | .... | .... | .... | .... | .... | .... | .... | .... | .... | .... |
| 2000-01 | Leduc Oil Kings | AMHL | 35 | 39 | 29 | 68 | 95 | .... | .... | .... | .... | .... | .... | .... | .... | .... | .... | .... | .... | .... | .... | .... | .... | .... | .... |
| 2001-02 | Drayton Valley | AJHL | 20 | 7 | 4 | 11 | 10 | .... | .... | .... | .... | .... | .... | .... | .... | .... | .... | .... | .... | .... | .... | .... | .... | .... | .... |
| | Vancouver Giants | WHL | 10 | 1 | 0 | 1 | 5 | .... | .... | .... | .... | .... | .... | .... | .... | .... | .... | .... | .... | .... | .... | .... | .... | .... | .... |
| 2002-03 | Kelowna Rockets | WHL | 39 | 4 | 12 | 16 | 39 | .... | .... | .... | .... | .... | .... | .... | .... | .... | .... | .... | .... | .... | .... | .... | .... | .... | .... |
| | Lethbridge | WHL | 30 | 5 | 8 | 13 | 45 | .... | .... | .... | .... | .... | .... | .... | .... | .... | .... | .... | .... | .... | .... | .... | .... | .... | .... |
| 2003-04 | Lethbridge | WHL | 71 | 26 | 23 | 49 | 108 | .... | .... | .... | .... | .... | .... | .... | .... | .... | .... | .... | .... | .... | .... | .... | .... | .... | .... |
| 2004-05 | Springfield | AHL | 80 | 7 | 10 | 17 | 176 | .... | .... | .... | .... | .... | .... | .... | .... | .... | .... | .... | .... | .... | .... | .... | .... | .... | .... |
| **2005-06** | **Tampa Bay** | **NHL** | **12** | **0** | **1** | **1** | **4** | **0** | **0** | **0** | **9** | **0.0** | **-3** | **15** | **40.0** | **4:40** | .... | .... | .... | .... | .... | .... | .... | .... | .... |
| | Springfield | AHL | 68 | 14 | 9 | 23 | 100 | .... | .... | .... | .... | .... | .... | .... | .... | .... | .... | .... | .... | .... | .... | .... | .... | .... | .... |
| **2006-07** | **Tampa Bay** | **NHL** | **77** | **5** | **4** | **9** | **80** | **0** | **0** | **1** | **41** | **12.2** | **-6** | **13** | **30.8** | **6:30** | **6** | **0** | **0** | **0** | **10** | **0** | **0** | **0** | **6:13** |
| **2007-08** | **Tampa Bay** | **NHL** | **80** | **6** | **4** | **10** | **78** | **1** | **0** | **1** | **91** | **6.6** | **-15** | **9** | **44.4** | **8:15** | .... | .... | .... | .... | .... | .... | .... | .... | .... |
| **2008-09** | **Nashville** | **NHL** | **11** | **0** | **1** | **1** | **17** | **0** | **0** | **0** | **6** | **0.0** | **1** | **0** | **0.0** | **5:38** | .... | .... | .... | .... | .... | .... | .... | .... | .... |
| | **Florida** | **NHL** | **34** | **1** | **5** | **6** | **33** | **0** | **0** | **0** | **32** | **3.1** | **-2** | **1** | **0.0** | **7:52** | .... | .... | .... | .... | .... | .... | .... | .... | .... |
| | **NHL Totals** | | **214** | **12** | **15** | **27** | **212** | **1** | **0** | **2** | **179** | **6.7** | | **38** | **36.8** | **7:13** | **6** | **0** | **0** | **0** | **10** | **0** | **0** | **0** | **6:13** |

Traded to **Nashville** by **Tampa Bay** for Nashville's 6th round choice (Jaroslav Janus) in 2009 Entry Draft, September 29, 2008. Traded to **Florida** by **Nashville** for Wade Belak, November 27, 2008.

## TARNSTROM, Dick
(TAHRN-struhm, DIHK)

Defense. Shoots left. 6'1", 205 lbs. Born, Sundbyberg, Sweden, January 20, 1975. NY Islanders' 12th choice, 272nd overall, in 1994 Entry Draft.

| Season | Club | League | GP | G | A | Pts | PIM | PP | SH | GW | S | % | +/- | TF | F% | Min | GP | G | A | Pts | PIM | PP | SH | GW | Min |
|---|---|---|---|---|---|---|---|---|---|---|---|---|---|---|---|---|---|---|---|---|---|---|---|---|---|
| 1992-93 | AIK Solna | Sweden | 3 | 0 | 0 | 0 | 0 | .... | .... | .... | .... | .... | .... | .... | .... | .... | .... | .... | .... | .... | .... | .... | .... | .... | .... |
| 1993-94 | AIK Solna | Sweden-2 | 33 | 1 | 4 | 5 | .... | .... | .... | .... | .... | .... | .... | .... | .... | .... | .... | .... | .... | .... | .... | .... | .... | .... | .... |
| 1994-95 | AIK Solna | Sweden | 37 | 8 | 4 | 12 | 26 | .... | .... | .... | .... | .... | .... | .... | .... | .... | .... | .... | .... | .... | .... | .... | .... | .... | .... |
| 1995-96 | AIK Solna | Sweden | 40 | 0 | 5 | 5 | 32 | .... | .... | .... | .... | .... | .... | .... | .... | .... | .... | .... | .... | .... | .... | .... | .... | .... | .... |
| 1996-97 | AIK Solna | Sweden | 49 | 5 | 3 | 8 | 38 | .... | .... | .... | .... | .... | .... | .... | .... | .... | 7 | 0 | 1 | 1 | 6 | .... | .... | .... | .... |
| 1997-98 | AIK Solna | Sweden | 45 | 2 | 12 | 14 | 30 | .... | .... | .... | .... | .... | .... | .... | .... | .... | .... | .... | .... | .... | .... | .... | .... | .... | .... |
| 1998-99 | AIK Solna | Sweden | 47 | 9 | 14 | 23 | 36 | .... | .... | .... | .... | .... | .... | .... | .... | .... | .... | .... | .... | .... | .... | .... | .... | .... | .... |
| 99-2000 | AIK Solna | Sweden | 42 | 7 | 15 | 22 | 20 | .... | .... | .... | .... | .... | .... | .... | .... | .... | .... | .... | .... | .... | .... | .... | .... | .... | .... |
| 2000-01 | AIK Solna | Sweden | 50 | 10 | 18 | 28 | 28 | .... | .... | .... | .... | .... | .... | .... | .... | .... | 5 | 0 | 0 | 0 | 8 | .... | .... | .... | .... |
| **2001-02** | **NY Islanders** | **NHL** | **62** | **3** | **16** | **19** | **38** | **0** | **0** | **0** | **59** | **5.1** | **-12** | **0** | **0.0** | **17:39** | **5** | **0** | **0** | **0** | **2** | **0** | **0** | **0** | **7:13** |
| | Bridgeport | AHL | 9 | 0 | 2 | 2 | 2 | .... | .... | .... | .... | .... | .... | .... | .... | .... | .... | .... | .... | .... | .... | .... | .... | .... | .... |
| **2002-03** | **Pittsburgh** | **NHL** | **61** | **7** | **34** | **41** | **50** | **3** | **0** | **0** | **115** | **6.1** | **-11** | **0** | **0.0** | **23:54** | .... | .... | .... | .... | .... | .... | .... | .... | .... |
| **2003-04** | **Pittsburgh** | **NHL** | **80** | **16** | **36** | **52** | **38** | **12** | **0** | **0** | **158** | **10.1** | **-37** | **0** | **0.0** | **24:03** | .... | .... | .... | .... | .... | .... | .... | .... | .... |
| 2004-05 | Sodertalje SK | Sweden | 50 | 7 | 18 | 25 | 46 | .... | .... | .... | .... | .... | .... | .... | .... | .... | 9 | 1 | 0 | 1 | 6 | .... | .... | .... | .... |
| **2005-06** | **Pittsburgh** | **NHL** | **33** | **5** | **5** | **10** | **52** | **4** | **0** | **0** | **40** | **12.5** | **-10** | **1** | **100.0** | **16:54** | .... | .... | .... | .... | .... | .... | .... | .... | .... |
| | **Edmonton** | **NHL** | **22** | **1** | **3** | **4** | **24** | **0** | **0** | **0** | **20** | **5.0** | **-5** | **0** | **0.0** | **16:58** | **12** | **0** | **2** | **2** | **10** | **0** | **0** | **0** | **14:00** |
| 2006-07 | HC Lugano | Swiss | 44 | 3 | 26 | 29 | 90 | .... | .... | .... | .... | .... | .... | .... | .... | .... | 5 | 1 | 6 | 7 | 8 | .... | .... | .... | .... |
| **2007-08** | **Edmonton** | **NHL** | **29** | **1** | **4** | **5** | **40** | **0** | **0** | **0** | **22** | **4.5** | **-6** | **0** | **0.0** | **19:35** | .... | .... | .... | .... | .... | .... | .... | .... | .... |
| | **Columbus** | **NHL** | **19** | **2** | **7** | **9** | **12** | **1** | **0** | **0** | **22** | **9.1** | **-5** | **0** | **0.0** | **19:03** | .... | .... | .... | .... | .... | .... | .... | .... | .... |
| 2008-09 | AIK IF Solna | Sweden-2 | 38 | 9 | 23 | 32 | 68 | .... | .... | .... | .... | .... | .... | .... | .... | .... | .... | .... | .... | .... | .... | .... | .... | .... | .... |
| | **NHL Totals** | | **306** | **35** | **105** | **140** | **254** | **20** | **0** | **0** | **436** | **8.0** | | **1** | **100.0** | **20:43** | **17** | **0** | **2** | **2** | **12** | **0** | **0** | **0** | **12:00** |

Claimed on waivers by **Pittsburgh** from **NY Islanders**, August 6, 2002. Signed as a free agent by **Sodertalje** (Sweden), August 9, 2004. Traded to **Edmonton** by **Pittsburgh** for Jani Rita and Cory Cross, January 26, 2006. Signed as a free agent by **Lugano** (Swiss), August 16, 2006. Signed as a free agent by **Edmonton**, July 1, 2007. Traded to **Columbus** by **Edmonton** for Curtis Glencross, February 1, 2008.

## THOMAS, Bill
(TAW-mas, BIHL)

Right wing. Shoots right. 6'1", 191 lbs. Born, Pittsburgh, PA, June 20, 1983.

| Season | Club | League | GP | G | A | Pts | PIM | PP | SH | GW | S | % | +/- | TF | F% | Min | GP | G | A | Pts | PIM | PP | SH | GW | Min |
|---|---|---|---|---|---|---|---|---|---|---|---|---|---|---|---|---|---|---|---|---|---|---|---|---|---|
| 2002-03 | Tri-City Storm | USHL | 60 | 29 | 21 | 50 | 20 | .... | .... | .... | .... | .... | .... | .... | .... | .... | 3 | 0 | 3 | 3 | 4 | .... | .... | .... | .... |
| 2003-04 | Tri-City Storm | USHL | 60 | 31 | 38 | 69 | 30 | .... | .... | .... | .... | .... | .... | .... | .... | .... | 11 | *9 | 7 | *16 | 4 | .... | .... | .... | .... |
| 2004-05 | Nebraska-Omaha | CCHA | 39 | 19 | 26 | 45 | 12 | .... | .... | .... | .... | .... | .... | .... | .... | .... | .... | .... | .... | .... | .... | .... | .... | .... | .... |
| **2005-06** | Nebraska-Omaha | CCHA | 41 | *27 | 23 | 50 | 43 | .... | .... | .... | .... | .... | .... | .... | .... | .... | .... | .... | .... | .... | .... | .... | .... | .... | .... |
| | **Phoenix** | **NHL** | **9** | **1** | **2** | **3** | **8** | **1** | **0** | **0** | **15** | **6.7** | **-2** | **2** | **50.0** | **13:30** | .... | .... | .... | .... | .... | .... | .... | .... | .... |
| **2006-07** | **Phoenix** | **NHL** | **24** | **8** | **6** | **14** | **2** | **4** | **0** | **1** | **60** | **13.3** | **-6** | **0** | **0.0** | **13:29** | .... | .... | .... | .... | .... | .... | .... | .... | .... |
| | San Antonio | AHL | 47 | 13 | 20 | 33 | 20 | .... | .... | .... | .... | .... | .... | .... | .... | .... | .... | .... | .... | .... | .... | .... | .... | .... | .... |
| **2007-08** | **Phoenix** | **NHL** | **7** | **0** | **0** | **0** | **0** | **0** | **0** | **0** | **9** | **0.0** | **-2** | **0** | **0.0** | **13:08** | .... | .... | .... | .... | .... | .... | .... | .... | .... |
| | San Antonio | AHL | 75 | 24 | 28 | 52 | 40 | .... | .... | .... | .... | .... | .... | .... | .... | .... | 7 | 1 | 2 | 3 | 0 | .... | .... | .... | .... |
| **2008-09** | **Pittsburgh** | **NHL** | **16** | **2** | **1** | **3** | **2** | **0** | **1** | **0** | **17** | **11.8** | **-4** | **101** | **51.5** | **9:31** | .... | .... | .... | .... | .... | .... | .... | .... | .... |
| | Wilkes-Barre | AHL | 39 | 8 | 10 | 18 | 24 | .... | .... | .... | .... | .... | .... | .... | .... | .... | 12 | 1 | 4 | 5 | 12 | .... | .... | .... | .... |
| | **NHL Totals** | | **56** | **11** | **9** | **20** | **12** | **5** | **1** | **1** | **101** | **10.9** | | **103** | **51.5** | **12:19** | .... | .... | .... | .... | .... | .... | .... | .... | .... |

CCHA All-Rookie Team (2005) • CCHA Rookie of the Year (2005) • CCHA Second All-Star Team (2005) • CCHA First All-Star Team (2006)

Signed as a free agent by **Phoenix**. March 27, 2006. Signed as a free agent by **Pittsburgh**. July 15, 2008.

## THOMPSON, Nate
(TAWM-suhn, NAYT) **NYI**

Center. Shoots left. 6', 207 lbs. Born, Anchorage, AK, October 5, 1984. Boston's 8th choice, 183rd overall, in 2003 Entry Draft.

| Season | Club | League | GP | G | A | Pts | PIM | PP | SH | GW | S | % | +/- | TF | F% | Min | GP | G | A | Pts | PIM | PP | SH | GW | Min |
|---|---|---|---|---|---|---|---|---|---|---|---|---|---|---|---|---|---|---|---|---|---|---|---|---|---|
| 2001-02 | Seattle | WHL | 69 | 13 | 26 | 39 | 42 | .... | .... | .... | .... | .... | .... | .... | .... | .... | 11 | 1 | 3 | 4 | 13 | .... | .... | .... | .... |
| 2002-03 | Seattle | WHL | 61 | 10 | 24 | 34 | 48 | .... | .... | .... | .... | .... | .... | .... | .... | .... | 15 | 5 | 4 | 9 | 6 | .... | .... | .... | .... |
| 2003-04 | Seattle | WHL | 65 | 13 | 23 | 36 | 24 | .... | .... | .... | .... | .... | .... | .... | .... | .... | .... | .... | .... | .... | .... | .... | .... | .... | .... |
| 2004-05 | Seattle | WHL | 58 | 19 | 15 | 34 | 39 | .... | .... | .... | .... | .... | .... | .... | .... | .... | 12 | 1 | 2 | 3 | 2 | .... | .... | .... | .... |
| | Providence Bruins | AHL | .... | .... | .... | .... | .... | .... | .... | .... | .... | .... | .... | .... | .... | .... | 11 | 0 | 1 | 1 | 6 | .... | .... | .... | .... |
| 2005-06 | Providence Bruins | AHL | 74 | 8 | 10 | 18 | 58 | .... | .... | .... | .... | .... | .... | .... | .... | .... | 3 | 0 | 0 | 0 | 10 | .... | .... | .... | .... |

| | | | Regular Season | | | | | | | | | | | | | | Playoffs | | | | | | | | |
|---|---|---|---|---|---|---|---|---|---|---|---|---|---|---|---|---|---|---|---|---|---|---|---|---|---|
| Season | Club | League | GP | G | A | Pts | PIM | PP | SH | GW | S | % | +/- | TF | F% | Min | GP | G | A | Pts | PIM | PP | SH | GW | Min |
| 2006-07 | Boston | NHL | 4 | 0 | 0 | 0 | 0 | 0 | 0 | 0 | 5 | 0.0 | 0 | 10 | 40.0 | 4:46 | .... | .... | .... | .... | .... | .... | .... | .... | .... |
| | Providence Bruins | AHL | 67 | 8 | 15 | 23 | 74 | .... | .... | .... | .... | .... | .... | .... | .... | .... | 13 | 0 | 2 | 2 | 9 | .... | .... | .... | .... |
| 2007-08 | Providence Bruins | AHL | 75 | 19 | 20 | 39 | 83 | .... | .... | .... | .... | .... | .... | .... | .... | .... | 10 | 2 | 3 | 5 | 4 | .... | .... | .... | .... |
| 2008-09 | NY Islanders | NHL | 43 | 2 | 2 | 4 | 49 | 0 | 1 | 0 | 56 | 3.6 | –11 | 429 | 50.4 | 12:05 | .... | .... | .... | .... | .... | .... | .... | .... | .... |
| | NHL Totals | | 47 | 2 | 2 | 4 | 49 | 0 | 1 | 0 | 61 | 3.3 | | 439 | 50.1 | 11:28 | .... | .... | .... | .... | .... | .... | .... | .... | .... |

Claimed on waivers by **NY Islanders** from **Boston**, October 8, 2008.

## THORBURN, Chris

(THOHR-buhrn, KRIHS) **ATL.**

Center. Shoots right. 6'3", 225 lbs. Born, Sault Ste. Marie, Ont., June 3, 1983. Buffalo's 3rd choice, 50th overall, in 2001 Entry Draft.

| Season | Club | League | GP | G | A | Pts | PIM | PP | SH | GW | S | % | +/- | TF | F% | Min | GP | G | A | Pts | PIM | PP | SH | GW | Min |
|---|---|---|---|---|---|---|---|---|---|---|---|---|---|---|---|---|---|---|---|---|---|---|---|---|---|
| 1998-99 | Elliot Lake Vikings | NOJHA | 40 | 21 | 12 | 33 | 28 | .... | .... | .... | .... | .... | .... | .... | .... | .... | .... | .... | .... | .... | .... | .... | .... | .... | .... |
| 99-2000 | North Bay | OHL | 56 | 12 | 8 | 20 | 33 | .... | .... | .... | .... | .... | .... | .... | .... | .... | 6 | 0 | 2 | 2 | 0 | .... | .... | .... | .... |
| 2000-01 | North Bay | OHL | 66 | 22 | 32 | 54 | 64 | .... | .... | .... | .... | .... | .... | .... | .... | .... | 4 | 0 | 1 | 1 | 9 | .... | .... | .... | .... |
| 2001-02 | North Bay | OHL | 67 | 15 | 43 | 58 | 112 | .... | .... | .... | .... | .... | .... | .... | .... | .... | 5 | 1 | 2 | 3 | 8 | .... | .... | .... | .... |
| 2002-03 | Saginaw Spirit | OHL | 37 | 19 | 19 | 38 | 68 | .... | .... | .... | .... | .... | .... | .... | .... | .... | .... | .... | .... | .... | .... | .... | .... | .... | .... |
| | Plymouth Whalers | OHL | 27 | 11 | 22 | 33 | 56 | .... | .... | .... | .... | .... | .... | .... | .... | .... | 18 | 11 | 9 | 20 | 10 | .... | .... | .... | .... |
| 2003-04 | Rochester | AHL | 58 | 6 | 16 | 22 | 77 | .... | .... | .... | .... | .... | .... | .... | .... | .... | 16 | 3 | 2 | 5 | 18 | .... | .... | .... | .... |
| 2004-05 | Rochester | AHL | 73 | 12 | 17 | 29 | 185 | .... | .... | .... | .... | .... | .... | .... | .... | .... | 4 | 0 | 1 | 1 | 2 | .... | .... | .... | .... |
| 2005-06 | Buffalo | NHL | 2 | 0 | 1 | 1 | 7 | 0 | 0 | 0 | 1 | 0.0 | –1 | 1 | 0.0 | 6:52 | .... | .... | .... | .... | .... | .... | .... | .... | .... |
| | Rochester | AHL | 77 | 23 | 27 | 50 | 134 | .... | .... | .... | .... | .... | .... | .... | .... | .... | .... | .... | .... | .... | .... | .... | .... | .... | .... |
| 2006-07 | Pittsburgh | NHL | 39 | 3 | 2 | 5 | 69 | 0 | 0 | 1 | 40 | 7.5 | 1 | 8 | 25.0 | 7:54 | .... | .... | .... | .... | .... | .... | .... | .... | .... |
| | Wilkes-Barre | AHL | 3 | 0 | 1 | 1 | 2 | .... | .... | .... | .... | .... | .... | .... | .... | .... | .... | .... | .... | .... | .... | .... | .... | .... | .... |
| 2007-08 | Atlanta | NHL | 73 | 5 | 13 | 18 | 92 | 0 | 0 | 1 | 72 | 6.9 | –4 | 20 | 60.0 | 8:56 | .... | .... | .... | .... | .... | .... | .... | .... | .... |
| 2008-09 | Atlanta | NHL | 82 | 7 | 8 | 15 | 104 | 0 | 0 | 1 | 85 | 8.2 | –10 | 37 | 40.5 | 9:35 | .... | .... | .... | .... | .... | .... | .... | .... | .... |
| | NHL Totals | | 196 | 15 | 24 | 39 | 272 | 0 | 0 | 3 | 198 | 7.6 | | 66 | 43.9 | 8:59 | .... | .... | .... | .... | .... | .... | .... | .... | .... |

Claimed on waivers by **Pittsburgh** from **Buffalo**, October 3, 2006. Traded to **Atlanta** by **Pittsburgh** for NY Rangers' 3rd round choice (previously acquired, Pittsburgh selected Robert Bortuzzo) in 2007 Entry Draft, June 22, 2007.

## THORESEN, Patrick

(THOR-eh-sehn, PAT-rihk) **PHI.**

Center. Shoots left. 5'11", 188 lbs. Born, Oslo, Norway, November 8, 1983.

| Season | Club | League | GP | G | A | Pts | PIM | PP | SH | GW | S | % | +/- | TF | F% | Min | GP | G | A | Pts | PIM | PP | SH | GW | Min |
|---|---|---|---|---|---|---|---|---|---|---|---|---|---|---|---|---|---|---|---|---|---|---|---|---|---|
| 99-2000 | Storhamar | Norway | 25 | 1 | 8 | 9 | 4 | .... | .... | .... | .... | .... | .... | .... | .... | .... | .... | .... | .... | .... | .... | .... | .... | .... | .... |
| | Norway | WJ18-B | 5 | 3 | 2 | 5 | 6 | .... | .... | .... | .... | .... | .... | .... | .... | .... | .... | .... | .... | .... | .... | .... | .... | .... | .... |
| 2000-01 | Storhamar | Norway | 40 | 18 | 27 | 45 | 24 | .... | .... | .... | .... | .... | .... | .... | .... | .... | .... | .... | .... | .... | .... | .... | .... | .... | .... |
| 2001-02 | Moncton Wildcats | QMJHL | 60 | 30 | 43 | 73 | 50 | .... | .... | .... | .... | .... | .... | .... | .... | .... | .... | .... | .... | .... | .... | .... | .... | .... | .... |
| 2002-03 | Baie-Comeau | QMJHL | 71 | 33 | *75 | 108 | 57 | .... | .... | .... | .... | .... | .... | .... | .... | .... | 12 | 2 | 8 | 10 | 8 | .... | .... | .... | .... |
| 2003-04 | Morrums GoIS IK | Sweden-2 | 38 | 19 | 22 | 41 | 40 | .... | .... | .... | .... | .... | .... | .... | .... | .... | .... | .... | .... | .... | .... | .... | .... | .... | .... |
| | Djurgarden | Sweden | 3 | 0 | 0 | 0 | 2 | .... | .... | .... | .... | .... | .... | .... | .... | .... | .... | .... | .... | .... | .... | .... | .... | .... | .... |
| 2004-05 | Djurgarden | Sweden | 30 | 10 | 7 | 17 | 33 | .... | .... | .... | .... | .... | .... | .... | .... | .... | 12 | 2 | 2 | 4 | 29 | .... | .... | .... | .... |
| 2005-06 | Djurgarden | Sweden | 50 | 17 | 19 | 36 | 44 | .... | .... | .... | .... | .... | .... | .... | .... | .... | .... | .... | .... | .... | .... | .... | .... | .... | .... |
| | Salzburg | Austria | .... | .... | .... | .... | .... | .... | .... | .... | .... | .... | .... | .... | .... | .... | 9 | 4 | 7 | 11 | 12 | .... | .... | .... | .... |
| 2006-07 | Edmonton | NHL | 68 | 4 | 12 | 16 | 52 | 0 | 1 | 2 | 73 | 5.5 | –1 | 82 | 51.2 | 11:25 | .... | .... | .... | .... | .... | .... | .... | .... | .... |
| | Wilkes-Barre | AHL | 5 | 1 | 5 | 6 | 4 | .... | .... | .... | .... | .... | .... | .... | .... | .... | .... | .... | .... | .... | .... | .... | .... | .... | .... |
| 2007-08 | Edmonton | NHL | 17 | 2 | 1 | 3 | 6 | 0 | 0 | 0 | 18 | 11.1 | –4 | 19 | 52.6 | 10:43 | .... | .... | .... | .... | .... | .... | .... | .... | .... |
| | Springfield | AHL | 29 | 13 | 13 | 26 | 13 | .... | .... | .... | .... | .... | .... | .... | .... | .... | .... | .... | .... | .... | .... | .... | .... | .... | .... |
| | Philadelphia | NHL | 21 | 0 | 5 | 5 | 8 | 0 | 0 | 0 | 21 | 0.0 | –6 | 81 | 38.3 | 12:36 | 14 | 0 | 2 | 2 | 4 | 0 | 0 | 0 | 9:22 |
| 2008-09 | HC Lugano | Swiss | 48 | 22 | 41 | 63 | 83 | .... | .... | .... | .... | .... | .... | .... | .... | .... | 7 | 1 | 7 | 8 | 2 | .... | .... | .... | .... |
| | NHL Totals | | 106 | 6 | 18 | 24 | 66 | 0 | 1 | 2 | 112 | 5.4 | | 182 | 45.6 | 11:32 | 14 | 0 | 2 | 2 | 4 | 0 | 0 | 0 | 9:22 |

Signed as a free agent by **Edmonton**, June 12, 2006. Claimed on waivers by **Philadelphia** from **Edmonton**, February 22, 2008. Signed as a free agent by **Lugano** (Swiss), July 14, 2008.

## THORNTON, Joe

(THOHRN-tuhn, JOH) **S.J.**

Center. Shoots left. 6'4", 235 lbs. Born, London, Ont., July 2, 1979. Boston's 1st choice, 1st overall, in 1997 Entry Draft.

| Season | Club | League | GP | G | A | Pts | PIM | PP | SH | GW | S | % | +/- | TF | F% | Min | GP | G | A | Pts | PIM | PP | SH | GW | Min |
|---|---|---|---|---|---|---|---|---|---|---|---|---|---|---|---|---|---|---|---|---|---|---|---|---|---|
| 1993-94 | Elgin-Middlesex | Minor-ON | 67 | *83 | *85 | *168 | 45 | .... | .... | .... | .... | .... | .... | .... | .... | .... | .... | .... | .... | .... | .... | .... | .... | .... | .... |
| | St. Thomas Stars | OHA-B | 6 | 2 | 6 | 8 | 2 | .... | .... | .... | .... | .... | .... | .... | .... | .... | .... | .... | .... | .... | .... | .... | .... | .... | .... |
| 1994-95 | St. Thomas Stars | OHA-B | 50 | 40 | 64 | 104 | 53 | .... | .... | .... | .... | .... | .... | .... | .... | .... | .... | .... | .... | .... | .... | .... | .... | .... | .... |
| 1995-96 | Sault Ste. Marie | OHL | 66 | 30 | 46 | 76 | 53 | .... | .... | .... | .... | .... | .... | .... | .... | .... | 4 | 1 | 1 | 2 | 11 | .... | .... | .... | .... |
| 1996-97 | Sault Ste. Marie | OHL | 59 | 41 | 81 | 122 | 123 | .... | .... | .... | .... | .... | .... | .... | .... | .... | 11 | 11 | 8 | 19 | 24 | .... | .... | .... | .... |
| 1997-98 | Boston | NHL | 55 | 3 | 4 | 7 | 19 | 0 | 0 | 1 | 33 | 9.1 | –6 | .... | .... | .... | 6 | 0 | 0 | 0 | 9 | 0 | 0 | 0 | .... |
| 1998-99 | Boston | NHL | 81 | 16 | 25 | 41 | 69 | 7 | 0 | 1 | 128 | 12.5 | 3 | 1073 | 48.7 | 15:21 | 11 | 3 | 6 | 9 | 4 | 2 | 0 | 2 | 19:52 |
| 99-2000 | Boston | NHL | 81 | 23 | 37 | 60 | 82 | 5 | 0 | 3 | 171 | 13.5 | –5 | 1861 | 49.5 | 21:18 | .... | .... | .... | .... | .... | .... | .... | .... | .... |
| 2000-01 | Boston | NHL | 72 | 37 | 34 | 71 | 107 | 19 | 1 | 5 | 181 | 20.4 | –4 | 1651 | 52.1 | 21:45 | .... | .... | .... | .... | .... | .... | .... | .... | .... |
| 2001-02 | Boston | NHL | 66 | 22 | 46 | 68 | 127 | 6 | 0 | 5 | 152 | 14.5 | 7 | 1341 | 49.1 | 19:59 | 6 | 2 | 4 | 6 | 10 | 0 | 0 | 0 | 21:09 |
| 2002-03 | Boston | NHL | 77 | 36 | 65 | 101 | 109 | 12 | 2 | 4 | 196 | 18.4 | 12 | 1766 | 49.5 | 22:33 | 5 | 1 | 2 | 3 | 4 | 1 | 0 | 0 | 20:13 |
| 2003-04 | Boston | NHL | 77 | 23 | 50 | 73 | 98 | 4 | 0 | 6 | 187 | 12.3 | 18 | 1671 | 56.3 | 21:38 | 7 | 0 | 0 | 0 | 14 | 0 | 0 | 0 | 21:30 |
| 2004-05 | HC Davos | Swiss | 40 | 10 | 44 | 54 | 80 | .... | .... | .... | .... | .... | .... | .... | .... | .... | 14 | 4 | *20 | *24 | 29 | .... | .... | .... | .... |
| 2005-06 | Boston | NHL | 23 | 9 | *24 | *33 | 6 | 3 | 0 | 2 | 60 | 15.0 | 0 | 511 | 52.3 | 21:33 | .... | .... | .... | .... | .... | .... | .... | .... | .... |
| | San Jose | NHL | 58 | 20 | *72 | *92 | 55 | 8 | 0 | 4 | 135 | 14.8 | 31 | 1287 | 50.9 | 21:15 | 11 | 2 | 7 | 9 | 12 | 1 | 0 | 1 | 25:09 |
| | Canada | Olympics | 6 | 1 | 2 | 3 | 0 | .... | .... | .... | .... | .... | .... | .... | .... | .... | .... | .... | .... | .... | .... | .... | .... | .... | .... |
| 2006-07 | San Jose | NHL | 82 | 22 | *92 | 114 | 44 | 10 | 0 | 5 | 213 | 10.3 | 24 | 1522 | 51.1 | 20:19 | 11 | 1 | 10 | 11 | 10 | 0 | 0 | 0 | 22:00 |
| 2007-08 | San Jose | NHL | 82 | 29 | *67 | 96 | 59 | 11 | 0 | 5 | 178 | 16.3 | 18 | 1485 | 52.9 | 21:24 | 13 | 2 | 8 | 10 | 2 | 1 | 0 | 1 | 24:42 |
| 2008-09 | San Jose | NHL | 82 | 25 | 61 | 86 | 56 | 11 | 0 | 3 | 139 | 18.0 | 16 | 1295 | 55.4 | 19:28 | 6 | 1 | 4 | 5 | 5 | 1 | 0 | 0 | 19:14 |
| | NHL Totals | | 836 | 265 | 577 | 842 | 831 | 96 | 3 | 44 | 1773 | 14.9 | | 15463 | 51.6 | 20:29 | 76 | 12 | 41 | 53 | 70 | 6 | 0 | 4 | 22:10 |

OHL All-Rookie Team (1996) • OHL Rookie of the Year (1996) • Canadian Major Junior Rookie of the Year (1996) • OHL Second All-Star Team (1997) • NHL Second All-Star Team (2003, 2008) • NHL First All-Star Team (2006) • Art Ross Trophy (2006) • Hart Memorial Trophy (2006)

Played in NHL All-Star Game (2002, 2003, 2004, 2007, 2008, 2009)

Signed as a free agent by **Davos** (Swiss), July 8, 2004. Traded to **San Jose** by **Boston** for Brad Stuart, Marco Sturm and Wayne Primeau, November 30, 2005.

## THORNTON, Shawn

(THOHRN-tuhn, SHAWN) **BOS.**

Right wing. Shoots right. 6'2", 217 lbs. Born, Oshawa, Ont., July 23, 1977. Toronto's 6th choice, 190th overall, in 1997 Entry Draft.

| Season | Club | League | GP | G | A | Pts | PIM | PP | SH | GW | S | % | +/- | TF | F% | Min | GP | G | A | Pts | PIM | PP | SH | GW | Min |
|---|---|---|---|---|---|---|---|---|---|---|---|---|---|---|---|---|---|---|---|---|---|---|---|---|---|
| 1995-96 | Peterborough | OHL | 63 | 4 | 10 | 14 | 192 | .... | .... | .... | .... | .... | .... | .... | .... | .... | 24 | 3 | 0 | 3 | 25 | .... | .... | .... | .... |
| 1996-97 | Peterborough | OHL | 61 | 19 | 10 | 29 | 204 | .... | .... | .... | .... | .... | .... | .... | .... | .... | 11 | 2 | 4 | 6 | 20 | .... | .... | .... | .... |
| 1997-98 | St. John's | AHL | 59 | 0 | 3 | 3 | 225 | .... | .... | .... | .... | .... | .... | .... | .... | .... | .... | .... | .... | .... | .... | .... | .... | .... | .... |
| 1998-99 | St. John's | AHL | 78 | 8 | 11 | 19 | 354 | .... | .... | .... | .... | .... | .... | .... | .... | .... | 5 | 0 | 0 | 0 | 9 | .... | .... | .... | .... |
| 99-2000 | St. John's | AHL | 60 | 4 | 12 | 16 | 316 | .... | .... | .... | .... | .... | .... | .... | .... | .... | .... | .... | .... | .... | .... | .... | .... | .... | .... |
| 2000-01 | St. John's | AHL | 79 | 5 | 12 | 17 | 320 | .... | .... | .... | .... | .... | .... | .... | .... | .... | 3 | 1 | 2 | 3 | 2 | .... | .... | .... | .... |
| 2001-02 | Norfolk Admirals | AHL | 70 | 8 | 14 | 22 | 281 | .... | .... | .... | .... | .... | .... | .... | .... | .... | 4 | 0 | 0 | 0 | 4 | .... | .... | .... | .... |
| 2002-03 | Chicago | NHL | 13 | 1 | 1 | 2 | 31 | 0 | 0 | 0 | 15 | 6.7 | –4 | 3 | 66.7 | 8:30 | .... | .... | .... | .... | .... | .... | .... | .... | .... |
| | Norfolk Admirals | AHL | 50 | 11 | 2 | 13 | 213 | .... | .... | .... | .... | .... | .... | .... | .... | .... | 9 | 0 | 2 | 2 | 28 | .... | .... | .... | .... |
| 2003-04 | Chicago | NHL | 8 | 1 | 0 | 1 | 23 | 0 | 0 | 0 | 14 | 7.1 | 2 | 19 | 42.1 | 11:14 | .... | .... | .... | .... | .... | .... | .... | .... | .... |
| | Norfolk Admirals | AHL | 64 | 6 | 11 | 17 | 259 | .... | .... | .... | .... | .... | .... | .... | .... | .... | 8 | 1 | 1 | 2 | 6 | .... | .... | .... | .... |
| 2004-05 | Norfolk Admirals | AHL | 71 | 5 | 9 | 14 | 253 | .... | .... | .... | .... | .... | .... | .... | .... | .... | 6 | 0 | 0 | 0 | 8 | .... | .... | .... | .... |
| 2005-06 | Chicago | NHL | 10 | 0 | 0 | 0 | 16 | 0 | 0 | 0 | 16 | 0.0 | –5 | 17 | 58.8 | 7:18 | .... | .... | .... | .... | .... | .... | .... | .... | .... |
| | Norfolk Admirals | AHL | 59 | 10 | 22 | 32 | 192 | .... | .... | .... | .... | .... | .... | .... | .... | .... | 4 | 0 | 0 | 0 | 35 | .... | .... | .... | .... |
| 2006-07♦ | Anaheim | NHL | 48 | 2 | 7 | 9 | 88 | 0 | 0 | 0 | 60 | 3.3 | 3 | 8 | 25.0 | 8:26 | 15 | 0 | 0 | 0 | 19 | 0 | 0 | 0 | 3:58 |
| | Portland Pirates | AHL | 15 | 4 | 4 | 8 | 55 | .... | .... | .... | .... | .... | .... | .... | .... | .... | .... | .... | .... | .... | .... | .... | .... | .... | .... |
| 2007-08 | Boston | NHL | 58 | 4 | 3 | 7 | 74 | 0 | 0 | 1 | 65 | 6.2 | –1 | 7 | 28.6 | 7:24 | 7 | 0 | 0 | 0 | 6 | 0 | 0 | 0 | 8:04 |
| 2008-09 | Boston | NHL | 79 | 6 | 5 | 11 | 123 | 0 | 0 | 2 | 136 | 4.4 | –2 | 5 | 20.0 | 10:02 | 10 | 1 | 0 | 1 | 6 | 0 | 0 | 0 | 9:07 |
| | NHL Totals | | 216 | 14 | 16 | 30 | 355 | 0 | 0 | 3 | 306 | 4.6 | | 59 | 42.4 | 8:48 | 32 | 1 | 0 | 1 | 31 | 0 | 0 | 0 | 6:28 |

Traded to **Chicago** by **Toronto** for Marty Wilford, September 30, 2001. Signed as a free agent by **Anaheim**, July 14, 2006. Signed as a free agent by **Boston**, July 1, 2007.

| | | | Regular Season | | | | | | | | | | | | | | Playoffs | | | | | | | | |
|---|---|---|---|---|---|---|---|---|---|---|---|---|---|---|---|---|---|---|---|---|---|---|---|---|---|
| Season | Club | League | GP | G | A | Pts | PIM | PP | SH | GW | S | % | +/- | TF | F% | Min | GP | G | A | Pts | PIM | PP | SH | GW | Min |

## TIKHONOV, Viktor

(TIHK-uh-nawf, VIHK-tohr) **PHX.**

Center. Shoots right. 6'2", 187 lbs. Born, Riga, Latvia, May 12, 1988. Phoenix's 2nd choice, 28th overall, in 2008 Entry Draft.

| | | | | | | | | | | | | | | | | | | | | | | | | | |
|---|---|---|---|---|---|---|---|---|---|---|---|---|---|---|---|---|---|---|---|---|---|---|---|---|---|
| 2004-05 | CSKA Moscow 2 | Russia-3 | STATISTICS NOT AVAILABLE | | | | | | | | | | | | | | | | | | | | | | |
| 2005-06 | CSKA Moscow 2 | Russia-3 | STATISTICS NOT AVAILABLE | | | | | | | | | | | | | | | | | | | | | | |
| | HK Dmitrov | Russia-2 | 36 | 6 | 8 | 14 | 10 | .... | .... | .... | .... | .... | .... | .... | .... | .... | .... | .... | .... | .... | .... | .... | .... | .... | .... |
| 2006-07 | Cherepovets 2 | Russia-3 | STATISTICS NOT AVAILABLE | | | | | | | | | | | | | | | | | | | | | | |
| | Cherepovets | Russia | 4 | 0 | 0 | 0 | 0 | .... | .... | .... | .... | .... | .... | .... | .... | .... | .... | .... | .... | .... | .... | .... | .... | .... | .... |
| 2007-08 | Cherepovets | Russia | 43 | 7 | 5 | 12 | 43 | .... | .... | .... | .... | .... | .... | .... | .... | .... | 8 | 0 | 1 | 1 | 4 | .... | .... | .... | .... |
| **2008-09** | **Phoenix** | **NHL** | **61** | **8** | **8** | **16** | **20** | **1** | **0** | **1** | **71** | **11.3** | **–3** | **60** | **38.3** | **12:08** | .... | .... | .... | .... | .... | .... | .... | .... | .... |
| | San Antonio | AHL | 4 | 2 | 1 | 3 | 0 | .... | .... | .... | .... | .... | .... | .... | .... | .... | .... | .... | .... | .... | .... | .... | .... | .... | .... |
| | **NHL Totals** | | **61** | **8** | **8** | **16** | **20** | **1** | **0** | **1** | **71** | **11.3** | | **60** | **38.3** | **12:08** | .... | .... | .... | .... | .... | .... | .... | .... | .... |

## TIMONEN, Kimmo

(TEEM-oh-nehn, KEE-moh) **PHI.**

Defense. Shoots left. 5'10", 194 lbs. Born, Kuopio, Finland, March 18, 1975. Los Angeles' 11th choice, 250th overall, in 1993 Entry Draft.

| | | | | | | | | | | | | | | | | | | | | | | | | | |
|---|---|---|---|---|---|---|---|---|---|---|---|---|---|---|---|---|---|---|---|---|---|---|---|---|---|
| 1990-91 | KalPa Kuopio Jr. | Fin-Jr. | 4 | 0 | 1 | 1 | 2 | .... | .... | .... | .... | .... | .... | .... | .... | .... | .... | .... | .... | .... | .... | .... | .... | .... | .... |
| 1991-92 | KalPa Kuopio Jr. | Fin-Jr. | 32 | 7 | 10 | 17 | 4 | .... | .... | .... | .... | .... | .... | .... | .... | .... | .... | .... | .... | .... | .... | .... | .... | .... | .... |
| | KalPa Kuopio | Finland | 5 | 0 | 0 | 0 | 0 | .... | .... | .... | .... | .... | .... | .... | .... | .... | .... | .... | .... | .... | .... | .... | .... | .... | .... |
| 1992-93 | KalPa Kuopio U18 | Fin-U18 | 3 | 0 | 5 | 5 | 0 | .... | .... | .... | .... | .... | .... | .... | .... | .... | .... | .... | .... | .... | .... | .... | .... | .... | .... |
| | KalPa Kuopio Jr. | Fin-Jr. | 16 | 9 | 15 | 24 | 10 | .... | .... | .... | .... | .... | .... | .... | .... | .... | .... | .... | .... | .... | .... | .... | .... | .... | .... |
| | KalPa Kuopio | Finland | 33 | 0 | 2 | 2 | 4 | .... | .... | .... | .... | .... | .... | .... | .... | .... | .... | .... | .... | .... | .... | .... | .... | .... | .... |
| 1993-94 | KalPa Kuopio Jr. | Fin-Jr. | 5 | 4 | 7 | 11 | 0 | .... | .... | .... | .... | .... | .... | .... | .... | .... | .... | .... | .... | .... | .... | .... | .... | .... | .... |
| | KalPa Kuopio | Finland | 46 | 6 | 7 | 13 | 55 | .... | .... | .... | .... | .... | .... | .... | .... | .... | .... | .... | .... | .... | .... | .... | .... | .... | .... |
| 1994-95 | TPS Turku Jr. | Fin-Jr. | 1 | 0 | 0 | 0 | 0 | .... | .... | .... | .... | .... | .... | .... | .... | .... | .... | .... | .... | .... | .... | .... | .... | .... | .... |
| | TPS Turku | Finland | 45 | 3 | 4 | 7 | 10 | .... | .... | .... | .... | .... | .... | .... | .... | .... | 13 | 0 | 1 | 1 | 6 | .... | .... | .... | .... |
| 1995-96 | TPS Turku | Finland | 48 | 3 | 21 | 24 | 22 | .... | .... | .... | .... | .... | .... | .... | .... | .... | 9 | 1 | 2 | 3 | 12 | .... | .... | .... | .... |
| 1996-97 | TPS Turku | Finland | 50 | 10 | 14 | 24 | 18 | .... | .... | .... | .... | .... | .... | .... | .... | .... | 12 | 2 | 7 | 9 | 6 | .... | .... | .... | .... |
| | TPS Turku | EuroHL | 6 | 1 | 0 | 1 | 27 | .... | .... | .... | .... | .... | .... | .... | .... | .... | 4 | 0 | 1 | 1 | 0 | .... | .... | .... | .... |
| 1997-98 | HIFK Helsinki | Finland | 45 | 10 | 15 | 25 | 24 | .... | .... | .... | .... | .... | .... | .... | .... | .... | 9 | 3 | 4 | 7 | 8 | .... | .... | .... | .... |
| | Finland | Olympics | 6 | 0 | 1 | 1 | 2 | .... | .... | .... | .... | .... | .... | .... | .... | .... | .... | .... | .... | .... | .... | .... | .... | .... | .... |
| **1998-99** | **Nashville** | **NHL** | **50** | **4** | **8** | **12** | **30** | **1** | **0** | **0** | **75** | **5.3** | **–4** | **0** | **0.0** | **19:04** | .... | .... | .... | .... | .... | .... | .... | .... | .... |
| | Milwaukee | IHL | 29 | 2 | 13 | 15 | 22 | .... | .... | .... | .... | .... | .... | .... | .... | .... | .... | .... | .... | .... | .... | .... | .... | .... | .... |
| **99-2000** | **Nashville** | **NHL** | **51** | **8** | **25** | **33** | **26** | **2** | **1** | **2** | **97** | **8.2** | **–5** | **0** | **0.0** | **21:06** | .... | .... | .... | .... | .... | .... | .... | .... | .... |
| **2000-01** | **Nashville** | **NHL** | **82** | **12** | **13** | **25** | **50** | **6** | **0** | **3** | **151** | **7.9** | **–6** | **2** | **50.0** | **23:11** | .... | .... | .... | .... | .... | .... | .... | .... | .... |
| **2001-02** | **Nashville** | **NHL** | **82** | **13** | **29** | **42** | **28** | **9** | **0** | **1** | **154** | **8.4** | **2** | **0** | **0.0** | **24:12** | .... | .... | .... | .... | .... | .... | .... | .... | .... |
| | Finland | Olympics | 4 | 0 | 1 | 1 | 2 | .... | .... | .... | .... | .... | .... | .... | .... | .... | .... | .... | .... | .... | .... | .... | .... | .... | .... |
| **2002-03** | **Nashville** | **NHL** | **72** | **6** | **34** | **40** | **46** | **4** | **0** | **0** | **144** | **4.2** | **–3** | **0** | **0.0** | **22:25** | .... | .... | .... | .... | .... | .... | .... | .... | .... |
| **2003-04** | **Nashville** | **NHL** | **77** | **12** | **32** | **44** | **52** | **8** | **0** | **1** | **180** | **6.7** | **–7** | **1** | **0.0** | **23:52** | **6** | **0** | **0** | **0** | **10** | **0** | **0** | **0** | **24:16** |
| 2004-05 | HC Lugano | Swiss | 3 | 0 | 1 | 1 | 0 | .... | .... | .... | .... | .... | .... | .... | .... | .... | .... | .... | .... | .... | .... | .... | .... | .... | .... |
| | Brynas IF Gavle | Sweden | 10 | 5 | 3 | 8 | 8 | .... | .... | .... | .... | .... | .... | .... | .... | .... | .... | .... | .... | .... | .... | .... | .... | .... | .... |
| | KalPa Kuopio | Finland-2 | 12 | 4 | 13 | 17 | 6 | .... | .... | .... | .... | .... | .... | .... | .... | .... | 8 | 3 | 7 | 10 | 4 | .... | .... | .... | .... |
| **2005-06** | **Nashville** | **NHL** | **79** | **11** | **39** | **50** | **74** | **8** | **0** | **1** | **156** | **7.1** | **–3** | **5** | **80.0** | **22:26** | **5** | **1** | **3** | **4** | **4** | **0** | **1** | **0** | **24:42** |
| | Finland | Olympics | 8 | 1 | 4 | 5 | 2 | .... | .... | .... | .... | .... | .... | .... | .... | .... | .... | .... | .... | .... | .... | .... | .... | .... | .... |
| **2006-07** | **Nashville** | **NHL** | **80** | **13** | **42** | **55** | **42** | **8** | **0** | **2** | **121** | **10.7** | **20** | **1** | **0.0** | **21:51** | **5** | **0** | **2** | **2** | **4** | **0** | **0** | **0** | **24:33** |
| **2007-08** | **Philadelphia** | **NHL** | **80** | **8** | **36** | **44** | **50** | **3** | **1** | **1** | **125** | **6.4** | **0** | **0** | **0.0** | **23:35** | **13** | **0** | **6** | **6** | **8** | **0** | **0** | **0** | **24:41** |
| **2008-09** | **Philadelphia** | **NHL** | **77** | **3** | **40** | **43** | **54** | **2** | **0** | **0** | **104** | **2.9** | **19** | **2** | **0.0** | **24:31** | **6** | **0** | **1** | **1** | **12** | **0** | **0** | **0** | **26:21** |
| | **NHL Totals** | | **730** | **90** | **298** | **388** | **452** | **51** | **2** | **11** | **1307** | **6.9** | | **11** | **45.5** | **22:49** | **35** | **1** | **12** | **13** | **38** | **0** | **1** | **0** | **24:53** |

Olympic Tournament All-Star Team (2006)

Played in NHL All-Star Game (2004, 2007, 2008)

Traded to **Nashville** by **Los Angeles** with Jan Vopat for future considerations, June 26, 1998. Signed as a free agent by **Lugano** (Swiss), October 31, 2004. Signed as a free agent by **Gavle** (Sweden), November 8, 2004. Signed as a free agent by **Kuopio** (Finland-2), January 3, 2005. Traded to **Philadelphia** by **Nashville** with Scott Hartnell for Nashville's 1st round choice (previously acquired, Nashville selected Jonathon Blum) in 2007 Entry Draft, June 18, 2007.



## TJARNQVIST, Daniel

(T'YAHRN-kvihst, DAN-yehl)

Defense. Shoots left. 6'1", 207 lbs. Born, Umea, Sweden, October 14, 1976. Florida's 5th choice, 88th overall, in 1995 Entry Draft.

| | | | | | | | | | | | | | | | | | | | | | | | | | |
|---|---|---|---|---|---|---|---|---|---|---|---|---|---|---|---|---|---|---|---|---|---|---|---|---|---|
| 1992-93 | Rogle Jr. | Swe-Jr. | 7 | 1 | 0 | 1 | 0 | .... | .... | .... | .... | .... | .... | .... | .... | .... | .... | .... | .... | .... | .... | .... | .... | .... | .... |
| 1993-94 | Rogle U18 | Swe-U18 | STATISTICS NOT AVAILABLE | | | | | | | | | | | | | | | | | | | | | | |
| 1994-95 | Rogle | Sweden | 18 | 0 | 1 | 1 | 2 | .... | .... | .... | .... | .... | .... | .... | .... | .... | .... | .... | .... | .... | .... | .... | .... | .... | .... |
| | Rogle | Sweden-Q | 15 | 2 | 3 | 5 | 0 | .... | .... | .... | .... | .... | .... | .... | .... | .... | .... | .... | .... | .... | .... | .... | .... | .... | .... |
| 1995-96 | Rogle | Sweden | 22 | 1 | 7 | 8 | 6 | .... | .... | .... | .... | .... | .... | .... | .... | .... | .... | .... | .... | .... | .... | .... | .... | .... | .... |
| 1996-97 | Jokerit Helsinki | Finland | 44 | 3 | 8 | 11 | 4 | .... | .... | .... | .... | .... | .... | .... | .... | .... | 9 | 0 | 3 | 3 | 4 | .... | .... | .... | .... |
| | Jokerit Helsinki | EuroHL | 6 | 1 | 1 | 2 | 2 | .... | .... | .... | .... | .... | .... | .... | .... | .... | .... | .... | .... | .... | .... | .... | .... | .... | .... |
| 1997-98 | Djurgarden | Sweden | 40 | 5 | 9 | 14 | 12 | .... | .... | .... | .... | .... | .... | .... | .... | .... | 15 | 1 | 1 | 2 | 2 | .... | .... | .... | .... |
| 1998-99 | Djurgarden | Sweden | 40 | 4 | 3 | 7 | 16 | .... | .... | .... | .... | .... | .... | .... | .... | .... | 4 | 0 | 0 | 0 | 2 | .... | .... | .... | .... |
| 99-2000 | Djurgarden | Sweden | 42 | 3 | 16 | 19 | 8 | .... | .... | .... | .... | .... | .... | .... | .... | .... | 5 | 0 | 0 | 0 | 2 | .... | .... | .... | .... |
| 2000-01 | Djurgarden | Sweden | 45 | 9 | 17 | 26 | 26 | .... | .... | .... | .... | .... | .... | .... | .... | .... | 16 | 6 | 5 | 11 | 2 | .... | .... | .... | .... |
| **2001-02** | **Atlanta** | **NHL** | **75** | **2** | **16** | **18** | **14** | **1** | **0** | **0** | **68** | **2.9** | **–22** | **4** | **25.0** | **21:32** | .... | .... | .... | .... | .... | .... | .... | .... | .... |
| **2002-03** | **Atlanta** | **NHL** | **75** | **3** | **12** | **15** | **26** | **1** | **0** | **0** | **65** | **4.6** | **–20** | **3** | **66.7** | **21:53** | .... | .... | .... | .... | .... | .... | .... | .... | .... |
| **2003-04** | **Atlanta** | **NHL** | **68** | **5** | **15** | **20** | **20** | **0** | **2** | **1** | **65** | **7.7** | **–4** | **4** | **25.0** | **22:17** | .... | .... | .... | .... | .... | .... | .... | .... | .... |
| 2004-05 | Djurgarden | Sweden | 49 | 12 | 12 | 24 | 30 | .... | .... | .... | .... | .... | .... | .... | .... | .... | 12 | 2 | 5 | 7 | 10 | .... | .... | .... | .... |
| **2005-06** | **Minnesota** | **NHL** | **60** | **3** | **15** | **18** | **32** | **3** | **0** | **1** | **54** | **5.6** | **–11** | **0** | **0.0** | **19:46** | .... | .... | .... | .... | .... | .... | .... | .... | .... |
| | Sweden | Olympics | 8 | 2 | 1 | 3 | 4 | .... | .... | .... | .... | .... | .... | .... | .... | .... | .... | .... | .... | .... | .... | .... | .... | .... | .... |
| **2006-07** | **Edmonton** | **NHL** | **37** | **3** | **12** | **15** | **30** | **2** | **0** | **0** | **33** | **9.1** | **3** | **0** | **0.0** | **22:42** | .... | .... | .... | .... | .... | .... | .... | .... | .... |
| 2007-08 | Yaroslavl | Russia | 18 | 1 | 2 | 3 | 14 | .... | .... | .... | .... | .... | .... | .... | .... | .... | 8 | 0 | 4 | 4 | 4 | .... | .... | .... | .... |
| **2008-09** | **Colorado** | **NHL** | **37** | **2** | **2** | **4** | **8** | **0** | **0** | **0** | **19** | **10.5** | **1** | **0** | **0.0** | **14:40** | .... | .... | .... | .... | .... | .... | .... | .... | .... |
| | **NHL Totals** | | **352** | **18** | **72** | **90** | **130** | **7** | **2** | **2** | **304** | **5.9** | | **11** | **36.4** | **20:51** | .... | .... | .... | .... | .... | .... | .... | .... | .... |

Traded to **Atlanta** by **Florida** with Gord Murphy, Herbert Vasiljevs and Ottawa's 6th round choice (previously acquired, later traded to Dallas – Dallas selected Justin Cox) in 1999 Entry Draft for Trevor Kidd, June 25, 1999. Signed as a free agent by **Djurgarden** (Sweden), September 16, 2004. Signed as a free agent by **Minnesota**, August 15, 2005. Signed as a free agent by **Edmonton**, July 6, 2006. • Missed majority of 2006-07 season recovering from recurring groin injury. Signed as a free agent by **Kazan** (Russia), August 23, 2007. Signed as a free agent by **Colorado**, July 3, 2008.

## TJARNQVIST, Mathias

(T'YAHRN-kvihst, MAT-ee-uhs)

Right wing. Shoots left. 6'2", 196 lbs. Born, Umea, Sweden, April 15, 1979. Dallas' 3rd choice, 96th overall, in 1999 Entry Draft.

| | | | | | | | | | | | | | | | | | | | | | | | | | |
|---|---|---|---|---|---|---|---|---|---|---|---|---|---|---|---|---|---|---|---|---|---|---|---|---|---|
| 1995-96 | Rogle Jr. | Swe-Jr. | 4 | 2 | 0 | 2 | 0 | .... | .... | .... | .... | .... | .... | .... | .... | .... | .... | .... | .... | .... | .... | .... | .... | .... | .... |
| 1996-97 | Rogle Jr. | Swe-Jr. | 18 | 5 | 8 | 13 | .... | .... | .... | .... | .... | .... | .... | .... | .... | .... | .... | .... | .... | .... | .... | .... | .... | .... | .... |
| | Rogle | Sweden-2 | 15 | 1 | 4 | 5 | 4 | .... | .... | .... | .... | .... | .... | .... | .... | .... | .... | .... | .... | .... | .... | .... | .... | .... | .... |
| 1997-98 | Rogle | Sweden-2 | 31 | 12 | 11 | 23 | 30 | .... | .... | .... | .... | .... | .... | .... | .... | .... | 4 | 2 | 0 | 2 | 6 | .... | .... | .... | .... |
| 1998-99 | Rogle | Sweden-2 | 34 | 18 | 16 | 34 | 44 | .... | .... | .... | .... | .... | .... | .... | .... | .... | 5 | 4 | 1 | 5 | 4 | .... | .... | .... | .... |
| 99-2000 | Djurgarden | Sweden | 50 | 12 | 12 | 24 | 20 | .... | .... | .... | .... | .... | .... | .... | .... | .... | 13 | 3 | 2 | 5 | 16 | .... | .... | .... | .... |
| 2000-01 | Djurgarden | Sweden | 47 | 11 | 8 | 19 | 53 | .... | .... | .... | .... | .... | .... | .... | .... | .... | 16 | 1 | 2 | 3 | 6 | .... | .... | .... | .... |
| 2001-02 | Djurgarden | Sweden | 6 | 0 | 1 | 1 | 4 | .... | .... | .... | .... | .... | .... | .... | .... | .... | 2 | 0 | 0 | 0 | 2 | .... | .... | .... | .... |
| 2002-03 | Djurgarden | Sweden | 38 | 11 | 13 | 24 | 30 | .... | .... | .... | .... | .... | .... | .... | .... | .... | 9 | 4 | 1 | 5 | 12 | .... | .... | .... | .... |
| **2003-04** | **Dallas** | **NHL** | **18** | **1** | **1** | **2** | **2** | **0** | **0** | **1** | **11** | **9.1** | **–6** | **4** | **25.0** | **9:43** | .... | .... | .... | .... | .... | .... | .... | .... | .... |
| | Utah Grizzlies | AHL | 60 | 15 | 13 | 28 | 51 | .... | .... | .... | .... | .... | .... | .... | .... | .... | .... | .... | .... | .... | .... | .... | .... | .... | .... |
| 2004-05 | HV 71 Jonkoping | Sweden | 46 | 8 | 9 | 17 | 18 | .... | .... | .... | .... | .... | .... | .... | .... | .... | .... | .... | .... | .... | .... | .... | .... | .... | .... |
| **2005-06** | **Dallas** | **NHL** | **33** | **2** | **4** | **6** | **18** | **0** | **0** | **0** | **36** | **5.6** | **4** | **4** | **75.0** | **8:10** | .... | .... | .... | .... | .... | .... | .... | .... | .... |
| | Iowa Stars | AHL | 34 | 17 | 12 | 29 | 28 | .... | .... | .... | .... | .... | .... | .... | .... | .... | 1 | 0 | 0 | 0 | 0 | .... | .... | .... | .... |
| **2006-07** | **Dallas** | **NHL** | **18** | **1** | **3** | **4** | **4** | **0** | **0** | **0** | **13** | **7.7** | **–3** | **7** | **42.9** | **9:15** | .... | .... | .... | .... | .... | .... | .... | .... | .... |
| | Iowa Stars | AHL | 2 | 1 | 1 | 2 | 0 | .... | .... | .... | .... | .... | .... | .... | .... | .... | .... | .... | .... | .... | .... | .... | .... | .... | .... |
| | **Phoenix** | **NHL** | **26** | **5** | **4** | **9** | **2** | **0** | **1** | **0** | **31** | **16.1** | **–2** | **11** | **54.6** | **14:50** | .... | .... | .... | .... | .... | .... | .... | .... | .... |
| **2007-08** | **Phoenix** | **NHL** | **78** | **4** | **7** | **11** | **34** | **0** | **0** | **0** | **90** | **4.4** | **–1** | **46** | **32.6** | **13:39** | .... | .... | .... | .... | .... | .... | .... | .... | .... |
| 2008-09 | Rogle | Sweden | 40 | 11 | 10 | 21 | 16 | .... | .... | .... | .... | .... | .... | .... | .... | .... | .... | .... | .... | .... | .... | .... | .... | .... | .... |
| | Rogle | Sweden-Q | 8 | 0 | 2 | 2 | 4 | .... | .... | .... | .... | .... | .... | .... | .... | .... | .... | .... | .... | .... | .... | .... | .... | .... | .... |
| | **NHL Totals** | | **173** | **13** | **19** | **32** | **60** | **0** | **1** | **1** | **181** | **7.2** | | **72** | **38.9** | **11:55** | .... | .... | .... | .... | .... | .... | .... | .... | .... |

Signed as a free agent by **Jonkoping** (Sweden), August 30, 2004. Traded to **Phoenix** by **Dallas** with Dallas' 1st round choice (later traded to Edmonton - Edmonton selected Riley Nash) in 2007 Entry Draft for Ladislav Nagy, February 12, 2007.

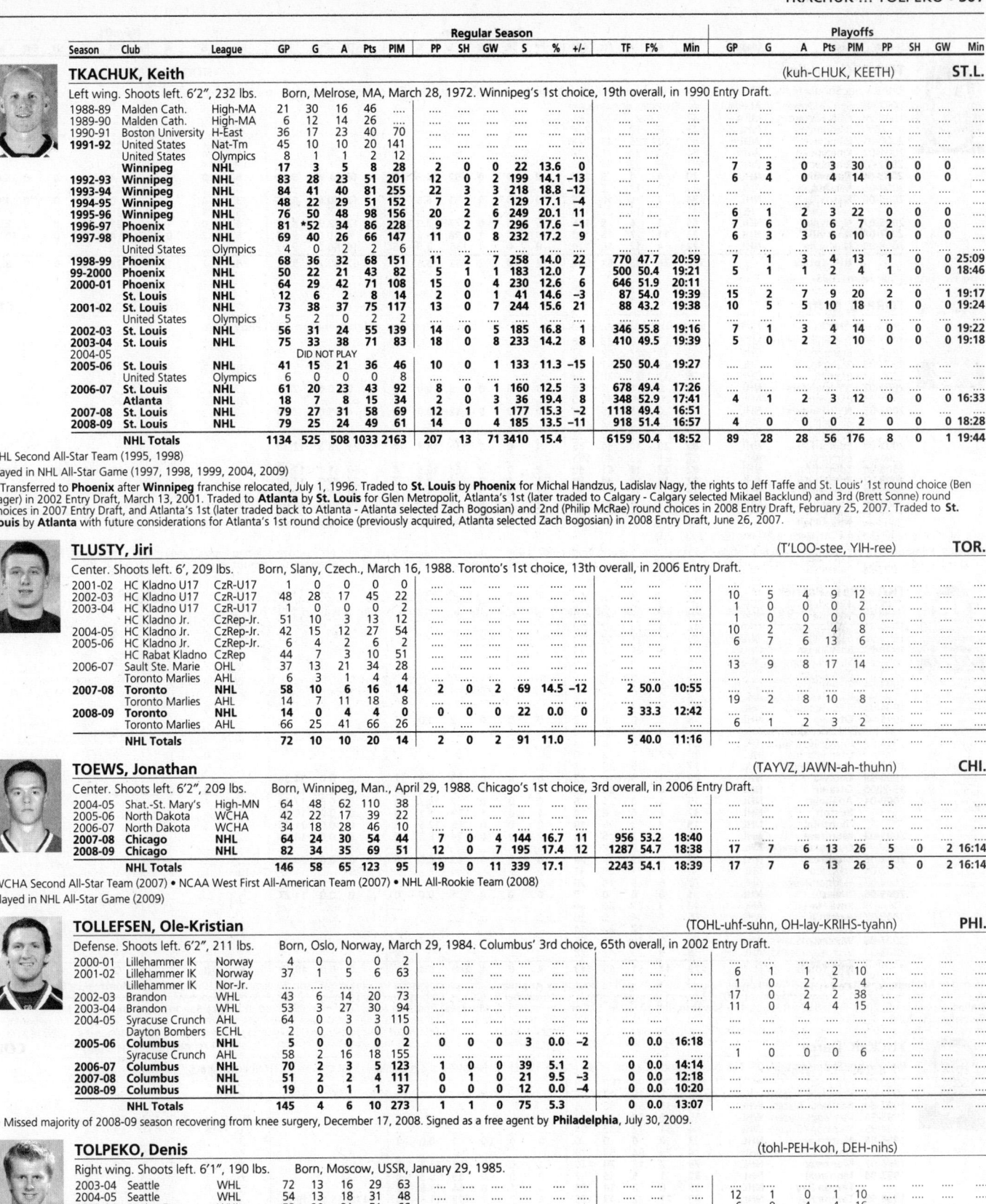

## TKACHUK, Keith
(kuh-CHUK, KEETH) **ST.L.**

Left wing. Shoots left. 6'2", 232 lbs. Born, Melrose, MA, March 28, 1972. Winnipeg's 1st choice, 19th overall, in 1990 Entry Draft.

| Season | Club | League | Regular Season GP | G | A | Pts | PIM | PP | SH | GW | S | % | +/- | TF | F% | Min | Playoffs GP | G | A | Pts | PIM | PP | SH | GW | Min |
|---|---|---|---|---|---|---|---|---|---|---|---|---|---|---|---|---|---|---|---|---|---|---|---|---|---|
| 1988-89 | Malden Cath. | High-MA | 21 | 30 | 16 | 46 | .... | .... | .... | .... | .... | .... | .... | .... | .... | .... | .... | .... | .... | .... | .... | .... | .... | .... | .... |
| 1989-90 | Malden Cath. | High-MA | 6 | 12 | 14 | 26 | .... | .... | .... | .... | .... | .... | .... | .... | .... | .... | .... | .... | .... | .... | .... | .... | .... | .... | .... |
| 1990-91 | Boston University | H-East | 36 | 17 | 23 | 40 | 70 | .... | .... | .... | .... | .... | .... | .... | .... | .... | .... | .... | .... | .... | .... | .... | .... | .... | .... |
| **1991-92** | United States | Nat-Tm | 45 | 10 | 10 | 20 | 141 | .... | .... | .... | .... | .... | .... | .... | .... | .... | .... | .... | .... | .... | .... | .... | .... | .... | .... |
| | United States | Olympics | 8 | 1 | 1 | 2 | 12 | .... | .... | .... | .... | .... | .... | .... | .... | .... | .... | .... | .... | .... | .... | .... | .... | .... | .... |
| | **Winnipeg** | **NHL** | **17** | **3** | **5** | **8** | **28** | **2** | **0** | **0** | **22** | **13.6** | **0** | .... | .... | .... | **7** | **3** | **0** | **3** | **30** | **0** | **0** | **0** | .... |
| **1992-93** | **Winnipeg** | **NHL** | **83** | **28** | **23** | **51** | **201** | **12** | **0** | **2** | **199** | **14.1** | **–13** | .... | .... | .... | **6** | **4** | **0** | **4** | **14** | **1** | **0** | **0** | .... |
| **1993-94** | **Winnipeg** | **NHL** | **84** | **41** | **40** | **81** | **255** | **22** | **3** | **3** | **218** | **18.8** | **–12** | .... | .... | .... | .... | .... | .... | .... | .... | .... | .... | .... | .... |
| **1994-95** | **Winnipeg** | **NHL** | **48** | **22** | **29** | **51** | **152** | **7** | **2** | **2** | **129** | **17.1** | **–4** | .... | .... | .... | .... | .... | .... | .... | .... | .... | .... | .... | .... |
| **1995-96** | **Winnipeg** | **NHL** | **76** | **50** | **48** | **98** | **156** | **20** | **2** | **6** | **249** | **20.1** | **11** | .... | .... | .... | **6** | **1** | **2** | **3** | **22** | **0** | **0** | **0** | .... |
| **1996-97** | **Phoenix** | **NHL** | **81** | ***52** | **34** | **86** | **228** | **9** | **2** | **7** | **296** | **17.6** | **–1** | .... | .... | .... | **7** | **6** | **0** | **6** | **7** | **2** | **0** | **0** | .... |
| **1997-98** | **Phoenix** | **NHL** | **69** | **40** | **26** | **66** | **147** | **11** | **0** | **8** | **232** | **17.2** | **9** | .... | .... | .... | **6** | **3** | **3** | **6** | **10** | **0** | **0** | **0** | .... |
| | United States | Olympics | 4 | 0 | 2 | 2 | 6 | .... | .... | .... | .... | .... | .... | .... | .... | .... | .... | .... | .... | .... | .... | .... | .... | .... | .... |
| **1998-99** | **Phoenix** | **NHL** | **68** | **36** | **32** | **68** | **151** | **11** | **2** | **7** | **258** | **14.0** | **22** | **770** | **47.7** | **20:59** | **7** | **1** | **3** | **4** | **13** | **1** | **0** | **0** | **25:09** |
| **99-2000** | **Phoenix** | **NHL** | **50** | **22** | **21** | **43** | **82** | **5** | **1** | **1** | **183** | **12.0** | **7** | **500** | **50.4** | **19:21** | **5** | **1** | **1** | **2** | **4** | **1** | **0** | **0** | **18:46** |
| **2000-01** | **Phoenix** | **NHL** | **64** | **29** | **42** | **71** | **108** | **15** | **0** | **4** | **230** | **12.6** | **6** | **646** | **51.9** | **20:11** | .... | .... | .... | .... | .... | .... | .... | .... | .... |
| | **St. Louis** | **NHL** | **12** | **6** | **2** | **8** | **14** | **2** | **0** | **1** | **41** | **14.6** | **–3** | **87** | **54.0** | **19:39** | **15** | **2** | **7** | **9** | **20** | **2** | **0** | **1** | **19:17** |
| **2001-02** | **St. Louis** | **NHL** | **73** | **38** | **37** | **75** | **117** | **13** | **0** | **7** | **244** | **15.6** | **21** | **88** | **43.2** | **19:38** | **10** | **5** | **5** | **10** | **18** | **1** | **0** | **0** | **19:24** |
| | United States | Olympics | 5 | 2 | 0 | 2 | 2 | .... | .... | .... | .... | .... | .... | .... | .... | .... | .... | .... | .... | .... | .... | .... | .... | .... | .... |
| **2002-03** | **St. Louis** | **NHL** | **56** | **31** | **24** | **55** | **139** | **14** | **0** | **5** | **185** | **16.8** | **1** | **346** | **55.8** | **19:16** | **7** | **1** | **3** | **4** | **14** | **0** | **0** | **0** | **19:22** |
| **2003-04** | **St. Louis** | **NHL** | **75** | **33** | **38** | **71** | **83** | **18** | **0** | **8** | **233** | **14.2** | **8** | **410** | **49.5** | **19:39** | **5** | **0** | **2** | **2** | **10** | **0** | **0** | **0** | **19:18** |
| 2004-05 | | | DID NOT PLAY | | | | | | | | | | | | | | | | | | | | | | |
| **2005-06** | **St. Louis** | **NHL** | **41** | **15** | **21** | **36** | **46** | **10** | **0** | **1** | **133** | **11.3** | **–15** | **250** | **50.4** | **19:27** | .... | .... | .... | .... | .... | .... | .... | .... | .... |
| | United States | Olympics | 6 | 0 | 0 | 0 | 8 | .... | .... | .... | .... | .... | .... | .... | .... | .... | .... | .... | .... | .... | .... | .... | .... | .... | .... |
| **2006-07** | **St. Louis** | **NHL** | **61** | **20** | **23** | **43** | **92** | **8** | **0** | **1** | **160** | **12.5** | **3** | **678** | **49.4** | **17:26** | .... | .... | .... | .... | .... | .... | .... | .... | .... |
| | **Atlanta** | **NHL** | **18** | **7** | **8** | **15** | **34** | **2** | **0** | **3** | **36** | **19.4** | **8** | **348** | **52.9** | **17:41** | **4** | **1** | **2** | **3** | **12** | **0** | **0** | **0** | **16:33** |
| **2007-08** | **St. Louis** | **NHL** | **79** | **27** | **31** | **58** | **69** | **12** | **1** | **1** | **177** | **15.3** | **–2** | **1118** | **49.4** | **16:51** | .... | .... | .... | .... | .... | .... | .... | .... | .... |
| **2008-09** | **St. Louis** | **NHL** | **79** | **25** | **24** | **49** | **61** | **14** | **0** | **4** | **185** | **13.5** | **–11** | **918** | **51.4** | **16:57** | **4** | **0** | **0** | **0** | **2** | **0** | **0** | **0** | **18:28** |
| | **NHL Totals** | | **1134** | **525** | **508** | **1033** | **2163** | **207** | **13** | **71** | **3410** | **15.4** | | **6159** | **50.4** | **18:52** | **89** | **28** | **28** | **56** | **176** | **8** | **0** | **1** | **19:44** |

NHL Second All-Star Team (1995, 1998)
Played in NHL All-Star Game (1997, 1998, 1999, 2004, 2009)

• Transferred to **Phoenix** after **Winnipeg** franchise relocated, July 1, 1996. Traded to **St. Louis** by **Phoenix** for Michal Handzus, Ladislav Nagy, the rights to Jeff Taffe and St. Louis' 1st round choice (Ben Eager) in 2002 Entry Draft, March 13, 2001. Traded to **Atlanta** by **St. Louis** for Glen Metropolit, Atlanta's 1st (later traded to Calgary - Calgary selected Mikael Backlund) and 3rd (Brett Sonne) round choices in 2007 Entry Draft, and Atlanta's 1st (later traded back to Atlanta - Atlanta selected Zach Bogosian) and 2nd (Philip McRae) round choices in 2008 Entry Draft, February 25, 2007. Traded to **St. Louis** by **Atlanta** with future considerations for Atlanta's 1st round choice (previously acquired, Atlanta selected Zach Bogosian) in 2008 Entry Draft, June 26, 2007.

## TLUSTY, Jiri
(T'LOO-stee, YIH-ree) **TOR.**

Center. Shoots left. 6', 209 lbs. Born, Slany, Czech., March 16, 1988. Toronto's 1st choice, 13th overall, in 2006 Entry Draft.

| Season | Club | League | GP | G | A | Pts | PIM | PP | SH | GW | S | % | +/- | TF | F% | Min | GP | G | A | Pts | PIM | PP | SH | GW | Min |
|---|---|---|---|---|---|---|---|---|---|---|---|---|---|---|---|---|---|---|---|---|---|---|---|---|---|
| 2001-02 | HC Kladno U17 | CzR-U17 | 1 | 0 | 0 | 0 | 0 | .... | .... | .... | .... | .... | .... | .... | .... | .... | .... | .... | .... | .... | .... | .... | .... | .... | .... |
| 2002-03 | HC Kladno U17 | CzR-U17 | 48 | 28 | 17 | 45 | 22 | .... | .... | .... | .... | .... | .... | .... | .... | .... | 10 | 5 | 4 | 9 | 12 | .... | .... | .... | .... |
| 2003-04 | HC Kladno U17 | CzR-U17 | 1 | 0 | 0 | 0 | 2 | .... | .... | .... | .... | .... | .... | .... | .... | .... | 1 | 0 | 0 | 0 | 2 | .... | .... | .... | .... |
| | HC Kladno Jr. | CzRep-Jr. | 51 | 10 | 3 | 13 | 12 | .... | .... | .... | .... | .... | .... | .... | .... | .... | 1 | 0 | 0 | 0 | 0 | .... | .... | .... | .... |
| 2004-05 | HC Kladno Jr. | CzRep-Jr. | 42 | 15 | 12 | 27 | 54 | .... | .... | .... | .... | .... | .... | .... | .... | .... | 10 | 2 | 2 | 4 | 8 | .... | .... | .... | .... |
| 2005-06 | HC Kladno Jr. | CzRep-Jr. | 6 | 4 | 2 | 6 | 2 | .... | .... | .... | .... | .... | .... | .... | .... | .... | 6 | 7 | 6 | 13 | 6 | .... | .... | .... | .... |
| | HC Rabat Kladno | CzRep | 44 | 7 | 3 | 10 | 51 | .... | .... | .... | .... | .... | .... | .... | .... | .... | .... | .... | .... | .... | .... | .... | .... | .... | .... |
| 2006-07 | Sault Ste. Marie | OHL | 37 | 13 | 21 | 34 | 28 | .... | .... | .... | .... | .... | .... | .... | .... | .... | 13 | 9 | 8 | 17 | 14 | .... | .... | .... | .... |
| | Toronto Marlies | AHL | 6 | 3 | 1 | 4 | 4 | .... | .... | .... | .... | .... | .... | .... | .... | .... | .... | .... | .... | .... | .... | .... | .... | .... | .... |
| **2007-08** | **Toronto** | **NHL** | **58** | **10** | **6** | **16** | **14** | **2** | **0** | **2** | **69** | **14.5** | **–12** | **2** | **50.0** | **10:55** | .... | .... | .... | .... | .... | .... | .... | .... | .... |
| | Toronto Marlies | AHL | 14 | 7 | 11 | 18 | 8 | .... | .... | .... | .... | .... | .... | .... | .... | .... | 19 | 2 | 8 | 10 | 8 | .... | .... | .... | .... |
| **2008-09** | **Toronto** | **NHL** | **14** | **0** | **4** | **4** | **0** | **0** | **0** | **0** | **22** | **0.0** | **0** | **3** | **33.3** | **12:42** | .... | .... | .... | .... | .... | .... | .... | .... | .... |
| | Toronto Marlies | AHL | 66 | 25 | 41 | 66 | 26 | .... | .... | .... | .... | .... | .... | .... | .... | .... | 6 | 1 | 2 | 3 | 2 | .... | .... | .... | .... |
| | **NHL Totals** | | **72** | **10** | **10** | **20** | **14** | **2** | **0** | **2** | **91** | **11.0** | | **5** | **40.0** | **11:16** | .... | .... | .... | .... | .... | .... | .... | .... | .... |

## TOEWS, Jonathan
(TAYVZ, JAWN-ah-thuhn) **CHI.**

Center. Shoots left. 6'2", 209 lbs. Born, Winnipeg, Man., April 29, 1988. Chicago's 1st choice, 3rd overall, in 2006 Entry Draft.

| Season | Club | League | GP | G | A | Pts | PIM | PP | SH | GW | S | % | +/- | TF | F% | Min | GP | G | A | Pts | PIM | PP | SH | GW | Min |
|---|---|---|---|---|---|---|---|---|---|---|---|---|---|---|---|---|---|---|---|---|---|---|---|---|---|
| 2004-05 | Shat.-St. Mary's | High-MN | 64 | 48 | 62 | 110 | 38 | .... | .... | .... | .... | .... | .... | .... | .... | .... | .... | .... | .... | .... | .... | .... | .... | .... | .... |
| 2005-06 | North Dakota | WCHA | 42 | 22 | 17 | 39 | 22 | .... | .... | .... | .... | .... | .... | .... | .... | .... | .... | .... | .... | .... | .... | .... | .... | .... | .... |
| 2006-07 | North Dakota | WCHA | 34 | 18 | 28 | 46 | 10 | .... | .... | .... | .... | .... | .... | .... | .... | .... | .... | .... | .... | .... | .... | .... | .... | .... | .... |
| **2007-08** | **Chicago** | **NHL** | **64** | **24** | **30** | **54** | **44** | **7** | **0** | **4** | **144** | **16.7** | **11** | **956** | **53.2** | **18:40** | .... | .... | .... | .... | .... | .... | .... | .... | .... |
| **2008-09** | **Chicago** | **NHL** | **82** | **34** | **35** | **69** | **51** | **12** | **0** | **7** | **195** | **17.4** | **12** | **1287** | **54.7** | **18:38** | **17** | **7** | **6** | **13** | **26** | **5** | **0** | **2** | **16:14** |
| | **NHL Totals** | | **146** | **58** | **65** | **123** | **95** | **19** | **0** | **11** | **339** | **17.1** | | **2243** | **54.1** | **18:39** | **17** | **7** | **6** | **13** | **26** | **5** | **0** | **2** | **16:14** |

WCHA Second All-Star Team (2007) • NCAA West First All-American Team (2007) • NHL All-Rookie Team (2008)
Played in NHL All-Star Game (2009)

## TOLLEFSEN, Ole-Kristian
(TOHL-uhf-suhn, OH-lay-KRIHS-tyahn) **PHI.**

Defense. Shoots left. 6'2", 211 lbs. Born, Oslo, Norway, March 29, 1984. Columbus' 3rd choice, 65th overall, in 2002 Entry Draft.

| Season | Club | League | GP | G | A | Pts | PIM | PP | SH | GW | S | % | +/- | TF | F% | Min | GP | G | A | Pts | PIM | PP | SH | GW | Min |
|---|---|---|---|---|---|---|---|---|---|---|---|---|---|---|---|---|---|---|---|---|---|---|---|---|---|
| 2000-01 | Lillehammer IK | Norway | 4 | 0 | 0 | 0 | 2 | .... | .... | .... | .... | .... | .... | .... | .... | .... | .... | .... | .... | .... | .... | .... | .... | .... | .... |
| 2001-02 | Lillehammer IK | Norway | 37 | 1 | 5 | 6 | 63 | .... | .... | .... | .... | .... | .... | .... | .... | .... | 6 | 1 | 1 | 2 | 10 | .... | .... | .... | .... |
| | Lillehammer IK | Nor-Jr. | .... | .... | .... | .... | .... | .... | .... | .... | .... | .... | .... | .... | .... | .... | 1 | 0 | 2 | 2 | 4 | .... | .... | .... | .... |
| 2002-03 | Brandon | WHL | 43 | 6 | 14 | 20 | 73 | .... | .... | .... | .... | .... | .... | .... | .... | .... | 17 | 0 | 2 | 2 | 38 | .... | .... | .... | .... |
| 2003-04 | Brandon | WHL | 53 | 3 | 27 | 30 | 94 | .... | .... | .... | .... | .... | .... | .... | .... | .... | 11 | 0 | 4 | 4 | 15 | .... | .... | .... | .... |
| 2004-05 | Syracuse Crunch | AHL | 64 | 0 | 3 | 3 | 115 | .... | .... | .... | .... | .... | .... | .... | .... | .... | .... | .... | .... | .... | .... | .... | .... | .... | .... |
| | Dayton Bombers | ECHL | 2 | 0 | 0 | 0 | 0 | .... | .... | .... | .... | .... | .... | .... | .... | .... | .... | .... | .... | .... | .... | .... | .... | .... | .... |
| **2005-06** | **Columbus** | **NHL** | **5** | **0** | **0** | **0** | **2** | **0** | **0** | **0** | **3** | **0.0** | **–2** | **0** | **0.0** | **16:18** | .... | .... | .... | .... | .... | .... | .... | .... | .... |
| | Syracuse Crunch | AHL | 58 | 2 | 16 | 18 | 155 | .... | .... | .... | .... | .... | .... | .... | .... | .... | 1 | 0 | 0 | 0 | 6 | .... | .... | .... | .... |
| **2006-07** | **Columbus** | **NHL** | **70** | **2** | **3** | **5** | **123** | **1** | **0** | **0** | **39** | **5.1** | **2** | **0** | **0.0** | **14:14** | .... | .... | .... | .... | .... | .... | .... | .... | .... |
| **2007-08** | **Columbus** | **NHL** | **51** | **2** | **2** | **4** | **111** | **0** | **1** | **0** | **21** | **9.5** | **–3** | **0** | **0.0** | **12:18** | .... | .... | .... | .... | .... | .... | .... | .... | .... |
| **2008-09** | **Columbus** | **NHL** | **19** | **0** | **1** | **1** | **37** | **0** | **0** | **0** | **12** | **0.0** | **–4** | **0** | **0.0** | **10:20** | .... | .... | .... | .... | .... | .... | .... | .... | .... |
| | **NHL Totals** | | **145** | **4** | **6** | **10** | **273** | **1** | **1** | **0** | **75** | **5.3** | | **0** | **0.0** | **13:07** | .... | .... | .... | .... | .... | .... | .... | .... | .... |

• Missed majority of 2008-09 season recovering from knee surgery, December 17, 2008. Signed as a free agent by **Philadelphia**, July 30, 2009.

## TOLPEKO, Denis
(tohl-PEH-koh, DEH-nihs)

Right wing. Shoots left. 6'1", 190 lbs. Born, Moscow, USSR, January 29, 1985.

| Season | Club | League | GP | G | A | Pts | PIM | PP | SH | GW | S | % | +/- | TF | F% | Min | GP | G | A | Pts | PIM | PP | SH | GW | Min |
|---|---|---|---|---|---|---|---|---|---|---|---|---|---|---|---|---|---|---|---|---|---|---|---|---|---|
| 2003-04 | Seattle | WHL | 72 | 13 | 16 | 29 | 63 | .... | .... | .... | .... | .... | .... | .... | .... | .... | .... | .... | .... | .... | .... | .... | .... | .... | .... |
| 2004-05 | Seattle | WHL | 54 | 13 | 18 | 31 | 48 | .... | .... | .... | .... | .... | .... | .... | .... | .... | 12 | 1 | 0 | 1 | 10 | .... | .... | .... | .... |
| 2005-06 | Regina Pats | WHL | 53 | 20 | 31 | 51 | 66 | .... | .... | .... | .... | .... | .... | .... | .... | .... | 6 | 0 | 4 | 4 | 16 | .... | .... | .... | .... |
| 2006-07 | Philadelphia | AHL | 58 | 11 | 19 | 30 | 58 | .... | .... | .... | .... | .... | .... | .... | .... | .... | .... | .... | .... | .... | .... | .... | .... | .... | .... |
| **2007-08** | **Philadelphia** | **NHL** | **26** | **1** | **5** | **6** | **24** | **0** | **0** | **0** | **24** | **4.2** | **–4** | **0** | **0.0** | **8:17** | .... | .... | .... | .... | .... | .... | .... | .... | .... |
| | Philadelphia | AHL | 24 | 8 | 9 | 17 | 26 | .... | .... | .... | .... | .... | .... | .... | .... | .... | .... | .... | .... | .... | .... | .... | .... | .... | .... |
| 2008-09 | Dynamo Moscow | Rus-KHL | 42 | 3 | 13 | 16 | 42 | .... | .... | .... | .... | .... | .... | .... | .... | .... | 11 | 2 | 1 | 3 | 36 | .... | .... | .... | .... |
| | **NHL Totals** | | **26** | **1** | **5** | **6** | **24** | **0** | **0** | **0** | **24** | **4.2** | | **0** | **0.0** | **8:17** | .... | .... | .... | .... | .... | .... | .... | .... | .... |

Signed as a free agent by **Philadelphia**, July 5, 2006.

| | | | Regular Season | | | | | | | | | | | | | | | Playoffs | | | | | | | | |
|---|---|---|---|---|---|---|---|---|---|---|---|---|---|---|---|---|---|---|---|---|---|---|---|---|---|
| Season | Club | League | GP | G | A | Pts | PIM | PP | SH | GW | S | % | +/- | TF | F% | Min | GP | G | A | Pts | PIM | PP | SH | GW | Min |

## TOOTOO, Jordin

(TOO-TOO, JOHR-dahn) **NSH.**

Right wing. Shoots right. 5'9", 200 lbs. Born, Churchill, Man., February 2, 1983. Nashville's 6th choice, 98th overall, in 2001 Entry Draft.

| Season | Club | League | GP | G | A | Pts | PIM | PP | SH | GW | S | % | +/- | TF | F% | Min | GP | G | A | Pts | PIM | PP | SH | GW | Min |
|---|---|---|---|---|---|---|---|---|---|---|---|---|---|---|---|---|---|---|---|---|---|---|---|---|---|
| 1997-98 | Spruce Grove | AMBHL | STATISTICS NOT AVAILABLE | | | | | | | | | | | | | | | | | | | | | | |
| 1998-99 | OCN Blizzard | MJHL | 47 | 16 | 21 | 37 | 251 | .... | .... | .... | .... | .... | .... | .... | .... | .... | .... | .... | .... | .... | .... | .... | .... | .... | .... |
| 99-2000 | Brandon | WHL | 45 | 6 | 10 | 16 | 214 | .... | .... | .... | .... | .... | .... | .... | .... | .... | .... | .... | .... | .... | .... | .... | .... | .... | .... |
| 2000-01 | Brandon | WHL | 60 | 20 | 28 | 48 | 172 | .... | .... | .... | .... | .... | .... | .... | .... | .... | 6 | 2 | 4 | 6 | 18 | .... | .... | .... | .... |
| 2001-02 | Brandon | WHL | 64 | 32 | 39 | 71 | 272 | .... | .... | .... | .... | .... | .... | .... | .... | .... | 16 | 4 | 3 | 7 | *58 | .... | .... | .... | .... |
| 2002-03 | Brandon | WHL | 51 | 35 | 39 | 74 | 216 | .... | .... | .... | .... | .... | .... | .... | .... | .... | 17 | 6 | 3 | 9 | 49 | .... | .... | .... | .... |
| **2003-04** | **Nashville** | **NHL** | **70** | **4** | **4** | **8** | **137** | **2** | **0** | **0** | **92** | **4.3** | **–6** | **18** | **55.6** | **8:29** | **5** | **0** | **0** | **0** | **4** | **0** | **0** | **0** | **5:09** |
| 2004-05 | Milwaukee | AHL | 59 | 10 | 12 | 22 | 266 | .... | .... | .... | .... | .... | .... | .... | .... | .... | 6 | 0 | 0 | 0 | 41 | .... | .... | .... | .... |
| **2005-06** | **Nashville** | **NHL** | **34** | **4** | **6** | **10** | **55** | **0** | **0** | **0** | **61** | **6.6** | **9** | **17** | **70.6** | **9:15** | **3** | **0** | **0** | **0** | **0** | **0** | **0** | **0** | **4:04** |
| | Milwaukee | AHL | 41 | 13 | 14 | 27 | 133 | .... | .... | .... | .... | .... | .... | .... | .... | .... | 15 | 9 | 2 | 11 | 35 | .... | .... | .... | .... |
| **2006-07** | **Nashville** | **NHL** | **65** | **3** | **6** | **9** | **116** | **0** | **0** | **0** | **77** | **3.9** | **–11** | **12** | **33.3** | **8:24** | **4** | **0** | **1** | **1** | **21** | **0** | **0** | **0** | **9:32** |
| **2007-08** | **Nashville** | **NHL** | **63** | **11** | **7** | **18** | **100** | **0** | **0** | **1** | **98** | **11.2** | **–8** | **4** | **50.0** | **9:54** | **6** | **2** | **0** | **2** | **4** | **0** | **0** | **0** | **12:31** |
| **2008-09** | **Nashville** | **NHL** | **72** | **4** | **12** | **16** | **124** | **0** | **0** | **1** | **138** | **2.9** | **–15** | **16** | **56.3** | **12:05** | .... | .... | .... | .... | .... | .... | .... | .... | .... |
| | **NHL Totals** | | **304** | **26** | **35** | **61** | **532** | **2** | **0** | **2** | **466** | **5.6** | | **67** | **55.2** | **9:42** | **18** | **2** | **1** | **3** | **29** | **0** | **0** | **0** | **8:24** |

WHL East First All-Star Team (2003)

## TORRES, Raffi

(TOHR-ehz, RA-fee) **CBJ**

Left wing. Shoots left. 6', 223 lbs. Born, Toronto, Ont., October 8, 1981. NY Islanders' 2nd choice, 5th overall, in 2000 Entry Draft.

| Season | Club | League | GP | G | A | Pts | PIM | PP | SH | GW | S | % | +/- | TF | F% | Min | GP | G | A | Pts | PIM | PP | SH | GW | Min |
|---|---|---|---|---|---|---|---|---|---|---|---|---|---|---|---|---|---|---|---|---|---|---|---|---|---|
| 1997-98 | Thornhill Rattlers | MTJHL | 46 | 17 | 16 | 33 | 90 | .... | .... | .... | .... | .... | .... | .... | .... | .... | .... | .... | .... | .... | .... | .... | .... | .... | .... |
| 1998-99 | Brampton | OHL | 62 | 35 | 27 | 62 | 32 | .... | .... | .... | .... | .... | .... | .... | .... | .... | .... | .... | .... | .... | .... | .... | .... | .... | .... |
| 99-2000 | Brampton | OHL | 68 | 43 | 48 | 91 | 40 | .... | .... | .... | .... | .... | .... | .... | .... | .... | 6 | 5 | 2 | 7 | 23 | .... | .... | .... | .... |
| 2000-01 | Brampton | OHL | 55 | 33 | 37 | 70 | 76 | .... | .... | .... | .... | .... | .... | .... | .... | .... | 8 | 7 | 4 | 11 | 19 | .... | .... | .... | .... |
| **2001-02** | **NY Islanders** | **NHL** | **14** | **0** | **1** | **1** | **6** | **0** | **0** | **0** | **9** | **0.0** | **2** | **0** | **0.0** | **7:35** | .... | .... | .... | .... | .... | .... | .... | .... | .... |
| | Bridgeport | AHL | 59 | 20 | 10 | 30 | 45 | .... | .... | .... | .... | .... | .... | .... | .... | .... | 20 | 8 | 9 | 17 | 26 | .... | .... | .... | .... |
| **2002-03** | **NY Islanders** | **NHL** | **17** | **0** | **5** | **5** | **10** | **0** | **0** | **0** | **12** | **0.0** | **0** | **4** | **25.0** | **7:40** | .... | .... | .... | .... | .... | .... | .... | .... | .... |
| | Bridgeport | AHL | 49 | 17 | 15 | 32 | 54 | .... | .... | .... | .... | .... | .... | .... | .... | .... | .... | .... | .... | .... | .... | .... | .... | .... | .... |
| | Hamilton | AHL | 11 | 1 | 7 | 8 | 14 | .... | .... | .... | .... | .... | .... | .... | .... | .... | 23 | 6 | 1 | 7 | 29 | .... | .... | .... | .... |
| **2003-04** | **Edmonton** | **NHL** | **80** | **20** | **14** | **34** | **65** | **5** | **0** | **3** | **136** | **14.7** | **12** | **21** | **28.6** | **12:38** | .... | .... | .... | .... | .... | .... | .... | .... | .... |
| 2004-05 | Edmonton | AHL | 67 | 21 | 25 | 46 | 165 | .... | .... | .... | .... | .... | .... | .... | .... | .... | .... | .... | .... | .... | .... | .... | .... | .... | .... |
| **2005-06** | **Edmonton** | **NHL** | **82** | **27** | **14** | **41** | **50** | **6** | **0** | **3** | **164** | **16.5** | **4** | **60** | **41.7** | **13:24** | **22** | **4** | **7** | **11** | **16** | **1** | **0** | **1** | **13:15** |
| **2006-07** | **Edmonton** | **NHL** | **82** | **15** | **19** | **34** | **88** | **1** | **0** | **0** | **154** | **9.7** | **–7** | **50** | **44.0** | **14:19** | .... | .... | .... | .... | .... | .... | .... | .... | .... |
| **2007-08** | **Edmonton** | **NHL** | **32** | **5** | **6** | **11** | **36** | **1** | **0** | **2** | **87** | **5.7** | **–4** | **20** | **65.0** | **17:01** | .... | .... | .... | .... | .... | .... | .... | .... | .... |
| **2008-09** | **Columbus** | **NHL** | **51** | **12** | **8** | **20** | **23** | **2** | **0** | **6** | **74** | **16.2** | **–4** | **19** | **57.9** | **12:06** | **4** | **0** | **2** | **2** | **2** | **0** | **0** | **0** | **12:04** |
| | **NHL Totals** | | **358** | **79** | **67** | **146** | **278** | **15** | **0** | **14** | **636** | **12.4** | | **174** | **44.8** | **13:05** | **26** | **4** | **9** | **13** | **18** | **1** | **0** | **1** | **13:04** |

OHL All-Rookie Team (1999) • OHL Second All-Star Team (2000, 2001)

Traded to **Edmonton** by **NY Islanders** with Brad Isbister for Janne Niinimaa and Washington's 2nd round choice (previously acquired, NY Islanders selected Evgeni Tunik) in 2003 Entry Draft, March 11, 2003. • Missed majority of 2007-08 season recovering from knee injury suffered in game vs. Detroit, December 15, 2007. Traded to **Columbus** by **Edmonton** for Gilbert Brule, July 1, 2008.

## TRAVERSE, Patrick

(tra-VAIRZ, PAT-rihk)

Defense. Shoots left. 6'4", 207 lbs. Born, Montreal, Que., March 14, 1974. Ottawa's 3rd choice, 50th overall, in 1992 Entry Draft.

| Season | Club | League | GP | G | A | Pts | PIM | PP | SH | GW | S | % | +/- | TF | F% | Min | GP | G | A | Pts | PIM | PP | SH | GW | Min |
|---|---|---|---|---|---|---|---|---|---|---|---|---|---|---|---|---|---|---|---|---|---|---|---|---|---|
| 1990-91 | Mtl-Bourassa | QAAA | 42 | 4 | 19 | 23 | 10 | .... | .... | .... | .... | .... | .... | .... | .... | .... | 5 | 0 | 3 | 3 | 2 | .... | .... | .... | .... |
| 1991-92 | Shawinigan | QMJHL | 59 | 3 | 11 | 14 | 12 | .... | .... | .... | .... | .... | .... | .... | .... | .... | 10 | 0 | 0 | 0 | 4 | .... | .... | .... | .... |
| 1992-93 | Shawinigan | QMJHL | 53 | 5 | 24 | 29 | 24 | .... | .... | .... | .... | .... | .... | .... | .... | .... | .... | .... | .... | .... | .... | .... | .... | .... | .... |
| | St-Jean Lynx | QMJHL | 15 | 1 | 6 | 7 | 0 | .... | .... | .... | .... | .... | .... | .... | .... | .... | 4 | 0 | 1 | 1 | 2 | .... | .... | .... | .... |
| | New Haven | AHL | 2 | 0 | 0 | 0 | 2 | .... | .... | .... | .... | .... | .... | .... | .... | .... | .... | .... | .... | .... | .... | .... | .... | .... | .... |
| 1993-94 | St-Jean Lynx | QMJHL | 66 | 15 | 37 | 52 | 30 | .... | .... | .... | .... | .... | .... | .... | .... | .... | 5 | 0 | 4 | 4 | 4 | .... | .... | .... | .... |
| | P.E.I. Senators | AHL | 3 | 0 | 1 | 1 | 2 | .... | .... | .... | .... | .... | .... | .... | .... | .... | .... | .... | .... | .... | .... | .... | .... | .... | .... |
| 1994-95 | P.E.I. Senators | AHL | 70 | 5 | 13 | 18 | 19 | .... | .... | .... | .... | .... | .... | .... | .... | .... | 7 | 0 | 2 | 2 | 0 | .... | .... | .... | .... |
| **1995-96** | **Ottawa** | **NHL** | **5** | **0** | **0** | **0** | **2** | **0** | **0** | **0** | **2** | **0.0** | **–1** | .... | .... | .... | .... | .... | .... | .... | .... | .... | .... | .... | .... |
| | P.E.I. Senators | AHL | 55 | 4 | 21 | 25 | 32 | .... | .... | .... | .... | .... | .... | .... | .... | .... | 5 | 1 | 2 | 3 | 2 | .... | .... | .... | .... |
| 1996-97 | Worcester IceCats | AHL | 24 | 0 | 4 | 4 | 23 | .... | .... | .... | .... | .... | .... | .... | .... | .... | .... | .... | .... | .... | .... | .... | .... | .... | .... |
| | Grand Rapids | IHL | 10 | 2 | 1 | 3 | 10 | .... | .... | .... | .... | .... | .... | .... | .... | .... | 2 | 0 | 1 | 1 | 2 | .... | .... | .... | .... |
| 1997-98 | Hershey Bears | AHL | 71 | 14 | 15 | 29 | 67 | .... | .... | .... | .... | .... | .... | .... | .... | .... | 7 | 1 | 3 | 4 | 4 | .... | .... | .... | .... |
| **1998-99** | **Ottawa** | **NHL** | **46** | **1** | **9** | **10** | **22** | **0** | **0** | **0** | **35** | **2.9** | **12** | **0** | **0.0** | **14:56** | .... | .... | .... | .... | .... | .... | .... | .... | .... |
| **99-2000** | **Ottawa** | **NHL** | **66** | **6** | **17** | **23** | **21** | **1** | **0** | **0** | **73** | **8.2** | **17** | **0** | **0.0** | **18:43** | **6** | **0** | **0** | **0** | **2** | **0** | **0** | **0** | **17:50** |
| **2000-01** | **Anaheim** | **NHL** | **15** | **1** | **0** | **1** | **6** | **0** | **0** | **0** | **7** | **14.3** | **–6** | **0** | **0.0** | **17:19** | .... | .... | .... | .... | .... | .... | .... | .... | .... |
| | **Boston** | **NHL** | **37** | **2** | **6** | **8** | **14** | **1** | **0** | **1** | **39** | **5.1** | **4** | **0** | **0.0** | **16:38** | .... | .... | .... | .... | .... | .... | .... | .... | .... |
| | **Montreal** | **NHL** | **19** | **2** | **3** | **5** | **10** | **0** | **0** | **0** | **16** | **12.5** | **–8** | **0** | **0.0** | **21:36** | .... | .... | .... | .... | .... | .... | .... | .... | .... |
| **2001-02** | **Montreal** | **NHL** | **25** | **2** | **3** | **5** | **14** | **2** | **0** | **0** | **24** | **8.3** | **–7** | **0** | **0.0** | **18:14** | .... | .... | .... | .... | .... | .... | .... | .... | .... |
| | Quebec Citadelles | AHL | 4 | 0 | 2 | 2 | 4 | .... | .... | .... | .... | .... | .... | .... | .... | .... | .... | .... | .... | .... | .... | .... | .... | .... | .... |
| **2002-03** | **Montreal** | **NHL** | **65** | **0** | **13** | **13** | **24** | **0** | **0** | **0** | **63** | **0.0** | **–9** | **0** | **0.0** | **20:12** | .... | .... | .... | .... | .... | .... | .... | .... | .... |
| 2003-04 | Hamilton | AHL | 80 | 5 | 21 | 26 | 31 | .... | .... | .... | .... | .... | .... | .... | .... | .... | 10 | 1 | 2 | 3 | 0 | .... | .... | .... | .... |
| 2004-05 | Houston Aeros | AHL | 72 | 6 | 9 | 15 | 28 | .... | .... | .... | .... | .... | .... | .... | .... | .... | 5 | 0 | 0 | 0 | 2 | .... | .... | .... | .... |
| **2005-06** | **Dallas** | **NHL** | **1** | **0** | **0** | **0** | **0** | **0** | **0** | **0** | **1** | **0.0** | **0** | **0** | **0.0** | **11:27** | .... | .... | .... | .... | .... | .... | .... | .... | .... |
| | Iowa Stars | AHL | 40 | 3 | 21 | 24 | 16 | .... | .... | .... | .... | .... | .... | .... | .... | .... | 7 | 1 | 2 | 3 | 2 | .... | .... | .... | .... |
| 2006-07 | Hamilton | AHL | 26 | 1 | 4 | 5 | 10 | .... | .... | .... | .... | .... | .... | .... | .... | .... | .... | .... | .... | .... | .... | .... | .... | .... | .... |
| | Worcester Sharks | AHL | 54 | 5 | 17 | 22 | 14 | .... | .... | .... | .... | .... | .... | .... | .... | .... | 6 | 0 | 2 | 2 | 2 | .... | .... | .... | .... |
| 2007-08 | Worcester Sharks | AHL | 65 | 6 | 19 | 25 | 52 | .... | .... | .... | .... | .... | .... | .... | .... | .... | .... | .... | .... | .... | .... | .... | .... | .... | .... |
| 2008-09 | Worcester Sharks | AHL | 78 | 9 | 33 | 42 | 28 | .... | .... | .... | .... | .... | .... | .... | .... | .... | 12 | 4 | 5 | 9 | 4 | .... | .... | .... | .... |
| | **NHL Totals** | | **279** | **14** | **51** | **65** | **113** | **4** | **0** | **1** | **260** | **5.4** | | **0** | **0.0** | **18:12** | **6** | **0** | **0** | **0** | **2** | **0** | **0** | **0** | **17:50** |

Traded to **Anaheim** by **Ottawa** for Joel Kwiatkowski, June 12, 2000. Traded to **Boston** by **Anaheim** with Andrei Nazarov for Samuel Pahlsson, November 18, 2000. Traded to **Montreal** by **Boston** for Eric Weinrich, February 21, 2001. • Missed majority of 2001-02 season recovering from knee (November 3, 2001 vs. Calgary) and head (January 10, 2002 vs. NY Islanders) injuries. Signed as a free agent by **Dallas**, September 9, 2004. Signed as a free agent by **San Jose**, July 10, 2006. Claimed on waivers by **Montreal** from **San Jose**, September 28, 2006. Traded to **San Jose** by **Montreal** for Mathieu Biron, December 15, 2006.

## TUCKER, Darcy

(TUH-kuhr, DAHR-see) **COL.**

Right wing. Shoots left. 5'10", 178 lbs. Born, Castor, Alta., March 15, 1975. Montreal's 8th choice, 151st overall, in 1993 Entry Draft.

| Season | Club | League | GP | G | A | Pts | PIM | PP | SH | GW | S | % | +/- | TF | F% | Min | GP | G | A | Pts | PIM | PP | SH | GW | Min |
|---|---|---|---|---|---|---|---|---|---|---|---|---|---|---|---|---|---|---|---|---|---|---|---|---|---|
| 1990-91 | Red Deer | AMHL | 47 | 70 | 90 | 160 | 48 | .... | .... | .... | .... | .... | .... | .... | .... | .... | .... | .... | .... | .... | .... | .... | .... | .... | .... |
| 1991-92 | Kamloops Blazers | WHL | 26 | 3 | 10 | 13 | 32 | .... | .... | .... | .... | .... | .... | .... | .... | .... | 9 | 0 | 1 | 1 | 16 | .... | .... | .... | .... |
| 1992-93 | Kamloops Blazers | WHL | 67 | 31 | 58 | 89 | 155 | .... | .... | .... | .... | .... | .... | .... | .... | .... | 13 | 7 | 6 | 13 | 34 | .... | .... | .... | .... |
| 1993-94 | Kamloops Blazers | WHL | 66 | 52 | 88 | 140 | 143 | .... | .... | .... | .... | .... | .... | .... | .... | .... | 19 | 9 | *18 | *27 | 43 | .... | .... | .... | .... |
| 1994-95 | Kamloops Blazers | WHL | 64 | 64 | 73 | 137 | 94 | .... | .... | .... | .... | .... | .... | .... | .... | .... | 21 | *16 | 15 | *31 | 19 | .... | .... | .... | .... |
| **1995-96** | **Montreal** | **NHL** | **3** | **0** | **0** | **0** | **0** | **0** | **0** | **0** | **1** | **0.0** | **–1** | .... | .... | .... | .... | .... | .... | .... | .... | .... | .... | .... | .... |
| | Fredericton | AHL | 74 | 29 | 64 | 93 | 174 | .... | .... | .... | .... | .... | .... | .... | .... | .... | 7 | 7 | 3 | 10 | 14 | .... | .... | .... | .... |
| **1996-97** | **Montreal** | **NHL** | **73** | **7** | **13** | **20** | **110** | **1** | **0** | **3** | **62** | **11.3** | **–5** | .... | .... | .... | **4** | **0** | **0** | **0** | **0** | **0** | **0** | **0** | |
| **1997-98** | **Montreal** | **NHL** | **39** | **1** | **5** | **6** | **57** | **0** | **0** | **0** | **19** | **5.3** | **–6** | .... | .... | .... | .... | .... | .... | .... | .... | .... | .... | .... | .... |
| | **Tampa Bay** | **NHL** | **35** | **6** | **8** | **14** | **89** | **1** | **1** | **0** | **44** | **13.6** | **–8** | .... | .... | .... | .... | .... | .... | .... | .... | .... | .... | .... | .... |
| **1998-99** | **Tampa Bay** | **NHL** | **82** | **21** | **22** | **43** | **176** | **8** | **2** | **3** | **178** | **11.8** | **–34** | **1470** | **45.6** | **19:24** | .... | .... | .... | .... | .... | .... | .... | .... | .... |
| **99-2000** | **Tampa Bay** | **NHL** | **50** | **14** | **20** | **34** | **108** | **1** | **0** | **2** | **98** | **14.3** | **–15** | **152** | **48.7** | **19:58** | .... | .... | .... | .... | .... | .... | .... | .... | .... |
| | **Toronto** | **NHL** | **27** | **7** | **10** | **17** | **55** | **0** | **2** | **3** | **40** | **17.5** | **3** | **11** | **54.6** | **16:41** | **12** | **4** | **2** | **6** | **15** | **1** | **0** | **2** | **17:23** |
| **2000-01** | **Toronto** | **NHL** | **82** | **16** | **21** | **37** | **141** | **2** | **0** | **4** | **122** | **13.1** | **6** | **413** | **47.0** | **16:09** | **11** | **0** | **2** | **2** | **6** | **0** | **0** | **0** | **13:59** |
| **2001-02** | **Toronto** | **NHL** | **77** | **24** | **35** | **59** | **92** | **7** | **0** | **5** | **124** | **19.4** | **24** | **138** | **43.5** | **16:59** | **17** | **4** | **4** | **8** | **38** | **1** | **0** | **1** | **16:50** |
| **2002-03** | **Toronto** | **NHL** | **77** | **10** | **26** | **36** | **119** | **4** | **1** | **2** | **108** | **9.3** | **–7** | **68** | **45.6** | **15:21** | **6** | **0** | **3** | **3** | **6** | **0** | **0** | **0** | **21:07** |
| **2003-04** | **Toronto** | **NHL** | **64** | **21** | **11** | **32** | **68** | **8** | **1** | **2** | **146** | **14.4** | **4** | **136** | **50.7** | **17:50** | **12** | **2** | **0** | **2** | **14** | **1** | **0** | **0** | **13:54** |
| 2004-05 | | | DID NOT PLAY | | | | | | | | | | | | | | | | | | | | | | |
| **2005-06** | **Toronto** | **NHL** | **74** | **28** | **33** | **61** | **100** | **18** | **0** | **4** | **189** | **14.8** | **–12** | **29** | **58.6** | **17:38** | .... | .... | .... | .... | .... | .... | .... | .... | .... |
| **2006-07** | **Toronto** | **NHL** | **56** | **24** | **19** | **43** | **81** | **15** | **0** | **6** | **143** | **16.8** | **–11** | **15** | **40.0** | **17:47** | .... | .... | .... | .... | .... | .... | .... | .... | .... |

| | | | Regular Season | | | | | | | | | | | | | | Playoffs | | | | | | | | |
|---|---|---|---|---|---|---|---|---|---|---|---|---|---|---|---|---|---|---|---|---|---|---|---|---|---|
| Season | Club | League | GP | G | A | Pts | PIM | PP | SH | GW | S | % | +/- | TF | F% | Min | GP | G | A | Pts | PIM | PP | SH | GW | Min |
| **2007-08** | **Toronto** | **NHL** | **74** | **18** | **16** | **34** | **100** | **7** | **0** | **3** | **152** | **11.8** | **–8** | **25** | **52.0** | **16:26** | .... | .... | .... | .... | .... | .... | .... | .... | .... |
| **2008-09** | **Colorado** | **NHL** | **63** | **8** | **8** | **16** | **67** | **2** | **0** | **1** | **94** | **8.5** | **–13** | **35** | **42.9** | **14:07** | .... | .... | .... | .... | .... | .... | .... | .... | .... |
| | **NHL Totals** | | **876** | **205** | **247** | **452** | **1363** | **74** | **7** | **38** | **1520** | **13.5** | | **2492** | **46.3** | **17:05** | **62** | **10** | **11** | **21** | **79** | **3** | **0** | **3** | **16:15** |

WHL West First All-Star Team (1994, 1995) • Canadian Major Junior First All-Star Team (1994) • Memorial Cup Tournament All-Star Team (1994, 1995) • Stafford Smythe Memorial Trophy (Memorial Cup Tournament - MVP) (1994) • Dudley "Red" Garrett Memorial Award (AHL – Rookie of the Year) (1996)

Traded to **Tampa Bay** by **Montreal** with Stephane Richer and David Wilkie for Patrick Poulin, Mick Vukota and Igor Ulanov, January 15, 1998. Traded to **Toronto** by **Tampa Bay** with Tampa Bay's 4th round choice (Miguel Delisle) in 2000 Entry Draft for Mike Johnson, Marek Posmyk and Toronto's 5th (Pavel Sedov) and 6th (Aaron Gionet) round choices in 2000 Entry Draft, February 9, 2000. Signed as a free agent by **Colorado**, July 1, 2008.

## TUKONEN, Lauri

(too-KOH-nehn, LOW-ree) **T.B.**

Right wing. Shoots right. 6'2", 200 lbs. Born, Hyvinkaa, Finland, September 1, 1986. Los Angeles' 1st choice, 11th overall, in 2004 Entry Draft.

| Season | Club | League | GP | G | A | Pts | PIM | PP | SH | GW | S | % | +/- | TF | F% | Min | GP | G | A | Pts | PIM | PP | SH | GW | Min |
|---|---|---|---|---|---|---|---|---|---|---|---|---|---|---|---|---|---|---|---|---|---|---|---|---|---|
| 2001-02 | Ahmat Jr. | Fin-Jr. | 2 | 4 | 0 | 4 | 2 | .... | .... | .... | .... | .... | .... | .... | .... | .... | .... | .... | .... | .... | .... | .... | .... | .... | .... |
| | Ahmat Hyvinkaa | Finland-2 | 24 | 7 | 4 | 11 | 6 | .... | .... | .... | .... | .... | .... | .... | .... | .... | .... | .... | .... | .... | .... | .... | .... | .... | .... |
| | HC Sunne | Sweden-3 | 2 | 4 | 0 | 4 | 2 | .... | .... | .... | .... | .... | .... | .... | .... | .... | .... | .... | .... | .... | .... | .... | .... | .... | .... |
| 2002-03 | Ahmat Jr. | Fin-Jr. | 4 | 3 | 1 | 4 | 2 | .... | .... | .... | .... | .... | .... | .... | .... | .... | .... | .... | .... | .... | .... | .... | .... | .... | .... |
| | Ahmat Hyvinkaa | Finland-2 | 12 | 2 | 2 | 4 | 2 | .... | .... | .... | .... | .... | .... | .... | .... | .... | .... | .... | .... | .... | .... | .... | .... | .... | .... |
| | Blues Espoo Jr. | Fin-Jr. | 17 | 6 | 6 | 12 | 18 | .... | .... | .... | .... | .... | .... | .... | .... | .... | 5 | 0 | 0 | 0 | 10 | .... | .... | .... | .... |
| 2003-04 | Suomi U20 | Finland-2 | 6 | 0 | 0 | 0 | 6 | .... | .... | .... | .... | .... | .... | .... | .... | .... | .... | .... | .... | .... | .... | .... | .... | .... | .... |
| | Blues Espoo Jr. | Fin-Jr. | 14 | 14 | 9 | 23 | 4 | .... | .... | .... | .... | .... | .... | .... | .... | .... | .... | .... | .... | .... | .... | .... | .... | .... | .... |
| | Blues Espoo | Finland | 35 | 3 | 3 | 6 | 16 | .... | .... | .... | .... | .... | .... | .... | .... | .... | 7 | 0 | 0 | 0 | 0 | .... | .... | .... | .... |
| 2004-05 | Blues Espoo Jr. | Fin-Jr. | 2 | 0 | 0 | 0 | 2 | .... | .... | .... | .... | .... | .... | .... | .... | .... | .... | .... | .... | .... | .... | .... | .... | .... | .... |
| | Blues Espoo | Finland | 43 | 5 | 5 | 10 | 10 | .... | .... | .... | .... | .... | .... | .... | .... | .... | .... | .... | .... | .... | .... | .... | .... | .... | .... |
| 2005-06 | Manchester | AHL | 62 | 14 | 22 | 36 | 20 | .... | .... | .... | .... | .... | .... | .... | .... | .... | .... | .... | .... | .... | .... | .... | .... | .... | .... |
| **2006-07** | **Los Angeles** | **NHL** | **4** | **0** | **0** | **0** | **0** | **0** | **0** | **0** | **1** | **0.0** | **–2** | **0** | **0.0** | **6:33** | .... | .... | .... | .... | .... | .... | .... | .... | .... |
| | Manchester | AHL | 61 | 13 | 19 | 32 | 30 | .... | .... | .... | .... | .... | .... | .... | .... | .... | 6 | 0 | 3 | 3 | 0 | .... | .... | .... | .... |
| **2007-08** | **Los Angeles** | **NHL** | **1** | **0** | **0** | **0** | **0** | **0** | **0** | **0** | **1** | **0.0** | **0** | **0** | **0.0** | **9:48** | .... | .... | .... | .... | .... | .... | .... | .... | .... |
| | Manchester | AHL | 62 | 9 | 26 | 35 | 24 | .... | .... | .... | .... | .... | .... | .... | .... | .... | 2 | 0 | 0 | 0 | 0 | .... | .... | .... | .... |
| 2008-09 | Ilves Tampere | Finland | 21 | 5 | 8 | 13 | 22 | .... | .... | .... | .... | .... | .... | .... | .... | .... | .... | .... | .... | .... | .... | .... | .... | .... | .... |
| | Lukko Rauma | Finland | 14 | 3 | 5 | 8 | 2 | .... | .... | .... | .... | .... | .... | .... | .... | .... | .... | .... | .... | .... | .... | .... | .... | .... | .... |
| | **NHL Totals** | | **5** | **0** | **0** | **0** | **0** | **0** | **0** | **0** | **2** | **0.0** | | **0** | **0.0** | **7:12** | .... | .... | .... | .... | .... | .... | .... | .... | .... |

Traded to **Dallas** by **Los Angeles** for Richard Clune, July 21, 2008. • Assigned to **Ilves Tampere** (Finland) by **Dallas**, September 26, 2008. Traded to **Tampa Bay** by **Dallas** for Andrew Hutchinson, November 30, 2008.

## TURRIS, Kyle

(TUH-rihs, KIGHL) **PHX.**

Center. Shoots right. 6'1", 180 lbs. Born, New Westminster, B.C., August 14, 1989. Phoenix's 1st choice, 3rd overall, in 2007 Entry Draft.

| Season | Club | League | GP | G | A | Pts | PIM | PP | SH | GW | S | % | +/- | TF | F% | Min | GP | G | A | Pts | PIM | PP | SH | GW | Min |
|---|---|---|---|---|---|---|---|---|---|---|---|---|---|---|---|---|---|---|---|---|---|---|---|---|---|
| 2004-05 | Grandview | Minor-BC | 30 | 13 | 20 | 33 | .... | .... | .... | .... | .... | .... | .... | .... | .... | .... | 12 | 3 | 6 | 9 | .... | .... | .... | .... | .... |
| 2005-06 | Burnaby Express | BCHL | 57 | 36 | 36 | 72 | 32 | .... | .... | .... | .... | .... | .... | .... | .... | .... | 20 | 10 | 13 | 23 | 6 | .... | .... | .... | .... |
| 2006-07 | Burnaby Express | BCHL | 53 | 66 | 55 | 121 | 83 | .... | .... | .... | .... | .... | .... | .... | .... | .... | 14 | 12 | 14 | 26 | 16 | .... | .... | .... | .... |
| **2007-08** | U. of Wisconsin | WCHA | 36 | 11 | 24 | 35 | 38 | .... | .... | .... | .... | .... | .... | .... | .... | .... | .... | .... | .... | .... | .... | .... | .... | .... | .... |
| | **Phoenix** | **NHL** | **3** | **0** | **1** | **1** | **2** | **0** | **0** | **0** | **11** | **0.0** | **–5** | **42** | **40.5** | **19:45** | .... | .... | .... | .... | .... | .... | .... | .... | .... |
| **2008-09** | **Phoenix** | **NHL** | **63** | **8** | **12** | **20** | **21** | **3** | **0** | **3** | **91** | **8.8** | **–15** | **567** | **42.9** | **12:55** | .... | .... | .... | .... | .... | .... | .... | .... | .... |
| | San Antonio | AHL | 8 | 4 | 3 | 7 | 6 | .... | .... | .... | .... | .... | .... | .... | .... | .... | .... | .... | .... | .... | .... | .... | .... | .... | .... |
| | **NHL Totals** | | **66** | **8** | **13** | **21** | **23** | **3** | **0** | **3** | **102** | **7.8** | | **609** | **42.7** | **13:14** | .... | .... | .... | .... | .... | .... | .... | .... | .... |

WCHA All-Rookie Team (2008)

## TYUTIN, Fedor

(T'YOO-tihn, FEH-duhr) **CBJ**

Defense. Shoots left. 6'3", 216 lbs. Born, Izhevsk, USSR, July 19, 1983. NY Rangers' 2nd choice, 40th overall, in 2001 Entry Draft.

| Season | Club | League | GP | G | A | Pts | PIM | PP | SH | GW | S | % | +/- | TF | F% | Min | GP | G | A | Pts | PIM | PP | SH | GW | Min |
|---|---|---|---|---|---|---|---|---|---|---|---|---|---|---|---|---|---|---|---|---|---|---|---|---|---|
| 1998-99 | Magnitogorsk 2 | Russia-4 | 7 | 0 | 1 | 1 | 2 | .... | .... | .... | .... | .... | .... | .... | .... | .... | .... | .... | .... | .... | .... | .... | .... | .... | .... |
| 99-2000 | Izhstal Izhevsk 2 | Russia-3 | 38 | 11 | 8 | 19 | 68 | .... | .... | .... | .... | .... | .... | .... | .... | .... | .... | .... | .... | .... | .... | .... | .... | .... | .... |
| | Izhstal Izhevsk | Russia-2 | 10 | 0 | 1 | 1 | 12 | .... | .... | .... | .... | .... | .... | .... | .... | .... | .... | .... | .... | .... | .... | .... | .... | .... | .... |
| 2000-01 | St. Petersburg | Russia | 34 | 2 | 4 | 6 | 20 | .... | .... | .... | .... | .... | .... | .... | .... | .... | .... | .... | .... | .... | .... | .... | .... | .... | .... |
| 2001-02 | Guelph Storm | OHL | 53 | 19 | 40 | 59 | 54 | .... | .... | .... | .... | .... | .... | .... | .... | .... | 9 | 2 | 8 | 10 | 8 | .... | .... | .... | .... |
| 2002-03 | St. Petersburg | Russia | 10 | 1 | 1 | 2 | 16 | .... | .... | .... | .... | .... | .... | .... | .... | .... | .... | .... | .... | .... | .... | .... | .... | .... | .... |
| | Ak Bars Kazan | Russia | 10 | 0 | 0 | 0 | 8 | .... | .... | .... | .... | .... | .... | .... | .... | .... | 5 | 0 | 0 | 0 | 4 | .... | .... | .... | .... |
| **2003-04** | **NY Rangers** | **NHL** | **25** | **2** | **5** | **7** | **14** | **0** | **1** | **0** | **33** | **6.1** | **–4** | **1** | **0.0** | **20:08** | .... | .... | .... | .... | .... | .... | .... | .... | .... |
| | Hartford | AHL | 43 | 5 | 9 | 14 | 50 | .... | .... | .... | .... | .... | .... | .... | .... | .... | 16 | 0 | 5 | 5 | 18 | .... | .... | .... | .... |
| 2004-05 | Hartford | AHL | 13 | 2 | 1 | 3 | 10 | .... | .... | .... | .... | .... | .... | .... | .... | .... | .... | .... | .... | .... | .... | .... | .... | .... | .... |
| | St. Petersburg | Russia | 35 | 5 | 3 | 8 | 24 | .... | .... | .... | .... | .... | .... | .... | .... | .... | .... | .... | .... | .... | .... | .... | .... | .... | .... |
| **2005-06** | **NY Rangers** | **NHL** | **77** | **6** | **19** | **25** | **58** | **4** | **0** | **2** | **102** | **5.9** | **1** | **1** | **0.0** | **20:33** | **4** | **0** | **1** | **1** | **0** | **0** | **0** | **0** | **17:50** |
| | Russia | Olympics | 8 | 0 | 1 | 1 | 4 | .... | .... | .... | .... | .... | .... | .... | .... | .... | .... | .... | .... | .... | .... | .... | .... | .... | .... |
| **2006-07** | **NY Rangers** | **NHL** | **66** | **2** | **12** | **14** | **44** | **1** | **1** | **0** | **75** | **2.7** | **–8** | **1** | **0.0** | **20:02** | **10** | **0** | **5** | **5** | **8** | **0** | **0** | **0** | **19:30** |
| **2007-08** | **NY Rangers** | **NHL** | **82** | **5** | **15** | **20** | **43** | **1** | **0** | **0** | **131** | **3.8** | **5** | **0** | **0.0** | **20:27** | **10** | **0** | **3** | **3** | **4** | **0** | **0** | **0** | **19:52** |
| **2008-09** | **Columbus** | **NHL** | **82** | **9** | **25** | **34** | **81** | **5** | **1** | **0** | **167** | **5.4** | **1** | **1** | **100.0** | **23:31** | **4** | **0** | **0** | **0** | **0** | **0** | **0** | **0** | **23:16** |
| | **NHL Totals** | | **332** | **24** | **76** | **100** | **240** | **11** | **3** | **2** | **508** | **4.7** | | **4** | **25.0** | **21:07** | **28** | **0** | **9** | **9** | **12** | **0** | **0** | **0** | **19:56** |

Signed as a free agent by **St. Petersburg** (Russia), November 11, 2004. Traded to **Columbus** by **NY Rangers** with Christian Backman for Nikolai Zherdev and Dan Fritsche, July 2, 2008.

## UMBERGER, R.J.

(UHM-buhr-guhr, AHR-JAY) **CBJ**

Center. Shoots left. 6'2", 215 lbs. Born, Pittsburgh, PA, May 3, 1982. Vancouver's 1st choice, 16th overall, in 2001 Entry Draft.

| Season | Club | League | GP | G | A | Pts | PIM | PP | SH | GW | S | % | +/- | TF | F% | Min | GP | G | A | Pts | PIM | PP | SH | GW | Min |
|---|---|---|---|---|---|---|---|---|---|---|---|---|---|---|---|---|---|---|---|---|---|---|---|---|---|
| 1997-98 | Plum Mustangs | High-PA | 26 | *60 | *56 | *116 | .... | .... | .... | .... | .... | .... | .... | .... | .... | .... | .... | .... | .... | .... | .... | .... | .... | .... | .... |
| 1998-99 | USNTDP | USHL | 5 | 2 | 2 | 4 | 0 | .... | .... | .... | .... | .... | .... | .... | .... | .... | .... | .... | .... | .... | .... | .... | .... | .... | .... |
| | USNTDP | NAHL | 50 | 21 | 21 | 42 | 32 | .... | .... | .... | .... | .... | .... | .... | .... | .... | .... | .... | .... | .... | .... | .... | .... | .... | .... |
| 99-2000 | USNTDP | U-18 | 6 | 1 | 0 | 1 | 2 | .... | .... | .... | .... | .... | .... | .... | .... | .... | .... | .... | .... | .... | .... | .... | .... | .... | .... |
| | USNTDP | USHL | 57 | 33 | 35 | 68 | 20 | .... | .... | .... | .... | .... | .... | .... | .... | .... | .... | .... | .... | .... | .... | .... | .... | .... | .... |
| 2000-01 | Ohio State | CCHA | 32 | 14 | 23 | 37 | 18 | .... | .... | .... | .... | .... | .... | .... | .... | .... | .... | .... | .... | .... | .... | .... | .... | .... | .... |
| 2001-02 | Ohio State | CCHA | 37 | 18 | 21 | 39 | 31 | .... | .... | .... | .... | .... | .... | .... | .... | .... | .... | .... | .... | .... | .... | .... | .... | .... | .... |
| 2002-03 | Ohio State | CCHA | 43 | 26 | 27 | 53 | 16 | .... | .... | .... | .... | .... | .... | .... | .... | .... | .... | .... | .... | .... | .... | .... | .... | .... | .... |
| 2003-04 | | | DID NOT PLAY | | | | | | | | | | | | | | | | | | | | | | |
| 2004-05 | Philadelphia | AHL | 80 | 21 | 44 | 65 | 36 | .... | .... | .... | .... | .... | .... | .... | .... | .... | 21 | 3 | 7 | 10 | 12 | .... | .... | .... | .... |
| **2005-06** | **Philadelphia** | **NHL** | **73** | **20** | **18** | **38** | **18** | **5** | **0** | **2** | **138** | **14.5** | **9** | **163** | **50.3** | **13:14** | **5** | **1** | **0** | **1** | **2** | **0** | **0** | **0** | **11:15** |
| | Philadelphia | AHL | 8 | 3 | 7 | 10 | 8 | .... | .... | .... | .... | .... | .... | .... | .... | .... | .... | .... | .... | .... | .... | .... | .... | .... | .... |
| **2006-07** | **Philadelphia** | **NHL** | **81** | **16** | **12** | **28** | **41** | **2** | **2** | **1** | **134** | **11.9** | **–32** | **535** | **44.5** | **14:32** | .... | .... | .... | .... | .... | .... | .... | .... | .... |
| **2007-08** | **Philadelphia** | **NHL** | **74** | **13** | **37** | **50** | **19** | **4** | **0** | **3** | **173** | **7.5** | **0** | **117** | **38.5** | **17:52** | **17** | **10** | **5** | **15** | **10** | **1** | **0** | **2** | **16:51** |
| **2008-09** | **Columbus** | **NHL** | **82** | **26** | **20** | **46** | **53** | **9** | **0** | **2** | **234** | **11.1** | **–10** | **841** | **48.0** | **18:46** | **4** | **3** | **0** | **3** | **0** | **2** | **0** | **0** | **16:22** |
| | **NHL Totals** | | **310** | **75** | **87** | **162** | **131** | **20** | **2** | **8** | **679** | **11.0** | | **1656** | **46.4** | **16:09** | **26** | **14** | **5** | **19** | **12** | **3** | **0** | **2** | **15:42** |

CCHA All-Rookie Team (2001) • CCHA Rookie of the Year (2001) • CCHA First All-Star Team (2003) • NCAA West Second All-American Team (2003)

• Missed entire 2003-04 season due to contract dispute. Traded to **NY Rangers** by **Vancouver** with Martin Grenier for Martin Rucinsky, March 9, 2004. Signed as a free agent by **Philadelphia**, June 16, 2004. Traded to **Columbus** by **Philadelphia** with Philadelphia's 4th round choice (Drew Olson) in 2008 Entry Draft for Colorado's 1st round choice (previously acquired, Philadelphia selected Luca Sbisa) in 2008 Entry Draft and Columbus's 3rd round choice (Marc-Andre Bourdon) in 2008 Entry Draft, June 20, 2008.

## UPSHALL, Scottie

(UHP-shuhl, SKAW-tee) **PHX.**

Left wing. Shoots left. 6', 197 lbs. Born, Fort McMurray, Alta., October 7, 1983. Nashville's 1st choice, 6th overall, in 2002 Entry Draft.

| Season | Club | League | GP | G | A | Pts | PIM | PP | SH | GW | S | % | +/- | TF | F% | Min | GP | G | A | Pts | PIM | PP | SH | GW | Min |
|---|---|---|---|---|---|---|---|---|---|---|---|---|---|---|---|---|---|---|---|---|---|---|---|---|---|
| 1998-99 | Fort McMurray | AMHL | 28 | 62 | 40 | 102 | 100 | .... | .... | .... | .... | .... | .... | .... | .... | .... | .... | .... | .... | .... | .... | .... | .... | .... | .... |
| 99-2000 | Fort McMurray | AJHL | 52 | 26 | 26 | 52 | 65 | .... | .... | .... | .... | .... | .... | .... | .... | .... | .... | .... | .... | .... | .... | .... | .... | .... | .... |
| 2000-01 | Kamloops Blazers | WHL | 70 | 42 | 45 | 87 | 111 | .... | .... | .... | .... | .... | .... | .... | .... | .... | 4 | 0 | 2 | 2 | 10 | .... | .... | .... | .... |
| 2001-02 | Kamloops Blazers | WHL | 61 | 32 | 51 | 83 | 139 | .... | .... | .... | .... | .... | .... | .... | .... | .... | 4 | 1 | 2 | 3 | 21 | .... | .... | .... | .... |
| **2002-03** | **Nashville** | **NHL** | **8** | **1** | **0** | **1** | **0** | **0** | **0** | **0** | **6** | **16.7** | **2** | **2** | **0.0** | **8:42** | .... | .... | .... | .... | .... | .... | .... | .... | .... |
| | Kamloops Blazers | WHL | 42 | 25 | 31 | 56 | 111 | .... | .... | .... | .... | .... | .... | .... | .... | .... | 6 | 0 | 2 | 2 | 34 | .... | .... | .... | .... |
| | Milwaukee | AHL | 2 | 1 | 0 | 1 | 2 | .... | .... | .... | .... | .... | .... | .... | .... | .... | 6 | 0 | 0 | 0 | 2 | .... | .... | .... | .... |
| **2003-04** | **Nashville** | **NHL** | **7** | **0** | **1** | **1** | **0** | **0** | **0** | **0** | **6** | **0.0** | **–2** | **8** | **37.5** | **9:11** | .... | .... | .... | .... | .... | .... | .... | .... | .... |
| | Milwaukee | AHL | 31 | 13 | 11 | 24 | 42 | .... | .... | .... | .... | .... | .... | .... | .... | .... | 8 | 3 | 0 | 3 | 4 | .... | .... | .... | .... |
| 2004-05 | Milwaukee | AHL | 62 | 19 | 27 | 46 | 108 | .... | .... | .... | .... | .... | .... | .... | .... | .... | 5 | 2 | 2 | 4 | 8 | .... | .... | .... | .... |
| **2005-06** | **Nashville** | **NHL** | **48** | **8** | **16** | **24** | **34** | **1** | **0** | **2** | **72** | **11.1** | **14** | **11** | **45.5** | **10:26** | **2** | **0** | **0** | **0** | **0** | **0** | **0** | **0** | **11:57** |
| | Milwaukee | AHL | 23 | 17 | 16 | 33 | 44 | .... | .... | .... | .... | .... | .... | .... | .... | .... | 14 | 6 | 10 | 16 | 20 | .... | .... | .... | .... |

| | | | Regular Season | | | | | | | | | | | | | | Playoffs | | | | | | | | |
|---|---|---|---|---|---|---|---|---|---|---|---|---|---|---|---|---|---|---|---|---|---|---|---|---|---|
| Season | Club | League | GP | G | A | Pts | PIM | PP | SH | GW | S | % | +/- | TF | F% | Min | GP | G | A | Pts | PIM | PP | SH | GW | Min |
| **2006-07** | **Nashville** | **NHL** | **14** | **2** | **1** | **3** | **18** | **0** | **0** | **2** | **27** | **7.4** | **–1** | **0** | **0.0** | **10:28** | | | | | | | | | |
| | Milwaukee | AHL | 5 | 0 | 1 | 1 | 6 | | | | | | | | | | | | | | | | | | |
| | **Philadelphia** | **NHL** | **18** | **6** | **7** | **13** | **8** | **1** | **1** | **2** | **60** | **10.0** | **4** | **18** | **44.4** | **18:05** | | | | | | | | | |
| **2007-08** | **Philadelphia** | **NHL** | **61** | **14** | **16** | **30** | **74** | **3** | **0** | **1** | **128** | **10.9** | **2** | **7** | **28.6** | **13:20** | **17** | **3** | **4** | **7** | ***44** | **1** | **0** | **1** | **13:57** |
| **2008-09** | **Philadelphia** | **NHL** | **55** | **7** | **14** | **21** | **63** | **2** | **0** | **0** | **126** | **5.6** | **5** | **10** | **10.0** | **13:13** | | | | | | | | | |
| | **Phoenix** | **NHL** | **19** | **8** | **5** | **13** | **26** | **3** | **0** | **1** | **66** | **12.1** | **2** | **9** | **44.4** | **18:35** | | | | | | | | | |
| | **NHL Totals** | | **230** | **46** | **60** | **106** | **223** | **10** | **1** | **8** | **491** | **9.4** | | **65** | **35.4** | **13:03** | **19** | **3** | **4** | **7** | **44** | **1** | **0** | **1** | **13:44** |

WHL All-Rookie Team (2001) • WHL Rookie of the Year (2001) • CHL All-Rookie Team (2001) • Canadian Major Junior Rookie of the Year (2001) • WHL West Second All-Star Team (2002)

• Missed majority of 2003-04 season recovering from knee injury suffered in game vs. Phoenix, December 22, 2003. Traded to **Philadelphia** by **Nashville** with Ryan Parent and Nashville's 1st (later traded back to Nashville - Nashville selected Jonathon Blum) and 3rd (later traded to Washington - Washington selected Phil Desimone) round choices in 2007 Entry Draft for Peter Forsberg, February 15, 2007. Traded to **Phoenix** by **Philadelphia** with Philadelphia's 2nd round choice in 2011 Entry Draft for Daniel Carcillo, March 4, 2009.

## VAANANEN, Ossi

(VAN-ih-nehn, AW-see)

Defense. Shoots left. 6'4", 215 lbs. Born, Vantaa, Finland, August 18, 1980. Phoenix's 2nd choice, 43rd overall, in 1998 Entry Draft.

| | | | | | | | | | | | | | | | | | | | | | | | | | |
|---|---|---|---|---|---|---|---|---|---|---|---|---|---|---|---|---|---|---|---|---|---|---|---|---|---|
| 1995-96 | Jokerit U18 | Fin-U18 | 8 | 0 | 0 | 0 | 2 | | | | | | | | | | 2 | 0 | 0 | 0 | 0 | | | | |
| 1996-97 | Jokerit U18 | Fin-U18 | 18 | 1 | 2 | 3 | 43 | | | | | | | | | | | | | | | | | | |
| | Jokerit Helsinki Jr. | Fin-Jr. | 1 | 0 | 0 | 0 | 0 | | | | | | | | | | | | | | | | | | |
| 1997-98 | Jokerit U18 | Fin-U18 | 7 | 3 | 3 | 6 | 8 | | | | | | | | | | | | | | | | | | |
| | Jokerit Helsinki Jr. | Fin-Jr. | 31 | 0 | 6 | 6 | 24 | | | | | | | | | | 7 | 0 | 2 | 2 | 16 | | | | |
| 1998-99 | Jokerit Helsinki Jr. | Fin-Jr. | 12 | 1 | 6 | 7 | 16 | | | | | | | | | | 6 | 1 | 0 | 1 | 12 | | | | |
| | Jokerit Helsinki | Finland | 48 | 0 | 1 | 1 | 42 | | | | | | | | | | 3 | 0 | 1 | 1 | 2 | | | | |
| | Jokerit Helsinki | EuroHL | 5 | 0 | 0 | 0 | 2 | | | | | | | | | | 1 | 0 | 1 | 1 | 2 | | | | |
| 99-2000 | Jokerit Helsinki | Finland | 49 | 1 | 6 | 7 | 46 | | | | | | | | | | 11 | 1 | 1 | 2 | 2 | | | | |
| **2000-01** | **Phoenix** | **NHL** | **81** | **4** | **12** | **16** | **90** | **0** | **0** | **2** | **69** | **5.8** | **9** | **0** | **0.0** | **19:09** | | | | | | | | | |
| **2001-02** | **Phoenix** | **NHL** | **76** | **2** | **12** | **14** | **74** | **0** | **1** | **0** | **41** | **4.9** | **6** | **0** | **0.0** | **20:13** | **5** | **0** | **0** | **0** | **6** | **0** | **0** | **0** | **20:33** |
| | Finland | Olympics | 2 | 0 | 1 | 1 | 0 | | | | | | | | | | | | | | | | | | |
| **2002-03** | **Phoenix** | **NHL** | **67** | **2** | **7** | **9** | **82** | **0** | **0** | **0** | **49** | **4.1** | **1** | **0** | **0.0** | **19:15** | | | | | | | | | |
| **2003-04** | **Phoenix** | **NHL** | **67** | **2** | **4** | **6** | **87** | **0** | **0** | **1** | **39** | **5.1** | **–10** | **0** | **0.0** | **19:21** | | | | | | | | | |
| | **Colorado** | **NHL** | **12** | **0** | **0** | **0** | **2** | **0** | **0** | **0** | **6** | **0.0** | **–4** | **0** | **0.0** | **18:36** | **11** | **0** | **1** | **1** | **18** | **0** | **0** | **0** | **22:06** |
| 2004-05 | Jokerit Helsinki | Finland | 28 | 2 | 2 | 4 | 30 | | | | | | | | | | 12 | 0 | 0 | 0 | 26 | | | | |
| **2005-06** | **Colorado** | **NHL** | **53** | **0** | **4** | **4** | **56** | **0** | **0** | **0** | **34** | **0.0** | **10** | **1** | **0.0** | **13:34** | **1** | **0** | **0** | **0** | **0** | **0** | **0** | **0** | **13:58** |
| **2006-07** | **Colorado** | **NHL** | **74** | **2** | **6** | **8** | **69** | **0** | **0** | **1** | **32** | **6.3** | **6** | **0** | **0.0** | **14:20** | | | | | | | | | |
| 2007-08 | Djurgarden | Sweden | 45 | 7 | 8 | 15 | 102 | | | | | | | | | | 5 | 0 | 0 | 0 | 2 | | | | |
| **2008-09** | **Philadelphia** | **NHL** | **46** | **1** | **9** | **10** | **22** | **0** | **0** | **0** | **18** | **5.6** | **7** | **0** | **0.0** | **18:28** | | | | | | | | | |
| | **Vancouver** | **NHL** | **3** | **0** | **1** | **1** | **0** | **0** | **0** | **0** | **2** | **0.0** | **1** | **0** | **0.0** | **9:28** | **3** | **0** | **0** | **0** | **2** | **0** | **0** | **0** | **9:14** |
| | **NHL Totals** | | **479** | **13** | **55** | **68** | **482** | **0** | **1** | **4** | **290** | **4.5** | | **1** | **0.0** | **17:52** | **20** | **0** | **1** | **1** | **26** | **0** | **0** | **0** | **19:23** |

Traded to **Colorado** by **Phoenix** with Chris Gratton and Phoenix's 2nd round choice (Paul Stastny) in 2005 Entry Draft for Derek Morris and Keith Ballard, March 9, 2004. Signed as a free agent by **Jokerit Helsinki** (Finland), December 1, 2004. Signed as a free agent by **Philadelphia**, July 1, 2008. Claimed on waivers by **Vancouver** from **Philadelphia**, February 27, 2009.

## VALABIK, Boris

(vuh-LA-bihk, BOHR-ihs) **ATL.**

Defense. Shoots left. 6'7", 240 lbs. Born, Nitra, Czech., February 14, 1986. Atlanta's 1st choice, 10th overall, in 2004 Entry Draft.

| | | | | | | | | | | | | | | | | | | | | | | | | | |
|---|---|---|---|---|---|---|---|---|---|---|---|---|---|---|---|---|---|---|---|---|---|---|---|---|---|
| 2002-03 | HKM Nitra Jr. | Slovak-Jr. | 46 | 2 | 12 | 14 | 145 | | | | | | | | | | | | | | | | | | |
| 2003-04 | Kitchener Rangers | OHL | 68 | 3 | 13 | 16 | 278 | | | | | | | | | | 5 | 0 | 0 | 0 | 8 | | | | |
| 2004-05 | Kitchener Rangers | OHL | 43 | 0 | 4 | 4 | 231 | | | | | | | | | | 15 | 0 | 0 | 0 | 56 | | | | |
| 2005-06 | Kitchener Rangers | OHL | 52 | 1 | 9 | 10 | 216 | | | | | | | | | | 5 | 0 | 2 | 2 | 14 | | | | |
| 2006-07 | Chicago Wolves | AHL | 50 | 2 | 7 | 9 | 184 | | | | | | | | | | 8 | 0 | 1 | 1 | 37 | | | | |
| **2007-08** | **Atlanta** | **NHL** | **7** | **0** | **0** | **0** | **42** | **0** | **0** | **0** | **5** | **0.0** | **–2** | **0** | **0.0** | **16:42** | | | | | | | | | |
| | Chicago Wolves | AHL | 58 | 1 | 7 | 8 | 229 | | | | | | | | | | 24 | 3 | 1 | 4 | 71 | | | | |
| **2008-09** | **Atlanta** | **NHL** | **50** | **0** | **5** | **5** | **132** | **0** | **0** | **0** | **16** | **0.0** | **–14** | **0** | **0.0** | **15:15** | | | | | | | | | |
| | Chicago Wolves | AHL | 11 | 1 | 2 | 3 | 21 | | | | | | | | | | | | | | | | | | |
| | **NHL Totals** | | **57** | **0** | **5** | **5** | **174** | **0** | **0** | **0** | **21** | **0.0** | | **0** | **0.0** | **15:25** | | | | | | | | | |

OHL All-Rookie Team (2004) • Canadian Major Junior All-Rookie Team (2004)

## VAN DER GULIK, David

(VAN DUHR-GOO-lihk, DAY-vihd) **CGY.**

Right wing. Shoots left. 5'10", 173 lbs. Born, Abbotsford, B.C., April 20, 1983. Calgary's 10th choice, 206th overall, in 2002 Entry Draft.

| | | | | | | | | | | | | | | | | | | | | | | | | | |
|---|---|---|---|---|---|---|---|---|---|---|---|---|---|---|---|---|---|---|---|---|---|---|---|---|---|
| 99-2000 | Chilliwack Chiefs | BCHL | 41 | 35 | 46 | 81 | | | | | | | | | | | | | | | | | | | |
| 2000-01 | Chilliwack Chiefs | BCHL | 60 | 42 | 38 | 80 | | | | | | | | | | | | | | | | | | | |
| 2001-02 | Chilliwack Chiefs | BCHL | 56 | 38 | 62 | 100 | 90 | | | | | | | | | | 13 | 8 | 11 | 19 | | | | | |
| 2002-03 | Boston University | H-East | 40 | 10 | 10 | 20 | 56 | | | | | | | | | | | | | | | | | | |
| 2003-04 | Boston University | H-East | 35 | 13 | 7 | 20 | 74 | | | | | | | | | | | | | | | | | | |
| 2004-05 | Boston University | H-East | 41 | 18 | 13 | 31 | 48 | | | | | | | | | | | | | | | | | | |
| 2005-06 | Boston University | H-East | 25 | 11 | 11 | 22 | 26 | | | | | | | | | | | | | | | | | | |
| 2006-07 | Omaha | AHL | 80 | 16 | 27 | 43 | 69 | | | | | | | | | | 6 | 0 | 2 | 2 | 4 | | | | |
| 2007-08 | Quad City Flames | AHL | 80 | 19 | 23 | 42 | 62 | | | | | | | | | | | | | | | | | | |
| **2008-09** | **Calgary** | **NHL** | **6** | **0** | **2** | **2** | **0** | **0** | **0** | **0** | **11** | **0.0** | **–1** | **1** | **0.0** | **8:29** | | | | | | | | | |
| | Quad City Flames | AHL | 73 | 17 | 19 | 36 | 58 | | | | | | | | | | | | | | | | | | |
| | **NHL Totals** | | **6** | **0** | **2** | **2** | **0** | **0** | **0** | **0** | **11** | **0.0** | | **1** | **0.0** | **8:29** | | | | | | | | | |

Hockey East All-Rookie Team (2003)

## VANDERMEER, Jim

(VAN-duhr-meer, JIHM) **PHX.**

Defense. Shoots left. 6'1", 211 lbs. Born, Caroline, Alta., February 21, 1980.

| | | | | | | | | | | | | | | | | | | | | | | | | | |
|---|---|---|---|---|---|---|---|---|---|---|---|---|---|---|---|---|---|---|---|---|---|---|---|---|---|
| 1997-98 | Red Deer | AMHL | 26 | 4 | 8 | 12 | 51 | | | | | | | | | | | | | | | | | | |
| | Red Deer Rebels | WHL | 35 | 0 | 3 | 3 | 55 | | | | | | | | | | 2 | 0 | 0 | 0 | 0 | | | | |
| 1998-99 | Red Deer Rebels | WHL | 70 | 5 | 23 | 28 | 258 | | | | | | | | | | 9 | 0 | 1 | 1 | 24 | | | | |
| 99-2000 | Red Deer Rebels | WHL | 71 | 8 | 30 | 38 | 221 | | | | | | | | | | 4 | 0 | 1 | 1 | 16 | | | | |
| 2000-01 | Red Deer Rebels | WHL | 72 | 21 | 44 | 65 | 180 | | | | | | | | | | 22 | 3 | 13 | 16 | 43 | | | | |
| 2001-02 | Philadelphia | AHL | 74 | 1 | 13 | 14 | 88 | | | | | | | | | | 5 | 0 | 2 | 2 | 14 | | | | |
| **2002-03** | **Philadelphia** | **NHL** | **24** | **2** | **1** | **3** | **27** | **0** | **0** | **0** | **22** | **9.1** | **9** | **0** | **0.0** | **13:42** | **8** | **0** | **1** | **1** | **9** | **0** | **0** | **0** | **12:42** |
| | Philadelphia | AHL | 48 | 4 | 8 | 12 | 122 | | | | | | | | | | | | | | | | | | |
| **2003-04** | **Philadelphia** | **NHL** | **23** | **3** | **2** | **5** | **25** | **0** | **0** | **1** | **24** | **12.5** | **–5** | **0** | **0.0** | **15:47** | | | | | | | | | |
| | Philadelphia | AHL | 26 | 1 | 6 | 7 | 120 | | | | | | | | | | | | | | | | | | |
| | **Chicago** | **NHL** | **23** | **2** | **10** | **12** | **58** | **1** | **1** | **0** | **37** | **5.4** | **–6** | **1** | **100.0** | **22:03** | | | | | | | | | |
| 2004-05 | Norfolk Admirals | AHL | 52 | 3 | 10 | 13 | 164 | | | | | | | | | | | | | | | | | | |
| **2005-06** | **Chicago** | **NHL** | **76** | **6** | **18** | **24** | **116** | **2** | **0** | **1** | **93** | **6.5** | **–2** | **1** | **100.0** | **21:47** | | | | | | | | | |
| **2006-07** | **Chicago** | **NHL** | **46** | **1** | **6** | **7** | **53** | **0** | **0** | **0** | **50** | **2.0** | **–3** | **0** | **0.0** | **17:50** | | | | | | | | | |
| **2007-08** | **Chicago** | **NHL** | **26** | **2** | **7** | **9** | **44** | **1** | **0** | **0** | **23** | **8.7** | **3** | **0** | **0.0** | **19:37** | | | | | | | | | |
| | **Philadelphia** | **NHL** | **28** | **1** | **5** | **6** | **27** | **1** | **0** | **0** | **26** | **3.8** | **–1** | **0** | **0.0** | **19:34** | | | | | | | | | |
| | **Calgary** | **NHL** | **21** | **0** | **2** | **2** | **39** | **0** | **0** | **0** | **23** | **0.0** | **4** | **0** | **0.0** | **19:44** | **7** | **0** | **0** | **0** | **4** | **0** | **0** | **0** | **16:18** |
| **2008-09** | **Calgary** | **NHL** | **45** | **1** | **6** | **7** | **108** | **0** | **0** | **0** | **31** | **3.2** | **1** | **0** | **0.0** | **16:01** | **6** | **0** | **1** | **1** | **4** | **0** | **0** | **0** | **16:33** |
| | **NHL Totals** | | **312** | **18** | **57** | **75** | **497** | **5** | **1** | **2** | **329** | **5.5** | | **2** | **100.0** | **18:48** | **21** | **0** | **2** | **2** | **17** | **0** | **0** | **0** | **15:00** |

WHL East First All-Star Team (2001) • Canadian Major Junior Humanitarian Player of the Year (2001)

Signed as a free agent by **Philadelphia**, December 21, 2000. Traded to **Chicago** by **Philadelphia** with the rights to Colin Fraser and Los Angeles' 2nd round choice (previously acquired, Chicago selected Bryan Bickell) in 2004 Entry Draft for Alex Zhamnov and Washington's 4th round choice (previously acquired, Philadelphia selected R.J. Anderson) in 2004 Entry Draft, February 19, 2004. Traded to **Philadelphia** by **Chicago** for Ben Eager, December 18, 2007. Traded to **Calgary** by **Philadelphia** for Calgary's 3rd round choice (Adam Morrison) in 2009 Entry Draft, February 20, 2008. Traded to **Phoenix** by **Calgary** for Brandon Prust, June 27. 2009.

## VANDERMEER, Peter

(VAN-duhr-meer, PEE-tuhr)

Left wing. Shoots left. 6', 209 lbs. Born, Caroline, Alta., October 14, 1975.

| | | | | | | | | | | | | | | | | | | | | | | | | | |
|---|---|---|---|---|---|---|---|---|---|---|---|---|---|---|---|---|---|---|---|---|---|---|---|---|---|
| 1992-93 | Red Deer | AMHL | 34 | 26 | 30 | 56 | 172 | | | | | | | | | | | | | | | | | | |
| | Red Deer Rebels | WHL | 2 | 0 | 0 | 0 | 2 | | | | | | | | | | | | | | | | | | |
| 1993-94 | Red Deer Rebels | WHL | 54 | 4 | 9 | 13 | 170 | | | | | | | | | | | | | | | | | | |
| 1994-95 | Red Deer Rebels | WHL | 61 | 16 | 16 | 32 | 218 | | | | | | | | | | | | | | | | | | |
| 1995-96 | Red Deer Rebels | WHL | 63 | 21 | 40 | 61 | 207 | | | | | | | | | | | | | | | | | | |
| 1996-97 | Columbus Chill | ECHL | 30 | 6 | 11 | 17 | 195 | | | | | | | | | | 7 | 2 | 1 | 3 | 26 | | | | |

| | | | Regular Season | | | | | | | | | | | | | | Playoffs | | | | | | | | |
|---|---|---|---|---|---|---|---|---|---|---|---|---|---|---|---|---|---|---|---|---|---|---|---|---|---|
| Season | Club | League | GP | G | A | Pts | PIM | PP | SH | GW | S | % | +/- | TF | F% | Min | GP | G | A | Pts | PIM | PP | SH | GW | Min |
| 1997-98 | Columbus Chill | ECHL | 20 | 4 | 7 | 11 | 78 | .... | .... | .... | .... | .... | .... | .... | .... | .... | .... | .... | .... | .... | .... | .... | .... | .... | .... |
| | Richmond | ECHL | 18 | 2 | 5 | 7 | 165 | .... | .... | .... | .... | .... | .... | .... | .... | .... | .... | .... | .... | .... | .... | .... | .... | .... | .... |
| | Rochester | AHL | 30 | 4 | 2 | 6 | 140 | .... | .... | .... | .... | .... | .... | .... | .... | .... | 4 | 1 | 0 | 1 | 13 | .... | .... | .... | .... |
| 1998-99 | Rochester | AHL | 2 | 1 | 0 | 1 | 16 | .... | .... | .... | .... | .... | .... | .... | .... | .... | 16 | 1 | 0 | 1 | 38 | .... | .... | .... | .... |
| | Binghamton | UHL | 62 | 15 | 21 | 36 | *390 | .... | .... | .... | .... | .... | .... | .... | .... | .... | 5 | 2 | 2 | 4 | 0 | .... | .... | .... | .... |
| 99-2000 | Wilkes-Barre | AHL | 4 | 0 | 0 | 0 | 7 | .... | .... | .... | .... | .... | .... | .... | .... | .... | .... | .... | .... | .... | .... | .... | .... | .... | .... |
| | Richmond | ECHL | 58 | 31 | 25 | 56 | *457 | .... | .... | .... | .... | .... | .... | .... | .... | .... | 3 | 0 | 1 | 1 | 20 | .... | .... | .... | .... |
| | Providence Bruins | AHL | .... | .... | .... | .... | .... | .... | .... | .... | .... | .... | .... | .... | .... | .... | 9 | 0 | 3 | 3 | 2 | .... | .... | .... | .... |
| 2000-01 | Providence Bruins | AHL | 62 | 19 | 18 | 37 | 240 | .... | .... | .... | .... | .... | .... | .... | .... | .... | 4 | 0 | 0 | 0 | 16 | .... | .... | .... | .... |
| 2001-02 | Philadelphia | AHL | 61 | 5 | 1 | 6 | 313 | .... | .... | .... | .... | .... | .... | .... | .... | .... | 5 | 0 | 0 | 0 | 8 | .... | .... | .... | .... |
| | Trenton Titans | ECHL | 2 | 0 | 1 | 1 | 2 | .... | .... | .... | .... | .... | .... | .... | .... | .... | .... | .... | .... | .... | .... | .... | .... | .... | .... |
| 2002-03 | Philadelphia | AHL | 77 | 5 | 8 | 13 | 335 | .... | .... | .... | .... | .... | .... | .... | .... | .... | .... | .... | .... | .... | .... | .... | .... | .... | .... |
| 2003-04 | Philadelphia | AHL | 71 | 5 | 8 | 13 | *398 | .... | .... | .... | .... | .... | .... | .... | .... | .... | 12 | 1 | 0 | 1 | 29 | .... | .... | .... | .... |
| 2004-05 | Grand Rapids | AHL | 73 | 4 | 13 | 17 | 310 | .... | .... | .... | .... | .... | .... | .... | .... | .... | .... | .... | .... | .... | .... | .... | .... | .... | .... |
| 2005-06 | Hamilton | AHL | 67 | 6 | 6 | 12 | 276 | .... | .... | .... | .... | .... | .... | .... | .... | .... | .... | .... | .... | .... | .... | .... | .... | .... | .... |
| 2006-07 | Hershey Bears | AHL | 26 | 2 | 5 | 7 | 129 | .... | .... | .... | .... | .... | .... | .... | .... | .... | 2 | 0 | 0 | 0 | 0 | .... | .... | .... | .... |
| **2007-08** | San Antonio | AHL | 38 | 2 | 6 | 8 | 332 | .... | .... | .... | .... | .... | .... | .... | .... | .... | .... | .... | .... | .... | .... | .... | .... | .... | .... |
| | **Phoenix** | **NHL** | **2** | **0** | **0** | **0** | **0** | **0** | **0** | **0** | **0** | **0.0** | **0** | **0** | **0.0** | **7:33** | .... | .... | .... | .... | .... | .... | .... | .... | .... |
| 2008-09 | Quad City Flames | AHL | 80 | 5 | 1 | 6 | 185 | .... | .... | .... | .... | .... | .... | .... | .... | .... | .... | .... | .... | .... | .... | .... | .... | .... | .... |
| | **NHL Totals** | | **2** | **0** | **0** | **0** | **0** | **0** | **0** | **0** | **0** | **0.0** | | **0** | **0.0** | **7:33** | .... | .... | .... | .... | .... | .... | .... | .... | .... |

Signed as a free agent by **Philadelphia**, July 6, 2001. Signed as a free agent by **Detroit**, August 16, 2004. Signed as a free agent by **Montreal**, August 2, 2005. Signed as a free agent by **Washington**, July 21, 2006. Signed as a free agent by **San Antonio** (AHL), August 16, 2007. Signed as a free agent by **Phoenix**, February 8, 2008. Signed as a free agent by **Calgary**, July 2, 2008.

## VANEK, Thomas

(VAN-ehk, TAW-muhs) **BUF.**

Left wing. Shoots right. 6'2", 208 lbs. Born, Vienna, Austria, January 19, 1984. Buffalo's 1st choice, 5th overall, in 2003 Entry Draft.

| Season | Club | League | GP | G | A | Pts | PIM | PP | SH | GW | S | % | +/- | TF | F% | Min | GP | G | A | Pts | PIM | PP | SH | GW | Min |
|---|---|---|---|---|---|---|---|---|---|---|---|---|---|---|---|---|---|---|---|---|---|---|---|---|---|
| 99-2000 | Sioux Falls | USHL | 35 | 15 | 18 | 33 | 12 | .... | .... | .... | .... | .... | .... | .... | .... | .... | 3 | 0 | 1 | 1 | 0 | .... | .... | .... | .... |
| 2000-01 | Sioux Falls | USHL | 20 | 19 | 10 | 29 | 15 | .... | .... | .... | .... | .... | .... | .... | .... | .... | 8 | 5 | 4 | 9 | 2 | .... | .... | .... | .... |
| 2001-02 | Sioux Falls | USHL | 53 | 46 | 45 | 91 | 54 | .... | .... | .... | .... | .... | .... | .... | .... | .... | 3 | 0 | 0 | 0 | 9 | .... | .... | .... | .... |
| 2002-03 | U. of Minnesota | WCHA | 45 | 31 | 31 | 62 | 60 | .... | .... | .... | .... | .... | .... | .... | .... | .... | .... | .... | .... | .... | .... | .... | .... | .... | .... |
| 2003-04 | U. of Minnesota | WCHA | 38 | 26 | 25 | 51 | 72 | .... | .... | .... | .... | .... | .... | .... | .... | .... | .... | .... | .... | .... | .... | .... | .... | .... | .... |
| 2004-05 | Rochester | AHL | 74 | 42 | 26 | 68 | 62 | .... | .... | .... | .... | .... | .... | .... | .... | .... | 5 | 2 | 3 | 5 | 10 | .... | .... | .... | .... |
| **2005-06** | **Buffalo** | **NHL** | **81** | **25** | **23** | **48** | **72** | **11** | **0** | **4** | **204** | **12.3** | **–11** | **23** | **21.7** | **14:44** | **10** | **2** | **0** | **2** | **6** | **2** | **0** | **0** | **10:45** |
| **2006-07** | **Buffalo** | **NHL** | **82** | **43** | **41** | **84** | **40** | **15** | **0** | **5** | **237** | **18.1** | **47** | **39** | **28.2** | **16:47** | **16** | **6** | **4** | **10** | **10** | **1** | **0** | **2** | **16:27** |
| **2007-08** | **Buffalo** | **NHL** | **82** | **36** | **28** | **64** | **64** | **19** | **0** | **9** | **240** | **15.0** | **–5** | **13** | **46.2** | **16:51** | .... | .... | .... | .... | .... | .... | .... | .... | .... |
| **2008-09** | **Buffalo** | **NHL** | **73** | **40** | **24** | **64** | **44** | **20** | **2** | **5** | **211** | **19.0** | **–1** | **6** | **16.7** | **17:12** | .... | .... | .... | .... | .... | .... | .... | .... | .... |
| | **NHL Totals** | | **318** | **144** | **116** | **260** | **220** | **65** | **2** | **23** | **892** | **16.1** | | **81** | **28.4** | **16:22** | **26** | **8** | **4** | **12** | **16** | **3** | **0** | **2** | **14:15** |

USHL First All-Star Team (2002) • USHL MVP (2002) • WCHA All-Rookie Team (2003) • WCHA Second All-Star Team (2003, 2004) • WCHA Rookie of the Year (2003) • NCAA Championship All-Tournament Team (2003) • NCAA Championship Tournament MVP (2003) • NCAA West Second All-American Team (2004) • AHL All-Rookie Team (2005) • NHL Second All-Star Team (2007)

Played in NHL All-Star Game (2009)

## VAN RYN, Mike

(VAN RIGHN, MIGHK) **TOR.**

Defense. Shoots right. 6'1", 198 lbs. Born, London, Ont., May 14, 1979. New Jersey's 1st choice, 26th overall, in 1998 Entry Draft.

| Season | Club | League | GP | G | A | Pts | PIM | PP | SH | GW | S | % | +/- | TF | F% | Min | GP | G | A | Pts | PIM | PP | SH | GW | Min |
|---|---|---|---|---|---|---|---|---|---|---|---|---|---|---|---|---|---|---|---|---|---|---|---|---|---|
| 1995-96 | London Nationals | OHA-B | 44 | 9 | 14 | 23 | 24 | .... | .... | .... | .... | .... | .... | .... | .... | .... | .... | .... | .... | .... | .... | .... | .... | .... | .... |
| 1996-97 | London Nationals | OHA-B | 46 | 14 | 31 | 45 | 32 | .... | .... | .... | .... | .... | .... | .... | .... | .... | .... | .... | .... | .... | .... | .... | .... | .... | .... |
| 1997-98 | U. of Michigan | CCHA | 38 | 4 | 14 | 18 | 44 | .... | .... | .... | .... | .... | .... | .... | .... | .... | .... | .... | .... | .... | .... | .... | .... | .... | .... |
| 1998-99 | U. of Michigan | CCHA | 37 | 10 | 13 | 23 | 52 | .... | .... | .... | .... | .... | .... | .... | .... | .... | .... | .... | .... | .... | .... | .... | .... | .... | .... |
| 99-2000 | Sarnia Sting | OHL | 61 | 6 | 35 | 41 | 34 | .... | .... | .... | .... | .... | .... | .... | .... | .... | 7 | 0 | 5 | 5 | 4 | .... | .... | .... | .... |
| **2000-01** | **St. Louis** | **NHL** | **1** | **0** | **0** | **0** | **0** | **0** | **0** | **0** | **1** | **0.0** | **–2** | **0** | **0.0** | **13:43** | .... | .... | .... | .... | .... | .... | .... | .... | .... |
| | Worcester IceCats | AHL | 37 | 3 | 10 | 13 | 12 | .... | .... | .... | .... | .... | .... | .... | .... | .... | 7 | 1 | 1 | 2 | 2 | .... | .... | .... | .... |
| **2001-02** | **St. Louis** | **NHL** | **48** | **2** | **8** | **10** | **18** | **0** | **0** | **1** | **52** | **3.8** | **10** | **0** | **0.0** | **16:23** | **9** | **0** | **0** | **0** | **0** | **0** | **0** | **0** | **16:04** |
| | Worcester IceCats | AHL | 24 | 2 | 7 | 9 | 17 | .... | .... | .... | .... | .... | .... | .... | .... | .... | .... | .... | .... | .... | .... | .... | .... | .... | .... |
| **2002-03** | **St. Louis** | **NHL** | **20** | **0** | **3** | **3** | **8** | **0** | **0** | **0** | **21** | **0.0** | **3** | **0** | **0.0** | **15:04** | .... | .... | .... | .... | .... | .... | .... | .... | .... |
| | Worcester IceCats | AHL | 33 | 2 | 8 | 10 | 16 | .... | .... | .... | .... | .... | .... | .... | .... | .... | .... | .... | .... | .... | .... | .... | .... | .... | .... |
| | San Antonio | AHL | 11 | 0 | 3 | 3 | 20 | .... | .... | .... | .... | .... | .... | .... | .... | .... | 3 | 0 | 0 | 0 | 0 | .... | .... | .... | .... |
| **2003-04** | **Florida** | **NHL** | **79** | **13** | **24** | **37** | **52** | **6** | **1** | **0** | **136** | **9.6** | **–16** | **3** | **33.3** | **24:26** | .... | .... | .... | .... | .... | .... | .... | .... | .... |
| 2004-05 | | | Did not play | | | | | | | | | | | | | | | | | | | | | | |
| **2005-06** | **Florida** | **NHL** | **80** | **8** | **29** | **37** | **90** | **3** | **0** | **2** | **154** | **5.2** | **15** | **0** | **0.0** | **22:36** | .... | .... | .... | .... | .... | .... | .... | .... | .... |
| **2006-07** | **Florida** | **NHL** | **78** | **4** | **25** | **29** | **64** | **1** | **0** | **0** | **121** | **3.3** | **–5** | **1** | **0.0** | **21:08** | .... | .... | .... | .... | .... | .... | .... | .... | .... |
| **2007-08** | **Florida** | **NHL** | **20** | **0** | **2** | **2** | **14** | **0** | **0** | **0** | **16** | **0.0** | **–2** | **0** | **0.0** | **17:49** | .... | .... | .... | .... | .... | .... | .... | .... | .... |
| **2008-09** | **Toronto** | **NHL** | **27** | **3** | **8** | **11** | **14** | **2** | **0** | **0** | **53** | **5.7** | **2** | **0** | **0.0** | **19:37** | .... | .... | .... | .... | .... | .... | .... | .... | .... |
| | **NHL Totals** | | **353** | **30** | **99** | **129** | **260** | **12** | **1** | **3** | **554** | **5.4** | | **4** | **25.0** | **20:54** | **9** | **0** | **0** | **0** | **0** | **0** | **0** | **0** | **16:04** |

OHA-B First All-Star Team (1997)

Signed as a free agent by **St. Louis**, June 30, 2000. • Missed majority of 2000-01 season recovering from a shoulder injury suffered in game vs. Phoenix, October 5, 2000. Traded to **Florida** by **St. Louis** for Valeri Bure and Florida's 5th round choice (Nikita Nikitin) in 2004 Entry Draft, March 11, 2003. • Missed majority of 2007-08 season recovering from off-season wrist surgery and recurring complications. Traded to **Toronto** by **Florida** for Bryan McCabe and Toronto's 4th round choice in 2010 Entry Draft, September 2, 2008. • Missed majority of 2008-09 season recovering from various injuries.

## VASICEK, Josef

(VAS-ih-chehk, YOH-zehf)

Center. Shoots left. 6'5", 214 lbs. Born, Havlickuv Brod, Czech., September 12, 1980. Carolina's 4th choice, 91st overall, in 1998 Entry Draft.

| Season | Club | League | GP | G | A | Pts | PIM | PP | SH | GW | S | % | +/- | TF | F% | Min | GP | G | A | Pts | PIM | PP | SH | GW | Min |
|---|---|---|---|---|---|---|---|---|---|---|---|---|---|---|---|---|---|---|---|---|---|---|---|---|---|
| 1995-96 | Havl. Brod U17 | CzR-U17 | 36 | 25 | 25 | 50 | .... | .... | .... | .... | .... | .... | .... | .... | .... | .... | .... | .... | .... | .... | .... | .... | .... | .... | .... |
| 1996-97 | Slavia U17 | CzR-U17 | 37 | 20 | 40 | 60 | .... | .... | .... | .... | .... | .... | .... | .... | .... | .... | .... | .... | .... | .... | .... | .... | .... | .... | .... |
| 1997-98 | Slavia Jr. | CzRep-Jr. | 34 | 13 | 20 | 33 | .... | .... | .... | .... | .... | .... | .... | .... | .... | .... | .... | .... | .... | .... | .... | .... | .... | .... | .... |
| 1998-99 | Sault Ste. Marie | OHL | 66 | 21 | 35 | 56 | 30 | .... | .... | .... | .... | .... | .... | .... | .... | .... | 5 | 3 | 0 | 3 | 10 | .... | .... | .... | .... |
| 99-2000 | Sault Ste. Marie | OHL | 54 | 26 | 46 | 72 | 49 | .... | .... | .... | .... | .... | .... | .... | .... | .... | 17 | 5 | 15 | 20 | 8 | .... | .... | .... | .... |
| **2000-01** | **Carolina** | **NHL** | **76** | **8** | **13** | **21** | **53** | **1** | **0** | **0** | **103** | **7.8** | **–8** | **786** | **46.6** | **11:49** | **6** | **2** | **0** | **2** | **0** | **0** | **0** | **0** | **13:56** |
| | Cincinnati | IHL | .... | .... | .... | .... | .... | .... | .... | .... | .... | .... | .... | .... | .... | .... | 3 | 0 | 0 | 0 | 0 | .... | .... | .... | .... |
| **2001-02** | **Carolina** | **NHL** | **78** | **14** | **17** | **31** | **53** | **3** | **0** | **3** | **117** | **12.0** | **–7** | **878** | **48.3** | **14:11** | **23** | **3** | **2** | **5** | **12** | **0** | **0** | **1** | **14:50** |
| **2002-03** | **Carolina** | **NHL** | **57** | **10** | **10** | **20** | **33** | **4** | **0** | **1** | **87** | **11.5** | **–19** | **652** | **49.5** | **15:57** | .... | .... | .... | .... | .... | .... | .... | .... | .... |
| **2003-04** | **Carolina** | **NHL** | **82** | **19** | **26** | **45** | **60** | **6** | **0** | **5** | **161** | **11.8** | **–3** | **262** | **48.9** | **17:06** | .... | .... | .... | .... | .... | .... | .... | .... | .... |
| 2004-05 | HC Slavia Praha | CzRep | 52 | 20 | 23 | 43 | 42 | .... | .... | .... | .... | .... | .... | .... | .... | .... | 7 | 1 | 6 | 7 | 10 | .... | .... | .... | .... |
| **2005-06**♦ | **Carolina** | **NHL** | **23** | **4** | **5** | **9** | **8** | **0** | **0** | **0** | **41** | **9.8** | **3** | **46** | **60.9** | **15:23** | **8** | **0** | **0** | **0** | **2** | **0** | **0** | **0** | **10:04** |
| **2006-07** | **Nashville** | **NHL** | **38** | **4** | **9** | **13** | **29** | **0** | **0** | **0** | **47** | **8.5** | **1** | **307** | **49.8** | **13:11** | .... | .... | .... | .... | .... | .... | .... | .... | .... |
| | **Carolina** | **NHL** | **25** | **2** | **7** | **9** | **22** | **0** | **0** | **0** | **30** | **6.7** | **–6** | **292** | **51.4** | **13:42** | .... | .... | .... | .... | .... | .... | .... | .... | .... |
| **2007-08** | **NY Islanders** | **NHL** | **81** | **16** | **19** | **35** | **53** | **0** | **2** | **2** | **126** | **12.7** | **1** | **1105** | **55.7** | **15:51** | .... | .... | .... | .... | .... | .... | .... | .... | .... |
| 2008-09 | Yaroslavl | Rus-KHL | 56 | 12 | 20 | 32 | 81 | .... | .... | .... | .... | .... | .... | .... | .... | .... | 19 | 5 | 10 | 15 | 20 | .... | .... | .... | .... |
| | **NHL Totals** | | **460** | **77** | **106** | **183** | **311** | **14** | **2** | **11** | **712** | **10.8** | | **4328** | **50.5** | **14:47** | **37** | **5** | **2** | **7** | **14** | **0** | **0** | **1** | **13:39** |

Signed as a free agent by **Slavia Praha** (CzRep), September 17, 2004. • Missed majority of 2005-06 season recovering from knee injury sufferd in game at Florida, November 11, 2005. Traded to **Nashville** by **Carolina** for Scott Walker, July 18, 2006. Traded to **Carolina** by **Nashville** for Eric Belanger, February 9, 2007. Signed as a free agent by **NY Islanders**, August 15, 2007.

## VEILLEUX, Stephane

(VAY-oo, STEH-fan) **T.B.**

Left wing. Shoots left. 6', 190 lbs. Born, Beauceville, Que., November 16, 1981. Minnesota's 4th choice, 93rd overall, in 2001 Entry Draft.

| Season | Club | League | GP | G | A | Pts | PIM | PP | SH | GW | S | % | +/- | TF | F% | Min | GP | G | A | Pts | PIM | PP | SH | GW | Min |
|---|---|---|---|---|---|---|---|---|---|---|---|---|---|---|---|---|---|---|---|---|---|---|---|---|---|
| 1997-98 | Beauce-Amiante | QAAA | 21 | 20 | 17 | 37 | .... | .... | .... | .... | .... | .... | .... | .... | .... | .... | .... | .... | .... | .... | .... | .... | .... | .... | .... |
| | Levis-Lauzon | QAAA | 14 | 3 | 5 | 8 | .... | .... | .... | .... | .... | .... | .... | .... | .... | .... | 1 | 0 | 0 | 0 | 0 | .... | .... | .... | .... |
| 1998-99 | Victoriaville Tigres | QMJHL | 65 | 6 | 13 | 19 | 35 | .... | .... | .... | .... | .... | .... | .... | .... | .... | 6 | 1 | 3 | 4 | 2 | .... | .... | .... | .... |
| 99-2000 | Victoriaville Tigres | QMJHL | 22 | 1 | 4 | 5 | 17 | .... | .... | .... | .... | .... | .... | .... | .... | .... | .... | .... | .... | .... | .... | .... | .... | .... | .... |
| | Val-d'Or Foreurs | QMJHL | 50 | 14 | 28 | 42 | 100 | .... | .... | .... | .... | .... | .... | .... | .... | .... | .... | .... | .... | .... | .... | .... | .... | .... | .... |
| 2000-01 | Val-d'Or Foreurs | QMJHL | 68 | 48 | 67 | 115 | 90 | .... | .... | .... | .... | .... | .... | .... | .... | .... | 21 | 15 | 18 | 33 | 42 | .... | .... | .... | .... |
| 2001-02 | Houston Aeros | AHL | 77 | 13 | 22 | 35 | 113 | .... | .... | .... | .... | .... | .... | .... | .... | .... | 14 | 2 | 4 | 6 | 20 | .... | .... | .... | .... |
| **2002-03** | **Minnesota** | **NHL** | **38** | **3** | **2** | **5** | **23** | **1** | **0** | **0** | **52** | **5.8** | **–6** | **13** | **7.7** | **12:08** | .... | .... | .... | .... | .... | .... | .... | .... | .... |
| | Houston Aeros | AHL | 29 | 8 | 4 | 12 | 43 | .... | .... | .... | .... | .... | .... | .... | .... | .... | 23 | 7 | 11 | 18 | 12 | .... | .... | .... | .... |
| **2003-04** | **Minnesota** | **NHL** | **19** | **2** | **8** | **10** | **20** | **1** | **1** | **1** | **37** | **5.4** | **0** | **10** | **40.0** | **14:20** | .... | .... | .... | .... | .... | .... | .... | .... | .... |
| | Houston Aeros | AHL | 64 | 13 | 25 | 38 | 66 | .... | .... | .... | .... | .... | .... | .... | .... | .... | 2 | 1 | 1 | 2 | 2 | .... | .... | .... | .... |
| 2004-05 | Houston Aeros | AHL | 59 | 15 | 24 | 39 | 35 | .... | .... | .... | .... | .... | .... | .... | .... | .... | .... | .... | .... | .... | .... | .... | .... | .... | .... |
| **2005-06** | **Minnesota** | **NHL** | **71** | **7** | **9** | **16** | **63** | **0** | **0** | **1** | **87** | **8.0** | **–13** | **33** | **33.3** | **12:58** | .... | .... | .... | .... | .... | .... | .... | .... | .... |
| **2006-07** | **Minnesota** | **NHL** | **75** | **7** | **11** | **18** | **47** | **0** | **0** | **1** | **84** | **8.3** | **3** | **32** | **21.9** | **12:17** | **5** | **0** | **0** | **0** | **4** | **0** | **0** | **0** | **12:40** |

| | | | Regular Season | | | | | | | | | | | | | | Playoffs | | | | | | | | |
|---|---|---|---|---|---|---|---|---|---|---|---|---|---|---|---|---|---|---|---|---|---|---|---|---|---|
| Season | Club | League | GP | G | A | Pts | PIM | PP | SH | GW | S | % | +/- | TF | F% | Min | GP | G | A | Pts | PIM | PP | SH | GW | Min |
| 2007-08 | Minnesota | NHL | 77 | 11 | 7 | 18 | 61 | 0 | 0 | 0 | 136 | 8.1 | −13 | 45 | 37.8 | 14:32 | 6 | 0 | 0 | 0 | 27 | 0 | 0 | 0 | 15:43 |
| 2008-09 | Minnesota | NHL | 81 | 13 | 10 | 23 | 40 | 0 | 1 | 1 | 146 | 8.9 | −17 | 22 | 27.3 | 15:48 | .... | .... | .... | .... | .... | .... | .... | .... | .... |
| | NHL Totals | | 361 | 43 | 47 | 90 | 254 | 2 | 2 | 4 | 542 | 7.9 | | 155 | 29.7 | 13:47 | 11 | 0 | 0 | 0 | 31 | 0 | 0 | 0 | 14:20 |

Signed as a free agent by **Tampa Bay**, July 7, 2009.

## VERMETTE, Antoine

(vuhr-MEHT, AN-twuhn) **CBJ**

Center. Shoots left. 6'1", 197 lbs. Born, St-Agapit, Que., July 20, 1982. Ottawa's 3rd choice, 55th overall, in 2000 Entry Draft.

| Season | Club | League | GP | G | A | Pts | PIM | PP | SH | GW | S | % | +/- | TF | F% | Min | GP | G | A | Pts | PIM | PP | SH | GW | Min |
|---|---|---|---|---|---|---|---|---|---|---|---|---|---|---|---|---|---|---|---|---|---|---|---|---|---|
| 1997-98 | Quebec Select | QAHA | 19 | 11 | 20 | 31 | 36 | .... | .... | .... | .... | .... | .... | .... | .... | .... | .... | .... | .... | .... | .... | .... | .... | .... | .... |
| | Levis-Lauzon | QAAA | 8 | 1 | 1 | 2 | 4 | .... | .... | .... | .... | .... | .... | .... | .... | .... | 1 | 0 | 0 | 0 | 0 | .... | .... | .... | .... |
| 1998-99 | Quebec Remparts | QMJHL | 57 | 9 | 17 | 26 | 32 | .... | .... | .... | .... | .... | .... | .... | .... | .... | 13 | 0 | 0 | 0 | 2 | .... | .... | .... | .... |
| 99-2000 | Victoriaville Tigres | QMJHL | 71 | 30 | 41 | 71 | 87 | .... | .... | .... | .... | .... | .... | .... | .... | .... | 6 | 0 | 1 | 1 | 6 | .... | .... | .... | .... |
| 2000-01 | Victoriaville Tigres | QMJHL | 71 | 57 | 62 | 119 | 102 | .... | .... | .... | .... | .... | .... | .... | .... | .... | 9 | 4 | 6 | 10 | 14 | .... | .... | .... | .... |
| 2001-02 | Victoriaville Tigres | QMJHL | 4 | 0 | 2 | 2 | 6 | .... | .... | .... | .... | .... | .... | .... | .... | .... | 22 | 10 | 16 | 26 | 10 | .... | .... | .... | .... |
| 2002-03 | Binghamton | AHL | 80 | 34 | 28 | 62 | 57 | .... | .... | .... | .... | .... | .... | .... | .... | .... | 14 | 2 | 9 | 11 | 10 | .... | .... | .... | .... |
| **2003-04** | **Ottawa** | **NHL** | **57** | **7** | **7** | **14** | **16** | **0** | **1** | **0** | **63** | **11.1** | **5** | **100** | **44.0** | **11:59** | **4** | **0** | **1** | **1** | **4** | **0** | **0** | **0** | **11:35** |
| | Binghamton | AHL | 3 | 0 | 0 | 0 | 6 | .... | .... | .... | .... | .... | .... | .... | .... | .... | .... | .... | .... | .... | .... | .... | .... | .... | .... |
| 2004-05 | Binghamton | AHL | 78 | 28 | 45 | 73 | 36 | .... | .... | .... | .... | .... | .... | .... | .... | .... | 6 | 1 | 4 | 5 | 10 | .... | .... | .... | .... |
| **2005-06** | **Ottawa** | **NHL** | **82** | **21** | **12** | **33** | **44** | **1** | **6** | **4** | **123** | **17.1** | **17** | **537** | **57.9** | **12:35** | **10** | **2** | **0** | **2** | **4** | **0** | **0** | **1** | **15:00** |
| **2006-07** | **Ottawa** | **NHL** | **77** | **19** | **20** | **39** | **52** | **2** | **3** | **2** | **151** | **12.6** | **−2** | **834** | **53.0** | **15:42** | **20** | **2** | **3** | **5** | **6** | **0** | **0** | **0** | **16:20** |
| **2007-08** | **Ottawa** | **NHL** | **81** | **24** | **29** | **53** | **51** | **4** | **3** | **3** | **175** | **13.7** | **3** | **1217** | **56.7** | **17:35** | **4** | **0** | **0** | **0** | **4** | **0** | **0** | **0** | **20:33** |
| **2008-09** | **Ottawa** | **NHL** | **62** | **9** | **19** | **28** | **42** | **2** | **0** | **0** | **141** | **6.4** | **−12** | **771** | **58.4** | **18:03** | .... | .... | .... | .... | .... | .... | .... | .... | .... |
| | **Columbus** | **NHL** | **17** | **7** | **6** | **13** | **8** | **1** | **1** | **1** | **33** | **21.2** | **5** | **341** | **56.3** | **19:29** | **4** | **0** | **0** | **0** | **10** | **0** | **0** | **0** | **16:47** |
| | **NHL Totals** | | **376** | **87** | **93** | **180** | **213** | **10** | **14** | **10** | **686** | **12.7** | | **3800** | **56.0** | **15:25** | **42** | **4** | **4** | **8** | **28** | **0** | **0** | **1** | **16:00** |

AHL All-Rookie Team (2003)

• Missed majority of 2001-02 season recovering from neck injury suffered at Team Canada Jr. Selection Camp, June 3, 2001. Traded to **Columbus** by **Ottawa** for Pascal Leclaire and Columbus' 2nd round choice (Robin Lehner) in 2009 Entry Draft, March 4, 2009.

## VERNACE, Michael

(vuhr-NAYS, MIGH-kuhl) **ATL.**

Defense. Shoots left. 6'2", 200 lbs. Born, Toronto, Ont., May 26, 1986. San Jose's 6th choice, 201st overall, in 2004 Entry Draft.

| Season | Club | League | GP | G | A | Pts | PIM | PP | SH | GW | S | % | +/- | TF | F% | Min | GP | G | A | Pts | PIM | PP | SH | GW | Min |
|---|---|---|---|---|---|---|---|---|---|---|---|---|---|---|---|---|---|---|---|---|---|---|---|---|---|
| 2003-04 | Bramalea Blues | OPJHL | 33 | 3 | 12 | 15 | 16 | .... | .... | .... | .... | .... | .... | .... | .... | .... | .... | .... | .... | .... | .... | .... | .... | .... | .... |
| | Brampton | OHL | 2 | 1 | 1 | 2 | 0 | .... | .... | .... | .... | .... | .... | .... | .... | .... | 11 | 2 | 3 | 5 | 8 | .... | .... | .... | .... |
| 2004-05 | Brampton | OHL | 68 | 12 | 38 | 50 | 42 | .... | .... | .... | .... | .... | .... | .... | .... | .... | 6 | 2 | 2 | 4 | 0 | .... | .... | .... | .... |
| 2005-06 | Brampton | OHL | 68 | 10 | 62 | 72 | 54 | .... | .... | .... | .... | .... | .... | .... | .... | .... | 11 | 1 | 5 | 6 | 6 | .... | .... | .... | .... |
| 2006-07 | Albany River Rats | AHL | 30 | 1 | 11 | 12 | 35 | .... | .... | .... | .... | .... | .... | .... | .... | .... | .... | .... | .... | .... | .... | .... | .... | .... | .... |
| | Arizona Sundogs | CHL | 24 | 3 | 11 | 14 | 20 | .... | .... | .... | .... | .... | .... | .... | .... | .... | .... | .... | .... | .... | .... | .... | .... | .... | .... |
| 2007-08 | Lake Erie | AHL | 79 | 3 | 26 | 29 | 59 | .... | .... | .... | .... | .... | .... | .... | .... | .... | .... | .... | .... | .... | .... | .... | .... | .... | .... |
| **2008-09** | **Colorado** | **NHL** | **12** | **0** | **0** | **0** | **8** | **0** | **0** | **0** | **9** | **0.0** | **−5** | **0** | **0.0** | **19:39** | .... | .... | .... | .... | .... | .... | .... | .... | .... |
| | Lake Erie | AHL | 65 | 3 | 14 | 17 | 52 | .... | .... | .... | .... | .... | .... | .... | .... | .... | .... | .... | .... | .... | .... | .... | .... | .... | .... |
| | **NHL Totals** | | **12** | **0** | **0** | **0** | **8** | **0** | **0** | **0** | **9** | **0.0** | | **0** | **0.0** | **19:39** | .... | .... | .... | .... | .... | .... | .... | .... | .... |

OHL All-Rookie Team (2005)

• Rights traded to **Colorado** by **San Jose** for Colorado's 6th round choice (Patrick Zackrisson) in 2007 Entry Draft, June 1, 2006. Signed as a free agent by **Atlanta**, July 30, 2009.

## VERSTEEG, Kris

(vuhr-STEEG, KRIHS) **CHI.**

Right wing. Shoots right. 5'10", 180 lbs. Born, Lethbridge, Alta., May 13, 1986. Boston's 4th choice, 134th overall, in 2004 Entry Draft.

| Season | Club | League | GP | G | A | Pts | PIM | PP | SH | GW | S | % | +/- | TF | F% | Min | GP | G | A | Pts | PIM | PP | SH | GW | Min |
|---|---|---|---|---|---|---|---|---|---|---|---|---|---|---|---|---|---|---|---|---|---|---|---|---|---|
| 2002-03 | Lethbridge | WHL | 57 | 8 | 10 | 18 | 32 | .... | .... | .... | .... | .... | .... | .... | .... | .... | .... | .... | .... | .... | .... | .... | .... | .... | .... |
| 2003-04 | Lethbridge | WHL | 68 | 16 | 33 | 49 | 85 | .... | .... | .... | .... | .... | .... | .... | .... | .... | .... | .... | .... | .... | .... | .... | .... | .... | .... |
| 2004-05 | Lethbridge | WHL | 68 | 22 | 30 | 52 | 68 | .... | .... | .... | .... | .... | .... | .... | .... | .... | 5 | 0 | 1 | 1 | 4 | .... | .... | .... | .... |
| 2005-06 | Kamloops Blazers | WHL | 14 | 6 | 6 | 12 | 24 | .... | .... | .... | .... | .... | .... | .... | .... | .... | .... | .... | .... | .... | .... | .... | .... | .... | .... |
| | Red Deer Rebels | WHL | 57 | 10 | 26 | 36 | 103 | .... | .... | .... | .... | .... | .... | .... | .... | .... | .... | .... | .... | .... | .... | .... | .... | .... | .... |
| | Providence Bruins | AHL | 13 | 2 | 4 | 6 | 13 | .... | .... | .... | .... | .... | .... | .... | .... | .... | 3 | 0 | 0 | 0 | 6 | .... | .... | .... | .... |
| 2006-07 | Providence Bruins | AHL | 43 | 22 | 27 | 49 | 19 | .... | .... | .... | .... | .... | .... | .... | .... | .... | .... | .... | .... | .... | .... | .... | .... | .... | .... |
| | Norfolk Admirals | AHL | 27 | 4 | 19 | 23 | 20 | .... | .... | .... | .... | .... | .... | .... | .... | .... | 2 | 0 | 0 | 0 | 2 | .... | .... | .... | .... |
| **2007-08** | **Chicago** | **NHL** | **13** | **2** | **2** | **4** | **6** | **0** | **0** | **0** | **21** | **9.5** | **−1** | **3** | **66.7** | **15:52** | .... | .... | .... | .... | .... | .... | .... | .... | .... |
| | Rockford IceHogs | AHL | 56 | 18 | 31 | 49 | 174 | .... | .... | .... | .... | .... | .... | .... | .... | .... | 12 | 6 | 5 | 11 | 6 | .... | .... | .... | .... |
| **2008-09** | **Chicago** | **NHL** | **78** | **22** | **31** | **53** | **55** | **6** | **4** | **3** | **139** | **15.8** | **15** | **266** | **46.6** | **17:02** | **17** | **4** | **8** | **12** | **22** | **3** | **0** | **0** | **16:14** |
| | **NHL Totals** | | **91** | **24** | **33** | **57** | **61** | **6** | **4** | **3** | **160** | **15.0** | | **269** | **46.8** | **16:52** | **17** | **4** | **8** | **12** | **22** | **3** | **0** | **0** | **16:14** |

NHL All-Rookie Team (2009)

Traded to **Chicago** by **Boston** with future considerations for Brandon Bochenski, February 3, 2007.

## VESCE, Ryan

(veks-KEE, RIGH-uhn) **S.J.**

Center. Shoots right. 5'8", 175 lbs. Born, Lloyd Harbor, NY, April 7, 1982.

| Season | Club | League | GP | G | A | Pts | PIM | PP | SH | GW | S | % | +/- | TF | F% | Min | GP | G | A | Pts | PIM | PP | SH | GW | Min |
|---|---|---|---|---|---|---|---|---|---|---|---|---|---|---|---|---|---|---|---|---|---|---|---|---|---|
| 2000-01 | Cornell Big Red | ECAC | 33 | 7 | 20 | 27 | 10 | .... | .... | .... | .... | .... | .... | .... | .... | .... | .... | .... | .... | .... | .... | .... | .... | .... | .... |
| 2001-02 | Cornell Big Red | ECAC | 35 | 10 | 20 | 30 | 10 | .... | .... | .... | .... | .... | .... | .... | .... | .... | .... | .... | .... | .... | .... | .... | .... | .... | .... |
| 2002-03 | Cornell Big Red | ECAC | 36 | 19 | 26 | 45 | 16 | .... | .... | .... | .... | .... | .... | .... | .... | .... | .... | .... | .... | .... | .... | .... | .... | .... | .... |
| 2003-04 | Cornell Big Red | ECAC | 27 | 10 | 16 | 26 | 14 | .... | .... | .... | .... | .... | .... | .... | .... | .... | .... | .... | .... | .... | .... | .... | .... | .... | .... |
| 2004-05 | Rogle | Sweden-2 | 43 | 20 | 25 | 45 | 51 | .... | .... | .... | .... | .... | .... | .... | .... | .... | .... | .... | .... | .... | .... | .... | .... | .... | .... |
| 2005-06 | Springfield | AHL | 80 | 18 | 49 | 67 | 50 | .... | .... | .... | .... | .... | .... | .... | .... | .... | .... | .... | .... | .... | .... | .... | .... | .... | .... |
| 2006-07 | Binghamton | AHL | 80 | 16 | 35 | 51 | 51 | .... | .... | .... | .... | .... | .... | .... | .... | .... | .... | .... | .... | .... | .... | .... | .... | .... | .... |
| 2007-08 | HIFK Helsinki | Finland | 56 | 26 | 18 | 44 | 42 | .... | .... | .... | .... | .... | .... | .... | .... | .... | 7 | 1 | 2 | 3 | 2 | .... | .... | .... | .... |
| **2008-09** | **San Jose** | **NHL** | **10** | **0** | **0** | **0** | **4** | **0** | **0** | **0** | **11** | **0.0** | **−2** | **64** | **46.9** | **9:45** | .... | .... | .... | .... | .... | .... | .... | .... | .... |
| | Worcester Sharks | AHL | 67 | 24 | 47 | 71 | 28 | .... | .... | .... | .... | .... | .... | .... | .... | .... | 12 | 3 | 7 | 10 | 22 | .... | .... | .... | .... |
| | **NHL Totals** | | **10** | **0** | **0** | **0** | **4** | **0** | **0** | **0** | **11** | **0.0** | | **64** | **46.9** | **9:45** | .... | .... | .... | .... | .... | .... | .... | .... | .... |

Signed as a free agent by **Ottawa**, July 17, 2006. Signed as a free agent by **HIFK Helsinki** (Finland), July 17, 2007. Signed as a free agent by **San Jose**, August 13, 2008.

## VISHNEVSKI, Vitaly

(vihsh-NEHV-skee, vih-TAL-ee)

Defense. Shoots left. 6'2", 215 lbs. Born, Kharkov, USSR, March 18, 1980. Anaheim's 1st choice, 5th overall, in 1998 Entry Draft.

| Season | Club | League | GP | G | A | Pts | PIM | PP | SH | GW | S | % | +/- | TF | F% | Min | GP | G | A | Pts | PIM | PP | SH | GW | Min |
|---|---|---|---|---|---|---|---|---|---|---|---|---|---|---|---|---|---|---|---|---|---|---|---|---|---|
| 1995-96 | Yaroslavl 2 | CIS-2 | 40 | 4 | 4 | 8 | 20 | .... | .... | .... | .... | .... | .... | .... | .... | .... | .... | .... | .... | .... | .... | .... | .... | .... | .... |
| 1996-97 | Yaroslavl 2 | Russia-3 | 45 | 0 | 2 | 2 | 30 | .... | .... | .... | .... | .... | .... | .... | .... | .... | .... | .... | .... | .... | .... | .... | .... | .... | .... |
| 1997-98 | Yaroslavl 2 | Russia-2 | 47 | 8 | 9 | 17 | 164 | .... | .... | .... | .... | .... | .... | .... | .... | .... | .... | .... | .... | .... | .... | .... | .... | .... | .... |
| 1998-99 | Yaroslavl | Russia | 34 | 3 | 4 | 7 | 38 | .... | .... | .... | .... | .... | .... | .... | .... | .... | 10 | 0 | 0 | 0 | 4 | .... | .... | .... | .... |
| **99-2000** | **Anaheim** | **NHL** | **31** | **1** | **1** | **2** | **26** | **1** | **0** | **0** | **17** | **5.9** | **0** | **0** | **0.0** | **16:38** | .... | .... | .... | .... | .... | .... | .... | .... | .... |
| | Cincinnati | AHL | 35 | 1 | 3 | 4 | 45 | .... | .... | .... | .... | .... | .... | .... | .... | .... | .... | .... | .... | .... | .... | .... | .... | .... | .... |
| **2000-01** | **Anaheim** | **NHL** | **76** | **1** | **10** | **11** | **99** | **0** | **0** | **0** | **49** | **2.0** | **−1** | **0** | **0.0** | **19:14** | .... | .... | .... | .... | .... | .... | .... | .... | .... |
| **2001-02** | **Anaheim** | **NHL** | **74** | **0** | **3** | **3** | **60** | **0** | **0** | **0** | **54** | **0.0** | **−10** | **0** | **0.0** | **17:36** | .... | .... | .... | .... | .... | .... | .... | .... | .... |
| **2002-03** | **Anaheim** | **NHL** | **80** | **2** | **6** | **8** | **76** | **0** | **1** | **0** | **65** | **3.1** | **−8** | **0** | **0.0** | **14:10** | **21** | **0** | **1** | **1** | **6** | **0** | **0** | **0** | **10:02** |
| **2003-04** | **Anaheim** | **NHL** | **73** | **6** | **10** | **16** | **51** | **0** | **0** | **0** | **86** | **7.0** | **0** | **0** | **0.0** | **17:10** | .... | .... | .... | .... | .... | .... | .... | .... | .... |
| 2004-05 | Voskresensk | Russia | 51 | 7 | 17 | 24 | 92 | .... | .... | .... | .... | .... | .... | .... | .... | .... | .... | .... | .... | .... | .... | .... | .... | .... | .... |
| **2005-06** | **Anaheim** | **NHL** | **82** | **1** | **7** | **8** | **91** | **0** | **0** | **0** | **90** | **1.1** | **8** | **1** | **100.0** | **16:26** | **16** | **0** | **4** | **4** | **10** | **0** | **0** | **0** | **13:41** |
| | Russia | Olympics | 8 | 0 | 1 | 1 | 4 | .... | .... | .... | .... | .... | .... | .... | .... | .... | .... | .... | .... | .... | .... | .... | .... | .... | .... |
| **2006-07** | **Atlanta** | **NHL** | **52** | **3** | **9** | **12** | **31** | **0** | **0** | **0** | **41** | **7.3** | **−5** | **0** | **0.0** | **19:18** | .... | .... | .... | .... | .... | .... | .... | .... | .... |
| | **Nashville** | **NHL** | **15** | **0** | **1** | **1** | **10** | **0** | **0** | **0** | **6** | **0.0** | **1** | **0** | **0.0** | **10:02** | .... | .... | .... | .... | .... | .... | .... | .... | .... |
| **2007-08** | **New Jersey** | **NHL** | **69** | **2** | **5** | **7** | **50** | **0** | **0** | **0** | **48** | **4.2** | **−12** | **0** | **0.0** | **15:32** | **3** | **0** | **0** | **0** | **2** | **0** | **0** | **0** | **13:29** |
| 2008-09 | Yaroslavl | Rus-KHL | 53 | 8 | 13 | 21 | 124 | .... | .... | .... | .... | .... | .... | .... | .... | .... | 19 | 2 | 7 | 9 | 44 | .... | .... | .... | .... |
| | **NHL Totals** | | **552** | **16** | **52** | **68** | **494** | **1** | **1** | **0** | **456** | **3.5** | | **1** | **100.0** | **16:44** | **40** | **0** | **5** | **5** | **18** | **0** | **0** | **0** | **11:45** |

Signed as a free agent by **Voskresensk** (Russia), August 25, 2004. Traded to **Atlanta** by **Anaheim** for Karl Stewart, Atlanta's 2nd round choice (later traded to Colorado - Colorado selected T.J. Galiardi) in 2007 Entry Draft and future considerations, August 17, 2006. Traded to **Nashville** by **Atlanta** for Eric Belanger, February 10, 2007. Signed as a free agent by **New Jersey**, July 10, 2007. Signed as a free agent by **Yaroslavl** (Rus-KHL). August 26, 2008.

## VISHNEVSKIY, Ivan

(vihsh-NEHV-skee, ee-VAHN) **DAL.**

Defense. Shoots left. 5'11", 176 lbs. Born, Barnaul, USSR, February 18, 1988. Dallas' 1st choice, 27th overall, in 2006 Entry Draft.

| | | | Regular Season | | | | | | | | | | | | | | | Playoffs | | | | | | | | |
|---|---|---|---|---|---|---|---|---|---|---|---|---|---|---|---|---|---|---|---|---|---|---|---|---|
| Season | Club | League | GP | G | A | Pts | PIM | PP | SH | GW | S | % | +/- | TF | F% | Min | GP | G | A | Pts | PIM | PP | SH | GW | Min |
| 2003-04 | Lada Togliatti 2 | Russia-3 | 16 | 0 | 0 | 0 | 10 | .... | .... | .... | .... | .... | .... | .... | .... | .... | .... | .... | .... | .... | .... | .... | .... | .... | .... |
| 2004-05 | Lada Togliatti 2 | Russia-3 | STATISTICS NOT AVAILABLE | | | | | | | | | | | | | | | | | | | | | | |
| 2005-06 | Rouyn-Noranda | QMJHL | 54 | 13 | 35 | 48 | 57 | .... | .... | .... | .... | .... | .... | .... | .... | .... | 5 | 2 | 1 | 3 | 2 | .... | .... | .... | .... |
| 2006-07 | Rouyn-Noranda | QMJHL | 60 | 14 | 37 | 51 | 90 | .... | .... | .... | .... | .... | .... | .... | .... | .... | 16 | 5 | 8 | 13 | 8 | .... | .... | .... | .... |
| 2007-08 | Rouyn-Noranda | QMJHL | 45 | 17 | 28 | 45 | 50 | .... | .... | .... | .... | .... | .... | .... | .... | .... | 17 | 0 | 6 | 6 | 16 | .... | .... | .... | .... |
| **2008-09** | **Dallas** | **NHL** | **3** | **0** | **2** | **2** | **2** | **0** | **0** | **0** | **9** | **0.0** | **1** | **0** | **0.0** | **19:33** | .... | .... | .... | .... | .... | .... | .... | .... | .... |
| | Peoria Rivermen | AHL | 67 | 6 | 13 | 19 | 28 | .... | .... | .... | .... | .... | .... | .... | .... | .... | 5 | 0 | 2 | 2 | 2 | .... | .... | .... | .... |
| | **NHL Totals** | | **3** | **0** | **2** | **2** | **2** | **0** | **0** | **0** | **9** | **0.0** | | **0** | **0.0** | **19:33** | .... | .... | .... | .... | .... | .... | .... | .... | .... |

QMJHL All-Rookie Team (2006) • QMJHL Second All-Star Team (2008)

## VISNOVSKY, Lubomir

(vihsh-NAWV-skee, LOO-boh-mihr) **EDM.**

Defense. Shoots left. 5'10", 188 lbs. Born, Topolcany, Czech., August 11, 1976. Los Angeles' 4th choice, 118th overall, in 2000 Entry Draft.

| | | | Regular Season | | | | | | | | | | | | | | | Playoffs | | | | | | | | |
|---|---|---|---|---|---|---|---|---|---|---|---|---|---|---|---|---|---|---|---|---|---|---|---|---|
| Season | Club | League | GP | G | A | Pts | PIM | PP | SH | GW | S | % | +/- | TF | F% | Min | GP | G | A | Pts | PIM | PP | SH | GW | Min |
| 1994-95 | Bratislava | Slovakia | 36 | 11 | 12 | 23 | 10 | .... | .... | .... | .... | .... | .... | .... | .... | .... | 9 | 1 | 3 | 4 | 2 | .... | .... | .... | .... |
| 1995-96 | Bratislava | Slovakia | 35 | 8 | 6 | 14 | 22 | .... | .... | .... | .... | .... | .... | .... | .... | .... | 13 | 1 | 5 | 6 | 2 | .... | .... | .... | .... |
| 1996-97 | Bratislava | Slovakia | 44 | 11 | 12 | 23 | .... | .... | .... | .... | .... | .... | .... | .... | .... | .... | 2 | 0 | 1 | 1 | .... | .... | .... | .... | .... |
| | Bratislava | EuroHL | 6 | 3 | 1 | 4 | 2 | .... | .... | .... | .... | .... | .... | .... | .... | .... | 2 | 0 | 0 | 0 | 6 | .... | .... | .... | .... |
| 1997-98 | Bratislava | Slovakia | 36 | 7 | 9 | 16 | 16 | .... | .... | .... | .... | .... | .... | .... | .... | .... | 11 | 2 | 4 | 6 | 8 | .... | .... | .... | .... |
| | Bratislava | EuroHL | 6 | 1 | 0 | 1 | 4 | .... | .... | .... | .... | .... | .... | .... | .... | .... | .... | .... | .... | .... | .... | .... | .... | .... | .... |
| | Slovakia | Olympics | 3 | 0 | 0 | 0 | 2 | .... | .... | .... | .... | .... | .... | .... | .... | .... | .... | .... | .... | .... | .... | .... | .... | .... | .... |
| 1998-99 | Bratislava | Slovakia | 40 | 9 | 10 | 19 | 31 | .... | .... | .... | .... | .... | .... | .... | .... | .... | 10 | 5 | 5 | 10 | 0 | .... | .... | .... | .... |
| | Bratislava | EuroHL | 6 | 0 | 3 | 3 | 4 | .... | .... | .... | .... | .... | .... | .... | .... | .... | .... | .... | .... | .... | .... | .... | .... | .... | .... |
| 99-2000 | Bratislava | Slovakia | 52 | 21 | 24 | 45 | 38 | .... | .... | .... | .... | .... | .... | .... | .... | .... | 8 | 5 | 3 | 8 | 16 | .... | .... | .... | .... |
| **2000-01** | **Los Angeles** | **NHL** | **81** | **7** | **32** | **39** | **36** | **3** | **0** | **3** | **105** | **6.7** | **16** | **0** | **0.0** | **16:58** | **8** | **0** | **0** | **0** | **0** | **0** | **0** | **0** | **13:57** |
| **2001-02** | **Los Angeles** | **NHL** | **72** | **4** | **17** | **21** | **14** | **1** | **0** | **2** | **95** | **4.2** | **–5** | **0** | **0.0** | **16:15** | **4** | **0** | **1** | **1** | **0** | **0** | **0** | **0** | **8:22** |
| | Slovakia | Olympics | 3 | 1 | 2 | 3 | 0 | .... | .... | .... | .... | .... | .... | .... | .... | .... | .... | .... | .... | .... | .... | .... | .... | .... | .... |
| **2002-03** | **Los Angeles** | **NHL** | **57** | **8** | **16** | **24** | **28** | **1** | **0** | **1** | **85** | **9.4** | **2** | **0** | **0.0** | **19:20** | .... | .... | .... | .... | .... | .... | .... | .... | .... |
| **2003-04** | **Los Angeles** | **NHL** | **58** | **8** | **21** | **29** | **26** | **5** | **0** | **0** | **114** | **7.0** | **8** | **0** | **0.0** | **24:02** | .... | .... | .... | .... | .... | .... | .... | .... | .... |
| 2004-05 | Bratislava | Slovakia | 43 | 13 | 25 | 38 | 40 | .... | .... | .... | .... | .... | .... | .... | .... | .... | 14 | 2 | 10 | 12 | 10 | .... | .... | .... | .... |
| **2005-06** | **Los Angeles** | **NHL** | **80** | **17** | **50** | **67** | **50** | **10** | **0** | **3** | **152** | **11.2** | **7** | **1** | **100.0** | **23:16** | .... | .... | .... | .... | .... | .... | .... | .... | .... |
| | Slovakia | Olympics | 6 | 1 | 1 | 2 | 0 | .... | .... | .... | .... | .... | .... | .... | .... | .... | .... | .... | .... | .... | .... | .... | .... | .... | .... |
| **2006-07** | **Los Angeles** | **NHL** | **69** | **18** | **40** | **58** | **26** | **8** | **0** | **0** | **159** | **11.3** | **1** | **6** | **33.3** | **24:27** | .... | .... | .... | .... | .... | .... | .... | .... | .... |
| **2007-08** | **Los Angeles** | **NHL** | **82** | **8** | **33** | **41** | **34** | **3** | **0** | **1** | **153** | **5.2** | **–18** | **8** | **12.5** | **23:00** | .... | .... | .... | .... | .... | .... | .... | .... | .... |
| **2008-09** | **Edmonton** | **NHL** | **50** | **8** | **23** | **31** | **30** | **5** | **0** | **1** | **86** | **9.3** | **6** | **0** | **0.0** | **23:01** | .... | .... | .... | .... | .... | .... | .... | .... | .... |
| | **NHL Totals** | | **549** | **78** | **232** | **310** | **244** | **36** | **0** | **11** | **949** | **8.2** | | **15** | **26.7** | **21:11** | **12** | **0** | **1** | **1** | **0** | **0** | **0** | **0** | **12:05** |

NHL All-Rookie Team (2001)
Played in NHL All-Star Game (2007)
Signed as a free agent by **Bratislava** (Slovakia), September 27, 2004. Traded to **Edmonton** by **Los Angeles** for Jarret Stoll and Matt Greene, June 29, 2008.

## VLASIC, Marc-Edouard

(vih-LASH-ihc, MAHRK-EHD-wahrd) **S.J.**

Defense. Shoots left. 6'1", 200 lbs. Born, Montreal, Que., March 30, 1987. San Jose's 2nd choice, 35th overall, in 2005 Entry Draft.

| | | | Regular Season | | | | | | | | | | | | | | | Playoffs | | | | | | | | |
|---|---|---|---|---|---|---|---|---|---|---|---|---|---|---|---|---|---|---|---|---|---|---|---|---|
| Season | Club | League | GP | G | A | Pts | PIM | PP | SH | GW | S | % | +/- | TF | F% | Min | GP | G | A | Pts | PIM | PP | SH | GW | Min |
| 2003-04 | Quebec Remparts | QMJHL | 41 | 1 | 9 | 10 | 4 | .... | .... | .... | .... | .... | .... | .... | .... | .... | 5 | 0 | 1 | 1 | 0 | .... | .... | .... | .... |
| 2004-05 | Quebec Remparts | QMJHL | 70 | 5 | 25 | 30 | 33 | .... | .... | .... | .... | .... | .... | .... | .... | .... | 13 | 2 | 7 | 9 | 2 | .... | .... | .... | .... |
| 2005-06 | Quebec Remparts | QMJHL | 66 | 16 | 57 | 73 | 57 | .... | .... | .... | .... | .... | .... | .... | .... | .... | 23 | 5 | 24 | 29 | 10 | .... | .... | .... | .... |
| **2006-07** | **San Jose** | **NHL** | **81** | **3** | **23** | **26** | **18** | **2** | **0** | **0** | **66** | **4.5** | **13** | **0** | **0.0** | **22:12** | **11** | **0** | **1** | **1** | **2** | **0** | **0** | **0** | **22:52** |
| **2007-08** | **San Jose** | **NHL** | **82** | **2** | **12** | **14** | **24** | **1** | **0** | **0** | **72** | **2.8** | **–12** | **0** | **0.0** | **21:37** | **13** | **0** | **1** | **1** | **0** | **0** | **0** | **0** | **24:39** |
| | Worcester Sharks | AHL | 1 | 0 | 2 | 2 | 0 | .... | .... | .... | .... | .... | .... | .... | .... | .... | .... | .... | .... | .... | .... | .... | .... | .... | .... |
| **2008-09** | **San Jose** | **NHL** | **82** | **6** | **30** | **36** | **42** | **3** | **0** | **1** | **104** | **5.8** | **15** | **0** | **0.0** | **23:54** | **6** | **0** | **1** | **1** | **0** | **0** | **0** | **0** | **20:39** |
| | **NHL Totals** | | **245** | **11** | **65** | **76** | **84** | **6** | **0** | **1** | **242** | **4.5** | | **0** | **0.0** | **22:34** | **30** | **0** | **3** | **3** | **2** | **0** | **0** | **0** | **23:12** |

NHL All-Rookie Team (2007)

## VOLCHENKOV, Anton

(vohl-chen-KAHF, AN-tawn) **OTT.**

Defense. Shoots left. 6'1", 226 lbs. Born, Moscow, USSR, February 25, 1982. Ottawa's 1st choice, 21st overall, in 2000 Entry Draft.

| | | | Regular Season | | | | | | | | | | | | | | | Playoffs | | | | | | | | |
|---|---|---|---|---|---|---|---|---|---|---|---|---|---|---|---|---|---|---|---|---|---|---|---|---|
| Season | Club | League | GP | G | A | Pts | PIM | PP | SH | GW | S | % | +/- | TF | F% | Min | GP | G | A | Pts | PIM | PP | SH | GW | Min |
| 99-2000 | HK Moscow 2 | Russia-3 | 6 | 0 | 1 | 1 | 10 | .... | .... | .... | .... | .... | .... | .... | .... | .... | .... | .... | .... | .... | .... | .... | .... | .... | .... |
| | HK Moscow | Russia-2 | 30 | 2 | 9 | 11 | 36 | .... | .... | .... | .... | .... | .... | .... | .... | .... | .... | .... | .... | .... | .... | .... | .... | .... | .... |
| 2000-01 | Krylja Sovetov | Russia-2 | 34 | 3 | 4 | 7 | 56 | .... | .... | .... | .... | .... | .... | .... | .... | .... | .... | .... | .... | .... | .... | .... | .... | .... | .... |
| 2001-02 | Krylja Sovetov 2 | Russia-3 | 1 | 0 | 0 | 0 | 0 | .... | .... | .... | .... | .... | .... | .... | .... | .... | .... | .... | .... | .... | .... | .... | .... | .... | .... |
| | Krylja Sovetov | Russia | 47 | 4 | 16 | 20 | 50 | .... | .... | .... | .... | .... | .... | .... | .... | .... | 3 | 0 | 0 | 0 | 29 | .... | .... | .... | .... |
| **2002-03** | **Ottawa** | **NHL** | **57** | **3** | **13** | **16** | **40** | **0** | **0** | **0** | **75** | **4.0** | **–4** | **0** | **0.0** | **15:30** | **17** | **1** | **1** | **2** | **4** | **0** | **0** | **1** | **13:31** |
| **2003-04** | **Ottawa** | **NHL** | **19** | **1** | **2** | **3** | **8** | **0** | **0** | **0** | **15** | **6.7** | **1** | **0** | **0.0** | **13:04** | **5** | **0** | **0** | **0** | **6** | **0** | **0** | **0** | **11:52** |
| 2004-05 | Binghamton | AHL | 69 | 10 | 35 | 45 | 62 | .... | .... | .... | .... | .... | .... | .... | .... | .... | 6 | 0 | 3 | 3 | 0 | .... | .... | .... | .... |
| **2005-06** | **Ottawa** | **NHL** | **75** | **4** | **13** | **17** | **53** | **0** | **0** | **0** | **82** | **4.9** | **21** | **0** | **0.0** | **18:03** | **9** | **0** | **4** | **4** | **8** | **0** | **0** | **0** | **13:53** |
| | Russia | Olympics | 8 | 0 | 0 | 0 | 2 | .... | .... | .... | .... | .... | .... | .... | .... | .... | .... | .... | .... | .... | .... | .... | .... | .... | .... |
| **2006-07** | **Ottawa** | **NHL** | **78** | **1** | **18** | **19** | **67** | **0** | **0** | **0** | **85** | **1.2** | **37** | **0** | **0.0** | **21:17** | **20** | **2** | **4** | **6** | **24** | **0** | **0** | **1** | **23:19** |
| **2007-08** | **Ottawa** | **NHL** | **67** | **1** | **14** | **15** | **55** | **0** | **0** | **1** | **71** | **1.4** | **14** | **0** | **0.0** | **20:31** | **4** | **0** | **1** | **1** | **2** | **0** | **0** | **0** | **17:11** |
| **2008-09** | **Ottawa** | **NHL** | **68** | **2** | **8** | **10** | **36** | **0** | **0** | **1** | **79** | **2.5** | **–10** | **0** | **0.0** | **20:08** | .... | .... | .... | .... | .... | .... | .... | .... | .... |
| | **NHL Totals** | | **364** | **12** | **68** | **80** | **259** | **0** | **0** | **2** | **407** | **2.9** | | **0** | **0.0** | **18:56** | **55** | **3** | **10** | **13** | **44** | **0** | **0** | **2** | **17:16** |

• Missed majority of 2003-04 season recovering from shoulder injury suffered in game vs. Boston, December 8, 2003.

## VORACEK, Jakub

(VOHR-rah-chehk, YA-kuhb) **CBJ**

Right wing. Shoots left. 6'1", 205 lbs. Born, Kladno, Czech., August 15, 1989. Columbus' 1st choice, 7th overall, in 2007 Entry Draft.

| | | | Regular Season | | | | | | | | | | | | | | | Playoffs | | | | | | | | |
|---|---|---|---|---|---|---|---|---|---|---|---|---|---|---|---|---|---|---|---|---|---|---|---|---|
| Season | Club | League | GP | G | A | Pts | PIM | PP | SH | GW | S | % | +/- | TF | F% | Min | GP | G | A | Pts | PIM | PP | SH | GW | Min |
| 2002-03 | HC Kladno U17 | CzR-U17 | 2 | 1 | 1 | 2 | 2 | .... | .... | .... | .... | .... | .... | .... | .... | .... | 2 | 1 | 1 | 2 | 0 | .... | .... | .... | .... |
| 2003-04 | HC Kladno U17 | CzR-U17 | 52 | 30 | 24 | 54 | 26 | .... | .... | .... | .... | .... | .... | .... | .... | .... | 2 | 0 | 0 | 0 | 2 | .... | .... | .... | .... |
| 2004-05 | HC Kladno U17 | CzR-U17 | 30 | 23 | 39 | 62 | 44 | .... | .... | .... | .... | .... | .... | .... | .... | .... | 7 | 5 | 4 | 9 | 14 | .... | .... | .... | .... |
| | HC Kladno Jr. | CzRep-Jr. | 16 | 5 | 7 | 12 | 6 | .... | .... | .... | .... | .... | .... | .... | .... | .... | 1 | 1 | 0 | 1 | 2 | .... | .... | .... | .... |
| 2005-06 | HC Kladno U17 | CzR-U17 | .... | .... | .... | .... | .... | .... | .... | .... | .... | .... | .... | .... | .... | .... | 2 | 1 | 3 | 4 | 31 | .... | .... | .... | .... |
| | HC Kladno Jr. | CzRep-Jr. | 46 | 21 | 38 | 59 | 54 | .... | .... | .... | .... | .... | .... | .... | .... | .... | 6 | 7 | 4 | 11 | 2 | .... | .... | .... | .... |
| | HC Rabat Kladno | CzRep | 1 | 0 | 0 | 0 | 0 | .... | .... | .... | .... | .... | .... | .... | .... | .... | .... | .... | .... | .... | .... | .... | .... | .... | .... |
| 2006-07 | Halifax | QMJHL | 59 | 23 | 63 | 86 | 26 | .... | .... | .... | .... | .... | .... | .... | .... | .... | 12 | 7 | 17 | 24 | 6 | .... | .... | .... | .... |
| 2007-08 | Halifax | QMJHL | 53 | 33 | 68 | 101 | 42 | .... | .... | .... | .... | .... | .... | .... | .... | .... | 15 | 5 | 13 | 18 | 14 | .... | .... | .... | .... |
| **2008-09** | **Columbus** | **NHL** | **80** | **9** | **29** | **38** | **44** | **0** | **0** | **1** | **101** | **8.9** | **11** | **3** | **0.0** | **12:40** | **4** | **0** | **1** | **1** | **8** | **0** | **0** | **0** | **12:06** |
| | **NHL Totals** | | **80** | **9** | **29** | **38** | **44** | **0** | **0** | **1** | **101** | **8.9** | | **3** | **0.0** | **12:40** | **4** | **0** | **1** | **1** | **8** | **0** | **0** | **0** | **12:06** |

QMJHL All-Rookie Team (2007) • QMJHL Rookie of the Year (2007) • QMJHL Second All-Star Team (2008)

## VOROS, Aaron

(VOH-ruhs, AIR-ruhn) **NYR**

Center. Shoots left. 6'3", 215 lbs. Born, Vancouver, B.C., July 2, 1981. New Jersey's 10th choice, 229th overall, in 2001 Entry Draft.

| | | | Regular Season | | | | | | | | | | | | | | | Playoffs | | | | | | | | |
|---|---|---|---|---|---|---|---|---|---|---|---|---|---|---|---|---|---|---|---|---|---|---|---|---|
| Season | Club | League | GP | G | A | Pts | PIM | PP | SH | GW | S | % | +/- | TF | F% | Min | GP | G | A | Pts | PIM | PP | SH | GW | Min |
| 99-2000 | Victoria Salsa | BCHL | 58 | 14 | 21 | 35 | 285 | .... | .... | .... | .... | .... | .... | .... | .... | .... | .... | .... | .... | .... | .... | .... | .... | .... | .... |
| 2000-01 | Victoria Salsa | BCHL | 57 | 34 | 34 | 68 | 196 | .... | .... | .... | .... | .... | .... | .... | .... | .... | 30 | 16 | 15 | 31 | .... | .... | .... | .... | .... |
| 2001-02 | Alaska | CCHA | 37 | 18 | 12 | 30 | *101 | .... | .... | .... | .... | .... | .... | .... | .... | .... | .... | .... | .... | .... | .... | .... | .... | .... | .... |
| 2002-03 | Alaska | CCHA | 16 | 2 | 5 | 7 | 42 | .... | .... | .... | .... | .... | .... | .... | .... | .... | .... | .... | .... | .... | .... | .... | .... | .... | .... |
| 2003-04 | Alaska | CCHA | 36 | 16 | 8 | 24 | *132 | .... | .... | .... | .... | .... | .... | .... | .... | .... | .... | .... | .... | .... | .... | .... | .... | .... | .... |
| | Albany River Rats | AHL | 9 | 2 | 1 | 3 | 14 | .... | .... | .... | .... | .... | .... | .... | .... | .... | .... | .... | .... | .... | .... | .... | .... | .... | .... |
| 2004-05 | Albany River Rats | AHL | 71 | 11 | 17 | 28 | 220 | .... | .... | .... | .... | .... | .... | .... | .... | .... | .... | .... | .... | .... | .... | .... | .... | .... | .... |
| 2005-06 | Albany River Rats | AHL | 73 | 16 | 14 | 30 | 180 | .... | .... | .... | .... | .... | .... | .... | .... | .... | .... | .... | .... | .... | .... | .... | .... | .... | .... |
| 2006-07 | Lowell Devils | AHL | 39 | 9 | 8 | 17 | 111 | .... | .... | .... | .... | .... | .... | .... | .... | .... | .... | .... | .... | .... | .... | .... | .... | .... | .... |
| | Houston Aeros | AHL | 19 | 2 | 3 | 5 | 58 | .... | .... | .... | .... | .... | .... | .... | .... | .... | .... | .... | .... | .... | .... | .... | .... | .... | .... |

| Season | Club | League | GP | G | A | Pts | PIM | PP | SH | GW | S | % | +/- | TF | F% | Min | GP | G | A | Pts | PIM | PP | SH | GW | Min |
|---|---|---|---|---|---|---|---|---|---|---|---|---|---|---|---|---|---|---|---|---|---|---|---|---|---|
| | | | Regular Season | | | | | | | | | | | | | | Playoffs | | | | | | | | |
| **2007-08** | **Minnesota** | **NHL** | **55** | **7** | **7** | **14** | **141** | **0** | **0** | **1** | **52** | **13.5** | **-7** | **15** | **20.0** | **9:11** | **5** | **1** | **0** | **1** | **16** | **0** | **0** | **0** | **10:39** |
| | Houston Aeros | AHL | 12 | 4 | 4 | 8 | 46 | .... | .... | .... | .... | .... | .... | .... | .... | .... | .... | .... | .... | .... | .... | .... | .... | .... | .... |
| **2008-09** | **NY Rangers** | **NHL** | **54** | **8** | **8** | **16** | **122** | **3** | **0** | **1** | **66** | **12.1** | **-9** | **10** | **40.0** | **11:11** | **4** | **0** | **0** | **0** | **14** | **0** | **0** | **0** | **6:51** |
| | **NHL Totals** | | **109** | **15** | **15** | **30** | **263** | **3** | **0** | **2** | **118** | **12.7** | | **25** | **28.0** | **10:10** | **9** | **1** | **0** | **1** | **30** | **0** | **0** | **0** | **8:58** |

CCHA All-Rookie Team (2002)

• Missed majority of 2002-03 season recovering from leg surgery, January 30, 2003. Traded to **Minnesota** by **New Jersey** for Minnesota's 7th round choice (Jean-Sebastien Berube) in 2008 Entry Draft, February 28, 2007. Signed as a free agent by **NY Rangers**, July 1, 2008.

## VRANA, Petr

(vuh-RA-nuh, PEE-tuhr) **N.J.**

Center. Shoots left. 5'10", 190 lbs. Born, Sternberk, Czech., March 29, 1985. New Jersey's 2nd choice, 42nd overall, in 2003 Entry Draft.

| Season | Club | League | GP | G | A | Pts | PIM | PP | SH | GW | S | % | +/- | TF | F% | Min | GP | G | A | Pts | PIM | PP | SH | GW | Min |
|---|---|---|---|---|---|---|---|---|---|---|---|---|---|---|---|---|---|---|---|---|---|---|---|---|---|
| 2001-02 | HC Havirov Jr. | CzRep-Jr. | 38 | 11 | 12 | 23 | .... | .... | .... | .... | .... | .... | .... | .... | .... | .... | .... | .... | .... | .... | .... | .... | .... | .... | .... |
| | HC Femax Havirov | CzRep | 6 | 0 | 0 | 0 | 4 | .... | .... | .... | .... | .... | .... | .... | .... | .... | .... | .... | .... | .... | .... | .... | .... | .... | .... |
| 2002-03 | Halifax | QMJHL | 72 | 37 | 46 | 83 | 32 | .... | .... | .... | .... | .... | .... | .... | .... | .... | 24 | 5 | 15 | 20 | 12 | .... | .... | .... | .... |
| 2003-04 | Halifax | QMJHL | 48 | 13 | 25 | 38 | 56 | .... | .... | .... | .... | .... | .... | .... | .... | .... | .... | .... | .... | .... | .... | .... | .... | .... | .... |
| 2004-05 | Halifax | QMJHL | 60 | 16 | 35 | 51 | 77 | .... | .... | .... | .... | .... | .... | .... | .... | .... | 12 | 10 | 4 | 14 | 12 | .... | .... | .... | .... |
| 2005-06 | Albany River Rats | AHL | 74 | 12 | 23 | 35 | 91 | .... | .... | .... | .... | .... | .... | .... | .... | .... | .... | .... | .... | .... | .... | .... | .... | .... | .... |
| 2006-07 | Lowell Devils | AHL | 61 | 13 | 19 | 32 | 44 | .... | .... | .... | .... | .... | .... | .... | .... | .... | .... | .... | .... | .... | .... | .... | .... | .... | .... |
| 2007-08 | Lowell Devils | AHL | 80 | 20 | 41 | 61 | 64 | .... | .... | .... | .... | .... | .... | .... | .... | .... | .... | .... | .... | .... | .... | .... | .... | .... | .... |
| **2008-09** | **New Jersey** | **NHL** | **16** | **1** | **0** | **1** | **2** | **0** | **0** | **0** | **6** | **16.7** | **-4** | **36** | **41.7** | **6:54** | .... | .... | .... | .... | .... | .... | .... | .... | .... |
| | Lowell Devils | AHL | 14 | 5 | 4 | 9 | 6 | .... | .... | .... | .... | .... | .... | .... | .... | .... | .... | .... | .... | .... | .... | .... | .... | .... | .... |
| | **NHL Totals** | | **16** | **1** | **0** | **1** | **2** | **0** | **0** | **0** | **6** | **16.7** | | **36** | **41.7** | **6:54** | .... | .... | .... | .... | .... | .... | .... | .... | .... |

QMJHL All-Rookie Team (2003) • QMJHL Rookie of the Year (2003)

## VRBATA, Radim

(vuhr-BA-tuh, RA-dihm) **PHX.**

Right wing. Shoots right. 6'1", 190 lbs. Born, Mlada Boleslav, Czech., June 13, 1981. Colorado's 10th choice, 212th overall, in 1999 Entry Draft.

| Season | Club | League | GP | G | A | Pts | PIM | PP | SH | GW | S | % | +/- | TF | F% | Min | GP | G | A | Pts | PIM | PP | SH | GW | Min |
|---|---|---|---|---|---|---|---|---|---|---|---|---|---|---|---|---|---|---|---|---|---|---|---|---|---|
| 1997-98 | Ml. Boleslav Jr. | CzRep-Jr. | 35 | 42 | 31 | 73 | 4 | .... | .... | .... | .... | .... | .... | .... | .... | .... | .... | .... | .... | .... | .... | .... | .... | .... | .... |
| 1998-99 | Hull Olympiques | QMJHL | 54 | 22 | 38 | 60 | 16 | .... | .... | .... | .... | .... | .... | .... | .... | .... | 23 | 6 | 13 | 19 | 6 | .... | .... | .... | .... |
| 99-2000 | Hull Olympiques | QMJHL | 58 | 29 | 45 | 74 | 26 | .... | .... | .... | .... | .... | .... | .... | .... | .... | 15 | 3 | 9 | 12 | 8 | .... | .... | .... | .... |
| 2000-01 | Shawinigan | QMJHL | 55 | 56 | 64 | 120 | 67 | .... | .... | .... | .... | .... | .... | .... | .... | .... | 10 | 4 | 7 | 11 | 4 | .... | .... | .... | .... |
| | Hershey Bears | AHL | .... | .... | .... | .... | .... | .... | .... | .... | .... | .... | .... | .... | .... | .... | 1 | 0 | 1 | 1 | 2 | .... | .... | .... | .... |
| **2001-02** | **Colorado** | **NHL** | **52** | **18** | **12** | **30** | **14** | **6** | **0** | **3** | **112** | **16.1** | **7** | **8** | **37.5** | **14:32** | **9** | **0** | **0** | **0** | **0** | **0** | **0** | **0** | **13:05** |
| | Hershey Bears | AHL | 20 | 8 | 14 | 22 | 8 | .... | .... | .... | .... | .... | .... | .... | .... | .... | .... | .... | .... | .... | .... | .... | .... | .... | .... |
| **2002-03** | **Colorado** | **NHL** | **66** | **11** | **19** | **30** | **16** | **3** | **0** | **4** | **171** | **6.4** | **0** | **14** | **50.0** | **13:55** | .... | .... | .... | .... | .... | .... | .... | .... | .... |
| | **Carolina** | **NHL** | **10** | **5** | **0** | **5** | **2** | **3** | **0** | **0** | **44** | **11.4** | **-7** | **15** | **46.7** | **19:00** | .... | .... | .... | .... | .... | .... | .... | .... | .... |
| **2003-04** | **Carolina** | **NHL** | **80** | **12** | **13** | **25** | **24** | **4** | **0** | **2** | **195** | **6.2** | **-10** | **21** | **38.1** | **13:42** | .... | .... | .... | .... | .... | .... | .... | .... | .... |
| 2004-05 | Liberec | CzRep | 45 | 18 | 21 | 39 | 91 | .... | .... | .... | .... | .... | .... | .... | .... | .... | 12 | 3 | 2 | 5 | 0 | .... | .... | .... | .... |
| **2005-06** | **Carolina** | **NHL** | **16** | **2** | **3** | **5** | **6** | **1** | **0** | **0** | **38** | **5.3** | **0** | **3** | **33.3** | **12:37** | .... | .... | .... | .... | .... | .... | .... | .... | .... |
| | **Chicago** | **NHL** | **45** | **13** | **21** | **34** | **16** | **5** | **0** | **0** | **147** | **8.8** | **4** | **6** | **50.0** | **15:43** | .... | .... | .... | .... | .... | .... | .... | .... | .... |
| **2006-07** | **Chicago** | **NHL** | **77** | **14** | **27** | **41** | **26** | **5** | **0** | **2** | **215** | **6.5** | **-4** | **12** | **33.3** | **16:53** | .... | .... | .... | .... | .... | .... | .... | .... | .... |
| **2007-08** | **Phoenix** | **NHL** | **76** | **27** | **29** | **56** | **14** | **7** | **3** | **5** | **246** | **11.0** | **6** | **19** | **36.8** | **18:12** | .... | .... | .... | .... | .... | .... | .... | .... | .... |
| **2008-09** | **Tampa Bay** | **NHL** | **18** | **3** | **3** | **6** | **8** | **1** | **0** | **0** | **41** | **7.3** | **-1** | **3** | **33.3** | **14:13** | .... | .... | .... | .... | .... | .... | .... | .... | .... |
| | BK Mlada Boleslav | CzRep | 11 | 5 | 3 | 8 | 18 | .... | .... | .... | .... | .... | .... | .... | .... | .... | .... | .... | .... | .... | .... | .... | .... | .... | .... |
| | Liberec | CzRep | 7 | 7 | 2 | 9 | 2 | .... | .... | .... | .... | .... | .... | .... | .... | .... | 3 | 0 | 1 | 1 | 2 | .... | .... | .... | .... |
| | **NHL Totals** | | **440** | **105** | **127** | **232** | **126** | **35** | **3** | **16** | **1209** | **8.7** | | **101** | **40.6** | **15:28** | **9** | **0** | **0** | **0** | **0** | **0** | **0** | **0** | **13:05** |

QMJHL First All-Star Team (2001)

Traded to **Carolina** by **Colorado** for Bates Battaglia, March 11, 2003. Signed as a free agent by **Liberec** (CzRep), September 4, 2004. Traded to **Chicago** by **Carolina** for Chicago's 4th round choice (later traded to St. Louis - St. Louis selected Cade Fairchild) in 2007 Entry Draft, December 29, 2005. Traded to **Phoenix** by **Chicago** for Kevyn Adams, August 11, 2007. Signed as a free agent by **Tampa Bay**, July 1, 2008. Traded to **Phoenix** by **Tampa Bay** for Todd Fedoruk and David Hale, July 21, 2009.

## VYBORNY, David

(vih-BOHR-nee, DAY-vihd)

Right wing. Shoots left. 5'10", 181 lbs. Born, Jihlava, Czech., January 22, 1975. Edmonton's 3rd choice, 33rd overall, in 1993 Entry Draft.

| Season | Club | League | GP | G | A | Pts | PIM | PP | SH | GW | S | % | +/- | TF | F% | Min | GP | G | A | Pts | PIM | PP | SH | GW | Min |
|---|---|---|---|---|---|---|---|---|---|---|---|---|---|---|---|---|---|---|---|---|---|---|---|---|---|
| 1991-92 | HC Sparta Praha | Czech | 32 | 6 | 9 | 15 | 2 | .... | .... | .... | .... | .... | .... | .... | .... | .... | .... | .... | .... | .... | .... | .... | .... | .... | .... |
| 1992-93 | HC Sparta Praha | Czech | 52 | 20 | 24 | 44 | .... | .... | .... | .... | .... | .... | .... | .... | .... | .... | .... | .... | .... | .... | .... | .... | .... | .... | .... |
| 1993-94 | HC Sparta Praha | CzRep | 44 | 15 | 20 | 35 | 0 | .... | .... | .... | .... | .... | .... | .... | .... | .... | 6 | 4 | 7 | 11 | 0 | .... | .... | .... | .... |
| 1994-95 | Cape Breton | AHL | 76 | 23 | 38 | 61 | 30 | .... | .... | .... | .... | .... | .... | .... | .... | .... | .... | .... | .... | .... | .... | .... | .... | .... | .... |
| 1995-96 | HC Sparta Praha | CzRep | 40 | 12 | 18 | 30 | .... | .... | .... | .... | .... | .... | .... | .... | .... | .... | 12 | 6 | 5 | 11 | .... | .... | .... | .... | .... |
| 1996-97 | HC Sparta Praha | CzRep | 47 | 20 | 29 | 49 | 14 | .... | .... | .... | .... | .... | .... | .... | .... | .... | 10 | 7 | 7 | 14 | 6 | .... | .... | .... | .... |
| 1997-98 | MoDo | Sweden | 45 | 16 | 21 | 37 | 34 | .... | .... | .... | .... | .... | .... | .... | .... | .... | 9 | 0 | 2 | 2 | 2 | .... | .... | .... | .... |
| 1998-99 | HC Sparta Praha | CzRep | 52 | 24 | *46 | *70 | 22 | .... | .... | .... | .... | .... | .... | .... | .... | .... | 8 | 1 | 3 | 4 | .... | .... | .... | .... | .... |
| 99-2000 | HC Sparta Praha | CzRep | 50 | 25 | 38 | 63 | 30 | .... | .... | .... | .... | .... | .... | .... | .... | .... | 9 | 3 | *8 | *11 | 4 | .... | .... | .... | .... |
| **2000-01** | **Columbus** | **NHL** | **79** | **13** | **19** | **32** | **22** | **5** | **0** | **1** | **125** | **10.4** | **-9** | **36** | **44.4** | **15:25** | .... | .... | .... | .... | .... | .... | .... | .... | .... |
| **2001-02** | **Columbus** | **NHL** | **75** | **13** | **18** | **31** | **6** | **6** | **0** | **2** | **103** | **12.6** | **-14** | **25** | **44.0** | **15:27** | .... | .... | .... | .... | .... | .... | .... | .... | .... |
| **2002-03** | **Columbus** | **NHL** | **79** | **20** | **26** | **46** | **16** | **4** | **1** | **4** | **125** | **16.0** | **12** | **46** | **32.6** | **16:20** | .... | .... | .... | .... | .... | .... | .... | .... | .... |
| **2003-04** | **Columbus** | **NHL** | **82** | **22** | **31** | **53** | **40** | **8** | **4** | **2** | **158** | **13.9** | **-26** | **97** | **21.7** | **20:23** | .... | .... | .... | .... | .... | .... | .... | .... | .... |
| 2004-05 | HC Sparta Praha | CzRep | 51 | 12 | 34 | 46 | 10 | .... | .... | .... | .... | .... | .... | .... | .... | .... | 5 | 2 | 5 | 7 | 4 | .... | .... | .... | .... |
| **2005-06** | **Columbus** | **NHL** | **80** | **22** | **43** | **65** | **50** | **5** | **2** | **6** | **145** | **15.2** | **-9** | **292** | **30.1** | **20:41** | .... | .... | .... | .... | .... | .... | .... | .... | .... |
| | Czech Republic | Olympics | 8 | 1 | 3 | 4 | 0 | .... | .... | .... | .... | .... | .... | .... | .... | .... | .... | .... | .... | .... | .... | .... | .... | .... | .... |
| **2006-07** | **Columbus** | **NHL** | **82** | **16** | **48** | **64** | **60** | **6** | **0** | **2** | **158** | **10.1** | **6** | **269** | **37.9** | **20:20** | .... | .... | .... | .... | .... | .... | .... | .... | .... |
| **2007-08** | **Columbus** | **NHL** | **66** | **7** | **19** | **26** | **34** | **2** | **0** | **0** | **106** | **6.6** | **-8** | **57** | **36.8** | **15:29** | .... | .... | .... | .... | .... | .... | .... | .... | .... |
| 2008-09 | HC Sparta Praha | CzRep | 52 | 15 | 28 | 43 | 14 | .... | .... | .... | .... | .... | .... | .... | .... | .... | 11 | 8 | 4 | 12 | 4 | .... | .... | .... | .... |
| | **NHL Totals** | | **543** | **113** | **204** | **317** | **228** | **36** | **7** | **17** | **920** | **12.3** | | **822** | **33.3** | **17:50** | .... | .... | .... | .... | .... | .... | .... | .... | .... |

Signed as a free agent by **Columbus**, June 8, 2000. Signed as a free agent by **Sparta Praha** (CzRep), August 9, 2004. Signed as a free agent by **Sparta Praha** (CzRep), April 22, 2008.

## WAGNER, Steve

(WAG-nuhr, STEEV) **ST.L.**

Defense. Shoots left. 6'2", 203 lbs. Born, Grand Rapids, MN, March 6, 1984.

| Season | Club | League | GP | G | A | Pts | PIM | PP | SH | GW | S | % | +/- | TF | F% | Min | GP | G | A | Pts | PIM | PP | SH | GW | Min |
|---|---|---|---|---|---|---|---|---|---|---|---|---|---|---|---|---|---|---|---|---|---|---|---|---|---|
| 2002-03 | Des Moines | USHL | 14 | 0 | 1 | 1 | 17 | .... | .... | .... | .... | .... | .... | .... | .... | .... | .... | .... | .... | .... | .... | .... | .... | .... | .... |
| | Tri-City Storm | USHL | 27 | 0 | 5 | 5 | 52 | .... | .... | .... | .... | .... | .... | .... | .... | .... | 3 | 1 | 0 | 1 | 0 | .... | .... | .... | .... |
| 2003-04 | Tri-City Storm | USHL | 43 | 3 | 19 | 22 | 52 | .... | .... | .... | .... | .... | .... | .... | .... | .... | 9 | 0 | 4 | 4 | 13 | .... | .... | .... | .... |
| 2004-05 | Minnesota State | WCHA | 37 | 1 | 9 | 10 | 40 | .... | .... | .... | .... | .... | .... | .... | .... | .... | .... | .... | .... | .... | .... | .... | .... | .... | .... |
| 2005-06 | Minnesota State | WCHA | 38 | 5 | 11 | 16 | 53 | .... | .... | .... | .... | .... | .... | .... | .... | .... | .... | .... | .... | .... | .... | .... | .... | .... | .... |
| 2006-07 | Minnesota State | WCHA | 38 | 6 | 23 | 29 | 63 | .... | .... | .... | .... | .... | .... | .... | .... | .... | .... | .... | .... | .... | .... | .... | .... | .... | .... |
| | Peoria Rivermen | AHL | 14 | 1 | 2 | 3 | 8 | .... | .... | .... | .... | .... | .... | .... | .... | .... | .... | .... | .... | .... | .... | .... | .... | .... | .... |
| **2007-08** | **St. Louis** | **NHL** | **24** | **2** | **6** | **8** | **8** | **1** | **0** | **0** | **25** | **8.0** | **-4** | **0** | **0.0** | **18:29** | .... | .... | .... | .... | .... | .... | .... | .... | .... |
| | Peoria Rivermen | AHL | 23 | 5 | 7 | 12 | 16 | .... | .... | .... | .... | .... | .... | .... | .... | .... | .... | .... | .... | .... | .... | .... | .... | .... | .... |
| **2008-09** | **St. Louis** | **NHL** | **22** | **2** | **2** | **4** | **18** | **0** | **0** | **0** | **16** | **12.5** | **-5** | **0** | **0.0** | **15:38** | .... | .... | .... | .... | .... | .... | .... | .... | .... |
| | Peoria Rivermen | AHL | 47 | 6 | 16 | 22 | 38 | .... | .... | .... | .... | .... | .... | .... | .... | .... | 7 | 1 | 3 | 4 | 4 | .... | .... | .... | .... |
| | **NHL Totals** | | **46** | **4** | **8** | **12** | **26** | **1** | **0** | **0** | **41** | **9.8** | | **0** | **0.0** | **17:07** | .... | .... | .... | .... | .... | .... | .... | .... | .... |

Signed as a free agent by **St. Louis**, March 20, 2007.

## WALKER, Matt

(WAH-kuhr, MAT) **T.B.**

Defense. Shoots right. 6'3", 214 lbs. Born, Beaverlodge, Alta., April 7, 1980. St. Louis' 3rd choice, 83rd overall, in 1998 Entry Draft.

| Season | Club | League | GP | G | A | Pts | PIM | PP | SH | GW | S | % | +/- | TF | F% | Min | GP | G | A | Pts | PIM | PP | SH | GW | Min |
|---|---|---|---|---|---|---|---|---|---|---|---|---|---|---|---|---|---|---|---|---|---|---|---|---|---|
| 1996-97 | Grand Prairie | AAHA | 68 | 22 | 62 | 74 | 186 | .... | .... | .... | .... | .... | .... | .... | .... | .... | .... | .... | .... | .... | .... | .... | .... | .... | .... |
| 1997-98 | Portland | WHL | 64 | 2 | 13 | 15 | 124 | .... | .... | .... | .... | .... | .... | .... | .... | .... | 16 | 0 | 0 | 0 | 21 | .... | .... | .... | .... |
| 1998-99 | Portland | WHL | 64 | 1 | 10 | 11 | 151 | .... | .... | .... | .... | .... | .... | .... | .... | .... | 4 | 0 | 1 | 1 | 6 | .... | .... | .... | .... |
| 99-2000 | Portland | WHL | 38 | 2 | 7 | 9 | 97 | .... | .... | .... | .... | .... | .... | .... | .... | .... | .... | .... | .... | .... | .... | .... | .... | .... | .... |
| | Kootenay Ice | WHL | 31 | 4 | 19 | 23 | 53 | .... | .... | .... | .... | .... | .... | .... | .... | .... | 21 | 5 | 13 | 18 | 24 | .... | .... | .... | .... |
| 2000-01 | Worcester IceCats | AHL | 61 | 4 | 8 | 12 | 131 | .... | .... | .... | .... | .... | .... | .... | .... | .... | 11 | 0 | 0 | 0 | 6 | .... | .... | .... | .... |
| | Peoria Rivermen | ECHL | 8 | 1 | 0 | 1 | 70 | .... | .... | .... | .... | .... | .... | .... | .... | .... | .... | .... | .... | .... | .... | .... | .... | .... | .... |
| 2001-02 | Worcester IceCats | AHL | 49 | 2 | 11 | 13 | 164 | .... | .... | .... | .... | .... | .... | .... | .... | .... | 3 | 0 | 0 | 0 | 8 | .... | .... | .... | .... |
| **2002-03** | **St. Louis** | **NHL** | **16** | **0** | **1** | **1** | **38** | **0** | **0** | **0** | **13** | **0.0** | **0** | **1** | **100.0** | **11:09** | .... | .... | .... | .... | .... | .... | .... | .... | .... |
| | Worcester IceCats | AHL | 40 | 1 | 8 | 9 | 58 | .... | .... | .... | .... | .... | .... | .... | .... | .... | .... | .... | .... | .... | .... | .... | .... | .... | .... |
| **2003-04** | **St. Louis** | **NHL** | **14** | **0** | **1** | **1** | **25** | **0** | **0** | **0** | **8** | **0.0** | **0** | **0** | **0.0** | **11:23** | **4** | **0** | **0** | **0** | **0** | **0** | **0** | **0** | **9:43** |
| | Worcester IceCats | AHL | 4 | 0 | 1 | 1 | 7 | .... | .... | .... | .... | .... | .... | .... | .... | .... | .... | .... | .... | .... | .... | .... | .... | .... | .... |
| 2004-05 | Worcester IceCats | AHL | 20 | 2 | 4 | 6 | 44 | .... | .... | .... | .... | .... | .... | .... | .... | .... | .... | .... | .... | .... | .... | .... | .... | .... | .... |

| Season | Club | League | GP | G | A | Pts | PIM | PP | SH | GW | S | % | +/- | TF | F% | Min | GP | G | A | Pts | PIM | PP | SH | GW | Min |
|---|---|---|---|---|---|---|---|---|---|---|---|---|---|---|---|---|---|---|---|---|---|---|---|---|---|
| | | | Regular Season | | | | | | | | | | | | | | Playoffs | | | | | | | | |
| **2005-06** | **St. Louis** | **NHL** | **54** | **0** | **2** | **2** | **79** | **0** | **0** | **0** | **59** | **0.0** | **–7** | **0** | **0.0** | **14:15** | .... | .... | .... | .... | .... | .... | .... | .... | .... |
| **2006-07** | **St. Louis** | **NHL** | **48** | **0** | **5** | **5** | **72** | **0** | **0** | **0** | **34** | **0.0** | **7** | **0** | **0.0** | **15:15** | .... | .... | .... | .... | .... | .... | .... | .... | .... |
| | Peoria Rivermen | AHL | 2 | 0 | 1 | 1 | 0 | .... | .... | .... | .... | .... | .... | .... | .... | .... | .... | .... | .... | .... | .... | .... | .... | .... | .... |
| **2007-08** | **St. Louis** | **NHL** | **43** | **1** | **1** | **2** | **61** | **0** | **0** | **0** | **47** | **2.1** | **–3** | **0** | **0.0** | **15:54** | .... | .... | .... | .... | .... | .... | .... | .... | .... |
| **2008-09** | **Chicago** | **NHL** | **65** | **1** | **13** | **14** | **79** | **0** | **0** | **0** | **83** | **1.2** | **7** | **0** | **0.0** | **16:38** | **17** | **0** | **2** | **2** | **14** | **0** | **0** | **0** | **15:21** |
| | **NHL Totals** | | **240** | **2** | **23** | **25** | **354** | **0** | **0** | **0** | **244** | **0.8** | | **1** | **100.0** | **15:01** | **21** | **0** | **2** | **2** | **14** | **0** | **0** | **0** | **14:17** |

• Missed majority of 2003-04 season recovering from groin injury suffered in training camp, September 23, 2003. Signed as a free agent by **Chicago**, July 7, 2008. Signed as a free agent by **Tampa Bay**, July 1, 2009.

## WALKER, Scott

(WAH-kuhr, SKAWT) **CAR.**

Right wing. Shoots right. 5'10", 196 lbs. Born, Cambridge, Ont., July 19, 1973. Vancouver's 4th choice, 124th overall, in 1993 Entry Draft.

| Season | Club | League | GP | G | A | Pts | PIM | PP | SH | GW | S | % | +/- | TF | F% | Min | GP | G | A | Pts | PIM | PP | SH | GW | Min |
|---|---|---|---|---|---|---|---|---|---|---|---|---|---|---|---|---|---|---|---|---|---|---|---|---|---|
| 1989-90 | Kitchener | OHA-B | 6 | 0 | 5 | 5 | 4 | .... | .... | .... | .... | .... | .... | .... | .... | .... | .... | .... | .... | .... | .... | .... | .... | .... | .... |
| | Cambridge | OHA-B | 27 | 7 | 22 | 29 | 87 | .... | .... | .... | .... | .... | .... | .... | .... | .... | .... | .... | .... | .... | .... | .... | .... | .... | .... |
| 1990-91 | Cambridge | OHA-B | 45 | 10 | 27 | 37 | 241 | .... | .... | .... | .... | .... | .... | .... | .... | .... | .... | .... | .... | .... | .... | .... | .... | .... | .... |
| 1991-92 | Owen Sound | OHL | 53 | 7 | 31 | 38 | 128 | .... | .... | .... | .... | .... | .... | .... | .... | .... | 5 | 0 | 7 | 7 | 8 | .... | .... | .... | .... |
| 1992-93 | Owen Sound | OHL | 57 | 23 | 68 | 91 | 110 | .... | .... | .... | .... | .... | .... | .... | .... | .... | 8 | 1 | 5 | 6 | 16 | .... | .... | .... | .... |
| 1993-94 | Hamilton | AHL | 77 | 10 | 29 | 39 | 272 | .... | .... | .... | .... | .... | .... | .... | .... | .... | 4 | 0 | 1 | 1 | 25 | .... | .... | .... | .... |
| **1994-95** | Syracuse Crunch | AHL | 74 | 14 | 38 | 52 | 334 | .... | .... | .... | .... | .... | .... | .... | .... | .... | .... | .... | .... | .... | .... | .... | .... | .... | .... |
| | **Vancouver** | **NHL** | **11** | **0** | **1** | **1** | **33** | **0** | **0** | **0** | **8** | **0.0** | **0** | .... | .... | .... | .... | .... | .... | .... | .... | .... | .... | .... | .... |
| **1995-96** | **Vancouver** | **NHL** | **63** | **4** | **8** | **12** | **137** | **0** | **1** | **1** | **45** | **8.9** | **–7** | .... | .... | .... | .... | .... | .... | .... | .... | .... | .... | .... | .... |
| | Syracuse Crunch | AHL | 15 | 3 | 12 | 15 | 52 | .... | .... | .... | .... | .... | .... | .... | .... | .... | 16 | 9 | 8 | 17 | 39 | .... | .... | .... | .... |
| **1996-97** | **Vancouver** | **NHL** | **64** | **3** | **15** | **18** | **132** | **0** | **0** | **0** | **55** | **5.5** | **2** | .... | .... | .... | .... | .... | .... | .... | .... | .... | .... | .... | .... |
| **1997-98** | **Vancouver** | **NHL** | **59** | **3** | **10** | **13** | **164** | **0** | **1** | **1** | **40** | **7.5** | **–8** | .... | .... | .... | .... | .... | .... | .... | .... | .... | .... | .... | .... |
| **1998-99** | **Nashville** | **NHL** | **71** | **15** | **25** | **40** | **103** | **0** | **1** | **2** | **96** | **15.6** | **0** | **265** | **48.3** | **16:21** | .... | .... | .... | .... | .... | .... | .... | .... | .... |
| **99-2000** | **Nashville** | **NHL** | **69** | **7** | **21** | **28** | **90** | **0** | **1** | **0** | **98** | **7.1** | **–16** | **30** | **36.7** | **15:49** | .... | .... | .... | .... | .... | .... | .... | .... | .... |
| **2000-01** | **Nashville** | **NHL** | **74** | **25** | **29** | **54** | **66** | **9** | **3** | **1** | **159** | **15.7** | **–2** | **541** | **51.4** | **19:17** | .... | .... | .... | .... | .... | .... | .... | .... | .... |
| **2001-02** | **Nashville** | **NHL** | **28** | **4** | **5** | **9** | **18** | **1** | **0** | **0** | **46** | **8.7** | **–13** | **149** | **38.9** | **18:38** | .... | .... | .... | .... | .... | .... | .... | .... | .... |
| **2002-03** | **Nashville** | **NHL** | **60** | **15** | **18** | **33** | **58** | **7** | **0** | **5** | **124** | **12.1** | **2** | **336** | **49.1** | **19:50** | .... | .... | .... | .... | .... | .... | .... | .... | .... |
| **2003-04** | **Nashville** | **NHL** | **75** | **25** | **42** | **67** | **94** | **9** | **3** | **3** | **157** | **15.9** | **4** | **367** | **41.4** | **20:03** | **6** | **0** | **1** | **1** | **6** | **0** | **0** | **0** | **20:10** |
| 2004-05 | Cambridge | OHA-Sr. | 5 | 2 | 6 | 8 | 4 | .... | .... | .... | .... | .... | .... | .... | .... | .... | .... | .... | .... | .... | .... | .... | .... | .... | .... |
| | Dundas | OHA-Sr. | 3 | 3 | 2 | 5 | 8 | .... | .... | .... | .... | .... | .... | .... | .... | .... | .... | .... | .... | .... | .... | .... | .... | .... | .... |
| **2005-06** | **Nashville** | **NHL** | **33** | **5** | **11** | **16** | **36** | **1** | **0** | **0** | **57** | **8.8** | **2** | **87** | **44.8** | **17:23** | **5** | **0** | **0** | **0** | **6** | **0** | **0** | **0** | **16:01** |
| **2006-07** | **Carolina** | **NHL** | **81** | **21** | **30** | **51** | **45** | **6** | **0** | **6** | **183** | **11.5** | **–10** | **95** | **42.1** | **16:10** | .... | .... | .... | .... | .... | .... | .... | .... | .... |
| **2007-08** | **Carolina** | **NHL** | **58** | **14** | **18** | **32** | **115** | **4** | **2** | **4** | **122** | **11.5** | **–3** | **48** | **43.8** | **16:37** | .... | .... | .... | .... | .... | .... | .... | .... | .... |
| **2008-09** | **Carolina** | **NHL** | **41** | **5** | **10** | **15** | **39** | **1** | **0** | **0** | **71** | **7.0** | **–4** | **4** | **50.0** | **13:20** | **18** | **1** | **6** | **7** | **19** | **0** | **0** | **1** | **11:31** |
| | **NHL Totals** | | **787** | **146** | **243** | **389** | **1130** | **38** | **12** | **23** | **1261** | **11.6** | | **1922** | **46.5** | **17:26** | **29** | **1** | **7** | **8** | **31** | **0** | **0** | **1** | **14:05** |

OHL Second All-Star Team (1993)

Claimed by **Nashville** from **Vancouver** in Expansion Draft, June 26, 1998. Signed as a free agent by **Cambridge** (OHA-Sr.), October 21, 2004. Signed as a free agent by **Dundas** (OHA-Sr.), February 10, 2005. • Missed majority of 2005-06 season recovering from sports hernia (October 25, 2005 vs. Chicago) and wrist (February 6, 2006 at Dallas) injuries. Traded to **Carolina** by **Nashville** for Josef Vasicek, July 18, 2006.

## WALLACE, Tim

(WAHL-las, TIHM) **PIT.**

Right wing. Shoots right. 6'1", 207 lbs. Born, Anchorage, AK, August 6, 1984.

| Season | Club | League | GP | G | A | Pts | PIM | PP | SH | GW | S | % | +/- | TF | F% | Min | GP | G | A | Pts | PIM | PP | SH | GW | Min |
|---|---|---|---|---|---|---|---|---|---|---|---|---|---|---|---|---|---|---|---|---|---|---|---|---|---|
| 2002-03 | U. of Notre Dame | CCHA | 40 | 6 | 5 | 11 | 28 | .... | .... | .... | .... | .... | .... | .... | .... | .... | .... | .... | .... | .... | .... | .... | .... | .... | .... |
| 2003-04 | U. of Notre Dame | CCHA | 39 | 3 | 8 | 11 | 10 | .... | .... | .... | .... | .... | .... | .... | .... | .... | .... | .... | .... | .... | .... | .... | .... | .... | .... |
| 2004-05 | U. of Notre Dame | CCHA | 38 | 5 | 9 | 14 | 20 | .... | .... | .... | .... | .... | .... | .... | .... | .... | .... | .... | .... | .... | .... | .... | .... | .... | .... |
| 2005-06 | U. of Notre Dame | CCHA | 36 | 11 | 12 | 23 | 28 | .... | .... | .... | .... | .... | .... | .... | .... | .... | .... | .... | .... | .... | .... | .... | .... | .... | .... |
| 2006-07 | Wilkes-Barre | AHL | 32 | 5 | 9 | 14 | 39 | .... | .... | .... | .... | .... | .... | .... | .... | .... | 11 | 1 | 1 | 2 | 2 | .... | .... | .... | .... |
| | Wheeling Nailers | ECHL | 19 | 6 | 11 | 17 | 23 | .... | .... | .... | .... | .... | .... | .... | .... | .... | .... | .... | .... | .... | .... | .... | .... | .... | .... |
| 2007-08 | Wilkes-Barre | AHL | 74 | 12 | 14 | 26 | 82 | .... | .... | .... | .... | .... | .... | .... | .... | .... | 23 | 2 | 6 | 8 | 21 | .... | .... | .... | .... |
| **2008-09** | **Pittsburgh** | **NHL** | **16** | **0** | **2** | **2** | **7** | **0** | **0** | **0** | **17** | **0.0** | **2** | **3** | **66.7** | **8:07** | .... | .... | .... | .... | .... | .... | .... | .... | .... |
| | Wilkes-Barre | AHL | 58 | 11 | 8 | 19 | 51 | .... | .... | .... | .... | .... | .... | .... | .... | .... | 7 | 0 | 2 | 2 | 2 | .... | .... | .... | .... |
| | **NHL Totals** | | **16** | **0** | **2** | **2** | **7** | **0** | **0** | **0** | **17** | **0.0** | | **3** | **66.7** | **8:07** | .... | .... | .... | .... | .... | .... | .... | .... | .... |

Signed as a free agent by **Pittsburgh**, May 29, 2007.

## WALLIN, Niclas

(WAHL-ihn, NIHK-luhs) **CAR.**

Defense. Shoots left. 6'3", 220 lbs. Born, Boden, Sweden, February 20, 1975. Carolina's 3rd choice, 97th overall, in 2000 Entry Draft.

| Season | Club | League | GP | G | A | Pts | PIM | PP | SH | GW | S | % | +/- | TF | F% | Min | GP | G | A | Pts | PIM | PP | SH | GW | Min |
|---|---|---|---|---|---|---|---|---|---|---|---|---|---|---|---|---|---|---|---|---|---|---|---|---|---|
| 1994-95 | Bodens IK | Swe-Jr. | 30 | 2 | 13 | 15 | 125 | .... | .... | .... | .... | .... | .... | .... | .... | .... | .... | .... | .... | .... | .... | .... | .... | .... | .... |
| | Bodens IK | Sweden-2 | 13 | 0 | 0 | 0 | 0 | .... | .... | .... | .... | .... | .... | .... | .... | .... | 2 | 0 | 0 | 0 | 0 | .... | .... | .... | .... |
| 1995-96 | Bodens IK | Swe-Jr. | 2 | 2 | 2 | 4 | 0 | .... | .... | .... | .... | .... | .... | .... | .... | .... | .... | .... | .... | .... | .... | .... | .... | .... | .... |
| | Bodens IK | Sweden-2 | 30 | 2 | 7 | 9 | 26 | .... | .... | .... | .... | .... | .... | .... | .... | .... | 2 | 0 | 1 | 1 | 2 | .... | .... | .... | .... |
| 1996-97 | Brynas IF Gavle | Sweden | 47 | 1 | 1 | 2 | 14 | .... | .... | .... | .... | .... | .... | .... | .... | .... | .... | .... | .... | .... | .... | .... | .... | .... | .... |
| 1997-98 | Brynas IF Gavle | Sweden | 44 | 2 | 3 | 5 | 57 | .... | .... | .... | .... | .... | .... | .... | .... | .... | 3 | 0 | 1 | 1 | 4 | .... | .... | .... | .... |
| 1998-99 | Brynas IF Gavle | Sweden | 46 | 2 | 4 | 6 | 52 | .... | .... | .... | .... | .... | .... | .... | .... | .... | 14 | 0 | 1 | 1 | 8 | .... | .... | .... | .... |
| 99-2000 | Brynas IF Gavle | Sweden | 48 | 7 | 9 | 16 | 73 | .... | .... | .... | .... | .... | .... | .... | .... | .... | 11 | 2 | 1 | 3 | 14 | .... | .... | .... | .... |
| | Brynas IF Gavle | EuroHL | 5 | 1 | 1 | 2 | 10 | .... | .... | .... | .... | .... | .... | .... | .... | .... | .... | .... | .... | .... | .... | .... | .... | .... | .... |
| **2000-01** | **Carolina** | **NHL** | **37** | **2** | **3** | **5** | **21** | **0** | **0** | **0** | **19** | **10.5** | **–11** | **0** | **0.0** | **14:57** | **3** | **0** | **0** | **0** | **2** | **0** | **0** | **0** | **19:10** |
| | Cincinnati | IHL | 8 | 1 | 2 | 3 | 4 | .... | .... | .... | .... | .... | .... | .... | .... | .... | 3 | 0 | 0 | 0 | 2 | .... | .... | .... | .... |
| **2001-02** | **Carolina** | **NHL** | **52** | **1** | **2** | **3** | **36** | **0** | **0** | **0** | **33** | **3.0** | **1** | **0** | **0.0** | **12:12** | **23** | **2** | **1** | **3** | **12** | **0** | **0** | **2** | **15:26** |
| **2002-03** | **Carolina** | **NHL** | **77** | **2** | **8** | **10** | **71** | **0** | **0** | **2** | **69** | **2.9** | **–19** | **0** | **0.0** | **16:12** | .... | .... | .... | .... | .... | .... | .... | .... | .... |
| **2003-04** | **Carolina** | **NHL** | **57** | **3** | **7** | **10** | **51** | **0** | **0** | **0** | **74** | **4.1** | **–8** | **0** | **0.0** | **18:40** | .... | .... | .... | .... | .... | .... | .... | .... | .... |
| 2004-05 | Lulea HF | Sweden | 39 | 6 | 7 | 13 | 89 | .... | .... | .... | .... | .... | .... | .... | .... | .... | 3 | 0 | 1 | 1 | 6 | .... | .... | .... | .... |
| **2005-06** ♦ | **Carolina** | **NHL** | **50** | **4** | **4** | **8** | **42** | **0** | **0** | **0** | **44** | **9.1** | **2** | **0** | **0.0** | **16:50** | **25** | **1** | **4** | **5** | **14** | **0** | **0** | **1** | **16:39** |
| **2006-07** | **Carolina** | **NHL** | **67** | **2** | **8** | **10** | **48** | **0** | **0** | **0** | **76** | **2.6** | **–2** | **0** | **0.0** | **18:33** | .... | .... | .... | .... | .... | .... | .... | .... | .... |
| **2007-08** | **Carolina** | **NHL** | **66** | **2** | **6** | **8** | **54** | **0** | **0** | **0** | **60** | **3.3** | **–18** | **1** | **0.0** | **18:08** | .... | .... | .... | .... | .... | .... | .... | .... | .... |
| **2008-09** | **Carolina** | **NHL** | **64** | **2** | **8** | **10** | **42** | **0** | **0** | **1** | **53** | **3.8** | **–1** | **1** | **0.0** | **16:16** | **18** | **0** | **0** | **0** | **4** | **0** | **0** | **0** | **13:46** |
| | **NHL Totals** | | **470** | **18** | **46** | **64** | **365** | **0** | **0** | **3** | **428** | **4.2** | | **2** | **0.0** | **16:38** | **69** | **3** | **5** | **8** | **32** | **0** | **0** | **3** | **15:36** |

Signed as a free agent by **Lulea** (Sweden), September 19, 2004.

## WALLIN, Rickard

(WAHL-ihn, RIH-kahrd) **TOR.**

Center. Shoots left. 6'2", 185 lbs. Born, Stockholm, Sweden, April 19, 1980. Phoenix's 8th choice, 160th overall, in 1998 Entry Draft.

| Season | Club | League | GP | G | A | Pts | PIM | PP | SH | GW | S | % | +/- | TF | F% | Min | GP | G | A | Pts | PIM | PP | SH | GW | Min |
|---|---|---|---|---|---|---|---|---|---|---|---|---|---|---|---|---|---|---|---|---|---|---|---|---|---|
| 1996-97 | Vasteras IK Jr. | Swe-Jr. | 26 | 3 | 3 | 6 | .... | .... | .... | .... | .... | .... | .... | .... | .... | .... | .... | .... | .... | .... | .... | .... | .... | .... | .... |
| 1997-98 | Farjestad Jr. | Swe-Jr. | 29 | 20 | 30 | 50 | 32 | .... | .... | .... | .... | .... | .... | .... | .... | .... | 2 | 1 | 1 | 2 | 2 | .... | .... | .... | .... |
| 1998-99 | Farjestad Jr. | Swe-Jr. | 21 | 11 | 15 | 26 | 30 | .... | .... | .... | .... | .... | .... | .... | .... | .... | .... | .... | .... | .... | .... | .... | .... | .... | .... |
| | Farjestad | Sweden | 5 | 0 | 0 | 0 | 0 | .... | .... | .... | .... | .... | .... | .... | .... | .... | .... | .... | .... | .... | .... | .... | .... | .... | .... |
| 99-2000 | IF Troja-Ljungby | Sweden-2 | 46 | 15 | 22 | 37 | 54 | .... | .... | .... | .... | .... | .... | .... | .... | .... | .... | .... | .... | .... | .... | .... | .... | .... | .... |
| 2000-01 | Farjestad | Sweden | 47 | 9 | 22 | 31 | 24 | .... | .... | .... | .... | .... | .... | .... | .... | .... | 16 | 11 | 3 | 14 | 4 | .... | .... | .... | .... |
| 2001-02 | Farjestad | Sweden | 50 | 12 | 31 | 43 | 56 | .... | .... | .... | .... | .... | .... | .... | .... | .... | 10 | 4 | 9 | 13 | 8 | .... | .... | .... | .... |
| **2002-03** | **Minnesota** | **NHL** | **4** | **1** | **0** | **1** | **0** | **0** | **0** | **1** | **1** | **100.0** | **1** | **28** | **53.6** | **7:44** | .... | .... | .... | .... | .... | .... | .... | .... | .... |
| | Houston Aeros | AHL | 52 | 13 | 22 | 35 | 70 | .... | .... | .... | .... | .... | .... | .... | .... | .... | 23 | 4 | 11 | 15 | 22 | .... | .... | .... | .... |
| **2003-04** | **Minnesota** | **NHL** | **15** | **5** | **4** | **9** | **14** | **3** | **0** | **1** | **16** | **31.3** | **1** | **189** | **45.5** | **14:20** | .... | .... | .... | .... | .... | .... | .... | .... | .... |
| | Houston Aeros | AHL | 47 | 14 | 18 | 32 | 36 | .... | .... | .... | .... | .... | .... | .... | .... | .... | 2 | 0 | 0 | 0 | 2 | .... | .... | .... | .... |
| 2004-05 | Houston Aeros | AHL | 79 | 12 | 31 | 43 | 61 | .... | .... | .... | .... | .... | .... | .... | .... | .... | 5 | 1 | 0 | 1 | 29 | .... | .... | .... | .... |
| 2005-06 | Farjestad | Sweden | 50 | 11 | 19 | 30 | 82 | .... | .... | .... | .... | .... | .... | .... | .... | .... | 18 | 6 | 3 | 9 | 28 | .... | .... | .... | .... |
| 2006-07 | HC Lugano | Swiss | 44 | 14 | 35 | 49 | 87 | .... | .... | .... | .... | .... | .... | .... | .... | .... | 6 | 3 | 3 | 6 | 16 | .... | .... | .... | .... |
| 2007-08 | Farjestad | Sweden | 55 | 17 | 23 | 40 | 54 | .... | .... | .... | .... | .... | .... | .... | .... | .... | 12 | 1 | 5 | 6 | 18 | .... | .... | .... | .... |
| 2008-09 | Farjestad | Sweden | 55 | 18 | 27 | 45 | 56 | .... | .... | .... | .... | .... | .... | .... | .... | .... | 13 | 1 | 4 | 5 | 8 | .... | .... | .... | .... |
| | **NHL Totals** | | **19** | **6** | **4** | **10** | **14** | **3** | **0** | **2** | **17** | **35.3** | | **217** | **46.5** | **12:56** | .... | .... | .... | .... | .... | .... | .... | .... | .... |

• Rights traded to **Minnesota** by **Phoenix** for Joe Juneau, June 23, 2000. • Reassigned to **Farjestad** (Sweden) by **Minnesota**, September 22, 2005. Signed as a free agent by **Lugano** (Swiss), July 23, 2006. Signed as a free agent by **Toronto**, July 10, 2009.

## WALSER, Derrick

(WAHL-zuhr, DAIR-ihk) **TOR.**

Defense. Shoots left. 5'10", 190 lbs. Born, New Glasgow, N.S., May 12, 1978.

| | | | Regular Season | | | | | | | | | | | | | | Playoffs | | | | | | | | |
|---|---|---|---|---|---|---|---|---|---|---|---|---|---|---|---|---|---|---|---|---|---|---|---|---|---|
| Season | Club | League | GP | G | A | Pts | PIM | PP | SH | GW | S | % | +/- | TF | F% | Min | GP | G | A | Pts | PIM | PP | SH | GW | Min |
| 1994-95 | Beauport | QMJHL | 48 | 4 | 18 | 22 | 34 | .... | .... | .... | .... | .... | .... | .... | .... | .... | 12 | 2 | 5 | 7 | 2 | .... | .... | .... | .... |
| 1995-96 | Beauport | QMJHL | 69 | 9 | 31 | 40 | 56 | .... | .... | .... | .... | .... | .... | .... | .... | .... | 20 | 2 | 11 | 13 | 16 | .... | .... | .... | .... |
| 1996-97 | Beauport | QMJHL | 37 | 13 | 25 | 38 | 26 | .... | .... | .... | .... | .... | .... | .... | .... | .... | .... | .... | .... | .... | .... | .... | .... | .... | .... |
| | Rimouski Oceanic | QMJHL | 31 | 15 | 30 | 45 | 44 | .... | .... | .... | .... | .... | .... | .... | .... | .... | 4 | 2 | 2 | 4 | 6 | .... | .... | .... | .... |
| 1997-98 | Rimouski Oceanic | QMJHL | 70 | 41 | 69 | 110 | 135 | .... | .... | .... | .... | .... | .... | .... | .... | .... | 18 | 10 | *26 | 36 | 49 | .... | .... | .... | .... |
| 1998-99 | Saint John Flames | AHL | 40 | 3 | 7 | 10 | 24 | .... | .... | .... | .... | .... | .... | .... | .... | .... | .... | .... | .... | .... | .... | .... | .... | .... | .... |
| | Johnstown Chiefs | ECHL | 24 | 8 | 12 | 20 | 29 | .... | .... | .... | .... | .... | .... | .... | .... | .... | .... | .... | .... | .... | .... | .... | .... | .... | .... |
| 99-2000 | Saint John Flames | AHL | 14 | 2 | 3 | 5 | 10 | .... | .... | .... | .... | .... | .... | .... | .... | .... | .... | .... | .... | .... | .... | .... | .... | .... | .... |
| | Johnstown Chiefs | ECHL | 54 | 17 | 26 | 43 | 104 | .... | .... | .... | .... | .... | .... | .... | .... | .... | 7 | 3 | 3 | 6 | 8 | .... | .... | .... | .... |
| 2000-01 | Saint John Flames | AHL | 76 | 19 | 36 | 55 | 36 | .... | .... | .... | .... | .... | .... | .... | .... | .... | 19 | 7 | 9 | 16 | 14 | .... | .... | .... | .... |
| **2001-02** | **Columbus** | **NHL** | **2** | **1** | **0** | **1** | **0** | **0** | **0** | **0** | **2** | **50.0** | **-2** | **0** | **0.0** | **16:18** | .... | .... | .... | .... | .... | .... | .... | .... | .... |
| | Syracuse Crunch | AHL | 73 | 23 | 38 | 61 | 70 | .... | .... | .... | .... | .... | .... | .... | .... | .... | 10 | 1 | 5 | 6 | 12 | .... | .... | .... | .... |
| **2002-03** | **Columbus** | **NHL** | **53** | **4** | **13** | **17** | **34** | **3** | **0** | **2** | **86** | **4.7** | **-9** | **1** | **100.0** | **14:52** | .... | .... | .... | .... | .... | .... | .... | .... | .... |
| | Syracuse Crunch | AHL | 28 | 7 | 14 | 21 | 30 | .... | .... | .... | .... | .... | .... | .... | .... | .... | .... | .... | .... | .... | .... | .... | .... | .... | .... |
| **2003-04** | **Columbus** | **NHL** | **27** | **1** | **8** | **9** | **22** | **1** | **0** | **0** | **35** | **2.9** | **-6** | **0** | **0.0** | **18:23** | .... | .... | .... | .... | .... | .... | .... | .... | .... |
| | Syracuse Crunch | AHL | 48 | 10 | 26 | 36 | 82 | .... | .... | .... | .... | .... | .... | .... | .... | .... | 3 | 1 | 1 | 2 | 4 | .... | .... | .... | .... |
| 2004-05 | Eisbaren Berlin | Germany | 50 | 9 | 14 | 23 | 143 | .... | .... | .... | .... | .... | .... | .... | .... | .... | 12 | 4 | 4 | 8 | 20 | .... | .... | .... | .... |
| 2005-06 | Eisbaren Berlin | Germany | 48 | 19 | 24 | 43 | 120 | .... | .... | .... | .... | .... | .... | .... | .... | .... | 11 | 6 | 1 | 7 | 20 | .... | .... | .... | .... |
| **2006-07** | Albany River Rats | AHL | 6 | 0 | 1 | 1 | 4 | .... | .... | .... | .... | .... | .... | .... | .... | .... | .... | .... | .... | .... | .... | .... | .... | .... | .... |
| | **Columbus** | **NHL** | **9** | **2** | **0** | **2** | **0** | **2** | **0** | **0** | **10** | **20.0** | **-1** | **0** | **0.0** | **12:14** | .... | .... | .... | .... | .... | .... | .... | .... | .... |
| | Syracuse Crunch | AHL | 49 | 9 | 27 | 36 | 59 | .... | .... | .... | .... | .... | .... | .... | .... | .... | .... | .... | .... | .... | .... | .... | .... | .... | .... |
| 2007-08 | Toronto Marlies | AHL | 77 | 16 | 29 | 45 | 82 | .... | .... | .... | .... | .... | .... | .... | .... | .... | 17 | 2 | 5 | 7 | 30 | .... | .... | .... | .... |
| 2008-09 | Vityaz Chekhov | Rus-KHL | 51 | 3 | 19 | 22 | 79 | .... | .... | .... | .... | .... | .... | .... | .... | .... | .... | .... | .... | .... | .... | .... | .... | .... | .... |
| | **NHL Totals** | | **91** | **8** | **21** | **29** | **56** | **6** | **0** | **2** | **133** | **6.0** | | **1** | **100.0** | **15:41** | .... | .... | .... | .... | .... | .... | .... | .... | .... |

QMJHL First All-Star Team (1997, 1998) • Emile Bouchard Trophy (QMJHL – Top Defenseman) (1998) • Canadian Major Junior First All-Star Team (1998) • Canadian Major Junior Defenseman of the Year (1998)

Signed as a free agent by **Calgary**, October 16, 1998. Signed as a free agent by **Columbus**, September 17, 2001. Signed as a free agent by **Berlin** (Germany), May 13, 2004. • Rights traded to **Carolina** by **Columbus** with Columbus' 4th round choice (later traded to Toronto - Toronto selected James Reimer) in 2006 Entry Draft for Carolina's 4th round choice (Jared Boll) in 2005 Entry Draft, July 30, 2005. Traded to **Columbus** by **Carolina** for Mark Flood, November 29, 2006. Signed a free agent by **Toronto**, July 18, 2007.

## WALTER, Ben

(WAHL-tuhr, BEHN) **N.J.**

Center. Shoots left. 6'1", 195 lbs. Born, Beaconsfield, Que., May 11, 1984. Boston's 5th choice, 160th overall, in 2004 Entry Draft.

| Season | Club | League | GP | G | A | Pts | PIM | PP | SH | GW | S | % | +/- | TF | F% | Min | GP | G | A | Pts | PIM | PP | SH | GW | Min |
|---|---|---|---|---|---|---|---|---|---|---|---|---|---|---|---|---|---|---|---|---|---|---|---|---|---|
| 2000-01 | Langley Hornets | BCHL | 50 | 8 | 22 | 30 | 19 | .... | .... | .... | .... | .... | .... | .... | .... | .... | .... | .... | .... | .... | .... | .... | .... | .... | .... |
| 2001-02 | Langley Hornets | BCHL | 50 | 29 | 47 | 76 | 29 | .... | .... | .... | .... | .... | .... | .... | .... | .... | .... | .... | .... | .... | .... | .... | .... | .... | .... |
| 2002-03 | U. Mass-Lowell | H-East | 35 | 5 | 12 | 17 | 12 | .... | .... | .... | .... | .... | .... | .... | .... | .... | .... | .... | .... | .... | .... | .... | .... | .... | .... |
| 2003-04 | U. Mass-Lowell | H-East | 36 | 18 | 16 | 34 | 18 | .... | .... | .... | .... | .... | .... | .... | .... | .... | .... | .... | .... | .... | .... | .... | .... | .... | .... |
| 2004-05 | U. Mass-Lowell | H-East | 36 | *26 | 13 | 39 | 28 | .... | .... | .... | .... | .... | .... | .... | .... | .... | .... | .... | .... | .... | .... | .... | .... | .... | .... |
| **2005-06** | **Boston** | **NHL** | **6** | **0** | **0** | **0** | **4** | **0** | **0** | **0** | **6** | **0.0** | **2** | **32** | **53.1** | **11:49** | .... | .... | .... | .... | .... | .... | .... | .... | .... |
| | Providence Bruins | AHL | 62 | 16 | 25 | 41 | 33 | .... | .... | .... | .... | .... | .... | .... | .... | .... | 3 | 2 | 0 | 2 | 2 | .... | .... | .... | .... |
| **2006-07** | **Boston** | **NHL** | **4** | **0** | **0** | **0** | **0** | **0** | **0** | **0** | **0** | **0.0** | **0** | **24** | **41.7** | **6:11** | .... | .... | .... | .... | .... | .... | .... | .... | .... |
| | Providence Bruins | AHL | 73 | 24 | 43 | 67 | 58 | .... | .... | .... | .... | .... | .... | .... | .... | .... | 13 | 4 | 4 | 8 | 6 | .... | .... | .... | .... |
| **2007-08** | **NY Islanders** | **NHL** | **8** | **1** | **0** | **1** | **0** | **1** | **0** | **0** | **6** | **16.7** | **-1** | **33** | **30.3** | **6:05** | .... | .... | .... | .... | .... | .... | .... | .... | .... |
| | Bridgeport | AHL | 68 | 20 | 46 | 66 | 31 | .... | .... | .... | .... | .... | .... | .... | .... | .... | .... | .... | .... | .... | .... | .... | .... | .... | .... |
| **2008-09** | **NY Islanders** | **NHL** | **4** | **0** | **0** | **0** | **0** | **0** | **0** | **0** | **2** | **0.0** | **-2** | **43** | **41.9** | **10:58** | .... | .... | .... | .... | .... | .... | .... | .... | .... |
| | Bridgeport | AHL | 65 | 20 | 30 | 50 | 10 | .... | .... | .... | .... | .... | .... | .... | .... | .... | 5 | 1 | 4 | 5 | 2 | .... | .... | .... | .... |
| | **NHL Totals** | | **22** | **1** | **0** | **1** | **4** | **1** | **0** | **0** | **14** | **7.1** | | **132** | **41.7** | **8:33** | .... | .... | .... | .... | .... | .... | .... | .... | .... |

Hockey East Second All-Star Team (2005)

Traded to **NY Islanders** by **Boston** with Boston's 2nd round choice (later traded to Columbus – Columbus selected Kevin Lynch) in 2009 Entry Draft for Petteri Nokelainen, September 11, 2007. Traded to **New Jersey** by **NY Islanders** with future considerations for the rights to Tony Romano, June 30, 2009.

## WANDELL, Tom

(VAHN-dehl, TAWM) **DAL.**

Center. Shoots left. 6'1", 183 lbs. Born, Sodertalje, Sweden, January 29, 1987. Dallas' 5th choice, 146th overall, in 2005 Entry Draft.

| Season | Club | League | GP | G | A | Pts | PIM | PP | SH | GW | S | % | +/- | TF | F% | Min | GP | G | A | Pts | PIM | PP | SH | GW | Min |
|---|---|---|---|---|---|---|---|---|---|---|---|---|---|---|---|---|---|---|---|---|---|---|---|---|---|
| 2002-03 | Sodertalje SK U18 | Swe-U18 | 13 | 8 | 7 | 15 | 6 | .... | .... | .... | .... | .... | .... | .... | .... | .... | .... | .... | .... | .... | .... | .... | .... | .... | .... |
| 2003-04 | Sodertalje SK U18 | Swe-U18 | 6 | 5 | 7 | 12 | 6 | .... | .... | .... | .... | .... | .... | .... | .... | .... | 2 | 0 | 0 | 0 | 0 | .... | .... | .... | .... |
| | Sodertalje SK Jr. | Swe-Jr. | 33 | 7 | 15 | 22 | 14 | .... | .... | .... | .... | .... | .... | .... | .... | .... | 2 | 0 | 0 | 0 | 0 | .... | .... | .... | .... |
| 2004-05 | Sodertalje SK Jr. | Swe-Jr. | 5 | 1 | 2 | 3 | 4 | .... | .... | .... | .... | .... | .... | .... | .... | .... | .... | .... | .... | .... | .... | .... | .... | .... | .... |
| 2005-06 | Sodertalje SK Jr. | Swe-Jr. | 41 | 19 | 20 | 39 | 45 | .... | .... | .... | .... | .... | .... | .... | .... | .... | 4 | 1 | 0 | 1 | 2 | .... | .... | .... | .... |
| | Sodertalje SK | Sweden | 6 | 0 | 0 | 0 | 0 | .... | .... | .... | .... | .... | .... | .... | .... | .... | .... | .... | .... | .... | .... | .... | .... | .... | .... |
| | Sodertalje SK | Sweden-Q | 1 | 1 | 0 | 1 | 0 | .... | .... | .... | .... | .... | .... | .... | .... | .... | .... | .... | .... | .... | .... | .... | .... | .... | .... |
| 2006-07 | Assat Pori Jr. | Fin-Jr. | 4 | 1 | 1 | 2 | 0 | .... | .... | .... | .... | .... | .... | .... | .... | .... | .... | .... | .... | .... | .... | .... | .... | .... | .... |
| | Assat Pori | Finland | 50 | 6 | 6 | 12 | 20 | .... | .... | .... | .... | .... | .... | .... | .... | .... | .... | .... | .... | .... | .... | .... | .... | .... | .... |
| 2007-08 | Iowa Stars | AHL | 53 | 10 | 9 | 19 | 16 | .... | .... | .... | .... | .... | .... | .... | .... | .... | .... | .... | .... | .... | .... | .... | .... | .... | .... |
| | Idaho Steelheads | ECHL | 3 | 3 | 0 | 3 | 2 | .... | .... | .... | .... | .... | .... | .... | .... | .... | .... | .... | .... | .... | .... | .... | .... | .... | .... |
| **2008-09** | Timra IK | Sweden | 51 | 15 | 26 | 41 | 26 | .... | .... | .... | .... | .... | .... | .... | .... | .... | 7 | 0 | 4 | 4 | 0 | .... | .... | .... | .... |
| | **Dallas** | **NHL** | **14** | **1** | **2** | **3** | **4** | **0** | **0** | **0** | **23** | **4.3** | **-1** | **113** | **51.3** | **11:09** | .... | .... | .... | .... | .... | .... | .... | .... | .... |
| | **NHL Totals** | | **14** | **1** | **2** | **3** | **4** | **0** | **0** | **0** | **23** | **4.3** | | **113** | **51.3** | **11:09** | .... | .... | .... | .... | .... | .... | .... | .... | .... |

## WANVIG, Kyle

(WEHN-vihg, KIGHL)

Right wing. Shoots right. 6'2", 210 lbs. Born, Calgary, Alta., January 29, 1981. Minnesota's 2nd choice, 36th overall, in 2001 Entry Draft.

| Season | Club | League | GP | G | A | Pts | PIM | PP | SH | GW | S | % | +/- | TF | F% | Min | GP | G | A | Pts | PIM | PP | SH | GW | Min |
|---|---|---|---|---|---|---|---|---|---|---|---|---|---|---|---|---|---|---|---|---|---|---|---|---|---|
| 1996-97 | Calgary Blazers | AMHL | 26 | 31 | 48 | 79 | 85 | .... | .... | .... | .... | .... | .... | .... | .... | .... | .... | .... | .... | .... | .... | .... | .... | .... | .... |
| 1997-98 | Edmonton Ice | WHL | 62 | 17 | 12 | 29 | 69 | .... | .... | .... | .... | .... | .... | .... | .... | .... | .... | .... | .... | .... | .... | .... | .... | .... | .... |
| 1998-99 | Kootenay Ice | WHL | 71 | 12 | 20 | 32 | 119 | .... | .... | .... | .... | .... | .... | .... | .... | .... | 7 | 1 | 3 | 4 | 18 | .... | .... | .... | .... |
| 99-2000 | Kootenay Ice | WHL | 6 | 2 | 2 | 4 | 12 | .... | .... | .... | .... | .... | .... | .... | .... | .... | .... | .... | .... | .... | .... | .... | .... | .... | .... |
| | Red Deer Rebels | WHL | 58 | 21 | 18 | 39 | 123 | .... | .... | .... | .... | .... | .... | .... | .... | .... | 4 | 1 | 0 | 1 | 4 | .... | .... | .... | .... |
| 2000-01 | Red Deer Rebels | WHL | 69 | 55 | 46 | 101 | 202 | .... | .... | .... | .... | .... | .... | .... | .... | .... | 22 | 10 | 12 | 22 | 47 | .... | .... | .... | .... |
| 2001-02 | Houston Aeros | AHL | 34 | 6 | 7 | 13 | 43 | .... | .... | .... | .... | .... | .... | .... | .... | .... | 9 | 0 | 1 | 1 | 23 | .... | .... | .... | .... |
| **2002-03** | **Minnesota** | **NHL** | **7** | **1** | **0** | **1** | **13** | **0** | **0** | **0** | **5** | **20.0** | **0** | **1** | **100.0** | **9:14** | .... | .... | .... | .... | .... | .... | .... | .... | .... |
| | Houston Aeros | AHL | 57 | 13 | 16 | 29 | 137 | .... | .... | .... | .... | .... | .... | .... | .... | .... | 21 | 6 | 4 | 10 | 27 | .... | .... | .... | .... |
| **2003-04** | **Minnesota** | **NHL** | **6** | **0** | **1** | **1** | **10** | **0** | **0** | **0** | **16** | **0.0** | **-2** | **4** | **75.0** | **13:48** | .... | .... | .... | .... | .... | .... | .... | .... | .... |
| | Houston Aeros | AHL | 72 | 25 | 16 | 41 | 147 | .... | .... | .... | .... | .... | .... | .... | .... | .... | 2 | 0 | 1 | 1 | 0 | .... | .... | .... | .... |
| 2004-05 | Houston Aeros | AHL | 76 | 13 | 17 | 30 | 158 | .... | .... | .... | .... | .... | .... | .... | .... | .... | 5 | 1 | 2 | 3 | 8 | .... | .... | .... | .... |
| **2005-06** | **Minnesota** | **NHL** | **51** | **4** | **8** | **12** | **64** | **1** | **0** | **0** | **55** | **7.3** | **-8** | **26** | **46.2** | **10:39** | .... | .... | .... | .... | .... | .... | .... | .... | .... |
| **2006-07** | Chicago Wolves | AHL | 26 | 10 | 11 | 21 | 61 | .... | .... | .... | .... | .... | .... | .... | .... | .... | .... | .... | .... | .... | .... | .... | .... | .... | .... |
| | **Tampa Bay** | **NHL** | **4** | **0** | **0** | **0** | **0** | **0** | **0** | **0** | **0** | **0.0** | **0** | **0** | **0.0** | **5:12** | .... | .... | .... | .... | .... | .... | .... | .... | .... |
| | Springfield | AHL | 23 | 11 | 7 | 18 | 40 | .... | .... | .... | .... | .... | .... | .... | .... | .... | .... | .... | .... | .... | .... | .... | .... | .... | .... |
| **2007-08** | **Tampa Bay** | **NHL** | **7** | **1** | **0** | **1** | **7** | **0** | **0** | **1** | **10** | **10.0** | **-1** | **1** | **100.0** | **10:09** | .... | .... | .... | .... | .... | .... | .... | .... | .... |
| | Norfolk Admirals | AHL | 62 | 23 | 33 | 56 | 110 | .... | .... | .... | .... | .... | .... | .... | .... | .... | .... | .... | .... | .... | .... | .... | .... | .... | .... |
| 2008-09 | Brynas IF Gavle | Sweden | 18 | 2 | 1 | 3 | 53 | .... | .... | .... | .... | .... | .... | .... | .... | .... | .... | .... | .... | .... | .... | .... | .... | .... | .... |
| | Amur Khabarovsk | Rus-KHL | 16 | 2 | 1 | 3 | 28 | .... | .... | .... | .... | .... | .... | .... | .... | .... | .... | .... | .... | .... | .... | .... | .... | .... | .... |
| | **NHL Totals** | | **75** | **6** | **9** | **15** | **94** | **1** | **0** | **1** | **86** | **7.0** | | **32** | **53.1** | **10:26** | .... | .... | .... | .... | .... | .... | .... | .... | .... |

• Re-entered NHL Entry Draft. Originally Boston's 3rd choice, 89th overall, in 1999 Entry Draft.

WHL East Second All-Star Team (2001) • Canadian Major Junior Second All-Star Team (2001) • Memorial Cup Tournament All-Star Team (2001) • Stafford Smythe Memorial Trophy (Memorial Cup Tournament - MVP) (2001)

• Missed majority of 2001-02 season recovering from ankle injury suffered in game vs. Grand Rapids (AHL), December 30, 2001. Signed as a free agent by **Atlanta**, July 18, 2006. Traded to **Tampa Bay** by **Atlanta** with Stephen Baby for Andy Delmore and Andre Deveaux, February 1, 2007.

| | | | Regular Season | | | | | | | | | | | | | | Playoffs | | | | | | | | |
|---|---|---|---|---|---|---|---|---|---|---|---|---|---|---|---|---|---|---|---|---|---|---|---|---|---|
| Season | Club | League | GP | G | A | Pts | PIM | PP | SH | GW | S | % | +/- | TF | F% | Min | GP | G | A | Pts | PIM | PP | SH | GW | Min |

## WARD, Aaron

(WOHRD, AIR-ruhn) **CAR.**

Defense. Shoots right. 6'2", 209 lbs. Born, Windsor, Ont., January 17, 1973. Winnipeg's 1st choice, 5th overall, in 1991 Entry Draft.

| | | | | | | | | | | | | | | | | | | | | | | | | | |
|---|---|---|---|---|---|---|---|---|---|---|---|---|---|---|---|---|---|---|---|---|---|---|---|---|---|
| 1988-89 | Nepean Raiders | CJHL | 54 | 1 | 14 | 15 | 40 | .... | .... | .... | .... | .... | .... | .... | .... | .... | .... | .... | .... | .... | .... | .... | .... | .... | .... |
| 1989-90 | Nepean Raiders | CJHL | 52 | 6 | 33 | 39 | 85 | .... | .... | .... | .... | .... | .... | .... | .... | .... | .... | .... | .... | .... | .... | .... | .... | .... | .... |
| 1990-91 | U. of Michigan | CCHA | 46 | 8 | 11 | 19 | 126 | .... | .... | .... | .... | .... | .... | .... | .... | .... | .... | .... | .... | .... | .... | .... | .... | .... | .... |
| 1991-92 | U. of Michigan | CCHA | 42 | 7 | 12 | 19 | 64 | .... | .... | .... | .... | .... | .... | .... | .... | .... | .... | .... | .... | .... | .... | .... | .... | .... | .... |
| 1992-93 | U. of Michigan | CCHA | 30 | 5 | 8 | 13 | 73 | .... | .... | .... | .... | .... | .... | .... | .... | .... | .... | .... | .... | .... | .... | .... | .... | .... | .... |
| **1993-94** | **Detroit** | **NHL** | **5** | **1** | **0** | **1** | **4** | **0** | **0** | **0** | **3** | **33.3** | **2** | .... | .... | .... | .... | .... | .... | .... | .... | .... | .... | .... | .... |
| | Adirondack | AHL | 58 | 4 | 12 | 16 | 87 | .... | .... | .... | .... | .... | .... | .... | .... | .... | 9 | 2 | 6 | 8 | 6 | .... | .... | .... | .... |
| **1994-95** | Adirondack | AHL | 76 | 11 | 24 | 35 | 87 | .... | .... | .... | .... | .... | .... | .... | .... | .... | 4 | 0 | 1 | 1 | 0 | .... | .... | .... | .... |
| | **Detroit** | **NHL** | **1** | **0** | **1** | **1** | **2** | **0** | **0** | **0** | **0** | **0.0** | **1** | .... | .... | .... | .... | .... | .... | .... | .... | .... | .... | .... | .... |
| 1995-96 | Adirondack | AHL | 74 | 5 | 10 | 15 | 133 | .... | .... | .... | .... | .... | .... | .... | .... | .... | 3 | 0 | 0 | 0 | 6 | .... | .... | .... | .... |
| **1996-97◆** | **Detroit** | **NHL** | **49** | **2** | **5** | **7** | **52** | **0** | **0** | **0** | **40** | **5.0** | **–9** | .... | .... | .... | **19** | **0** | **0** | **0** | **17** | **0** | **0** | **0** | .... |
| **1997-98◆** | **Detroit** | **NHL** | **52** | **5** | **5** | **10** | **47** | **0** | **0** | **1** | **47** | **10.6** | **–1** | .... | .... | .... | .... | .... | .... | .... | .... | .... | .... | .... | .... |
| **1998-99** | **Detroit** | **NHL** | **60** | **3** | **8** | **11** | **52** | **0** | **0** | **0** | **46** | **6.5** | **–5** | **0** | **0.0** | **13:55** | **8** | **0** | **1** | **1** | **8** | **0** | **0** | **0** | **10:15** |
| **99-2000** | **Detroit** | **NHL** | **36** | **1** | **3** | **4** | **24** | **0** | **0** | **0** | **25** | **4.0** | **–4** | **0** | **0.0** | **12:36** | **3** | **0** | **0** | **0** | **0** | **0** | **0** | **0** | **7:36** |
| **2000-01** | **Detroit** | **NHL** | **73** | **4** | **5** | **9** | **57** | **0** | **0** | **1** | **48** | **8.3** | **–4** | **0** | **0.0** | **17:00** | .... | .... | .... | .... | .... | .... | .... | .... | .... |
| **2001-02** | **Carolina** | **NHL** | **79** | **3** | **11** | **14** | **74** | **0** | **0** | **2** | **69** | **4.3** | **0** | **1** | **100.0** | **19:40** | **23** | **1** | **1** | **2** | **22** | **0** | **0** | **0** | **21:12** |
| **2002-03** | **Carolina** | **NHL** | **77** | **3** | **6** | **9** | **90** | **0** | **0** | **1** | **66** | **4.5** | **–23** | **0** | **0.0** | **18:43** | .... | .... | .... | .... | .... | .... | .... | .... | .... |
| **2003-04** | **Carolina** | **NHL** | **49** | **3** | **5** | **8** | **37** | **2** | **0** | **0** | **51** | **5.9** | **1** | **0** | **0.0** | **17:52** | .... | .... | .... | .... | .... | .... | .... | .... | .... |
| 2004-05 | ERC Ingolstadt | Germany | 8 | 0 | 3 | 3 | 16 | .... | .... | .... | .... | .... | .... | .... | .... | .... | 11 | 1 | 1 | 2 | 16 | .... | .... | .... | .... |
| **2005-06◆** | **Carolina** | **NHL** | **71** | **6** | **19** | **25** | **62** | **0** | **0** | **1** | **60** | **10.0** | **2** | **1** | **0.0** | **19:07** | **25** | **2** | **3** | **5** | **18** | **0** | **0** | **0** | **21:42** |
| **2006-07** | **NY Rangers** | **NHL** | **60** | **3** | **10** | **13** | **57** | **0** | **0** | **0** | **45** | **6.7** | **–3** | **0** | **0.0** | **19:42** | .... | .... | .... | .... | .... | .... | .... | .... | .... |
| | **Boston** | **NHL** | **20** | **1** | **2** | **3** | **18** | **0** | **0** | **0** | **17** | **5.9** | **–8** | **0** | **0.0** | **21:36** | .... | .... | .... | .... | .... | .... | .... | .... | .... |
| **2007-08** | **Boston** | **NHL** | **65** | **5** | **8** | **13** | **54** | **0** | **0** | **3** | **68** | **7.4** | **9** | **0** | **0.0** | **20:45** | **6** | **0** | **1** | **1** | **6** | **0** | **0** | **0** | **22:20** |
| **2008-09** | **Boston** | **NHL** | **65** | **3** | **7** | **10** | **44** | **0** | **1** | **0** | **53** | **5.7** | **16** | **0** | **0.0** | **19:01** | **11** | **1** | **0** | **1** | **2** | **0** | **0** | **0** | **19:41** |
| | **NHL Totals** | | **762** | **43** | **95** | **138** | **674** | **2** | **1** | **9** | **638** | **6.7** | | **2** | **50.0** | **18:15** | **95** | **4** | **6** | **10** | **73** | **0** | **0** | **0** | **19:33** |

Traded to **Detroit** by **Winnipeg** with Toronto's 4th round choice (previously acquired, Detroit selected John Jakopin) in 1993 Entry Draft for Paul Ysebaert and future considerations (Alan Kerr, June 18, 1993), June 11, 1993. • Missed majority of 1999-2000 season recovering from shoulder injury suffered in game vs. Vancouver, January 19, 2000. Traded to **Carolina** by **Detroit** for Carolina's 2nd round choice (Jiri Hudler) in 2002 Entry Draft, July 9, 2001. Signed as a free agent by **Ingolstadt** (Germany), February 15, 2005. Signed as a free agent by **NY Rangers**, July 3, 2006. Traded to **Boston** by **NY Rangers** for Paul Mara, February 27, 2007. Traded to **Carolina** by **Boston** for Patrick Eaves and Carolina's 4th round choice in 2010 Entry Draft, July 24, 2009.

## WARD, Jason

(WOHRD, JAY-suhn) **PHI.**

Right wing. Shoots right. 6'2", 208 lbs. Born, Chapleau, Ont., January 16, 1979. Montreal's 1st choice, 11th overall, in 1997 Entry Draft.

| | | | | | | | | | | | | | | | | | | | | | | | | | |
|---|---|---|---|---|---|---|---|---|---|---|---|---|---|---|---|---|---|---|---|---|---|---|---|---|---|
| 1994-95 | Oshawa | OHA-B | 47 | 30 | 31 | 61 | 75 | .... | .... | .... | .... | .... | .... | .... | .... | .... | .... | .... | .... | .... | .... | .... | .... | .... | .... |
| 1995-96 | Niagara Falls | OHL | 64 | 15 | 35 | 50 | 139 | .... | .... | .... | .... | .... | .... | .... | .... | .... | 10 | 6 | 4 | 10 | 23 | .... | .... | .... | .... |
| 1996-97 | Erie Otters | OHL | 58 | 25 | 39 | 64 | 137 | .... | .... | .... | .... | .... | .... | .... | .... | .... | 5 | 1 | 2 | 3 | 2 | .... | .... | .... | .... |
| 1997-98 | Erie Otters | OHL | 21 | 7 | 9 | 16 | 42 | .... | .... | .... | .... | .... | .... | .... | .... | .... | .... | .... | .... | .... | .... | .... | .... | .... | .... |
| | Windsor Spitfires | OHL | 26 | 19 | 27 | 46 | 34 | .... | .... | .... | .... | .... | .... | .... | .... | .... | .... | .... | .... | .... | .... | .... | .... | .... | .... |
| | Fredericton | AHL | 7 | 1 | 0 | 1 | 2 | .... | .... | .... | .... | .... | .... | .... | .... | .... | 1 | 0 | 0 | 0 | 2 | .... | .... | .... | .... |
| 1998-99 | Windsor Spitfires | OHL | 12 | 8 | 11 | 19 | 25 | .... | .... | .... | .... | .... | .... | .... | .... | .... | .... | .... | .... | .... | .... | .... | .... | .... | .... |
| | Plymouth Whalers | OHL | 23 | 14 | 13 | 27 | 28 | .... | .... | .... | .... | .... | .... | .... | .... | .... | 11 | 6 | 8 | 14 | 12 | .... | .... | .... | .... |
| | Fredericton | AHL | .... | .... | .... | .... | .... | .... | .... | .... | .... | .... | .... | .... | .... | .... | 10 | 4 | 2 | 6 | 22 | .... | .... | .... | .... |
| **99-2000** | **Montreal** | **NHL** | **32** | **2** | **1** | **3** | **10** | **1** | **0** | **0** | **24** | **8.3** | **–1** | **86** | **44.2** | **9:10** | .... | .... | .... | .... | .... | .... | .... | .... | .... |
| | Quebec Citadelles | AHL | 40 | 14 | 12 | 26 | 30 | .... | .... | .... | .... | .... | .... | .... | .... | .... | 3 | 2 | 1 | 3 | 4 | .... | .... | .... | .... |
| **2000-01** | **Montreal** | **NHL** | **12** | **0** | **0** | **0** | **12** | **0** | **0** | **0** | **4** | **0.0** | **3** | **2** | **50.0** | **8:16** | .... | .... | .... | .... | .... | .... | .... | .... | .... |
| | Quebec Citadelles | AHL | 23 | 7 | 12 | 19 | 69 | .... | .... | .... | .... | .... | .... | .... | .... | .... | .... | .... | .... | .... | .... | .... | .... | .... | .... |
| 2001-02 | Quebec Citadelles | AHL | 78 | 24 | 33 | 57 | 128 | .... | .... | .... | .... | .... | .... | .... | .... | .... | 3 | 0 | 0 | 0 | 2 | .... | .... | .... | .... |
| **2002-03** | **Montreal** | **NHL** | **8** | **3** | **2** | **5** | **0** | **0** | **0** | **0** | **10** | **30.0** | **3** | **6** | **50.0** | **11:17** | .... | .... | .... | .... | .... | .... | .... | .... | .... |
| | Hamilton | AHL | 69 | 31 | 41 | 72 | 78 | .... | .... | .... | .... | .... | .... | .... | .... | .... | 23 | *12 | 9 | *21 | 20 | .... | .... | .... | .... |
| **2003-04** | **Montreal** | **NHL** | **53** | **5** | **7** | **12** | **21** | **2** | **0** | **1** | **56** | **8.9** | **3** | **98** | **41.8** | **12:39** | **5** | **0** | **2** | **2** | **2** | **0** | **0** | **0** | **15:39** |
| | Hamilton | AHL | 2 | 0 | 3 | 3 | 17 | .... | .... | .... | .... | .... | .... | .... | .... | .... | .... | .... | .... | .... | .... | .... | .... | .... | .... |
| 2004-05 | Hamilton | AHL | 77 | 20 | 34 | 54 | 66 | .... | .... | .... | .... | .... | .... | .... | .... | .... | 4 | 2 | 1 | 3 | 2 | .... | .... | .... | .... |
| **2005-06** | **NY Rangers** | **NHL** | **81** | **10** | **18** | **28** | **44** | **0** | **2** | **1** | **125** | **8.0** | **–4** | **153** | **47.7** | **13:12** | **1** | **0** | **0** | **0** | **2** | **0** | **0** | **0** | **2:39** |
| **2006-07** | **NY Rangers** | **NHL** | **46** | **4** | **6** | **10** | **26** | **0** | **1** | **1** | **68** | **5.9** | **–3** | **191** | **41.9** | **12:19** | .... | .... | .... | .... | .... | .... | .... | .... | .... |
| | **Los Angeles** | **NHL** | **7** | **0** | **1** | **1** | **4** | **0** | **0** | **0** | **2** | **0.0** | **–1** | **7** | **14.3** | **4:51** | .... | .... | .... | .... | .... | .... | .... | .... | .... |
| | **Tampa Bay** | **NHL** | **17** | **4** | **4** | **8** | **10** | **0** | **0** | **0** | **38** | **10.5** | **–11** | **16** | **37.5** | **16:38** | **6** | **0** | **1** | **1** | **6** | **0** | **0** | **0** | **20:03** |
| **2007-08** | **Tampa Bay** | **NHL** | **79** | **8** | **6** | **14** | **42** | **1** | **1** | **0** | **85** | **9.4** | **–18** | **45** | **40.0** | **12:33** | .... | .... | .... | .... | .... | .... | .... | .... | .... |
| **2008-09** | **Tampa Bay** | **NHL** | **1** | **0** | **0** | **0** | **2** | **0** | **0** | **0** | **1** | **0.0** | **0** | **0** | **0.0** | **9:31** | .... | .... | .... | .... | .... | .... | .... | .... | .... |
| | Norfolk Admirals | AHL | 21 | 2 | 7 | 9 | 16 | .... | .... | .... | .... | .... | .... | .... | .... | .... | .... | .... | .... | .... | .... | .... | .... | .... | .... |
| | **NHL Totals** | | **336** | **36** | **45** | **81** | **171** | **4** | **4** | **3** | **413** | **8.7** | | **604** | **43.2** | **12:13** | **12** | **0** | **3** | **3** | **10** | **0** | **0** | **0** | **16:46** |

AHL First All-Star Team (2003) • Les Cunningham Award (AHL – MVP) (2003)

• Missed majority of 2000-01 season recovering from knee injury suffered in game vs. Carolina, January 16, 2001. Signed as a free agent by **Hamilton** (AHL), October 19, 2004. Signed as a free agent by **NY Rangers**, August 4, 2005. Traded to **Los Angeles** by **NY Rangers** with Jan Marek, Marc-Andre Cliche and NY Rangers' 3rd round choice (later traded to Buffalo - Buffalo selected Corey Fienhage) in 2008 Entry Draft for Sean Avery and John Seymour, February 5, 2007. Traded to **Tampa Bay** by **Los Angeles** for Tampa Bay's 5th round choice (Joshua Turnbull) in 2007 Entry Draft, February 27, 2007. • Missed majority of 2008-09 season recovering from lower body injury suffered in game at Portland (AHL), December 31, 2008. Signed as a free agent by **Philadelphia**, July 23, 2009.

## WARD, Joel

(WOHRD, JOHL) **NSH.**

Right wing. Shoots right. 6'1", 220 lbs. Born, Toronto, Ont., December 2, 1980.

| | | | | | | | | | | | | | | | | | | | | | | | | | |
|---|---|---|---|---|---|---|---|---|---|---|---|---|---|---|---|---|---|---|---|---|---|---|---|---|---|
| 1997-98 | Owen Sound | OHL | 47 | 8 | 4 | 12 | 14 | .... | .... | .... | .... | .... | .... | .... | .... | .... | 11 | 1 | 1 | 2 | 5 | .... | .... | .... | .... |
| 1998-99 | Owen Sound | OHL | 58 | 19 | 16 | 35 | 23 | .... | .... | .... | .... | .... | .... | .... | .... | .... | 16 | 2 | 4 | 6 | 0 | .... | .... | .... | .... |
| 99-2000 | Owen Sound | OHL | 63 | 23 | 20 | 43 | 51 | .... | .... | .... | .... | .... | .... | .... | .... | .... | .... | .... | .... | .... | .... | .... | .... | .... | .... |
| 2000-01 | Owen Sound | OHL | 67 | 26 | 36 | 62 | 45 | .... | .... | .... | .... | .... | .... | .... | .... | .... | 5 | 2 | 4 | 6 | 4 | .... | .... | .... | .... |
| | Long Beach | WCHL | .... | .... | .... | .... | .... | .... | .... | .... | .... | .... | .... | .... | .... | .... | 8 | 0 | 0 | 0 | 0 | .... | .... | .... | .... |
| 2001-02 | U. of P.E.I. | CIS | 22 | 13 | 14 | 27 | 16 | .... | .... | .... | .... | .... | .... | .... | .... | .... | .... | .... | .... | .... | .... | .... | .... | .... | .... |
| 2002-03 | U. of P.E.I. | CIS | 19 | 11 | 15 | 26 | 24 | .... | .... | .... | .... | .... | .... | .... | .... | .... | .... | .... | .... | .... | .... | .... | .... | .... | .... |
| 2003-04 | U. of P.E.I. | CIS | 27 | 14 | 24 | 38 | 42 | .... | .... | .... | .... | .... | .... | .... | .... | .... | .... | .... | .... | .... | .... | .... | .... | .... | .... |
| 2004-05 | U. of P.E.I. | CIS | 28 | 16 | 28 | 44 | 42 | .... | .... | .... | .... | .... | .... | .... | .... | .... | .... | .... | .... | .... | .... | .... | .... | .... | .... |
| 2005-06 | Houston Aeros | AHL | 66 | 8 | 14 | 22 | 34 | .... | .... | .... | .... | .... | .... | .... | .... | .... | 8 | 4 | 2 | 6 | 4 | .... | .... | .... | .... |
| **2006-07** | **Minnesota** | **NHL** | **11** | **0** | **1** | **1** | **0** | **0** | **0** | **0** | **12** | **0.0** | **0** | **1** | **0.0** | **7:42** | .... | .... | .... | .... | .... | .... | .... | .... | .... |
| | Houston Aeros | AHL | 64 | 9 | 14 | 23 | 45 | .... | .... | .... | .... | .... | .... | .... | .... | .... | .... | .... | .... | .... | .... | .... | .... | .... | .... |
| 2007-08 | Houston Aeros | AHL | 79 | 21 | 20 | 41 | 47 | .... | .... | .... | .... | .... | .... | .... | .... | .... | 4 | 0 | 2 | 2 | 0 | .... | .... | .... | .... |
| **2008-09** | **Nashville** | **NHL** | **79** | **17** | **18** | **35** | **29** | **3** | **2** | **2** | **133** | **12.8** | **1** | **46** | **43.5** | **16:01** | .... | .... | .... | .... | .... | .... | .... | .... | .... |
| | **NHL Totals** | | **90** | **17** | **19** | **36** | **29** | **3** | **2** | **2** | **145** | **11.7** | | **47** | **42.6** | **15:00** | .... | .... | .... | .... | .... | .... | .... | .... | .... |

Signed as a free agent by **Houston** (AHL), December 4, 2005. Signed as a free agent by **Minnesota**, September 27, 2006. Signed as a free agent by **Nashville**, July 14, 2008.

## WEAVER, Mike

(WEE-vuhr, MIGHK) **ST.L.**

Defense. Shoots right. 5'9", 188 lbs. Born, Bramalea, Ont., May 2, 1978.

| | | | | | | | | | | | | | | | | | | | | | | | | | |
|---|---|---|---|---|---|---|---|---|---|---|---|---|---|---|---|---|---|---|---|---|---|---|---|---|---|
| 1995-96 | Bramalea Blues | OPJHL | 48 | 10 | 39 | 49 | 103 | .... | .... | .... | .... | .... | .... | .... | .... | .... | .... | .... | .... | .... | .... | .... | .... | .... | .... |
| 1996-97 | Michigan State | CCHA | 39 | 0 | 7 | 7 | 46 | .... | .... | .... | .... | .... | .... | .... | .... | .... | .... | .... | .... | .... | .... | .... | .... | .... | .... |
| 1997-98 | Michigan State | CCHA | 44 | 4 | 22 | 26 | 68 | .... | .... | .... | .... | .... | .... | .... | .... | .... | .... | .... | .... | .... | .... | .... | .... | .... | .... |
| 1998-99 | Michigan State | CCHA | 42 | 1 | 6 | 7 | 54 | .... | .... | .... | .... | .... | .... | .... | .... | .... | .... | .... | .... | .... | .... | .... | .... | .... | .... |
| 99-2000 | Michigan State | CCHA | 26 | 0 | 7 | 7 | 20 | .... | .... | .... | .... | .... | .... | .... | .... | .... | .... | .... | .... | .... | .... | .... | .... | .... | .... |
| 2000-01 | Orlando | IHL | 68 | 0 | 8 | 8 | 34 | .... | .... | .... | .... | .... | .... | .... | .... | .... | 16 | 0 | 2 | 2 | 8 | .... | .... | .... | .... |
| **2001-02** | **Atlanta** | **NHL** | **16** | **0** | **1** | **1** | **10** | **0** | **0** | **0** | **9** | **0.0** | **0** | **0** | **0.0** | **13:54** | .... | .... | .... | .... | .... | .... | .... | .... | .... |
| | Chicago Wolves | AHL | 58 | 2 | 8 | 10 | 67 | .... | .... | .... | .... | .... | .... | .... | .... | .... | 25 | 1 | 3 | 4 | 21 | .... | .... | .... | .... |
| **2002-03** | **Atlanta** | **NHL** | **40** | **0** | **5** | **5** | **20** | **0** | **0** | **0** | **21** | **0.0** | **–5** | **0** | **0.0** | **18:38** | .... | .... | .... | .... | .... | .... | .... | .... | .... |
| | Chicago Wolves | AHL | 33 | 2 | 2 | 4 | 32 | .... | .... | .... | .... | .... | .... | .... | .... | .... | 9 | 0 | 3 | 3 | 4 | .... | .... | .... | .... |
| **2003-04** | **Atlanta** | **NHL** | **1** | **0** | **0** | **0** | **0** | **0** | **0** | **0** | **0** | **0.0** | **–1** | **0** | **0.0** | **8:28** | .... | .... | .... | .... | .... | .... | .... | .... | .... |
| | Chicago Wolves | AHL | 78 | 3 | 14 | 17 | 89 | .... | .... | .... | .... | .... | .... | .... | .... | .... | 9 | 2 | 2 | 4 | 20 | .... | .... | .... | .... |
| 2004-05 | Manchester | AHL | 79 | 1 | 22 | 23 | 61 | .... | .... | .... | .... | .... | .... | .... | .... | .... | 6 | 0 | 1 | 1 | 0 | .... | .... | .... | .... |
| **2005-06** | **Los Angeles** | **NHL** | **53** | **0** | **9** | **9** | **14** | **0** | **0** | **0** | **21** | **0.0** | **–3** | **0** | **0.0** | **15:03** | .... | .... | .... | .... | .... | .... | .... | .... | .... |
| **2006-07** | **Los Angeles** | **NHL** | **39** | **3** | **6** | **9** | **16** | **1** | **0** | **1** | **22** | **13.6** | **–4** | **3** | **66.7** | **15:20** | .... | .... | .... | .... | .... | .... | .... | .... | .... |
| | Manchester | AHL | 7 | 1 | 3 | 4 | 2 | .... | .... | .... | .... | .... | .... | .... | .... | .... | .... | .... | .... | .... | .... | .... | .... | .... | .... |

| Season | Club | League | GP | G | A | Pts | PIM | PP | SH | GW | S | % | +/- | TF | F% | Min | Playoffs GP | G | A | Pts | PIM | PP | SH | GW | Min |
|---|---|---|---|---|---|---|---|---|---|---|---|---|---|---|---|---|---|---|---|---|---|---|---|---|---|
| 2007-08 | **Vancouver** | **NHL** | **55** | **0** | **1** | **1** | **33** | **0** | **0** | **0** | **33** | **0.0** | **1** | **1** | **0.0** | **14:02** | .... | .... | .... | .... | .... | .... | .... | .... | .... |
| 2008-09 | **St. Louis** | **NHL** | **58** | **0** | **7** | **7** | **12** | **0** | **0** | **0** | **36** | **0.0** | **–3** | **0** | **0.0** | **17:16** | **4** | **0** | **0** | **0** | **0** | **0** | **0** | **0** | **17:02** |
| | **NHL Totals** | | **262** | **3** | **29** | **32** | **105** | **1** | **0** | **1** | **142** | **2.1** | | **4** | **50.0** | **15:49** | **4** | **0** | **0** | **0** | **0** | **0** | **0** | **0** | **17:02** |

OPJHL Defenseman of the Year (1996) • CCHA All-Tournament Team (1997) • CCHA First All-Star Team (1999, 2000) • CCHA Best Defensive Defenseman Award (1999, 2000) • NCAA West Second All-American Team (1999, 2000)

Signed as a free agent by **Atlanta**, June 15, 2000. Signed as a free agent by **Los Angeles**, July 16, 2004. Signed as a free agent by **Pittsburgh**, August 8, 2007. Claimed on waivers by **Vancouver** from **Pittsburgh**, October 2, 2007. Signed as a free agent by **St. Louis**, July 10, 2008.

### WEBER, Mike

(WEH-buhr, MIGHK) **BUF.**

Defense. Shoots left. 6'2", 211 lbs. Born, Pittsburgh, PA, December 16, 1987. Buffalo's 3rd choice, 57th overall, in 2006 Entry Draft.

| Season | Club | League | GP | G | A | Pts | PIM | PP | SH | GW | S | % | +/- | TF | F% | Min | Playoffs GP | G | A | Pts | PIM | PP | SH | GW | Min |
|---|---|---|---|---|---|---|---|---|---|---|---|---|---|---|---|---|---|---|---|---|---|---|---|---|---|
| 2002-03 | Jr. Penguins | EmJHL | 28 | 4 | 11 | 15 | 109 | .... | .... | .... | .... | .... | .... | .... | .... | .... | 3 | 0 | 0 | 0 | 20 | .... | .... | .... | .... |
| 2003-04 | Windsor Spitfires | OHL | 65 | 0 | 2 | 2 | 49 | .... | .... | .... | .... | .... | .... | .... | .... | .... | .... | .... | .... | .... | .... | .... | .... | .... | .... |
| 2004-05 | Windsor Spitfires | OHL | 68 | 2 | 6 | 8 | 132 | .... | .... | .... | .... | .... | .... | .... | .... | .... | 11 | 0 | 1 | 1 | 18 | .... | .... | .... | .... |
| 2005-06 | Windsor Spitfires | OHL | 68 | 5 | 21 | 26 | 181 | .... | .... | .... | .... | .... | .... | .... | .... | .... | 7 | 0 | 0 | 0 | 12 | .... | .... | .... | .... |
| 2006-07 | Windsor Spitfires | OHL | 30 | 3 | 16 | 19 | 86 | .... | .... | .... | .... | .... | .... | .... | .... | .... | .... | .... | .... | .... | .... | .... | .... | .... | .... |
| | Barrie Colts | OHL | 30 | 3 | 12 | 15 | 86 | .... | .... | .... | .... | .... | .... | .... | .... | .... | 7 | 0 | 6 | 6 | 10 | .... | .... | .... | .... |
| **2007-08** | **Buffalo** | **NHL** | **16** | **0** | **3** | **3** | **14** | **0** | **0** | **0** | **12** | **0.0** | **12** | **0** | **0.0** | **16:41** | .... | .... | .... | .... | .... | .... | .... | .... | .... |
| | Rochester | AHL | 59 | 1 | 13 | 14 | 178 | .... | .... | .... | .... | .... | .... | .... | .... | .... | .... | .... | .... | .... | .... | .... | .... | .... | .... |
| **2008-09** | **Buffalo** | **NHL** | **7** | **0** | **0** | **0** | **19** | **0** | **0** | **0** | **2** | **0.0** | **–3** | **0** | **0.0** | **14:10** | .... | .... | .... | .... | .... | .... | .... | .... | .... |
| | Portland Pirates | AHL | 42 | 1 | 7 | 8 | 94 | .... | .... | .... | .... | .... | .... | .... | .... | .... | .... | .... | .... | .... | .... | .... | .... | .... | .... |
| | **NHL Totals** | | **23** | **0** | **3** | **3** | **33** | **0** | **0** | **0** | **14** | **0.0** | | **0** | **0.0** | **15:55** | .... | .... | .... | .... | .... | .... | .... | .... | .... |

### WEBER, Shea

(WEH-buhr, SHAY) **NSH.**

Defense. Shoots right. 6'4", 230 lbs. Born, Sicamous, B.C., August 14, 1985. Nashville's 4th choice, 49th overall, in 2003 Entry Draft.

| Season | Club | League | GP | G | A | Pts | PIM | PP | SH | GW | S | % | +/- | TF | F% | Min | Playoffs GP | G | A | Pts | PIM | PP | SH | GW | Min |
|---|---|---|---|---|---|---|---|---|---|---|---|---|---|---|---|---|---|---|---|---|---|---|---|---|---|
| 2001-02 | Sicamous Eagles | KIJHL | 47 | 9 | 33 | 42 | 87 | .... | .... | .... | .... | .... | .... | .... | .... | .... | .... | .... | .... | .... | .... | .... | .... | .... | .... |
| | Kelowna Rockets | WHL | 5 | 0 | 0 | 0 | 0 | .... | .... | .... | .... | .... | .... | .... | .... | .... | .... | .... | .... | .... | .... | .... | .... | .... | .... |
| 2002-03 | Kelowna Rockets | WHL | 70 | 2 | 16 | 18 | 167 | .... | .... | .... | .... | .... | .... | .... | .... | .... | 19 | 1 | 4 | 5 | 26 | .... | .... | .... | .... |
| 2003-04 | Kelowna Rockets | WHL | 60 | 12 | 20 | 32 | 126 | .... | .... | .... | .... | .... | .... | .... | .... | .... | 17 | 3 | 14 | 17 | 16 | .... | .... | .... | .... |
| 2004-05 | Kelowna Rockets | WHL | 55 | 12 | 29 | 41 | 95 | .... | .... | .... | .... | .... | .... | .... | .... | .... | 18 | 9 | 8 | 17 | 25 | .... | .... | .... | .... |
| **2005-06** | **Nashville** | **NHL** | **28** | **2** | **8** | **10** | **42** | **2** | **0** | **1** | **46** | **4.3** | **8** | **0** | **0.0** | **17:00** | **4** | **2** | **0** | **2** | **8** | **1** | **0** | **0** | **14:12** |
| | Milwaukee | AHL | 46 | 12 | 15 | 27 | 49 | .... | .... | .... | .... | .... | .... | .... | .... | .... | 14 | 6 | 5 | 11 | 16 | .... | .... | .... | .... |
| **2006-07** | **Nashville** | **NHL** | **79** | **17** | **23** | **40** | **60** | **6** | **0** | **2** | **152** | **11.2** | **13** | **0** | **0.0** | **19:23** | **5** | **0** | **3** | **3** | **2** | **0** | **0** | **0** | **21:41** |
| **2007-08** | **Nashville** | **NHL** | **54** | **6** | **14** | **20** | **49** | **5** | **0** | **2** | **152** | **3.9** | **–6** | **0** | **0.0** | **19:30** | **6** | **1** | **3** | **4** | **6** | **0** | **0** | **0** | **19:30** |
| **2008-09** | **Nashville** | **NHL** | **81** | **23** | **30** | **53** | **80** | **10** | **1** | **4** | **251** | **9.2** | **1** | **0** | **0.0** | **23:58** | .... | .... | .... | .... | .... | .... | .... | .... | .... |
| | **NHL Totals** | | **242** | **48** | **75** | **123** | **231** | **23** | **1** | **9** | **601** | **8.0** | | **0** | **0.0** | **20:40** | **15** | **3** | **6** | **9** | **16** | **1** | **0** | **0** | **18:49** |

WHL West Second All-Star Team (2004) • Memorial Cup Tournament All-Star Team (2004) • WHL West First All-Star Team (2005) • Canadian Major Junior Second All-Star Team (2005)

Played in NHL All-Star Game (2009)

### WEBER, Yannick

(WEH-buhr, YAH-nihk) **MTL.**

Defense. Shoots right. 5'11", 197 lbs. Born, Morges, Switz., September 23, 1988. Montreal's 5th choice, 73rd overall, in 2007 Entry Draft.

| Season | Club | League | GP | G | A | Pts | PIM | PP | SH | GW | S | % | +/- | TF | F% | Min | Playoffs GP | G | A | Pts | PIM | PP | SH | GW | Min |
|---|---|---|---|---|---|---|---|---|---|---|---|---|---|---|---|---|---|---|---|---|---|---|---|---|---|
| 2003-04 | SC Bern Jr. | Swiss-Jr. | 32 | 2 | 3 | 5 | 39 | .... | .... | .... | .... | .... | .... | .... | .... | .... | 8 | 2 | 0 | 2 | 8 | .... | .... | .... | .... |
| 2004-05 | SC Bern Jr. | Swiss-Jr. | 37 | 5 | 4 | 9 | 62 | .... | .... | .... | .... | .... | .... | .... | .... | .... | 5 | 0 | 0 | 0 | 22 | .... | .... | .... | .... |
| 2005-06 | SC Bern Future Jr. | Swiss-Jr. | 17 | 1 | 6 | 7 | 46 | .... | .... | .... | .... | .... | .... | .... | .... | .... | .... | .... | .... | .... | .... | .... | .... | .... | .... |
| | SC Langenthal | Swiss-2 | 28 | 3 | 0 | 3 | 8 | .... | .... | .... | .... | .... | .... | .... | .... | .... | .... | .... | .... | .... | .... | .... | .... | .... | .... |
| 2006-07 | SC Bern Future Jr. | Swiss-Jr. | 1 | 0 | 0 | 0 | 2 | .... | .... | .... | .... | .... | .... | .... | .... | .... | .... | .... | .... | .... | .... | .... | .... | .... | .... |
| | Kitchener Rangers | OHL | 51 | 13 | 28 | 41 | 42 | .... | .... | .... | .... | .... | .... | .... | .... | .... | 9 | 3 | 6 | 9 | 8 | .... | .... | .... | .... |
| 2007-08 | Kitchener Rangers | OHL | 59 | 20 | 35 | 55 | 79 | .... | .... | .... | .... | .... | .... | .... | .... | .... | 17 | 4 | 13 | 17 | 24 | .... | .... | .... | .... |
| **2008-09** | **Montreal** | **NHL** | **3** | **0** | **1** | **1** | **2** | **0** | **0** | **0** | **6** | **0.0** | **–1** | **0** | **0.0** | **15:06** | **3** | **1** | **1** | **2** | **0** | **0** | **0** | **0** | **13:36** |
| | Hamilton | AHL | 68 | 16 | 28 | 44 | 42 | .... | .... | .... | .... | .... | .... | .... | .... | .... | 2 | 0 | 1 | 1 | 10 | .... | .... | .... | .... |
| | **NHL Totals** | | **3** | **0** | **1** | **1** | **2** | **0** | **0** | **0** | **6** | **0.0** | | **0** | **0.0** | **15:06** | **3** | **1** | **1** | **2** | **0** | **0** | **0** | **0** | **13:36** |

OHL Second All-Star Team (2008) • AHL All-Rookie Team (2009)

### WEIGHT, Doug

(WAYT, DUHG) **NYI**

Center. Shoots left. 5'11", 196 lbs. Born, Warren, MI, January 21, 1971. NY Rangers' 2nd choice, 34th overall, in 1990 Entry Draft.

| Season | Club | League | GP | G | A | Pts | PIM | PP | SH | GW | S | % | +/- | TF | F% | Min | Playoffs GP | G | A | Pts | PIM | PP | SH | GW | Min |
|---|---|---|---|---|---|---|---|---|---|---|---|---|---|---|---|---|---|---|---|---|---|---|---|---|---|
| 1988-89 | Bloomfield Jets | NAHL | 34 | 26 | 53 | 79 | 105 | .... | .... | .... | .... | .... | .... | .... | .... | .... | .... | .... | .... | .... | .... | .... | .... | .... | .... |
| 1989-90 | Lake Superior | CCHA | 46 | 21 | 48 | 69 | 44 | .... | .... | .... | .... | .... | .... | .... | .... | .... | .... | .... | .... | .... | .... | .... | .... | .... | .... |
| **1990-91** | Lake Superior | CCHA | 42 | 29 | 46 | 75 | 86 | .... | .... | .... | .... | .... | .... | .... | .... | .... | .... | .... | .... | .... | .... | .... | .... | .... | .... |
| | **NY Rangers** | **NHL** | .... | .... | .... | .... | .... | .... | .... | .... | .... | .... | .... | .... | .... | .... | **1** | **0** | **0** | **0** | **0** | **0** | **0** | **0** | .... |
| **1991-92** | **NY Rangers** | **NHL** | **53** | **8** | **22** | **30** | **23** | **0** | **0** | **2** | **72** | **11.1** | **–3** | .... | .... | .... | **7** | **2** | **2** | **4** | **0** | **1** | **0** | **0** | .... |
| | Binghamton | AHL | 9 | 3 | 14 | 17 | 2 | .... | .... | .... | .... | .... | .... | .... | .... | .... | 4 | 1 | 4 | 5 | 6 | .... | .... | .... | .... |
| **1992-93** | **NY Rangers** | **NHL** | **65** | **15** | **25** | **40** | **55** | **3** | **0** | **1** | **90** | **16.7** | **4** | .... | .... | .... | .... | .... | .... | .... | .... | .... | .... | .... | .... |
| | **Edmonton** | **NHL** | **13** | **2** | **6** | **8** | **10** | **0** | **0** | **0** | **35** | **5.7** | **–2** | .... | .... | .... | .... | .... | .... | .... | .... | .... | .... | .... | .... |
| **1993-94** | **Edmonton** | **NHL** | **84** | **24** | **50** | **74** | **47** | **4** | **1** | **1** | **188** | **12.8** | **–22** | .... | .... | .... | .... | .... | .... | .... | .... | .... | .... | .... | .... |
| **1994-95** | Rosenheim | Germany | 8 | 2 | 3 | 5 | 18 | .... | .... | .... | .... | .... | .... | .... | .... | .... | .... | .... | .... | .... | .... | .... | .... | .... | .... |
| | **Edmonton** | **NHL** | **48** | **7** | **33** | **40** | **69** | **1** | **0** | **1** | **104** | **6.7** | **–17** | .... | .... | .... | .... | .... | .... | .... | .... | .... | .... | .... | .... |
| **1995-96** | **Edmonton** | **NHL** | **82** | **25** | **79** | **104** | **95** | **9** | **0** | **2** | **204** | **12.3** | **–19** | .... | .... | .... | .... | .... | .... | .... | .... | .... | .... | .... | .... |
| **1996-97** | **Edmonton** | **NHL** | **80** | **21** | **61** | **82** | **80** | **4** | **0** | **2** | **235** | **8.9** | **1** | .... | .... | .... | **12** | **3** | **8** | **11** | **8** | **0** | **0** | **0** | .... |
| **1997-98** | **Edmonton** | **NHL** | **79** | **26** | **44** | **70** | **69** | **9** | **0** | **4** | **205** | **12.7** | **1** | .... | .... | .... | **12** | **2** | **7** | **9** | **14** | **2** | **0** | **1** | .... |
| | United States | Olympics | 4 | 0 | 2 | 2 | 2 | .... | .... | .... | .... | .... | .... | .... | .... | .... | .... | .... | .... | .... | .... | .... | .... | .... | .... |
| **1998-99** | **Edmonton** | **NHL** | **43** | **6** | **31** | **37** | **12** | **1** | **0** | **0** | **79** | **7.6** | **–8** | **853** | **49.5** | **19:51** | **4** | **1** | **1** | **2** | **15** | **0** | **0** | **0** | **14:43** |
| **99-2000** | **Edmonton** | **NHL** | **77** | **21** | **51** | **72** | **54** | **3** | **1** | **4** | **167** | **12.6** | **6** | **1588** | **50.4** | **20:35** | **5** | **3** | **2** | **5** | **4** | **2** | **0** | **1** | **21:05** |
| **2000-01** | **Edmonton** | **NHL** | **82** | **25** | **65** | **90** | **91** | **8** | **0** | **3** | **188** | **13.3** | **12** | **1514** | **51.3** | **22:08** | **6** | **1** | **5** | **6** | **17** | **0** | **0** | **0** | **22:45** |
| **2001-02** | **St. Louis** | **NHL** | **61** | **15** | **34** | **49** | **40** | **3** | **0** | **1** | **131** | **11.5** | **20** | **1123** | **49.2** | **19:48** | **10** | **1** | **1** | **2** | **4** | **1** | **0** | **1** | **16:26** |
| | United States | Olympics | 6 | 0 | 3 | 3 | 4 | .... | .... | .... | .... | .... | .... | .... | .... | .... | .... | .... | .... | .... | .... | .... | .... | .... | .... |
| **2002-03** | **St. Louis** | **NHL** | **70** | **15** | **52** | **67** | **52** | **7** | **0** | **3** | **182** | **8.2** | **–6** | **1048** | **50.4** | **20:23** | **7** | **5** | **8** | **13** | **2** | **5** | **0** | **1** | **22:26** |
| **2003-04** | **St. Louis** | **NHL** | **75** | **14** | **51** | **65** | **37** | **6** | **0** | **5** | **198** | **7.1** | **–3** | **1115** | **50.4** | **20:25** | **5** | **2** | **1** | **3** | **6** | **1** | **1** | **0** | **19:24** |
| 2004-05 | Frankfurt Lions | Germany | 7 | 6 | 9 | 15 | 26 | .... | .... | .... | .... | .... | .... | .... | .... | .... | 11 | 2 | 10 | 12 | 8 | .... | .... | .... | .... |
| **2005-06** | **St. Louis** | **NHL** | **47** | **11** | **33** | **44** | **50** | **7** | **0** | **1** | **123** | **8.9** | **–11** | **638** | **49.8** | **22:17** | .... | .... | .... | .... | .... | .... | .... | .... | .... |
| | ♦ **Carolina** | **NHL** | **23** | **4** | **9** | **13** | **25** | **2** | **0** | **0** | **52** | **7.7** | **–6** | **256** | **46.1** | **17:35** | **23** | **3** | **13** | **16** | **20** | **2** | **0** | **0** | **15:27** |
| | United States | Olympics | 6 | 0 | 3 | 3 | 4 | .... | .... | .... | .... | .... | .... | .... | .... | .... | .... | .... | .... | .... | .... | .... | .... | .... | .... |
| **2006-07** | **St. Louis** | **NHL** | **82** | **16** | **43** | **59** | **56** | **5** | **0** | **3** | **123** | **13.0** | **10** | **1025** | **47.7** | **18:17** | .... | .... | .... | .... | .... | .... | .... | .... | .... |
| **2007-08** | **St. Louis** | **NHL** | **29** | **4** | **7** | **11** | **12** | **0** | **0** | **0** | **47** | **8.5** | **4** | **289** | **49.5** | **16:11** | .... | .... | .... | .... | .... | .... | .... | .... | .... |
| | **Anaheim** | **NHL** | **38** | **6** | **8** | **14** | **20** | **2** | **0** | **1** | **49** | **12.2** | **0** | **325** | **45.2** | **13:25** | **5** | **0** | **1** | **1** | **4** | **0** | **0** | **0** | **7:39** |
| **2008-09** | **NY Islanders** | **NHL** | **53** | **10** | **28** | **38** | **55** | **5** | **0** | **0** | **96** | **10.4** | **–15** | **679** | **45.1** | **18:17** | .... | .... | .... | .... | .... | .... | .... | .... | .... |
| | **NHL Totals** | | **1184** | **275** | **732** | **1007** | **952** | **79** | **2** | **34** | **2568** | **10.7** | | **10453** | **49.4** | **19:35** | **97** | **23** | **49** | **72** | **94** | **14** | **1** | **4** | **17:07** |

CCHA First All-Star Team (1991) • NCAA West Second All-American Team (1991)

Played in NHL All-Star Game (1996, 1998, 2001, 2003)

Traded to **Edmonton** by **NY Rangers** for Esa Tikkanen, March 17, 1993. Traded to **St. Louis** by **Edmonton** with Michel Riesen for Marty Reasoner, Jochen Hecht and Jan Horacek, July 1, 2001. Signed as a free agent by **Frankfurt** (Germany), February 11, 2005. Traded to **Carolina** by **St. Louis** with Erkki Rajamaki for Jesse Boulerice, Mike Zigomanis, the rights to Magnus Kahnberg, Carolina's 1st round choice (later traded to New Jersey - New Jersey selected Matthew Corrente) in 2006 Entry Draft, Toronto's 4th round choice (previously acquired, St. Louis selected Reto Berra) in 2006 Entry Draft and Chicago's 4th round choice (previously acquired, St. Louis selected Cade Fairchild) in 2007 Entry Draft, January 30, 2006. Signed as a free agent by **St. Louis**, July 2, 2006. Traded to **Anaheim** by **St. Louis** with Michal Birner and St. Louis' 7th round choice (later traded to Los Angeles - later traded back to St. Louis - St. Louis selected Paul Karpowich) in 2008 Entry Draft for Andy McDonald, December 14, 2007. Signed as a free agent by **NY Islanders**, July 2, 2008.

### WEISS, Stephen

(WIGHS, STEE-vehn) **FLA.**

Center. Shoots left. 5'11", 185 lbs. Born, Toronto, Ont., April 3, 1983. Florida's 1st choice, 4th overall, in 2001 Entry Draft.

| Season | Club | League | GP | G | A | Pts | PIM | PP | SH | GW | S | % | +/- | TF | F% | Min | Playoffs GP | G | A | Pts | PIM | PP | SH | GW | Min |
|---|---|---|---|---|---|---|---|---|---|---|---|---|---|---|---|---|---|---|---|---|---|---|---|---|---|
| 1997-98 | Tor. Young Nats | MTHL | 48 | 51 | 58 | 109 | .... | .... | .... | .... | .... | .... | .... | .... | .... | .... | .... | .... | .... | .... | .... | .... | .... | .... | .... |
| 1998-99 | North York | OPJHL | 35 | 15 | 22 | 37 | 10 | .... | .... | .... | .... | .... | .... | .... | .... | .... | .... | .... | .... | .... | .... | .... | .... | .... | .... |
| 99-2000 | Plymouth Whalers | OHL | 64 | 24 | 42 | 66 | 35 | .... | .... | .... | .... | .... | .... | .... | .... | .... | 23 | 8 | 18 | 26 | 18 | .... | .... | .... | .... |
| 2000-01 | Plymouth Whalers | OHL | 62 | 40 | 47 | 87 | 45 | .... | .... | .... | .... | .... | .... | .... | .... | .... | 18 | 7 | 16 | 23 | 10 | .... | .... | .... | .... |
| **2001-02** | **Florida** | **NHL** | **7** | **1** | **1** | **2** | **0** | **1** | **0** | **0** | **15** | **6.7** | **0** | **107** | **52.3** | **16:14** | .... | .... | .... | .... | .... | .... | .... | .... | .... |
| | Plymouth Whalers | OHL | 46 | 25 | 45 | 70 | 69 | .... | .... | .... | .... | .... | .... | .... | .... | .... | 6 | 2 | 7 | 9 | 13 | .... | .... | .... | .... |
| **2002-03** | **Florida** | **NHL** | **77** | **6** | **15** | **21** | **17** | **0** | **0** | **2** | **87** | **6.9** | **–13** | **1065** | **46.3** | **14:17** | .... | .... | .... | .... | .... | .... | .... | .... | .... |

| | | | Regular Season | | | | | | | | | | | | | | Playoffs | | | | | | | | |
|---|---|---|---|---|---|---|---|---|---|---|---|---|---|---|---|---|---|---|---|---|---|---|---|---|---|
| Season | Club | League | GP | G | A | Pts | PIM | PP | SH | GW | S | % | +/- | TF | F% | Min | GP | G | A | Pts | PIM | PP | SH | GW | Min |
| **2003-04** | **Florida** | **NHL** | **50** | **12** | **17** | **29** | **10** | **3** | **0** | **2** | **82** | **14.6** | **–10** | **799** | **44.9** | **17:42** | .... | .... | .... | .... | .... | .... | .... | .... | .... |
| | San Antonio | AHL | 10 | 6 | 3 | 9 | 14 | .... | .... | .... | .... | .... | .... | .... | .... | .... | .... | .... | .... | .... | .... | .... | .... | .... | .... |
| 2004-05 | San Antonio | AHL | 62 | 15 | 23 | 38 | 38 | .... | .... | .... | .... | .... | .... | .... | .... | .... | .... | .... | .... | .... | .... | .... | .... | .... | .... |
| | Chicago Wolves | AHL | 18 | 7 | 9 | 16 | 12 | .... | .... | .... | .... | .... | .... | .... | .... | .... | 18 | 2 | 7 | 9 | 17 | .... | .... | .... | .... |
| **2005-06** | **Florida** | **NHL** | **41** | **9** | **12** | **21** | **22** | **5** | **0** | **1** | **74** | **12.2** | **–2** | **514** | **49.6** | **15:15** | .... | .... | .... | .... | .... | .... | .... | .... | .... |
| **2006-07** | **Florida** | **NHL** | **74** | **20** | **28** | **48** | **28** | **10** | **0** | **1** | **176** | **11.4** | **–1** | **1182** | **45.9** | **17:07** | .... | .... | .... | .... | .... | .... | .... | .... | .... |
| **2007-08** | **Florida** | **NHL** | **74** | **13** | **29** | **42** | **40** | **4** | **0** | **4** | **132** | **9.8** | **14** | **1198** | **51.2** | **17:35** | .... | .... | .... | .... | .... | .... | .... | .... | .... |
| **2008-09** | **Florida** | **NHL** | **78** | **14** | **47** | **61** | **22** | **4** | **1** | **4** | **154** | **9.1** | **19** | **1277** | **50.9** | **17:48** | .... | .... | .... | .... | .... | .... | .... | .... | .... |
| | **NHL Totals** | | **401** | **75** | **149** | **224** | **139** | **27** | **1** | **14** | **720** | **10.4** | | **6142** | **48.3** | **16:40** | .... | .... | .... | .... | .... | .... | .... | .... | .... |

OHL All-Rookie Team (2000)
• Loaned to **Chicago** (AHL) by **San Antonio** (AHL) for cash, March 8, 2005.

## WELCH, Noah

(WEHLCH, NOH-uh) **ATL.**

Defense. Shoots left. 6'4", 220 lbs. Born, Brighton, MA, August 26, 1982. Pittsburgh's 2nd choice, 54th overall, in 2001 Entry Draft.

| | | | | | | | | | | | | | | | | | | | | | | | | | |
|---|---|---|---|---|---|---|---|---|---|---|---|---|---|---|---|---|---|---|---|---|---|---|---|---|---|
| 99-2000 | St. Sebastian's | High-MA | 26 | 4 | 11 | 15 | 35 | .... | .... | .... | .... | .... | .... | .... | .... | .... | .... | .... | .... | .... | .... | .... | .... | .... | .... |
| | Eastern-Mass | MBAHL | 4 | 0 | 3 | 3 | 6 | .... | .... | .... | .... | .... | .... | .... | .... | .... | .... | .... | .... | .... | .... | .... | .... | .... | .... |
| 2000-01 | St. Sebastian's | High-MA | 30 | 11 | 20 | 31 | 37 | .... | .... | .... | .... | .... | .... | .... | .... | .... | .... | .... | .... | .... | .... | .... | .... | .... | .... |
| 2001-02 | Harvard Crimson | ECAC | 27 | 5 | 6 | 11 | 56 | .... | .... | .... | .... | .... | .... | .... | .... | .... | .... | .... | .... | .... | .... | .... | .... | .... | .... |
| 2002-03 | Harvard Crimson | ECAC | 34 | 6 | 22 | 28 | 70 | .... | .... | .... | .... | .... | .... | .... | .... | .... | .... | .... | .... | .... | .... | .... | .... | .... | .... |
| 2003-04 | Harvard Crimson | ECAC | 34 | 6 | 13 | 19 | 58 | .... | .... | .... | .... | .... | .... | .... | .... | .... | .... | .... | .... | .... | .... | .... | .... | .... | .... |
| 2004-05 | Harvard Crimson | ECAC | 34 | 6 | 12 | 18 | *86 | .... | .... | .... | .... | .... | .... | .... | .... | .... | .... | .... | .... | .... | .... | .... | .... | .... | .... |
| **2005-06** | **Pittsburgh** | **NHL** | **5** | **1** | **3** | **4** | **2** | **0** | **0** | **0** | **5** | **20.0** | **0** | **0** | **0.0** | **17:24** | .... | .... | .... | .... | .... | .... | .... | .... | .... |
| | Wilkes-Barre | AHL | 77 | 9 | 20 | 29 | 99 | .... | .... | .... | .... | .... | .... | .... | .... | .... | 11 | 1 | 0 | 1 | 18 | .... | .... | .... | .... |
| **2006-07** | **Pittsburgh** | **NHL** | **22** | **1** | **1** | **2** | **22** | **0** | **0** | **0** | **14** | **7.1** | **1** | **0** | **0.0** | **13:34** | .... | .... | .... | .... | .... | .... | .... | .... | .... |
| | Wilkes-Barre | AHL | 27 | 5 | 16 | 21 | 24 | .... | .... | .... | .... | .... | .... | .... | .... | .... | .... | .... | .... | .... | .... | .... | .... | .... | .... |
| | **Florida** | **NHL** | **2** | **1** | **0** | **1** | **2** | **0** | **0** | **0** | **4** | **25.0** | **3** | **0** | **0.0** | **18:08** | .... | .... | .... | .... | .... | .... | .... | .... | .... |
| | Rochester | AHL | 11 | 2 | 4 | 6 | 21 | .... | .... | .... | .... | .... | .... | .... | .... | .... | 6 | 0 | 2 | 2 | 12 | .... | .... | .... | .... |
| **2007-08** | **Florida** | **NHL** | **4** | **0** | **0** | **0** | **7** | **0** | **0** | **0** | **0** | **0.0** | **1** | **0** | **0.0** | **8:04** | .... | .... | .... | .... | .... | .... | .... | .... | .... |
| **2008-09** | **Florida** | **NHL** | **23** | **1** | **1** | **2** | **11** | **0** | **0** | **0** | **11** | **9.1** | **–5** | **0** | **0.0** | **6:38** | .... | .... | .... | .... | .... | .... | .... | .... | .... |
| | Rochester | AHL | 7 | 0 | 3 | 3 | 10 | .... | .... | .... | .... | .... | .... | .... | .... | .... | .... | .... | .... | .... | .... | .... | .... | .... | .... |
| | **Tampa Bay** | **NHL** | **17** | **0** | **0** | **0** | **14** | **0** | **0** | **0** | **11** | **0.0** | **–4** | **0** | **0.0** | **16:45** | .... | .... | .... | .... | .... | .... | .... | .... | .... |
| | **NHL Totals** | | **73** | **4** | **5** | **9** | **58** | **0** | **0** | **0** | **45** | **8.9** | | **0** | **0.0** | **12:13** | .... | .... | .... | .... | .... | .... | .... | .... | .... |

ECAC All-Rookie Team (2002) • ECAC Second All-Star Team (2002, 2003) • NCAA East Second All-American Team (2003) • ECAC First All-Star Team (2005) • NCAA East First All-American Team (2005)
Traded to **Florida** by **Pittsburgh** for Gary Roberts, February 27, 2007. • Missed remainder of 2007-08 season recovering from shoulder injury suffered in game at Montreal, October 16, 2007. Traded to **Tampa Bay** by **Florida** with Florida's 3rd round choice (later traded to Detroit – Detroit selected Andrej Nestrasil) in 2009 Entry Draft for Steve Eminger, March 4, 2009. Signed as a free agent by **Atlanta**, July 13, 2009.

## WELLER, Craig

(WEHL-uhr, KRAIG) **MIN.**

Right wing. Shoots right. 6'4", 220 lbs. Born, Calgary, Alta., January 17, 1981. St. Louis' 6th choice, 167th overall, in 2000 Entry Draft.

| | | | | | | | | | | | | | | | | | | | | | | | | | |
|---|---|---|---|---|---|---|---|---|---|---|---|---|---|---|---|---|---|---|---|---|---|---|---|---|---|
| 1997-98 | Cgy. AAA Flames | AMHL | 33 | 2 | 10 | 12 | 65 | .... | .... | .... | .... | .... | .... | .... | .... | .... | 3 | 0 | 1 | 1 | 2 | .... | .... | .... | .... |
| 1998-99 | Calgary Canucks | AJHL | 49 | 4 | 14 | 18 | 80 | .... | .... | .... | .... | .... | .... | .... | .... | .... | 13 | 0 | 1 | 1 | 10 | .... | .... | .... | .... |
| 99-2000 | Calgary Canucks | AJHL | 53 | 3 | 14 | 17 | 100 | .... | .... | .... | .... | .... | .... | .... | .... | .... | 4 | 0 | 0 | 0 | 4 | .... | .... | .... | .... |
| 2000-01 | U. Minn-Duluth | WCHA | 6 | 0 | 1 | 1 | 0 | .... | .... | .... | .... | .... | .... | .... | .... | .... | .... | .... | .... | .... | .... | .... | .... | .... | .... |
| | Kootenay Ice | WHL | 30 | 1 | 5 | 6 | 40 | .... | .... | .... | .... | .... | .... | .... | .... | .... | 11 | 0 | 2 | 2 | 26 | .... | .... | .... | .... |
| 2001-02 | Kootenay Ice | WHL | 69 | 5 | 13 | 18 | 127 | .... | .... | .... | .... | .... | .... | .... | .... | .... | 22 | 3 | 7 | 10 | 27 | .... | .... | .... | .... |
| 2002-03 | Hartford | AHL | 11 | 0 | 0 | 0 | 8 | .... | .... | .... | .... | .... | .... | .... | .... | .... | 2 | 0 | 0 | 0 | 0 | .... | .... | .... | .... |
| | Charlotte | ECHL | 48 | 3 | 11 | 14 | 84 | .... | .... | .... | .... | .... | .... | .... | .... | .... | .... | .... | .... | .... | .... | .... | .... | .... | .... |
| 2003-04 | Hartford | AHL | 68 | 5 | 9 | 14 | 86 | .... | .... | .... | .... | .... | .... | .... | .... | .... | 16 | 2 | 2 | 4 | 30 | .... | .... | .... | .... |
| 2004-05 | Hartford | AHL | 76 | 10 | 9 | 19 | 182 | .... | .... | .... | .... | .... | .... | .... | .... | .... | 6 | 0 | 1 | 1 | 6 | .... | .... | .... | .... |
| 2005-06 | Hartford | AHL | 80 | 12 | 21 | 33 | 152 | .... | .... | .... | .... | .... | .... | .... | .... | .... | 13 | 2 | 3 | 5 | 44 | .... | .... | .... | .... |
| 2006-07 | Hartford | AHL | 56 | 11 | 6 | 17 | 96 | .... | .... | .... | .... | .... | .... | .... | .... | .... | 4 | 0 | 0 | 0 | 4 | .... | .... | .... | .... |
| **2007-08** | **Phoenix** | **NHL** | **59** | **3** | **8** | **11** | **80** | **0** | **0** | **1** | **72** | **4.2** | **–7** | **2** | **0.0** | **10:23** | .... | .... | .... | .... | .... | .... | .... | .... | .... |
| **2008-09** | **Minnesota** | **NHL** | **36** | **1** | **2** | **3** | **47** | **1** | **0** | **0** | **27** | **3.7** | **–3** | **5** | **0.0** | **6:57** | .... | .... | .... | .... | .... | .... | .... | .... | .... |
| | **NHL Totals** | | **95** | **4** | **10** | **14** | **127** | **1** | **0** | **1** | **99** | **4.0** | | **7** | **0.0** | **9:05** | .... | .... | .... | .... | .... | .... | .... | .... | .... |

WHL West Second All-Star Team (2002)
• Left **University of Minnesota-Duluth** (WCHA) and signed as a free agent by **Kootenay** (WHL), January 7, 2001. Signed as a free agent by **NY Rangers**, July 11, 2002. Signed as a free agent by **Phoenix**, July 19, 2007. Signed as a free agent by **Minnesota**, July 1, 2008. • Missed majority of 2008-09 season recovering from various injuries and serving as a healthy reserve.

## WELLWOOD, Kyle

(WEHL-wud, KIGHL) **VAN.**

Center. Shoots right. 5'10", 180 lbs. Born, Windsor, Ont., May 16, 1983. Toronto's 6th choice, 134th overall, in 2001 Entry Draft.

| | | | | | | | | | | | | | | | | | | | | | | | | | |
|---|---|---|---|---|---|---|---|---|---|---|---|---|---|---|---|---|---|---|---|---|---|---|---|---|---|
| 1998-99 | Tecumseh | OHA-B | 51 | 22 | 41 | 63 | 12 | .... | .... | .... | .... | .... | .... | .... | .... | .... | .... | .... | .... | .... | .... | .... | .... | .... | .... |
| 99-2000 | Belleville Bulls | OHL | 65 | 14 | 37 | 51 | 14 | .... | .... | .... | .... | .... | .... | .... | .... | .... | 16 | 3 | 7 | 10 | 6 | .... | .... | .... | .... |
| 2000-01 | Belleville Bulls | OHL | 68 | 35 | *83 | *118 | 24 | .... | .... | .... | .... | .... | .... | .... | .... | .... | 10 | 3 | 16 | 19 | 4 | .... | .... | .... | .... |
| 2001-02 | Belleville Bulls | OHL | 28 | 16 | 24 | 40 | 4 | .... | .... | .... | .... | .... | .... | .... | .... | .... | .... | .... | .... | .... | .... | .... | .... | .... | .... |
| | Windsor Spitfires | OHL | 26 | 14 | 21 | 35 | 0 | .... | .... | .... | .... | .... | .... | .... | .... | .... | 16 | 12 | 12 | 24 | 0 | .... | .... | .... | .... |
| 2002-03 | Windsor Spitfires | OHL | 57 | 41 | 59 | 100 | 0 | .... | .... | .... | .... | .... | .... | .... | .... | .... | 7 | 5 | 9 | 14 | 0 | .... | .... | .... | .... |
| **2003-04** | **Toronto** | **NHL** | **1** | **0** | **0** | **0** | **0** | **0** | **0** | **0** | **1** | **0.0** | **–1** | **13** | **30.8** | **7:56** | .... | .... | .... | .... | .... | .... | .... | .... | .... |
| | St. John's | AHL | 76 | 20 | 35 | 55 | 6 | .... | .... | .... | .... | .... | .... | .... | .... | .... | .... | .... | .... | .... | .... | .... | .... | .... | .... |
| 2004-05 | St. John's | AHL | 80 | 38 | 49 | 87 | 20 | .... | .... | .... | .... | .... | .... | .... | .... | .... | 5 | 2 | 2 | 4 | 2 | .... | .... | .... | .... |
| **2005-06** | **Toronto** | **NHL** | **81** | **11** | **34** | **45** | **14** | **3** | **0** | **0** | **117** | **9.4** | **0** | **593** | **56.3** | **12:47** | .... | .... | .... | .... | .... | .... | .... | .... | .... |
| **2006-07** | **Toronto** | **NHL** | **48** | **12** | **30** | **42** | **0** | **7** | **0** | **2** | **99** | **12.1** | **3** | **291** | **56.4** | **16:38** | .... | .... | .... | .... | .... | .... | .... | .... | .... |
| **2007-08** | **Toronto** | **NHL** | **59** | **8** | **13** | **21** | **0** | **5** | **0** | **1** | **57** | **14.0** | **–12** | **325** | **54.8** | **12:39** | .... | .... | .... | .... | .... | .... | .... | .... | .... |
| **2008-09** | **Vancouver** | **NHL** | **74** | **18** | **9** | **27** | **4** | **10** | **0** | **3** | **94** | **19.1** | **2** | **621** | **57.5** | **13:48** | **10** | **1** | **5** | **6** | **0** | **0** | **0** | **0** | **15:05** |
| | **NHL Totals** | | **263** | **49** | **86** | **135** | **18** | **25** | **0** | **6** | **368** | **13.3** | | **1843** | **56.3** | **13:43** | **10** | **1** | **5** | **6** | **0** | **0** | **0** | **0** | **15:05** |

OHL First All-Star Team (2001) • Canadian Major Junior Sportsman of the Year (2003)
Claimed on waivers by **Vancouver** from **Toronto**, June 25, 2008.

## WESTCOTT, Duvie

(WEST-koht, DOO-vee)

Defense. Shoots right. 5'11", 197 lbs. Born, Winnipeg, Man., October 30, 1977.

| | | | | | | | | | | | | | | | | | | | | | | | | | |
|---|---|---|---|---|---|---|---|---|---|---|---|---|---|---|---|---|---|---|---|---|---|---|---|---|---|
| 1996-97 | Winnipeg South | MJHL | 52 | 12 | 47 | 59 | .... | .... | .... | .... | .... | .... | .... | .... | .... | .... | .... | .... | .... | .... | .... | .... | .... | .... | .... |
| 1997-98 | Alaska Anchorage | WCHA | 25 | 3 | 5 | 8 | 43 | .... | .... | .... | .... | .... | .... | .... | .... | .... | .... | .... | .... | .... | .... | .... | .... | .... | .... |
| | Omaha Lancers | USHL | 12 | 3 | 3 | 6 | 31 | .... | .... | .... | .... | .... | .... | .... | .... | .... | 14 | 0 | 8 | 8 | 84 | .... | .... | .... | .... |
| 1998-99 | St. Cloud State | WCHA | DID NOT PLAY – TRANSFERRED COLLEGES | | | | | | | | | | | | | | | | | | | | | | |
| 99-2000 | St. Cloud State | WCHA | 36 | 1 | 18 | 19 | 67 | .... | .... | .... | .... | .... | .... | .... | .... | .... | .... | .... | .... | .... | .... | .... | .... | .... | .... |
| 2000-01 | St. Cloud State | WCHA | 38 | 10 | 24 | 34 | 116 | .... | .... | .... | .... | .... | .... | .... | .... | .... | .... | .... | .... | .... | .... | .... | .... | .... | .... |
| **2001-02** | **Columbus** | **NHL** | **4** | **0** | **0** | **0** | **2** | **0** | **0** | **0** | **3** | **0.0** | **–2** | **0** | **0.0** | **15:08** | .... | .... | .... | .... | .... | .... | .... | .... | .... |
| | Syracuse Crunch | AHL | 68 | 4 | 29 | 33 | 99 | .... | .... | .... | .... | .... | .... | .... | .... | .... | 10 | 0 | 1 | 1 | 12 | .... | .... | .... | .... |
| **2002-03** | **Columbus** | **NHL** | **39** | **0** | **7** | **7** | **77** | **0** | **0** | **0** | **27** | **0.0** | **–3** | **0** | **0.0** | **18:41** | .... | .... | .... | .... | .... | .... | .... | .... | .... |
| | Syracuse Crunch | AHL | 22 | 1 | 10 | 11 | 54 | .... | .... | .... | .... | .... | .... | .... | .... | .... | .... | .... | .... | .... | .... | .... | .... | .... | .... |
| **2003-04** | **Columbus** | **NHL** | **34** | **0** | **7** | **7** | **39** | **0** | **0** | **0** | **43** | **0.0** | **–15** | **0** | **0.0** | **21:11** | .... | .... | .... | .... | .... | .... | .... | .... | .... |
| 2004-05 | JYP Jyvaskyla | Finland | 46 | 11 | 7 | 18 | 106 | .... | .... | .... | .... | .... | .... | .... | .... | .... | 1 | 2 | 0 | 2 | 25 | .... | .... | .... | .... |
| **2005-06** | **Columbus** | **NHL** | **78** | **6** | **22** | **28** | **133** | **1** | **1** | **0** | **113** | **5.3** | **1** | **0** | **0.0** | **22:34** | .... | .... | .... | .... | .... | .... | .... | .... | .... |
| **2006-07** | **Columbus** | **NHL** | **23** | **4** | **6** | **10** | **18** | **2** | **0** | **1** | **34** | **11.8** | **–13** | **0** | **0.0** | **22:09** | .... | .... | .... | .... | .... | .... | .... | .... | .... |
| **2007-08** | **Columbus** | **NHL** | **23** | **1** | **3** | **4** | **30** | **1** | **0** | **0** | **27** | **3.7** | **–10** | **0** | **0.0** | **16:25** | .... | .... | .... | .... | .... | .... | .... | .... | .... |
| | Syracuse Crunch | AHL | 37 | 4 | 23 | 27 | 77 | .... | .... | .... | .... | .... | .... | .... | .... | .... | 13 | 2 | 4 | 6 | 10 | .... | .... | .... | .... |
| 2008-09 | Dynamo Riga | Rus-KHL | 51 | 2 | 18 | 20 | 124 | .... | .... | .... | .... | .... | .... | .... | .... | .... | 2 | 0 | 0 | 0 | 33 | .... | .... | .... | .... |
| | **NHL Totals** | | **201** | **11** | **45** | **56** | **299** | **4** | **1** | **1** | **247** | **4.5** | | **0** | **0.0** | **20:41** | .... | .... | .... | .... | .... | .... | .... | .... | .... |

WCHA Second All-Star Team (2001)
Signed as a free agent by **Columbus**, May 10, 2001. • Missed majority of 2003-04 season recovering from ankle (October 13, 2003 vs. Vancouver) and hand (January 31, 2004 vs. Minnesota) injuries. Signed as a free agent by **Jyvaskyla** (Finland), September 30, 2004. • Missed majority of 2006-07 season recovering from finger (November 3, 2006 vs. Calgary) and head (January 6, 2007 vs. San Jose) injuries.

## WESTGARTH, Kevin

(WEHST-garth, KEH-vihn) **L.A.**

Right wing. Shoots right. 6'5", 241 lbs. Born, Amherstburg, Ont., February 7, 1984.

| Season | Club | League | GP | G | A | Pts | PIM | PP | SH | GW | S | % | +/- | TF | F% | Min | GP | G | A | Pts | PIM | PP | SH | GW | Min |
|---|---|---|---|---|---|---|---|---|---|---|---|---|---|---|---|---|---|---|---|---|---|---|---|---|---|
| | | | Regular Season | | | | | | | | | | | | | | Playoffs | | | | | | | | |
| 2003-04 | Princeton | ECAC | 25 | 3 | 3 | 6 | 48 | | | | | | | | | | | | | | | | | | |
| 2004-05 | Princeton | ECAC | 29 | 4 | 3 | 7 | 36 | | | | | | | | | | | | | | | | | | |
| 2005-06 | Princeton | ECAC | 29 | 10 | 13 | 23 | 36 | | | | | | | | | | | | | | | | | | |
| 2006-07 | Princeton | ECAC | 33 | 8 | 16 | 24 | 40 | | | | | | | | | | | | | | | | | | |
| | Manchester | AHL | 14 | 1 | 2 | 3 | 44 | | | | | | | | | | | | | | | | | | |
| 2007-08 | Manchester | AHL | 69 | 6 | 6 | 12 | 191 | | | | | | | | | | 4 | 0 | 0 | 0 | 6 | | | | |
| **2008-09** | **Los Angeles** | **NHL** | **9** | **0** | **0** | **0** | **9** | **0** | **0** | **0** | **1** | **0.0** | **1** | **1** | **0.0** | **5:02** | | | | | | | | | |
| | Manchester | AHL | 65 | 4 | 6 | 10 | 165 | | | | | | | | | | | | | | | | | | |
| | **NHL Totals** | | **9** | **0** | **0** | **0** | **9** | **0** | **0** | **0** | **1** | **0.0** | | **1** | **0.0** | **5:02** | | | | | | | | | |

Signed as a free agent by **Los Angeles**, March 16, 2007.

## WHEELER, Blake

(WEE-luhr, BLAYK) **BOS.**

Right wing. Shoots right. 6'5", 205 lbs. Born, Robbinsdale, MN, August 31, 1986. Phoenix's 1st choice, 5th overall, in 2004 Entry Draft.

| Season | Club | League | GP | G | A | Pts | PIM | PP | SH | GW | S | % | +/- | TF | F% | Min | GP | G | A | Pts | PIM | PP | SH | GW | Min |
|---|---|---|---|---|---|---|---|---|---|---|---|---|---|---|---|---|---|---|---|---|---|---|---|---|---|
| 2002-03 | Breck Mustangs | High-MN | 26 | 15 | 27 | 42 | | | | | | | | | | | | | | | | | | | |
| 2003-04 | Team Northwest | UMEHL | 24 | 5 | 6 | 11 | | | | | | | | | | | | | | | | | | | |
| | Breck Mustangs | High-MN | 27 | 39 | 50 | 89 | 34 | | | | | | | | | | 3 | 6 | 5 | 11 | 0 | | | | |
| 2004-05 | Green Bay | USHL | 58 | 19 | 28 | 47 | 43 | | | | | | | | | | | | | | | | | | |
| 2005-06 | U. of Minnesota | WCHA | 39 | 9 | 14 | 23 | 41 | | | | | | | | | | | | | | | | | | |
| 2006-07 | U. of Minnesota | WCHA | 44 | 18 | 20 | 38 | 42 | | | | | | | | | | | | | | | | | | |
| 2007-08 | U. of Minnesota | WCHA | 44 | 15 | 20 | 35 | 72 | | | | | | | | | | | | | | | | | | |
| **2008-09** | **Boston** | **NHL** | **81** | **21** | **24** | **45** | **46** | **3** | **2** | **3** | **150** | **14.0** | **36** | **34** | **38.2** | **13:41** | **8** | **0** | **0** | **0** | **0** | **0** | **0** | **0** | **12:08** |
| | **NHL Totals** | | **81** | **21** | **24** | **45** | **46** | **3** | **2** | **3** | **150** | **14.0** | | **34** | **38.2** | **13:41** | **8** | **0** | **0** | **0** | **0** | **0** | **0** | **0** | **12:08** |

USHL All-Rookie Team (2005)

Signed as a free agent by **Boston**, July 1, 2008.

## WHITE, Colin

(WIGHT, KAW-lihn) **N.J.**

Defense. Shoots left. 6'4", 215 lbs. Born, New Glasgow, N.S., December 12, 1977. New Jersey's 5th choice, 49th overall, in 1996 Entry Draft.

| Season | Club | League | GP | G | A | Pts | PIM | PP | SH | GW | S | % | +/- | TF | F% | Min | GP | G | A | Pts | PIM | PP | SH | GW | Min |
|---|---|---|---|---|---|---|---|---|---|---|---|---|---|---|---|---|---|---|---|---|---|---|---|---|---|
| 1994-95 | Laval Titan | QMJHL | 7 | 0 | 1 | 1 | 32 | | | | | | | | | | | | | | | | | | |
| | Hull Olympiques | QMJHL | 5 | 0 | 1 | 1 | 4 | | | | | | | | | | 12 | 0 | 0 | 0 | 23 | | | | |
| 1995-96 | Hull Olympiques | QMJHL | 62 | 2 | 8 | 10 | 303 | | | | | | | | | | 18 | 0 | 4 | 4 | 42 | | | | |
| 1996-97 | Hull Olympiques | QMJHL | 63 | 3 | 12 | 15 | 297 | | | | | | | | | | 14 | 3 | 12 | 15 | 65 | | | | |
| 1997-98 | Albany River Rats | AHL | 76 | 3 | 13 | 16 | 235 | | | | | | | | | | 13 | 0 | 0 | 0 | 55 | | | | |
| 1998-99 | Albany River Rats | AHL | 77 | 2 | 12 | 14 | 265 | | | | | | | | | | 5 | 0 | 1 | 1 | 8 | | | | |
| **99-2000♦** | **New Jersey** | **NHL** | **21** | **2** | **1** | **3** | **40** | **0** | **0** | **1** | **29** | **6.9** | **3** | **0** | **0.0** | **14:45** | **23** | **1** | **5** | **6** | **18** | **0** | **0** | **1** | **14:25** |
| | Albany River Rats | AHL | 52 | 5 | 21 | 26 | 176 | | | | | | | | | | | | | | | | | | |
| **2000-01** | **New Jersey** | **NHL** | **82** | **1** | **19** | **20** | **155** | **0** | **0** | **1** | **114** | **0.9** | **32** | **0** | **0.0** | **19:06** | **25** | **0** | **3** | **3** | **42** | **0** | **0** | **0** | **16:45** |
| **2001-02** | **New Jersey** | **NHL** | **73** | **2** | **3** | **5** | **133** | **0** | **0** | **0** | **81** | **2.5** | **6** | **0** | **0.0** | **20:06** | **6** | **0** | **0** | **0** | **2** | **0** | **0** | **0** | **21:50** |
| **2002-03♦** | **New Jersey** | **NHL** | **72** | **5** | **8** | **13** | **98** | **0** | **0** | **1** | **81** | **6.2** | **19** | **0** | **0.0** | **19:41** | **24** | **0** | **5** | **5** | **29** | **0** | **0** | **0** | **22:02** |
| **2003-04** | **New Jersey** | **NHL** | **75** | **2** | **11** | **13** | **96** | **0** | **0** | **0** | **61** | **3.3** | **10** | **0** | **0.0** | **21:02** | **5** | **0** | **0** | **0** | **4** | **0** | **0** | **0** | **19:40** |
| 2004-05 | | | DID NOT PLAY | | | | | | | | | | | | | | | | | | | | | | |
| **2005-06** | **New Jersey** | **NHL** | **73** | **3** | **14** | **17** | **91** | **1** | **0** | **1** | **60** | **5.0** | **–2** | **0** | **0.0** | **21:48** | **4** | **0** | **0** | **0** | **4** | **0** | **0** | **0** | **17:39** |
| **2006-07** | **New Jersey** | **NHL** | **69** | **0** | **8** | **8** | **69** | **0** | **0** | **0** | **47** | **0.0** | **–8** | **0** | **0.0** | **22:28** | **7** | **0** | **0** | **0** | **6** | **0** | **0** | **0** | **21:16** |
| **2007-08** | **New Jersey** | **NHL** | **57** | **2** | **8** | **10** | **26** | **0** | **0** | **1** | **27** | **7.4** | **–5** | **0** | **0.0** | **19:40** | **5** | **0** | **0** | **0** | **6** | **0** | **0** | **0** | **20:27** |
| **2008-09** | **New Jersey** | **NHL** | **71** | **1** | **17** | **18** | **46** | **0** | **0** | **0** | **68** | **1.5** | **18** | **1** | **0.0** | **19:01** | **7** | **0** | **1** | **1** | **6** | **0** | **0** | **0** | **19:46** |
| | **NHL Totals** | | **593** | **18** | **89** | **107** | **754** | **1** | **0** | **5** | **568** | **3.2** | | **1** | **0.0** | **20:09** | **106** | **1** | **14** | **15** | **117** | **0** | **0** | **1** | **18:34** |

QMJHL All-Rookie Team (1996) • NHL All-Rookie Team (2001)

## WHITE, Ian

(WIGHT, EE-an) **TOR.**

Defense. Shoots right. 5'10", 185 lbs. Born, Steinbach, Man., June 4, 1984. Toronto's 6th choice, 191st overall, in 2002 Entry Draft.

| Season | Club | League | GP | G | A | Pts | PIM | PP | SH | GW | S | % | +/- | TF | F% | Min | GP | G | A | Pts | PIM | PP | SH | GW | Min |
|---|---|---|---|---|---|---|---|---|---|---|---|---|---|---|---|---|---|---|---|---|---|---|---|---|---|
| 99-2000 | Eastman Selects | MAHA | 32 | 29 | 33 | 62 | 36 | | | | | | | | | | | | | | | | | | |
| 2000-01 | Swift Current | WHL | 69 | 12 | 31 | 43 | 24 | | | | | | | | | | | | | | | | | | |
| 2001-02 | Swift Current | WHL | 70 | 32 | 47 | 79 | 40 | | | | | | | | | | 12 | 4 | 5 | 9 | 12 | | | | |
| 2002-03 | Swift Current | WHL | 64 | 24 | 44 | 68 | 44 | | | | | | | | | | 4 | 0 | 4 | 4 | 0 | | | | |
| 2003-04 | Swift Current | WHL | 43 | 9 | 23 | 32 | 32 | | | | | | | | | | 5 | 1 | 3 | 4 | 8 | | | | |
| | St. John's | AHL | 8 | 0 | 4 | 4 | 2 | | | | | | | | | | | | | | | | | | |
| 2004-05 | St. John's | AHL | 78 | 4 | 22 | 26 | 54 | | | | | | | | | | 5 | 0 | 2 | 2 | 2 | | | | |
| **2005-06** | **Toronto** | **NHL** | **12** | **1** | **5** | **6** | **10** | **0** | **0** | **0** | **21** | **4.8** | **2** | **0** | **0.0** | **19:07** | | | | | | | | | |
| | Toronto Marlies | AHL | 59 | 7 | 30 | 37 | 42 | | | | | | | | | | 5 | 1 | 4 | 5 | 4 | | | | |
| **2006-07** | **Toronto** | **NHL** | **76** | **3** | **23** | **26** | **40** | **1** | **0** | **1** | **138** | **2.2** | **8** | **0** | **0.0** | **18:32** | | | | | | | | | |
| **2007-08** | **Toronto** | **NHL** | **81** | **5** | **16** | **21** | **44** | **0** | **0** | **2** | **116** | **4.3** | **–9** | **0** | **0.0** | **18:48** | | | | | | | | | |
| **2008-09** | **Toronto** | **NHL** | **71** | **10** | **16** | **26** | **57** | **2** | **0** | **2** | **158** | **6.3** | **6** | **0** | **0.0** | **22:51** | | | | | | | | | |
| | **NHL Totals** | | **240** | **19** | **60** | **79** | **151** | **3** | **0** | **5** | **433** | **4.4** | | **0** | **0.0** | **19:56** | | | | | | | | | |

WHL East Second All-Star Team (2002) • WHL East First All-Star Team (2003) • Canadian Major Junior Second All-Star Team (2003)

## WHITE, Todd

(WIGHT, TAWD) **ATL.**

Center. Shoots left. 5'10", 195 lbs. Born, Kanata, Ont., May 21, 1975.

| Season | Club | League | GP | G | A | Pts | PIM | PP | SH | GW | S | % | +/- | TF | F% | Min | GP | G | A | Pts | PIM | PP | SH | GW | Min |
|---|---|---|---|---|---|---|---|---|---|---|---|---|---|---|---|---|---|---|---|---|---|---|---|---|---|
| 1990-91 | Powassan | NOJHA | 38 | 34 | 38 | 72 | 118 | | | | | | | | | | | | | | | | | | |
| 1991-92 | Kanata Valley | CJHL | 55 | 39 | 49 | 88 | 30 | | | | | | | | | | | | | | | | | | |
| 1992-93 | Kanata Valley | CJHL | 49 | 51 | 87 | 138 | 46 | | | | | | | | | | | | | | | | | | |
| 1993-94 | Clarkson Knights | ECAC | 33 | 10 | 12 | 22 | 28 | | | | | | | | | | | | | | | | | | |
| 1994-95 | Clarkson Knights | ECAC | 34 | 13 | 16 | 29 | 44 | | | | | | | | | | | | | | | | | | |
| 1995-96 | Clarkson Knights | ECAC | 38 | 29 | 43 | 72 | 36 | | | | | | | | | | | | | | | | | | |
| 1996-97 | Clarkson Knights | ECAC | 37 | *38 | *36 | *74 | 22 | | | | | | | | | | | | | | | | | | |
| **1997-98** | **Chicago** | **NHL** | **7** | **1** | **0** | **1** | **2** | **0** | **0** | **0** | **3** | **33.3** | **0** | | | | | | | | | | | | |
| | Indianapolis Ice | IHL | 65 | 46 | 36 | 82 | 28 | | | | | | | | | | 5 | 2 | 3 | 5 | 4 | | | | |
| **1998-99** | **Chicago** | **NHL** | **35** | **5** | **8** | **13** | **20** | **2** | **0** | **0** | **43** | **11.6** | **–1** | **452** | **46.0** | **13:39** | | | | | | | | | |
| | Chicago Wolves | IHL | 25 | 11 | 13 | 24 | 8 | | | | | | | | | | 10 | 1 | 4 | 5 | 8 | | | | |
| **99-2000** | **Chicago** | **NHL** | **1** | **0** | **0** | **0** | **0** | **0** | **0** | **0** | **0** | **0.0** | **0** | **9** | **55.6** | **13:02** | | | | | | | | | |
| | Cleveland | IHL | 42 | 21 | 30 | 51 | 32 | | | | | | | | | | | | | | | | | | |
| | **Philadelphia** | **NHL** | **3** | **1** | **0** | **1** | **0** | **0** | **0** | **0** | **4** | **25.0** | **–1** | **25** | **40.0** | **10:29** | | | | | | | | | |
| | Philadelphia | AHL | 32 | 19 | 24 | 43 | 12 | | | | | | | | | | 5 | 2 | 1 | 3 | 8 | | | | |
| **2000-01** | **Ottawa** | **NHL** | **16** | **4** | **1** | **5** | **4** | **0** | **0** | **0** | **12** | **33.3** | **5** | **133** | **57.1** | **8:33** | **2** | **0** | **0** | **0** | **0** | **0** | **0** | **0** | **7:29** |
| | Grand Rapids | IHL | 64 | 22 | 32 | 54 | 20 | | | | | | | | | | 10 | 4 | 4 | 8 | 10 | | | | |
| **2001-02** | **Ottawa** | **NHL** | **81** | **20** | **30** | **50** | **24** | **4** | **0** | **1** | **147** | **13.6** | **12** | **1508** | **50.5** | **18:22** | **12** | **2** | **2** | **4** | **6** | **0** | **0** | **0** | **18:57** |
| **2002-03** | **Ottawa** | **NHL** | **80** | **25** | **35** | **60** | **28** | **8** | **1** | **5** | **144** | **17.4** | **19** | **1396** | **50.5** | **17:58** | **18** | **5** | **1** | **6** | **6** | **1** | **1** | **2** | **16:59** |
| **2003-04** | **Ottawa** | **NHL** | **53** | **9** | **20** | **29** | **22** | **1** | **1** | **2** | **98** | **9.2** | **12** | **879** | **52.0** | **17:32** | **7** | **1** | **0** | **1** | **4** | **0** | **0** | **0** | **18:04** |
| 2004-05 | Sodertalje SK | Sweden | 1 | 0 | 1 | 1 | 4 | | | | | | | | | | | | | | | | | | |
| **2005-06** | **Minnesota** | **NHL** | **61** | **19** | **21** | **40** | **18** | **5** | **0** | **0** | **109** | **17.4** | **–1** | **886** | **49.1** | **17:12** | | | | | | | | | |
| **2006-07** | **Minnesota** | **NHL** | **77** | **13** | **31** | **44** | **24** | **6** | **1** | **1** | **162** | **8.0** | **8** | **1051** | **49.2** | **17:13** | **4** | **0** | **0** | **0** | **0** | **0** | **0** | **0** | **14:18** |
| **2007-08** | **Atlanta** | **NHL** | **74** | **14** | **23** | **37** | **36** | **6** | **1** | **4** | **111** | **12.6** | **–12** | **1166** | **46.6** | **18:26** | | | | | | | | | |
| **2008-09** | **Atlanta** | **NHL** | **82** | **22** | **51** | **73** | **24** | **12** | **1** | **0** | **150** | **14.7** | **–9** | **1329** | **50.6** | **18:04** | | | | | | | | | |
| | **NHL Totals** | | **570** | **133** | **220** | **353** | **202** | **44** | **5** | **13** | **983** | **13.5** | | **8834** | **49.7** | **17:17** | **43** | **8** | **3** | **11** | **16** | **1** | **1** | **2** | **17:01** |

ECAC Second All-Star Team (1996) • NCAA East Second All-American Team (1996) • ECAC First All-Star Team (1997) • ECAC Player of the Year (1997) • NCAA East First All-American Team (1997) • Garry F. Longman Memorial Trophy (IHL – Rookie of the Year) (1998)

Signed as a free agent by **Chicago**, August 27, 1997. Traded to **Philadelphia** by **Chicago** for future considerations, January 26, 2000. Signed as a free agent by **Ottawa**, July 12, 2000. Signed as a free agent by **Sodertalje** (Sweden), December 21, 2004. Traded to **Minnesota** by **Ottawa** for Colorado's 4th round choice (previously acquired, Ottawa selected Cody Bass) in 2005 Entry Draft, July 30, 2005. Signed as a free agent by **Atlanta**, July 1, 2007.

## WHITFIELD, Trent

(WHIHT-feeld, TREHNT) **BOS.**

Center. Shoots left. 5'11", 209 lbs. Born, Estevan, Sask., June 17, 1977. Boston's 5th choice, 100th overall, in 1996 Entry Draft.

| Season | Club | League | GP | G | A | Pts | PIM | PP | SH | GW | S | % | +/- | TF | F% | Min | Playoffs GP | G | A | Pts | PIM | PP | SH | GW | Min |
|---|---|---|---|---|---|---|---|---|---|---|---|---|---|---|---|---|---|---|---|---|---|---|---|---|---|
| 1993-94 | Saskatoon Blazers | SMHL | 36 | 26 | 22 | 48 | 42 | | | | | | | | | | | | | | | | | | |
| | Spokane Chiefs | WHL | 5 | 1 | 1 | 2 | 0 | | | | | | | | | | | | | | | | | | |
| 1994-95 | Spokane Chiefs | WHL | 48 | 8 | 17 | 25 | 26 | | | | | | | | | | 11 | 7 | 6 | 13 | 5 | | | | |
| 1995-96 | Spokane Chiefs | WHL | 72 | 33 | 51 | 84 | 75 | | | | | | | | | | 18 | 8 | 10 | 18 | 10 | | | | |
| 1996-97 | Spokane Chiefs | WHL | 58 | 34 | 42 | 76 | 74 | | | | | | | | | | 9 | 5 | 7 | 12 | 10 | | | | |
| 1997-98 | Spokane Chiefs | WHL | 65 | 38 | 44 | 82 | 97 | | | | | | | | | | 18 | 9 | 10 | 19 | 15 | | | | |
| 1998-99 | Portland Pirates | AHL | 50 | 10 | 8 | 18 | 20 | | | | | | | | | | | | | | | | | | |
| | Hampton Roads | ECHL | 19 | 13 | 12 | 25 | 12 | | | | | | | | | | 4 | 2 | 0 | 2 | 14 | | | | |
| 99-2000 | Portland Pirates | AHL | 79 | 18 | 35 | 53 | 52 | | | | | | | | | | 3 | 1 | 1 | 2 | 2 | | | | |
| | Washington | NHL | | | | | | | | | | | | | | | 3 | 0 | 0 | 0 | 0 | 0 | 0 | 0 | 5:47 |
| 2000-01 | Washington | NHL | 61 | 2 | 4 | 6 | 35 | 0 | 0 | 0 | 47 | 4.3 | 3 | 520 | 51.9 | 9:39 | 5 | 0 | 0 | 0 | 2 | 0 | 0 | 0 | 7:07 |
| | Portland Pirates | AHL | 19 | 9 | 11 | 20 | 27 | | | | | | | | | | | | | | | | | | |
| 2001-02 | Washington | NHL | 24 | 0 | 1 | 1 | 28 | 0 | 0 | 0 | 15 | 0.0 | -3 | 189 | 54.0 | 7:06 | | | | | | | | | |
| | Portland Pirates | AHL | 10 | 4 | 4 | 8 | 8 | | | | | | | | | | | | | | | | | | |
| | NY Rangers | NHL | 1 | 0 | 0 | 0 | 0 | 0 | 0 | 0 | 0 | 0.0 | 1 | 18 | 50.0 | 12:44 | | | | | | | | | |
| | Portland Pirates | AHL | 24 | 10 | 16 | 26 | 16 | | | | | | | | | | | | | | | | | | |
| 2002-03 | Washington | NHL | 14 | 1 | 1 | 2 | 6 | 0 | 0 | 1 | 4 | 25.0 | 1 | 124 | 57.3 | 8:30 | 6 | 0 | 0 | 0 | 10 | 0 | 0 | 0 | 11:01 |
| | Portland Pirates | AHL | 64 | 27 | 34 | 61 | 42 | | | | | | | | | | | | | | | | | | |
| 2003-04 | Washington | NHL | 44 | 6 | 5 | 11 | 14 | 0 | 1 | 2 | 38 | 15.8 | -2 | 598 | 55.4 | 12:48 | | | | | | | | | |
| | Portland Pirates | AHL | 24 | 8 | 7 | 15 | 22 | | | | | | | | | | | | | | | | | | |
| 2004-05 | Portland Pirates | AHL | 67 | 17 | 38 | 55 | 75 | | | | | | | | | | | | | | | | | | |
| 2005-06 | St. Louis | NHL | 30 | 2 | 5 | 7 | 14 | 1 | 0 | 0 | 41 | 4.9 | -3 | 330 | 54.6 | 11:56 | | | | | | | | | |
| | Peoria Rivermen | AHL | 41 | 19 | 34 | 53 | 18 | | | | | | | | | | | | | | | | | | |
| 2006-07 | Peoria Rivermen | AHL | 79 | 33 | 45 | 78 | 70 | | | | | | | | | | | | | | | | | | |
| 2007-08 | Peoria Rivermen | AHL | 80 | 22 | 30 | 52 | 51 | | | | | | | | | | | | | | | | | | |
| 2008-09 | St. Louis | NHL | 3 | 0 | 1 | 1 | 0 | 0 | 0 | 0 | 4 | 0.0 | 2 | 26 | 73.1 | 11:03 | | | | | | | | | |
| | Peoria Rivermen | AHL | 69 | 20 | 30 | 50 | 37 | | | | | | | | | | 7 | 2 | 1 | 3 | 0 | | | | |
| | NHL Totals | | 177 | 11 | 17 | 28 | 97 | 1 | 1 | 3 | 149 | 7.4 | | 1805 | 54.4 | 10:25 | 14 | 0 | 0 | 0 | 12 | 0 | 0 | 0 | 8:30 |

WHL West First All-Star Team (1997) • WHL West Second All-Star Team (1998)

Signed as a free agent by **Washington**, September 1, 1998. Claimed on waivers by **NY Rangers** from **Washington**, January 16, 2002. Claimed on waivers by **Washington** from **NY Rangers**, February 1, 2002. Signed as a free agent by **St. Louis**, August 2, 2005. Signed as a free agent by **Boston**, July 13, 2009.

## WHITNEY, Ray

(WHIHT-nee, RAY) **CAR.**

Left wing. Shoots right. 5'10", 180 lbs. Born, Fort Saskatchewan, Alta., May 8, 1972. San Jose's 2nd choice, 23rd overall, in 1991 Entry Draft.

| Season | Club | League | GP | G | A | Pts | PIM | PP | SH | GW | S | % | +/- | TF | F% | Min | Playoffs GP | G | A | Pts | PIM | PP | SH | GW | Min |
|---|---|---|---|---|---|---|---|---|---|---|---|---|---|---|---|---|---|---|---|---|---|---|---|---|---|
| 1987-88 | Ft. Saskatchewan | AMHL | 71 | 80 | 155 | 235 | 119 | | | | | | | | | | | | | | | | | | |
| 1988-89 | Spokane Chiefs | WHL | 71 | 17 | 33 | 50 | 16 | | | | | | | | | | | | | | | | | | |
| 1989-90 | Spokane Chiefs | WHL | 71 | 57 | 56 | 113 | 50 | | | | | | | | | | 6 | 3 | 4 | 7 | 6 | | | | |
| 1990-91 | Spokane Chiefs | WHL | 72 | 67 | 118 | *185 | 36 | | | | | | | | | | 15 | 13 | 18 | *31 | 12 | | | | |
| 1991-92 | Kolner EC | Germany | 10 | 3 | 6 | 9 | 4 | | | | | | | | | | | | | | | | | | |
| | Canada | Nat-Tm | 5 | 1 | 0 | 1 | 6 | | | | | | | | | | | | | | | | | | |
| | San Jose | NHL | 2 | 0 | 3 | 3 | 0 | 0 | 0 | 0 | 4 | 0.0 | -1 | | | | | | | | | | | | |
| | San Diego Gulls | IHL | 63 | 36 | 54 | 90 | 12 | | | | | | | | | | 4 | 0 | 0 | 0 | 0 | | | | |
| 1992-93 | San Jose | NHL | 26 | 4 | 6 | 10 | 4 | 1 | 0 | 0 | 24 | 16.7 | -14 | | | | | | | | | | | | |
| | Kansas City | IHL | 46 | 20 | 33 | 53 | 14 | | | | | | | | | | 12 | 5 | 7 | 12 | 2 | | | | |
| 1993-94 | San Jose | NHL | 61 | 14 | 26 | 40 | 14 | 1 | 0 | 0 | 82 | 17.1 | 2 | | | | 14 | 0 | 4 | 4 | 8 | 0 | 0 | 0 | |
| 1994-95 | San Jose | NHL | 39 | 13 | 12 | 25 | 14 | 4 | 0 | 1 | 67 | 19.4 | -7 | | | | 11 | 4 | 4 | 8 | 2 | 0 | 0 | 1 | |
| 1995-96 | San Jose | NHL | 60 | 17 | 24 | 41 | 16 | 4 | 2 | 2 | 106 | 16.0 | -23 | | | | | | | | | | | | |
| 1996-97 | San Jose | NHL | 12 | 0 | 2 | 2 | 4 | 0 | 0 | 0 | 24 | 0.0 | -6 | | | | | | | | | | | | |
| | Kentucky | AHL | 9 | 1 | 7 | 8 | 2 | | | | | | | | | | | | | | | | | | |
| | Utah Grizzlies | IHL | 43 | 13 | 35 | 48 | 34 | | | | | | | | | | 7 | 3 | 1 | 4 | 6 | | | | |
| 1997-98 | Edmonton | NHL | 9 | 1 | 3 | 4 | 0 | 0 | 0 | 0 | 19 | 5.3 | -1 | | | | | | | | | | | | |
| | Florida | NHL | 68 | 32 | 29 | 61 | 28 | 12 | 0 | 2 | 156 | 20.5 | 10 | | | | | | | | | | | | |
| 1998-99 | Florida | NHL | 81 | 26 | 38 | 64 | 18 | 7 | 0 | 6 | 193 | 13.5 | -3 | 144 | 43.8 | 18:20 | | | | | | | | | |
| 99-2000 | Florida | NHL | 81 | 29 | 42 | 71 | 35 | 5 | 0 | 3 | 198 | 14.6 | 16 | 198 | 49.0 | 18:41 | 4 | 1 | 0 | 1 | 4 | 0 | 0 | 0 | 18:13 |
| 2000-01 | Florida | NHL | 43 | 10 | 21 | 31 | 28 | 5 | 0 | 0 | 117 | 8.5 | -16 | 38 | 39.5 | 17:41 | | | | | | | | | |
| | Columbus | NHL | 3 | 0 | 3 | 3 | 2 | 0 | 0 | 0 | 3 | 0.0 | -1 | 19 | 36.8 | 20:17 | | | | | | | | | |
| 2001-02 | Columbus | NHL | 67 | 21 | 40 | 61 | 12 | 6 | 0 | 3 | 210 | 10.0 | -22 | 21 | 47.6 | 20:13 | | | | | | | | | |
| 2002-03 | Columbus | NHL | 81 | 24 | 52 | 76 | 22 | 8 | 2 | 2 | 235 | 10.2 | -26 | 29 | 44.8 | 21:00 | | | | | | | | | |
| 2003-04 | Detroit | NHL | 67 | 14 | 29 | 43 | 22 | 3 | 1 | 4 | 119 | 11.8 | 7 | 18 | 38.9 | 16:24 | 12 | 1 | 3 | 4 | 4 | 0 | 0 | 1 | 11:56 |
| 2004-05 | | | DID NOT PLAY | | | | | | | | | | | | | | | | | | | | | | |
| 2005-06♦ | Carolina | NHL | 63 | 17 | 38 | 55 | 42 | 12 | 0 | 2 | 147 | 11.6 | 0 | 13 | 38.5 | 17:11 | 24 | 9 | 6 | 15 | 14 | 5 | 0 | 1 | 14:07 |
| 2006-07 | Carolina | NHL | 81 | 32 | 51 | 83 | 46 | 6 | 0 | 6 | 215 | 14.9 | -5 | 7 | 28.6 | 18:42 | | | | | | | | | |
| 2007-08 | Carolina | NHL | 66 | 25 | 36 | 61 | 30 | 6 | 0 | 4 | 204 | 12.3 | -6 | 5 | 60.0 | 18:56 | | | | | | | | | |
| 2008-09 | Carolina | NHL | 82 | 24 | 53 | 77 | 32 | 7 | 0 | 2 | 219 | 11.0 | 2 | 4 | 50.0 | 18:25 | 18 | 3 | 8 | 11 | 4 | 0 | 0 | 1 | 18:36 |
| | NHL Totals | | 992 | 303 | 508 | 811 | 369 | 87 | 5 | 37 | 2342 | 12.9 | | 496 | 45.2 | 18:39 | 83 | 18 | 25 | 43 | 36 | 5 | 0 | 4 | 15:20 |

WHL West First All-Star Team (1991) • WHL Player of the Year (1991) • Memorial Cup Tournament All-Star Team (1991) • George Parsons Trophy (Memorial Cup Tournament - Most Sportsmanlike Player) (1991)

Played in NHL All-Star Game (2000, 2003)

Signed as a free agent by **Edmonton**, October 1, 1997. Claimed on waivers by **Florida** from **Edmonton**, November 6, 1997. Traded to **Columbus** by **Florida** with future considerations for Kevyn Adams and Columbus's 4th round choice (Michael Woodford) in 2001 Entry Draft, March 13, 2001. Signed as a free agent by **Detroit**, July 30, 2003. Signed as a free agent by **Carolina**, August 7, 2005.

## WHITNEY, Ryan

(WHIHT-nee, RIGH-uhn) **ANA.**

Defense. Shoots left. 6'4", 219 lbs. Born, Boston, MA, February 19, 1983. Pittsburgh's 1st choice, 5th overall, in 2002 Entry Draft.

| Season | Club | League | GP | G | A | Pts | PIM | PP | SH | GW | S | % | +/- | TF | F% | Min | Playoffs GP | G | A | Pts | PIM | PP | SH | GW | Min |
|---|---|---|---|---|---|---|---|---|---|---|---|---|---|---|---|---|---|---|---|---|---|---|---|---|---|
| 99-2000 | Thayer Academy | High-MA | 22 | 5 | 33 | 38 | | | | | | | | | | | | | | | | | | | |
| 2000-01 | USNTDP | U-18 | 40 | 7 | 23 | 30 | 64 | | | | | | | | | | | | | | | | | | |
| | USNTDP | USHL | 20 | 2 | 8 | 10 | 22 | | | | | | | | | | | | | | | | | | |
| 2001-02 | Boston University | H-East | 35 | 4 | 17 | 21 | 46 | | | | | | | | | | | | | | | | | | |
| 2002-03 | Boston University | H-East | 34 | 3 | 10 | 13 | 48 | | | | | | | | | | | | | | | | | | |
| 2003-04 | Boston University | H-East | 38 | 9 | 16 | 25 | 56 | | | | | | | | | | | | | | | | | | |
| | Wilkes-Barre | AHL | | | | | | | | | | | | | | | 20 | 1 | 9 | 10 | 6 | | | | |
| 2004-05 | Wilkes-Barre | AHL | 80 | 6 | 35 | 41 | 101 | | | | | | | | | | 11 | 2 | 7 | 9 | 12 | | | | |
| 2005-06 | Pittsburgh | NHL | 68 | 6 | 32 | 38 | 85 | 2 | 0 | 1 | 113 | 5.3 | -7 | 1 | 0.0 | 23:50 | | | | | | | | | |
| | Wilkes-Barre | AHL | 9 | 5 | 9 | 14 | 6 | | | | | | | | | | 11 | 1 | 4 | 5 | 8 | | | | |
| 2006-07 | Pittsburgh | NHL | 81 | 14 | 45 | 59 | 77 | 9 | 0 | 2 | 129 | 10.9 | 9 | 5 | 20.0 | 23:56 | 5 | 1 | 1 | 2 | 6 | 1 | 0 | 0 | 22:51 |
| 2007-08 | Pittsburgh | NHL | 76 | 12 | 28 | 40 | 45 | 7 | 1 | 1 | 119 | 10.1 | -2 | 0 | 0.0 | 22:27 | 20 | 1 | 5 | 6 | 25 | 1 | 0 | 0 | 20:46 |
| 2008-09 | Pittsburgh | NHL | 28 | 2 | 11 | 13 | 16 | 1 | 0 | 0 | 42 | 4.8 | -15 | 0 | 0.0 | 24:34 | | | | | | | | | |
| | Wilkes-Barre | AHL | 1 | 0 | 1 | 1 | 2 | | | | | | | | | | | | | | | | | | |
| | Anaheim | NHL | 20 | 0 | 10 | 10 | 12 | 0 | 0 | 0 | 29 | 0.0 | 1 | 0 | 0.0 | 22:53 | 13 | 1 | 5 | 6 | 9 | 1 | 0 | 0 | 21:34 |
| | NHL Totals | | 273 | 34 | 126 | 160 | 235 | 19 | 1 | 4 | 432 | 7.9 | | 6 | 16.7 | 23:29 | 38 | 3 | 11 | 14 | 40 | 3 | 0 | 0 | 21:19 |

Hockey East All-Rookie Team (2002)

Traded to **Anaheim** by **Pittsburgh** for Chris Kunitz and Eric Tangradi, February 26, 2009.

## WIDEMAN, Dennis

(WIGHD-muhn, DEH-nihs) **BOS.**

Defense. Shoots right. 6', 196 lbs. Born, Kitchener, Ont., March 20, 1983. Buffalo's 9th choice, 241st overall, in 2002 Entry Draft.

| Season | Club | League | GP | G | A | Pts | PIM | PP | SH | GW | S | % | +/- | TF | F% | Min | Playoffs GP | G | A | Pts | PIM | PP | SH | GW | Min |
|---|---|---|---|---|---|---|---|---|---|---|---|---|---|---|---|---|---|---|---|---|---|---|---|---|---|
| 1998-99 | Elmira | OHA-B | 47 | 18 | 30 | 48 | 142 | | | | | | | | | | | | | | | | | | |
| 99-2000 | Sudbury Wolves | OHL | 63 | 10 | 26 | 36 | 64 | | | | | | | | | | 12 | 1 | 2 | 3 | 22 | | | | |
| 2000-01 | Sudbury Wolves | OHL | 25 | 7 | 11 | 18 | 37 | | | | | | | | | | | | | | | | | | |
| | London Knights | OHL | 24 | 8 | 8 | 16 | 38 | | | | | | | | | | 5 | 0 | 4 | 4 | 6 | | | | |
| 2001-02 | London Knights | OHL | 65 | 27 | 42 | 69 | 141 | | | | | | | | | | 12 | 4 | 9 | 13 | 26 | | | | |
| 2002-03 | London Knights | OHL | 55 | 20 | 27 | 47 | 83 | | | | | | | | | | 14 | 6 | 6 | 12 | 10 | | | | |
| 2003-04 | London Knights | OHL | 60 | 24 | 41 | 65 | 85 | | | | | | | | | | 15 | 7 | 10 | 17 | 17 | | | | |
| 2004-05 | Worcester IceCats | AHL | 79 | 13 | 30 | 43 | 65 | | | | | | | | | | | | | | | | | | |
| 2005-06 | St. Louis | NHL | 67 | 8 | 16 | 24 | 83 | 5 | 1 | 1 | 150 | 5.3 | -31 | 1 | 0.0 | 21:41 | | | | | | | | | |
| | Peoria Rivermen | AHL | 12 | 2 | 4 | 6 | 31 | | | | | | | | | | | | | | | | | | |

| | | | Regular Season | | | | | | | | | | | | | | Playoffs | | | | | | | | |
|---|---|---|---|---|---|---|---|---|---|---|---|---|---|---|---|---|---|---|---|---|---|---|---|---|---|
| Season | Club | League | GP | G | A | Pts | PIM | PP | SH | GW | S | % | +/- | TF | F% | Min | GP | G | A | Pts | PIM | PP | SH | GW | Min |
| **2006-07** | **St. Louis** | **NHL** | **55** | **5** | **17** | **22** | **44** | **4** | **0** | **1** | **94** | **5.3** | **–7** | **0** | **0.0** | **20:12** | .... | .... | .... | .... | .... | .... | .... | .... | .... |
| | **Boston** | **NHL** | **20** | **1** | **2** | **3** | **27** | **0** | **0** | **0** | **28** | **3.6** | **–3** | **1** | **0.0** | **17:20** | .... | .... | .... | .... | .... | .... | .... | .... | .... |
| **2007-08** | **Boston** | **NHL** | **81** | **13** | **23** | **36** | **70** | **9** | **0** | **1** | **171** | **7.6** | **11** | **0** | **0.0** | **25:09** | **6** | **0** | **3** | **3** | **0** | **0** | **0** | **0** | **24:21** |
| **2008-09** | **Boston** | **NHL** | **79** | **13** | **37** | **50** | **34** | **6** | **1** | **2** | **169** | **7.7** | **32** | **0** | **0.0** | **24:39** | **11** | **0** | **7** | **7** | **4** | **0** | **0** | **0** | **24:42** |
| | **NHL Totals** | | **302** | **40** | **95** | **135** | **258** | **24** | **2** | **5** | **612** | **6.5** | | **2** | **0.0** | **22:50** | **17** | **0** | **10** | **10** | **4** | **0** | **0** | **0** | **24:35** |

OHL First All-Star Team (2004) • Canadian Major Junior Second All-Star Team (2004)

Signed as a free agent by **St. Louis**, June 30, 2004. Traded to **Boston** by **St. Louis** for Brad Boyes, February 27, 2007.

## WILLIAMS, Jason

(WIHL-yuhms, JAY-suhn) **DET.**

Center. Shoots right. 5'11", 185 lbs. Born, London, Ont., August 11, 1980.

| Season | Club | League | GP | G | A | Pts | PIM | PP | SH | GW | S | % | +/- | TF | F% | Min | GP | G | A | Pts | PIM | PP | SH | GW | Min |
|---|---|---|---|---|---|---|---|---|---|---|---|---|---|---|---|---|---|---|---|---|---|---|---|---|---|
| 1995-96 | Mount Brydges | OHA-D | 36 | 31 | 28 | 59 | 18 | .... | .... | .... | .... | .... | .... | .... | .... | .... | .... | .... | .... | .... | .... | .... | .... | .... | .... |
| 1996-97 | Peterborough | OHL | 60 | 4 | 8 | 12 | 8 | .... | .... | .... | .... | .... | .... | .... | .... | .... | 10 | 1 | 0 | 1 | 2 | .... | .... | .... | .... |
| 1997-98 | Peterborough | OHL | 55 | 8 | 27 | 35 | 31 | .... | .... | .... | .... | .... | .... | .... | .... | .... | 4 | 0 | 1 | 1 | 2 | .... | .... | .... | .... |
| 1998-99 | Peterborough | OHL | 68 | 26 | 48 | 74 | 42 | .... | .... | .... | .... | .... | .... | .... | .... | .... | 5 | 1 | 2 | 3 | 2 | .... | .... | .... | .... |
| 99-2000 | Peterborough | OHL | 66 | 36 | 37 | 75 | 64 | .... | .... | .... | .... | .... | .... | .... | .... | .... | 5 | 2 | 1 | 3 | 2 | .... | .... | .... | .... |
| **2000-01** | **Detroit** | **NHL** | **5** | **0** | **3** | **3** | **2** | **0** | **0** | **0** | **7** | **0.0** | **1** | **56** | **39.3** | **12:24** | **2** | **0** | **0** | **0** | **0** | **0** | **0** | **0** | **11:45** |
| | Cincinnati | AHL | 76 | 24 | 45 | 69 | 48 | .... | .... | .... | .... | .... | .... | .... | .... | .... | 1 | 0 | 0 | 0 | 2 | .... | .... | .... | .... |
| **2001-02♦** | **Detroit** | **NHL** | **25** | **8** | **2** | **10** | **4** | **4** | **0** | **0** | **32** | **25.0** | **2** | **208** | **47.6** | **10:50** | **9** | **0** | **0** | **0** | **2** | **0** | **0** | **0** | **6:12** |
| | Cincinnati | AHL | 52 | 23 | 27 | 50 | 27 | .... | .... | .... | .... | .... | .... | .... | .... | .... | 3 | 0 | 1 | 1 | 6 | .... | .... | .... | .... |
| **2002-03** | **Detroit** | **NHL** | **16** | **3** | **3** | **6** | **2** | **1** | **0** | **0** | **20** | **15.0** | **3** | **78** | **51.3** | **10:43** | .... | .... | .... | .... | .... | .... | .... | .... | .... |
| | Grand Rapids | AHL | 45 | 23 | 22 | 45 | 18 | .... | .... | .... | .... | .... | .... | .... | .... | .... | 15 | 1 | 7 | 8 | 16 | .... | .... | .... | .... |
| **2003-04** | **Detroit** | **NHL** | **49** | **6** | **7** | **13** | **15** | **0** | **0** | **0** | **44** | **13.6** | **1** | **315** | **49.2** | **9:27** | **3** | **0** | **0** | **0** | **2** | **0** | **0** | **0** | **6:11** |
| 2004-05 | Assat Pori | Finland | 43 | 26 | 17 | 43 | 52 | .... | .... | .... | .... | .... | .... | .... | .... | .... | 2 | 1 | 1 | 2 | 4 | .... | .... | .... | .... |
| **2005-06** | **Detroit** | **NHL** | **80** | **21** | **37** | **58** | **26** | **6** | **0** | **4** | **177** | **11.9** | **4** | **29** | **55.2** | **14:55** | **6** | **1** | **1** | **2** | **6** | **0** | **0** | **0** | **18:10** |
| **2006-07** | **Detroit** | **NHL** | **58** | **11** | **15** | **26** | **24** | **3** | **0** | **2** | **111** | **9.9** | **7** | **11** | **45.5** | **14:26** | .... | .... | .... | .... | .... | .... | .... | .... | .... |
| | **Chicago** | **NHL** | **20** | **4** | **2** | **6** | **20** | **2** | **1** | **0** | **38** | **10.5** | **–6** | **193** | **42.5** | **18:17** | .... | .... | .... | .... | .... | .... | .... | .... | .... |
| **2007-08** | **Chicago** | **NHL** | **43** | **13** | **23** | **36** | **22** | **6** | **0** | **4** | **101** | **12.9** | **–2** | **15** | **60.0** | **16:35** | .... | .... | .... | .... | .... | .... | .... | .... | .... |
| **2008-09** | **Atlanta** | **NHL** | **41** | **7** | **11** | **18** | **8** | **4** | **0** | **2** | **79** | **8.9** | **–9** | **381** | **49.1** | **16:05** | .... | .... | .... | .... | .... | .... | .... | .... | .... |
| | **Columbus** | **NHL** | **39** | **12** | **17** | **29** | **16** | **3** | **0** | **2** | **74** | **16.2** | **5** | **237** | **40.9** | **15:38** | **4** | **0** | **1** | **1** | **2** | **0** | **0** | **0** | **14:12** |
| | **NHL Totals** | | **376** | **85** | **120** | **205** | **139** | **29** | **1** | **14** | **683** | **12.4** | | **1523** | **46.7** | **14:13** | **24** | **1** | **2** | **3** | **12** | **0** | **0** | **0** | **10:59** |

Signed as a free agent by **Detroit**, September 18, 2000. Signed as a free agent by **Pori** (Finland), October 18, 2004. Traded to **Chicago** by **Detroit** for Kyle Calder, February 26, 2007. Signed as a free agent by **Atlanta**, July 14, 2008. Traded to **Columbus** by **Atlanta** for Clay Wilson and San Jose's 6th round choice (previously acquired, later traded to Chicago – Chicago selected David Pacan) in 2009 Entry Draft, January 14, 2009. Signed as a free agent by **Detroit**, August 6. 2009.

## WILLIAMS, Jeremy

(WIHL-yuhms, JAIR-eh-mee) **DET.**

Center. Shoots right. 5'11", 190 lbs. Born, Regina, Sask., January 26, 1984. Toronto's 5th choice, 220th overall, in 2003 Entry Draft.

| Season | Club | League | GP | G | A | Pts | PIM | PP | SH | GW | S | % | +/- | TF | F% | Min | GP | G | A | Pts | PIM | PP | SH | GW | Min |
|---|---|---|---|---|---|---|---|---|---|---|---|---|---|---|---|---|---|---|---|---|---|---|---|---|---|
| 2001-02 | Swift Current | SMMHL | 24 | 18 | 23 | 41 | 64 | .... | .... | .... | .... | .... | .... | .... | .... | .... | .... | .... | .... | .... | .... | .... | .... | .... | .... |
| | Swift Current | WHL | 32 | 6 | 7 | 13 | 30 | .... | .... | .... | .... | .... | .... | .... | .... | .... | 12 | 1 | 0 | 1 | 4 | .... | .... | .... | .... |
| 2002-03 | Swift Current | WHL | 72 | 41 | 52 | 93 | 117 | .... | .... | .... | .... | .... | .... | .... | .... | .... | 4 | 1 | 0 | 1 | 6 | .... | .... | .... | .... |
| 2003-04 | Swift Current | WHL | 68 | *52 | 49 | 101 | 82 | .... | .... | .... | .... | .... | .... | .... | .... | .... | 5 | 2 | 1 | 3 | 12 | .... | .... | .... | .... |
| | St. John's | AHL | 4 | 0 | 2 | 2 | 0 | .... | .... | .... | .... | .... | .... | .... | .... | .... | .... | .... | .... | .... | .... | .... | .... | .... | .... |
| 2004-05 | St. John's | AHL | 75 | 16 | 20 | 36 | 24 | .... | .... | .... | .... | .... | .... | .... | .... | .... | 5 | 0 | 0 | 0 | 0 | .... | .... | .... | .... |
| **2005-06** | **Toronto** | **NHL** | **1** | **1** | **0** | **1** | **0** | **0** | **0** | **0** | **1** | **100.0** | **0** | **0** | **0.0** | **9:31** | .... | .... | .... | .... | .... | .... | .... | .... | .... |
| | Toronto Marlies | AHL | 55 | 23 | 33 | 56 | 62 | .... | .... | .... | .... | .... | .... | .... | .... | .... | 5 | 1 | 0 | 1 | 6 | .... | .... | .... | .... |
| **2006-07** | **Toronto** | **NHL** | **1** | **1** | **0** | **1** | **0** | **0** | **0** | **0** | **3** | **33.3** | **1** | **1** | **0.0** | **7:18** | .... | .... | .... | .... | .... | .... | .... | .... | .... |
| | Toronto Marlies | AHL | 23 | 6 | 9 | 15 | 27 | .... | .... | .... | .... | .... | .... | .... | .... | .... | .... | .... | .... | .... | .... | .... | .... | .... | .... |
| **2007-08** | **Toronto** | **NHL** | **18** | **2** | **0** | **2** | **4** | **0** | **0** | **0** | **16** | **12.5** | **–3** | **4** | **0.0** | **7:20** | .... | .... | .... | .... | .... | .... | .... | .... | .... |
| | Toronto Marlies | AHL | 49 | 18 | 15 | 33 | 36 | .... | .... | .... | .... | .... | .... | .... | .... | .... | .... | .... | .... | .... | .... | .... | .... | .... | .... |
| **2008-09** | **Toronto** | **NHL** | **11** | **5** | **2** | **7** | **2** | **0** | **0** | **0** | **21** | **23.8** | **2** | **1** | **0.0** | **13:26** | .... | .... | .... | .... | .... | .... | .... | .... | .... |
| | Toronto Marlies | AHL | 46 | 27 | 13 | 40 | 29 | .... | .... | .... | .... | .... | .... | .... | .... | .... | 6 | 0 | 1 | 1 | 6 | .... | .... | .... | .... |
| | **NHL Totals** | | **31** | **9** | **2** | **11** | **6** | **0** | **0** | **0** | **41** | **22.0** | | **6** | **0.0** | **9:34** | .... | .... | .... | .... | .... | .... | .... | .... | .... |

WHL East First All-Star Team (2004) • Canadian Major Junior First All-Star Team (2004)

Signed as a free agent by **Detroit**, July 7, 2009.

## WILLIAMS, Justin

(WIHL-yuhms, JUHS-tihn) **L.A.**

Right wing. Shoots right. 6'1", 195 lbs. Born, Cobourg, Ont., October 4, 1981. Philadelphia's 1st choice, 28th overall, in 2000 Entry Draft.

| Season | Club | League | GP | G | A | Pts | PIM | PP | SH | GW | S | % | +/- | TF | F% | Min | GP | G | A | Pts | PIM | PP | SH | GW | Min |
|---|---|---|---|---|---|---|---|---|---|---|---|---|---|---|---|---|---|---|---|---|---|---|---|---|---|
| 1997-98 | Colborne Colts | OHA-C | 36 | 32 | 35 | 67 | 26 | .... | .... | .... | .... | .... | .... | .... | .... | .... | .... | .... | .... | .... | .... | .... | .... | .... | .... |
| | Cobourg Cougars | OPJHL | 17 | 0 | 3 | 3 | 5 | .... | .... | .... | .... | .... | .... | .... | .... | .... | .... | .... | .... | .... | .... | .... | .... | .... | .... |
| 1998-99 | Plymouth Whalers | OHL | 47 | 4 | 8 | 12 | 28 | .... | .... | .... | .... | .... | .... | .... | .... | .... | 7 | 1 | 2 | 3 | 0 | .... | .... | .... | .... |
| 99-2000 | Plymouth Whalers | OHL | 68 | 37 | 46 | 83 | 46 | .... | .... | .... | .... | .... | .... | .... | .... | .... | 23 | *14 | 16 | *30 | 10 | .... | .... | .... | .... |
| **2000-01** | **Philadelphia** | **NHL** | **63** | **12** | **13** | **25** | **22** | **0** | **0** | **0** | **99** | **12.1** | **6** | **13** | **53.9** | **12:31** | .... | .... | .... | .... | .... | .... | .... | .... | .... |
| **2001-02** | **Philadelphia** | **NHL** | **75** | **17** | **23** | **40** | **32** | **0** | **0** | **1** | **162** | **10.5** | **11** | **16** | **25.0** | **14:27** | **5** | **0** | **0** | **0** | **4** | **0** | **0** | **0** | **16:42** |
| **2002-03** | **Philadelphia** | **NHL** | **41** | **8** | **16** | **24** | **22** | **0** | **0** | **2** | **105** | **7.6** | **15** | **16** | **50.0** | **15:57** | **12** | **1** | **5** | **6** | **8** | **0** | **0** | **1** | **14:11** |
| **2003-04** | **Philadelphia** | **NHL** | **47** | **6** | **20** | **26** | **32** | **3** | **0** | **1** | **107** | **5.6** | **10** | **38** | **31.6** | **15:30** | .... | .... | .... | .... | .... | .... | .... | .... | .... |
| | **Carolina** | **NHL** | **32** | **5** | **13** | **18** | **32** | **1** | **0** | **0** | **96** | **5.2** | **2** | **25** | **36.0** | **18:52** | .... | .... | .... | .... | .... | .... | .... | .... | .... |
| 2004-05 | Lulea HF | Sweden | 49 | 14 | 18 | 32 | 61 | .... | .... | .... | .... | .... | .... | .... | .... | .... | 4 | 0 | 1 | 1 | 29 | .... | .... | .... | .... |
| **2005-06♦** | **Carolina** | **NHL** | **82** | **31** | **45** | **76** | **60** | **8** | **4** | **4** | **255** | **12.2** | **1** | **17** | **29.4** | **21:08** | **25** | **7** | **11** | **18** | **34** | **0** | **1** | **1** | **21:36** |
| **2006-07** | **Carolina** | **NHL** | **82** | **33** | **34** | **67** | **73** | **12** | **2** | **8** | **258** | **12.8** | **–11** | **24** | **37.5** | **20:51** | .... | .... | .... | .... | .... | .... | .... | .... | .... |
| **2007-08** | **Carolina** | **NHL** | **37** | **9** | **21** | **30** | **43** | **2** | **0** | **0** | **106** | **8.5** | **2** | **13** | **38.5** | **19:18** | .... | .... | .... | .... | .... | .... | .... | .... | .... |
| **2008-09** | **Carolina** | **NHL** | **32** | **3** | **7** | **10** | **9** | **2** | **0** | **0** | **80** | **3.8** | **–9** | **20** | **30.0** | **15:08** | .... | .... | .... | .... | .... | .... | .... | .... | .... |
| | **Los Angeles** | **NHL** | **12** | **1** | **3** | **4** | **8** | **1** | **0** | **0** | **28** | **3.6** | **1** | **2** | **50.0** | **17:51** | .... | .... | .... | .... | .... | .... | .... | .... | .... |
| | **NHL Totals** | | **503** | **125** | **195** | **320** | **333** | **29** | **6** | **16** | **1296** | **9.6** | | **184** | **35.9** | **17:20** | **42** | **8** | **16** | **24** | **46** | **0** | **1** | **2** | **18:54** |

Played in NHL All-Star Game (2007)

• Missed majority of 2002-03 season recovering from shoulder (November 15, 2002 vs. Carolina) and knee (January 18, 2003 vs. Tampa Bay) injuries. Traded to **Carolina** by **Philadelphia** for Danny Markov, January 20, 2004. Signed as a free agent by **Lulea** (Sweden), September 21, 2004. • Missed majority of 2007-08 season recovering from knee injury suffered in game at Florida, December 20, 2007. Traded to **Los Angeles** by **Carolina** for Patrick O'Sullivan and Calgary's 2nd round choice (previously acquired, Carolina selected Brian Dumoulin) in 2009 Entry Draft, March 4. 2009.

## WILLSIE, Brian

(WIHL-see, BRIGH-uhn) **COL.**

Right wing. Shoots right. 6'1", 202 lbs. Born, Belmont, Ont., March 16, 1978. Colorado's 7th choice, 146th overall, in 1996 Entry Draft.

| Season | Club | League | GP | G | A | Pts | PIM | PP | SH | GW | S | % | +/- | TF | F% | Min | GP | G | A | Pts | PIM | PP | SH | GW | Min |
|---|---|---|---|---|---|---|---|---|---|---|---|---|---|---|---|---|---|---|---|---|---|---|---|---|---|
| 1993-94 | Belmont Bombers | OHA-D | 13 | 9 | 5 | 14 | 14 | .... | .... | .... | .... | .... | .... | .... | .... | .... | .... | .... | .... | .... | .... | .... | .... | .... | .... |
| 1994-95 | St. Thomas Stars | OHA-B | 45 | 35 | 47 | 82 | 47 | .... | .... | .... | .... | .... | .... | .... | .... | .... | .... | .... | .... | .... | .... | .... | .... | .... | .... |
| 1995-96 | Guelph Storm | OHL | 65 | 13 | 21 | 34 | 18 | .... | .... | .... | .... | .... | .... | .... | .... | .... | 16 | 4 | 2 | 6 | 6 | .... | .... | .... | .... |
| 1996-97 | Guelph Storm | OHL | 64 | 37 | 31 | 68 | 37 | .... | .... | .... | .... | .... | .... | .... | .... | .... | 18 | 15 | 4 | 19 | 10 | .... | .... | .... | .... |
| 1997-98 | Guelph Storm | OHL | 57 | 45 | 31 | 76 | 41 | .... | .... | .... | .... | .... | .... | .... | .... | .... | 12 | 9 | 5 | 14 | 18 | .... | .... | .... | .... |
| 1998-99 | Hershey Bears | AHL | 72 | 19 | 10 | 29 | 28 | .... | .... | .... | .... | .... | .... | .... | .... | .... | 3 | 1 | 0 | 1 | 0 | .... | .... | .... | .... |
| **99-2000** | **Colorado** | **NHL** | **1** | **0** | **0** | **0** | **0** | **0** | **0** | **0** | **1** | **0.0** | **0** | **0** | **0.0** | **8:16** | .... | .... | .... | .... | .... | .... | .... | .... | .... |
| | Hershey Bears | AHL | 78 | 20 | 39 | 59 | 44 | .... | .... | .... | .... | .... | .... | .... | .... | .... | 12 | 2 | 6 | 8 | 8 | .... | .... | .... | .... |
| 2000-01 | Hershey Bears | AHL | 48 | 18 | 23 | 41 | 20 | .... | .... | .... | .... | .... | .... | .... | .... | .... | 12 | 7 | 2 | 9 | 14 | .... | .... | .... | .... |
| **2001-02** | **Colorado** | **NHL** | **56** | **7** | **7** | **14** | **14** | **2** | **0** | **1** | **66** | **10.6** | **4** | **8** | **12.5** | **11:24** | **4** | **0** | **1** | **1** | **2** | **0** | **0** | **0** | **11:54** |
| **2002-03** | **Colorado** | **NHL** | **12** | **0** | **1** | **1** | **15** | **0** | **0** | **0** | **12** | **0.0** | **0** | **7** | **14.3** | **9:36** | **6** | **1** | **0** | **1** | **2** | **0** | **0** | **1** | **10:48** |
| | Hershey Bears | AHL | 59 | 29 | 28 | 57 | 49 | .... | .... | .... | .... | .... | .... | .... | .... | .... | .... | .... | .... | .... | .... | .... | .... | .... | .... |
| **2003-04** | **Washington** | **NHL** | **49** | **10** | **5** | **15** | **18** | **1** | **1** | **1** | **85** | **11.8** | **–7** | **46** | **34.8** | **12:42** | .... | .... | .... | .... | .... | .... | .... | .... | .... |
| 2004-05 | Ljubljana | Slovenia | 2 | 0 | 3 | 3 | 4 | .... | .... | .... | .... | .... | .... | .... | .... | .... | .... | .... | .... | .... | .... | .... | .... | .... | .... |
| | Ljubljana | Interliga | 12 | 7 | 6 | 13 | 34 | .... | .... | .... | .... | .... | .... | .... | .... | .... | .... | .... | .... | .... | .... | .... | .... | .... | .... |
| | Portland Pirates | AHL | 53 | 23 | 17 | 40 | 47 | .... | .... | .... | .... | .... | .... | .... | .... | .... | .... | .... | .... | .... | .... | .... | .... | .... | .... |
| **2005-06** | **Washington** | **NHL** | **82** | **19** | **22** | **41** | **77** | **8** | **1** | **2** | **185** | **10.3** | **–19** | **52** | **51.9** | **16:40** | .... | .... | .... | .... | .... | .... | .... | .... | .... |
| **2006-07** | **Los Angeles** | **NHL** | **81** | **11** | **10** | **21** | **49** | **2** | **0** | **1** | **131** | **8.4** | **–20** | **201** | **45.3** | **13:23** | .... | .... | .... | .... | .... | .... | .... | .... | .... |
| **2007-08** | **Los Angeles** | **NHL** | **53** | **4** | **8** | **12** | **30** | **0** | **0** | **0** | **62** | **6.5** | **–8** | **24** | **58.3** | **10:38** | .... | .... | .... | .... | .... | .... | .... | .... | .... |
| **2008-09** | **Colorado** | **NHL** | **42** | **1** | **3** | **4** | **14** | **0** | **0** | **0** | **59** | **1.7** | **–6** | **89** | **33.7** | **11:47** | .... | .... | .... | .... | .... | .... | .... | .... | .... |
| | Lake Erie | AHL | 12 | 8 | 6 | 14 | 8 | .... | .... | .... | .... | .... | .... | .... | .... | .... | .... | .... | .... | .... | .... | .... | .... | .... | .... |
| | **NHL Totals** | | **376** | **52** | **56** | **108** | **217** | **13** | **2** | **5** | **601** | **8.7** | | **427** | **42.2** | **13:01** | **10** | **1** | **1** | **2** | **4** | **0** | **0** | **1** | **11:14** |

OHL First All-Star Team (1998)

Claimed by **Washington** from **Colorado** in Waiver Draft, October 3, 2003. Signed as a free agent by **Ljubljana** (Slovenia), October 8, 2004. Signed as a free agent by **Portland** (AHL), December 15, 2004. Signed as a free agent by **Los Angeles**, July 4, 2006. Signed as a free agent by **Colorado**, July 15, 2008.

## WILSON, Clay
(WIHL-suhn, KLAY) **FLA.**

Defense. Shoots left. 6', 195 lbs. Born, Sturgeon Lake, MN, April 5, 1983.

| | | | Regular Season | | | | | | | | | | | | | | Playoffs | | | | | | | | |
|---|---|---|---|---|---|---|---|---|---|---|---|---|---|---|---|---|---|---|---|---|---|---|---|---|---|
| Season | Club | League | GP | G | A | Pts | PIM | PP | SH | GW | S | % | +/- | TF | F% | Min | GP | G | A | Pts | PIM | PP | SH | GW | Min |
| 2001-02 | Michigan Tech | WCHA | 38 | 4 | 8 | 12 | 18 | | | | | | | | | | | | | | | | | | |
| 2002-03 | Michigan Tech | WCHA | 38 | 8 | 17 | 25 | 37 | | | | | | | | | | | | | | | | | | |
| 2003-04 | Michigan Tech | WCHA | 37 | 2 | 11 | 13 | 22 | | | | | | | | | | | | | | | | | | |
| 2004-05 | Michigan Tech | WCHA | 35 | 3 | 4 | 7 | 42 | | | | | | | | | | | | | | | | | | |
| | Muskegon Fury | UHL | 14 | 3 | 3 | 6 | 2 | | | | | | | | | | 17 | 0 | 2 | 2 | 8 | | | | |
| 2005-06 | Muskegon Fury | UHL | 13 | 3 | 9 | 12 | 9 | | | | | | | | | | | | | | | | | | |
| | Grand Rapids | AHL | 60 | 10 | 27 | 37 | 40 | | | | | | | | | | 16 | 0 | 3 | 3 | 8 | | | | |
| 2006-07 | Portland Pirates | AHL | 79 | 9 | 34 | 43 | 52 | | | | | | | | | | | | | | | | | | |
| **2007-08** | Portland Pirates | AHL | 14 | 3 | 5 | 8 | 6 | | | | | | | | | | | | | | | | | | |
| | **Columbus** | **NHL** | **7** | **1** | **1** | **2** | **2** | **0** | **0** | **0** | **12** | **8.3** | **3** | **0** | **0.0** | **16:55** | | | | | | | | | |
| | Syracuse Crunch | AHL | 57 | 11 | 28 | 39 | 29 | | | | | | | | | | 13 | 2 | 5 | 7 | 4 | | | | |
| **2008-09** | **Columbus** | **NHL** | **5** | **0** | **1** | **1** | **0** | **0** | **0** | **0** | **9** | **0.0** | **–2** | **0** | **0.0** | **9:26** | | | | | | | | | |
| | Syracuse Crunch | AHL | 33 | 8 | 12 | 20 | 6 | | | | | | | | | | | | | | | | | | |
| | **Atlanta** | **NHL** | **2** | **0** | **0** | **0** | **0** | **0** | **0** | **0** | **4** | **0.0** | **–1** | **0** | **0.0** | **15:55** | | | | | | | | | |
| | Chicago Wolves | AHL | 37 | 6 | 18 | 24 | 10 | | | | | | | | | | | | | | | | | | |
| | **NHL Totals** | | **14** | **1** | **2** | **3** | **2** | **0** | **0** | **0** | **25** | **4.0** | | **0** | **0.0** | **14:06** | | | | | | | | | |

Signed as a free agent by **Anaheim**, July 11, 2006. Traded to **Columbus** by **Anaheim** with Aaron Rome for Geoff Platt, November 15, 2007. Traded to **Atlanta** by **Columbus** with San Jose's 6th round choice (previously acquired, later traded to Chicago – Chicago selected David Pacan) in 2009 Entry Draft for Jason Williams, January 14, 2009. Signed as a free agent by **Florida**, July 2, 2009.

## WILSON, Landon
(WIHL-suhn, LAN-duhn)

Right wing. Shoots right. 6'3", 224 lbs. Born, St. Louis, MO, March 13, 1975. Toronto's 2nd choice, 19th overall, in 1993 Entry Draft.

| | | | Regular Season | | | | | | | | | | | | | | Playoffs | | | | | | | | |
|---|---|---|---|---|---|---|---|---|---|---|---|---|---|---|---|---|---|---|---|---|---|---|---|---|---|
| Season | Club | League | GP | G | A | Pts | PIM | PP | SH | GW | S | % | +/- | TF | F% | Min | GP | G | A | Pts | PIM | PP | SH | GW | Min |
| 1991-92 | California | WSJHL | 38 | 50 | 42 | 92 | 135 | | | | | | | | | | | | | | | | | | |
| 1992-93 | Dubuque | USHL | 43 | 29 | 36 | 65 | 284 | | | | | | | | | | | | | | | | | | |
| 1993-94 | North Dakota | WCHA | 35 | 18 | 15 | 33 | *147 | | | | | | | | | | | | | | | | | | |
| 1994-95 | North Dakota | WCHA | 31 | 7 | 16 | 23 | 141 | | | | | | | | | | | | | | | | | | |
| | Cornwall Aces | AHL | 8 | 4 | 4 | 8 | 25 | | | | | | | | | | 13 | 3 | 4 | 7 | 68 | | | | |
| **1995-96** | **Colorado** | **NHL** | **7** | **1** | **0** | **1** | **6** | **0** | **0** | **0** | **6** | **16.7** | **3** | | | | | | | | | | | | |
| | Cornwall Aces | AHL | 53 | 21 | 13 | 34 | 154 | | | | | | | | | | 8 | 1 | 3 | 4 | 22 | | | | |
| **1996-97** | **Colorado** | **NHL** | **9** | **1** | **2** | **3** | **23** | **0** | **0** | **0** | **7** | **14.3** | **1** | | | | | | | | | | | | |
| | **Boston** | **NHL** | **40** | **7** | **10** | **17** | **49** | **0** | **0** | **0** | **76** | **9.2** | **–6** | | | | | | | | | | | | |
| | Providence Bruins | AHL | 2 | 2 | 1 | 3 | 2 | | | | | | | | | | 10 | 3 | 4 | 7 | 16 | | | | |
| **1997-98** | **Boston** | **NHL** | **28** | **1** | **5** | **6** | **7** | **0** | **0** | **0** | **26** | **3.8** | **3** | | | | **1** | **0** | **0** | **0** | **0** | **0** | **0** | **0** | |
| | Providence Bruins | AHL | 42 | 18 | 10 | 28 | 146 | | | | | | | | | | | | | | | | | | |
| **1998-99** | **Boston** | **NHL** | **22** | **3** | **3** | **6** | **17** | **0** | **0** | **0** | **32** | **9.4** | **0** | **3** | **0.0** | **10:04** | **8** | **1** | **1** | **2** | **8** | **1** | **0** | **1** | **13:41** |
| | Providence Bruins | AHL | 48 | 31 | 22 | 53 | 89 | | | | | | | | | | 11 | 7 | 1 | 8 | 19 | | | | |
| **99-2000** | **Boston** | **NHL** | **40** | **1** | **3** | **4** | **18** | **0** | **0** | **0** | **67** | **1.5** | **–6** | **14** | **42.9** | **10:09** | | | | | | | | | |
| | Providence Bruins | AHL | 17 | 5 | 5 | 10 | 45 | | | | | | | | | | 9 | 2 | 3 | 5 | 38 | | | | |
| **2000-01** | **Phoenix** | **NHL** | **70** | **18** | **13** | **31** | **92** | **2** | **0** | **3** | **123** | **14.6** | **3** | **13** | **46.2** | **11:26** | | | | | | | | | |
| **2001-02** | **Phoenix** | **NHL** | **47** | **7** | **12** | **19** | **46** | **1** | **0** | **0** | **100** | **7.0** | **4** | **15** | **53.3** | **12:51** | **4** | **0** | **0** | **0** | **12** | **0** | **0** | **0** | **12:03** |
| | Springfield | AHL | 2 | 2 | 1 | 3 | 2 | | | | | | | | | | | | | | | | | | |
| **2002-03** | **Phoenix** | **NHL** | **31** | **6** | **8** | **14** | **26** | **0** | **0** | **3** | **92** | **6.5** | **1** | **35** | **54.3** | **12:11** | | | | | | | | | |
| **2003-04** | **Phoenix** | **NHL** | **35** | **1** | **3** | **4** | **16** | **0** | **0** | **0** | **41** | **2.4** | **–3** | **44** | **31.8** | **9:51** | | | | | | | | | |
| | **Pittsburgh** | **NHL** | **19** | **5** | **1** | **6** | **31** | **2** | **0** | **0** | **35** | **14.3** | **0** | **2** | **0.0** | **11:21** | | | | | | | | | |
| 2004-05 | Blues Espoo | Finland | 37 | 8 | 11 | 19 | 80 | | | | | | | | | | | | | | | | | | |
| 2005-06 | HC Davos | Swiss | 36 | 27 | 14 | 41 | 142 | | | | | | | | | | 11 | 5 | 3 | 8 | 40 | | | | |
| 2006-07 | HC Lugano | Swiss | 35 | 20 | 11 | 31 | 67 | | | | | | | | | | 6 | 3 | 2 | 5 | 12 | | | | |
| 2007-08 | HC Lugano | Swiss | 30 | 13 | 7 | 20 | 67 | | | | | | | | | | 3 | 4 | 0 | 4 | 2 | | | | |
| **2008-09** | **Dallas** | **NHL** | **27** | **2** | **6** | **8** | **21** | **0** | **0** | **0** | **34** | **5.9** | **5** | **3** | **0.0** | **9:14** | | | | | | | | | |
| | Grand Rapids | AHL | 15 | 8 | 7 | 15 | 37 | | | | | | | | | | | | | | | | | | |
| | **NHL Totals** | | **375** | **53** | **66** | **119** | **352** | **5** | **0** | **6** | **639** | **8.3** | | **129** | **41.1** | **11:04** | **13** | **1** | **1** | **2** | **20** | **1** | **0** | **1** | **13:08** |

WCHA Rookie of the Year (1994) • AHL First All-Star Team (1999)

Traded to **Quebec** by **Toronto** with Wendel Clark, Sylvain Lefebvre and Toronto's 1st round choice (Jeffrey Kealty) in 1994 Entry Draft for Mats Sundin, Garth Butcher, Todd Warriner and Philadelphia's 1st round choice (previously acquired, later traded to Washington – Washington selected Nolan Baumgartner) in 1994 Entry Draft, June 28, 1994. Transferred to **Colorado** after **Quebec** franchise relocated, June 21, 1995. Traded to **Boston** by **Colorado** with Anders Myrvold for Boston's 1st round choice (Robyn Regehr) in 1998 Entry Draft, November 22, 1996. Signed as a free agent by **Phoenix**, July 7, 2000. • Missed majority of 2002-03 season recovering from eye injury suffered in game vs. Washington, December 13, 2002. Traded to **Pittsburgh** by **Phoenix** for future considerations, February 22, 2004. Signed as a free agent by **Espoo** (Finland), June 23, 2004. Signed as a free agent by **Davos** (Swiss), August 31, 2005. Signed as a free agent by **Lugano** (Swiss), July 17, 2006. Signed as a free agent by **Dallas**, July 3, 2008.

## WINCHESTER, Brad
(WIHN-chehst-uhr, BRAD) **ST.L.**

Center/left wing. Shoots left. 6'5", 228 lbs. Born, Madison, WI, March 1, 1981. Edmonton's 2nd choice, 35th overall, in 2000 Entry Draft.

| | | | Regular Season | | | | | | | | | | | | | | Playoffs | | | | | | | | |
|---|---|---|---|---|---|---|---|---|---|---|---|---|---|---|---|---|---|---|---|---|---|---|---|---|---|
| Season | Club | League | GP | G | A | Pts | PIM | PP | SH | GW | S | % | +/- | TF | F% | Min | GP | G | A | Pts | PIM | PP | SH | GW | Min |
| 1997-98 | USNTDP | U-17 | 24 | 8 | 5 | 13 | 64 | | | | | | | | | | | | | | | | | | |
| | USNTDP | USHL | 5 | 2 | 1 | 3 | 6 | | | | | | | | | | | | | | | | | | |
| | USNTDP | NAHL | 40 | 11 | 17 | 28 | 84 | | | | | | | | | | 5 | 1 | 0 | 1 | 8 | | | | |
| 1998-99 | USNTDP | U-18 | 6 | 0 | 3 | 3 | 6 | | | | | | | | | | | | | | | | | | |
| | USNTDP | USHL | 48 | 14 | 23 | 37 | 103 | | | | | | | | | | | | | | | | | | |
| 99-2000 | U. of Wisconsin | WCHA | 33 | 9 | 9 | 18 | 48 | | | | | | | | | | | | | | | | | | |
| 2000-01 | U. of Wisconsin | WCHA | 41 | 7 | 9 | 16 | 71 | | | | | | | | | | | | | | | | | | |
| 2001-02 | U. of Wisconsin | WCHA | 38 | 14 | 20 | 34 | 38 | | | | | | | | | | | | | | | | | | |
| 2002-03 | U. of Wisconsin | WCHA | 38 | 10 | 6 | 16 | 58 | | | | | | | | | | | | | | | | | | |
| 2003-04 | Toronto | AHL | 65 | 13 | 6 | 19 | 85 | | | | | | | | | | 3 | 0 | 0 | 0 | 2 | | | | |
| 2004-05 | Edmonton | AHL | 76 | 22 | 18 | 40 | 143 | | | | | | | | | | | | | | | | | | |
| **2005-06** | **Edmonton** | **NHL** | **19** | **0** | **1** | **1** | **21** | **0** | **0** | **0** | **19** | **0.0** | **–2** | **2** | **100.0** | **6:05** | **10** | **1** | **2** | **3** | **4** | **0** | **0** | **1** | **9:14** |
| | Hamilton | AHL | 40 | 26 | 14 | 40 | 118 | | | | | | | | | | | | | | | | | | |
| **2006-07** | **Edmonton** | **NHL** | **59** | **4** | **5** | **9** | **86** | **0** | **0** | **0** | **66** | **6.1** | **–10** | **3** | **33.3** | **8:04** | | | | | | | | | |
| **2007-08** | **Dallas** | **NHL** | **41** | **1** | **2** | **3** | **46** | **0** | **0** | **0** | **36** | **2.8** | **–9** | **2** | **0.0** | **7:34** | **6** | **0** | **0** | **0** | **8** | **0** | **0** | **0** | **6:50** |
| | Iowa Stars | AHL | 1 | 0 | 0 | 0 | 2 | | | | | | | | | | | | | | | | | | |
| **2008-09** | **St. Louis** | **NHL** | **64** | **13** | **8** | **21** | **89** | **5** | **0** | **3** | **82** | **15.9** | **–1** | **20** | **45.0** | **12:10** | **4** | **0** | **0** | **0** | **10** | **0** | **0** | **0** | **11:42** |
| | Peoria Rivermen | AHL | 13 | 4 | 2 | 6 | 46 | | | | | | | | | | | | | | | | | | |
| | **NHL Totals** | | **183** | **18** | **16** | **34** | **242** | **5** | **0** | **3** | **203** | **8.9** | | **27** | **44.4** | **9:11** | **20** | **1** | **2** | **3** | **22** | **0** | **0** | **1** | **9:00** |

Signed as a free agent by **Dallas**, July 6, 2007. Signed as a free agent by **St. Louis**, July 16, 2008.

## WINCHESTER, Jesse
(WIHN-chehst-uhr, JEH-see) **OTT.**

Center. Shoots right. 6'1", 204 lbs. Born, Long Sault, Ont., October 4, 1983.

| | | | Regular Season | | | | | | | | | | | | | | Playoffs | | | | | | | | |
|---|---|---|---|---|---|---|---|---|---|---|---|---|---|---|---|---|---|---|---|---|---|---|---|---|---|
| Season | Club | League | GP | G | A | Pts | PIM | PP | SH | GW | S | % | +/- | TF | F% | Min | GP | G | A | Pts | PIM | PP | SH | GW | Min |
| 2004-05 | Colgate | ECAC | 28 | 2 | 2 | 4 | 22 | | | | | | | | | | | | | | | | | | |
| 2005-06 | Colgate | ECAC | 37 | 14 | 22 | 36 | 31 | | | | | | | | | | | | | | | | | | |
| 2006-07 | Colgate | ECAC | 37 | 16 | 21 | 37 | 52 | | | | | | | | | | | | | | | | | | |
| **2007-08** | Colgate | ECAC | 40 | 8 | *29 | 37 | 51 | | | | | | | | | | | | | | | | | | |
| | **Ottawa** | **NHL** | **1** | **0** | **0** | **0** | **2** | **0** | **0** | **0** | **1** | **0.0** | **0** | **0** | **0.0** | **14:00** | | | | | | | | | |
| **2008-09** | **Ottawa** | **NHL** | **76** | **3** | **15** | **18** | **33** | **0** | **0** | **1** | **115** | **2.6** | **0** | **199** | **56.8** | **10:35** | | | | | | | | | |
| | **NHL Totals** | | **77** | **3** | **15** | **18** | **35** | **0** | **0** | **1** | **116** | **2.6** | | **199** | **56.8** | **10:38** | | | | | | | | | |

Signed as a free agent by **Ottawa**, March 24, 2008.

## WINNIK, Daniel
(WIHN-ihk, DAN-yehl) **PHX.**

Center/Left wing. Shoots right. 6'2", 210 lbs. Born, Toronto, Ont., March 6, 1985. Phoenix's 10th choice, 265th overall, in 2004 Entry Draft.

| | | | Regular Season | | | | | | | | | | | | | | Playoffs | | | | | | | | |
|---|---|---|---|---|---|---|---|---|---|---|---|---|---|---|---|---|---|---|---|---|---|---|---|---|---|
| Season | Club | League | GP | G | A | Pts | PIM | PP | SH | GW | S | % | +/- | TF | F% | Min | GP | G | A | Pts | PIM | PP | SH | GW | Min |
| 2002-03 | Wexford | OPJHL | 47 | 20 | 33 | 53 | 70 | | | | | | | | | | 18 | 11 | 11 | 22 | 24 | | | | |
| 2003-04 | New Hampshire | H-East | 38 | 4 | 10 | 14 | 12 | | | | | | | | | | | | | | | | | | |
| 2004-05 | New Hampshire | H-East | 42 | 18 | 22 | 40 | 26 | | | | | | | | | | | | | | | | | | |
| 2005-06 | New Hampshire | H-East | 39 | 15 | 26 | 41 | 44 | | | | | | | | | | | | | | | | | | |
| | San Antonio | AHL | 7 | 1 | 1 | 2 | 8 | | | | | | | | | | | | | | | | | | |
| 2006-07 | San Antonio | AHL | 66 | 9 | 12 | 21 | 34 | | | | | | | | | | | | | | | | | | |
| | Phoenix | ECHL | 5 | 0 | 6 | 6 | 9 | | | | | | | | | | | | | | | | | | |
| **2007-08** | **Phoenix** | **NHL** | **79** | **11** | **15** | **26** | **25** | **0** | **0** | **1** | **122** | **9.0** | **–3** | **154** | **42.2** | **14:06** | | | | | | | | | |

| | | | Regular Season | | | | | | | | | | | | | | Playoffs | | | | | | | | |
|---|---|---|---|---|---|---|---|---|---|---|---|---|---|---|---|---|---|---|---|---|---|---|---|---|---|
| Season | Club | League | GP | G | A | Pts | PIM | PP | SH | GW | S | % | +/- | TF | F% | Min | GP | G | A | Pts | PIM | PP | SH | GW | Min |
| **2008-09** | **Phoenix** | **NHL** | **49** | **3** | **4** | **7** | **63** | **0** | **0** | **0** | **66** | **4.5** | **1** | **138** | **37.0** | **13:04** | .... | .... | .... | .... | .... | .... | .... | .... | .... |
| | San Antonio | AHL | 5 | 0 | 0 | 0 | 4 | .... | .... | .... | .... | .... | .... | .... | .... | .... | .... | .... | .... | .... | .... | .... | .... | .... | .... |
| | **NHL Totals** | | **128** | **14** | **19** | **33** | **88** | **0** | **0** | **1** | **188** | **7.4** | | **292** | **39.7** | **13:42** | .... | .... | .... | .... | .... | .... | .... | .... | .... |

Hockey East Second All-Star Team (2006)

## WIRTANEN, Petteri

(WEER-tah-nehn, PEH-tuh-ree) **ANA.**

Center. Shoots left. 6'1", 207 lbs. Born, Hyvinkaa, Finland, May 28, 1986. Anaheim's 5th choice, 172nd overall, in 2006 Entry Draft.

| Season | Club | League | GP | G | A | Pts | PIM | PP | SH | GW | S | % | +/- | TF | F% | Min | GP | G | A | Pts | PIM | PP | SH | GW | Min |
|---|---|---|---|---|---|---|---|---|---|---|---|---|---|---|---|---|---|---|---|---|---|---|---|---|---|
| 2001-02 | Ahmat Jr. | Fin-Jr. | 1 | 1 | 0 | 1 | 2 | .... | .... | .... | .... | .... | .... | .... | .... | .... | .... | .... | .... | .... | .... | .... | .... | .... | .... |
| 2002-03 | HPK U18 | Fin-U18 | 27 | 17 | 12 | 29 | 36 | .... | .... | .... | .... | .... | .... | .... | .... | .... | 2 | 0 | 0 | 0 | 2 | .... | .... | .... | .... |
| | HPK Jr. | Fin-Jr. | 2 | 1 | 0 | 1 | 0 | .... | .... | .... | .... | .... | .... | .... | .... | .... | .... | .... | .... | .... | .... | .... | .... | .... | .... |
| 2003-04 | HPK U18 | Fin-U18 | 7 | 2 | 3 | 5 | 10 | .... | .... | .... | .... | .... | .... | .... | .... | .... | 2 | 0 | 0 | 0 | 0 | .... | .... | .... | .... |
| | HPK Jr. | Fin-Jr. | 40 | 7 | 11 | 18 | 26 | .... | .... | .... | .... | .... | .... | .... | .... | .... | .... | .... | .... | .... | .... | .... | .... | .... | .... |
| 2004-05 | HPK Jr. | Fin-Jr. | 43 | 14 | 25 | 39 | 42 | .... | .... | .... | .... | .... | .... | .... | .... | .... | 2 | 0 | 0 | 0 | 10 | .... | .... | .... | .... |
| | HPK Hameenlinna | Finland | 8 | 0 | 0 | 0 | 0 | .... | .... | .... | .... | .... | .... | .... | .... | .... | .... | .... | .... | .... | .... | .... | .... | .... | .... |
| 2005-06 | Suomi U20 | Finland-2 | 2 | 2 | 0 | 2 | 2 | .... | .... | .... | .... | .... | .... | .... | .... | .... | .... | .... | .... | .... | .... | .... | .... | .... | .... |
| | HPK Jr. | Fin-Jr. | 3 | 4 | 2 | 6 | 4 | .... | .... | .... | .... | .... | .... | .... | .... | .... | .... | .... | .... | .... | .... | .... | .... | .... | .... |
| | HPK Hameenlinna | Finland | 50 | 8 | 3 | 11 | 24 | .... | .... | .... | .... | .... | .... | .... | .... | .... | 13 | 1 | 0 | 1 | 12 | .... | .... | .... | .... |
| 2006-07 | Portland Pirates | AHL | 67 | 7 | 11 | 18 | 40 | .... | .... | .... | .... | .... | .... | .... | .... | .... | .... | .... | .... | .... | .... | .... | .... | .... | .... |
| **2007-08** | **Anaheim** | **NHL** | **3** | **1** | **0** | **1** | **2** | **0** | **0** | **1** | **1** | **100.0** | **1** | **11** | **45.5** | **4:11** | .... | .... | .... | .... | .... | .... | .... | .... | .... |
| | Portland Pirates | AHL | 78 | 10 | 27 | 37 | 58 | .... | .... | .... | .... | .... | .... | .... | .... | .... | 18 | 0 | 0 | 0 | 14 | .... | .... | .... | .... |
| 2008-09 | Iowa Chops | AHL | 78 | 15 | 26 | 41 | 50 | .... | .... | .... | .... | .... | .... | .... | .... | .... | .... | .... | .... | .... | .... | .... | .... | .... | .... |
| | **NHL Totals** | | **3** | **1** | **0** | **1** | **2** | **0** | **0** | **1** | **1** | **100.0** | | **11** | **45.5** | **4:11** | .... | .... | .... | .... | .... | .... | .... | .... | .... |

## WISEMAN, Chad

(WIGHZ-man, CHAD)

Left wing. Shoots left. 6'1", 210 lbs. Born, Burlington, Ont., March 25, 1981. San Jose's 8th choice, 246th overall, in 2000 Entry Draft.

| Season | Club | League | GP | G | A | Pts | PIM | PP | SH | GW | S | % | +/- | TF | F% | Min | GP | G | A | Pts | PIM | PP | SH | GW | Min |
|---|---|---|---|---|---|---|---|---|---|---|---|---|---|---|---|---|---|---|---|---|---|---|---|---|---|
| 1997-98 | Burlington | OPJHL | 50 | 28 | 36 | 64 | 31 | .... | .... | .... | .... | .... | .... | .... | .... | .... | .... | .... | .... | .... | .... | .... | .... | .... | .... |
| 1998-99 | Mississauga | OHL | 64 | 11 | 25 | 36 | 29 | .... | .... | .... | .... | .... | .... | .... | .... | .... | .... | .... | .... | .... | .... | .... | .... | .... | .... |
| 99-2000 | Mississauga | OHL | 68 | 23 | 45 | 68 | 53 | .... | .... | .... | .... | .... | .... | .... | .... | .... | .... | .... | .... | .... | .... | .... | .... | .... | .... |
| 2000-01 | Mississauga | OHL | 30 | 15 | 29 | 44 | 22 | .... | .... | .... | .... | .... | .... | .... | .... | .... | .... | .... | .... | .... | .... | .... | .... | .... | .... |
| | Plymouth Whalers | OHL | 32 | 11 | 16 | 27 | 12 | .... | .... | .... | .... | .... | .... | .... | .... | .... | 19 | 12 | 8 | 20 | 22 | .... | .... | .... | .... |
| 2001-02 | Cleveland Barons | AHL | 76 | 21 | 29 | 50 | 61 | .... | .... | .... | .... | .... | .... | .... | .... | .... | .... | .... | .... | .... | .... | .... | .... | .... | .... |
| **2002-03** | **San Jose** | **NHL** | **4** | **0** | **0** | **0** | **4** | **0** | **0** | **0** | **1** | **0.0** | **–2** | **0** | **0.0** | **9:19** | .... | .... | .... | .... | .... | .... | .... | .... | .... |
| | Cleveland Barons | AHL | 77 | 17 | 35 | 52 | 44 | .... | .... | .... | .... | .... | .... | .... | .... | .... | .... | .... | .... | .... | .... | .... | .... | .... | .... |
| **2003-04** | **NY Rangers** | **NHL** | **4** | **1** | **0** | **1** | **0** | **0** | **0** | **0** | **3** | **33.3** | **–1** | **0** | **0.0** | **8:49** | .... | .... | .... | .... | .... | .... | .... | .... | .... |
| | Hartford | AHL | 62 | 25 | 27 | 52 | 45 | .... | .... | .... | .... | .... | .... | .... | .... | .... | 15 | 5 | 6 | 11 | 12 | .... | .... | .... | .... |
| 2004-05 | Hartford | AHL | 60 | 17 | 16 | 33 | 74 | .... | .... | .... | .... | .... | .... | .... | .... | .... | 6 | 1 | 1 | 2 | 6 | .... | .... | .... | .... |
| **2005-06** | **NY Rangers** | **NHL** | **1** | **0** | **1** | **1** | **4** | **0** | **0** | **0** | **1** | **0.0** | **2** | **0** | **0.0** | **8:47** | **1** | **0** | **0** | **0** | **2** | **0** | **0** | **0** | **6:00** |
| | Hartford | AHL | 69 | 19 | 35 | 54 | 65 | .... | .... | .... | .... | .... | .... | .... | .... | .... | 11 | 3 | 6 | 9 | 22 | .... | .... | .... | .... |
| 2006-07 | Hershey Bears | AHL | 48 | 15 | 20 | 35 | 80 | .... | .... | .... | .... | .... | .... | .... | .... | .... | 16 | 2 | 6 | 8 | 16 | .... | .... | .... | .... |
| 2007-08 | Wolfsburg | Germany | 28 | 10 | 13 | 23 | 41 | .... | .... | .... | .... | .... | .... | .... | .... | .... | .... | .... | .... | .... | .... | .... | .... | .... | .... |
| 2008-09 | Lowell Devils | AHL | 23 | 9 | 10 | 19 | 23 | .... | .... | .... | .... | .... | .... | .... | .... | .... | .... | .... | .... | .... | .... | .... | .... | .... | .... |
| | **NHL Totals** | | **9** | **1** | **1** | **2** | **8** | **0** | **0** | **0** | **5** | **20.0** | | **0** | **0.0** | **9:02** | **1** | **0** | **0** | **0** | **2** | **0** | **0** | **0** | **6:00** |

Traded to **NY Rangers** by **San Jose** for Nils Ekman, August 12, 2003. Signed as a free agent by **Washington**, July 14, 2006. Signed as a free agent by **Wolfsburg** (Germany), July 9, 2007. Signed as a free agent by **New Jersey**, July 17, 2008. • Missed majority of 2007-08 and 2008-09 seasons recovering from three sports hernia surgeries.

## WISHART, Ty

(wih-SHAHRT, TIGH) **T.B.**

Defense. Shoots left. 6'4", 205 lbs. Born, Belleville, Ont., May 19, 1988. San Jose's 1st choice, 16th overall, in 2006 Entry Draft.

| Season | Club | League | GP | G | A | Pts | PIM | PP | SH | GW | S | % | +/- | TF | F% | Min | GP | G | A | Pts | PIM | PP | SH | GW | Min |
|---|---|---|---|---|---|---|---|---|---|---|---|---|---|---|---|---|---|---|---|---|---|---|---|---|---|
| 2003-04 | Comox Valley | Minor-BC | 47 | 26 | 27 | 53 | 48 | .... | .... | .... | .... | .... | .... | .... | .... | .... | .... | .... | .... | .... | .... | .... | .... | .... | .... |
| 2004-05 | Prince George | WHL | 58 | 1 | 7 | 8 | 41 | .... | .... | .... | .... | .... | .... | .... | .... | .... | .... | .... | .... | .... | .... | .... | .... | .... | .... |
| 2005-06 | Prince George | WHL | 70 | 5 | 32 | 37 | 68 | .... | .... | .... | .... | .... | .... | .... | .... | .... | 5 | 0 | 0 | 0 | 4 | .... | .... | .... | .... |
| 2006-07 | Prince George | WHL | 62 | 11 | 38 | 49 | 59 | .... | .... | .... | .... | .... | .... | .... | .... | .... | 15 | 3 | 8 | 11 | 6 | .... | .... | .... | .... |
| 2007-08 | Prince George | WHL | 40 | 12 | 28 | 40 | 34 | .... | .... | .... | .... | .... | .... | .... | .... | .... | .... | .... | .... | .... | .... | .... | .... | .... | .... |
| | Moose Jaw | WHL | 32 | 4 | 23 | 27 | 18 | .... | .... | .... | .... | .... | .... | .... | .... | .... | 6 | 1 | 3 | 4 | 2 | .... | .... | .... | .... |
| | Worcester Sharks | AHL | 5 | 0 | 0 | 0 | 0 | .... | .... | .... | .... | .... | .... | .... | .... | .... | .... | .... | .... | .... | .... | .... | .... | .... | .... |
| **2008-09** | **Tampa Bay** | **NHL** | **5** | **0** | **1** | **1** | **0** | **0** | **0** | **0** | **2** | **0.0** | **0** | **0** | **0.0** | **10:07** | .... | .... | .... | .... | .... | .... | .... | .... | .... |
| | Norfolk Admirals | AHL | 61 | 1 | 6 | 7 | 25 | .... | .... | .... | .... | .... | .... | .... | .... | .... | .... | .... | .... | .... | .... | .... | .... | .... | .... |
| | **NHL Totals** | | **5** | **0** | **1** | **1** | **0** | **0** | **0** | **0** | **2** | **0.0** | | **0** | **0.0** | **10:07** | .... | .... | .... | .... | .... | .... | .... | .... | .... |

WHL West Second All-Star Team (2007) • WHL East Second All-Star Team (2008)

Traded to **Tampa Bay** by **San Jose** with Matt Carle, San Jose's 1st round choice (later traded to Ottawa, later traded to NY Islanders, later traded to Columbus, later traded to Anaheim - Anaheim selected Kyle Palmieri) in 2009 Entry Draft and San Jose's 4th round choice in 2010 Entry Draft for Dan Boyle and Brad Lukowich, July 4, 2008.

## WISNIEWSKI, James

(wihz-NOO-skee, JAYMZ) **ANA.**

Defense. Shoots right. 6', 207 lbs. Born, Canton, MI, February 21, 1984. Chicago's 5th choice, 156th overall, in 2002 Entry Draft.

| Season | Club | League | GP | G | A | Pts | PIM | PP | SH | GW | S | % | +/- | TF | F% | Min | GP | G | A | Pts | PIM | PP | SH | GW | Min |
|---|---|---|---|---|---|---|---|---|---|---|---|---|---|---|---|---|---|---|---|---|---|---|---|---|---|
| 99-2000 | Det. Compuware | NAHL | 50 | 5 | 11 | 16 | 67 | .... | .... | .... | .... | .... | .... | .... | .... | .... | 5 | 0 | 3 | 3 | 4 | .... | .... | .... | .... |
| 2000-01 | Plymouth Whalers | OHL | 53 | 6 | 23 | 29 | 72 | .... | .... | .... | .... | .... | .... | .... | .... | .... | 19 | 3 | 10 | 13 | 34 | .... | .... | .... | .... |
| 2001-02 | Plymouth Whalers | OHL | 62 | 11 | 25 | 36 | 100 | .... | .... | .... | .... | .... | .... | .... | .... | .... | 6 | 1 | 2 | 3 | 6 | .... | .... | .... | .... |
| 2002-03 | Plymouth Whalers | OHL | 52 | 18 | 34 | 52 | 60 | .... | .... | .... | .... | .... | .... | .... | .... | .... | 18 | 2 | 10 | 12 | 14 | .... | .... | .... | .... |
| 2003-04 | Plymouth Whalers | OHL | 50 | 17 | 53 | 70 | 63 | .... | .... | .... | .... | .... | .... | .... | .... | .... | 9 | 3 | 7 | 10 | 8 | .... | .... | .... | .... |
| 2004-05 | Norfolk Admirals | AHL | 66 | 7 | 18 | 25 | 110 | .... | .... | .... | .... | .... | .... | .... | .... | .... | 5 | 1 | 3 | 4 | 2 | .... | .... | .... | .... |
| **2005-06** | **Chicago** | **NHL** | **19** | **2** | **5** | **7** | **36** | **0** | **0** | **0** | **25** | **8.0** | **0** | **1** | **0.0** | **15:52** | .... | .... | .... | .... | .... | .... | .... | .... | .... |
| | Norfolk Admirals | AHL | 61 | 7 | 28 | 35 | 67 | .... | .... | .... | .... | .... | .... | .... | .... | .... | 4 | 1 | 2 | 3 | 6 | .... | .... | .... | .... |
| **2006-07** | **Chicago** | **NHL** | **50** | **2** | **8** | **10** | **39** | **0** | **0** | **0** | **55** | **3.6** | **3** | **1** | **0.0** | **19:00** | .... | .... | .... | .... | .... | .... | .... | .... | .... |
| | Norfolk Admirals | AHL | 10 | 0 | 6 | 6 | 8 | .... | .... | .... | .... | .... | .... | .... | .... | .... | .... | .... | .... | .... | .... | .... | .... | .... | .... |
| **2007-08** | **Chicago** | **NHL** | **68** | **7** | **19** | **26** | **103** | **1** | **1** | **0** | **82** | **8.5** | **12** | **0** | **0.0** | **17:00** | .... | .... | .... | .... | .... | .... | .... | .... | .... |
| **2008-09** | **Chicago** | **NHL** | **31** | **2** | **11** | **13** | **14** | **1** | **0** | **0** | **70** | **2.9** | **6** | **0** | **0.0** | **19:15** | .... | .... | .... | .... | .... | .... | .... | .... | .... |
| | Rockford IceHogs | AHL | 2 | 3 | 1 | 4 | 0 | .... | .... | .... | .... | .... | .... | .... | .... | .... | .... | .... | .... | .... | .... | .... | .... | .... | .... |
| | **Anaheim** | **NHL** | **17** | **1** | **10** | **11** | **16** | **0** | **0** | **0** | **19** | **5.3** | **3** | **0** | **0.0** | **20:57** | **12** | **1** | **2** | **3** | **10** | **0** | **0** | **0** | **20:22** |
| | **NHL Totals** | | **185** | **14** | **53** | **67** | **208** | **2** | **1** | **0** | **251** | **5.6** | | **2** | **0.0** | **18:10** | **12** | **1** | **2** | **3** | **10** | **0** | **0** | **0** | **20:22** |

OHL First All-Star Team (2004) • OHL Defenseman of the Year (2004) • Canadian Major Junior First All-Star Team (2004) • Canadian Major Junior Defenseman of the Year (2004)

Traded to **Anaheim** by **Chicago** with Petri Kontiola for Samuel Pahlsson, Logan Stephenson and future considerations, March 4, 2009.

## WITT, Brendan

(WIHT, BREHN-duhn) **NYI**

Defense. Shoots left. 6'2", 223 lbs. Born, Humboldt, Sask., February 20, 1975. Washington's 1st choice, 11th overall, in 1993 Entry Draft.

| Season | Club | League | GP | G | A | Pts | PIM | PP | SH | GW | S | % | +/- | TF | F% | Min | GP | G | A | Pts | PIM | PP | SH | GW | Min |
|---|---|---|---|---|---|---|---|---|---|---|---|---|---|---|---|---|---|---|---|---|---|---|---|---|---|
| 1990-91 | Saskatoon Blazers | SMHL | 31 | 5 | 13 | 18 | 42 | .... | .... | .... | .... | .... | .... | .... | .... | .... | .... | .... | .... | .... | .... | .... | .... | .... | .... |
| | Seattle | WHL | .... | .... | .... | .... | .... | .... | .... | .... | .... | .... | .... | .... | .... | .... | 1 | 0 | 0 | 0 | 0 | .... | .... | .... | .... |
| 1991-92 | Seattle | WHL | 67 | 3 | 9 | 12 | 212 | .... | .... | .... | .... | .... | .... | .... | .... | .... | 15 | 1 | 1 | 2 | 84 | .... | .... | .... | .... |
| 1992-93 | Seattle | WHL | 70 | 2 | 26 | 28 | 239 | .... | .... | .... | .... | .... | .... | .... | .... | .... | 5 | 1 | 2 | 3 | 30 | .... | .... | .... | .... |
| 1993-94 | Seattle | WHL | 56 | 8 | 31 | 39 | 235 | .... | .... | .... | .... | .... | .... | .... | .... | .... | 9 | 3 | 8 | 11 | 23 | .... | .... | .... | .... |
| 1994-95 | | | DID NOT PLAY | | | | | | | | | | | | | | | | | | | | | | |
| **1995-96** | **Washington** | **NHL** | **48** | **2** | **3** | **5** | **85** | **0** | **0** | **1** | **44** | **4.5** | **–4** | .... | .... | .... | .... | .... | .... | .... | .... | .... | .... | .... | .... |
| **1996-97** | **Washington** | **NHL** | **44** | **3** | **2** | **5** | **88** | **0** | **0** | **0** | **41** | **7.3** | **–20** | .... | .... | .... | .... | .... | .... | .... | .... | .... | .... | .... | .... |
| | Portland Pirates | AHL | 30 | 2 | 4 | 6 | 56 | .... | .... | .... | .... | .... | .... | .... | .... | .... | 5 | 1 | 0 | 1 | 30 | .... | .... | .... | .... |
| **1997-98** | **Washington** | **NHL** | **64** | **1** | **7** | **8** | **112** | **0** | **0** | **0** | **68** | **1.5** | **–11** | .... | .... | .... | **16** | **1** | **0** | **1** | **14** | **0** | **0** | **0** | .... |
| **1998-99** | **Washington** | **NHL** | **54** | **2** | **5** | **7** | **87** | **0** | **0** | **0** | **51** | **3.9** | **–6** | **0** | **0.0** | **15:50** | .... | .... | .... | .... | .... | .... | .... | .... | .... |
| **99-2000** | **Washington** | **NHL** | **77** | **1** | **7** | **8** | **114** | **0** | **0** | **0** | **64** | **1.6** | **5** | **2** | **50.0** | **20:56** | **3** | **0** | **0** | **0** | **0** | **0** | **0** | **0** | **20:52** |
| **2000-01** | **Washington** | **NHL** | **72** | **3** | **3** | **6** | **101** | **0** | **0** | **0** | **87** | **3.4** | **2** | **1** | **100.0** | **20:41** | **6** | **2** | **0** | **2** | **12** | **1** | **0** | **0** | **20:50** |
| **2001-02** | **Washington** | **NHL** | **68** | **3** | **7** | **10** | **78** | **0** | **0** | **0** | **81** | **3.7** | **–1** | **1** | **100.0** | **20:03** | .... | .... | .... | .... | .... | .... | .... | .... | .... |
| **2002-03** | **Washington** | **NHL** | **69** | **2** | **9** | **11** | **106** | **0** | **0** | **0** | **80** | **2.5** | **12** | **0** | **0.0** | **20:55** | **6** | **1** | **0** | **1** | **0** | **0** | **0** | **0** | **23:33** |
| **2003-04** | **Washington** | **NHL** | **72** | **2** | **10** | **12** | **123** | **0** | **0** | **0** | **91** | **2.2** | **–22** | **3** | **66.7** | **22:48** | .... | .... | .... | .... | .... | .... | .... | .... | .... |
| 2004-05 | Bracknell Bees | Britain-2 | 3 | 1 | 4 | 5 | 0 | .... | .... | .... | .... | .... | .... | .... | .... | .... | .... | .... | .... | .... | .... | .... | .... | .... | .... |
| **2005-06** | **Washington** | **NHL** | **58** | **1** | **10** | **11** | **141** | **0** | **0** | **0** | **62** | **1.6** | **–5** | **0** | **0.0** | **21:41** | .... | .... | .... | .... | .... | .... | .... | .... | .... |
| | **Nashville** | **NHL** | **17** | **0** | **3** | **3** | **68** | **0** | **0** | **0** | **13** | **0.0** | **5** | **0** | **0.0** | **17:29** | **5** | **0** | **0** | **0** | **12** | **0** | **0** | **0** | **17:07** |
| **2006-07** | **NY Islanders** | **NHL** | **81** | **1** | **13** | **14** | **131** | **0** | **0** | **0** | **75** | **1.3** | **14** | **0** | **0.0** | **21:39** | **5** | **0** | **1** | **1** | **6** | **0** | **0** | **0** | **20:06** |

| | | | Regular Season | | | | | | | | | | | | | | Playoffs | | | | | | | | |
|---|---|---|---|---|---|---|---|---|---|---|---|---|---|---|---|---|---|---|---|---|---|---|---|---|---|
| Season | Club | League | GP | G | A | Pts | PIM | PP | SH | GW | S | % | +/- | TF | F% | Min | GP | G | A | Pts | PIM | PP | SH | GW | Min |
| **2007-08** | **NY Islanders** | **NHL** | **59** | **2** | **5** | **7** | **51** | **0** | **0** | **0** | **58** | **3.4** | **-8** | **0** | **0.0** | **21:46** | .... | .... | .... | .... | .... | .... | .... | .... | .... |
| **2008-09** | **NY Islanders** | **NHL** | **65** | **0** | **9** | **9** | **94** | **0** | **0** | **0** | **52** | **0.0** | **-34** | **2** | **50.0** | **20:18** | .... | .... | .... | .... | .... | .... | .... | .... | .... |
| | **NHL Totals** | | **848** | **23** | **93** | **116** | **1379** | **0** | **0** | **1** | **867** | **2.7** | | **9** | **66.7** | **20:41** | **41** | **4** | **1** | **5** | **44** | **1** | **0** | **0** | **20:36** |

WHL West First All-Star Team (1993, 1994) • Canadian Major Junior First All-Star Team (1994)

• Missed entire 1994-95 season after failing to come to contract terms with **Washington**. Signed as a free agent by **Bracknell** (Britain-2), December 21, 2004. Traded to **Nashville** by **Washington** for Kris Beech and Nashville's 1st round choice (Semyon Varlamov) in 2006 Entry Draft, March 9, 2006. Signed as a free agent by **NY Islanders**, July 3, 2006.

## WOLSKI, Wojtek

(WOHL-skee, VOI-tehk) **COL.**

Left wing. Shoots left. 6'3", 210 lbs. Born, Zabrze, Poland, February 24, 1986. Colorado's 1st choice, 21st overall, in 2004 Entry Draft.

| Season | Club | League | GP | G | A | Pts | PIM | PP | SH | GW | S | % | +/- | TF | F% | Min | GP | G | A | Pts | PIM | PP | SH | GW | Min |
|---|---|---|---|---|---|---|---|---|---|---|---|---|---|---|---|---|---|---|---|---|---|---|---|---|---|
| 2001-02 | St. Mike's B's | OPJHL | 33 | 16 | 33 | 49 | 40 | .... | .... | .... | .... | .... | .... | .... | .... | .... | .... | .... | .... | .... | .... | .... | .... | .... | .... |
| 2002-03 | Brampton | OHL | 64 | 25 | 32 | 57 | 26 | .... | .... | .... | .... | .... | .... | .... | .... | .... | 11 | 5 | 0 | 5 | 6 | .... | .... | .... | .... |
| 2003-04 | Brampton | OHL | 66 | 29 | 41 | 70 | 30 | .... | .... | .... | .... | .... | .... | .... | .... | .... | 12 | 5 | 3 | 8 | 8 | .... | .... | .... | .... |
| 2004-05 | Brampton | OHL | 67 | 29 | 44 | 73 | 41 | .... | .... | .... | .... | .... | .... | .... | .... | .... | 6 | 2 | 5 | 7 | 6 | .... | .... | .... | .... |
| **2005-06** | **Colorado** | **NHL** | **9** | **2** | **4** | **6** | **4** | **2** | **0** | **0** | **9** | **22.2** | **-5** | **4** | **0.0** | **9:44** | **8** | **1** | **3** | **4** | **2** | **0** | **0** | **0** | **12:06** |
| | Brampton | OHL | 56 | 47 | 81 | 128 | 46 | .... | .... | .... | .... | .... | .... | .... | .... | .... | 11 | 7 | 11 | 18 | 4 | .... | .... | .... | .... |
| **2006-07** | **Colorado** | **NHL** | **76** | **22** | **28** | **50** | **14** | **7** | **0** | **2** | **165** | **13.3** | **2** | **3** | **100.0** | **15:31** | .... | .... | .... | .... | .... | .... | .... | .... | .... |
| **2007-08** | **Colorado** | **NHL** | **77** | **18** | **30** | **48** | **14** | **4** | **0** | **6** | **158** | **11.4** | **10** | **48** | **50.0** | **15:56** | **7** | **2** | **3** | **5** | **2** | **1** | **0** | **1** | **13:15** |
| **2008-09** | **Colorado** | **NHL** | **78** | **14** | **28** | **42** | **28** | **2** | **1** | **3** | **169** | **8.3** | **-13** | **515** | **48.2** | **18:23** | .... | .... | .... | .... | .... | .... | .... | .... | .... |
| | **NHL Totals** | | **240** | **56** | **90** | **146** | **60** | **15** | **1** | **11** | **501** | **11.2** | | **570** | **48.2** | **16:22** | **15** | **3** | **6** | **9** | **4** | **1** | **0** | **1** | **12:38** |

OHL First All-Star Team (2004) • OHL Second All-Star Team (2006)

## WOYWITKA, Jeff

(WOI-wiht-ka, JEHF) **DAL.**

Defense. Shoots left. 6'2", 217 lbs. Born, Vermilion, Alta., September 1, 1983. Philadelphia's 1st choice, 27th overall, in 2001 Entry Draft.

| Season | Club | League | GP | G | A | Pts | PIM | PP | SH | GW | S | % | +/- | TF | F% | Min | GP | G | A | Pts | PIM | PP | SH | GW | Min |
|---|---|---|---|---|---|---|---|---|---|---|---|---|---|---|---|---|---|---|---|---|---|---|---|---|---|
| 1998-99 | Wainwright | AAHA | 26 | 7 | 15 | 22 | 60 | .... | .... | .... | .... | .... | .... | .... | .... | .... | .... | .... | .... | .... | .... | .... | .... | .... | .... |
| 99-2000 | Red Deer Rebels | WHL | 67 | 4 | 12 | 16 | 40 | .... | .... | .... | .... | .... | .... | .... | .... | .... | 4 | 0 | 3 | 3 | 2 | .... | .... | .... | .... |
| 2000-01 | Red Deer Rebels | WHL | 72 | 7 | 28 | 35 | 113 | .... | .... | .... | .... | .... | .... | .... | .... | .... | 22 | 2 | 8 | 10 | 25 | .... | .... | .... | .... |
| 2001-02 | Red Deer Rebels | WHL | 72 | 14 | 23 | 37 | 109 | .... | .... | .... | .... | .... | .... | .... | .... | .... | 23 | 2 | 10 | 12 | 22 | .... | .... | .... | .... |
| 2002-03 | Red Deer Rebels | WHL | 57 | 16 | 36 | 52 | 65 | .... | .... | .... | .... | .... | .... | .... | .... | .... | 23 | 1 | 9 | 10 | 25 | .... | .... | .... | .... |
| 2003-04 | Philadelphia | AHL | 29 | 0 | 6 | 6 | 51 | .... | .... | .... | .... | .... | .... | .... | .... | .... | .... | .... | .... | .... | .... | .... | .... | .... | .... |
| | Toronto | AHL | 53 | 4 | 18 | 22 | 41 | .... | .... | .... | .... | .... | .... | .... | .... | .... | 3 | 0 | 0 | 0 | 2 | .... | .... | .... | .... |
| 2004-05 | Edmonton | AHL | 80 | 6 | 20 | 26 | 84 | .... | .... | .... | .... | .... | .... | .... | .... | .... | .... | .... | .... | .... | .... | .... | .... | .... | .... |
| **2005-06** | **St. Louis** | **NHL** | **26** | **0** | **2** | **2** | **25** | **0** | **0** | **0** | **23** | **0.0** | **-12** | **0** | **0.0** | **10:38** | .... | .... | .... | .... | .... | .... | .... | .... | .... |
| | Peoria Rivermen | AHL | 53 | 1 | 14 | 15 | 58 | .... | .... | .... | .... | .... | .... | .... | .... | .... | 4 | 0 | 0 | 0 | 4 | .... | .... | .... | .... |
| **2006-07** | **St. Louis** | **NHL** | **34** | **1** | **6** | **7** | **12** | **0** | **0** | **0** | **28** | **3.6** | **4** | **0** | **0.0** | **14:45** | .... | .... | .... | .... | .... | .... | .... | .... | .... |
| | Peoria Rivermen | AHL | 41 | 0 | 18 | 18 | 20 | .... | .... | .... | .... | .... | .... | .... | .... | .... | .... | .... | .... | .... | .... | .... | .... | .... | .... |
| **2007-08** | **St. Louis** | **NHL** | **27** | **2** | **6** | **8** | **12** | **0** | **0** | **0** | **25** | **8.0** | **2** | **0** | **0.0** | **16:04** | .... | .... | .... | .... | .... | .... | .... | .... | .... |
| | Peoria Rivermen | AHL | 52 | 10 | 20 | 30 | 35 | .... | .... | .... | .... | .... | .... | .... | .... | .... | .... | .... | .... | .... | .... | .... | .... | .... | .... |
| **2008-09** | **St. Louis** | **NHL** | **65** | **3** | **15** | **18** | **57** | **2** | **0** | **1** | **71** | **4.2** | **8** | **0** | **0.0** | **18:29** | **4** | **0** | **0** | **0** | **0** | **0** | **0** | **0** | **18:48** |
| | Peoria Rivermen | AHL | 7 | 0 | 7 | 7 | 2 | .... | .... | .... | .... | .... | .... | .... | .... | .... | .... | .... | .... | .... | .... | .... | .... | .... | .... |
| | **NHL Totals** | | **152** | **6** | **29** | **35** | **106** | **2** | **0** | **1** | **147** | **4.1** | | **0** | **0.0** | **15:53** | **4** | **0** | **0** | **0** | **0** | **0** | **0** | **0** | **18:48** |

WHL East Second All-Star Team (2002) • WHL East First All-Star Team (2003)

Traded to **Edmonton** by **Philadelphia** with Philadelphia's 1st round choice (Rob Schremp) in 2004 Entry Draft and Philadelphia's 3rd round choice (Danny Syvret) in 2005 Entry Draft for Mike Comrie, December 16, 2003. Traded to **St. Louis** by **Edmonton** with Eric Brewer and Doug Lynch for Chris Pronger, August 2, 2005. Signed as a free agent by **Dallas**, July 7, 2009.

## WOZNIEWSKI, Andy

(wuhz-NYOO-skee, AN-dee)

Defense. Shoots left. 6'5", 225 lbs. Born, Buffalo Grove, IL, May 25, 1980.

| Season | Club | League | GP | G | A | Pts | PIM | PP | SH | GW | S | % | +/- | TF | F% | Min | GP | G | A | Pts | PIM | PP | SH | GW | Min |
|---|---|---|---|---|---|---|---|---|---|---|---|---|---|---|---|---|---|---|---|---|---|---|---|---|---|
| 99-2000 | U. Mass-Lowell | H-East | 17 | 1 | 1 | 2 | 8 | .... | .... | .... | .... | .... | .... | .... | .... | .... | .... | .... | .... | .... | .... | .... | .... | .... | .... |
| 2000-01 | Texas Tornado | NAHL | 54 | 10 | 34 | 44 | 98 | .... | .... | .... | .... | .... | .... | .... | .... | .... | 8 | 2 | 7 | 9 | 12 | .... | .... | .... | .... |
| 2001-02 | U. of Wisconsin | WCHA | 39 | 3 | 13 | 16 | 54 | .... | .... | .... | .... | .... | .... | .... | .... | .... | .... | .... | .... | .... | .... | .... | .... | .... | .... |
| 2002-03 | U. of Wisconsin | WCHA | 33 | 1 | 7 | 8 | 47 | .... | .... | .... | .... | .... | .... | .... | .... | .... | .... | .... | .... | .... | .... | .... | .... | .... | .... |
| 2003-04 | U. of Wisconsin | WCHA | 43 | 6 | 8 | 14 | *104 | .... | .... | .... | .... | .... | .... | .... | .... | .... | .... | .... | .... | .... | .... | .... | .... | .... | .... |
| | St. John's | AHL | 3 | 0 | 1 | 1 | 0 | .... | .... | .... | .... | .... | .... | .... | .... | .... | .... | .... | .... | .... | .... | .... | .... | .... | .... |
| 2004-05 | St. John's | AHL | 28 | 1 | 4 | 5 | 20 | .... | .... | .... | .... | .... | .... | .... | .... | .... | .... | .... | .... | .... | .... | .... | .... | .... | .... |
| **2005-06** | **Toronto** | **NHL** | **13** | **0** | **1** | **1** | **13** | **0** | **0** | **0** | **6** | **0.0** | **-8** | **0** | **0.0** | **17:55** | .... | .... | .... | .... | .... | .... | .... | .... | .... |
| | Toronto Marlies | AHL | 31 | 4 | 11 | 15 | 42 | .... | .... | .... | .... | .... | .... | .... | .... | .... | .... | .... | .... | .... | .... | .... | .... | .... | .... |
| **2006-07** | **Toronto** | **NHL** | **15** | **0** | **2** | **2** | **14** | **0** | **0** | **0** | **10** | **0.0** | **-1** | **0** | **0.0** | **13:55** | .... | .... | .... | .... | .... | .... | .... | .... | .... |
| | Toronto Marlies | AHL | 5 | 0 | 3 | 3 | 8 | .... | .... | .... | .... | .... | .... | .... | .... | .... | .... | .... | .... | .... | .... | .... | .... | .... | .... |
| **2007-08** | **Toronto** | **NHL** | **48** | **2** | **7** | **9** | **54** | **0** | **0** | **0** | **34** | **5.9** | **5** | **0** | **0.0** | **14:10** | .... | .... | .... | .... | .... | .... | .... | .... | .... |
| | Toronto Marlies | AHL | 33 | 7 | 10 | 17 | 26 | .... | .... | .... | .... | .... | .... | .... | .... | .... | 19 | 4 | 5 | 9 | 14 | .... | .... | .... | .... |
| **2008-09** | **St. Louis** | **NHL** | **1** | **0** | **0** | **0** | **0** | **0** | **0** | **0** | **0** | **0.0** | **0** | **0** | **0.0** | **6:44** | .... | .... | .... | .... | .... | .... | .... | .... | .... |
| | Peoria Rivermen | AHL | 56 | 1 | 16 | 17 | 56 | .... | .... | .... | .... | .... | .... | .... | .... | .... | .... | .... | .... | .... | .... | .... | .... | .... | .... |
| | Wilkes-Barre | AHL | 18 | 2 | 2 | 4 | 26 | .... | .... | .... | .... | .... | .... | .... | .... | .... | 6 | 1 | 1 | 2 | 2 | .... | .... | .... | .... |
| | **NHL Totals** | | **77** | **2** | **10** | **12** | **81** | **0** | **0** | **0** | **50** | **4.0** | | **0** | **0.0** | **14:40** | .... | .... | .... | .... | .... | .... | .... | .... | .... |

Signed as a free agent by **Toronto**, May 27, 2004. • Missed majority of 2006-07 season recovering from shoulder surgery, October 10, 2006. Signed as a free agent by **St. Louis**, July 17, 2008. Traded to **Pittsburgh** by **St. Louis** for Danny Richmond, March 4, 2009.

## YABLONSKI, Jeremy

(ya-BLAWN-skee, JAIR-eh-mee) **OTT.**

Left wing. Shoots right. 6', 240 lbs. Born, Meadow Lake, Sask., March 21, 1980.

| Season | Club | League | GP | G | A | Pts | PIM | PP | SH | GW | S | % | +/- | TF | F% | Min | GP | G | A | Pts | PIM | PP | SH | GW | Min |
|---|---|---|---|---|---|---|---|---|---|---|---|---|---|---|---|---|---|---|---|---|---|---|---|---|---|
| 1996-97 | Beardy's | SMHL | 38 | 7 | 3 | 10 | 284 | .... | .... | .... | .... | .... | .... | .... | .... | .... | .... | .... | .... | .... | .... | .... | .... | .... | .... |
| 1997-98 | Edmonton Ice | WHL | 47 | 3 | 0 | 3 | 143 | .... | .... | .... | .... | .... | .... | .... | .... | .... | .... | .... | .... | .... | .... | .... | .... | .... | .... |
| 1998-99 | Kootenay Ice | WHL | 27 | 1 | 1 | 2 | 77 | .... | .... | .... | .... | .... | .... | .... | .... | .... | .... | .... | .... | .... | .... | .... | .... | .... | .... |
| 99-2000 | Kootenay Ice | WHL | DID NOT PLAY – INJURED | | | | | | | | | | | | | | | | | | | | | | |
| 2000-01 | Phoenix | WCHL | 44 | 2 | 1 | 3 | 169 | .... | .... | .... | .... | .... | .... | .... | .... | .... | .... | .... | .... | .... | .... | .... | .... | .... | .... |
| 2001-02 | Idaho Steelheads | WCHL | 69 | 2 | 1 | 3 | 303 | .... | .... | .... | .... | .... | .... | .... | .... | .... | .... | .... | .... | .... | .... | .... | .... | .... | .... |
| 2002-03 | Peoria Rivermen | ECHL | 24 | 1 | 2 | 3 | 154 | .... | .... | .... | .... | .... | .... | .... | .... | .... | .... | .... | .... | .... | .... | .... | .... | .... | .... |
| | Cincinnati | AHL | 9 | 0 | 0 | 0 | 42 | .... | .... | .... | .... | .... | .... | .... | .... | .... | .... | .... | .... | .... | .... | .... | .... | .... | .... |
| | Worcester IceCats | AHL | 20 | 1 | 0 | 1 | 50 | .... | .... | .... | .... | .... | .... | .... | .... | .... | .... | .... | .... | .... | .... | .... | .... | .... | .... |
| **2003-04** | Worcester IceCats | AHL | 6 | 0 | 0 | 0 | 19 | .... | .... | .... | .... | .... | .... | .... | .... | .... | .... | .... | .... | .... | .... | .... | .... | .... | .... |
| | **St. Louis** | **NHL** | **1** | **0** | **0** | **0** | **5** | **0** | **0** | **0** | **1** | **0.0** | **-1** | **0** | **0.0** | **7:53** | .... | .... | .... | .... | .... | .... | .... | .... | .... |
| | Peoria Rivermen | ECHL | 13 | 0 | 2 | 2 | 62 | .... | .... | .... | .... | .... | .... | .... | .... | .... | .... | .... | .... | .... | .... | .... | .... | .... | .... |
| | Milwaukee | AHL | 2 | 0 | 0 | 0 | 11 | .... | .... | .... | .... | .... | .... | .... | .... | .... | .... | .... | .... | .... | .... | .... | .... | .... | .... |
| 2004-05 | Milwaukee | AHL | 32 | 3 | 2 | 5 | 116 | .... | .... | .... | .... | .... | .... | .... | .... | .... | .... | .... | .... | .... | .... | .... | .... | .... | .... |
| 2005-06 | Milwaukee | AHL | 30 | 0 | 1 | 1 | 82 | .... | .... | .... | .... | .... | .... | .... | .... | .... | .... | .... | .... | .... | .... | .... | .... | .... | .... |
| | Idaho Steelheads | ECHL | 3 | 0 | 1 | 1 | 25 | .... | .... | .... | .... | .... | .... | .... | .... | .... | .... | .... | .... | .... | .... | .... | .... | .... | .... |
| 2006-07 | Idaho Steelheads | ECHL | 41 | 3 | 3 | 6 | 163 | .... | .... | .... | .... | .... | .... | .... | .... | .... | .... | .... | .... | .... | .... | .... | .... | .... | .... |
| 2007-08 | Binghamton | AHL | 76 | 3 | 10 | 13 | 228 | .... | .... | .... | .... | .... | .... | .... | .... | .... | .... | .... | .... | .... | .... | .... | .... | .... | .... |
| 2008-09 | Binghamton | AHL | 64 | 1 | 2 | 3 | 215 | .... | .... | .... | .... | .... | .... | .... | .... | .... | .... | .... | .... | .... | .... | .... | .... | .... | .... |
| | **NHL Totals** | | **1** | **0** | **0** | **0** | **5** | **0** | **0** | **0** | **1** | **0.0** | | **0** | **0.0** | **7:53** | .... | .... | .... | .... | .... | .... | .... | .... | .... |

• Missed majority of 1998-99 season and entire 1999-2000 season recovering from head injury suffered in practice, January 3, 1999. Signed as a free agent by **Worcester** (AHL), July 17, 2003. Signed as a free agent by **St. Louis**, December 30, 2003. Claimed on waivers by **Nashville** from **St. Louis**, January 30, 2004. Signed as a free agent by **Binghamton** (AHL), August 9, 2007. Signed as a free agent by **Ottawa**, June 30, 2008.

## YANDLE, Keith

(Yan-duhl, KEETH) **PHX.**

Defense. Shoots left. 6'2", 195 lbs. Born, Boston, MA, September 9, 1986. Phoenix's 3rd choice, 105th overall, in 2005 Entry Draft.

| Season | Club | League | GP | G | A | Pts | PIM | PP | SH | GW | S | % | +/- | TF | F% | Min | GP | G | A | Pts | PIM | PP | SH | GW | Min |
|---|---|---|---|---|---|---|---|---|---|---|---|---|---|---|---|---|---|---|---|---|---|---|---|---|---|
| 2004-05 | Cushing | High-MA | 34 | 14 | 40 | 54 | 52 | .... | .... | .... | .... | .... | .... | .... | .... | .... | .... | .... | .... | .... | .... | .... | .... | .... | .... |
| 2005-06 | Moncton Wildcats | QMJHL | 66 | 25 | 59 | 84 | 109 | .... | .... | .... | .... | .... | .... | .... | .... | .... | 21 | 6 | 14 | 20 | 36 | .... | .... | .... | .... |
| **2006-07** | **Phoenix** | **NHL** | **7** | **0** | **2** | **2** | **8** | **0** | **0** | **0** | **10** | **0.0** | **0** | **0** | **0.0** | **20:10** | .... | .... | .... | .... | .... | .... | .... | .... | .... |
| | San Antonio | AHL | 69 | 6 | 27 | 33 | 97 | .... | .... | .... | .... | .... | .... | .... | .... | .... | .... | .... | .... | .... | .... | .... | .... | .... | .... |
| **2007-08** | **Phoenix** | **NHL** | **43** | **5** | **7** | **12** | **14** | **4** | **0** | **0** | **72** | **6.9** | **-12** | **0** | **0.0** | **14:04** | .... | .... | .... | .... | .... | .... | .... | .... | .... |
| | San Antonio | AHL | 30 | 1 | 14 | 15 | 80 | .... | .... | .... | .... | .... | .... | .... | .... | .... | 5 | 0 | 0 | 0 | 8 | .... | .... | .... | .... |
| **2008-09** | **Phoenix** | **NHL** | **69** | **4** | **26** | **30** | **37** | **1** | **0** | **0** | **118** | **3.4** | **-4** | **0** | **0.0** | **16:37** | .... | .... | .... | .... | .... | .... | .... | .... | .... |
| | **NHL Totals** | | **119** | **9** | **35** | **44** | **59** | **5** | **0** | **0** | **200** | **4.5** | | **0** | **0.0** | **15:54** | .... | .... | .... | .... | .... | .... | .... | .... | .... |

QMJHL First All-Star Team (2006) • Canadian Major Junior First All-Star Team (2006) • Canadian Major Junior Defenseman of the Year (2006)

## YELLE, Stephane

(YEHL, STEH-fan)

Center. Shoots left. 6'2", 182 lbs. Born, Ottawa, Ont., May 9, 1974. New Jersey's 9th choice, 186th overall, in 1992 Entry Draft.

| | | | Regular Season | | | | | | | | | | | | | | Playoffs | | | | | | | | |
|---|---|---|---|---|---|---|---|---|---|---|---|---|---|---|---|---|---|---|---|---|---|---|---|---|---|
| Season | Club | League | GP | G | A | Pts | PIM | PP | SH | GW | S | % | +/- | TF | F% | Min | GP | G | A | Pts | PIM | PP | SH | GW | Min |
| 1990-91 | Cumberland | OHA-B | 33 | 20 | 30 | 50 | 16 | .... | .... | .... | .... | .... | .... | .... | .... | .... | .... | .... | .... | .... | .... | .... | .... | .... | .... |
| 1991-92 | Oshawa Generals | OHL | 55 | 12 | 14 | 26 | 20 | .... | .... | .... | .... | .... | .... | .... | .... | .... | 7 | 2 | 0 | 2 | 2 | .... | .... | .... | .... |
| 1992-93 | Oshawa Generals | OHL | 66 | 24 | 50 | 74 | 20 | .... | .... | .... | .... | .... | .... | .... | .... | .... | 10 | 2 | 4 | 6 | 4 | .... | .... | .... | .... |
| 1993-94 | Oshawa Generals | OHL | 66 | 35 | 69 | 104 | 22 | .... | .... | .... | .... | .... | .... | .... | .... | .... | 5 | 1 | 7 | 8 | 2 | .... | .... | .... | .... |
| 1994-95 | Cornwall Aces | AHL | 40 | 18 | 15 | 33 | 22 | .... | .... | .... | .... | .... | .... | .... | .... | .... | 13 | 7 | 7 | 14 | 8 | .... | .... | .... | .... |
| **1995-96 ◆** | **Colorado** | **NHL** | **71** | **13** | **14** | **27** | **30** | **0** | **2** | **1** | **93** | **14.0** | **15** | .... | .... | .... | **22** | **1** | **4** | **5** | **8** | **0** | **1** | **0** | .... |
| **1996-97** | **Colorado** | **NHL** | **79** | **9** | **17** | **26** | **38** | **0** | **1** | **1** | **89** | **10.1** | **1** | .... | .... | .... | **12** | **1** | **6** | **7** | **2** | **0** | **0** | **0** | .... |
| **1997-98** | **Colorado** | **NHL** | **81** | **7** | **15** | **22** | **48** | **0** | **1** | **0** | **93** | **7.5** | **–10** | .... | .... | .... | **7** | **1** | **0** | **1** | **12** | **0** | **0** | **0** | .... |
| **1998-99** | **Colorado** | **NHL** | **72** | **8** | **7** | **15** | **40** | **1** | **0** | **0** | **99** | **8.1** | **–8** | **1201** | **51.2** | **15:15** | **10** | **0** | **1** | **1** | **6** | **0** | **0** | **0** | **15:13** |
| **99-2000** | **Colorado** | **NHL** | **79** | **8** | **14** | **22** | **28** | **0** | **1** | **1** | **90** | **8.9** | **9** | **1294** | **52.2** | **15:51** | **17** | **1** | **2** | **3** | **4** | **0** | **0** | **0** | **15:38** |
| **2000-01 ◆** | **Colorado** | **NHL** | **50** | **4** | **10** | **14** | **20** | **0** | **1** | **0** | **54** | **7.4** | **–3** | **736** | **56.4** | **14:28** | **23** | **1** | **2** | **3** | **8** | **0** | **0** | **1** | **13:52** |
| **2001-02** | **Colorado** | **NHL** | **73** | **5** | **12** | **17** | **48** | **0** | **1** | **1** | **71** | **7.0** | **1** | **1036** | **51.8** | **14:02** | **20** | **0** | **2** | **2** | **14** | **0** | **0** | **0** | **13:26** |
| **2002-03** | **Calgary** | **NHL** | **82** | **10** | **15** | **25** | **50** | **3** | **0** | **3** | **121** | **8.3** | **–10** | **1494** | **53.4** | **18:06** | .... | .... | .... | .... | .... | .... | .... | .... | .... |
| **2003-04** | **Calgary** | **NHL** | **53** | **4** | **13** | **17** | **24** | **1** | **0** | **0** | **76** | **5.3** | **1** | **996** | **56.6** | **15:48** | **23** | **3** | **3** | **6** | **16** | **0** | **1** | **1** | **17:04** |
| 2004-05 | | | DID NOT PLAY | | | | | | | | | | | | | | | | | | | | | | |
| **2005-06** | **Calgary** | **NHL** | **74** | **4** | **14** | **18** | **48** | **1** | **1** | **1** | **93** | **4.3** | **10** | **1072** | **55.4** | **14:27** | **7** | **1** | **0** | **1** | **8** | **0** | **0** | **0** | **15:28** |
| **2006-07** | **Calgary** | **NHL** | **56** | **10** | **14** | **24** | **32** | **1** | **1** | **1** | **55** | **18.2** | **5** | **808** | **50.4** | **14:37** | **6** | **0** | **0** | **0** | **2** | **0** | **0** | **0** | **15:13** |
| **2007-08** | **Calgary** | **NHL** | **74** | **3** | **9** | **12** | **20** | **0** | **1** | **0** | **62** | **4.8** | **–4** | **381** | **49.9** | **11:57** | **7** | **2** | **0** | **2** | **6** | **0** | **0** | **1** | **14:35** |
| **2008-09** | **Boston** | **NHL** | **77** | **7** | **11** | **18** | **32** | **1** | **0** | **2** | **72** | **9.7** | **6** | **792** | **52.0** | **13:16** | **11** | **0** | **1** | **1** | **2** | **0** | **0** | **0** | **12:30** |
| | **NHL Totals** | | **921** | **92** | **165** | **257** | **458** | **8** | **10** | **11** | **1068** | **8.6** | | **9810** | **53.1** | **14:48** | **165** | **11** | **21** | **32** | **88** | **0** | **2** | **3** | **14:49** |

Traded to **Quebec** by **New Jersey** with New Jersey's 11th round choice (Steven Low) in 1994 Entry Draft for Quebec's 11th round choice (Mike Hanson) in 1994 Entry Draft, June 1, 1994. Transferred to **Colorado** after **Quebec** franchise relocated, June 21, 1995. Traded to **Calgary** by **Colorado** with Chris Drury for Derek Morris, Jeff Shantz and Dean McAmmond, October 1, 2002. Signed as a free agent by **Boston**, September 3, 2008.

## YONKMAN, Nolan

(YAWNK-man, NOH-luhn) **NSH.**

Defense. Shoots right. 6'6", 245 lbs. Born, Punnichy, Sask., April 1, 1981. Washington's 5th choice, 37th overall, in 1999 Entry Draft.

| | | | | | | | | | | | | | | | | | | | | | | | | | |
|---|---|---|---|---|---|---|---|---|---|---|---|---|---|---|---|---|---|---|---|---|---|---|---|---|---|
| 1996-97 | Naicam Vikings | SAHA | 64 | 15 | 23 | 38 | 36 | .... | .... | .... | .... | .... | .... | .... | .... | .... | .... | .... | .... | .... | .... | .... | .... | .... | .... |
| | Kelowna Rockets | WHL | 4 | 0 | 0 | 0 | 0 | .... | .... | .... | .... | .... | .... | .... | .... | .... | .... | .... | .... | .... | .... | .... | .... | .... | .... |
| 1997-98 | Kelowna Rockets | WHL | 65 | 0 | 2 | 2 | 36 | .... | .... | .... | .... | .... | .... | .... | .... | .... | 7 | 0 | 0 | 0 | 2 | .... | .... | .... | .... |
| 1998-99 | Kelowna Rockets | WHL | 61 | 1 | 6 | 7 | 129 | .... | .... | .... | .... | .... | .... | .... | .... | .... | 6 | 0 | 0 | 0 | 6 | .... | .... | .... | .... |
| 99-2000 | Kelowna Rockets | WHL | 71 | 5 | 7 | 12 | 153 | .... | .... | .... | .... | .... | .... | .... | .... | .... | 5 | 0 | 0 | 0 | 8 | .... | .... | .... | .... |
| 2000-01 | Kelowna Rockets | WHL | 7 | 0 | 1 | 1 | 19 | .... | .... | .... | .... | .... | .... | .... | .... | .... | .... | .... | .... | .... | .... | .... | .... | .... | .... |
| | Brandon | WHL | 51 | 6 | 10 | 16 | 94 | .... | .... | .... | .... | .... | .... | .... | .... | .... | 6 | 0 | 1 | 1 | 12 | .... | .... | .... | .... |
| **2001-02** | **Washington** | **NHL** | **11** | **1** | **0** | **1** | **4** | **0** | **0** | **0** | **7** | **14.3** | **3** | **0** | **0.0** | **12:44** | .... | .... | .... | .... | .... | .... | .... | .... | .... |
| | Portland Pirates | AHL | 59 | 4 | 3 | 7 | 116 | .... | .... | .... | .... | .... | .... | .... | .... | .... | .... | .... | .... | .... | .... | .... | .... | .... | .... |
| 2002-03 | Portland Pirates | AHL | 24 | 1 | 4 | 5 | 40 | .... | .... | .... | .... | .... | .... | .... | .... | .... | 3 | 0 | 1 | 1 | 2 | .... | .... | .... | .... |
| **2003-04** | **Washington** | **NHL** | **1** | **0** | **0** | **0** | **0** | **0** | **0** | **0** | **0** | **0.0** | **0** | **0** | **0.0** | **5:00** | .... | .... | .... | .... | .... | .... | .... | .... | .... |
| | Portland Pirates | AHL | 4 | 0 | 0 | 0 | 11 | .... | .... | .... | .... | .... | .... | .... | .... | .... | .... | .... | .... | .... | .... | .... | .... | .... | .... |
| 2004-05 | Portland Pirates | AHL | 32 | 0 | 3 | 3 | 68 | .... | .... | .... | .... | .... | .... | .... | .... | .... | .... | .... | .... | .... | .... | .... | .... | .... | .... |
| **2005-06** | **Washington** | **NHL** | **38** | **0** | **7** | **7** | **86** | **0** | **0** | **0** | **14** | **0.0** | **1** | **0** | **0.0** | **8:13** | .... | .... | .... | .... | .... | .... | .... | .... | .... |
| | Hershey Bears | AHL | 6 | 0 | 0 | 0 | 15 | .... | .... | .... | .... | .... | .... | .... | .... | .... | .... | .... | .... | .... | .... | .... | .... | .... | .... |
| 2006-07 | Milwaukee | AHL | 77 | 3 | 10 | 13 | 113 | .... | .... | .... | .... | .... | .... | .... | .... | .... | 4 | 0 | 0 | 0 | 2 | .... | .... | .... | .... |
| 2007-08 | Milwaukee | AHL | 69 | 0 | 7 | 7 | 103 | .... | .... | .... | .... | .... | .... | .... | .... | .... | 6 | 0 | 1 | 1 | 18 | .... | .... | .... | .... |
| 2008-09 | Milwaukee | AHL | 61 | 3 | 7 | 10 | 80 | .... | .... | .... | .... | .... | .... | .... | .... | .... | 11 | 0 | 0 | 0 | 15 | .... | .... | .... | .... |
| | **NHL Totals** | | **50** | **1** | **7** | **8** | **90** | **0** | **0** | **0** | **21** | **4.8** | | **0** | **0.0** | **9:09** | .... | .... | .... | .... | .... | .... | .... | .... | .... |

• Missed majority of 2002-03 season recovering from abdominal injury suffered in training camp, September 25, 2002. • Missed majority of 2003-04 and 2004-05 seasons recovering from knee injury suffered in game vs. Worcester (AHL), October 23, 2003. Signed as a free agent by **Nashville**, July 17, 2006.

## YORK, Mike

(YOHRK, MIGHK)

Left wing. Shoots right. 5'10", 185 lbs. Born, Waterford, MI, January 3, 1978. NY Rangers' 7th choice, 136th overall, in 1997 Entry Draft.

| | | | | | | | | | | | | | | | | | | | | | | | | | |
|---|---|---|---|---|---|---|---|---|---|---|---|---|---|---|---|---|---|---|---|---|---|---|---|---|---|
| 1992-93 | Michigan | MNHL | 50 | 45 | 50 | 95 | .... | .... | .... | .... | .... | .... | .... | .... | .... | .... | .... | .... | .... | .... | .... | .... | .... | .... | .... |
| 1993-94 | Det. Compuware | MNHL | 85 | 136 | 140 | 276 | .... | .... | .... | .... | .... | .... | .... | .... | .... | .... | .... | .... | .... | .... | .... | .... | .... | .... | .... |
| 1994-95 | Thornhill Islanders | MTJHL | 49 | 39 | 54 | *93 | 44 | .... | .... | .... | .... | .... | .... | .... | .... | .... | 11 | 7 | 6 | 13 | 0 | .... | .... | .... | .... |
| 1995-96 | Michigan State | CCHA | 39 | 12 | 27 | 39 | 20 | .... | .... | .... | .... | .... | .... | .... | .... | .... | .... | .... | .... | .... | .... | .... | .... | .... | .... |
| 1996-97 | Michigan State | CCHA | 37 | 18 | 29 | 47 | 42 | .... | .... | .... | .... | .... | .... | .... | .... | .... | .... | .... | .... | .... | .... | .... | .... | .... | .... |
| 1997-98 | Michigan State | CCHA | 40 | 27 | 34 | 61 | 38 | .... | .... | .... | .... | .... | .... | .... | .... | .... | .... | .... | .... | .... | .... | .... | .... | .... | .... |
| 1998-99 | Michigan State | CCHA | 42 | 22 | 32 | *54 | 41 | .... | .... | .... | .... | .... | .... | .... | .... | .... | .... | .... | .... | .... | .... | .... | .... | .... | .... |
| | Hartford | AHL | 3 | 2 | 2 | 4 | 0 | .... | .... | .... | .... | .... | .... | .... | .... | .... | 6 | 3 | 1 | 4 | 0 | .... | .... | .... | .... |
| **99-2000** | **NY Rangers** | **NHL** | **82** | **26** | **24** | **50** | **18** | **8** | **0** | **4** | **177** | **14.7** | **–17** | **1131** | **48.1** | **1:35** | .... | .... | .... | .... | .... | .... | .... | .... | .... |
| **2000-01** | **NY Rangers** | **NHL** | **79** | **14** | **17** | **31** | **20** | **3** | **2** | **4** | **171** | **8.2** | **1** | **1098** | **46.9** | **17:45** | .... | .... | .... | .... | .... | .... | .... | .... | .... |
| **2001-02** | **NY Rangers** | **NHL** | **69** | **18** | **39** | **57** | **16** | **2** | **0** | **5** | **188** | **9.6** | **8** | **267** | **43.1** | **20:24** | .... | .... | .... | .... | .... | .... | .... | .... | .... |
| | United States | Olympics | 6 | 0 | 1 | 1 | 0 | .... | .... | .... | .... | .... | .... | .... | .... | .... | .... | .... | .... | .... | .... | .... | .... | .... | .... |
| | **Edmonton** | **NHL** | **12** | **2** | **2** | **4** | **0** | **1** | **0** | **1** | **30** | **6.7** | **–1** | **100** | **56.0** | **16:35** | .... | .... | .... | .... | .... | .... | .... | .... | .... |
| **2002-03** | **Edmonton** | **NHL** | **71** | **22** | **29** | **51** | **10** | **7** | **2** | **4** | **177** | **12.4** | **–8** | **390** | **43.9** | **19:04** | **6** | **0** | **2** | **2** | **2** | **0** | **0** | **0** | **14:20** |
| **2003-04** | **Edmonton** | **NHL** | **61** | **16** | **26** | **42** | **15** | **1** | **2** | **0** | **144** | **11.1** | **18** | **656** | **45.9** | **19:17** | .... | .... | .... | .... | .... | .... | .... | .... | .... |
| 2004-05 | Iserlohn Roosters | Germany | 52 | 16 | 46 | 62 | 77 | .... | .... | .... | .... | .... | .... | .... | .... | .... | .... | .... | .... | .... | .... | .... | .... | .... | .... |
| **2005-06** | **NY Islanders** | **NHL** | **75** | **13** | **39** | **52** | **30** | **4** | **1** | **2** | **146** | **8.9** | **–9** | **1289** | **46.1** | **19:55** | .... | .... | .... | .... | .... | .... | .... | .... | .... |
| **2006-07** | **NY Islanders** | **NHL** | **32** | **6** | **7** | **13** | **14** | **2** | **0** | **1** | **46** | **13.0** | **–9** | **432** | **45.6** | **14:47** | .... | .... | .... | .... | .... | .... | .... | .... | .... |
| | **Philadelphia** | **NHL** | **34** | **4** | **4** | **8** | **8** | **0** | **0** | **1** | **41** | **9.8** | **–9** | **272** | **47.8** | **10:22** | .... | .... | .... | .... | .... | .... | .... | .... | .... |
| **2007-08** | **Phoenix** | **NHL** | **63** | **6** | **8** | **14** | **4** | **4** | **0** | **1** | **85** | **7.1** | **–8** | **205** | **50.7** | **11:59** | .... | .... | .... | .... | .... | .... | .... | .... | .... |
| **2008-09** | **Columbus** | **NHL** | **1** | **0** | **0** | **0** | **0** | **0** | **0** | **0** | **1** | **0.0** | **0** | **0** | **0.0** | **13:15** | .... | .... | .... | .... | .... | .... | .... | .... | .... |
| | Syracuse Crunch | AHL | 75 | 11 | 47 | 58 | 30 | .... | .... | .... | .... | .... | .... | .... | .... | .... | .... | .... | .... | .... | .... | .... | .... | .... | .... |
| | **NHL Totals** | | **579** | **127** | **195** | **322** | **135** | **32** | **7** | **23** | **1206** | **10.5** | | **5840** | **46.7** | **15:07** | **6** | **0** | **2** | **2** | **2** | **0** | **0** | **0** | **14:20** |

CCHA Second All-Star Team (1998) • NCAA West First All-American Team (1998, 1999) • CCHA First All-Star Team (1999) • CCHA Player of the Year (1999) • NHL All-Rookie Team (2000)

Played in NHL All-Star Game (2002)

Traded to **Edmonton** by **NY Rangers** with NY Rangers' 4th round choice (Ivan Koltsov) in 2002 Entry Draft for Tom Poti and Rem Murray, March 19, 2002. Signed as a free agent by **Iserlohn** (Germany), February 25, 2005. Traded to **NY Islanders** by **Edmonton** with Edmonton's 4th round choice (later traded to Colorado - Colorado selected Kevin Montgomery) in 2006 Entry Draft for Michael Peca, August 3, 2005. Traded to **Philadelphia** by **NY Islanders** for Randy Robitaille and Philadelphia's 5th round choice (Matthew Martin) in 2008 Entry Draft, December 20, 2006. Signed as a free agent by **Phoenix**, July 9, 2007. Signed as a free agent by **Columbus**, July 25, 2008.

## YOUNG, Bryan

(YUHNG, BRIGH-uhn)

Defense. Shoots left. 6'1", 191 lbs. Born, Kitchener, Ont., August 6, 1986. Edmonton's 6th choice, 146th overall, in 2004 Entry Draft.

| | | | | | | | | | | | | | | | | | | | | | | | | | |
|---|---|---|---|---|---|---|---|---|---|---|---|---|---|---|---|---|---|---|---|---|---|---|---|---|---|
| 2002-03 | Lindsay Muskies | OPJHL | 47 | 1 | 9 | 10 | 56 | .... | .... | .... | .... | .... | .... | .... | .... | .... | .... | .... | .... | .... | .... | .... | .... | .... | .... |
| | Peterborough | OHL | 2 | 0 | 0 | 0 | 0 | .... | .... | .... | .... | .... | .... | .... | .... | .... | .... | .... | .... | .... | .... | .... | .... | .... | .... |
| 2003-04 | Peterborough | OHL | 60 | 0 | 8 | 8 | 63 | .... | .... | .... | .... | .... | .... | .... | .... | .... | .... | .... | .... | .... | .... | .... | .... | .... | .... |
| 2004-05 | Peterborough | OHL | 60 | 1 | 11 | 12 | 44 | .... | .... | .... | .... | .... | .... | .... | .... | .... | 14 | 0 | 1 | 1 | 10 | .... | .... | .... | .... |
| 2005-06 | Peterborough | OHL | 64 | 0 | 10 | 10 | 113 | .... | .... | .... | .... | .... | .... | .... | .... | .... | 19 | 0 | 0 | 0 | 37 | .... | .... | .... | .... |
| **2006-07** | **Edmonton** | **NHL** | **15** | **0** | **0** | **0** | **10** | **0** | **0** | **0** | **2** | **0.0** | **–8** | **0** | **0.0** | **10:06** | .... | .... | .... | .... | .... | .... | .... | .... | .... |
| | Milwaukee | AHL | 22 | 0 | 0 | 0 | 6 | .... | .... | .... | .... | .... | .... | .... | .... | .... | .... | .... | .... | .... | .... | .... | .... | .... | .... |
| | Stockton Thunder | ECHL | 17 | 0 | 4 | 4 | 24 | .... | .... | .... | .... | .... | .... | .... | .... | .... | .... | .... | .... | .... | .... | .... | .... | .... | .... |
| | Wilkes-Barre | AHL | 10 | 0 | 1 | 1 | 2 | .... | .... | .... | .... | .... | .... | .... | .... | .... | 4 | 0 | 1 | 1 | 2 | .... | .... | .... | .... |
| **2007-08** | **Edmonton** | **NHL** | **2** | **0** | **0** | **0** | **0** | **0** | **0** | **0** | **0** | **0.0** | **–1** | **0** | **0.0** | **2:08** | .... | .... | .... | .... | .... | .... | .... | .... | .... |
| | Springfield | AHL | 74 | 0 | 7 | 7 | 62 | .... | .... | .... | .... | .... | .... | .... | .... | .... | .... | .... | .... | .... | .... | .... | .... | .... | .... |
| 2008-09 | Springfield | AHL | 63 | 3 | 7 | 10 | 64 | .... | .... | .... | .... | .... | .... | .... | .... | .... | .... | .... | .... | .... | .... | .... | .... | .... | .... |
| | **NHL Totals** | | **17** | **0** | **0** | **0** | **10** | **0** | **0** | **0** | **2** | **0.0** | | **0** | **0.0** | **9:10** | .... | .... | .... | .... | .... | .... | .... | .... | .... |

## ZAJAC, Travis
(ZAY-jak, TRA-vihs) **N.J.**

Center. Shoots right. 6'3", 195 lbs. Born, Winnipeg, Man., May 13, 1985. New Jersey's 1st choice, 20th overall, in 2004 Entry Draft.

| Season | Club | League | GP | G | A | Pts | PIM | PP | SH | GW | S | % | +/- | TF | F% | Min | GP | G | A | Pts | PIM | PP | SH | GW | Min |
|---|---|---|---|---|---|---|---|---|---|---|---|---|---|---|---|---|---|---|---|---|---|---|---|---|---|
| | | | Regular Season | | | | | | | | | | | | | | Playoffs | | | | | | | | |
| 2002-03 | Salmon Arm | BCHL | 59 | 16 | 36 | 52 | 27 | .... | .... | .... | .... | .... | .... | .... | .... | .... | 11 | 2 | 4 | 6 | 6 | .... | .... | .... | .... |
| 2003-04 | Salmon Arm | BCHL | 59 | 43 | 69 | 112 | 110 | .... | .... | .... | .... | .... | .... | .... | .... | .... | 14 | 10 | 13 | 23 | 10 | .... | .... | .... | .... |
| 2004-05 | North Dakota | WCHA | 45 | 20 | 19 | 39 | 16 | .... | .... | .... | .... | .... | .... | .... | .... | .... | .... | .... | .... | .... | .... | .... | .... | .... | .... |
| 2005-06 | North Dakota | WCHA | 46 | 18 | 29 | 47 | 20 | .... | .... | .... | .... | .... | .... | .... | .... | .... | .... | .... | .... | .... | .... | .... | .... | .... | .... |
| | Albany River Rats | AHL | 2 | 0 | 1 | 1 | 2 | .... | .... | .... | .... | .... | .... | .... | .... | .... | .... | .... | .... | .... | .... | .... | .... | .... | .... |
| **2006-07** | **New Jersey** | **NHL** | **80** | **17** | **25** | **42** | **16** | **6** | **0** | **2** | **134** | **12.7** | **1** | **904** | **46.9** | **16:03** | **11** | **1** | **4** | **5** | **4** | **0** | **0** | **0** | **16:22** |
| **2007-08** | **New Jersey** | **NHL** | **82** | **14** | **20** | **34** | **31** | **5** | **0** | **1** | **155** | **9.0** | **-11** | **1032** | **51.2** | **16:44** | **5** | **0** | **1** | **1** | **4** | **0** | **0** | **0** | **13:35** |
| **2008-09** | **New Jersey** | **NHL** | **82** | **20** | **42** | **62** | **29** | **5** | **1** | **2** | **185** | **10.8** | **33** | **1287** | **53.1** | **18:39** | **7** | **1** | **3** | **4** | **6** | **0** | **0** | **1** | **17:51** |
| | **NHL Totals** | | **244** | **51** | **87** | **138** | **76** | **16** | **1** | **5** | **474** | **10.8** | | **3223** | **50.7** | **17:09** | **23** | **2** | **8** | **10** | **14** | **0** | **0** | **1** | **16:13** |

WCHA All-Rookie Team (2005) • NCAA Championship All-Tournament Team (2005)

## ZANON, Greg
(ZA-nuhn, GREHG) **MIN.**

Defense. Shoots left. 5'11", 201 lbs. Born, Burnaby, B.C., June 5, 1980. Ottawa's 6th choice, 156th overall, in 2000 Entry Draft.

| Season | Club | League | GP | G | A | Pts | PIM | PP | SH | GW | S | % | +/- | TF | F% | Min | GP | G | A | Pts | PIM | PP | SH | GW | Min |
|---|---|---|---|---|---|---|---|---|---|---|---|---|---|---|---|---|---|---|---|---|---|---|---|---|---|
| 1995-96 | Burnaby Beavers | Minor-BC | 49 | 16 | 27 | 43 | 142 | .... | .... | .... | .... | .... | .... | .... | .... | .... | .... | .... | .... | .... | .... | .... | .... | .... | .... |
| 1996-97 | Victoria Salsa | BCHL | 53 | 4 | 13 | 17 | 124 | .... | .... | .... | .... | .... | .... | .... | .... | .... | .... | .... | .... | .... | .... | .... | .... | .... | .... |
| 1997-98 | Victoria Salsa | BCHL | 59 | 11 | 21 | 32 | 108 | .... | .... | .... | .... | .... | .... | .... | .... | .... | 7 | 0 | 2 | 2 | 10 | .... | .... | .... | .... |
| 1998-99 | South Surrey | BCHL | 59 | 17 | 54 | 71 | 154 | .... | .... | .... | .... | .... | .... | .... | .... | .... | .... | .... | .... | .... | .... | .... | .... | .... | .... |
| 99-2000 | Nebraska-Omaha | CCHA | 42 | 3 | 26 | 29 | 56 | .... | .... | .... | .... | .... | .... | .... | .... | .... | .... | .... | .... | .... | .... | .... | .... | .... | .... |
| 2000-01 | Nebraska-Omaha | CCHA | 39 | 12 | 16 | 28 | 64 | .... | .... | .... | .... | .... | .... | .... | .... | .... | .... | .... | .... | .... | .... | .... | .... | .... | .... |
| 2001-02 | Nebraska-Omaha | CCHA | 41 | 9 | 16 | 25 | 54 | .... | .... | .... | .... | .... | .... | .... | .... | .... | .... | .... | .... | .... | .... | .... | .... | .... | .... |
| 2002-03 | Nebraska-Omaha | CCHA | 32 | 6 | 19 | 25 | 44 | .... | .... | .... | .... | .... | .... | .... | .... | .... | .... | .... | .... | .... | .... | .... | .... | .... | .... |
| 2003-04 | Milwaukee | AHL | 62 | 4 | 12 | 16 | 59 | .... | .... | .... | .... | .... | .... | .... | .... | .... | 22 | 2 | 6 | 8 | 31 | .... | .... | .... | .... |
| 2004-05 | Milwaukee | AHL | 80 | 2 | 17 | 19 | 59 | .... | .... | .... | .... | .... | .... | .... | .... | .... | 7 | 0 | 1 | 1 | 10 | .... | .... | .... | .... |
| **2005-06** | **Nashville** | **NHL** | **4** | **0** | **2** | **2** | **6** | **0** | **0** | **0** | **3** | **0.0** | **0** | **0** | **0.0** | **17:19** | .... | .... | .... | .... | .... | .... | .... | .... | .... |
| | Milwaukee | AHL | 71 | 8 | 27 | 35 | 55 | .... | .... | .... | .... | .... | .... | .... | .... | .... | 21 | 1 | 7 | 8 | 24 | .... | .... | .... | .... |
| **2006-07** | **Nashville** | **NHL** | **66** | **3** | **5** | **8** | **32** | **0** | **0** | **0** | **43** | **7.0** | **16** | **0** | **0.0** | **17:20** | **5** | **0** | **2** | **2** | **2** | **0** | **0** | **0** | **20:44** |
| | Milwaukee | AHL | 2 | 0 | 2 | 2 | 0 | .... | .... | .... | .... | .... | .... | .... | .... | .... | .... | .... | .... | .... | .... | .... | .... | .... | .... |
| **2007-08** | **Nashville** | **NHL** | **78** | **0** | **5** | **5** | **24** | **0** | **0** | **0** | **38** | **0.0** | **-5** | **0** | **0.0** | **18:28** | **6** | **0** | **2** | **2** | **4** | **0** | **0** | **0** | **18:45** |
| **2008-09** | **Nashville** | **NHL** | **82** | **4** | **7** | **11** | **38** | **0** | **0** | **1** | **54** | **7.4** | **8** | **0** | **0.0** | **20:51** | .... | .... | .... | .... | .... | .... | .... | .... | .... |
| | **NHL Totals** | | **230** | **7** | **19** | **26** | **100** | **0** | **0** | **1** | **138** | **5.1** | | **0** | **0.0** | **18:58** | **11** | **0** | **4** | **4** | **6** | **0** | **0** | **0** | **19:39** |

CCHA First All-Star Team (2001) • NCAA West Second All-American Team (2001, 2002) • CCHA Second All-Star Team (2002)

Signed as a free agent by **Nashville**, July 9, 2004. Signed as a free agent by **Minnesota**, July 1, 2009.

## ZEDNIK, Richard
(ZEHD-nihk, RIH-chuhrd)

Right wing. Shoots left. 6', 200 lbs. Born, Banska Bystrica, Czech., January 6, 1976. Washington's 10th choice, 249th overall, in 1994 Entry Draft.

| Season | Club | League | GP | G | A | Pts | PIM | PP | SH | GW | S | % | +/- | TF | F% | Min | GP | G | A | Pts | PIM | PP | SH | GW | Min |
|---|---|---|---|---|---|---|---|---|---|---|---|---|---|---|---|---|---|---|---|---|---|---|---|---|---|
| 1993-94 | B. Bystrica | Slovak-2 | 25 | 3 | 6 | 9 | .... | .... | .... | .... | .... | .... | .... | .... | .... | .... | .... | .... | .... | .... | .... | .... | .... | .... | .... |
| 1994-95 | Portland | WHL | 65 | 35 | 51 | 86 | 89 | .... | .... | .... | .... | .... | .... | .... | .... | .... | 9 | 5 | 5 | 10 | 20 | .... | .... | .... | .... |
| **1995-96** | Portland | WHL | 61 | 44 | 37 | 81 | 154 | .... | .... | .... | .... | .... | .... | .... | .... | .... | 7 | 8 | 4 | 12 | 23 | .... | .... | .... | .... |
| | **Washington** | **NHL** | **1** | **0** | **0** | **0** | **0** | **0** | **0** | **0** | **0** | **0.0** | **0** | .... | .... | .... | .... | .... | .... | .... | .... | .... | .... | .... | .... |
| | Portland Pirates | AHL | 1 | 1 | 1 | 2 | 0 | .... | .... | .... | .... | .... | .... | .... | .... | .... | 21 | 4 | 5 | 9 | 26 | .... | .... | .... | .... |
| **1996-97** | **Washington** | **NHL** | **11** | **2** | **1** | **3** | **4** | **1** | **0** | **0** | **21** | **9.5** | **-5** | .... | .... | .... | .... | .... | .... | .... | .... | .... | .... | .... | .... |
| | Portland Pirates | AHL | 56 | 15 | 20 | 35 | 70 | .... | .... | .... | .... | .... | .... | .... | .... | .... | 5 | 1 | 0 | 1 | 6 | .... | .... | .... | .... |
| **1997-98** | **Washington** | **NHL** | **65** | **17** | **9** | **26** | **28** | **2** | **0** | **2** | **148** | **11.5** | **-2** | .... | .... | .... | **17** | **7** | **3** | **10** | **16** | **2** | **0** | **0** | .... |
| **1998-99** | **Washington** | **NHL** | **63** | **9** | **8** | **17** | **50** | **1** | **0** | **2** | **115** | **7.8** | **-6** | **2** | **0.0** | **15:08** | .... | .... | .... | .... | .... | .... | .... | .... | .... |
| **99-2000** | **Washington** | **NHL** | **69** | **19** | **16** | **35** | **54** | **1** | **0** | **2** | **179** | **10.6** | **6** | **1** | **100.0** | **15:34** | **5** | **0** | **0** | **0** | **5** | **0** | **0** | **0** | **16:57** |
| **2000-01** | **Washington** | **NHL** | **62** | **16** | **19** | **35** | **61** | **4** | **0** | **3** | **155** | **10.3** | **-2** | **1** | **0.0** | **15:32** | .... | .... | .... | .... | .... | .... | .... | .... | .... |
| | **Montreal** | **NHL** | **12** | **3** | **6** | **9** | **10** | **1** | **0** | **0** | **23** | **13.0** | **-2** | **0** | **0.0** | **18:29** | .... | .... | .... | .... | .... | .... | .... | .... | .... |
| **2001-02** | **Montreal** | **NHL** | **82** | **22** | **22** | **44** | **59** | **4** | **0** | **3** | **249** | **8.8** | **-3** | **10** | **30.0** | **17:39** | **4** | **4** | **4** | **8** | **6** | **2** | **0** | **0** | **21:19** |
| **2002-03** | **Montreal** | **NHL** | **80** | **31** | **19** | **50** | **79** | **9** | **0** | **2** | **250** | **12.4** | **4** | **10** | **30.0** | **18:25** | .... | .... | .... | .... | .... | .... | .... | .... | .... |
| **2003-04** | **Montreal** | **NHL** | **81** | **26** | **24** | **50** | **63** | **7** | **0** | **9** | **218** | **11.9** | **5** | **6** | **50.0** | **17:30** | **11** | **3** | **3** | **6** | **2** | **0** | **0** | **1** | **18:52** |
| 2004-05 | HKm Zvolen | Slovakia | 36 | 15 | 19 | 34 | 56 | .... | .... | .... | .... | .... | .... | .... | .... | .... | 17 | 9 | 10 | 19 | 12 | .... | .... | .... | .... |
| **2005-06** | **Montreal** | **NHL** | **67** | **16** | **14** | **30** | **48** | **6** | **0** | **4** | **161** | **9.9** | **-2** | **6** | **16.7** | **15:46** | **6** | **2** | **0** | **2** | **4** | **1** | **0** | **0** | **15:13** |
| | Slovakia | Olympics | 6 | 1 | 0 | 1 | 12 | .... | .... | .... | .... | .... | .... | .... | .... | .... | .... | .... | .... | .... | .... | .... | .... | .... | .... |
| **2006-07** | **Washington** | **NHL** | **32** | **6** | **12** | **18** | **16** | **1** | **0** | **1** | **68** | **8.8** | **-4** | **3** | **33.3** | **15:42** | .... | .... | .... | .... | .... | .... | .... | .... | .... |
| | **NY Islanders** | **NHL** | **10** | **1** | **2** | **3** | **2** | **0** | **0** | **0** | **15** | **6.7** | **-2** | **1** | **0.0** | **12:51** | **5** | **0** | **0** | **0** | **8** | **0** | **0** | **0** | **10:45** |
| **2007-08** | **Florida** | **NHL** | **54** | **15** | **11** | **26** | **43** | **6** | **0** | **5** | **140** | **10.7** | **-5** | **2** | **0.0** | **17:35** | .... | .... | .... | .... | .... | .... | .... | .... | .... |
| **2008-09** | **Florida** | **NHL** | **70** | **17** | **16** | **33** | **46** | **3** | **0** | **4** | **153** | **11.1** | **2** | **1** | **0.0** | **15:35** | .... | .... | .... | .... | .... | .... | .... | .... | .... |
| | **NHL Totals** | | **745** | **200** | **179** | **379** | **563** | **46** | **0** | **37** | **1895** | **10.6** | | **43** | **27.9** | **16:34** | **48** | **16** | **10** | **26** | **41** | **5** | **0** | **1** | **16:51** |

WHL West Second All-Star Team (1996)

Traded to **Montreal** by **Washington** with Jan Bulis and Washington's 1st round choice (Alexander Perezhogin) in 2001 Entry Draft for Trevor Linden, Dainius Zubrus and New Jersey's 2nd round choice (previously acquired, later traded to Tampa Bay – Tampa Bay selected Andreas Holmqvist) in 2001 Entry Draft, March 13, 2001. Signed as a free agent by **Zvolen** (Slovakia), October 7, 2004. Traded to **Washington** by **Montreal** for Wahington's 3rd round choice (Olivier Fortier) in 2007 Entry Draft, July 12, 2006. Traded to **NY Islanders** by **Washington** for NY Islanders' 2nd round choice (Theo Ruth) in 2007 Entry Draft, February 26, 2007. Signed as a free agent by **Florida**, July 1, 2007. Signed as a free agent by **Lokomotiv** (KHL), April 30, 2009.

## ZEILER, John
(ZIGH-luhr, JAHN) **L.A.**

Right wing. Shoots right. 6', 204 lbs. Born, Jefferson Hills, PA, November 21, 1982. Phoenix's 7th choice, 132nd overall, in 2002 Entry Draft.

| Season | Club | League | GP | G | A | Pts | PIM | PP | SH | GW | S | % | +/- | TF | F% | Min | GP | G | A | Pts | PIM | PP | SH | GW | Min |
|---|---|---|---|---|---|---|---|---|---|---|---|---|---|---|---|---|---|---|---|---|---|---|---|---|---|
| 99-2000 | Pittsburgh | PAHA | 27 | 17 | 15 | 32 | 94 | .... | .... | .... | .... | .... | .... | .... | .... | .... | .... | .... | .... | .... | .... | .... | .... | .... | .... |
| 2000-01 | Sioux City | USHL | 56 | 8 | 20 | 28 | 45 | .... | .... | .... | .... | .... | .... | .... | .... | .... | 2 | 0 | 0 | 0 | 26 | .... | .... | .... | .... |
| 2001-02 | Sioux City | USHL | 60 | 23 | 27 | 50 | 116 | .... | .... | .... | .... | .... | .... | .... | .... | .... | 12 | 2 | 3 | 5 | 25 | .... | .... | .... | .... |
| 2002-03 | St. Lawrence | ECAC | 37 | 10 | 17 | 27 | 28 | .... | .... | .... | .... | .... | .... | .... | .... | .... | .... | .... | .... | .... | .... | .... | .... | .... | .... |
| 2003-04 | St. Lawrence | ECAC | 41 | 8 | *28 | 36 | 42 | .... | .... | .... | .... | .... | .... | .... | .... | .... | .... | .... | .... | .... | .... | .... | .... | .... | .... |
| 2004-05 | St. Lawrence | ECAC | 38 | 9 | 23 | 32 | 42 | .... | .... | .... | .... | .... | .... | .... | .... | .... | .... | .... | .... | .... | .... | .... | .... | .... | .... |
| 2005-06 | St. Lawrence | ECAC | 28 | 13 | 15 | 28 | 28 | .... | .... | .... | .... | .... | .... | .... | .... | .... | .... | .... | .... | .... | .... | .... | .... | .... | .... |
| | San Antonio | AHL | 8 | 0 | 1 | 1 | 10 | .... | .... | .... | .... | .... | .... | .... | .... | .... | .... | .... | .... | .... | .... | .... | .... | .... | .... |
| | Lubbock | CHL | 4 | 2 | 0 | 2 | 16 | .... | .... | .... | .... | .... | .... | .... | .... | .... | .... | .... | .... | .... | .... | .... | .... | .... | .... |
| **2006-07** | Manchester | AHL | 56 | 12 | 16 | 28 | 70 | .... | .... | .... | .... | .... | .... | .... | .... | .... | 16 | 3 | 2 | 5 | 14 | .... | .... | .... | .... |
| | **Los Angeles** | **NHL** | **23** | **1** | **2** | **3** | **22** | **0** | **0** | **0** | **12** | **8.3** | **-2** | **22** | **40.9** | **8:36** | .... | .... | .... | .... | .... | .... | .... | .... | .... |
| **2007-08** | **Los Angeles** | **NHL** | **36** | **0** | **1** | **1** | **23** | **0** | **0** | **0** | **18** | **0.0** | **-6** | **31** | **38.7** | **8:29** | .... | .... | .... | .... | .... | .... | .... | .... | .... |
| | Manchester | AHL | 45 | 6 | 5 | 11 | 40 | .... | .... | .... | .... | .... | .... | .... | .... | .... | 4 | 0 | 2 | 2 | 8 | .... | .... | .... | .... |
| **2008-09** | **Los Angeles** | **NHL** | **27** | **0** | **1** | **1** | **42** | **0** | **0** | **0** | **3** | **0.0** | **-2** | **5** | **60.0** | **6:33** | .... | .... | .... | .... | .... | .... | .... | .... | .... |
| | Manchester | AHL | 2 | 0 | 1 | 1 | 4 | .... | .... | .... | .... | .... | .... | .... | .... | .... | .... | .... | .... | .... | .... | .... | .... | .... | .... |
| | **NHL Totals** | | **86** | **1** | **4** | **5** | **87** | **0** | **0** | **0** | **33** | **3.0** | | **58** | **41.4** | **7:54** | .... | .... | .... | .... | .... | .... | .... | .... | .... |

ECAC All-Rookie Team (2003)

Signed as a free agent by **San Antonio** (AHL), March 18, 2006. Signed as a free agent by **Los Angeles**, February 17, 2007. • Missed majority of 2008-09 season recovering from pre-season groin injury and serving as a healthy reserve.

## ZETTERBERG, Henrik
(ZEH-tuhr-buhrg, HEHN-rihk) **DET.**

Left wing. Shoots left. 5'11", 195 lbs. Born, Njurunda, Sweden, October 9, 1980. Detroit's 4th choice, 210th overall, in 1999 Entry Draft.

| Season | Club | League | GP | G | A | Pts | PIM | PP | SH | GW | S | % | +/- | TF | F% | Min | GP | G | A | Pts | PIM | PP | SH | GW | Min |
|---|---|---|---|---|---|---|---|---|---|---|---|---|---|---|---|---|---|---|---|---|---|---|---|---|---|
| 1997-98 | Timra IK Jr. | Swe-Jr. | 18 | 9 | 5 | 14 | 4 | .... | .... | .... | .... | .... | .... | .... | .... | .... | .... | .... | .... | .... | .... | .... | .... | .... | .... |
| | Timra IK | Sweden-2 | 16 | 1 | 2 | 3 | 4 | .... | .... | .... | .... | .... | .... | .... | .... | .... | 4 | 0 | 1 | 1 | 0 | .... | .... | .... | .... |
| 1998-99 | Timra IK | Sweden-2 | 37 | 15 | 13 | 28 | 2 | .... | .... | .... | .... | .... | .... | .... | .... | .... | 4 | 2 | 1 | 3 | 2 | .... | .... | .... | .... |
| 99-2000 | Timra IK | Sweden-2 | 32 | 20 | 14 | 34 | 20 | .... | .... | .... | .... | .... | .... | .... | .... | .... | 10 | 10 | 4 | 14 | 4 | .... | .... | .... | .... |
| 2000-01 | Timra IK | Sweden | 47 | 15 | 31 | 46 | 24 | .... | .... | .... | .... | .... | .... | .... | .... | .... | .... | .... | .... | .... | .... | .... | .... | .... | .... |
| 2001-02 | Timra IK | Sweden | 48 | 10 | 22 | 32 | 20 | .... | .... | .... | .... | .... | .... | .... | .... | .... | .... | .... | .... | .... | .... | .... | .... | .... | .... |
| | Sweden | Olympics | 4 | 0 | 1 | 1 | 0 | .... | .... | .... | .... | .... | .... | .... | .... | .... | .... | .... | .... | .... | .... | .... | .... | .... | .... |
| **2002-03** | **Detroit** | **NHL** | **79** | **22** | **22** | **44** | **8** | **5** | **1** | **4** | **135** | **16.3** | **6** | **401** | **46.1** | **16:19** | **4** | **1** | **0** | **1** | **0** | **0** | **0** | **0** | **18:19** |
| **2003-04** | **Detroit** | **NHL** | **61** | **15** | **28** | **43** | **14** | **7** | **1** | **2** | **137** | **10.9** | **15** | **627** | **45.6** | **18:15** | **12** | **2** | **2** | **4** | **4** | **0** | **0** | **0** | **17:17** |
| 2004-05 | Timra IK | Sweden | 50 | 19 | 31 | *50 | 24 | .... | .... | .... | .... | .... | .... | .... | .... | .... | 7 | 6 | 2 | 8 | 2 | .... | .... | .... | .... |
| **2005-06** | **Detroit** | **NHL** | **77** | **39** | **46** | **85** | **30** | **17** | **1** | **9** | **270** | **14.4** | **29** | **583** | **50.3** | **18:57** | **6** | **6** | **0** | **6** | **2** | **4** | **0** | **0** | **21:43** |
| | Sweden | Olympics | 8 | 3 | 3 | 6 | 0 | .... | .... | .... | .... | .... | .... | .... | .... | .... | .... | .... | .... | .... | .... | .... | .... | .... | .... |
| **2006-07** | **Detroit** | **NHL** | **63** | **33** | **35** | **68** | **36** | **11** | **1** | **10** | **224** | **14.7** | **26** | **888** | **52.5** | **20:50** | **18** | **6** | **8** | **14** | **12** | **3** | **0** | **1** | **22:45** |

| Season | Club | League | GP | G | A | Pts | PIM | PP | SH | GW | S | % | +/- | TF | F% | Min | Playoffs GP | G | A | Pts | PIM | PP | SH | GW | Min |
|---|---|---|---|---|---|---|---|---|---|---|---|---|---|---|---|---|---|---|---|---|---|---|---|---|---|
| 2007-08♦ | Detroit | NHL | 75 | 43 | 49 | 92 | 34 | 16 | 1 | 7 | 358 | 12.0 | 30 | 1210 | 55.0 | 22:04 | 22 | *13 | 14 | *27 | 16 | 4 | 2 | 4 | 22:36 |
| 2008-09 | Detroit | NHL | 77 | 31 | 42 | 73 | 36 | 12 | 2 | 5 | 309 | 10.0 | 13 | 1189 | 53.3 | 19:53 | 23 | 11 | 13 | 24 | 13 | 4 | 0 | 0 | 22:10 |
| | NHL Totals | | 432 | 183 | 222 | 405 | 158 | 68 | 7 | 37 | 1433 | 12.8 | | 4898 | 51.7 | 19:21 | 85 | 39 | 37 | 76 | 47 | 15 | 2 | 5 | 21:30 |

Swedish Elite League Rookie of the Year (2001) • NHL All-Rookie Team (2003) • NHL Second All-Star Team (2008) • Conn Smythe Trophy (2008)
Signed as a free agent by **Timra** (Sweden), September 20, 2004.

## ZHERDEV, Nikolai
(ZHAIR-dehv, NIH-koh-ligh)

Wing. Shoots right. 6'2", 203 lbs. Born, Kiev, USSR, November 5, 1984. Columbus' 1st choice, 4th overall, in 2003 Entry Draft.

| Season | Club | League | GP | G | A | Pts | PIM | PP | SH | GW | S | % | +/- | TF | F% | Min | Playoffs GP | G | A | Pts | PIM | PP | SH | GW | Min |
|---|---|---|---|---|---|---|---|---|---|---|---|---|---|---|---|---|---|---|---|---|---|---|---|---|---|
| 99-2000 | Elektrostal 2 | Russia-3 | 21 | 10 | 7 | 17 | 26 | .... | .... | .... | .... | .... | .... | .... | .... | .... | 7 | 0 | 0 | 0 | 0 | .... | .... | .... | .... |
| 2000-01 | Elektrostal | Russia-2 | 18 | 5 | 8 | 13 | 12 | .... | .... | .... | .... | .... | .... | .... | .... | .... | .... | .... | .... | .... | .... | .... | .... | .... | .... |
| | Russia | Exhib. | 17 | 10 | 11 | 21 | 17 | .... | .... | .... | .... | .... | .... | .... | .... | .... | .... | .... | .... | .... | .... | .... | .... | .... | .... |
| 2001-02 | Elektrostal | Russia-2 | 53 | 13 | 15 | 28 | 62 | .... | .... | .... | .... | .... | .... | .... | .... | .... | .... | .... | .... | .... | .... | .... | .... | .... | .... |
| | Elektrostal 2 | Russia-3 | 1 | 1 | 0 | 1 | 4 | .... | .... | .... | .... | .... | .... | .... | .... | .... | .... | .... | .... | .... | .... | .... | .... | .... | .... |
| 2002-03 | CSKA Moscow | Russia | 44 | 12 | 12 | 24 | 34 | .... | .... | .... | .... | .... | .... | .... | .... | .... | .... | .... | .... | .... | .... | .... | .... | .... | .... |
| 2003-04 | CSKA Moscow | Russia | 20 | 2 | 2 | 4 | 14 | .... | .... | .... | .... | .... | .... | .... | .... | .... | .... | .... | .... | .... | .... | .... | .... | .... | .... |
| | Columbus | NHL | 57 | 13 | 21 | 34 | 54 | 5 | 0 | 1 | 137 | 9.5 | –11 | 9 | 11.1 | 16:11 | .... | .... | .... | .... | .... | .... | .... | .... | .... |
| 2004-05 | CSKA Moscow | Russia | 51 | 19 | 21 | 40 | 62 | .... | .... | .... | .... | .... | .... | .... | .... | .... | .... | .... | .... | .... | .... | .... | .... | .... | .... |
| 2005-06 | Columbus | NHL | 73 | 27 | 27 | 54 | 50 | 10 | 0 | 0 | 194 | 13.9 | –13 | 20 | 10.0 | 17:36 | .... | .... | .... | .... | .... | .... | .... | .... | .... |
| | Syracuse Crunch | AHL | 2 | 1 | 0 | 1 | 0 | .... | .... | .... | .... | .... | .... | .... | .... | .... | .... | .... | .... | .... | .... | .... | .... | .... | .... |
| 2006-07 | Mytischi | Russia | 8 | 2 | 4 | 6 | 10 | .... | .... | .... | .... | .... | .... | .... | .... | .... | .... | .... | .... | .... | .... | .... | .... | .... | .... |
| | Columbus | NHL | 71 | 10 | 22 | 32 | 26 | 3 | 0 | 2 | 164 | 6.1 | –19 | 17 | 23.5 | 16:13 | .... | .... | .... | .... | .... | .... | .... | .... | .... |
| 2007-08 | Columbus | NHL | 82 | 26 | 35 | 61 | 34 | 7 | 0 | 3 | 254 | 10.2 | –9 | 29 | 41.4 | 19:22 | .... | .... | .... | .... | .... | .... | .... | .... | .... |
| 2008-09 | NY Rangers | NHL | 82 | 23 | 35 | 58 | 39 | 4 | 1 | 3 | 219 | 10.5 | 6 | 11 | 9.1 | 16:50 | 7 | 0 | 0 | 0 | 2 | 0 | 0 | 0 | 12:33 |
| | NHL Totals | | 365 | 99 | 140 | 239 | 203 | 29 | 1 | 9 | 968 | 10.2 | | 86 | 23.3 | 17:20 | 7 | 0 | 0 | 0 | 2 | 0 | 0 | 0 | 12:33 |

Signed as a free agent by **CSKA Moscow** (Russia), July 27, 2004. Signed as a free agent by **Mystichi** (Russia), July 20, 2006. Traded to **NY Rangers** by **Columbus** with Dan Fritsche for Fedor Tyutin and Christian Backman, July 2, 2008.

## ZIDLICKY, Marek
(zihd-LIH-kee, MAIR-ehk) **MIN.**

Defense. Shoots right. 5'11", 190 lbs. Born, Most, Czech., February 3, 1977. NY Rangers' 6th choice, 176th overall, in 2001 Entry Draft.

| Season | Club | League | GP | G | A | Pts | PIM | PP | SH | GW | S | % | +/- | TF | F% | Min | Playoffs GP | G | A | Pts | PIM | PP | SH | GW | Min |
|---|---|---|---|---|---|---|---|---|---|---|---|---|---|---|---|---|---|---|---|---|---|---|---|---|---|
| 1994-95 | HC Kladno | CzRep | 30 | 2 | 2 | 4 | 38 | .... | .... | .... | .... | .... | .... | .... | .... | .... | 11 | 1 | 1 | 2 | 10 | .... | .... | .... | .... |
| 1995-96 | HC Poldi Kladno | CzRep | 37 | 4 | 5 | 9 | 74 | .... | .... | .... | .... | .... | .... | .... | .... | .... | 7 | 1 | 1 | 2 | 8 | .... | .... | .... | .... |
| 1996-97 | HC Poldi Kladno | CzRep | 49 | 5 | 16 | 21 | 60 | .... | .... | .... | .... | .... | .... | .... | .... | .... | 2 | 0 | 0 | 0 | 0 | .... | .... | .... | .... |
| 1997-98 | Kladno | CzRep | 51 | 2 | 13 | 15 | 121 | .... | .... | .... | .... | .... | .... | .... | .... | .... | .... | .... | .... | .... | .... | .... | .... | .... | .... |
| 1998-99 | Kladno | CzRep | 50 | 10 | 12 | 22 | 94 | .... | .... | .... | .... | .... | .... | .... | .... | .... | .... | .... | .... | .... | .... | .... | .... | .... | .... |
| 99-2000 | HIFK Helsinki | Finland | 47 | 4 | 16 | 20 | 66 | .... | .... | .... | .... | .... | .... | .... | .... | .... | 9 | 3 | 2 | 5 | 24 | .... | .... | .... | .... |
| | HIFK Helsinki | EuroHL | 4 | 2 | 2 | 4 | 10 | .... | .... | .... | .... | .... | .... | .... | .... | .... | 1 | 0 | 0 | 0 | 0 | .... | .... | .... | .... |
| 2000-01 | HIFK Helsinki | Finland | 51 | 12 | 25 | 37 | 146 | .... | .... | .... | .... | .... | .... | .... | .... | .... | 5 | 0 | 1 | 1 | 6 | .... | .... | .... | .... |
| 2001-02 | HIFK Helsinki | Finland | 56 | 11 | 29 | 40 | 107 | .... | .... | .... | .... | .... | .... | .... | .... | .... | .... | .... | .... | .... | .... | .... | .... | .... | .... |
| 2002-03 | HIFK Helsinki | Finland | 54 | 10 | 37 | 47 | 79 | .... | .... | .... | .... | .... | .... | .... | .... | .... | 4 | 0 | 0 | 0 | 4 | .... | .... | .... | .... |
| 2003-04 | Nashville | NHL | 82 | 14 | 39 | 53 | 82 | 9 | 0 | 4 | 143 | 9.8 | –16 | 0 | 0.0 | 20:02 | 1 | 0 | 0 | 0 | 0 | 0 | 0 | 0 | 2:16 |
| 2004-05 | HIFK Helsinki | Finland | 49 | 11 | 20 | 31 | 91 | .... | .... | .... | .... | .... | .... | .... | .... | .... | 5 | 0 | 3 | 3 | 14 | .... | .... | .... | .... |
| 2005-06 | Nashville | NHL | 67 | 12 | 37 | 49 | 82 | 10 | 0 | 1 | 113 | 10.6 | 8 | 0 | 0.0 | 20:04 | 2 | 0 | 1 | 1 | 2 | 0 | 0 | 0 | 15:19 |
| | Czech Republic | Olympics | 7 | 4 | 1 | 5 | 16 | .... | .... | .... | .... | .... | .... | .... | .... | .... | .... | .... | .... | .... | .... | .... | .... | .... | .... |
| 2006-07 | Nashville | NHL | 79 | 4 | 26 | 30 | 72 | 2 | 0 | 1 | 114 | 3.5 | 8 | 0 | 0.0 | 19:43 | 5 | 0 | 2 | 2 | 4 | 0 | 0 | 0 | 19:19 |
| 2007-08 | Nashville | NHL | 79 | 5 | 38 | 43 | 63 | 4 | 0 | 0 | 122 | 4.1 | –5 | 0 | 0.0 | 20:50 | 6 | 0 | 3 | 3 | 8 | 0 | 0 | 0 | 19:04 |
| 2008-09 | Minnesota | NHL | 76 | 12 | 30 | 42 | 76 | 10 | 0 | 3 | 147 | 8.2 | –12 | 0 | 0.0 | 22:07 | .... | .... | .... | .... | .... | .... | .... | .... | .... |
| | NHL Totals | | 383 | 47 | 170 | 217 | 375 | 35 | 0 | 9 | 639 | 7.4 | | 0 | 0.0 | 20:33 | 14 | 0 | 6 | 6 | 14 | 0 | 0 | 0 | 17:25 |

Traded to **Nashville** by **NY Rangers** with Rem Murray and Tomas Kloucek for Mike Dunham, December 12, 2002. Signed as a free agent by **HIFK Helsinki** (Finland), September 17, 2004. Traded to **Minnesota** by **Nashville** for Ryan Jones and Minnesota's 2nd round choice (Charles-Olivier Roussel) in 2009 Entry Draft, July 1, 2008.

## ZIGOMANIS, Mike
(zih-goh-MAN-ihs, MIGHK)

Center. Shoots right. 6', 200 lbs. Born, Toronto, Ont., January 17, 1981. Carolina's 2nd choice, 46th overall, in 2001 Entry Draft.

| Season | Club | League | GP | G | A | Pts | PIM | PP | SH | GW | S | % | +/- | TF | F% | Min | Playoffs GP | G | A | Pts | PIM | PP | SH | GW | Min |
|---|---|---|---|---|---|---|---|---|---|---|---|---|---|---|---|---|---|---|---|---|---|---|---|---|---|
| 1996-97 | Wexford Raiders | MTHL | 40 | 37 | 48 | 85 | 23 | .... | .... | .... | .... | .... | .... | .... | .... | .... | .... | .... | .... | .... | .... | .... | .... | .... | .... |
| | Wexford Raiders | MTJHL | 8 | 2 | 5 | 7 | 2 | .... | .... | .... | .... | .... | .... | .... | .... | .... | .... | .... | .... | .... | .... | .... | .... | .... | .... |
| 1997-98 | Kingston | OHL | 62 | 23 | 51 | 74 | 30 | .... | .... | .... | .... | .... | .... | .... | .... | .... | 12 | 1 | 6 | 7 | 2 | .... | .... | .... | .... |
| 1998-99 | Kingston | OHL | 67 | 29 | 56 | 85 | 36 | .... | .... | .... | .... | .... | .... | .... | .... | .... | 5 | 1 | 7 | 8 | 2 | .... | .... | .... | .... |
| 99-2000 | Kingston | OHL | 59 | 40 | 54 | 94 | 49 | .... | .... | .... | .... | .... | .... | .... | .... | .... | 5 | 0 | 4 | 4 | 0 | .... | .... | .... | .... |
| 2000-01 | Kingston | OHL | 52 | 40 | 37 | 77 | 44 | .... | .... | .... | .... | .... | .... | .... | .... | .... | .... | .... | .... | .... | .... | .... | .... | .... | .... |
| 2001-02 | Lowell | AHL | 79 | 18 | 30 | 48 | 24 | .... | .... | .... | .... | .... | .... | .... | .... | .... | 5 | 1 | 1 | 2 | 2 | .... | .... | .... | .... |
| 2002-03 | Carolina | NHL | 19 | 2 | 1 | 3 | 0 | 1 | 1 | 0 | 19 | 10.5 | –4 | 147 | 59.2 | 9:43 | .... | .... | .... | .... | .... | .... | .... | .... | .... |
| | Lowell | AHL | 38 | 13 | 18 | 31 | 19 | .... | .... | .... | .... | .... | .... | .... | .... | .... | .... | .... | .... | .... | .... | .... | .... | .... | .... |
| 2003-04 | Carolina | NHL | 17 | 0 | 3 | 3 | 2 | 0 | 0 | 0 | 13 | 0.0 | –1 | 108 | 53.7 | 8:37 | .... | .... | .... | .... | .... | .... | .... | .... | .... |
| | Lowell | AHL | 61 | 17 | 35 | 52 | 56 | .... | .... | .... | .... | .... | .... | .... | .... | .... | .... | .... | .... | .... | .... | .... | .... | .... | .... |
| 2004-05 | Lowell | AHL | 76 | 29 | 31 | 60 | 71 | .... | .... | .... | .... | .... | .... | .... | .... | .... | 11 | 4 | 7 | 11 | 8 | .... | .... | .... | .... |
| 2005-06 | Carolina | NHL | 21 | 1 | 0 | 1 | 4 | 0 | 0 | 0 | 16 | 6.3 | 1 | 72 | 50.0 | 9:25 | .... | .... | .... | .... | .... | .... | .... | .... | .... |
| | Lowell | AHL | 11 | 6 | 7 | 13 | 19 | .... | .... | .... | .... | .... | .... | .... | .... | .... | .... | .... | .... | .... | .... | .... | .... | .... | .... |
| | St. Louis | NHL | 2 | 0 | 0 | 0 | 0 | 0 | 0 | 0 | 1 | 0.0 | 0 | 1 | 100.0 | 7:39 | .... | .... | .... | .... | .... | .... | .... | .... | .... |
| | Peoria Rivermen | AHL | 28 | 10 | 18 | 28 | 16 | .... | .... | .... | .... | .... | .... | .... | .... | .... | 4 | 2 | 4 | 6 | 6 | .... | .... | .... | .... |
| 2006-07 | Phoenix | NHL | 75 | 14 | 9 | 23 | 46 | 2 | 1 | 0 | 142 | 9.9 | –8 | 1010 | 56.2 | 14:53 | .... | .... | .... | .... | .... | .... | .... | .... | .... |
| 2007-08 | Phoenix | NHL | 33 | 2 | 1 | 3 | 6 | 0 | 0 | 0 | 35 | 5.7 | –7 | 328 | 59.8 | 12:24 | .... | .... | .... | .... | .... | .... | .... | .... | .... |
| | San Antonio | AHL | 27 | 10 | 15 | 25 | 14 | .... | .... | .... | .... | .... | .... | .... | .... | .... | 7 | 0 | 5 | 5 | 10 | .... | .... | .... | .... |
| 2008-09♦ | Pittsburgh | NHL | 22 | 2 | 4 | 6 | 27 | 0 | 0 | 0 | 23 | 8.7 | –2 | 251 | 63.0 | 11:26 | .... | .... | .... | .... | .... | .... | .... | .... | .... |
| | NHL Totals | | 189 | 21 | 18 | 39 | 85 | 3 | 2 | 0 | 249 | 8.4 | | 1917 | 57.6 | 12:17 | .... | .... | .... | .... | .... | .... | .... | .... | .... |

• Re-entered NHL Entry Draft. Originally Buffalo's 4th choice, 64th overall, in 1999 Entry Draft.

Traded to **St. Louis** by **Carolina** with Jesse Boulerice, the rights to Magnus Kahnberg, Carolina's 1st round choice (later traded to New Jersey - New Jersey selected Matthew Corrente) in 2006 Entry Draft, Toronto's 4th round choice (previously acquired, St. Louis selected Reto Berra) in 2006 Entry Draft and Chicago's 4th round choice (previously acquired, St. Louis selected Cade Fairchild) in 2007 Entry Draft for Doug Weight and Erkki Rajamaki, January 30, 2006. Signed as a free agent by **Phoenix**, July 21, 2006. Traded to **Pittsburgh** by **Phoenix** for future considerations, October 9, 2008. • Missed majority of 2008-09 season recovering from shoulder surgery.

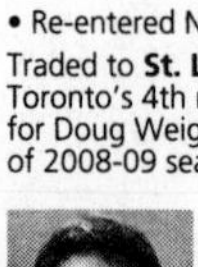

## ZUBOV, Ilya
(ZOO-bahf, IHL-yah) **OTT.**

Center. Shoots left. 6', 200 lbs. Born, Chelyabinsk, USSR, February 14, 1987. Ottawa's 4th choice, 98th overall, in 2005 Entry Draft.

| Season | Club | League | GP | G | A | Pts | PIM | PP | SH | GW | S | % | +/- | TF | F% | Min | Playoffs GP | G | A | Pts | PIM | PP | SH | GW | Min |
|---|---|---|---|---|---|---|---|---|---|---|---|---|---|---|---|---|---|---|---|---|---|---|---|---|---|
| 2003-04 | Chelyabinsk | Russia-2 | 33 | 7 | 7 | 14 | 16 | .... | .... | .... | .... | .... | .... | .... | .... | .... | 8 | 2 | 1 | 3 | 2 | .... | .... | .... | .... |
| 2004-05 | Chelyabinsk | Russia-2 | 40 | 9 | 8 | 17 | 36 | .... | .... | .... | .... | .... | .... | .... | .... | .... | .... | .... | .... | .... | .... | .... | .... | .... | .... |
| | Chelyabinsk 2 | Russia-3 | 1 | 0 | 0 | 0 | 0 | .... | .... | .... | .... | .... | .... | .... | .... | .... | .... | .... | .... | .... | .... | .... | .... | .... | .... |
| 2005-06 | Spartak 2 | Russia-3 | 1 | 0 | 1 | 1 | 4 | .... | .... | .... | .... | .... | .... | .... | .... | .... | .... | .... | .... | .... | .... | .... | .... | .... | .... |
| | Spartak Moscow | Russia | 43 | 4 | 8 | 12 | 12 | .... | .... | .... | .... | .... | .... | .... | .... | .... | 3 | 2 | 2 | 4 | 0 | .... | .... | .... | .... |
| 2006-07 | Mytischi | Russia | 16 | 1 | 1 | 2 | 4 | .... | .... | .... | .... | .... | .... | .... | .... | .... | .... | .... | .... | .... | .... | .... | .... | .... | .... |
| | Ufa | Russia | 26 | 3 | 7 | 10 | 4 | .... | .... | .... | .... | .... | .... | .... | .... | .... | 8 | 2 | 3 | 5 | 2 | .... | .... | .... | .... |
| 2007-08 | Ottawa | NHL | 1 | 0 | 0 | 0 | 0 | 0 | 0 | 0 | 0 | 0.0 | 0 | 5 | 40.0 | 14:38 | .... | .... | .... | .... | .... | .... | .... | .... | .... |
| | Binghamton | AHL | 74 | 15 | 23 | 38 | 18 | .... | .... | .... | .... | .... | .... | .... | .... | .... | .... | .... | .... | .... | .... | .... | .... | .... | .... |
| 2008-09 | Ottawa | NHL | 10 | 0 | 2 | 2 | 0 | 0 | 0 | 0 | 11 | 0.0 | –1 | 1 | 0.0 | 10:17 | .... | .... | .... | .... | .... | .... | .... | .... | .... |
| | Binghamton | AHL | 63 | 14 | 38 | 52 | 26 | .... | .... | .... | .... | .... | .... | .... | .... | .... | .... | .... | .... | .... | .... | .... | .... | .... | .... |
| | NHL Totals | | 11 | 0 | 2 | 2 | 0 | 0 | 0 | 0 | 11 | 0.0 | | 6 | 33.3 | 10:40 | .... | .... | .... | .... | .... | .... | .... | .... | .... |

## ZUBOV, Sergei
(ZOO-bahf, SAIR-gay)

Defense. Shoots right. 6'1", 198 lbs. Born, Moscow, USSR, July 22, 1970. NY Rangers' 6th choice, 85th overall, in 1990 Entry Draft.

| Season | Club | League | GP | G | A | Pts | PIM | PP | SH | GW | S | % | +/- | TF | F% | Min | Playoffs GP | G | A | Pts | PIM | PP | SH | GW | Min |
|---|---|---|---|---|---|---|---|---|---|---|---|---|---|---|---|---|---|---|---|---|---|---|---|---|---|
| 1988-89 | CSKA Moscow | USSR | 29 | 1 | 4 | 5 | 10 | .... | .... | .... | .... | .... | .... | .... | .... | .... | .... | .... | .... | .... | .... | .... | .... | .... | .... |
| 1989-90 | CSKA Moscow | USSR | 48 | 6 | 2 | 8 | 16 | .... | .... | .... | .... | .... | .... | .... | .... | .... | .... | .... | .... | .... | .... | .... | .... | .... | .... |
| 1990-91 | CSKA Moscow | USSR | 41 | 6 | 5 | 11 | 12 | .... | .... | .... | .... | .... | .... | .... | .... | .... | .... | .... | .... | .... | .... | .... | .... | .... | .... |
| | CSKA Moscow | Super-S | 7 | 0 | 1 | 1 | 0 | .... | .... | .... | .... | .... | .... | .... | .... | .... | .... | .... | .... | .... | .... | .... | .... | .... | .... |
| 1991-92 | CSKA Moscow | CIS | 44 | 4 | 7 | 11 | 8 | .... | .... | .... | .... | .... | .... | .... | .... | .... | .... | .... | .... | .... | .... | .... | .... | .... | .... |
| | Russia | Olympics | 8 | 0 | 1 | 1 | 0 | .... | .... | .... | .... | .... | .... | .... | .... | .... | .... | .... | .... | .... | .... | .... | .... | .... | .... |

| | | | Regular Season | | | | | | | | | | | | | | Playoffs | | | | | | | | |
|---|---|---|---|---|---|---|---|---|---|---|---|---|---|---|---|---|---|---|---|---|---|---|---|---|---|
| **Season** | **Club** | **League** | **GP** | **G** | **A** | **Pts** | **PIM** | **PP** | **SH** | **GW** | **S** | **%** | **+/-** | **TF** | **F%** | **Min** | **GP** | **G** | **A** | **Pts** | **PIM** | **PP** | **SH** | **GW** | **Min** |
| **1992-93** | CSKA Moscow | CIS | 1 | 0 | 1 | 1 | 0 | .... | .... | .... | .... | .... | .... | .... | .... | .... | .... | .... | .... | .... | .... | .... | .... | .... | .... |
| | **NY Rangers** | **NHL** | **49** | **8** | **23** | **31** | **4** | **3** | **0** | **0** | **93** | **8.6** | **–1** | .... | .... | .... | .... | .... | .... | .... | .... | .... | .... | .... | .... |
| | Binghamton | AHL | 30 | 7 | 29 | 36 | 14 | .... | .... | .... | .... | .... | .... | .... | .... | .... | 11 | 5 | 5 | 10 | 2 | .... | .... | .... | .... |
| **1993-94**♦ | **NY Rangers** | **NHL** | **78** | **12** | **77** | **89** | **39** | **9** | **0** | **1** | **222** | **5.4** | **20** | .... | .... | .... | **22** | **5** | **14** | **19** | **0** | **2** | **0** | **0** | .... |
| | Binghamton | AHL | 2 | 1 | 2 | 3 | 0 | .... | .... | .... | .... | .... | .... | .... | .... | .... | .... | .... | .... | .... | .... | .... | .... | .... | .... |
| **1994-95** | **NY Rangers** | **NHL** | **38** | **10** | **26** | **36** | **18** | **6** | **0** | **0** | **116** | **8.6** | **–2** | .... | .... | .... | **10** | **3** | **8** | **11** | **2** | **1** | **0** | **0** | .... |
| **1995-96** | **Pittsburgh** | **NHL** | **64** | **11** | **55** | **66** | **22** | **3** | **2** | **1** | **141** | **7.8** | **28** | .... | .... | .... | **18** | **1** | **14** | **15** | **26** | **1** | **0** | **0** | .... |
| **1996-97** | **Dallas** | **NHL** | **78** | **13** | **30** | **43** | **24** | **1** | **0** | **3** | **133** | **9.8** | **19** | .... | .... | .... | **7** | **0** | **3** | **3** | **2** | **0** | **0** | **0** | .... |
| **1997-98** | **Dallas** | **NHL** | **73** | **10** | **47** | **57** | **16** | **5** | **1** | **2** | **148** | **6.8** | **16** | .... | .... | .... | **17** | **4** | **5** | **9** | **2** | **3** | **0** | **1** | .... |
| **1998-99**♦ | **Dallas** | **NHL** | **81** | **10** | **41** | **51** | **20** | **5** | **0** | **3** | **155** | **6.5** | **9** | **0** | **0.0** | **24:14** | **23** | **1** | **12** | **13** | **4** | **0** | **0** | **0** | **30:16** |
| **99-2000** | **Dallas** | **NHL** | **77** | **9** | **33** | **42** | **18** | **3** | **1** | **3** | **179** | **5.0** | **–2** | **0** | **0.0** | **28:50** | **18** | **2** | **7** | **9** | **6** | **1** | **1** | **0** | **26:28** |
| **2000-01** | **Dallas** | **NHL** | **79** | **10** | **41** | **51** | **24** | **6** | **0** | **1** | **173** | **5.8** | **22** | **0** | **0.0** | **26:37** | **10** | **1** | **5** | **6** | **4** | **0** | **0** | **0** | **30:37** |
| **2001-02** | **Dallas** | **NHL** | **80** | **12** | **32** | **44** | **22** | **8** | **0** | **2** | **198** | **6.1** | **–4** | **0** | **0.0** | **26:46** | .... | .... | .... | .... | .... | .... | .... | .... | .... |
| **2002-03** | **Dallas** | **NHL** | **82** | **11** | **44** | **55** | **26** | **8** | **0** | **2** | **158** | **7.0** | **21** | **0** | **0.0** | **25:50** | **12** | **4** | **10** | **14** | **4** | **2** | **0** | **0** | **30:45** |
| **2003-04** | **Dallas** | **NHL** | **77** | **7** | **35** | **42** | **20** | **4** | **1** | **1** | **154** | **4.5** | **0** | **0** | **0.0** | **25:50** | **5** | **1** | **1** | **2** | **0** | **1** | **0** | **0** | **28:01** |
| 2004-05 | | | DID NOT PLAY | | | | | | | | | | | | | | | | | | | | | | |
| **2005-06** | **Dallas** | **NHL** | **78** | **13** | **58** | **71** | **46** | **9** | **0** | **0** | **141** | **9.2** | **20** | **0** | **0.0** | **26:27** | **5** | **1** | **5** | **6** | **6** | **1** | **0** | **0** | **29:42** |
| **2006-07** | **Dallas** | **NHL** | **78** | **12** | **42** | **54** | **26** | **9** | **0** | **3** | **156** | **7.7** | **0** | **1** | **100.0** | **25:57** | **6** | **0** | **4** | **4** | **2** | **0** | **0** | **0** | **30:51** |
| **2007-08** | **Dallas** | **NHL** | **46** | **4** | **31** | **35** | **12** | **2** | **0** | **0** | **84** | **4.8** | **6** | **0** | **0.0** | **25:42** | **11** | **1** | **5** | **6** | **4** | **1** | **0** | **0** | **26:01** |
| **2008-09** | **Dallas** | **NHL** | **10** | **0** | **4** | **4** | **0** | **0** | **0** | **0** | **15** | **0.0** | **–4** | **0** | **0.0** | **24:18** | .... | .... | .... | .... | .... | .... | .... | .... | .... |
| | **NHL Totals** | | **1068** | **152** | **619** | **771** | **337** | **81** | **5** | **22** | **2266** | **6.7** | | **1** | **100.0** | **26:14** | **164** | **24** | **93** | **117** | **62** | **13** | **1** | **1** | **28:58** |

NHL Second All-Star Team (2006)

Played in NHL All-Star Game (1998, 1999, 2000)

Traded to **Pittsburgh** by **NY Rangers** with Petr Nedved for Luc Robitaille and Ulf Samuelsson, August 31, 1995. Traded to **Dallas** by **Pittsburgh** for Kevin Hatcher, June 22, 1996. • Missed majority of 2008-09 season recovering from recurring hip injury. Signed as a free agent by **St. Petersburg** (Rus-KHL), July 31, 2009.

## ZUBRUS, Dainius (ZOO-bruhs, DAYN-ihs) **N.J.**

Center/Right wing. Shoots left. 6'5", 225 lbs. Born, Elektrenai, USSR, June 16, 1978. Philadelphia's 1st choice, 15th overall, in 1996 Entry Draft.

| **Season** | **Club** | **League** | **GP** | **G** | **A** | **Pts** | **PIM** | **PP** | **SH** | **GW** | **S** | **%** | **+/-** | **TF** | **F%** | **Min** | **GP** | **G** | **A** | **Pts** | **PIM** | **PP** | **SH** | **GW** | **Min** |
|---|---|---|---|---|---|---|---|---|---|---|---|---|---|---|---|---|---|---|---|---|---|---|---|---|---|
| 1995-96 | Pembroke | CJHL | 28 | 19 | 13 | 32 | 73 | .... | .... | .... | .... | .... | .... | .... | .... | .... | .... | .... | .... | .... | .... | .... | .... | .... | .... |
| | Caledon | MTJHL | 7 | 3 | 7 | 10 | 2 | .... | .... | .... | .... | .... | .... | .... | .... | .... | 17 | 11 | 12 | 23 | 4 | .... | .... | .... | .... |
| **1996-97** | **Philadelphia** | **NHL** | **68** | **8** | **13** | **21** | **22** | **1** | **0** | **2** | **71** | **11.3** | **3** | .... | .... | .... | **19** | **5** | **4** | **9** | **12** | **1** | **0** | **1** | .... |
| **1997-98** | **Philadelphia** | **NHL** | **69** | **8** | **25** | **33** | **42** | **1** | **0** | **5** | **101** | **7.9** | **29** | .... | .... | .... | **5** | **0** | **1** | **1** | **2** | **0** | **0** | **0** | .... |
| **1998-99** | **Philadelphia** | **NHL** | **63** | **3** | **5** | **8** | **25** | **0** | **1** | **0** | **49** | **6.1** | **–5** | **29** | **51.7** | **11:00** | .... | .... | .... | .... | .... | .... | .... | .... | .... |
| | **Montreal** | **NHL** | **17** | **3** | **5** | **8** | **4** | **0** | **0** | **1** | **31** | **9.7** | **–3** | **2** | **50.0** | **16:53** | .... | .... | .... | .... | .... | .... | .... | .... | .... |
| **99-2000** | **Montreal** | **NHL** | **73** | **14** | **28** | **42** | **54** | **3** | **0** | **1** | **139** | **10.1** | **–1** | **212** | **39.2** | **17:37** | .... | .... | .... | .... | .... | .... | .... | .... | .... |
| **2000-01** | **Montreal** | **NHL** | **49** | **12** | **12** | **24** | **30** | **3** | **0** | **0** | **70** | **17.1** | **–7** | **190** | **41.1** | **18:30** | .... | .... | .... | .... | .... | .... | .... | .... | .... |
| | **Washington** | **NHL** | **12** | **1** | **1** | **2** | **7** | **1** | **0** | **0** | **13** | **7.7** | **–4** | **0** | **0.0** | **13:05** | **6** | **0** | **0** | **0** | **2** | **0** | **0** | **0** | **17:24** |
| **2001-02** | **Washington** | **NHL** | **71** | **17** | **26** | **43** | **38** | **4** | **0** | **3** | **138** | **12.3** | **5** | **131** | **37.4** | **18:52** | .... | .... | .... | .... | .... | .... | .... | .... | .... |
| **2002-03** | **Washington** | **NHL** | **63** | **13** | **22** | **35** | **43** | **2** | **0** | **0** | **104** | **12.5** | **15** | **565** | **50.3** | **16:26** | **6** | **2** | **2** | **4** | **4** | **1** | **0** | **0** | **21:30** |
| **2003-04** | **Washington** | **NHL** | **54** | **12** | **15** | **27** | **38** | **6** | **1** | **2** | **115** | **10.4** | **–16** | **916** | **48.0** | **19:32** | .... | .... | .... | .... | .... | .... | .... | .... | .... |
| 2004-05 | Lada Togliatti | Russia | 42 | 8 | 11 | 19 | 85 | .... | .... | .... | .... | .... | .... | .... | .... | .... | 10 | 3 | 1 | 4 | 22 | .... | .... | .... | .... |
| **2005-06** | **Washington** | **NHL** | **71** | **23** | **34** | **57** | **84** | **13** | **0** | **5** | **181** | **12.7** | **3** | **1118** | **50.3** | **20:22** | .... | .... | .... | .... | .... | .... | .... | .... | .... |
| **2006-07** | **Washington** | **NHL** | **60** | **20** | **32** | **52** | **50** | **9** | **0** | **4** | **127** | **15.7** | **–16** | **1096** | **49.7** | **19:51** | .... | .... | .... | .... | .... | .... | .... | .... | .... |
| | **Buffalo** | **NHL** | **19** | **4** | **4** | **8** | **12** | **1** | **0** | **0** | **31** | **12.9** | **–3** | **69** | **39.1** | **18:22** | **15** | **0** | **8** | **8** | **8** | **0** | **0** | **0** | **18:38** |
| **2007-08** | **New Jersey** | **NHL** | **82** | **13** | **25** | **38** | **38** | **4** | **0** | **2** | **128** | **10.2** | **2** | **144** | **55.6** | **15:42** | **5** | **0** | **1** | **1** | **8** | **0** | **0** | **0** | **16:18** |
| **2008-09** | **New Jersey** | **NHL** | **82** | **15** | **25** | **40** | **69** | **1** | **0** | **3** | **130** | **11.5** | **6** | **923** | **51.3** | **15:16** | **7** | **0** | **1** | **1** | **10** | **0** | **0** | **0** | **13:57** |
| | **NHL Totals** | | **853** | **166** | **272** | **438** | **556** | **49** | **2** | **28** | **1428** | **11.6** | | **5395** | **48.9** | **17:09** | **63** | **7** | **17** | **24** | **46** | **2** | **0** | **1** | **17:45** |

Traded to **Montreal** by **Philadelphia** with Philadelphia's 2nd round choice (Matt Carkner) in 1999 Entry Draft and NY Islanders' 6th round choice (previously acquired, Montreal selected Scott Selig) in 2000 Entry Draft for Mark Recchi, March 10, 1999. Traded to **Washington** by **Montreal** with Trevor Linden and New Jersey's 2nd round choice (previously acquired, later traded to Tampa Bay – Tampa Bay selected Andreas Holmqvist) in 2001 Entry Draft for Richard Zednik, Jan Bulis and Washington's 1st round choice (Alexander Perezhogin) in 2001 Entry Draft, March 13, 2001. Signed as a free agent by **Togliatti** (Russia), July 1, 2004. Traded to **Buffalo** by **Washington** with Timo Helbling for Jiri Novotny and Buffalo's 1st round choice (later traded to San Jose - San Jose selected Nicholas Petrecki) in 2007 Entry Draft, February 27, 2007. Signed as a free agent by **New Jersey**, July 3, 2007.

# NHL Goaltenders

Craig Anderson · Jean-Sebastien Aubin · Alex Auld · Jason Bacashihua · Niklas Backstrom · Jonathan Bernier · Martin Biron · Brian Boucher · Martin Brodeur · Barry Brust

Ilya Bryzgalov · Peter Budaj · Sebastian Caron · Scott Clemmensen · Matt Climie · Ty Conklin · John Curry · Yann Danis · Marc Denis · Rick DiPietro

Jeff Drouin-Deslauriers · Wade Dubielewicz · Dan Ellis · Ray Emery · Erik Ersberg · Robert Esche · Manny Fernandez · Marc-Andre Fleury · Mathieu Garon · Martin Gerber

Jean-Sebastien Giguere · John Grahame · Jaroslav Halak · Josh Harding · Johan Hedberg · Jonas Hiller · Johan Holmqvist · Jimmy Howard · Cristobal Huet · Brent Johnson

Nikolai Khabibulin · Miikka Kiprusoff · Olaf Kolzig · Jason LaBarbera · Patrick Lalime · Pascal Leclaire · Manny Legace · Kari Lehtonen · Michael Leighton · David LeNeveu

Henrik Lundqvist · Roberto Luongo · Joey MacDonald · Chris Mason · Steve Mason · Curtis McElhinney · Mike McKenna · Ryan Miller · Al Montoya · Evgeni Nabokov

Antti Niemi · Antero Niittymaki · Fredrik Norrena · Chris Osgood · Ondrej Pavelec · Justin Pogge · Carey Price · Karri Ramo · Tuukka Rask · Andrew Raycroft

Pekka Rinne · Dwayne Roloson · Dany Sabourin · Curtis Sanford · Nolan Schaefer · Cory Schneider · Marek Schwarz · Mike Smith · Tobias Stephan · Mikael Tellqvist

Jose Theodore · Tim Thomas · Hannu Toivonen · Vesa Toskala · Marty Turco · Steve Valiquette · Semyon Varlamov · Tomas Vokoun · Cam Ward · Kevin Weekes

# 2009-10 Goaltender Register

**Note:** The 2009-10 Goaltender Register lists all active NHL goaltenders, every goaltender drafted in the 2009 Entry Draft, goaltenders on NHL Reserve Lists and other goaltenders.

Trades and roster changes are current as of August 10, 2009.

To calculate a goaltender's goals-against per game average **(Avg)**, divide goals against **(GA)** by minutes played **(Mins)** and multiply this result by **60**.

**Abbreviations: GP** – games played; **W** – wins; **L** – losses; **O/T** – overtime losses/ties; **Mins** – minutes played; **GA** – goals against; **SO** – shutouts; **Avg** – goals-against-per-game average; * – league-leading total
♦ – member of Stanley Cup-winning team.

**NHL Player Register begins on page 352.**
**Prospect Register begins on page 279.**
**League Abbreviations are listed on page 662.**

## AEBISCHER, David (A-bih-shuhr, DAY-vihd)

Goaltender. Catches left. 6'1", 185 lbs. Born, Fribourg, Switz., February 7, 1978.
(Colorado's 7th choice, 161st overall, in 1997 Entry Draft).

| | | | Regular Season | | | | | | | | Playoffs | | | | | | |
|---|---|---|---|---|---|---|---|---|---|---|---|---|---|---|---|---|---|
| Season | Club | League | GP | W | L | O/T | Mins | GA | SO | Avg | GP | W | L | Mins | GA | SO | Avg |
| 1996-97 | Fribourg | Swiss | 10 | .... | .... | .... | 577 | 34 | 0 | 3.54 | 3 | 1 | 2 | 184 | 13 | 0 | 4.24 |
| 1997-98 | Chesapeake | ECHL | 17 | 5 | 7 | 2 | 930 | 52 | 0 | 3.35 | .... | .... | .... | .... | .... | .... | .... |
| | Wheeling Nailers | ECHL | 10 | 5 | 3 | 1 | 564 | 30 | 1 | 3.19 | .... | .... | .... | .... | .... | .... | .... |
| | Hershey Bears | AHL | 2 | 0 | 0 | 1 | 79 | 5 | 0 | 3.76 | .... | .... | .... | .... | .... | .... | .... |
| | Fribourg | Swiss | 1 | 1 | 0 | 0 | 60 | 1 | 0 | 1.00 | 4 | .... | .... | 240 | 17 | .... | 4.25 |
| 1998-99 | Hershey Bears | AHL | 38 | 17 | 10 | 5 | 1932 | 79 | 2 | 2.45 | 3 | 1 | 2 | 152 | 6 | 0 | 2.37 |
| 99-2000 | Hershey Bears | AHL | 58 | 29 | 23 | 2 | 3259 | 180 | 1 | 3.31 | 14 | 7 | 6 | 788 | 40 | 2 | 3.05 |
| **2000-01** ♦ | **Colorado** | **NHL** | **26** | **12** | **7** | **3** | **1393** | **52** | **3** | **2.24** | **1** | **0** | **0** | **1** | **0** | **0** | **0.00** |
| **2001-02** | **Colorado** | **NHL** | **21** | **13** | **6** | **0** | **1184** | **37** | **2** | **1.88** | **1** | **0** | **0** | **34** | **1** | **0** | **1.76** |
| | Switzerland | Olympics | 2 | 1 | 0 | 0 | 81 | 6 | 0 | 4.43 | .... | .... | .... | .... | .... | .... | .... |
| **2002-03** | **Colorado** | **NHL** | **22** | **7** | **12** | **0** | **1235** | **50** | **1** | **2.43** | .... | .... | .... | .... | .... | .... | .... |
| **2003-04** | **Colorado** | **NHL** | **62** | **32** | **19** | **9** | **3703** | **129** | **4** | **2.09** | **11** | **6** | **5** | **662** | **23** | **1** | **2.08** |
| 2004-05 | HC Lugano | Swiss | 18 | 12 | 2 | 3 | 1019 | 41 | 0 | 2.41 | 4 | 1 | 3 | 240 | 10 | 0 | 2.50 |
| | EHC Chur | Swiss-2 | .... | .... | .... | .... | .... | .... | .... | .... | 2 | .... | .... | 130 | 4 | 0 | 1.84 |
| **2005-06** | **Colorado** | **NHL** | **43** | **25** | **14** | **2** | **2477** | **123** | **3** | **2.98** | .... | .... | .... | .... | .... | .... | .... |
| | Switzerland | Olympics | 4 | 1 | 0 | 2 | 200 | 7 | 0 | 2.10 | .... | .... | .... | .... | .... | .... | .... |
| | **Montreal** | **NHL** | **7** | **4** | **3** | **0** | **418** | **26** | **0** | **3.73** | .... | .... | .... | .... | .... | .... | .... |
| **2006-07** | **Montreal** | **NHL** | **32** | **13** | **12** | **3** | **1760** | **93** | **0** | **3.17** | .... | .... | .... | .... | .... | .... | .... |
| **2007-08** | **Phoenix** | **NHL** | **1** | **0** | **1** | **0** | **60** | **3** | **0** | **3.00** | .... | .... | .... | .... | .... | .... | .... |
| | San Antonio | AHL | 5 | 2 | 3 | 0 | 302 | 13 | 0 | 2.58 | .... | .... | .... | .... | .... | .... | .... |
| | HC Lugano | Swiss | 26 | 12 | 14 | 0 | 1576 | 69 | 2 | 2.63 | 5 | 4 | 1 | 301 | 14 | 0 | 2.79 |
| 2008-09 | HC Lugano | Swiss | 49 | 27 | 22 | 0 | 2953 | 140 | 2 | 2.84 | 7 | 3 | 4 | 452 | 26 | 0 | 3.45 |
| | **NHL Totals** | | **214** | **106** | **74** | **17** | **12230** | **513** | **13** | **2.52** | **13** | **6** | **5** | **697** | **24** | **1** | **2.07** |

Signed as a free agent by **Lugano** (Swiss), September 17, 2004. Traded to **Montreal** by **Colorado** for Jose Theodore, March 8, 2006. Signed as a free agent by **Phoenix**, July 19, 2007. • Loaned to **Lugano** (Swiss) by **Phoenix**, November 23, 2007.

## AKERLUND, Magnus (AK-uhr-luhnd, MAG-nuhs) CAR.

Goaltender. Catches right. 6'1", 183 lbs. Born, Osby, Sweden, April 25, 1986.
(Carolina's 5th choice, 137th overall, in 2004 Entry Draft).

| | | | Regular Season | | | | | | | | Playoffs | | | | | | |
|---|---|---|---|---|---|---|---|---|---|---|---|---|---|---|---|---|---|
| Season | Club | League | GP | W | L | O/T | Mins | GA | SO | Avg | GP | W | L | Mins | GA | SO | Avg |
| 2002-03 | HV 71 Jr. | Swe-Jr. | 18 | .... | .... | .... | 861 | 44 | 1 | 3.07 | 2 | .... | .... | 80 | 6 | 0 | 4.50 |
| 2003-04 | HV 71 Jr. | Swe-Jr. | 26 | .... | .... | .... | 1556 | 85 | 1 | 3.28 | 2 | .... | .... | 119 | 10 | 0 | 5.04 |
| 2004-05 | HV 71 Jr. | Swe-Jr. | 19 | .... | .... | .... | 1096 | 48 | 1 | 2.63 | .... | .... | .... | .... | .... | .... | .... |
| | HV 71 Jonkoping | Sweden | 3 | .... | .... | .... | 185 | 9 | 0 | 2.92 | .... | .... | .... | .... | .... | .... | .... |
| | Skovde IK | Sweden-2 | 22 | .... | .... | .... | 1290 | 55 | 1 | 2.56 | .... | .... | .... | .... | .... | .... | .... |
| 2005-06 | HV 71 Jr. | Swe-Jr. | 4 | .... | .... | .... | 214 | 17 | 0 | 4.76 | .... | .... | .... | .... | .... | .... | .... |
| | Nykoping | Sweden-2 | 21 | .... | .... | .... | 1236 | 67 | 0 | 3.25 | .... | .... | .... | .... | .... | .... | .... |
| 2006-07 | Skovde IK | Sweden-3 | 38 | .... | .... | .... | 2293 | 91 | 6 | 2.38 | .... | .... | .... | .... | .... | .... | .... |
| | HV 71 Jonkoping | Sweden | 1 | .... | .... | .... | 65 | 1 | 0 | 0.92 | .... | .... | .... | .... | .... | .... | .... |
| 2007-08 | Timra IK | Sweden | 9 | .... | .... | .... | 512 | 25 | 1 | 2.93 | .... | .... | .... | .... | .... | .... | .... |
| | Sundsvall | Sweden-2 | 5 | .... | .... | .... | 305 | 16 | 0 | 3.15 | .... | .... | .... | .... | .... | .... | .... |
| 2008-09 | Sundsvall | Sweden-2 | 3 | .... | .... | .... | 180 | 1 | 2 | 0.33 | .... | .... | .... | .... | .... | .... | .... |
| | Timra IK | Sweden | 7 | .... | .... | .... | 375 | 13 | 0 | 2.08 | 2 | .... | .... | 123 | 4 | 0 | 1.96 |

## ALLEN, Jake (A-lehn, JAYK) ST.L.

Goaltender. Catches left. 6'2", 185 lbs. Born, Fredericton, N.B., August 7, 1990.
(St. Louis' 3rd choice, 34th overall, in 2008 Entry Draft).

| | | | Regular Season | | | | | | | | Playoffs | | | | | | |
|---|---|---|---|---|---|---|---|---|---|---|---|---|---|---|---|---|---|
| Season | Club | League | GP | W | L | O/T | Mins | GA | SO | Avg | GP | W | L | Mins | GA | SO | Avg |
| 2006-07 | Fredericton | NBPEI | | | | | STATISTICS NOT AVAILABLE | | | | | | | | | | |
| 2007-08 | St. John's | QMJHL | 30 | 9 | 12 | .... | 1507 | 79 | 2 | 3.14 | 4 | 2 | 1 | 128 | 8 | 0 | 3.74 |
| 2008-09 | Montreal | QMJHL | 53 | 28 | 25 | .... | 3023 | 144 | 3 | 2.86 | 10 | 4 | 6 | 585 | 35 | 1 | 3.59 |

## ANDERSON, Craig (AN-duhr-suhn, KRAYG) COL.

Goaltender. Catches left. 6'2", 180 lbs. Born, Park Ridge, IL, May 21, 1981.
(Chicago's 4th choice, 73rd overall, in 2001 Entry Draft).

| | | | Regular Season | | | | | | | | Playoffs | | | | | | |
|---|---|---|---|---|---|---|---|---|---|---|---|---|---|---|---|---|---|
| Season | Club | League | GP | W | L | O/T | Mins | GA | SO | Avg | GP | W | L | Mins | GA | SO | Avg |
| 1997-98 | Chicago Jets | MEHL | 50 | .... | .... | .... | 2991 | 143 | 2 | 2.86 | .... | .... | .... | .... | .... | .... | .... |
| 1998-99 | Chicago Freeze | NAHL | 14 | 11 | 3 | 0 | 840 | 40 | 0 | 2.56 | .... | .... | .... | .... | .... | .... | .... |
| | Guelph Storm | OHL | 21 | 12 | 5 | 1 | 1006 | 52 | 1 | 3.10 | 3 | 0 | 2 | 114 | 9 | 0 | 4.74 |
| 99-2000 | Guelph Storm | OHL | 38 | 12 | 17 | 2 | 1955 | 117 | 0 | 3.59 | 3 | 0 | 1 | 110 | 5 | 0 | 2.73 |
| 2000-01 | Guelph Storm | OHL | 59 | 30 | 19 | 9 | 3555 | 156 | 3 | 2.63 | 4 | 0 | 4 | 240 | 17 | 0 | 4.25 |
| 2001-02 | Norfolk Admirals | AHL | 28 | 9 | 13 | 4 | 1568 | 77 | 2 | 2.95 | 1 | 0 | 1 | 21 | 1 | 0 | 2.83 |
| **2002-03** | **Chicago** | **NHL** | **6** | **0** | **3** | **2** | **270** | **18** | **0** | **4.00** | .... | .... | .... | .... | .... | .... | .... |
| | Norfolk Admirals | AHL | 32 | 15 | 11 | 5 | 1795 | 58 | 4 | 1.94 | 5 | 2 | 3 | 345 | 15 | 0 | 2.61 |
| **2003-04** | **Chicago** | **NHL** | **21** | **6** | **14** | **0** | **1205** | **57** | **1** | **2.84** | .... | .... | .... | .... | .... | .... | .... |
| | Norfolk Admirals | AHL | 37 | 17 | 20 | 0 | 2108 | 74 | 3 | 2.11 | 5 | 2 | 3 | 327 | 10 | 0 | 1.84 |
| 2004-05 | Norfolk Admirals | AHL | 15 | 9 | 4 | 1 | 886 | 27 | 2 | 1.83 | 6 | 2 | 4 | 356 | 14 | 0 | 2.36 |
| **2005-06** | **Chicago** | **NHL** | **29** | **6** | **12** | **4** | **1554** | **86** | **1** | **3.32** | .... | .... | .... | .... | .... | .... | .... |
| **2006-07** | **Florida** | **NHL** | **5** | **1** | **1** | **1** | **217** | **8** | **0** | **2.21** | .... | .... | .... | .... | .... | .... | .... |
| | Rochester | AHL | 34 | 23 | 10 | 1 | 2060 | 88 | 1 | 2.56 | 6 | 2 | 4 | 376 | 18 | 0 | 2.87 |
| **2007-08** | **Florida** | **NHL** | **17** | **8** | **6** | **1** | **935** | **35** | **2** | **2.25** | .... | .... | .... | .... | .... | .... | .... |
| **2008-09** | **Florida** | **NHL** | **31** | **15** | **7** | **5** | **1636** | **74** | **3** | **2.71** | .... | .... | .... | .... | .... | .... | .... |
| | **NHL Totals** | | **109** | **36** | **43** | **13** | **5817** | **278** | **7** | **2.87** | .... | .... | .... | .... | .... | .... | .... |

• Re-entered NHL Entry Draft. Originally Calgary's 3rd choice, 77th overall, in 1999 Entry Draft.

OHL First All-Star Team (2001)

Claimed on waivers by **Boston** from **Chicago**, January 19, 2006. Claimed on waivers by **St. Louis** from **Boston**, January 31, 2006. Claimed on waivers by **Chicago** from **St. Louis**, February 3, 2006. Traded to **Florida** by **Chicago** for Florida's 6th round choice (later traded to Tampa Bay - Tampa Bay selected Luke Witkowski) in 2008 Entry Draft, June 24, 2006. Signed as a free agent by **Colorado**, July 1, 2009.

## AUBIN, Jean-Sebastien (oh-BEHN, ZHAWN-suh-BAS-tee-yeh)

Goaltender. Catches right. 5'11", 180 lbs. Born, Montreal, Que., July 19, 1977.
(Pittsburgh's 2nd choice, 76th overall, in 1995 Entry Draft).

| | | | Regular Season | | | | | | | | Playoffs | | | | | | |
|---|---|---|---|---|---|---|---|---|---|---|---|---|---|---|---|---|---|
| Season | Club | League | GP | W | L | O/T | Mins | GA | SO | Avg | GP | W | L | Mins | GA | SO | Avg |
| 1993-94 | Montreal-Bourassa | QAAA | 27 | 14 | 13 | 0 | 1524 | 96 | 1 | 3.74 | 4 | 1 | 3 | 222 | 19 | 0 | 5.14 |
| 1994-95 | Sherbrooke | QMJHL | 27 | 13 | 10 | 1 | 1287 | 73 | 1 | 3.40 | 3 | 1 | 2 | 185 | 11 | 0 | 3.57 |
| 1995-96 | Sherbrooke | QMJHL | 40 | 18 | 14 | 2 | 2140 | 127 | 0 | 3.57 | 4 | 1 | 3 | 238 | 23 | 0 | 5.55 |
| 1996-97 | Sherbrooke | QMJHL | 4 | 3 | 1 | 0 | 249 | 8 | 0 | 1.93 | 1 | 0 | 1 | 60 | 4 | 0 | 4.00 |
| | Moncton Wildcats | QMJHL | 22 | 9 | 12 | 0 | 1252 | 67 | 1 | 3.21 | .... | .... | .... | .... | .... | .... | .... |
| | Laval Titan | QMJHL | 11 | 2 | 6 | 1 | 532 | 41 | 0 | 4.62 | .... | .... | .... | .... | .... | .... | .... |
| 1997-98 | Syracuse Crunch | AHL | 8 | 2 | 4 | 1 | 380 | 26 | 0 | 4.10 | .... | .... | .... | .... | .... | .... | .... |
| | Dayton Bombers | ECHL | 21 | 15 | 2 | 2 | 1177 | 59 | 1 | 3.01 | 3 | 1 | 1 | 142 | 4 | 0 | 1.69 |
| **1998-99** | **Pittsburgh** | **NHL** | **17** | **4** | **3** | **6** | **756** | **28** | **2** | **2.22** | .... | .... | .... | .... | .... | .... | .... |
| | Kansas City Blades | IHL | 13 | 5 | 7 | 1 | 751 | 41 | 0 | 3.28 | .... | .... | .... | .... | .... | .... | .... |
| **99-2000** | **Pittsburgh** | **NHL** | **51** | **23** | **21** | **3** | **2789** | **120** | **2** | **2.58** | .... | .... | .... | .... | .... | .... | .... |
| | Wilkes-Barre | AHL | 11 | 2 | 8 | 0 | 538 | 39 | 0 | 4.35 | .... | .... | .... | .... | .... | .... | .... |
| **2000-01** | **Pittsburgh** | **NHL** | **36** | **20** | **14** | **1** | **2050** | **107** | **0** | **3.13** | **1** | **0** | **0** | **1** | **0** | **0** | **0.00** |
| **2001-02** | **Pittsburgh** | **NHL** | **21** | **3** | **12** | **1** | **1094** | **65** | **0** | **3.56** | .... | .... | .... | .... | .... | .... | .... |
| **2002-03** | **Pittsburgh** | **NHL** | **21** | **6** | **13** | **0** | **1132** | **59** | **1** | **3.13** | .... | .... | .... | .... | .... | .... | .... |
| | Wilkes-Barre | AHL | 16 | 8 | 6 | 1 | 919 | 29 | 3 | 1.89 | 6 | 3 | 3 | 356 | 12 | 0 | 2.02 |
| **2003-04** | **Pittsburgh** | **NHL** | **22** | **7** | **9** | **0** | **1067** | **53** | **1** | **2.98** | .... | .... | .... | .... | .... | .... | .... |
| | Wilkes-Barre | AHL | 13 | 4 | 5 | 2 | 670 | 31 | 0 | 2.78 | .... | .... | .... | .... | .... | .... | .... |
| 2004-05 | St. John's | AHL | 23 | 12 | 9 | 0 | 1336 | 64 | 3 | 2.87 | 1 | 0 | 0 | 47 | 1 | 0 | 1.27 |
| **2005-06** | **Toronto** | **NHL** | **11** | **9** | **0** | **2** | **677** | **25** | **1** | **2.22** | .... | .... | .... | .... | .... | .... | .... |
| | Toronto Marlies | AHL | 46 | 19 | 18 | 2 | 2491 | 126 | 2 | 3.03 | 5 | 1 | 4 | 359 | 17 | 0 | 2.84 |
| **2006-07** | **Toronto** | **NHL** | **20** | **3** | **5** | **2** | **804** | **46** | **0** | **3.43** | .... | .... | .... | .... | .... | .... | .... |
| **2007-08** | **Los Angeles** | **NHL** | **19** | **5** | **6** | **1** | **828** | **44** | **0** | **3.19** | .... | .... | .... | .... | .... | .... | .... |
| | Manchester | AHL | 1 | 0 | 0 | 0 | 9 | 4 | 0 | 27.69 | .... | .... | .... | .... | .... | .... | .... |
| | Portland Pirates | AHL | 11 | 6 | 4 | 0 | 645 | 18 | 3 | 1.67 | 12 | 9 | 3 | 757 | 29 | 0 | 2.30 |
| 2008-09 | Philadelphia | AHL | 23 | 10 | 10 | 1 | 1252 | 70 | 0 | 3.36 | 1 | 0 | 1 | 58 | 1 | 0 | 1.03 |
| | **NHL Totals** | | **218** | **80** | **83** | **16** | **11197** | **547** | **7** | **2.93** | **1** | **0** | **0** | **1** | **0** | **0** | **0.00** |

Signed to a PTO (tryout) contract by **St. John's** (AHL), November 13, 2004. Signed as a free agent by **Toronto**, August 18, 2005. Signed as a free agent by **Los Angeles**, August 28, 2007. Traded to **Anaheim** by **Los Angeles** for St. Louis' 7th round choice (previously acquired, later traded back to St. Louis - St. Louis selected Paul Karpowich) in 2008 Entry Draft, February 26, 2008. Signed as a free agent by **Philadelphia**, September 18, 2008.

## AULD, Alex (AWLD, AL-ehx) DAL.

Goaltender. Catches left. 6'4", 223 lbs. Born, Cold Lake, Alta., January 7, 1981.
(Florida's 2nd choice, 40th overall, in 1999 Entry Draft).

| | | | Regular Season | | | | | | | | Playoffs | | | | | | |
|---|---|---|---|---|---|---|---|---|---|---|---|---|---|---|---|---|---|
| Season | Club | League | GP | W | L | O/T | Mins | GA | SO | Avg | GP | W | L | Mins | GA | SO | Avg |
| 1996-97 | Thunder Bay Kings | TBMHL | 35 | .... | .... | .... | 2100 | 46 | 10 | 1.35 | .... | .... | .... | .... | .... | .... | .... |
| 1997-98 | Sturgeon Falls Lynx | NOJHA | 11 | 4 | 6 | 0 | 611 | 46 | 0 | 4.52 | .... | .... | .... | .... | .... | .... | .... |
| | North Bay | OHL | 6 | 0 | 4 | 0 | 206 | 17 | 0 | 4.95 | .... | .... | .... | .... | .... | .... | .... |
| 1998-99 | North Bay | OHL | 37 | 9 | 20 | 1 | 1894 | 106 | 1 | 3.36 | 3 | 0 | 3 | 170 | 10 | 0 | 3.53 |
| 99-2000 | North Bay | OHL | 55 | 21 | 26 | 6 | 3047 | 167 | 2 | 3.29 | 6 | 2 | 4 | 374 | 12 | 0 | *1.93 |
| 2000-01 | North Bay | OHL | 40 | 22 | 11 | 5 | 2319 | 98 | 1 | 2.54 | 4 | 0 | 4 | 240 | 15 | 0 | 3.75 |
| **2001-02** | **Vancouver** | **NHL** | **1** | **1** | **0** | **0** | **60** | **2** | **0** | **2.00** | .... | .... | .... | .... | .... | .... | .... |
| | Columbia Inferno | ECHL | 6 | 3 | 1 | 2 | 375 | 12 | 0 | 1.92 | .... | .... | .... | .... | .... | .... | .... |
| | Manitoba Moose | AHL | 21 | 11 | 9 | 0 | 1104 | 65 | 1 | 3.53 | 1 | 0 | 0 | 20 | 0 | 0 | 0.00 |
| **2002-03** | **Vancouver** | **NHL** | **7** | **3** | **3** | **0** | **382** | **10** | **1** | **1.57** | **1** | **0** | **0** | **20** | **1** | **0** | **3.00** |
| | Manitoba Moose | AHL | 37 | 15 | 19 | 3 | 2209 | 97 | 3 | 2.64 | .... | .... | .... | .... | .... | .... | .... |
| **2003-04** | **Vancouver** | **NHL** | **6** | **2** | **2** | **2** | **349** | **12** | **0** | **2.06** | **3** | **1** | **2** | **222** | **9** | **0** | **2.43** |
| | Manitoba Moose | AHL | 40 | 18 | 16 | 4 | 2329 | 99 | 4 | 2.55 | .... | .... | .... | .... | .... | .... | .... |
| 2004-05 | Manitoba Moose | AHL | 50 | 25 | 18 | 4 | 2764 | 118 | 2 | 2.56 | 3 | 0 | 2 | 128 | 7 | 0 | 3.29 |

| | | | | | | | | | | | | | | | | | |
|---|---|---|---|---|---|---|---|---|---|---|---|---|---|---|---|---|---|
| 2005-06 | Vancouver | NHL | 67 | 33 | 26 | 6 | 3859 | 189 | 0 | 2.94 | .... | .... | .... | .... | .... | .... | .... |
| 2006-07 | Florida | NHL | 27 | 7 | 13 | 5 | 1471 | 82 | 1 | 3.34 | .... | .... | .... | .... | .... | .... | .... |
| 2007-08 | Phoenix | NHL | 9 | 3 | 6 | 0 | 509 | 30 | 1 | 3.54 | .... | .... | .... | .... | .... | .... | .... |
| | San Antonio | AHL | 2 | 1 | 1 | 0 | 119 | 5 | 1 | 2.53 | .... | .... | .... | .... | .... | .... | .... |
| | Boston | NHL | 23 | 9 | 7 | 5 | 1213 | 47 | 2 | 2.32 | .... | .... | .... | .... | .... | .... | .... |
| 2008-09 | Ottawa | NHL | 43 | 16 | 18 | 7 | 2449 | 101 | 1 | 2.47 | .... | .... | .... | .... | .... | .... | .... |
| | NHL Totals | | 183 | 74 | 75 | 25 | 10292 | 473 | 6 | 2.76 | 4 | 1 | 2 | 242 | 10 | 0 | 2.48 |

• Rights traded to **Vancouver** by **Florida** for Vancouver's 2nd round compensatory choice (later traded to New Jersey – New Jersey selected Tuomas Pihlman) in 2001 Entry Draft and Vancouver's 3rd round choice (later traded to Atlanta – later traded to Buffalo – Buffalo selected John Adams) in 2002 Entry Draft, May 31, 2001. Traded to **Florida** by **Vancouver** with Todd Bertuzzi and Bryan Allen for Roberto Luongo, Lukas Krajicek and Florida's 6th round choice (Sergei Shirokov) in 2006 Entry Draft, June 23, 2006. Signed as a free agent by **Phoenix**, August 13, 2007. Traded to **Boston** by **Phoenix** for Nate DiCasmirro and Boston's 5th round choice (later traded to Ottawa – Ottawa selected Jeff Costello) in 2009 Entry Draft, December 6, 2007. Signed as a free agent by **Ottawa**, July 1, 2008. Traded to **Dallas** by **Ottawa** for San Jose's 6th round choice (previously acquired) in 2010 Entry Draft, July 8, 2009.

## BACASHIHUA, Jason (buh-KAH-shoo-wuh, JAY-suhn)

Goaltender. Catches left. 5'11", 177 lbs. Born, Garden City, MI, September 20, 1982.
(Dallas' 1st choice, 26th overall, in 2001 Entry Draft).

| | | | Regular Season | | | | | | | | Playoffs | | | | | | |
|---|---|---|---|---|---|---|---|---|---|---|---|---|---|---|---|---|---|
| Season | Club | League | GP | W | L | O/T | Mins | GA | SO | Avg | GP | W | L | Mins | GA | SO | Avg |
| 99-2000 | Chicago Freeze | NAHL | 41 | 20 | 19 | 2 | 2432 | 118 | 2 | 2.91 | 2 | 0 | 2 | 103 | 12 | 0 | 6.97 |
| 2000-01 | Chicago Freeze | NAHL | 39 | 24 | 14 | 0 | 2246 | 121 | 1 | 3.23 | 3 | 1 | 2 | 190 | 12 | 0 | 3.79 |
| 2001-02 | Plymouth Whalers | OHL | 46 | 26 | 12 | 7 | 2688 | 105 | *5 | 2.34 | 6 | 2 | 4 | 360 | 15 | 0 | 2.50 |
| | Utah Grizzlies | AHL | 1 | 0 | 1 | 0 | 61 | 3 | 0 | 2.97 | .... | .... | .... | .... | .... | .... | .... |
| 2002-03 | Utah Grizzlies | AHL | 39 | 18 | 18 | 2 | 2245 | 118 | 3 | 3.15 | 1 | 0 | 1 | 59 | 2 | 0 | 2.05 |
| 2003-04 | Utah Grizzlies | AHL | 39 | 13 | 19 | 5 | 2234 | 99 | 3 | 2.66 | .... | .... | .... | .... | .... | .... | .... |
| 2004-05 | Worcester IceCats | AHL | 35 | 18 | 13 | 1 | 1909 | 80 | 2 | 2.51 | .... | .... | .... | .... | .... | .... | .... |
| 2005-06 | St. Louis | NHL | 19 | 4 | 10 | 1 | 966 | 52 | 0 | 3.23 | .... | .... | .... | .... | .... | .... | .... |
| | Peoria Rivermen | AHL | 15 | 9 | 4 | 0 | 820 | 36 | 2 | 2.63 | .... | .... | .... | .... | .... | .... | .... |
| 2006-07 | St. Louis | NHL | 19 | 3 | 7 | 3 | 894 | 47 | 0 | 3.15 | .... | .... | .... | .... | .... | .... | .... |
| | Peoria Rivermen | AHL | 20 | 5 | 10 | 4 | 1139 | 55 | 1 | 2.90 | .... | .... | .... | .... | .... | .... | .... |
| 2007-08 | Peoria Rivermen | AHL | 4 | 1 | 3 | 0 | 208 | 11 | 0 | 3.17 | .... | .... | .... | .... | .... | .... | .... |
| | Johnstown Chiefs | ECHL | 1 | 1 | 0 | 0 | 65 | 4 | 0 | 3.70 | .... | .... | .... | .... | .... | .... | .... |
| | Lake Erie Monsters | AHL | 19 | 5 | 11 | 2 | 1074 | 60 | 1 | 3.35 | .... | .... | .... | .... | .... | .... | .... |
| 2008-09 | Lake Erie Monsters | AHL | 39 | 13 | 21 | 3 | 2255 | 104 | 2 | 2.77 | .... | .... | .... | .... | .... | .... | .... |
| | NHL Totals | | 38 | 7 | 17 | 4 | 1860 | 99 | 0 | 3.19 | .... | .... | .... | .... | .... | .... | .... |

Traded to **St. Louis** by **Dallas** for the rights to Shawn Belle, June 25, 2004. Traded to **Colorado** by **St. Louis** for future considerations, November 8, 2007. Signed as a free agent by **Hershey** (AHL), July 31, 2009.

## BACHMAN, Richard (BAWK-mahn, RIH-chuhrd) DAL.

Goaltender. Catches left. 5'11", 160 lbs. Born, Salt Lake City, UT, July 25, 1987.
(Dallas' 3rd choice, 120th overall, in 2006 Entry Draft).

| | | | Regular Season | | | | | | | | Playoffs | | | | | | |
|---|---|---|---|---|---|---|---|---|---|---|---|---|---|---|---|---|---|
| Season | Club | League | GP | W | L | O/T | Mins | GA | SO | Avg | GP | W | L | Mins | GA | SO | Avg |
| 2004-05 | Cushing | High-MA | 28 | .... | .... | .... | 1498 | 53 | 3 | 1.89 | .... | .... | .... | .... | .... | .... | .... |
| | Boston Jr. Bruins | EmJHL | 25 | .... | .... | .... | .... | .... | .... | .... | .... | .... | .... | .... | .... | .... | .... |
| 2005-06 | Cushing | High-MA | 30 | .... | .... | .... | 1598 | 60 | 4 | 2.25 | .... | .... | .... | .... | .... | .... | .... |
| | Boston Jr. Bruins | EmJHL | .... | 31 | 1 | 2 | .... | .... | .... | 1.69 | .... | .... | .... | .... | .... | .... | .... |
| 2006-07 | Chicago Steel | USHL | 7 | 2 | 5 | 0 | 359 | 29 | 0 | 4.85 | .... | .... | .... | .... | .... | .... | .... |
| | Cedar Rapids | USHL | 26 | 14 | 10 | 2 | 1565 | 78 | 4 | 2.99 | 6 | 4 | 1 | 329 | 7 | *2 | *1.28 |
| 2007-08 | Colorado College | WCHA | 35 | 25 | 9 | 1 | 2103 | 65 | 4 | 1.85 | .... | .... | .... | .... | .... | .... | .... |
| 2008-09 | Colorado College | WCHA | 35 | 14 | 11 | 10 | 2073 | 91 | 3 | 2.63 | .... | .... | .... | .... | .... | .... | .... |

WCHA All-Rookie Team (2008) • WCHA First All-Star Team (2008) • WCHA Rookie of the Year (2008) • WCHA Player of the Year (2008) • NCAA West First All-American Team (2008)

## BACKSTROM, Niklas (BAK-struhm, NIHK-luhs) MIN.

Goaltender. Catches left. 6'1", 189 lbs. Born, Helsinki, Finland, February 13, 1978.

| | | | Regular Season | | | | | | | | Playoffs | | | | | | |
|---|---|---|---|---|---|---|---|---|---|---|---|---|---|---|---|---|---|
| Season | Club | League | GP | W | L | O/T | Mins | GA | SO | Avg | GP | W | L | Mins | GA | SO | Avg |
| 1994-95 | HIFK Helsinki U18 | Fin-U18 | STATISTICS NOT AVAILABLE | | | | | | | | | | | | | | |
| 1995-96 | HIFK Helsinki U18 | Fin-U18 | 12 | .... | .... | .... | 699 | 44 | .... | 3.77 | 4 | .... | .... | 203 | 9 | .... | 2.66 |
| 1996-97 | HIFK Helsinki Jr. | Fin-Jr. | 21 | .... | .... | .... | 1243 | 57 | .... | 2.75 | .... | .... | .... | .... | .... | .... | .... |
| | PiTa Helsinki | Finland-2 | 8 | .... | .... | .... | 390 | 24 | .... | 3.69 | .... | .... | .... | .... | .... | .... | .... |
| | HIFK Helsinki | Finland | 2 | 0 | 0 | 0 | 30 | 3 | 0 | 5.85 | .... | .... | .... | .... | .... | .... | .... |
| 1997-98 | HIFK Helsinki Jr. | Fin-Jr. | 14 | 7 | 7 | 0 | 847 | 42 | .... | 2.98 | .... | .... | .... | .... | .... | .... | .... |
| | Hermes Kokkola | Finland-2 | 9 | 4 | 3 | 1 | 468 | 23 | 1 | 2.95 | .... | .... | .... | .... | .... | .... | .... |
| 1998-99 | HIFK Helsinki | Finland | 16 | 9 | 5 | 1 | 923 | 26 | 1 | *1.69 | .... | .... | .... | .... | .... | .... | .... |
| | HIFK Helsinki Jr. | Fin-Jr. | 15 | 7 | 7 | 1 | 898 | 45 | 1 | 3.01 | .... | .... | .... | .... | .... | .... | .... |
| 99-2000 | HIFK Helsinki | Finland | 4 | 0 | 4 | 0 | 155 | 17 | 0 | 6.58 | .... | .... | .... | .... | .... | .... | .... |
| | FPS Forssa | Finland-2 | 22 | 13 | 8 | 1 | 1320 | 50 | 1 | 2.27 | 3 | 1 | 2 | 178 | 8 | 0 | 2.69 |
| 2000-01 | SaiPa | Finland | 49 | 22 | 24 | 3 | 2826 | 120 | 2 | 2.55 | .... | .... | .... | .... | .... | .... | .... |
| 2001-02 | AIK Solna | Sweden | 40 | .... | .... | .... | 2186 | 111 | 1 | 3.05 | .... | .... | .... | .... | .... | .... | .... |
| | AIK Solna | Sweden-Q | 9 | .... | .... | .... | 543 | 20 | 0 | 2.21 | .... | .... | .... | .... | .... | .... | .... |
| 2002-03 | Karpat Oulu | Finland | 36 | 16 | 8 | 9 | 2136 | 77 | 4 | 2.16 | *15 | 7 | 8 | *990 | 33 | 1 | 2.00 |
| 2003-04 | Karpat Oulu | Finland | 43 | 24 | 8 | 0 | 2572 | 87 | 7 | 2.03 | *15 | *9 | 6 | *927 | 36 | 1 | 2.33 |
| 2004-05 | Karpat Oulu | Finland | 47 | 27 | 10 | 10 | 2819 | 102 | 7 | 2.17 | *12 | *10 | 2 | 720 | 15 | *3 | *1.25 |
| 2005-06 | Karpat Oulu | Finland | 51 | *32 | 9 | 10 | 3077 | 86 | *10 | *1.68 | 4 | 3 | 1 | 195 | 6 | 0 | 1.84 |
| | Finland | Olympics | DID NOT PLAY – SPARE GOALTENDER | | | | | | | | | | | | | | |
| 2006-07 | Minnesota | NHL | 41 | 23 | 8 | 6 | 2227 | 73 | 5 | *1.97 | 5 | 1 | 4 | 297 | 11 | 0 | 2.22 |
| 2007-08 | Minnesota | NHL | 58 | 33 | 13 | 8 | 3409 | 131 | 4 | 2.31 | 6 | 2 | 4 | 361 | 17 | 0 | 2.83 |
| 2008-09 | Minnesota | NHL | 71 | 37 | 24 | 8 | 4088 | 159 | 8 | 2.33 | .... | .... | .... | .... | .... | .... | .... |
| | NHL Totals | | 170 | 93 | 45 | 22 | 9724 | 363 | 17 | 2.24 | 11 | 3 | 8 | 658 | 28 | 0 | 2.55 |

MBNA Roger Crozier Saving Grace Award (2007) • William M. Jennings Trophy (2007) (shared with Manny Fernandez)

Played in NHL All-Star Game (2009)

Signed as a free agent by **Minnesota**, June 1, 2006.

## BARULIN, Konstantin (bah-ROO-lihn, KAWN-stan-tihn) ST.L.

Goaltender. Catches left. 6', 180 lbs. Born, Karaganda, USSR, September 4, 1984.
(St. Louis' 3rd choice, 84th overall, in 2003 Entry Draft).

| | | | Regular Season | | | | | | | | Playoffs | | | | | | |
|---|---|---|---|---|---|---|---|---|---|---|---|---|---|---|---|---|---|
| Season | Club | League | GP | W | L | O/T | Mins | GA | SO | Avg | GP | W | L | Mins | GA | SO | Avg |
| 2001-02 | Gazovik Tyumen | Russia-2 | 4 | .... | .... | .... | 190 | 15 | 0 | 4.73 | .... | .... | .... | .... | .... | .... | .... |
| 2002-03 | Gazovik Tyumen | Russia-2 | 41 | .... | .... | .... | 2361 | 67 | 5 | 1.70 | .... | .... | .... | .... | .... | .... | .... |
| 2003-04 | Gazovik Tyumen | Russia-2 | 11 | .... | .... | .... | 663 | 24 | .... | 2.17 | .... | .... | .... | .... | .... | .... | .... |
| | SKA St. Petersburg | Russia | 1 | .... | .... | .... | 1 | 0 | 0 | 0.00 | .... | .... | .... | .... | .... | .... | .... |
| | St. Petersburg 2 | Russia-3 | 11 | .... | .... | .... | 668 | 24 | 1 | 2.15 | .... | .... | .... | .... | .... | .... | .... |
| 2004-05 | Gazovik Tyumen | Russia-2 | 30 | .... | .... | .... | 1773 | 59 | 6 | 2.00 | 3 | .... | .... | 136 | 9 | 0 | 3.97 |
| 2005-06 | Spartak Moscow | Russia | 36 | .... | .... | .... | 2102 | 75 | 2 | 2.14 | 2 | .... | .... | 104 | 4 | 0 | 2.30 |
| 2006-07 | Mytischi | Russia | 26 | .... | .... | .... | 1249 | 45 | 1 | 2.16 | 1 | .... | .... | 48 | 3 | 0 | 3.76 |
| 2007-08 | Mytischi | Russia | 11 | .... | .... | .... | 434 | 20 | 0 | 2.77 | .... | .... | .... | .... | .... | .... | .... |
| 2008-09 | CSKA Moscow | Rus-KHL | 41 | .... | .... | .... | 2443 | 100 | 2 | 2.46 | 2 | .... | .... | 100 | 9 | 0 | 5.40 |

## BECKFORD-TSEU, Chris (BEHK-fuhrd-TSEW, KRIHS) FLA.

Goaltender. Catches left. 6'2", 201 lbs. Born, Toronto, Ont., June 22, 1984.
(St. Louis' 8th choice, 159th overall, in 2003 Entry Draft).

| | | | Regular Season | | | | | | | | Playoffs | | | | | | |
|---|---|---|---|---|---|---|---|---|---|---|---|---|---|---|---|---|---|
| Season | Club | League | GP | W | L | O/T | Mins | GA | SO | Avg | GP | W | L | Mins | GA | SO | Avg |
| 2000-01 | St. Mike's B's | OPJHL | 25 | 9 | 15 | 1 | 1506 | 119 | 1 | 4.75 | 4 | 1 | 3 | 240 | 10 | 0 | 2.50 |
| 2001-02 | Oshawa | OPJHL | STATISTICS NOT AVAILABLE | | | | | | | | | | | | | | |
| | Guelph Storm | OHL | 5 | 2 | 0 | 0 | 207 | 16 | 0 | 4.64 | .... | .... | .... | .... | .... | .... | .... |
| | Oshawa Generals | OHL | 7 | 2 | 3 | 0 | 341 | 19 | 0 | 3.34 | 5 | 1 | 4 | 310 | 16 | 0 | 3.10 |
| 2002-03 | Oshawa Generals | OHL | 54 | 25 | 26 | 2 | 2978 | 157 | 4 | 3.16 | 13 | 6 | 7 | 727 | 48 | 1 | 3.96 |
| 2003-04 | Oshawa Generals | OHL | 9 | 1 | 5 | 2 | 495 | 28 | 0 | 3.39 | .... | .... | .... | .... | .... | .... | .... |
| | Kingston | OHL | 40 | 16 | 19 | 2 | 2226 | 121 | 3 | 3.26 | 5 | 1 | 4 | 303 | 18 | 0 | 3.56 |
| 2004-05 | Worcester IceCats | AHL | 1 | 0 | 0 | 0 | 29 | 0 | 0 | 0.00 | .... | .... | .... | .... | .... | .... | .... |
| | Peoria Rivermen | ECHL | 29 | 11 | 12 | 3 | 1594 | 72 | 1 | 2.71 | .... | .... | .... | .... | .... | .... | .... |
| 2005-06 | Peoria Rivermen | AHL | 16 | 7 | 5 | 1 | 737 | 38 | 0 | 3.10 | 4 | 0 | 4 | 238 | 15 | 0 | 3.78 |
| | Alaska Aces | ECHL | 19 | 16 | 1 | 2 | 1152 | 36 | 2 | 1.87 | 12 | 8 | 4 | 795 | 27 | *3 | *2.04 |
| 2006-07 | Peoria Rivermen | AHL | 29 | 12 | 11 | 4 | 1654 | 75 | 1 | 2.72 | .... | .... | .... | .... | .... | .... | .... |
| | Alaska Aces | ECHL | 7 | 7 | 0 | 0 | 426 | 9 | 2 | 1.27 | .... | .... | .... | .... | .... | .... | .... |
| 2007-08 | St. Louis | NHL | 1 | 0 | 0 | 0 | 27 | 1 | 0 | 2.22 | .... | .... | .... | .... | .... | .... | .... |
| | Peoria Rivermen | AHL | 34 | 15 | 14 | 2 | 1871 | 82 | 1 | 2.63 | .... | .... | .... | .... | .... | .... | .... |
| | Alaska Aces | ECHL | 16 | 12 | 4 | 0 | 921 | 36 | 1 | 2.34 | 2 | 0 | 2 | 98 | 7 | 0 | 4.27 |
| 2008-09 | Rochester | AHL | 22 | 3 | 14 | 1 | 1112 | 73 | 0 | 3.94 | .... | .... | .... | .... | .... | .... | .... |
| | Florida Everblades | ECHL | 1 | 0 | 0 | 1 | 65 | 5 | 0 | 4.62 | .... | .... | .... | .... | .... | .... | .... |
| | Phoenix | ECHL | 11 | 2 | 7 | 1 | 577 | 49 | 0 | 5.09 | .... | .... | .... | .... | .... | .... | .... |
| | NHL Totals | | 1 | 0 | 0 | 0 | 27 | 1 | 0 | 2.22 | .... | .... | .... | .... | .... | .... | .... |

Signed as a free agent by **Florida**, July 3, 2008.

## BENNETT, Brett (BEHN-neht, BREHT) PHX.

Goaltender. Catches left. 6'1", 185 lbs. Born, Buffalo, NY, March 8, 1988.
(Phoenix's 4th choice, 130th overall, in 2006 Entry Draft).

| | | | Regular Season | | | | | | | | Playoffs | | | | | | |
|---|---|---|---|---|---|---|---|---|---|---|---|---|---|---|---|---|---|
| Season | Club | League | GP | W | L | O/T | Mins | GA | SO | Avg | GP | W | L | Mins | GA | SO | Avg |
| 2003-04 | Det. Honeybaked | MWEHL | 31 | .... | .... | .... | .... | .... | .... | .... | .... | .... | .... | .... | .... | .... | .... |
| 2004-05 | USNTDP | U-17 | 14 | 10 | 6 | 1 | 930 | 41 | 0 | 2.65 | .... | .... | .... | .... | .... | .... | .... |
| | USNTDP | NAHL | 23 | 10 | 7 | 1 | 1217 | 56 | 1 | 2.76 | 10 | 7 | 3 | 598 | 20 | 3 | 2.01 |
| 2005-06 | USNTDP | U-18 | 12 | 7 | 2 | 0 | 593 | 24 | 0 | 2.43 | .... | .... | .... | .... | .... | .... | .... |
| | USNTDP | NAHL | 5 | 3 | 0 | 0 | 238 | 5 | 0 | 1.26 | .... | .... | .... | .... | .... | .... | .... |
| 2006-07 | Boston University | H-East | 1 | 1 | 0 | 0 | 60 | 1 | 0 | 1.00 | .... | .... | .... | .... | .... | .... | .... |
| 2007-08 | Boston University | H-East | 31 | 16 | 10 | 3 | 1780 | 78 | *3 | 2.63 | .... | .... | .... | .... | .... | .... | .... |
| 2008-09 | Indiana Ice | USHL | *54 | *35 | 17 | 2 | *3110 | 134 | *4 | 2.59 | *13 | *9 | 4 | *789 | 31 | *1 | *2.36 |

## BERKHOEL, Adam (BUHRK-uhl, A-duhm)

Goaltender. Catches left. 5'11", 185 lbs. Born, St. Paul, MN, May 16, 1981.
(Chicago's 12th choice, 240th overall, in 2000 Entry Draft).

| | | | Regular Season | | | | | | | | Playoffs | | | | | | |
|---|---|---|---|---|---|---|---|---|---|---|---|---|---|---|---|---|---|
| Season | Club | League | GP | W | L | O/T | Mins | GA | SO | Avg | GP | W | L | Mins | GA | SO | Avg |
| 99-2000 | Twin Cities | USHL | 49 | 25 | 15 | 7 | 2848 | 129 | 0 | 2.72 | 13 | 7 | 6 | 797 | 43 | 0 | 3.24 |
| 2000-01 | U. of Denver | WCHA | 15 | 7 | 6 | 1 | 745 | 38 | 1 | 3.06 | .... | .... | .... | .... | .... | .... | .... |
| 2001-02 | U. of Denver | WCHA | 18 | 12 | 4 | 1 | 1026 | 40 | 1 | 2.34 | .... | .... | .... | .... | .... | .... | .... |
| 2002-03 | U. of Denver | WCHA | 26 | 12 | 6 | 4 | 1436 | 55 | 3 | *2.30 | .... | .... | .... | .... | .... | .... | .... |
| 2003-04 | U. of Denver | WCHA | 39 | 24 | 11 | 4 | 2225 | 91 | *7 | 2.45 | .... | .... | .... | .... | .... | .... | .... |
| 2004-05 | Chicago Wolves | AHL | 1 | 0 | 1 | 0 | 59 | 4 | 0 | 4.04 | .... | .... | .... | .... | .... | .... | .... |
| | Gwinnett | ECHL | 24 | 9 | 10 | 5 | 1458 | 59 | 2 | 2.43 | 7 | 4 | 1 | 353 | 9 | 0 | *1.53 |
| 2005-06 | Atlanta | NHL | 9 | 2 | 4 | 1 | 473 | 30 | 0 | 3.81 | .... | .... | .... | .... | .... | .... | .... |
| | Chicago Wolves | AHL | 11 | 3 | 6 | 0 | 526 | 32 | 0 | 3.65 | .... | .... | .... | .... | .... | .... | .... |
| | Gwinnett | ECHL | 15 | 10 | 4 | 1 | 902 | 41 | 1 | 2.73 | 9 | 6 | 3 | 551 | 30 | 0 | 3.27 |
| 2006-07 | Rochester | AHL | 6 | 2 | 3 | 0 | 316 | 17 | 0 | 3.22 | .... | .... | .... | .... | .... | .... | .... |
| | Dayton Bombers | ECHL | 43 | 23 | 17 | 3 | 2584 | 105 | 5 | 2.44 | *22 | 12 | 10 | 1385 | 59 | *3 | 2.56 |
| 2007-08 | Grand Rapids | AHL | 31 | 10 | 14 | 4 | 1697 | 83 | 1 | 2.93 | .... | .... | .... | .... | .... | .... | .... |
| 2008-09 | Wilkes-Barre | AHL | 28 | 15 | 11 | 2 | 1635 | 69 | 4 | 2.53 | 6 | 3 | 2 | 340 | 12 | 0 | 2.12 |
| | NHL Totals | | 9 | 2 | 4 | 1 | 473 | 30 | 0 | 3.81 | .... | .... | .... | .... | .... | .... | .... |

USHL All-Rookie Team (2000) • USHL Second All-Star Team (2000) • NCAA Championship All-Tournament Team (2004) • NCAA Championship Tournament MVP (2004) • ECHL First All-Star Team (2007) • ECHL Goaltender of the Year (2007)

Traded to **Atlanta** by **Chicago** for Atlanta's 7th round choice (Adam Hobson) in 2005 Entry Draft, June 27, 2004. Signed as a free agent by **Detroit**, July 3, 2007.

## BERNIER, Jonathan (BAIRN-yay, JAWN-ah-thuhn) L.A.

Goaltender. Catches left. 6', 185 lbs. Born, Laval, Que., August 7, 1988.
(Los Angeles' 1st choice, 11th overall, in 2006 Entry Draft).

| | | | Regular Season | | | | | | | | Playoffs | | | | | | |
|---|---|---|---|---|---|---|---|---|---|---|---|---|---|---|---|---|---|
| Season | Club | League | GP | W | L | O/T | Mins | GA | SO | Avg | GP | W | L | Mins | GA | SO | Avg |
| 2003-04 | Laval Regents | QAAA | 27 | 16 | 4 | 0 | 1329 | 62 | 2 | 2.80 | 3 | 1 | 2 | 180 | 5 | 0 | 1.70 |
| 2004-05 | Lewiston | QMJHL | 23 | 7 | 12 | 3 | 1353 | 67 | 0 | 2.97 | 1 | 0 | 0 | 20 | 0 | 0 | 0.00 |
| 2005-06 | Lewiston | QMJHL | 54 | 27 | 26 | 0 | 3241 | 146 | 2 | 2.70 | 6 | 2 | 4 | 359 | 17 | 1 | 2.84 |
| 2006-07 | Lewiston | QMJHL | 37 | 26 | 10 | .... | 2186 | 94 | 2 | 2.58 | 17 | *16 | 1 | 1025 | 40 | 1 | 2.34 |
| 2007-08 | Los Angeles | NHL | 4 | 1 | 3 | 0 | 238 | 16 | 0 | 4.03 | .... | .... | .... | .... | .... | .... | .... |
| | Lewiston | QMJHL | 34 | 18 | 15 | .... | 2024 | 92 | 0 | 2.73 | 6 | 2 | 4 | 348 | 17 | 0 | 2.93 |
| | Manchester | AHL | 3 | 1 | 1 | 1 | 184 | 5 | 0 | 1.63 | 3 | 0 | 3 | 195 | 9 | 0 | 2.76 |
| 2008-09 | Manchester | AHL | 54 | 23 | 24 | 4 | 3101 | 124 | 5 | 2.40 | .... | .... | .... | .... | .... | .... | .... |
| | NHL Totals | | 4 | 1 | 3 | 0 | 238 | 16 | 0 | 4.03 | .... | .... | .... | .... | .... | .... | .... |

QMJHL Second All-Star Team (2007) • Canadian Major Junior Second All-Star Team (2007)

## BERRA, Reto (BAIR-ruh, REH-toh) ST.L.

Goaltender. Catches left. 6'4", 209 lbs. Born, Bulach, Switz., January 3, 1987.
(St. Louis' 6th choice, 106th overall, in 2006 Entry Draft).

| | | | Regular Season | | | | | | | | Playoffs | | | | | | |
|---|---|---|---|---|---|---|---|---|---|---|---|---|---|---|---|---|---|
| Season | Club | League | GP | W | L | O/T | Mins | GA | SO | Avg | GP | W | L | Mins | GA | SO | Avg |
| 2004-05 | GCK Zurich Jr. | Swiss-Jr. | 22 | .... | .... | .... | .... | .... | .... | .... | .... | .... | .... | .... | .... | .... | .... |
| | GCK Lions Zurich | Swiss-2 | 3 | .... | .... | .... | 180 | 12 | 0 | 4.00 | .... | .... | .... | .... | .... | .... | .... |
| | EHC Dubendorf | Swiss-3 | STATISTICS NOT AVAILABLE | | | | | | | | | | | | | | |
| 2005-06 | GCK Zurich Jr. | Swiss-Jr. | 23 | .... | .... | .... | .... | .... | .... | .... | .... | .... | .... | .... | .... | .... | .... |
| | GCK Lions Zurich | Swiss-2 | 15 | .... | .... | .... | 835 | 51 | 1 | 3.56 | .... | .... | .... | .... | .... | .... | .... |
| | ZSC Lions Zurich | Swiss | 2 | 0 | 1 | 0 | 90 | 6 | 0 | 3.99 | .... | .... | .... | .... | .... | .... | .... |
| 2006-07 | Switzerland U20 | Swiss-2 | 3 | 0 | 3 | 0 | 179 | 13 | 0 | 4.69 | .... | .... | .... | .... | .... | .... | .... |
| | GCK Lions Zurich | Swiss-2 | 6 | 4 | 2 | 0 | 359 | 18 | 0 | 3.01 | .... | .... | .... | .... | .... | .... | .... |
| | ZSC Lions Zurich | Swiss | 2 | 1 | 0 | 0 | 78 | 4 | 0 | 3.08 | 4 | 0 | 3 | 188 | 9 | 0 | 2.87 |
| 2007-08 | HC Davos | Swiss | 16 | 9 | 7 | 0 | 966 | 44 | 0 | 2.73 | .... | .... | .... | .... | .... | .... | .... |
| 2008-09 | EV Zug | Swiss | 6 | 1 | 5 | 0 | 368 | 17 | 0 | 2.77 | .... | .... | .... | .... | .... | .... | .... |
| | SCL Tigers Langnau | Swiss | 2 | 1 | 1 | 0 | 120 | 9 | 0 | 4.50 | .... | .... | .... | .... | .... | .... | .... |
| | HC Davos | Swiss | 8 | 3 | 4 | 0 | 445 | 20 | 0 | 2.70 | 4 | 3 | 1 | 216 | 5 | 0 | 1.39 |

## BERUBE, Jean-Francois (beh-ROO-bay, ZHAWN-fran-SWUH) L.A.

Goaltender. Catches left. 6'1", 155 lbs. Born, Repentigny, Que., July 13, 1991.
(Los Angeles' 4th choice, 95th overall, in 2009 Entry Draft).

| | | | Regular Season | | | | | | | | Playoffs | | | | | | |
|---|---|---|---|---|---|---|---|---|---|---|---|---|---|---|---|---|---|
| Season | Club | League | GP | W | L | O/T | Mins | GA | SO | Avg | GP | W | L | Mins | GA | SO | Avg |
| 2007-08 | Laurentides | QAAA | 10 | 0 | 6 | 1 | 511 | 35 | 0 | 4.11 | .... | .... | .... | .... | .... | .... | .... |
| | Lachute Stars | QueAA | STATISTICS NOT AVAILABLE | | | | | | | | | | | | | | |
| 2008-09 | Montreal | QMJHL | 20 | 6 | 9 | .... | 1059 | 51 | 1 | 2.89 | 1 | 0 | 0 | 20 | 1 | 0 | 3.00 |

## BESKOROWANY, Tyler (behs-koor-WAH-nee, TIGH-luhr) DAL.

Goaltender. Catches left. 6'4", 203 lbs. Born, Sudbury, Ont., April 28, 1990.
(Dallas' 1st choice, 59th overall, in 2008 Entry Draft).

| | | | Regular Season | | | | | | | | Playoffs | | | | | | |
|---|---|---|---|---|---|---|---|---|---|---|---|---|---|---|---|---|---|
| Season | Club | League | GP | W | L | O/T | Mins | GA | SO | Avg | GP | W | L | Mins | GA | SO | Avg |
| 2006-07 | Valley East Cobras | GNML | 32 | .... | .... | .... | 1443 | 80 | 1 | 3.33 | 7 | .... | .... | 410 | 22 | 2 | 3.22 |
| 2007-08 | Owen Sound | OHL | 35 | 12 | 19 | 3 | 2021 | 136 | 0 | 4.04 | .... | .... | .... | .... | .... | .... | .... |
| 2008-09 | Owen Sound | OHL | 37 | 11 | 12 | 10 | 2160 | 131 | 1 | 3.64 | 1 | 0 | 1 | 27 | 5 | 0 | 11.16 |

## BIRON, Martin (BEE-rawn, MAHR-tihn) NYI

Goaltender. Catches left. 6'3", 180 lbs. Born, Lac-St-Charles, Que., August 15, 1977.
(Buffalo's 2nd choice, 16th overall, in 1995 Entry Draft).

| | | | Regular Season | | | | | | | | Playoffs | | | | | | |
|---|---|---|---|---|---|---|---|---|---|---|---|---|---|---|---|---|---|
| Season | Club | League | GP | W | L | O/T | Mins | GA | SO | Avg | GP | W | L | Mins | GA | SO | Avg |
| 1993-94 | Trois-Rivieres | QAAA | 23 | 14 | 8 | 1 | 1412 | 80 | 1 | 3.40 | 2 | 1 | 1 | 112 | 7 | 0 | 3.73 |
| 1994-95 | Beauport Harfangs | QMJHL | 56 | 29 | 16 | 9 | 3193 | 132 | 3 | *2.48 | 16 | 8 | 7 | 900 | 37 | *4 | 2.47 |
| 1995-96 | Beauport Harfangs | QMJHL | 55 | 29 | 17 | 7 | 3201 | 152 | 1 | 2.85 | *19 | *12 | 7 | 1134 | 64 | 0 | 3.39 |
| | Buffalo | NHL | 3 | 0 | 2 | 0 | 119 | 10 | 0 | 5.04 | .... | .... | .... | .... | .... | .... | .... |
| 1996-97 | Beauport Harfangs | QMJHL | 18 | 6 | 9 | 1 | 928 | 61 | 1 | 3.94 | .... | .... | .... | .... | .... | .... | .... |
| | Hull Olympiques | QMJHL | 16 | 11 | 4 | 1 | 974 | 43 | 2 | 2.65 | 6 | 3 | 1 | 325 | 19 | 0 | 3.51 |
| 1997-98 | South Carolina | ECHL | 2 | 0 | 1 | 1 | 86 | 3 | 0 | 2.09 | .... | .... | .... | .... | .... | .... | .... |
| | Rochester | AHL | 41 | 14 | 18 | 6 | 2312 | 113 | *5 | 2.93 | 4 | 1 | 3 | 239 | 16 | 0 | 4.01 |
| 1998-99 | Buffalo | NHL | 6 | 1 | 2 | 1 | 281 | 10 | 0 | 2.14 | .... | .... | .... | .... | .... | .... | .... |
| | Rochester | AHL | 52 | 36 | 13 | 3 | 3129 | 108 | *6 | *2.07 | *20 | 12 | 8 | 1167 | 42 | 1 | *2.16 |
| 99-2000 | Buffalo | NHL | 41 | 19 | 18 | 2 | 2229 | 90 | 5 | 2.42 | .... | .... | .... | .... | .... | .... | .... |
| | Rochester | AHL | 6 | 6 | 0 | 0 | 344 | 12 | 1 | 2.09 | .... | .... | .... | .... | .... | .... | .... |
| 2000-01 | Buffalo | NHL | 18 | 7 | 7 | 1 | 918 | 39 | 2 | 2.55 | .... | .... | .... | .... | .... | .... | .... |
| | Rochester | AHL | 4 | 3 | 1 | 0 | 239 | 4 | 1 | 1.00 | .... | .... | .... | .... | .... | .... | .... |
| 2001-02 | Buffalo | NHL | 72 | 31 | 28 | 10 | 4085 | 151 | 4 | 2.22 | .... | .... | .... | .... | .... | .... | .... |
| 2002-03 | Buffalo | NHL | 54 | 17 | 28 | 6 | 3170 | 135 | 4 | 2.56 | .... | .... | .... | .... | .... | .... | .... |
| 2003-04 | Buffalo | NHL | 52 | 26 | 18 | 5 | 2972 | 125 | 2 | 2.52 | .... | .... | .... | .... | .... | .... | .... |
| 2004-05 | | | | | | | DID NOT PLAY | | | | | | | | | | |
| 2005-06 | Buffalo | NHL | 35 | 21 | 8 | 3 | 1934 | 93 | 1 | 2.89 | .... | .... | .... | .... | .... | .... | .... |
| 2006-07 | Buffalo | NHL | 19 | 12 | 4 | 1 | 1066 | 54 | 0 | 3.04 | .... | .... | .... | .... | .... | .... | .... |
| | Philadelphia | NHL | 16 | 6 | 8 | 2 | 935 | 47 | 0 | 3.02 | .... | .... | .... | .... | .... | .... | .... |
| 2007-08 | Philadelphia | NHL | 62 | 30 | 20 | 9 | 3539 | 153 | 5 | 2.59 | 17 | 9 | 8 | 1049 | 52 | 1 | 2.97 |
| 2008-09 | Philadelphia | NHL | 55 | 29 | 19 | 5 | 3177 | 146 | 2 | 2.76 | 6 | 2 | 4 | 375 | 16 | 1 | 2.56 |
| | **NHL Totals** | | **433** | **199** | **162** | **45** | **24425** | **1053** | **25** | **2.59** | **23** | **11** | **12** | **1424** | **68** | **2** | **2.87** |

QMJHL All-Rookie Team (1995) • Canadian Major Junior First All-Star Team (1995) • Canadian Major Junior Goaltender of the Year (1995) • AHL First All-Star Team (1999) • Harry "Hap" Holmes Memorial Award (AHL – fewest goals against) (1999) (shared with Tom Draper) • Aldege "Baz" Bastien Memorial Award (AHL – Outstanding Goaltender) (1999)

Traded to **Philadelphia** by **Buffalo** for Philadelphia's 2nd round choice (T.J. Brennan) in 2007 Entry Draft, February 27, 2007. Signed as a free agent by **NY Islanders**, July 22, 2009.

## BISHOP, Ben (BIH-shuhp, BEHN) ST.L.

Goaltender. Catches left. 6'7", 210 lbs. Born, Denver, CO, November 21, 1986.
(St. Louis' 3rd choice, 85th overall, in 2005 Entry Draft).

| | | | Regular Season | | | | | | | | Playoffs | | | | | | |
|---|---|---|---|---|---|---|---|---|---|---|---|---|---|---|---|---|---|
| Season | Club | League | GP | W | L | O/T | Mins | GA | SO | Avg | GP | W | L | Mins | GA | SO | Avg |
| 2003-04 | St.L. AAA Blues | MAHL | 11 | 8 | 1 | 2 | 660 | 19 | 1 | 1.73 | .... | .... | .... | .... | .... | .... | .... |
| | St.L. AAA Blues | Exhib. | 26 | 15 | 7 | 4 | 1480 | 62 | 3 | 2.51 | .... | .... | .... | .... | .... | .... | .... |
| 2004-05 | Texas Tornado | NAHL | 45 | *35 | 8 | 0 | 2577 | 83 | 5 | 1.93 | *11 | *9 | 2 | *660 | 30 | 0 | 2.73 |
| 2005-06 | University of Maine | H-East | 31 | 21 | 8 | 2 | 1788 | 68 | 0 | 2.28 | .... | .... | .... | .... | .... | .... | .... |
| 2006-07 | University of Maine | H-East | 34 | 21 | 9 | 2 | 1907 | 68 | 3 | 2.14 | .... | .... | .... | .... | .... | .... | .... |
| 2007-08 | University of Maine | H-East | 34 | 13 | 18 | 3 | 1972 | 80 | 2 | 2.43 | .... | .... | .... | .... | .... | .... | .... |
| | Peoria Rivermen | AHL | 5 | 2 | 2 | 1 | 302 | 12 | 0 | 2.38 | .... | .... | .... | .... | .... | .... | .... |
| 2008-09 | St. Louis | NHL | 6 | 1 | 1 | 1 | 245 | 12 | 0 | 2.94 | .... | .... | .... | .... | .... | .... | .... |
| | Peoria Rivermen | AHL | 33 | 15 | 16 | 1 | 1898 | 89 | 1 | 2.81 | .... | .... | .... | .... | .... | .... | .... |
| | **NHL Totals** | | **6** | **1** | **1** | **1** | **245** | **12** | **0** | **2.94** | .... | .... | .... | .... | .... | .... | .... |

Hockey East All-Rookie Team (2006) • Hockey East Second All-Star Team (2008)

## BJURLING, Bjorn (b-YUHR-lihng, b-YOHRN) EDM.

Goaltender. Catches left. 6', 205 lbs. Born, Stockholm, Sweden, August 21, 1979.
(Edmonton's 10th choice, 274th overall, in 2004 Entry Draft).

| | | | Regular Season | | | | | | | | Playoffs | | | | | | |
|---|---|---|---|---|---|---|---|---|---|---|---|---|---|---|---|---|---|
| Season | Club | League | GP | W | L | O/T | Mins | GA | SO | Avg | GP | W | L | Mins | GA | SO | Avg |
| 2000-01 | Bodens IK | Sweden-2 | 32 | .... | .... | .... | 1914 | 80 | 0 | 2.51 | 6 | .... | .... | 398 | 16 | 1 | 2.41 |
| 2001-02 | Bodens IK | Sweden-2 | 43 | .... | .... | .... | 2568 | 128 | 2 | 2.99 | 9 | .... | .... | 508 | 36 | 0 | 4.25 |
| 2002-03 | Bodens IK | Sweden-2 | 3 | .... | .... | .... | 179 | 7 | 1 | 2.35 | .... | .... | .... | .... | .... | .... | .... |
| | Djurgarden | Sweden | 15 | .... | .... | .... | 571 | 21 | 2 | 2.21 | .... | .... | .... | .... | .... | .... | .... |
| 2003-04 | Djurgarden | Sweden | 45 | .... | .... | .... | 2601 | 100 | 4 | 2.31 | 2 | .... | .... | 100 | 15 | 0 | 9.00 |
| 2004-05 | Djurgarden | Sweden | 24 | .... | .... | .... | 1441 | 61 | 1 | 2.54 | .... | .... | .... | .... | .... | .... | .... |
| 2005-06 | Salzburg | Austria | 23 | .... | .... | .... | 1367 | 78 | 1 | 3.42 | .... | .... | .... | .... | .... | .... | .... |
| | Geneve | Swiss | 7 | 2 | 2 | 2 | 430 | 24 | 1 | 3.35 | .... | .... | .... | .... | .... | .... | .... |
| 2006-07 | Valerengen IF Oslo | Norway | 35 | .... | .... | .... | 2027 | 69 | 5 | 2.04 | 15 | .... | .... | 907 | 32 | 1 | 2.11 |
| 2007-08 | Sodertalje SK | Sweden | 30 | .... | .... | .... | 1752 | 70 | 2 | 2.40 | .... | .... | .... | .... | .... | .... | .... |
| 2008-09 | Sodertalje SK | Sweden | 36 | .... | .... | .... | 2168 | 110 | 0 | 3.04 | .... | .... | .... | .... | .... | .... | .... |
| | Sodertalje SK | Sweden-Q | 2 | .... | .... | .... | 105 | 6 | 0 | 3.43 | .... | .... | .... | .... | .... | .... | .... |

## BOBKOV, Igor (bawb-KAWF, EE-gohr) ANA.

Goaltender. Catches left. 6'4", 192 lbs. Born, Surgut, USSR, January 2, 1991.
(Anaheim's 4th choice, 76th overall, in 2009 Entry Draft).

| | | | Regular Season | | | | | | | | Playoffs | | | | | | |
|---|---|---|---|---|---|---|---|---|---|---|---|---|---|---|---|---|---|
| Season | Club | League | GP | W | L | O/T | Mins | GA | SO | Avg | GP | W | L | Mins | GA | SO | Avg |
| 2008-09 | Magnitogorsk 2 | Russia-3 | 9 | .... | .... | .... | .... | 24 | .... | .... | .... | .... | .... | .... | .... | .... | .... |

## BOUCHER, Brian (BOO-shay, BRIGH-uhn) PHI.

Goaltender. Catches left. 6'2", 200 lbs. Born, Woonsocket, RI, January 2, 1977.
(Philadelphia's 1st choice, 22nd overall, in 1995 Entry Draft).

| | | | Regular Season | | | | | | | | Playoffs | | | | | | |
|---|---|---|---|---|---|---|---|---|---|---|---|---|---|---|---|---|---|
| Season | Club | League | GP | W | L | O/T | Mins | GA | SO | Avg | GP | W | L | Mins | GA | SO | Avg |
| 1993-94 | Mount St. Charles | High-RI | 15 | *14 | 0 | 1 | *504 | *8 | *9 | *0.57 | 4 | *4 | 0 | *180 | *6 | *1 | *1.20 |
| 1994-95 | Wexford Raiders | MTJHL | 8 | .... | .... | .... | 425 | 23 | 0 | 3.25 | .... | .... | .... | .... | .... | .... | .... |
| | Tri-City Americans | WHL | 35 | 17 | 11 | 2 | 1969 | 108 | 1 | 3.29 | 13 | 6 | 5 | 795 | 50 | 0 | 3.77 |
| 1995-96 | Tri-City Americans | WHL | 55 | 33 | 19 | 2 | 3183 | 181 | 1 | 3.41 | 11 | 6 | 5 | 653 | 37 | *2 | 3.40 |
| 1996-97 | Tri-City Americans | WHL | 41 | 10 | 24 | 6 | 2458 | 149 | 1 | 3.64 | .... | .... | .... | .... | .... | .... | .... |
| 1997-98 | Philadelphia | AHL | 34 | 16 | 12 | 3 | 1901 | 101 | 0 | 3.19 | 2 | 0 | 0 | 30 | 1 | 0 | 1.95 |
| 1998-99 | Philadelphia | AHL | 36 | 20 | 8 | 5 | 2061 | 89 | 2 | 2.59 | 16 | 9 | 7 | 947 | 45 | 0 | 2.85 |
| 99-2000 | Philadelphia | NHL | 35 | 20 | 10 | 3 | 2038 | 65 | 4 | *1.91 | 18 | 11 | 7 | 1183 | 40 | 1 | 2.03 |
| | Philadelphia | AHL | 1 | 0 | 0 | 1 | 65 | 3 | 0 | 2.77 | .... | .... | .... | .... | .... | .... | .... |
| 2000-01 | Philadelphia | NHL | 27 | 8 | 12 | 5 | 1470 | 80 | 1 | 3.27 | 1 | 0 | 0 | 37 | 3 | 0 | 4.86 |
| 2001-02 | Philadelphia | NHL | 41 | 18 | 16 | 4 | 2295 | 92 | 2 | 2.41 | 2 | 0 | 1 | 88 | 2 | 0 | 1.36 |
| 2002-03 | Phoenix | NHL | 45 | 15 | 20 | 8 | 2544 | 128 | 0 | 3.02 | .... | .... | .... | .... | .... | .... | .... |
| 2003-04 | Phoenix | NHL | 40 | 10 | 19 | 10 | 2364 | 108 | 5 | 2.74 | .... | .... | .... | .... | .... | .... | .... |
| 2004-05 | HV 71 Jonkoping | Sweden | 4 | .... | .... | .... | 235 | 13 | 0 | 3.32 | .... | .... | .... | .... | .... | .... | .... |
| 2005-06 | Phoenix | NHL | 11 | 3 | 6 | 0 | 512 | 33 | 0 | 3.87 | .... | .... | .... | .... | .... | .... | .... |
| | San Antonio | AHL | 6 | 2 | 3 | 0 | 345 | 8 | 0 | 1.39 | .... | .... | .... | .... | .... | .... | .... |
| | Calgary | NHL | 3 | 1 | 2 | 0 | 182 | 15 | 0 | 4.95 | .... | .... | .... | .... | .... | .... | .... |
| 2006-07 | Chicago | NHL | 15 | 1 | 10 | 3 | 827 | 45 | 1 | 3.26 | .... | .... | .... | .... | .... | .... | .... |
| | Columbus | NHL | 3 | 1 | 1 | 0 | 142 | 9 | 0 | 3.80 | .... | .... | .... | .... | .... | .... | .... |
| 2007-08 | Philadelphia | AHL | 42 | 23 | 16 | 1 | 2288 | 94 | 4 | 2.47 | .... | .... | .... | .... | .... | .... | .... |
| | San Jose | NHL | 5 | 3 | 1 | 1 | 238 | 7 | 1 | 1.76 | 1 | 0 | 0 | 2 | 0 | 0 | 0.00 |
| 2008-09 | San Jose | NHL | 22 | 12 | 6 | 3 | 1291 | 47 | 2 | 2.18 | .... | .... | .... | .... | .... | .... | .... |
| | **NHL Totals** | | **247** | **92** | **103** | **37** | **13903** | **629** | **16** | **2.71** | **22** | **11** | **8** | **1310** | **45** | **1** | **2.06** |

WHL West Second All-Star Team (1996) • WHL West First All-Star Team (1997) • WHL Goaltender of the Year (1997) • NHL All-Rookie Team (2000)

Traded to **Phoenix** by **Philadelphia** with Nashville's 3rd round choice (previously acquired, Phoenix selected Joe Callahan) in 2002 Entry Draft for Michal Handzus and Robert Esche, June 12, 2002. Signed as a free agent by **Jonkoping** (Sweden), October 20, 2004. Traded to **Calgary** by **Phoenix** with Mike Leclerc for Steve Reinprecht and Philippe Sauve, February 2, 2006. Signed as a free agent by **Chicago**, September 24, 2006. Claimed on waivers by **Columbus** from **Chicago**, February 27, 2007. Signed as a free agent by **Philadelphia** (AHL), July 23, 2007. Signed as a free agent by **San Jose**, February 26, 2008. Signed as a free agent by **Philadelphia**, July 1, 2009.

## BRODEUR, Martin (broh-DUHR, MAHR-tihn) N.J.

Goaltender. Catches left. 6'2", 215 lbs. Born, Montreal, Que., May 6, 1972.
(New Jersey's 1st choice, 20th overall, in 1990 Entry Draft).

| | | | Regular Season | | | | | | | | Playoffs | | | | | | |
|---|---|---|---|---|---|---|---|---|---|---|---|---|---|---|---|---|---|
| Season | Club | League | GP | W | L | O/T | Mins | GA | SO | Avg | GP | W | L | Mins | GA | SO | Avg |
| 1988-89 | Montreal-Bourassa | QAAA | 27 | 13 | 12 | 1 | 1580 | 98 | 0 | 3.72 | 3 | 0 | 3 | 210 | 14 | 0 | 3.99 |
| 1989-90 | St-Hyacinthe Laser | QMJHL | 42 | 23 | 13 | 2 | 2333 | 156 | 0 | 4.01 | 12 | 5 | 7 | 678 | 46 | 0 | 4.07 |
| 1990-91 | St-Hyacinthe Laser | QMJHL | 52 | 22 | 24 | 4 | 2946 | 162 | 2 | 3.30 | 4 | 0 | 4 | 232 | 16 | 0 | 4.14 |
| 1991-92 | St-Hyacinthe Laser | QMJHL | 48 | 27 | 16 | 4 | 2846 | 161 | 2 | 3.39 | 5 | 2 | 3 | 317 | 14 | 0 | 2.65 |
| | New Jersey | NHL | 4 | 2 | 1 | 0 | 179 | 10 | 0 | 3.35 | 1 | 0 | 1 | 32 | 3 | 0 | 5.63 |
| 1992-93 | Utica Devils | AHL | 32 | 14 | 13 | 5 | 1952 | 131 | 0 | 4.03 | 4 | 1 | 3 | 258 | 18 | 0 | 4.19 |
| 1993-94 | New Jersey | NHL | 47 | 27 | 11 | 8 | 2625 | 105 | 3 | 2.40 | 17 | 8 | 9 | 1171 | 38 | 1 | 1.95 |
| 1994-95 ♦ | New Jersey | NHL | 40 | 19 | 11 | 6 | 2184 | 89 | 3 | 2.45 | *20 | *16 | 4 | *1222 | 34 | *3 | *1.67 |
| 1995-96 | New Jersey | NHL | 77 | 34 | 30 | 12 | *4433 | 173 | 6 | 2.34 | .... | .... | .... | .... | .... | .... | .... |
| 1996-97 | New Jersey | NHL | 67 | 37 | 14 | 13 | 3838 | 120 | *10 | *1.88 | 10 | 5 | 5 | 659 | 19 | 2 | *1.73 |
| 1997-98 | New Jersey | NHL | 70 | *43 | 17 | 8 | 4128 | 130 | 10 | 1.89 | 6 | 2 | 4 | 366 | 12 | 0 | 1.97 |
| 1998-99 | New Jersey | NHL | *70 | *39 | 21 | 10 | *4239 | 162 | 4 | 2.29 | 7 | 3 | 4 | 425 | 20 | 0 | 2.82 |
| 99-2000 ♦ | New Jersey | NHL | 72 | *43 | 20 | 8 | 4312 | 161 | 6 | 2.24 | *23 | *16 | 7 | *1450 | 39 | 2 | *1.61 |
| 2000-01 | New Jersey | NHL | 72 | *42 | 17 | 11 | 4297 | 166 | 9 | 2.32 | *25 | 15 | 10 | *1505 | 52 | *4 | 2.07 |
| 2001-02 | New Jersey | NHL | *73 | 38 | 26 | 9 | *4347 | 156 | 4 | 2.15 | 6 | 2 | 4 | 381 | 9 | 1 | 1.42 |
| | Canada | Olympics | 5 | *4 | 0 | 1 | 300 | 9 | 0 | *1.80 | .... | .... | .... | .... | .... | .... | .... |
| 2002-03 ♦ | New Jersey | NHL | 73 | *41 | 23 | 9 | 4374 | 147 | *9 | 2.02 | *24 | *16 | 8 | *1491 | 41 | *7 | 1.65 |
| 2003-04 | New Jersey | NHL | *75 | *38 | 26 | 11 | *4555 | 154 | *11 | 2.03 | 5 | 1 | 4 | 298 | 13 | 0 | 2.62 |
| 2004-05 | | | | | | | DID NOT PLAY | | | | | | | | | | |
| 2005-06 | New Jersey | NHL | 73 | *43 | 23 | 7 | 4365 | 187 | 5 | 2.57 | 9 | 5 | 4 | 533 | 20 | 1 | 2.25 |
| | Canada | Olympics | 4 | 2 | 2 | 0 | 239 | 8 | 0 | 2.01 | .... | .... | .... | .... | .... | .... | .... |
| 2006-07 | New Jersey | NHL | *78 | *48 | 23 | 7 | *4697 | 171 | *12 | 2.18 | 11 | 5 | 6 | 688 | 28 | 1 | 2.44 |
| 2007-08 | New Jersey | NHL | *77 | 44 | 27 | 6 | *4635 | 168 | 4 | 2.17 | 5 | 1 | 4 | 301 | 16 | 0 | 3.19 |
| 2008-09 | New Jersey | NHL | 31 | 19 | 9 | 3 | 1814 | 73 | 5 | 2.41 | 7 | 3 | 4 | 427 | 17 | 1 | 2.39 |
| | **NHL Totals** | | **999** | **557** | **299** | **128** | **59022** | **2172** | **101** | **2.21** | **176** | **98** | **78** | **10949** | **361** | **23** | **1.98** |

QMJHL All-Rookie Team (1990) • QMJHL Second All-Star Team (1992) • NHL All-Rookie Team (1994) • Calder Memorial Trophy (1994) • NHL Second All-Star Team (1997, 1998, 2006, 2008) • William M. Jennings Trophy (1997) (shared with Mike Dunham) • William M. Jennings Trophy (1998, 2004) • NHL First All-Star Team (2003, 2004, 2007) • William M. Jennings Trophy (2003) (tied with Roman Cechmanek/Robert Esche) • Vezina Trophy (2003, 2004, 2007, 2008)

Played in NHL All-Star Game (1996, 1997, 1998, 1999, 2000, 2001, 2003, 2004, 2007)

• Scored a goal in playoffs vs. Montreal, April 17, 1997. • Missed majority of 2008-09 season recovering from elbow injury suffered in game vs. Atlanta, November 1, 2008 and resulting surgery, November 6, 2008.

## BRODEUR, Mike (broh-DUHR, MIGHK) OTT.

Goaltender. Catches left. 6'2", 171 lbs. Born, Calgary, Alta., March 30, 1983.
(Chicago's 7th choice, 211th overall, in 2003 Entry Draft).

| | | | Regular Season | | | | | | | | Playoffs | | | | | | |
|---|---|---|---|---|---|---|---|---|---|---|---|---|---|---|---|---|---|
| Season | Club | League | GP | W | L | O/T | Mins | GA | SO | Avg | GP | W | L | Mins | GA | SO | Avg |
| 2000-01 | Cgy. AAA Flames | AMHL | 21 | 11 | 8 | 3 | 1231 | 54 | 1 | 2.63 | 10 | 6 | 4 | 620 | 31 | 0 | 3.00 |
| 2001-02 | Camrose Kodiaks | AJHL | 24 | 13 | 9 | 1 | 1299 | 65 | 1 | 2.91 | .... | .... | .... | .... | .... | .... | .... |
| 2002-03 | Camrose Kodiaks | AJHL | 48 | 28 | 16 | 2 | 2570 | 113 | 2 | 2.64 | 21 | 16 | 5 | 1378 | 48 | 4 | 2.09 |
| 2003-04 | Moose Jaw | WHL | 41 | 23 | 12 | 5 | 2385 | 84 | 5 | 2.11 | 10 | 6 | 4 | 624 | 18 | 1 | *1.73 |
| 2004-05 | Norfolk Admirals | AHL | 1 | 0 | 1 | 0 | 39 | 4 | 0 | 6.17 | .... | .... | .... | .... | .... | .... | .... |
| | Greenville Grrrowl | ECHL | 35 | 19 | 15 | 1 | 2081 | 93 | 2 | 2.68 | 5 | 2 | 3 | 302 | 10 | 1 | 1.98 |
| 2005-06 | Greenville Grrrowl | ECHL | 24 | 14 | 8 | 2 | 1466 | 63 | 1 | 2.58 | .... | .... | .... | .... | .... | .... | .... |
| 2006-07 | Norfolk Admirals | AHL | 10 | 4 | 3 | 0 | 495 | 28 | 0 | 3.39 | 1 | 0 | 0 | 8 | 2 | 0 | 14.17 |
| | Augusta Lynx | ECHL | 2 | 2 | 0 | 0 | 120 | 4 | 1 | 2.00 | .... | .... | .... | .... | .... | .... | .... |
| | Toledo Storm | ECHL | 5 | 3 | 2 | 0 | 300 | 10 | 2 | 2.00 | .... | .... | .... | .... | .... | .... | .... |
| 2007-08 | Rockford IceHogs | AHL | 8 | 2 | 3 | 0 | 341 | 16 | 0 | 2.81 | .... | .... | .... | .... | .... | .... | .... |
| | Pensacola Ice Pilots | ECHL | 26 | 10 | 9 | 5 | 1504 | 71 | 1 | 2.83 | .... | .... | .... | .... | .... | .... | .... |
| 2008-09 | Rochester | AHL | 38 | 18 | 13 | 4 | 2127 | 87 | 2 | 2.45 | .... | .... | .... | .... | .... | .... | .... |
| | Augusta Lynx | ECHL | 8 | 2 | 4 | 1 | 457 | 23 | 1 | 3.02 | .... | .... | .... | .... | .... | .... | .... |

Signed as a free agent by **Ottawa**, July 1, 2009.

## BROWN, David (BROWN, DAY-vihd)

Goaltender. Catches left. 6', 185 lbs. Born, Stoney Creek, Ont., February 11, 1985.
(Pittsburgh's 11th choice, 228th overall, in 2004 Entry Draft).

| | | | Regular Season | | | | | | | | Playoffs | | | | | | |
|---|---|---|---|---|---|---|---|---|---|---|---|---|---|---|---|---|---|
| Season | Club | League | GP | W | L | O/T | Mins | GA | SO | Avg | GP | W | L | Mins | GA | SO | Avg |
| 2002-03 | Hamilton Kilty B's | OPJHL | 35 | .... | .... | .... | .... | .... | .... | 3.11 | .... | .... | .... | .... | .... | .... | .... |
| 2003-04 | U. of Notre Dame | CCHA | 26 | 14 | 7 | 3 | 1445 | 56 | 5 | 2.32 | .... | .... | .... | .... | .... | .... | .... |
| 2004-05 | U. of Notre Dame | CCHA | 15 | 2 | 10 | 1 | 767 | 55 | 0 | 4.30 | .... | .... | .... | .... | .... | .... | .... |
| 2005-06 | U. of Notre Dame | CCHA | 31 | 9 | 15 | 4 | 1724 | 71 | 0 | 2.47 | .... | .... | .... | .... | .... | .... | .... |
| 2006-07 | U. of Notre Dame | CCHA | 39 | *30 | 6 | 3 | 2390 | 63 | *6 | *1.58 | .... | .... | .... | .... | .... | .... | .... |
| 2007-08 | Wilkes-Barre | AHL | 19 | 9 | 7 | 1 | 1050 | 41 | 0 | 2.34 | 1 | 0 | 0 | 20 | 1 | 0 | 3.00 |
| | Wheeling Nailers | ECHL | 13 | 6 | 6 | 1 | 707 | 39 | 0 | 3.31 | .... | .... | .... | .... | .... | .... | .... |
| 2008-09 | Wilkes-Barre | AHL | 4 | 1 | 2 | 0 | 198 | 13 | 0 | 3.94 | .... | .... | .... | .... | .... | .... | .... |
| | Wheeling Nailers | ECHL | 24 | 14 | 6 | 2 | 1355 | 69 | 0 | 3.06 | 1 | 0 | 0 | 12 | 1 | 0 | 5.11 |

CCHA First All-Star Team (2007) • CCHA Player of the Year (2007) • NCAA West First All-American Team (2007)

## BRUST, Barry (BRUHST, BAIR-ree) MIN.

Goaltender. Catches left. 6'2", 235 lbs. Born, Swan River, Man., August 8, 1983.
(Minnesota's 4th choice, 73rd overall, in 2002 Entry Draft).

| | | | Regular Season | | | | | | | | Playoffs | | | | | | |
|---|---|---|---|---|---|---|---|---|---|---|---|---|---|---|---|---|---|
| Season | Club | League | GP | W | L | O/T | Mins | GA | SO | Avg | GP | W | L | Mins | GA | SO | Avg |
| 99-2000 | Swan Valley | MJHL | 19 | 10 | 9 | 0 | 1140 | 67 | 0 | 3.50 | .... | .... | .... | .... | .... | .... | .... |
| 2000-01 | Spokane Chiefs | WHL | 16 | 4 | 6 | 1 | 777 | 42 | 0 | 3.24 | .... | .... | .... | .... | .... | .... | .... |
| 2001-02 | Spokane Chiefs | WHL | 60 | 28 | 21 | 10 | 3540 | 152 | 1 | 2.58 | 11 | 6 | 5 | 677 | 23 | 0 | 2.04 |
| 2002-03 | Spokane Chiefs | WHL | *59 | 22 | 31 | 4 | *3385 | 194 | 0 | 3.44 | 11 | 4 | 7 | 722 | 37 | 0 | 3.07 |
| 2003-04 | Spokane Chiefs | WHL | 27 | 10 | 13 | 2 | 1505 | 75 | 0 | 2.99 | .... | .... | .... | .... | .... | .... | .... |
| | Calgary Hitmen | WHL | 25 | 12 | 8 | 3 | 1448 | 54 | 2 | 2.24 | 7 | 3 | 4 | 457 | 15 | 2 | 1.97 |
| 2004-05 | Reading Royals | ECHL | 42 | 27 | 9 | 4 | 2413 | 79 | 4 | 1.96 | 8 | 4 | 4 | 481 | 14 | 2 | 1.74 |
| 2005-06 | Manchester | AHL | 35 | 19 | 14 | 1 | 1971 | 89 | 2 | 2.71 | 5 | 2 | 2 | 279 | 17 | 1 | 3.66 |
| | Reading Royals | ECHL | 6 | 3 | 3 | 0 | 361 | 18 | 0 | 3.00 | .... | .... | .... | .... | .... | .... | .... |
| 2006-07 | Los Angeles | NHL | 11 | 2 | 4 | 1 | 486 | 30 | 0 | 3.70 | .... | .... | .... | .... | .... | .... | .... |
| | Manchester | AHL | 18 | 9 | 7 | 0 | 951 | 38 | 2 | 2.40 | 5 | 2 | 1 | 199 | 6 | 0 | 1.81 |
| 2007-08 | Houston Aeros | AHL | 43 | 24 | 16 | 3 | 2380 | 90 | 4 | 2.27 | 3 | 1 | 2 | 202 | 6 | 1 | 1.78 |

| | | | | | | | | | | | | | | | | | |
|---|---|---|---|---|---|---|---|---|---|---|---|---|---|---|---|---|---|
| 2008-09 | Houston Aeros | AHL | 28 | 9 | 9 | 3 | 1548 | 65 | 0 | 2.52 | .... | .... | .... | .... | .... | .... | .... |
| | **NHL Totals** | | **11** | **2** | **4** | **1** | **486** | **30** | **0** | **3.70** | .... | .... | .... | .... | .... | .... | .... |

WHL West First All-Star Team (2002) • Harry "Hap" Holmes Memorial Award (AHL – fewest goals against) (2008) (shared with Nolan Schaefer)

Signed as a free agent by **Los Angeles**, June 10, 2004. Signed as a free agent by **Minnesota**, July 6, 2008.

## BRYZGALOV, Ilya (breez-GAH-lahf, IHL-yah) PHX.

Goaltender. Catches left. 6'3", 199 lbs. Born, Togliatti, USSR, June 22, 1980.
(Anaheim's 2nd choice, 44th overall, in 2000 Entry Draft).

| | | | Regular Season | | | | | | | | Playoffs | | | | | | |
|---|---|---|---|---|---|---|---|---|---|---|---|---|---|---|---|---|---|
| Season | Club | League | GP | W | L | O/T | Mins | GA | SO | Avg | GP | W | L | Mins | GA | SO | Avg |
| 1996-97 | Lada Togliatti 2 | Russia-3 | 5 | .... | .... | .... | .... | .... | .... | .... | .... | .... | .... | .... | .... | .... | .... |
| 1997-98 | Lada Togliatti 2 | Russia-3 | 8 | .... | .... | .... | .... | 28 | .... | .... | .... | .... | .... | .... | .... | .... | .... |
| 1998-99 | Lada Togliatti 2 | Russia-4 | 20 | .... | .... | .... | .... | 43 | .... | .... | .... | .... | .... | .... | .... | .... | .... |
| 99-2000 | Spartak Moscow | Russia-2 | 10 | .... | .... | .... | 500 | 21 | .... | 2.52 | .... | .... | .... | .... | .... | .... | .... |
| | Lada Togliatti 2 | Russia-3 | 2 | .... | .... | .... | .... | 5 | .... | .... | .... | .... | .... | .... | .... | .... | .... |
| | Lada Togliatti | Russia | 14 | .... | .... | .... | 796 | 18 | 3 | 1.36 | 7 | .... | .... | 407 | 10 | 1 | 1.47 |
| 2000-01 | Lada Togliatti | Russia | 34 | .... | .... | .... | 1992 | 61 | 8 | 1.84 | 5 | .... | .... | 249 | 8 | 0 | 1.93 |
| **2001-02** | **Anaheim** | **NHL** | **1** | **0** | **0** | **0** | **32** | **1** | **0** | **1.88** | .... | .... | .... | .... | .... | .... | .... |
| | Cincinnati | AHL | 45 | 20 | 16 | 4 | 2399 | 99 | 4 | 2.48 | .... | .... | .... | .... | .... | .... | .... |
| | Russia | Olympics | DID NOT PLAY – SPARE GOALTENDER | | | | | | | | | | | | | | |
| 2002-03 | Cincinnati | AHL | 54 | 12 | 26 | 9 | 3020 | 142 | 1 | 2.82 | .... | .... | .... | .... | .... | .... | .... |
| **2003-04** | **Anaheim** | **NHL** | **1** | **1** | **0** | **0** | **60** | **2** | **0** | **2.00** | .... | .... | .... | .... | .... | .... | .... |
| | Cincinnati | AHL | *64 | 27 | 25 | 10 | *3748 | 145 | 6 | 2.32 | 9 | 5 | 4 | 536 | 27 | 1 | 3.02 |
| 2004-05 | Cincinnati | AHL | 36 | 17 | 13 | 1 | 2007 | 87 | 4 | 2.60 | 7 | 3 | 3 | 314 | 13 | 0 | 2.48 |
| **2005-06** | **Anaheim** | **NHL** | **31** | **13** | **12** | **1** | **1575** | **66** | **1** | **2.51** | **11** | **6** | **4** | **659** | **16** | ***3** | ***1.46** |
| | Russia | Olympics | 1 | 0 | 1 | 0 | 60 | 5 | 0 | 5.00 | .... | .... | .... | .... | .... | .... | .... |
| **2006-07** ♦ | **Anaheim** | **NHL** | **27** | **10** | **8** | **6** | **1509** | **62** | **1** | **2.47** | **5** | **3** | **1** | **267** | **10** | **0** | **2.25** |
| **2007-08** | **Anaheim** | **NHL** | **9** | **2** | **3** | **1** | **447** | **19** | **0** | **2.55** | .... | .... | .... | .... | .... | .... | .... |
| | **Phoenix** | **NHL** | **55** | **26** | **22** | **5** | **3167** | **128** | **3** | **2.43** | .... | .... | .... | .... | .... | .... | .... |
| **2008-09** | **Phoenix** | **NHL** | **65** | **26** | **31** | **6** | **3760** | **187** | **3** | **2.98** | .... | .... | .... | .... | .... | .... | .... |
| | **NHL Totals** | | **189** | **78** | **76** | **19** | **10550** | **465** | **8** | **2.64** | **16** | **9** | **5** | **926** | **26** | **3** | **1.68** |

Claimed on waivers by **Phoenix** from **Anaheim**, November 17, 2007.

## BUDAJ, Peter (BOO-digh, PEE-tuhr) COL.

Goaltender. Catches left. 6'1", 200 lbs. Born, Banska Bystrica, Czech., September 18, 1982.
(Colorado's 1st choice, 63rd overall, in 2001 Entry Draft).

| | | | Regular Season | | | | | | | | Playoffs | | | | | | |
|---|---|---|---|---|---|---|---|---|---|---|---|---|---|---|---|---|---|
| Season | Club | League | GP | W | L | O/T | Mins | GA | SO | Avg | GP | W | L | Mins | GA | SO | Avg |
| 99-2000 | St. Michael's | OHL | 34 | 6 | 18 | 1 | 1676 | 112 | 1 | 4.01 | .... | .... | .... | .... | .... | .... | .... |
| 2000-01 | St. Michael's | OHL | 37 | 17 | 12 | 3 | 1996 | 95 | 3 | 2.86 | 11 | 6 | 4 | 621 | 26 | 1 | 2.51 |
| 2001-02 | St. Michael's | OHL | 42 | 26 | 9 | 5 | 2329 | 89 | 2 | *2.29 | 12 | 5 | 6 | 620 | 34 | *1 | 3.29 |
| 2002-03 | Hershey Bears | AHL | 28 | 10 | 10 | 2 | 1467 | 65 | 2 | 2.66 | 1 | 0 | 0 | 6 | 2 | 0 | 20.81 |
| 2003-04 | Hershey Bears | AHL | 46 | 17 | 20 | 6 | 2574 | 120 | 3 | 2.80 | .... | .... | .... | .... | .... | .... | .... |
| 2004-05 | Hershey Bears | AHL | 59 | 29 | 25 | 2 | 3356 | 148 | 5 | 2.65 | .... | .... | .... | .... | .... | .... | .... |
| **2005-06** | **Colorado** | **NHL** | **34** | **14** | **10** | **6** | **1803** | **86** | **2** | **2.86** | .... | .... | .... | .... | .... | .... | .... |
| | Slovakia | Olympics | 3 | 2 | 1 | 0 | 179 | 6 | 0 | 2.01 | .... | .... | .... | .... | .... | .... | .... |
| **2006-07** | **Colorado** | **NHL** | **57** | **31** | **16** | **6** | **3199** | **143** | **3** | **2.68** | .... | .... | .... | .... | .... | .... | .... |
| **2007-08** | **Colorado** | **NHL** | **35** | **16** | **10** | **4** | **1912** | **82** | **0** | **2.57** | **3** | **0** | **0** | **108** | **6** | **0** | **3.33** |
| **2008-09** | **Colorado** | **NHL** | **56** | **20** | **29** | **5** | **3232** | **154** | **2** | **2.86** | .... | .... | .... | .... | .... | .... | .... |
| | **NHL Totals** | | **182** | **81** | **65** | **21** | **10146** | **465** | **7** | **2.75** | **3** | **0** | **0** | **108** | **6** | **0** | **3.33** |

OHL Second All-Star Team (2002)

## CANN, Trevor (KAN, TREH-vuhr) COL.

Goaltender. Catches left. 5'11", 199 lbs. Born, Oakville, Ont., March 30, 1989.
(Colorado's 3rd choice, 49th overall, in 2007 Entry Draft).

| | | | Regular Season | | | | | | | | Playoffs | | | | | | |
|---|---|---|---|---|---|---|---|---|---|---|---|---|---|---|---|---|---|
| Season | Club | League | GP | W | L | O/T | Mins | GA | SO | Avg | GP | W | L | Mins | GA | SO | Avg |
| 2005-06 | Peterborough | OHL | 20 | 16 | 2 | 0 | 1176 | 52 | 1 | 2.65 | 1 | 0 | 0 | 35 | 3 | 0 | 5.14 |
| 2006-07 | Peterborough | OHL | *62 | 23 | 32 | 5 | 3565 | 219 | 0 | 3.69 | .... | .... | .... | .... | .... | .... | .... |
| 2007-08 | Peterborough | OHL | 51 | 20 | 28 | 3 | 2976 | 178 | 2 | 3.59 | 5 | 1 | 4 | 317 | 21 | 0 | 3.98 |
| 2008-09 | Peterborough | OHL | 10 | 5 | 5 | 0 | 545 | 28 | 1 | 3.08 | .... | .... | .... | .... | .... | .... | .... |
| | London Knights | OHL | 42 | 30 | 10 | 1 | 2482 | 104 | 5 | 2.51 | 13 | 9 | 4 | 805 | 38 | 0 | 2.83 |

## CANNATA, Joe (ka-NA-tuh, JOH) VAN.

Goaltender. Catches left. 6'1", 200 lbs. Born, Wakefield, MA, January 2, 1990.
(Vancouver's 6th choice, 173rd overall, in 2009 Entry Draft).

| | | | Regular Season | | | | | | | | Playoffs | | | | | | |
|---|---|---|---|---|---|---|---|---|---|---|---|---|---|---|---|---|---|
| Season | Club | League | GP | W | L | O/T | Mins | GA | SO | Avg | GP | W | L | Mins | GA | SO | Avg |
| 2007-08 | USNTDP | NAHL | 5 | 3 | 1 | 1 | 307 | 12 | 0 | 2.35 | .... | .... | .... | .... | .... | .... | .... |
| | USNTDP | U-18 | 28 | 13 | 13 | 2 | 1474 | 64 | 1 | 2.61 | .... | .... | .... | .... | .... | .... | .... |
| 2008-09 | Merrimack College | H-East | 23 | 7 | 11 | 4 | 1353 | 53 | 2 | 2.35 | .... | .... | .... | .... | .... | .... | .... |

## CARON, Sebastien (KAIR-aw, suh-BAS-tee-yeh)

Goaltender. Catches left. 6'1", 170 lbs. Born, Amqui, Que., June 25, 1980.
(Pittsburgh's 4th choice, 86th overall, in 1999 Entry Draft).

| | | | Regular Season | | | | | | | | Playoffs | | | | | | |
|---|---|---|---|---|---|---|---|---|---|---|---|---|---|---|---|---|---|
| Season | Club | League | GP | W | L | O/T | Mins | GA | SO | Avg | GP | W | L | Mins | GA | SO | Avg |
| 1997-98 | TGV Pentagone | QAHA | 17 | .... | .... | .... | 762 | 48 | 1 | 2.84 | .... | .... | .... | .... | .... | .... | .... |
| 1998-99 | Rimouski Oceanic | QMJHL | 30 | 13 | 10 | 3 | 1570 | 85 | 0 | 3.25 | 2 | 1 | 0 | 68 | 0 | 0 | 0.00 |
| 99-2000 | Rimouski Oceanic | QMJHL | 54 | *38 | 11 | 3 | 3040 | 179 | 1 | 3.53 | 14 | *12 | 2 | 828 | 50 | 0 | 3.62 |
| 2000-01 | Wilkes-Barre | AHL | 30 | 12 | 14 | 3 | 1746 | 103 | 4 | 3.54 | .... | .... | .... | .... | .... | .... | .... |
| 2001-02 | Wilkes-Barre | AHL | 46 | 14 | 22 | 8 | 2671 | 139 | 1 | 3.12 | .... | .... | .... | .... | .... | .... | .... |
| **2002-03** | **Pittsburgh** | **NHL** | **24** | **7** | **14** | **2** | **1408** | **62** | **2** | **2.64** | .... | .... | .... | .... | .... | .... | .... |
| | Wilkes-Barre | AHL | 27 | 12 | 14 | 1 | 1561 | 81 | 1 | 3.11 | .... | .... | .... | .... | .... | .... | .... |
| **2003-04** | **Pittsburgh** | **NHL** | **40** | **9** | **24** | **5** | **2213** | **138** | **1** | **3.74** | .... | .... | .... | .... | .... | .... | .... |
| | Wilkes-Barre | AHL | 14 | 7 | 3 | 4 | 811 | 26 | 2 | 1.92 | 7 | 3 | 4 | 395 | 23 | 0 | 3.50 |
| 2004-05 | Saguenay Fjord | QNAHL | STATISTICS NOT AVAILABLE | | | | | | | | | | | | | | |
| **2005-06** | **Pittsburgh** | **NHL** | **26** | **8** | **9** | **5** | **1312** | **87** | **1** | **3.98** | .... | .... | .... | .... | .... | .... | .... |
| | Wilkes-Barre | AHL | 6 | 3 | 3 | 0 | 357 | 7 | 2 | 1.18 | .... | .... | .... | .... | .... | .... | .... |
| **2006-07** | **Chicago** | **NHL** | **1** | **1** | **0** | **0** | **60** | **1** | **0** | **1.00** | .... | .... | .... | .... | .... | .... | .... |
| | Norfolk Admirals | AHL | 9 | 4 | 4 | 0 | 506 | 34 | 0 | 4.03 | .... | .... | .... | .... | .... | .... | .... |
| | **Anaheim** | **NHL** | **1** | **0** | **0** | **0** | **28** | **1** | **0** | **2.14** | .... | .... | .... | .... | .... | .... | .... |
| | Portland Pirates | AHL | 17 | 7 | 6 | 4 | 1025 | 40 | 0 | 2.34 | .... | .... | .... | .... | .... | .... | .... |
| 2007-08 | Fribourg | Swiss | 48 | 24 | 24 | 0 | 2851 | 144 | 5 | 3.03 | 7 | 4 | 3 | 437 | 21 | 0 | 2.88 |
| 2008-09 | Fribourg | Swiss | 39 | 21 | 17 | 0 | 2265 | 101 | 4 | 2.68 | 11 | 7 | 3 | 668 | 19 | 2 | 1.71 |
| | **NHL Totals** | | **92** | **25** | **47** | **12** | **5021** | **289** | **4** | **3.45** | .... | .... | .... | .... | .... | .... | .... |

Memorial Cup Tournament All-Star Team (2000) • Hap Emms Memorial Trophy (Memorial Cup Tournament - Top Goaltender) (2000) • NHL All-Rookie Team (2003)

Signed as a free agent by **Saguenay** (QNAHL), September 21, 2004. Signed as a free agent by **Chicago**, August 8, 2006. Traded to **Anaheim** by **Chicago** with Matt Keith and Chris Durno for P. A. Parenteau and Bruno St. Jacques, December 28, 2006. Signed as a free agent by **Fribourg** (Swiss), June 21, 2007.

## CARROZZI, Christopher (ka-ROH-zee, KRIHS-toh-fuhr) ATL.

Goaltender. Catches left. 6'3", 185 lbs. Born, Ottawa, Ont., March 2, 1990.
(Atlanta's 6th choice, 154th overall, in 2008 Entry Draft).

| | | | Regular Season | | | | | | | | Playoffs | | | | | | |
|---|---|---|---|---|---|---|---|---|---|---|---|---|---|---|---|---|---|
| Season | Club | League | GP | W | L | O/T | Mins | GA | SO | Avg | GP | W | L | Mins | GA | SO | Avg |
| 2005-06 | Nepean Raiders | Minor-ON | 23 | .... | .... | .... | .... | 42 | 4 | 1.82 | .... | .... | .... | .... | .... | .... | .... |
| 2006-07 | St. Michael's | OHL | 25 | 6 | 7 | 2 | 1130 | 81 | 0 | 4.30 | .... | .... | .... | .... | .... | .... | .... |
| 2007-08 | St. Michael's | OHL | 47 | 25 | 18 | 2 | 2505 | 115 | *4 | 2.75 | 4 | 0 | 4 | 240 | 18 | 0 | 4.50 |
| 2008-09 | St. Michael's | OHL | 47 | 27 | 14 | 3 | 2715 | 133 | 2 | 2.94 | 2 | 0 | 0 | 33 | 3 | 0 | 5.52 |

## CARUSO, Dave (kah-ROO-soh, DAYV)

Goaltender. Catches left. 6'1", 210 lbs. Born, Queens, NY, June 18, 1982.

| | | | Regular Season | | | | | | | | Playoffs | | | | | | |
|---|---|---|---|---|---|---|---|---|---|---|---|---|---|---|---|---|---|
| Season | Club | League | GP | W | L | O/T | Mins | GA | SO | Avg | GP | W | L | Mins | GA | SO | Avg |
| 2002-03 | Ohio State | CCHA | 8 | 5 | 2 | 0 | 460 | 12 | 2 | 1.56 | .... | .... | .... | .... | .... | .... | .... |
| 2003-04 | Ohio State | CCHA | 14 | 9 | 3 | 0 | 762 | 25 | 2 | *1.97 | .... | .... | .... | .... | .... | .... | .... |
| 2004-05 | Ohio State | CCHA | 38 | 25 | 9 | 4 | 2272 | 81 | 2 | 2.14 | .... | .... | .... | .... | .... | .... | .... |
| 2005-06 | Ohio State | CCHA | 36 | 13 | 18 | 5 | 2146 | 77 | *5 | 2.15 | .... | .... | .... | .... | .... | .... | .... |
| 2006-07 | Chicago Wolves | AHL | 1 | 1 | 0 | 0 | 36 | 4 | 0 | 6.75 | .... | .... | .... | .... | .... | .... | .... |
| | Gwinnett | ECHL | 38 | 23 | 11 | 4 | 2297 | 120 | 1 | 3.13 | 3 | 1 | 2 | 200 | 9 | 0 | 2.71 |
| 2007-08 | Lowell Devils | AHL | 16 | 7 | 8 | 0 | 930 | 51 | 0 | 3.29 | .... | .... | .... | .... | .... | .... | .... |
| | Trenton Devils | ECHL | 34 | 13 | 16 | 4 | 1972 | 85 | 2 | 2.59 | .... | .... | .... | .... | .... | .... | .... |
| 2008-09 | Lowell Devils | AHL | 16 | 1 | 11 | 0 | 721 | 42 | 0 | 3.49 | .... | .... | .... | .... | .... | .... | .... |
| | Trenton Devils | ECHL | 1 | 0 | 0 | 1 | 65 | 4 | 0 | 3.69 | .... | .... | .... | .... | .... | .... | .... |

Signed as a free agent by **Atlanta**, July 6, 2006. Signed as a free agent by **New Jersey**, August 10, 2007.

## CHEVERIE, Marc (she-VEH-ree, MAHRK) FLA.

Goaltender. Catches left. 6'3", 183 lbs. Born, Cole Harbour, N.S., February 22, 1987.
(Florida's 6th choice, 193rd overall, in 2006 Entry Draft).

| | | | Regular Season | | | | | | | | Playoffs | | | | | | |
|---|---|---|---|---|---|---|---|---|---|---|---|---|---|---|---|---|---|
| Season | Club | League | GP | W | L | O/T | Mins | GA | SO | Avg | GP | W | L | Mins | GA | SO | Avg |
| 2003-04 | Dartmouth | NSMHL | .... | 19 | 4 | 2 | 1521 | 76 | 1 | 2.99 | .... | .... | .... | .... | .... | .... | .... |
| 2004-05 | Notre Dame | SMHL | 25 | .... | .... | .... | .... | .... | .... | 2.25 | .... | .... | .... | .... | .... | .... | .... |
| 2005-06 | Nanaimo Clippers | BCHL | 46 | 23 | 9 | 0 | 2032 | 86 | 4 | 2.54 | .... | .... | .... | .... | .... | .... | .... |
| 2006-07 | Nanaimo Clippers | BCHL | 34 | 21 | 9 | 2 | 2015 | 104 | 3 | 3.10 | .... | .... | .... | .... | .... | .... | .... |
| 2007-08 | U. of Denver | WCHA | 5 | 1 | 0 | 0 | 141 | 4 | 0 | 1.70 | .... | .... | .... | .... | .... | .... | .... |
| 2008-09 | U. of Denver | WCHA | 40 | 23 | 12 | 5 | 2383 | 93 | 4 | 2.34 | .... | .... | .... | .... | .... | .... | .... |

WCHA Second All-Star Team (2009)

## CLARK, Morgan (KLAHRK, MOHR-guhn) VAN.

Goaltender. Catches left. 5'11", 160 lbs. Born, Toronto, Ont., February 17, 1990.
(Vancouver's 5th choice, 191st overall, in 2008 Entry Draft).

| | | | Regular Season | | | | | | | | Playoffs | | | | | | |
|---|---|---|---|---|---|---|---|---|---|---|---|---|---|---|---|---|---|
| Season | Club | League | GP | W | L | O/T | Mins | GA | SO | Avg | GP | W | L | Mins | GA | SO | Avg |
| 2006-07 | Red Deer Rebels | WHL | 21 | 9 | 5 | 2 | 1015 | 55 | 1 | 3.25 | .... | .... | .... | .... | .... | .... | .... |
| 2007-08 | Red Deer Rebels | WHL | 47 | 10 | 30 | 0 | 2513 | 155 | 1 | 3.70 | .... | .... | .... | .... | .... | .... | .... |
| 2008-09 | Red Deer Rebels | WHL | 20 | 4 | 9 | 2 | 957 | 60 | 0 | 3.76 | .... | .... | .... | .... | .... | .... | .... |
| | Swift Current | WHL | 8 | 3 | 2 | 1 | 406 | 28 | 0 | 4.14 | .... | .... | .... | .... | .... | .... | .... |

## CLEMMENSEN, Scott (KLEH-mehn-sehn, SKAWT) FLA.

Goaltender. Catches left. 6'3", 205 lbs. Born, Des Moines, IA, July 23, 1977.
(New Jersey's 7th choice, 215th overall, in 1997 Entry Draft).

| | | | Regular Season | | | | | | | | Playoffs | | | | | | |
|---|---|---|---|---|---|---|---|---|---|---|---|---|---|---|---|---|---|
| Season | Club | League | GP | W | L | O/T | Mins | GA | SO | Avg | GP | W | L | Mins | GA | SO | Avg |
| 1995-96 | Dubuque | USHL | 20 | 10 | 7 | 1 | 1082 | 62 | 0 | 3.44 | .... | .... | .... | .... | .... | .... | .... |
| 1996-97 | Des Moines | USHL | 36 | 22 | 9 | 2 | 2042 | 111 | 1 | 3.26 | 4 | 1 | 2 | 200 | 9 | 1 | 2.70 |
| 1997-98 | Boston College | H-East | 37 | 24 | 9 | 4 | 2205 | 102 | *4 | 2.78 | .... | .... | .... | .... | .... | .... | .... |
| 1998-99 | Boston College | H-East | *42 | 26 | 12 | 4 | *2507 | 120 | 1 | 2.87 | .... | .... | .... | .... | .... | .... | .... |
| 99-2000 | Boston College | H-East | 29 | 19 | 7 | 0 | 1610 | 59 | *5 | 2.20 | .... | .... | .... | .... | .... | .... | .... |
| 2000-01 | Boston College | H-East | *39 | *30 | 7 | 2 | *2312 | 82 | 3 | 2.13 | .... | .... | .... | .... | .... | .... | .... |
| **2001-02** | **New Jersey** | **NHL** | **2** | **0** | **0** | **0** | **20** | **1** | **0** | **3.00** | .... | .... | .... | .... | .... | .... | .... |
| | Albany River Rats | AHL | 29 | 5 | 19 | 4 | 1677 | 92 | 0 | 3.29 | .... | .... | .... | .... | .... | .... | .... |
| 2002-03 | Albany River Rats | AHL | 47 | 12 | 24 | 8 | 2694 | 119 | 1 | 2.65 | .... | .... | .... | .... | .... | .... | .... |
| **2003-04** | **New Jersey** | **NHL** | **4** | **3** | **1** | **0** | **238** | **4** | **2** | **1.01** | .... | .... | .... | .... | .... | .... | .... |
| | Albany River Rats | AHL | 22 | 5 | 12 | 4 | 1309 | 67 | 0 | 3.07 | .... | .... | .... | .... | .... | .... | .... |
| 2004-05 | Albany River Rats | AHL | 46 | 13 | 25 | 5 | 2645 | 124 | 2 | 2.81 | .... | .... | .... | .... | .... | .... | .... |
| **2005-06** | **New Jersey** | **NHL** | **13** | **3** | **4** | **2** | **627** | **35** | **0** | **3.35** | **1** | **0** | **0** | **7** | **0** | **0** | **0.00** |
| | Albany River Rats | AHL | 1 | 0 | 1 | 0 | 59 | 5 | 0 | 5.05 | .... | .... | .... | .... | .... | .... | .... |
| **2006-07** | **New Jersey** | **NHL** | **6** | **1** | **1** | **2** | **305** | **16** | **0** | **3.15** | .... | .... | .... | .... | .... | .... | .... |
| | Lowell Devils | AHL | 1 | 1 | 0 | 0 | 60 | 0 | 1 | 0.00 | .... | .... | .... | .... | .... | .... | .... |
| **2007-08** | **Toronto** | **NHL** | **3** | **1** | **1** | **0** | **154** | **10** | **0** | **3.90** | .... | .... | .... | .... | .... | .... | .... |
| | Toronto Marlies | AHL | 40 | 23 | 14 | 2 | 2363 | 96 | 1 | 2.44 | 17 | 8 | 9 | 992 | 50 | 0 | 3.02 |
| **2008-09** | **New Jersey** | **NHL** | **40** | **25** | **13** | **1** | **2356** | **94** | **2** | **2.39** | .... | .... | .... | .... | .... | .... | .... |
| | Lowell Devils | AHL | 12 | 6 | 5 | 1 | 707 | 40 | 0 | 3.39 | .... | .... | .... | .... | .... | .... | .... |
| | **NHL Totals** | | **68** | **33** | **20** | **5** | **3700** | **160** | **4** | **2.59** | **1** | **0** | **0** | **7** | **0** | **0** | **0.00** |

NCAA Championship All-Tournament Team (2001)

Signed as a free agent by **Toronto**, July 6, 2007. Signed as a free agent by **New Jersey**, July 10, 2008. Signed as a free agent by **Florida**, July 1, 2009.

## CLIMIE, Matt (KLIGH-mee, MAT) DAL.

Goaltender. Catches left. 6'3", 185 lbs. Born, Leduc, Alta., February 11, 1983.

| | | | Regular Season | | | | | | | | Playoffs | | | | | | |
|---|---|---|---|---|---|---|---|---|---|---|---|---|---|---|---|---|---|
| Season | Club | League | GP | W | L | O/T | Mins | GA | SO | Avg | GP | W | L | Mins | GA | SO | Avg |
| 2002-03 | Truro Bearcats | MJrHL | STATISTICS NOT AVAILABLE | | | | | | | | | | | | | | |
| 2003-04 | Truro Bearcats | MJrHL | 45 | 30 | 10 | 0 | 2731 | 119 | 0 | 2.61 | .... | .... | .... | .... | .... | .... | .... |
| 2004-05 | Bemidji State | CHA | 21 | 12 | 5 | 1 | 1167 | 35 | 4 | 1.80 | .... | .... | .... | .... | .... | .... | .... |
| 2005-06 | Bemidji State | CHA | 18 | 8 | 7 | 2 | 1065 | 48 | 1 | 2.70 | .... | .... | .... | .... | .... | .... | .... |
| 2006-07 | Bemidji State | CHA | 29 | 11 | 10 | 5 | 1666 | 84 | 2 | 3.03 | .... | .... | .... | .... | .... | .... | .... |
| 2007-08 | Bemidji State | CHA | 27 | 14 | 8 | 3 | 1529 | 55 | 5 | 2.16 | .... | .... | .... | .... | .... | .... | .... |
| | Iowa Stars | AHL | 6 | 1 | 4 | 1 | 346 | 23 | 0 | .... | .... | .... | .... | .... | .... | .... | .... |
| **2008-09** | **Dallas** | **NHL** | **3** | **2** | **1** | **0** | **185** | **9** | **0** | **2.92** | .... | .... | .... | .... | .... | .... | .... |
| | Idaho Steelheads | ECHL | 42 | 27 | 12 | 1 | 2404 | 92 | 4 | 2.30 | 4 | 0 | 3 | 199 | 8 | 0 | 2.41 |
| | Houston Aeros | AHL | .... | .... | .... | .... | .... | .... | .... | .... | 5 | 1 | 1 | 191 | 6 | 0 | 1.88 |
| | **NHL Totals** | | **3** | **2** | **1** | **0** | **185** | **9** | **0** | **2.92** | .... | .... | .... | .... | .... | .... | .... |

CHA Second All-Star Team (2008)

Signed as a free agent by **Dallas**, March 20, 2008.

## COLEMAN, Gerald (KOHL-man, JAIR-uhld) N.J.

Goaltender. Catches left. 6'4", 214 lbs. Born, Romeoville, IL, April 3, 1985.
(Tampa Bay's 5th choice, 224th overall, in 2003 Entry Draft).

| | | | Regular Season | | | | | | | | Playoffs | | | | | | |
|---|---|---|---|---|---|---|---|---|---|---|---|---|---|---|---|---|---|
| Season | Club | League | GP | W | L | O/T | Mins | GA | SO | Avg | GP | W | L | Mins | GA | SO | Avg |
| 99-2000 | Chicago | MEHL | 26 | .... | .... | .... | 1560 | 65 | 0 | 2.50 | .... | .... | .... | .... | .... | .... | .... |
| 2000-01 | USNTDP | U-17 | 9 | 3 | 0 | 4 | 527 | 26 | 0 | 2.96 | .... | .... | .... | .... | .... | .... | .... |
| | USNTDP | NAHL | 36 | 8 | 23 | 1 | 1859 | 132 | 0 | 4.26 | .... | .... | .... | .... | .... | .... | .... |
| 2001-02 | USNTDP | U-18 | 13 | 8 | 1 | 3 | 667 | 38 | 1 | 3.42 | .... | .... | .... | .... | .... | .... | .... |
| | USNTDP | USHL | 2 | 1 | 1 | 0 | 76 | 4 | 0 | 3.15 | .... | .... | .... | .... | .... | .... | .... |
| | USNTDP | NAHL | 22 | 5 | 14 | 2 | 1263 | 75 | 0 | 3.56 | .... | .... | .... | .... | .... | .... | .... |

| Season | Club | League | GP | W | L | O/T | Mins | GA | SO | Avg | GP | W | L | Mins | GA | SO | Avg |
|---|---|---|---|---|---|---|---|---|---|---|---|---|---|---|---|---|---|
| 2002-03 | London Knights | OHL | 26 | 6 | 9 | 3 | 1074 | 59 | 1 | 3.30 | | | | | | | |
| 2003-04 | London Knights | OHL | 33 | 24 | 8 | 0 | 1852 | 68 | *5 | 2.20 | 8 | 5 | 2 | 442 | 19 | 1 | 2.58 |
| 2004-05 | London Knights | OHL | 38 | *32 | 2 | 2 | 2224 | 63 | *8 | *1.70 | 8 | 7 | 1 | 455 | 13 | 0 | *1.71 |
| 2005-06 | Tampa Bay | NHL | 2 | 0 | 0 | 1 | 43 | 2 | 0 | 2.79 | | | | | | | |
| | Springfield Falcons | AHL | 43 | 14 | 21 | 3 | 2413 | 156 | 2 | 3.88 | | | | | | | |
| 2006-07 | Springfield Falcons | AHL | 3 | 2 | 1 | 0 | 179 | 6 | 0 | 2.01 | | | | | | | |
| | Johnstown Chiefs | ECHL | 17 | 7 | 9 | 0 | 914 | 52 | 0 | 3.41 | | | | | | | |
| | Portland Pirates | AHL | 11 | 4 | 5 | 0 | 603 | 29 | 0 | 2.89 | | | | | | | |
| 2007-08 | Portland Pirates | AHL | 18 | 8 | 7 | 1 | 968 | 47 | 2 | 2.91 | 1 | 0 | 0 | 39 | 4 | 0 | 6.09 |
| | Augusta Lynx | ECHL | 9 | 2 | 5 | 0 | 500 | 22 | 0 | 2.64 | | | | | | | |
| 2008-09 | Worcester Sharks | AHL | 3 | 0 | 2 | 0 | 112 | 6 | 0 | 3.23 | | | | | | | |
| | Phoenix | ECHL | 4 | 2 | 1 | 1 | 244 | 6 | 1 | 1.48 | | | | | | | |
| | Trenton Devils | ECHL | 40 | 27 | 8 | 2 | 2322 | 92 | 3 | 2.38 | 3 | 1 | 1 | 246 | 15 | 0 | 3.66 |
| | NHL Totals | | 2 | 0 | 0 | 1 | 43 | 2 | 0 | 2.79 | | | | | | | |

ECHL Second All-Star Team (2009)

Traded to **Anaheim** by **Tampa Bay** with Tampa Bay's 1st round choice (later traded to Minnesota - Minnesota selected Colton Gillies) in 2007 Entry Draft for Shane O'Brien and Colorado's 3rd round choice (previously acquired, Tampa Bay selected Luca Cunti) in 2007 Entry Draft, February 24, 2007. Signed as a free agent by **New Jersey**, July 31, 2009.

## CONKLIN, Ty (KAWN-klihn, TIGH) ST.L.

Goaltender. Catches left. 6', 184 lbs. Born, Anchorage, AK, March 30, 1976.

| | | | Regular Season | | | | | | | | Playoffs | | | | | | |
|---|---|---|---|---|---|---|---|---|---|---|---|---|---|---|---|---|---|
| Season | Club | League | GP | W | L | O/T | Mins | GA | SO | Avg | GP | W | L | Mins | GA | SO | Avg |
| 1995-96 | Green Bay | USHL | 30 | | | | 1727 | 82 | 1 | 2.85 | | | | | | | |
| 1996-97 | Alaska Anchorage | WCHA | DID NOT PLAY – FRESHMAN | | | | | | | | | | | | | | |
| | Green Bay | USHL | 30 | 19 | 7 | 1 | 1609 | 86 | 1 | 3.21 | 17 | 8 | 9 | 980 | 56 | 1 | 3.43 |
| 1997-98 | New Hampshire | H-East | DID NOT PLAY – TRANSFERRED COLLEGES | | | | | | | | | | | | | | |
| 1998-99 | New Hampshire | H-East | 22 | 18 | 3 | 1 | 1338 | 41 | 0 | *1.84 | | | | | | | |
| 99-2000 | New Hampshire | H-East | *37 | *22 | 8 | 6 | *2194 | 91 | 2 | 2.49 | | | | | | | |
| 2000-01 | New Hampshire | H-East | 34 | 17 | 12 | 5 | 2048 | 70 | *5 | *2.05 | | | | | | | |
| 2001-02 | Edmonton | NHL | 4 | 2 | 0 | 0 | 148 | 4 | 0 | 1.62 | | | | | | | |
| | Hamilton Bulldogs | AHL | 37 | 13 | 12 | 8 | 2043 | 89 | 1 | 2.61 | 7 | 4 | 2 | 416 | 18 | 0 | 2.60 |
| 2002-03 | Hamilton Bulldogs | AHL | 38 | 19 | 13 | 3 | 2140 | 91 | 4 | 2.55 | 17 | 9 | 6 | 1024 | 38 | 1 | 2.23 |
| 2003-04 | Edmonton | NHL | 38 | 17 | 14 | 4 | 2086 | 84 | 1 | 2.42 | | | | | | | |
| 2004-05 | Wolfsburg | Germany | 11 | | | | 623 | 31 | 0 | 2.99 | 7 | | | 414 | 11 | 2 | 1.59 |
| 2005-06 | Edmonton | NHL | 18 | 8 | 5 | 1 | 922 | 43 | 1 | 2.80 | 1 | 0 | 1 | 6 | 1 | 0 | 10.00 |
| | Hamilton Bulldogs | AHL | 3 | 1 | 2 | 0 | 152 | 8 | 0 | 3.17 | | | | | | | |
| | Hartford Wolf Pack | AHL | 2 | 1 | 0 | 1 | 130 | 5 | 0 | 2.31 | | | | | | | |
| 2006-07 | Columbus | NHL | 11 | 2 | 3 | 2 | 491 | 27 | 0 | 3.30 | | | | | | | |
| | Syracuse Crunch | AHL | 19 | 3 | 12 | 3 | 1085 | 60 | 0 | 3.32 | | | | | | | |
| | Buffalo | NHL | 5 | 1 | 2 | 0 | 227 | 13 | 0 | 3.44 | | | | | | | |
| 2007-08 | Pittsburgh | NHL | 33 | 18 | 8 | 5 | 1866 | 78 | 2 | 2.51 | | | | | | | |
| | Wilkes-Barre | AHL | 18 | 11 | 7 | 0 | 1058 | 39 | 2 | 2.21 | | | | | | | |
| 2008-09 | Detroit | NHL | 40 | 25 | 11 | 2 | 2246 | 94 | 6 | 2.51 | 1 | 0 | 0 | 20 | 0 | 0 | 0.00 |
| | NHL Totals | | 149 | 73 | 43 | 14 | 7986 | 343 | 10 | 2.58 | 2 | 0 | 1 | 26 | 1 | 0 | 2.31 |

USHL Second All-Star Team (1996) • Hockey East All-Rookie Team (1999) • Hockey East Second All-Star Team (1999) • Hockey East First All-Star Team (2000, 2001) • Hockey East Player of the Year (2000) (co-winner - Mike Mottau) • NCAA East Second All-American Team (2000) • NCAA East First All-American Team (2001)

• Left **Alaska-Anchorage** (WCHA) and returned to **Green Bay** (USHL), November 14, 1996. Signed as a free agent by **Edmonton**, April 18, 2001. Signed as a free agent by **Wolfsburg** (Germany), January 25, 2005. • Loaned to **Hartford** (AHL) by **Edmonton**, March 8, 2006. Signed as a free agent by **Columbus**, July 6, 2006. Traded to **Buffalo** by **Columbus** for Buffalo's 5th round choice (later traded to Dallas - Dallas selected Michael Neal) in 2007 Entry Draft, February 27, 2007. Signed as a free agent by **Pittsburgh**, July 19, 2007. Signed as a free agent by **Detroit**, July 1, 2008. Signed as a free agent by **St. Louis**, July 1, 2009.

## COURCHAINE, Adam (KOOR-shayn, A-duhm) BOS.

Goaltender. Catches left. 6'2", 188 lbs. Born, Calgary, Alta., February 20, 1989.

| | | | Regular Season | | | | | | | | Playoffs | | | | | | |
|---|---|---|---|---|---|---|---|---|---|---|---|---|---|---|---|---|---|
| Season | Club | League | GP | W | L | O/T | Mins | GA | SO | Avg | GP | W | L | Mins | GA | SO | Avg |
| 2006-07 | Orleans Blues | CJHL | 39 | 19 | 11 | 5 | 2285 | 119 | 1 | 3.12 | 6 | 2 | 2 | 372 | 16 | 0 | 2.58 |
| 2007-08 | Ottawa 67's | OHL | 48 | 17 | 25 | 4 | 2813 | 152 | 2 | 3.24 | 4 | 0 | 4 | 158 | 12 | 0 | 4.56 |
| | Providence Bruins | AHL | 3 | 2 | 0 | 0 | 144 | 4 | 0 | 1.67 | | | | | | | |
| 2008-09 | Ottawa 67's | OHL | 30 | 13 | 11 | 2 | 1520 | 83 | 2 | 3.28 | 5 | 2 | 3 | 280 | 14 | *1 | 3.00 |
| | Providence Bruins | AHL | 1 | 0 | 1 | 0 | 60 | 3 | 0 | 3.00 | | | | | | | |

Signed as a free agent by **Boston**, September 30, 2007.

## COUSINEAU, Marco (KOO-zih-noh, MAHR-koh) ANA.

Goaltender. Catches left. 6', 195 lbs. Born, St.Lazare, Que., November 9, 1989.
(Anaheim's 6th choice, 83rd overall, in 2008 Entry Draft).

| | | | Regular Season | | | | | | | | Playoffs | | | | | | |
|---|---|---|---|---|---|---|---|---|---|---|---|---|---|---|---|---|---|
| Season | Club | League | GP | W | L | O/T | Mins | GA | SO | Avg | GP | W | L | Mins | GA | SO | Avg |
| 2006-07 | Baie-Comeau | QMJHL | 23 | 4 | 12 | | 1015 | 71 | 0 | 4.20 | 1 | 0 | 0 | 10 | 2 | 0 | 11.88 |
| 2007-08 | Baie-Comeau | QMJHL | 58 | 34 | 19 | | 3227 | 151 | 4 | 2.81 | 5 | 1 | 4 | 305 | 11 | 0 | *2.17 |
| 2008-09 | Baie-Comeau | QMJHL | 34 | 9 | 25 | | 1878 | 115 | 1 | 3.67 | | | | | | | |
| | Drummondville | QMJHL | 16 | 12 | 4 | | 919 | 36 | 0 | 2.35 | 17 | *13 | 3 | 1009 | 41 | 0 | 2.44 |

QMJHL Second All-Star Team (2008)

## CRAWFORD, Corey (KRAW-fohrd, KOH-ree) CHI.

Goaltender. Catches left. 6'2", 183 lbs. Born, Montreal, Que., December 31, 1984.
(Chicago's 2nd choice, 52nd overall, in 2003 Entry Draft).

| | | | Regular Season | | | | | | | | Playoffs | | | | | | |
|---|---|---|---|---|---|---|---|---|---|---|---|---|---|---|---|---|---|
| Season | Club | League | GP | W | L | O/T | Mins | GA | SO | Avg | GP | W | L | Mins | GA | SO | Avg |
| 2000-01 | Gatineau Intrepide | QAAA | 21 | 17 | 3 | 1 | 1260 | 40 | 2 | 1.92 | | | | | | | |
| 2001-02 | Moncton Wildcats | QMJHL | 38 | 9 | 20 | 3 | 1863 | 116 | 1 | 3.74 | | | | | | | |
| 2002-03 | Moncton Wildcats | QMJHL | 50 | 24 | 17 | 6 | 2855 | 130 | 2 | 2.73 | 6 | 2 | 3 | 303 | 20 | 0 | 3.97 |
| 2003-04 | Moncton Wildcats | QMJHL | 54 | *35 | 15 | 3 | 3019 | 132 | 2 | 2.62 | *20 | *13 | 6 | *1170 | 42 | 0 | 2.15 |
| 2004-05 | Moncton Wildcats | QMJHL | 51 | 28 | 16 | 6 | 2942 | 121 | *6 | 2.47 | 12 | 6 | 6 | 725 | 33 | *1 | 2.73 |
| 2005-06 | Chicago | NHL | 2 | 0 | 1 | 0 | 86 | 5 | 0 | 3.49 | | | | | | | |
| | Norfolk Admirals | AHL | 48 | 22 | 23 | 1 | 2734 | 134 | 1 | 2.94 | 1 | 0 | 0 | 17 | 1 | 0 | 3.49 |
| 2006-07 | Norfolk Admirals | AHL | 60 | 38 | 20 | 2 | 3467 | 164 | 1 | 2.84 | 6 | 2 | 4 | 363 | 20 | 0 | 3.31 |
| 2007-08 | Chicago | NHL | 5 | 1 | 2 | 0 | 224 | 8 | 1 | 2.14 | | | | | | | |
| | Rockford IceHogs | AHL | 55 | 29 | 19 | 5 | 3028 | 143 | 3 | 2.83 | 12 | 7 | 5 | 741 | 27 | 0 | 2.19 |
| 2008-09 | Rockford IceHogs | AHL | 47 | 22 | 20 | 3 | 2686 | 116 | 2 | 2.59 | 2 | 0 | 2 | 117 | 5 | 0 | 2.57 |
| | Chicago | NHL | | | | | | | | | 1 | 0 | 0 | 16 | 1 | 0 | 3.75 |
| | NHL Totals | | 7 | 1 | 2 | 1 | 310 | 13 | 1 | 2.52 | 1 | 0 | 0 | 16 | 1 | 0 | 3.75 |

QMJHL Second All-Star Team (2004, 2005)

## CURRY, John (KUH-ree, JAWN) PIT.

Goaltender. Catches left. 5'11", 185 lbs. Born, Shorewood, MN, February 27, 1984.

| | | | Regular Season | | | | | | | | Playoffs | | | | | | |
|---|---|---|---|---|---|---|---|---|---|---|---|---|---|---|---|---|---|
| Season | Club | League | GP | W | L | O/T | Mins | GA | SO | Avg | GP | W | L | Mins | GA | SO | Avg |
| 2003-04 | Boston University | H-East | 1 | 0 | 0 | 0 | 5 | 0 | 0 | 0.00 | | | | | | | |
| 2004-05 | Boston University | H-East | 33 | 18 | 11 | 3 | 1950 | 64 | 3 | 1.97 | | | | | | | |
| 2005-06 | Boston University | H-East | 37 | 24 | 8 | 4 | 2166 | 81 | 3 | 2.24 | | | | | | | |
| 2006-07 | Boston University | H-East | 36 | 17 | 10 | 8 | 2154 | 72 | 7 | 2.01 | | | | | | | |
| 2007-08 | Wilkes-Barre | AHL | 40 | 24 | 12 | 3 | 2343 | 87 | 3 | 2.23 | 23 | 14 | 9 | 1358 | 64 | 1 | 2.83 |
| | Las Vegas | ECHL | 6 | 4 | 1 | 0 | 342 | 16 | 0 | 2.81 | | | | | | | |
| | Wheeling Nailers | ECHL | 1 | 0 | 1 | 0 | 60 | 4 | 0 | 4.00 | | | | | | | |
| 2008-09 | Pittsburgh | NHL | 3 | 2 | 1 | 0 | 150 | 6 | 0 | 2.40 | | | | | | | |
| | Wilkes-Barre | AHL | 50 | 33 | 15 | 1 | 2996 | 119 | 4 | 2.38 | 7 | 4 | 3 | 393 | 22 | 0 | 3.36 |
| | NHL Totals | | 3 | 2 | 1 | 0 | 150 | 6 | 0 | 2.40 | | | | | | | |

NCAA East Second All-American Team (2006) • NCAA East First All-American Team (2007)

Signed as a free agent by **Pittsburgh**, July 13, 2007.

## DAKERS, Taylor (DAY-kuhrs, TAY-luhr)

Goaltender. Catches left. 6'1", 175 lbs. Born, Richmond, B.C., September 14, 1986.
(San Jose's 4th choice, 140th overall, in 2005 Entry Draft).

| | | | Regular Season | | | | | | | | Playoffs | | | | | | |
|---|---|---|---|---|---|---|---|---|---|---|---|---|---|---|---|---|---|
| Season | Club | League | GP | W | L | O/T | Mins | GA | SO | Avg | GP | W | L | Mins | GA | SO | Avg |
| 2002-03 | Columbia Valley | KIJHL | 37 | | | | 2077 | 93 | 4 | 2.68 | | | | | | | |
| 2003-04 | Kootenay Ice | WHL | 19 | 6 | 10 | 0 | 856 | 48 | 1 | 3.36 | | | | | | | |
| 2004-05 | Kootenay Ice | WHL | 23 | 13 | 7 | 2 | 1303 | 44 | 4 | 2.03 | | | | | | | |
| 2005-06 | Kootenay Ice | WHL | 47 | 30 | 15 | 1 | 2671 | 94 | 8 | 2.11 | 6 | 2 | 4 | 378 | 23 | 0 | 3.65 |
| 2006-07 | Kootenay Ice | WHL | 48 | 33 | 10 | 4 | 2831 | 102 | 5 | 2.16 | 7 | 3 | 4 | 429 | 18 | 1 | 2.52 |
| 2007-08 | Worcester Sharks | AHL | 22 | 7 | 11 | 1 | 1226 | 64 | 0 | 3.13 | | | | | | | |
| | Phoenix | ECHL | 15 | 6 | 7 | 2 | 899 | 35 | 0 | 2.34 | | | | | | | |
| 2008-09 | Worcester Sharks | AHL | 21 | 11 | 9 | 0 | 1220 | 58 | 1 | 2.85 | | | | | | | |

WHL East Second All-Star Team (2007)

## DALTON, Matt (DAWL-tuhn, MAT) BOS.

Goaltender. Catches left. 6'1", 194 lbs. Born, Clinton, Ont., July 4, 1986.

| | | | Regular Season | | | | | | | | Playoffs | | | | | | |
|---|---|---|---|---|---|---|---|---|---|---|---|---|---|---|---|---|---|
| Season | Club | League | GP | W | L | O/T | Mins | GA | SO | Avg | GP | W | L | Mins | GA | SO | Avg |
| 2006-07 | Des Moines | USHL | *53 | *27 | 15 | 9 | *3030 | 143 | *5 | 2.83 | *8 | 6 | 2 | *540 | 14 | 1 | 1.56 |
| 2007-08 | Bemidji State | CHA | 5 | 1 | 3 | 0 | 233 | 12 | 1 | 3.09 | | | | | | | |
| 2008-09 | Bemidji State | CHA | 31 | *19 | 11 | 1 | 1861 | 68 | 2 | 2.19 | | | | | | | |

CHA Second All-Star Team (2009)

Signed as a free agent by **Boston**, April 22, 2009.

## DANIS, Yann (DA-nihs, YAN) N.J.

Goaltender. Catches left. 6', 180 lbs. Born, Lafontaine, Que., June 21, 1981.

| | | | Regular Season | | | | | | | | Playoffs | | | | | | |
|---|---|---|---|---|---|---|---|---|---|---|---|---|---|---|---|---|---|
| Season | Club | League | GP | W | L | O/T | Mins | GA | SO | Avg | GP | W | L | Mins | GA | SO | Avg |
| 99-2000 | St-Jerome | QJHL | STATISTICS NOT AVAILABLE | | | | | | | | | | | | | | |
| | Cornwall Colts | CJHL | 26 | | | | 1367 | 71 | 0 | 3.12 | | | | | | | |
| 2000-01 | Brown U. | ECAC | 12 | 2 | 8 | 1 | 667 | 40 | 0 | 3.60 | | | | | | | |
| 2001-02 | Brown U. | ECAC | 24 | 11 | 10 | 2 | 1451 | 45 | 3 | 1.86 | | | | | | | |
| 2002-03 | Brown U. | ECAC | *34 | 15 | 14 | 5 | *2074 | 80 | 5 | 2.31 | | | | | | | |
| 2003-04 | Brown U. | ECAC | 30 | 15 | 11 | 4 | 1821 | 55 | *5 | *1.81 | | | | | | | |
| | Hamilton Bulldogs | AHL | 2 | 2 | 0 | 0 | 120 | 3 | 1 | 1.50 | 1 | 0 | 0 | 12 | 0 | 0 | 0.00 |
| 2004-05 | Hamilton Bulldogs | AHL | 53 | 28 | 17 | 6 | 3075 | 120 | 5 | 2.34 | 4 | 0 | 4 | 237 | 13 | 0 | 3.29 |
| 2005-06 | Montreal | NHL | 6 | 3 | 2 | 0 | 312 | 14 | 1 | 2.69 | | | | | | | |
| | Hamilton Bulldogs | AHL | 39 | 17 | 17 | 3 | 2242 | 111 | 0 | 2.97 | | | | | | | |
| 2006-07 | Hamilton Bulldogs | AHL | 44 | 23 | 14 | 5 | 2540 | 119 | 1 | 2.81 | 1 | 1 | 0 | 54 | 1 | 0 | 1.12 |
| 2007-08 | Hamilton Bulldogs | AHL | 38 | 11 | 19 | 4 | 2064 | 113 | 0 | 3.28 | | | | | | | |
| 2008-09 | NY Islanders | NHL | 31 | 10 | 17 | 3 | 1760 | 84 | 2 | 2.86 | | | | | | | |
| | Bridgeport | AHL | 10 | 7 | 3 | 0 | 611 | 23 | 0 | 2.26 | | | | | | | |
| | NHL Totals | | 37 | 13 | 19 | 3 | 2072 | 98 | 3 | 2.84 | | | | | | | |

ECAC Second All-Star Team (2002, 2003) • ECAC First All-Star Team (2004) • ECAC Goaltender of the Year (2004) • ECAC Player of the Year (2004) • NCAA East First All-American Team (2004)

Signed as a free agent by **Montreal**, March 19, 2004. Signed as a free agent by **NY Islanders**, July 2, 2008. Signed as a free agent by **New Jersey**, July 10, 2009.

## DARLING, Scott (DAHR-lihng, SKAWT) PHX.

Goaltender. Catches left. 6'6", 190 lbs. Born, Lemont, IL, December 22, 1988.
(Phoenix's 7th choice, 153rd overall, in 2007 Entry Draft).

| | | | Regular Season | | | | | | | | Playoffs | | | | | | |
|---|---|---|---|---|---|---|---|---|---|---|---|---|---|---|---|---|---|
| Season | Club | League | GP | W | L | O/T | Mins | GA | SO | Avg | GP | W | L | Mins | GA | SO | Avg |
| 2005-06 | Chicago | MWEHL | 2 | 0 | 2 | 0 | 120 | 10 | 0 | 5.00 | | | | | | | |
| | North Iowa | NAHL | 8 | 2 | 4 | 0 | 405 | 28 | 0 | 4.15 | | | | | | | |
| 2006-07 | Capital District | EJHL | 22 | 9 | 9 | 3 | 1243 | 70 | 1 | 3.38 | | | | | | | |
| | North Iowa | NAHL | 1 | 0 | 0 | 0 | 15 | 3 | 0 | 12.00 | | | | | | | |
| 2007-08 | Indiana Ice | USHL | 42 | 27 | 10 | 2 | 2391 | 121 | 1 | 3.04 | 3 | 1 | 2 | 179 | 11 | 0 | 3.69 |
| 2008-09 | University of Maine | H-East | 27 | 10 | 14 | 3 | 1566 | 72 | *3 | 2.76 | | | | | | | |

## DEKANICH, Mark (deh-KAN-ihch, MAHRK) NSH.

Goaltender. Catches left. 6'2", 190 lbs. Born, N. Vancouver, B.C., May 10, 1986.
(Nashville's 3rd choice, 146th overall, in 2006 Entry Draft).

| | | | Regular Season | | | | | | | | Playoffs | | | | | | |
|---|---|---|---|---|---|---|---|---|---|---|---|---|---|---|---|---|---|
| Season | Club | League | GP | W | L | O/T | Mins | GA | SO | Avg | GP | W | L | Mins | GA | SO | Avg |
| 2003-04 | Coquitlam Express | BCHL | 30 | 13 | 15 | 1 | 1647 | 89 | 2 | 3.24 | | | | | | | |
| 2004-05 | Colgate | ECAC | 5 | 1 | 1 | 0 | 162 | 5 | 0 | 1.85 | | | | | | | |
| 2005-06 | Colgate | ECAC | 36 | 18 | 11 | 6 | 2126 | 81 | 4 | 2.29 | | | | | | | |
| 2006-07 | Colgate | ECAC | 36 | 15 | 17 | 4 | 2136 | 83 | 1 | 2.33 | | | | | | | |
| 2007-08 | Colgate | ECAC | *41 | 18 | 16 | 6 | *2389 | 86 | *6 | 2.16 | | | | | | | |
| 2008-09 | Milwaukee | AHL | 30 | 15 | 10 | 2 | 1663 | 58 | 1 | 2.09 | | | | | | | |

ECAC First All-Star Team (2006) • ECAC Second All-Star Team (2007)

## DELMAS, Peter (DEHL-mas, PEE-tuhr) COL.

Goaltender. Catches left. 6'2", 169 lbs. Born, Alliston, Ont., February 16, 1990.
(Colorado's 2nd choice, 61st overall, in 2008 Entry Draft).

| | | | Regular Season | | | | | | | | Playoffs | | | | | | |
|---|---|---|---|---|---|---|---|---|---|---|---|---|---|---|---|---|---|
| Season | Club | League | GP | W | L | O/T | Mins | GA | SO | Avg | GP | W | L | Mins | GA | SO | Avg |
| 2006-07 | Lewiston | QMJHL | 34 | 23 | 10 | | 1983 | 93 | 3 | 2.81 | | | | | | | |
| 2007-08 | Lewiston | QMJHL | 34 | 17 | 17 | | 1987 | 94 | 0 | 2.84 | | | | | | | |
| 2008-09 | Lewiston | QMJHL | 38 | 9 | 27 | | 2090 | 146 | 0 | 4.19 | 2 | 0 | 2 | 75 | 15 | 0 | 11.96 |

QMJHL All-Rookie Team (2007)

## DENIS, Marc (deh-NEE, MAHRK)

Goaltender. Catches left. 6'1", 193 lbs. Born, Montreal, Que., August 1, 1977.
(Colorado's 1st choice, 25th overall, in 1995 Entry Draft).

| | | | Regular Season | | | | | | | | Playoffs | | | | | | |
|---|---|---|---|---|---|---|---|---|---|---|---|---|---|---|---|---|---|
| Season | Club | League | GP | W | L | O/T | Mins | GA | SO | Avg | GP | W | L | Mins | GA | SO | Avg |
| 1992-93 | Montreal-Bourassa | QAAA | 26 | | | | 1559 | 74 | 5 | 2.87 | | | | | | | |
| 1993-94 | Trois-Rivieres | QAAA | 36 | 10 | 22 | 3 | 2093 | 158 | 0 | 4.53 | 4 | 1 | 3 | 249 | 20 | 0 | 4.83 |
| 1994-95 | Chicoutimi | QMJHL | 32 | 17 | 9 | 1 | 1688 | 98 | 0 | 3.48 | 6 | 4 | 2 | 372 | 19 | 1 | 3.06 |
| 1995-96 | Chicoutimi | QMJHL | 51 | 23 | 21 | 4 | 2951 | 157 | 2 | 3.19 | 16 | 8 | 8 | 957 | 69 | 0 | 4.33 |
| 1996-97 | Chicoutimi | QMJHL | 41 | 22 | 15 | 2 | 2323 | 104 | 4 | *2.69 | *21 | *11 | 10 | *1229 | 70 | *1 | 3.42 |
| | Colorado | NHL | 1 | 0 | 1 | 0 | 60 | 3 | 0 | 3.00 | | | | | | | |
| | Hershey Bears | AHL | | | | | | | | | 4 | 1 | 0 | 56 | 1 | 0 | 1.08 |
| 1997-98 | Hershey Bears | AHL | 47 | 17 | 23 | 4 | 2588 | 125 | 1 | 2.90 | 6 | 3 | 3 | 346 | 15 | 0 | 2.59 |

| | | | | | | | | | | | | | | | | | |
|---|---|---|---|---|---|---|---|---|---|---|---|---|---|---|---|---|---|
| 1998-99 | Colorado | NHL | 4 | 1 | 1 | 1 | 217 | 9 | 0 | 2.49 | .... | .... | .... | .... | .... | .... | .... |
| | Hershey Bears | AHL | 52 | 20 | 23 | 5 | 2908 | 137 | 4 | 2.83 | 3 | 1 | 1 | 143 | 7 | 0 | 2.93 |
| 99-2000 | Colorado | NHL | 23 | 9 | 8 | 3 | 1203 | 51 | 3 | 2.54 | .... | .... | .... | .... | .... | .... | .... |
| 2000-01 | Columbus | NHL | 32 | 6 | 20 | 4 | 1830 | 99 | 0 | 3.25 | .... | .... | .... | .... | .... | .... | .... |
| 2001-02 | Columbus | NHL | 42 | 9 | 24 | 5 | 2335 | 121 | 1 | 3.11 | .... | .... | .... | .... | .... | .... | .... |
| 2002-03 | Columbus | NHL | *77 | 27 | 41 | 8 | *4511 | 232 | 5 | 3.09 | .... | .... | .... | .... | .... | .... | .... |
| 2003-04 | Columbus | NHL | 66 | 21 | 36 | 7 | 3796 | 162 | 5 | 2.56 | .... | .... | .... | .... | .... | .... | .... |
| 2004-05 | | | | | | | DID NOT PLAY | | | | | | | | | | |
| 2005-06 | Columbus | NHL | 49 | 21 | 25 | 1 | 2786 | 151 | 1 | 3.25 | .... | .... | .... | .... | .... | .... | .... |
| 2006-07 | Tampa Bay | NHL | 44 | 17 | 18 | 2 | 2353 | 125 | 1 | 3.19 | .... | .... | .... | .... | .... | .... | .... |
| 2007-08 | Tampa Bay | NHL | 10 | 1 | 5 | 0 | 415 | 28 | 0 | 4.05 | .... | .... | .... | .... | .... | .... | .... |
| | Norfolk Admirals | AHL | 32 | 11 | 17 | 2 | 1832 | 89 | 1 | 2.91 | .... | .... | .... | .... | .... | .... | .... |
| 2008-09 | Montreal | NHL | 1 | 0 | 0 | 0 | 20 | 1 | 0 | 3.00 | .... | .... | .... | .... | .... | .... | .... |
| | Hamilton Bulldogs | AHL | 46 | 27 | 18 | 0 | 2659 | 109 | 5 | 2.46 | 6 | 2 | 4 | 359 | 20 | 0 | 3.34 |
| | NHL Totals | | 349 | 112 | 179 | 31 | 19526 | 982 | 16 | 3.02 | .... | .... | .... | .... | .... | .... | .... |

QMJHL First All-Star Team (1997) • Canadian Major Junior First All-Star Team (1997) • Canadian Major Junior Goaltender of the Year (1997)

Traded to **Columbus** by **Colorado** for Columbus' 2nd round choice (later traded to Carolina – Carolina selected Tomas Kurka) in 2000 Entry Draft, June 7, 2000. Traded to **Tampa Bay** by **Columbus** for Fredrik Modin and Fredrik Norrena, June 30, 2006. Signed as a free agent by **Montreal**, July 3, 2008.

## DENNIS, Adam (DEH-nihs, A-duhm)

Goaltender. Catches left. 5'11", 183 lbs. Born, Toronto, Ont., February 8, 1985.
(Buffalo's 6th choice, 182nd overall, in 2005 Entry Draft).

| | | | Regular Season | | | | | | | | Playoffs | | | | | | |
|---|---|---|---|---|---|---|---|---|---|---|---|---|---|---|---|---|---|
| Season | Club | League | GP | W | L | O/T | Mins | GA | SO | Avg | GP | W | L | Mins | GA | SO | Avg |
| 2002-03 | Guelph Storm | OHL | 18 | 6 | 7 | 1 | 846 | 45 | 0 | 3.19 | .... | .... | .... | .... | .... | .... | .... |
| 2003-04 | Guelph Storm | OHL | 46 | *33 | 10 | 2 | 2662 | 111 | 3 | 2.50 | 20 | *15 | 5 | 1205 | 40 | 1 | *1.99 |
| 2004-05 | Guelph Storm | OHL | 23 | 5 | 11 | 6 | 1372 | 57 | 3 | 2.49 | .... | .... | .... | .... | .... | .... | .... |
| | London Knights | OHL | 16 | 12 | 4 | 0 | 920 | 23 | 3 | 1.50 | 11 | 9 | 1 | 629 | 22 | *2 | 2.10 |
| 2005-06 | London Knights | OHL | 57 | *44 | 9 | 4 | *3444 | 162 | 1 | 2.82 | 18 | 12 | 6 | 1090 | 59 | 0 | 3.25 |
| 2006-07 | Rochester | AHL | 35 | 18 | 17 | 0 | 2068 | 115 | 1 | 3.34 | .... | .... | .... | .... | .... | .... | .... |
| 2007-08 | Rochester | AHL | 46 | 17 | 26 | 2 | 2601 | 138 | 3 | 3.18 | .... | .... | .... | .... | .... | .... | .... |
| 2008-09 | Portland Pirates | AHL | 13 | 7 | 6 | 0 | 709 | 33 | 0 | 2.79 | .... | .... | .... | .... | .... | .... | .... |

OHL First All-Star Team (2005, 2006) • Memorial Cup Tournament All-Star Team (2005) • Hap Emms Memorial Trophy (Memorial Cup Tournament - Top Goaltender) (2005) • Canadian Major Junior Second All-Star Team (2006)

Signed as a free agent by **Fassa** (Italy), August 2, 2009.

## DESERRES, Jacob (deh-SAIR, JAY-kawb) PHI.

Goaltender. Catches left. 6'2", 195 lbs. Born, East York, Ont., March 18, 1990.
(Philadelphia's 3rd choice, 84th overall, in 2008 Entry Draft).

| | | | Regular Season | | | | | | | | Playoffs | | | | | | |
|---|---|---|---|---|---|---|---|---|---|---|---|---|---|---|---|---|---|
| Season | Club | League | GP | W | L | O/T | Mins | GA | SO | Avg | GP | W | L | Mins | GA | SO | Avg |
| 2005-06 | Calgary Buffaloes | AMHL | 21 | 11 | 7 | 3 | 1246 | 55 | .... | 2.65 | 11 | 9 | 2 | 698 | 19 | .... | 1.63 |
| | Seattle | WHL | 3 | 3 | 0 | 0 | 183 | 5 | 0 | 1.64 | .... | .... | .... | .... | .... | .... | .... |
| 2006-07 | Seattle | WHL | 20 | 7 | 9 | 2 | 1076 | 50 | 3 | 2.79 | 2 | 0 | 0 | 31 | 4 | 0 | 7.67 |
| 2007-08 | Seattle | WHL | 34 | 20 | 11 | 0 | 1972 | 75 | 3 | 2.28 | 5 | 1 | 2 | 208 | 10 | 0 | 2.88 |
| 2008-09 | Seattle | WHL | 32 | 11 | 16 | 0 | 1582 | 90 | 1 | 3.41 | .... | .... | .... | .... | .... | .... | .... |

## DESJARDINS, Cedrick (deh-ZHAHR-dai, SEH-DRIHK) MTL.

Goaltender. Catches left. 6', 183 lbs. Born, Edmunston, N.B., September 30, 1985.

| | | | Regular Season | | | | | | | | Playoffs | | | | | | |
|---|---|---|---|---|---|---|---|---|---|---|---|---|---|---|---|---|---|
| Season | Club | League | GP | W | L | O/T | Mins | GA | SO | Avg | GP | W | L | Mins | GA | SO | Avg |
| 2002-03 | Coaticook | QJHL | | | | | STATISTICS NOT AVAILABLE | | | | | | | | | | |
| | Rimouski Oceanic | QMJHL | 23 | 1 | 19 | 0 | 1239 | 109 | 0 | 5.28 | .... | .... | .... | .... | .... | .... | .... |
| 2003-04 | Rimouski Oceanic | QMJHL | 20 | 8 | 11 | 0 | 1119 | 72 | 0 | 3.86 | 1 | 0 | 0 | 14 | 0 | 0 | 0.00 |
| 2004-05 | Rimouski Oceanic | QMJHL | 44 | *30 | 7 | 4 | 2439 | 120 | 2 | 2.95 | 13 | *12 | 1 | *767 | 34 | *1 | 2.66 |
| 2005-06 | Quebec Remparts | QMJHL | 41 | 28 | 10 | 0 | 2254 | 111 | *5 | 2.95 | *23 | 14 | 9 | *1413 | 60 | 1 | 2.55 |
| 2006-07 | Hamilton Bulldogs | AHL | 3 | 0 | 2 | 0 | 142 | 7 | 0 | 2.96 | .... | .... | .... | .... | .... | .... | .... |
| | Cincinnati | ECHL | 45 | 24 | 19 | 1 | 2648 | 112 | 4 | 2.54 | .... | .... | .... | .... | .... | .... | .... |
| 2007-08 | Hamilton Bulldogs | AHL | 12 | 4 | 3 | 2 | 572 | 29 | 0 | 3.04 | .... | .... | .... | .... | .... | .... | .... |
| | Cincinnati | ECHL | 22 | 16 | 4 | 2 | 1285 | 41 | *5 | 1.91 | 16 | 11 | 4 | 947 | 29 | 1 | *1.83 |
| 2008-09 | Hamilton Bulldogs | AHL | 30 | 16 | 12 | 0 | 1718 | 73 | 4 | 2.55 | .... | .... | .... | .... | .... | .... | .... |

Memorial Cup Tournament All-Star Team (2006) • Hap Emms Memorial Trophy (Memorial Cup Tournament - Top Goaltender) (2006) • ECHL All-Rookie-Team (2007) • ECHL Playoff MVP (2009)

Signed as a free agent by **Hamilton** (AHL), July 26, 2006. Signed as a free agent by **Montreal**, July 3, 2008.

## DESLAURIERS, Jeff (duh-LAW-ree-yay, JEHF) EDM.

Goaltender. Catches right. 6'4", 200 lbs. Born, St-Jean-Richelieu, Que., May 15, 1984.
(Edmonton's 2nd choice, 31st overall, in 2002 Entry Draft).

| | | | Regular Season | | | | | | | | Playoffs | | | | | | |
|---|---|---|---|---|---|---|---|---|---|---|---|---|---|---|---|---|---|
| Season | Club | League | GP | W | L | O/T | Mins | GA | SO | Avg | GP | W | L | Mins | GA | SO | Avg |
| 2000-01 | Gatineau Intrepide | QAAA | 22 | 10 | 9 | 2 | 1194 | 61 | 2 | 3.07 | 2 | 1 | 0 | 125 | 6 | 0 | 2.89 |
| 2001-02 | Chicoutimi | QMJHL | 51 | 28 | 20 | 1 | 2909 | 170 | 1 | 3.51 | 4 | 0 | 3 | 197 | 20 | 0 | 6.11 |
| 2002-03 | Chicoutimi | QMJHL | 54 | 18 | 24 | 1 | 2582 | 164 | 0 | 3.81 | 4 | 0 | 4 | 240 | 15 | 0 | 9.00 |
| 2003-04 | Chicoutimi | QMJHL | 50 | 21 | 20 | 6 | 2701 | 129 | 1 | 2.87 | 18 | 10 | 8 | 956 | 50 | 1 | 3.14 |
| 2004-05 | Edmonton | AHL | 22 | 6 | 13 | 2 | 1258 | 62 | 0 | 2.96 | .... | .... | .... | .... | .... | .... | .... |
| | Greenville Grrrowl | ECHL | 11 | 7 | 3 | 1 | 673 | 26 | 1 | 2.32 | .... | .... | .... | .... | .... | .... | .... |
| 2005-06 | Hamilton Bulldogs | AHL | 13 | 4 | 7 | 0 | 666 | 35 | 0 | 3.15 | .... | .... | .... | .... | .... | .... | .... |
| | Greenville Grrrowl | ECHL | 6 | 2 | 4 | 0 | 335 | 17 | 0 | 3.05 | .... | .... | .... | .... | .... | .... | .... |
| 2006-07 | Wilkes-Barre | AHL | 40 | 22 | 12 | 3 | 2231 | 92 | 4 | 2.47 | .... | .... | .... | .... | .... | .... | .... |
| 2007-08 | Springfield Falcons | AHL | 57 | 26 | 23 | 5 | 3045 | 147 | 0 | 2.90 | .... | .... | .... | .... | .... | .... | .... |
| 2008-09 | Edmonton | NHL | 10 | 4 | 3 | 0 | 540 | 30 | 0 | 3.33 | .... | .... | .... | .... | .... | .... | .... |
| | Springfield Falcons | AHL | 5 | 1 | 4 | 0 | 286 | 13 | 0 | 2.73 | .... | .... | .... | .... | .... | .... | .... |
| | NHL Totals | | 10 | 4 | 3 | 0 | 540 | 30 | 0 | 3.33 | .... | .... | .... | .... | .... | .... | .... |

QMJHL All-Rookie Team (2002)

## DiPIETRO, Rick (dee-pee-EHT-roh, RIHK) NYI

Goaltender. Catches right. 6'1", 210 lbs. Born, Winthrop, MA, September 19, 1981.
(NY Islanders' 1st choice, 1st overall, in 2000 Entry Draft).

| | | | Regular Season | | | | | | | | Playoffs | | | | | | |
|---|---|---|---|---|---|---|---|---|---|---|---|---|---|---|---|---|---|
| Season | Club | League | GP | W | L | O/T | Mins | GA | SO | Avg | GP | W | L | Mins | GA | SO | Avg |
| 1997-98 | USNTDP | U-17 | 10 | 6 | 4 | 0 | 800 | 31 | 0 | 2.33 | .... | .... | .... | .... | .... | .... | .... |
| | USNTDP | USHL | 3 | 0 | 2 | 0 | 117 | 8 | 0 | 4.09 | .... | .... | .... | .... | .... | .... | .... |
| | USNTDP | NAHL | 30 | 13 | 12 | 0 | 1602 | 85 | 1 | 3.18 | 3 | 2 | 1 | 179 | 7 | 1 | 2.35 |
| 1998-99 | USNTDP | U-18 | 16 | 9 | 5 | 1 | 1027 | 46 | .... | 2.69 | .... | .... | .... | .... | .... | .... | .... |
| | USNTDP | USHL | 30 | 22 | 6 | 1 | 1733 | 67 | 3 | 2.32 | .... | .... | .... | .... | .... | .... | .... |
| 99-2000 | Boston University | H-East | 29 | 18 | 5 | 5 | 1790 | 73 | 2 | 2.45 | .... | .... | .... | .... | .... | .... | .... |
| 2000-01 | NY Islanders | NHL | 20 | 3 | 15 | 1 | 1083 | 63 | 0 | 3.49 | .... | .... | .... | .... | .... | .... | .... |
| | Chicago Wolves | IHL | 14 | 4 | 5 | 2 | 778 | 44 | 0 | 3.39 | .... | .... | .... | .... | .... | .... | .... |
| 2001-02 | Bridgeport | AHL | 59 | *30 | 22 | 7 | 3472 | 134 | 4 | 2.32 | 20 | 12 | 8 | *1270 | 45 | *3 | 2.13 |
| 2002-03 | NY Islanders | NHL | 10 | 2 | 5 | 2 | 585 | 29 | 0 | 2.97 | 1 | 0 | 0 | 15 | 0 | 0 | 0.00 |
| | Bridgeport | AHL | 34 | 16 | 10 | 8 | 2044 | 73 | 3 | 2.14 | 5 | 2 | 3 | 299 | 10 | 1 | 2.01 |
| 2003-04 | NY Islanders | NHL | 50 | 23 | 18 | 5 | 2844 | 112 | 5 | 2.36 | 5 | 1 | 4 | 303 | 11 | 1 | 2.18 |
| | Bridgeport | AHL | 2 | 0 | 2 | 0 | 119 | 3 | 0 | 1.51 | .... | .... | .... | .... | .... | .... | .... |
| 2004-05 | | | | | | | DID NOT PLAY | | | | | | | | | | |
| 2005-06 | NY Islanders | NHL | 63 | 30 | 24 | 5 | 3572 | 180 | 1 | 3.02 | .... | .... | .... | .... | .... | .... | .... |
| | United States | Olympics | 4 | 1 | 3 | 0 | 237 | 9 | 0 | 2.28 | .... | .... | .... | .... | .... | .... | .... |
| 2006-07 | NY Islanders | NHL | 62 | 32 | 19 | 9 | 3627 | 156 | 5 | 2.58 | 4 | 1 | 3 | 236 | 13 | 0 | 3.31 |
| 2007-08 | NY Islanders | NHL | 63 | 26 | 28 | 7 | 3707 | 174 | 3 | 2.82 | .... | .... | .... | .... | .... | .... | .... |
| 2008-09 | NY Islanders | NHL | 5 | 1 | 3 | 0 | 256 | 15 | 0 | 3.52 | .... | .... | .... | .... | .... | .... | .... |
| | NHL Totals | | 273 | 117 | 112 | 29 | 15674 | 729 | 14 | 2.79 | 10 | 2 | 7 | 554 | 24 | 1 | 2.60 |

Hockey East Second All-Star Team (2000) • Hockey East Rookie of the Year (2000)

Played in NHL All-Star Game (2008)

• Missed majority of 2008-09 season recovering from arthroscopic knee surgery, October 31, 2008.

## DUBIELEWICZ, Wade (DOO-bih-wihtz, WAYD) MIN.

Goaltender. Catches left. 5'10", 185 lbs. Born, Invermere, B.C., January 30, 1979.

| | | | Regular Season | | | | | | | | Playoffs | | | | | | |
|---|---|---|---|---|---|---|---|---|---|---|---|---|---|---|---|---|---|
| Season | Club | League | GP | W | L | O/T | Mins | GA | SO | Avg | GP | W | L | Mins | GA | SO | Avg |
| 1997-98 | Trail Smoke Eaters | BCHL | 41 | .... | .... | .... | 2225 | 118 | 0 | 3.18 | .... | .... | .... | .... | .... | .... | .... |
| 1998-99 | Trail Smoke Eaters | BCHL | | | | | STATISTICS NOT AVAILABLE | | | | | | | | | | |
| | Chilliwack Chiefs | BCHL | 14 | 10 | 4 | 0 | 834 | .... | 0 | .... | .... | .... | .... | .... | .... | .... | .... |
| 99-2000 | U. of Denver | WCHA | 13 | 3 | 5 | 1 | 596 | 27 | 1 | 2.72 | .... | .... | .... | .... | .... | .... | .... |
| 2000-01 | U. of Denver | WCHA | 29 | 12 | 9 | 3 | 1542 | 59 | 2 | 2.30 | .... | .... | .... | .... | .... | .... | .... |
| 2001-02 | U. of Denver | WCHA | 24 | 20 | 4 | 0 | 1431 | 41 | 2 | *1.72 | .... | .... | .... | .... | .... | .... | .... |
| 2002-03 | U. of Denver | WCHA | 19 | 9 | 8 | 2 | 1060 | 43 | 3 | 2.43 | .... | .... | .... | .... | .... | .... | .... |
| 2003-04 | NY Islanders | NHL | 2 | 1 | 0 | 1 | 105 | 3 | 0 | 1.71 | .... | .... | .... | .... | .... | .... | .... |
| | Bridgeport | AHL | 33 | 20 | 8 | 5 | 1959 | 45 | 9 | *1.38 | 3 | 2 | 1 | 181 | 11 | 0 | 3.64 |
| 2004-05 | Bridgeport | AHL | 43 | 18 | 23 | 1 | 2539 | 113 | 1 | 2.67 | .... | .... | .... | .... | .... | .... | .... |
| 2005-06 | NY Islanders | NHL | 7 | 2 | 3 | 0 | 310 | 15 | 0 | 2.90 | .... | .... | .... | .... | .... | .... | .... |
| | Bridgeport | AHL | 46 | 20 | 21 | 2 | 2575 | 134 | 3 | 3.12 | 7 | 3 | 4 | 435 | 16 | 0 | 2.21 |
| 2006-07 | NY Islanders | NHL | 8 | 4 | 1 | 0 | 379 | 13 | 0 | 2.06 | 1 | 0 | 1 | 59 | 4 | 0 | 4.07 |
| | Bridgeport | AHL | 40 | 22 | 12 | 5 | 2405 | 108 | 2 | 2.69 | .... | .... | .... | .... | .... | .... | .... |
| 2007-08 | NY Islanders | NHL | 20 | 9 | 9 | 1 | 1132 | 51 | 0 | 2.70 | .... | .... | .... | .... | .... | .... | .... |
| | Bridgeport | AHL | 2 | 1 | 1 | 0 | 124 | 5 | 0 | 2.42 | .... | .... | .... | .... | .... | .... | .... |
| 2008-09 | Ak Bars Kazan | Rus-KHL | 21 | .... | .... | .... | 1236 | 58 | 0 | 2.82 | .... | .... | .... | .... | .... | .... | .... |
| | Columbus | NHL | 3 | 1 | 2 | 0 | 169 | 10 | 0 | 3.55 | .... | .... | .... | .... | .... | .... | .... |
| | NHL Totals | | 40 | 17 | 15 | 2 | 2095 | 92 | 0 | 2.63 | 1 | 0 | 1 | 59 | 4 | 0 | 4.07 |

WCHA Second All-Star Team (2001, 2003) • WCHA First All-Star Team (2002) • AHL All-Rookie Team (2004) • AHL Second All-Star Team (2004) • Dudley "Red" Garrett Memorial Award (AHL - Rookie of the Year) (2004) • Harry "Hap" Holmes Memorial Award (AHL - fewest goals against) (2004) (shared with Dieter Kochan)

Signed as a free agent by **NY Islanders**, May 25, 2003. Signed as a free agent by **Kazan** (Rus-KHL), June 25. 2008. Signed as a free agent by **NY Islanders**, January 15, 2009. Claimed on waivers by **Columbus** from **NY Islanders**, January 17, 2009. Signed as a free agent by **Minnesota**, July 17, 2009.

## DUBNYK, Devan (DOOB-nihk, DEH-vuhn) EDM.

Goaltender. Catches left. 6'5", 194 lbs. Born, Regina, Sask., May 4, 1986.
(Edmonton's 1st choice, 14th overall, in 2004 Entry Draft).

| | | | Regular Season | | | | | | | | Playoffs | | | | | | |
|---|---|---|---|---|---|---|---|---|---|---|---|---|---|---|---|---|---|
| Season | Club | League | GP | W | L | O/T | Mins | GA | SO | Avg | GP | W | L | Mins | GA | SO | Avg |
| 2000-01 | Calgary Bruins | CBHL | 14 | .... | .... | .... | 815 | 39 | 2 | 3.10 | .... | .... | .... | .... | .... | .... | .... |
| 2001-02 | Calgary Bruins | CBHL | 18 | 7 | 9 | 2 | 1105 | 68 | 1 | 3.69 | .... | .... | .... | .... | .... | .... | .... |
| | Titaanit Kotka Jr. | Fin-Jr. | 5 | 5 | 0 | 0 | 300 | 7 | .... | 1.40 | .... | .... | .... | .... | .... | .... | .... |
| | Kamloops Blazers | WHL | 3 | 1 | 1 | 0 | 143 | 13 | 0 | 5.45 | .... | .... | .... | .... | .... | .... | .... |
| 2002-03 | Kamloops Blazers | WHL | 26 | 12 | 8 | 1 | 1279 | 68 | 2 | 3.19 | .... | .... | .... | .... | .... | .... | .... |
| 2003-04 | Kamloops Blazers | WHL | 44 | 20 | 18 | 5 | 2533 | 106 | 6 | 2.51 | 4 | 1 | 3 | 245 | 12 | 0 | 2.94 |
| 2004-05 | Kamloops Blazers | WHL | *65 | 23 | 34 | 7 | 3699 | 166 | 6 | 2.69 | 6 | 2 | 4 | 363 | 22 | 0 | 3.64 |
| 2005-06 | Kamloops Blazers | WHL | 54 | 27 | 26 | 1 | 3207 | 136 | 1 | 2.54 | .... | .... | .... | .... | .... | .... | .... |
| 2006-07 | Wilkes-Barre | AHL | 4 | 2 | 1 | 0 | 204 | 10 | 0 | 2.94 | .... | .... | .... | .... | .... | .... | .... |
| | Stockton Thunder | ECHL | 43 | 24 | 11 | 7 | 2529 | 108 | 2 | 2.56 | 6 | 2 | 4 | 395 | 18 | 0 | 2.73 |
| 2007-08 | Springfield Falcons | AHL | 33 | 9 | 17 | 0 | 1772 | 92 | 0 | 3.12 | .... | .... | .... | .... | .... | .... | .... |
| 2008-09 | Springfield Falcons | AHL | *62 | 18 | 41 | 2 | *3635 | 180 | 3 | 2.97 | .... | .... | .... | .... | .... | .... | .... |

Canadian Major Junior Scholastic Player of the Year (2004)

## DUCHESNE, Jeremy (DOO-shayn, JAIR-eh-mee) PHI.

Goaltender. Catches left. 6', 218 lbs. Born, Silver Spring, MD, October 17, 1986.
(Philadelphia's 3rd choice, 119th overall, in 2005 Entry Draft).

| | | | Regular Season | | | | | | | | Playoffs | | | | | | |
|---|---|---|---|---|---|---|---|---|---|---|---|---|---|---|---|---|---|
| Season | Club | League | GP | W | L | O/T | Mins | GA | SO | Avg | GP | W | L | Mins | GA | SO | Avg |
| 2002-03 | St-Francois Blizzard | QAAA | 26 | 7 | 11 | 5 | 1341 | 75 | 0 | 3.35 | .... | .... | .... | .... | .... | .... | .... |
| 2003-04 | Victoriaville Tigres | QMJHL | 17 | 3 | 8 | 1 | 870 | 60 | 0 | 4.14 | .... | .... | .... | .... | .... | .... | .... |
| 2004-05 | Victoriaville Tigres | QMJHL | 15 | 2 | 9 | 0 | 711 | 41 | 2 | *3.46 | .... | .... | .... | .... | .... | .... | .... |
| | Halifax | QMJHL | 18 | 12 | 0 | 2 | 921 | 23 | 3 | *1.50 | 12 | 8 | 4 | 723 | 33 | *1 | 2.74 |
| 2005-06 | Halifax | QMJHL | 55 | 25 | 29 | 0 | 3175 | 185 | 4 | 3.50 | 11 | 5 | 6 | 626 | 34 | 1 | 3.26 |
| 2006-07 | Halifax | QMJHL | 28 | 12 | 15 | .... | 1580 | 97 | 1 | 3.68 | .... | .... | .... | .... | .... | .... | .... |
| | Val-d'Or Foreurs | QMJHL | 24 | 13 | 10 | .... | 1356 | 66 | 1 | 2.92 | *18 | 11 | 7 | *1157 | 56 | 0 | 2.90 |
| 2007-08 | Philadelphia | AHL | 2 | 1 | 0 | 0 | 80 | 6 | 0 | 4.50 | .... | .... | .... | .... | .... | .... | .... |
| | Dayton Bombers | ECHL | 31 | 13 | 13 | 5 | 1838 | 91 | 1 | 2.97 | .... | .... | .... | .... | .... | .... | .... |
| 2008-09 | Mississippi | ECHL | 13 | 3 | 7 | 2 | 718 | 57 | 1 | 4.77 | .... | .... | .... | .... | .... | .... | .... |
| | South Carolina | ECHL | 5 | 2 | 2 | 0 | 206 | 17 | 0 | 4.94 | .... | .... | .... | .... | .... | .... | .... |

## DUNN, Dan (DUHN, DAN) WSH.

Goaltender. Catches left. 6'5", 204 lbs. Born, Oshawa, Ont., June 20, 1988.
(Washington's 7th choice, 154th overall, in 2007 Entry Draft).

| | | | Regular Season | | | | | | | | Playoffs | | | | | | |
|---|---|---|---|---|---|---|---|---|---|---|---|---|---|---|---|---|---|
| Season | Club | League | GP | W | L | O/T | Mins | GA | SO | Avg | GP | W | L | Mins | GA | SO | Avg |
| 2005-06 | Oshawa | OPJHL | 10 | 2 | 4 | 2 | 494 | 29 | 1 | 3.52 | .... | .... | .... | .... | .... | .... | .... |
| | Cobourg Cougars | OPJHL | 6 | 0 | 5 | 0 | 277 | 33 | 0 | 7.14 | .... | .... | .... | .... | .... | .... | .... |
| 2006-07 | Wellington Dukes | OPJHL | 27 | 19 | 4 | 2 | 1546 | 50 | 2 | 1.94 | .... | .... | .... | .... | .... | .... | .... |
| 2007-08 | St. Cloud State | WCHA | 9 | 3 | 2 | 2 | 433 | 19 | 0 | 2.63 | .... | .... | .... | .... | .... | .... | .... |
| 2008-09 | St. Cloud State | WCHA | 9 | 2 | 4 | 1 | 393 | 17 | 0 | 2.60 | .... | .... | .... | .... | .... | .... | .... |

## EHELECHNER, Patrick (eh-heh-LEHCH-nuhr, PAT-rihk) PIT.

Goaltender. Catches left. 6'2", 169 lbs. Born, Rosenheim, West Germany, September 23, 1984.
(San Jose's 5th choice, 139th overall, in 2003 Entry Draft).

| | | | Regular Season | | | | | | | | Playoffs | | | | | | |
|---|---|---|---|---|---|---|---|---|---|---|---|---|---|---|---|---|---|
| Season | Club | League | GP | W | L | O/T | Mins | GA | SO | Avg | GP | W | L | Mins | GA | SO | Avg |
| 2000-01 | Jung. Mannheim | German-4 | 40 | .... | .... | .... | 2423 | 171 | 2 | 4.23 | .... | .... | .... | .... | .... | .... | .... |
| 2001-02 | EV Landshut | German-3 | 2 | .... | .... | .... | 130 | 6 | 0 | 2.77 | .... | .... | .... | .... | .... | .... | .... |
| | Hannover | Germany | 8 | .... | .... | .... | 475 | 24 | 0 | 3.03 | .... | .... | .... | .... | .... | .... | .... |
| 2002-03 | ESC Wedemark | German-4 | | | | | STATISTICS NOT AVAILABLE | | | | | | | | | | |
| | Hannover | Germany | 4 | .... | .... | .... | 162 | 16 | 0 | 5.90 | .... | .... | .... | .... | .... | .... | .... |
| 2003-04 | Sudbury Wolves | OHL | 56 | 22 | 26 | 6 | 3089 | 148 | 3 | 2.87 | 7 | 2 | 4 | 390 | 14 | 2 | 2.15 |
| 2004-05 | Sudbury Wolves | OHL | 51 | 23 | 21 | 4 | 2997 | 128 | 3 | 2.56 | 10 | 4 | 5 | 497 | 29 | 0 | 3.50 |
| 2005-06 | Adler Mannheim | Germany | 1 | .... | .... | .... | 59 | 5 | 0 | 5.02 | .... | .... | .... | .... | .... | .... | .... |
| | Fuchse Duisburg | Germany | 26 | .... | .... | .... | 1243 | 75 | 2 | 3.62 | .... | .... | .... | .... | .... | .... | .... |
| 2006-07 | Fuchse Duisburg | Germany | 6 | .... | .... | .... | 244 | 28 | 0 | 6.89 | .... | .... | .... | .... | .... | .... | .... |
| 2007-08 | Nurnberg | Germany | 15 | 10 | 4 | 0 | 820 | 37 | 0 | 2.71 | 2 | 0 | 0 | 17 | 1 | 0 | 3.57 |

| | | | | | | | | | | | | | | | | | |
|---|---|---|---|---|---|---|---|---|---|---|---|---|---|---|---|---|---|
| 2008-09 | Nurnberg | Germany | 7 | 4 | 3 | .... | 428 | 15 | 0 | 2.10 | .... | .... | .... | .... | .... | .... | .... |

OHL Second All-Star Team (2004)

Signed as a free agent by **Mannheim** (Germany), April 25, 2005. Traded to **Pittsburgh** by **San Jose** with Nils Ekman for Carolina's 2nd round choice (previously acquired, later traded to Philadelphia - Philadelphia selected Kevin Marshall) in 2007 Entry Draft, July 20, 2006.

## EIDSNESS, Bradley (IGHD-nehz, BRAD-lee) BUF.

Goaltender. Catches left. 6', 190 lbs. Born, Chestermere, Alta., June 2, 1989.
(Buffalo's 4th choice, 139th overall, in 2007 Entry Draft).

| | | | Regular Season | | | | | | | | Playoffs | | | | | | |
|---|---|---|---|---|---|---|---|---|---|---|---|---|---|---|---|---|---|
| **Season** | **Club** | **League** | **GP** | **W** | **L** | **O/T** | **Mins** | **GA** | **SO** | **Avg** | **GP** | **W** | **L** | **Mins** | **GA** | **SO** | **Avg** |
| 2005-06 | Okotoks Oilers | AJHL | 4 | 3 | 1 | 0 | 238 | 4 | 2 | 1.01 | .... | .... | .... | .... | .... | .... | .... |
| | UFA Bisons | AMHL | 18 | 12 | 4 | 2 | 1046 | 45 | .... | 2.58 | 8 | 5 | 3 | 512 | 14 | .... | 1.64 |
| 2006-07 | Okotoks Oilers | AJHL | 48 | 24 | 18 | 2 | 2658 | 127 | 4 | 2.87 | .... | .... | .... | .... | .... | .... | .... |
| 2007-08 | Okotoks Oilers | AJHL | .... | 29 | 4 | 4 | 2264 | 80 | 3 | 2.12 | 9 | 4 | 5 | 547 | 25 | 0 | 2.74 |
| 2008-09 | North Dakota | WCHA | 41 | *24 | 12 | 0 | 2441 | 104 | 1 | 2.56 | .... | .... | .... | .... | .... | .... | .... |

WCHA All-Rookie Team (2009)

## ELLIOTT, Brian (EHL-lee-awt, BRIGH-uhn) OTT.

Goaltender. Catches left. 6'2", 199 lbs. Born, Newmarket, Ont., April 9, 1985.
(Ottawa's 9th choice, 291st overall, in 2003 Entry Draft).

| | | | Regular Season | | | | | | | | Playoffs | | | | | | |
|---|---|---|---|---|---|---|---|---|---|---|---|---|---|---|---|---|---|
| **Season** | **Club** | **League** | **GP** | **W** | **L** | **O/T** | **Mins** | **GA** | **SO** | **Avg** | **GP** | **W** | **L** | **Mins** | **GA** | **SO** | **Avg** |
| 2002-03 | Ajax Axemen | OPJHL | 39 | .... | .... | .... | 2097 | 135 | 0 | 3.86 | .... | .... | .... | .... | .... | .... | .... |
| 2003-04 | U. of Wisconsin | WCHA | 6 | 3 | 3 | 0 | 336 | 12 | 0 | 2.14 | .... | .... | .... | .... | .... | .... | .... |
| 2004-05 | U. of Wisconsin | WCHA | 9 | 6 | 2 | 1 | 467 | 9 | 3 | 1.16 | .... | .... | .... | .... | .... | .... | .... |
| 2005-06 | U. of Wisconsin | WCHA | 35 | *27 | 5 | 3 | 2128 | 55 | *8 | *1.55 | .... | .... | .... | .... | .... | .... | .... |
| 2006-07 | U. of Wisconsin | WCHA | 36 | 15 | 17 | 2 | 2053 | 72 | *5 | 2.10 | .... | .... | .... | .... | .... | .... | .... |
| | Binghamton | AHL | 8 | 3 | 4 | 0 | 425 | 30 | 0 | 4.24 | .... | .... | .... | .... | .... | .... | .... |
| **2007-08** | **Ottawa** | **NHL** | **1** | **1** | **0** | **0** | **60** | **1** | **0** | **1.00** | .... | .... | .... | .... | .... | .... | .... |
| | Binghamton | AHL | 44 | 18 | 19 | 1 | 2394 | 112 | 2 | 2.81 | .... | .... | .... | .... | .... | .... | .... |
| **2008-09** | **Ottawa** | **NHL** | **31** | **16** | **8** | **3** | **1667** | **77** | **1** | **2.77** | .... | .... | .... | .... | .... | .... | .... |
| | Binghamton | AHL | 30 | 18 | 8 | 1 | 1691 | 65 | 2 | 2.31 | .... | .... | .... | .... | .... | .... | .... |
| | **NHL Totals** | | **32** | **17** | **8** | **3** | **1727** | **78** | **1** | **2.71** | .... | .... | .... | .... | .... | .... | .... |

WCHA Second All-Star Team (2006, 2007) • NCAA West First All-American Team (2006) • NCAA Championship All-Tournament Team (2006)

## ELLIS, Dan (EHL-ihs, DAN) NSH.

Goaltender. Catches left. 6', 188 lbs. Born, Orangeville, Ont., June 19, 1980.
(Dallas' 2nd choice, 60th overall, in 2000 Entry Draft).

| | | | Regular Season | | | | | | | | Playoffs | | | | | | |
|---|---|---|---|---|---|---|---|---|---|---|---|---|---|---|---|---|---|
| **Season** | **Club** | **League** | **GP** | **W** | **L** | **O/T** | **Mins** | **GA** | **SO** | **Avg** | **GP** | **W** | **L** | **Mins** | **GA** | **SO** | **Avg** |
| 1998-99 | Newmarket | OPJHL | 28 | 24 | 3 | 1 | 1670 | 63 | 3 | 2.25 | .... | .... | .... | .... | .... | .... | .... |
| 99-2000 | Omaha Lancers | USHL | 55 | *34 | 16 | 4 | *3274 | 123 | *11 | *2.25 | 4 | 1 | 3 | 238 | 10 | 0 | 2.52 |
| 2000-01 | Nebraska-Omaha | CCHA | 40 | 21 | 14 | 3 | 2285 | 95 | 2 | 2.49 | .... | .... | .... | .... | .... | .... | .... |
| 2001-02 | Nebraska-Omaha | CCHA | 40 | 20 | 15 | 4 | 2405 | 97 | 3 | 2.42 | .... | .... | .... | .... | .... | .... | .... |
| 2002-03 | Nebraska-Omaha | CCHA | 39 | 11 | 21 | 5 | 2211 | 117 | 3 | 3.18 | .... | .... | .... | .... | .... | .... | .... |
| **2003-04** | **Dallas** | **NHL** | **1** | **1** | **0** | **0** | **60** | **3** | **0** | **3.00** | .... | .... | .... | .... | .... | .... | .... |
| | Utah Grizzlies | AHL | 20 | 5 | 14 | 0 | 1130 | 55 | 2 | 2.92 | .... | .... | .... | .... | .... | .... | .... |
| | Idaho Steelheads | ECHL | 23 | 13 | 8 | 1 | 1334 | 57 | 2 | 2.56 | *16 | *13 | 3 | *966 | 30 | *3 | *1.86 |
| 2004-05 | Hamilton Bulldogs | AHL | 31 | 10 | 19 | 0 | 1774 | 82 | 1 | 2.77 | .... | .... | .... | .... | .... | .... | .... |
| 2005-06 | Iowa Stars | AHL | 34 | 16 | 13 | 1 | 1857 | 86 | 2 | 2.78 | .... | .... | .... | .... | .... | .... | .... |
| 2006-07 | Iowa Stars | AHL | 55 | 30 | 21 | 1 | 3194 | 148 | 4 | 2.78 | 12 | 6 | 6 | 679 | 35 | 0 | 3.09 |
| **2007-08** | **Nashville** | **NHL** | **44** | **23** | **10** | **3** | **2229** | **87** | **6** | **2.34** | **6** | **2** | **4** | **357** | **15** | **0** | **2.52** |
| **2008-09** | **Nashville** | **NHL** | **35** | **11** | **19** | **4** | **1965** | **96** | **3** | **2.93** | .... | .... | .... | .... | .... | .... | .... |
| | **NHL Totals** | | **80** | **35** | **29** | **7** | **4254** | **186** | **9** | **2.62** | **6** | **2** | **4** | **357** | **15** | **0** | **2.52** |

USHL First All-Star Team (2000) • USHL Goaltender of the Year (2000) • USHL Player of the Year (2000) • CCHA Second All-Star Team (2002) • ECHL Playoff MVP (2004)

Signed as a free agent by **Nashville**, July 5, 2007.

## ELLIS, Julien (EHL-ihs, JEW-lee-ehn)

Goaltender. Catches left. 6', 186 lbs. Born, Sorel, Que., January 27, 1986.
(Vancouver's 5th choice, 189th overall, in 2004 Entry Draft).

| | | | Regular Season | | | | | | | | Playoffs | | | | | | |
|---|---|---|---|---|---|---|---|---|---|---|---|---|---|---|---|---|---|
| **Season** | **Club** | **League** | **GP** | **W** | **L** | **O/T** | **Mins** | **GA** | **SO** | **Avg** | **GP** | **W** | **L** | **Mins** | **GA** | **SO** | **Avg** |
| 2001-02 | Antoine-Girouard | QAAA | 22 | 16 | 2 | 1 | 1227 | 55 | 2 | 2.69 | .... | .... | .... | .... | .... | .... | .... |
| 2002-03 | Antoine-Girouard | QAAA | 16 | 11 | 4 | 1 | 966 | 29 | 4 | 1.80 | .... | .... | .... | .... | .... | .... | .... |
| | Shawinigan | QMJHL | 7 | 2 | 3 | 0 | 365 | 21 | 0 | 3.45 | .... | .... | .... | .... | .... | .... | .... |
| 2003-04 | Shawinigan | QMJHL | *59 | 32 | 18 | 2 | *3287 | 156 | 1 | 2.85 | 10 | 3 | 6 | 569 | 33 | 0 | 3.48 |
| 2004-05 | Shawinigan | QMJHL | *59 | 27 | 21 | 11 | *3480 | 140 | 4 | 2.41 | 4 | 0 | 3 | 175 | 10 | 0 | 3.43 |
| 2005-06 | Shawinigan | QMJHL | 48 | 27 | 19 | 0 | 2680 | 154 | 3 | 3.45 | 7 | 4 | 3 | 412 | 18 | *2 | 2.62 |
| 2006-07 | Manitoba Moose | AHL | 8 | 1 | 7 | 0 | 463 | 26 | 0 | 3.37 | .... | .... | .... | .... | .... | .... | .... |
| | Victoria | ECHL | 37 | 21 | 14 | 2 | 2190 | 117 | 1 | 3.21 | 4 | 1 | 3 | 213 | 15 | 0 | 4.23 |
| 2007-08 | Manitoba Moose | AHL | 1 | 0 | 0 | 0 | 40 | 1 | 0 | 1.50 | .... | .... | .... | .... | .... | .... | .... |
| | Victoria | ECHL | 42 | 24 | 11 | 5 | 2412 | 128 | 2 | 3.18 | 3 | 1 | 1 | 136 | 9 | 0 | 3.97 |
| 2008-09 | Manitoba Moose | AHL | 2 | 0 | 1 | 0 | 80 | 6 | 0 | 4.50 | .... | .... | .... | .... | .... | .... | .... |
| | Victoria | ECHL | 23 | 11 | 8 | 4 | 1398 | 63 | 1 | 2.70 | 3 | 1 | 1 | 139 | 8 | 1 | 3.45 |

QMJHL All-Rookie Team (2004) • QMJHL First All-Star Team (2005) • Canadian Major Junior Second All-Star Team (2005)

## EMERY, Ray (EH-muhr-ee, RAY) PHI.

Goaltender. Catches left. 6'2", 196 lbs. Born, Cayuga, Ont., September 28, 1982.
(Ottawa's 4th choice, 99th overall, in 2001 Entry Draft).

| | | | Regular Season | | | | | | | | Playoffs | | | | | | |
|---|---|---|---|---|---|---|---|---|---|---|---|---|---|---|---|---|---|
| **Season** | **Club** | **League** | **GP** | **W** | **L** | **O/T** | **Mins** | **GA** | **SO** | **Avg** | **GP** | **W** | **L** | **Mins** | **GA** | **SO** | **Avg** |
| 1998-99 | Dunnville Terriers | OJHL-C | 22 | 3 | 19 | 0 | 1320 | 140 | 0 | 6.37 | .... | .... | .... | .... | .... | .... | .... |
| 99-2000 | Welland Cougars | OHA-B | 23 | 13 | 10 | 1 | 1323 | 62 | 1 | 2.68 | .... | .... | .... | .... | .... | .... | .... |
| | Sault Ste. Marie | OHL | 16 | 9 | 3 | 0 | 716 | 36 | 1 | 3.02 | 15 | 8 | 7 | 883 | 33 | *3 | 2.24 |
| 2000-01 | Sault Ste. Marie | OHL | 52 | 18 | 29 | 2 | 2938 | 174 | 1 | 3.55 | .... | .... | .... | .... | .... | .... | .... |
| 2001-02 | Sault Ste. Marie | OHL | *59 | *33 | 17 | 9 | *3477 | 158 | 4 | 2.73 | 6 | 2 | 4 | 360 | 19 | *1 | 3.17 |
| **2002-03** | **Ottawa** | **NHL** | **3** | **1** | **0** | **0** | **85** | **2** | **0** | **1.41** | .... | .... | .... | .... | .... | .... | .... |
| | Binghamton | AHL | 50 | 27 | 17 | 6 | 2924 | 118 | *7 | 2.42 | 14 | 8 | 6 | 848 | 40 | *2 | 2.83 |
| **2003-04** | **Ottawa** | **NHL** | **3** | **2** | **0** | **0** | **126** | **5** | **0** | **2.38** | .... | .... | .... | .... | .... | .... | .... |
| | Binghamton | AHL | 53 | 21 | 23 | 7 | 3109 | 128 | 3 | 2.47 | 2 | 0 | 2 | 120 | 6 | 0 | 3.01 |
| 2004-05 | Binghamton | AHL | 51 | 28 | 18 | 5 | 2993 | 132 | 0 | 2.65 | 6 | 2 | 4 | 409 | 14 | 0 | 2.05 |
| **2005-06** | **Ottawa** | **NHL** | **39** | **23** | **11** | **4** | **2168** | **102** | **3** | **2.82** | **10** | **5** | **5** | **604** | **29** | **0** | **2.88** |
| **2006-07** | **Ottawa** | **NHL** | **58** | **33** | **16** | **6** | **3351** | **138** | **5** | **2.47** | ***20** | ***13** | **7** | ***1249** | **47** | ***3** | **2.26** |
| **2007-08** | **Ottawa** | **NHL** | **31** | **12** | **13** | **4** | **1689** | **88** | **0** | **3.13** | .... | .... | .... | .... | .... | .... | .... |
| | Binghamton | AHL | 2 | 1 | 1 | 0 | 120 | 6 | 0 | 3.00 | .... | .... | .... | .... | .... | .... | .... |
| 2008-09 | Mytischi | Rus-KHL | 36 | .... | .... | .... | 2070 | 73 | 2 | 2.12 | 7 | .... | .... | 419 | 13 | 1 | 1.86 |
| | **NHL Totals** | | **134** | **71** | **40** | **14** | **7419** | **335** | **8** | **2.71** | **30** | **18** | **12** | **1853** | **76** | **3** | **2.46** |

OHL First All-Star Team (2002) • Canadian Major Junior First All-Star Team (2002) • Canadian Major Junior Goaltender of the Year (2002) • AHL All-Rookie Team (2003)

Signed as a free agent by **Mytischi** (Rus-KHL), July 9, 2008. Signed as a free agent by **Philadelphia** June 10, 2009.

## ENGREN, Atte (EHN-grehn, AH-tay) NSH.

Goaltender. Catches left. 6'1", 184 lbs. Born, Rauma, Finland, February 19, 1988.
(Nashville's 9th choice, 204th overall, in 2007 Entry Draft).

| | | | Regular Season | | | | | | | | Playoffs | | | | | | |
|---|---|---|---|---|---|---|---|---|---|---|---|---|---|---|---|---|---|
| **Season** | **Club** | **League** | **GP** | **W** | **L** | **O/T** | **Mins** | **GA** | **SO** | **Avg** | **GP** | **W** | **L** | **Mins** | **GA** | **SO** | **Avg** |
| 2004-05 | Lukko Rauma U18 | Fin-U18 | 10 | .... | .... | .... | 603 | 22 | 0 | 2.19 | .... | .... | .... | .... | .... | .... | .... |
| 2005-06 | Lukko Rauma U18 | Fin-U18 | 16 | .... | .... | .... | 966 | 44 | 0 | 2.73 | .... | .... | .... | .... | .... | .... | .... |
| | Lukko Rauma Jr. | Fin-Jr. | 11 | .... | .... | .... | 637 | 30 | 0 | 2.83 | 9 | .... | .... | 509 | 27 | 0 | 3.18 |
| 2006-07 | Lukko Rauma Jr. | Fin-Jr. | 38 | .... | .... | .... | 2277 | 115 | 1 | 3.03 | .... | .... | .... | .... | .... | .... | .... |
| | Suomi U20 | Finland-2 | 2 | .... | .... | .... | 100 | 7 | 0 | 4.20 | .... | .... | .... | .... | .... | .... | .... |
| 2007-08 | Hokki Kajaani | Finland-2 | 1 | 0 | 0 | 0 | 15 | 4 | 0 | 15.70 | .... | .... | .... | .... | .... | .... | .... |
| | Lukko Rauma | Finland | 1 | 0 | 1 | 0 | 59 | 3 | 0 | 3.04 | .... | .... | .... | .... | .... | .... | .... |
| | Lukko Rauma Jr. | Fin-Jr. | 31 | 14 | 13 | 0 | 1791 | 89 | 1 | 2.98 | 2 | 2 | 0 | 120 | 3 | 0 | 1.50 |
| 2008-09 | TPS Turku Jr. | Fin-Jr. | 4 | 3 | 1 | 0 | 240 | 11 | 0 | 2.75 | .... | .... | .... | .... | .... | .... | .... |
| | Kiekko-Vantaa | Finland-2 | 5 | 3 | 2 | 0 | 264 | 9 | 0 | 2.05 | .... | .... | .... | .... | .... | .... | .... |
| | TPS Turku | Finland | 6 | 1 | 4 | 1 | 317 | 17 | 1 | 3.22 | .... | .... | .... | .... | .... | .... | .... |

## ENO, Nick (EE-noh, NIHK) BUF.

Goaltender. Catches left. 6'3", 190 lbs. Born, Howell, MI, February 12, 1989.
(Buffalo's 7th choice, 187th overall, in 2007 Entry Draft).

| | | | Regular Season | | | | | | | | Playoffs | | | | | | |
|---|---|---|---|---|---|---|---|---|---|---|---|---|---|---|---|---|---|
| **Season** | **Club** | **League** | **GP** | **W** | **L** | **O/T** | **Mins** | **GA** | **SO** | **Avg** | **GP** | **W** | **L** | **Mins** | **GA** | **SO** | **Avg** |
| 2005-06 | Howell | High-MI | 25 | .... | .... | .... | 1020 | 52 | 5 | 2.29 | .... | .... | .... | .... | .... | .... | .... |
| 2006-07 | Green Mountain | EJHL | 25 | 9 | 14 | 2 | 1398 | 84 | 1 | 3.60 | .... | .... | .... | .... | .... | .... | .... |
| 2007-08 | Bowling Green | CCHA | 22 | 12 | 10 | 0 | 1269 | 59 | 0 | 2.79 | .... | .... | .... | .... | .... | .... | .... |
| 2008-09 | Bowling Green | CCHA | 7 | 0 | 5 | 0 | 328 | 25 | 0 | 4.58 | .... | .... | .... | .... | .... | .... | .... |

CCHA All-Rookie Team (2008)

## ENROTH, Jhonas (EHN-rawth, YOH-nuhs) BUF.

Goaltender. Catches left. 5'10", 174 lbs. Born, Stockholm, Sweden, June 25, 1988.
(Buffalo's 2nd choice, 46th overall, in 2006 Entry Draft).

| | | | Regular Season | | | | | | | | Playoffs | | | | | | |
|---|---|---|---|---|---|---|---|---|---|---|---|---|---|---|---|---|---|
| **Season** | **Club** | **League** | **GP** | **W** | **L** | **O/T** | **Mins** | **GA** | **SO** | **Avg** | **GP** | **W** | **L** | **Mins** | **GA** | **SO** | **Avg** |
| 2003-04 | Huddinge IK U18 | Swe-U18 | 6 | .... | .... | .... | 324 | 15 | 0 | 2.77 | .... | .... | .... | .... | .... | .... | .... |
| 2004-05 | Huddinge IK Jr. | Swe-Jr. | 19 | .... | .... | .... | 1144 | 49 | 3 | 2.57 | 3 | .... | .... | 186 | 6 | 1 | 1.93 |
| | Huddinge IK U18 | Swe-U18 | 2 | .... | .... | .... | 125 | 5 | 0 | 2.40 | .... | .... | .... | .... | .... | .... | .... |
| | Huddinge IK | Sweden-2 | 2 | .... | .... | .... | 51 | 6 | 0 | 6.95 | .... | .... | .... | .... | .... | .... | .... |
| 2005-06 | Sodertalje SK Jr. | Swe-Jr. | 39 | .... | .... | .... | 2378 | 86 | 1 | 2.17 | 4 | .... | .... | 243 | 9 | 0 | 2.22 |
| | Sodertalje SK U18 | Swe-U18 | 2 | .... | .... | .... | 120 | 5 | 0 | 2.50 | .... | .... | .... | .... | .... | .... | .... |
| 2006-07 | Sodertalje SK Jr. | Swe-Jr. | 3 | .... | .... | .... | 180 | 4 | 0 | 1.33 | .... | .... | .... | .... | .... | .... | .... |
| | Sodertalje SK | Sweden-2 | 33 | .... | .... | .... | 1938 | 57 | 3 | 1.76 | .... | .... | .... | .... | .... | .... | .... |
| 2007-08 | Sodertalje SK Jr. | Swe-Jr. | 1 | .... | .... | .... | 59 | 4 | 0 | 4.05 | .... | .... | .... | .... | .... | .... | .... |
| | Sodertalje SK | Sweden | 27 | .... | .... | .... | 1578 | 56 | 2 | *2.13 | .... | .... | .... | .... | .... | .... | .... |
| 2008-09 | Portland Pirates | AHL | 58 | 26 | 23 | 6 | 3424 | 157 | 3 | 2.75 | 5 | 1 | 4 | 264 | 10 | 1 | 2.27 |

## ERIKSSON, Joacim (AIR-ihk-suhn, YOH-a-kihm) PHI.

Goaltender. Catches right. 6'1", 189 lbs. Born, Gavle, Sweden, April 9, 1990.
(Philadelphia's 5th choice, 196th overall, in 2008 Entry Draft).

| | | | Regular Season | | | | | | | | Playoffs | | | | | | |
|---|---|---|---|---|---|---|---|---|---|---|---|---|---|---|---|---|---|
| **Season** | **Club** | **League** | **GP** | **W** | **L** | **O/T** | **Mins** | **GA** | **SO** | **Avg** | **GP** | **W** | **L** | **Mins** | **GA** | **SO** | **Avg** |
| 2006-07 | Valbo AIF Jr. | Swe-Jr. | 18 | .... | .... | .... | 1072 | 55 | .... | 3.08 | .... | .... | .... | .... | .... | .... | .... |
| | Valbo AIF | Sweden-3 | 1 | .... | .... | .... | 34 | 2 | 0 | 3.51 | .... | .... | .... | .... | .... | .... | .... |
| 2007-08 | Brynas U18 | Swe-U18 | 9 | .... | .... | .... | 545 | 21 | 2 | 2.31 | 5 | .... | .... | 296 | 7 | 2 | 1.42 |
| | Brynas IF Gavle Jr. | Swe-Jr. | 16 | .... | .... | .... | 960 | 53 | 0 | 3.31 | 7 | .... | .... | 426 | 13 | 1 | 1.83 |
| | Valbo HC | Sweden-3 | 2 | .... | .... | .... | 123 | 8 | 0 | 3.91 | .... | .... | .... | .... | .... | .... | .... |
| 2008-09 | Brynas IF Gavle Jr. | Swe-Jr. | 33 | .... | .... | .... | 1962 | 65 | 6 | 1.99 | 7 | .... | .... | 468 | 19 | 0 | 2.43 |

## ERSBERG, Erik (AIRZH-buhrg, AIR-ihk) L.A.

Goaltender. Catches left. 6', 168 lbs. Born, Sala, Sweden, March 8, 1982.

| | | | Regular Season | | | | | | | | Playoffs | | | | | | |
|---|---|---|---|---|---|---|---|---|---|---|---|---|---|---|---|---|---|
| **Season** | **Club** | **League** | **GP** | **W** | **L** | **O/T** | **Mins** | **GA** | **SO** | **Avg** | **GP** | **W** | **L** | **Mins** | **GA** | **SO** | **Avg** |
| 99-2000 | Vasteras IK U18 | Swe-U18 | 1 | .... | .... | .... | 60 | 2 | 0 | 2.00 | 2 | .... | .... | 119 | 10 | 0 | 5.02 |
| | Vasteras IK Jr. | Swe-Jr. | 16 | .... | .... | .... | 885 | 36 | 0 | 2.44 | .... | .... | .... | .... | .... | .... | .... |
| 2000-01 | Vasteras | Sweden-4 | 33 | .... | .... | .... | .... | .... | .... | 1.48 | .... | .... | .... | .... | .... | .... | .... |
| 2001-02 | Vasteras Jr. | Swe-Jr. | .... | .... | .... | .... | .... | .... | .... | .... | 2 | .... | .... | 118 | 11 | 0 | 5.61 |
| | Vasteras | Sweden-3 | 37 | .... | .... | .... | .... | .... | .... | .... | .... | .... | .... | .... | .... | .... | .... |
| 2002-03 | Vasteras | Sweden-2 | 32 | .... | .... | .... | 1920 | 91 | 1 | 2.84 | .... | .... | .... | .... | .... | .... | .... |
| 2003-04 | Vasteras | Sweden-2 | 32 | .... | .... | .... | 1850 | 79 | 3 | 2.56 | .... | .... | .... | .... | .... | .... | .... |
| 2004-05 | Vasteras | Sweden-2 | 37 | .... | .... | .... | 2189 | 76 | 3 | 2.08 | 5 | .... | .... | 308 | 8 | 2 | 1.56 |
| 2005-06 | VIK Vasteras HK | Sweden-2 | 2 | .... | .... | .... | 118 | 4 | 0 | 2.02 | .... | .... | .... | .... | .... | .... | .... |
| | HV 71 Jonkoping | Sweden | 10 | .... | .... | .... | 602 | 18 | 2 | 1.79 | 2 | .... | .... | 79 | 4 | 0 | 3.05 |
| | HV 71 Jr. | Swe-Jr. | 1 | .... | .... | .... | 60 | 1 | 0 | 1.00 | .... | .... | .... | .... | .... | .... | .... |
| 2006-07 | HV 71 Jonkoping | Sweden | 41 | .... | .... | .... | 2455 | 98 | 4 | 2.39 | 14 | .... | .... | 834 | 39 | 0 | 2.81 |
| **2007-08** | **Los Angeles** | **NHL** | **14** | **6** | **5** | **3** | **799** | **33** | **2** | **2.48** | .... | .... | .... | .... | .... | .... | .... |
| | Manchester | AHL | 30 | 10 | 13 | 2 | 1540 | 75 | 1 | 2.92 | .... | .... | .... | .... | .... | .... | .... |
| **2008-09** | **Los Angeles** | **NHL** | **28** | **8** | **11** | **5** | **1477** | **65** | **0** | **2.64** | .... | .... | .... | .... | .... | .... | .... |
| | **NHL Totals** | | **42** | **14** | **16** | **8** | **2276** | **98** | **2** | **2.58** | .... | .... | .... | .... | .... | .... | .... |

Signed as a free agent by **Los Angeles**, May 31, 2007.

## ESCHE, Robert (EHSH, RAW-buhrt)

Goaltender. Catches left. 6'1", 210 lbs. Born, Whitesboro, NY, January 22, 1978.
(Phoenix's 5th choice, 139th overall, in 1996 Entry Draft).

| | | | Regular Season | | | | | | | | Playoffs | | | | | | |
|---|---|---|---|---|---|---|---|---|---|---|---|---|---|---|---|---|---|
| **Season** | **Club** | **League** | **GP** | **W** | **L** | **O/T** | **Mins** | **GA** | **SO** | **Avg** | **GP** | **W** | **L** | **Mins** | **GA** | **SO** | **Avg** |
| 1994-95 | Gloucester | CJHL | 20 | 10 | 6 | 0 | 1034 | 70 | 0 | 4.06 | .... | .... | .... | .... | .... | .... | .... |
| 1995-96 | Detroit Jr. Whalers | OHL | 23 | 13 | 6 | 0 | 1219 | 76 | 1 | 3.74 | 3 | 0 | 2 | 105 | 4 | 0 | 2.29 |
| 1996-97 | Detroit Jr. Whalers | OHL | 58 | 24 | 28 | 2 | 3241 | 206 | 2 | 3.81 | 5 | 1 | 4 | 317 | 19 | 0 | 3.60 |
| 1997-98 | Plymouth Whalers | OHL | 48 | 29 | 13 | 4 | 2810 | 135 | 3 | 2.88 | 15 | 8 | 7 | 869 | 45 | 0 | 3.11 |
| **1998-99** | **Phoenix** | **NHL** | **3** | **0** | **1** | **0** | **130** | **7** | **0** | **3.23** | .... | .... | .... | .... | .... | .... | .... |
| | Springfield Falcons | AHL | 55 | 24 | 20 | 6 | 2957 | 138 | 1 | 2.80 | 1 | 0 | 1 | 60 | 4 | 0 | 4.02 |
| **99-2000** | **Phoenix** | **NHL** | **8** | **2** | **5** | **0** | **408** | **23** | **0** | **3.38** | .... | .... | .... | .... | .... | .... | .... |
| | Houston Aeros | IHL | 7 | 4 | 2 | 1 | 419 | 16 | 2 | 2.29 | .... | .... | .... | .... | .... | .... | .... |
| | Springfield Falcons | AHL | 21 | 9 | 9 | 2 | 1207 | 61 | 2 | 3.03 | 3 | 1 | 2 | 180 | 12 | 0 | 4.01 |
| **2000-01** | **Phoenix** | **NHL** | **25** | **10** | **8** | **4** | **1350** | **68** | **2** | **3.02** | .... | .... | .... | .... | .... | .... | .... |
| **2001-02** | **Phoenix** | **NHL** | **22** | **6** | **10** | **2** | **1145** | **52** | **1** | **2.72** | .... | .... | .... | .... | .... | .... | .... |
| | Springfield Falcons | AHL | 1 | 1 | 0 | 0 | 60 | 0 | 1 | 0.00 | .... | .... | .... | .... | .... | .... | .... |
| **2002-03** | **Philadelphia** | **NHL** | **30** | **12** | **9** | **3** | **1638** | **60** | **2** | **2.20** | **1** | **0** | **0** | **30** | **1** | **0** | **2.00** |
| **2003-04** | **Philadelphia** | **NHL** | **40** | **21** | **11** | **7** | **2322** | **79** | **3** | **2.04** | **18** | **11** | **7** | **1061** | **41** | **1** | **2.32** |
| 2004-05 | | | | | | | DID NOT PLAY | | | | | | | | | | |
| **2005-06** | **Philadelphia** | **NHL** | **40** | **22** | **11** | **5** | **2286** | **113** | **1** | **2.97** | **6** | **2** | **4** | **314** | **22** | **0** | **4.20** |
| | United States | Olympics | 1 | 0 | 1 | 0 | 59 | 5 | 0 | 5.10 | .... | .... | .... | .... | .... | .... | .... |
| **2006-07** | **Philadelphia** | **NHL** | **18** | **5** | **9** | **1** | **860** | **62** | **1** | **4.33** | .... | .... | .... | .... | .... | .... | .... |
| 2007-08 | Ak Bars Kazan | Russia | 18 | .... | .... | .... | 1095 | 34 | 3 | 1.86 | 10 | .... | .... | 609 | 25 | 1 | 2.46 |
| 2008-09 | SKA St. Petersburg | Rus-KHL | 38 | .... | .... | .... | 2183 | 71 | *9 | 1.95 | 3 | .... | .... | 185 | 8 | 0 | 2.59 |
| | **NHL Totals** | | **186** | **78** | **64** | **22** | **10139** | **464** | **10** | **2.75** | **25** | **13** | **11** | **1405** | **64** | **1** | **2.73** |

OHL Second All-Star Team (1998) • AHL All-Rookie Team (1999) • William M. Jennings Trophy (2003) (shared with Roman Cechmanek) (tied with Martin Brodeur)

Traded to **Philadelphia** by **Phoenix** with Michal Handzus for Brian Boucher and Nashville's 3rd round choice (previously acquired, Phoenix selected Joe Callahan) in 2002 Entry Draft, June 12, 2002. Signed as a free agent by **Kazan** (Russia), October 18, 2007.

## FALLON, Joseph (FA-luhn, JOH-sehf) CHI.

Goaltender. Catches left. 6'3", 203 lbs. Born, Bemidji, MN, February 1, 1985.
(Chicago's 9th choice, 167th overall, in 2005 Entry Draft).

| Season | Club | League | Regular Season GP | W | L | O/T | Mins | GA | SO | Avg | Playoffs GP | W | L | Mins | GA | SO | Avg |
|---|---|---|---|---|---|---|---|---|---|---|---|---|---|---|---|---|---|
| 2001-02 | Rochester | USHL | 27 | 7 | 16 | 1 | 1484 | 93 | 0 | 3.76 | | | | | | | |
| 2002-03 | Cedar Rapids | USHL | 42 | 20 | 15 | 6 | 2495 | 108 | 2 | 2.60 | 7 | 3 | 4 | 426 | 21 | 0 | 2.96 |
| 2003-04 | Cedar Rapids | USHL | 42 | 25 | 13 | 2 | 2370 | 108 | 4 | 2.73 | 4 | 1 | 3 | 237 | 9 | 0 | 2.28 |
| 2004-05 | U. of Vermont | ECAC | 32 | 17 | 10 | 4 | 1932 | 63 | 5 | 1.96 | | | | | | | |
| 2005-06 | U. of Vermont | H-East | 33 | 14 | 14 | 5 | 1931 | 65 | 6 | 2.02 | | | | | | | |
| 2006-07 | U. of Vermont | H-East | 34 | 17 | 14 | 3 | 1997 | 62 | 6 | *1.86 | | | | | | | |
| 2007-08 | U. of Vermont | H-East | 33 | 15 | 13 | 5 | 1942 | 77 | *3 | 2.38 | | | | | | | |
| 2008-09 | Rockford IceHogs | AHL | 2 | 0 | 0 | 0 | 63 | 1 | 0 | 0.95 | | | | | | | |
| | Fresno Falcons | ECHL | 13 | 8 | 4 | 1 | 747 | 32 | 1 | 2.57 | | | | | | | |
| | Gwinnett | ECHL | 22 | 10 | 10 | 1 | 1246 | 67 | 1 | 3.23 | | | | | | | |

ECAC All-Rookie Team (2005) • ECAC Rookie of the Year (2005)

## FERNANDEZ, Manny (fuhr-NAN-dehz, MAN-ee)

Goaltender. Catches left. 6', 207 lbs. Born, Etobicoke, Ont., August 27, 1974.
(Quebec's 4th choice, 52nd overall, in 1992 Entry Draft).

| Season | Club | League | Regular Season GP | W | L | O/T | Mins | GA | SO | Avg | Playoffs GP | W | L | Mins | GA | SO | Avg |
|---|---|---|---|---|---|---|---|---|---|---|---|---|---|---|---|---|---|
| 1990-91 | Lac St-Louis Lions | QAAA | 20 | 13 | 5 | 0 | 1176 | 69 | *3 | 3.52 | 3 | 2 | 1 | 181 | 12 | 0 | 3.98 |
| 1991-92 | Laval Titan | QMJHL | 31 | 14 | 13 | 2 | 1593 | 99 | 1 | 3.73 | 9 | 3 | 5 | 468 | 39 | 0 | 5.00 |
| 1992-93 | Laval Titan | QMJHL | 43 | 26 | 14 | 2 | 2347 | 141 | 1 | 3.60 | 13 | *12 | 1 | 818 | 42 | 0 | 3.08 |
| 1993-94 | Laval Titan | QMJHL | 51 | 29 | 14 | 1 | 2776 | 143 | *5 | 3.09 | 19 | 14 | 5 | 1116 | 49 | *1 | *2.63 |
| 1994-95 | Kalamazoo Wings | IHL | 46 | 21 | 10 | 9 | 2470 | 115 | 2 | 2.79 | 14 | 10 | 2 | 753 | 34 | 1 | 2.71 |
| | Dallas | NHL | 1 | 0 | 1 | 0 | 59 | 3 | 0 | 3.05 | | | | | | | |
| 1995-96 | Dallas | NHL | 5 | 0 | 1 | 1 | 249 | 19 | 0 | 4.58 | | | | | | | |
| | Michigan K-Wings | IHL | 47 | 22 | 15 | 9 | 2664 | 133 | *4 | 3.00 | 6 | 5 | 1 | 372 | 14 | 0 | *2.26 |
| 1996-97 | Michigan K-Wings | IHL | 48 | 20 | 24 | 2 | 2720 | 142 | 2 | 3.13 | 4 | 1 | 3 | 277 | 15 | 0 | 3.25 |
| 1997-98 | Dallas | NHL | 2 | 1 | 0 | 0 | 69 | 2 | 0 | 1.74 | 1 | 0 | 0 | 2 | 0 | 0 | 0.00 |
| | Michigan K-Wings | IHL | 55 | 27 | 17 | 5 | 3022 | 139 | 5 | 2.76 | 2 | 0 | 2 | 88 | 7 | 0 | 4.73 |
| 1998-99 | Dallas | NHL | 1 | 0 | 1 | 0 | 60 | 2 | 0 | 2.00 | | | | | | | |
| | Houston Aeros | IHL | 50 | 34 | 6 | 9 | 2949 | 116 | 2 | 2.36 | *19 | *11 | 8 | *1126 | 49 | 1 | 2.61 |
| 99-2000 | Dallas | NHL | 24 | 11 | 8 | 3 | 1353 | 48 | 1 | 2.13 | 1 | 0 | 0 | 17 | 1 | 0 | 3.53 |
| 2000-01 | Minnesota | NHL | 42 | 19 | 17 | 4 | 2461 | 92 | 4 | 2.24 | | | | | | | |
| 2001-02 | Minnesota | NHL | 44 | 12 | 24 | 5 | 2463 | 125 | 1 | 3.05 | | | | | | | |
| 2002-03 | Minnesota | NHL | 35 | 19 | 13 | 2 | 1979 | 74 | 2 | 2.24 | 9 | 3 | 4 | 552 | 18 | 0 | 1.96 |
| 2003-04 | Minnesota | NHL | 37 | 11 | 14 | 9 | 2166 | 90 | 2 | 2.49 | | | | | | | |
| 2004-05 | Lulea HF | Sweden | 19 | | | | 1083 | 50 | 2 | 2.77 | 3 | | | 159 | 13 | 0 | 4.90 |
| 2005-06 | Minnesota | NHL | 58 | 30 | 18 | 7 | 3411 | 130 | 1 | 2.29 | | | | | | | |
| 2006-07 | Minnesota | NHL | 44 | 22 | 16 | 1 | 2422 | 103 | 2 | 2.55 | | | | | | | |
| 2007-08 | Boston | NHL | 4 | 2 | 2 | 0 | 244 | 16 | 1 | 3.93 | | | | | | | |
| 2008-09 | Boston | NHL | 28 | 16 | 8 | 3 | 1644 | 71 | 1 | 2.59 | | | | | | | |
| | **NHL Totals** | | **325** | **143** | **123** | **35** | **18580** | **775** | **15** | **2.50** | **11** | **3** | **4** | **571** | **19** | **0** | **2.00** |

QMJHL First All-Star Team (1994) • QMJHL MVP (1994) • IHL Second All-Star Team (1995) • William M. Jennings Trophy (2007) (shared with Niklas Backstrom) • William M. Jennings Trophy (2009) (shared with Tim Thomas)

• Rights traded to **Dallas** by **Quebec** for Tommy Sjodin and Dallas' 3rd round choice (Chris Drury) in 1994 Entry Draft, February 13, 1994. Traded to **Minnesota** by **Dallas** with Brad Lukowich for Minnesota's 3rd round choice (Joel Lundqvist) in 2000 Entry Draft and Minnesota's 4th round choice (later traded back to Minnesota – later traded to Los Angeles – Los Angeles selected Aaron Rome) in 2002 Entry Draft, June 12, 2000. Signed as a free agent by **Lulea** (Sweden), December 18, 2004. Traded to **Boston** by **Minnesota** for Petr Kalus and Boston's 4th round choice (Alexander Fallstrom) in 2009 Entry Draft, July 1, 2007. • Missed majority of 2007-08 season recovering from back and knee injuries.

## FLEURY, Marc-Andre (fluh-REE, MAHRK-AWN-dray) PIT.

Goaltender. Catches left. 6'2", 180 lbs. Born, Sorel, Que., November 28, 1984.
(Pittsburgh's 1st choice, 1st overall, in 2003 Entry Draft).

| Season | Club | League | Regular Season GP | W | L | O/T | Mins | GA | SO | Avg | Playoffs GP | W | L | Mins | GA | SO | Avg |
|---|---|---|---|---|---|---|---|---|---|---|---|---|---|---|---|---|---|
| 99-2000 | Charles-Lemoyne | QAAA | 15 | 4 | 9 | 0 | 780 | 36 | 1 | 2.77 | | | | | | | |
| 2000-01 | Cape Breton | QMJHL | 35 | 12 | 13 | 2 | 1705 | 115 | 0 | 4.05 | 2 | 0 | 1 | 32 | 4 | 0 | 7.50 |
| 2001-02 | Cape Breton | QMJHL | 55 | 26 | 14 | 8 | 3043 | 141 | 2 | 2.78 | 16 | 9 | 7 | 1003 | 55 | 0 | 3.29 |
| 2002-03 | Cape Breton | QMJHL | 51 | 17 | 24 | 6 | 2889 | 162 | 2 | 3.36 | 4 | 0 | 4 | 228 | 17 | 0 | 4.47 |
| 2003-04 | Pittsburgh | NHL | 21 | 4 | 14 | 2 | 1154 | 70 | 1 | 3.64 | | | | | | | |
| | Cape Breton | QMJHL | 10 | 8 | 1 | 1 | 606 | 20 | 0 | 1.98 | 4 | 1 | 3 | 251 | 13 | 0 | 3.10 |
| | Wilkes-Barre | AHL | | | | | | | | | 2 | 0 | 1 | 92 | 6 | 0 | 3.90 |
| 2004-05 | Wilkes-Barre | AHL | 54 | 26 | 19 | 4 | 3029 | 127 | 5 | 2.52 | 4 | 0 | 2 | 151 | 11 | 0 | 4.36 |
| 2005-06 | Pittsburgh | NHL | 50 | 13 | 27 | 6 | 2809 | 152 | 1 | 3.25 | | | | | | | |
| | Wilkes-Barre | AHL | 12 | 10 | 2 | 0 | 727 | 19 | 0 | 1.57 | 5 | 2 | 3 | 311 | 18 | 0 | 3.48 |
| 2006-07 | Pittsburgh | NHL | 67 | 40 | 16 | 9 | 3905 | 184 | 5 | 2.83 | 5 | 1 | 4 | 287 | 18 | 0 | 3.76 |
| 2007-08 | Pittsburgh | NHL | 35 | 19 | 10 | 2 | 1857 | 72 | 4 | 2.33 | *20 | *14 | 6 | *1251 | 41 | *3 | 1.97 |
| | Wilkes-Barre | AHL | 5 | 3 | 2 | 0 | 297 | 7 | 0 | 1.41 | | | | | | | |
| 2008-09♦ | Pittsburgh | NHL | 62 | 35 | 18 | 7 | 3641 | 162 | 4 | 2.67 | *24 | *16 | 8 | *1447 | 63 | 0 | 2.61 |
| | **NHL Totals** | | **235** | **111** | **85** | **26** | **13366** | **640** | **15** | **2.87** | **49** | **31** | **18** | **2985** | **122** | **3** | **2.45** |

QMJHL Second All-Star Team (2003)

## FOSTER, Brian (FAW-stuhr, BRIGH-uhn) FLA.

Goaltender. Catches left. 6'1", 155 lbs. Born, Pembroke, NH, February 4, 1987.
(Florida's 6th choice, 161st overall, in 2005 Entry Draft).

| Season | Club | League | Regular Season GP | W | L | O/T | Mins | GA | SO | Avg | Playoffs GP | W | L | Mins | GA | SO | Avg |
|---|---|---|---|---|---|---|---|---|---|---|---|---|---|---|---|---|---|
| 2003-04 | N.H. Jr. Monarchs | EJHL | STATISTICS NOT AVAILABLE | | | | | | | | | | | | | | |
| 2004-05 | N.H. Jr. Monarchs | EJHL | 41 | 30 | 6 | 4 | 2339 | | 3 | 2.51 | | | | | | | |
| 2005-06 | Des Moines | USHL | 26 | 12 | 9 | 3 | 1516 | 71 | 0 | 2.81 | 1 | 0 | 0 | 12 | 0 | 0 | 0.00 |
| 2006-07 | New Hampshire | H-East | 7 | 2 | 2 | 0 | 298 | 11 | 2 | 2.21 | | | | | | | |
| 2007-08 | New Hampshire | H-East | 6 | 2 | 2 | 2 | 372 | 19 | 0 | 3.06 | | | | | | | |
| 2008-09 | New Hampshire | H-East | 35 | 19 | 11 | 4 | 2080 | 93 | *3 | 2.68 | | | | | | | |

## FRAZEE, Jeff (FRAY-zee, JEHF) N.J.

Goaltender. Catches left. 6', 195 lbs. Born, Edina, MN, May 13, 1987.
(New Jersey's 2nd choice, 38th overall, in 2005 Entry Draft).

| Season | Club | League | Regular Season GP | W | L | O/T | Mins | GA | SO | Avg | Playoffs GP | W | L | Mins | GA | SO | Avg |
|---|---|---|---|---|---|---|---|---|---|---|---|---|---|---|---|---|---|
| 2001-02 | Holy Angels | High-MN | 6 | 6 | 0 | 0 | | | | | | | | | | | |
| 2002-03 | Holy Angels | High-MN | 16 | 14 | 1 | 1 | | | | | | | | | | | |
| 2003-04 | USNTDP | U-17 | 16 | 9 | 3 | 0 | 781 | 31 | | 2.38 | | | | | | | |
| | USNTDP | NAHL | 25 | 14 | 8 | 3 | 1463 | 71 | 3 | 2.91 | | | | | | | |
| 2004-05 | USNTDP | U-18 | 24 | | | | 1309 | 59 | 3 | 2.71 | | | | | | | |
| | USNTDP | NAHL | 9 | 8 | 1 | 0 | 500 | 18 | 1 | 2.16 | | | | | | | |
| 2005-06 | U. of Minnesota | WCHA | 12 | 6 | 3 | 2 | 660 | 26 | 2 | 2.36 | | | | | | | |
| 2006-07 | U. of Minnesota | WCHA | 20 | 14 | 3 | 1 | 1148 | 45 | 1 | 2.35 | | | | | | | |
| 2007-08 | U. of Minnesota | WCHA | 14 | 6 | 7 | 0 | 798 | 39 | 1 | 2.93 | | | | | | | |
| | Lowell Devils | AHL | 1 | 0 | 1 | 0 | 40 | 3 | 0 | 4.50 | | | | | | | |
| 2008-09 | Lowell Devils | AHL | 58 | 28 | 22 | 6 | 3407 | 149 | 4 | 2.62 | | | | | | | |
| | Trenton Devils | ECHL | 5 | 2 | 2 | 0 | 272 | 12 | 0 | 2.65 | 4 | 2 | 2 | 271 | 10 | 0 | 2.22 |

## FUKUFUJI, Yutaka (foo-koo-FOO-jee, yoo-TA-ka)

Goaltender. Catches left. 6'1", 180 lbs. Born, Tokyo, Japan, September 17, 1982.
(Los Angeles' 9th choice, 238th overall, in 2004 Entry Draft).

| Season | Club | League | Regular Season GP | W | L | O/T | Mins | GA | SO | Avg | Playoffs GP | W | L | Mins | GA | SO | Avg |
|---|---|---|---|---|---|---|---|---|---|---|---|---|---|---|---|---|---|
| 2003-04 | Kokudo Toyko | AsianHL | 7 | | | | 420 | 13 | | 1.86 | | | | | | | |
| | Kokudo Toyko | Japan | 7 | | | | 430 | 12 | | 1.67 | | | | | | | |
| 2004-05 | Bakersfield | ECHL | 44 | 27 | 9 | 5 | 2517 | 104 | 3 | 2.48 | | | | | | | |
| 2005-06 | Manchester | AHL | 2 | 1 | 1 | 0 | 120 | 6 | 0 | 3.00 | | | | | | | |
| | Reading Royals | ECHL | 29 | 15 | 9 | 4 | 1691 | 82 | 1 | 2.91 | 4 | 1 | 2 | 196 | 11 | 0 | 3.36 |
| 2006-07 | Los Angeles | NHL | 4 | 0 | 3 | 0 | 96 | 7 | 0 | 4.38 | | | | | | | |
| | Manchester | AHL | 5 | 3 | 1 | 0 | 261 | 4 | 1 | 0.92 | 1 | 0 | 0 | 0 | 0 | 0 | 0.00 |
| | Reading Royals | ECHL | 28 | 13 | 10 | 0 | 1522 | 75 | 1 | 2.96 | | | | | | | |
| 2007-08 | Bakersfield | ECHL | 46 | 18 | 18 | 1 | 2427 | 137 | 1 | 3.39 | 6 | 2 | 2 | 372 | 22 | 0 | 3.55 |
| 2008-09 | Bakersfield | ECHL | 35 | 18 | 12 | 1 | 1821 | 100 | 0 | 3.29 | 7 | 3 | 4 | 432 | 25 | 0 | 3.47 |
| | **NHL Totals** | | **4** | **0** | **3** | **0** | **96** | **7** | **0** | **4.38** | | | | | | | |

## GARON, Mathieu (gah-ROHN, MA-tyew) CBJ

Goaltender. Catches right. 6'2", 199 lbs. Born, Chandler, Que., January 9, 1978.
(Montreal's 2nd choice, 44th overall, in 1996 Entry Draft).

| Season | Club | League | Regular Season GP | W | L | O/T | Mins | GA | SO | Avg | Playoffs GP | W | L | Mins | GA | SO | Avg |
|---|---|---|---|---|---|---|---|---|---|---|---|---|---|---|---|---|---|
| 1993-94 | Jonquiere Elites | QAAA | 17 | 0 | 13 | 0 | 834 | 88 | 0 | 6.33 | | | | | | | |
| 1994-95 | Jonquiere Elites | QAAA | 27 | 13 | 13 | 1 | 1554 | 94 | 0 | 3.63 | 9 | 6 | 2 | 467 | 26 | 0 | 3.34 |
| 1995-96 | Victoriaville Tigres | QMJHL | 51 | 18 | 27 | 0 | 2709 | 189 | 1 | 4.19 | 12 | 7 | 4 | 676 | 38 | 1 | 3.39 |
| 1996-97 | Victoriaville Tigres | QMJHL | 53 | 29 | 18 | 3 | 3032 | 150 | *6 | 2.97 | 6 | 2 | 4 | 330 | 23 | 0 | 4.18 |
| 1997-98 | Victoriaville Tigres | QMJHL | 47 | 27 | 18 | 2 | 2802 | 125 | 5 | 2.68 | 6 | 2 | 4 | 345 | 22 | 0 | 3.82 |
| 1998-99 | Fredericton | AHL | 40 | 14 | 22 | 2 | 2222 | 114 | 3 | 3.08 | 6 | 1 | 1 | 208 | 12 | 0 | 3.47 |
| 99-2000 | Quebec Citadelles | AHL | 53 | 17 | 28 | 3 | 2884 | 149 | 2 | 3.10 | 1 | 0 | 0 | 20 | 3 | 0 | 8.82 |
| 2000-01 | Montreal | NHL | 11 | 4 | 5 | 1 | 589 | 24 | 2 | 2.44 | | | | | | | |
| | Quebec Citadelles | AHL | 31 | 16 | 13 | 1 | 1768 | 86 | 1 | 2.92 | 8 | 4 | 4 | 459 | 22 | 1 | 2.88 |
| 2001-02 | Montreal | NHL | 5 | 1 | 4 | 0 | 261 | 19 | 0 | 4.37 | | | | | | | |
| | Quebec Citadelles | AHL | 50 | 21 | 15 | 12 | 2988 | 136 | 2 | 2.73 | 3 | 0 | 3 | 198 | 12 | 0 | 3.63 |
| 2002-03 | Montreal | NHL | 8 | 3 | 5 | 0 | 482 | 16 | 2 | 1.99 | | | | | | | |
| | Hamilton Bulldogs | AHL | 20 | 15 | 2 | 2 | 1150 | 34 | 4 | 1.77 | | | | | | | |
| 2003-04 | Montreal | NHL | 19 | 8 | 6 | 2 | 1003 | 38 | 0 | 2.27 | 1 | 0 | 0 | 12 | 0 | 0 | 0.00 |
| 2004-05 | Manchester | AHL | 52 | 32 | 14 | 4 | 2969 | 105 | 8 | 2.12 | 6 | 2 | 4 | 285 | 17 | 0 | 3.58 |
| 2005-06 | Los Angeles | NHL | 63 | 31 | 26 | 3 | 3446 | 185 | 4 | 3.22 | | | | | | | |
| 2006-07 | Los Angeles | NHL | 32 | 13 | 10 | 6 | 1779 | 79 | 2 | 2.66 | | | | | | | |
| 2007-08 | Edmonton | NHL | 47 | 26 | 18 | 1 | 2658 | 118 | 4 | 2.66 | | | | | | | |
| 2008-09 | Edmonton | NHL | 15 | 6 | 8 | 0 | 815 | 43 | 0 | 3.17 | | | | | | | |
| | ♦ Pittsburgh | NHL | 4 | 2 | 1 | 0 | 206 | 10 | 0 | 2.91 | 1 | 0 | 0 | 24 | 0 | 0 | 0.00 |
| | **NHL Totals** | | **204** | **94** | **83** | **13** | **11239** | **532** | **14** | **2.84** | **2** | **0** | **0** | **36** | **0** | **0** | **0.00** |

QMJHL All-Rookie Team (1996) • QMJHL Defensive Rookie of the Year (1996) • QMJHL First All-Star Team (1998) • Canadian Major Junior First All-Star Team (1998) • Canadian Major Junior Goaltender of the Year (1998)

Traded to **Los Angeles** by **Montreal** with San Jose's 3rd round choice (previously acquired, Los Angeles selected Paul Baier) in 2004 Entry Draft for Radek Bonk and Cristobal Huet, June 26, 2004. Signed as a free agent by **Edmonton**, July 3, 2007. Traded to **Pittsburgh** by **Edmonton** for Dany Sabourin, Ryan Stone and Pittsburgh's 4th round choice in 2011 Entry Draft, January 17, 2009. Signed as a free agent by **Columbus**, July 1, 2009.

## GAYDUCHENKO, Sergei (gay-doo-CHEHN-koh, SAIR-gay) FLA.

Goaltender. Catches left. 6'5", 222 lbs. Born, Kiev, USSR, June 6, 1989.
(Florida's 8th choice, 202nd overall, in 2007 Entry Draft).

| Season | Club | League | Regular Season GP | W | L | O/T | Mins | GA | SO | Avg | Playoffs GP | W | L | Mins | GA | SO | Avg |
|---|---|---|---|---|---|---|---|---|---|---|---|---|---|---|---|---|---|
| 2006-07 | Yaroslavl 2 | Russia-3 | 23 | | | | 1180 | 57 | 3 | 2.90 | | | | | | | |
| 2007-08 | Novokuznetsk 2 | Russia-3 | 2 | | | | | 5 | | | | | | | | | |
| | Novokuznetsk | Russia | 11 | | | | 533 | 27 | 0 | 3.04 | | | | | | | |
| 2008-09 | Yaroslavl 2 | Russia-3 | STATISTICS NOT AVAILABLE | | | | | | | | | | | | | | |
| | Yaroslavl | Rus-KHL | 3 | | | | 185 | 6 | 0 | 1.95 | | | | | | | |

## GERBER, Martin (GUHR-buhr, MAHR-tihn)

Goaltender. Catches left. 5'11", 199 lbs. Born, Burgdorf, Switz., September 3, 1974.
(Anaheim's 10th choice, 232nd overall, in 2001 Entry Draft).

| Season | Club | League | Regular Season GP | W | L | O/T | Mins | GA | SO | Avg | Playoffs GP | W | L | Mins | GA | SO | Avg |
|---|---|---|---|---|---|---|---|---|---|---|---|---|---|---|---|---|---|
| 1996-97 | SC Langnau | Swiss-2 | 38 | | | | 2286 | 121 | 0 | 3.18 | 8 | | | 488 | 29 | 0 | 3.57 |
| 1997-98 | SC Langnau | Swiss-2 | 40 | | | | 2430 | 141 | 2 | 3.48 | 16 | | | 961 | 42 | 0 | 2.62 |
| 1998-99 | SC Langnau | Swiss | 42 | | | | 2521 | 203 | 1 | 4.83 | 11 | | | 664 | 50 | 0 | 4.52 |
| 99-2000 | SC Langnau | Swiss | 44 | | | | 2652 | 161 | 3 | 3.64 | 6 | | | 360 | 13 | *2 | *2.17 |
| 2000-01 | SCL Tigers Langnau | Swiss | *44 | | | | 2671 | 114 | 3 | 2.56 | 5 | | | 319 | 7 | 1 | 1.32 |
| 2001-02 | Farjestad | Sweden | 44 | | | | 2664 | 87 | *4 | *1.96 | *10 | | | *657 | 18 | *2 | *1.64 |
| | Switzerland | Olympics | 3 | 1 | 1 | 1 | 158 | 4 | 0 | 1.52 | | | | | | | |
| 2002-03 | Anaheim | NHL | 22 | 6 | 11 | 3 | 1203 | 39 | 1 | 1.95 | 2 | 0 | 0 | 20 | 1 | 0 | 3.00 |
| | Cincinnati | AHL | 1 | 1 | 0 | 0 | 60 | 2 | 0 | 2.00 | | | | | | | |
| 2003-04 | Anaheim | NHL | 32 | 11 | 12 | 4 | 1698 | 64 | 2 | 2.26 | | | | | | | |
| 2004-05 | SCL Tigers Langnau | Swiss | 20 | 6 | 10 | 4 | 1220 | 59 | 0 | 2.90 | | | | | | | |
| | Farjestad | Sweden | 30 | 20 | 6 | 4 | 1827 | 58 | 4 | 1.90 | *15 | 9 | 6 | *900 | 36 | 1 | 2.40 |
| 2005-06♦ | Carolina | NHL | 60 | 38 | 14 | 6 | 3493 | 162 | 3 | 2.78 | 6 | 1 | 1 | 221 | 13 | 1 | 3.53 |
| | Switzerland | Olympics | 3 | 1 | 2 | 0 | 160 | 11 | 1 | 4.13 | | | | | | | |
| 2006-07 | Ottawa | NHL | 29 | 15 | 9 | 3 | 1599 | 74 | 1 | 2.78 | | | | | | | |
| 2007-08 | Ottawa | NHL | 57 | 30 | 18 | 4 | 3197 | 145 | 2 | 2.72 | 4 | 0 | 4 | 238 | 14 | 0 | 3.53 |
| 2008-09 | Ottawa | NHL | 14 | 4 | 9 | 1 | 839 | 40 | 1 | 2.86 | | | | | | | |
| | Binghamton | AHL | 14 | 6 | 7 | 0 | 783 | 38 | 1 | 2.91 | | | | | | | |
| | Toronto | NHL | 12 | 6 | 5 | 0 | 706 | 38 | 0 | 3.23 | | | | | | | |
| | **NHL Totals** | | **226** | **110** | **78** | **21** | **12735** | **562** | **10** | **2.65** | **12** | **1** | **5** | **479** | **28** | **1** | **3.51** |

• Scored a goal in playoffs vs. Martigny (Swiss-2), February 27, 1997. Traded to **Carolina** by **Anaheim** for Tomas Malec and Carolina's 3rd round choice (Kyle Klubertanz) in 2004 Entry Draft, June 18, 2004. Signed as a free agent by **Langnau** (Swiss), September 17, 2004. Signed as a free agent by **Farjestad** (Sweden), November 7, 2004. Signed as a free agent by **Ottawa**, July 1, 2006. Claimed on waivers by **Toronto** from **Ottawa**, March 4, 2009. Signed as a free agent by **Mytischi** (Rus-KHL), July 21, 2009.

## GIGUERE, Jean-Sebastien (zhih-GAIR, ZHAWN-suh-BAS-tee-yehn) ANA.

Goaltender. Catches left. 6'1", 201 lbs. Born, Montreal, Que., May 16, 1977.
(Hartford's 1st choice, 13th overall, in 1995 Entry Draft).

| Season | Club | League | Regular Season GP | W | L | O/T | Mins | GA | SO | Avg | Playoffs GP | W | L | Mins | GA | SO | Avg |
|---|---|---|---|---|---|---|---|---|---|---|---|---|---|---|---|---|---|
| 1992-93 | Laval-Laurentides | QAAA | 25 | 12 | 11 | 2 | 1498 | 76 | 0 | 3.02 | 11 | 6 | 5 | 654 | 38 | 0 | 3.49 |
| 1993-94 | Verdun | QMJHL | 25 | 13 | 5 | 2 | 1234 | 66 | 1 | 3.21 | | | | | | | |
| 1994-95 | Halifax | QMJHL | 47 | 14 | 27 | 5 | 2755 | 181 | 2 | 3.94 | 7 | 3 | 4 | 417 | 17 | 1 | *2.45 |
| 1995-96 | Halifax | QMJHL | 55 | 26 | 23 | 2 | 3230 | 185 | 1 | 3.44 | 6 | 1 | 5 | 354 | 24 | 0 | 4.07 |
| 1996-97 | Hartford | NHL | 8 | 1 | 4 | 0 | 394 | 24 | 0 | 3.65 | | | | | | | |
| | Halifax | QMJHL | 50 | 28 | 19 | 3 | 3014 | 170 | 2 | 3.38 | 16 | 9 | 7 | 954 | 58 | 0 | 3.65 |
| 1997-98 | Saint John Flames | AHL | 31 | 16 | 10 | 3 | 1758 | 72 | 2 | 2.46 | 10 | 5 | 3 | 536 | 27 | 0 | 3.02 |
| 1998-99 | Calgary | NHL | 15 | 6 | 7 | 1 | 860 | 46 | 0 | 3.21 | | | | | | | |
| | Saint John Flames | AHL | 39 | 18 | 16 | 3 | 2145 | 123 | 3 | 3.44 | 7 | 3 | 2 | 304 | 21 | 0 | 4.14 |
| 99-2000 | Calgary | NHL | 7 | 1 | 3 | 1 | 330 | 15 | 0 | 2.73 | | | | | | | |
| | Saint John Flames | AHL | 41 | 17 | 17 | 3 | 2243 | 114 | 0 | 3.05 | 3 | 0 | 3 | 178 | 9 | 0 | 3.03 |

| | | | | | | | | | | | | | | | | | |
|---|---|---|---|---|---|---|---|---|---|---|---|---|---|---|---|---|---|
| 2000-01 | Anaheim | NHL | 34 | 11 | 17 | 5 | 2031 | 87 | 4 | 2.57 | .... | .... | .... | .... | .... | .... | .... |
| | Cincinnati | AHL | 23 | 12 | 7 | 2 | 1306 | 53 | 0 | 2.43 | .... | .... | .... | .... | .... | .... | .... |
| 2001-02 | Anaheim | NHL | 53 | 20 | 25 | 6 | 3127 | 111 | 4 | 2.13 | .... | .... | .... | .... | .... | .... | .... |
| 2002-03 | Anaheim | NHL | 65 | 34 | 22 | 6 | 3775 | 145 | 8 | 2.30 | 21 | 15 | 6 | 1407 | 38 | 5 | *1.62 |
| 2003-04 | Anaheim | NHL | 55 | 17 | 31 | 6 | 3210 | 140 | 3 | 2.62 | .... | .... | .... | .... | .... | .... | .... |
| 2004-05 | Hamburg Freezers | Germany | 6 | .... | .... | .... | 301 | 12 | 0 | 2.39 | 2 | .... | .... | 100 | 7 | 0 | 4.20 |
| 2005-06 | Anaheim | NHL | 60 | 30 | 15 | 11 | 3381 | 150 | 2 | 2.66 | 6 | 3 | 3 | 318 | 18 | 0 | 3.40 |
| 2006-07 ♦ | Anaheim | NHL | 56 | 36 | 10 | 8 | 3245 | 122 | 4 | 2.26 | 18 | *13 | 4 | 1067 | 35 | 1 | 1.97 |
| 2007-08 | Anaheim | NHL | 58 | 35 | 17 | 6 | 3310 | 117 | 4 | 2.12 | 6 | 2 | 4 | 358 | 19 | 0 | 3.18 |
| 2008-09 | Anaheim | NHL | 46 | 19 | 18 | 6 | 2458 | 127 | 2 | 3.10 | 1 | 0 | 0 | 17 | 0 | 0 | 0.00 |
| | **NHL Totals** | | **457** | **210** | **169** | **56** | **26121** | **1084** | **31** | **2.49** | **52** | **33** | **17** | **3167** | **110** | **6** | **2.08** |

QMJHL Second All-Star Team (1997) • AHL All-Rookie Team (1998) • Harry ''Hap'' Holmes Memorial Award (AHL – fewest goals against) (1998) (shared with Tyler Moss) • Conn Smythe Trophy (2003)

Played in NHL All-Star Game (2009)

• Transferred to **Carolina** after **Hartford** franchise relocated, June 25, 1997. Traded to **Calgary** by **Carolina** with Andrew Cassels for Gary Roberts and Trevor Kidd, August 25, 1997. Traded to **Anaheim** by **Calgary** for Anaheim's 2nd round choice (later traded to Washington – Washington selected Matt Pettinger) in 2000 Entry Draft, June 10, 2000. Signed as a free agent by **Hamburg** (Germany), January 31, 2005.

## GISTEDT, Joel (JIHZ-tehd, JOHL) PHX.

Goaltender. Catches left. 5'11", 176 lbs. Born, Uddevalla, Sweden, December 7, 1987.
(Phoenix's 4th choice, 36th overall, in 2007 Entry Draft).

| | | | Regular Season | | | | | | | | Playoffs | | | | | | |
|---|---|---|---|---|---|---|---|---|---|---|---|---|---|---|---|---|---|
| **Season** | **Club** | **League** | **GP** | **W** | **L** | **O/T** | **Mins** | **GA** | **SO** | **Avg** | **GP** | **W** | **L** | **Mins** | **GA** | **SO** | **Avg** |
| 2003-04 | V.Frolunda U18 | Swe-U18 | 21 | .... | .... | .... | 1258 | 49 | 1 | 2.34 | 7 | .... | .... | 422 | 11 | 2 | 1.57 |
| 2004-05 | Frolunda U18 | Swe-U18 | 2 | .... | .... | .... | 120 | 6 | 0 | 3.00 | 6 | .... | .... | 366 | 14 | 1 | 2.30 |
| | Frolunda Jr. | Swe-Jr. | 8 | .... | .... | .... | 485 | 14 | 0 | 1.73 | .... | .... | .... | .... | .... | .... | .... |
| 2005-06 | Frolunda Jr. | Swe-Jr. | 32 | .... | .... | .... | 1926 | 76 | 5 | 2.37 | 7 | .... | .... | 434 | 18 | 0 | 2.49 |
| | Frolunda | Sweden | 3 | .... | .... | .... | 181 | 5 | 1 | 1.66 | .... | .... | .... | .... | .... | .... | .... |
| 2006-07 | Frolunda Jr. | Swe-Jr. | 2 | .... | .... | .... | 120 | 3 | 1 | 1.50 | 8 | .... | .... | 484 | 15 | 0 | 1.86 |
| | Frolunda | Sweden | 35 | .... | .... | .... | 2050 | 88 | 2 | 2.58 | .... | .... | .... | .... | .... | .... | .... |
| 2007-08 | Frolunda Jr. | Swe-Jr. | 5 | .... | .... | .... | 303 | 7 | 0 | 1.38 | .... | .... | .... | .... | .... | .... | .... |
| | Frolunda | Sweden | 11 | .... | .... | .... | 578 | 37 | 0 | 3.84 | .... | .... | .... | .... | .... | .... | .... |
| 2008-09 | Arizona Sundogs | CHL | 29 | 10 | 15 | 1 | 1533 | 106 | 0 | 4.15 | .... | .... | .... | .... | .... | .... | .... |
| | San Antonio | AHL | 1 | 0 | 0 | 0 | 20 | 2 | 0 | 6.00 | .... | .... | .... | .... | .... | .... | .... |

## GLASS, Jeff (GLAS, JEHF)

Goaltender. Catches left. 6'3", 206 lbs. Born, Calgary, Alta., November 19, 1985.
(Ottawa's 5th choice, 89th overall, in 2004 Entry Draft).

| | | | Regular Season | | | | | | | | Playoffs | | | | | | |
|---|---|---|---|---|---|---|---|---|---|---|---|---|---|---|---|---|---|
| **Season** | **Club** | **League** | **GP** | **W** | **L** | **O/T** | **Mins** | **GA** | **SO** | **Avg** | **GP** | **W** | **L** | **Mins** | **GA** | **SO** | **Avg** |
| 2001-02 | Crowsnest Pass | AJHL | 34 | .... | .... | .... | 1802 | 126 | 0 | 4.20 | .... | .... | .... | .... | .... | .... | .... |
| 2002-03 | Kootenay Ice | WHL | 35 | 15 | 16 | 3 | 1884 | 77 | 4 | 2.45 | 9 | 4 | 5 | 643 | 23 | 0 | 2.15 |
| 2003-04 | Kootenay Ice | WHL | 57 | 26 | 20 | 6 | 3263 | 128 | 5 | 2.35 | 4 | 0 | 4 | 239 | 14 | 0 | 3.51 |
| 2004-05 | Kootenay Ice | WHL | 51 | 34 | 11 | 5 | 3061 | 90 | 8 | 1.76 | 16 | 10 | 6 | 1027 | 39 | 0 | 2.28 |
| 2005-06 | Binghamton | AHL | 6 | 1 | 4 | 0 | 312 | 20 | 0 | 3.85 | .... | .... | .... | .... | .... | .... | .... |
| | Charlotte Checkers | ECHL | 39 | 19 | 15 | 4 | 2221 | 119 | 2 | 3.22 | 3 | 1 | 2 | 178 | 11 | 0 | 3.71 |
| 2006-07 | Binghamton | AHL | 43 | 9 | 24 | 2 | 2174 | 149 | 1 | 4.11 | .... | .... | .... | .... | .... | .... | .... |
| 2007-08 | Binghamton | AHL | 45 | 15 | 20 | 4 | 2313 | 111 | 2 | 2.88 | .... | .... | .... | .... | .... | .... | .... |
| 2008-09 | Binghamton | AHL | 41 | 17 | 19 | 3 | 2219 | 119 | 0 | 3.22 | .... | .... | .... | .... | .... | .... | .... |

WHL West First All-Star Team (2005) • WHL Goaltender of the Year (2005) • Canadian Major Junior First All-Star Team (2005) • Canadian Major Junior Goaltender of the Year (2005)

## GOEHRING, Karl (GAIR-ihng, KAHRL)

Goaltender. Catches left. 5'8", 160 lbs. Born, Apple Valley, MN, August 23, 1978.

| | | | Regular Season | | | | | | | | Playoffs | | | | | | |
|---|---|---|---|---|---|---|---|---|---|---|---|---|---|---|---|---|---|
| **Season** | **Club** | **League** | **GP** | **W** | **L** | **O/T** | **Mins** | **GA** | **SO** | **Avg** | **GP** | **W** | **L** | **Mins** | **GA** | **SO** | **Avg** |
| 1996-97 | Fargo-Moorhead | USHL | 32 | 13 | 18 | 1 | 1909 | 79 | *4 | *2.48 | 5 | 2 | 3 | 251 | 15 | 1 | 3.58 |
| 1997-98 | North Dakota | WCHA | 27 | 23 | 3 | 1 | 1504 | 57 | 1 | *2.27 | .... | .... | .... | .... | .... | .... | .... |
| 1998-99 | North Dakota | WCHA | 31 | 22 | 5 | 2 | 1774 | 71 | 3 | 2.40 | .... | .... | .... | .... | .... | .... | .... |
| 99-2000 | North Dakota | WCHA | 30 | 19 | 6 | 4 | 1747 | 55 | *8 | *1.89 | .... | .... | .... | .... | .... | .... | .... |
| 2000-01 | North Dakota | WCHA | 30 | 16 | 6 | 6 | 1662 | 66 | *3 | 2.38 | .... | .... | .... | .... | .... | .... | .... |
| 2001-02 | Syracuse Crunch | AHL | 15 | 5 | 6 | 3 | 891 | 37 | 1 | 2.49 | .... | .... | .... | .... | .... | .... | .... |
| | Dayton Bombers | ECHL | 23 | 11 | 9 | 3 | 1393 | 52 | 2 | 2.24 | *14 | 9 | 5 | *866 | 35 | 1 | 2.43 |
| 2002-03 | Syracuse Crunch | AHL | 49 | 18 | 21 | 4 | 2608 | 116 | 4 | 2.67 | .... | .... | .... | .... | .... | .... | .... |
| 2003-04 | Syracuse Crunch | AHL | 38 | 17 | 14 | 6 | 2234 | 97 | 1 | 2.60 | 5 | 2 | 2 | 295 | 16 | 0 | 3.26 |
| 2004-05 | Syracuse Crunch | AHL | 49 | 23 | 22 | 0 | 2788 | 128 | 3 | 2.75 | .... | .... | .... | .... | .... | .... | .... |
| 2005-06 | Jokerit Helsinki | Finland | 19 | 5 | 10 | 3 | 1076 | 57 | 2 | 3.18 | .... | .... | .... | .... | .... | .... | .... |
| | San Antonio | AHL | 23 | 4 | 16 | 1 | 1250 | 65 | 1 | 3.12 | .... | .... | .... | .... | .... | .... | .... |
| 2006-07 | Milwaukee | AHL | 44 | 22 | 15 | 4 | 2524 | 113 | 1 | 2.69 | .... | .... | .... | .... | .... | .... | .... |
| 2007-08 | Wilkes-Barre | AHL | 2 | 0 | 1 | 0 | 85 | 3 | 0 | 2.11 | .... | .... | .... | .... | .... | .... | .... |
| | Norfolk Admirals | AHL | 1 | 0 | 0 | 0 | 25 | 3 | 0 | 7.30 | .... | .... | .... | .... | .... | .... | .... |
| | Syracuse Crunch | AHL | 26 | 15 | 8 | 2 | 1471 | 52 | 2 | 2.12 | 13 | 7 | 6 | 829 | 33 | 0 | 2.39 |
| 2008-09 | Manitoba Moose | AHL | 26 | 15 | 9 | 2 | 1522 | 64 | 0 | 2.52 | .... | .... | .... | .... | .... | .... | .... |
| | San Antonio | AHL | 5 | 4 | 1 | 0 | 302 | 15 | 0 | 2.99 | .... | .... | .... | .... | .... | .... | .... |

USHL Rookie of the Year (1997) • USHL Goaltender of the Year (1997) • USHL Player of the Year (1997) (co-winner - Jeff Panzer) • WCHA First All-Star Team (1998, 2000) • WCHA Rookie of the Year (1998) • NCAA West First All-American Team (1998, 2000) • WCHA Second All-Star Team (1999) • Harry "Hap" Holmes Memorial Award (AHL – fewest goals against) (2009) (shared with Cory Schneider)

Signed as a free agent by **Columbus**, May 7, 2001. Signed as a free agent by **Jokerit Helsinki** (Finland), September 16, 2005. Signed as a free agent by **Nashville**, July 17, 2006. Signed as a free agent by **Wilkes-Barre** (AHL), October 3, 2007.

## GRAHAME, John (GRAY-uhm, JAWN)

Goaltender. Catches left. 6'3", 220 lbs. Born, Denver, CO, August 31, 1975.
(Boston's 7th choice, 229th overall, in 1994 Entry Draft).

| | | | Regular Season | | | | | | | | Playoffs | | | | | | |
|---|---|---|---|---|---|---|---|---|---|---|---|---|---|---|---|---|---|
| **Season** | **Club** | **League** | **GP** | **W** | **L** | **O/T** | **Mins** | **GA** | **SO** | **Avg** | **GP** | **W** | **L** | **Mins** | **GA** | **SO** | **Avg** |
| 1993-94 | Sioux City | USHL | 20 | .... | .... | .... | 1200 | 73 | 0 | 3.70 | .... | .... | .... | .... | .... | .... | .... |
| 1994-95 | Lake Superior State | CCHA | 28 | 16 | 7 | 3 | 1616 | 75 | 2 | 2.79 | .... | .... | .... | .... | .... | .... | .... |
| 1995-96 | Lake Superior State | CCHA | 29 | 21 | 4 | 2 | 1558 | 66 | 2 | 2.54 | .... | .... | .... | .... | .... | .... | .... |
| 1996-97 | Lake Superior State | CCHA | 37 | 19 | 13 | 4 | 2197 | 134 | 3 | 3.66 | .... | .... | .... | .... | .... | .... | .... |
| 1997-98 | Providence Bruins | AHL | 55 | 15 | 31 | 4 | 3053 | 164 | 3 | 3.22 | .... | .... | .... | .... | .... | .... | .... |
| 1998-99 | Providence Bruins | AHL | 48 | *37 | 9 | 1 | 2771 | 134 | 3 | 2.90 | 19 | *15 | 4 | *1209 | 48 | 1 | 2.38 |
| 99-2000 | Boston | NHL | 24 | 7 | 10 | 5 | 1344 | 55 | 2 | 2.46 | .... | .... | .... | .... | .... | .... | .... |
| | Providence Bruins | AHL | 27 | 11 | 13 | 2 | 1528 | 86 | 1 | 3.38 | 13 | 10 | 3 | 839 | 35 | 0 | 2.50 |
| 2000-01 | Boston | NHL | 10 | 3 | 4 | 0 | 471 | 28 | 0 | 3.57 | .... | .... | .... | .... | .... | .... | .... |
| | Providence Bruins | AHL | 16 | 4 | 7 | 3 | 893 | 47 | 0 | 3.16 | 17 | 8 | 9 | 1043 | 46 | 2 | 2.65 |
| 2001-02 | Boston | NHL | 19 | 8 | 7 | 2 | 1079 | 52 | 1 | 2.89 | .... | .... | .... | .... | .... | .... | .... |
| 2002-03 | Boston | NHL | 23 | 11 | 9 | 2 | 1352 | 61 | 1 | 2.71 | .... | .... | .... | .... | .... | .... | .... |
| | Tampa Bay | NHL | 17 | 6 | 5 | 4 | 914 | 34 | 2 | 2.23 | 1 | 0 | 1 | 111 | 2 | 0 | 1.08 |
| 2003-04 ♦ | Tampa Bay | NHL | 29 | 18 | 9 | 1 | 1688 | 58 | 1 | 2.06 | 1 | 0 | 0 | 34 | 2 | 0 | 3.53 |
| 2004-05 | | | | | | | DID NOT PLAY | | | | | | | | | | |
| 2005-06 | Tampa Bay | NHL | 57 | 29 | 22 | 1 | 3152 | 161 | 5 | 3.06 | 4 | 1 | 3 | 188 | 15 | 0 | 4.79 |
| | United States | Olympics | 1 | 0 | 0 | 1 | 60 | 3 | 0 | 3.00 | .... | .... | .... | .... | .... | .... | .... |
| 2006-07 | Carolina | NHL | 28 | 10 | 13 | 2 | 1515 | 72 | 0 | 2.85 | .... | .... | .... | .... | .... | .... | .... |
| 2007-08 | Carolina | NHL | 17 | 5 | 7 | 1 | 848 | 53 | 0 | 3.75 | .... | .... | .... | .... | .... | .... | .... |
| | Albany River Rats | AHL | 7 | 4 | 3 | 0 | 415 | 21 | 0 | 3.04 | .... | .... | .... | .... | .... | .... | .... |
| 2008-09 | Omsk | Rus-KHL | 20 | 9 | 10 | 0 | 1195 | 57 | 3 | 2.86 | .... | .... | .... | .... | .... | .... | .... |
| | **NHL Totals** | | **224** | **97** | **86** | **18** | **12363** | **574** | **12** | **2.79** | **6** | **1** | **4** | **333** | **19** | **0** | **3.42** |

Traded to **Tampa Bay** by **Boston** for Tampa Bay's 4th round choice (later traded to San Jose – San Jose selected Jason Churchill) in 2004 Entry Draft, January 13, 2003. Signed as a free agent by **Carolina**, July 1, 2006. Signed as a free agent by **Omsk** (Rus-KHL), May 17, 2008.

## GREISS, Thomas (GRIGHS, TAW-muhs) S.J.

Goaltender. Catches left. 6'1", 210 lbs. Born, Straubing, West Germany, January 29, 1986.
(San Jose's 2nd choice, 94th overall, in 2004 Entry Draft).

| | | | Regular Season | | | | | | | | Playoffs | | | | | | |
|---|---|---|---|---|---|---|---|---|---|---|---|---|---|---|---|---|---|
| **Season** | **Club** | **League** | **GP** | **W** | **L** | **O/T** | **Mins** | **GA** | **SO** | **Avg** | **GP** | **W** | **L** | **Mins** | **GA** | **SO** | **Avg** |
| 2001-02 | EV Fussen Jr. | Ger-Jr. | | | | | STATISTICS NOT AVAILABLE | | | | | | | | | | |
| 2002-03 | Koln Jr. | Ger-Jr. | 25 | .... | .... | .... | 1613 | 58 | 0 | 2.16 | 3 | 1 | 2 | 180 | 8 | 1 | 2.67 |
| 2003-04 | Koln Jr. | Ger-Jr. | 24 | .... | .... | .... | 1286 | 56 | .... | 2.61 | .... | .... | .... | .... | .... | .... | .... |
| | Kolner Haie | Germany | 1 | .... | .... | .... | 20 | 4 | 0 | 12.00 | .... | .... | .... | .... | .... | .... | .... |
| 2004-05 | Kolner Haie | Germany | 8 | .... | .... | .... | 459 | 16 | 0 | 2.09 | .... | .... | .... | .... | .... | .... | .... |
| | Regensburg | German-2 | 1 | .... | .... | .... | 60 | 2 | 0 | 2.00 | 2 | .... | .... | 56 | 2 | 0 | 2.14 |
| 2005-06 | Kolner Haie | Germany | 27 | .... | .... | .... | 1560 | 64 | 1 | 2.46 | 9 | .... | .... | 533 | 27 | *1 | 3.04 |
| | Germany | Olympics | 1 | 0 | 1 | 0 | 60 | 5 | 0 | 5.00 | .... | .... | .... | .... | .... | .... | .... |
| 2006-07 | Worcester Sharks | AHL | 43 | 26 | 15 | 2 | 2555 | 111 | 0 | 2.61 | 3 | 0 | 3 | 172 | 12 | 0 | 4.18 |
| | Fresno Falcons | ECHL | 3 | 1 | 2 | 0 | 180 | 7 | 0 | 2.34 | .... | .... | .... | .... | .... | .... | .... |
| 2007-08 | San Jose | NHL | 3 | 0 | 1 | 1 | 129 | 7 | 0 | 3.26 | .... | .... | .... | .... | .... | .... | .... |
| | Worcester Sharks | AHL | 41 | 18 | 21 | 2 | 2424 | 125 | 0 | 3.09 | .... | .... | .... | .... | .... | .... | .... |
| 2008-09 | Worcester Sharks | AHL | 57 | 30 | 24 | 2 | 3346 | 138 | 1 | 2.47 | 12 | 6 | 6 | 742 | 30 | 2 | 2.43 |
| | **NHL Totals** | | **3** | **0** | **1** | **1** | **129** | **7** | **0** | **3.26** | .... | .... | .... | .... | .... | .... | .... |

## GUSTAVSSON, Jonas (YOH-nuhs, GUHS-tahv-suhn) TOR.

Goaltender. Catches left. 6'3", 192 lbs. Born, Stockholm, Sweden, October 24, 1984.

| | | | Regular Season | | | | | | | | Playoffs | | | | | | |
|---|---|---|---|---|---|---|---|---|---|---|---|---|---|---|---|---|---|
| **Season** | **Club** | **League** | **GP** | **W** | **L** | **O/T** | **Mins** | **GA** | **SO** | **Avg** | **GP** | **W** | **L** | **Mins** | **GA** | **SO** | **Avg** |
| 2000-01 | AIK Solna U18 | Swe-U18 | 12 | .... | .... | .... | 667 | 42 | 1 | 3.78 | .... | .... | .... | .... | .... | .... | .... |
| 2001-02 | AIK Solna U18 | Swe-U18 | 8 | .... | .... | .... | 439 | 13 | 2 | 1.78 | 4 | .... | .... | 239 | 12 | 0 | 3.01 |
| 2002-03 | AIK Solna Jr. | Swe-Jr. | 21 | .... | .... | .... | 1261 | 69 | 0 | 3.28 | 4 | .... | .... | 198 | 9 | 0 | 2.72 |
| 2003-04 | AIK Solna Jr. | Swe-Jr. | 9 | .... | .... | .... | 505 | 24 | 0 | 2.85 | .... | .... | .... | .... | .... | .... | .... |
| | AIK Solna | Sweden-2 | 1 | .... | .... | .... | 20 | 1 | 0 | 2.95 | .... | .... | .... | .... | .... | .... | .... |
| 2004-05 | AIK Solna Jr. | Swe-Jr. | 10 | .... | .... | .... | 557 | 32 | 0 | 3.45 | .... | .... | .... | .... | .... | .... | .... |
| | AIK Solna | Sweden-3 | 22 | .... | .... | .... | 1270 | 32 | 4 | 1.51 | .... | .... | .... | .... | .... | .... | .... |
| 2005-06 | AIK Solna Jr. | Swe-Jr. | 5 | .... | .... | .... | 258 | 14 | 0 | 3.26 | .... | .... | .... | .... | .... | .... | .... |
| | AIK Solna | Sweden-2 | 6 | .... | .... | .... | 351 | 14 | 0 | 2.39 | .... | .... | .... | .... | .... | .... | .... |
| 2006-07 | AIK IF Solna | Sweden-2 | 23 | .... | .... | .... | 1269 | 59 | 2 | 2.79 | .... | .... | .... | .... | .... | .... | .... |
| 2007-08 | Skare BK | Sweden-3 | 6 | .... | .... | .... | 368 | 16 | 0 | 2.61 | .... | .... | .... | .... | .... | .... | .... |
| | Farjestad | Sweden | 20 | .... | .... | .... | 1102 | 44 | 2 | 2.40 | 10 | .... | .... | 517 | 31 | 0 | 3.60 |
| 2008-09 | Farjestad | Sweden | 42 | .... | .... | .... | 2475 | 81 | 3 | *1.96 | 13 | .... | .... | 819 | 14 | *5 | *1.03 |

Signed as a free agent by **Toronto**, July 7, 2009.

## HACKETT, Matt (HA-keht, MA-thew) MIN.

Goaltender. Catches left. 6'2", 170 lbs. Born, London, Ont., March 7, 1990.
(Minnesota's 2nd choice, 77th overall, in 2009 Entry Draft).

| | | | Regular Season | | | | | | | | Playoffs | | | | | | |
|---|---|---|---|---|---|---|---|---|---|---|---|---|---|---|---|---|---|
| **Season** | **Club** | **League** | **GP** | **W** | **L** | **O/T** | **Mins** | **GA** | **SO** | **Avg** | **GP** | **W** | **L** | **Mins** | **GA** | **SO** | **Avg** |
| 2006-07 | London Jr. Knights | Minor-ON | 38 | 28 | 7 | 3 | .... | 52 | 20 | 1.39 | 6 | 5 | 1 | .... | 12 | 2 | 2.00 |
| | St. Catharines | OJHL-B | 16 | 7 | 7 | 0 | 902 | 63 | 0 | 4.19 | .... | .... | .... | .... | .... | .... | .... |
| | Windsor Spitfires | OHL | 7 | 0 | 7 | 0 | 429 | 36 | 0 | 5.04 | .... | .... | .... | .... | .... | .... | .... |
| 2007-08 | Windsor Spitfires | OHL | 4 | 1 | 1 | 0 | 130 | 10 | 0 | 4.61 | .... | .... | .... | .... | .... | .... | .... |
| | Plymouth Whalers | OHL | 18 | 6 | 9 | 1 | 978 | 56 | 0 | 3.44 | 1 | 0 | 0 | 16 | 0 | 0 | 0.00 |
| 2008-09 | Plymouth Whalers | OHL | 55 | 34 | 15 | 3 | 3036 | 154 | 2 | 3.04 | 11 | 6 | 5 | 638 | 32 | *1 | 3.01 |

## HALAK, Jaroslav (HAH-lak, YAHR-roh-slav) MTL.

Goaltender. Catches left. 5'11", 182 lbs. Born, Bratislava, Czech., May 13, 1985.
(Montreal's 11th choice, 271st overall, in 2003 Entry Draft).

| | | | Regular Season | | | | | | | | Playoffs | | | | | | |
|---|---|---|---|---|---|---|---|---|---|---|---|---|---|---|---|---|---|
| **Season** | **Club** | **League** | **GP** | **W** | **L** | **O/T** | **Mins** | **GA** | **SO** | **Avg** | **GP** | **W** | **L** | **Mins** | **GA** | **SO** | **Avg** |
| 2001-02 | Bratislava Jr. | Slovak-Jr. | 22 | .... | .... | .... | 1257 | 41 | 0 | 1.96 | 6 | 6 | 0 | 353 | 7 | 2 | 1.19 |
| 2002-03 | Bratislava Jr. | Slovak-Jr. | 20 | 13 | 3 | 3 | 1200 | 41 | 1 | 2.02 | .... | .... | .... | .... | .... | .... | .... |
| 2003-04 | Bratislava Jr. | Slovak-Jr. | 29 | .... | .... | .... | 1694 | 51 | .... | 1.81 | .... | .... | .... | .... | .... | .... | .... |
| | HK 91 Senica | Slovak-2 | 21 | .... | .... | .... | 1240 | 54 | .... | 2.61 | .... | .... | .... | .... | .... | .... | .... |
| | Bratislava | Slovakia | 12 | .... | .... | .... | 650 | 18 | 0 | 1.66 | 1 | .... | .... | 45 | 6 | 0 | 8.00 |
| 2004-05 | Lewiston | QMJHL | 47 | 24 | 17 | 4 | 2697 | 125 | 4 | 2.78 | 8 | 4 | 4 | 460 | 27 | 0 | 3.52 |
| 2005-06 | Hamilton Bulldogs | AHL | 13 | 7 | 6 | 0 | 786 | 30 | 3 | 2.29 | .... | .... | .... | .... | .... | .... | .... |
| | Long Beach | ECHL | 20 | 11 | 4 | 2 | 1026 | 35 | 2 | 2.05 | 4 | 2 | 2 | 252 | 13 | 0 | 3.10 |
| 2006-07 | Montreal | NHL | 16 | 10 | 6 | 0 | 912 | 44 | 2 | 2.89 | .... | .... | .... | .... | .... | .... | .... |
| | Hamilton Bulldogs | AHL | 28 | 16 | 11 | 0 | 1618 | 54 | 6 | *2.00 | .... | .... | .... | .... | .... | .... | .... |
| 2007-08 | Montreal | NHL | 6 | 2 | 1 | 1 | 285 | 10 | 1 | 2.11 | 2 | 0 | 1 | 77 | 3 | 0 | 2.34 |
| | Hamilton Bulldogs | AHL | 28 | 15 | 10 | 2 | 1630 | 57 | 2 | 2.10 | .... | .... | .... | .... | .... | .... | .... |
| 2008-09 | Montreal | NHL | 34 | 18 | 14 | 1 | 1931 | 92 | 1 | 2.86 | 1 | 0 | 0 | 20 | 0 | 0 | 0.00 |
| | **NHL Totals** | | **56** | **30** | **21** | **2** | **3128** | **146** | **4** | **2.80** | **3** | **0** | **1** | **97** | **3** | **0** | **1.86** |

AHL All-Rookie Team (2007)

## HARDING, Josh (HAHR-dihng, JAWSH) MIN.

Goaltender. Catches right. 6'1", 197 lbs. Born, Regina, Sask., June 18, 1984.
(Minnesota's 2nd choice, 38th overall, in 2002 Entry Draft).

| | | | Regular Season | | | | | | | | Playoffs | | | | | | |
|---|---|---|---|---|---|---|---|---|---|---|---|---|---|---|---|---|---|
| **Season** | **Club** | **League** | **GP** | **W** | **L** | **O/T** | **Mins** | **GA** | **SO** | **Avg** | **GP** | **W** | **L** | **Mins** | **GA** | **SO** | **Avg** |
| 2000-01 | Reg. Pat Cdns. | SMHL | 36 | 17 | 13 | 0 | 2106 | 96 | 2 | 2.75 | 3 | 1 | 2 | 170 | 11 | 0 | 3.88 |
| 2001-02 | Regina Pats | WHL | 42 | 27 | 13 | 1 | 2389 | 95 | *4 | 2.39 | 6 | 2 | 4 | 325 | 16 | 0 | 2.95 |
| 2002-03 | Regina Pats | WHL | 57 | 18 | 24 | 13 | *3385 | 155 | 3 | 2.75 | 5 | 1 | 4 | 321 | 13 | 0 | 2.43 |
| 2003-04 | Regina Pats | WHL | 28 | 12 | 14 | 2 | 1665 | 67 | 2 | 2.41 | .... | .... | .... | .... | .... | .... | .... |
| | Brandon | WHL | 27 | 13 | 11 | 3 | 1612 | 65 | 5 | 2.42 | 11 | 5 | 6 | 660 | 36 | 0 | 3.27 |
| 2004-05 | Houston Aeros | AHL | 42 | 21 | 16 | 3 | 2388 | 80 | 4 | 2.01 | 2 | 0 | 2 | 119 | 8 | 0 | 4.03 |
| 2005-06 | Minnesota | NHL | 3 | 2 | 1 | 0 | 185 | 8 | 1 | 2.59 | .... | .... | .... | .... | .... | .... | .... |
| | Houston Aeros | AHL | 38 | 29 | 8 | 0 | 2215 | 99 | 2 | 2.68 | 8 | 4 | 4 | 476 | 30 | 0 | 3.79 |
| 2006-07 | Minnesota | NHL | 7 | 3 | 2 | 1 | 361 | 7 | 1 | 1.16 | .... | .... | .... | .... | .... | .... | .... |
| | Houston Aeros | AHL | 38 | 17 | 16 | 4 | 2270 | 94 | 1 | 2.48 | .... | .... | .... | .... | .... | .... | .... |
| 2007-08 | Minnesota | NHL | 29 | 11 | 15 | 2 | 1571 | 77 | 1 | 2.94 | 1 | 0 | 0 | 20 | 0 | 0 | 0.00 |
| 2008-09 | Minnesota | NHL | 19 | 3 | 9 | 1 | 870 | 32 | 0 | 2.21 | .... | .... | .... | .... | .... | .... | .... |
| | **NHL Totals** | | **58** | **19** | **27** | **4** | **2987** | **124** | **3** | **2.49** | **1** | **0** | **0** | **20** | **0** | **0** | **0.00** |

WHL East Second All-Star Team (2002) • WHL East First All-Star Team (2003) • WHL Goaltender of the Year (2003) • WHL Player of the Year (2003) • Canadian Major Junior Second All-Star Team (2003)

## HEDBERG, Johan (HEHD-buhrg, YOH-han) ATL.

Goaltender. Catches left. 6', 190 lbs. Born, Leksand, Sweden, May 5, 1973.
(Philadelphia's 8th choice, 218th overall, in 1994 Entry Draft).

| | | | Regular Season | | | | | | | | Playoffs | | | | | | |
|---|---|---|---|---|---|---|---|---|---|---|---|---|---|---|---|---|---|
| **Season** | **Club** | **League** | **GP** | **W** | **L** | **O/T** | **Mins** | **GA** | **SO** | **Avg** | **GP** | **W** | **L** | **Mins** | **GA** | **SO** | **Avg** |
| 1992-93 | Leksands IF | Sweden | 10 | .... | .... | .... | 600 | 24 | .... | 2.40 | .... | .... | .... | .... | .... | .... | .... |
| 1993-94 | Leksands IF | Sweden | 17 | .... | .... | .... | 1020 | 48 | .... | 2.82 | .... | .... | .... | .... | .... | .... | .... |
| 1994-95 | Leksands IF | Sweden | 17 | .... | .... | .... | 986 | 58 | .... | 3.53 | .... | .... | .... | .... | .... | .... | .... |

| | | | | | | | | | | | | | | | | | |
|---|---|---|---|---|---|---|---|---|---|---|---|---|---|---|---|---|---|
| 1995-96 | Leksands IF | Sweden | 34 | .... | .... | .... | 2013 | 95 | .... | 2.83 | 4 | .... | .... | 240 | 13 | .... | 3.25 |
| 1996-97 | Leksands IF | Sweden | 38 | .... | .... | .... | 2260 | 95 | 3 | 2.52 | 8 | .... | .... | 581 | 18 | 1 | 1.86 |
| 1997-98 | Detroit Vipers | IHL | 16 | 7 | 2 | 2 | 726 | 32 | 1 | 2.64 | .... | .... | .... | .... | .... | .... | .... |
| | Baton Rouge | ECHL | 2 | 1 | 1 | 0 | 100 | 7 | 0 | 4.20 | .... | .... | .... | .... | .... | .... | .... |
| | Manitoba Moose | IHL | 14 | 8 | 4 | 1 | 745 | 32 | 1 | 2.58 | 2 | 0 | 2 | 105 | 6 | 0 | 3.40 |
| | Sweden | Olympics | | | | | DID NOT PLAY – SPARE GOALTENDER | | | | | | | | | | |
| 1998-99 | Leksands IF | Sweden | *48 | .... | .... | .... | *2940 | 140 | 0 | 2.86 | 4 | .... | .... | 255 | 15 | 0 | 3.53 |
| 99-2000 | Kentucky | AHL | 33 | 18 | 9 | 5 | 1973 | 88 | 3 | 2.68 | 5 | 3 | 2 | 311 | 10 | 1 | 1.93 |
| **2000-01** | Manitoba Moose | IHL | 46 | 23 | 13 | 7 | 2697 | 115 | 1 | 2.56 | .... | .... | .... | .... | .... | .... | .... |
| | **Pittsburgh** | **NHL** | **9** | **7** | **1** | **1** | **545** | **24** | **0** | **2.64** | **18** | **9** | **9** | **1123** | **43** | **2** | **2.30** |
| **2001-02** | **Pittsburgh** | **NHL** | **66** | **25** | **34** | **7** | **3877** | **178** | **6** | **2.75** | .... | .... | .... | .... | .... | .... | .... |
| | Sweden | Olympics | 1 | 1 | 0 | 0 | 60 | 1 | 0 | 1.00 | .... | .... | .... | .... | .... | .... | .... |
| **2002-03** | **Pittsburgh** | **NHL** | **41** | **14** | **22** | **4** | **2410** | **126** | **1** | **3.14** | .... | .... | .... | .... | .... | .... | .... |
| **2003-04** | **Vancouver** | **NHL** | **21** | **8** | **6** | **2** | **1098** | **46** | **3** | **2.51** | **2** | **1** | **1** | **98** | **4** | **0** | **2.45** |
| | Manitoba Moose | AHL | 2 | 0 | 2 | 0 | 125 | 9 | 0 | 4.32 | .... | .... | .... | .... | .... | .... | .... |
| 2004-05 | Leksands IF | Sweden-2 | 21 | .... | .... | .... | 1274 | 45 | 1 | 2.12 | .... | .... | .... | .... | .... | .... | .... |
| **2005-06** | **Dallas** | **NHL** | **19** | **12** | **4** | **1** | **1079** | **48** | **0** | **2.67** | .... | .... | .... | .... | .... | .... | .... |
| **2006-07** | **Atlanta** | **NHL** | **21** | **9** | **4** | **2** | **1057** | **51** | **0** | **2.89** | **2** | **0** | **2** | **117** | **5** | **0** | **2.56** |
| **2007-08** | **Atlanta** | **NHL** | **36** | **14** | **15** | **3** | **1927** | **111** | **1** | **3.46** | .... | .... | .... | .... | .... | .... | .... |
| **2008-09** | **Atlanta** | **NHL** | **33** | **13** | **12** | **3** | **1717** | **100** | **0** | **3.49** | .... | .... | .... | .... | .... | .... | .... |
| | **NHL Totals** | | **246** | **102** | **98** | **23** | **13710** | **684** | **11** | **2.99** | **22** | **10** | **12** | **1338** | **52** | **2** | **2.33** |

• Rights traded to **San Jose** by **Philadelphia** for San Jose's 7th round choice (Pavel Kasparik) in 1999 Entry Draft, August 6, 1998. Traded to **Pittsburgh** by **San Jose** with Bobby Dollas for Jeff Norton, March 12, 2001. Traded to **Vancouver** by **Pittsburgh** for Vancouver's 2nd round choice (Alex Goligoski) in 2004 Entry Draft, August 25, 2003. Signed as a free agent by **Leksands** (Sweden-2), August 1, 2004. Signed as a free agent by **Dallas**, August 5, 2005. Signed as a free agent by **Atlanta**, July 1, 2006.

## HELENIUS, Riku (heh-lehn-NEE-uhs, REE-koo) T.B.

Goaltender. Catches left. 6'3", 202 lbs. Born, Palkane, Finland, March 1, 1988.
(Tampa Bay's 1st choice, 15th overall, in 2006 Entry Draft).

| | | | Regular Season | | | | | | | | Playoffs | | | | | | |
|---|---|---|---|---|---|---|---|---|---|---|---|---|---|---|---|---|---|
| **Season** | **Club** | **League** | **GP** | **W** | **L** | **O/T** | **Mins** | **GA** | **SO** | **Avg** | **GP** | **W** | **L** | **Mins** | **GA** | **SO** | **Avg** |
| 2004-05 | Ilves Tampere U18 | Fin-U18 | 16 | .... | .... | .... | 903 | 30 | 3 | 1.99 | 5 | .... | .... | 295 | 15 | 0 | 3.05 |
| | Ilves Tampere Jr. | Fin-Jr. | 2 | .... | .... | .... | 86 | 4 | 0 | 2.77 | .... | .... | .... | .... | .... | .... | .... |
| 2005-06 | Suomi U20 | Finland-2 | 1 | .... | .... | .... | 60 | 3 | 0 | 3.00 | .... | .... | .... | .... | .... | .... | .... |
| | Ilves Tampere U18 | Fin-U18 | 2 | .... | .... | .... | 120 | 2 | 0 | 1.00 | 5 | .... | .... | 300 | 13 | 0 | 2.60 |
| | Ilves Tampere Jr. | Fin-Jr. | 26 | .... | .... | .... | 1565 | 70 | 4 | 2.68 | 2 | .... | .... | 135 | 7 | 0 | 3.11 |
| 2006-07 | Ilves Tampere Jr. | Fin-Jr. | 2 | 2 | 0 | 0 | 120 | 4 | 0 | 2.00 | .... | .... | .... | .... | .... | .... | .... |
| 2007-08 | Seattle | WHL | 41 | 22 | 12 | 6 | 2358 | 95 | 3 | 2.42 | 9 | 4 | 5 | 534 | 24 | 0 | 2.70 |
| **2008-09** | **Tampa Bay** | **NHL** | **1** | **0** | **0** | **0** | **7** | **0** | **0** | **0.00** | .... | .... | .... | .... | .... | .... | .... |
| | Norfolk Admirals | AHL | 25 | 9 | 15 | 0 | 1388 | 63 | 1 | 2.72 | .... | .... | .... | .... | .... | .... | .... |
| | Augusta Lynx | ECHL | 8 | 3 | 4 | 1 | 463 | 34 | 0 | 4.41 | .... | .... | .... | .... | .... | .... | .... |
| | Mississippi | ECHL | 3 | 1 | 1 | 1 | 184 | 7 | 0 | 2.28 | .... | .... | .... | .... | .... | .... | .... |
| | Elmira Jackals | ECHL | .... | .... | .... | .... | .... | .... | .... | .... | 2 | 0 | 1 | 87 | 10 | 0 | 6.91 |
| | **NHL Totals** | | **1** | **0** | **0** | **0** | **7** | **0** | **0** | **0.00** | .... | .... | .... | .... | .... | .... | .... |

## HILLER, Jonas (HIHL-uhr, YOH-nuhs) ANA.

Goaltender. Catches right. 6'2", 193 lbs. Born, Felben Wellhausen, Switz., February 12, 1982.

| | | | Regular Season | | | | | | | | Playoffs | | | | | | |
|---|---|---|---|---|---|---|---|---|---|---|---|---|---|---|---|---|---|
| **Season** | **Club** | **League** | **GP** | **W** | **L** | **O/T** | **Mins** | **GA** | **SO** | **Avg** | **GP** | **W** | **L** | **Mins** | **GA** | **SO** | **Avg** |
| 2000-01 | HC Davos | Swiss | 1 | 0 | 0 | 0 | 9 | 0 | 0 | 0.00 | .... | .... | .... | .... | .... | .... | .... |
| 2001-02 | HC Davos | Swiss | | | | | DID NOT PLAY | | | | | | | | | | |
| 2002-03 | HC Davos | Swiss | | | | | DID NOT PLAY | | | | | | | | | | |
| 2003-04 | Lausanne HC | Swiss | 21 | .... | .... | .... | 1161 | 64 | 1 | 3.31 | .... | .... | .... | .... | .... | .... | .... |
| | Chaux-de-Fonds | Swiss-2 | 1 | 0 | 1 | 0 | 60 | 4 | 0 | 4.00 | .... | .... | .... | .... | .... | .... | .... |
| | Lausanne HC | Swiss-Q | .... | .... | .... | .... | .... | .... | .... | .... | 4 | 4 | 0 | 251 | 7 | 0 | 1.67 |
| 2004-05 | HC Davos | Swiss | 43 | 26 | 12 | 4 | 2519 | 95 | *8 | 2.26 | *15 | 12 | 3 | *932 | 34 | 0 | *2.19 |
| 2005-06 | HC Davos | Swiss | *44 | 23 | 16 | 5 | *2676 | 110 | 3 | 2.47 | 15 | 9 | 6 | 900 | 45 | 1 | 3.00 |
| 2006-07 | HC Davos | Swiss | *44 | *28 | 16 | 0 | *2656 | 115 | 3 | 2.60 | *19 | *12 | 7 | *1138 | 39 | 3 | 2.05 |
| **2007-08** | **Anaheim** | **NHL** | **23** | **10** | **7** | **1** | **1223** | **42** | **0** | **2.06** | .... | .... | .... | .... | .... | .... | .... |
| | Portland Pirates | AHL | 6 | 3 | 2 | 1 | 370 | 13 | 0 | 2.11 | .... | .... | .... | .... | .... | .... | .... |
| **2008-09** | **Anaheim** | **NHL** | **46** | **23** | **15** | **1** | **2486** | **99** | **4** | **2.39** | **13** | **7** | **6** | **807** | **30** | ***2** | **2.23** |
| | **NHL Totals** | | **69** | **33** | **22** | **2** | **3709** | **141** | **4** | **2.28** | **13** | **7** | **6** | **807** | **30** | **2** | **2.23** |

Signed as a free agent by **Anaheim**, May 25, 2007.

## HOLMQVIST, Johan (HOHLM-kvihst, YOH-han)

Goaltender. Catches left. 6'3", 198 lbs. Born, Tolfta, Sweden, May 24, 1978.
(NY Rangers' 9th choice, 175th overall, in 1997 Entry Draft).

| | | | Regular Season | | | | | | | | Playoffs | | | | | | |
|---|---|---|---|---|---|---|---|---|---|---|---|---|---|---|---|---|---|
| **Season** | **Club** | **League** | **GP** | **W** | **L** | **O/T** | **Mins** | **GA** | **SO** | **Avg** | **GP** | **W** | **L** | **Mins** | **GA** | **SO** | **Avg** |
| 1996-97 | Brynas IF Gavle | Sweden | 2 | 0 | 0 | 0 | 80 | 4 | 0 | 3.00 | .... | .... | .... | .... | .... | .... | .... |
| 1997-98 | Brynas IF Gavle | Sweden | 33 | .... | .... | .... | 1897 | 82 | .... | 2.59 | 3 | 0 | 3 | 180 | 14 | .... | 4.67 |
| 1998-99 | Brynas IF Gavle | Sweden | 41 | .... | .... | .... | 2383 | 111 | 4 | 2.79 | *14 | 9 | 5 | *855 | 34 | 0 | 2.39 |
| 99-2000 | Brynas IF Gavle | Sweden | 41 | .... | .... | .... | 2402 | 104 | 4 | 2.60 | 11 | .... | .... | 671 | 30 | 1 | 2.68 |
| **2000-01** | **NY Rangers** | **NHL** | **2** | **0** | **2** | **0** | **119** | **10** | **0** | **5.04** | .... | .... | .... | .... | .... | .... | .... |
| | Hartford Wolf Pack | AHL | 43 | 19 | 14 | 4 | 2305 | 111 | 2 | 2.89 | 5 | 2 | 3 | 314 | 13 | 0 | 2.48 |
| **2001-02** | **NY Rangers** | **NHL** | **1** | **0** | **0** | **0** | **9** | **0** | **0** | **0.00** | .... | .... | .... | .... | .... | .... | .... |
| | Hartford Wolf Pack | AHL | 48 | 26 | 12 | 6 | 2734 | 140 | 1 | 3.07 | 4 | 1 | 2 | 163 | 12 | 0 | 4.41 |
| **2002-03** | **NY Rangers** | **NHL** | **1** | **0** | **1** | **0** | **39** | **2** | **0** | **3.08** | .... | .... | .... | .... | .... | .... | .... |
| | Hartford Wolf Pack | AHL | 35 | 14 | 13 | 5 | 1904 | 84 | 2 | 2.65 | .... | .... | .... | .... | .... | .... | .... |
| | Charlotte Checkers | ECHL | 1 | 1 | 0 | 0 | 60 | 2 | 0 | 2.00 | .... | .... | .... | .... | .... | .... | .... |
| | Houston Aeros | AHL | 8 | 5 | 3 | 0 | 479 | 23 | 1 | 2.88 | *23 | *15 | 8 | *1499 | 50 | 1 | 2.00 |
| 2003-04 | Houston Aeros | AHL | 59 | 23 | 27 | 7 | 3467 | 148 | 4 | 2.56 | .... | .... | .... | .... | .... | .... | .... |
| 2004-05 | Brynas IF Gavle | Sweden | 42 | .... | .... | .... | 2445 | 138 | 1 | 3.39 | .... | .... | .... | .... | .... | .... | .... |
| 2005-06 | Brynas IF Gavle | Sweden | 26 | .... | .... | .... | 1539 | 50 | 3 | *1.95 | 4 | .... | .... | 194 | 13 | 0 | 4.02 |
| **2006-07** | **Tampa Bay** | **NHL** | **48** | **27** | **15** | **3** | **2548** | **121** | **1** | **2.85** | **6** | **2** | **4** | **370** | **18** | **0** | **2.92** |
| **2007-08** | **Tampa Bay** | **NHL** | **45** | **20** | **16** | **6** | **2469** | **124** | **2** | **3.01** | .... | .... | .... | .... | .... | .... | .... |
| | **Dallas** | **NHL** | **2** | **1** | **0** | **0** | **80** | **5** | **0** | **3.75** | .... | .... | .... | .... | .... | .... | .... |
| 2008-09 | Frolunda | Sweden | *49 | .... | .... | .... | 2799 | 101 | 2 | 2.17 | 11 | .... | .... | 623 | 25 | 1 | 2.41 |
| | **NHL Totals** | | **99** | **48** | **34** | **9** | **5264** | **262** | **3** | **2.99** | **6** | **2** | **4** | **370** | **18** | **0** | **2.92** |

Jack A. Butterfield Trophy (AHL –Playoff MVP) (2003)

Traded to **Minnesota** by **NY Rangers** for Lawrence Nycholat, March 11, 2003. Signed as a free agent by **Gavle** (Sweden), July 29, 2004. Signed as a free agent by **Tampa Bay**, June 1, 2006. Traded to **Dallas** by **Tampa Bay** with Brad Richards for Jussi Jokinen, Jeff Halpern, Mike Smith and Dallas' 4th round choice (later traded to Minnesota – later traded to Edmonton – Edmonton selected Kyle Bigos) in 2009 Entry Draft, February 26, 2008.

## HOLT, Chris (HOHLT, KRIHS) ST.L.

Goaltender. Catches left. 6'3", 221 lbs. Born, Vancouver, B.C., June 5, 1985.
(NY Rangers' 8th choice, 180th overall, in 2003 Entry Draft).

| | | | Regular Season | | | | | | | | Playoffs | | | | | | |
|---|---|---|---|---|---|---|---|---|---|---|---|---|---|---|---|---|---|
| **Season** | **Club** | **League** | **GP** | **W** | **L** | **O/T** | **Mins** | **GA** | **SO** | **Avg** | **GP** | **W** | **L** | **Mins** | **GA** | **SO** | **Avg** |
| 2001-02 | Billings Bulls | AWHL | 24 | 13 | 7 | 1 | 1184 | 59 | 2 | 2.99 | .... | .... | .... | .... | .... | .... | .... |
| 2002-03 | USNTDP | U-18 | 27 | 7 | 12 | 2 | 1519 | 81 | 1 | 3.20 | .... | .... | .... | .... | .... | .... | .... |
| | USNTDP | NAHL | 5 | 2 | 3 | 0 | 255 | 14 | 0 | 3.30 | .... | .... | .... | .... | .... | .... | .... |
| 2003-04 | Nebraska-Omaha | CCHA | 27 | 5 | 17 | 2 | 1499 | 81 | 0 | 3.24 | .... | .... | .... | .... | .... | .... | .... |
| 2004-05 | Nebraska-Omaha | CCHA | 37 | 19 | 14 | 4 | 2190 | 106 | 1 | 2.90 | .... | .... | .... | .... | .... | .... | .... |
| **2005-06** | **NY Rangers** | **NHL** | **1** | **0** | **0** | **0** | **10** | **0** | **0** | **0.00** | .... | .... | .... | .... | .... | .... | .... |
| | Hartford Wolf Pack | AHL | 9 | 3 | 2 | 1 | 459 | 31 | 0 | 4.06 | 8 | 4 | 4 | 487 | 24 | 0 | 2.96 |
| | Charlotte Checkers | ECHL | 23 | 7 | 11 | 1 | 1229 | 84 | 0 | 4.10 | .... | .... | .... | .... | .... | .... | .... |
| 2006-07 | Hartford Wolf Pack | AHL | 6 | 2 | 1 | 0 | 240 | 8 | 0 | 2.00 | 1 | 0 | 0 | 26 | 1 | 0 | 2.28 |
| | Charlotte Checkers | ECHL | 45 | 24 | 18 | 2 | 2650 | 139 | 1 | 3.15 | 4 | 2 | 2 | 223 | 11 | 0 | 2.97 |
| 2007-08 | Hartford Wolf Pack | AHL | 9 | 5 | 3 | 0 | 447 | 18 | 0 | 2.42 | .... | .... | .... | .... | .... | .... | .... |
| | Charlotte Checkers | ECHL | 32 | 15 | 13 | 2 | 1808 | 82 | 3 | 2.72 | 3 | 0 | 3 | 179 | 10 | 0 | 3.35 |
| **2008-09** | **St. Louis** | **NHL** | **1** | **0** | **0** | **0** | **19** | **0** | **0** | **0.00** | .... | .... | .... | .... | .... | .... | .... |
| | Peoria Rivermen | AHL | 20 | 10 | 6 | 2 | 1111 | 32 | 1 | 1.73 | .... | .... | .... | .... | .... | .... | .... |
| | Alaska Aces | ECHL | 5 | 3 | 2 | 0 | 300 | 9 | 1 | 1.80 | .... | .... | .... | .... | .... | .... | .... |
| | **NHL Totals** | | **2** | **0** | **0** | **0** | **29** | **0** | **0** | **0.00** | .... | .... | .... | .... | .... | .... | .... |

Signed as a free agent by **St. Louis**, October 30, 2008.

## HOLTBY, Braden (HOHLT-bee, BRAY-duhn) WSH.

Goaltender. Catches left. 6'1", 206 lbs. Born, Lloydminster, Sask., September 16, 1989.
(Washington's 5th choice, 93rd overall, in 2008 Entry Draft).

| | | | Regular Season | | | | | | | | Playoffs | | | | | | |
|---|---|---|---|---|---|---|---|---|---|---|---|---|---|---|---|---|---|
| **Season** | **Club** | **League** | **GP** | **W** | **L** | **O/T** | **Mins** | **GA** | **SO** | **Avg** | **GP** | **W** | **L** | **Mins** | **GA** | **SO** | **Avg** |
| 2005-06 | Saskatoon Blazers | SMHL | | | | | STATISTICS NOT AVAILABLE | | | | | | | | | | |
| | Saskatoon Blades | WHL | 1 | 0 | 1 | 0 | 59 | 4 | 0 | 4.07 | .... | .... | .... | .... | .... | .... | .... |
| 2006-07 | Saskatoon Blades | WHL | 51 | 17 | 29 | 3 | 2725 | 146 | 0 | 3.21 | .... | .... | .... | .... | .... | .... | .... |
| 2007-08 | Saskatoon Blades | WHL | *64 | 25 | 29 | 0 | 3632 | 172 | 1 | 2.84 | .... | .... | .... | .... | .... | .... | .... |
| 2008-09 | Saskatoon Blades | WHL | *61 | 40 | 16 | 4 | *3571 | 156 | 6 | 2.62 | 7 | 3 | 4 | 414 | 16 | 0 | 2.32 |

WHL East First All-Star Team (2009)

## HOVINEN, Niko (HOH-vih-nehn, NEE-KOH) MIN.

Goaltender. Catches left. 6'6", 208 lbs. Born, Helsinki, Finland, March 16, 1988.
(Minnesota's 5th choice, 132nd overall, in 2006 Entry Draft).

| | | | Regular Season | | | | | | | | Playoffs | | | | | | |
|---|---|---|---|---|---|---|---|---|---|---|---|---|---|---|---|---|---|
| **Season** | **Club** | **League** | **GP** | **W** | **L** | **O/T** | **Mins** | **GA** | **SO** | **Avg** | **GP** | **W** | **L** | **Mins** | **GA** | **SO** | **Avg** |
| 2004-05 | Jokerit U18 | Fin-U18 | 20 | .... | .... | .... | 1166 | 38 | 3 | 1.95 | 4 | .... | .... | 246 | 9 | 1 | 2.20 |
| | Jokerit Helsinki Jr. | Fin-Jr. | 4 | .... | .... | .... | 242 | 13 | 0 | 3.21 | .... | .... | .... | .... | .... | .... | .... |
| 2005-06 | Jokerit Helsinki Jr. | Fin-Jr. | 26 | .... | .... | .... | 1480 | 77 | 0 | 3.12 | .... | .... | .... | .... | .... | .... | .... |
| | Jokerit U18 | Fin-U18 | 11 | .... | .... | .... | 637 | 34 | 1 | 3.20 | 4 | .... | .... | 232 | 14 | 1 | 3.62 |
| | Suomi U20 | Finland-2 | 1 | .... | .... | .... | 60 | 4 | 0 | 4.00 | .... | .... | .... | .... | .... | .... | .... |
| 2006-07 | Jokerit Helsinki Jr. | Fin-Jr. | 27 | 13 | 10 | 0 | 1641 | 74 | 1 | 2.71 | 5 | 2 | 3 | 303 | 12 | 1 | 2.38 |
| | Suomi U20 | Finland-2 | 6 | 1 | 2 | 0 | 329 | 18 | 0 | 3.28 | .... | .... | .... | .... | .... | .... | .... |
| | Jokerit Helsinki | Finland | 1 | 0 | 1 | 0 | 60 | 4 | 0 | 4.00 | .... | .... | .... | .... | .... | .... | .... |
| 2007-08 | Suomi U20 | Finland-2 | 3 | 2 | 1 | 0 | 180 | 12 | 0 | 4.00 | .... | .... | .... | .... | .... | .... | .... |
| | Jokerit Helsinki | Finland | 4 | 0 | 1 | 0 | 125 | 12 | 0 | 5.78 | .... | .... | .... | .... | .... | .... | .... |
| | Jokerit Helsinki Jr. | Fin-Jr. | 22 | 13 | 8 | 0 | 1272 | 58 | 2 | 2.74 | 3 | 1 | 2 | 182 | 14 | 0 | 4.62 |
| 2008-09 | HeKi Heinola | Finland-2 | 1 | 0 | 1 | 0 | 41 | 4 | 0 | 5.81 | .... | .... | .... | .... | .... | .... | .... |
| | Pelicans Lahti Jr. | Fin-Jr. | 13 | 9 | 4 | 0 | 786 | 26 | 1 | 1.99 | 3 | 1 | 2 | 180 | 13 | 0 | 4.33 |
| | Pelicans Lahti | Finland | 21 | 7 | 12 | 1 | 1110 | 54 | 2 | 2.92 | 1 | 0 | 0 | 11 | 3 | 0 | 15.72 |

## HOWARD, Jimmy (HOW-uhrd, JAYMZ) DET.

Goaltender. Catches left. 6', 218 lbs. Born, Syracuse, NY, March 26, 1984.
(Detroit's 1st choice, 64th overall, in 2003 Entry Draft).

| | | | Regular Season | | | | | | | | Playoffs | | | | | | |
|---|---|---|---|---|---|---|---|---|---|---|---|---|---|---|---|---|---|
| **Season** | **Club** | **League** | **GP** | **W** | **L** | **O/T** | **Mins** | **GA** | **SO** | **Avg** | **GP** | **W** | **L** | **Mins** | **GA** | **SO** | **Avg** |
| 2001-02 | USNTDP | U-18 | 19 | 15 | 4 | 1 | 1170 | 37 | 4 | 1.90 | .... | .... | .... | .... | .... | .... | .... |
| | USNTDP | USHL | 8 | 4 | 3 | 0 | 425 | 14 | 0 | 1.98 | .... | .... | .... | .... | .... | .... | .... |
| | USNTDP | NAHL | 8 | 3 | 4 | 0 | 381 | 25 | 0 | 3.93 | .... | .... | .... | .... | .... | .... | .... |
| 2002-03 | University of Maine | H-East | 21 | 14 | 6 | 0 | 1151 | 47 | 3 | 2.45 | .... | .... | .... | .... | .... | .... | .... |
| 2003-04 | University of Maine | H-East | 23 | 14 | 4 | 3 | 1364 | 27 | *6 | *1.19 | .... | .... | .... | .... | .... | .... | .... |
| 2004-05 | University of Maine | H-East | *39 | *19 | 13 | 7 | *2310 | 74 | *6 | 1.92 | .... | .... | .... | .... | .... | .... | .... |
| **2005-06** | **Detroit** | **NHL** | **4** | **1** | **2** | **0** | **201** | **10** | **0** | **2.99** | .... | .... | .... | .... | .... | .... | .... |
| | Grand Rapids | AHL | 38 | 27 | 6 | 2 | 2140 | 92 | 2 | 2.58 | 13 | 5 | 7 | 763 | 44 | 0 | 3.46 |
| 2006-07 | Grand Rapids | AHL | 49 | 21 | 21 | 3 | 2776 | 125 | 6 | 2.70 | 7 | 3 | 4 | 434 | 14 | 0 | 1.93 |
| **2007-08** | **Detroit** | **NHL** | **4** | **0** | **2** | **0** | **197** | **7** | **0** | **2.13** | .... | .... | .... | .... | .... | .... | .... |
| | Grand Rapids | AHL | 54 | 21 | 28 | 2 | 3097 | 146 | 2 | 2.83 | .... | .... | .... | .... | .... | .... | .... |
| **2008-09** | **Detroit** | **NHL** | **1** | **0** | **1** | **0** | **59** | **4** | **0** | **4.07** | .... | .... | .... | .... | .... | .... | .... |
| | Grand Rapids | AHL | 45 | 21 | 18 | 4 | 2644 | 112 | 4 | 2.54 | 10 | 4 | 6 | 598 | 24 | 0 | 2.41 |
| | **NHL Totals** | | **9** | **1** | **5** | **0** | **457** | **21** | **0** | **2.76** | .... | .... | .... | .... | .... | .... | .... |

Hockey East All-Rookie Team (2003) • Hockey East Rookie of the Year (2003) • Hockey East First All-Star Team (2004) • NCAA East Second All-American Team (2004) • AHL All-Rookie Team (2006)

## HUET, Cristobal (hew-AY, KRIHS-toh-bahl) CHI.

Goaltender. Catches left. 6'1", 205 lbs. Born, St. Martin d'Heres, France, September 3, 1975.
(Los Angeles' 9th choice, 214th overall, in 2001 Entry Draft).

| | | | Regular Season | | | | | | | | Playoffs | | | | | | |
|---|---|---|---|---|---|---|---|---|---|---|---|---|---|---|---|---|---|
| **Season** | **Club** | **League** | **GP** | **W** | **L** | **O/T** | **Mins** | **GA** | **SO** | **Avg** | **GP** | **W** | **L** | **Mins** | **GA** | **SO** | **Avg** |
| 1997-98 | CSG Grenoble | France | | | | | STATISTICS NOT AVAILABLE | | | | | | | | | | |
| | France | Olympics | 2 | 1 | 1 | 0 | 120 | 5 | 0 | 2.50 | .... | .... | .... | .... | .... | .... | .... |
| 1998-99 | HC Lugano | Swiss | 21 | .... | .... | .... | 1275 | 58 | 1 | 2.73 | 10 | .... | .... | 628 | 18 | 1 | *1.72 |
| 99-2000 | HC Lugano | Swiss | 31 | .... | .... | .... | 1886 | 50 | *8 | *1.59 | 13 | .... | .... | 783 | 29 | 0 | 2.22 |
| 2000-01 | HC Lugano | Swiss | 39 | .... | .... | .... | 2365 | 77 | *6 | *1.95 | *18 | .... | .... | *1141 | 39 | 2 | 2.05 |
| 2001-02 | HC Lugano | Swiss | 39 | .... | .... | .... | 2313 | 107 | *4 | 2.78 | 1 | 0 | 1 | 60 | 3 | 0 | 3.00 |
| | France | Olympics | 3 | 0 | 2 | 1 | 179 | 10 | 0 | 3.36 | .... | .... | .... | .... | .... | .... | .... |
| | France | WC-B | 5 | 4 | 1 | 0 | 299 | 5 | 2 | 1.00 | .... | .... | .... | .... | .... | .... | .... |
| **2002-03** | **Los Angeles** | **NHL** | **12** | **4** | **4** | **1** | **541** | **21** | **1** | **2.33** | .... | .... | .... | .... | .... | .... | .... |
| | Manchester | AHL | 30 | 16 | 8 | 5 | 1784 | 68 | 1 | 2.29 | 1 | 0 | 1 | 30 | 4 | 0 | 8.08 |
| **2003-04** | **Los Angeles** | **NHL** | **41** | **10** | **16** | **10** | **2199** | **89** | **3** | **2.43** | .... | .... | .... | .... | .... | .... | .... |
| 2004-05 | Adler Mannheim | Germany | 36 | .... | .... | .... | 2001 | 93 | 1 | 2.79 | *14 | .... | .... | *850 | 40 | 2 | 2.82 |
| **2005-06** | **Montreal** | **NHL** | **36** | **18** | **11** | **4** | **2103** | **77** | **7** | **2.20** | **6** | **2** | **4** | **386** | **15** | **0** | **2.33** |
| | Hamilton Bulldogs | AHL | 4 | 0 | 4 | 0 | 237 | 15 | 0 | 3.79 | .... | .... | .... | .... | .... | .... | .... |
| **2006-07** | **Montreal** | **NHL** | **42** | **19** | **16** | **3** | **2286** | **107** | **2** | **2.81** | .... | .... | .... | .... | .... | .... | .... |
| **2007-08** | **Montreal** | **NHL** | **39** | **21** | **12** | **6** | **2278** | **97** | **2** | **2.55** | .... | .... | .... | .... | .... | .... | .... |
| | **Washington** | **NHL** | **13** | **11** | **2** | **0** | **771** | **21** | **2** | **1.63** | **7** | **3** | **4** | **451** | **22** | **0** | **2.93** |
| **2008-09** | **Chicago** | **NHL** | **41** | **20** | **15** | **4** | **2351** | **99** | **3** | **2.53** | **3** | **1** | **2** | **130** | **7** | **0** | **3.23** |
| | **NHL Totals** | | **224** | **103** | **76** | **28** | **12529** | **511** | **20** | **2.45** | **16** | **6** | **10** | **967** | **44** | **0** | **2.73** |

Played in NHL All-Star Game (2007)

Traded to **Montreal** by **Los Angeles** with Radek Bonk for Mathieu Garon and San Jose's 3rd round choice (previously acquired, Los Angeles selected Piaul Baier) in 2004 Entry Draft, June 26, 2004. Signed as a free agent by **Mannheim** (Germany), September 14, 2004. Traded to **Washington** by **Montreal** for Anaheim's 2nd round choice (previously acquired, later traded to Atlanta – Atlanta selected Jeremy Morin) in 2009 Entry Draft, February 26, 2008. Signed as a free agent by **Chicago**, July 1, 2008.

## HUTCHINSON, Michael (HUH-chihn-suhn, MIGH-kuhl) BOS.

Goaltender. Catches right. 6'3", 185 lbs. Born, Barrie, Ont., March 2, 1990.
(Boston's 3rd choice, 77th overall, in 2008 Entry Draft).

| | | | Regular Season | | | | | | | | Playoffs | | | | | | |
|---|---|---|---|---|---|---|---|---|---|---|---|---|---|---|---|---|---|
| **Season** | **Club** | **League** | **GP** | **W** | **L** | **O/T** | **Mins** | **GA** | **SO** | **Avg** | **GP** | **W** | **L** | **Mins** | **GA** | **SO** | **Avg** |
| 2006-07 | Orangeville | OPJHL | 8 | 1 | 4 | 0 | 289 | 24 | 0 | 4.99 | .... | .... | .... | .... | .... | .... | .... |
| | Barrie Colts | OHL | 14 | 8 | 3 | 0 | 768 | 27 | 0 | 2.11 | 1 | 1 | 0 | 45 | 1 | 0 | 1.33 |
| 2007-08 | Barrie Colts | OHL | 32 | 12 | 15 | 4 | 1826 | 92 | 1 | 3.02 | 8 | 4 | 4 | 500 | 22 | 1 | 2.64 |
| 2008-09 | Barrie Colts | OHL | 38 | 15 | 20 | 1 | 2146 | 108 | 5 | 3.02 | 3 | 0 | 2 | 112 | 10 | 0 | 5.37 |

## IRVING, Leland (UHR-vihng, LEE-land) CGY.

Goaltender. Catches left. 6', 177 lbs. Born, Barrhead, Alta., April 11, 1988.
(Calgary's 1st choice, 26th overall, in 2006 Entry Draft).

| | | | Regular Season | | | | | | | | Playoffs | | | | | | |
|---|---|---|---|---|---|---|---|---|---|---|---|---|---|---|---|---|---|
| Season | Club | League | GP | W | L | O/T | Mins | GA | SO | Avg | GP | W | L | Mins | GA | SO | Avg |
| 2002-03 | Spruce Grove | AMBHL | .... | 11 | 11 | 4 | 1559 | 94 | .... | 3.62 | .... | .... | .... | .... | .... | .... | .... |
| 2003-04 | Spruce Grove | RAMHL | 19 | .... | .... | .... | 1017 | 44 | 1 | 2.60 | .... | .... | .... | .... | .... | .... | .... |
| | Everett Silvertips | WHL | 1 | 0 | 0 | 0 | 8 | 0 | 0 | 0.00 | .... | .... | .... | .... | .... | .... | .... |
| 2004-05 | Everett Silvertips | WHL | 23 | 9 | 8 | 1 | 1132 | 34 | 2 | 1.80 | .... | .... | .... | .... | .... | .... | .... |
| 2005-06 | Everett Silvertips | WHL | *67 | 37 | 22 | 4 | *3791 | 121 | 4 | 1.92 | 12 | 8 | 4 | 747 | 21 | 3 | 1.69 |
| 2006-07 | Everett Silvertips | WHL | 48 | 34 | 9 | 3 | 2802 | 87 | *11 | 1.86 | 12 | 6 | 5 | 639 | 30 | 0 | 2.82 |
| 2007-08 | Everett Silvertips | WHL | 56 | 27 | 24 | 0 | 3258 | 133 | 4 | 2.45 | 3 | 0 | 3 | 139 | 10 | 0 | 4.32 |
| 2008-09 | Quad City Flames | AHL | 47 | 24 | 18 | 2 | 2658 | 99 | 1 | 2.23 | .... | .... | .... | .... | .... | .... | .... |

WHL West Second All-Star Team (2006, 2007)

## JANUS, Jaroslav (YA-nuhs, YAHR-roh-slav) T.B.

Goaltender. Catches left. 5'11", 192 lbs. Born, Presov, Czechoslovakia, September 21, 1989.
(Tampa Bay's 6th choice, 162nd overall, in 2009 Entry Draft).

| | | | Regular Season | | | | | | | | Playoffs | | | | | | |
|---|---|---|---|---|---|---|---|---|---|---|---|---|---|---|---|---|---|
| Season | Club | League | GP | W | L | O/T | Mins | GA | SO | Avg | GP | W | L | Mins | GA | SO | Avg |
| 2003-04 | Presov U18 | Svk-U18 | 14 | .... | .... | .... | .... | .... | .... | .... | .... | .... | .... | .... | .... | .... | .... |
| 2004-05 | PHK Presov U18 | Svk-U18 | 34 | .... | .... | .... | 1743 | 53 | 3 | 1.82 | .... | .... | .... | .... | .... | .... | .... |
| | PHK Presov Jr. | Slovak-Jr. | 1 | .... | .... | .... | 60 | 7 | 0 | 7.00 | 1 | .... | .... | 23 | 1 | 0 | 2.61 |
| 2005-06 | Bratislava U18 | Svk-U18 | 37 | .... | .... | .... | 1913 | 92 | 2 | 2.89 | 8 | .... | .... | 486 | 19 | 0 | 2.34 |
| | Bratislava Jr. | Slovak-Jr. | 13 | .... | .... | .... | 609 | 25 | 0 | 2.46 | .... | .... | .... | .... | .... | .... | .... |
| 2006-07 | Bratislava U18 | Svk-U18 | 35 | .... | .... | .... | 2010 | 84 | 1 | 2.51 | .... | .... | .... | .... | .... | .... | .... |
| | Bratislava Jr. | Slovak-Jr. | 24 | .... | .... | .... | 1355 | 49 | 4 | 2.17 | 1 | .... | .... | 33 | 4 | 0 | 7.28 |
| 2007-08 | Erie Otters | OHL | 48 | 13 | 29 | 3 | 2740 | 201 | 0 | 4.40 | .... | .... | .... | .... | .... | .... | .... |
| 2008-09 | Erie Otters | OHL | 49 | 25 | 20 | 4 | 2818 | 152 | 3 | 3.24 | 5 | 1 | 4 | 285 | 20 | *1 | 4.21 |

## JOHNSON, Brent (JAWN-suhn, BREHNT) PIT.

Goaltender. Catches left. 6'3", 199 lbs. Born, Farmington, MI, March 12, 1977.
(Colorado's 5th choice, 129th overall, in 1995 Entry Draft).

| | | | Regular Season | | | | | | | | Playoffs | | | | | | |
|---|---|---|---|---|---|---|---|---|---|---|---|---|---|---|---|---|---|
| Season | Club | League | GP | W | L | O/T | Mins | GA | SO | Avg | GP | W | L | Mins | GA | SO | Avg |
| 1993-94 | Det. Compuware | NAHL | 18 | .... | .... | .... | 1024 | 49 | 1 | 3.52 | .... | .... | .... | .... | .... | .... | .... |
| 1994-95 | Owen Sound | OHL | 18 | 3 | 9 | 1 | 904 | 75 | 0 | 4.98 | .... | .... | .... | .... | .... | .... | .... |
| 1995-96 | Owen Sound | OHL | 58 | 24 | 28 | 1 | 3211 | 243 | 1 | 4.54 | 6 | 2 | 4 | 371 | 29 | 0 | 4.69 |
| 1996-97 | Owen Sound | OHL | 50 | 20 | 28 | 1 | 2798 | 201 | 1 | 4.31 | 4 | 0 | 4 | 253 | 24 | 0 | 5.69 |
| 1997-98 | Worcester IceCats | AHL | 42 | 14 | 15 | 7 | 2240 | 119 | 0 | 3.19 | 6 | 3 | 2 | 332 | 19 | 0 | 3.43 |
| **1998-99** | **St. Louis** | **NHL** | **6** | **3** | **2** | **0** | **286** | **10** | **0** | **2.10** | .... | .... | .... | .... | .... | .... | .... |
| | Worcester IceCats | AHL | 49 | 22 | 22 | 4 | 2925 | 146 | 2 | 2.99 | 4 | 1 | 3 | 238 | 12 | 0 | 3.02 |
| 99-2000 | Worcester IceCats | AHL | 58 | 24 | 27 | 5 | 3319 | 161 | 3 | 2.91 | 9 | 4 | 5 | 561 | 23 | 1 | 2.46 |
| **2000-01** | **St. Louis** | **NHL** | **31** | **19** | **9** | **2** | **1744** | **63** | **4** | **2.17** | **2** | **0** | **1** | **62** | **2** | **0** | **1.94** |
| **2001-02** | **St. Louis** | **NHL** | **58** | **34** | **20** | **4** | **3491** | **127** | **5** | **2.18** | **10** | **5** | **5** | **590** | **18** | **3** | **1.83** |
| **2002-03** | **St. Louis** | **NHL** | **38** | **16** | **13** | **5** | **2042** | **84** | **2** | **2.47** | .... | .... | .... | .... | .... | .... | .... |
| | Worcester IceCats | AHL | 2 | 0 | 1 | 1 | 125 | 8 | 0 | 3.84 | .... | .... | .... | .... | .... | .... | .... |
| **2003-04** | **St. Louis** | **NHL** | **10** | **4** | **3** | **1** | **493** | **20** | **1** | **2.43** | .... | .... | .... | .... | .... | .... | .... |
| | Worcester IceCats | AHL | 8 | 2 | 2 | 2 | 365 | 14 | 0 | 2.30 | .... | .... | .... | .... | .... | .... | .... |
| | **Phoenix** | **NHL** | **8** | **1** | **6** | **1** | **486** | **21** | **0** | **2.59** | .... | .... | .... | .... | .... | .... | .... |
| 2004-05 | | | | | | | DID NOT PLAY | | | | | | | | | | |
| **2005-06** | **Washington** | **NHL** | **26** | **9** | **12** | **1** | **1413** | **81** | **1** | **3.44** | .... | .... | .... | .... | .... | .... | .... |
| **2006-07** | **Washington** | **NHL** | **30** | **6** | **15** | **7** | **1644** | **99** | **0** | **3.61** | .... | .... | .... | .... | .... | .... | .... |
| **2007-08** | **Washington** | **NHL** | **19** | **7** | **8** | **2** | **1032** | **46** | **0** | **2.67** | .... | .... | .... | .... | .... | .... | .... |
| | Hershey Bears | AHL | 1 | 0 | 1 | 0 | 59 | 3 | 0 | 3.04 | .... | .... | .... | .... | .... | .... | .... |
| **2008-09** | **Washington** | **NHL** | **21** | **12** | **6** | **2** | **1131** | **53** | **0** | **2.81** | .... | .... | .... | .... | .... | .... | .... |
| | **NHL Totals** | | **247** | **111** | **94** | **25** | **13762** | **604** | **13** | **2.63** | **12** | **5** | **6** | **652** | **20** | **3** | **1.84** |

Traded to **St. Louis** by **Colorado** for San Jose's 3rd round choice (previously acquired, Colorado selected Rick Berry) in 1997 Entry Draft, May 30, 1997. Traded to **Phoenix** by **St. Louis** for Mike Sillinger, March 4, 2004. Signed as a free agent by **Vancouver**, September 1, 2005. Claimed on waivers by **Washington** from **Vancouver**, October 4, 2005. Signed as a free agent by **Pittsburgh**, July 21, 2009.

## JOHNSON, Chad (JAWN-suhn, CHAD) NYR

Goaltender. Catches left. 6'2", 175 lbs. Born, Calgary, Alta., June 10, 1986.
(Pittsburgh's 4th choice, 125th overall, in 2006 Entry Draft).

| | | | Regular Season | | | | | | | | Playoffs | | | | | | |
|---|---|---|---|---|---|---|---|---|---|---|---|---|---|---|---|---|---|
| Season | Club | League | GP | W | L | O/T | Mins | GA | SO | Avg | GP | W | L | Mins | GA | SO | Avg |
| 2002-03 | Calgary Buffaloes | AMHL | .... | 8 | 8 | 2 | 1145 | 62 | .... | 3.25 | 1 | 0 | 1 | 60 | 3 | 0 | 3.00 |
| 2003-04 | Brooks Bandits | AJHL | 31 | 6 | 20 | 3 | 1782 | 117 | 0 | 3.94 | .... | .... | .... | .... | .... | .... | .... |
| 2004-05 | Brooks Bandits | AJHL | 43 | 25 | 16 | 2 | 2505 | 109 | 2 | 2.61 | 119 | 4 | 5 | 493 | .... | .... | .... |
| 2005-06 | Alaska | CCHA | 18 | 6 | 7 | 4 | 985 | 42 | 0 | 2.56 | .... | .... | .... | .... | .... | .... | .... |
| 2006-07 | Alaska | CCHA | 19 | 5 | 6 | 2 | 1002 | 52 | 1 | 3.11 | .... | .... | .... | .... | .... | .... | .... |
| 2007-08 | Alaska | CCHA | 7 | 0 | 6 | 0 | 357 | 20 | 0 | 3.36 | .... | .... | .... | .... | .... | .... | .... |
| 2008-09 | Alaska | CCHA | 35 | 14 | 16 | 5 | 2062 | 57 | 6 | *1.66 | .... | .... | .... | .... | .... | .... | .... |

AJHL South Division First All-Star Team (2005) • CCHA First All-Star Team (2009) • CCHA Rookie of the Year (2009) • NCAA West Second All-American Team (2009)

Traded to **NY Rangers** by **Pittsburgh** for Pittsburgh's 5th round choice (previously acquired, Pittsburgh selected Andy Bathgate) in 2009 Entry Draft, June 27, 2009.

## JONES, Martin (JOHNZ, MAR-tihn) L.A.

Goaltender. Catches left. 6'3", 181 lbs. Born, North Vancouver, B.C., January 10, 1990.

| | | | Regular Season | | | | | | | | Playoffs | | | | | | |
|---|---|---|---|---|---|---|---|---|---|---|---|---|---|---|---|---|---|
| Season | Club | League | GP | W | L | O/T | Mins | GA | SO | Avg | GP | W | L | Mins | GA | SO | Avg |
| 2006-07 | Calgary Hitmen | WHL | 18 | 9 | 4 | 3 | 1029 | 52 | 0 | 3.03 | .... | .... | .... | .... | .... | .... | .... |
| 2007-08 | Calgary Hitmen | WHL | 27 | 18 | 8 | 1 | 1529 | 54 | 1 | 2.12 | 5 | 2 | 1 | 250 | 12 | 0 | 2.88 |
| 2008-09 | Calgary Hitmen | WHL | 55 | *45 | 5 | 4 | 3295 | 114 | *7 | 2.08 | 18 | 14 | 4 | 1095 | 34 | 2 | 1.86 |

WHL East Second All-Star Team (2009)

Signed as a free agent by **Los Angeles**, October 2, 2008.

## JOSEPH, Curtis (JOH-sehf, KUHR-tihs)

Goaltender. Catches left. 5'11", 193 lbs. Born, Keswick, Ont., April 29, 1967.

| | | | Regular Season | | | | | | | | Playoffs | | | | | | |
|---|---|---|---|---|---|---|---|---|---|---|---|---|---|---|---|---|---|
| Season | Club | League | GP | W | L | O/T | Mins | GA | SO | Avg | GP | W | L | Mins | GA | SO | Avg |
| 1984-85 | King City Dukes | OHA-B | 18 | .... | .... | .... | 947 | 76 | 0 | 4.82 | .... | .... | .... | .... | .... | .... | .... |
| | Newmarket Flyers | OPJHL | 2 | 1 | 1 | 0 | 120 | 16 | 0 | 8.00 | .... | .... | .... | .... | .... | .... | .... |
| 1985-86 | Richmond Hill | OPJHL | 33 | 12 | 18 | 0 | 1716 | 156 | 1 | 5.45 | .... | .... | .... | .... | .... | .... | .... |
| 1986-87 | Richmond Hill | OPJHL | 30 | 14 | 7 | 6 | 1764 | 128 | 1 | 4.35 | .... | .... | .... | .... | .... | .... | .... |
| 1987-88 | Notre Dame | SJHL | 36 | 25 | 4 | 7 | 2174 | 94 | 1 | 2.59 | .... | .... | .... | .... | .... | .... | .... |
| 1988-89 | U. of Wisconsin | WCHA | 38 | 21 | 11 | 5 | 2267 | 94 | 1 | 2.49 | .... | .... | .... | .... | .... | .... | .... |
| **1989-90** | **St. Louis** | **NHL** | **15** | **9** | **5** | **1** | **852** | **48** | **0** | **3.38** | **6** | **4** | **1** | **327** | **18** | **0** | **3.30** |
| | Peoria Rivermen | IHL | 23 | 10 | 8 | 2 | 1241 | 80 | 0 | 3.87 | .... | .... | .... | .... | .... | .... | .... |
| **1990-91** | **St. Louis** | **NHL** | **30** | **16** | **10** | **2** | **1710** | **89** | **0** | **3.12** | .... | .... | .... | .... | .... | .... | .... |
| **1991-92** | **St. Louis** | **NHL** | **60** | **27** | **20** | **10** | **3494** | **175** | **2** | **3.01** | **6** | **2** | **4** | **379** | **23** | **0** | **3.64** |
| **1992-93** | **St. Louis** | **NHL** | **68** | **29** | **28** | **9** | **3890** | **196** | **1** | **3.02** | **11** | **7** | **4** | **715** | **27** | ***2** | **2.27** |
| **1993-94** | **St. Louis** | **NHL** | **71** | **36** | **23** | **11** | **4127** | **213** | **1** | **3.10** | **4** | **0** | **4** | **246** | **15** | **0** | **3.66** |
| **1994-95** | **St. Louis** | **NHL** | **36** | **20** | **10** | **1** | **1914** | **89** | **1** | **2.79** | **7** | **3** | **3** | **392** | **24** | **0** | **3.67** |
| **1995-96** | Las Vegas Thunder | IHL | 15 | 12 | 2 | 1 | 874 | 29 | 1 | 1.99 | .... | .... | .... | .... | .... | .... | .... |
| | **Edmonton** | **NHL** | **34** | **15** | **16** | **2** | **1936** | **111** | **0** | **3.44** | .... | .... | .... | .... | .... | .... | .... |
| **1996-97** | **Edmonton** | **NHL** | **72** | **32** | **29** | **9** | **4100** | **200** | **6** | **2.93** | **12** | **5** | **7** | **767** | **36** | **2** | **2.82** |
| **1997-98** | **Edmonton** | **NHL** | **71** | **29** | **31** | **9** | **4132** | **181** | **8** | **2.63** | **12** | **5** | **7** | **716** | **23** | **3** | **1.93** |
| **1998-99** | **Toronto** | **NHL** | **67** | **35** | **24** | **7** | **4001** | **171** | **3** | **2.56** | **17** | **9** | **8** | **1011** | **41** | **1** | **2.43** |
| **99-2000** | **Toronto** | **NHL** | **63** | **36** | **20** | **7** | **3801** | **158** | **4** | **2.49** | **12** | **6** | **6** | **729** | **25** | **1** | **2.06** |
| **2000-01** | **Toronto** | **NHL** | **68** | **33** | **27** | **8** | **4100** | **163** | **6** | **2.39** | **11** | **7** | **4** | **685** | **24** | **3** | **2.10** |
| **2001-02** | **Toronto** | **NHL** | **51** | **29** | **17** | **5** | **3065** | **114** | **4** | **2.23** | **20** | **10** | **10** | **1253** | **48** | **3** | **2.30** |
| | Canada | Olympics | 1 | 0 | 1 | 0 | 60 | 5 | 0 | 5.00 | .... | .... | .... | .... | .... | .... | .... |
| **2002-03** | **Detroit** | **NHL** | **61** | **34** | **19** | **6** | **3566** | **148** | **5** | **2.49** | **4** | **0** | **4** | **289** | **10** | **0** | **2.08** |
| **2003-04** | **Detroit** | **NHL** | **31** | **16** | **10** | **3** | **1708** | **68** | **2** | **2.39** | **9** | **4** | **4** | **518** | **12** | **1** | ***1.39** |
| | Grand Rapids | AHL | 1 | 1 | 0 | 0 | 60 | 1 | 0 | 1.00 | .... | .... | .... | .... | .... | .... | .... |
| 2004-05 | | | | | | | DID NOT PLAY | | | | | | | | | | |
| **2005-06** | **Phoenix** | **NHL** | **60** | **32** | **21** | **3** | **3424** | **166** | **4** | **2.91** | .... | .... | .... | .... | .... | .... | .... |
| **2006-07** | **Phoenix** | **NHL** | **55** | **18** | **31** | **2** | **2993** | **159** | **4** | **3.19** | .... | .... | .... | .... | .... | .... | .... |
| **2007-08** | **Calgary** | **NHL** | **9** | **3** | **2** | **0** | **400** | **17** | **0** | **2.55** | **2** | **1** | **0** | **79** | **1** | **0** | **0.76** |
| **2008-09** | **Toronto** | **NHL** | **21** | **5** | **9** | **1** | **841** | **50** | **0** | **3.57** | .... | .... | .... | .... | .... | .... | .... |
| | **NHL Totals** | | **943** | **454** | **352** | **96** | **54054** | **2516** | **51** | **2.79** | **133** | **63** | **66** | **8106** | **327** | **16** | **2.42** |

WCHA First All-Star Team (1989) • WCHA Freshman of the Year (1989) • WCHA Most Valuable Player (1989) • NCAA West Second All-American Team (1989) • King Clancy Memorial Trophy (2000)

Played in NHL All-Star Game (1994, 2000)

Signed as a free agent by **St. Louis**, June 16, 1989. Traded to **Edmonton** by **St. Louis** with the rights to Mike Grier for St. Louis' 1st round choices (previously acquired) in 1996 (Marty Reasoner) and 1997 (later traded to Los Angeles – Los Angeles selected Matt Zultek) Entry Drafts, August 4, 1995. Signed as a free agent by **Toronto**, July 15, 1998. Traded to **Calgary** by **Toronto** for Calgary's 3rd round choice (later traded to Minnesota – Minnesota selected Danny Irmen) in 2003 Entry Draft and future considerations, June 30, 2002. Signed as a free agent by **Detroit**, July 2, 2002. Signed as a free agent by **Phoenix**, August 17, 2005. Signed as a free agent by **Calgary**, January 17, 2008. Signed as a free agent by **Toronto**, July 1, 2008.

## KANGAS, Alex (KANG-uhs, AL-ehx) ATL.

Goaltender. Catches left. 6'2", 175 lbs. Born, Rochester, NY, May 28, 1987.
(Atlanta's 4th choice, 135th overall, in 2006 Entry Draft).

| | | | Regular Season | | | | | | | | Playoffs | | | | | | |
|---|---|---|---|---|---|---|---|---|---|---|---|---|---|---|---|---|---|
| Season | Club | League | GP | W | L | O/T | Mins | GA | SO | Avg | GP | W | L | Mins | GA | SO | Avg |
| 2001-02 | Rochester Century | High-MN | 3 | 3 | 0 | 0 | .... | 3 | 2 | 1.00 | .... | .... | .... | .... | .... | .... | .... |
| 2002-03 | Rochester Century | High-MN | 27 | 17 | 9 | 0 | .... | 50 | 6 | 1.76 | .... | .... | .... | .... | .... | .... | .... |
| 2003-04 | Rochester Century | High-MN | 28 | 15 | 12 | 1 | .... | 59 | 3 | 2.08 | .... | .... | .... | .... | .... | .... | .... |
| 2004-05 | Rochester Century | High-MN | 30 | 23 | 4 | 3 | .... | 55 | 7 | 1.86 | .... | .... | .... | .... | .... | .... | .... |
| 2005-06 | Sioux Falls | USHL | 29 | 20 | 6 | 3 | 1733 | 62 | 3 | 2.15 | 6 | 4 | 2 | 359 | 17 | 0 | 2.84 |
| 2006-07 | Indiana Ice | USHL | 46 | 19 | 19 | 5 | 2467 | 136 | 1 | 3.31 | 7 | 6 | 1 | 434 | 18 | 0 | 2.49 |
| 2007-08 | U. of Minnesota | WCHA | 31 | 12 | 10 | 9 | 1967 | 65 | 0 | 1.98 | .... | .... | .... | .... | .... | .... | .... |
| 2008-09 | U. of Minnesota | WCHA | 36 | 17 | 11 | 6 | 2019 | 94 | 3 | 2.79 | .... | .... | .... | .... | .... | .... | .... |

USHL All-Rookie Team (2006)

## KARPOWICH, Paul (KAHR-puh-wihch, PAWL) ST.L.

Goaltender. Catches left. 6'2", 190 lbs. Born, Thunder Bay, Ont., October 25, 1988.
(St. Louis' 10th choice, 185th overall, in 2008 Entry Draft).

| | | | Regular Season | | | | | | | | Playoffs | | | | | | |
|---|---|---|---|---|---|---|---|---|---|---|---|---|---|---|---|---|---|
| Season | Club | League | GP | W | L | O/T | Mins | GA | SO | Avg | GP | W | L | Mins | GA | SO | Avg |
| 2004-05 | Thunder Bay Kings | Minor-ON | 38 | 25 | 7 | 3 | 2057 | 103 | 2 | 3.00 | .... | .... | .... | .... | .... | .... | .... |
| 2005-06 | Thunder Bay Kings | Minor-ON | 42 | 29 | 8 | 3 | 2280 | 91 | 6 | 2.39 | .... | .... | .... | .... | .... | .... | .... |
| 2006-07 | Brooks Bandits | AJHL | 18 | 6 | 6 | 2 | 1010 | 59 | 0 | 3.51 | 2 | 1 | 0 | 92 | 8 | 0 | 5.21 |
| 2007-08 | Wellington Dukes | OPJHL | 22 | 15 | 3 | 2 | 1202 | 43 | 3 | 2.15 | 13 | 9 | 4 | 771 | 35 | 1 | 2.72 |
| 2008-09 | Clarkson Knights | ECAC | 27 | 7 | 14 | 4 | 1516 | 72 | 1 | 2.85 | .... | .... | .... | .... | .... | .... | .... |

## KEETLEY, Matt (KEET-lee, MAT) CGY.

Goaltender. Catches right. 6'1", 187 lbs. Born, Medicine Hat, Alta., April 27, 1986.
(Calgary's 6th choice, 158th overall, in 2005 Entry Draft).

| | | | Regular Season | | | | | | | | Playoffs | | | | | | |
|---|---|---|---|---|---|---|---|---|---|---|---|---|---|---|---|---|---|
| Season | Club | League | GP | W | L | O/T | Mins | GA | SO | Avg | GP | W | L | Mins | GA | SO | Avg |
| 2003-04 | Medicine Hat | AMHL | .... | 7 | 4 | 2 | 813 | 48 | .... | 3.54 | .... | .... | .... | .... | .... | .... | .... |
| | Medicine Hat | WHL | 3 | 0 | 1 | 0 | 72 | 5 | 0 | 4.17 | 2 | 0 | 0 | 15 | 1 | 0 | 4.00 |
| 2004-05 | Medicine Hat | WHL | 32 | 21 | 5 | 3 | 1846 | 51 | 6 | *1.66 | 3 | 1 | 0 | 103 | 8 | 0 | 4.66 |
| 2005-06 | Medicine Hat | WHL | 62 | *42 | 13 | 6 | 3741 | 130 | 6 | 2.09 | 13 | 9 | 4 | 864 | 30 | 0 | 2.08 |
| 2006-07 | Medicine Hat | WHL | 55 | *42 | 11 | 1 | 3258 | 119 | 6 | 2.19 | *23 | *16 | 7 | *1407 | 51 | *4 | 2.18 |
| **2007-08** | **Calgary** | **NHL** | **1** | **0** | **0** | **0** | **9** | **0** | **0** | **0.00** | .... | .... | .... | .... | .... | .... | .... |
| | Quad City Flames | AHL | 26 | 10 | 8 | 3 | 1393 | 54 | 1 | 2.33 | .... | .... | .... | .... | .... | .... | .... |
| 2008-09 | Quad City Flames | AHL | 33 | 8 | 18 | 4 | 1853 | 88 | 2 | 2.85 | .... | .... | .... | .... | .... | .... | .... |
| | Las Vegas | ECHL | 7 | 1 | 3 | 3 | 429 | 19 | 0 | 2.66 | .... | .... | .... | .... | .... | .... | .... |
| | **NHL Totals** | | **1** | **0** | **0** | **0** | **9** | **0** | **0** | **0.00** | .... | .... | .... | .... | .... | .... | .... |

WHL East Second All-Star Team (2006) • WHL East First All-Star Team (2007) • Memorial Cup Tournament All-Star Team (2007) • Hap Emms Memorial Trophy (Memorial Cup Tournament - Top Goaltender) (2007)

## KHABIBULIN, Nikolai (khah-bee-BOO-lihn, NIH-koh-ligh) EDM.

Goaltender. Catches left. 6'1", 209 lbs. Born, Sverdlovsk, USSR, January 13, 1973.
(Winnipeg's 8th choice, 204th overall, in 1992 Entry Draft).

| | | | Regular Season | | | | | | | | Playoffs | | | | | | |
|---|---|---|---|---|---|---|---|---|---|---|---|---|---|---|---|---|---|
| Season | Club | League | GP | W | L | O/T | Mins | GA | SO | Avg | GP | W | L | Mins | GA | SO | Avg |
| 1988-89 | Sverdlovsk | USSR | 1 | .... | .... | .... | 3 | 0 | 0 | 0.00 | .... | .... | .... | .... | .... | .... | .... |
| 1989-90 | Luch Sverdlovsk | USSR-2 | | | | | STATISTICS NOT AVAILABLE | | | | | | | | | | |
| 1990-91 | Nizhny Tagil | USSR-3 | 10 | .... | .... | .... | .... | .... | .... | .... | .... | .... | .... | .... | .... | .... | .... |
| | Sverdlovsk | USSR-Q | 2 | .... | .... | .... | .... | 7 | .... | .... | .... | .... | .... | .... | .... | .... | .... |
| 1991-92 | CSKA Moscow 2 | CIS-3 | 11 | .... | .... | .... | .... | .... | .... | .... | .... | .... | .... | .... | .... | .... | .... |
| | CSKA Moscow | CIS | 2 | .... | .... | .... | 34 | 2 | 0 | 3.53 | .... | .... | .... | .... | .... | .... | .... |
| | Russia | Olympics | | | | | DID NOT PLAY – SPARE GOALTENDER | | | | | | | | | | |
| 1992-93 | CSKA Moscow | CIS | 13 | .... | .... | .... | 491 | 27 | .... | 3.29 | .... | .... | .... | .... | .... | .... | .... |
| | Serov | CIS-2 | 18 | .... | .... | .... | .... | .... | .... | .... | .... | .... | .... | .... | .... | .... | .... |
| 1993-94 | CSKA Moscow | CIS | 46 | .... | .... | .... | 2625 | 116 | .... | 2.65 | .... | .... | .... | .... | .... | .... | .... |
| | Russian Penguins | IHL | 12 | 2 | 7 | 2 | 639 | 47 | 0 | 4.41 | .... | .... | .... | .... | .... | .... | .... |
| **1994-95** | Springfield Indians | AHL | 23 | 9 | 9 | 3 | 1240 | 80 | 0 | 3.87 | .... | .... | .... | .... | .... | .... | .... |
| | **Winnipeg** | **NHL** | **26** | **8** | **9** | **4** | **1339** | **76** | **0** | **3.41** | .... | .... | .... | .... | .... | .... | .... |
| **1995-96** | **Winnipeg** | **NHL** | **53** | **26** | **20** | **3** | **2914** | **152** | **2** | **3.13** | **6** | **2** | **4** | **359** | **19** | **0** | **3.18** |
| **1996-97** | **Phoenix** | **NHL** | **72** | **30** | **33** | **6** | **4091** | **193** | **7** | **2.83** | **7** | **3** | **4** | **426** | **15** | **1** | **2.11** |
| **1997-98** | **Phoenix** | **NHL** | **70** | **30** | **28** | **10** | **4026** | **184** | **4** | **2.74** | **4** | **2** | **1** | **185** | **13** | **0** | **4.22** |
| **1998-99** | **Phoenix** | **NHL** | **63** | **32** | **23** | **7** | **3657** | **130** | **8** | **2.13** | **7** | **3** | **4** | **449** | **18** | **0** | **2.41** |
| 99-2000 | Long Beach | IHL | 33 | 21 | 11 | 1 | 1936 | 59 | 5 | *1.83 | 5 | 2 | 3 | 321 | 15 | 0 | 2.81 |
| **2000-01** | **Tampa Bay** | **NHL** | **2** | **1** | **1** | **0** | **123** | **6** | **0** | **2.93** | .... | .... | .... | .... | .... | .... | .... |
| **2001-02** | **Tampa Bay** | **NHL** | **70** | **24** | **32** | **10** | **3896** | **153** | **7** | **2.36** | .... | .... | .... | .... | .... | .... | .... |
| | Russia | Olympics | 6 | 3 | 2 | 1 | *359 | 14 | *1 | 2.34 | .... | .... | .... | .... | .... | .... | .... |
| **2002-03** | **Tampa Bay** | **NHL** | **65** | **30** | **22** | **11** | **3787** | **156** | **4** | **2.47** | **10** | **5** | **5** | **644** | **26** | **0** | **2.42** |
| **2003-04** ♦ | **Tampa Bay** | **NHL** | **55** | **28** | **19** | **7** | **3274** | **127** | **3** | **2.33** | **23** | ***16** | **7** | **1401** | **40** | ***5** | **1.71** |
| 2004-05 | Ak Bars Kazan | Russia | 24 | .... | .... | .... | 1457 | 40 | 5 | 1.65 | 2 | .... | .... | 118 | 6 | 0 | 3.04 |
| **2005-06** | **Chicago** | **NHL** | **50** | **17** | **26** | **6** | **2815** | **157** | **0** | **3.35** | .... | .... | .... | .... | .... | .... | .... |
| | Russia | Olympics | | | | | DID NOT PLAY – INJURED | | | | | | | | | | |
| **2006-07** | **Chicago** | **NHL** | **60** | **25** | **26** | **5** | **3425** | **163** | **1** | **2.86** | .... | .... | .... | .... | .... | .... | .... |
| **2007-08** | **Chicago** | **NHL** | **50** | **23** | **20** | **6** | **2892** | **127** | **2** | **2.63** | .... | .... | .... | .... | .... | .... | .... |

| | | | | | | | | | | | | | | | | | |
|---|---|---|---|---|---|---|---|---|---|---|---|---|---|---|---|---|---|
| 2008-09 | Chicago | NHL | 42 | 25 | 8 | 7 | 2467 | 96 | 3 | 2.33 | 15 | 8 | 6 | 881 | 43 | 0 | 2.93 |
| | NHL Totals | | 678 | 299 | 267 | 82 | 38706 | 1720 | 41 | 2.67 | 72 | 39 | 31 | 4345 | 174 | 6 | 2.40 |

James Gatschene Memorial Trophy (IHL – MVP) (2000) (co-winner - Frederic Chabot)

Played in NHL All-Star Game (1998, 1999, 2002, 2003)

• Transferred to **Phoenix** after **Winnipeg** franchise relocated, July 1, 1996. • Missed entire 1999-2000 NHL season and majority of 2000-01 season after failing to come to contract terms with **Phoenix**. Signed as a free agent by **Long Beach** (IHL) with **Phoenix** retaining NHL rights, January 14, 2000. Traded to **Tampa Bay** by **Phoenix** with Stan Neckar for Mike Johnson, Paul Mara, Ruslan Zainullin and NY Islanders' 2nd round choice (previously acquired, Phoenix selected Matthew Spiller) in 2001 Entry Draft, March 5, 2001. Signed as a free agent by **Kazan** (Russia), November 8, 2004. Signed as a free agent by **Chicago**, August 5, 2005. Signed as a free agent by **Edmonton**, July 1, 2009.

## KHUDOBIN, Anton (khuh-DAW-bihn, AN-tawn) MIN.

Goaltender. Catches left. 5'11", 176 lbs. Born, Ust-Kamenogorsk, USSR, May 7, 1986.
(Minnesota's 11th choice, 206th overall, in 2004 Entry Draft).

| | | | Regular Season | | | | | | | | Playoffs | | | | | | |
|---|---|---|---|---|---|---|---|---|---|---|---|---|---|---|---|---|---|
| Season | Club | League | GP | W | L | O/T | Mins | GA | SO | Avg | GP | W | L | Mins | GA | SO | Avg |
| 2003-04 | Magnitogorsk 2 | Russia-3 | 38 | .... | .... | .... | .... | 80 | .... | .... | .... | .... | .... | .... | .... | .... | .... |
| 2004-05 | Magnitogorsk | Russia | 4 | .... | .... | .... | 133 | 0 | 1 | 0.00 | .... | .... | .... | .... | .... | .... | .... |
| | Magnitogorsk 2 | Russia-3 | 27 | .... | .... | .... | .... | 52 | .... | .... | .... | .... | .... | .... | .... | .... | .... |
| 2005-06 | Saskatoon Blades | WHL | 44 | 23 | 13 | 3 | 2362 | 114 | 4 | 2.90 | 10 | 4 | 6 | 685 | 32 | 0 | 2.80 |
| 2006-07 | Magnitogorsk | Russia | 16 | .... | .... | .... | 618 | 28 | 0 | 2.72 | 3 | .... | .... | 26 | 1 | 0 | 2.30 |
| 2007-08 | Houston Aeros | AHL | 12 | 2 | 2 | 1 | 482 | 16 | 1 | 1.99 | .... | .... | .... | .... | .... | .... | .... |
| | Texas Wildcatters | ECHL | 27 | 20 | 1 | 4 | 1549 | 51 | 3 | 1.98 | 9 | 5 | 2 | 547 | 20 | 1 | 2.19 |
| 2008-09 | Houston Aeros | AHL | 10 | 3 | 6 | 1 | 512 | 26 | 0 | 3.04 | 17 | 8 | 8 | 890 | 40 | 2 | 2.70 |
| | Florida Everblades | ECHL | 33 | 18 | 10 | 1 | 1706 | 77 | 4 | 2.71 | .... | .... | .... | .... | .... | .... | .... |

ECHL First All-Star Team (2008) • ECHL Goalie of the Year (2008)

## KILLEEN, Patrick (kih-LEEN, PAT-rihk) PIT.

Goaltender. Catches left. 6'4", 194 lbs. Born, Almonte, Ont., April 15, 1990.
(Pittsburgh's 3rd choice, 180th overall, in 2008 Entry Draft).

| | | | Regular Season | | | | | | | | Playoffs | | | | | | |
|---|---|---|---|---|---|---|---|---|---|---|---|---|---|---|---|---|---|
| Season | Club | League | GP | W | L | O/T | Mins | GA | SO | Avg | GP | W | L | Mins | GA | SO | Avg |
| 2006-07 | Ottawa Jr. Sens | CJHL | 7 | 5 | 1 | 0 | 376 | 20 | 0 | 3.19 | .... | .... | .... | .... | .... | .... | .... |
| | Brampton Battalion | OHL | 8 | 1 | 3 | 0 | 304 | 29 | 0 | 5.72 | .... | .... | .... | .... | .... | .... | .... |
| 2007-08 | Brampton Battalion | OHL | 34 | 20 | 9 | 2 | 1959 | 90 | 1 | 2.76 | .... | .... | .... | .... | .... | .... | .... |
| 2008-09 | Brampton Battalion | OHL | 34 | 19 | 11 | 2 | 1916 | 91 | 2 | 2.85 | 2 | 0 | 0 | 26 | 4 | 0 | 9.27 |

## KIPRUSOFF, Miikka (KIHP-roo-sawf, MEE-kah) CGY.

Goaltender. Catches left. 6'1", 184 lbs. Born, Turku, Finland, October 26, 1976.
(San Jose's 5th choice, 116th overall, in 1995 Entry Draft).

| | | | Regular Season | | | | | | | | Playoffs | | | | | | |
|---|---|---|---|---|---|---|---|---|---|---|---|---|---|---|---|---|---|
| Season | Club | League | GP | W | L | O/T | Mins | GA | SO | Avg | GP | W | L | Mins | GA | SO | Avg |
| 1993-94 | TPS Turku Jr. | Fin-Jr. | 35 | 20 | 9 | 5 | 2101 | 100 | 0 | 2.85 | 6 | 3 | 3 | 369 | 26 | 0 | 4.23 |
| 1994-95 | TPS Turku Jr. | Fin-Jr. | 31 | 13 | 14 | 4 | 1896 | 92 | 2 | 2.91 | .... | .... | .... | .... | .... | .... | .... |
| | Kiekko-67 Turku | Finland-2 | 1 | 0 | 1 | 0 | 60 | 6 | 0 | 6.00 | .... | .... | .... | .... | .... | .... | .... |
| | TPS Turku | Finland | 4 | 3 | 1 | 0 | 240 | 12 | 0 | 3.00 | 2 | 2 | 0 | 120 | 7 | 0 | 3.50 |
| 1995-96 | TPS Turku Jr. | Fin-Jr. | 3 | 1 | 2 | 0 | 180 | 9 | 0 | 3.00 | .... | .... | .... | .... | .... | .... | .... |
| | Kiekko-67 Turku | Finland-2 | 5 | 5 | 0 | 0 | 300 | 7 | 1 | 1.40 | .... | .... | .... | .... | .... | .... | .... |
| | TPS Turku | Finland | 12 | 5 | 3 | 1 | 550 | 38 | 0 | 4.14 | 3 | 0 | 1 | 113 | 4 | 0 | 2.12 |
| 1996-97 | AIK Solna | Sweden | 42 | .... | .... | .... | 2440 | 93 | 3 | 2.29 | 7 | .... | .... | 420 | 22 | 0 | 3.14 |
| 1997-98 | AIK Solna | Sweden | 43 | .... | .... | .... | 2517 | 111 | 1 | 2.65 | .... | .... | .... | .... | .... | .... | .... |
| | AIK Solna | Sweden-Q | 9 | .... | .... | .... | 540 | 15 | 2 | 1.67 | .... | .... | .... | .... | .... | .... | .... |
| 1998-99 | TPS Turku | Finland | 39 | 26 | 6 | 6 | 2259 | 70 | 4 | 1.86 | 10 | 9 | 1 | 580 | 15 | 3 | 1.55 |
| 99-2000 | Kentucky | AHL | 47 | 23 | 19 | 4 | 2759 | 114 | 3 | 2.48 | 5 | 1 | 3 | 239 | 13 | 0 | 3.27 |
| **2000-01** | **San Jose** | **NHL** | **5** | **2** | **1** | **0** | **154** | **5** | **0** | **1.95** | **3** | **1** | **1** | **149** | **5** | **0** | **2.01** |
| | Kentucky | AHL | 36 | 19 | 9 | 6 | 2038 | 76 | 2 | 2.24 | .... | .... | .... | .... | .... | .... | .... |
| **2001-02** | **San Jose** | **NHL** | **20** | **7** | **6** | **3** | **1037** | **43** | **2** | **2.49** | **1** | **0** | **0** | **8** | **0** | **0** | **0.00** |
| | Cleveland Barons | AHL | 4 | 4 | 0 | 0 | 242 | 7 | 0 | 1.73 | .... | .... | .... | .... | .... | .... | .... |
| **2002-03** | **San Jose** | **NHL** | **22** | **5** | **14** | **0** | **1199** | **65** | **1** | **3.25** | .... | .... | .... | .... | .... | .... | .... |
| **2003-04** | **Calgary** | **NHL** | **38** | **24** | **10** | **4** | **2301** | **65** | **4** | ***1.69** | ***26** | **15** | **11** | ***1655** | **51** | ***5** | **1.85** |
| 2004-05 | Timra IK | Sweden | 46 | .... | .... | .... | 2719 | 97 | 5 | 2.14 | 6 | .... | .... | 356 | 13 | 0 | 2.19 |
| **2005-06** | **Calgary** | **NHL** | **74** | **42** | **20** | **11** | ***4380** | **151** | ***10** | ***2.07** | **7** | **3** | **4** | **428** | **16** | **0** | **2.24** |
| | Finland | Olympics | DID NOT PLAY – INJURED | | | | | | | | | | | | | | |
| **2006-07** | **Calgary** | **NHL** | **74** | **40** | **24** | **9** | **4419** | **181** | **7** | **2.46** | **6** | **2** | **4** | **384** | **18** | **0** | **2.81** |
| **2007-08** | **Calgary** | **NHL** | **76** | **39** | **26** | **10** | **4398** | **197** | **2** | **2.69** | **7** | **2** | **4** | **336** | **18** | **1** | **3.21** |
| **2008-09** | **Calgary** | **NHL** | ***76** | ***45** | **24** | **5** | ***4418** | **209** | **4** | **2.84** | **6** | **2** | **4** | **324** | **19** | **0** | **3.52** |
| | **NHL Totals** | | **385** | **204** | **125** | **42** | **22306** | **916** | **30** | **2.46** | **56** | **25** | **28** | **3284** | **127** | **6** | **2.32** |

NHL First All-Star Team (2006) • Vezina Trophy (2006)

Played in NHL All-Star Game (2007)

Traded to **Calgary** by **San Jose** for Calgary's 2nd round choice (Marc-Edouard Vlasic) in 2005 Entry Draft, November 16, 2003. Signed as a free agent by **Timra** (Sweden), September 20, 2004.

## KNAPP, Connor (NAP, KAW-nuhr) BUF.

Goaltender. Catches left. 6'5", 215 lbs. Born, New York, NY, May 1, 1990.
(Buffalo's 5th choice, 164th overall, in 2009 Entry Draft).

| | | | Regular Season | | | | | | | | Playoffs | | | | | | |
|---|---|---|---|---|---|---|---|---|---|---|---|---|---|---|---|---|---|
| Season | Club | League | GP | W | L | O/T | Mins | GA | SO | Avg | GP | W | L | Mins | GA | SO | Avg |
| 2006-07 | Bos. Jr. Bruins | EmJHL | 23 | *22 | 1 | 0 | 1340 | 37 | 3 | *1.66 | 5 | 5 | 0 | 290 | 6 | *2 | *1.24 |
| 2007-08 | Bos. Jr. Bruins | EJHL | .... | 14 | 7 | 2 | 1307 | .... | .... | 1.92 | .... | .... | .... | .... | .... | .... | .... |
| 2008-09 | Miami U. | CCHA | 23 | 13 | 5 | 3 | 1350 | 47 | 2 | 2.09 | .... | .... | .... | .... | .... | .... | .... |

## KOLZIG, Olaf (KOHL-zihg, OH-lahf)

Goaltender. Catches left. 6'3", 224 lbs. Born, Johannesburg, South Africa, April 6, 1970.
(Washington's 1st choice, 19th overall, in 1989 Entry Draft).

| | | | Regular Season | | | | | | | | Playoffs | | | | | | |
|---|---|---|---|---|---|---|---|---|---|---|---|---|---|---|---|---|---|
| Season | Club | League | GP | W | L | O/T | Mins | GA | SO | Avg | GP | W | L | Mins | GA | SO | Avg |
| 1986-87 | Abbotsford Pilots | Minor-BC | 17 | 5 | 9 | 0 | 857 | 81 | 0 | 5.67 | .... | .... | .... | .... | .... | .... | .... |
| 1987-88 | New Westminster | WHL | 15 | 6 | 5 | 0 | 650 | 48 | 1 | 4.43 | 3 | 0 | 3 | 149 | 11 | 0 | 4.43 |
| 1988-89 | Tri-City Americans | WHL | 30 | 16 | 10 | 2 | 1671 | 97 | 1 | *3.48 | .... | .... | .... | .... | .... | .... | .... |
| **1989-90** | **Washington** | **NHL** | **2** | **0** | **2** | **0** | **120** | **12** | **0** | **6.00** | .... | .... | .... | .... | .... | .... | .... |
| | Tri-City Americans | WHL | 48 | 21 | 18 | 3 | 2504 | 187 | 1 | 4.48 | 6 | 4 | 0 | 318 | 27 | 0 | 5.09 |
| 1990-91 | Baltimore Skipjacks | AHL | 26 | 10 | 12 | 1 | 1367 | 72 | 0 | 3.16 | .... | .... | .... | .... | .... | .... | .... |
| | Hampton Roads | ECHL | 21 | 11 | 9 | 1 | 1248 | 71 | 2 | 3.41 | 3 | 1 | 2 | 180 | 14 | 0 | 4.66 |
| 1991-92 | Baltimore Skipjacks | AHL | 28 | 5 | 17 | 2 | 1503 | 105 | 1 | 4.19 | .... | .... | .... | .... | .... | .... | .... |
| | Hampton Roads | ECHL | 14 | 11 | 3 | 0 | 847 | 41 | 0 | 2.90 | .... | .... | .... | .... | .... | .... | .... |
| **1992-93** | **Washington** | **NHL** | **1** | **0** | **0** | **0** | **20** | **2** | **0** | **6.00** | .... | .... | .... | .... | .... | .... | .... |
| | Rochester | AHL | 49 | 25 | 16 | 4 | 2737 | 168 | 0 | 3.68 | *17 | 9 | 8 | *1040 | 61 | 0 | 3.52 |
| **1993-94** | **Washington** | **NHL** | **7** | **0** | **3** | **0** | **224** | **20** | **0** | **5.36** | .... | .... | .... | .... | .... | .... | .... |
| | Portland Pirates | AHL | 29 | 16 | 8 | 5 | 1725 | 88 | 3 | 3.06 | 17 | *12 | 5 | 1035 | 44 | 0 | *2.55 |
| **1994-95** | **Washington** | **NHL** | **14** | **2** | **8** | **2** | **724** | **30** | **0** | **2.49** | **2** | **1** | **0** | **44** | **1** | **0** | **1.36** |
| | Portland Pirates | AHL | 2 | 1 | 0 | 1 | 125 | 3 | 0 | 1.44 | .... | .... | .... | .... | .... | .... | .... |
| **1995-96** | **Washington** | **NHL** | **18** | **4** | **8** | **2** | **897** | **46** | **0** | **3.08** | **5** | **2** | **3** | **341** | **11** | **0** | ***1.94** |
| | Portland Pirates | AHL | 5 | 5 | 0 | 0 | 300 | 7 | 1 | 1.40 | .... | .... | .... | .... | .... | .... | .... |
| **1996-97** | **Washington** | **NHL** | **29** | **8** | **15** | **4** | **1645** | **71** | **2** | **2.59** | .... | .... | .... | .... | .... | .... | .... |
| **1997-98** | **Washington** | **NHL** | **64** | **33** | **18** | **10** | **3788** | **139** | **5** | **2.20** | **21** | **12** | **9** | **1351** | **44** | ***4** | **1.95** |
| | Germany | Olympics | 2 | 2 | 0 | 0 | 120 | 2 | 1 | 1.00 | .... | .... | .... | .... | .... | .... | .... |
| **1998-99** | **Washington** | **NHL** | **64** | **26** | **31** | **3** | **3586** | **154** | **4** | **2.58** | .... | .... | .... | .... | .... | .... | .... |
| **99-2000** | **Washington** | **NHL** | **73** | **41** | **20** | **11** | ***4371** | **163** | **5** | **2.24** | **5** | **1** | **4** | **284** | **16** | **0** | **3.38** |
| **2000-01** | **Washington** | **NHL** | **72** | **37** | **26** | **8** | **4279** | **177** | **5** | **2.48** | **6** | **2** | **4** | **375** | **14** | **1** | **2.24** |
| **2001-02** | **Washington** | **NHL** | **71** | **31** | **29** | **8** | **4131** | **192** | **6** | **2.79** | .... | .... | .... | .... | .... | .... | .... |
| **2002-03** | **Washington** | **NHL** | **66** | **33** | **25** | **6** | **3894** | **156** | **4** | **2.40** | **6** | **2** | **4** | **404** | **14** | **1** | **2.08** |
| **2003-04** | **Washington** | **NHL** | **63** | **19** | **35** | **9** | **3738** | **180** | **2** | **2.89** | .... | .... | .... | .... | .... | .... | .... |
| 2004-05 | Eisbaren Berlin | Germany | 8 | .... | .... | .... | 452 | 19 | 2 | 2.52 | .... | .... | .... | .... | .... | .... | .... |
| **2005-06** | **Washington** | **NHL** | **59** | **20** | **28** | **11** | **3506** | **206** | **0** | **3.53** | .... | .... | .... | .... | .... | .... | .... |
| | Germany | Olympics | 3 | 0 | 1 | 2 | 179 | 8 | 0 | 2.68 | .... | .... | .... | .... | .... | .... | .... |
| **2006-07** | **Washington** | **NHL** | **54** | **22** | **24** | **6** | **3184** | **159** | **1** | **3.00** | .... | .... | .... | .... | .... | .... | .... |
| **2007-08** | **Washington** | **NHL** | **54** | **25** | **21** | **6** | **3154** | **153** | **1** | **2.91** | .... | .... | .... | .... | .... | .... | .... |
| **2008-09** | **Tampa Bay** | **NHL** | **8** | **2** | **4** | **1** | **410** | **25** | **0** | **3.66** | .... | .... | .... | .... | .... | .... | .... |
| | **NHL Totals** | | **719** | **303** | **297** | **87** | **41671** | **1885** | **35** | **2.71** | **45** | **20** | **24** | **2799** | **100** | **6** | **2.14** |

WHL West Second All-Star Team (1989) • Harry "Hap" Holmes Memorial Award (AHL – fewest goals against) (1994) (shared with Byron Dafoe) • Jack A. Butterfield Trophy (AHL – Playoff MVP) (1994) • NHL First All-Star Team (2000) • Vezina Trophy (2000) • King Clancy Memorial Trophy (2006)

Played in NHL All-Star Game (1998, 2000)

• Scored a goal while with Tri-City (WHL), November 29, 1989. Signed as a free agent by **Berlin** (Germany), February 2, 2005. Signed as a free agent by **Tampa Bay**, July 1, 2008. • Missed majority of 2008-09 season recovering from arm injury suffered in practice, December 17, 2008. Traded to **Toronto** by **Tampa Bay** with Jamie Heward, Andy Rogers and Carolina's 4th round choice (previously acquired – later forfeited) in 2009 Entry Draft for Richard Petiot, March 4, 2009.

## KOSHECHKIN, Vasily (KOH-shech-kihn, va-SEE-lee) T.B.

Goaltender. Catches left. 6'6", 210 lbs. Born, Togliatti, USSR, March 27, 1983.
(Tampa Bay's 9th choice, 233rd overall, in 2002 Entry Draft).

| | | | Regular Season | | | | | | | | Playoffs | | | | | | |
|---|---|---|---|---|---|---|---|---|---|---|---|---|---|---|---|---|---|
| Season | Club | League | GP | W | L | O/T | Mins | GA | SO | Avg | GP | W | L | Mins | GA | SO | Avg |
| 1998-99 | Lada Togliatti 2 | Russia-4 | 8 | .... | .... | .... | .... | 8 | .... | .... | .... | .... | .... | .... | .... | .... | .... |
| 99-2000 | Lada Togliatti 2 | Russia-3 | 18 | .... | .... | .... | .... | 20 | .... | .... | .... | .... | .... | .... | .... | .... | .... |
| 2000-01 | Lada Togliatti 2 | Russia-3 | STATISTICS NOT AVAILABLE | | | | | | | | | | | | | | |
| 2001-02 | Lada Togliatti 2 | Russia-3 | STATISTICS NOT AVAILABLE | | | | | | | | | | | | | | |
| 2002-03 | Lada Togliatti 2 | Russia-3 | STATISTICS NOT AVAILABLE | | | | | | | | | | | | | | |
| | Kirovo-Chepetsk | Russia-2 | 10 | .... | .... | .... | 613 | 14 | 3 | 1.37 | .... | .... | .... | .... | .... | .... | .... |
| | Almetjevsk | Russia-2 | 14 | .... | .... | .... | 675 | 29 | 1 | 2.58 | .... | .... | .... | .... | .... | .... | .... |
| 2003-04 | Lada Togliatti 2 | Russia-3 | 13 | .... | .... | .... | .... | 19 | 1 | .... | 3 | .... | .... | .... | .... | .... | .... |
| | Lada Togliatti | Russia | 8 | .... | .... | .... | 247 | 10 | 0 | 2.43 | 1 | .... | .... | 40 | 3 | 0 | 4.50 |
| 2004-05 | Lada Togliatti | Russia | 4 | .... | .... | .... | 121 | 5 | 0 | 2.47 | .... | .... | .... | .... | .... | .... | .... |
| | Lada Togliatti | Russia | 4 | .... | .... | .... | 121 | 5 | 0 | 2.47 | .... | .... | .... | .... | .... | .... | .... |
| 2005-06 | Lada Togliatti | Russia | 41 | .... | .... | .... | 2375 | 63 | 9 | 1.59 | 8 | .... | .... | 474 | 20 | 1 | 2.53 |
| 2006-07 | Lada Togliatti | Russia | 42 | .... | .... | .... | 2430 | 82 | 5 | 2.02 | 3 | .... | .... | 179 | 13 | 0 | 4.35 |
| 2007-08 | Ak Bars Kazan | Russia | 19 | .... | .... | .... | 990 | 45 | 0 | 2.73 | .... | .... | .... | .... | .... | .... | .... |
| 2008-09 | Lada Togliatti | Rus-KHL | 43 | .... | .... | .... | 2404 | 67 | 8 | 1.67 | 5 | .... | .... | 280 | 9 | 1 | 1.93 |

## KOSKINEN, Mikko (KAWS-kih-nehn, MEE-koh) NYI

Goaltender. Catches left. 6'5", 187 lbs. Born, Vantaa, Finland, July 18, 1988.
(NY Islanders' 3rd choice, 31st overall, in 2009 Entry Draft).

| | | | Regular Season | | | | | | | | Playoffs | | | | | | |
|---|---|---|---|---|---|---|---|---|---|---|---|---|---|---|---|---|---|
| Season | Club | League | GP | W | L | O/T | Mins | GA | SO | Avg | GP | W | L | Mins | GA | SO | Avg |
| 2004-05 | Blues-T U18 | Fin-U18 | 21 | .... | .... | .... | 1138 | 67 | 0 | 3.53 | .... | .... | .... | .... | .... | .... | .... |
| 2005-06 | Blues Espoo U18 | Fin-U18 | 3 | .... | .... | .... | 142 | 12 | 0 | 5.07 | .... | .... | .... | .... | .... | .... | .... |
| 2006-07 | Kiekko-Vantaa Jr. | Fin-Jr. | 27 | 16 | 8 | 0 | 1567 | 62 | 3 | 2.37 | .... | .... | .... | .... | .... | .... | .... |
| 2007-08 | Blues Espoo Jr. | Fin-Jr. | 20 | 12 | 4 | 0 | 1176 | 45 | 2 | 2.30 | 2 | 0 | 2 | 81 | 7 | 0 | 5.18 |
| | Blues Espoo | Finland | 1 | 1 | 0 | 0 | 60 | 0 | 1 | 0.00 | .... | .... | .... | .... | .... | .... | .... |
| 2008-09 | Blues Espoo Jr. | Fin-Jr. | 9 | 9 | 0 | 0 | 545 | 15 | 2 | 1.65 | .... | .... | .... | .... | .... | .... | .... |
| | Blues Espoo | Finland | 33 | 17 | 9 | 7 | 1921 | 61 | 1 | 1.91 | 14 | 6 | 8 | 856 | 37 | 0 | 2.59 |

## KOVAR, Jakub (KOH-vahr, YA-kuhb) PHI.

Goaltender. Catches left. 6', 193 lbs. Born, Pisek, Czech., July 19, 1988.
(Philadelphia's 7th choice, 109th overall, in 2006 Entry Draft).

| | | | Regular Season | | | | | | | | Playoffs | | | | | | |
|---|---|---|---|---|---|---|---|---|---|---|---|---|---|---|---|---|---|
| Season | Club | League | GP | W | L | O/T | Mins | GA | SO | Avg | GP | W | L | Mins | GA | SO | Avg |
| 2004-05 | IHC Pisek U17 | CzR-U17 | 40 | .... | .... | .... | 2298 | 137 | 4 | 3.58 | .... | .... | .... | .... | .... | .... | .... |
| 2005-06 | C. Budejovice Jr. | CzRep-Jr. | 19 | .... | .... | .... | 1048 | 39 | 2 | 2.23 | 5 | .... | .... | 304 | 8 | 0 | 1.58 |
| 2006-07 | C. Budejovice Jr. | CzRep-Jr. | 38 | .... | .... | .... | 2231 | 77 | 3 | 2.07 | 3 | .... | .... | 160 | 16 | 0 | 6.00 |
| 2007-08 | Oshawa Generals | OHL | 16 | 12 | 3 | 0 | 917 | 48 | 0 | 3.14 | .... | .... | .... | .... | .... | .... | .... |
| | Windsor Spitfires | OHL | 20 | 14 | 3 | 3 | 1194 | 68 | 1 | 3.42 | 4 | 1 | 2 | 188 | 13 | 0 | 4.15 |
| 2008-09 | C. Budejovice | CzRep | 25 | .... | .... | .... | 1355 | 63 | 0 | 2.79 | .... | .... | .... | .... | .... | .... | .... |

## KRAHN, Brent (KRAWN, BREHNT) DAL.

Goaltender. Catches left. 6'5", 220 lbs. Born, Winnipeg, Man., April 2, 1982.
(Calgary's 1st choice, 9th overall, in 2000 Entry Draft).

| | | | Regular Season | | | | | | | | Playoffs | | | | | | |
|---|---|---|---|---|---|---|---|---|---|---|---|---|---|---|---|---|---|
| Season | Club | League | GP | W | L | O/T | Mins | GA | SO | Avg | GP | W | L | Mins | GA | SO | Avg |
| 1997-98 | Pembina Valley | MMMHL | 22 | 20 | 0 | 1 | 1265 | 40 | 3 | 1.90 | 2 | 2 | 0 | 120 | 2 | 1 | 1.00 |
| 1998-99 | Pembina Valley | MMMHL | 13 | 10 | 3 | 0 | 770 | 30 | 2 | 2.34 | .... | .... | .... | .... | .... | .... | .... |
| 99-2000 | Calgary Hitmen | WHL | 39 | 33 | 6 | 0 | 2315 | 92 | 4 | 2.38 | 5 | 2 | 2 | 266 | 13 | 0 | 2.93 |
| 2000-01 | Calgary Hitmen | WHL | 37 | 22 | 10 | 3 | 2087 | 104 | 1 | 2.99 | .... | .... | .... | .... | .... | .... | .... |
| 2001-02 | Calgary Hitmen | WHL | 18 | 8 | 6 | 2 | 1033 | 61 | 0 | 3.54 | 2 | 1 | 1 | 119 | 6 | 0 | 3.03 |
| 2002-03 | Calgary Hitmen | WHL | 23 | 11 | 10 | 2 | 1343 | 72 | 2 | 3.22 | .... | .... | .... | .... | .... | .... | .... |
| | Seattle | WHL | 5 | 5 | 0 | 0 | 302 | 9 | 2 | 1.79 | 15 | 9 | 6 | 960 | 38 | 2 | 2.38 |
| 2003-04 | San Antonio | AHL | 14 | 3 | 7 | 1 | 715 | 41 | 0 | 3.44 | .... | .... | .... | .... | .... | .... | .... |
| | Lowell | AHL | 7 | 2 | 3 | 0 | 344 | 15 | 0 | 2.62 | .... | .... | .... | .... | .... | .... | .... |
| | Las Vegas | ECHL | 14 | 7 | 5 | 2 | 828 | 36 | 0 | 2.61 | .... | .... | .... | .... | .... | .... | .... |
| 2004-05 | Lowell | AHL | 35 | 20 | 11 | 2 | 1998 | 83 | 6 | 2.49 | 1 | 0 | 0 | 1 | 0 | 0 | 0.00 |
| 2005-06 | Omaha | AHL | 57 | 26 | 20 | 9 | 3241 | 135 | 3 | 2.50 | .... | .... | .... | .... | .... | .... | .... |
| 2006-07 | Omaha | AHL | 28 | 14 | 12 | 0 | 1564 | 63 | 2 | 2.42 | 1 | 0 | 1 | 59 | 3 | 0 | 3.06 |
| 2007-08 | Quad City Flames | AHL | 14 | 6 | 6 | 2 | 795 | 33 | 0 | 2.49 | .... | .... | .... | .... | .... | .... | .... |
| **2008-09** | **Dallas** | **NHL** | **1** | **0** | **0** | **0** | **20** | **3** | **0** | **9.00** | .... | .... | .... | .... | .... | .... | .... |
| | Chicago Wolves | AHL | 13 | 6 | 6 | 0 | 738 | 26 | 2 | 2.11 | .... | .... | .... | .... | .... | .... | .... |
| | Las Vegas | ECHL | 6 | 1 | 4 | 1 | 342 | 23 | 0 | 4.04 | .... | .... | .... | .... | .... | .... | .... |
| | **NHL Totals** | | **1** | **0** | **0** | **0** | **20** | **3** | **0** | **9.00** | .... | .... | .... | .... | .... | .... | .... |

Signed as a free agent by **Dallas**, September 24, 2008.

## KUEMPER, Darcy (KEHM-puhr, DAHR-see) MIN.

Goaltender. Catches left. 6'4", 195 lbs. Born, Saskatoon, Sask., May 5, 1990.
(Minnesota's 5th choice, 161st overall, in 2009 Entry Draft).

| | | | Regular Season | | | | | | | | Playoffs | | | | | | |
|---|---|---|---|---|---|---|---|---|---|---|---|---|---|---|---|---|---|
| Season | Club | League | GP | W | L | O/T | Mins | GA | SO | Avg | GP | W | L | Mins | GA | SO | Avg |
| 2006-07 | Sask. Contacts | SMHL | 25 | 8 | 14 | 3 | 1489 | 87 | 1 | 3.51 | 4 | 1 | 3 | 200 | 19 | 0 | 5.70 |
| | Spokane Chiefs | WHL | .... | .... | .... | .... | .... | .... | .... | .... | 1 | 0 | 0 | 0 | 0 | 0 | 0.00 |
| 2007-08 | Saskatoon Blazers | SMHL | 26 | 15 | 7 | 4 | 1578 | 62 | 1 | 2.36 | 13 | 7 | 6 | 781 | 34 | 1 | 2.61 |
| 2008-09 | Red Deer Rebels | WHL | 55 | 21 | 25 | 8 | 3167 | 156 | 3 | 2.96 | .... | .... | .... | .... | .... | .... | .... |

## LaBARBERA, Jason (luh-BAHR-buhr-ah, JAY-suhn) PHX.

Goaltender. Catches left. 6'3", 225 lbs. Born, Burnaby, B.C., January 18, 1980.
(NY Rangers' 3rd choice, 66th overall, in 1998 Entry Draft).

| | | | Regular Season | | | | | | | | Playoffs | | | | | | |
|---|---|---|---|---|---|---|---|---|---|---|---|---|---|---|---|---|---|
| Season | Club | League | GP | W | L | O/T | Mins | GA | SO | Avg | GP | W | L | Mins | GA | SO | Avg |
| 1995-96 | Prince George | Minor-BC | 31 | .... | .... | .... | 1860 | 83 | 0 | 2.68 | .... | .... | .... | .... | .... | .... | .... |

| | | | | | | | | | | | | | | | | | |
|---|---|---|---|---|---|---|---|---|---|---|---|---|---|---|---|---|---|
| 1996-97 | Tri-City Americans | WHL | 2 | 1 | 0 | 0 | 63 | 4 | 0 | 3.81 | .... | .... | .... | .... | .... | .... | .... |
| | Portland | WHL | 9 | 5 | 1 | 1 | 443 | 18 | 0 | 2.44 | .... | .... | .... | .... | .... | .... | .... |
| 1997-98 | Portland | WHL | 23 | 18 | 4 | 0 | 1305 | 72 | 1 | 3.31 | .... | .... | .... | .... | .... | .... | .... |
| 1998-99 | Portland | WHL | 51 | 18 | 23 | 9 | 2991 | 170 | 4 | 3.41 | 4 | 0 | 4 | 252 | 19 | 0 | 4.52 |
| 99-2000 | Portland | WHL | 34 | 8 | 24 | 2 | 2005 | 123 | 1 | 3.68 | .... | .... | .... | .... | .... | .... | .... |
| | Spokane Chiefs | WHL | 21 | 12 | 6 | 2 | 1146 | 50 | 0 | 2.62 | 9 | 6 | 1 | 435 | 18 | 1 | 2.48 |
| **2000-01** | **NY Rangers** | **NHL** | **1** | **0** | **0** | **0** | **10** | **0** | **0** | **0.00** | .... | .... | .... | .... | .... | .... | .... |
| | Hartford Wolf Pack | AHL | 4 | 1 | 1 | 0 | 156 | 12 | 0 | 4.61 | .... | .... | .... | .... | .... | .... | .... |
| | Charlotte Checkers | ECHL | 35 | 18 | 10 | 7 | 2100 | 112 | 1 | 3.20 | 2 | 1 | 1 | 143 | 5 | 0 | 2.09 |
| 2001-02 | Hartford Wolf Pack | AHL | 20 | 7 | 11 | 1 | 1058 | 55 | 0 | 3.12 | .... | .... | .... | .... | .... | .... | .... |
| | Charlotte Checkers | ECHL | 13 | 9 | 3 | 1 | 744 | 29 | 0 | 2.34 | 4 | 2 | 2 | 212 | 12 | 0 | 3.39 |
| 2002-03 | Hartford Wolf Pack | AHL | 46 | 18 | 17 | 6 | 2452 | 105 | 2 | 2.57 | 2 | 0 | 2 | 117 | 6 | 0 | 3.07 |
| **2003-04** | **NY Rangers** | **NHL** | **4** | **1** | **2** | **0** | **198** | **16** | **0** | **4.85** | .... | .... | .... | .... | .... | .... | .... |
| | Hartford Wolf Pack | AHL | 59 | 34 | 9 | 9 | 3393 | 90 | *13 | 1.59 | 16 | 11 | 5 | 1043 | 30 | *3 | *1.73 |
| 2004-05 | Hartford Wolf Pack | AHL | 53 | 31 | 16 | 2 | 2937 | 90 | 6 | 1.84 | 4 | 1 | 3 | 238 | 9 | 0 | 2.27 |
| **2005-06** | **Los Angeles** | **NHL** | **29** | **11** | **9** | **2** | **1433** | **69** | **1** | **2.89** | .... | .... | .... | .... | .... | .... | .... |
| | Manchester | AHL | 3 | 1 | 1 | 1 | 185 | 10 | 0 | 3.25 | .... | .... | .... | .... | .... | .... | .... |
| 2006-07 | Manchester | AHL | *62 | *39 | 20 | 1 | *3619 | 133 | *7 | 2.21 | 13 | 6 | 7 | 824 | 38 | 1 | 2.77 |
| **2007-08** | **Los Angeles** | **NHL** | **45** | **17** | **23** | **2** | **2421** | **121** | **1** | **3.00** | .... | .... | .... | .... | .... | .... | .... |
| **2008-09** | **Los Angeles** | **NHL** | **19** | **5** | **8** | **4** | **995** | **47** | **2** | **2.83** | .... | .... | .... | .... | .... | .... | .... |
| | **Vancouver** | **NHL** | **9** | **3** | **2** | **2** | **451** | **20** | **0** | **2.66** | .... | .... | .... | .... | .... | .... | .... |
| | **NHL Totals** | | **107** | **37** | **44** | **10** | **5508** | **273** | **4** | **2.97** | .... | .... | .... | .... | .... | .... | .... |

AHL First All-Star Team (2004, 2007) • Aldege "Baz" Bastien Memorial Award (AHL - Outstanding Goaltender) (2004, 2007) • Les Cunningham Award (AHL - MVP) (2004) • Harry "Hap" Holmes Memorial Trophy (AHL - fewest goals against) (2005) (shared with Steve Valiquette) • Harry "Hap" Holmes Memorial Trophy (AHL - fewest goals against) (2007)

Signed as a free agent by **Los Angeles**, August 2, 2005. Traded to **Vancouver** by **Los Angeles** for Vancouver's 7th round choice (later traded to Atlanta – Atlanta selected Jordan Samuels-Thomas) in 2009 Entry Draft, December 30, 2008. Signed as a free agent by **Phoenix**, July 1, 2009.

## LACASSE, Loic (luh-KAS, LOIK)

Goaltender. Catches left. 6'3", 178 lbs. Born, Granby, Que., April 23, 1986.
(Montreal's 5th choice, 181st overall, in 2004 Entry Draft).

| | | | Regular Season | | | | | | | | Playoffs | | | | | | |
|---|---|---|---|---|---|---|---|---|---|---|---|---|---|---|---|---|---|
| Season | Club | League | GP | W | L | O/T | Mins | GA | SO | Avg | GP | W | L | Mins | GA | SO | Avg |
| 2002-03 | Antoine-Girouard | QAAA | 24 | 22 | 1 | 1 | 1453 | 50 | 1 | 2.07 | .... | .... | .... | .... | .... | .... | .... |
| 2003-04 | Baie-Comeau | QMJHL | 41 | 9 | 15 | 4 | 1758 | 117 | 0 | 3.99 | 4 | 0 | 4 | 172 | 16 | 0 | 5.57 |
| 2004-05 | Baie-Comeau | QMJHL | 39 | 10 | 22 | 2 | 2001 | 138 | 1 | 4.14 | 2 | 0 | 1 | 54 | 2 | 0 | 2.21 |
| 2005-06 | Baie-Comeau | QMJHL | 27 | 10 | 12 | 0 | 1394 | 94 | 1 | 4.05 | .... | .... | .... | .... | .... | .... | .... |
| | Drummondville | QMJHL | 6 | 2 | 3 | 0 | 272 | 18 | 0 | 3.97 | 5 | 3 | 2 | 280 | 13 | 0 | 2.78 |
| 2006-07 | Oshawa Generals | OHL | 33 | 16 | 12 | 5 | 1964 | 129 | 3 | 3.94 | 9 | 3 | 5 | 523 | 43 | 0 | 4.93 |
| 2007-08 | Bloomington | IHL | 47 | 18 | 17 | 5 | 2558 | 138 | 1 | 3.24 | .... | .... | .... | .... | .... | .... | .... |
| 2008-09 | Hamilton Bulldogs | AHL | 8 | 6 | 1 | 0 | 436 | 15 | 2 | 2.07 | .... | .... | .... | .... | .... | .... | .... |
| | Cincinnati | ECHL | 21 | 11 | 6 | 1 | 1128 | 51 | 1 | 2.71 | 11 | 5 | 5 | 536 | 29 | 0 | 3.25 |

## LaCOSTA, Dan (luh-KAWS-tah, DAN) CBJ

Goaltender. Catches left. 6'2", 194 lbs. Born, Labrador City, Nfld., March 28, 1986.
(Columbus' 4th choice, 93rd overall, in 2004 Entry Draft).

| | | | Regular Season | | | | | | | | Playoffs | | | | | | |
|---|---|---|---|---|---|---|---|---|---|---|---|---|---|---|---|---|---|
| Season | Club | League | GP | W | L | O/T | Mins | GA | SO | Avg | GP | W | L | Mins | GA | SO | Avg |
| 2001-02 | Wellington Dukes | OPJHL | 24 | 19 | 2 | 3 | 1377 | 44 | 2 | *1.92 | .... | .... | .... | .... | .... | .... | .... |
| 2002-03 | Owen Sound | OHL | 28 | 8 | 10 | 3 | 1321 | 82 | 0 | 3.72 | .... | .... | .... | .... | .... | .... | .... |
| 2003-04 | Owen Sound | OHL | 37 | 17 | 10 | 1 | 1810 | 82 | 4 | 2.72 | .... | .... | .... | .... | .... | .... | .... |
| 2004-05 | Owen Sound | OHL | 25 | 15 | 7 | 2 | 1423 | 70 | 0 | 2.95 | .... | .... | .... | .... | .... | .... | .... |
| | Barrie Colts | OHL | 21 | 10 | 5 | 2 | 1054 | 48 | 1 | 2.73 | 5 | 1 | 2 | 215 | 11 | 0 | 3.07 |
| 2005-06 | Barrie Colts | OHL | *59 | 36 | 17 | 4 | 3340 | 142 | 6 | 2.55 | 11 | 5 | 5 | 654 | 34 | 0 | 3.12 |
| 2006-07 | Syracuse Crunch | AHL | 19 | 5 | 7 | 1 | 852 | 40 | 3 | 2.82 | .... | .... | .... | .... | .... | .... | .... |
| | Dayton Bombers | ECHL | 10 | 3 | 5 | 1 | 556 | 32 | 0 | 3.45 | .... | .... | .... | .... | .... | .... | .... |
| **2007-08** | **Columbus** | **NHL** | **1** | **0** | **0** | **0** | **13** | **0** | **0** | **0.00** | .... | .... | .... | .... | .... | .... | .... |
| | Syracuse Crunch | AHL | 15 | 9 | 2 | 3 | 848 | 30 | 1 | 2.12 | .... | .... | .... | .... | .... | .... | .... |
| | Elmira Jackals | ECHL | 14 | 7 | 4 | 1 | 754 | 27 | 0 | 2.15 | .... | .... | .... | .... | .... | .... | .... |
| **2008-09** | **Columbus** | **NHL** | **3** | **2** | **0** | **0** | **156** | **4** | **1** | **1.54** | .... | .... | .... | .... | .... | .... | .... |
| | Syracuse Crunch | AHL | 45 | 19 | 18 | 2 | 2469 | 115 | 2 | 2.79 | .... | .... | .... | .... | .... | .... | .... |
| | **NHL Totals** | | **4** | **2** | **0** | **0** | **169** | **4** | **1** | **1.42** | .... | .... | .... | .... | .... | .... | .... |

## LALANDE, Kevin (lah-LAWND, KEH-vihn) CBJ

Goaltender. Catches left. 6', 175 lbs. Born, Kingston, Ont., February 19, 1987.
(Calgary's 5th choice, 128th overall, in 2005 Entry Draft).

| | | | Regular Season | | | | | | | | Playoffs | | | | | | |
|---|---|---|---|---|---|---|---|---|---|---|---|---|---|---|---|---|---|
| Season | Club | League | GP | W | L | O/T | Mins | GA | SO | Avg | GP | W | L | Mins | GA | SO | Avg |
| 2003-04 | Hawkesbury | CJHL | 35 | .... | .... | .... | 2010 | 105 | 3 | 3.13 | 6 | .... | .... | 286 | 19 | 0 | 3.99 |
| | Belleville Bulls | OHL | 3 | 1 | 2 | 0 | 133 | 15 | 0 | 6.77 | .... | .... | .... | .... | .... | .... | .... |
| 2004-05 | Belleville Bulls | OHL | 30 | 15 | 11 | 3 | 1797 | 79 | 1 | 2.64 | 2 | 0 | 2 | 120 | 8 | 0 | 4.00 |
| 2005-06 | Belleville Bulls | OHL | 50 | 24 | 17 | 5 | 2789 | 143 | 3 | 3.08 | .... | .... | .... | .... | .... | .... | .... |
| 2006-07 | Belleville Bulls | OHL | 48 | 27 | 17 | 3 | 2772 | 139 | 3 | 3.01 | 15 | 10 | 5 | 989 | 42 | *1 | 2.55 |
| 2007-08 | Quad City Flames | AHL | 7 | 2 | 3 | 0 | 360 | 20 | 0 | 3.34 | .... | .... | .... | .... | .... | .... | .... |
| | Las Vegas | ECHL | 27 | 17 | 5 | 4 | 1607 | 55 | 3 | 2.05 | *20 | *13 | 6 | 1142 | 48 | 3 | 2.52 |
| 2008-09 | Quad City Flames | AHL | 6 | 4 | 1 | 1 | 340 | 11 | 1 | 1.94 | .... | .... | .... | .... | .... | .... | .... |
| | Las Vegas | ECHL | 21 | 9 | 8 | 2 | 1181 | 47 | 3 | 2.39 | .... | .... | .... | .... | .... | .... | .... |
| | Syracuse Crunch | AHL | 15 | 9 | 5 | 1 | 848 | 32 | 0 | 2.26 | .... | .... | .... | .... | .... | .... | .... |

Traded to **Columbus** by **Calgary** for Columbus' 4th round choice (later traded to Los Angeles – later traded to Florida – Florida selected Garrett Wilson) in 2009 Entry Draft, March 4, 2009.

## LALIME, Patrick (lah-LEEM, PAT-rihk) BUF.

Goaltender. Catches left. 6'3", 189 lbs. Born, St-Bonaventure, Que., July 7, 1974.
(Pittsburgh's 6th choice, 156th overall, in 1993 Entry Draft).

| | | | Regular Season | | | | | | | | Playoffs | | | | | | |
|---|---|---|---|---|---|---|---|---|---|---|---|---|---|---|---|---|---|
| Season | Club | League | GP | W | L | O/T | Mins | GA | SO | Avg | GP | W | L | Mins | GA | SO | Avg |
| 1990-91 | Abitibi Forestiers | QAAA | 26 | 9 | 17 | 0 | 1595 | 151 | 0 | 5.81 | .... | .... | .... | .... | .... | .... | .... |
| 1991-92 | Shawinigan | QMJHL | 6 | .... | .... | .... | 272 | 25 | 0 | 5.50 | .... | .... | .... | .... | .... | .... | .... |
| 1992-93 | Shawinigan | QMJHL | 44 | 10 | 24 | 4 | 2467 | 192 | 0 | 4.67 | .... | .... | .... | .... | .... | .... | .... |
| 1993-94 | Shawinigan | QMJHL | 48 | 22 | 20 | 0 | 2733 | 192 | 1 | 4.22 | 5 | 1 | 3 | 223 | 25 | 0 | 6.73 |
| 1994-95 | Hampton Roads | ECHL | 26 | 15 | 7 | 3 | 1470 | 82 | 2 | 3.35 | .... | .... | .... | .... | .... | .... | .... |
| | Cleveland | IHL | 23 | 7 | 10 | 4 | 1230 | 91 | 0 | 4.44 | .... | .... | .... | .... | .... | .... | .... |
| 1995-96 | Cleveland | IHL | 41 | 20 | 12 | 7 | 2314 | 149 | 0 | 3.86 | .... | .... | .... | .... | .... | .... | .... |
| **1996-97** | **Pittsburgh** | **NHL** | **39** | **21** | **12** | **2** | **2058** | **101** | **3** | **2.94** | .... | .... | .... | .... | .... | .... | .... |
| | Cleveland | IHL | 14 | 6 | 6 | 2 | 834 | 45 | 1 | 3.24 | .... | .... | .... | .... | .... | .... | .... |
| 1997-98 | Grand Rapids | IHL | 31 | 10 | 10 | 9 | 1749 | 76 | 2 | 2.61 | 1 | 0 | 1 | 77 | 4 | 0 | 3.11 |
| 1998-99 | Kansas City Blades | IHL | *66 | *39 | 20 | 4 | *3789 | 190 | 2 | 3.01 | 3 | 1 | 2 | 179 | 6 | 1 | 2.01 |
| **99-2000** | **Ottawa** | **NHL** | **38** | **19** | **14** | **3** | **2038** | **79** | **3** | **2.33** | .... | .... | .... | .... | .... | .... | .... |
| **2000-01** | **Ottawa** | **NHL** | **60** | **36** | **19** | **5** | **3607** | **141** | **7** | **2.35** | **4** | **0** | **4** | **251** | **10** | **0** | **2.39** |
| **2001-02** | **Ottawa** | **NHL** | **61** | **27** | **24** | **8** | **3583** | **148** | **7** | **2.48** | **12** | **7** | **5** | **778** | **18** | **4** | ***1.39** |
| **2002-03** | **Ottawa** | **NHL** | **67** | **39** | **20** | **7** | **3943** | **142** | **8** | **2.16** | **18** | **11** | **7** | **1122** | **34** | **1** | **1.82** |
| **2003-04** | **Ottawa** | **NHL** | **57** | **25** | **23** | **7** | **3324** | **127** | **5** | **2.29** | **7** | **3** | **4** | **398** | **13** | **0** | **1.96** |
| 2004-05 | | | | | | | | DID NOT PLAY | | | | | | | | | |
| **2005-06** | **St. Louis** | **NHL** | **31** | **4** | **18** | **8** | **1699** | **103** | **0** | **3.64** | .... | .... | .... | .... | .... | .... | .... |
| | Peoria Rivermen | AHL | 14 | 6 | 6 | 1 | 798 | 38 | 1 | 2.86 | .... | .... | .... | .... | .... | .... | .... |
| **2006-07** | **Chicago** | **NHL** | **12** | **4** | **6** | **1** | **645** | **33** | **1** | **3.07** | .... | .... | .... | .... | .... | .... | .... |
| | Norfolk Admirals | AHL | 4 | 3 | 1 | 0 | 241 | 10 | 0 | 2.49 | .... | .... | .... | .... | .... | .... | .... |
| **2007-08** | **Chicago** | **NHL** | **32** | **16** | **12** | **2** | **1828** | **86** | **1** | **2.82** | .... | .... | .... | .... | .... | .... | .... |
| **2008-09** | **Buffalo** | **NHL** | **24** | **5** | **13** | **3** | **1297** | **67** | **0** | **3.10** | .... | .... | .... | .... | .... | .... | .... |
| | **NHL Totals** | | **421** | **196** | **161** | **46** | **24022** | **1027** | **35** | **2.57** | **41** | **21** | **20** | **2549** | **75** | **5** | **1.77** |

NHL All-Rookie Team (1997) • IHL First All-Star Team (1999)

Played in NHL All-Star Game (2003)

• Rights traded to **Anaheim** by **Pittsburgh** for Sean Pronger, March 24, 1998. Traded to **Ottawa** by **Anaheim** for Ted Donato and the rights to Antti-Jussi Niemi, June 18, 1999. Traded to **St. Louis** by **Ottawa** for St. Louis' 4th round choice (Ilya Zubov) in 2005 Entry Draft, June 27, 2004. Signed as a free agent by **Chicago**, July 1, 2006. Signed as a free agent by **Buffalo**, July 1, 2008.

## LARSSON, Daniel (LAR-suhn, DAN-yehl) DET.

Goaltender. Catches left. 6', 180 lbs. Born, Boden, Sweden, February 7, 1986.
(Detroit's 4th choice, 92nd overall, in 2006 Entry Draft).

| | | | Regular Season | | | | | | | | Playoffs | | | | | | |
|---|---|---|---|---|---|---|---|---|---|---|---|---|---|---|---|---|---|
| Season | Club | League | GP | W | L | O/T | Mins | GA | SO | Avg | GP | W | L | Mins | GA | SO | Avg |
| 2002-03 | Lulea HF U18 | Swe-U18 | 12 | .... | .... | .... | 731 | 50 | 0 | 4.10 | .... | .... | .... | .... | .... | .... | .... |
| 2003-04 | Lulea HF Jr. | Swe-Jr. | 4 | .... | .... | .... | 239 | 12 | 0 | 3.01 | .... | .... | .... | .... | .... | .... | .... |
| | Bodens IK | Sweden-2 | 1 | .... | .... | .... | 20 | 1 | 0 | 3.00 | .... | .... | .... | .... | .... | .... | .... |
| 2004-05 | Bodens IK | Sweden-2 | 28 | .... | .... | .... | 1514 | 97 | 1 | 3.84 | .... | .... | .... | .... | .... | .... | .... |
| 2005-06 | Hammarby Jr. | Swe-Jr. | 9 | .... | .... | .... | 548 | 24 | 1 | 2.63 | .... | .... | .... | .... | .... | .... | .... |
| | Hammarby | Sweden-2 | 36 | .... | .... | .... | 2001 | 90 | 0 | 2.70 | .... | .... | .... | .... | .... | .... | .... |
| 2006-07 | Djurgarden | Sweden | 24 | .... | .... | .... | 1259 | 53 | 3 | 2.53 | .... | .... | .... | .... | .... | .... | .... |
| 2007-08 | Djurgarden | Sweden | 46 | .... | .... | .... | 2721 | 104 | 6 | 2.29 | 5 | .... | .... | 295 | 13 | 0 | 2.64 |
| 2008-09 | Grand Rapids | AHL | 40 | 22 | 12 | 2 | 2152 | 99 | 5 | 2.76 | .... | .... | .... | .... | .... | .... | .... |

## LAWSON, Nathan (LAW-suhn, NAY-thuhn) NYI

Goaltender. Catches . 6'2", 191 lbs. Born, Calgary, Alta., September 29, 1983.

| | | | Regular Season | | | | | | | | Playoffs | | | | | | |
|---|---|---|---|---|---|---|---|---|---|---|---|---|---|---|---|---|---|
| Season | Club | League | GP | W | L | O/T | Mins | GA | SO | Avg | GP | W | L | Mins | GA | SO | Avg |
| 2004-05 | Alaska Anchorage | WCHA | 27 | 7 | 15 | 3 | 1482 | 82 | 1 | 3.32 | .... | .... | .... | .... | .... | .... | .... |
| 2005-06 | Alaska Anchorage | WCHA | 21 | 4 | 11 | 3 | 1063 | 61 | 1 | 3.44 | .... | .... | .... | .... | .... | .... | .... |
| 2006-07 | Alaska Anchorage | WCHA | 27 | 10 | 15 | 2 | 1523 | 77 | 0 | 3.03 | .... | .... | .... | .... | .... | .... | .... |
| 2007-08 | Phoenix | ECHL | 5 | 3 | 2 | 0 | 279 | 14 | 1 | 3.01 | .... | .... | .... | .... | .... | .... | .... |
| | Utah Grizzlies | ECHL | 24 | 14 | 7 | 1 | 1390 | 67 | 1 | 2.89 | 10 | 5 | 4 | 543 | 26 | 2 | 2.87 |
| 2008-09 | Bridgeport | AHL | 31 | 19 | 9 | 2 | 1723 | 62 | 2 | 2.16 | 2 | 0 | 2 | 123 | 8 | 0 | 3.89 |
| | Utah Grizzlies | ECHL | 3 | 2 | 0 | 0 | 158 | 6 | 0 | 2.28 | .... | .... | .... | .... | .... | .... | .... |

Signed as a free agent by **NY Islanders**, March 2, 2008.

## LECLAIRE, Pascal (luh-KLAIR, pas-KAL) OTT.

Goaltender. Catches left. 6'2", 200 lbs. Born, Repentigny, Que., November 7, 1982.
(Columbus' 1st choice, 8th overall, in 2001 Entry Draft).

| | | | Regular Season | | | | | | | | Playoffs | | | | | | |
|---|---|---|---|---|---|---|---|---|---|---|---|---|---|---|---|---|---|
| Season | Club | League | GP | W | L | O/T | Mins | GA | SO | Avg | GP | W | L | Mins | GA | SO | Avg |
| 1997-98 | Cap-d-Madeleine | QAAA | 26 | 6 | 17 | 3 | 1580 | 127 | 0 | 4.90 | .... | .... | .... | .... | .... | .... | .... |
| 1998-99 | Halifax | QMJHL | 33 | 19 | 11 | 1 | 1828 | 96 | 2 | 3.15 | 1 | 0 | 0 | 17 | 2 | 0 | 7.06 |
| 99-2000 | Halifax | QMJHL | 31 | 16 | 8 | 4 | 1729 | 103 | 1 | 3.57 | 5 | 1 | 2 | 198 | 12 | 0 | 3.65 |
| 2000-01 | Halifax | QMJHL | 35 | 14 | 16 | 5 | 2111 | 126 | 1 | 3.58 | 2 | 0 | 2 | 109 | 10 | 0 | 5.49 |
| 2001-02 | Montreal Rocket | QMJHL | 45 | 15 | 23 | 4 | 2513 | 138 | 1 | 3.29 | 7 | 3 | 4 | 441 | 15 | 0 | *2.04 |
| 2002-03 | Syracuse Crunch | AHL | 36 | 8 | 21 | 3 | 1886 | 112 | 0 | 3.56 | .... | .... | .... | .... | .... | .... | .... |
| **2003-04** | **Columbus** | **NHL** | **2** | **0** | **2** | **0** | **119** | **7** | **0** | **3.53** | .... | .... | .... | .... | .... | .... | .... |
| | Syracuse Crunch | AHL | 44 | 21 | 16 | 3 | 2447 | 125 | 2 | 3.06 | 3 | 1 | 2 | 142 | 12 | 0 | 5.07 |
| 2004-05 | Syracuse Crunch | AHL | 14 | 5 | 6 | 3 | 845 | 33 | 2 | 2.34 | .... | .... | .... | .... | .... | .... | .... |
| **2005-06** | **Columbus** | **NHL** | **33** | **11** | **15** | **3** | **1804** | **97** | **0** | **3.23** | .... | .... | .... | .... | .... | .... | .... |
| | Syracuse Crunch | AHL | 7 | 3 | 3 | 0 | 340 | 16 | 1 | 2.82 | 5 | 2 | 3 | 288 | 11 | 1 | 2.29 |
| **2006-07** | **Columbus** | **NHL** | **24** | **6** | **15** | **2** | **1315** | **65** | **1** | **2.97** | .... | .... | .... | .... | .... | .... | .... |
| **2007-08** | **Columbus** | **NHL** | **54** | **24** | **17** | **6** | **2986** | **112** | **9** | **2.25** | .... | .... | .... | .... | .... | .... | .... |
| **2008-09** | **Columbus** | **NHL** | **12** | **4** | **6** | **1** | **674** | **43** | **0** | **3.83** | .... | .... | .... | .... | .... | .... | .... |
| | **NHL Totals** | | **125** | **45** | **55** | **12** | **6898** | **324** | **10** | **2.82** | .... | .... | .... | .... | .... | .... | .... |

• Missed majority of 2008-09 season recovering from ankle injury suffered in game vs. Minnesota, October 25, 2008. Traded to **Ottawa** by **Columbus** with Columbus' 2nd round choice (Robin Lehner) in 2009 Entry Draft for Antoine Vermette, March 4, 2009.

## LEE, Michael (LEE, MIGH-kuhl) PHX.

Goaltender. Catches left. 6'1", 185 lbs. Born, Fargo, ND, October 5, 1990.
(Phoenix's 3rd choice, 91st overall, in 2009 Entry Draft).

| | | | Regular Season | | | | | | | | Playoffs | | | | | | |
|---|---|---|---|---|---|---|---|---|---|---|---|---|---|---|---|---|---|
| Season | Club | League | GP | W | L | O/T | Mins | GA | SO | Avg | GP | W | L | Mins | GA | SO | Avg |
| 2006-07 | Roseau Rams | High-MN | 12 | 12 | 0 | 0 | 612 | 9 | 6 | 0.75 | .... | .... | .... | .... | .... | .... | .... |
| 2007-08 | Roseau Rams | High-MN | 29 | 27 | 2 | 0 | 1482 | 32 | 12 | 1.10 | 1 | 0 | 0 | 16 | 0 | 0 | 0.00 |
| 2008-09 | Fargo Force | USHL | 48 | 26 | 15 | 4 | 2745 | 110 | 3 | 2.40 | 10 | 7 | 3 | 546 | 24 | *1 | 2.64 |

USHL All-Rookie Team (2009) • USHL Goaltender of the Year (2009)

• Signed Letter of Intent to attend **St. Cloud State University** (WCHA) in fall of 2009.

## LEGACE, Manny (LEH-gah-see, MAN-ee)

Goaltender. Catches left. 5'10", 200 lbs. Born, Toronto, Ont., February 4, 1973.
(Hartford's 5th choice, 188th overall, in 1993 Entry Draft).

| | | | Regular Season | | | | | | | | Playoffs | | | | | | |
|---|---|---|---|---|---|---|---|---|---|---|---|---|---|---|---|---|---|
| Season | Club | League | GP | W | L | O/T | Mins | GA | SO | Avg | GP | W | L | Mins | GA | SO | Avg |
| 1987-88 | Alliston Hornets | OJHL-C | 16 | 7 | 9 | 0 | 960 | 83 | 0 | 5.17 | .... | .... | .... | .... | .... | .... | .... |
| 1988-89 | Vaughan Raiders | MTJHL | 23 | .... | .... | .... | 1303 | 92 | 1 | 4.24 | .... | .... | .... | .... | .... | .... | .... |
| 1989-90 | Vaughan Raiders | MTJHL | 21 | 8 | 11 | 1 | 1180 | 89 | 1 | 4.53 | .... | .... | .... | .... | .... | .... | .... |
| | Thornhill | OHA-B | 8 | 3 | 3 | 2 | 480 | 30 | 0 | 3.75 | .... | .... | .... | .... | .... | .... | .... |
| 1990-91 | Niagara Falls | OHL | 30 | 13 | 11 | 2 | 1515 | 107 | 0 | 4.24 | 4 | 1 | 1 | 119 | 10 | 0 | 5.04 |
| 1991-92 | Niagara Falls | OHL | 43 | 21 | 16 | 3 | 2384 | 143 | 0 | 3.60 | 14 | 8 | 5 | 791 | 56 | 0 | 4.25 |
| 1992-93 | Niagara Falls | OHL | 48 | 22 | 19 | 3 | 2630 | 171 | 0 | 3.90 | 4 | 0 | 4 | 240 | 18 | 0 | 4.50 |
| 1993-94 | Canada | Nat-Tm | 16 | 8 | 6 | 0 | 859 | 36 | 2 | 2.51 | .... | .... | .... | .... | .... | .... | .... |
| 1994-95 | Springfield Indians | AHL | 39 | 12 | 17 | 6 | 2169 | 128 | 2 | 3.54 | .... | .... | .... | .... | .... | .... | .... |
| 1995-96 | Springfield Falcons | AHL | 37 | 20 | 12 | 4 | 2196 | 83 | *5 | *2.27 | 4 | 1 | 3 | 220 | 18 | 0 | 4.91 |
| 1996-97 | Springfield Falcons | AHL | 36 | 17 | 14 | 5 | 2119 | 107 | 1 | 3.03 | 12 | 9 | 3 | 745 | 25 | *2 | 2.01 |
| | Richmond | ECHL | 3 | 2 | 1 | 0 | 157 | 8 | 0 | 3.05 | .... | .... | .... | .... | .... | .... | .... |
| 1997-98 | Springfield Falcons | AHL | 6 | 4 | 2 | 0 | 345 | 16 | 0 | 2.78 | .... | .... | .... | .... | .... | .... | .... |
| | Las Vegas Thunder | IHL | 41 | 18 | 16 | 4 | 2106 | 111 | 1 | 3.16 | 4 | 1 | 3 | 237 | 16 | 0 | 4.05 |
| **1998-99** | **Los Angeles** | **NHL** | **17** | **2** | **9** | **2** | **899** | **39** | **0** | **2.60** | .... | .... | .... | .... | .... | .... | .... |
| | Long Beach | IHL | 33 | 22 | 8 | 1 | 1796 | 67 | 2 | 2.24 | 6 | 4 | 2 | 338 | 9 | 0 | *1.60 |
| **99-2000** | **Detroit** | **NHL** | **4** | **4** | **0** | **0** | **240** | **11** | **0** | **2.75** | .... | .... | .... | .... | .... | .... | .... |
| | Manitoba Moose | IHL | 42 | 17 | 18 | 5 | 2409 | 104 | 2 | 2.59 | 2 | 0 | 2 | 141 | 7 | 0 | 2.97 |
| **2000-01** | **Detroit** | **NHL** | **39** | **24** | **5** | **5** | **2136** | **73** | **2** | **2.05** | .... | .... | .... | .... | .... | .... | .... |
| **2001-02** ♦ | **Detroit** | **NHL** | **20** | **10** | **6** | **2** | **1117** | **45** | **1** | **2.42** | **1** | **0** | **0** | **11** | **1** | **0** | **5.45** |
| **2002-03** | **Detroit** | **NHL** | **25** | **14** | **5** | **4** | **1406** | **51** | **0** | **2.18** | .... | .... | .... | .... | .... | .... | .... |
| **2003-04** | **Detroit** | **NHL** | **41** | **23** | **10** | **5** | **2325** | **82** | **3** | **2.12** | **4** | **2** | **2** | **220** | **8** | **0** | **2.18** |
| 2004-05 | Voskresensk | Russia | 2 | .... | .... | .... | 89 | 10 | 0 | 6.73 | .... | .... | .... | .... | .... | .... | .... |
| **2005-06** | **Detroit** | **NHL** | **51** | **37** | **8** | **3** | **2905** | **106** | **7** | **2.19** | **6** | **2** | **4** | **408** | **18** | **0** | **2.65** |
| | Grand Rapids | AHL | 1 | 1 | 0 | 0 | 60 | 2 | 0 | 2.00 | .... | .... | .... | .... | .... | .... | .... |
| **2006-07** | **St. Louis** | **NHL** | **45** | **23** | **15** | **5** | **2522** | **109** | **5** | **2.59** | .... | .... | .... | .... | .... | .... | .... |
| **2007-08** | **St. Louis** | **NHL** | **66** | **27** | **25** | **8** | **3666** | **147** | **5** | **2.41** | .... | .... | .... | .... | .... | .... | .... |

| | | | Regular Season | | | | | | | | Playoffs | | | | | | |
|---|---|---|---|---|---|---|---|---|---|---|---|---|---|---|---|---|---|
| 2008-09 | St. Louis | NHL | 29 | 13 | 9 | 2 | 1452 | 77 | 0 | 3.18 | .... | .... | .... | .... | .... | .... | .... |
| | Peoria Rivermen | AHL | 23 | 14 | 7 | 1 | 1290 | 43 | 3 | 2.00 | 7 | 3 | 4 | 429 | 18 | 0 | 2.52 |
| | NHL Totals | | 337 | 177 | 92 | 36 | 18668 | 740 | 23 | 2.38 | 11 | 4 | 6 | 639 | 27 | 0 | 2.54 |

OHL First All-Star Team (1993) • AHL First All-Star Team (1996) • Harry "Hap" Holmes Memorial Award (AHL – fewest goals against) (1996) (shared with Scott Langkow) • Aldege "Baz" Bastien Memorial Award (AHL – Outstanding Goaltender) (1996)

Played in NHL All-Star Game (2008)

• Rights transferred to **Carolina** after **Hartford** franchise relocated, June 25, 1997. Traded to **Los Angeles** by **Carolina** for future considerations, July 31, 1998. Signed as a free agent by **Detroit**, August 9, 1999. Claimed on waivers by **Vancouver** from **Detroit**, September 30, 1999. Claimed on waivers by **Detroit** from **Vancouver**, October 13, 1999. Signed as a free agent by **Voskresensk** (Russia), December 20, 2004. Signed as a free agent by **St. Louis**, August 8, 2006.

## LEHNER, Robin (LEH-nuhr, RAW-bihn) OTT.

Goaltender. Catches left. 6'4", 225 lbs. Born, Goteborg, Sweden, July 24, 1991.
(Ottawa's 3rd choice, 46th overall, in 2009 Entry Draft).

| | | | Regular Season | | | | | | | | Playoffs | | | | | | |
|---|---|---|---|---|---|---|---|---|---|---|---|---|---|---|---|---|---|
| Season | Club | League | GP | W | L | O/T | Mins | GA | SO | Avg | GP | W | L | Mins | GA | SO | Avg |
| 2007-08 | Frolunda U18 | Swe-U18 | 19 | .... | .... | .... | 1147 | 34 | 6 | 1.78 | 4 | .... | .... | 243 | 15 | 0 | 3.70 |
| 2008-09 | Frolunda U18 | Swe-U18 | 2 | .... | .... | .... | 117 | 5 | 0 | 2.56 | 7 | .... | .... | 438 | 19 | 0 | 2.60 |
| | Frolunda Jr. | Swe-Jr. | 22 | .... | .... | .... | 1318 | 67 | 1 | 3.05 | 1 | .... | .... | 58 | 3 | 0 | 3.08 |

## LEHTONEN, Kari (LEH-tuh-nehn, KAH-ree) ATL.

Goaltender. Catches left. 6'4", 215 lbs. Born, Helsinki, Finland, November 16, 1983.
(Atlanta's 1st choice, 2nd overall, in 2002 Entry Draft).

| | | | Regular Season | | | | | | | | Playoffs | | | | | | |
|---|---|---|---|---|---|---|---|---|---|---|---|---|---|---|---|---|---|
| Season | Club | League | GP | W | L | O/T | Mins | GA | SO | Avg | GP | W | L | Mins | GA | SO | Avg |
| 1998-99 | Jokerit U18 | Fin-U18 | 2 | .... | .... | .... | .... | .... | .... | .... | 4 | 2 | 2 | 240 | 7 | 0 | 1.75 |
| 99-2000 | Jokerit Helsinki Jr. | Fin-Jr. | 33 | 21 | 9 | 3 | 1974 | 86 | 2 | 2.61 | 12 | 9 | 3 | 758 | 14 | 4 | 1.11 |
| 2000-01 | Jokerit U18 | Fin-U18 | .... | .... | .... | .... | .... | .... | .... | .... | 6 | .... | .... | .... | .... | .... | .... |
| | Jokerit Helsinki Jr. | Fin-Jr. | 31 | 20 | 9 | 1 | 1799 | 71 | 3 | 2.37 | 1 | 0 | 1 | 54 | 4 | 0 | 4.44 |
| | Jokerit Helsinki | Finland | 4 | 3 | 1 | 0 | 189 | 6 | 0 | 1.90 | .... | .... | .... | .... | .... | .... | .... |
| 2001-02 | Jokerit Helsinki Jr. | Fin-Jr. | 6 | 5 | 1 | 0 | 360 | 11 | 1 | 1.83 | .... | .... | .... | .... | .... | .... | .... |
| | Jokerit Helsinki | Finland | 23 | 13 | 5 | 2 | 1242 | 37 | 4 | 1.79 | 11 | 8 | 2 | 623 | 18 | 3 | 1.73 |
| 2002-03 | Jokerit Helsinki | Finland | 45 | 23 | 14 | 6 | 2634 | 87 | 5 | 1.98 | 10 | 6 | 4 | 626 | 17 | 2 | 1.63 |
| 2003-04 | Atlanta | NHL | 4 | 4 | 0 | 0 | 240 | 5 | 1 | 1.25 | .... | .... | .... | .... | .... | .... | .... |
| | Chicago Wolves | AHL | 39 | 20 | 14 | 2 | 2192 | 88 | 3 | 2.41 | 10 | 6 | 4 | 663 | 23 | 1 | 2.08 |
| 2004-05 | Chicago Wolves | AHL | 57 | 38 | 17 | 2 | 3378 | 128 | 5 | 2.27 | 16 | 10 | 6 | 983 | 28 | 2 | *1.71 |
| 2005-06 | Atlanta | NHL | 38 | 20 | 15 | 0 | 2166 | 106 | 2 | 2.94 | .... | .... | .... | .... | .... | .... | .... |
| 2006-07 | Atlanta | NHL | 68 | 34 | 24 | 9 | 3934 | 183 | 4 | 2.79 | 2 | 0 | 2 | 118 | 11 | 0 | 5.59 |
| 2007-08 | Atlanta | NHL | 48 | 17 | 22 | 5 | 2707 | 131 | 4 | 2.90 | .... | .... | .... | .... | .... | .... | .... |
| | Chicago Wolves | AHL | 2 | 2 | 0 | 0 | 124 | 4 | 0 | 1.93 | .... | .... | .... | .... | .... | .... | .... |
| 2008-09 | Atlanta | NHL | 46 | 19 | 22 | 3 | 2624 | 134 | 3 | 3.06 | .... | .... | .... | .... | .... | .... | .... |
| | NHL Totals | | 204 | 94 | 83 | 17 | 11671 | 559 | 14 | 2.87 | 2 | 0 | 2 | 118 | 11 | 0 | 5.59 |

AHL Second All-Star Team (2005)

## LEIGHTON, Michael (LAY-tohn, MIGH-kuhl) CAR.

Goaltender. Catches left. 6'3", 190 lbs. Born, Petrolia, Ont., May 19, 1981.
(Chicago's 5th choice, 165th overall, in 1999 Entry Draft).

| | | | Regular Season | | | | | | | | Playoffs | | | | | | |
|---|---|---|---|---|---|---|---|---|---|---|---|---|---|---|---|---|---|
| Season | Club | League | GP | W | L | O/T | Mins | GA | SO | Avg | GP | W | L | Mins | GA | SO | Avg |
| 1997-98 | Petrolia Jets | OHA-B | 30 | .... | .... | .... | 1583 | 87 | 2 | 3.30 | .... | .... | .... | .... | .... | .... | .... |
| 1998-99 | Windsor Spitfires | OHL | 28 | 4 | 17 | 2 | 1389 | 112 | 0 | 4.84 | 3 | 0 | 1 | 80 | 10 | 0 | 7.50 |
| 99-2000 | Windsor Spitfires | OHL | 42 | 17 | 17 | 2 | 2272 | 118 | 1 | 3.12 | 12 | 5 | 6 | 616 | 32 | 0 | 3.12 |
| 2000-01 | Windsor Spitfires | OHL | 54 | 32 | 13 | 5 | 3035 | 138 | 2 | 2.73 | 9 | 4 | 5 | 519 | 27 | 1 | 3.12 |
| 2001-02 | Norfolk Admirals | AHL | 52 | 27 | 16 | 8 | 3114 | 111 | 6 | 2.14 | 4 | 1 | 2 | 238 | 8 | 0 | 2.02 |
| 2002-03 | Chicago | NHL | 8 | 2 | 3 | 2 | 447 | 21 | 1 | 2.82 | .... | .... | .... | .... | .... | .... | .... |
| | Norfolk Admirals | AHL | 36 | 18 | 13 | 5 | 2184 | 91 | 4 | 2.50 | 4 | 3 | 1 | 240 | 7 | 1 | 1.75 |
| 2003-04 | Chicago | NHL | 34 | 6 | 18 | 8 | 1988 | 99 | 2 | 2.99 | .... | .... | .... | .... | .... | .... | .... |
| | Norfolk Admirals | AHL | 18 | 10 | 7 | 1 | 1081 | 33 | 1 | 1.83 | 4 | 2 | 1 | 212 | 2 | 2 | 0.57 |
| 2004-05 | Norfolk Admirals | AHL | 41 | 20 | 16 | 3 | 2319 | 78 | 7 | 2.02 | .... | .... | .... | .... | .... | .... | .... |
| 2005-06 | Rochester | AHL | 40 | 15 | 22 | 1 | 2318 | 124 | 2 | 3.21 | .... | .... | .... | .... | .... | .... | .... |
| 2006-07 | Portland Pirates | AHL | 16 | 8 | 6 | 1 | 962 | 37 | 2 | 2.31 | .... | .... | .... | .... | .... | .... | .... |
| | Nashville | NHL | 1 | 0 | 0 | 0 | 20 | 2 | 0 | 6.00 | .... | .... | .... | .... | .... | .... | .... |
| | Philadelphia | NHL | 4 | 2 | 2 | 0 | 195 | 12 | 0 | 3.69 | .... | .... | .... | .... | .... | .... | .... |
| | Philadelphia | AHL | 5 | 2 | 0 | 2 | 270 | 7 | 0 | 1.56 | .... | .... | .... | .... | .... | .... | .... |
| 2007-08 | Carolina | NHL | 3 | 1 | 1 | 0 | 158 | 7 | 0 | 2.66 | .... | .... | .... | .... | .... | .... | .... |
| | Albany River Rats | AHL | 58 | 28 | 25 | 4 | 3451 | 121 | *7 | 2.10 | 7 | 3 | 4 | 510 | 10 | *2 | *1.18 |
| 2008-09 | Carolina | NHL | 19 | 6 | 7 | 2 | 1029 | 50 | 0 | 2.92 | .... | .... | .... | .... | .... | .... | .... |
| | NHL Totals | | 69 | 17 | 31 | 12 | 3837 | 191 | 3 | 2.99 | .... | .... | .... | .... | .... | .... | .... |

AHL All-Rookie Team (2002) • AHL First All-Star Team (2008) • Aldege "Baz" Bastien Memorial Award (AHL – Outstanding Goaltender) (2008)

Traded to **Buffalo** by **Chicago** for Milan Bartovic, October 4, 2005. Signed as a free agent by **Anaheim**, July 13, 2006. Claimed on waivers by **Nashville** from **Anaheim**, November 27, 2006. Claimed on waivers by **Philadelphia** from **Nashville**, January 11, 2007. Claimed on waivers by **Montreal** from **Philadelphia**, February 27, 2007. Traded to **Carolina** by **Montreal** for Carolina's 7th round choice (Scott Kishel) in 2007 Entry Draft, June 23, 2007.

## LeNEVEU, David (LEH-neh-voo, DAY-vihd)

Goaltender. Catches left. 6'1", 187 lbs. Born, Fernie, B.C., May 23, 1983.
(Phoenix's 3rd choice, 46th overall, in 2002 Entry Draft).

| | | | Regular Season | | | | | | | | Playoffs | | | | | | |
|---|---|---|---|---|---|---|---|---|---|---|---|---|---|---|---|---|---|
| Season | Club | League | GP | W | L | O/T | Mins | GA | SO | Avg | GP | W | L | Mins | GA | SO | Avg |
| 99-2000 | Fernie Ghostriders | AWHL | 22 | 15 | 2 | 0 | 1140 | 48 | 0 | 2.49 | .... | .... | .... | .... | .... | .... | .... |
| 2000-01 | Nanaimo Clippers | BCHL | 41 | .... | .... | .... | 2330 | 127 | 6 | 3.29 | .... | .... | .... | .... | .... | .... | .... |
| 2001-02 | Cornell Big Red | ECAC | 14 | 11 | 2 | 1 | 842 | 21 | 2 | *1.50 | .... | .... | .... | .... | .... | .... | .... |
| 2002-03 | Cornell Big Red | ECAC | 32 | *28 | 3 | 1 | 1946 | 39 | *9 | *1.20 | .... | .... | .... | .... | .... | .... | .... |
| 2003-04 | Springfield Falcons | AHL | 38 | 16 | 19 | 3 | 2217 | 102 | 1 | 2.76 | .... | .... | .... | .... | .... | .... | .... |
| 2004-05 | Utah Grizzlies | AHL | 48 | 11 | 32 | 3 | 2702 | 132 | 0 | 2.93 | .... | .... | .... | .... | .... | .... | .... |
| 2005-06 | Phoenix | NHL | 15 | 3 | 8 | 2 | 814 | 44 | 0 | 3.24 | .... | .... | .... | .... | .... | .... | .... |
| | San Antonio | AHL | 28 | 10 | 16 | 2 | 1646 | 80 | 2 | 2.92 | .... | .... | .... | .... | .... | .... | .... |
| 2006-07 | Phoenix | NHL | 6 | 2 | 1 | 0 | 233 | 15 | 0 | 3.86 | .... | .... | .... | .... | .... | .... | .... |
| | San Antonio | AHL | 37 | 13 | 20 | 2 | 2101 | 104 | 2 | 2.97 | .... | .... | .... | .... | .... | .... | .... |
| 2007-08 | San Antonio | AHL | 21 | 9 | 7 | 3 | 1172 | 52 | 1 | 2.66 | .... | .... | .... | .... | .... | .... | .... |
| | Hartford Wolf Pack | AHL | 13 | 8 | 3 | 2 | 786 | 24 | 1 | 1.83 | 4 | 1 | 3 | 266 | 11 | 0 | 2.48 |
| 2008-09 | Iowa Chops | AHL | 46 | 20 | 19 | 6 | 2627 | 129 | 0 | 2.95 | .... | .... | .... | .... | .... | .... | .... |
| | NHL Totals | | 21 | 5 | 9 | 2 | 1047 | 59 | 0 | 3.38 | .... | .... | .... | .... | .... | .... | .... |

ECAC All-Rookie Team (2002) • ECAC First All-Star Team (2003) • ECAC Goaltender of the Year (2003) • ECAC Player of the Year (2003) (co-winner - Christopher Higgins) • NCAA East First All-American Team (2003)

Traded to **NY Rangers** by **Phoenix** with Josh Gratton, Fredrik Sjostrom and Phoenix's 5th round choice (Roman Horak) in 2009 Entry Draft for Marcel Hossa and Al Montoya, February 26, 2008. Signed as a free agent by **Anaheim**, July 7, 2008.

## LEVASSEUR, Jean-Philippe (leh-VAH-soor, ZHAWN-fihl-EEP) ANA.

Goaltender. Catches right. 6'1", 205 lbs. Born, Victoriaville, Que., January 15, 1987.
(Anaheim's 6th choice, 197th overall, in 2005 Entry Draft).

| | | | Regular Season | | | | | | | | Playoffs | | | | | | |
|---|---|---|---|---|---|---|---|---|---|---|---|---|---|---|---|---|---|
| Season | Club | League | GP | W | L | O/T | Mins | GA | SO | Avg | GP | W | L | Mins | GA | SO | Avg |
| 2002-03 | Magog | QAAA | 28 | 15 | 10 | 1 | 1563 | 71 | 3 | 2.73 | .... | .... | .... | .... | .... | .... | .... |
| 2003-04 | Magog | QAAA | 24 | 12 | 11 | 2 | 1424 | 86 | 0 | 3.62 | 13 | 7 | 5 | 762 | 35 | 0 | 2.80 |
| | Rouyn-Noranda | QMJHL | 3 | 0 | 2 | 1 | 184 | 14 | 0 | 4.57 | .... | .... | .... | .... | .... | .... | .... |
| 2004-05 | Rouyn-Noranda | QMJHL | 29 | 8 | 14 | 3 | 1393 | 89 | 0 | 3.83 | 3 | 0 | 0 | 48 | 3 | 0 | 3.76 |
| 2005-06 | Rouyn-Noranda | QMJHL | 58 | *35 | 19 | 0 | 3125 | 178 | 2 | 3.42 | 5 | 1 | 4 | 297 | 16 | 0 | 3.23 |
| 2006-07 | Rouyn-Noranda | QMJHL | 58 | *31 | 21 | .... | 3118 | 182 | 1 | 3.50 | 15 | 8 | 6 | 852 | 51 | 0 | 3.59 |
| 2007-08 | Portland Pirates | AHL | 10 | 4 | 5 | 1 | 600 | 25 | 1 | 2.50 | .... | .... | .... | .... | .... | .... | .... |
| | Augusta Lynx | ECHL | 29 | 10 | 11 | 2 | 1527 | 76 | 1 | 2.99 | 1 | 0 | 1 | 59 | 2 | 0 | 2.02 |
| 2008-09 | Iowa Chops | AHL | 41 | 13 | 18 | 4 | 2217 | 115 | 0 | 3.11 | .... | .... | .... | .... | .... | .... | .... |

## LINDBACK, Anders (LIHND-bak, AN-duhrs) NSH.

Goaltender. Catches left. 6'6", 205 lbs. Born, Gavle, Sweden, May 3, 1988.
(Nashville's 7th choice, 207th overall, in 2008 Entry Draft).

| | | | Regular Season | | | | | | | | Playoffs | | | | | | |
|---|---|---|---|---|---|---|---|---|---|---|---|---|---|---|---|---|---|
| Season | Club | League | GP | W | L | O/T | Mins | GA | SO | Avg | GP | W | L | Mins | GA | SO | Avg |
| 2003-04 | Brynas U18 | Swe-U18 | 3 | .... | .... | .... | 178 | 13 | 0 | 4.38 | .... | .... | .... | .... | .... | .... | .... |
| 2004-05 | Brynas U18 | Swe-U18 | 49 | .... | .... | .... | 2940 | 108 | 7 | 2.20 | .... | .... | .... | .... | .... | .... | .... |
| 2005-06 | Brynas U18 | Swe-U18 | 11 | .... | .... | .... | 666 | 36 | 2 | 3.24 | .... | .... | .... | .... | .... | .... | .... |
| | Brynas IF Gavle Jr. | Swe-Jr. | 5 | .... | .... | .... | 257 | 7 | 2 | 1.64 | .... | .... | .... | .... | .... | .... | .... |
| 2006-07 | Brynas IF Gavle Jr. | Swe-Jr. | 36 | .... | .... | .... | 2143 | 81 | 5 | 2.27 | 3 | .... | .... | 180 | 6 | 0 | 2.00 |
| 2007-08 | Almtuna | Sweden-2 | 18 | .... | .... | .... | 1034 | 53 | 0 | 3.07 | .... | .... | .... | .... | .... | .... | .... |
| 2008-09 | Brynas IF Gavle Jr. | Swe-Jr. | 3 | .... | .... | .... | 179 | 7 | 0 | 2.35 | .... | .... | .... | .... | .... | .... | .... |
| | Brynas IF Gavle | Sweden | 24 | .... | .... | .... | 1332 | 57 | 1 | 2.57 | 3 | .... | .... | 177 | 7 | 0 | 2.37 |

## LUNDQVIST, Henrik (LUHND-kvihst, HEHN-rihk) NYR

Goaltender. Catches left. 6'1", 195 lbs. Born, Are, Sweden, March 2, 1982.
(NY Rangers' 7th choice, 205th overall, in 2000 Entry Draft).

| | | | Regular Season | | | | | | | | Playoffs | | | | | | |
|---|---|---|---|---|---|---|---|---|---|---|---|---|---|---|---|---|---|
| Season | Club | League | GP | W | L | O/T | Mins | GA | SO | Avg | GP | W | L | Mins | GA | SO | Avg |
| 1998-99 | V.Frolunda Jr. | Swe-Jr. | 35 | .... | .... | .... | 2100 | 95 | 0 | 2.73 | .... | .... | .... | .... | .... | .... | .... |
| 99-2000 | V.Frolunda Jr. | Swe-Jr. | 30 | .... | .... | .... | 1726 | 73 | 0 | 2.54 | 5 | 4 | 1 | 300 | 7 | 2 | 1.40 |
| 2000-01 | V.Frolunda U18 | Swe-U18 | 2 | .... | .... | .... | 120 | 5 | 0 | 2.50 | 3 | 2 | 1 | 182 | 5 | 0 | 1.62 |
| | V.Frolunda Jr. | Swe-Jr. | 19 | .... | .... | .... | 1140 | 50 | 2 | 2.64 | .... | .... | .... | .... | .... | .... | .... |
| | IF Molndal Hockey | Sweden-2 | 7 | .... | .... | .... | 420 | 29 | 0 | 4.22 | .... | .... | .... | .... | .... | .... | .... |
| | V.Frolunda | Sweden | 4 | .... | .... | .... | 190 | 11 | 0 | 3.47 | .... | .... | .... | .... | .... | .... | .... |
| 2001-02 | V.Frolunda | Sweden | 20 | .... | .... | .... | 1152 | 52 | 2 | 2.71 | 8 | 8 | 0 | 489 | 18 | *2 | 2.21 |
| | V.Frolunda Jr. | Swe-Jr. | 1 | 1 | 0 | 0 | 60 | 4 | 0 | 4.00 | .... | .... | .... | .... | .... | .... | .... |
| 2002-03 | V.Frolunda | Sweden | 28 | .... | .... | .... | 1650 | 40 | *6 | *1.45 | 12 | .... | .... | 739 | 26 | *2 | 2.11 |
| | V.Frolunda Jr. | Swe-Jr. | 1 | 1 | 0 | 0 | 60 | 4 | 0 | 4.00 | .... | .... | .... | .... | .... | .... | .... |
| 2003-04 | V.Frolunda | Sweden | *48 | .... | .... | .... | *2897 | 105 | 7 | 2.17 | 10 | .... | .... | 610 | 20 | 0 | 1.97 |
| 2004-05 | Frolunda | Sweden | 44 | *33 | 8 | 3 | 2642 | 79 | *6 | *1.79 | *14 | *12 | 2 | 854 | 15 | *6 | *1.05 |
| 2005-06 | NY Rangers | NHL | 53 | 30 | 12 | 9 | 3112 | 116 | 2 | 2.24 | 3 | 0 | 3 | 177 | 13 | 0 | 4.41 |
| | Sweden | Olympics | 6 | 5 | 1 | 0 | 360 | 14 | 0 | 2.33 | .... | .... | .... | .... | .... | .... | .... |
| 2006-07 | NY Rangers | NHL | 70 | 37 | 22 | 8 | 4109 | 160 | 5 | 2.34 | 10 | 6 | 4 | 637 | 22 | 1 | 2.07 |
| 2007-08 | NY Rangers | NHL | 72 | 37 | 24 | 10 | 4305 | 160 | *10 | 2.23 | 10 | 5 | 5 | 608 | 26 | 1 | 2.57 |
| 2008-09 | NY Rangers | NHL | 70 | 38 | 25 | 7 | 4153 | 168 | 3 | 2.43 | 7 | 3 | 4 | 380 | 19 | 1 | 3.00 |
| | NHL Totals | | 265 | 142 | 83 | 34 | 15679 | 604 | 20 | 2.31 | 30 | 14 | 16 | 1802 | 80 | 3 | 2.66 |

NHL All-Rookie Team (2006)

Played in NHL All-Star Game (2009)

## LUONGO, Roberto (loo-WAHN-goh, roh-BUHR-toh) VAN.

Goaltender. Catches left. 6'3", 205 lbs. Born, Montreal, Que., April 4, 1979.
(NY Islanders' 1st choice, 4th overall, in 1997 Entry Draft).

| | | | Regular Season | | | | | | | | Playoffs | | | | | | |
|---|---|---|---|---|---|---|---|---|---|---|---|---|---|---|---|---|---|
| Season | Club | League | GP | W | L | O/T | Mins | GA | SO | Avg | GP | W | L | Mins | GA | SO | Avg |
| 1994-95 | Montreal-Bourassa | QAAA | 25 | 10 | 14 | 0 | 1465 | 94 | 0 | 3.85 | .... | .... | .... | .... | .... | .... | .... |
| 1995-96 | Val-d'Or Foreurs | QMJHL | 23 | 6 | 11 | 4 | 1201 | 74 | 0 | 3.70 | 3 | 0 | 1 | 68 | 5 | 0 | 4.41 |
| 1996-97 | Val-d'Or Foreurs | QMJHL | 60 | 32 | 22 | 2 | 3305 | 171 | 2 | 3.10 | 13 | 8 | 5 | 777 | 44 | 0 | 3.40 |
| 1997-98 | Val-d'Or Foreurs | QMJHL | 54 | 27 | 20 | 5 | 3046 | 157 | *7 | 3.09 | *17 | *14 | 3 | *1019 | 37 | *2 | *2.18 |
| 1998-99 | Val-d'Or Foreurs | QMJHL | 21 | 6 | 10 | 2 | 1176 | 77 | 1 | 3.93 | .... | .... | .... | .... | .... | .... | .... |
| | Acadie-Bathurst | QMJHL | 22 | 14 | 7 | 1 | 1340 | 74 | 0 | 3.31 | *23 | *16 | 6 | *1400 | 64 | 0 | 2.74 |
| 99-2000 | NY Islanders | NHL | 24 | 7 | 14 | 1 | 1292 | 70 | 1 | 3.25 | .... | .... | .... | .... | .... | .... | .... |
| | Lowell | AHL | 26 | 10 | 12 | 4 | 1517 | 74 | 1 | 2.93 | 6 | 3 | 3 | 359 | 18 | 0 | 3.01 |
| 2000-01 | Florida | NHL | 47 | 12 | 24 | 7 | 2628 | 107 | 5 | 2.44 | .... | .... | .... | .... | .... | .... | .... |
| | Louisville Panthers | AHL | 3 | 1 | 2 | 0 | 178 | 10 | 0 | 3.38 | .... | .... | .... | .... | .... | .... | .... |
| 2001-02 | Florida | NHL | 58 | 16 | 33 | 4 | 3030 | 140 | 4 | 2.77 | .... | .... | .... | .... | .... | .... | .... |
| 2002-03 | Florida | NHL | 65 | 20 | 34 | 7 | 3627 | 164 | 6 | 2.71 | .... | .... | .... | .... | .... | .... | .... |
| 2003-04 | Florida | NHL | 72 | 25 | 33 | 14 | 4252 | 172 | 7 | 2.43 | .... | .... | .... | .... | .... | .... | .... |
| 2004-05 | | | | | | | DID NOT PLAY | | | | | | | | | | |
| 2005-06 | Florida | NHL | *75 | 35 | 30 | 9 | 4305 | 213 | 4 | 2.97 | .... | .... | .... | .... | .... | .... | .... |
| | Canada | Olympics | 2 | 1 | 1 | 0 | 119 | 3 | 0 | 1.51 | .... | .... | .... | .... | .... | .... | .... |
| 2006-07 | Vancouver | NHL | 76 | 47 | 22 | 6 | 4490 | 171 | 5 | 2.29 | 12 | 5 | 7 | 847 | 25 | 0 | 1.77 |
| 2007-08 | Vancouver | NHL | 73 | 35 | 29 | 9 | 4233 | 168 | 6 | 2.38 | .... | .... | .... | .... | .... | .... | .... |
| 2008-09 | Vancouver | NHL | 54 | 33 | 13 | 7 | 3181 | 124 | 9 | 2.34 | 10 | 6 | 4 | 618 | 26 | 1 | 2.52 |
| | NHL Totals | | 544 | 230 | 232 | 64 | 31038 | 1329 | 47 | 2.57 | 22 | 11 | 11 | 1465 | 51 | 1 | 2.09 |

NHL Second All-Star Team (2004, 2007)

Played in NHL All-Star Game (2004, 2007, 2009)

Traded to **Florida** by **NY Islanders** with Olli Jokinen for Mark Parrish and Oleg Kvasha, June 24, 2000. Traded to **Vancouver** by **Florida** with Lukas Krajicek and Florida's 6th round choice (Sergei Shirokov) in 2006 Entry Draft for Todd Bertuzzi, Bryan Allen and Alex Auld, June 23, 2006.

## MacDONALD, Joey (MAK-DAWN-uhld, JOH-ee) TOR.

Goaltender. Catches left. 6', 197 lbs. Born, Pictou, N.S., February 7, 1980.

| | | | Regular Season | | | | | | | | Playoffs | | | | | | |
|---|---|---|---|---|---|---|---|---|---|---|---|---|---|---|---|---|---|
| Season | Club | League | GP | W | L | O/T | Mins | GA | SO | Avg | GP | W | L | Mins | GA | SO | Avg |
| 1997-98 | Halifax | QMJHL | 17 | 3 | 12 | 0 | 815 | 54 | 0 | 3.97 | 3 | 1 | 2 | 140 | 15 | 0 | 6.43 |
| 1998-99 | Peterborough | OHL | 47 | 22 | 15 | 2 | 2483 | 123 | 3 | 2.97 | 3 | 0 | 2 | 145 | 13 | 0 | 5.38 |
| 99-2000 | Peterborough | OHL | 48 | 20 | 15 | 6 | 2641 | 125 | 2 | 2.84 | 5 | 1 | 4 | 280 | 16 | 1 | 3.43 |
| 2000-01 | Peterborough | OHL | 57 | 25 | 21 | 7 | 3284 | 161 | 1 | 2.94 | 7 | 3 | 4 | 425 | 18 | 0 | 2.54 |
| 2001-02 | Toledo Storm | ECHL | 38 | 12 | 15 | 7 | 2084 | 100 | 1 | 2.88 | .... | .... | .... | .... | .... | .... | .... |
| 2002-03 | Grand Rapids | AHL | 25 | 14 | 6 | 0 | 1337 | 49 | 3 | 2.20 | 1 | 0 | 0 | 8 | 1 | 0 | 7.95 |
| 2003-04 | Grand Rapids | AHL | 39 | 22 | 12 | 3 | 2249 | 74 | 6 | 1.97 | 1 | 0 | 1 | 40 | 4 | 0 | 6.04 |
| 2004-05 | Grand Rapids | AHL | *66 | 34 | 29 | 2 | *3755 | 143 | 5 | 2.29 | .... | .... | .... | .... | .... | .... | .... |
| 2005-06 | Grand Rapids | AHL | 32 | 17 | 9 | 2 | 1745 | 91 | 2 | 3.13 | .... | .... | .... | .... | .... | .... | .... |
| | Toledo Storm | ECHL | 1 | 1 | 0 | 0 | 60 | 1 | 0 | 1.00 | .... | .... | .... | .... | .... | .... | .... |
| 2006-07 | Detroit | NHL | 8 | 1 | 5 | 1 | 468 | 27 | 0 | 3.46 | .... | .... | .... | .... | .... | .... | .... |
| | Grand Rapids | AHL | 2 | 1 | 1 | 0 | 123 | 6 | 0 | 2.93 | .... | .... | .... | .... | .... | .... | .... |
| | Boston | NHL | 7 | 2 | 2 | 1 | 358 | 16 | 0 | 2.68 | .... | .... | .... | .... | .... | .... | .... |
| 2007-08 | NY Islanders | NHL | 2 | 0 | 1 | 1 | 120 | 6 | 0 | 3.00 | .... | .... | .... | .... | .... | .... | .... |
| | Bridgeport | AHL | 38 | 16 | 19 | 2 | 2266 | 109 | 2 | 2.89 | .... | .... | .... | .... | .... | .... | .... |

| | | | | | | | | | | | | | | | | | |
|---|---|---|---|---|---|---|---|---|---|---|---|---|---|---|---|---|---|
| **2008-09** | **NY Islanders** | **NHL** | **49** | **14** | **26** | **6** | **2792** | **157** | **1** | **3.37** | .... | .... | .... | .... | .... | .... | .... |
| | **NHL Totals** | | **66** | **17** | **34** | **9** | **3738** | **206** | **1** | **3.31** | .... | .... | .... | .... | .... | .... | .... |

Harry "Hap" Holmes Memorial Award (AHL – fewest goals against) (2003) (shared with Marc Lamothe)

Signed as a free agent by **Detroit**, December 21, 2001. Claimed on waivers by **Boston** from **Detroit**, February 24, 2007. Signed as a free agent by **NY Islanders**, July 7, 2007. Signed as a free agent by **Toronto**, August 10, 2009.

## MACHESNEY, Daren (muh-KEHS-nee, DAIR-ehn)

Goaltender. Catches left. 6', 182 lbs. Born, Hamilton, Ont., December 13, 1986.
(Washington's 5th choice, 143rd overall, in 2005 Entry Draft).

| | | | Regular Season | | | | | | | | Playoffs | | | | | | |
|---|---|---|---|---|---|---|---|---|---|---|---|---|---|---|---|---|---|
| **Season** | **Club** | **League** | **GP** | **W** | **L** | **O/T** | **Mins** | **GA** | **SO** | **Avg** | **GP** | **W** | **L** | **Mins** | **GA** | **SO** | **Avg** |
| 2003-04 | Newmarket | OPJHL | 32 | .... | .... | .... | 1868 | 82 | 1 | 2.63 | .... | .... | .... | .... | .... | .... | .... |
| | Brampton Battalion | OHL | 5 | 3 | 2 | 0 | 300 | 15 | 0 | 3.00 | .... | .... | .... | .... | .... | .... | .... |
| 2004-05 | Brampton Battalion | OHL | 38 | 16 | 13 | 6 | 2166 | 99 | 1 | 2.74 | 5 | 2 | 3 | 331 | 15 | 0 | 2.72 |
| 2005-06 | Brampton Battalion | OHL | 49 | 28 | 17 | 3 | 2830 | 143 | 3 | 3.03 | 11 | 5 | 6 | 633 | 32 | 0 | 3.03 |
| 2006-07 | Hershey Bears | AHL | 10 | 3 | 3 | 1 | 377 | 20 | 0 | 3.18 | .... | .... | .... | .... | .... | .... | .... |
| | South Carolina | ECHL | 15 | 5 | 8 | 2 | 836 | 46 | 1 | 3.30 | .... | .... | .... | .... | .... | .... | .... |
| 2007-08 | Hershey Bears | AHL | 38 | 22 | 10 | 2 | 2139 | 91 | 1 | 2.55 | 2 | 0 | 1 | 21 | 3 | 0 | 8.54 |
| 2008-09 | Hershey Bears | AHL | 36 | 19 | 12 | 1 | 1981 | 107 | 3 | 3.24 | .... | .... | .... | .... | .... | .... | .... |

OHL All-Rookie Team (2005)

Signed as a free agent by **Manitoba** (AHL), July 20, 2009.

## MacINTYRE, Drew (MAK-ihn-tighr, DROO) ATL.

Goaltender. Catches left. 6'2", 185 lbs. Born, Charlottetown, P.E.I., June 24, 1983.
(Detroit's 2nd choice, 121st overall, in 2001 Entry Draft).

| | | | Regular Season | | | | | | | | Playoffs | | | | | | |
|---|---|---|---|---|---|---|---|---|---|---|---|---|---|---|---|---|---|
| **Season** | **Club** | **League** | **GP** | **W** | **L** | **O/T** | **Mins** | **GA** | **SO** | **Avg** | **GP** | **W** | **L** | **Mins** | **GA** | **SO** | **Avg** |
| 1998-99 | Trenton Sting | OPJHL | 20 | .... | .... | .... | 1173 | 71 | 2 | 3.63 | .... | .... | .... | .... | .... | .... | .... |
| 99-2000 | Sherbrooke | QMJHL | 24 | 10 | 7 | 2 | 1253 | 67 | 0 | 3.21 | .... | .... | .... | .... | .... | .... | .... |
| 2000-01 | Sherbrooke | QMJHL | 48 | 17 | 22 | 3 | 2552 | 139 | 4 | 3.27 | 4 | 0 | 4 | 238 | 19 | 0 | 4.78 |
| 2001-02 | Sherbrooke | QMJHL | 55 | 15 | 34 | 3 | 3028 | 201 | 1 | 3.98 | .... | .... | .... | .... | .... | .... | .... |
| 2002-03 | Sherbrooke | QMJHL | *61 | 31 | 24 | 5 | *3515 | 161 | 2 | 2.75 | 12 | 5 | 7 | 767 | 52 | 0 | 4.07 |
| 2003-04 | Toledo Storm | ECHL | 11 | 6 | 4 | 0 | 574 | 25 | 0 | 2.61 | .... | .... | .... | .... | .... | .... | .... |
| 2004-05 | Grand Rapids | AHL | 24 | 7 | 8 | 0 | 1049 | 47 | 1 | 2.69 | .... | .... | .... | .... | .... | .... | .... |
| | Toledo Storm | ECHL | 2 | 0 | 1 | 0 | 87 | 6 | 0 | 4.12 | .... | .... | .... | .... | .... | .... | .... |
| 2005-06 | Grand Rapids | AHL | 13 | 8 | 4 | 0 | 681 | 33 | 0 | 2.91 | 5 | 3 | 1 | 260 | 7 | 0 | 1.62 |
| | Toledo Storm | ECHL | 33 | 24 | 7 | 2 | 1981 | 68 | 2 | *2.06 | 6 | 5 | 1 | 360 | 12 | 0 | 2.00 |
| 2006-07 | Manitoba Moose | AHL | 41 | 24 | 12 | 2 | 2290 | 83 | 3 | 2.17 | 11 | 4 | 6 | 633 | 21 | 1 | 1.99 |
| **2007-08** | **Vancouver** | **NHL** | **2** | **0** | **1** | **0** | **61** | **3** | **0** | **2.95** | .... | .... | .... | .... | .... | .... | .... |
| | Manitoba Moose | AHL | 46 | 25 | 18 | 2 | 2736 | 106 | 2 | 2.32 | 1 | 1 | 0 | 31 | 2 | 0 | 3.93 |
| 2008-09 | Milwaukee | AHL | 55 | *34 | 15 | 4 | 3180 | 122 | 4 | 2.30 | 11 | 7 | 4 | 655 | 18 | 1 | *1.65 |
| | **NHL Totals** | | **2** | **0** | **1** | **0** | **61** | **3** | **0** | **2.95** | .... | .... | .... | .... | .... | .... | .... |

AHL Second All-Star Team (2008, 2009)

• Missed majority of 2003-04 season recovering from thigh injury suffered in practice, December 27, 2003. Traded to **Vancouver** by **Detroit** for future considerations, September 12, 2006. Signed as a free agent by **Nashville**, July 1, 2008. Signed as a free agent by **Atlanta**, July 6, 2009.

## MANNINO, Peter (ma-NEE-noh, PE-tuhr) ATL.

Goaltender. Catches right. 6', 200 lbs. Born, Farmington Hills, MI, February 17, 1984.

| | | | Regular Season | | | | | | | | Playoffs | | | | | | |
|---|---|---|---|---|---|---|---|---|---|---|---|---|---|---|---|---|---|
| **Season** | **Club** | **League** | **GP** | **W** | **L** | **O/T** | **Mins** | **GA** | **SO** | **Avg** | **GP** | **W** | **L** | **Mins** | **GA** | **SO** | **Avg** |
| 2001-02 | Pittsburgh Forge | NAHL | 11 | .... | .... | .... | .... | .... | .... | .... | .... | .... | .... | .... | .... | .... | .... |
| 2002-03 | Pittsburgh Forge | NAHL | 45 | .... | .... | .... | .... | .... | .... | .... | .... | .... | .... | .... | .... | .... | .... |
| 2003-04 | Tri-City Storm | USHL | 38 | 26 | 7 | 0 | 1988 | 70 | 5 | *2.11 | 7 | 4 | 1 | 334 | 12 | *1 | 2.15 |
| 2004-05 | U. of Denver | WCHA | 21 | 16 | 4 | 1 | 1224 | 46 | *5 | 2.25 | .... | .... | .... | .... | .... | .... | .... |
| 2005-06 | U. of Denver | WCHA | 22 | 12 | 8 | 1 | 1241 | 56 | 1 | 2.71 | .... | .... | .... | .... | .... | .... | .... |
| 2006-07 | U. of Denver | WCHA | 18 | 8 | 6 | 2 | 1021 | 39 | 3 | 2.29 | .... | .... | .... | .... | .... | .... | .... |
| 2007-08 | U. of Denver | WCHA | 40 | 25 | 14 | 1 | 2302 | 87 | *6 | 2.27 | .... | .... | .... | .... | .... | .... | .... |
| **2008-09** | **NY Islanders** | **NHL** | **3** | **1** | **1** | **0** | **133** | **10** | **0** | **4.51** | .... | .... | .... | .... | .... | .... | .... |
| | Bridgeport | AHL | 34 | 17 | 12 | 2 | 1959 | 96 | 1 | 2.94 | 3 | 1 | 2 | 189 | 10 | 0 | 3.18 |
| | Utah Grizzlies | ECHL | 9 | 4 | 3 | 2 | 549 | 25 | 0 | 2.73 | .... | .... | .... | .... | .... | .... | .... |
| | **NHL Totals** | | **3** | **1** | **1** | **0** | **133** | **10** | **0** | **4.51** | .... | .... | .... | .... | .... | .... | .... |

Signed as a free agent by **NY Islanders**, July 3, 2008. Signed as a free agent by **Atlanta**, July 6, 2009.

## MANZATO, Daniel (man-ZA-toh, DAN-yehl)

Goaltender. Catches left. 6', 178 lbs. Born, Fribourg, Switz., January 17, 1984.
(Carolina's 3rd choice, 160th overall, in 2002 Entry Draft).

| | | | Regular Season | | | | | | | | Playoffs | | | | | | |
|---|---|---|---|---|---|---|---|---|---|---|---|---|---|---|---|---|---|
| **Season** | **Club** | **League** | **GP** | **W** | **L** | **O/T** | **Mins** | **GA** | **SO** | **Avg** | **GP** | **W** | **L** | **Mins** | **GA** | **SO** | **Avg** |
| 2000-01 | Fribourg Jr. | Swiss-Jr. | 36 | .... | .... | .... | 2160 | 32 | 6 | 0.91 | .... | .... | .... | .... | .... | .... | .... |
| 2001-02 | Victoriaville Tigres | QMJHL | 36 | 20 | 8 | 2 | 1894 | 102 | 0 | 3.23 | 6 | 3 | 0 | 249 | 17 | 0 | 4.09 |
| 2002-03 | Victoriaville Tigres | QMJHL | 48 | 23 | 18 | 5 | 2756 | 155 | 3 | 3.37 | 3 | 0 | 3 | 125 | 11 | 0 | 5.27 |
| 2003-04 | Victoriaville Tigres | QMJHL | 23 | 7 | 13 | 0 | 1170 | 78 | 0 | 4.00 | .... | .... | .... | .... | .... | .... | .... |
| | Kloten Flyers | Swiss | 15 | .... | .... | .... | 912 | 39 | 1 | 2.57 | .... | .... | .... | .... | .... | .... | .... |
| 2004-05 | HC Ambri-Piotta | Swiss | 25 | .... | .... | .... | 1446 | 65 | 1 | 2.70 | .... | .... | .... | .... | .... | .... | .... |
| 2005-06 | EHC Basel | Swiss | 41 | 18 | 14 | 9 | 2449 | 107 | *5 | 2.62 | 5 | 1 | 4 | 280 | 22 | 0 | 4.71 |
| 2006-07 | EHC Basel | Swiss | 43 | 13 | 30 | 0 | 2590 | 157 | 1 | 3.64 | 13 | 7 | 6 | 795 | 41 | 2 | 3.09 |
| 2007-08 | Albany River Rats | AHL | 1 | 0 | 1 | 0 | 59 | 5 | 0 | 5.07 | .... | .... | .... | .... | .... | .... | .... |
| | Charlotte Checkers | ECHL | 2 | 2 | 0 | 0 | 120 | 4 | 0 | 2.00 | .... | .... | .... | .... | .... | .... | .... |
| | Las Vegas | ECHL | 33 | 22 | 5 | 6 | 1985 | 79 | 3 | 2.39 | 2 | 1 | 0 | 97 | 4 | 0 | 2.48 |
| 2008-09 | Albany River Rats | AHL | 32 | 14 | 12 | 0 | 1597 | 85 | 0 | 3.19 | .... | .... | .... | .... | .... | .... | .... |

Signed as a free agent by **Kloten** (Swiss), January 5, 2004, following release by **Victoriaville** (QMJHL), January 4, 2004. Signed as a free agent by **Ambri-Piotta** (Swiss), August 5, 2004. Signed as a free agent by **Basel** (Swiss), August, 2005.

## MARKSTROM, Jacob (MAHRK-struhm, JAY-kawb) FLA.

Goaltender. Catches left. 6'3", 178 lbs. Born, Gavle, Sweden, January 31, 1990.
(Florida's 1st choice, 31st overall, in 2008 Entry Draft).

| | | | Regular Season | | | | | | | | Playoffs | | | | | | |
|---|---|---|---|---|---|---|---|---|---|---|---|---|---|---|---|---|---|
| **Season** | **Club** | **League** | **GP** | **W** | **L** | **O/T** | **Mins** | **GA** | **SO** | **Avg** | **GP** | **W** | **L** | **Mins** | **GA** | **SO** | **Avg** |
| 2006-07 | Brynas U18 | Swe-U18 | 13 | .... | .... | .... | 789 | 27 | 0 | 2.05 | 3 | .... | .... | 193 | 6 | 1 | 1.86 |
| | Brynas IF Gavle Jr. | Swe-Jr. | 1 | .... | .... | .... | 65 | 3 | 0 | 2.77 | 1 | .... | .... | 25 | 4 | 0 | 9.76 |
| 2007-08 | Brynas U18 | Swe-U18 | 1 | .... | .... | .... | 60 | 3 | 0 | 3.00 | .... | .... | .... | .... | .... | .... | .... |
| | Brynas IF Gavle Jr. | Swe-Jr. | 22 | .... | .... | .... | 1320 | 44 | 2 | 2.00 | .... | .... | .... | .... | .... | .... | .... |
| | Brynas IF Gavle | Sweden | 7 | .... | .... | .... | 423 | 22 | 0 | 3.12 | .... | .... | .... | .... | .... | .... | .... |
| | Brynas IF Gavle | Sweden-Q | 9 | .... | .... | .... | 505 | 15 | 2 | 1.78 | .... | .... | .... | .... | .... | .... | .... |
| 2008-09 | Brynas IF Gavle | Sweden | 35 | .... | .... | .... | 1992 | 79 | 3 | 2.38 | 1 | .... | .... | 59 | 2 | 0 | 2.02 |

## MASON, Chris (MAY-sohn, KRIHS) ST.L.

Goaltender. Catches left. 6', 195 lbs. Born, Red Deer, Alta., April 20, 1976.
(New Jersey's 7th choice, 122nd overall, in 1995 Entry Draft).

| | | | Regular Season | | | | | | | | Playoffs | | | | | | |
|---|---|---|---|---|---|---|---|---|---|---|---|---|---|---|---|---|---|
| **Season** | **Club** | **League** | **GP** | **W** | **L** | **O/T** | **Mins** | **GA** | **SO** | **Avg** | **GP** | **W** | **L** | **Mins** | **GA** | **SO** | **Avg** |
| 1992-93 | Red Deer | AMHL | 20 | .... | .... | .... | 1280 | 76 | 0 | 3.35 | .... | .... | .... | .... | .... | .... | .... |
| 1993-94 | Victoria Cougars | WHL | 5 | 1 | 4 | 0 | 237 | 27 | 0 | 6.84 | .... | .... | .... | .... | .... | .... | .... |
| 1994-95 | Prince George | WHL | 44 | 8 | 30 | 1 | 2288 | 192 | 1 | 5.03 | .... | .... | .... | .... | .... | .... | .... |
| 1995-96 | Prince George | WHL | 59 | 16 | 37 | 1 | 3289 | 236 | 1 | 4.31 | .... | .... | .... | .... | .... | .... | .... |
| 1996-97 | Prince George | WHL | 50 | 19 | 24 | 4 | 2851 | 172 | 2 | 3.62 | 15 | 9 | 6 | 938 | 44 | *1 | 2.81 |
| 1997-98 | Cincinnati | AHL | 47 | 13 | 19 | 7 | 2368 | 136 | 0 | 3.45 | .... | .... | .... | .... | .... | .... | .... |
| **1998-99** | **Nashville** | **NHL** | **3** | **0** | **0** | **0** | **69** | **6** | **0** | **5.22** | .... | .... | .... | .... | .... | .... | .... |
| | Milwaukee | IHL | 34 | 15 | 12 | 6 | 1901 | 92 | 1 | 2.90 | .... | .... | .... | .... | .... | .... | .... |
| 99-2000 | Milwaukee | IHL | 53 | 20 | 21 | 8 | 2952 | 137 | 2 | 2.78 | 3 | 1 | 2 | 252 | 11 | 0 | 2.62 |
| **2000-01** | **Nashville** | **NHL** | **1** | **0** | **1** | **0** | **59** | **2** | **0** | **2.03** | .... | .... | .... | .... | .... | .... | .... |
| | Milwaukee | IHL | 37 | 17 | 14 | 5 | 2226 | 87 | 5 | 2.35 | 4 | 1 | 3 | 239 | 12 | 0 | 3.02 |
| 2001-02 | Milwaukee | AHL | 48 | 17 | 21 | 7 | 2755 | 116 | 2 | 2.53 | .... | .... | .... | .... | .... | .... | .... |
| 2002-03 | San Antonio | AHL | 50 | 25 | 18 | 6 | 2914 | 122 | 1 | 2.51 | 3 | 0 | 3 | 195 | 9 | 0 | 2.77 |
| **2003-04** | **Nashville** | **NHL** | **17** | **4** | **4** | **1** | **744** | **27** | **1** | **2.18** | .... | .... | .... | .... | .... | .... | .... |
| | Milwaukee | AHL | 1 | 1 | 0 | 0 | 60 | 2 | 0 | 2.00 | .... | .... | .... | .... | .... | .... | .... |
| 2004-05 | Valerengen IF Oslo | Norway | 20 | .... | .... | .... | 1204 | 36 | 1 | 1.79 | 11 | .... | .... | 657 | 22 | 1 | 2.01 |
| **2005-06** | **Nashville** | **NHL** | **23** | **12** | **5** | **1** | **1227** | **52** | **2** | **2.54** | **5** | **1** | **4** | **296** | **17** | **0** | **3.45** |
| **2006-07** | **Nashville** | **NHL** | **40** | **24** | **11** | **4** | **2342** | **93** | **5** | **2.38** | .... | .... | .... | .... | .... | .... | .... |
| **2007-08** | **Nashville** | **NHL** | **51** | **18** | **22** | **6** | **2692** | **130** | **4** | **2.90** | .... | .... | .... | .... | .... | .... | .... |
| **2008-09** | **St. Louis** | **NHL** | **57** | **27** | **21** | **7** | **3215** | **129** | **6** | **2.41** | **4** | **0** | **4** | **256** | **10** | **0** | **2.34** |
| | **NHL Totals** | | **192** | **85** | **64** | **19** | **10348** | **439** | **18** | **2.55** | **9** | **1** | **8** | **552** | **27** | **0** | **2.93** |

Signed as a free agent by **Anaheim**, June 27, 1997. Traded to **Nashville** by **Anaheim** with Marc Moro for Dominic Roussel, October 5, 1998. Signed as a free agent by **Florida**, August 20, 2002. Claimed by **Nashville** from **Florida** in Waiver Draft, October 3, 2003. Signed as a free agent by **Oslo** (Norway), November 30, 2004. Traded to **St. Louis** by **Nashville** for NY Rangers' 4th round choice (previously acquired, later traded back to NY Rangers - NY Rangers selected Dale Weise) in 2008 Entry Draft, June 20, 2008.

## MASON, Steve (MAY-sohn, STEEV) CBJ

Goaltender. Catches right. 6'4", 212 lbs. Born, Oakville, Ont., May 29, 1988.
(Columbus' 2nd choice, 69th overall, in 2006 Entry Draft).

| | | | Regular Season | | | | | | | | Playoffs | | | | | | |
|---|---|---|---|---|---|---|---|---|---|---|---|---|---|---|---|---|---|
| **Season** | **Club** | **League** | **GP** | **W** | **L** | **O/T** | **Mins** | **GA** | **SO** | **Avg** | **GP** | **W** | **L** | **Mins** | **GA** | **SO** | **Avg** |
| 2004-05 | Grimsby | OJHL-C | 45 | .... | .... | .... | 2800 | .... | 6 | 1.75 | .... | .... | .... | .... | .... | .... | .... |
| 2005-06 | Petrolia Jets | OJHL-B | 9 | 6 | 3 | 0 | 521 | .... | 1 | 2.53 | .... | .... | .... | .... | .... | .... | .... |
| | London Knights | OHL | 12 | 5 | 3 | 0 | 497 | 22 | 0 | 2.66 | 4 | 0 | 1 | 150 | 7 | 0 | 2.80 |
| 2006-07 | London Knights | OHL | *62 | *45 | 13 | 4 | *3733 | 199 | 2 | 3.20 | 16 | 9 | 7 | 931 | 54 | 0 | 3.48 |
| 2007-08 | London Knights | OHL | 26 | 19 | 4 | 3 | 1569 | 73 | 2 | 2.79 | .... | .... | .... | .... | .... | .... | .... |
| | Kitchener Rangers | OHL | 16 | 13 | 3 | 0 | 961 | 33 | 1 | 2.06 | 5 | 5 | 0 | 313 | 10 | 1 | 1.92 |
| **2008-09** | **Columbus** | **NHL** | **61** | **33** | **20** | **7** | **3664** | **140** | ***10** | **2.29** | **4** | **0** | **4** | **239** | **17** | **0** | **4.27** |
| | Syracuse Crunch | AHL | 3 | 2 | 1 | 0 | 184 | 5 | 0 | 1.63 | .... | .... | .... | .... | .... | .... | .... |
| | **NHL Totals** | | **61** | **33** | **20** | **7** | **3664** | **140** | **10** | **2.29** | **4** | **0** | **4** | **239** | **17** | **0** | **4.27** |

OHL First All-Star Team (2007) • OHL Second All-Star Team (2008) • NHL All-Rookie Team (2009) • NHL Second All-Star Team (2009) • Calder Memorial Trophy (2009)

## MAXWELL, Brandon (MAX-wehl, BRAN-duhn) COL.

Goaltender. Catches left. 6', 195 lbs. Born, Winter Park, FL, March 22, 1991.
(Colorado's 6th choice, 154th overall, in 2009 Entry Draft).

| | | | Regular Season | | | | | | | | Playoffs | | | | | | |
|---|---|---|---|---|---|---|---|---|---|---|---|---|---|---|---|---|---|
| **Season** | **Club** | **League** | **GP** | **W** | **L** | **O/T** | **Mins** | **GA** | **SO** | **Avg** | **GP** | **W** | **L** | **Mins** | **GA** | **SO** | **Avg** |
| 2007-08 | USNTDP | NAHL | 21 | 8 | 10 | 1 | 1201 | 68 | 1 | 3.40 | .... | .... | .... | .... | .... | .... | .... |
| | USNTDP | U-17 | 5 | 3 | 2 | 0 | .... | .... | 0 | .... | .... | .... | .... | .... | .... | .... | .... |
| | USNTDP | U-18 | 13 | 9 | 3 | 1 | .... | .... | 1 | 1.91 | .... | .... | .... | .... | .... | .... | .... |
| 2008-09 | USNTDP | NAHL | 11 | 7 | 3 | 1 | 666 | 35 | 0 | 3.15 | 9 | 5 | 4 | 535 | 23 | 0 | 2.58 |
| | USNTDP | U-17 | 15 | 8 | 6 | 1 | 900 | 43 | 0 | 2.87 | .... | .... | .... | .... | .... | .... | .... |
| | USNTDP | U-18 | 3 | 3 | 0 | 0 | 185 | 8 | 0 | 2.59 | .... | .... | .... | .... | .... | .... | .... |

## MAYER, Robert (MAY-uhr, RAW-buhrt) MTL.

Goaltender. Catches left. 6'1", 190 lbs. Born, Havirov, Czech., October 9, 1989.

| | | | Regular Season | | | | | | | | Playoffs | | | | | | |
|---|---|---|---|---|---|---|---|---|---|---|---|---|---|---|---|---|---|
| **Season** | **Club** | **League** | **GP** | **W** | **L** | **O/T** | **Mins** | **GA** | **SO** | **Avg** | **GP** | **W** | **L** | **Mins** | **GA** | **SO** | **Avg** |
| 2005-06 | ESV Kaufbeuren | German-2 | 3 | .... | .... | .... | .... | .... | .... | .... | .... | .... | .... | .... | .... | .... | .... |
| 2006-07 | ESV Kaufbeuren | German-2 | 7 | .... | .... | .... | .... | .... | .... | .... | .... | .... | .... | .... | .... | .... | .... |
| | Kloten Flyers | Swiss | 1 | 0 | 0 | 0 | 10 | 1 | 0 | 6.00 | .... | .... | .... | .... | .... | .... | .... |
| 2007-08 | Saint John | QMJHL | 32 | 16 | 10 | 1 | 1669 | 105 | 2 | 3.77 | .... | .... | .... | .... | .... | .... | .... |
| 2008-09 | Saint John | QMJHL | 57 | 26 | 28 | .... | 3155 | 169 | 2 | 3.21 | 4 | 0 | 3 | 204 | 16 | 0 | 4.70 |

Signed as a free agent by **Montreal**, September 25, 2008.

## McCOLLUM, Thomas (muk-KAWL-uhm, TAW-muhs) DET.

Goaltender. Catches left. 6'2", 205 lbs. Born, Amherst, NY, December 7, 1989.
(Detroit's 1st choice, 30th overall, in 2008 Entry Draft).

| | | | Regular Season | | | | | | | | Playoffs | | | | | | |
|---|---|---|---|---|---|---|---|---|---|---|---|---|---|---|---|---|---|
| **Season** | **Club** | **League** | **GP** | **W** | **L** | **O/T** | **Mins** | **GA** | **SO** | **Avg** | **GP** | **W** | **L** | **Mins** | **GA** | **SO** | **Avg** |
| 2005-06 | Wheatfield Blades | EmJHL | 24 | 2 | 19 | 3 | 1448 | 109 | 1 | 4.52 | .... | .... | .... | .... | .... | .... | .... |
| 2006-07 | Guelph Storm | OHL | 55 | 26 | 18 | 10 | 3158 | 126 | *5 | 2.39 | 4 | 0 | 4 | 233 | 17 | 0 | 4.38 |
| 2007-08 | Guelph Storm | OHL | 51 | 25 | 17 | 6 | 2978 | 124 | *4 | 2.50 | 10 | 5 | 5 | 596 | 19 | 1 | 1.91 |
| 2008-09 | Guelph Storm | OHL | 31 | 17 | 10 | 4 | 1859 | 69 | *3 | 2.23 | .... | .... | .... | .... | .... | .... | .... |
| | Brampton Battalion | OHL | 23 | 17 | 6 | 0 | 1333 | 43 | *4 | 1.94 | *21 | 13 | 8 | *1284 | 62 | *1 | 2.90 |

OHL Second All-Star Team (2009)

## McELHINNEY, Curtis (MAK-IHL-ehn-ee, KUHR-this) CGY.

Goaltender. Catches left. 6'2", 193 lbs. Born, London, Ont., May 23, 1983.
(Calgary's 9th choice, 176th overall, in 2002 Entry Draft).

| | | | Regular Season | | | | | | | | Playoffs | | | | | | |
|---|---|---|---|---|---|---|---|---|---|---|---|---|---|---|---|---|---|
| **Season** | **Club** | **League** | **GP** | **W** | **L** | **O/T** | **Mins** | **GA** | **SO** | **Avg** | **GP** | **W** | **L** | **Mins** | **GA** | **SO** | **Avg** |
| 2000-01 | Notre Dame | SJHL | | | | | STATISTICS NOT AVAILABLE | | | | | | | | | | |
| 2001-02 | Colorado College | WCHA | 9 | 6 | 0 | 1 | 441 | 15 | 1 | 2.04 | .... | .... | .... | .... | .... | .... | .... |
| 2002-03 | Colorado College | WCHA | *37 | *25 | 6 | 5 | *2147 | 85 | *4 | 2.37 | .... | .... | .... | .... | .... | .... | .... |
| 2003-04 | Colorado College | WCHA | 19 | 10 | 6 | 1 | 1015 | 41 | 2 | 2.42 | .... | .... | .... | .... | .... | .... | .... |
| 2004-05 | Colorado College | WCHA | 26 | *21 | 4 | 1 | 1550 | 58 | 2 | 2.24 | .... | .... | .... | .... | .... | .... | .... |
| 2005-06 | Omaha | AHL | 33 | 9 | 14 | 2 | 1621 | 68 | 3 | 2.52 | .... | .... | .... | .... | .... | .... | .... |
| 2006-07 | Omaha | AHL | 57 | 35 | 17 | 1 | 3181 | 113 | *7 | 2.13 | 5 | 2 | 3 | 311 | 11 | 0 | 2.12 |
| **2007-08** | **Calgary** | **NHL** | **5** | **0** | **2** | **0** | **150** | **5** | **0** | **2.00** | .... | .... | .... | .... | .... | .... | .... |
| | Quad City Flames | AHL | 41 | 20 | 18 | 2 | 2320 | 88 | 3 | 2.28 | .... | .... | .... | .... | .... | .... | .... |
| **2008-09** | **Calgary** | **NHL** | **14** | **1** | **6** | **1** | **518** | **31** | **0** | **3.59** | **1** | **0** | **0** | **34** | **1** | **0** | **1.76** |
| | **NHL Totals** | | **19** | **1** | **8** | **1** | **668** | **36** | **0** | **3.23** | **1** | **0** | **0** | **34** | **1** | **0** | **1.76** |

WCHA First All-Star Team (2003, 2005) • NCAA West Second All-American Team (2003) • NCAA West First All-American Team (2005) • AHL Second All-Star Team (2007)

## McGANN, Pat (muh-GAN, PAT) DAL.

Goaltender. Catches right. 5'11", 160 lbs. Born, Evergreen Park, IL, January 27, 1987.
(Dallas' 7th choice, 223rd overall, in 2005 Entry Draft).

| | | | Regular Season | | | | | | | | Playoffs | | | | | | |
|---|---|---|---|---|---|---|---|---|---|---|---|---|---|---|---|---|---|
| **Season** | **Club** | **League** | **GP** | **W** | **L** | **O/T** | **Mins** | **GA** | **SO** | **Avg** | **GP** | **W** | **L** | **Mins** | **GA** | **SO** | **Avg** |
| 2003-04 | Chicago Chill | MAHL | 31 | 14 | 16 | 1 | .... | .... | .... | 3.40 | .... | .... | .... | .... | .... | .... | .... |
| 2004-05 | Team Illinois | MWEHL | 50 | 31 | 18 | 1 | .... | 91 | 5 | 2.21 | .... | .... | .... | .... | .... | .... | .... |
| 2005-06 | Cedar Rapids | USHL | 17 | 5 | 8 | 3 | 998 | 49 | 1 | 2.95 | .... | .... | .... | .... | .... | .... | .... |
| 2006-07 | Cedar Rapids | USHL | 6 | 3 | 3 | 0 | 357 | 22 | 0 | 3.70 | .... | .... | .... | .... | .... | .... | .... |
| | Chicago Steel | USHL | 17 | 2 | 14 | 1 | 935 | 67 | 0 | 4.30 | .... | .... | .... | .... | .... | .... | .... |
| 2007-08 | Quinnipiac | ECAC | 8 | 2 | 1 | 0 | 242 | 19 | 0 | 4.72 | .... | .... | .... | .... | .... | .... | .... |
| 2008-09 | Quinnipiac | ECAC | | | | | DID NOT PLAY – SPARE GOALTENDER | | | | | | | | | | |

## McKENNA, Mike (mih-KEHN-ah, MIGHK)

Goaltender. Catches right. 6'3", 187 lbs. Born, St. Louis, MO, April 11, 1983.
(Nashville's 4th choice, 172nd overall, in 2002 Entry Draft).

| | | | Regular Season | | | | | | | | Playoffs | | | | | | |
|---|---|---|---|---|---|---|---|---|---|---|---|---|---|---|---|---|---|
| Season | Club | League | GP | W | L | O/T | Mins | GA | SO | Avg | GP | W | L | Mins | GA | SO | Avg |
| 2001-02 | St. Lawrence | ECAC | 20 | 7 | 10 | 1 | 1121 | 59 | 0 | 3.16 | .... | .... | .... | .... | .... | .... | .... |
| 2002-03 | St. Lawrence | ECAC | 15 | 1 | 7 | 2 | 618 | 38 | 0 | 3.69 | .... | .... | .... | .... | .... | .... | .... |
| 2003-04 | St. Lawrence | ECAC | 27 | 9 | 10 | 3 | 1475 | 60 | 3 | 2.44 | .... | .... | .... | .... | .... | .... | .... |
| 2004-05 | St. Lawrence | ECAC | 35 | 15 | 17 | 2 | 2022 | 92 | 3 | 2.73 | .... | .... | .... | .... | .... | .... | .... |
| 2005-06 | Norfolk Admirals | AHL | 7 | 4 | 2 | 1 | 388 | 25 | 0 | 3.86 | .... | .... | .... | .... | .... | .... | .... |
| | Las Vegas | ECHL | 25 | 19 | 2 | 1 | 1383 | 49 | 1 | 2.13 | 4 | 1 | 1 | 173 | 9 | 0 | 3.12 |
| 2006-07 | Las Vegas | ECHL | 38 | 27 | 4 | 7 | 2258 | 83 | 5 | *2.21 | 6 | 3 | 3 | 358 | 15 | 0 | 2.51 |
| | Milwaukee | AHL | 1 | 0 | 0 | 0 | 11 | 3 | 0 | 15.72 | .... | .... | .... | .... | .... | .... | .... |
| | Omaha | AHL | 2 | 0 | 1 | 0 | 96 | 6 | 0 | 3.74 | .... | .... | .... | .... | .... | .... | .... |
| 2007-08 | Portland Pirates | AHL | 41 | 24 | 13 | 1 | 2269 | 103 | 3 | 2.72 | 6 | 2 | 4 | 320 | 18 | 0 | 3.38 |
| **2008-09** | **Tampa Bay** | **NHL** | **15** | **4** | **8** | **1** | **776** | **46** | **1** | **3.56** | .... | .... | .... | .... | .... | .... | .... |
| | Norfolk Admirals | AHL | 24 | 11 | 10 | 1 | 1315 | 65 | 1 | 2.97 | .... | .... | .... | .... | .... | .... | .... |
| | **NHL Totals** | | **15** | **4** | **8** | **1** | **776** | **46** | **1** | **3.56** | .... | .... | .... | .... | .... | .... | .... |

ECHL Second All-Star Team (2007)

Signed as a free agent by **Tampa Bay**, February 3, 2009.

## MENSATOR, Lukas (MEHN-suh-tohr, LOO-kahsh) VAN.

Goaltender. Catches left. 5'8", 180 lbs. Born, Sokolov, Czech., August 18, 1984.
(Vancouver's 4th choice, 83rd overall, in 2002 Entry Draft).

| | | | Regular Season | | | | | | | | Playoffs | | | | | | |
|---|---|---|---|---|---|---|---|---|---|---|---|---|---|---|---|---|---|
| Season | Club | League | GP | W | L | O/T | Mins | GA | SO | Avg | GP | W | L | Mins | GA | SO | Avg |
| 99-2000 | Karlovy Vary U17 | CzR-U17 | 42 | .... | .... | .... | 2406 | 160 | 0 | 3.99 | .... | .... | .... | .... | .... | .... | .... |
| | Karlovy Vary Jr. | CzRep-Jr. | 1 | 1 | 0 | 0 | 60 | 3 | 0 | 3.00 | .... | .... | .... | .... | .... | .... | .... |
| 2000-01 | Karlovy Vary U17 | CzR-U17 | 6 | .... | .... | .... | 360 | 15 | 0 | 2.50 | .... | .... | .... | .... | .... | .... | .... |
| | Karlovy Vary Jr. | CzRep-Jr. | 19 | .... | .... | .... | 1085 | 60 | 0 | 3.32 | .... | .... | .... | .... | .... | .... | .... |
| 2001-02 | Karlovy Vary Jr. | CzRep-Jr. | 31 | .... | .... | .... | 1809 | 93 | 0 | 3.08 | 9 | .... | .... | 459 | 17 | 0 | 2.22 |
| | Banik CHZ Sokolov | CzRep-3 | 3 | .... | .... | .... | 180 | 12 | 0 | 4.00 | .... | .... | .... | .... | .... | .... | .... |
| 2002-03 | Ottawa 67's | OHL | 42 | 26 | 8 | 5 | 2395 | 122 | 0 | 3.06 | *23 | 13 | 8 | *1381 | 63 | *2 | 2.74 |
| 2003-04 | Ottawa 67's | OHL | 50 | 18 | 22 | 7 | 2924 | 162 | 0 | 3.32 | 7 | 3 | 4 | 447 | 23 | 0 | 3.09 |
| 2004-05 | Karlovy Vary | CzRep | 13 | .... | .... | .... | 686 | 34 | 1 | 2.97 | .... | .... | .... | .... | .... | .... | .... |
| | IHC Pisek | CzRep-2 | 14 | .... | .... | .... | 808 | 41 | 1 | 3.04 | .... | .... | .... | .... | .... | .... | .... |
| | BK Mlada Boleslav | CzRep-2 | 17 | .... | .... | .... | 991 | 34 | 4 | 2.06 | 7 | .... | .... | 393 | 17 | 1 | 2.60 |
| 2005-06 | Karlovy Vary | CzRep | 36 | .... | .... | .... | 1981 | 69 | 5 | 2.09 | .... | .... | .... | .... | .... | .... | .... |
| | SK Kadan | CzRep-2 | 1 | .... | .... | .... | 49 | 5 | 0 | 6.12 | .... | .... | .... | .... | .... | .... | .... |
| 2006-07 | Karlovy Vary | CzRep | 22 | .... | .... | .... | 1166 | 47 | 1 | 2.42 | .... | .... | .... | .... | .... | .... | .... |
| 2007-08 | Karlovy Vary | CzRep | 38 | .... | .... | .... | 2254 | 94 | 3 | 2.50 | *19 | .... | .... | *1149 | 47 | 2 | 2.45 |
| 2008-09 | Karlovy Vary | CzRep | 49 | .... | .... | .... | 2868 | 120 | 1 | 2.51 | 16 | .... | .... | *1003 | 38 | 0 | 2.27 |

Signed as a free agent by **Karlovy Vary** (CzRep), May 17, 2004.

## MILLAN, Kieran (MIH-luhn, KEER-uhn) COL.

Goaltender. Catches left. 6', 190 lbs. Born, Edmonton, Alta., August 31, 1989.
(Colorado's 5th choice, 124th overall, in 2009 Entry Draft).

| | | | Regular Season | | | | | | | | Playoffs | | | | | | |
|---|---|---|---|---|---|---|---|---|---|---|---|---|---|---|---|---|---|
| Season | Club | League | GP | W | L | O/T | Mins | GA | SO | Avg | GP | W | L | Mins | GA | SO | Avg |
| 2006-07 | Spruce Grove | AJHL | 32 | 20 | 7 | 4 | 1883 | 82 | 3 | 2.61 | 4 | 2 | 2 | 200 | 10 | 1 | 3.00 |
| 2007-08 | Spruce Grove | AJHL | 43 | 21 | 12 | 8 | 2391 | 121 | 1 | 3.04 | 15 | 8 | 7 | 931 | 34 | 1 | 2.19 |
| 2008-09 | Boston University | H-East | 35 | 29 | 2 | 3 | 2073 | 67 | 3 | 1.94 | .... | .... | .... | .... | .... | .... | .... |

## MILLER, Ryan (MIHL-luhr, RIGH-uhn) BUF.

Goaltender. Catches left. 6'2", 170 lbs. Born, East Lansing, MI, July 17, 1980.
(Buffalo's 7th choice, 138th overall, in 1999 Entry Draft).

| | | | Regular Season | | | | | | | | Playoffs | | | | | | |
|---|---|---|---|---|---|---|---|---|---|---|---|---|---|---|---|---|---|
| Season | Club | League | GP | W | L | O/T | Mins | GA | SO | Avg | GP | W | L | Mins | GA | SO | Avg |
| 1997-98 | Soo Indians | NAHL | 37 | 21 | 14 | 0 | 2113 | 82 | 3 | 2.33 | 2 | 0 | 2 | 158 | 7 | 0 | 2.66 |
| 1998-99 | Soo Indians | NAHL | 47 | 31 | 14 | 1 | 2711 | 104 | 8 | 2.30 | 4 | 2 | 2 | 218 | 10 | 1 | 2.76 |
| 99-2000 | Michigan State | CCHA | 26 | 16 | 5 | 3 | 1525 | 39 | *8 | *1.53 | .... | .... | .... | .... | .... | .... | .... |
| 2000-01 | Michigan State | CCHA | 40 | *31 | 5 | 4 | 2447 | 54 | *10 | *1.32 | .... | .... | .... | .... | .... | .... | .... |
| 2001-02 | Michigan State | CCHA | 40 | 26 | 9 | 5 | 2411 | 71 | *8 | *1.77 | .... | .... | .... | .... | .... | .... | .... |
| **2002-03** | **Buffalo** | **NHL** | **15** | **6** | **8** | **1** | **912** | **40** | **1** | **2.63** | .... | .... | .... | .... | .... | .... | .... |
| | Rochester | AHL | 47 | 23 | 18 | 5 | 2817 | 110 | 2 | 2.34 | 3 | 1 | 2 | 190 | 13 | 0 | 4.11 |
| **2003-04** | **Buffalo** | **NHL** | **3** | **0** | **3** | **0** | **178** | **15** | **0** | **5.06** | .... | .... | .... | .... | .... | .... | .... |
| | Rochester | AHL | 60 | 27 | 25 | 7 | 3579 | 132 | 5 | 2.21 | 14 | 7 | 7 | 857 | 26 | 2 | 1.82 |
| 2004-05 | Rochester | AHL | 63 | *41 | 17 | 4 | 3741 | 153 | 8 | 2.45 | 9 | 5 | 4 | 547 | 24 | 0 | 2.63 |
| **2005-06** | **Buffalo** | **NHL** | **48** | **30** | **14** | **3** | **2862** | **124** | **1** | **2.60** | **18** | **11** | **7** | **1123** | **48** | **1** | **2.56** |
| | Rochester | AHL | 2 | 1 | 1 | 0 | 120 | 5 | 0 | 2.50 | .... | .... | .... | .... | .... | .... | .... |
| **2006-07** | **Buffalo** | **NHL** | **63** | **40** | **16** | **6** | **3692** | **168** | **2** | **2.73** | **16** | **9** | **7** | **1029** | **38** | **0** | **2.22** |
| **2007-08** | **Buffalo** | **NHL** | **76** | **36** | **27** | **10** | **4474** | **197** | **3** | **2.64** | .... | .... | .... | .... | .... | .... | .... |
| **2008-09** | **Buffalo** | **NHL** | **59** | **34** | **18** | **6** | **3443** | **145** | **5** | **2.53** | .... | .... | .... | .... | .... | .... | .... |
| | **NHL Totals** | | **264** | **146** | **86** | **26** | **15561** | **689** | **12** | **2.66** | **34** | **20** | **14** | **2152** | **86** | **1** | **2.40** |

CCHA Second All-Star Team (2000) • CCHA First All-Star Team (2001, 2002) • NCAA West First All-American Team (2001, 2002) • CCHA Player of the Year (2001, 2002) • Hobey Baker Memorial Award (Top U.S. Collegiate Player) (2001) • AHL First All-Star Team (2005) • Aldege "Baz" Bastien Memorial Award (AHL – Outstanding Goaltender) (2005)

Played in NHL All-Star Game (2007)

## MISSIAEN, Jason (MIHS-ee-ehn, JAY-suhn) MTL.

Goaltender. Catches left. 6'9", 217 lbs. Born, Chatham, Ont., April 25, 1990.
(Montreal's 3rd choice, 116th overall, in 2008 Entry Draft).

| | | | Regular Season | | | | | | | | Playoffs | | | | | | |
|---|---|---|---|---|---|---|---|---|---|---|---|---|---|---|---|---|---|
| Season | Club | League | GP | W | L | O/T | Mins | GA | SO | Avg | GP | W | L | Mins | GA | SO | Avg |
| 2004-05 | Dresden Kings | OHA-C | 16 | 11 | 4 | 1 | 919 | 47 | 1 | 3.07 | .... | .... | .... | .... | .... | .... | .... |
| 2005-06 | Dresden Kings | OHA-C | 26 | 13 | 8 | 2 | 1560 | 76 | 1 | 2.93 | .... | .... | .... | .... | .... | .... | .... |
| 2006-07 | Peterborough | OHL | 12 | 1 | 7 | 0 | 559 | 48 | 0 | 5.15 | .... | .... | .... | .... | .... | .... | .... |
| 2007-08 | Peterborough | OHL | 22 | 8 | 8 | 1 | 1134 | 62 | 1 | 3.28 | .... | .... | .... | .... | .... | .... | .... |
| 2008-09 | Peterborough | OHL | 38 | 12 | 21 | 2 | 2221 | 141 | 1 | 3.81 | 4 | 0 | 4 | 241 | 17 | 0 | 4.23 |

## MODIG, Mattias (moh-DIHG, mat-TEE-uhs) ANA.

Goaltender. Catches left. 6', 180 lbs. Born, Lulea, Sweden, April 1, 1987.
(Anaheim's 7th choice, 121st overall, in 2007 Entry Draft).

| | | | Regular Season | | | | | | | | Playoffs | | | | | | |
|---|---|---|---|---|---|---|---|---|---|---|---|---|---|---|---|---|---|
| Season | Club | League | GP | W | L | O/T | Mins | GA | SO | Avg | GP | W | L | Mins | GA | SO | Avg |
| 2002-03 | Lulea HF U18 | Swe-U18 | 2 | .... | .... | .... | 120 | 4 | 0 | 2.00 | .... | .... | .... | .... | .... | .... | .... |
| 2003-04 | Lulea HF U18 | Swe-U18 | 14 | .... | .... | .... | 854 | 30 | 2 | 2.11 | 7 | .... | .... | 449 | 14 | 0 | 1.87 |
| | Lulea HF Jr. | Swe-Jr. | 2 | .... | .... | .... | 66 | 2 | 0 | 1.81 | .... | .... | .... | .... | .... | .... | .... |
| 2004-05 | Lulea HF U18 | Swe-U18 | 2 | .... | .... | .... | 120 | 4 | 0 | 2.00 | .... | .... | .... | .... | .... | .... | .... |
| | Lulea HF Jr. | Swe-Jr. | 14 | .... | .... | .... | 819 | 42 | 2 | 3.08 | 5 | .... | .... | 306 | 16 | 0 | 3.14 |
| 2005-06 | Lulea HF Jr. | Swe-Jr. | 19 | .... | .... | .... | 1154 | 42 | 1 | 2.18 | 3 | .... | .... | 175 | 10 | 0 | 3.43 |
| | Lulea HF | Sweden | 2 | .... | .... | .... | 66 | 3 | 0 | 2.74 | .... | .... | .... | .... | .... | .... | .... |
| 2006-07 | Lulea HF Jr. | Swe-Jr. | 2 | .... | .... | .... | 120 | 7 | 0 | 3.50 | .... | .... | .... | .... | .... | .... | .... |
| | Lulea HF | Sweden | 32 | .... | .... | .... | 1636 | 69 | 1 | 2.53 | 1 | .... | .... | 20 | 1 | 0 | 3.00 |
| 2007-08 | Lulea HF Jr. | Swe-Jr. | 5 | .... | .... | .... | 297 | 14 | 0 | 2.83 | .... | .... | .... | .... | .... | .... | .... |
| | Lulea HF | Sweden | 13 | .... | .... | .... | 696 | 41 | 1 | 3.53 | .... | .... | .... | .... | .... | .... | .... |
| 2008-09 | Lulea HF | Sweden | 40 | .... | .... | .... | 2268 | 85 | *4 | 2.25 | 4 | .... | .... | 238 | 13 | 0 | 3.28 |

## MOLE, Mike (MOHL, MIGHK)

Goaltender. Catches right. 6', 183 lbs. Born, Orleans, Ont., October 12, 1982.

| | | | Regular Season | | | | | | | | Playoffs | | | | | | |
|---|---|---|---|---|---|---|---|---|---|---|---|---|---|---|---|---|---|
| Season | Club | League | GP | W | L | O/T | Mins | GA | SO | Avg | GP | W | L | Mins | GA | SO | Avg |
| 99-2000 | Mississauga | OHL | 37 | 5 | 28 | 0 | 2007 | 173 | 0 | 5.17 | .... | .... | .... | .... | .... | .... | .... |
| 2000-01 | Mississauga | OHL | 45 | 2 | 35 | 4 | 2435 | 219 | 0 | 5.40 | .... | .... | .... | .... | .... | .... | .... |
| 2001-02 | Mississauga | OHL | 23 | 5 | 15 | 2 | 1342 | 96 | 0 | 4.29 | .... | .... | .... | .... | .... | .... | .... |
| | Belleville Bulls | OHL | 26 | 20 | 4 | 2 | 1575 | 66 | 2 | 2.51 | 11 | 6 | 5 | 685 | 25 | *1 | 2.19 |
| 2002-03 | Belleville Bulls | OHL | 54 | 25 | 23 | 5 | 3138 | 153 | 1 | 2.93 | 7 | 3 | 4 | 400 | 21 | 0 | 3.15 |
| | Lowell | AHL | 1 | 0 | 0 | 0 | 20 | 4 | 0 | 12.00 | .... | .... | .... | .... | .... | .... | .... |
| 2003-04 | St. FX University | AUAA | 22 | 16 | 3 | 2 | 1301 | 54 | 3 | 2.49 | .... | .... | .... | .... | .... | .... | .... |
| 2004-05 | St. FX University | AUAA | 25 | 10 | 11 | 4 | 1496 | 58 | 3 | 2.33 | .... | .... | .... | .... | .... | .... | .... |
| 2005-06 | Phoenix | ECHL | *48 | 15 | 27 | 3 | 2617 | 142 | 2 | 3.26 | .... | .... | .... | .... | .... | .... | .... |
| | San Diego Gulls | ECHL | *9 | 4 | 3 | 2 | 549 | 24 | 0 | 2.62 | .... | .... | .... | .... | .... | .... | .... |
| 2006-07 | Bridgeport | AHL | 15 | 3 | 8 | 0 | 762 | 41 | 0 | 3.23 | .... | .... | .... | .... | .... | .... | .... |
| | Pensacola Ice Pilots | ECHL | 39 | 13 | 18 | 3 | 2189 | 144 | 0 | 3.95 | .... | .... | .... | .... | .... | .... | .... |
| 2007-08 | Utah Grizzlies | ECHL | 37 | 18 | 13 | 5 | 2208 | 121 | 0 | 3.29 | 8 | 3 | 1 | 410 | 18 | 1 | 2.64 |
| 2008-09 | Bridgeport | AHL | 1 | 0 | 1 | 0 | 59 | 3 | 0 | 3.04 | .... | .... | .... | .... | .... | .... | .... |
| | Utah Grizzlies | ECHL | 49 | 17 | 32 | 0 | 2919 | 162 | 0 | 3.33 | .... | .... | .... | .... | .... | .... | .... |

Signed as a free agent by **NY Islanders**, October 5, 2006.

## MONTOYA, Al (mawn-TOI-uh, AL) PHX.

Goaltender. Catches left. 6'2", 185 lbs. Born, Chicago, IL, February 13, 1985.
(NY Rangers' 1st choice, 6th overall, in 2004 Entry Draft).

| | | | Regular Season | | | | | | | | Playoffs | | | | | | |
|---|---|---|---|---|---|---|---|---|---|---|---|---|---|---|---|---|---|
| Season | Club | League | GP | W | L | O/T | Mins | GA | SO | Avg | GP | W | L | Mins | GA | SO | Avg |
| 99-2000 | Loyola Academy | High-MN | 28 | 12 | 13 | 3 | 1685 | 56 | 1 | 2.01 | .... | .... | .... | .... | .... | .... | .... |
| 2000-01 | Texas Tornado | NAHL | 15 | 10 | 3 | 0 | 780 | 38 | 0 | 2.92 | 1 | 1 | 0 | 60 | 2 | 0 | 2.00 |
| | United States | Nat-Tm | 2 | 2 | 0 | 0 | 120 | 4 | 0 | 2.00 | .... | .... | .... | .... | .... | .... | .... |
| 2001-02 | USNTDP | U-17 | 10 | 5 | 5 | 0 | 570 | 24 | 0 | 2.53 | .... | .... | .... | .... | .... | .... | .... |
| | USNTDP | NAHL | 24 | 6 | 11 | 4 | 1344 | 79 | 0 | 3.53 | .... | .... | .... | .... | .... | .... | .... |
| 2002-03 | U. of Michigan | CCHA | *43 | *30 | 10 | 3 | *2547 | 99 | 4 | 2.33 | .... | .... | .... | .... | .... | .... | .... |
| 2003-04 | U. of Michigan | CCHA | *40 | *26 | 12 | 2 | *2340 | 87 | 6 | 2.23 | .... | .... | .... | .... | .... | .... | .... |
| 2004-05 | U. of Michigan | CCHA | *40 | *30 | 7 | 3 | *2359 | 99 | 3 | 2.52 | .... | .... | .... | .... | .... | .... | .... |
| 2005-06 | Hartford Wolf Pack | AHL | 40 | 23 | 9 | 1 | 2094 | 91 | 2 | 2.61 | 5 | 2 | 1 | 257 | 8 | 1 | 1.87 |
| | Charlotte Checkers | ECHL | 2 | 1 | 1 | 0 | 123 | 8 | 0 | 3.92 | .... | .... | .... | .... | .... | .... | .... |
| 2006-07 | Hartford Wolf Pack | AHL | 48 | 27 | 17 | 0 | 2556 | 98 | 6 | 2.30 | 7 | 3 | 4 | 391 | 20 | 1 | 3.07 |
| 2007-08 | Hartford Wolf Pack | AHL | 31 | 16 | 8 | 3 | 1704 | 72 | 0 | 2.54 | .... | .... | .... | .... | .... | .... | .... |
| | San Antonio | AHL | 14 | 8 | 6 | 0 | 789 | 34 | 1 | 2.59 | 1 | 0 | 1 | 59 | 4 | 0 | 4.04 |
| **2008-09** | **Phoenix** | **NHL** | **5** | **3** | **1** | **0** | **259** | **9** | **1** | **2.08** | .... | .... | .... | .... | .... | .... | .... |
| | San Antonio | AHL | 29 | 7 | 17 | 2 | 1562 | 84 | 0 | 3.23 | .... | .... | .... | .... | .... | .... | .... |
| | **NHL Totals** | | **5** | **3** | **1** | **0** | **259** | **9** | **1** | **2.08** | .... | .... | .... | .... | .... | .... | .... |

CCHA All-Rookie Team (2003) • NCAA West Second All-American Team (2004)

Traded to **Phoenix** by **NY Rangers** with Marcel Hossa for Josh Gratton, David LeNeveu, Fredrik Sjostrom and Phoenix's 5th round choice (Roman Horak) in 2009 Entry Draft, February 26, 2008.

## MORRISON, Adam (MOHR_ih-suhn, A-duhm) PHI.

Goaltender. Catches left. 6'3", 166 lbs. Born, Edmonton, Alta., February 9, 1991.
(Philadelphia's 1st choice, 81st overall, in 2009 Entry Draft).

| | | | Regular Season | | | | | | | | Playoffs | | | | | | |
|---|---|---|---|---|---|---|---|---|---|---|---|---|---|---|---|---|---|
| Season | Club | League | GP | W | L | O/T | Mins | GA | SO | Avg | GP | W | L | Mins | GA | SO | Avg |
| 2007-08 | Valley West Hawks | Minor-BC | .... | 12 | 6 | 2 | .... | .... | .... | 2.92 | .... | .... | .... | .... | .... | .... | .... |
| 2008-09 | Saskatoon Blades | WHL | 13 | 9 | 1 | 1 | 746 | 31 | 1 | 2.49 | .... | .... | .... | .... | .... | .... | .... |

## MUNCE, Ryan (MUNTS, RIGH-uhn)

Goaltender. Catches left. 6'2", 180 lbs. Born, Mississauga, Ont., April 16, 1985.
(Los Angeles' 5th choice, 82nd overall, in 2003 Entry Draft).

| | | | Regular Season | | | | | | | | Playoffs | | | | | | |
|---|---|---|---|---|---|---|---|---|---|---|---|---|---|---|---|---|---|
| Season | Club | League | GP | W | L | O/T | Mins | GA | SO | Avg | GP | W | L | Mins | GA | SO | Avg |
| 2002-03 | Sarnia Sting | OHL | 27 | 15 | 7 | 0 | 1410 | 62 | 3 | 2.64 | 4 | 1 | 1 | 149 | 8 | 1 | 3.22 |
| 2003-04 | Sarnia Sting | OHL | 54 | 28 | 21 | 4 | 3160 | 158 | 2 | 3.00 | 5 | 1 | 4 | 298 | 17 | 0 | 3.42 |
| 2004-05 | Sarnia Sting | OHL | 55 | 12 | 32 | 6 | 3090 | 163 | 0 | 3.17 | .... | .... | .... | .... | .... | .... | .... |
| 2005-06 | Bakersfield | ECHL | 55 | 30 | 18 | 5 | *3234 | 150 | 2 | 2.78 | 11 | 5 | 5 | 642 | 36 | 0 | 3.36 |
| 2006-07 | Reading Royals | ECHL | 17 | 5 | 6 | 4 | 837 | 46 | 0 | 3.30 | .... | .... | .... | .... | .... | .... | .... |
| | Johnstown Chiefs | ECHL | 14 | 6 | 3 | 1 | 652 | 28 | 0 | 2.58 | 1 | 0 | 1 | 59 | 4 | 0 | 4.08 |
| 2007-08 | Norfolk Admirals | AHL | 10 | 3 | 6 | 0 | 502 | 25 | 0 | 2.99 | .... | .... | .... | .... | .... | .... | .... |
| | Mississippi | ECHL | 35 | 19 | 16 | 0 | 2067 | 97 | 3 | 2.82 | 4 | 1 | 3 | 242 | 16 | 0 | 3.97 |
| 2008-09 | Syracuse Crunch | AHL | 3 | 0 | 2 | 0 | 141 | 7 | 0 | 2.99 | .... | .... | .... | .... | .... | .... | .... |
| | Mississippi | ECHL | *54 | 24 | 24 | 5 | *3219 | 172 | 1 | 3.21 | .... | .... | .... | .... | .... | .... | .... |

Traded to **Tampa Bay** by **Los Angeles** for Tampa Bay's 4th round choice (later traded to San Jose - San Jose selected Samuel Groulx) in 2008 Entry Draft, January 20, 2007.

## MUNRO, Adam (muhn-ROH, A-duhm)

Goaltender. Catches left. 6'2", 219 lbs. Born, St. George, Ont., November 12, 1982.
(Chicago's 1st choice, 29th overall, in 2001 Entry Draft).

| | | | Regular Season | | | | | | | | Playoffs | | | | | | |
|---|---|---|---|---|---|---|---|---|---|---|---|---|---|---|---|---|---|
| Season | Club | League | GP | W | L | O/T | Mins | GA | SO | Avg | GP | W | L | Mins | GA | SO | Avg |
| 1997-98 | Brantford Classics | Minor-ON | 15 | 13 | 2 | 0 | 660 | 20 | *4 | *1.36 | .... | .... | .... | .... | .... | .... | .... |
| 1998-99 | Brant County | OJHL-B | 10 | .... | .... | .... | 348 | 30 | 0 | 5.17 | .... | .... | .... | .... | .... | .... | .... |
| | Bowmanville | OPJHL | 14 | .... | .... | .... | 816 | 50 | 0 | 3.68 | .... | .... | .... | .... | .... | .... | .... |
| | Erie Otters | OHL | 1 | 0 | 0 | 0 | 1 | 0 | 0 | 0.00 | .... | .... | .... | .... | .... | .... | .... |
| 99-2000 | Bowmanville | OPJHL | 2 | 2 | 0 | 0 | 125 | 5 | 0 | 2.40 | .... | .... | .... | .... | .... | .... | .... |
| | Erie Otters | OHL | 22 | 8 | 7 | 1 | 948 | 48 | 1 | 3.04 | 1 | 0 | 0 | 5 | 1 | 0 | 12.00 |
| 2000-01 | Erie Otters | OHL | 41 | 26 | 6 | 6 | 2283 | 88 | *4 | 2.31 | 10 | 6 | 2 | 509 | 27 | 1 | 3.18 |
| 2001-02 | Erie Otters | OHL | 43 | 24 | 13 | 1 | 2277 | 128 | 3 | 3.37 | 6 | 4 | 2 | 361 | 17 | 0 | 2.83 |
| 2002-03 | Erie Otters | OHL | 8 | 2 | 6 | 0 | 426 | 24 | 1 | 3.38 | .... | .... | .... | .... | .... | .... | .... |
| | Sault Ste. Marie | OHL | 42 | 20 | 20 | 2 | 2494 | 160 | 1 | 3.85 | 4 | 0 | 4 | 240 | 12 | 0 | 3.00 |
| **2003-04** | **Chicago** | **NHL** | **7** | **1** | **5** | **1** | **426** | **26** | **0** | **3.66** | .... | .... | .... | .... | .... | .... | .... |
| | Norfolk Admirals | AHL | 12 | 5 | 4 | 1 | 695 | 26 | 0 | 2.24 | .... | .... | .... | .... | .... | .... | .... |
| | Gwinnett | ECHL | 6 | 4 | 1 | 1 | 370 | 17 | 0 | 2.76 | 1 | 0 | 1 | 60 | 2 | 0 | 2.01 |
| 2004-05 | Norfolk Admirals | AHL | 30 | 14 | 10 | 2 | 1595 | 66 | 4 | 2.48 | .... | .... | .... | .... | .... | .... | .... |
| | Atlantic City | ECHL | 5 | 2 | 2 | 1 | 272 | 9 | 0 | 1.99 | .... | .... | .... | .... | .... | .... | .... |
| **2005-06** | **Chicago** | **NHL** | **10** | **3** | **5** | **2** | **501** | **25** | **1** | **2.99** | .... | .... | .... | .... | .... | .... | .... |
| | Norfolk Admirals | AHL | 28 | 17 | 8 | 1 | 1612 | 73 | 1 | 2.72 | 4 | 0 | 4 | 239 | 15 | 0 | 3.77 |
| 2006-07 | Fribourg | Swiss | 41 | 12 | 28 | 0 | 2488 | 149 | 0 | 3.59 | .... | .... | .... | .... | .... | .... | .... |
| 2007-08 | Syracuse Crunch | AHL | 25 | 13 | 9 | 1 | 1414 | 57 | 2 | 2.42 | 1 | 0 | 0 | 20 | 4 | 0 | 12.04 |
| 2008-09 | Toronto Marlies | AHL | 26 | 12 | 11 | 2 | 1511 | 61 | 2 | 2.42 | 1 | 0 | 1 | 58 | 4 | 0 | 4.11 |
| | **NHL Totals** | | **17** | **4** | **10** | **3** | **927** | **51** | **1** | **3.30** | .... | .... | .... | .... | .... | .... | .... |

Signed as a free agent by **Fribourg** (Swiss), July 7, 2006. Signed as a free agent by **Syracuse** (AHL), July 23, 2007.

## MUNROE, Scott (muhn-ROH, SKAWT) NYI

Goaltender. Catches left. 6'2", 210 lbs. Born, Moose Jaw, Sask., January 20, 1982.

| | | | Regular Season | | | | | | | | Playoffs | | | | | | |
|---|---|---|---|---|---|---|---|---|---|---|---|---|---|---|---|---|---|
| Season | Club | League | GP | W | L | O/T | Mins | GA | SO | Avg | GP | W | L | Mins | GA | SO | Avg |
| 2002-03 | AL-Huntsville | CHA | 20 | 11 | 6 | 1 | 1049 | 49 | 1 | 2.80 | .... | .... | .... | .... | .... | .... | .... |
| 2003-04 | AL-Huntsville | CHA | 17 | 5 | 9 | 1 | 891 | 47 | 0 | 3.16 | .... | .... | .... | .... | .... | .... | .... |
| 2004-05 | AL-Huntsville | CHA | 31 | 16 | 10 | 4 | 1805 | 69 | 3 | 2.29 | .... | .... | .... | .... | .... | .... | .... |
| 2005-06 | AL-Huntsville | CHA | 31 | 17 | 11 | 2 | 1813 | 91 | 0 | 3.01 | .... | .... | .... | .... | .... | .... | .... |
| | Philadelphia | AHL | 2 | 0 | 2 | 0 | 119 | 7 | 0 | 3.54 | .... | .... | .... | .... | .... | .... | .... |

| | | | | | | | | | | | | | | | | | |
|---|---|---|---|---|---|---|---|---|---|---|---|---|---|---|---|---|---|
| 2006-07 | Philadelphia | AHL | 40 | 15 | 19 | 2 | 2298 | 117 | 2 | 3.05 | .... | .... | .... | .... | .... | .... | .... |
| 2007-08 | Philadelphia | AHL | 36 | 18 | 8 | 2 | 1779 | 68 | 4 | 2.29 | 12 | 5 | 7 | 784 | 29 | *2 | 2.22 |
| 2008-09 | Philadelphia | AHL | 56 | 31 | 19 | 4 | 3271 | 134 | 4 | 2.46 | 3 | 0 | 3 | 180 | 12 | 0 | 4.01 |

CHA All-Rookie Team (2003) • CHA Rookie of the Year (2003)

Signed as a free agent by **Philadelphia** (AHL), March 18, 2006. Signed as a free agent by **NY Islanders**, July 2, 2009.

## MURPHY, Mike (MUHR-phee, MIGHK) CAR.

Goaltender. Catches left. 5'11", 165 lbs. Born, Kingston, Ont., January 15, 1989.
(Carolina's 4th choice, 165th overall, in 2008 Entry Draft).

| | | | Regular Season | | | | | | | | Playoffs | | | | | | |
|---|---|---|---|---|---|---|---|---|---|---|---|---|---|---|---|---|---|
| Season | Club | League | GP | W | L | O/T | Mins | GA | SO | Avg | GP | W | L | Mins | GA | SO | Avg |
| 2005-06 | Kingston | OPJHL | 33 | 16 | 13 | 2 | .... | 102 | 3 | 3.30 | 4 | 0 | 3 | 174 | 19 | 0 | 6.55 |
| | Belleville Bulls | OHL | 3 | 1 | 1 | 0 | 93 | 9 | 0 | 5.81 | .... | .... | .... | .... | .... | .... | .... |
| 2006-07 | Belleville Bulls | OHL | 18 | 8 | 6 | 2 | 995 | 61 | 0 | 3.68 | .... | .... | .... | .... | .... | .... | .... |
| 2007-08 | Belleville Bulls | OHL | 49 | 36 | 7 | 4 | 2942 | 110 | 3 | *2.24 | *19 | *14 | 4 | *1085 | 42 | 1 | 2.32 |
| 2008-09 | Belleville Bulls | OHL | 54 | 40 | 9 | 4 | 3169 | 110 | 5 | *2.08 | 17 | 10 | 7 | 1007 | 43 | 0 | 2.56 |

OHL First All-Star Team (2008, 2009) • Canadian Major Junior Second All-Star Team (2008) • Canadian Major Junior First All-Star Team (2009)

## NABOKOV, Evgeni (na-BAW-kahv, ehv-GEH-nee) S.J.

Goaltender. Catches left. 6', 205 lbs. Born, Ust-Kamenogorsk, USSR, July 25, 1975.
(San Jose's 9th choice, 219th overall, in 1994 Entry Draft).

| | | | Regular Season | | | | | | | | Playoffs | | | | | | |
|---|---|---|---|---|---|---|---|---|---|---|---|---|---|---|---|---|---|
| Season | Club | League | GP | W | L | O/T | Mins | GA | SO | Avg | GP | W | L | Mins | GA | SO | Avg |
| 1991-92 | Ust-Kamenogorsk | CIS | 1 | .... | .... | .... | 20 | 1 | 0 | 3.00 | .... | .... | .... | .... | .... | .... | .... |
| 1992-93 | Ust-Kam'gorsk 2 | CIS-2 | 19 | .... | .... | .... | .... | .... | .... | .... | .... | .... | .... | .... | .... | .... | .... |
| | Ust-Kamenogorsk | CIS | 4 | .... | .... | .... | 109 | 5 | 0 | 2.75 | .... | .... | .... | .... | .... | .... | .... |
| 1993-94 | Ust-Kamenogorsk | CIS | 11 | .... | .... | .... | 539 | 29 | .... | 3.23 | .... | .... | .... | .... | .... | .... | .... |
| 1994-95 | Dynamo Moscow | CIS | 24 | .... | .... | .... | 1326 | 40 | 3 | 1.81 | 13 | .... | .... | 806 | 30 | 2 | 2.23 |
| 1995-96 | Dynamo Moscow | CIS | 39 | .... | .... | .... | 2008 | 67 | 5 | 2.00 | .... | .... | .... | .... | .... | .... | .... |
| 1996-97 | Dynamo Moscow | Russia | 27 | .... | .... | .... | 1588 | 56 | 2 | 2.11 | 4 | .... | .... | 255 | 12 | 0 | 2.82 |
| | Dynamo Moscow 2 | Russia-3 | 1 | .... | .... | .... | .... | 2 | .... | .... | .... | .... | .... | .... | .... | .... | .... |
| 1997-98 | Kentucky | AHL | 33 | 10 | 21 | 2 | 1866 | 122 | 0 | 3.92 | 1 | 0 | 0 | 23 | 1 | 0 | 2.59 |
| 1998-99 | Kentucky | AHL | 43 | 26 | 14 | 1 | 2429 | 106 | 5 | 2.62 | 11 | 6 | 5 | 599 | 30 | *2 | 3.00 |
| **99-2000** | **San Jose** | **NHL** | **11** | **2** | **2** | **1** | **414** | **15** | **1** | **2.17** | **1** | **0** | **0** | **20** | **0** | **0** | **0.00** |
| | Kentucky | AHL | 2 | 1 | 1 | 0 | 120 | 3 | 1 | 1.50 | .... | .... | .... | .... | .... | .... | .... |
| | Cleveland | IHL | 20 | 12 | 4 | 3 | 1164 | 52 | 0 | 2.68 | .... | .... | .... | .... | .... | .... | .... |
| **2000-01** | **San Jose** | **NHL** | **66** | **32** | **21** | **7** | **3700** | **135** | **6** | **2.19** | **4** | **1** | **3** | **218** | **10** | **1** | **2.75** |
| **2001-02** | **San Jose** | **NHL** | **67** | **37** | **24** | **5** | **3901** | **149** | **7** | **2.29** | **12** | **7** | **5** | **712** | **31** | **0** | **2.61** |
| **2002-03** | **San Jose** | **NHL** | **55** | **19** | **28** | **8** | **3227** | **146** | **3** | **2.71** | .... | .... | .... | .... | .... | .... | .... |
| **2003-04** | **San Jose** | **NHL** | **59** | **31** | **19** | **8** | **3456** | **127** | **9** | **2.20** | **17** | **10** | **7** | **1052** | **30** | **3** | **1.71** |
| 2004-05 | Magnitogorsk | Russia | 14 | .... | .... | .... | 808 | 27 | 3 | 2.00 | 5 | .... | .... | 307 | 13 | 0 | 2.53 |
| **2005-06** | **San Jose** | **NHL** | **45** | **16** | **19** | **7** | **2575** | **133** | **1** | **3.10** | **1** | **0** | **0** | **12** | **1** | **0** | **5.00** |
| | Russia | Olympics | 7 | 4 | 2 | 0 | 359 | 8 | 3 | 1.34 | .... | .... | .... | .... | .... | .... | .... |
| **2006-07** | **San Jose** | **NHL** | **50** | **25** | **16** | **4** | **2778** | **106** | **7** | **2.29** | **11** | **6** | **5** | **701** | **26** | **1** | **2.23** |
| **2007-08** | **San Jose** | **NHL** | ***77** | ***46** | **21** | **8** | **4561** | **163** | **6** | **2.14** | **13** | **6** | **7** | **853** | **31** | **1** | **2.18** |
| **2008-09** | **San Jose** | **NHL** | **62** | **41** | **12** | **8** | **3686** | **150** | **7** | **2.44** | **6** | **2** | **4** | **362** | **17** | **0** | **2.82** |
| | **NHL Totals** | | **492** | **249** | **162** | **56** | **28298** | **1124** | **47** | **2.38** | **65** | **32** | **31** | **3930** | **146** | **6** | **2.23** |

NHL All-Rookie Team (2001) • Calder Memorial Trophy (2001) • NHL First All-Star Team (2008)

Played in NHL All-Star Game (2001, 2008)

• Scored a goal vs. Vancouver, March 10, 2002. Signed as a free agent by **Magnitogorsk** (Russia), December 2, 2004.

## NEUVIRTH, Michal (NOI-vihrt, MEE-khahl) WSH.

Goaltender. Catches left. 6'1", 199 lbs. Born, Usti nad Labem, Czech., March 23, 1988.
(Washington's 3rd choice, 34th overall, in 2006 Entry Draft).

| | | | Regular Season | | | | | | | | Playoffs | | | | | | |
|---|---|---|---|---|---|---|---|---|---|---|---|---|---|---|---|---|---|
| Season | Club | League | GP | W | L | O/T | Mins | GA | SO | Avg | GP | W | L | Mins | GA | SO | Avg |
| 2003-04 | Sparta U17 | CzR-U17 | 55 | .... | .... | .... | 3137 | 96 | 5 | 1.84 | 3 | .... | .... | 180 | 13 | 0 | 4.33 |
| 2004-05 | Sparta U17 | CzR-U17 | 20 | .... | .... | .... | 1178 | 49 | 3 | 2.50 | 8 | .... | .... | 482 | 17 | 0 | 2.12 |
| | Sparta Jr. | CzRep-Jr. | 10 | .... | .... | .... | 501 | 20 | 1 | 2.40 | .... | .... | .... | .... | .... | .... | .... |
| 2005-06 | Sparta Jr. | CzRep-Jr. | 42 | .... | .... | .... | 2516 | 82 | 5 | 1.96 | 3 | .... | .... | 179 | 9 | 0 | 3.02 |
| 2006-07 | Plymouth Whalers | OHL | 41 | 26 | 8 | 4 | 2223 | 86 | 4 | 2.32 | 18 | 14 | 4 | 1080 | 44 | 0 | 2.44 |
| 2007-08 | Plymouth Whalers | OHL | 10 | 5 | 4 | 1 | 600 | 26 | 0 | 2.60 | .... | .... | .... | .... | .... | .... | .... |
| | Windsor Spitfires | OHL | 8 | 6 | 1 | 1 | 482 | 17 | 0 | 2.12 | .... | .... | .... | .... | .... | .... | .... |
| | Oshawa Generals | OHL | 15 | 6 | 2 | 6 | 844 | 57 | 0 | 4.05 | 9 | 7 | 2 | 507 | 21 | 0 | 2.49 |
| **2008-09** | **Washington** | **NHL** | **5** | **2** | **1** | **0** | **220** | **11** | **0** | **3.00** | .... | .... | .... | .... | .... | .... | .... |
| | Hershey Bears | AHL | 17 | 9 | 5 | 2 | 1001 | 45 | 1 | 2.70 | 22 | 16 | 6 | 1346 | 43 | 4 | 1.92 |
| | South Carolina | ECHL | 13 | 6 | 7 | 0 | 762 | 29 | 2 | 2.28 | .... | .... | .... | .... | .... | .... | .... |
| | **NHL Totals** | | **5** | **2** | **1** | **0** | **220** | **11** | **0** | **3.00** | .... | .... | .... | .... | .... | .... | .... |

OHL Second All-Star Team (2007)

## NIEMI, Antti (nee-YEH-mee, AN-tee) CHI.

Goaltender. Catches left. 6'1", 200 lbs. Born, Vantaa, Finland, August 29, 1983.

| | | | Regular Season | | | | | | | | Playoffs | | | | | | |
|---|---|---|---|---|---|---|---|---|---|---|---|---|---|---|---|---|---|
| Season | Club | League | GP | W | L | O/T | Mins | GA | SO | Avg | GP | W | L | Mins | GA | SO | Avg |
| 2000-01 | Kiekko-Vantaa Jr. | Fin-Jr. | 4 | .... | .... | .... | .... | .... | .... | 6.86 | .... | .... | .... | .... | .... | .... | .... |
| 2001-02 | Kiekko-Vantaa | Finland-2 | 24 | .... | .... | .... | .... | .... | .... | .... | 3 | .... | .... | .... | .... | .... | .... |
| 2002-03 | Kiekko-Vantaa | Finland-2 | .... | .... | .... | .... | 364 | 16 | 0 | 2.63 | .... | .... | .... | .... | .... | .... | .... |
| 2003-04 | Kiekko-Vantaa | Finland-2 | 19 | .... | .... | .... | 1048 | 47 | 1 | 2.52 | 3 | .... | .... | 187 | 13 | 0 | 4.17 |
| | Kiekko-Vantaa Jr. | Fin-Jr. | 19 | .... | .... | .... | 1095 | 58 | 2 | 3.18 | .... | .... | .... | .... | .... | .... | .... |
| 2004-05 | Kiekko-Vantaa | Finland-2 | 38 | .... | .... | .... | 2261 | 95 | 1 | 2.52 | 3 | .... | .... | 187 | 13 | 0 | 4.17 |
| 2005-06 | Pelicans Lahti | Finland | 40 | 12 | 17 | 8 | 2263 | 103 | 3 | 2.73 | .... | .... | .... | .... | .... | .... | .... |
| 2006-07 | Pelicans Lahti | Finland | 48 | 18 | 21 | 7 | 2780 | 119 | 3 | 2.57 | 6 | 2 | 4 | 371 | 9 | 1 | 1.46 |
| 2007-08 | Pelicans Lahti | Finland | 49 | 26 | 14 | 6 | 2778 | 109 | 4 | 2.35 | 6 | 2 | 3 | 327 | 21 | 0 | 3.85 |
| **2008-09** | **Chicago** | **NHL** | **3** | **1** | **1** | **1** | **141** | **8** | **0** | **3.40** | .... | .... | .... | .... | .... | .... | .... |
| | Rockford IceHogs | AHL | 38 | 18 | 14 | 3 | 2095 | 85 | 2 | 2.43 | 2 | 0 | 2 | 115 | 7 | 0 | 3.65 |
| | **NHL Totals** | | **3** | **1** | **1** | **1** | **141** | **8** | **0** | **3.40** | .... | .... | .... | .... | .... | .... | .... |

Signed as a free agent by **Chicago**, May 5, 2008.

## NIITTYMAKI, Antero (nih-tih-MA-kee, AN-tehr-oh) T.B.

Goaltender. Catches left. 6'1", 195 lbs. Born, Turku, Finland, June 18, 1980.
(Philadelphia's 7th choice, 168th overall, in 1998 Entry Draft).

| | | | Regular Season | | | | | | | | Playoffs | | | | | | |
|---|---|---|---|---|---|---|---|---|---|---|---|---|---|---|---|---|---|
| Season | Club | League | GP | W | L | O/T | Mins | GA | SO | Avg | GP | W | L | Mins | GA | SO | Avg |
| 1997-98 | TPS Turku U18 | Fin-U18 | 12 | .... | .... | .... | .... | .... | .... | .... | 1 | 1 | 0 | 60 | 1 | 0 | 1.00 |
| | TPS Turku Jr. | Fin-Jr. | 19 | 10 | 8 | 1 | 1131 | 34 | .... | 1.80 | 4 | 3 | 1 | 220 | 7 | 0 | 1.91 |
| 1998-99 | TPS Turku Jr. | Fin-Jr. | 35 | 27 | 8 | 0 | 2095 | 60 | 3 | 1.72 | 6 | 3 | 3 | 362 | 14 | 0 | 2.32 |
| 99-2000 | TPS Turku Jr. | Fin-Jr. | 1 | 1 | 0 | 0 | 60 | 1 | 0 | 1.00 | 1 | 0 | 1 | 60 | 5 | 0 | 5.00 |
| | TPS Turku | Finland | 32 | 23 | 6 | 3 | 1899 | 68 | 3 | 2.15 | 8 | 6 | 2 | 453 | 13 | 0 | 1.72 |
| 2000-01 | TPS Turku Jr. | Fin-Jr. | .... | .... | .... | .... | .... | .... | .... | .... | 2 | 1 | 1 | 120 | 4 | 1 | 2.00 |
| | TPS Turku | Finland | 21 | 10 | 5 | 1 | 1112 | 46 | 2 | 2.48 | .... | .... | .... | .... | .... | .... | .... |
| 2001-02 | TPS Turku | Finland | 27 | 16 | 8 | 1 | 1498 | 46 | 3 | 1.84 | 4 | 2 | 2 | 295 | 11 | 0 | 2.24 |
| 2002-03 | Philadelphia | AHL | 40 | 14 | 21 | 2 | 2283 | 98 | 0 | 2.58 | .... | .... | .... | .... | .... | .... | .... |
| **2003-04** | **Philadelphia** | **NHL** | **3** | **3** | **0** | **0** | **180** | **3** | **0** | **1.00** | .... | .... | .... | .... | .... | .... | .... |
| | Philadelphia | AHL | 49 | 24 | 13 | 6 | 2728 | 92 | 7 | 2.02 | 12 | 6 | 6 | 796 | 24 | 0 | 1.81 |
| 2004-05 | Philadelphia | AHL | 58 | 33 | 21 | 4 | 3453 | 119 | 6 | 2.07 | *21 | *15 | 5 | *1269 | 37 | *3 | 1.75 |
| **2005-06** | **Philadelphia** | **NHL** | **46** | **23** | **15** | **6** | **2690** | **133** | **2** | **2.97** | **2** | **0** | **0** | **73** | **5** | **0** | **4.11** |
| | Finland | Olympics | 6 | 5 | 1 | 0 | 359 | 8 | 3 | 1.34 | .... | .... | .... | .... | .... | .... | .... |
| **2006-07** | **Philadelphia** | **NHL** | **52** | **9** | **29** | **9** | **2943** | **166** | **0** | **3.38** | .... | .... | .... | .... | .... | .... | .... |
| **2007-08** | **Philadelphia** | **NHL** | **28** | **12** | **9** | **2** | **1424** | **69** | **1** | **2.91** | .... | .... | .... | .... | .... | .... | .... |
| **2008-09** | **Philadelphia** | **NHL** | **32** | **15** | **8** | **6** | **1805** | **83** | **1** | **2.76** | .... | .... | .... | .... | .... | .... | .... |
| | **NHL Totals** | | **161** | **62** | **61** | **23** | **9042** | **454** | **4** | **3.01** | **2** | **0** | **0** | **73** | **5** | **0** | **4.11** |

Jack A. Butterfield Trophy (AHL – Playoff MVP) (2005) • Olympic Tournament All-Star Team (2006) • Olympic Tournament Best Goaltender (2006) • Olympic Tournament MVP (2006)

Signed as a free agent by **Tampa Bay**, July 10, 2009.

## NILSSON, Anders (NIHL-suhn, AN-duhrz) NYI

Goaltender. Catches left. 6'5", 220 lbs. Born, Lulea, Sweden, March 19, 1990.
(NY Islanders' 4th choice, 62nd overall, in 2009 Entry Draft).

| | | | Regular Season | | | | | | | | Playoffs | | | | | | |
|---|---|---|---|---|---|---|---|---|---|---|---|---|---|---|---|---|---|
| Season | Club | League | GP | W | L | O/T | Mins | GA | SO | Avg | GP | W | L | Mins | GA | SO | Avg |
| 2004-05 | Lulea HF Jr. | Swe-Jr. | 1 | .... | .... | .... | 24 | 4 | 0 | 9.90 | .... | .... | .... | .... | .... | .... | .... |
| 2007-08 | Lulea HF U18 | Swe-U18 | 11 | .... | .... | .... | 625 | 31 | 0 | 2.97 | .... | .... | .... | .... | .... | .... | .... |
| | Lulea HF Jr. | Swe-Jr. | 16 | .... | .... | .... | 898 | 31 | 2 | 2.07 | 1 | .... | .... | 60 | 6 | 0 | 6.00 |
| 2008-09 | Lulea HF Jr. | Swe-Jr. | 37 | .... | .... | .... | 2199 | 75 | 4 | 2.05 | 6 | .... | .... | 357 | 14 | 1 | 2.35 |
| | Kalix Ungdoms HC | Sweden-3 | 1 | .... | .... | .... | 59 | 3 | 0 | 3.05 | .... | .... | .... | .... | .... | .... | .... |
| | Lulea HF | Sweden | 1 | .... | .... | .... | 28 | 0 | 0 | 0.00 | .... | .... | .... | .... | .... | .... | .... |

## NORRENA, Fredrik (noh-REH-nah, FREHD-rihk)

Goaltender. Catches left. 6', 189 lbs. Born, Pietarsaari, Finland, November 29, 1973.
(Tampa Bay's 8th choice, 213th overall, in 2002 Entry Draft).

| | | | Regular Season | | | | | | | | Playoffs | | | | | | |
|---|---|---|---|---|---|---|---|---|---|---|---|---|---|---|---|---|---|
| Season | Club | League | GP | W | L | O/T | Mins | GA | SO | Avg | GP | W | L | Mins | GA | SO | Avg |
| 1989-90 | LIFK Leppalahti | Finland-3 | 36 | .... | .... | .... | .... | .... | .... | .... | .... | .... | .... | .... | .... | .... | .... |
| 1990-91 | LIFK Leppalahti | Finland-3 | 36 | .... | .... | .... | .... | .... | .... | .... | .... | .... | .... | .... | .... | .... | .... |
| 1991-92 | LIFK Leppalahti | Finland-3 | 35 | .... | .... | .... | .... | .... | .... | .... | .... | .... | .... | .... | .... | .... | .... |
| 1992-93 | TPS Turku Jr. | Fin-Jr. | 25 | 15 | 9 | 1 | 1449 | 74 | 1 | 3.06 | 5 | .... | .... | 307 | 11 | 1 | 2.14 |
| | TPS Turku | Finland | 2 | 0 | 1 | 0 | 30 | 1 | 0 | 2.00 | .... | .... | .... | .... | .... | .... | .... |
| 1993-94 | TPS Turku Jr. | Fin-Jr. | 2 | 0 | 1 | 0 | 80 | 5 | 0 | 3.75 | 1 | 0 | 1 | 58 | 4 | 0 | 4.10 |
| | TPS Turku | Finland | 10 | 3 | 3 | 0 | 387 | 19 | 0 | 2.94 | .... | .... | .... | .... | .... | .... | .... |
| | Kiekko-67 Turku | Finland-2 | 15 | 7 | 7 | 1 | 884 | 43 | 2 | 2.92 | .... | .... | .... | .... | .... | .... | .... |
| 1994-95 | TPS Turku | Finland | 22 | 14 | 6 | 2 | 1328 | 60 | 1 | 2.71 | 11 | 7 | 4 | 666 | 27 | 1 | 2.43 |
| | Kiekko-67 Turku | Finland-2 | 15 | .... | .... | .... | 828 | 34 | 0 | 2.46 | .... | .... | .... | .... | .... | .... | .... |
| 1995-96 | TPS Turku | Finland | 26 | 14 | 8 | 3 | 1539 | 68 | 0 | 2.65 | .... | .... | .... | .... | .... | .... | .... |
| 1996-97 | Kiekko-67 Turku | Finland-2 | 12 | .... | .... | .... | 725 | 36 | 0 | 2.98 | .... | .... | .... | .... | .... | .... | .... |
| | AIK Solna | Sweden | 5 | .... | .... | .... | 274 | 21 | 1 | 4.60 | .... | .... | .... | .... | .... | .... | .... |
| 1997-98 | Lukko Rauma | Finland | 37 | 12 | 19 | 4 | 2174 | 105 | 0 | 2.90 | .... | .... | .... | .... | .... | .... | .... |
| 1998-99 | TPS Turku | Finland | 20 | 11 | 4 | 1 | 1010 | 35 | 2 | 2.08 | 1 | 0 | 0 | 20 | 2 | 0 | 6.00 |
| 99-2000 | TPS Turku | Finland | 21 | 15 | 4 | 0 | 1175 | 35 | 2 | 1.79 | 4 | 3 | 0 | 234 | 10 | 0 | 2.56 |
| | TuTo Turku | Finland-2 | 2 | 1 | 1 | 0 | 118 | 7 | 0 | 3.54 | .... | .... | .... | .... | .... | .... | .... |
| 2000-01 | TPS Turku | Finland | 39 | 26 | 10 | 3 | 2266 | 66 | 6 | 1.75 | 10 | 9 | 1 | 603 | 13 | 2 | 1.29 |
| 2001-02 | TPS Turku | Finland | 32 | 14 | 11 | 5 | 1878 | 62 | 2 | 1.98 | 4 | 1 | 3 | 256 | 7 | 1 | 1.64 |
| 2002-03 | V.Frolunda | Sweden | 23 | .... | .... | .... | 1386 | 56 | 1 | 2.42 | 4 | .... | .... | 288 | 6 | 1 | 1.25 |
| 2003-04 | Linkopings HC | Sweden | 40 | .... | .... | .... | 2414 | 68 | 9 | 1.69 | 3 | .... | .... | 176 | 6 | 0 | 2.05 |
| 2004-05 | Linkopings HC | Sweden | 43 | .... | .... | .... | 2522 | 78 | 5 | 1.86 | 6 | .... | .... | 383 | 13 | 0 | 2.03 |
| 2005-06 | Linkopings HC | Sweden | 36 | .... | .... | .... | 2170 | 78 | 4 | 2.16 | 11 | .... | .... | 693 | 22 | 2 | *1.90 |
| | Finland | Olympics | 2 | 2 | 0 | 0 | 120 | 0 | 2 | 0.00 | .... | .... | .... | .... | .... | .... | .... |
| **2006-07** | **Columbus** | **NHL** | **55** | **24** | **23** | **3** | **2952** | **137** | **3** | **2.78** | .... | .... | .... | .... | .... | .... | .... |
| **2007-08** | **Columbus** | **NHL** | **37** | **10** | **19** | **6** | **1960** | **89** | **2** | **2.72** | .... | .... | .... | .... | .... | .... | .... |
| **2008-09** | **Columbus** | **NHL** | **8** | **1** | **3** | **2** | **323** | **17** | **0** | **3.16** | .... | .... | .... | .... | .... | .... | .... |
| | Ak Bars Kazan | Rus-KHL | 11 | .... | .... | .... | 669 | 18 | 1 | 1.61 | 15 | .... | .... | 892 | 29 | 2 | 1.95 |
| | **NHL Totals** | | **100** | **35** | **45** | **11** | **5235** | **243** | **5** | **2.79** | .... | .... | .... | .... | .... | .... | .... |

Traded to **Columbus** by **Tampa Bay** with Fredrik Modin for Marc Denis, June 30, 2006. Signed as a free agent by **Kazan** (Rus-KHL), December 20, 2008.

## ORTIO, Joni (OHR-tee-oh, YOH-nee) CGY.

Goaltender. Catches left. 6'1", 181 lbs. Born, Turku, Finland, April 16, 1991.
(Calgary's 5th choice, 171st overall, in 2009 Entry Draft).

| | | | Regular Season | | | | | | | | Playoffs | | | | | | |
|---|---|---|---|---|---|---|---|---|---|---|---|---|---|---|---|---|---|
| Season | Club | League | GP | W | L | O/T | Mins | GA | SO | Avg | GP | W | L | Mins | GA | SO | Avg |
| 2007-08 | TuTo Turku U18 | Fin-U18 | 7 | 1 | 6 | 0 | 392 | 34 | 0 | 5.20 | .... | .... | .... | .... | .... | .... | .... |
| | TuTo Turku Jr. | Fin-Jr. | 5 | 1 | 3 | 0 | 302 | 16 | 0 | 3.18 | .... | .... | .... | .... | .... | .... | .... |
| 2008-09 | TPS Turku U18 | Fin-U18 | 1 | 1 | 0 | 0 | 60 | 4 | 0 | 4.00 | .... | .... | .... | .... | .... | .... | .... |
| | TPS Turku Jr. | Fin-Jr. | 26 | 18 | 8 | 0 | 1573 | 69 | 1 | 2.63 | 12 | 6 | 6 | 716 | 23 | 0 | 1.93 |

## OSGOOD, Chris (AWS-gud, KRIHS) DET.

Goaltender. Catches left. 5'10", 178 lbs. Born, Peace River, Alta., November 26, 1972.
(Detroit's 3rd choice, 54th overall, in 1991 Entry Draft).

| | | | Regular Season | | | | | | | | Playoffs | | | | | | |
|---|---|---|---|---|---|---|---|---|---|---|---|---|---|---|---|---|---|
| Season | Club | League | GP | W | L | O/T | Mins | GA | SO | Avg | GP | W | L | Mins | GA | SO | Avg |
| 1988-89 | Medicine Hat | AMHL | 26 | .... | .... | .... | 1441 | 88 | 0 | 3.66 | .... | .... | .... | .... | .... | .... | .... |
| 1989-90 | Medicine Hat | WHL | 57 | 24 | 28 | 2 | 3094 | 228 | 0 | 4.42 | 3 | 0 | 3 | 173 | 17 | 0 | 5.91 |
| 1990-91 | Medicine Hat | WHL | 46 | 23 | 18 | 3 | 2630 | 173 | 2 | 3.95 | 12 | 7 | 5 | 712 | 42 | 0 | 3.54 |
| 1991-92 | Medicine Hat | WHL | 15 | 10 | 3 | 0 | 819 | 44 | 0 | 3.22 | .... | .... | .... | .... | .... | .... | .... |
| | Brandon | WHL | 16 | 3 | 10 | 1 | 890 | 60 | 1 | 4.04 | .... | .... | .... | .... | .... | .... | .... |
| | Seattle | WHL | 21 | 12 | 7 | 1 | 1217 | 65 | 1 | 3.20 | 15 | 9 | 6 | 904 | 51 | 0 | 3.38 |
| 1992-93 | Adirondack | AHL | 45 | 19 | 19 | 4 | 2438 | 159 | 0 | 3.91 | 1 | 0 | 1 | 59 | 2 | 0 | 2.03 |
| **1993-94** | **Detroit** | **NHL** | **41** | **23** | **8** | **5** | **2206** | **105** | **2** | **2.86** | **6** | **3** | **2** | **307** | **12** | **1** | **2.35** |
| | Adirondack | AHL | 4 | 3 | 1 | 0 | 239 | 13 | 0 | 3.26 | .... | .... | .... | .... | .... | .... | .... |
| **1994-95** | **Detroit** | **NHL** | **19** | **14** | **5** | **0** | **1087** | **41** | **1** | **2.26** | **2** | **0** | **0** | **68** | **2** | **0** | **1.76** |
| | Adirondack | AHL | 2 | 1 | 1 | 0 | 120 | 6 | 0 | 3.00 | .... | .... | .... | .... | .... | .... | .... |
| **1995-96** | **Detroit** | **NHL** | **50** | ***39** | **6** | **5** | **2933** | **106** | **5** | **2.17** | **15** | **8** | **7** | **936** | **33** | **2** | **2.12** |
| **1996-97 ♦** | **Detroit** | **NHL** | **47** | **23** | **13** | **9** | **2769** | **106** | **6** | **2.30** | **2** | **0** | **0** | **47** | **2** | **0** | **2.55** |
| **1997-98 ♦** | **Detroit** | **NHL** | **64** | **33** | **20** | **11** | **3807** | **140** | **6** | **2.21** | ***22** | ***16** | **6** | ***1361** | **48** | **2** | **2.12** |
| **1998-99** | **Detroit** | **NHL** | **63** | **34** | **25** | **4** | **3691** | **149** | **3** | **2.42** | **6** | **4** | **2** | **358** | **14** | **1** | **2.35** |
| **99-2000** | **Detroit** | **NHL** | **53** | **30** | **14** | **8** | **3148** | **126** | **6** | **2.40** | **9** | **5** | **4** | **547** | **18** | **2** | **1.97** |
| **2000-01** | **Detroit** | **NHL** | **52** | **25** | **19** | **4** | **2834** | **127** | **1** | **2.69** | **6** | **2** | **4** | **365** | **15** | **1** | **2.47** |
| **2001-02** | **NY Islanders** | **NHL** | **66** | **32** | **25** | **6** | **3743** | **156** | **4** | **2.50** | **7** | **3** | **4** | **392** | **17** | **0** | **2.60** |
| **2002-03** | **NY Islanders** | **NHL** | **37** | **17** | **14** | **4** | **1993** | **97** | **2** | **2.92** | .... | .... | .... | .... | .... | .... | .... |
| | **St. Louis** | **NHL** | **9** | **4** | **3** | **2** | **532** | **27** | **2** | **3.05** | **7** | **3** | **4** | **417** | **17** | **1** | **2.45** |
| **2003-04** | **St. Louis** | **NHL** | **67** | **31** | **25** | **8** | **3861** | **144** | **3** | **2.24** | **5** | **1** | **4** | **287** | **12** | **0** | **2.51** |
| 2004-05 | | | | | | | | DID NOT PLAY | | | | | | | | | |
| **2005-06** | **Detroit** | **NHL** | **32** | **20** | **6** | **5** | **1846** | **85** | **2** | **2.76** | .... | .... | .... | .... | .... | .... | .... |
| | Grand Rapids | AHL | 3 | 2 | 1 | 0 | 180 | 10 | 0 | 3.34 | .... | .... | .... | .... | .... | .... | .... |
| **2006-07** | **Detroit** | **NHL** | **21** | **11** | **3** | **6** | **1161** | **46** | **0** | **2.38** | .... | .... | .... | .... | .... | .... | .... |
| **2007-08 ♦** | **Detroit** | **NHL** | **43** | **27** | **9** | **4** | **2409** | **84** | **4** | ***2.09** | **19** | ***14** | **4** | **1160** | **30** | ***3** | ***1.55** |
| **2008-09** | **Detroit** | **NHL** | **46** | **26** | **9** | **8** | **2663** | **137** | **2** | **3.09** | **23** | **15** | **8** | **1406** | **47** | ***2** | **2.01** |
| | **NHL Totals** | | **710** | **389** | **204** | **89** | **40683** | **1676** | **49** | **2.47** | **129** | **74** | **49** | **7651** | **267** | **15** | **2.09** |

WHL East Second All-Star Team (1991) • NHL Second All-Star Team (1996) • William M. Jennings Trophy (1996) (shared with Mike Vernon) • William M. Jennings Trophy (2008) (shared with Dominik Hasek)

Played in NHL All-Star Game (1996, 2008)

• Scored a goal while with Medicine Hat (WHL), January 3, 1991. • Scored a goal vs. Hartford, March 6, 1996. Claimed by **NY Islanders** from **Detroit** in Waiver Draft, September 28, 2001. Traded to **St. Louis** by **NY Islanders** with NY Islanders' 3rd round choice (Konstantin Barulin) in 2003 Entry Draft for Justin Papineau and St. Louis' 2nd round choice (Jeremy Colliton) in 2003 Entry Draft, March 11, 2003. Signed as a free agent by **Detroit**, August 8, 2005.

## PALMER, Joe (PAHL-muhr, JOH) CHI.

Goaltender. Catches left. 6'1", 205 lbs. Born, Yorkville, NY, February 19, 1988.
(Chicago's 6th choice, 96th overall, in 2006 Entry Draft).

| | | | Regular Season | | | | | | | | Playoffs | | | | | | |
|---|---|---|---|---|---|---|---|---|---|---|---|---|---|---|---|---|---|
| Season | Club | League | GP | W | L | O/T | Mins | GA | SO | Avg | GP | W | L | Mins | GA | SO | Avg |
| 2003-04 | Syracuse Jr. Stars | EmJHL | 31 | .... | .... | .... | 1147 | 69 | 1 | 3.61 | 6 | .... | .... | 368 | 19 | 0 | 3.10 |
| | USNTDP | U-17 | 1 | 0 | 0 | 0 | 11 | 2 | 0 | 10.91 | .... | .... | .... | .... | .... | .... | .... |
| 2004-05 | USNTDP | U-17 | 8 | 6 | 1 | 1 | 495 | 22 | 0 | 2.67 | .... | .... | .... | .... | .... | .... | .... |
| | USNTDP | NAHL | 19 | 10 | 8 | 1 | 1020 | 56 | 0 | 3.29 | .... | .... | .... | .... | .... | .... | .... |
| 2005-06 | USNTDP | U-18 | 33 | 16 | 14 | 3 | 1900 | 99 | 0 | 3.13 | .... | .... | .... | .... | .... | .... | .... |
| | USNTDP | NAHL | 14 | 13 | 1 | 0 | 776 | 22 | 1 | 1.70 | .... | .... | .... | .... | .... | .... | .... |
| 2006-07 | Ohio State | CCHA | 34 | 15 | 15 | 4 | 1968 | 97 | 1 | 2.96 | .... | .... | .... | .... | .... | .... | .... |
| 2007-08 | Ohio State | CCHA | 34 | 10 | 19 | 4 | 1980 | 103 | 1 | 3.12 | .... | .... | .... | .... | .... | .... | .... |
| 2008-09 | Ohio State | CCHA | 3 | 0 | 2 | 1 | 122 | 11 | 0 | 5.40 | .... | .... | .... | .... | .... | .... | .... |

## PASQUALE, Edward (pas-KWAHL-ee, EHD-wuhrd) ATL.

Goaltender. Catches left. 6'2", 218 lbs. Born, Toronto, Ont., November 20, 1990.
(Atlanta's 4th choice, 117th overall, in 2009 Entry Draft).

| | | | Regular Season | | | | | | | | Playoffs | | | | | | |
|---|---|---|---|---|---|---|---|---|---|---|---|---|---|---|---|---|---|
| Season | Club | League | GP | W | L | O/T | Mins | GA | SO | Avg | GP | W | L | Mins | GA | SO | Avg |
| 2006-07 | Wellington Dukes | OPJHL | 18 | 13 | 3 | 2 | 1091 | 35 | 1 | 1.92 | .... | .... | .... | .... | .... | .... | .... |
| | Belleville Bulls | OHL | 7 | 4 | 1 | 0 | 367 | 19 | 0 | 3.11 | .... | .... | .... | .... | .... | .... | .... |
| 2007-08 | Belleville Bulls | OHL | 10 | 4 | 4 | 2 | 558 | 27 | 1 | 2.90 | .... | .... | .... | .... | .... | .... | .... |
| | Saginaw Spirit | OHL | 13 | 8 | 5 | 0 | 661 | 39 | 0 | 3.54 | 2 | 0 | 1 | 97 | 5 | 0 | 3.09 |
| 2008-09 | Saginaw Spirit | OHL | *61 | 32 | 21 | 6 | *3536 | 178 | 0 | 3.02 | 8 | 4 | 4 | 530 | 34 | 0 | 3.85 |

## PATTERSON, Kent (PA-tuhr-suhn, KEHNT) COL.

Goaltender. Catches left. 6', 184 lbs. Born, St. Louis Park, MN, September 15, 1989.
(Colorado's 6th choice, 113th overall, in 2007 Entry Draft).

| | | | Regular Season | | | | | | | | Playoffs | | | | | | |
|---|---|---|---|---|---|---|---|---|---|---|---|---|---|---|---|---|---|
| Season | Club | League | GP | W | L | O/T | Mins | GA | SO | Avg | GP | W | L | Mins | GA | SO | Avg |
| 2004-05 | Blake Bears | High-MN | 14 | 9 | 4 | 1 | 673 | 27 | .... | 2.05 | .... | .... | .... | .... | .... | .... | .... |
| 2005-06 | Blake Bears | High-MN | 25 | 14 | 8 | 2 | 1249 | 66 | .... | 2.70 | .... | .... | .... | .... | .... | .... | .... |
| 2006-07 | Cedar Rapids | USHL | 29 | 20 | 5 | 3 | 1710 | 83 | 2 | 2.91 | 1 | 0 | 1 | 41 | 6 | 0 | 8.78 |
| 2007-08 | Cedar Rapids | USHL | 20 | 10 | 6 | 1 | 1110 | 46 | 1 | 2.49 | .... | .... | .... | .... | .... | .... | .... |
| 2008-09 | U. of Minnesota | WCHA | 7 | 0 | 2 | 1 | 231 | 9 | 0 | 2.34 | .... | .... | .... | .... | .... | .... | .... |

USHL All-Rookie Team (2007)

## PATZOLD, Dimitri (PATZ-ohld, dih-MEE-tree)

Goaltender. Catches left. 6', 195 lbs. Born, Ust-Kamenogorsk, USSR, February 3, 1983.
(San Jose's 3rd choice, 107th overall, in 2001 Entry Draft).

| | | | Regular Season | | | | | | | | Playoffs | | | | | | |
|---|---|---|---|---|---|---|---|---|---|---|---|---|---|---|---|---|---|
| Season | Club | League | GP | W | L | O/T | Mins | GA | SO | Avg | GP | W | L | Mins | GA | SO | Avg |
| 99-2000 | Kolner EC Jr. | Ger-Jr. | 38 | .... | .... | .... | 2131 | 73 | 0 | 2.06 | .... | .... | .... | .... | .... | .... | .... |
| | Kolner Haie 2 | German-5 | 16 | .... | .... | .... | 896 | 58 | 0 | 3.88 | .... | .... | .... | .... | .... | .... | .... |
| 2000-01 | EV Duisburg | German-3 | 6 | .... | .... | .... | 360 | 17 | 0 | 2.83 | .... | .... | .... | .... | .... | .... | .... |
| | Erding Jets | German-2 | 24 | .... | .... | .... | 1378 | 89 | 0 | 3.88 | .... | .... | .... | .... | .... | .... | .... |
| 2001-02 | Kolner Haie | Germany | 7 | .... | .... | .... | 260 | 16 | 0 | 3.69 | .... | .... | .... | .... | .... | .... | .... |
| | EV Duisburg | German-2 | 6 | .... | .... | .... | 360 | 17 | 0 | 2.83 | .... | .... | .... | .... | .... | .... | .... |
| 2002-03 | Adler Mannheim | Germany | 15 | .... | .... | .... | 817 | 35 | 0 | 2.57 | 2 | .... | .... | 34 | 2 | 0 | 3.53 |
| 2003-04 | Cleveland Barons | AHL | 27 | 10 | 15 | 0 | 1457 | 70 | 3 | 2.88 | .... | .... | .... | .... | .... | .... | .... |
| | Johnstown Chiefs | ECHL | 8 | 7 | 0 | 0 | 443 | 20 | 0 | 2.71 | 1 | 0 | 1 | 59 | 2 | 0 | 2.02 |
| 2004-05 | Cleveland Barons | AHL | 41 | 18 | 16 | 5 | 2418 | 104 | 1 | 2.58 | .... | .... | .... | .... | .... | .... | .... |
| 2005-06 | Cleveland Barons | AHL | 33 | 10 | 21 | 0 | 1876 | 124 | 0 | 3.97 | .... | .... | .... | .... | .... | .... | .... |
| 2006-07 | Worcester Sharks | AHL | 24 | 10 | 8 | 3 | 1378 | 77 | 0 | 3.35 | 4 | 2 | 1 | 256 | 8 | 0 | 1.87 |
| | Fresno Falcons | ECHL | 4 | 2 | 2 | 0 | 239 | 8 | 0 | 2.01 | .... | .... | .... | .... | .... | .... | .... |
| **2007-08** | **San Jose** | **NHL** | **3** | **0** | **0** | **0** | **44** | **4** | **0** | **5.45** | .... | .... | .... | .... | .... | .... | .... |
| | Worcester Sharks | AHL | 21 | 7 | 10 | 3 | 1184 | 56 | 1 | 2.84 | .... | .... | .... | .... | .... | .... | .... |
| 2008-09 | Vityaz Chekhov | Rus-KHL | 1 | .... | .... | .... | 52 | 5 | 0 | 5.80 | .... | .... | .... | .... | .... | .... | .... |
| | Hannover Scorp. | Germany | 26 | 18 | 7 | .... | 1454 | 68 | 0 | 2.81 | 10 | 6 | 4 | 625 | 24 | 1 | 2.30 |
| | **NHL Totals** | | **3** | **0** | **0** | **0** | **44** | **4** | **0** | **5.45** | .... | .... | .... | .... | .... | .... | .... |

## PAVELEC, Ondrej (pah-vah-LEK, AWN-dray) ATL.

Goaltender. Catches left. 6'2", 215 lbs. Born, Kladno, Czech., August 31, 1987.
(Atlanta's 2nd choice, 41st overall, in 2005 Entry Draft).

| | | | Regular Season | | | | | | | | Playoffs | | | | | | |
|---|---|---|---|---|---|---|---|---|---|---|---|---|---|---|---|---|---|
| Season | Club | League | GP | W | L | O/T | Mins | GA | SO | Avg | GP | W | L | Mins | GA | SO | Avg |
| 2003-04 | HC Kladno U17 | CzR-U17 | 38 | .... | .... | .... | 2079 | 77 | 3 | 2.22 | 2 | .... | .... | 67 | 7 | 0 | 6.27 |
| 2004-05 | HC Kladno Jr. | CzRep-Jr. | 39 | .... | .... | .... | 2218 | 85 | 7 | 2.30 | 10 | .... | .... | 587 | 24 | 1 | 2.45 |
| | HK LEV Slany | CzRep-3 | 1 | .... | .... | .... | 60 | 4 | 0 | 4.00 | .... | .... | .... | .... | .... | .... | .... |
| 2005-06 | Cape Breton | QMJHL | 47 | 27 | 18 | 0 | 2578 | 108 | 3 | 2.51 | 9 | 4 | 5 | 507 | 19 | 0 | *2.25 |
| 2006-07 | Cape Breton | QMJHL | 43 | 28 | 11 | .... | 2335 | 98 | 1 | *2.52 | 16 | 11 | 5 | 970 | 37 | *2 | *2.29 |
| **2007-08** | **Atlanta** | **NHL** | **7** | **3** | **3** | **0** | **347** | **18** | **0** | **3.11** | .... | .... | .... | .... | .... | .... | .... |
| | Chicago Wolves | AHL | 52 | 33 | 16 | 3 | 3033 | 140 | 2 | 2.77 | *24 | *16 | 8 | *1438 | 56 | *2 | 2.34 |
| **2008-09** | **Atlanta** | **NHL** | **12** | **3** | **7** | **0** | **599** | **36** | **0** | **3.61** | .... | .... | .... | .... | .... | .... | .... |
| | Chicago Wolves | AHL | 40 | 18 | 20 | 2 | 2417 | 104 | 3 | 2.58 | .... | .... | .... | .... | .... | .... | .... |
| | **NHL Totals** | | **19** | **6** | **10** | **0** | **946** | **54** | **0** | **3.42** | .... | .... | .... | .... | .... | .... | .... |

QMJHL All-Rookie Team (2006) • QMJHL First All-Star Team (2006, 2007) • QMJHL Defensive Rookie of the Year (2006)

## PEARCE, Jordan (PEERS-JOHR-dahn) DET.

Goaltender. Catches left. 6'1", 206 lbs. Born, Anchorage, AK, October 10, 1986.

| | | | Regular Season | | | | | | | | Playoffs | | | | | | |
|---|---|---|---|---|---|---|---|---|---|---|---|---|---|---|---|---|---|
| Season | Club | League | GP | W | L | O/T | Mins | GA | SO | Avg | GP | W | L | Mins | GA | SO | Avg |
| 2004-05 | Lincoln Stars | USHL | 38 | 22 | 10 | 4 | 2227 | 114 | 0 | 3.07 | 2 | 0 | 1 | 69 | 7 | 0 | 6.06 |
| 2005-06 | U. of Notre Dame | CCHA | 9 | 4 | 4 | 0 | 442 | 24 | 1 | 3.25 | .... | .... | .... | .... | .... | .... | .... |
| 2006-07 | U. of Notre Dame | CCHA | 3 | 2 | 1 | 0 | 180 | 6 | 1 | 2.01 | .... | .... | .... | .... | .... | .... | .... |
| 2007-08 | U. of Notre Dame | CCHA | *43 | 23 | 15 | 4 | *2558 | 87 | 2 | 2.04 | .... | .... | .... | .... | .... | .... | .... |
| 2008-09 | U. of Notre Dame | CCHA | *39 | *30 | 6 | 3 | *2326 | 65 | 8 | 1.68 | .... | .... | .... | .... | .... | .... | .... |
| | Grand Rapids | AHL | 1 | 0 | 1 | 0 | 59 | 5 | 0 | 5.11 | .... | .... | .... | .... | .... | .... | .... |

Signed as a free agent by **Detroit**, April 10, 2009.

## PECHURSKI, Alexander (puh-CHUHR-skee, al-ehx-AN-duhr) PIT.

Goaltender. Catches left. 6', 187 lbs. Born, Magnitogorsk, USSR, June 4, 1990.
(Pittsburgh's 2nd choice, 150th overall, in 2008 Entry Draft).

| | | | Regular Season | | | | | | | | Playoffs | | | | | | |
|---|---|---|---|---|---|---|---|---|---|---|---|---|---|---|---|---|---|
| Season | Club | League | GP | W | L | O/T | Mins | GA | SO | Avg | GP | W | L | Mins | GA | SO | Avg |
| 2007-08 | Magnitogorsk 2 | Russia-3 | 27 | .... | .... | .... | .... | 62 | .... | .... | .... | .... | .... | .... | .... | .... | .... |
| | Magnitogorsk | Russia | 1 | .... | .... | .... | 1 | 0 | 0 | 0.00 | .... | .... | .... | .... | .... | .... | .... |
| 2008-09 | Magnitogorsk 2 | Russia-3 | 20 | .... | .... | .... | .... | 54 | .... | .... | .... | .... | .... | .... | .... | .... | .... |

## PETERS, Justin (PEE-tuhrz, JUHS-tihn) CAR.

Goaltender. Catches left. 6'1", 205 lbs. Born, Blyth, Ont., August 30, 1986.
(Carolina's 2nd choice, 38th overall, in 2004 Entry Draft).

| | | | Regular Season | | | | | | | | Playoffs | | | | | | |
|---|---|---|---|---|---|---|---|---|---|---|---|---|---|---|---|---|---|
| Season | Club | League | GP | W | L | O/T | Mins | GA | SO | Avg | GP | W | L | Mins | GA | SO | Avg |
| 2001-02 | Huron-Perth | Minor-ON | 17 | 11 | 2 | 4 | 810 | 32 | 1 | 1.89 | 13 | 9 | 4 | 285 | 30 | 1 | 2.31 |
| 2002-03 | St. Michael's | OHL | 23 | 6 | 10 | 1 | 1052 | 54 | 0 | 3.08 | 7 | 1 | 0 | 126 | 4 | 0 | 1.90 |
| 2003-04 | St. Michael's | OHL | 53 | 30 | 16 | 6 | 3149 | 139 | 4 | 2.65 | 18 | 10 | 8 | 1109 | 37 | 4 | 2.00 |
| 2004-05 | St. Michael's | OHL | 58 | 23 | 23 | 5 | 3150 | 146 | 3 | 2.78 | 10 | 4 | 4 | 524 | 25 | 0 | 2.86 |
| 2005-06 | St. Michael's | OHL | 20 | 10 | 6 | 3 | 1174 | 75 | 0 | 3.83 | .... | .... | .... | .... | .... | .... | .... |
| | Plymouth Whalers | OHL | 35 | 19 | 15 | 1 | 2073 | 95 | 1 | 2.75 | 13 | 6 | 7 | 789 | 42 | 0 | 3.19 |
| 2006-07 | Albany River Rats | AHL | 34 | 10 | 18 | 0 | 1765 | 96 | 1 | 3.26 | .... | .... | .... | .... | .... | .... | .... |
| | Florida Everblades | ECHL | 1 | 0 | 0 | 1 | 65 | 6 | 0 | 5.54 | .... | .... | .... | .... | .... | .... | .... |
| 2007-08 | Albany River Rats | AHL | 11 | 7 | 3 | 0 | 645 | 29 | 0 | 2.70 | .... | .... | .... | .... | .... | .... | .... |
| | Florida Everblades | ECHL | 31 | 18 | 10 | 2 | 1846 | 79 | 1 | 2.57 | .... | .... | .... | .... | .... | .... | .... |
| 2008-09 | Albany River Rats | AHL | 56 | 19 | 30 | 4 | 3178 | 153 | 4 | 2.89 | .... | .... | .... | .... | .... | .... | .... |

## PHILLIPS, Brad (FIHL-ihps , BRAD) PHI.

Goaltender. Catches left. 6'2", 163 lbs. Born, Allen Park, MI, April 22, 1989.
(Philadelphia's 7th choice, 182nd overall, in 2007 Entry Draft).

| | | | Regular Season | | | | | | | | Playoffs | | | | | | |
|---|---|---|---|---|---|---|---|---|---|---|---|---|---|---|---|---|---|
| Season | Club | League | GP | W | L | O/T | Mins | GA | SO | Avg | GP | W | L | Mins | GA | SO | Avg |
| 2004-05 | Det. Honeybaked | MWEHL | 38 | 32 | 3 | 3 | .... | 50 | 10 | 1.32 | .... | .... | .... | .... | .... | .... | .... |
| 2005-06 | USNTDP | U-17 | 13 | 8 | 5 | 0 | 610 | 28 | .... | 2.75 | .... | .... | .... | .... | .... | .... | .... |
| | USNTDP | NAHL | 21 | 12 | 6 | 3 | 1261 | 51 | 0 | 2.43 | 4 | 1 | 3 | 254 | 12 | 0 | 2.83 |
| 2006-07 | USNTDP | U-18 | 12 | 7 | 1 | 2 | 706 | 29 | 0 | 2.46 | .... | .... | .... | .... | .... | .... | .... |
| | USNTDP | NAHL | 11 | 8 | 3 | 0 | 660 | 24 | 2 | 2.18 | 1 | 0 | 1 | 60 | 3 | 0 | 3.00 |
| 2007-08 | U. of Notre Dame | CCHA | 5 | 4 | 1 | 0 | 275 | 7 | 1 | 1.53 | .... | .... | .... | .... | .... | .... | .... |
| 2008-09 | U. of Notre Dame | CCHA | | | | | DID NOT PLAY – INJURED | | | | | | | | | | |

• Missed entire 2008-09 season recovering from pre-season knee injury.

## PICKARD, Chet (PIH-kuhrd, CHEHT) NSH.

Goaltender. Catches left. 6'2", 210 lbs. Born, Moncton, N.B., November 29, 1989.
(Nashville's 2nd choice, 18th overall, in 2008 Entry Draft).

| | | | Regular Season | | | | | | | | Playoffs | | | | | | |
|---|---|---|---|---|---|---|---|---|---|---|---|---|---|---|---|---|---|
| Season | Club | League | GP | W | L | O/T | Mins | GA | SO | Avg | GP | W | L | Mins | GA | SO | Avg |
| 2004-05 | Wpg. Monarchs | MMHL | 22 | .... | .... | .... | 1264 | 55 | 2 | 2.61 | .... | .... | .... | .... | .... | .... | .... |
| 2005-06 | Tri-City Americans | WHL | 26 | 9 | 9 | 1 | 1270 | 62 | 3 | 2.93 | .... | .... | .... | .... | .... | .... | .... |
| 2006-07 | Tri-City Americans | WHL | 29 | 17 | 10 | 1 | 1577 | 75 | 1 | 2.85 | 1 | 0 | 0 | 20 | 1 | 0 | 3.00 |
| 2007-08 | Tri-City Americans | WHL | *64 | *46 | 12 | 4 | *3779 | 146 | 2 | 2.32 | 16 | 11 | 5 | 1010 | 30 | *3 | 1.78 |
| 2008-09 | Tri-City Americans | WHL | 50 | 35 | 12 | 3 | 2947 | 112 | 6 | 2.28 | 11 | 6 | 5 | 650 | 37 | 0 | 3.41 |

WHL West First All-Star Team (2008, 2009) • WHL Goaltender of the Year (2008, 2009) • Canadian Major Junior First All-Star Team (2008) • Canadian Major Junior Goaltender of the Year (2008)

## PIELMEIER, Timo (PEEL-migh-uhr, TEE-moh) ANA.

Goaltender. Catches left. 6', 194 lbs. Born, Deggendorf, West Germany, July 7, 1989.
(San Jose's 3rd choice, 83rd overall, in 2007 Entry Draft).

| | | | Regular Season | | | | | | | | Playoffs | | | | | | |
|---|---|---|---|---|---|---|---|---|---|---|---|---|---|---|---|---|---|
| Season | Club | League | GP | W | L | O/T | Mins | GA | SO | Avg | GP | W | L | Mins | GA | SO | Avg |
| 2004-05 | Mannheimer ERC | German-5 | 1 | .... | .... | .... | .... | .... | .... | 8.15 | .... | .... | .... | .... | .... | .... | .... |
| | Mannheim Jr. | Ger-Jr. | 10 | .... | .... | .... | 568 | 33 | .... | 3.49 | .... | .... | .... | .... | .... | .... | .... |
| 2005-06 | Koln Jr. | Ger-Jr. | 8 | .... | .... | .... | 459 | 52 | .... | 6.79 | 2 | .... | .... | 100 | 17 | .... | 10.20 |
| 2006-07 | Koln Jr. | Ger-Jr. | 20 | .... | .... | .... | 1159 | 77 | .... | 3.99 | 6 | .... | .... | 370 | 17 | .... | 2.76 |
| 2007-08 | St. John's | QMJHL | 50 | 23 | 26 | .... | 2719 | 133 | 1 | 2.94 | 5 | 0 | 3 | 231 | 22 | 0 | 5.71 |
| 2008-09 | Shawinigan | QMJHL | 43 | 29 | 11 | .... | 2407 | 106 | 2 | 2.64 | *18 | 12 | 5 | 1021 | 47 | 0 | 2.76 |

Traded to **Anaheim** by **San Jose** with Nick Bonino and future considerations for Travis Moen and Kent Huskins, March 4, 2009.

## PITTON, Bryan (PIH-tuhn, BRIGH-uhn) EDM.

Goaltender. Catches left. 6'2", 176 lbs. Born, Mississauga, Ont., January 26, 1988.
(Edmonton's 3rd choice, 133rd overall, in 2006 Entry Draft).

| | | | Regular Season | | | | | | | | Playoffs | | | | | | |
|---|---|---|---|---|---|---|---|---|---|---|---|---|---|---|---|---|---|
| Season | Club | League | GP | W | L | O/T | Mins | GA | SO | Avg | GP | W | L | Mins | GA | SO | Avg |
| 2004-05 | Wellington Dukes | OPJHL | .... | 24 | 7 | 3 | .... | .... | 2 | 2.93 | .... | .... | .... | .... | .... | .... | .... |
| 2005-06 | Brampton Battalion | OHL | 24 | 16 | 4 | 0 | 1293 | 74 | 0 | 3.43 | 2 | 0 | 0 | 45 | 5 | 0 | 6.67 |
| 2006-07 | Brampton Battalion | OHL | 61 | 26 | 29 | 4 | 3494 | 208 | 0 | 3.57 | 4 | 0 | 4 | 270 | 15 | 0 | 3.33 |
| 2007-08 | Brampton Battalion | OHL | 39 | 22 | 13 | 2 | 2153 | 91 | *4 | 2.54 | 5 | 1 | 4 | 333 | 10 | 0 | *1.80 |
| | Springfield Falcons | AHL | 1 | 0 | 0 | 0 | 12 | 1 | 0 | 4.88 | .... | .... | .... | .... | .... | .... | .... |
| 2008-09 | Stockton Thunder | ECHL | 34 | 9 | 19 | 3 | 1949 | 110 | 0 | 3.39 | 3 | 1 | 2 | 144 | 12 | 0 | 5.01 |

## PLANTE, Tyler (PLAWNT, TIGH-luhr) FLA.

Goaltender. Catches left. 6'3", 191 lbs. Born, Milwaukee, WI, April 16, 1987.
(Florida's 2nd choice, 32nd overall, in 2005 Entry Draft).

| | | | Regular Season | | | | | | | | Playoffs | | | | | | |
|---|---|---|---|---|---|---|---|---|---|---|---|---|---|---|---|---|---|
| Season | Club | League | GP | W | L | O/T | Mins | GA | SO | Avg | GP | W | L | Mins | GA | SO | Avg |
| 2003-04 | Brandon | WHL | 2 | 0 | 0 | 1 | 58 | 2 | 0 | 2.07 | .... | .... | .... | .... | .... | .... | .... |
| 2004-05 | Brandon | WHL | 48 | 34 | 11 | 2 | 2833 | 122 | 6 | 2.58 | *24 | *13 | 11 | *1408 | 69 | 0 | 2.94 |
| 2005-06 | Brandon | WHL | 60 | 25 | 24 | 9 | 3414 | 189 | 2 | 3.32 | 6 | 2 | 4 | 360 | 18 | 0 | 3.00 |
| 2006-07 | Brandon | WHL | 54 | 30 | 14 | 9 | 3215 | 145 | 4 | 2.71 | 11 | 6 | 5 | 659 | 37 | 0 | 3.37 |
| 2007-08 | Rochester | AHL | 25 | 6 | 16 | 1 | 1451 | 86 | 0 | 3.56 | .... | .... | .... | .... | .... | .... | .... |
| | Florida Everblades | ECHL | 10 | 4 | 5 | 1 | 598 | 28 | 1 | 2.81 | .... | .... | .... | .... | .... | .... | .... |
| 2008-09 | Rochester | AHL | 19 | 5 | 10 | 1 | 904 | 49 | 0 | 3.25 | .... | .... | .... | .... | .... | .... | .... |
| | Dayton Bombers | ECHL | 19 | 6 | 11 | 1 | 1076 | 60 | 0 | 3.35 | .... | .... | .... | .... | .... | .... | .... |

WHL Rookie of the Year (2005) • Canadian Major Junior All-Rookie Team (2005)

## POGGE, Justin (POH-gee, JUHS-tihn) ANA.

Goaltender. Catches left. 6'3", 200 lbs. Born, Ft. McMurray, Alta., April 22, 1986.
(Toronto's 1st choice, 90th overall, in 2004 Entry Draft).

| | | | Regular Season | | | | | | | | Playoffs | | | | | | |
|---|---|---|---|---|---|---|---|---|---|---|---|---|---|---|---|---|---|
| Season | Club | League | GP | W | L | O/T | Mins | GA | SO | Avg | GP | W | L | Mins | GA | SO | Avg |
| 2002-03 | Summerland Sting | KIJHL | 30 | .... | .... | .... | 1761 | 91 | 0 | 3.13 | .... | .... | .... | .... | .... | .... | .... |
| 2003-04 | Prince George | WHL | 44 | 17 | 18 | 2 | 2271 | 107 | 3 | 2.83 | .... | .... | .... | .... | .... | .... | .... |
| 2004-05 | Prince George | WHL | 24 | 10 | 9 | 2 | 1198 | 56 | 4 | 2.80 | .... | .... | .... | .... | .... | .... | .... |
| | Calgary Hitmen | WHL | 29 | 14 | 12 | 3 | 1727 | 66 | 2 | 2.29 | 12 | 7 | 5 | 742 | 24 | 1 | 1.94 |
| 2005-06 | Calgary Hitmen | WHL | 54 | 38 | 10 | 6 | 3237 | 93 | *11 | *1.72 | 13 | 7 | 6 | 802 | 34 | 2 | 2.54 |
| 2006-07 | Toronto Marlies | AHL | 48 | 19 | 25 | 2 | 2812 | 142 | 3 | 3.03 | .... | .... | .... | .... | .... | .... | .... |
| 2007-08 | Toronto Marlies | AHL | 41 | 26 | 10 | 4 | 2415 | 94 | 4 | 2.34 | 4 | 1 | 1 | 172 | 6 | 0 | 2.09 |
| **2008-09** | **Toronto** | **NHL** | **7** | **1** | **4** | **1** | **372** | **27** | **0** | **4.35** | .... | .... | .... | .... | .... | .... | .... |
| | Toronto Marlies | AHL | 53 | 26 | 21 | 5 | 3155 | 142 | 0 | 2.70 | 5 | 2 | 3 | 304 | 16 | 0 | 3.15 |
| | **NHL Totals** | | **7** | **1** | **4** | **1** | **372** | **27** | **0** | **4.35** | .... | .... | .... | .... | .... | .... | .... |

WHL East First All-Star Team (2006) • WHL Goaltender of the Year (2006) • WHL Player of the Year (2006) • Canadian Major Junior First All-Star Team (2006) • Canadian Major Junior Goaltender of the Year (2006)

Traded to **Anaheim** by **Toronto** for future considerations, August 10, 2009.

## POPPERLE, Tomas (PAW-puhr-lay, TAW-mahsh)

Goaltender. Catches left. 6'1", 187 lbs. Born, Broumov, Czech., October 10, 1984.
(Columbus' 5th choice, 131st overall, in 2005 Entry Draft).

| | | | Regular Season | | | | | | | | Playoffs | | | | | | |
|---|---|---|---|---|---|---|---|---|---|---|---|---|---|---|---|---|---|
| Season | Club | League | GP | W | L | O/T | Mins | GA | SO | Avg | GP | W | L | Mins | GA | SO | Avg |
| 2001-02 | Sparta Jr. | CzRep-Jr. | 29 | .... | .... | .... | 1653 | 65 | 2 | 2.36 | 5 | .... | .... | 320 | 15 | 0 | 2.81 |
| 2002-03 | Sparta Jr. | CzRep-Jr. | 28 | .... | .... | .... | 1500 | 52 | 2 | 2.08 | .... | .... | .... | .... | .... | .... | .... |
| 2003-04 | Sparta Jr. | CzRep-Jr. | 30 | .... | .... | .... | 1778 | 60 | 4 | 2.02 | .... | .... | .... | .... | .... | .... | .... |
| | HC Pribram | CzRep-3 | 2 | .... | .... | .... | 60 | 2 | 0 | 2.00 | .... | .... | .... | .... | .... | .... | .... |
| | Beroun | CzRep-2 | 5 | .... | .... | .... | 305 | 7 | 0 | 1.38 | 2 | .... | .... | 120 | 4 | 0 | 2.00 |
| | HC Sparta Praha | CzRep | .... | .... | .... | .... | .... | .... | .... | .... | 1 | .... | .... | 11 | 0 | 0 | 0.00 |

| Season | Club | League | GP | W | L | O/T | Mins | GA | SO | Avg | GP | W | L | Mins | GA | SO | Avg |
|---|---|---|---|---|---|---|---|---|---|---|---|---|---|---|---|---|---|
| 2004-05 | Beroun | CzRep-2 | 16 | .... | .... | .... | 966 | 29 | 1 | 1.80 | 2 | .... | .... | 120 | 5 | 0 | 2.50 |
| | HC Sparta Praha | CzRep | 25 | .... | .... | .... | 1325 | 35 | 4 | *1.58 | 2 | .... | .... | 12 | 4 | 0 | 20.00 |
| 2005-06 | Eisbaren Berlin | Germany | 31 | .... | .... | .... | 1845 | 67 | 3 | 2.18 | 11 | .... | .... | 655 | 23 | *1 | *2.11 |
| **2006-07** | **Columbus** | **NHL** | **2** | **0** | **0** | **0** | **45** | **1** | **0** | **1.33** | .... | .... | .... | .... | .... | .... | .... |
| | Syracuse Crunch | AHL | 49 | 25 | 19 | 4 | 2833 | 135 | 4 | 2.86 | .... | .... | .... | .... | .... | .... | .... |
| 2007-08 | Syracuse Crunch | AHL | 17 | 7 | 8 | 0 | 890 | 44 | 1 | 2.97 | .... | .... | .... | .... | .... | .... | .... |
| 2008-09 | HC Sparta Praha | CzRep | 41 | .... | .... | .... | 2361 | 106 | 2 | 2.69 | 1 | .... | .... | 32 | 4 | 0 | 7.50 |
| | **NHL Totals** | | **2** | **0** | **0** | **0** | **45** | **1** | **0** | **1.33** | .... | .... | .... | .... | .... | .... | .... |

## POULIN, Kevin (POO-lihn, KEH-vihn) NYI

Goaltender. Catches left. 6'2", 210 lbs. Born, Montreal, Que., April 12, 1990.
(NY Islanders' 10th choice, 126th overall, in 2008 Entry Draft).

| | | | Regular Season | | | | | | | | Playoffs | | | | | | |
|---|---|---|---|---|---|---|---|---|---|---|---|---|---|---|---|---|---|
| Season | Club | League | GP | W | L | O/T | Mins | GA | SO | Avg | GP | W | L | Mins | GA | SO | Avg |
| 2005-06 | C.C. Lemoyne | QAAA | 27 | 13 | 8 | 2 | 1440 | 71 | 1 | 2.96 | 7 | 4 | 3 | 373 | 16 | 1 | 2.57 |
| 2006-07 | Victoriaville Tigres | QMJHL | 24 | 10 | 6 | .... | 1220 | 68 | 0 | 3.34 | 2 | 0 | 0 | 42 | 5 | 0 | 7.20 |
| 2007-08 | Victoriaville Tigres | QMJHL | 52 | 18 | 24 | .... | 2734 | 168 | 0 | 3.69 | 6 | 2 | 4 | 279 | 27 | 0 | 5.80 |
| 2008-09 | Victoriaville Tigres | QMJHL | 39 | 18 | 19 | .... | 2273 | 120 | 1 | 3.17 | 4 | 0 | 4 | 249 | 18 | 0 | 4.34 |

## PRICE, Carey (PRIGHS, KAIR-ee) MTL.

Goaltender. Catches left. 6'3", 219 lbs. Born, Vancouver, B.C., August 16, 1987.
(Montreal's 1st choice, 5th overall, in 2005 Entry Draft).

| | | | Regular Season | | | | | | | | Playoffs | | | | | | |
|---|---|---|---|---|---|---|---|---|---|---|---|---|---|---|---|---|---|
| Season | Club | League | GP | W | L | O/T | Mins | GA | SO | Avg | GP | W | L | Mins | GA | SO | Avg |
| 2002-03 | Williams Lake | Minor-BC | 18 | .... | .... | .... | 1050 | 48 | 1 | 2.70 | .... | .... | .... | .... | .... | .... | .... |
| | Tri-City Americans | WHL | 1 | 0 | 0 | 0 | 20 | 2 | 0 | 6.00 | .... | .... | .... | .... | .... | .... | .... |
| 2003-04 | Tri-City Americans | WHL | 28 | 8 | 9 | 3 | 1363 | 54 | 1 | 2.38 | 8 | 5 | 3 | 470 | 19 | 0 | 2.43 |
| 2004-05 | Tri-City Americans | WHL | 63 | 24 | 31 | 8 | 3712 | 145 | 8 | 2.34 | 5 | 1 | 4 | 325 | 12 | 0 | 2.22 |
| 2005-06 | Tri-City Americans | WHL | 55 | 21 | 25 | 6 | 3072 | 147 | 3 | 2.87 | 5 | 1 | 4 | 302 | 12 | 0 | 2.38 |
| 2006-07 | Tri-City Americans | WHL | 46 | 30 | 13 | 1 | 2722 | 111 | 3 | 2.45 | 6 | 2 | 4 | 348 | 17 | 0 | 2.93 |
| | Hamilton Bulldogs | AHL | 2 | 1 | 1 | 0 | 117 | 3 | 0 | 1.53 | *22 | *15 | 6 | *1314 | 45 | *2 | 2.06 |
| **2007-08** | **Montreal** | **NHL** | **41** | **24** | **12** | **3** | **2413** | **103** | **3** | **2.56** | **11** | **5** | **6** | **648** | **30** | **2** | **2.78** |
| | Hamilton Bulldogs | AHL | 10 | 6 | 4 | 0 | 581 | 26 | 1 | 2.69 | .... | .... | .... | .... | .... | .... | .... |
| **2008-09** | **Montreal** | **NHL** | **52** | **23** | **16** | **10** | **3036** | **143** | **1** | **2.83** | **4** | **0** | **4** | **219** | **15** | **0** | **4.11** |
| | **NHL Totals** | | **93** | **47** | **28** | **13** | **5449** | **246** | **4** | **2.71** | **15** | **5** | **10** | **867** | **45** | **2** | **3.11** |

WHL West First All-Star Team (2007) • WHL Goaltender of the Year (2007) • Canadian Major Junior First All-Star Team (2007) • Canadian Major Junior Goaltender of the Year (2007) • Jack A. Butterfield Trophy (AHL - Playoff MVP) (2007) • NHL All-Rookie Team (2008)

Played in NHL All-Star Game (2009)

## QUICK, Jonathan (KWIHK, JAWN-ah-thuhn) L.A.

Goaltender. Catches left. 6'1", 216 lbs. Born, Milford, CT, January 21, 1986.
(Los Angeles' 4th choice, 72nd overall, in 2005 Entry Draft).

| | | | Regular Season | | | | | | | | Playoffs | | | | | | |
|---|---|---|---|---|---|---|---|---|---|---|---|---|---|---|---|---|---|
| Season | Club | League | GP | W | L | O/T | Mins | GA | SO | Avg | GP | W | L | Mins | GA | SO | Avg |
| 2002-03 | Avon Old Farms | High-CT | 13 | 8 | 5 | 0 | 780 | 38 | 0 | 2.92 | .... | .... | .... | .... | .... | .... | .... |
| 2003-04 | Avon Old Farms | High-CT | 21 | 20 | 1 | 0 | 1260 | 26 | 2 | 1.71 | .... | .... | .... | .... | .... | .... | .... |
| 2004-05 | Avon Old Farms | High-CT | 27 | 25 | 2 | 0 | 1413 | 1.14 | 9 | 1.14 | .... | .... | .... | .... | .... | .... | .... |
| 2005-06 | Massachusetts | H-East | 17 | 4 | 10 | 1 | 905 | 45 | 0 | 2.98 | .... | .... | .... | .... | .... | .... | .... |
| 2006-07 | Massachusetts | H-East | 37 | 19 | 12 | 5 | 2224 | 80 | 3 | 2.16 | .... | .... | .... | .... | .... | .... | .... |
| **2007-08** | **Los Angeles** | **NHL** | **3** | **1** | **2** | **0** | **141** | **9** | **0** | **3.83** | .... | .... | .... | .... | .... | .... | .... |
| | Manchester | AHL | 19 | 11 | 8 | 0 | 1085 | 42 | 3 | 2.32 | 1 | 0 | 1 | 59 | 1 | 0 | 1.02 |
| | Reading Royals | ECHL | 38 | 23 | 11 | 3 | 2257 | 105 | 1 | 2.79 | .... | .... | .... | .... | .... | .... | .... |
| **2008-09** | **Los Angeles** | **NHL** | **44** | **21** | **18** | **2** | **2495** | **103** | **4** | **2.48** | .... | .... | .... | .... | .... | .... | .... |
| | Manchester | AHL | 14 | 6 | 5 | 2 | 827 | 37 | 0 | 2.68 | .... | .... | .... | .... | .... | .... | .... |
| | **NHL Totals** | | **47** | **22** | **20** | **2** | **2636** | **112** | **4** | **2.55** | .... | .... | .... | .... | .... | .... | .... |

Hockey East Second All-Star Team (2007) • NCAA East Second All-American Team (2007)

## RAMO, Karri (RAH-moh, KAH-ree) T.B.

Goaltender. Catches left. 6'2", 201 lbs. Born, Asikkala, Finland, July 1, 1986.
(Tampa Bay's 7th choice, 191st overall, in 2004 Entry Draft).

| | | | Regular Season | | | | | | | | Playoffs | | | | | | |
|---|---|---|---|---|---|---|---|---|---|---|---|---|---|---|---|---|---|
| Season | Club | League | GP | W | L | O/T | Mins | GA | SO | Avg | GP | W | L | Mins | GA | SO | Avg |
| 2002-03 | K-Reipas U18 | Fin-U18 | 19 | 12 | 3 | 2 | 1013 | 47 | 0 | 2.78 | 4 | 2 | 2 | 182 | 11 | 0 | 3.62 |
| 2003-04 | Pelicans Lahti U18 | Fin-U18 | 3 | 3 | 0 | 0 | 180 | 7 | 0 | 2.33 | 5 | 2 | 2 | 268 | 10 | 0 | 2.24 |
| | Pelicans Lahti Jr. | Fin-Jr. | 18 | 5 | 9 | 2 | 960 | 53 | 0 | 3.31 | 2 | 2 | 0 | 120 | 1 | 1 | 0.50 |
| | Pelicans Lahti | Finland | 3 | 0 | 2 | 0 | 138 | 10 | 0 | 4.34 | .... | .... | .... | .... | .... | .... | .... |
| 2004-05 | Pelicans Lahti Jr. | Fin-Jr. | 21 | 10 | 5 | 6 | 1269 | 36 | 6 | 1.70 | 4 | 1 | 3 | 206 | 16 | 0 | 4.66 |
| | Pelicans Lahti | Finland | 26 | 4 | 12 | 4 | 1267 | 84 | 1 | 3.98 | .... | .... | .... | .... | .... | .... | .... |
| 2005-06 | Haukat Jarvenpaa | Finland-2 | 1 | .... | .... | .... | 60 | 5 | 0 | 5.00 | .... | .... | .... | .... | .... | .... | .... |
| | Suomi U20 | Finland-2 | 3 | .... | .... | .... | 183 | 12 | 0 | 3.93 | .... | .... | .... | .... | .... | .... | .... |
| | HPK Hameenlinna | Finland | 24 | 7 | 8 | 7 | 1359 | 49 | 2 | 2.16 | 3 | 2 | 1 | 204 | 5 | 1 | 1.46 |
| **2006-07** | **Tampa Bay** | **NHL** | **2** | **0** | **0** | **0** | **70** | **4** | **0** | **3.43** | .... | .... | .... | .... | .... | .... | .... |
| | Springfield Falcons | AHL | 45 | 15 | 24 | 1 | 2432 | 127 | 1 | 3.13 | .... | .... | .... | .... | .... | .... | .... |
| **2007-08** | **Tampa Bay** | **NHL** | **22** | **7** | **11** | **3** | **1269** | **64** | **0** | **3.03** | .... | .... | .... | .... | .... | .... | .... |
| | Norfolk Admirals | AHL | 6 | 2 | 4 | 0 | 342 | 19 | 0 | 3.33 | .... | .... | .... | .... | .... | .... | .... |
| **2008-09** | **Tampa Bay** | **NHL** | **24** | **4** | **10** | **7** | **1312** | **80** | **0** | **3.66** | .... | .... | .... | .... | .... | .... | .... |
| | Norfolk Admirals | AHL | 26 | 7 | 14 | 4 | 1507 | 95 | 0 | 3.78 | .... | .... | .... | .... | .... | .... | .... |
| | **NHL Totals** | | **48** | **11** | **21** | **10** | **2651** | **148** | **0** | **3.35** | .... | .... | .... | .... | .... | .... | .... |

Signed as a free agent by **Omsk** (Rus-KHL), June 23, 2009.

## RASK, Tuukka (RASK, TU-kah) BOS.

Goaltender. Catches left. 6'2", 169 lbs. Born, Savonlinna, Finland, March 10, 1987.
(Toronto's 1st choice, 21st overall, in 2005 Entry Draft).

| | | | Regular Season | | | | | | | | Playoffs | | | | | | |
|---|---|---|---|---|---|---|---|---|---|---|---|---|---|---|---|---|---|
| Season | Club | League | GP | W | L | O/T | Mins | GA | SO | Avg | GP | W | L | Mins | GA | SO | Avg |
| 2003-04 | Ilves Tampere U18 | Fin-U18 | 9 | 4 | 3 | 2 | 533 | 25 | 0 | 2.81 | .... | .... | .... | .... | .... | .... | .... |
| | Ilves Tampere Jr. | Fin-Jr. | 30 | 12 | 10 | 7 | 1767 | 65 | 2 | 2.21 | 3 | 1 | 2 | 178 | 6 | 0 | 2.02 |
| 2004-05 | Ilves Tampere Jr. | Fin-Jr. | 26 | 17 | 3 | 4 | 1517 | 47 | 2 | 1.86 | 10 | 9 | 1 | 619 | 9 | 6 | 0.87 |
| | Ilves Tampere | Finland | 4 | 0 | 1 | 1 | 201 | 15 | 0 | 4.46 | .... | .... | .... | .... | .... | .... | .... |
| 2005-06 | Ilves Tampere Jr. | Fin-Jr. | 1 | .... | .... | .... | 60 | 2 | 0 | 2.00 | .... | .... | .... | .... | .... | .... | .... |
| | Suomi U20 | Finland-2 | 3 | .... | .... | .... | 179 | 6 | 0 | 2.01 | .... | .... | .... | .... | .... | .... | .... |
| | Ilves Tampere | Finland | 30 | 12 | 8 | 7 | 1724 | 60 | 2 | 2.09 | 3 | 0 | 3 | 180 | 7 | 0 | 2.33 |
| 2006-07 | Suomi U20 | Finland-2 | 1 | 0 | 1 | 0 | 58 | 4 | 0 | 4.14 | .... | .... | .... | .... | .... | .... | .... |
| | Ilves Tampere | Finland | 49 | 18 | 18 | 10 | 2872 | 114 | 3 | 2.38 | 7 | 2 | 5 | 397 | 20 | 0 | 3.02 |
| **2007-08** | **Boston** | **NHL** | **4** | **2** | **1** | **1** | **184** | **10** | **0** | **3.26** | .... | .... | .... | .... | .... | .... | .... |
| | Providence Bruins | AHL | 45 | 27 | 13 | 2 | 2570 | 100 | 1 | 2.33 | 10 | 6 | 4 | 605 | 22 | *2 | 2.18 |
| **2008-09** | **Boston** | **NHL** | **1** | **1** | **0** | **0** | **60** | **0** | **1** | **0.00** | .... | .... | .... | .... | .... | .... | .... |
| | Providence Bruins | AHL | 57 | 33 | 20 | 4 | 3340 | 139 | 4 | 2.50 | 16 | 9 | 7 | 977 | 36 | 0 | 2.21 |
| | **NHL Totals** | | **5** | **3** | **1** | **1** | **244** | **10** | **1** | **2.46** | .... | .... | .... | .... | .... | .... | .... |

Traded to **Boston** by **Toronto** for Andrew Raycroft, June 24, 2006.

## RAYCROFT, Andrew (RAY-krawft, AN-droo) VAN.

Goaltender. Catches left. 6', 185 lbs. Born, Belleville, Ont., May 4, 1980.
(Boston's 4th choice, 135th overall, in 1998 Entry Draft).

| | | | Regular Season | | | | | | | | Playoffs | | | | | | |
|---|---|---|---|---|---|---|---|---|---|---|---|---|---|---|---|---|---|
| Season | Club | League | GP | W | L | O/T | Mins | GA | SO | Avg | GP | W | L | Mins | GA | SO | Avg |
| 1996-97 | Wellington Dukes | MTJHL | 27 | .... | .... | .... | 1402 | 92 | 0 | 3.94 | .... | .... | .... | .... | .... | .... | .... |
| 1997-98 | Sudbury Wolves | OHL | 33 | 8 | 16 | 5 | 1802 | 125 | 0 | 4.16 | 2 | 0 | 1 | 89 | 8 | 0 | 5.39 |
| 1998-99 | Sudbury Wolves | OHL | 45 | 17 | 22 | 5 | 2528 | 173 | 1 | 4.11 | 3 | 0 | 2 | 96 | 13 | 0 | 8.13 |
| 99-2000 | Kingston | OHL | *61 | 33 | 20 | 5 | 3340 | 191 | 0 | 3.43 | 5 | 1 | 4 | 300 | 21 | 0 | 4.20 |
| **2000-01** | **Boston** | **NHL** | **15** | **4** | **6** | **0** | **649** | **32** | **0** | **2.96** | .... | .... | .... | .... | .... | .... | .... |
| | Providence Bruins | AHL | 26 | 8 | 14 | 4 | 1459 | 82 | 1 | 3.37 | .... | .... | .... | .... | .... | .... | .... |
| **2001-02** | **Boston** | **NHL** | **1** | **0** | **0** | **1** | **65** | **3** | **0** | **2.77** | .... | .... | .... | .... | .... | .... | .... |
| | Providence Bruins | AHL | 56 | 25 | 24 | 6 | 3317 | 142 | 4 | 2.57 | 2 | 0 | 2 | 119 | 5 | 0 | 2.52 |
| **2002-03** | **Boston** | **NHL** | **5** | **2** | **3** | **0** | **300** | **12** | **0** | **2.40** | .... | .... | .... | .... | .... | .... | .... |
| | Providence Bruins | AHL | 39 | 23 | 10 | 3 | 2255 | 94 | 1 | 2.50 | 4 | 1 | 3 | 264 | 6 | 1 | *1.36 |
| **2003-04** | **Boston** | **NHL** | **57** | **29** | **18** | **9** | **3420** | **117** | **3** | **2.05** | **7** | **3** | **4** | **447** | **16** | **1** | **2.15** |
| 2004-05 | Tappara Tampere | Finland | 11 | 4 | 5 | 2 | 657 | 32 | 1 | 2.92 | 3 | 0 | 2 | 104 | 11 | 0 | 6.36 |
| **2005-06** | **Boston** | **NHL** | **30** | **8** | **19** | **2** | **1619** | **100** | **0** | **3.71** | .... | .... | .... | .... | .... | .... | .... |
| | Providence Bruins | AHL | 1 | 1 | 0 | 0 | 64 | 3 | 0 | 2.80 | .... | .... | .... | .... | .... | .... | .... |
| **2006-07** | **Toronto** | **NHL** | **72** | **37** | **25** | **9** | **4108** | **205** | **2** | **2.99** | .... | .... | .... | .... | .... | .... | .... |
| **2007-08** | **Toronto** | **NHL** | **19** | **2** | **9** | **5** | **965** | **63** | **1** | **3.92** | .... | .... | .... | .... | .... | .... | .... |
| **2008-09** | **Colorado** | **NHL** | **31** | **12** | **16** | **0** | **1722** | **90** | **0** | **3.14** | .... | .... | .... | .... | .... | .... | .... |
| | **NHL Totals** | | **230** | **94** | **96** | **26** | **12848** | **622** | **6** | **2.90** | **7** | **3** | **4** | **447** | **16** | **1** | **2.15** |

OHL First All-Star Team (2000) • Canadian Major Junior First All-Star Team (2000) • Canadian Major Junior Goaltender of the Year (2000) • NHL All-Rookie Team (2004) • Calder Memorial Trophy (2004)

Signed as a free agent by **Tappara Tampere** (Finland), January 17, 2005. Traded to **Toronto** by **Boston** for Tuukka Rask, June 24, 2006. Signed as a free agent by **Colorado**, July 1, 2008. Signed as a free agent by **Vancouver**, July 6, 2009.

## REGAN, Kevin (REE-guhn, KEH-vihn) BOS.

Goaltender. Catches left. 6', 195 lbs. Born, Boston, MA, July 25, 1984.
(Boston's 10th choice, 277th overall, in 2003 Entry Draft).

| | | | Regular Season | | | | | | | | Playoffs | | | | | | |
|---|---|---|---|---|---|---|---|---|---|---|---|---|---|---|---|---|---|
| Season | Club | League | GP | W | L | O/T | Mins | GA | SO | Avg | GP | W | L | Mins | GA | SO | Avg |
| 2001-02 | St. Sebastian's | High-MA | 31 | 27 | 4 | 0 | 1860 | 56 | 0 | 1.91 | .... | .... | .... | .... | .... | .... | .... |
| | USNTDP | U-18 | 1 | 0 | 0 | 0 | 12 | 0 | 0 | 0.00 | .... | .... | .... | .... | .... | .... | .... |
| | South Boston | USHA | 3 | 3 | 0 | 0 | 158 | 8 | 0 | 2.58 | .... | .... | .... | .... | .... | .... | .... |
| 2002-03 | St. Sebastian's | High-MA | 28 | .... | .... | .... | 1215 | 47 | 4 | 1.81 | .... | .... | .... | .... | .... | .... | .... |
| 2003-04 | Waterloo | USHL | 50 | *28 | 19 | 1 | 0 | 111 | *6 | 2.37 | *12 | *9 | 3 | *735 | 19 | *1 | *1.55 |
| 2004-05 | New Hampshire | H-East | 23 | 15 | 4 | 2 | 1276 | 50 | 0 | 2.35 | .... | .... | .... | .... | .... | .... | .... |
| 2005-06 | New Hampshire | H-East | 23 | 8 | 8 | 5 | 1299 | 57 | 3 | 2.63 | .... | .... | .... | .... | .... | .... | .... |
| 2006-07 | New Hampshire | H-East | 35 | 24 | 9 | 2 | 2066 | 71 | 3 | 2.06 | .... | .... | .... | .... | .... | .... | .... |
| 2007-08 | New Hampshire | H-East | 32 | 23 | 8 | 1 | 1958 | 72 | *3 | 2.21 | .... | .... | .... | .... | .... | .... | .... |
| | Providence Bruins | AHL | 1 | 0 | 0 | 0 | 60 | 0 | 1 | 0.00 | .... | .... | .... | .... | .... | .... | .... |
| 2008-09 | Providence Bruins | AHL | 21 | 9 | 7 | 2 | 1124 | 56 | 0 | 2.99 | .... | .... | .... | .... | .... | .... | .... |
| | Gwinnett | ECHL | 2 | 1 | 1 | 0 | 120 | 5 | 0 | 2.50 | .... | .... | .... | .... | .... | .... | .... |
| | Alaska Aces | ECHL | 4 | 2 | 2 | 0 | 243 | 10 | 0 | 2.47 | .... | .... | .... | .... | .... | .... | .... |

Hockey East All-Rookie Team (2005) (co-winners - Cory Schneider and Peter Vetri) • Hockey East First All-Star Team (2008) • Hockey East Player of the Year (2008) • NCAA East First All-American Team (2008)

## REIMER, James (RIGH-muhr, JAYMZ) TOR.

Goaltender. Catches left. 6'2", 208 lbs. Born, Winnipeg, Man., March 15, 1988.
(Toronto's 3rd choice, 99th overall, in 2006 Entry Draft).

| | | | Regular Season | | | | | | | | Playoffs | | | | | | |
|---|---|---|---|---|---|---|---|---|---|---|---|---|---|---|---|---|---|
| Season | Club | League | GP | W | L | O/T | Mins | GA | SO | Avg | GP | W | L | Mins | GA | SO | Avg |
| 2003-04 | Interlake Lightning | MMHL | 27 | 6 | 5 | 2 | 863 | 41 | 1 | 2.85 | .... | .... | .... | .... | .... | .... | .... |
| 2004-05 | Interlake Lightning | MMHL | 37 | 19 | 6 | 2 | 1646 | 58 | 4 | 2.11 | 435 | 26 | 0 | 3.59 | .... | .... | .... |
| 2005-06 | Red Deer Rebels | WHL | 34 | 7 | 18 | 3 | 1709 | 80 | 0 | 2.81 | .... | .... | .... | .... | .... | .... | .... |
| 2006-07 | Red Deer Rebels | WHL | 60 | 26 | 23 | 7 | 3339 | 148 | 3 | 2.66 | 7 | 3 | 4 | 417 | 27 | 0 | 3.88 |
| 2007-08 | Red Deer Rebels | WHL | 30 | 8 | 15 | 0 | 1668 | 76 | 1 | 2.73 | .... | .... | .... | .... | .... | .... | .... |
| 2008-09 | Toronto Marlies | AHL | 3 | 1 | 2 | 0 | 183 | 10 | 0 | 3.28 | .... | .... | .... | .... | .... | .... | .... |
| | Reading Royals | ECHL | 22 | 10 | 7 | 3 | 1236 | 68 | 0 | 3.30 | .... | .... | .... | .... | .... | .... | .... |
| | South Carolina | ECHL | 6 | 6 | 0 | 0 | 363 | 8 | 2 | 1.32 | 8 | 4 | 1 | 497 | 18 | 1 | 2.17 |

ECHL Playoff MVP (2009)

## RICHARDS, Alec (RIH-chuhrds, ALEHK) CHI.

Goaltender. Catches . 6'4", 190 lbs. Born, Robbinsdale, MN, June 29, 1987.

| | | | Regular Season | | | | | | | | Playoffs | | | | | | |
|---|---|---|---|---|---|---|---|---|---|---|---|---|---|---|---|---|---|
| Season | Club | League | GP | W | L | O/T | Mins | GA | SO | Avg | GP | W | L | Mins | GA | SO | Avg |
| 2003-04 | Breck Mustangs | High-MN | .... | 19 | 1 | 1 | .... | .... | .... | 1.70 | .... | .... | .... | .... | .... | .... | .... |
| 2004-05 | Breck Mustangs | High-MN | .... | 15 | 2 | 2 | .... | .... | .... | 1.90 | .... | .... | .... | .... | .... | .... | .... |
| | Indiana Ice | USHL | 4 | 1 | 2 | 1 | 241 | 14 | 0 | 3.47 | .... | .... | .... | .... | .... | .... | .... |
| 2005-06 | Yale | ECAC | 29 | 8 | 15 | 3 | 1686 | 85 | 1 | 3.02 | .... | .... | .... | .... | .... | .... | .... |
| 2006-07 | Yale | ECAC | 26 | 9 | 15 | 2 | 1518 | 79 | 0 | 3.12 | .... | .... | .... | .... | .... | .... | .... |
| 2007-08 | Yale | ECAC | 11 | 3 | 4 | 0 | 563 | 19 | 1 | 2.02 | .... | .... | .... | .... | .... | .... | .... |
| 2008-09 | Yale | ECAC | 25 | 19 | 5 | 1 | 1458 | 50 | 4 | 2.06 | .... | .... | .... | .... | .... | .... | .... |

Signed as a free agent by **Chicago**, June 8, 2009.

## RIDDERWALL, Stefan (RIH-duhr-vahl, STEH-fan) NYI

Goaltender. Catches left. 6'1", 189 lbs. Born, Stockholm, Sweden, March 5, 1988.
(NY Islanders' 12th choice, 173rd overall, in 2006 Entry Draft).

| | | | Regular Season | | | | | | | | Playoffs | | | | | | |
|---|---|---|---|---|---|---|---|---|---|---|---|---|---|---|---|---|---|
| Season | Club | League | GP | W | L | O/T | Mins | GA | SO | Avg | GP | W | L | Mins | GA | SO | Avg |
| 2003-04 | Huddinge IK U18 | Swe-U18 | 7 | .... | .... | .... | 345 | 31 | 0 | 5.38 | .... | .... | .... | .... | .... | .... | .... |
| 2004-05 | Djurgarden U18 | Swe-U18 | 3 | .... | .... | .... | 154 | 8 | 0 | 3.10 | 4 | .... | .... | 234 | 11 | 0 | 2.81 |
| | Djurgarden Jr. | Swe-Jr. | 16 | .... | .... | .... | 972 | 51 | 0 | 3.15 | .... | .... | .... | .... | .... | .... | .... |
| 2005-06 | Djurgarden Jr. | Swe-Jr. | 18 | .... | .... | .... | 1073 | 43 | 3 | 2.40 | 4 | .... | .... | 242 | 13 | 1 | 3.22 |
| | Djurgarden | Sweden | 1 | .... | .... | .... | 4 | 0 | 0 | 0.00 | .... | .... | .... | .... | .... | .... | .... |
| 2006-07 | Djurgarden Jr. | Swe-Jr. | 28 | .... | .... | .... | 1690 | 50 | 4 | 1.78 | 7 | .... | .... | 417 | 10 | 1 | 1.44 |
| 2007-08 | Nykoping | Sweden-2 | 1 | .... | .... | .... | 58 | 5 | 0 | 5.14 | .... | .... | .... | .... | .... | .... | .... |
| | Almtuna | Sweden-2 | 3 | .... | .... | .... | 182 | 10 | 0 | 3.29 | .... | .... | .... | .... | .... | .... | .... |
| | Djurgarden | Sweden | 11 | .... | .... | .... | 605 | 27 | 0 | 2.68 | .... | .... | .... | .... | .... | .... | .... |
| | Djurgarden Jr. | Swe-Jr. | 8 | .... | .... | .... | 479 | 14 | 1 | 1.75 | 4 | .... | .... | 254 | 7 | 0 | 1.65 |
| 2008-09 | Djurgarden | Sweden | 27 | .... | .... | .... | 1470 | 71 | 0 | 2.90 | .... | .... | .... | .... | .... | .... | .... |

## RINNE, Pekka (RIH-neh, PEH-kuh) NSH.

Goaltender. Catches left. 6'5", 206 lbs. Born, Kempele, Finland, November 3, 1982.
(Nashville's 10th choice, 258th overall, in 2004 Entry Draft).

| | | | Regular Season | | | | | | | | Playoffs | | | | | | |
|---|---|---|---|---|---|---|---|---|---|---|---|---|---|---|---|---|---|
| Season | Club | League | GP | W | L | O/T | Mins | GA | SO | Avg | GP | W | L | Mins | GA | SO | Avg |
| 2000-01 | Karpat Oulu Jr. | Fin-Jr. | 20 | 9 | 4 | 5 | 1148 | 63 | 0 | 3.29 | .... | .... | .... | .... | .... | .... | .... |
| 2001-02 | Karpat Oulu Jr. | Fin-Jr. | 30 | 19 | 7 | 3 | 1724 | 61 | 3 | 2.12 | 3 | 1 | 2 | 184 | 10 | 1 | 3.26 |
| 2002-03 | Karpat Oulu Jr. | Fin-Jr. | 25 | 14 | 8 | 3 | 1479 | 48 | 5 | 1.95 | 4 | 1 | 3 | 238 | 7 | 0 | 1.76 |
| | Karpat Oulu | Finland | 1 | 0 | 1 | 0 | 60 | 7 | 0 | 7.00 | .... | .... | .... | .... | .... | .... | .... |
| 2003-04 | Karpat Oulu | Finland | 14 | 5 | 4 | 4 | 824 | 41 | 0 | 2.99 | 2 | 1 | 0 | 22 | 0 | 0 | 0.00 |
| | Hokki Kajaani | Finland-2 | 8 | 5 | 2 | 1 | 463 | 16 | 2 | 2.07 | .... | .... | .... | .... | .... | .... | .... |
| 2004-05 | Karpat Oulu | Finland | 10 | 8 | 0 | 1 | 571 | 16 | 0 | 1.68 | .... | .... | .... | .... | .... | .... | .... |
| **2005-06** | **Nashville** | **NHL** | **2** | **1** | **1** | **0** | **63** | **4** | **0** | **3.81** | .... | .... | .... | .... | .... | .... | .... |
| | Milwaukee | AHL | 51 | 30 | 18 | 2 | 2960 | 139 | 2 | 2.82 | 14 | 10 | 4 | 734 | 35 | 3 | 2.86 |
| 2006-07 | Milwaukee | AHL | 29 | 15 | 7 | 6 | 1670 | 65 | 3 | 2.34 | 4 | 0 | 4 | 247 | 12 | 0 | 2.91 |
| **2007-08** | **Nashville** | **NHL** | **1** | **0** | **0** | **0** | **29** | **0** | **0** | **0.00** | .... | .... | .... | .... | .... | .... | .... |
| | Milwaukee | AHL | *65 | *36 | 24 | 3 | *3840 | 158 | 5 | 2.47 | 6 | 2 | 4 | 358 | 15 | 1 | 2.51 |
| **2008-09** | **Nashville** | **NHL** | **52** | **29** | **15** | **4** | **2999** | **119** | **7** | **2.38** | .... | .... | .... | .... | .... | .... | .... |
| | **NHL Totals** | | **55** | **30** | **16** | **4** | **3091** | **123** | **7** | **2.39** | .... | .... | .... | .... | .... | .... | .... |

## RIOPEL, Nicola (ree-OH-pehl, NIH-koh-la) PHI.

Goaltender. Catches left. 6', 175 lbs. Born, St-Pie de Bagot, Que., February 20, 1989.
(Philadelphia's 3rd choice, 142nd overall, in 2009 Entry Draft).

| | | | Regular Season | | | | | | | | Playoffs | | | | | | |
|---|---|---|---|---|---|---|---|---|---|---|---|---|---|---|---|---|---|
| **Season** | **Club** | **League** | **GP** | **W** | **L** | **O/T** | **Mins** | **GA** | **SO** | **Avg** | **GP** | **W** | **L** | **Mins** | **GA** | **SO** | **Avg** |
| 2006-07 | Moncton Wildcats | QMJHL | 37 | 17 | 12 | .... | 1914 | 107 | 1 | 3.35 | 4 | 1 | 3 | 185 | 16 | 0 | 5.19 |
| 2007-08 | Moncton Wildcats | QMJHL | 47 | 15 | 29 | .... | 2662 | 135 | 1 | 3.04 | .... | .... | .... | .... | .... | .... | .... |
| 2008-09 | Moncton Wildcats | QMJHL | *59 | *43 | 15 | .... | *3487 | 117 | 5 | *2.01 | 10 | 5 | 5 | 620 | 21 | *2 | *2.03 |

QMJHL All-Rookie Team (2009) • QMJHL First All-Star Team (2009) • Canadian Major Junior Second All-Star Team (2009)

## ROLLHEISER, Grant (rohl-HIGH-zuhr, GRANT) TOR.

Goaltender. Catches left. 6'4", 195 lbs. Born, Chilliwak, B.C., July 24, 1989.
(Toronto's 7th choice, 158th overall, in 2008 Entry Draft).

| | | | Regular Season | | | | | | | | Playoffs | | | | | | |
|---|---|---|---|---|---|---|---|---|---|---|---|---|---|---|---|---|---|
| **Season** | **Club** | **League** | **GP** | **W** | **L** | **O/T** | **Mins** | **GA** | **SO** | **Avg** | **GP** | **W** | **L** | **Mins** | **GA** | **SO** | **Avg** |
| 2006-07 | Nelson Leafs | KIJHL | 35 | 25 | 8 | 0 | 1990 | 110 | 2 | 3.32 | 15 | 9 | 6 | 907 | 35 | 2 | 2.31 |
| 2007-08 | Trail Smoke Eaters | BCHL | 46 | 19 | 26 | 0 | 2557 | 136 | 2 | 3.19 | 3 | 0 | 3 | 159 | 13 | 0 | 4.90 |
| 2008-09 | Boston University | H-East | 12 | 6 | 4 | 1 | 648 | 23 | 1 | 2.13 | .... | .... | .... | .... | .... | .... | .... |

## ROLOSON, Dwayne (ROH-loh-suhn, DWAYN) NYI

Goaltender. Catches left. 6'1", 180 lbs. Born, Simcoe, Ont., October 12, 1969.

| | | | Regular Season | | | | | | | | Playoffs | | | | | | |
|---|---|---|---|---|---|---|---|---|---|---|---|---|---|---|---|---|---|
| **Season** | **Club** | **League** | **GP** | **W** | **L** | **O/T** | **Mins** | **GA** | **SO** | **Avg** | **GP** | **W** | **L** | **Mins** | **GA** | **SO** | **Avg** |
| 1984-85 | Simcoe Penguins | OJHL-C | 3 | .... | .... | .... | 100 | 21 | 0 | 12.60 | .... | .... | .... | .... | .... | .... | .... |
| 1985-86 | Simcoe Rams | OJHL-C | 1 | .... | .... | .... | 60 | 6 | 0 | 6.00 | .... | .... | .... | .... | .... | .... | .... |
| 1986-87 | Norwich | OJHL-C | 19 | .... | .... | .... | 1091 | 55 | 0 | *3.03 | .... | .... | .... | .... | .... | .... | .... |
| 1987-88 | Belleville Bobcats | OJHL-B | 21 | 9 | 6 | 1 | 1070 | 60 | *2 | 3.36 | .... | .... | .... | .... | .... | .... | .... |
| 1988-89 | Thorold | OJHL-B | 27 | 15 | 6 | 4 | 1490 | 82 | 0 | 3.30 | .... | .... | .... | .... | .... | .... | .... |
| 1989-90 | Thorold | OHA-B | 30 | 18 | 8 | 1 | 1683 | 108 | 0 | 3.85 | .... | .... | .... | .... | .... | .... | .... |
| 1990-91 | U. Mass-Lowell | H-East | 15 | 5 | 9 | 0 | 823 | 63 | 0 | 4.59 | .... | .... | .... | .... | .... | .... | .... |
| 1991-92 | U. Mass-Lowell | H-East | 12 | 3 | 8 | 0 | 660 | 52 | 0 | 4.73 | .... | .... | .... | .... | .... | .... | .... |
| 1992-93 | U. Mass-Lowell | H-East | *39 | 20 | 17 | 2 | *2342 | 150 | 0 | 3.84 | .... | .... | .... | .... | .... | .... | .... |
| 1993-94 | U. Mass-Lowell | H-East | *40 | *23 | 10 | 7 | *2305 | 106 | 0 | 2.76 | .... | .... | .... | .... | .... | .... | .... |
| 1994-95 | Saint John Flames | AHL | 46 | 16 | 21 | 8 | 2734 | 156 | 1 | 3.42 | 5 | 1 | 4 | 298 | 13 | 0 | 2.61 |
| 1995-96 | Saint John Flames | AHL | 67 | *33 | 22 | 11 | 4026 | 190 | 1 | 2.83 | 16 | 10 | 6 | 1027 | 49 | 1 | 2.86 |
| **1996-97** | **Calgary** | **NHL** | **31** | **9** | **14** | **3** | **1618** | **78** | **1** | **2.89** | .... | .... | .... | .... | .... | .... | .... |
| | Saint John Flames | AHL | 8 | 6 | 2 | 0 | 481 | 22 | 1 | 2.75 | .... | .... | .... | .... | .... | .... | .... |
| **1997-98** | **Calgary** | **NHL** | **39** | **11** | **16** | **8** | **2205** | **110** | **0** | **2.99** | .... | .... | .... | .... | .... | .... | .... |
| | Saint John Flames | AHL | 4 | 3 | 0 | 1 | 245 | 8 | 0 | 1.96 | .... | .... | .... | .... | .... | .... | .... |
| **1998-99** | **Buffalo** | **NHL** | **18** | **6** | **8** | **2** | **911** | **42** | **1** | **2.77** | **4** | **1** | **1** | **139** | **10** | **0** | **4.32** |
| | Rochester | AHL | 2 | 2 | 0 | 0 | 120 | 4 | 0 | 2.00 | .... | .... | .... | .... | .... | .... | .... |
| **99-2000** | **Buffalo** | **NHL** | **14** | **1** | **7** | **3** | **677** | **32** | **0** | **2.84** | .... | .... | .... | .... | .... | .... | .... |
| 2000-01 | Worcester IceCats | AHL | 52 | *32 | 15 | 5 | *3127 | 113 | *6 | *2.17 | 11 | 6 | 5 | 697 | 23 | 1 | 1.98 |
| **2001-02** | **Minnesota** | **NHL** | **45** | **14** | **20** | **7** | **2506** | **112** | **5** | **2.68** | .... | .... | .... | .... | .... | .... | .... |
| **2002-03** | **Minnesota** | **NHL** | **50** | **23** | **16** | **8** | **2945** | **98** | **4** | **2.00** | **11** | **5** | **6** | **579** | **25** | **0** | **2.59** |
| **2003-04** | **Minnesota** | **NHL** | **48** | **19** | **18** | **11** | **2847** | **89** | **5** | **1.88** | .... | .... | .... | .... | .... | .... | .... |
| 2004-05 | Lukko Rauma | Finland | 34 | 20 | 10 | 4 | 2048 | 70 | 4 | 2.05 | 9 | 4 | 5 | 512 | 18 | 2 | 2.11 |
| **2005-06** | **Minnesota** | **NHL** | **24** | **6** | **17** | **1** | **1361** | **68** | **1** | **3.00** | .... | .... | .... | .... | .... | .... | .... |
| | **Edmonton** | **NHL** | **19** | **8** | **7** | **4** | **1163** | **47** | **1** | **2.42** | **18** | **12** | **5** | **1160** | **45** | **1** | **2.33** |
| **2006-07** | **Edmonton** | **NHL** | **68** | **27** | **34** | **6** | **3932** | **180** | **4** | **2.75** | .... | .... | .... | .... | .... | .... | .... |
| **2007-08** | **Edmonton** | **NHL** | **43** | **15** | **17** | **5** | **2340** | **119** | **0** | **3.05** | .... | .... | .... | .... | .... | .... | .... |
| **2008-09** | **Edmonton** | **NHL** | **63** | **28** | **24** | **9** | **3597** | **166** | **1** | **2.77** | .... | .... | .... | .... | .... | .... | .... |
| | **NHL Totals** | | **462** | **167** | **198** | **67** | **26102** | **1141** | **23** | **2.62** | **33** | **18** | **12** | **1878** | **80** | **1** | **2.56** |

Hockey East First All-Star Team (1994) • Hockey East Player of the Year (1994) • NCAA East First All-American Team (1994) • AHL First All-Star Team (2001) • Aldege "Baz" Bastien Memorial Award (AHL – Outstanding Goaltender) (2001) • MBNA/Mastercard Roger Crozier Saving Grace Award (2004)

Played in NHL All-Star Game (2004)

Signed as a free agent by **Calgary**, July 4, 1994. Signed as a free agent by **Buffalo**, July 15, 1998. Claimed by **Columbus** from **Buffalo** in Expansion Draft, June 23, 2000. Signed as a free agent by **St. Louis**, July 14, 2000. Signed as a free agent by **Minnesota**, July 2, 2001. Signed as a free agent by **Rauma** (Finland), October 18, 2004. Traded to **Edmonton** by **Minnesota** for Edmonton's 1st round choice (later traded to Los Angeles - Los Angeles selected Trevor Lewis) in 2006 Entry Draft and Edmonton's 3rd round choice (later traded to Atlanta - Atlanta selected Spencer Machacek) in 2007 Entry Draft, March 8, 2006. Signed as a free agent by **NY Islanders**, July 1, 2009.

## ROY, Olivier (WAH, oh-LIHV-ee-ay) EDM.

Goaltender. Catches left. 6', 165 lbs. Born, Amqui, Que., July 12, 1991.
(Edmonton's 7th choice, 133rd overall, in 2009 Entry Draft).

| | | | Regular Season | | | | | | | | Playoffs | | | | | | |
|---|---|---|---|---|---|---|---|---|---|---|---|---|---|---|---|---|---|
| **Season** | **Club** | **League** | **GP** | **W** | **L** | **O/T** | **Mins** | **GA** | **SO** | **Avg** | **GP** | **W** | **L** | **Mins** | **GA** | **SO** | **Avg** |
| 2006-07 | Ecole Notre Dame | QAAA | 27 | 15 | 8 | 0 | 1459 | 65 | 2 | 2.67 | 4 | 2 | 1 | 206 | 13 | 0 | 3.79 |
| 2007-08 | Cape Breton | QMJHL | 47 | 27 | 15 | .... | 2428 | 116 | 4 | 2.87 | 11 | 5 | 6 | 707 | 30 | 1 | 2.55 |
| 2008-09 | Cape Breton | QMJHL | 54 | 35 | 13 | .... | 2935 | 137 | 3 | 2.80 | 11 | 7 | 4 | 740 | 30 | 0 | 2.43 |

QMJHL All-Rookie Team (2008)

## SABOURIN, Dany (SA-boo-rihn, DA-nee) BOS.

Goaltender. Catches left. 6'4", 200 lbs. Born, Val-d'Or, Que., September 2, 1980.
(Calgary's 5th choice, 108th overall, in 1998 Entry Draft).

| | | | Regular Season | | | | | | | | Playoffs | | | | | | |
|---|---|---|---|---|---|---|---|---|---|---|---|---|---|---|---|---|---|
| **Season** | **Club** | **League** | **GP** | **W** | **L** | **O/T** | **Mins** | **GA** | **SO** | **Avg** | **GP** | **W** | **L** | **Mins** | **GA** | **SO** | **Avg** |
| 1996-97 | Amos Forestiers | QAAA | 24 | 6 | 16 | 0 | 1440 | 107 | 0 | 4.48 | .... | .... | .... | .... | .... | .... | .... |
| 1997-98 | Sherbrooke | QMJHL | 37 | 15 | 15 | 2 | 1906 | 128 | 1 | 4.03 | .... | .... | .... | .... | .... | .... | .... |
| 1998-99 | Sherbrooke | QMJHL | 30 | 8 | 13 | 2 | 1477 | 102 | 1 | 4.14 | 1 | 0 | 1 | 49 | 2 | 0 | 2.45 |
| | Saint John Flames | AHL | .... | .... | .... | .... | .... | .... | .... | .... | 1 | 0 | 1 | 57 | 4 | 0 | 4.19 |
| 99-2000 | Sherbrooke | QMJHL | 55 | 25 | 22 | 5 | 3067 | 181 | 1 | 3.54 | 5 | 1 | 4 | 324 | 18 | 0 | 3.33 |
| 2000-01 | Saint John Flames | AHL | 1 | 1 | 0 | 0 | 40 | 0 | 0 | 0.00 | .... | .... | .... | .... | .... | .... | .... |
| | Johnstown Chiefs | ECHL | 19 | 4 | 9 | 1 | 903 | 56 | 0 | 3.72 | 1 | 0 | 0 | 40 | 2 | 0 | 3.00 |
| 2001-02 | Johnstown Chiefs | ECHL | 27 | 14 | 10 | 1 | 1539 | 84 | 0 | 3.28 | 3 | 0 | 2 | 137 | 5 | 0 | 2.18 |
| 2002-03 | Saint John Flames | AHL | 41 | 15 | 17 | 4 | 2220 | 100 | 4 | 2.70 | .... | .... | .... | .... | .... | .... | .... |
| **2003-04** | **Calgary** | **NHL** | **4** | **0** | **3** | **0** | **169** | **10** | **0** | **3.55** | .... | .... | .... | .... | .... | .... | .... |
| | Lowell | AHL | 14 | 5 | 7 | 2 | 821 | 39 | 0 | 2.85 | .... | .... | .... | .... | .... | .... | .... |
| | Las Vegas | ECHL | 10 | 6 | 3 | 1 | 613 | 24 | 0 | 2.35 | 1 | 0 | 1 | 58 | 2 | 0 | 2.07 |
| 2004-05 | Wilkes-Barre | AHL | 20 | 8 | 8 | 2 | 1029 | 38 | 1 | 2.22 | .... | .... | .... | .... | .... | .... | .... |
| | Wheeling Nailers | ECHL | 27 | 19 | 6 | 1 | 1579 | 44 | 5 | *1.67 | .... | .... | .... | .... | .... | .... | .... |
| **2005-06** | **Pittsburgh** | **NHL** | **1** | **0** | **1** | **0** | **21** | **4** | **0** | **11.43** | .... | .... | .... | .... | .... | .... | .... |
| | Wilkes-Barre | AHL | 49 | 30 | 14 | 4 | 2943 | 111 | 4 | *2.26 | 6 | 2 | 4 | 362 | 13 | 1 | 2.15 |
| **2006-07** | **Vancouver** | **NHL** | **9** | **2** | **4** | **1** | **480** | **21** | **0** | **2.63** | **2** | **0** | **0** | **14** | **1** | **0** | **4.29** |
| | Manitoba Moose | AHL | 2 | 1 | 1 | 0 | 119 | 4 | 1 | 2.01 | .... | .... | .... | .... | .... | .... | .... |
| **2007-08** | **Pittsburgh** | **NHL** | **24** | **10** | **9** | **1** | **1242** | **57** | **2** | **2.75** | .... | .... | .... | .... | .... | .... | .... |
| **2008-09** | **Pittsburgh** | **NHL** | **19** | **6** | **8** | **2** | **989** | **47** | **0** | **2.85** | .... | .... | .... | .... | .... | .... | .... |
| | Springfield Falcons | AHL | 13 | 5 | 6 | 2 | 795 | 42 | 0 | 3.17 | .... | .... | .... | .... | .... | .... | .... |
| | **NHL Totals** | | **57** | **18** | **25** | **4** | **2901** | **139** | **2** | **2.87** | **2** | **0** | **0** | **14** | **1** | **0** | **4.29** |

AHL First All-Star Team (2006) • Aldege "Baz" Bastien Memorial Award (AHL – Outstanding Goaltender) (2006)

Signed as a free agent by **Pittsburgh**, August 10, 2005. Claimed on waivers by **Vancouver** from **Pittsburgh**, October 4, 2006. Signed as a free agent by **Pittsburgh**, July 1, 2007. Traded to **Edmonton** by **Pittsburgh** with Ryan Stone and Pittsburgh's 4th round choice in 2011 Entry Draft for Mathieu Garon, January 17, 2009. Signed as a free agent by **Boston**, July 7, 2009.

## SALAK, Alexander (SAL-ak, al-EHX-AN-duhr) FLA.

Goaltender. Catches left. 6'1", 189 lbs. Born, Strakonice, Czech., January 5, 1987.

| | | | Regular Season | | | | | | | | Playoffs | | | | | | |
|---|---|---|---|---|---|---|---|---|---|---|---|---|---|---|---|---|---|
| **Season** | **Club** | **League** | **GP** | **W** | **L** | **O/T** | **Mins** | **GA** | **SO** | **Avg** | **GP** | **W** | **L** | **Mins** | **GA** | **SO** | **Avg** |
| 2006-07 | Jokipojat Joensuu | Finland-2 | 35 | .... | .... | .... | .... | .... | .... | 2.81 | .... | .... | .... | .... | .... | .... | .... |
| 2007-08 | TPS Turku | Finland | 31 | .... | .... | .... | 1757 | 76 | 1 | 2.59 | .... | .... | .... | .... | .... | .... | .... |
| 2008-09 | TPS Turku | Finland | 52 | 20 | 20 | 9 | 2981 | 119 | 4 | 2.40 | 8 | 4 | 4 | 489 | 16 | 0 | 1.96 |

Signed as a free agent by **Florida**, May 29, 2009.

## SANFORD, Curtis (SAN-fohrd, KUHR-this) MTL.

Goaltender. Catches left. 5'10", 187 lbs. Born, Owen Sound, Ont., October 5, 1979.

| | | | Regular Season | | | | | | | | Playoffs | | | | | | |
|---|---|---|---|---|---|---|---|---|---|---|---|---|---|---|---|---|---|
| **Season** | **Club** | **League** | **GP** | **W** | **L** | **O/T** | **Mins** | **GA** | **SO** | **Avg** | **GP** | **W** | **L** | **Mins** | **GA** | **SO** | **Avg** |
| 1994-95 | Wiarton Wolves | OJHL-C | 18 | .... | .... | .... | 949 | 98 | 0 | 6.20 | .... | .... | .... | .... | .... | .... | .... |
| 1995-96 | Collingwood | OJHL | 21 | .... | .... | .... | 2128 | 74 | 0 | 3.54 | .... | .... | .... | .... | .... | .... | .... |
| 1996-97 | Owen Sound | OHL | 19 | 4 | 8 | 1 | 847 | 77 | 0 | 5.45 | .... | .... | .... | .... | .... | .... | .... |
| | Owen Sound | OJHL-B | 6 | .... | .... | .... | 360 | 28 | 0 | 4.68 | .... | .... | .... | .... | .... | .... | .... |
| 1997-98 | Owen Sound | OHL | 30 | 13 | 10 | 2 | 1542 | 114 | 1 | 4.44 | 9 | 4 | 4 | 456 | 30 | 1 | 3.95 |
| 1998-99 | Owen Sound | OHL | 56 | 30 | 16 | 5 | 2998 | 191 | 2 | 3.82 | 16 | 9 | 7 | 960 | 58 | 0 | 3.63 |
| 99-2000 | Owen Sound | OHL | 53 | 18 | 26 | 6 | 3124 | 198 | 1 | 3.80 | .... | .... | .... | .... | .... | .... | .... |
| | Missouri | UHL | 6 | 3 | 1 | 0 | 237 | 6 | 0 | 1.52 | .... | .... | .... | .... | .... | .... | .... |
| 2000-01 | Worcester IceCats | AHL | 5 | 3 | 0 | 1 | 237 | 16 | 0 | 4.06 | .... | .... | .... | .... | .... | .... | .... |
| | Peoria Rivermen | ECHL | 27 | 15 | 7 | 4 | 1511 | 48 | 3 | *1.91 | 14 | 9 | 4 | 813 | 28 | *2 | 2.07 |
| 2001-02 | Worcester IceCats | AHL | 9 | 5 | 4 | 0 | 537 | 22 | 0 | 2.46 | .... | .... | .... | .... | .... | .... | .... |
| | Peoria Rivermen | ECHL | 24 | 13 | 8 | 2 | 1418 | 58 | 1 | 2.45 | .... | .... | .... | .... | .... | .... | .... |
| **2002-03** | **St. Louis** | **NHL** | **8** | **5** | **1** | **0** | **397** | **13** | **1** | **1.96** | .... | .... | .... | .... | .... | .... | .... |
| | Worcester IceCats | AHL | 41 | 18 | 14 | 8 | 2317 | 93 | 3 | 2.41 | 3 | 0 | 3 | 179 | 8 | 0 | 2.68 |
| 2003-04 | Worcester IceCats | AHL | 43 | 20 | 16 | 3 | 2367 | 84 | 5 | 2.13 | 9 | 4 | 5 | 569 | 24 | 0 | 2.53 |
| 2004-05 | Worcester IceCats | AHL | 50 | 19 | 25 | 2 | 2743 | 123 | 2 | 2.69 | .... | .... | .... | .... | .... | .... | .... |
| **2005-06** | **St. Louis** | **NHL** | **34** | **13** | **13** | **5** | **1830** | **81** | **3** | **2.66** | .... | .... | .... | .... | .... | .... | .... |
| | Peoria Rivermen | AHL | 6 | 4 | 2 | 0 | 358 | 11 | 2 | 1.84 | .... | .... | .... | .... | .... | .... | .... |
| **2006-07** | **St. Louis** | **NHL** | **31** | **8** | **12** | **5** | **1492** | **79** | **0** | **3.18** | .... | .... | .... | .... | .... | .... | .... |
| | Peoria Rivermen | AHL | 2 | 1 | 1 | 0 | 119 | 5 | 0 | 2.52 | .... | .... | .... | .... | .... | .... | .... |
| **2007-08** | **Vancouver** | **NHL** | **16** | **4** | **3** | **1** | **679** | **32** | **0** | **2.83** | .... | .... | .... | .... | .... | .... | .... |
| **2008-09** | **Vancouver** | **NHL** | **19** | **7** | **8** | **0** | **973** | **42** | **1** | **2.59** | .... | .... | .... | .... | .... | .... | .... |
| | Manitoba Moose | AHL | 16 | 7 | 3 | 3 | 865 | 25 | 2 | 1.73 | 1 | 0 | 1 | 43 | 1 | 0 | 1.40 |
| | **NHL Totals** | | **108** | **37** | **37** | **11** | **5371** | **247** | **5** | **2.76** | .... | .... | .... | .... | .... | .... | .... |

ECHL Second All-Star Team (2001)

Signed as a free agent by **St. Louis**, October 1, 2000. Signed as a free agent by **Vancouver**, July 2, 2007. Signed as a free agent by **Montreal**, July 20, 2009.

## SATERI, Harri (SA-teh-ree, HAR-ree) S.J.

Goaltender. Catches left. 6'1", 190 lbs. Born, Toijala, Finland, December 29, 1989.
(San Jose's 3rd choice, 106th overall, in 2008 Entry Draft).

| | | | Regular Season | | | | | | | | Playoffs | | | | | | |
|---|---|---|---|---|---|---|---|---|---|---|---|---|---|---|---|---|---|
| **Season** | **Club** | **League** | **GP** | **W** | **L** | **O/T** | **Mins** | **GA** | **SO** | **Avg** | **GP** | **W** | **L** | **Mins** | **GA** | **SO** | **Avg** |
| 2005-06 | HPK U18 | Fin-U18 | 27 | .... | .... | .... | 1515 | 66 | 5 | 2.61 | 2 | .... | .... | 118 | 10 | 0 | 5.08 |
| | HPK Jr. | Fin-Jr. | 1 | .... | .... | .... | 50 | 3 | 0 | 3.60 | .... | .... | .... | .... | .... | .... | .... |
| 2006-07 | Tappara U18 | Fin-U18 | 2 | .... | .... | .... | 119 | 4 | 0 | 2.02 | .... | .... | .... | .... | .... | .... | .... |
| | Tappara Jr. | Fin-Jr. | 23 | .... | .... | .... | 1346 | 59 | 2 | 2.63 | 10 | .... | .... | 614 | 31 | 0 | 3.03 |
| 2007-08 | Tappara Jr. | Fin-Jr. | 34 | 13 | 17 | 0 | 2048 | 102 | 1 | 2.99 | 3 | 0 | 3 | 178 | 8 | 0 | 2.70 |
| 2008-09 | Suomi U20 | Finland-2 | 4 | 2 | 2 | 0 | 247 | 12 | 0 | 2.91 | .... | .... | .... | .... | .... | .... | .... |

## SAUER, Billy (SAW-uhr, BIHL-lee) COL.

Goaltender. Catches left. 6'2", 180 lbs. Born, Rochester, NY, January 6, 1988.
(Colorado's 6th choice, 201st overall, in 2006 Entry Draft).

| | | | Regular Season | | | | | | | | Playoffs | | | | | | |
|---|---|---|---|---|---|---|---|---|---|---|---|---|---|---|---|---|---|
| **Season** | **Club** | **League** | **GP** | **W** | **L** | **O/T** | **Mins** | **GA** | **SO** | **Avg** | **GP** | **W** | **L** | **Mins** | **GA** | **SO** | **Avg** |
| 2004-05 | Chicago Steel | USHL | 30 | 12 | 12 | 2 | 1592 | 81 | 2 | 3.05 | .... | .... | .... | .... | .... | .... | .... |
| 2005-06 | U. of Michigan | CCHA | 23 | 11 | 6 | 4 | 1281 | 65 | 1 | 3.04 | .... | .... | .... | .... | .... | .... | .... |
| 2006-07 | U. of Michigan | CCHA | 40 | 25 | 14 | 1 | 2354 | 119 | 1 | 3.03 | .... | .... | .... | .... | .... | .... | .... |
| 2007-08 | U. of Michigan | CCHA | 38 | 30 | 4 | 3 | 2272 | 74 | *4 | 1.95 | .... | .... | .... | .... | .... | .... | .... |
| 2008-09 | U. of Michigan | CCHA | 13 | 5 | 6 | 0 | 653 | 22 | 2 | 2.02 | .... | .... | .... | .... | .... | .... | .... |

## SCHAEFER, Nolan (SHAY-fuhr, NOH-luhn)

Goaltender. Catches right. 6'2", 195 lbs. Born, Regina, Sask., January 15, 1980.
(San Jose's 4th choice, 166th overall, in 2000 Entry Draft).

| | | | Regular Season | | | | | | | | Playoffs | | | | | | |
|---|---|---|---|---|---|---|---|---|---|---|---|---|---|---|---|---|---|
| **Season** | **Club** | **League** | **GP** | **W** | **L** | **O/T** | **Mins** | **GA** | **SO** | **Avg** | **GP** | **W** | **L** | **Mins** | **GA** | **SO** | **Avg** |
| 1996-97 | Yorkton Mallers | SMHL | 36 | .... | .... | .... | 1854 | 132 | 0 | 4.27 | .... | .... | .... | .... | .... | .... | .... |
| 1997-98 | Yorkton Mallers | SMHL | 5 | .... | .... | .... | 239 | 17 | 0 | 4.25 | .... | .... | .... | .... | .... | .... | .... |
| | Nipawin Hawks | SJHL | 21 | 12 | 4 | 3 | 1080 | 42 | *3 | *2.33 | .... | .... | .... | .... | .... | .... | .... |
| 1998-99 | Nipawin Hawks | SJHL | 46 | .... | .... | .... | 2478 | 165 | 0 | 3.60 | .... | .... | .... | .... | .... | .... | .... |
| 99-2000 | Providence College | H-East | 14 | 6 | 5 | 1 | 778 | 42 | 0 | 3.24 | .... | .... | .... | .... | .... | .... | .... |
| 2000-01 | Providence College | H-East | 25 | 15 | 8 | 2 | 1529 | 63 | 3 | 2.47 | .... | .... | .... | .... | .... | .... | .... |
| 2001-02 | Providence College | H-East | *35 | 11 | 18 | 5 | *2062 | 113 | 0 | 3.29 | .... | .... | .... | .... | .... | .... | .... |
| 2002-03 | Providence College | H-East | 25 | 13 | 8 | 2 | 1440 | 71 | 0 | 2.96 | .... | .... | .... | .... | .... | .... | .... |
| 2003-04 | Cleveland Barons | AHL | 27 | 14 | 9 | 3 | 1592 | 62 | 2 | 2.34 | 9 | 4 | 5 | 573 | 24 | 0 | 2.51 |
| | Fresno Falcons | ECHL | 12 | 5 | 5 | 0 | 654 | 34 | 1 | 3.12 | .... | .... | .... | .... | .... | .... | .... |
| 2004-05 | Cleveland Barons | AHL | 43 | 17 | 23 | 1 | 2418 | 110 | 3 | 2.73 | .... | .... | .... | .... | .... | .... | .... |
| **2005-06** | **San Jose** | **NHL** | **7** | **5** | **1** | **0** | **352** | **11** | **1** | **1.88** | .... | .... | .... | .... | .... | .... | .... |
| | Cleveland Barons | AHL | 36 | 12 | 21 | 2 | 2058 | 118 | 2 | 3.44 | .... | .... | .... | .... | .... | .... | .... |
| 2006-07 | Worcester Sharks | AHL | 16 | 5 | 8 | 3 | 921 | 43 | 0 | 2.80 | .... | .... | .... | .... | .... | .... | .... |
| | Hershey Bears | AHL | 3 | 0 | 3 | 0 | 162 | 10 | 0 | 3.70 | .... | .... | .... | .... | .... | .... | .... |
| | Wilkes-Barre | AHL | 15 | 9 | 5 | 0 | 804 | 30 | 1 | 2.24 | 11 | 5 | 6 | 699 | 32 | 0 | 2.75 |
| 2007-08 | Houston Aeros | AHL | 34 | 19 | 13 | 0 | 1980 | 68 | 6 | *2.06 | 2 | 0 | 2 | 117 | 4 | 0 | 2.05 |
| 2008-09 | Houston Aeros | AHL | 51 | 26 | 17 | 5 | 2711 | 114 | 1 | 2.52 | 4 | 1 | 1 | 148 | 11 | 0 | 4.46 |
| | **NHL Totals** | | **7** | **5** | **1** | **0** | **352** | **11** | **1** | **1.88** | .... | .... | .... | .... | .... | .... | .... |

Hockey East Second All-Star Team (2001) • NCAA East Second All-American Team (2001) • Harry "Hap" Holmes Memorial Award (AHL – fewest goals against) (2008) (shared with Barry Brust)

Traded to **Pittsburgh** by **San Jose** for Pittsburgh's 7th round choice (Justin Braun) in 2007 Entry Draft, February 27, 2007. Signed as a free agent by **Minnesota**, July 3, 2007.

## SCHNEIDER, Cory (SHNIGH-duhr, KOHR-ee) VAN.

Goaltender. Catches left. 6'2", 202 lbs. Born, Marblehead, MA, March 18, 1986.
(Vancouver's 1st choice, 26th overall, in 2004 Entry Draft).

| | | | Regular Season | | | | | | | | Playoffs | | | | | | |
|---|---|---|---|---|---|---|---|---|---|---|---|---|---|---|---|---|---|
| **Season** | **Club** | **League** | **GP** | **W** | **L** | **O/T** | **Mins** | **GA** | **SO** | **Avg** | **GP** | **W** | **L** | **Mins** | **GA** | **SO** | **Avg** |
| 2002-03 | Andover | High-MA | 23 | 13 | 7 | 2 | 1385 | 39 | 3 | 1.69 | .... | .... | .... | .... | .... | .... | .... |
| 2003-04 | Andover | High-MA | 24 | 17 | 5 | 2 | 1336 | 32 | 6 | 1.42 | .... | .... | .... | .... | .... | .... | .... |
| | USNTDP | U-18 | 10 | 9 | 1 | 0 | 559 | 15 | 1 | 1.61 | .... | .... | .... | .... | .... | .... | .... |
| | USNTDP | NAHL | 2 | 2 | 0 | 0 | 120 | 6 | 0 | 3.00 | .... | .... | .... | .... | .... | .... | .... |
| 2004-05 | Boston College | H-East | 18 | 13 | 1 | 4 | 1102 | 35 | 1 | 1.90 | .... | .... | .... | .... | .... | .... | .... |
| 2005-06 | Boston College | H-East | *39 | *24 | 13 | 2 | *2362 | 83 | *8 | 2.11 | .... | .... | .... | .... | .... | .... | .... |
| 2006-07 | Boston College | H-East | *42 | *29 | 12 | 1 | *2517 | 90 | 6 | 2.15 | .... | .... | .... | .... | .... | .... | .... |
| 2007-08 | Manitoba Moose | AHL | 36 | 21 | 12 | 2 | 2054 | 78 | 3 | 2.28 | 6 | 1 | 4 | 375 | 12 | 0 | 1.92 |

| | | | | | | | | | | | | | | | | | |
|---|---|---|---|---|---|---|---|---|---|---|---|---|---|---|---|---|---|
| **2008-09** | **Vancouver** | **NHL** | **8** | **2** | **4** | **1** | **355** | **20** | **0** | **3.38** | .... | .... | .... | .... | .... | .... | .... |
| | Manitoba Moose | AHL | 40 | 28 | 10 | 1 | 2324 | 79 | 5 | *2.04 | *22 | 14 | 7 | 1315 | 47 | 0 | 2.15 |
| | **NHL Totals** | | **8** | **2** | **4** | **1** | **355** | **20** | **0** | **3.38** | .... | .... | .... | .... | .... | .... | .... |

Hockey East All-Rookie Team (2005) (co-winners - Kevin Regan and Peter Vetri) • Hockey East Second All-Star Team (2006) • NCAA East First All-American Team (2006) • AHL First All-Star Team (2009) • Harry "Hap" Holmes Memorial Award (AHL – fewest goals against) (2009) (shared with Karl Goehring) • Aldege "Baz" Bastien Memorial Award (AHL – Outstanding Goaltender) (2009)

## SCHWARZ, Marek (SHWAHRTS, MAIR-ehk)

Goaltender. Catches right. 6', 180 lbs. Born, Mlada Boleslav, Czech., April 1, 1986.
(St. Louis' 1st choice, 17th overall, in 2004 Entry Draft).

| | | | Regular Season | | | | | | | | Playoffs | | | | | | |
|---|---|---|---|---|---|---|---|---|---|---|---|---|---|---|---|---|---|
| Season | Club | League | GP | W | L | O/T | Mins | GA | SO | Avg | GP | W | L | Mins | GA | SO | Avg |
| 2000-01 | Ml. Boleslav Jr. | CzRep-Jr. | 45 | .... | .... | .... | 1969 | 154 | 0 | 4.69 | .... | .... | .... | .... | .... | .... | .... |
| 2001-02 | Sparta Jr. | CzRep-Jr. | 46 | .... | .... | .... | 2692 | 86 | 9 | 1.92 | 6 | .... | .... | 368 | 16 | 0 | 2.61 |
| 2002-03 | Sparta Jr. | CzRep-Jr. | 34 | .... | .... | .... | 1778 | 57 | 3 | 1.92 | 2 | .... | .... | 120 | 5 | 0 | 2.50 |
| | HC Sparta Praha | CzRep | 1 | .... | .... | .... | 1 | 0 | 0 | 0.00 | .... | .... | .... | .... | .... | .... | .... |
| 2003-04 | Sparta Jr. | CzRep-Jr. | 7 | .... | .... | .... | 352 | 14 | 2 | 2.39 | .... | .... | .... | .... | .... | .... | .... |
| | Plzen | CzRep | 10 | .... | .... | .... | 603 | 33 | 0 | 3.28 | .... | .... | .... | .... | .... | .... | .... |
| | HC Sparta Praha | CzRep | 8 | .... | .... | .... | 335 | 20 | 0 | 3.58 | .... | .... | .... | .... | .... | .... | .... |
| | HC Ocelari Trinec | CzRep | 5 | .... | .... | .... | 280 | 12 | 0 | 2.57 | .... | .... | .... | .... | .... | .... | .... |
| | BK Mlada Boleslav | CzRep-2 | 1 | .... | .... | .... | 63 | 6 | 0 | 5.71 | .... | .... | .... | .... | .... | .... | .... |
| 2004-05 | Vancouver Giants | WHL | 56 | 26 | 24 | 4 | 3304 | 147 | 2 | 2.67 | 6 | 2 | 4 | 378 | 18 | 0 | 2.86 |
| 2005-06 | Sparta Jr. | CzRep-Jr. | 3 | .... | .... | .... | 178 | 5 | 0 | 1.69 | .... | .... | .... | .... | .... | .... | .... |
| | HC Sparta Praha | CzRep | 15 | .... | .... | .... | 746 | 32 | 1 | 2.57 | 1 | .... | .... | 1 | 0 | 0 | 0.00 |
| | Beroun | CzRep-2 | 4 | .... | .... | .... | 229 | 17 | 0 | 4.45 | .... | .... | .... | .... | .... | .... | .... |
| **2006-07** | **St. Louis** | **NHL** | **2** | **0** | **1** | **0** | **60** | **3** | **0** | **3.00** | .... | .... | .... | .... | .... | .... | .... |
| | Peoria Rivermen | AHL | 34 | 19 | 13 | 0 | 1912 | 88 | 1 | 2.76 | .... | .... | .... | .... | .... | .... | .... |
| **2007-08** | **St. Louis** | **NHL** | **2** | **0** | **1** | **0** | **50** | **6** | **0** | **7.20** | .... | .... | .... | .... | .... | .... | .... |
| | Peoria Rivermen | AHL | 33 | 14 | 14 | 2 | 1808 | 84 | 0 | 2.79 | .... | .... | .... | .... | .... | .... | .... |
| | Alaska Aces | ECHL | 6 | 6 | 0 | 0 | 375 | 13 | 0 | 2.08 | 8 | 5 | 2 | 468 | 25 | 0 | 3.21 |
| **2008-09** | **St. Louis** | **NHL** | **2** | **0** | **0** | **0** | **15** | **0** | **0** | **0.00** | .... | .... | .... | .... | .... | .... | .... |
| | Peoria Rivermen | AHL | 10 | 4 | 4 | 0 | 523 | 31 | 0 | 3.56 | .... | .... | .... | .... | .... | .... | .... |
| | Alaska Aces | ECHL | 5 | 2 | 2 | 1 | 304 | 16 | 0 | 3.15 | .... | .... | .... | .... | .... | .... | .... |
| | BK Mlada Boleslav | CzRep | 19 | .... | .... | .... | 1132 | 49 | 3 | 2.60 | .... | .... | .... | .... | .... | .... | .... |
| | BK Mlada Boleslav | CzRep-Q | 4 | .... | .... | .... | 249 | 2 | 2 | 0.48 | .... | .... | .... | .... | .... | .... | .... |
| | **NHL Totals** | | **6** | **0** | **2** | **0** | **125** | **9** | **0** | **4.32** | .... | .... | .... | .... | .... | .... | .... |

## SEXSMITH, Tyson (SEHX-smihth, TIGH-suhn) S.J.

Goaltender. Catches left. 5'11", 210 lbs. Born, Calgary, Alta., March 19, 1989.
(San Jose's 4th choice, 91st overall, in 2007 Entry Draft).

| | | | Regular Season | | | | | | | | Playoffs | | | | | | |
|---|---|---|---|---|---|---|---|---|---|---|---|---|---|---|---|---|---|
| Season | Club | League | GP | W | L | O/T | Mins | GA | SO | Avg | GP | W | L | Mins | GA | SO | Avg |
| 2004-05 | Olds Grizzlys | AJHL | | | | | STATISTICS NOT AVAILABLE | | | | | | | | | | |
| | Medicine Hat | WHL | 1 | 0 | 0 | 0 | 5 | 0 | 0 | 0.00 | .... | .... | .... | .... | .... | .... | .... |
| | Vancouver Giants | WHL | 2 | 1 | 0 | 0 | 80 | 4 | 0 | 3.00 | .... | .... | .... | .... | .... | .... | .... |
| 2005-06 | Vancouver Giants | WHL | 11 | 6 | 3 | 1 | 547 | 21 | 1 | 2.30 | .... | .... | .... | .... | .... | .... | .... |
| 2006-07 | Vancouver Giants | WHL | 51 | 31 | 12 | 8 | 3047 | 91 | 10 | *1.79 | 22 | 14 | 7 | 1339 | 40 | *4 | *1.79 |
| 2007-08 | Vancouver Giants | WHL | 62 | 43 | 11 | 0 | 3678 | 116 | *9 | *1.89 | 10 | 6 | 4 | 658 | 20 | 0 | 1.82 |
| 2008-09 | Vancouver Giants | WHL | 52 | 39 | 9 | 4 | 3109 | 117 | 6 | 2.26 | 17 | 10 | 5 | .... | 36 | 1 | 1.88 |

WHL West Second All-Star Team (2008)

## SHANTZ, David (SHAWNTS, DAY-vihd)

Goaltender. Catches left. 6'1", 202 lbs. Born, Burlington, Ont., May 5, 1986.
(Florida's 2nd choice, 37th overall, in 2004 Entry Draft).

| | | | Regular Season | | | | | | | | Playoffs | | | | | | |
|---|---|---|---|---|---|---|---|---|---|---|---|---|---|---|---|---|---|
| Season | Club | League | GP | W | L | O/T | Mins | GA | SO | Avg | GP | W | L | Mins | GA | SO | Avg |
| 2002-03 | Thorold | OJHL-B | 36 | 30 | 3 | 3 | 2107 | 63 | 8 | 1.79 | .... | .... | .... | .... | .... | .... | .... |
| 2003-04 | Mississauga | OHL | 43 | 21 | 18 | 3 | 2483 | 120 | 1 | 2.90 | *24 | 12 | 12 | *1449 | 49 | *5 | 2.03 |
| 2004-05 | Mississauga | OHL | 27 | 10 | 11 | 3 | 1524 | 72 | 0 | 2.83 | 2 | 0 | 1 | 80 | 2 | 0 | 1.50 |
| 2005-06 | Peterborough | OHL | 49 | 31 | 14 | 3 | 2946 | 141 | 2 | 2.87 | *19 | *16 | 3 | *1239 | 54 | 1 | 2.62 |
| 2006-07 | Rochester | AHL | 2 | 1 | 1 | 0 | 120 | 9 | 0 | 4.51 | .... | .... | .... | .... | .... | .... | .... |
| | Florida Everblades | ECHL | 23 | 13 | 7 | 1 | 1338 | 66 | 0 | 2.96 | 1 | 0 | 0 | 20 | 1 | 0 | 3.00 |
| 2007-08 | Rochester | AHL | 14 | 1 | 10 | 1 | 780 | 53 | 0 | 4.07 | .... | .... | .... | .... | .... | .... | .... |
| | Florida Everblades | ECHL | 20 | 11 | 5 | 3 | 1101 | 47 | 0 | 2.56 | 2 | 0 | 1 | 77 | 3 | 0 | 2.33 |
| 2008-09 | Rochester | AHL | 12 | 3 | 6 | 2 | 690 | 30 | 1 | 2.61 | .... | .... | .... | .... | .... | .... | .... |
| | Elmira Jackals | ECHL | 11 | 5 | 4 | 1 | 645 | 31 | 1 | 2.88 | .... | .... | .... | .... | .... | .... | .... |
| | Dayton Bombers | ECHL | 23 | 10 | 9 | 3 | 1326 | 69 | 1 | 3.12 | .... | .... | .... | .... | .... | .... | .... |

OHL All-Rookie Team (2004) • Canadian Major Junior All-Rookie Team (2004)

## SIMILA, Petteri (sih-MIH-la, PEH-tuhr-ree) MTL.

Goaltender. Catches left. 6'5", 188 lbs. Born, Oulu, Finland, April 9, 1990.
(Montreal's 8th choice, 211th overall, in 2009 Entry Draft).

| | | | Regular Season | | | | | | | | Playoffs | | | | | | |
|---|---|---|---|---|---|---|---|---|---|---|---|---|---|---|---|---|---|
| Season | Club | League | GP | W | L | O/T | Mins | GA | SO | Avg | GP | W | L | Mins | GA | SO | Avg |
| 2006-07 | Karpat Oulu U18 | Fin-U18 | 15 | 7 | 5 | 0 | 826 | 46 | 0 | 3.34 | .... | .... | .... | .... | .... | .... | .... |
| 2007-08 | Karpat Oulu U18 | Fin-U18 | 12 | 4 | 3 | 0 | 738 | 35 | 0 | 2.84 | 3 | 0 | 2 | 162 | 9 | 0 | 3.33 |
| 2008-09 | Karpat Oulu Jr. | Fin-Jr. | 18 | 7 | 9 | 0 | 980 | 58 | 0 | 3.55 | .... | .... | .... | .... | .... | .... | .... |

## SMITH, Jeremy (SMIHTH, JAIR-eh-mee) NSH.

Goaltender. Catches left. 6', 168 lbs. Born, Dearborn, MI, April 13, 1989.
(Nashville's 2nd choice, 54th overall, in 2007 Entry Draft).

| | | | Regular Season | | | | | | | | Playoffs | | | | | | |
|---|---|---|---|---|---|---|---|---|---|---|---|---|---|---|---|---|---|
| Season | Club | League | GP | W | L | O/T | Mins | GA | SO | Avg | GP | W | L | Mins | GA | SO | Avg |
| 2005-06 | Det. Compuware | MWEHL | 13 | 5 | 6 | 0 | 696 | 31 | 0 | 2.67 | .... | .... | .... | .... | .... | .... | .... |
| | Det. Compuware | Exhib. | 3 | 2 | 1 | 0 | 178 | 8 | 0 | 2.70 | .... | .... | .... | .... | .... | .... | .... |
| | Plymouth Whalers | OHL | 5 | 0 | 2 | 0 | 111 | 11 | 0 | 5.95 | .... | .... | .... | .... | .... | .... | .... |
| 2006-07 | Plymouth Whalers | OHL | 34 | 23 | 6 | 1 | 1901 | 82 | 4 | 2.59 | 3 | 2 | 0 | 149 | 8 | 0 | 3.22 |
| 2007-08 | Plymouth Whalers | OHL | 40 | 23 | 13 | 4 | 2431 | 116 | 3 | 2.86 | 4 | 0 | 4 | 224 | 29 | 0 | 7.77 |
| 2008-09 | Plymouth Whalers | OHL | 17 | 3 | 9 | 2 | 901 | 72 | 0 | 4.80 | .... | .... | .... | .... | .... | .... | .... |
| | Niagara Ice Dogs | OHL | 26 | 12 | 9 | 3 | 1488 | 79 | 1 | 3.19 | 12 | 5 | 7 | 724 | 45 | *1 | 3.73 |

## SMITH, Mike (SMIHTH, MIGHK) T.B.

Goaltender. Catches left. 6'4", 218 lbs. Born, Kingston, Ont., March 22, 1982.
(Dallas' 5th choice, 161st overall, in 2001 Entry Draft).

| | | | Regular Season | | | | | | | | Playoffs | | | | | | |
|---|---|---|---|---|---|---|---|---|---|---|---|---|---|---|---|---|---|
| Season | Club | League | GP | W | L | O/T | Mins | GA | SO | Avg | GP | W | L | Mins | GA | SO | Avg |
| 1998-99 | Kingston | OPJHL | 16 | .... | .... | .... | 906 | 53 | 0 | 3.51 | .... | .... | .... | .... | .... | .... | .... |
| 99-2000 | Kingston | OHL | 15 | 4 | 5 | 0 | 666 | 42 | 0 | 3.78 | .... | .... | .... | .... | .... | .... | .... |
| 2000-01 | Kingston | OHL | 3 | 0 | 0 | 2 | 136 | 8 | 0 | 3.53 | .... | .... | .... | .... | .... | .... | .... |
| | Sudbury Wolves | OHL | 43 | 22 | 13 | 7 | 2571 | 108 | 3 | 2.52 | 12 | 7 | 5 | 735 | 26 | 2 | *2.12 |
| 2001-02 | Sudbury Wolves | OHL | 53 | 19 | 28 | 5 | 3082 | 157 | 3 | 3.06 | 5 | 1 | 4 | 302 | 15 | 0 | 2.98 |
| 2002-03 | Lexington | ECHL | 27 | 11 | 10 | 4 | 1553 | 66 | 1 | 2.55 | 2 | 0 | 1 | 93 | 8 | 0 | 5.14 |
| | Utah Grizzlies | AHL | 11 | 5 | 5 | 0 | 614 | 33 | 0 | 3.23 | .... | .... | .... | .... | .... | .... | .... |
| 2003-04 | Utah Grizzlies | AHL | 21 | 8 | 11 | 0 | 1186 | 56 | 2 | 2.83 | .... | .... | .... | .... | .... | .... | .... |
| 2004-05 | Houston Aeros | AHL | 45 | 19 | 17 | 3 | 2408 | 97 | 5 | 2.42 | 3 | 1 | 2 | 181 | 4 | 0 | 1.33 |
| 2005-06 | Iowa Stars | AHL | 50 | 25 | 19 | 6 | 2998 | 125 | 3 | 2.50 | 7 | 3 | 4 | 417 | 19 | 0 | 2.74 |
| **2006-07** | **Dallas** | **NHL** | **23** | **12** | **5** | **2** | **1213** | **45** | **3** | **2.23** | .... | .... | .... | .... | .... | .... | .... |
| **2007-08** | **Dallas** | **NHL** | **21** | **12** | **9** | **0** | **1172** | **48** | **2** | **2.46** | .... | .... | .... | .... | .... | .... | .... |
| | **Tampa Bay** | **NHL** | **13** | **3** | **10** | **0** | **774** | **36** | **1** | **2.79** | .... | .... | .... | .... | .... | .... | .... |
| **2008-09** | **Tampa Bay** | **NHL** | **41** | **14** | **18** | **9** | **2471** | **108** | **2** | **2.62** | .... | .... | .... | .... | .... | .... | .... |
| | **NHL Totals** | | **98** | **41** | **42** | **11** | **5630** | **237** | **8** | **2.53** | .... | .... | .... | .... | .... | .... | .... |

NHL All-Rookie Team (2007)

Traded to **Tampa Bay** by **Dallas** with Jussi Jokinen, Jeff Halpern and Dallas' 4th round choice (later traded to Minnesota – later traded to Edmonton – Edmonton selected Kyle Bigos) in 2009 Entry Draft for Brad Richards and Johan Holmqvist, February 26, 2008.

## STAJCER, Scott (STA-chuhr, SKAWT) NYR

Goaltender. Catches left. 6'3", 180 lbs. Born, Cambridge, Ont., June 14, 1991.
(NY Rangers' 5th choice, 140th overall, in 2009 Entry Draft).

| | | | Regular Season | | | | | | | | Playoffs | | | | | | |
|---|---|---|---|---|---|---|---|---|---|---|---|---|---|---|---|---|---|
| Season | Club | League | GP | W | L | O/T | Mins | GA | SO | Avg | GP | W | L | Mins | GA | SO | Avg |
| 2007-08 | Owen Sound | OJHL-B | 32 | 8 | 21 | 2 | 1862 | 130 | 0 | 3.90 | .... | .... | .... | .... | .... | .... | .... |
| | Owen Sound | OHL | 6 | 1 | 3 | 1 | 306 | 22 | 0 | 4.31 | .... | .... | .... | .... | .... | .... | .... |
| 2008-09 | Owen Sound | OHL | 35 | 15 | 15 | 5 | 1969 | 117 | 0 | 3.57 | 4 | 0 | 3 | 211 | 20 | 0 | 5.70 |

## STALOCK, Alex (STAY-lahk, AL-ehx) S.J.

Goaltender. Catches left. 5'11", 170 lbs. Born, St. Paul, MN, July 28, 1987.
(San Jose's 3rd choice, 112th overall, in 2005 Entry Draft).

| | | | Regular Season | | | | | | | | Playoffs | | | | | | |
|---|---|---|---|---|---|---|---|---|---|---|---|---|---|---|---|---|---|
| Season | Club | League | GP | W | L | O/T | Mins | GA | SO | Avg | GP | W | L | Mins | GA | SO | Avg |
| 2003-04 | South St. Paul | High-MN | 31 | 23 | 7 | 1 | .... | .... | .... | 2.20 | .... | .... | .... | .... | .... | .... | .... |
| 2004-05 | Cedar Rapids | USHL | 32 | 19 | 9 | 3 | 1801 | 82 | 1 | 2.73 | 9 | 7 | 2 | 582 | 14 | *1 | *1.44 |
| 2005-06 | Cedar Rapids | USHL | 44 | *28 | 13 | 3 | 2641 | 112 | 4 | 2.54 | 8 | 3 | 5 | 472 | 25 | 0 | 3.18 |
| 2006-07 | U. Minn-Duluth | WCHA | 23 | 5 | 14 | 3 | 1364 | 76 | 1 | 3.34 | .... | .... | .... | .... | .... | .... | .... |
| 2007-08 | U. Minn-Duluth | WCHA | 36 | 13 | 17 | 6 | 2170 | 85 | 3 | 2.35 | .... | .... | .... | .... | .... | .... | .... |
| 2008-09 | U. Minn-Duluth | WCHA | *42 | 21 | 13 | 8 | *2534 | 90 | *5 | *2.13 | .... | .... | .... | .... | .... | .... | .... |

USHL Playoff MVP (2005) • USHL First All-Star Team (2006) • USHL Goaltender of the Year (2006) • WCHA All-Rookie Team (2007) • WCHA First All-Star Team (2009) • NCAA West First All-American Team (2009)

## STEFANISZIN, Sebastian steh-fan-IHSH-ihn,suh-BAS-tee-yehn ANA.

Goaltender. Catches left. 6', 190 lbs. Born, Berlin, East Germany, July 22, 1987.
(Anaheim's 6th choice, 98th overall, in 2007 Entry Draft).

| | | | Regular Season | | | | | | | | Playoffs | | | | | | |
|---|---|---|---|---|---|---|---|---|---|---|---|---|---|---|---|---|---|
| Season | Club | League | GP | W | L | O/T | Mins | GA | SO | Avg | GP | W | L | Mins | GA | SO | Avg |
| 2002-03 | Eisb. Jrs. Berl. Jr. | Ger-Jr. | 12 | .... | .... | .... | .... | .... | .... | .... | .... | .... | .... | .... | .... | .... | .... |
| 2003-04 | Eisb. Jrs. Berl. Jr. | Ger-Jr. | 23 | .... | .... | .... | .... | .... | .... | 2.87 | 3 | .... | .... | .... | .... | .... | 5.45 |
| 2004-05 | Eisb. Jrs. Berlin | German-3 | 4 | .... | .... | .... | 183 | 10 | 1 | 3.28 | .... | .... | .... | .... | .... | .... | .... |
| | Eisb. Jrs. Berl. Jr. | Ger-Jr. | 20 | .... | .... | .... | 1048 | 55 | 1 | 3.15 | 4 | .... | .... | 240 | 21 | 0 | 5.25 |
| 2005-06 | Eisbaren Berlin | Germany | 3 | .... | .... | .... | 175 | 11 | 0 | 3.77 | .... | .... | .... | .... | .... | .... | .... |
| | Eisb. Jrs. Berlin | German-3 | 16 | .... | .... | .... | 818 | 57 | 0 | 4.18 | .... | .... | .... | .... | .... | .... | .... |
| | Hamburg Freezers | Germany | 4 | .... | .... | .... | 240 | 8 | 0 | 2.00 | .... | .... | .... | .... | .... | .... | .... |
| 2006-07 | Eisbaren Berlin | Germany | 2 | .... | .... | .... | 39 | 3 | 0 | 4.59 | .... | .... | .... | .... | .... | .... | .... |
| | Eisb. Jrs. Berlin | German-3 | 36 | .... | .... | .... | 2005 | 130 | 1 | 3.89 | 2 | .... | .... | 120 | 11 | 0 | 5.50 |
| 2007-08 | Essen | German-2 | 10 | 0 | 5 | 0 | 492 | 37 | 0 | 4.51 | .... | .... | .... | .... | .... | .... | .... |
| | Iserlohn Roosters | Germany | 9 | 1 | 6 | 0 | 467 | 35 | 0 | 4.50 | .... | .... | .... | .... | .... | .... | .... |
| 2008-09 | Iserlohn Roosters | Germany | 23 | 8 | 12 | 0 | 1275 | 71 | 0 | 3.34 | .... | .... | .... | .... | .... | .... | .... |

## STEPHAN, Tobias (STEH-fan, toh-BUY-uhs)

Goaltender. Catches left. 6'2", 180 lbs. Born, Zurich, Switz., January 21, 1984.
(Dallas' 3rd choice, 34th overall, in 2002 Entry Draft).

| | | | Regular Season | | | | | | | | Playoffs | | | | | | |
|---|---|---|---|---|---|---|---|---|---|---|---|---|---|---|---|---|---|
| Season | Club | League | GP | W | L | O/T | Mins | GA | SO | Avg | GP | W | L | Mins | GA | SO | Avg |
| 2000-01 | Kloten Flyers Jr. | Swiss-Jr. | | | | | STATISTICS NOT AVAILABLE | | | | | | | | | | |
| 2001-02 | EHC Chur | Swiss | 23 | .... | .... | .... | 1396 | 80 | 0 | 3.44 | 10 | .... | .... | 604 | 39 | 0 | 3.87 |
| 2002-03 | Kloten Flyers | Swiss | *44 | .... | .... | .... | 2670 | 125 | 2 | 2.81 | 5 | .... | .... | 292 | 20 | 0 | 4.11 |
| 2003-04 | Kloten Flyers | Swiss | 26 | .... | .... | .... | 1547 | 61 | 5 | 2.37 | .... | .... | .... | .... | .... | .... | .... |
| 2004-05 | Kloten Flyers | Swiss | *44 | .... | .... | .... | 2580 | 123 | 4 | 2.86 | 5 | .... | .... | 301 | 11 | 0 | 2.19 |
| 2005-06 | Kloten Flyers | Swiss | *44 | 16 | 19 | 8 | 2663 | 125 | *5 | 2.82 | 11 | 5 | 6 | 683 | 34 | 0 | 2.98 |
| 2006-07 | Iowa Stars | AHL | 27 | 10 | 15 | 0 | 1396 | 67 | 1 | 2.88 | 2 | 0 | 0 | 52 | 3 | 0 | 3.46 |
| **2007-08** | **Dallas** | **NHL** | **1** | **0** | **0** | **1** | **61** | **2** | **0** | **1.97** | .... | .... | .... | .... | .... | .... | .... |
| | Iowa Stars | AHL | 60 | 27 | 25 | 2 | 3329 | 147 | 6 | 2.65 | .... | .... | .... | .... | .... | .... | .... |
| **2008-09** | **Dallas** | **NHL** | **10** | **1** | **3** | **1** | **438** | **27** | **0** | **3.70** | .... | .... | .... | .... | .... | .... | .... |
| | Bridgeport | AHL | 5 | 4 | 0 | 1 | 313 | 10 | 0 | 1.91 | .... | .... | .... | .... | .... | .... | .... |
| | **NHL Totals** | | **11** | **1** | **3** | **2** | **499** | **29** | **0** | **3.49** | .... | .... | .... | .... | .... | .... | .... |

## TAYLOR, Daniel (TAY-luhr, DAN-yehl)

Goaltender. Catches left. 5'11", 179 lbs. Born, Plymouth, England, April 28, 1986.
(Los Angeles' 8th choice, 221st overall, in 2004 Entry Draft).

| | | | Regular Season | | | | | | | | Playoffs | | | | | | |
|---|---|---|---|---|---|---|---|---|---|---|---|---|---|---|---|---|---|
| Season | Club | League | GP | W | L | O/T | Mins | GA | SO | Avg | GP | W | L | Mins | GA | SO | Avg |
| 2002-03 | Cumberland Grads | CJHL | 23 | 13 | 3 | 1 | 1009 | 41 | 1 | 2.44 | 6 | 3 | 3 | 432 | 17 | 0 | 2.36 |
| 2003-04 | Guelph Storm | OHL | 26 | 16 | 4 | 3 | 1462 | 66 | 0 | 2.71 | 3 | 1 | 1 | 159 | 9 | 0 | 3.40 |
| 2004-05 | Guelph Storm | OHL | 31 | 13 | 14 | 3 | 1821 | 80 | 2 | 2.64 | 1 | 0 | 1 | 59 | 4 | 0 | 4.07 |
| 2005-06 | Kingston | OHL | 57 | 32 | 15 | 6 | 3319 | 172 | 3 | 3.11 | .... | .... | .... | .... | .... | .... | .... |
| 2006-07 | Bakersfield | ECHL | 17 | 7 | 7 | 2 | 969 | 70 | 0 | 4.33 | .... | .... | .... | .... | .... | .... | .... |
| | Wheeling Nailers | ECHL | 1 | 0 | 0 | 1 | 62 | 4 | 0 | 3.86 | .... | .... | .... | .... | .... | .... | .... |
| | Texas Wildcatters | ECHL | 2 | 0 | 1 | 0 | 74 | 2 | 0 | 1.61 | .... | .... | .... | .... | .... | .... | .... |
| **2007-08** | **Los Angeles** | **NHL** | **1** | **0** | **0** | **0** | **20** | **2** | **0** | **6.00** | .... | .... | .... | .... | .... | .... | .... |
| | Manchester | AHL | 23 | 13 | 5 | 2 | 1275 | 51 | 4 | 2.40 | .... | .... | .... | .... | .... | .... | .... |
| | Reading Royals | ECHL | 5 | 3 | 0 | 0 | 182 | 8 | 0 | 2.63 | 13 | 7 | 6 | 815 | 38 | 1 | 2.80 |
| 2008-09 | Manchester | AHL | 15 | 7 | 4 | 2 | 744 | 33 | 0 | 2.66 | .... | .... | .... | .... | .... | .... | .... |
| | **NHL Totals** | | **1** | **0** | **0** | **0** | **20** | **2** | **0** | **6.00** | .... | .... | .... | .... | .... | .... | .... |

## TELLQVIST, Mikael (TEHL-kvihst, MIGH-kuhl)

Goaltender. Catches left. 5'11", 185 lbs. Born, Sundbyberg, Sweden, September 19, 1979.
(Toronto's 3rd choice, 70th overall, in 2000 Entry Draft).

| | | | Regular Season | | | | | | | | Playoffs | | | | | | |
|---|---|---|---|---|---|---|---|---|---|---|---|---|---|---|---|---|---|
| Season | Club | League | GP | W | L | O/T | Mins | GA | SO | Avg | GP | W | L | Mins | GA | SO | Avg |
| 1997-98 | Djurgarden Jr. | Swe-Jr. | 23 | .... | .... | .... | 1380 | 55 | .... | 2.39 | 2 | 0 | 2 | 120 | 8 | 0 | 4.00 |
| 1998-99 | Djurgarden | Sweden | 3 | 1 | 2 | 0 | 124 | 8 | 0 | 3.87 | 4 | .... | .... | 240 | 11 | 0 | 2.75 |
| | Djurgarden | EuroHL | 3 | 2 | 1 | 0 | 180 | 8 | .... | 2.33 | .... | .... | .... | .... | .... | .... | .... |
| 99-2000 | Huddinge IK | Sweden-2 | 11 | 4 | 7 | 0 | 660 | 33 | .... | 3.30 | .... | .... | .... | .... | .... | .... | .... |
| | Djurgarden | Sweden | 30 | .... | .... | .... | 1909 | 66 | 2 | *2.07 | *13 | .... | .... | *814 | 21 | *3 | *1.55 |
| 2000-01 | Djurgarden | Sweden | 43 | .... | .... | .... | 2622 | 91 | *5 | *2.08 | *16 | .... | .... | *1006 | 45 | *1 | 2.68 |
| 2001-02 | St. John's | AHL | 28 | 8 | 11 | 6 | 1521 | 79 | 0 | 3.12 | 1 | 1 | 0 | 15 | 0 | 0 | 0.00 |
| | Sweden | Olympics | | | | | DID NOT PLAY – SPARE GOALTENDER | | | | | | | | | | |
| **2002-03** | **Toronto** | **NHL** | **3** | **1** | **1** | **0** | **86** | **4** | **0** | **2.79** | .... | .... | .... | .... | .... | .... | .... |
| | St. John's | AHL | 47 | 17 | 25 | 3 | 2651 | 148 | 1 | 3.35 | .... | .... | .... | .... | .... | .... | .... |
| **2003-04** | **Toronto** | **NHL** | **11** | **5** | **3** | **2** | **647** | **31** | **0** | **2.87** | .... | .... | .... | .... | .... | .... | .... |
| | St. John's | AHL | 23 | 10 | 11 | 1 | 1343 | 59 | 1 | 2.64 | .... | .... | .... | .... | .... | .... | .... |
| 2004-05 | St. John's | AHL | 45 | 24 | 16 | 4 | 2600 | 115 | 0 | 2.65 | 5 | 1 | 4 | 253 | 15 | 0 | 3.56 |
| **2005-06** | **Toronto** | **NHL** | **25** | **10** | **11** | **2** | **1399** | **73** | **2** | **3.13** | .... | .... | .... | .... | .... | .... | .... |
| | Sweden | Olympics | 1 | 0 | 1 | 0 | 60 | 3 | 0 | 3.00 | .... | .... | .... | .... | .... | .... | .... |
| **2006-07** | **Toronto** | **NHL** | **1** | **0** | **1** | **0** | **59** | **2** | **0** | **2.03** | .... | .... | .... | .... | .... | .... | .... |
| | Toronto Marlies | AHL | 3 | 2 | 1 | 0 | 182 | 12 | 0 | 3.95 | .... | .... | .... | .... | .... | .... | .... |
| | **Phoenix** | **NHL** | **30** | **11** | **11** | **3** | **1591** | **90** | **2** | **3.39** | .... | .... | .... | .... | .... | .... | .... |
| **2007-08** | **Phoenix** | **NHL** | **22** | **9** | **8** | **2** | **1224** | **56** | **2** | **2.75** | .... | .... | .... | .... | .... | .... | .... |

| Season | Club | League | GP | W | L | O/T | Mins | GA | SO | Avg | GP | W | L | Mins | GA | SO | Avg |
|---|---|---|---|---|---|---|---|---|---|---|---|---|---|---|---|---|---|
| 2008-09 | Phoenix | NHL | 15 | 7 | 5 | 1 | 798 | 38 | 0 | 2.86 | .... | .... | .... | .... | .... | .... | .... |
| | Buffalo | NHL | 6 | 2 | 1 | 0 | 230 | 9 | 0 | 2.35 | .... | .... | .... | .... | .... | .... | .... |
| | NHL Totals | | 113 | 45 | 41 | 10 | 6034 | 303 | 6 | 3.01 | .... | .... | .... | .... | .... | .... | .... |

Traded to **Phoenix** by **Toronto** for Tyson Nash and Boston's 4th round choice (previously acquired, Toronto selected Matt Frattin) in 2007 Entry Draft, November 28, 2006. Traded to **Buffalo** by **Phoenix** for Buffalo's 4th round choice in 2010 Entry Draft, March 4, 2009. Signed as a free agent by **Kazan** (Rus - KHL), May 1, 2009.

## TESLAK, Michael (TEHZ-lak, MIGH-kuhl)

Goaltender. Catches left. 6'2", 192 lbs. Born, Fernie, B.C., December 2, 1985.

| | | | Regular Season | | | | | | | | Playoffs | | | | | | |
|---|---|---|---|---|---|---|---|---|---|---|---|---|---|---|---|---|---|
| Season | Club | League | GP | W | L | O/T | Mins | GA | SO | Avg | GP | W | L | Mins | GA | SO | Avg |
| 2003-04 | Alberni Valley | BCHL | 22 | 8 | 11 | 0 | 1139 | 77 | 0 | 4.05 | .... | .... | .... | .... | .... | .... | .... |
| 2004-05 | Prince George | BCHL | 33 | 21 | 9 | 0 | 1920 | 79 | 1 | 2.47 | .... | .... | .... | .... | .... | .... | .... |
| 2005-06 | Michigan Tech | WCHA | 26 | 7 | 14 | 4 | 1437 | 88 | 0 | 3.68 | .... | .... | .... | .... | .... | .... | .... |
| 2006-07 | Michigan Tech | WCHA | 22 | 11 | 8 | 3 | 1259 | 42 | 4 | 2.00 | .... | .... | .... | .... | .... | .... | .... |
| 2007-08 | Michigan Tech | WCHA | 25 | 8 | 11 | 4 | 1389 | 51 | 1 | 2.20 | .... | .... | .... | .... | .... | .... | .... |
| | Philadelphia | AHL | 5 | 2 | 2 | 0 | 236 | 10 | 0 | 2.54 | 1 | 0 | 0 | 27 | 3 | 0 | 6.55 |
| 2008-09 | Philadelphia | AHL | 6 | 2 | 3 | 0 | 332 | 18 | 0 | 3.25 | .... | .... | .... | .... | .... | .... | .... |
| | Mississippi | ECHL | 1 | 0 | 1 | 0 | 60 | 4 | 0 | 4.00 | .... | .... | .... | .... | .... | .... | .... |
| | Elmira Jackals | ECHL | 32 | 17 | 9 | 4 | 1824 | 86 | 1 | 2.83 | 10 | 4 | 3 | 671 | 29 | 1 | 2.59 |

Signed as a free agent by **Philadelphia**, March 18, 2008.

## THEODORE, Jose (THEE-uh-dohr, joh-SAY) WSH.

Goaltender. Catches right. 5'11", 182 lbs. Born, Laval, Que., September 13, 1976.
(Montreal's 2nd choice, 44th overall, in 1994 Entry Draft).

| | | | Regular Season | | | | | | | | Playoffs | | | | | | |
|---|---|---|---|---|---|---|---|---|---|---|---|---|---|---|---|---|---|
| Season | Club | League | GP | W | L | O/T | Mins | GA | SO | Avg | GP | W | L | Mins | GA | SO | Avg |
| 1990-91 | Richelieu | QAHA | 42 | .... | .... | .... | 2520 | 80 | 0 | 1.90 | .... | .... | .... | .... | .... | .... | .... |
| 1991-92 | Richelieu Riverains | QAAA | 24 | 9 | 13 | 2 | 1440 | 96 | 0 | 3.99 | 5 | 2 | 3 | 295 | 26 | 0 | 5.28 |
| 1992-93 | St-Jean Lynx | QMJHL | 34 | 12 | 16 | 2 | 1776 | 112 | 0 | 3.78 | 3 | 0 | 2 | 175 | 11 | 0 | 3.77 |
| 1993-94 | St-Jean Lynx | QMJHL | 57 | 20 | 29 | 6 | 3225 | 194 | 0 | 3.61 | 5 | 1 | 4 | 296 | 18 | 0 | 3.65 |
| 1994-95 | Hull Olympiques | QMJHL | *58 | *32 | 22 | 2 | *3348 | 193 | 5 | 3.46 | *21 | *15 | 6 | *1263 | 59 | *1 | 2.80 |
| | Fredericton | AHL | .... | .... | .... | .... | .... | .... | .... | .... | 1 | 0 | 1 | 60 | 3 | 0 | 3.00 |
| 1995-96 | Montreal | NHL | 1 | 0 | 0 | 0 | 9 | 1 | 0 | 6.67 | .... | .... | .... | .... | .... | .... | .... |
| | Hull Olympiques | QMJHL | 48 | 33 | 11 | 2 | 2807 | 158 | 0 | 3.38 | 5 | 2 | 3 | 299 | 20 | 0 | 4.01 |
| 1996-97 | Montreal | NHL | 16 | 5 | 6 | 2 | 821 | 53 | 0 | 3.87 | 2 | 1 | 1 | 168 | 7 | 0 | 2.50 |
| | Fredericton | AHL | 26 | 12 | 12 | 0 | 1469 | 87 | 0 | 3.55 | .... | .... | .... | .... | .... | .... | .... |
| 1997-98 | Fredericton | AHL | 53 | 20 | 23 | 8 | 3053 | 145 | 2 | 2.85 | 4 | 1 | 3 | 237 | 13 | 0 | 3.28 |
| | Montreal | NHL | .... | .... | .... | .... | .... | .... | .... | .... | 3 | 0 | 1 | 120 | 1 | 0 | 0.50 |
| 1998-99 | Montreal | NHL | 18 | 4 | 12 | 0 | 913 | 50 | 1 | 3.29 | .... | .... | .... | .... | .... | .... | .... |
| | Fredericton | AHL | 27 | 12 | 13 | 2 | 1609 | 77 | 2 | 2.87 | 13 | 8 | 5 | 694 | 35 | 1 | 3.03 |
| 99-2000 | Montreal | NHL | 30 | 12 | 13 | 2 | 1655 | 58 | 5 | 2.10 | .... | .... | .... | .... | .... | .... | .... |
| 2000-01 | Montreal | NHL | 59 | 20 | 29 | 5 | 3298 | 141 | 2 | 2.57 | .... | .... | .... | .... | .... | .... | .... |
| | Quebec Citadelles | AHL | 3 | 3 | 0 | 0 | 180 | 9 | 0 | 3.00 | .... | .... | .... | .... | .... | .... | .... |
| 2001-02 | Montreal | NHL | 67 | 30 | 24 | 10 | 3864 | 136 | 7 | 2.11 | 12 | 6 | 6 | 686 | 35 | 0 | 3.06 |
| 2002-03 | Montreal | NHL | 57 | 20 | 31 | 6 | 3419 | 165 | 2 | 2.90 | .... | .... | .... | .... | .... | .... | .... |
| 2003-04 | Montreal | NHL | 67 | 33 | 28 | 5 | 3961 | 150 | 6 | 2.27 | 11 | 4 | 7 | 678 | 27 | 1 | 2.39 |
| 2004-05 | Djurgarden | Sweden | 17 | .... | .... | .... | 1024 | 42 | 0 | 2.46 | 12 | .... | .... | 728 | 27 | 0 | 2.23 |
| 2005-06 | Montreal | NHL | 38 | 17 | 15 | 5 | 2114 | 122 | 0 | 3.46 | .... | .... | .... | .... | .... | .... | .... |
| | Colorado | NHL | 5 | 1 | 3 | 1 | 296 | 15 | 0 | 3.04 | 9 | 4 | 5 | 573 | 29 | 0 | 3.04 |
| 2006-07 | Colorado | NHL | 33 | 13 | 15 | 1 | 1748 | 95 | 0 | 3.26 | .... | .... | .... | .... | .... | .... | .... |
| 2007-08 | Colorado | NHL | 53 | 28 | 21 | 3 | 3028 | 123 | 3 | 2.44 | 10 | 4 | 6 | 514 | 27 | 0 | 3.15 |
| | Lake Erie Monsters | AHL | 1 | 0 | 1 | 0 | 60 | 3 | 0 | 3.02 | .... | .... | .... | .... | .... | .... | .... |
| 2008-09 | Washington | NHL | 57 | 32 | 17 | 5 | 3287 | 157 | 2 | 2.87 | 2 | 0 | 1 | 97 | 6 | 0 | 3.71 |
| | NHL Totals | | 501 | 215 | 214 | 45 | 28413 | 1266 | 28 | 2.67 | 49 | 19 | 27 | 2836 | 132 | 1 | 2.79 |

QMJHL Second All-Star Team (1995, 1996) • NHL Second All-Star Team (2002) • MBNA Roger Crozier Saving Grace Award (2002) • Vezina Trophy (2002) • Hart Memorial Trophy (2002)

Played in NHL All-Star Game (2002, 2004)

• Scored a goal vs. NY Islanders, January 2, 2001. Signed as a free agent by **Djurgarden** (Sweden), December 20, 2004. Traded to **Colorado** by **Montreal** for David Aebischer, March 8, 2006. Signed as a free agent by **Washington**, July 1, 2008.

## THOMAS, Tim (TAW-mas, TIHM) BOS.

Goaltender. Catches left. 5'11", 208 lbs. Born, Flint, MI, April 15, 1974.
(Quebec's 11th choice, 217th overall, in 1994 Entry Draft).

| | | | Regular Season | | | | | | | | Playoffs | | | | | | |
|---|---|---|---|---|---|---|---|---|---|---|---|---|---|---|---|---|---|
| Season | Club | League | GP | W | L | O/T | Mins | GA | SO | Avg | GP | W | L | Mins | GA | SO | Avg |
| 1992-93 | Davison High | High-MI | 27 | .... | .... | .... | 1580 | 87 | .... | 3.30 | .... | .... | .... | .... | .... | .... | .... |
| 1993-94 | U. of Vermont | ECAC | *33 | 15 | 12 | 6 | 1864 | 94 | 0 | 3.03 | .... | .... | .... | .... | .... | .... | .... |
| 1994-95 | U. of Vermont | ECAC | 34 | 18 | 13 | 2 | 2010 | 90 | *4 | *2.69 | .... | .... | .... | .... | .... | .... | .... |
| 1995-96 | U. of Vermont | ECAC | 37 | *26 | 7 | 4 | *2254 | 88 | *3 | *2.34 | .... | .... | .... | .... | .... | .... | .... |
| 1996-97 | U. of Vermont | ECAC | 36 | 22 | 11 | 3 | 2158 | 101 | 2 | 2.81 | .... | .... | .... | .... | .... | .... | .... |
| 1997-98 | Birmingham Bulls | ECHL | 6 | 4 | 1 | 1 | 360 | 13 | 1 | 2.17 | .... | .... | .... | .... | .... | .... | .... |
| | Houston Aeros | IHL | 1 | 0 | 1 | 0 | 59 | 4 | 0 | 4.01 | .... | .... | .... | .... | .... | .... | .... |
| | HIFK Helsinki | Finland | 18 | 13 | 4 | 1 | 1034 | 28 | 2 | 1.62 | 9 | 9 | 0 | 551 | 14 | 3 | 1.52 |
| 1998-99 | Hamilton Bulldogs | AHL | 15 | 6 | 8 | 0 | 837 | 45 | 0 | 3.23 | .... | .... | .... | .... | .... | .... | .... |
| | HIFK Helsinki | Finland | 14 | 8 | 3 | 3 | 833 | 31 | 2 | 2.23 | 11 | 7 | 4 | 658 | 25 | 0 | 2.28 |
| 99-2000 | Detroit Vipers | IHL | 36 | 10 | 21 | 3 | 2020 | 120 | 1 | 3.56 | .... | .... | .... | .... | .... | .... | .... |
| 2000-01 | AIK Solna | Sweden | 43 | .... | .... | .... | 2542 | 105 | 3 | 2.48 | 5 | .... | .... | 299 | 20 | 0 | 4.01 |
| 2001-02 | Karpat Oulu | Finland | 32 | 15 | 12 | 5 | 1937 | 79 | 4 | 2.44 | 3 | 1 | 2 | 180 | 12 | 0 | 4.00 |
| 2002-03 | Boston | NHL | 4 | 3 | 1 | 0 | 220 | 11 | 0 | 3.00 | .... | .... | .... | .... | .... | .... | .... |
| | Providence Bruins | AHL | 35 | 18 | 12 | 5 | 2049 | 98 | 1 | 2.87 | .... | .... | .... | .... | .... | .... | .... |
| 2003-04 | Providence Bruins | AHL | 43 | 20 | 16 | 6 | 2544 | 78 | 9 | 1.84 | 2 | 0 | 2 | 84 | 10 | 0 | 7.13 |
| 2004-05 | Jokerit Helsinki | Finland | 54 | 34 | 13 | 7 | 3266 | 86 | 15 | 1.58 | 12 | 8 | 4 | 720 | 22 | 0 | 1.83 |
| 2005-06 | Boston | NHL | 38 | 12 | 13 | 10 | 2187 | 101 | 1 | 2.77 | .... | .... | .... | .... | .... | .... | .... |
| | Providence Bruins | AHL | 26 | 15 | 11 | 0 | 1515 | 57 | 1 | 2.26 | .... | .... | .... | .... | .... | .... | .... |
| 2006-07 | Boston | NHL | 66 | 30 | 29 | 4 | 3619 | 189 | 3 | 3.13 | .... | .... | .... | .... | .... | .... | .... |
| 2007-08 | Boston | NHL | 57 | 28 | 19 | 6 | 3342 | 136 | 3 | 2.44 | 7 | 3 | 4 | 430 | 19 | 0 | 2.65 |
| 2008-09 | Boston | NHL | 54 | 36 | 11 | 7 | 3259 | 114 | 5 | *2.10 | 11 | 7 | 4 | 680 | 21 | 1 | *1.85 |
| | NHL Totals | | 219 | 109 | 73 | 27 | 12627 | 551 | 12 | 2.62 | 18 | 10 | 8 | 1110 | 40 | 1 | 2.16 |

ECAC First All-Star Team (1995, 1996) • ECAC Goaltender of the Year (1996) • NCAA East Second All-American Team (1995) • NCAA East First All-American Team (1996) • NHL First All-Star Team (2009) • William M. Jennings Trophy (2009) (shared with Manny Fernandez) • Vezina Trophy (2009)

Played in NHL All-Star Game (2008, 2009)

Signed as a free agent by **Edmonton**, June 4, 1998. Signed as a free agent by **Boston**, August 8, 2002. Signed as a free agent by **Jokerit Helsinki** (Finland), May 17, 2004. Signed as a free agent by **Boston**, September 14, 2005.

## TOIVONEN, Hannu (TOI-voh-nuhn, HA-noo) ST.L.

Goaltender. Catches left. 6'2", 200 lbs. Born, Kalvola, Finland, May 18, 1984.
(Boston's 1st choice, 29th overall, in 2002 Entry Draft).

| | | | Regular Season | | | | | | | | Playoffs | | | | | | |
|---|---|---|---|---|---|---|---|---|---|---|---|---|---|---|---|---|---|
| Season | Club | League | GP | W | L | O/T | Mins | GA | SO | Avg | GP | W | L | Mins | GA | SO | Avg |
| 2000-01 | HPK U18 | Fin-U18 | .... | .... | .... | .... | .... | .... | .... | .... | .... | .... | .... | .... | .... | .... | .... |
| 2001-02 | HPK U18 | Fin-U18 | 5 | 4 | 1 | 0 | 277 | 14 | 0 | 3.03 | .... | .... | .... | .... | .... | .... | .... |
| | HPK Jr. | Fin-Jr. | 31 | 15 | 12 | 4 | 1877 | 103 | 2 | 3.29 | 7 | 3 | 4 | 440 | 31 | 0 | 4.23 |
| 2002-03 | HPK Jr. | Fin-Jr. | 6 | 3 | 3 | 0 | 359 | 20 | 0 | 3.34 | .... | .... | .... | .... | .... | .... | .... |
| | HPK Hameenlinna | Finland | 24 | 16 | 2 | 4 | 1432 | 54 | 2 | 2.26 | 2 | 1 | 1 | 117 | 3 | 1 | 1.53 |
| 2003-04 | Providence Bruins | AHL | 36 | 15 | 16 | 4 | 2162 | 83 | 2 | 2.30 | 0 | 0 | 0 | 0 | 0 | 0 | 0.00 |
| 2004-05 | Providence Bruins | AHL | 54 | 29 | 18 | 3 | 3017 | 103 | 7 | 2.05 | 17 | 10 | 7 | 1038 | 42 | 0 | 2.43 |
| 2005-06 | Boston | NHL | 20 | 9 | 5 | 4 | 1163 | 51 | 1 | 2.63 | .... | .... | .... | .... | .... | .... | .... |
| 2006-07 | Boston | NHL | 18 | 3 | 9 | 1 | 894 | 63 | 0 | 4.23 | .... | .... | .... | .... | .... | .... | .... |
| | Providence Bruins | AHL | 27 | 13 | 13 | 1 | 1618 | 64 | 2 | 2.37 | 13 | 6 | 7 | 742 | 36 | 0 | 2.91 |
| 2007-08 | St. Louis | NHL | 23 | 6 | 10 | 5 | 1202 | 69 | 0 | 3.44 | .... | .... | .... | .... | .... | .... | .... |
| | Peoria Rivermen | AHL | 11 | 6 | 4 | 0 | 627 | 33 | 0 | 3.16 | .... | .... | .... | .... | .... | .... | .... |
| 2008-09 | Ilves Tampere | Finland | 52 | 19 | 23 | 9 | 2913 | 130 | 3 | 2.68 | 3 | 1 | 2 | 198 | 6 | 1 | 1.82 |
| | NHL Totals | | 61 | 18 | 24 | 10 | 3259 | 183 | 1 | 3.37 | .... | .... | .... | .... | .... | .... | .... |

Traded to **St. Louis** by **Boston** for Carl Soderberg, July 23, 2007. Signed as a free agent by **Ilves Tampere** (Finland), July 15, 2008. Signed as a free agent by **St. Louis**, July 9, 2009.

## TOKARSKI, Dustin (toh-KAHR-skee, DUHS-tihn) T.B.

Goaltender. Catches left. 5'11", 185 lbs. Born, Humboldt, Sask., September 16, 1989.
(Tampa Bay's 3rd choice, 122nd overall, in 2008 Entry Draft).

| | | | Regular Season | | | | | | | | Playoffs | | | | | | |
|---|---|---|---|---|---|---|---|---|---|---|---|---|---|---|---|---|---|
| Season | Club | League | GP | W | L | O/T | Mins | GA | SO | Avg | GP | W | L | Mins | GA | SO | Avg |
| 2006-07 | Spokane Chiefs | WHL | 30 | 13 | 11 | 2 | 1674 | 78 | 2 | 2.80 | 6 | 2 | 4 | 364 | 17 | 0 | 2.80 |
| 2007-08 | Spokane Chiefs | WHL | 45 | 30 | 10 | 0 | 2543 | 87 | 6 | 2.05 | *21 | *16 | 5 | *1352 | 31 | *3 | *1.38 |
| 2008-09 | Spokane Chiefs | WHL | 54 | 34 | 18 | 2 | 3264 | 107 | *7 | *1.97 | 12 | 7 | 5 | 812 | 23 | 1 | *1.70 |

Memorial Cup All-Star Team (2008) • Hap Emms Memorial Trophy (Memorial Cup Tournament - Top Goaltender) (2008) • Stafford Smythe Memorial Trophy (Memorial Cup Tournament - MVP) (2008) • WHL West Second All-Star Team (2009)

## TORDJMAN, Josh (TOHRJ-man, JAWSH) PHX.

Goaltender. Catches left. 6'1", 155 lbs. Born, Montreal, Que., January 11, 1985.

| | | | Regular Season | | | | | | | | Playoffs | | | | | | |
|---|---|---|---|---|---|---|---|---|---|---|---|---|---|---|---|---|---|
| Season | Club | League | GP | W | L | O/T | Mins | GA | SO | Avg | GP | W | L | Mins | GA | SO | Avg |
| 2002-03 | Valleyfield Braves | QJHL | STATISTICS NOT AVAILABLE | | | | | | | | | | | | | | |
| | Victoriaville Tigres | QMJHL | 10 | 4 | 3 | 0 | 432 | 24 | 1 | 3.33 | 2 | 0 | 1 | 112 | 12 | 0 | 6.46 |
| 2003-04 | Victoriaville Tigres | QMJHL | 42 | 10 | 24 | 4 | 2177 | 143 | 2 | 3.94 | .... | .... | .... | .... | .... | .... | .... |
| 2004-05 | Victoriaville Tigres | QMJHL | 56 | 22 | 28 | 4 | 3185 | 171 | 5 | 3.22 | 7 | 3 | 4 | 435 | 24 | 0 | 3.31 |
| 2005-06 | Victoriaville Tigres | QMJHL | 31 | 13 | 17 | 0 | 1792 | 106 | 2 | 3.55 | .... | .... | .... | .... | .... | .... | .... |
| | Moncton Wildcats | QMJHL | 25 | 18 | 6 | 0 | 1427 | 55 | 2 | *2.31 | 21 | *15 | 5 | 1238 | 48 | *2 | 2.33 |
| 2006-07 | San Antonio | AHL | 37 | 15 | 18 | 2 | 2114 | 91 | 1 | 2.58 | .... | .... | .... | .... | .... | .... | .... |
| | Phoenix | ECHL | 9 | 4 | 4 | 0 | 480 | 25 | 0 | 3.12 | .... | .... | .... | .... | .... | .... | .... |
| 2007-08 | San Antonio | AHL | 43 | 22 | 14 | 4 | 2466 | 109 | 1 | 2.65 | 6 | 3 | 3 | 357 | 11 | 1 | 1.85 |
| 2008-09 | Phoenix | NHL | 2 | 0 | 2 | 0 | 118 | 8 | 0 | 4.07 | .... | .... | .... | .... | .... | .... | .... |
| | San Antonio | AHL | 51 | 25 | 22 | 2 | 2921 | 127 | 6 | 2.61 | .... | .... | .... | .... | .... | .... | .... |
| | NHL Totals | | 2 | 0 | 2 | 0 | 118 | 8 | 0 | 4.07 | .... | .... | .... | .... | .... | .... | .... |

QMJHL Second All-Star Team (2006)

Signed as a free agent by **Phoenix**, July 2, 2006.

## TOSKALA, Vesa (TAWS-kah-lah, VEH-sa) TOR.

Goaltender. Catches left. 5'10", 195 lbs. Born, Tampere, Finland, May 20, 1977.
(San Jose's 4th choice, 90th overall, in 1995 Entry Draft).

| | | | Regular Season | | | | | | | | Playoffs | | | | | | |
|---|---|---|---|---|---|---|---|---|---|---|---|---|---|---|---|---|---|
| Season | Club | League | GP | W | L | O/T | Mins | GA | SO | Avg | GP | W | L | Mins | GA | SO | Avg |
| 1994-95 | Ilves Tampere Jr. | Fin-Jr. | 17 | 10 | 5 | 1 | 956 | 36 | 2 | 2.26 | 7 | .... | .... | 393 | 22 | .... | 3.36 |
| 1995-96 | Ilves Tampere Jr. | Fin-Jr. | 3 | 3 | 0 | 0 | 180 | 3 | 0 | 1.00 | .... | .... | .... | .... | .... | .... | .... |
| | KooVee Tampere | Finland-2 | 2 | 1 | 1 | 0 | 119 | 5 | 1 | 2.51 | .... | .... | .... | .... | .... | .... | .... |
| | Ilves Tampere | Finland | 37 | 14 | 14 | 7 | 2072 | 109 | 1 | 3.16 | 2 | 0 | 2 | 78 | 11 | 0 | 8.46 |
| 1996-97 | Ilves Tampere Jr. | Fin-Jr. | 3 | .... | .... | .... | 184 | .... | .... | 2.93 | .... | .... | .... | .... | .... | .... | .... |
| | Ilves Tampere | Finland | 40 | 22 | 12 | 5 | 2270 | 108 | 0 | 2.85 | 8 | 3 | 5 | 479 | 29 | 0 | 3.63 |
| 1997-98 | Ilves Tampere Jr. | Fin-Jr. | 2 | 2 | 0 | 0 | 120 | 4 | 0 | 2.00 | .... | .... | .... | .... | .... | .... | .... |
| | Ilves Tampere | Finland | 43 | 26 | 13 | 3 | 2554 | 118 | 1 | 2.77 | 9 | 6 | 3 | 519 | 18 | 1 | 2.08 |
| 1998-99 | Ilves Tampere | Finland | 33 | 21 | 12 | 0 | 1966 | 70 | 5 | 2.14 | 4 | 1 | 3 | 248 | 14 | 0 | 3.39 |
| 99-2000 | Farjestad | Sweden | 44 | .... | .... | .... | 2652 | 118 | 3 | 2.67 | 7 | .... | .... | 439 | 19 | 0 | 2.59 |
| 2000-01 | Kentucky | AHL | 44 | 22 | 13 | 5 | 2466 | 114 | 2 | 2.77 | 3 | 0 | 3 | 197 | 8 | 0 | 2.43 |
| 2001-02 | San Jose | NHL | 1 | 0 | 0 | 0 | 10 | 0 | 0 | 0.00 | .... | .... | .... | .... | .... | .... | .... |
| | Cleveland Barons | AHL | *62 | 19 | 33 | 7 | *3574 | 178 | 3 | 2.99 | .... | .... | .... | .... | .... | .... | .... |
| 2002-03 | San Jose | NHL | 11 | 4 | 3 | 1 | 537 | 21 | 1 | 2.35 | .... | .... | .... | .... | .... | .... | .... |
| | Cleveland Barons | AHL | 49 | 15 | 30 | 2 | 2824 | 151 | 1 | 3.21 | .... | .... | .... | .... | .... | .... | .... |
| 2003-04 | San Jose | NHL | 28 | 12 | 8 | 4 | 1541 | 53 | 1 | 2.06 | .... | .... | .... | .... | .... | .... | .... |
| 2004-05 | Ilves Tampere | Finland | 3 | 0 | 1 | 2 | 186 | 8 | 0 | 2.58 | 6 | 3 | 3 | 357 | 19 | 0 | 3.19 |
| 2005-06 | San Jose | NHL | 37 | 23 | 7 | 4 | 2039 | 87 | 2 | 2.56 | 11 | 6 | 5 | 686 | 28 | 1 | 2.45 |
| | Cleveland Barons | AHL | 1 | 0 | 0 | 1 | 65 | 0 | 1 | 0.00 | .... | .... | .... | .... | .... | .... | .... |
| 2006-07 | San Jose | NHL | 38 | 26 | 10 | 1 | 2142 | 84 | 4 | 2.35 | .... | .... | .... | .... | .... | .... | .... |
| 2007-08 | Toronto | NHL | 66 | 33 | 25 | 6 | 3837 | 175 | 3 | 2.74 | .... | .... | .... | .... | .... | .... | .... |
| 2008-09 | Toronto | NHL | 53 | 22 | 17 | 11 | 3056 | 166 | 1 | 3.26 | .... | .... | .... | .... | .... | .... | .... |
| | NHL Totals | | 234 | 120 | 70 | 27 | 13162 | 586 | 12 | 2.67 | 11 | 6 | 5 | 686 | 28 | 1 | 2.45 |

Signed as a free agent by **Ilves Tampere** (Finland), January 31, 2005. Traded to **Toronto** by **San Jose** with Mark Bell for Toronto's 1st (later traded to St. Louis – St. Louis selected Lars Eller) and 2nd (later traded to St. Louis – St. Louis selected Aaron Palushaj) round choices in 2007 Entry Draft and Toronto's 4th round choice (later traded to Nashville – Nashville selected Craig Smith) in 2009 Entry Draft, June 22, 2007.

## TURCO, Marty (TUHR-koh, MAHR-tee) DAL.

Goaltender. Catches left. 5'11", 185 lbs. Born, Sault Ste. Marie, Ont., August 13, 1975.
(Dallas' 4th choice, 124th overall, in 1994 Entry Draft).

| | | | Regular Season | | | | | | | | Playoffs | | | | | | |
|---|---|---|---|---|---|---|---|---|---|---|---|---|---|---|---|---|---|
| Season | Club | League | GP | W | L | O/T | Mins | GA | SO | Avg | GP | W | L | Mins | GA | SO | Avg |
| 1993-94 | Cambridge | OJHL-B | 34 | 19 | 10 | 3 | 1973 | 114 | 0 | 3.47 | .... | .... | .... | .... | .... | .... | .... |
| 1994-95 | U. of Michigan | CCHA | 37 | *27 | 7 | 1 | 2063 | 95 | 1 | 2.76 | .... | .... | .... | .... | .... | .... | .... |
| 1995-96 | U. of Michigan | CCHA | *42 | *34 | 7 | 1 | *2335 | 84 | *5 | *2.16 | .... | .... | .... | .... | .... | .... | .... |
| 1996-97 | U. of Michigan | CCHA | *41 | *33 | 4 | 4 | *2296 | 87 | *4 | *2.27 | .... | .... | .... | .... | .... | .... | .... |
| 1997-98 | U. of Michigan | CCHA | *45 | *33 | 10 | 1 | *2640 | 95 | 4 | 2.16 | .... | .... | .... | .... | .... | .... | .... |
| 1998-99 | Michigan K-Wings | IHL | 54 | 24 | 17 | 10 | 3127 | 136 | 1 | 2.61 | 5 | 2 | 3 | 300 | 14 | 0 | 2.80 |
| 99-2000 | Michigan K-Wings | IHL | 60 | 23 | 27 | *7 | 3399 | 139 | *7 | 2.45 | .... | .... | .... | .... | .... | .... | .... |
| 2000-01 | Dallas | NHL | 26 | 13 | 6 | 1 | 1266 | 40 | 3 | *1.90 | .... | .... | .... | .... | .... | .... | .... |
| 2001-02 | Dallas | NHL | 31 | 15 | 6 | 2 | 1519 | 53 | 2 | 2.09 | .... | .... | .... | .... | .... | .... | .... |
| 2002-03 | Dallas | NHL | 55 | 31 | 10 | 10 | 3203 | 92 | 7 | *1.72 | 12 | 6 | 6 | 798 | 25 | 0 | 1.88 |
| 2003-04 | Dallas | NHL | 73 | 37 | 21 | 13 | 4359 | 144 | 9 | 1.98 | 5 | 1 | 4 | 325 | 18 | 0 | 3.32 |
| 2004-05 | Djurgarden | Sweden | 6 | .... | .... | .... | 356 | 12 | 1 | 2.02 | .... | .... | .... | .... | .... | .... | .... |
| 2005-06 | Dallas | NHL | 68 | 41 | 19 | 5 | 3910 | 166 | 3 | 2.55 | 5 | 1 | 4 | 319 | 18 | 0 | 3.39 |
| | Canada | Olympics | DID NOT PLAY – SPARE GOALTENDER | | | | | | | | | | | | | | |
| 2006-07 | Dallas | NHL | 67 | 38 | 20 | 5 | 3764 | 140 | 6 | 2.23 | 7 | 3 | 4 | 509 | 11 | 3 | *1.30 |
| 2007-08 | Dallas | NHL | 62 | 32 | 21 | 6 | 3629 | 140 | 3 | 2.31 | 18 | 10 | 8 | 1152 | 40 | 1 | 2.08 |
| 2008-09 | Dallas | NHL | 74 | 33 | 31 | 10 | 4327 | 203 | 3 | 2.81 | .... | .... | .... | .... | .... | .... | .... |
| | NHL Totals | | 456 | 240 | 134 | 52 | 25977 | 978 | 36 | 2.26 | 47 | 21 | 26 | 3103 | 112 | 4 | 2.17 |

CCHA Rookie of the Year (1995) • NCAA Championship All-Tournament Team (1996, 1998) • CCHA First All-Star Team (1997) • NCAA West First All-American Team (1997) • CCHA Second All-Star Team (1998) • NCAA Championship Tournament MVP (1998) • Garry F. Longman Memorial Trophy (IHL – Rookie of the Year) (1999) • MBNA Roger Crozier Saving Grace Award (2001, 2003) • NHL Second All-Star Team (2003)

Played in NHL All-Star Game (2003, 2004, 2007)

Signed as a free agent by **Djurgarden** (Sweden), November 13, 2004.

## TURPLE, Dan
(TUHR-puhl, DAN)

Goaltender. Catches left. 6'6", 210 lbs. Born, Oakville, Ont., January 1, 1985.
(Atlanta's 6th choice, 186th overall, in 2004 Entry Draft).

| | | | Regular Season | | | | | | | | Playoffs | | | | | | |
|---|---|---|---|---|---|---|---|---|---|---|---|---|---|---|---|---|---|
| Season | Club | League | GP | W | L | O/T | Mins | GA | SO | Avg | GP | W | L | Mins | GA | SO | Avg |
| 2002-03 | Kingston | OHL | 12 | 2 | 8 | 0 | 449 | 42 | 0 | 5.61 | | | | | | | |
| 2003-04 | Kingston | OHL | 9 | 4 | 4 | 1 | 534 | 29 | 0 | 3.26 | | | | | | | |
| | Oshawa Generals | OHL | 35 | 20 | 7 | 3 | 1843 | 81 | 2 | 2.64 | 7 | 3 | 4 | 443 | 19 | 1 | 2.57 |
| 2004-05 | Oshawa Generals | OHL | 10 | 4 | 4 | 0 | 469 | 29 | 0 | 3.71 | | | | | | | |
| | Kitchener Rangers | OHL | 40 | 17 | 16 | 5 | 2335 | 92 | 3 | 2.36 | 3 | 0 | 2 | 162 | 9 | 0 | 3.33 |
| 2005-06 | Kitchener Rangers | OHL | 57 | 40 | 15 | 2 | 3306 | 124 | *7 | *2.25 | 5 | 1 | 4 | 326 | 20 | 0 | 3.68 |
| 2006-07 | Gwinnett | ECHL | 34 | 18 | 13 | 3 | 2052 | 129 | 1 | 3.77 | 1 | 0 | 1 | 73 | 5 | 0 | 4.11 |
| 2007-08 | Grand Rapids | AHL | 1 | 0 | 0 | 0 | 20 | 1 | 0 | 3.00 | | | | | | | |
| | Gwinnett | ECHL | 30 | 15 | 12 | 3 | 1786 | 94 | 0 | 3.16 | 1 | 1 | 0 | 60 | 1 | 0 | 1.00 |
| 2008-09 | Chicago Wolves | AHL | 14 | 5 | 8 | 0 | 699 | 34 | 0 | 2.92 | | | | | | | |
| | Utah Grizzlies | ECHL | 2 | 0 | 0 | 2 | 130 | 8 | 0 | 3.69 | | | | | | | |
| | Gwinnett | ECHL | 8 | 2 | 4 | 1 | 441 | 28 | 0 | 3.81 | | | | | | | |

OHL Second All-Star Team (2006)

## VALIQUETTE, Steve
(val-ih-KEHT, STEEV) **NYR**

Goaltender. Catches left. 6'6", 210 lbs. Born, Etobicoke, Ont., August 20, 1977.
(Los Angeles' 8th choice, 190th overall, in 1996 Entry Draft).

| | | | Regular Season | | | | | | | | Playoffs | | | | | | |
|---|---|---|---|---|---|---|---|---|---|---|---|---|---|---|---|---|---|
| Season | Club | League | GP | W | L | O/T | Mins | GA | SO | Avg | GP | W | L | Mins | GA | SO | Avg |
| 1993-94 | Burlington | OPJHL | 30 | .... | .... | .... | 1663 | 112 | 1 | 4.04 | | | | | | | |
| 1994-95 | Rayside-Balfour | NOJHA | 2 | 0 | 2 | 0 | 89 | 12 | 0 | 8.09 | | | | | | | |
| | Smiths Falls Bears | CJHL | 21 | 10 | 8 | 3 | 1275 | 75 | 0 | 3.53 | | | | | | | |
| | Sudbury Wolves | OHL | 4 | 2 | 0 | 0 | 138 | 6 | 0 | 2.61 | | | | | | | |
| 1995-96 | Sudbury Wolves | OHL | 39 | 13 | 16 | 2 | 1887 | 123 | 0 | 3.91 | | | | | | | |
| 1996-97 | Sudbury Wolves | OHL | *61 | 21 | 29 | 7 | 3311 | 232 | 1 | 4.20 | | | | | | | |
| | Dayton Bombers | ECHL | 3 | 1 | 0 | 0 | 89 | 6 | 0 | 4.03 | 2 | 1 | 1 | 118 | 5 | 0 | 2.54 |
| 1997-98 | Sudbury Wolves | OHL | 14 | 5 | 7 | 1 | 807 | 50 | 0 | 3.72 | | | | | | | |
| | Erie Otters | OHL | 28 | 16 | 7 | 3 | 1525 | 65 | 3 | 2.56 | 7 | 3 | 4 | 467 | 15 | 1 | 1.93 |
| 1998-99 | Lowell | AHL | 1 | 0 | 1 | 0 | 59 | 3 | 0 | 3.05 | | | | | | | |
| | Hampton Roads | ECHL | 31 | 18 | 7 | 3 | 1713 | 84 | 1 | 2.94 | 2 | 0 | 1 | 60 | 7 | 0 | 7.00 |
| **99-2000** | **NY Islanders** | **NHL** | **6** | **2** | **0** | **0** | **193** | **6** | **0** | **1.87** | | | | | | | |
| | Lowell | AHL | 14 | 8 | 5 | 0 | 727 | 36 | 0 | 2.97 | | | | | | | |
| | Providence Bruins | AHL | 1 | 1 | 0 | 0 | 60 | 3 | 0 | 3.00 | | | | | | | |
| | Trenton Titans | ECHL | 12 | 5 | 6 | 1 | 692 | 36 | 1 | 3.12 | | | | | | | |
| 2000-01 | Springfield Falcons | AHL | 20 | 7 | 10 | 1 | 1066 | 54 | 0 | 3.04 | | | | | | | |
| 2001-02 | Bridgeport | AHL | 20 | 10 | 5 | 1 | 1071 | 45 | 2 | 2.52 | 1 | 0 | 0 | 18 | 1 | 0 | 3.30 |
| 2002-03 | Bridgeport | AHL | 34 | 15 | 14 | 3 | 1962 | 86 | 2 | 2.63 | 4 | 3 | 1 | 253 | 9 | 0 | 2.13 |
| **2003-04** | **Edmonton** | **NHL** | **1** | **0** | **0** | **0** | **14** | **2** | **0** | **8.57** | | | | | | | |
| | Toronto | AHL | 35 | 14 | 14 | 5 | 2064 | 89 | 2 | 2.59 | | | | | | | |
| | **NY Rangers** | **NHL** | **2** | **1** | **1** | **0** | **120** | **6** | **0** | **3.00** | | | | | | | |
| | Hartford Wolf Pack | AHL | 7 | 2 | 4 | 1 | 400 | 15 | 1 | 2.25 | 1 | 0 | 0 | 11 | 0 | 0 | 0.00 |
| 2004-05 | Hartford Wolf Pack | AHL | 35 | 19 | 11 | 1 | 1900 | 56 | 7 | *1.77 | 2 | 1 | 1 | 118 | 4 | 0 | 2.03 |
| 2005-06 | Yaroslavl | Russia | 45 | .... | .... | .... | 2734 | 89 | 4 | 1.95 | 8 | .... | .... | 458 | 23 | 0 | 3.01 |
| **2006-07** | **NY Rangers** | **NHL** | **3** | **1** | **2** | **0** | **115** | **6** | **0** | **3.13** | | | | | | | |
| | Hartford Wolf Pack | AHL | 30 | 17 | 12 | 0 | 1694 | 66 | 2 | 2.34 | | | | | | | |
| **2007-08** | **NY Rangers** | **NHL** | **13** | **5** | **3** | **3** | **686** | **25** | **2** | **2.19** | | | | | | | |
| **2008-09** | **NY Rangers** | **NHL** | **15** | **5** | **5** | **2** | **823** | **39** | **1** | **2.84** | **2** | **0** | **0** | **40** | **0** | **0** | **0.00** |
| | **NHL Totals** | | **40** | **14** | **11** | **5** | **1951** | **84** | **3** | **2.58** | **2** | **0** | **0** | **40** | **0** | **0** | **0.00** |

Harry "Hap" Holmes Memorial Trophy (AHL - fewest goals against) (2005) (shared with Jason LaBarbera)

Signed as a free agent by **NY Islanders**, August 18, 1998. Signed as a free agent by **Edmonton**, July 20, 2003. Claimed by **Florida** from **Edmonton** in Waiver Draft, October 3, 2003. Claimed on waivers by **Edmonton** from **Florida**, October 9, 2003. Traded to **NY Rangers** by **Edmonton** with Dwight Helminen and Edmonton's 2nd round compensatory choice (Dane Byers) in 2004 Entry Draft for Petr Nedved and Jussi Markkanen, March 3, 2004. Signed as a free agent by **Yaroslavl** (Russia), April 26, 2005. Signed as a free agent by **NY Rangers**, July 1, 2006.

## VARLAMOV, Semyon
(vahr-LA-mawv, sehm-YAWN) **WSH.**

Goaltender. Catches left. 6'1", 201 lbs. Born, Kuybyshev, USSR, April 27, 1988.
(Washington's 2nd choice, 23rd overall, in 2006 Entry Draft).

| | | | Regular Season | | | | | | | | Playoffs | | | | | | |
|---|---|---|---|---|---|---|---|---|---|---|---|---|---|---|---|---|---|
| Season | Club | League | GP | W | L | O/T | Mins | GA | SO | Avg | GP | W | L | Mins | GA | SO | Avg |
| 2004-05 | Yaroslavl 2 | Russia-3 | 8 | .... | .... | .... | 369 | 15 | 1 | 2.43 | | | | | | | |
| 2005-06 | Yaroslavl 2 | Russia-3 | 33 | .... | .... | .... | 1782 | 60 | 8 | 2.02 | | | | | | | |
| 2006-07 | Yaroslavl 2 | Russia-3 | 2 | .... | .... | .... | 120 | 3 | 0 | 1.50 | | | | | | | |
| | Yaroslavl | Russia | 33 | .... | .... | .... | 1936 | 70 | 3 | 2.17 | 6 | .... | .... | 368 | 18 | 0 | 2.94 |
| 2007-08 | Yaroslavl | Russia | 44 | .... | .... | .... | 2592 | 106 | 3 | 2.45 | *16 | .... | .... | *924 | 25 | *5 | 1.62 |
| **2008-09** | **Washington** | **NHL** | **6** | **4** | **0** | **1** | **329** | **13** | **0** | **2.37** | **13** | **7** | **6** | **759** | **32** | ***2** | **2.53** |
| | Hershey Bears | AHL | 27 | 19 | 7 | 1 | 1551 | 62 | 2 | 2.40 | | | | | | | |
| | **NHL Totals** | | **6** | **4** | **0** | **1** | **329** | **13** | **0** | **2.37** | **13** | **7** | **6** | **759** | **32** | **2** | **2.53** |

## VOKOUN, Tomas
(voh-KOON, TAW-mas) **FLA.**

Goaltender. Catches right. 6', 195 lbs. Born, Karlovy Vary, Czech., July 2, 1976.
(Montreal's 11th choice, 226th overall, in 1994 Entry Draft).

| | | | Regular Season | | | | | | | | Playoffs | | | | | | |
|---|---|---|---|---|---|---|---|---|---|---|---|---|---|---|---|---|---|
| Season | Club | League | GP | W | L | O/T | Mins | GA | SO | Avg | GP | W | L | Mins | GA | SO | Avg |
| 1993-94 | HC Kladno | CzRep | 1 | 0 | 0 | 0 | 20 | 2 | 0 | 6.01 | | | | | | | |
| 1994-95 | HC Kladno | CzRep | 26 | .... | .... | .... | 1368 | 70 | .... | 3.07 | 5 | .... | .... | 240 | 19 | .... | 4.75 |
| 1995-96 | Wheeling | ECHL | 35 | 20 | 10 | 2 | 1912 | 117 | 0 | 3.67 | 7 | 4 | 3 | 436 | 19 | 0 | 2.61 |
| | Fredericton | AHL | | | | | | | | | 1 | 0 | 1 | 59 | 4 | 0 | 4.09 |
| **1996-97** | **Montreal** | **NHL** | **1** | **0** | **0** | **0** | **20** | **4** | **0** | **12.00** | | | | | | | |
| | Fredericton | AHL | 47 | 12 | 26 | 7 | 2645 | 154 | 2 | 3.49 | | | | | | | |
| 1997-98 | Fredericton | AHL | 31 | 13 | 13 | 2 | 1735 | 90 | 0 | 3.11 | | | | | | | |
| **1998-99** | **Nashville** | **NHL** | **37** | **12** | **18** | **4** | **1954** | **96** | **1** | **2.95** | | | | | | | |
| | Milwaukee | IHL | 9 | 3 | 2 | 4 | 539 | 22 | 1 | 2.45 | 2 | 0 | 2 | 149 | 8 | 0 | 3.22 |
| **99-2000** | **Nashville** | **NHL** | **33** | **9** | **20** | **1** | **1879** | **87** | **1** | **2.78** | | | | | | | |
| | Milwaukee | IHL | 7 | 5 | 2 | 0 | 364 | 17 | 0 | 2.80 | | | | | | | |
| **2000-01** | **Nashville** | **NHL** | **37** | **13** | **17** | **5** | **2088** | **85** | **2** | **2.44** | | | | | | | |
| **2001-02** | **Nashville** | **NHL** | **29** | **5** | **14** | **4** | **1471** | **66** | **2** | **2.69** | | | | | | | |
| **2002-03** | **Nashville** | **NHL** | **69** | **25** | **31** | **11** | **3974** | **146** | **3** | **2.20** | | | | | | | |
| **2003-04** | **Nashville** | **NHL** | **73** | **34** | **29** | **10** | **4221** | **178** | **3** | **2.53** | **6** | **2** | **4** | **356** | **12** | **1** | **2.02** |
| 2004-05 | Znojmo | CzRep | 27 | .... | .... | .... | 1599 | 69 | 3 | 2.59 | | | | | | | |
| | HIFK Helsinki | Finland | 19 | 11 | 4 | 4 | 1149 | 35 | 2 | 1.83 | 4 | 0 | 3 | 205 | 12 | 0 | 3.51 |
| **2005-06** | **Nashville** | **NHL** | **61** | **36** | **18** | **7** | **3601** | **160** | **4** | **2.67** | | | | | | | |
| | Czech Republic | Olympics | 7 | 3 | 4 | 0 | 342 | 14 | 1 | 2.46 | | | | | | | |
| **2006-07** | **Nashville** | **NHL** | **44** | **27** | **12** | **4** | **2601** | **104** | **5** | **2.40** | **5** | **1** | **4** | **324** | **16** | **0** | **2.96** |
| **2007-08** | **Florida** | **NHL** | **69** | **30** | **29** | **8** | **4031** | **180** | **4** | **2.68** | | | | | | | |
| **2008-09** | **Florida** | **NHL** | **59** | **26** | **23** | **6** | **3324** | **138** | **6** | **2.49** | | | | | | | |
| | **NHL Totals** | | **512** | **217** | **211** | **60** | **29164** | **1244** | **31** | **2.56** | **11** | **3** | **8** | **680** | **28** | **1** | **2.47** |

Played in NHL All-Star Game (2004, 2008)

Claimed by **Nashville** from **Montreal** in Expansion Draft, June 26, 1998. Signed as a free agent by **Znojmo** (CzRep), September 6, 2004. Signed as a free agent by **HIFK Helsinki** (Finland), December 20, 2004. Traded to **Florida** by **Nashville** for Detroit's 2nd round choice (previously acquired, Nashville selected Nick Spaling) in 2007 Entry Draft and Florida's 1st (later traded to NY Islanders - NY Islanders selected Joshua Bailey) and 2nd (later traded to NY Islanders - NY Islanders selected Aaron Ness) round choices in 2008 Entry Draft, June 22, 2007.

## WARD, Cam
(WOHRD, KAM) **CAR.**

Goaltender. Catches left. 6'1", 200 lbs. Born, Saskatoon, Sask., February 29, 1984.
(Carolina's 1st choice, 25th overall, in 2002 Entry Draft).

| | | | Regular Season | | | | | | | | Playoffs | | | | | | |
|---|---|---|---|---|---|---|---|---|---|---|---|---|---|---|---|---|---|
| Season | Club | League | GP | W | L | O/T | Mins | GA | SO | Avg | GP | W | L | Mins | GA | SO | Avg |
| 1998-99 | Sherwood Park | ABHL | 24 | 13 | 7 | 4 | 1403 | 85 | 0 | 3.64 | | | | | | | |
| 99-2000 | Sherwood Park | AMHL | 20 | 9 | 5 | 1 | 1194 | 71 | 0 | 3.57 | 7 | 4 | 3 | 262 | 22 | 0 | 3.57 |
| 2000-01 | Sherwood Park | AMHL | 25 | 14 | 6 | 3 | 1449 | 70 | 0 | 2.90 | | | | | | | |
| | Red Deer Rebels | WHL | 1 | 1 | 0 | 0 | 60 | 0 | 1 | 0.00 | | | | | | | |
| 2001-02 | Red Deer Rebels | WHL | 46 | 30 | 11 | 4 | 2694 | 102 | 1 | *2.27 | *23 | 14 | 9 | *1502 | 53 | *2 | 2.12 |
| 2002-03 | Red Deer Rebels | WHL | 57 | *40 | 13 | 3 | 3368 | 118 | 5 | 2.10 | *23 | 14 | 9 | *1407 | 49 | 3 | 2.09 |
| 2003-04 | Red Deer Rebels | WHL | 56 | 31 | 16 | 8 | 3338 | 114 | 4 | 2.05 | 19 | 10 | 9 | 1200 | 37 | 3 | 1.85 |
| 2004-05 | Lowell | AHL | 50 | 27 | 17 | 3 | 2829 | 94 | 6 | 1.99 | 11 | 5 | 6 | 664 | 28 | 2 | 2.53 |
| **2005-06 ◆** | **Carolina** | **NHL** | **28** | **14** | **8** | **2** | **1484** | **91** | **0** | **3.68** | ***23** | ***15** | **8** | ***1320** | **47** | **2** | **2.14** |
| | Lowell | AHL | 2 | 0 | 2 | 0 | 118 | 5 | 0 | 2.54 | | | | | | | |
| **2006-07** | **Carolina** | **NHL** | **60** | **30** | **21** | **6** | **3422** | **167** | **2** | **2.93** | | | | | | | |
| **2007-08** | **Carolina** | **NHL** | **69** | **37** | **25** | **5** | **3930** | **180** | **4** | **2.75** | | | | | | | |
| **2008-09** | **Carolina** | **NHL** | **68** | **39** | **23** | **5** | **3928** | **160** | **6** | **2.44** | **18** | **8** | **10** | **1101** | **49** | ***2** | **2.67** |
| | **NHL Totals** | | **225** | **120** | **77** | **18** | **12764** | **598** | **12** | **2.81** | **41** | **23** | **18** | **2421** | **96** | **4** | **2.38** |

WHL East First All-Star Team (2002, 2004) • Canadian Major Junior Second All-Star Team (2002) • WHL East Second All-Star Team (2003) • WHL Goaltender of the Year (2002, 2004) • WHL Player of the Year (2004) • Canadian Major Junior First All-Star Team (2004) • Canadian Major Junior Goaltender of the Year (2004) • AHL All-Rookie Team (2005) • Conn Smythe Trophy (2006)

## WEEKES, Kevin
(WEEKS, KEH-vihn)

Goaltender. Catches left. 6'2", 215 lbs. Born, Toronto, Ont., April 4, 1975.
(Florida's 2nd choice, 41st overall, in 1993 Entry Draft).

| | | | Regular Season | | | | | | | | Playoffs | | | | | | |
|---|---|---|---|---|---|---|---|---|---|---|---|---|---|---|---|---|---|
| Season | Club | League | GP | W | L | O/T | Mins | GA | SO | Avg | GP | W | L | Mins | GA | SO | Avg |
| 1990-91 | Tor. Red Wings | MTHL | STATISTICS NOT AVAILABLE | | | | | | | | | | | | | | |
| | St. Mike's B's | MTJHL | 1 | 0 | 0 | 0 | 41 | 1 | 0 | 1.46 | | | | | | | |
| 1991-92 | Tor. Red Wings | MTHL | 35 | .... | .... | .... | 1575 | 68 | 4 | 1.94 | | | | | | | |
| | St. Mike's B's | MTJHL | 2 | 0 | 1 | 1 | 127 | 11 | 0 | 5.20 | 4 | 1 | 2 | 214 | 15 | 1 | 4.21 |
| 1992-93 | Owen Sound | OHL | 29 | 9 | 12 | 5 | 1645 | 143 | 0 | 5.22 | 1 | 0 | 0 | 26 | 5 | 0 | 11.50 |
| 1993-94 | Owen Sound | OHL | 34 | 13 | 19 | 1 | 1974 | 158 | 0 | 4.80 | | | | | | | |
| 1994-95 | Ottawa 67's | OHL | 41 | 13 | 23 | 4 | 2266 | 153 | 1 | 4.05 | | | | | | | |
| 1995-96 | Carolina Panthers | AHL | 60 | 24 | 25 | 8 | 3404 | 229 | 2 | 4.04 | | | | | | | |
| 1996-97 | Carolina Monarchs | AHL | 51 | 17 | 28 | 4 | 2899 | 172 | 1 | 3.56 | | | | | | | |
| **1997-98** | **Florida** | **NHL** | **11** | **0** | **5** | **1** | **485** | **32** | **0** | **3.96** | | | | | | | |
| | Fort Wayne | IHL | 12 | 9 | 2 | 1 | 719 | 34 | 1 | 2.84 | | | | | | | |
| 1998-99 | Detroit Vipers | IHL | 33 | 19 | 5 | 7 | 1857 | 64 | *4 | *2.07 | | | | | | | |
| | **Vancouver** | **NHL** | **11** | **0** | **8** | **1** | **532** | **34** | **0** | **3.83** | | | | | | | |
| **99-2000** | **Vancouver** | **NHL** | **20** | **6** | **7** | **4** | **987** | **47** | **1** | **2.86** | | | | | | | |
| | **NY Islanders** | **NHL** | **36** | **10** | **20** | **4** | **2026** | **115** | **1** | **3.41** | | | | | | | |
| **2000-01** | **Tampa Bay** | **NHL** | **61** | **20** | **33** | **3** | **3378** | **177** | **4** | **3.14** | | | | | | | |
| **2001-02** | **Tampa Bay** | **NHL** | **19** | **3** | **9** | **0** | **830** | **40** | **2** | **2.89** | | | | | | | |
| | **Carolina** | **NHL** | **2** | **2** | **0** | **0** | **120** | **3** | **0** | **1.50** | **8** | **3** | **2** | **408** | **11** | **2** | **1.62** |
| **2002-03** | **Carolina** | **NHL** | **51** | **14** | **24** | **9** | **2965** | **126** | **5** | **2.55** | | | | | | | |
| **2003-04** | **Carolina** | **NHL** | **66** | **23** | **30** | **11** | **3765** | **146** | **6** | **2.33** | | | | | | | |
| 2004-05 | | | DID NOT PLAY | | | | | | | | | | | | | | |
| **2005-06** | **NY Rangers** | **NHL** | **32** | **14** | **14** | **3** | **1850** | **91** | **0** | **2.95** | **1** | **0** | **1** | **60** | **4** | **0** | **4.00** |
| **2006-07** | **NY Rangers** | **NHL** | **14** | **4** | **6** | **2** | **761** | **43** | **0** | **3.39** | | | | | | | |
| **2007-08** | **New Jersey** | **NHL** | **9** | **2** | **2** | **1** | **343** | **17** | **0** | **2.97** | | | | | | | |
| **2008-09** | **New Jersey** | **NHL** | **16** | **7** | **5** | **0** | **795** | **32** | **0** | **2.42** | | | | | | | |
| | **NHL Totals** | | **348** | **105** | **163** | **39** | **18837** | **903** | **19** | **2.88** | **9** | **3** | **3** | **468** | **15** | **2** | **1.92** |

James Norris Memorial Trophy (IHL – fewest goals against) (1999) (shared with Andrei Trefilov)

Traded to **Vancouver** by **Florida** with Ed Jovanovski, Dave Gagner, Mike Brown and Florida's 1st round choice (Nathan Smith) in 2000 Entry Draft for Pavel Bure, Bret Hedican, Brad Ference and Vancouver's 3rd round choice (Robert Fried) in 2000 Entry Draft, January 17, 1999. Traded to **NY Islanders** by **Vancouver** with Dave Scatchard and Bill Muckalt for Felix Potvin, NY Islanders' 2nd round compensatory choice (later traded to New Jersey – New Jersey selected Teemu Laine) in 2000 Entry Draft and NY Islanders' 3rd round choice (Thatcher Bell) in 2000 Entry Draft, December 19, 1999. Traded to **Tampa Bay** by **NY Islanders** with the rights to Kristian Kudroc and NY Islanders' 2nd round choice (later traded to Phoenix – Phoenix selected Matthew Spiller) in 2001 Entry Draft for Tampa Bay's 1st round choice (Raffi Torres) in 2000 Entry Draft, Calgary's 4th round choice (previously acquired, NY Islanders selected Vladimir Gorbunov) in 2000 Entry Draft and NY Islanders' 7th round choice (previously acquired, NY Islanders selected Ryan Caldwell) in 2000 Entry Draft, June 24, 2000. Traded to **Carolina** by **Tampa Bay** for Shane Willis and Chris Dingman, March 5, 2002. Signed as a free agent by **NY Rangers**, August 26, 2004. Signed as a free agent by **New Jersey**, July 5, 2007.

## WEIMAN, Tyler
(WIGH-muhn, TIGH-luhr) **COL.**

Goaltender. Catches left. 5'11", 180 lbs. Born, Saskatoon, Sask., June 5, 1984.
(Colorado's 6th choice, 164th overall, in 2002 Entry Draft).

| | | | Regular Season | | | | | | | | Playoffs | | | | | | |
|---|---|---|---|---|---|---|---|---|---|---|---|---|---|---|---|---|---|
| Season | Club | League | GP | W | L | O/T | Mins | GA | SO | Avg | GP | W | L | Mins | GA | SO | Avg |
| 99-2000 | Ft. Saskatchewan | AMBHL | 21 | 15 | 4 | 2 | 1239 | 60 | 0 | 2.91 | | | | | | | |
| 2000-01 | Tri-City Americans | WHL | 44 | 10 | 25 | 4 | 2464 | 155 | 0 | 3.77 | | | | | | | |
| 2001-02 | Tri-City Americans | WHL | 47 | 18 | 17 | 5 | 2492 | 149 | 2 | 3.59 | 5 | 1 | 4 | 300 | 14 | 0 | 2.80 |
| 2002-03 | Tri-City Americans | WHL | 55 | 16 | 34 | 2 | 3129 | 207 | 1 | 3.97 | | | | | | | |
| 2003-04 | Tri-City Americans | WHL | 54 | 23 | 21 | 7 | 3023 | 134 | 1 | 2.66 | 5 | 1 | 2 | 234 | 11 | 0 | 2.82 |
| 2004-05 | Colorado Eagles | CHL | 44 | *33 | 6 | 5 | 2630 | 79 | *8 | *1.80 | *13 | *8 | 4 | *744 | 32 | 1 | 2.58 |
| 2005-06 | Lowell | AHL | 14 | 6 | 6 | 1 | 844 | 36 | 0 | 2.56 | | | | | | | |
| | San Diego Gulls | ECHL | 32 | 14 | 12 | 3 | 1797 | 84 | 1 | 2.81 | 4 | 0 | 4 | 251 | 15 | 0 | 3.59 |
| 2006-07 | Albany River Rats | AHL | 54 | 27 | 22 | 3 | 3047 | 152 | 2 | 2.99 | 5 | 1 | 4 | 294 | 17 | 0 | 3.47 |
| **2007-08** | **Colorado** | **NHL** | **1** | **0** | **0** | **0** | **16** | **0** | **0** | **0.00** | | | | | | | |
| | Lake Erie Monsters | AHL | 31 | 9 | 19 | 1 | 1769 | 98 | 2 | 3.32 | | | | | | | |
| 2008-09 | Lake Erie Monsters | AHL | 44 | 21 | 20 | 2 | 2559 | 105 | *8 | 2.46 | | | | | | | |
| | **NHL Totals** | | **1** | **0** | **0** | **0** | **16** | **0** | **0** | **0.00** | | | | | | | |

## WESLOSKY, Jase
(wehs-LAWZ-kee, JAYS) **NYI**

Goaltender. Catches left. 6'2", 170 lbs. Born, St. Albert, Alta., August 14, 1988.
(NY Islanders' 5th choice, 108th overall, in 2006 Entry Draft).

| | | | Regular Season | | | | | | | | Playoffs | | | | | | |
|---|---|---|---|---|---|---|---|---|---|---|---|---|---|---|---|---|---|
| Season | Club | League | GP | W | L | O/T | Mins | GA | SO | Avg | GP | W | L | Mins | GA | SO | Avg |
| 2004-05 | St. Albert Blues | EMHA | .... | 13 | 3 | 2 | 1043 | 38 | .... | 2.19 | | | | | | | |
| 2005-06 | Sherwood Park | AJHL | 58 | .... | .... | .... | 2123 | 110 | 2 | 3.11 | | | | | | | |
| 2006-07 | St. Cloud State | WCHA | 6 | 5 | 1 | 0 | 359 | 16 | 1 | 2.67 | | | | | | | |
| 2007-08 | St. Cloud State | WCHA | 33 | 16 | 13 | 2 | 1901 | 67 | 3 | 2.11 | | | | | | | |
| 2008-09 | St. Cloud State | WCHA | 33 | 16 | 13 | 2 | 1889 | 85 | 2 | 2.70 | | | | | | | |

## WIIKMAN, Miika
(VEEK-man, MEE-kah) **NYR**

Goaltender. Catches left. 5'11", 187 lbs. Born, Toreboda, Sweden, October 17, 1984.

| | | | Regular Season | | | | | | | | Playoffs | | | | | | |
|---|---|---|---|---|---|---|---|---|---|---|---|---|---|---|---|---|---|
| Season | Club | League | GP | W | L | O/T | Mins | GA | SO | Avg | GP | W | L | Mins | GA | SO | Avg |
| 99-2000 | HV 71 U18 | Swe-U18 | 4 | .... | .... | .... | 240 | 23 | 0 | 5.75 | | | | | | | |
| | HV 71 Jr. | Swe-Jr. | 1 | .... | .... | .... | 20 | 0 | 0 | 0.00 | | | | | | | |
| 2000-01 | HV 71 U18 | Swe-U18 | 13 | .... | .... | .... | 740 | 45 | 1 | 3.65 | 2 | .... | .... | 120 | 12 | 0 | 6.00 |
| | HV 71 Jr. | Swe-Jr. | 3 | .... | .... | .... | 100 | 6 | 0 | 3.60 | | | | | | | |
| 2001-02 | HV 71 U18 | Swe-U18 | 7 | .... | .... | .... | 416 | 33 | 0 | 4.76 | | | | | | | |
| | HV 71 Jr. | Swe-Jr. | 9 | .... | .... | .... | 501 | 28 | 0 | 3.36 | | | | | | | |

| | | | | | | | | | | | | | | | | | |
|---|---|---|---|---|---|---|---|---|---|---|---|---|---|---|---|---|---|
| 2002-03 | HV 71 Jr. | Swe-Jr. | 27 | .... | .... | .... | 1569 | 72 | 1 | 2.75 | 7 | .... | .... | 423 | 28 | 0 | 3.97 |
| 2003-04 | Suomi U20 | Finland-2 | 4 | .... | .... | .... | 240 | 9 | 1 | 2.25 | .... | .... | .... | .... | .... | .... | .... |
| | Hermes Kokkola | Finland-2 | 31 | .... | .... | .... | 1845 | 67 | 3 | 2.18 | 6 | .... | .... | 375 | 15 | 0 | 2.40 |
| 2004-05 | HPK Hameenlinna | Finland | 23 | 9 | 5 | 9 | 1361 | 54 | 2 | 2.38 | 2 | 1 | 1 | 118 | 4 | 0 | 2.03 |
| 2005-06 | HPK Hameenlinna | Finland | 34 | 21 | 5 | 7 | 1949 | 68 | 3 | 2.09 | 11 | 8 | 2 | 607 | 20 | 3 | 1.98 |
| 2006-07 | HPK Hameenlinna | Finland | 18 | 8 | 6 | 4 | 1066 | 46 | 0 | 2.59 | .... | .... | .... | .... | .... | .... | .... |
| 2007-08 | Hartford Wolf Pack | AHL | 34 | 21 | 8 | 3 | 1907 | 73 | 2 | 2.30 | 1 | 0 | 1 | 59 | 3 | 0 | 3.07 |
| | Charlotte Checkers | ECHL | 4 | 1 | 1 | 2 | 254 | 10 | 0 | 2.36 | .... | .... | .... | .... | .... | .... | .... |
| 2008-09 | Hartford Wolf Pack | AHL | 43 | 21 | 18 | 4 | 2463 | 111 | 2 | 2.70 | .... | .... | .... | .... | .... | .... | .... |

Signed as a free agent by **NY Rangers**, April 24, 2008.

## YORK, Allen (YOHRK, AL-ihn) CBJ

Goaltender. Catches left. 6'4", 185 lbs. Born, Wetaskiwin, Alta., June 17, 1989.
(Columbus' 6th choice, 158th overall, in 2007 Entry Draft).

| | | | Regular Season | | | | | | | | Playoffs | | | | | | |
|---|---|---|---|---|---|---|---|---|---|---|---|---|---|---|---|---|---|
| **Season** | **Club** | **League** | **GP** | **W** | **L** | **O/T** | **Mins** | **GA** | **SO** | **Avg** | **GP** | **W** | **L** | **Mins** | **GA** | **SO** | **Avg** |
| 2006-07 | Camrose Kodiaks | AJHL | 32 | 23 | 4 | 0 | 1661 | 60 | 2 | 2.17 | 22 | 16 | 6 | 1391 | 46 | 4 | 1.98 |
| 2007-08 | Camrose Kodiaks | AJHL | .... | 24 | 5 | 3 | 2005 | 75 | 3 | 2.24 | .... | .... | .... | .... | .... | .... | .... |
| 2008-09 | RPI Engineers | ECAC | 16 | 5 | 10 | 0 | 913 | 46 | 1 | 3.02 | .... | .... | .... | .... | .... | .... | .... |

## ZABA, Matt (ZA-buh, MAT) NYR

Goaltender. Catches left. 6'1", 185 lbs. Born, Yorkton, Sask., July 14, 1983.
(Los Angeles' 8th choice, 231st overall, in 2003 Entry Draft).

| | | | Regular Season | | | | | | | | Playoffs | | | | | | |
|---|---|---|---|---|---|---|---|---|---|---|---|---|---|---|---|---|---|
| **Season** | **Club** | **League** | **GP** | **W** | **L** | **O/T** | **Mins** | **GA** | **SO** | **Avg** | **GP** | **W** | **L** | **Mins** | **GA** | **SO** | **Avg** |
| 2000-01 | Yorkton Mallers | SMHL | 26 | 13 | 10 | 3 | 1480 | 79 | 0 | 3.20 | .... | .... | .... | .... | .... | .... | .... |
| 2001-02 | Penticton Panthers | BCHL | 33 | .... | .... | .... | 1980 | 128 | 0 | 3.69 | .... | .... | .... | .... | .... | .... | .... |
| 2002-03 | Vernon Vipers | BCHL | 44 | 34 | 9 | 0 | 2012 | 96 | 2 | 2.21 | 17 | 14 | 3 | 1006 | 25 | 3 | 1.49 |
| 2003-04 | Colorado College | WCHA | 23 | 10 | 10 | 2 | 1323 | 50 | 1 | 2.27 | .... | .... | .... | .... | .... | .... | .... |
| 2004-05 | Colorado College | WCHA | 18 | 10 | 5 | 2 | 1050 | 43 | 2 | 2.46 | .... | .... | .... | .... | .... | .... | .... |
| 2005-06 | Colorado College | WCHA | 36 | 20 | 14 | 2 | 2068 | 87 | 4 | 2.52 | .... | .... | .... | .... | .... | .... | .... |
| 2006-07 | Colorado College | WCHA | 33 | 15 | 13 | 4 | 1908 | 76 | 3 | 2.39 | .... | .... | .... | .... | .... | .... | .... |
| 2007-08 | Charlotte Checkers | ECHL | 9 | 3 | 4 | 1 | 496 | 30 | 0 | 3.63 | .... | .... | .... | .... | .... | .... | .... |
| | Idaho Steelheads | ECHL | 19 | 12 | 4 | 1 | 1070 | 39 | 3 | 2.19 | 2 | 0 | 1 | 129 | 6 | 0 | 2.78 |
| 2008-09 | Hartford Wolf Pack | AHL | 41 | 25 | 10 | 0 | 2262 | 88 | 2 | 2.33 | 6 | 2 | 4 | 378 | 20 | 1 | 3.17 |

WCHA All-Rookie Team (2004)

Signed as a free agent by **NY Rangers** , August 20, 2007.

## ZADOR, Michael (ZAY-dohr, MIGH-kuhl) T.B.

Goaltender. Catches left. 6'2", 172 lbs. Born, Toronto, Ont., May 8, 1991.
(Tampa Bay's 5th choice, 148th overall, in 2009 Entry Draft).

| | | | Regular Season | | | | | | | | Playoffs | | | | | | |
|---|---|---|---|---|---|---|---|---|---|---|---|---|---|---|---|---|---|
| **Season** | **Club** | **League** | **GP** | **W** | **L** | **O/T** | **Mins** | **GA** | **SO** | **Avg** | **GP** | **W** | **L** | **Mins** | **GA** | **SO** | **Avg** |
| 2007-08 | Petrolia Jets | OJHL-B | 17 | 0 | 16 | 0 | 917 | 122 | 0 | 7.98 | .... | .... | .... | .... | .... | .... | .... |
| | London Knights | OHL | 1 | 0 | 1 | 0 | 20 | 3 | 0 | 9.00 | .... | .... | .... | .... | .... | .... | .... |
| 2008-09 | St. Mary's Lincolns | OJHL-B | 5 | 4 | 1 | 0 | 300 | 14 | 0 | 2.80 | .... | .... | .... | .... | .... | .... | .... |
| | London Knights | OHL | 10 | 6 | 1 | 0 | 462 | 28 | 0 | 3.64 | .... | .... | .... | .... | .... | .... | .... |
| | Oshawa Generals | OHL | 18 | 5 | 12 | 1 | 1002 | 61 | 0 | 3.65 | .... | .... | .... | .... | .... | .... | .... |

## ZATKOFF, Jeff (ZAT-kawf, JEHF) L.A.

Goaltender. Catches left. 6'2", 170 lbs. Born, Detroit, MI, June 9, 1987.
(Los Angeles' 4th choice, 74th overall, in 2006 Entry Draft).

| | | | Regular Season | | | | | | | | Playoffs | | | | | | |
|---|---|---|---|---|---|---|---|---|---|---|---|---|---|---|---|---|---|
| **Season** | **Club** | **League** | **GP** | **W** | **L** | **O/T** | **Mins** | **GA** | **SO** | **Avg** | **GP** | **W** | **L** | **Mins** | **GA** | **SO** | **Avg** |
| 2004-05 | Sioux City | USHL | 24 | 13 | 6 | 3 | 1271 | 54 | 1 | 2.55 | 2 | 0 | 0 | 68 | 10 | 0 | 8.88 |
| 2005-06 | Miami U. | CCHA | 20 | 14 | 5 | 1 | 1217 | 41 | 3 | 2.02 | .... | .... | .... | .... | .... | .... | .... |
| 2006-07 | Miami U. | CCHA | 26 | 14 | 8 | 3 | 1542 | 58 | 1 | 2.26 | .... | .... | .... | .... | .... | .... | .... |
| 2007-08 | Miami U. | CCHA | 36 | 27 | 8 | 1 | 2161 | 62 | 3 | *1.72 | .... | .... | .... | .... | .... | .... | .... |
| 2008-09 | Manchester | AHL | 3 | 1 | 2 | 0 | 182 | 7 | 0 | 2.31 | .... | .... | .... | .... | .... | .... | .... |
| | Ontario Reign | ECHL | 37 | 17 | 15 | 3 | 2164 | 107 | 1 | 2.97 | 7 | 3 | 3 | 418 | 26 | 0 | 3.73 |

CCHA Second All-Star Team (2008)

# Late Additions to Player Register

## FREE AGENT SIGNINGS

### BANNISTER, DREW (BAN-ihs-tuhr, DROO) OTT

Defense. Shoots right. 6'2", 198 lbs. Born, Belleville, Ontario, April 9, 1974.

| | | | Regular Season | | | | | Playoffs | | | | |
|---|---|---|---|---|---|---|---|---|---|---|---|---|
| Season | Club | League | GP | G | A | Pts | PIM | GP | G | A | Pts | PIM |
| 1989-90 | Sudbury Legion | NOHA | 26 | 13 | 14 | 27 | 98 | .... | .... | .... | .... | .... |
| 1990-91 | Sault Ste. Marie | OHL | 41 | 2 | 8 | 10 | 51 | 4 | 0 | 0 | 0 | 0 |
| 1991-92 | Sault Ste. Marie | OHL | 64 | 4 | 21 | 25 | 122 | 16 | 3 | 10 | 13 | 36 |
| 1992-93 | Sault Ste. Marie | OHL | 59 | 5 | 28 | 3 | 114 | 18 | 2 | 7 | 9 | 12 |
| 1993-94 | Sault Ste. Marie | OHL | 58 | 7 | 43 | 50 | 108 | 14 | 6 | 9 | 15 | 20 |
| 1994-95 | Atlanta Knights | IHL | 72 | 5 | 7 | 12 | 74 | 5 | 0 | 2 | 2 | 22 |
| **1995-96** | **Tampa Bay** | **NHL** | **13** | **0** | **1** | **1** | **4** | .... | .... | .... | .... | .... |
| | Atlanta Knights | IHL | 61 | 3 | 13 | 16 | 105 | 3 | 0 | 0 | 0 | 4 |
| **1996-97** | **Tampa Bay** | **NHL** | **64** | **4** | **13** | **17** | **44** | .... | .... | .... | .... | .... |
| | **Edmonton** | **NHL** | **1** | **0** | **1** | **1** | **0** | **12** | **0** | **0** | **0** | **30** |
| **1997-98** | **Edmonton** | **NHL** | **34** | **0** | **2** | **2** | **42** | .... | .... | .... | .... | .... |
| | **Anaheim** | **NHL** | **27** | **0** | **6** | **6** | **47** | .... | .... | .... | .... | .... |
| 1998-99 | Las Vegas | IHL | 16 | 2 | 1 | 3 | 73 | .... | .... | .... | .... | .... |
| | **Tampa Bay** | **NHL** | **21** | **1** | **2** | **3** | **24** | .... | .... | .... | .... | .... |
| 99-2000 | Hartford | AHL | 44 | 6 | 14 | 20 | 121 | 18 | 2 | 9 | 11 | 53 |
| **2000-01** | **NY Rangers** | **NHL** | **3** | **0** | **0** | **0** | **0** | .... | .... | .... | .... | .... |
| | Hartford | AHL | 73 | 9 | 30 | 39 | 143 | 5 | 0 | 2 | 2 | 6 |
| **2001-02** | **Anaheim** | **NHL** | **1** | **0** | **0** | **0** | **0** | .... | .... | .... | .... | .... |
| | Cincinnati | AHL | 30 | 1 | 10 | 11 | 57 | 3 | 0 | 1 | 1 | 6 |
| 2002-03 | Karpat Oulu | Finland | 41 | 2 | 12 | 14 | 81 | 14 | 2 | 0 | 2 | *42 |
| 2003-04 | Espoo Blues | Finland | 36 | 2 | 8 | 10 | 42 | 9 | 0 | 3 | 3 | 26 |
| | Cherepovets | Russia | 3 | 0 | 0 | 0 | 4 | .... | .... | .... | .... | .... |
| 2004-05 | Nurnberg | Germany | 46 | 1 | 12 | 13 | 97 | .... | .... | .... | .... | .... |
| 2005-06 | Kassel Huskies | Germany | 44 | 9 | 12 | 21 | 79 | 5 | 2 | 6 | 8 | 8 |
| 2006-07 | Kassel Huskies | German-2 | 43 | 9 | 32 | 41 | .... | .... | .... | .... | .... | .... |
| 2007-08 | Kassel Huskies | German-2 | 41 | 11 | 27 | 38 | 73 | 15 | 4 | 12 | 16 | 28 |
| 2008-09 | Kassel Huskies | Germany | 34 | 2 | 15 | 17 | 84 | .... | .... | .... | .... | .... |
| | **NHL Totals** | | **164** | **5** | **25** | **30** | **161** | **12** | **0** | **0** | **0** | **30** |

Memorial Cup All-Star Team (1993) • OHL Second All-Star Team (1994)

Traded to **Edmonton** by **Tampa Bay** with Tampa Bay's 6th round choice (Peter Sarno) in 1997 Entry Draft for Jeff Norton, March 18, 1997. Traded to **Anaheim** by **Edmonton** for Bobby Dollas, January 9, 1998. Traded to **Tampa Bay** by **Anaheim** for Tampa Bay's 5th round choice (Peter Podhradsky) in 2000 Entry Draft, December 10, 1998. Signed as a free agent by **NY Rangers**, October 3, 1999. Signed as a free agent by **Anaheim**, July 27, 2001. • Missed majority of 2001-02 season recovering from shoulder injury suffered in game vs. Utah (AHL), November 30, 2001. Signed by **Karpat Oulu** (Finland), October 20, 2002. Signed as a free agent by **Ottawa**, August 6, 2009.

### DIDIOMETE, Devin (dih-dee-OH-meht, DEH-vihn) NYR

Left wing. Shoots left. 5'11", 200 lbs. Born, Stratford, Ontario, May 9, 1988.
(Calgary's 7th choice, 187th overall, in 2006 Entry Draft).

| | | | Regular Season | | | | | Playoffs | | | | |
|---|---|---|---|---|---|---|---|---|---|---|---|---|
| Season | Club | League | GP | G | A | Pts | PIM | GP | G | A | Pts | PIM |
| 2004-05 | Sudbury | OHL | 58 | 7 | 8 | 15 | 113 | 11 | 0 | 1 | 1 | 11 |
| 2005-06 | Sudbury | OHL | 60 | 15 | 21 | 36 | 202 | 10 | 0 | 4 | 4 | 26 |
| 2006-07 | Sudbury | OHL | 62 | 21 | 19 | 40 | 205 | 21 | 6 | 6 | 12 | 62 |
| 2007-08 | Sarnia | OHL | 56 | 23 | 33 | 56 | 216 | 9 | 1 | 2 | 3 | 40 |
| 2008-09 | Hartford | AHL | 73 | 4 | 5 | 9 | 239 | 4 | 0 | 0 | 0 | 6 |

Signed as a free agent by **NY Rangers**, October 20, 2008.

### KARLSSON, Henrik (KARL-suhn, HEHN-rihk) S.J.

Goaltender. Catches left. 6'6", 215 lbs. Born, Stockholm, Sweden, November 27, 1983.

| | | | Regular Season | | | | | | | | Playoffs | | | | | | |
|---|---|---|---|---|---|---|---|---|---|---|---|---|---|---|---|---|---|
| Season | Club | League | GP | W | L | O/T | Mins | GA | SO | Avg | GP | W | L | Mins | GA | SO | Avg |
| 2000-01 | Hammarby U18 | Swe-U18 | 2 | ... | ... | ... | 120 | 7 | 0 | 3.50 | ... | ... | ... | ... | ... | ... | ... |
| | Hammarby Jr. | Swe-Jr. | 13 | ... | ... | ... | 706 | 56 | 0 | 4.76 | ... | ... | ... | ... | ... | ... | ... |
| 2001-02 | Hammarby Jr. | Swe-Jr. | 23 | ... | ... | ... | 1356 | 97 | 1 | 4.29 | ... | ... | ... | ... | ... | ... | ... |
| 2002-03 | Botkyrka | Sweden-3 | ... | ... | ... | ... | ... | ... | ... | 2.58 | ... | ... | ... | ... | ... | ... | ... |
| 2003-04 | Botkyrka | Sweden-3 | 21 | ... | ... | ... | ... | ... | ... | 2.49 | 6 | ... | ... | 236 | 15 | 0 | 3.82 |
| 2004-05 | Olofstrom | Sweden-3 | 1 | ... | ... | ... | 60 | 0 | 1 | 0.00 | ... | ... | ... | ... | ... | ... | ... |
| | Oskarshamn | Sweden-2 | 11 | ... | ... | ... | 613 | 25 | 1 | 2.45 | 2 | | | 109 | 7 | 0 | 3.87 |
| 2005-06 | Oskarshamn | Sweden-2 | 1 | ... | ... | ... | 40 | 3 | 0 | 4.54 | ... | ... | ... | ... | ... | ... | ... |
| | Malarh/Bre | Sweden-3 | 17 | ... | ... | ... | 982 | 50 | 0 | 3.06 | ... | ... | ... | ... | ... | ... | ... |
| 2006-07 | Hammarby Jr. | Swe-Jr. | 1 | ... | ... | ... | 59 | 2 | 0 | 2.04 | ... | ... | ... | ... | ... | ... | ... |
| | Hammarby | Sweden-2 | 35 | ... | ... | ... | 1893 | 111 | 1 | 3.52 | ... | ... | ... | ... | ... | ... | ... |
| 2007-08 | Hammarby | Sweden-2 | 29 | ... | ... | ... | 1692 | 109 | 1 | 3.86 | ... | ... | ... | ... | ... | ... | ... |
| | Malmo | Sweden-2 | 3 | ... | ... | ... | 180 | 8 | 0 | 2.67 | ... | ... | ... | ... | ... | ... | ... |
| 2008-09 | Malmo | Sweden-2 | 32 | ... | ... | ... | 1888 | 77 | 4 | 2.45 | ... | ... | ... | ... | ... | ... | ... |
| | Sodertalje | Sweden | 7 | ... | ... | ... | 410 | 17 | 0 | 2.49 | ... | ... | ... | ... | ... | ... | ... |
| | Sodertalje | Sweden-Q | 8 | ... | ... | ... | 483 | 16 | 0 | 1.99 | ... | ... | ... | ... | ... | ... | ... |

Signed as a free agent by **San Jose**, August 12, 2009.

### OWENS, Jordan (OH-wehnz, JOHR-dan) NYR

Left wing. Shoots left. 6', 166 lbs. Born, Niagara Falls, Ontario, May 1, 1986.

| | | | Regular Season | | | | | Playoffs | | | | |
|---|---|---|---|---|---|---|---|---|---|---|---|---|
| Season | Club | League | GP | G | A | Pts | PIM | GP | G | A | Pts | PIM |
| 2004-05 | Mississauga | OHL | 66 | 11 | 14 | 25 | 45 | 5 | 0 | 0 | 0 | 2 |
| 2005-06 | Mississauga | OHL | 66 | 26 | 28 | 54 | 47 | .... | .... | .... | .... | .... |
| 2006-07 | Mississauga | OHL | 60 | 32 | 42 | 74 | 51 | 5 | 1 | 2 | 3 | 6 |
| | Hartford | AHL | 2 | 0 | 0 | 0 | 0 | 6 | 0 | 0 | 0 | 9 |
| 2007-08 | Hartford | AHL | 41 | 7 | 7 | 14 | 44 | 5 | 0 | 0 | 0 | 0 |
| | Charlotte | ECHL | 20 | 3 | 10 | 13 | 28 | 2 | 0 | 0 | 0 | 0 |
| 2008-09 | Hartford | AHL | 67 | 12 | 25 | 37 | 66 | 6 | 1 | 2 | 3 | 0 |

Signed as a free agent by **NY Rangers**, May 5, 2009.

### BRULE, Gilbert (*see page 377 for data panel*) EDM

Center. Re-signed as a free agent by **Edmonton**, August 12, 2009.

### GREISS, Thomas (*see page 593 for data panel*) S.J.

Goaltender. Re-signed as a free agent by **San Jose**, August 10, 2009.

### SMID, Ladislav (*see page 377 for data panel*) EDM

Defense. Re-signed as a free agent by **Edmonton**, August 12, 2009.

### STONE, Ryan (*see page 551 for data panel*) EDM

Center. Re-signed as a free agent by **Edmonton**, August 12, 2009.

*Art Alexandre*

*Perry Anderson*

*Peter Andersson*

*Syl Apps*

# Retired NHL Player Index

**Abbreviations**: Teams/Cities: – **Ana**. – Anaheim; **Atl**. – Atlanta; **Bos**. – Boston; **Bro**. – Brooklyn; **Buf**. – Buffalo; **Cal**. – California; **Cgy**. – Calgary; **Car**. – Carolina; **Chi**. – Chicago; **Cle**. – Cleveland; **Col**. – Colorado; **CBJ** – Columbus; **Dal**. – Dallas; **Det**. – Detroit; **Edm**. – Edmonton; **Fla**. – Florida; **Ham**. – Hamilton; **Hfd**. – Hartford; **K.C.** – Kansas City; **L.A.** – Los Angeles; **Min**. – Minnesota; **Mtl**. – Montreal; **Mtl.M.** – Montreal Maroons; **Mtl.W.** – Montreal Wanderers; **Nsh**. – Nashville; **N.J.** – New Jersey; **NYA** – NY Americans; **NYI** – NY Islanders; **NYR** – New York Rangers; **Oak**. – Oakland; **Ott**. – Ottawa; **Phi**. – Philadelphia; **Phx**. – Phoenix; **Pit**. – Pittsburgh; **Que**. – Quebec; **St.L.** – St. Louis; **S.J.** – San Jose; **T.B.** – Tampa Bay; **Tor.** – Toronto; **Van**. – Vancouver; **Wpg**. – Winnipeg; **Wsh**. – Washington

**A** – assists; **G** – goals; **GP** – games played; **PIM** – penalties in minutes; **TP** – total points.
● – deceased. Assists not recorded during 1917-18 season ‡ – Remains active in other leagues.

**NHL Seasons** – A player or goaltender who does not play in a regular season but who does appear in that year's playoffs is credited with an NHL Season in this Index. Total seasons are rounded off to the nearest full season.

| | | | Regular Schedule | | | | | Playoffs | | | | | NHL | First | Last |
|---|---|---|---|---|---|---|---|---|---|---|---|---|---|---|---|
| Name | NHL Teams | NHL Seasons | GP | G | A | TP | PIM | GP | G | A | TP | PIM | Cup Wins | NHL Season | NHL Season |
| **A** | | | | | | | | | | | | | | | |
| Aalto, Antti | Ana. | 4 | 151 | 11 | 17 | 28 | 52 | 4 | 0 | 0 | 0 | 2 | .... | 1997-98 | 2000-01 |
| Abbott, Reg | Mtl. | 1 | 3 | 0 | 0 | 0 | 0 | .... | .... | .... | .... | .... | .... | 1952-53 | 1952-53 |
| ● Abel, Clarence | NYR, Chi. | 8 | 333 | 19 | 18 | 37 | 359 | 38 | 1 | 1 | 2 | 58 | 2 | 1926-27 | 1933-34 |
| Abel, Gerry | Det. | 1 | 1 | 0 | 0 | 0 | 0 | .... | .... | .... | .... | .... | .... | 1966-67 | 1966-67 |
| ● Abel, Sid | Det., Chi. | 14 | 612 | 189 | 283 | 472 | 376 | 97 | 28 | 30 | 58 | 79 | 3 | 1938-39 | 1953-54 |
| Abgrall, Dennis | L.A. | 1 | 13 | 0 | 2 | 2 | 4 | .... | .... | .... | .... | .... | .... | 1975-76 | 1975-76 |
| ‡ Abid, Ramzi | Phx., Pit., Atl., Nsh. | 4 | 68 | 14 | 16 | 30 | 78 | 2 | 0 | 0 | 0 | 0 | .... | 2002-03 | 2006-07 |
| Abrahamsson, Thommy | Hfd. | 1 | 32 | 6 | 11 | 17 | 16 | .... | .... | .... | .... | .... | .... | 1980-81 | 1980-81 |
| Achtymichuk, Gene | Mtl., Det. | 4 | 32 | 3 | 5 | 8 | 2 | .... | .... | .... | .... | .... | .... | 1951-52 | 1958-59 |
| Acomb, Doug | Tor. | 1 | 2 | 0 | 1 | 1 | 0 | .... | .... | .... | .... | .... | .... | 1969-70 | 1969-70 |
| Acton, Keith | Mtl., Min., Edm., Phi., Wsh., NYI | 15 | 1023 | 226 | 358 | 584 | 1172 | 66 | 12 | 21 | 33 | 88 | 1 | 1979-80 | 1993-94 |
| ● Adam, Douglas | NYR | 1 | 4 | 0 | 1 | 1 | 0 | .... | .... | .... | .... | .... | .... | 1949-50 | 1949-50 |
| Adam, Russ | Tor. | 1 | 8 | 1 | 2 | 3 | 11 | .... | .... | .... | .... | .... | .... | 1982-83 | 1982-83 |
| ‡ Adams, Bryan | Atl. | 2 | 11 | 0 | 1 | 1 | 2 | .... | .... | .... | .... | .... | .... | 1999-00 | 2000-01 |
| Adams, Greg | Phi., Hfd., Wsh., Edm., Van., Que., Det. | 10 | 545 | 84 | 143 | 227 | 1173 | 43 | 2 | 11 | 13 | 153 | .... | 1980-81 | 1989-90 |
| Adams, Greg | N.J., Van., Dal., Phx., Fla. | 17 | 1056 | 355 | 388 | 743 | 326 | 81 | 20 | 22 | 42 | 16 | .... | 1984-85 | 2000-01 |
| ● Adams, Jack | Tor., Ott. | 7 | 173 | 83 | 32 | 115 | 366 | 10 | 2 | 0 | 2 | 13 | 2 | 1917-18 | 1926-27 |
| Adams, John | Mtl. | 1 | 42 | 6 | 12 | 18 | 11 | 3 | 0 | 0 | 0 | 0 | .... | 1940-41 | 1940-41 |
| Adams, Kevyn | Tor., CBJ, Fla., Car., Phx., Chi. | 10 | 540 | 59 | 77 | 136 | 317 | 67 | 2 | 2 | 4 | 39 | 1 | 1997-98 | 2007-08 |
| ● Adams, Stew | Chi., Tor. | 4 | 95 | 9 | 26 | 35 | 60 | 11 | 3 | 3 | 6 | 14 | .... | 1929-30 | 1932-33 |
| Adduono, Rick | Bos., Atl. | 2 | 4 | 0 | 0 | 0 | 2 | .... | .... | .... | .... | .... | .... | 1975-76 | 1979-80 |
| ‡ Afanasenkov, Dmitry | T.B., Phi. | 5 | 227 | 27 | 27 | 54 | 52 | 28 | 1 | 3 | 4 | 8 | 1 | 2000-01 | 2006-07 |
| Affleck, Bruce | St.L., Van., NYI | 7 | 280 | 14 | 66 | 80 | 86 | 8 | 0 | 0 | 0 | 0 | .... | 1974-75 | 1983-84 |
| Agnew, Jim | Van., Hfd. | 6 | 81 | 0 | 1 | 1 | 257 | 4 | 0 | 0 | 0 | 6 | .... | 1986-87 | 1992-93 |
| Ahern, Fred | Cal., Cle., Col. | 4 | 146 | 31 | 30 | 61 | 130 | 2 | 0 | 1 | 1 | 2 | .... | 1974-75 | 1977-78 |
| ● Ahlin, Rudy | Chi. | 1 | 1 | 0 | 0 | 0 | 0 | .... | .... | .... | .... | .... | .... | 1937-38 | 1937-38 |
| Ahola, Peter | L.A., Pit., S.J., Cgy. | 3 | 123 | 10 | 17 | 27 | 137 | 6 | 0 | 0 | 0 | 2 | .... | 1991-92 | 1993-94 |
| Ahrens, Chris | Min. | 6 | 52 | 0 | 3 | 3 | 84 | 1 | 0 | 0 | 0 | 0 | .... | 1972-73 | 1977-78 |
| ● Ailsby, Lloyd | NYR | 1 | 3 | 0 | 0 | 0 | 2 | .... | .... | .... | .... | .... | .... | 1951-52 | 1951-52 |
| Aitken, Brad | Pit., Edm. | 2 | 14 | 1 | 3 | 4 | 25 | .... | .... | .... | .... | .... | .... | 1987-88 | 1990-91 |
| Aitken, Johnathan | Bos., Chi. | 2 | 44 | 0 | 1 | 1 | 70 | .... | .... | .... | .... | .... | .... | 1999-00 | 2003-04 |
| Aivazoff, Micah | Det., Edm., NYI | 3 | 92 | 4 | 6 | 10 | 46 | .... | .... | .... | .... | .... | .... | 1993-94 | 1995-96 |
| Alatalo, Mika | Phx. | 2 | 152 | 17 | 29 | 46 | 58 | 5 | 0 | 0 | 0 | 2 | .... | 1999-00 | 2000-01 |
| Albelin, Tommy | Que., N.J., Cgy. | 18 | 952 | 44 | 211 | 255 | 417 | 81 | 7 | 15 | 22 | 22 | 2 | 1987-88 | 2005-06 |
| ● Albright, Clint | NYR | 1 | 59 | 14 | 5 | 19 | 19 | .... | .... | .... | .... | .... | .... | 1948-49 | 1948-49 |
| Aldcorn, Gary | Tor., Det., Bos. | 5 | 226 | 41 | 56 | 97 | 78 | 6 | 1 | 2 | 3 | 4 | .... | 1956-57 | 1960-61 |
| Aldridge, Keith | Dal. | 1 | 4 | 0 | 0 | 0 | 0 | .... | .... | .... | .... | .... | .... | 1999-00 | 1999-00 |
| Alexander, Claire | Tor., Van. | 4 | 155 | 18 | 47 | 65 | 36 | 16 | 2 | 4 | 6 | 4 | .... | 1974-75 | 1977-78 |
| ● Alexandre, Art | Mtl. | 2 | 11 | 0 | 2 | 2 | 8 | 4 | 0 | 0 | 0 | 0 | .... | 1931-32 | 1932-33 |
| ‡ Alexeev, Nikita | T.B., Chi. | 3 | 159 | 20 | 17 | 37 | 28 | 11 | 1 | 0 | 1 | 0 | .... | 2001-02 | 2006-07 |
| Allan, Jeff | Cle. | 1 | 4 | 0 | 0 | 0 | 2 | .... | .... | .... | .... | .... | .... | 1977-78 | 1977-78 |
| Allen, Bobby | Edm., Bos. | 3 | 51 | 0 | 3 | 3 | 12 | .... | .... | .... | .... | .... | .... | 2002-03 | 2007-08 |
| Allen, Chris | Fla. | 2 | 2 | 0 | 0 | 0 | 2 | .... | .... | .... | .... | .... | .... | 1997-98 | 1998-99 |
| ● Allen, George | NYR, Chi., Mtl. | 8 | 339 | 82 | 115 | 197 | 179 | 41 | 9 | 10 | 19 | 32 | .... | 1938-39 | 1946-47 |
| Allen, Keith | Det. | 2 | 28 | 0 | 4 | 4 | 8 | 5 | 0 | 0 | 0 | 0 | 1 | 1953-54 | 1954-55 |
| Allen, Peter | Pit. | 1 | 8 | 0 | 0 | 0 | 8 | .... | .... | .... | .... | .... | .... | 1995-96 | 1995-96 |
| ● Allen, Viv | NYA | 1 | 6 | 0 | 1 | 1 | 0 | .... | .... | .... | .... | .... | .... | 1940-41 | 1940-41 |
| Alley, Steve | Hfd. | 2 | 15 | 3 | 3 | 6 | 11 | 3 | 0 | 1 | 1 | 0 | .... | 1979-80 | 1980-81 |
| Allison, Dave | Mtl. | 1 | 3 | 0 | 0 | 0 | 12 | .... | .... | .... | .... | .... | .... | 1983-84 | 1983-84 |
| Allison, Jamie | Cgy., Chi., CBJ, Nsh., Fla. | 10 | 372 | 7 | 23 | 30 | 639 | .... | .... | .... | .... | .... | .... | 1994-95 | 2005-06 |
| Allison, Jason | Wsh., Bos., L.A., Tor. | 12 | 552 | 154 | 331 | 485 | 441 | 25 | 7 | 18 | 25 | 14 | .... | 1993-94 | 2005-06 |
| Allison, Mike | NYR, Tor., L.A. | 10 | 499 | 102 | 166 | 268 | 630 | 82 | 9 | 17 | 26 | 135 | .... | 1980-81 | 1989-90 |
| Allison, Ray | Hfd., Phi. | 7 | 238 | 64 | 93 | 157 | 223 | 12 | 2 | 3 | 5 | 20 | .... | 1979-80 | 1986-87 |
| ● Allum, Bill | NYR | 1 | 1 | 0 | 1 | 1 | 0 | .... | .... | .... | .... | .... | .... | 1940-41 | 1940-41 |
| ● Amadio, Dave | Det., L.A. | 3 | 125 | 5 | 11 | 16 | 163 | 16 | 1 | 2 | 3 | 18 | .... | 1957-58 | 1968-69 |
| Ambroziak, Peter | Buf. | 1 | 12 | 0 | 1 | 1 | 0 | .... | .... | .... | .... | .... | .... | 1994-95 | 1994-95 |
| Amodeo, Mike | Wpg. | 1 | 19 | 0 | 0 | 0 | 2 | .... | .... | .... | .... | .... | .... | 1979-80 | 1979-80 |
| Amonte, Tony | NYR, Chi., Phx., Phi., Cgy. | 16 | 1174 | 416 | 484 | 900 | 752 | 99 | 22 | 33 | 55 | 56 | .... | 1990-91 | 2006-07 |
| ● Anderson, Bill | Bos. | 1 | .... | .... | .... | .... | .... | 1 | 0 | 0 | 0 | 0 | .... | 1942-43 | 1942-43 |
| Anderson, Dale | Det. | 1 | 13 | 0 | 0 | 0 | 6 | 2 | 0 | 0 | 0 | 0 | .... | 1956-57 | 1956-57 |
| Anderson, Doug | Mtl.. | 1 | .... | .... | .... | .... | .... | 2 | 0 | 0 | 0 | 0 | .... | 1952-53 | 1952-53 |
| Anderson, Earl | Det., Bos. | 3 | 109 | 19 | 19 | 38 | 22 | 5 | 0 | 1 | 1 | 0 | .... | 1974-75 | 1976-77 |
| Anderson, Glenn | Edm., Tor., NYR, St.L. | 16 | 1129 | 498 | 601 | 1099 | 1120 | 225 | 93 | 121 | 214 | 442 | 6 | 1980-81 | 1995-96 |
| Anderson, Jim | L.A. | 1 | 7 | 1 | 2 | 3 | 2 | .... | .... | .... | .... | .... | .... | 1967-68 | 1967-68 |
| Anderson, John | Tor., Que., Hfd. | 12 | 814 | 282 | 349 | 631 | 263 | 37 | 9 | 18 | 27 | 2 | .... | 1977-78 | 1988-89 |
| Anderson, Murray | Wsh. | 1 | 40 | 0 | 1 | 1 | 68 | .... | .... | .... | .... | .... | .... | 1974-75 | 1974-75 |
| Anderson, Perry | St.L., N.J., S.J. | 10 | 400 | 50 | 59 | 109 | 1051 | 36 | 2 | 1 | 3 | 161 | .... | 1981-82 | 1991-92 |
| Anderson, Ron | Det., L.A., St.L., Buf. | 5 | 251 | 28 | 30 | 58 | 146 | 5 | 0 | 0 | 0 | 4 | .... | 1967-68 | 1971-72 |
| Anderson, Ron | Wsh. | 1 | 28 | 9 | 7 | 16 | 8 | .... | .... | .... | .... | .... | .... | 1974-75 | 1974-75 |
| Anderson, Russ | Pit., Hfd., L.A. | 9 | 519 | 22 | 99 | 121 | 1086 | 10 | 0 | 3 | 3 | 28 | .... | 1976-77 | 1984-85 |
| Anderson, Shawn | Buf., Que., Wsh., Phi. | 8 | 255 | 11 | 51 | 62 | 117 | 19 | 1 | 1 | 2 | 16 | .... | 1986-87 | 1994-95 |
| ● Anderson, Tom | Det., NYA, Bro. | 8 | 319 | 62 | 127 | 189 | 180 | 16 | 2 | 7 | 9 | 8 | .... | 1934-35 | 1941-42 |
| Andersson, Erik | Cgy. | 1 | 12 | 2 | 1 | 3 | 8 | .... | .... | .... | .... | .... | .... | 1997-98 | 1997-98 |
| Andersson, Kent-Erik | Min., NYR | 7 | 456 | 72 | 103 | 175 | 78 | 50 | 4 | 11 | 15 | 4 | .... | 1977-78 | 1983-84 |
| Andersson, Mikael | Buf., Hfd., T.B., Phi., NYI | 15 | 761 | 95 | 169 | 264 | 134 | 25 | 2 | 7 | 9 | 10 | .... | 1985-86 | 1999-00 |
| ‡ Andersson, Niklas | Que., NYI, S.J., Nsh., Cgy. | 6 | 164 | 29 | 53 | 82 | 85 | .... | .... | .... | .... | .... | .... | 1992-93 | 2000-01 |
| Andersson, Peter | Wsh., Que. | 3 | 172 | 10 | 41 | 51 | 81 | 7 | 0 | 2 | 2 | 2 | .... | 1983-84 | 1985-86 |
| Andersson, Peter | NYR, Fla. | 2 | 47 | 6 | 13 | 19 | 20 | .... | .... | .... | .... | .... | .... | 1992-93 | 1993-94 |
| Andrascik, Steve | NYR | 1 | .... | .... | .... | .... | .... | 1 | 0 | 0 | 0 | 0 | .... | 1971-72 | 1971-72 |
| Andrea, Paul | NYR, Pit., Cal., Buf. | 4 | 150 | 31 | 49 | 80 | 10 | .... | .... | .... | .... | .... | .... | 1965-66 | 1970-71 |
| ● Andrews, Lloyd | Tor. | 4 | 53 | 8 | 5 | 13 | 10 | 2 | 0 | 0 | 0 | 0 | 1 | 1921-22 | 1924-25 |
| Andreychuk, Dave | Buf., Tor., N.J., Bos., Col., T.B. | 23 | 1639 | 640 | 698 | 1338 | 1125 | 162 | 43 | 54 | 97 | 162 | 1 | 1982-83 | 2005-06 |
| Andrievski, Alexander | Chi. | 1 | 1 | 0 | 0 | 0 | 0 | .... | .... | .... | .... | .... | .... | 1992-93 | 1992-93 |
| Andruff, Ron | Mtl., Col. | 5 | 153 | 19 | 36 | 55 | 54 | 2 | 0 | 0 | 0 | 0 | .... | 1974-75 | 1978-79 |
| Andrusak, Greg | Pit., Tor. | 5 | 28 | 0 | 6 | 6 | 16 | 15 | 1 | 0 | 1 | 8 | .... | 1993-94 | 1999-00 |
| Angelstad, Mel | Wsh. | 1 | 2 | 0 | 0 | 0 | 2 | .... | .... | .... | .... | .... | .... | 2003-04 | 2003-04 |
| Angotti, Lou | NYR, Chi., Phi., Pit., St.L. | 10 | 653 | 103 | 186 | 289 | 228 | 65 | 8 | 8 | 16 | 17 | .... | 1964-65 | 1973-74 |
| Anholt, Darrel | Chi. | 1 | 1 | 0 | 0 | 0 | 0 | .... | .... | .... | .... | .... | .... | 1983-84 | 1983-84 |
| ● Anslow, Hub | NYR | 1 | 2 | 0 | 0 | 0 | 0 | .... | .... | .... | .... | .... | .... | 1947-48 | 1947-48 |
| Antonovich, Mike | Min., Hfd., N.J. | 5 | 87 | 10 | 15 | 25 | 37 | .... | .... | .... | .... | .... | .... | 1975-76 | 1983-84 |
| Antoski, Shawn | Van., Phi., Pit., Ana. | 8 | 183 | 3 | 5 | 8 | 599 | 36 | 1 | 3 | 4 | 74 | .... | 1990-91 | 1997-98 |
| ● Apps, Syl | Tor. | 10 | 423 | 201 | 231 | 432 | 56 | 69 | 25 | 29 | 54 | 8 | 3 | 1936-37 | 1947-48 |
| Apps, Syl | NYR, Pit., L.A. | 10 | 727 | 183 | 423 | 606 | 311 | 23 | 5 | 5 | 10 | 23 | .... | 1970-71 | 1979-80 |
| Arbour, Al | Det., Chi., Tor., St.L. | 16 | 626 | 12 | 58 | 70 | 617 | 86 | 1 | 8 | 9 | 92 | 4 | 1953-54 | 1970-71 |
| ● Arbour, Amos | Mtl., Ham., Tor. | 6 | 113 | 52 | 20 | 72 | 77 | .... | .... | .... | .... | .... | .... | 1918-19 | 1923-24 |
| ● Arbour, Jack | Det., Tor. | 2 | 47 | 5 | 1 | 6 | 56 | .... | .... | .... | .... | .... | .... | 1926-27 | 1928-29 |
| Arbour, John | Bos., Pit., Van., St.L. | 5 | 106 | 1 | 9 | 10 | 149 | 5 | 0 | 0 | 0 | 0 | .... | 1965-66 | 1971-72 |
| ● Arbour, Ty | Pit., Chi. | 5 | 207 | 28 | 28 | 56 | 112 | 11 | 2 | 0 | 2 | 6 | .... | 1926-27 | 1930-31 |
| Archambault, Michel | Chi. | 1 | 3 | 0 | 0 | 0 | 0 | .... | .... | .... | .... | .... | .... | 1976-77 | 1976-77 |
| Archibald, Dave | Min., NYR, Ott., NYI | 8 | 323 | 57 | 67 | 124 | 139 | 5 | 0 | 1 | 1 | 0 | .... | 1987-88 | 1996-97 |
| Archibald, Jim | Min. | 3 | 16 | 1 | 2 | 3 | 45 | .... | .... | .... | .... | .... | .... | 1984-85 | 1986-87 |

| Name | NHL Teams | NHL Seasons | Regular Schedule GP | G | A | TP | PIM | Playoffs GP | G | A | TP | PIM | NHL Cup Wins | First NHL Season | Last NHL Season |
|---|---|---|---|---|---|---|---|---|---|---|---|---|---|---|---|
| Areshenkoff, Ron | Edm. | 1 | 4 | 0 | 0 | 0 | 0 | .... | .... | .... | .... | .... | .... | 1979-80 | 1979-80 |
| ‡ Arkhipov, Denis | Nsh., Chi. | 5 | 352 | 56 | 82 | 138 | 128 | .... | .... | .... | .... | .... | .... | 2000-01 | 2006-07 |
| Armstrong, Bill | Phi. | 1 | 1 | 0 | 1 | 1 | 0 | .... | .... | .... | .... | .... | .... | 1990-91 | 1990-91 |
| • Armstrong, Bob | Bos. | 12 | 542 | 13 | 86 | 99 | 671 | 42 | 1 | 7 | 8 | 28 | .... | 1950-51 | 1961-62 |
| ‡ Armstrong, Chris | Min., Ana. | 2 | 7 | 0 | 1 | 1 | 0 | .... | .... | .... | .... | .... | .... | 2000-01 | 2003-04 |
| Armstrong, George | Tor. | 21 | 1187 | 296 | 417 | 713 | 721 | 110 | 26 | 34 | 60 | 52 | 4 | 1949-50 | 1970-71 |
| Armstrong, Murray | Tor., NYA, Bro., Det. | 8 | 270 | 67 | 121 | 188 | 72 | 30 | 4 | 6 | 10 | 2 | .... | 1937-38 | 1945-46 |
| • Armstrong, Norm | Tor. | 1 | 7 | 1 | 1 | 2 | 2 | .... | .... | .... | .... | .... | .... | 1962-63 | 1962-63 |
| Armstrong, Tim | Tor. | 1 | 11 | 1 | 0 | 1 | 6 | .... | .... | .... | .... | .... | .... | 1988-89 | 1988-89 |
| Arnason, Chuck | Mtl., Atl., Pit., K.C., Col., Cle., Min., Wsh. | 8 | 401 | 109 | 90 | 199 | 122 | 9 | 2 | 4 | 6 | 4 | .... | 1971-72 | 1978-79 |
| Arniel, Scott | Wpg., Buf., Bos. | 12 | 730 | 149 | 189 | 338 | 599 | 34 | 3 | 3 | 6 | 39 | .... | 1981-82 | 1991-92 |
| Arthur, Fred | Hfd., Phi. | 3 | 80 | 1 | 8 | 9 | 49 | 4 | 0 | 0 | 0 | 2 | .... | 1980-81 | 1982-83 |
| • Arundel, John | Tor. | 1 | 3 | 0 | 0 | 0 | 9 | .... | .... | .... | .... | .... | .... | 1949-50 | 1949-50 |
| Arvedson, Magnus | Ott., Van. | 7 | 434 | 100 | 125 | 225 | 241 | 52 | 3 | 8 | 11 | 34 | .... | 1997-98 | 2003-04 |
| • Ashbee, Barry | Bos., Phi. | 5 | 284 | 15 | 70 | 85 | 291 | 17 | 0 | 4 | 4 | 22 | 1 | 1965-66 | 1973-74 |
| • Ashby, Don | Tor., Col., Edm. | 6 | 188 | 40 | 56 | 96 | 40 | 12 | 1 | 0 | 1 | 4 | .... | 1975-76 | 1980-81 |
| Ashton, Brent | Van., Col., N.J., Min., Que., Det., Wpg., Bos., Cgy. | 14 | 998 | 284 | 345 | 629 | 635 | 85 | 24 | 25 | 49 | 70 | .... | 1979-80 | 1992-93 |
| Ashworth, Frank | Chi. | 1 | 18 | 5 | 4 | 9 | 2 | .... | .... | .... | .... | .... | .... | 1946-47 | 1946-47 |
| • Asmundson, Oscar | NYR, Det., St.L., NYA, Mtl. | 5 | 111 | 11 | 23 | 34 | 30 | 9 | 0 | 2 | 2 | 4 | 1 | 1932-33 | 1937-38 |
| ‡ Astashenko, Kaspars | T.B. | 2 | 23 | 1 | 2 | 3 | 8 | .... | .... | .... | .... | .... | .... | 1999-00 | 2000-01 |
| Astley, Mark | Buf. | 3 | 75 | 4 | 19 | 23 | 92 | 2 | 0 | 0 | 0 | 0 | .... | 1993-94 | 1995-96 |
| • Atanas, Walt | NYR | 1 | 49 | 13 | 8 | 21 | 40 | .... | .... | .... | .... | .... | .... | 1944-45 | 1944-45 |
| Atcheynum, Blair | Ott., St.L., Nsh., Chi. | 5 | 196 | 27 | 33 | 60 | 36 | 23 | 1 | 3 | 4 | 8 | .... | 1992-93 | 2000-01 |
| • Atkinson, Steve | Bos., Buf., Wsh. | 6 | 302 | 60 | 51 | 111 | 104 | 1 | 0 | 0 | 0 | 0 | .... | 1968-69 | 1974-75 |
| Attwell, Bob | Col. | 2 | 22 | 1 | 5 | 6 | 0 | .... | .... | .... | .... | .... | .... | 1979-80 | 1980-81 |
| Attwell, Ron | St.L., NYR | 1 | 22 | 1 | 7 | 8 | 8 | .... | .... | .... | .... | .... | .... | 1967-68 | 1967-68 |
| Aubin, Norm | Tor. | 2 | 69 | 18 | 13 | 31 | 30 | 1 | 0 | 0 | 0 | 0 | .... | 1981-82 | 1982-83 |
| ‡ Aubin, Serge | Col., CBJ, Atl. | 7 | 374 | 44 | 64 | 108 | 361 | 22 | 0 | 1 | 1 | 10 | .... | 1998-99 | 2005-06 |
| Aubry, Pierre | Que., Det. | 5 | 202 | 24 | 26 | 50 | 133 | 20 | 1 | 1 | 2 | 32 | .... | 1980-81 | 1984-85 |
| Aubuchon, Ossie | Bos., NYR | 2 | 50 | 20 | 12 | 32 | 4 | 6 | 1 | 0 | 1 | 0 | .... | 1942-43 | 1943-44 |
| Audet, Philippe | Det. | 1 | 4 | 0 | 0 | 0 | 0 | .... | .... | .... | .... | .... | .... | 1998-99 | 1998-99 |
| Audette, Donald | Buf., L.A., Atl., Dal., Mtl., Fla. | 15 | 735 | 260 | 249 | 509 | 584 | 73 | 21 | 27 | 48 | 46 | .... | 1989-90 | 2003-04 |
| • Auge, Les | Col. | 1 | 6 | 0 | 3 | 3 | 4 | .... | .... | .... | .... | .... | .... | 1980-81 | 1980-81 |
| Augusta, Patrik | Tor., Wsh. | 2 | 4 | 0 | 0 | 0 | 0 | .... | .... | .... | .... | .... | .... | 1993-94 | 1998-99 |
| Aulin, Jared | L.A. | 1 | 17 | 2 | 2 | 4 | 0 | .... | .... | .... | .... | .... | .... | 2002-03 | 2002-03 |
| • Aurie, Larry | Det. | 12 | 489 | 147 | 129 | 276 | 279 | 24 | 6 | 9 | 15 | 10 | 2 | 1927-28 | 1938-39 |
| Awrey, Don | Bos., St.L., Mtl., Pit., NYR, Col. | 16 | 979 | 31 | 158 | 189 | 1065 | 71 | 0 | 18 | 18 | 150 | 2 | 1963-64 | 1978-79 |
| • Ayres, Vern | NYA, Mtl.M., St.L., NYR | 6 | 211 | 6 | 11 | 17 | 350 | .... | .... | .... | .... | .... | .... | 1930-31 | 1935-36 |

## B

| Name | NHL Teams | NHL Seasons | Regular Schedule GP | G | A | TP | PIM | Playoffs GP | G | A | TP | PIM | NHL Cup Wins | First NHL Season | Last NHL Season |
|---|---|---|---|---|---|---|---|---|---|---|---|---|---|---|---|
| Babando, Pete | Bos., Det., Chi., NYR | 6 | 351 | 86 | 73 | 159 | 194 | 17 | 3 | 3 | 6 | 6 | 1 | 1947-48 | 1952-53 |
| Babcock, Bobby | Wsh. | 2 | 2 | 0 | 0 | 0 | 2 | .... | .... | .... | .... | .... | .... | 1990-91 | 1992-93 |
| Babe, Warren | Min. | 3 | 21 | 2 | 5 | 7 | 23 | 2 | 0 | 0 | 0 | 0 | .... | 1987-88 | 1990-91 |
| ‡ Babenko, Yuri | Col. | 1 | 3 | 0 | 0 | 0 | 0 | .... | .... | .... | .... | .... | .... | 2000-01 | 2000-01 |
| Babin, Mitch | St.L. | 1 | 8 | 0 | 0 | 0 | 0 | .... | .... | .... | .... | .... | .... | 1975-76 | 1975-76 |
| Baby, John | Cle., Min. | 2 | 26 | 2 | 8 | 10 | 26 | .... | .... | .... | .... | .... | .... | 1977-78 | 1978-79 |
| Babych, Dave | Wpg., Hfd., Van., Phi., L.A. | 19 | 1195 | 142 | 581 | 723 | 970 | 114 | 21 | 41 | 62 | 113 | .... | 1980-81 | 1998-99 |
| Babych, Wayne | St.L., Pit., Que., Hfd. | 9 | 519 | 192 | 246 | 438 | 498 | 41 | 7 | 9 | 16 | 24 | .... | 1978-79 | 1986-87 |
| Baca, Jergus | Hfd. | 2 | 10 | 0 | 2 | 2 | 14 | .... | .... | .... | .... | .... | .... | 1990-91 | 1991-92 |
| Backman, Mike | NYR | 3 | 18 | 1 | 6 | 7 | 18 | 10 | 2 | 2 | 4 | 2 | .... | 1981-82 | 1983-84 |
| • Backor, Pete | Tor. | 1 | 36 | 4 | 5 | 9 | 6 | .... | .... | .... | .... | .... | 1 | 1944-45 | 1944-45 |
| Backstrom, Ralph | Mtl., L.A., Chi. | 17 | 1032 | 278 | 361 | 639 | 386 | 116 | 27 | 32 | 59 | 68 | 6 | 1956-57 | 1972-73 |
| • Bailey, Ace | Tor. | 8 | 313 | 111 | 82 | 193 | 472 | 21 | 3 | 4 | 7 | 12 | 1 | 1926-27 | 1933-34 |
| • Bailey, Bob | Tor., Det., Chi. | 5 | 150 | 15 | 21 | 36 | 207 | 15 | 0 | 4 | 4 | 22 | .... | 1953-54 | 1957-58 |
| • Bailey, Garnet | Bos., Det., St.L., Wsh. | 10 | 568 | 107 | 171 | 278 | 633 | 15 | 2 | 4 | 6 | 28 | 2 | 1968-69 | 1977-78 |
| Bailey, Reid | Phi., Tor., Hfd. | 4 | 40 | 1 | 3 | 4 | 105 | 16 | 0 | 2 | 2 | 25 | .... | 1980-81 | 1983-84 |
| Baillargeon, Joel | Wpg., Que. | 3 | 20 | 0 | 2 | 2 | 31 | .... | .... | .... | .... | .... | .... | 1986-87 | 1988-89 |
| Baird, Ken | Cal. | 1 | 10 | 0 | 2 | 2 | 15 | .... | .... | .... | .... | .... | .... | 1971-72 | 1971-72 |
| Baker, Bill | Mtl., Col., St.L., NYR | 3 | 143 | 7 | 25 | 32 | 175 | 6 | 0 | 0 | 0 | 0 | .... | 1980-81 | 1982-83 |
| Baker, Jamie | Que., Ott., S.J., Tor. | 9 | 404 | 71 | 79 | 150 | 271 | 25 | 5 | 4 | 9 | 42 | .... | 1989-90 | 1998-99 |
| Bakovic, Peter | Van. | 1 | 10 | 2 | 0 | 2 | 48 | .... | .... | .... | .... | .... | .... | 1987-88 | 1987-88 |
| ‡ Bala, Chris | Ott. | 1 | 6 | 0 | 1 | 1 | 0 | .... | .... | .... | .... | .... | .... | 2001-02 | 2001-02 |
| ‡ Balastik, Jaroslav | CBJ | 2 | 74 | 13 | 11 | 24 | 30 | .... | .... | .... | .... | .... | .... | 2005-06 | 2006-07 |
| Balderis, Helmut | Min. | 1 | 26 | 3 | 6 | 9 | 2 | .... | .... | .... | .... | .... | .... | 1989-90 | 1989-90 |
| • Baldwin, Doug | Tor., Det., Chi. | 3 | 24 | 0 | 1 | 1 | 8 | .... | .... | .... | .... | .... | .... | 1945-46 | 1947-48 |
| ‡ Balej, Jozef | Mtl., NYR, Van. | 2 | 18 | 1 | 5 | 6 | 4 | .... | .... | .... | .... | .... | .... | 2003-04 | 2005-06 |
| Balfour, Earl | Tor., Chi. | 7 | 288 | 30 | 22 | 52 | 78 | 26 | 0 | 3 | 3 | 4 | 1 | 1951-52 | 1960-61 |
| • Balfour, Murray | Mtl., Chi., Bos. | 8 | 306 | 67 | 90 | 157 | 393 | 40 | 9 | 10 | 19 | 45 | 1 | 1956-57 | 1964-65 |
| Ball, Terry | Phi., Buf. | 4 | 74 | 7 | 19 | 26 | 26 | .... | .... | .... | .... | .... | .... | 1967-68 | 1971-72 |
| Balmochnykh, Maxim | Ana. | 1 | 6 | 0 | 1 | 1 | 2 | .... | .... | .... | .... | .... | .... | 1999-00 | 1999-00 |
| • Balon, Dave | NYR, Mtl., Min., Van. | 14 | 776 | 192 | 222 | 414 | 607 | 78 | 14 | 21 | 35 | 109 | 2 | 1959-60 | 1972-73 |
| Baltimore, Bryon | Edm. | 1 | 2 | 0 | 0 | 0 | 4 | .... | .... | .... | .... | .... | .... | 1979-80 | 1979-80 |
| Baluik, Stan | Bos. | 1 | 7 | 0 | 0 | 0 | 2 | .... | .... | .... | .... | .... | .... | 1959-60 | 1959-60 |
| Bancroft, Steve | Chi., S.J. | 2 | 6 | 0 | 1 | 1 | 2 | .... | .... | .... | .... | .... | .... | 1992-93 | 2001-02 |
| Bandura, Jeff | NYR | 1 | 2 | 0 | 1 | 1 | 0 | .... | .... | .... | .... | .... | .... | 1980-81 | 1980-81 |
| Banham, Frank | Ana., Phx. | 4 | 32 | 9 | 2 | 11 | 16 | .... | .... | .... | .... | .... | .... | 1996-97 | 2002-03 |
| Banks, Darren | Bos. | 2 | 20 | 2 | 2 | 4 | 73 | .... | .... | .... | .... | .... | .... | 1992-93 | 1993-94 |
| ‡ Bannister, Drew | T.B., Edm., Ana., NYR | 6 | 164 | 5 | 25 | 30 | 161 | 12 | 0 | 0 | 0 | 30 | .... | 1995-96 | 2001-02 |
| Barahona, Ralph | Bos. | 2 | 6 | 2 | 2 | 4 | 0 | .... | .... | .... | .... | .... | .... | 1990-91 | 1991-92 |
| • Barbe, Andy | Tor. | 1 | 1 | 0 | 0 | 0 | 2 | .... | .... | .... | .... | .... | .... | 1950-51 | 1950-51 |
| Barber, Bill | Phi. | 14 | 903 | 420 | 463 | 883 | 623 | 129 | 53 | 55 | 108 | 109 | 2 | 1972-73 | 1983-84 |
| Barber, Don | Min., Wpg., Que., S.J. | 4 | 115 | 25 | 32 | 57 | 64 | 11 | 4 | 4 | 8 | 10 | .... | 1988-89 | 1991-92 |
| • Barilko, Bill | Tor. | 5 | 252 | 26 | 36 | 62 | 456 | 47 | 5 | 7 | 12 | 104 | 4 | 1946-47 | 1950-51 |
| ‡ Barinka, Michal | Chi. | 2 | 34 | 0 | 2 | 2 | 26 | .... | .... | .... | .... | .... | .... | 2003-04 | 2005-06 |
| Barkley, Doug | Chi., Det. | 6 | 253 | 24 | 80 | 104 | 382 | 30 | 0 | 9 | 9 | 63 | .... | 1957-58 | 1965-66 |
| Barlow, Bob | Min. | 2 | 77 | 16 | 17 | 33 | 10 | 6 | 2 | 2 | 4 | 6 | .... | 1969-70 | 1970-71 |
| Barnaby, Matthew | Buf., Pit., T.B., NYR, Col., Chi., Dal. | 14 | 834 | 113 | 187 | 300 | 2562 | 62 | 7 | 15 | 22 | 170 | .... | 1992-93 | 2006-07 |
| Barnes, Blair | L.A. | 1 | 1 | 0 | 0 | 0 | 0 | .... | .... | .... | .... | .... | .... | 1982-83 | 1982-83 |
| Barnes, Norm | Phi., Hfd. | 5 | 156 | 6 | 38 | 44 | 178 | 12 | 0 | 0 | 0 | 8 | .... | 1976-77 | 1981-82 |
| Barnes, Ryan | Det. | 1 | 2 | 0 | 0 | 0 | 0 | .... | .... | .... | .... | .... | .... | 2003-04 | 2003-04 |
| Barnes, Stu | Wpg., Fla., Pit., Buf., Dal. | 16 | 1136 | 261 | 336 | 597 | 438 | 116 | 30 | 32 | 62 | 24 | .... | 1991-92 | 2007-08 |
| ‡ Barney, Scott | L.A., Atl. | 3 | 27 | 5 | 6 | 11 | 4 | .... | .... | .... | .... | .... | .... | 2002-03 | 2005-06 |
| Baron, Murray | Phi., St.L., Mtl., Phx., Van. | 15 | 988 | 35 | 94 | 129 | 1309 | 73 | 2 | 8 | 10 | 78 | .... | 1989-90 | 2003-04 |
| Baron, Normand | Mtl., St.L. | 2 | 27 | 2 | 0 | 2 | 51 | 3 | 0 | 0 | 0 | 22 | .... | 1983-84 | 1985-86 |
| Barr, Dave | Bos., NYR, St.L., Hfd., Det., N.J., Dal. | 13 | 614 | 128 | 204 | 332 | 520 | 71 | 12 | 10 | 22 | 70 | .... | 1981-82 | 1993-94 |
| Barrault, Doug | Min., Fla. | 2 | 4 | 0 | 0 | 0 | 2 | .... | .... | .... | .... | .... | .... | 1992-93 | 1993-94 |
| Barrett, Fred | Min., L.A. | 13 | 745 | 25 | 123 | 148 | 671 | 44 | 0 | 2 | 2 | 60 | .... | 1970-71 | 1983-84 |
| Barrett, John | Det., Wsh., Min. | 8 | 488 | 20 | 77 | 97 | 604 | 16 | 2 | 2 | 4 | 50 | .... | 1980-81 | 1987-88 |
| Barrie, Doug | Pit., Buf., L.A. | 3 | 158 | 10 | 42 | 52 | 268 | .... | .... | .... | .... | .... | .... | 1968-69 | 1971-72 |
| Barrie, Len | Phi., Fla., Pit., L.A. | 7 | 184 | 19 | 45 | 64 | 290 | 8 | 1 | 0 | 1 | 8 | .... | 1989-90 | 2000-01 |
| Barry, Ed | Bos. | 1 | 19 | 1 | 3 | 4 | 2 | .... | .... | .... | .... | .... | .... | 1946-47 | 1946-47 |
| • Barry, Marty | NYA, Bos., Det., Mtl. | 12 | 509 | 195 | 192 | 387 | 231 | 43 | 15 | 18 | 33 | 34 | 2 | 1927-28 | 1939-40 |
| Barry, Ray | Bos. | 1 | 18 | 1 | 2 | 3 | 6 | .... | .... | .... | .... | .... | .... | 1951-52 | 1951-52 |
| ‡ Bartecko, Lubos | St.L., Atl. | 5 | 257 | 46 | 65 | 111 | 107 | 12 | 1 | 1 | 2 | 2 | .... | 1998-99 | 2002-03 |
| Bartel, Robin | Cgy., Van. | 2 | 41 | 0 | 1 | 1 | 14 | 6 | 0 | 0 | 0 | 16 | .... | 1985-86 | 1986-87 |
| Bartlett, Jim | Mtl., NYR, Bos. | 5 | 191 | 34 | 23 | 57 | 273 | 2 | 0 | 0 | 0 | 0 | .... | 1954-55 | 1960-61 |
| • Barton, Cliff | Pit., Phi., NYR | 3 | 85 | 10 | 9 | 19 | 22 | .... | .... | .... | .... | .... | .... | 1929-30 | 1939-40 |
| ‡ Bartos, Peter | Min. | 1 | 13 | 4 | 2 | 6 | 6 | .... | .... | .... | .... | .... | .... | 2000-01 | 2000-01 |
| ‡ Bartovic, Milan | Buf., Chi. | 3 | 50 | 3 | 14 | 17 | 26 | .... | .... | .... | .... | .... | .... | 2002-03 | 2005-06 |
| ‡ Bashkirov, Andrei | Mtl. | 3 | 30 | 0 | 3 | 3 | 0 | .... | .... | .... | .... | .... | .... | 1998-99 | 2000-01 |
| Bassen, Bob | NYI, Chi., St.L., Que., Dal., Cgy. | 15 | 765 | 88 | 144 | 232 | 1004 | 93 | 9 | 15 | 24 | 134 | .... | 1985-86 | 1999-00 |
| Bast, Ryan | Phi. | 1 | 2 | 0 | 1 | 1 | 0 | .... | .... | .... | .... | .... | .... | 1998-99 | 1998-99 |
| ‡ Bates, Shawn | Bos., NYI | 10 | 465 | 72 | 126 | 198 | 266 | 29 | 3 | 4 | 7 | 19 | .... | 1997-98 | 2007-08 |
| Bathe, Frank | Det., Phi. | 9 | 224 | 3 | 28 | 31 | 542 | 27 | 1 | 3 | 4 | 42 | .... | 1974-75 | 1983-84 |
| Bathgate, Andy | NYR, Tor., Det., Pit. | 17 | 1069 | 349 | 624 | 973 | 624 | 54 | 21 | 14 | 35 | 76 | 1 | 1952-53 | 1970-71 |
| Bathgate, Frank | NYR | 1 | 2 | 0 | 0 | 0 | 2 | .... | .... | .... | .... | .... | .... | 1952-53 | 1952-53 |
| • Batters, Jeff | St.L. | 2 | 16 | 0 | 0 | 0 | 28 | .... | .... | .... | .... | .... | .... | 1993-94 | 1994-95 |
| Batyrshin, Ruslan | L.A. | 1 | 2 | 0 | 0 | 0 | 6 | .... | .... | .... | .... | .... | .... | 1995-96 | 1995-96 |
| • Bauer, Bobby | Bos. | 9 | 327 | 123 | 137 | 260 | 36 | 48 | 11 | 8 | 19 | 6 | 2 | 1936-37 | 1951-52 |
| Baumgartner, Ken | L.A., NYI, Tor., Ana., Bos. | 12 | 696 | 13 | 41 | 54 | 2244 | 51 | 1 | 2 | 3 | 106 | .... | 1987-88 | 1998-99 |
| Baumgartner, Mike | K.C. | 1 | 17 | 0 | 0 | 0 | 0 | .... | .... | .... | .... | .... | .... | 1974-75 | 1974-75 |
| Baun, Bob | Tor., Oak., Det. | 17 | 964 | 37 | 187 | 224 | 1493 | 96 | 3 | 12 | 15 | 171 | 4 | 1956-57 | 1972-73 |
| Bautin, Sergei | Wpg., Det., S.J. | 3 | 132 | 5 | 25 | 30 | 176 | 6 | 0 | 0 | 0 | 2 | .... | 1992-93 | 1995-96 |

Patrik Augusta

Pete Babando

Reid Bailey

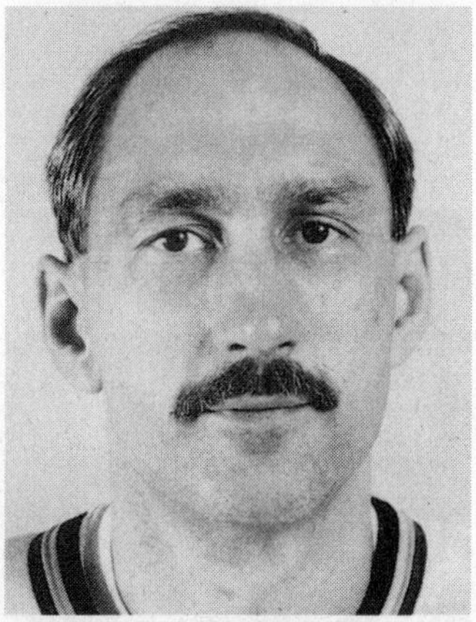
Helmut Balderis

Bill Barber

Stu Barnes

Andy Bathgate

Red Beattie

| | | | Regular Schedule | | | | | Playoffs | | | | | NHL | First | Last |
|---|---|---|---|---|---|---|---|---|---|---|---|---|---|---|---|
| Name | NHL Teams | NHL Seasons | GP | G | A | TP | PIM | GP | G | A | TP | PIM | Cup Wins | NHL Season | NHL Season |
| Bawa, Robin | Wsh., Van., S.J., Ana. | 4 | 61 | 6 | 1 | 7 | 60 | 1 | 0 | 0 | 0 | 0 | .... | 1989-90 | 1993-94 |
| Baxter, Paul | Que., Pit., Cgy. | 8 | 472 | 48 | 121 | 169 | 1564 | 40 | 0 | 5 | 5 | 162 | .... | 1979-80 | 1986-87 |
| Beadle, Sandy | Wpg. | 1 | 6 | 1 | 0 | 1 | 2 | .... | .... | .... | .... | .... | .... | 1980-81 | 1980-81 |
| Beaton, Frank | NYR | 2 | 25 | 1 | 1 | 2 | 43 | .... | .... | .... | .... | .... | .... | 1978-79 | 1979-80 |
| • Beattie, Red | Bos., Det., NYA | 9 | 334 | 62 | 85 | 147 | 137 | 24 | 4 | 2 | 6 | 8 | .... | 1930-31 | 1938-39 |
| Beaudin, Norm | St.L., Min. | 2 | 25 | 1 | 2 | 3 | 4 | .... | .... | .... | .... | .... | .... | 1967-68 | 1970-71 |
| ‡ Beaudoin, Eric | Fla. | 3 | 53 | 3 | 8 | 11 | 41 | .... | .... | .... | .... | .... | .... | 2001-02 | 2003-04 |
| Beaudoin, Serge | Atl. | 1 | 3 | 0 | 0 | 0 | 0 | .... | .... | .... | .... | .... | .... | 1979-80 | 1979-80 |
| Beaudoin, Yves | Wsh. | 3 | 11 | 0 | 0 | 0 | 5 | .... | .... | .... | .... | .... | .... | 1985-86 | 1987-88 |
| ‡ Beaufait, Mark | S.J. | 1 | 5 | 1 | 0 | 1 | 0 | .... | .... | .... | .... | .... | .... | 1992-93 | 1992-93 |
| Beck, Barry | Col., NYR, L.A. | 10 | 615 | 104 | 251 | 355 | 1016 | 51 | 10 | 23 | 33 | 77 | .... | 1977-78 | 1989-90 |
| Beckett, Bob | Bos. | 4 | 68 | 7 | 6 | 13 | 18 | .... | .... | .... | .... | .... | .... | 1956-57 | 1963-64 |
| Bedard, James | Chi. | 2 | 22 | 1 | 1 | 2 | 8 | .... | .... | .... | .... | .... | .... | 1949-50 | 1950-51 |
| Beddoes, Clayton | Bos. | 2 | 60 | 2 | 8 | 10 | 57 | .... | .... | .... | .... | .... | .... | 1995-96 | 1996-97 |
| ‡ Bednar, Jaroslav | L.A., Fla. | 3 | 102 | 10 | 25 | 35 | 30 | 3 | 0 | 0 | 0 | 0 | .... | 2001-02 | 2003-04 |
| Bednarski, John | NYR, Edm. | 4 | 100 | 2 | 18 | 20 | 114 | 1 | 0 | 0 | 0 | 17 | .... | 1974-75 | 1979-80 |
| Beers, Bob | Bos., T.B., Edm., NYI | 8 | 258 | 28 | 79 | 107 | 225 | 21 | 1 | 1 | 2 | 22 | .... | 1989-90 | 1996-97 |
| Beers, Eddy | Cgy., St.L. | 5 | 250 | 94 | 116 | 210 | 256 | 41 | 7 | 10 | 17 | 47 | .... | 1981-82 | 1985-86 |
| • Behling, Dick | Det. | 2 | 5 | 1 | 0 | 1 | 2 | .... | .... | .... | .... | .... | .... | 1940-41 | 1942-43 |
| • Beisler, Frank | NYA | 2 | 2 | 0 | 0 | 0 | 0 | .... | .... | .... | .... | .... | .... | 1936-37 | 1939-40 |
| Bekar, Derek | St.L., L.A., NYI | 3 | 11 | 0 | 0 | 0 | 6 | .... | .... | .... | .... | .... | .... | 1999-00 | 2003-04 |
| Belanger, Alain | Tor. | 1 | 9 | 0 | 1 | 1 | 6 | .... | .... | .... | .... | .... | .... | 1977-78 | 1977-78 |
| Belanger, Francis | Mtl. | 1 | 10 | 0 | 0 | 0 | 29 | .... | .... | .... | .... | .... | .... | 2000-01 | 2000-01 |
| Belanger, Jesse | Mtl., Fla., Van., Edm., NYI | 8 | 246 | 59 | 76 | 135 | 56 | 12 | 0 | 3 | 3 | 2 | 1 | 1991-92 | 2000-01 |
| Belanger, Ken | Tor., NYI, Bos., L.A. | 11 | 248 | 11 | 12 | 23 | 695 | 12 | 1 | 0 | 1 | 16 | .... | 1994-95 | 2005-06 |
| Belanger, Roger | Pit. | 1 | 44 | 3 | 5 | 8 | 32 | .... | .... | .... | .... | .... | .... | 1984-85 | 1984-85 |
| Belisle, Danny | NYR | 1 | 4 | 2 | 0 | 2 | 0 | .... | .... | .... | .... | .... | .... | 1960-61 | 1960-61 |
| Beliveau, Jean | Mtl. | 20 | 1125 | 507 | 712 | 1219 | 1029 | 162 | 79 | 97 | 176 | 211 | 10 | 1950-51 | 1970-71 |
| • Bell, Billy | Mtl.W., Mtl., Ott. | 6 | 66 | 3 | 2 | 5 | 14 | 5 | 0 | 0 | 0 | 0 | 1 | 1917-18 | 1923-24 |
| Bell, Bruce | Que., St.L., NYR, Edm. | 5 | 209 | 12 | 64 | 76 | 113 | 34 | 3 | 5 | 8 | 41 | .... | 1984-85 | 1989-90 |
| Bell, Harry | NYR | 1 | 1 | 0 | 1 | 1 | 0 | .... | .... | .... | .... | .... | .... | 1946-47 | 1946-47 |
| Bell, Joe | NYR | 2 | 62 | 8 | 9 | 17 | 18 | .... | .... | .... | .... | .... | .... | 1942-43 | 1946-47 |
| Belland, Neil | Van., Pit. | 6 | 109 | 13 | 32 | 45 | 54 | 21 | 2 | 9 | 11 | 23 | .... | 1981-82 | 1986-87 |
| ‡ Bellefeuille, Blake | CBJ | 2 | 5 | 0 | 1 | 1 | 0 | .... | .... | .... | .... | .... | .... | 2001-02 | 2002-03 |
| • Bellefeuille, Pete | Tor., Det. | 4 | 92 | 26 | 4 | 30 | 58 | .... | .... | .... | .... | .... | .... | 1925-26 | 1929-30 |
| • Bellemer, Andy | Mtl.M. | 1 | 15 | 0 | 0 | 0 | 0 | .... | .... | .... | .... | .... | .... | 1932-33 | 1932-33 |
| Bellows, Brian | Min., Mtl., T.B., Ana., Wsh. | 17 | 1188 | 485 | 537 | 1022 | 718 | 143 | 51 | 71 | 122 | 143 | 1 | 1982-83 | 1998-99 |
| • Bend, Lin | NYR | 1 | 8 | 3 | 1 | 4 | 2 | .... | .... | .... | .... | .... | .... | 1942-43 | 1942-43 |
| ‡ Benda, Jan | Wsh. | 1 | 9 | 0 | 3 | 3 | 6 | .... | .... | .... | .... | .... | .... | 1997-98 | 1997-98 |
| Bennett, Adam | Chi., Edm. | 3 | 69 | 3 | 8 | 11 | 69 | .... | .... | .... | .... | .... | .... | 1991-92 | 1993-94 |
| Bennett, Bill | Bos., Hfd. | 2 | 31 | 4 | 7 | 11 | 65 | .... | .... | .... | .... | .... | .... | 1978-79 | 1979-80 |
| Bennett, Curt | St.L., NYR, Atl. | 10 | 580 | 152 | 182 | 334 | 347 | 21 | 1 | 1 | 2 | 57 | .... | 1970-71 | 1979-80 |
| Bennett, Frank | Det. | 1 | 7 | 0 | 1 | 1 | 2 | .... | .... | .... | .... | .... | .... | 1943-44 | 1943-44 |
| Bennett, Harvey | Pit., Wsh., Phi., Min., St.L. | 5 | 268 | 44 | 46 | 90 | 347 | 4 | 0 | 0 | 0 | 2 | .... | 1974-75 | 1978-79 |
| • Bennett, Max | Mtl. | 1 | 1 | 0 | 0 | 0 | 0 | .... | .... | .... | .... | .... | .... | 1935-36 | 1935-36 |
| Bennett, Rick | NYR | 3 | 15 | 1 | 1 | 2 | 13 | .... | .... | .... | .... | .... | .... | 1989-90 | 1991-92 |
| Benning, Brian | St.L., L.A., Phi., Edm., Fla. | 11 | 568 | 63 | 233 | 296 | 963 | 48 | 3 | 20 | 23 | 74 | .... | 1984-85 | 1994-95 |
| Benning, Jim | Tor., Van. | 9 | 605 | 52 | 191 | 243 | 461 | 7 | 1 | 1 | 2 | 2 | .... | 1981-82 | 1989-90 |
| • Benoit, Joe | Mtl. | 5 | 185 | 75 | 69 | 144 | 94 | 11 | 6 | 3 | 9 | 11 | 1 | 1940-41 | 1946-47 |
| Benson, Bill | NYA, Bro. | 2 | 67 | 11 | 25 | 36 | 35 | .... | .... | .... | .... | .... | .... | 1940-41 | 1941-42 |
| • Benson, Bobby | Bos. | 1 | 8 | 0 | 1 | 1 | 4 | .... | .... | .... | .... | .... | .... | 1924-25 | 1924-25 |
| • Bentley, Doug | Chi., NYR | 13 | 566 | 219 | 324 | 543 | 217 | 23 | 9 | 8 | 17 | 12 | .... | 1939-40 | 1953-54 |
| • Bentley, Max | Chi., Tor., NYR | 12 | 646 | 245 | 299 | 544 | 179 | 51 | 18 | 27 | 45 | 14 | 3 | 1940-41 | 1953-54 |
| • Bentley, Reg | Chi. | 1 | 11 | 1 | 2 | 3 | 2 | .... | .... | .... | .... | .... | .... | 1942-43 | 1942-43 |
| ‡ Benysek, Ladislav | Edm., Min. | 4 | 161 | 3 | 12 | 15 | 74 | .... | .... | .... | .... | .... | .... | 1997-98 | 2002-03 |
| Beraldo, Paul | Bos. | 2 | 10 | 0 | 0 | 0 | 4 | .... | .... | .... | .... | .... | .... | 1987-88 | 1988-89 |
| ‡ Beranek, Josef | Edm., Phi., Van., Pit. | 9 | 531 | 118 | 144 | 262 | 398 | 57 | 5 | 8 | 13 | 24 | .... | 1991-92 | 2000-01 |
| Berehowsky, Drake | Tor., Pit., Edm., Nsh., Van., Phx. | 13 | 549 | 37 | 112 | 149 | 848 | 22 | 1 | 3 | 4 | 30 | .... | 1990-91 | 2003-04 |
| Berenson, Red | Mtl., NYR, St.L., Det. | 17 | 987 | 261 | 397 | 658 | 305 | 85 | 23 | 14 | 37 | 49 | 1 | 1961-62 | 1977-78 |
| Berenzweig, Bubba | Nsh. | 4 | 37 | 3 | 7 | 10 | 14 | .... | .... | .... | .... | .... | .... | 1999-00 | 2002-03 |
| Berezan, Perry | Cgy., Min., S.J. | 9 | 378 | 61 | 75 | 136 | 279 | 31 | 4 | 7 | 11 | 34 | .... | 1984-85 | 1992-93 |
| Berezin, Sergei | Tor., Phx., Mtl., Chi., Wsh. | 7 | 502 | 160 | 126 | 286 | 54 | 52 | 13 | 17 | 30 | 6 | .... | 1996-97 | 2002-03 |
| ‡ Berg, Aki | L.A., Tor. | 9 | 606 | 15 | 70 | 85 | 374 | 54 | 1 | 7 | 8 | 47 | .... | 1995-96 | 2005-06 |
| Berg, Bill | NYI, Tor., NYR, Ott. | 10 | 546 | 55 | 67 | 122 | 488 | 61 | 3 | 4 | 7 | 34 | .... | 1988-89 | 1998-99 |
| • Bergdinon, Fred | Bos. | 1 | 2 | 0 | 0 | 0 | 0 | .... | .... | .... | .... | .... | .... | 1925-26 | 1925-26 |
| Bergen, Todd | Phi. | 1 | 14 | 11 | 5 | 16 | 4 | 17 | 4 | 9 | 13 | 8 | .... | 1984-85 | 1984-85 |
| Berger, Mike | Min. | 2 | 30 | 3 | 1 | 4 | 67 | .... | .... | .... | .... | .... | .... | 1987-88 | 1988-89 |
| Bergeron, Michel | Det., NYI, Wsh. | 5 | 229 | 80 | 58 | 138 | 165 | .... | .... | .... | .... | .... | .... | 1974-75 | 1978-79 |
| Bergeron, Yves | Pit. | 2 | 3 | 0 | 0 | 0 | 0 | .... | .... | .... | .... | .... | .... | 1974-75 | 1976-77 |
| Bergevin, Marc | Chi., NYI, Hfd., T.B., Det., St.L., Pit., Van. | 20 | 1191 | 36 | 145 | 181 | 1090 | 80 | 3 | 6 | 9 | 52 | .... | 1984-85 | 2003-04 |
| Bergkvist, Stefan | Pit. | 2 | 7 | 0 | 0 | 0 | 9 | 4 | 0 | 0 | 0 | 2 | .... | 1995-96 | 1996-97 |
| Bergland, Tim | Wsh., T.B. | 5 | 182 | 17 | 26 | 43 | 75 | 26 | 2 | 2 | 4 | 22 | .... | 1989-90 | 1993-94 |
| Bergloff, Bob | Min. | 1 | 2 | 0 | 0 | 0 | 5 | .... | .... | .... | .... | .... | .... | 1982-83 | 1982-83 |
| Berglund, Bo | Que., Min., Phi. | 3 | 130 | 28 | 39 | 67 | 40 | 9 | 2 | 0 | 2 | 6 | .... | 1983-84 | 1985-86 |
| ‡ Berglund, Christian | N.J., Fla. | 3 | 86 | 11 | 16 | 27 | 42 | 3 | 0 | 0 | 0 | 2 | .... | 2001-02 | 2003-04 |
| • Bergman, Gary | Det., Min., K.C. | 12 | 838 | 68 | 299 | 367 | 1249 | 21 | 0 | 5 | 5 | 20 | .... | 1964-65 | 1975-76 |
| Bergman, Thommie | Det. | 6 | 246 | 21 | 44 | 65 | 243 | 7 | 0 | 2 | 2 | 2 | .... | 1972-73 | 1979-80 |
| Bergqvist, Jonas | Cgy. | 1 | 22 | 2 | 5 | 7 | 10 | .... | .... | .... | .... | .... | .... | 1989-90 | 1989-90 |
| • Berlinguette, Louis | Mtl., Mtl.M., Pit. | 8 | 193 | 45 | 33 | 78 | 129 | 11 | 0 | 5 | 5 | 9 | .... | 1917-18 | 1925-26 |
| Bernier, Serge | Phi., L.A., Que. | 7 | 302 | 78 | 119 | 197 | 234 | 5 | 1 | 1 | 2 | 0 | .... | 1968-69 | 1980-81 |
| Berry, Bob | Mtl., L.A. | 8 | 541 | 159 | 191 | 350 | 344 | 26 | 2 | 6 | 8 | 6 | .... | 1968-69 | 1976-77 |
| Berry, Brad | Wpg., Min., Dal. | 8 | 241 | 4 | 28 | 32 | 323 | 13 | 0 | 1 | 1 | 16 | .... | 1985-86 | 1993-94 |
| Berry, Doug | Col. | 2 | 121 | 10 | 33 | 43 | 25 | .... | .... | .... | .... | .... | .... | 1979-80 | 1980-81 |
| Berry, Fred | Det. | 1 | 3 | 0 | 0 | 0 | 0 | .... | .... | .... | .... | .... | .... | 1976-77 | 1976-77 |
| Berry, Ken | Edm., Van. | 4 | 55 | 8 | 10 | 18 | 30 | .... | .... | .... | .... | .... | .... | 1981-82 | 1988-89 |
| ‡ Berry, Rick | Col., Pit., Wsh. | 4 | 197 | 2 | 13 | 15 | 314 | .... | .... | .... | .... | .... | .... | 2000-01 | 2003-04 |
| ‡ Bertrand, Eric | N.J., Atl., Mtl. | 2 | 15 | 0 | 0 | 0 | 4 | .... | .... | .... | .... | .... | .... | 1999-00 | 2000-01 |
| Berube, Craig | Phi., Tor., Cgy., Wsh., NYI | 17 | 1054 | 61 | 98 | 159 | 3149 | 89 | 3 | 1 | 4 | 211 | .... | 1986-87 | 2002-03 |
| • Besler, Phil | Bos., Chi., Det. | 2 | 30 | 1 | 4 | 5 | 18 | .... | .... | .... | .... | .... | .... | 1935-36 | 1938-39 |
| • Bessone, Pete | Det. | 1 | 6 | 0 | 1 | 1 | 6 | .... | .... | .... | .... | .... | .... | 1937-38 | 1937-38 |
| Bethel, John | Wpg. | 1 | 17 | 0 | 2 | 2 | 4 | .... | .... | .... | .... | .... | .... | 1979-80 | 1979-80 |
| Betik, Karel | T.B. | 1 | 3 | 0 | 2 | 2 | 2 | .... | .... | .... | .... | .... | .... | 1998-99 | 1998-99 |
| Bets, Maxim | Ana. | 1 | 3 | 0 | 0 | 0 | 0 | .... | .... | .... | .... | .... | .... | 1993-94 | 1993-94 |
| • Bettio, Sam | Bos. | 1 | 44 | 9 | 12 | 21 | 32 | .... | .... | .... | .... | .... | .... | 1949-50 | 1949-50 |
| Beukeboom, Jeff | Edm., NYR | 14 | 804 | 30 | 129 | 159 | 1890 | 99 | 3 | 16 | 19 | 197 | 4 | 1985-86 | 1998-99 |
| Beverley, Nick | Bos., Pit., NYR, Min., L.A., Col. | 11 | 502 | 18 | 94 | 112 | 156 | 7 | 0 | 1 | 1 | 0 | .... | 1966-67 | 1979-80 |
| ‡ Bezina, Goran | Phx. | 1 | 3 | 0 | 0 | 0 | 2 | .... | .... | .... | .... | .... | .... | 2003-04 | 2003-04 |
| Bialowas, Dwight | Atl., Min. | 4 | 164 | 11 | 46 | 57 | 46 | .... | .... | .... | .... | .... | .... | 1973-74 | 1976-77 |
| Bialowas, Frank | Tor. | 1 | 3 | 0 | 0 | 0 | 12 | .... | .... | .... | .... | .... | .... | 1993-94 | 1993-94 |
| Bianchin, Wayne | Pit., Edm. | 7 | 276 | 68 | 41 | 109 | 137 | 3 | 0 | 1 | 1 | 6 | .... | 1973-74 | 1979-80 |
| Bicanek, Radim | Ott., Chi., CBJ | 7 | 122 | 1 | 11 | 12 | 62 | 7 | 0 | 0 | 0 | 8 | .... | 1994-95 | 2001-02 |
| ‡ Bicek, Jiri | N.J. | 4 | 62 | 6 | 7 | 13 | 29 | 7 | 0 | 0 | 0 | 0 | 1 | 2000-01 | 2003-04 |
| Bidner, Todd | Wsh. | 1 | 12 | 2 | 1 | 3 | 7 | .... | .... | .... | .... | .... | .... | 1981-82 | 1981-82 |
| Biggs, Don | Min., Phi. | 2 | 12 | 2 | 0 | 2 | 8 | .... | .... | .... | .... | .... | .... | 1984-85 | 1989-90 |
| Bignell, Larry | Pit. | 2 | 20 | 0 | 3 | 3 | 2 | 3 | 0 | 0 | 0 | 2 | .... | 1973-74 | 1974-75 |
| • Bilodeau, Gilles | Que. | 1 | 9 | 0 | 1 | 1 | 25 | .... | .... | .... | .... | .... | .... | 1979-80 | 1979-80 |
| • Bionda, Jack | Tor., Bos. | 4 | 93 | 3 | 9 | 12 | 113 | 11 | 0 | 1 | 1 | 14 | .... | 1955-56 | 1958-59 |
| ‡ Biron, Mathieu | NYI, T.B., Fla., Wsh. | 6 | 253 | 12 | 32 | 44 | 177 | .... | .... | .... | .... | .... | .... | 1999-00 | 2005-06 |
| ‡ Bishai, Mike | Edm. | 1 | 14 | 0 | 2 | 2 | 19 | .... | .... | .... | .... | .... | .... | 2003-04 | 2003-04 |
| Bissett, Tom | Det. | 1 | 5 | 0 | 0 | 0 | 0 | .... | .... | .... | .... | .... | .... | 1990-91 | 1990-91 |
| Bjugstad, Scott | Min., Pit., L.A. | 9 | 317 | 76 | 68 | 144 | 144 | 9 | 0 | 1 | 1 | 2 | .... | 1983-84 | 1991-92 |
| Black, James | Hfd., Min., Dal., Buf., Chi., Wsh. | 11 | 352 | 58 | 57 | 115 | 84 | 13 | 2 | 1 | 3 | 4 | .... | 1989-90 | 2000-01 |
| • Black, Steve | Det., Chi. | 2 | 113 | 11 | 20 | 31 | 77 | 13 | 0 | 0 | 0 | 13 | 1 | 1949-50 | 1950-51 |
| Blackburn, Bob | NYR, Pit. | 3 | 135 | 8 | 12 | 20 | 105 | 6 | 0 | 0 | 0 | 4 | .... | 1968-69 | 1970-71 |
| Blackburn, Don | Bos., Phi., NYR, NYI, Min. | 6 | 185 | 23 | 44 | 67 | 87 | 12 | 3 | 0 | 3 | 10 | .... | 1962-63 | 1972-73 |
| • Blade, Hank | Chi. | 2 | 24 | 2 | 3 | 5 | 2 | .... | .... | .... | .... | .... | .... | 1946-47 | 1947-48 |
| Bladon, Tom | Phi., Pit., Edm., Wpg., Det. | 9 | 610 | 73 | 197 | 270 | 392 | 86 | 8 | 29 | 37 | 70 | 2 | 1972-73 | 1980-81 |
| • Blaine, Garry | Mtl. | 1 | 1 | 0 | 0 | 0 | 0 | .... | .... | .... | .... | .... | .... | 1954-55 | 1954-55 |
| • Blair, Andy | Tor., Chi. | 9 | 402 | 74 | 86 | 160 | 323 | 38 | 6 | 6 | 12 | 32 | 1 | 1928-29 | 1936-37 |
| • Blair, Chuck | Tor. | 1 | 1 | 0 | 0 | 0 | 0 | .... | .... | .... | .... | .... | .... | 1948-49 | 1948-49 |
| Blair, Dusty | Tor. | 1 | 2 | 0 | 0 | 0 | 0 | .... | .... | .... | .... | .... | .... | 1950-51 | 1950-51 |
| Blaisdell, Mike | Det., NYR, Pit., Tor. | 9 | 343 | 70 | 84 | 154 | 166 | 6 | 1 | 2 | 3 | 10 | .... | 1980-81 | 1988-89 |
| • Blake, Bob | Bos. | 1 | 12 | 0 | 0 | 0 | 0 | .... | .... | .... | .... | .... | .... | 1935-36 | 1935-36 |
| • Blake, Mickey | Mtl.M., St.L., Tor. | 3 | 10 | 1 | 1 | 2 | 4 | .... | .... | .... | .... | .... | .... | 1932-33 | 1935-36 |
| • Blake, Toe | Mtl.M., Mtl. | 14 | 577 | 235 | 292 | 527 | 272 | 58 | 25 | 37 | 62 | 23 | 3 | 1934-35 | 1947-48 |

| | | | Regular Schedule | | | | | Playoffs | | | | | | | |
|---|---|---|---|---|---|---|---|---|---|---|---|---|---|---|---|
| Name | NHL Teams | NHL Seasons | GP | G | A | TP | PIM | GP | G | A | TP | PIM | NHL Cup Wins | First NHL Season | Last NHL Season |
| ‡ Blatny, Zdenek | Atl., Bos. | 3 | 25 | 3 | 0 | 3 | 8 | .... | .... | .... | .... | .... | .... | 2002-03 | 2005-06 |
| • Blight, Rick | Van., L.A. | 7 | 326 | 96 | 125 | 221 | 170 | 5 | 0 | 5 | 5 | 2 | .... | 1975-76 | 1982-83 |
| • Blinco, Russ | Mtl.M., Chi. | 6 | 268 | 59 | 66 | 125 | 24 | 19 | 3 | 3 | 6 | 4 | 1 | 1933-34 | 1938-39 |
| Block, Ken | Van. | 1 | 1 | 0 | 0 | 0 | 0 | .... | .... | .... | .... | .... | .... | 1970-71 | 1970-71 |
| Bloemberg, Jeff | NYR | 4 | 43 | 3 | 6 | 9 | 25 | 7 | 0 | 3 | 3 | 5 | .... | 1988-89 | 1991-92 |
| Blomqvist, Timo | Wsh., N.J. | 5 | 243 | 4 | 53 | 57 | 293 | 13 | 0 | 0 | 0 | 24 | .... | 1981-82 | 1986-87 |
| Blomsten, Arto | Wpg., L.A. | 3 | 25 | 0 | 4 | 4 | 8 | .... | .... | .... | .... | .... | .... | 1993-94 | 1995-96 |
| Bloom, Mike | Wsh., Det. | 3 | 201 | 30 | 47 | 77 | 215 | .... | .... | .... | .... | .... | .... | 1974-75 | 1976-77 |
| ‡ Blouin, Sylvain | NYR, Mtl., Min. | 6 | 115 | 3 | 4 | 7 | 336 | .... | .... | .... | .... | .... | .... | 1996-97 | 2002-03 |
| Blum, John | Edm., Bos., Wsh., Det. | 8 | 250 | 7 | 34 | 41 | 610 | 20 | 0 | 2 | 2 | 27 | .... | 1982-83 | 1989-90 |
| Bodak, Bob | Cgy., Hfd. | 2 | 4 | 0 | 0 | 0 | 29 | .... | .... | .... | .... | .... | .... | 1987-88 | 1989-90 |
| Boddy, Gregg | Van. | 5 | 273 | 23 | 44 | 67 | 263 | 3 | 0 | 0 | 0 | 0 | .... | 1971-72 | 1975-76 |
| Bodger, Doug | Pit., Buf., S.J., N.J., L.A., Van. | 16 | 1071 | 106 | 422 | 528 | 1007 | 47 | 6 | 18 | 24 | 25 | .... | 1984-85 | 1999-00 |
| • Bodnar, Gus | Tor., Chi., Bos. | 12 | 667 | 142 | 254 | 396 | 207 | 32 | 4 | 3 | 7 | 10 | 2 | 1943-44 | 1954-55 |
| Boehm, Ron | Oak. | 1 | 16 | 2 | 1 | 3 | 10 | .... | .... | .... | .... | .... | .... | 1967-68 | 1967-68 |
| • Boesch, Garth | Tor. | 4 | 197 | 9 | 28 | 37 | 205 | 34 | 2 | 5 | 7 | 18 | 3 | 1946-47 | 1949-50 |
| Boh, Rick | Min. | 1 | 8 | 2 | 1 | 3 | 4 | .... | .... | .... | .... | .... | .... | 1987-88 | 1987-88 |
| Bohonos, Lonny | Van., Tor. | 4 | 83 | 19 | 16 | 35 | 22 | 9 | 3 | 6 | 9 | 2 | .... | 1995-96 | 1998-99 |
| Boikov, Alexandre | Nsh. | 2 | 10 | 0 | 0 | 0 | 15 | .... | .... | .... | .... | .... | .... | 1999-00 | 2000-01 |
| • Boileau, Marc | Det. | 1 | 54 | 5 | 6 | 11 | 8 | .... | .... | .... | .... | .... | .... | 1961-62 | 1961-62 |
| Boileau, Patrick | Wsh., Det., Pit. | 5 | 48 | 5 | 11 | 16 | 26 | .... | .... | .... | .... | .... | .... | 1996-97 | 2003-04 |
| • Boileau, Rene | NYA | 1 | 7 | 0 | 0 | 0 | 0 | .... | .... | .... | .... | .... | .... | 1925-26 | 1925-26 |
| Boimistruck, Fred | Tor. | 2 | 83 | 4 | 14 | 18 | 45 | .... | .... | .... | .... | .... | .... | 1981-82 | 1982-83 |
| Boisvert, Serge | Tor., Mtl. | 5 | 46 | 5 | 7 | 12 | 8 | 23 | 3 | 7 | 10 | 4 | 1 | 1982-83 | 1987-88 |
| Boivin, Claude | Phi., Ott. | 4 | 132 | 12 | 19 | 31 | 364 | .... | .... | .... | .... | .... | .... | 1991-92 | 1994-95 |
| Boivin, Leo | Tor., Bos., Det., Pit., Min. | 19 | 1150 | 72 | 250 | 322 | 1192 | 54 | 3 | 10 | 13 | 59 | .... | 1951-52 | 1969-70 |
| Boland, Mike | Phi. | 1 | 2 | 0 | 0 | 0 | 0 | .... | .... | .... | .... | .... | .... | 1974-75 | 1974-75 |
| Boland, Mike | K.C., Buf. | 2 | 23 | 1 | 2 | 3 | 29 | 3 | 1 | 0 | 1 | 2 | .... | 1974-75 | 1978-79 |
| Boldirev, Ivan | Bos., Cal., Chi., Atl., Van., Det. | 15 | 1052 | 361 | 505 | 866 | 507 | 48 | 13 | 20 | 33 | 14 | 1 | 1969-70 | 1984-85 |
| Bolduc, Danny | Det., Cgy. | 3 | 102 | 22 | 19 | 41 | 33 | 1 | 0 | 0 | 0 | 0 | .... | 1978-79 | 1983-84 |
| Bolduc, Michel | Que. | 2 | 10 | 0 | 0 | 0 | 6 | .... | .... | .... | .... | .... | .... | 1981-82 | 1982-83 |
| • Boll, Buzz | Tor., NYA, Bro., Bos. | 12 | 437 | 133 | 130 | 263 | 148 | 31 | 7 | 3 | 10 | 13 | .... | 1932-33 | 1943-44 |
| Bolonchuk, Larry | Van., Wsh. | 4 | 74 | 3 | 9 | 12 | 97 | .... | .... | .... | .... | .... | .... | 1972-73 | 1977-78 |
| • Bolton, Hugh | Tor. | 8 | 235 | 10 | 51 | 61 | 221 | 17 | 0 | 5 | 5 | 14 | 1 | 1949-50 | 1956-57 |
| Bombardir, Brad | N.J., Min., Nsh. | 7 | 356 | 8 | 46 | 54 | 127 | 16 | 0 | 1 | 1 | 2 | 1 | 1997-98 | 2003-04 |
| Bonar, Dan | L.A. | 3 | 170 | 25 | 39 | 64 | 208 | 14 | 3 | 4 | 7 | 22 | .... | 1980-81 | 1982-83 |
| Bondra, Peter | Wsh., Ott., Atl., Chi. | 16 | 1081 | 503 | 389 | 892 | 761 | 80 | 30 | 26 | 56 | 60 | .... | 1990-91 | 2006-07 |
| Bonin, Brian | Pit., Min. | 2 | 12 | 0 | 0 | 0 | 0 | 3 | 0 | 0 | 0 | 0 | .... | 1998-99 | 2000-01 |
| Bonin, Marcel | Det., Bos., Mtl. | 9 | 454 | 97 | 175 | 272 | 336 | 50 | 11 | 14 | 25 | 51 | 4 | 1952-53 | 1961-62 |
| Bonni, Ryan | Van. | 1 | 3 | 0 | 0 | 0 | 0 | .... | .... | .... | .... | .... | .... | 1999-00 | 1999-00 |
| Bonsignore, Jason | Edm., T.B. | 4 | 79 | 3 | 13 | 16 | 34 | .... | .... | .... | .... | .... | .... | 1994-95 | 1998-99 |
| Bonvie, Dennis | Edm., Chi., Pit., Bos., Ott., Col. | 9 | 92 | 1 | 2 | 3 | 311 | 1 | 0 | 0 | 0 | 0 | .... | 1994-95 | 2003-04 |
| Boo, Jim | Min. | 1 | 6 | 0 | 0 | 0 | 22 | .... | .... | .... | .... | .... | .... | 1977-78 | 1977-78 |
| • Boone, Buddy | Bos. | 2 | 34 | 5 | 3 | 8 | 28 | 22 | 2 | 1 | 3 | 25 | .... | 1956-57 | 1957-58 |
| • Boothman, George | Tor. | 2 | 58 | 17 | 19 | 36 | 18 | 5 | 2 | 1 | 3 | 2 | .... | 1942-43 | 1943-44 |
| Bordeleau, Christian | Mtl., St.L., Chi. | 4 | 205 | 38 | 65 | 103 | 82 | 19 | 4 | 7 | 11 | 17 | 1 | 1968-69 | 1971-72 |
| Bordeleau, J.P. | Chi. | 10 | 519 | 97 | 126 | 223 | 143 | 48 | 3 | 6 | 9 | 12 | .... | 1969-70 | 1979-80 |
| Bordeleau, Paulin | Van. | 3 | 183 | 33 | 56 | 89 | 47 | 5 | 2 | 1 | 3 | 0 | .... | 1973-74 | 1975-76 |
| ‡ Bordeleau, Sebastien | Mtl., Nsh., Min., Phx. | 7 | 251 | 37 | 61 | 98 | 118 | 5 | 0 | 0 | 0 | 2 | .... | 1995-96 | 2001-02 |
| Borotsik, Jack | St.L. | 1 | 1 | 0 | 0 | 0 | 0 | .... | .... | .... | .... | .... | .... | 1974-75 | 1974-75 |
| Borsato, Luciano | Wpg. | 5 | 203 | 35 | 55 | 90 | 113 | 7 | 1 | 0 | 1 | 4 | .... | 1990-91 | 1994-95 |
| Borschevsky, Nikolai | Tor., Cgy., Dal. | 4 | 162 | 49 | 73 | 122 | 44 | 31 | 4 | 9 | 13 | 4 | .... | 1992-93 | 1995-96 |
| Boschman, Laurie | Tor., Edm., Wpg., N.J., Ott. | 14 | 1009 | 229 | 348 | 577 | 2265 | 57 | 8 | 13 | 21 | 140 | .... | 1979-80 | 1992-93 |
| Bossy, Mike | NYI | 10 | 752 | 573 | 553 | 1126 | 210 | 129 | 85 | 75 | 160 | 38 | 4 | 1977-78 | 1986-87 |
| • Bostrom, Helge | Chi. | 4 | 96 | 3 | 3 | 6 | 58 | 13 | 0 | 0 | 0 | 16 | .... | 1929-30 | 1932-33 |
| Botell, Mark | Phi. | 1 | 32 | 4 | 10 | 14 | 31 | .... | .... | .... | .... | .... | .... | 1981-82 | 1981-82 |
| Bothwell, Tim | NYR, St.L., Hfd. | 12 | 502 | 28 | 93 | 121 | 382 | 49 | 0 | 3 | 3 | 56 | .... | 1978-79 | 1988-89 |
| Botterill, Jason | Dal., Atl., Cgy., Buf. | 6 | 88 | 5 | 9 | 14 | 89 | .... | .... | .... | .... | .... | .... | 1997-98 | 2003-04 |
| Botting, Cam | Atl. | 1 | 2 | 0 | 1 | 1 | 0 | .... | .... | .... | .... | .... | .... | 1975-76 | 1975-76 |
| Boucha, Henry | Det., Min., K.C., Col. | 6 | 247 | 53 | 49 | 102 | 157 | .... | .... | .... | .... | .... | .... | 1971-72 | 1976-77 |
| Bouchard, Butch | Mtl. | 15 | 785 | 49 | 144 | 193 | 863 | 113 | 11 | 21 | 32 | 121 | 4 | 1941-42 | 1955-56 |
| • Bouchard, Dick | NYR | 1 | 1 | 0 | 0 | 0 | 0 | .... | .... | .... | .... | .... | .... | 1954-55 | 1954-55 |
| • Bouchard, Edmond | Mtl., Ham., NYA, Pit. | 8 | 211 | 19 | 21 | 40 | 117 | .... | .... | .... | .... | .... | .... | 1921-22 | 1928-29 |
| Bouchard, Joel | Cgy., Nsh., Dal., Phx., N.J., NYR, Pit., NYI | 11 | 364 | 22 | 53 | 75 | 264 | .... | .... | .... | .... | .... | .... | 1994-95 | 2005-06 |
| Bouchard, Pierre | Mtl., Wsh. | 12 | 595 | 24 | 82 | 106 | 433 | 76 | 3 | 10 | 13 | 56 | 5 | 1970-71 | 1981-82 |
| • Boucher, Billy | Mtl., Bos., NYA | 7 | 213 | 93 | 38 | 131 | 409 | 14 | 3 | 0 | 3 | 17 | 1 | 1921-22 | 1927-28 |
| • Boucher, Bobby | Mtl. | 1 | 11 | 1 | 0 | 1 | 0 | 2 | 0 | 0 | 0 | 0 | 1 | 1923-24 | 1923-24 |
| • Boucher, Clarence | NYA | 2 | 47 | 2 | 2 | 4 | 133 | .... | .... | .... | .... | .... | .... | 1926-27 | 1927-28 |
| • Boucher, Frank | Ott., NYR | 14 | 557 | 160 | 263 | 423 | 119 | 55 | 16 | 20 | 36 | 12 | 2 | 1921-22 | 1943-44 |
| • Boucher, Georges | Ott., Mtl.M., Chi. | 15 | 449 | 117 | 87 | 204 | 838 | 28 | 5 | 3 | 8 | 88 | 4 | 1917-18 | 1931-32 |
| Boudreau, Bruce | Tor., Chi. | 8 | 141 | 28 | 42 | 70 | 46 | 9 | 2 | 0 | 2 | 0 | .... | 1976-77 | 1985-86 |
| Boudrias, Andre | Mtl., Min., Chi., St.L., Van. | 12 | 662 | 151 | 340 | 491 | 216 | 34 | 6 | 10 | 16 | 12 | .... | 1963-64 | 1975-76 |
| Boughner, Barry | Oak., Cal. | 2 | 20 | 0 | 0 | 0 | 11 | .... | .... | .... | .... | .... | .... | 1969-70 | 1970-71 |
| Boughner, Bob | Buf., Nsh., Pit., Cgy., Car., Col. | 10 | 630 | 15 | 57 | 72 | 1382 | 65 | 0 | 12 | 12 | 67 | .... | 1995-96 | 2005-06 |
| Bourbonnais, Dan | Hfd. | 2 | 59 | 3 | 25 | 28 | 11 | .... | .... | .... | .... | .... | .... | 1981-82 | 1983-84 |
| Bourbonnais, Rick | St.L. | 3 | 71 | 9 | 15 | 24 | 29 | 4 | 0 | 1 | 1 | 0 | .... | 1975-76 | 1977-78 |
| • Bourcier, Conrad | Mtl. | 1 | 6 | 0 | 0 | 0 | 0 | .... | .... | .... | .... | .... | .... | 1935-36 | 1935-36 |
| • Bourcier, Jean | Mtl. | 1 | 9 | 0 | 1 | 1 | 0 | .... | .... | .... | .... | .... | .... | 1935-36 | 1935-36 |
| • Bourdon, Luc | Van. | 2 | 36 | 2 | 0 | 2 | 24 | .... | .... | .... | .... | .... | .... | 2006-07 | 2007-08 |
| • Bourgeault, Leo | Tor., NYR, Ott., Mtl. | 8 | 307 | 24 | 20 | 44 | 334 | 24 | 1 | 1 | 2 | 18 | 1 | 1926-27 | 1934-35 |
| Bourgeois, Charlie | Cgy., St.L., Hfd. | 7 | 290 | 16 | 54 | 70 | 788 | 40 | 2 | 3 | 5 | 194 | .... | 1981-82 | 1987-88 |
| Bourne, Bob | NYI, L.A. | 14 | 964 | 258 | 324 | 582 | 605 | 139 | 40 | 56 | 96 | 108 | 4 | 1974-75 | 1987-88 |
| Bourque, Phil | Pit., NYR, Ott. | 12 | 477 | 88 | 111 | 199 | 516 | 56 | 13 | 12 | 25 | 107 | 2 | 1983-84 | 1995-96 |
| Bourque, Raymond | Bos., Col. | 22 | 1612 | 410 | 1169 | 1579 | 1141 | 214 | 41 | 139 | 180 | 171 | 1 | 1979-80 | 2000-01 |
| Boutette, Pat | Tor., Hfd., Pit. | 10 | 756 | 171 | 282 | 453 | 1354 | 46 | 10 | 14 | 24 | 109 | .... | 1975-76 | 1984-85 |
| Boutilier, Paul | NYI, Bos., Min., NYR, Wpg. | 8 | 288 | 27 | 83 | 110 | 358 | 41 | 1 | 9 | 10 | 45 | 1 | 1981-82 | 1988-89 |
| Bowen, Jason | Phi., Edm. | 6 | 77 | 2 | 6 | 8 | 109 | .... | .... | .... | .... | .... | .... | 1992-93 | 1997-98 |
| Bowler, Bill | CBJ | 1 | 9 | 0 | 2 | 2 | 8 | .... | .... | .... | .... | .... | .... | 2000-01 | 2000-01 |
| Bowman, Kirk | Chi. | 3 | 88 | 11 | 17 | 28 | 19 | 7 | 1 | 0 | 1 | 0 | .... | 1976-77 | 1978-79 |
| • Bowman, Ralph | Ott., St.L., Det. | 7 | 274 | 8 | 17 | 25 | 260 | 22 | 2 | 2 | 4 | 6 | 2 | 1933-34 | 1939-40 |
| Bownass, Jack | Mtl., NYR | 4 | 80 | 3 | 8 | 11 | 58 | .... | .... | .... | .... | .... | .... | 1957-58 | 1961-62 |
| Bowness, Rick | Atl., Det., St.L., Wpg. | 7 | 173 | 18 | 37 | 55 | 191 | 5 | 0 | 0 | 0 | 2 | .... | 1975-76 | 1981-82 |
| • Boyd, Bill | NYR, NYA | 4 | 138 | 15 | 7 | 22 | 72 | 10 | 0 | 0 | 0 | 4 | 1 | 1926-27 | 1929-30 |
| • Boyd, Irwin | Bos., Det. | 4 | 96 | 10 | 10 | 20 | 30 | 5 | 0 | 1 | 1 | 4 | .... | 1931-32 | 1943-44 |
| Boyd, Randy | Pit., Chi., NYI, Van. | 8 | 257 | 20 | 67 | 87 | 328 | 13 | 0 | 2 | 2 | 26 | .... | 1981-82 | 1988-89 |
| Boyer, Wally | Tor., Chi., Oak., Pit. | 7 | 365 | 54 | 105 | 159 | 163 | 15 | 1 | 3 | 4 | 0 | .... | 1965-66 | 1971-72 |
| Boyer, Zac | Dal. | 2 | 3 | 0 | 0 | 0 | 0 | 2 | 0 | 0 | 0 | 0 | .... | 1994-95 | 1995-96 |
| Boyko, Darren | Wpg. | 1 | 1 | 0 | 0 | 0 | 0 | .... | .... | .... | .... | .... | .... | 1988-89 | 1988-89 |
| Bozek, Steve | L.A., Cgy., St.L., Van., S.J. | 11 | 641 | 164 | 167 | 331 | 309 | 58 | 12 | 11 | 23 | 69 | .... | 1981-82 | 1991-92 |
| Bozon, Philippe | St.L. | 4 | 144 | 16 | 25 | 41 | 101 | 19 | 2 | 0 | 2 | 31 | .... | 1991-92 | 1994-95 |
| • Brackenborough, John | Bos. | 1 | 7 | 0 | 0 | 0 | 0 | .... | .... | .... | .... | .... | .... | 1925-26 | 1925-26 |
| Brackenbury, Curt | Que., Edm., St.L. | 4 | 141 | 9 | 17 | 26 | 226 | 2 | 0 | 0 | 0 | 0 | .... | 1979-80 | 1982-83 |
| • Bradley, Bart | Bos. | 1 | 1 | 0 | 0 | 0 | 0 | .... | .... | .... | .... | .... | .... | 1949-50 | 1949-50 |
| Bradley, Brian | Cgy., Van., Tor., T.B. | 13 | 651 | 182 | 321 | 503 | 528 | 13 | 3 | 7 | 10 | 16 | .... | 1985-86 | 1997-98 |
| Bradley, Lyle | Cal., Cle. | 2 | 6 | 1 | 0 | 1 | 2 | .... | .... | .... | .... | .... | .... | 1973-74 | 1976-77 |
| Brady, Neil | N.J., Ott., Dal. | 5 | 89 | 9 | 22 | 31 | 95 | .... | .... | .... | .... | .... | .... | 1989-90 | 1993-94 |
| Bragnalo, Rick | Wsh. | 4 | 145 | 15 | 35 | 50 | 46 | .... | .... | .... | .... | .... | .... | 1975-76 | 1978-79 |
| ‡ Brandner, Christoph | Min. | 1 | 35 | 4 | 5 | 9 | 8 | .... | .... | .... | .... | .... | .... | 2003-04 | 2003-04 |
| • Branigan, Andy | NYA, Bro. | 2 | 27 | 1 | 2 | 3 | 31 | .... | .... | .... | .... | .... | .... | 1940-41 | 1941-42 |
| Brasar, Per-Olov | Min., Van. | 5 | 348 | 64 | 142 | 206 | 33 | 13 | 1 | 2 | 3 | 0 | .... | 1977-78 | 1981-82 |
| • Brayshaw, Russ | Chi. | 1 | 43 | 5 | 9 | 14 | 24 | .... | .... | .... | .... | .... | .... | 1944-45 | 1944-45 |
| Breault, Francois | L.A. | 3 | 27 | 2 | 4 | 6 | 42 | .... | .... | .... | .... | .... | .... | 1990-91 | 1992-93 |
| Breitenbach, Ken | Buf. | 3 | 68 | 1 | 13 | 14 | 49 | 8 | 0 | 1 | 1 | 4 | .... | 1975-76 | 1978-79 |
| ‡ Bremberg, Fredrik | Edm. | 1 | 8 | 0 | 0 | 0 | 2 | .... | .... | .... | .... | .... | .... | 1998-99 | 1998-99 |
| ‡ Brendl, Pavel | Phi., Car., Phx. | 4 | 78 | 11 | 11 | 22 | 16 | 2 | 0 | 0 | 0 | 0 | .... | 2001-02 | 2005-06 |
| Brennan, Dan | L.A. | 2 | 8 | 0 | 1 | 1 | 9 | .... | .... | .... | .... | .... | .... | 1983-84 | 1985-86 |
| • Brennan, Doug | NYR | 3 | 123 | 9 | 7 | 16 | 152 | 16 | 1 | 0 | 1 | 21 | 1 | 1931-32 | 1933-34 |
| Brennan, Rich | Col., S.J., NYR, L.A., Nsh., Bos. | 6 | 50 | 2 | 6 | 8 | 33 | .... | .... | .... | .... | .... | .... | 1996-97 | 2002-03 |
| • Brennan, Tom | Bos. | 2 | 12 | 2 | 2 | 4 | 2 | .... | .... | .... | .... | .... | .... | 1943-44 | 1944-45 |
| Brenneman, John | Chi., NYR, Tor., Det., Oak. | 5 | 152 | 21 | 19 | 40 | 46 | .... | .... | .... | .... | .... | 1 | 1964-65 | 1968-69 |
| • Bretto, Joe | Chi. | 1 | 3 | 0 | 0 | 0 | 4 | .... | .... | .... | .... | .... | .... | 1944-45 | 1944-45 |
| • Brewer, Carl | Tor., Det., St.L. | 12 | 604 | 25 | 198 | 223 | 1037 | 72 | 3 | 17 | 20 | 146 | 3 | 1957-58 | 1979-80 |
| Brickley, Andy | Phi., Pit., N.J., Bos., Wpg. | 11 | 385 | 82 | 140 | 222 | 81 | 17 | 1 | 4 | 5 | 4 | .... | 1982-83 | 1993-94 |
| • Briden, Archie | Bos., Det., Pit. | 2 | 71 | 9 | 5 | 14 | 56 | .... | .... | .... | .... | .... | .... | 1926-27 | 1929-30 |
| Bridgman, Mel | Phi., Cgy., N.J., Det., Van. | 14 | 977 | 252 | 449 | 701 | 1625 | 125 | 28 | 39 | 67 | 298 | .... | 1975-76 | 1988-89 |

*Danny Belisle*

*Doug Bentley*

*Scott Bjugstad*

*John Blum*

Luc Bourdon

Gordie Bruce

Roy Burmister

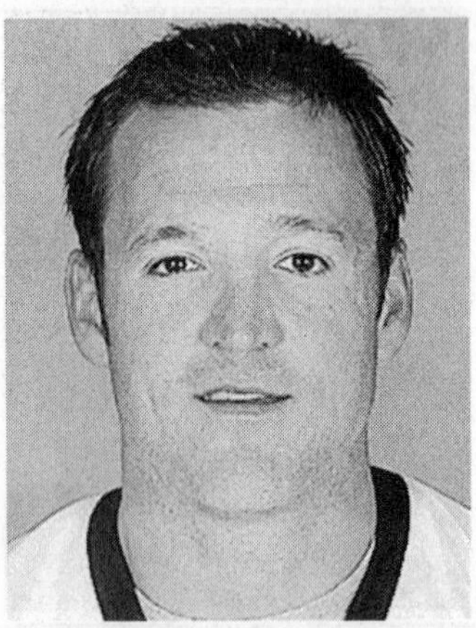

Dan Bylsma

| | | | Regular Schedule | | | | | Playoffs | | | | | NHL | First | Last |
|---|---|---|---|---|---|---|---|---|---|---|---|---|---|---|---|
| | Name | NHL Teams | NHL Seasons | GP | G | A | TP | PIM | GP | G | A | TP | PIM | Cup Wins | NHL Season | NHL Season |
| • | Briere, Michel | Pit. | 1 | 76 | 12 | 32 | 44 | 20 | 10 | 5 | 3 | 8 | 17 | .... | 1969-70 | 1969-70 |
| ‡ | Brigley, Travis | Cgy., Col. | 3 | 55 | 3 | 6 | 9 | 16 | .... | .... | .... | .... | .... | .... | 1997-98 | 2003-04 |
| ‡ | Brimanis, Aris | Phi., NYI, Ana., St.L. | 7 | 113 | 2 | 12 | 14 | 57 | .... | .... | .... | .... | .... | .... | 1993-94 | 2003-04 |
| | Brindley, Doug | Tor. | 1 | 3 | 0 | 0 | 0 | 0 | .... | .... | .... | .... | .... | .... | 1970-71 | 1970-71 |
| • | Brink, Milt | Chi. | 1 | 5 | 0 | 0 | 0 | 0 | .... | .... | .... | .... | .... | .... | 1936-37 | 1936-37 |
| | Brisson, Gerry | Mtl. | 1 | 4 | 0 | 2 | 2 | 4 | .... | .... | .... | .... | .... | .... | 1962-63 | 1962-63 |
| | Britz, Greg | Tor., Hfd. | 3 | 8 | 0 | 0 | 0 | 4 | .... | .... | .... | .... | .... | .... | 1983-84 | 1986-87 |
| • | Broadbent, Punch | Ott., Mtl.M., NYA | 11 | 303 | 121 | 51 | 172 | 564 | 23 | 4 | 6 | 10 | 60 | 4 | 1918-19 | 1928-29 |
| | Brochu, Stephane | NYR | 1 | 1 | 0 | 0 | 0 | 0 | .... | .... | .... | .... | .... | .... | 1988-89 | 1988-89 |
| | Broden, Connie | Mtl. | 3 | 6 | 2 | 1 | 3 | 2 | 7 | 0 | 1 | 1 | 0 | 2 | 1955-56 | 1957-58 |
| | Brooke, Bob | NYR, Min., N.J. | 7 | 447 | 69 | 97 | 166 | 520 | 34 | 9 | 9 | 18 | 59 | .... | 1983-84 | 1989-90 |
| | Brooks, Gord | St.L., Wsh. | 3 | 70 | 7 | 18 | 25 | 37 | .... | .... | .... | .... | .... | .... | 1971-72 | 1974-75 |
| • | Brophy, Bernie | Mtl.M., Det. | 3 | 62 | 4 | 4 | 8 | 25 | 2 | 0 | 0 | 0 | 2 | 1 | 1925-26 | 1929-30 |
| | Brossart, Willie | Phi., Tor., Wsh. | 6 | 129 | 1 | 14 | 15 | 88 | 1 | 0 | 0 | 0 | 0 | .... | 1970-71 | 1975-76 |
| | Broten, Aaron | Col., N.J., Min., Que., Tor., Wpg. | 12 | 748 | 186 | 329 | 515 | 441 | 34 | 7 | 18 | 25 | 40 | .... | 1980-81 | 1991-92 |
| | Broten, Neal | Min., Dal., N.J., L.A. | 17 | 1099 | 289 | 634 | 923 | 569 | 135 | 35 | 63 | 98 | 77 | 1 | 1980-81 | 1996-97 |
| | Broten, Paul | NYR, Dal., St.L. | 7 | 322 | 46 | 55 | 101 | 264 | 38 | 4 | 6 | 10 | 18 | .... | 1989-90 | 1995-96 |
| | Brousseau, Paul | Col., T.B., Fla. | 4 | 26 | 1 | 3 | 4 | 29 | .... | .... | .... | .... | .... | .... | 1995-96 | 2000-01 |
| • | Brown, Adam | Det., Chi., Bos. | 10 | 391 | 104 | 113 | 217 | 378 | 26 | 2 | 4 | 6 | 14 | 1 | 1941-42 | 1951-52 |
| | Brown, Arnie | Tor., NYR, Det., NYI, Atl. | 12 | 681 | 44 | 141 | 185 | 738 | 22 | 0 | 6 | 6 | 23 | .... | 1961-62 | 1973-74 |
| ‡ | Brown, Brad | Mtl., Chi., NYR, Min., Buf. | 7 | 330 | 2 | 27 | 29 | 747 | 11 | 0 | 0 | 0 | 16 | .... | 1996-97 | 2003-04 |
| | Brown, Cam | Van. | 1 | 1 | 0 | 0 | 0 | 7 | .... | .... | .... | .... | .... | .... | 1990-91 | 1990-91 |
| • | Brown, Connie | Det. | 5 | 73 | 15 | 24 | 39 | 12 | 14 | 2 | 3 | 5 | 0 | 1 | 1938-39 | 1942-43 |
| | Brown, Dave | Phi., Edm., S.J. | 14 | 729 | 45 | 52 | 97 | 1789 | 80 | 2 | 3 | 5 | 209 | 1 | 1982-83 | 1995-96 |
| | Brown, Doug | N.J., Pit., Det. | 15 | 854 | 160 | 214 | 374 | 210 | 109 | 23 | 23 | 46 | 26 | 2 | 1986-87 | 2000-01 |
| • | Brown, Fred | Mtl.M. | 1 | 19 | 1 | 0 | 1 | 0 | 9 | 0 | 0 | 0 | 0 | .... | 1927-28 | 1927-28 |
| | Brown, George | Mtl. | 3 | 79 | 6 | 22 | 28 | 34 | 7 | 0 | 0 | 0 | 2 | .... | 1936-37 | 1938-39 |
| • | Brown, Gerry | Det. | 2 | 23 | 4 | 5 | 9 | 2 | 12 | 2 | 1 | 3 | 4 | .... | 1941-42 | 1945-46 |
| | Brown, Greg | Buf., Pit., Wpg. | 4 | 94 | 4 | 14 | 18 | 86 | 6 | 0 | 1 | 1 | 4 | .... | 1990-91 | 1994-95 |
| | Brown, Harold | NYR | 1 | 13 | 2 | 1 | 3 | 2 | .... | .... | .... | .... | .... | .... | 1945-46 | 1945-46 |
| | Brown, Jeff | Que., St.L., Van., Hfd., Car., Tor., Wsh. | 13 | 747 | 154 | 430 | 584 | 498 | 87 | 20 | 45 | 65 | 59 | .... | 1985-86 | 1997-98 |
| | Brown, Jim | L.A. | 1 | 3 | 0 | 1 | 1 | 5 | .... | .... | .... | .... | .... | .... | 1982-83 | 1982-83 |
| | Brown, Keith | Chi., Fla. | 16 | 876 | 68 | 274 | 342 | 916 | 103 | 4 | 32 | 36 | 184 | .... | 1979-80 | 1994-95 |
| | Brown, Kevin | L.A., Hfd., Car., Edm. | 6 | 64 | 7 | 9 | 16 | 28 | 1 | 0 | 0 | 0 | 0 | .... | 1994-95 | 1999-00 |
| | Brown, Larry | NYR, Det., Phi., L.A. | 9 | 455 | 7 | 53 | 60 | 180 | 35 | 0 | 4 | 4 | 10 | .... | 1969-70 | 1977-78 |
| | Brown, Mike | Van., Ana., Chi. | 3 | 34 | 1 | 2 | 3 | 130 | .... | .... | .... | .... | .... | .... | 2000-01 | 2005-06 |
| | Brown, Rob | Pit., Hfd., Chi., Dal., L.A. | 11 | 543 | 190 | 248 | 438 | 599 | 54 | 12 | 14 | 26 | 45 | .... | 1987-88 | 1999-00 |
| ‡ | Brown, Sean | Edm., Bos., N.J., Van. | 9 | 436 | 14 | 43 | 57 | 907 | 9 | 0 | 0 | 0 | 37 | .... | 1996-97 | 2005-06 |
| • | Brown, Stan | NYR, Det. | 2 | 48 | 8 | 2 | 10 | 18 | 2 | 0 | 0 | 0 | 0 | .... | 1926-27 | 1927-28 |
| | Brown, Wayne | Bos. | 1 | .... | .... | .... | .... | .... | 4 | 0 | 0 | 0 | 2 | .... | 1953-54 | 1953-54 |
| • | Browne, Cecil | Chi. | 1 | 13 | 2 | 0 | 2 | 4 | .... | .... | .... | .... | .... | .... | 1927-28 | 1927-28 |
| | Brownschidle, Jack | St.L., Hfd. | 9 | 494 | 39 | 162 | 201 | 151 | 26 | 0 | 5 | 5 | 18 | .... | 1977-78 | 1985-86 |
| • | Brownschidle, Jeff | Hfd. | 2 | 7 | 0 | 1 | 1 | 2 | .... | .... | .... | .... | .... | .... | 1981-82 | 1982-83 |
| | Brubaker, Jeff | Hfd., Mtl., Cgy., Tor., Edm., NYR, Det. | 8 | 178 | 16 | 9 | 25 | 512 | 2 | 0 | 0 | 0 | 27 | .... | 1979-80 | 1988-89 |
| | Bruce, David | Van., St.L., S.J. | 8 | 234 | 48 | 39 | 87 | 338 | 3 | 0 | 0 | 0 | 2 | .... | 1985-86 | 1993-94 |
| • | Bruce, Gordie | Bos. | 3 | 28 | 4 | 9 | 13 | 13 | 7 | 2 | 3 | 5 | 4 | .... | 1940-41 | 1945-46 |
| • | Bruce, Morley | Ott. | 4 | 71 | 8 | 3 | 11 | 27 | 3 | 0 | 0 | 0 | 2 | 2 | 1917-18 | 1921-22 |
| | Brule, Steve | N.J., Col. | 2 | 2 | 0 | 0 | 0 | 0 | 1 | 0 | 0 | 0 | 0 | 1 | 1999-00 | 2002-03 |
| | Brumwell, Murray | Min., N.J. | 7 | 128 | 12 | 31 | 43 | 70 | 2 | 0 | 0 | 0 | 2 | .... | 1980-81 | 1987-88 |
| | Brunet, Benoit | Mtl., Dal., Ott. | 13 | 539 | 101 | 161 | 262 | 229 | 54 | 5 | 20 | 25 | 32 | 1 | 1988-89 | 2001-02 |
| • | Bruneteau, Eddie | Det. | 7 | 180 | 40 | 42 | 82 | 35 | 31 | 7 | 6 | 13 | 0 | .... | 1940-41 | 1948-49 |
| • | Bruneteau, Mud | Det. | 11 | 411 | 139 | 138 | 277 | 80 | 77 | 23 | 14 | 37 | 22 | 3 | 1935-36 | 1945-46 |
| • | Brydge, Bill | Tor., Det., NYA | 9 | 368 | 26 | 52 | 78 | 506 | 2 | 0 | 0 | 0 | 4 | .... | 1926-27 | 1935-36 |
| | Brydges, Paul | Buf. | 1 | 15 | 2 | 2 | 4 | 6 | .... | .... | .... | .... | .... | .... | 1986-87 | 1986-87 |
| • | Brydson, Glenn | Mtl.M., St.L., NYR, Chi. | 8 | 299 | 56 | 79 | 135 | 203 | 11 | 0 | 0 | 0 | 8 | .... | 1930-31 | 1937-38 |
| • | Brydson, Gord | Tor. | 1 | 8 | 2 | 0 | 2 | 8 | .... | .... | .... | .... | .... | .... | 1929-30 | 1929-30 |
| | Bubla, Jiri | Van. | 5 | 256 | 17 | 101 | 118 | 202 | 6 | 0 | 0 | 0 | 7 | .... | 1981-82 | 1985-86 |
| • | Buchanan, Al | Tor. | 2 | 4 | 0 | 1 | 1 | 2 | .... | .... | .... | .... | .... | .... | 1948-49 | 1949-50 |
| • | Buchanan, Bucky | NYR | 1 | 2 | 0 | 0 | 0 | 0 | .... | .... | .... | .... | .... | .... | 1948-49 | 1948-49 |
| | Buchanan, Jeff | Col. | 1 | 6 | 0 | 0 | 0 | 6 | .... | .... | .... | .... | .... | .... | 1998-99 | 1998-99 |
| | Buchanan, Mike | Chi. | 1 | 1 | 0 | 0 | 0 | 0 | .... | .... | .... | .... | .... | .... | 1951-52 | 1951-52 |
| | Buchanan, Ron | Bos., St.L. | 2 | 5 | 0 | 0 | 0 | 0 | .... | .... | .... | .... | .... | .... | 1966-67 | 1969-70 |
| | Buchberger, Kelly | Edm., Atl., L.A., Phx., Pit. | 18 | 1182 | 105 | 204 | 309 | 2297 | 97 | 10 | 15 | 25 | 129 | 2 | 1986-87 | 2003-04 |
| | Bucyk, John | Det., Bos. | 23 | 1540 | 556 | 813 | 1369 | 497 | 124 | 41 | 62 | 103 | 42 | 2 | 1955-56 | 1977-78 |
| | Bucyk, Randy | Mtl., Cgy. | 2 | 19 | 4 | 2 | 6 | 8 | 2 | 0 | 0 | 0 | 0 | .... | 1985-86 | 1987-88 |
| • | Buhr, Doug | K.C. | 1 | 6 | 0 | 2 | 2 | 4 | .... | .... | .... | .... | .... | .... | 1974-75 | 1974-75 |
| | Bukovich, Tony | Det. | 2 | 17 | 7 | 3 | 10 | 6 | 6 | 0 | 1 | 1 | 0 | .... | 1943-44 | 1944-45 |
| ‡ | Bulis, Jan | Wsh., Mtl., Van. | 9 | 552 | 96 | 149 | 245 | 268 | 35 | 3 | 3 | 6 | 14 | .... | 1997-98 | 2006-07 |
| | Bullard, Mike | Pit., Cgy., St.L., Phi., Tor. | 11 | 727 | 329 | 345 | 674 | 703 | 40 | 11 | 18 | 29 | 44 | .... | 1980-81 | 1991-92 |
| • | Buller, Hy | Det., NYR | 5 | 188 | 22 | 58 | 80 | 215 | .... | .... | .... | .... | .... | .... | 1943-44 | 1953-54 |
| | Bulley, Ted | Chi., Wsh., Pit. | 8 | 414 | 101 | 113 | 214 | 704 | 29 | 5 | 5 | 10 | 24 | .... | 1976-77 | 1983-84 |
| | Burakovsky, Robert | Ott. | 1 | 23 | 2 | 3 | 5 | 6 | .... | .... | .... | .... | .... | .... | 1993-94 | 1993-94 |
| • | Burch, Billy | Ham., NYA, Bos., Chi. | 11 | 390 | 137 | 61 | 198 | 255 | 2 | 0 | 0 | 0 | 0 | .... | 1922-23 | 1932-33 |
| • | Burchell, Fred | Mtl. | 2 | 4 | 0 | 0 | 0 | 2 | .... | .... | .... | .... | .... | .... | 1950-51 | 1953-54 |
| | Burdon, Glen | K.C. | 1 | 11 | 0 | 2 | 2 | 0 | .... | .... | .... | .... | .... | .... | 1974-75 | 1974-75 |
| | Bure, Pavel | Van., Fla., NYR | 12 | 702 | 437 | 342 | 779 | 484 | 64 | 35 | 35 | 70 | 74 | .... | 1991-92 | 2002-03 |
| | Bure, Valeri | Mtl., Cgy., Fla., St.L., Dal. | 10 | 621 | 174 | 226 | 400 | 221 | 22 | 0 | 7 | 7 | 16 | .... | 1994-95 | 2003-04 |
| | Bureau, Marc | Cgy., Min., T.B., Mtl., Phi. | 11 | 567 | 55 | 83 | 138 | 327 | 50 | 5 | 7 | 12 | 46 | .... | 1989-90 | 1999-00 |
| | Burega, Bill | Tor. | 1 | 4 | 0 | 1 | 1 | 4 | .... | .... | .... | .... | .... | .... | 1955-56 | 1955-56 |
| • | Burke, Eddie | Bos., NYA | 4 | 106 | 29 | 20 | 49 | 55 | .... | .... | .... | .... | .... | .... | 1931-32 | 1934-35 |
| • | Burke, Marty | Mtl., Pit., Ott., Chi. | 11 | 494 | 19 | 47 | 66 | 560 | 31 | 2 | 4 | 6 | 44 | 2 | 1927-28 | 1937-38 |
| • | Burmister, Roy | NYA | 3 | 67 | 4 | 3 | 7 | 2 | .... | .... | .... | .... | .... | .... | 1929-30 | 1931-32 |
| | Burnett, Garrett | Ana. | 1 | 39 | 1 | 2 | 3 | 184 | .... | .... | .... | .... | .... | .... | 2003-04 | 2003-04 |
| | Burnett, Kelly | NYR | 1 | 3 | 1 | 0 | 1 | 0 | .... | .... | .... | .... | .... | .... | 1952-53 | 1952-53 |
| • | Burns, Bobby | Chi. | 3 | 20 | 1 | 0 | 1 | 8 | .... | .... | .... | .... | .... | .... | 1927-28 | 1929-30 |
| | Burns, Charlie | Det., Bos., Oak., Pit., Min. | 11 | 749 | 106 | 198 | 304 | 252 | 31 | 5 | 4 | 9 | 6 | .... | 1958-59 | 1972-73 |
| | Burns, Gary | NYR | 2 | 11 | 2 | 2 | 4 | 18 | 5 | 0 | 0 | 0 | 2 | .... | 1980-81 | 1981-82 |
| • | Burns, Norm | NYR | 1 | 11 | 0 | 4 | 4 | 2 | .... | .... | .... | .... | .... | .... | 1941-42 | 1941-42 |
| | Burns, Robin | Pit., K.C. | 5 | 190 | 31 | 38 | 69 | 139 | .... | .... | .... | .... | .... | .... | 1970-71 | 1975-76 |
| | Burr, Shawn | Det., T.B., S.J. | 16 | 878 | 181 | 259 | 440 | 1069 | 91 | 16 | 19 | 35 | 95 | .... | 1984-85 | 1999-00 |
| | Burridge, Randy | Bos., Wsh., L.A., Buf. | 13 | 706 | 199 | 251 | 450 | 458 | 107 | 18 | 34 | 52 | 103 | .... | 1985-86 | 1997-98 |
| | Burrows, Dave | Pit., Tor. | 10 | 724 | 29 | 135 | 164 | 373 | 29 | 1 | 5 | 6 | 25 | .... | 1971-72 | 1980-81 |
| • | Burry, Bert | Ott. | 1 | 4 | 0 | 0 | 0 | 0 | .... | .... | .... | .... | .... | .... | 1932-33 | 1932-33 |
| | Burt, Adam | Hfd., Car., Phi., Atl. | 13 | 737 | 37 | 115 | 152 | 961 | 21 | 0 | 1 | 1 | 8 | .... | 1988-89 | 2000-01 |
| | Burton, Cummy | Det. | 3 | 43 | 0 | 2 | 2 | 21 | 3 | 0 | 0 | 0 | 0 | .... | 1955-56 | 1958-59 |
| | Burton, Nelson | Wsh. | 2 | 8 | 1 | 0 | 1 | 21 | .... | .... | .... | .... | .... | .... | 1977-78 | 1978-79 |
| • | Bush, Eddie | Det. | 2 | 26 | 4 | 6 | 10 | 40 | 11 | 1 | 6 | 7 | 23 | .... | 1938-39 | 1941-42 |
| | Buskas, Rod | Pit., Van., L.A., Chi. | 11 | 556 | 19 | 63 | 82 | 1294 | 18 | 0 | 3 | 3 | 45 | .... | 1982-83 | 1992-93 |
| | Busniuk, Mike | Phi. | 2 | 143 | 3 | 23 | 26 | 297 | 25 | 2 | 5 | 7 | 34 | .... | 1979-80 | 1980-81 |
| | Busniuk, Ron | Buf. | 2 | 6 | 0 | 3 | 3 | 13 | .... | .... | .... | .... | .... | .... | 1972-73 | 1973-74 |
| • | Buswell, Walt | Det., Mtl. | 8 | 368 | 10 | 40 | 50 | 164 | 24 | 2 | 1 | 3 | 10 | .... | 1932-33 | 1939-40 |
| | Butcher, Garth | Van., St.L., Que., Tor. | 14 | 897 | 48 | 158 | 206 | 2302 | 50 | 6 | 5 | 11 | 122 | .... | 1981-82 | 1994-95 |
| ‡ | Butenschon, Sven | Pit., Edm., NYI, Van. | 8 | 140 | 2 | 12 | 14 | 86 | 4 | 0 | 0 | 0 | 0 | .... | 1997-98 | 2005-06 |
| • | Butler, Dick | Chi. | 1 | 7 | 2 | 0 | 2 | 0 | .... | .... | .... | .... | .... | .... | 1947-48 | 1947-48 |
| | Butler, Jerry | NYR, St.L., Tor., Van., Wpg. | 11 | 641 | 99 | 120 | 219 | 515 | 48 | 3 | 3 | 6 | 79 | .... | 1972-73 | 1982-83 |
| | Butsayev, Viacheslav | Phi., S.J., Ana., Fla., Ott., T.B. | 6 | 132 | 17 | 26 | 43 | 133 | .... | .... | .... | .... | .... | .... | 1992-93 | 1999-00 |
| ‡ | Butsayev, Yuri | Det., Atl. | 4 | 99 | 10 | 4 | 14 | 28 | .... | .... | .... | .... | .... | .... | 1999-00 | 2002-03 |
| | Butters, Bill | Min. | 2 | 72 | 1 | 4 | 5 | 77 | .... | .... | .... | .... | .... | .... | 1977-78 | 1978-79 |
| | Buttrey, Gord | Chi. | 1 | 10 | 0 | 0 | 0 | 0 | .... | .... | .... | .... | .... | .... | 1943-44 | 1943-44 |
| | Buynak, Gord | St.L. | 1 | 4 | 0 | 0 | 0 | 2 | .... | .... | .... | .... | .... | .... | 1974-75 | 1974-75 |
| | Buzek, Petr | Dal., Atl., Cgy. | 6 | 157 | 9 | 22 | 31 | 94 | .... | .... | .... | .... | .... | .... | 1997-98 | 2002-03 |
| | Byakin, Ilja | Edm., S.J. | 2 | 57 | 8 | 25 | 33 | 44 | .... | .... | .... | .... | .... | .... | 1993-94 | 1994-95 |
| | Byce, John | Bos. | 3 | 21 | 2 | 3 | 5 | 6 | 8 | 2 | 0 | 2 | 2 | .... | 1989-90 | 1991-92 |
| • | Byers, Gord | Bos. | 1 | 1 | 0 | 1 | 1 | 0 | .... | .... | .... | .... | .... | .... | 1949-50 | 1949-50 |
| • | Byers, Jerry | Min., Atl., NYR | 4 | 43 | 3 | 4 | 7 | 15 | .... | .... | .... | .... | .... | .... | 1972-73 | 1977-78 |
| | Byers, Lyndon | Bos., S.J. | 10 | 279 | 28 | 43 | 71 | 1081 | 37 | 2 | 2 | 4 | 96 | .... | 1983-84 | 1992-93 |
| | Byers, Mike | Tor., Phi., L.A., Buf. | 4 | 166 | 42 | 34 | 76 | 39 | 4 | 0 | 1 | 1 | 0 | .... | 1967-68 | 1971-72 |
| ‡ | Bykov, Dmitri | Det. | 1 | 71 | 2 | 10 | 12 | 43 | 4 | 0 | 0 | 0 | 0 | .... | 2002-03 | 2002-03 |
| | Bylsma, Dan | L.A., Ana. | 9 | 429 | 19 | 43 | 62 | 184 | 16 | 0 | 1 | 1 | 2 | .... | 1995-96 | 2003-04 |
| | Byram, Shawn | NYI, Chi. | 2 | 5 | 0 | 0 | 0 | 14 | .... | .... | .... | .... | .... | .... | 1990-91 | 1991-92 |

## C

| | Name | NHL Teams | NHL Seasons | GP | G | A | TP | PIM | GP | G | A | TP | PIM | NHL Cup Wins | First NHL Season | Last NHL Season |
|---|---|---|---|---|---|---|---|---|---|---|---|---|---|---|---|---|
| • | Caffery, Jack | Tor., Bos. | 3 | 57 | 3 | 2 | 5 | 22 | 10 | 1 | 0 | 1 | 4 | .... | 1954-55 | 1957-58 |
| | Caffery, Terry | Chi., Min. | 2 | 14 | 0 | 0 | 0 | 0 | 1 | 0 | 0 | 0 | 0 | .... | 1969-70 | 1970-71 |
| • | Cahan, Larry | Tor., NYR, Oak., L.A. | 13 | 666 | 38 | 92 | 130 | 700 | 29 | 1 | 1 | 2 | 38 | .... | 1954-55 | 1970-71 |

| Name | NHL Teams | NHL Seasons | Regular Schedule GP | G | A | TP | PIM | Playoffs GP | G | A | TP | PIM | NHL Cup Wins | First NHL Season | Last NHL Season |
|---|---|---|---|---|---|---|---|---|---|---|---|---|---|---|---|
| • Cahill, Charles | Bos. | 2 | 32 | 0 | 1 | 1 | 4 | .... | .... | .... | .... | .... | .... | 1925-26 | 1926-27 |
| • Cain, Francis | Mtl.M., Tor. | 2 | 61 | 4 | 0 | 4 | 35 | .... | .... | .... | .... | .... | .... | 1924-25 | 1925-26 |
| • Cain, Herb | Mtl.M., Mtl., Bos. | 13 | 570 | 206 | 194 | 400 | 178 | 67 | 16 | 13 | 29 | 13 | 2 | 1933-34 | 1945-46 |
| Cairns, Don | K.C., Col. | 2 | 9 | 0 | 1 | 1 | 2 | .... | .... | .... | .... | .... | .... | 1975-76 | 1976-77 |
| Cairns, Eric | NYR, NYI, Fla., Pit. | 10 | 457 | 10 | 32 | 42 | 1182 | 16 | 0 | 0 | 0 | 28 | .... | 1996-97 | 2006-07 |
| ‡ Cajanek, Petr | St.L. | 4 | 269 | 46 | 107 | 153 | 144 | 7 | 0 | 2 | 2 | 4 | .... | 2002-03 | 2006-07 |
| Calder, Eric | Wsh. | 2 | 2 | 0 | 0 | 0 | 0 | .... | .... | .... | .... | .... | .... | 1981-82 | 1982-83 |
| • Calladine, Norm | Bos. | 3 | 63 | 19 | 29 | 48 | 8 | .... | .... | .... | .... | .... | .... | 1942-43 | 1944-45 |
| Callander, Drew | Phi., Van. | 4 | 39 | 6 | 2 | 8 | 7 | .... | .... | .... | .... | .... | .... | 1976-77 | 1979-80 |
| Callander, Jock | Pit., T.B. | 5 | 109 | 22 | 29 | 51 | 116 | 22 | 3 | 8 | 11 | 12 | 1 | 1987-88 | 1992-93 |
| Callighen, Brett | Edm. | 3 | 160 | 56 | 89 | 145 | 132 | 14 | 4 | 6 | 10 | 8 | .... | 1979-80 | 1981-82 |
| • Callighen, Patsy | NYR | 1 | 36 | 0 | 0 | 0 | 32 | 9 | 0 | 0 | 0 | 0 | 1 | 1927-28 | 1927-28 |
| ‡ Caloun, Jan | S.J., CBJ | 3 | 24 | 8 | 6 | 14 | 2 | .... | .... | .... | .... | .... | .... | 1995-96 | 2000-01 |
| Camazzola, James | Chi. | 2 | 3 | 0 | 0 | 0 | 0 | .... | .... | .... | .... | .... | .... | 1983-84 | 1986-87 |
| Camazzola, Tony | Wsh. | 1 | 3 | 0 | 0 | 0 | 4 | .... | .... | .... | .... | .... | .... | 1981-82 | 1981-82 |
| Cameron, Al | Det., Wpg. | 6 | 282 | 11 | 44 | 55 | 356 | 7 | 0 | 1 | 1 | 2 | .... | 1975-76 | 1980-81 |
| • Cameron, Billy | Mtl., NYA | 2 | 39 | 0 | 0 | 0 | 2 | 2 | 0 | 0 | 0 | 0 | 1 | 1923-24 | 1925-26 |
| Cameron, Craig | Det., St.L., Min., NYI | 9 | 552 | 87 | 65 | 152 | 196 | 27 | 3 | 1 | 4 | 17 | .... | 1966-67 | 1975-76 |
| Cameron, Dave | Col., N.J. | 3 | 168 | 25 | 28 | 53 | 238 | .... | .... | .... | .... | .... | .... | 1981-82 | 1983-84 |
| • Cameron, Harry | Tor., Ott., Mtl. | 6 | 128 | 88 | 51 | 139 | 189 | 11 | 5 | 4 | 9 | 16 | 2 | 1917-18 | 1922-23 |
| • Cameron, Scotty | NYR | 1 | 35 | 8 | 11 | 19 | 0 | .... | .... | .... | .... | .... | .... | 1942-43 | 1942-43 |
| Campbell, Bryan | L.A., Chi. | 5 | 260 | 35 | 71 | 106 | 74 | 22 | 3 | 4 | 7 | 2 | .... | 1967-68 | 1971-72 |
| Campbell, Colin | Pit., Col., Edm., Van., Det. | 11 | 636 | 25 | 103 | 128 | 1292 | 45 | 4 | 10 | 14 | 181 | .... | 1974-75 | 1984-85 |
| • Campbell, Dave | Mtl. | 1 | 2 | 0 | 0 | 0 | 0 | .... | .... | .... | .... | .... | .... | 1920-21 | 1920-21 |
| Campbell, Don | Chi. | 1 | 17 | 1 | 3 | 4 | 8 | .... | .... | .... | .... | .... | .... | 1943-44 | 1943-44 |
| • Campbell, Earl | Ott., NYA | 3 | 76 | 6 | 3 | 9 | 14 | 1 | 0 | 0 | 0 | 6 | .... | 1923-24 | 1925-26 |
| Campbell, Jim | Ana., St.L., Mtl., Chi., Fla., T.B. | 9 | 285 | 61 | 75 | 136 | 268 | 14 | 8 | 3 | 11 | 18 | .... | 1995-96 | 2005-06 |
| Campbell, Scott | Wpg., St.L. | 3 | 80 | 4 | 21 | 25 | 243 | .... | .... | .... | .... | .... | .... | 1979-80 | 1981-82 |
| Campbell, Wade | Wpg., Bos. | 6 | 213 | 9 | 27 | 36 | 305 | 10 | 0 | 0 | 0 | 20 | .... | 1982-83 | 1987-88 |
| Campeau, Tod | Mtl. | 3 | 42 | 5 | 9 | 14 | 16 | 1 | 0 | 0 | 0 | 0 | .... | 1943-44 | 1948-49 |
| Campedelli, Dom | Mtl. | 1 | 2 | 0 | 0 | 0 | 0 | .... | .... | .... | .... | .... | .... | 1985-86 | 1985-86 |
| Capuano, Dave | Pit., Van., T.B., S.J. | 4 | 104 | 17 | 38 | 55 | 56 | 6 | 1 | 1 | 2 | 5 | .... | 1989-90 | 1993-94 |
| Capuano, Jack | Tor., Van., Bos. | 3 | 6 | 0 | 0 | 0 | 0 | .... | .... | .... | .... | .... | .... | 1989-90 | 1991-92 |
| • Carbol, Leo | Chi. | 1 | 6 | 0 | 1 | 1 | 4 | .... | .... | .... | .... | .... | .... | 1942-43 | 1942-43 |
| Carbonneau, Guy | Mtl., St.L., Dal. | 19 | 1318 | 260 | 403 | 663 | 820 | 231 | 38 | 55 | 93 | 161 | 3 | 1980-81 | 1999-00 |
| Cardin, Claude | St.L. | 1 | 1 | 0 | 0 | 0 | 0 | .... | .... | .... | .... | .... | .... | 1967-68 | 1967-68 |
| Cardwell, Steve | Pit. | 3 | 53 | 9 | 11 | 20 | 35 | 4 | 0 | 0 | 0 | 2 | .... | 1970-71 | 1972-73 |
| • Carey, George | Que., Ham., Tor. | 5 | 72 | 21 | 12 | 33 | 20 | .... | .... | .... | .... | .... | .... | 1919-20 | 1923-24 |
| Carkner, Terry | NYR, Que., Phi., Det., Fla. | 13 | 858 | 42 | 188 | 230 | 1588 | 54 | 1 | 9 | 10 | 48 | .... | 1986-87 | 1998-99 |
| Carleton, Wayne | Tor., Bos., Cal. | 7 | 278 | 55 | 73 | 128 | 172 | 18 | 2 | 4 | 6 | 14 | 1 | 1965-66 | 1971-72 |
| Carlin, Brian | L.A. | 1 | 5 | 1 | 0 | 1 | 0 | .... | .... | .... | .... | .... | .... | 1971-72 | 1971-72 |
| Carlson, Jack | Min., St.L. | 6 | 236 | 30 | 15 | 45 | 417 | 25 | 1 | 2 | 3 | 72 | .... | 1978-79 | 1986-87 |
| Carlson, Kent | Mtl., St.L., Wsh. | 5 | 113 | 7 | 11 | 18 | 148 | 8 | 0 | 0 | 0 | 13 | .... | 1983-84 | 1988-89 |
| Carlson, Steve | L.A. | 1 | 52 | 9 | 12 | 21 | 23 | 4 | 1 | 1 | 2 | 7 | .... | 1979-80 | 1979-80 |
| Carlsson, Anders | N.J. | 3 | 104 | 7 | 26 | 33 | 34 | 3 | 1 | 0 | 1 | 2 | .... | 1986-87 | 1988-89 |
| Carlyle, Randy | Tor., Pit., Wpg. | 18 | 1055 | 148 | 499 | 647 | 1400 | 69 | 9 | 24 | 33 | 120 | .... | 1976-77 | 1992-93 |
| Carnback, Patrik | Mtl., Ana. | 4 | 154 | 24 | 38 | 62 | 122 | .... | .... | .... | .... | .... | .... | 1992-93 | 1995-96 |
| Carney, Keith | Buf., Chi., Phx., Ana., Van., Min. | 14 | 1018 | 45 | 183 | 228 | 904 | 91 | 3 | 19 | 22 | 67 | .... | 1991-92 | 2007-08 |
| • Caron, Alain | Oak., Mtl. | 2 | 60 | 9 | 13 | 22 | 18 | .... | .... | .... | .... | .... | .... | 1967-68 | 1968-69 |
| Carpenter, Bob | Wsh., NYR, L.A., Bos., N.J. | 19 | 1178 | 320 | 408 | 728 | 919 | 140 | 21 | 38 | 59 | 136 | 1 | 1981-82 | 1998-99 |
| • Carpenter, Ed | Que., Ham. | 2 | 45 | 10 | 5 | 15 | 41 | .... | .... | .... | .... | .... | .... | 1919-20 | 1920-21 |
| Carr, Gene | St.L., NYR, L.A., Pit., Atl. | 8 | 465 | 79 | 136 | 215 | 365 | 35 | 5 | 8 | 13 | 66 | .... | 1971-72 | 1978-79 |
| • Carr, Lorne | NYR, NYA, Tor. | 13 | 580 | 204 | 222 | 426 | 132 | 53 | 10 | 9 | 19 | 13 | 2 | 1933-34 | 1945-46 |
| Carr, Red | Tor. | 1 | 5 | 0 | 1 | 1 | 2 | .... | .... | .... | .... | .... | .... | 1943-44 | 1943-44 |
| Carriere, Larry | Buf., Atl., Van., L.A., Tor. | 7 | 367 | 16 | 74 | 90 | 462 | 27 | 0 | 3 | 3 | 42 | .... | 1972-73 | 1979-80 |
| • Carrigan, Gene | NYR, Det., St.L. | 3 | 37 | 2 | 1 | 3 | 13 | 4 | 0 | 0 | 0 | 0 | .... | 1930-31 | 1934-35 |
| Carroll, Billy | NYI, Edm., Det. | 7 | 322 | 30 | 54 | 84 | 113 | 71 | 6 | 12 | 18 | 18 | 4 | 1980-81 | 1986-87 |
| • Carroll, George | Mtl.M., Bos. | 1 | 16 | 0 | 0 | 0 | 11 | .... | .... | .... | .... | .... | .... | 1924-25 | 1924-25 |
| Carroll, Greg | Wsh., Det., Hfd. | 2 | 131 | 20 | 34 | 54 | 44 | .... | .... | .... | .... | .... | .... | 1978-79 | 1979-80 |
| Carruthers, Dwight | Det., Phi. | 2 | 2 | 0 | 0 | 0 | 0 | .... | .... | .... | .... | .... | .... | 1965-66 | 1967-68 |
| • Carse, Bill | NYR, Chi. | 4 | 124 | 28 | 43 | 71 | 38 | 13 | 3 | 2 | 5 | 0 | .... | 1938-39 | 1941-42 |
| • Carse, Bob | Chi., Mtl. | 5 | 167 | 32 | 55 | 87 | 52 | 10 | 0 | 2 | 2 | 2 | .... | 1939-40 | 1947-48 |
| • Carson, Bill | Tor., Bos. | 4 | 159 | 54 | 24 | 78 | 156 | 11 | 3 | 0 | 3 | 14 | 1 | 1926-27 | 1929-30 |
| • Carson, Frank | Mtl.M., NYA, Det. | 7 | 248 | 42 | 48 | 90 | 166 | 27 | 0 | 2 | 2 | 9 | 1 | 1925-26 | 1933-34 |
| • Carson, Gerry | Mtl., NYR, Mtl.M. | 6 | 261 | 12 | 11 | 23 | 205 | 22 | 0 | 0 | 0 | 12 | 1 | 1928-29 | 1936-37 |
| Carson, Jimmy | L.A., Edm., Det., Van., Hfd. | 10 | 626 | 275 | 286 | 561 | 254 | 55 | 17 | 15 | 32 | 22 | .... | 1986-87 | 1995-96 |
| Carson, Lindsay | Phi., Hfd. | 7 | 373 | 66 | 80 | 146 | 524 | 49 | 4 | 10 | 14 | 56 | .... | 1981-82 | 1987-88 |
| Carter, Anson | Wsh., Bos., Edm., NYR, L.A., Van., CBJ, Car. | 10 | 674 | 202 | 219 | 421 | 229 | 24 | 8 | 5 | 13 | 4 | .... | 1996-97 | 2006-07 |
| Carter, Billy | Mtl., Bos. | 3 | 16 | 0 | 0 | 0 | 6 | .... | .... | .... | .... | .... | .... | 1957-58 | 1961-62 |
| Carter, John | Bos., S.J. | 8 | 244 | 40 | 50 | 90 | 201 | 31 | 7 | 5 | 12 | 51 | .... | 1985-86 | 1992-93 |
| Carter, Ron | Edm. | 1 | 2 | 0 | 0 | 0 | 0 | .... | .... | .... | .... | .... | .... | 1979-80 | 1979-80 |
| • Carveth, Joe | Det., Bos., Mtl. | 11 | 504 | 150 | 189 | 339 | 81 | 69 | 21 | 16 | 37 | 28 | 2 | 1940-41 | 1950-51 |
| Cashman, Wayne | Bos. | 17 | 1027 | 277 | 516 | 793 | 1041 | 145 | 31 | 57 | 88 | 250 | 2 | 1964-65 | 1982-83 |
| Casselman, Mike | Fla. | 1 | 3 | 0 | 0 | 0 | 0 | .... | .... | .... | .... | .... | .... | 1995-96 | 1995-96 |
| Cassels, Andrew | Mtl., Hfd., Cgy., Van., CBJ, Wsh. | 16 | 1015 | 204 | 528 | 732 | 410 | 21 | 4 | 7 | 11 | 8 | .... | 1989-90 | 2005-06 |
| Cassidy, Bruce | Chi. | 7 | 36 | 4 | 13 | 17 | 10 | 1 | 0 | 0 | 0 | 0 | .... | 1983-84 | 1989-90 |
| Cassidy, Tom | Pit. | 1 | 26 | 3 | 4 | 7 | 15 | .... | .... | .... | .... | .... | .... | 1977-78 | 1977-78 |
| Cassolato, Tony | Wsh. | 3 | 23 | 1 | 6 | 7 | 4 | .... | .... | .... | .... | .... | .... | 1979-80 | 1981-82 |
| Caufield, Jay | NYR, Min., Pit. | 7 | 208 | 5 | 8 | 13 | 759 | 17 | 0 | 0 | 0 | 42 | 2 | 1986-87 | 1992-93 |
| Cavallini, Gino | Cgy., St.L., Que. | 9 | 593 | 114 | 159 | 273 | 507 | 74 | 14 | 19 | 33 | 66 | .... | 1984-85 | 1992-93 |
| Cavallini, Paul | Wsh., St.L., Dal. | 10 | 564 | 56 | 177 | 233 | 750 | 69 | 8 | 27 | 35 | 114 | .... | 1986-87 | 1995-96 |
| Ceresino, Ray | Tor. | 1 | 12 | 1 | 1 | 2 | 2 | .... | .... | .... | .... | .... | .... | 1948-49 | 1948-49 |
| Cernik, Frantisek | Det. | 1 | 49 | 5 | 4 | 9 | 13 | .... | .... | .... | .... | .... | .... | 1984-85 | 1984-85 |
| Chabot, John | Mtl., Pit., Det. | 8 | 508 | 84 | 228 | 312 | 85 | 33 | 6 | 20 | 26 | 2 | .... | 1983-84 | 1990-91 |
| • Chad, John | Chi. | 3 | 80 | 15 | 22 | 37 | 29 | 10 | 0 | 1 | 1 | 2 | .... | 1939-40 | 1945-46 |
| • Chalmers, Chick | NYR | 1 | 1 | 0 | 0 | 0 | 0 | .... | .... | .... | .... | .... | .... | 1953-54 | 1953-54 |
| Chalupa, Milan | Det. | 1 | 14 | 0 | 5 | 5 | 6 | .... | .... | .... | .... | .... | .... | 1984-85 | 1984-85 |
| • Chamberlain, Murph | Tor., Mtl., Bro., Bos. | 12 | 510 | 100 | 175 | 275 | 769 | 66 | 14 | 17 | 31 | 96 | 2 | 1937-38 | 1948-49 |
| Chambers, Shawn | Min., Wsh., T.B., N.J., Dal. | 13 | 625 | 50 | 185 | 235 | 364 | 94 | 7 | 26 | 33 | 72 | 2 | 1987-88 | 1999-00 |
| Champagne, Andre | Tor. | 1 | 2 | 0 | 0 | 0 | 0 | .... | .... | .... | .... | .... | .... | 1962-63 | 1962-63 |
| Chapdelaine, Rene | L.A. | 3 | 32 | 0 | 2 | 2 | 32 | .... | .... | .... | .... | .... | .... | 1990-91 | 1992-93 |
| • Chapman, Art | Bos., NYA | 10 | 438 | 62 | 176 | 238 | 140 | 26 | 1 | 5 | 6 | 9 | .... | 1930-31 | 1939-40 |
| Chapman, Blair | Pit., St.L. | 7 | 402 | 106 | 125 | 231 | 158 | 25 | 4 | 6 | 10 | 15 | .... | 1976-77 | 1982-83 |
| Chapman, Brian | Hfd. | 1 | 3 | 0 | 0 | 0 | 29 | .... | .... | .... | .... | .... | .... | 1990-91 | 1990-91 |
| Charbonneau, Jose | Mtl., Van. | 4 | 71 | 9 | 13 | 22 | 67 | 11 | 1 | 0 | 1 | 8 | .... | 1987-88 | 1994-95 |
| Charbonneau, Stephane | Que. | 1 | 2 | 0 | 0 | 0 | 0 | .... | .... | .... | .... | .... | .... | 1991-92 | 1991-92 |
| Charlebois, Bob | Min. | 1 | 7 | 1 | 0 | 1 | 0 | .... | .... | .... | .... | .... | .... | 1967-68 | 1967-68 |
| Charlesworth, Todd | Pit., NYR | 6 | 93 | 3 | 9 | 12 | 47 | .... | .... | .... | .... | .... | .... | 1983-84 | 1989-90 |
| Charron, Eric | Mtl., T.B., Wsh., Cgy. | 8 | 130 | 2 | 7 | 9 | 127 | 6 | 0 | 0 | 0 | 8 | .... | 1992-93 | 1999-00 |
| Charron, Guy | Mtl., Det., K.C., Wsh. | 12 | 734 | 221 | 309 | 530 | 146 | .... | .... | .... | .... | .... | .... | 1969-70 | 1980-81 |
| Chartier, Dave | Wpg. | 1 | 1 | 0 | 0 | 0 | 0 | .... | .... | .... | .... | .... | .... | 1980-81 | 1980-81 |
| Chartrand, Brad | L.A. | 5 | 215 | 25 | 25 | 50 | 122 | 11 | 1 | 1 | 2 | 8 | .... | 1999-00 | 2003-04 |
| Chartraw, Rick | Mtl., L.A., NYR, Edm. | 10 | 420 | 28 | 64 | 92 | 399 | 75 | 7 | 9 | 16 | 80 | 4 | 1974-75 | 1983-84 |
| Chase, Kelly | St.L., Hfd., Tor. | 11 | 458 | 17 | 36 | 53 | 2017 | 27 | 1 | 1 | 2 | 100 | .... | 1989-90 | 1999-00 |
| Chasse, Denis | St.L., Wsh., Wpg., Ott. | 4 | 132 | 11 | 14 | 25 | 292 | 7 | 1 | 7 | 8 | 23 | .... | 1993-94 | 1996-97 |
| ‡ Chebaturkin, Vladimir | NYI, St.L., Chi. | 5 | 62 | 2 | 7 | 9 | 52 | 3 | 0 | 0 | 0 | 2 | .... | 1997-98 | 2001-02 |
| • Check, Lude | Det., Chi. | 2 | 27 | 6 | 2 | 8 | 4 | .... | .... | .... | .... | .... | .... | 1943-44 | 1944-45 |
| Chernoff, Mike | Min. | 1 | 1 | 0 | 0 | 0 | 0 | .... | .... | .... | .... | .... | .... | 1968-69 | 1968-69 |
| Chernomaz, Rich | Col., N.J., Cgy. | 7 | 51 | 9 | 7 | 16 | 18 | .... | .... | .... | .... | .... | .... | 1981-82 | 1991-92 |
| Cherry, Dick | Bos., Phi. | 3 | 145 | 12 | 10 | 22 | 45 | 4 | 1 | 0 | 1 | 4 | .... | 1956-57 | 1969-70 |
| Cherry, Don | Bos. | 1 | .... | .... | .... | .... | .... | 1 | 0 | 0 | 0 | 0 | .... | 1954-55 | 1954-55 |
| Chervyakov, Denis | Bos. | 1 | 2 | 0 | 0 | 0 | 2 | .... | .... | .... | .... | .... | .... | 1992-93 | 1992-93 |
| • Chevrefils, Real | Bos., Det. | 8 | 387 | 104 | 97 | 201 | 185 | 30 | 5 | 4 | 9 | 20 | .... | 1951-52 | 1958-59 |
| • Chiasson, Steve | Det., Cgy., Hfd., Car. | 13 | 751 | 93 | 305 | 398 | 1107 | 63 | 16 | 19 | 35 | 119 | .... | 1986-87 | 1998-99 |
| Chibirev, Igor | Hfd. | 2 | 45 | 7 | 12 | 19 | 2 | .... | .... | .... | .... | .... | .... | 1993-94 | 1994-95 |
| Chicoine, Dan | Cle., Min. | 3 | 31 | 1 | 2 | 3 | 12 | 1 | 0 | 0 | 0 | 0 | .... | 1977-78 | 1979-80 |
| Chinnick, Rick | Min. | 2 | 4 | 0 | 2 | 2 | 0 | .... | .... | .... | .... | .... | .... | 1973-74 | 1974-75 |
| Chipperfield, Ron | Edm., Que. | 2 | 83 | 22 | 24 | 46 | 34 | .... | .... | .... | .... | .... | .... | 1979-80 | 1980-81 |
| Chisholm, Art | Bos. | 1 | 3 | 0 | 0 | 0 | 0 | .... | .... | .... | .... | .... | .... | 1960-61 | 1960-61 |
| Chisholm, Colin | Min. | 1 | 1 | 0 | 0 | 0 | 0 | .... | .... | .... | .... | .... | .... | 1986-87 | 1986-87 |
| • Chisholm, Lex | Tor. | 2 | 54 | 10 | 8 | 18 | 19 | 3 | 1 | 0 | 1 | 0 | .... | 1939-40 | 1940-41 |
| ‡ Chistov, Stanislav | Ana., Bos. | 3 | 196 | 19 | 42 | 61 | 116 | 21 | 4 | 2 | 6 | 8 | .... | 2002-03 | 2006-07 |
| Chorney, Marc | Pit., L.A. | 4 | 210 | 8 | 27 | 35 | 209 | 7 | 0 | 1 | 1 | 2 | .... | 1980-81 | 1983-84 |
| Chorske, Tom | Mtl., N.J., Ott., NYI, Wsh., Cgy., Pit. | 11 | 596 | 115 | 122 | 237 | 225 | 50 | 5 | 12 | 17 | 10 | 1 | 1989-90 | 1999-00 |
| ‡ Chouinard, Eric | Mtl., Phi., Min. | 4 | 90 | 11 | 11 | 22 | 16 | .... | .... | .... | .... | .... | .... | 2000-01 | 2005-06 |

Herb Cain

Gene Carrigan

Joe Carveth

Art Chapman

*Don Cherry*

*Marc Chorney*

*Joe Cirella*

*Sprague Cleghorn*

| | | | Regular Schedule | | | | | Playoffs | | | | | NHL | First | Last |
|---|---|---|---|---|---|---|---|---|---|---|---|---|---|---|---|
| **Name** | **NHL Teams** | **NHL Seasons** | **GP** | **G** | **A** | **TP** | **PIM** | **GP** | **G** | **A** | **TP** | **PIM** | **Cup Wins** | **NHL Season** | **NHL Season** |
| • Chouinard, Gene | Ott. | 1 | 8 | 0 | 0 | 0 | 0 | .... | .... | .... | .... | .... | .... | 1927-28 | 1927-28 |
| Chouinard, Guy | Atl., Cgy., St.L. | 10 | 578 | 205 | 370 | 575 | 120 | 46 | 9 | 28 | 37 | 12 | .... | 1974-75 | 1983-84 |
| ‡ Chouinard, Marc | Ana., Min., Van. | 6 | 320 | 37 | 41 | 78 | 123 | 15 | 1 | 0 | 1 | 0 | .... | 2000-01 | 2006-07 |
| Christian, Dave | Wpg., Wsh., Bos., St.L., Chi. | 15 | 1009 | 340 | 433 | 773 | 284 | 102 | 32 | 25 | 57 | 27 | .... | 1979-80 | 1993-94 |
| Christian, Jeff | N.J., Pit., Phx. | 5 | 18 | 2 | 2 | 4 | 17 | .... | .... | .... | .... | .... | .... | 1991-92 | 1997-98 |
| Christie, Mike | Cal., Cle., Col., Van. | 7 | 412 | 15 | 101 | 116 | 550 | 2 | 0 | 0 | 0 | 0 | .... | 1974-75 | 1980-81 |
| Christie, Ryan | Dal., Cgy. | 2 | 7 | 0 | 0 | 0 | 0 | .... | .... | .... | .... | .... | .... | 1999-00 | 2001-02 |
| Christoff, Steve | Min., Cgy., L.A. | 5 | 248 | 77 | 64 | 141 | 108 | 35 | 16 | 12 | 28 | 25 | .... | 1979-80 | 1983-84 |
| Chrystal, Bob | NYR | 2 | 132 | 11 | 14 | 25 | 112 | .... | .... | .... | .... | .... | .... | 1953-54 | 1954-55 |
| ‡ Chubarov, Artem | Van. | 5 | 228 | 25 | 33 | 58 | 40 | 27 | 0 | 4 | 4 | 4 | .... | 1999-00 | 2003-04 |
| Church, Brad | Wsh. | 1 | 2 | 0 | 0 | 0 | 0 | .... | .... | .... | .... | .... | .... | 1997-98 | 1997-98 |
| • Church, Jack | Tor., Bro., Bos. | 5 | 130 | 4 | 19 | 23 | 154 | 25 | 1 | 1 | 2 | 18 | .... | 1938-39 | 1945-46 |
| Churla, Shane | Hfd., Cgy., Min., Dal., L.A., NYR | 11 | 488 | 26 | 45 | 71 | 2301 | 78 | 5 | 7 | 12 | 282 | .... | 1986-87 | 1996-97 |
| Chychrun, Jeff | Phi., L.A., Pit., Edm. | 8 | 262 | 3 | 22 | 25 | 744 | 19 | 0 | 2 | 2 | 65 | 1 | 1986-87 | 1993-94 |
| Chynoweth, Dean | NYI, Bos. | 9 | 241 | 4 | 18 | 22 | 667 | 6 | 0 | 0 | 0 | 26 | .... | 1988-89 | 1997-98 |
| Chyzowski, Dave | NYI, Chi. | 6 | 126 | 15 | 16 | 31 | 144 | 2 | 0 | 0 | 0 | 0 | .... | 1989-90 | 1996-97 |
| Ciavaglia, Peter | Buf. | 2 | 5 | 0 | 0 | 0 | 0 | .... | .... | .... | .... | .... | .... | 1991-92 | 1992-93 |
| ‡ Cibak, Martin | T.B. | 3 | 154 | 5 | 18 | 23 | 60 | 11 | 0 | 1 | 1 | 0 | 1 | 2001-02 | 2005-06 |
| Ciccarelli, Dino | Min., Wsh., Det., T.B., Fla. | 19 | 1232 | 608 | 592 | 1200 | 1425 | 141 | 73 | 45 | 118 | 211 | .... | 1980-81 | 1998-99 |
| Ciccone, Enrico | Min., Wsh., T.B., Chi., Car., Van., Mtl. | 9 | 374 | 10 | 18 | 28 | 1469 | 13 | 1 | 0 | 1 | 48 | .... | 1991-92 | 2000-01 |
| Cichocki, Chris | Det., N.J. | 4 | 68 | 11 | 12 | 23 | 27 | .... | .... | .... | .... | .... | .... | 1985-86 | 1988-89 |
| ‡ Ciernik, Ivan | Ott., Wsh. | 5 | 89 | 12 | 14 | 26 | 32 | 2 | 0 | 1 | 1 | 6 | .... | 1997-98 | 2003-04 |
| ‡ Cierny, Jozef | Edm. | 1 | 1 | 0 | 0 | 0 | 0 | .... | .... | .... | .... | .... | .... | 1993-94 | 1993-94 |
| • Ciesla, Hank | Chi., NYR | 4 | 269 | 26 | 51 | 77 | 87 | 6 | 0 | 2 | 2 | 0 | .... | 1955-56 | 1958-59 |
| Ciger, Zdeno | N.J., Edm., NYR, T.B. | 7 | 352 | 94 | 134 | 228 | 101 | 13 | 2 | 6 | 8 | 4 | .... | 1990-91 | 2001-02 |
| Cimellaro, Tony | Ott. | 1 | 2 | 0 | 0 | 0 | 0 | .... | .... | .... | .... | .... | .... | 1992-93 | 1992-93 |
| Cimetta, Rob | Bos., Tor. | 4 | 103 | 16 | 16 | 32 | 66 | 1 | 0 | 0 | 0 | 15 | .... | 1988-89 | 1991-92 |
| Cirella, Joe | Col., N.J., Que., NYR, Fla., Ott. | 15 | 828 | 64 | 211 | 275 | 1446 | 38 | 0 | 13 | 13 | 98 | .... | 1981-82 | 1995-96 |
| Cirone, Jason | Wpg. | 1 | 3 | 0 | 0 | 0 | 2 | .... | .... | .... | .... | .... | .... | 1991-92 | 1991-92 |
| Cisar, Marian | Nsh. | 3 | 73 | 13 | 17 | 30 | 57 | .... | .... | .... | .... | .... | .... | 1999-00 | 2001-02 |
| Clackson, Kim | Pit., Que. | 2 | 106 | 0 | 8 | 8 | 370 | 8 | 0 | 0 | 0 | 70 | .... | 1979-80 | 1980-81 |
| • Clancy, King | Ott., Tor. | 16 | 592 | 136 | 147 | 283 | 914 | 55 | 8 | 8 | 16 | 88 | 3 | 1921-22 | 1936-37 |
| Clancy, Terry | Oak., Tor. | 4 | 93 | 6 | 6 | 12 | 39 | .... | .... | .... | .... | .... | .... | 1967-68 | 1972-73 |
| • Clapper, Dit | Bos. | 20 | 833 | 228 | 246 | 474 | 462 | 82 | 13 | 17 | 30 | 50 | 3 | 1927-28 | 1946-47 |
| Clark, Dan | NYR | 1 | 4 | 0 | 1 | 1 | 6 | .... | .... | .... | .... | .... | .... | 1978-79 | 1978-79 |
| Clark, Dean | Edm. | 1 | 1 | 0 | 0 | 0 | 0 | .... | .... | .... | .... | .... | .... | 1983-84 | 1983-84 |
| Clark, Gordie | Bos. | 2 | 8 | 0 | 1 | 1 | 0 | 1 | 0 | 0 | 0 | 0 | .... | 1974-75 | 1975-76 |
| • Clark, Nobby | Bos. | 1 | 5 | 0 | 0 | 0 | 0 | .... | .... | .... | .... | .... | .... | 1927-28 | 1927-28 |
| Clark, Wendel | Tor., Que., NYI, T.B., Det., Chi. | 15 | 793 | 330 | 234 | 564 | 1690 | 95 | 37 | 32 | 69 | 201 | .... | 1985-86 | 1999-00 |
| Clarke, Bobby | Phi. | 15 | 1144 | 358 | 852 | 1210 | 1453 | 136 | 42 | 77 | 119 | 152 | 2 | 1969-70 | 1983-84 |
| ‡ Clarke, Dale | St.L. | 1 | 3 | 0 | 0 | 0 | 0 | .... | .... | .... | .... | .... | .... | 2000-01 | 2000-01 |
| ‡ Classen, Greg | Nsh. | 3 | 90 | 7 | 10 | 17 | 48 | .... | .... | .... | .... | .... | .... | 2000-01 | 2002-03 |
| • Cleghorn, Odie | Mtl., Pit. | 10 | 181 | 95 | 34 | 129 | 142 | 12 | 7 | 2 | 9 | 5 | 1 | 1918-19 | 1927-28 |
| • Cleghorn, Sprague | Ott., Tor., Mtl., Bos. | 10 | 259 | 83 | 55 | 138 | 538 | 21 | 4 | 3 | 7 | 26 | 2 | 1918-19 | 1927-28 |
| Clement, Bill | Phi., Wsh., Atl., Cgy. | 11 | 719 | 148 | 208 | 356 | 383 | 50 | 5 | 3 | 8 | 26 | 2 | 1971-72 | 1981-82 |
| Cline, Bruce | NYR | 1 | 30 | 2 | 3 | 5 | 10 | .... | .... | .... | .... | .... | .... | 1956-57 | 1956-57 |
| Clippingdale, Steve | L.A., Wsh. | 2 | 19 | 1 | 2 | 3 | 9 | 1 | 0 | 0 | 0 | 0 | .... | 1976-77 | 1979-80 |
| Cloutier, Real | Que., Buf. | 6 | 317 | 146 | 198 | 344 | 119 | 25 | 7 | 5 | 12 | 20 | .... | 1979-80 | 1984-85 |
| Cloutier, Rejean | Det. | 2 | 5 | 0 | 2 | 2 | 2 | .... | .... | .... | .... | .... | .... | 1979-80 | 1981-82 |
| Cloutier, Roland | Det., Que. | 3 | 34 | 8 | 9 | 17 | 2 | .... | .... | .... | .... | .... | .... | 1977-78 | 1979-80 |
| Cloutier, Sylvain | Chi. | 1 | 7 | 0 | 0 | 0 | 0 | .... | .... | .... | .... | .... | .... | 1998-99 | 1998-99 |
| • Clune, Wally | Mtl. | 1 | 5 | 0 | 0 | 0 | 6 | .... | .... | .... | .... | .... | .... | 1955-56 | 1955-56 |
| Coalter, Gary | Cal., K.C. | 2 | 34 | 2 | 4 | 6 | 2 | .... | .... | .... | .... | .... | .... | 1973-74 | 1974-75 |
| Coates, Steve | Det. | 1 | 5 | 1 | 0 | 1 | 24 | .... | .... | .... | .... | .... | .... | 1976-77 | 1976-77 |
| Cochrane, Glen | Phi., Van., Chi., Edm. | 10 | 411 | 17 | 72 | 89 | 1556 | 18 | 1 | 1 | 2 | 31 | .... | 1978-79 | 1988-89 |
| Coffey, Paul | Edm., Pit., L.A., Det., Hfd., Phi., Chi., Car., Bos. | 21 | 1409 | 396 | 1135 | 1531 | 1802 | 194 | 59 | 137 | 196 | 264 | 4 | 1980-81 | 2000-01 |
| Coflin, Hugh | Chi. | 1 | 31 | 0 | 3 | 3 | 33 | .... | .... | .... | .... | .... | .... | 1950-51 | 1950-51 |
| Cole, Danton | Wpg., T.B., N.J., NYI, Chi. | 7 | 318 | 58 | 60 | 118 | 125 | 1 | 0 | 0 | 0 | 0 | 1 | 1989-90 | 1995-96 |
| Colley, Kevin | NYI | 1 | 16 | 0 | 0 | 0 | 52 | .... | .... | .... | .... | .... | .... | 2005-06 | 2005-06 |
| Colley, Tom | Min. | 1 | 1 | 0 | 0 | 0 | 2 | .... | .... | .... | .... | .... | .... | 1974-75 | 1974-75 |
| Collings, Norm | Mtl. | 1 | 1 | 0 | 1 | 1 | 0 | .... | .... | .... | .... | .... | .... | 1934-35 | 1934-35 |
| Collins, Bill | Min., Mtl., Det., St.L., NYR, Phi., Wsh. | 11 | 768 | 157 | 154 | 311 | 415 | 18 | 3 | 5 | 8 | 12 | .... | 1967-68 | 1977-78 |
| Collins, Gary | Tor. | 1 | .... | .... | .... | .... | .... | 2 | 0 | 0 | 0 | 0 | .... | 1958-59 | 1958-59 |
| ‡ Collins, Rob | NYI | 1 | 8 | 1 | 1 | 2 | 0 | .... | .... | .... | .... | .... | .... | 2005-06 | 2005-06 |
| Collyard, Bob | St.L. | 1 | 10 | 1 | 3 | 4 | 4 | .... | .... | .... | .... | .... | .... | 1973-74 | 1973-74 |
| • Colman, Michael | S.J. | 1 | 15 | 0 | 1 | 1 | 32 | .... | .... | .... | .... | .... | .... | 1991-92 | 1991-92 |
| • Colville, Mac | NYR | 9 | 353 | 71 | 104 | 175 | 130 | 40 | 9 | 10 | 19 | 14 | 1 | 1935-36 | 1946-47 |
| • Colville, Neil | NYR | 12 | 464 | 99 | 166 | 265 | 213 | 46 | 7 | 19 | 26 | 32 | 1 | 1935-36 | 1948-49 |
| Colwill, Les | NYR | 1 | 69 | 7 | 6 | 13 | 16 | .... | .... | .... | .... | .... | .... | 1958-59 | 1958-59 |
| Comeau, Rey | Mtl., Atl., Col. | 9 | 564 | 98 | 141 | 239 | 175 | 9 | 2 | 1 | 3 | 8 | .... | 1971-72 | 1979-80 |
| Comrie, Paul | Edm. | 1 | 15 | 1 | 2 | 3 | 4 | .... | .... | .... | .... | .... | .... | 1999-00 | 1999-00 |
| Conacher, Brian | Tor., Det. | 5 | 155 | 28 | 28 | 56 | 84 | 12 | 3 | 2 | 5 | 21 | 1 | 1961-62 | 1971-72 |
| • Conacher, Charlie | Tor., Det., NYA | 12 | 459 | 225 | 173 | 398 | 523 | 49 | 17 | 18 | 35 | 49 | 1 | 1929-30 | 1940-41 |
| Conacher, Jim | Det., Chi., NYR | 8 | 328 | 85 | 117 | 202 | 91 | 19 | 5 | 2 | 7 | 4 | .... | 1945-46 | 1952-53 |
| • Conacher, Lionel | Pit., NYA, Mtl.M., Chi. | 12 | 498 | 80 | 105 | 185 | 882 | 35 | 2 | 2 | 4 | 34 | 2 | 1925-26 | 1936-37 |
| Conacher, Pat | NYR, Edm., N.J., L.A., Cgy., NYI | 13 | 521 | 63 | 76 | 139 | 235 | 67 | 11 | 10 | 21 | 40 | 1 | 1979-80 | 1995-96 |
| Conacher, Pete | Chi., NYR, Tor. | 6 | 229 | 47 | 39 | 86 | 57 | 7 | 0 | 0 | 0 | 0 | .... | 1951-52 | 1957-58 |
| • Conacher, Roy | Bos., Det., Chi. | 11 | 490 | 226 | 200 | 426 | 90 | 42 | 15 | 15 | 30 | 14 | 2 | 1938-39 | 1951-52 |
| • Conn, Red | NYA | 2 | 96 | 9 | 28 | 37 | 22 | .... | .... | .... | .... | .... | .... | 1933-34 | 1934-35 |
| Conn, Rob | Chi., Buf. | 2 | 30 | 2 | 5 | 7 | 20 | .... | .... | .... | .... | .... | .... | 1991-92 | 1995-96 |
| • Connelly, Bert | NYR, Chi. | 3 | 87 | 13 | 15 | 28 | 37 | 14 | 1 | 0 | 1 | 0 | 1 | 1934-35 | 1937-38 |
| Connelly, Wayne | Mtl., Bos., Min., Det., St.L., Van. | 10 | 543 | 133 | 174 | 307 | 156 | 24 | 11 | 7 | 18 | 4 | .... | 1960-61 | 1971-72 |
| Connor, Cam | Mtl., Edm., NYR | 5 | 89 | 9 | 22 | 31 | 256 | 20 | 5 | 0 | 5 | 6 | 1 | 1978-79 | 1982-83 |
| • Connor, Harry | Bos., NYA, Ott. | 4 | 134 | 16 | 5 | 21 | 149 | 10 | 0 | 0 | 0 | 2 | .... | 1927-28 | 1930-31 |
| • Connors, Bob | NYA, Det. | 3 | 78 | 17 | 10 | 27 | 110 | 2 | 0 | 0 | 0 | 10 | .... | 1926-27 | 1929-30 |
| Conroy, Al | Phi. | 3 | 114 | 9 | 14 | 23 | 156 | .... | .... | .... | .... | .... | .... | 1991-92 | 1993-94 |
| Contini, Joe | Col., Min. | 3 | 68 | 17 | 21 | 38 | 34 | 2 | 0 | 0 | 0 | 0 | .... | 1977-78 | 1980-81 |
| Convery, Brandon | Tor., Van., L.A. | 4 | 72 | 9 | 19 | 28 | 36 | 5 | 0 | 0 | 0 | 2 | .... | 1995-96 | 1998-99 |
| • Convey, Eddie | NYA | 3 | 36 | 1 | 1 | 2 | 33 | .... | .... | .... | .... | .... | .... | 1930-31 | 1932-33 |
| • Cook, Bill | NYR | 11 | 474 | 229 | 138 | 367 | 386 | 46 | 13 | 11 | 24 | 68 | 2 | 1926-27 | 1936-37 |
| • Cook, Bob | Van., Det., NYI, Min. | 4 | 72 | 13 | 9 | 22 | 22 | .... | .... | .... | .... | .... | .... | 1970-71 | 1974-75 |
| • Cook, Bud | Bos., Ott., St.L. | 3 | 50 | 5 | 4 | 9 | 22 | .... | .... | .... | .... | .... | .... | 1931-32 | 1934-35 |
| • Cook, Bun | NYR, Bos. | 11 | 473 | 158 | 144 | 302 | 444 | 46 | 15 | 3 | 18 | 50 | 2 | 1926-27 | 1936-37 |
| • Cook, Lloyd | Bos. | 1 | 4 | 1 | 0 | 1 | 0 | .... | .... | .... | .... | .... | .... | 1924-25 | 1924-25 |
| • Cook, Tom | Chi., Mtl.M. | 9 | 349 | 77 | 98 | 175 | 184 | 24 | 2 | 4 | 6 | 19 | 1 | 1929-30 | 1937-38 |
| • Cooper, Carson | Bos., Mtl., Det. | 8 | 294 | 110 | 57 | 167 | 111 | 7 | 0 | 0 | 0 | 2 | .... | 1924-25 | 1931-32 |
| Cooper, David | Tor. | 3 | 30 | 3 | 7 | 10 | 24 | .... | .... | .... | .... | .... | .... | 1996-97 | 2000-01 |
| Cooper, Ed | Col. | 2 | 49 | 8 | 7 | 15 | 46 | .... | .... | .... | .... | .... | .... | 1980-81 | 1981-82 |
| • Cooper, Hal | NYR | 1 | 8 | 0 | 0 | 0 | 2 | .... | .... | .... | .... | .... | .... | 1944-45 | 1944-45 |
| • Cooper, Joe | NYR, Chi. | 11 | 420 | 30 | 66 | 96 | 442 | 35 | 3 | 5 | 8 | 58 | .... | 1935-36 | 1946-47 |
| • Copp, Bobby | Tor. | 2 | 40 | 3 | 9 | 12 | 26 | .... | .... | .... | .... | .... | .... | 1942-43 | 1950-51 |
| • Corbeau, Bert | Mtl., Ham., Tor. | 10 | 258 | 63 | 49 | 112 | 629 | 9 | 2 | 2 | 4 | 38 | .... | 1917-18 | 1926-27 |
| Corbet, Rene | Que., Col., Cgy., Pit. | 8 | 362 | 58 | 74 | 132 | 420 | 53 | 7 | 6 | 13 | 52 | 1 | 1993-94 | 2000-01 |
| • Corbett, Mike | L.A. | 1 | .... | .... | .... | .... | .... | 2 | 0 | 1 | 1 | 2 | .... | 1967-68 | 1967-68 |
| Corcoran, Norm | Bos., Det., Chi. | 4 | 29 | 1 | 3 | 4 | 21 | 4 | 0 | 0 | 0 | 6 | .... | 1949-50 | 1955-56 |
| Corkum, Bob | Buf., Ana., Phi., Phx., L.A., N.J., Atl. | 12 | 720 | 97 | 103 | 200 | 281 | 62 | 7 | 7 | 14 | 24 | .... | 1989-90 | 2001-02 |
| • Cormier, Roger | Mtl. | 1 | 1 | 0 | 0 | 0 | 0 | .... | .... | .... | .... | .... | .... | 1925-26 | 1925-26 |
| Cornforth, Mark | Bos. | 1 | 6 | 0 | 0 | 0 | 4 | .... | .... | .... | .... | .... | .... | 1995-96 | 1995-96 |
| • Corrigan, Chuck | Tor., NYA | 2 | 19 | 2 | 2 | 4 | 2 | .... | .... | .... | .... | .... | .... | 1937-38 | 1940-41 |
| Corrigan, Mike | L.A., Van., Pit. | 10 | 594 | 152 | 195 | 347 | 698 | 17 | 2 | 3 | 5 | 20 | .... | 1967-68 | 1977-78 |
| Corrinet, Chris | Wsh. | 1 | 8 | 0 | 1 | 1 | 6 | .... | .... | .... | .... | .... | .... | 2001-02 | 2001-02 |
| • Corriveau, Andre | Mtl. | 1 | 3 | 0 | 1 | 1 | 0 | .... | .... | .... | .... | .... | .... | 1953-54 | 1953-54 |
| Corriveau, Yvon | Wsh., Hfd., S.J. | 9 | 280 | 48 | 40 | 88 | 310 | 29 | 5 | 7 | 12 | 50 | .... | 1985-86 | 1993-94 |
| ‡ Corso, Daniel | St.L., Atl. | 4 | 77 | 14 | 11 | 25 | 20 | 14 | 0 | 1 | 1 | 0 | .... | 2000-01 | 2003-04 |
| Corson, Shayne | Mtl., Edm., St.L., Tor., Dal. | 19 | 1156 | 273 | 420 | 693 | 2357 | 140 | 38 | 49 | 87 | 291 | .... | 1985-86 | 2003-04 |
| Cory, Ross | Wpg. | 2 | 51 | 2 | 10 | 12 | 41 | .... | .... | .... | .... | .... | .... | 1979-80 | 1980-81 |
| Cossette, Jacques | Pit. | 3 | 64 | 8 | 6 | 14 | 29 | 3 | 0 | 1 | 1 | 4 | .... | 1975-76 | 1978-79 |
| • Costello, Les | Tor. | 3 | 15 | 2 | 3 | 5 | 11 | 6 | 2 | 2 | 4 | 2 | 1 | 1947-48 | 1949-50 |
| Costello, Murray | Chi., Bos., Det. | 4 | 162 | 13 | 19 | 32 | 54 | 5 | 0 | 0 | 0 | 2 | .... | 1953-54 | 1956-57 |
| Costello, Rich | Tor. | 2 | 12 | 2 | 2 | 4 | 2 | .... | .... | .... | .... | .... | .... | 1983-84 | 1985-86 |
| • Cotch, Charlie | Ham., Tor. | 1 | 12 | 1 | 0 | 1 | 0 | .... | .... | .... | .... | .... | .... | 1924-25 | 1924-25 |
| Cote, Alain | Que. | 10 | 696 | 103 | 190 | 293 | 383 | 67 | 9 | 15 | 24 | 44 | .... | 1979-80 | 1988-89 |
| Cote, Alain | Bos., Wsh., Mtl., T.B., Que. | 9 | 119 | 2 | 18 | 20 | 124 | 11 | 0 | 2 | 2 | 26 | .... | 1985-86 | 1993-94 |
| ‡ Cote, Patrick | Dal., Nsh., Edm. | 6 | 105 | 1 | 2 | 3 | 377 | .... | .... | .... | .... | .... | .... | 1995-96 | 2000-01 |
| Cote, Ray | Edm. | 3 | 15 | 0 | 0 | 0 | 4 | 14 | 3 | 2 | 5 | 0 | .... | 1982-83 | 1984-85 |

| | | | Regular Schedule | | | | | Playoffs | | | | | NHL | First | Last |
|---|---|---|---|---|---|---|---|---|---|---|---|---|---|---|---|
| Name | NHL Teams | NHL Seasons | GP | G | A | TP | PIM | GP | G | A | TP | PIM | Cup Wins | NHL Season | NHL Season |
| Cote, Sylvain | Hfd., Wsh., Tor., Chi., Dal. | 19 | 1171 | 122 | 313 | 435 | 545 | 102 | 11 | 22 | 33 | 62 | .... | 1984-85 | 2002-03 |
| ● Cotton, Baldy | Pit., Tor., NYA | 12 | 503 | 101 | 103 | 204 | 419 | 43 | 4 | 9 | 13 | 46 | 1 | 1925-26 | 1936-37 |
| ● Coughlin, Jack | Tor., Que., Mtl., Ham. | 3 | 19 | 2 | 0 | 2 | 3 | .... | .... | .... | .... | .... | 1 | 1917-18 | 1920-21 |
| Coulis, Tim | Wsh., Min. | 4 | 47 | 4 | 5 | 9 | 138 | 3 | 1 | 0 | 1 | 2 | .... | 1979-80 | 1985-86 |
| ‡ Coulombe, Patrick | Van. | 1 | 7 | 0 | 1 | 1 | 4 | .... | .... | .... | .... | .... | .... | 2006-07 | 2006-07 |
| ● Coulson, D'arcy | Phi. | 1 | 28 | 0 | 0 | 0 | 103 | .... | .... | .... | .... | .... | .... | 1930-31 | 1930-31 |
| ● Coulter, Art | Chi., NYR | 11 | 465 | 30 | 82 | 112 | 543 | 49 | 4 | 5 | 9 | 61 | 2 | 1931-32 | 1941-42 |
| Coulter, Neal | NYI | 3 | 26 | 5 | 5 | 10 | 11 | .... | .... | .... | .... | .... | .... | 1985-86 | 1987-88 |
| ● Coulter, Thomas | Chi. | 1 | 2 | 0 | 0 | 0 | 0 | .... | .... | .... | .... | .... | .... | 1933-34 | 1933-34 |
| Cournoyer, Yvan | Mtl. | 16 | 968 | 428 | 435 | 863 | 255 | 147 | 64 | 63 | 127 | 47 | 10 | 1963-64 | 1978-79 |
| Courteau, Yves | Cgy., Hfd. | 3 | 22 | 2 | 5 | 7 | 4 | 1 | 0 | 0 | 0 | 0 | .... | 1984-85 | 1986-87 |
| Courtenay, Ed | S.J. | 2 | 44 | 7 | 13 | 20 | 10 | .... | .... | .... | .... | .... | .... | 1991-92 | 1992-93 |
| Courtnall, Geoff | Bos., Edm., Wsh., St.L., Van. | 17 | 1048 | 367 | 432 | 799 | 1465 | 156 | 39 | 70 | 109 | 262 | 1 | 1983-84 | 1999-00 |
| Courtnall, Russ | Tor., Mtl., Min., Dal., Van., NYR, L.A. | 16 | 1029 | 297 | 447 | 744 | 557 | 129 | 39 | 44 | 83 | 83 | .... | 1983-84 | 1998-99 |
| ‡ Courville, Larry | Van. | 3 | 33 | 1 | 2 | 3 | 16 | .... | .... | .... | .... | .... | .... | 1995-96 | 1997-98 |
| ● Coutu, Billy | Mtl., Ham., Bos. | 10 | 244 | 33 | 21 | 54 | 478 | 19 | 1 | 1 | 2 | 39 | 1 | 1917-18 | 1926-27 |
| ● Couture, Gerry | Det., Mtl., Chi. | 10 | 385 | 86 | 70 | 156 | 89 | 45 | 9 | 7 | 16 | 4 | 1 | 1944-45 | 1953-54 |
| ● Couture, Rosie | Chi., Mtl. | 8 | 309 | 48 | 56 | 104 | 184 | 23 | 1 | 5 | 6 | 15 | 1 | 1928-29 | 1935-36 |
| Couturier, Sylvain | L.A. | 3 | 33 | 4 | 5 | 9 | 4 | .... | .... | .... | .... | .... | .... | 1988-89 | 1991-92 |
| Cowick, Bruce | Phi., Wsh., St.L. | 3 | 70 | 5 | 6 | 11 | 43 | 8 | 0 | 0 | 0 | 9 | 1 | 1973-74 | 1975-76 |
| Cowie, Rob | L.A. | 2 | 78 | 7 | 12 | 19 | 52 | .... | .... | .... | .... | .... | .... | 1994-95 | 1995-96 |
| ● Cowley, Bill | St.L., Bos. | 13 | 549 | 195 | 353 | 548 | 143 | 64 | 12 | 34 | 46 | 22 | 2 | 1934-35 | 1946-47 |
| ● Cox, Danny | Tor., Ott., Det., NYR | 8 | 319 | 47 | 49 | 96 | 128 | 10 | 0 | 1 | 1 | 6 | .... | 1926-27 | 1933-34 |
| Coxe, Craig | Van., Cgy., St.L., S.J. | 8 | 235 | 14 | 31 | 45 | 713 | 5 | 1 | 0 | 1 | 18 | .... | 1984-85 | 1991-92 |
| Craig, Mike | Min., Dal., Tor., S.J. | 9 | 423 | 71 | 97 | 168 | 550 | 26 | 2 | 2 | 4 | 49 | .... | 1990-91 | 2001-02 |
| Craighead, John | Tor. | 1 | 5 | 0 | 0 | 0 | 10 | .... | .... | .... | .... | .... | .... | 1996-97 | 1996-97 |
| Craigwell, Dale | S.J. | 3 | 98 | 11 | 18 | 29 | 28 | .... | .... | .... | .... | .... | .... | 1991-92 | 1993-94 |
| Crashley, Bart | Det., K.C., L.A. | 6 | 140 | 7 | 36 | 43 | 50 | .... | .... | .... | .... | .... | .... | 1965-66 | 1975-76 |
| Craven, Murray | Det., Phi., Hfd., Van., Chi., S.J. | 18 | 1071 | 266 | 493 | 759 | 524 | 118 | 27 | 43 | 70 | 64 | .... | 1982-83 | 1999-00 |
| Crawford, Bob | St.L., Hfd., NYR, Wsh. | 7 | 246 | 71 | 71 | 142 | 72 | 11 | 0 | 1 | 1 | 8 | .... | 1979-80 | 1986-87 |
| Crawford, Bobby | Col., Det. | 2 | 16 | 1 | 3 | 4 | 6 | .... | .... | .... | .... | .... | .... | 1980-81 | 1982-83 |
| ● Crawford, Jack | Bos. | 13 | 548 | 38 | 140 | 178 | 202 | 66 | 3 | 13 | 16 | 36 | 2 | 1937-38 | 1949-50 |
| Crawford, Lou | Bos. | 2 | 26 | 2 | 1 | 3 | 29 | 1 | 0 | 0 | 0 | 0 | .... | 1989-90 | 1991-92 |
| Crawford, Marc | Van. | 6 | 176 | 19 | 31 | 50 | 229 | 20 | 1 | 2 | 3 | 44 | .... | 1981-82 | 1986-87 |
| ● Crawford, Rusty | Ott., Tor. | 2 | 38 | 10 | 8 | 18 | 117 | 2 | 2 | 1 | 3 | 9 | 1 | 1917-18 | 1918-19 |
| Creighton, Adam | Buf., Chi., NYI, T.B., St.L. | 14 | 708 | 187 | 216 | 403 | 1077 | 61 | 11 | 14 | 25 | 137 | .... | 1983-84 | 1996-97 |
| Creighton, Dave | Bos., Tor., Chi., NYR | 12 | 616 | 140 | 174 | 314 | 223 | 51 | 11 | 13 | 24 | 20 | .... | 1948-49 | 1959-60 |
| ● Creighton, Jimmy | Det. | 1 | 11 | 1 | 0 | 1 | 2 | .... | .... | .... | .... | .... | .... | 1930-31 | 1930-31 |
| Cressman, Dave | Min. | 2 | 85 | 6 | 8 | 14 | 37 | .... | .... | .... | .... | .... | .... | 1974-75 | 1975-76 |
| Cressman, Glen | Mtl. | 1 | 4 | 0 | 0 | 0 | 2 | .... | .... | .... | .... | .... | .... | 1956-57 | 1956-57 |
| Crisp, Terry | Bos., St.L., NYI, Phi. | 11 | 536 | 67 | 134 | 201 | 135 | 110 | 15 | 28 | 43 | 40 | 2 | 1965-66 | 1976-77 |
| Cristofoli, Ed | Mtl. | 1 | 9 | 0 | 1 | 1 | 4 | .... | .... | .... | .... | .... | .... | 1989-90 | 1989-90 |
| ● Croghan, Maurice | Mtl.M. | 1 | 16 | 0 | 0 | 0 | 4 | .... | .... | .... | .... | .... | .... | 1937-38 | 1937-38 |
| Crombeen, Mike | Cle., St.L., Hfd. | 8 | 475 | 55 | 68 | 123 | 218 | 27 | 6 | 2 | 8 | 32 | .... | 1977-78 | 1984-85 |
| Cronin, Shawn | Wsh., Wpg., Phi., S.J. | 7 | 292 | 3 | 18 | 21 | 877 | 32 | 1 | 0 | 1 | 38 | .... | 1988-89 | 1994-95 |
| Cross, Cory | T.B., Tor., NYR, Edm., Pit., Det. | 12 | 659 | 34 | 97 | 131 | 684 | 47 | 2 | 4 | 6 | 62 | .... | 1993-94 | 2005-06 |
| ● Crossett, Stan | Phi. | 1 | 21 | 0 | 0 | 0 | 10 | .... | .... | .... | .... | .... | .... | 1930-31 | 1930-31 |
| Crossman, Doug | Chi., Phi., L.A., NYI, Hfd., Det., T.B., St.L. | 14 | 914 | 105 | 359 | 464 | 534 | 97 | 12 | 39 | 51 | 105 | .... | 1980-81 | 1993-94 |
| Croteau, Gary | L.A., Det., Cal., K.C., Col. | 12 | 684 | 144 | 175 | 319 | 143 | 11 | 3 | 2 | 5 | 8 | .... | 1968-69 | 1979-80 |
| Crowder, Bruce | Bos., Pit. | 4 | 243 | 47 | 51 | 98 | 156 | 31 | 8 | 4 | 12 | 41 | .... | 1981-82 | 1984-85 |
| Crowder, Keith | Bos., L.A. | 10 | 662 | 223 | 271 | 494 | 1354 | 85 | 14 | 22 | 36 | 218 | .... | 1980-81 | 1989-90 |
| Crowder, Troy | N.J., Det., L.A., Van. | 7 | 150 | 9 | 7 | 16 | 433 | 4 | 0 | 0 | 0 | 22 | .... | 1987-88 | 1996-97 |
| Crowe, Phil | L.A., Phi., Ott., Nsh. | 6 | 94 | 4 | 5 | 9 | 173 | 3 | 0 | 0 | 0 | 16 | .... | 1993-94 | 1999-00 |
| Crowley, Mike | Ana. | 3 | 67 | 5 | 15 | 20 | 44 | .... | .... | .... | .... | .... | .... | 1997-98 | 2000-01 |
| Crowley, Ted | Hfd., Col., NYI | 2 | 34 | 2 | 4 | 6 | 12 | .... | .... | .... | .... | .... | .... | 1993-94 | 1998-99 |
| Crozier, Greg | Pit. | 1 | 1 | 0 | 0 | 0 | 0 | .... | .... | .... | .... | .... | .... | 2000-01 | 2000-01 |
| Crozier, Joe | Tor. | 1 | 5 | 0 | 3 | 3 | 2 | .... | .... | .... | .... | .... | .... | 1959-60 | 1959-60 |
| ● Crutchfield, Nels | Mtl. | 1 | 41 | 5 | 5 | 10 | 20 | 2 | 0 | 1 | 1 | 22 | .... | 1934-35 | 1934-35 |
| Culhane, Jim | Hfd. | 1 | 6 | 0 | 1 | 1 | 4 | .... | .... | .... | .... | .... | .... | 1989-90 | 1989-90 |
| Cullen, Barry | Tor., Det. | 5 | 219 | 32 | 52 | 84 | 111 | 6 | 0 | 0 | 0 | 2 | .... | 1955-56 | 1959-60 |
| Cullen, Brian | Tor., NYR | 7 | 326 | 56 | 100 | 156 | 92 | 19 | 3 | 0 | 3 | 2 | .... | 1954-55 | 1960-61 |
| ‡ Cullen, David | Phx., Min. | 2 | 19 | 0 | 0 | 0 | 6 | .... | .... | .... | .... | .... | .... | 2000-01 | 2001-02 |
| Cullen, John | Pit., Hfd., Tor., T.B. | 11 | 621 | 187 | 363 | 550 | 898 | 53 | 12 | 22 | 34 | 58 | .... | 1988-89 | 1998-99 |
| Cullen, Ray | NYR, Det., Min., Van. | 6 | 313 | 92 | 123 | 215 | 120 | 20 | 3 | 10 | 13 | 2 | .... | 1965-66 | 1970-71 |
| Cummins, Barry | Cal. | 1 | 36 | 1 | 2 | 3 | 39 | .... | .... | .... | .... | .... | .... | 1973-74 | 1973-74 |
| Cummins, Jim | Det., Phi., T.B., Chi., Phx., Mtl., Ana., NYI, Col. | 12 | 511 | 24 | 36 | 60 | 1538 | 37 | 1 | 2 | 3 | 43 | .... | 1991-92 | 2003-04 |
| Cunneyworth, Randy | Buf., Pit., Wpg., Hfd., Chi., Ott. | 16 | 866 | 189 | 225 | 414 | 1280 | 45 | 7 | 7 | 14 | 61 | .... | 1980-81 | 1998-99 |
| Cunningham, Bob | NYR | 2 | 4 | 0 | 1 | 1 | 0 | .... | .... | .... | .... | .... | .... | 1960-61 | 1961-62 |
| Cunningham, Jim | Phi. | 1 | 1 | 0 | 0 | 0 | 4 | .... | .... | .... | .... | .... | .... | 1977-78 | 1977-78 |
| ● Cunningham, Les | NYA, Chi. | 2 | 60 | 7 | 19 | 26 | 21 | 1 | 0 | 0 | 0 | 0 | .... | 1936-37 | 1939-40 |
| ● Cupolo, Bill | Bos. | 1 | 47 | 11 | 13 | 24 | 10 | 7 | 1 | 2 | 3 | 0 | .... | 1944-45 | 1944-45 |
| Curran, Brian | Bos., NYI, Tor., Buf., Wsh. | 10 | 381 | 7 | 33 | 40 | 1461 | 24 | 0 | 1 | 1 | 122 | .... | 1983-84 | 1993-94 |
| Currie, Dan | Edm., L.A. | 4 | 22 | 2 | 1 | 3 | 4 | .... | .... | .... | .... | .... | .... | 1990-91 | 1993-94 |
| Currie, Glen | Wsh., L.A. | 8 | 326 | 39 | 79 | 118 | 100 | 12 | 1 | 3 | 4 | 4 | .... | 1979-80 | 1987-88 |
| Currie, Hugh | Mtl. | 1 | 1 | 0 | 0 | 0 | 0 | .... | .... | .... | .... | .... | .... | 1950-51 | 1950-51 |
| Currie, Tony | St.L., Van., Hfd. | 8 | 290 | 92 | 119 | 211 | 83 | 16 | 4 | 12 | 16 | 14 | .... | 1977-78 | 1984-85 |
| ● Curry, Floyd | Mtl. | 11 | 601 | 105 | 99 | 204 | 147 | 91 | 23 | 17 | 40 | 38 | 4 | 1947-48 | 1957-58 |
| Curtale, Tony | Cgy. | 1 | 2 | 0 | 0 | 0 | 0 | .... | .... | .... | .... | .... | .... | 1980-81 | 1980-81 |
| Curtis, Paul | Mtl., L.A., St.L. | 4 | 185 | 3 | 34 | 37 | 161 | 5 | 0 | 0 | 0 | 2 | .... | 1969-70 | 1972-73 |
| Cushenan, Ian | Chi., Mtl., NYR, Det. | 5 | 129 | 3 | 11 | 14 | 134 | .... | .... | .... | .... | .... | 1 | 1956-57 | 1963-64 |
| Cusson, Jean | Oak. | 1 | 2 | 0 | 0 | 0 | 0 | .... | .... | .... | .... | .... | .... | 1967-68 | 1967-68 |
| ‡ Cutta, Jakub | Wsh. | 3 | 8 | 0 | 0 | 0 | 0 | .... | .... | .... | .... | .... | .... | 2000-01 | 2003-04 |
| Cyr, Denis | Cgy., Chi., St.L. | 6 | 193 | 41 | 43 | 84 | 36 | 4 | 0 | 0 | 0 | 0 | .... | 1980-81 | 1985-86 |
| Cyr, Paul | Buf., NYR, Hfd. | 9 | 470 | 101 | 140 | 241 | 623 | 24 | 4 | 6 | 10 | 31 | .... | 1982-83 | 1991-92 |
| ‡ Czerkawski, Mariusz | Bos., Edm., NYI, Mtl., Tor. | 12 | 745 | 215 | 220 | 435 | 274 | 42 | 8 | 7 | 15 | 18 | .... | 1993-94 | 2005-06 |

## D

| | | | | | | | | | | | | | | | |
|---|---|---|---|---|---|---|---|---|---|---|---|---|---|---|---|
| ‡ Dackell, Andreas | Ott., Mtl. | 8 | 613 | 91 | 159 | 250 | 162 | 44 | 5 | 5 | 10 | 10 | .... | 1996-97 | 2003-04 |
| ‡ Dagenais, Pierre | N.J., Fla., Mtl. | 5 | 142 | 35 | 23 | 58 | 58 | 8 | 0 | 1 | 1 | 6 | .... | 2000-01 | 2005-06 |
| Dahl, Kevin | Cgy., Phx., Tor., CBJ | 8 | 188 | 7 | 22 | 29 | 153 | 16 | 0 | 2 | 2 | 12 | .... | 1992-93 | 2000-01 |
| Dahlen, Ulf | NYR, Min., Dal., S.J., Chi., Wsh. | 14 | 966 | 301 | 354 | 655 | 230 | 85 | 15 | 25 | 40 | 12 | .... | 1987-88 | 2002-03 |
| Dahlin, Kjell | Mtl. | 3 | 166 | 57 | 59 | 116 | 10 | 35 | 6 | 11 | 17 | 6 | 1 | 1985-86 | 1987-88 |
| ‡ Dahlman, Toni | Ott. | 2 | 22 | 1 | 1 | 2 | 0 | .... | .... | .... | .... | .... | .... | 2001-02 | 2002-03 |
| Dahlquist, Chris | Pit., Min., Cgy., Ott. | 11 | 532 | 19 | 71 | 90 | 488 | 39 | 4 | 7 | 11 | 30 | .... | 1985-86 | 1995-96 |
| ● Dahlstrom, Cully | Chi. | 8 | 342 | 88 | 118 | 206 | 58 | 29 | 6 | 8 | 14 | 4 | 1 | 1937-38 | 1944-45 |
| Daigle, Alain | Chi. | 6 | 389 | 56 | 50 | 106 | 122 | 17 | 0 | 1 | 1 | 0 | .... | 1974-75 | 1979-80 |
| ‡ Daigle, Alexandre | Ott., Phi., T.B., NYR, Pit., Min. | 10 | 616 | 129 | 198 | 327 | 186 | 12 | 0 | 2 | 2 | 2 | .... | 1993-94 | 2005-06 |
| Daigneault, J.J. | Van., Phi., Mtl., St.L., Pit., Ana., NYI, Nsh., Phx., Min. | 16 | 899 | 53 | 197 | 250 | 687 | 99 | 5 | 26 | 31 | 100 | 1 | 1984-85 | 2000-01 |
| Dailey, Bob | Van., Phi. | 9 | 561 | 94 | 231 | 325 | 814 | 63 | 12 | 34 | 46 | 105 | .... | 1973-74 | 1981-82 |
| ● Daley, Frank | Det. | 1 | 5 | 0 | 0 | 0 | 0 | 2 | 0 | 0 | 0 | 0 | .... | 1928-29 | 1928-29 |
| Daley, Pat | Wpg. | 2 | 12 | 1 | 0 | 1 | 13 | .... | .... | .... | .... | .... | .... | 1979-80 | 1980-81 |
| Dalgarno, Brad | NYI | 10 | 321 | 49 | 71 | 120 | 332 | 27 | 2 | 4 | 6 | 37 | .... | 1985-86 | 1995-96 |
| Dallman, Marty | Tor. | 2 | 6 | 0 | 1 | 1 | 0 | .... | .... | .... | .... | .... | .... | 1987-88 | 1988-89 |
| Dallman, Rod | NYI, Phi. | 4 | 6 | 1 | 0 | 1 | 26 | 1 | 0 | 1 | 1 | 0 | .... | 1987-88 | 1991-92 |
| ● Dame, Bunny | Mtl. | 1 | 34 | 2 | 5 | 7 | 4 | .... | .... | .... | .... | .... | .... | 1941-42 | 1941-42 |
| ● Damore, Hank | NYR | 1 | 4 | 1 | 0 | 1 | 2 | .... | .... | .... | .... | .... | .... | 1943-44 | 1943-44 |
| Damphousse, Vincent | Tor., Edm., Mtl., S.J. | 18 | 1378 | 432 | 773 | 1205 | 1190 | 140 | 41 | 63 | 104 | 144 | 1 | 1986-87 | 2003-04 |
| Daneyko, Ken | N.J. | 20 | 1283 | 36 | 142 | 178 | 2519 | 175 | 5 | 17 | 22 | 296 | 3 | 1983-84 | 2002-03 |
| Daniels, Jeff | Pit., Fla., Hfd., Car., Nsh. | 12 | 425 | 17 | 26 | 43 | 83 | 41 | 3 | 5 | 8 | 2 | 1 | 1990-91 | 2002-03 |
| ‡ Daniels, Kimbi | Phi. | 2 | 27 | 1 | 2 | 3 | 4 | .... | .... | .... | .... | .... | .... | 1990-91 | 1991-92 |
| Daniels, Scott | Hfd., Phi., N.J. | 6 | 149 | 8 | 12 | 20 | 667 | 1 | 0 | 0 | 0 | 0 | .... | 1992-93 | 1998-99 |
| Danton, Mike | N.J., St.L. | 3 | 87 | 9 | 5 | 14 | 182 | 5 | 1 | 0 | 1 | 2 | .... | 2000-01 | 2003-04 |
| Daoust, Dan | Mtl., Tor. | 8 | 522 | 87 | 167 | 254 | 544 | 32 | 7 | 5 | 12 | 83 | .... | 1982-83 | 1989-90 |
| ‡ Darby, Craig | Mtl., NYI, Phi., N.J. | 9 | 196 | 21 | 35 | 56 | 32 | .... | .... | .... | .... | .... | .... | 1994-95 | 2003-04 |
| Dark, Michael | St.L. | 2 | 43 | 5 | 6 | 11 | 14 | .... | .... | .... | .... | .... | .... | 1986-87 | 1987-88 |
| ● Darragh, Harold | Pit., Phi., Bos., Tor. | 8 | 308 | 68 | 49 | 117 | 50 | 16 | 1 | 3 | 4 | 4 | 1 | 1925-26 | 1932-33 |
| ● Darragh, Jack | Ott. | 6 | 121 | 66 | 46 | 112 | 113 | 11 | 3 | 0 | 3 | 9 | 3 | 1917-18 | 1923-24 |
| David, Richard | Que. | 3 | 31 | 4 | 4 | 8 | 10 | 1 | 0 | 0 | 0 | 0 | .... | 1979-80 | 1982-83 |
| ● Davidson, Bob | Tor. | 12 | 491 | 94 | 160 | 254 | 398 | 79 | 5 | 17 | 22 | 76 | 2 | 1934-35 | 1945-46 |
| ● Davidson, Gord | NYR | 2 | 51 | 3 | 6 | 9 | 8 | .... | .... | .... | .... | .... | .... | 1942-43 | 1943-44 |
| Davidson, Matt | CBJ | 3 | 56 | 5 | 7 | 12 | 28 | .... | .... | .... | .... | .... | .... | 2000-01 | 2002-03 |
| ‡ Davidsson, Johan | Ana., NYI | 2 | 83 | 6 | 9 | 15 | 16 | 1 | 0 | 0 | 0 | 0 | .... | 1998-99 | 1999-00 |

Cam Connor

Marc Crawford

Ray Cullen

Bob Davidson

Butch Deadmarsh

Kevin Devine

Cecil Dillon

Dave Downie

| | | | Regular Schedule | | | | | Playoffs | | | | | NHL | First | Last |
|---|---|---|---|---|---|---|---|---|---|---|---|---|---|---|---|
| Name | NHL Teams | NHL Seasons | GP | G | A | TP | PIM | GP | G | A | TP | PIM | Cup Wins | NHL Season | NHL Season |
| • Davie, Bob | Bos. | 3 | 41 | 0 | 1 | 1 | 25 | .... | .... | .... | .... | .... | .... | 1933-34 | 1935-36 |
| • Davies, Buck | NYR | 1 | .... | .... | .... | .... | .... | 1 | 0 | 0 | 0 | 0 | .... | 1947-48 | 1947-48 |
| • Davis, Bob | Det. | 1 | 3 | 0 | 0 | 0 | 0 | .... | .... | .... | .... | .... | .... | 1932-33 | 1932-33 |
| Davis, Kim | Pit., Tor. | 4 | 36 | 5 | 7 | 12 | 51 | 4 | 0 | 0 | 0 | 0 | .... | 1977-78 | 1980-81 |
| • Davis, Lorne | Mtl., Chi., Det., Bos. | 6 | 95 | 8 | 12 | 20 | 20 | 18 | 3 | 1 | 4 | 10 | 1 | 1951-52 | 1959-60 |
| Davis, Mal | Det., Buf. | 6 | 100 | 31 | 22 | 53 | 34 | 7 | 1 | 0 | 1 | 0 | .... | 1978-79 | 1985-86 |
| • Davison, Murray | Bos. | 1 | 1 | 0 | 0 | 0 | 0 | .... | .... | .... | .... | .... | .... | 1965-66 | 1965-66 |
| Davydov, Evgeny | Wpg., Fla., Ott. | 4 | 155 | 40 | 39 | 79 | 120 | 11 | 2 | 2 | 4 | 2 | .... | 1991-92 | 1994-95 |
| Daw, Jeff | Col. | 1 | 1 | 0 | 1 | 1 | 0 | .... | .... | .... | .... | .... | .... | 2001-02 | 2001-02 |
| Dawe, Jason | Buf., NYI, Mtl., NYR | 8 | 366 | 86 | 90 | 176 | 162 | 22 | 4 | 3 | 7 | 18 | .... | 1993-94 | 2001-02 |
| • Dawes, Bob | Tor., Mtl. | 4 | 32 | 2 | 7 | 9 | 6 | 10 | 0 | 0 | 0 | 2 | 1 | 1946-47 | 1950-51 |
| • Day, Hap | Tor., NYA | 14 | 581 | 86 | 116 | 202 | 601 | 53 | 4 | 7 | 11 | 56 | 1 | 1924-25 | 1937-38 |
| Day, Joe | Hfd., NYI | 3 | 72 | 1 | 10 | 11 | 87 | .... | .... | .... | .... | .... | .... | 1991-92 | 1993-94 |
| Daze, Eric | Chi. | 11 | 601 | 226 | 172 | 398 | 176 | 37 | 5 | 7 | 12 | 8 | .... | 1994-95 | 2005-06 |
| Dea, Billy | NYR, Det., Chi., Pit. | 8 | 397 | 67 | 54 | 121 | 44 | 11 | 2 | 1 | 3 | 6 | .... | 1953-54 | 1970-71 |
| • Deacon, Don | Det. | 3 | 30 | 6 | 4 | 10 | 6 | 2 | 2 | 1 | 3 | 0 | .... | 1936-37 | 1939-40 |
| Deadmarsh, Adam | Que., Col., L.A. | 10 | 567 | 184 | 189 | 373 | 819 | 105 | 26 | 40 | 66 | 100 | 1 | 1994-95 | 2003-04 |
| Deadmarsh, Butch | Buf., Atl., K.C. | 5 | 137 | 12 | 5 | 17 | 155 | 4 | 0 | 0 | 0 | 17 | .... | 1970-71 | 1974-75 |
| Dean, Barry | Col., Phi. | 3 | 165 | 25 | 56 | 81 | 146 | .... | .... | .... | .... | .... | .... | 1976-77 | 1978-79 |
| Dean, Kevin | N.J., Atl., Dal., Chi. | 7 | 331 | 7 | 48 | 55 | 138 | 16 | 2 | 2 | 4 | 2 | 1 | 1994-95 | 2000-01 |
| Debenedet, Nelson | Det., Pit. | 2 | 46 | 10 | 4 | 14 | 13 | .... | .... | .... | .... | .... | .... | 1973-74 | 1974-75 |
| DeBlois, Lucien | NYR, Col., Wpg., Mtl., Que., Tor. | 15 | 993 | 249 | 276 | 525 | 814 | 52 | 7 | 6 | 13 | 38 | 1 | 1977-78 | 1991-92 |
| Debol, Dave | Hfd. | 2 | 92 | 26 | 26 | 52 | 4 | 3 | 0 | 0 | 0 | 0 | .... | 1979-80 | 1980-81 |
| DeBrusk, Louie | Edm., T.B., Phx., Chi. | 11 | 401 | 24 | 17 | 41 | 1161 | 15 | 2 | 0 | 2 | 10 | .... | 1991-92 | 2002-03 |
| DeFauw, Brad | Car. | 1 | 9 | 3 | 0 | 3 | 2 | .... | .... | .... | .... | .... | .... | 2002-03 | 2002-03 |
| Defazio, Dean | Pit. | 1 | 22 | 0 | 2 | 2 | 28 | .... | .... | .... | .... | .... | .... | 1983-84 | 1983-84 |
| DeGray, Dale | Cgy., Tor., L.A., Buf. | 5 | 153 | 18 | 47 | 65 | 195 | 13 | 1 | 3 | 4 | 28 | .... | 1985-86 | 1989-90 |
| • Delisle, Jonathan | Mtl. | 1 | 1 | 0 | 0 | 0 | 0 | .... | .... | .... | .... | .... | .... | 1998-99 | 1998-99 |
| Delisle, Xavier | T.B., Mtl. | 2 | 16 | 3 | 2 | 5 | 6 | .... | .... | .... | .... | .... | .... | 1998-99 | 2000-01 |
| • Delmonte, Armand | Bos. | 1 | 1 | 0 | 0 | 0 | 0 | .... | .... | .... | .... | .... | .... | 1945-46 | 1945-46 |
| Delorme, Gilbert | Mtl., St.L., Que., Det., Pit. | 9 | 541 | 31 | 92 | 123 | 520 | 56 | 1 | 9 | 10 | 56 | .... | 1981-82 | 1989-90 |
| Delorme, Ron | Col., Van. | 9 | 524 | 83 | 83 | 166 | 667 | 25 | 1 | 2 | 3 | 59 | .... | 1976-77 | 1984-85 |
| Delory, Val | NYR | 1 | 1 | 0 | 0 | 0 | 0 | .... | .... | .... | .... | .... | .... | 1948-49 | 1948-49 |
| Delparte, Guy | Col. | 1 | 48 | 1 | 8 | 9 | 18 | .... | .... | .... | .... | .... | .... | 1976-77 | 1976-77 |
| Delvecchio, Alex | Det. | 24 | 1549 | 456 | 825 | 1281 | 383 | 121 | 35 | 69 | 104 | 29 | 3 | 1950-51 | 1973-74 |
| • DeMarco, Ab | Chi., Tor., Bos., NYR | 7 | 209 | 72 | 93 | 165 | 53 | 11 | 3 | 0 | 3 | 2 | .... | 1938-39 | 1946-47 |
| DeMarco, Ab | NYR, St.L., Pit., Van., L.A., Bos. | 9 | 344 | 44 | 80 | 124 | 75 | 25 | 1 | 2 | 3 | 17 | .... | 1969-70 | 1978-79 |
| • Demers, Tony | Mtl., NYR | 6 | 83 | 20 | 22 | 42 | 23 | 2 | 0 | 0 | 0 | 0 | .... | 1937-38 | 1943-44 |
| ‡ Dempsey, Nathan | Tor., Chi., L.A., Bos. | 8 | 260 | 21 | 67 | 88 | 120 | 6 | 0 | 2 | 2 | 0 | .... | 1996-97 | 2006-07 |
| Denis, Jean-Paul | NYR | 2 | 10 | 0 | 2 | 2 | 2 | .... | .... | .... | .... | .... | .... | 1946-47 | 1949-50 |
| Denis, Lulu | Mtl. | 2 | 3 | 0 | 1 | 1 | 0 | .... | .... | .... | .... | .... | .... | 1949-50 | 1950-51 |
| • Denneny, Corb | Tor., Ham., Chi. | 9 | 176 | 103 | 42 | 145 | 148 | 6 | 1 | 0 | 1 | 7 | 2 | 1917-18 | 1927-28 |
| • Denneny, Cy | Ott., Bos. | 12 | 328 | 248 | 85 | 333 | 301 | 25 | 16 | 2 | 18 | 23 | 5 | 1917-18 | 1928-29 |
| Dennis, Norm | St.L. | 4 | 12 | 3 | 0 | 3 | 11 | 5 | 0 | 0 | 0 | 2 | .... | 1968-69 | 1971-72 |
| • Denoird, Gerry | Tor. | 1 | 17 | 0 | 1 | 1 | 0 | .... | .... | .... | .... | .... | .... | 1922-23 | 1922-23 |
| DePalma, Larry | Min., S.J., Pit. | 7 | 148 | 21 | 20 | 41 | 408 | 3 | 0 | 0 | 0 | 6 | .... | 1985-86 | 1993-94 |
| Derlago, Bill | Van., Tor., Bos., Wpg., Que. | 9 | 555 | 189 | 227 | 416 | 247 | 13 | 5 | 0 | 5 | 8 | .... | 1978-79 | 1986-87 |
| • Desaulniers, Gerard | Mtl. | 3 | 8 | 0 | 2 | 2 | 4 | .... | .... | .... | .... | .... | .... | 1950-51 | 1953-54 |
| ‡ Descoteaux, Matthieu | Mtl. | 1 | 5 | 1 | 1 | 2 | 4 | .... | .... | .... | .... | .... | .... | 2000-01 | 2000-01 |
| • Desilets, Joffre | Mtl., Chi. | 5 | 192 | 37 | 45 | 82 | 57 | 7 | 1 | 0 | 1 | 7 | .... | 1935-36 | 1939-40 |
| Desjardins, Eric | Mtl., Phi. | 17 | 1143 | 136 | 439 | 575 | 757 | 168 | 23 | 57 | 80 | 93 | 1 | 1988-89 | 2005-06 |
| Desjardins, Martin | Mtl. | 1 | 8 | 0 | 2 | 2 | 2 | .... | .... | .... | .... | .... | .... | 1989-90 | 1989-90 |
| • Desjardins, Vic | Chi., NYR | 2 | 87 | 6 | 15 | 21 | 27 | 16 | 0 | 0 | 0 | 0 | .... | 1930-31 | 1931-32 |
| Deslauriers, Jacques | Mtl. | 1 | 2 | 0 | 0 | 0 | 0 | .... | .... | .... | .... | .... | .... | 1955-56 | 1955-56 |
| Deuling, Jarrett | NYI | 2 | 15 | 0 | 1 | 1 | 11 | .... | .... | .... | .... | .... | .... | 1995-96 | 1996-97 |
| Devine, Kevin | NYI | 1 | 2 | 0 | 1 | 1 | 8 | .... | .... | .... | .... | .... | .... | 1982-83 | 1982-83 |
| • Dewar, Tom | NYR | 1 | 9 | 0 | 2 | 2 | 4 | .... | .... | .... | .... | .... | .... | 1943-44 | 1943-44 |
| • Dewsbury, Al | Det., Chi. | 9 | 347 | 30 | 78 | 108 | 365 | 14 | 1 | 5 | 6 | 16 | 1 | 1946-47 | 1955-56 |
| Deziel, Michel | Buf. | 1 | .... | .... | .... | .... | .... | 1 | 0 | 0 | 0 | 0 | .... | 1974-75 | 1974-75 |
| • Dheere, Marcel | Mtl. | 1 | 11 | 1 | 2 | 3 | 2 | 5 | 0 | 0 | 0 | 6 | .... | 1942-43 | 1942-43 |
| Diachuk, Edward | Det. | 1 | 12 | 0 | 0 | 0 | 19 | .... | .... | .... | .... | .... | .... | 1960-61 | 1960-61 |
| • Dick, Harry | Chi. | 1 | 12 | 0 | 1 | 1 | 12 | .... | .... | .... | .... | .... | .... | 1946-47 | 1946-47 |
| • Dickens, Ernie | Tor., Chi. | 6 | 278 | 12 | 44 | 56 | 98 | 13 | 0 | 0 | 0 | 4 | 1 | 1941-42 | 1950-51 |
| Dickenson, Herb | NYR | 2 | 48 | 18 | 17 | 35 | 10 | .... | .... | .... | .... | .... | .... | 1951-52 | 1952-53 |
| Diduck, Gerald | NYI, Mtl., Van., Chi., Hfd., Phx., Tor., Dal. | 17 | 932 | 56 | 156 | 212 | 1612 | 114 | 8 | 16 | 24 | 212 | .... | 1984-85 | 2000-01 |
| Dietrich, Don | Chi., N.J. | 2 | 28 | 0 | 7 | 7 | 10 | .... | .... | .... | .... | .... | .... | 1983-84 | 1985-86 |
| • Dill, Bob | NYR | 2 | 76 | 15 | 15 | 30 | 135 | .... | .... | .... | .... | .... | .... | 1943-44 | 1944-45 |
| • Dillabough, Bob | Det., Bos., Pit., Oak. | 9 | 283 | 32 | 54 | 86 | 76 | 17 | 3 | 0 | 3 | 0 | .... | 1961-62 | 1969-70 |
| • Dillon, Cecil | NYR, Det. | 10 | 453 | 167 | 131 | 298 | 105 | 43 | 14 | 9 | 23 | 14 | 1 | 1930-31 | 1939-40 |
| Dillon, Gary | Col. | 1 | 13 | 1 | 1 | 2 | 29 | .... | .... | .... | .... | .... | .... | 1980-81 | 1980-81 |
| Dillon, Wayne | NYR, Wpg. | 4 | 229 | 43 | 66 | 109 | 60 | 3 | 0 | 1 | 1 | 0 | .... | 1975-76 | 1979-80 |
| DiMaio, Rob | NYI, T.B., Phi., Bos., NYR, Car., Dal. | 17 | 894 | 106 | 171 | 277 | 840 | 62 | 7 | 9 | 16 | 40 | .... | 1988-89 | 2005-06 |
| Dineen, Bill | Det., Chi. | 5 | 323 | 51 | 44 | 95 | 122 | 37 | 1 | 1 | 2 | 18 | 2 | 1953-54 | 1957-58 |
| • Dineen, Gary | Min. | 1 | 4 | 0 | 1 | 1 | 0 | .... | .... | .... | .... | .... | .... | 1968-69 | 1968-69 |
| Dineen, Gord | NYI, Min., Pit., Ott. | 13 | 528 | 16 | 90 | 106 | 695 | 40 | 1 | 7 | 8 | 68 | .... | 1982-83 | 1994-95 |
| Dineen, Kevin | Hfd., Phi., Car., Ott., CBJ | 19 | 1188 | 355 | 405 | 760 | 2229 | 59 | 23 | 18 | 41 | 127 | .... | 1984-85 | 2002-03 |
| Dineen, Peter | L.A., Det. | 2 | 13 | 0 | 2 | 2 | 13 | .... | .... | .... | .... | .... | .... | 1986-87 | 1989-90 |
| Dingman, Chris | Cgy., Col., Car., T.B. | 8 | 385 | 15 | 19 | 34 | 769 | 52 | 2 | 5 | 7 | 100 | 2 | 1997-98 | 2005-06 |
| • Dinsmore, Chuck | Mtl.M. | 4 | 100 | 6 | 2 | 8 | 50 | 8 | 1 | 0 | 1 | 2 | 1 | 1924-25 | 1929-30 |
| Dionne, Gilbert | Mtl., Phi., Fla. | 6 | 223 | 61 | 79 | 140 | 108 | 39 | 10 | 12 | 22 | 34 | 1 | 1990-91 | 1995-96 |
| Dionne, Marcel | Det., L.A., NYR | 18 | 1348 | 731 | 1040 | 1771 | 600 | 49 | 21 | 24 | 45 | 17 | .... | 1971-72 | 1988-89 |
| ‡ DiPietro, Paul | Mtl., Tor., L.A. | 6 | 192 | 31 | 49 | 80 | 96 | 31 | 11 | 10 | 21 | 10 | 1 | 1991-92 | 1996-97 |
| Dirk, Robert | St.L., Van., Chi., Ana., Mtl. | 9 | 402 | 13 | 29 | 42 | 786 | 39 | 0 | 1 | 1 | 56 | .... | 1987-88 | 1995-96 |
| ‡ Divisek, Tomas | Phi. | 2 | 5 | 1 | 0 | 1 | 0 | .... | .... | .... | .... | .... | .... | 2000-01 | 2001-02 |
| Djoos, Per | Det., NYR | 3 | 82 | 2 | 31 | 33 | 58 | .... | .... | .... | .... | .... | .... | 1990-91 | 1992-93 |
| Doak, Gary | Det., Bos., Van., NYR | 16 | 789 | 23 | 107 | 130 | 908 | 78 | 2 | 4 | 6 | 121 | 1 | 1965-66 | 1980-81 |
| Dobbin, Brian | Phi., Bos. | 5 | 63 | 7 | 8 | 15 | 61 | 2 | 0 | 0 | 0 | 17 | .... | 1986-87 | 1991-92 |
| Dobson, Jim | Min., Col., Que. | 4 | 12 | 0 | 0 | 0 | 6 | .... | .... | .... | .... | .... | .... | 1979-80 | 1983-84 |
| • Doherty, Fred | Mtl. | 1 | 1 | 0 | 0 | 0 | 0 | .... | .... | .... | .... | .... | .... | 1918-19 | 1918-19 |
| ‡ Doig, Jason | Wpg., Phx., NYR, Wsh. | 7 | 158 | 6 | 18 | 24 | 285 | 6 | 0 | 1 | 1 | 6 | .... | 1995-96 | 2003-04 |
| Dollas, Bobby | Wpg., Que., Det., Ana., Edm., Pit., Ott., Cgy., S.J. | 16 | 646 | 42 | 96 | 138 | 467 | 47 | 2 | 1 | 3 | 41 | .... | 1983-84 | 2000-01 |
| ‡ Dome, Robert | Pit., Cgy. | 3 | 53 | 7 | 7 | 14 | 12 | .... | .... | .... | .... | .... | .... | 1997-98 | 2002-03 |
| ‡ Domenichelli, Hnat | Hfd., Cgy., Atl., Min. | 7 | 267 | 52 | 61 | 113 | 104 | .... | .... | .... | .... | .... | .... | 1996-97 | 2002-03 |
| Domi, Tie | Tor., NYR, Wpg. | 16 | 1020 | 104 | 141 | 245 | 3515 | 98 | 7 | 12 | 19 | 238 | .... | 1989-90 | 2005-06 |
| Donaldson, Gary | Chi. | 1 | 1 | 0 | 0 | 0 | 0 | .... | .... | .... | .... | .... | .... | 1973-74 | 1973-74 |
| Donatelli, Clark | Min., Bos. | 2 | 35 | 3 | 4 | 7 | 39 | 2 | 0 | 0 | 0 | 0 | .... | 1989-90 | 1991-92 |
| Donato, Ted | Bos., NYI, Ott., Ana., Dal., St.L., L.A., NYR | 13 | 796 | 150 | 197 | 347 | 396 | 58 | 8 | 10 | 18 | 22 | .... | 1991-92 | 2003-04 |
| • Donnelly, Babe | Mtl.M. | 1 | 34 | 0 | 1 | 1 | 14 | 2 | 0 | 0 | 0 | 0 | .... | 1926-27 | 1926-27 |
| Donnelly, Dave | Bos., Chi., Edm. | 5 | 137 | 15 | 24 | 39 | 150 | 5 | 0 | 0 | 0 | 0 | .... | 1983-84 | 1987-88 |
| Donnelly, Gord | Que., Wpg., Buf., Dal. | 12 | 554 | 28 | 41 | 69 | 2069 | 26 | 0 | 2 | 2 | 61 | .... | 1983-84 | 1994-95 |
| Donnelly, Mike | NYR, Buf., L.A., Dal., NYI | 11 | 465 | 114 | 121 | 235 | 255 | 47 | 12 | 12 | 24 | 30 | .... | 1986-87 | 1996-97 |
| ‡ Dopita, Jiri | Phi., Edm. | 2 | 73 | 12 | 21 | 33 | 19 | .... | .... | .... | .... | .... | .... | 2001-02 | 2002-03 |
| • Doran, John | NYA, Det., Mtl. | 5 | 98 | 5 | 10 | 15 | 110 | 3 | 0 | 0 | 0 | 0 | .... | 1933-34 | 1939-40 |
| • Doran, Lloyd | Det. | 1 | 24 | 3 | 2 | 5 | 10 | .... | .... | .... | .... | .... | .... | 1946-47 | 1946-47 |
| • Doraty, Ken | Chi., Tor., Det. | 5 | 103 | 15 | 26 | 41 | 24 | 15 | 7 | 2 | 9 | 2 | .... | 1926-27 | 1937-38 |
| Dore, Andre | NYR, St.L., Que. | 7 | 257 | 14 | 81 | 95 | 261 | 23 | 1 | 2 | 3 | 32 | .... | 1978-79 | 1984-85 |
| Dore, Daniel | Que. | 2 | 17 | 2 | 3 | 5 | 59 | .... | .... | .... | .... | .... | .... | 1989-90 | 1990-91 |
| Dorey, Jim | Tor., NYR | 4 | 232 | 25 | 74 | 99 | 553 | 11 | 0 | 2 | 2 | 40 | .... | 1968-69 | 1971-72 |
| Dorion, Dan | N.J. | 2 | 4 | 1 | 1 | 2 | 2 | .... | .... | .... | .... | .... | .... | 1985-86 | 1987-88 |
| Dornhoefer, Gary | Bos., Phi. | 14 | 787 | 214 | 328 | 542 | 1291 | 80 | 17 | 19 | 36 | 203 | 2 | 1963-64 | 1977-78 |
| Dorohoy, Eddie | Mtl. | 1 | 16 | 0 | 0 | 0 | 6 | .... | .... | .... | .... | .... | .... | 1948-49 | 1948-49 |
| Douglas, Jordy | Hfd., Min., Wpg. | 6 | 268 | 76 | 62 | 138 | 160 | 6 | 0 | 0 | 0 | 4 | .... | 1979-80 | 1984-85 |
| • Douglas, Kent | Tor., Oak., Det. | 7 | 428 | 33 | 115 | 148 | 631 | 19 | 1 | 3 | 4 | 33 | 3 | 1962-63 | 1968-69 |
| • Douglas, Les | Det. | 4 | 52 | 6 | 12 | 18 | 8 | 10 | 3 | 2 | 5 | 2 | 1 | 1940-41 | 1946-47 |
| Doull, Doug | Bos., Wsh. | 2 | 37 | 0 | 1 | 1 | 151 | .... | .... | .... | .... | .... | .... | 2003-04 | 2005-06 |
| Douris, Peter | Wpg., Bos., Ana., Dal. | 11 | 321 | 54 | 67 | 121 | 80 | 27 | 3 | 5 | 8 | 14 | .... | 1985-86 | 1997-98 |
| Dowd, Jim | N.J., Van., NYI, Cgy., Edm., Min., Mtl., Chi., Col., Phi. | 16 | 728 | 71 | 168 | 239 | 390 | 99 | 9 | 17 | 26 | 50 | 1 | 1991-92 | 2007-08 |
| • Downie, Dave | Tor. | 1 | 11 | 0 | 1 | 1 | 2 | .... | .... | .... | .... | .... | .... | 1932-33 | 1932-33 |
| Doyon, Mario | Chi., Que. | 3 | 28 | 3 | 4 | 7 | 16 | .... | .... | .... | .... | .... | .... | 1988-89 | 1990-91 |
| ‡ Drake, Dallas | Det., Wpg., Phx., St.L. | 15 | 1009 | 177 | 300 | 477 | 885 | 90 | 14 | 19 | 33 | 79 | 1 | 1992-93 | 2007-08 |
| • Draper, Bruce | Tor. | 1 | 1 | 0 | 0 | 0 | 0 | .... | .... | .... | .... | .... | .... | 1962-63 | 1962-63 |
| • Drillon, Gordie | Tor., Mtl. | 7 | 311 | 155 | 139 | 294 | 56 | 50 | 26 | 15 | 41 | 10 | 1 | 1936-37 | 1942-43 |

| Name | NHL Teams | NHL Seasons | Regular Schedule | | | | | Playoffs | | | | | NHL Cup Wins | First NHL Season | Last NHL Season |
|---|---|---|---|---|---|---|---|---|---|---|---|---|---|---|---|
| | | | GP | G | A | TP | PIM | GP | G | A | TP | PIM | | | |
| Driscoll, Peter | Edm. | 2 | 60 | 3 | 8 | 11 | 97 | 3 | 0 | 0 | 0 | 0 | .... | 1979-80 | 1980-81 |
| Driver, Bruce | N.J., NYR | 15 | 922 | 96 | 390 | 486 | 670 | 108 | 10 | 40 | 50 | 64 | 1 | 1983-84 | 1997-98 |
| Drolet, Rene | Phi., Det. | 2 | 2 | 0 | 0 | 0 | 0 | .... | .... | .... | .... | .... | .... | 1971-72 | 1974-75 |
| ‡ Droppa, Ivan | Chi. | 2 | 19 | 0 | 1 | 1 | 14 | .... | .... | .... | .... | .... | .... | 1993-94 | 1995-96 |
| • Drouillard, Clarence | Det. | 1 | 10 | 0 | 1 | 1 | 0 | .... | .... | .... | .... | .... | .... | 1937-38 | 1937-38 |
| Drouin, Jude | Mtl., Min., NYI, Wpg. | 12 | 666 | 151 | 305 | 456 | 346 | 72 | 27 | 41 | 68 | 33 | .... | 1968-69 | 1980-81 |
| Drouin, P.C. | Bos. | 1 | 3 | 0 | 0 | 0 | 0 | .... | .... | .... | .... | .... | .... | 1996-97 | 1996-97 |
| • Drouin, Polly | Mtl. | 7 | 160 | 23 | 50 | 73 | 80 | 5 | 0 | 1 | 1 | 5 | .... | 1934-35 | 1940-41 |
| Druce, John | Wsh., Wpg., L.A., Phi. | 10 | 531 | 113 | 126 | 239 | 347 | 53 | 17 | 6 | 23 | 38 | .... | 1988-89 | 1997-98 |
| Druken, Harold | Van., Car., Tor. | 5 | 146 | 27 | 36 | 63 | 36 | 4 | 0 | 1 | 1 | 0 | .... | 1999-00 | 2003-04 |
| Drulia, Stan | T.B. | 3 | 126 | 15 | 27 | 42 | 52 | .... | .... | .... | .... | .... | .... | 1992-93 | 2000-01 |
| • Drummond, Jim | NYR | 1 | 2 | 0 | 0 | 0 | 0 | .... | .... | .... | .... | .... | .... | 1944-45 | 1944-45 |
| • Drury, Herb | Pit., Phi. | 6 | 213 | 24 | 13 | 37 | 203 | 4 | 1 | 1 | 2 | 0 | .... | 1925-26 | 1930-31 |
| Drury, Ted | Cgy., Hfd., Ott., Ana., NYI, CBJ | 8 | 414 | 41 | 52 | 93 | 367 | 14 | 1 | 0 | 1 | 4 | .... | 1993-94 | 2000-01 |
| ‡ Dube, Christian | NYR | 2 | 33 | 1 | 1 | 2 | 4 | 3 | 0 | 0 | 0 | 0 | .... | 1996-97 | 1998-99 |
| Dube, Gilles | Mtl., Det. | 2 | 12 | 1 | 2 | 3 | 2 | 2 | 0 | 0 | 0 | 0 | 1 | 1949-50 | 1953-54 |
| Dube, Norm | K.C. | 2 | 57 | 8 | 10 | 18 | 54 | .... | .... | .... | .... | .... | .... | 1974-75 | 1975-76 |
| Duberman, Justin | Pit. | 1 | 4 | 0 | 0 | 0 | 0 | .... | .... | .... | .... | .... | .... | 1993-94 | 1993-94 |
| Dubinsky, Steve | Chi., Cgy., Nsh., St.L. | 10 | 375 | 25 | 45 | 70 | 164 | 10 | 1 | 0 | 1 | 14 | .... | 1993-94 | 2002-03 |
| • Duchesne, Gaetan | Wsh., Que., Min., S.J., Fla. | 14 | 1028 | 179 | 254 | 433 | 617 | 84 | 14 | 13 | 27 | 97 | .... | 1981-82 | 1994-95 |
| Duchesne, Steve | L.A., Phi., Que., St.L., Ott., Det. | 16 | 1113 | 227 | 525 | 752 | 824 | 121 | 16 | 61 | 77 | 96 | 1 | 1986-87 | 2001-02 |
| Dudley, Rick | Buf., Wpg. | 6 | 309 | 75 | 99 | 174 | 292 | 25 | 7 | 2 | 9 | 69 | .... | 1972-73 | 1980-81 |
| Duerden, Dave | Fla. | 1 | 2 | 0 | 0 | 0 | 0 | .... | .... | .... | .... | .... | .... | 1999-00 | 1999-00 |
| Duff, Dick | Tor., NYR, Mtl., L.A., Buf. | 18 | 1030 | 283 | 289 | 572 | 743 | 114 | 30 | 49 | 79 | 78 | 6 | 1954-55 | 1971-72 |
| Dufour, Luc | Bos., Que., St.L. | 3 | 167 | 23 | 21 | 44 | 199 | 18 | 1 | 0 | 1 | 32 | .... | 1982-83 | 1984-85 |
| Dufour, Marc | NYR, L.A. | 3 | 14 | 1 | 0 | 1 | 2 | .... | .... | .... | .... | .... | .... | 1963-64 | 1968-69 |
| Dufresne, Donald | Mtl., T.B., L.A., St.L., Edm. | 9 | 268 | 6 | 36 | 42 | 258 | 34 | 1 | 3 | 4 | 47 | 1 | 1988-89 | 1996-97 |
| • Duggan, John | Ott. | 1 | 27 | 0 | 0 | 0 | 0 | 2 | 0 | 0 | 0 | 0 | .... | 1925-26 | 1925-26 |
| Duggan, Ken | Min. | 1 | 1 | 0 | 0 | 0 | 0 | .... | .... | .... | .... | .... | .... | 1987-88 | 1987-88 |
| Duguay, Ron | NYR, Det., Pit., L.A. | 12 | 864 | 274 | 346 | 620 | 582 | 89 | 31 | 22 | 53 | 118 | .... | 1977-78 | 1988-89 |
| • Duguid, Lorne | Mtl.M., Det., Bos. | 6 | 135 | 9 | 15 | 24 | 57 | 4 | 1 | 0 | 1 | 6 | .... | 1931-32 | 1936-37 |
| • Dukowski, Duke | Chi., NYA, NYR | 5 | 200 | 16 | 30 | 46 | 172 | 6 | 0 | 0 | 0 | 6 | .... | 1926-27 | 1933-34 |
| • Dumart, Woody | Bos. | 16 | 772 | 211 | 218 | 429 | 99 | 88 | 12 | 15 | 27 | 23 | 2 | 1935-36 | 1953-54 |
| Dunbar, Dale | Van., Bos. | 2 | 2 | 0 | 0 | 0 | 2 | .... | .... | .... | .... | .... | .... | 1985-86 | 1988-89 |
| • Duncan, Art | Det., Tor. | 5 | 156 | 18 | 16 | 34 | 225 | 5 | 0 | 0 | 0 | 4 | .... | 1926-27 | 1930-31 |
| Duncan, Iain | Wpg. | 4 | 127 | 34 | 55 | 89 | 149 | 11 | 0 | 3 | 3 | 6 | .... | 1986-87 | 1990-91 |
| Duncanson, Craig | L.A., Wpg., NYR | 7 | 38 | 5 | 4 | 9 | 61 | .... | .... | .... | .... | .... | .... | 1985-86 | 1992-93 |
| Dundas, Rocky | Tor. | 1 | 5 | 0 | 0 | 0 | 14 | .... | .... | .... | .... | .... | .... | 1989-90 | 1989-90 |
| • Dunlap, Frank | Tor. | 1 | 15 | 0 | 1 | 1 | 2 | .... | .... | .... | .... | .... | .... | 1943-44 | 1943-44 |
| Dunlop, Blake | Min., Phi., St.L., Det. | 11 | 550 | 130 | 274 | 404 | 172 | 40 | 4 | 10 | 14 | 18 | .... | 1973-74 | 1983-84 |
| Dunn, Dave | Van., Tor. | 3 | 184 | 14 | 41 | 55 | 313 | 10 | 1 | 1 | 2 | 41 | .... | 1973-74 | 1975-76 |
| Dunn, Richie | Buf., Cgy., Hfd. | 12 | 483 | 36 | 140 | 176 | 314 | 36 | 3 | 15 | 18 | 24 | .... | 1977-78 | 1988-89 |
| Dupere, Denis | Tor., Wsh., St.L., K.C., Col. | 8 | 421 | 80 | 99 | 179 | 66 | 16 | 1 | 0 | 1 | 0 | .... | 1970-71 | 1977-78 |
| Dupont, Andre | NYR, St.L., Phi., Que. | 13 | 800 | 59 | 185 | 244 | 1986 | 140 | 14 | 18 | 32 | 352 | 2 | 1970-71 | 1982-83 |
| Dupont, Jerome | Chi., Tor. | 6 | 214 | 7 | 29 | 36 | 468 | 20 | 0 | 2 | 2 | 56 | .... | 1981-82 | 1986-87 |
| Dupont, Norm | Mtl., Wpg., Hfd. | 5 | 256 | 55 | 85 | 140 | 52 | 13 | 4 | 2 | 6 | 0 | .... | 1979-80 | 1983-84 |
| • Dupre, Yanick | Phi. | 3 | 35 | 2 | 0 | 2 | 16 | .... | .... | .... | .... | .... | .... | 1991-92 | 1995-96 |
| • Durbano, Steve | St.L., Pit., K.C., Col. | 6 | 220 | 13 | 60 | 73 | 1127 | 5 | 0 | 2 | 2 | 8 | .... | 1972-73 | 1978-79 |
| Duris, Vitezslav | Tor. | 2 | 89 | 3 | 20 | 23 | 62 | 3 | 0 | 1 | 1 | 2 | .... | 1980-81 | 1982-83 |
| Dusablon, Benoit | NYR | 1 | 3 | 0 | 0 | 0 | 2 | .... | .... | .... | .... | .... | .... | 2003-04 | 2003-04 |
| Dussault, Norm | Mtl. | 4 | 206 | 31 | 62 | 93 | 47 | 7 | 3 | 1 | 4 | 0 | .... | 1947-48 | 1950-51 |
| • Dutton, Red | Mtl.M., NYA | 10 | 449 | 29 | 67 | 96 | 871 | 18 | 1 | 0 | 1 | 33 | .... | 1926-27 | 1935-36 |
| • Dvorak, Miroslav | Phi. | 3 | 193 | 11 | 74 | 85 | 51 | 18 | 0 | 2 | 2 | 6 | .... | 1982-83 | 1984-85 |
| ‡ Dwyer, Gordie | T.B., NYR, Mtl. | 5 | 108 | 0 | 5 | 5 | 394 | .... | .... | .... | .... | .... | .... | 1999-00 | 2003-04 |
| Dwyer, Mike | Col., Cgy. | 4 | 31 | 2 | 6 | 8 | 25 | 1 | 1 | 0 | 1 | 0 | .... | 1978-79 | 1981-82 |
| • Dyck, Henry | NYR | 1 | 1 | 0 | 0 | 0 | 0 | .... | .... | .... | .... | .... | .... | 1943-44 | 1943-44 |
| • Dye, Babe | Tor., Ham., Chi., NYA | 11 | 271 | 201 | 47 | 248 | 221 | 10 | 2 | 0 | 2 | 11 | 1 | 1919-20 | 1930-31 |
| Dykhuis, Karl | Chi., Phi., T.B., Mtl. | 12 | 644 | 42 | 91 | 133 | 495 | 62 | 8 | 10 | 18 | 50 | .... | 1991-92 | 2003-04 |
| Dykstra, Steve | Buf., Edm., Pit., Hfd. | 5 | 217 | 8 | 32 | 40 | 545 | 1 | 0 | 0 | 0 | 2 | .... | 1985-86 | 1989-90 |
| • Dyte, Jack | Chi. | 1 | 27 | 1 | 0 | 1 | 31 | .... | .... | .... | .... | .... | .... | 1943-44 | 1943-44 |
| Dziedzic, Joe | Pit., Phx. | 3 | 130 | 14 | 14 | 28 | 131 | 21 | 1 | 3 | 4 | 23 | .... | 1995-96 | 1998-99 |

## E

| Name | NHL Teams | NHL Seasons | GP | G | A | TP | PIM | GP | G | A | TP | PIM | NHL Cup Wins | First NHL Season | Last NHL Season |
|---|---|---|---|---|---|---|---|---|---|---|---|---|---|---|---|
| Eagles, Mike | Que., Chi., Wpg., Wsh. | 16 | 853 | 74 | 122 | 196 | 928 | 44 | 2 | 6 | 8 | 34 | .... | 1982-83 | 1999-00 |
| Eakin, Bruce | Cgy., Det. | 4 | 13 | 2 | 2 | 4 | 4 | .... | .... | .... | .... | .... | .... | 1981-82 | 1985-86 |
| Eakins, Dallas | Wpg., Fla., St.L., Phx., NYR, Tor., NYI, Cgy. | 10 | 120 | 0 | 9 | 9 | 208 | 5 | 0 | 0 | 0 | 4 | .... | 1992-93 | 2001-02 |
| Eastwood, Mike | Tor., Wpg., Phx., NYR, St.L., Chi., Pit. | 13 | 783 | 87 | 149 | 236 | 354 | 97 | 8 | 11 | 19 | 64 | .... | 1991-92 | 2003-04 |
| Eatough, Jeff | Buf. | 1 | 1 | 0 | 0 | 0 | 0 | .... | .... | .... | .... | .... | .... | 1981-82 | 1981-82 |
| Eaves, Mike | Min., Cgy. | 8 | 324 | 83 | 143 | 226 | 80 | 43 | 7 | 10 | 17 | 14 | .... | 1978-79 | 1985-86 |
| Eaves, Murray | Wpg., Det. | 8 | 57 | 4 | 13 | 17 | 9 | 4 | 0 | 1 | 1 | 2 | .... | 1980-81 | 1989-90 |
| Ecclestone, Tim | St.L., Det., Tor., Atl. | 11 | 692 | 126 | 233 | 359 | 344 | 48 | 6 | 11 | 17 | 76 | .... | 1967-68 | 1977-78 |
| Edberg, Rolf | Wsh. | 3 | 184 | 45 | 58 | 103 | 24 | .... | .... | .... | .... | .... | .... | 1978-79 | 1980-81 |
| • Eddolls, Frank | Mtl., NYR | 8 | 317 | 23 | 43 | 66 | 114 | 31 | 0 | 2 | 2 | 10 | 1 | 1944-45 | 1951-52 |
| Edestrand, Darryl | St.L., Phi., Pit., Bos., L.A. | 10 | 455 | 34 | 90 | 124 | 404 | 42 | 3 | 9 | 12 | 57 | .... | 1967-68 | 1978-79 |
| Edmundson, Garry | Mtl., Tor. | 3 | 43 | 4 | 6 | 10 | 49 | 11 | 0 | 1 | 1 | 8 | .... | 1951-52 | 1960-61 |
| Edur, Tom | Col., Pit. | 2 | 158 | 17 | 70 | 87 | 67 | .... | .... | .... | .... | .... | .... | 1976-77 | 1977-78 |
| • Egan, Pat | NYA, Bro., Det., Bos., NYR | 11 | 554 | 77 | 153 | 230 | 776 | 46 | 9 | 4 | 13 | 48 | .... | 1939-40 | 1950-51 |
| Egeland, Allan | T.B. | 3 | 17 | 0 | 0 | 0 | 16 | .... | .... | .... | .... | .... | .... | 1995-96 | 1997-98 |
| Egers, Jack | NYR, St.L., Wsh. | 7 | 284 | 64 | 69 | 133 | 154 | 32 | 5 | 6 | 11 | 32 | .... | 1969-70 | 1975-76 |
| • Ehman, Gerry | Bos., Det., Tor., Oak., Cal. | 9 | 429 | 96 | 118 | 214 | 100 | 41 | 10 | 10 | 20 | 12 | 1 | 1957-58 | 1970-71 |
| Eisenhut, Neil | Van., Cgy. | 2 | 16 | 1 | 3 | 4 | 21 | .... | .... | .... | .... | .... | .... | 1993-94 | 1994-95 |
| Eklund, Pelle | Phi., Dal. | 9 | 594 | 120 | 335 | 455 | 109 | 66 | 10 | 36 | 46 | 8 | .... | 1985-86 | 1993-94 |
| ‡ Ekman, Nils | T.B., S.J., Pit. | 5 | 264 | 60 | 91 | 151 | 188 | 28 | 2 | 5 | 7 | 16 | .... | 1999-00 | 2006-07 |
| Eldebrink, Anders | Van., Que. | 2 | 55 | 3 | 11 | 14 | 29 | 14 | 0 | 0 | 0 | 10 | .... | 1981-82 | 1982-83 |
| Elich, Matt | T.B. | 2 | 16 | 1 | 1 | 2 | 0 | .... | .... | .... | .... | .... | .... | 1999-00 | 2000-01 |
| Elik, Bo | Det. | 1 | 3 | 0 | 0 | 0 | 0 | .... | .... | .... | .... | .... | .... | 1962-63 | 1962-63 |
| Elik, Todd | L.A., Min., Edm., S.J., St.L., Bos. | 8 | 448 | 110 | 219 | 329 | 453 | 52 | 15 | 27 | 42 | 48 | .... | 1989-90 | 1996-97 |
| Ellett, Dave | Wpg., Tor., N.J., Bos., St.L. | 16 | 1129 | 153 | 415 | 568 | 985 | 116 | 11 | 46 | 57 | 87 | .... | 1984-85 | 1999-00 |
| • Elliott, Fred | Ott. | 1 | 43 | 2 | 0 | 2 | 6 | .... | .... | .... | .... | .... | .... | 1928-29 | 1928-29 |
| Ellis, Ron | Tor. | 16 | 1034 | 332 | 308 | 640 | 207 | 70 | 18 | 8 | 26 | 20 | 1 | 1963-64 | 1980-81 |
| Elomo, Miika | Wsh. | 1 | 2 | 0 | 1 | 1 | 2 | .... | .... | .... | .... | .... | .... | 1999-00 | 1999-00 |
| Eloranta, Kari | Cgy., St.L. | 5 | 267 | 13 | 103 | 116 | 155 | 26 | 1 | 7 | 8 | 19 | .... | 1981-82 | 1986-87 |
| Eloranta, Mikko | Bos., L.A. | 4 | 264 | 32 | 44 | 76 | 186 | 7 | 1 | 1 | 2 | 2 | .... | 1999-00 | 2002-03 |
| Elynuik, Pat | Wpg., Wsh., T.B., Ott. | 9 | 506 | 154 | 188 | 342 | 459 | 20 | 6 | 9 | 15 | 25 | .... | 1987-88 | 1995-96 |
| • Emberg, Eddie | Mtl. | 1 | .... | .... | .... | .... | .... | 2 | 1 | 0 | 1 | 0 | .... | 1944-45 | 1944-45 |
| Emerson, Nelson | St.L., Wpg., Hfd., Car., Chi., Ott., Atl., L.A. | 12 | 771 | 195 | 293 | 488 | 575 | 40 | 7 | 15 | 22 | 33 | .... | 1990-91 | 2001-02 |
| Emma, David | N.J., Bos., Fla. | 5 | 34 | 5 | 6 | 11 | 2 | .... | .... | .... | .... | .... | .... | 1992-93 | 2000-01 |
| Emmons, Gary | S.J. | 1 | 3 | 1 | 0 | 1 | 0 | .... | .... | .... | .... | .... | .... | 1993-94 | 1993-94 |
| Emmons, John | Ott., T.B., Bos. | 3 | 85 | 2 | 4 | 6 | 64 | .... | .... | .... | .... | .... | .... | 1999-00 | 2001-02 |
| • Emms, Hap | Mtl.M., NYA, Det., Bos. | 10 | 320 | 36 | 53 | 89 | 311 | 14 | 0 | 0 | 0 | 12 | .... | 1926-27 | 1937-38 |
| Endean, Craig | Wpg. | 1 | 2 | 0 | 1 | 1 | 0 | .... | .... | .... | .... | .... | .... | 1986-87 | 1986-87 |
| ‡ Endicott, Shane | Pit. | 2 | 45 | 1 | 2 | 3 | 47 | .... | .... | .... | .... | .... | .... | 2001-02 | 2005-06 |
| Engblom, Brian | Mtl., Wsh., L.A., Buf., Cgy. | 11 | 659 | 29 | 177 | 206 | 599 | 48 | 3 | 9 | 12 | 43 | 2 | 1976-77 | 1986-87 |
| Engele, Jerry | Min. | 3 | 100 | 2 | 13 | 15 | 162 | 2 | 0 | 1 | 1 | 0 | .... | 1975-76 | 1977-78 |
| English, John | L.A. | 1 | 3 | 1 | 3 | 4 | 4 | 1 | 0 | 0 | 0 | 0 | .... | 1987-88 | 1987-88 |
| Ennis, Jim | Edm. | 1 | 5 | 1 | 0 | 1 | 10 | .... | .... | .... | .... | .... | .... | 1987-88 | 1987-88 |
| Erickson, Aut | Bos., Chi., Tor., Oak. | 7 | 226 | 7 | 24 | 31 | 182 | 7 | 0 | 0 | 0 | 2 | 1 | 1959-60 | 1969-70 |
| Erickson, Bryan | Wsh., L.A., Pit., Wpg. | 9 | 351 | 80 | 125 | 205 | 141 | 14 | 3 | 4 | 7 | 7 | .... | 1983-84 | 1993-94 |
| Erickson, Grant | Bos., Min. | 2 | 6 | 1 | 0 | 1 | 0 | .... | .... | .... | .... | .... | .... | 1968-69 | 1969-70 |
| Eriksson, Peter | Edm. | 1 | 20 | 3 | 3 | 6 | 24 | .... | .... | .... | .... | .... | .... | 1989-90 | 1989-90 |
| Eriksson, Roland | Min., Van. | 3 | 193 | 48 | 95 | 143 | 26 | 2 | 1 | 0 | 1 | 0 | .... | 1976-77 | 1978-79 |
| Eriksson, Thomas | Phi. | 5 | 208 | 22 | 76 | 98 | 107 | 19 | 0 | 3 | 3 | 12 | .... | 1980-81 | 1985-86 |
| Erixon, Jan | NYR | 10 | 556 | 57 | 159 | 216 | 167 | 58 | 7 | 7 | 14 | 16 | .... | 1983-84 | 1992-93 |
| Errey, Bob | Pit., Buf., S.J., Det., Dal., NYR | 15 | 895 | 170 | 212 | 382 | 1005 | 99 | 13 | 16 | 29 | 109 | 2 | 1983-84 | 1997-98 |
| Esau, Len | Tor., Que., Cgy., Edm. | 4 | 27 | 0 | 10 | 10 | 24 | .... | .... | .... | .... | .... | .... | 1991-92 | 1994-95 |
| Esposito, Phil | Chi., Bos., NYR | 18 | 1282 | 717 | 873 | 1590 | 910 | 130 | 61 | 76 | 137 | 138 | 2 | 1963-64 | 1980-81 |
| • Evans, Chris | Tor., Buf., St.L., Det., K.C. | 5 | 241 | 19 | 42 | 61 | 143 | 12 | 1 | 1 | 2 | 8 | .... | 1969-70 | 1974-75 |
| Evans, Daryl | L.A., Wsh., Tor. | 6 | 113 | 22 | 30 | 52 | 25 | 11 | 5 | 8 | 13 | 12 | .... | 1981-82 | 1986-87 |
| Evans, Doug | St.L., Wpg., Phi. | 8 | 355 | 48 | 87 | 135 | 502 | 22 | 3 | 4 | 7 | 38 | .... | 1985-86 | 1992-93 |
| • Evans, Jack | NYR, Chi. | 14 | 752 | 19 | 80 | 99 | 989 | 56 | 2 | 2 | 4 | 97 | 1 | 1948-49 | 1962-63 |
| Evans, John Paul | Phi. | 3 | 103 | 14 | 25 | 39 | 34 | 1 | 0 | 0 | 0 | 0 | .... | 1978-79 | 1982-83 |
| Evans, Kevin | Min., S.J. | 2 | 9 | 0 | 1 | 1 | 44 | .... | .... | .... | .... | .... | .... | 1990-91 | 1991-92 |
| Evans, Paul | Tor. | 2 | 11 | 1 | 1 | 2 | 21 | 2 | 0 | 0 | 0 | 0 | .... | 1976-77 | 1977-78 |

Dallas Drake

Steve Durbano

John Paul Evans

Paul Evans

Dave Farrish

Ray Ferraro

Reggie Fleming

Jeff Friesen

| Name | NHL Teams | NHL Seasons | Regular Schedule GP | G | A | TP | PIM | Playoffs GP | G | A | TP | PIM | NHL Cup Wins | First NHL Season | Last NHL Season |
|---|---|---|---|---|---|---|---|---|---|---|---|---|---|---|---|
| Evans, Shawn | St.L., NYI | 2 | 9 | 1 | 0 | 1 | 2 | .... | .... | .... | .... | .... | .... | 1985-86 | 1989-90 |
| • Evans, Stewart | Det., Mtl.M., Mtl. | 8 | 367 | 28 | 49 | 77 | 425 | 26 | 0 | 0 | 0 | 20 | 1 | 1930-31 | 1938-39 |
| Evason, Dean | Wsh., Hfd., S.J., Dal., Cgy. | 13 | 803 | 139 | 233 | 372 | 1002 | 55 | 9 | 20 | 29 | 132 | .... | 1983-84 | 1995-96 |
| Ewen, Todd | St.L., Mtl., Ana., S.J. | 11 | 518 | 36 | 40 | 76 | 1911 | 26 | 0 | 0 | 0 | 87 | 1 | 1986-87 | 1996-97 |
| Ezinicki, Bill | Tor., Bos., NYR | 9 | 368 | 79 | 105 | 184 | 713 | 40 | 5 | 8 | 13 | 87 | 3 | 1944-45 | 1954-55 |

## F

| Name | NHL Teams | NHL Seasons | Regular Schedule GP | G | A | TP | PIM | Playoffs GP | G | A | TP | PIM | NHL Cup Wins | First NHL Season | Last NHL Season |
|---|---|---|---|---|---|---|---|---|---|---|---|---|---|---|---|
| Fahey, Trevor | NYR | 1 | 1 | 0 | 0 | 0 | 0 | .... | .... | .... | .... | .... | .... | 1964-65 | 1964-65 |
| Fairbairn, Bill | NYR, Min., St.L. | 11 | 658 | 162 | 261 | 423 | 173 | 54 | 13 | 22 | 35 | 42 | .... | 1968-69 | 1978-79 |
| Fairchild, Kelly | Tor., Dal., Col. | 4 | 34 | 2 | 3 | 5 | 6 | .... | .... | .... | .... | .... | .... | 1995-96 | 2001-02 |
| Falkenberg, Bob | Det. | 5 | 54 | 1 | 5 | 6 | 26 | .... | .... | .... | .... | .... | .... | 1966-67 | 1971-72 |
| Falloon, Pat | S.J., Phi., Ott., Edm., Pit. | 9 | 575 | 143 | 179 | 322 | 141 | 66 | 11 | 7 | 18 | 16 | .... | 1991-92 | 1999-00 |
| Farkas, Jeff | Tor., Atl. | 4 | 11 | 0 | 2 | 2 | 6 | 5 | 1 | 0 | 1 | 0 | .... | 1999-00 | 2002-03 |
| • Farrant, Walt | Chi. | 1 | 1 | 0 | 0 | 0 | 0 | .... | .... | .... | .... | .... | .... | 1943-44 | 1943-44 |
| Farrell, Mike | Wsh., Nsh. | 3 | 13 | 0 | 0 | 0 | 2 | .... | .... | .... | .... | .... | .... | 2001-02 | 2003-04 |
| Farrish, Dave | NYR, Que., Tor. | 7 | 430 | 17 | 110 | 127 | 440 | 14 | 0 | 2 | 2 | 24 | .... | 1976-77 | 1983-84 |
| Fashoway, Gordie | Chi. | 1 | 13 | 3 | 2 | 5 | 14 | .... | .... | .... | .... | .... | .... | 1950-51 | 1950-51 |
| ‡ Fast, Brad | Car. | 1 | 1 | 1 | 0 | 1 | 0 | .... | .... | .... | .... | .... | .... | 2003-04 | 2003-04 |
| ‡ Fata, Rico | Cgy., NYR, Pit., Atl., Wsh. | 8 | 230 | 27 | 36 | 63 | 104 | .... | .... | .... | .... | .... | .... | 1998-99 | 2006-07 |
| Faubert, Mario | Pit. | 7 | 231 | 21 | 90 | 111 | 292 | 10 | 2 | 2 | 4 | 6 | .... | 1974-75 | 1981-82 |
| Faulkner, Alex | Tor., Det. | 3 | 101 | 15 | 17 | 32 | 15 | 12 | 5 | 0 | 5 | 2 | .... | 1961-62 | 1963-64 |
| Fauss, Ted | Tor. | 2 | 28 | 0 | 2 | 2 | 15 | .... | .... | .... | .... | .... | .... | 1986-87 | 1987-88 |
| Faust, Andre | Phi. | 2 | 47 | 10 | 7 | 17 | 14 | .... | .... | .... | .... | .... | .... | 1992-93 | 1993-94 |
| Feamster, Dave | Chi. | 4 | 169 | 13 | 24 | 37 | 154 | 33 | 3 | 5 | 8 | 61 | .... | 1981-82 | 1984-85 |
| Featherstone, Glen | St.L., Bos., NYR, Hfd., Cgy. | 9 | 384 | 19 | 61 | 80 | 939 | 28 | 0 | 2 | 2 | 103 | .... | 1988-89 | 1996-97 |
| Featherstone, Tony | Oak., Cal., Min. | 3 | 130 | 17 | 21 | 38 | 65 | 2 | 0 | 0 | 0 | 0 | .... | 1969-70 | 1973-74 |
| Federko, Bernie | St.L., Det. | 14 | 1000 | 369 | 761 | 1130 | 487 | 91 | 35 | 66 | 101 | 83 | .... | 1976-77 | 1989-90 |
| ‡ Fedorov, Fedor | Van., NYR | 3 | 18 | 0 | 2 | 2 | 14 | .... | .... | .... | .... | .... | .... | 2002-03 | 2005-06 |
| Fedotov, Anatoli | Wpg., Ana. | 2 | 4 | 0 | 2 | 2 | 0 | .... | .... | .... | .... | .... | .... | 1992-93 | 1993-94 |
| Fedyk, Brent | Det., Phi., Dal., NYR | 10 | 470 | 97 | 112 | 209 | 308 | 16 | 3 | 2 | 5 | 12 | .... | 1987-88 | 1998-99 |
| Felix, Chris | Wsh. | 4 | 35 | 1 | 12 | 13 | 10 | 2 | 0 | 1 | 1 | 0 | .... | 1987-88 | 1990-91 |
| Felsner, Brian | Chi. | 1 | 12 | 1 | 3 | 4 | 12 | .... | .... | .... | .... | .... | .... | 1997-98 | 1997-98 |
| Felsner, Denny | St.L. | 4 | 18 | 1 | 4 | 5 | 6 | 10 | 2 | 3 | 5 | 2 | .... | 1991-92 | 1994-95 |
| Feltrin, Tony | Pit., NYR | 4 | 48 | 3 | 3 | 6 | 65 | .... | .... | .... | .... | .... | .... | 1980-81 | 1985-86 |
| Fenton, Paul | Hfd., NYR, L.A., Wpg., Tor., Cgy., S.J. | 8 | 411 | 100 | 83 | 183 | 198 | 17 | 4 | 1 | 5 | 27 | .... | 1984-85 | 1991-92 |
| Fenyves, David | Buf., Phi. | 9 | 206 | 3 | 32 | 35 | 119 | 11 | 0 | 0 | 0 | 9 | .... | 1982-83 | 1990-91 |
| Ference, Brad | Fla., Phx., Cgy. | 6 | 250 | 4 | 30 | 34 | 565 | .... | .... | .... | .... | .... | .... | 1999-00 | 2006-07 |
| Fergus, Tom | Bos., Tor., Van. | 12 | 726 | 235 | 346 | 581 | 499 | 65 | 21 | 17 | 38 | 48 | .... | 1981-82 | 1992-93 |
| Ferguson, Craig | Mtl., Cgy., Fla. | 5 | 27 | 1 | 1 | 2 | 6 | .... | .... | .... | .... | .... | .... | 1993-94 | 1999-00 |
| Ferguson, George | Tor., Pit., Min. | 12 | 797 | 160 | 238 | 398 | 431 | 86 | 14 | 23 | 37 | 44 | .... | 1972-73 | 1983-84 |
| • Ferguson, John | Mtl. | 8 | 500 | 145 | 158 | 303 | 1214 | 85 | 20 | 18 | 38 | 260 | 5 | 1963-64 | 1970-71 |
| • Ferguson, Lorne | Bos., Det., Chi. | 8 | 422 | 82 | 80 | 162 | 193 | 31 | 6 | 3 | 9 | 24 | .... | 1949-50 | 1958-59 |
| Ferguson, Norm | Oak., Cal. | 4 | 279 | 73 | 66 | 139 | 72 | 10 | 1 | 4 | 5 | 7 | .... | 1968-69 | 1971-72 |
| ‡ Ferguson, Scott | Edm., Ana., Min. | 5 | 218 | 7 | 14 | 21 | 310 | 11 | 0 | 0 | 0 | 8 | .... | 1997-98 | 2005-06 |
| Ferner, Mark | Buf., Wsh., Ana., Det. | 6 | 91 | 3 | 10 | 13 | 51 | .... | .... | .... | .... | .... | .... | 1986-87 | 1994-95 |
| ‡ Ferraro, Chris | NYR, Pit., Edm., NYI, Wsh. | 6 | 74 | 7 | 9 | 16 | 57 | .... | .... | .... | .... | .... | .... | 1995-96 | 2001-02 |
| ‡ Ferraro, Peter | NYR, Pit., Bos., Wsh. | 6 | 92 | 9 | 15 | 24 | 58 | 2 | 0 | 0 | 0 | 0 | .... | 1995-96 | 2001-02 |
| Ferraro, Ray | Hfd., NYI, NYR, L.A., Atl., St.L. | 18 | 1258 | 408 | 490 | 898 | 1288 | 68 | 21 | 22 | 43 | 54 | .... | 1984-85 | 2001-02 |
| Fetisov, Viacheslav | N.J., Det. | 9 | 546 | 36 | 192 | 228 | 656 | 116 | 2 | 26 | 28 | 147 | 2 | 1989-90 | 1997-98 |
| ‡ Fibiger, Jesse | S.J. | 1 | 16 | 0 | 0 | 0 | 2 | .... | .... | .... | .... | .... | .... | 2002-03 | 2002-03 |
| Fidler, Mike | Cle., Min., Hfd., Chi. | 7 | 271 | 84 | 97 | 181 | 124 | .... | .... | .... | .... | .... | .... | 1976-77 | 1982-83 |
| • Field, Wilf | NYA, Bro., Mtl., Chi. | 6 | 219 | 17 | 25 | 42 | 151 | 2 | 0 | 0 | 0 | 2 | .... | 1936-37 | 1944-45 |
| Fielder, Guyle | Chi., Det., Bos. | 4 | 9 | 0 | 0 | 0 | 2 | 6 | 0 | 0 | 0 | 2 | .... | 1950-51 | 1957-58 |
| Filimonov, Dmitri | Ott. | 1 | 30 | 1 | 4 | 5 | 18 | .... | .... | .... | .... | .... | .... | 1993-94 | 1993-94 |
| Fillion, Bob | Mtl. | 7 | 327 | 42 | 61 | 103 | 84 | 33 | 7 | 4 | 11 | 10 | 2 | 1943-44 | 1949-50 |
| • Fillion, Marcel | Bos. | 1 | 1 | 0 | 0 | 0 | 0 | .... | .... | .... | .... | .... | .... | 1944-45 | 1944-45 |
| • Filmore, Tommy | Det., NYA, Bos. | 4 | 117 | 15 | 12 | 27 | 33 | .... | .... | .... | .... | .... | .... | 1930-31 | 1933-34 |
| • Finkbeiner, Lloyd | NYA | 1 | 2 | 0 | 0 | 0 | 0 | .... | .... | .... | .... | .... | .... | 1940-41 | 1940-41 |
| Finley, Jeff | NYI, Phi., Wpg., Phx., NYR, St.L. | 15 | 708 | 13 | 70 | 83 | 457 | 52 | 1 | 6 | 7 | 38 | .... | 1987-88 | 2003-04 |
| Finn, Steven | Que., T.B., L.A. | 12 | 725 | 34 | 78 | 112 | 1724 | 23 | 0 | 4 | 4 | 39 | .... | 1985-86 | 1996-97 |
| • Finney, Sid | Chi. | 3 | 59 | 10 | 7 | 17 | 4 | 7 | 0 | 2 | 2 | 0 | .... | 1951-52 | 1953-54 |
| • Finnigan, Ed | St.L., Bos. | 2 | 15 | 1 | 1 | 2 | 2 | .... | .... | .... | .... | .... | .... | 1934-35 | 1935-36 |
| • Finnigan, Frank | Ott., Tor., St.L. | 14 | 553 | 115 | 88 | 203 | 407 | 38 | 6 | 9 | 15 | 22 | 2 | 1923-24 | 1936-37 |
| Fiorentino, Peter | NYR | 1 | 1 | 0 | 0 | 0 | 0 | .... | .... | .... | .... | .... | .... | 1991-92 | 1991-92 |
| Fischer, Jiri | Det. | 6 | 305 | 11 | 49 | 60 | 295 | 38 | 4 | 3 | 7 | 55 | 1 | 1999-00 | 2005-06 |
| ‡ Fischer, Patrick | Phx. | 1 | 27 | 4 | 6 | 10 | 24 | .... | .... | .... | .... | .... | .... | 2006-07 | 2006-07 |
| Fischer, Ron | Buf. | 2 | 18 | 0 | 7 | 7 | 6 | .... | .... | .... | .... | .... | .... | 1981-82 | 1982-83 |
| • Fisher, Alvin | Tor. | 1 | 9 | 1 | 0 | 1 | 4 | .... | .... | .... | .... | .... | .... | 1924-25 | 1924-25 |
| Fisher, Craig | Phi., Wpg., Fla. | 4 | 12 | 0 | 0 | 0 | 2 | .... | .... | .... | .... | .... | .... | 1989-90 | 1996-97 |
| Fisher, Dunc | NYR, Bos., Det. | 7 | 275 | 45 | 70 | 115 | 104 | 21 | 4 | 4 | 8 | 14 | .... | 1947-48 | 1958-59 |
| • Fisher, Joe | Det. | 4 | 65 | 8 | 12 | 20 | 13 | 12 | 2 | 1 | 3 | 6 | 1 | 1939-40 | 1942-43 |
| Fitchner, Bob | Que. | 2 | 78 | 12 | 20 | 32 | 59 | 3 | 0 | 0 | 0 | 10 | .... | 1979-80 | 1980-81 |
| Fitzgerald, Rusty | Pit. | 2 | 25 | 2 | 2 | 4 | 12 | 5 | 0 | 0 | 0 | 4 | .... | 1994-95 | 1995-96 |
| Fitzgerald, Tom | NYI, Fla., Col., Nsh., Chi., Tor., Bos. | 17 | 1097 | 139 | 190 | 329 | 776 | 78 | 7 | 12 | 19 | 90 | .... | 1988-89 | 2005-06 |
| Fitzpatrick, Ross | Phi. | 4 | 20 | 5 | 2 | 7 | 0 | .... | .... | .... | .... | .... | .... | 1982-83 | 1985-86 |
| Fitzpatrick, Sandy | NYR, Min. | 2 | 22 | 3 | 6 | 9 | 8 | 12 | 0 | 0 | 0 | 0 | .... | 1964-65 | 1967-68 |
| Flaman, Fern | Bos., Tor. | 17 | 910 | 34 | 174 | 208 | 1370 | 63 | 4 | 8 | 12 | 93 | 1 | 1944-45 | 1960-61 |
| Flatley, Pat | NYI, NYR | 14 | 780 | 170 | 340 | 510 | 686 | 70 | 18 | 15 | 33 | 75 | .... | 1983-84 | 1996-97 |
| Fleming, Gerry | Mtl. | 2 | 11 | 0 | 0 | 0 | 42 | .... | .... | .... | .... | .... | .... | 1993-94 | 1994-95 |
| • Fleming, Reggie | Mtl., Chi., Bos., NYR, Phi., Buf. | 12 | 749 | 108 | 132 | 240 | 1468 | 50 | 3 | 6 | 9 | 106 | 1 | 1959-60 | 1970-71 |
| Flesch, John | Min., Pit., Col. | 4 | 124 | 18 | 23 | 41 | 117 | .... | .... | .... | .... | .... | .... | 1974-75 | 1979-80 |
| Fletcher, Steven | Mtl., Wpg. | 2 | 3 | 0 | 0 | 0 | 5 | 1 | 0 | 0 | 0 | 5 | .... | 1987-88 | 1988-89 |
| • Flett, Bill | L.A., Phi., Tor., Atl., Edm. | 11 | 689 | 202 | 215 | 417 | 501 | 52 | 7 | 16 | 23 | 42 | 1 | 1967-68 | 1979-80 |
| Fleury, Theoren | Cgy., Col., NYR, Chi. | 15 | 1084 | 455 | 633 | 1088 | 1840 | 77 | 34 | 45 | 79 | 116 | 1 | 1988-89 | 2002-03 |
| Flichel, Todd | Wpg. | 3 | 6 | 0 | 1 | 1 | 4 | .... | .... | .... | .... | .... | .... | 1987-88 | 1989-90 |
| Flockhart, Rob | Van., Min. | 5 | 55 | 2 | 5 | 7 | 14 | 1 | 1 | 0 | 1 | 2 | .... | 1976-77 | 1980-81 |
| Flockhart, Ron | Phi., Pit., Mtl., St.L., Bos. | 9 | 453 | 145 | 183 | 328 | 208 | 19 | 4 | 6 | 10 | 14 | .... | 1980-81 | 1988-89 |
| Floyd, Larry | N.J. | 2 | 12 | 2 | 3 | 5 | 9 | .... | .... | .... | .... | .... | .... | 1982-83 | 1983-84 |
| Focht, Dan | Phx., Pit. | 3 | 82 | 2 | 6 | 8 | 145 | 1 | 0 | 1 | 1 | 0 | .... | 2001-02 | 2003-04 |
| • Fogarty, Bryan | Que., Pit., Mtl. | 6 | 156 | 22 | 52 | 74 | 119 | .... | .... | .... | .... | .... | .... | 1989-90 | 1994-95 |
| • Fogolin, Lee | Det., Chi. | 9 | 427 | 10 | 48 | 58 | 575 | 28 | 0 | 2 | 2 | 30 | 1 | 1947-48 | 1955-56 |
| Fogolin, Lee | Buf., Edm. | 13 | 924 | 44 | 195 | 239 | 1318 | 108 | 5 | 19 | 24 | 173 | 2 | 1974-75 | 1986-87 |
| Folco, Peter | Van. | 1 | 2 | 0 | 0 | 0 | 0 | .... | .... | .... | .... | .... | .... | 1973-74 | 1973-74 |
| Foley, Gerry | Tor., NYR, L.A. | 4 | 142 | 9 | 14 | 23 | 99 | 9 | 0 | 1 | 1 | 2 | .... | 1954-55 | 1968-69 |
| Foley, Rick | Chi., Phi., Det. | 3 | 67 | 11 | 26 | 37 | 180 | 4 | 0 | 1 | 1 | 4 | .... | 1970-71 | 1973-74 |
| Foligno, Mike | Det., Buf., Tor., Fla. | 15 | 1018 | 355 | 372 | 727 | 2049 | 57 | 15 | 17 | 32 | 185 | .... | 1979-80 | 1993-94 |
| Folk, Bill | Det. | 2 | 12 | 0 | 0 | 0 | 4 | .... | .... | .... | .... | .... | .... | 1951-52 | 1952-53 |
| Fontaine, Len | Det. | 2 | 46 | 8 | 11 | 19 | 10 | .... | .... | .... | .... | .... | .... | 1972-73 | 1973-74 |
| Fontas, Jon | Min. | 2 | 2 | 0 | 0 | 0 | 0 | .... | .... | .... | .... | .... | .... | 1979-80 | 1980-81 |
| Fonteyne, Val | Det., NYR, Pit. | 13 | 820 | 75 | 154 | 229 | 26 | 59 | 3 | 10 | 13 | 8 | .... | 1959-60 | 1971-72 |
| Fontinato, Lou | NYR, Mtl. | 9 | 535 | 26 | 78 | 104 | 1247 | 21 | 0 | 2 | 2 | 42 | .... | 1954-55 | 1962-63 |
| ‡ Forbes, Colin | Phi., T.B., Ott., NYR, Wsh. | 9 | 311 | 33 | 28 | 61 | 213 | 13 | 1 | 0 | 1 | 16 | .... | 1996-97 | 2005-06 |
| Forbes, Dave | Bos., Wsh. | 6 | 363 | 64 | 64 | 128 | 341 | 45 | 1 | 4 | 5 | 13 | .... | 1973-74 | 1978-79 |
| Forbes, Mike | Bos., Edm. | 3 | 50 | 1 | 11 | 12 | 41 | .... | .... | .... | .... | .... | .... | 1977-78 | 1981-82 |
| Forey, Connie | St.L. | 1 | 4 | 0 | 0 | 0 | 2 | .... | .... | .... | .... | .... | .... | 1973-74 | 1973-74 |
| Forsberg, Peter | Que., Col., Phi., Nsh. | 13 | 706 | 249 | 636 | 885 | 686 | 151 | 64 | 107 | 171 | 163 | 2 | 1994-95 | 2007-08 |
| • Forsey, Jack | Tor. | 1 | 19 | 7 | 9 | 16 | 10 | 3 | 0 | 1 | 1 | 0 | .... | 1942-43 | 1942-43 |
| • Forslund, Gus | Ott. | 1 | 48 | 4 | 9 | 13 | 2 | .... | .... | .... | .... | .... | .... | 1932-33 | 1932-33 |
| Forslund, Tomas | Cgy. | 2 | 44 | 5 | 11 | 16 | 12 | .... | .... | .... | .... | .... | .... | 1991-92 | 1992-93 |
| Forsyth, Alex | Wsh. | 1 | 1 | 0 | 0 | 0 | 0 | .... | .... | .... | .... | .... | .... | 1976-77 | 1976-77 |
| Fortier, Dave | Tor., NYI, Van. | 4 | 205 | 8 | 21 | 29 | 335 | 20 | 0 | 2 | 2 | 33 | .... | 1972-73 | 1976-77 |
| Fortier, Marc | Que., Ott., L.A. | 6 | 212 | 42 | 60 | 102 | 135 | .... | .... | .... | .... | .... | .... | 1987-88 | 1992-93 |
| ‡ Fortin, Jean-Francois | Wsh. | 3 | 71 | 1 | 4 | 5 | 42 | .... | .... | .... | .... | .... | .... | 2001-02 | 2003-04 |
| Fortin, Ray | St.L. | 3 | 92 | 2 | 6 | 8 | 33 | 6 | 0 | 0 | 0 | 8 | .... | 1967-68 | 1969-70 |
| Foster, Corey | N.J., Phi., Pit., NYI | 4 | 45 | 5 | 6 | 11 | 24 | 3 | 0 | 0 | 0 | 4 | .... | 1988-89 | 1996-97 |
| Foster, Dwight | Bos., Col., N.J., Det. | 10 | 541 | 111 | 163 | 274 | 420 | 35 | 5 | 12 | 17 | 4 | .... | 1977-78 | 1986-87 |
| • Foster, Herb | NYR | 2 | 6 | 1 | 0 | 1 | 5 | .... | .... | .... | .... | .... | .... | 1940-41 | 1947-48 |
| • Foster, Yip | NYR, Bos., Det. | 4 | 83 | 3 | 2 | 5 | 32 | .... | .... | .... | .... | .... | .... | 1929-30 | 1934-35 |
| Fotiu, Nick | NYR, Hfd., Cgy., Phi., Edm. | 13 | 646 | 60 | 77 | 137 | 1362 | 38 | 0 | 4 | 4 | 67 | .... | 1976-77 | 1988-89 |
| • Fowler, Jimmy | Tor. | 3 | 135 | 18 | 29 | 47 | 39 | 18 | 0 | 3 | 3 | 2 | .... | 1936-37 | 1938-39 |
| Fowler, Tom | Chi. | 1 | 24 | 0 | 1 | 1 | 18 | .... | .... | .... | .... | .... | .... | 1946-47 | 1946-47 |
| Fox, Greg | Atl., Chi., Pit. | 8 | 494 | 14 | 92 | 106 | 637 | 44 | 1 | 9 | 10 | 67 | .... | 1977-78 | 1984-85 |
| Fox, Jim | L.A. | 9 | 578 | 186 | 293 | 479 | 143 | 22 | 4 | 8 | 12 | 0 | .... | 1980-81 | 1989-90 |
| • Foyston, Frank | Det. | 2 | 64 | 17 | 7 | 24 | 32 | .... | .... | .... | .... | .... | .... | 1926-27 | 1927-28 |
| Frampton, Bob | Mtl. | 1 | 2 | 0 | 0 | 0 | 0 | 3 | 0 | 0 | 0 | 0 | .... | 1949-50 | 1949-50 |

| Name | NHL Teams | NHL Seasons | Regular Schedule GP | G | A | TP | PIM | Playoffs GP | G | A | TP | PIM | NHL Cup Wins | First NHL Season | Last NHL Season |
|---|---|---|---|---|---|---|---|---|---|---|---|---|---|---|---|
| Franceschetti, Lou | Wsh., Tor., Buf. | 10 | 459 | 59 | 81 | 140 | 747 | 44 | 3 | 2 | 5 | 111 | .... | 1981-82 | 1991-92 |
| Francis, Bobby | Det. | 1 | 14 | 2 | 0 | 2 | 0 | .... | .... | .... | .... | .... | .... | 1982-83 | 1982-83 |
| Francis, Ron | Hfd., Pit., Car., Tor. | 23 | 1731 | 549 | 1249 | 1798 | 979 | 171 | 46 | 97 | 143 | 95 | 2 | 1981-82 | 2003-04 |
| • Fraser, Archie | NYR | 1 | 3 | 0 | 1 | 1 | 0 | .... | .... | .... | .... | .... | .... | 1943-44 | 1943-44 |
| • Fraser, Charles | Ham. | 1 | 1 | 0 | 0 | 0 | 0 | .... | .... | .... | .... | .... | .... | 1923-24 | 1923-24 |
| Fraser, Curt | Van., Chi., Min. | 12 | 704 | 193 | 240 | 433 | 1306 | 65 | 15 | 18 | 33 | 198 | .... | 1978-79 | 1989-90 |
| • Fraser, Gord | Chi., Det., Mtl., Pit., Phi. | 5 | 144 | 24 | 12 | 36 | 224 | 2 | 1 | 0 | 1 | 6 | .... | 1926-27 | 1930-31 |
| • Fraser, Harvey | Chi. | 1 | 21 | 5 | 4 | 9 | 0 | .... | .... | .... | .... | .... | .... | 1944-45 | 1944-45 |
| Fraser, Iain | NYI, Que., Dal., Edm., Wpg., S.J. | 5 | 94 | 23 | 23 | 46 | 31 | 4 | 0 | 0 | 0 | 0 | .... | 1992-93 | 1996-97 |
| Fraser, Scott | Mtl., Edm., NYR | 3 | 72 | 16 | 15 | 31 | 24 | 11 | 1 | 1 | 2 | 0 | .... | 1995-96 | 1998-99 |
| Frawley, Dan | Chi., Pit. | 6 | 273 | 37 | 40 | 77 | 674 | 1 | 0 | 0 | 0 | 0 | .... | 1983-84 | 1988-89 |
| Freadrich, Kyle | T.B. | 2 | 23 | 0 | 1 | 1 | 75 | .... | .... | .... | .... | .... | .... | 1999-00 | 2000-01 |
| • Fredrickson, Frank | Det., Bos., Pit. | 5 | 161 | 39 | 34 | 73 | 206 | 10 | 2 | 3 | 5 | 24 | .... | 1926-27 | 1930-31 |
| Freer, Mark | Phi., Ott., Cgy. | 7 | 124 | 16 | 23 | 39 | 61 | .... | .... | .... | .... | .... | .... | 1986-87 | 1993-94 |
| • Frew, Irv | Mtl.M., St.L., Mtl. | 3 | 96 | 2 | 5 | 7 | 146 | 4 | 0 | 0 | 0 | 6 | .... | 1933-34 | 1935-36 |
| Friday, Tim | Det. | 1 | 23 | 0 | 3 | 3 | 6 | .... | .... | .... | .... | .... | .... | 1985-86 | 1985-86 |
| Fridgen, Dan | Hfd. | 2 | 13 | 2 | 3 | 5 | 2 | .... | .... | .... | .... | .... | .... | 1981-82 | 1982-83 |
| Friedman, Doug | Edm., Nsh. | 2 | 18 | 0 | 1 | 1 | 34 | .... | .... | .... | .... | .... | .... | 1997-98 | 1998-99 |
| Friesen, Jeff | S.J., Ana., N.J., Wsh., Cgy. | 12 | 893 | 218 | 298 | 516 | 488 | 84 | 18 | 15 | 33 | 48 | 1 | 1994-95 | 2006-07 |
| Friest, Ron | Min. | 3 | 64 | 7 | 7 | 14 | 191 | 6 | 1 | 0 | 1 | 7 | .... | 1980-81 | 1982-83 |
| Frig, Len | Chi., Cal., Cle., St.L. | 7 | 311 | 13 | 51 | 64 | 479 | 14 | 2 | 1 | 3 | 0 | .... | 1972-73 | 1979-80 |
| • Frost, Harry | Bos. | 1 | 4 | 0 | 0 | 0 | 0 | 1 | 0 | 0 | 0 | 0 | 1 | 1938-39 | 1938-39 |
| Frycer, Miroslav | Que., Tor., Det., Edm. | 8 | 415 | 147 | 183 | 330 | 486 | 17 | 3 | 8 | 11 | 16 | .... | 1981-82 | 1988-89 |
| • Fryday, Bob | Mtl. | 2 | 5 | 1 | 0 | 1 | 0 | .... | .... | .... | .... | .... | .... | 1949-50 | 1951-52 |
| Ftorek, Robbie | Det., Que., NYR | 8 | 334 | 77 | 150 | 227 | 262 | 19 | 9 | 6 | 15 | 28 | .... | 1972-73 | 1984-85 |
| Fullan, Larry | Wsh. | 1 | 4 | 1 | 0 | 1 | 0 | .... | .... | .... | .... | .... | .... | 1974-75 | 1974-75 |
| Fusco, Mark | Hfd. | 2 | 80 | 3 | 12 | 15 | 42 | .... | .... | .... | .... | .... | .... | 1983-84 | 1984-85 |
| ‡ Fussey, Owen | Wsh. | 1 | 4 | 0 | 1 | 1 | 0 | .... | .... | .... | .... | .... | .... | 2003-04 | 2003-04 |

## G

| Name | NHL Teams | NHL Seasons | Regular Schedule GP | G | A | TP | PIM | Playoffs GP | G | A | TP | PIM | NHL Cup Wins | First NHL Season | Last NHL Season |
|---|---|---|---|---|---|---|---|---|---|---|---|---|---|---|---|
| Gadsby, Bill | Chi., NYR, Det. | 20 | 1248 | 130 | 438 | 568 | 1539 | 67 | 4 | 23 | 27 | 92 | .... | 1946-47 | 1965-66 |
| Gaetz, Link | Min., S.J. | 3 | 65 | 6 | 8 | 14 | 412 | .... | .... | .... | .... | .... | .... | 1988-89 | 1991-92 |
| Gage, Jody | Det., Buf. | 6 | 68 | 14 | 15 | 29 | 26 | .... | .... | .... | .... | .... | .... | 1980-81 | 1991-92 |
| • Gagne, Art | Mtl., Bos., Ott., Det. | 6 | 228 | 67 | 33 | 100 | 257 | 11 | 2 | 1 | 3 | 20 | .... | 1926-27 | 1931-32 |
| Gagne, Paul | Col., N.J., Tor., NYI | 8 | 390 | 110 | 101 | 211 | 127 | .... | .... | .... | .... | .... | .... | 1980-81 | 1989-90 |
| Gagne, Pierre | Bos. | 1 | 2 | 0 | 0 | 0 | 0 | .... | .... | .... | .... | .... | .... | 1959-60 | 1959-60 |
| Gagner, Dave | NYR, Min., Dal., Tor., Cgy., Fla., Van. | 15 | 946 | 318 | 401 | 719 | 1018 | 57 | 22 | 26 | 48 | 64 | .... | 1984-85 | 1998-99 |
| Gagnon, Germain | Mtl., NYI, Chi., K.C. | 5 | 259 | 40 | 101 | 141 | 72 | 19 | 2 | 3 | 5 | 2 | .... | 1971-72 | 1975-76 |
| • Gagnon, Johnny | Mtl., Bos., NYA | 10 | 454 | 120 | 141 | 261 | 295 | 32 | 12 | 12 | 24 | 37 | 1 | 1930-31 | 1939-40 |
| Gagnon, Sean | Phx., Ott. | 3 | 12 | 0 | 1 | 1 | 34 | .... | .... | .... | .... | .... | .... | 1997-98 | 2000-01 |
| Gainey, Bob | Mtl. | 16 | 1160 | 239 | 262 | 501 | 585 | 182 | 25 | 48 | 73 | 151 | 5 | 1973-74 | 1988-89 |
| Gainey, Steve | Dal., Phx. | 4 | 33 | 0 | 2 | 2 | 34 | .... | .... | .... | .... | .... | .... | 2000-01 | 2005-06 |
| • Gainor, Dutch | Bos., NYR, Ott., Mtl.M. | 7 | 246 | 51 | 56 | 107 | 129 | 22 | 2 | 1 | 3 | 14 | 2 | 1927-28 | 1934-35 |
| ‡ Galanov, Maxim | NYR, Pit., Atl., T.B. | 4 | 122 | 8 | 12 | 20 | 44 | 1 | 0 | 0 | 0 | 0 | .... | 1997-98 | 2000-01 |
| Galarneau, Michel | Hfd. | 3 | 78 | 7 | 10 | 17 | 34 | .... | .... | .... | .... | .... | .... | 1980-81 | 1982-83 |
| • Galbraith, Percy | Bos., Ott. | 8 | 347 | 29 | 31 | 60 | 224 | 31 | 4 | 7 | 11 | 24 | 1 | 1926-27 | 1933-34 |
| • Gallagher, John | Mtl.M., Det., NYA | 7 | 205 | 14 | 19 | 33 | 153 | 24 | 2 | 3 | 5 | 27 | 1 | 1930-31 | 1938-39 |
| Gallant, Gerard | Det., T.B. | 11 | 615 | 211 | 269 | 480 | 1674 | 58 | 18 | 21 | 39 | 178 | .... | 1984-85 | 1994-95 |
| Galley, Garry | L.A., Wsh., Bos., Phi., Buf., NYI | 17 | 1149 | 125 | 475 | 600 | 1218 | 89 | 7 | 23 | 30 | 119 | .... | 1984-85 | 2000-01 |
| Gallimore, Jamie | Min. | 1 | 2 | 0 | 0 | 0 | 0 | .... | .... | .... | .... | .... | .... | 1977-78 | 1977-78 |
| • Gallinger, Don | Bos. | 5 | 222 | 65 | 88 | 153 | 89 | 23 | 5 | 5 | 10 | 19 | .... | 1942-43 | 1947-48 |
| ‡ Gamache, Simon | Atl., Nsh., St.L., Tor. | 4 | 48 | 6 | 7 | 13 | 18 | .... | .... | .... | .... | .... | .... | 2002-03 | 2007-08 |
| Gamble, Dick | Mtl., Chi., Tor. | 8 | 195 | 41 | 41 | 82 | 66 | 14 | 1 | 2 | 3 | 4 | 1 | 1950-51 | 1966-67 |
| Gambucci, Gary | Min. | 2 | 51 | 2 | 7 | 9 | 9 | .... | .... | .... | .... | .... | .... | 1971-72 | 1973-74 |
| Ganchar, Perry | St.L., Mtl., Pit. | 4 | 42 | 3 | 7 | 10 | 36 | 7 | 3 | 1 | 4 | 0 | .... | 1983-84 | 1988-89 |
| Gans, Dave | L.A. | 2 | 6 | 0 | 0 | 0 | 2 | .... | .... | .... | .... | .... | .... | 1982-83 | 1985-86 |
| Gardiner, Bruce | Ott., T.B., CBJ, N.J. | 6 | 312 | 34 | 54 | 88 | 263 | 21 | 1 | 4 | 5 | 8 | .... | 1996-97 | 2001-02 |
| • Gardiner, Herb | Mtl., Chi. | 3 | 108 | 10 | 9 | 19 | 52 | 9 | 0 | 1 | 1 | 16 | .... | 1926-27 | 1928-29 |
| Gardner, Bill | Chi., Hfd. | 9 | 380 | 73 | 115 | 188 | 68 | 45 | 3 | 8 | 11 | 17 | .... | 1980-81 | 1988-89 |
| • Gardner, Cal | NYR, Tor., Chi., Bos. | 12 | 696 | 154 | 238 | 392 | 517 | 61 | 7 | 10 | 17 | 20 | 2 | 1945-46 | 1956-57 |
| Gardner, Dave | Mtl., St.L., Cal., Cle., Phi. | 7 | 350 | 75 | 115 | 190 | 41 | .... | .... | .... | .... | .... | .... | 1972-73 | 1979-80 |
| Gardner, Paul | Col., Tor., Pit., Wsh., Buf. | 10 | 447 | 201 | 201 | 402 | 207 | 16 | 2 | 6 | 8 | 14 | .... | 1976-77 | 1985-86 |
| Gare, Danny | Buf., Det., Edm. | 13 | 827 | 354 | 331 | 685 | 1285 | 64 | 25 | 21 | 46 | 195 | .... | 1974-75 | 1986-87 |
| Gariepy, Ray | Bos., Tor. | 2 | 36 | 1 | 6 | 7 | 43 | .... | .... | .... | .... | .... | .... | 1953-54 | 1955-56 |
| • Garland, Scott | Tor., L.A. | 3 | 91 | 13 | 24 | 37 | 115 | 7 | 1 | 2 | 3 | 35 | .... | 1975-76 | 1978-79 |
| Garner, Rob | Pit. | 1 | 1 | 0 | 0 | 0 | 0 | .... | .... | .... | .... | .... | .... | 1982-83 | 1982-83 |
| Garpenlov, Johan | Det., S.J., Fla., Atl. | 10 | 609 | 114 | 197 | 311 | 276 | 44 | 10 | 9 | 19 | 22 | .... | 1990-91 | 1999-00 |
| • Garrett, Red | NYR | 1 | 23 | 1 | 1 | 2 | 18 | .... | .... | .... | .... | .... | .... | 1942-43 | 1942-43 |
| Gartner, Mike | Wsh., Min., NYR, Tor., Phx. | 19 | 1432 | 708 | 627 | 1335 | 1159 | 122 | 43 | 50 | 93 | 125 | .... | 1979-80 | 1997-98 |
| • Gassoff, Bob | St.L. | 4 | 245 | 11 | 47 | 58 | 866 | 9 | 0 | 1 | 1 | 16 | .... | 1973-74 | 1976-77 |
| Gassoff, Brad | Van. | 4 | 122 | 19 | 17 | 36 | 163 | 3 | 0 | 0 | 0 | 0 | .... | 1975-76 | 1978-79 |
| Gatzos, Steve | Pit. | 4 | 89 | 15 | 20 | 35 | 83 | 1 | 0 | 0 | 0 | 0 | .... | 1981-82 | 1984-85 |
| Gaudreau, Rob | S.J., Ott. | 4 | 231 | 51 | 54 | 105 | 69 | 14 | 2 | 0 | 2 | 0 | .... | 1992-93 | 1995-96 |
| Gaudreault, Armand | Bos. | 1 | 44 | 15 | 9 | 24 | 27 | 7 | 0 | 2 | 2 | 8 | .... | 1944-45 | 1944-45 |
| • Gaudreault, Leo | Mtl. | 3 | 67 | 8 | 4 | 12 | 30 | .... | .... | .... | .... | .... | .... | 1927-28 | 1932-33 |
| Gaul, Mike | Col., CBJ | 2 | 3 | 0 | 0 | 0 | 4 | .... | .... | .... | .... | .... | .... | 1998-99 | 2000-01 |
| Gaulin, Jean-Marc | Que. | 4 | 26 | 4 | 3 | 7 | 8 | 1 | 0 | 0 | 0 | 0 | .... | 1982-83 | 1985-86 |
| Gaume, Dallas | Hfd. | 1 | 4 | 1 | 1 | 2 | 0 | .... | .... | .... | .... | .... | .... | 1988-89 | 1988-89 |
| • Gauthier, Art | Mtl. | 1 | 13 | 0 | 0 | 0 | 0 | 1 | 0 | 0 | 0 | 0 | .... | 1926-27 | 1926-27 |
| Gauthier, Daniel | Chi. | 1 | 5 | 0 | 0 | 0 | 0 | .... | .... | .... | .... | .... | .... | 1994-95 | 1994-95 |
| • Gauthier, Fern | NYR, Mtl., Det. | 6 | 229 | 46 | 50 | 96 | 35 | 22 | 5 | 1 | 6 | 7 | .... | 1943-44 | 1948-49 |
| Gauthier, Jean | Mtl., Phi., Bos. | 10 | 166 | 6 | 29 | 35 | 150 | 14 | 1 | 3 | 4 | 22 | 1 | 1960-61 | 1969-70 |
| Gauthier, Luc | Mtl. | 1 | 3 | 0 | 0 | 0 | 2 | .... | .... | .... | .... | .... | .... | 1990-91 | 1990-91 |
| Gauvreau, Jocelyn | Mtl. | 1 | 2 | 0 | 0 | 0 | 0 | .... | .... | .... | .... | .... | .... | 1983-84 | 1983-84 |
| Gavey, Aaron | T.B., Cgy., Dal., Min., Tor., Ana. | 9 | 360 | 41 | 50 | 91 | 272 | 19 | 1 | 2 | 3 | 14 | .... | 1995-96 | 2005-06 |
| Gavin, Stew | Tor., Hfd., Min. | 13 | 768 | 130 | 155 | 285 | 584 | 66 | 14 | 20 | 34 | 75 | .... | 1980-81 | 1992-93 |
| Geale, Bob | Pit. | 1 | 1 | 0 | 0 | 0 | 2 | .... | .... | .... | .... | .... | .... | 1984-85 | 1984-85 |
| • Gee, George | Chi., Det. | 9 | 551 | 135 | 183 | 318 | 345 | 41 | 6 | 13 | 19 | 32 | 1 | 1945-46 | 1953-54 |
| Geldart, Gary | Min. | 1 | 4 | 0 | 0 | 0 | 5 | .... | .... | .... | .... | .... | .... | 1970-71 | 1970-71 |
| ‡ Gelinas, Martin | Edm., Que., Van., Car., Cgy., Fla., Nsh. | 19 | 1273 | 309 | 351 | 660 | 820 | 147 | 23 | 33 | 56 | 120 | 1 | 1988-89 | 2007-08 |
| Gendron, Jean-Guy | NYR, Bos., Mtl., Phi. | 14 | 863 | 182 | 201 | 383 | 701 | 42 | 7 | 4 | 11 | 47 | .... | 1955-56 | 1971-72 |
| ‡ Gendron, Martin | Wsh., Chi. | 3 | 30 | 4 | 2 | 6 | 10 | .... | .... | .... | .... | .... | .... | 1994-95 | 1997-98 |
| • Geoffrion, Bernie | Mtl., NYR | 16 | 883 | 393 | 429 | 822 | 689 | 132 | 58 | 60 | 118 | 88 | 6 | 1950-51 | 1967-68 |
| Geoffrion, Danny | Mtl., Wpg. | 3 | 111 | 20 | 32 | 52 | 99 | 2 | 0 | 0 | 0 | 7 | .... | 1979-80 | 1981-82 |
| • Geran, Gerry | Mtl.W., Bos. | 2 | 37 | 5 | 1 | 6 | 6 | .... | .... | .... | .... | .... | .... | 1917-18 | 1925-26 |
| • Gerard, Eddie | Ott. | 6 | 128 | 50 | 48 | 98 | 108 | 11 | 4 | 0 | 4 | 17 | 3 | 1917-18 | 1922-23 |
| Germain, Eric | L.A. | 1 | 4 | 0 | 1 | 1 | 13 | 1 | 0 | 0 | 0 | 4 | .... | 1987-88 | 1987-88 |
| Gernander, Ken | NYR | 3 | 12 | 2 | 3 | 5 | 6 | 15 | 0 | 0 | 0 | 0 | .... | 1995-96 | 2003-04 |
| • Getliffe, Ray | Bos., Mtl. | 10 | 393 | 136 | 137 | 273 | 250 | 45 | 9 | 10 | 19 | 30 | 2 | 1935-36 | 1944-45 |
| Giallonardo, Mario | Col. | 2 | 23 | 0 | 3 | 3 | 6 | .... | .... | .... | .... | .... | .... | 1979-80 | 1980-81 |
| Gibbs, Barry | Bos., Min., Atl., St.L., L.A. | 13 | 797 | 58 | 224 | 282 | 945 | 36 | 4 | 2 | 6 | 67 | .... | 1967-68 | 1979-80 |
| Gibson, Don | Van. | 1 | 14 | 0 | 3 | 3 | 20 | .... | .... | .... | .... | .... | .... | 1990-91 | 1990-91 |
| Gibson, Doug | Bos., Wsh. | 3 | 63 | 9 | 19 | 28 | 0 | 1 | 0 | 0 | 0 | 0 | .... | 1973-74 | 1977-78 |
| Gibson, John | L.A., Tor., Wpg. | 3 | 48 | 0 | 2 | 2 | 120 | .... | .... | .... | .... | .... | .... | 1980-81 | 1983-84 |
| • Giesebrecht, Gus | Det. | 4 | 135 | 27 | 51 | 78 | 13 | 17 | 2 | 3 | 5 | 0 | .... | 1938-39 | 1941-42 |
| Giffin, Lee | Pit. | 2 | 27 | 1 | 3 | 4 | 9 | .... | .... | .... | .... | .... | .... | 1986-87 | 1987-88 |
| Gilbert, Ed | K.C., Pit. | 3 | 166 | 21 | 31 | 52 | 22 | .... | .... | .... | .... | .... | .... | 1974-75 | 1976-77 |
| Gilbert, Greg | NYI, Chi., NYR, St.L. | 15 | 837 | 150 | 228 | 378 | 576 | 133 | 17 | 33 | 50 | 162 | 3 | 1981-82 | 1995-96 |
| Gilbert, Jeannot | Bos. | 2 | 9 | 0 | 1 | 1 | 4 | .... | .... | .... | .... | .... | .... | 1962-63 | 1964-65 |
| Gilbert, Rod | NYR | 18 | 1065 | 406 | 615 | 1021 | 508 | 79 | 34 | 33 | 67 | 43 | .... | 1960-61 | 1977-78 |
| Gilbertson, Stan | Cal., St.L., Wsh., Pit. | 6 | 428 | 85 | 89 | 174 | 148 | 3 | 1 | 1 | 2 | 2 | .... | 1971-72 | 1976-77 |
| Gilchrist, Brent | Mtl., Edm., Min., Dal., Det., Nsh. | 15 | 792 | 135 | 170 | 305 | 400 | 90 | 17 | 14 | 31 | 48 | 1 | 1988-89 | 2002-03 |
| Giles, Curt | Min., NYR, St.L. | 14 | 895 | 43 | 199 | 242 | 733 | 103 | 6 | 16 | 22 | 118 | .... | 1979-80 | 1992-93 |
| Gilhen, Randy | Hfd., Wpg., Pit., L.A., NYR, T.B., Fla. | 11 | 457 | 55 | 60 | 115 | 314 | 33 | 3 | 2 | 5 | 26 | 1 | 1982-83 | 1995-96 |
| Gill, Todd | Tor., S.J., St.L., Det., Phx., Col., Chi. | 19 | 1007 | 82 | 272 | 354 | 1214 | 103 | 7 | 30 | 37 | 193 | .... | 1984-85 | 2002-03 |
| Gillen, Don | Phi., Hfd. | 2 | 35 | 2 | 4 | 6 | 22 | .... | .... | .... | .... | .... | .... | 1979-80 | 1981-82 |
| • Gillie, Farrand | Det. | 1 | 1 | 0 | 0 | 0 | 0 | .... | .... | .... | .... | .... | .... | 1928-29 | 1928-29 |
| Gillies, Clark | NYI, Buf. | 14 | 958 | 319 | 378 | 697 | 1023 | 164 | 47 | 47 | 94 | 287 | 4 | 1974-75 | 1987-88 |
| Gillis, Jere | Van., NYR, Que., Buf., Phi. | 9 | 386 | 78 | 95 | 173 | 230 | 19 | 4 | 7 | 11 | 9 | .... | 1977-78 | 1986-87 |
| Gillis, Mike | Col., Bos. | 6 | 246 | 33 | 43 | 76 | 186 | 27 | 2 | 5 | 7 | 10 | .... | 1978-79 | 1983-84 |
| Gillis, Paul | Que., Chi., Hfd. | 11 | 624 | 88 | 154 | 242 | 1498 | 42 | 3 | 14 | 17 | 156 | .... | 1982-83 | 1992-93 |
| Gilmour, Doug | St.L., Cgy., Tor., N.J., Chi., Buf., Mtl. | 20 | 1474 | 450 | 964 | 1414 | 1301 | 182 | 60 | 128 | 188 | 235 | 1 | 1983-84 | 2002-03 |
| Gingras, Gaston | Mtl., Tor., St.L. | 10 | 476 | 61 | 174 | 235 | 161 | 52 | 6 | 18 | 24 | 20 | 1 | 1979-80 | 1988-89 |
| Girard, Bob | Cal., Cle., Wsh. | 5 | 305 | 45 | 69 | 114 | 140 | .... | .... | .... | .... | .... | .... | 1975-76 | 1979-80 |
| Girard, Jonathan | Bos. | 5 | 150 | 10 | 34 | 44 | 46 | 3 | 0 | 1 | 1 | 2 | .... | 1998-99 | 2002-03 |

Bob Fryday

Art Gagne

Paul Gagne

Steve Gatzos

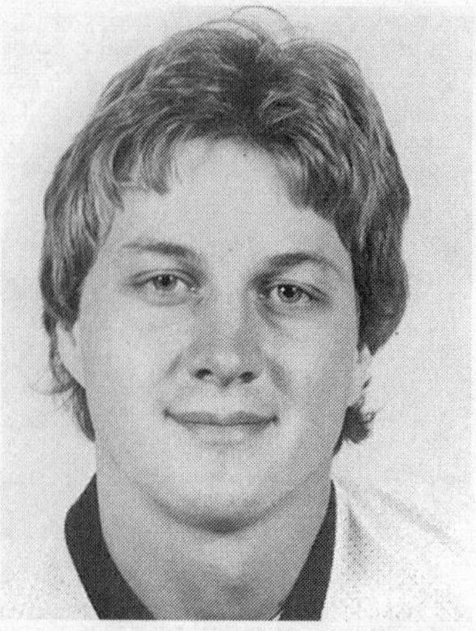

Mike Gillis

Warren Godfrey

Ebbie Goodfellow

John Grisdale

| | | | Regular Schedule | | | | | Playoffs | | | | | | | |
|---|---|---|---|---|---|---|---|---|---|---|---|---|---|---|---|
| Name | NHL Teams | NHL Seasons | GP | G | A | TP | PIM | GP | G | A | TP | PIM | NHL Cup Wins | First NHL Season | Last NHL Season |
| Girard, Kenny | Tor. | 3 | 7 | 0 | 1 | 1 | 2 | .... | .... | .... | .... | .... | .... | 1956-57 | 1959-60 |
| • Giroux, Art | Mtl., Bos., Det. | 3 | 54 | 6 | 4 | 10 | 14 | 2 | 0 | 0 | 0 | 0 | .... | 1932-33 | 1935-36 |
| Giroux, Larry | St.L., K.C., Det., Hfd. | 7 | 274 | 15 | 74 | 89 | 333 | 5 | 0 | 0 | 0 | 4 | .... | 1973-74 | 1979-80 |
| Giroux, Pierre | L.A. | 1 | 6 | 1 | 0 | 1 | 17 | .... | .... | .... | .... | .... | .... | 1982-83 | 1982-83 |
| ‡ Giroux, Raymond | NYI, N.J. | 4 | 38 | 0 | 13 | 13 | 22 | 4 | 0 | 0 | 0 | 0 | .... | 1999-00 | 2003-04 |
| Gladney, Bob | L.A., Pit. | 2 | 14 | 1 | 5 | 6 | 4 | .... | .... | .... | .... | .... | .... | 1982-83 | 1983-84 |
| Gladu, Jean-Paul | Bos. | 1 | 40 | 6 | 14 | 20 | 2 | 7 | 2 | 2 | 4 | 0 | .... | 1944-45 | 1944-45 |
| Glennie, Brian | Tor., L.A. | 10 | 572 | 14 | 100 | 114 | 621 | 32 | 0 | 1 | 1 | 66 | .... | 1969-70 | 1978-79 |
| Glennon, Matt | Bos. | 1 | 3 | 0 | 0 | 0 | 2 | .... | .... | .... | .... | .... | .... | 1991-92 | 1991-92 |
| Gloeckner, Lorry | Det. | 1 | 13 | 0 | 2 | 2 | 6 | .... | .... | .... | .... | .... | .... | 1978-79 | 1978-79 |
| Gloor, Dan | Van. | 1 | 2 | 0 | 0 | 0 | 0 | .... | .... | .... | .... | .... | .... | 1973-74 | 1973-74 |
| • Glover, Fred | Det., Chi. | 5 | 92 | 13 | 11 | 24 | 62 | 8 | 0 | 0 | 0 | 0 | 1 | 1948-49 | 1952-53 |
| Glover, Howie | Chi., Det., NYR, Mtl. | 5 | 144 | 29 | 17 | 46 | 101 | 11 | 1 | 2 | 3 | 2 | .... | 1958-59 | 1968-69 |
| Glynn, Brian | Cgy., Min., Edm., Ott., Van., Hfd. | 10 | 431 | 25 | 79 | 104 | 410 | 57 | 6 | 10 | 16 | 40 | .... | 1987-88 | 1996-97 |
| ‡ Goc, Sascha | N.J., T.B. | 2 | 22 | 0 | 0 | 0 | 4 | .... | .... | .... | .... | .... | .... | 2000-01 | 2001-02 |
| Godden, Ernie | Tor. | 1 | 5 | 1 | 1 | 2 | 6 | .... | .... | .... | .... | .... | .... | 1981-82 | 1981-82 |
| • Godfrey, Warren | Bos., Det. | 16 | 786 | 32 | 125 | 157 | 752 | 52 | 1 | 4 | 5 | 42 | .... | 1952-53 | 1967-68 |
| Godin, Eddy | Wsh. | 2 | 27 | 3 | 6 | 9 | 12 | .... | .... | .... | .... | .... | .... | 1977-78 | 1978-79 |
| • Godin, Sam | Ott., Mtl. | 3 | 83 | 4 | 3 | 7 | 36 | .... | .... | .... | .... | .... | .... | 1927-28 | 1933-34 |
| Godynyuk, Alexander | Tor., Cgy., Fla., Hfd. | 7 | 223 | 10 | 39 | 49 | 224 | .... | .... | .... | .... | .... | .... | 1990-91 | 1996-97 |
| • Goegan, Pete | Det., NYR, Min. | 11 | 383 | 19 | 67 | 86 | 365 | 33 | 1 | 3 | 4 | 61 | .... | 1957-58 | 1967-68 |
| Goertz, Dave | Pit. | 1 | 2 | 0 | 0 | 0 | 2 | .... | .... | .... | .... | .... | .... | 1987-88 | 1987-88 |
| • Goldham, Bob | Tor., Chi., Det. | 12 | 650 | 28 | 143 | 171 | 400 | 66 | 3 | 14 | 17 | 53 | 5 | 1941-42 | 1955-56 |
| Goldmann, Erich | Ott. | 1 | 1 | 0 | 0 | 0 | 0 | .... | .... | .... | .... | .... | .... | 1999-00 | 1999-00 |
| • Goldsworthy, Bill | Bos., Min., NYR | 14 | 771 | 283 | 258 | 541 | 793 | 40 | 18 | 19 | 37 | 30 | .... | 1964-65 | 1977-78 |
| • Goldsworthy, Leroy | NYR, Det., Chi., Mtl., Bos., NYA | 10 | 336 | 66 | 57 | 123 | 79 | 24 | 1 | 0 | 1 | 4 | 1 | 1928-29 | 1938-39 |
| Goldup, Glenn | Mtl., L.A. | 9 | 291 | 52 | 67 | 119 | 303 | 16 | 4 | 3 | 7 | 22 | .... | 1973-74 | 1981-82 |
| • Goldup, Hank | Tor., NYR | 6 | 202 | 63 | 80 | 143 | 97 | 26 | 5 | 1 | 6 | 6 | 1 | 1939-40 | 1945-46 |
| Golubovsky, Yan | Det., Fla. | 4 | 56 | 1 | 7 | 8 | 32 | .... | .... | .... | .... | .... | .... | 1997-98 | 2000-01 |
| Goneau, Daniel | NYR | 3 | 53 | 12 | 3 | 15 | 14 | .... | .... | .... | .... | .... | .... | 1996-97 | 1999-00 |
| • Gooden, Bill | NYR | 2 | 53 | 9 | 11 | 20 | 15 | .... | .... | .... | .... | .... | .... | 1942-43 | 1943-44 |
| Goodenough, Larry | Phi., Van. | 6 | 242 | 22 | 77 | 99 | 179 | 22 | 3 | 15 | 18 | 10 | 1 | 1974-75 | 1979-80 |
| • Goodfellow, Ebbie | Det. | 14 | 557 | 134 | 190 | 324 | 511 | 45 | 8 | 8 | 16 | 65 | 3 | 1929-30 | 1942-43 |
| Gordiouk, Viktor | Buf. | 2 | 26 | 3 | 8 | 11 | 0 | .... | .... | .... | .... | .... | .... | 1992-93 | 1994-95 |
| • Gordon, Fred | Det., Bos. | 2 | 81 | 8 | 7 | 15 | 68 | 2 | 0 | 0 | 0 | 0 | .... | 1926-27 | 1927-28 |
| Gordon, Jack | NYR | 3 | 36 | 3 | 10 | 13 | 0 | 9 | 1 | 1 | 2 | 7 | .... | 1948-49 | 1950-51 |
| Gordon, Robb | Van. | 1 | 4 | 0 | 0 | 0 | 2 | .... | .... | .... | .... | .... | .... | 1998-99 | 1998-99 |
| ‡ Goren, Lee | Bos., Fla., Van. | 5 | 67 | 5 | 4 | 9 | 44 | 5 | 0 | 0 | 0 | 5 | .... | 2000-01 | 2006-07 |
| Gorence, Tom | Phi., Edm. | 6 | 303 | 58 | 53 | 111 | 89 | 37 | 9 | 6 | 15 | 47 | .... | 1978-79 | 1983-84 |
| Goring, Butch | L.A., NYI, Bos. | 16 | 1107 | 375 | 513 | 888 | 102 | 134 | 38 | 50 | 88 | 32 | 4 | 1969-70 | 1984-85 |
| Gorman, Dave | Atl. | 1 | 3 | 0 | 0 | 0 | 0 | .... | .... | .... | .... | .... | .... | 1979-80 | 1979-80 |
| • Gorman, Ed | Ott., Tor. | 4 | 111 | 14 | 6 | 20 | 108 | 8 | 0 | 0 | 0 | 2 | 1 | 1924-25 | 1927-28 |
| Gosselin, Benoit | NYR | 1 | 7 | 0 | 0 | 0 | 33 | .... | .... | .... | .... | .... | .... | 1977-78 | 1977-78 |
| Gosselin, David | Nsh. | 2 | 13 | 2 | 1 | 3 | 11 | .... | .... | .... | .... | .... | .... | 1999-00 | 2001-02 |
| Gosselin, Guy | Wpg. | 1 | 5 | 0 | 0 | 0 | 6 | .... | .... | .... | .... | .... | .... | 1987-88 | 1987-88 |
| Gotaas, Steve | Pit., Min. | 3 | 49 | 6 | 9 | 15 | 53 | 3 | 0 | 1 | 1 | 5 | .... | 1987-88 | 1990-91 |
| • Gottselig, Johnny | Chi. | 16 | 589 | 176 | 195 | 371 | 203 | 43 | 13 | 13 | 26 | 18 | 2 | 1928-29 | 1944-45 |
| Gould, Bobby | Atl., Cgy., Wsh., Bos. | 11 | 697 | 145 | 159 | 304 | 572 | 78 | 15 | 13 | 28 | 58 | .... | 1979-80 | 1989-90 |
| Gould, John | Buf., Van., Atl. | 9 | 504 | 131 | 138 | 269 | 113 | 14 | 3 | 2 | 5 | 4 | .... | 1971-72 | 1979-80 |
| Gould, Larry | Van. | 1 | 2 | 0 | 0 | 0 | 0 | .... | .... | .... | .... | .... | .... | 1973-74 | 1973-74 |
| Goulet, Michel | Que., Chi. | 15 | 1089 | 548 | 604 | 1152 | 825 | 92 | 39 | 39 | 78 | 110 | .... | 1979-80 | 1993-94 |
| • Goupille, Red | Mtl. | 8 | 222 | 12 | 28 | 40 | 256 | 8 | 2 | 0 | 2 | 6 | .... | 1935-36 | 1942-43 |
| Govedaris, Chris | Hfd., Tor. | 4 | 45 | 4 | 6 | 10 | 24 | 4 | 0 | 0 | 0 | 2 | .... | 1989-90 | 1993-94 |
| Goyer, Gerry | Chi. | 1 | 40 | 1 | 2 | 3 | 4 | 3 | 0 | 0 | 0 | 2 | .... | 1967-68 | 1967-68 |
| Goyette, Phil | Mtl., NYR, St.L., Buf. | 16 | 941 | 207 | 467 | 674 | 131 | 94 | 17 | 29 | 46 | 26 | 4 | 1956-57 | 1971-72 |
| • Graboski, Tony | Mtl. | 3 | 66 | 6 | 10 | 16 | 24 | 3 | 0 | 0 | 0 | 6 | .... | 1940-41 | 1942-43 |
| • Gracie, Bob | Tor., Bos., NYA, Mtl.M., Mtl., Chi. | 9 | 379 | 82 | 109 | 191 | 205 | 33 | 4 | 7 | 11 | 4 | 2 | 1930-31 | 1938-39 |
| Gradin, Thomas | Van., Bos. | 9 | 677 | 209 | 384 | 593 | 298 | 42 | 17 | 25 | 42 | 20 | .... | 1978-79 | 1986-87 |
| Graham, Dirk | Min., Chi. | 12 | 772 | 219 | 270 | 489 | 917 | 90 | 17 | 27 | 44 | 92 | .... | 1983-84 | 1994-95 |
| • Graham, Leth | Ott., Ham. | 6 | 27 | 3 | 0 | 3 | 0 | 1 | 0 | 0 | 0 | 0 | 1 | 1920-21 | 1925-26 |
| Graham, Pat | Pit., Tor. | 3 | 103 | 11 | 17 | 28 | 136 | 4 | 0 | 0 | 0 | 2 | .... | 1981-82 | 1983-84 |
| Graham, Rod | Bos. | 1 | 14 | 2 | 1 | 3 | 7 | .... | .... | .... | .... | .... | .... | 1974-75 | 1974-75 |
| • Graham, Ted | Chi., Mtl.M., Det., St.L., Bos., NYA | 9 | 346 | 14 | 25 | 39 | 300 | 24 | 3 | 1 | 4 | 30 | .... | 1927-28 | 1936-37 |
| Granato, Tony | NYR, L.A., S.J. | 14 | 773 | 248 | 244 | 492 | 1425 | 79 | 16 | 27 | 43 | 141 | .... | 1988-89 | 2000-01 |
| ‡ Grand-Pierre, Jean-Luc | Buf., CBJ, Atl., Wsh. | 6 | 269 | 7 | 13 | 20 | 311 | 4 | 0 | 0 | 0 | 4 | .... | 1998-99 | 2003-04 |
| Grant, Danny | Mtl., Min., Det., L.A. | 13 | 736 | 263 | 273 | 536 | 239 | 43 | 10 | 14 | 24 | 19 | 1 | 1965-66 | 1978-79 |
| ‡ Gratton, Benoit | Wsh., Cgy., Mtl. | 6 | 58 | 6 | 10 | 16 | 58 | .... | .... | .... | .... | .... | .... | 1997-98 | 2003-04 |
| Gratton, Dan | L.A. | 1 | 7 | 1 | 0 | 1 | 5 | .... | .... | .... | .... | .... | .... | 1987-88 | 1987-88 |
| Gratton, Norm | NYR, Atl., Buf., Min. | 5 | 201 | 39 | 44 | 83 | 64 | 6 | 0 | 1 | 1 | 2 | .... | 1971-72 | 1975-76 |
| Gravelle, Leo | Mtl., Det. | 5 | 223 | 44 | 34 | 78 | 42 | 17 | 4 | 1 | 5 | 2 | .... | 1946-47 | 1950-51 |
| Graves, Adam | Det., Edm., NYR, S.J. | 16 | 1152 | 329 | 287 | 616 | 1224 | 125 | 38 | 27 | 65 | 119 | 2 | 1987-88 | 2002-03 |
| Graves, Hilliard | Cal., Atl., Van., Wpg. | 9 | 556 | 118 | 163 | 281 | 209 | 2 | 0 | 0 | 0 | 0 | .... | 1970-71 | 1979-80 |
| Graves, Steve | Edm. | 3 | 35 | 5 | 4 | 9 | 10 | .... | .... | .... | .... | .... | .... | 1983-84 | 1987-88 |
| • Gray, Alex | NYR, Tor. | 2 | 50 | 7 | 0 | 7 | 32 | 13 | 1 | 0 | 1 | 0 | 1 | 1927-28 | 1928-29 |
| Gray, Terry | Bos., Mtl., L.A., St.L. | 6 | 147 | 26 | 28 | 54 | 64 | 35 | 5 | 5 | 10 | 22 | .... | 1961-62 | 1970-71 |
| ‡ Green, Mike | Fla., NYR | 1 | 24 | 1 | 3 | 4 | 4 | .... | .... | .... | .... | .... | .... | 2003-04 | 2003-04 |
| • Green, Red | Ham., NYA, Bos., Det. | 6 | 195 | 59 | 26 | 85 | 290 | 1 | 0 | 0 | 0 | 0 | 1 | 1923-24 | 1928-29 |
| Green, Rick | Wsh., Mtl., Det., NYI | 15 | 845 | 43 | 220 | 263 | 588 | 100 | 3 | 16 | 19 | 73 | 1 | 1976-77 | 1991-92 |
| • Green, Shorty | Ham., NYA | 4 | 103 | 33 | 20 | 53 | 151 | .... | .... | .... | .... | .... | .... | 1923-24 | 1926-27 |
| Green, Ted | Bos. | 11 | 620 | 48 | 206 | 254 | 1029 | 31 | 4 | 8 | 12 | 54 | 1 | 1960-61 | 1971-72 |
| Green, Travis | NYI, Ana., Phx., Tor., Bos. | 14 | 970 | 193 | 262 | 455 | 764 | 56 | 10 | 11 | 21 | 60 | .... | 1992-93 | 2006-07 |
| Greenlaw, Jeff | Wsh., Fla. | 6 | 57 | 3 | 6 | 9 | 108 | 2 | 0 | 0 | 0 | 21 | .... | 1986-87 | 1993-94 |
| Gregg, Randy | Edm., Van. | 10 | 474 | 41 | 152 | 193 | 333 | 137 | 13 | 38 | 51 | 127 | 5 | 1981-82 | 1991-92 |
| • Greig, Bruce | Cal. | 2 | 9 | 0 | 1 | 1 | 46 | .... | .... | .... | .... | .... | .... | 1973-74 | 1974-75 |
| Greig, Mark | Hfd., Tor., Cgy., Phi. | 9 | 125 | 13 | 27 | 40 | 90 | 5 | 0 | 1 | 1 | 0 | .... | 1990-91 | 2002-03 |
| Grenier, Lucien | Mtl., L.A. | 4 | 151 | 14 | 14 | 28 | 18 | 2 | 0 | 0 | 0 | 0 | .... | 1968-69 | 1971-72 |
| ‡ Grenier, Martin | Phx., Van., Phi. | 4 | 18 | 1 | 0 | 1 | 14 | .... | .... | .... | .... | .... | .... | 2001-02 | 2006-07 |
| Grenier, Richard | NYI | 1 | 10 | 1 | 1 | 2 | 2 | .... | .... | .... | .... | .... | .... | 1972-73 | 1972-73 |
| Greschner, Ron | NYR | 16 | 982 | 179 | 431 | 610 | 1226 | 84 | 17 | 32 | 49 | 106 | .... | 1974-75 | 1989-90 |
| Gretzky, Brent | T.B. | 2 | 13 | 1 | 3 | 4 | 2 | .... | .... | .... | .... | .... | .... | 1993-94 | 1994-95 |
| Gretzky, Wayne | Edm., L.A., St.L., NYR | 20 | 1487 | 894 | 1963 | 2857 | 577 | 208 | 122 | 260 | 382 | 66 | 4 | 1979-80 | 1998-99 |
| Grieve, Brent | NYI, Edm., Chi., L.A. | 4 | 97 | 20 | 16 | 36 | 87 | .... | .... | .... | .... | .... | .... | 1993-94 | 1996-97 |
| • Grigor, George | Chi. | 1 | 2 | 1 | 0 | 1 | 0 | 1 | 0 | 0 | 0 | 0 | .... | 1943-44 | 1943-44 |
| Grimson, Stu | Cgy., Chi., Ana., Det., Hfd., Car., L.A., Nsh. | 14 | 729 | 17 | 22 | 39 | 2113 | 42 | 1 | 1 | 2 | 120 | .... | 1988-89 | 2001-02 |
| Grisdale, John | Tor., Van. | 6 | 250 | 4 | 39 | 43 | 346 | 10 | 0 | 1 | 1 | 15 | .... | 1972-73 | 1978-79 |
| ‡ Groleau, Francois | Mtl. | 3 | 8 | 0 | 1 | 1 | 6 | .... | .... | .... | .... | .... | .... | 1995-96 | 1997-98 |
| ‡ Gron, Stanislav | N.J. | 1 | 1 | 0 | 0 | 0 | 0 | .... | .... | .... | .... | .... | .... | 2000-01 | 2000-01 |
| Gronman, Tuomas | Chi., Pit. | 2 | 38 | 1 | 3 | 4 | 38 | 1 | 0 | 0 | 0 | 0 | .... | 1996-97 | 1997-98 |
| • Gronsdahl, Lloyd | Bos. | 1 | 10 | 1 | 2 | 3 | 0 | .... | .... | .... | .... | .... | .... | 1941-42 | 1941-42 |
| Gronstrand, Jari | Min., NYR, Que., NYI | 5 | 185 | 8 | 26 | 34 | 135 | 3 | 0 | 0 | 0 | 4 | .... | 1986-87 | 1990-91 |
| ‡ Grosek, Michal | Wpg., Buf., Chi., NYR, Bos. | 11 | 526 | 84 | 137 | 221 | 509 | 45 | 9 | 11 | 20 | 77 | .... | 1993-94 | 2003-04 |
| • Gross, Lloyd | Tor., NYA, Bos., Det. | 3 | 52 | 11 | 5 | 16 | 20 | 1 | 0 | 0 | 0 | 0 | .... | 1926-27 | 1934-35 |
| • Grosso, Don | Det., Chi., Bos. | 9 | 336 | 87 | 117 | 204 | 90 | 48 | 15 | 14 | 29 | 63 | 1 | 1938-39 | 1946-47 |
| • Grosvenor, Len | Ott., NYA, Mtl. | 6 | 149 | 9 | 11 | 20 | 78 | 4 | 0 | 0 | 0 | 2 | .... | 1927-28 | 1932-33 |
| Groulx, Wayne | Que. | 1 | 1 | 0 | 0 | 0 | 0 | .... | .... | .... | .... | .... | .... | 1984-85 | 1984-85 |
| Gruden, John | Bos., Ott., Wsh. | 6 | 92 | 1 | 8 | 9 | 46 | 3 | 0 | 1 | 1 | 0 | .... | 1993-94 | 2003-04 |
| Gruen, Danny | Det., Col. | 3 | 49 | 9 | 13 | 22 | 19 | .... | .... | .... | .... | .... | .... | 1972-73 | 1976-77 |
| Gruhl, Scott | L.A., Pit. | 3 | 20 | 3 | 3 | 6 | 6 | .... | .... | .... | .... | .... | .... | 1981-82 | 1987-88 |
| Gryp, Bob | Bos., Wsh. | 3 | 74 | 11 | 13 | 24 | 33 | .... | .... | .... | .... | .... | .... | 1973-74 | 1975-76 |
| Guay, Francois | Buf. | 1 | 1 | 0 | 0 | 0 | 0 | .... | .... | .... | .... | .... | .... | 1989-90 | 1989-90 |
| Guay, Paul | Phi., L.A., Bos., NYI | 7 | 117 | 11 | 23 | 34 | 92 | 9 | 0 | 1 | 1 | 12 | .... | 1983-84 | 1990-91 |
| Guerard, Daniel | Ott. | 1 | 2 | 0 | 0 | 0 | 0 | .... | .... | .... | .... | .... | .... | 1994-95 | 1994-95 |
| Guerard, Stephane | Que. | 2 | 34 | 0 | 0 | 0 | 40 | .... | .... | .... | .... | .... | .... | 1987-88 | 1989-90 |
| Guevremont, Jocelyn | Van., Buf., NYR | 9 | 571 | 84 | 223 | 307 | 319 | 40 | 4 | 17 | 21 | 18 | .... | 1971-72 | 1979-80 |
| Guidolin, Aldo | NYR | 4 | 182 | 9 | 15 | 24 | 117 | .... | .... | .... | .... | .... | .... | 1952-53 | 1955-56 |
| • Guidolin, Bep | Bos., Det., Chi. | 9 | 519 | 107 | 171 | 278 | 606 | 24 | 5 | 7 | 12 | 35 | .... | 1942-43 | 1951-52 |
| Guindon, Bobby | Wpg. | 1 | 6 | 0 | 1 | 1 | 0 | .... | .... | .... | .... | .... | .... | 1979-80 | 1979-80 |
| Guolla, Steve | S.J., T.B., Atl., N.J. | 6 | 205 | 40 | 46 | 86 | 60 | .... | .... | .... | .... | .... | .... | 1996-97 | 2002-03 |
| ‡ Guren, Miloslav | Mtl. | 2 | 36 | 1 | 3 | 4 | 16 | .... | .... | .... | .... | .... | .... | 1998-99 | 1999-00 |
| Gusarov, Alexei | Que., Col., NYR, St.L. | 11 | 607 | 39 | 128 | 167 | 313 | 68 | 0 | 14 | 14 | 38 | 1 | 1990-91 | 2000-01 |
| Gusev, Sergey | Dal., T.B. | 4 | 89 | 4 | 10 | 14 | 34 | .... | .... | .... | .... | .... | .... | 1997-98 | 2000-01 |
| ‡ Gusmanov, Ravil | Wpg. | 1 | 4 | 0 | 0 | 0 | 0 | .... | .... | .... | .... | .... | .... | 1995-96 | 1995-96 |
| Gustafsson, Bengt-Ake | Wsh. | 9 | 629 | 196 | 359 | 555 | 196 | 32 | 9 | 19 | 28 | 16 | .... | 1979-80 | 1988-89 |
| ‡ Gustafsson, Per | Fla., Tor., Ott. | 2 | 89 | 8 | 27 | 35 | 38 | 1 | 0 | 0 | 0 | 0 | .... | 1996-97 | 1997-98 |
| Gustavsson, Peter | Col. | 1 | 2 | 0 | 0 | 0 | 0 | .... | .... | .... | .... | .... | .... | 1981-82 | 1981-82 |

| Name | NHL Teams | NHL Seasons | Regular Schedule | | | | | Playoffs | | | | | NHL Cup Wins | First NHL Season | Last NHL Season |
|---|---|---|---|---|---|---|---|---|---|---|---|---|---|---|---|
| | | | GP | G | A | TP | PIM | GP | G | A | TP | PIM | | | |
| Guy, Kevan | Cgy., Van. | 6 | 156 | 5 | 20 | 25 | 138 | 5 | 0 | 1 | 1 | 23 | .... | 1986-87 | 1991-92 |

## H

| Name | NHL Teams | NHL Seasons | GP | G | A | TP | PIM | GP | G | A | TP | PIM | NHL Cup Wins | First NHL Season | Last NHL Season |
|---|---|---|---|---|---|---|---|---|---|---|---|---|---|---|---|
| ‡ Haakana, Kari | Edm. | 1 | 13 | 0 | 0 | 0 | 4 | .... | .... | .... | .... | .... | .... | 2002-03 | 2002-03 |
| Haanpaa, Ari | NYI | 3 | 60 | 6 | 11 | 17 | 37 | 6 | 0 | 0 | 0 | 10 | .... | 1985-86 | 1987-88 |
| Haas, David | Edm., Cgy. | 2 | 7 | 2 | 1 | 3 | 7 | .... | .... | .... | .... | .... | .... | 1990-91 | 1993-94 |
| Habscheid, Marc | Edm., Min., Det., Cgy. | 11 | 345 | 72 | 91 | 163 | 171 | 12 | 1 | 3 | 4 | 13 | .... | 1981-82 | 1991-92 |
| Hachborn, Len | Phi., L.A. | 3 | 102 | 20 | 39 | 59 | 29 | 7 | 0 | 3 | 3 | 7 | .... | 1983-84 | 1985-86 |
| Haddon, Lloyd | Det. | 1 | 8 | 0 | 0 | 0 | 2 | 1 | 0 | 0 | 0 | 0 | .... | 1959-60 | 1959-60 |
| Hadfield, Vic | NYR, Pit. | 16 | 1002 | 323 | 389 | 712 | 1154 | 73 | 27 | 21 | 48 | 117 | .... | 1961-62 | 1976-77 |
| • Haggarty, Jim | Mtl. | 1 | 5 | 1 | 1 | 2 | 0 | 3 | 2 | 1 | 3 | 0 | .... | 1941-42 | 1941-42 |
| Haggerty, Sean | Tor., NYI, Nsh. | 4 | 14 | 1 | 2 | 3 | 4 | .... | .... | .... | .... | .... | .... | 1995-96 | 2000-01 |
| • Hagglund, Roger | Que. | 1 | 3 | 0 | 0 | 0 | 0 | .... | .... | .... | .... | .... | .... | 1984-85 | 1984-85 |
| Hagman, Matti | Bos., Edm. | 4 | 237 | 56 | 89 | 145 | 36 | 20 | 5 | 2 | 7 | 6 | .... | 1976-77 | 1981-82 |
| ‡ Hahl, Riku | Col. | 3 | 92 | 5 | 8 | 13 | 38 | 34 | 2 | 4 | 6 | 4 | .... | 2001-02 | 2003-04 |
| • Haidy, Gord | Det. | 1 | .... | .... | .... | .... | .... | 1 | 0 | 0 | 0 | 0 | .... | 1949-50 | 1949-50 |
| Hajdu, Richard | Buf. | 2 | 5 | 0 | 0 | 0 | 4 | .... | .... | .... | .... | .... | .... | 1985-86 | 1986-87 |
| Hajt, Bill | Buf. | 14 | 854 | 42 | 202 | 244 | 433 | 80 | 2 | 16 | 18 | 70 | .... | 1973-74 | 1986-87 |
| Hajt, Chris | Edm., Wsh. | 2 | 6 | 0 | 0 | 0 | 2 | .... | .... | .... | .... | .... | .... | 2000-01 | 2003-04 |
| Hakansson, Anders | Min., Pit., L.A. | 5 | 330 | 52 | 46 | 98 | 141 | 6 | 0 | 0 | 0 | 2 | .... | 1981-82 | 1985-86 |
| • Halderson, Harold | Det., Tor. | 1 | 44 | 3 | 2 | 5 | 65 | .... | .... | .... | .... | .... | .... | 1926-27 | 1926-27 |
| Hale, Larry | Phi. | 4 | 196 | 5 | 37 | 42 | 90 | 8 | 0 | 0 | 0 | 12 | .... | 1968-69 | 1971-72 |
| Haley, Len | Det. | 2 | 30 | 2 | 2 | 4 | 14 | 6 | 1 | 3 | 4 | 6 | .... | 1959-60 | 1960-61 |
| Halkidis, Bob | Buf., L.A., Tor., Det., T.B., NYI | 11 | 256 | 8 | 32 | 40 | 825 | 20 | 0 | 1 | 1 | 51 | .... | 1984-85 | 1995-96 |
| Halko, Steven | Car. | 6 | 155 | 0 | 15 | 15 | 71 | 4 | 0 | 0 | 0 | 2 | .... | 1997-98 | 2002-03 |
| • Hall, Bob | NYA | 1 | 8 | 0 | 0 | 0 | 0 | .... | .... | .... | .... | .... | .... | 1925-26 | 1925-26 |
| Hall, Del | Cal. | 3 | 9 | 2 | 0 | 2 | 2 | .... | .... | .... | .... | .... | .... | 1971-72 | 1973-74 |
| • Hall, Joe | Mtl. | 2 | 37 | 15 | 9 | 24 | 235 | 7 | 0 | 1 | 1 | 38 | .... | 1917-18 | 1918-19 |
| Hall, Murray | Chi., Det., Min., Van. | 9 | 164 | 35 | 48 | 83 | 46 | 6 | 0 | 0 | 0 | 0 | .... | 1961-62 | 1971-72 |
| Hall, Taylor | Van., Bos. | 5 | 41 | 7 | 9 | 16 | 29 | .... | .... | .... | .... | .... | .... | 1983-84 | 1987-88 |
| Hall, Wayne | NYR | 1 | 4 | 0 | 0 | 0 | 0 | .... | .... | .... | .... | .... | .... | 1960-61 | 1960-61 |
| Haller, Kevin | Buf., Mtl., Phi., Hfd., Car., Ana., NYI | 13 | 642 | 41 | 97 | 138 | 907 | 64 | 7 | 16 | 23 | 71 | 1 | 1989-90 | 2001-02 |
| • Halliday, Milt | Ott. | 3 | 67 | 1 | 0 | 1 | 4 | 6 | 0 | 0 | 0 | 0 | 1 | 1926-27 | 1928-29 |
| Hallin, Mats | NYI, Min. | 5 | 152 | 17 | 14 | 31 | 193 | 15 | 1 | 0 | 1 | 13 | 1 | 1982-83 | 1986-87 |
| Halverson, Trevor | Wsh. | 1 | 17 | 0 | 4 | 4 | 28 | .... | .... | .... | .... | .... | .... | 1998-99 | 1998-99 |
| Halward, Doug | Bos., L.A., Van., Det., Edm. | 14 | 653 | 69 | 224 | 293 | 774 | 47 | 7 | 10 | 17 | 113 | .... | 1975-76 | 1988-89 |
| Hamel, Gilles | Buf., Wpg., L.A. | 9 | 519 | 127 | 147 | 274 | 276 | 27 | 4 | 5 | 9 | 10 | .... | 1980-81 | 1988-89 |
| • Hamel, Herb | Tor. | 1 | 2 | 0 | 0 | 0 | 4 | .... | .... | .... | .... | .... | .... | 1930-31 | 1930-31 |
| Hamel, Jean | St.L., Det., Que., Mtl. | 12 | 699 | 26 | 95 | 121 | 766 | 33 | 0 | 2 | 2 | 44 | .... | 1972-73 | 1983-84 |
| • Hamill, Red | Bos., Chi. | 12 | 419 | 128 | 94 | 222 | 160 | 24 | 1 | 2 | 3 | 20 | 1 | 1937-38 | 1950-51 |
| Hamilton, Al | NYR, Buf., Edm. | 7 | 257 | 10 | 78 | 88 | 258 | 7 | 0 | 0 | 0 | 2 | .... | 1965-66 | 1979-80 |
| Hamilton, Chuck | Mtl., St.L. | 2 | 4 | 0 | 2 | 2 | 2 | .... | .... | .... | .... | .... | .... | 1961-62 | 1972-73 |
| • Hamilton, Jack | Tor. | 3 | 102 | 28 | 32 | 60 | 20 | 11 | 2 | 1 | 3 | 0 | .... | 1942-43 | 1945-46 |
| Hamilton, Jim | Pit. | 8 | 95 | 14 | 18 | 32 | 28 | 6 | 3 | 0 | 3 | 0 | .... | 1977-78 | 1984-85 |
| • Hamilton, Reg | Tor., Chi. | 12 | 424 | 21 | 87 | 108 | 412 | 64 | 3 | 8 | 11 | 46 | 2 | 1935-36 | 1946-47 |
| Hammarstrom, Inge | Tor., St.L. | 6 | 427 | 116 | 123 | 239 | 86 | 13 | 2 | 3 | 5 | 4 | .... | 1973-74 | 1978-79 |
| Hammond, Ken | L.A., Edm., NYR, Tor., Bos., S.J., Van., Ott. | 8 | 193 | 18 | 29 | 47 | 290 | 15 | 0 | 0 | 0 | 24 | .... | 1984-85 | 1992-93 |
| Hampson, Gord | Cgy. | 1 | 4 | 0 | 0 | 0 | 5 | .... | .... | .... | .... | .... | .... | 1982-83 | 1982-83 |
| Hampson, Ted | Tor., NYR, Det., Oak., Cal., Min. | 14 | 676 | 108 | 245 | 353 | 94 | 35 | 7 | 10 | 17 | 2 | .... | 1959-60 | 1971-72 |
| Hampton, Rick | Cal., Cle., L.A. | 6 | 337 | 59 | 113 | 172 | 147 | 2 | 0 | 0 | 0 | 0 | .... | 1974-75 | 1979-80 |
| ‡ Hamr, Radek | Ott. | 2 | 11 | 0 | 0 | 0 | 0 | .... | .... | .... | .... | .... | .... | 1992-93 | 1993-94 |
| Hamway, Mark | NYI | 3 | 53 | 5 | 13 | 18 | 9 | 1 | 0 | 0 | 0 | 0 | .... | 1984-85 | 1986-87 |
| Handy, Ron | NYI, St.L. | 2 | 14 | 0 | 3 | 3 | 0 | .... | .... | .... | .... | .... | .... | 1984-85 | 1987-88 |
| Hangsleben, Al | Hfd., Wsh., L.A. | 3 | 185 | 21 | 48 | 69 | 396 | .... | .... | .... | .... | .... | .... | 1979-80 | 1981-82 |
| Hankinson, Ben | N.J., T.B. | 3 | 43 | 3 | 3 | 6 | 45 | 2 | 1 | 0 | 1 | 4 | .... | 1992-93 | 1994-95 |
| Hankinson, Casey | Chi., Ana. | 3 | 18 | 0 | 1 | 1 | 13 | .... | .... | .... | .... | .... | .... | 2000-01 | 2003-04 |
| • Hanna, John | NYR, Mtl., Phi. | 5 | 198 | 6 | 26 | 32 | 206 | .... | .... | .... | .... | .... | .... | 1958-59 | 1967-68 |
| Hannan, Dave | Pit., Edm., Tor., Buf., Col., Ott. | 16 | 841 | 114 | 191 | 305 | 942 | 63 | 6 | 7 | 13 | 46 | 2 | 1981-82 | 1996-97 |
| • Hannigan, Gord | Tor. | 4 | 161 | 29 | 31 | 60 | 117 | 9 | 2 | 0 | 2 | 8 | .... | 1952-53 | 1955-56 |
| • Hannigan, Pat | Tor., NYR, Phi. | 5 | 182 | 30 | 39 | 69 | 116 | 11 | 1 | 2 | 3 | 11 | .... | 1959-60 | 1968-69 |
| Hannigan, Ray | Tor. | 1 | 3 | 0 | 0 | 0 | 2 | .... | .... | .... | .... | .... | .... | 1948-49 | 1948-49 |
| Hansen, Richie | NYI, St.L. | 4 | 20 | 2 | 8 | 10 | 4 | .... | .... | .... | .... | .... | .... | 1976-77 | 1981-82 |
| Hansen, Tavis | Wpg., Phx. | 5 | 34 | 2 | 1 | 3 | 16 | 2 | 0 | 0 | 0 | 0 | .... | 1994-95 | 2000-01 |
| Hanson, Dave | Det., Min. | 2 | 33 | 1 | 1 | 2 | 65 | .... | .... | .... | .... | .... | .... | 1978-79 | 1979-80 |
| • Hanson, Emil | Det. | 1 | 7 | 0 | 0 | 0 | 6 | .... | .... | .... | .... | .... | .... | 1932-33 | 1932-33 |
| Hanson, Keith | Cgy. | 1 | 25 | 0 | 2 | 2 | 77 | .... | .... | .... | .... | .... | .... | 1983-84 | 1983-84 |
| • Hanson, Oscar | Chi. | 1 | 8 | 0 | 0 | 0 | 0 | .... | .... | .... | .... | .... | .... | 1937-38 | 1937-38 |
| Harbaruk, Nick | Pit., St.L. | 5 | 364 | 45 | 75 | 120 | 273 | 14 | 3 | 1 | 4 | 20 | .... | 1969-70 | 1973-74 |
| Harding, Jeff | Phi. | 2 | 15 | 0 | 0 | 0 | 47 | .... | .... | .... | .... | .... | .... | 1988-89 | 1989-90 |
| Hardy, Joe | Oak., Cal. | 2 | 63 | 9 | 14 | 23 | 51 | 4 | 0 | 0 | 0 | 0 | .... | 1969-70 | 1970-71 |
| Hardy, Mark | L.A., NYR, Min. | 15 | 915 | 62 | 306 | 368 | 1293 | 67 | 5 | 16 | 21 | 158 | .... | 1979-80 | 1993-94 |
| Hargreaves, Jim | Van. | 2 | 66 | 1 | 7 | 8 | 105 | .... | .... | .... | .... | .... | .... | 1970-71 | 1972-73 |
| Harkins, Brett | Bos., Fla., CBJ | 4 | 78 | 6 | 30 | 36 | 22 | .... | .... | .... | .... | .... | .... | 1994-95 | 2001-02 |
| Harkins, Todd | Cgy., Hfd. | 3 | 48 | 3 | 3 | 6 | 78 | .... | .... | .... | .... | .... | .... | 1991-92 | 1993-94 |
| Harlock, David | Tor., Wsh., NYI, Atl. | 8 | 212 | 2 | 14 | 16 | 188 | .... | .... | .... | .... | .... | .... | 1993-94 | 2001-02 |
| Harlow, Scott | St.L. | 1 | 1 | 0 | 1 | 1 | 0 | .... | .... | .... | .... | .... | .... | 1987-88 | 1987-88 |
| • Harmon, Glen | Mtl. | 9 | 452 | 50 | 96 | 146 | 334 | 53 | 5 | 10 | 15 | 37 | 2 | 1942-43 | 1950-51 |
| • Harms, John | Chi. | 2 | 44 | 5 | 5 | 10 | 21 | 4 | 3 | 0 | 3 | 2 | .... | 1943-44 | 1944-45 |
| • Harnott, Walter | Bos. | 1 | 6 | 0 | 0 | 0 | 2 | .... | .... | .... | .... | .... | .... | 1933-34 | 1933-34 |
| Harper, Terry | Mtl., L.A., Det., St.L., Col. | 19 | 1066 | 35 | 221 | 256 | 1362 | 112 | 4 | 13 | 17 | 140 | 5 | 1962-63 | 1980-81 |
| Harrer, Tim | Cgy. | 1 | 3 | 0 | 0 | 0 | 2 | .... | .... | .... | .... | .... | .... | 1982-83 | 1982-83 |
| • Harrington, Hago | Bos., Mtl. | 3 | 72 | 9 | 3 | 12 | 15 | 4 | 1 | 0 | 1 | 2 | .... | 1925-26 | 1932-33 |
| • Harris, Billy | Tor., Det., Oak., Pit. | 13 | 769 | 126 | 219 | 345 | 205 | 62 | 8 | 10 | 18 | 30 | 3 | 1955-56 | 1968-69 |
| Harris, Billy | NYI, L.A., Tor. | 12 | 897 | 231 | 327 | 558 | 394 | 71 | 19 | 19 | 38 | 48 | .... | 1972-73 | 1983-84 |
| Harris, Duke | Min., Tor. | 1 | 26 | 1 | 4 | 5 | 4 | .... | .... | .... | .... | .... | .... | 1967-68 | 1967-68 |
| • Harris, Henry | Bos. | 1 | 32 | 2 | 4 | 6 | 20 | .... | .... | .... | .... | .... | .... | 1930-31 | 1930-31 |
| Harris, Hugh | Buf. | 1 | 60 | 12 | 26 | 38 | 17 | 3 | 0 | 0 | 0 | 0 | .... | 1972-73 | 1972-73 |
| Harris, Ron | Det., Oak., Atl., NYR | 11 | 476 | 20 | 91 | 111 | 474 | 28 | 4 | 3 | 7 | 33 | .... | 1962-63 | 1975-76 |
| • Harris, Smokey | Bos. | 1 | 6 | 3 | 1 | 4 | 8 | .... | .... | .... | .... | .... | .... | 1924-25 | 1924-25 |
| Harris, Ted | Mtl., Min., Det., St.L., Phi. | 12 | 788 | 30 | 168 | 198 | 1000 | 100 | 1 | 22 | 23 | 230 | 5 | 1963-64 | 1974-75 |
| Harrison, Ed | Bos., NYR | 4 | 194 | 27 | 24 | 51 | 53 | 9 | 1 | 0 | 1 | 2 | .... | 1947-48 | 1950-51 |
| Harrison, Jim | Bos., Tor., Chi., Edm. | 8 | 324 | 67 | 86 | 153 | 435 | 13 | 1 | 1 | 2 | 43 | .... | 1968-69 | 1979-80 |
| Hart, Gerry | Det., NYI, Que., St.L. | 15 | 730 | 29 | 150 | 179 | 1240 | 78 | 3 | 12 | 15 | 175 | .... | 1968-69 | 1982-83 |
| • Hart, Gizzy | Det., Mtl. | 3 | 104 | 6 | 8 | 14 | 12 | 8 | 0 | 1 | 1 | 0 | .... | 1926-27 | 1932-33 |
| Hartman, Mike | Buf., Wpg., T.B., NYR | 9 | 397 | 43 | 35 | 78 | 1388 | 21 | 0 | 0 | 0 | 106 | 1 | 1986-87 | 1994-95 |
| Hartsburg, Craig | Min. | 10 | 570 | 98 | 315 | 413 | 818 | 61 | 15 | 27 | 42 | 70 | .... | 1979-80 | 1988-89 |
| • Harvey, Buster | Min., Atl., K.C., Det. | 7 | 407 | 90 | 118 | 208 | 131 | 14 | 0 | 2 | 2 | 8 | .... | 1970-71 | 1976-77 |
| • Harvey, Doug | Mtl., NYR, Det., St.L. | 20 | 1113 | 88 | 452 | 540 | 1216 | 137 | 8 | 64 | 72 | 152 | 6 | 1947-48 | 1968-69 |
| Harvey, Hugh | K.C. | 2 | 18 | 1 | 1 | 2 | 4 | .... | .... | .... | .... | .... | .... | 1974-75 | 1975-76 |
| Harvey, Todd | Dal., NYR, S.J., Edm. | 11 | 671 | 91 | 132 | 223 | 950 | 68 | 3 | 6 | 9 | 52 | .... | 1994-95 | 2005-06 |
| Hassard, Bob | Tor., Chi. | 5 | 126 | 9 | 28 | 37 | 22 | .... | .... | .... | .... | .... | 1 | 1949-50 | 1954-55 |
| Hatcher, Derian | Min., Dal., Det., Phi. | 16 | 1045 | 80 | 251 | 331 | 1581 | 133 | 7 | 26 | 33 | 248 | 1 | 1991-92 | 2007-08 |
| Hatcher, Kevin | Wsh., Dal., Pit., NYR, Car. | 17 | 1157 | 227 | 450 | 677 | 1392 | 118 | 22 | 37 | 59 | 252 | .... | 1984-85 | 2000-01 |
| Hatoum, Ed | Det., Van. | 3 | 47 | 3 | 6 | 9 | 25 | .... | .... | .... | .... | .... | .... | 1968-69 | 1970-71 |
| ‡ Hauer, Brett | Edm., Nsh. | 3 | 37 | 4 | 4 | 8 | 38 | .... | .... | .... | .... | .... | .... | 1995-96 | 2001-02 |
| Hawerchuk, Dale | Wpg., Buf., St.L., Phi. | 16 | 1188 | 518 | 891 | 1409 | 730 | 97 | 30 | 69 | 99 | 67 | .... | 1981-82 | 1996-97 |
| Hawgood, Greg | Bos., Edm., Phi., Fla., Pit., S.J., Van., Dal. | 12 | 474 | 60 | 164 | 224 | 426 | 42 | 2 | 8 | 10 | 37 | .... | 1987-88 | 2001-02 |
| Hawkins, Todd | Van., Tor. | 3 | 10 | 0 | 0 | 0 | 15 | .... | .... | .... | .... | .... | .... | 1988-89 | 1991-92 |
| Haworth, Alan | Buf., Wsh., Que. | 8 | 524 | 189 | 211 | 400 | 425 | 42 | 12 | 16 | 28 | 28 | .... | 1980-81 | 1987-88 |
| Haworth, Gord | NYR | 1 | 2 | 0 | 1 | 1 | 0 | .... | .... | .... | .... | .... | .... | 1952-53 | 1952-53 |
| Hawryliw, Neil | NYI | 1 | 1 | 0 | 0 | 0 | 0 | .... | .... | .... | .... | .... | .... | 1981-82 | 1981-82 |
| Hay, Bill | Chi. | 8 | 506 | 113 | 273 | 386 | 244 | 67 | 15 | 21 | 36 | 62 | 1 | 1959-60 | 1966-67 |
| Hay, Dwayne | Wsh., Fla., T.B., Cgy. | 4 | 79 | 2 | 4 | 6 | 22 | .... | .... | .... | .... | .... | .... | 1997-98 | 2000-01 |
| • Hay, George | Chi., Det. | 7 | 239 | 74 | 60 | 134 | 84 | 8 | 2 | 3 | 5 | 2 | .... | 1926-27 | 1933-34 |
| Hay, Jim | Det. | 3 | 75 | 1 | 5 | 6 | 22 | 9 | 1 | 0 | 1 | 2 | 1 | 1952-53 | 1954-55 |
| Hayek, Peter | Min. | 1 | 1 | 0 | 0 | 0 | 0 | .... | .... | .... | .... | .... | .... | 1981-82 | 1981-82 |
| Hayes, Chris | Bos. | 1 | .... | .... | .... | .... | .... | 1 | 0 | 0 | 0 | 0 | .... | 1971-72 | 1971-72 |
| • Haynes, Paul | Mtl.M., Bos., Mtl. | 11 | 391 | 61 | 134 | 195 | 164 | 24 | 2 | 8 | 10 | 13 | .... | 1930-31 | 1940-41 |
| Hayward, Rick | L.A. | 1 | 4 | 0 | 0 | 0 | 5 | .... | .... | .... | .... | .... | .... | 1990-91 | 1990-91 |
| Hazlett, Steve | Van. | 1 | 1 | 0 | 0 | 0 | 0 | .... | .... | .... | .... | .... | .... | 1979-80 | 1979-80 |
| Head, Galen | Det. | 1 | 1 | 0 | 0 | 0 | 0 | .... | .... | .... | .... | .... | .... | 1967-68 | 1967-68 |
| • Headley, Fern | Bos., Mtl. | 1 | 30 | 1 | 3 | 4 | 10 | 1 | 0 | 0 | 0 | 0 | .... | 1924-25 | 1924-25 |
| ‡ Healey, Eric | Bos. | 1 | 2 | 0 | 0 | 0 | 2 | .... | .... | .... | .... | .... | .... | 2005-06 | 2005-06 |

Jocelyn Guevremont

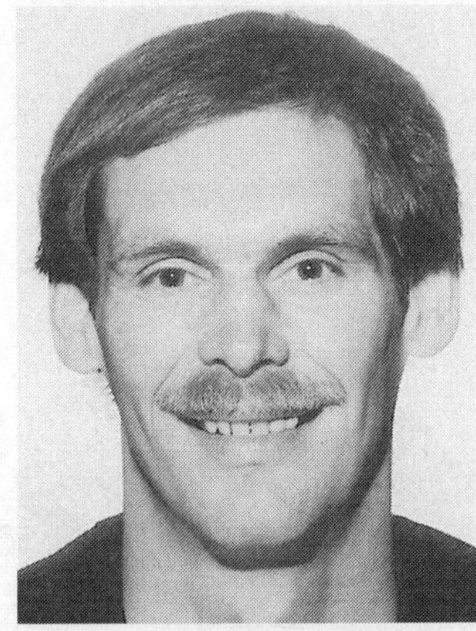

Bill Hajt

Steven Halko

Pat Hannigan

Ott Heller

Lorne Henning

Mel Hill

Chuck Holmes

| | | | Regular Schedule | | | | | Playoffs | | | | | | | |
|---|---|---|---|---|---|---|---|---|---|---|---|---|---|---|---|
| Name | NHL Teams | NHL Seasons | GP | G | A | TP | PIM | GP | G | A | TP | PIM | NHL Cup Wins | First NHL Season | Last NHL Season |
| ‡ Healey, Paul | Phi., Tor., NYR, Col. | 6 | 77 | 6 | 14 | 20 | 44 | 22 | 0 | 2 | 2 | 4 | .... | 1996-97 | 2005-06 |
| Healey, Rich | Det. | 1 | 1 | 0 | 0 | 0 | 2 | .... | .... | .... | .... | .... | .... | 1960-61 | 1960-61 |
| Heaphy, Shawn | Cgy. | 1 | 1 | 0 | 0 | 0 | 0 | .... | .... | .... | .... | .... | .... | 1992-93 | 1992-93 |
| Heaslip, Mark | NYR, L.A. | 3 | 117 | 10 | 19 | 29 | 110 | 5 | 0 | 0 | 0 | 2 | .... | 1976-77 | 1978-79 |
| Heath, Randy | NYR | 2 | 13 | 2 | 4 | 6 | 15 | .... | .... | .... | .... | .... | .... | 1984-85 | 1985-86 |
| Hebenton, Andy | NYR, Bos. | 9 | 630 | 189 | 202 | 391 | 83 | 22 | 6 | 5 | 11 | 8 | .... | 1955-56 | 1963-64 |
| Hecl, Radoslav | Buf. | 1 | 14 | 0 | 0 | 0 | 2 | .... | .... | .... | .... | .... | .... | 2002-03 | 2002-03 |
| Hedberg, Anders | NYR | 7 | 465 | 172 | 225 | 397 | 144 | 58 | 22 | 24 | 46 | 31 | .... | 1978-79 | 1984-85 |
| ‡ Hedin, Pierre | Tor. | 1 | 3 | 0 | 1 | 1 | 0 | .... | .... | .... | .... | .... | .... | 2003-04 | 2003-04 |
| ‡ Hedstrom, Jonathan | Ana. | 2 | 83 | 13 | 14 | 27 | 48 | 3 | 0 | 1 | 1 | 2 | .... | 2002-03 | 2005-06 |
| ‡ Heerema, Jeff | Car., St.L. | 2 | 32 | 4 | 2 | 6 | 6 | .... | .... | .... | .... | .... | .... | 2002-03 | 2003-04 |
| • Heffernan, Frank | Tor. | 1 | 19 | 0 | 1 | 1 | 10 | .... | .... | .... | .... | .... | .... | 1919-20 | 1919-20 |
| • Heffernan, Gerry | Mtl. | 3 | 83 | 33 | 35 | 68 | 27 | 11 | 3 | 3 | 6 | 8 | 1 | 1941-42 | 1943-44 |
| Heidt, Mike | L.A. | 1 | 6 | 0 | 1 | 1 | 7 | .... | .... | .... | .... | .... | .... | 1983-84 | 1983-84 |
| • Heindl, Bill | Min., NYR | 3 | 18 | 2 | 1 | 3 | 0 | .... | .... | .... | .... | .... | .... | 1970-71 | 1972-73 |
| Heinrich, Lionel | Bos. | 1 | 35 | 1 | 1 | 2 | 33 | .... | .... | .... | .... | .... | .... | 1955-56 | 1955-56 |
| ‡ Heins, Shawn | S.J., Pit., Atl. | 6 | 125 | 4 | 12 | 16 | 154 | 2 | 0 | 0 | 0 | 0 | .... | 1998-99 | 2003-04 |
| Heinze, Steve | Bos., CBJ, Buf., L.A. | 12 | 694 | 178 | 158 | 336 | 379 | 69 | 11 | 15 | 26 | 48 | .... | 1991-92 | 2002-03 |
| Heiskala, Earl | Phi. | 3 | 127 | 13 | 11 | 24 | 294 | .... | .... | .... | .... | .... | .... | 1968-69 | 1970-71 |
| ‡ Heisten, Barrett | NYR | 1 | 10 | 0 | 0 | 0 | 2 | .... | .... | .... | .... | .... | .... | 2001-02 | 2001-02 |
| Helander, Peter | L.A. | 1 | 7 | 0 | 1 | 1 | 0 | .... | .... | .... | .... | .... | .... | 1982-83 | 1982-83 |
| ‡ Helbling, Timo | T.B., Wsh. | 2 | 11 | 0 | 1 | 1 | 8 | .... | .... | .... | .... | .... | .... | 2005-06 | 2006-07 |
| ‡ Helenius, Sami | Cgy., T.B., Col., Dal., Chi. | 6 | 155 | 2 | 4 | 6 | 260 | 1 | 0 | 0 | 0 | 0 | .... | 1996-97 | 2002-03 |
| • Heller, Ott | NYR | 15 | 647 | 55 | 176 | 231 | 465 | 61 | 6 | 8 | 14 | 61 | 2 | 1931-32 | 1945-46 |
| • Helman, Harry | Ott. | 3 | 44 | 1 | 0 | 1 | 7 | 2 | 0 | 0 | 0 | 0 | 1 | 1922-23 | 1924-25 |
| ‡ Helminen, Raimo | NYR, Min., NYI | 3 | 117 | 13 | 46 | 59 | 16 | 2 | 0 | 0 | 0 | 0 | .... | 1985-86 | 1988-89 |
| Hemingway, Colin | St.L. | 1 | 3 | 0 | 0 | 0 | 0 | .... | .... | .... | .... | .... | .... | 2005-06 | 2005-06 |
| • Hemmerling, Tony | NYA | 2 | 22 | 3 | 3 | 6 | 4 | .... | .... | .... | .... | .... | .... | 1935-36 | 1936-37 |
| Henderson, Archie | Wsh., Min., Hfd. | 3 | 23 | 3 | 1 | 4 | 92 | .... | .... | .... | .... | .... | .... | 1980-81 | 1982-83 |
| ‡ Henderson, Jay | Bos. | 4 | 33 | 1 | 3 | 4 | 37 | .... | .... | .... | .... | .... | .... | 1998-99 | 2001-02 |
| Henderson, Matt | Nsh., Chi. | 2 | 6 | 0 | 1 | 1 | 2 | .... | .... | .... | .... | .... | .... | 1998-99 | 2001-02 |
| Henderson, Murray | Bos. | 8 | 405 | 24 | 62 | 86 | 305 | 41 | 2 | 3 | 5 | 23 | .... | 1944-45 | 1951-52 |
| Henderson, Paul | Det., Tor., Atl. | 13 | 707 | 236 | 241 | 477 | 304 | 56 | 11 | 14 | 25 | 28 | .... | 1962-63 | 1979-80 |
| Hendrickson, Darby | Tor., NYI, Van., Min., Col. | 11 | 518 | 65 | 64 | 129 | 370 | 25 | 3 | 3 | 6 | 6 | .... | 1993-94 | 2003-04 |
| Hendrickson, John | Det. | 3 | 5 | 0 | 0 | 0 | 4 | .... | .... | .... | .... | .... | .... | 1957-58 | 1961-62 |
| Henning, Lorne | NYI | 9 | 543 | 73 | 111 | 184 | 102 | 81 | 7 | 7 | 14 | 8 | 2 | 1972-73 | 1980-81 |
| Henry, Burke | Chi. | 2 | 39 | 2 | 6 | 8 | 33 | .... | .... | .... | .... | .... | .... | 2002-03 | 2003-04 |
| • Henry, Camille | NYR, Chi., St.L. | 14 | 727 | 279 | 249 | 528 | 88 | 47 | 6 | 12 | 18 | 7 | .... | 1953-54 | 1969-70 |
| Henry, Dale | NYI | 6 | 132 | 13 | 26 | 39 | 263 | 14 | 1 | 0 | 1 | 19 | .... | 1984-85 | 1989-90 |
| ‡ Hentunen, Jukka | Cgy., Nsh. | 1 | 38 | 4 | 5 | 9 | 4 | .... | .... | .... | .... | .... | .... | 2001-02 | 2001-02 |
| Hepple, Alan | N.J. | 3 | 3 | 0 | 0 | 0 | 7 | .... | .... | .... | .... | .... | .... | 1983-84 | 1985-86 |
| Herbers, Ian | Edm., T.B., NYI | 2 | 65 | 0 | 5 | 5 | 79 | .... | .... | .... | .... | .... | .... | 1993-94 | 1999-00 |
| • Herberts, Jimmy | Bos., Tor., Det. | 6 | 206 | 83 | 31 | 114 | 253 | 9 | 3 | 0 | 3 | 10 | .... | 1924-25 | 1929-30 |
| • Herchenratter, Art | Det. | 1 | 10 | 1 | 2 | 3 | 2 | .... | .... | .... | .... | .... | .... | 1940-41 | 1940-41 |
| Hergerts, Fred | NYA | 2 | 20 | 2 | 4 | 6 | 2 | .... | .... | .... | .... | .... | .... | 1934-35 | 1935-36 |
| • Hergesheimer, Phil | Chi., Bos. | 4 | 125 | 21 | 41 | 62 | 19 | 6 | 0 | 0 | 0 | 2 | .... | 1939-40 | 1942-43 |
| Hergesheimer, Wally | NYR, Chi. | 7 | 351 | 114 | 85 | 199 | 106 | 5 | 1 | 0 | 1 | 0 | .... | 1951-52 | 1958-59 |
| • Heron, Red | Tor., Bro., Mtl. | 4 | 106 | 21 | 19 | 40 | 38 | 21 | 2 | 2 | 4 | 6 | .... | 1938-39 | 1941-42 |
| Heroux, Yves | Que. | 1 | 1 | 0 | 0 | 0 | 0 | .... | .... | .... | .... | .... | .... | 1986-87 | 1986-87 |
| ‡ Herperger, Chris | Chi., Ott., Atl. | 4 | 169 | 18 | 25 | 43 | 75 | .... | .... | .... | .... | .... | .... | 1999-00 | 2002-03 |
| Herr, Matt | Wsh., Fla., Bos. | 4 | 58 | 4 | 5 | 9 | 25 | .... | .... | .... | .... | .... | .... | 1998-99 | 2002-03 |
| Herter, Jason | NYI | 1 | 1 | 0 | 1 | 1 | 0 | .... | .... | .... | .... | .... | .... | 1995-96 | 1995-96 |
| Hervey, Matt | Wpg., Bos., T.B. | 3 | 35 | 0 | 5 | 5 | 97 | 5 | 0 | 0 | 0 | 6 | .... | 1988-89 | 1992-93 |
| Hess, Bob | St.L., Buf., Hfd. | 8 | 329 | 27 | 95 | 122 | 178 | 4 | 1 | 1 | 2 | 2 | .... | 1974-75 | 1983-84 |
| • Heximer, Obs | NYR, Bos., NYA | 3 | 84 | 13 | 7 | 20 | 16 | 5 | 0 | 0 | 0 | 2 | .... | 1929-30 | 1934-35 |
| • Hextall, Bryan | NYR | 11 | 449 | 187 | 175 | 362 | 227 | 37 | 8 | 9 | 17 | 19 | 1 | 1936-37 | 1947-48 |
| Hextall, Bryan | NYR, Pit., Atl., Det., Min. | 8 | 549 | 99 | 161 | 260 | 738 | 18 | 0 | 4 | 4 | 59 | .... | 1962-63 | 1975-76 |
| Hextall, Dennis | NYR, L.A., Cal., Min., Det., Wsh. | 13 | 681 | 153 | 350 | 503 | 1398 | 22 | 3 | 3 | 6 | 45 | .... | 1967-68 | 1979-80 |
| • Heyliger, Vic | Chi. | 2 | 33 | 2 | 3 | 5 | 2 | .... | .... | .... | .... | .... | .... | 1937-38 | 1943-44 |
| • Hicke, Bill | Mtl., NYR, Oak., Cal., Pit. | 14 | 729 | 168 | 234 | 402 | 395 | 42 | 3 | 10 | 13 | 41 | 2 | 1958-59 | 1971-72 |
| Hicke, Ernie | Cal., Atl., NYI, Min., L.A. | 8 | 520 | 132 | 140 | 272 | 407 | 2 | 1 | 0 | 1 | 0 | .... | 1970-71 | 1977-78 |
| Hickey, Greg | NYR | 1 | 1 | 0 | 0 | 0 | 0 | .... | .... | .... | .... | .... | .... | 1977-78 | 1977-78 |
| Hickey, Pat | NYR, Col., Tor., Que., St.L. | 10 | 646 | 192 | 212 | 404 | 351 | 55 | 5 | 11 | 16 | 37 | .... | 1975-76 | 1984-85 |
| Hicks, Alex | Ana., Pit., S.J., Fla. | 5 | 258 | 25 | 54 | 79 | 247 | 15 | 0 | 2 | 2 | 8 | .... | 1995-96 | 1999-00 |
| Hicks, Doug | Min., Chi., Edm., Wsh. | 9 | 561 | 37 | 131 | 168 | 442 | 18 | 2 | 1 | 3 | 15 | .... | 1974-75 | 1982-83 |
| Hicks, Glenn | Det. | 2 | 108 | 6 | 12 | 18 | 127 | .... | .... | .... | .... | .... | .... | 1979-80 | 1980-81 |
| • Hicks, Henry | Mtl.M., Det. | 3 | 96 | 7 | 2 | 9 | 72 | .... | .... | .... | .... | .... | .... | 1928-29 | 1930-31 |
| Hicks, Wayne | Chi., Bos., Mtl., Phi., Pit. | 5 | 115 | 13 | 23 | 36 | 22 | 2 | 0 | 1 | 1 | 2 | 1 | 1959-60 | 1967-68 |
| Hidi, Andre | Wsh. | 2 | 7 | 2 | 1 | 3 | 9 | 2 | 0 | 0 | 0 | 0 | .... | 1983-84 | 1984-85 |
| Hiemer, Uli | N.J. | 3 | 143 | 19 | 54 | 73 | 176 | .... | .... | .... | .... | .... | .... | 1984-85 | 1986-87 |
| ‡ Higgins, Matt | Mtl. | 4 | 57 | 1 | 2 | 3 | 6 | .... | .... | .... | .... | .... | .... | 1997-98 | 2000-01 |
| Higgins, Paul | Tor. | 2 | 25 | 0 | 0 | 0 | 152 | 1 | 0 | 0 | 0 | 0 | .... | 1981-82 | 1982-83 |
| Higgins, Tim | Chi., N.J., Det. | 11 | 706 | 154 | 198 | 352 | 719 | 65 | 5 | 8 | 13 | 77 | .... | 1978-79 | 1988-89 |
| • Hildebrand, Ike | NYR, Chi. | 2 | 41 | 7 | 11 | 18 | 16 | .... | .... | .... | .... | .... | .... | 1953-54 | 1954-55 |
| Hill, Al | Phi. | 8 | 221 | 40 | 55 | 95 | 227 | 51 | 8 | 11 | 19 | 43 | .... | 1976-77 | 1987-88 |
| Hill, Brian | Hfd. | 1 | 19 | 1 | 1 | 2 | 4 | .... | .... | .... | .... | .... | .... | 1979-80 | 1979-80 |
| • Hill, Mel | Bos., Bro., Tor. | 9 | 324 | 89 | 109 | 198 | 128 | 43 | 12 | 7 | 19 | 18 | 3 | 1937-38 | 1945-46 |
| ‡ Hill, Sean | Mtl., Ana., Ott., Car., St.L., Fla., NYI, Min. | 17 | 876 | 62 | 236 | 298 | 1008 | 55 | 5 | 5 | 10 | 42 | 1 | 1990-91 | 2007-08 |
| • Hiller, Dutch | NYR, Det., Bos., Mtl. | 9 | 383 | 91 | 113 | 204 | 163 | 48 | 9 | 8 | 17 | 21 | 2 | 1937-38 | 1945-46 |
| Hiller, Jim | L.A., Det., NYR | 2 | 63 | 8 | 12 | 20 | 116 | 2 | 0 | 0 | 0 | 4 | .... | 1992-93 | 1993-94 |
| Hillier, Randy | Bos., Pit., NYI, Buf. | 11 | 543 | 16 | 110 | 126 | 906 | 28 | 0 | 2 | 2 | 93 | 1 | 1981-82 | 1991-92 |
| Hillman, Floyd | Bos. | 1 | 6 | 0 | 0 | 0 | 10 | .... | .... | .... | .... | .... | .... | 1956-57 | 1956-57 |
| Hillman, Larry | Det., Bos., Tor., Min., Mtl., Phi., L.A., Buf. | 19 | 790 | 36 | 196 | 232 | 579 | 74 | 2 | 9 | 11 | 30 | 6 | 1954-55 | 1972-73 |
| • Hillman, Wayne | Chi., NYR, Min., Phi. | 13 | 691 | 18 | 86 | 104 | 534 | 28 | 0 | 3 | 3 | 19 | 1 | 1960-61 | 1972-73 |
| Hilworth, John | Det. | 3 | 57 | 1 | 1 | 2 | 89 | .... | .... | .... | .... | .... | .... | 1977-78 | 1979-80 |
| • Himes, Normie | NYA | 9 | 402 | 106 | 113 | 219 | 127 | 2 | 0 | 0 | 0 | 0 | .... | 1926-27 | 1934-35 |
| Hindmarch, Dave | Cgy. | 4 | 99 | 21 | 17 | 38 | 25 | 10 | 0 | 0 | 0 | 6 | .... | 1980-81 | 1983-84 |
| Hinse, Andre | Tor. | 1 | 4 | 0 | 0 | 0 | 0 | .... | .... | .... | .... | .... | .... | 1967-68 | 1967-68 |
| Hinton, Dan | Chi. | 1 | 14 | 0 | 0 | 0 | 16 | .... | .... | .... | .... | .... | .... | 1976-77 | 1976-77 |
| Hirsch, Tom | Min. | 3 | 31 | 1 | 7 | 8 | 30 | 12 | 0 | 0 | 0 | 6 | .... | 1983-84 | 1987-88 |
| • Hirschfeld, Bert | Mtl. | 2 | 33 | 1 | 4 | 5 | 2 | 5 | 1 | 0 | 1 | 0 | .... | 1949-50 | 1950-51 |
| Hislop, Jamie | Que., Cgy. | 5 | 345 | 75 | 103 | 178 | 86 | 28 | 3 | 2 | 5 | 11 | .... | 1979-80 | 1983-84 |
| • Hitchman, Lionel | Ott., Bos. | 12 | 417 | 28 | 34 | 62 | 523 | 35 | 2 | 2 | 4 | 73 | 2 | 1922-23 | 1933-34 |
| • Hlinka, Ivan | Van. | 2 | 137 | 42 | 81 | 123 | 28 | 16 | 3 | 10 | 13 | 8 | .... | 1981-82 | 1982-83 |
| ‡ Hlinka, Jaroslav | Col. | 1 | 63 | 8 | 20 | 28 | 16 | 1 | 0 | 0 | 0 | 0 | .... | 2007-08 | 2007-08 |
| ‡ Hlushko, Todd | Phi., Cgy., Pit. | 6 | 79 | 8 | 13 | 21 | 84 | 3 | 0 | 0 | 0 | 2 | .... | 1993-94 | 1998-99 |
| Hocking, Justin | L.A. | 1 | 1 | 0 | 0 | 0 | 0 | .... | .... | .... | .... | .... | .... | 1993-94 | 1993-94 |
| Hodge, Ken | Chi., Bos., NYR | 14 | 881 | 328 | 472 | 800 | 779 | 97 | 34 | 47 | 81 | 120 | 2 | 1964-65 | 1977-78 |
| Hodge, Ken | Min., Bos., T.B. | 4 | 142 | 39 | 48 | 87 | 32 | 15 | 4 | 6 | 10 | 6 | .... | 1988-89 | 1992-93 |
| Hodgson, Dan | Tor., Van. | 4 | 114 | 29 | 45 | 74 | 64 | .... | .... | .... | .... | .... | .... | 1985-86 | 1988-89 |
| Hodgson, Rick | Hfd. | 1 | 6 | 0 | 0 | 0 | 6 | 1 | 0 | 0 | 0 | 0 | .... | 1979-80 | 1979-80 |
| Hodgson, Ted | Bos. | 1 | 4 | 0 | 0 | 0 | 0 | .... | .... | .... | .... | .... | .... | 1966-67 | 1966-67 |
| Hoekstra, Cec | Mtl. | 1 | 4 | 0 | 0 | 0 | 0 | .... | .... | .... | .... | .... | .... | 1959-60 | 1959-60 |
| Hoekstra, Ed | Phi. | 1 | 70 | 15 | 21 | 36 | 6 | 7 | 0 | 1 | 1 | 0 | .... | 1967-68 | 1967-68 |
| Hoene, Phil | L.A. | 3 | 37 | 2 | 4 | 6 | 22 | .... | .... | .... | .... | .... | .... | 1972-73 | 1974-75 |
| • Hoffinger, Val | Chi. | 2 | 28 | 0 | 1 | 1 | 30 | .... | .... | .... | .... | .... | .... | 1927-28 | 1928-29 |
| Hoffman, Mike | Hfd. | 3 | 9 | 1 | 3 | 4 | 2 | .... | .... | .... | .... | .... | .... | 1982-83 | 1985-86 |
| Hoffmeyer, Bob | Chi., Phi., N.J. | 6 | 198 | 14 | 52 | 66 | 325 | 3 | 0 | 1 | 1 | 25 | .... | 1977-78 | 1984-85 |
| Hofford, Jim | Buf., L.A. | 3 | 18 | 0 | 0 | 0 | 47 | .... | .... | .... | .... | .... | .... | 1985-86 | 1988-89 |
| Hogaboam, Bill | Atl., Det., Min. | 8 | 332 | 80 | 109 | 189 | 100 | 2 | 0 | 0 | 0 | 0 | .... | 1972-73 | 1979-80 |
| Hoganson, Dale | L.A., Mtl., Que. | 7 | 343 | 13 | 77 | 90 | 186 | 11 | 0 | 3 | 3 | 12 | .... | 1969-70 | 1981-82 |
| ‡ Hoglund, Jonas | Cgy., Mtl., Tor. | 7 | 545 | 117 | 145 | 262 | 112 | 59 | 8 | 11 | 19 | 8 | .... | 1996-97 | 2002-03 |
| Hogue, Benoit | Buf., NYI, Tor., Dal., T.B., Phx., Bos., Wsh. | 15 | 863 | 222 | 321 | 543 | 877 | 92 | 17 | 16 | 33 | 124 | 1 | 1987-88 | 2001-02 |
| Holan, Milos | Phi., Ana. | 3 | 49 | 5 | 11 | 16 | 42 | .... | .... | .... | .... | .... | .... | 1993-94 | 1995-96 |
| Holbrook, Terry | Min. | 2 | 43 | 3 | 6 | 9 | 4 | 6 | 0 | 0 | 0 | 0 | .... | 1972-73 | 1973-74 |
| ‡ Holden, Josh | Van., Car., Tor. | 6 | 60 | 5 | 9 | 14 | 16 | .... | .... | .... | .... | .... | .... | 1998-99 | 2003-04 |
| ‡ Holland, Jason | NYI, Buf., L.A. | 7 | 81 | 4 | 5 | 9 | 36 | 1 | 0 | 0 | 0 | 0 | .... | 1996-97 | 2003-04 |
| Holland, Jerry | NYR | 2 | 37 | 8 | 4 | 12 | 6 | .... | .... | .... | .... | .... | .... | 1974-75 | 1975-76 |
| • Hollett, Flash | Tor., Ott., Bos., Det. | 13 | 562 | 132 | 181 | 313 | 358 | 79 | 8 | 26 | 34 | 38 | 2 | 1933-34 | 1945-46 |
| Hollinger, Terry | St.L. | 2 | 7 | 0 | 0 | 0 | 2 | .... | .... | .... | .... | .... | .... | 1993-94 | 1994-95 |
| • Hollingworth, Gord | Chi., Det. | 4 | 163 | 4 | 14 | 18 | 201 | 3 | 0 | 0 | 0 | 2 | .... | 1954-55 | 1957-58 |
| Holloway, Bruce | Van. | 1 | 2 | 0 | 0 | 0 | 0 | .... | .... | .... | .... | .... | .... | 1984-85 | 1984-85 |
| • Holmes, Bill | Mtl., NYA | 3 | 52 | 6 | 4 | 10 | 35 | .... | .... | .... | .... | .... | .... | 1925-26 | 1929-30 |

| Name | NHL Teams | NHL Seasons | Regular Schedule GP | G | A | TP | PIM | Playoffs GP | G | A | TP | PIM | NHL Cup Wins | First NHL Season | Last NHL Season |
|---|---|---|---|---|---|---|---|---|---|---|---|---|---|---|---|
| Holmes, Chuck | Det. | 2 | 23 | 1 | 3 | 4 | 10 | .... | .... | .... | .... | .... | .... | 1958-59 | 1961-62 |
| Holmes, Lou | Chi. | 2 | 59 | 1 | 4 | 5 | 6 | 2 | 0 | 0 | 0 | 2 | .... | 1931-32 | 1932-33 |
| Holmes, Warren | L.A. | 3 | 45 | 8 | 18 | 26 | 7 | .... | .... | .... | .... | .... | .... | 1981-82 | 1983-84 |
| Holmgren, Paul | Phi., Min. | 10 | 527 | 144 | 179 | 323 | 1684 | 82 | 19 | 32 | 51 | 195 | .... | 1975-76 | 1984-85 |
| ‡ Holmqvist, Michael | Ana., Chi. | 3 | 156 | 18 | 17 | 35 | 72 | .... | .... | .... | .... | .... | .... | 2003-04 | 2006-07 |
| • Holota, John | Det. | 2 | 15 | 2 | 0 | 2 | 0 | .... | .... | .... | .... | .... | .... | 1942-43 | 1945-46 |
| Holst, Greg | NYR | 3 | 11 | 0 | 0 | 0 | 0 | .... | .... | .... | .... | .... | .... | 1975-76 | 1977-78 |
| Holt, Gary | Cal., Cle., St.L. | 5 | 101 | 13 | 11 | 24 | 133 | .... | .... | .... | .... | .... | .... | 1973-74 | 1977-78 |
| Holt, Randy | Chi., Cle., Van., L.A., Cgy., Wsh., Phi. | 10 | 395 | 4 | 37 | 41 | 1438 | 21 | 2 | 3 | 5 | 83 | .... | 1974-75 | 1983-84 |
| • Holway, Albert | Tor., Mtl.M., Pit. | 5 | 112 | 7 | 2 | 9 | 48 | 6 | 0 | 0 | 0 | 0 | 1 | 1923-24 | 1928-29 |
| Holzinger, Brian | Buf., T.B., Pit., CBJ | 10 | 547 | 93 | 145 | 238 | 339 | 52 | 11 | 18 | 29 | 61 | .... | 1994-95 | 2003-04 |
| Homenuke, Ron | Van. | 1 | 1 | 0 | 0 | 0 | 0 | .... | .... | .... | .... | .... | .... | 1972-73 | 1972-73 |
| Hoover, Ron | Bos., St.L. | 3 | 18 | 4 | 0 | 4 | 31 | 8 | 0 | 0 | 0 | 18 | .... | 1989-90 | 1991-92 |
| Hopkins, Dean | L.A., Edm., Que. | 6 | 223 | 23 | 51 | 74 | 306 | 18 | 1 | 5 | 6 | 29 | .... | 1979-80 | 1988-89 |
| Hopkins, Larry | Tor., Wpg. | 4 | 60 | 13 | 16 | 29 | 26 | 6 | 0 | 0 | 0 | 2 | .... | 1977-78 | 1982-83 |
| Horacek, Tony | Phi., Chi. | 5 | 154 | 10 | 19 | 29 | 316 | 2 | 1 | 0 | 1 | 2 | .... | 1989-90 | 1994-95 |
| Horava, Miloslav | NYR | 3 | 80 | 5 | 17 | 22 | 38 | 2 | 0 | 1 | 1 | 0 | .... | 1988-89 | 1990-91 |
| Horbul, Doug | K.C. | 1 | 4 | 1 | 0 | 1 | 2 | .... | .... | .... | .... | .... | .... | 1974-75 | 1974-75 |
| Hordy, Mike | NYI | 2 | 11 | 0 | 0 | 0 | 7 | .... | .... | .... | .... | .... | .... | 1978-79 | 1979-80 |
| Horeck, Pete | Chi., Det., Bos. | 8 | 426 | 106 | 118 | 224 | 340 | 34 | 6 | 8 | 14 | 43 | .... | 1944-45 | 1951-52 |
| • Horne, George | Mtl.M., Tor. | 3 | 54 | 9 | 3 | 12 | 34 | 4 | 0 | 0 | 0 | 4 | 1 | 1925-26 | 1928-29 |
| • Horner, Red | Tor. | 12 | 490 | 42 | 110 | 152 | 1254 | 71 | 7 | 10 | 17 | 170 | 1 | 1928-29 | 1939-40 |
| • Hornung, Larry | St.L. | 2 | 48 | 2 | 9 | 11 | 10 | 11 | 0 | 2 | 2 | 2 | .... | 1970-71 | 1971-72 |
| • Horton, Tim | Tor., NYR, Pit., Buf. | 24 | 1446 | 115 | 403 | 518 | 1611 | 126 | 11 | 39 | 50 | 183 | 4 | 1949-50 | 1973-74 |
| Horvath, Bronco | NYR, Mtl., Bos., Chi., Tor., Min. | 9 | 434 | 141 | 185 | 326 | 319 | 36 | 12 | 9 | 21 | 18 | .... | 1955-56 | 1967-68 |
| Hospodar, Ed | NYR, Hfd., Phi., Min., Buf. | 9 | 450 | 17 | 51 | 68 | 1314 | 44 | 4 | 1 | 5 | 208 | .... | 1979-80 | 1987-88 |
| Hostak, Martin | Phi. | 2 | 55 | 3 | 11 | 14 | 24 | .... | .... | .... | .... | .... | .... | 1990-91 | 1991-92 |
| Hotham, Greg | Tor., Pit. | 6 | 230 | 15 | 74 | 89 | 139 | 5 | 0 | 3 | 3 | 6 | .... | 1979-80 | 1984-85 |
| Houck, Paul | Min. | 3 | 16 | 1 | 2 | 3 | 2 | .... | .... | .... | .... | .... | .... | 1985-86 | 1987-88 |
| Houda, Doug | Det., Hfd., L.A., Buf., NYI, Ana. | 15 | 561 | 19 | 63 | 82 | 1104 | 18 | 0 | 3 | 3 | 21 | .... | 1985-86 | 2002-03 |
| Houde, Claude | K.C. | 2 | 59 | 3 | 6 | 9 | 40 | .... | .... | .... | .... | .... | .... | 1974-75 | 1975-76 |
| ‡ Houde, Eric | Mtl. | 3 | 30 | 2 | 3 | 5 | 4 | .... | .... | .... | .... | .... | .... | 1996-97 | 1998-99 |
| Hough, Mike | Que., Fla., NYI | 13 | 707 | 100 | 156 | 256 | 675 | 44 | 5 | 5 | 10 | 38 | .... | 1984-85 | 1998-99 |
| Houlder, Bill | Wsh., Buf., Ana., St.L., T.B., S.J., Nsh. | 16 | 846 | 59 | 191 | 250 | 412 | 30 | 5 | 6 | 11 | 14 | .... | 1987-88 | 2002-03 |
| Houle, Rejean | Mtl. | 11 | 635 | 161 | 247 | 408 | 395 | 90 | 14 | 34 | 48 | 66 | 5 | 1969-70 | 1982-83 |
| Housley, Phil | Buf., Wpg., St.L., Cgy., N.J., Wsh., Chi., Tor. | 21 | 1495 | 338 | 894 | 1232 | 822 | 85 | 13 | 43 | 56 | 36 | .... | 1982-83 | 2002-03 |
| Houston, Ken | Atl., Cgy., Wsh., L.A. | 9 | 570 | 161 | 167 | 328 | 624 | 35 | 10 | 9 | 19 | 66 | .... | 1975-76 | 1983-84 |
| Howard, Jack | Tor. | 1 | 2 | 0 | 0 | 0 | 0 | .... | .... | .... | .... | .... | .... | 1936-37 | 1936-37 |
| Howatt, Garry | NYI, Hfd., N.J. | 12 | 720 | 112 | 156 | 268 | 1836 | 87 | 12 | 14 | 26 | 289 | 2 | 1972-73 | 1983-84 |
| Howe, Gordie | Det., Hfd. | 26 | 1767 | 801 | 1049 | 1850 | 1685 | 157 | 68 | 92 | 160 | 220 | 4 | 1946-47 | 1979-80 |
| Howe, Mark | Hfd., Phi., Det. | 16 | 929 | 197 | 545 | 742 | 455 | 101 | 10 | 51 | 61 | 34 | .... | 1979-80 | 1994-95 |
| Howe, Marty | Hfd., Bos. | 6 | 197 | 2 | 29 | 31 | 99 | 15 | 1 | 2 | 3 | 9 | .... | 1979-80 | 1984-85 |
| • Howe, Syd | Ott., Phi., Tor., St.L., Det. | 17 | 698 | 237 | 291 | 528 | 212 | 70 | 17 | 27 | 44 | 10 | 3 | 1929-30 | 1945-46 |
| Howe, Vic | NYR | 3 | 33 | 3 | 4 | 7 | 10 | .... | .... | .... | .... | .... | .... | 1950-51 | 1954-55 |
| Howell, Harry | NYR, Oak., Cal., L.A. | 21 | 1411 | 94 | 324 | 418 | 1298 | 38 | 3 | 3 | 6 | 32 | .... | 1952-53 | 1972-73 |
| • Howell, Ron | NYR | 2 | 4 | 0 | 0 | 0 | 0 | .... | .... | .... | .... | .... | .... | 1954-55 | 1955-56 |
| Howse, Don | L.A. | 1 | 33 | 2 | 5 | 7 | 6 | 2 | 0 | 0 | 0 | 0 | .... | 1979-80 | 1979-80 |
| Howson, Scott | NYI | 2 | 18 | 5 | 3 | 8 | 4 | .... | .... | .... | .... | .... | .... | 1984-85 | 1985-86 |
| Hoyda, Dave | Phi., Wpg. | 4 | 132 | 6 | 17 | 23 | 299 | 12 | 0 | 0 | 0 | 17 | .... | 1977-78 | 1980-81 |
| ‡ Hrdina, Jan | Pit., Phx., N.J., CBJ | 7 | 513 | 101 | 196 | 297 | 341 | 45 | 12 | 14 | 26 | 24 | .... | 1998-99 | 2005-06 |
| Hrdina, Jiri | Cgy., Pit. | 5 | 250 | 45 | 85 | 130 | 92 | 46 | 2 | 5 | 7 | 24 | 3 | 1987-88 | 1991-92 |
| Hrechkosy, Dave | Cal., St.L. | 4 | 140 | 42 | 24 | 66 | 41 | 3 | 1 | 0 | 1 | 2 | .... | 1973-74 | 1976-77 |
| Hrkac, Tony | St.L., Que., S.J., Chi., Dal., Edm., NYI, Ana., Atl. | 13 | 758 | 132 | 239 | 371 | 173 | 41 | 7 | 7 | 14 | 12 | 1 | 1986-87 | 2002-03 |
| Hrycuik, Jim | Wsh. | 1 | 21 | 5 | 5 | 10 | 12 | .... | .... | .... | .... | .... | .... | 1974-75 | 1974-75 |
| Hrymnak, Steve | Chi., Det. | 2 | 18 | 2 | 1 | 3 | 4 | 2 | 0 | 0 | 0 | 0 | .... | 1951-52 | 1952-53 |
| Hrynewich, Tim | Pit. | 2 | 55 | 6 | 8 | 14 | 82 | .... | .... | .... | .... | .... | .... | 1982-83 | 1983-84 |
| Huard, Bill | Bos., Ott., Que., Dal., Edm., L.A. | 8 | 223 | 16 | 18 | 34 | 594 | 5 | 0 | 0 | 0 | 2 | .... | 1992-93 | 1999-00 |
| • Huard, Rolly | Tor. | 1 | 1 | 1 | 0 | 1 | 0 | .... | .... | .... | .... | .... | .... | 1930-31 | 1930-31 |
| ‡ Hubacek, Petr | Phi. | 1 | 6 | 1 | 0 | 1 | 2 | .... | .... | .... | .... | .... | .... | 2000-01 | 2000-01 |
| Huber, Willie | Det., NYR, Van., Phi. | 10 | 655 | 104 | 217 | 321 | 950 | 33 | 5 | 5 | 10 | 35 | .... | 1978-79 | 1987-88 |
| Hubick, Greg | Tor., Van. | 2 | 77 | 6 | 9 | 15 | 10 | .... | .... | .... | .... | .... | .... | 1975-76 | 1979-80 |
| Huck, Fran | Mtl., St.L. | 3 | 94 | 24 | 30 | 54 | 38 | 11 | 3 | 4 | 7 | 2 | .... | 1969-70 | 1972-73 |
| Hucul, Fred | Chi., St.L. | 5 | 164 | 11 | 30 | 41 | 113 | 6 | 1 | 0 | 1 | 10 | .... | 1950-51 | 1967-68 |
| Huddy, Charlie | Edm., L.A., Buf., St.L. | 17 | 1017 | 99 | 354 | 453 | 785 | 183 | 19 | 66 | 85 | 135 | 5 | 1980-81 | 1996-97 |
| Hudson, Dave | NYI, K.C., Col. | 6 | 409 | 59 | 124 | 183 | 89 | 2 | 1 | 1 | 2 | 0 | .... | 1972-73 | 1977-78 |
| Hudson, Lex | Pit. | 1 | 2 | 0 | 0 | 0 | 0 | 2 | 0 | 0 | 0 | 0 | .... | 1978-79 | 1978-79 |
| Hudson, Mike | Chi., Edm., NYR, Pit., Tor., St.L., Phx. | 9 | 416 | 49 | 87 | 136 | 414 | 49 | 4 | 10 | 14 | 64 | 1 | 1988-89 | 1996-97 |
| Hudson, Ron | Det. | 2 | 33 | 5 | 2 | 7 | 2 | .... | .... | .... | .... | .... | .... | 1937-38 | 1939-40 |
| Huffman, Kerry | Phi., Que., Ott. | 10 | 401 | 37 | 108 | 145 | 361 | 11 | 0 | 0 | 0 | 2 | .... | 1986-87 | 1995-96 |
| Huggins, Al | Mtl.M. | 1 | 20 | 1 | 1 | 2 | 2 | .... | .... | .... | .... | .... | .... | 1930-31 | 1930-31 |
| • Hughes, Albert | NYA | 2 | 60 | 6 | 8 | 14 | 22 | .... | .... | .... | .... | .... | .... | 1930-31 | 1931-32 |
| Hughes, Brent | L.A., Phi., St.L., Det., K.C. | 8 | 435 | 15 | 117 | 132 | 440 | 22 | 1 | 3 | 4 | 53 | .... | 1967-68 | 1974-75 |
| Hughes, Brent | Wpg., Bos., Buf., NYI | 8 | 357 | 41 | 39 | 80 | 831 | 29 | 4 | 1 | 5 | 53 | .... | 1988-89 | 1996-97 |
| Hughes, Frank | Cal. | 1 | 5 | 0 | 0 | 0 | 0 | .... | .... | .... | .... | .... | .... | 1971-72 | 1971-72 |
| Hughes, Howie | L.A. | 3 | 168 | 25 | 32 | 57 | 30 | 14 | 2 | 0 | 2 | 2 | .... | 1967-68 | 1969-70 |
| Hughes, Jack | Col. | 2 | 46 | 2 | 5 | 7 | 104 | .... | .... | .... | .... | .... | .... | 1980-81 | 1981-82 |
| • Hughes, James | Det. | 1 | 40 | 0 | 1 | 1 | 48 | .... | .... | .... | .... | .... | .... | 1929-30 | 1929-30 |
| Hughes, John | Van., Edm., NYR | 2 | 70 | 2 | 14 | 16 | 211 | 7 | 0 | 1 | 1 | 16 | .... | 1979-80 | 1980-81 |
| Hughes, Pat | Mtl., Pit., Edm., Buf., St.L., Hfd. | 10 | 573 | 130 | 128 | 258 | 646 | 71 | 8 | 25 | 33 | 77 | 3 | 1977-78 | 1986-87 |
| Hughes, Ryan | Bos. | 1 | 3 | 0 | 0 | 0 | 0 | .... | .... | .... | .... | .... | .... | 1995-96 | 1995-96 |
| Hulbig, Joe | Edm., Bos. | 5 | 55 | 4 | 4 | 8 | 16 | 6 | 0 | 1 | 1 | 2 | .... | 1996-97 | 2000-01 |
| Hull, Bobby | Chi., Wpg., Hfd. | 16 | 1063 | 610 | 560 | 1170 | 640 | 119 | 62 | 67 | 129 | 102 | 1 | 1957-58 | 1979-80 |
| Hull, Brett | Cgy., St.L., Dal., Det., Phx. | 20 | 1269 | 741 | 650 | 1391 | 458 | 202 | 103 | 87 | 190 | 73 | 2 | 1985-86 | 2005-06 |
| Hull, Dennis | Chi., Det. | 14 | 959 | 303 | 351 | 654 | 261 | 104 | 33 | 34 | 67 | 30 | .... | 1964-65 | 1977-78 |
| Hull, Jody | Hfd., NYR, Ott., Fla., T.B., Phi. | 16 | 831 | 124 | 137 | 261 | 156 | 69 | 4 | 5 | 9 | 14 | .... | 1988-89 | 2003-04 |
| Hulse, Cale | N.J., Cgy., Nsh., Phx., CBJ | 10 | 619 | 16 | 79 | 95 | 1000 | 1 | 0 | 0 | 0 | 0 | .... | 1995-96 | 2005-06 |
| ‡ Huml, Ivan | Bos. | 3 | 49 | 6 | 12 | 18 | 36 | .... | .... | .... | .... | .... | .... | 2001-02 | 2003-04 |
| • Hunt, Fred | NYA, NYR | 2 | 59 | 15 | 14 | 29 | 6 | .... | .... | .... | .... | .... | .... | 1940-41 | 1944-45 |
| Hunter, Dale | Que., Wsh., Col. | 19 | 1407 | 323 | 697 | 1020 | 3565 | 186 | 42 | 76 | 118 | 729 | .... | 1980-81 | 1998-99 |
| Hunter, Dave | Edm., Pit., Wpg. | 10 | 746 | 133 | 190 | 323 | 918 | 105 | 16 | 24 | 40 | 211 | 3 | 1979-80 | 1988-89 |
| Hunter, Mark | Mtl., St.L., Cgy., Hfd., Wsh. | 12 | 628 | 213 | 171 | 384 | 1426 | 79 | 18 | 20 | 38 | 230 | 1 | 1981-82 | 1992-93 |
| Hunter, Tim | Cgy., Que., Van., S.J. | 16 | 815 | 62 | 76 | 138 | 3146 | 132 | 5 | 7 | 12 | 426 | 1 | 1981-82 | 1996-97 |
| Huras, Larry | NYR | 1 | 2 | 0 | 0 | 0 | 0 | .... | .... | .... | .... | .... | .... | 1976-77 | 1976-77 |
| Hurlburt, Bob | Van. | 1 | 1 | 0 | 0 | 0 | 2 | .... | .... | .... | .... | .... | .... | 1974-75 | 1974-75 |
| Hurlbut, Mike | NYR, Que., Buf. | 5 | 29 | 1 | 8 | 9 | 20 | .... | .... | .... | .... | .... | .... | 1992-93 | 1999-00 |
| Hurley, Paul | Bos. | 1 | 1 | 0 | 1 | 1 | 0 | .... | .... | .... | .... | .... | .... | 1968-69 | 1968-69 |
| Hurst, Ron | Tor. | 2 | 64 | 9 | 7 | 16 | 70 | 3 | 0 | 2 | 2 | 4 | .... | 1955-56 | 1956-57 |
| Huscroft, Jamie | N.J., Bos., Cgy., T.B., Van., Phx., Wsh. | 10 | 352 | 5 | 33 | 38 | 1065 | 21 | 0 | 1 | 1 | 46 | .... | 1988-89 | 1999-00 |
| Huska, Ryan | Chi. | 1 | 1 | 0 | 0 | 0 | 0 | .... | .... | .... | .... | .... | .... | 1997-98 | 1997-98 |
| ‡ Hussey, Matt | Pit., Det. | 3 | 21 | 2 | 2 | 4 | 2 | .... | .... | .... | .... | .... | .... | 2003-04 | 2006-07 |
| Huston, Ron | Cal. | 2 | 79 | 15 | 31 | 46 | 8 | .... | .... | .... | .... | .... | .... | 1973-74 | 1974-75 |
| Hutchinson, Ron | NYR | 1 | 9 | 0 | 0 | 0 | 0 | .... | .... | .... | .... | .... | .... | 1960-61 | 1960-61 |
| Hutchison, Dave | L.A., Tor., Chi., N.J. | 10 | 584 | 19 | 97 | 116 | 1550 | 48 | 2 | 12 | 14 | 149 | .... | 1974-75 | 1983-84 |
| • Hutton, Bill | Bos., Ott., Phi. | 2 | 64 | 3 | 2 | 5 | 8 | 2 | 0 | 0 | 0 | 0 | .... | 1929-30 | 1930-31 |
| • Hyland, Harry | Mtl.W., Ott. | 1 | 17 | 14 | 2 | 16 | 65 | .... | .... | .... | .... | .... | .... | 1917-18 | 1917-18 |
| Hynes, Dave | Bos. | 2 | 22 | 4 | 0 | 4 | 2 | .... | .... | .... | .... | .... | .... | 1973-74 | 1974-75 |
| Hynes, Gord | Bos., Phi. | 2 | 52 | 3 | 9 | 12 | 22 | 12 | 1 | 2 | 3 | 6 | .... | 1991-92 | 1992-93 |
| ‡ Hyvonen, Hannes | S.J., CBJ | 2 | 42 | 4 | 5 | 9 | 22 | .... | .... | .... | .... | .... | .... | 2001-02 | 2002-03 |

# I

| Name | NHL Teams | NHL Seasons | Regular Schedule GP | G | A | TP | PIM | Playoffs GP | G | A | TP | PIM | NHL Cup Wins | First NHL Season | Last NHL Season |
|---|---|---|---|---|---|---|---|---|---|---|---|---|---|---|---|
| Iafrate, Al | Tor., Wsh., Bos., S.J. | 12 | 799 | 152 | 311 | 463 | 1301 | 71 | 19 | 16 | 35 | 77 | .... | 1984-85 | 1997-98 |
| Ignatjev, Victor | Pit. | 1 | 11 | 0 | 1 | 1 | 6 | 1 | 0 | 0 | 0 | 2 | .... | 1998-99 | 1998-99 |
| Ihnacak, Miroslav | Tor., Det. | 3 | 56 | 8 | 9 | 17 | 39 | 1 | 0 | 0 | 0 | 0 | .... | 1985-86 | 1988-89 |
| Ihnacak, Peter | Tor. | 8 | 417 | 102 | 165 | 267 | 175 | 28 | 4 | 10 | 14 | 25 | .... | 1982-83 | 1989-90 |
| Imlach, Brent | Tor. | 2 | 3 | 0 | 0 | 0 | 2 | .... | .... | .... | .... | .... | .... | 1965-66 | 1966-67 |
| ‡ Immonen, Jarkko | NYR | 2 | 20 | 3 | 5 | 8 | 4 | .... | .... | .... | .... | .... | .... | 2005-06 | 2006-07 |
| Ingarfield, Earl | NYR, Pit., Oak., Cal. | 13 | 746 | 179 | 226 | 405 | 239 | 21 | 9 | 8 | 17 | 10 | .... | 1958-59 | 1970-71 |
| Ingarfield, Earl | Atl., Cgy., Det. | 2 | 39 | 4 | 4 | 8 | 22 | 2 | 0 | 1 | 1 | 0 | .... | 1979-80 | 1980-81 |
| Inglis, Billy | L.A., Buf. | 3 | 36 | 1 | 3 | 4 | 4 | 11 | 1 | 2 | 3 | 4 | .... | 1967-68 | 1970-71 |
| • Ingoldsby, Johnny | Tor. | 2 | 29 | 5 | 1 | 6 | 15 | .... | .... | .... | .... | .... | .... | 1942-43 | 1943-44 |
| • Ingram, Frank | Chi. | 3 | 101 | 24 | 16 | 40 | 69 | 11 | 0 | 1 | 1 | 2 | .... | 1929-30 | 1931-32 |
| • Ingram, John | Bos. | 1 | 1 | 0 | 0 | 0 | 0 | .... | .... | .... | .... | .... | .... | 1924-25 | 1924-25 |
| • Ingram, Ron | Chi., Det., NYR | 4 | 114 | 5 | 15 | 20 | 81 | 2 | 0 | 0 | 0 | 0 | .... | 1956-57 | 1964-65 |

Rejean Houle

Charlie Huddy

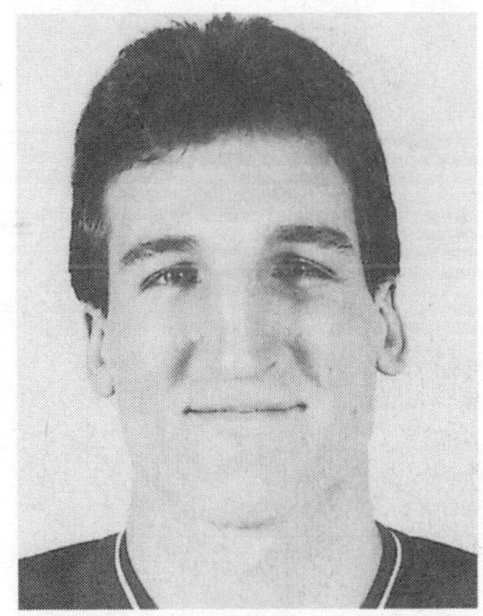
Tim Hunter

Earl Ingarfield

Doug Jarrett

Joe Jerwa

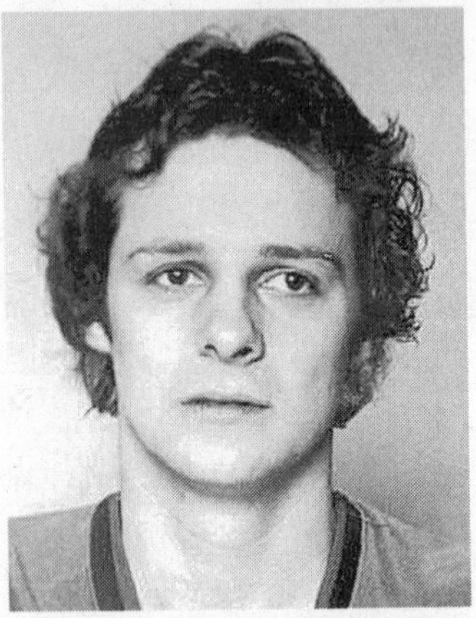

Rick Jodzio

Roger Johansson

| | | | Regular Schedule | | | | | Playoffs | | | | | NHL Cup | First NHL | Last NHL |
|---|---|---|---|---|---|---|---|---|---|---|---|---|---|---|---|
| Name | NHL Teams | NHL Seasons | GP | G | A | TP | PIM | GP | G | A | TP | PIM | Wins | Season | Season |
| Intranuovo, Ralph | Edm., Tor. | 3 | 22 | 2 | 4 | 6 | 4 | .... | .... | .... | .... | .... | .... | 1994-95 | 1996-97 |
| • Irvin, Dick | Chi. | 3 | 94 | 29 | 23 | 52 | 78 | 2 | 2 | 0 | 2 | 4 | .... | 1926-27 | 1928-29 |
| Irvine, Ted | Bos., L.A., NYR, St.L. | 11 | 724 | 154 | 177 | 331 | 657 | 83 | 16 | 24 | 40 | 115 | .... | 1963-64 | 1976-77 |
| Irwin, Ivan | Mtl., NYR | 5 | 155 | 2 | 27 | 29 | 214 | 5 | 0 | 0 | 0 | 8 | .... | 1952-53 | 1957-58 |
| • Isaksson, Ulf | L.A. | 1 | 50 | 7 | 15 | 22 | 10 | .... | .... | .... | .... | .... | .... | 1982-83 | 1982-83 |
| Issel, Kim | Edm. | 1 | 4 | 0 | 0 | 0 | 0 | .... | .... | .... | .... | .... | .... | 1988-89 | 1988-89 |

## *J*

| | | | | | | | | | | | | | | | |
|---|---|---|---|---|---|---|---|---|---|---|---|---|---|---|---|
| ‡ Jacina, Greg | Fla. | 2 | 14 | 0 | 1 | 1 | 6 | .... | .... | .... | .... | .... | .... | 2005-06 | 2006-07 |
| ‡ Jackman, Ric | Dal., Bos., Tor., Pit., Fla., Ana. | 7 | 231 | 19 | 58 | 77 | 166 | 7 | 1 | 1 | 2 | 2 | 1 | 1999-00 | 2006-07 |
| • Jackson, Art | Tor., Bos., NYA | 11 | 468 | 123 | 178 | 301 | 144 | 52 | 8 | 12 | 20 | 29 | 2 | 1934-35 | 1944-45 |
| • Jackson, Busher | Tor., NYA, Bos. | 15 | 633 | 241 | 234 | 475 | 437 | 71 | 18 | 12 | 30 | 53 | 1 | 1929-30 | 1943-44 |
| Jackson, Dane | Van., Buf., NYI | 4 | 45 | 12 | 6 | 18 | 58 | 6 | 0 | 0 | 0 | 10 | .... | 1993-94 | 1997-98 |
| Jackson, Don | Min., Edm., NYR | 10 | 311 | 16 | 52 | 68 | 640 | 53 | 4 | 5 | 9 | 147 | 2 | 1977-78 | 1986-87 |
| • Jackson, Harold | Chi., Det. | 8 | 219 | 17 | 34 | 51 | 208 | 31 | 1 | 2 | 3 | 33 | 2 | 1936-37 | 1946-47 |
| Jackson, Jack | Chi. | 1 | 48 | 2 | 5 | 7 | 38 | .... | .... | .... | .... | .... | .... | 1946-47 | 1946-47 |
| Jackson, Jeff | Tor., NYR, Que., Chi. | 8 | 263 | 38 | 48 | 86 | 313 | 6 | 1 | 1 | 2 | 16 | .... | 1984-85 | 1991-92 |
| Jackson, Jim | Cgy., Buf. | 4 | 112 | 17 | 30 | 47 | 20 | 14 | 3 | 2 | 5 | 6 | .... | 1982-83 | 1987-88 |
| • Jackson, Lloyd | NYA | 1 | 14 | 1 | 1 | 2 | 0 | .... | .... | .... | .... | .... | .... | 1936-37 | 1936-37 |
| • Jackson, Stan | Tor., Bos., Ott. | 5 | 86 | 9 | 6 | 15 | 75 | .... | .... | .... | .... | .... | 1 | 1921-22 | 1926-27 |
| Jackson, Walter | NYA, Bos. | 4 | 84 | 16 | 11 | 27 | 18 | .... | .... | .... | .... | .... | .... | 1932-33 | 1935-36 |
| • Jacobs, Paul | Tor. | 1 | 1 | 0 | 0 | 0 | 0 | .... | .... | .... | .... | .... | .... | 1918-19 | 1918-19 |
| Jacobs, Tim | Cal. | 1 | 46 | 0 | 10 | 10 | 35 | .... | .... | .... | .... | .... | .... | 1975-76 | 1975-76 |
| ‡ Jagr, Jaromir | Pit., Wsh., NYR | 17 | 1273 | 646 | 953 | 1599 | 907 | 169 | 77 | 104 | 181 | 149 | 2 | 1990-91 | 2007-08 |
| Jakopin, John | Fla., Pit., S.J. | 6 | 113 | 1 | 6 | 7 | 145 | .... | .... | .... | .... | .... | .... | 1997-98 | 2002-03 |
| Jalo, Risto | Edm. | 1 | 3 | 0 | 3 | 3 | 0 | .... | .... | .... | .... | .... | .... | 1985-86 | 1985-86 |
| Jalonen, Kari | Cgy., Edm. | 2 | 37 | 9 | 6 | 15 | 4 | 5 | 1 | 0 | 1 | 0 | .... | 1982-83 | 1983-84 |
| James, Gerry | Tor. | 5 | 149 | 14 | 26 | 40 | 257 | 15 | 1 | 0 | 1 | 8 | .... | 1954-55 | 1959-60 |
| James, Val | Buf., Tor. | 2 | 11 | 0 | 0 | 0 | 30 | 3 | 0 | 0 | 0 | 0 | .... | 1981-82 | 1986-87 |
| Jamieson, Jim | NYR | 1 | 1 | 0 | 1 | 1 | 0 | .... | .... | .... | .... | .... | .... | 1943-44 | 1943-44 |
| Jankowski, Lou | Det., Chi. | 4 | 127 | 19 | 18 | 37 | 15 | 1 | 0 | 0 | 0 | 0 | .... | 1950-51 | 1954-55 |
| Janney, Craig | Bos., St.L., S.J., Wpg., Phx., T.B., NYI | 12 | 760 | 188 | 563 | 751 | 170 | 120 | 24 | 86 | 110 | 53 | .... | 1987-88 | 1998-99 |
| Janssens, Mark | NYR, Min., Hfd., Ana., NYI, Phx., Chi. | 14 | 711 | 40 | 73 | 113 | 1422 | 27 | 5 | 1 | 6 | 33 | .... | 1987-88 | 2000-01 |
| ‡ Jantunen, Marko | Cgy. | 1 | 3 | 0 | 0 | 0 | 0 | .... | .... | .... | .... | .... | .... | 1996-97 | 1996-97 |
| Jardine, Ryan | Fla. | 1 | 8 | 0 | 2 | 2 | 2 | .... | .... | .... | .... | .... | .... | 2001-02 | 2001-02 |
| ‡ Jarrett, Cole | NYI | 1 | 1 | 0 | 0 | 0 | 0 | .... | .... | .... | .... | .... | .... | 2005-06 | 2005-06 |
| Jarrett, Doug | Chi., NYR | 13 | 775 | 38 | 182 | 220 | 631 | 99 | 7 | 16 | 23 | 82 | .... | 1964-65 | 1976-77 |
| Jarrett, Gary | Tor., Det., Oak., Cal. | 7 | 341 | 72 | 92 | 164 | 131 | 11 | 3 | 1 | 4 | 9 | .... | 1960-61 | 1971-72 |
| Jarry, Pierre | NYR, Tor., Det., Min. | 7 | 344 | 88 | 117 | 205 | 142 | 5 | 0 | 1 | 1 | 0 | .... | 1971-72 | 1977-78 |
| Jarvenpaa, Hannu | Wpg. | 3 | 114 | 11 | 26 | 37 | 83 | .... | .... | .... | .... | .... | .... | 1986-87 | 1988-89 |
| ‡ Jarventie, Martti | Mtl. | 1 | 1 | 0 | 0 | 0 | 0 | .... | .... | .... | .... | .... | .... | 2001-02 | 2001-02 |
| Jarvi, Iiro | Que. | 2 | 116 | 18 | 43 | 61 | 58 | .... | .... | .... | .... | .... | .... | 1988-89 | 1989-90 |
| Jarvis, Doug | Mtl., Wsh., Hfd. | 13 | 964 | 139 | 264 | 403 | 263 | 105 | 14 | 27 | 41 | 42 | 4 | 1975-76 | 1987-88 |
| • Jarvis, James | Pit., Phi., Tor. | 3 | 112 | 17 | 15 | 32 | 62 | .... | .... | .... | .... | .... | .... | 1929-30 | 1936-37 |
| Jarvis, Wes | Wsh., Min., L.A., Tor. | 9 | 237 | 31 | 55 | 86 | 98 | 2 | 0 | 0 | 0 | 2 | .... | 1979-80 | 1987-88 |
| ‡ Jaspers, Jason | Phx. | 3 | 9 | 0 | 1 | 1 | 6 | .... | .... | .... | .... | .... | .... | 2001-02 | 2003-04 |
| Javanainen, Arto | Pit. | 1 | 14 | 4 | 1 | 5 | 2 | .... | .... | .... | .... | .... | .... | 1984-85 | 1984-85 |
| Jay, Bob | L.A. | 1 | 3 | 0 | 1 | 1 | 0 | .... | .... | .... | .... | .... | .... | 1993-94 | 1993-94 |
| Jeffrey, Larry | Det., Tor., NYR | 8 | 368 | 39 | 62 | 101 | 293 | 38 | 4 | 10 | 14 | 42 | 1 | 1961-62 | 1968-69 |
| Jelinek, Tomas | Ott. | 1 | 49 | 7 | 6 | 13 | 52 | .... | .... | .... | .... | .... | .... | 1992-93 | 1992-93 |
| Jenkins, Dean | L.A. | 1 | 5 | 0 | 0 | 0 | 2 | .... | .... | .... | .... | .... | .... | 1983-84 | 1983-84 |
| • Jenkins, Roger | Chi., Tor., Mtl., Bos., Mtl.M., NYA | 8 | 325 | 15 | 39 | 54 | 253 | 27 | 1 | 7 | 8 | 12 | 2 | 1930-31 | 1938-39 |
| Jennings, Bill | Det., Bos. | 5 | 108 | 32 | 33 | 65 | 45 | 20 | 4 | 4 | 8 | 6 | .... | 1940-41 | 1944-45 |
| Jennings, Grant | Wsh., Hfd., Pit., Tor., Buf. | 9 | 389 | 14 | 43 | 57 | 804 | 54 | 2 | 1 | 3 | 68 | 2 | 1987-88 | 1995-96 |
| Jensen, Chris | NYR, Phi. | 6 | 74 | 9 | 12 | 21 | 27 | .... | .... | .... | .... | .... | .... | 1985-86 | 1991-92 |
| Jensen, David | Min. | 3 | 18 | 0 | 2 | 2 | 11 | .... | .... | .... | .... | .... | .... | 1983-84 | 1985-86 |
| Jensen, David | Hfd., Wsh. | 4 | 69 | 9 | 13 | 22 | 22 | 11 | 0 | 0 | 0 | 2 | .... | 1984-85 | 1987-88 |
| Jensen, Steve | Min., L.A. | 7 | 438 | 113 | 107 | 220 | 318 | 12 | 0 | 3 | 3 | 9 | .... | 1975-76 | 1981-82 |
| • Jeremiah, Ed | NYA, Bos. | 1 | 15 | 0 | 1 | 1 | 0 | .... | .... | .... | .... | .... | .... | 1931-32 | 1931-32 |
| Jerrard, Paul | Min. | 1 | 5 | 0 | 0 | 0 | 4 | .... | .... | .... | .... | .... | .... | 1988-89 | 1988-89 |
| • Jerwa, Frank | Bos., St.L. | 4 | 81 | 11 | 16 | 27 | 53 | .... | .... | .... | .... | .... | .... | 1931-32 | 1934-35 |
| • Jerwa, Joe | NYR, Bos., NYA | 7 | 234 | 29 | 58 | 87 | 309 | 17 | 2 | 3 | 5 | 16 | .... | 1930-31 | 1938-39 |
| Jirik, Jaroslav | St.L. | 1 | 3 | 0 | 0 | 0 | 0 | .... | .... | .... | .... | .... | .... | 1969-70 | 1969-70 |
| • Joanette, Rosario | Mtl. | 1 | 2 | 0 | 1 | 1 | 4 | .... | .... | .... | .... | .... | .... | 1944-45 | 1944-45 |
| Jodzio, Rick | Col., Cle. | 1 | 70 | 2 | 8 | 10 | 71 | .... | .... | .... | .... | .... | .... | 1977-78 | 1977-78 |
| Johannesen, Glenn | NYI | 1 | 2 | 0 | 0 | 0 | 0 | .... | .... | .... | .... | .... | .... | 1985-86 | 1985-86 |
| Johannson, John | N.J. | 1 | 5 | 0 | 0 | 0 | 0 | .... | .... | .... | .... | .... | .... | 1983-84 | 1983-84 |
| • Johansen, Bill | Tor. | 1 | 1 | 0 | 0 | 0 | 0 | .... | .... | .... | .... | .... | .... | 1949-50 | 1949-50 |
| Johansen, Trevor | Tor., Col., L.A. | 5 | 286 | 11 | 46 | 57 | 282 | 13 | 0 | 3 | 3 | 21 | .... | 1977-78 | 1981-82 |
| ‡ Johansson, Andreas | NYI, Pit., Ott., T.B., Cgy., NYR, Nsh. | 8 | 377 | 81 | 88 | 169 | 190 | 9 | 0 | 0 | 0 | 0 | .... | 1995-96 | 2003-04 |
| Johansson, Bjorn | Cle. | 2 | 15 | 1 | 1 | 2 | 10 | .... | .... | .... | .... | .... | .... | 1976-77 | 1977-78 |
| Johansson, Calle | Buf., Wsh., Tor. | 17 | 1109 | 119 | 416 | 535 | 519 | 105 | 12 | 43 | 55 | 44 | .... | 1987-88 | 2003-04 |
| ‡ Johansson, Jonas | Wsh. | 1 | 1 | 0 | 0 | 0 | 2 | .... | .... | .... | .... | .... | .... | 2005-06 | 2005-06 |
| ‡ Johansson, Magnus | Chi., Fla. | 1 | 45 | 0 | 14 | 14 | 18 | .... | .... | .... | .... | .... | .... | 2007-08 | 2007-08 |
| ‡ Johansson, Mathias | Cgy., Pit. | 1 | 58 | 5 | 10 | 15 | 16 | .... | .... | .... | .... | .... | .... | 2002-03 | 2002-03 |
| Johansson, Roger | Cgy., Chi. | 4 | 161 | 9 | 34 | 43 | 163 | 5 | 0 | 1 | 1 | 2 | .... | 1989-90 | 1994-95 |
| Johns, Don | NYR, Mtl., Min. | 6 | 153 | 2 | 21 | 23 | 76 | .... | .... | .... | .... | .... | .... | 1960-61 | 1967-68 |
| Johnson, Allan | Mtl., Det. | 4 | 105 | 21 | 28 | 49 | 30 | 11 | 2 | 2 | 4 | 6 | .... | 1956-57 | 1962-63 |
| Johnson, Brian | Det. | 1 | 3 | 0 | 0 | 0 | 5 | .... | .... | .... | .... | .... | .... | 1983-84 | 1983-84 |
| • Johnson, Ching | NYR, NYA | 12 | 436 | 38 | 48 | 86 | 808 | 61 | 5 | 2 | 7 | 161 | 2 | 1926-27 | 1937-38 |
| Johnson, Craig | St.L., L.A., Ana., Tor., Wsh. | 10 | 557 | 75 | 98 | 173 | 260 | 16 | 3 | 2 | 5 | 10 | .... | 1994-95 | 2003-04 |
| • Johnson, Danny | Tor., Van., Det. | 3 | 121 | 18 | 19 | 37 | 24 | .... | .... | .... | .... | .... | .... | 1969-70 | 1971-72 |
| Johnson, Earl | Det. | 1 | 1 | 0 | 0 | 0 | 0 | .... | .... | .... | .... | .... | 1 | 1953-54 | 1953-54 |
| Johnson, Greg | Det., Pit., Chi., Nsh. | 12 | 785 | 145 | 224 | 369 | 345 | 37 | 7 | 6 | 13 | 14 | .... | 1993-94 | 2005-06 |
| Johnson, Jim | NYR, Phi., L.A. | 8 | 302 | 75 | 111 | 186 | 73 | 7 | 0 | 2 | 2 | 2 | .... | 1964-65 | 1971-72 |
| Johnson, Jim | Pit., Min., Dal., Wsh., Phx. | 13 | 829 | 29 | 166 | 195 | 1197 | 51 | 1 | 11 | 12 | 132 | .... | 1985-86 | 1997-98 |
| Johnson, Mark | Pit., Min., Hfd., St.L., N.J. | 11 | 669 | 203 | 305 | 508 | 260 | 37 | 16 | 12 | 28 | 10 | .... | 1979-80 | 1989-90 |
| Johnson, Matt | L.A., Atl., Min. | 10 | 473 | 23 | 20 | 43 | 1523 | 16 | 0 | 0 | 0 | 31 | .... | 1994-95 | 2003-04 |
| ‡ Johnson, Mike | Tor., T.B., Phx., Mtl., St.L. | 11 | 661 | 129 | 246 | 375 | 315 | 22 | 4 | 3 | 7 | 10 | .... | 1996-97 | 2007-08 |
| Johnson, Norm | Bos., Chi. | 3 | 61 | 5 | 20 | 25 | 41 | 14 | 4 | 0 | 4 | 6 | .... | 1957-58 | 1959-60 |
| Johnson, Terry | Que., St.L., Cgy., Tor. | 9 | 285 | 3 | 24 | 27 | 580 | 38 | 0 | 4 | 4 | 118 | .... | 1979-80 | 1987-88 |
| • Johnson, Tom | Mtl., Bos. | 17 | 978 | 51 | 213 | 264 | 960 | 111 | 8 | 15 | 23 | 109 | 6 | 1947-48 | 1964-65 |
| • Johnson, Virgil | Chi. | 3 | 75 | 1 | 11 | 12 | 27 | 19 | 0 | 3 | 3 | 4 | 1 | 1937-38 | 1944-45 |
| Johnston, Bernie | Hfd. | 2 | 57 | 12 | 24 | 36 | 16 | 3 | 0 | 1 | 1 | 0 | .... | 1979-80 | 1980-81 |
| • Johnston, George | Chi. | 4 | 58 | 20 | 12 | 32 | 2 | .... | .... | .... | .... | .... | .... | 1941-42 | 1946-47 |
| Johnston, Greg | Bos., Tor. | 9 | 187 | 26 | 29 | 55 | 124 | 22 | 2 | 1 | 3 | 12 | .... | 1983-84 | 1991-92 |
| Johnston, Jay | Wsh. | 2 | 8 | 0 | 0 | 0 | 13 | .... | .... | .... | .... | .... | .... | 1980-81 | 1981-82 |
| Johnston, Joey | Min., Cal., Chi. | 6 | 331 | 85 | 106 | 191 | 320 | .... | .... | .... | .... | .... | .... | 1968-69 | 1975-76 |
| Johnston, Larry | L.A., Det., K.C., Col. | 7 | 320 | 9 | 64 | 73 | 580 | .... | .... | .... | .... | .... | .... | 1967-68 | 1976-77 |
| Johnston, Marshall | Min., Cal. | 7 | 251 | 14 | 52 | 66 | 58 | 6 | 0 | 0 | 0 | 2 | .... | 1967-68 | 1973-74 |
| Johnston, Randy | NYI | 1 | 4 | 0 | 0 | 0 | 4 | .... | .... | .... | .... | .... | .... | 1979-80 | 1979-80 |
| Johnstone, Eddie | NYR, Det. | 10 | 426 | 122 | 136 | 258 | 375 | 55 | 13 | 10 | 23 | 83 | .... | 1975-76 | 1986-87 |
| Johnstone, Ross | Tor. | 2 | 42 | 5 | 4 | 9 | 14 | 3 | 0 | 0 | 0 | 0 | 1 | 1943-44 | 1944-45 |
| ‡ Jokela, Mikko | Van. | 1 | 1 | 0 | 0 | 0 | 0 | .... | .... | .... | .... | .... | .... | 2002-03 | 2002-03 |
| • Joliat, Aurel | Mtl. | 16 | 655 | 270 | 190 | 460 | 771 | 45 | 9 | 13 | 22 | 66 | 3 | 1922-23 | 1937-38 |
| • Joliat, Rene | Mtl. | 1 | 1 | 0 | 0 | 0 | 0 | .... | .... | .... | .... | .... | .... | 1924-25 | 1924-25 |
| Joly, Greg | Wsh., Det. | 9 | 365 | 21 | 76 | 97 | 250 | 5 | 0 | 0 | 0 | 8 | .... | 1974-75 | 1982-83 |
| Joly, Yvan | Mtl. | 3 | 2 | 0 | 0 | 0 | 0 | 1 | 0 | 0 | 0 | 0 | .... | 1979-80 | 1982-83 |
| Jomphe, Jean-Francois | Ana., Phx., Mtl. | 4 | 111 | 10 | 29 | 39 | 102 | .... | .... | .... | .... | .... | .... | 1995-96 | 1998-99 |
| Jonathan, Stan | Bos., Pit. | 8 | 411 | 91 | 110 | 201 | 751 | 63 | 8 | 4 | 12 | 137 | .... | 1975-76 | 1982-83 |
| Jones, Bob | NYR | 1 | 2 | 0 | 0 | 0 | 0 | .... | .... | .... | .... | .... | .... | 1968-69 | 1968-69 |
| Jones, Brad | Wpg., L.A., Phi. | 6 | 148 | 25 | 31 | 56 | 122 | 9 | 1 | 1 | 2 | 2 | .... | 1986-87 | 1991-92 |
| • Jones, Buck | Det., Tor. | 4 | 50 | 2 | 2 | 4 | 36 | 12 | 0 | 1 | 1 | 18 | .... | 1938-39 | 1942-43 |
| Jones, Jim | Cal. | 1 | 2 | 0 | 0 | 0 | 0 | .... | .... | .... | .... | .... | .... | 1971-72 | 1971-72 |
| Jones, Jimmy | Tor. | 3 | 148 | 13 | 18 | 31 | 68 | 19 | 1 | 5 | 6 | 11 | .... | 1977-78 | 1979-80 |
| Jones, Keith | Wsh., Col., Phi. | 9 | 491 | 117 | 141 | 258 | 765 | 63 | 12 | 12 | 24 | 120 | .... | 1992-93 | 2000-01 |
| Jones, Ron | Bos., Pit., Wsh. | 5 | 54 | 1 | 4 | 5 | 31 | .... | .... | .... | .... | .... | .... | 1971-72 | 1975-76 |
| Jones, Ty | Chi., Fla. | 2 | 14 | 0 | 0 | 0 | 19 | .... | .... | .... | .... | .... | .... | 1998-99 | 2003-04 |
| ‡ Jonsson, Hans | Pit. | 4 | 242 | 10 | 38 | 48 | 92 | 27 | 0 | 1 | 1 | 14 | .... | 1999-00 | 2002-03 |
| ‡ Jonsson, Jorgen | NYI, Ana. | 1 | 81 | 12 | 19 | 31 | 16 | .... | .... | .... | .... | .... | .... | 1999-00 | 1999-00 |
| Jonsson, Kenny | Tor., NYI | 10 | 686 | 63 | 204 | 267 | 298 | 19 | 1 | 3 | 4 | 6 | .... | 1994-95 | 2003-04 |
| ‡ Jonsson, Lars | Phi. | 1 | 8 | 0 | 2 | 2 | 6 | .... | .... | .... | .... | .... | .... | 2006-07 | 2006-07 |
| Jonsson, Tomas | NYI, Edm. | 8 | 552 | 85 | 259 | 344 | 482 | 80 | 11 | 26 | 37 | 97 | 2 | 1981-82 | 1988-89 |
| Joseph, Chris | Pit., Edm., T.B., Van., Phi., Phx., Atl. | 14 | 510 | 39 | 112 | 151 | 567 | 31 | 3 | 4 | 7 | 24 | .... | 1987-88 | 2000-01 |
| Joseph, Tony | Wpg. | 1 | 2 | 1 | 0 | 1 | 0 | .... | .... | .... | .... | .... | .... | 1988-89 | 1988-89 |

| | | | Regular Schedule | | | | | Playoffs | | | | | | | |
|---|---|---|---|---|---|---|---|---|---|---|---|---|---|---|---|
| Name | NHL Teams | NHL Seasons | GP | G | A | TP | PIM | GP | G | A | TP | PIM | NHL Cup Wins | First NHL Season | Last NHL Season |
| Joyal, Eddie | Det., Tor., L.A., Phi. | 9 | 466 | 128 | 134 | 262 | 103 | 50 | 11 | 8 | 19 | 18 | .... | 1962-63 | 1971-72 |
| Joyce, Bob | Bos., Wsh., Wpg. | 6 | 158 | 34 | 49 | 83 | 90 | 46 | 15 | 9 | 24 | 29 | .... | 1987-88 | 1992-93 |
| Joyce, Duane | Dal. | 1 | 3 | 0 | 0 | 0 | 0 | .... | .... | .... | .... | .... | .... | 1993-94 | 1993-94 |
| • Juckes, Bing | NYR | 2 | 16 | 2 | 1 | 3 | 6 | .... | .... | .... | .... | .... | .... | 1947-48 | 1949-50 |
| Juhlin, Patrik | Phi. | 2 | 56 | 7 | 6 | 13 | 23 | 13 | 1 | 0 | 1 | 2 | .... | 1994-95 | 1995-96 |
| Julien, Claude | Que. | 2 | 14 | 0 | 1 | 1 | 25 | .... | .... | .... | .... | .... | .... | 1984-85 | 1985-86 |
| Juneau, Joe | Bos., Wsh., Buf., Ott., Phx., Mtl. | 13 | 828 | 156 | 416 | 572 | 272 | 112 | 25 | 54 | 79 | 69 | .... | 1991-92 | 2003-04 |
| Junker, Steve | NYI | 2 | 5 | 0 | 0 | 0 | 0 | 3 | 0 | 1 | 1 | 0 | .... | 1992-93 | 1993-94 |
| Jutila, Timo | Buf. | 1 | 10 | 1 | 5 | 6 | 13 | .... | .... | .... | .... | .... | .... | 1984-85 | 1984-85 |
| • Juzda, Bill | NYR, Tor. | 9 | 398 | 14 | 54 | 68 | 398 | 42 | 0 | 3 | 3 | 46 | 2 | 1940-41 | 1951-52 |

## K

| | | | Regular Schedule | | | | | Playoffs | | | | | | | |
|---|---|---|---|---|---|---|---|---|---|---|---|---|---|---|---|
| Name | NHL Teams | NHL Seasons | GP | G | A | TP | PIM | GP | G | A | TP | PIM | NHL Cup Wins | First NHL Season | Last NHL Season |
| Kabel, Bob | NYR | 2 | 48 | 5 | 13 | 18 | 34 | .... | .... | .... | .... | .... | .... | 1959-60 | 1960-61 |
| Kachowski, Mark | Pit. | 3 | 64 | 6 | 5 | 11 | 209 | .... | .... | .... | .... | .... | .... | 1987-88 | 1989-90 |
| Kachur, Ed | Chi. | 2 | 96 | 10 | 14 | 24 | 35 | .... | .... | .... | .... | .... | .... | 1956-57 | 1957-58 |
| Kaese, Trent | Buf. | 1 | 1 | 0 | 0 | 0 | 0 | .... | .... | .... | .... | .... | .... | 1988-89 | 1988-89 |
| Kaiser, Vern | Mtl. | 1 | 50 | 7 | 5 | 12 | 33 | 2 | 0 | 0 | 0 | 0 | .... | 1950-51 | 1950-51 |
| • Kalbfleisch, Walter | Ott., St.L., NYA, Bos. | 4 | 36 | 0 | 4 | 4 | 32 | 5 | 0 | 0 | 0 | 2 | .... | 1933-34 | 1936-37 |
| • Kaleta, Alex | Chi., NYR | 7 | 387 | 92 | 121 | 213 | 190 | 17 | 1 | 6 | 7 | 2 | .... | 1941-42 | 1950-51 |
| ‡ Kallio, Tomi | Atl., CBJ, Phi. | 3 | 140 | 24 | 31 | 55 | 48 | .... | .... | .... | .... | .... | .... | 2000-01 | 2002-03 |
| Kallur, Anders | NYI | 6 | 383 | 101 | 110 | 211 | 149 | 78 | 12 | 23 | 35 | 32 | 4 | 1979-80 | 1984-85 |
| Kamensky, Valeri | Que., Col., NYR, Dal., N.J. | 11 | 637 | 200 | 301 | 501 | 383 | 66 | 25 | 35 | 60 | 72 | 1 | 1991-92 | 2001-02 |
| Kaminski, Kevin | Min., Que., Wsh. | 7 | 139 | 3 | 10 | 13 | 528 | 8 | 0 | 0 | 0 | 52 | .... | 1988-89 | 1996-97 |
| • Kaminsky, Max | Ott., St.L., Bos., Mtl.M. | 4 | 130 | 22 | 34 | 56 | 38 | 4 | 0 | 0 | 0 | 0 | .... | 1933-34 | 1936-37 |
| Kaminsky, Yan | Wpg., NYI | 2 | 26 | 3 | 2 | 5 | 4 | 2 | 0 | 0 | 0 | 4 | .... | 1993-94 | 1994-95 |
| • Kampman, Bingo | Tor. | 5 | 189 | 14 | 30 | 44 | 287 | 47 | 1 | 4 | 5 | 38 | 1 | 1937-38 | 1941-42 |
| Kane, Francis | Det. | 1 | 2 | 0 | 0 | 0 | 0 | .... | .... | .... | .... | .... | .... | 1943-44 | 1943-44 |
| ‡ Kanko, Petr | L.A. | 1 | 10 | 1 | 0 | 1 | 0 | .... | .... | .... | .... | .... | .... | 2005-06 | 2005-06 |
| Kannegiesser, Gord | St.L. | 2 | 23 | 0 | 1 | 1 | 15 | .... | .... | .... | .... | .... | .... | 1967-68 | 1971-72 |
| Kannegiesser, Sheldon | Pit., NYR, L.A., Van. | 8 | 366 | 14 | 67 | 81 | 292 | 18 | 0 | 2 | 2 | 10 | .... | 1970-71 | 1977-78 |
| ‡ Kapanen, Sami | Hfd., Car., Phi. | 12 | 831 | 189 | 269 | 458 | 175 | 87 | 13 | 22 | 35 | 22 | .... | 1995-96 | 2007-08 |
| Karabin, Ladislav | Pit. | 1 | 9 | 0 | 0 | 0 | 2 | .... | .... | .... | .... | .... | .... | 1993-94 | 1993-94 |
| ‡ Karalahti, Jere | L.A., Nsh. | 3 | 149 | 8 | 19 | 27 | 97 | 17 | 0 | 1 | 1 | 20 | .... | 1999-00 | 2001-02 |
| Karamnov, Vitali | St.L. | 3 | 92 | 12 | 20 | 32 | 65 | 2 | 0 | 0 | 0 | 2 | .... | 1992-93 | 1994-95 |
| Kariya, Steve | Van. | 3 | 65 | 9 | 18 | 27 | 32 | .... | .... | .... | .... | .... | .... | 1999-00 | 2001-02 |
| Karjalainen, Kyosti | L.A. | 1 | 28 | 1 | 8 | 9 | 12 | 3 | 0 | 1 | 1 | 2 | .... | 1991-92 | 1991-92 |
| Karlander, Al | Det. | 4 | 212 | 36 | 56 | 92 | 70 | 4 | 0 | 1 | 1 | 0 | .... | 1969-70 | 1972-73 |
| ‡ Karlsson, Andreas | Atl., T.B. | 5 | 264 | 16 | 35 | 51 | 72 | 6 | 0 | 0 | 0 | 0 | .... | 1999-00 | 2007-08 |
| Karpa, Dave | Que., Ana., Car., NYR | 12 | 557 | 18 | 80 | 98 | 1374 | 19 | 1 | 1 | 2 | 39 | .... | 1991-92 | 2002-03 |
| Karpov, Valeri | Ana. | 3 | 76 | 14 | 15 | 29 | 32 | .... | .... | .... | .... | .... | .... | 1994-95 | 1996-97 |
| ‡ Karpovtsev, Alexander | NYR, Tor., Chi., NYI, Fla. | 12 | 596 | 34 | 154 | 188 | 430 | 74 | 4 | 14 | 18 | 52 | 1 | 1993-94 | 2005-06 |
| Kasatonov, Alexei | N.J., Ana., St.L., Bos. | 7 | 383 | 38 | 122 | 160 | 326 | 33 | 4 | 7 | 11 | 40 | .... | 1989-90 | 1995-96 |
| ‡ Kasparaitis, Darius | NYI, Pit., Col., NYR | 14 | 863 | 27 | 136 | 163 | 1379 | 83 | 2 | 10 | 12 | 107 | .... | 1992-93 | 2006-07 |
| Kasper, Steve | Bos., L.A., Phi., T.B. | 13 | 821 | 177 | 291 | 468 | 554 | 94 | 20 | 28 | 48 | 82 | .... | 1980-81 | 1992-93 |
| Kastelic, Ed | Wsh., Hfd. | 7 | 220 | 11 | 10 | 21 | 719 | 8 | 1 | 0 | 1 | 32 | .... | 1985-86 | 1991-92 |
| Kaszycki, Mike | NYI, Wsh., Tor. | 5 | 226 | 42 | 80 | 122 | 108 | 19 | 2 | 6 | 8 | 10 | .... | 1977-78 | 1982-83 |
| ‡ Kavanagh, Pat | Van., Phi. | 4 | 14 | 2 | 0 | 2 | 4 | 3 | 0 | 0 | 0 | 2 | .... | 2000-01 | 2005-06 |
| • Kea, Ed | Atl., St.L. | 10 | 583 | 30 | 145 | 175 | 508 | 32 | 2 | 4 | 6 | 39 | .... | 1973-74 | 1982-83 |
| ‡ Keane, Mike | Mtl., Col., NYR, Dal., St.L., Van. | 16 | 1161 | 168 | 302 | 470 | 881 | 220 | 34 | 40 | 74 | 135 | 3 | 1988-89 | 2003-04 |
| Kearns, Dennis | Van. | 10 | 677 | 31 | 290 | 321 | 386 | 11 | 1 | 2 | 3 | 8 | .... | 1971-72 | 1980-81 |
| • Keating, Jack | Det. | 2 | 11 | 3 | 0 | 3 | 4 | .... | .... | .... | .... | .... | .... | 1938-39 | 1939-40 |
| • Keating, John | NYA | 2 | 35 | 5 | 5 | 10 | 17 | .... | .... | .... | .... | .... | .... | 1931-32 | 1932-33 |
| Keating, Mike | NYR | 1 | 1 | 0 | 0 | 0 | 0 | .... | .... | .... | .... | .... | .... | 1977-78 | 1977-78 |
| • Keats, Duke | Bos., Det., Chi. | 3 | 82 | 30 | 19 | 49 | 113 | .... | .... | .... | .... | .... | .... | 1926-27 | 1928-29 |
| Keczmer, Dan | Min., Hfd., Cgy., Dal., Nsh. | 10 | 235 | 8 | 38 | 46 | 212 | 12 | 0 | 1 | 1 | 8 | .... | 1990-91 | 1999-00 |
| Keefe, Sheldon | T.B. | 3 | 125 | 12 | 12 | 24 | 78 | .... | .... | .... | .... | .... | .... | 2000-01 | 2002-03 |
| • Keeling, Butch | Tor., NYR | 12 | 525 | 157 | 63 | 220 | 331 | 47 | 11 | 11 | 22 | 34 | 1 | 1926-27 | 1937-38 |
| Keenan, Larry | Tor., St.L., Buf., Phi. | 6 | 233 | 38 | 64 | 102 | 28 | 46 | 15 | 16 | 31 | 12 | .... | 1961-62 | 1971-72 |
| Kehoe, Rick | Tor., Pit. | 14 | 906 | 371 | 396 | 767 | 120 | 39 | 4 | 17 | 21 | 4 | .... | 1971-72 | 1984-85 |
| Kekalainen, Jarmo | Bos., Ott. | 5 | 55 | 5 | 8 | 13 | 28 | .... | .... | .... | .... | .... | .... | 1989-90 | 1993-94 |
| Kelleher, Chris | Bos. | 1 | 1 | 0 | 0 | 0 | 0 | .... | .... | .... | .... | .... | .... | 2001-02 | 2001-02 |
| Keller, Ralph | NYR | 1 | 3 | 1 | 0 | 1 | 6 | .... | .... | .... | .... | .... | .... | 1962-63 | 1962-63 |
| Kellgren, Christer | Col. | 1 | 5 | 0 | 0 | 0 | 0 | .... | .... | .... | .... | .... | .... | 1981-82 | 1981-82 |
| Kelly, Bob | Phi., Wsh. | 12 | 837 | 154 | 208 | 362 | 1454 | 101 | 9 | 14 | 23 | 172 | 2 | 1970-71 | 1981-82 |
| Kelly, Bob | St.L., Pit., Chi. | 6 | 425 | 87 | 109 | 196 | 687 | 23 | 6 | 3 | 9 | 40 | .... | 1973-74 | 1978-79 |
| Kelly, Dave | Det. | 1 | 16 | 2 | 0 | 2 | 4 | .... | .... | .... | .... | .... | .... | 1976-77 | 1976-77 |
| Kelly, John Paul | L.A. | 7 | 400 | 54 | 70 | 124 | 366 | 18 | 1 | 1 | 2 | 41 | .... | 1979-80 | 1985-86 |
| • Kelly, Pep | Tor., Chi., Bro. | 8 | 288 | 74 | 53 | 127 | 105 | 38 | 7 | 6 | 13 | 10 | .... | 1934-35 | 1941-42 |
| • Kelly, Pete | St.L., Det., NYA, Bro. | 7 | 177 | 21 | 38 | 59 | 68 | 19 | 3 | 1 | 4 | 2 | 2 | 1934-35 | 1941-42 |
| Kelly, Red | Det., Tor. | 20 | 1316 | 281 | 542 | 823 | 327 | 164 | 33 | 59 | 92 | 51 | 8 | 1947-48 | 1966-67 |
| • Kemp, Kevin | Hfd. | 1 | 3 | 0 | 0 | 0 | 4 | .... | .... | .... | .... | .... | .... | 1980-81 | 1980-81 |
| Kemp, Stan | Tor. | 1 | 1 | 0 | 0 | 0 | 2 | .... | .... | .... | .... | .... | .... | 1948-49 | 1948-49 |
| Kenady, Chris | St.L., NYR | 2 | 7 | 0 | 2 | 2 | 0 | .... | .... | .... | .... | .... | .... | 1997-98 | 1999-00 |
| • Kendall, Bill | Chi., Tor. | 5 | 131 | 16 | 10 | 26 | 28 | 6 | 0 | 0 | 0 | 0 | 1 | 1933-34 | 1937-38 |
| Kennedy, Dean | L.A., NYR, Buf., Wpg., Edm. | 12 | 717 | 26 | 108 | 134 | 1118 | 36 | 1 | 7 | 8 | 59 | .... | 1982-83 | 1994-95 |
| Kennedy, Forbes | Chi., Det., Bos., Phi., Tor. | 11 | 603 | 70 | 108 | 178 | 988 | 12 | 2 | 4 | 6 | 64 | .... | 1956-57 | 1968-69 |
| ‡ Kennedy, Mike | Dal., Tor., NYI | 5 | 145 | 16 | 36 | 52 | 112 | 5 | 0 | 0 | 0 | 9 | .... | 1994-95 | 1998-99 |
| Kennedy, Sheldon | Det., Cgy., Bos. | 8 | 310 | 49 | 58 | 107 | 233 | 24 | 6 | 4 | 10 | 20 | .... | 1989-90 | 1996-97 |
| Kennedy, Ted | Tor. | 14 | 696 | 231 | 329 | 560 | 432 | 78 | 29 | 31 | 60 | 32 | 5 | 1942-43 | 1956-57 |
| • Kenny, Ernest | NYR, Chi. | 2 | 10 | 0 | 0 | 0 | 18 | .... | .... | .... | .... | .... | .... | 1930-31 | 1934-35 |
| Keon, Dave | Tor., Hfd. | 18 | 1296 | 396 | 590 | 986 | 117 | 92 | 32 | 36 | 68 | 6 | 4 | 1960-61 | 1981-82 |
| Kerch, Alexander | Edm. | 1 | 5 | 0 | 0 | 0 | 2 | .... | .... | .... | .... | .... | .... | 1993-94 | 1993-94 |
| Kerr, Alan | NYI, Det., Wpg. | 9 | 391 | 72 | 94 | 166 | 826 | 38 | 5 | 4 | 9 | 70 | .... | 1984-85 | 1992-93 |
| Kerr, Reg | Cle., Chi., Edm. | 6 | 263 | 66 | 94 | 160 | 169 | 7 | 1 | 0 | 1 | 7 | .... | 1977-78 | 1983-84 |
| Kerr, Tim | Phi., NYR, Hfd. | 13 | 655 | 370 | 304 | 674 | 596 | 81 | 40 | 31 | 71 | 58 | .... | 1980-81 | 1992-93 |
| Kesa, Dan | Van., Dal., Pit., T.B. | 4 | 139 | 8 | 22 | 30 | 66 | 13 | 1 | 0 | 1 | 0 | .... | 1993-94 | 1999-00 |
| Kessell, Rick | Pit., Cal. | 5 | 135 | 4 | 24 | 28 | 6 | .... | .... | .... | .... | .... | .... | 1969-70 | 1973-74 |
| Ketola, Veli-Pekka | Col. | 1 | 44 | 9 | 5 | 14 | 4 | .... | .... | .... | .... | .... | .... | 1981-82 | 1981-82 |
| Ketter, Kerry | Atl. | 1 | 41 | 0 | 2 | 2 | 58 | .... | .... | .... | .... | .... | .... | 1972-73 | 1972-73 |
| Kharin, Sergei | Wpg. | 1 | 7 | 2 | 3 | 5 | 2 | .... | .... | .... | .... | .... | .... | 1990-91 | 1990-91 |
| ‡ Kharitonov, Alexander | T.B., NYI | 2 | 71 | 7 | 15 | 22 | 12 | .... | .... | .... | .... | .... | .... | 2000-01 | 2001-02 |
| Khavanov, Alexander | St.L., Tor. | 5 | 348 | 27 | 75 | 102 | 233 | 26 | 5 | 5 | 10 | 18 | .... | 2000-01 | 2005-06 |
| Khmylev, Yuri | Buf., St.L. | 5 | 263 | 64 | 88 | 152 | 133 | 26 | 8 | 6 | 14 | 24 | .... | 1992-93 | 1996-97 |
| Khristich, Dmitri | Wsh., L.A., Bos., Tor. | 12 | 811 | 259 | 337 | 596 | 422 | 75 | 15 | 25 | 40 | 41 | .... | 1990-91 | 2001-02 |
| Kidd, Ian | Van. | 2 | 20 | 4 | 7 | 11 | 25 | .... | .... | .... | .... | .... | .... | 1987-88 | 1988-89 |
| Kiessling, Udo | Min. | 1 | 1 | 0 | 0 | 0 | 2 | .... | .... | .... | .... | .... | .... | 1981-82 | 1981-82 |
| Kilger, Chad | Ana., Wpg., Phx., Chi., Edm., Mtl., Tor. | 12 | 714 | 107 | 111 | 218 | 363 | 36 | 3 | 2 | 5 | 13 | .... | 1995-96 | 2007-08 |
| Kilrea, Brian | Det., L.A. | 2 | 26 | 3 | 5 | 8 | 12 | .... | .... | .... | .... | .... | .... | 1957-58 | 1967-68 |
| • Kilrea, Hec | Ott., Det., Tor. | 15 | 633 | 167 | 129 | 296 | 438 | 48 | 8 | 7 | 15 | 18 | 3 | 1925-26 | 1939-40 |
| • Kilrea, Ken | Det. | 5 | 91 | 16 | 23 | 39 | 8 | 15 | 2 | 2 | 4 | 4 | .... | 1938-39 | 1943-44 |
| • Kilrea, Wally | Ott., Phi., NYA, Mtl.M., Det. | 9 | 329 | 35 | 58 | 93 | 87 | 25 | 2 | 4 | 6 | 6 | 2 | 1929-30 | 1937-38 |
| Kimble, Darin | Que., St.L., Bos., Chi. | 7 | 311 | 23 | 20 | 43 | 1082 | 23 | 0 | 0 | 0 | 52 | .... | 1988-89 | 1994-95 |
| Kindrachuk, Orest | Phi., Pit., Wsh. | 10 | 508 | 118 | 261 | 379 | 648 | 76 | 20 | 20 | 40 | 53 | 2 | 1972-73 | 1981-82 |
| King, Derek | NYI, Hfd., Tor., St.L. | 14 | 830 | 261 | 351 | 612 | 417 | 47 | 4 | 17 | 21 | 24 | .... | 1986-87 | 1999-00 |
| King, Frank | Mtl. | 1 | 10 | 1 | 0 | 1 | 2 | .... | .... | .... | .... | .... | .... | 1950-51 | 1950-51 |
| King, Kris | Det., NYR, Wpg., Phx., Tor., Chi. | 14 | 849 | 66 | 85 | 151 | 2030 | 67 | 8 | 5 | 13 | 142 | .... | 1987-88 | 2000-01 |
| King, Steven | NYR, Ana. | 3 | 67 | 17 | 8 | 25 | 75 | .... | .... | .... | .... | .... | .... | 1992-93 | 1995-96 |
| King, Wayne | Cal. | 3 | 73 | 5 | 18 | 23 | 34 | .... | .... | .... | .... | .... | .... | 1973-74 | 1975-76 |
| Kinnear, Geordie | Atl. | 1 | 4 | 0 | 0 | 0 | 13 | .... | .... | .... | .... | .... | .... | 1999-00 | 1999-00 |
| Kinsella, Brian | Wsh. | 2 | 10 | 0 | 1 | 1 | 0 | .... | .... | .... | .... | .... | .... | 1975-76 | 1976-77 |
| • Kinsella, Ray | Ott. | 1 | 14 | 0 | 0 | 0 | 0 | .... | .... | .... | .... | .... | .... | 1930-31 | 1930-31 |
| ‡ Kiprusoff, Marko | Mtl., NYI | 2 | 51 | 0 | 10 | 10 | 12 | .... | .... | .... | .... | .... | .... | 1995-96 | 2001-02 |
| • Kirk, Bobby | NYR | 1 | 39 | 4 | 8 | 12 | 14 | .... | .... | .... | .... | .... | .... | 1937-38 | 1937-38 |
| Kirkpatrick, Bob | NYR | 1 | 49 | 12 | 12 | 24 | 6 | .... | .... | .... | .... | .... | .... | 1942-43 | 1942-43 |
| Kirton, Mark | Tor., Det., Van. | 6 | 266 | 57 | 56 | 113 | 121 | 4 | 1 | 2 | 3 | 7 | .... | 1979-80 | 1984-85 |
| Kisio, Kelly | Det., NYR, S.J., Cgy. | 13 | 761 | 229 | 429 | 658 | 768 | 39 | 6 | 15 | 21 | 52 | .... | 1982-83 | 1994-95 |
| Kitchen, Bill | Mtl., Tor. | 4 | 41 | 1 | 4 | 5 | 40 | 3 | 0 | 1 | 1 | 0 | .... | 1981-82 | 1984-85 |
| • Kitchen, Hobie | Mtl.M., Det. | 2 | 47 | 5 | 4 | 9 | 58 | .... | .... | .... | .... | .... | 1 | 1925-26 | 1926-27 |
| Kitchen, Mike | Col., N.J. | 8 | 474 | 12 | 62 | 74 | 370 | 2 | 0 | 0 | 0 | 2 | .... | 1976-77 | 1983-84 |
| Kjellberg, Patric | Mtl., Nsh., Ana. | 6 | 394 | 64 | 96 | 160 | 84 | 10 | 0 | 0 | 0 | 0 | .... | 1992-93 | 2002-03 |
| Klassen, Ralph | Cal., Cle., Col., St.L. | 9 | 497 | 52 | 93 | 145 | 120 | 26 | 4 | 2 | 6 | 12 | .... | 1975-76 | 1983-84 |
| Klatt, Trent | Min., Dal., Phi., Van., L.A. | 13 | 782 | 143 | 200 | 343 | 307 | 74 | 16 | 9 | 25 | 20 | .... | 1991-92 | 2003-04 |
| • Klein, Lloyd | Bos., NYA | 8 | 164 | 30 | 24 | 54 | 68 | 5 | 0 | 0 | 0 | 2 | 1 | 1928-29 | 1937-38 |
| Kleinendorst, Scot | NYR, Hfd., Wsh. | 8 | 281 | 12 | 46 | 58 | 452 | 26 | 2 | 7 | 9 | 40 | .... | 1982-83 | 1989-90 |
| ‡ Klemm, Jon | Que., Col., Chi., Dal., L.A. | 15 | 773 | 42 | 100 | 142 | 436 | 105 | 7 | 7 | 14 | 47 | 2 | 1991-92 | 2007-08 |

*Yan Kaminsky*

*Red Kelly*

*Chad Kilger*

*Joe Klukay*

Gord Kluzak

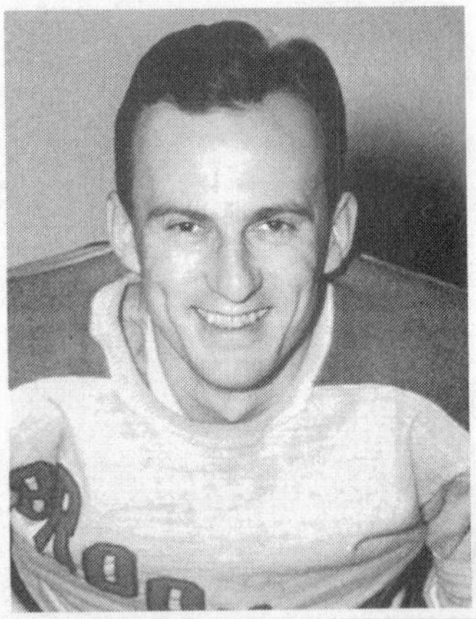

Joe Krol

Yvon Lambert

Daniel Laperriere

| Name | NHL Teams | NHL Seasons | Regular Schedule GP | G | A | TP | PIM | Playoffs GP | G | A | TP | PIM | NHL Cup Wins | First NHL Season | Last NHL Season |
|---|---|---|---|---|---|---|---|---|---|---|---|---|---|---|---|
| Klima, Petr | Det., Edm., T.B., L.A., Pit. | 13 | 786 | 313 | 260 | 573 | 671 | 95 | 28 | 24 | 52 | 83 | 1 | 1985-86 | 1998-99 |
| Klimovich, Sergei | Chi. | 1 | 1 | 0 | 0 | 0 | 2 | .... | .... | .... | .... | .... | .... | 1996-97 | 1996-97 |
| • Klingbeil, Ike | Chi. | 1 | 5 | 1 | 2 | 3 | 2 | .... | .... | .... | .... | .... | .... | 1936-37 | 1936-37 |
| ‡ Kloucek, Tomas | NYR, Nsh., Atl. | 5 | 141 | 2 | 8 | 10 | 250 | .... | .... | .... | .... | .... | .... | 2000-01 | 2005-06 |
| • Klukay, Joe | Tor., Bos. | 11 | 566 | 109 | 127 | 236 | 189 | 71 | 13 | 10 | 23 | 23 | 4 | 1942-43 | 1955-56 |
| Kluzak, Gord | Bos. | 7 | 299 | 25 | 98 | 123 | 543 | 46 | 6 | 13 | 19 | 129 | .... | 1982-83 | 1990-91 |
| • Knibbs, Bill | Bos. | 1 | 53 | 7 | 10 | 17 | 4 | .... | .... | .... | .... | .... | .... | 1964-65 | 1964-65 |
| Knipscheer, Fred | Bos., St.L. | 3 | 28 | 6 | 3 | 9 | 18 | 16 | 2 | 1 | 3 | 6 | .... | 1993-94 | 1995-96 |
| • Knott, Nick | Bro. | 1 | 14 | 3 | 1 | 4 | 9 | .... | .... | .... | .... | .... | .... | 1941-42 | 1941-42 |
| Knox, Paul | Tor. | 1 | 1 | 0 | 0 | 0 | 0 | .... | .... | .... | .... | .... | .... | 1954-55 | 1954-55 |
| Knutsen, Espen | Ana., CBJ | 5 | 207 | 30 | 81 | 111 | 105 | .... | .... | .... | .... | .... | .... | 1997-98 | 2003-04 |
| Koalska, Matt | NYI | 1 | 3 | 0 | 0 | 0 | 2 | .... | .... | .... | .... | .... | .... | 2005-06 | 2005-06 |
| Kocur, Joe | Det., NYR, Van. | 15 | 820 | 80 | 82 | 162 | 2519 | 118 | 10 | 12 | 22 | 231 | 3 | 1984-85 | 1998-99 |
| Koehler, Greg | Car. | 1 | 1 | 0 | 0 | 0 | 0 | .... | .... | .... | .... | .... | .... | 2000-01 | 2000-01 |
| ‡ Kohn, Ladislav | Cgy., Tor., Ana., Atl., Det. | 7 | 186 | 14 | 28 | 42 | 125 | 2 | 0 | 0 | 0 | 5 | .... | 1995-96 | 2002-03 |
| ‡ Koivisto, Tom | St.L. | 1 | 22 | 2 | 4 | 6 | 10 | .... | .... | .... | .... | .... | .... | 2002-03 | 2002-03 |
| ‡ Kolarik, Pavel | Bos. | 2 | 23 | 0 | 0 | 0 | 10 | .... | .... | .... | .... | .... | .... | 2000-01 | 2001-02 |
| Kolesar, Mark | Tor. | 2 | 28 | 2 | 2 | 4 | 14 | 3 | 1 | 0 | 1 | 2 | .... | 1995-96 | 1996-97 |
| ‡ Kolnik, Juraj | NYI, Fla. | 6 | 240 | 46 | 49 | 95 | 84 | .... | .... | .... | .... | .... | .... | 2000-01 | 2006-07 |
| Kolstad, Dean | Min., S.J. | 3 | 40 | 1 | 7 | 8 | 69 | .... | .... | .... | .... | .... | .... | 1988-89 | 1992-93 |
| ‡ Koltsov, Konstantin | Pit. | 3 | 144 | 12 | 26 | 38 | 50 | .... | .... | .... | .... | .... | .... | 2002-03 | 2005-06 |
| Komadoski, Neil | L.A., St.L. | 8 | 502 | 16 | 76 | 92 | 632 | 23 | 0 | 2 | 2 | 47 | .... | 1972-73 | 1979-80 |
| Komarniski, Zenith | Van., CBJ | 3 | 21 | 1 | 1 | 2 | 10 | .... | .... | .... | .... | .... | .... | 1999-00 | 2003-04 |
| ‡ Kondratiev, Maxim | Tor., NYR, Ana. | 3 | 40 | 1 | 2 | 3 | 24 | .... | .... | .... | .... | .... | .... | 2003-04 | 2007-08 |
| Konik, George | Pit. | 1 | 52 | 7 | 8 | 15 | 26 | .... | .... | .... | .... | .... | .... | 1967-68 | 1967-68 |
| Konowalchuk, Steve | Wsh., Col. | 14 | 790 | 171 | 225 | 396 | 703 | 52 | 9 | 12 | 21 | 60 | .... | 1991-92 | 2005-06 |
| Konroyd, Steve | Cgy., NYI, Chi., Hfd., Det., Ott. | 15 | 895 | 41 | 195 | 236 | 863 | 97 | 10 | 15 | 25 | 99 | .... | 1980-81 | 1994-95 |
| Konstantinov, Vladimir | Det. | 6 | 446 | 47 | 128 | 175 | 838 | 82 | 5 | 14 | 19 | 107 | 1 | 1991-92 | 1996-97 |
| Kontos, Chris | NYR, Pit., L.A., T.B. | 8 | 230 | 54 | 69 | 123 | 103 | 20 | 11 | 0 | 11 | 12 | .... | 1982-83 | 1992-93 |
| • Kopak, Russ | Bos. | 1 | 24 | 7 | 9 | 16 | 0 | .... | .... | .... | .... | .... | .... | 1943-44 | 1943-44 |
| Korab, Jerry | Chi., Van., Buf., L.A. | 15 | 975 | 114 | 341 | 455 | 1629 | 93 | 8 | 18 | 26 | 201 | .... | 1970-71 | 1984-85 |
| Kordic, Dan | Phi. | 6 | 197 | 4 | 8 | 12 | 584 | 12 | 1 | 0 | 1 | 22 | .... | 1991-92 | 1998-99 |
| • Kordic, John | Mtl., Tor., Wsh., Que. | 7 | 244 | 17 | 18 | 35 | 997 | 41 | 4 | 3 | 7 | 131 | 1 | 1985-86 | 1991-92 |
| Korn, Jim | Det., Tor., Buf., N.J., Cgy. | 10 | 597 | 66 | 122 | 188 | 1801 | 16 | 1 | 2 | 3 | 109 | .... | 1979-80 | 1989-90 |
| Korney, Mike | Det., NYR | 4 | 77 | 9 | 10 | 19 | 59 | .... | .... | .... | .... | .... | .... | 1973-74 | 1978-79 |
| Korolev, Evgeny | NYI | 3 | 42 | 1 | 4 | 5 | 20 | 2 | 0 | 0 | 0 | 0 | .... | 1999-00 | 2001-02 |
| ‡ Korolev, Igor | St.L., Wpg., Phx., Tor., Chi. | 12 | 795 | 119 | 227 | 346 | 330 | 41 | 0 | 8 | 8 | 6 | .... | 1992-93 | 2003-04 |
| Koroll, Cliff | Chi. | 11 | 814 | 208 | 254 | 462 | 376 | 85 | 19 | 29 | 48 | 67 | .... | 1969-70 | 1979-80 |
| ‡ Korolyuk, Alexander | S.J. | 6 | 296 | 62 | 80 | 142 | 140 | 34 | 6 | 8 | 14 | 18 | .... | 1997-98 | 2003-04 |
| Kortko, Roger | NYI | 2 | 79 | 7 | 17 | 24 | 28 | 10 | 0 | 3 | 3 | 17 | .... | 1984-85 | 1985-86 |
| Kostynski, Doug | Bos. | 2 | 15 | 3 | 1 | 4 | 4 | .... | .... | .... | .... | .... | .... | 1983-84 | 1984-85 |
| Kotanen, Dick | NYR | 1 | 1 | 0 | 0 | 0 | 0 | .... | .... | .... | .... | .... | .... | 1950-51 | 1950-51 |
| Kotsopoulos, Chris | NYR, Hfd., Tor., Det. | 10 | 479 | 44 | 109 | 153 | 827 | 31 | 1 | 3 | 4 | 91 | .... | 1980-81 | 1989-90 |
| ‡ Kovalenko, Andrei | Que., Col., Mtl., Edm., Phi., Car., Bos. | 9 | 620 | 173 | 206 | 379 | 389 | 33 | 5 | 6 | 11 | 20 | .... | 1992-93 | 2000-01 |
| Kowal, Joe | Buf. | 2 | 22 | 0 | 5 | 5 | 13 | 2 | 0 | 0 | 0 | 0 | .... | 1976-77 | 1977-78 |
| Kozak, Don | L.A., Van. | 7 | 437 | 96 | 86 | 182 | 480 | 29 | 7 | 2 | 9 | 69 | .... | 1972-73 | 1978-79 |
| Kozak, Les | Tor. | 1 | 12 | 1 | 0 | 1 | 2 | .... | .... | .... | .... | .... | .... | 1961-62 | 1961-62 |
| ‡ Kraft, Milan | Pit. | 4 | 207 | 41 | 41 | 82 | 52 | 8 | 0 | 0 | 0 | 2 | .... | 2000-01 | 2003-04 |
| Kraft, Ryan | S.J. | 1 | 7 | 0 | 1 | 1 | 0 | .... | .... | .... | .... | .... | .... | 2002-03 | 2002-03 |
| • Kraftcheck, Stephen | Bos., NYR, Tor. | 4 | 157 | 11 | 18 | 29 | 83 | 6 | 0 | 0 | 0 | 7 | .... | 1950-51 | 1958-59 |
| Krake, Skip | Bos., L.A., Buf. | 7 | 249 | 23 | 40 | 63 | 182 | 10 | 1 | 0 | 1 | 17 | .... | 1963-64 | 1970-71 |
| Kravchuk, Igor | Chi., Edm., St.L., Ott., Cgy., Fla. | 12 | 699 | 64 | 210 | 274 | 251 | 51 | 6 | 15 | 21 | 18 | .... | 1991-92 | 2002-03 |
| Kravets, Mikhail | S.J. | 2 | 2 | 0 | 0 | 0 | 0 | .... | .... | .... | .... | .... | .... | 1991-92 | 1992-93 |
| Krentz, Dale | Det. | 3 | 30 | 5 | 3 | 8 | 9 | 2 | 0 | 0 | 0 | 0 | .... | 1986-87 | 1988-89 |
| ‡ Krestanovich, Jordan | Col. | 2 | 22 | 0 | 2 | 2 | 6 | .... | .... | .... | .... | .... | .... | 2001-02 | 2003-04 |
| ‡ Kristek, Jaroslav | Buf. | 1 | 6 | 0 | 0 | 0 | 4 | .... | .... | .... | .... | .... | .... | 2002-03 | 2002-03 |
| ‡ Krivokrasov, Sergei | Chi., Nsh., Cgy., Min., Ana. | 10 | 450 | 86 | 109 | 195 | 288 | 21 | 2 | 0 | 2 | 14 | .... | 1992-93 | 2001-02 |
| • Krol, Joe | NYR, Bro. | 3 | 26 | 10 | 4 | 14 | 8 | .... | .... | .... | .... | .... | .... | 1936-37 | 1941-42 |
| Kromm, Richard | Cgy., NYI | 9 | 372 | 70 | 103 | 173 | 138 | 36 | 2 | 6 | 8 | 22 | .... | 1983-84 | 1992-93 |
| Kron, Robert | Van., Hfd., Car., CBJ | 12 | 771 | 144 | 194 | 338 | 119 | 16 | 3 | 2 | 5 | 2 | .... | 1990-91 | 2001-02 |
| Krook, Kevin | Col. | 1 | 3 | 0 | 0 | 0 | 2 | .... | .... | .... | .... | .... | .... | 1978-79 | 1978-79 |
| ‡ Kroupa, Vlastimil | S.J., N.J. | 5 | 105 | 4 | 19 | 23 | 66 | 20 | 1 | 2 | 3 | 25 | .... | 1993-94 | 1997-98 |
| Krulicki, Jim | NYR, Det. | 1 | 41 | 0 | 3 | 3 | 6 | .... | .... | .... | .... | .... | .... | 1970-71 | 1970-71 |
| Krupp, Uwe | Buf., NYI, Que., Col., Det., Atl. | 15 | 729 | 69 | 212 | 281 | 660 | 81 | 6 | 23 | 29 | 86 | 1 | 1986-87 | 2002-03 |
| Kruppke, Gord | Det. | 3 | 23 | 0 | 0 | 0 | 32 | .... | .... | .... | .... | .... | .... | 1990-91 | 1993-94 |
| Kruse, Paul | Cgy., NYI, Buf., S.J. | 11 | 423 | 38 | 33 | 71 | 1074 | 28 | 5 | 2 | 7 | 36 | .... | 1990-91 | 2000-01 |
| Krushelnyski, Mike | Bos., Edm., L.A., Tor., Det. | 14 | 897 | 241 | 328 | 569 | 699 | 139 | 29 | 43 | 72 | 106 | 3 | 1981-82 | 1994-95 |
| Krutov, Vladimir | Van. | 1 | 61 | 11 | 23 | 34 | 20 | .... | .... | .... | .... | .... | .... | 1989-90 | 1989-90 |
| Krygier, Todd | Hfd., Wsh., Ana. | 9 | 543 | 100 | 143 | 243 | 533 | 48 | 10 | 7 | 17 | 40 | .... | 1989-90 | 1997-98 |
| Kryskow, Dave | Chi., Wsh., Det., Atl. | 4 | 231 | 33 | 56 | 89 | 174 | 12 | 2 | 0 | 2 | 4 | .... | 1972-73 | 1975-76 |
| • Kryzanowski, Ed | Bos., Chi. | 5 | 237 | 15 | 22 | 37 | 65 | 18 | 0 | 1 | 1 | 4 | .... | 1948-49 | 1952-53 |
| Kucera, Frantisek | Chi., Hfd., Van., Phi., CBJ, Pit., Wsh. | 9 | 465 | 24 | 95 | 119 | 251 | 12 | 0 | 1 | 1 | 0 | .... | 1990-91 | 2001-02 |
| ‡ Kudashov, Alexei | Tor. | 1 | 25 | 1 | 0 | 1 | 4 | .... | .... | .... | .... | .... | .... | 1993-94 | 1993-94 |
| Kudelski, Bob | L.A., Ott., Fla. | 9 | 442 | 139 | 102 | 241 | 218 | 22 | 4 | 4 | 8 | 4 | .... | 1987-88 | 1995-96 |
| ‡ Kudroc, Kristian | T.B., Fla. | 3 | 26 | 2 | 2 | 4 | 38 | .... | .... | .... | .... | .... | .... | 2000-01 | 2003-04 |
| • Kuhn, Gord | NYA | 1 | 12 | 1 | 1 | 2 | 4 | .... | .... | .... | .... | .... | .... | 1932-33 | 1932-33 |
| • Kukulowicz, Aggie | NYR | 2 | 4 | 1 | 0 | 1 | 0 | .... | .... | .... | .... | .... | .... | 1952-53 | 1953-54 |
| Kulak, Stu | Van., Edm., NYR, Que., Wpg. | 4 | 90 | 8 | 4 | 12 | 130 | 3 | 0 | 0 | 0 | 2 | .... | 1982-83 | 1988-89 |
| Kuleshov, Mikhail | Col. | 1 | 3 | 0 | 0 | 0 | 0 | .... | .... | .... | .... | .... | .... | 2003-04 | 2003-04 |
| • Kullman, Arnie | Bos. | 2 | 13 | 0 | 1 | 1 | 11 | .... | .... | .... | .... | .... | .... | 1947-48 | 1949-50 |
| • Kullman, Eddie | NYR | 6 | 343 | 56 | 70 | 126 | 298 | 6 | 1 | 0 | 1 | 2 | .... | 1947-48 | 1953-54 |
| ‡ Kultanen, Jarno | Bos. | 3 | 102 | 2 | 11 | 13 | 59 | .... | .... | .... | .... | .... | .... | 2000-01 | 2002-03 |
| Kumpel, Mark | Que., Det., Wpg. | 6 | 288 | 38 | 46 | 84 | 113 | 39 | 6 | 4 | 10 | 14 | .... | 1984-85 | 1990-91 |
| • Kuntz, Alan | NYR | 2 | 45 | 10 | 12 | 22 | 12 | 6 | 1 | 0 | 1 | 2 | .... | 1941-42 | 1945-46 |
| Kuntz, Murray | St.L. | 1 | 7 | 1 | 2 | 3 | 0 | .... | .... | .... | .... | .... | .... | 1974-75 | 1974-75 |
| ‡ Kurka, Tomas | Car. | 2 | 17 | 3 | 2 | 5 | 2 | .... | .... | .... | .... | .... | .... | 2002-03 | 2003-04 |
| Kurri, Jari | Edm., L.A., NYR, Ana., Col. | 17 | 1251 | 601 | 797 | 1398 | 545 | 200 | 106 | 127 | 233 | 123 | 5 | 1980-81 | 1997-98 |
| Kurtenbach, Orland | NYR, Bos., Tor., Van. | 13 | 639 | 119 | 213 | 332 | 628 | 19 | 2 | 4 | 6 | 70 | .... | 1960-61 | 1973-74 |
| Kurtz, Justin | Van. | 1 | 27 | 3 | 5 | 8 | 14 | .... | .... | .... | .... | .... | .... | 2001-02 | 2001-02 |
| Kurvers, Tom | Mtl., Buf., N.J., Tor., Van., NYI, Ana. | 11 | 659 | 93 | 328 | 421 | 350 | 57 | 8 | 22 | 30 | 68 | 1 | 1984-85 | 1994-95 |
| Kuryluk, Merv | Chi. | 1 | .... | .... | .... | .... | .... | 2 | 0 | 0 | 0 | 0 | .... | 1961-62 | 1961-62 |
| Kushner, Dale | NYI, Phi. | 3 | 84 | 10 | 13 | 23 | 215 | .... | .... | .... | .... | .... | .... | 1989-90 | 1991-92 |
| ‡ Kutlak, Zdenek | Bos. | 3 | 16 | 1 | 2 | 3 | 4 | .... | .... | .... | .... | .... | .... | 2000-01 | 2003-04 |
| ‡ Kuznetsov, Maxim | Det., L.A. | 4 | 136 | 2 | 8 | 10 | 137 | .... | .... | .... | .... | .... | .... | 2000-01 | 2003-04 |
| Kuznik, Greg | Car. | 1 | 1 | 0 | 0 | 0 | 0 | .... | .... | .... | .... | .... | .... | 2000-01 | 2000-01 |
| Kuzyk, Ken | Cle. | 2 | 41 | 5 | 9 | 14 | 8 | .... | .... | .... | .... | .... | .... | 1976-77 | 1977-78 |
| Kvartalnov, Dmitri | Bos. | 2 | 112 | 42 | 49 | 91 | 26 | 4 | 0 | 0 | 0 | 0 | .... | 1992-93 | 1993-94 |
| ‡ Kvasha, Oleg | Fla., NYI, Phx. | 7 | 493 | 81 | 136 | 217 | 335 | 21 | 1 | 2 | 3 | 8 | .... | 1998-99 | 2005-06 |
| Kwong, Larry | NYR | 1 | 1 | 0 | 0 | 0 | 0 | .... | .... | .... | .... | .... | .... | 1947-48 | 1947-48 |
| • Kyle, Bill | NYR | 2 | 3 | 0 | 3 | 3 | 0 | .... | .... | .... | .... | .... | .... | 1949-50 | 1950-51 |
| • Kyle, Gus | NYR, Bos. | 3 | 203 | 6 | 20 | 26 | 362 | 14 | 1 | 2 | 3 | 34 | .... | 1949-50 | 1951-52 |
| Kyllonen, Markku | Wpg. | 1 | 9 | 0 | 2 | 2 | 2 | .... | .... | .... | .... | .... | .... | 1988-89 | 1988-89 |
| Kypreos, Nick | Wsh., Hfd., NYR, Tor. | 8 | 442 | 46 | 44 | 90 | 1210 | 34 | 1 | 3 | 4 | 65 | 1 | 1989-90 | 1996-97 |
| Kyte, Jim | Wpg., Pit., Cgy., Ott., S.J. | 13 | 598 | 17 | 49 | 66 | 1342 | 42 | 0 | 6 | 6 | 94 | .... | 1982-83 | 1995-96 |
| **L** | | | | | | | | | | | | | | | |
| ‡ Laaksonen, Antti | Bos., Min., Col. | 8 | 483 | 81 | 87 | 168 | 152 | 25 | 1 | 5 | 6 | 6 | .... | 1998-99 | 2006-07 |
| Labadie, Mike | NYR | 1 | 3 | 0 | 0 | 0 | 0 | .... | .... | .... | .... | .... | .... | 1952-53 | 1952-53 |
| Labatte, Neil | St.L. | 2 | 26 | 0 | 2 | 2 | 19 | .... | .... | .... | .... | .... | .... | 1978-79 | 1981-82 |
| L'Abbe, Moe | Chi. | 1 | 5 | 0 | 1 | 1 | 0 | .... | .... | .... | .... | .... | .... | 1972-73 | 1972-73 |
| Labelle, Marc | Dal. | 1 | 9 | 0 | 0 | 0 | 46 | .... | .... | .... | .... | .... | .... | 1996-97 | 1996-97 |
| • Labine, Leo | Bos., Det. | 11 | 643 | 128 | 193 | 321 | 730 | 60 | 12 | 11 | 23 | 82 | .... | 1951-52 | 1961-62 |
| Labossiere, Gord | NYR, L.A., Min. | 6 | 215 | 44 | 62 | 106 | 75 | 10 | 2 | 3 | 5 | 28 | .... | 1963-64 | 1971-72 |
| Labovitch, Max | NYR | 1 | 5 | 0 | 0 | 0 | 4 | .... | .... | .... | .... | .... | .... | 1943-44 | 1943-44 |
| Labraaten, Dan | Det., Cgy. | 4 | 268 | 71 | 73 | 144 | 47 | 8 | 1 | 0 | 1 | 4 | .... | 1978-79 | 1981-82 |
| Labre, Yvon | Pit., Wsh. | 9 | 371 | 14 | 87 | 101 | 788 | .... | .... | .... | .... | .... | .... | 1970-71 | 1980-81 |
| Labrie, Guy | Bos., NYR | 2 | 42 | 4 | 9 | 13 | 16 | .... | .... | .... | .... | .... | .... | 1943-44 | 1944-45 |
| Lach, Elmer | Mtl. | 14 | 664 | 215 | 408 | 623 | 478 | 76 | 19 | 45 | 64 | 36 | 3 | 1940-41 | 1953-54 |
| Lachance, Michel | Col. | 1 | 21 | 0 | 4 | 4 | 22 | .... | .... | .... | .... | .... | .... | 1978-79 | 1978-79 |
| Lachance, Scott | NYI, Mtl., Van., CBJ | 13 | 819 | 31 | 112 | 143 | 567 | 11 | 1 | 2 | 3 | 6 | .... | 1991-92 | 2003-04 |
| Lacombe, Francois | Oak., Buf., Que. | 4 | 78 | 2 | 17 | 19 | 54 | 3 | 1 | 0 | 1 | 0 | .... | 1968-69 | 1979-80 |
| Lacombe, Normand | Buf., Edm., Phi. | 7 | 319 | 53 | 62 | 115 | 196 | 26 | 5 | 1 | 6 | 49 | 1 | 1984-85 | 1990-91 |
| Lacroix, Andre | Phi., Chi., Hfd. | 6 | 325 | 79 | 119 | 198 | 44 | 16 | 2 | 5 | 7 | 0 | .... | 1967-68 | 1979-80 |
| Lacroix, Daniel | NYR, Bos., Phi., Edm., NYI | 7 | 188 | 11 | 7 | 18 | 379 | 16 | 0 | 1 | 1 | 26 | .... | 1993-94 | 1999-00 |
| Lacroix, Eric | Tor., L.A., Col., NYR, Ott. | 8 | 472 | 67 | 70 | 137 | 361 | 30 | 1 | 5 | 6 | 25 | .... | 1993-94 | 2000-01 |

| | | NHL | Regular Schedule | | | | | Playoffs | | | | | NHL Cup | First NHL | Last NHL |
|---|---|---|---|---|---|---|---|---|---|---|---|---|---|---|---|
| **Name** | **NHL Teams** | **Seasons** | **GP** | **G** | **A** | **TP** | **PIM** | **GP** | **G** | **A** | **TP** | **PIM** | **Wins** | **Season** | **Season** |
| Lacroix, Pierre | Que., Hfd. | 4 | 274 | 24 | 108 | 132 | 197 | 8 | 0 | 2 | 2 | 10 | .... | 1979-80 | 1982-83 |
| Ladouceur, Randy | Det., Hfd., Ana. | 14 | 930 | 30 | 126 | 156 | 1322 | 40 | 5 | 8 | 13 | 59 | .... | 1982-83 | 1995-96 |
| LaFayette, Nathan | St.L., Van., NYR, L.A. | 6 | 187 | 17 | 20 | 37 | 103 | 32 | 2 | 7 | 9 | 8 | .... | 1993-94 | 1998-99 |
| ‡ Laflamme, Christian | Chi., Edm., Mtl., St.L. | 8 | 324 | 2 | 45 | 47 | 282 | 9 | 0 | 1 | 1 | 6 | .... | 1996-97 | 2003-04 |
| Lafleur, Guy | Mtl., NYR, Que. | 17 | 1126 | 560 | 793 | 1353 | 399 | 128 | 58 | 76 | 134 | 67 | 5 | 1971-72 | 1990-91 |
| • Lafleur, Roland | Mtl. | 1 | 1 | 0 | 0 | 0 | 0 | .... | .... | .... | .... | .... | .... | 1924-25 | 1924-25 |
| LaFontaine, Pat | NYI, Buf., NYR | 15 | 865 | 468 | 545 | 1013 | 552 | 69 | 26 | 36 | 62 | 36 | .... | 1983-84 | 1997-98 |
| Laforce, Ernie | Mtl. | 1 | 1 | 0 | 0 | 0 | 0 | .... | .... | .... | .... | .... | .... | 1942-43 | 1942-43 |
| LaForest, Bob | L.A. | 1 | 5 | 1 | 0 | 1 | 2 | .... | .... | .... | .... | .... | .... | 1983-84 | 1983-84 |
| Laforge, Claude | Mtl., Det., Phi. | 8 | 193 | 24 | 33 | 57 | 82 | 5 | 1 | 2 | 3 | 15 | .... | 1957-58 | 1968-69 |
| Laforge, Marc | Hfd., Edm. | 2 | 14 | 0 | 0 | 0 | 64 | .... | .... | .... | .... | .... | .... | 1989-90 | 1993-94 |
| Laframboise, Pete | Cal., Wsh., Pit. | 4 | 227 | 33 | 55 | 88 | 70 | 9 | 1 | 0 | 1 | 0 | .... | 1971-72 | 1974-75 |
| Lafrance, Adie | Mtl. | 1 | 3 | 0 | 0 | 0 | 2 | 2 | 0 | 0 | 0 | 0 | .... | 1933-34 | 1933-34 |
| • Lafrance, Leo | Mtl., Chi. | 2 | 33 | 2 | 0 | 2 | 6 | .... | .... | .... | .... | .... | .... | 1926-27 | 1927-28 |
| Lafreniere, Jason | Que., NYR, T.B. | 5 | 146 | 34 | 53 | 87 | 22 | 15 | 1 | 5 | 6 | 19 | .... | 1986-87 | 1993-94 |
| Lafreniere, Roger | Det., St.L. | 2 | 13 | 0 | 0 | 0 | 4 | .... | .... | .... | .... | .... | .... | 1962-63 | 1972-73 |
| Lagace, Jean-Guy | Pit., Buf., K.C. | 6 | 197 | 9 | 39 | 48 | 251 | .... | .... | .... | .... | .... | .... | 1968-69 | 1975-76 |
| Laidlaw, Tom | NYR, L.A. | 10 | 705 | 25 | 139 | 164 | 717 | 69 | 4 | 17 | 21 | 78 | .... | 1980-81 | 1989-90 |
| Laird, Robbie | Min. | 1 | 1 | 0 | 0 | 0 | 0 | .... | .... | .... | .... | .... | .... | 1979-80 | 1979-80 |
| Lajeunesse, Serge | Det., Phi. | 5 | 103 | 1 | 4 | 5 | 103 | .... | .... | .... | .... | .... | .... | 1970-71 | 1974-75 |
| Lakovic, Sasha | Cgy., N.J. | 3 | 37 | 0 | 4 | 4 | 118 | .... | .... | .... | .... | .... | .... | 1996-97 | 1998-99 |
| Lalande, Hec | Chi., Det. | 4 | 151 | 21 | 39 | 60 | 120 | .... | .... | .... | .... | .... | .... | 1953-54 | 1957-58 |
| Lalonde, Bobby | Van., Atl., Bos., Cgy. | 11 | 641 | 124 | 210 | 334 | 298 | 16 | 4 | 2 | 6 | 6 | .... | 1971-72 | 1981-82 |
| • Lalonde, Newsy | Mtl., NYA | 6 | 99 | 125 | 41 | 166 | 183 | 7 | 15 | 4 | 19 | 32 | .... | 1917-18 | 1926-27 |
| Lalonde, Ron | Pit., Wsh. | 7 | 397 | 45 | 78 | 123 | 106 | .... | .... | .... | .... | .... | .... | 1972-73 | 1978-79 |
| Lalor, Mike | Mtl., St.L., Wsh., Wpg., S.J., Dal. | 12 | 687 | 17 | 88 | 105 | 677 | 92 | 5 | 10 | 15 | 167 | 1 | 1985-86 | 1996-97 |
| • Lamb, Joe | Mtl.M., Ott., NYA, Bos., Mtl., St.L., Det. | 11 | 443 | 108 | 101 | 209 | 601 | 18 | 1 | 1 | 2 | 51 | .... | 1927-28 | 1937-38 |
| Lamb, Mark | Cgy., Det., Edm., Ott., Phi., Mtl. | 11 | 403 | 46 | 100 | 146 | 291 | 70 | 7 | 19 | 26 | 51 | 1 | 1985-86 | 1995-96 |
| ‡ Lambert, Dan | Que. | 2 | 29 | 6 | 9 | 15 | 22 | .... | .... | .... | .... | .... | .... | 1990-91 | 1991-92 |
| Lambert, Denny | Ana., Ott., Nsh., Atl. | 8 | 487 | 27 | 66 | 93 | 1391 | 17 | 0 | 1 | 1 | 28 | .... | 1994-95 | 2001-02 |
| Lambert, Lane | Det., NYR, Que. | 6 | 283 | 58 | 66 | 124 | 521 | 17 | 2 | 4 | 6 | 40 | .... | 1983-84 | 1988-89 |
| Lambert, Yvon | Mtl., Buf. | 10 | 683 | 206 | 273 | 479 | 340 | 90 | 27 | 22 | 49 | 67 | 4 | 1972-73 | 1981-82 |
| Lamby, Dick | St.L. | 3 | 22 | 0 | 5 | 5 | 22 | .... | .... | .... | .... | .... | .... | 1978-79 | 1980-81 |
| • Lamirande, Jean-Paul | NYR, Mtl. | 4 | 49 | 5 | 5 | 10 | 26 | 8 | 0 | 0 | 0 | 4 | .... | 1946-47 | 1954-55 |
| Lammens, Hank | Ott. | 1 | 27 | 1 | 2 | 3 | 22 | .... | .... | .... | .... | .... | .... | 1993-94 | 1993-94 |
| • Lamoureux, Leo | Mtl. | 6 | 235 | 19 | 79 | 98 | 175 | 28 | 1 | 6 | 7 | 16 | 2 | 1941-42 | 1946-47 |
| Lamoureux, Mitch | Pit., Phi. | 3 | 73 | 11 | 9 | 20 | 59 | .... | .... | .... | .... | .... | .... | 1983-84 | 1987-88 |
| Lampman, Mike | St.L., Van., Wsh. | 4 | 96 | 17 | 20 | 37 | 34 | .... | .... | .... | .... | .... | .... | 1972-73 | 1976-77 |
| Lancien, Jack | NYR | 4 | 63 | 1 | 5 | 6 | 35 | 6 | 0 | 1 | 1 | 2 | .... | 1946-47 | 1950-51 |
| Landon, Larry | Mtl., Tor. | 2 | 9 | 0 | 0 | 0 | 2 | .... | .... | .... | .... | .... | .... | 1983-84 | 1984-85 |
| ‡ Landry, Eric | Cgy., Mtl. | 4 | 68 | 5 | 9 | 14 | 47 | .... | .... | .... | .... | .... | .... | 1997-98 | 2001-02 |
| Lane, Gord | Wsh., NYI | 10 | 539 | 19 | 94 | 113 | 1228 | 75 | 3 | 14 | 17 | 214 | 4 | 1975-76 | 1984-85 |
| • Lane, Myles | NYR, Bos. | 3 | 71 | 4 | 1 | 5 | 41 | 11 | 0 | 0 | 0 | 0 | 1 | 1928-29 | 1933-34 |
| Langdon, Darren | NYR, Car., Van., Mtl., N.J. | 11 | 521 | 16 | 23 | 39 | 1251 | 25 | 1 | 0 | 1 | 20 | .... | 1994-95 | 2005-06 |
| Langdon, Steve | Bos. | 3 | 7 | 0 | 1 | 1 | 2 | 4 | 0 | 0 | 0 | 0 | .... | 1974-75 | 1977-78 |
| Langelle, Pete | Tor. | 4 | 136 | 22 | 51 | 73 | 11 | 39 | 5 | 9 | 14 | 4 | 1 | 1938-39 | 1941-42 |
| Langevin, Chris | Buf. | 2 | 22 | 3 | 1 | 4 | 22 | .... | .... | .... | .... | .... | .... | 1983-84 | 1985-86 |
| Langevin, Dave | NYI, Min., L.A. | 8 | 513 | 12 | 107 | 119 | 530 | 87 | 2 | 17 | 19 | 106 | 4 | 1979-80 | 1986-87 |
| Langlais, Alain | Min. | 2 | 25 | 4 | 4 | 8 | 10 | .... | .... | .... | .... | .... | .... | 1973-74 | 1974-75 |
| Langlois, Albert | Mtl., NYR, Det., Bos. | 9 | 497 | 21 | 91 | 112 | 488 | 53 | 1 | 5 | 6 | 50 | 3 | 1957-58 | 1965-66 |
| • Langlois, Charlie | Ham., NYA, Pit., Mtl. | 4 | 151 | 22 | 5 | 27 | 189 | 2 | 0 | 0 | 0 | 0 | .... | 1924-25 | 1927-28 |
| Langway, Rod | Mtl., Wsh. | 15 | 994 | 51 | 278 | 329 | 849 | 104 | 5 | 22 | 27 | 97 | 1 | 1978-79 | 1992-93 |
| Lank, Jeff | Phi. | 1 | 2 | 0 | 0 | 0 | 2 | .... | .... | .... | .... | .... | .... | 1999-00 | 1999-00 |
| Lanthier, Jean-Marc | Van. | 4 | 105 | 16 | 16 | 32 | 29 | .... | .... | .... | .... | .... | .... | 1983-84 | 1987-88 |
| • Lanyon, Ted | Pit. | 1 | 5 | 0 | 0 | 0 | 4 | .... | .... | .... | .... | .... | .... | 1967-68 | 1967-68 |
| Lanz, Rick | Van., Tor., Chi. | 10 | 569 | 65 | 221 | 286 | 448 | 28 | 3 | 8 | 11 | 35 | .... | 1980-81 | 1991-92 |
| Laperriere, Daniel | St.L., Ott. | 4 | 48 | 2 | 5 | 7 | 27 | .... | .... | .... | .... | .... | .... | 1992-93 | 1995-96 |
| Laperriere, Jacques | Mtl. | 12 | 691 | 40 | 242 | 282 | 674 | 88 | 9 | 22 | 31 | 101 | 6 | 1962-63 | 1973-74 |
| Laplante, Darryl | Det. | 3 | 35 | 0 | 6 | 6 | 10 | .... | .... | .... | .... | .... | .... | 1997-98 | 1999-00 |
| Lapointe, Claude | Que., Col., Cgy., NYI, Phi. | 14 | 879 | 127 | 178 | 305 | 721 | 34 | 4 | 7 | 11 | 44 | .... | 1990-91 | 2003-04 |
| Lapointe, Guy | Mtl., St.L., Bos. | 16 | 884 | 171 | 451 | 622 | 893 | 123 | 26 | 44 | 70 | 138 | 6 | 1968-69 | 1983-84 |
| Lapointe, Martin | Det., Bos., Chi., Ott. | 16 | 991 | 181 | 200 | 381 | 1417 | 108 | 19 | 24 | 43 | 202 | 2 | 1991-92 | 2007-08 |
| • Lapointe, Rick | Det., Phi., St.L., Que., L.A. | 11 | 664 | 44 | 176 | 220 | 831 | 46 | 2 | 7 | 9 | 64 | .... | 1975-76 | 1985-86 |
| Lappin, Peter | Min., S.J. | 2 | 7 | 0 | 0 | 0 | 2 | .... | .... | .... | .... | .... | .... | 1989-90 | 1991-92 |
| Laprade, Edgar | NYR | 10 | 500 | 108 | 172 | 280 | 42 | 18 | 4 | 9 | 13 | 4 | .... | 1945-46 | 1954-55 |
| • LaPrairie, Benjamin | Chi. | 1 | 7 | 0 | 0 | 0 | 0 | .... | .... | .... | .... | .... | .... | 1936-37 | 1936-37 |
| Larionov, Igor | Van., S.J., Det., Fla., N.J. | 14 | 921 | 169 | 475 | 644 | 474 | 150 | 30 | 67 | 97 | 60 | 3 | 1989-90 | 2003-04 |
| Lariviere, Garry | Que., Edm. | 4 | 219 | 6 | 57 | 63 | 167 | 14 | 0 | 5 | 5 | 8 | .... | 1979-80 | 1982-83 |
| Larmer, Jeff | Col., N.J., Chi. | 5 | 158 | 37 | 51 | 88 | 57 | 5 | 1 | 0 | 1 | 2 | .... | 1981-82 | 1985-86 |
| Larmer, Steve | Chi., NYR | 15 | 1006 | 441 | 571 | 1012 | 532 | 140 | 56 | 75 | 131 | 89 | 1 | 1980-81 | 1994-95 |
| • Larochelle, Wildor | Mtl., Chi. | 12 | 474 | 92 | 74 | 166 | 211 | 34 | 6 | 4 | 10 | 24 | 2 | 1925-26 | 1936-37 |
| Larocque, Denis | L.A. | 1 | 8 | 0 | 1 | 1 | 18 | .... | .... | .... | .... | .... | .... | 1987-88 | 1987-88 |
| Larocque, Mario | T.B. | 1 | 5 | 0 | 0 | 0 | 16 | .... | .... | .... | .... | .... | .... | 1998-99 | 1998-99 |
| • Larose, Bonner | Bos. | 1 | 6 | 0 | 0 | 0 | 0 | .... | .... | .... | .... | .... | .... | 1925-26 | 1925-26 |
| Larose, Claude | Mtl., Min., St.L. | 16 | 943 | 226 | 257 | 483 | 887 | 97 | 14 | 18 | 32 | 143 | 5 | 1962-63 | 1977-78 |
| Larose, Claude | NYR | 2 | 25 | 4 | 7 | 11 | 2 | 2 | 0 | 0 | 0 | 0 | .... | 1979-80 | 1981-82 |
| Larose, Guy | Wpg., Tor., Cgy., Bos. | 6 | 70 | 10 | 9 | 19 | 63 | 4 | 0 | 0 | 0 | 0 | .... | 1988-89 | 1994-95 |
| Larouche, Pierre | Pit., Mtl., Hfd., NYR | 14 | 812 | 395 | 427 | 822 | 237 | 64 | 20 | 34 | 54 | 16 | 2 | 1974-75 | 1987-88 |
| Larouche, Steve | Ott., NYR, L.A. | 2 | 26 | 9 | 9 | 18 | 10 | .... | .... | .... | .... | .... | .... | 1994-95 | 1995-96 |
| • Larson, Norm | NYA, Bro., NYR | 3 | 89 | 25 | 18 | 43 | 12 | .... | .... | .... | .... | .... | .... | 1940-41 | 1946-47 |
| Larson, Reed | Det., Bos., Edm., NYI, Min., Buf. | 14 | 904 | 222 | 463 | 685 | 1391 | 32 | 4 | 7 | 11 | 63 | .... | 1976-77 | 1989-90 |
| Larter, Tyler | Wsh. | 1 | 1 | 0 | 0 | 0 | 0 | .... | .... | .... | .... | .... | .... | 1989-90 | 1989-90 |
| Latal, Jiri | Phi. | 3 | 92 | 12 | 36 | 48 | 24 | .... | .... | .... | .... | .... | .... | 1989-90 | 1991-92 |
| Latos, James | NYR | 1 | 1 | 0 | 0 | 0 | 0 | .... | .... | .... | .... | .... | .... | 1988-89 | 1988-89 |
| Latreille, Phil | NYR | 1 | 4 | 0 | 0 | 0 | 2 | .... | .... | .... | .... | .... | .... | 1960-61 | 1960-61 |
| Latta, David | Que. | 4 | 36 | 4 | 8 | 12 | 4 | .... | .... | .... | .... | .... | .... | 1985-86 | 1990-91 |
| • Lauder, Martin | Bos. | 1 | 3 | 0 | 0 | 0 | 2 | .... | .... | .... | .... | .... | .... | 1927-28 | 1927-28 |
| Lauen, Mike | Wpg. | 1 | 4 | 0 | 1 | 1 | 0 | .... | .... | .... | .... | .... | .... | 1983-84 | 1983-84 |
| Lauer, Brad | NYI, Chi., Ott., Pit. | 9 | 323 | 44 | 67 | 111 | 218 | 34 | 7 | 5 | 12 | 24 | .... | 1986-87 | 1995-96 |
| Laughlin, Craig | Mtl., Wsh., L.A., Tor. | 8 | 549 | 136 | 205 | 341 | 364 | 33 | 6 | 6 | 12 | 20 | .... | 1981-82 | 1988-89 |
| Laughton, Mike | Oak., Cal. | 4 | 189 | 39 | 48 | 87 | 101 | 11 | 3 | 4 | 7 | 0 | .... | 1967-68 | 1970-71 |
| Laukkanen, Janne | Que., Col., Ott., Pit., T.B. | 9 | 407 | 22 | 99 | 121 | 335 | 59 | 7 | 9 | 16 | 46 | .... | 1994-95 | 2002-03 |
| Laurence, Don | Atl., St.L. | 2 | 79 | 15 | 22 | 37 | 14 | .... | .... | .... | .... | .... | .... | 1978-79 | 1979-80 |
| Laus, Paul | Fla. | 9 | 530 | 14 | 58 | 72 | 1702 | 30 | 2 | 7 | 9 | 74 | .... | 1993-94 | 2001-02 |
| LaVallee, Kevin | Cgy., L.A., St.L., Pit. | 7 | 366 | 110 | 125 | 235 | 85 | 32 | 5 | 8 | 13 | 21 | .... | 1980-81 | 1986-87 |
| LaVarre, Mark | Chi. | 3 | 78 | 9 | 16 | 25 | 58 | 1 | 0 | 0 | 0 | 2 | .... | 1985-86 | 1987-88 |
| Lavender, Brian | St.L., NYI, Det., Cal. | 4 | 184 | 16 | 26 | 42 | 174 | 3 | 0 | 0 | 0 | 2 | .... | 1971-72 | 1974-75 |
| Lavigne, Eric | L.A. | 1 | 1 | 0 | 0 | 0 | 0 | .... | .... | .... | .... | .... | .... | 1994-95 | 1994-95 |
| • Laviolette, Jack | Mtl. | 1 | 18 | 2 | 1 | 3 | 6 | 2 | 0 | 0 | 0 | 0 | .... | 1917-18 | 1917-18 |
| Laviolette, Peter | NYR | 1 | 12 | 0 | 0 | 0 | 6 | .... | .... | .... | .... | .... | .... | 1988-89 | 1988-89 |
| Lavoie, Dominic | St.L., Ott., Bos., L.A. | 6 | 38 | 5 | 8 | 13 | 32 | .... | .... | .... | .... | .... | .... | 1988-89 | 1993-94 |
| ‡ Law, Kirby | Phi. | 3 | 9 | 0 | 1 | 1 | 4 | .... | .... | .... | .... | .... | .... | 2000-01 | 2003-04 |
| Lawless, Paul | Hfd., Phi., Van., Tor. | 7 | 239 | 49 | 77 | 126 | 54 | 3 | 0 | 2 | 2 | 2 | .... | 1982-83 | 1989-90 |
| Lawrence, Mark | Dal., NYI | 6 | 142 | 18 | 26 | 44 | 115 | .... | .... | .... | .... | .... | .... | 1994-95 | 2000-01 |
| • Lawson, Danny | Det., Min., Buf. | 5 | 219 | 28 | 29 | 57 | 61 | 16 | 0 | 1 | 1 | 2 | .... | 1967-68 | 1971-72 |
| Lawton, Brian | Min., NYR, Hfd., Que., Bos., S.J. | 9 | 483 | 112 | 154 | 266 | 401 | 11 | 1 | 1 | 2 | 12 | .... | 1983-84 | 1992-93 |
| Laxdal, Derek | Tor., NYI | 6 | 67 | 12 | 7 | 19 | 88 | 1 | 0 | 2 | 2 | 2 | .... | 1984-85 | 1990-91 |
| • Laycoe, Hal | NYR, Mtl., Bos. | 11 | 531 | 25 | 77 | 102 | 292 | 40 | 2 | 5 | 7 | 39 | .... | 1945-46 | 1955-56 |
| Lazaro, Jeff | Bos., Ott. | 3 | 102 | 14 | 23 | 37 | 114 | 28 | 3 | 3 | 6 | 32 | .... | 1990-91 | 1992-93 |
| Leach, Jamie | Pit., Hfd., Fla. | 5 | 81 | 11 | 9 | 20 | 12 | .... | .... | .... | .... | .... | 1 | 1989-90 | 1993-94 |
| Leach, Larry | Bos. | 3 | 126 | 13 | 29 | 42 | 91 | 7 | 1 | 1 | 2 | 8 | .... | 1958-59 | 1961-62 |
| Leach, Reggie | Bos., Cal., Phi., Det. | 13 | 934 | 381 | 285 | 666 | 387 | 94 | 47 | 22 | 69 | 22 | 1 | 1970-71 | 1982-83 |
| Leach, Stephen | Wsh., Bos., St.L., Car., Ott., Phx., Pit. | 15 | 702 | 130 | 153 | 283 | 978 | 92 | 15 | 11 | 26 | 87 | .... | 1985-86 | 1999-00 |
| ‡ Leahy, Patrick | Bos., Nsh. | 3 | 50 | 4 | 4 | 8 | 19 | .... | .... | .... | .... | .... | .... | 2003-04 | 2006-07 |
| Leavins, Jim | Det., NYR | 2 | 41 | 2 | 12 | 14 | 30 | .... | .... | .... | .... | .... | .... | 1985-86 | 1986-87 |
| Lebeau, Patrick | Mtl., Cgy., Fla., Pit. | 4 | 15 | 3 | 2 | 5 | 6 | .... | .... | .... | .... | .... | .... | 1990-91 | 1998-99 |
| Lebeau, Stephan | Mtl., Ana. | 7 | 373 | 118 | 159 | 277 | 105 | 30 | 9 | 7 | 16 | 12 | 1 | 1988-89 | 1994-95 |
| LeBlanc, Fern | Det. | 3 | 34 | 5 | 6 | 11 | 0 | .... | .... | .... | .... | .... | .... | 1976-77 | 1978-79 |
| LeBlanc, J.P. | Chi., Det. | 5 | 153 | 14 | 30 | 44 | 87 | 2 | 0 | 0 | 0 | 0 | .... | 1968-69 | 1978-79 |
| LeBlanc, John | Van., Edm., Wpg. | 7 | 83 | 26 | 13 | 39 | 28 | 1 | 0 | 0 | 0 | 0 | .... | 1986-87 | 1994-95 |
| LeBoutillier, Peter | Ana. | 2 | 35 | 2 | 1 | 3 | 176 | .... | .... | .... | .... | .... | .... | 1996-97 | 1997-98 |
| LeBrun, Al | NYR | 2 | 6 | 0 | 2 | 2 | 4 | .... | .... | .... | .... | .... | .... | 1960-61 | 1965-66 |
| Lecaine, Bill | Pit. | 1 | 4 | 0 | 0 | 0 | 0 | .... | .... | .... | .... | .... | .... | 1968-69 | 1968-69 |
| Leclair, Jackie | Mtl. | 3 | 160 | 20 | 40 | 60 | 56 | 20 | 6 | 1 | 7 | 6 | 1 | 1954-55 | 1956-57 |
| LeClair, John | Mtl., Phi., Pit. | 16 | 967 | 406 | 413 | 819 | 501 | 154 | 42 | 47 | 89 | 94 | 1 | 1990-91 | 2006-07 |
| Leclerc, Mike | Ana., Phx., Cgy. | 9 | 341 | 64 | 94 | 158 | 288 | 26 | 2 | 9 | 11 | 14 | .... | 1996-97 | 2005-06 |

*Guy Lapointe*

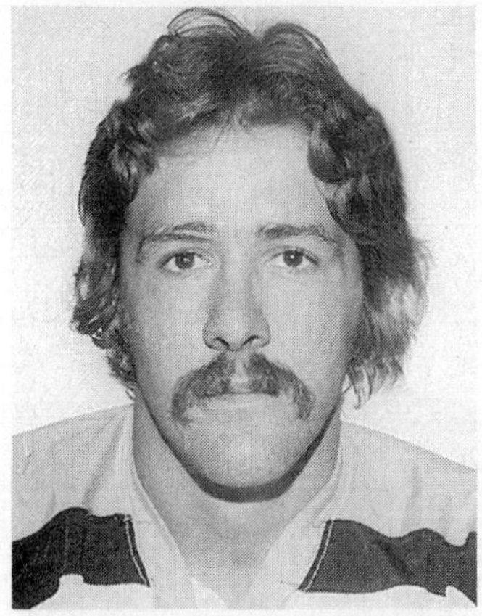

*Rich LeDuc*

*Dave Lewis*

*Trevor Linden*

*Willy Lindstrom*

*Ross Lonsberry*

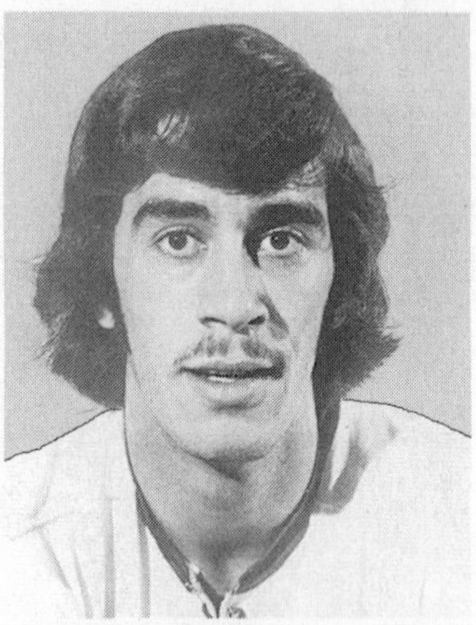

*Gilles Lupien*

*Vic Lynn*

| | | | Regular Schedule | | | | | Playoffs | | | | | NHL | First | Last |
|---|---|---|---|---|---|---|---|---|---|---|---|---|---|---|---|
| Name | NHL Teams | NHL Seasons | GP | G | A | TP | PIM | GP | G | A | TP | PIM | Cup Wins | NHL Season | NHL Season |
| Leclerc, Rene | Det. | 2 | 87 | 10 | 11 | 21 | 105 | .... | .... | .... | .... | .... | .... | 1968-69 | 1970-71 |
| Lecuyer, Doug | Chi., Wpg., Pit. | 4 | 126 | 11 | 31 | 42 | 178 | 7 | 4 | 0 | 4 | 15 | .... | 1978-79 | 1982-83 |
| Ledingham, Walt | Chi., NYI | 3 | 15 | 0 | 2 | 2 | 4 | .... | .... | .... | .... | .... | .... | 1972-73 | 1976-77 |
| • Leduc, Albert | Mtl., Ott., NYR | 10 | 383 | 57 | 35 | 92 | 614 | 28 | 5 | 6 | 11 | 32 | 2 | 1925-26 | 1934-35 |
| LeDuc, Rich | Bos., Que. | 4 | 130 | 28 | 38 | 66 | 69 | 5 | 0 | 0 | 0 | 9 | .... | 1972-73 | 1980-81 |
| Ledyard, Grant | NYR, L.A., Wsh., Buf., Dal., Van., Bos., Ott., T.B. | 18 | 1028 | 90 | 276 | 366 | 766 | 83 | 6 | 12 | 18 | 96 | .... | 1984-85 | 2001-02 |
| • Lee, Bobby | Mtl. | 1 | 1 | 0 | 0 | 0 | 0 | .... | .... | .... | .... | .... | .... | 1942-43 | 1942-43 |
| Lee, Edward | Que. | 1 | 2 | 0 | 0 | 0 | 5 | .... | .... | .... | .... | .... | .... | 1984-85 | 1984-85 |
| Lee, Peter | Pit. | 6 | 431 | 114 | 131 | 245 | 257 | 19 | 0 | 8 | 8 | 4 | .... | 1977-78 | 1982-83 |
| ‡ Leeb, Brad | Van., Tor. | 3 | 5 | 0 | 0 | 0 | 2 | .... | .... | .... | .... | .... | .... | 1999-00 | 2003-04 |
| ‡ Leeb, Greg | Dal. | 1 | 2 | 0 | 0 | 0 | 0 | .... | .... | .... | .... | .... | .... | 2000-01 | 2000-01 |
| Leeman, Gary | Tor., Cgy., Mtl., Van., St.L. | 14 | 667 | 199 | 267 | 466 | 531 | 36 | 8 | 16 | 24 | 36 | 1 | 1982-83 | 1996-97 |
| Leetch, Brian | NYR, Tor., Bos. | 18 | 1205 | 247 | 781 | 1028 | 571 | 95 | 28 | 69 | 97 | 36 | 1 | 1987-88 | 2005-06 |
| ‡ Lefebvre, Guillaume | Phi., Pit. | 3 | 38 | 2 | 4 | 6 | 13 | .... | .... | .... | .... | .... | .... | 2001-02 | 2005-06 |
| ‡ Lefebvre, Patrice | Wsh. | 1 | 3 | 0 | 0 | 0 | 2 | .... | .... | .... | .... | .... | .... | 1998-99 | 1998-99 |
| Lefebvre, Sylvain | Mtl., Tor., Que., Col., NYR | 14 | 945 | 30 | 154 | 184 | 674 | 129 | 4 | 14 | 18 | 101 | 1 | 1989-90 | 2002-03 |
| • Lefley, Bryan | NYI, K.C., Col. | 5 | 228 | 7 | 29 | 36 | 101 | 2 | 0 | 0 | 0 | 0 | .... | 1972-73 | 1977-78 |
| Lefley, Chuck | Mtl., St.L. | 9 | 407 | 128 | 164 | 292 | 137 | 29 | 5 | 8 | 13 | 10 | 2 | 1970-71 | 1980-81 |
| • Leger, Roger | NYR, Mtl. | 5 | 187 | 18 | 53 | 71 | 71 | 20 | 0 | 7 | 7 | 14 | .... | 1943-44 | 1949-50 |
| Legge, Barry | Que., Wpg. | 3 | 107 | 1 | 11 | 12 | 144 | .... | .... | .... | .... | .... | .... | 1979-80 | 1981-82 |
| Legge, Randy | NYR | 1 | 12 | 0 | 2 | 2 | 2 | .... | .... | .... | .... | .... | .... | 1972-73 | 1972-73 |
| Lehman, Tommy | Bos., Edm. | 3 | 36 | 5 | 5 | 10 | 16 | .... | .... | .... | .... | .... | .... | 1987-88 | 1989-90 |
| Lehto, Petteri | Pit. | 1 | 6 | 0 | 0 | 0 | 4 | .... | .... | .... | .... | .... | .... | 1984-85 | 1984-85 |
| Lehtonen, Antero | Wsh. | 1 | 65 | 9 | 12 | 21 | 14 | .... | .... | .... | .... | .... | .... | 1979-80 | 1979-80 |
| ‡ Lehtonen, Mikko | Nsh. | 1 | 15 | 1 | 2 | 3 | 8 | .... | .... | .... | .... | .... | .... | 2006-07 | 2006-07 |
| Lehvonen, Henry | K.C. | 1 | 4 | 0 | 0 | 0 | 0 | .... | .... | .... | .... | .... | .... | 1974-75 | 1974-75 |
| Leier, Edward | Chi. | 2 | 16 | 2 | 1 | 3 | 2 | .... | .... | .... | .... | .... | .... | 1949-50 | 1950-51 |
| Leinonen, Mikko | NYR, Wsh. | 4 | 162 | 31 | 78 | 109 | 71 | 20 | 2 | 11 | 13 | 28 | .... | 1981-82 | 1984-85 |
| Leiter, Bobby | Bos., Pit., Atl. | 10 | 447 | 98 | 126 | 224 | 144 | 8 | 3 | 0 | 3 | 2 | .... | 1962-63 | 1975-76 |
| Leiter, Ken | NYI, Min. | 5 | 143 | 14 | 36 | 50 | 62 | 15 | 0 | 6 | 6 | 8 | .... | 1984-85 | 1989-90 |
| Lemaire, Jacques | Mtl. | 12 | 853 | 366 | 469 | 835 | 217 | 145 | 61 | 78 | 139 | 63 | 8 | 1967-68 | 1978-79 |
| Lemay, Moe | Van., Edm., Bos., Wpg. | 8 | 317 | 72 | 94 | 166 | 442 | 28 | 6 | 3 | 9 | 55 | 1 | 1981-82 | 1988-89 |
| Lemelin, Roger | K.C., Col. | 4 | 36 | 1 | 2 | 3 | 27 | .... | .... | .... | .... | .... | .... | 1974-75 | 1977-78 |
| Lemieux, Alain | St.L., Que., Pit. | 6 | 119 | 28 | 44 | 72 | 38 | 19 | 4 | 6 | 10 | 0 | .... | 1981-82 | 1986-87 |
| Lemieux, Bob | Oak. | 1 | 19 | 0 | 1 | 1 | 12 | .... | .... | .... | .... | .... | .... | 1967-68 | 1967-68 |
| Lemieux, Jacques | L.A. | 3 | 19 | 0 | 4 | 4 | 8 | 1 | 0 | 0 | 0 | 0 | .... | 1967-68 | 1969-70 |
| Lemieux, Jean | Atl., Wsh. | 5 | 204 | 23 | 63 | 86 | 39 | 3 | 1 | 1 | 2 | 0 | .... | 1973-74 | 1977-78 |
| Lemieux, Jocelyn | St.L., Mtl., Chi., Hfd., N.J., Cgy., Phx. | 12 | 598 | 80 | 84 | 164 | 740 | 60 | 5 | 10 | 15 | 88 | .... | 1986-87 | 1997-98 |
| Lemieux, Mario | Pit. | 18 | 915 | 690 | 1033 | 1723 | 834 | 107 | 76 | 96 | 172 | 87 | 2 | 1984-85 | 2005-06 |
| • Lemieux, Real | Det., L.A., NYR, Buf. | 8 | 456 | 51 | 104 | 155 | 262 | 18 | 2 | 4 | 6 | 10 | .... | 1966-67 | 1973-74 |
| Lemieux, Rich | Van., K.C., Atl. | 5 | 274 | 39 | 82 | 121 | 132 | 2 | 0 | 0 | 0 | 0 | .... | 1971-72 | 1975-76 |
| Lenardon, Tim | N.J., Van. | 2 | 15 | 2 | 1 | 3 | 4 | .... | .... | .... | .... | .... | .... | 1986-87 | 1989-90 |
| • Lepine, Hec | Mtl. | 1 | 33 | 5 | 2 | 7 | 2 | .... | .... | .... | .... | .... | .... | 1925-26 | 1925-26 |
| • Lepine, Pit | Mtl. | 13 | 526 | 143 | 98 | 241 | 392 | 41 | 7 | 5 | 12 | 26 | 2 | 1925-26 | 1937-38 |
| Leroux, Francois | Edm., Ott., Pit., Col. | 10 | 249 | 3 | 20 | 23 | 577 | 33 | 1 | 3 | 4 | 34 | .... | 1988-89 | 1997-98 |
| Leroux, Gaston | Mtl. | 1 | 2 | 0 | 0 | 0 | 0 | .... | .... | .... | .... | .... | .... | 1935-36 | 1935-36 |
| ‡ Leroux, Jean-Yves | Chi. | 5 | 220 | 16 | 22 | 38 | 146 | .... | .... | .... | .... | .... | .... | 1996-97 | 2000-01 |
| Leschyshyn, Curtis | Que., Col., Wsh., Hfd., Car., Min., Ott. | 16 | 1033 | 47 | 165 | 212 | 669 | 68 | 2 | 6 | 8 | 34 | 1 | 1988-89 | 2003-04 |
| • Lesieur, Art | Mtl., Chi. | 4 | 100 | 4 | 2 | 6 | 50 | 14 | 0 | 0 | 0 | 4 | 1 | 1928-29 | 1935-36 |
| Lessard, Rick | Cgy., S.J. | 3 | 15 | 0 | 4 | 4 | 18 | .... | .... | .... | .... | .... | .... | 1988-89 | 1991-92 |
| Lesuk, Bill | Bos., Phi., L.A., Wsh., Wpg. | 8 | 388 | 44 | 63 | 107 | 368 | 9 | 1 | 0 | 1 | 12 | 1 | 1968-69 | 1979-80 |
| • Leswick, Jack | Chi. | 1 | 37 | 1 | 7 | 8 | 16 | .... | .... | .... | .... | .... | 1 | 1933-34 | 1933-34 |
| • Leswick, Pete | NYA, Bos. | 2 | 3 | 1 | 0 | 1 | 0 | .... | .... | .... | .... | .... | .... | 1936-37 | 1944-45 |
| • Leswick, Tony | NYR, Det., Chi. | 12 | 740 | 165 | 159 | 324 | 900 | 59 | 13 | 10 | 23 | 91 | 3 | 1945-46 | 1957-58 |
| ‡ Letang, Alan | Dal., Cgy., NYI | 3 | 14 | 0 | 0 | 0 | 2 | .... | .... | .... | .... | .... | .... | 1999-00 | 2002-03 |
| • Levandoski, Joe | NYR | 1 | 8 | 1 | 1 | 2 | 0 | .... | .... | .... | .... | .... | .... | 1946-47 | 1946-47 |
| Leveille, Normand | Bos. | 2 | 75 | 17 | 25 | 42 | 49 | .... | .... | .... | .... | .... | .... | 1981-82 | 1982-83 |
| • Leveque, Guy | L.A. | 2 | 17 | 2 | 2 | 4 | 21 | .... | .... | .... | .... | .... | .... | 1992-93 | 1993-94 |
| Lever, Don | Van., Atl., Cgy., Col., N.J., Buf. | 15 | 1020 | 313 | 367 | 680 | 593 | 30 | 7 | 10 | 17 | 26 | .... | 1972-73 | 1986-87 |
| Levie, Craig | Wpg., Min., St.L., Van. | 6 | 183 | 22 | 53 | 75 | 177 | 16 | 2 | 3 | 5 | 32 | .... | 1981-82 | 1986-87 |
| Levins, Scott | Wpg., Fla., Ott., Phx. | 5 | 124 | 13 | 20 | 33 | 316 | .... | .... | .... | .... | .... | .... | 1992-93 | 1997-98 |
| • Levinsky, Alex | Tor., NYR, Chi. | 9 | 367 | 19 | 49 | 68 | 307 | 37 | 2 | 1 | 3 | 26 | 2 | 1930-31 | 1938-39 |
| Levo, Tapio | Col., N.J. | 2 | 107 | 16 | 53 | 69 | 36 | .... | .... | .... | .... | .... | .... | 1981-82 | 1982-83 |
| Lewicki, Danny | Tor., NYR, Chi. | 9 | 461 | 105 | 135 | 240 | 177 | 28 | 0 | 4 | 4 | 8 | 1 | 1950-51 | 1958-59 |
| Lewis, Dale | NYR | 1 | 8 | 0 | 0 | 0 | 0 | .... | .... | .... | .... | .... | .... | 1975-76 | 1975-76 |
| Lewis, Dave | NYI, L.A., N.J., Det. | 15 | 1008 | 36 | 187 | 223 | 953 | 91 | 1 | 20 | 21 | 143 | .... | 1973-74 | 1987-88 |
| • Lewis, Doug | Mtl. | 1 | 3 | 0 | 0 | 0 | 0 | .... | .... | .... | .... | .... | .... | 1946-47 | 1946-47 |
| • Lewis, Herbie | Det. | 11 | 483 | 148 | 161 | 309 | 248 | 38 | 13 | 10 | 23 | 6 | 2 | 1928-29 | 1938-39 |
| Ley, Rick | Tor., Hfd. | 6 | 310 | 12 | 72 | 84 | 528 | 14 | 0 | 2 | 2 | 20 | .... | 1968-69 | 1980-81 |
| Liba, Igor | NYR, L.A. | 1 | 37 | 7 | 18 | 25 | 36 | 2 | 0 | 0 | 0 | 2 | .... | 1988-89 | 1988-89 |
| Libby, Jeff | NYI | 1 | 1 | 0 | 0 | 0 | 0 | .... | .... | .... | .... | .... | .... | 1997-98 | 1997-98 |
| Libett, Nick | Det., Pit. | 14 | 982 | 237 | 268 | 505 | 472 | 16 | 6 | 2 | 8 | 2 | .... | 1967-68 | 1980-81 |
| Licari, Tony | Det. | 1 | 9 | 0 | 1 | 1 | 0 | .... | .... | .... | .... | .... | .... | 1946-47 | 1946-47 |
| Liddington, Bob | Tor. | 1 | 11 | 0 | 1 | 1 | 2 | .... | .... | .... | .... | .... | .... | 1970-71 | 1970-71 |
| Lidster, Doug | Van., NYR, St.L., Dal. | 16 | 897 | 75 | 268 | 343 | 679 | 80 | 6 | 15 | 21 | 64 | 1 | 1983-84 | 1998-99 |
| ‡ Liffiton, David | NYR | 2 | 3 | 0 | 0 | 0 | 9 | .... | .... | .... | .... | .... | .... | 2005-06 | 2006-07 |
| Lilley, John | Ana. | 3 | 23 | 3 | 8 | 11 | 13 | .... | .... | .... | .... | .... | .... | 1993-94 | 1995-96 |
| ‡ Lind, Juha | Dal., Mtl. | 3 | 133 | 9 | 13 | 22 | 20 | 15 | 2 | 2 | 4 | 8 | .... | 1997-98 | 2000-01 |
| Lindberg, Chris | Cgy., Que. | 3 | 116 | 17 | 25 | 42 | 47 | 2 | 0 | 1 | 1 | 2 | .... | 1991-92 | 1993-94 |
| Lindbom, Johan | NYR | 1 | 38 | 1 | 3 | 4 | 28 | .... | .... | .... | .... | .... | .... | 1997-98 | 1997-98 |
| Linden, Jamie | Fla. | 1 | 4 | 0 | 0 | 0 | 17 | .... | .... | .... | .... | .... | .... | 1994-95 | 1994-95 |
| Linden, Trevor | Van., NYI, Mtl., Wsh. | 19 | 1382 | 375 | 492 | 867 | 895 | 124 | 34 | 65 | 99 | 104 | .... | 1988-89 | 2007-08 |
| Lindgren, Lars | Van., Min. | 6 | 394 | 25 | 113 | 138 | 325 | 40 | 5 | 6 | 11 | 20 | .... | 1978-79 | 1983-84 |
| Lindgren, Mats | Edm., NYI, Van. | 8 | 387 | 54 | 74 | 128 | 146 | 24 | 1 | 5 | 6 | 10 | .... | 1996-97 | 2003-04 |
| Lindholm, Mikael | L.A. | 1 | 18 | 2 | 2 | 4 | 2 | .... | .... | .... | .... | .... | .... | 1989-90 | 1989-90 |
| Lindros, Brett | NYI | 2 | 51 | 2 | 5 | 7 | 147 | .... | .... | .... | .... | .... | .... | 1994-95 | 1995-96 |
| Lindros, Eric | Phi., NYR, Tor., Dal. | 14 | 760 | 372 | 493 | 865 | 1398 | 53 | 24 | 33 | 57 | 122 | .... | 1992-93 | 2006-07 |
| Lindsay, Bill | Que., Fla., Cgy., S.J., Mtl., Atl. | 13 | 777 | 83 | 141 | 224 | 922 | 42 | 7 | 8 | 15 | 44 | .... | 1991-92 | 2003-04 |
| Lindsay, Ted | Det., Chi. | 17 | 1068 | 379 | 472 | 851 | 1808 | 133 | 47 | 49 | 96 | 194 | 4 | 1944-45 | 1964-65 |
| Lindstrom, Willy | Wpg., Edm., Pit. | 8 | 582 | 161 | 162 | 323 | 200 | 57 | 14 | 18 | 32 | 24 | 2 | 1979-80 | 1986-87 |
| ‡ Ling, David | Mtl., CBJ | 5 | 93 | 4 | 4 | 8 | 191 | .... | .... | .... | .... | .... | .... | 1996-97 | 2003-04 |
| Linseman, Ken | Phi., Edm., Bos., Tor. | 14 | 860 | 256 | 551 | 807 | 1727 | 113 | 43 | 77 | 120 | 325 | 1 | 1978-79 | 1991-92 |
| ‡ Lintner, Richard | Nsh., NYR, Pit. | 3 | 112 | 8 | 12 | 20 | 54 | .... | .... | .... | .... | .... | .... | 1999-00 | 2002-03 |
| Lipuma, Chris | T.B., S.J. | 5 | 72 | 0 | 9 | 9 | 146 | .... | .... | .... | .... | .... | .... | 1992-93 | 1996-97 |
| • Liscombe, Carl | Det. | 9 | 373 | 137 | 140 | 277 | 117 | 59 | 22 | 19 | 41 | 20 | 1 | 1937-38 | 1945-46 |
| Litzenberger, Ed | Mtl., Chi., Det., Tor. | 12 | 618 | 178 | 238 | 416 | 283 | 40 | 5 | 13 | 18 | 34 | 4 | 1952-53 | 1963-64 |
| Loach, Lonnie | Ott., L.A., Ana. | 2 | 56 | 10 | 13 | 23 | 29 | 1 | 0 | 0 | 0 | 0 | .... | 1992-93 | 1993-94 |
| • Locas, Jacques | Mtl. | 2 | 59 | 7 | 8 | 15 | 66 | .... | .... | .... | .... | .... | .... | 1947-48 | 1948-49 |
| Lochead, Bill | Det., Col., NYR | 6 | 330 | 69 | 62 | 131 | 180 | 7 | 3 | 0 | 3 | 6 | .... | 1974-75 | 1979-80 |
| • Locking, Norm | Chi. | 2 | 48 | 2 | 6 | 8 | 26 | .... | .... | .... | .... | .... | .... | 1934-35 | 1935-36 |
| Loewen, Darcy | Buf., Ott. | 5 | 135 | 4 | 8 | 12 | 211 | .... | .... | .... | .... | .... | .... | 1989-90 | 1993-94 |
| Lofthouse, Mark | Wsh., Det. | 6 | 181 | 42 | 38 | 80 | 73 | .... | .... | .... | .... | .... | .... | 1977-78 | 1982-83 |
| Logan, Dave | Chi., Van. | 6 | 218 | 5 | 29 | 34 | 470 | 12 | 0 | 0 | 0 | 10 | .... | 1975-76 | 1980-81 |
| Logan, Robert | Buf., L.A. | 3 | 42 | 10 | 5 | 15 | 0 | .... | .... | .... | .... | .... | .... | 1986-87 | 1988-89 |
| Loiselle, Claude | Det., N.J., Que., Tor., NYI | 13 | 616 | 92 | 117 | 209 | 1149 | 41 | 4 | 11 | 15 | 58 | .... | 1981-82 | 1993-94 |
| • Lomakin, Andrei | Phi., Fla. | 4 | 215 | 42 | 62 | 104 | 92 | .... | .... | .... | .... | .... | .... | 1991-92 | 1994-95 |
| Loney, Brian | Van. | 1 | 12 | 2 | 3 | 5 | 6 | .... | .... | .... | .... | .... | .... | 1995-96 | 1995-96 |
| Loney, Troy | Pit., Ana., NYI, NYR | 12 | 624 | 87 | 110 | 197 | 1091 | 67 | 8 | 14 | 22 | 97 | 2 | 1983-84 | 1994-95 |
| Long, Barry | L.A., Det., Wpg. | 5 | 280 | 11 | 68 | 79 | 250 | 5 | 0 | 1 | 1 | 18 | .... | 1972-73 | 1981-82 |
| • Long, Stan | Mtl. | 1 | .... | .... | .... | .... | .... | 3 | 0 | 0 | 0 | 0 | .... | 1951-52 | 1951-52 |
| Lonsberry, Ross | Bos., L.A., Phi., Pit. | 15 | 968 | 256 | 310 | 566 | 806 | 100 | 21 | 25 | 46 | 87 | 2 | 1966-67 | 1980-81 |
| Loob, Hakan | Cgy. | 6 | 450 | 193 | 236 | 429 | 189 | 73 | 26 | 28 | 54 | 16 | 1 | 1983-84 | 1988-89 |
| Loob, Peter | Que. | 1 | 8 | 1 | 2 | 3 | 0 | .... | .... | .... | .... | .... | .... | 1984-85 | 1984-85 |
| Lorentz, Jim | Bos., St.L., NYR, Buf. | 10 | 659 | 161 | 238 | 399 | 208 | 54 | 12 | 10 | 22 | 30 | 1 | 1968-69 | 1977-78 |
| Lorimer, Bob | NYI, Col., N.J. | 10 | 529 | 22 | 90 | 112 | 431 | 49 | 3 | 10 | 13 | 83 | 2 | 1976-77 | 1985-86 |
| • Lorrain, Rod | Mtl. | 6 | 179 | 28 | 39 | 67 | 30 | 11 | 0 | 3 | 3 | 0 | .... | 1935-36 | 1941-42 |
| • Loughlin, Clem | Det., Chi. | 3 | 101 | 8 | 6 | 14 | 77 | .... | .... | .... | .... | .... | .... | 1926-27 | 1928-29 |
| • Loughlin, Wilf | Tor. | 1 | 14 | 0 | 0 | 0 | 2 | .... | .... | .... | .... | .... | .... | 1923-24 | 1923-24 |
| Lovsin, Ken | Wsh. | 1 | 1 | 0 | 0 | 0 | 0 | .... | .... | .... | .... | .... | .... | 1990-91 | 1990-91 |
| Low, Reed | St.L., Chi. | 5 | 256 | 3 | 16 | 19 | 725 | .... | .... | .... | .... | .... | .... | 2000-01 | 2006-07 |
| Lowdermilk, Dwayne | Wsh. | 1 | 2 | 0 | 1 | 1 | 2 | .... | .... | .... | .... | .... | .... | 1980-81 | 1980-81 |
| Lowe, Darren | Pit. | 1 | 8 | 1 | 2 | 3 | 0 | .... | .... | .... | .... | .... | .... | 1983-84 | 1983-84 |
| Lowe, Kevin | Edm., NYR | 19 | 1254 | 84 | 347 | 431 | 1498 | 214 | 10 | 48 | 58 | 192 | 6 | 1979-80 | 1997-98 |
| Lowe, Odie | NYR | 1 | 4 | 1 | 1 | 2 | 0 | .... | .... | .... | .... | .... | .... | 1949-50 | 1949-50 |
| • Lowe, Ross | Bos., Mtl. | 3 | 77 | 6 | 8 | 14 | 82 | 2 | 0 | 0 | 0 | 0 | .... | 1949-50 | 1951-52 |

| Name | NHL Teams | NHL Seasons | Regular Schedule GP | G | A | TP | PIM | Playoffs GP | G | A | TP | PIM | NHL Cup Wins | First NHL Season | Last NHL Season |
|---|---|---|---|---|---|---|---|---|---|---|---|---|---|---|---|
| • Lowrey, Ed | Ott., Ham. | 3 | 27 | 2 | 2 | 4 | 6 | .... | .... | .... | .... | .... | .... | 1917-18 | 1920-21 |
| • Lowrey, Fred | Mtl.M., Pit. | 2 | 53 | 1 | 1 | 2 | 10 | 2 | 0 | 0 | 0 | 6 | .... | 1924-25 | 1925-26 |
| • Lowrey, Gerry | Tor., Pit., Phi., Chi., Ott. | 6 | 211 | 48 | 48 | 96 | 148 | 2 | 1 | 0 | 1 | 2 | .... | 1927-28 | 1932-33 |
| Lowry, Dave | Van., St.L., Fla., S.J., Cgy. | 19 | 1084 | 164 | 187 | 351 | 1191 | 111 | 16 | 20 | 36 | 181 | .... | 1985-86 | 2003-04 |
| ‡ Loyns, Lynn | S.J., Cgy. | 3 | 34 | 3 | 2 | 5 | 21 | .... | .... | .... | .... | .... | .... | 2002-03 | 2005-06 |
| Lucas, Danny | Phi. | 1 | 6 | 1 | 0 | 1 | 0 | .... | .... | .... | .... | .... | .... | 1978-79 | 1978-79 |
| Lucas, Dave | Det. | 1 | 1 | 0 | 0 | 0 | 0 | .... | .... | .... | .... | .... | .... | 1962-63 | 1962-63 |
| Luce, Don | NYR, Det., Buf., L.A., Tor. | 13 | 894 | 225 | 329 | 554 | 364 | 71 | 17 | 22 | 39 | 52 | .... | 1969-70 | 1981-82 |
| Ludvig, Jan | N.J., Buf. | 7 | 314 | 54 | 87 | 141 | 418 | .... | .... | .... | .... | .... | .... | 1982-83 | 1988-89 |
| Ludwig, Craig | Mtl., NYI, Min., Dal. | 17 | 1256 | 38 | 184 | 222 | 1437 | 177 | 4 | 25 | 29 | 244 | 2 | 1982-83 | 1998-99 |
| Ludzik, Steve | Chi., Buf. | 9 | 424 | 46 | 93 | 139 | 333 | 44 | 4 | 8 | 12 | 70 | .... | 1981-82 | 1989-90 |
| Luhning, Warren | NYI, Dal. | 3 | 29 | 0 | 1 | 1 | 21 | .... | .... | .... | .... | .... | .... | 1997-98 | 1999-00 |
| Lukowich, Bernie | Pit., St.L. | 2 | 79 | 13 | 15 | 28 | 34 | 2 | 0 | 0 | 0 | 0 | .... | 1973-74 | 1974-75 |
| Lukowich, Morris | Wpg., Bos., L.A. | 8 | 582 | 199 | 219 | 418 | 584 | 11 | 0 | 2 | 2 | 24 | .... | 1979-80 | 1986-87 |
| Luksa, Charlie | Hfd. | 1 | 8 | 0 | 1 | 1 | 4 | .... | .... | .... | .... | .... | .... | 1979-80 | 1979-80 |
| Lumley, Dave | Mtl., Edm., Hfd. | 9 | 437 | 98 | 160 | 258 | 680 | 61 | 6 | 8 | 14 | 131 | 2 | 1978-79 | 1986-87 |
| Lumme, Jyrki | Mtl., Van., Phx., Dal., Tor. | 15 | 985 | 114 | 354 | 468 | 620 | 105 | 9 | 35 | 44 | 52 | .... | 1988-89 | 2002-03 |
| Lund, Pentti | Bos., NYR | 7 | 259 | 44 | 55 | 99 | 40 | 19 | 7 | 5 | 12 | 0 | .... | 1946-47 | 1952-53 |
| Lundberg, Brian | Pit. | 1 | 1 | 0 | 0 | 0 | 2 | .... | .... | .... | .... | .... | .... | 1982-83 | 1982-83 |
| Lunde, Len | Det., Chi., Min., Van. | 8 | 321 | 39 | 83 | 122 | 75 | 20 | 3 | 2 | 5 | 2 | .... | 1958-59 | 1970-71 |
| Lundholm, Bengt | Wpg. | 5 | 275 | 48 | 95 | 143 | 72 | 14 | 3 | 4 | 7 | 14 | .... | 1981-82 | 1985-86 |
| Lundrigan, Joe | Tor., Wsh. | 2 | 52 | 2 | 8 | 10 | 22 | .... | .... | .... | .... | .... | .... | 1972-73 | 1974-75 |
| Lundstrom, Tord | Det. | 1 | 11 | 1 | 1 | 2 | 0 | .... | .... | .... | .... | .... | .... | 1973-74 | 1973-74 |
| • Lundy, Pat | Det., Chi. | 5 | 150 | 37 | 32 | 69 | 31 | 16 | 2 | 2 | 4 | 2 | .... | 1945-46 | 1950-51 |
| ‡ Luoma, Mikko | Edm. | 1 | 3 | 0 | 1 | 1 | 0 | .... | .... | .... | .... | .... | .... | 2003-04 | 2003-04 |
| Luongo, Chris | Det., Ott., NYI | 5 | 218 | 8 | 23 | 31 | 176 | .... | .... | .... | .... | .... | .... | 1990-91 | 1995-96 |
| ‡ Lupaschuk, Ross | Pit. | 1 | 3 | 0 | 0 | 0 | 4 | .... | .... | .... | .... | .... | .... | 2002-03 | 2002-03 |
| Lupien, Gilles | Mtl., Pit., Hfd. | 5 | 226 | 5 | 25 | 30 | 416 | 25 | 0 | 0 | 0 | 21 | 2 | 1977-78 | 1981-82 |
| • Lupul, Gary | Van. | 7 | 293 | 70 | 75 | 145 | 243 | 25 | 4 | 7 | 11 | 11 | .... | 1979-80 | 1985-86 |
| • Lyashenko, Roman | Dal., NYR | 4 | 139 | 14 | 9 | 23 | 55 | 17 | 2 | 1 | 3 | 0 | .... | 1999-00 | 2002-03 |
| Lyle, George | Det., Hfd. | 4 | 99 | 24 | 38 | 62 | 51 | .... | .... | .... | .... | .... | .... | 1979-80 | 1982-83 |
| ‡ Lynch, Doug | Edm. | 1 | 2 | 0 | 0 | 0 | 0 | .... | .... | .... | .... | .... | .... | 2003-04 | 2003-04 |
| Lynch, Jack | Pit., Det., Wsh. | 7 | 382 | 24 | 106 | 130 | 336 | .... | .... | .... | .... | .... | .... | 1972-73 | 1978-79 |
| Lynn, Vic | NYR, Det., Mtl., Tor., Bos., Chi. | 11 | 327 | 49 | 76 | 125 | 274 | 47 | 7 | 10 | 17 | 46 | 3 | 1942-43 | 1953-54 |
| Lyon, Steve | Pit. | 1 | 3 | 0 | 0 | 0 | 2 | .... | .... | .... | .... | .... | .... | 1976-77 | 1976-77 |
| • Lyons, Ron | Bos., Phi. | 1 | 36 | 2 | 4 | 6 | 27 | 5 | 0 | 0 | 0 | 0 | .... | 1930-31 | 1930-31 |
| ‡ Lysak, Brett | Car. | 1 | 2 | 0 | 0 | 0 | 2 | .... | .... | .... | .... | .... | .... | 2003-04 | 2003-04 |
| Lysiak, Tom | Atl., Chi. | 13 | 919 | 292 | 551 | 843 | 567 | 76 | 25 | 38 | 63 | 49 | .... | 1973-74 | 1985-86 |

## M

| Name | NHL Teams | NHL Seasons | Regular Schedule GP | G | A | TP | PIM | Playoffs GP | G | A | TP | PIM | NHL Cup Wins | First NHL Season | Last NHL Season |
|---|---|---|---|---|---|---|---|---|---|---|---|---|---|---|---|
| MacAdam, Al | Phi., Cal., Cle., Min., Van. | 12 | 864 | 240 | 351 | 591 | 509 | 64 | 20 | 24 | 44 | 21 | .... | 1973-74 | 1984-85 |
| MacDermid, Paul | Hfd., Wpg., Wsh., Que. | 14 | 690 | 116 | 142 | 258 | 1303 | 43 | 5 | 11 | 16 | 116 | .... | 1981-82 | 1994-95 |
| MacDonald, Blair | Edm., Van. | 4 | 219 | 91 | 100 | 191 | 65 | 11 | 0 | 6 | 6 | 2 | .... | 1979-80 | 1982-83 |
| MacDonald, Brett | Van. | 1 | 1 | 0 | 0 | 0 | 0 | .... | .... | .... | .... | .... | .... | 1987-88 | 1987-88 |
| MacDonald, Doug | Buf. | 3 | 11 | 1 | 0 | 1 | 2 | .... | .... | .... | .... | .... | .... | 1992-93 | 1994-95 |
| MacDonald, Jason | NYR | 1 | 4 | 0 | 0 | 0 | 19 | .... | .... | .... | .... | .... | .... | 2003-04 | 2003-04 |
| MacDonald, Kevin | Ott. | 1 | 1 | 0 | 0 | 0 | 2 | .... | .... | .... | .... | .... | .... | 1993-94 | 1993-94 |
| • MacDonald, Kilby | NYR | 4 | 151 | 36 | 34 | 70 | 47 | 15 | 1 | 2 | 3 | 4 | 1 | 1939-40 | 1944-45 |
| MacDonald, Lowell | Det., L.A., Pit. | 13 | 506 | 180 | 210 | 390 | 92 | 30 | 11 | 11 | 22 | 12 | .... | 1961-62 | 1977-78 |
| MacDonald, Parker | Tor., NYR, Det., Bos., Min. | 14 | 676 | 144 | 179 | 323 | 253 | 75 | 14 | 14 | 28 | 20 | .... | 1952-53 | 1968-69 |
| MacDougall, Kim | Min. | 1 | 1 | 0 | 0 | 0 | 0 | .... | .... | .... | .... | .... | .... | 1974-75 | 1974-75 |
| MacEachern, Shane | St.L. | 1 | 1 | 0 | 0 | 0 | 0 | .... | .... | .... | .... | .... | .... | 1987-88 | 1987-88 |
| • Macey, Hub | NYR, Mtl. | 3 | 30 | 6 | 9 | 15 | 0 | 8 | 0 | 0 | 0 | 0 | .... | 1941-42 | 1946-47 |
| MacGregor, Bruce | Det., NYR | 14 | 893 | 213 | 257 | 470 | 217 | 107 | 19 | 28 | 47 | 44 | .... | 1960-61 | 1973-74 |
| MacGregor, Randy | Hfd. | 1 | 2 | 1 | 1 | 2 | 2 | .... | .... | .... | .... | .... | .... | 1981-82 | 1981-82 |
| MacGuigan, Garth | NYI | 2 | 5 | 0 | 1 | 1 | 2 | .... | .... | .... | .... | .... | .... | 1979-80 | 1983-84 |
| MacInnis, Al | Cgy., St.L. | 23 | 1416 | 340 | 934 | 1274 | 1511 | 177 | 39 | 121 | 160 | 255 | 1 | 1981-82 | 2003-04 |
| MacIntosh, Ian | NYR | 1 | 4 | 0 | 0 | 0 | 4 | .... | .... | .... | .... | .... | .... | 1952-53 | 1952-53 |
| MacIver, Don | Wpg. | 1 | 6 | 0 | 0 | 0 | 2 | .... | .... | .... | .... | .... | .... | 1979-80 | 1979-80 |
| Maciver, Norm | NYR, Hfd., Edm., Ott., Pit., Wpg., Phx. | 12 | 500 | 55 | 230 | 285 | 350 | 56 | 3 | 11 | 14 | 32 | .... | 1986-87 | 1997-98 |
| MacKasey, Blair | Tor. | 1 | 1 | 0 | 0 | 0 | 2 | .... | .... | .... | .... | .... | .... | 1976-77 | 1976-77 |
| • MacKay, Calum | Det., Mtl. | 8 | 237 | 50 | 55 | 105 | 214 | 38 | 5 | 13 | 18 | 20 | 1 | 1946-47 | 1954-55 |
| MacKay, Dave | Chi. | 1 | 29 | 3 | 0 | 3 | 26 | 5 | 0 | 1 | 1 | 2 | .... | 1940-41 | 1940-41 |
| • MacKay, Mickey | Chi., Pit., Bos. | 4 | 147 | 44 | 19 | 63 | 79 | 11 | 0 | 0 | 0 | 6 | 1 | 1926-27 | 1929-30 |
| • MacKay, Murdo | Mtl. | 4 | 19 | 0 | 3 | 3 | 0 | 15 | 1 | 2 | 3 | 0 | .... | 1945-46 | 1948-49 |
| MacKell, Fleming | Tor., Bos. | 13 | 665 | 149 | 220 | 369 | 562 | 80 | 22 | 41 | 63 | 75 | 2 | 1947-48 | 1959-60 |
| • MacKell, Jack | Ott. | 2 | 45 | 4 | 2 | 6 | 59 | 2 | 0 | 0 | 0 | 0 | 2 | 1919-20 | 1920-21 |
| MacKenzie, Barry | Min. | 1 | 6 | 0 | 1 | 1 | 6 | .... | .... | .... | .... | .... | .... | 1968-69 | 1968-69 |
| • MacKenzie, Bill | Chi., Mtl.M., NYR, Mtl. | 7 | 264 | 15 | 14 | 29 | 145 | 21 | 1 | 1 | 2 | 11 | 1 | 1932-33 | 1939-40 |
| Mackey, David | Chi., Min., St.L. | 6 | 126 | 8 | 12 | 20 | 305 | 3 | 0 | 0 | 0 | 2 | .... | 1987-88 | 1993-94 |
| • Mackey, Reg | NYR | 1 | 34 | 0 | 0 | 0 | 16 | 1 | 0 | 0 | 0 | 0 | .... | 1926-27 | 1926-27 |
| • Mackie, Howie | Det. | 2 | 20 | 1 | 0 | 1 | 4 | 8 | 0 | 0 | 0 | 0 | 1 | 1936-37 | 1937-38 |
| MacKinnon, Paul | Wsh. | 5 | 147 | 5 | 23 | 28 | 91 | .... | .... | .... | .... | .... | .... | 1979-80 | 1983-84 |
| ‡ MacLean, Don | L.A., Tor., CBJ, Det., Phx. | 6 | 41 | 8 | 5 | 13 | 6 | 3 | 0 | 0 | 0 | 0 | .... | 1997-98 | 2006-07 |
| MacLean, John | N.J., S.J., NYR, Dal. | 18 | 1194 | 413 | 429 | 842 | 1328 | 104 | 35 | 48 | 83 | 152 | 1 | 1983-84 | 2001-02 |
| MacLean, Paul | St.L., Wpg., Det. | 11 | 719 | 324 | 349 | 673 | 968 | 53 | 21 | 14 | 35 | 110 | .... | 1980-81 | 1990-91 |
| MacLeish, Rick | Phi., Hfd., Pit., Det. | 14 | 846 | 349 | 410 | 759 | 434 | 114 | 54 | 53 | 107 | 38 | 2 | 1970-71 | 1983-84 |
| MacLellan, Brian | L.A., NYR, Min., Cgy., Det. | 10 | 606 | 172 | 241 | 413 | 551 | 47 | 5 | 9 | 14 | 42 | 1 | 1982-83 | 1991-92 |
| MacLeod, Pat | Min., S.J., Dal. | 4 | 53 | 5 | 13 | 18 | 14 | .... | .... | .... | .... | .... | .... | 1990-91 | 1995-96 |
| MacMillan, Billy | Tor., Atl., NYI | 7 | 446 | 74 | 77 | 151 | 184 | 53 | 6 | 6 | 12 | 40 | .... | 1970-71 | 1976-77 |
| MacMillan, Bob | NYR, St.L., Atl., Cgy., Col., N.J., Chi. | 11 | 753 | 228 | 349 | 577 | 260 | 31 | 8 | 11 | 19 | 16 | .... | 1974-75 | 1984-85 |
| MacMillan, Jeff | Dal. | 1 | 4 | 0 | 0 | 0 | 0 | .... | .... | .... | .... | .... | .... | 2003-04 | 2003-04 |
| MacMillan, John | Tor., Det. | 5 | 104 | 5 | 10 | 15 | 32 | 12 | 0 | 1 | 1 | 2 | 2 | 1960-61 | 1964-65 |
| MacNeil, Al | Tor., Mtl., Chi., NYR, Pit. | 11 | 524 | 17 | 75 | 92 | 617 | 37 | 0 | 4 | 4 | 67 | .... | 1955-56 | 1967-68 |
| MacNeil, Bernie | St.L. | 1 | 4 | 0 | 0 | 0 | 0 | .... | .... | .... | .... | .... | .... | 1973-74 | 1973-74 |
| MacNeil, Ian | Phi. | 1 | 2 | 0 | 0 | 0 | 0 | .... | .... | .... | .... | .... | .... | 2002-03 | 2002-03 |
| Macoun, Jamie | Cgy., Tor., Det. | 16 | 1128 | 76 | 282 | 358 | 1208 | 159 | 10 | 32 | 42 | 169 | 2 | 1982-83 | 1998-99 |
| • MacPherson, Bud | Mtl. | 7 | 259 | 5 | 33 | 38 | 233 | 29 | 0 | 3 | 3 | 21 | 1 | 1948-49 | 1956-57 |
| • MacSweyn, Ralph | Phi. | 5 | 47 | 0 | 5 | 5 | 10 | 8 | 0 | 0 | 0 | 6 | .... | 1967-68 | 1971-72 |
| MacTavish, Craig | Bos., Edm., NYR, Phi., St.L. | 17 | 1093 | 213 | 267 | 480 | 891 | 193 | 20 | 38 | 58 | 218 | 4 | 1979-80 | 1996-97 |
| MacWilliam, Mike | NYI | 1 | 6 | 0 | 0 | 0 | 14 | .... | .... | .... | .... | .... | .... | 1995-96 | 1995-96 |
| Madigan, Connie | St.L. | 1 | 20 | 0 | 3 | 3 | 25 | 5 | 0 | 0 | 0 | 4 | .... | 1972-73 | 1972-73 |
| Madill, Jeff | N.J. | 1 | 14 | 4 | 0 | 4 | 46 | 7 | 0 | 2 | 2 | 8 | .... | 1990-91 | 1990-91 |
| Magee, Dean | Min. | 1 | 7 | 0 | 0 | 0 | 4 | .... | .... | .... | .... | .... | .... | 1977-78 | 1977-78 |
| Maggs, Daryl | Chi., Cal., Tor. | 3 | 135 | 14 | 19 | 33 | 54 | 4 | 0 | 0 | 0 | 0 | .... | 1971-72 | 1979-80 |
| Magnan, Marc | Tor. | 1 | 4 | 0 | 1 | 1 | 5 | .... | .... | .... | .... | .... | .... | 1982-83 | 1982-83 |
| • Magnuson, Keith | Chi. | 11 | 589 | 14 | 125 | 139 | 1442 | 68 | 3 | 9 | 12 | 164 | .... | 1969-70 | 1979-80 |
| Maguire, Kevin | Tor., Buf., Phi. | 6 | 260 | 29 | 30 | 59 | 782 | 11 | 0 | 0 | 0 | 86 | .... | 1986-87 | 1991-92 |
| Mahaffy, John | Mtl., NYR | 3 | 37 | 11 | 25 | 36 | 4 | 1 | 0 | 1 | 1 | 0 | .... | 1942-43 | 1944-45 |
| Mahovlich, Frank | Tor., Det., Mtl. | 18 | 1181 | 533 | 570 | 1103 | 1056 | 137 | 51 | 67 | 118 | 163 | 6 | 1956-57 | 1973-74 |
| Mahovlich, Pete | Det., Mtl., Pit. | 16 | 884 | 288 | 485 | 773 | 916 | 88 | 30 | 42 | 72 | 134 | 4 | 1965-66 | 1980-81 |
| Mailhot, Jacques | Que. | 1 | 5 | 0 | 0 | 0 | 33 | .... | .... | .... | .... | .... | .... | 1988-89 | 1988-89 |
| • Mailley, Frank | Mtl. | 1 | 1 | 0 | 0 | 0 | 0 | .... | .... | .... | .... | .... | .... | 1942-43 | 1942-43 |
| Mair, Jim | Phi., NYI, Van. | 5 | 76 | 4 | 15 | 19 | 49 | 3 | 1 | 2 | 3 | 4 | .... | 1970-71 | 1974-75 |
| • Majeau, Fern | Mtl. | 2 | 56 | 22 | 24 | 46 | 43 | 1 | 0 | 0 | 0 | 0 | 1 | 1943-44 | 1944-45 |
| ‡ Majesky, Ivan | Fla., Atl., Wsh. | 3 | 202 | 8 | 23 | 31 | 234 | .... | .... | .... | .... | .... | .... | 2002-03 | 2005-06 |
| Major, Bruce | Que. | 1 | 4 | 0 | 0 | 0 | 0 | .... | .... | .... | .... | .... | .... | 1990-91 | 1990-91 |
| Major, Mark | Det. | 1 | 2 | 0 | 0 | 0 | 5 | .... | .... | .... | .... | .... | .... | 1996-97 | 1996-97 |
| Makarov, Sergei | Cgy., S.J., Dal. | 7 | 424 | 134 | 250 | 384 | 317 | 34 | 12 | 11 | 23 | 8 | .... | 1989-90 | 1996-97 |
| Makela, Mikko | NYI, L.A., Buf., Bos. | 7 | 423 | 118 | 147 | 265 | 139 | 18 | 3 | 8 | 11 | 14 | .... | 1985-86 | 1994-95 |
| Maki, Chico | Chi. | 15 | 841 | 143 | 292 | 435 | 345 | 113 | 17 | 36 | 53 | 43 | 1 | 1960-61 | 1975-76 |
| • Maki, Wayne | Chi., St.L., Van. | 6 | 246 | 57 | 79 | 136 | 184 | 2 | 1 | 0 | 1 | 2 | .... | 1967-68 | 1972-73 |
| Makkonen, Kari | Edm. | 1 | 9 | 2 | 2 | 4 | 0 | .... | .... | .... | .... | .... | .... | 1979-80 | 1979-80 |
| Malakhov, Vladimir | NYI, Mtl., N.J., NYR, Phi. | 13 | 712 | 86 | 260 | 346 | 697 | 75 | 8 | 19 | 27 | 64 | 1 | 1992-93 | 2005-06 |
| ‡ Malec, Tomas | Car., Ott. | 4 | 46 | 0 | 2 | 2 | 47 | .... | .... | .... | .... | .... | .... | 2002-03 | 2006-07 |
| Maley, David | Mtl., N.J., Edm., S.J., NYI | 9 | 466 | 43 | 81 | 124 | 1043 | 46 | 5 | 5 | 10 | 111 | 1 | 1985-86 | 1993-94 |
| Malgunas, Stewart | Phi., Wpg., Wsh., Cgy. | 7 | 129 | 1 | 5 | 6 | 144 | .... | .... | .... | .... | .... | .... | 1993-94 | 1999-00 |
| Malinowski, Merlin | Col., N.J., Hfd. | 5 | 282 | 54 | 111 | 165 | 121 | .... | .... | .... | .... | .... | .... | 1978-79 | 1982-83 |
| Malkoc, Dean | Van., Bos., NYI | 4 | 116 | 1 | 3 | 4 | 299 | .... | .... | .... | .... | .... | .... | 1995-96 | 1998-99 |
| Mallette, Troy | NYR, Edm., N.J., Ott., Bos., T.B. | 9 | 456 | 51 | 68 | 119 | 1226 | 15 | 2 | 2 | 4 | 99 | .... | 1989-90 | 1997-98 |
| ‡ Malmivaara, Olli | N.J. | 1 | 2 | 0 | 0 | 0 | 0 | .... | .... | .... | .... | .... | .... | 2007-08 | 2007-08 |
| • Malone, Cliff | Mtl. | 1 | 3 | 0 | 0 | 0 | 0 | .... | .... | .... | .... | .... | .... | 1951-52 | 1951-52 |
| Malone, Greg | Pit., Hfd., Que. | 11 | 704 | 191 | 310 | 501 | 661 | 20 | 3 | 5 | 8 | 32 | .... | 1976-77 | 1986-87 |
| • Malone, Joe | Mtl., Que., Ham. | 7 | 126 | 143 | 32 | 175 | 57 | 9 | 6 | 2 | 8 | 6 | 1 | 1917-18 | 1923-24 |
| Maloney, Dan | Chi., L.A., Det., Tor. | 11 | 737 | 192 | 259 | 451 | 1489 | 40 | 4 | 7 | 11 | 35 | .... | 1970-71 | 1981-82 |

*John MacMillan*

*Craig MacTavish*

*Sergei Makarov*

*Grant Marshall*

Clare Martin

Pit Martin

Eddie Mazur

Thomas McCarthy

| | | | Regular Schedule | | | | | Playoffs | | | | | | | |
|---|---|---|---|---|---|---|---|---|---|---|---|---|---|---|---|
| Name | NHL Teams | NHL Seasons | GP | G | A | TP | PIM | GP | G | A | TP | PIM | NHL Cup Wins | First NHL Season | Last NHL Season |
| Maloney, Dave | NYR, Buf. | 11 | 657 | 71 | 246 | 317 | 1154 | 49 | 7 | 17 | 24 | 91 | .... | 1974-75 | 1984-85 |
| Maloney, Don | NYR, Hfd., NYI | 13 | 765 | 214 | 350 | 564 | 815 | 94 | 22 | 35 | 57 | 101 | .... | 1978-79 | 1990-91 |
| Maloney, Phil | Bos., Tor., Chi. | 5 | 158 | 28 | 43 | 71 | 16 | 6 | 0 | 0 | 0 | 0 | .... | 1949-50 | 1959-60 |
| Maltais, Steve | Wsh., Min., T.B., Det., CBJ | 6 | 120 | 9 | 18 | 27 | 53 | 1 | 0 | 0 | 0 | 0 | .... | 1989-90 | 2000-01 |
| Maluta, Ray | Bos. | 2 | 25 | 2 | 3 | 5 | 6 | 2 | 0 | 0 | 0 | 0 | .... | 1975-76 | 1976-77 |
| Manastersky, Tom | Mtl. | 1 | 6 | 0 | 0 | 0 | 11 | .... | .... | .... | .... | .... | .... | 1950-51 | 1950-51 |
| • Mancuso, Gus | Mtl., NYR | 4 | 42 | 7 | 9 | 16 | 17 | .... | .... | .... | .... | .... | .... | 1937-38 | 1942-43 |
| Manderville, Kent | Tor., Edm., Hfd., Car., Phi., Pit. | 12 | 646 | 37 | 67 | 104 | 348 | 67 | 3 | 3 | 6 | 44 | .... | 1991-92 | 2002-03 |
| Mandich, Dan | Min. | 4 | 111 | 5 | 11 | 16 | 303 | 7 | 0 | 0 | 0 | 2 | .... | 1982-83 | 1985-86 |
| ‡ Maneluk, Mike | Phi., Chi., NYR, CBJ | 3 | 85 | 11 | 10 | 21 | 57 | .... | .... | .... | .... | .... | .... | 1998-99 | 2000-01 |
| Manery, Kris | Cle., Min., Van., Wpg. | 4 | 250 | 63 | 64 | 127 | 91 | .... | .... | .... | .... | .... | .... | 1977-78 | 1980-81 |
| Manery, Randy | Det., Atl., L.A. | 10 | 582 | 50 | 206 | 256 | 415 | 13 | 0 | 2 | 2 | 12 | .... | 1970-71 | 1979-80 |
| Manlow, Eric | Bos., NYI | 4 | 37 | 2 | 4 | 6 | 8 | .... | .... | .... | .... | .... | .... | 2000-01 | 2003-04 |
| ‡ Mann, Cameron | Bos., Nsh. | 5 | 93 | 14 | 10 | 24 | 40 | 1 | 0 | 0 | 0 | 0 | .... | 1997-98 | 2002-03 |
| Mann, Jack | NYR | 2 | 9 | 3 | 4 | 7 | 0 | .... | .... | .... | .... | .... | .... | 1943-44 | 1944-45 |
| Mann, Jimmy | Wpg., Que., Pit. | 8 | 293 | 10 | 20 | 30 | 895 | 22 | 0 | 0 | 0 | 89 | .... | 1979-80 | 1987-88 |
| Mann, Ken | Det. | 1 | 1 | 0 | 0 | 0 | 0 | .... | .... | .... | .... | .... | .... | 1975-76 | 1975-76 |
| • Mann, Norm | Tor. | 3 | 31 | 0 | 3 | 3 | 4 | 2 | 0 | 0 | 0 | 0 | .... | 1935-36 | 1940-41 |
| • Manners, Rennison | Pit., Phi. | 2 | 37 | 3 | 2 | 5 | 14 | .... | .... | .... | .... | .... | .... | 1929-30 | 1930-31 |
| ‡ Manning, Paul | CBJ | 1 | 8 | 0 | 0 | 0 | 2 | .... | .... | .... | .... | .... | .... | 2002-03 | 2002-03 |
| Manno, Bob | Van., Tor., Det. | 8 | 371 | 41 | 131 | 172 | 274 | 17 | 2 | 4 | 6 | 12 | .... | 1976-77 | 1984-85 |
| Manson, Dave | Chi., Edm., Wpg., Phx., Mtl., Dal., Tor. | 16 | 1103 | 102 | 288 | 390 | 2792 | 112 | 7 | 24 | 31 | 343 | .... | 1986-87 | 2001-02 |
| Manson, Ray | Bos., NYR | 2 | 2 | 0 | 1 | 1 | 0 | .... | .... | .... | .... | .... | .... | 1947-48 | 1948-49 |
| • Mantha, Georges | Mtl. | 13 | 488 | 89 | 102 | 191 | 148 | 36 | 6 | 2 | 8 | 24 | 2 | 1928-29 | 1940-41 |
| Mantha, Moe | Wpg., Pit., Edm., Min., Phi. | 12 | 656 | 81 | 289 | 370 | 501 | 17 | 5 | 10 | 15 | 18 | .... | 1980-81 | 1991-92 |
| • Mantha, Sylvio | Mtl., Bos. | 14 | 542 | 63 | 78 | 141 | 671 | 39 | 5 | 5 | 10 | 64 | 3 | 1923-24 | 1936-37 |
| ‡ Mapletoft, Justin | NYI | 2 | 38 | 3 | 6 | 9 | 8 | 2 | 0 | 0 | 0 | 0 | .... | 2002-03 | 2003-04 |
| • Maracle, Bud | NYR | 1 | 11 | 1 | 3 | 4 | 4 | 4 | 0 | 0 | 0 | 0 | .... | 1930-31 | 1930-31 |
| Marcetta, Milan | Tor., Min. | 3 | 54 | 7 | 15 | 22 | 10 | 17 | 7 | 7 | 14 | 4 | 1 | 1966-67 | 1968-69 |
| • March, Mush | Chi. | 17 | 759 | 153 | 230 | 383 | 540 | 45 | 12 | 15 | 27 | 41 | 2 | 1928-29 | 1944-45 |
| Marchinko, Brian | Tor., NYI | 4 | 47 | 2 | 6 | 8 | 0 | .... | .... | .... | .... | .... | .... | 1970-71 | 1973-74 |
| Marchment, Bryan | Wpg., Chi., Hfd., Edm., T.B., S.J., Col., Tor., Cgy. | 17 | 926 | 40 | 142 | 182 | 2307 | 83 | 4 | 3 | 7 | 102 | .... | 1988-89 | 2005-06 |
| Marcinyshyn, Dave | N.J., Que., NYR | 3 | 16 | 0 | 1 | 1 | 49 | .... | .... | .... | .... | .... | .... | 1990-91 | 1992-93 |
| Marcon, Lou | Det. | 3 | 60 | 0 | 4 | 4 | 42 | .... | .... | .... | .... | .... | .... | 1958-59 | 1962-63 |
| Marcotte, Don | Bos. | 15 | 868 | 230 | 254 | 484 | 317 | 132 | 34 | 27 | 61 | 81 | 2 | 1965-66 | 1981-82 |
| ‡ Marha, Josef | Col., Ana., Chi. | 6 | 159 | 21 | 32 | 53 | 32 | .... | .... | .... | .... | .... | .... | 1995-96 | 2000-01 |
| Marini, Hector | NYI, N.J. | 5 | 154 | 27 | 46 | 73 | 246 | 10 | 3 | 6 | 9 | 14 | 2 | 1978-79 | 1983-84 |
| Marinucci, Chris | NYI, L.A. | 2 | 13 | 1 | 4 | 5 | 2 | .... | .... | .... | .... | .... | .... | 1994-95 | 1996-97 |
| • Mario, Frank | Bos. | 2 | 53 | 9 | 19 | 28 | 24 | .... | .... | .... | .... | .... | .... | 1941-42 | 1944-45 |
| • Mariucci, John | Chi. | 5 | 223 | 11 | 34 | 45 | 308 | 12 | 0 | 3 | 3 | 26 | .... | 1940-41 | 1947-48 |
| ‡ Marjamaki, Masi | NYI | 1 | 1 | 0 | 0 | 0 | 0 | .... | .... | .... | .... | .... | .... | 2005-06 | 2005-06 |
| Mark, Gordon | N.J., Edm. | 4 | 85 | 3 | 10 | 13 | 187 | .... | .... | .... | .... | .... | .... | 1986-87 | 1994-95 |
| Markell, John | Wpg., St.L., Min. | 4 | 55 | 11 | 10 | 21 | 36 | .... | .... | .... | .... | .... | .... | 1979-80 | 1984-85 |
| • Marker, Gus | Det., Mtl.M., Tor., Bro. | 10 | 322 | 64 | 69 | 133 | 133 | 46 | 5 | 7 | 12 | 36 | 1 | 1932-33 | 1941-42 |
| Markham, Ray | NYR | 1 | 14 | 1 | 1 | 2 | 21 | 7 | 1 | 0 | 1 | 24 | .... | 1979-80 | 1979-80 |
| • Markle, Jack | Tor. | 1 | 8 | 0 | 1 | 1 | 0 | .... | .... | .... | .... | .... | .... | 1935-36 | 1935-36 |
| ‡ Markov, Danny | Tor., Phx., Car., Phi., Nsh., Det. | 9 | 538 | 29 | 118 | 147 | 456 | 81 | 2 | 12 | 14 | 84 | .... | 1997-98 | 2006-07 |
| • Marks, Jack | Mtl.W., Tor., Que. | 2 | 7 | 0 | 0 | 0 | 4 | .... | .... | .... | .... | .... | 1 | 1917-18 | 1919-20 |
| Marks, John | Chi. | 10 | 657 | 112 | 163 | 275 | 330 | 57 | 5 | 9 | 14 | 60 | .... | 1972-73 | 1981-82 |
| Markwart, Nevin | Bos., Cgy. | 8 | 309 | 41 | 68 | 109 | 794 | 19 | 1 | 0 | 1 | 33 | .... | 1983-84 | 1991-92 |
| Marois, Daniel | Tor., NYI, Bos., Dal. | 8 | 350 | 117 | 93 | 210 | 419 | 19 | 3 | 3 | 6 | 28 | .... | 1987-88 | 1995-96 |
| Marois, Mario | NYR, Van., Que., Wpg., St.L. | 15 | 955 | 76 | 357 | 433 | 1746 | 100 | 4 | 34 | 38 | 182 | .... | 1977-78 | 1991-92 |
| • Marotte, Gilles | Bos., Chi., L.A., NYR, St.L. | 12 | 808 | 56 | 265 | 321 | 919 | 29 | 3 | 3 | 6 | 26 | .... | 1965-66 | 1976-77 |
| Marquess, Mark | Bos. | 1 | 27 | 5 | 4 | 9 | 6 | 4 | 0 | 0 | 0 | 0 | .... | 1946-47 | 1946-47 |
| Marsh, Brad | Atl., Cgy., Phi., Tor., Det., Ott. | 15 | 1086 | 23 | 175 | 198 | 1241 | 97 | 6 | 18 | 24 | 124 | .... | 1978-79 | 1992-93 |
| Marsh, Gary | Det., Tor. | 2 | 7 | 1 | 3 | 4 | 4 | .... | .... | .... | .... | .... | .... | 1967-68 | 1968-69 |
| Marsh, Peter | Wpg., Chi. | 5 | 278 | 48 | 71 | 119 | 224 | 26 | 1 | 5 | 6 | 33 | .... | 1979-80 | 1983-84 |
| Marshall, Bert | Det., Oak., Cal., NYR, NYI | 14 | 868 | 17 | 181 | 198 | 926 | 72 | 4 | 22 | 26 | 99 | .... | 1965-66 | 1978-79 |
| Marshall, Don | Mtl., NYR, Buf., Tor. | 19 | 1176 | 265 | 324 | 589 | 127 | 94 | 8 | 15 | 23 | 14 | 5 | 1951-52 | 1971-72 |
| Marshall, Grant | Dal., CBJ, N.J. | 11 | 700 | 92 | 147 | 239 | 793 | 90 | 6 | 11 | 17 | 95 | 2 | 1994-95 | 2005-06 |
| Marshall, Jason | St.L., Ana., Wsh., Min., S.J. | 12 | 526 | 16 | 51 | 67 | 1004 | 43 | 2 | 3 | 5 | 55 | .... | 1991-92 | 2005-06 |
| Marshall, Paul | Pit., Tor., Hfd. | 4 | 95 | 15 | 18 | 33 | 17 | 1 | 0 | 0 | 0 | 0 | .... | 1979-80 | 1982-83 |
| Marshall, Willie | Tor. | 4 | 33 | 1 | 5 | 6 | 2 | .... | .... | .... | .... | .... | .... | 1952-53 | 1958-59 |
| Marson, Mike | Wsh., L.A. | 6 | 196 | 24 | 24 | 48 | 233 | .... | .... | .... | .... | .... | .... | 1974-75 | 1979-80 |
| ‡ Martensson, Tony | Ana. | 1 | 6 | 1 | 1 | 2 | 0 | .... | .... | .... | .... | .... | .... | 2003-04 | 2003-04 |
| • Martin, Clare | Bos., Det., Chi., NYR | 6 | 237 | 12 | 28 | 40 | 78 | 27 | 0 | 2 | 2 | 6 | 1 | 1941-42 | 1951-52 |
| Martin, Craig | Wpg., Fla. | 2 | 21 | 0 | 1 | 1 | 24 | .... | .... | .... | .... | .... | .... | 1994-95 | 1996-97 |
| • Martin, Frank | Bos., Chi. | 6 | 282 | 11 | 46 | 57 | 122 | 10 | 0 | 2 | 2 | 2 | .... | 1952-53 | 1957-58 |
| Martin, Grant | Van., Wsh. | 4 | 44 | 0 | 4 | 4 | 55 | 1 | 1 | 0 | 1 | 2 | .... | 1983-84 | 1986-87 |
| Martin, Jack | Tor. | 1 | 1 | 0 | 0 | 0 | 0 | .... | .... | .... | .... | .... | .... | 1960-61 | 1960-61 |
| Martin, Matt | Tor. | 4 | 76 | 0 | 5 | 5 | 71 | .... | .... | .... | .... | .... | .... | 1993-94 | 1996-97 |
| • Martin, Pit | Det., Bos., Chi., Van. | 17 | 1101 | 324 | 485 | 809 | 609 | 100 | 27 | 31 | 58 | 56 | .... | 1961-62 | 1978-79 |
| Martin, Rick | Buf., L.A. | 11 | 685 | 384 | 317 | 701 | 477 | 63 | 24 | 29 | 53 | 74 | .... | 1971-72 | 1981-82 |
| • Martin, Ron | NYA | 2 | 94 | 13 | 16 | 29 | 36 | .... | .... | .... | .... | .... | .... | 1932-33 | 1933-34 |
| Martin, Terry | Buf., Que., Tor., Edm., Min. | 10 | 479 | 104 | 101 | 205 | 202 | 21 | 4 | 2 | 6 | 26 | .... | 1975-76 | 1984-85 |
| Martin, Tom | Tor. | 1 | 3 | 1 | 0 | 1 | 0 | .... | .... | .... | .... | .... | .... | 1967-68 | 1967-68 |
| Martin, Tom | Wpg., Hfd., Min. | 6 | 92 | 12 | 11 | 23 | 249 | 4 | 0 | 0 | 0 | 6 | .... | 1984-85 | 1989-90 |
| • Martineau, Don | Atl., Min., Det. | 4 | 90 | 6 | 10 | 16 | 63 | .... | .... | .... | .... | .... | .... | 1973-74 | 1976-77 |
| Martini, Darcy | Edm. | 1 | 2 | 0 | 0 | 0 | 0 | .... | .... | .... | .... | .... | .... | 1993-94 | 1993-94 |
| ‡ Martins, Steve | Hfd., Car., Ott., T.B., NYI, St.L. | 10 | 267 | 21 | 25 | 46 | 142 | 5 | 0 | 1 | 1 | 0 | .... | 1995-96 | 2005-06 |
| Martinson, Steve | Det., Mtl., Min. | 4 | 49 | 2 | 1 | 3 | 244 | 1 | 0 | 0 | 0 | 10 | .... | 1987-88 | 1991-92 |
| Maruk, Dennis | Cal., Cle., Min., Wsh. | 14 | 888 | 356 | 522 | 878 | 761 | 34 | 14 | 22 | 36 | 26 | .... | 1975-76 | 1988-89 |
| Masnick, Paul | Mtl., Chi., Tor. | 6 | 232 | 18 | 41 | 59 | 139 | 33 | 4 | 5 | 9 | 27 | 1 | 1950-51 | 1957-58 |
| • Mason, Charley | NYR, NYA, Det., Chi. | 4 | 95 | 7 | 18 | 25 | 44 | 4 | 0 | 1 | 1 | 0 | .... | 1934-35 | 1938-39 |
| • Massecar, George | NYA | 3 | 100 | 12 | 11 | 23 | 46 | .... | .... | .... | .... | .... | .... | 1929-30 | 1931-32 |
| Masters, Jamie | St.L. | 3 | 33 | 1 | 13 | 14 | 2 | 2 | 0 | 0 | 0 | 0 | .... | 1975-76 | 1978-79 |
| • Masterton, Bill | Min. | 1 | 38 | 4 | 8 | 12 | 4 | .... | .... | .... | .... | .... | .... | 1967-68 | 1967-68 |
| • Mathers, Frank | Tor. | 3 | 23 | 1 | 3 | 4 | 4 | .... | .... | .... | .... | .... | .... | 1948-49 | 1951-52 |
| Mathiasen, Dwight | Pit. | 3 | 33 | 1 | 7 | 8 | 18 | .... | .... | .... | .... | .... | .... | 1985-86 | 1987-88 |
| Mathieson, Jim | Wsh. | 1 | 2 | 0 | 0 | 0 | 4 | .... | .... | .... | .... | .... | .... | 1989-90 | 1989-90 |
| Mathieu, Marquis | Bos. | 3 | 16 | 0 | 2 | 2 | 14 | .... | .... | .... | .... | .... | .... | 1998-99 | 2000-01 |
| Matte, Christian | Col., Min. | 5 | 25 | 2 | 3 | 5 | 12 | .... | .... | .... | .... | .... | .... | 1996-97 | 2000-01 |
| • Matte, Joe | Tor., Ham., Bos., Mtl. | 4 | 68 | 17 | 15 | 32 | 54 | .... | .... | .... | .... | .... | .... | 1919-20 | 1925-26 |
| • Matte, Joe | Det., Chi. | 2 | 24 | 0 | 3 | 3 | 8 | .... | .... | .... | .... | .... | .... | 1929-30 | 1942-43 |
| Matteau, Stephane | Cgy., Chi., NYR, St.L., S.J., Fla. | 13 | 848 | 144 | 172 | 316 | 742 | 109 | 12 | 22 | 34 | 80 | 1 | 1990-91 | 2002-03 |
| Matteucci, Mike | Min. | 2 | 6 | 0 | 0 | 0 | 4 | .... | .... | .... | .... | .... | .... | 2000-01 | 2001-02 |
| Mattiussi, Dick | Pit., Oak., Cal. | 4 | 200 | 8 | 31 | 39 | 124 | 8 | 0 | 1 | 1 | 6 | .... | 1967-68 | 1970-71 |
| Matvichuk, Richard | Min., Dal., N.J. | 14 | 796 | 39 | 139 | 178 | 624 | 123 | 5 | 19 | 24 | 128 | 1 | 1992-93 | 2006-07 |
| • Matz, Johnny | Mtl. | 1 | 30 | 2 | 3 | 5 | 0 | 1 | 0 | 0 | 0 | 0 | .... | 1924-25 | 1924-25 |
| Maxner, Wayne | Bos. | 2 | 62 | 8 | 9 | 17 | 48 | .... | .... | .... | .... | .... | .... | 1964-65 | 1965-66 |
| Maxwell, Brad | Min., Que., Tor., Van., NYR | 10 | 612 | 98 | 270 | 368 | 1292 | 79 | 12 | 49 | 61 | 178 | .... | 1977-78 | 1986-87 |
| Maxwell, Bryan | Min., St.L., Wpg., Pit. | 8 | 331 | 18 | 77 | 95 | 745 | 15 | 1 | 1 | 2 | 86 | .... | 1977-78 | 1984-85 |
| Maxwell, Kevin | Min., Col., N.J. | 3 | 66 | 6 | 15 | 21 | 61 | 16 | 3 | 4 | 7 | 24 | .... | 1980-81 | 1983-84 |
| Maxwell, Wally | Tor. | 1 | 2 | 0 | 0 | 0 | 0 | .... | .... | .... | .... | .... | .... | 1952-53 | 1952-53 |
| May, Alan | Bos., Edm., Wsh., Dal., Cgy. | 8 | 393 | 31 | 45 | 76 | 1348 | 40 | 1 | 2 | 3 | 80 | .... | 1987-88 | 1994-95 |
| Mayer, Derek | Ott. | 1 | 17 | 2 | 2 | 4 | 8 | .... | .... | .... | .... | .... | .... | 1993-94 | 1993-94 |
| Mayer, Jim | NYR | 1 | 4 | 0 | 0 | 0 | 0 | .... | .... | .... | .... | .... | .... | 1979-80 | 1979-80 |
| Mayer, Pat | Pit. | 1 | 1 | 0 | 0 | 0 | 4 | .... | .... | .... | .... | .... | .... | 1987-88 | 1987-88 |
| • Mayer, Shep | Tor. | 1 | 12 | 1 | 2 | 3 | 4 | .... | .... | .... | .... | .... | .... | 1942-43 | 1942-43 |
| • Mazur, Eddie | Mtl., Chi. | 6 | 107 | 8 | 20 | 28 | 120 | 25 | 4 | 5 | 9 | 22 | 1 | 1950-51 | 1956-57 |
| Mazur, Jay | Van. | 4 | 47 | 11 | 7 | 18 | 20 | 6 | 0 | 1 | 1 | 8 | .... | 1988-89 | 1991-92 |
| McAdam, Gary | Buf., Pit., Det., Cgy., Wsh., N.J., Tor. | 11 | 534 | 96 | 132 | 228 | 243 | 30 | 6 | 5 | 11 | 16 | .... | 1975-76 | 1985-86 |
| • McAdam, Sam | NYR | 1 | 5 | 0 | 0 | 0 | 0 | .... | .... | .... | .... | .... | .... | 1930-31 | 1930-31 |
| ‡ McAllister, Chris | Van., Tor., Phi., Col., NYR | 7 | 301 | 4 | 17 | 21 | 634 | 9 | 0 | 1 | 1 | 4 | .... | 1997-98 | 2003-04 |
| McAlpine, Chris | N.J., St.L., T.B., Atl., Chi., L.A. | 8 | 289 | 6 | 24 | 30 | 245 | 28 | 0 | 1 | 1 | 18 | 1 | 1994-95 | 2002-03 |
| • McAndrew, Hazen | Bro. | 1 | 7 | 0 | 1 | 1 | 6 | .... | .... | .... | .... | .... | .... | 1941-42 | 1941-42 |
| McAneeley, Ted | Cal. | 3 | 158 | 8 | 35 | 43 | 141 | .... | .... | .... | .... | .... | .... | 1972-73 | 1974-75 |
| McAtee, Jud | Det. | 3 | 46 | 15 | 13 | 28 | 6 | 14 | 2 | 1 | 3 | 0 | .... | 1942-43 | 1944-45 |
| McAtee, Norm | Bos. | 1 | 13 | 0 | 1 | 1 | 0 | .... | .... | .... | .... | .... | .... | 1946-47 | 1946-47 |
| • McAvoy, George | Mtl. | 1 | .... | .... | .... | .... | .... | 4 | 0 | 0 | 0 | 0 | .... | 1954-55 | 1954-55 |
| McBain, Andrew | Wpg., Pit., Van., Ott. | 11 | 608 | 129 | 172 | 301 | 633 | 24 | 5 | 7 | 12 | 39 | .... | 1983-84 | 1993-94 |
| McBain, Jason | Hfd. | 2 | 9 | 0 | 0 | 0 | 0 | .... | .... | .... | .... | .... | .... | 1995-96 | 1996-97 |
| McBain, Mike | T.B. | 2 | 64 | 0 | 7 | 7 | 22 | .... | .... | .... | .... | .... | .... | 1997-98 | 1998-99 |
| McBean, Wayne | L.A., NYI, Wpg. | 6 | 211 | 10 | 39 | 49 | 168 | 2 | 1 | 1 | 2 | 0 | .... | 1987-88 | 1993-94 |
| McBride, Cliff | Mtl.M., Tor. | 2 | 2 | 0 | 0 | 0 | 0 | .... | .... | .... | .... | .... | .... | 1928-29 | 1929-30 |

| Name | NHL Teams | NHL Seasons | Regular Schedule GP | G | A | TP | PIM | Playoffs GP | G | A | TP | PIM | NHL Cup Wins | First NHL Season | Last NHL Season |
|---|---|---|---|---|---|---|---|---|---|---|---|---|---|---|---|
| McBurney, Jim | Chi. | 1 | 1 | 0 | 1 | 1 | 0 | .... | .... | .... | .... | .... | .... | 1952-53 | 1952-53 |
| • McCabe, Stan | Det., Mtl.M. | 4 | 78 | 9 | 4 | 13 | 49 | .... | .... | .... | .... | .... | .... | 1929-30 | 1933-34 |
| • McCaffrey, Bert | Tor., Pit., Mtl. | 7 | 260 | 43 | 30 | 73 | 202 | 8 | 2 | 1 | 3 | 10 | 1 | 1924-25 | 1930-31 |
| McCahill, John | Col. | 1 | 1 | 0 | 0 | 0 | 0 | .... | .... | .... | .... | .... | .... | 1977-78 | 1977-78 |
| • McCaig, Doug | Det., Chi. | 7 | 263 | 8 | 21 | 29 | 255 | 7 | 0 | 1 | 1 | 10 | .... | 1941-42 | 1950-51 |
| • McCallum, Dunc | NYR, Pit. | 5 | 187 | 14 | 35 | 49 | 230 | 10 | 1 | 2 | 3 | 12 | .... | 1965-66 | 1970-71 |
| • McCalmon, Eddie | Chi., Phi. | 2 | 39 | 5 | 0 | 5 | 14 | .... | .... | .... | .... | .... | .... | 1927-28 | 1930-31 |
| McCann, Rick | Det. | 6 | 43 | 1 | 4 | 5 | 6 | .... | .... | .... | .... | .... | .... | 1967-68 | 1974-75 |
| McCarthy, Dan | NYR | 1 | 5 | 4 | 0 | 4 | 4 | .... | .... | .... | .... | .... | .... | 1980-81 | 1980-81 |
| McCarthy, Kevin | Phi., Van., Pit. | 10 | 537 | 67 | 191 | 258 | 527 | 21 | 2 | 3 | 5 | 20 | .... | 1977-78 | 1986-87 |
| McCarthy, Sandy | Cgy., T.B., Phi., Car., NYR, Bos. | 11 | 736 | 72 | 76 | 148 | 1534 | 23 | 0 | 2 | 2 | 61 | .... | 1993-94 | 2003-04 |
| • McCarthy, Thomas | Que., Ham. | 2 | 35 | 22 | 7 | 29 | 10 | .... | .... | .... | .... | .... | .... | 1919-20 | 1920-21 |
| McCarthy, Tom | Det., Bos. | 4 | 60 | 8 | 9 | 17 | 8 | .... | .... | .... | .... | .... | .... | 1956-57 | 1960-61 |
| McCarthy, Tom | Min., Bos. | 9 | 460 | 178 | 221 | 399 | 330 | 68 | 12 | 26 | 38 | 67 | .... | 1979-80 | 1987-88 |
| • McCartney, Walt | Mtl. | 1 | 2 | 0 | 0 | 0 | 0 | .... | .... | .... | .... | .... | .... | 1932-33 | 1932-33 |
| McCaskill, Ted | Min. | 1 | 4 | 0 | 2 | 2 | 0 | .... | .... | .... | .... | .... | .... | 1967-68 | 1967-68 |
| McCauley, Alyn | Tor., S.J., L.A. | 9 | 488 | 69 | 97 | 166 | 116 | 52 | 7 | 12 | 19 | 18 | .... | 1997-98 | 2006-07 |
| McClanahan, Rob | Buf., Hfd., NYR | 5 | 224 | 38 | 63 | 101 | 126 | 34 | 4 | 12 | 16 | 31 | .... | 1979-80 | 1983-84 |
| McCleary, Trent | Ott., Bos., Mtl. | 4 | 192 | 8 | 15 | 23 | 134 | .... | .... | .... | .... | .... | .... | 1995-96 | 1999-00 |
| McClelland, Kevin | Pit., Edm., Det., Tor., Wpg. | 12 | 588 | 68 | 112 | 180 | 1672 | 98 | 11 | 18 | 29 | 281 | 4 | 1981-82 | 1993-94 |
| McCord, Bob | Bos., Det., Min., St.L. | 7 | 316 | 10 | 58 | 68 | 262 | 14 | 2 | 5 | 7 | 10 | .... | 1963-64 | 1972-73 |
| • McCord, Dennis | Van. | 1 | 3 | 0 | 0 | 0 | 6 | .... | .... | .... | .... | .... | .... | 1973-74 | 1973-74 |
| McCormack, John | Tor., Mtl., Chi. | 8 | 311 | 25 | 49 | 74 | 35 | 22 | 1 | 1 | 2 | 0 | 2 | 1947-48 | 1954-55 |
| McCosh, Shawn | L.A., NYR | 2 | 9 | 1 | 0 | 1 | 6 | .... | .... | .... | .... | .... | .... | 1991-92 | 1994-95 |
| McCourt, Dale | Det., Buf., Tor. | 7 | 532 | 194 | 284 | 478 | 124 | 21 | 9 | 7 | 16 | 6 | .... | 1977-78 | 1983-84 |
| McCreary, Bill | NYR, Det., Mtl., St.L. | 8 | 309 | 53 | 62 | 115 | 108 | 48 | 6 | 16 | 22 | 14 | .... | 1953-54 | 1970-71 |
| McCreary, Bill | Tor. | 1 | 12 | 1 | 0 | 1 | 4 | .... | .... | .... | .... | .... | .... | 1980-81 | 1980-81 |
| • McCreary, Keith | Mtl., Pit., Atl. | 10 | 532 | 131 | 112 | 243 | 294 | 16 | 0 | 4 | 4 | 6 | .... | 1961-62 | 1974-75 |
| • McCreedy, John | Tor. | 2 | 64 | 17 | 12 | 29 | 25 | 21 | 4 | 3 | 7 | 16 | 2 | 1941-42 | 1944-45 |
| McCrimmon, Brad | Bos., Phi., Cgy., Det., Hfd., Phx. | 18 | 1222 | 81 | 322 | 403 | 1416 | 116 | 11 | 18 | 29 | 176 | 1 | 1979-80 | 1996-97 |
| McCrimmon, Jim | St.L. | 1 | 2 | 0 | 0 | 0 | 0 | .... | .... | .... | .... | .... | .... | 1974-75 | 1974-75 |
| • McCulley, Bob | Mtl. | 1 | 1 | 0 | 0 | 0 | 0 | .... | .... | .... | .... | .... | .... | 1934-35 | 1934-35 |
| • McCurry, Duke | Pit. | 4 | 148 | 21 | 11 | 32 | 119 | 4 | 0 | 2 | 2 | 2 | .... | 1925-26 | 1928-29 |
| McCutcheon, Brian | Det. | 3 | 37 | 3 | 1 | 4 | 7 | .... | .... | .... | .... | .... | .... | 1974-75 | 1976-77 |
| McCutcheon, Darwin | Tor. | 1 | 1 | 0 | 0 | 0 | 2 | .... | .... | .... | .... | .... | .... | 1981-82 | 1981-82 |
| McDill, Jeff | Chi. | 1 | 1 | 0 | 0 | 0 | 0 | .... | .... | .... | .... | .... | .... | 1976-77 | 1976-77 |
| McDonagh, Bill | NYR | 1 | 4 | 0 | 0 | 0 | 2 | .... | .... | .... | .... | .... | .... | 1949-50 | 1949-50 |
| McDonald, Ab | Mtl., Chi., Bos., Det., Pit., St.L. | 15 | 762 | 182 | 248 | 430 | 200 | 84 | 21 | 29 | 50 | 42 | 4 | 1957-58 | 1971-72 |
| McDonald, Brian | Chi., Buf. | 2 | 12 | 0 | 0 | 0 | 29 | 8 | 0 | 0 | 0 | 2 | .... | 1967-68 | 1970-71 |
| • McDonald, Bucko | Det., Tor., NYR | 11 | 446 | 35 | 88 | 123 | 206 | 50 | 6 | 1 | 7 | 24 | 3 | 1934-35 | 1944-45 |
| • McDonald, Butch | Det., Chi. | 2 | 66 | 8 | 20 | 28 | 2 | 5 | 0 | 2 | 2 | 10 | .... | 1939-40 | 1944-45 |
| McDonald, Gerry | Hfd. | 2 | 8 | 0 | 0 | 0 | 4 | .... | .... | .... | .... | .... | .... | 1981-82 | 1983-84 |
| • McDonald, Jack | Mtl.W., Mtl., Que., Tor. | 5 | 69 | 26 | 14 | 40 | 30 | 7 | 1 | 3 | 4 | 3 | .... | 1917-18 | 1921-22 |
| McDonald, Jack | NYR | 1 | 43 | 10 | 9 | 19 | 6 | .... | .... | .... | .... | .... | .... | 1943-44 | 1943-44 |
| McDonald, Lanny | Tor., Col., Cgy. | 16 | 1111 | 500 | 506 | 1006 | 899 | 117 | 44 | 40 | 84 | 120 | 1 | 1973-74 | 1988-89 |
| McDonald, Robert | NYR | 1 | 1 | 0 | 0 | 0 | 0 | .... | .... | .... | .... | .... | .... | 1943-44 | 1943-44 |
| McDonald, Terry | K.C. | 1 | 8 | 0 | 1 | 1 | 6 | .... | .... | .... | .... | .... | .... | 1975-76 | 1975-76 |
| ‡ McDonell, Kent | CBJ | 2 | 32 | 1 | 2 | 3 | 36 | .... | .... | .... | .... | .... | .... | 2002-03 | 2003-04 |
| McDonnell, Joe | Van., Pit. | 3 | 50 | 2 | 10 | 12 | 34 | .... | .... | .... | .... | .... | .... | 1981-82 | 1985-86 |
| • McDonnell, Moylan | Ham. | 1 | 22 | 1 | 2 | 3 | 2 | .... | .... | .... | .... | .... | .... | 1920-21 | 1920-21 |
| McDonough, Al | L.A., Pit., Atl., Det. | 5 | 237 | 73 | 88 | 161 | 73 | 8 | 0 | 1 | 1 | 2 | .... | 1970-71 | 1977-78 |
| McDonough, Hubie | L.A., NYI, S.J. | 5 | 195 | 40 | 26 | 66 | 67 | 5 | 1 | 0 | 1 | 4 | .... | 1988-89 | 1992-93 |
| McDougal, Mike | NYR, Hfd. | 4 | 61 | 8 | 10 | 18 | 43 | .... | .... | .... | .... | .... | .... | 1978-79 | 1982-83 |
| McDougall, Bill | Det., Edm., T.B. | 3 | 28 | 5 | 5 | 10 | 12 | 1 | 0 | 0 | 0 | 0 | .... | 1990-91 | 1993-94 |
| McEachern, Shawn | Pit., L.A., Bos., Ott., Atl. | 14 | 911 | 256 | 323 | 579 | 506 | 97 | 12 | 25 | 37 | 62 | 1 | 1991-92 | 2005-06 |
| McElmury, Jim | Min., K.C., Col. | 5 | 180 | 14 | 47 | 61 | 49 | .... | .... | .... | .... | .... | .... | 1972-73 | 1977-78 |
| McEwen, Mike | NYR, Col., NYI, L.A., Wsh., Det., Hfd. | 12 | 716 | 108 | 296 | 404 | 460 | 78 | 12 | 36 | 48 | 48 | 3 | 1976-77 | 1987-88 |
| • McFadden, Jim | Det., Chi. | 8 | 412 | 100 | 126 | 226 | 89 | 49 | 10 | 9 | 19 | 30 | 1 | 1946-47 | 1953-54 |
| • McFadyen, Don | Chi. | 4 | 179 | 12 | 33 | 45 | 77 | 11 | 2 | 2 | 4 | 5 | 1 | 1932-33 | 1935-36 |
| McFall, Dan | Wpg. | 2 | 9 | 0 | 1 | 1 | 0 | .... | .... | .... | .... | .... | .... | 1984-85 | 1985-86 |
| • McFarlane, Gord | Chi. | 1 | 2 | 0 | 0 | 0 | 0 | .... | .... | .... | .... | .... | .... | 1926-27 | 1926-27 |
| McGeough, Jim | Wsh., Pit. | 4 | 57 | 7 | 10 | 17 | 32 | .... | .... | .... | .... | .... | .... | 1981-82 | 1986-87 |
| • McGibbon, Irv | Mtl. | 1 | 1 | 0 | 0 | 0 | 2 | .... | .... | .... | .... | .... | .... | 1942-43 | 1942-43 |
| McGill, Bob | Tor., Chi., S.J., Det., NYI, Hfd. | 13 | 705 | 17 | 55 | 72 | 1766 | 49 | 0 | 0 | 0 | 88 | .... | 1981-82 | 1993-94 |
| • McGill, Jack | Mtl. | 3 | 134 | 27 | 10 | 37 | 71 | 3 | 2 | 0 | 2 | 0 | .... | 1934-35 | 1936-37 |
| • McGill, Jack | Bos. | 4 | 97 | 23 | 36 | 59 | 42 | 27 | 7 | 4 | 11 | 17 | .... | 1941-42 | 1946-47 |
| McGill, Ryan | Chi., Phi., Edm. | 4 | 151 | 4 | 15 | 19 | 391 | .... | .... | .... | .... | .... | .... | 1991-92 | 1994-95 |
| ‡ McGillis, Dan | Edm., Phi., S.J., Bos., N.J. | 9 | 634 | 56 | 182 | 238 | 570 | 64 | 8 | 14 | 22 | 76 | .... | 1996-97 | 2005-06 |
| McGregor, Sandy | NYR | 1 | 2 | 0 | 0 | 0 | 2 | .... | .... | .... | .... | .... | .... | 1963-64 | 1963-64 |
| • McGuire, Mickey | Pit. | 2 | 36 | 3 | 0 | 3 | 6 | .... | .... | .... | .... | .... | .... | 1926-27 | 1927-28 |
| McHugh, Mike | Min., S.J. | 4 | 20 | 1 | 0 | 1 | 16 | .... | .... | .... | .... | .... | .... | 1988-89 | 1991-92 |
| McIlhargey, Jack | Phi., Van., Hfd. | 8 | 393 | 11 | 36 | 47 | 1102 | 27 | 0 | 3 | 3 | 68 | .... | 1974-75 | 1981-82 |
| • McInenly, Bert | Det., NYA, Ott., Bos. | 6 | 166 | 19 | 15 | 34 | 144 | 4 | 0 | 0 | 0 | 2 | .... | 1930-31 | 1935-36 |
| McInnis, Marty | NYI, Cgy., Ana., Bos. | 12 | 796 | 170 | 250 | 420 | 330 | 22 | 3 | 2 | 5 | 4 | .... | 1991-92 | 2002-03 |
| McIntosh, Bruce | Min. | 1 | 2 | 0 | 0 | 0 | 0 | .... | .... | .... | .... | .... | .... | 1972-73 | 1972-73 |
| McIntosh, Paul | Buf. | 2 | 48 | 0 | 2 | 2 | 66 | 2 | 0 | 0 | 0 | 7 | .... | 1974-75 | 1975-76 |
| • McIntyre, Jack | Bos., Chi., Det. | 11 | 499 | 109 | 102 | 211 | 173 | 29 | 7 | 6 | 13 | 4 | .... | 1949-50 | 1959-60 |
| McIntyre, John | Tor., L.A., NYR, Van. | 6 | 351 | 24 | 54 | 78 | 516 | 44 | 0 | 6 | 6 | 54 | .... | 1989-90 | 1994-95 |
| McIntyre, Larry | Tor. | 2 | 41 | 0 | 3 | 3 | 26 | .... | .... | .... | .... | .... | .... | 1969-70 | 1972-73 |
| McKay, Doug | Det. | 1 | .... | .... | .... | .... | .... | 1 | 0 | 0 | 0 | 0 | 1 | 1949-50 | 1949-50 |
| McKay, Randy | Det., N.J., Dal., Mtl. | 15 | 932 | 162 | 201 | 363 | 1731 | 123 | 20 | 23 | 43 | 123 | 2 | 1988-89 | 2002-03 |
| McKay, Ray | Chi., Buf., Cal. | 6 | 140 | 2 | 16 | 18 | 102 | 1 | 0 | 0 | 0 | 0 | .... | 1968-69 | 1973-74 |
| McKay, Scott | Ana. | 1 | 1 | 0 | 0 | 0 | 0 | .... | .... | .... | .... | .... | .... | 1993-94 | 1993-94 |
| McKechnie, Walt | Min., Cal., Bos., Det., Wsh., Cle., Tor., Col. | 16 | 955 | 214 | 392 | 606 | 469 | 15 | 7 | 5 | 12 | 7 | .... | 1967-68 | 1982-83 |
| McKee, Mike | Que. | 1 | 48 | 3 | 12 | 15 | 41 | .... | .... | .... | .... | .... | .... | 1993-94 | 1993-94 |
| McKegney, Ian | Chi. | 1 | 3 | 0 | 0 | 0 | 2 | .... | .... | .... | .... | .... | .... | 1976-77 | 1976-77 |
| McKegney, Tony | Buf., Que., Min., NYR, St.L., Det., Chi. | 13 | 912 | 320 | 319 | 639 | 517 | 79 | 24 | 23 | 47 | 56 | .... | 1978-79 | 1990-91 |
| McKendry, Alex | NYI, Cgy. | 4 | 46 | 3 | 6 | 9 | 21 | 6 | 2 | 2 | 4 | 0 | 1 | 1977-78 | 1980-81 |
| McKenna, Sean | Buf., L.A., Tor. | 9 | 414 | 82 | 80 | 162 | 181 | 15 | 1 | 2 | 3 | 2 | .... | 1981-82 | 1989-90 |
| McKenna, Steve | L.A., Min., Pit., NYR | 8 | 373 | 18 | 14 | 32 | 824 | 3 | 0 | 1 | 1 | 8 | .... | 1996-97 | 2003-04 |
| McKenney, Don | Bos., NYR, Tor., Det., St.L. | 13 | 798 | 237 | 345 | 582 | 211 | 58 | 18 | 29 | 47 | 10 | 1 | 1954-55 | 1967-68 |
| McKenny, Jim | Tor., Min. | 14 | 604 | 82 | 247 | 329 | 294 | 37 | 7 | 9 | 16 | 10 | .... | 1965-66 | 1978-79 |
| McKenzie, Brian | Pit. | 1 | 6 | 1 | 1 | 2 | 4 | .... | .... | .... | .... | .... | .... | 1971-72 | 1971-72 |
| McKenzie, Jim | Hfd., Dal., Pit., Wpg., Phx., Ana., Wsh., N.J., Nsh. | 15 | 880 | 48 | 52 | 100 | 1739 | 51 | 0 | 0 | 0 | 38 | 1 | 1989-90 | 2003-04 |
| McKenzie, John | Chi., Det., NYR, Bos. | 12 | 691 | 206 | 268 | 474 | 917 | 69 | 15 | 32 | 47 | 133 | 2 | 1958-59 | 1971-72 |
| McKim, Andrew | Bos., Det. | 3 | 38 | 1 | 4 | 5 | 6 | .... | .... | .... | .... | .... | .... | 1992-93 | 1994-95 |
| • McKinnon, Alex | Ham., NYA, Chi. | 5 | 193 | 19 | 11 | 30 | 237 | .... | .... | .... | .... | .... | .... | 1924-25 | 1928-29 |
| • McKinnon, John | Mtl., Pit., Phi. | 6 | 208 | 28 | 11 | 39 | 224 | 2 | 0 | 0 | 0 | 4 | .... | 1925-26 | 1930-31 |
| McLaren, Steve | St.L. | 1 | 6 | 0 | 0 | 0 | 25 | .... | .... | .... | .... | .... | .... | 2003-04 | 2003-04 |
| McLean, Don | Wsh. | 1 | 9 | 0 | 0 | 0 | 6 | .... | .... | .... | .... | .... | .... | 1975-76 | 1975-76 |
| • McLean, Fred | Que., Ham. | 2 | 8 | 0 | 0 | 0 | 2 | .... | .... | .... | .... | .... | .... | 1919-20 | 1920-21 |
| • McLean, Jack | Tor. | 3 | 67 | 14 | 24 | 38 | 76 | 13 | 2 | 2 | 4 | 8 | 1 | 1942-43 | 1944-45 |
| • McLean, Jeff | S.J. | 1 | 6 | 1 | 0 | 1 | 0 | .... | .... | .... | .... | .... | .... | 1993-94 | 1993-94 |
| • McLellan, John | Tor. | 1 | 2 | 0 | 0 | 0 | 0 | .... | .... | .... | .... | .... | .... | 1951-52 | 1951-52 |
| McLellan, Scott | Bos. | 1 | 2 | 0 | 0 | 0 | 0 | .... | .... | .... | .... | .... | .... | 1982-83 | 1982-83 |
| McLellan, Todd | NYI | 1 | 5 | 1 | 1 | 2 | 0 | .... | .... | .... | .... | .... | .... | 1987-88 | 1987-88 |
| • McLenahan, Rollie | Det. | 1 | 9 | 2 | 1 | 3 | 10 | 2 | 0 | 0 | 0 | 0 | .... | 1945-46 | 1945-46 |
| McLeod, Al | Det. | 1 | 26 | 2 | 2 | 4 | 24 | .... | .... | .... | .... | .... | .... | 1973-74 | 1973-74 |
| McLeod, Jackie | NYR | 5 | 106 | 14 | 23 | 37 | 12 | 7 | 0 | 0 | 0 | 0 | .... | 1949-50 | 1954-55 |
| ‡ McLlwain, Dave | Pit., Wpg., Buf., NYI, Tor., Ott. | 10 | 501 | 100 | 107 | 207 | 292 | 20 | 0 | 2 | 2 | 2 | .... | 1987-88 | 1996-97 |
| • McMahon, Mike | Mtl., Bos. | 3 | 57 | 7 | 18 | 25 | 102 | 13 | 1 | 2 | 3 | 30 | 1 | 1942-43 | 1945-46 |
| McMahon, Mike | NYR, Min., Chi., Det., Pit., Buf. | 8 | 224 | 15 | 68 | 83 | 171 | 14 | 3 | 7 | 10 | 4 | .... | 1963-64 | 1971-72 |
| McManama, Bob | Pit. | 3 | 99 | 11 | 25 | 36 | 28 | 8 | 0 | 1 | 1 | 6 | .... | 1973-74 | 1975-76 |
| • McManus, Sammy | Mtl.M., Bos. | 2 | 26 | 0 | 1 | 1 | 8 | 1 | 0 | 0 | 0 | 0 | 1 | 1934-35 | 1936-37 |
| McMorrow, Sean | Buf. | 1 | 1 | 0 | 0 | 0 | 0 | .... | .... | .... | .... | .... | .... | 2002-03 | 2002-03 |
| McMurchy, Tom | Chi., Edm. | 4 | 55 | 8 | 4 | 12 | 65 | .... | .... | .... | .... | .... | .... | 1983-84 | 1987-88 |
| • McNab, Max | Det. | 4 | 128 | 16 | 19 | 35 | 24 | 25 | 1 | 0 | 1 | 4 | 1 | 1947-48 | 1950-51 |
| McNab, Peter | Buf., Bos., Van., N.J. | 14 | 954 | 363 | 450 | 813 | 179 | 107 | 40 | 42 | 82 | 20 | .... | 1973-74 | 1986-87 |
| • McNabney, Sid | Mtl. | 1 | .... | .... | .... | .... | .... | 5 | 0 | 1 | 1 | 2 | .... | 1950-51 | 1950-51 |
| • McNamara, Howard | Mtl. | 1 | 10 | 1 | 0 | 1 | 4 | .... | .... | .... | .... | .... | .... | 1919-20 | 1919-20 |
| • McNaughton, George | Que. | 1 | 1 | 0 | 0 | 0 | 0 | .... | .... | .... | .... | .... | .... | 1919-20 | 1919-20 |
| • McNeill, Billy | Det. | 6 | 257 | 21 | 46 | 67 | 142 | 4 | 1 | 1 | 2 | 4 | .... | 1956-57 | 1963-64 |
| ‡ McNeill, Grant | Fla. | 1 | 3 | 0 | 0 | 0 | 5 | .... | .... | .... | .... | .... | .... | 2003-04 | 2003-04 |
| McNeill, Mike | Chi., Que. | 2 | 63 | 5 | 11 | 16 | 18 | .... | .... | .... | .... | .... | .... | 1990-91 | 1991-92 |

*Jim McCrimmon*

*Jack McDonald*

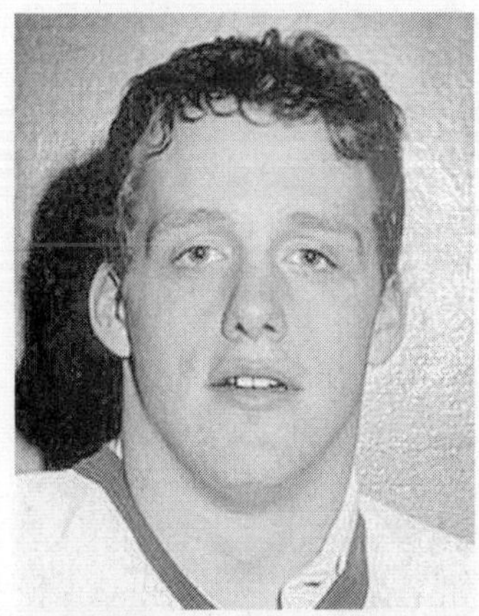
*Scott Metcalfe*

*Art Michaluk*

*Larry Mickey*

*Carl Mokosak*

*Armand Mondou*

*Bill Mosienko*

| | | | Regular Schedule | | | | | Playoffs | | | | | | | |
|---|---|---|---|---|---|---|---|---|---|---|---|---|---|---|---|
| Name | NHL Teams | NHL Seasons | GP | G | A | TP | PIM | GP | G | A | TP | PIM | NHL Cup Wins | First NHL Season | Last NHL Season |
| McNeill, Stu | Det. | 3 | 10 | 1 | 1 | 2 | 2 | .... | .... | .... | .... | .... | .... | 1957-58 | 1959-60 |
| McPhee, George | NYR, N.J. | 7 | 115 | 24 | 25 | 49 | 257 | 29 | 5 | 3 | 8 | 69 | .... | 1982-83 | 1988-89 |
| McPhee, Mike | Mtl., Min., Dal. | 11 | 744 | 200 | 199 | 399 | 661 | 134 | 28 | 27 | 55 | 193 | 1 | 1983-84 | 1993-94 |
| McRae, Basil | Que., Tor., Det., Min., T.B., St.L., Chi. | 16 | 576 | 53 | 83 | 136 | 2457 | 78 | 8 | 4 | 12 | 349 | .... | 1981-82 | 1996-97 |
| McRae, Chris | Tor., Det. | 3 | 21 | 1 | 0 | 1 | 122 | .... | .... | .... | .... | .... | .... | 1987-88 | 1989-90 |
| McRae, Ken | Que., Tor. | 7 | 137 | 14 | 21 | 35 | 364 | 6 | 0 | 0 | 0 | 4 | .... | 1987-88 | 1993-94 |
| ● McReavy, Pat | Bos., Det. | 4 | 55 | 5 | 10 | 15 | 4 | 22 | 3 | 3 | 6 | 9 | 1 | 1938-39 | 1941-42 |
| McReynolds, Brian | Wpg., NYR, L.A. | 3 | 30 | 1 | 5 | 6 | 8 | .... | .... | .... | .... | .... | .... | 1989-90 | 1993-94 |
| McSheffrey, Bryan | Van., Buf. | 3 | 90 | 13 | 7 | 20 | 44 | .... | .... | .... | .... | .... | .... | 1972-73 | 1974-75 |
| McSorley, Marty | Pit., Edm., L.A., NYR, S.J., Bos. | 17 | 961 | 108 | 251 | 359 | 3381 | 115 | 10 | 19 | 29 | 374 | 2 | 1983-84 | 1999-00 |
| McSween, Don | Buf., Ana. | 5 | 47 | 3 | 10 | 13 | 55 | .... | .... | .... | .... | .... | .... | 1987-88 | 1995-96 |
| McTaggart, Jim | Wsh. | 2 | 71 | 3 | 10 | 13 | 205 | .... | .... | .... | .... | .... | .... | 1980-81 | 1981-82 |
| ‡ McTavish, Dale | Cgy. | 1 | 9 | 1 | 2 | 3 | 2 | .... | .... | .... | .... | .... | .... | 1996-97 | 1996-97 |
| McTavish, Gord | St.L., Wpg. | 2 | 11 | 1 | 3 | 4 | 2 | .... | .... | .... | .... | .... | .... | 1978-79 | 1979-80 |
| ● McVeigh, Charley | Chi., NYA | 9 | 397 | 84 | 88 | 172 | 138 | 4 | 0 | 0 | 0 | 2 | .... | 1926-27 | 1934-35 |
| ● McVicar, Jack | Mtl.M. | 2 | 88 | 2 | 4 | 6 | 63 | 6 | 0 | 0 | 0 | 2 | .... | 1930-31 | 1931-32 |
| Meagher, Rick | Mtl., Hfd., N.J., St.L. | 12 | 691 | 144 | 165 | 309 | 383 | 62 | 8 | 7 | 15 | 41 | .... | 1979-80 | 1990-91 |
| Meehan, Gerry | Tor., Phi., Buf., Van., Atl., Wsh. | 10 | 670 | 180 | 243 | 423 | 111 | 10 | 0 | 1 | 1 | 0 | .... | 1968-69 | 1978-79 |
| Meeke, Brent | Cal., Cle. | 5 | 75 | 9 | 22 | 31 | 8 | .... | .... | .... | .... | .... | .... | 1972-73 | 1976-77 |
| Meeker, Howie | Tor. | 8 | 346 | 83 | 102 | 185 | 329 | 42 | 6 | 9 | 15 | 50 | 4 | 1946-47 | 1953-54 |
| Meeker, Mike | Pit. | 1 | 4 | 0 | 0 | 0 | 5 | .... | .... | .... | .... | .... | .... | 1978-79 | 1978-79 |
| ● Meeking, Harry | Tor., Det., Bos. | 3 | 64 | 18 | 12 | 30 | 66 | 9 | 3 | 0 | 3 | 6 | .... | 1917-18 | 1926-27 |
| Meger, Paul | Mtl. | 6 | 212 | 39 | 52 | 91 | 118 | 35 | 3 | 8 | 11 | 16 | 1 | 1949-50 | 1954-55 |
| Meighan, Ron | Min., Pit. | 2 | 48 | 3 | 7 | 10 | 18 | .... | .... | .... | .... | .... | .... | 1981-82 | 1982-83 |
| Meissner, Barrie | Min. | 2 | 6 | 0 | 1 | 1 | 4 | .... | .... | .... | .... | .... | .... | 1967-68 | 1968-69 |
| ● Meissner, Dick | Bos., NYR | 5 | 171 | 11 | 15 | 26 | 37 | .... | .... | .... | .... | .... | .... | 1959-60 | 1964-65 |
| Melametsa, Anssi | Wpg. | 1 | 27 | 0 | 3 | 3 | 2 | .... | .... | .... | .... | .... | .... | 1985-86 | 1985-86 |
| Melanson, Dean | Buf., Wsh. | 2 | 9 | 0 | 0 | 0 | 8 | .... | .... | .... | .... | .... | .... | 1994-95 | 2001-02 |
| ‡ Melin, Bjorn | Ana. | 1 | 3 | 1 | 0 | 1 | 0 | .... | .... | .... | .... | .... | .... | 2006-07 | 2006-07 |
| Melin, Roger | Min. | 2 | 3 | 0 | 0 | 0 | 0 | .... | .... | .... | .... | .... | .... | 1980-81 | 1981-82 |
| Mellanby, Scott | Phi., Edm., Fla., St.L., Atl. | 21 | 1431 | 364 | 476 | 840 | 2479 | 136 | 24 | 29 | 53 | 220 | .... | 1985-86 | 2006-07 |
| Mellor, Tom | Det. | 2 | 26 | 2 | 4 | 6 | 25 | .... | .... | .... | .... | .... | .... | 1973-74 | 1974-75 |
| ● Melnyk, Gerry | Det., Chi., St.L. | 6 | 269 | 39 | 77 | 116 | 34 | 53 | 6 | 6 | 12 | 6 | .... | 1955-56 | 1967-68 |
| Melnyk, Larry | Bos., Edm., NYR, Van. | 10 | 432 | 11 | 63 | 74 | 686 | 66 | 2 | 9 | 11 | 127 | 1 | 1980-81 | 1989-90 |
| ‡ Meloche, Eric | Pit., Phi. | 3 | 74 | 9 | 11 | 20 | 36 | .... | .... | .... | .... | .... | .... | 2001-02 | 2006-07 |
| Melrose, Barry | Wpg., Tor., Det. | 6 | 300 | 10 | 23 | 33 | 728 | 7 | 0 | 2 | 2 | 38 | .... | 1979-80 | 1985-86 |
| Menard, Hillary | Chi. | 1 | 1 | 0 | 0 | 0 | 0 | .... | .... | .... | .... | .... | .... | 1953-54 | 1953-54 |
| Menard, Howie | Det., L.A., Chi., Oak. | 4 | 151 | 23 | 42 | 65 | 87 | 19 | 3 | 7 | 10 | 36 | .... | 1963-64 | 1969-70 |
| Mercredi, Vic | Atl. | 1 | 2 | 0 | 0 | 0 | 0 | .... | .... | .... | .... | .... | .... | 1974-75 | 1974-75 |
| Meredith, Greg | Cgy. | 2 | 38 | 6 | 4 | 10 | 8 | 5 | 3 | 1 | 4 | 4 | .... | 1980-81 | 1982-83 |
| Merkosky, Glenn | Hfd., N.J., Det. | 5 | 66 | 5 | 12 | 17 | 22 | .... | .... | .... | .... | .... | .... | 1981-82 | 1989-90 |
| ● Meronek, Bill | Mtl. | 2 | 19 | 5 | 8 | 13 | 0 | 1 | 0 | 0 | 0 | 0 | .... | 1939-40 | 1942-43 |
| Merrick, Wayne | St.L., Cal., Cle., NYI | 12 | 774 | 191 | 265 | 456 | 303 | 102 | 19 | 30 | 49 | 30 | 4 | 1972-73 | 1983-84 |
| ● Merrill, Horace | Ott. | 2 | 8 | 0 | 0 | 0 | 3 | .... | .... | .... | .... | .... | 1 | 1917-18 | 1919-20 |
| Mertzig, Jan | NYR | 1 | 23 | 0 | 2 | 2 | 8 | .... | .... | .... | .... | .... | .... | 1998-99 | 1998-99 |
| Messier, Eric | Col., Fla. | 8 | 406 | 25 | 50 | 75 | 146 | 72 | 3 | 5 | 8 | 22 | 1 | 1996-97 | 2003-04 |
| Messier, Joby | NYR | 3 | 25 | 0 | 4 | 4 | 24 | .... | .... | .... | .... | .... | .... | 1992-93 | 1994-95 |
| Messier, Mark | Edm., NYR, Van. | 25 | 1756 | 694 | 1193 | 1887 | 1910 | 236 | 109 | 186 | 295 | 244 | 6 | 1979-80 | 2003-04 |
| Messier, Mitch | Min. | 4 | 20 | 0 | 2 | 2 | 11 | .... | .... | .... | .... | .... | .... | 1987-88 | 1990-91 |
| Messier, Paul | Col. | 1 | 9 | 0 | 0 | 0 | 4 | .... | .... | .... | .... | .... | .... | 1978-79 | 1978-79 |
| Metcalfe, Scott | Edm., Buf. | 3 | 19 | 1 | 2 | 3 | 18 | .... | .... | .... | .... | .... | .... | 1987-88 | 1989-90 |
| ● Metz, Don | Tor. | 9 | 172 | 20 | 35 | 55 | 42 | 42 | 7 | 8 | 15 | 12 | 5 | 1938-39 | 1948-49 |
| ● Metz, Nick | Tor. | 12 | 518 | 131 | 119 | 250 | 149 | 76 | 19 | 20 | 39 | 31 | 4 | 1934-35 | 1947-48 |
| ● Michaluk, Art | Chi. | 1 | 5 | 0 | 0 | 0 | 0 | .... | .... | .... | .... | .... | .... | 1947-48 | 1947-48 |
| Michaluk, John | Chi. | 1 | 1 | 0 | 0 | 0 | 0 | .... | .... | .... | .... | .... | .... | 1950-51 | 1950-51 |
| Michayluk, Dave | Phi., Pit. | 3 | 14 | 2 | 6 | 8 | 8 | 7 | 1 | 1 | 2 | 0 | 1 | 1981-82 | 1991-92 |
| Micheletti, Joe | St.L., Col. | 3 | 158 | 11 | 60 | 71 | 114 | 11 | 1 | 11 | 12 | 10 | .... | 1979-80 | 1981-82 |
| Micheletti, Pat | Min. | 1 | 12 | 2 | 0 | 2 | 8 | .... | .... | .... | .... | .... | .... | 1987-88 | 1987-88 |
| ● Mickey, Larry | Chi., NYR, Tor., Mtl., L.A., Phi., Buf. | 11 | 292 | 39 | 53 | 92 | 160 | 9 | 1 | 0 | 1 | 10 | .... | 1964-65 | 1974-75 |
| ● Mickoski, Nick | NYR, Chi., Det., Bos. | 13 | 703 | 158 | 185 | 343 | 319 | 18 | 1 | 6 | 7 | 6 | .... | 1947-48 | 1959-60 |
| Middendorf, Max | Que., Edm. | 4 | 13 | 2 | 4 | 6 | 6 | .... | .... | .... | .... | .... | .... | 1986-87 | 1990-91 |
| Middleton, Rick | NYR, Bos. | 14 | 1005 | 448 | 540 | 988 | 157 | 114 | 45 | 55 | 100 | 19 | .... | 1974-75 | 1987-88 |
| Miehm, Kevin | St.L. | 2 | 22 | 1 | 4 | 5 | 8 | 2 | 0 | 1 | 1 | 0 | .... | 1992-93 | 1993-94 |
| Migay, Rudy | Tor. | 10 | 418 | 59 | 92 | 151 | 293 | 15 | 1 | 0 | 1 | 20 | .... | 1949-50 | 1959-60 |
| Mika, Petr | NYI | 1 | 3 | 0 | 0 | 0 | 0 | .... | .... | .... | .... | .... | .... | 1999-00 | 1999-00 |
| Mikita, Stan | Chi. | 22 | 1394 | 541 | 926 | 1467 | 1270 | 155 | 59 | 91 | 150 | 169 | 1 | 1958-59 | 1979-80 |
| Mikkelson, Bill | L.A., NYI, Wsh. | 4 | 147 | 4 | 18 | 22 | 105 | .... | .... | .... | .... | .... | .... | 1971-72 | 1976-77 |
| Mikol, Jim | Tor., NYR | 2 | 34 | 1 | 4 | 5 | 8 | .... | .... | .... | .... | .... | .... | 1962-63 | 1964-65 |
| Mikulchik, Oleg | Wpg., Ana. | 3 | 37 | 0 | 3 | 3 | 33 | .... | .... | .... | .... | .... | .... | 1993-94 | 1995-96 |
| Milbury, Mike | Bos. | 12 | 754 | 49 | 189 | 238 | 1552 | 86 | 4 | 24 | 28 | 219 | .... | 1975-76 | 1986-87 |
| ● Milks, Hib | Pit., Phi., NYR, Ott. | 8 | 317 | 87 | 41 | 128 | 179 | 11 | 0 | 0 | 0 | 2 | .... | 1925-26 | 1932-33 |
| Millar, Craig | Edm., Nsh., T.B. | 5 | 114 | 8 | 14 | 22 | 73 | .... | .... | .... | .... | .... | .... | 1996-97 | 2000-01 |
| ● Millar, Hugh | Det. | 1 | 4 | 0 | 0 | 0 | 0 | 1 | 0 | 0 | 0 | 0 | .... | 1946-47 | 1946-47 |
| Millar, Mike | Hfd., Wsh., Bos., Tor. | 5 | 78 | 18 | 18 | 36 | 12 | .... | .... | .... | .... | .... | .... | 1986-87 | 1990-91 |
| Millen, Corey | NYR, L.A., N.J., Dal., Cgy. | 8 | 335 | 90 | 119 | 209 | 236 | 47 | 5 | 7 | 12 | 22 | .... | 1989-90 | 1996-97 |
| Miller, Aaron | Que., Col., L.A., Van. | 14 | 677 | 25 | 94 | 119 | 422 | 80 | 3 | 9 | 12 | 40 | .... | 1993-94 | 2007-08 |
| ● Miller, Bill | Mtl.M., Mtl. | 3 | 95 | 7 | 3 | 10 | 16 | 12 | 0 | 0 | 0 | 0 | 1 | 1934-35 | 1936-37 |
| Miller, Bob | Bos., Col., L.A. | 6 | 404 | 75 | 119 | 194 | 220 | 36 | 4 | 7 | 11 | 27 | .... | 1977-78 | 1984-85 |
| Miller, Brad | Buf., Ott., Cgy. | 6 | 82 | 1 | 5 | 6 | 321 | .... | .... | .... | .... | .... | .... | 1988-89 | 1993-94 |
| ● Miller, Earl | Chi., Tor. | 5 | 109 | 19 | 14 | 33 | 124 | 10 | 1 | 0 | 1 | 6 | 1 | 1927-28 | 1931-32 |
| Miller, Jack | Chi. | 2 | 17 | 0 | 0 | 0 | 4 | .... | .... | .... | .... | .... | .... | 1949-50 | 1950-51 |
| Miller, Jason | N.J. | 3 | 6 | 0 | 0 | 0 | 0 | .... | .... | .... | .... | .... | .... | 1990-91 | 1992-93 |
| Miller, Jay | Bos., L.A. | 7 | 446 | 40 | 44 | 84 | 1723 | 48 | 2 | 3 | 5 | 243 | .... | 1985-86 | 1991-92 |
| Miller, Kelly | NYR, Wsh. | 15 | 1057 | 181 | 282 | 463 | 512 | 119 | 20 | 34 | 54 | 65 | .... | 1984-85 | 1998-99 |
| Miller, Kevin | NYR, Det., Wsh., St.L., S.J., Pit., Chi., NYI, Ott. | 13 | 620 | 150 | 185 | 335 | 429 | 61 | 7 | 10 | 17 | 49 | .... | 1988-89 | 2003-04 |
| Miller, Kip | Que., Min., S.J., NYI, Chi., Pit., Ana., Wsh. | 12 | 449 | 74 | 165 | 239 | 105 | 25 | 6 | 11 | 17 | 23 | .... | 1990-91 | 2003-04 |
| Miller, Paul | Col. | 1 | 3 | 0 | 3 | 3 | 0 | .... | .... | .... | .... | .... | .... | 1981-82 | 1981-82 |
| Miller, Perry | Det. | 4 | 217 | 10 | 51 | 61 | 387 | .... | .... | .... | .... | .... | .... | 1977-78 | 1980-81 |
| Miller, Tom | Det., NYI | 4 | 118 | 16 | 25 | 41 | 34 | .... | .... | .... | .... | .... | .... | 1970-71 | 1974-75 |
| Miller, Warren | NYR, Hfd. | 4 | 262 | 40 | 50 | 90 | 137 | 6 | 1 | 0 | 1 | 0 | .... | 1979-80 | 1982-83 |
| ‡ Milley, Norm | Buf., T.B. | 4 | 29 | 2 | 4 | 6 | 12 | .... | .... | .... | .... | .... | .... | 2001-02 | 2005-06 |
| Mills, Craig | Wpg., Chi. | 3 | 31 | 0 | 5 | 5 | 36 | 1 | 0 | 0 | 0 | 0 | .... | 1995-96 | 1998-99 |
| Miner, John | Edm. | 1 | 14 | 2 | 3 | 5 | 16 | .... | .... | .... | .... | .... | .... | 1987-88 | 1987-88 |
| Minor, Gerry | Van. | 5 | 140 | 11 | 21 | 32 | 173 | 12 | 1 | 3 | 4 | 25 | .... | 1979-80 | 1983-84 |
| Mironov, Boris | Wpg., Edm., Chi., NYR | 11 | 716 | 76 | 231 | 307 | 891 | 25 | 5 | 11 | 16 | 45 | .... | 1993-94 | 2003-04 |
| Mironov, Dmitri | Tor., Pit., Ana., Det., Wsh. | 10 | 556 | 54 | 206 | 260 | 568 | 75 | 10 | 26 | 36 | 48 | 1 | 1991-92 | 2000-01 |
| Miszuk, John | Det., Chi., Phi., Min. | 6 | 237 | 7 | 39 | 46 | 232 | 19 | 0 | 3 | 3 | 19 | .... | 1963-64 | 1969-70 |
| Mitchell, Bill | Det. | 1 | 1 | 0 | 0 | 0 | 0 | .... | .... | .... | .... | .... | .... | 1963-64 | 1963-64 |
| ● Mitchell, Herb | Bos. | 2 | 44 | 6 | 0 | 6 | 36 | .... | .... | .... | .... | .... | .... | 1924-25 | 1925-26 |
| Mitchell, Jeff | Dal. | 1 | 7 | 0 | 0 | 0 | 7 | .... | .... | .... | .... | .... | .... | 1997-98 | 1997-98 |
| ● Mitchell, Red | Chi. | 3 | 83 | 4 | 5 | 9 | 67 | .... | .... | .... | .... | .... | .... | 1941-42 | 1944-45 |
| Mitchell, Roy | Min. | 1 | 3 | 0 | 0 | 0 | 0 | .... | .... | .... | .... | .... | .... | 1992-93 | 1992-93 |
| ● Moe, Bill | NYR | 5 | 261 | 11 | 42 | 53 | 163 | 1 | 0 | 0 | 0 | 0 | .... | 1944-45 | 1948-49 |
| Moffat, Lyle | Tor., Wpg. | 3 | 97 | 12 | 16 | 28 | 51 | .... | .... | .... | .... | .... | .... | 1972-73 | 1979-80 |
| ● Moffat, Ron | Det. | 3 | 37 | 1 | 1 | 2 | 8 | 7 | 0 | 0 | 0 | 0 | .... | 1932-33 | 1934-35 |
| Moger, Sandy | Bos., L.A. | 5 | 236 | 41 | 38 | 79 | 212 | 5 | 2 | 2 | 4 | 12 | .... | 1994-95 | 1998-99 |
| Mogilny, Alexander | Buf., Van., N.J., Tor. | 16 | 990 | 473 | 559 | 1032 | 432 | 124 | 39 | 47 | 86 | 58 | 1 | 1989-90 | 2005-06 |
| Moher, Mike | N.J. | 1 | 9 | 0 | 1 | 1 | 28 | .... | .... | .... | .... | .... | .... | 1982-83 | 1982-83 |
| Mohns, Doug | Bos., Chi., Min., Atl., Wsh. | 22 | 1390 | 248 | 462 | 710 | 1250 | 94 | 14 | 36 | 50 | 122 | .... | 1953-54 | 1974-75 |
| ● Mohns, Lloyd | NYR | 1 | 1 | 0 | 0 | 0 | 0 | .... | .... | .... | .... | .... | .... | 1943-44 | 1943-44 |
| Mokosak, Carl | Cgy., L.A., Phi., Pit., Bos. | 6 | 83 | 11 | 15 | 26 | 170 | 1 | 0 | 0 | 0 | 0 | .... | 1981-82 | 1988-89 |
| Mokosak, John | Det. | 2 | 41 | 0 | 2 | 2 | 96 | .... | .... | .... | .... | .... | .... | 1988-89 | 1989-90 |
| Molin, Lars | Van. | 3 | 172 | 33 | 65 | 98 | 37 | 19 | 2 | 9 | 11 | 7 | .... | 1981-82 | 1983-84 |
| Moller, Mike | Buf., Edm. | 7 | 134 | 15 | 28 | 43 | 41 | 3 | 0 | 1 | 1 | 0 | .... | 1980-81 | 1986-87 |
| Moller, Randy | Que., NYR, Buf., Fla. | 14 | 815 | 45 | 180 | 225 | 1692 | 78 | 6 | 16 | 22 | 197 | .... | 1981-82 | 1994-95 |
| Molloy, Mitch | Buf. | 1 | 2 | 0 | 0 | 0 | 10 | .... | .... | .... | .... | .... | .... | 1989-90 | 1989-90 |
| ● Molyneaux, Larry | NYR | 2 | 45 | 0 | 1 | 1 | 20 | 10 | 0 | 0 | 0 | 8 | .... | 1937-38 | 1938-39 |
| Momesso, Sergio | Mtl., St.L., Van., Tor., NYR | 13 | 710 | 152 | 193 | 345 | 1557 | 119 | 18 | 26 | 44 | 311 | .... | 1983-84 | 1996-97 |
| Monahan, Garry | Mtl., Det., L.A., Tor., Van. | 12 | 748 | 116 | 169 | 285 | 484 | 22 | 3 | 1 | 4 | 13 | .... | 1967-68 | 1978-79 |
| Monahan, Hartland | Cal., NYR, Wsh., Pit., L.A., St.L. | 7 | 334 | 61 | 80 | 141 | 163 | 6 | 0 | 0 | 0 | 4 | .... | 1973-74 | 1980-81 |
| ● Mondou, Armand | Mtl. | 12 | 386 | 47 | 71 | 118 | 99 | 32 | 3 | 5 | 8 | 12 | 2 | 1928-29 | 1939-40 |
| Mondou, Pierre | Mtl. | 9 | 548 | 194 | 262 | 456 | 179 | 69 | 17 | 28 | 45 | 26 | 3 | 1976-77 | 1984-85 |
| Mongeau, Michel | St.L., T.B. | 4 | 54 | 6 | 19 | 25 | 10 | 2 | 0 | 1 | 1 | 0 | .... | 1989-90 | 1992-93 |
| Mongrain, Bob | Buf., L.A. | 6 | 81 | 13 | 14 | 27 | 14 | 11 | 1 | 2 | 3 | 2 | .... | 1979-80 | 1985-86 |

| Name | NHL Teams | NHL Seasons | Regular Schedule GP | G | A | TP | PIM | Playoffs GP | G | A | TP | PIM | NHL Cup Wins | First NHL Season | Last NHL Season |
|---|---|---|---|---|---|---|---|---|---|---|---|---|---|---|---|
| Monteith, Hank | Det. | 3 | 77 | 5 | 12 | 17 | 6 | 4 | 0 | 0 | 0 | 0 | .... | 1968-69 | 1970-71 |
| Montgomery, Jim | St.L., Mtl., Phi., S.J., Dal. | 6 | 122 | 9 | 25 | 34 | 80 | 8 | 1 | 0 | 1 | 2 | .... | 1993-94 | 2002-03 |
| Moore, Barrie | Buf., Edm., Wsh. | 3 | 39 | 2 | 6 | 8 | 18 | .... | .... | .... | .... | .... | .... | 1995-96 | 1999-00 |
| Moore, Dickie | Mtl., Tor., St.L. | 14 | 719 | 261 | 347 | 608 | 652 | 135 | 46 | 64 | 110 | 122 | 6 | 1951-52 | 1967-68 |
| Moore, Steve | Col. | 3 | 69 | 5 | 7 | 12 | 41 | .... | .... | .... | .... | .... | .... | 2001-02 | 2003-04 |
| ● Moran, Amby | Mtl., Chi. | 2 | 35 | 1 | 1 | 2 | 24 | .... | .... | .... | .... | .... | .... | 1926-27 | 1927-28 |
| ‡ Moran, Brad | CBJ, Van. | 3 | 8 | 1 | 2 | 3 | 4 | .... | .... | .... | .... | .... | .... | 2001-02 | 2006-07 |
| ‡ Moran, Ian | Pit., Bos., Ana. | 12 | 489 | 21 | 50 | 71 | 321 | 66 | 1 | 7 | 8 | 24 | .... | 1994-95 | 2006-07 |
| ‡ Moravec, David | Buf. | 1 | 1 | 0 | 0 | 0 | 0 | .... | .... | .... | .... | .... | .... | 1999-00 | 1999-00 |
| More, Jay | NYR, Min., S.J., Phx., Chi., Nsh. | 10 | 406 | 18 | 54 | 72 | 702 | 31 | 0 | 6 | 6 | 45 | .... | 1988-89 | 1998-99 |
| ● Morenz, Howie | Mtl., Chi., NYR | 14 | 550 | 271 | 201 | 472 | 546 | 39 | 13 | 9 | 22 | 58 | 3 | 1923-24 | 1936-37 |
| Moretto, Angelo | Cle. | 1 | 5 | 1 | 2 | 3 | 2 | .... | .... | .... | .... | .... | .... | 1976-77 | 1976-77 |
| Morgan, Gavin | Dal. | 1 | 6 | 0 | 0 | 0 | 21 | .... | .... | .... | .... | .... | .... | 2003-04 | 2003-04 |
| ‡ Morgan, Jason | L.A., Cgy., Nsh., Chi., Min. | 5 | 44 | 2 | 5 | 7 | 18 | .... | .... | .... | .... | .... | .... | 1996-97 | 2006-07 |
| ● Morin, Pete | Mtl. | 1 | 31 | 10 | 12 | 22 | 7 | 1 | 0 | 0 | 0 | 0 | .... | 1941-42 | 1941-42 |
| ● Morin, Stephane | Que., Van. | 5 | 90 | 16 | 39 | 55 | 52 | .... | .... | .... | .... | .... | .... | 1989-90 | 1993-94 |
| Morisset, Dave | Fla. | 1 | 4 | 0 | 0 | 0 | 5 | .... | .... | .... | .... | .... | .... | 2001-02 | 2001-02 |
| Morissette, Dave | Mtl. | 2 | 11 | 0 | 0 | 0 | 57 | .... | .... | .... | .... | .... | .... | 1998-99 | 1999-00 |
| Moro, Marc | Ana., Nsh., Tor. | 4 | 30 | 0 | 0 | 0 | 77 | .... | .... | .... | .... | .... | .... | 1997-98 | 2001-02 |
| ‡ Morozov, Aleksey | Pit. | 7 | 451 | 84 | 135 | 219 | 98 | 39 | 4 | 5 | 9 | 8 | .... | 1997-98 | 2003-04 |
| ● Morris, Bernie | Bos. | 1 | 6 | 1 | 0 | 1 | 0 | .... | .... | .... | .... | .... | .... | 1924-25 | 1924-25 |
| Morris, Jon | N.J., S.J., Bos. | 6 | 103 | 16 | 33 | 49 | 47 | 11 | 1 | 7 | 8 | 25 | .... | 1988-89 | 1993-94 |
| ● Morris, Moe | Tor., NYR | 4 | 135 | 13 | 29 | 42 | 58 | 18 | 4 | 2 | 6 | 16 | 1 | 1943-44 | 1948-49 |
| Morrison, Dave | L.A., Van. | 4 | 39 | 3 | 3 | 6 | 4 | .... | .... | .... | .... | .... | .... | 1980-81 | 1984-85 |
| ● Morrison, Don | Det., Chi. | 3 | 112 | 18 | 28 | 46 | 12 | 3 | 0 | 1 | 1 | 0 | .... | 1947-48 | 1950-51 |
| Morrison, Doug | Bos. | 4 | 23 | 7 | 3 | 10 | 15 | .... | .... | .... | .... | .... | .... | 1979-80 | 1984-85 |
| Morrison, Gary | Phi. | 3 | 43 | 1 | 15 | 16 | 70 | 5 | 0 | 1 | 1 | 2 | .... | 1979-80 | 1981-82 |
| ● Morrison, George | St.L. | 2 | 115 | 17 | 21 | 38 | 13 | 3 | 0 | 0 | 0 | 0 | .... | 1970-71 | 1971-72 |
| Morrison, Jim | Bos., Tor., Det., NYR, Pit. | 12 | 704 | 40 | 160 | 200 | 542 | 36 | 0 | 12 | 12 | 38 | .... | 1951-52 | 1970-71 |
| ● Morrison, John | NYA | 1 | 18 | 0 | 0 | 0 | 0 | .... | .... | .... | .... | .... | .... | 1925-26 | 1925-26 |
| Morrison, Kevin | Col. | 1 | 41 | 4 | 11 | 15 | 23 | .... | .... | .... | .... | .... | .... | 1979-80 | 1979-80 |
| Morrison, Lew | Phi., Atl., Wsh., Pit. | 9 | 564 | 39 | 52 | 91 | 107 | 17 | 0 | 0 | 0 | 2 | .... | 1969-70 | 1977-78 |
| Morrison, Mark | NYR | 2 | 10 | 1 | 1 | 2 | 0 | .... | .... | .... | .... | .... | .... | 1981-82 | 1983-84 |
| ● Morrison, Rod | Det. | 1 | 34 | 8 | 7 | 15 | 4 | 3 | 0 | 0 | 0 | 0 | .... | 1947-48 | 1947-48 |
| Morrow, Ken | NYI | 10 | 550 | 17 | 88 | 105 | 309 | 127 | 11 | 22 | 33 | 97 | 4 | 1979-80 | 1988-89 |
| Morrow, Scott | Cgy. | 1 | 4 | 0 | 0 | 0 | 0 | .... | .... | .... | .... | .... | .... | 1994-95 | 1994-95 |
| Morton, Dean | Det. | 1 | 1 | 1 | 0 | 1 | 2 | .... | .... | .... | .... | .... | .... | 1989-90 | 1989-90 |
| Mortson, Gus | Tor., Chi., Det. | 13 | 797 | 46 | 152 | 198 | 1380 | 54 | 5 | 8 | 13 | 68 | 4 | 1946-47 | 1958-59 |
| ● Mosdell, Ken | Bro., Mtl., Chi. | 16 | 693 | 141 | 168 | 309 | 475 | 80 | 16 | 13 | 29 | 48 | 4 | 1941-42 | 1958-59 |
| ● Mosienko, Bill | Chi. | 14 | 711 | 258 | 282 | 540 | 121 | 22 | 10 | 4 | 14 | 15 | .... | 1941-42 | 1954-55 |
| Mott, Morris | Cal. | 3 | 199 | 18 | 32 | 50 | 49 | .... | .... | .... | .... | .... | .... | 1972-73 | 1974-75 |
| ● Motter, Alex | Bos., Det. | 8 | 255 | 39 | 64 | 103 | 135 | 41 | 3 | 9 | 12 | 41 | 1 | 1934-35 | 1942-43 |
| Moxey, Jim | Cal., Cle., L.A. | 3 | 127 | 22 | 27 | 49 | 59 | .... | .... | .... | .... | .... | .... | 1974-75 | 1976-77 |
| Mrozik, Rick | Cgy. | 1 | 2 | 0 | 0 | 0 | 0 | .... | .... | .... | .... | .... | .... | 2002-03 | 2002-03 |
| Muckalt, Bill | Van., NYI, Ott., Min. | 5 | 256 | 40 | 57 | 97 | 204 | 5 | 0 | 0 | 0 | 0 | .... | 1998-99 | 2002-03 |
| ‡ Muir, Bryan | Edm., N.J., Chi., T.B., Col., L.A., Wsh. | 11 | 279 | 16 | 37 | 53 | 281 | 29 | 0 | 0 | 0 | 6 | 1 | 1995-96 | 2006-07 |
| Mulhern, Richard | Atl., L.A., Tor., Wpg. | 6 | 303 | 27 | 93 | 120 | 217 | 7 | 0 | 3 | 3 | 5 | .... | 1975-76 | 1980-81 |
| Mulhern, Ryan | Wsh. | 1 | 3 | 0 | 0 | 0 | 0 | .... | .... | .... | .... | .... | .... | 1997-98 | 1997-98 |
| Mullen, Brian | Wpg., NYR, S.J., NYI | 11 | 832 | 260 | 362 | 622 | 414 | 62 | 12 | 18 | 30 | 30 | .... | 1982-83 | 1992-93 |
| Mullen, Joe | St.L., Cgy., Pit., Bos. | 17 | 1062 | 502 | 561 | 1063 | 241 | 143 | 60 | 46 | 106 | 42 | 3 | 1979-80 | 1996-97 |
| Muller, Kirk | N.J., Mtl., NYI, Tor., Fla., Dal. | 19 | 1349 | 357 | 602 | 959 | 1223 | 127 | 33 | 36 | 69 | 153 | 1 | 1984-85 | 2002-03 |
| Muloin, Wayne | Det., Oak., Cal., Min. | 3 | 147 | 3 | 21 | 24 | 93 | 11 | 0 | 0 | 0 | 2 | .... | 1963-64 | 1970-71 |
| Mulvenna, Glenn | Pit., Phi. | 2 | 2 | 0 | 0 | 0 | 4 | .... | .... | .... | .... | .... | .... | 1991-92 | 1992-93 |
| Mulvey, Grant | Chi., N.J. | 10 | 586 | 149 | 135 | 284 | 816 | 42 | 10 | 5 | 15 | 70 | .... | 1974-75 | 1983-84 |
| Mulvey, Paul | Wsh., Pit., L.A. | 4 | 225 | 30 | 51 | 81 | 613 | .... | .... | .... | .... | .... | .... | 1978-79 | 1981-82 |
| ● Mummery, Harry | Tor., Que., Mtl., Ham. | 6 | 106 | 33 | 19 | 52 | 226 | 2 | 1 | 1 | 2 | 17 | .... | 1917-18 | 1922-23 |
| Muni, Craig | Tor., Edm., Chi., Buf., Wpg., Pit., Dal. | 16 | 819 | 28 | 119 | 147 | 775 | 113 | 0 | 17 | 17 | 108 | 3 | 1981-82 | 1997-98 |
| ● Munro, Dunc | Mtl.M., Mtl. | 8 | 239 | 28 | 18 | 46 | 172 | 21 | 2 | 2 | 4 | 18 | 1 | 1924-25 | 1931-32 |
| ● Munro, Gerry | Mtl.M., Tor. | 2 | 34 | 1 | 0 | 1 | 37 | .... | .... | .... | .... | .... | .... | 1924-25 | 1925-26 |
| Murdoch, Bob | Mtl., L.A., Atl., Cgy. | 12 | 757 | 60 | 218 | 278 | 764 | 69 | 4 | 18 | 22 | 92 | 2 | 1970-71 | 1981-82 |
| Murdoch, Bob | Cal., Cle., St.L. | 4 | 260 | 72 | 85 | 157 | 127 | .... | .... | .... | .... | .... | .... | 1975-76 | 1978-79 |
| Murdoch, Don | NYR, Edm., Det. | 6 | 320 | 121 | 117 | 238 | 155 | 24 | 10 | 8 | 18 | 16 | .... | 1976-77 | 1981-82 |
| ● Murdoch, Murray | NYR | 11 | 508 | 84 | 108 | 192 | 197 | 55 | 9 | 12 | 21 | 28 | 2 | 1926-27 | 1936-37 |
| Murphy, Brian | Det. | 1 | 1 | 0 | 0 | 0 | 0 | .... | .... | .... | .... | .... | .... | 1974-75 | 1974-75 |
| ‡ Murphy, Curtis | Min. | 1 | 1 | 0 | 0 | 0 | 0 | .... | .... | .... | .... | .... | .... | 2002-03 | 2002-03 |
| Murphy, Gord | Phi., Bos., Fla., Atl. | 14 | 862 | 85 | 238 | 323 | 668 | 53 | 3 | 16 | 19 | 35 | .... | 1988-89 | 2001-02 |
| Murphy, Joe | Det., Edm., Chi., St.L., S.J., Bos., Wsh. | 15 | 779 | 233 | 295 | 528 | 810 | 120 | 34 | 43 | 77 | 185 | 1 | 1986-87 | 2000-01 |
| Murphy, Larry | L.A., Wsh., Min., Pit., Tor., Det. | 21 | 1615 | 287 | 929 | 1216 | 1084 | 215 | 37 | 115 | 152 | 201 | 4 | 1980-81 | 2000-01 |
| Murphy, Mike | St.L., NYR, L.A. | 12 | 831 | 238 | 318 | 556 | 514 | 66 | 13 | 23 | 36 | 54 | .... | 1971-72 | 1982-83 |
| Murphy, Rob | Van., Ott., L.A. | 7 | 125 | 9 | 12 | 21 | 152 | 4 | 0 | 0 | 0 | 2 | .... | 1987-88 | 1993-94 |
| Murphy, Ron | NYR, Chi., Det., Bos. | 18 | 889 | 205 | 274 | 479 | 460 | 53 | 7 | 8 | 15 | 26 | 2 | 1952-53 | 1969-70 |
| ● Murray, Allan | NYA | 7 | 271 | 5 | 9 | 14 | 163 | 14 | 0 | 0 | 0 | 10 | .... | 1933-34 | 1939-40 |
| Murray, Bob | Atl., Van. | 4 | 194 | 6 | 16 | 22 | 98 | 10 | 1 | 1 | 2 | 15 | .... | 1973-74 | 1976-77 |
| Murray, Bob | Chi. | 15 | 1008 | 132 | 382 | 514 | 873 | 112 | 19 | 37 | 56 | 106 | .... | 1975-76 | 1989-90 |
| Murray, Chris | Mtl., Hfd., Car., Ott., Chi., Dal. | 6 | 242 | 16 | 18 | 34 | 550 | 15 | 1 | 0 | 1 | 12 | .... | 1994-95 | 1999-00 |
| Murray, Glen | Bos., Pit., L.A. | 16 | 1009 | 337 | 314 | 651 | 679 | 94 | 20 | 22 | 42 | 66 | .... | 1991-92 | 2007-08 |
| Murray, Jim | L.A. | 1 | 30 | 0 | 2 | 2 | 14 | .... | .... | .... | .... | .... | .... | 1967-68 | 1967-68 |
| Murray, Ken | Tor., NYI, Det., K.C. | 5 | 106 | 1 | 10 | 11 | 135 | .... | .... | .... | .... | .... | .... | 1969-70 | 1975-76 |
| ● Murray, Leo | Mtl. | 1 | 6 | 0 | 0 | 0 | 2 | .... | .... | .... | .... | .... | .... | 1932-33 | 1932-33 |
| Murray, Mike | Phi. | 1 | 1 | 0 | 0 | 0 | 0 | .... | .... | .... | .... | .... | .... | 1987-88 | 1987-88 |
| Murray, Pat | Phi. | 2 | 25 | 3 | 1 | 4 | 15 | .... | .... | .... | .... | .... | .... | 1990-91 | 1991-92 |
| Murray, Randy | Tor. | 1 | 3 | 0 | 0 | 0 | 2 | .... | .... | .... | .... | .... | .... | 1969-70 | 1969-70 |
| ‡ Murray, Rem | Edm., NYR, Nsh. | 9 | 560 | 94 | 121 | 215 | 161 | 62 | 5 | 12 | 17 | 18 | .... | 1996-97 | 2005-06 |
| Murray, Rob | Wsh., Wpg., Phx. | 8 | 107 | 4 | 15 | 19 | 111 | 9 | 0 | 0 | 0 | 18 | .... | 1989-90 | 1998-99 |
| Murray, Terry | Cal., Phi., Det., Wsh. | 8 | 302 | 4 | 76 | 80 | 199 | 18 | 2 | 2 | 4 | 10 | .... | 1972-73 | 1981-82 |
| Murray, Troy | Chi., Wpg., Ott., Pit., Col. | 15 | 915 | 230 | 354 | 584 | 875 | 113 | 17 | 26 | 43 | 145 | 1 | 1981-82 | 1995-96 |
| Murzyn, Dana | Hfd., Cgy., Van. | 14 | 838 | 52 | 152 | 204 | 1571 | 82 | 9 | 10 | 19 | 166 | 1 | 1985-86 | 1998-99 |
| Musil, Frantisek | Min., Cgy., Ott., Edm. | 15 | 797 | 34 | 106 | 140 | 1241 | 42 | 2 | 4 | 6 | 47 | .... | 1986-87 | 2000-01 |
| Myers, Hap | Buf. | 1 | 13 | 0 | 0 | 0 | 6 | .... | .... | .... | .... | .... | .... | 1970-71 | 1970-71 |
| Myhres, Brantt | T.B., Phi., S.J., Nsh., Wsh., Bos. | 7 | 154 | 6 | 2 | 8 | 687 | .... | .... | .... | .... | .... | .... | 1994-95 | 2002-03 |
| ● Myles, Vic | NYR | 1 | 45 | 6 | 9 | 15 | 57 | .... | .... | .... | .... | .... | .... | 1942-43 | 1942-43 |
| ‡ Myrvold, Anders | Col., Bos., NYI, Det. | 4 | 33 | 0 | 5 | 5 | 12 | .... | .... | .... | .... | .... | .... | 1995-96 | 2003-04 |

## N

| Name | NHL Teams | NHL Seasons | Regular Schedule GP | G | A | TP | PIM | Playoffs GP | G | A | TP | PIM | NHL Cup Wins | First NHL Season | Last NHL Season |
|---|---|---|---|---|---|---|---|---|---|---|---|---|---|---|---|
| ‡ Nabokov, Dmitri | Chi., NYI | 3 | 55 | 11 | 13 | 24 | 28 | .... | .... | .... | .... | .... | .... | 1997-98 | 1999-00 |
| Nachbaur, Don | Hfd., Edm., Phi. | 8 | 223 | 23 | 46 | 69 | 465 | 11 | 1 | 1 | 2 | 24 | .... | 1980-81 | 1989-90 |
| Nahrgang, Jim | Det. | 3 | 57 | 5 | 12 | 17 | 34 | .... | .... | .... | .... | .... | .... | 1974-75 | 1976-77 |
| Namestnikov, John | Van., NYI, Nsh. | 6 | 43 | 0 | 9 | 9 | 24 | 2 | 0 | 0 | 0 | 2 | .... | 1993-94 | 1999-00 |
| Nanne, Lou | Min. | 11 | 635 | 68 | 157 | 225 | 356 | 32 | 4 | 10 | 14 | 8 | .... | 1967-68 | 1977-78 |
| Nantais, Rich | Min. | 3 | 63 | 5 | 4 | 9 | 79 | .... | .... | .... | .... | .... | .... | 1974-75 | 1976-77 |
| Napier, Mark | Mtl., Min., Edm., Buf. | 11 | 767 | 235 | 306 | 541 | 157 | 82 | 18 | 24 | 42 | 11 | 2 | 1978-79 | 1988-89 |
| ‡ Nash, Tyson | St.L., Phx. | 7 | 374 | 27 | 37 | 64 | 673 | 23 | 3 | 2 | 5 | 52 | .... | 1998-99 | 2005-06 |
| Naslund, Mats | Mtl., Bos. | 9 | 651 | 251 | 383 | 634 | 111 | 102 | 35 | 57 | 92 | 33 | 1 | 1982-83 | 1994-95 |
| ‡ Nasreddine, Alain | Chi., Mtl., NYI, Pit. | 5 | 74 | 1 | 4 | 5 | 84 | .... | .... | .... | .... | .... | .... | 1998-99 | 2007-08 |
| Nattrass, Ralph | Chi. | 4 | 223 | 18 | 38 | 56 | 308 | .... | .... | .... | .... | .... | .... | 1946-47 | 1949-50 |
| Nattress, Ric | Mtl., St.L., Cgy., Tor., Phi. | 11 | 536 | 29 | 135 | 164 | 377 | 67 | 5 | 10 | 15 | 60 | 1 | 1982-83 | 1992-93 |
| Natyshak, Mike | Que. | 1 | 4 | 0 | 0 | 0 | 0 | .... | .... | .... | .... | .... | .... | 1987-88 | 1987-88 |
| Nazarov, Andrei | S.J., T.B., Cgy., Ana., Bos., Phx., Min. | 12 | 571 | 53 | 71 | 124 | 1409 | 9 | 0 | 0 | 0 | 11 | .... | 1993-94 | 2005-06 |
| Ndur, Rumun | Buf., NYR, Atl. | 4 | 69 | 2 | 3 | 5 | 137 | .... | .... | .... | .... | .... | .... | 1996-97 | 1999-00 |
| Neaton, Pat | Pit. | 1 | 9 | 1 | 1 | 2 | 12 | .... | .... | .... | .... | .... | .... | 1993-94 | 1993-94 |
| Nechayev, Viktor | L.A. | 1 | 3 | 1 | 0 | 1 | 0 | .... | .... | .... | .... | .... | .... | 1982-83 | 1982-83 |
| Neckar, Stan | Ott., NYR, Phx., T.B., Nsh. | 10 | 510 | 12 | 41 | 53 | 316 | 29 | 0 | 3 | 3 | 8 | 1 | 1994-95 | 2003-04 |
| Nedomansky, Vaclav | Det., NYR, St.L. | 6 | 421 | 122 | 156 | 278 | 88 | 7 | 3 | 5 | 8 | 0 | .... | 1977-78 | 1982-83 |
| ‡ Nedorost, Andrej | CBJ | 3 | 28 | 2 | 3 | 5 | 12 | .... | .... | .... | .... | .... | .... | 2001-02 | 2003-04 |
| ‡ Nedorost, Vaclav | Col., Fla. | 3 | 99 | 10 | 10 | 20 | 34 | .... | .... | .... | .... | .... | .... | 2001-02 | 2003-04 |
| ‡ Nedved, Petr | Van., St.L., NYR, Pit., Edm., Phx., Phi. | 15 | 982 | 310 | 407 | 717 | 708 | 71 | 19 | 23 | 42 | 64 | .... | 1990-91 | 2006-07 |
| Nedved, Zdenek | Tor. | 3 | 31 | 4 | 6 | 10 | 14 | .... | .... | .... | .... | .... | .... | 1994-95 | 1996-97 |
| Needham, Mike | Pit., Dal. | 3 | 86 | 9 | 5 | 14 | 16 | 14 | 2 | 0 | 2 | 4 | 1 | 1991-92 | 1993-94 |
| Neely, Bob | Tor., Col. | 5 | 283 | 39 | 59 | 98 | 266 | 26 | 5 | 7 | 12 | 15 | .... | 1973-74 | 1977-78 |
| Neely, Cam | Van., Bos. | 13 | 726 | 395 | 299 | 694 | 1241 | 93 | 57 | 32 | 89 | 168 | .... | 1983-84 | 1995-96 |
| Neilson, Jim | NYR, Cal., Cle. | 16 | 1023 | 69 | 299 | 368 | 904 | 65 | 1 | 17 | 18 | 61 | .... | 1962-63 | 1977-78 |
| Nelson, Gordie | Tor. | 1 | 3 | 0 | 0 | 0 | 11 | .... | .... | .... | .... | .... | .... | 1969-70 | 1969-70 |
| Nelson, Jeff | Wsh., Nsh. | 3 | 52 | 3 | 8 | 11 | 20 | 3 | 0 | 0 | 0 | 4 | .... | 1994-95 | 1998-99 |
| Nelson, Todd | Pit., Wsh. | 2 | 3 | 1 | 0 | 1 | 2 | 4 | 0 | 0 | 0 | 0 | .... | 1991-92 | 1993-94 |
| Nemchinov, Sergei | NYR, Van., NYI, N.J. | 11 | 761 | 152 | 193 | 345 | 251 | 105 | 11 | 20 | 31 | 24 | 2 | 1991-92 | 2001-02 |

Don Murdoch

Glen Murray

Ric Nattress

Dan Newman

Gary Nylund

Jeff O'Neill

Terry O'Reilly

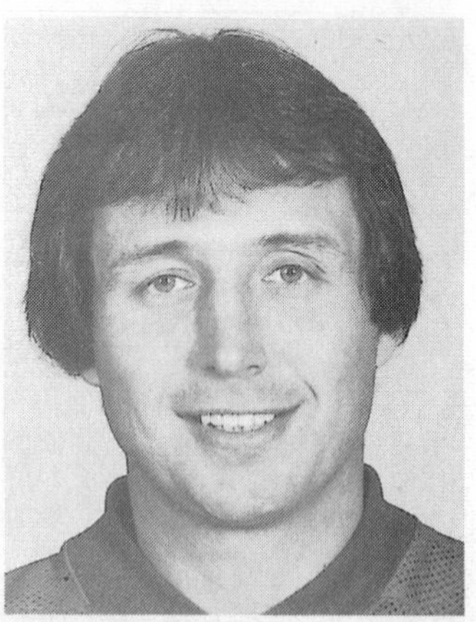

Brad Park

| Name | NHL Teams | NHL Seasons | Regular Schedule GP | G | A | TP | PIM | Playoffs GP | G | A | TP | PIM | NHL Cup Wins | First NHL Season | Last NHL Season |
|---|---|---|---|---|---|---|---|---|---|---|---|---|---|---|---|
| Nemecek, Jan | L.A. | 2 | 7 | 1 | 0 | 1 | 4 | .... | .... | .... | .... | .... | .... | 1998-99 | 1999-00 |
| Nemeth, Steve | NYR | 1 | 12 | 2 | 0 | 2 | 2 | .... | .... | .... | .... | .... | .... | 1987-88 | 1987-88 |
| ‡ Nemirovsky, David | Fla. | 4 | 91 | 16 | 22 | 38 | 42 | 3 | 1 | 0 | 1 | 0 | .... | 1995-96 | 1998-99 |
| Nesterenko, Eric | Tor., Chi. | 21 | 1219 | 250 | 324 | 574 | 1273 | 124 | 13 | 24 | 37 | 127 | 1 | 1951-52 | 1971-72 |
| Nethery, Lance | NYR, Edm. | 2 | 41 | 11 | 14 | 25 | 14 | 14 | 5 | 3 | 8 | 9 | .... | 1980-81 | 1981-82 |
| Neufeld, Ray | Hfd., Wpg., Bos. | 11 | 595 | 157 | 200 | 357 | 816 | 28 | 8 | 6 | 14 | 55 | .... | 1979-80 | 1989-90 |
| • Neville, Mike | Tor., NYA | 3 | 65 | 5 | 5 | 10 | 14 | 2 | 0 | 0 | 0 | 0 | .... | 1924-25 | 1930-31 |
| Nevin, Bob | Tor., NYR, Min., L.A. | 18 | 1128 | 307 | 419 | 726 | 211 | 84 | 16 | 18 | 34 | 24 | 2 | 1957-58 | 1975-76 |
| Newberry, John | Mtl., Hfd. | 4 | 22 | 0 | 4 | 4 | 6 | 2 | 0 | 0 | 0 | 0 | .... | 1982-83 | 1985-86 |
| Newell, Rick | Det. | 2 | 6 | 0 | 0 | 0 | 0 | .... | .... | .... | .... | .... | .... | 1972-73 | 1973-74 |
| Newman, Dan | NYR, Mtl., Edm. | 4 | 126 | 17 | 24 | 41 | 63 | 3 | 0 | 0 | 0 | 4 | .... | 1976-77 | 1979-80 |
| • Newman, John | Det. | 1 | 8 | 1 | 1 | 2 | 0 | .... | .... | .... | .... | .... | .... | 1930-31 | 1930-31 |
| Nicholls, Bernie | L.A., NYR, Edm., N.J., Chi., S.J. | 18 | 1127 | 475 | 734 | 1209 | 1292 | 118 | 42 | 72 | 114 | 164 | .... | 1981-82 | 1998-99 |
| • Nicholson, Al | Bos. | 2 | 19 | 0 | 1 | 1 | 4 | .... | .... | .... | .... | .... | .... | 1955-56 | 1956-57 |
| • Nicholson, Ed | Det. | 1 | 1 | 0 | 0 | 0 | 0 | .... | .... | .... | .... | .... | .... | 1947-48 | 1947-48 |
| • Nicholson, Hickey | Chi. | 1 | 2 | 1 | 0 | 1 | 0 | .... | .... | .... | .... | .... | .... | 1937-38 | 1937-38 |
| Nicholson, Neil | Oak., NYI | 4 | 39 | 3 | 1 | 4 | 23 | 2 | 0 | 0 | 0 | 0 | .... | 1969-70 | 1977-78 |
| Nicholson, Paul | Wsh. | 3 | 62 | 4 | 8 | 12 | 18 | .... | .... | .... | .... | .... | .... | 1974-75 | 1976-77 |
| ‡ Nickulas, Eric | Bos., St.L., Chi. | 6 | 118 | 15 | 23 | 38 | 82 | 1 | 0 | 0 | 0 | 2 | .... | 1998-99 | 2005-06 |
| Nicolson, Graeme | Bos., Col., NYR | 3 | 52 | 2 | 7 | 9 | 60 | .... | .... | .... | .... | .... | .... | 1978-79 | 1982-83 |
| Nieckar, Barry | Hfd., Cgy., Ana. | 4 | 8 | 0 | 0 | 0 | 21 | .... | .... | .... | .... | .... | .... | 1992-93 | 1997-98 |
| Niekamp, Jim | Det. | 2 | 29 | 0 | 2 | 2 | 37 | .... | .... | .... | .... | .... | .... | 1970-71 | 1971-72 |
| Nielsen, Chris | CBJ | 2 | 52 | 6 | 8 | 14 | 8 | .... | .... | .... | .... | .... | .... | 2000-01 | 2001-02 |
| Nielsen, Jeff | NYR, Ana., Min. | 5 | 252 | 20 | 27 | 47 | 70 | 4 | 0 | 0 | 0 | 2 | .... | 1996-97 | 2000-01 |
| Nielsen, Kirk | Bos. | 1 | 6 | 0 | 0 | 0 | 0 | .... | .... | .... | .... | .... | .... | 1997-98 | 1997-98 |
| ‡ Niemi, Antti-Jussi | Ana. | 2 | 29 | 1 | 1 | 2 | 22 | .... | .... | .... | .... | .... | .... | 2000-01 | 2001-02 |
| ‡ Nieminen, Ville | Col., Pit., Chi., Cgy., NYR, S.J., St.L. | 7 | 385 | 48 | 69 | 117 | 333 | 58 | 8 | 12 | 20 | 99 | 1 | 1999-00 | 2006-07 |
| Nienhuis, Kraig | Bos. | 3 | 87 | 20 | 16 | 36 | 39 | 2 | 0 | 0 | 0 | 14 | .... | 1985-86 | 1987-88 |
| Nieuwendyk, Joe | Cgy., Dal., N.J., Tor., Fla. | 20 | 1257 | 564 | 562 | 1126 | 677 | 158 | 66 | 50 | 116 | 91 | 3 | 1986-87 | 2006-07 |
| • Nighbor, Frank | Ott., Tor. | 13 | 349 | 139 | 98 | 237 | 249 | 20 | 4 | 9 | 13 | 13 | 4 | 1917-18 | 1929-30 |
| Nigro, Frank | Tor. | 2 | 68 | 8 | 18 | 26 | 39 | 3 | 0 | 0 | 0 | 2 | .... | 1982-83 | 1983-84 |
| ‡ Niinimaa, Janne | Phi., Edm., NYI, Dal., Mtl. | 10 | 741 | 54 | 265 | 319 | 733 | 59 | 3 | 21 | 24 | 60 | .... | 1996-97 | 2006-07 |
| ‡ Nikolishin, Andrei | Hfd., Wsh., Chi., Col. | 10 | 628 | 93 | 187 | 280 | 270 | 43 | 1 | 17 | 18 | 22 | .... | 1994-95 | 2003-04 |
| Nikulin, Igor | Ana. | 1 | .... | .... | .... | .... | .... | 1 | 0 | 0 | 0 | 0 | .... | 1996-97 | 1996-97 |
| Nilan, Chris | Mtl., NYR, Bos. | 13 | 688 | 110 | 115 | 225 | 3043 | 111 | 8 | 9 | 17 | 541 | 1 | 1979-80 | 1991-92 |
| Nill, Jim | St.L., Van., Bos., Wpg., Det. | 9 | 524 | 58 | 87 | 145 | 854 | 59 | 10 | 5 | 15 | 203 | .... | 1981-82 | 1989-90 |
| Nilsson, Kent | Atl., Cgy., Min., Edm. | 9 | 553 | 264 | 422 | 686 | 116 | 59 | 11 | 41 | 52 | 14 | 1 | 1979-80 | 1994-95 |
| Nilsson, Ulf | NYR | 4 | 170 | 57 | 112 | 169 | 85 | 25 | 8 | 14 | 22 | 27 | .... | 1978-79 | 1982-83 |
| Nistico, Lou | Col. | 1 | 3 | 0 | 0 | 0 | 0 | .... | .... | .... | .... | .... | .... | 1977-78 | 1977-78 |
| • Noble, Reg | Tor., Mtl.M., Det. | 16 | 510 | 168 | 106 | 274 | 916 | 18 | 2 | 2 | 4 | 33 | 3 | 1917-18 | 1932-33 |
| Noel, Claude | Wsh. | 1 | 7 | 0 | 0 | 0 | 0 | .... | .... | .... | .... | .... | .... | 1979-80 | 1979-80 |
| • Nolan, Paddy | Tor. | 1 | 2 | 0 | 0 | 0 | 0 | .... | .... | .... | .... | .... | .... | 1921-22 | 1921-22 |
| Nolan, Ted | Det., Pit. | 3 | 78 | 6 | 16 | 22 | 105 | .... | .... | .... | .... | .... | .... | 1981-82 | 1985-86 |
| Nolet, Simon | Phi., K.C., Pit., Col. | 10 | 562 | 150 | 182 | 332 | 187 | 34 | 6 | 3 | 9 | 8 | 1 | 1967-68 | 1976-77 |
| Noonan, Brian | Chi., NYR, St.L., Van., Phx. | 12 | 629 | 116 | 159 | 275 | 518 | 71 | 17 | 19 | 36 | 77 | 1 | 1987-88 | 1998-99 |
| ‡ Nordgren, Niklas | Car., Pit. | 1 | 58 | 4 | 2 | 6 | 34 | .... | .... | .... | .... | .... | .... | 2005-06 | 2005-06 |
| Nordmark, Robert | St.L., Van. | 4 | 236 | 13 | 70 | 83 | 254 | 7 | 3 | 2 | 5 | 8 | .... | 1987-88 | 1990-91 |
| ‡ Nordqvist, Jonas | Chi. | 1 | 3 | 0 | 2 | 2 | 2 | .... | .... | .... | .... | .... | .... | 2006-07 | 2006-07 |
| ‡ Nordstrom, Peter | Bos. | 1 | 2 | 0 | 0 | 0 | 0 | .... | .... | .... | .... | .... | .... | 1998-99 | 1998-99 |
| Noris, Joe | Pit., St.L., Buf. | 3 | 55 | 2 | 5 | 7 | 22 | .... | .... | .... | .... | .... | .... | 1971-72 | 1973-74 |
| Norris, Dwayne | Que., Ana. | 3 | 20 | 2 | 4 | 6 | 8 | .... | .... | .... | .... | .... | .... | 1993-94 | 1995-96 |
| Norrish, Rod | Min. | 2 | 21 | 3 | 3 | 6 | 2 | .... | .... | .... | .... | .... | .... | 1973-74 | 1974-75 |
| Norstrom, Mattias | NYR, L.A., Dal. | 14 | 903 | 18 | 147 | 165 | 661 | 56 | 2 | 5 | 7 | 54 | .... | 1993-94 | 2007-08 |
| • Northcott, Baldy | Mtl.M., Chi. | 11 | 446 | 133 | 112 | 245 | 273 | 31 | 8 | 5 | 13 | 14 | 1 | 1928-29 | 1938-39 |
| ‡ Norton, Brad | Fla., L.A., Wsh., Ott., Det., S.J. | 5 | 124 | 3 | 8 | 11 | 287 | .... | .... | .... | .... | .... | .... | 2001-02 | 2007-08 |
| Norton, Jeff | NYI, S.J., St.L., Edm., T.B., Fla., Pit., Bos. | 15 | 799 | 52 | 332 | 384 | 615 | 65 | 4 | 21 | 25 | 89 | .... | 1987-88 | 2001-02 |
| Norwich, Craig | Wpg., St.L., Col. | 2 | 104 | 17 | 58 | 75 | 60 | .... | .... | .... | .... | .... | .... | 1979-80 | 1980-81 |
| Norwood, Lee | Que., Wsh., St.L., Det., N.J., Hfd., Cgy. | 12 | 503 | 58 | 153 | 211 | 1099 | 65 | 6 | 22 | 28 | 171 | .... | 1980-81 | 1993-94 |
| ‡ Novak, Filip | Ott., CBJ | 2 | 17 | 0 | 0 | 0 | 6 | .... | .... | .... | .... | .... | .... | 2005-06 | 2006-07 |
| ‡ Novoseltsev, Ivan | Fla., Phx. | 5 | 234 | 31 | 44 | 75 | 112 | .... | .... | .... | .... | .... | .... | 1999-00 | 2003-04 |
| Novy, Milan | Wsh. | 1 | 73 | 18 | 30 | 48 | 16 | 2 | 0 | 0 | 0 | 0 | .... | 1982-83 | 1982-83 |
| Nowak, Hank | Pit., Det., Bos. | 4 | 180 | 26 | 29 | 55 | 161 | 13 | 1 | 0 | 1 | 8 | .... | 1973-74 | 1976-77 |
| ‡ Nummelin, Petteri | CBJ, Min. | 3 | 139 | 9 | 36 | 45 | 34 | 7 | 1 | 2 | 3 | 0 | .... | 2000-01 | 2007-08 |
| ‡ Nurminen, Kai | L.A., Min. | 2 | 69 | 17 | 11 | 28 | 24 | .... | .... | .... | .... | .... | .... | 1996-97 | 2000-01 |
| Nykoluk, Mike | Tor. | 1 | 32 | 3 | 1 | 4 | 20 | .... | .... | .... | .... | .... | .... | 1956-57 | 1956-57 |
| Nylund, Gary | Tor., Chi., NYI | 11 | 608 | 32 | 139 | 171 | 1235 | 24 | 0 | 6 | 6 | 63 | .... | 1982-83 | 1992-93 |
| • Nyrop, Bill | Mtl., Min. | 4 | 207 | 12 | 51 | 63 | 101 | 35 | 1 | 7 | 8 | 22 | 3 | 1975-76 | 1981-82 |
| Nystrom, Bob | NYI | 14 | 900 | 235 | 278 | 513 | 1248 | 157 | 39 | 44 | 83 | 236 | 4 | 1972-73 | 1985-86 |

## *O*

| Name | NHL Teams | NHL Seasons | Regular Schedule GP | G | A | TP | PIM | Playoffs GP | G | A | TP | PIM | NHL Cup Wins | First NHL Season | Last NHL Season |
|---|---|---|---|---|---|---|---|---|---|---|---|---|---|---|---|
| Oates, Adam | Det., St.L., Bos., Wsh., Phi., Ana., Edm. | 19 | 1337 | 341 | 1079 | 1420 | 415 | 163 | 42 | 114 | 156 | 66 | .... | 1985-86 | 2003-04 |
| • Oatman, Russell | Det., Mtl.M., NYR | 3 | 120 | 20 | 9 | 29 | 100 | 15 | 1 | 0 | 1 | 18 | .... | 1926-27 | 1928-29 |
| O'Brien, Dennis | Min., Col., Cle., Bos. | 10 | 592 | 31 | 91 | 122 | 1017 | 34 | 1 | 2 | 3 | 101 | .... | 1970-71 | 1979-80 |
| O'Brien, Ellard | Bos. | 1 | 2 | 0 | 0 | 0 | 0 | .... | .... | .... | .... | .... | .... | 1955-56 | 1955-56 |
| ‡ Obsut, Jaroslav | St.L., Col. | 2 | 7 | 0 | 0 | 0 | 2 | .... | .... | .... | .... | .... | .... | 2000-01 | 2001-02 |
| O'Callahan, Jack | Chi., N.J. | 7 | 389 | 27 | 104 | 131 | 541 | 32 | 4 | 11 | 15 | 41 | .... | 1982-83 | 1988-89 |
| O'Connell, Mike | Chi., Bos., Det. | 13 | 860 | 105 | 334 | 439 | 605 | 82 | 8 | 24 | 32 | 64 | .... | 1977-78 | 1989-90 |
| • O'Connor, Buddy | Mtl., NYR | 10 | 509 | 140 | 257 | 397 | 34 | 53 | 15 | 21 | 36 | 6 | 2 | 1941-42 | 1950-51 |
| O'Connor, Myles | N.J., Ana. | 4 | 43 | 3 | 4 | 7 | 69 | .... | .... | .... | .... | .... | .... | 1990-91 | 1993-94 |
| Oddleifson, Chris | Bos., Van. | 9 | 524 | 95 | 191 | 286 | 464 | 14 | 1 | 6 | 7 | 8 | .... | 1972-73 | 1980-81 |
| Odelein, Lyle | Mtl., N.J., Phx., CBJ, Chi., Dal., Fla., Pit. | 16 | 1056 | 50 | 202 | 252 | 2316 | 86 | 5 | 13 | 18 | 209 | 1 | 1989-90 | 2005-06 |
| Odelein, Selmar | Edm. | 3 | 18 | 0 | 2 | 2 | 35 | .... | .... | .... | .... | .... | .... | 1985-86 | 1988-89 |
| Odgers, Jeff | S.J., Bos., Col., Atl. | 12 | 821 | 75 | 70 | 145 | 2364 | 47 | 2 | 1 | 3 | 73 | .... | 1991-92 | 2002-03 |
| Odjick, Gino | Van., NYI, Phi., Mtl. | 12 | 605 | 64 | 73 | 137 | 2567 | 44 | 4 | 1 | 5 | 142 | .... | 1990-91 | 2001-02 |
| O'Donnell, Fred | Bos. | 2 | 115 | 15 | 11 | 26 | 98 | 5 | 0 | 1 | 1 | 5 | .... | 1972-73 | 1973-74 |
| • O'Donoghue, Don | Oak., Cal. | 3 | 125 | 18 | 17 | 35 | 35 | 3 | 0 | 0 | 0 | 0 | .... | 1969-70 | 1971-72 |
| Odrowski, Gerry | Det., Oak., St.L. | 6 | 309 | 12 | 19 | 31 | 111 | 30 | 0 | 1 | 1 | 16 | .... | 1960-61 | 1971-72 |
| O'Dwyer, Bill | L.A., Bos. | 5 | 120 | 9 | 13 | 22 | 108 | 10 | 0 | 0 | 0 | 2 | .... | 1983-84 | 1989-90 |
| O'Flaherty, Gerry | Tor., Van., Atl. | 8 | 438 | 99 | 95 | 194 | 168 | 7 | 2 | 2 | 4 | 6 | .... | 1971-72 | 1978-79 |
| • O'Flaherty, Peanuts | NYA, Bro. | 2 | 21 | 5 | 1 | 6 | 0 | .... | .... | .... | .... | .... | .... | 1940-41 | 1941-42 |
| Ogilvie, Brian | Chi., St.L. | 6 | 90 | 15 | 21 | 36 | 29 | .... | .... | .... | .... | .... | .... | 1972-73 | 1978-79 |
| • O'Grady, George | Mtl.W. | 1 | 4 | 0 | 0 | 0 | 0 | .... | .... | .... | .... | .... | .... | 1917-18 | 1917-18 |
| Ogrodnick, John | Det., Que., NYR | 14 | 928 | 402 | 425 | 827 | 260 | 41 | 18 | 8 | 26 | 6 | .... | 1979-80 | 1992-93 |
| ‡ Ojanen, Janne | N.J. | 4 | 98 | 21 | 23 | 44 | 28 | 3 | 0 | 2 | 2 | 0 | .... | 1988-89 | 1992-93 |
| Okerlund, Todd | NYI | 1 | 4 | 0 | 0 | 0 | 2 | .... | .... | .... | .... | .... | .... | 1987-88 | 1987-88 |
| Oksiuta, Roman | Edm., Van., Ana., Pit. | 4 | 153 | 46 | 41 | 87 | 100 | 10 | 2 | 3 | 5 | 0 | .... | 1993-94 | 1996-97 |
| Olausson, Fredrik | Wpg., Edm., Ana., Pit., Det. | 16 | 1022 | 147 | 434 | 581 | 450 | 71 | 6 | 23 | 29 | 28 | 1 | 1986-87 | 2002-03 |
| Olczyk, Ed | Chi., Tor., Wpg., NYR, L.A., Pit. | 16 | 1031 | 342 | 452 | 794 | 874 | 57 | 19 | 15 | 34 | 57 | 1 | 1984-85 | 1999-00 |
| Oliver, David | Edm., NYR, Ott., Phx., Dal. | 9 | 233 | 49 | 49 | 98 | 84 | 10 | 0 | 0 | 0 | 2 | .... | 1994-95 | 2005-06 |
| • Oliver, Harry | Bos., NYA | 11 | 463 | 127 | 85 | 212 | 147 | 35 | 10 | 6 | 16 | 24 | 1 | 1926-27 | 1936-37 |
| Oliver, Murray | Det., Bos., Tor., Min. | 17 | 1127 | 274 | 454 | 728 | 320 | 35 | 9 | 16 | 25 | 10 | .... | 1957-58 | 1974-75 |
| Oliwa, Krzysztof | N.J., CBJ, Pit., NYR, Bos., Cgy. | 9 | 410 | 17 | 28 | 45 | 1447 | 32 | 2 | 0 | 2 | 47 | 1 | 1996-97 | 2005-06 |
| Olmstead, Bert | Chi., Mtl., Tor. | 14 | 848 | 181 | 421 | 602 | 884 | 115 | 16 | 43 | 59 | 101 | 5 | 1948-49 | 1961-62 |
| Olsen, Darryl | Cgy. | 1 | 1 | 0 | 0 | 0 | 0 | .... | .... | .... | .... | .... | .... | 1991-92 | 1991-92 |
| Olson, Dennis | Det. | 1 | 4 | 0 | 0 | 0 | 0 | .... | .... | .... | .... | .... | .... | 1957-58 | 1957-58 |
| ‡ Olson, Josh | Fla. | 1 | 5 | 1 | 0 | 1 | 0 | .... | .... | .... | .... | .... | .... | 2003-04 | 2003-04 |
| Olsson, Christer | St.L., Ott. | 2 | 56 | 4 | 12 | 16 | 24 | 3 | 0 | 0 | 0 | 0 | .... | 1995-96 | 1996-97 |
| ‡ Olvestad, Jimmie | T.B. | 2 | 111 | 3 | 14 | 17 | 40 | .... | .... | .... | .... | .... | .... | 2001-02 | 2002-03 |
| • O'Neil, Jim | Bos., Mtl. | 6 | 156 | 6 | 30 | 36 | 109 | 9 | 1 | 1 | 2 | 13 | .... | 1933-34 | 1941-42 |
| O'Neil, Paul | Van., Bos. | 2 | 6 | 0 | 0 | 0 | 0 | .... | .... | .... | .... | .... | .... | 1973-74 | 1975-76 |
| O'Neill, Jeff | Hfd., Car., Tor. | 11 | 821 | 237 | 259 | 496 | 670 | 34 | 9 | 8 | 17 | 37 | .... | 1995-96 | 2006-07 |
| • O'Neill, Tom | Tor. | 2 | 66 | 10 | 12 | 22 | 53 | 4 | 0 | 0 | 0 | 6 | 1 | 1943-44 | 1944-45 |
| Orban, Bill | Chi., Min. | 3 | 114 | 8 | 15 | 23 | 67 | 3 | 0 | 0 | 0 | 0 | .... | 1967-68 | 1969-70 |
| O'Ree, Willie | Bos. | 2 | 45 | 4 | 10 | 14 | 26 | .... | .... | .... | .... | .... | .... | 1957-58 | 1960-61 |
| O'Regan, Tom | Pit. | 3 | 61 | 5 | 12 | 17 | 10 | .... | .... | .... | .... | .... | .... | 1983-84 | 1985-86 |
| O'Reilly, Terry | Bos. | 14 | 891 | 204 | 402 | 606 | 2095 | 108 | 25 | 42 | 67 | 335 | .... | 1971-72 | 1984-85 |
| Orlando, Gates | Buf. | 3 | 98 | 18 | 26 | 44 | 51 | 5 | 0 | 4 | 4 | 14 | .... | 1984-85 | 1986-87 |
| • Orlando, Jimmy | Det. | 6 | 199 | 6 | 25 | 31 | 375 | 36 | 0 | 9 | 9 | 105 | 1 | 1936-37 | 1942-43 |
| Orleski, Dave | Mtl. | 2 | 2 | 0 | 0 | 0 | 0 | .... | .... | .... | .... | .... | .... | 1980-81 | 1981-82 |
| Orr, Bobby | Bos., Chi. | 12 | 657 | 270 | 645 | 915 | 953 | 74 | 26 | 66 | 92 | 107 | 2 | 1966-67 | 1978-79 |
| Orszagh, Vladimir | NYI, Nsh., St.L. | 7 | 289 | 54 | 65 | 119 | 194 | 6 | 2 | 0 | 2 | 4 | .... | 1997-98 | 2005-06 |
| Osborne, Keith | St.L., T.B. | 2 | 16 | 1 | 3 | 4 | 16 | .... | .... | .... | .... | .... | .... | 1989-90 | 1992-93 |
| Osborne, Mark | Det., NYR, Tor., Wpg. | 14 | 919 | 212 | 319 | 531 | 1152 | 87 | 12 | 16 | 28 | 141 | .... | 1981-82 | 1994-95 |

| | | | Regular Schedule | | | | | Playoffs | | | | | | | |
|---|---|---|---|---|---|---|---|---|---|---|---|---|---|---|---|
| Name | NHL Teams | NHL Seasons | GP | G | A | TP | PIM | GP | G | A | TP | PIM | NHL Cup Wins | First NHL Season | Last NHL Season |
| Osburn, Randy | Tor., Phi. | 2 | 27 | 0 | 2 | 2 | 0 | .... | .... | .... | .... | .... | .... | 1972-73 | 1974-75 |
| O'Shea, Danny | Min., Chi., St.L. | 5 | 369 | 64 | 115 | 179 | 265 | 39 | 3 | 7 | 10 | 61 | .... | 1968-69 | 1972-73 |
| O'Shea, Kevin | Buf., St.L. | 3 | 134 | 13 | 18 | 31 | 85 | 12 | 2 | 1 | 3 | 10 | .... | 1970-71 | 1972-73 |
| Osiecki, Mark | Cgy., Ott., Wpg., Min. | 2 | 93 | 3 | 11 | 14 | 43 | .... | .... | .... | .... | .... | .... | 1991-92 | 1992-93 |
| O'Sullivan, Chris | Cgy., Van., Ana. | 5 | 62 | 2 | 17 | 19 | 16 | .... | .... | .... | .... | .... | .... | 1996-97 | 2002-03 |
| Otevrel, Jaroslav | S.J. | 2 | 16 | 3 | 4 | 7 | 2 | .... | .... | .... | .... | .... | .... | 1992-93 | 1993-94 |
| Otto, Joel | Cgy., Phi. | 14 | 943 | 195 | 313 | 508 | 1934 | 122 | 27 | 47 | 74 | 207 | 1 | 1984-85 | 1997-98 |
| Ouellette, Eddie | Chi. | 1 | 43 | 3 | 2 | 5 | 11 | 1 | 0 | 0 | 0 | 0 | .... | 1935-36 | 1935-36 |
| Ouellette, Gerry | Bos. | 1 | 34 | 5 | 4 | 9 | 0 | .... | .... | .... | .... | .... | .... | 1960-61 | 1960-61 |
| Owchar, Dennis | Pit., Col. | 6 | 288 | 30 | 85 | 115 | 200 | 10 | 1 | 1 | 2 | 8 | .... | 1974-75 | 1979-80 |
| • Owen, George | Bos. | 5 | 183 | 44 | 33 | 77 | 151 | 21 | 2 | 5 | 7 | 25 | 1 | 1928-29 | 1932-33 |
| Ozolinsh, Sandis | S.J., Col., Car., Fla., Ana., NYR | 15 | 875 | 167 | 397 | 564 | 638 | 137 | 23 | 67 | 90 | 131 | 1 | 1992-93 | 2007-08 |

## P

| Name | NHL Teams | NHL Seasons | GP | G | A | TP | PIM | GP | G | A | TP | PIM | NHL Cup Wins | First NHL Season | Last NHL Season |
|---|---|---|---|---|---|---|---|---|---|---|---|---|---|---|---|
| Pachal, Clayton | Bos., Col. | 3 | 35 | 2 | 3 | 5 | 95 | .... | .... | .... | .... | .... | .... | 1976-77 | 1978-79 |
| Paddock, John | Wsh., Phi., Que. | 5 | 87 | 8 | 14 | 22 | 86 | 5 | 2 | 0 | 2 | 0 | .... | 1975-76 | 1982-83 |
| Paek, Jim | Pit., L.A., Ott. | 5 | 217 | 5 | 29 | 34 | 155 | 27 | 1 | 4 | 5 | 8 | 2 | 1990-91 | 1994-95 |
| Paiement, Rosaire | Phi., Van. | 5 | 190 | 48 | 52 | 100 | 343 | 3 | 3 | 0 | 3 | 0 | .... | 1967-68 | 1971-72 |
| Paiement, Wilf | K.C., Col., Tor., Que., NYR, Buf., Pit. | 14 | 946 | 356 | 458 | 814 | 1757 | 69 | 18 | 17 | 35 | 185 | .... | 1974-75 | 1987-88 |
| • Palangio, Pete | Mtl., Det., Chi. | 5 | 71 | 13 | 10 | 23 | 28 | 7 | 0 | 0 | 0 | 0 | 1 | 1926-27 | 1937-38 |
| • Palazzari, Aldo | Bos., NYR | 1 | 35 | 8 | 3 | 11 | 4 | .... | .... | .... | .... | .... | .... | 1943-44 | 1943-44 |
| Palazzari, Doug | St.L. | 4 | 108 | 18 | 20 | 38 | 23 | 2 | 0 | 0 | 0 | 0 | .... | 1974-75 | 1978-79 |
| ‡ Palffy, Ziggy | NYI, L.A., Pit. | 12 | 684 | 329 | 384 | 713 | 322 | 24 | 9 | 10 | 19 | 8 | .... | 1993-94 | 2005-06 |
| Palmer, Brad | Min., Bos. | 3 | 168 | 32 | 38 | 70 | 58 | 29 | 9 | 5 | 14 | 16 | .... | 1980-81 | 1982-83 |
| Palmer, Rob | Chi. | 3 | 16 | 0 | 3 | 3 | 2 | .... | .... | .... | .... | .... | .... | 1973-74 | 1975-76 |
| Palmer, Robert | L.A., N.J. | 7 | 320 | 9 | 101 | 110 | 115 | 8 | 1 | 2 | 3 | 6 | .... | 1977-78 | 1983-84 |
| • Panagabko, Ed | Bos. | 2 | 29 | 0 | 3 | 3 | 38 | .... | .... | .... | .... | .... | .... | 1955-56 | 1956-57 |
| Pandolfo, Mike | CBJ | 1 | 3 | 0 | 0 | 0 | 0 | .... | .... | .... | .... | .... | .... | 2003-04 | 2003-04 |
| ‡ Pankewicz, Greg | Ott., Cgy. | 2 | 21 | 0 | 3 | 3 | 22 | .... | .... | .... | .... | .... | .... | 1993-94 | 1998-99 |
| Panteleev, Grigori | Bos., NYI | 4 | 54 | 8 | 6 | 14 | 12 | .... | .... | .... | .... | .... | .... | 1992-93 | 1995-96 |
| • Papike, Joe | Chi. | 3 | 20 | 3 | 3 | 6 | 4 | 5 | 0 | 2 | 2 | 0 | .... | 1940-41 | 1944-45 |
| ‡ Papineau, Justin | St.L., NYI | 3 | 81 | 11 | 8 | 19 | 12 | 1 | 0 | 0 | 0 | 0 | .... | 2001-02 | 2003-04 |
| Pappin, Jim | Tor., Chi., Cal., Cle. | 14 | 767 | 278 | 295 | 573 | 667 | 92 | 33 | 34 | 67 | 101 | 2 | 1963-64 | 1976-77 |
| Paradise, Bob | Min., Atl., Pit., Wsh. | 8 | 368 | 8 | 54 | 62 | 393 | 12 | 0 | 1 | 1 | 19 | .... | 1971-72 | 1978-79 |
| • Pargeter, George | Mtl. | 1 | 4 | 0 | 0 | 0 | 0 | .... | .... | .... | .... | .... | .... | 1946-47 | 1946-47 |
| Parise, J.P. | Bos., Tor., Min., NYI, Cle. | 14 | 890 | 238 | 356 | 594 | 706 | 86 | 27 | 31 | 58 | 87 | .... | 1965-66 | 1978-79 |
| Parizeau, Michel | St.L., Phi. | 1 | 58 | 3 | 14 | 17 | 18 | .... | .... | .... | .... | .... | .... | 1971-72 | 1971-72 |
| Park, Brad | NYR, Bos., Det. | 17 | 1113 | 213 | 683 | 896 | 1429 | 161 | 35 | 90 | 125 | 217 | .... | 1968-69 | 1984-85 |
| Parker, Jeff | Buf., Hfd. | 5 | 141 | 16 | 19 | 35 | 163 | 5 | 0 | 0 | 0 | 26 | .... | 1986-87 | 1990-91 |
| Parker, Scott | Col., S.J. | 8 | 308 | 7 | 14 | 21 | 699 | 5 | 0 | 0 | 0 | 4 | 1 | 1998-99 | 2007-08 |
| • Parkes, Ernie | Mtl.M. | 1 | 17 | 0 | 0 | 0 | 2 | .... | .... | .... | .... | .... | .... | 1924-25 | 1924-25 |
| Parks, Greg | NYI | 3 | 23 | 1 | 2 | 3 | 6 | 2 | 0 | 0 | 0 | 0 | .... | 1990-91 | 1992-93 |
| • Parsons, George | Tor. | 3 | 78 | 12 | 13 | 25 | 20 | 7 | 3 | 2 | 5 | 11 | .... | 1936-37 | 1938-39 |
| ‡ Parssinen, Timo | Ana. | 1 | 17 | 0 | 3 | 3 | 2 | .... | .... | .... | .... | .... | .... | 2001-02 | 2001-02 |
| • Pasek, Dusan | Min. | 1 | 48 | 4 | 10 | 14 | 30 | 2 | 1 | 0 | 1 | 0 | .... | 1988-89 | 1988-89 |
| Pasin, Dave | Bos., L.A. | 2 | 76 | 18 | 19 | 37 | 50 | 3 | 0 | 1 | 1 | 0 | .... | 1985-86 | 1988-89 |
| Paslawski, Greg | Mtl., St.L., Wpg., Buf., Que., Phi., Cgy. | 11 | 650 | 187 | 185 | 372 | 169 | 60 | 19 | 13 | 32 | 25 | .... | 1983-84 | 1993-94 |
| ‡ Patera, Pavel | Dal., Min. | 2 | 32 | 2 | 7 | 9 | 8 | .... | .... | .... | .... | .... | .... | 1999-00 | 2000-01 |
| Paterson, Joe | Det., Phi., L.A., NYR | 9 | 291 | 19 | 37 | 56 | 829 | 22 | 3 | 4 | 7 | 77 | .... | 1980-81 | 1988-89 |
| Paterson, Mark | Hfd. | 4 | 29 | 3 | 3 | 6 | 33 | .... | .... | .... | .... | .... | .... | 1982-83 | 1985-86 |
| Paterson, Rick | Chi. | 9 | 430 | 50 | 43 | 93 | 136 | 61 | 7 | 10 | 17 | 51 | .... | 1978-79 | 1986-87 |
| Patey, Doug | Wsh. | 3 | 45 | 4 | 2 | 6 | 8 | .... | .... | .... | .... | .... | .... | 1976-77 | 1978-79 |
| Patey, Larry | Cal., St.L., NYR | 12 | 717 | 153 | 163 | 316 | 631 | 40 | 8 | 10 | 18 | 57 | .... | 1973-74 | 1984-85 |
| Patrick, Craig | Cal., St.L., K.C., Wsh. | 8 | 401 | 72 | 91 | 163 | 61 | 2 | 0 | 1 | 1 | 0 | .... | 1971-72 | 1978-79 |
| Patrick, Glenn | St.L., Cal., Cle. | 4 | 38 | 2 | 3 | 5 | 72 | .... | .... | .... | .... | .... | .... | 1973-74 | 1976-77 |
| Patrick, James | NYR, Hfd., Cgy., Buf. | 21 | 1280 | 149 | 490 | 639 | 759 | 117 | 6 | 32 | 38 | 86 | .... | 1983-84 | 2003-04 |
| • Patrick, Lester | NYR | 1 | 1 | 0 | 0 | 0 | 2 | .... | .... | .... | .... | .... | .... | 1926-27 | 1926-27 |
| • Patrick, Lynn | NYR | 10 | 455 | 145 | 190 | 335 | 240 | 44 | 10 | 6 | 16 | 22 | 1 | 1934-35 | 1945-46 |
| • Patrick, Muzz | NYR | 5 | 166 | 5 | 26 | 31 | 133 | 25 | 4 | 0 | 4 | 34 | 1 | 1937-38 | 1945-46 |
| Patrick, Steve | Buf., NYR, Que. | 6 | 250 | 40 | 68 | 108 | 242 | 12 | 0 | 1 | 1 | 12 | .... | 1980-81 | 1985-86 |
| Patterson, Colin | Cgy., Buf. | 10 | 504 | 96 | 109 | 205 | 239 | 85 | 12 | 17 | 29 | 57 | 1 | 1983-84 | 1992-93 |
| Patterson, Dennis | K.C., Phi. | 3 | 138 | 6 | 22 | 28 | 67 | .... | .... | .... | .... | .... | .... | 1974-75 | 1979-80 |
| Patterson, Ed | Pit. | 3 | 68 | 3 | 3 | 6 | 56 | .... | .... | .... | .... | .... | .... | 1993-94 | 1996-97 |
| • Patterson, George | Tor., Mtl., NYA, Bos., Det., St.L. | 9 | 284 | 51 | 27 | 78 | 218 | 3 | 0 | 0 | 0 | 2 | .... | 1926-27 | 1934-35 |
| • Paul, Butch | Det. | 1 | 3 | 0 | 0 | 0 | 0 | .... | .... | .... | .... | .... | .... | 1964-65 | 1964-65 |
| ‡ Paul, Jeff | Col. | 1 | 2 | 0 | 0 | 0 | 7 | .... | .... | .... | .... | .... | .... | 2002-03 | 2002-03 |
| • Paulhus, Rollie | Mtl. | 1 | 33 | 0 | 0 | 0 | 0 | .... | .... | .... | .... | .... | .... | 1925-26 | 1925-26 |
| Pavelich, Mark | NYR, Min., S.J. | 7 | 355 | 137 | 192 | 329 | 340 | 23 | 7 | 17 | 24 | 14 | .... | 1981-82 | 1991-92 |
| Pavelich, Marty | Det. | 10 | 634 | 93 | 159 | 252 | 454 | 91 | 13 | 15 | 28 | 74 | 4 | 1947-48 | 1956-57 |
| Pavese, Jim | St.L., NYR, Det., Hfd. | 8 | 328 | 13 | 44 | 57 | 689 | 36 | 0 | 6 | 6 | 81 | .... | 1981-82 | 1988-89 |
| • Payer, Evariste | Mtl. | 1 | 1 | 0 | 0 | 0 | 0 | .... | .... | .... | .... | .... | .... | 1917-18 | 1917-18 |
| Payne, Davis | Bos. | 2 | 22 | 0 | 1 | 1 | 14 | .... | .... | .... | .... | .... | .... | 1995-96 | 1996-97 |
| Payne, Steve | Min. | 10 | 613 | 228 | 238 | 466 | 435 | 71 | 35 | 35 | 70 | 60 | .... | 1978-79 | 1987-88 |
| Paynter, Kent | Chi., Wsh., Wpg., Ott. | 7 | 37 | 1 | 3 | 4 | 69 | 4 | 0 | 0 | 0 | 10 | .... | 1987-88 | 1993-94 |
| Peake, Pat | Wsh. | 5 | 134 | 28 | 41 | 69 | 105 | 13 | 2 | 2 | 4 | 20 | .... | 1993-94 | 1997-98 |
| • Pearson, Mel | NYR, Pit. | 5 | 38 | 2 | 6 | 8 | 25 | .... | .... | .... | .... | .... | .... | 1959-60 | 1967-68 |
| Pearson, Rob | Tor., Wsh., St.L. | 6 | 269 | 56 | 54 | 110 | 645 | 33 | 4 | 2 | 6 | 94 | .... | 1991-92 | 1996-97 |
| Pearson, Scott | Tor., Que., Edm., Buf., NYI | 10 | 292 | 56 | 42 | 98 | 615 | 10 | 2 | 0 | 2 | 14 | .... | 1988-89 | 1999-00 |
| Peat, Stephen | Wsh. | 4 | 130 | 8 | 2 | 10 | 234 | .... | .... | .... | .... | .... | .... | 2001-02 | 2005-06 |
| Pedersen, Allen | Bos., Min., Hfd. | 8 | 428 | 5 | 36 | 41 | 487 | 64 | 0 | 0 | 0 | 91 | .... | 1986-87 | 1993-94 |
| Pederson, Barry | Bos., Van., Pit., Hfd. | 12 | 701 | 238 | 416 | 654 | 472 | 34 | 22 | 30 | 52 | 25 | 1 | 1980-81 | 1991-92 |
| ‡ Pederson, Denis | N.J., Van., Phx., Nsh. | 8 | 435 | 57 | 71 | 128 | 398 | 27 | 1 | 5 | 6 | 8 | .... | 1995-96 | 2002-03 |
| Pederson, Mark | Mtl., Phi., S.J., Det. | 5 | 169 | 35 | 50 | 85 | 77 | 2 | 0 | 0 | 0 | 0 | .... | 1989-90 | 1993-94 |
| Pederson, Tom | S.J., Tor. | 5 | 240 | 20 | 49 | 69 | 142 | 24 | 1 | 11 | 12 | 10 | .... | 1992-93 | 1996-97 |
| • Peer, Bert | Det. | 1 | 1 | 0 | 0 | 0 | 0 | .... | .... | .... | .... | .... | .... | 1939-40 | 1939-40 |
| Peirson, Johnny | Bos. | 11 | 545 | 153 | 173 | 326 | 315 | 49 | 10 | 16 | 26 | 26 | .... | 1946-47 | 1957-58 |
| Pelensky, Perry | Chi. | 1 | 4 | 0 | 0 | 0 | 5 | .... | .... | .... | .... | .... | .... | 1983-84 | 1983-84 |
| Pellerin, Scott | N.J., St.L., Min., Car., Bos., Dal., Phx. | 11 | 536 | 72 | 126 | 198 | 320 | 37 | 1 | 2 | 3 | 26 | .... | 1992-93 | 2003-04 |
| Pelletier, Roger | Phi. | 1 | 1 | 0 | 0 | 0 | 0 | .... | .... | .... | .... | .... | .... | 1967-68 | 1967-68 |
| Peloffy, Andre | Wsh. | 1 | 9 | 0 | 0 | 0 | 0 | .... | .... | .... | .... | .... | .... | 1974-75 | 1974-75 |
| Peluso, Mike | Chi., Ott., N.J., St.L., Cgy. | 9 | 458 | 38 | 52 | 90 | 1951 | 62 | 3 | 4 | 7 | 107 | 1 | 1989-90 | 1997-98 |
| Peluso, Mike | Chi., Phi. | 2 | 38 | 4 | 2 | 6 | 19 | .... | .... | .... | .... | .... | .... | 2001-02 | 2003-04 |
| Pelyk, Mike | Tor. | 9 | 441 | 26 | 88 | 114 | 566 | 40 | 0 | 3 | 3 | 41 | .... | 1967-68 | 1977-78 |
| Penney, Chad | Ott. | 1 | 3 | 0 | 0 | 0 | 2 | .... | .... | .... | .... | .... | .... | 1993-94 | 1993-94 |
| Pennington, Cliff | Mtl., Bos. | 3 | 101 | 17 | 42 | 59 | 6 | .... | .... | .... | .... | .... | .... | 1960-61 | 1962-63 |
| Peplinski, Jim | Cgy. | 11 | 711 | 161 | 263 | 424 | 1467 | 99 | 15 | 31 | 46 | 382 | 1 | 1980-81 | 1994-95 |
| Perlini, Fred | Tor. | 2 | 8 | 2 | 3 | 5 | 0 | .... | .... | .... | .... | .... | .... | 1981-82 | 1983-84 |
| Perreault, Fern | NYR | 2 | 3 | 0 | 0 | 0 | 0 | .... | .... | .... | .... | .... | .... | 1947-48 | 1949-50 |
| Perreault, Gilbert | Buf. | 17 | 1191 | 512 | 814 | 1326 | 500 | 90 | 33 | 70 | 103 | 44 | .... | 1970-71 | 1986-87 |
| Perreault, Yanic | Tor., L.A., Mtl., Nsh., Phx., Chi. | 14 | 859 | 247 | 269 | 516 | 402 | 54 | 11 | 19 | 30 | 18 | .... | 1993-94 | 2007-08 |
| ‡ Perrott, Nathan | Nsh., Tor., Dal. | 4 | 89 | 4 | 5 | 9 | 251 | .... | .... | .... | .... | .... | .... | 2001-02 | 2005-06 |
| Perry, Brian | Oak., Buf. | 3 | 96 | 16 | 29 | 45 | 24 | 8 | 1 | 1 | 2 | 4 | .... | 1968-69 | 1970-71 |
| Persson, Ricard | N.J., St.L., Ott. | 7 | 229 | 10 | 44 | 54 | 262 | 26 | 1 | 3 | 4 | 59 | .... | 1995-96 | 2001-02 |
| Persson, Stefan | NYI | 9 | 622 | 52 | 317 | 369 | 574 | 102 | 7 | 50 | 57 | 69 | 4 | 1977-78 | 1985-86 |
| Pesut, George | Cal. | 2 | 92 | 3 | 22 | 25 | 130 | .... | .... | .... | .... | .... | .... | 1974-75 | 1975-76 |
| • Peters, Frank | NYR | 1 | 43 | 0 | 0 | 0 | 59 | 4 | 0 | 0 | 0 | 2 | .... | 1930-31 | 1930-31 |
| Peters, Garry | Mtl., NYR, Phi., Bos. | 8 | 311 | 34 | 34 | 68 | 261 | 9 | 2 | 2 | 4 | 31 | 1 | 1964-65 | 1971-72 |
| • Peters, Jimmy | Mtl., Bos., Det., Chi. | 9 | 574 | 125 | 150 | 275 | 186 | 60 | 5 | 9 | 14 | 22 | 3 | 1945-46 | 1953-54 |
| Peters, Jimmy | Det., L.A. | 9 | 309 | 37 | 36 | 73 | 48 | 11 | 0 | 2 | 2 | 2 | .... | 1964-65 | 1974-75 |
| Peters, Steve | Col. | 1 | 2 | 0 | 1 | 1 | 0 | .... | .... | .... | .... | .... | .... | 1979-80 | 1979-80 |
| Peterson, Brent | Det., Buf., Van., Hfd. | 11 | 620 | 72 | 141 | 213 | 484 | 31 | 4 | 4 | 8 | 65 | .... | 1978-79 | 1988-89 |
| Peterson, Brent | T.B. | 3 | 56 | 9 | 1 | 10 | 6 | .... | .... | .... | .... | .... | .... | 1996-97 | 1998-99 |
| Petit, Michel | Van., NYR, Que., Tor., Cgy., L.A., T.B., Edm., Phi., Phx. | 16 | 827 | 90 | 238 | 328 | 1839 | 19 | 0 | 2 | 2 | 61 | .... | 1982-83 | 1997-98 |
| Petrenko, Sergei | Buf. | 1 | 14 | 0 | 4 | 4 | 0 | .... | .... | .... | .... | .... | .... | 1993-94 | 1993-94 |
| ‡ Petrov, Oleg | Mtl., Nsh. | 8 | 382 | 72 | 115 | 187 | 101 | 20 | 1 | 6 | 7 | 2 | .... | 1992-93 | 2002-03 |
| ‡ Petrovicky, Robert | Hfd., Dal., St.L., T.B., NYI | 8 | 208 | 27 | 38 | 65 | 118 | 2 | 0 | 0 | 0 | 0 | .... | 1992-93 | 2000-01 |
| ‡ Petrovicky, Ronald | Cgy., NYR, Atl., Pit. | 6 | 342 | 41 | 51 | 92 | 429 | 3 | 0 | 0 | 0 | 2 | .... | 2000-01 | 2006-07 |
| Pettersson, Jorgen | St.L., Hfd., Wsh. | 6 | 435 | 174 | 192 | 366 | 117 | 44 | 15 | 12 | 27 | 4 | .... | 1980-81 | 1985-86 |
| ‡ Pettinen, Tomi | NYI | 3 | 24 | 0 | 0 | 0 | 18 | .... | .... | .... | .... | .... | .... | 2002-03 | 2005-06 |
| • Pettinger, Eric | Bos., Tor., Ott. | 3 | 98 | 7 | 12 | 19 | 83 | 4 | 1 | 0 | 1 | 8 | .... | 1928-29 | 1930-31 |
| • Pettinger, Gord | NYR, Det., Bos. | 8 | 292 | 42 | 74 | 116 | 77 | 47 | 4 | 5 | 9 | 11 | 4 | 1932-33 | 1939-40 |
| Phair, Lyle | L.A. | 3 | 48 | 6 | 7 | 13 | 12 | 1 | 0 | 0 | 0 | 0 | .... | 1985-86 | 1987-88 |
| Phillipoff, Harold | Atl., Chi. | 3 | 141 | 26 | 57 | 83 | 267 | 6 | 0 | 2 | 2 | 9 | .... | 1977-78 | 1979-80 |
| • Phillips, Bill | Mtl.M. | 1 | 27 | 1 | 1 | 2 | 6 | 4 | 0 | 0 | 0 | 2 | .... | 1929-30 | 1929-30 |

Yanic Perreault

Noel Picard

Mark Plantery

Larry Pleau

Poul Popiel

Tom Price

Fido Purpur

Yip Radley

| | | | Regular Schedule | | | | | Playoffs | | | | | | | |
|---|---|---|---|---|---|---|---|---|---|---|---|---|---|---|---|
| Name | NHL Teams | NHL Seasons | GP | G | A | TP | PIM | GP | G | A | TP | PIM | NHL Cup Wins | First NHL Season | Last NHL Season |
| • Phillips, Charlie | Mtl. | 1 | 17 | 0 | 0 | 0 | 6 | .... | .... | .... | .... | .... | .... | 1942-43 | 1942-43 |
| • Phillips, Merlyn | Mtl.M., NYA | 8 | 302 | 52 | 31 | 83 | 232 | 24 | 5 | 1 | 6 | 19 | 1 | 1925-26 | 1932-33 |
| Picard, Michel | Hfd., S.J., Ott., St.L., Edm., Phi. | 9 | 166 | 28 | 42 | 70 | 103 | 5 | 0 | 0 | 0 | 2 | .... | 1990-91 | 2000-01 |
| Picard, Noel | Mtl., St.L., Atl. | 7 | 335 | 12 | 63 | 75 | 616 | 50 | 2 | 11 | 13 | 167 | 1 | 1964-65 | 1972-73 |
| Picard, Robert | Wsh., Tor., Mtl., Wpg., Que., Det. | 13 | 899 | 104 | 319 | 423 | 1025 | 36 | 5 | 15 | 20 | 39 | .... | 1977-78 | 1989-90 |
| Picard, Roger | St.L. | 1 | 15 | 2 | 2 | 4 | 21 | .... | .... | .... | .... | .... | .... | 1967-68 | 1967-68 |
| Pichette, Dave | Que., St.L., N.J., NYR | 7 | 322 | 41 | 140 | 181 | 348 | 28 | 3 | 7 | 10 | 54 | .... | 1980-81 | 1987-88 |
| Picketts, Hal | NYA | 1 | 48 | 3 | 1 | 4 | 32 | .... | .... | .... | .... | .... | .... | 1933-34 | 1933-34 |
| Pidhirny, Harry | Bos. | 1 | 2 | 0 | 0 | 0 | 0 | .... | .... | .... | .... | .... | .... | 1957-58 | 1957-58 |
| Pierce, Randy | Col., N.J., Hfd. | 8 | 277 | 62 | 76 | 138 | 223 | 2 | 0 | 0 | 0 | 0 | .... | 1977-78 | 1984-85 |
| • Pike, Alf | NYR | 6 | 234 | 42 | 77 | 119 | 145 | 21 | 4 | 2 | 6 | 12 | 1 | 1939-40 | 1946-47 |
| ‡ Pilar, Karel | Tor. | 3 | 90 | 6 | 24 | 30 | 42 | 12 | 1 | 4 | 5 | 12 | .... | 2001-02 | 2003-04 |
| Pilon, Rich | NYI, NYR, St.L. | 14 | 631 | 8 | 69 | 77 | 1745 | 15 | 0 | 0 | 0 | 50 | .... | 1988-89 | 2001-02 |
| Pilote, Pierre | Chi., Tor. | 14 | 890 | 80 | 418 | 498 | 1251 | 86 | 8 | 53 | 61 | 102 | 1 | 1955-56 | 1968-69 |
| Pinder, Gerry | Chi., Cal. | 3 | 223 | 55 | 69 | 124 | 135 | 17 | 0 | 4 | 4 | 6 | .... | 1969-70 | 1971-72 |
| ‡ Pirjeta, Lasse | CBJ, Pit. | 3 | 146 | 23 | 27 | 50 | 50 | .... | .... | .... | .... | .... | .... | 2002-03 | 2005-06 |
| ‡ Pirnes, Esa | L.A. | 1 | 57 | 3 | 8 | 11 | 12 | .... | .... | .... | .... | .... | .... | 2003-04 | 2003-04 |
| ‡ Piros, Kamil | Atl., Fla. | 3 | 28 | 4 | 4 | 8 | 10 | .... | .... | .... | .... | .... | .... | 2001-02 | 2003-04 |
| Pirus, Alex | Min., Det. | 4 | 159 | 30 | 28 | 58 | 94 | 2 | 0 | 1 | 1 | 2 | .... | 1976-77 | 1979-80 |
| ‡ Pisa, Ales | Edm., NYR | 2 | 53 | 1 | 3 | 4 | 26 | .... | .... | .... | .... | .... | .... | 2001-02 | 2002-03 |
| Pitlick, Lance | Ott., Fla. | 8 | 393 | 16 | 33 | 49 | 298 | 24 | 0 | 2 | 2 | 21 | .... | 1994-95 | 2001-02 |
| • Pitre, Didier | Mtl. | 6 | 127 | 64 | 33 | 97 | 87 | 9 | 2 | 4 | 6 | 19 | .... | 1917-18 | 1922-23 |
| Pittis, Domenic | Pit., Buf., Edm., Nsh. | 7 | 86 | 5 | 11 | 16 | 71 | 3 | 0 | 0 | 0 | 2 | .... | 1996-97 | 2003-04 |
| ‡ Pivko, Libor | Nsh. | 1 | 1 | 0 | 0 | 0 | 0 | .... | .... | .... | .... | .... | .... | 2003-04 | 2003-04 |
| Pivonka, Michal | Wsh. | 13 | 825 | 181 | 418 | 599 | 478 | 95 | 19 | 36 | 55 | 86 | .... | 1986-87 | 1998-99 |
| • Plager, Barclay | St.L. | 10 | 614 | 44 | 187 | 231 | 1115 | 68 | 3 | 20 | 23 | 182 | .... | 1967-68 | 1976-77 |
| Plager, Bill | Min., St.L., Atl. | 9 | 263 | 4 | 34 | 38 | 294 | 31 | 0 | 2 | 2 | 26 | .... | 1967-68 | 1975-76 |
| Plager, Bob | NYR, St.L. | 14 | 644 | 20 | 126 | 146 | 802 | 74 | 2 | 17 | 19 | 195 | .... | 1964-65 | 1977-78 |
| Plamondon, Gerry | Mtl. | 5 | 74 | 7 | 13 | 20 | 10 | 11 | 5 | 2 | 7 | 2 | 1 | 1945-46 | 1950-51 |
| Plante, Cam | Tor. | 1 | 2 | 0 | 0 | 0 | 0 | .... | .... | .... | .... | .... | .... | 1984-85 | 1984-85 |
| Plante, Dan | NYI | 4 | 159 | 9 | 14 | 23 | 135 | 1 | 1 | 0 | 1 | 2 | .... | 1993-94 | 1997-98 |
| Plante, Derek | Buf., Dal., Chi., Phi. | 8 | 450 | 96 | 152 | 248 | 138 | 41 | 6 | 10 | 16 | 18 | 1 | 1993-94 | 2000-01 |
| Plante, Pierre | Phi., St.L., Chi., NYR, Que. | 9 | 599 | 125 | 172 | 297 | 599 | 33 | 2 | 6 | 8 | 51 | .... | 1971-72 | 1979-80 |
| Plantery, Mark | Wpg. | 1 | 25 | 1 | 5 | 6 | 14 | .... | .... | .... | .... | .... | .... | 1980-81 | 1980-81 |
| Plavsic, Adrien | St.L., Van., T.B., Ana. | 8 | 214 | 16 | 56 | 72 | 161 | 13 | 1 | 7 | 8 | 4 | .... | 1989-90 | 1996-97 |
| • Plaxton, Hugh | Mtl.M. | 1 | 15 | 1 | 2 | 3 | 4 | .... | .... | .... | .... | .... | .... | 1932-33 | 1932-33 |
| Playfair, Jim | Edm., Chi. | 3 | 21 | 2 | 4 | 6 | 51 | .... | .... | .... | .... | .... | .... | 1983-84 | 1988-89 |
| Playfair, Larry | Buf., L.A. | 12 | 688 | 26 | 94 | 120 | 1812 | 43 | 0 | 6 | 6 | 111 | .... | 1978-79 | 1989-90 |
| Pleau, Larry | Mtl. | 3 | 94 | 9 | 15 | 24 | 27 | 4 | 0 | 0 | 0 | 0 | .... | 1969-70 | 1971-72 |
| ‡ Pletka, Vaclav | Phi. | 1 | 1 | 0 | 0 | 0 | 0 | .... | .... | .... | .... | .... | .... | 2001-02 | 2001-02 |
| • Pletsch, Charles | Ham. | 1 | 1 | 0 | 0 | 0 | 0 | .... | .... | .... | .... | .... | .... | 1920-21 | 1920-21 |
| Plett, Willi | Atl., Cgy., Min., Bos. | 13 | 834 | 222 | 215 | 437 | 2572 | 83 | 24 | 22 | 46 | 466 | .... | 1975-76 | 1987-88 |
| Plumb, Rob | Det. | 2 | 14 | 3 | 2 | 5 | 2 | .... | .... | .... | .... | .... | .... | 1977-78 | 1978-79 |
| Plumb, Ron | Hfd. | 1 | 26 | 3 | 4 | 7 | 14 | .... | .... | .... | .... | .... | .... | 1979-80 | 1979-80 |
| Poapst, Steve | Wsh., Chi., Pit., St.L. | 7 | 307 | 8 | 28 | 36 | 173 | 11 | 0 | 0 | 0 | 0 | .... | 1995-96 | 2005-06 |
| Pocza, Harvie | Wsh. | 2 | 3 | 0 | 0 | 0 | 2 | .... | .... | .... | .... | .... | .... | 1979-80 | 1981-82 |
| • Poddubny, Walt | Edm., Tor., NYR, Que., N.J. | 11 | 468 | 184 | 238 | 422 | 454 | 19 | 7 | 2 | 9 | 12 | .... | 1981-82 | 1991-92 |
| Podein, Shjon | Edm., Phi., Col., St.L. | 11 | 699 | 100 | 106 | 206 | 439 | 127 | 14 | 13 | 27 | 132 | 1 | 1992-93 | 2002-03 |
| ‡ Podkonicky, Andrej | Fla., Wsh. | 2 | 8 | 1 | 0 | 1 | 2 | .... | .... | .... | .... | .... | .... | 2000-01 | 2003-04 |
| Podloski, Ray | Bos. | 1 | 8 | 0 | 1 | 1 | 17 | .... | .... | .... | .... | .... | .... | 1988-89 | 1988-89 |
| Podollan, Jason | Fla., Tor., L.A., NYI | 4 | 41 | 1 | 5 | 6 | 19 | .... | .... | .... | .... | .... | .... | 1996-97 | 2001-02 |
| Podolsky, Nels | Det. | 1 | 1 | 0 | 0 | 0 | 0 | 7 | 0 | 0 | 0 | 4 | .... | 1948-49 | 1948-49 |
| Poeschek, Rudy | NYR, Wpg., T.B., St.L. | 12 | 364 | 6 | 25 | 31 | 817 | 5 | 0 | 0 | 0 | 18 | .... | 1987-88 | 1999-00 |
| • Poeta, Tony | Chi. | 1 | 1 | 0 | 0 | 0 | 0 | .... | .... | .... | .... | .... | .... | 1951-52 | 1951-52 |
| • Poile, Bud | Tor., Chi., Det., NYR, Bos. | 7 | 311 | 107 | 122 | 229 | 91 | 23 | 4 | 5 | 9 | 8 | 1 | 1942-43 | 1949-50 |
| Poile, Don | Det. | 2 | 66 | 7 | 9 | 16 | 12 | 4 | 0 | 0 | 0 | 0 | .... | 1954-55 | 1957-58 |
| • Poirier, Gordie | Mtl. | 1 | 10 | 0 | 0 | 0 | 0 | .... | .... | .... | .... | .... | .... | 1939-40 | 1939-40 |
| Polanic, Tom | Min. | 2 | 19 | 0 | 2 | 2 | 53 | 5 | 1 | 1 | 2 | 4 | .... | 1969-70 | 1970-71 |
| • Polich, John | NYR | 2 | 3 | 0 | 1 | 1 | 0 | .... | .... | .... | .... | .... | .... | 1939-40 | 1940-41 |
| Polich, Mike | Mtl., Min. | 5 | 226 | 24 | 29 | 53 | 57 | 23 | 2 | 1 | 3 | 2 | 1 | 1976-77 | 1980-81 |
| Polis, Greg | Pit., St.L., NYR, Wsh. | 10 | 615 | 174 | 169 | 343 | 391 | 7 | 0 | 2 | 2 | 6 | .... | 1970-71 | 1979-80 |
| Poliziani, Dan | Bos. | 1 | 1 | 0 | 0 | 0 | 0 | 3 | 0 | 0 | 0 | 0 | .... | 1958-59 | 1958-59 |
| ‡ Pollock, Jame | St.L. | 1 | 9 | 0 | 0 | 0 | 6 | .... | .... | .... | .... | .... | .... | 2003-04 | 2003-04 |
| Polonich, Dennis | Det. | 8 | 390 | 59 | 82 | 141 | 1242 | 7 | 1 | 0 | 1 | 19 | .... | 1974-75 | 1982-83 |
| Pooley, Paul | Wpg. | 2 | 15 | 0 | 3 | 3 | 0 | .... | .... | .... | .... | .... | .... | 1984-85 | 1985-86 |
| Popein, Larry | NYR, Oak. | 8 | 449 | 80 | 141 | 221 | 162 | 16 | 1 | 4 | 5 | 6 | .... | 1954-55 | 1967-68 |
| Popiel, Poul | Bos., L.A., Det., Van., Edm. | 7 | 224 | 13 | 41 | 54 | 210 | 4 | 1 | 0 | 1 | 4 | .... | 1965-66 | 1979-80 |
| Popovic, Peter | Mtl., NYR, Pit., Bos. | 8 | 485 | 10 | 63 | 73 | 291 | 35 | 1 | 4 | 5 | 18 | .... | 1993-94 | 2000-01 |
| • Portland, Jack | Mtl., Bos., Chi. | 10 | 381 | 15 | 56 | 71 | 323 | 33 | 1 | 3 | 4 | 25 | 1 | 1933-34 | 1942-43 |
| Porvari, Jukka | Col., N.J. | 2 | 39 | 3 | 9 | 12 | 4 | .... | .... | .... | .... | .... | .... | 1981-82 | 1982-83 |
| Posa, Victor | Chi. | 1 | 2 | 0 | 0 | 0 | 2 | .... | .... | .... | .... | .... | .... | 1985-86 | 1985-86 |
| Posavad, Mike | St.L. | 2 | 8 | 0 | 0 | 0 | 0 | .... | .... | .... | .... | .... | .... | 1985-86 | 1986-87 |
| ‡ Posmyk, Marek | T.B. | 2 | 19 | 1 | 2 | 3 | 20 | .... | .... | .... | .... | .... | .... | 1999-00 | 2000-01 |
| Potomski, Barry | L.A., S.J. | 3 | 68 | 6 | 5 | 11 | 227 | .... | .... | .... | .... | .... | .... | 1995-96 | 1997-98 |
| Potvin, Denis | NYI | 15 | 1060 | 310 | 742 | 1052 | 1356 | 185 | 56 | 108 | 164 | 253 | 4 | 1973-74 | 1987-88 |
| Potvin, Jean | L.A., Phi., NYI, Cle., Min. | 11 | 613 | 63 | 224 | 287 | 478 | 39 | 2 | 9 | 11 | 17 | 2 | 1970-71 | 1980-81 |
| • Potvin, Marc | Det., L.A., Hfd., Bos. | 6 | 121 | 3 | 5 | 8 | 456 | 13 | 0 | 1 | 1 | 50 | .... | 1990-91 | 1995-96 |
| Poudrier, Daniel | Que. | 3 | 25 | 1 | 5 | 6 | 10 | .... | .... | .... | .... | .... | .... | 1985-86 | 1987-88 |
| Poulin, Daniel | Min. | 1 | 3 | 1 | 1 | 2 | 2 | .... | .... | .... | .... | .... | .... | 1981-82 | 1981-82 |
| Poulin, Dave | Phi., Bos., Wsh. | 13 | 724 | 205 | 325 | 530 | 482 | 129 | 31 | 42 | 73 | 132 | .... | 1982-83 | 1994-95 |
| Poulin, Patrick | Hfd., Chi., T.B., Mtl. | 11 | 634 | 101 | 134 | 235 | 299 | 32 | 6 | 2 | 8 | 8 | .... | 1991-92 | 2001-02 |
| Pouzar, Jaroslav | Edm. | 4 | 186 | 34 | 48 | 82 | 135 | 29 | 6 | 4 | 10 | 16 | 3 | 1982-83 | 1986-87 |
| • Powell, Ray | Chi. | 1 | 31 | 7 | 15 | 22 | 2 | .... | .... | .... | .... | .... | .... | 1950-51 | 1950-51 |
| • Powis, Geoff | Chi. | 1 | 2 | 0 | 0 | 0 | 0 | .... | .... | .... | .... | .... | .... | 1967-68 | 1967-68 |
| Powis, Lynn | Chi., K.C. | 2 | 130 | 19 | 33 | 52 | 25 | 1 | 0 | 0 | 0 | 0 | .... | 1973-74 | 1974-75 |
| Prajsler, Petr | L.A., Bos. | 4 | 46 | 3 | 10 | 13 | 51 | 4 | 0 | 0 | 0 | 0 | .... | 1987-88 | 1991-92 |
| • Pratt, Babe | NYR, Tor., Bos. | 12 | 517 | 83 | 209 | 292 | 463 | 63 | 12 | 17 | 29 | 90 | 2 | 1935-36 | 1946-47 |
| • Pratt, Jack | Bos. | 2 | 37 | 2 | 0 | 2 | 42 | 4 | 0 | 0 | 0 | 0 | .... | 1930-31 | 1931-32 |
| Pratt, Kelly | Pit. | 1 | 22 | 0 | 6 | 6 | 15 | .... | .... | .... | .... | .... | .... | 1974-75 | 1974-75 |
| Pratt, Tracy | Oak., Pit., Buf., Van., Col., Tor. | 10 | 580 | 17 | 97 | 114 | 1026 | 25 | 0 | 1 | 1 | 62 | .... | 1967-68 | 1976-77 |
| Prentice, Dean | NYR, Bos., Det., Pit., Min. | 22 | 1378 | 391 | 469 | 860 | 484 | 54 | 13 | 17 | 30 | 38 | .... | 1952-53 | 1973-74 |
| • Prentice, Eric | Tor. | 1 | 5 | 0 | 0 | 0 | 4 | .... | .... | .... | .... | .... | .... | 1943-44 | 1943-44 |
| Presley, Wayne | Chi., S.J., Buf., NYR, Tor. | 12 | 684 | 155 | 147 | 302 | 953 | 83 | 26 | 17 | 43 | 142 | .... | 1984-85 | 1995-96 |
| Preston, Rich | Chi., N.J. | 8 | 580 | 127 | 164 | 291 | 348 | 47 | 4 | 18 | 22 | 56 | .... | 1979-80 | 1986-87 |
| Preston, Yves | Phi. | 2 | 28 | 7 | 3 | 10 | 4 | .... | .... | .... | .... | .... | .... | 1978-79 | 1980-81 |
| Priakin, Sergei | Cgy. | 3 | 46 | 3 | 8 | 11 | 2 | 3 | 0 | 0 | 0 | 0 | .... | 1988-89 | 1990-91 |
| Price, Jack | Chi. | 3 | 57 | 4 | 6 | 10 | 24 | 4 | 0 | 0 | 0 | 0 | .... | 1951-52 | 1953-54 |
| Price, Noel | Tor., NYR, Det., Mtl., Pit., L.A., Atl. | 14 | 499 | 14 | 114 | 128 | 333 | 12 | 0 | 1 | 1 | 8 | 1 | 1957-58 | 1975-76 |
| Price, Pat | NYI, Edm., Pit., Que., NYR, Min. | 13 | 726 | 43 | 218 | 261 | 1456 | 74 | 2 | 10 | 12 | 195 | .... | 1975-76 | 1987-88 |
| Price, Tom | Cal., Cle., Pit. | 5 | 29 | 0 | 2 | 2 | 12 | .... | .... | .... | .... | .... | .... | 1974-75 | 1978-79 |
| Priestlay, Ken | Buf., Pit. | 6 | 168 | 27 | 34 | 61 | 63 | 14 | 0 | 0 | 0 | 21 | 1 | 1986-87 | 1991-92 |
| • Primeau, Joe | Tor. | 9 | 310 | 66 | 177 | 243 | 105 | 38 | 5 | 18 | 23 | 12 | 1 | 1927-28 | 1935-36 |
| Primeau, Keith | Det., Hfd., Car., Phi. | 15 | 909 | 266 | 353 | 619 | 1541 | 128 | 18 | 39 | 57 | 213 | .... | 1990-91 | 2005-06 |
| Primeau, Kevin | Van. | 1 | 2 | 0 | 0 | 0 | 4 | .... | .... | .... | .... | .... | .... | 1980-81 | 1980-81 |
| • Pringle, Ellie | NYA | 1 | 6 | 0 | 0 | 0 | 0 | .... | .... | .... | .... | .... | .... | 1930-31 | 1930-31 |
| ‡ Printz, David | Phi. | 2 | 13 | 0 | 0 | 0 | 4 | .... | .... | .... | .... | .... | .... | 2005-06 | 2006-07 |
| Probert, Bob | Det., Chi. | 16 | 935 | 163 | 221 | 384 | 3300 | 81 | 16 | 32 | 48 | 274 | .... | 1985-86 | 2001-02 |
| ‡ Prochazka, Martin | Tor., Atl. | 2 | 32 | 2 | 5 | 7 | 8 | .... | .... | .... | .... | .... | .... | 1997-98 | 1999-00 |
| • Prodger, Goldie | Tor., Ham. | 6 | 111 | 63 | 29 | 92 | 39 | .... | .... | .... | .... | .... | .... | 1919-20 | 1924-25 |
| Prokhorov, Vitali | St.L. | 3 | 83 | 19 | 11 | 30 | 35 | 4 | 0 | 0 | 0 | 0 | .... | 1992-93 | 1994-95 |
| Prokopec, Mike | Chi. | 2 | 15 | 0 | 0 | 0 | 11 | .... | .... | .... | .... | .... | .... | 1995-96 | 1996-97 |
| Pronger, Sean | Ana., Pit., NYR, L.A., Bos., CBJ, Van. | 8 | 260 | 23 | 36 | 59 | 159 | 14 | 0 | 2 | 2 | 8 | .... | 1995-96 | 2003-04 |
| Pronovost, Andre | Mtl., Bos., Det., Min. | 10 | 556 | 94 | 104 | 198 | 408 | 70 | 11 | 11 | 22 | 58 | 4 | 1956-57 | 1967-68 |
| Pronovost, Jean | Pit., Atl., Wsh. | 14 | 998 | 391 | 383 | 774 | 413 | 35 | 11 | 9 | 20 | 14 | .... | 1968-69 | 1981-82 |
| Pronovost, Marcel | Det., Tor. | 21 | 1206 | 88 | 257 | 345 | 851 | 134 | 8 | 23 | 31 | 104 | 5 | 1949-50 | 1969-70 |
| Propp, Brian | Phi., Bos., Min., Hfd. | 15 | 1016 | 425 | 579 | 1004 | 830 | 160 | 64 | 84 | 148 | 151 | .... | 1979-80 | 1993-94 |
| Proulx, Christian | Mtl. | 1 | 7 | 1 | 2 | 3 | 20 | .... | .... | .... | .... | .... | .... | 1993-94 | 1993-94 |
| • Provost, Claude | Mtl. | 15 | 1005 | 254 | 335 | 589 | 469 | 126 | 25 | 38 | 63 | 86 | 9 | 1955-56 | 1969-70 |
| Prpic, Joel | Bos., Col. | 3 | 18 | 0 | 3 | 3 | 4 | .... | .... | .... | .... | .... | .... | 1997-98 | 2000-01 |
| Pryor, Chris | Min., NYI | 6 | 82 | 1 | 4 | 5 | 122 | .... | .... | .... | .... | .... | .... | 1984-85 | 1989-90 |
| Prystai, Metro | Chi., Det. | 11 | 674 | 151 | 179 | 330 | 231 | 43 | 12 | 14 | 26 | 8 | 2 | 1947-48 | 1957-58 |
| • Pudas, Al | Tor. | 1 | 4 | 0 | 0 | 0 | 0 | .... | .... | .... | .... | .... | .... | 1926-27 | 1926-27 |
| Pulford, Bob | Tor., L.A. | 16 | 1079 | 281 | 362 | 643 | 792 | 89 | 25 | 26 | 51 | 126 | 4 | 1956-57 | 1971-72 |
| Pulkkinen, Dave | NYI | 1 | 2 | 0 | 0 | 0 | 0 | .... | .... | .... | .... | .... | .... | 1972-73 | 1972-73 |
| Purinton, Dale | NYR | 5 | 181 | 4 | 16 | 20 | 578 | .... | .... | .... | .... | .... | .... | 1999-00 | 2003-04 |
| • Purpur, Fido | St.L., Chi., Det. | 5 | 144 | 25 | 35 | 60 | 46 | 16 | 1 | 2 | 3 | 4 | .... | 1934-35 | 1944-45 |

| | | | Regular Schedule | | | | | Playoffs | | | | | | | |
|---|---|---|---|---|---|---|---|---|---|---|---|---|---|---|---|
| Name | NHL Teams | NHL Seasons | GP | G | A | TP | PIM | GP | G | A | TP | PIM | NHL Cup Wins | First NHL Season | Last NHL Season |
| Purves, John | Wsh. | 1 | 7 | 1 | 0 | 1 | 0 | .... | .... | .... | .... | .... | .... | 1990-91 | 1990-91 |
| Pushor, Jamie | Det., Ana., Dal., CBJ, Pit., NYR | 10 | 521 | 14 | 46 | 60 | 648 | 14 | 0 | 1 | 1 | 16 | 1 | 1995-96 | 2005-06 |
| • Pusie, Jean | Mtl., NYR, Bos. | 5 | 61 | 1 | 4 | 5 | 28 | 7 | 0 | 0 | 0 | 0 | 1 | 1930-31 | 1935-36 |
| Pyatt, Nelson | Det., Wsh., Col. | 7 | 296 | 71 | 63 | 134 | 69 | .... | .... | .... | .... | .... | .... | 1973-74 | 1979-80 |
| **Q** | | | | | | | | | | | | | | | |
| • Quackenbush, Bill | Det., Bos. | 14 | 774 | 62 | 222 | 284 | 95 | 80 | 2 | 19 | 21 | 8 | .... | 1942-43 | 1955-56 |
| Quackenbush, Max | Bos., Chi. | 2 | 61 | 4 | 7 | 11 | 30 | 6 | 0 | 0 | 0 | 4 | .... | 1950-51 | 1951-52 |
| Quenneville, Joel | Tor., Col., N.J., Hfd., Wsh. | 13 | 803 | 54 | 136 | 190 | 705 | 32 | 0 | 8 | 8 | 22 | .... | 1978-79 | 1990-91 |
| • Quenneville, Leo | NYR | 1 | 25 | 0 | 3 | 3 | 10 | 3 | 0 | 0 | 0 | 0 | .... | 1929-30 | 1929-30 |
| • Quilty, John | Mtl., Bos. | 4 | 125 | 36 | 34 | 70 | 81 | 13 | 3 | 5 | 8 | 9 | .... | 1940-41 | 1947-48 |
| Quinn, Dan | Cgy., Pit., Van., St.L., Phi., Min., Ott., L.A. | 14 | 805 | 266 | 419 | 685 | 533 | 65 | 22 | 26 | 48 | 62 | .... | 1983-84 | 1996-97 |
| Quinn, Pat | Tor., Van., Atl. | 9 | 606 | 18 | 113 | 131 | 950 | 11 | 0 | 1 | 1 | 21 | .... | 1968-69 | 1976-77 |
| Quinney, Ken | Que. | 3 | 59 | 7 | 13 | 20 | 23 | .... | .... | .... | .... | .... | .... | 1986-87 | 1990-91 |
| ‡ Quint, Deron | Wpg., Phx., N.J., CBJ, Chi., NYI | 10 | 463 | 46 | 97 | 143 | 166 | 7 | 0 | 2 | 2 | 0 | .... | 1995-96 | 2006-07 |
| Quintal, Stephane | Bos., St.L., Wpg., Mtl., NYR, Chi. | 16 | 1037 | 63 | 180 | 243 | 1320 | 52 | 2 | 10 | 12 | 51 | .... | 1988-89 | 2003-04 |
| Quintin, Jean-Francois | S.J. | 2 | 22 | 5 | 5 | 10 | 4 | .... | .... | .... | .... | .... | .... | 1991-92 | 1992-93 |
| **R** | | | | | | | | | | | | | | | |
| Racine, Yves | Det., Phi., Mtl., S.J., Cgy., T.B. | 9 | 508 | 37 | 194 | 231 | 439 | 25 | 5 | 4 | 9 | 37 | .... | 1989-90 | 1997-98 |
| • Radley, Yip | NYA, Mtl.M. | 2 | 18 | 0 | 1 | 1 | 13 | .... | .... | .... | .... | .... | .... | 1930-31 | 1936-37 |
| ‡ Radulov, Igor | Chi. | 2 | 43 | 9 | 7 | 16 | 22 | .... | .... | .... | .... | .... | .... | 2002-03 | 2003-04 |
| Raglan, Herb | St.L., Que., T.B., Ott. | 9 | 343 | 33 | 56 | 89 | 775 | 32 | 3 | 6 | 9 | 50 | .... | 1985-86 | 1993-94 |
| • Raglan, Rags | Det., Chi. | 3 | 100 | 4 | 9 | 13 | 52 | 3 | 0 | 0 | 0 | 0 | .... | 1950-51 | 1952-53 |
| ‡ Ragnarsson, Marcus | S.J., Phi. | 9 | 632 | 37 | 140 | 177 | 482 | 68 | 2 | 13 | 15 | 60 | .... | 1995-96 | 2003-04 |
| Raleigh, Don | NYR | 10 | 535 | 101 | 219 | 320 | 96 | 18 | 6 | 5 | 11 | 6 | .... | 1943-44 | 1955-56 |
| ‡ Ralph, Brad | Phx. | 1 | 1 | 0 | 0 | 0 | 0 | .... | .... | .... | .... | .... | .... | 2000-01 | 2000-01 |
| Ramage, Rob | Col., St.L., Cgy., Tor., Min., T.B., Mtl., Phi. | 15 | 1044 | 139 | 425 | 564 | 2226 | 84 | 8 | 42 | 50 | 218 | 2 | 1979-80 | 1993-94 |
| • Ramsay, Beattie | Tor. | 1 | 43 | 0 | 2 | 2 | 10 | .... | .... | .... | .... | .... | .... | 1927-28 | 1927-28 |
| Ramsay, Craig | Buf. | 14 | 1070 | 252 | 420 | 672 | 201 | 89 | 17 | 31 | 48 | 27 | .... | 1971-72 | 1984-85 |
| Ramsay, Les | Chi. | 1 | 11 | 2 | 2 | 4 | 2 | .... | .... | .... | .... | .... | .... | 1944-45 | 1944-45 |
| Ramsey, Mike | Buf., Pit., Det. | 18 | 1070 | 79 | 266 | 345 | 1012 | 115 | 8 | 29 | 37 | 176 | .... | 1979-80 | 1996-97 |
| Ramsey, Wayne | Buf. | 1 | 2 | 0 | 0 | 0 | 0 | .... | .... | .... | .... | .... | .... | 1977-78 | 1977-78 |
| • Randall, Ken | Tor., Ham., NYA | 10 | 218 | 68 | 50 | 118 | 533 | 6 | 2 | 1 | 3 | 27 | 2 | 1917-18 | 1926-27 |
| Ranheim, Paul | Cgy., Hfd., Car., Phi., Phx. | 15 | 1013 | 161 | 199 | 360 | 288 | 36 | 3 | 8 | 11 | 6 | .... | 1988-89 | 2002-03 |
| Ranieri, George | Bos. | 1 | 2 | 0 | 0 | 0 | 0 | .... | .... | .... | .... | .... | .... | 1956-57 | 1956-57 |
| ‡ Ratchuk, Peter | Fla. | 2 | 32 | 1 | 1 | 2 | 10 | .... | .... | .... | .... | .... | .... | 1998-99 | 2000-01 |
| Ratelle, Jean | NYR, Bos. | 21 | 1281 | 491 | 776 | 1267 | 276 | 123 | 32 | 66 | 98 | 24 | .... | 1960-61 | 1980-81 |
| Rathje, Mike | S.J., Phi. | 13 | 768 | 30 | 150 | 180 | 491 | 77 | 9 | 14 | 23 | 51 | .... | 1993-94 | 2006-07 |
| Rathwell, Jake | Bos. | 1 | 1 | 0 | 0 | 0 | 0 | .... | .... | .... | .... | .... | .... | 1974-75 | 1974-75 |
| Ratushny, Dan | Van. | 1 | 1 | 0 | 1 | 1 | 2 | .... | .... | .... | .... | .... | .... | 1992-93 | 1992-93 |
| Rausse, Errol | Wsh. | 3 | 31 | 7 | 3 | 10 | 0 | .... | .... | .... | .... | .... | .... | 1979-80 | 1981-82 |
| Rautakallio, Pekka | Atl., Cgy. | 3 | 235 | 33 | 121 | 154 | 122 | 23 | 2 | 5 | 7 | 8 | .... | 1979-80 | 1981-82 |
| Ravlich, Matt | Bos., Chi., Det., L.A. | 10 | 410 | 12 | 78 | 90 | 364 | 24 | 1 | 5 | 6 | 16 | .... | 1962-63 | 1972-73 |
| Ray, Rob | Buf., Ott. | 15 | 900 | 41 | 50 | 91 | 3207 | 55 | 3 | 2 | 5 | 169 | .... | 1989-90 | 2003-04 |
| • Raymond, Armand | Mtl. | 2 | 22 | 0 | 2 | 2 | 10 | .... | .... | .... | .... | .... | .... | 1937-38 | 1939-40 |
| • Raymond, Paul | Mtl. | 4 | 76 | 2 | 3 | 5 | 6 | 5 | 0 | 0 | 0 | 2 | .... | 1932-33 | 1938-39 |
| • Read, Mel | NYR | 1 | 1 | 0 | 0 | 0 | 0 | .... | .... | .... | .... | .... | .... | 1946-47 | 1946-47 |
| ‡ Ready, Ryan | Phi. | 1 | 7 | 0 | 1 | 1 | 0 | .... | .... | .... | .... | .... | .... | 2005-06 | 2005-06 |
| • Reardon, Ken | Mtl. | 7 | 341 | 26 | 96 | 122 | 604 | 31 | 2 | 5 | 7 | 62 | 1 | 1940-41 | 1949-50 |
| • Reardon, Terry | Bos., Mtl. | 7 | 193 | 47 | 53 | 100 | 73 | 30 | 8 | 10 | 18 | 12 | 1 | 1938-39 | 1946-47 |
| Reaume, Marc | Tor., Det., Mtl., Van. | 9 | 344 | 8 | 43 | 51 | 273 | 21 | 0 | 2 | 2 | 8 | .... | 1954-55 | 1970-71 |
| • Reay, Billy | Det., Mtl. | 10 | 479 | 105 | 162 | 267 | 202 | 63 | 13 | 16 | 29 | 43 | 2 | 1943-44 | 1952-53 |
| Redahl, Gord | Bos. | 1 | 18 | 0 | 1 | 1 | 2 | .... | .... | .... | .... | .... | .... | 1958-59 | 1958-59 |
| • Redding, George | Bos. | 2 | 55 | 3 | 2 | 5 | 23 | .... | .... | .... | .... | .... | .... | 1924-25 | 1925-26 |
| Redmond, Craig | L.A., Edm. | 5 | 191 | 16 | 68 | 84 | 134 | 3 | 1 | 0 | 1 | 2 | .... | 1984-85 | 1988-89 |
| Redmond, Dick | Min., Cal., Chi., St.L., Atl., Bos. | 13 | 771 | 133 | 312 | 445 | 504 | 66 | 9 | 22 | 31 | 27 | .... | 1969-70 | 1981-82 |
| Redmond, Keith | L.A. | 1 | 12 | 1 | 0 | 1 | 20 | .... | .... | .... | .... | .... | .... | 1993-94 | 1993-94 |
| Redmond, Mickey | Mtl., Det. | 9 | 538 | 233 | 195 | 428 | 219 | 16 | 2 | 3 | 5 | 2 | 2 | 1967-68 | 1975-76 |
| Reeds, Mark | St.L., Hfd. | 8 | 365 | 45 | 114 | 159 | 135 | 53 | 8 | 9 | 17 | 23 | .... | 1981-82 | 1988-89 |
| Reekie, Joe | Buf., NYI, T.B., Wsh., Chi. | 17 | 902 | 25 | 139 | 164 | 1326 | 51 | 3 | 4 | 7 | 63 | .... | 1985-86 | 2001-02 |
| • Regan, Bill | NYR, NYA | 3 | 67 | 3 | 2 | 5 | 67 | 8 | 0 | 0 | 0 | 2 | .... | 1929-30 | 1932-33 |
| • Regan, Larry | Bos., Tor. | 5 | 280 | 41 | 95 | 136 | 71 | 42 | 7 | 14 | 21 | 18 | .... | 1956-57 | 1960-61 |
| ‡ Regehr, Richie | Cgy. | 2 | 20 | 1 | 3 | 4 | 6 | .... | .... | .... | .... | .... | .... | 2005-06 | 2006-07 |
| Regier, Darcy | Cle., NYI | 3 | 26 | 0 | 2 | 2 | 35 | .... | .... | .... | .... | .... | .... | 1977-78 | 1983-84 |
| • Reibel, Dutch | Det., Chi., Bos. | 6 | 409 | 84 | 161 | 245 | 75 | 39 | 6 | 14 | 20 | 4 | 2 | 1953-54 | 1958-59 |
| ‡ Reichel, Robert | Cgy., NYI, Phx., Tor. | 11 | 830 | 252 | 378 | 630 | 388 | 70 | 8 | 23 | 31 | 20 | .... | 1990-91 | 2003-04 |
| Reichert, Craig | Ana. | 1 | 3 | 0 | 0 | 0 | 0 | .... | .... | .... | .... | .... | .... | 1996-97 | 1996-97 |
| ‡ Reid, Brandon | Van. | 3 | 13 | 2 | 4 | 6 | 0 | 10 | 0 | 2 | 2 | 0 | .... | 2002-03 | 2006-07 |
| • Reid, Dave | Tor. | 3 | 7 | 0 | 0 | 0 | 0 | .... | .... | .... | .... | .... | .... | 1952-53 | 1955-56 |
| Reid, Dave | Bos., Tor., Dal., Col. | 18 | 961 | 165 | 204 | 369 | 253 | 118 | 9 | 26 | 35 | 34 | 2 | 1983-84 | 2000-01 |
| Reid, Gerry | Det. | 1 | .... | .... | .... | .... | .... | 2 | 0 | 0 | 0 | 2 | .... | 1948-49 | 1948-49 |
| Reid, Gord | NYA | 1 | 1 | 0 | 0 | 0 | 2 | .... | .... | .... | .... | .... | .... | 1936-37 | 1936-37 |
| • Reid, Reg | Tor. | 2 | 39 | 1 | 0 | 1 | 4 | 2 | 0 | 0 | 0 | 0 | .... | 1924-25 | 1925-26 |
| Reid, Tom | Chi., Min. | 11 | 701 | 17 | 113 | 130 | 654 | 42 | 1 | 13 | 14 | 49 | .... | 1967-68 | 1977-78 |
| Reierson, Dave | Cgy. | 1 | 2 | 0 | 0 | 0 | 2 | .... | .... | .... | .... | .... | .... | 1988-89 | 1988-89 |
| • Reigle, Ed | Bos. | 1 | 17 | 0 | 2 | 2 | 25 | .... | .... | .... | .... | .... | .... | 1950-51 | 1950-51 |
| Reinhart, Paul | Atl., Cgy., Van. | 11 | 648 | 133 | 426 | 559 | 277 | 83 | 23 | 54 | 77 | 42 | .... | 1979-80 | 1989-90 |
| • Reinikka, Ollie | NYR | 1 | 16 | 0 | 0 | 0 | 0 | .... | .... | .... | .... | .... | .... | 1926-27 | 1926-27 |
| Reirden, Todd | Edm., St.L., Atl., Phx. | 5 | 183 | 11 | 35 | 46 | 181 | 5 | 0 | 1 | 1 | 0 | .... | 1998-99 | 2003-04 |
| • Reise, Leo | Ham., NYA, NYR | 8 | 223 | 36 | 29 | 65 | 181 | 6 | 0 | 0 | 0 | 16 | .... | 1920-21 | 1929-30 |
| Reise, Leo | Chi., Det., NYR | 9 | 494 | 28 | 81 | 109 | 399 | 52 | 8 | 5 | 13 | 68 | 2 | 1945-46 | 1953-54 |
| Renaud, Mark | Hfd., Buf. | 5 | 152 | 6 | 50 | 56 | 86 | .... | .... | .... | .... | .... | .... | 1979-80 | 1983-84 |
| ‡ Renberg, Mikael | Phi., T.B., Phx., Tor. | 10 | 661 | 190 | 274 | 464 | 372 | 67 | 16 | 22 | 38 | 42 | .... | 1993-94 | 2003-04 |
| Reynolds, Bobby | Tor. | 1 | 7 | 1 | 1 | 2 | 0 | .... | .... | .... | .... | .... | .... | 1989-90 | 1989-90 |
| Ribble, Pat | Atl., Chi., Tor., Wsh., Cgy. | 8 | 349 | 19 | 60 | 79 | 365 | 8 | 0 | 1 | 1 | 12 | .... | 1975-76 | 1982-83 |
| Ricci, Mike | Phi., Que., Col., S.J., Phx. | 16 | 1099 | 243 | 362 | 605 | 974 | 110 | 23 | 43 | 66 | 77 | 1 | 1990-91 | 2006-07 |
| Rice, Steven | NYR, Edm., Hfd., Car. | 8 | 329 | 64 | 61 | 125 | 275 | 2 | 2 | 1 | 3 | 6 | .... | 1990-91 | 1997-98 |
| Richard, Henri | Mtl. | 20 | 1256 | 358 | 688 | 1046 | 928 | 180 | 49 | 80 | 129 | 181 | 11 | 1955-56 | 1974-75 |
| • Richard, Jacques | Atl., Buf., Que. | 10 | 556 | 160 | 187 | 347 | 307 | 35 | 5 | 5 | 10 | 34 | .... | 1972-73 | 1982-83 |
| Richard, Jean-Marc | Que. | 2 | 5 | 2 | 1 | 3 | 2 | .... | .... | .... | .... | .... | .... | 1987-88 | 1989-90 |
| • Richard, Maurice | Mtl. | 18 | 978 | 544 | 421 | 965 | 1285 | 133 | 82 | 44 | 126 | 188 | 8 | 1942-43 | 1959-60 |
| ‡ Richard, Mike | Wsh. | 2 | 7 | 0 | 2 | 2 | 0 | .... | .... | .... | .... | .... | .... | 1987-88 | 1989-90 |
| Richards, Todd | Hfd. | 2 | 8 | 0 | 4 | 4 | 4 | 11 | 0 | 3 | 3 | 6 | .... | 1990-91 | 1991-92 |
| Richards, Travis | Dal. | 2 | 3 | 0 | 0 | 0 | 2 | .... | .... | .... | .... | .... | .... | 1994-95 | 1995-96 |
| Richardson, Dave | NYR, Chi., Det. | 4 | 45 | 3 | 2 | 5 | 27 | .... | .... | .... | .... | .... | .... | 1963-64 | 1967-68 |
| Richardson, Glen | Van. | 1 | 24 | 3 | 6 | 9 | 19 | .... | .... | .... | .... | .... | .... | 1975-76 | 1975-76 |
| Richardson, Ken | St.L. | 3 | 49 | 8 | 13 | 21 | 16 | .... | .... | .... | .... | .... | .... | 1974-75 | 1978-79 |
| Richer, Bob | Buf. | 1 | 3 | 0 | 0 | 0 | 0 | .... | .... | .... | .... | .... | .... | 1972-73 | 1972-73 |
| Richer, Stephane | Mtl., N.J., T.B., St.L., Pit. | 17 | 1054 | 421 | 398 | 819 | 614 | 134 | 53 | 45 | 98 | 61 | 2 | 1984-85 | 2001-02 |
| Richer, Stephane | T.B., Bos., Fla. | 3 | 27 | 1 | 5 | 6 | 20 | 3 | 0 | 0 | 0 | 0 | .... | 1992-93 | 1994-95 |
| Richmond, Steve | NYR, Det., N.J., L.A. | 5 | 159 | 4 | 23 | 27 | 514 | 4 | 0 | 0 | 0 | 12 | .... | 1983-84 | 1988-89 |
| ‡ Richter, Barry | NYR, Bos., NYI, Mtl. | 5 | 151 | 11 | 34 | 45 | 76 | .... | .... | .... | .... | .... | .... | 1995-96 | 2000-01 |
| Richter, Dave | Min., Phi., Van., St.L. | 9 | 365 | 9 | 40 | 49 | 1030 | 22 | 1 | 0 | 1 | 80 | .... | 1981-82 | 1989-90 |
| Ridley, Mike | NYR, Wsh., Tor., Van. | 12 | 866 | 292 | 466 | 758 | 424 | 104 | 28 | 50 | 78 | 70 | .... | 1985-86 | 1996-97 |
| ‡ Riesen, Michel | Edm. | 1 | 12 | 0 | 1 | 1 | 4 | .... | .... | .... | .... | .... | .... | 2000-01 | 2000-01 |
| Riley, Bill | Wsh., Wpg. | 5 | 139 | 31 | 30 | 61 | 320 | .... | .... | .... | .... | .... | .... | 1974-75 | 1979-80 |
| • Riley, Jack | Det., Mtl., Bos. | 4 | 104 | 10 | 22 | 32 | 8 | 4 | 0 | 3 | 3 | 0 | .... | 1932-33 | 1935-36 |
| • Riley, Jim | Chi., Det. | 1 | 9 | 0 | 2 | 2 | 14 | .... | .... | .... | .... | .... | .... | 1926-27 | 1926-27 |
| Riopelle, Rip | Mtl. | 3 | 169 | 27 | 16 | 43 | 73 | 8 | 1 | 1 | 2 | 2 | .... | 1947-48 | 1949-50 |
| Rioux, Gerry | Wpg. | 1 | 8 | 0 | 0 | 0 | 6 | .... | .... | .... | .... | .... | .... | 1979-80 | 1979-80 |
| Rioux, Pierre | Cgy. | 1 | 14 | 1 | 2 | 3 | 4 | .... | .... | .... | .... | .... | .... | 1982-83 | 1982-83 |
| • Ripley, Vic | Chi., Bos., NYR, St.L. | 7 | 278 | 51 | 49 | 100 | 173 | 20 | 4 | 1 | 5 | 10 | .... | 1928-29 | 1934-35 |
| Risebrough, Doug | Mtl., Cgy. | 13 | 740 | 185 | 286 | 471 | 1542 | 124 | 21 | 37 | 58 | 238 | 4 | 1974-75 | 1986-87 |
| Rissling, Gary | Wsh., Pit. | 7 | 221 | 23 | 30 | 53 | 1008 | 5 | 0 | 1 | 1 | 4 | .... | 1978-79 | 1984-85 |
| ‡ Rita, Jani | Edm., Pit. | 4 | 66 | 9 | 5 | 14 | 10 | .... | .... | .... | .... | .... | .... | 2001-02 | 2005-06 |
| Ritchie, Bob | Phi., Det. | 2 | 29 | 8 | 4 | 12 | 10 | .... | .... | .... | .... | .... | .... | 1976-77 | 1977-78 |
| • Ritchie, Dave | Mtl.W., Ott., Tor., Que., Mtl. | 6 | 58 | 15 | 6 | 21 | 50 | 1 | 0 | 0 | 0 | 0 | .... | 1917-18 | 1925-26 |
| Ritson, Alex | NYR | 1 | 1 | 0 | 0 | 0 | 0 | .... | .... | .... | .... | .... | .... | 1944-45 | 1944-45 |
| Rittinger, Alan | Bos. | 1 | 19 | 3 | 7 | 10 | 0 | .... | .... | .... | .... | .... | .... | 1943-44 | 1943-44 |
| Rivard, Bob | Pit. | 1 | 27 | 5 | 12 | 17 | 4 | .... | .... | .... | .... | .... | .... | 1967-68 | 1967-68 |
| • Rivers, Gus | Mtl. | 3 | 88 | 4 | 5 | 9 | 12 | 16 | 2 | 0 | 2 | 2 | 2 | 1929-30 | 1931-32 |

*Billy Reay*

*Stephane Richer*

*Doug Risebrough*

*Shawn Rivers*

Jim Roberts

Warren Rychel

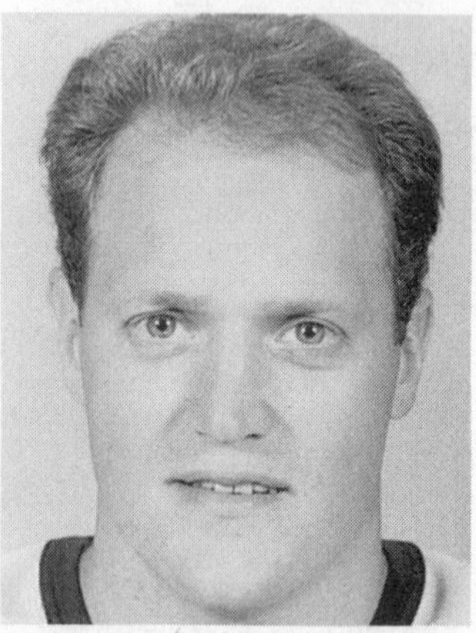

David Sacco

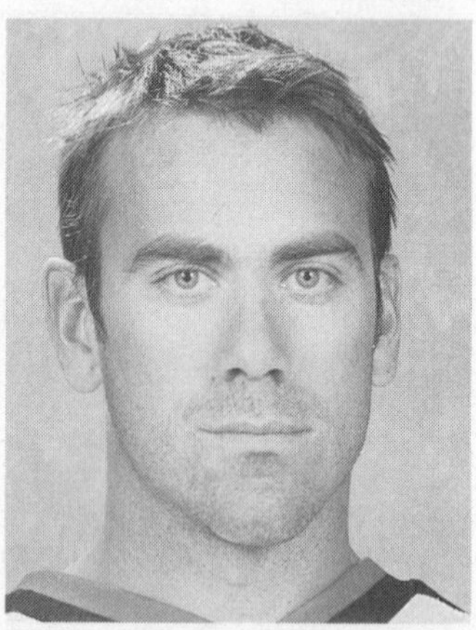

Geoff Sanderson

| | | | Regular Schedule | | | | | Playoffs | | | | | | | |
|---|---|---|---|---|---|---|---|---|---|---|---|---|---|---|---|
| Name | NHL Teams | NHL Seasons | GP | G | A | TP | PIM | GP | G | A | TP | PIM | NHL Cup Wins | First NHL Season | Last NHL Season |
| Rivers, Shawn | T.B. | 1 | 4 | 0 | 2 | 2 | 2 | .... | .... | .... | .... | .... | .... | 1992-93 | 1992-93 |
| Rivers, Wayne | Det., Bos., St.L., NYR | 7 | 108 | 15 | 30 | 45 | 94 | .... | .... | .... | .... | .... | .... | 1961-62 | 1968-69 |
| Rizzuto, Garth | Van. | 1 | 37 | 3 | 4 | 7 | 16 | .... | .... | .... | .... | .... | .... | 1970-71 | 1970-71 |
| ‡ Roach, Andy | St.L. | 1 | 5 | 1 | 2 | 3 | 10 | .... | .... | .... | .... | .... | .... | 2005-06 | 2005-06 |
| • Roach, Mickey | Tor., Ham., NYA | 8 | 211 | 77 | 34 | 111 | 54 | .... | .... | .... | .... | .... | .... | 1919-20 | 1926-27 |
| Roberge, Mario | Mtl. | 5 | 112 | 7 | 7 | 14 | 314 | 15 | 0 | 0 | 0 | 24 | 1 | 1990-91 | 1994-95 |
| Roberge, Serge | Que. | 1 | 9 | 0 | 0 | 0 | 24 | .... | .... | .... | .... | .... | .... | 1990-91 | 1990-91 |
| • Robert, Claude | Mtl. | 1 | 23 | 1 | 0 | 1 | 9 | .... | .... | .... | .... | .... | .... | 1950-51 | 1950-51 |
| Robert, Rene | Tor., Pit., Buf., Col. | 12 | 744 | 284 | 418 | 702 | 597 | 50 | 22 | 19 | 41 | 73 | .... | 1970-71 | 1981-82 |
| Roberto, Phil | Mtl., St.L., Det., K.C., Col., Cle. | 8 | 385 | 75 | 106 | 181 | 464 | 31 | 9 | 8 | 17 | 69 | 1 | 1969-70 | 1976-77 |
| Roberts, David | St.L., Edm., Van. | 5 | 125 | 20 | 33 | 53 | 85 | 9 | 0 | 0 | 0 | 16 | .... | 1993-94 | 1997-98 |
| Roberts, Doug | Det., Oak., Cal., Bos. | 10 | 419 | 43 | 104 | 147 | 342 | 16 | 2 | 3 | 5 | 46 | .... | 1965-66 | 1974-75 |
| Roberts, Gordie | Hfd., Min., Phi., St.L., Pit., Bos. | 15 | 1097 | 61 | 359 | 420 | 1582 | 153 | 10 | 47 | 57 | 273 | 2 | 1979-80 | 1993-94 |
| Roberts, Jim | Min. | 3 | 106 | 17 | 23 | 40 | 33 | 2 | 0 | 0 | 0 | 0 | .... | 1976-77 | 1978-79 |
| Roberts, Jimmy | Mtl., St.L. | 15 | 1006 | 126 | 194 | 320 | 621 | 153 | 20 | 16 | 36 | 160 | 5 | 1963-64 | 1977-78 |
| • Robertson, Fred | Tor., Det. | 2 | 34 | 1 | 0 | 1 | 35 | 7 | 0 | 0 | 0 | 0 | 1 | 1931-32 | 1933-34 |
| Robertson, Geordie | Buf. | 1 | 5 | 1 | 2 | 3 | 7 | .... | .... | .... | .... | .... | .... | 1982-83 | 1982-83 |
| • Robertson, George | Mtl. | 2 | 31 | 2 | 5 | 7 | 6 | .... | .... | .... | .... | .... | .... | 1947-48 | 1948-49 |
| Robertson, Torrie | Wsh., Hfd., Det. | 10 | 442 | 49 | 99 | 148 | 1751 | 22 | 2 | 1 | 3 | 90 | .... | 1980-81 | 1989-90 |
| Robertsson, Bert | Van., Edm., NYR | 4 | 123 | 4 | 10 | 14 | 75 | 5 | 0 | 0 | 0 | 0 | .... | 1997-98 | 2000-01 |
| Robidoux, Florent | Chi. | 3 | 52 | 7 | 4 | 11 | 75 | .... | .... | .... | .... | .... | .... | 1980-81 | 1983-84 |
| Robinson, Doug | Chi., NYR, L.A. | 7 | 239 | 44 | 67 | 111 | 34 | 11 | 4 | 3 | 7 | 0 | .... | 1963-64 | 1970-71 |
| • Robinson, Earl | Mtl.M., Chi., Mtl. | 11 | 417 | 83 | 98 | 181 | 133 | 25 | 5 | 4 | 9 | 0 | 1 | 1928-29 | 1939-40 |
| Robinson, Larry | Mtl., L.A. | 20 | 1384 | 208 | 750 | 958 | 793 | 227 | 28 | 116 | 144 | 211 | 6 | 1972-73 | 1991-92 |
| Robinson, Moe | Mtl. | 1 | 1 | 0 | 0 | 0 | 0 | .... | .... | .... | .... | .... | .... | 1979-80 | 1979-80 |
| ‡ Robinson, Nathan | Det., Bos. | 2 | 7 | 0 | 0 | 0 | 2 | .... | .... | .... | .... | .... | .... | 2003-04 | 2005-06 |
| Robinson, Rob | St.L. | 1 | 22 | 0 | 1 | 1 | 8 | .... | .... | .... | .... | .... | .... | 1991-92 | 1991-92 |
| Robinson, Scott | Min. | 1 | 1 | 0 | 0 | 0 | 2 | .... | .... | .... | .... | .... | .... | 1989-90 | 1989-90 |
| ‡ Robitaille, Louis | Wsh. | 1 | 2 | 0 | 0 | 0 | 5 | .... | .... | .... | .... | .... | .... | 2005-06 | 2005-06 |
| Robitaille, Luc | L.A., Pit., NYR, Det. | 19 | 1431 | 668 | 726 | 1394 | 1177 | 159 | 58 | 69 | 127 | 174 | 1 | 1986-87 | 2005-06 |
| Robitaille, Mike | NYR, Det., Buf., Van. | 8 | 382 | 23 | 105 | 128 | 280 | 13 | 0 | 1 | 1 | 4 | .... | 1969-70 | 1976-77 |
| Roche, Dave | Pit., Cgy., NYI | 5 | 171 | 15 | 15 | 30 | 334 | 16 | 2 | 7 | 9 | 26 | .... | 1995-96 | 2001-02 |
| • Roche, Des | Mtl.M., Ott., St.L., Mtl., Det. | 4 | 113 | 20 | 18 | 38 | 44 | .... | .... | .... | .... | .... | .... | 1930-31 | 1934-35 |
| • Roche, Earl | Mtl.M., Bos., Ott., St.L., Det. | 4 | 147 | 25 | 27 | 52 | 48 | 2 | 0 | 0 | 0 | 0 | .... | 1930-31 | 1934-35 |
| Roche, Ernie | Mtl. | 1 | 4 | 0 | 0 | 0 | 2 | .... | .... | .... | .... | .... | .... | 1950-51 | 1950-51 |
| Rochefort, Dave | Det. | 1 | 1 | 0 | 0 | 0 | 0 | .... | .... | .... | .... | .... | .... | 1966-67 | 1966-67 |
| Rochefort, Leon | NYR, Mtl., Phi., L.A., Det., Atl., Van. | 15 | 617 | 121 | 147 | 268 | 93 | 39 | 4 | 4 | 8 | 16 | 2 | 1960-61 | 1975-76 |
| Rochefort, Normand | Que., NYR, T.B. | 13 | 598 | 39 | 119 | 158 | 570 | 69 | 7 | 5 | 12 | 82 | .... | 1980-81 | 1993-94 |
| • Rockburn, Harvey | Det., Ott. | 3 | 94 | 4 | 2 | 6 | 254 | .... | .... | .... | .... | .... | .... | 1929-30 | 1932-33 |
| • Rodden, Eddie | Chi., Tor., Bos., NYR | 4 | 97 | 6 | 14 | 20 | 60 | 2 | 0 | 1 | 1 | 0 | .... | 1926-27 | 1930-31 |
| Rodgers, Marc | Det. | 1 | 21 | 1 | 1 | 2 | 10 | .... | .... | .... | .... | .... | .... | 1999-00 | 1999-00 |
| Roest, Stacy | Det., Min. | 5 | 244 | 28 | 48 | 76 | 54 | 3 | 0 | 0 | 0 | 0 | .... | 1998-99 | 2002-03 |
| Rogers, John | Min. | 2 | 14 | 2 | 4 | 6 | 0 | .... | .... | .... | .... | .... | .... | 1973-74 | 1974-75 |
| Rogers, Mike | Hfd., NYR, Edm. | 7 | 484 | 202 | 317 | 519 | 184 | 17 | 1 | 13 | 14 | 6 | .... | 1979-80 | 1985-86 |
| Rohlicek, Jeff | Van. | 2 | 9 | 0 | 0 | 0 | 8 | .... | .... | .... | .... | .... | .... | 1987-88 | 1988-89 |
| Rohlin, Leif | Van. | 2 | 96 | 8 | 24 | 32 | 40 | 5 | 0 | 0 | 0 | 0 | .... | 1995-96 | 1996-97 |
| Rohloff, Jon | Bos. | 3 | 150 | 7 | 25 | 32 | 129 | 10 | 1 | 2 | 3 | 8 | .... | 1994-95 | 1996-97 |
| Rohloff, Todd | Wsh., CBJ | 2 | 75 | 0 | 6 | 6 | 40 | .... | .... | .... | .... | .... | .... | 2001-02 | 2003-04 |
| Rolfe, Dale | Bos., L.A., Det., NYR | 9 | 509 | 25 | 125 | 150 | 556 | 71 | 5 | 24 | 29 | 89 | .... | 1959-60 | 1974-75 |
| Romanchych, Larry | Chi., Atl. | 6 | 298 | 68 | 97 | 165 | 102 | 7 | 2 | 2 | 4 | 4 | .... | 1970-71 | 1976-77 |
| Romaniuk, Russell | Wpg., Phi. | 5 | 102 | 13 | 14 | 27 | 63 | 2 | 0 | 0 | 0 | 0 | .... | 1991-92 | 1995-96 |
| Rombough, Doug | Buf., NYI, Min. | 4 | 150 | 24 | 27 | 51 | 80 | .... | .... | .... | .... | .... | .... | 1972-73 | 1975-76 |
| Rominski, Dale | T.B. | 1 | 3 | 0 | 1 | 1 | 2 | .... | .... | .... | .... | .... | .... | 1999-00 | 1999-00 |
| • Romnes, Doc | Chi., Tor., NYA | 10 | 360 | 68 | 136 | 204 | 42 | 43 | 7 | 18 | 25 | 4 | 2 | 1930-31 | 1939-40 |
| Ronan, Ed | Mtl., Wpg., Buf. | 6 | 182 | 13 | 23 | 36 | 101 | 27 | 4 | 3 | 7 | 16 | 1 | 1991-92 | 1996-97 |
| • Ronan, Skene | Ott. | 1 | 11 | 0 | 0 | 0 | 6 | .... | .... | .... | .... | .... | .... | 1918-19 | 1918-19 |
| Ronning, Cliff | St.L., Van., Phx., Nsh., L.A., Min., NYI | 18 | 1137 | 306 | 563 | 869 | 453 | 126 | 29 | 57 | 86 | 72 | .... | 1985-86 | 2003-04 |
| Ronnqvist, Jonas | Ana. | 1 | 38 | 0 | 4 | 4 | 14 | .... | .... | .... | .... | .... | .... | 2000-01 | 2000-01 |
| Ronson, Len | NYR, Oak. | 2 | 18 | 2 | 1 | 3 | 10 | .... | .... | .... | .... | .... | .... | 1960-61 | 1968-69 |
| Ronty, Paul | Bos., NYR, Mtl. | 8 | 488 | 101 | 211 | 312 | 103 | 21 | 1 | 7 | 8 | 6 | .... | 1947-48 | 1954-55 |
| Rooney, Steve | Mtl., Wpg., N.J. | 5 | 154 | 15 | 13 | 28 | 496 | 25 | 3 | 2 | 5 | 86 | 1 | 1984-85 | 1988-89 |
| Root, Bill | Mtl., Tor., St.L., Phi. | 6 | 247 | 11 | 23 | 34 | 180 | 22 | 1 | 2 | 3 | 25 | .... | 1982-83 | 1987-88 |
| ‡ Rosa, Pavel | L.A. | 4 | 36 | 5 | 13 | 18 | 6 | .... | .... | .... | .... | .... | .... | 1998-99 | 2003-04 |
| • Ross, Art | Mtl.W. | 1 | 3 | 1 | 0 | 1 | 12 | .... | .... | .... | .... | .... | .... | 1917-18 | 1917-18 |
| Ross, Jim | NYR | 2 | 62 | 2 | 11 | 13 | 29 | .... | .... | .... | .... | .... | .... | 1951-52 | 1952-53 |
| Rossignol, Roly | Det., Mtl. | 3 | 14 | 3 | 5 | 8 | 6 | 1 | 0 | 0 | 0 | 2 | .... | 1943-44 | 1945-46 |
| Rossiter, Kyle | Fla., Atl. | 3 | 11 | 0 | 1 | 1 | 9 | .... | .... | .... | .... | .... | .... | 2001-02 | 2003-04 |
| Rota, Darcy | Chi., Atl., Van. | 11 | 794 | 256 | 239 | 495 | 973 | 60 | 14 | 7 | 21 | 147 | .... | 1973-74 | 1983-84 |
| Rota, Randy | Mtl., L.A., K.C., Col. | 5 | 212 | 38 | 39 | 77 | 60 | 5 | 0 | 1 | 1 | 0 | .... | 1972-73 | 1976-77 |
| • Rothschild, Sam | Mtl.M., Pit., NYA | 4 | 100 | 8 | 6 | 14 | 25 | 6 | 0 | 0 | 0 | 0 | 1 | 1924-25 | 1927-28 |
| • Roulston, Rolly | Det. | 3 | 24 | 0 | 6 | 6 | 10 | .... | .... | .... | .... | .... | 1 | 1935-36 | 1937-38 |
| Roulston, Tom | Edm., Pit. | 5 | 195 | 47 | 49 | 96 | 74 | 21 | 2 | 2 | 4 | 2 | .... | 1980-81 | 1985-86 |
| Roupe, Magnus | Phi. | 2 | 40 | 3 | 5 | 8 | 42 | .... | .... | .... | .... | .... | .... | 1987-88 | 1988-89 |
| Rouse, Bob | Min., Wsh., Tor., Det., S.J. | 17 | 1061 | 37 | 181 | 218 | 1559 | 136 | 7 | 21 | 28 | 198 | 2 | 1983-84 | 1999-00 |
| Rousseau, Bobby | Mtl., Min., NYR | 15 | 942 | 245 | 458 | 703 | 359 | 128 | 27 | 57 | 84 | 69 | 4 | 1960-61 | 1974-75 |
| Rousseau, Guy | Mtl. | 2 | 4 | 0 | 1 | 1 | 0 | .... | .... | .... | .... | .... | .... | 1954-55 | 1956-57 |
| Rousseau, Roland | Mtl. | 1 | 2 | 0 | 0 | 0 | 0 | .... | .... | .... | .... | .... | .... | 1952-53 | 1952-53 |
| Routhier, Jean-Marc | Que. | 1 | 8 | 0 | 0 | 0 | 9 | .... | .... | .... | .... | .... | .... | 1989-90 | 1989-90 |
| • Rowe, Bobby | Bos. | 1 | 4 | 1 | 0 | 1 | 0 | .... | .... | .... | .... | .... | .... | 1924-25 | 1924-25 |
| Rowe, Mike | Pit. | 3 | 11 | 0 | 0 | 0 | 11 | .... | .... | .... | .... | .... | .... | 1984-85 | 1986-87 |
| • Rowe, Ron | NYR | 1 | 5 | 1 | 0 | 1 | 0 | .... | .... | .... | .... | .... | .... | 1947-48 | 1947-48 |
| Rowe, Tom | Wsh., Hfd., Det. | 7 | 357 | 85 | 100 | 185 | 615 | 3 | 2 | 0 | 2 | 0 | .... | 1976-77 | 1982-83 |
| Roy, Jean-Yves | NYR, Ott., Bos. | 4 | 61 | 12 | 16 | 28 | 26 | .... | .... | .... | .... | .... | .... | 1994-95 | 1997-98 |
| Roy, Stephane | Min. | 1 | 12 | 1 | 0 | 1 | 0 | .... | .... | .... | .... | .... | .... | 1987-88 | 1987-88 |
| Royer, Gaetan | T.B. | 1 | 3 | 0 | 0 | 0 | 2 | .... | .... | .... | .... | .... | .... | 2001-02 | 2001-02 |
| Royer, Remi | Chi. | 1 | 18 | 0 | 0 | 0 | 67 | .... | .... | .... | .... | .... | .... | 1998-99 | 1998-99 |
| • Rozzini, Gino | Bos. | 1 | 31 | 5 | 10 | 15 | 20 | 6 | 1 | 2 | 3 | 6 | .... | 1944-45 | 1944-45 |
| Rucchin, Steve | Ana., NYR, Atl. | 12 | 735 | 171 | 318 | 489 | 164 | 37 | 9 | 8 | 17 | 12 | .... | 1994-95 | 2006-07 |
| Rucinski, Mike | Chi. | 2 | 1 | 0 | 0 | 0 | 0 | 2 | 0 | 0 | 0 | 0 | .... | 1987-88 | 1988-89 |
| Rucinski, Mike | Car. | 3 | 26 | 0 | 2 | 2 | 10 | .... | .... | .... | .... | .... | .... | 1997-98 | 2000-01 |
| ‡ Rucinsky, Martin | Edm., Que., Col., Mtl., Dal., NYR, St.L., Van. | 16 | 961 | 241 | 371 | 612 | 821 | 37 | 9 | 5 | 14 | 24 | .... | 1991-92 | 2007-08 |
| • Ruelle, Bernie | Det. | 1 | 2 | 1 | 0 | 1 | 0 | .... | .... | .... | .... | .... | .... | 1943-44 | 1943-44 |
| Ruff, Jason | St.L., T.B. | 2 | 14 | 3 | 3 | 6 | 10 | .... | .... | .... | .... | .... | .... | 1992-93 | 1993-94 |
| Ruff, Lindy | Buf., NYR | 12 | 691 | 105 | 195 | 300 | 1264 | 52 | 11 | 13 | 24 | 193 | .... | 1979-80 | 1990-91 |
| Ruhnke, Kent | Bos. | 1 | 2 | 0 | 1 | 1 | 0 | .... | .... | .... | .... | .... | .... | 1975-76 | 1975-76 |
| Rumble, Darren | Phi., Ott., St.L., T.B. | 8 | 193 | 10 | 26 | 36 | 216 | .... | .... | .... | .... | .... | 1 | 1990-91 | 2003-04 |
| Rundqvist, Thomas | Mtl. | 1 | 2 | 0 | 1 | 1 | 0 | .... | .... | .... | .... | .... | .... | 1984-85 | 1984-85 |
| • Runge, Paul | Bos., Mtl.M., Mtl. | 7 | 140 | 18 | 22 | 40 | 57 | 7 | 0 | 0 | 0 | 6 | .... | 1930-31 | 1937-38 |
| Ruotsalainen, Reijo | NYR, Edm., N.J. | 7 | 446 | 107 | 237 | 344 | 180 | 86 | 15 | 32 | 47 | 44 | 2 | 1981-82 | 1989-90 |
| Rupp, Duane | NYR, Tor., Min., Pit. | 10 | 374 | 24 | 93 | 117 | 220 | 10 | 2 | 2 | 4 | 8 | .... | 1962-63 | 1972-73 |
| Ruskowski, Terry | Chi., L.A., Pit., Min. | 10 | 630 | 113 | 313 | 426 | 1354 | 21 | 1 | 6 | 7 | 86 | .... | 1979-80 | 1988-89 |
| Russell, Cam | Chi., Col. | 10 | 396 | 9 | 21 | 30 | 872 | 44 | 0 | 5 | 5 | 16 | .... | 1989-90 | 1998-99 |
| • Russell, Church | NYR | 3 | 90 | 20 | 16 | 36 | 12 | .... | .... | .... | .... | .... | .... | 1945-46 | 1947-48 |
| Russell, Phil | Chi., Atl., Cgy., N.J., Buf. | 15 | 1016 | 99 | 325 | 424 | 2038 | 73 | 4 | 22 | 26 | 202 | .... | 1972-73 | 1986-87 |
| Ruuttu, Christian | Buf., Chi., Van. | 9 | 621 | 134 | 298 | 432 | 714 | 42 | 4 | 9 | 13 | 49 | .... | 1986-87 | 1994-95 |
| Ruzicka, Vladimir | Edm., Bos., Ott. | 5 | 233 | 82 | 85 | 167 | 129 | 30 | 4 | 14 | 18 | 2 | .... | 1989-90 | 1993-94 |
| ‡ Ryan, Matt | L.A. | 1 | 12 | 0 | 1 | 1 | 2 | .... | .... | .... | .... | .... | .... | 2005-06 | 2005-06 |
| ‡ Ryan, Prestin | Van. | 1 | 1 | 0 | 0 | 0 | 2 | .... | .... | .... | .... | .... | .... | 2005-06 | 2005-06 |
| Ryan, Terry | Mtl. | 3 | 8 | 0 | 0 | 0 | 36 | .... | .... | .... | .... | .... | .... | 1996-97 | 1998-99 |
| Rychel, Warren | Chi., L.A., Tor., Col., Ana. | 9 | 406 | 38 | 39 | 77 | 1422 | 70 | 8 | 13 | 21 | 121 | 1 | 1988-89 | 1998-99 |
| Rycroft, Mark | St.L., Col. | 4 | 226 | 21 | 25 | 46 | 113 | 3 | 0 | 0 | 0 | 2 | .... | 2001-02 | 2006-07 |
| Rymsha, Andy | Que. | 1 | 6 | 0 | 0 | 0 | 23 | .... | .... | .... | .... | .... | .... | 1991-92 | 1991-92 |

## S

| | | | | | | | | | | | | | | | |
|---|---|---|---|---|---|---|---|---|---|---|---|---|---|---|---|
| Saarinen, Simo | NYR | 1 | 8 | 0 | 0 | 0 | 0 | .... | .... | .... | .... | .... | .... | 1984-85 | 1984-85 |
| Sabol, Shaun | Phi. | 1 | 2 | 0 | 0 | 0 | 0 | .... | .... | .... | .... | .... | .... | 1989-90 | 1989-90 |
| Sabourin, Bob | Tor. | 1 | 1 | 0 | 0 | 0 | 2 | .... | .... | .... | .... | .... | .... | 1951-52 | 1951-52 |
| Sabourin, Gary | St.L., Tor., Cal., Cle. | 10 | 627 | 169 | 188 | 357 | 397 | 62 | 19 | 11 | 30 | 58 | .... | 1967-68 | 1976-77 |
| Sabourin, Ken | Cgy., Wsh. | 4 | 74 | 2 | 8 | 10 | 201 | 12 | 0 | 0 | 0 | 34 | .... | 1988-89 | 1991-92 |
| Sacco, David | Tor., Ana. | 3 | 35 | 5 | 13 | 18 | 22 | .... | .... | .... | .... | .... | .... | 1993-94 | 1995-96 |
| Sacco, Joe | Tor., Ana., NYI, Wsh., Phi. | 13 | 738 | 94 | 119 | 213 | 421 | 26 | 2 | 0 | 2 | 8 | .... | 1990-91 | 2002-03 |
| Sacharuk, Larry | NYR, St.L. | 5 | 151 | 29 | 33 | 62 | 42 | 2 | 1 | 1 | 2 | 2 | .... | 1972-73 | 1976-77 |
| ‡ Safronov, Kirill | Phx., Atl. | 2 | 35 | 2 | 2 | 4 | 16 | .... | .... | .... | .... | .... | .... | 2001-02 | 2002-03 |
| Saganiuk, Rocky | Tor., Pit. | 6 | 259 | 57 | 65 | 122 | 201 | 6 | 1 | 0 | 1 | 15 | .... | 1978-79 | 1983-84 |

| | | | Regular Schedule | | | | | Playoffs | | | | | NHL | First | Last |
|---|---|---|---|---|---|---|---|---|---|---|---|---|---|---|---|
| Name | NHL Teams | NHL Seasons | GP | G | A | TP | PIM | GP | G | A | TP | PIM | Cup Wins | NHL Season | NHL Season |
| Saleski, Don | Phi., Col. | 9 | 543 | 128 | 125 | 253 | 629 | 82 | 13 | 17 | 30 | 131 | 2 | 1971-72 | 1979-80 |
| ‡ Salmelainen, Tony | Edm., Chi. | 2 | 70 | 6 | 12 | 18 | 30 | .... | .... | .... | .... | .... | .... | 2003-04 | 2006-07 |
| Salming, Borje | Tor., Det. | 17 | 1148 | 150 | 637 | 787 | 1344 | 81 | 12 | 37 | 49 | 91 | .... | 1973-74 | 1989-90 |
| ‡ Salomonsson, Andreas | N.J., Wsh. | 2 | 71 | 5 | 9 | 14 | 36 | 4 | 0 | 1 | 1 | 0 | .... | 2001-02 | 2002-03 |
| Salovaara, Barry | Det. | 2 | 90 | 2 | 13 | 15 | 70 | .... | .... | .... | .... | .... | .... | 1974-75 | 1975-76 |
| Salvian, Dave | NYI | 1 | .... | .... | .... | .... | .... | 1 | 0 | 1 | 1 | 2 | .... | 1976-77 | 1976-77 |
| Samis, Phil | Tor. | 2 | 2 | 0 | 0 | 0 | 0 | 5 | 0 | 1 | 1 | 2 | 1 | 1947-48 | 1949-50 |
| Sampson, Gary | Wsh. | 4 | 105 | 13 | 22 | 35 | 25 | 12 | 1 | 0 | 1 | 0 | .... | 1983-84 | 1986-87 |
| Samuelsson, Kjell | NYR, Phi., Pit., T.B. | 14 | 813 | 48 | 138 | 186 | 1225 | 123 | 4 | 20 | 24 | 178 | 1 | 1985-86 | 1998-99 |
| Samuelsson, Martin | Bos. | 2 | 14 | 0 | 1 | 1 | 2 | .... | .... | .... | .... | .... | .... | 2002-03 | 2003-04 |
| Samuelsson, Ulf | Hfd., Pit., NYR, Det., Phi. | 16 | 1080 | 57 | 275 | 332 | 2453 | 132 | 7 | 27 | 34 | 272 | 2 | 1984-85 | 1999-00 |
| Sandelin, Scott | Mtl., Phi., Min. | 4 | 25 | 0 | 4 | 4 | 2 | .... | .... | .... | .... | .... | .... | 1986-87 | 1991-92 |
| Sanderson, Derek | Bos., NYR, St.L., Van., Pit. | 13 | 598 | 202 | 250 | 452 | 911 | 56 | 18 | 12 | 30 | 187 | 2 | 1965-66 | 1977-78 |
| Sanderson, Geoff | Hfd., Car., Van., Buf., CBJ, Phx., Phi., Edm. | 17 | 1104 | 355 | 345 | 700 | 511 | 55 | 9 | 10 | 19 | 32 | .... | 1990-91 | 2007-08 |
| Sandford, Ed | Bos., Det., Chi. | 9 | 502 | 106 | 145 | 251 | 355 | 42 | 13 | 11 | 24 | 27 | .... | 1947-48 | 1955-56 |
| Sandlak, Jim | Van., Hfd. | 11 | 549 | 110 | 119 | 229 | 821 | 33 | 7 | 10 | 17 | 30 | .... | 1985-86 | 1995-96 |
| ● Sands, Charlie | Tor., Bos., Mtl., NYR | 12 | 427 | 99 | 109 | 208 | 58 | 34 | 6 | 6 | 12 | 4 | 1 | 1932-33 | 1943-44 |
| Sandstrom, Tomas | NYR, L.A., Pit., Det., Ana. | 15 | 983 | 394 | 462 | 856 | 1193 | 139 | 32 | 49 | 81 | 183 | 1 | 1984-85 | 1998-99 |
| Sandwith, Terran | Edm. | 1 | 8 | 0 | 0 | 0 | 6 | .... | .... | .... | .... | .... | .... | 1997-98 | 1997-98 |
| Sanipass, Everett | Chi., Que. | 5 | 164 | 25 | 34 | 59 | 358 | 5 | 2 | 0 | 2 | 4 | .... | 1986-87 | 1990-91 |
| ‡ Santala, Tommi | Atl., Van. | 2 | 63 | 2 | 7 | 9 | 46 | 1 | 0 | 0 | 0 | 0 | .... | 2003-04 | 2006-07 |
| ‡ Saprykin, Oleg | Cgy., Phx., Ott. | 7 | 325 | 55 | 82 | 137 | 240 | 41 | 4 | 4 | 8 | 18 | .... | 1999-00 | 2006-07 |
| ‡ Sarault, Yves | Mtl., Cgy., Col., Ott., Atl., Nsh. | 8 | 106 | 10 | 10 | 20 | 51 | 5 | 0 | 0 | 0 | 2 | .... | 1994-95 | 2001-02 |
| Sargent, Gary | L.A., Min. | 8 | 402 | 61 | 161 | 222 | 273 | 20 | 5 | 7 | 12 | 8 | .... | 1975-76 | 1982-83 |
| Sarner, Craig | Bos. | 1 | 7 | 0 | 0 | 0 | 0 | .... | .... | .... | .... | .... | .... | 1974-75 | 1974-75 |
| ‡ Sarno, Peter | Edm., CBJ | 2 | 7 | 1 | 0 | 1 | 2 | .... | .... | .... | .... | .... | .... | 2003-04 | 2005-06 |
| Sarrazin, Dick | Phi. | 3 | 100 | 20 | 35 | 55 | 22 | 4 | 0 | 0 | 0 | 0 | .... | 1968-69 | 1971-72 |
| Sasakamoose, Fred | Chi. | 1 | 11 | 0 | 0 | 0 | 6 | .... | .... | .... | .... | .... | .... | 1953-54 | 1953-54 |
| Sasser, Grant | Pit. | 1 | 3 | 0 | 0 | 0 | 0 | .... | .... | .... | .... | .... | .... | 1983-84 | 1983-84 |
| Sather, Glen | Bos., Pit., NYR, St.L., Mtl., Min. | 10 | 658 | 80 | 113 | 193 | 724 | 72 | 1 | 5 | 6 | 86 | .... | 1966-67 | 1975-76 |
| Saunders, Bernie | Que. | 2 | 10 | 0 | 1 | 1 | 8 | .... | .... | .... | .... | .... | .... | 1979-80 | 1980-81 |
| Saunders, David | Van. | 1 | 56 | 7 | 13 | 20 | 10 | .... | .... | .... | .... | .... | .... | 1987-88 | 1987-88 |
| ● Saunders, Ted | Ott. | 1 | 18 | 1 | 3 | 4 | 4 | .... | .... | .... | .... | .... | .... | 1933-34 | 1933-34 |
| Sauve, Jean-Francois | Buf., Que. | 7 | 290 | 65 | 138 | 203 | 114 | 36 | 9 | 12 | 21 | 10 | .... | 1980-81 | 1986-87 |
| ‡ Savage, Andre | Bos., Phi. | 4 | 66 | 10 | 14 | 24 | 14 | .... | .... | .... | .... | .... | .... | 1998-99 | 2002-03 |
| Savage, Brian | Mtl., Phx., St.L., Phi. | 12 | 674 | 192 | 167 | 359 | 321 | 39 | 3 | 8 | 11 | 12 | .... | 1993-94 | 2005-06 |
| Savage, Joel | Buf. | 1 | 3 | 0 | 1 | 1 | 0 | .... | .... | .... | .... | .... | .... | 1990-91 | 1990-91 |
| Savage, Reggie | Wsh., Que. | 3 | 34 | 5 | 7 | 12 | 28 | .... | .... | .... | .... | .... | .... | 1990-91 | 1993-94 |
| ● Savage, Tony | Bos., Mtl. | 1 | 49 | 1 | 5 | 6 | 6 | 2 | 0 | 0 | 0 | 0 | .... | 1934-35 | 1934-35 |
| Savard, Andre | Bos., Buf., Que. | 12 | 790 | 211 | 271 | 482 | 411 | 85 | 13 | 18 | 31 | 77 | .... | 1973-74 | 1984-85 |
| Savard, Denis | Chi., Mtl., T.B. | 17 | 1196 | 473 | 865 | 1338 | 1336 | 169 | 66 | 109 | 175 | 256 | 1 | 1980-81 | 1996-97 |
| Savard, Jean | Chi., Hfd. | 3 | 43 | 7 | 12 | 19 | 29 | .... | .... | .... | .... | .... | .... | 1977-78 | 1979-80 |
| Savard, Serge | Mtl., Wpg. | 17 | 1040 | 106 | 333 | 439 | 592 | 130 | 19 | 49 | 68 | 88 | 7 | 1966-67 | 1982-83 |
| ‡ Savoia, Ryan | Pit. | 1 | 3 | 0 | 0 | 0 | 0 | .... | .... | .... | .... | .... | .... | 1998-99 | 1998-99 |
| Sawyer, Kevin | St.L., Bos., Phx., Ana. | 6 | 110 | 3 | 3 | 6 | 403 | .... | .... | .... | .... | .... | .... | 1995-96 | 2002-03 |
| Scamurra, Peter | Wsh. | 4 | 132 | 8 | 25 | 33 | 59 | .... | .... | .... | .... | .... | .... | 1975-76 | 1979-80 |
| Scatchard, Dave | Van., NYI, Bos., Phx. | 9 | 635 | 125 | 138 | 263 | 1017 | 17 | 2 | 2 | 4 | 34 | .... | 1997-98 | 2006-07 |
| Sceviour, Darin | Chi. | 1 | 1 | 0 | 0 | 0 | 0 | .... | .... | .... | .... | .... | .... | 1986-87 | 1986-87 |
| ● Schaeffer, Butch | Chi. | 1 | 5 | 0 | 0 | 0 | 6 | .... | .... | .... | .... | .... | .... | 1936-37 | 1936-37 |
| Schamehorn, Kevin | Det., L.A. | 3 | 10 | 0 | 0 | 0 | 17 | .... | .... | .... | .... | .... | .... | 1976-77 | 1980-81 |
| ‡ Schastlivy, Petr | Ott., Ana. | 5 | 129 | 18 | 22 | 40 | 30 | 1 | 0 | 0 | 0 | 0 | .... | 1999-00 | 2003-04 |
| Schella, John | Van. | 2 | 115 | 2 | 18 | 20 | 224 | .... | .... | .... | .... | .... | .... | 1970-71 | 1971-72 |
| Scherza, Chuck | Bos., NYR | 2 | 36 | 6 | 6 | 12 | 35 | .... | .... | .... | .... | .... | .... | 1943-44 | 1944-45 |
| Schinkel, Ken | NYR, Pit. | 12 | 636 | 127 | 198 | 325 | 163 | 19 | 7 | 2 | 9 | 4 | .... | 1959-60 | 1972-73 |
| Schlegel, Brad | Wsh., Cgy. | 3 | 48 | 1 | 8 | 9 | 10 | 7 | 0 | 1 | 1 | 2 | .... | 1991-92 | 1993-94 |
| Schliebener, Andy | Van. | 3 | 84 | 2 | 11 | 13 | 74 | 6 | 0 | 0 | 0 | 0 | .... | 1981-82 | 1984-85 |
| Schmautz, Bobby | Chi., Van., Bos., Edm., Col. | 13 | 764 | 271 | 286 | 557 | 988 | 84 | 28 | 33 | 61 | 92 | .... | 1967-68 | 1980-81 |
| ● Schmautz, Cliff | Buf., Phi. | 1 | 56 | 13 | 19 | 32 | 33 | .... | .... | .... | .... | .... | .... | 1970-71 | 1970-71 |
| ‡ Schmidt, Chris | L.A. | 1 | 10 | 0 | 2 | 2 | 5 | .... | .... | .... | .... | .... | .... | 2002-03 | 2002-03 |
| ● Schmidt, Clarence | Bos. | 1 | 7 | 1 | 0 | 1 | 2 | .... | .... | .... | .... | .... | .... | 1943-44 | 1943-44 |
| Schmidt, Jackie | Bos. | 1 | 45 | 6 | 7 | 13 | 6 | 5 | 0 | 0 | 0 | 0 | .... | 1942-43 | 1942-43 |
| Schmidt, Milt | Bos. | 16 | 776 | 229 | 346 | 575 | 466 | 86 | 24 | 25 | 49 | 60 | 2 | 1936-37 | 1954-55 |
| Schmidt, Norm | Pit. | 4 | 125 | 23 | 33 | 56 | 73 | .... | .... | .... | .... | .... | .... | 1983-84 | 1987-88 |
| Schmidt, Otto | Bos. | 1 | 2 | 0 | 0 | 0 | 0 | .... | .... | .... | .... | .... | .... | 1943-44 | 1943-44 |
| ‡ Schnabel, Robert | Nsh. | 3 | 22 | 0 | 3 | 3 | 34 | .... | .... | .... | .... | .... | .... | 2001-02 | 2003-04 |
| ● Schnarr, Werner | Bos. | 2 | 26 | 0 | 0 | 0 | 0 | .... | .... | .... | .... | .... | .... | 1924-25 | 1925-26 |
| ‡ Schneider, Andy | Ott. | 1 | 10 | 0 | 0 | 0 | 15 | .... | .... | .... | .... | .... | .... | 1993-94 | 1993-94 |
| Schock, Danny | Bos., Phi. | 2 | 20 | 1 | 2 | 3 | 0 | 1 | 0 | 0 | 0 | 0 | 1 | 1969-70 | 1970-71 |
| Schock, Ron | Bos., St.L., Pit., Buf. | 15 | 909 | 166 | 351 | 517 | 260 | 55 | 4 | 16 | 20 | 29 | .... | 1963-64 | 1977-78 |
| Schoenfeld, Jim | Buf., Det., Bos. | 13 | 719 | 51 | 204 | 255 | 1132 | 75 | 3 | 13 | 16 | 151 | .... | 1972-73 | 1984-85 |
| Schofield, Dwight | Det., Mtl., St.L., Wsh., Pit., Wpg. | 7 | 211 | 8 | 22 | 30 | 631 | 9 | 0 | 0 | 0 | 55 | .... | 1976-77 | 1987-88 |
| Schreiber, Wally | Min. | 2 | 41 | 8 | 10 | 18 | 12 | .... | .... | .... | .... | .... | .... | 1987-88 | 1988-89 |
| ● Schriner, Sweeney | NYA, Tor. | 11 | 484 | 201 | 204 | 405 | 148 | 59 | 18 | 11 | 29 | 54 | 2 | 1934-35 | 1945-46 |
| Schulte, Paxton | Que., Cgy. | 2 | 2 | 0 | 0 | 0 | 4 | .... | .... | .... | .... | .... | .... | 1993-94 | 1996-97 |
| Schultz, Dave | Phi., L.A., Pit., Buf. | 9 | 535 | 79 | 121 | 200 | 2294 | 73 | 8 | 12 | 20 | 412 | 2 | 1971-72 | 1979-80 |
| Schultz, Ray | NYI | 6 | 45 | 0 | 4 | 4 | 155 | 2 | 0 | 0 | 0 | 2 | .... | 1997-98 | 2002-03 |
| Schurman, Maynard | Hfd. | 1 | 7 | 0 | 0 | 0 | 0 | .... | .... | .... | .... | .... | .... | 1979-80 | 1979-80 |
| Schutt, Rod | Mtl., Pit., Tor. | 8 | 286 | 77 | 92 | 169 | 177 | 22 | 8 | 6 | 14 | 26 | .... | 1977-78 | 1985-86 |
| Scissons, Scott | NYI | 3 | 2 | 0 | 0 | 0 | 0 | 1 | 0 | 0 | 0 | 0 | .... | 1990-91 | 1993-94 |
| Sclisizzi, Enio | Det., Chi. | 6 | 81 | 12 | 11 | 23 | 26 | 13 | 0 | 0 | 0 | 6 | 1 | 1946-47 | 1952-53 |
| ● Scott, Ganton | Tor., Ham., Mtl.M. | 3 | 57 | 1 | 1 | 2 | 0 | .... | .... | .... | .... | .... | .... | 1922-23 | 1924-25 |
| ● Scott, Laurie | NYA, NYR | 2 | 62 | 6 | 3 | 9 | 28 | .... | .... | .... | .... | .... | .... | 1926-27 | 1927-28 |
| Scott, Richard | NYR | 2 | 10 | 0 | 0 | 0 | 28 | .... | .... | .... | .... | .... | .... | 2001-02 | 2003-04 |
| Scoville, Darrel | Cgy., CBJ | 3 | 16 | 0 | 1 | 1 | 12 | .... | .... | .... | .... | .... | .... | 1999-00 | 2003-04 |
| Scremin, Claudio | S.J. | 2 | 17 | 0 | 1 | 1 | 29 | .... | .... | .... | .... | .... | .... | 1991-92 | 1992-93 |
| Scruton, Howard | L.A. | 1 | 4 | 0 | 4 | 4 | 9 | .... | .... | .... | .... | .... | .... | 1982-83 | 1982-83 |
| Seabrooke, Glen | Phi. | 3 | 19 | 1 | 6 | 7 | 4 | .... | .... | .... | .... | .... | .... | 1986-87 | 1988-89 |
| Secord, Al | Bos., Chi., Tor., Phi. | 12 | 766 | 273 | 222 | 495 | 2093 | 102 | 21 | 34 | 55 | 382 | .... | 1978-79 | 1989-90 |
| Sedlbauer, Ron | Van., Chi., Tor. | 7 | 430 | 143 | 86 | 229 | 210 | 19 | 1 | 3 | 4 | 27 | .... | 1974-75 | 1980-81 |
| Seftel, Steve | Wsh. | 1 | 4 | 0 | 0 | 0 | 2 | .... | .... | .... | .... | .... | .... | 1990-91 | 1990-91 |
| Seguin, Dan | Min., Van. | 2 | 37 | 2 | 6 | 8 | 50 | .... | .... | .... | .... | .... | .... | 1970-71 | 1973-74 |
| Seguin, Steve | L.A. | 1 | 5 | 0 | 0 | 0 | 9 | .... | .... | .... | .... | .... | .... | 1984-85 | 1984-85 |
| ● Seibert, Earl | NYR, Chi., Det. | 15 | 645 | 89 | 187 | 276 | 746 | 66 | 11 | 8 | 19 | 76 | 2 | 1931-32 | 1945-46 |
| Seiling, Ric | Buf., Det. | 10 | 738 | 179 | 208 | 387 | 573 | 62 | 14 | 14 | 28 | 36 | .... | 1977-78 | 1986-87 |
| Seiling, Rod | Tor., NYR, Wsh., St.L., Atl. | 17 | 979 | 62 | 269 | 331 | 601 | 77 | 4 | 8 | 12 | 55 | .... | 1962-63 | 1978-79 |
| Sejba, Jiri | Buf. | 1 | 11 | 0 | 2 | 2 | 8 | .... | .... | .... | .... | .... | .... | 1990-91 | 1990-91 |
| ‡ Sejna, Peter | St.L. | 4 | 49 | 7 | 4 | 11 | 12 | .... | .... | .... | .... | .... | .... | 2002-03 | 2006-07 |
| ‡ Sekeras, Lubomir | Min., Dal. | 4 | 213 | 18 | 53 | 71 | 122 | 15 | 1 | 1 | 2 | 6 | .... | 2000-01 | 2003-04 |
| Selby, Brit | Tor., Phi., St.L. | 8 | 350 | 55 | 62 | 117 | 163 | 16 | 1 | 1 | 2 | 8 | .... | 1964-65 | 1971-72 |
| Self, Steve | Wsh. | 1 | 3 | 0 | 0 | 0 | 0 | .... | .... | .... | .... | .... | .... | 1976-77 | 1976-77 |
| ‡ Selivanov, Alex | T.B., Edm., CBJ | 7 | 459 | 121 | 114 | 235 | 379 | 13 | 2 | 3 | 5 | 16 | .... | 1994-95 | 2000-01 |
| ‡ Sellars, Luke | Atl. | 1 | 1 | 0 | 0 | 0 | 2 | .... | .... | .... | .... | .... | .... | 2001-02 | 2001-02 |
| ‡ Selmser, Sean | CBJ | 1 | 1 | 0 | 0 | 0 | 5 | .... | .... | .... | .... | .... | .... | 2000-01 | 2000-01 |
| Selwood, Brad | Tor., L.A. | 3 | 163 | 7 | 40 | 47 | 153 | 6 | 0 | 0 | 0 | 4 | .... | 1970-71 | 1979-80 |
| Semak, Alexander | N.J., T.B., NYI, Van. | 6 | 289 | 83 | 91 | 174 | 187 | 8 | 1 | 1 | 2 | 0 | .... | 1991-92 | 1996-97 |
| Semchuk, Brandy | L.A. | 1 | 1 | 0 | 0 | 0 | 2 | .... | .... | .... | .... | .... | .... | 1992-93 | 1992-93 |
| Semenko, Dave | Edm., Hfd., Tor. | 9 | 575 | 65 | 88 | 153 | 1175 | 73 | 6 | 6 | 12 | 208 | 2 | 1979-80 | 1987-88 |
| Semenov, Anatoli | Edm., T.B., Van., Ana., Phi., Buf. | 8 | 362 | 68 | 126 | 194 | 122 | 49 | 9 | 13 | 22 | 12 | .... | 1989-90 | 1996-97 |
| ● Senick, George | NYR | 1 | 13 | 2 | 3 | 5 | 8 | .... | .... | .... | .... | .... | .... | 1952-53 | 1952-53 |
| Seppa, Jyrki | Wpg. | 1 | 13 | 0 | 2 | 2 | 6 | .... | .... | .... | .... | .... | .... | 1983-84 | 1983-84 |
| Serafini, Ron | Cal. | 1 | 2 | 0 | 0 | 0 | 2 | .... | .... | .... | .... | .... | .... | 1973-74 | 1973-74 |
| Serowik, Jeff | Tor., Bos., Pit. | 3 | 28 | 0 | 6 | 6 | 16 | .... | .... | .... | .... | .... | .... | 1990-91 | 1998-99 |
| Servinis, George | Min. | 1 | 5 | 0 | 0 | 0 | 0 | .... | .... | .... | .... | .... | .... | 1987-88 | 1987-88 |
| Sevcik, Jaroslav | Que. | 1 | 13 | 0 | 2 | 2 | 2 | .... | .... | .... | .... | .... | .... | 1989-90 | 1989-90 |
| ‡ Severson, Cam | Ana., CBJ | 3 | 37 | 3 | 0 | 3 | 63 | 1 | 0 | 0 | 0 | 0 | .... | 2002-03 | 2005-06 |
| Severyn, Brent | Que., Fla., NYI, Col., Ana., Dal. | 7 | 328 | 10 | 30 | 40 | 825 | 8 | 0 | 0 | 0 | 12 | 1 | 1989-90 | 1998-99 |
| ‡ Sevigny, Pierre | Mtl., NYR | 4 | 78 | 4 | 5 | 9 | 64 | 3 | 0 | 1 | 1 | 0 | .... | 1993-94 | 1997-98 |
| Shack, Eddie | NYR, Tor., Bos., L.A., Buf., Pit. | 17 | 1047 | 239 | 226 | 465 | 1437 | 74 | 6 | 7 | 13 | 151 | 4 | 1958-59 | 1974-75 |
| ● Shack, Joe | NYR | 2 | 70 | 9 | 27 | 36 | 20 | .... | .... | .... | .... | .... | .... | 1942-43 | 1944-45 |
| Shafranov, Konstantin | St.L. | 1 | 5 | 2 | 1 | 3 | 0 | .... | .... | .... | .... | .... | .... | 1996-97 | 1996-97 |
| Shakes, Paul | Cal. | 1 | 21 | 0 | 4 | 4 | 12 | .... | .... | .... | .... | .... | .... | 1973-74 | 1973-74 |
| Shaldybin, Yevgeny | Bos. | 1 | 3 | 1 | 0 | 1 | 0 | .... | .... | .... | .... | .... | .... | 1996-97 | 1996-97 |
| Shanahan, Sean | Mtl., Col., Bos. | 3 | 40 | 1 | 3 | 4 | 47 | .... | .... | .... | .... | .... | .... | 1975-76 | 1977-78 |
| Shand, Dave | Atl., Tor., Wsh. | 8 | 421 | 19 | 84 | 103 | 544 | 26 | 1 | 2 | 3 | 83 | .... | 1976-77 | 1984-85 |
| Shank, Daniel | Det., Hfd. | 3 | 77 | 13 | 14 | 27 | 175 | 5 | 0 | 0 | 0 | 22 | .... | 1989-90 | 1991-92 |

*Dick Sarrazin*

*Joel Savage*

*Jim Schoenfeld*

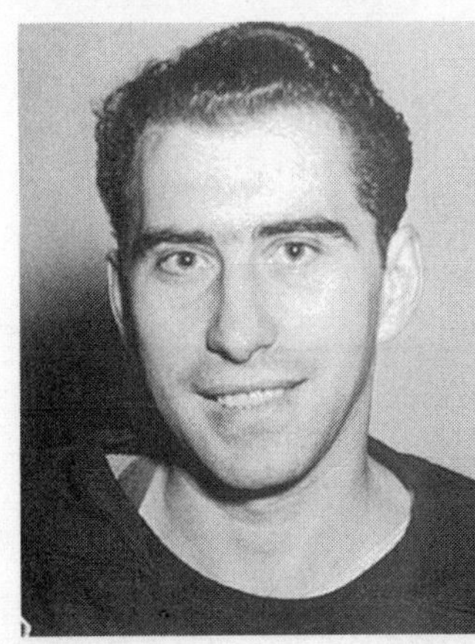
*Joe Shack*

*Cully Simon*

*Ed Slowinski*

*Dale Smedsmo*

*Floyd Smith*

| | | | Regular Schedule | | | | | Playoffs | | | | | | | |
|---|---|---|---|---|---|---|---|---|---|---|---|---|---|---|---|
| Name | NHL Teams | NHL Seasons | GP | G | A | TP | PIM | GP | G | A | TP | PIM | NHL Cup Wins | First NHL Season | Last NHL Season |
| • Shannon, Chuck | NYA | 1 | 4 | 0 | 0 | 0 | 2 | .... | .... | .... | .... | .... | .... | 1939-40 | 1939-40 |
| Shannon, Darrin | Buf., Wpg., Phx. | 10 | 506 | 87 | 163 | 250 | 344 | 45 | 7 | 10 | 17 | 38 | .... | 1988-89 | 1997-98 |
| Shannon, Darryl | Tor., Wpg., Buf., Atl., Cgy., Mtl. | 13 | 544 | 28 | 111 | 139 | 523 | 29 | 4 | 7 | 11 | 16 | .... | 1988-89 | 2000-01 |
| • Shannon, Gerry | Ott., St.L., Bos., Mtl.M. | 5 | 180 | 23 | 29 | 52 | 80 | 9 | 0 | 1 | 1 | 2 | .... | 1933-34 | 1937-38 |
| Shantz, Jeff | Chi., Cgy., Col. | 10 | 642 | 72 | 139 | 211 | 341 | 44 | 5 | 8 | 13 | 24 | .... | 1993-94 | 2002-03 |
| Sharifijanov, Vadim | N.J., Van. | 3 | 92 | 16 | 21 | 37 | 50 | 4 | 0 | 0 | 0 | 0 | .... | 1996-97 | 1999-00 |
| Sharples, Jeff | Det. | 3 | 105 | 14 | 35 | 49 | 70 | 7 | 0 | 3 | 3 | 6 | .... | 1986-87 | 1988-89 |
| Sharpley, Glen | Min., Chi. | 6 | 389 | 117 | 161 | 278 | 199 | 27 | 7 | 11 | 18 | 24 | .... | 1976-77 | 1981-82 |
| Shaunessy, Scott | Que. | 2 | 7 | 0 | 0 | 0 | 23 | .... | .... | .... | .... | .... | .... | 1986-87 | 1988-89 |
| Shaw, Brad | Hfd., Ott., Wsh., St.L. | 11 | 377 | 22 | 137 | 159 | 208 | 23 | 4 | 8 | 12 | 6 | .... | 1985-86 | 1998-99 |
| Shaw, David | Que., NYR, Edm., Min., Bos., T.B. | 16 | 769 | 41 | 153 | 194 | 906 | 45 | 3 | 9 | 12 | 81 | .... | 1982-83 | 1997-98 |
| • Shay, Norm | Bos., Tor. | 2 | 53 | 5 | 3 | 8 | 34 | .... | .... | .... | .... | .... | .... | 1924-25 | 1925-26 |
| • Shea, Pat | Chi. | 1 | 10 | 1 | 0 | 1 | 0 | .... | .... | .... | .... | .... | .... | 1931-32 | 1931-32 |
| Shearer, Rob | Col. | 1 | 2 | 0 | 0 | 0 | 0 | .... | .... | .... | .... | .... | .... | 2000-01 | 2000-01 |
| Shedden, Doug | Pit., Det., Que., Tor. | 8 | 416 | 139 | 186 | 325 | 176 | .... | .... | .... | .... | .... | .... | 1981-82 | 1990-91 |
| Sheehan, Bobby | Mtl., Cal., Chi., Det., NYR, Col., L.A. | 9 | 310 | 48 | 63 | 111 | 40 | 25 | 4 | 3 | 7 | 8 | 1 | 1969-70 | 1981-82 |
| Sheehy, Neil | Cgy., Hfd., Wsh. | 9 | 379 | 18 | 47 | 65 | 1311 | 54 | 0 | 3 | 3 | 241 | .... | 1983-84 | 1991-92 |
| Sheehy, Tim | Det., Hfd. | 2 | 27 | 2 | 1 | 3 | 0 | .... | .... | .... | .... | .... | .... | 1977-78 | 1979-80 |
| Shelton, Doug | Chi. | 1 | 5 | 0 | 1 | 1 | 2 | .... | .... | .... | .... | .... | .... | 1967-68 | 1967-68 |
| • Sheppard, Frank | Det. | 1 | 8 | 1 | 1 | 2 | 0 | .... | .... | .... | .... | .... | .... | 1927-28 | 1927-28 |
| Sheppard, Gregg | Bos., Pit. | 10 | 657 | 205 | 293 | 498 | 243 | 82 | 32 | 40 | 72 | 31 | .... | 1972-73 | 1981-82 |
| • Sheppard, Johnny | Det., NYA, Bos., Chi. | 8 | 308 | 68 | 58 | 126 | 224 | 10 | 0 | 0 | 0 | 0 | 1 | 1926-27 | 1933-34 |
| Sheppard, Ray | Buf., NYR, Det., S.J., Fla., Car. | 13 | 817 | 357 | 300 | 657 | 212 | 81 | 30 | 20 | 50 | 21 | .... | 1987-88 | 1999-00 |
| • Sherf, John | Det. | 5 | 19 | 0 | 0 | 0 | 8 | 8 | 0 | 1 | 1 | 2 | 1 | 1935-36 | 1943-44 |
| • Shero, Fred | NYR | 3 | 145 | 6 | 14 | 20 | 137 | 13 | 0 | 2 | 2 | 8 | .... | 1947-48 | 1949-50 |
| • Sherritt, Gordon | Det. | 1 | 8 | 0 | 0 | 0 | 12 | .... | .... | .... | .... | .... | .... | 1943-44 | 1943-44 |
| Sherven, Gord | Edm., Min., Hfd. | 5 | 97 | 13 | 22 | 35 | 33 | 3 | 0 | 0 | 0 | 0 | .... | 1983-84 | 1987-88 |
| Shevalier, Jeff | L.A., T.B. | 3 | 32 | 5 | 9 | 14 | 8 | .... | .... | .... | .... | .... | .... | 1994-95 | 1999-00 |
| • Shewchuk, Jack | Bos. | 6 | 187 | 9 | 19 | 28 | 160 | 20 | 0 | 1 | 1 | 19 | 1 | 1938-39 | 1944-45 |
| • Shibicky, Alex | NYR | 8 | 324 | 110 | 91 | 201 | 161 | 39 | 12 | 12 | 24 | 12 | 1 | 1935-36 | 1945-46 |
| • Shields, Al | Ott., Phi., NYA, Mtl.M., Bos. | 11 | 459 | 42 | 46 | 88 | 637 | 17 | 0 | 1 | 1 | 14 | 1 | 1927-28 | 1937-38 |
| • Shill, Bill | Bos. | 3 | 79 | 21 | 13 | 34 | 18 | 7 | 1 | 2 | 3 | 2 | .... | 1942-43 | 1946-47 |
| • Shill, Jack | Tor., Bos., NYA, Chi. | 6 | 160 | 15 | 20 | 35 | 70 | 25 | 1 | 6 | 7 | 23 | 1 | 1933-34 | 1938-39 |
| Shinske, Rick | Cle., St.L. | 3 | 63 | 5 | 16 | 21 | 10 | .... | .... | .... | .... | .... | .... | 1976-77 | 1978-79 |
| Shires, Jim | Det., St.L., Pit. | 3 | 56 | 3 | 6 | 9 | 32 | .... | .... | .... | .... | .... | .... | 1970-71 | 1972-73 |
| ‡ Shishkanov, Timofei | Nsh., St.L. | 2 | 24 | 3 | 2 | 5 | 6 | .... | .... | .... | .... | .... | .... | 2003-04 | 2005-06 |
| • Shmyr, Paul | Chi., Cal., Min., Hfd. | 7 | 343 | 13 | 72 | 85 | 528 | 34 | 3 | 3 | 6 | 44 | .... | 1968-69 | 1981-82 |
| Shoebottom, Bruce | Bos. | 4 | 35 | 1 | 4 | 5 | 53 | 14 | 1 | 2 | 3 | 77 | .... | 1987-88 | 1990-91 |
| • Shore, Eddie | Bos., NYA | 14 | 550 | 105 | 179 | 284 | 1047 | 55 | 7 | 12 | 19 | 181 | 2 | 1926-27 | 1939-40 |
| • Shore, Hamby | Ott. | 1 | 18 | 3 | 8 | 11 | 51 | .... | .... | .... | .... | .... | .... | 1917-18 | 1917-18 |
| Short, Steve | L.A., Det. | 2 | 6 | 0 | 0 | 0 | 2 | .... | .... | .... | .... | .... | .... | 1977-78 | 1978-79 |
| Shuchuk, Gary | Det., L.A. | 5 | 142 | 13 | 26 | 39 | 70 | 20 | 2 | 2 | 4 | 12 | .... | 1990-91 | 1995-96 |
| Shudra, Ron | Edm. | 1 | 10 | 0 | 5 | 5 | 6 | .... | .... | .... | .... | .... | .... | 1987-88 | 1987-88 |
| Shutt, Steve | Mtl., L.A. | 13 | 930 | 424 | 393 | 817 | 410 | 99 | 50 | 48 | 98 | 65 | 5 | 1972-73 | 1984-85 |
| ‡ Shvidki, Denis | Fla. | 4 | 76 | 11 | 14 | 25 | 30 | .... | .... | .... | .... | .... | .... | 2000-01 | 2003-04 |
| • Siebert, Babe | Mtl.M., NYR, Bos., Mtl. | 14 | 592 | 140 | 156 | 296 | 982 | 49 | 7 | 5 | 12 | 62 | 2 | 1925-26 | 1938-39 |
| ‡ Siklenka, Mike | Phi., NYR | 2 | 2 | 0 | 0 | 0 | 0 | .... | .... | .... | .... | .... | .... | 2002-03 | 2003-04 |
| Silk, Dave | NYR, Bos., Det., Wpg. | 7 | 249 | 54 | 59 | 113 | 271 | 13 | 2 | 4 | 6 | 13 | .... | 1979-80 | 1985-86 |
| Siltala, Mike | Wsh., NYR | 3 | 7 | 1 | 0 | 1 | 2 | .... | .... | .... | .... | .... | .... | 1981-82 | 1987-88 |
| Siltanen, Risto | Edm., Hfd., Que. | 8 | 562 | 90 | 265 | 355 | 266 | 32 | 6 | 12 | 18 | 30 | .... | 1979-80 | 1986-87 |
| Sim, Trevor | Edm. | 1 | 3 | 0 | 1 | 1 | 2 | .... | .... | .... | .... | .... | .... | 1989-90 | 1989-90 |
| Simard, Martin | Cgy., T.B. | 3 | 44 | 1 | 5 | 6 | 183 | .... | .... | .... | .... | .... | .... | 1990-91 | 1992-93 |
| ‡ Simicek, Roman | Pit., Min. | 2 | 63 | 7 | 10 | 17 | 59 | .... | .... | .... | .... | .... | .... | 2000-01 | 2001-02 |
| Simmer, Charlie | Cal., Cle., L.A., Bos., Pit. | 14 | 712 | 342 | 369 | 711 | 544 | 24 | 9 | 9 | 18 | 32 | .... | 1974-75 | 1987-88 |
| Simmons, Al | Cal., Bos. | 3 | 11 | 0 | 1 | 1 | 21 | 1 | 0 | 0 | 0 | 0 | .... | 1971-72 | 1975-76 |
| ‡ Simon, Chris | Que., Col., Wsh., Chi., NYR, Cgy., NYI, Min. | 15 | 782 | 144 | 161 | 305 | 1824 | 75 | 10 | 7 | 17 | 191 | 1 | 1992-93 | 2007-08 |
| • Simon, Cully | Det., Chi. | 3 | 130 | 4 | 11 | 15 | 121 | 14 | 1 | 0 | 1 | 6 | 1 | 1942-43 | 1944-45 |
| ‡ Simon, Jason | NYI, Phx. | 2 | 5 | 0 | 0 | 0 | 34 | .... | .... | .... | .... | .... | .... | 1993-94 | 1996-97 |
| • Simon, Thain | Det. | 1 | 3 | 0 | 0 | 0 | 0 | .... | .... | .... | .... | .... | .... | 1946-47 | 1946-47 |
| Simon, Todd | Buf. | 1 | 15 | 0 | 1 | 1 | 0 | 5 | 1 | 0 | 1 | 0 | .... | 1993-94 | 1993-94 |
| Simonetti, Frank | Bos. | 4 | 115 | 5 | 8 | 13 | 76 | 12 | 0 | 1 | 1 | 8 | .... | 1984-85 | 1987-88 |
| Simpson, Bobby | Atl., St.L., Pit. | 5 | 175 | 35 | 29 | 64 | 98 | 6 | 0 | 1 | 1 | 2 | .... | 1976-77 | 1982-83 |
| • Simpson, Cliff | Det. | 2 | 6 | 0 | 1 | 1 | 0 | 2 | 0 | 0 | 0 | 2 | .... | 1946-47 | 1947-48 |
| Simpson, Craig | Pit., Edm., Buf. | 10 | 634 | 247 | 250 | 497 | 659 | 67 | 36 | 32 | 68 | 56 | 2 | 1985-86 | 1994-95 |
| • Simpson, Joe | NYA | 6 | 228 | 21 | 19 | 40 | 156 | 2 | 0 | 0 | 0 | 0 | .... | 1925-26 | 1930-31 |
| Simpson, Reid | Phi., Min., N.J., Chi., T.B., St.L., Mtl., Nsh., Pit. | 12 | 301 | 18 | 18 | 36 | 838 | 10 | 0 | 0 | 0 | 31 | .... | 1991-92 | 2003-04 |
| Simpson, Todd | Cgy., Fla., Phx., Ana., Ott., Chi., Mtl. | 10 | 580 | 14 | 63 | 77 | 1357 | 9 | 0 | 2 | 2 | 10 | .... | 1995-96 | 2005-06 |
| Sims, Al | Bos., Hfd., L.A. | 10 | 475 | 49 | 116 | 165 | 286 | 41 | 0 | 2 | 2 | 14 | .... | 1973-74 | 1982-83 |
| Sinclair, Reg | NYR, Det. | 3 | 208 | 49 | 43 | 92 | 139 | 3 | 1 | 0 | 1 | 0 | .... | 1950-51 | 1952-53 |
| • Singbush, Alex | Mtl. | 1 | 32 | 0 | 5 | 5 | 15 | 3 | 0 | 0 | 0 | 4 | .... | 1940-41 | 1940-41 |
| Sinisalo, Ilkka | Phi., Min., L.A. | 11 | 582 | 204 | 222 | 426 | 208 | 68 | 21 | 11 | 32 | 6 | .... | 1981-82 | 1991-92 |
| Siren, Ville | Pit., Min. | 5 | 290 | 14 | 68 | 82 | 276 | 7 | 0 | 0 | 0 | 6 | .... | 1985-86 | 1989-90 |
| Sirois, Bob | Phi., Wsh. | 6 | 286 | 92 | 120 | 212 | 42 | .... | .... | .... | .... | .... | .... | 1974-75 | 1979-80 |
| Sittler, Darryl | Tor., Phi., Det. | 15 | 1096 | 484 | 637 | 1121 | 948 | 76 | 29 | 45 | 74 | 137 | .... | 1970-71 | 1984-85 |
| ‡ Sivek, Michal | Pit. | 1 | 38 | 3 | 3 | 6 | 14 | .... | .... | .... | .... | .... | .... | 2002-03 | 2002-03 |
| • Sjoberg, Lars-Erik | Wpg. | 1 | 79 | 7 | 27 | 34 | 48 | .... | .... | .... | .... | .... | .... | 1979-80 | 1979-80 |
| ‡ Sjodin, Tommy | Min., Dal., Que. | 2 | 106 | 8 | 40 | 48 | 52 | .... | .... | .... | .... | .... | .... | 1992-93 | 1993-94 |
| • Skaare, Bjorn | Det. | 1 | 1 | 0 | 0 | 0 | 0 | .... | .... | .... | .... | .... | .... | 1978-79 | 1978-79 |
| ‡ Skalde, Jarrod | N.J., Ana., Cgy., S.J., Chi., Dal., Atl., Phi. | 9 | 115 | 13 | 21 | 34 | 62 | .... | .... | .... | .... | .... | .... | 1990-91 | 2001-02 |
| Skarda, Randy | St.L. | 2 | 26 | 0 | 5 | 5 | 11 | .... | .... | .... | .... | .... | .... | 1989-90 | 1991-92 |
| • Skilton, Raymie | Mtl.W. | 1 | 1 | 0 | 0 | 0 | 0 | .... | .... | .... | .... | .... | .... | 1917-18 | 1917-18 |
| • Skinner, Alf | Tor., Bos., Mtl.M., Pit. | 4 | 71 | 26 | 10 | 36 | 87 | 2 | 0 | 1 | 1 | 9 | 1 | 1917-18 | 1925-26 |
| Skinner, Larry | Col. | 4 | 47 | 10 | 12 | 22 | 8 | 2 | 0 | 0 | 0 | 0 | .... | 1976-77 | 1979-80 |
| ‡ Skolney, Wade | Phi. | 1 | 1 | 0 | 0 | 0 | 2 | .... | .... | .... | .... | .... | .... | 2005-06 | 2005-06 |
| ‡ Skopintsev, Andrei | T.B., Atl. | 3 | 40 | 2 | 4 | 6 | 32 | .... | .... | .... | .... | .... | .... | 1998-99 | 2000-01 |
| Skov, Glen | Det., Chi., Mtl. | 12 | 650 | 106 | 136 | 242 | 413 | 53 | 7 | 7 | 14 | 48 | 3 | 1949-50 | 1960-61 |
| ‡ Skrbek, Pavel | Pit., Nsh. | 3 | 12 | 0 | 0 | 0 | 8 | .... | .... | .... | .... | .... | .... | 1998-99 | 2001-02 |
| Skriko, Petri | Van., Bos., Wpg., S.J. | 9 | 541 | 183 | 222 | 405 | 246 | 28 | 5 | 9 | 14 | 4 | .... | 1984-85 | 1992-93 |
| Skrlac, Rob | N.J. | 1 | 8 | 1 | 0 | 1 | 22 | .... | .... | .... | .... | .... | .... | 2003-04 | 2003-04 |
| Skrudland, Brian | Mtl., Cgy., Fla., NYR, Dal. | 15 | 881 | 124 | 219 | 343 | 1107 | 164 | 15 | 46 | 61 | 323 | 2 | 1985-86 | 1999-00 |
| ‡ Slaney, John | Wsh., Col., L.A., Phx., Nsh., Pit., Phi. | 9 | 268 | 22 | 69 | 91 | 99 | 14 | 2 | 1 | 3 | 4 | .... | 1993-94 | 2003-04 |
| • Sleaver, John | Chi. | 2 | 13 | 1 | 0 | 1 | 6 | .... | .... | .... | .... | .... | .... | 1953-54 | 1956-57 |
| ‡ Slegr, Jiri | Van., Edm., Pit., Atl., Det., Bos. | 11 | 622 | 56 | 193 | 249 | 838 | 42 | 4 | 14 | 18 | 39 | 1 | 1992-93 | 2005-06 |
| Sleigher, Louis | Que., Bos. | 6 | 194 | 46 | 53 | 99 | 146 | 17 | 1 | 1 | 2 | 64 | .... | 1979-80 | 1985-86 |
| ‡ Sloan, Blake | Dal., CBJ, Cgy. | 6 | 290 | 11 | 32 | 43 | 162 | 35 | 0 | 2 | 2 | 20 | 1 | 1998-99 | 2003-04 |
| Sloan, Tod | Tor., Chi. | 13 | 745 | 220 | 262 | 482 | 831 | 47 | 9 | 12 | 21 | 47 | 2 | 1947-48 | 1960-61 |
| • Slobodian, Peter | NYA | 1 | 41 | 3 | 2 | 5 | 54 | .... | .... | .... | .... | .... | .... | 1940-41 | 1940-41 |
| • Slowinski, Ed | NYR | 6 | 291 | 58 | 74 | 132 | 63 | 16 | 2 | 6 | 8 | 6 | .... | 1947-48 | 1952-53 |
| • Sly, Darryl | Tor., Min., Van. | 4 | 79 | 1 | 2 | 3 | 20 | .... | .... | .... | .... | .... | .... | 1965-66 | 1970-71 |
| Smail, Doug | Wpg., Min., Que., Ott. | 13 | 845 | 210 | 249 | 459 | 602 | 42 | 9 | 2 | 11 | 49 | .... | 1980-81 | 1992-93 |
| • Smart, Alex | Mtl. | 1 | 8 | 5 | 2 | 7 | 0 | .... | .... | .... | .... | .... | .... | 1942-43 | 1942-43 |
| Smedsmo, Dale | Tor. | 1 | 4 | 0 | 0 | 0 | 0 | .... | .... | .... | .... | .... | .... | 1972-73 | 1972-73 |
| Smehlik, Richard | Buf., Atl., N.J. | 10 | 644 | 49 | 146 | 195 | 415 | 88 | 1 | 14 | 15 | 40 | 1 | 1992-93 | 2002-03 |
| • Smillie, Don | Bos. | 1 | 12 | 2 | 2 | 4 | 4 | .... | .... | .... | .... | .... | .... | 1933-34 | 1933-34 |
| ‡ Smirnov, Alexei | Ana. | 2 | 52 | 3 | 3 | 6 | 20 | 4 | 0 | 0 | 0 | 2 | .... | 2002-03 | 2003-04 |
| • Smith, Alex | Ott., Det., Bos., NYA | 11 | 443 | 41 | 50 | 91 | 645 | 19 | 0 | 2 | 2 | 26 | 1 | 1924-25 | 1934-35 |
| • Smith, Art | Tor., Ott. | 4 | 144 | 15 | 10 | 25 | 249 | 4 | 1 | 1 | 2 | 8 | .... | 1927-28 | 1930-31 |
| Smith, Barry | Bos., Col. | 3 | 114 | 7 | 7 | 14 | 10 | .... | .... | .... | .... | .... | .... | 1975-76 | 1980-81 |
| Smith, Bobby | Min., Mtl. | 15 | 1077 | 357 | 679 | 1036 | 917 | 184 | 64 | 96 | 160 | 245 | 1 | 1978-79 | 1992-93 |
| Smith, Brad | Van., Atl., Cgy., Det., Tor. | 9 | 222 | 28 | 34 | 62 | 591 | 20 | 3 | 3 | 6 | 49 | .... | 1978-79 | 1986-87 |
| ‡ Smith, Brandon | Bos., NYI | 4 | 33 | 3 | 4 | 7 | 10 | .... | .... | .... | .... | .... | .... | 1998-99 | 2002-03 |
| Smith, Brian | Det. | 3 | 61 | 2 | 8 | 10 | 12 | 5 | 0 | 0 | 0 | 0 | .... | 1957-58 | 1960-61 |
| • Smith, Brian | L.A., Min. | 2 | 67 | 10 | 10 | 20 | 33 | 7 | 0 | 0 | 0 | 0 | .... | 1967-68 | 1968-69 |
| • Smith, Carl | Det. | 1 | 7 | 1 | 1 | 2 | 2 | .... | .... | .... | .... | .... | .... | 1943-44 | 1943-44 |
| • Smith, Clint | NYR, Chi. | 11 | 483 | 161 | 236 | 397 | 24 | 42 | 10 | 14 | 24 | 2 | 1 | 1936-37 | 1946-47 |
| Smith, D.J. | Tor., Col. | 3 | 45 | 1 | 1 | 2 | 67 | .... | .... | .... | .... | .... | .... | 1996-97 | 2002-03 |
| Smith, Dallas | Bos., NYR | 16 | 890 | 55 | 252 | 307 | 959 | 86 | 3 | 29 | 32 | 128 | 2 | 1959-60 | 1977-78 |
| Smith, Dennis | Wsh., L.A. | 2 | 8 | 0 | 0 | 0 | 4 | .... | .... | .... | .... | .... | .... | 1989-90 | 1990-91 |
| Smith, Derek | Buf., Det. | 8 | 335 | 78 | 116 | 194 | 60 | 30 | 9 | 14 | 23 | 13 | .... | 1975-76 | 1982-83 |
| Smith, Derrick | Phi., Min., Dal. | 10 | 537 | 82 | 92 | 174 | 373 | 82 | 14 | 11 | 25 | 79 | .... | 1984-85 | 1993-94 |
| • Smith, Des | Mtl.M., Mtl., Chi., Bos. | 5 | 196 | 22 | 25 | 47 | 236 | 25 | 1 | 4 | 5 | 18 | 1 | 1937-38 | 1941-42 |
| • Smith, Don | Mtl. | 1 | 12 | 1 | 0 | 1 | 6 | .... | .... | .... | .... | .... | .... | 1919-20 | 1919-20 |
| • Smith, Don | NYR | 1 | 11 | 1 | 1 | 2 | 0 | 1 | 0 | 0 | 0 | 0 | .... | 1949-50 | 1949-50 |

| Name | NHL Teams | NHL Seasons | Regular Schedule GP | G | A | TP | PIM | Playoffs GP | G | A | TP | PIM | NHL Cup Wins | First NHL Season | Last NHL Season |
|---|---|---|---|---|---|---|---|---|---|---|---|---|---|---|---|
| Smith, Doug | L.A., Buf., Edm., Van., Pit. | 9 | 535 | 115 | 138 | 253 | 624 | 18 | 4 | 2 | 6 | 21 | .... | 1981-82 | 1989-90 |
| Smith, Floyd | Bos., NYR, Det., Tor., Buf. | 13 | 616 | 129 | 178 | 307 | 207 | 48 | 12 | 11 | 23 | 16 | .... | 1954-55 | 1971-72 |
| Smith, Geoff | Edm., Fla., NYR | 10 | 462 | 18 | 73 | 91 | 282 | 13 | 0 | 1 | 1 | 8 | 1 | 1989-90 | 1998-99 |
| Smith, Glen | Chi. | 1 | 2 | 0 | 0 | 0 | 0 | .... | .... | .... | .... | .... | .... | 1950-51 | 1950-51 |
| • Smith, Glenn | Tor. | 1 | 9 | 0 | 0 | 0 | 0 | .... | .... | .... | .... | .... | .... | 1921-22 | 1921-22 |
| Smith, Gord | Wsh., Wpg. | 6 | 299 | 9 | 30 | 39 | 284 | .... | .... | .... | .... | .... | .... | 1974-75 | 1979-80 |
| Smith, Greg | Cal., Cle., Min., Det., Wsh. | 13 | 829 | 56 | 232 | 288 | 1110 | 63 | 4 | 7 | 11 | 106 | .... | 1975-76 | 1987-88 |
| • Smith, Hooley | Ott., Mtl.M., Bos., NYA | 17 | 715 | 200 | 225 | 425 | 1013 | 54 | 11 | 8 | 19 | 109 | 2 | 1924-25 | 1940-41 |
| • Smith, Ken | Bos. | 7 | 331 | 78 | 93 | 171 | 49 | 30 | 8 | 13 | 21 | 6 | .... | 1944-45 | 1950-51 |
| • Smith, Nakina | Det. | 1 | 10 | 1 | 2 | 3 | 0 | .... | .... | .... | .... | .... | .... | 1943-44 | 1943-44 |
| Smith, Nick | Fla. | 1 | 15 | 0 | 0 | 0 | 0 | .... | .... | .... | .... | .... | .... | 2001-02 | 2001-02 |
| Smith, Randy | Min. | 2 | 3 | 0 | 0 | 0 | 0 | .... | .... | .... | .... | .... | .... | 1985-86 | 1986-87 |
| Smith, Rick | Bos., Cal., St.L., Det., Wsh. | 11 | 687 | 52 | 167 | 219 | 560 | 78 | 3 | 23 | 26 | 73 | 1 | 1968-69 | 1980-81 |
| • Smith, Rodger | Pit., Phi. | 6 | 210 | 20 | 4 | 24 | 172 | 4 | 3 | 0 | 3 | 0 | .... | 1925-26 | 1930-31 |
| Smith, Ron | NYI | 1 | 11 | 1 | 1 | 2 | 14 | .... | .... | .... | .... | .... | .... | 1972-73 | 1972-73 |
| • Smith, Sid | Tor. | 12 | 601 | 186 | 183 | 369 | 94 | 44 | 17 | 10 | 27 | 2 | 3 | 1946-47 | 1957-58 |
| Smith, Stan | NYR | 2 | 9 | 2 | 1 | 3 | 0 | 1 | 0 | 0 | 0 | 0 | 1 | 1939-40 | 1940-41 |
| Smith, Steve | Phi., Buf. | 6 | 18 | 0 | 1 | 1 | 15 | .... | .... | .... | .... | .... | .... | 1981-82 | 1988-89 |
| Smith, Steve | Edm., Chi., Cgy. | 16 | 804 | 72 | 303 | 375 | 2139 | 134 | 11 | 41 | 52 | 288 | 3 | 1984-85 | 2000-01 |
| Smith, Stu | Mtl. | 2 | 4 | 2 | 2 | 4 | 2 | 1 | 0 | 0 | 0 | 0 | .... | 1940-41 | 1941-42 |
| Smith, Stu | Hfd. | 4 | 77 | 2 | 10 | 12 | 95 | .... | .... | .... | .... | .... | .... | 1979-80 | 1982-83 |
| • Smith, Tommy | Que. | 1 | 10 | 0 | 1 | 1 | 11 | .... | .... | .... | .... | .... | .... | 1919-20 | 1919-20 |
| Smith, Vern | NYI | 1 | 1 | 0 | 0 | 0 | 0 | .... | .... | .... | .... | .... | .... | 1984-85 | 1984-85 |
| Smith, Wayne | Chi. | 1 | 2 | 1 | 1 | 2 | 2 | 1 | 0 | 0 | 0 | 0 | .... | 1966-67 | 1966-67 |
| ‡ Smolinski, Bryan | Bos., Pit., NYI, L.A., Ott., Chi., Van., Mtl. | 15 | 1056 | 274 | 377 | 651 | 606 | 123 | 23 | 29 | 52 | 60 | .... | 1992-93 | 2007-08 |
| ‡ Smrek, Peter | St.L., NYR | 2 | 28 | 2 | 4 | 6 | 18 | .... | .... | .... | .... | .... | .... | 2000-01 | 2001-02 |
| Smrke, John | St.L., Que. | 3 | 103 | 11 | 17 | 28 | 33 | .... | .... | .... | .... | .... | .... | 1977-78 | 1979-80 |
| • Smrke, Stan | Mtl. | 2 | 9 | 0 | 3 | 3 | 0 | .... | .... | .... | .... | .... | .... | 1956-57 | 1957-58 |
| Smyl, Stan | Van. | 13 | 896 | 262 | 411 | 673 | 1556 | 41 | 16 | 17 | 33 | 64 | .... | 1978-79 | 1990-91 |
| • Smylie, Rod | Tor., Ott. | 6 | 74 | 4 | 2 | 6 | 12 | 4 | 0 | 0 | 0 | 2 | 1 | 1920-21 | 1925-26 |
| ‡ Smyth, Brad | Fla., L.A., NYR, Nsh., Ott. | 6 | 88 | 15 | 13 | 28 | 109 | .... | .... | .... | .... | .... | .... | 1995-96 | 2002-03 |
| Smyth, Greg | Phi., Que., Cgy., Fla., Tor., Chi. | 10 | 229 | 4 | 16 | 20 | 783 | 12 | 0 | 0 | 0 | 40 | .... | 1986-87 | 1996-97 |
| Smyth, Kevin | Hfd. | 3 | 58 | 6 | 8 | 14 | 31 | .... | .... | .... | .... | .... | .... | 1993-94 | 1995-96 |
| Snell, Chris | Tor., L.A. | 2 | 34 | 2 | 7 | 9 | 24 | .... | .... | .... | .... | .... | .... | 1993-94 | 1994-95 |
| Snell, Ron | Pit. | 2 | 7 | 3 | 2 | 5 | 6 | .... | .... | .... | .... | .... | .... | 1968-69 | 1969-70 |
| Snell, Ted | Pit., K.C., Det. | 2 | 104 | 7 | 18 | 25 | 22 | .... | .... | .... | .... | .... | .... | 1973-74 | 1974-75 |
| Snepsts, Harold | Van., Min., Det., St.L. | 17 | 1033 | 38 | 195 | 233 | 2009 | 93 | 1 | 14 | 15 | 231 | .... | 1974-75 | 1990-91 |
| Snow, Sandy | Det. | 1 | 3 | 0 | 0 | 0 | 2 | .... | .... | .... | .... | .... | .... | 1968-69 | 1968-69 |
| Snuggerud, Dave | Buf., S.J., Phi. | 4 | 265 | 30 | 54 | 84 | 127 | 12 | 1 | 3 | 4 | 6 | .... | 1989-90 | 1992-93 |
| • Snyder, Dan | Atl. | 3 | 49 | 11 | 5 | 16 | 64 | .... | .... | .... | .... | .... | .... | 2000-01 | 2002-03 |
| Sobchuk, Dennis | Det., Que. | 2 | 35 | 5 | 6 | 11 | 2 | .... | .... | .... | .... | .... | .... | 1979-80 | 1982-83 |
| Sobchuk, Gene | Van. | 1 | 1 | 0 | 0 | 0 | 0 | .... | .... | .... | .... | .... | .... | 1973-74 | 1973-74 |
| Solheim, Ken | Chi., Min., Det., Edm. | 5 | 135 | 19 | 20 | 39 | 34 | 3 | 1 | 1 | 2 | 2 | .... | 1980-81 | 1985-86 |
| Solinger, Bob | Tor., Det. | 5 | 99 | 10 | 11 | 21 | 19 | .... | .... | .... | .... | .... | .... | 1951-52 | 1959-60 |
| • Somers, Art | Chi., NYR | 6 | 222 | 33 | 56 | 89 | 189 | 30 | 1 | 5 | 6 | 20 | 1 | 1929-30 | 1934-35 |
| ‡ Somik, Radovan | Phi. | 2 | 113 | 12 | 20 | 32 | 27 | 15 | 2 | 2 | 4 | 10 | .... | 2002-03 | 2003-04 |
| Sommer, Roy | Edm. | 1 | 3 | 1 | 0 | 1 | 7 | .... | .... | .... | .... | .... | .... | 1980-81 | 1980-81 |
| Songin, Tom | Bos. | 3 | 43 | 5 | 5 | 10 | 22 | .... | .... | .... | .... | .... | .... | 1978-79 | 1980-81 |
| Sonmor, Glen | NYR | 2 | 28 | 2 | 0 | 2 | 21 | .... | .... | .... | .... | .... | .... | 1953-54 | 1954-55 |
| ‡ Sonnenberg, Martin | Pit., Cgy. | 3 | 63 | 2 | 3 | 5 | 21 | 7 | 0 | 0 | 0 | 0 | .... | 1998-99 | 2003-04 |
| Sorochan, Lee | Cgy. | 2 | 3 | 0 | 0 | 0 | 0 | .... | .... | .... | .... | .... | .... | 1998-99 | 1999-00 |
| • Sorrell, John | Det., NYA | 11 | 490 | 127 | 119 | 246 | 100 | 42 | 12 | 15 | 27 | 10 | 2 | 1930-31 | 1940-41 |
| Spanhel, Martin | CBJ | 2 | 10 | 2 | 0 | 2 | 4 | .... | .... | .... | .... | .... | .... | 2000-01 | 2001-02 |
| • Sparrow, Emory | Bos. | 1 | 8 | 0 | 0 | 0 | 4 | .... | .... | .... | .... | .... | .... | 1924-25 | 1924-25 |
| Speck, Fred | Det., Van. | 3 | 28 | 1 | 2 | 3 | 2 | .... | .... | .... | .... | .... | .... | 1968-69 | 1971-72 |
| • Speer, Bill | Pit., Bos. | 4 | 130 | 5 | 20 | 25 | 79 | 8 | 1 | 0 | 1 | 4 | 1 | 1967-68 | 1970-71 |
| Speers, Ted | Det. | 1 | 4 | 1 | 1 | 2 | 0 | .... | .... | .... | .... | .... | .... | 1985-86 | 1985-86 |
| • Spence, Gordon | Tor. | 1 | 3 | 0 | 0 | 0 | 0 | .... | .... | .... | .... | .... | .... | 1925-26 | 1925-26 |
| • Spencer, Brian | Tor., NYI, Buf., Pit. | 10 | 553 | 80 | 143 | 223 | 634 | 37 | 1 | 5 | 6 | 29 | .... | 1969-70 | 1978-79 |
| • Spencer, Irv | NYR, Bos., Det. | 8 | 230 | 12 | 38 | 50 | 127 | 16 | 0 | 0 | 0 | 8 | .... | 1959-60 | 1967-68 |
| • Speyer, Chris | Tor., NYA | 3 | 14 | 0 | 0 | 0 | 0 | .... | .... | .... | .... | .... | .... | 1923-24 | 1933-34 |
| Spring, Corey | T.B. | 2 | 16 | 1 | 1 | 2 | 12 | .... | .... | .... | .... | .... | .... | 1997-98 | 1998-99 |
| Spring, Don | Wpg. | 4 | 259 | 1 | 54 | 55 | 80 | 6 | 0 | 0 | 0 | 10 | .... | 1980-81 | 1983-84 |
| Spring, Frank | Bos., St.L., Cal., Cle. | 5 | 61 | 14 | 20 | 34 | 12 | .... | .... | .... | .... | .... | .... | 1969-70 | 1976-77 |
| • Spring, Jesse | Ham., Pit., Tor., NYA | 6 | 133 | 11 | 4 | 15 | 74 | 2 | 0 | 2 | 2 | 2 | .... | 1923-24 | 1929-30 |
| Spruce, Andy | Van., Col. | 3 | 172 | 31 | 42 | 73 | 111 | 2 | 0 | 2 | 2 | 0 | .... | 1976-77 | 1978-79 |
| Srsen, Tomas | Edm. | 1 | 2 | 0 | 0 | 0 | 0 | .... | .... | .... | .... | .... | .... | 1990-91 | 1990-91 |
| St. Amour, Martin | Ott. | 1 | 1 | 0 | 0 | 0 | 2 | .... | .... | .... | .... | .... | .... | 1992-93 | 1992-93 |
| St. Laurent, Andre | NYI, Det., L.A., Pit. | 11 | 644 | 129 | 187 | 316 | 749 | 59 | 8 | 12 | 20 | 48 | .... | 1973-74 | 1983-84 |
| St. Laurent, Dollard | Mtl., Chi. | 12 | 652 | 29 | 133 | 162 | 496 | 92 | 2 | 22 | 24 | 87 | 5 | 1950-51 | 1961-62 |
| St. Marseille, Frank | St.L., L.A. | 10 | 707 | 140 | 285 | 425 | 242 | 88 | 20 | 25 | 45 | 18 | .... | 1967-68 | 1976-77 |
| St. Sauveur, Claude | Atl. | 1 | 79 | 24 | 24 | 48 | 23 | 2 | 0 | 0 | 0 | 0 | .... | 1975-76 | 1975-76 |
| Stackhouse, Ron | Cal., Det., Pit. | 12 | 889 | 87 | 372 | 459 | 824 | 32 | 5 | 8 | 13 | 38 | .... | 1970-71 | 1981-82 |
| • Stackhouse, Ted | Tor. | 1 | 13 | 0 | 0 | 0 | 2 | 1 | 0 | 0 | 0 | 0 | 1 | 1921-22 | 1921-22 |
| • Stahan, Butch | Mtl. | 1 | .... | .... | .... | .... | .... | 3 | 0 | 1 | 1 | 2 | .... | 1944-45 | 1944-45 |
| Stajduhar, Nick | Edm. | 1 | 2 | 0 | 0 | 0 | 4 | .... | .... | .... | .... | .... | .... | 1995-96 | 1995-96 |
| Staley, Al | NYR | 1 | 1 | 0 | 1 | 1 | 0 | .... | .... | .... | .... | .... | .... | 1948-49 | 1948-49 |
| Stamler, Lorne | L.A., Tor., Wpg. | 4 | 116 | 14 | 11 | 25 | 16 | .... | .... | .... | .... | .... | .... | 1976-77 | 1979-80 |
| Standing, George | Min. | 1 | 2 | 0 | 0 | 0 | 0 | .... | .... | .... | .... | .... | .... | 1967-68 | 1967-68 |
| Stanfield, Fred | Chi., Bos., Min., Buf. | 14 | 914 | 211 | 405 | 616 | 134 | 106 | 21 | 35 | 56 | 10 | 2 | 1964-65 | 1977-78 |
| Stanfield, Jack | Chi. | 1 | .... | .... | .... | .... | .... | 1 | 0 | 0 | 0 | 0 | .... | 1965-66 | 1965-66 |
| Stanfield, Jim | L.A. | 3 | 7 | 0 | 1 | 1 | 0 | .... | .... | .... | .... | .... | .... | 1969-70 | 1971-72 |
| Stankiewicz, Ed | Det. | 2 | 6 | 0 | 0 | 0 | 2 | .... | .... | .... | .... | .... | .... | 1953-54 | 1955-56 |
| Stankiewicz, Myron | St.L., Phi. | 1 | 35 | 0 | 7 | 7 | 36 | 1 | 0 | 0 | 0 | 0 | .... | 1968-69 | 1968-69 |
| Stanley, Allan | NYR, Chi., Bos., Tor., Phi. | 21 | 1244 | 100 | 333 | 433 | 792 | 109 | 7 | 36 | 43 | 80 | 4 | 1948-49 | 1968-69 |
| • Stanley, Barney | Chi. | 1 | 1 | 0 | 0 | 0 | 0 | .... | .... | .... | .... | .... | .... | 1927-28 | 1927-28 |
| Stanley, Daryl | Phi., Van. | 6 | 189 | 8 | 17 | 25 | 408 | 17 | 0 | 0 | 0 | 30 | .... | 1983-84 | 1989-90 |
| Stanowski, Wally | Tor., NYR | 10 | 428 | 23 | 88 | 111 | 160 | 60 | 3 | 14 | 17 | 13 | 4 | 1939-40 | 1950-51 |
| Stanton, Paul | Pit., Bos., NYI | 5 | 295 | 14 | 49 | 63 | 262 | 44 | 2 | 10 | 12 | 66 | 2 | 1990-91 | 1994-95 |
| Stapleton, Brian | Wsh. | 1 | 1 | 0 | 0 | 0 | 0 | .... | .... | .... | .... | .... | .... | 1975-76 | 1975-76 |
| Stapleton, Mike | Chi., Pit., Edm., Wpg., Phx., Atl., NYI, Van. | 14 | 697 | 71 | 111 | 182 | 342 | 34 | 1 | 0 | 1 | 39 | .... | 1986-87 | 2000-01 |
| Stapleton, Pat | Bos., Chi. | 10 | 635 | 43 | 294 | 337 | 353 | 65 | 10 | 39 | 49 | 38 | .... | 1961-62 | 1972-73 |
| Starikov, Sergei | N.J. | 1 | 16 | 0 | 1 | 1 | 8 | .... | .... | .... | .... | .... | .... | 1989-90 | 1989-90 |
| • Starr, Harold | Ott., Mtl.M., Mtl., NYR | 7 | 205 | 6 | 5 | 11 | 186 | 15 | 1 | 0 | 1 | 4 | .... | 1929-30 | 1935-36 |
| • Starr, Wilf | NYA, Det. | 4 | 87 | 8 | 6 | 14 | 25 | 7 | 0 | 2 | 2 | 2 | .... | 1932-33 | 1935-36 |
| Stasiuk, Vic | Chi., Det., Bos. | 14 | 745 | 183 | 254 | 437 | 669 | 69 | 16 | 18 | 34 | 40 | 2 | 1949-50 | 1962-63 |
| Stastny, Anton | Que. | 9 | 650 | 252 | 384 | 636 | 150 | 66 | 20 | 32 | 52 | 31 | .... | 1980-81 | 1988-89 |
| Stastny, Marian | Que., Tor. | 5 | 322 | 121 | 173 | 294 | 110 | 32 | 5 | 17 | 22 | 7 | .... | 1981-82 | 1985-86 |
| Stastny, Peter | Que., N.J., St.L. | 15 | 977 | 450 | 789 | 1239 | 824 | 93 | 33 | 72 | 105 | 123 | .... | 1980-81 | 1994-95 |
| Staszak, Ray | Det. | 1 | 4 | 0 | 1 | 1 | 7 | .... | .... | .... | .... | .... | .... | 1985-86 | 1985-86 |
| • Steele, Frank | Det. | 1 | 1 | 0 | 0 | 0 | 0 | .... | .... | .... | .... | .... | .... | 1930-31 | 1930-31 |
| Steen, Anders | Wpg. | 1 | 42 | 5 | 11 | 16 | 22 | .... | .... | .... | .... | .... | .... | 1980-81 | 1980-81 |
| Steen, Thomas | Wpg. | 14 | 950 | 264 | 553 | 817 | 753 | 56 | 12 | 32 | 44 | 62 | .... | 1981-82 | 1994-95 |
| ‡ Stefan, Patrik | Atl., Dal. | 7 | 455 | 64 | 124 | 188 | 158 | .... | .... | .... | .... | .... | .... | 1999-00 | 2006-07 |
| Stefaniw, Morris | Atl. | 1 | 13 | 1 | 1 | 2 | 2 | .... | .... | .... | .... | .... | .... | 1972-73 | 1972-73 |
| Stefanski, Bud | NYR | 1 | 1 | 0 | 0 | 0 | 0 | .... | .... | .... | .... | .... | .... | 1977-78 | 1977-78 |
| Stemkowski, Pete | Tor., Det., NYR, L.A. | 15 | 967 | 206 | 349 | 555 | 866 | 83 | 25 | 29 | 54 | 136 | 1 | 1963-64 | 1977-78 |
| Stenlund, Vern | Cle. | 1 | 4 | 0 | 0 | 0 | 0 | .... | .... | .... | .... | .... | .... | 1976-77 | 1976-77 |
| ‡ Stephens, Charlie | Col. | 2 | 8 | 0 | 2 | 2 | 4 | .... | .... | .... | .... | .... | .... | 2002-03 | 2003-04 |
| Stephenson, Bob | Hfd., Tor. | 1 | 18 | 2 | 3 | 5 | 4 | .... | .... | .... | .... | .... | .... | 1979-80 | 1979-80 |
| ‡ Stephenson, Shay | L.A. | 1 | 2 | 0 | 0 | 0 | 0 | .... | .... | .... | .... | .... | .... | 2006-07 | 2006-07 |
| Stern, Ron | Van., Cgy., S.J. | 12 | 638 | 75 | 86 | 161 | 2077 | 43 | 7 | 7 | 14 | 119 | .... | 1987-88 | 1999-00 |
| Sterner, Ulf | NYR | 1 | 4 | 0 | 0 | 0 | 0 | .... | .... | .... | .... | .... | .... | 1964-65 | 1964-65 |
| Stevens, John | Phi., Hfd. | 5 | 53 | 0 | 10 | 10 | 48 | .... | .... | .... | .... | .... | .... | 1986-87 | 1993-94 |
| Stevens, Kevin | Pit., Bos., L.A., NYR, Phi. | 15 | 874 | 329 | 397 | 726 | 1470 | 103 | 46 | 60 | 106 | 170 | 2 | 1987-88 | 2001-02 |
| Stevens, Mike | Van., Bos., NYI, Tor. | 4 | 23 | 1 | 4 | 5 | 29 | .... | .... | .... | .... | .... | .... | 1984-85 | 1989-90 |
| • Stevens, Phil | Mtl.W., Mtl., Bos. | 3 | 25 | 1 | 0 | 1 | 3 | .... | .... | .... | .... | .... | .... | 1917-18 | 1925-26 |
| Stevens, Scott | Wsh., St.L., N.J. | 22 | 1635 | 196 | 712 | 908 | 2785 | 233 | 26 | 92 | 118 | 402 | 3 | 1982-83 | 2003-04 |
| ‡ Stevenson, Jeremy | Ana., Nsh., Min., Dal. | 9 | 207 | 19 | 19 | 38 | 451 | 21 | 0 | 5 | 5 | 20 | .... | 1995-96 | 2005-06 |
| Stevenson, Shayne | Bos., T.B. | 3 | 27 | 0 | 2 | 2 | 35 | .... | .... | .... | .... | .... | .... | 1990-91 | 1992-93 |
| Stevenson, Turner | Mtl., N.J., Phi. | 13 | 644 | 75 | 115 | 190 | 969 | 67 | 6 | 12 | 18 | 66 | 1 | 1992-93 | 2005-06 |
| Stewart, Allan | N.J., Bos. | 6 | 64 | 6 | 4 | 10 | 243 | .... | .... | .... | .... | .... | .... | 1985-86 | 1991-92 |
| Stewart, Bill | Buf., St.L., Tor., Min. | 8 | 261 | 7 | 64 | 71 | 424 | 13 | 1 | 3 | 4 | 11 | .... | 1977-78 | 1985-86 |
| Stewart, Blair | Det., Wsh., Que. | 7 | 229 | 34 | 44 | 78 | 326 | .... | .... | .... | .... | .... | .... | 1973-74 | 1979-80 |

*Sid Smith*

*Dave Snuggerud*

*Rich Sutter*

*Magnus Svensson*

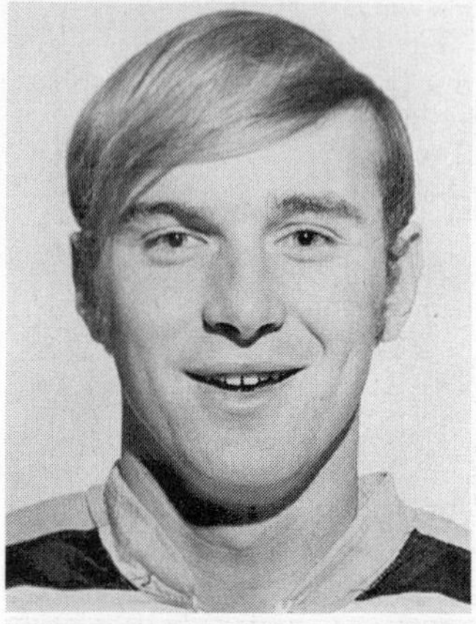

*Don Tannahill*

*Scott Thornton*

*Dave Tippett*

*Walt Tkaczuk*

| Name | NHL Teams | NHL Seasons | Regular Schedule GP | G | A | TP | PIM | Playoffs GP | G | A | TP | PIM | NHL Cup Wins | First NHL Season | Last NHL Season |
|---|---|---|---|---|---|---|---|---|---|---|---|---|---|---|---|
| Stewart, Bob | Bos., Cal., Cle., St.L., Pit. | 9 | 575 | 27 | 101 | 128 | 809 | 5 | 1 | 1 | 2 | 2 | .... | 1971-72 | 1979-80 |
| Stewart, Cam | Bos., Fla., Min. | 6 | 202 | 16 | 23 | 39 | 120 | 13 | 1 | 3 | 4 | 9 | .... | 1993-94 | 2001-02 |
| Stewart, Gaye | Tor., Chi., Det., NYR, Mtl. | 11 | 502 | 185 | 159 | 344 | 274 | 25 | 2 | 9 | 11 | 16 | 2 | 1941-42 | 1953-54 |
| • Stewart, Jack | Det., Chi. | 12 | 565 | 31 | 84 | 115 | 765 | 80 | 5 | 14 | 19 | 143 | 2 | 1938-39 | 1951-52 |
| Stewart, John | Pit., Atl., Cal. | 5 | 258 | 58 | 60 | 118 | 158 | 4 | 0 | 0 | 0 | 10 | .... | 1970-71 | 1974-75 |
| Stewart, John | Que. | 1 | 2 | 0 | 0 | 0 | 0 | .... | .... | .... | .... | .... | .... | 1979-80 | 1979-80 |
| Stewart, Ken | Chi. | 1 | 6 | 1 | 1 | 2 | 2 | .... | .... | .... | .... | .... | .... | 1941-42 | 1941-42 |
| • Stewart, Nels | Mtl.M., Bos., NYA | 15 | 650 | 324 | 191 | 515 | 953 | 50 | 9 | 12 | 21 | 47 | 1 | 1925-26 | 1939-40 |
| Stewart, Paul | Que. | 1 | 21 | 2 | 0 | 2 | 74 | .... | .... | .... | .... | .... | .... | 1979-80 | 1979-80 |
| Stewart, Ralph | Van., NYI | 7 | 252 | 57 | 73 | 130 | 28 | 19 | 4 | 4 | 8 | 2 | .... | 1970-71 | 1977-78 |
| Stewart, Ron | Tor., Bos., St.L., NYR, Van., NYI | 21 | 1353 | 276 | 253 | 529 | 560 | 119 | 14 | 21 | 35 | 60 | 3 | 1952-53 | 1972-73 |
| Stewart, Ryan | Wpg. | 1 | 3 | 1 | 0 | 1 | 0 | .... | .... | .... | .... | .... | .... | 1985-86 | 1985-86 |
| Stienburg, Trevor | Que. | 4 | 71 | 8 | 4 | 12 | 161 | 1 | 0 | 0 | 0 | 0 | .... | 1985-86 | 1988-89 |
| Stiles, Tony | Cgy. | 1 | 30 | 2 | 7 | 9 | 20 | .... | .... | .... | .... | .... | .... | 1983-84 | 1983-84 |
| Stock, P.J. | NYR, Mtl., Phi., Bos. | 7 | 235 | 5 | 21 | 26 | 523 | 8 | 1 | 0 | 1 | 19 | .... | 1997-98 | 2003-04 |
| Stoddard, Jack | NYR | 2 | 80 | 16 | 15 | 31 | 31 | .... | .... | .... | .... | .... | .... | 1951-52 | 1952-53 |
| Stojanov, Alek | Van., Pit. | 3 | 107 | 2 | 5 | 7 | 222 | 14 | 0 | 0 | 0 | 21 | .... | 1994-95 | 1996-97 |
| Stoltz, Roland | Wsh. | 1 | 14 | 2 | 2 | 4 | 14 | .... | .... | .... | .... | .... | .... | 1981-82 | 1981-82 |
| Stone, Steve | Van. | 1 | 2 | 0 | 0 | 0 | 0 | .... | .... | .... | .... | .... | .... | 1973-74 | 1973-74 |
| Storm, Jim | Hfd., Dal. | 3 | 84 | 7 | 15 | 22 | 44 | .... | .... | .... | .... | .... | .... | 1993-94 | 1995-96 |
| Stothers, Mike | Phi., Tor. | 4 | 30 | 0 | 2 | 2 | 65 | 5 | 0 | 0 | 0 | 11 | .... | 1984-85 | 1987-88 |
| Stoughton, Blaine | Pit., Tor., Hfd., NYR | 8 | 526 | 258 | 191 | 449 | 204 | 8 | 4 | 2 | 6 | 2 | .... | 1973-74 | 1983-84 |
| Stoyanovich, Steve | Hfd. | 1 | 23 | 3 | 5 | 8 | 11 | .... | .... | .... | .... | .... | .... | 1983-84 | 1983-84 |
| • Strain, Neil | NYR | 1 | 52 | 11 | 13 | 24 | 12 | .... | .... | .... | .... | .... | .... | 1952-53 | 1952-53 |
| ‡ Straka, Martin | Pit., Ott., NYI, Fla., L.A., NYR | 15 | 954 | 257 | 460 | 717 | 360 | 106 | 26 | 44 | 70 | 52 | .... | 1992-93 | 2007-08 |
| Strate, Gord | Det. | 3 | 61 | 0 | 0 | 0 | 34 | .... | .... | .... | .... | .... | .... | 1956-57 | 1958-59 |
| Stratton, Art | NYR, Det., Chi., Pit., Phi. | 4 | 95 | 18 | 33 | 51 | 24 | 5 | 0 | 0 | 0 | 0 | .... | 1959-60 | 1967-68 |
| ‡ Strbak, Martin | L.A., Pit. | 1 | 49 | 5 | 11 | 16 | 46 | .... | .... | .... | .... | .... | .... | 2003-04 | 2003-04 |
| • Strobel, Art | NYR | 1 | 7 | 0 | 0 | 0 | 0 | .... | .... | .... | .... | .... | .... | 1943-44 | 1943-44 |
| Strong, Ken | Tor. | 3 | 15 | 2 | 2 | 4 | 6 | .... | .... | .... | .... | .... | .... | 1982-83 | 1984-85 |
| Stroshein, Garret | Wsh. | 1 | 3 | 0 | 0 | 0 | 14 | .... | .... | .... | .... | .... | .... | 2003-04 | 2003-04 |
| Struch, David | Cgy. | 1 | 4 | 0 | 0 | 0 | 4 | .... | .... | .... | .... | .... | .... | 1993-94 | 1993-94 |
| Strueby, Todd | Edm. | 3 | 5 | 0 | 1 | 1 | 2 | .... | .... | .... | .... | .... | .... | 1981-82 | 1983-84 |
| • Stuart, Billy | Tor., Bos. | 7 | 195 | 30 | 20 | 50 | 151 | 12 | 1 | 1 | 2 | 6 | 1 | 1920-21 | 1926-27 |
| ‡ Stuart, Mike | St.L. | 2 | 3 | 0 | 0 | 0 | 0 | .... | .... | .... | .... | .... | .... | 2003-04 | 2005-06 |
| ‡ Stumpel, Jozef | Bos., L.A., Fla. | 16 | 957 | 196 | 481 | 677 | 245 | 55 | 6 | 24 | 30 | 24 | .... | 1991-92 | 2007-08 |
| Stumpf, Bob | St.L., Pit. | 1 | 10 | 1 | 1 | 2 | 20 | .... | .... | .... | .... | .... | .... | 1974-75 | 1974-75 |
| Sturgeon, Peter | Col. | 2 | 6 | 0 | 1 | 1 | 2 | .... | .... | .... | .... | .... | .... | 1979-80 | 1980-81 |
| Stutzel, Mike | Phx. | 1 | 9 | 0 | 0 | 0 | 0 | .... | .... | .... | .... | .... | .... | 2003-04 | 2003-04 |
| ‡ Suchy, Radoslav | Phx., CBJ | 6 | 451 | 13 | 58 | 71 | 104 | 10 | 1 | 1 | 2 | 0 | .... | 1999-00 | 2005-06 |
| ‡ Suglobov, Alexander | N.J., Tor. | 3 | 18 | 1 | 0 | 1 | 4 | .... | .... | .... | .... | .... | .... | 2003-04 | 2006-07 |
| Suikkanen, Kai | Buf. | 2 | 2 | 0 | 0 | 0 | 0 | .... | .... | .... | .... | .... | .... | 1981-82 | 1982-83 |
| Sulliman, Doug | NYR, Hfd., N.J., Phi. | 11 | 631 | 160 | 168 | 328 | 175 | 16 | 1 | 3 | 4 | 2 | .... | 1979-80 | 1989-90 |
| • Sullivan, Barry | Det. | 1 | 1 | 0 | 0 | 0 | 0 | .... | .... | .... | .... | .... | .... | 1947-48 | 1947-48 |
| Sullivan, Bob | Hfd. | 1 | 62 | 18 | 19 | 37 | 18 | .... | .... | .... | .... | .... | .... | 1982-83 | 1982-83 |
| Sullivan, Brian | N.J. | 1 | 2 | 0 | 1 | 1 | 0 | .... | .... | .... | .... | .... | .... | 1992-93 | 1992-93 |
| • Sullivan, Frank | Tor., Chi. | 4 | 8 | 0 | 0 | 0 | 2 | .... | .... | .... | .... | .... | .... | 1949-50 | 1955-56 |
| Sullivan, Mike | S.J., Cgy., Bos., Phx. | 11 | 709 | 54 | 82 | 136 | 203 | 34 | 4 | 8 | 12 | 14 | .... | 1991-92 | 2001-02 |
| Sullivan, Peter | Wpg. | 2 | 126 | 28 | 54 | 82 | 40 | .... | .... | .... | .... | .... | .... | 1979-80 | 1980-81 |
| Sullivan, Red | Bos., Chi., NYR | 11 | 557 | 107 | 239 | 346 | 441 | 18 | 1 | 2 | 3 | 6 | .... | 1949-50 | 1960-61 |
| Summanen, Raimo | Edm., Van. | 5 | 151 | 36 | 40 | 76 | 35 | 10 | 2 | 5 | 7 | 0 | .... | 1983-84 | 1987-88 |
| • Summerhill, Bill | Mtl., Bro. | 4 | 72 | 14 | 17 | 31 | 70 | 3 | 0 | 0 | 0 | 2 | .... | 1937-38 | 1941-42 |
| ‡ Sundblad, Niklas | Cgy. | 1 | 2 | 0 | 0 | 0 | 0 | .... | .... | .... | .... | .... | .... | 1995-96 | 1995-96 |
| ‡ Sundin, Ronnie | NYR | 1 | 1 | 0 | 0 | 0 | 0 | .... | .... | .... | .... | .... | .... | 1997-98 | 1997-98 |
| ‡ Sundstrom, Niklas | NYR, S.J., Mtl. | 10 | 750 | 117 | 232 | 349 | 256 | 59 | 6 | 22 | 28 | 22 | .... | 1995-96 | 2005-06 |
| Sundstrom, Patrik | Van., N.J. | 10 | 679 | 219 | 369 | 588 | 349 | 37 | 9 | 17 | 26 | 25 | .... | 1982-83 | 1991-92 |
| Sundstrom, Peter | NYR, Wsh., N.J. | 6 | 338 | 61 | 83 | 144 | 120 | 23 | 3 | 3 | 6 | 8 | .... | 1983-84 | 1989-90 |
| Suomi, Al | Chi. | 1 | 5 | 0 | 0 | 0 | 0 | .... | .... | .... | .... | .... | .... | 1936-37 | 1936-37 |
| Surma, Damian | Car. | 2 | 2 | 1 | 1 | 2 | 0 | .... | .... | .... | .... | .... | .... | 2002-03 | 2003-04 |
| ‡ Surovy, Tomas | Pit. | 3 | 126 | 27 | 32 | 59 | 71 | .... | .... | .... | .... | .... | .... | 2002-03 | 2005-06 |
| ‡ Sushinsky, Maxim | Min. | 1 | 30 | 7 | 4 | 11 | 29 | .... | .... | .... | .... | .... | .... | 2000-01 | 2000-01 |
| Suter, Gary | Cgy., Chi., S.J. | 17 | 1145 | 203 | 641 | 844 | 1349 | 108 | 17 | 56 | 73 | 120 | 1 | 1985-86 | 2001-02 |
| Sutherland, Bill | Mtl., Phi., Tor., St.L., Det. | 6 | 250 | 70 | 58 | 128 | 99 | 14 | 2 | 4 | 6 | 0 | .... | 1962-63 | 1971-72 |
| • Sutherland, Max | Bos. | 1 | 2 | 0 | 0 | 0 | 0 | .... | .... | .... | .... | .... | .... | 1931-32 | 1931-32 |
| Sutter, Brent | NYI, Chi. | 18 | 1111 | 363 | 466 | 829 | 1054 | 144 | 30 | 44 | 74 | 164 | 2 | 1980-81 | 1997-98 |
| Sutter, Brian | St.L. | 12 | 779 | 303 | 333 | 636 | 1786 | 65 | 21 | 21 | 42 | 249 | .... | 1976-77 | 1987-88 |
| Sutter, Darryl | Chi. | 8 | 406 | 161 | 118 | 279 | 288 | 51 | 24 | 19 | 43 | 26 | .... | 1979-80 | 1986-87 |
| Sutter, Duane | NYI, Chi. | 11 | 731 | 139 | 203 | 342 | 1333 | 161 | 26 | 32 | 58 | 405 | 4 | 1979-80 | 1989-90 |
| Sutter, Rich | Pit., Phi., Van., St.L., Chi., T.B., Tor. | 13 | 874 | 149 | 166 | 315 | 1411 | 78 | 13 | 5 | 18 | 133 | .... | 1982-83 | 1994-95 |
| Sutter, Ron | Phi., St.L., Que., NYI, Bos., S.J., Cgy. | 19 | 1093 | 205 | 329 | 534 | 1352 | 104 | 8 | 32 | 40 | 193 | .... | 1982-83 | 2000-01 |
| Sutton, Ken | Buf., Edm., St.L., N.J., S.J., NYI | 11 | 388 | 23 | 80 | 103 | 338 | 32 | 3 | 4 | 7 | 29 | 1 | 1990-91 | 2001-02 |
| Suzor, Mark | Phi., Col. | 2 | 64 | 4 | 16 | 20 | 60 | .... | .... | .... | .... | .... | .... | 1976-77 | 1977-78 |
| ‡ Svartvadet, Per | Atl. | 4 | 247 | 17 | 34 | 51 | 58 | .... | .... | .... | .... | .... | .... | 1999-00 | 2002-03 |
| Svehla, Robert | Fla., Tor. | 9 | 655 | 68 | 267 | 335 | 649 | 38 | 1 | 14 | 15 | 42 | .... | 1994-95 | 2002-03 |
| Svejkovsky, Jaroslav | Wsh., T.B. | 4 | 113 | 23 | 19 | 42 | 56 | 1 | 0 | 0 | 0 | 2 | .... | 1996-97 | 1999-00 |
| Svensson, Leif | Wsh. | 2 | 121 | 6 | 40 | 46 | 49 | .... | .... | .... | .... | .... | .... | 1978-79 | 1979-80 |
| Svensson, Magnus | Fla. | 2 | 46 | 4 | 14 | 18 | 31 | .... | .... | .... | .... | .... | .... | 1994-95 | 1995-96 |
| ‡ Svoboda, Jaroslav | Car., Dal. | 4 | 134 | 12 | 17 | 29 | 62 | 25 | 1 | 4 | 5 | 30 | .... | 2001-02 | 2005-06 |
| Svoboda, Petr | Mtl., Buf., Phi., T.B. | 17 | 1028 | 58 | 341 | 399 | 1605 | 127 | 4 | 45 | 49 | 140 | 1 | 1984-85 | 2000-01 |
| Svoboda, Petr | Tor. | 1 | 18 | 1 | 2 | 3 | 10 | .... | .... | .... | .... | .... | .... | 2000-01 | 2000-01 |
| Swain, Garry | Pit. | 1 | 9 | 1 | 1 | 2 | 0 | .... | .... | .... | .... | .... | .... | 1968-69 | 1968-69 |
| ‡ Swanson, Brian | Edm., Atl. | 4 | 70 | 4 | 13 | 17 | 16 | .... | .... | .... | .... | .... | .... | 2000-01 | 2003-04 |
| Swarbrick, George | Oak., Pit., Phi. | 4 | 132 | 17 | 25 | 42 | 173 | .... | .... | .... | .... | .... | .... | 1967-68 | 1970-71 |
| • Sweeney, Bill | NYR | 1 | 4 | 1 | 0 | 1 | 0 | .... | .... | .... | .... | .... | .... | 1959-60 | 1959-60 |
| Sweeney, Bob | Bos., Buf., NYI, Cgy. | 10 | 639 | 125 | 163 | 288 | 799 | 103 | 15 | 18 | 33 | 197 | .... | 1986-87 | 1995-96 |
| Sweeney, Don | Bos., Dal. | 16 | 1115 | 52 | 221 | 273 | 681 | 108 | 9 | 10 | 19 | 81 | .... | 1988-89 | 2003-04 |
| Sweeney, Tim | Cgy., Bos., Ana., NYR | 8 | 291 | 55 | 83 | 138 | 123 | 4 | 0 | 0 | 0 | 2 | .... | 1990-91 | 1997-98 |
| Sykes, Bob | Tor. | 1 | 2 | 0 | 0 | 0 | 0 | .... | .... | .... | .... | .... | .... | 1974-75 | 1974-75 |
| Sykes, Phil | L.A., Wpg. | 10 | 456 | 79 | 85 | 164 | 519 | 26 | 0 | 3 | 3 | 29 | .... | 1982-83 | 1991-92 |
| Sykora, Michal | S.J., Chi., T.B., Phi. | 7 | 267 | 15 | 54 | 69 | 185 | 7 | 0 | 1 | 1 | 0 | .... | 1993-94 | 2000-01 |
| ‡ Sykora, Petr | Nsh., Wsh. | 2 | 12 | 2 | 2 | 4 | 6 | .... | .... | .... | .... | .... | .... | 1998-99 | 2005-06 |
| Sylvester, Dean | Buf., Atl. | 3 | 96 | 21 | 16 | 37 | 32 | 4 | 0 | 0 | 0 | 0 | .... | 1998-99 | 2000-01 |
| • Szura, Joe | Oak. | 2 | 90 | 10 | 15 | 25 | 30 | 7 | 2 | 3 | 5 | 2 | .... | 1967-68 | 1968-69 |

## T

| Name | NHL Teams | NHL Seasons | Regular Schedule GP | G | A | TP | PIM | Playoffs GP | G | A | TP | PIM | NHL Cup Wins | First NHL Season | Last NHL Season |
|---|---|---|---|---|---|---|---|---|---|---|---|---|---|---|---|
| Taft, John | Det. | 1 | 15 | 0 | 2 | 2 | 4 | .... | .... | .... | .... | .... | .... | 1978-79 | 1978-79 |
| Taglianetti, Peter | Wpg., Min., Pit., T.B. | 11 | 451 | 18 | 74 | 92 | 1106 | 53 | 2 | 8 | 10 | 103 | 2 | 1984-85 | 1994-95 |
| Talafous, Dean | Atl., Min., NYR | 8 | 497 | 104 | 154 | 258 | 163 | 21 | 4 | 7 | 11 | 11 | .... | 1974-75 | 1981-82 |
| • Talakoski, Ron | NYR | 2 | 9 | 0 | 1 | 1 | 33 | .... | .... | .... | .... | .... | .... | 1986-87 | 1987-88 |
| Talbot, Jean-Guy | Mtl., Min., Det., St.L., Buf. | 17 | 1056 | 43 | 242 | 285 | 1006 | 150 | 4 | 26 | 30 | 142 | 7 | 1954-55 | 1970-71 |
| Tallon, Dale | Van., Chi., Pit. | 10 | 642 | 98 | 238 | 336 | 568 | 33 | 2 | 10 | 12 | 45 | .... | 1970-71 | 1979-80 |
| Tambellini, Steve | NYI, Col., N.J., Cgy., Van. | 10 | 553 | 160 | 150 | 310 | 105 | 2 | 0 | 1 | 1 | 0 | 1 | 1978-79 | 1987-88 |
| Tamer, Chris | Pit., NYR, Atl. | 11 | 644 | 21 | 64 | 85 | 1183 | 37 | 0 | 8 | 8 | 52 | .... | 1993-94 | 2003-04 |
| Tanabe, David | Car., Phx., Bos. | 8 | 449 | 30 | 84 | 114 | 245 | 7 | 2 | 1 | 3 | 12 | .... | 1999-00 | 2007-08 |
| Tancill, Chris | Hfd., Det., Dal., S.J. | 8 | 134 | 17 | 32 | 49 | 54 | 11 | 1 | 1 | 2 | 8 | .... | 1990-91 | 1997-98 |
| Tanguay, Christian | Que. | 1 | 2 | 0 | 0 | 0 | 0 | .... | .... | .... | .... | .... | .... | 1981-82 | 1981-82 |
| Tannahill, Don | Van. | 2 | 111 | 30 | 33 | 63 | 25 | .... | .... | .... | .... | .... | .... | 1972-73 | 1973-74 |
| Tanti, Tony | Chi., Van., Pit., Buf. | 11 | 697 | 287 | 273 | 560 | 661 | 30 | 3 | 12 | 15 | 27 | .... | 1981-82 | 1991-92 |
| ‡ Tapper, Brad | Atl. | 3 | 71 | 14 | 11 | 25 | 72 | .... | .... | .... | .... | .... | .... | 2000-01 | 2002-03 |
| Tardif, Marc | Mtl., Que. | 8 | 517 | 194 | 207 | 401 | 443 | 62 | 13 | 15 | 28 | 75 | 2 | 1969-70 | 1982-83 |
| Tardif, Patrice | St.L., L.A. | 2 | 65 | 7 | 11 | 18 | 78 | .... | .... | .... | .... | .... | .... | 1994-95 | 1995-96 |
| Tatarinov, Mikhail | Wsh., Que., Bos. | 4 | 161 | 21 | 48 | 69 | 184 | .... | .... | .... | .... | .... | .... | 1990-91 | 1993-94 |
| • Tatchell, Spence | NYR | 1 | 1 | 0 | 0 | 0 | 0 | .... | .... | .... | .... | .... | .... | 1942-43 | 1942-43 |
| ‡ Taticek, Petr | Fla. | 1 | 3 | 0 | 0 | 0 | 0 | .... | .... | .... | .... | .... | .... | 2005-06 | 2005-06 |
| • Taylor, Billy | Tor., Det., Bos., NYR | 7 | 323 | 87 | 180 | 267 | 120 | 33 | 6 | 18 | 24 | 13 | 1 | 1939-40 | 1947-48 |
| • Taylor, Billy | NYR | 1 | 2 | 0 | 0 | 0 | 0 | .... | .... | .... | .... | .... | .... | 1964-65 | 1964-65 |
| • Taylor, Bob | Bos. | 1 | 8 | 0 | 0 | 0 | 6 | .... | .... | .... | .... | .... | .... | 1929-30 | 1929-30 |
| ‡ Taylor, Chris | NYI, Bos., Buf. | 8 | 149 | 11 | 21 | 32 | 48 | 2 | 0 | 0 | 0 | 2 | .... | 1994-95 | 2003-04 |
| Taylor, Dave | L.A. | 17 | 1111 | 431 | 638 | 1069 | 1589 | 92 | 26 | 33 | 59 | 145 | .... | 1977-78 | 1993-94 |
| Taylor, Harry | Tor., Chi. | 3 | 66 | 5 | 10 | 15 | 30 | 1 | 0 | 0 | 0 | 0 | 1 | 1946-47 | 1951-52 |
| Taylor, Mark | Phi., Pit., Wsh. | 5 | 209 | 42 | 68 | 110 | 73 | 6 | 0 | 0 | 0 | 0 | .... | 1981-82 | 1985-86 |
| • Taylor, Ralph | Chi., NYR | 3 | 99 | 4 | 1 | 5 | 169 | 4 | 0 | 0 | 0 | 10 | .... | 1927-28 | 1929-30 |
| Taylor, Ted | NYR, Det., Min., Van. | 6 | 166 | 23 | 35 | 58 | 181 | .... | .... | .... | .... | .... | .... | 1964-65 | 1971-72 |
| Taylor, Tim | Det., Bos., NYR, T.B. | 13 | 746 | 73 | 94 | 167 | 433 | 89 | 2 | 12 | 14 | 73 | 2 | 1993-94 | 2006-07 |
| Teal, Jeff | Mtl. | 1 | 6 | 0 | 1 | 1 | 0 | .... | .... | .... | .... | .... | .... | 1984-85 | 1984-85 |

| Name | NHL Teams | NHL Seasons | Regular Schedule GP | G | A | TP | PIM | Playoffs GP | G | A | TP | PIM | NHL Cup Wins | First NHL Season | Last NHL Season |
|---|---|---|---|---|---|---|---|---|---|---|---|---|---|---|---|
| • Teal, Skip | Bos. | 1 | 1 | 0 | 0 | 0 | 0 | .... | .... | .... | .... | .... | .... | 1954-55 | 1954-55 |
| Teal, Vic | NYI | 1 | 1 | 0 | 0 | 0 | 0 | .... | .... | .... | .... | .... | .... | 1973-74 | 1973-74 |
| Tebbutt, Greg | Que., Pit. | 2 | 26 | 0 | 3 | 3 | 35 | .... | .... | .... | .... | .... | .... | 1979-80 | 1983-84 |
| ‡ Tenkrat, Petr | Ana., Nsh., Bos. | 3 | 177 | 22 | 30 | 52 | 84 | .... | .... | .... | .... | .... | .... | 2000-01 | 2006-07 |
| ‡ Tenute, Joey | Wsh. | 1 | 1 | 0 | 0 | 0 | 0 | .... | .... | .... | .... | .... | .... | 2005-06 | 2005-06 |
| Tepper, Stephen | Chi. | 1 | 1 | 0 | 0 | 0 | 0 | .... | .... | .... | .... | .... | .... | 1992-93 | 1992-93 |
| Terbenche, Paul | Chi., Buf. | 5 | 189 | 5 | 26 | 31 | 28 | 12 | 0 | 0 | 0 | 0 | .... | 1967-68 | 1973-74 |
| Terrion, Greg | L.A., Tor. | 8 | 561 | 93 | 150 | 243 | 339 | 35 | 2 | 9 | 11 | 41 | .... | 1980-81 | 1987-88 |
| Terry, Bill | Min. | 1 | 5 | 0 | 0 | 0 | 0 | .... | .... | .... | .... | .... | .... | 1987-88 | 1987-88 |
| • Tertyshny, Dmitri | Phi. | 1 | 62 | 2 | 8 | 10 | 30 | 1 | 0 | 0 | 0 | 0 | .... | 1998-99 | 1998-99 |
| Tessier, Orval | Mtl., Bos. | 3 | 59 | 5 | 7 | 12 | 6 | .... | .... | .... | .... | .... | .... | 1954-55 | 1960-61 |
| Tetarenko, Joey | Fla., Ott., Car. | 4 | 73 | 4 | 1 | 5 | 176 | .... | .... | .... | .... | .... | .... | 2000-01 | 2003-04 |
| ‡ Tezikov, Alexei | Wsh., Van. | 3 | 30 | 1 | 1 | 2 | 2 | .... | .... | .... | .... | .... | .... | 1998-99 | 2001-02 |
| Theberge, Greg | Wsh. | 5 | 153 | 15 | 63 | 78 | 73 | 4 | 0 | 1 | 1 | 0 | .... | 1979-80 | 1983-84 |
| Thelin, Mats | Bos. | 3 | 163 | 8 | 19 | 27 | 107 | 5 | 0 | 0 | 0 | 6 | .... | 1984-85 | 1986-87 |
| Thelven, Michael | Bos. | 5 | 207 | 20 | 80 | 100 | 217 | 34 | 4 | 10 | 14 | 34 | .... | 1985-86 | 1989-90 |
| Therien, Chris | Phi., Dal. | 11 | 764 | 29 | 130 | 159 | 585 | 104 | 4 | 10 | 14 | 68 | .... | 1994-95 | 2005-06 |
| Therrien, Gaston | Que. | 3 | 22 | 0 | 8 | 8 | 12 | 9 | 0 | 1 | 1 | 4 | .... | 1980-81 | 1982-83 |
| Thibaudeau, Gilles | Mtl., NYI, Tor. | 5 | 119 | 25 | 37 | 62 | 40 | 8 | 3 | 3 | 6 | 2 | .... | 1986-87 | 1990-91 |
| Thibeault, Lorrain | Det., Mtl. | 2 | 5 | 0 | 2 | 2 | 2 | .... | .... | .... | .... | .... | .... | 1944-45 | 1945-46 |
| Thiffault, Leo | Min. | 1 | .... | .... | .... | .... | .... | 5 | 0 | 0 | 0 | 0 | .... | 1967-68 | 1967-68 |
| • Thomas, Cy | Chi., Tor. | 1 | 14 | 2 | 2 | 4 | 12 | .... | .... | .... | .... | .... | .... | 1947-48 | 1947-48 |
| Thomas, Reg | Que. | 1 | 39 | 9 | 7 | 16 | 6 | .... | .... | .... | .... | .... | .... | 1979-80 | 1979-80 |
| Thomas, Scott | Buf., L.A. | 3 | 63 | 6 | 4 | 10 | 32 | 12 | 1 | 0 | 1 | 4 | .... | 1992-93 | 2000-01 |
| Thomas, Steve | Tor., Chi., NYI, N.J., Ana., Det. | 20 | 1235 | 421 | 512 | 933 | 1306 | 174 | 54 | 53 | 107 | 187 | .... | 1984-85 | 2003-04 |
| Thomlinson, Dave | St.L., Bos., L.A. | 5 | 42 | 1 | 3 | 4 | 50 | 9 | 3 | 1 | 4 | 4 | .... | 1989-90 | 1994-95 |
| Thompson, Brent | L.A., Wpg., Phx. | 6 | 121 | 1 | 10 | 11 | 352 | 4 | 0 | 0 | 0 | 4 | .... | 1991-92 | 1996-97 |
| • Thompson, Cliff | Bos. | 2 | 13 | 0 | 1 | 1 | 2 | .... | .... | .... | .... | .... | .... | 1941-42 | 1948-49 |
| Thompson, Errol | Tor., Det., Pit. | 10 | 599 | 208 | 185 | 393 | 184 | 34 | 7 | 5 | 12 | 11 | .... | 1970-71 | 1980-81 |
| • Thompson, Ken | Mtl.W. | 1 | 1 | 0 | 0 | 0 | 0 | .... | .... | .... | .... | .... | .... | 1917-18 | 1917-18 |
| • Thompson, Paul | NYR, Chi. | 13 | 582 | 153 | 179 | 332 | 336 | 48 | 11 | 11 | 22 | 54 | 3 | 1926-27 | 1938-39 |
| Thompson, Rocky | Cgy., Fla. | 4 | 25 | 0 | 0 | 0 | 117 | .... | .... | .... | .... | .... | .... | 1997-98 | 2001-02 |
| • Thoms, Bill | Tor., Chi., Bos. | 13 | 548 | 135 | 206 | 341 | 154 | 44 | 6 | 10 | 16 | 6 | .... | 1932-33 | 1944-45 |
| • Thomson, Bill | Det. | 2 | 9 | 2 | 2 | 4 | 0 | 2 | 0 | 0 | 0 | 0 | .... | 1938-39 | 1943-44 |
| Thomson, Floyd | St.L. | 8 | 411 | 56 | 97 | 153 | 341 | 10 | 0 | 2 | 2 | 6 | .... | 1971-72 | 1979-80 |
| Thomson, Jim | Wsh., Hfd., N.J., L.A., Ott., Ana. | 7 | 115 | 4 | 3 | 7 | 416 | 1 | 0 | 0 | 0 | 0 | .... | 1986-87 | 1993-94 |
| • Thomson, Jimmy | Tor., Chi. | 13 | 787 | 19 | 215 | 234 | 920 | 63 | 2 | 13 | 15 | 135 | 4 | 1945-46 | 1957-58 |
| • Thomson, Rhys | Mtl., Tor. | 2 | 25 | 0 | 2 | 2 | 38 | .... | .... | .... | .... | .... | .... | 1939-40 | 1942-43 |
| Thornbury, Tom | Pit. | 1 | 14 | 1 | 8 | 9 | 16 | .... | .... | .... | .... | .... | .... | 1983-84 | 1983-84 |
| Thornton, Scott | Tor., Edm., Mtl., Dal., S.J., L.A. | 17 | 941 | 144 | 141 | 285 | 1459 | 79 | 13 | 14 | 27 | 82 | .... | 1990-91 | 2007-08 |
| • Thorsteinson, Joe | NYA | 1 | 4 | 0 | 0 | 0 | 0 | .... | .... | .... | .... | .... | .... | 1932-33 | 1932-33 |
| • Thurier, Fred | NYA, Bro., NYR | 3 | 80 | 25 | 27 | 52 | 18 | .... | .... | .... | .... | .... | .... | 1940-41 | 1944-45 |
| Thurlby, Tom | Oak. | 1 | 20 | 1 | 1 | 2 | 4 | .... | .... | .... | .... | .... | .... | 1967-68 | 1967-68 |
| Thyer, Mario | Min. | 1 | 5 | 0 | 0 | 0 | 0 | 1 | 0 | 0 | 0 | 2 | .... | 1989-90 | 1989-90 |
| Tibbetts, Billy | Pit., Phi., NYR | 3 | 82 | 2 | 8 | 10 | 269 | .... | .... | .... | .... | .... | .... | 2000-01 | 2002-03 |
| Tichy, Milan | Chi., NYI | 3 | 23 | 0 | 5 | 5 | 40 | .... | .... | .... | .... | .... | .... | 1992-93 | 1995-96 |
| Tidey, Alex | Buf., Edm. | 3 | 9 | 0 | 0 | 0 | 8 | 2 | 0 | 0 | 0 | 0 | .... | 1976-77 | 1979-80 |
| Tikkanen, Esa | Edm., NYR, St.L., N.J., Van., Fla., Wsh. | 15 | 877 | 244 | 386 | 630 | 1077 | 186 | 72 | 60 | 132 | 275 | 5 | 1984-85 | 1998-99 |
| Tiley, Brad | Phx., Phi. | 3 | 11 | 0 | 0 | 0 | 0 | 1 | 0 | 0 | 0 | 0 | .... | 1997-98 | 2000-01 |
| Tilley, Tom | St.L. | 4 | 174 | 4 | 38 | 42 | 89 | 14 | 1 | 3 | 4 | 19 | .... | 1988-89 | 1993-94 |
| ‡ Timander, Mattias | Bos., CBJ, NYI, Phi. | 8 | 419 | 13 | 57 | 70 | 165 | 23 | 3 | 5 | 8 | 8 | .... | 1996-97 | 2003-04 |
| • Timgren, Ray | Tor., Chi. | 6 | 251 | 14 | 44 | 58 | 70 | 30 | 3 | 9 | 12 | 6 | 2 | 1948-49 | 1954-55 |
| ‡ Timonen, Jussi | Phi. | 1 | 14 | 0 | 4 | 4 | 6 | .... | .... | .... | .... | .... | .... | 2006-07 | 2006-07 |
| Tinordi, Mark | NYR, Min., Dal., Wsh. | 12 | 663 | 52 | 148 | 200 | 1514 | 70 | 7 | 11 | 18 | 165 | .... | 1987-88 | 1998-99 |
| Tippett, Dave | Hfd., Wsh., Pit., Phi. | 12 | 721 | 93 | 169 | 262 | 317 | 62 | 6 | 16 | 22 | 34 | .... | 1983-84 | 1993-94 |
| Titanic, Morris | Buf. | 2 | 19 | 0 | 0 | 0 | 0 | .... | .... | .... | .... | .... | .... | 1974-75 | 1975-76 |
| Titov, German | Cgy., Pit., Edm., Ana. | 9 | 624 | 157 | 220 | 377 | 311 | 34 | 11 | 12 | 23 | 18 | .... | 1993-94 | 2001-02 |
| ‡ Tkaczuk, Daniel | Cgy. | 1 | 19 | 4 | 7 | 11 | 14 | .... | .... | .... | .... | .... | .... | 2000-01 | 2000-01 |
| Tkaczuk, Walt | NYR | 14 | 945 | 227 | 451 | 678 | 556 | 93 | 19 | 32 | 51 | 119 | .... | 1967-68 | 1980-81 |
| Toal, Mike | Edm. | 1 | 3 | 0 | 0 | 0 | 0 | .... | .... | .... | .... | .... | .... | 1979-80 | 1979-80 |
| ‡ Tobler, Ryan | T.B. | 1 | 4 | 0 | 0 | 0 | 5 | .... | .... | .... | .... | .... | .... | 2001-02 | 2001-02 |
| Tocchet, Rick | Phi., Pit., L.A., Bos., Wsh., Phx. | 18 | 1144 | 440 | 512 | 952 | 2972 | 145 | 52 | 60 | 112 | 471 | 1 | 1984-85 | 2001-02 |
| Todd, Kevin | N.J., Edm., Chi., L.A., Ana. | 9 | 383 | 70 | 133 | 203 | 225 | 12 | 3 | 2 | 5 | 16 | .... | 1988-89 | 1997-98 |
| Tomalty, Glenn | Wpg. | 1 | 1 | 0 | 0 | 0 | 0 | .... | .... | .... | .... | .... | .... | 1979-80 | 1979-80 |
| Tomlak, Mike | Hfd. | 4 | 141 | 15 | 22 | 37 | 103 | 10 | 0 | 1 | 1 | 4 | .... | 1989-90 | 1993-94 |
| Tomlinson, Dave | Tor., Wpg., Fla. | 4 | 42 | 1 | 3 | 4 | 28 | .... | .... | .... | .... | .... | .... | 1991-92 | 1994-95 |
| Tomlinson, Kirk | Min. | 1 | 1 | 0 | 0 | 0 | 0 | .... | .... | .... | .... | .... | .... | 1987-88 | 1987-88 |
| ‡ Toms, Jeff | T.B., Wsh., NYI, NYR, Pit., Fla. | 8 | 236 | 22 | 33 | 55 | 59 | 1 | 0 | 0 | 0 | 0 | .... | 1995-96 | 2002-03 |
| • Tomson, Jack | NYA | 3 | 15 | 1 | 1 | 2 | 0 | 2 | 0 | 0 | 0 | 0 | .... | 1938-39 | 1940-41 |
| Tonelli, John | NYI, Cgy., L.A., Chi., Que. | 14 | 1028 | 325 | 511 | 836 | 911 | 172 | 40 | 75 | 115 | 200 | 4 | 1978-79 | 1991-92 |
| Tookey, Tim | Wsh., Que., Pit., Phi., L.A. | 7 | 106 | 22 | 36 | 58 | 71 | 10 | 1 | 3 | 4 | 2 | .... | 1980-81 | 1988-89 |
| Toomey, Sean | Min. | 1 | 1 | 0 | 0 | 0 | 0 | .... | .... | .... | .... | .... | .... | 1986-87 | 1986-87 |
| ‡ Toporowski, Shayne | Tor. | 1 | 3 | 0 | 0 | 0 | 7 | .... | .... | .... | .... | .... | .... | 1996-97 | 1996-97 |
| Toppazzini, Jerry | Bos., Chi., Det. | 12 | 783 | 163 | 244 | 407 | 436 | 40 | 13 | 9 | 22 | 13 | .... | 1952-53 | 1963-64 |
| • Toppazzini, Zellio | Bos., NYR, Chi. | 5 | 123 | 21 | 22 | 43 | 49 | 2 | 0 | 0 | 0 | 0 | .... | 1948-49 | 1956-57 |
| Torgaev, Pavel | Cgy., T.B. | 2 | 55 | 6 | 14 | 20 | 20 | 1 | 0 | 0 | 0 | 0 | .... | 1995-96 | 1999-00 |
| Torkki, Jari | Chi. | 1 | 4 | 1 | 0 | 1 | 0 | .... | .... | .... | .... | .... | .... | 1988-89 | 1988-89 |
| Tormanen, Antti | Ott. | 1 | 50 | 7 | 8 | 15 | 28 | .... | .... | .... | .... | .... | .... | 1995-96 | 1995-96 |
| • Touhey, Bill | Mtl.M., Ott., Bos. | 7 | 280 | 65 | 40 | 105 | 107 | 2 | 1 | 0 | 1 | 0 | .... | 1927-28 | 1933-34 |
| • Toupin, Jacques | Chi. | 1 | 8 | 1 | 2 | 3 | 0 | 4 | 0 | 0 | 0 | 0 | .... | 1943-44 | 1943-44 |
| • Townsend, Art | Chi. | 1 | 5 | 0 | 0 | 0 | 0 | .... | .... | .... | .... | .... | .... | 1926-27 | 1926-27 |
| Townshend, Graeme | Bos., NYI, Ott. | 5 | 45 | 3 | 7 | 10 | 28 | .... | .... | .... | .... | .... | .... | 1989-90 | 1993-94 |
| Trader, Larry | Det., St.L., Mtl. | 4 | 91 | 5 | 13 | 18 | 74 | 3 | 0 | 0 | 0 | 0 | .... | 1982-83 | 1987-88 |
| • Trainor, Wes | NYR | 1 | 17 | 1 | 2 | 3 | 6 | .... | .... | .... | .... | .... | .... | 1948-49 | 1948-49 |
| • Trapp, Bob | Chi. | 2 | 82 | 4 | 4 | 8 | 129 | 2 | 0 | 0 | 0 | 4 | .... | 1926-27 | 1927-28 |
| Trapp, Doug | Buf. | 1 | 2 | 0 | 0 | 0 | 0 | .... | .... | .... | .... | .... | .... | 1986-87 | 1986-87 |
| • Traub, Percy | Chi., Det. | 3 | 130 | 3 | 3 | 6 | 217 | 4 | 0 | 0 | 0 | 6 | .... | 1926-27 | 1928-29 |
| Trebil, Dan | Ana., Pit., St.L. | 5 | 85 | 4 | 4 | 8 | 32 | 10 | 0 | 1 | 1 | 8 | .... | 1996-97 | 2000-01 |
| Tredway, Brock | L.A. | 1 | .... | .... | .... | .... | .... | 1 | 0 | 0 | 0 | 0 | .... | 1981-82 | 1981-82 |
| Tremblay, Brent | Wsh. | 2 | 10 | 1 | 0 | 1 | 6 | .... | .... | .... | .... | .... | .... | 1978-79 | 1979-80 |
| Tremblay, Gilles | Mtl. | 9 | 509 | 168 | 162 | 330 | 161 | 48 | 9 | 14 | 23 | 4 | 4 | 1960-61 | 1968-69 |
| • Tremblay, J.C. | Mtl. | 13 | 794 | 57 | 306 | 363 | 204 | 108 | 14 | 51 | 65 | 58 | 5 | 1959-60 | 1971-72 |
| • Tremblay, Marcel | Mtl. | 1 | 10 | 0 | 2 | 2 | 0 | .... | .... | .... | .... | .... | .... | 1938-39 | 1938-39 |
| Tremblay, Mario | Mtl. | 12 | 852 | 258 | 326 | 584 | 1043 | 101 | 20 | 29 | 49 | 187 | 5 | 1974-75 | 1985-86 |
| • Tremblay, Nils | Mtl. | 2 | 3 | 0 | 1 | 1 | 0 | 2 | 0 | 0 | 0 | 0 | .... | 1944-45 | 1945-46 |
| Tremblay, Yannick | Tor., Atl., Van. | 9 | 390 | 38 | 87 | 125 | 178 | .... | .... | .... | .... | .... | .... | 1996-97 | 2006-07 |
| ‡ Trepanier, Pascal | Col., Ana., Nsh. | 6 | 229 | 12 | 22 | 34 | 252 | 2 | 0 | 0 | 0 | 0 | .... | 1997-98 | 2002-03 |
| Trimper, Tim | Chi., Wpg., Min. | 6 | 190 | 30 | 36 | 66 | 153 | 2 | 0 | 0 | 0 | 2 | .... | 1979-80 | 1984-85 |
| ‡ Tripp, John | NYR, L.A. | 2 | 43 | 2 | 7 | 9 | 35 | .... | .... | .... | .... | .... | .... | 2002-03 | 2003-04 |
| ‡ Trnka, Pavel | Ana., Fla. | 7 | 411 | 14 | 63 | 77 | 323 | 4 | 0 | 1 | 1 | 2 | .... | 1997-98 | 2003-04 |
| Trottier, Bryan | NYI, Pit. | 18 | 1279 | 524 | 901 | 1425 | 912 | 221 | 71 | 113 | 184 | 277 | 6 | 1975-76 | 1993-94 |
| • Trottier, Dave | Mtl.M., Det. | 11 | 446 | 121 | 113 | 234 | 517 | 31 | 4 | 3 | 7 | 39 | 1 | 1928-29 | 1938-39 |
| Trottier, Guy | NYR, Tor. | 3 | 115 | 28 | 17 | 45 | 37 | 9 | 1 | 0 | 1 | 16 | .... | 1968-69 | 1971-72 |
| Trottier, Rocky | N.J. | 2 | 38 | 6 | 4 | 10 | 2 | .... | .... | .... | .... | .... | .... | 1983-84 | 1984-85 |
| ‡ Trudel, Jean-Guy | Phx., Min. | 3 | 5 | 0 | 0 | 0 | 4 | .... | .... | .... | .... | .... | .... | 1999-00 | 2002-03 |
| • Trudel, Lou | Chi., Mtl. | 8 | 306 | 49 | 69 | 118 | 122 | 24 | 1 | 3 | 4 | 4 | 2 | 1933-34 | 1940-41 |
| • Trudell, Rene | NYR | 3 | 129 | 24 | 28 | 52 | 72 | 5 | 0 | 0 | 0 | 2 | .... | 1945-46 | 1947-48 |
| Tselios, Nikos | Car. | 1 | 2 | 0 | 0 | 0 | 6 | .... | .... | .... | .... | .... | .... | 2001-02 | 2001-02 |
| ‡ Tsulygin, Nikolai | Ana. | 1 | 22 | 0 | 1 | 1 | 8 | .... | .... | .... | .... | .... | .... | 1996-97 | 1996-97 |
| Tsygurov, Denis | Buf., L.A. | 3 | 51 | 1 | 5 | 6 | 45 | .... | .... | .... | .... | .... | .... | 1993-94 | 1995-96 |
| Tsyplakov, Vladimir | L.A., Buf. | 6 | 331 | 69 | 101 | 170 | 90 | 18 | 1 | 2 | 3 | 16 | .... | 1995-96 | 2000-01 |
| Tucker, John | Buf., Wsh., NYI, T.B. | 12 | 656 | 177 | 259 | 436 | 285 | 31 | 10 | 18 | 28 | 24 | .... | 1983-84 | 1995-96 |
| • Tudin, Connie | Mtl. | 1 | 4 | 0 | 1 | 1 | 4 | .... | .... | .... | .... | .... | .... | 1941-42 | 1941-42 |
| Tudor, Rob | Van., St.L. | 3 | 28 | 4 | 4 | 8 | 19 | 3 | 0 | 0 | 0 | 0 | .... | 1978-79 | 1982-83 |
| Tuer, Allan | L.A., Min., Hfd. | 4 | 57 | 1 | 1 | 2 | 208 | .... | .... | .... | .... | .... | .... | 1985-86 | 1989-90 |
| Tuomainen, Marko | Edm., L.A., NYI | 4 | 79 | 9 | 9 | 18 | 84 | 1 | 0 | 0 | 0 | 0 | .... | 1994-95 | 2001-02 |
| Turcotte, Alfie | Mtl., Wpg., Wsh. | 7 | 112 | 17 | 29 | 46 | 49 | 5 | 0 | 0 | 0 | 0 | .... | 1983-84 | 1990-91 |
| Turcotte, Darren | NYR, Hfd., Wpg., S.J., St.L., Nsh. | 12 | 635 | 195 | 216 | 411 | 301 | 35 | 6 | 8 | 14 | 12 | .... | 1988-89 | 1999-00 |
| Turgeon, Pierre | Buf., NYI, Mtl., St.L., Dal., Col. | 19 | 1294 | 515 | 812 | 1327 | 452 | 109 | 35 | 62 | 97 | 36 | .... | 1987-88 | 2006-07 |
| Turgeon, Sylvain | Hfd., N.J., Mtl., Ott. | 12 | 669 | 269 | 226 | 495 | 691 | 36 | 4 | 7 | 11 | 22 | .... | 1983-84 | 1994-95 |
| Turlick, Gord | Bos. | 1 | 2 | 0 | 0 | 0 | 2 | .... | .... | .... | .... | .... | .... | 1959-60 | 1959-60 |
| Turnbull, Ian | Tor., L.A., Pit. | 10 | 628 | 123 | 317 | 440 | 736 | 55 | 13 | 32 | 45 | 94 | .... | 1973-74 | 1982-83 |
| Turnbull, Perry | St.L., Mtl., Wpg. | 9 | 608 | 188 | 163 | 351 | 1245 | 34 | 6 | 7 | 13 | 86 | .... | 1979-80 | 1987-88 |
| Turnbull, Randy | Cgy. | 1 | 1 | 0 | 0 | 0 | 2 | .... | .... | .... | .... | .... | .... | 1981-82 | 1981-82 |
| • Turner, Bob | Mtl., Chi. | 8 | 478 | 19 | 51 | 70 | 307 | 68 | 1 | 4 | 5 | 44 | 5 | 1955-56 | 1962-63 |
| Turner, Brad | NYI | 1 | 3 | 0 | 0 | 0 | 0 | .... | .... | .... | .... | .... | .... | 1991-92 | 1991-92 |

*Brock Tredway*

*Guy Trottier*

*Ian Turnbull*

*Ed Van Impe*

*David Volek*

*Kurt Walker*

*Wes Walz*

*Grant Warwick*

| | | | Regular Schedule | | | | | Playoffs | | | | | | | |
|---|---|---|---|---|---|---|---|---|---|---|---|---|---|---|---|
| Name | NHL Teams | NHL Seasons | GP | G | A | TP | PIM | GP | G | A | TP | PIM | NHL Cup Wins | First NHL Season | Last NHL Season |
| Turner, Dean | NYR, Col., L.A. | 4 | 35 | 1 | 0 | 1 | 59 | .... | .... | .... | .... | .... | .... | 1978-79 | 1982-83 |
| • Tustin, Norm | NYR | 1 | 18 | 2 | 4 | 6 | 0 | .... | .... | .... | .... | .... | .... | 1941-42 | 1941-42 |
| • Tuten, Aud | Chi. | 2 | 39 | 4 | 8 | 12 | 48 | .... | .... | .... | .... | .... | .... | 1941-42 | 1942-43 |
| Tutt, Brian | Wsh. | 1 | 7 | 1 | 0 | 1 | 2 | .... | .... | .... | .... | .... | .... | 1989-90 | 1989-90 |
| Tuttle, Steve | St.L. | 3 | 144 | 28 | 28 | 56 | 12 | 17 | 1 | 6 | 7 | 2 | .... | 1988-89 | 1990-91 |
| ‡ Tuzzolino, Tony | Ana., NYR, Bos. | 3 | 9 | 0 | 0 | 0 | 7 | .... | .... | .... | .... | .... | .... | 1997-98 | 2001-02 |
| ‡ Tverdovsky, Oleg | Ana., Wpg., Phx., N.J., Car., L.A. | 11 | 713 | 77 | 240 | 317 | 291 | 45 | 0 | 14 | 14 | 6 | 2 | 1994-95 | 2006-07 |
| ‡ Tvrdon, Roman | Wsh. | 1 | 9 | 0 | 1 | 1 | 2 | .... | .... | .... | .... | .... | .... | 2003-04 | 2003-04 |
| Twist, Tony | St.L., Que. | 10 | 445 | 10 | 18 | 28 | 1121 | 18 | 1 | 1 | 2 | 22 | .... | 1989-90 | 1998-99 |

## U V

| Name | NHL Teams | NHL Seasons | GP | G | A | TP | PIM | GP | G | A | TP | PIM | NHL Cup Wins | First NHL Season | Last NHL Season |
|---|---|---|---|---|---|---|---|---|---|---|---|---|---|---|---|
| Ubriaco, Gene | Pit., Oak., Chi. | 3 | 177 | 39 | 35 | 74 | 50 | 11 | 2 | 0 | 2 | 4 | .... | 1967-68 | 1969-70 |
| ‡ Ulanov, Igor | Wpg., Wsh., Chi., T.B., Mtl., Edm., NYR, Fla. | 14 | 739 | 27 | 135 | 162 | 1151 | 39 | 1 | 4 | 5 | 84 | .... | 1991-92 | 2005-06 |
| Ullman, Norm | Det., Tor. | 20 | 1410 | 490 | 739 | 1229 | 712 | 106 | 30 | 53 | 83 | 67 | .... | 1955-56 | 1974-75 |
| ‡ Ulmer, Jeff | NYR | 1 | 21 | 3 | 0 | 3 | 8 | .... | .... | .... | .... | .... | .... | 2000-01 | 2000-01 |
| ‡ Ulmer, Layne | NYR | 1 | 1 | 0 | 0 | 0 | 0 | .... | .... | .... | .... | .... | .... | 2003-04 | 2003-04 |
| Unger, Garry | Tor., Det., St.L., Atl., L.A., Edm. | 16 | 1105 | 413 | 391 | 804 | 1075 | 52 | 12 | 18 | 30 | 105 | .... | 1967-68 | 1982-83 |
| ‡ Ustorf, Stefan | Wsh. | 2 | 54 | 7 | 10 | 17 | 16 | 5 | 0 | 0 | 0 | 0 | .... | 1995-96 | 1996-97 |
| Vachon, Nick | NYI | 1 | 1 | 0 | 0 | 0 | 0 | .... | .... | .... | .... | .... | .... | 1996-97 | 1996-97 |
| Vadnais, Carol | Mtl., Oak., Cal., Bos., NYR, N.J. | 17 | 1087 | 169 | 418 | 587 | 1813 | 106 | 10 | 40 | 50 | 185 | 2 | 1966-67 | 1982-83 |
| ‡ Vaic, Lubomir | Van. | 2 | 9 | 1 | 1 | 2 | 2 | .... | .... | .... | .... | .... | .... | 1997-98 | 1999-00 |
| Vail, Eric | Atl., Cgy., Det. | 9 | 591 | 216 | 260 | 476 | 281 | 20 | 5 | 6 | 11 | 6 | .... | 1973-74 | 1981-82 |
| • Vail, Sparky | NYR | 2 | 50 | 4 | 1 | 5 | 18 | 10 | 0 | 0 | 0 | 2 | .... | 1928-29 | 1929-30 |
| Vaive, Rick | Van., Tor., Chi., Buf. | 13 | 876 | 441 | 347 | 788 | 1445 | 54 | 27 | 16 | 43 | 111 | .... | 1979-80 | 1991-92 |
| Valentine, Chris | Wsh. | 3 | 105 | 43 | 52 | 95 | 127 | 2 | 0 | 0 | 0 | 4 | .... | 1981-82 | 1983-84 |
| Valicevic, Rob | Nsh., L.A., Ana., Dal. | 6 | 193 | 28 | 20 | 48 | 61 | .... | .... | .... | .... | .... | .... | 1998-99 | 2003-04 |
| Valiquette, Jack | Tor., Col. | 7 | 350 | 84 | 134 | 218 | 79 | 23 | 3 | 6 | 9 | 4 | .... | 1974-75 | 1980-81 |
| Valk, Garry | Van., Ana., Pit., Tor., Chi. | 13 | 777 | 100 | 156 | 256 | 747 | 61 | 6 | 7 | 13 | 79 | .... | 1990-91 | 2002-03 |
| Vallis, Lindsay | Mtl. | 1 | 1 | 0 | 0 | 0 | 0 | .... | .... | .... | .... | .... | .... | 1993-94 | 1993-94 |
| Van Allen, Shaun | Edm., Ana., Ott., Dal., Mtl. | 13 | 794 | 84 | 185 | 269 | 481 | 61 | 1 | 7 | 8 | 45 | .... | 1990-91 | 2003-04 |
| Van Boxmeer, John | Mtl., Col., Buf., Que. | 11 | 588 | 84 | 274 | 358 | 465 | 38 | 5 | 15 | 20 | 37 | .... | 1973-74 | 1983-84 |
| Van Dorp, Wayne | Edm., Pit., Chi., Que. | 6 | 125 | 12 | 12 | 24 | 565 | 27 | 0 | 1 | 1 | 42 | .... | 1986-87 | 1991-92 |
| Van Drunen, David | Ott. | 1 | 1 | 0 | 0 | 0 | 0 | .... | .... | .... | .... | .... | .... | 1999-00 | 1999-00 |
| ‡ Van Impe, Darren | Ana., Bos., NYR, Fla., NYI, CBJ | 9 | 411 | 25 | 90 | 115 | 397 | 33 | 3 | 9 | 12 | 28 | .... | 1994-95 | 2002-03 |
| Van Impe, Ed | Chi., Phi., Pit. | 11 | 700 | 27 | 126 | 153 | 1025 | 66 | 1 | 12 | 13 | 131 | 2 | 1966-67 | 1976-77 |
| VandenBussche, Ryan | NYR, Chi., Pit. | 9 | 310 | 10 | 10 | 20 | 702 | 1 | 0 | 0 | 0 | 0 | .... | 1996-97 | 2005-06 |
| ‡ Varada, Vaclav | Buf., Ott. | 10 | 493 | 58 | 125 | 183 | 410 | 87 | 11 | 19 | 30 | 82 | .... | 1995-96 | 2005-06 |
| ‡ Varis, Petri | Chi. | 1 | 1 | 0 | 0 | 0 | 0 | .... | .... | .... | .... | .... | .... | 1997-98 | 1997-98 |
| ‡ Varlamov, Sergei | Cgy., St.L. | 4 | 63 | 8 | 7 | 15 | 26 | 1 | 0 | 0 | 0 | 2 | .... | 1997-98 | 2002-03 |
| Varvio, Jarkko | Dal. | 2 | 13 | 3 | 4 | 7 | 4 | .... | .... | .... | .... | .... | .... | 1993-94 | 1994-95 |
| Vasilevski, Alexander | St.L. | 2 | 4 | 0 | 0 | 0 | 2 | .... | .... | .... | .... | .... | .... | 1995-96 | 1996-97 |
| Vasiliev, Alexei | NYR | 1 | 1 | 0 | 0 | 0 | 2 | .... | .... | .... | .... | .... | .... | 1999-00 | 1999-00 |
| ‡ Vasiljevs, Herbert | Fla., Atl., Van. | 4 | 51 | 8 | 7 | 15 | 22 | .... | .... | .... | .... | .... | .... | 1998-99 | 2001-02 |
| Vasilyev, Andrei | NYI, Phx. | 4 | 16 | 2 | 5 | 7 | 6 | .... | .... | .... | .... | .... | .... | 1994-95 | 1998-99 |
| Vaske, Dennis | NYI, Bos. | 9 | 235 | 5 | 41 | 46 | 253 | 22 | 0 | 7 | 7 | 16 | .... | 1990-91 | 1998-99 |
| • Vasko, Moose | Chi., Min. | 13 | 786 | 34 | 166 | 200 | 719 | 78 | 2 | 7 | 9 | 73 | 1 | 1956-57 | 1969-70 |
| Vasko, Rick | Det. | 3 | 31 | 3 | 7 | 10 | 29 | .... | .... | .... | .... | .... | .... | 1977-78 | 1980-81 |
| ‡ Vauclair, Julien | Ott. | 1 | 1 | 0 | 0 | 0 | 2 | .... | .... | .... | .... | .... | .... | 2003-04 | 2003-04 |
| Vautour, Yvon | NYI, Col., N.J., Que. | 6 | 204 | 26 | 33 | 59 | 401 | .... | .... | .... | .... | .... | .... | 1979-80 | 1984-85 |
| Vaydik, Greg | Chi. | 1 | 5 | 0 | 0 | 0 | 0 | .... | .... | .... | .... | .... | .... | 1976-77 | 1976-77 |
| Veitch, Darren | Wsh., Det., Tor. | 10 | 511 | 48 | 209 | 257 | 296 | 33 | 4 | 11 | 15 | 33 | .... | 1980-81 | 1990-91 |
| Velischek, Randy | Min., N.J., Que. | 10 | 509 | 21 | 76 | 97 | 401 | 44 | 2 | 5 | 7 | 32 | .... | 1982-83 | 1991-92 |
| Vellucci, Mike | Hfd. | 1 | 2 | 0 | 0 | 0 | 11 | .... | .... | .... | .... | .... | .... | 1987-88 | 1987-88 |
| Venasky, Vic | L.A. | 7 | 430 | 61 | 101 | 162 | 66 | 21 | 1 | 5 | 6 | 12 | .... | 1972-73 | 1978-79 |
| Veneruzzo, Gary | St.L. | 2 | 7 | 1 | 1 | 2 | 0 | 9 | 0 | 2 | 2 | 2 | .... | 1967-68 | 1971-72 |
| Verbeek, Pat | N.J., Hfd., NYR, Dal., Det. | 20 | 1424 | 522 | 541 | 1063 | 2905 | 117 | 26 | 36 | 62 | 225 | 1 | 1982-83 | 2001-02 |
| Vermette, Mark | Que. | 4 | 67 | 5 | 13 | 18 | 33 | .... | .... | .... | .... | .... | .... | 1988-89 | 1991-92 |
| ‡ Vernarsky, Kris | Bos. | 2 | 17 | 1 | 0 | 1 | 2 | .... | .... | .... | .... | .... | .... | 2002-03 | 2003-04 |
| ‡ Verot, Darcy | Wsh. | 1 | 37 | 0 | 2 | 2 | 135 | .... | .... | .... | .... | .... | .... | 2003-04 | 2003-04 |
| Verret, Claude | Buf. | 2 | 14 | 2 | 5 | 7 | 2 | .... | .... | .... | .... | .... | .... | 1983-84 | 1984-85 |
| Verstraete, Leigh | Tor. | 3 | 8 | 0 | 1 | 1 | 14 | .... | .... | .... | .... | .... | .... | 1982-83 | 1987-88 |
| Ververgaert, Dennis | Van., Phi., Wsh. | 8 | 583 | 176 | 216 | 392 | 247 | 8 | 1 | 2 | 3 | 6 | .... | 1973-74 | 1980-81 |
| Vesey, Jim | St.L., Bos. | 3 | 15 | 1 | 2 | 3 | 7 | .... | .... | .... | .... | .... | .... | 1988-89 | 1991-92 |
| Veysey, Sid | Van. | 1 | 1 | 0 | 0 | 0 | 0 | .... | .... | .... | .... | .... | .... | 1977-78 | 1977-78 |
| Vial, Dennis | NYR, Det., Ott. | 8 | 242 | 4 | 15 | 19 | 794 | .... | .... | .... | .... | .... | .... | 1990-91 | 1997-98 |
| Vickers, Steve | NYR | 10 | 698 | 246 | 340 | 586 | 330 | 68 | 24 | 25 | 49 | 58 | .... | 1972-73 | 1981-82 |
| ‡ Vigier, J.P. | Atl. | 6 | 213 | 23 | 23 | 46 | 97 | .... | .... | .... | .... | .... | .... | 2000-01 | 2006-07 |
| Vigneault, Alain | St.L. | 2 | 42 | 2 | 5 | 7 | 82 | 4 | 0 | 1 | 1 | 26 | .... | 1981-82 | 1982-83 |
| ‡ Viitakoski, Vesa | Cgy. | 3 | 23 | 2 | 4 | 6 | 8 | .... | .... | .... | .... | .... | .... | 1993-94 | 1995-96 |
| Vilgrain, Claude | Van., N.J., Phi. | 5 | 89 | 21 | 32 | 53 | 78 | 11 | 1 | 1 | 2 | 17 | .... | 1987-88 | 1993-94 |
| Vincelette, Dan | Chi., Que. | 6 | 193 | 20 | 22 | 42 | 351 | 12 | 0 | 0 | 0 | 4 | .... | 1986-87 | 1991-92 |
| Vipond, Pete | Cal. | 1 | 3 | 0 | 0 | 0 | 0 | .... | .... | .... | .... | .... | .... | 1972-73 | 1972-73 |
| Virta, Hannu | Buf. | 5 | 245 | 25 | 101 | 126 | 66 | 17 | 1 | 3 | 4 | 6 | .... | 1981-82 | 1985-86 |
| ‡ Virta, Tony | Min. | 1 | 8 | 2 | 3 | 5 | 0 | .... | .... | .... | .... | .... | .... | 2001-02 | 2001-02 |
| Virtue, Terry | Bos., NYR | 2 | 5 | 0 | 0 | 0 | 0 | .... | .... | .... | .... | .... | .... | 1998-99 | 1999-00 |
| Visheau, Mark | Wpg., L.A. | 2 | 29 | 1 | 3 | 4 | 107 | .... | .... | .... | .... | .... | .... | 1993-94 | 1998-99 |
| Vitolinsh, Harijs | Wpg. | 1 | 8 | 0 | 0 | 0 | 4 | .... | .... | .... | .... | .... | .... | 1993-94 | 1993-94 |
| Viveiros, Emanuel | Min. | 3 | 29 | 1 | 11 | 12 | 6 | .... | .... | .... | .... | .... | .... | 1985-86 | 1987-88 |
| ‡ Vlasak, Tomas | L.A. | 1 | 10 | 1 | 3 | 4 | 2 | .... | .... | .... | .... | .... | .... | 2000-01 | 2000-01 |
| • Vokes, Ed | Chi. | 1 | 5 | 0 | 0 | 0 | 0 | .... | .... | .... | .... | .... | .... | 1930-31 | 1930-31 |
| Volcan, Mickey | Hfd., Cgy. | 4 | 162 | 8 | 33 | 41 | 146 | .... | .... | .... | .... | .... | .... | 1980-81 | 1983-84 |
| Volchkov, Alexandre | Wsh. | 1 | 3 | 0 | 0 | 0 | 0 | .... | .... | .... | .... | .... | .... | 1999-00 | 1999-00 |
| Volek, David | NYI | 6 | 396 | 95 | 154 | 249 | 201 | 15 | 5 | 5 | 10 | 2 | .... | 1988-89 | 1993-94 |
| Volmar, Doug | Det., L.A. | 4 | 62 | 13 | 8 | 21 | 26 | 2 | 1 | 0 | 1 | 0 | .... | 1969-70 | 1972-73 |
| ‡ Von Arx, Reto | Chi. | 1 | 19 | 3 | 1 | 4 | 4 | .... | .... | .... | .... | .... | .... | 2000-01 | 2000-01 |
| Von Stefenelli, Phil | Bos., Ott. | 2 | 33 | 0 | 5 | 5 | 23 | .... | .... | .... | .... | .... | .... | 1995-96 | 1996-97 |
| Vopat, Jan | L.A., Nsh. | 5 | 126 | 11 | 20 | 31 | 70 | 2 | 0 | 1 | 1 | 2 | .... | 1995-96 | 1999-00 |
| Vopat, Roman | St.L., L.A., Chi., Phi. | 4 | 133 | 6 | 14 | 20 | 253 | .... | .... | .... | .... | .... | .... | 1995-96 | 1998-99 |
| ‡ Vorobiev, Pavel | Chi. | 2 | 57 | 10 | 15 | 25 | 38 | .... | .... | .... | .... | .... | .... | 2003-04 | 2005-06 |
| ‡ Vorobiev, Vladimir | NYR, Edm. | 3 | 33 | 9 | 7 | 16 | 14 | 1 | 0 | 0 | 0 | 0 | .... | 1996-97 | 1998-99 |
| • Voss, Carl | Tor., NYR, Det., Ott., St.L., NYA, Mtl.M., Chi. | 8 | 261 | 34 | 70 | 104 | 50 | 24 | 5 | 3 | 8 | 0 | 1 | 1926-27 | 1937-38 |
| Vujtek, Vladimir | Mtl., Edm., T.B., Atl., Pit. | 6 | 110 | 7 | 30 | 37 | 38 | .... | .... | .... | .... | .... | .... | 1991-92 | 2002-03 |
| Vukota, Mick | NYI, T.B., Mtl. | 11 | 574 | 17 | 29 | 46 | 2071 | 23 | 0 | 0 | 0 | 73 | .... | 1987-88 | 1997-98 |
| Vyazmikin, Igor | Edm. | 1 | 4 | 1 | 0 | 1 | 0 | .... | .... | .... | .... | .... | .... | 1990-91 | 1990-91 |
| ‡ Vyshedkevich, Sergei | Atl. | 2 | 30 | 2 | 5 | 7 | 16 | .... | .... | .... | .... | .... | .... | 1999-00 | 2000-01 |

## W

| Name | NHL Teams | NHL Seasons | GP | G | A | TP | PIM | GP | G | A | TP | PIM | NHL Cup Wins | First NHL Season | Last NHL Season |
|---|---|---|---|---|---|---|---|---|---|---|---|---|---|---|---|
| Waddell, Don | L.A. | 1 | 1 | 0 | 0 | 0 | 0 | .... | .... | .... | .... | .... | .... | 1980-81 | 1980-81 |
| • Waite, Frank | NYR | 1 | 17 | 1 | 3 | 4 | 4 | .... | .... | .... | .... | .... | .... | 1930-31 | 1930-31 |
| Walker, Gord | NYR, L.A. | 4 | 31 | 3 | 4 | 7 | 23 | .... | .... | .... | .... | .... | .... | 1986-87 | 1989-90 |
| Walker, Howard | Wsh., Cgy. | 3 | 83 | 2 | 13 | 15 | 133 | .... | .... | .... | .... | .... | .... | 1980-81 | 1982-83 |
| • Walker, Jack | Det. | 2 | 80 | 5 | 8 | 13 | 18 | .... | .... | .... | .... | .... | .... | 1926-27 | 1927-28 |
| Walker, Kurt | Tor. | 3 | 71 | 4 | 5 | 9 | 142 | 16 | 0 | 0 | 0 | 34 | .... | 1975-76 | 1977-78 |
| Walker, Russ | L.A. | 2 | 17 | 1 | 0 | 1 | 41 | .... | .... | .... | .... | .... | .... | 1976-77 | 1977-78 |
| Wall, Bob | Det., L.A., St.L. | 8 | 322 | 30 | 55 | 85 | 155 | 22 | 0 | 3 | 3 | 2 | .... | 1964-65 | 1971-72 |
| Wallin, Jesse | Det. | 4 | 49 | 0 | 2 | 2 | 34 | .... | .... | .... | .... | .... | .... | 1999-00 | 2002-03 |
| Wallin, Peter | NYR | 2 | 52 | 3 | 14 | 17 | 14 | 14 | 2 | 6 | 8 | 6 | .... | 1980-81 | 1981-82 |
| Walsh, Jim | Buf. | 1 | 4 | 0 | 1 | 1 | 4 | .... | .... | .... | .... | .... | .... | 1981-82 | 1981-82 |
| Walsh, Mike | NYI | 2 | 14 | 2 | 0 | 2 | 4 | .... | .... | .... | .... | .... | .... | 1987-88 | 1988-89 |
| Walter, Ryan | Wsh., Mtl., Van. | 15 | 1003 | 264 | 382 | 646 | 946 | 113 | 16 | 35 | 51 | 62 | 1 | 1978-79 | 1992-93 |
| • Walton, Bobby | Mtl. | 1 | 4 | 0 | 0 | 0 | 0 | .... | .... | .... | .... | .... | .... | 1943-44 | 1943-44 |
| Walton, Mike | Tor., Bos., Van., St.L., Chi. | 12 | 588 | 201 | 247 | 448 | 357 | 47 | 14 | 10 | 24 | 45 | 2 | 1965-66 | 1978-79 |
| Walz, Wes | Bos., Phi., Cgy., Det., Min. | 13 | 607 | 109 | 151 | 260 | 343 | 32 | 10 | 7 | 17 | 20 | .... | 1989-90 | 2007-08 |
| Wappel, Gord | Atl., Cgy. | 3 | 20 | 1 | 1 | 2 | 10 | 2 | 0 | 0 | 0 | 4 | .... | 1979-80 | 1981-82 |
| Ward, Dixon | Van., L.A., Tor., Buf., Bos., NYR | 10 | 537 | 95 | 129 | 224 | 431 | 62 | 14 | 20 | 34 | 46 | .... | 1992-93 | 2002-03 |
| • Ward, Don | Chi., Bos. | 2 | 34 | 0 | 1 | 1 | 16 | .... | .... | .... | .... | .... | .... | 1957-58 | 1959-60 |
| Ward, Ed | Que., Cgy., Atl., Ana., N.J. | 8 | 278 | 23 | 26 | 49 | 354 | .... | .... | .... | .... | .... | .... | 1993-94 | 2000-01 |
| • Ward, Jimmy | Mtl.M., Mtl. | 12 | 527 | 147 | 127 | 274 | 455 | 36 | 4 | 4 | 8 | 26 | 1 | 1927-28 | 1938-39 |
| Ward, Joe | Col. | 1 | 4 | 0 | 0 | 0 | 2 | .... | .... | .... | .... | .... | .... | 1980-81 | 1980-81 |
| ‡ Ward, Lance | Fla., Ana. | 4 | 209 | 4 | 12 | 16 | 391 | .... | .... | .... | .... | .... | .... | 2000-01 | 2003-04 |
| Ward, Ron | Tor., Van. | 2 | 89 | 2 | 5 | 7 | 6 | .... | .... | .... | .... | .... | .... | 1969-70 | 1971-72 |
| Ware, Jeff | Tor., Fla. | 3 | 21 | 0 | 1 | 1 | 12 | .... | .... | .... | .... | .... | .... | 1996-97 | 1998-99 |

| Name | NHL Teams | NHL Seasons | Regular Schedule | | | | | Playoffs | | | | | NHL Cup Wins | First NHL Season | Last NHL Season |
|---|---|---|---|---|---|---|---|---|---|---|---|---|---|---|---|
| | | | GP | G | A | TP | PIM | GP | G | A | TP | PIM | | | |
| Ware, Michael | Edm. | 2 | 5 | 0 | 1 | 1 | 15 | .... | .... | .... | .... | .... | .... | 1988-89 | 1989-90 |
| • Wares, Eddie | NYR, Det., Chi. | 9 | 321 | 60 | 102 | 162 | 161 | 45 | 5 | 7 | 12 | 34 | 1 | 1936-37 | 1946-47 |
| Warner, Bob | Tor. | 2 | 10 | 1 | 1 | 2 | 4 | 4 | 0 | 0 | 0 | 0 | .... | 1975-76 | 1976-77 |
| Warner, Jim | Hfd. | 1 | 32 | 0 | 3 | 3 | 10 | .... | .... | .... | .... | .... | .... | 1979-80 | 1979-80 |
| Warrener, Rhett | Fla., Buf., Cgy. | 12 | 714 | 24 | 82 | 106 | 899 | 101 | 1 | 7 | 8 | 68 | .... | 1995-96 | 2007-08 |
| Warriner, Todd | Tor., T.B., Phx., Van., Phi., Nsh. | 9 | 453 | 65 | 89 | 154 | 249 | 21 | 2 | 1 | 3 | 6 | .... | 1994-95 | 2002-03 |
| • Warwick, Billy | NYR | 2 | 14 | 3 | 3 | 6 | 16 | .... | .... | .... | .... | .... | .... | 1942-43 | 1943-44 |
| • Warwick, Grant | NYR, Bos., Mtl. | 9 | 395 | 147 | 142 | 289 | 220 | 16 | 2 | 4 | 6 | 6 | .... | 1941-42 | 1949-50 |
| Washburn, Steve | Fla., Van., Phi. | 6 | 93 | 14 | 15 | 29 | 42 | 1 | 0 | 1 | 1 | 0 | .... | 1995-96 | 2000-01 |
| • Wasnie, Nick | Chi., Mtl., NYA, Ott., St.L. | 7 | 248 | 57 | 34 | 91 | 176 | 20 | 6 | 3 | 9 | 20 | 2 | 1927-28 | 1934-35 |
| Watson, Bill | Chi. | 4 | 115 | 23 | 36 | 59 | 12 | 6 | 0 | 2 | 2 | 0 | .... | 1985-86 | 1988-89 |
| Watson, Bryan | Mtl., Det., Oak., Pit., St.L., Wsh. | 16 | 878 | 17 | 135 | 152 | 2212 | 32 | 2 | 0 | 2 | 70 | 1 | 1963-64 | 1978-79 |
| Watson, Dave | Col. | 2 | 18 | 0 | 1 | 1 | 10 | .... | .... | .... | .... | .... | .... | 1979-80 | 1980-81 |
| • Watson, Harry | Bro., Det., Tor., Chi. | 14 | 809 | 236 | 207 | 443 | 150 | 62 | 16 | 9 | 25 | 27 | 5 | 1941-42 | 1956-57 |
| Watson, Jim | Det., Buf. | 8 | 221 | 4 | 19 | 23 | 345 | .... | .... | .... | .... | .... | .... | 1963-64 | 1971-72 |
| Watson, Jimmy | Phi. | 10 | 613 | 38 | 148 | 186 | 492 | 101 | 5 | 34 | 39 | 89 | 2 | 1972-73 | 1981-82 |
| Watson, Joe | Bos., Phi., Col. | 14 | 835 | 38 | 178 | 216 | 447 | 84 | 3 | 12 | 15 | 82 | 2 | 1964-65 | 1978-79 |
| • Watson, Phil | NYR, Mtl. | 13 | 590 | 144 | 265 | 409 | 532 | 54 | 10 | 25 | 35 | 67 | 2 | 1935-36 | 1947-48 |
| ‡ Watt, Mike | Edm., NYI, Nsh., Car. | 5 | 157 | 15 | 26 | 41 | 41 | .... | .... | .... | .... | .... | .... | 1997-98 | 2002-03 |
| Watters, Tim | Wpg., L.A. | 14 | 741 | 26 | 151 | 177 | 1289 | 82 | 1 | 5 | 6 | 115 | .... | 1981-82 | 1994-95 |
| Watts, Brian | Det. | 1 | 4 | 0 | 0 | 0 | 0 | .... | .... | .... | .... | .... | .... | 1975-76 | 1975-76 |
| Webb, Steve | NYI, Pit. | 8 | 321 | 5 | 13 | 18 | 532 | 14 | 0 | 0 | 0 | 28 | .... | 1996-97 | 2003-04 |
| • Webster, Aubrey | Phi., Mtl.M. | 2 | 5 | 0 | 0 | 0 | 0 | .... | .... | .... | .... | .... | .... | 1930-31 | 1934-35 |
| • Webster, Don | Tor. | 1 | 27 | 7 | 6 | 13 | 28 | 5 | 0 | 0 | 0 | 12 | .... | 1943-44 | 1943-44 |
| Webster, John | NYR | 1 | 14 | 0 | 0 | 0 | 4 | .... | .... | .... | .... | .... | .... | 1949-50 | 1949-50 |
| Webster, Tom | Bos., Det., Cal. | 5 | 102 | 33 | 42 | 75 | 61 | 1 | 0 | 0 | 0 | 0 | .... | 1968-69 | 1979-80 |
| • Weiland, Cooney | Bos., Ott., Det. | 11 | 509 | 173 | 160 | 333 | 147 | 45 | 12 | 10 | 22 | 12 | 2 | 1928-29 | 1938-39 |
| ‡ Weinhandl, Mattias | NYI, Min. | 4 | 182 | 19 | 37 | 56 | 70 | 5 | 0 | 0 | 0 | 2 | .... | 2002-03 | 2006-07 |
| Weinrich, Eric | N.J., Hfd., Chi., Mtl., Bos., Phi., St.L., Van. | 17 | 1157 | 70 | 318 | 388 | 825 | 81 | 6 | 23 | 29 | 67 | .... | 1988-89 | 2005-06 |
| Weir, Stan | Cal., Tor., Edm., Col., Det. | 10 | 642 | 139 | 207 | 346 | 183 | 37 | 6 | 5 | 11 | 4 | .... | 1972-73 | 1982-83 |
| Weir, Wally | Que., Hfd., Pit. | 6 | 320 | 21 | 45 | 66 | 625 | 23 | 0 | 1 | 1 | 96 | .... | 1979-80 | 1984-85 |
| • Wellington, Alex | Que. | 1 | 1 | 0 | 0 | 0 | 0 | .... | .... | .... | .... | .... | .... | 1919-20 | 1919-20 |
| Wells, Chris | Pit., Fla. | 5 | 195 | 9 | 20 | 29 | 193 | 3 | 0 | 0 | 0 | 0 | .... | 1995-96 | 1999-00 |
| Wells, Jay | L.A., Phi., Buf., NYR, St.L., T.B. | 18 | 1098 | 47 | 216 | 263 | 2359 | 114 | 3 | 14 | 17 | 213 | 1 | 1979-80 | 1996-97 |
| Wensink, John | St.L., Bos., Que., Col., N.J. | 8 | 403 | 70 | 68 | 138 | 840 | 43 | 2 | 6 | 8 | 86 | .... | 1973-74 | 1982-83 |
| • Wentworth, Cy | Chi., Mtl.M., Mtl. | 13 | 575 | 39 | 68 | 107 | 355 | 35 | 5 | 6 | 11 | 20 | 1 | 1927-28 | 1939-40 |
| Werenka, Brad | Edm., Que., Chi., Pit., Cgy. | 7 | 320 | 19 | 61 | 80 | 299 | 19 | 2 | 1 | 3 | 14 | .... | 1992-93 | 2000-01 |
| Wesenberg, Brian | Phi. | 1 | 1 | 0 | 0 | 0 | 5 | .... | .... | .... | .... | .... | .... | 1998-99 | 1998-99 |
| Wesley, Blake | Phi., Hfd., Que., Tor. | 7 | 298 | 18 | 46 | 64 | 486 | 19 | 2 | 2 | 4 | 30 | .... | 1979-80 | 1985-86 |
| Wesley, Glen | Bos., Hfd., Car., Tor. | 20 | 1457 | 128 | 409 | 537 | 1045 | 169 | 15 | 37 | 52 | 141 | 1 | 1987-88 | 2007-08 |
| Westfall, Ed | Bos., NYI | 18 | 1226 | 231 | 394 | 625 | 544 | 95 | 22 | 37 | 59 | 41 | 2 | 1961-62 | 1978-79 |
| Westlund, Tommy | Car. | 4 | 203 | 9 | 13 | 22 | 48 | 25 | 1 | 0 | 1 | 17 | .... | 1999-00 | 2002-03 |
| ‡ Westrum, Erik | Phx., Min., Tor. | 3 | 27 | 1 | 2 | 3 | 22 | .... | .... | .... | .... | .... | .... | 2003-04 | 2006-07 |
| Wharram, Kenny | Chi. | 14 | 766 | 252 | 281 | 533 | 222 | 80 | 16 | 27 | 43 | 38 | 1 | 1951-52 | 1968-69 |
| • Wharton, Len | NYR | 1 | 1 | 0 | 0 | 0 | 0 | .... | .... | .... | .... | .... | .... | 1944-45 | 1944-45 |
| Wheeldon, Simon | NYR, Wpg. | 3 | 15 | 0 | 2 | 2 | 10 | .... | .... | .... | .... | .... | .... | 1987-88 | 1990-91 |
| • Wheldon, Don | St.L. | 1 | 2 | 0 | 0 | 0 | 0 | .... | .... | .... | .... | .... | .... | 1974-75 | 1974-75 |
| Whelton, Bill | Wpg. | 1 | 2 | 0 | 0 | 0 | 0 | .... | .... | .... | .... | .... | .... | 1980-81 | 1980-81 |
| Whistle, Rob | NYR, St.L. | 2 | 51 | 7 | 5 | 12 | 16 | 4 | 0 | 0 | 0 | 2 | .... | 1985-86 | 1987-88 |
| White, Bill | L.A., Chi. | 9 | 604 | 50 | 215 | 265 | 495 | 91 | 7 | 32 | 39 | 76 | .... | 1967-68 | 1975-76 |
| ‡ White, Brian | Col. | 1 | 2 | 0 | 0 | 0 | 0 | .... | .... | .... | .... | .... | .... | 1998-99 | 1998-99 |
| White, Moe | Mtl. | 1 | 4 | 0 | 1 | 1 | 2 | .... | .... | .... | .... | .... | .... | 1945-46 | 1945-46 |
| White, Peter | Edm., Tor., Phi., Chi. | 9 | 220 | 23 | 37 | 60 | 36 | 19 | 0 | 2 | 2 | 0 | .... | 1993-94 | 2003-04 |
| • White, Sherman | NYR | 2 | 4 | 0 | 2 | 2 | 0 | .... | .... | .... | .... | .... | .... | 1946-47 | 1949-50 |
| • White, Tex | Pit., NYA, Phi. | 6 | 203 | 33 | 12 | 45 | 141 | 4 | 0 | 0 | 0 | 4 | .... | 1925-26 | 1930-31 |
| White, Tony | Wsh., Min. | 5 | 164 | 37 | 28 | 65 | 104 | .... | .... | .... | .... | .... | .... | 1974-75 | 1979-80 |
| Whitelaw, Bob | Det. | 2 | 32 | 0 | 2 | 2 | 2 | 8 | 0 | 0 | 0 | 0 | .... | 1940-41 | 1941-42 |
| Whitlock, Bob | Min. | 1 | 1 | 0 | 0 | 0 | 0 | .... | .... | .... | .... | .... | .... | 1969-70 | 1969-70 |
| Whyte, Sean | L.A. | 2 | 21 | 0 | 2 | 2 | 12 | .... | .... | .... | .... | .... | .... | 1991-92 | 1992-93 |
| • Wickenheiser, Doug | Mtl., St.L., Van., NYR, Wsh. | 10 | 556 | 111 | 165 | 276 | 286 | 41 | 4 | 7 | 11 | 18 | .... | 1980-81 | 1989-90 |
| • Widing, Juha | NYR, L.A., Cle. | 8 | 575 | 144 | 226 | 370 | 208 | 8 | 1 | 2 | 3 | 2 | .... | 1969-70 | 1976-77 |
| Widmer, Jason | NYI, S.J. | 3 | 7 | 0 | 1 | 1 | 7 | .... | .... | .... | .... | .... | .... | 1994-95 | 1996-97 |
| • Wiebe, Art | Chi. | 11 | 414 | 14 | 27 | 41 | 201 | 31 | 1 | 3 | 4 | 10 | 1 | 1932-33 | 1943-44 |
| Wiemer, Jason | T.B., Cgy., Fla., NYI, Min., N.J. | 11 | 726 | 90 | 112 | 202 | 1420 | 19 | 1 | 0 | 1 | 67 | .... | 1994-95 | 2005-06 |
| Wiemer, Jim | Buf., NYR, Edm., L.A., Bos. | 11 | 325 | 29 | 72 | 101 | 378 | 62 | 5 | 8 | 13 | 63 | .... | 1982-83 | 1993-94 |
| • Wilcox, Archie | Mtl.M., Bos., St.L. | 6 | 208 | 8 | 14 | 22 | 158 | 12 | 1 | 0 | 1 | 8 | .... | 1929-30 | 1934-35 |
| Wilcox, Barry | Van. | 2 | 33 | 3 | 2 | 5 | 15 | .... | .... | .... | .... | .... | .... | 1972-73 | 1974-75 |
| • Wilder, Arch | Det. | 1 | 18 | 0 | 2 | 2 | 2 | .... | .... | .... | .... | .... | .... | 1940-41 | 1940-41 |
| Wiley, Jim | Pit., Van. | 5 | 63 | 4 | 10 | 14 | 8 | .... | .... | .... | .... | .... | .... | 1972-73 | 1976-77 |
| Wilkie, Bob | Det., Phi. | 2 | 18 | 2 | 5 | 7 | 10 | .... | .... | .... | .... | .... | .... | 1990-91 | 1993-94 |
| Wilkie, David | Mtl., T.B., NYR | 6 | 167 | 10 | 26 | 36 | 165 | 8 | 1 | 2 | 3 | 14 | .... | 1994-95 | 2000-01 |
| Wilkins, Barry | Bos., Van., Pit. | 9 | 418 | 27 | 125 | 152 | 663 | 6 | 0 | 1 | 1 | 4 | .... | 1966-67 | 1975-76 |
| • Wilkinson, John | Bos. | 1 | 9 | 0 | 0 | 0 | 6 | .... | .... | .... | .... | .... | .... | 1943-44 | 1943-44 |
| Wilkinson, Neil | Min., S.J., Chi., Wpg., Pit. | 10 | 460 | 16 | 67 | 83 | 813 | 53 | 3 | 6 | 9 | 41 | .... | 1989-90 | 1998-99 |
| Wilks, Brian | L.A. | 4 | 48 | 4 | 8 | 12 | 27 | .... | .... | .... | .... | .... | .... | 1984-85 | 1988-89 |
| Willard, Rod | Tor. | 1 | 1 | 0 | 0 | 0 | 0 | .... | .... | .... | .... | .... | .... | 1982-83 | 1982-83 |
| • Williams, Burr | Det., St.L., Bos. | 3 | 19 | 0 | 1 | 1 | 28 | 7 | 0 | 0 | 0 | 8 | .... | 1933-34 | 1936-37 |
| Williams, Butch | St.L., Cal. | 3 | 108 | 14 | 35 | 49 | 131 | .... | .... | .... | .... | .... | .... | 1973-74 | 1975-76 |
| Williams, Darryl | L.A. | 1 | 2 | 0 | 0 | 0 | 10 | .... | .... | .... | .... | .... | .... | 1992-93 | 1992-93 |
| Williams, David | S.J., Ana. | 4 | 173 | 11 | 53 | 64 | 157 | .... | .... | .... | .... | .... | .... | 1991-92 | 1994-95 |
| Williams, Fred | Det. | 1 | 44 | 2 | 5 | 7 | 10 | .... | .... | .... | .... | .... | .... | 1976-77 | 1976-77 |
| Williams, Gord | Phi. | 2 | 2 | 0 | 0 | 0 | 2 | .... | .... | .... | .... | .... | .... | 1981-82 | 1982-83 |
| Williams, Sean | Chi. | 1 | 2 | 0 | 0 | 0 | 4 | .... | .... | .... | .... | .... | .... | 1991-92 | 1991-92 |
| Williams, Tiger | Tor., Van., Det., L.A., Hfd. | 14 | 962 | 241 | 272 | 513 | 3966 | 83 | 12 | 23 | 35 | 455 | .... | 1974-75 | 1987-88 |
| Williams, Tom | NYR, L.A. | 8 | 397 | 115 | 138 | 253 | 73 | 29 | 8 | 7 | 15 | 4 | .... | 1971-72 | 1978-79 |
| • Williams, Tommy | Bos., Min., Cal., Wsh. | 13 | 663 | 161 | 269 | 430 | 177 | 10 | 2 | 5 | 7 | 2 | .... | 1961-62 | 1975-76 |
| ‡ Willis, Shane | Car., T.B. | 5 | 174 | 31 | 43 | 74 | 77 | 2 | 0 | 0 | 0 | 0 | .... | 1998-99 | 2003-04 |
| Willson, Don | Mtl. | 2 | 22 | 2 | 7 | 9 | 0 | 3 | 0 | 0 | 0 | 0 | .... | 1937-38 | 1938-39 |
| ‡ Wilm, Clarke | Cgy., Nsh., Tor. | 7 | 455 | 37 | 60 | 97 | 336 | 5 | 0 | 1 | 1 | 2 | .... | 1998-99 | 2005-06 |
| Wilson, Behn | Phi., Chi. | 9 | 601 | 98 | 260 | 358 | 1480 | 67 | 12 | 29 | 41 | 190 | .... | 1978-79 | 1987-88 |
| • Wilson, Bert | NYR, St.L., L.A., Cgy. | 8 | 478 | 37 | 44 | 81 | 646 | 21 | 0 | 2 | 2 | 42 | .... | 1973-74 | 1980-81 |
| Wilson, Bob | Chi. | 1 | 1 | 0 | 0 | 0 | 0 | .... | .... | .... | .... | .... | .... | 1953-54 | 1953-54 |
| Wilson, Carey | Cgy., Hfd., NYR | 10 | 552 | 169 | 258 | 427 | 314 | 52 | 11 | 13 | 24 | 14 | .... | 1983-84 | 1992-93 |
| • Wilson, Cully | Tor., Mtl., Ham., Chi. | 5 | 127 | 59 | 28 | 87 | 243 | 2 | 1 | 0 | 1 | 6 | .... | 1919-20 | 1926-27 |
| Wilson, Doug | Chi., S.J. | 16 | 1024 | 237 | 590 | 827 | 830 | 95 | 19 | 61 | 80 | 88 | .... | 1977-78 | 1992-93 |
| Wilson, Gord | Bos. | 1 | .... | .... | .... | .... | .... | 2 | 0 | 0 | 0 | 0 | .... | 1954-55 | 1954-55 |
| • Wilson, Hub | NYA | 1 | 2 | 0 | 0 | 0 | 0 | .... | .... | .... | .... | .... | .... | 1931-32 | 1931-32 |
| Wilson, Jerry | Mtl. | 1 | 3 | 0 | 0 | 0 | 2 | .... | .... | .... | .... | .... | .... | 1956-57 | 1956-57 |
| Wilson, Johnny | Det., Chi., Tor., NYR | 13 | 688 | 161 | 171 | 332 | 190 | 66 | 14 | 13 | 27 | 11 | 4 | 1949-50 | 1961-62 |
| • Wilson, Larry | Det., Chi. | 6 | 152 | 21 | 48 | 69 | 75 | 4 | 0 | 0 | 0 | 0 | 1 | 1949-50 | 1955-56 |
| Wilson, Mike | Buf., Fla., Pit., NYR | 8 | 336 | 16 | 41 | 57 | 264 | 29 | 0 | 2 | 2 | 15 | .... | 1995-96 | 2002-03 |
| Wilson, Mitch | N.J., Pit. | 2 | 26 | 2 | 3 | 5 | 104 | .... | .... | .... | .... | .... | .... | 1984-85 | 1986-87 |
| Wilson, Murray | Mtl., L.A. | 7 | 386 | 94 | 95 | 189 | 162 | 53 | 5 | 14 | 19 | 32 | 4 | 1972-73 | 1978-79 |
| Wilson, Rick | Mtl., St.L., Det. | 4 | 239 | 6 | 26 | 32 | 165 | 3 | 0 | 0 | 0 | 0 | .... | 1973-74 | 1976-77 |
| Wilson, Rik | St.L., Cgy., Chi. | 6 | 251 | 25 | 65 | 90 | 220 | 22 | 0 | 4 | 4 | 23 | .... | 1981-82 | 1987-88 |
| Wilson, Roger | Chi. | 1 | 7 | 0 | 2 | 2 | 6 | .... | .... | .... | .... | .... | .... | 1974-75 | 1974-75 |
| Wilson, Ron | Tor., Min. | 7 | 177 | 26 | 67 | 93 | 68 | 20 | 4 | 13 | 17 | 8 | .... | 1977-78 | 1987-88 |
| Wilson, Ron | Wpg., St.L., Mtl. | 14 | 832 | 110 | 216 | 326 | 415 | 63 | 10 | 12 | 22 | 64 | .... | 1979-80 | 1993-94 |
| • Wilson, Wally | Bos. | 1 | 53 | 11 | 8 | 19 | 18 | 1 | 0 | 0 | 0 | 0 | .... | 1947-48 | 1947-48 |
| Wing, Murray | Det. | 1 | 1 | 0 | 1 | 1 | 0 | .... | .... | .... | .... | .... | .... | 1973-74 | 1973-74 |
| Winnes, Chris | Bos., Phi. | 4 | 33 | 1 | 6 | 7 | 6 | 1 | 0 | 0 | 0 | 0 | .... | 1990-91 | 1993-94 |
| Wiseman, Brian | Tor. | 1 | 3 | 0 | 0 | 0 | 0 | .... | .... | .... | .... | .... | .... | 1996-97 | 1996-97 |
| • Wiseman, Eddie | Det., NYA, Bos. | 10 | 456 | 115 | 165 | 280 | 136 | 43 | 10 | 10 | 20 | 16 | 1 | 1932-33 | 1941-42 |
| Wiste, Jim | Chi., Van. | 3 | 52 | 1 | 10 | 11 | 8 | .... | .... | .... | .... | .... | .... | 1968-69 | 1970-71 |
| Witehall, Johan | NYR, Mtl. | 3 | 54 | 2 | 5 | 7 | 16 | .... | .... | .... | .... | .... | .... | 1998-99 | 2000-01 |
| Witherspoon, Jim | L.A. | 1 | 2 | 0 | 0 | 0 | 2 | .... | .... | .... | .... | .... | .... | 1975-76 | 1975-76 |
| Witiuk, Steve | Chi. | 1 | 33 | 3 | 8 | 11 | 14 | .... | .... | .... | .... | .... | .... | 1951-52 | 1951-52 |
| Woit, Benny | Det., Chi. | 7 | 334 | 7 | 26 | 33 | 170 | 41 | 2 | 6 | 8 | 18 | 3 | 1950-51 | 1956-57 |
| Wojciechowski, Steve | Det. | 2 | 54 | 19 | 20 | 39 | 17 | 6 | 0 | 1 | 1 | 0 | .... | 1944-45 | 1946-47 |
| Wolanin, Craig | N.J., Que., Col., T.B., Tor. | 13 | 695 | 40 | 133 | 173 | 894 | 35 | 4 | 6 | 10 | 67 | 1 | 1985-86 | 1997-98 |
| Wolf, Bennett | Pit. | 3 | 30 | 0 | 1 | 1 | 133 | .... | .... | .... | .... | .... | .... | 1980-81 | 1982-83 |
| Wong, Mike | Det. | 1 | 22 | 1 | 1 | 2 | 12 | .... | .... | .... | .... | .... | .... | 1975-76 | 1975-76 |
| Wood, Dody | S.J. | 5 | 106 | 8 | 10 | 18 | 471 | .... | .... | .... | .... | .... | .... | 1992-93 | 1997-98 |
| Wood, Randy | NYI, Buf., Tor., Dal. | 11 | 741 | 175 | 159 | 334 | 603 | 51 | 8 | 9 | 17 | 40 | .... | 1986-87 | 1996-97 |
| • Wood, Robert | NYR | 1 | 1 | 0 | 0 | 0 | 0 | .... | .... | .... | .... | .... | .... | 1950-51 | 1950-51 |

*Aubrey Webster*

*Sean Whyte*

*Cully Wilson*

*Randy Wood*

Ken Yackel

Peter Zezel

| | | | Regular Schedule | | | | | Playoffs | | | | | NHL | First | Last |
|---|---|---|---|---|---|---|---|---|---|---|---|---|---|---|---|
| **Name** | **NHL Teams** | **NHL Seasons** | **GP** | **G** | **A** | **TP** | **PIM** | **GP** | **G** | **A** | **TP** | **PIM** | **Cup Wins** | **NHL Season** | **NHL Season** |
| Woodley, Dan | Van. | 1 | 5 | 2 | 0 | 2 | 17 | .... | .... | .... | .... | .... | .... | 1987-88 | 1987-88 |
| Woods, Paul | Det. | 7 | 501 | 72 | 124 | 196 | 276 | 7 | 0 | 5 | 5 | 4 | .... | 1977-78 | 1983-84 |
| Woolley, Jason | Wsh., Fla., Pit., Buf., Det. | 14 | 718 | 68 | 246 | 314 | 430 | 79 | 11 | 36 | 47 | 44 | .... | 1991-92 | 2005-06 |
| Worrell, Peter | Fla., Col. | 7 | 391 | 19 | 27 | 46 | 1554 | 4 | 1 | 0 | 1 | 8 | .... | 1997-98 | 2003-04 |
| Wortman, Kevin | Cgy. | 1 | 5 | 0 | 0 | 0 | 2 | .... | .... | .... | .... | .... | .... | 1993-94 | 1993-94 |
| ‡ Wotton, Mark | Van., Dal. | 4 | 43 | 3 | 6 | 9 | 25 | 5 | 0 | 0 | 0 | 4 | .... | 1994-95 | 2000-01 |
| • Woytowich, Bob | Bos., Min., Pit., L.A. | 8 | 503 | 32 | 126 | 158 | 352 | 24 | 1 | 3 | 4 | 20 | .... | 1964-65 | 1971-72 |
| ‡ Wren, Bob | Ana., Tor. | 3 | 5 | 0 | 0 | 0 | 0 | 1 | 0 | 0 | 0 | 0 | .... | 1997-98 | 2001-02 |
| ‡ Wright, Jamie | Dal., Cgy., Phi. | 6 | 124 | 12 | 20 | 32 | 54 | 5 | 0 | 0 | 0 | 0 | .... | 1997-98 | 2002-03 |
| Wright, John | Van., St.L., K.C. | 3 | 127 | 16 | 36 | 52 | 67 | .... | .... | .... | .... | .... | .... | 1972-73 | 1974-75 |
| Wright, Keith | Phi. | 1 | 1 | 0 | 0 | 0 | 0 | .... | .... | .... | .... | .... | .... | 1967-68 | 1967-68 |
| Wright, Larry | Phi., Cal., Det. | 5 | 106 | 4 | 8 | 12 | 19 | .... | .... | .... | .... | .... | .... | 1971-72 | 1977-78 |
| Wright, Tyler | Edm., Pit., CBJ, Ana. | 13 | 613 | 79 | 70 | 149 | 854 | 30 | 3 | 2 | 5 | 40 | .... | 1992-93 | 2005-06 |
| • Wycherley, Ralph | NYA, Bro. | 2 | 28 | 4 | 7 | 11 | 6 | .... | .... | .... | .... | .... | .... | 1940-41 | 1941-42 |
| • Wylie, Bill | NYR | 1 | 1 | 0 | 0 | 0 | 0 | .... | .... | .... | .... | .... | .... | 1950-51 | 1950-51 |
| Wylie, Duane | Chi. | 2 | 14 | 3 | 3 | 6 | 2 | .... | .... | .... | .... | .... | .... | 1974-75 | 1976-77 |
| Wyrozub, Randy | Buf. | 4 | 100 | 8 | 10 | 18 | 10 | .... | .... | .... | .... | .... | .... | 1970-71 | 1973-74 |

## Y Z

| | | | | | | | | | | | | | | | |
|---|---|---|---|---|---|---|---|---|---|---|---|---|---|---|---|
| ‡ Yachmenev, Vitali | L.A., Nsh. | 8 | 487 | 83 | 133 | 216 | 88 | .... | .... | .... | .... | .... | .... | 1995-96 | 2002-03 |
| • Yackel, Ken | Bos. | 1 | 6 | 0 | 0 | 0 | 2 | 2 | 0 | 0 | 0 | 2 | .... | 1958-59 | 1958-59 |
| Yake, Terry | Hfd., Ana., Tor., St.L., Wsh. | 11 | 403 | 77 | 120 | 197 | 220 | 32 | 4 | 4 | 8 | 36 | .... | 1988-89 | 2000-01 |
| ‡ Yakubov, Mikhail | Chi., Fla. | 2 | 53 | 2 | 10 | 12 | 20 | .... | .... | .... | .... | .... | .... | 2003-04 | 2005-06 |
| Yakushin, Dmitri | Tor. | 1 | 2 | 0 | 0 | 0 | 2 | .... | .... | .... | .... | .... | .... | 1999-00 | 1999-00 |
| Yaremchuk, Gary | Tor. | 4 | 34 | 1 | 4 | 5 | 28 | .... | .... | .... | .... | .... | .... | 1981-82 | 1984-85 |
| Yaremchuk, Ken | Chi., Tor. | 6 | 235 | 36 | 56 | 92 | 106 | 31 | 6 | 8 | 14 | 49 | .... | 1983-84 | 1988-89 |
| ‡ Yashin, Alexei | Ott., NYI | 12 | 850 | 337 | 444 | 781 | 401 | 48 | 11 | 16 | 27 | 24 | .... | 1993-94 | 2006-07 |
| Yates, Ross | Hfd. | 1 | 7 | 1 | 1 | 2 | 4 | .... | .... | .... | .... | .... | .... | 1983-84 | 1983-84 |
| Yawney, Trent | Chi., Cgy., St.L. | 12 | 593 | 27 | 102 | 129 | 783 | 60 | 9 | 17 | 26 | 81 | .... | 1987-88 | 1998-99 |
| • Yegorov, Alexei | S.J. | 2 | 11 | 3 | 3 | 6 | 2 | .... | .... | .... | .... | .... | .... | 1995-96 | 1996-97 |
| Ylonen, Juha | Phx., T.B., Ott. | 6 | 341 | 26 | 76 | 102 | 90 | 15 | 0 | 7 | 7 | 4 | .... | 1996-97 | 2001-02 |
| York, Harry | St.L., NYR, Pit., Van. | 4 | 244 | 29 | 46 | 75 | 99 | 5 | 0 | 0 | 0 | 2 | .... | 1996-97 | 1999-00 |
| York, Jason | Det., Ana., Ott., Nsh., Bos. | 13 | 757 | 42 | 187 | 229 | 621 | 34 | 2 | 7 | 9 | 25 | .... | 1992-93 | 2006-07 |
| • Young, B.J. | Det. | 1 | 1 | 0 | 0 | 0 | 0 | .... | .... | .... | .... | .... | .... | 1999-00 | 1999-00 |
| Young, Brian | Chi. | 1 | 8 | 0 | 2 | 2 | 6 | .... | .... | .... | .... | .... | .... | 1980-81 | 1980-81 |
| Young, C.J. | Cgy., Bos. | 1 | 43 | 7 | 7 | 14 | 32 | .... | .... | .... | .... | .... | .... | 1992-93 | 1992-93 |
| • Young, Doug | Det., Mtl. | 10 | 388 | 35 | 45 | 80 | 303 | 28 | 1 | 5 | 6 | 16 | 2 | 1931-32 | 1940-41 |
| • Young, Howie | Det., Chi., Van. | 8 | 336 | 12 | 62 | 74 | 851 | 19 | 2 | 4 | 6 | 46 | .... | 1960-61 | 1970-71 |
| Young, Scott | Hfd., Pit., Que., Col., Ana., St.L., Dal. | 17 | 1181 | 342 | 415 | 757 | 448 | 141 | 44 | 43 | 87 | 64 | 2 | 1987-88 | 2005-06 |
| Young, Tim | Min., Wpg., Phi. | 10 | 628 | 195 | 341 | 536 | 438 | 36 | 7 | 24 | 31 | 27 | .... | 1975-76 | 1984-85 |
| Young, Warren | Min., Pit., Det. | 7 | 236 | 72 | 77 | 149 | 472 | .... | .... | .... | .... | .... | .... | 1981-82 | 1987-88 |
| Younghans, Tom | Min., NYR | 6 | 429 | 44 | 41 | 85 | 373 | 24 | 2 | 1 | 3 | 21 | .... | 1976-77 | 1981-82 |
| Ysebaert, Paul | N.J., Det., Wpg., Chi., T.B. | 11 | 532 | 149 | 187 | 336 | 217 | 30 | 4 | 3 | 7 | 20 | .... | 1988-89 | 1998-99 |
| Yushkevich, Dmitry | Phi., Tor., Fla., L.A. | 11 | 786 | 43 | 182 | 225 | 659 | 72 | 4 | 19 | 23 | 52 | .... | 1992-93 | 2002-03 |
| Yzerman, Steve | Det. | 22 | 1514 | 692 | 1063 | 1755 | 924 | 196 | 70 | 115 | 185 | 84 | 3 | 1983-84 | 2005-06 |
| Zabransky, Libor | St.L. | 2 | 40 | 1 | 6 | 7 | 50 | .... | .... | .... | .... | .... | .... | 1996-97 | 1997-98 |
| Zaharko, Miles | Atl., Chi. | 4 | 129 | 5 | 32 | 37 | 84 | 3 | 0 | 0 | 0 | 0 | .... | 1977-78 | 1981-82 |
| Zaine, Rod | Pit., Buf. | 2 | 61 | 10 | 6 | 16 | 25 | .... | .... | .... | .... | .... | .... | 1970-71 | 1971-72 |
| ‡ Zalapski, Zarley | Pit., Hfd., Cgy., Mtl., Phi. | 12 | 637 | 99 | 285 | 384 | 684 | 48 | 4 | 23 | 27 | 47 | .... | 1987-88 | 1999-00 |
| ‡ Zalesak, Miroslav | S.J. | 2 | 12 | 1 | 2 | 3 | 0 | .... | .... | .... | .... | .... | .... | 2002-03 | 2003-04 |
| Zamuner, Rob | NYR, T.B., Ott., Bos. | 13 | 798 | 139 | 172 | 311 | 467 | 34 | 4 | 5 | 9 | 26 | .... | 1991-92 | 2003-04 |
| Zanussi, Joe | NYR, Bos., St.L. | 3 | 87 | 1 | 13 | 14 | 46 | 4 | 0 | 1 | 1 | 2 | .... | 1974-75 | 1976-77 |
| Zanussi, Ron | Min., Tor. | 5 | 299 | 52 | 83 | 135 | 373 | 17 | 0 | 4 | 4 | 17 | .... | 1977-78 | 1981-82 |
| Zavisha, Brad | Edm. | 1 | 2 | 0 | 0 | 0 | 0 | .... | .... | .... | .... | .... | .... | 1993-94 | 1993-94 |
| ‡ Zehr, Jeff | Bos. | 1 | 4 | 0 | 0 | 0 | 2 | .... | .... | .... | .... | .... | .... | 1999-00 | 1999-00 |
| Zeidel, Larry | Det., Chi., Phi. | 5 | 158 | 3 | 16 | 19 | 198 | 12 | 0 | 1 | 1 | 12 | 1 | 1951-52 | 1968-69 |
| Zelepukin, Valeri | N.J., Edm., Phi., Chi. | 10 | 595 | 117 | 177 | 294 | 527 | 85 | 13 | 13 | 26 | 48 | 1 | 1991-92 | 2000-01 |
| Zemlak, Richard | Que., Min., Pit., Cgy. | 5 | 132 | 2 | 12 | 14 | 587 | 1 | 0 | 0 | 0 | 10 | .... | 1986-87 | 1991-92 |
| • Zeniuk, Ed | Det. | 1 | 2 | 0 | 0 | 0 | 0 | .... | .... | .... | .... | .... | .... | 1954-55 | 1954-55 |
| Zent, Jason | Ott., Phi. | 3 | 27 | 3 | 3 | 6 | 13 | .... | .... | .... | .... | .... | .... | 1996-97 | 1998-99 |
| Zetterstrom, Lars | Van. | 1 | 14 | 0 | 1 | 1 | 2 | .... | .... | .... | .... | .... | .... | 1978-79 | 1978-79 |
| Zettler, Rob | Min., S.J., Phi., Tor., Nsh., Wsh. | 14 | 569 | 5 | 65 | 70 | 920 | 14 | 0 | 0 | 0 | 4 | .... | 1988-89 | 2001-02 |
| • Zezel, Peter | Phi., St.L., Wsh., Tor., Dal., N.J., Van. | 15 | 873 | 219 | 389 | 608 | 435 | 131 | 25 | 39 | 64 | 83 | .... | 1984-85 | 1998-99 |
| Zhamnov, Alex | Wpg., Chi., Phi., Bos. | 13 | 807 | 249 | 470 | 719 | 668 | 35 | 6 | 13 | 19 | 18 | .... | 1992-93 | 2005-06 |
| ‡ Zhitnik, Alexei | L.A., Buf., NYI, Phi., Atl. | 15 | 1085 | 96 | 375 | 471 | 1268 | 98 | 9 | 30 | 39 | 168 | .... | 1992-93 | 2007-08 |
| • Zholtok, Sergei | Bos., Ott., Mtl., Edm., Min., Nsh. | 10 | 588 | 111 | 147 | 258 | 166 | 45 | 4 | 14 | 18 | 0 | .... | 1992-93 | 2003-04 |
| ‡ Ziegler, Thomas | T.B. | 1 | 5 | 0 | 0 | 0 | 0 | .... | .... | .... | .... | .... | .... | 2000-01 | 2000-01 |
| ‡ Zinger, Dwayne | Wsh. | 1 | 7 | 0 | 1 | 1 | 9 | .... | .... | .... | .... | .... | .... | 2003-04 | 2003-04 |
| ‡ Zinovjev, Sergei | Bos. | 1 | 10 | 0 | 1 | 1 | 2 | .... | .... | .... | .... | .... | .... | 2003-04 | 2003-04 |
| ‡ Zizka, Tomas | L.A. | 2 | 25 | 2 | 6 | 8 | 16 | .... | .... | .... | .... | .... | .... | 2002-03 | 2003-04 |
| Zmolek, Doug | S.J., Dal., L.A., Chi. | 8 | 467 | 11 | 53 | 64 | 905 | 14 | 0 | 1 | 1 | 16 | .... | 1992-93 | 1999-00 |
| Zoborosky, Marty | Chi. | 1 | 1 | 0 | 0 | 0 | 2 | .... | .... | .... | .... | .... | .... | 1944-45 | 1944-45 |
| Zombo, Rick | Det., St.L., Bos. | 12 | 652 | 24 | 130 | 154 | 728 | 60 | 1 | 11 | 12 | 127 | .... | 1984-85 | 1995-96 |
| Zuke, Mike | St.L., Hfd. | 8 | 455 | 86 | 196 | 282 | 220 | 26 | 6 | 6 | 12 | 12 | .... | 1978-79 | 1985-86 |
| • Zunich, Rudy | Det. | 1 | 2 | 0 | 0 | 0 | 2 | .... | .... | .... | .... | .... | .... | 1943-44 | 1943-44 |
| ‡ Zyuzin, Andrei | S.J., T.B., N.J., Min., Cgy., Chi. | 10 | 496 | 38 | 82 | 120 | 446 | 29 | 2 | 1 | 3 | 30 | .... | 1997-98 | 2007-08 |

*Billy Mosienko celebrates his record three goals in 21 seconds, March 23, 1952. (Record listed on page 181.)*

# Retired Players, Goaltenders and Coaches Research Project

Throughout the Retired Players and Retired Goaltenders sections of this book, you will notice many players with a bullet (•) by their names. These players, according to our records, are deceased. The editors recognize that our information on the death dates of NHLers is incomplete. If you have documented information on the passing of any player not marked with a bullet (•) in this edition, we would like to hear from you. We also welcome information on deceased NHL head coaches. Please send this information to:

Retired Player Research Project
c/o NHL Publishing
194 Dovercourt Road
Toronto, Ontario
M6J 3C8 Canada
**Fax: 416/531-3939**

**Many thanks to the following contributors . . .**

Tim Bateman, Corey Bryant, Paul R. Carroll, Jr., Bob Duff, Peter Fillman, Ernie Fitzsimmons, Chris Gory, Calvin McLellan, Gary J. Pearce, Martin Schmid, Al Tario, Drew "Whitey" White.

# Retired NHL Goaltender Index

**Abbreviations**: Teams/Cities: – **Ana.** – Anaheim; **Atl.** – Atlanta; **Bos.** – Boston; **Bro.** – Brooklyn; **Buf.** – Buffalo; **Cal.** – California; **Cgy.** – Calgary; **Car.** – Carolina; **Chi.** – Chicago; **Cle.** – Cleveland; **Col.** – Colorado; **CBJ** – Columbus; **Dal.** – Dallas; **Det.** – Detroit; **Edm.** – Edmonton; **Fla.** – Florida; **Ham.** – Hamilton; **Hfd.** – Hartford; **K.C.** – Kansas City; **L.A.** – Los Angeles; **Min.** – Minnesota; **Mtl.** – Montreal; **Mtl.M.** – Montreal Maroons; **Mtl.W.** – Montreal Wanderers; **Nsh.** – Nashville; **N.J.** – New Jersey; **NYA** – NY Americans; **NYI** – NY Islanders; **NYR** – New York Rangers; **Oak.** – Oakland; **Ott.** – Ottawa; **Phi.** – Philadelphia; **Phx.** – Phoenix; **Pit.** – Pittsburgh; **Que.** – Quebec; **St.L.** – St. Louis; **S.J.** – San Jose; **T.B.** – Tampa Bay; **Tor.** – Toronto; **Van.** – Vancouver; **Wpg.** – Winnipeg; **Wsh.** – Washington

**Avg.** – goals against per 60 minutes played; **GA** – goals agains; **GP** – games played; **Mins** – minutes played; **SO** – shutouts.
• – deceased. § – Forward, defenseman or coach who appeared in goal. For complete career, see Retired Player Index. ‡ – Remains active in other leagues.

**NHL Seasons** – A player or goaltender who does not play in a regular season but who does appear in that year's playoffs is credited with an NHL Season in this Index. Total seasons are rounded off to the nearest full season.

| | | | Regular Schedule | | | | | | | | Playoffs | | | | | | | | | | |
|---|---|---|---|---|---|---|---|---|---|---|---|---|---|---|---|---|---|---|---|---|---|
| Name | NHL Teams | NHL Seasons | GP | W | L | T | Mins | GA | SO | Avg | GP | W | L | T | Mins | GA | SO | Avg | NHL Cup Wins | First NHL Season | Last NHL Season |
| Abbott, George | Bos. | 1 | 1 | 0 | 1 | 0 | 60 | 7 | 0 | 7.00 | .... | .... | .... | .... | .... | .... | .... | .... | | 1943-44 | 1943-44 |
| Adams, John | Bos., Wsh. | 2 | 22 | 9 | 10 | 1 | 1180 | 85 | 1 | 4.32 | .... | .... | .... | .... | .... | .... | .... | .... | 1 | 1969-70 | 1974-75 |
| Aiken, Don | Mtl. | 1 | 1 | 0 | 1 | 0 | 34 | 6 | 0 | 10.59 | .... | .... | .... | .... | .... | .... | .... | .... | | 1957-58 | 1957-58 |
| • Aitkenhead, Andy | NYR | 3 | 106 | 47 | 43 | 16 | 6570 | 257 | 11 | 2.35 | 10 | 6 | 2 | 2 | 608 | 15 | 3 | 1.48 | 1 | 1932-33 | 1934-35 |
| • Almas, Red | Det., Chi. | 3 | 3 | 0 | 2 | 1 | 180 | 13 | 0 | 4.33 | 5 | 1 | 3 | .... | 263 | 13 | 0 | 2.97 | | 1946-47 | 1952-53 |
| • Anderson, Lorne | NYR | 1 | 3 | 1 | 2 | 0 | 180 | 18 | 0 | 6.00 | .... | .... | .... | .... | .... | .... | .... | .... | | 1951-52 | 1951-52 |
| Askey, Tom | Ana. | 2 | 7 | 0 | 1 | 2 | 273 | 12 | 0 | 2.64 | 1 | 0 | 1 | .... | 30 | 2 | 0 | 4.00 | | 1997-98 | 1998-99 |
| Astrom, Hardy | NYR, Col. | 3 | 83 | 17 | 44 | 12 | 4456 | 278 | 0 | 3.74 | .... | .... | .... | .... | .... | .... | .... | .... | | 1977-78 | 1980-81 |
| Bach, Ryan | L.A. | 1 | 3 | 0 | 3 | 0 | 108 | 8 | 0 | 4.44 | .... | .... | .... | .... | .... | .... | .... | .... | | 1998-99 | 1998-99 |
| Bailey, Scott | Bos. | 2 | 19 | 6 | 6 | 2 | 965 | 55 | 0 | 3.42 | .... | .... | .... | .... | .... | .... | .... | .... | | 1995-96 | 1996-97 |
| Baker, Steve | NYR | 4 | 57 | 20 | 20 | 11 | 3081 | 190 | 3 | 3.70 | 14 | 7 | 7 | .... | 826 | 55 | 0 | 4.00 | | 1979-80 | 1982-83 |
| Bales, Mike | Bos., Ott. | 4 | 23 | 2 | 15 | 1 | 1120 | 77 | 0 | 4.13 | .... | .... | .... | .... | .... | .... | .... | .... | | 1992-93 | 1996-97 |
| Bannerman, Murray | Van., Chi. | 8 | 289 | 116 | 125 | 33 | 16470 | 1051 | 8 | 3.83 | 40 | 20 | 18 | .... | 2322 | 165 | 0 | 4.26 | | 1977-78 | 1986-87 |
| Baron, Marco | Bos., L.A., Edm. | 6 | 86 | 34 | 38 | 9 | 4822 | 292 | 1 | 3.63 | 1 | 0 | 1 | .... | 20 | 3 | 0 | 9.00 | | 1979-80 | 1984-85 |
| Barrasso, Tom | Buf., Pit., Ott., Car., Tor., St.L. | 19 | 777 | 369 | 277 | 86 | 44180 | 2385 | 38 | 3.24 | 119 | 61 | 54 | .... | 6953 | 349 | 6 | 3.01 | 2 | 1983-84 | 2002-03 |
| Bassen, Hank | Chi., Det., Pit. | 9 | 156 | 46 | 66 | 31 | 8759 | 434 | 5 | 2.97 | 5 | 1 | 3 | .... | 274 | 11 | 0 | 2.41 | | 1954-55 | 1967-68 |
| • Bastien, Baz | Tor. | 1 | 5 | 0 | 4 | 1 | 300 | 20 | 0 | 4.00 | .... | .... | .... | .... | .... | .... | .... | .... | | 1945-46 | 1945-46 |
| • Bauman, Garry | Mtl., Min. | 3 | 35 | 5 | 16 | 6 | 1719 | 102 | 0 | 3.56 | .... | .... | .... | .... | .... | .... | .... | .... | | 1966-67 | 1968-69 |
| Beaupre, Don | Min., Wsh., Ott., Tor. | 17 | 667 | 268 | 277 | 75 | 37396 | 2151 | 17 | 3.45 | 72 | 33 | 31 | .... | 3943 | 220 | 3 | 3.35 | | 1980-81 | 1996-97 |
| Beauregard, Stephane | Wpg., Phi. | 5 | 90 | 19 | 39 | 11 | 4402 | 268 | 2 | 3.65 | 4 | 1 | 3 | .... | 238 | 12 | 0 | 3.03 | | 1989-90 | 1993-94 |
| Bedard, Jim | Wsh. | 2 | 73 | 17 | 40 | 13 | 4232 | 278 | 1 | 3.94 | .... | .... | .... | .... | .... | .... | .... | .... | | 1977-78 | 1978-79 |
| Behrend, Marc | Wpg. | 3 | 39 | 12 | 19 | 3 | 1991 | 160 | 1 | 4.82 | 7 | 1 | 3 | .... | 312 | 19 | 0 | 3.65 | | 1983-84 | 1985-86 |
| Belanger, Yves | St.L., Atl., Bos. | 6 | 78 | 29 | 33 | 6 | 4134 | 259 | 2 | 3.76 | .... | .... | .... | .... | .... | .... | .... | .... | | 1974-75 | 1979-80 |
| Belfour, Ed | Chi., S.J., Dal., Tor., Fla. | 18 | 963 | 484 | 320 | 125 | 55695 | 2317 | 76 | 2.50 | 161 | 88 | 68 | .... | 9945 | 359 | 14 | 2.17 | 1 | 1988-89 | 2006-07 |
| Belhumeur, Michel | Phi., Wsh. | 3 | 65 | 9 | 36 | 7 | 3306 | 254 | 0 | 4.61 | 1 | 0 | 0 | .... | 10 | 1 | 0 | 6.00 | | 1972-73 | 1975-76 |
| • Bell, Gordie | Tor., NYR | 2 | 8 | 3 | 5 | 0 | 480 | 31 | 0 | 3.88 | 2 | 1 | 1 | .... | 120 | 9 | 0 | 4.50 | | 1945-46 | 1955-56 |
| • Benedict, Clint | Ott., Mtl.M. | 13 | 362 | 190 | 143 | 28 | 22367 | 863 | 57 | 2.32 | 28 | 11 | 12 | 5 | 1707 | 53 | 9 | 1.86 | 4 | 1917-18 | 1929-30 |
| • Bennett, Harvey | Bos. | 1 | 25 | 10 | 12 | 2 | 1470 | 103 | 0 | 4.20 | .... | .... | .... | .... | .... | .... | .... | .... | | 1944-45 | 1944-45 |
| Bergeron, Jean-Claude | Mtl., T.B., L.A. | 6 | 72 | 21 | 33 | 7 | 3772 | 232 | 1 | 3.69 | .... | .... | .... | .... | .... | .... | .... | .... | | 1990-91 | 1996-97 |
| Bernhardt, Tim | Cgy., Tor. | 4 | 67 | 17 | 36 | 7 | 3748 | 267 | 0 | 4.27 | .... | .... | .... | .... | .... | .... | .... | .... | | 1982-83 | 1986-87 |
| Berthiaume, Daniel | Wpg., Min., L.A., Bos., Ott. | 9 | 215 | 81 | 90 | 21 | 11662 | 714 | 5 | 3.67 | 14 | 5 | 9 | .... | 807 | 50 | 0 | 3.72 | | 1985-86 | 1993-94 |
| Bester, Allan | Tor., Det., Dal. | 10 | 219 | 73 | 99 | 17 | 11773 | 786 | 7 | 4.01 | 11 | 2 | 6 | .... | 508 | 37 | 0 | 4.37 | | 1983-84 | 1995-96 |
| • Beveridge, Bill | Det., Ott., St.L., Mtl.M., NYR | 9 | 297 | 87 | 166 | 42 | 18375 | 879 | 18 | 2.87 | 5 | 2 | 3 | .... | 300 | 11 | 0 | 2.20 | | 1929-30 | 1942-43 |
| • Bibeault, Paul | Mtl., Tor., Bos., Chi. | 7 | 214 | 81 | 107 | 25 | 12890 | 785 | 10 | 3.65 | 20 | 6 | 14 | .... | 1237 | 71 | 2 | 3.44 | | 1940-41 | 1946-47 |
| Bierk, Zac | T.B., Min., Phx. | 6 | 47 | 9 | 20 | 5 | 2135 | 113 | 1 | 3.18 | .... | .... | .... | .... | .... | .... | .... | .... | | 1997-98 | 2003-04 |
| Billington, Craig | N.J., Ott., Bos., Col., Wsh. | 15 | 332 | 110 | 149 | 31 | 17097 | 1034 | 9 | 3.63 | 8 | 0 | 2 | .... | 213 | 15 | 0 | 4.23 | | 1985-86 | 2002-03 |
| Binette, Andre | Mtl. | 1 | 1 | 1 | 0 | 0 | 60 | 4 | 0 | 4.00 | .... | .... | .... | .... | .... | .... | .... | .... | | 1954-55 | 1954-55 |
| Binkley, Les | Pit. | 5 | 196 | 58 | 94 | 34 | 11046 | 575 | 11 | 3.12 | 7 | 5 | 2 | .... | 428 | 15 | 0 | 2.10 | | 1967-68 | 1971-72 |
| • Bittner, Richard | Bos. | 1 | 1 | 0 | 0 | 1 | 60 | 3 | 0 | 3.00 | .... | .... | .... | .... | .... | .... | .... | .... | | 1949-50 | 1949-50 |
| Blackburn, Dan | NYR | 2 | 63 | 20 | 32 | 4 | 3499 | 188 | 1 | 3.22 | .... | .... | .... | .... | .... | .... | .... | .... | | 2001-02 | 2002-03 |
| Blake, Mike | L.A. | 3 | 40 | 13 | 15 | 5 | 2117 | 150 | 0 | 4.25 | .... | .... | .... | .... | .... | .... | .... | .... | | 1981-82 | 1983-84 |
| Blue, John | Bos., Buf. | 3 | 46 | 16 | 18 | 7 | 2521 | 126 | 1 | 3.00 | 2 | 0 | 1 | .... | 96 | 5 | 0 | 3.13 | | 1992-93 | 1995-96 |
| Boisvert, Gilles | Det. | 1 | 3 | 0 | 3 | 0 | 180 | 9 | 0 | 3.00 | .... | .... | .... | .... | .... | .... | .... | .... | | 1959-60 | 1959-60 |
| Bouchard, Dan | Atl., Cgy., Que., Wpg. | 14 | 655 | 286 | 232 | 113 | 37919 | 2061 | 27 | 3.26 | 43 | 13 | 30 | .... | 2549 | 147 | 1 | 3.46 | | 1972-73 | 1985-86 |
| • Bourque, Claude | Mtl., Det. | 2 | 62 | 16 | 38 | 8 | 3830 | 193 | 4 | 3.02 | 3 | 1 | 2 | .... | 188 | 8 | 1 | 2.55 | | 1938-39 | 1939-40 |
| Boutin, Rollie | Wsh. | 3 | 22 | 7 | 10 | 1 | 1137 | 75 | 0 | 3.96 | .... | .... | .... | .... | .... | .... | .... | .... | | 1978-79 | 1980-81 |
| • Bouvrette, Lionel | NYR | 1 | 1 | 0 | 1 | 0 | 60 | 6 | 0 | 6.00 | .... | .... | .... | .... | .... | .... | .... | .... | | 1942-43 | 1942-43 |
| Bower, Johnny | NYR, Tor. | 15 | 552 | 250 | 195 | 90 | 32016 | 1340 | 37 | 2.51 | 74 | 35 | 34 | .... | 4378 | 180 | 5 | 2.47 | 4 | 1953-54 | 1969-70 |
| § • Branigan, Andy | NYA | 1 | 1 | 0 | 0 | 0 | 7 | 0 | 0 | 0.00 | .... | .... | .... | .... | .... | .... | .... | .... | | 1940-41 | 1940-41 |
| ‡ Brathwaite, Fred | Edm., Cgy., St.L., CBJ | 9 | 254 | 81 | 99 | 37 | 13840 | 629 | 15 | 2.73 | 1 | 0 | 0 | .... | 1 | 0 | 0 | 0.00 | | 1993-94 | 2003-04 |
| • Brimsek, Frank | Bos., Chi. | 10 | 514 | 252 | 182 | 80 | 31210 | 1404 | 40 | 2.70 | 68 | 32 | 36 | .... | 4395 | 186 | 2 | 2.54 | 2 | 1938-39 | 1949-50 |
| Brochu, Martin | Wsh., Van., Pit. | 3 | 9 | 0 | 5 | 0 | 369 | 22 | 0 | 3.58 | .... | .... | .... | .... | .... | .... | .... | .... | | 1998-99 | 2003-04 |
| • Broda, Turk | Tor. | 14 | 629 | 302 | 224 | 101 | 38167 | 1609 | 62 | 2.53 | 101 | 60 | 39 | .... | 6389 | 211 | 13 | 1.98 | 5 | 1936-37 | 1951-52 |
| Broderick, Ken | Min., Bos. | 3 | 27 | 11 | 12 | 1 | 1464 | 74 | 1 | 3.03 | .... | .... | .... | .... | .... | .... | .... | .... | | 1969-70 | 1974-75 |
| Broderick, Len | Mtl. | 1 | 1 | 1 | 0 | 0 | 60 | 2 | 0 | 2.00 | .... | .... | .... | .... | .... | .... | .... | .... | | 1957-58 | 1957-58 |
| Brodeur, Richard | NYI, Van., Hfd. | 9 | 385 | 131 | 175 | 62 | 21968 | 1410 | 6 | 3.85 | 33 | 13 | 20 | .... | 2009 | 111 | 1 | 3.32 | | 1979-80 | 1987-88 |
| Bromley, Gary | Buf., Van. | 6 | 136 | 54 | 44 | 28 | 7427 | 425 | 7 | 3.43 | 7 | 2 | 5 | .... | 360 | 25 | 0 | 4.17 | | 1973-74 | 1980-81 |
| • Brooks, Art | Tor. | 1 | 4 | 2 | 2 | 0 | 220 | 23 | 0 | 6.27 | .... | .... | .... | .... | .... | .... | .... | .... | | 1917-18 | 1917-18 |
| Brooks, Ross | Bos. | 3 | 54 | 37 | 7 | 6 | 3047 | 134 | 4 | 2.64 | 1 | 0 | 0 | .... | 20 | 3 | 0 | 9.00 | | 1972-73 | 1974-75 |
| • Brophy, Frank | Que. | 1 | 21 | 3 | 18 | 0 | 1249 | 148 | 0 | 7.11 | .... | .... | .... | .... | .... | .... | .... | .... | | 1919-20 | 1919-20 |
| Brown, Andy | Det., Pit. | 3 | 62 | 22 | 26 | 9 | 3373 | 213 | 1 | 3.79 | .... | .... | .... | .... | .... | .... | .... | .... | | 1971-72 | 1973-74 |
| Brown, Ken | Chi. | 1 | 1 | 0 | 0 | 0 | 18 | 1 | 0 | 3.33 | .... | .... | .... | .... | .... | .... | .... | .... | | 1970-71 | 1970-71 |
| Brunetta, Mario | Que. | 3 | 40 | 12 | 17 | 1 | 1967 | 128 | 0 | 3.90 | .... | .... | .... | .... | .... | .... | .... | .... | | 1987-88 | 1989-90 |
| Bullock, Bruce | Van. | 3 | 16 | 3 | 9 | 3 | 927 | 74 | 0 | 4.79 | .... | .... | .... | .... | .... | .... | .... | .... | | 1972-73 | 1976-77 |
| Burke, Sean | N.J., Hfd., Car., Van., Phi., Fla., Phx., T.B., L.A. | 18 | 820 | 324 | 341 | 110 | 46442 | 2290 | 38 | 2.96 | 38 | 12 | 23 | .... | 2151 | 119 | 1 | 3.32 | | 1987-88 | 2006-07 |
| • Buzinski, Steve | NYR | 1 | 9 | 2 | 6 | 1 | 560 | 55 | 0 | 5.89 | .... | .... | .... | .... | .... | .... | .... | .... | | 1942-43 | 1942-43 |
| Caley, Don | St.L. | 1 | 1 | 0 | 0 | 0 | 30 | 3 | 0 | 6.00 | .... | .... | .... | .... | .... | .... | .... | .... | | 1967-68 | 1967-68 |
| Caprice, Frank | Van. | 6 | 102 | 31 | 46 | 11 | 5589 | 391 | 1 | 4.20 | .... | .... | .... | .... | .... | .... | .... | .... | | 1982-83 | 1987-88 |
| Carey, Jim | Wsh., Bos., St.L. | 5 | 172 | 79 | 65 | 16 | 9668 | 416 | 16 | 2.58 | 10 | 2 | 5 | .... | 455 | 35 | 0 | 4.62 | | 1994-95 | 1998-99 |
| Caron, Jacques | L.A., St.L., Van. | 5 | 72 | 24 | 29 | 11 | 3846 | 211 | 2 | 3.29 | 12 | 4 | 7 | .... | 639 | 34 | 0 | 3.19 | | 1967-68 | 1973-74 |
| Carter, Lyle | Cal. | 1 | 15 | 4 | 7 | 0 | 721 | 50 | 0 | 4.16 | .... | .... | .... | .... | .... | .... | .... | .... | | 1971-72 | 1971-72 |
| Casey, Jon | Min., Bos., St.L. | 12 | 425 | 170 | 157 | 55 | 23255 | 1246 | 16 | 3.21 | 66 | 32 | 31 | .... | 3743 | 192 | 3 | 3.08 | | 1983-84 | 1996-97 |
| ‡ Cassivi, Frederic | Atl., Wsh. | 4 | 13 | 3 | 6 | 1 | 628 | 38 | 0 | 3.63 | .... | .... | .... | .... | .... | .... | .... | .... | | 2001-02 | 2006-07 |
| Cechmanek, Roman | Phi., L.A. | 4 | 212 | 110 | 64 | 28 | 12085 | 419 | 25 | 2.08 | 23 | 9 | 14 | .... | 1441 | 56 | 3 | 2.33 | | 2000-01 | 2003-04 |
| Centomo, Sebastien | Tor. | 1 | 1 | 0 | 0 | 0 | 40 | 3 | 0 | 4.50 | .... | .... | .... | .... | .... | .... | .... | .... | | 2001-02 | 2001-02 |
| Chabot, Frederic | Mtl., Phi., L.A. | 5 | 32 | 4 | 8 | 4 | 1262 | 62 | 0 | 2.95 | .... | .... | .... | .... | .... | .... | .... | .... | | 1990-91 | 1998-99 |
| • Chabot, Lorne | NYR, Tor., Mtl., Chi., Mtl.M., NYA | 11 | 412 | 201 | 147 | 62 | 25411 | 859 | 71 | 2.03 | 37 | 13 | 17 | 6 | 2498 | 64 | 5 | 1.54 | 2 | 1926-27 | 1936-37 |
| Chadwick, Ed | Tor., Bos. | 6 | 184 | 57 | 92 | 35 | 11040 | 541 | 14 | 2.94 | .... | .... | .... | .... | .... | .... | .... | .... | | 1955-56 | 1961-62 |
| Champoux, Bob | Det., Cal. | 2 | 17 | 2 | 11 | 3 | 923 | 80 | 0 | 5.20 | 1 | 1 | 0 | .... | 55 | 4 | 0 | 4.36 | | 1963-64 | 1973-74 |
| Charpentier, Sebastien | Wsh. | 3 | 26 | 6 | 14 | 1 | 1350 | 66 | 0 | 2.93 | .... | .... | .... | .... | .... | .... | .... | .... | | 2001-02 | 2003-04 |
| Cheevers, Gerry | Tor., Bos. | 13 | 418 | 230 | 102 | 74 | 24394 | 1174 | 26 | 2.89 | 88 | 53 | 34 | .... | 5396 | 242 | 8 | 2.69 | 2 | 1961-62 | 1979-80 |
| Cheveldae, Tim | Det., Wpg., Bos. | 9 | 340 | 149 | 136 | 37 | 19172 | 1116 | 10 | 3.49 | 25 | 9 | 15 | .... | 1418 | 71 | 2 | 3.00 | | 1988-89 | 1996-97 |
| Chevrier, Alain | N.J., Wpg., Chi., Pit., Det. | 6 | 234 | 91 | 100 | 14 | 12202 | 845 | 2 | 4.16 | 16 | 9 | 7 | .... | 1013 | 44 | 0 | 2.61 | | 1985-86 | 1990-91 |
| ‡ Chiodo, Andy | Pit. | 1 | 8 | 3 | 4 | 1 | 486 | 28 | 0 | 3.46 | .... | .... | .... | .... | .... | .... | .... | .... | | 2003-04 | 2003-04 |
| Chouinard, Mathieu | L.A. | 1 | 1 | 0 | 0 | 0 | 3 | 0 | 0 | 0.00 | .... | .... | .... | .... | .... | .... | .... | .... | | 2003-04 | 2003-04 |
| § • Clancy, King | Ott., Tor. | 2 | 2 | 0 | 0 | 0 | 3 | 1 | 0 | 20.00 | .... | .... | .... | .... | .... | .... | .... | .... | | 1924-25 | 1931-32 |
| § • Cleghorn, Odie | Pit. | 1 | 1 | 1 | 0 | 0 | 60 | 2 | 0 | 2.00 | .... | .... | .... | .... | .... | .... | .... | .... | | 1925-26 | 1925-26 |
| § • Cleghorn, Sprague | Ott., Mtl. | 2 | 2 | 0 | 0 | 0 | 5 | 0 | 0 | 0.00 | .... | .... | .... | .... | .... | .... | .... | .... | | 1918-19 | 1921-22 |
| Clifford, Chris | Chi. | 2 | 2 | 0 | 0 | 0 | 24 | 0 | 0 | 0.00 | .... | .... | .... | .... | .... | .... | .... | .... | | 1984-85 | 1988-89 |
| Cloutier, Dan | NYR, T.B., Van., L.A. | 10 | 351 | 139 | 142 | 37 | 18927 | 874 | 15 | 2.77 | 25 | 10 | 13 | .... | 1361 | 75 | 0 | 3.31 | | 1997-98 | 2007-08 |
| Cloutier, Jacques | Buf., Chi., Que. | 12 | 255 | 82 | 102 | 24 | 12826 | 778 | 3 | 3.64 | 8 | 1 | 5 | .... | 413 | 18 | 1 | 2.62 | | 1981-82 | 1993-94 |
| • Colvin, Les | Bos. | 1 | 1 | 0 | 1 | 0 | 60 | 4 | 0 | 4.00 | .... | .... | .... | .... | .... | .... | .... | .... | | 1948-49 | 1948-49 |

| Name | NHL Teams | NHL Seasons | Regular Schedule GP | W | L | T | Mins | GA | SO | Avg | Playoffs GP | W | L | T | Mins | GA | SO | Avg | NHL Cup Wins | First NHL Season | Last NHL Season |
|---|---|---|---|---|---|---|---|---|---|---|---|---|---|---|---|---|---|---|---|---|---|
| § • Conacher, Charlie | Tor., Det. | 3 | 4 | 0 | 0 | 0 | 10 | 0 | 0 | 0.00 | .... | .... | .... | .... | .... | .... | .... | .... | | 1932-33 | 1938-39 |
| • Connell, Alec | Ott., Det., NYA, Mtl.M. | 12 | 417 | 193 | 156 | 67 | 26050 | 830 | 81 | 1.91 | 21 | 8 | 5 | 8 | 1309 | 26 | 4 | 1.19 | 2 | 1924-25 | 1936-37 |
| Corsi, Jim | Edm. | 1 | 26 | 8 | 14 | 3 | 1366 | 83 | 0 | 3.65 | .... | .... | .... | .... | .... | .... | .... | .... | | 1979-80 | 1979-80 |
| • Courteau, Maurice | Bos. | 1 | 6 | 2 | 4 | 0 | 360 | 33 | 0 | 5.50 | .... | .... | .... | .... | .... | .... | .... | .... | | 1943-44 | 1943-44 |
| Cousineau, Marcel | Tor., NYI, L.A. | 4 | 26 | 4 | 10 | 1 | 1047 | 51 | 1 | 2.92 | .... | .... | .... | .... | .... | .... | .... | .... | | 1996-97 | 1999-00 |
| Cowley, Wayne | Edm. | 1 | 1 | 0 | 1 | 0 | 57 | 3 | 0 | 3.16 | .... | .... | .... | .... | .... | .... | .... | .... | | 1993-94 | 1993-94 |
| • Cox, Abbie | Mtl.M., NYA, Det., Mtl. | 3 | 5 | 1 | 1 | 2 | 263 | 11 | 0 | 2.51 | .... | .... | .... | .... | .... | .... | .... | .... | | 1929-30 | 1935-36 |
| Craig, Jim | Atl., Bos., Min. | 3 | 30 | 11 | 10 | 7 | 1588 | 100 | 0 | 3.78 | .... | .... | .... | .... | .... | .... | .... | .... | | 1979-80 | 1983-84 |
| Crha, Jiri | Tor. | 2 | 69 | 28 | 27 | 11 | 3942 | 261 | 0 | 3.97 | 5 | 0 | 4 | .... | 186 | 21 | 0 | 6.77 | | 1979-80 | 1980-81 |
| • Crozier, Roger | Det., Buf., Wsh. | 14 | 518 | 206 | 197 | 70 | 28567 | 1446 | 30 | 3.04 | 32 | 14 | 16 | .... | 1789 | 82 | 1 | 2.75 | | 1963-64 | 1976-77 |
| • Cude, Wilf | Phi., Bos., Chi., Mtl., Det. | 10 | 282 | 100 | 132 | 49 | 17586 | 798 | 24 | 2.72 | 19 | 7 | 11 | 1 | 1257 | 51 | 1 | 2.43 | | 1930-31 | 1940-41 |
| Cutts, Don | Edm. | 1 | 6 | 1 | 2 | 1 | 269 | 16 | 0 | 3.57 | .... | .... | .... | .... | .... | .... | .... | .... | | 1979-80 | 1979-80 |
| • Cyr, Claude | Mtl. | 1 | 1 | 0 | 0 | 0 | 20 | 1 | 0 | 3.00 | .... | .... | .... | .... | .... | .... | .... | .... | | 1958-59 | 1958-59 |
| Dadswell, Doug | Cgy. | 2 | 27 | 8 | 8 | 3 | 1346 | 99 | 0 | 4.41 | .... | .... | .... | .... | .... | .... | .... | .... | | 1986-87 | 1987-88 |
| Dafoe, Byron | Wsh., L.A., Bos., Atl. | 12 | 415 | 171 | 170 | 56 | 23478 | 1051 | 26 | 2.69 | 27 | 10 | 16 | .... | 1686 | 65 | 3 | 2.31 | | 1992-93 | 2003-04 |
| D'Alessio, Corrie | Hfd. | 1 | 1 | 0 | 0 | 0 | 11 | 0 | 0 | 0.00 | .... | .... | .... | .... | .... | .... | .... | .... | | 1992-93 | 1992-93 |
| Daley, Joe | Pit., Buf., Det. | 4 | 105 | 34 | 44 | 19 | 5836 | 326 | 3 | 3.35 | .... | .... | .... | .... | .... | .... | .... | .... | | 1968-69 | 1971-72 |
| • Damore, Nick | Bos. | 1 | 1 | 1 | 0 | 0 | 60 | 3 | 0 | 3.00 | .... | .... | .... | .... | .... | .... | .... | .... | | 1941-42 | 1941-42 |
| D'Amour, Marc | Cgy., Phi. | 2 | 16 | 2 | 4 | 2 | 579 | 32 | 0 | 3.32 | .... | .... | .... | .... | .... | .... | .... | .... | | 1985-86 | 1988-89 |
| Damphousse, Jean-Fr. | N.J. | 1 | 6 | 1 | 3 | 0 | 294 | 12 | 0 | 2.45 | .... | .... | .... | .... | .... | .... | .... | .... | | 2001-02 | 2001-02 |
| § • Darragh, Jack | Ott. | 1 | 1 | 0 | 0 | 0 | 2 | 0 | 0 | 0.00 | .... | .... | .... | .... | .... | .... | .... | .... | | 1919-20 | 1919-20 |
| Daskalakis, Cleon | Bos. | 3 | 12 | 3 | 4 | 1 | 506 | 41 | 0 | 4.86 | .... | .... | .... | .... | .... | .... | .... | .... | | 1984-85 | 1986-87 |
| Davidson, John | St.L., NYR | 10 | 301 | 123 | 124 | 39 | 17109 | 1004 | 7 | 3.52 | 31 | 16 | 14 | .... | 1862 | 77 | 1 | 2.48 | | 1973-74 | 1982-83 |
| Decourcy, Bob | NYR | 1 | 1 | 0 | 1 | 0 | 29 | 6 | 0 | 12.41 | .... | .... | .... | .... | .... | .... | .... | .... | | 1947-48 | 1947-48 |
| Defelice, Norm | Bos. | 1 | 10 | 3 | 5 | 2 | 600 | 30 | 0 | 3.00 | .... | .... | .... | .... | .... | .... | .... | .... | | 1956-57 | 1956-57 |
| DeJordy, Denis | Chi., L.A., Mtl., Det. | 12 | 316 | 124 | 128 | 51 | 17798 | 929 | 15 | 3.13 | 18 | 6 | 9 | .... | 946 | 55 | 0 | 3.49 | 1 | 1960-61 | 1973-74 |
| DelGuidice, Matt | Bos. | 2 | 11 | 2 | 5 | 1 | 434 | 28 | 0 | 3.87 | .... | .... | .... | .... | .... | .... | .... | .... | | 1990-91 | 1991-92 |
| DeRouville, Philippe | Pit. | 2 | 3 | 1 | 2 | 0 | 171 | 9 | 0 | 3.16 | .... | .... | .... | .... | .... | .... | .... | .... | | 1994-95 | 1996-97 |
| Desjardins, Gerry | L.A., Chi., NYI, Buf. | 10 | 331 | 122 | 153 | 44 | 19014 | 1042 | 12 | 3.29 | 35 | 15 | 15 | .... | 1874 | 108 | 0 | 3.46 | | 1968-69 | 1977-78 |
| ‡ DesRochers, Patrick | Phx., Car. | 2 | 11 | 2 | 6 | 1 | 540 | 33 | 0 | 3.67 | .... | .... | .... | .... | .... | .... | .... | .... | | 2001-02 | 2002-03 |
| • Dickie, Bill | Chi. | 1 | 1 | 1 | 0 | 0 | 60 | 3 | 0 | 3.00 | .... | .... | .... | .... | .... | .... | .... | .... | | 1941-42 | 1941-42 |
| Dion, Connie | Det. | 2 | 38 | 23 | 11 | 4 | 2280 | 119 | 1 | 3.13 | 5 | 1 | 4 | .... | 300 | 17 | 0 | 3.40 | | 1943-44 | 1944-45 |
| Dion, Michel | Que., Wpg., Pit. | 6 | 227 | 60 | 118 | 32 | 12695 | 898 | 2 | 4.24 | 5 | 2 | 3 | .... | 304 | 22 | 0 | 4.34 | | 1979-80 | 1984-85 |
| ‡ Divis, Reinhard | St.L. | 4 | 28 | 6 | 9 | 3 | 1212 | 67 | 0 | 3.32 | 1 | 0 | 0 | .... | 18 | 0 | 0 | 0.00 | | 2001-02 | 2005-06 |
| • Dolson, Dolly | Det. | 3 | 93 | 35 | 41 | 17 | 5820 | 192 | 16 | 1.98 | 2 | 0 | 2 | 0 | 120 | 7 | 0 | 3.50 | | 1928-29 | 1930-31 |
| Dopson, Rob | Pit. | 1 | 2 | 0 | 0 | 0 | 45 | 3 | 0 | 4.00 | .... | .... | .... | .... | .... | .... | .... | .... | | 1993-94 | 1993-94 |
| Dowie, Bruce | Tor. | 1 | 2 | 0 | 1 | 0 | 72 | 4 | 0 | 3.33 | .... | .... | .... | .... | .... | .... | .... | .... | | 1983-84 | 1983-84 |
| Draper, Tom | Wpg., Buf., NYI | 6 | 53 | 19 | 23 | 5 | 2807 | 173 | 1 | 3.70 | 7 | 3 | 4 | .... | 433 | 19 | 1 | 2.63 | | 1988-89 | 1995-96 |
| Dryden, Dave | NYR, Chi., Buf., Edm. | 9 | 203 | 66 | 76 | 31 | 10424 | 555 | 9 | 3.19 | 3 | 0 | 2 | .... | 133 | 9 | 0 | 4.06 | | 1961-62 | 1979-80 |
| Dryden, Ken | Mtl. | 8 | 397 | 258 | 57 | 74 | 23352 | 870 | 46 | 2.24 | 112 | 80 | 32 | .... | 6846 | 274 | 10 | 2.40 | 6 | 1970-71 | 1978-79 |
| Duffus, Parris | Phx. | 1 | 1 | 0 | 0 | 0 | 29 | 1 | 0 | 2.07 | .... | .... | .... | .... | .... | .... | .... | .... | | 1996-97 | 1996-97 |
| Dumas, Michel | Chi. | 3 | 8 | 2 | 1 | 2 | 362 | 24 | 0 | 3.98 | 1 | 0 | 0 | .... | 19 | 1 | 0 | 3.16 | | 1974-75 | 1976-77 |
| Dunham, Mike | N.J., Nsh., NYR, Atl., NYI | 10 | 394 | 141 | 178 | 44 | 21653 | 989 | 19 | 2.74 | .... | .... | .... | .... | .... | .... | .... | .... | | 1996-97 | 2006-07 |
| Dupuis, Bob | Edm. | 1 | 1 | 0 | 1 | 0 | 60 | 4 | 0 | 4.00 | .... | .... | .... | .... | .... | .... | .... | .... | | 1979-80 | 1979-80 |
| • Durnan, Bill | Mtl. | 7 | 383 | 208 | 112 | 62 | 22945 | 901 | 34 | 2.36 | 45 | 27 | 18 | .... | 2871 | 99 | 2 | 2.07 | 2 | 1943-44 | 1949-50 |
| Dyck, Ed | Van. | 3 | 49 | 8 | 28 | 5 | 2453 | 178 | 1 | 4.35 | .... | .... | .... | .... | .... | .... | .... | .... | | 1971-72 | 1973-74 |
| Edwards, Don | Buf., Cgy., Tor. | 10 | 459 | 208 | 155 | 74 | 26181 | 1449 | 16 | 3.32 | 42 | 16 | 21 | .... | 2302 | 132 | 1 | 3.44 | | 1976-77 | 1985-86 |
| Edwards, Gary | St.L., L.A., Cle., Min., Edm., Pit. | 13 | 286 | 88 | 125 | 51 | 16002 | 973 | 10 | 3.65 | 11 | 5 | 4 | .... | 537 | 34 | 0 | 3.80 | | 1968-69 | 1981-82 |
| Edwards, Marv | Pit., Tor., Cal. | 4 | 61 | 15 | 34 | 7 | 3467 | 218 | 2 | 3.77 | .... | .... | .... | .... | .... | .... | .... | .... | | 1968-69 | 1973-74 |
| • Edwards, Roy | Chi., Det., Pit. | 7 | 236 | 97 | 88 | 38 | 13109 | 637 | 12 | 2.92 | 4 | 0 | 3 | .... | 206 | 11 | 0 | 3.20 | 1 | 1960-61 | 1973-74 |
| Eklund, Brian | T.B. | 1 | 1 | 0 | 1 | 0 | 58 | 3 | 0 | 3.10 | .... | .... | .... | .... | .... | .... | .... | .... | | 2005-06 | 2005-06 |
| Eliot, Darren | L.A., Det., Buf. | 5 | 89 | 25 | 41 | 12 | 4931 | 377 | 1 | 4.59 | 1 | 0 | 0 | .... | 40 | 7 | 0 | 10.50 | | 1984-85 | 1988-89 |
| Ellacott, Ken | Van. | 1 | 12 | 2 | 3 | 4 | 555 | 41 | 0 | 4.43 | .... | .... | .... | .... | .... | .... | .... | .... | | 1982-83 | 1982-83 |
| Erickson, Chad | N.J. | 1 | 2 | 1 | 1 | 0 | 120 | 9 | 0 | 4.50 | .... | .... | .... | .... | .... | .... | .... | .... | | 1991-92 | 1991-92 |
| Esposito, Tony | Mtl., Chi. | 16 | 886 | 423 | 306 | 151 | 52585 | 2563 | 76 | 2.92 | 99 | 45 | 53 | .... | 6017 | 308 | 6 | 3.07 | 1 | 1968-69 | 1983-84 |
| Essensa, Bob | Wpg., Det., Edm., Phx., Van., Buf. | 12 | 446 | 173 | 176 | 47 | 24215 | 1270 | 18 | 3.15 | 16 | 4 | 9 | .... | 864 | 51 | 0 | 3.54 | | 1988-89 | 2001-02 |
| • Evans, Claude | Mtl., Bos. | 2 | 5 | 1 | 2 | 1 | 260 | 16 | 0 | 3.69 | .... | .... | .... | .... | .... | .... | .... | .... | | 1954-55 | 1957-58 |
| Exelby, Randy | Mtl., Edm. | 2 | 2 | 0 | 1 | 0 | 63 | 5 | 0 | 4.76 | .... | .... | .... | .... | .... | .... | .... | .... | | 1988-89 | 1989-90 |
| Fankhouser, Scott | Atl. | 2 | 23 | 4 | 12 | 2 | 1180 | 65 | 0 | 3.31 | .... | .... | .... | .... | .... | .... | .... | .... | | 1999-00 | 2000-01 |
| Farr, Rocky | Buf. | 3 | 19 | 2 | 6 | 3 | 722 | 42 | 0 | 3.49 | .... | .... | .... | .... | .... | .... | .... | .... | | 1972-73 | 1974-75 |
| Favell, Doug | Phi., Tor., Col. | 12 | 373 | 123 | 153 | 69 | 20771 | 1096 | 18 | 3.17 | 21 | 6 | 15 | .... | 1270 | 66 | 1 | 3.12 | | 1967-68 | 1978-79 |
| ‡ Fichaud, Eric | NYI, Nsh., Car., Mtl. | 6 | 95 | 22 | 47 | 10 | 4799 | 251 | 2 | 3.14 | .... | .... | .... | .... | .... | .... | .... | .... | | 1995-96 | 2000-01 |
| Finley, Brian | Nsh., Bos. | 3 | 4 | 0 | 2 | 0 | 166 | 13 | 0 | 4.70 | .... | .... | .... | .... | .... | .... | .... | .... | | 2002-03 | 2006-07 |
| Fiset, Stephane | Que., Col., L.A., Mtl. | 13 | 390 | 164 | 153 | 44 | 21785 | 1114 | 16 | 3.07 | 14 | 1 | 7 | .... | 563 | 37 | 0 | 3.94 | 1 | 1989-90 | 2001-02 |
| Fitzpatrick, Mark | L.A., NYI, Fla., T.B., Chi., Car. | 12 | 329 | 113 | 136 | 49 | 18329 | 953 | 8 | 3.12 | 9 | 0 | 3 | .... | 289 | 23 | 0 | 4.78 | | 1988-89 | 1999-00 |
| Flaherty, Wade | S.J., NYI, T.B., Fla., Nsh. | 11 | 120 | 27 | 56 | 9 | 5941 | 348 | 5 | 3.51 | 7 | 2 | 3 | .... | 377 | 31 | 0 | 4.93 | | 1991-92 | 2002-03 |
| • Forbes, Jake | Tor., Ham., NYA, Phi. | 13 | 210 | 85 | 114 | 11 | 12922 | 594 | 19 | 2.76 | 2 | 0 | 2 | 0 | 120 | 7 | 0 | 3.50 | | 1919-20 | 1932-33 |
| Ford, Brian | Que., Pit. | 2 | 11 | 3 | 7 | 0 | 580 | 61 | 0 | 6.31 | .... | .... | .... | .... | .... | .... | .... | .... | | 1983-84 | 1984-85 |
| Foster, Norm | Bos., Edm. | 2 | 13 | 7 | 4 | 0 | 623 | 34 | 0 | 3.27 | .... | .... | .... | .... | .... | .... | .... | .... | | 1990-91 | 1991-92 |
| ‡ Fountain, Mike | Van., Car., Ott. | 4 | 11 | 2 | 6 | 0 | 483 | 28 | 1 | 3.48 | .... | .... | .... | .... | .... | .... | .... | .... | | 1996-97 | 2000-01 |
| • Fowler, Hec | Bos. | 1 | 7 | 1 | 6 | 0 | 409 | 42 | 0 | 6.16 | .... | .... | .... | .... | .... | .... | .... | .... | | 1924-25 | 1924-25 |
| Francis, Emile | Chi., NYR | 6 | 95 | 31 | 52 | 11 | 5660 | 355 | 1 | 3.76 | .... | .... | .... | .... | .... | .... | .... | .... | | 1946-47 | 1951-52 |
| • Franks, Jimmy | Det., NYR, Bos. | 4 | 42 | 12 | 23 | 7 | 2520 | 181 | 1 | 4.31 | 1 | 0 | 1 | .... | 30 | 2 | 0 | 4.00 | 1 | 1936-37 | 1943-44 |
| • Frederick, Ray | Chi. | 1 | 5 | 0 | 4 | 1 | 300 | 22 | 0 | 4.40 | .... | .... | .... | .... | .... | .... | .... | .... | | 1954-55 | 1954-55 |
| Friesen, Karl | N.J. | 1 | 4 | 0 | 2 | 1 | 130 | 16 | 0 | 7.38 | .... | .... | .... | .... | .... | .... | .... | .... | | 1986-87 | 1986-87 |
| Froese, Bob | Phi., NYR | 8 | 242 | 128 | 72 | 20 | 13451 | 694 | 13 | 3.10 | 18 | 3 | 9 | .... | 830 | 55 | 0 | 3.98 | | 1982-83 | 1989-90 |
| Fuhr, Grant | Edm., Tor., Buf., L.A., St.L., Cgy. | 19 | 868 | 403 | 295 | 114 | 48945 | 2756 | 25 | 3.38 | 150 | 92 | 50 | .... | 8834 | 430 | 6 | 2.92 | 5 | 1981-82 | 1999-00 |
| Gage, Joaquin | Edm. | 3 | 23 | 4 | 12 | 1 | 1076 | 67 | 0 | 3.74 | .... | .... | .... | .... | .... | .... | .... | .... | | 1994-95 | 2000-01 |
| Gagnon, David | Det. | 1 | 2 | 0 | 1 | 0 | 35 | 6 | 0 | 10.29 | .... | .... | .... | .... | .... | .... | .... | .... | | 1990-91 | 1990-91 |
| • Gamble, Bruce | NYR, Bos., Tor., Phi. | 10 | 327 | 110 | 150 | 46 | 18442 | 988 | 22 | 3.21 | 5 | 0 | 4 | .... | 206 | 25 | 0 | 7.28 | | 1958-59 | 1971-72 |
| Gamble, Troy | Van. | 4 | 72 | 22 | 29 | 9 | 3804 | 229 | 1 | 3.61 | 4 | 1 | 3 | .... | 249 | 16 | 0 | 3.86 | | 1986-87 | 1991-92 |
| • Gardiner, Bert | NYR, Mtl., Chi., Bos. | 6 | 144 | 49 | 68 | 27 | 8760 | 554 | 3 | 3.79 | 9 | 4 | 5 | .... | 647 | 20 | 0 | 1.85 | | 1935-36 | 1943-44 |
| • Gardiner, Charlie | Chi. | 7 | 316 | 112 | 152 | 52 | 19687 | 664 | 42 | 2.02 | 21 | 12 | 6 | 3 | 1472 | 35 | 5 | 1.43 | 1 | 1927-28 | 1933-34 |
| • Gardner, George | Det., Van. | 5 | 66 | 16 | 30 | 6 | 3313 | 207 | 0 | 3.75 | .... | .... | .... | .... | .... | .... | .... | .... | | 1965-66 | 1971-72 |
| Garner, Tyrone | Cgy. | 1 | 3 | 0 | 2 | 0 | 139 | 12 | 0 | 5.18 | .... | .... | .... | .... | .... | .... | .... | .... | | 1998-99 | 1998-99 |
| ‡ Garnett, Michael | Atl. | 1 | 24 | 10 | 7 | 4 | 1271 | 73 | 2 | 3.45 | .... | .... | .... | .... | .... | .... | .... | .... | | 2005-06 | 2005-06 |
| Garrett, John | Hfd., Que., Van. | 6 | 207 | 68 | 91 | 37 | 11763 | 837 | 1 | 4.27 | 9 | 4 | 3 | .... | 461 | 33 | 0 | 4.30 | | 1979-80 | 1984-85 |
| Gatherum, Dave | Det. | 1 | 3 | 2 | 0 | 1 | 180 | 3 | 1 | 1.00 | .... | .... | .... | .... | .... | .... | .... | .... | 1 | 1953-54 | 1953-54 |
| Gauthier, Paul | Mtl. | 1 | 1 | 0 | 0 | 1 | 70 | 2 | 0 | 1.71 | .... | .... | .... | .... | .... | .... | .... | .... | | 1937-38 | 1937-38 |
| Gauthier, Sean | S.J. | 1 | 1 | 0 | 0 | 0 | 3 | 0 | 0 | 0.00 | .... | .... | .... | .... | .... | .... | .... | .... | | 1998-99 | 1998-99 |
| • Gelineau, Jack | Bos., Chi. | 4 | 143 | 46 | 64 | 33 | 8580 | 447 | 7 | 3.13 | 4 | 1 | 2 | .... | 260 | 7 | 1 | 1.62 | | 1948-49 | 1953-54 |
| Giacomin, Ed | NYR, Det. | 13 | 609 | 289 | 209 | 96 | 35633 | 1672 | 54 | 2.82 | 65 | 29 | 35 | .... | 3838 | 180 | 1 | 2.81 | | 1965-66 | 1977-78 |
| Gilbert, Gilles | Min., Bos., Det. | 14 | 416 | 192 | 143 | 60 | 23677 | 1290 | 18 | 3.27 | 32 | 17 | 15 | .... | 1919 | 97 | 3 | 3.03 | | 1969-70 | 1982-83 |
| Gill, Andre | Bos. | 1 | 5 | 3 | 2 | 0 | 270 | 13 | 1 | 2.89 | .... | .... | .... | .... | .... | .... | .... | .... | | 1967-68 | 1967-68 |
| • Goodman, Paul | Chi. | 3 | 52 | 23 | 20 | 9 | 3240 | 117 | 6 | 2.17 | 3 | 0 | 3 | .... | 187 | 10 | 0 | 3.21 | 1 | 1937-38 | 1940-41 |
| Gordon, Scott | Que. | 2 | 23 | 2 | 16 | 0 | 1082 | 101 | 0 | 5.60 | .... | .... | .... | .... | .... | .... | .... | .... | | 1989-90 | 1990-91 |
| Gosselin, Mario | Que., L.A., Hfd. | 9 | 241 | 91 | 107 | 14 | 12857 | 801 | 6 | 3.74 | 32 | 16 | 15 | .... | 1816 | 99 | 0 | 3.27 | | 1983-84 | 1993-94 |
| Goverde, David | L.A. | 3 | 5 | 1 | 4 | 0 | 278 | 29 | 0 | 6.26 | .... | .... | .... | .... | .... | .... | .... | .... | | 1991-92 | 1993-94 |
| Grahame, Ron | Bos., L.A., Que. | 4 | 114 | 50 | 43 | 15 | 6472 | 409 | 5 | 3.79 | 4 | 2 | 1 | .... | 202 | 7 | 0 | 2.08 | | 1977-78 | 1980-81 |
| • Grant, Benny | Tor., NYA, Bos. | 6 | 52 | 17 | 27 | 4 | 3036 | 188 | 4 | 3.72 | .... | .... | .... | .... | .... | .... | .... | .... | | 1928-29 | 1943-44 |
| Grant, Doug | Det., St.L. | 7 | 77 | 27 | 34 | 8 | 4199 | 280 | 2 | 4.00 | .... | .... | .... | .... | .... | .... | .... | .... | | 1973-74 | 1979-80 |
| Gratton, Gilles | St.L., NYR | 2 | 47 | 13 | 18 | 9 | 2299 | 154 | 0 | 4.02 | .... | .... | .... | .... | .... | .... | .... | .... | | 1975-76 | 1976-77 |
| Gray, Gerry | Det., NYI | 2 | 8 | 1 | 5 | 1 | 440 | 35 | 0 | 4.77 | .... | .... | .... | .... | .... | .... | .... | .... | | 1970-71 | 1972-73 |
| Gray, Harrison | Det. | 1 | 1 | 0 | 1 | 0 | 40 | 5 | 0 | 7.50 | .... | .... | .... | .... | .... | .... | .... | .... | | 1963-64 | 1963-64 |
| Greenlay, Mike | Edm. | 1 | 2 | 0 | 0 | 0 | 20 | 4 | 0 | 12.00 | .... | .... | .... | .... | .... | .... | .... | .... | | 1989-90 | 1989-90 |
| Guenette, Steve | Pit., Cgy. | 5 | 35 | 19 | 16 | 0 | 1958 | 122 | 1 | 3.74 | .... | .... | .... | .... | .... | .... | .... | .... | | 1986-87 | 1990-91 |
| ‡ Gustafson, Derek | Min. | 2 | 5 | 1 | 3 | 0 | 265 | 10 | 0 | 2.26 | .... | .... | .... | .... | .... | .... | .... | .... | | 2000-01 | 2001-02 |
| Hackett, Jeff | NYI, S.J., Chi., Mtl., Bos., Phi. | 15 | 500 | 166 | 244 | 56 | 28125 | 1361 | 26 | 2.90 | 12 | 3 | 7 | .... | 610 | 36 | 0 | 3.54 | | 1988-89 | 2003-04 |

| | | | Regular Schedule | | | | | | | | Playoffs | | | | | | | | | | |
|---|---|---|---|---|---|---|---|---|---|---|---|---|---|---|---|---|---|---|---|---|---|
| Name | NHL Teams | NHL Seasons | GP | W | L | T | Mins | GA | SO | Avg | GP | W | L | T | Mins | GA | SO | Avg | NHL Cup Wins | First NHL Season | Last NHL Season |
| • Hainsworth, George | Mtl., Tor. | 11 | 465 | 246 | 145 | 74 | 29087 | 937 | 94 | 1.93 | 52 | 22 | 25 | 5 | 3486 | 112 | 8 | 1.93 | 2 | 1926-27 | 1936-37 |
| Hall, Glenn | Det., Chi., St.L. | 19 | 906 | 407 | 326 | 163 | 53484 | 2222 | 84 | 2.49 | 115 | 49 | 65 | .... | 6899 | 320 | 6 | 2.78 | 2 | 1951-52 | 1970-71 |
| Hamel, Pierre | Tor., Wpg. | 4 | 69 | 13 | 41 | 7 | 3766 | 276 | 0 | 4.40 | .... | .... | .... | .... | .... | .... | .... | .... | | 1974-75 | 1980-81 |
| Hanlon, Glen | Van., St.L., NYR, Det. | 15 | 477 | 167 | 202 | 61 | 26037 | 1561 | 13 | 3.60 | 35 | 11 | 15 | .... | 1756 | 92 | 4 | 3.14 | | 1977-78 | 1990-91 |
| Harrison, Paul | Min., Tor., Pit., Buf. | 7 | 109 | 28 | 59 | 9 | 5806 | 408 | 2 | 4.22 | 4 | 0 | 1 | .... | 157 | 9 | 0 | 3.44 | | 1975-76 | 1981-82 |
| ‡ Hasek, Dominik | Chi., Buf., Det., Ott. | 16 | 735 | 389 | 223 | 95 | 42837 | 1572 | 81 | 2.20 | 119 | 65 | 49 | .... | 7318 | 246 | 14 | 2.02 | 2 | 1990-91 | 2007-08 |
| ‡ Hauser, Adam | L.A. | 1 | 1 | 0 | 0 | 0 | 51 | 6 | 0 | 7.06 | .... | .... | .... | .... | .... | .... | .... | .... | | 2005-06 | 2005-06 |
| Hayward, Brian | Wpg., Mtl., Min., S.J. | 11 | 357 | 143 | 156 | 37 | 20025 | 1242 | 8 | 3.72 | 37 | 11 | 18 | .... | 1803 | 104 | 0 | 3.46 | | 1982-83 | 1992-93 |
| Head, Don | Bos. | 1 | 38 | 9 | 26 | 3 | 2280 | 158 | 2 | 4.16 | .... | .... | .... | .... | .... | .... | .... | .... | | 1961-62 | 1961-62 |
| Healy, Glenn | L.A., NYI, NYR, Tor. | 15 | 437 | 166 | 190 | 47 | 24256 | 1361 | 13 | 3.37 | 37 | 13 | 15 | .... | 1930 | 108 | 0 | 3.36 | 1 | 1985-86 | 2000-01 |
| Hebert, Guy | St.L., Ana., NYR | 10 | 491 | 191 | 222 | 56 | 27889 | 1307 | 28 | 2.81 | 14 | 4 | 7 | .... | 744 | 33 | 1 | 2.66 | | 1991-92 | 2000-01 |
| • Hebert, Sammy | Tor., Ott. | 2 | 4 | 2 | 1 | 0 | 200 | 19 | 0 | 5.70 | .... | .... | .... | .... | .... | .... | .... | .... | 1 | 1917-18 | 1923-24 |
| Heinz, Rick | St.L., Van. | 5 | 49 | 14 | 19 | 5 | 2356 | 159 | 2 | 4.05 | 1 | 0 | 0 | .... | 8 | 1 | 0 | 7.50 | | 1980-81 | 1984-85 |
| Henderson, John | Bos. | 2 | 46 | 15 | 15 | 15 | 2688 | 113 | 5 | 2.52 | 2 | 0 | 2 | .... | 120 | 8 | 0 | 4.00 | | 1954-55 | 1955-56 |
| • Henry, Gord | Bos. | 4 | 3 | 1 | 2 | 0 | 180 | 5 | 1 | 1.67 | 5 | 0 | 4 | .... | 283 | 21 | 0 | 4.45 | | 1948-49 | 1952-53 |
| • Henry, Jim | NYR, Chi., Bos. | 9 | 406 | 161 | 173 | 70 | 24355 | 1166 | 28 | 2.87 | 29 | 11 | 18 | .... | 1741 | 81 | 2 | 2.79 | | 1941-42 | 1954-55 |
| Herron, Denis | Pit., K.C., Mtl. | 14 | 462 | 146 | 203 | 76 | 25608 | 1579 | 10 | 3.70 | 15 | 5 | 10 | .... | 901 | 50 | 0 | 3.33 | | 1972-73 | 1985-86 |
| Hextall, Ron | Phi., Que., NYI | 13 | 608 | 296 | 214 | 69 | 34750 | 1723 | 23 | 2.97 | 93 | 47 | 43 | .... | 5456 | 276 | 2 | 3.04 | | 1986-87 | 1998-99 |
| • Highton, Hec | Chi. | 1 | 24 | 10 | 14 | 0 | 1440 | 108 | 0 | 4.50 | .... | .... | .... | .... | .... | .... | .... | .... | | 1943-44 | 1943-44 |
| § • Himes, Normie | NYA | 2 | 2 | 0 | 1 | 0 | 79 | 3 | 0 | 2.28 | .... | .... | .... | .... | .... | .... | .... | .... | | 1927-28 | 1928-29 |
| Hirsch, Corey | NYR, Van., Wsh., Dal. | 7 | 108 | 34 | 45 | 14 | 5775 | 301 | 4 | 3.13 | 6 | 2 | 3 | .... | 338 | 21 | 0 | 3.73 | | 1992-93 | 2002-03 |
| ‡ Hnilicka, Milan | NYR, Atl., L.A. | 5 | 121 | 29 | 67 | 13 | 6509 | 359 | 5 | 3.31 | .... | .... | .... | .... | .... | .... | .... | .... | | 1999-00 | 2003-04 |
| Hodge, Charlie | Mtl., Oak., Van. | 14 | 358 | 150 | 125 | 61 | 20573 | 925 | 24 | 2.70 | 16 | 7 | 8 | .... | 804 | 32 | 2 | 2.39 | 6 | 1954-55 | 1970-71 |
| Hodson, Kevin | Det., T.B. | 6 | 71 | 17 | 18 | 10 | 2910 | 134 | 4 | 2.76 | 1 | 0 | 0 | .... | 1 | 0 | 0 | 0.00 | 2 | 1995-96 | 2002-03 |
| Hoffort, Bruce | Phi. | 2 | 9 | 4 | 0 | 3 | 368 | 22 | 0 | 3.59 | .... | .... | .... | .... | .... | .... | .... | .... | | 1989-90 | 1990-91 |
| Hoganson, Paul | Pit. | 1 | 2 | 0 | 1 | 0 | 57 | 7 | 0 | 7.37 | .... | .... | .... | .... | .... | .... | .... | .... | | 1970-71 | 1970-71 |
| Hogosta, Goran | NYI, Que. | 2 | 22 | 5 | 12 | 3 | 1208 | 83 | 1 | 4.12 | .... | .... | .... | .... | .... | .... | .... | .... | | 1977-78 | 1979-80 |
| Holden, Mark | Mtl., Wpg. | 4 | 8 | 2 | 2 | 1 | 372 | 25 | 0 | 4.03 | .... | .... | .... | .... | .... | .... | .... | .... | | 1981-82 | 1984-85 |
| Holland, Ken | Hfd., Det. | 2 | 4 | 0 | 2 | 1 | 206 | 17 | 0 | 4.95 | .... | .... | .... | .... | .... | .... | .... | .... | | 1980-81 | 1983-84 |
| Holland, Rob | Pit. | 2 | 44 | 11 | 22 | 9 | 2513 | 171 | 1 | 4.08 | .... | .... | .... | .... | .... | .... | .... | .... | | 1979-80 | 1980-81 |
| • Holmes, Hap | Tor., Det. | 4 | 103 | 39 | 54 | 10 | 6510 | 264 | 17 | 2.43 | 2 | 1 | 1 | 0 | 120 | 7 | 0 | 3.50 | 1 | 1917-18 | 1927-28 |
| § • Horner, Red | Tor. | 1 | 2 | 0 | 0 | 0 | 3 | 1 | 0 | 20.00 | .... | .... | .... | .... | .... | .... | .... | .... | | 1928-29 | 1931-32 |
| ‡ Houle, Martin | Phi. | 1 | 1 | 0 | 0 | 0 | 2 | 1 | 0 | 30.00 | .... | .... | .... | .... | .... | .... | .... | .... | | 2006-07 | 2006-07 |
| Hrivnak, Jim | Wsh., Wpg., St.L. | 5 | 85 | 34 | 30 | 3 | 4217 | 262 | 0 | 3.73 | .... | .... | .... | .... | .... | .... | .... | .... | | 1989-90 | 1993-94 |
| Hrudey, Kelly | NYI, L.A., S.J. | 15 | 677 | 271 | 265 | 88 | 38084 | 2174 | 17 | 3.43 | 85 | 36 | 46 | .... | 5163 | 283 | 0 | 3.29 | | 1983-84 | 1997-98 |
| Hurme, Jani | Ott., Fla. | 4 | 76 | 29 | 25 | 11 | 4041 | 176 | 6 | 2.61 | .... | .... | .... | .... | .... | .... | .... | .... | | 1999-00 | 2002-03 |
| Ing, Peter | Tor., Edm., Det. | 4 | 74 | 20 | 37 | 9 | 3941 | 266 | 1 | 4.05 | .... | .... | .... | .... | .... | .... | .... | .... | | 1989-90 | 1993-94 |
| Inness, Gary | Pit., Phi., Wsh. | 7 | 162 | 58 | 61 | 27 | 8710 | 494 | 2 | 3.40 | 9 | 5 | 4 | .... | 540 | 24 | 0 | 2.67 | | 1973-74 | 1980-81 |
| Irbe, Arturs | S.J., Dal., Van., Car. | 13 | 568 | 218 | 236 | 79 | 32066 | 1513 | 33 | 2.83 | 51 | 23 | 27 | .... | 2981 | 142 | 1 | 2.86 | | 1991-92 | 2003-04 |
| Ireland, Randy | Buf. | 1 | 2 | 0 | 0 | 0 | 30 | 3 | 0 | 6.00 | .... | .... | .... | .... | .... | .... | .... | .... | | 1978-79 | 1978-79 |
| Irons, Robbie | St.L. | 1 | 1 | 0 | 0 | 0 | 3 | 0 | 0 | 0.00 | .... | .... | .... | .... | .... | .... | .... | .... | | 1968-69 | 1968-69 |
| • Ironstone, Joe | Ott., NYA, Tor. | 3 | 2 | 0 | 0 | 1 | 110 | 3 | 1 | 1.64 | .... | .... | .... | .... | .... | .... | .... | .... | | 1924-25 | 1927-28 |
| Jablonski, Pat | St.L., T.B., Mtl., Phx., Car. | 8 | 128 | 28 | 62 | 18 | 6634 | 413 | 1 | 3.74 | 4 | 0 | 0 | .... | 139 | 6 | 0 | 2.59 | | 1989-90 | 1997-98 |
| Jackson, Doug | Chi. | 1 | 6 | 2 | 3 | 1 | 360 | 42 | 0 | 7.00 | .... | .... | .... | .... | .... | .... | .... | .... | | 1947-48 | 1947-48 |
| Jackson, Percy | Bos., NYA, NYR | 4 | 7 | 1 | 3 | 1 | 392 | 26 | 0 | 3.98 | .... | .... | .... | .... | .... | .... | .... | .... | | 1931-32 | 1935-36 |
| Jaks, Pauli | L.A. | 1 | 1 | 0 | 0 | 0 | 40 | 2 | 0 | 3.00 | .... | .... | .... | .... | .... | .... | .... | .... | | 1994-95 | 1994-95 |
| Janaszak, Steve | Min., Col. | 2 | 3 | 0 | 1 | 1 | 160 | 15 | 0 | 5.63 | .... | .... | .... | .... | .... | .... | .... | .... | | 1979-80 | 1981-82 |
| Janecyk, Bob | Chi., L.A. | 6 | 110 | 43 | 47 | 13 | 6250 | 432 | 2 | 4.15 | 3 | 0 | 3 | .... | 184 | 10 | 0 | 3.26 | | 1983-84 | 1988-89 |
| § • Jenkins, Roger | NYA | 1 | 1 | 0 | 1 | 0 | 30 | 7 | 0 | 14.00 | .... | .... | .... | .... | .... | .... | .... | .... | | 1938-39 | 1938-39 |
| Jensen, Al | Det., Wsh., L.A. | 7 | 179 | 95 | 53 | 18 | 9974 | 557 | 8 | 3.35 | 12 | 5 | 5 | .... | 598 | 32 | 0 | 3.21 | | 1980-81 | 1986-87 |
| Jensen, Darren | Phi. | 2 | 30 | 15 | 10 | 1 | 1496 | 95 | 2 | 3.81 | .... | .... | .... | .... | .... | .... | .... | .... | | 1984-85 | 1985-86 |
| Johnson, Bob | St.L., Pit. | 2 | 24 | 9 | 9 | 1 | 1059 | 66 | 0 | 3.74 | .... | .... | .... | .... | .... | .... | .... | .... | | 1972-73 | 1974-75 |
| Johnston, Eddie | Bos., Tor., St.L., Chi. | 16 | 592 | 234 | 257 | 80 | 34216 | 1852 | 32 | 3.25 | 18 | 7 | 10 | .... | 1023 | 57 | 1 | 3.34 | 2 | 1962-63 | 1977-78 |
| Junkin, Joe | Bos. | 1 | 1 | 0 | 0 | 0 | 8 | 0 | 0 | 0.00 | .... | .... | .... | .... | .... | .... | .... | .... | | 1968-69 | 1968-69 |
| Kaarela, Jari | Col. | 1 | 5 | 2 | 2 | 0 | 220 | 22 | 0 | 6.00 | .... | .... | .... | .... | .... | .... | .... | .... | | 1980-81 | 1980-81 |
| Kamppuri, Hannu | N.J. | 1 | 13 | 1 | 10 | 1 | 645 | 54 | 0 | 5.02 | .... | .... | .... | .... | .... | .... | .... | .... | | 1984-85 | 1984-85 |
| • Karakas, Mike | Chi., Mtl. | 8 | 336 | 114 | 169 | 53 | 20614 | 1002 | 28 | 2.92 | 23 | 11 | 12 | 0 | 1434 | 72 | 3 | 3.01 | 1 | 1935-36 | 1945-46 |
| Keans, Doug | L.A., Bos. | 9 | 210 | 96 | 64 | 26 | 11388 | 666 | 4 | 3.51 | 9 | 2 | 6 | .... | 432 | 34 | 0 | 4.72 | | 1979-80 | 1987-88 |
| • Keenan, Don | Bos. | 1 | 1 | 0 | 1 | 0 | 60 | 4 | 0 | 4.00 | .... | .... | .... | .... | .... | .... | .... | .... | | 1958-59 | 1958-59 |
| • Kerr, Dave | Mtl.M., NYA, NYR | 11 | 427 | 203 | 148 | 75 | 26639 | 954 | 51 | 2.15 | 40 | 18 | 19 | 3 | 2616 | 76 | 8 | 1.74 | 1 | 1930-31 | 1940-41 |
| Kidd, Trevor | Cgy., Car., Fla., Tor. | 12 | 387 | 140 | 162 | 52 | 21426 | 1014 | 19 | 2.84 | 10 | 3 | 5 | .... | 550 | 36 | 1 | 3.93 | | 1991-92 | 2003-04 |
| King, Scott | Det. | 2 | 2 | 0 | 0 | 0 | 61 | 3 | 0 | 2.95 | .... | .... | .... | .... | .... | .... | .... | .... | | 1990-91 | 1991-92 |
| Kleisinger, Terry | NYR | 1 | 4 | 0 | 2 | 0 | 191 | 14 | 0 | 4.40 | .... | .... | .... | .... | .... | .... | .... | .... | | 1985-86 | 1985-86 |
| Klymkiw, Julian | NYR | 1 | 1 | 0 | 0 | 0 | 19 | 2 | 0 | 6.32 | .... | .... | .... | .... | .... | .... | .... | .... | | 1958-59 | 1958-59 |
| Knickle, Rick | L.A. | 2 | 14 | 7 | 6 | 0 | 706 | 44 | 0 | 3.74 | .... | .... | .... | .... | .... | .... | .... | .... | | 1992-93 | 1993-94 |
| Kochan, Dieter | T.B., Min. | 4 | 21 | 1 | 11 | 1 | 849 | 56 | 0 | 3.96 | .... | .... | .... | .... | .... | .... | .... | .... | | 1999-00 | 2002-03 |
| ‡ Kolesnik, Vitali | Col. | 1 | 8 | 3 | 3 | 0 | 370 | 20 | 0 | 3.24 | .... | .... | .... | .... | .... | .... | .... | .... | | 2005-06 | 2005-06 |
| Konstantinov, Evgeny | T.B. | 2 | 2 | 0 | 0 | 0 | 21 | 1 | 0 | 2.86 | .... | .... | .... | .... | .... | .... | .... | .... | | 2000-01 | 2002-03 |
| Kuntar, Les | Mtl. | 1 | 6 | 2 | 2 | 0 | 302 | 16 | 0 | 3.18 | .... | .... | .... | .... | .... | .... | .... | .... | | 1993-94 | 1993-94 |
| Kurt, Gary | Cal. | 1 | 16 | 1 | 7 | 5 | 838 | 60 | 0 | 4.30 | .... | .... | .... | .... | .... | .... | .... | .... | | 1971-72 | 1971-72 |
| Labbe, Jean-Francois | NYR, CBJ | 3 | 15 | 3 | 6 | 0 | 628 | 36 | 0 | 3.44 | .... | .... | .... | .... | .... | .... | .... | .... | | 1999-00 | 2002-03 |
| Labrecque, Patrick | Mtl. | 1 | 2 | 0 | 1 | 0 | 98 | 7 | 0 | 4.29 | .... | .... | .... | .... | .... | .... | .... | .... | | 1995-96 | 1995-96 |
| Lacher, Blaine | Bos. | 2 | 47 | 22 | 16 | 4 | 2636 | 123 | 4 | 2.80 | 5 | 1 | 4 | .... | 283 | 12 | 0 | 2.54 | | 1994-95 | 1995-96 |
| • Lacroix, Frenchy | Mtl. | 2 | 5 | 1 | 4 | 0 | 280 | 16 | 0 | 3.43 | .... | .... | .... | .... | .... | .... | .... | .... | | 1925-26 | 1926-27 |
| LaFerriere, Rick | Col. | 1 | 1 | 0 | 0 | 0 | 20 | 1 | 0 | 3.00 | .... | .... | .... | .... | .... | .... | .... | .... | | 1981-82 | 1981-82 |
| LaForest, Mark | Det., Phi., Tor., Ott. | 6 | 103 | 25 | 54 | 4 | 5032 | 354 | 2 | 4.22 | 2 | 1 | 0 | .... | 48 | 1 | 0 | 1.25 | | 1985-86 | 1993-94 |
| Lajeunesse, Simon | Ott. | 1 | 1 | 0 | 0 | 0 | 24 | 0 | 0 | 0.00 | .... | .... | .... | .... | .... | .... | .... | .... | | 2001-02 | 2001-02 |
| Lamothe, Marc | Chi., Det. | 2 | 4 | 2 | 1 | 1 | 241 | 13 | 0 | 3.24 | .... | .... | .... | .... | .... | .... | .... | .... | | 1999-00 | 2003-04 |
| Langkow, Scott | Wpg., Phx., Atl. | 4 | 20 | 3 | 12 | 1 | 943 | 68 | 0 | 4.33 | .... | .... | .... | .... | .... | .... | .... | .... | | 1995-96 | 1999-00 |
| • Larocque, Michel | Mtl., Tor., Phi., St.L. | 11 | 312 | 160 | 89 | 45 | 17615 | 978 | 17 | 3.33 | 14 | 6 | 6 | .... | 759 | 37 | 1 | 2.92 | 4 | 1973-74 | 1983-84 |
| Larocque, Michel | Chi. | 1 | 3 | 0 | 2 | 0 | 152 | 9 | 0 | 3.55 | .... | .... | .... | .... | .... | .... | .... | .... | | 2000-01 | 2000-01 |
| ‡ Lasak, Jan | Nsh. | 2 | 6 | 0 | 4 | 0 | 267 | 18 | 0 | 4.04 | .... | .... | .... | .... | .... | .... | .... | .... | | 2001-02 | 2002-03 |
| Laskoski, Gary | L.A. | 2 | 59 | 19 | 27 | 5 | 2942 | 228 | 0 | 4.65 | .... | .... | .... | .... | .... | .... | .... | .... | | 1982-83 | 1983-84 |
| Laxton, Gord | Pit. | 4 | 17 | 4 | 9 | 0 | 800 | 74 | 0 | 5.55 | .... | .... | .... | .... | .... | .... | .... | .... | | 1975-76 | 1978-79 |
| LeBlanc, Ray | Chi. | 1 | 1 | 1 | 0 | 0 | 60 | 1 | 0 | 1.00 | .... | .... | .... | .... | .... | .... | .... | .... | | 1991-92 | 1991-92 |
| § • Leduc, Albert | Mtl. | 1 | 1 | 0 | 0 | 0 | 2 | 1 | 0 | 30.00 | .... | .... | .... | .... | .... | .... | .... | .... | | 1931-32 | 1931-32 |
| Legris, Claude | Det. | 2 | 4 | 0 | 1 | 1 | 91 | 4 | 0 | 2.64 | .... | .... | .... | .... | .... | .... | .... | .... | | 1980-81 | 1981-82 |
| • Lehman, Hugh | Chi. | 2 | 48 | 20 | 24 | 4 | 3047 | 136 | 6 | 2.68 | 2 | 0 | 1 | 1 | 120 | 10 | 0 | 5.00 | | 1926-27 | 1927-28 |
| Lemelin, Reggie | Atl., Cgy., Bos. | 15 | 507 | 236 | 162 | 63 | 28006 | 1613 | 12 | 3.46 | 59 | 23 | 25 | .... | 3119 | 186 | 2 | 3.58 | | 1978-79 | 1992-93 |
| Lenarduzzi, Mike | Hfd. | 2 | 4 | 1 | 1 | 1 | 189 | 10 | 0 | 3.17 | .... | .... | .... | .... | .... | .... | .... | .... | | 1992-93 | 1993-94 |
| Lessard, Mario | L.A. | 6 | 240 | 92 | 97 | 39 | 13529 | 843 | 9 | 3.74 | 20 | 6 | 12 | .... | 1136 | 83 | 0 | 4.38 | | 1978-79 | 1983-84 |
| Levasseur, Jean-Louis | Min. | 1 | 1 | 0 | 1 | 0 | 60 | 7 | 0 | 7.00 | .... | .... | .... | .... | .... | .... | .... | .... | | 1979-80 | 1979-80 |
| § • Levinsky, Alex | Tor. | 1 | 1 | 0 | 0 | 0 | 1 | 1 | 0 | 60.00 | .... | .... | .... | .... | .... | .... | .... | .... | | 1931-32 | 1931-32 |
| • Lindbergh, Pelle | Phi. | 5 | 157 | 87 | 49 | 15 | 9150 | 503 | 7 | 3.30 | 23 | 12 | 10 | .... | 1214 | 63 | 3 | 3.11 | | 1981-82 | 1985-86 |
| • Lindsay, Bert | Mtl.W., Tor. | 2 | 20 | 6 | 14 | 0 | 1238 | 118 | 0 | 5.72 | .... | .... | .... | .... | .... | .... | .... | .... | | 1917-18 | 1918-19 |
| Little, Neil | Phi. | 2 | 2 | 0 | 2 | 0 | 93 | 6 | 0 | 3.87 | .... | .... | .... | .... | .... | .... | .... | .... | | 2001-02 | 2003-04 |
| Littman, David | Buf., T.B. | 3 | 3 | 0 | 2 | 0 | 141 | 14 | 0 | 5.96 | .... | .... | .... | .... | .... | .... | .... | .... | | 1990-91 | 1992-93 |
| Liut, Mike | St.L., Hfd., Wsh. | 13 | 664 | 294 | 271 | 74 | 38215 | 2221 | 25 | 3.49 | 67 | 29 | 32 | .... | 3814 | 215 | 2 | 3.38 | | 1979-80 | 1991-92 |
| Lockett, Ken | Van. | 2 | 55 | 13 | 15 | 8 | 2348 | 131 | 2 | 3.35 | 1 | 0 | 1 | .... | 60 | 6 | 0 | 6.00 | | 1974-75 | 1975-76 |
| • Lockhart, Howard | Tor., Que., Ham., Bos. | 5 | 59 | 16 | 41 | 0 | 3413 | 287 | 1 | 5.05 | .... | .... | .... | .... | .... | .... | .... | .... | | 1919-20 | 1924-25 |
| LoPresti, Pete | Min., Edm. | 6 | 175 | 43 | 102 | 20 | 9858 | 668 | 5 | 4.07 | 2 | 0 | 2 | .... | 77 | 6 | 0 | 4.68 | | 1974-75 | 1980-81 |
| • LoPresti, Sam | Chi. | 2 | 74 | 30 | 38 | 6 | 4530 | 236 | 4 | 3.13 | 8 | 3 | 5 | .... | 530 | 17 | 1 | 1.92 | | 1940-41 | 1941-42 |
| Lorenz, Danny | NYI | 3 | 8 | 1 | 5 | 0 | 357 | 25 | 0 | 4.20 | .... | .... | .... | .... | .... | .... | .... | .... | | 1990-91 | 1992-93 |
| Loustel, Ron | Wpg. | 1 | 1 | 0 | 1 | 0 | 60 | 10 | 0 | 10.00 | .... | .... | .... | .... | .... | .... | .... | .... | | 1980-81 | 1980-81 |
| Low, Ron | Tor., Wsh., Det., Que., Edm., N.J. | 11 | 382 | 102 | 203 | 38 | 20502 | 1463 | 4 | 4.28 | 7 | 1 | 6 | .... | 452 | 29 | 0 | 3.85 | | 1972-73 | 1984-85 |
| Lozinski, Larry | Det. | 1 | 30 | 6 | 11 | 7 | 1459 | 105 | 0 | 4.32 | .... | .... | .... | .... | .... | .... | .... | .... | | 1980-81 | 1980-81 |
| • Lumley, Harry | Det., NYR, Chi., Tor., Bos. | 16 | 803 | 330 | 329 | 142 | 48044 | 2206 | 71 | 2.75 | 76 | 29 | 47 | .... | 4778 | 198 | 7 | 2.49 | 1 | 1943-44 | 1959-60 |
| MacKenzie, Shawn | N.J. | 1 | 4 | 0 | 1 | 0 | 130 | 15 | 0 | 6.92 | .... | .... | .... | .... | .... | .... | .... | .... | | 1982-83 | 1982-83 |

| Name | NHL Teams | NHL Seasons | Regular Schedule GP | W | L | T | Mins | GA | SO | Avg | Playoffs GP | W | L | T | Mins | GA | SO | Avg | NHL Cup Wins | First NHL Season | Last NHL Season |
|---|---|---|---|---|---|---|---|---|---|---|---|---|---|---|---|---|---|---|---|---|---|
| Madeley, Darrin | Ott. | 3 | 39 | 4 | 23 | 5 | 1928 | 140 | 0 | 4.36 | .... | .... | .... | .... | .... | .... | .... | .... | | 1992-93 | 1994-95 |
| Malarchuk, Clint | Que., Wsh., Buf. | 11 | 338 | 141 | 130 | 45 | 19030 | 1100 | 12 | 3.47 | 15 | 2 | 9 | .... | 781 | 56 | 0 | 4.30 | | 1981-82 | 1991-92 |
| Maneluk, George | NYI | 1 | 4 | 1 | 1 | 0 | 140 | 15 | 0 | 6.43 | .... | .... | .... | .... | .... | .... | .... | .... | | 1990-91 | 1990-91 |
| Maniago, Cesare | Tor., Mtl., NYR, Min., Van. | 15 | 568 | 190 | 257 | 97 | 32569 | 1773 | 30 | 3.27 | 36 | 15 | 21 | .... | 2247 | 100 | 3 | 2.67 | | 1960-61 | 1977-78 |
| ‡ Maracle, Norm | Det., Atl. | 5 | 66 | 14 | 33 | 8 | 3430 | 177 | 1 | 3.10 | 2 | 0 | 0 | .... | 58 | 3 | 0 | 3.10 | | 1997-98 | 2001-02 |
| ‡ Markkanen, Jussi | Edm., NYR | 5 | 128 | 43 | 47 | 15 | 6610 | 297 | 7 | 2.70 | 7 | 3 | 3 | .... | 374 | 14 | 1 | 2.25 | | 2001-02 | 2006-07 |
| Marois, Jean | Tor., Chi. | 2 | 3 | 1 | 2 | 0 | 180 | 15 | 0 | 5.00 | .... | .... | .... | .... | .... | .... | .... | .... | | 1943-44 | 1953-54 |
| Martin, Seth | St.L. | 1 | 30 | 8 | 10 | 7 | 1552 | 67 | 1 | 2.59 | 2 | 0 | 0 | .... | 73 | 5 | 0 | 4.11 | | 1967-68 | 1967-68 |
| Mason, Bob | Wsh., Chi., Que., Van. | 8 | 145 | 55 | 65 | 16 | 7988 | 500 | 1 | 3.76 | 5 | 2 | 3 | .... | 369 | 12 | 1 | 1.95 | | 1983-84 | 1990-91 |
| Mattsson, Markus | Wpg., Min., L.A. | 4 | 92 | 21 | 46 | 14 | 5007 | 343 | 6 | 4.11 | .... | .... | .... | .... | .... | .... | .... | .... | | 1979-80 | 1983-84 |
| May, Darrell | St.L. | 2 | 6 | 1 | 5 | 0 | 364 | 31 | 0 | 5.11 | .... | .... | .... | .... | .... | .... | .... | .... | | 1985-86 | 1987-88 |
| Mayer, Gilles | Tor. | 4 | 9 | 2 | 6 | 1 | 540 | 24 | 0 | 2.67 | .... | .... | .... | .... | .... | .... | .... | .... | | 1949-50 | 1955-56 |
| • McAuley, Ken | NYR | 2 | 96 | 17 | 64 | 15 | 5740 | 537 | 1 | 5.61 | .... | .... | .... | .... | .... | .... | .... | .... | | 1943-44 | 1944-45 |
| McCartan, Jack | NYR | 2 | 12 | 2 | 7 | 3 | 680 | 42 | 1 | 3.71 | .... | .... | .... | .... | .... | .... | .... | .... | | 1959-60 | 1960-61 |
| • McCool, Frank | Tor. | 2 | 72 | 34 | 31 | 7 | 4320 | 242 | 4 | 3.36 | 13 | 8 | 5 | .... | 807 | 30 | 4 | 2.23 | 1 | 1944-45 | 1945-46 |
| McDuffe, Peter | St.L., NYR, K.C., Det. | 5 | 57 | 11 | 36 | 6 | 3207 | 218 | 0 | 4.08 | 1 | 0 | 1 | .... | 60 | 7 | 0 | 7.00 | | 1971-72 | 1975-76 |
| McGrattan, Tom | Det. | 1 | 1 | 0 | 0 | 0 | 8 | 1 | 0 | 7.50 | .... | .... | .... | .... | .... | .... | .... | .... | | 1947-48 | 1947-48 |
| McKay, Ross | Hfd. | 1 | 1 | 0 | 0 | 0 | 35 | 3 | 0 | 5.14 | .... | .... | .... | .... | .... | .... | .... | .... | | 1990-91 | 1990-91 |
| McKenzie, Bill | Det., K.C., Col. | 6 | 91 | 18 | 49 | 13 | 4776 | 326 | 2 | 4.10 | .... | .... | .... | .... | .... | .... | .... | .... | | 1973-74 | 1979-80 |
| McKichan, Steve | Van. | 1 | 1 | 0 | 0 | 0 | 20 | 2 | 0 | 6.00 | .... | .... | .... | .... | .... | .... | .... | .... | | 1990-91 | 1990-91 |
| McLachlan, Murray | Tor. | 1 | 2 | 0 | 1 | 0 | 25 | 4 | 0 | 9.60 | .... | .... | .... | .... | .... | .... | .... | .... | | 1970-71 | 1970-71 |
| McLean, Kirk | N.J., Van., Car., Fla., NYR | 16 | 612 | 245 | 262 | 72 | 35090 | 1904 | 22 | 3.26 | 68 | 34 | 34 | .... | 4189 | 198 | 6 | 2.84 | | 1985-86 | 2000-01 |
| McLelland, Dave | Van. | 1 | 2 | 1 | 1 | 0 | 120 | 10 | 0 | 5.00 | .... | .... | .... | .... | .... | .... | .... | .... | | 1972-73 | 1972-73 |
| McLennan, Jamie | NYI, St.L., Min., Cgy., NYR, Fla. | 11 | 254 | 80 | 109 | 36 | 13834 | 617 | 13 | 2.68 | 5 | 0 | 2 | .... | 134 | 7 | 0 | 3.13 | | 1993-94 | 2006-07 |
| McLeod, Don | Det., Phi. | 2 | 18 | 3 | 10 | 1 | 879 | 74 | 0 | 5.05 | .... | .... | .... | .... | .... | .... | .... | .... | | 1970-71 | 1971-72 |
| McLeod, Jim | St.L. | 1 | 16 | 6 | 6 | 4 | 880 | 44 | 0 | 3.00 | .... | .... | .... | .... | .... | .... | .... | .... | | 1971-72 | 1971-72 |
| McNamara, Gerry | Tor. | 2 | 7 | 2 | 2 | 1 | 323 | 14 | 0 | 2.60 | .... | .... | .... | .... | .... | .... | .... | .... | | 1960-61 | 1969-70 |
| • McNeil, Gerry | Mtl. | 8 | 276 | 119 | 105 | 52 | 16535 | 649 | 28 | 2.36 | 35 | 17 | 18 | .... | 2284 | 72 | 5 | 1.89 | 3 | 1947-48 | 1957-58 |
| McRae, Gord | Tor. | 5 | 71 | 30 | 22 | 10 | 3799 | 221 | 1 | 3.49 | 8 | 2 | 5 | .... | 454 | 22 | 0 | 2.91 | | 1972-73 | 1977-78 |
| ‡ McVicar, Rob | Van. | 1 | 1 | 0 | 0 | 0 | 3 | 0 | 0 | 0.00 | .... | .... | .... | .... | .... | .... | .... | .... | | 2005-06 | 2005-06 |
| Melanson, Roland | NYI, Min., L.A., N.J., Mtl. | 11 | 291 | 129 | 106 | 33 | 16452 | 995 | 6 | 3.63 | 23 | 4 | 9 | .... | 801 | 59 | 0 | 4.42 | 3 | 1980-81 | 1991-92 |
| Meloche, Gilles | Chi., Cal., Cle., Min., Pit. | 18 | 788 | 270 | 351 | 131 | 45401 | 2756 | 20 | 3.64 | 45 | 21 | 19 | .... | 2464 | 143 | 2 | 3.48 | | 1970-71 | 1987-88 |
| Micalef, Corrado | Det. | 5 | 113 | 26 | 59 | 15 | 5794 | 409 | 2 | 4.24 | 3 | 0 | 0 | .... | 49 | 8 | 0 | 9.80 | | 1981-82 | 1985-86 |
| Michaud, Alfie | Van. | 1 | 2 | 0 | 1 | 0 | 69 | 5 | 0 | 4.35 | .... | .... | .... | .... | .... | .... | .... | .... | | 1999-00 | 1999-00 |
| ‡ Michaud, Olivier | Mtl. | 1 | 1 | 0 | 0 | 0 | 18 | 0 | 0 | 0.00 | .... | .... | .... | .... | .... | .... | .... | .... | | 2001-02 | 2001-02 |
| Middlebrook, Lindsay | Wpg., Min., N.J., Edm. | 4 | 37 | 3 | 23 | 6 | 1845 | 152 | 0 | 4.94 | .... | .... | .... | .... | .... | .... | .... | .... | | 1979-80 | 1982-83 |
| • Millar, Al | Bos. | 1 | 6 | 1 | 4 | 1 | 360 | 25 | 0 | 4.17 | .... | .... | .... | .... | .... | .... | .... | .... | | 1957-58 | 1957-58 |
| Millen, Greg | Pit., Hfd., St.L., Que., Chi., Det. | 14 | 604 | 215 | 284 | 89 | 35377 | 2281 | 17 | 3.87 | 59 | 27 | 29 | .... | 3383 | 193 | 0 | 3.42 | | 1978-79 | 1991-92 |
| • Miller, Joe | NYA, NYR, Pit., Phi. | 4 | 127 | 24 | 87 | 16 | 7871 | 383 | 16 | 2.92 | 3 | 2 | 1 | 0 | 180 | 3 | 1 | 1.00 | 1 | 1927-28 | 1930-31 |
| Minard, Mike | Edm. | 1 | 1 | 1 | 0 | 0 | 60 | 3 | 0 | 3.00 | .... | .... | .... | .... | .... | .... | .... | .... | | 1999-00 | 1999-00 |
| Mio, Eddie | Edm., NYR, Det. | 7 | 192 | 64 | 73 | 30 | 10428 | 705 | 4 | 4.06 | 17 | 9 | 7 | .... | 986 | 63 | 0 | 3.83 | | 1979-80 | 1985-86 |
| • Mitchell, Ivan | Tor. | 3 | 22 | 10 | 9 | 0 | 1190 | 88 | 0 | 4.44 | .... | .... | .... | .... | .... | .... | .... | .... | 1 | 1919-20 | 1921-22 |
| Moffat, Mike | Bos. | 3 | 19 | 7 | 7 | 2 | 979 | 70 | 0 | 4.29 | 11 | 6 | 5 | .... | 663 | 38 | 0 | 3.44 | | 1981-82 | 1983-84 |
| Moog, Andy | Edm., Bos., Dal., Mtl. | 18 | 713 | 372 | 209 | 88 | 40151 | 2097 | 28 | 3.13 | 132 | 68 | 57 | .... | 7452 | 377 | 4 | 3.04 | 3 | 1980-81 | 1997-98 |
| • Moore, Alfie | NYA, Chi., Det. | 4 | 21 | 7 | 14 | 0 | 1290 | 81 | 1 | 3.77 | 3 | 1 | 2 | .... | 180 | 7 | 0 | 2.33 | 1 | 1936-37 | 1939-40 |
| Moore, Robbie | Phi., Wsh. | 2 | 6 | 3 | 1 | 1 | 257 | 8 | 2 | 1.87 | 5 | 3 | 2 | .... | 268 | 18 | 0 | 4.03 | | 1978-79 | 1982-83 |
| Morissette, Jean-Guy | Mtl. | 1 | 1 | 0 | 1 | 0 | 36 | 4 | 0 | 6.67 | .... | .... | .... | .... | .... | .... | .... | .... | | 1963-64 | 1963-64 |
| ‡ Morrison, Mike | Edm., Ott., Phx. | 2 | 29 | 11 | 7 | 3 | 1226 | 67 | 0 | 3.28 | .... | .... | .... | .... | .... | .... | .... | .... | | 2005-06 | 2006-07 |
| Moss, Tyler | Cgy., Car., Van. | 4 | 30 | 6 | 16 | 1 | 1496 | 81 | 0 | 3.25 | .... | .... | .... | .... | .... | .... | .... | .... | | 1997-98 | 2002-03 |
| • Mowers, Johnny | Det. | 4 | 152 | 65 | 61 | 26 | 9350 | 399 | 15 | 2.56 | 32 | 19 | 13 | .... | 2000 | 85 | 2 | 2.55 | 1 | 1940-41 | 1946-47 |
| Mrazek, Jerome | Phi. | 1 | 1 | 0 | 0 | 0 | 6 | 1 | 0 | 10.00 | .... | .... | .... | .... | .... | .... | .... | .... | | 1975-76 | 1975-76 |
| § • Mummery, Harry | Que., Ham. | 2 | 4 | 2 | 1 | 0 | 192 | 20 | 0 | 6.25 | .... | .... | .... | .... | .... | .... | .... | .... | | 1919-20 | 1921-22 |
| § • Munro, Dunc | Mtl.M. | 1 | 1 | 0 | 0 | 0 | 2 | 0 | 0 | 0.00 | .... | .... | .... | .... | .... | .... | .... | .... | | 1924-25 | 1924-25 |
| • Murphy, Hal | Mtl. | 1 | 1 | 1 | 0 | 0 | 60 | 4 | 0 | 4.00 | .... | .... | .... | .... | .... | .... | .... | .... | | 1952-53 | 1952-53 |
| • Murray, Mickey | Mtl. | 1 | 1 | 0 | 1 | 0 | 60 | 4 | 0 | 4.00 | .... | .... | .... | .... | .... | .... | .... | .... | | 1929-30 | 1929-30 |
| Muzzatti, Jason | Cgy., Hfd., NYR, S.J. | 5 | 62 | 13 | 25 | 10 | 3014 | 167 | 1 | 3.32 | .... | .... | .... | .... | .... | .... | .... | .... | | 1993-94 | 1997-98 |
| Myllys, Jarmo | Min., S.J. | 4 | 39 | 4 | 27 | 1 | 1846 | 161 | 0 | 5.23 | .... | .... | .... | .... | .... | .... | .... | .... | | 1988-89 | 1991-92 |
| Mylnikov, Sergei | Que. | 1 | 10 | 1 | 7 | 2 | 568 | 47 | 0 | 4.96 | .... | .... | .... | .... | .... | .... | .... | .... | | 1989-90 | 1989-90 |
| Myre, Phil | Mtl., Atl., St.L., Phi., Col., Buf. | 14 | 439 | 149 | 198 | 76 | 25220 | 1482 | 14 | 3.53 | 12 | 6 | 5 | .... | 747 | 41 | 1 | 3.29 | | 1969-70 | 1982-83 |
| Naumenko, Gregg | Ana. | 1 | 2 | 0 | 1 | 0 | 70 | 7 | 0 | 6.00 | .... | .... | .... | .... | .... | .... | .... | .... | | 2000-01 | 2000-01 |
| Newton, Cam | Pit. | 2 | 16 | 4 | 7 | 1 | 814 | 51 | 0 | 3.76 | .... | .... | .... | .... | .... | .... | .... | .... | | 1970-71 | 1972-73 |
| ‡ Noronen, Mika | Buf., Van. | 5 | 71 | 23 | 32 | 6 | 3652 | 163 | 3 | 2.68 | .... | .... | .... | .... | .... | .... | .... | .... | | 2000-01 | 2005-06 |
| Norris, Jack | Bos., Chi., L.A. | 4 | 58 | 20 | 25 | 4 | 3119 | 202 | 2 | 3.89 | .... | .... | .... | .... | .... | .... | .... | .... | | 1964-65 | 1970-71 |
| Nurminen, Pasi | Atl. | 3 | 125 | 48 | 54 | 12 | 7059 | 338 | 5 | 2.87 | .... | .... | .... | .... | .... | .... | .... | .... | | 2001-02 | 2003-04 |
| Oleschuk, Bill | K.C., Col. | 4 | 55 | 7 | 28 | 10 | 2835 | 188 | 1 | 3.98 | .... | .... | .... | .... | .... | .... | .... | .... | | 1975-76 | 1979-80 |
| Olesevich, Dan | NYR | 1 | 1 | 0 | 0 | 1 | 29 | 2 | 0 | 4.14 | .... | .... | .... | .... | .... | .... | .... | .... | | 1961-62 | 1961-62 |
| O'Neill, Mike | Wpg., Ana. | 4 | 21 | 0 | 9 | 2 | 855 | 61 | 0 | 4.28 | .... | .... | .... | .... | .... | .... | .... | .... | | 1991-92 | 1996-97 |
| ‡ Ouellet, Maxime | Phi., Wsh., Van. | 3 | 12 | 2 | 6 | 2 | 663 | 34 | 1 | 3.08 | .... | .... | .... | .... | .... | .... | .... | .... | | 2000-01 | 2005-06 |
| Ouimet, Ted | St.L. | 1 | 1 | 0 | 1 | 0 | 60 | 2 | 0 | 2.00 | .... | .... | .... | .... | .... | .... | .... | .... | | 1968-69 | 1968-69 |
| Pageau, Paul | L.A. | 1 | 1 | 0 | 1 | 0 | 60 | 8 | 0 | 8.00 | .... | .... | .... | .... | .... | .... | .... | .... | | 1980-81 | 1980-81 |
| • Paille, Marcel | NYR | 7 | 107 | 32 | 52 | 22 | 6342 | 362 | 2 | 3.42 | .... | .... | .... | .... | .... | .... | .... | .... | | 1957-58 | 1964-65 |
| Palmateer, Mike | Tor., Wsh. | 8 | 356 | 149 | 138 | 52 | 20131 | 1183 | 17 | 3.53 | 29 | 12 | 17 | .... | 1765 | 89 | 2 | 3.03 | | 1976-77 | 1983-84 |
| Pang, Darren | Chi. | 3 | 81 | 27 | 35 | 7 | 4252 | 287 | 0 | 4.05 | 6 | 1 | 3 | .... | 250 | 18 | 0 | 4.32 | | 1984-85 | 1988-89 |
| Parent, Bernie | Bos., Phi., Tor. | 13 | 608 | 271 | 198 | 121 | 35136 | 1493 | 54 | 2.55 | 71 | 38 | 33 | .... | 4302 | 174 | 6 | 2.43 | 2 | 1965-66 | 1978-79 |
| Parent, Bob | Tor. | 2 | 3 | 0 | 2 | 0 | 160 | 15 | 0 | 5.63 | .... | .... | .... | .... | .... | .... | .... | .... | | 1981-82 | 1982-83 |
| Parent, Rich | St.L., T.B., Pit. | 4 | 32 | 7 | 11 | 5 | 1561 | 82 | 1 | 3.15 | .... | .... | .... | .... | .... | .... | .... | .... | | 1997-98 | 2000-01 |
| Parro, Dave | Wsh. | 4 | 77 | 21 | 36 | 10 | 4015 | 274 | 2 | 4.09 | .... | .... | .... | .... | .... | .... | .... | .... | | 1980-81 | 1983-84 |
| Passmore, Steve | Edm., Chi., L.A. | 6 | 93 | 23 | 44 | 12 | 5045 | 235 | 2 | 2.79 | 3 | 0 | 2 | .... | 138 | 6 | 0 | 2.61 | | 1998-99 | 2003-04 |
| § • Patrick, Lester | NYR | 1 | .... | .... | .... | .... | .... | .... | .... | .... | 1 | 1 | 0 | 0 | 46 | 1 | 0 | 1.30 | 1 | 1927-28 | 1927-28 |
| Peeters, Pete | Phi., Bos., Wsh. | 13 | 489 | 246 | 155 | 51 | 27699 | 1424 | 21 | 3.08 | 71 | 35 | 35 | .... | 4200 | 232 | 2 | 3.31 | | 1978-79 | 1990-91 |
| ‡ Pelletier, Jean-Marc | Phi., Phx. | 3 | 7 | 1 | 4 | 0 | 354 | 23 | 0 | 3.90 | .... | .... | .... | .... | .... | .... | .... | .... | | 1998-99 | 2003-04 |
| Pelletier, Marcel | Chi., NYR | 2 | 8 | 1 | 6 | 0 | 395 | 32 | 0 | 4.86 | .... | .... | .... | .... | .... | .... | .... | .... | | 1950-51 | 1962-63 |
| Penney, Steve | Mtl., Wpg. | 5 | 91 | 35 | 38 | 12 | 5194 | 313 | 1 | 3.62 | 27 | 15 | 12 | .... | 1604 | 72 | 4 | 2.69 | | 1983-84 | 1987-88 |
| • Perreault, Bob | Mtl., Det., Bos. | 3 | 31 | 8 | 16 | 7 | 1827 | 103 | 3 | 3.38 | .... | .... | .... | .... | .... | .... | .... | .... | | 1955-56 | 1962-63 |
| Pettie, Jim | Bos. | 3 | 21 | 9 | 7 | 2 | 1157 | 71 | 1 | 3.68 | .... | .... | .... | .... | .... | .... | .... | .... | | 1976-77 | 1978-79 |
| Pietrangelo, Frank | Pit., Hfd. | 7 | 141 | 46 | 59 | 6 | 7141 | 490 | 1 | 4.12 | 12 | 7 | 5 | .... | 713 | 34 | 1 | 2.86 | 1 | 1987-88 | 1993-94 |
| • Plante, Jacques | Mtl., NYR, St.L., Tor., Bos. | 18 | 837 | 437 | 246 | 145 | 49533 | 1964 | 82 | 2.38 | 112 | 71 | 36 | .... | 6651 | 237 | 14 | 2.14 | 6 | 1952-53 | 1972-73 |
| • Plasse, Michel | St.L., Mtl., K.C., Pit., Col., Que. | 11 | 299 | 92 | 136 | 54 | 16760 | 1058 | 2 | 3.79 | 4 | 1 | 2 | .... | 195 | 9 | 1 | 2.77 | 1 | 1970-71 | 1981-82 |
| § • Plaxton, Hugh | Mtl.M. | 1 | 1 | 0 | 1 | 0 | 57 | 5 | 0 | 5.26 | .... | .... | .... | .... | .... | .... | .... | .... | | 1932-33 | 1932-33 |
| Potvin, Felix | Tor., NYI, Van., L.A., Bos. | 13 | 635 | 266 | 260 | 85 | 36765 | 1694 | 32 | 2.76 | 72 | 35 | 37 | .... | 4435 | 195 | 8 | 2.64 | | 1991-92 | 2003-04 |
| Pronovost, Claude | Bos., Mtl. | 2 | 3 | 1 | 1 | 0 | 120 | 7 | 1 | 3.50 | .... | .... | .... | .... | .... | .... | .... | .... | | 1955-56 | 1958-59 |
| ‡ Prusek, Martin | Ott., CBJ | 4 | 57 | 31 | 12 | 4 | 2898 | 114 | 3 | 2.36 | 1 | 0 | 0 | .... | 40 | 1 | 0 | 1.50 | | 2001-02 | 2005-06 |
| Puppa, Daren | Buf., Tor., T.B. | 15 | 429 | 179 | 161 | 54 | 23819 | 1204 | 19 | 3.03 | 16 | 4 | 9 | .... | 786 | 51 | 0 | 3.89 | | 1985-86 | 1999-00 |
| Pusey, Chris | Det. | 1 | 1 | 0 | 0 | 0 | 40 | 3 | 0 | 4.50 | .... | .... | .... | .... | .... | .... | .... | .... | | 1985-86 | 1985-86 |
| Racicot, Andre | Mtl. | 5 | 68 | 26 | 23 | 8 | 3357 | 196 | 2 | 3.50 | 4 | 0 | 1 | .... | 31 | 4 | 0 | 7.74 | 1 | 1989-90 | 1993-94 |
| Racine, Bruce | St.L. | 1 | 11 | 0 | 3 | 0 | 230 | 12 | 0 | 3.13 | 1 | 0 | 0 | .... | 1 | 0 | 0 | 0.00 | | 1995-96 | 1995-96 |
| Ram, Jamie | NYR | 1 | 1 | 0 | 0 | 0 | 27 | 0 | 0 | 0.00 | .... | .... | .... | .... | .... | .... | .... | .... | | 1995-96 | 1995-96 |
| Ranford, Bill | Bos., Edm., Wsh., T.B., Det. | 15 | 647 | 240 | 279 | 76 | 35936 | 2042 | 15 | 3.41 | 53 | 28 | 25 | .... | 3110 | 159 | 4 | 3.07 | 2 | 1985-86 | 1999-00 |
| Raymond, Alain | Wsh. | 1 | 1 | 0 | 1 | 0 | 40 | 2 | 0 | 3.00 | .... | .... | .... | .... | .... | .... | .... | .... | | 1987-88 | 1987-88 |
| • Rayner, Chuck | NYA, Bro., NYR | 10 | 424 | 138 | 208 | 77 | 25491 | 1294 | 25 | 3.05 | 18 | 9 | 9 | .... | 1135 | 46 | 1 | 2.43 | | 1940-41 | 1952-53 |
| Reaugh, Daryl | Edm., Hfd. | 3 | 27 | 8 | 9 | 1 | 1246 | 72 | 1 | 3.47 | .... | .... | .... | .... | .... | .... | .... | .... | | 1984-85 | 1990-91 |
| Reddick, Pokey | Wpg., Edm., Fla. | 6 | 132 | 46 | 58 | 16 | 7162 | 443 | 0 | 3.71 | 4 | 0 | 2 | .... | 168 | 10 | 0 | 3.57 | 1 | 1986-87 | 1993-94 |
| § • Redding, George | Bos. | 1 | 1 | 0 | 0 | 0 | 11 | 1 | 0 | 5.45 | .... | .... | .... | .... | .... | .... | .... | .... | | 1924-25 | 1924-25 |
| Redquest, Greg | Pit. | 1 | 1 | 0 | 0 | 0 | 13 | 3 | 0 | 13.85 | .... | .... | .... | .... | .... | .... | .... | .... | | 1977-78 | 1977-78 |
| Reece, Dave | Bos. | 1 | 14 | 7 | 5 | 2 | 777 | 43 | 2 | 3.32 | .... | .... | .... | .... | .... | .... | .... | .... | | 1975-76 | 1975-76 |
| Reese, Jeff | Tor., Cgy., Hfd., T.B., N.J. | 11 | 174 | 53 | 65 | 17 | 8667 | 529 | 5 | 3.66 | 11 | 3 | 5 | .... | 515 | 35 | 0 | 4.08 | | 1987-88 | 1998-99 |
| Resch, Glenn | NYI, Col., N.J., Phi. | 14 | 571 | 231 | 224 | 82 | 32279 | 1761 | 26 | 3.27 | 41 | 17 | 17 | .... | 2044 | 85 | 2 | 2.50 | 1 | 1973-74 | 1986-87 |
| • Rheaume, Herb | Mtl. | 1 | 31 | 10 | 20 | 1 | 1889 | 92 | 0 | 2.92 | .... | .... | .... | .... | .... | .... | .... | .... | | 1925-26 | 1925-26 |

| Name | NHL Teams | NHL Seasons | Regular Schedule | | | | | | | | Playoffs | | | | | | | | NHL Cup Wins | First NHL Season | Last NHL Season |
|---|---|---|---|---|---|---|---|---|---|---|---|---|---|---|---|---|---|---|---|---|---|
| | | | GP | W | L | T | Mins | GA | SO | Avg | GP | W | L | T | Mins | GA | SO | Avg | | | |
| Rhodes, Damian | Tor., Ott., Atl. | 10 | 309 | 99 | 140 | 48 | 17339 | 820 | 12 | 2.84 | 13 | 5 | 7 | .... | 741 | 27 | 0 | 2.19 | | 1990-91 | 2001-02 |
| Ricci, Nick | Pit. | 4 | 19 | 7 | 12 | 0 | 1087 | 79 | 0 | 4.36 | .... | .... | .... | .... | .... | .... | .... | .... | | 1979-80 | 1982-83 |
| Richardson, Terry | Det., St.L. | 5 | 20 | 3 | 11 | 0 | 906 | 85 | 0 | 5.63 | .... | .... | .... | .... | .... | .... | .... | .... | | 1973-74 | 1978-79 |
| Richter, Mike | NYR | 15 | 666 | 301 | 258 | 73 | 38183 | 1840 | 24 | 2.89 | 76 | 41 | 33 | .... | 4514 | 202 | 9 | 2.68 | 1 | 1988-89 | 2002-03 |
| Ridley, Curt | NYR, Van., Tor. | 6 | 104 | 27 | 47 | 16 | 5498 | 355 | 1 | 3.87 | 2 | 0 | 2 | .... | 120 | 8 | 0 | 4.00 | | 1974-75 | 1980-81 |
| Riendeau, Vincent | Mtl., St.L., Det., Bos. | 8 | 184 | 85 | 65 | 20 | 10423 | 573 | 5 | 3.30 | 25 | 11 | 12 | .... | 1277 | 71 | 1 | 3.34 | | 1987-88 | 1994-95 |
| Riggin, Dennis | Det. | 2 | 18 | 6 | 10 | 2 | 999 | 52 | 1 | 3.12 | .... | .... | .... | .... | .... | .... | .... | .... | | 1959-60 | 1962-63 |
| Riggin, Pat | Atl., Cgy., Wsh., Bos., Pit. | 9 | 350 | 153 | 120 | 52 | 19872 | 1135 | 11 | 3.43 | 25 | 8 | 13 | .... | 1336 | 72 | 0 | 3.23 | | 1979-80 | 1987-88 |
| Ring, Bob | Bos. | 1 | 1 | 0 | 0 | 0 | 33 | 4 | 0 | 7.27 | .... | .... | .... | .... | .... | .... | .... | .... | | 1965-66 | 1965-66 |
| Rivard, Fern | Min. | 4 | 55 | 9 | 27 | 11 | 2865 | 190 | 2 | 3.98 | .... | .... | .... | .... | .... | .... | .... | .... | | 1968-69 | 1974-75 |
| • Roach, John Ross | Tor., NYR, Det. | 14 | 492 | 219 | 204 | 68 | 30444 | 1246 | 58 | 2.46 | 29 | 12 | 14 | 3 | 1901 | 60 | 7 | 1.89 | 1 | 1921-22 | 1934-35 |
| • Roberts, Moe | Bos., NYA, Chi. | 4 | 10 | 3 | 5 | 0 | 501 | 31 | 0 | 3.71 | .... | .... | .... | .... | .... | .... | .... | .... | | 1925-26 | 1951-52 |
| • Robertson, Earl | Det., NYA, Bro. | 6 | 190 | 60 | 95 | 34 | 11820 | 575 | 16 | 2.92 | 15 | 7 | 7 | .... | 995 | 29 | 2 | 1.75 | 1 | 1936-37 | 1941-42 |
| • Rollins, Al | Tor., Chi., NYR | 9 | 430 | 141 | 205 | 83 | 25723 | 1192 | 28 | 2.78 | 13 | 6 | 7 | .... | 755 | 30 | 0 | 2.38 | 1 | 1949-50 | 1959-60 |
| Romano, Roberto | Pit., Bos. | 6 | 126 | 46 | 63 | 8 | 7111 | 471 | 4 | 3.97 | .... | .... | .... | .... | .... | .... | .... | .... | | 1982-83 | 1993-94 |
| Rosati, Mike | Wsh. | 1 | 1 | 1 | 0 | 0 | 28 | 0 | 0 | 0.00 | .... | .... | .... | .... | .... | .... | .... | .... | | 1998-99 | 1998-99 |
| Roussel, Dominic | Phi., Wpg., Ana., Edm. | 8 | 205 | 77 | 70 | 23 | 10665 | 555 | 7 | 3.12 | 1 | 0 | 0 | .... | 23 | 0 | 0 | 0.00 | | 1991-92 | 2000-01 |
| Roy, Patrick | Mtl., Col. | 19 | 1029 | 551 | 315 | 131 | 60235 | 2546 | 66 | 2.54 | 247 | 151 | 94 | .... | 15209 | 584 | 23 | 2.30 | 4 | 1984-85 | 2002-03 |
| ‡ Rudkowsky, Cody | St.L. | 1 | 1 | 1 | 0 | 0 | 30 | 0 | 0 | 0.00 | .... | .... | .... | .... | .... | .... | .... | .... | | 2002-03 | 2002-03 |
| • Rupp, Pat | Det. | 1 | 1 | 0 | 1 | 0 | 60 | 4 | 0 | 4.00 | .... | .... | .... | .... | .... | .... | .... | .... | | 1963-64 | 1963-64 |
| Rutherford, Jim | Det., Pit., Tor., L.A. | 13 | 457 | 151 | 227 | 59 | 25895 | 1576 | 14 | 3.65 | 8 | 2 | 5 | .... | 440 | 28 | 0 | 3.82 | | 1970-71 | 1982-83 |
| • Rutledge, Wayne | L.A. | 3 | 82 | 28 | 37 | 9 | 4325 | 241 | 2 | 3.34 | 8 | 2 | 4 | .... | 378 | 20 | 0 | 3.17 | | 1967-68 | 1969-70 |
| St. Croix, Rick | Phi., Tor. | 8 | 130 | 49 | 54 | 18 | 7295 | 451 | 2 | 3.71 | 11 | 4 | 6 | .... | 562 | 29 | 1 | 3.10 | | 1977-78 | 1984-85 |
| St. Laurent, Sam | N.J., Det. | 5 | 34 | 7 | 12 | 4 | 1572 | 92 | 1 | 3.51 | 1 | 0 | 0 | .... | 10 | 1 | 0 | 6.00 | | 1985-86 | 1989-90 |
| Salo, Tommy | NYI, Edm., Col. | 10 | 526 | 210 | 225 | 73 | 30436 | 1296 | 37 | 2.55 | 22 | 5 | 16 | .... | 1369 | 58 | 0 | 2.54 | | 1994-95 | 2003-04 |
| § • Sands, Charlie | Mtl. | 1 | 1 | 0 | 0 | 0 | 25 | 5 | 0 | 12.00 | .... | .... | .... | .... | .... | .... | .... | .... | | 1939-40 | 1939-40 |
| Sands, Mike | Min. | 2 | 6 | 0 | 5 | 0 | 302 | 26 | 0 | 5.17 | .... | .... | .... | .... | .... | .... | .... | .... | | 1984-85 | 1986-87 |
| Sarjeant, Geoff | St.L., S.J. | 2 | 8 | 1 | 2 | 1 | 291 | 20 | 0 | 4.12 | .... | .... | .... | .... | .... | .... | .... | .... | | 1994-95 | 1995-96 |
| Sauve, Bob | Buf., Det., Chi., N.J. | 13 | 420 | 182 | 154 | 54 | 23711 | 1377 | 8 | 3.48 | 34 | 15 | 16 | .... | 1850 | 95 | 4 | 3.08 | | 1976-77 | 1988-89 |
| Sauve, Philippe | Col., Cgy., Phx., Bos. | 3 | 32 | 10 | 14 | 3 | 1616 | 93 | 0 | 3.45 | .... | .... | .... | .... | .... | .... | .... | .... | | 2003-04 | 2006-07 |
| • Sawchuk, Terry | Det., Bos., Tor., L.A., NYR | 21 | 971 | 447 | 330 | 172 | 57194 | 2389 | 103 | 2.51 | 106 | 54 | 48 | .... | 6290 | 266 | 12 | 2.54 | 4 | 1949-50 | 1969-70 |
| • Schaefer, Joe | NYR | 2 | 2 | 0 | 2 | 0 | 86 | 8 | 0 | 5.58 | .... | .... | .... | .... | .... | .... | .... | .... | | 1959-60 | 1960-61 |
| Schafer, Paxton | Bos. | 1 | 3 | 0 | 0 | 0 | 77 | 6 | 0 | 4.68 | .... | .... | .... | .... | .... | .... | .... | .... | | 1996-97 | 1996-97 |
| Schwab, Corey | N.J., T.B., Van., Tor. | 8 | 147 | 42 | 63 | 13 | 7476 | 360 | 6 | 2.89 | 3 | 0 | 0 | .... | 40 | 0 | 0 | 0.00 | 1 | 1995-96 | 2003-04 |
| Scott, Ron | NYR, L.A. | 5 | 28 | 8 | 13 | 4 | 1450 | 91 | 0 | 3.77 | 1 | 0 | 0 | .... | 32 | 4 | 0 | 7.50 | | 1983-84 | 1989-90 |
| Scott, Travis | L.A. | 1 | 1 | 0 | 0 | 0 | 25 | 3 | 0 | 7.20 | .... | .... | .... | .... | .... | .... | .... | .... | | 2000-01 | 2000-01 |
| Sevigny, Richard | Mtl., Que. | 9 | 176 | 80 | 54 | 20 | 9485 | 507 | 5 | 3.21 | 4 | 0 | 3 | .... | 208 | 13 | 0 | 3.75 | 1 | 1978-79 | 1986-87 |
| Sharples, Scott | Cgy. | 1 | 1 | 0 | 0 | 1 | 65 | 4 | 0 | 3.69 | .... | .... | .... | .... | .... | .... | .... | .... | | 1991-92 | 1991-92 |
| § • Shields, Al | NYA | 1 | 2 | 0 | 0 | 0 | 41 | 9 | 0 | 13.17 | .... | .... | .... | .... | .... | .... | .... | .... | | 1931-32 | 1931-32 |
| Shields, Steve | Buf., S.J., Ana., Bos., Fla., Atl. | 10 | 246 | 80 | 104 | 40 | 13630 | 606 | 10 | 2.67 | 25 | 9 | 16 | .... | 1445 | 74 | 1 | 3.07 | | 1995-96 | 2005-06 |
| Shtalenkov, Mikhail | Ana., Edm., Phx., Fla. | 7 | 190 | 62 | 82 | 19 | 9966 | 480 | 8 | 2.89 | 4 | 0 | 3 | .... | 211 | 10 | 0 | 2.84 | | 1993-94 | 1999-00 |
| Shulmistra, Richard | N.J., Fla. | 2 | 2 | 1 | 1 | 0 | 122 | 3 | 0 | 1.48 | .... | .... | .... | .... | .... | .... | .... | .... | | 1997-98 | 1999-00 |
| Sidorkiewicz, Peter | Hfd., Ott., N.J. | 8 | 246 | 79 | 128 | 27 | 13884 | 832 | 8 | 3.60 | 15 | 5 | 10 | .... | 912 | 55 | 0 | 3.62 | | 1987-88 | 1997-98 |
| Sigalet, Jordan | Bos. | 1 | 1 | 0 | 0 | 0 | 1 | 0 | 0 | 0.00 | .... | .... | .... | .... | .... | .... | .... | .... | | 2005-06 | 2005-06 |
| Simmons, Don | Bos., Tor., NYR | 11 | 249 | 101 | 101 | 41 | 14555 | 701 | 20 | 2.89 | 24 | 13 | 11 | .... | 1436 | 62 | 3 | 2.59 | 3 | 1956-57 | 1968-69 |
| Simmons, Gary | Cal., Cle., L.A. | 4 | 107 | 30 | 57 | 15 | 6162 | 366 | 5 | 3.56 | 1 | 0 | 0 | .... | 20 | 1 | 0 | 3.00 | | 1974-75 | 1977-78 |
| Skidmore, Paul | St.L. | 1 | 2 | 1 | 1 | 0 | 120 | 6 | 0 | 3.00 | .... | .... | .... | .... | .... | .... | .... | .... | | 1981-82 | 1981-82 |
| Skorodenski, Warren | Chi., Edm. | 5 | 35 | 12 | 11 | 4 | 1732 | 100 | 2 | 3.46 | 2 | 0 | 0 | .... | 33 | 6 | 0 | 10.91 | | 1981-82 | 1987-88 |
| Skudra, Peter | Pit., Buf., Bos., Van. | 6 | 146 | 51 | 47 | 20 | 7162 | 326 | 6 | 2.73 | 3 | 0 | 1 | .... | 116 | 6 | 0 | 3.10 | | 1997-98 | 2002-03 |
| • Smith, Al | Tor., Pit., Det., Buf., Hfd., Col. | 10 | 233 | 74 | 99 | 36 | 12752 | 735 | 10 | 3.46 | 6 | 1 | 4 | .... | 317 | 21 | 0 | 3.97 | | 1965-66 | 1980-81 |
| Smith, Billy | L.A., NYI | 18 | 680 | 305 | 233 | 105 | 38431 | 2031 | 22 | 3.17 | 132 | 88 | 36 | .... | 7645 | 348 | 5 | 2.73 | 4 | 1971-72 | 1988-89 |
| Smith, Gary | Tor., Oak., Cal., Chi., Van., Min., Wsh., Wpg. | 14 | 532 | 173 | 261 | 74 | 29619 | 1675 | 26 | 3.39 | 20 | 5 | 13 | .... | 1153 | 62 | 1 | 3.23 | | 1965-66 | 1979-80 |
| • Smith, Normie | Mtl.M., Det. | 8 | 199 | 81 | 83 | 35 | 12357 | 479 | 17 | 2.33 | 12 | 9 | 2 | 0 | 820 | 18 | 3 | 1.32 | 2 | 1931-32 | 1944-45 |
| Sneddon, Bob | Cal. | 1 | 5 | 0 | 2 | 0 | 225 | 21 | 0 | 5.60 | .... | .... | .... | .... | .... | .... | .... | .... | | 1970-71 | 1970-71 |
| Snow, Garth | Que., Phi., Van., Pit., NYI | 12 | 368 | 135 | 147 | 44 | 19837 | 925 | 16 | 2.80 | 20 | 9 | 8 | .... | 1040 | 48 | 1 | 2.77 | | 1993-94 | 2005-06 |
| Soderstrom, Tommy | Phi., NYI | 5 | 156 | 45 | 69 | 19 | 8189 | 496 | 10 | 3.63 | .... | .... | .... | .... | .... | .... | .... | .... | | 1992-93 | 1996-97 |
| Soetaert, Doug | NYR, Wpg., Mtl. | 12 | 284 | 110 | 104 | 42 | 15583 | 1030 | 6 | 3.97 | 5 | 1 | 2 | .... | 180 | 14 | 0 | 4.67 | 1 | 1975-76 | 1986-87 |
| Soucy, Christian | Chi. | 1 | 1 | 0 | 0 | 0 | 3 | 0 | 0 | 0.00 | .... | .... | .... | .... | .... | .... | .... | .... | | 1993-94 | 1993-94 |
| • Spooner, Red | Pit. | 1 | 1 | 0 | 1 | 0 | 60 | 6 | 0 | 6.00 | .... | .... | .... | .... | .... | .... | .... | .... | | 1929-30 | 1929-30 |
| § • Spring, Jesse | Ham. | 1 | 1 | 0 | 0 | 0 | 2 | 0 | 0 | 0.00 | .... | .... | .... | .... | .... | .... | .... | .... | | 1924-25 | 1924-25 |
| ‡ Stana, Rastislav | Wsh. | 1 | 6 | 1 | 2 | 0 | 211 | 11 | 0 | 3.13 | .... | .... | .... | .... | .... | .... | .... | .... | | 2003-04 | 2003-04 |
| Staniowski, Ed | St.L., Wpg., Hfd. | 10 | 219 | 67 | 104 | 21 | 12075 | 818 | 2 | 4.06 | 8 | 1 | 6 | .... | 428 | 28 | 0 | 3.93 | | 1975-76 | 1984-85 |
| § • Starr, Harold | Mtl.M. | 1 | 1 | 0 | 0 | 0 | 3 | 0 | 0 | 0.00 | .... | .... | .... | .... | .... | .... | .... | .... | | 1931-32 | 1931-32 |
| Stauber, Robb | L.A., Buf. | 4 | 62 | 21 | 23 | 9 | 3295 | 209 | 1 | 3.81 | 4 | 3 | 1 | .... | 240 | 16 | 0 | 4.00 | | 1989-90 | 1994-95 |
| Stefan, Greg | Det. | 9 | 299 | 115 | 127 | 30 | 16333 | 1068 | 5 | 3.92 | 30 | 12 | 17 | .... | 1681 | 99 | 1 | 3.53 | | 1981-82 | 1989-90 |
| • Stein, Phil | Tor. | 1 | 1 | 0 | 0 | 1 | 70 | 2 | 0 | 1.71 | .... | .... | .... | .... | .... | .... | .... | .... | | 1939-40 | 1939-40 |
| Stephenson, Wayne | St.L., Phi., Wsh. | 10 | 328 | 146 | 103 | 49 | 18343 | 937 | 14 | 3.06 | 26 | 11 | 12 | .... | 1522 | 79 | 2 | 3.11 | 1 | 1971-72 | 1980-81 |
| • Stevenson, Doug | NYR, Chi. | 3 | 8 | 2 | 6 | 0 | 480 | 39 | 0 | 4.88 | .... | .... | .... | .... | .... | .... | .... | .... | | 1944-45 | 1945-46 |
| • Stewart, Charles | Bos. | 3 | 77 | 30 | 41 | 5 | 4742 | 194 | 10 | 2.45 | .... | .... | .... | .... | .... | .... | .... | .... | | 1924-25 | 1926-27 |
| Stewart, Jim | Bos. | 1 | 1 | 0 | 1 | 0 | 20 | 5 | 0 | 15.00 | .... | .... | .... | .... | .... | .... | .... | .... | | 1979-80 | 1979-80 |
| ‡ Storr, Jamie | L.A., Car. | 10 | 219 | 85 | 86 | 23 | 11512 | 488 | 16 | 2.54 | 5 | 0 | 3 | .... | 182 | 11 | 0 | 3.63 | | 1994-95 | 2003-04 |
| • Stuart, Herb | Det. | 1 | 3 | 1 | 2 | 0 | 180 | 5 | 0 | 1.67 | .... | .... | .... | .... | .... | .... | .... | .... | | 1926-27 | 1926-27 |
| Sylvestri, Don | Bos. | 1 | 3 | 0 | 0 | 2 | 102 | 6 | 0 | 3.53 | .... | .... | .... | .... | .... | .... | .... | .... | | 1984-85 | 1984-85 |
| Tabaracci, Rick | Pit., Wpg., Wsh., Cgy., T.B., Atl., Col. | 11 | 286 | 93 | 125 | 30 | 15255 | 760 | 15 | 2.99 | 17 | 4 | 12 | .... | 1025 | 53 | 0 | 3.10 | | 1988-89 | 1999-00 |
| Takko, Kari | Min., Edm. | 6 | 142 | 37 | 71 | 14 | 7317 | 475 | 1 | 3.90 | 4 | 0 | 1 | .... | 109 | 7 | 0 | 3.85 | | 1985-86 | 1990-91 |
| Tallas, Robbie | Bos., Chi. | 6 | 99 | 28 | 42 | 10 | 5069 | 246 | 3 | 2.91 | .... | .... | .... | .... | .... | .... | .... | .... | | 1995-96 | 2000-01 |
| Tanner, John | Que. | 3 | 21 | 2 | 11 | 5 | 1084 | 65 | 1 | 3.60 | .... | .... | .... | .... | .... | .... | .... | .... | | 1989-90 | 1991-92 |
| Tataryn, Dave | NYR | 1 | 2 | 1 | 1 | 0 | 80 | 10 | 0 | 7.50 | .... | .... | .... | .... | .... | .... | .... | .... | | 1976-77 | 1976-77 |
| Taylor, Bobby | Phi., Pit. | 5 | 46 | 15 | 17 | 6 | 2268 | 155 | 0 | 4.10 | .... | .... | .... | .... | .... | .... | .... | .... | 1 | 1971-72 | 1975-76 |
| • Teno, Harvey | Det. | 1 | 5 | 2 | 3 | 0 | 300 | 15 | 0 | 3.00 | .... | .... | .... | .... | .... | .... | .... | .... | | 1938-39 | 1938-39 |
| Terreri, Chris | N.J., S.J., Chi., NYI | 14 | 406 | 151 | 172 | 43 | 22369 | 1143 | 9 | 3.07 | 29 | 12 | 12 | .... | 1523 | 86 | 0 | 3.39 | 2 | 1986-87 | 2000-01 |
| Thibault, Jocelyn | Que., Col., Mtl., Chi., Pit., Buf. | 14 | 586 | 238 | 238 | 75 | 32892 | 1508 | 39 | 2.75 | 18 | 4 | 11 | .... | 848 | 50 | 0 | 3.54 | | 1993-94 | 2007-08 |
| Thomas, Wayne | Mtl., Tor., NYR | 9 | 243 | 103 | 93 | 34 | 13768 | 766 | 10 | 3.34 | 15 | 6 | 8 | .... | 849 | 50 | 1 | 3.53 | | 1972-73 | 1980-81 |
| • Thompson, Tiny | Bos., Det. | 12 | 553 | 284 | 194 | 75 | 34175 | 1183 | 81 | 2.08 | 44 | 20 | 24 | 0 | 2974 | 93 | 7 | 1.88 | 1 | 1928-29 | 1939-40 |
| § Toppazzini, Jerry | Bos. | 1 | 1 | 0 | 0 | 0 | 1 | 0 | 0 | 0.00 | .... | .... | .... | .... | .... | .... | .... | .... | | 1960-61 | 1960-61 |
| Torchia, Mike | Dal. | 1 | 6 | 3 | 2 | 1 | 327 | 18 | 0 | 3.30 | .... | .... | .... | .... | .... | .... | .... | .... | | 1994-95 | 1994-95 |
| Trefilov, Andrei | Cgy., Buf., Chi. | 7 | 54 | 12 | 25 | 4 | 2663 | 153 | 2 | 3.45 | 1 | 0 | 0 | .... | 5 | 0 | 0 | 0.00 | | 1992-93 | 1998-99 |
| Tremblay, Vincent | Tor., Pit. | 5 | 58 | 12 | 26 | 8 | 2785 | 223 | 1 | 4.80 | .... | .... | .... | .... | .... | .... | .... | .... | | 1979-80 | 1983-84 |
| Tucker, Ted | Cal. | 1 | 5 | 1 | 1 | 1 | 177 | 10 | 0 | 3.39 | .... | .... | .... | .... | .... | .... | .... | .... | | 1973-74 | 1973-74 |
| Tugnutt, Ron | Que., Edm., Ana., Mtl., Ott., Pit., CBJ, Dal. | 16 | 537 | 186 | 239 | 62 | 29486 | 1497 | 26 | 3.05 | 25 | 9 | 13 | .... | 1482 | 56 | 3 | 2.27 | | 1987-88 | 2003-04 |
| ‡ Turek, Roman | Dal., St.L., Cgy. | 8 | 328 | 159 | 115 | 43 | 19095 | 734 | 27 | 2.31 | 22 | 12 | 9 | .... | 1342 | 50 | 0 | 2.24 | 1 | 1996-97 | 2003-04 |
| • Turner, Joe | Det. | 1 | 1 | 0 | 0 | 1 | 70 | 3 | 0 | 2.57 | .... | .... | .... | .... | .... | .... | .... | .... | | 1941-42 | 1941-42 |
| Underhill, Matt | Chi. | 1 | 1 | 0 | 1 | 0 | 61 | 4 | 0 | 3.93 | .... | .... | .... | .... | .... | .... | .... | .... | | 2003-04 | 2003-04 |
| Vachon, Rogie | Mtl., L.A., Det., Bos. | 16 | 795 | 355 | 291 | 127 | 46298 | 2310 | 51 | 2.99 | 48 | 23 | 23 | .... | 2876 | 133 | 2 | 2.77 | 3 | 1966-67 | 1981-82 |
| Vanbiesbrouck, John | NYR, Fla., Phi., NYI, N.J. | 20 | 882 | 374 | 346 | 119 | 50475 | 2503 | 40 | 2.98 | 71 | 28 | 38 | .... | 3969 | 177 | 5 | 2.68 | | 1981-82 | 2001-02 |
| Veisor, Mike | Chi., Hfd., Wpg. | 10 | 139 | 41 | 62 | 26 | 7806 | 532 | 5 | 4.09 | 4 | 0 | 2 | .... | 180 | 15 | 0 | 5.00 | | 1973-74 | 1983-84 |
| Vernon, Mike | Cgy., Det., S.J., Fla. | 19 | 781 | 385 | 273 | 92 | 44449 | 2206 | 27 | 2.98 | 138 | 77 | 56 | .... | 8214 | 367 | 6 | 2.68 | 2 | 1982-83 | 2001-02 |
| • Vezina, Georges | Mtl. | 9 | 190 | 103 | 81 | 5 | 11592 | 633 | 13 | 3.28 | 13 | 10 | 3 | 0 | 780 | 35 | 2 | 2.69 | 1 | 1917-18 | 1925-26 |
| Villemure, Gilles | NYR, Chi. | 10 | 205 | 100 | 64 | 29 | 11581 | 542 | 13 | 2.81 | 14 | 5 | 5 | .... | 656 | 32 | 0 | 2.93 | | 1963-64 | 1976-77 |
| Waite, Jimmy | Chi., S.J., Phx. | 11 | 106 | 28 | 41 | 12 | 5253 | 293 | 4 | 3.35 | 6 | 0 | 3 | .... | 211 | 14 | 0 | 3.98 | | 1988-89 | 1998-99 |
| Wakaluk, Darcy | Buf., Min., Dal., Phx. | 8 | 191 | 67 | 75 | 21 | 9756 | 524 | 9 | 3.22 | 8 | 4 | 2 | .... | 364 | 18 | 0 | 2.97 | | 1988-89 | 1996-97 |
| Wakely, Ernie | Mtl., St.L. | 5 | 113 | 41 | 42 | 17 | 6244 | 290 | 8 | 2.79 | 10 | 2 | 6 | .... | 509 | 37 | 1 | 4.36 | 2 | 1962-63 | 1971-72 |
| Wall, Michael | Ana. | 1 | 4 | 2 | 2 | 0 | 202 | 10 | 0 | 2.97 | .... | .... | .... | .... | .... | .... | .... | .... | | 2006-07 | 2006-07 |
| • Walsh, Flat | Mtl.M., NYA | 7 | 108 | 48 | 43 | 16 | 6641 | 256 | 12 | 2.31 | 8 | 2 | 4 | 2 | 570 | 16 | 2 | 1.68 | | 1926-27 | 1932-33 |
| Wamsley, Rick | Mtl., St.L., Cgy., Tor. | 13 | 407 | 204 | 131 | 46 | 23123 | 1287 | 12 | 3.34 | 27 | 7 | 18 | .... | 1397 | 81 | 0 | 3.48 | 1 | 1980-81 | 1992-93 |
| Watt, Jim | St.L. | 1 | 1 | 0 | 0 | 0 | 20 | 2 | 0 | 6.00 | .... | .... | .... | .... | .... | .... | .... | .... | | 1973-74 | 1973-74 |

| Name | NHL Teams | NHL Seasons | Regular Schedule GP | W | L | T | Mins | GA | SO | Avg | Playoffs GP | W | L | T | Mins | GA | SO | Avg | NHL Cup Wins | First NHL Season | Last NHL Season |
|---|---|---|---|---|---|---|---|---|---|---|---|---|---|---|---|---|---|---|---|---|---|
| Weeks, Steve | NYR, Hfd., Van., NYI, L.A., Ott. | 18 | 290 | 111 | 119 | 33 | 15879 | 989 | 5 | 3.74 | 12 | 3 | 5 | .... | 486 | 27 | 0 | 3.33 | | 1980-81 | 1992-93 |
| Wetzel, Carl | Det., Min. | 2 | 7 | 1 | 4 | 1 | 301 | 22 | 0 | 4.39 | .... | .... | .... | .... | .... | .... | .... | .... | | 1964-65 | 1967-68 |
| Whitmore, Kay | Hfd., Van., Bos., Cgy. | 9 | 155 | 60 | 64 | 16 | 8596 | 508 | 4 | 3.55 | 4 | 0 | 2 | .... | 174 | 13 | 0 | 4.48 | | 1988-89 | 2001-02 |
| Wilkinson, Derek | T.B. | 4 | 22 | 3 | 12 | 3 | 933 | 57 | 0 | 3.67 | .... | .... | .... | .... | .... | .... | .... | .... | | 1995-96 | 1998-99 |
| Willis, Jordan | Dal. | 1 | 1 | 0 | 1 | 0 | 19 | 1 | 0 | 3.16 | .... | .... | .... | .... | .... | .... | .... | .... | | 1995-96 | 1995-96 |
| Wilson, Dunc | Phi., Van., Tor., NYR, Pit. | 10 | 287 | 80 | 150 | 33 | 15851 | 988 | 8 | 3.74 | .... | .... | .... | .... | .... | .... | .... | .... | | 1969-70 | 1978-79 |
| • Wilson, Lefty | Det., Tor., Bos. | 3 | 3 | 0 | 0 | 1 | 81 | 1 | 0 | 0.74 | .... | .... | .... | .... | .... | .... | .... | .... | | 1953-54 | 1957-58 |
| • Winkler, Hal | NYR, Bos. | 2 | 75 | 35 | 26 | 14 | 4739 | 126 | 21 | 1.60 | 10 | 2 | 3 | 5 | 640 | 18 | 2 | 1.69 | | 1926-27 | 1927-28 |
| Wolfe, Bernie | Wsh. | 4 | 120 | 20 | 61 | 21 | 6104 | 424 | 1 | 4.17 | .... | .... | .... | .... | .... | .... | .... | .... | | 1975-76 | 1978-79 |
| • Wood, Alex | NYA | 1 | 1 | 0 | 1 | 0 | 70 | 3 | 0 | 2.57 | .... | .... | .... | .... | .... | .... | .... | .... | | 1936-37 | 1936-37 |
| • Worsley, Gump | NYR, Mtl., Min. | 21 | 861 | 335 | 352 | 150 | 50183 | 2407 | 43 | 2.88 | 70 | 40 | 26 | .... | 4084 | 189 | 5 | 2.78 | 4 | 1952-53 | 1973-74 |
| • Worters, Roy | Pit., NYA, Mtl. | 12 | 484 | 171 | 229 | 83 | 30175 | 1143 | 67 | 2.27 | 11 | 3 | 6 | 2 | 690 | 24 | 3 | 2.09 | | 1925-26 | 1936-37 |
| • Worthy, Chris | Oak., Cal. | 3 | 26 | 5 | 10 | 4 | 1326 | 98 | 0 | 4.43 | .... | .... | .... | .... | .... | .... | .... | .... | | 1968-69 | 1970-71 |
| Wregget, Ken | Tor., Phi., Pit., Cgy., Det. | 17 | 575 | 225 | 248 | 53 | 31663 | 1917 | 9 | 3.63 | 56 | 28 | 25 | .... | 3341 | 160 | 3 | 2.87 | 1 | 1983-84 | 1999-00 |
| Yeats, Matthew | Wsh. | 1 | 5 | 1 | 3 | 0 | 258 | 13 | 0 | 3.02 | .... | .... | .... | .... | .... | .... | .... | .... | | 2003-04 | 2003-04 |
| Yeremeyev, Vitali | NYR | 1 | 4 | 0 | 4 | 0 | 212 | 16 | 0 | 4.53 | .... | .... | .... | .... | .... | .... | .... | .... | | 2000-01 | 2000-01 |
| § • Young, Doug | Det. | 1 | 1 | 0 | 0 | 0 | 21 | 1 | 0 | 2.86 | .... | .... | .... | .... | .... | .... | .... | .... | | 1933-34 | 1933-34 |
| Young, Wendell | Van., Phi., Pit., T.B. | 10 | 187 | 59 | 86 | 12 | 9410 | 618 | 2 | 3.94 | 2 | 0 | 1 | .... | 99 | 6 | 0 | 3.64 | 2 | 1985-86 | 1994-95 |
| Zanier, Mike | Edm. | 1 | 3 | 1 | 1 | 1 | 185 | 12 | 0 | 3.89 | .... | .... | .... | .... | .... | .... | .... | .... | | 1984-85 | 1984-85 |

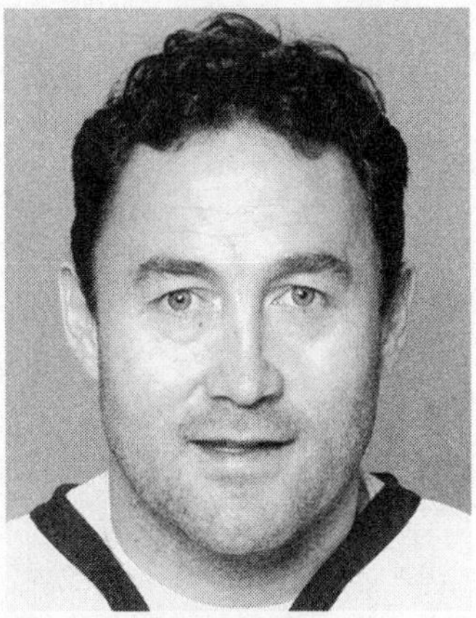

*Ed Belfour*

*Charlie Hodge*

*Marcel Paille*

*Gerry Desjardins*

*Michel Larocque*

*Jim Rutherford*

*Wade Flaherty*

*Greg Millen*

*Lefty Wilson*

# 2008-09
# NHL Player of the Week/Month Award Winners

## Player of the Week/Month

| Period Ending | First Star | Second Star | Third Star |
|---|---|---|---|
| Oct. 12 | **Daniel Sedin**, VAN | **David Booth**, FLA | **Martin Brodeur**, N.J. |
| Oct. 19 | **Thomas Vanek, BUF** | **Niklas Backstrom, MIN** | **Fabian Brunnstrom**, DAL |
| Oct. 26 | **Jarome Iginla**, CGY | **Peter Budaj**, COL | **Marian Hossa**, DET |
| **October** | **Alexander Semin**, WSH | **Henrik Lundqvist**, NYR | **Shea Webber**, NSH |
| Nov. 2 | **Getzlaf/Perry/Selanne**, ANA | **Tim Thomas**, BOS | **Simon Gagne**, PHI |
| Nov. 9 | **Roberto Luongo**, VAN | **Steve Mason**, CBJ | **Brent Johnson**, WSH |
| Nov. 16 | **Nicklas Backstrom**, WSH | **Alex Ovechkin**, WSH | **Dan Ellis**, NSH |
| Nov. 23 | **Marc Savard**, BOS | **Henrik Sedin**, VAN | **Nikolai Khabibulin** , CHI |
| Nov. 30 | **Sidney Crosby**, PIT | **Jonas Hiller**, ANA | **Chris Mason**, STL |
| **November** | **Alex Ovechkin**, WSH | **Evgeni Malkin**, PIT | **Joey MacDonald**, NYI |
| Dec. 7 | **Pekka Rinne**, NSH | **Jonathan Toews**, CHI | **Jason Spezza**, OTT |
| Dec. 14 | **Phil Kessel**, BOS | **Petr Sykora**, PIT | **Thomas Vanek**, BUF |
| Dec. 21 | **Loui Eriksson**, DAL | **Jeff Carter**, PHI | **Patrik Elias**, N.J. |
| Dec. 28 | **Alex Ovechkin**, WSH | **Bryan Little**, ATL | **Jonathan Quick**, L.A. |
| **December** | **Fernandez/Thomas**, BOS | **Jeff Carter**, PHI | **Alex Ovechkin**, WSH |
| Jan. 4 | **Rick Nash**, CBJ | **Brian Rafalski**, DET | **Cam Ward**, CAR |
| Jan. 11 | **Wojtek Wolski**, COL | **Bobby Ryan**, ANA | **Gregory Campbell**, FLA |
| Jan. 18 | **Pavel Datsyuk**, DET | **Mike Cammalleri**, CGY | **Rich Peverley**, ATL |
| Jan. 25 | **Dustin Brown**, L.A. | **Cam Ward**, CAR | **Ales Hemsky**, EDM |
| **January** | **Jamie Langenbrunner**, N.J. | **Scott Niedermayer**, ANA | **Ryan Miller**, BUF |
| Feb. 1 | **Jamie Langenbrunner**, N.J. | **Sidney Crosby**, PIT | **Mike Green**, WSH |
| Feb. 8 | **Jonathan Quick**, L.A. | **Marian Hossa**, DET | **Mike Green**, WSH |
| Feb. 15 | **Zach Parise**, N.J. | **Matthew Lombardi**, ATL | **Ilya Kovalchuk**, ATL |
| Feb. 22 | **Mike Richards**, PHI | **Tomas Vokoun**, FLA | **Cristobal Huet**, CHI |
| **February** | **Ilya Kovalchuk**, ATL | **Mike Green**, WSH | **Chris Mason**, STL |
| Mar. 1 | **Martin Brodeur**, N.J. | **Jarome Iginla**, CGY | **Ilya Kovalchuk**, ATL |
| Mar. 8 | **Eric Staal**, CAR | **Marc-Andre Fleury**, PIT | **Rick Nash**, CBJ |
| Mar. 15 | **Martin Brodeur**, N.J. | **Olli Jokinen**, CGY | **Sidney Crosby**, PIT |
| Mar. 22 | **Cam Ward**, CAR | **Evgeni Malkin**, PIT | **Shane Doan**, PHX |
| Mar. 29 | **Chris Mason**, STL | **Daniel Sedin**, VAN | **Cam Ward**, CAR |
| **March** | **Cam Ward**, CAR | **Henrik Sedin**, VAN | **Rick Nash**, CBJ |
| Apr. 5 | **Alex Kovalev**, MTL | **Nikolai Khabibulin** , CHI | **David Backes**, STL |
| Apr. 12 | **Roberto Luongo**, VAN | **Chris Mason**, STL | **Phil Kessel**, BOS |

## Rookie of the Month

| Month | Player |
|---|---|
| October | **Derick Brassard**, Columbus |
| November | **Steve Mason**, Columbus |
| December | **Steve Mason**, Columbus |
| January | **Bobby Ryan**, Anaheim |
| February | **Pekka Rinne**, Nashville |
| March | **T.J. Oshie**, St. Louis |

*Alexander Semin (above) of the Washington Capitals was the NHL's first star of the month for October of 2008. Semin led all NHL scorers with 16 points (eight goals, eight assists) during the opening month of the 2008-09 season. Boston's Phil Kessel (right) ran his scoring streak to 15 games with three goals and five assists in four games to be named first star of the week for the week ending December 14. Nashville goalie Pekka Rinne (far right) posted a record of 9-2-1 with two shutouts and a 1.72 goals-against average to be named rookie of the month in February of 2009.*

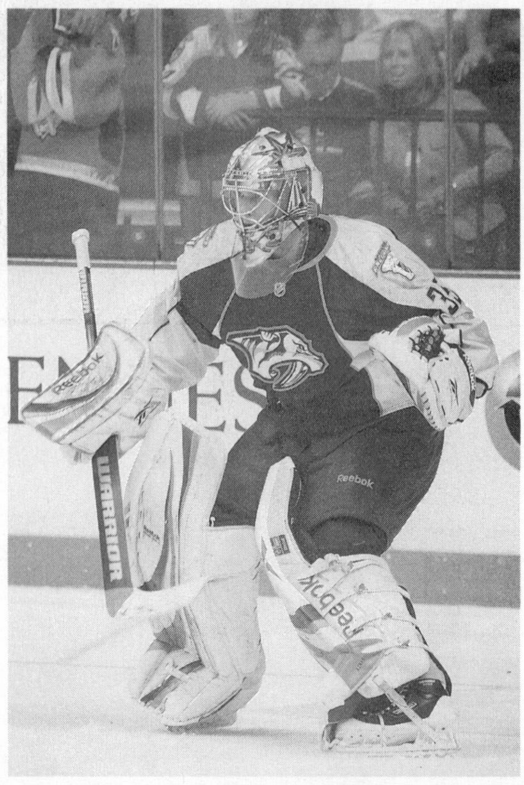

Brett Hull

Lou Lamoriello

Brian Leetch

Luc Robitaille

Steve Yzerman

# 2009 Hockey Hall of Fame Inductees

*THREE OF THE GREATEST GOAL SCORERS IN HOCKEY, as well as a two-time winner of the Norris Trophy and an architect of one of the most successful teams in recent history, are the Hockey Hall of Fame's 2009 inductees.*

*Though he was the son of a hockey legend and a big scorer in junior and university hockey, **Brett Hull** was not regarded as a top prospect. After a decent rookie season with the Calgary Flames, he blossomed with the St. Louis Blues, scoring 70 goals or more for three straight seasons from 1989 to 1992. Later, a Stanley Cup champion in Dallas and Detroit, Hull would score 741 goals in his career to rank third all-time in NHL history.*

***Lou Lamoriello** was a player, coach and administrator for 20 years at Providence College, sending many players on to the NHL before arriving himself in 1987 as president and general manager of the New Jersey Devils. A struggling franchise when he came on board, Lamoriello has built a team that annually contends for top spot in the NHL and has won the Stanley Cup in 1995, 2000 and 2003.*

***Brian Leetch** was a high school, university and U.S. National Team star who entered the NHL with the New York Rangers shortly after the 1988 Olympics. He spent 16+ of his 18 seasons as a high-scoring defenseman with the Rangers, winning the Calder Trophy in 1989, the Norris Trophy in 1992 and 1997 and the Conn Smythe Trophy as playoff MVP in 1994 when the Rangers won the Stanley Cup for the first time in 54 years.*

***Luc Robitaille** wasn't selected until the 171st pick in the 1984 Entry Draft yet scored 45 goals and won the Calder Trophy when he entered the NHL with the Los Angeles Kings in 1986-87. It was the first of eight consecutive seasons with 40-or-more goals, including a career-best 63 in 1992-93. His 125 points that season are the most ever scored by an NHL left winger. Robitaille scored 668 goals in his career, and won the Stanley Cup in 2002 as a member of the Detroit Red Wings.*

*Steve Yzerman was selected fourth overall in the 1983 NHL Entry Draft and immediately embarked on a career that would see him play 22 seasons, all with the Detroit Red Wings. Yzerman was captain of the team from 1986 to 2006, making him the longest-serving team leader in league history. A high-scoring center who totalled 692 goals and 1,063 assists in his career, Yzerman's hard work to become a two-way player resulted in three Stanley Cup victories between 1997 and 2002.*

*Also honored are John Davidson, winner of the Foster Hewitt Memorial Award for excellence in hockey broadcasting, and Dave Molinari, winner of the Elmer Ferguson Memorial Award for excellence in hockey journalism.*

# Free Agent Signing Register, 2009

| SIGNING DATE | POS. | PLAYER | SIGNED BY | PREVIOUS ORGANIZATION |
|---|---|---|---|---|
| June 29 – | RW | Craig Adams | Pittsburgh | Pittsburgh |
| – | LW | Jussi Jokinen | Carolina | Carolina |
| – | C | David Bolland | Chicago | Chicago |
| – | G | Peter Budaj | Colorado | Colorado |
| – | LW | Brad Winchester | St. Louis | St. Louis |
| – | D | Mike Weaver | St. Louis | St. Louis |
| – | RW | Bill Guerin | Pittsburgh | Pittsburgh |
| June 30 – | D | Rob Blake | San Jose | San Jose |
| – | D | Johnny Oduya | New Jersey | New Jersey |
| – | RW | Jere Lehtinen | Dallas | Dallas |
| – | D | Jay Bouwmeester | Calgary | Florida |
| July 1 – | C | Erik Christensen | Anaheim | Anaheim |
| – | LW | Daniel Sedin | Vancouver | Vancouver |
| – | C | Henrik Sedin | Vancouver | Vancouver |
| – | D | Mattias Ohlund | Tampa Bay | Vancouver |
| – | RW | Radek Dvorak | Florida | Florida |
| – | RW | Colton Orr | Toronto | NY Rangers |
| – | RW | Marian Hossa | Chicago | Detroit |
| – | LW | David Booth | Florida | Florida |
| – | G | Craig Anderson | Colorado | Florida |
| – | G | Ty Conklin | St. Louis | Detroit |
| – | G | Dwayne Roloson | NY Islanders | Edmonton |
| – | D | Andy Greene | New Jersey | New Jersey |
| – | RW | Mike Knuble | Washington | Philadelphia |
| – | D | Steve Montador | Buffalo | Boston |
| – | RW | Joel Ward | Nashville | Nashville |
| – | D | Scott Niedermayer | Anaheim | Anaheim |
| – | LW | Donald Brashear | NY Rangers | Washington |
| – | D | Matt Walker | Tampa Bay | Chicago |
| – | C | Tomas Kopecky | Chicago | Detroit |
| – | D | Aaron Rome | Vancouver | Columbus |
| – | D | Jaroslav Spacek | Montreal | Buffalo |
| – | G | Brian Boucher | Philadelphia | San Jose |
| – | LW | Erik Cole | Carolina | Carolina |
| – | G | Nikolai Khabibulin | Edmonton | Chicago |
| – | G | Scott Clemmensen | Florida | New Jersey |
| – | RW | Ian Laperriere | Philadelphia | Colorado |
| – | C | Mike Rupp | Pittsburgh | New Jersey |
| – | D | Hal Gill | Montreal | Pittsburgh |
| – | D | Adam Pardy | Calgary | Calgary |
| – | D | Kent Huskins | San Jose | San Jose |
| – | LW | David Koci | Colorado | Tampa Bay |
| – | C | Mike Cammalleri | Montreal | Calgary |
| – | D | Mike Komisarek | Toronto | Montreal |
| – | RW | Byron Bitz | Boston | Boston |
| – | D | Greg Zanon | Minnesota | Nashville |
| – | C | Vern Fiddler | Phoenix | Nashville |
| – | LW | Steve Begin | Boston | Dallas |
| – | LW | Steve Sullivan | Nashville | Nashville |
| – | C | Sammy Pahlsson | Columbus | Chicago |
| – | D | Jason Strudwick | Edmonton | Edmonton |
| – | G | Mathieu Garon | Columbus | Pittsburgh |
| – | RW | Marian Gaborik | NY Rangers | Minnesota |
| – | G | Jason LaBarbera | Phoenix | Vancouver |
| – | RW | Fredrik Sjostrom | Calgary | NY Rangers |
| – | RW | Chris Neil | Ottawa | Ottawa |
| – | C | John Madden | Chicago | New Jersey |
| – | RW | Brian Gionta | Montreal | New Jersey |
| – | RW | Martin Havlat | Minnesota | Chicago |
| – | D | Johnny Boychuk | Boston | Boston |
| July 2 – | D | Clay Wilson | Florida | Atlanta |
| – | C | Mike Glumac | Montreal | Montreal |
| – | LW | Mathieu Darche | Montreal | Buffalo |
| – | D | Nolan Baumgartner | Vancouver | Vancouver |
| – | D | Lawrence Nycholat | Vancouver | Colorado |
| – | RW | Chris Thorburn | Atlanta | Atlanta |
| – | RW | Mark Recchi | Boston | Boston |
| – | C | Nik Antropov | Atlanta | NY Rangers |
| – | D | Adrian Aucoin | Phoenix | Calgary |
| – | D | Karlis Skrastins | Dallas | Florida |
| – | C | Garth Murray | Calgary | Phoenix |
| – | C | Riley Armstrong | Calgary | San Jose |
| – | G | Scott Munroe | NY Islanders | Philadelphia |
| – | D | Brett Westgarth | NY Islanders | San Jose |
| – | C | Jeremy Reich | NY Islanders | Boston |
| – | C | Mikhail Grabovski | Toronto | Toronto |
| – | D | Rob Scuderi | Los Angeles | Pittsburgh |
| – | D | Jordan Leopold | Florida | Calgary |
| – | C | Chad LaRose | Carolina | Carolina |
| – | LW | Stefan Meyer | Phoenix | Phoenix |
| – | RW | Kevin Westgarth | Los Angeles | Los Angeles |
| July 3 – | D | Nate Guenin | Pittsburgh | Philadelphia |
| – | C | Tyler Arnason | NY Rangers | Colorado |
| – | C | Corey Locke | NY Rangers | Minnesota |
| – | F | Pierre Parenteau | NY Rangers | NY Rangers |
| – | RW | Mikael Samuelsson | Vancouver | Detroit |
| – | LW | Ryane Clowe | San Jose | San Jose |
| – | D | Shane Hnidy | Minnesota | Boston |
| – | LW | Ruslan Fedotenko | Pittsburgh | Pittsburgh |
| – | D | Shaun Heshka | Phoenix | Phoenix |
| July 5 – | D | Chris Lee | Pittsburgh | NY Islanders |
| – | RW | Chris Conner | Pittsburgh | Dallas Stars |
| July 6 – | RW | B.J. Crombeen | St. Louis | St. Louis |
| – | RW | David Jones | Colorado | Colorado |
| – | RW | Darren Haydar | Colorado | Detroit |
| – | LW | Chris Higgins | NY Rangers | Montreal |
| – | G | Andrew Raycroft | Vancouver | Colorado |
| – | D | Shane O'Brien | Vancouver | Vancouver |
| – | RW | Alex Kovalev | Ottawa | Montreal |
| – | LW | Ville Leino | Detroit | Detroit |
| – | D | Francois Beauchemin | Toronto | Anaheim |
| – | C | Colin Fraser | Chicago | Chicago |
| – | LW | Ben Eager | Chicago | Chicago |
| – | G | Corey Crawford | Chicago | Chicago |
| – | RW | Troy Brouwer | Chicago | Chicago |
| – | D | Aaron Johnson | Chicago | Chicago |
| – | LW | Warren Peters | Dallas | Calgary |
| – | C | Jason Krog | Atlanta | Vancouver |
| – | G | Drew MacIntyre | Atlanta | Vancouver |
| – | G | Peter Mannino | Atlanta | NY Islanders |
| – | RW | Greg Moore | NY Islanders | NY Rangers |
| – | LW | Matt Moulson | NY Islanders | Los Angeles |
| – | F | Greg Mauldin | NY Islanders | Ottawa |
| – | D | Mark Flood | NY Islanders | Carolina |
| – | D | Brian Salcido | Anaheim | Anaheim |
| – | D | Cam Barker | Chicago | Chicago |
| July 7 – | LW | Jason Jaffray | Calgary | Vancouver |
| – | C | Jamie Lundmark | Calgary | Calgary |
| – | RW | Jeremy Williams | Detroit | Toronto |
| – | C | Kris Newbury | Detroit | Toronto |
| – | C | Todd Marchant | Anaheim | Anaheim |
| – | LW | Stephane Veilleux | Tampa Bay | Minnesota |
| – | D | Jeff Woywitka | Dallas | St. Louis |
| – | G | Dany Sabourin | Boston | Edmonton |
| – | D | Drew Fata | Boston | Ottawa |
| – | LW | Jeff Taffe | Florida | Pittsburgh |
| July 8 – | RW | Kris Versteeg | Chicago | Chicago |
| – | C | Brian Boyle | NY Rangers | Los Angeles |
| – | D | Doug Janik | Detroit | NY Rangers |
| – | C | Saku Koivu | Anaheim | Montreal |
| – | RW | Steven Goertzen | Carolina | Phoenix |
| – | C | Jim Slater | Atlanta | Atlanta |
| – | G | Justin Peters | Carolina | Carolina |
| – | D | Casey Borer | Carolina | Carolina |
| – | C | Philippe Dupuis | Colorado | Colorado |
| – | D | Brett Skinner | Colorado | Atlanta |
| – | D | Kurtis Foster | Tampa Bay | Minnesota |
| – | D | Mark Fistric | Dallas | Dallas |

| SIGNING DATE | POS. | PLAYER | SIGNED BY | PREVIOUS ORGANIZATION |
|---|---|---|---|---|
| July 9 – | D | Nick Boynton | Anaheim | Florida |
| – | F | Scott Parse | Los Angeles | Los Angeles |
| – | RW | Ales Kotalik | NY Rangers | Edmonton |
| – | F | Carsen Germyn | Calgary | Calgary |
| – | D | Richard Petiot | Chicago | Tampa Bay |
| – | D | Jay Harrison | Carolina | Toronto |
| – | LW | Matt Ellis | Buffalo | Buffalo |
| July 10 – | G | Antero Niittymaki | Tampa Bay | Philadelphia |
| – | G | Yann Danis | New Jersey | NY Islanders |
| – | D | Paul Mara | Montreal | NY Rangers |
| – | D | Jonathan Sigalet | Columbus | Columbus |
| – | C | Brendan Morrison | Washington | Dallas |
| – | D | Jay McKee | Pittsburgh | St. Louis |
| – | LW | Travis Moen | Montreal | San Jose |
| – | D | Kyle Cumiskey | Colorado | Colorado |
| July 11 – | C | Kyle Chipchura | Montreal | Montreal |
| – | RW | Brian McGrattan | Calgary | Phoenix |
| July 13 – | D | Nolan Yonkman | Nashville | Nashville |
| – | D | James Wisniewski | Anaheim | Anaheim |
| – | RW | Brandon Segal | Los Angeles | Tampa Bay |
| – | D | Noah Welch | Atlanta | Tampa Bay |
| – | F | Anthony Stewart | Atlanta | Florida |
| – | C | Boyd Gordon | Washington | Washington |
| – | C | Drew Larman | Boston | Florida |
| – | C | Trent Whitfield | Boston | St. Louis |
| – | F | Chris Minard | Edmonton | Pittsburgh |
| – | RW | Ryan Callahan | NY Rangers | NY Rangers |
| July 14 – | RW | Ben Guite | Nashville | Colorado |
| – | D | Mathieu Roy | Columbus | Edmonton |
| – | F | Ryan Maki | Nashville | Nashville |
| – | D | Corey Potter | NY Rangers | NY Rangers |
| – | D | Staffan Kronwall | Calgary | Washington |
| – | RW | Tom Kostopoulos | Hurricanes | Montreal |
| – | D | Ben Lovejoy | Pittsburgh | Pittsburgh |
| July 15 – | F | Tim Wallace | Pittsburgh | Pittsburgh |
| – | D | Shawn Belle | Montreal | Montreal |
| – | RW | Guillaume Latendresse | Montreal | Montreal |
| – | F | Mike Angelidis | Carolina | Carolina |
| – | D | Zack Fitzgerald | Carolina | Vancouver |
| – | RW | Patrick Kaleta | Buffalo | Buffalo |
| – | D | Andrew Alberts | Carolina | Philadelphia |
| – | C | Scott Nichol | San Jose | Nashville |
| – | LW | Lauri Korpikoski | Phoenix | NY Rangers |
| – | LW | Robbie Earl | Minnesota | Minnesota |
| – | RW | Danny Irmen | Minnesota | Minnesota |
| – | LW | Benoit Pouliot | Minnesota | Minnesota |
| – | D | Clayton Stoner | Minnesota | Minnesota |
| – | F | Steve Pinizzotto | Washington | Washington |
| – | C | Kyle Wilson | Washington | Washington |
| – | LW | Chris Bourque | Washington | Washington |
| – | RW | Eric Fehr | Washington | Washington |
| – | D | Shaone Morrisonn | Washington | Washington |
| – | G | Kari Lehtonen | Atlanta | Atlanta |
| July 16 – | LW | Peter Olvecky | Nashville | Minnesota |
| – | D | Jeff Schultz | Washington | Washington |
| – | RW | Colby Armstrong | Atlanta | Atlanta |
| – | G | Devan Dubnyk | Edmonton | Edmonton |
| – | D | Keith Yandle | Phoenix | Phoenix |
| – | C | Blair Jones | Tampa Bay | Tampa Bay |
| – | RW | Lauri Tukonen | Tampa Bay | Tampa Bay |
| – | D | Joe Callahan | San Jose | Nashville |
| – | RW | Ryan Vesce | San Jose | San Jose |
| – | RW | Jed Ortmeyer | San Jose | Nashville |
| – | C | Dwight Helminen | San Jose | Carolina |
| July 17 – | D | Cory Murphy | New Jersey | Tampa Bay |
| – | RW | Jon DiSalvatore | Minnesota | New Jersey |
| – | G | Wade Dubielewicz | Minnesota | Columbus |
| – | D | Jack Johnson | Los Angeles | Los Angeles |
| – | F | Tim Stapleton | Atlanta | Toronto |
| – | D | Scott Lehman | Atlanta | Atlanta |
| – | D | Grant Lewis | Atlanta | Atlanta |
| – | D | Bryan Rodney | Carolina | Carolina |
| July 20 – | D | Brett Carson | Carolina | Carolina |
| – | RW | Danny Bois | Chicago | Ottawa |
| – | F | Clarke MacArthur | Buffalo | Buffalo |
| – | D | Andrej Sekera | Buffalo | Buffalo |
| – | LW | Nigel Dawes | Calgary | Phoenix |
| – | D | Drew Bagnall | Los Angeles | Los Angeles |
| – | RW | Teddy Purcell | Los Angeles | Los Angeles |
| – | G | Curtis Sanford | Montreal | Vancouver |
| – | D | Matt Hunwick | Boston | Boston |
| – | D | Sean Sullivan | Phoenix | Phoenix |
| – | F | David Spina | Phoenix | Phoenix |
| – | RW | Jeff Hoggan | Phoenix | Phoenix |
| July 21 – | D | Boris Valabik | Atlanta | Atlanta |
| – | G | Brent Johnson | Pittsburgh | Washington |
| – | F | Enver Lisin | NY Rangers | Phoenix |
| – | LW | Mike Blunden | Columbus | Columbus |
| – | D | Steve Wagner | St. Louis | St. Louis |
| – | C | Tomas Plekanec | Montreal | Montreal |
| – | F | Andre Deveaux | Toronto | Toronto |
| – | D | Denis Grebeshkov | Edmonton | Edmonton |
| July 22 – | C | Travis Zajac | New Jersey | New Jersey |
| – | F | Alex Foster | Toronto | Toronto |
| – | F | Darryl Boyce | Toronto | Toronto |
| – | D | Marc Methot | Columbus | Columbus |
| – | F | Ryan Oulahen | Detroit | Detroit |
| – | F | Evan McGrath | Detroit | Detroit |
| – | D | Mike Funk | Vancouver | Buffalo |
| – | F | Tanner Glass | Vancouver | Florida |
| – | C | Nathan Smith | Minnesota | Colorado |
| – | G | Martin Biron | NY Islanders | Philadelphia |
| July 23 – | F | Tuomo Ruutu | Carolina | Carolina |
| – | D | Ryan Lannon | Minnesota | Phoenix |
| – | C | Kyle Brodziak | Minnesota | Edmonton |
| – | RW | Adam Cracknell | St. Louis | Calgary |
| – | RW | Barry Tallackson | St. Louis | New Jersey |
| – | F | Kris Chucko | Calgary | Calgary |
| – | RW | Jason Ward | Philadelphia | Tampa Bay |
| – | C | Krys Kolanos | Philadelphia | Minnesota |
| – | LW | Lukas Kasper | Philadelphia | San Jose |
| July 24 – | F | Daniel Winnik | Phoenix | Phoenix |
| July 25 – | D | Derek Morris | Boston | NY Rangers |
| – | D | Roman Polak | St. Louis | St. Louis |
| – | C | Nate Thompson | NY Islanders | NY Islanders |
| July 26 – | D | Matt Smaby | Tampa Bay | Tampa Bay |
| July 28 – | G | Dan LaCosta | Columbus | Columbus |
| July 29 – | G | Josh Harding | Minnesota | Minnesota |
| – | F | Jeremy Yablonski | Ottawa | Ottawa |
| – | D | Derek Smith | Ottawa | Ottawa |
| – | C | Ryan Potulny | Edmonton | Edmonton |
| – | LW | Liam Reddox | Edmonton | Edmonton |
| – | G | Josh Tordjman | Phoenix | Phoenix |
| – | LW | Scottie Upshall | Phoenix | Phoenix |
| – | D | Jack Hillen | NY Islanders | NY Islanders |
| July 30 – | D | Mike Vernace | Atlanta | Colorado |
| – | F | Josh Gratton | Atlanta | Philadelphia |
| – | C | Kyle Wellwood | Vancouver | Vancouver |
| – | F | Dustin Boyd | Calgary | Calgary |
| – | D | Ole-Kristian Tollefsen | Philadelphia | Columbus |
| July 31 – | D | Milan Jurcina | Washington | Washington |
| – | D | Brendan Bell | St. Louis | Ottawa |
| Aug. 1 – | C | Cody McCormick | Buffalo | Colorado |
| – | G | John Curry | Pittsburgh | Pittsburgh |
| Aug. 3 – | F | Blake Comeau | NY Islanders | NY Islanders |
| Aug. 4 – | G | Brian Elliott | Ottawa | Ottawa |
| – | RW | Patrick Eaves | Detroit | Carolina |
| Aug. 5 – | RW | Jannik Hansen | Vancouver | Vancouver |
| Aug. 6 – | F | Jason Williams | Detroit | Columbus |
| Aug 10 – | RW | Mike Grier | Buffalo | San Jose |
| – | RW | Ryan Jones | Nashville | Nashville |
| – | G | Joey MacDonald | Toronto | NY Islanders |
| – | LW | Gregory Stewart | Montreal | Montreal |

# Trade Register, 2008-09

## September 2008

2– Vancouver traded RW **Ryan Shannon** to Ottawa for D **Lawrence Nycholat**.

2– Toronto traded D **Bryan McCabe** and its 4th-round choice in the 2010 Entry Draft to Florida for D **Mike Van Ryn**.

11– Phoenix traded LW **Kevin Cormier** to New Jersey for D **Sean Zimmerman**.

12– Chicago traded C **Robert Lang** to Montreal for Toronto's 2nd-round choice (previously acquired) in the 2010 Entry Draft.

26– Anaheim traded D **Mathieu Schneider** to Atlanta for D **Ken Klee**, LW **Brad Larsen** and LW **Chad Painchaud**.

29– Tampa Bay traded C **Nick Tarnasky** to Nashville for Nashville's 6th-round choice (G **Jaroslav Janus**) in the 2009 Entry Draft.

30– Anaheim traded D **Sean O'Donnell** to Los Angeles for future considerations.

## October 2008

1– Pittsburgh traded D **Michal Sersen** to Tampa Bay for Tampa Bay's 5th-round choice (D **Alex Velischek**) in the 2009 Entry Draft.

6– Tampa Bay traded D **Shane O'Brien** and RW **Michel Ouellet** to Vancouver for D **Lukas Krajicek** and LW **Juraj Simek**.

8– Chicago traded D **Doug Janik** to Dallas for a conditional choice in the 2010 Entry Draft.

9– Phoenix traded C **Michael Zigomanis** to Pittsburgh for future considerations.

13– Boston traded D **Andrew Alberts** to Philadelphia for Philadelphia's 4th-round choice (LW **Lane MacDermid**) in the 2009 Entry Draft and LW **Ned Lukacevic**.

30– Philadelphia traded D **Tim Ramholt** to Nashville for LW **Josh Gratton**.

30– NY Rangers traded RW **Hugh Jessiman** to Nashville for future considerations.

## November 2008

3– Phoenix traded D **Drew Fata** to Ottawa for C **Alexander Nikulin**.

7– Tampa Bay traded D **Matt Carle** and San Jose's 3rd-round choice (previously acquired, Philadelphia seleced D **Simon Bertilsson**) in the 2009 Entry Draft to Philadelphia for D **Steve Eminger**, RW **Steve Downie** and Tampa Bay's 4th-round choice (previously acquired, Tampa Bay selected LW **Alex Hutchings**) in 2009.

16– Pittsburgh traded D **Darryl Sydor** to Dallas for D **Philippe Boucher**.

24– Toronto traded D **Carlo Colaiacovo** and C **Alex Steen** to St. Louis for RW **Lee Stempniak**.

25– Tampa Bay traded C **Wyatt Smith** to Phoenix for future considerations.

27– Nashville traded C **Nick Tarnasky** to Florida for RW **Wade Belak**.

30– Tampa Bay traded D **Andrew Hutchinson** to Dallas for RW **Lauri Tukonen**.

## December 2008

3– Phoenix traded D **Logan Stephenson** to Anaheim for C **Joakim Lindstrom**.

8– Vancouver traded D **James Sharrow** to Chicago for future considerations.

14– Anaheim traded C **Brian Sutherby** to Dallas for C **David McIntyre** and a conditional choice in the 2010 Entry Draft.

19– Pittsburgh traded RW **Jonathan Filewich** to St. Louis for conditional choice in the 2010 Entry Draft.

30– Los Angeles traded G **Jason LaBarbera** to Vancouver for Vancouver's 7th-round choice (later traded to Atlanta – Atlanta selected LW **Jordan Samuels-Thomas**) in the 2009 Entry Draft.

## January 2009

5– Pittsburgh traded D **T.J. Kemp** to Montreal for a conditional choice in the 2010 Entry Draft.

7– Anaheim traded LW **Brad May** to Toronto for a conditional choice in the 2010 Entry Draft.

10– Chicago traded LW **Michael Blunden** to Columbus for RW **Adam Pineault**.

13– Atlanta traded D **Brett Skinner** to NY Islanders for RW **Junior Lessard**.

14– Atlanta traded C **Jason Williams** to Columbus for D **Clay Wilson** and San Jose's 6th-round choice (previously acquired, later traded to Chicago – Chicago selected C **David Pacan**) in the 2009 Entry Draft .

17– Edmonton traded G **Mathieu Garon** to Pittsburgh for G **Dany Sabourin**, C **Ryan Stone** and a 4th-round choice in the 2011 Entry Draft.

21– Minnesota traded LW **Ryan Hamilton** to Toronto for LW **Robbie Earl**.

29– NY Rangers traded C/LW **Dan Fritsche** to Minnesota for D **Erik Reitz**.

## February 2009

3– Anaheim traded C **David McIntyre** to New Jersey for D **Sheldon Brookbank**.

4– Anaheim traded D **Nathan McIver** to Vancouver for RW **Mike Brown**.

7– Carolina traded LW **Wade Brookbank**, D **Josef Melichar** and future considerations to Tampa Bay for LW **Jussi Jokinen**.

16– Atlanta traded D **Mathieu Schneider** and its 3rd-round choice (C **Joonas Nattinen**) in the 2009 Entry Draft to Montreal for Anaheim's 2nd-round choice (previously acquired, Atlanta selected LW **Jeremy Morin**) in 2009 and Montreal's 3rd-round choice in 2010.

20– NY Islanders traded C **Mike Comrie** and D **Chris Campoli** to Ottawa for C **Dean McAmmond** and San Jose's 1st-round choice (previously acquired, later traded to Columbus, later traded to Anaheim – Anaheim selected C/RW **Kyle Palmieri**) in the 2009 Entry Draft.

26– Anaheim traded LW **Chris Kunitz** and LW **Eric Tangradi** to Pittsburgh for D **Ryan Whitney**.

26– Dallas traded D **Doug Janik** to Montreal for C **Steve Begin**.

## March 2009

2– Atlanta traded D **Niclas Havelid** and LW **Myles Stoesz** to New Jersey for D **Anssi Salmela**.

4– Anaheim traded LW **Travis Moen** and D **Kent Huskins** to San Jose for G **Timo Pielmeier**, C **Nick Bonino** and conditional choices.

4– Anaheim traded C **Samuel Pahlsson**, D **Logan Stephenson** and future considerations to Chicago for D **James Wisniewski** and C **Petri Kontiola**.

4– Anaheim traded C **Eric O'Dell** to Atlanta for C **Erik Christensen**.

4– Boston traded C **Petteri Nokelainen** to Anaheim for D **Steve Montador**.

4– Boston traded D **Matt Lashoff** and RW **Martins Karsums** to Tampa Bay for RW **Mark Recchi** and Tampa Bay's 2nd-round choice in the 2010 Entry Draft.

4– Buffalo traded RW **Ales Kotalik** to Edmonton for Carolina's 2nd-round choice (previously acquired, later traded to Toronto – Toronto selected D **Jesse Blacker**) in the 2009 Entry Draft.

4– Calgary traded C **Matthew Lombardi**, LW **Brandon Prust** and its 1st-round choice in the 2010 Entry Draft to Phoenix for C **Olli Jokinen** and Phoenix's 3rd-round choice (later traded to Florida – Florida selected RW **Josh Birkholz**) in 2009.

4– Calgary traded D **Ryan Wilson**, D **Lawrence Nycholat** and Montreal's 2nd-round choice (previously acquired, Colorado selected D **Stefan Elliott**) in the 2009 Entry Draft to Colorado for D **Jordan Leopold**.

4– Calgary traded G **Kevin Lalande** to Columbus for Columbus' 4th-round choice (later traded to Los Angeles, later traded to Florida – Florida selected LW **Garrett Wilson**) in the 2009 Entry Draft.

4– Carolina traded RW **Justin Williams** to Los Angeles for C **Patrick O'Sullivan** and Calgary's 2nd-round choice (previously acquired, Carolina selected D **Brian Dumoulin**) in the 2009 Entry Draft .

4– Carolina traded C **Patrick O'Sullivan** and its 2nd-round choice (later traded to Buffalo, later traded to Toronto – Toronto selected D **Jesse Blacker**) in the 2009 Entry Draft to Edmonton for LW **Erik Cole** and Edmonton's 5th-round choice (RW **Matt Kennedy**) in 2009.

4– Columbus traded G **Pascal Leclaire** and its 2nd-round choice (G **Robin Lehner**) in the 2009 Entry Draft to Ottawa for LW **Antoine Vermette**.

4– Florida traded D **Noah Welch** and its 3rd-round choice (later traded to Detroit – Detroit selected C/RW **Andrej Nestrasil**) in the 2009 Entry Draft to Tampa Bay for D **Steve Eminger**.

4– NY Islanders traded RW **Bill Guerin** to Pittsburgh for Pittsburgh's 3rd-round choice (later traded to Phoenix – Phoenix selected G **Michael Lee**) in the 2009 Entry Draft.

4– NY Rangers traded D **Dmitri Kalinin**, LW **Nigel Dawes** and RW **Petr Prucha** to Phoenix for D **Derek Morris**.

4– Philadelphia traded LW **Scottie Upshall** and its 2nd-round choice in the 2011 Entry Draft to Phoenix for LW **Daniel Carcillo**.

4– Phoenix traded G **Mikael Tellqvist** to Buffalo for Buffalo's 4th-round choice in the 2010 Entry Draft.

4– Pittsburgh traded D **Danny Richmond** to St. Louis for D **Andy Wozniewski**.

4– Tampa Bay traded G **Olaf Kolzig**, D **Jamie Heward**, D **Andy Rogers** and Carolina's 4th-round choice (previously acquired – later forfeited) in the 2009 Entry Draft to Toronto for D **Richard Petiot**.

4– Toronto traded C **Nik Antropov** to NY Rangers for the Rangers' 2nd-round choice (RW **Kenny Ryan**) in the 2009 Entry Draft and a conditional choice in 2010.

4– Toronto traded C **Dominic Moore** to Buffalo for Carolina's 2nd-round choice (previously acquired, Toronto selected D **Jesse Blacker**) in the 2009 Entry Draft.

## June 2009

19– Florida traded C **Stefan Meyer** to Phoenix for C **Steve Reinprecht**.

26– Anaheim traded D **Chris Pronger** and C **Ryan Dingle** to Philadelphia for RW **Joffrey Lupul**, D **Luca Sbisa**, Philadelphia's 1st-round choice (later traded to Columbus – Columbus selected D **John Moore**) in the 2009 Entry Draft, 1st-round choice in 2010 and a conditional choice in the 2010 or 2011 Entry Draft.

26– Columbus traded choices #16 (later traded to Minnesota – Minnesota selected D **Nick Leddy**) and #77 (later traded to Minnesota – Minnesota selected G **Matthew Hackett**) in the 2009 Entry Draft to NY Islanders for choices #26 (later traded to Anaheim – Anaheim selected C/RW **Kyle Palmieri**), #37 (later traded to Anaheim – Anaheim selected D **Matt Clark**), #62 (G **Anders Nilsson**) and #92 (C **Casey Cizikas**) in 2009.

26– Minnesota traded choice #12 (D **Calvin De Haan**) in the 2009 Entry Draft to NY Islanders for choices #16 (D **Nick Leddy**), #77 (G **Matthew Hackett**) and #182 (LW **Erik Haula**) in 2009.

26– Calgary traded choice #20 (C **Jacob Josefson**) in the 2009 Entry Draft to New Jersey for choices #23 (D **Tim Erixon**) and #84 (later traded to Los Angeles – Los Angeles selcted D **Nicolas Deslauriers**) in 2009.

26– Anaheim traded choice #21 (D **John Moore**) in the 2009 Entry Draft to Columbus for choices #26 (C/RW **Kyle Palmieri**) and #37 (D **Matt Clark**) in 2009.

26– Detroit traded choice #29 (RW **Carter Ashton**) in the 2009 Entry Draft to Tampa Bay for choices #32 (C **Landon Ferraro**) and #75 (C/RW **Andrej Nestrasil**) in 2009.

27– NY Islanders traded choice #56 (C **Kevin Lynch**) in the 2009 Entry Draft to Columbus for choices #62 (G **Anders Nilsson**) and #92 (C **Casey Cizikas**) in 2009.

27– Florida traded D **Jay Bouwmeester** to Calgary for D **Jordan Leopold** and choice #67 (RW **Josh Birkholz**) in the 2009 Entry Draft.

27– Calgary traded choices #84 (D **Nicolas Deslauriers**) and #107 (later traded to Florida – Florida selected LW **Garrett Wilson**) in the 2009 Entry Draft to Los Angeles for choice #74 (LW **Ryan House**) in 2009.

27– NY Islanders traded choice #91 (G **Michael Lee**) in the 2009 Entry Draft to Phoenix for a 3rd-round choice in 2010.

27– Atlanta traded choice #95 (G **Jean-Francois Berube**) in the 2009 Entry Draft to Los Angeles for choices #117 (G **Edward Pasquale**), #120 (D **Ben Chiarot**) and #203 (LW **Jordan Samuels-Thomas**) in 2009.

27– Minnesota traded choices #99 (D **Kyle Bigos**) and #133 (G **Olivier Roy**) in the 2009 Entry Draft to Edmonton for C **Kyle Brodziak** and choice #161 (G **Darcy Kuemper**) in 2009.

27– Los Angeles traded choices #107 (LW **Garrett Wilson**) and #138 (C **Wade Megan**) in the 2009 Entry Draft to Florida for Florida's 3rd-round choice in 2010.

27– Washington traded D **Sami Lepisto** to Phoenix for Phoenix's 5th-round choice in the 2010 Entry Draft.

27– Pittsburgh traded unsigned draft choice G **Chad Johnson** to NY Rangers for choice #151 (C **Andy Bathgate**) in the 2009 Entry Draft.

27– Nashville traded choice #148 (G **Michael Zador**) in the 2009 Entry Draft to Tampa Bay for a 5th-round choice in 2010.

27– Los Angeles traded C **Brian Boyle** to NY Rangers for a 3rd-round choice in the 2010 Entry Draft.

27– Calgary traded D **Jim Vandermeer** to Phoenix for C **Brandon Prust**.

27– Atlanta traded choice #177 (C **David Pacan**) in the 2009 Entry Draft to Chicago for a 5th-round choice in 2010.

27– Dallas traded choice #189 (C **Marek Viedensky**) in the 2009 Entry Draft to San Jose for San Jose's 6th-round choice in 2010.

27– Phoenix traded choice #187 (LW **Steven Anthony**) in the 2009 Entry Draft to Vancouver for the rights to D **Shaun Heshka**.

27– Edmonton traded choice #191 (D **Michael Sdao**) in the 2009 Entry Draft to Ottawa for a 6th-round choice in 2010.

27– Nashville traded choice #202 (C **Maxwell Tardy**) in the 2009 Entry Draft to St. Louis for St. Louis' 7th-round choice in 2010.

27– Pittsburgh traded choice #211 (G **Petteri Simila**) in the 2009 Entry Draft to Montreal for a 6th-round choice in 2010.

30– Montreal traded LW **Chris Higgins**, D **Ryan McDonagh**, D **Pavel Valentenko** and D **Doug Janik** to NY Rangers for C **Scott Gomez**, C **Tom Pyatt** and D **Michael Busto**.

30– New Jersey traded C **Tony Romano** to NY Islanders for C **Ben Walter** and a conditional choice in the 2012 Entry Draft.

## July 2009

1– Atlanta traded D **Garnet Exelby** and LW **Colin Stuart** to Toronto for D **Pavel Kubina** and RW **Tim Stapleton**.

3– Colorado traded LW **Ryan Smyth** to Los Angeles for D **Kyle Quincey**, D **Tom Preissing** and a 5th-round choice in the 2010 Entry Draft.

8– Ottawa traded G **Alex Auld** to Dallas for a 6th-round choice in the 2010 Entry Draft.

9– Edmonton traded D **Tim Sestito** to New Jersey for a conditional choice in the 2010 Entry Draft.

13– NY Rangers traded LW **Lauri Korpikoski** to Phoenix for RW **Enver Lisin**.

16– Colorado traded D **Nigel Williams** to NY Rangers for D **Brian Fahey**.

17– Washington traded D **Keith Seabrook** to Calgary for a 7th-round choice in the 2012 Entry Draft.

21– Phoenix traded LW **Todd Fedoruk** and D **David Hale** to Tampa Bay for RW **Radim Vrbata**.

24– Boston traded D **Aaron Ward** to Carolina for RW **Patrick Eaves** and a 4th-round choice in the 2010 Entry Draft.

27– Calgary traded C **Wayne Primeau** and its 2nd-round choice in the 2011 Entry Draft to Toronto for D **Anton Stralman**, LW **Colin Stuart** and Toronto's 7th-round choice in the 2012 Entry Draft.

Trades and free agent signings after August 10, 2009 are listed on page 609.

# League Abbreviations

AAHA............Alberta Amateur Hockey Association
AAHL............Alaska Amateur Hockey League
AASHA...........Alaska All-Stars Hockey Association
ACHA............American Collegiate Hockey Association
ACHL............Atlantic Coast Hockey League
AFHL............American Frontier Hockey League
AH..............Atlantic Hockey
AHL.............American Hockey League
AJHL............Alberta Junior Hockey League
ALIH............Asia League Ice Hockey
Alpenliga.......Alpenliga (Austria, Italy, Slovenia 1994-1999)
AMHA............Alberta Minor Hockey Association
AMBHL...........Alberta Major Bantam Hockey League
AMHL............Alberta Midget AAA Hockey League
AUAA............Atlantic University Athletic Association
AtJHL...........Atlantic Junior Hockey League
AWHL............American West Hockey League
AYHL............Atlantic Youth Hockey League
BCAHA...........British Columbia Amateur Hockey Association
BCHL............British Columbia (Junior) Hockey League (also BCJHL)
CABHL...........Central Alberta Bantam Hockey League
CBHL............Calgary Bantam Hockey League
CCHA............Central Collegiate Hockey Association
CEGEP...........Quebec College Prep
CHA.............College Hockey America
CHL.............Central Hockey League
CIS.............Commonwealth of Independent States
CIS.............Canadian Interuniversity Sport
CJHL............Central Junior A Hockey League
CMHA............Calgary Minor Hockey Association
ColHL...........Colonial Hockey League
CSHL............Central States Hockey League
CSJHL...........Central States Junior Hockey League
CWUAA...........Canadian Western University Athletic Association
ECAC............Eastern College Athletic Conference
ECACHL..........ECAC Hockey League
ECHL............East Coast Hockey League
EEHL............Eastern European Hockey League
EJHL............Eastern Junior Hockey League
EMHA............Edmonton Minor Hockey Association
EmJHL...........Empire Junior B Hockey League
EuroHL..........European Hockey League
Exhib. .........Exhibition Games, Series or Season
GLHL............Great Lakes Hockey League
GNML............Greater North Midget League
GPAC............Great Plains Athletic Conference
GTHL............Greater Toronto Hockey League
H-East..........Hockey East
HJHL............Heritage Junior Hockey League
High-(XX).......High School (state/province)
IEHL............Internationale Eishockey Liga
IHL.............International Hockey League
KIJHL...........Kootenay International Junior B Hockey League
LCJHL...........Little Caesar's Junior Hockey League
MAAC............Metro Atlantic Athletic Conference
MAHA............Manitoba Amateur Hockey Association
MAHL............Mid America Hockey League
MBAHL...........Metropolitan Boston Amateur Hockey League
MBHL............Metropolitan Boston Hockey League
MEHL............Midwest Elite Hockey League
Metro-HL........Metro Hockey League
MIAC............Minnesota Intercollegiate Athletic Conference
Minor-(XX)......Minor/Youth hockey (state/province)
MJHL............Manitoba Junior Hockey League
MJrHL...........Maritime Junior A Hockey League
MMBHL...........Manitoba Major Bantam Hockey League
MMHL............Manitoba Midget AAA Hockey League
MMHL............Michigan Minor Hockey League
MMMHL...........Manitoba Minor Midget Hockey League
MNHL............Michigan National Hockey League
MtJHL...........Metropolitan Junior Hockey League (New York)
MTJHL...........Metropolitan Toronto Junior Hockey League
MTHL............Metro Toronto Hockey League
MWEHL...........Midwest Elite Hockey League
NAHL............North American Hockey League (Tier I Junior)
NAJHL...........North American Junior Hockey League
Nat-Team........National Team (also Nt.-Team)
NBAHA...........New Brunswick Amateur Hockey Association
NBMHL...........New Brunswick Midget Hockey League
NBPEI...........New Brunswick Prince Edward Island Midget Hockey League
NCAA............National Collegiate Athletic Association
NCHA............Northern Collegiate Hockey Association
NEJHL...........New England Junior Hockey League
NFAHA...........Newfoundland Amateur Hockey Association
NHL.............National Hockey League
NJCAA...........National Junior Collegiate Athletic Association
NOBHL...........Northern Ontario Bantam Hockey League
NOHA............Northern Ontario Hockey Association
NOJHA...........Northern Ontario Junior Hockey Association
NOJHL...........Northern Ontario Junior Hockey League
NSBHL...........Nova Scotia Bantam Hockey League
NSMHL...........Nova Scotia Midget AAA Hockey League
NTHL............North Texas Hockey League
NWJHL...........Northwest Junior B Hockey League
NYJHL...........New York Junior Hockey League
OCJHL...........Ontario Central Junior A Hockey League
OHA.............Ontario Hockey Association
OHL.............Ontario Hockey League
OJHL-B..........Ontario Junior B Hockey Leagues
OMJHL...........Ontario Major Junior Hockey League
OPJHL...........Ontario Provincial Junior A Hockey League
OUAA............Ontario Universities Athletic Association
PAHA............Pennsylvania Amateur Hockey Association
PCJHL...........Pacific Coast Junior Hockey League
PEIHA...........Prince Edward Island Hockey Association
PIJHL...........Pacific International Junior Hockey League
QAA.............Quebec Junior AA
QAAA............Quebec Amateur Athletic Association
QAHA............Quebec Amateur Hockey Association
QJHL............Quebec Junior Hockey League
QMJHL...........Quebec Major Junior Hockey League
QNAHL...........(Quebec) North American Hockey League
Q-RHL...........(Quebec) Richelieu Elite Hockey League
QSPHL...........Quebec Semi-Pro Hockey League
RAMHL...........Rural Alberta Midget Hockey League
RMJHL...........Rocky Mountain Junior Hockey League
SAHA............Saskatchewan Amateur Hockey Association
SAMHL...........Southern Alberta Midget Hockey League
SBHL............Saskatchewan Bantam Hockey League
SCAHA...........Southern California Amateur Hockey Association
SIJHL...........Superior International Junior Hockey League
SJHL............Saskatchewan Junior Hockey League
SMBHL...........Saskatchewan Major Bantam Hockey League
SMHL............Saskatchewan Midget AAA Hockey League
SMMHL...........Saskatchewan Minor Midget Hockey League
SPHL............Southern Professional Hockey League
SSJHL...........South Saskatchewan Junior B Hockey League
SSMHL...........South Saskatchewan Minor Hockey League
SunHL...........Sunshine Hockey League
T1EHL...........Tier 1 Elite Hockey League
TBAHA...........Thunder Bay Amateur Hockey Association
TBJHL...........Thunder Bay Junior Hockey League
TBMHL...........Thunder Bay Midget Hockey League
U-17............Under 17
U-18............Under 18
UHL.............United Hockey League
UMEHL...........Upper Midwest Elite Hockey League
UMHSEL..........Upper Midwest High School Elite League
USAHA...........United States Amateur Hockey Association
USHL............United States (Junior A) Hockey League
VIJHL...........Vancouver Island Junior Hockey League
WCHA............Western Collegiate Hockey Association
WCHL............West Coast Hockey League
WHL.............Western Hockey League
WNYHA...........Western New York Hockey Association
WPHL............Western Professional Hockey League
WSJHL...........Western States Junior Hockey League
WMHA............Winnipeg Minor Hockey Association

## Contributors

**The NHL Official Guide & Record Book is produced with the help of many. Special thanks to:** Mark Adams, Chico Adrahtas, Manny Almela, Mike Amundson, Andy Baggot, Dennis Barban, Dana Barbin, Randy Bedard, Jim Bennett, Mac Bennett, Larissa Blue, Bob Borgen, Minako Borgen, Mike Bortolussi, Dean Boyle, Kelly Butt, John Caldarozzi, Craig Campbell, Hugh Campbell, Paul Capizzano, Jack Carnefix (ECHL), Jason Chaimovitch (AHL), Ben Chiarot, Michael Chraba, Al Clark, Dave Clarke, Valerie Clement, Carmen Cogliano, Rusty Coleman, Ken Coleman, Ben Cook, Kory Cooper, John Craig, Fred Devereaux, Al Doria, Christine Dupuis, Bob Fallen, Dave Feltham, Tom Ferguson, Mike Fiorino, Dave Fischer (USA Hockey), Cory Flett (WHL), Paul Flindall, Jack Forsythe, Jon Frape, Rob Gagnon, John Gardner, Jamie Gilliam (CHA), Keegan Goodrich, Bob Grove, Stu Hackel, Anthony Hamburg, Ed Hansen, Rick Harkins, Tim Harwood, Jeff Hicks, Hockey Hall of Fame, Todd Hoffman, Nick Huras, Randy Jacobs, Peter Jagla, Karl Jahnke (QMJHL), Christy Jeffries (USA Hockey), Larry Johnson, Jim Johnson, Dave Kapp, Marc Kapsalis, Jay Keller, Chris Koper, Vladislav Korloev, Edward Krajewski (ECAC), Brian Lavelle, Eric Lindquist, Paul MacDermid, Paul Maciejewski, James Mancuso, Geoff Marottolo, Chris Masters, Bob McAfee, Brian McClary, Tracy McDonald, Penny McEwen (SJHL), Ray McIsaac, Curtis McKenzie, Len McNeely, Wade Megan, Adam Mitchell, Deb Moffatt, Herb Morell (OHL), NCAA Conference and School Sports Information Departments, NHL Broadcasters' Association, NHL Central Registry, NHL Officiating, NHL Players' Association, James Naylor, Denise Olsen, Dale Parker, Chris Peters (U.S. National Team Development Program), Lindsay Pink, Dan Plaster, Fred Pletsch (CCHA), Steven Poapst, Phil Pritchard, Pearl Rajwanth, Tara Renaud, Dave Rendall, Doug Reynolds, Alex Riazanova, Rick Rogers, David Rourke (AH), Max Saegert, Larry Sanderson, Martin Schmid, Mary E. Schneider, Jack Schoenmakers, Bruce Shatel, Ralph Slate, Lee Smith, Craig Smith, Susan Snow, SIHR, Peter Souris (Hockey East), Doug Spencer (WCHA), Matt Trevor, Dan Ukrainetz, Dennis Vaske, Rosemary Voulelikas, Randy Watt, Ryan Watters, Jesse Watts (WHL), Dan Whalen, Damon White, Paul Wilkinson (OPJHL), Bob Woods, Ankie Yip.

## Photo Credits

Hockey Hall of Fame: Various Collections. Getty Images: Graig Abel, Claus Andersen, Scott Audette, Steve Babineau, Bruce Bennett, Frederick Breedon, Mark Buckner, Scott Cunningham, Gregg Forwerck, Noah Graham, Norm Hall, Grant Halverson, Glenn James, Bruce Kluckhohn, Mitchell Layton, Scott Levy, Andy Marlin, Michael Martin, Doug Pensinger, Len Redkoles, Dave Reginek, Andre Ringuette, Debora Robinson, John Russell, Jamie Sabau, Joe Sargent, Gregory Shamus, Bill Smith, Dave Sandford, Mike Stobe, Gerry Thomas, Jeff Vinnick, Bill Wippert. Additional NHL team photographers: Rudy Ayasse, Brian Babineau, Greg Bartram, Will Bennett, Andrew D. Bernstein, Frederick Breedon, Tim DeFrisco, Mark Dellas, Andy Devlin, Noah Graham, Bob Fisher, Tim Heitman, Scott Iskowitz, Aimee Rickert, Al Ruelle, Don Smith, Rocky Widner

Special thanks to Paul Michinard, Getty Images.

**Researchers and historians:** contact the Society for International Hockey Research www.sihrhockey.org